Baldwin's
OHIO PRACTICE

Merrick-Rippner Probate Laws & Rules Annotated

2007

Ohio Revised Code complete to February 28, 2007
Ohio Court Rules complete to February 1, 2007
Local Court Rules complete to February 1, 2007

Mat #40513251

© 2007 Thomson/West
All Rights Reserved.

This publication was created to provide you with accurate and authoritative information concerning the subject matter covered; however, this publication was not necessarily prepared by persons licensed to practice law in a particular jurisdiction. The publisher is not engaged in rendering legal or other professional advice, and this publication is not a substitute for the advice of an attorney. If you require legal or other expert advice, you should seek the services of a competent attorney or other professional.

Reprinted from
BALDWIN'S™ OHIO REVISED CODE ANNOTATED

Merrick-Rippner Probate Law
    (including Merrick-Rippner Probate Laws & Rules Annotated)

ISBN: 978–0–8322–0872–0

West's and Westlaw are registered in the U.S. Patent and Trademark Office.

Foreword

Baldwin's Ohio Practice, *Merrick–Rippner Probate Laws & Rules Annotated* is the companion softcover volume to Baldwin's Ohio Practice, *Merrick–Rippner Probate Law*—Ohio's most popular work on probate law and practice.

This 2007 Edition contains selected provisions of the Ohio Constitution, Ohio Revised Code, and Court Rules, arranged in numerical order and cross referenced to Baldwin's Ohio Practice, *Merrick–Rippner Probate Law*.

Many key statutory provisions are included, especially Revised Code Title 21, "Courts—Probate—Juvenile" with annotations to both reported and unreported cases. This Title is of paramount importance to probate and juvenile judges, as well as magistrates and practitioners, who will turn to it often in their practice and judicial decisionmaking.

Included in the 2007 Edition are all relevant laws passed by the Ohio General Assembly complete to February 28, 2007, including:

- All new sections enacted and amended by 2006 HB 416, the Ohio Trust Code, including new Title 58
- Amendments to RC 4717.21 and RC 4717.22, as affected by 2006 HB 426, regarding the right of disposition of remains, including cremation

The Rules of Juvenile Procedure with commentary and selected Rules of Superintendence for the Courts of Ohio, complete to February 1, 2007, are reprinted from *Baldwin's Ohio Revised Code Annotated*. Local rules of the Probate Division for Cuyahoga, Franklin, Hamilton, Lucas, Montgomery, Stark, and Summit Counties, complete to February 1, 2007, are also included.

A comprehensive subject index facilitates access to all materials in this volume by topic.

Baldwin's Ohio Practice, *Merrick–Rippner Probate Laws & Rules Annotated* will aid the probate and juvenile law benches and bars in further research of the issues discussed in Baldwin's Ohio Practice, *Merrick–Rippner Probate Law*.

We acknowledge with appreciation the work of our editorial and production staffs—particularly Heather Day DiFranco, Esq., Mark Knaus, Suzanne Meleney, Diona Shaw, and Nancy Spino—for their efforts in compiling this new volume. If you have any comments or suggestions for future editions please contact us.

THE PUBLISHER

MARCH 2007

*

RELATED PRODUCTS FROM WEST

Baldwin's Ohio Practice, Business Organizations
Jason C. Blackford

Baldwin's Ohio Practice, Civil Practice
James M. Klein, Stanton G. Darling II & Dennis G. Terez

Baldwin's Ohio Practice, Criminal Law 2d
Lewis R. Katz, Paul C. Giannelli,
Beverly J. Blair, Judith P. Lipton

Baldwin's Ohio Practice, Ohio Criminal Justice
Lewis R. Katz, Paul C. Giannelli & Case Western Reserve University

Baldwin's Ohio Practice, Ohio Statutory Charges
Dennis G. Terez

Baldwin's Ohio Practice, Domestic Relations Law 4th
Beatrice K. Sowald & Stanley Morganstern

Baldwin's Ohio Practice, Evidence 2d
Paul C. Giannelli & Barbara Rook Snyder

Baldwin's Ohio Practice, Rules of Evidence Handbook
Paul C. Giannelli & Barbara Rook Snyder

Baldwin's Ohio Practice, Merrick–Rippner Probate Law 6th
Angela G. Carlin

Baldwin's Ohio Practice, Local Government Law—Township
Rebecca C. Princehorn

Baldwin's Ohio Practice, Local Government—Municipal
John E. Gotherman, Harold W. Babbit, & James F. Lang

Baldwin's Ohio Practice, Local Government—County
William T. Conard II

Ohio Appellate Practice
Judge Mark P. Painter and Douglas R. Dennis

Ohio Arrest, Search and Seizure
Lewis R. Katz

Ohio Consumer Law
Legal Aid Society of Cleveland,
Harold L. Williams, Ed.

Ohio Domestic Violence Law
Judge Ronald B. Adrine & Alexandria M. Ruden

Ohio Driving Under the Influence Law
Judge Mark P. Painter

RELATED PRODUCTS

Ohio Employment Practices Law
Bradd N. Siegel & John M. Stephen

Ohio Felony Sentencing Law
Judge Burt W. Griffin & Lewis R. Katz

Ohio Juvenile Law
Paul C. Giannelli &
Patricia McCloud Yeomans

Ohio Landlord Tenant Law
Frederic White

Ohio Personal Injury Practice

Ohio Planning and Zoning Law
Stuart Meck & Kenneth Pearlman

Ohio School Law Handbook
Susan C. Hastings, Richard D. Manoloff,
Timothy J. Sheeran & Gregory W. Stype

Trial Handbook for Ohio Lawyers
Richard M. Markus

Baldwin's Ohio School Law Journal
Mary A. Lentz, Ed.

Code News
David S. Collins, Ed.

Domestic Relations Journal of Ohio
Stanley Morganstern, Ed.

Finley's Ohio Municipal Service
Price D. Finley, Ed.

Probate Law Journal of Ohio
Robert M. Brucken, Ed.

Workers' Compensation Journal of Ohio
Jerald D. Harris, Ed.

Baldwin's Ohio School Law
Susan C. Hastings, Richard D. Manoloff,
Timothy J. Sheeran & Gregory W. Stype

Baldwin's Ohio Tax Law and Rules

Ohio Building Code and Related Codes

Know Your Code: A Guide to the OBC
The PREVIEW Group, Inc.

Ohio Workers' Compensation Law Practice Guide

RELATED PRODUCTS

Jo Ann Wasil, Mark E. Mastrangelo & Robert E. DeRose

Ohio Forms Legal and Business

Ohio Forms and Transactions

Ohio Jurisprudence Pleading and Practice Forms (CD–ROM)

Ohio Criminal Defense Motions (CD–ROM)

Michael C. Hennenberg & Harry R. Reinhart

Baldwin's Ohio Revised Code Annotated

Baldwin's Ohio Legislative Service Annotated

Ohio Administrative Code

Ohio Administrative Law Handbook and Agency Directory

Frederick A. Vierow & Michael B. Lepp, Eds.

Ohio Monthly Record

West's Ohio Cases

Ohio State Reports, 3d

Ohio Appellate Reports, 3d

Ohio Miscellaneous Reports, 2d

West's Ohio Digest

Ohio Rules of Court, Federal

Ohio Rules of Court, State

Ohio Rules of Court, Local

Westlaw®

West CD–ROM Libraries™

WestCheck.com™

For more information about any of these Ohio practice tools, please call your West representative or 1–800–328–9352.

RELATED PRODUCTS

NEED RESEARCH HELP?

You can get quality research results with free help—call the West Reference Attorneys when you have questions concerning Westlaw or West Publications at 1–800–733–2889.

INTERNET ACCESS

Contact the West Editorial Department directly with your questions and suggestions by e-mail at west.editor@thomson.com.
Visit West's home page at west.thomson.com.

WESTLAW ELECTRONIC RESEARCH GUIDE

Westlaw—Expanding the Reach of Your Library

Westlaw is West's online legal research service. With Westlaw, you experience the same quality and integrity that you have come to expect from West books, plus quick, easy access to West's vast collection of statutes, case law materials, public records, and other legal resources, in addition to current news articles and business information. For the most current and comprehensive legal research, combine the strengths of West books and Westlaw.

When you research with westlaw.com you get the convenience of the Internet combined with comprehensive and accurate Westlaw content, including exclusive editorial enhancements, plus features found only in westlaw.com such as ResultsPlus™ or StatutesPlus.™

Accessing Databases Using the Westlaw Directory

The Westlaw Directory lists all databases on Westlaw and contains links to detailed information relating to the content of each database. Click Directory on the westlaw.com toolbar. There are several ways to access a database even when you don't know the database identifier. Browse a directory view. Scan the directory. Type all or part of a database name in the Search these Databases box. The Find a Database Wizard can help you select relevant databases for your search. You can access up to ten databases at one time for user defined multibase searching.

Retrieving a Specific Document

To retrieve a specific document by citation or title on westlaw.com click **Find&Print** on the toolbar to display the Find a Document page. If you are unsure of the correct citation format, type the publication abbreviation, e.g., **xx st** (where xx is a state's two-letter postal abbreviation), in the Enter Citation box and click **Go** to display a fill-in-the blank template. To retrieve a specific case when you know one or more parties' names, click **Find a Case by Party Name**.

KeyCite®

KeyCite, the citation research service on Westlaw, makes it easy to trace the history of your case, statute, administrative decision or regulation to determine if there are recent updates, and to find other documents that cite your document. KeyCite will also find pending legislation relating to federal or state statutes. Access the powerful features of KeyCite from the westlaw.com toolbar, the **Links** tab, or KeyCite flags in a document display. KeyCite's red and yellow warning flags tell you at a glance whether your document has negative history. Depth-of-treatment stars help you focus on the most important citing references. KeyCite Alert allows you to monitor the status of your case, statute or rule, and automatically sends you updates at the frequency you specify.

ResultsPlus™

ResultsPlus is a Westlaw technology that automatically suggests additional information related to your search. The suggested materials are accessible by a set of links that appear to the right of your westlaw.com search results:

- Go directly to relevant ALR® articles and Am Jur® annotations.
- Find on-point resources by key number.

WESTLAW GUIDE

- See information from related treatises and law reviews.

StatutesPlus™

When you access a statutes database in westlaw.com you are brought to a powerful Search Center which collects, on one toolbar, the tools that are most useful for fast, efficient retrieval of statutes documents:
- Have a few key terms? Click **Index**.
- Know the common name? Click **Popular Name Table**.
- Familiar with the subject matter? Click **Table of Contents**.
- Have a citation or section number? Click **Find by Citation**.
- Or, simply search with Natural Language or **Terms and Connectors**.

When you access a statutes section, click on the **Links** tab for all relevant links for the current document that will also include a KeyCite section with a description of the KeyCite status flag. Depending on your document, links may also include administrative, bill text, and other sources that were previously only available by accessing and searching other databases.

Additional Information

Westlaw is available on the Web at www.westlaw.com.

For search assistance, call the West Reference Attorneys at 1–800–REF–ATTY (1–800–733–2889).

For technical assistance, call West Customer Technical Support at 1–800–WESTLAW (1–800–937–8529).

Table of Contents

CONSTITUTION OF THE STATE OF OHIO (Selected Provisions)		1
Article		
I	Bill of Rights	1
II	Legislative	7
IV	Judicial	7
XII	Finance and Taxation	10
XV	Miscellaneous	10
XVIII	Municipal Corporations	10
OHIO REVISED CODE—TITLES 1 TO 17 (Selected Provisions)		13
Chapter		
163	Appropriation of Property	13
1335	Statute of Frauds	27
1336	Ohio Uniform Fraudulent Transfer Act	29
1337	Power of Attorney	33
1339	Fiduciary Law	54
1340	Fiduciary Law	59
1548	Watercraft Certificates of Title	63
1709	Uniform Transfer–On–Death Security Registration Act	64
OHIO REVISED CODE—TITLE 21, COURTS—PROBATE—JUVENILE		67
2101	Probate Court—Jurisdiction; Procedure	67
2103	Dower	122
2105	Descent and Distribution	134
2106	Rights of Surviving Spouses	176
2107	Wills	214
2108	Human Bodies or Parts Thereof	325
2109	Fiduciaries	347
2111	Guardians; Conservatorships	444
2113	Executors and Administrators—Appointment; Powers; Duties	506
2115	Executors and Administrators—Inventory	580
2117	Presentment of Claims Against Estate	593
2119	Trustee for Absentee	651
2121	Presumed Decedents' Law	653
2123	Determination of Heirship	659
2125	Action for Wrongful Death	664
2127	Sale of Lands	716
2129	Ancillary Administration	756
2131	Miscellaneous	769
2133	Modified Uniform Rights of the Terminally Ill Act and the DNR Identification and Do-Not-Resuscitate Order Law	788
2135	Declarations for Mental Health Treatment	812
2151	Juvenile Courts—General Provisions	818
2152	Juvenile Courts—Criminal Provisions	1156
2153	Cuyahoga County Juvenile Court	1243

TABLE OF CONTENTS

OHIO REVISED CODE—TITLES 23 TO 57 (Selected Provisions)		1249
2301	Organization	1249
2305	Jurisdiction; Limitation of Actions	1260
2717	Change of Name	1267
2901	General Provisions	1267
2945	Trial	1277
3103	Husband and Wife	1289
3105	Divorce, Legal Separation, Annulment, Dissolution of Marriage	1291
3107	Adoption	1294
3109	Children	1331
3111	Parentage	1360
3705	Vital Statistics	1391
3923	Sickness and Accident Insurance	1393
4505	Certificate of Motor Vehicle Title Law	1394
4507	Driver's License Law	1398
4511	Traffic Laws—Operation of Motor Vehicles	1403
5101	Job and Family Services Department—General Provisions	1427
5103	Placement of Children	1433
5122	Hospitalization of Mentally Ill	1446
5123	Department of Mental Retardation and Developmental Disabilities	1465
5126	County Boards of Mental Retardation and Developmental Disabilities	1528
5302	Statutory Forms of Land Conveyance	1532
5305	Dower	1536
5731	Estate Tax	1540
5747	Income Tax	1564
OHIO REVISED CODE—TITLE 58—TRUSTS		1611
5801	General Provisions	1611
5802	Judicial Proceedings	1617
5803	Representation	1618
5804	Creation, Validity, Modification and Termination of Trust	1619
5805	Spendthrift and Discretionary Trusts	1624
5806	Revocable Trusts	1627
5807	Office of Trustee	1628
5808	Powers and Duties of Trustee	1631
5809	Prudent Investor Act	1637
5810	Remedies for Breach of Trust	1640
5811	Miscellaneous Provisions	1644
5812	Uniform Principal and Income Act (1997)	1645
5813	Institutional Trust Funds Act	1657
5814	Ohio Transfers to Minors Act	1660
5815	Fiduciary Law	1666
OHIO COURT RULES		1691
	Rules of Juvenile Procedure	1693
	Rules of Superintendence for the Courts of Ohio	1819

TABLE OF CONTENTS

COMMON PLEAS COURT LOCAL RULES—PROBATE DIVISION (Selected Counties)	1881
Cuyahoga County Court of Common Pleas	1883
Franklin County Court of Common Pleas	1888
Hamilton County Court of Common Pleas	1901
Lucas County Court of Common Pleas	1912
Montgomery County Court of Common Pleas	1922
Local Rules of Court, Stark County Court of Common Pleas	1937
Summit County Court of Common Pleas	1946
INDEX	Index–1

*

CONSTITUTION OF THE STATE OF OHIO
(Selected Provisions)

Complete to February 28, 2007

ARTICLE
- I   Bill of Rights
- II Legislative
- IV Judicial

ARTICLE
- XII   Finance and Taxation
- XV   Miscellaneous
- XVIII Municipal Corporations

ARTICLE I

BILL OF RIGHTS

Section
- O Const I Sec 2   Equal protection and benefit
- O Const I Sec 5   Right of trial by jury
- O Const I Sec 9   Bail; cruel and unusual punishments
- O Const I Sec 12   No transportation or forfeiture for crime
- O Const I Sec 15   No imprisonment for debt
- O Const I Sec 16   Redress for injury; due process
- O Const I Sec 19   Eminent domain
- O Const I Sec 19a Wrongful death

Library References

Constitutional Law ⚖82(1), 83(1), 86, 87.

Westlaw Topic No. 92.

C.J.S. Constitutional Law §§ 445, 447 to 454, 460, 465, 467, 471 to 481, 505 to 512.

O Const I Sec. 2   Equal protection and benefit

All political power is inherent in the people. Government is instituted for their equal protection and benefit, and they have the right to alter, reform, or abolish the same, whenever they may deem it necessary; and no special privileges or immunities shall ever be granted, that may not be altered, revoked, or repealed by the General Assembly.

(1851 constitutional convention, adopted eff. 9–1–1851)

Uncodified Law

2003 S 86, § 3, eff. 7–12–04, reads:

(A) As used in this section, "health care professional," "health care worker," "indigent and uninsured person," "nonprofit health care referral organization," and "volunteer" have the same meanings as in section 2305.234 of the Revised Code, as amended by this act.

(B) The Ohio Medical Malpractice Commission created by Section 4 of Am. Sub. S.B. 281 of the 124th General Assembly shall have the following duties, in addition to the other duties provided by law for the Commission:

(1) To study the affordability and availability of medical malpractice insurance for health care professionals and health care workers who are volunteers and for nonprofit health care referral organizations;

(2) To study the feasibility of whether the state of Ohio should provide catastrophic claims coverage, or an insurance pool of any kind, for health care professionals and health care workers to utilize as volunteers in providing medical, dental, or other health-related diagnosis, care, or treatment to indigent and uninsured persons;

(3) To study the feasibility of whether the state of Ohio should create a fund to provide compensation to indigent and uninsured persons who receive medical, dental, or other health-related diagnosis, care, or treatment from health care professionals or health care workers who are volunteers, for any injury, death, or loss to person or property as a result of the negligence or other misconduct by those health care professionals or workers;

(4) To study whether the Good Samaritan laws of other states offer approaches that are materially different from the Ohio Good Samaritan Law as amended by this act, as contained in section 2305.234 of the Revised Code.

(C) The Commission shall submit a report of its findings regarding all of the matters provided in division (B) of this section to the members of the General Assembly not later than two years after the effective date of this act.

(D) The Department of Insurance shall provide any technical, professional, and clerical employees that are necessary for the Commission to perform its duties under this section.

2002 S 281, § 3, eff. 4–11–03, reads:

The General Assembly makes the following statement of findings and intent:

(A) The General Assembly finds:

(1) Medical malpractice litigation represents an increasing danger to the availability and quality of health care in Ohio.

(2) The number of medical malpractice claims resulting in payments to plaintiffs has remained relatively constant. However, the average award to plaintiffs has risen dramatically. Payments to plaintiffs at or exceeding one million dollars have doubled in the past three years.

(3) This state has a rational and legitimate state interest in stabilizing the cost of health care delivery by limiting the amount of compensatory damages representing noneconomic loss awards in medical malpractice actions. The overall cost of health care to the consumer has been driven up by the fact that malpractice litigation causes health care providers to over prescribe, over treat, and over test their patients. The General Assembly bases its finding on this state interest upon the following evidence:

(a) The Superintendent of Insurance has stated that medical malpractice insurers' investments are not to blame for the increase in medical malpractice insurance premiums. The vast majority of these insurers' assets are invested in bonds and other fixed income investments, not in stocks. Investment income declined by less than one per cent from 1996 to 2001.

(b) Many medical malpractice insurers left the Ohio market as they faced increasing losses, largely as a consequence of rapidly rising compensatory damages and noneconomic loss awards in medical malpractice actions. The Department of Insurance reports that only six admitted carriers continue to actively write coverage in Ohio at this time.

(c) As insurers have left the market, physicians, hospitals, and other health care practitioners have had an increasingly difficult time finding affordable medical malpractice insurance. Some health care practitioners, including a large number of specialists, have been forced out of the practice of medicine altogether as a consequence. The Ohio State Medical Association reports fifteen per cent of Ohio's physicians are considering or have already relocated their practices due to rising medical malpractice insurance costs.

(d) As stated in testimony provided by Lawrence E. Smarr, President of the Physician Insurers Association of America, medical malpractice costs have increased even while sixty-one per cent of all claims filed against individual practitioners are dropped or dismissed by the court and even while the defendants win eighty per cent of all claims that are continued through trial to verdict.

(e) The U.S. Department of Health and Human Services published a report in 2002 stating that health care practitioners in states with effective caps on noneconomic damages are experiencing premium increases in the twelve to fifteen per cent range, as compared to an average forty-four per cent increase in states that do not cap noneconomic damage awards.

(4)(a) The distinction among claimants with a permanent physical functional loss strikes a reasonable balance between potential plaintiffs and defendants in consideration of the intent of an award for noneconomic losses, while treating similar plaintiffs equally, acknowledging that such distinctions do not limit the award of actual economic damages.

(b) The limits on compensatory damages representing noneconomic loss as specified in section 2323.43 of the Revised Code, as enacted by this act, are based on testimony asking the members of the General Assembly to recognize these distinctions and stating that the cap amounts are similar to caps on awards adopted by other states.

(c) In *Evans v. State* (Sup. Ct. Alaska, August 30, 2002), No. 5618, 2002 Alas. LEXIS 135, one of the issues addressed by the Alaska Supreme Court is whether the caps on noneconomic and punitive damages constitute a violation of the right to a trial by jury granted by the Alaska Constitution and the Seventh Amendment to the United States Constitution. The Court held that the damages caps do not violate the constitutional right to a trial by jury and agreed with the reasoning by the Third Circuit Court of Appeals in *Davis v. Omitowoju* (3d Cir. 1989), 883 F.2d 1155, which interpreted the Seventh Amendment to the United States Constitution to allow damages caps. The Alaska Supreme Court relied on the *Davis* holding that a damages cap did not intrude on the jury's fact-finding function, because the cap was a "policy decision" applied after the jury's determination and did not constitute a re-examination of the factual question of damages. *Evans v. State, supra*, at pp. 11–12.

It is the intent of the General Assembly that as a matter of policy, the limits on compensatory damages for noneconomic loss are applied after a jury's determination of the factual question of damages.

(d) A report from the U.S. Department of Health and Human Services, *Update on the Medical Litigation Crisis: Not the Result of the Insurance Cycle* (Sept. 25, 2002), states that among states that have adopted a two hundred fifty thousand dollar cap on noneconomic damages are: Indiana, Colorado, California, Nebraska, Utah, and Montana. These states, as well as others that have imposed meaningful caps on noneconomic damages, report significantly lower increases in average premium rates than those states without caps. Limits on damages have been upheld by other state supreme courts, as in *Fein v. Permanente Medical Group* (1985), 38 Cal.3d 137, 695 P.2d 665, *Johnson v. St. Vincent Hospital, Inc.* (1980), 273 Ind. 374, 404 N.E.2d 585, and *Evans v. State, supra*.

(5) This legislation does not affect the award of economic damages, such as for lost wages and medical care.

(6)(a) That a statute of repose on medical, dental, optometric, and chiropractic claims strikes a rational balance between the rights of prospective claimants and the rights of hospitals and health care practitioners;

(b) Over time, the availability of relevant evidence pertaining to an incident and the availability of witnesses knowledgeable with respect to the diagnosis, care, or treatment of a prospective claimant becomes problematic.

(c) The maintenance of records and other documentation related to the delivery of medical services, for a period of time in excess of the time period presented in the statute of repose, presents an unacceptable burden to hospitals and health care practitioners.

(d) Over time, the standards of care pertaining to various health care services may change dramatically due to advances being made in health care, science, and technology, thereby making it difficult for expert witnesses and triers of fact to discern the standard of care relevant to the point in time when the relevant health care services were delivered.

(e) This legislation precludes unfair and unconstitutional aspects of state litigation but does not affect timely medical malpractice actions brought to redress legitimate grievances.

(f) This legislation addresses the aspects of current division (B) of section 2305.11 of the Revised Code, the application of which was found by the Ohio Supreme Court to be unconstitutional in *Gaines v. Preterm–Cleveland, Inc.* (1987), 33 Ohio St.3d 54. In *Dunn v. St. Francis Hospital, Inc.* (Del. 1982), 401 Atl.2d 77, the Delaware Supreme Court found the Delaware three-year statute of repose constitutional as not violative of the Delaware Constitution's open courts provision.

(B) In consideration of these findings, the General Assembly declares its intent to accomplish all of the following by the enactment of this act:

(1) To stem the exodus of medical malpractice insurers from the Ohio market;

(2) To increase the availability of medical malpractice insurance to Ohio's hospitals, physicians, and other health care practitioners, thus ensuring the availability of quality health care for the citizens of this state;

(3) To continue to hold negligent health care providers accountable for their actions;

(4) To preserve the right of patients to seek legal recourse for medical malpractice.

(5)(a) To abrogate the common law collateral source rules as adopted by the Ohio Supreme Court in *Pryor v. Webber* (1970), 23 Ohio St.2d 104, and reaffirmed in *Sorrell v. Thevenir* (1994), 69 Ohio St.3d 415;

(b) To address the aspects of former section 2317.45 of the Revised Code that the Supreme Court found in *Sorrell v. Thevenir* (1994), 69 Ohio St.3d 415, *May v. Tandy Corp.* (1994), 69 Ohio St.3d 415, and *DePew v. Ogella* (1994), 69 Ohio St.3d 610, to be unconstitutional as being violative of the equal protection provision of Section 2, the right to a trial by jury provision of Section 5, and the due course of law, right to a remedy, and open court provision of Section 16 of Article I of the Ohio Constitution.

(C)(1) The Ohio General Assembly respectfully requests the Ohio Supreme Court to uphold this intent in the courts of Ohio, to reconsider its holding on damage caps in *State v. Sheward* (1999), Ohio St.3d 451, to reconsider its holding on the deductibility of collateral source benefits in *Sorrel v. Thevenir* (1994), 69 Ohio St.3d 415, and to reconsider its holding on statutes of repose in *Sedar v. Knowlton Constr. Co.* (1990), 49 Ohio St.3d 193, thereby providing health care practitioners with access to affordable medical malpractice insurance and maintaining the provision of quality health care in Ohio.

(2) The General Assembly acknowledges the Court's authority in prescribing rules governing practice and procedure in the courts of this state as provided by Section 5 of Article IV of the Ohio Constitution.

2002 S 281, § 4, eff. 4–11–03, reads:

(A) There is hereby created the Ohio Medical Malpractice Commission consisting of nine members. The President of the Senate shall appoint three of the members, and the Speaker of the House of Representatives shall appoint three of the members. The minority leader of the Senate shall appoint one member and the minority leader of the House of Representatives shall appoint one member. The Director of the Department of Insurance or the Director's designee shall be the ninth member of the Commission. Of the six members appointed by the President of the Senate and the Speaker of the House of Representatives, one shall represent the Ohio State Bar Association, one shall represent the Ohio State Medical Association, and one shall represent the insurance companies in Ohio, and all of them shall have expertise in medical malpractice insurance issues.

(B) The Commission shall do all of the following:

(1) Study the effects of this act;

(2) Investigate the problems posed by, and the issues surrounding, medical malpractice;

(3) Submit a report of its findings to the members of the General Assembly not later than two years after the effective date of this act.

(C) Any vacancy in the membership of the Commission shall be filled in the same manner in which the original appointment was made.

(D) The members of the Commission shall by majority vote elect a chairperson from among themselves.

(E) The Department of Insurance shall provide any technical, professional, and clerical employees that are necessary for the Commission to perform its duties.

Library References

Constitutional Law ⊕82(8), 205(1), 209.
Westlaw Topic No. 92.

C.J.S. Constitutional Law §§ 461 to 462, 612, 614 to 619, 624 to 626, 652 to 653, 680, 700 to 701, 704, 706.

O Const I Sec. 5 Right of trial by jury

The right of trial by jury shall be inviolate, except that, in civil cases, laws may be passed to authorize the rendering of a verdict by the concurrence of not less than three-fourths of the jury.

(1912 constitutional convention, am. eff. 1–1–13; 1851 constitutional convention, adopted eff. 9–1–1851)

Library References

Jury ⚖9, 32(4).
Westlaw Topic No. 230.
C.J.S. Juries §§ 7 to 9, 12 to 20, 28 to 29, 31 to 32, 177, 244, 247, 267.

O Const I Sec. 9 Bail; cruel and unusual punishments

All persons shall be bailable by sufficient sureties, except for a person who is charged with a capital offense where the proof is evident or the presumption great, and except for a person who is charged with a felony where the proof is evident or the presumption great and where the person poses a substantial risk of serious physical harm to any person or to the community. Where a person is charged with any offense for which the person may be incarcerated, the court may determine at any time the type, amount, and conditions of bail. Excessive bail shall not be required; nor excessive fines imposed; nor cruel and unusual punishments inflicted.

The general assembly shall fix by law standards to determine whether a person who is charged with a felony where the proof is evident or the presumption great poses a substantial risk of serious physical harm to any person or to the community. Procedures for establishing the amount and conditions of bail shall be established pursuant to Article IV, Section 5(B) of the Constitution of the state of Ohio.

(1997 HJR 5, am. eff. 1–1–98; 1851 constitutional convention, adopted eff. 9–1–1851)

Library References

Bail ⚖42, 52.
Sentencing and Punishment ⚖1433 to 1607.
Westlaw Topic Nos. 49, 350H.
C.J.S. Bail.
C.J.S. Release and Detention Pending Proceedings §§ 6, 9 to 11, 13 to 15, 17, 19, 24 to 29, 31 to 32, 69.
C.J.S. Criminal Law §§ 1459, 1461, 1463, 1469, 1472, 1593 to 1603, 1605 to 1609.

O Const I Sec. 12 No transportation or forfeiture for crime

No person shall be transported out of the State, for any offense committed within the same; and no conviction shall work corruption of blood, or forfeiture of estate.

(1851 constitutional convention, adopted eff. 9–1–1851)

Library References

Forfeitures ⚖1.
Sentencing and Punishment ⚖2045 to 2047.
Westlaw Topic Nos. 180, 350H.
C.J.S. Criminal Law §§ 1459, 1461.
C.J.S. RICO (Racketeer Influenced and Corrupt Organizations) § 30.

O Const I Sec. 15 No imprisonment for debt

No person shall be imprisoned for debt in any civil action, on mesne or final process, unless in cases of fraud.

(1851 constitutional convention, adopted eff. 9–1–1851)

Library References

Constitutional Law ⚖83(3).
Westlaw Topic No. 92.
C.J.S. Constitutional Law §§ 487 to 490.

O Const I Sec. 16 Redress for injury; due process

All courts shall be open, and every person, for an injury done him in his land, goods, person, or reputation, shall have remedy by due course of law, and shall have justice administered without denial or delay. Suits may be brought against the state, in such courts and in such manner, as may be provided by law.

(1912 constitutional convention, am. eff. 1–1–13; 1851 constitutional convention, adopted eff. 9–1–1851)

Uncodified Law

2003 S 86, § 3, eff. 7–12–04, reads:

(A) As used in this section, "health care professional," "health care worker," "indigent and uninsured person," "nonprofit health care referral organization," and "volunteer" have the same meanings as in section 2305.234 of the Revised Code, as amended by this act.

(B) The Ohio Medical Malpractice Commission created by Section 4 of Am. Sub. S.B. 281 of the 124th General Assembly shall have the following duties, in addition to the other duties provided by law for the Commission:

(1) To study the affordability and availability of medical malpractice insurance for health care professionals and health care workers who are volunteers and for nonprofit health care referral organizations;

(2) To study the feasibility of whether the state of Ohio should provide catastrophic claims coverage, or an insurance pool of any kind, for health care professionals and health care workers to utilize as volunteers in providing medical, dental, or other health-related diagnosis, care, or treatment to indigent and uninsured persons;

(3) To study the feasibility of whether the state of Ohio should create a fund to provide compensation to indigent and uninsured persons who receive medical, dental, or other health-related diagnosis, care, or treatment from health care professionals or health care workers who are volunteers, for any injury, death, or loss to person or property as a result of the negligence or other misconduct by those health care professionals or workers;

(4) To study whether the Good Samaritan laws of other states offer approaches that are materially different from the Ohio Good Samaritan Law as amended by this act, as contained in section 2305.234 of the Revised Code.

(C) The Commission shall submit a report of its findings regarding all of the matters provided in division (B) of this section to the members of the General Assembly not later than two years after the effective date of this act.

(D) The Department of Insurance shall provide any technical, professional, and clerical employees that are necessary for the Commission to perform its duties under this section.

2002 S 281, § 3, eff. 4–11–03, reads:

The General Assembly makes the following statement of findings and intent:

(A) The General Assembly finds:

(1) Medical malpractice litigation represents an increasing danger to the availability and quality of health care in Ohio.

(2) The number of medical malpractice claims resulting in payments to plaintiffs has remained relatively constant. However, the average award to plaintiffs has risen dramatically. Payments to plaintiffs at or exceeding one million dollars have doubled in the past three years.

(3) This state has a rational and legitimate state interest in stabilizing the cost of health care delivery by limiting the amount of compensatory damages representing noneconomic loss awards in medical malpractice actions. The overall cost of health care to the consumer has been driven up by the fact that malpractice litigation causes health care providers to over prescribe, over treat, and over test their patients. The General Assembly bases its finding on this state interest upon the following evidence:

(a) The Superintendent of Insurance has stated that medical malpractice insurers' investments are not to blame for the increase in medical malpractice insurance premiums. The vast majority of these insurers' assets are invested in bonds and other fixed income investments, not in stocks. Investment income declined by less than one per cent from 1996 to 2001.

(b) Many medical malpractice insurers left the Ohio market as they faced increasing losses, largely as a consequence of rapidly rising compensatory damages and noneconomic loss awards in medical malpractice actions. The Department of Insurance reports that only six admitted carriers continue to actively write coverage in Ohio at this time.

(c) As insurers have left the market, physicians, hospitals, and other health care practitioners have had an increasingly difficult time finding affordable medical malpractice insurance. Some health care practitioners, including a large number of specialists, have been forced out of the practice of medicine altogether as a consequence. The Ohio State Medical Association reports fifteen per cent of Ohio's physicians are considering or have already relocated their practices due to rising medical malpractice insurance costs.

(d) As stated in testimony provided by Lawrence E. Smarr, President of the Physician Insurers Association of America, medical malpractice costs have increased even while sixty-one per cent of all claims filed against individual practitioners are dropped or dismissed by the court and even while the defendants win eighty per cent of all claims that are continued through trial to verdict.

(e) The U.S. Department of Health and Human Services published a report in 2002 stating that health care practitioners in states with effective caps on noneconomic damages are experiencing premium increases in the twelve to fifteen per cent range, as compared to an average forty-four per cent increase in states that do not cap noneconomic damage awards.

(4)(a) The distinction among claimants with a permanent physical functional loss strikes a reasonable balance between potential plaintiffs and defendants in consideration of the intent of an award for noneconomic losses, while treating similar plaintiffs equally, acknowledging that such distinctions do not limit the award of actual economic damages.

(b) The limits on compensatory damages representing noneconomic loss as specified in section 2323.43 of the Revised Code, as enacted by this act, are based on testimony asking the members of the General Assembly to recognize these distinctions and stating that the cap amounts are similar to caps on awards adopted by other states.

(c) In *Evans v. State* (Sup. Ct. Alaska, August 30, 2002), No. 5618, 2002 Alas. LEXIS 135, one of the issues addressed by the Alaska Supreme Court is whether the caps on noneconomic and punitive damages constitute a violation of the right to a trial by jury granted by the Alaska Constitution and the Seventh Amendment to the United States Constitution. The Court held that the damages caps do not violate the constitutional right to a trial by jury and agreed with the reasoning by the Third Circuit Court of Appeals in *Davis v. Omitowoju* (3d Cir. 1989), 883 F.2d 1155, which interpreted the Seventh Amendment to the United States Constitution to allow damages caps. The Alaska Supreme Court relied on the *Davis* holding that a damages cap did not intrude on the jury's fact-finding function, because the cap was a "policy decision" applied after the jury's determination and did not constitute a re-examination of the factual question of damages. *Evans v. State, supra*, at pp. 11–12.

It is the intent of the General Assembly that as a matter of policy, the limits on compensatory damages for noneconomic loss are applied after a jury's determination of the factual question of damages.

(d) A report from the U.S. Department of Health and Human Services, *Update on the Medical Litigation Crisis: Not the Result of the Insurance Cycle* (Sept. 25, 2002), states that among states that have adopted a two hundred fifty thousand dollar cap on noneconomic damages are: Indiana, Colorado, California, Nebraska, Utah, and Montana. These states, as well as others that have imposed meaningful caps on noneconomic damages, report significantly lower increases in average premium rates than those states without caps. Limits on damages have been upheld by other state supreme courts, as in *Fein v. Permanente Medical Group* (1985), 38 Cal.3d 137, 695 P.2d 665, *Johnson v. St. Vincent Hospital, Inc.* (1980), 273 Ind. 374, 404 N.E.2d 585, and *Evans v. State, supra*.

(5) This legislation does not affect the award of economic damages, such as for lost wages and medical care.

(6)(a) That a statute of repose on medical, dental, optometric, and chiropractic claims strikes a rational balance between the rights of prospective claimants and the rights of hospitals and health care practitioners;

(b) Over time, the availability of relevant evidence pertaining to an incident and the availability of witnesses knowledgeable with respect to the diagnosis, care, or treatment of a prospective claimant becomes problematic.

(c) The maintenance of records and other documentation related to the delivery of medical services, for a period of time in excess of the time period presented in the statute of repose, presents an unacceptable burden to hospitals and health care practitioners.

(d) Over time, the standards of care pertaining to various health care services may change dramatically due to advances being made in health care, science, and technology, thereby making it difficult for expert witnesses and triers of fact to discern the standard of care relevant to the point in time when the relevant health care services were delivered.

(e) This legislation precludes unfair and unconstitutional aspects of state litigation but does not affect timely medical malpractice actions brought to redress legitimate grievances.

(f) This legislation addresses the aspects of current division (B) of section 2305.11 of the Revised Code, the application of which was found by the Ohio Supreme Court to be unconstitutional in *Gaines v. Preterm–Cleveland, Inc.* (1987), 33 Ohio St.3d 54. In *Dunn v. St. Francis Hospital, Inc.* (Del. 1982), 401 Atl.2d 77, the Delaware Supreme Court found the Delaware three-year statute of repose constitutional as not violative of the Delaware Constitution's open courts provision.

(B) In consideration of these findings, the General Assembly declares its intent to accomplish all of the following by the enactment of this act:

(1) To stem the exodus of medical malpractice insurers from the Ohio market;

(2) To increase the availability of medical malpractice insurance to Ohio's hospitals, physicians, and other health care practitioners, thus ensuring the availability of quality health care for the citizens of this state;

(3) To continue to hold negligent health care providers accountable for their actions;

(4) To preserve the right of patients to seek legal recourse for medical malpractice.

(5)(a) To abrogate the common law collateral source rules as adopted by the Ohio Supreme Court in *Pryor v. Webber* (1970), 23 Ohio St.2d 104, and reaffirmed in *Sorrell v. Thevenir* (1994), 69 Ohio St.3d 415;

(b) To address the aspects of former section 2317.45 of the Revised Code that the Supreme Court found in *Sorrell v. Thevenir* (1994), 69 Ohio St.3d 415, *May v. Tandy Corp.* (1994), 69 Ohio St.3d 415, and *DePew v. Ogella* (1994), 69 Ohio St.3d 610, to be unconstitutional as being violative of the equal protection provision of Section 2, the right to a trial by jury provision of Section 5, and the due course of law, right to a remedy, and open court provision of Section 16 of Article I of the Ohio Constitution.

(C)(1) The Ohio General Assembly respectfully requests the Ohio Supreme Court to uphold this intent in the courts of Ohio, to reconsider its holding on damage caps in *State v. Sheward* (1999), Ohio St.3d 451, to reconsider its holding on the deductibility of collateral source benefits in *Sorrel v. Thevenir* (1994), 69 Ohio St.3d 415, and to reconsider its holding on statutes of repose in *Sedar v. Knowlton Constr. Co.* (1990), 49 Ohio St.3d 193, thereby providing health care practitioners with access to affordable medical malpractice insurance and maintaining the provision of quality health care in Ohio.

(2) The General Assembly acknowledges the Court's authority in prescribing rules governing practice and procedure in the courts of this state as provided by Section 5 of Article IV of the Ohio Constitution.

2002 S 281, § 4, eff. 4–11–03, reads:

(A) There is hereby created the Ohio Medical Malpractice Commission consisting of nine members. The President of the Senate shall appoint three of the members, and the Speaker of the House of Representatives shall appoint three of the members. The minority leader of the Senate shall appoint one member and the minority leader of the House of Representatives shall appoint one member. The Director of the Department of Insurance or the Director's designee shall be the ninth member of the Commission. Of the six members appointed by the President of the Senate and the Speaker of the House of Representatives, one shall represent the Ohio State Bar Association, one shall represent the Ohio State Medical Association, and one shall represent the insurance companies in Ohio, and all of them shall have expertise in medical malpractice insurance issues.

(B) The Commission shall do all of the following:

(1) Study the effects of this act;

(2) Investigate the problems posed by, and the issues surrounding, medical malpractice;

(3) Submit a report of its findings to the members of the General Assembly not later than two years after the effective date of this act.

(C) Any vacancy in the membership of the Commission shall be filled in the same manner in which the original appointment was made.

(D) The members of the Commission shall by majority vote elect a chairperson from among themselves.

(E) The Department of Insurance shall provide any technical, professional, and clerical employees that are necessary for the Commission to perform its duties.

1999 S 30, § 3, eff. 9–29–99, reads:

In amending sections 2329.13, 2329.14, 2329.26, and 2329.27 of the Revised Code in this act to require that a written notice of the date, time, and place of an execution sale of real or personal property be given to certain parties to the underlying action, it is the intent of the General Assembly to respond to the holdings of the Ohio Supreme Court in *Central Trust Co., N.A. v. Jensen* (1993), 67 Ohio St. 3d 140, the Court of Appeals of Clark County in *In re Foreclosure of Liens for Delinquent Taxes* (1992), 79 Ohio App. 3d 766, the Court of Appeals of Columbiana County in *Perpetual Savings Bank v. Samuelson* (1992), 1992 WL 380301, and the Court of Appeals of Hamilton County in *Central Trust Co., N.A. v. Spencer* (1987), 41 Ohio App. 3d 237, that publication notice of an execution sale of property may not afford interested parties with actual notice that is reasonably calculated, under all the circumstances, to apprise them of the pendency of the sale and to afford them an opportunity to take appropriate action to protect their interests and that satisfies the due process of law requirements of the Fourteenth Amendment to the United States Constitution and of Section 16 of Article I of the Ohio Constitution.

1995 H 371, § 2, eff. 8–16–95, reads: This act is hereby declared to be an emergency measure necessary for the immediate preservation of the public peace, health, and safety. The reason for the necessity is that, due to the decision of the United States Supreme Court in *Bendix Autolite Corp. v. Midwesco Enterprises, Inc.* (1988), 486 U.S. 888, that declared Ohio's tolling provisions pertaining to out-of-state defendants in section 2305.15(A) of the Revised Code to be unconstitutional as impermissibly burdening interstate commerce and due to the decision of the United States Supreme Court in *Reynoldsville Casket Co. v. Hyde* (1995), 1995 WL 283463, that declared that those tolling provisions did not continue to apply to tort claims that accrued before the decision in *Bendix* despite a contrary decision of the Ohio Supreme Court in *Hyde v. Reynoldsville Casket Co.* (1994), 68 Ohio St. 3d 240, an immediate, reasonable extension of the statutes of limitations for the commencement of a tort action based on bodily injury or an action for wrongful death is necessary so that claimants who filed a claim in the A.H. Robins Bankruptcy Reorganization in reliance on the tolling provisions of section 2305.15(A) of the Revised Code are not denied their right-to-remedy by due course of law under Section 16 of Article I of the Ohio Constitution because of the unanticipated, broad consequences of the holdings in *Bendix and Reynoldsville Casket Co.* that otherwise could bar claimants from commencing actions in Ohio courts against the Dalkon Shield Claimants Trust for bodily injury or wrongful death caused by the effects of the Dalkon Shield intrauterine device. Therefore, this act shall go into immediate effect.

Library References

Constitutional Law ⇐305(2), 321, 328.
Westlaw Topic No. 92.
C.J.S. Constitutional Law §§ 1141, 1165 to 1166, 1428 to 1432.

O Const I Sec. 19   Eminent domain

Private property shall ever be held inviolate, but subservient to the public welfare. When taken in time of war or other public exigency, imperatively requiring its immediate seizure, or for the purpose of making or repairing roads, which shall be open to the public, without charge, a compensation shall be made to the owner, in money, and in all other cases, where private property shall be taken for public use, a compensation therefor shall first be made in money, or first secured by a deposit of money, and such compensation shall be assessed by a jury, without deduction for benefits to any property of the owner.

(1851 constitutional convention, adopted eff. 9–1–1851)

Uncodified Law

2005 S 167, § 1 through 7, eff. 11–16–05, reads:

SECTION 1. As used in Sections 2 to 7 of this act:

(A) "Blighted area" has the same meaning as in section 303.26 of the Revised Code, but also includes an area in a municipal corporation.

(B) "Public body" means any entity of the state government, and any county, municipal corporation, township, commission, district, authority, or other political subdivision of the state, that has the power to take private property by eminent domain.

SECTION 2. (A) Notwithstanding any provision of the Revised Code to the contrary, until December 31, 2006, no public body shall use eminent domain to take, without the consent of the owner, private property that is not within a blighted area, as determined by the public body, when the primary purpose for the taking is economic development that will ultimately result in ownership of that property being vested in another private person.

(B)(1) Until December 31, 2006, if any public body uses eminent domain to take, without the consent of the owner, private property that is not within a blighted area, as determined by the public body, when the primary purpose for the taking is economic development that will ultimately result in ownership of that property being vested in another private person, each of the following shall apply:

(a) The Ohio Public Works Commission shall not award or distribute to the public body any funding under a capital improvement program created under Chapter 164. of the Revised Code.

(b) The Department of Development shall not award or distribute to the public body any funding under a shovel ready sites program created under section 122.083 of the Revised Code.

(c) The public body shall not receive any funding designated for capital purposes in any act of the General Assembly.

(2) Until December 31, 2006, any public body seeking to obtain funds described in division (B)(1) of this section, shall certify in writing to the grantor of the funds that the public body has not used its eminent domain authority on or after the effective date of this act to take private property in violation of the moratorium established by this act.

(C) Divisions (A) and (B) of this section do not apply to the use of eminent domain for the taking of private property to be used as follows:

(1) In the construction, maintenance, or repair of streets, roads, or walkways, paths, or other ways open to the public's use, including rights of way immediately adjacent to those public ways, including, but not limited to, such use pursuant to authority granted under Title LV of the Revised Code;

(2) For a public utility purpose;

(3) By a common carrier;

(4) For parks or recreation areas open to the public;

(5) In the construction, maintenance, or repair of buildings and grounds used for governmental purposes.

SECTION 3. (A) There is hereby created the Legislative Task Force to Study Eminent Domain and Its Use and Application in the State. The Task Force shall consist of the following twenty-five members:

(1) Three members of the House of Representatives, appointed by the Speaker of the House of Representatives in consultation with the Minority Leader of the House of Representatives. The Speaker of the House of Representatives shall designate one of the members the Speaker appoints to serve as co-chairperson of the Task Force.

(2) Three members of the Senate, appointed by the President of the Senate in consultation with the Minority Leader of the Senate. The President of the Senate shall designate one of the members the President appoints to serve as co-chairperson of the Task Force.

(3) One member representing the home building industry in the state, appointed jointly by the Speaker of the House of Representatives and the President of the Senate;

(4) One member who shall be a statewide advocate on the issues raised in *Kelo v. City of New London* (2005), 125 S. Ct. 2655, insofar as they affect

eminent domain, appointed jointly by the Speaker of the House of Representatives and the President of the Senate;

(5) One member representing the agricultural industry in the state, appointed jointly by the Speaker of the House of Representatives and the President of the Senate;

(6) One member representing the commercial real estate industry in the state, appointed jointly by the Speaker of the House of Representatives and the President of the Senate;

(7) One member representing licensed realtors in the state, appointed jointly by the Speaker of the House of Representatives and the President of the Senate;

(8) One member representing the Ohio Prosecuting Attorneys Association or the Ohio Association of Probate Judges, appointed jointly by the Speaker of the House of Representatives and the President of the Senate;

(9) One member who shall be an attorney who is knowledgeable on the issues confronting the Task Force and who represents persons who own property and reside within Ohio, appointed jointly by the Speaker of the House of Representatives and the President of the Senate;

(10) One member knowledgeable on the issues confronting the Task Force who represents persons who own property and reside within Ohio, appointed jointly by the Speaker of the House of Representatives and the President of the Senate;

(11) One member representing the planning industry in the state, one member representing an Ohio labor organization, one member representing a statewide historic preservation organization that works within commercial districts, one member representing municipal corporations, one member representing counties, and one member representing townships, each appointed by the Governor;

(12) The Director of Development or the Director's designee;

(13) The Director of Transportation or the Director's designee;

(14) Two members who shall be attorneys with expertise in eminent domain issues, each appointed by the Attorney General;

(15) One member representing small businesses, appointed jointly by the Speaker of the House of Representatives and the President of the Senate.

(B) Appointments to the Task Force shall be made not later than thirty days after the effective date of this section. Any vacancy in the membership of the Task Force shall be filled in the same manner as the original appointment. Members of the Task Force shall serve without compensation.

(C)(1) The Task Force shall study each of the following:

(a) The use of eminent domain and its impact on the state;

(b) How the decision of the United States Supreme Court in *Kelo v. City of New London* (2005), 125 S. Ct. 2655, affects state law governing the use of eminent domain in the state;

(c) The overall impact of state laws governing the use of eminent domain on economic development, residents, and local governments in Ohio.

(2) The Task Force shall prepare and submit to the General Assembly by not later than April 1, 2006, a report that shall include the findings of its study and recommendations concerning the use of eminent domain and its impact on the state, and by not later than August 1, 2006, a report that shall include findings and recommendations regarding the updating of state law governing eminent domain. On submission of the report due not later than August 1, 2006, the Task Force shall cease to exist.

(D) The Legislative Service Commission shall provide any technical, professional, and clerical employees that are necessary for the Task Force to perform its duties.

(E) All meetings of the Task Force are declared to be public meetings open to the public at all times. A member of the Task Force shall be present in person at a meeting that is open to the public in order to be considered present or to vote at the meeting and for the purposes of determining whether a quorum is present. The Task Force shall promptly prepare and maintain the minutes of its meetings, which shall be public records under section 149.43 of the Revised Code. The Task Force shall give reasonable notice of its meetings so that any person may determine the time and place of all scheduled meetings. The Task Force shall not hold a meeting unless it gives at least twenty-four hours advance notification to the news media organizations that have requested such notification.

SECTION 4. The General Assembly hereby makes the following statements of findings and intent:

(A) On June 23, 2005, the United States Supreme Court rendered its decision in *Kelo v. City of New London* (2005), 125 S. Ct. 2655, which allows the taking of private property that is not within a blighted area by eminent domain for the purpose of economic development even when the ultimate result of the taking is ownership of the property being vested in another private person. As a result of this decision, the General Assembly believes the interpretation and use of the state's eminent domain law could be expanded to allow the taking of private property that is not within a blighted area, ultimately resulting in ownership of that property being vested in another private person in violation of Sections 1 and 19 of Article I, Ohio Constitution, which protect the rights of Ohio citizens to maintain property as inviolate, subservient only to the public welfare. Thus, the General Assembly finds it is necessary to enact a moratorium on any takings of this nature by any public body until further legislative remedies may be considered.

(B) The General Assembly finds that it is a matter of statewide concern to enact the moratorium. The moratorium is necessary to protect the general welfare and the rights of citizens under Sections 1 and 19 of Article I, Ohio Constitution, and to ensure that these rights are not violated due to the *Kelo* decision. In enacting this provision, the General Assembly wishes to ensure uniformity throughout the state.

SECTION 5. Section 2 of this act applies only to taking actions initiated on or after the effective date of this act. As used in this section, "initiated" means the adoption of a resolution or ordinance of necessity by the public body or filing of a court action, but excludes taking actions for which a resolution or ordinance of necessity or other official action of a public body has been taken and public funds have been expended in connection with that taking action prior to the effective date of this act.

SECTION 6. If any item of law that constitutes the whole or part of an uncodified section of law contained in this act, or if any application of any item of law that constitutes the whole or part of an uncodified section of law contained in this act, is held invalid, the invalidity does not affect other items of law or applications of items of law that can be given effect without the invalid item of law or application. To this end, the items of law of which the uncodified sections contained in this act are composed, and their applications, are independent and severable.

SECTION 7. Nothing in this act shall be construed to imply that any public body with eminent domain authority has prior to the enactment of this act abused that authority or engaged in any wrongdoing in the exercise of its eminent domain authority conferred by statute or the Ohio Constitution.

Library References

Eminent Domain ⚖1.
Westlaw Topic No. 148.
C.J.S. Eminent Domain §§ 2 to 3.

O Const I Sec. 19a   Wrongful death

The amount of damages recoverable by civil action in the courts for death caused by the wrongful act, neglect, or default of another, shall not be limited by law.

(1912 constitutional convention, adopted eff. 1–1–13)

Library References

Death ⚖95(1), 96.
Westlaw Topic No. 117.
C.J.S. Death §§ 175, 192 to 195, 197 to 199.

ARTICLE II

LEGISLATIVE

Section
O Const II Sec 28   Retroactive laws; laws impairing obligation of contracts

O Const II Sec. 28   Retroactive laws; laws impairing obligation of contracts

The general assembly shall have no power to pass retroactive laws, or laws impairing the obligation of contracts; but may, by general laws, authorize courts to carry into effect, upon such terms as shall be just and equitable, the manifest intention of parties, and officers, by curing omissions, defects, and errors, in instruments and proceedings, arising out of their want of conformity with the laws of this state.

(1851 constitutional convention, adopted eff. 9-1-1851)

Uncodified Law

2002 S 180, § 4, eff. 4–9–03, reads, in part:

(C) It is the intent of the General Assembly to exercise its authority under Ohio Constitution, Article II, Section 28, to pass a general law authorizing courts to carry into effect, upon such terms as are just and equitable, the manifest intention of parties, and officers, by curing omissions, defects, and errors in instruments and proceedings arising out of their want of conformity with the laws of this state. This section is remedial legislation and does not affect pending or past complaints where jurisdiction over a complainant absolutely vested with a county board of revision. It is the intent of the General Assembly that if a board of revision never had jurisdiction over a complainant because the complainant's previous complaint failed to vest jurisdictional validity because of an unauthorized practice of law violation, then no rights have vested with respect to the determination of the total valuation or assessment of a commercial parcel owned by the complainant, and, as such, there is not a reasonable expectation of finality with regard to said determination. Further, it is the intent of the General Assembly that this section merely modifies the existing right of a property owner, granted under sections 5715.13 and 5715.19 of the Revised Code, to file a complaint against a determination of the total valuation or assessment of a commercial parcel owned by the complainant, by expanding the statute of limitations under which a complaint can be filed.

2002 S 180, § 5, eff. 4–9–03, reads:

Section 4 of this act is hereby repealed on the first day of the seventh month beginning after the effective date of this section.

Library References

Constitutional Law ⚖113, 186 to 198.

Statutes ⚖261 to 278.

Westlaw Topic Nos. 92, 361.

C.J.S. Constitutional Law §§ 277, 390 to 404, 406 to 413, 421, 424 to 426.
C.J.S. Statutes §§ 407 to 431.

ARTICLE IV

JUDICIAL

Section
O Const IV Sec 1   Judicial power vested in courts
O Const IV Sec 2   Organization and jurisdiction of supreme court
O Const IV Sec 3   Organization and jurisdiction of courts of appeals
O Const IV Sec 4   Organization and jurisdiction of common pleas courts
O Const IV Sec 5   Powers and duties of supreme court; superintendence of courts; rules

Historical and Statutory Notes

Ed. Note: Effective date and repeal date for revision of O Const Art IV by 132 v HJR 42 is May 7, 1968. See Euclid v Heaton, 15 OS(2d) 65, 238 NE(2d) 790 (1968).

Library References

Constitutional Law ⚖67.
Courts ⚖150, 206(15.1).
Westlaw Topic Nos. 92, 106.
C.J.S. Constitutional Law §§ 169 to 173.

O Const IV Sec. 1   Judicial power vested in courts

The judicial power of the state is vested in a supreme court, courts of appeals, courts of common pleas and divisions thereof, and such other courts inferior to the supreme court as may from time to time be established by law.

(1973 SJR 30, am. eff. 11-6-73; 132 v HJR 42, am. eff. 5-7-68; 1912 constitutional convention, am. eff. 1-1-13; 80 v 382, am. eff. 10-9-1883; 1851 constitutional convention, adopted eff. 9-1-1851)

Historical and Statutory Notes

Ed. Note: Effective date and repeal date for revision of O Const Art IV by 132 v HJR 42 is May 7, 1968. See Euclid v Heaton, 15 OS(2d) 65, 238 NE(2d) 790 (1968).

Library References

Courts ⚖206(15.1), 240.
Westlaw Topic No. 106.

O Const IV Sec. 2   Organization and jurisdiction of supreme court

(A) The supreme court shall, until otherwise provided by law, consist of seven judges, who shall be known as the chief justice and justices. In case of the absence or disability of the chief justice, the judge having the period of longest total service upon the court shall be the acting chief justice. If any member of the court shall be unable, by reason of illness, disability or disqualification, to hear, consider and decide a cause or causes, the chief justice or the acting chief justice may direct any judge of any court of appeals to sit with the judges of the supreme court in the place and stead of the absent judge. A majority of the supreme court shall be necessary to constitute a quorum or to render a judgment.

(B) (1) The supreme court shall have original jurisdiction in the following:

(a) Quo warranto;

(b) Mandamus;

(c) Habeas corpus;

(d) Prohibition;

(e) Procedendo;

(f) In any cause on review as may be necessary to its complete determination;

(g) Admission to the practice of law, the discipline of persons so admitted, and all other matters relating to the practice of law.

(2) The supreme court shall have appellate jurisdiction as follows:

(a) In appeals from the courts of appeals as a matter of right in the following:

(i) Cases originating in the courts of appeals;

(ii) Cases involving questions arising under the constitution of the United States or of this state.

(b) In appeals from the courts of appeals in cases of felony on leave first obtained,

(c) In direct appeals from the courts of common pleas or other courts of record inferior to the court of appeals as a matter of right in cases in which the death penalty has been imposed;

(d) Such revisory jurisdiction of the proceedings of administrative officers or agencies as may be conferred by law;

(e) In cases of public or great general interest, the supreme court may direct any court of appeals to certify its record to the supreme court, and may review and affirm, modify, or reverse the judgment of the court of appeals;

(f) The supreme court shall review and affirm, modify, or reverse the judgment in any case certified by any court of appeals pursuant to section 3 (B)(4) of this article.

(3) No law shall be passed or rule made whereby any person shall be prevented from invoking the original jurisdiction of the supreme court.

(C) The decisions in all cases in the supreme court shall be reported, together with the reasons therefor.

(1994 HJR 15, am. eff. 1–1–95; 132 v HJR 42, am. eff. 5–7–68; 120 v 743, am. eff. 11–7–44; 1912 constitutional convention, am. eff. 1–1–13; 80 v 382, am. eff. 10–9–1883; 1851 constitutional convention, adopted eff. 9–1–1851)

Uncodified Law

1995 H 167, § 3, eff. 10–25–95, reads: The General Assembly hereby requests the Supreme Court to promptly adopt rules pursuant to its authority under Ohio Constitution, Article IV, Section 2(B)(1)(g) and consistent with section 4705.021 of the Revised Code that would include as attorney misconduct for which an attorney may be disciplined situations in which a person licensed to practice law in the State of Ohio has been determined pursuant to division (B) of section 3113.21 of the Revised Code by a court or child support enforcement agency to be in default under a child support order.

Historical and Statutory Notes

Ed. Note: Effective date and repeal date for revision of O Const Art IV by 132 v HJR 42 is May 7, 1968. See Euclid v Heaton, 15 OS(2d) 65, 238 NE(2d) 790 (1968).

Library References

Courts ⇌206(15.1), 240.

Westlaw Topic No. 106.

O Const IV Sec. 3 Organization and jurisdiction of courts of appeals

(A) The state shall be divided by law into compact appellate districts in each of which there shall be a court of appeals consisting of three judges. Laws may be passed increasing the number of judges in any district wherein the volume of business may require such additional judge or judges. In districts having additional judges, three judges shall participate in the hearing and disposition of each case. The court shall hold sessions in each county of the district as the necessity arises. The county commissioners of each county shall provide a proper and convenient place for the court of appeals to hold court.

(B) (1) The courts of appeals shall have original jurisdiction in the following:

(a) Quo warranto;

(b) Mandamus;

(c) Habeas corpus;

(d) Prohibition;

(e) Procedendo;

(f) In any cause on review as may be necessary to its complete determination.

(2) Courts of appeals shall have such jurisdiction as may be provided by law to review and affirm, modify, or reverse judgments or final orders of the courts of record inferior to the court of appeals within the district, except that courts of appeals shall not have jurisdiction to review on direct appeal a judgment that imposes a sentence of death. Courts of appeals shall have such appellate jurisdiction as may be provided by law to review and affirm, modify, or reverse final orders or actions of administrative officers or agencies.

(3) A majority of the judges hearing the cause shall be necessary to render a judgment. Judgments of the courts of appeals are final except as provided in section 2 (B) (2) of this article. No judgment resulting from a trial by jury shall be reversed on the weight of the evidence except by the concurrence of all three judges hearing the cause.

(4) Whenever the judges of a court of appeals find that a judgment upon which they have agreed is in conflict with a judgment pronounced upon the same question by any other court of appeals of the state, the judges shall certify the record of the case to the supreme court for review and final determination.

(C) Laws may be passed providing for the reporting of cases in the courts of appeals.

(1994 HJR 15, am. eff. 1–1–95; 132 v HJR 42, adopted eff. 5–7–68)

Historical and Statutory Notes

Ed. Note: Former Art IV, § 3 repealed by 132 v HJR 42, eff. 5–7–68; 1912 constitutional convention, am. eff. 1–1–13; 1851 constitutional convention, adopted eff. 9–1–1851.

Ed. Note: Effective date and repeal date for revision of O Const Art IV by 132 v HJR 42 is May 7, 1968. See Euclid v Heaton, 15 OS(2d) 65, 238 NE(2d) 790 (1968).

Library References

Courts ⇌206(15.1), 240.

Westlaw Topic No. 106.

O Const IV Sec. 4 Organization and jurisdiction of common pleas courts

(A) There shall be a court of common pleas and such divisions thereof as may be established by law serving each county of the state. Any judge of a court of common pleas or a division thereof may temporarily hold court in any county. In the interests of the fair, impartial, speedy, and sure administration of justice, each county shall have one or more resident judges, or two or more counties may be combined into districts having one or more judges resident in the district and serving the common pleas courts of all counties in the district, as may be provided by law. Judges serving a district shall sit in each county in the district as the business of the court requires. In counties or districts having more than one judge of the court of common pleas, the judges shall select one of their number to act as presiding judge, to serve at their pleasure. If the judges are unable because of equal division of the vote to make such selection, the judge having the longest total service on the court of common pleas shall serve as presiding judge until selection is made by vote. The presiding judge shall have such duties and exercise such powers as are prescribed by rule of the supreme court.

(B) The courts of common pleas and divisions thereof shall have such original jurisdiction over all justiciable matters and such powers of review of proceedings of administrative officers and agencies as may be provided by law.

(C) Unless otherwise provided by law, there shall be a probate division and such other divisions of the courts of common pleas as may be provided by law. Judges shall be elected specifically to such probate division and to such other divisions. The judges of the probate division shall be empowered to employ and control the clerks, employees, deputies, and referees of such probate division of the common pleas courts.

(1973 SJR 30, am. eff. 11–6–73; 132 v HJR 42, adopted eff. 5–7–68)

Historical and Statutory Notes

Ed. Note: Former Art IV, § 4 repealed by 132 v HJR 42, eff. 5–7–68; 1851 constitutional convention, adopted eff. 9–1–1851.

Ed. Note: Art IV, § 4 contains provisions analogous to former Art IV, § 7, 8, and 12, repealed by 132 v HJR 42, eff. 5–7–68.

Ed. Note: Effective date and repeal date for revision of O Const Art IV by 132 v HJR 42 is May 7, 1968. See Euclid v Heaton, 15 OS(2d) 65, 238 NE(2d) 790 (1968).

Library References

Courts ⚖150.
Westlaw Topic No. 106.

O Const IV Sec. 5 Powers and duties of supreme court; superintendence of courts; rules

(A) (1) In addition to all other powers vested by this article in the supreme court, the supreme court shall have general superintendence over all courts in the state. Such general superintending power shall be exercised by the chief justice in accordance with rules promulgated by the supreme court.

(2) The supreme court shall appoint an administrative director who shall assist the chief justice and who shall serve at the pleasure of the court. The compensation and duties of the administrative director shall be determined by the court.

(3) The chief justice or acting chief justice, as necessity arises, shall assign any judge of a court of common pleas or a division thereof temporarily to sit or hold court on any other court of common pleas or division thereof or any court of appeals or shall assign any judge of a court of appeals temporarily to sit or hold court on any other court of appeals or any court of common pleas or division thereof and upon such assignment said judge shall serve in such assigned capacity until the termination of the assignment. Rules may be adopted to provide for the temporary assignment of judges to sit and hold court in any court established by law.

(B) The supreme court shall prescribe rules governing practice and procedure in all courts of the state, which rules shall not abridge, enlarge, or modify any substantive right. Proposed rules shall be filed by the court, not later than the fifteenth day of January, with the clerk of each house of the general assembly during a regular session thereof, and amendments to any such proposed rules may be so filed not later than the first day of May in that session. Such rules shall take effect on the following first day of July, unless prior to such day the general assembly adopts a concurrent resolution of disapproval. All laws in conflict with such rules shall be of no further force or effect after such rules have taken effect.

Courts may adopt additional rules concerning local practice in their respective courts which are not inconsistent with the rules promulgated by the supreme court. The supreme court may make rules to require uniform record keeping for all courts of the state, and shall make rules governing the admission to the practice of law and discipline of persons so admitted.

(C) The chief justice of the supreme court or any judge of that court designated by him shall pass upon the disqualification of any judge of the courts of appeals or courts of common pleas or division thereof. Rules may be adopted to provide for the hearing of disqualification matters involving judges of courts established by law.

(1973 SJR 30, am. eff. 11–6–73; 132 v HJR 42, adopted eff. 5–7–68)

Uncodified Law

1997 H 215, § 163, eff. 6–30–97, reads:

The General Assembly hereby requests that the Supreme Court adopt, pursuant to its authority under Ohio Constitution, Article IV, Section 5, rules governing procedure in juvenile courts of the state that address the placement of children in foster homes in a county other than the county in which the child resided at the time of the removal.

1990 H 346, § 4, eff. 5–31–90, reads: The General Assembly hereby requests the supreme court to exercise its general superintendence authority over courts in this state, pursuant to section 5(A)(1) of Article IV, Ohio Constitution, to adopt standard probate forms that provide notice, to all distributees of an estate when assets are distributed prior to the one-year bar on claims established under section 2117.06 of the Revised Code, of their potential liabilities with respect to claims filed within the statutory time limitation.

Historical and Statutory Notes

Ed. Note: Former Art IV, § 5 repealed by 80 v 382, eff. 10–9–1883; 1851 constitutional convention, adopted eff. 9–1–1851.

Ed. Note: Effective date and repeal date for revision of O Const Art IV by 132 v HJR 42 is May 7, 1968. See Euclid v Heaton, 15 OS(2d) 65, 238 NE(2d) 790 (1968).

Ed. Note: Guidelines for Assignment of Judges were announced by the Chief Justice of the Ohio Supreme Court on 5–24–88, and revised 2–25–94 and 3–25–94, but not adopted as rules pursuant to O Const Art IV §5. For the full text, see 37 OS(3d) xxxix, 61 OBar A–2 (6–13–88) and 69 OS(3d) XCIX, and 67 OBar xiii (4–18–94).

Library References

Courts ⚖78 to 86.
Westlaw Topic No. 106.
C.J.S. Courts §§ 7, 124 to 134.

ARTICLE XII

FINANCE AND TAXATION

Section
O Const XII Sec 3   Estate and inheritance taxes; income taxes; excise and franchise taxes

O Const XII Sec. 3   Estate and inheritance taxes; income taxes; excise and franchise taxes

Laws may be passed providing for:

(A) The taxation of decedents' estates or of the right to receive or succeed to such estates, and the rates of such taxation may be uniform or may be graduated based on the value of the estate, inheritance, or succession. Such tax may also be levied at different rates upon collateral and direct inheritances, and a portion of each estate may be exempt from such taxation as provided by law.

(B) The taxation of incomes, and the rates of such taxation may be either uniform or graduated, and may be applied to such incomes and with such exemptions as may be provided by law.

(C) Excise and franchise taxes and for the imposition of taxes upon the production of coal, oil, gas, and other minerals; except that no excise tax shall be levied or collected upon the sale or purchase of food for human consumption off the premises where sold.

(1976 HJR 15, adopted eff. 6–8–76)

Historical and Statutory Notes

Ed. Note: Art XII, § 3 contains provisions analogous to former Art XII, § 7, 8, 10, and 12, repealed by 1976 HJR 15, eff. 6–8–76.

Ed. Note: Former Art XII, § 3 repealed by 113 v 790, eff. 1–1–31; 1851 constitutional convention, adopted eff. 9–1–1851.

Library References

Mines and Minerals ⟾87.
Taxation ⟾856, 931 to 933, 1201 to 1205.
Westlaw Topic Nos. 260, 371.
C.J.S. Mines and Minerals §§ 334, 373 to 374.
C.J.S. Taxation §§ 1693 to 1694, 1696, 1785, 1990 to 1994.

ARTICLE XV

MISCELLANEOUS

Section
O Const XV Sec 11   Defense of marriage

O Const XV Sec. 11   Defense of marriage

Only a union between one man and one woman may be a marriage valid in or recognized by this state and its political subdivisions. This state and its political subdivisions shall not create or recognize a legal status for relationships of unmarried individuals that intends to approximate the design, qualities, significance or effect of marriage.

(Adopted by initiative petition, eff. 12–2–04)

ARTICLE XVIII

MUNICIPAL CORPORATIONS

Section
O Const XVIII Sec 3   Municipal powers of local self-government
O Const XVIII Sec 10   Acquiring property exceeding public needs

O Const XVIII Sec. 3   Municipal powers of local self-government

Municipalities shall have authority to exercise all powers of local self-government and to adopt and enforce within their limits such local police, sanitary and other similar regulations, as are not in conflict with general laws.

(1912 constitutional convention, adopted eff. 11–15–12)

Uncodified Law

2002 H 386, § 3, eff. 5–24–02, reads:

(A) The provisions of the Revised Code, including, but not limited to, Titles XI, XIII, XVII, and XLVII, relating to the origination, granting, servicing, and collection of loans and other forms of credit prescribe rules of conduct upon citizens generally, comprise a comprehensive regulatory framework intended to operate uniformly throughout the state under the same circumstances and conditions, and constitute general laws within the meaning of Section 3 of Article XVIII of the Ohio Constitution.

(B) The provisions of the Revised Code, including, but not limited to, Titles XI, XIII, XVII, and XLVII, relating to the origination, granting, servicing, and collection of loans and other forms of credit have been enacted in furtherance of the police powers of the state.

(C) Silence in the Revised Code, including, but not limited to, Titles XI, XIII, XVII, and XLVII, with respect to any act or practice in the origination, granting, servicing, or collection of loans or other forms of credit shall not be interpreted to mean that the state has not completely occupied the field or has only set minimum standards in its regulation of lending and other credit activities.

(D) It is the intent of the General Assembly to entirely preempt municipal corporations and other political subdivisions from the regulation and licensing of lending and other credit activities.

Library References

Municipal Corporations ⟾57 to 61.
Westlaw Topic No. 268.
C.J.S. Municipal Corporations §§ 104, 106 to 108, 110 to 122, 134, 136 to 138, 143, 145 to 146, 150 to 151, 156 to 158, 160 to 161.

O Const XVIII Sec. 10   Acquiring property exceeding public needs

A municipality appropriating or otherwise acquiring property for public use may in furtherance of such public use appropriate or acquire an excess over that actually to be occupied by the improvement, and may sell such excess with such restrictions as shall be appropriate to preserve the improvement made. Bonds may be issued to supply the funds in whole or in part to pay for the excess property so appropriated or otherwise acquired, but said bonds shall be a lien only against the property so acquired for the improvement and excess, and they shall not be a liability of the municipality nor be included in any limitation of the bonded indebtedness of such municipality prescribed by law.

(1912 constitutional convention, adopted eff. 11–15–12)

Uncodified Law

2005 S 167, § 1 through 7, eff. 11–16–05, reads:

SECTION 1. As used in Sections 2 to 7 of this act:

(A) "Blighted area" has the same meaning as in section 303.26 of the Revised Code, but also includes an area in a municipal corporation.

(B) "Public body" means any entity of the state government, and any county, municipal corporation, township, commission, district, authority, or other political subdivision of the state, that has the power to take private property by eminent domain.

SECTION 2. (A) Notwithstanding any provision of the Revised Code to the contrary, until December 31, 2006, no public body shall use eminent domain to take, without the consent of the owner, private property that is not within a blighted area, as determined by the public body, when the primary purpose for the taking is economic development that will ultimately result in ownership of that property being vested in another private person.

(B)(1) Until December 31, 2006, if any public body uses eminent domain to take, without the consent of the owner, private property that is not within a blighted area, as determined by the public body, when the primary purpose for the taking is economic development that will ultimately result in ownership of that property being vested in another private person, each of the following shall apply:

(a) The Ohio Public Works Commission shall not award or distribute to the public body any funding under a capital improvement program created under Chapter 164. of the Revised Code.

(b) The Department of Development shall not award or distribute to the public body any funding under a shovel ready sites program created under section 122.083 of the Revised Code.

(c) The public body shall not receive any funding designated for capital purposes in any act of the General Assembly.

(2) Until December 31, 2006, any public body seeking to obtain funds described in division (B)(1) of this section, shall certify in writing to the grantor of the funds that the public body has not used its eminent domain authority on or after the effective date of this act to take private property in violation of the moratorium established by this act.

(C) Divisions (A) and (B) of this section do not apply to the use of eminent domain for the taking of private property to be used as follows:

(1) In the construction, maintenance, or repair of streets, roads, or walkways, paths, or other ways open to the public's use, including rights of way immediately adjacent to those public ways, including, but not limited to, such use pursuant to authority granted under Title LV of the Revised Code;

(2) For a public utility purpose;

(3) By a common carrier;

(4) For parks or recreation areas open to the public;

(5) In the construction, maintenance, or repair of buildings and grounds used for governmental purposes.

SECTION 3. (A) There is hereby created the Legislative Task Force to Study Eminent Domain and Its Use and Application in the State. The Task Force shall consist of the following twenty-five members:

(1) Three members of the House of Representatives, appointed by the Speaker of the House of Representatives in consultation with the Minority Leader of the House of Representatives. The Speaker of the House of Representatives shall designate one of the members the Speaker appoints to serve as co-chairperson of the Task Force.

(2) Three members of the Senate, appointed by the President of the Senate in consultation with the Minority Leader of the Senate. The President of the Senate shall designate one of the members the President appoints to serve as co-chairperson of the Task Force.

(3) One member representing the home building industry in the state, appointed jointly by the Speaker of the House of Representatives and the President of the Senate;

(4) One member who shall be a statewide advocate on the issues raised in *Kelo v. City of New London* (2005), 125 S. Ct. 2655, insofar as they affect eminent domain, appointed jointly by the Speaker of the House of Representatives and the President of the Senate;

(5) One member representing the agricultural industry in the state, appointed jointly by the Speaker of the House of Representatives and the President of the Senate;

(6) One member representing the commercial real estate industry in the state, appointed jointly by the Speaker of the House of Representatives and the President of the Senate;

(7) One member representing licensed realtors in the state, appointed jointly by the Speaker of the House of Representatives and the President of the Senate;

(8) One member representing the Ohio Prosecuting Attorneys Association or the Ohio Association of Probate Judges, appointed jointly by the Speaker of the House of Representatives and the President of the Senate;

(9) One member who shall be an attorney who is knowledgeable on the issues confronting the Task Force and who represents persons who own property and reside within Ohio, appointed jointly by the Speaker of the House of Representatives and the President of the Senate;

(10) One member knowledgeable on the issues confronting the Task Force who represents persons who own property and reside within Ohio, appointed jointly by the Speaker of the House of Representatives and the President of the Senate;

(11) One member representing the planning industry in the state, one member representing an Ohio labor organization, one member representing a statewide historic preservation organization that works within commercial districts, one member representing municipal corporations, one member representing counties, and one member representing townships, each appointed by the Governor;

(12) The Director of Development or the Director's designee;

(13) The Director of Transportation or the Director's designee;

(14) Two members who shall be attorneys with expertise in eminent domain issues, each appointed by the Attorney General;

(15) One member representing small businesses, appointed jointly by the Speaker of the House of Representatives and the President of the Senate.

(B) Appointments to the Task Force shall be made not later than thirty days after the effective date of this section. Any vacancy in the membership of the Task Force shall be filled in the same manner as the original appointment. Members of the Task Force shall serve without compensation.

(C)(1) The Task Force shall study each of the following:

(a) The use of eminent domain and its impact on the state;

(b) How the decision of the United States Supreme Court in *Kelo v. City of New London* (2005), 125 S. Ct. 2655, affects state law governing the use of eminent domain in the state;

(c) The overall impact of state laws governing the use of eminent domain on economic development, residents, and local governments in Ohio.

(2) The Task Force shall prepare and submit to the General Assembly by not later than April 1, 2006, a report that shall include the findings of its study and recommendations concerning the use of eminent domain and its impact on the state, and by not later than August 1, 2006, a report that shall include findings and recommendations regarding the updating of state law governing eminent domain. On submission of the report due not later than August 1, 2006, the Task Force shall cease to exist.

(D) The Legislative Service Commission shall provide any technical, professional, and clerical employees that are necessary for the Task Force to perform its duties.

(E) All meetings of the Task Force are declared to be public meetings open to the public at all times. A member of the Task Force shall be present in person at a meeting that is open to the public in order to be considered present or to vote at the meeting and for the purposes of determining whether a quorum is present. The Task Force shall promptly prepare and maintain the minutes of its meetings, which shall be public records under section 149.43 of the Revised Code. The Task Force shall give reasonable notice of its meetings so that any person may determine the time and place of all scheduled meetings. The Task Force shall not hold a meeting unless it gives at least twenty-four hours advance notification to the news media organizations that have requested such notification.

SECTION 4. The General Assembly hereby makes the following statements of findings and intent:

(A) On June 23, 2005, the United States Supreme Court rendered its decision in *Kelo v. City of New London* (2005), 125 S. Ct. 2655, which allows the taking of private property that is not within a blighted area by eminent domain for the purpose of economic development even when the ultimate result of the taking is ownership of the property being vested in another private person. As a result of this decision, the General Assembly believes the interpretation and use of the state's eminent domain law could be expanded to allow the taking of private property that is not within a blighted area, ultimately resulting in ownership of that property being vested in another private person in violation of Sections 1 and 19 of Article I, Ohio Constitution, which protect the rights of Ohio citizens to maintain property as inviolate, subservient only to the public welfare. Thus, the General Assembly finds it is necessary to enact a moratorium on any takings of this nature by any public body until further legislative remedies may be considered.

(B) The General Assembly finds that it is a matter of statewide concern to enact the moratorium. The moratorium is necessary to protect the general welfare and the rights of citizens under Sections 1 and 19 of Article I, Ohio Constitution, and to ensure that these rights are not violated due to the *Kelo* decision. In enacting this provision, the General Assembly wishes to ensure uniformity throughout the state.

SECTION 5. Section 2 of this act applies only to taking actions initiated on or after the effective date of this act. As used in this section, "initiated" means the adoption of a resolution or ordinance of necessity by the public body or filing of a court action, but excludes taking actions for which a resolution or ordinance of necessity or other official action of a public body has been taken and public funds have been expended in connection with that taking action prior to the effective date of this act.

SECTION 6. If any item of law that constitutes the whole or part of an uncodified section of law contained in this act, or if any application of any item of law that constitutes the whole or part of an uncodified section of law contained in this act, is held invalid, the invalidity does not affect other items of law or applications of items of law that can be given effect without the invalid item of law or application. To this end, the items of law of which the uncodified sections contained in this act are composed, and their applications, are independent and severable.

SECTION 7. Nothing in this act shall be construed to imply that any public body with eminent domain authority has prior to the enactment of this act abused that authority or engaged in any wrongdoing in the exercise of its eminent domain authority conferred by statute or the Ohio Constitution.

Library References

Eminent Domain ⚖12 to 60.
Municipal Corporations ⚖221 to 225.
Westlaw Topic Nos. 148, 268.
C.J.S. Eminent Domain §§ 24, 27, 29 to 69.
C.J.S. Municipal Corporations §§ 873 to 882.

OHIO REVISED CODE
TITLES 1 TO 17
(Selected Provisions)

Complete to February 28, 2007

CHAPTER		CHAPTER	
163	Appropriation of Property	1339	Fiduciary Law
1335	Statute of Frauds	1340	Fiduciary Law
1336	Ohio Uniform Fraudulent Transfer Act	1548	Watercraft Certificates of Title
1337	Power of Attorney	1709	Uniform Transfer–On–Death Security Registration Act

CHAPTER 163

APPROPRIATION OF PROPERTY

GENERAL PROVISIONS

Section
- 163.01 Definitions
- 163.02 Applicability of chapter; exceptions
- 163.03 Entry for surveys, examinations, etc.; notice; restitution for damages
- 163.04 Limitations

CIVIL ACTIONS; PROCEDURE

- 163.05 Petition for appropriation
- 163.06 Deposit with court; appraisal of structures
- 163.07 Service of summons and copy of petition to owners
- 163.08 Answer by owner; making roads open to public without charge; construction plans as presumptive evidence
- 163.09 Declaration of value and damages; time for assessment of compensation by jury; hearings
- 163.10 Selection of jury
- 163.11 Appointment of guardian ad litem
- 163.12 View of premises; defect in proceedings; new parties
- 163.13 Delay; retention of deposit until rights of parties determined
- 163.14 Jury; verdict
- 163.15 When agency entitled to possession; filing of journal entry with auditor
- 163.16 Court costs; confession of judgment
- 163.17 Withdrawal of deposit by owner; accrual of interest; deposit on appeal; refund
- 163.18 Notice of deposit or payment; motion for distribution
- 163.19 Appeals
- 163.20 Appropriation to perfect title
- 163.21 Abandonment of proceedings
- 163.22 Laws and rules applicable to civil actions to govern; advancement

ADVERTISING DEVICES

- 163.31 Definitions
- 163.32 Order for removal of advertising device; interests deemed taken; action to appropriate
- 163.33 Payment to owner of land and of device before removal; exception

RELOCATION ASSISTANCE

- 163.51 Definitions
- 163.52 Validity of acquisition; elements of value or damage not affected

Section
- 163.53 Application for relocation payments; eligibility; relocation of utility facility
- 163.54 Additional payment for replacement dwelling
- 163.55 Additional payment for rental dwelling or down payment on house
- 163.56 Relocation assistance advisory program
- 163.57 Replacement housing
- 163.58 Regulations and procedures; rulemaking powers
- 163.59 Policies for public land acquisition
- 163.60 Payment for buildings, structures and improvements on real property
- 163.61 Payment for other incidental expenses
- 163.62 Award by court having jurisdiction

Historical and Statutory Notes

Ed. Note: Chapter 163 contains provisions analogous to former 123.22 to 123.38 repealed by 131 v S 94, eff. 1–1–66.

Ed. Note: Chapter 163 contains provisions analogous to former Chapter 2709, repealed by 131 v S 94, eff. 1–1–66.

Comparative Laws

Cal.—West's Ann.Cal.Civ.Proc.Code § 1245.010 et seq.
Del.—29 Del.C. § 9301 et seq.
Ind.—West's A.I.C. 32–11–1–1.
Iowa—I.C.A. § 6B.1 et seq.
Mass.—M.G.L.A. c. 79A, § 1 et seq.
Mont.—MCA 70–31–101 et seq.

GENERAL PROVISIONS

163.01 Definitions

As used in sections 163.01 to 163.22 of the Revised Code:

(A) "Public agency" means any governmental corporation, unit, organization, or officer authorized by law to appropriate property in the courts of this state. "Private agency" means any other corporation, firm, partnership, voluntary association, joint-stock association, or company authorized by law to appropriate property in the courts of this state. "Agency" includes any public agency or private agency.

(B) "Court" includes the court of common pleas and the probate court of any county in which the property sought to be appropriated is located in whole or in part.

(C) "Owner" includes any individual, partnership, association, or corporation having any estate, title, or interest in any real property sought to be appropriated.

(D) "Real property," "land," or "property" includes any estate, title, or interest in any real property which is authorized to be appropriated by the agency in question, unless the context otherwise requires.

(1991 H 201, eff. 6–30–91; 131 v S 94)

Uncodified Law

2005 S 167, § 1 through 7, eff. 11–16–05, reads:

SECTION 1. As used in Sections 2 to 7 of this act:

(A) "Blighted area" has the same meaning as in section 303.26 of the Revised Code, but also includes an area in a municipal corporation.

(B) "Public body" means any entity of the state government, and any county, municipal corporation, township, commission, district, authority, or other political subdivision of the state, that has the power to take private property by eminent domain.

SECTION 2. (A) Notwithstanding any provision of the Revised Code to the contrary, until December 31, 2006, no public body shall use eminent domain to take, without the consent of the owner, private property that is not within a blighted area, as determined by the public body, when the primary purpose for the taking is economic development that will ultimately result in ownership of that property being vested in another private person.

(B)(1) Until December 31, 2006, if any public body uses eminent domain to take, without the consent of the owner, private property that is not within a blighted area, as determined by the public body, when the primary purpose for the taking is economic development that will ultimately result in ownership of that property being vested in another private person, each of the following shall apply:

(a) The Ohio Public Works Commission shall not award or distribute to the public body any funding under a capital improvement program created under Chapter 164. of the Revised Code.

(b) The Department of Development shall not award or distribute to the public body any funding under a shovel ready sites program created under section 122.083 of the Revised Code.

(c) The public body shall not receive any funding designated for capital purposes in any act of the General Assembly.

(2) Until December 31, 2006, any public body seeking to obtain funds described in division (B)(1) of this section, shall certify in writing to the grantor of the funds that the public body has not used its eminent domain authority on or after the effective date of this act to take private property in violation of the moratorium established by this act.

(C) Divisions (A) and (B) of this section do not apply to the use of eminent domain for the taking of private property to be used as follows:

(1) In the construction, maintenance, or repair of streets, roads, or walkways, paths, or other ways open to the public's use, including rights of way immediately adjacent to those public ways, including, but not limited to, such use pursuant to authority granted under Title LV of the Revised Code;

(2) For a public utility purpose;

(3) By a common carrier;

(4) For parks or recreation areas open to the public;

(5) In the construction, maintenance, or repair of buildings and grounds used for governmental purposes.

SECTION 3. (A) There is hereby created the Legislative Task Force to Study Eminent Domain and Its Use and Application in the State. The Task Force shall consist of the following twenty-five members:

(1) Three members of the House of Representatives, appointed by the Speaker of the House of Representatives in consultation with the Minority Leader of the House of Representatives. The Speaker of the House of Representatives shall designate one of the members the Speaker appoints to serve as co-chairperson of the Task Force.

(2) Three members of the Senate, appointed by the President of the Senate in consultation with the Minority Leader of the Senate. The President of the Senate shall designate one of the members the President appoints to serve as co-chairperson of the Task Force.

(3) One member representing the home building industry in the state, appointed jointly by the Speaker of the House of Representatives and the President of the Senate;

(4) One member who shall be a statewide advocate on the issues raised in *Kelo v. City of New London* (2005), 125 S. Ct. 2655, insofar as they affect eminent domain, appointed jointly by the Speaker of the House of Representatives and the President of the Senate;

(5) One member representing the agricultural industry in the state, appointed jointly by the Speaker of the House of Representatives and the President of the Senate;

(6) One member representing the commercial real estate industry in the state, appointed jointly by the Speaker of the House of Representatives and the President of the Senate;

(7) One member representing licensed realtors in the state, appointed jointly by the Speaker of the House of Representatives and the President of the Senate;

(8) One member representing the Ohio Prosecuting Attorneys Association or the Ohio Association of Probate Judges, appointed jointly by the Speaker of the House of Representatives and the President of the Senate;

(9) One member who shall be an attorney who is knowledgeable on the issues confronting the Task Force and who represents persons who own property and reside within Ohio, appointed jointly by the Speaker of the House of Representatives and the President of the Senate;

(10) One member knowledgeable on the issues confronting the Task Force who represents persons who own property and reside within Ohio, appointed jointly by the Speaker of the House of Representatives and the President of the Senate;

(11) One member representing the planning industry in the state, one member representing an Ohio labor organization, one member representing a statewide historic preservation organization that works within commercial districts, one member representing municipal corporations, one member representing counties, and one member representing townships, each appointed by the Governor;

(12) The Director of Development or the Director's designee;

(13) The Director of Transportation or the Director's designee;

(14) Two members who shall be attorneys with expertise in eminent domain issues, each appointed by the Attorney General;

(15) One member representing small businesses, appointed jointly by the Speaker of the House of Representatives and the President of the Senate.

(B) Appointments to the Task Force shall be made not later than thirty days after the effective date of this section. Any vacancy in the membership of the Task Force shall be filled in the same manner as the original appointment. Members of the Task Force shall serve without compensation.

(C)(1) The Task Force shall study each of the following:

(a) The use of eminent domain and its impact on the state;

(b) How the decision of the United States Supreme Court in *Kelo v. City of New London* (2005), 125 S. Ct. 2655, affects state law governing the use of eminent domain in the state;

(c) The overall impact of state laws governing the use of eminent domain on economic development, residents, and local governments in Ohio.

(2) The Task Force shall prepare and submit to the General Assembly by not later than April 1, 2006, a report that shall include the findings of its study and recommendations concerning the use of eminent domain and its impact on the state, and by not later than August 1, 2006, a report that shall include findings and recommendations regarding the updating of state law governing eminent domain. On submission of the report due not later than August 1, 2006, the Task Force shall cease to exist.

(D) The Legislative Service Commission shall provide any technical, professional, and clerical employees that are necessary for the Task Force to perform its duties.

(E) All meetings of the Task Force are declared to be public meetings open to the public at all times. A member of the Task Force shall be present in person at a meeting that is open to the public in order to be considered present or to vote at the meeting and for the purposes of determining whether a quorum is present. The Task Force shall promptly prepare and maintain the minutes of its meetings, which shall be public records under section 149.43 of the Revised Code. The Task Force shall give reasonable notice of its meetings so that any person may determine the time and place of all scheduled meetings. The Task Force shall not hold a meeting unless it gives at least twenty-four hours advance notification to the news media organizations that have requested such notification.

SECTION 4. The General Assembly hereby makes the following statements of findings and intent:

(A) On June 23, 2005, the United States Supreme Court rendered its decision in *Kelo v. City of New London* (2005), 125 S. Ct. 2655, which allows the taking of private property that is not within a blighted area by eminent domain for the purpose of economic development even when the ultimate result of the taking is ownership of the property being vested in another private person. As a result of this decision, the General Assembly believes the interpretation and use of the state's eminent domain law could be expanded to allow the taking of private property that is not within a blighted area, ultimately resulting in ownership of that property being vested in another private person in violation of Sections 1 and 19 of Article I, Ohio Constitution, which protect the rights of Ohio citizens to maintain property as inviolate, subservient only to the public welfare. Thus, the General Assembly finds it is necessary to enact a moratorium on any takings of this nature by any public body until further legislative remedies may be considered.

(B) The General Assembly finds that it is a matter of statewide concern to enact the moratorium. The moratorium is necessary to protect the general welfare and the rights of citizens under Sections 1 and 19 of Article I, Ohio Constitution, and to ensure that these rights are not violated due to the *Kelo* decision. In enacting this provision, the General Assembly wishes to ensure uniformity throughout the state.

SECTION 5. Section 2 of this act applies only to taking actions initiated on or after the effective date of this act. As used in this section, "initiated" means the adoption of a resolution or ordinance of necessity by the public body or filing of a court action, but excludes taking actions for which a resolution or ordinance of necessity or other official action of a public body has been taken and public funds have been expended in connection with that taking action prior to the effective date of this act.

SECTION 6. If any item of law that constitutes the whole or part of an uncodified section of law contained in this act, or if any application of any item of law that constitutes the whole or part of an uncodified section of law contained in this act, is held invalid, the invalidity does not affect other items of law or applications of items of law that can be given effect without the invalid item of law or application. To this end, the items of law of which the uncodified sections contained in this act are composed, and their applications, are independent and severable.

SECTION 7. Nothing in this act shall be construed to imply that any public body with eminent domain authority has prior to the enactment of this act abused that authority or engaged in any wrongdoing in the exercise of its eminent domain authority conferred by statute or the Ohio Constitution.

1994 S 182, § 5, eff. 10–20–94, reads:

As used in this section, "agency" has the same meaning as in section 163.01 of the Revised Code.

In the event of an appropriation where an agency otherwise would appropriate real property containing a lot devoted to residential use and the appropriation would cause any building on that lot to be closer to the property line resulting from the appropriation than is permissible under local zoning regulations, the agency shall appropriate the entire lot, or shall be required to pay compensation or damages sufficient in amount to relocate the building on the lot to such a location that the building is not closer to the resulting property line than is permissible under local zoning regulations.

This section applies to condemnation proceedings in progress on the effective date of this act, provided a verdict has not been issued on or before that date, under any section of the Revised Code providing for appropriations of real property.

163.02 Applicability of chapter; exceptions

(A) Except as provided in divisions (B), (C), (D), and (F) of this section, all appropriations of real property shall be made pursuant to sections 163.01 to 163.22 of the Revised Code.

(B) Subject to division (E) of this section, the director of transportation may appropriate real property pursuant to sections 163.01 to 163.22 of the Revised Code or as otherwise provided by law.

(C) Subject to division (E) of this section, a conservancy district may appropriate real property by procedures prescribed in Chapter 6101. of the Revised Code.

(D) Subject to division (E) of this section, a sanitary district may appropriate real property by procedures prescribed in Chapter 6115. of the Revised Code.

(E) When the director of transportation, a conservancy district, or a sanitary district proceeds to appropriate real property other than under sections 163.01 to 163.22 of the Revised Code, the proceedings are subject to division (B) of section 163.21 of the Revised Code.

(F) A county, township that has adopted a limited home rule government, conservancy district, sanitary district, county sewer district, or a regional water and sewer district also may appropriate real property in the manner prescribed in division (B) of section 307.08, 6101.181, 6115.221, 6117.39, or 6119.11 or division (D) of section 504.19 of the Revised Code, as applicable.

(G) Any instrument by which the state or an agency of the state acquires real property pursuant to this section shall identify the agency of the state that has the use and benefit of the real property as specified in section 5301.012 of the Revised Code.

(2004 H 411, eff. 5–6–05; 1999 H 19, eff. 10–26–99; 1987 H 57, eff. 9–10–87; 1973 H 200; 131 v S 94)

Historical and Statutory Notes

Amendment Note: 2004 H 411 inserted ", and (F)" in division (A); added new content in division (F); renumbered former division (F) as new (G); and made other nonsubstantive changes.

Amendment Note: 1999 H 19 added division (F).

Library References

Eminent Domain ⚖167(1, 3, 4).
Westlaw Topic No. 148.
C.J.S. Eminent Domain § 201–202, 204–205.

163.03 Entry for surveys, examinations, etc.; notice; restitution for damages

Any agency may, upon the notice prescribed in this section, prior to or subsequent to the filing of a petition pursuant to section 163.05 of the Revised Code, enter upon any lands, waters, and premises for the purpose of making such surveys, soundings, drillings, appraisals, and examinations as are necessary or proper for the purpose of the agency under sections 163.01 to 163.22, inclusive, of the Revised Code, and such entry shall not constitute a trespass. Notice of such proposed entry shall be given to the owner or the person in possession by such means as are reasonably available not less than forty-eight hours nor more than thirty days prior to the date of such entry.

The agency shall make restitution or reimbursement for any actual damage resulting to such lands, waters, and premises and to improvements or personal property located in, on, along, over, or under such lands, waters, and premises, as a result of such activities. If the parties are unable to agree upon restitution or other settlement, damages are recoverable by civil action to which the state or agency hereby consents.

(131 v S 94, eff. 1–1–66)

Library References

Eminent Domain ⚖179.1–184, 186.
Westlaw Topic No. 148.
C.J.S. Eminent Domain § 220, 237–246.

163.04 Limitations

Appropriations shall be made only after the agency is unable to agree, for any reason, with the owner, or if more than one, any owner, or his guardian or trustee, or when any owner is incapable of contracting in person or by agent and has no guardian or trustee, or is unknown, or is not a resident of this state, or his residence is unknown to the agency and cannot with reasonable diligence be ascertained.

(131 v S 94, eff. 1–1–66)

Library References

Eminent Domain ⚖170.
Westlaw Topic No. 148.
C.J.S. Eminent Domain § 215–218.

CIVIL ACTIONS; PROCEDURE

163.05 Petition for appropriation

An agency which has met the requirements of section 163.04 of the Revised Code, may commence proceedings in a proper court by filing a petition for appropriation of each parcel or contiguous parcels in a single common ownership, or interest or right therein. The petition of a private agency shall be verified as in a civil action and all petitions shall contain:

(A) A description of each parcel of land or interest or right therein sought to be appropriated, such as will permit ready identification of the land involved;

(B) In the case of a private agency, a statement that such appropriation is necessary, and, in the case of a public agency, a copy of the resolution of the public agency to appropriate;

(C) A statement of the purpose of the appropriation;

(D) A statement of the estate or interest sought to be appropriated;

(E) The names and addresses of the owners, so far as they can be ascertained;

(F) A statement showing requirements of section 163.04 of the Revised Code have been met;

(G) A prayer for the appropriation;

(H) In the event of an appropriation where the agency would require less than the whole of any parcel containing a residence structure and the required portion would remove a garage and sufficient land that a replacement garage could not be lawfully or practically attached, the appropriation shall be for the whole parcel and all structures.

In the event of the appropriation of less than the fee of any parcel or of a fee in less than the whole of any parcel of property, the agency shall either make available to the owner or shall file in the office of the county engineer, a description of the nature of the improvement or use which requires the appropriation, including any specifications, elevations, and grade changes already determined at the time of the filing of the petition, in sufficient detail to permit a determination of the nature, extent, and effect of the taking and improvement. A set of highway construction plans shall be acceptable in providing such description for the purposes of the preceding sentence in the appropriation of land for highway purposes.

(1994 H 790, eff. 9–12–94; 132 v H 132, eff. 8–8–67; 131 v S 94)

Historical and Statutory Notes

Amendment Note: 1994 H 790 added division (H).

Library References

Eminent Domain ⚖191.
Westlaw Topic No. 148.
C.J.S. Eminent Domain § 249.

163.06 Deposit with court; appraisal of structures

(A) A public agency, other than an agency appropriating property for the purposes described in division (B) of this section, which qualifies pursuant to Section 19 of Article I, Ohio Constitution, may deposit with the court at the time of filing the petition the value of such property appropriated together with the damages, if any, to the residue, as determined by the public agency, and thereupon take possession of and enter upon the property appropriated. The right of possession upon deposit as provided in this division shall not extend to structures.

(B) A public agency appropriating property for the purpose of making or repairing roads which shall be open to the public, without charge, or for the purpose of implementing rail service under Chapter 4981. of the Revised Code, may deposit with the court at the time of filing the petition the value of such property appropriated together with the damages, if any, to the residue, as determined by the public agency, and stated in an attached declaration of intention to obtain possession and thereupon take possession of and enter upon the property appropriated, including structures situated upon the land appropriated for such purpose or situated partly upon the land appropriated therefor and partly upon adjoining land, so that such structures cannot be divided upon the line between such lands without manifest injury thereto. The jury, in assessing compensation to any owner of land appropriated under this division shall assess the value thereof in accordance with section 163.14 of the Revised Code. The owner or occupant of such structures shall vacate the same within sixty days after service of summons as required under section 163.07 of the Revised Code, at no cost to the appropriating agency, after which time the agency may remove said structures. In the event such structures are to be removed before the jury has fixed the value of the same, the court, upon motion of the agency, shall:

(1) Order appraisals to be made by three persons, one to be named by the owner, one by the county auditor, and one by the agency. Such appraisals may be used as evidence by the owner or the agency in the trial of said case but shall not be binding on said owner, agency, or the jury, and the expense of said appraisals shall be approved by the court and charged as costs in said case.

(2) Cause pictures to be taken of all sides of said structures;

(3) Compile a complete description of said structures, which shall be preserved as evidence in said case to which the owner or occupants shall have access.

(C) Any time after the deposit is made by the public agency under division (A) or (B) of this section, the owner may apply to the court to withdraw the deposit, and such withdrawal shall in no way interfere with the action except that the sum so withdrawn shall be deducted from the sum of the final verdict or award. Upon such application being made the court shall direct that the sum be paid to such owner subject to the rights of other parties in interest provided such parties make timely application as provided in section 163.18 of the Revised Code. Interest shall not accrue on any sums withdrawable as provided in this division.

(1994 H 250, eff. 10–20–94; 1986 S 289, eff. 6–24–86; 132 v H 188, H 132, H 1; 131 v S 94)

Historical and Statutory Notes

Amendment Note: 1994 H 250 deleted "intercity passenger" before "rail service" in division (B).

Library References

Eminent Domain ⇌188.
Westlaw Topic No. 148.
C.J.S. Eminent Domain § 221.

163.07 Service of summons and copy of petition to owners

When the residence of the owners is known and is within this state, notice of the filing of a petition as provided in section 163.05 of the Revised Code shall be given to all such owners by serving a summons and a copy of such petition in the manner of service of summons in civil actions. When the residence of the owners is unknown, and as to all who cannot be served within the state, notice shall be given by publishing the substance of the petition, and a statement of the date of the filing thereof and of the date on and after which the matter may be heard, once a week for two consecutive weeks, in a newspaper of general circulation in the county, or shall be given by registered mail. When service is made by publication, section 2703.16 [1] of the Revised Code shall be complied with.

Unless a person acquiring any interest in any property described in an appropriation petition after the filing thereof moves to be made an additional party defendant prior to the date that the case is set for the jury trial on compensation or to any journalization of a settlement entry, he shall be bound by the final judgment, without right of appeal except as to distribution, and shall receive such compensation as was awarded to his predecessor in interest to the extent that he has succeeded thereto.

(131 v S 94, eff. 1–1–66)

[1] So in original; 2703.16 repealed by 1970 H 1201, eff. 7–1–71; see now Civ R 4.4 for provisions analogous to former 2703.16.

Library References

Eminent Domain ⇌182.
Westlaw Topic No. 148.
C.J.S. Eminent Domain § 240–243.

163.08 Answer by owner; making roads open to public without charge; construction plans as presumptive evidence

Any owner may file an answer to such petition. Such answer shall be verified as in a civil action and shall contain a general denial or specific denial of each material allegation not admitted. The agency's right to make the appropriation, the inability of the parties to agree, and the necessity for the appropriation shall be resolved by the court in favor of the agency unless such matters are specifically denied in the answer and the facts relied upon in support of such denial are set forth therein, provided, when taken in time of war or other public exigency, imperatively requiring its immediate seizure or for the purpose of making or repairing roads, which shall be open to the public, without charge, an answer may not deny the right to make the appropriation, the inability of the parties to agree, or the necessity for the appropriation. A petition for appropriation, filed by the director of transportation, which contains a declaration and journalization of his intent to construct a state highway or interstate highway, shall constitute a presumption that such appropriation is for the purpose of making or repairing roads which shall be open to the public without charge. At a hearing on an issue whether a taking sought by the director of transportation is for the purpose of making or repairing roads open to the public without charge, a set of construction plans made by or for the director and showing the proposed use of the property in connection with the construction or repair of such a road is presumptive evidence of such purpose, notwithstanding that no money has been appropriated for such construction or repair.

An answer shall be served in accordance with Civil Rule 12. If the agency involved in the action is a private agency, no more than one extension of the time authorized by Civil Rule 12 for serving an answer shall be granted pursuant to Civil Rule 6, and that extension shall not exceed thirty days.

(1983 H 373, eff. 7–1–83; 1981 S 61; 131 v S 94)

Library References

Eminent Domain ⇌186, 192.
Westlaw Topic No. 148.
C.J.S. Eminent Domain § 220, 261–263.

163.09 Declaration of value and damages; time for assessment of compensation by jury; hearings

(A) If no answer is filed pursuant to section 163.08 of the Revised Code, and no approval ordered by the court to a settlement of the rights of all necessary parties, the court, on motion of a public agency, shall declare the value of the property taken and the damages, if any, to the residue to be as set forth in any document properly filed with the clerk of the court of common pleas by the public agency. In all other cases, the court shall fix a time, within twenty days from the last date that the answer could have been filed, for the assessment of compensation by a jury.

(B) When an answer is filed pursuant to section 163.08 of the Revised Code and any of the matters relating to the right to make the appropriation, the inability of the parties to agree, or the necessity for the appropriation are specifically denied in the manner provided in that section, the court shall set a day, not less than five or more than fifteen days from the date the answer was filed, to hear those matters. Upon those matters, the burden of proof is upon the owner. A resolution or ordinance of the governing or controlling body, council, or board of the agency declaring the necessity for the appropriation shall be prima-facie evidence of that necessity in the absence of proof showing an abuse of discretion by the agency in determining that necessity. If, as to any or all of the property or other interests sought to be appropriated, the court determines the matters in favor of the agency, the court shall set a time for the assessment of compensation by the jury within twenty days from the date of the journalization of that determination. An order of the court in favor of the agency on any of the matters or on qualification under section 163.06 of the Revised Code shall not be a final order for purposes of appeal. An order of the court against the agency on any of the matters or on the question of qualification under section 163.06 of the Revised Code shall be a final order for purposes of appeal. If a public agency has taken possession prior to such an order and such an order, after any appeal, is against the agency on any of the matters, the agency shall restore the property to the owner in its original condition or respond in damages, which may include the items set forth in division (A)(2) of section 163.21 of the Revised Code, recoverable by civil action, to which the state consents.

(C) When an answer is filed pursuant to section 163.08 of the Revised Code, and none of the matters set forth in division (B) of this section is specifically denied, the court shall fix a time within twenty days from the date the answer was filed for the assessment of compensation by a jury.

(D) If answers are filed pursuant to divisions (B) and (C) of this section, or an answer is filed on behalf of fewer than all the named owners, the court shall set the hearing or hearings at such times as are reasonable under all the circumstances, but in no event later than twenty days after the issues are joined as to all necessary parties or twenty days after rule therefor, whichever is earlier.

(E) The court, with the consent of the parties, may order two or more cases to be consolidated and tried together, but the rights of each owner to compensation, damages, or both shall be separately determined by the jury in its verdict.

(F) If an answer is filed under section 163.08 of the Revised Code with respect to the value of property appropriated under section 307.08, 504.19, 6101.181, 6115.221, 6117.39, or 6119.11 of the Revised Code as the result of a public exigency, the burden of proof with respect to that value is on the party or parties to the appropriation other than the property owners.

(2004 H 411, eff. 5–6–05; 1987 H 57, eff. 9–10–87; 1969 H 1; 132 v H 188, H 132; 131 v S 94)

Historical and Statutory Notes

Amendment Note: 2004 H 411 substituted "and no" for "nor", inserted "the residue" and substituted "the court of common pleas" for "courts" in division (A); added division (F); and made other nonsubstantive changes throughout.

Library References

Eminent Domain ⇔198–223.
Westlaw Topic No. 148.
C.J.S. Eminent Domain § 171, 267–268, 270–280, 282–286, 288, 290–315, 320.

163.10 Selection of jury

The assessment of compensation may be made at a regular or special term of court. The jury shall be selected from the jurors drawn as prescribed in sections 2313.19 to 2313.26 of the Revised Code, and qualified as in civil actions. However, it shall be grounds for challenge for cause if a juror has served in two appropriation trials in the current term of court.

(2001 H 73, eff. 6–29–01; 1973 H 200, eff. 9–28–73; 131 v S 94)

Historical and Statutory Notes

Amendment Note: 2001 H 73 deleted the last three sentences of the section, which prior thereto read:

"Depositions may be taken as in other civil cases, subject to the requirements of section 5501.21 of the Revised Code. Depositions of the officers, agents, or employees of the agency or owner shall be taken as on cross-examination. No evidence may be adduced or elicited in depositions as to value or appraisals on cross-examination, unless raised by direct examination."

Library References

Eminent Domain ⇔209.
Westlaw Topic No. 148.
C.J.S. Eminent Domain § 290.

163.11 Appointment of guardian ad litem

If it appears that any of the owners is an infant or otherwise incompetent, and has no guardian, a guardian ad litem shall be appointed in his behalf.

(131 v S 94, eff. 1–1–66)

Library References

Infants ⇔78(1).
Westlaw Topic No. 211.
C.J.S. Infants § 223–229.

163.12 View of premises; defect in proceedings; new parties

(A) A view of the premises to be appropriated or of premises appropriated shall be ordered by the court when demanded by a party to the proceedings.

(B) The property owners shall open and close the case except that, if the premises are appropriated under section 307.08, 504.19, 6101.181, 6115.221, 6117.39, or 6119.11 of the Revised Code as the result of a public exigency, the party or parties other than the owners shall open and close the case.

(C) The court may amend any defect or informality in proceedings under sections 163.01 to 163.22 of the Revised Code. The court may cause new parties to be added and direct further notice to be given to a party in interest as the court considers proper.

(D) No part of the pleadings, other than the petition, shall be read or exhibited to the jury.

(2004 H 411, eff. 5–6–05; 131 v S 94, eff. 1–1–66)

Historical and Statutory Notes

Amendment Note: 2004 H 411 designated divisions (A) through (D); inserted "or of premises appropriated" in division (A); inserted the text after "case" in division (B); deleted ", inclusive," and substituted "considers" for "deems" in division (C); and made other nonsubstantive changes throughout.

Library References

Eminent Domain ⇔175.1, 178, 220.
Westlaw Topic No. 148.
C.J.S. Eminent Domain § 228, 232–233, 302.

163.13 Delay; retention of deposit until rights of parties determined

No delay in the proceedings shall be occasioned by doubt as to the ownership of any property, or as to the interest of the respective owners, but in such cases the court may require the retention of the deposit or award or such portion thereof as the court deems appropriate, until the rights of the respective parties have been determined.

(131 v S 94, eff. 1–1–66)

Library References

Eminent Domain ⇔188, 198(1).
Westlaw Topic No. 148.
C.J.S. Eminent Domain § 221, 267, 270.

163.14 Jury; verdict

In appropriation proceedings the jury shall be sworn to impartially assess the compensation and damages, if any, without deductions for general benefits as to the property of the owner.

The jury, in its verdict, shall assess the compensation for the property appropriated and damages, if any, to the residue, to be paid to the owners. When a building or other structure is on the property appropriated or when a building or other structure is situated partly upon the land appropriated and partly upon adjoining land so that the structure cannot be divided upon the line between such lands without manifest injury thereto, the jury, in assessing compensation to any owner of the land, shall assess the value thereof, as part of the compensation. The title to said structure shall vest in the agency which shall have the right to enter upon the adjoining land upon which any part of the structure is located for the purpose of removing said structure therefrom, after deposit in accordance with the verdict. Such removal shall be made within ninety days after taking title to the property appropriated; provided, that the court may extend removal time upon such conditions as the court requires.

The verdict shall be signed by at least three-fourths of the members of the jury.

If a jury is discharged without rendering a verdict, another shall be impaneled at the earliest convenient time and shall make the inquiry and assessment.

(132 v H 132, eff. 8–8–67; 131 v S 94)

Library References

Eminent Domain ⟐209, 223.
Westlaw Topic No. 148.
C.J.S. Eminent Domain § 290, 312–314.

163.15 When agency entitled to possession; filing of journal entry with auditor

As soon as the agency pays to the party entitled thereto or deposits with the court the amount of the award and the costs assessed against the agency, it may take possession; provided, that this shall not be construed to limit the right of a public agency to enter and take possession, as provided in section 163.06 of the Revised Code. When the agency is entitled to possession the court shall enter an order to such effect upon the record and, if necessary, process shall be issued to place the agency in possession. Whenever a final journal entry in an appropriation proceeding, granting to this state a fee title or any lesser estate or interest in real property is filed and journalized by the clerk of courts, the clerk of courts shall forthwith transmit to the county auditor a certified copy of said final journal entry who shall transfer the property on his books and transmit said entry with proper endorsement to the county recorder for recording. The costs of filing such final journal entry with the county auditor and the county recorder shall be taxed as costs in the appropriation proceedings the same as other costs are taxed under section 163.16 of the Revised Code.

(132 v S 38, eff. 4–29–68; 131 v S 94)

Library References

Eminent Domain ⟐187.
Westlaw Topic No. 148.
C.J.S. Eminent Domain § 210–212.

163.16 Court costs; confession of judgment

The court costs, including jury fees, of any proceeding shall be paid as the court directs, except as may be provided for in cases subject to division (A)(2) or (B)(1) of section 163.21 of the Revised Code. The agency may offer to confess judgment for the amount to be stated and the court costs then made in favor of any owner who in any manner enters an appearance or upon whom service has been made. If such owner refuses to accept such offer and as a result of the trial does not receive more, he shall pay all court costs accruing after the offer.

(1987 H 57, eff. 9–10–87; 131 v S 94)

Library References

Eminent Domain ⟐265.
Westlaw Topic No. 148.
C.J.S. Eminent Domain § 366.

163.17 Withdrawal of deposit by owner; accrual of interest; deposit on appeal; refund

Where the agency has the right to take possession of the property before the verdict upon payment into court of a deposit, and a portion of said deposit may be withdrawn immediately by the owner, the amount of the verdict which exceeds the portion of the deposit withdrawable shall be subject to interest from the date of taking to the date of actual payment of the award.

Where the agency has no right to take possession of the property before the verdict, if the award is not paid to the owner or deposited in court within twenty-one days after journalization of the verdict, interest thereafter shall accrue, except that where the owner appeals, interest shall not accrue until the agency takes possession.

If the owner appeals and is granted a larger award, interest shall be paid on the additional amount awarded from the date of taking possession to the date of actual payment or date of deposit with immediate right of withdrawal.

If the agency wishes to appeal, it may require the deposit to remain with the court pending final disposition of the case provided it pays interest on the final award from date of taking possession to the date the money is actually paid or made available to the owner; provided, the owner may withdraw the entire award upon posting an appropriate refund bond set by the court; and provided, that where a building or other structure is taken, the court may, on application of the owner, permit the owner to withdraw a reasonable portion of the award allocable to the building without giving bond.

If the amount of any deposit actually withdrawn by the owner exceeds the final award from which no appeal is or can be taken, then the owner at the time of entry of judgment on such award shall refund at once to the court for the account of the agency the amount of such excess plus interest on such excess from the date of withdrawal of such excess until the date of such refund, and upon the failure of the owner to make such refund, the agency shall be entitled to a money judgment against the owner.

Except for cases involving the department of transportation, interest as provided for in this section shall be at the rate of interest for judgments as set forth in section 1343.03 of the Revised Code. In a case involving the appropriation of property by the department of transportation, and the department is the sole public agency seeking to appropriate property in the case, interest as provided for in this section shall be at the per annum rate of either the interest rate as defined and established in division (B) of section 5703.47 of the Revised Code, or ten per cent, whichever is less.

(2001 S 108, § 2.01, eff. 7–6–01; 2001 S 108, § 2.02, eff. 7–6–01; 1996 H 350, eff. 1–27–97 [1]*; 1993 H 154, eff. 6–30–93; 1981 S 62; 131 v S 94)*

[1] See *Baldwin's Ohio Revised Code Annotated*, Notes of Decisions, *State ex rel. Ohio Academy of Trial Lawyers v. Sheward* (Ohio 1999), 86 Ohio St.3d 451, 715 N.E.2d 1062.

Uncodified Law

2001 S 108, § 1, eff. 7–6–01, reads:

It is the intent of this act (1) to repeal the Tort Reform Act, Am. Sub. H.B. 350 of the 121st General Assembly, 146 Ohio Laws 3867, in conformity with the Supreme Court of Ohio's decision in *State, ex rel. Ohio Academy of Trial Lawyers, v. Sheward* (1999), 86 Ohio St.3d 451; (2) to clarify the status of the law; and (3) to revive the law as it existed prior to the Tort Reform Act.

2001 S 108, § 3, eff. 7–6–01, reads, in part:

(A) In Section 2.01 of this act:

(4) Sections 163.17, 723.01, 1343.03, 1775.14, 2305.01, 2305.11, 2305.35, 2307.33, 2307.71, 2307.72, 2307.73, 2307.78, 2315.20, 2317.62, 2323.51, 2744.04, 4112.99, 4909.42, 5591.36, and 5591.37 of the Revised Code are

revived and supersede the versions of the same sections that are repealed by Section 2.02 of this act.

Historical and Statutory Notes

Ed. Note: The amendment of this section by 1996 H 350, eff. 1–27–97, was repealed by 2001 S 108, § 2.02, eff. 7–6–01. See *Baldwin's Ohio Legislative Service Annotated*, 1996, page 10/L–3356, and 2001, page 6/L–1441, or the OH–LEGIS or OH–LEGIS–OLD database on WESTLAW, for original versions of these Acts.

Amendment Note: 1996 H 350 substituted "the rate specified in division (A) of section 1343.03" for "the rate of interest for judgments as set forth in section 1343.03" in the sixth paragraph; and made other nonsubstantive changes.

Amendment Note: 1993 H 154 rewrote the final paragraph, which previously read:

"Interest as provided for in this section shall be at the rate of interest for judgments as set forth in section 1343.03 of the Revised Code."

Library References

Eminent Domain ⚖188, 247.
Westlaw Topic No. 148.
C.J.S. Eminent Domain § 221, 352, 355.

163.18   Notice of deposit or payment; motion for distribution

At the time the agency makes a deposit or pays into court the jury award, the clerk of courts shall give notice by ordinary mail of such payment to the counsel of record of each owner and to the known address of owners not represented. Thereupon any owner may file with the court a motion for distribution. After reasonable notice to all parties and to any additional interested parties who become known to the court, the court shall hear evidence as to the respective interests of the owners in the property and may make distribution of the deposit or award accordingly.

(131 v S 94, eff. 1–1–66)

Library References

Eminent Domain ⚖188, 245.
Westlaw Topic No. 148.
C.J.S. Eminent Domain § 221, 349.

163.19   Appeals

Subject to sections 163.07 and 163.09 of the Revised Code, any party may prosecute appeals as in other civil actions from the judgment of the court. The trial court upon proper terms may suspend the execution of any order; but in all cases where the agency pays or deposits the amount of the award assessed and gives adequate security for any further compensation and costs, as required by the court, the right to take and use the property appropriated shall not be affected by such review by the appellate courts.

(131 v S 94, eff. 1–1–66)

Library References

Eminent Domain ⚖250–263.
Westlaw Topic No. 148.

163.20   Appropriation to perfect title

An agency may appropriate in accordance with sections 163.01 to 163.22, inclusive, of the Revised Code, any property in which an interest has been appropriated, in order to perfect title in itself.

(131 v S 94, eff. 1–1–66)

Library References

Eminent Domain ⚖17, 45.
Westlaw Topic No. 148.
C.J.S. Eminent Domain § 24, 52, 55–56.

163.21   Abandonment of proceedings

(A) (1) If it has not taken possession of property that is appropriated, an agency may abandon appropriation proceedings under sections 163.01 to 163.22 of the Revised Code at any time after the proceedings are commenced but not later than ninety days after the final determination of the cause.

(2) In all cases of abandonment as described in division (A)(1) of this section, the court shall enter a judgment against the agency for costs, including jury fees, and shall enter a judgment in favor of each affected owner, in amounts that the court considers to be just, for each of the following that the owner incurred:

(a) Witness fees, including expert witness fees;

(b) Attorney's fees;

(c) Other actual expenses.

(B)(1) Except as provided in division (B)(2) of this section, if in appropriation proceedings under sections 163.01 to 163.22 of the Revised Code or, as authorized by divisions (B), (C), and (D) of section 163.02 of the Revised Code, in appropriation proceedings under other sections of the Revised Code, the court determines that an agency is not entitled to appropriate particular property, the court shall enter both of the following:

(a) A judgment against the agency for costs, including jury fees;

(b) A judgment in favor of each affected owner, in amounts that the court considers to be just, for witness fees, including expert witness fees, for attorney's fees, and for other actual expenses that the owner incurred in connection with the proceedings.

(2) This division does not apply to a state agency that is subject to section 163.62 of the Revised Code in connection with condemnation proceedings.

(1987 H 57, eff. 9–10–87; 131 v S 94)

Uncodified Law

1987 H 57, § 3, eff. 9–10–87, reads:

(A) It is the intent of the General Assembly in the enactment of new division (B) of section 163.21 of the Revised Code in this act to add the necessary provisions in sections 163.01 to 163.22 of the Revised Code to address the holding of the Supreme Court of Ohio in *Ohio Edison Co. v. Franklin Paper Co.*, 18 Ohio St.3d 15 (1985) that an award of attorney's fees and expenses was not authorized when an agency did not prevail in appropriation proceedings under those sections.

(B) It is the intent of the General Assembly in the revisions to former divisions (A) and (B) of section 163.21 of the Revised Code made in this act to consolidate abandonment of appropriation proceedings provisions and to codify court clarifications of those provisions, including the clarifications of the Supreme Court of Ohio in *Ohio Edison Co. v. Franklin Paper Co.*, 18 Ohio St.3d 15 (1985) and of the Court of Appeals for Ashland County in *Dept. of Natural Resources v. Sellers*, 14 Ohio App.2d 132 (1968).

Library References

Eminent Domain ⚖246.
Westlaw Topic No. 148.
C.J.S. Eminent Domain § 362.

163.22 Laws and rules applicable to civil actions to govern; advancement

All proceedings brought under sections 163.01 to 163.22 of the Revised Code shall be governed by the law applicable in civil actions and the Rules of Civil Procedure, including, but not limited to, the rules governing discovery, except as otherwise provided in those sections. The proceedings shall be advanced as a matter of immediate public interest and concern and shall be heard by the court at the earliest practicable moment.

(2001 H 73, eff. 6–29–01; 132 v H 1, eff. 2–21–67; 131 v S 94)

Historical and Statutory Notes

Amendment Note: 2001 H 73 rewrote this section, which prior thereto read:

"All proceedings brought under sections 163.01 to 163.22, inclusive, of the Revised Code, shall be governed by the law applicable in civil actions in the court of common pleas except as otherwise provided in such sections. Such proceedings shall be advanced as a matter of immediate public interest and concern and shall be heard by the court at the earliest practicable moment."

Library References

Eminent Domain ⚖166.
Westlaw Topic No. 148.
C.J.S. Eminent Domain § 201, 209.

ADVERTISING DEVICES

163.31 Definitions

As used in sections 163.31 to 163.33 of the Revised Code:

(A) "Advertising device" includes any legally erected and maintained outdoor sign, display, device, figure, painting, drawing, message, placard, poster, billboard, or other contrivance designed, intended, or used to advertise or to give information in the nature of advertising, or any part of any such contrivance, the advertisement on which is visible from the traveled way of any street, road, or highway in this state.

(B) "Erect" means to construct or allow to be constructed, but does not include any activity performed incident to a change of an advertisement or normal maintenance of an advertising device.

(C) "Just compensation" means the payment of compensation by a public agency that orders the removal of an advertising device, in the same manner as it would for other property acquired pursuant to this chapter.

(D) "Maintain" means to preserve, keep in repair, continue, allow to exist, or restore if destroyed by an act of God or vandalism.

(E) "Public agency" has the same meaning as in section 163.01 of the Revised Code.

(F) "Visible" means capable of being seen, whether or not legible, without visual aid by a person of normal acuity.

(1981 H 146, eff. 10–9–81)

163.32 Order for removal of advertising device; interests deemed taken; action to appropriate

Any removal of an advertising device that is ordered by a public agency pursuant to law or ordinance, or to the exercise of any power or authority possessed by the public agency, shall be deemed to constitute the taking of all right, title, and interest in the advertising device, including any leasehold interest, of the owner of the advertising device and of the right of the owner of the real property on which the advertising device is located to erect and maintain the advertising device on it. If the public agency and any such owner of a compensable right, title, or interest do not reach agreement as to the amount of just compensation to be paid for the right, title, or interest, the public agency shall institute an action to appropriate it in accordance with this chapter.

(1981 H 146, eff. 10–9–81)

Library References

Eminent Domain ⚖2(1.1, 1.2, 5, 6).
Westlaw Topic No. 148.
C.J.S. Eminent Domain § 7, 9, 12–13, 82–83, 87–88, 97, 104, 106–108.
C.J.S. Zoning and Land Planning § 24.

163.33 Payment to owner of land and of device before removal; exception

(A) Before any advertising device is removed by a public agency pursuant to any law or ordinance, or to the exercise of any power or authority possessed by the public agency, the owner of the advertising device and the owner of the real property upon which the advertising device is located shall be paid just compensation.

(B) Sections 163.31 to 163.33 of the Revised Code do not apply to any action taken pursuant to Chapter 5516. of the Revised Code.

(1981 H 146, eff. 10–9–81)

RELOCATION ASSISTANCE

163.51 Definitions

As used in sections 163.51 to 163.62 of the Revised Code:

(A) "State agency" means any department, agency, or instrumentality of a state or of a political subdivision of a state; any department, agency, or instrumentality of two or more states or of two or more political subdivisions of a state or states; or any community urban redevelopment corporation organized pursuant to Chapter 1728. of the Revised Code; and any person who has the authority to acquire property by eminent domain under state law.

(B) "Displacing agency" means any state agency or person carrying out a program or project with federal assistance, or carrying out any state highway project that causes a person to be a displaced person.

(C) "Federal financial assistance" means a grant, loan, or contribution provided by the United States.

(D) "Person" includes any individual, partnership, corporation, or association.

(E)(1) Except as provided in divisions (E)(2) and (3) of this section, "displaced person" means any person who moves from real property, or moves his personal property from real property, as a direct result of a written notice of intent to acquire or the acquisition of such real property, in whole or in part, under a program or project undertaken by a state agency with federal financial assistance or with the rights and powers granted to a community urban redevelopment corporation by the provisions of Chapter 1728. of the Revised Code, or for any state highway project; or as a direct result of rehabilitation, demolition, or other displacing activity on real property undertaken by such state agencies, on which such person is a residential tenant or conducts a business or farm operation, where the head of the displacing agency determines that the displacement is permanent.

(2) Solely for the purpose of establishing eligibility for moving expenses and advisory assistance under sections 163.53 and 163.56 of the Revised Code, "displaced person" includes any person who moves from real property, or moves personal property from real

property; as a direct result of a written notice of intent to acquire or the acquisition of other real property, in whole or in part, on which such person conducts a business or farm operation, under a program or project undertaken by a state agency with federal financial assistance or with the rights and powers granted to a community urban redevelopment corporation by the provisions of Chapter 1728. of the Revised Code, or for any state highway project; or as a direct result of rehabilitation, demolition, or other displacing activity undertaken by such state agencies on such other real property, where the head of the displacing agency determines that the displacement is permanent.

(3) "Displaced person" does not include a person who has been determined, according to criteria established by the head of the displacing agency, to be either in unlawful occupancy of the displacement dwelling or to have occupied such dwelling for the purpose of obtaining assistance under this chapter; or a person who became an occupant of the dwelling after its acquisition and whose occupancy is on a rental basis for a short term or a period subject to termination when the property is needed for the program or project.

(F) "Business" means any lawful activity, excepting a farm operation, conducted primarily for one or more of the following:

(1) The purchase, sale, lease, and rental of personal and real property, and for the manufacture, processing, or marketing of products, commodities, or any other personal property;

(2) The sale of services to the public;

(3) By a nonprofit organization;

(4) Solely for the purposes of section 163.53 of the Revised Code, for assisting in the purchase, sale, resale, manufacture, processing, or marketing of products, commodities, personal property, or services by the erection and maintenance of an outdoor advertising display or displays, whether or not such display or displays are located on the premises on which any of the above activities are conducted.

(G) "Farm operation" means any activity conducted solely or primarily for the production of one or more agricultural products or commodities, including timber, for sale or home use, and customarily producing such products or commodities in sufficient quantity to be capable of contributing materially to the operator's support.

(H) "Mortgage" means such classes of liens as are commonly given to secure advances on, or the unpaid purchase price of, real property, under the laws of Ohio, together with the credit instruments, if any, secured thereby.

(I) "Comparable replacement dwelling" means any dwelling that is decent, safe, and sanitary; adequate in size to accommodate the occupants; within the financial means of the displaced person; functionally equivalent to the displaced person's dwelling; in an area not subject to unreasonable adverse environmental conditions; and in a location generally not less desirable than the location of the displaced person's dwelling with respect to public utilities, facilities, services, and the displaced person's place of employment.

(J) "Acquiring agency" means both of the following:

(1) A state agency with authority to acquire property by eminent domain under state law;

(2) A state agency or person without such authority, to the extent provided by the head of the lead agency by rule.

(1989 H 381, eff. 7–1–89; 1989 H 295; 1973 S 90; 1971 H 295)

Uncodified Law

1987 H 57, § 3: See Uncodified Law under 163.21.

Historical and Statutory Notes

Ed. Note: 163.51 contains provisions analogous to former 5520.01, repealed by 1971 H 295, eff. 6–11–71.

Library References

States ⇌123.
Westlaw Topic No. 360.
C.J.S. States § 226.

163.52 Validity of acquisition; elements of value or damage not affected

(A) The failure of an acquiring agency to satisfy a requirement of section 163.59 of the Revised Code does not affect the validity of any property acquisition by purchase or condemnation.

(B) Nothing in sections 163.51 to 163.62 of the Revised Code shall be construed as creating, in any condemnation proceeding brought under the power of eminent domain, any element of value or damage not in existence immediately prior to June 11, 1971.

(2002 H 426, eff. 9–6–02; 1971 H 295, eff. 6–11–71)

Historical and Statutory Notes

Ed. Note: 163.52 contains provisions analogous to former 5520.07, repealed by 1971 H 295, eff. 6–11–71.

Amendment Note: 2002 H 426 rewrote the section, which prior thereto read:

"(A) Section 163.59 of the Revised Code creates no rights or liabilities and shall not affect the validity of any property acquisitions by purchase or condemnation.

"(B) Nothing in sections 163.51 to 163.62, inclusive, of the Revised Code, shall be construed as creating in any condemnation proceeding brought under the power of eminent domain, any element of value or damage not in existence immediately prior to the effective date of such sections."

163.53 Application for relocation payments; eligibility; relocation of utility facility

(A) Whenever the acquisition of real property for a program or project undertaken by a displacing agency will result in the displacement of any person, the head of the agency shall make a payment to any displaced person, upon proper application as approved by such agency head, for all of the following:

(1) Actual reasonable expenses in moving himself, his family, business, farm operation, or other personal property;

(2) Actual direct losses of tangible personal property as a result of moving or discontinuing a business or farm operation, but not to exceed an amount equal to the reasonable expenses that would have been required to relocate such property, as determined by the head of the displacing agency;

(3) Actual reasonable expenses in searching for a replacement business or farm;

(4) Actual and reasonable expenses necessary to reestablish a displaced farm, nonprofit organization, or small business at its new site, but not to exceed ten thousand dollars.

(B) Any displaced person eligible for payments under division (A) of this section who is displaced from a dwelling and who elects to accept the payments authorized by this division in lieu of the payments authorized by division (A) of this section may receive an expense and dislocation allowance, determined according to a schedule established by the head of the displacing agency.

(C) Any displaced person eligible for payments under division (A) of this section who is displaced from his place of business or from his farm operation may qualify for the payment authorized by this division in lieu of the payment authorized by division (A) of this section. The payment authorized by this division shall consist of a fixed payment in an amount to be determined according to criteria established by the head of the lead agency, except that such payment shall be not less than one thousand dollars nor more than twenty thousand dollars. A person whose sole business at the displacement dwelling is the rental of such property to others does not qualify for a payment under this division.

(D)(1) Except as provided in section 5501.51 of the Revised Code, if a program or project undertaken by a displacing agency results in the relocation of a utility facility, and the purpose of the program or project was not to relocate or reconstruct any utility facility; and if the owner of the utility facility which is being relocated under such program or project has entered into a franchise or similar agreement with the state or local government on whose property, easement, or right-of-way such facility is located with respect to the use of such property, easement, or right-of-way; and if the relocation of such facility results in such owner incurring an extraordinary cost in connection with such relocation; then the displacing agency may, in accordance with such rules as the head of the lead agency may adopt, provide to such owner a relocation payment which may not exceed the amount of such extraordinary cost, less any increase in the value of the new utility facility above the value of the old utility facility, and less any salvage value derived from the old utility facility.

(2) As used in division (D) of this section:

(a) "Extraordinary cost in connection with a relocation" means any cost incurred by the owner of a utility facility in connection with relocation of such facility that is determined by the head of the displacing agency, under such rules as the head of the lead agency shall adopt, to be a nonroutine relocation expense, to be a cost that owner ordinarily does not include in its annual budget as an expense of operation, and to meet such other requirements as the lead agency may prescribe in such rules.

(b) "Utility facility" means any electric, gas, water, steam power, or materials transmission or distribution system; any transportation system; any communications system, including cable television; and any fixture, equipment, or other property associated with the operation, maintenance, or repair of any such system; which is located on property owned by a state or local government or over which a state or local government has an easement or right-of-way. A utility facility may be publicly, privately, or cooperatively owned.

(1989 H 295, eff. 3–21–89; 1971 H 295)

Historical and Statutory Notes

Ed. Note: 163.53 contains provisions analogous to former 5520.02, repealed by 1971 H 295, eff. 6–11–71.

Comparative Laws

Alaska—AS 34.60.010 et seq.
Ariz.—A.R.S. § 28-1841 et seq.
Cal.—West's Ann.Cal.Gov.Code § 7260 et seq.
Colo.—West's C.R.S.A. 24–56–101.
Conn.—C.G.S.A. § 8-266 et seq.
Fla.—West's F.S.A. § 421.55.
Ga.—O.C.G.A. § 32-8-1.
Hawaii—HRS § 264–33, 264–34.
Ill.—ILCS 65 5/11–91.1–1 et seq.
Iowa—I.C.A. § 316.1 et seq.
Kan.—K.S.A. 58-3501 et seq.
Ky.—Baldwin's KRS 56.610 et seq.
La.—LSA-R.S. 38:3101 et seq.
Md.—Code, Transportation, § 8–503, 8–506.
Me.—1 M.R.S.A. § 901 et seq.
Mich.—M.C.L.A. § 252.131 et seq.
Minn.—M.S.A. § 117.52 et seq.
Miss.—Code 1972, § 43–39–1 et seq.
N.C.—G.S. § 133-5 et seq.
N.D.—NDCC 54–01.1–01 et seq.
N.H.—RSA 124:10.
N.J.—N.J.S.A. 20:4-1 et seq.
N.M.—NMSA 1978, § 42–3–1 et seq.
Ore.—ORS 366.324.
Pa.—35 P.S. § 1700–11.
R.I.—Gen.Laws 1956, § 37–6.1–1.
S.C.—Code 1976, § 28–11–10 et seq.
S.D.—SDCL 5–2–18.
Tenn.—T.C.A. § 13-11-101 et seq.
Utah—U.C.A.1953, 57–12–1 et seq.
Va.—Code 1950, § 25–235 et seq.
Wash.—West's RCWA 8.26.010 et seq.
W.Va.—Code, 54–3–1 et seq.

Library References

States ⚖123.
Westlaw Topic No. 360.
C.J.S. States § 226.

163.54 Additional payment for replacement dwelling

(A) In addition to payments otherwise authorized by sections 163.51 to 163.62 of the Revised Code, the head of the displacing agency shall make an additional payment not to exceed twenty-two thousand five hundred dollars to any displaced person who is displaced from a dwelling actually owned and occupied by him for not less than one hundred eighty days prior to the initiation of negotiations for the acquisition of the property. Such additional payment shall include the following elements:

(1) The amount, if any, which when added to the acquisition cost of the dwelling acquired by the displacing agency, equals the reasonable cost of a comparable replacement dwelling.

(2) The amount, if any, which will compensate the displaced person for any increased interest costs and other debt service costs which the person is required to pay for financing the acquisition of a comparable replacement dwelling. This amount shall be paid only if the dwelling acquired by the displacing agency was encumbered by a bona fide mortgage which was a valid lien on the dwelling for not less than one hundred eighty days prior to the initiation of negotiations for the acquisition of the dwelling.

(3) Reasonable expenses incurred by the displaced person for evidence of title, recording fees, and other closing costs incident to the purchase of the replacement dwelling, but not including prepaid expenses.

(B) The additional payment authorized by this section shall be made only to a displaced person who purchases and occupies a replacement dwelling which is decent, safe, and sanitary not later than the end of the one-year period beginning on the date on which he receives from the displacing agency final payment of all costs of the acquired dwelling, or on the date on which the displacing agency's obligation under division (B)(3) of section 163.56 of the Revised Code is met, whichever is later, except that the displacing agency may extend the period for good cause. If the period is extended, the payment under this section shall be based on the costs of relocating the person to a comparable replacement dwelling within one year after the displaced person receives from the displacing agency final payment of all costs of the acquired dwelling.

(1989 H 295, eff. 3–21–89; 1971 H 295)

Historical and Statutory Notes

Ed. Note: 163.54 contains provisions analogous to former 5520.03 and 5520.04, repealed by 1971 H 295, eff. 6–11–71.

Library References

States ⚖123.
Westlaw Topic No. 360.
C.J.S. States § 226.

163.55 Additional payment for rental dwelling or down payment on house

(A) In addition to amounts otherwise authorized by sections 163.51 to 163.62 of the Revised Code, the head of a displacing agency shall make a payment to or for any displaced person displaced from any dwelling not eligible to receive a payment under section 163.54 of the Revised Code which dwelling was actually and lawfully occupied by such displaced person for not less than ninety days prior to the initiation of negotiations for acquisition of such dwelling, or in any case in which displacement is not a direct result of acquisition, not less than ninety days prior to such other event as the head of the lead agency shall prescribe. The payment shall consist of the amount necessary to enable the displaced person to lease or rent for a period not to exceed forty-two months, a comparable replacement dwelling, but not to exceed five thousand two hundred fifty dollars. At the discretion of the head of the displacing agency, a payment under this division may be made in periodic installments. Computation of a payment under this division to a low-income displaced person shall take into account the person's income.

(B) Any person eligible for a payment under division (A) of this section may elect to apply the payment to a down payment on, and other incidental expenses pursuant to, the purchase of a decent, safe, and sanitary replacement dwelling. The person may, under criteria established by the head of the displacing agency, be eligible under this division for the maximum payment allowed under division (A) of this section, except that, in the case of a displaced homeowner who has owned and occupied the displacement dwelling for at least ninety days but not more than one hundred eighty days immediately prior to the initiation of negotiations for the acquisition of such dwelling, the payment shall not exceed the payment the person would otherwise have received under section 163.54 of the Revised Code had the person owned and occupied the displacement dwelling one hundred eighty days immediately prior to the initiation of the negotiations.

(1989 H 295, eff. 3–21–89; 1971 H 295)

Historical and Statutory Notes

Ed. Note: 163.55 contains provisions analogous to former 5520.03, repealed by 1971 H 295, eff. 6–11–71.

Library References

States ⚖123.
Westlaw Topic No. 360.
C.J.S. States § 226.

163.56 Relocation assistance advisory program

(A)(1) Projects or programs that cause persons to be displaced persons shall be planned in a manner that recognizes, at an early stage in the planning of such programs or projects and before the commencement of any actions that will cause displacements, the problems associated with the displacement of individuals, families, businesses, and farm operations, and in a manner that provides for the resolution of such problems in order to minimize adverse impacts on displaced persons and to expedite program or project advancement and completion.

(2) Whenever a program or project undertaken by a displacing agency will result in the displacement of any person, the head of the displacing agency shall provide a relocation assistance advisory program for displaced persons which shall offer the services described in division (B) of this section. If the head of the displacing agency determines that any person occupying property immediately adjacent to the real property acquired is caused substantial economic injury because of the acquisition, he may offer that person relocation advisory services under the program.

(B) Each relocation assistance advisory program required by division (A) of this section shall include such measures, facilities, or services as may be necessary or appropriate in order to do all of the following:

(1) Determine the need, if any, of displaced persons for relocation assistance;

(2) Provide current and continuing information on the availability, prices, and rentals, of comparable decent, safe, and sanitary sales and rental housing, and of suitable commercial properties and locations for displaced businesses and farm operations;

(3) Assure that, within a reasonable period of time, prior to displacement there will be available comparable replacement dwellings, as defined by the head of the displacing agency, equal in number to the number of and available to the displaced persons who require such dwellings, except that the head of the displacing agency may prescribe by regulation situations when such assurances may be waived;

(4) Assist a displaced person displaced from his business or farm operation in obtaining and becoming established in a suitable replacement location;

(5) Supply information concerning federal and state housing programs, disaster loan programs, and other federal or state programs offering assistance to displaced persons;

(6) Provide other advisory services to displaced persons in order to minimize hardships to them in adjusting to relocation.

(1989 H 295, eff. 3–21–89; 1971 H 295)

Historical and Statutory Notes

Ed. Note: 163.56 contains provisions analogous to former 5520.05, repealed by 1971 H 295, eff. 6–11–71.

163.57 Replacement housing

(A) If a project cannot proceed to actual construction because comparable replacement sale or rental housing is not available, and the head of the displacing agency determines that such housing cannot otherwise be made available, he may take such action as is necessary or appropriate to provide such housing by use of funds authorized for such project. The head of the displacing agency may use this section to exceed the maximum amounts which may be paid under sections 163.54 and 163.55 of the Revised Code on a case-by-case basis for good cause as determined in accordance with rules adopted under Chapter 119. of the Revised Code by the head of the lead agency.

(B) No person shall be required to move from his dwelling on account of any project, unless the displacing agency head is satisfied that replacement housing, in accordance with section 163.56 of the Revised Code, is available to such person.

(C) The acquisition of replacement housing sites and the acquisition, rehabilitation, relocation, and construction of replacement housing shall be considered to be for a public purpose, and displacing agencies may properly expend their respective funds to carry out the purposes of sections 163.51 to 163.62 of the Revised Code.

(D) In order to prevent unnecessary expenses and duplications of functions, and to promote uniform and effective administration of relocation assistance programs for displaced persons under sections 163.51 to 163.62 of the Revised Code, a displacing agency may enter into contracts with any individual, firm, association, or corporation for services in connection with such programs, or may carry out its functions under sections 163.51 to 163.62 of the Revised Code through any federal or state governmental agency or instrumentality having an established organization for conducting relocation assistance programs. The displacing agency shall, in carrying out the relocation assistance activities described in this section, whenever practicable, utilize the services of state or local housing agencies, or other agencies having experience in the administration or conduct of similar housing assistance activities.

(1989 H 295, eff. 3-21-89; 1971 H 295)

Historical and Statutory Notes

Ed. Note: 163.57 contains provisions analogous to former 5520.06, repealed by 1971 H 295, eff. 6-11-71.

Library References

States ⚖︎123.
Westlaw Topic No. 360.
C.J.S. States § 226.

163.58 Regulations and procedures; rulemaking powers

(A) Except as otherwise provided in rules adopted under division (B) of this section, the head of each displacing agency is authorized to establish such regulations and procedures as he may determine to be necessary to assure:

(1) That the payments and assistance authorized by sections 163.51 to 163.62 of the Revised Code shall be administered in a manner which is fair and reasonable, and as uniform as practicable;

(2) That a displaced person who makes proper application for a payment authorized for such person by sections 163.51 to 163.62 of the Revised Code shall be paid promptly after a move or, in hardship cases, be paid in advance;

(3) That any person aggrieved by a determination as to eligibility for a payment authorized by such sections, or the amount of a payment, may have his application reviewed by the head of the displacing agency having authority over the applicable program or project.

(B) Notwithstanding any provision of the Revised Code to the contrary, the lead agency shall adopt such rules as may be necessary to implement sections 163.51 to 163.62 of the Revised Code in a manner which is as fair, reasonable, and uniform as practicable. As used in this section, "lead agency" means the state agency that the governor shall designate to carry out the duties prescribed by this division.

(1989 H 295, eff. 3-21-89; 1971 H 295)

Historical and Statutory Notes

Ed. Note: 163.58 contains provisions analogous to former 5520.06, repealed by 1971 H 295, eff. 6-11-71.

163.59 Policies for public land acquisition

In order to encourage and expedite the acquisition of real property by agreements with owners, to avoid litigation and relieve congestion in the courts, to assure consistent treatment for owners in the many state and federally assisted programs, and to promote public confidence in public land acquisition practices, heads of acquiring agencies shall do or ensure the acquisition satisfies all of the following:

(A) The head of an acquiring agency shall make every reasonable effort to acquire expeditiously real property by negotiation.

(B) In order for an acquiring agency to acquire real property, the acquisition shall be for a defined public purpose that is to be achieved in a defined and reasonable period of time. An acquisition of real property that complies with section 5501.31 of the Revised Code satisfies the defined public purpose requirement of this division.

(C) Real property to be acquired shall be appraised before the initiation of negotiations, and the owner or the owner's designated representative shall be given a reasonable opportunity to accompany the appraiser during the appraiser's inspection of the property, except that the head of the lead agency may prescribe a procedure to waive the appraisal in cases involving the acquisition by sale or donation of property with a low fair market value. If the appraisal values the property to be acquired at more than ten thousand dollars, the head of the acquiring agency concerned shall make every reasonable effort to provide a copy of the appraisal to the owner. As used in this section, "appraisal" means a written statement independently and impartially prepared by a qualified appraiser, or a written statement prepared by an employee of the acquiring agency who is a qualified appraiser, setting forth an opinion of defined value of an adequately described property as of a specified date, supported by the presentation and analysis of relevant market information.

(D) Before the initiation of negotiations for real property, the head of the acquiring agency concerned shall establish an amount that the head of the acquiring agency believes to be just compensation for the property and shall make a prompt offer to acquire the property for no less than the full amount so established. In no event shall that amount be less than the agency's approved appraisal of the fair market value of the property. Any decrease or increase in the fair market value of real property prior to the date of valuation caused by the public improvement for which the property is acquired, or by the likelihood that the property would be acquired for that improvement, other than that due to physical deterioration within the reasonable control of the owner, will be disregarded in determining the compensation for the property.

The head of the acquiring agency concerned shall provide the owner of real property to be acquired with a written statement of, and summary of the basis for, the amount that the head of the acquiring agency established as just compensation. Where appropriate, the just compensation for real property acquired and for damages to remaining real property shall be separately stated.

The owner shall be given a reasonable opportunity to consider the offer of the acquiring agency for the real property, to present material that the owner believes is relevant to determining the fair market value of the property, and to suggest modification in the proposed terms and conditions of the acquisition. The acquiring agency shall consider the owner's presentation and suggestions.

(E) If information presented by the owner or a material change in the character or condition of the real property indicates the need for new appraisal information, or if a period of more than two years has elapsed since the time of the appraisal of the property, the head of the acquiring agency concerned shall have the appraisal updated or obtain a new appraisal. If updated appraisal information or a new appraisal indicates that a change in the acquisition offer is warranted, the head of the acquiring agency shall promptly reestablish the amount of the just compensation for the property and offer that amount to the owner in writing.

(F) No owner shall be required to surrender possession of real property before the acquiring agency concerned pays the agreed purchase price, or deposits with the court for the benefit of the owner an amount not less than the agency's approved appraisal of the fair market value of the property, or the amount of the award of compensation in the condemnation proceeding for the property.

(G) The construction or development of a public improvement shall be so scheduled that no person lawfully occupying real property shall be required to move from a dwelling, or to move the person's business or farm operation, without at least ninety days' written notice from the head of the acquiring agency concerned of the date by which the move is required.

(H) If the head of an acquiring agency permits an owner or tenant to occupy the real property acquired on a rental basis for a short term or for a period subject to termination on short notice, the amount of rent required shall not exceed the fair rental value of the property to a short-term occupier.

(I) In no event shall the head of an acquiring agency either advance the time of condemnation, or defer negotiations or condemnation and the deposit of funds in court for the use of the owner, or take any other action coercive in nature, in order to compel an agreement on the price to be paid for the real property.

(J) When any interest in real property is acquired by exercise of the power of eminent domain, the head of the acquiring agency concerned shall institute the formal condemnation proceedings. No head of an acquiring agency shall intentionally make it necessary for an owner to institute legal proceedings to prove the fact of the taking of the owner's real property.

(K) If the acquisition of only part of a property would leave its owner with an uneconomic remnant, the head of the acquiring agency concerned shall offer to acquire that remnant. For the purposes of this division, an uneconomic remnant is a parcel of real property in which the owner is left with an interest after the partial acquisition of the owner's property and which the head of the agency concerned has determined has little or no value or utility to the owner.

An acquisition of real property may continue while an acquiring agency carries out the requirements of divisions (A) to (K) of this section.

This section applies only when the acquisition of real property may result in an exercise of the power of eminent domain.

(2002 H 426, eff. 9-6-02; 1990 S 185, eff. 6-21-90; 1989 H 295; 1971 H 295)

Historical and Statutory Notes

Amendment Note: 2002 H 426 rewrote the section, which prior thereto read:

"In order to encourage and expedite the acquisition of real property by agreements with owners, to avoid litigation and relieve congestion in the courts, to assure consistent treatment for owners in the many state and federally assisted programs, and to promote public confidence in public land acquisition practices, heads of acquiring agencies shall, to the greatest extent practicable, be guided by the following policies:

"(A) The head of an acquiring agency shall make every reasonable effort to acquire expeditiously real property by negotiation.

"(B) Real property shall be appraised before the initiation of negotiations, and the owner or his designated representative shall be given an opportunity to accompany the appraiser during his inspection of the property, except that the head of the lead agency may prescribe a procedure to waive the appraisal in cases involving the acquisition by sale or donation of property with a low fair market value. As used in this section, 'appraisal' means a written statement independently and impartially prepared by a qualified appraiser setting forth an opinion of defined value of an adequately described property as of a specified date, supported by the presentation and analysis of relevant market information.

"(C) Before the initiation of negotiations for real property, the head of the acquiring agency concerned shall establish an amount which he believes to be just compensation therefor and shall make a prompt offer to acquire the property for the full amount so established. In no event shall such amount be less than the agency's approved appraisal of the fair market value of such property. Any decrease or increase in the fair market value of real property prior to the date of valuation caused by the public improvement for which such property is acquired, or by the likelihood that the property would be acquired for such improvement, other than that due to physical deterioration within the reasonable control of the owner, will be disregarded in determining the compensation for the property. The head of the acquiring agency concerned shall provide the owner of real property to be acquired with a written statement of, and summary of the basis for, the amount he established as just compensation. Where appropriate the just compensation for the real property acquired and for damages to remaining real property shall be separately stated.

"(D) No owner shall be required to surrender possession of real property before the acquiring agency concerned pays the agreed purchase price, or deposits with the court for the benefit of the owner, an amount not less than the agency's approved appraisal of the fair market value of such property, or the amount of the award of compensation in the condemnation proceeding for such property.

"(E) The construction or development of a public improvement shall be so scheduled that no person lawfully occupying real property shall be required to move from a dwelling, or to move his business or farm operation, without at least ninety days' written notice from the head of the acquiring agency concerned, of the date by which such move is required.

"(F) If the head of an acquiring agency permits an owner or tenant to occupy the real property acquired on a rental basis for a short term or for a period subject to termination on short notice, the amount of rent required shall not exceed the fair rental value of the property to a short-term occupier.

"(G) In no event shall the head of an acquiring agency either advance the time of condemnation, or defer negotiations or condemnation and the deposit of funds in court for the use of the owner, or take any other action coercive in nature, in order to compel an agreement on the price to be paid for the property.

"(H) If any interest in real property is to be acquired by exercise of the power of eminent domain, the head of the acquiring agency concerned shall institute formal condemnation proceedings. No acquiring agency head shall intentionally make it necessary for an owner to institute legal proceedings to prove the fact of the taking of his real property.

"(I) If the acquisition of only part of a property would leave its owner with an uneconomic remnant, the head of the acquiring agency concerned shall offer to acquire that remnant. For the purposes of this division, an uneconomic remnant is a parcel of real property in which the owner is left with an interest after the partial acquisition of the owner's property and which the head of the agency concerned has determined has little or no value or utility to the owner."

Library References

Eminent Domain ⟸170.
Westlaw Topic No. 148.
C.J.S. Eminent Domain § 215–218.

163.60 Payment for buildings, structures and improvements on real property

(A) If the head of a state agency acquires any interest in real property, he shall acquire at least an equal interest in all buildings, structures, or other improvements located upon the real property so acquired and which he requires to be removed from such real property or which he determines will be adversely affected by the use to which such real property will be put.

(B) For the purpose of determining the just compensation to be paid for any building, structure, or other improvement required to be acquired by division (A) of this section, such building, structure, or other improvement shall be deemed to be a part of the real property to be acquired notwithstanding the right or obligation of a tenant, as against the owner of any other interest in the real property, to remove such building, structure, or improvement at the expiration of his term, and the fair market value which such building, structure, or improvement contributes to the fair market value of the real property to be acquired, or the fair market value of such building, structure, or improvement for removal from the real property, whichever is the greater, shall be paid to the tenant therefor.

(C) Payment under this section shall not result in duplication of any payments otherwise authorized by law. No such payment shall be made unless the owner of the land involved disclaims all interest in the improvements of the tenant. In consideration for any such payment, the tenant shall assign, transfer, and release all his right, title, and interest in and to such improvements.

(1971 H 295, eff. 6–11–71)

Library References

Eminent Domain ⟲202.
Westlaw Topic No. 148.
C.J.S. Eminent Domain § 274.

163.61 Payment for other incidental expenses

The head of a state agency, as soon as practicable after the date of payment of the purchase price or the date of deposit in court of funds to satisfy the award of compensation in a condemnation proceeding to acquire real property, whichever is the earlier, shall reimburse the owner, to the extent the head of such agency considers fair and reasonable, for expenses he necessarily incurred for:

(A) Transfer taxes, and similar expenses incidental to conveying such real property to the state agency;

(B) Penalty costs for prepayment of any pre-existing recorded mortgage entered into in good faith encumbering such real property;

(C) The pro rata portion of any real property taxes paid which are allocable to a period subsequent to the date of vesting title in the state or state agency, or the effective date of possession of such real property by the agency, whichever is the earlier.

(1971 H 295, eff. 6–11–71)

Historical and Statutory Notes

Ed. Note: 163.61 contains provisions analogous to former 5520.04, repealed by 1971 H 295, eff. 6–11–71.

163.62 Award by court having jurisdiction

(A) The court having jurisdiction of a proceeding instituted by a state agency to acquire real property by condemnation shall award the owner of any right, or title to, or interest in, such real property such sum as will in the opinion of the court reimburse such owner for his reasonable costs, disbursements, and expenses, including reasonable attorney, appraisal, and engineering fees, actually incurred because of the condemnation proceeding, if either:

(1) The final judgment is that the agency cannot acquire the real property by condemnation; or

(2) The proceeding is abandoned by the state agency.

(B) Any award made pursuant to division (A) of this section shall be paid by the head of the agency for whose benefit the condemnation proceeding was instituted.

(1971 H 295, eff. 6–11–71)

Uncodified Law

1987 H 57, § 3: See Uncodified Law under 163.21.

Library References

Eminent Domain ⟲241.
Westlaw Topic No. 148.
C.J.S. Eminent Domain § 339–344.

CHAPTER 1335

STATUTE OF FRAUDS

Section
1335.01 Deeds made in trust for grantor; reservations permitted; legal and equitable titles not merging—Repealed
1335.02 Loan agreements
1335.04 Interest in land to be granted in writing
1335.05 Certain agreements to be in writing

Comparative Laws

Ala.—Code 1975, § 35–4–20.
Alaska—AS 09.25.010.
Ariz.—A.R.S. § 44–101.
Del.—6 Del.C. § 2711 to 2715.
Hawaii—HRS § 656–1.
Iowa—I.C.A. § 622.32.
La.—LSA-C.C. art. 2278.
Mich.—M.C.L.A. § 566.106.
N.H.—RSA 506:1, 506:2.
Okl.—15 Okl.St.Ann. § 136.

1335.01 Deeds made in trust for grantor; reservations permitted; legal and equitable titles not merging—Repealed

(2006 H 416, eff. 1–1–07; 1992 H 427, eff. 10–8–92; 1991 H 90; 130 v H 1; 129 v 7; 1953 H 1; GC 8617)

Uncodified Law

1992 H 427, § 4, eff. 10–8–92, reads: In amending sections 1335.01 and 2107.63 of the Revised Code, the General Assembly hereby declares its intent to supersede the effect of the holding of the Probate Court of Cuyahoga County on August 3, 1965, in *Knowles, Exrx. v. Knowles*, 4 Ohio Misc. 153, that a testamentary pour-over to an inter vivos trust is valid only if the trust has a corpus to which the decedent's assets may be added.

1991 H 90, § 3, eff. 10–10–91, reads: In enacting division (C) of section 1335.01 of the Revised Code, the General Assembly hereby declares its intent to supersede the effect of the holding of the Fifth District Court of Appeals in the March 1, 1990, decision of *Mathias v. Fantine*, 1990 Ohio App. Lexis 826 [No. 89-AP-080063 (5th Dist Ct App, Tuscawaras, 3–1–90), *Mathias v Fantine*].

Historical and Statutory Notes

Pre–1953 H 1 Amendments: 109 v 215; RS 4195

1335.02 Loan agreements

(A) As used in this section:

(1) "Debtor" means a person that obtains credit or seeks a loan agreement with a financial institution or owes money to a financial institution.

(2) "Financial institution" means either of the following:

(a) A federally or state-chartered bank, savings bank, savings and loan association, or credit union, or a holding company, subsidiary, or affiliate of a bank, savings bank, or savings and loan association;

(b) A licensee under sections 1321.01 to 1321.19 of the Revised Code, or a registrant under sections 1321.51 to 1321.60 of the Revised Code, or a parent company, subsidiary, or affiliate of a licensee or registrant.

(3) "Loan agreement" means one or more promises, promissory notes, agreements, undertakings, security agreements, mortgages, or other documents or commitments, or any combination of these documents or commitments, pursuant to which a financial institution loans or delays, or agrees to loan or delay, repayment of money, goods, or anything of value, or otherwise extends credit or makes a financial accommodation. "Loan agreement" does not include a promise, promissory note, agreement, undertaking, or other document or commitment relating to a credit card, a charge card, a revolving budget agreement subject to section 1317.11 of the Revised Code, an open-end loan agreement subject to section 1321.16 or 1321.58 of the Revised Code, or an open-end credit agreement subject to section 1109.18 of the Revised Code.

(B) No party to a loan agreement may bring an action on a loan agreement unless the agreement is in writing and is signed by the party against whom the action is brought or by the authorized representative of the party against whom the action is brought. However, a loan agreement need not be signed by an officer or other authorized representative of a financial institution, if the loan agreement is in the form of a promissory note or other document or commitment that describes the credit or loan and the loan agreement, by its terms, satisfies all of the following conditions:

(1) The loan agreement is intended by the parties to be signed by the debtor but not by an officer or other authorized representative of the financial institution.

(2) The loan agreement has been signed by the debtor.

(3) The delivery of the loan agreement has been accepted by the financial institution.

(C) The terms of a loan agreement subject to this section, including the rights and obligations of the parties to the loan agreement, shall be determined solely from the written loan agreement, and shall not be varied by any oral agreements that are made or discussions that occur before or contemporaneously with the execution of the loan agreement. Any prior oral agreements between the parties are superseded by the loan agreement.

(D) This section does not apply to any loan agreement in which the proceeds of the loan agreement are used by the debtor primarily for personal, household, or family purposes and either of the following applies:

(1) The proceeds of the loan agreement are less than forty thousand dollars;

(2) A security interest securing the loan agreement is or will be acquired in the primary residence of the debtor.

(1996 H 538, eff. 1–1–97; 1992 H 373, eff. 4–9–93)

Historical and Statutory Notes

Ed. Note: Former 1335.02 repealed by 129 v 1006, eff. 10–23–61; 1953 H 1; GC 8618; see now 1336.01 et seq for provisions analogous to former 1335.02.

Pre–1953 H 1 Amendments: RS 4196

Amendment Note: 1996 H 538 substituted "1109.18" for "1107.27" in division (A)(3).

Library References

Frauds, Statute Of ⇐115.1 to 115.3(1).
Westlaw Topic No. 185.

1335.04 Interest in land to be granted in writing

No lease, estate, or interest, either of freehold or term of years, or any uncertain interest of, in, or out of lands, tenements, or hereditaments, shall be assigned or granted except by deed, or note in writing, signed by the party assigning or granting it, or his agent thereunto lawfully authorized, by writing, or by act and operation of law.

(1953 H 1, eff. 10–1–53; GC 8620)

Historical and Statutory Notes

Pre–1953 H 1 Amendments: RS 4198

Comparative Laws

Ariz.—A.R.S. § 33–401.
Ill.—ILCS 765 5/1.
Ind.—West's A.I.C. 32–1–2–4.
Me.—33 M.R.S.A. § 162.
Wash.—West's RCWA 64.04.020.

Library References

Frauds, Statute Of ⇐56 to 58.
Westlaw Topic No. 185.

1335.05 Certain agreements to be in writing

No action shall be brought whereby to charge the defendant, upon a special promise, to answer for the debt, default, or miscarriage of another person; nor to charge an executor or administrator upon a special promise to answer damages out of his own estate; nor to charge a person upon an agreement made upon consideration of marriage, or upon a contract or sale of lands, tenements, or hereditaments, or interest in or concerning them, or upon an agreement that is not to be performed within one year from the making thereof; unless the agreement upon which such action is brought, or some memorandum or note thereof, is in writing and signed by the party to be charged therewith or some other person thereunto by him or her lawfully authorized.

No action shall be brought to charge a person licensed by Chapter 4731. of the Revised Code to practice medicine or surgery, osteopathic medicine or surgery, or podiatric medicine and surgery in this state, upon any promise or agreement relating to a medical prognosis unless the promise or agreement is in writing and signed by the party to be charged therewith.

(1976 H 1426, eff. 7–1–76; 1975 H 682; 1953 H 1; GC 8621)

Historical and Statutory Notes

Pre–1953 H 1 Amendments: 114 v 110; 111 v 104; RS 4199

Comparative Laws

Ark.—A.C.A. § 4–59–101.
Conn.—C.G.S.A. § 52–550.
Ga.—O.C.G.A. § 13–5–30.
Ill.—ILCS 740 80/1.
Ky.—Baldwin's KRS 371.010.
Mass.—M.G.L.A. c. 259, § 1.
Me.—33 M.R.S.A. § 51.
Mo.—V.A.M.S. § 432.010.
N.D.—NDCC 9–06–04.
Neb.—R.R.S.1943, § 36–202.
Nev.—N.R.S. 111.220.
N.Y.—McKinney's General Obligations Law § 5–701 et seq.
Pa.—33 P.S. § 1 et seq.
S.C.—Code 1976, § 32–3–10.
S.D.—SDCL 53–8–2.
Tex.—V.T.C.A. Bus. & C. § 26.01.
Va.—Code 1950, § 11–2.
Vt.—12 V.S.A. § 181.
Wash.—West's RCWA 19.36.010.
Wis.—W.S.A. 241.02.
W.Va.—Code, 55–1–1.

Library References

Frauds, Statute Of ⇐14 to 36, 50(1), 115.1.
Westlaw Topic No. 185.

CHAPTER 1336

OHIO UNIFORM FRAUDULENT TRANSFER ACT

Section
1336.01 Definitions
1336.02 Insolvency
1336.03 Value
1336.04 Intent to defraud; property depletion; debts incurred beyond ability to pay
1336.05 Fraudulent transfers and obligations as to creditors with pre-existing claims
1336.06 Effectiveness of transfer or obligation
1336.07 Remedies
1336.08 Defenses; recovery by creditors; rights of good faith transferees and obligees
1336.09 Limitation of actions
1336.10 Effect of other laws
1336.11 Short title

Comparative Laws
Uniform Fraudulent Transfer Act
Table of Jurisdictions Wherein Act Has Been Adopted.

For text of Uniform Act, and variation notes and annotation materials for adopting jurisdictions, see Uniform Laws Annotated, Master Edition, Volume 7A.

Jurisdiction	Statutory Citation
Alabama	Code 1975, § 8–9A–1 to 8–9A–12.
Arizona	A.R.S. § 44–1001 to 44–1010.
Arkansas	A.C.A. § 4–59–201 to 4–59–213.
California	West's Ann.Cal.Civ. Code, § 3439 to 3439.12.
Colorado	West's C.R.S.A. § 38–8–101 to 38–8–112.
Connecticut	C.G.S.A. § 52–552a to 52–552l.
Delaware	6 Del.C. § 1301 to 1311.
District of Columbia	D.C. Official Code, 2001 Ed. § 28–3101 to 28–3111.
Florida	West's F.S.A. § 726.101 to 726.112.
Georgia	O.C.G.A. § 18–2–70 to 18–2–80.
Hawaii	HRS § 651C–1 to 651C–10.
Idaho	I.C. § 55–910 to 55–921.
Illinois	S.H.A. 740 ILCS 160/1 to 160/12.
Indiana	West's A.I.C. § 32–18–2–1 to 32–18–2–21.
Iowa	I.C.A. § 684.1 to 684.12.
Kansas	K.S.A. § 33–201 to 33–212.
Louisiana	LSA-R.S. 9:2790.1 to 9:2790.12.
Maine	14 M.R.S.A. § 3571 to 3582.
Massachusetts	M.G.L.A. c. 109A, § 1 to 12.
Michigan	M.C.L.A. § 566.31 to 566.43.
Minnesota	M.S.A. § 513.41 to 513.51.
Missouri	V.A.M.S. § 428.005 to 428.059.
Montana	MCA 31–2–326 to 31–2–342.
Nebraska	R.R.S.1943, § 36–701 to 36–712.
Nevada	N.R.S. 112.140 to 112.250.
New Hampshire	RSA 545–A:1 to 545–A:12.
New Jersey	N.J.S.A. 25:2–20 to 25:2–34.
New Mexico	NMSA 1978, § 56–10–14 to 56–10–25.
North Carolina	G.S. § 39–23.1 to 39–23.12.
North Dakota	NDCC 13–02.1–01 to 13–02.1–10.
Oklahoma	24 Okl.St.Ann. § 112 to 123.
Oregon	ORS 95.200 to 95.310.
Pennsylvania	12 Pa.C.S.A. § 5101 to 5110.
Rhode Island	Gen. Laws 1956, § 6–16–1 to 6–16–12.
South Dakota	SDCL 54–8A–1 to 54–8A–12.
Tennessee	T.C.A. § 66–3–301 to 66–3–313.
Texas	V.T.C.A. Bus. & C. § 24.001 to 24.013.
Utah	U.C.A. 1953, 25–6–1 to 25–6–14.
Vermont	9 V.S.A. § 2285 to 2295.
Washington	West's RCWA 19.40.011 to 19.40.903.
West Virginia	Code, 40–1A–1 to 40–1A–12.
Wisconsin	W.S.A. 242.01 to 242.11.

1336.01 Definitions

As used in this chapter:

(A) "Affiliate" means any of the following:

(1) A person who directly or indirectly owns, controls, or holds with power to vote, twenty per cent or more of the outstanding voting securities of the debtor, other than a person who holds the securities in either of the following manners:

(a) As a fiduciary or agent without sole discretionary power to vote the securities;

(b) Solely to secure a debt, if the person has not exercised the power to vote.

(2) A corporation twenty per cent or more of the outstanding voting securities of which are directly or indirectly owned, controlled, or held with power to vote, by the debtor or a person who directly or indirectly owns, controls, or holds with power to vote, twenty per cent or more of the outstanding voting securities of the debtor, other than a person who holds the securities in either of the following manners:

(a) As a fiduciary or agent without sole discretionary power to vote the securities;

(b) Solely to secure a debt, if the person has not exercised the power to vote.

(3) A person whose business is operated by the debtor under a lease or other agreement, or a person substantially all of whose assets are controlled by the debtor;

(4) A person who operates the business of the debtor under a lease or other agreement, or controls substantially all of the assets of the debtor.

(B) "Asset" means property of a debtor, but does not include any of the following:

(1) Property to the extent it is encumbered by a valid lien;

(2) Property to the extent it generally is exempt under non-bankruptcy law, including, but not limited to, section 2329.66 of the Revised Code;

(3) An interest in property held in the form of a tenancy by the entireties created under section 5302.17 of the Revised Code prior to April 4, 1985, to the extent it is not subject to process by a creditor holding a claim against only one tenant.

(C) "Claim" means a right to payment, whether or not the right is reduced to judgment, liquidated, unliquidated, fixed, contingent, matured, unmatured, disputed, undisputed, legal, equitable, secured, or unsecured.

(D) "Creditor" means a person who has a claim.

(E) "Debt" means liability on a claim.

(F) "Debtor" means a person who is liable on a claim.

(G) "Insider" includes all of the following:

(1) If the debtor is an individual, any of the following:

(a) A relative of the debtor or of a general partner of the debtor;

(b) A partnership in which the debtor is a general partner;

(c) A general partner in a partnership described in division (G)(1)(b) of this section;

(d) A corporation of which the debtor is a director, officer, or person in control.

(2) If the debtor is a corporation, any of the following:

(a) A director of the debtor;

(b) An officer of the debtor;

(c) A person in control of the debtor;

(d) A partnership in which the debtor is a general partner;

(e) A general partner in a partnership described in division (G)(2)(d) of this section;

(f) A relative of a general partner, director, officer, or person in control of the debtor.

(3) If the debtor is a partnership, any of the following:

(a) A general partner in the debtor;

(b) A relative of a general partner in, a general partner of, or a person in control of the debtor;

(c) Another partnership in which the debtor is a general partner;

(d) A general partner in a partnership described in division (G)(3)(c) of this section;

(e) A person in control of the debtor.

(4) An affiliate, or an insider of an affiliate as if the affiliate were the debtor;

(5) A managing agent of the debtor.

(H) "Lien" means a charge against or an interest in property to secure payment of a debt or performance of an obligation, and includes a security interest created by agreement, a judicial lien obtained by legal or equitable process or proceedings, a common law lien, or a statutory lien.

(I) "Person" means an individual, partnership, corporation, association, organization, government or governmental subdivision or agency, business trust, estate, trust, or any other legal or commercial entity.

(J) "Property" means anything that may be the subject of ownership.

(K) "Relative" means an individual related by consanguinity within the third degree as determined by the common law, a spouse, or an individual related to a spouse within the third degree as so determined, and includes an individual in an adoptive relationship within the third degree.

(L) "Transfer" means every direct or indirect, absolute or conditional, and voluntary or involuntary method of disposing of or parting with an asset or an interest in an asset, and includes payment of money, release, lease, and creation of a lien or other encumbrance.

(M) "Valid lien" means a lien that is effective against the holder of a judicial lien subsequently obtained by legal or equitable process or proceedings.

(1990 H 506, eff. 9–28–90)

Historical and Statutory Notes

Ed. Note: Former 1336.01 repealed by 1990 H 506, eff. 9–28–90; 130 v H 1; 129 v 1006.

1336.02 Insolvency

(A)(1) A debtor is insolvent if the sum of the debts of the debtor is greater than all of the assets of the debtor at a fair valuation.

(2) A debtor who generally is not paying his debts as they become due is presumed to be insolvent.

(B) A partnership is insolvent under division (A)(1) of this section if the sum of the debts of the partnership is greater than the aggregate, at a fair valuation, of all of the assets of the partnership and the sum of the excess of the value of the nonpartnership assets of each general partner over the nonpartnership debts of the general partner.

(C) For purposes of this section:

(1) "Assets" do not include property that has been transferred, concealed, or removed with intent to hinder, delay, or defraud creditors, or that has been transferred in a manner making the transfer fraudulent under section 1336.04 or 1336.05 of the Revised Code.

(2) "Debts" do not include an obligation to the extent that it is secured by a valid lien on property of the debtor not included as an asset.

(1990 H 506, eff. 9–28–90)

Historical and Statutory Notes

Ed. Note: Former 1336.02 repealed by 1990 H 506, eff. 9–28–90; 129 v 1006.

Library References

Fraudulent Conveyances ⚛57(1) to 62.
Westlaw Topic No. 186.

1336.03 Value

(A) Value is given for a transfer or an obligation if, in exchange for the transfer or obligation, property is transferred or an antecedent debt is secured or satisfied, but value does not include an unperformed promise made otherwise than in the ordinary course of the business of the promisor to furnish support to the debtor or another person.

(B) For the purposes of division (A)(2) of section 1336.04 and division (A) of section 1336.05 of the Revised Code, a person gives a reasonably equivalent value if the person acquires an interest of the debtor in an asset pursuant to a regularly conducted, noncollusive foreclosure sale or execution of power of sale for the acquisition or disposition of the interest of the debtor upon default under a mortgage, deed of trust, or security agreement.

(C) A transfer is made for present value if the exchange between the debtor and the transferee is intended by them to be contemporaneous and in fact is substantially contemporaneous.

(1990 H 506, eff. 9–28–90)

Historical and Statutory Notes

Ed. Note: Former 1336.03 repealed by 1990 H 506, eff. 9–28–90; 129 v 1006.

Library References

Fraudulent Conveyances ⚛77.
Westlaw Topic No. 186.

1336.04 Intent to defraud; property depletion; debts incurred beyond ability to pay

(A) A transfer made or an obligation incurred by a debtor is fraudulent as to a creditor, whether the claim of the creditor arose before or after the transfer was made or the obligation was incurred, if the debtor made the transfer or incurred the obligation in either of the following ways:

(1) With actual intent to hinder, delay, or defraud any creditor of the debtor;

(2) Without receiving a reasonably equivalent value in exchange for the transfer or obligation, and if either of the following applies:

(a) The debtor was engaged or was about to engage in a business or a transaction for which the remaining assets of the debtor were unreasonably small in relation to the business or transaction;

(b) The debtor intended to incur, or believed or reasonably should have believed that he would incur, debts beyond his ability to pay as they became due.

(B) In determining actual intent under division (A)(1) of this section, consideration may be given to all relevant factors, including, but not limited to, the following:

(1) Whether the transfer or obligation was to an insider;

(2) Whether the debtor retained possession or control of the property transferred after the transfer;

(3) Whether the transfer or obligation was disclosed or concealed;

(4) Whether before the transfer was made or the obligation was incurred, the debtor had been sued or threatened with suit;

(5) Whether the transfer was of substantially all of the assets of the debtor;

(6) Whether the debtor absconded;

(7) Whether the debtor removed or concealed assets;

(8) Whether the value of the consideration received by the debtor was reasonably equivalent to the value of the asset transferred or the amount of the obligation incurred;

(9) Whether the debtor was insolvent or became insolvent shortly after the transfer was made or the obligation was incurred;

(10) Whether the transfer occurred shortly before or shortly after a substantial debt was incurred;

(11) Whether the debtor transferred the essential assets of the business to a lienholder who transferred the assets to an insider of the debtor.

(1990 H 506, eff. 9–28–90)

Historical and Statutory Notes

Ed. Note: Former 1336.04 repealed by 1990 H 506, eff. 9–28–90; 129 v 1006.

Library References

Fraudulent Conveyances ⚖57(3), 63 to 69(1).
Westlaw Topic No. 186.

1336.05 Fraudulent transfers and obligations as to creditors with pre-existing claims

(A) A transfer made or an obligation incurred by a debtor is fraudulent as to a creditor whose claim arose before the transfer was made or the obligation was incurred if the debtor made the transfer or incurred the obligation without receiving a reasonably equivalent value in exchange for the transfer or obligation and the debtor was insolvent at that time or the debtor became insolvent as a result of the transfer or obligation.

(B) A transfer made or an obligation incurred by a debtor is fraudulent as to a creditor whose claim arose before the transfer was made or the obligation was incurred if the transfer was made to or the obligation was incurred with respect to an insider for an antecedent debt, the debtor was insolvent at that time, and the insider had reasonable cause to believe that the debtor was insolvent.

(1990 H 506, eff. 9–28–90)

Historical and Statutory Notes

Ed. Note: Former 1336.05 repealed by 1990 H 506, eff. 9–28–90; 129 v 1006.

Library References

Fraudulent Conveyances ⚖74(2).
Westlaw Topic No. 186.

1336.06 Effectiveness of transfer or obligation

For the purposes of this chapter:

(A)(1) A transfer is made if either of the following applies:

(a) With respect to an asset that is real property other than a fixture, but including the interest of a seller or purchaser under a contract for the sale of the asset, when the transfer is so far perfected that a good faith purchaser of the asset from the debtor against whom applicable law permits the transfer to be perfected cannot acquire an interest in the asset that is superior to the interest of the transferee;

(b) With respect to an asset that is not real property or that is a fixture, when the transfer is so far perfected that a creditor on a simple contract cannot acquire a judicial lien otherwise than under this chapter that is superior to the interest of the transferee.

(2)(a) If applicable law permits the transfer to be perfected as provided in division (A) of this section and the transfer is not so perfected before the commencement of an action for relief arising out of a transfer that is fraudulent under section 1336.04 or 1336.05 of the Revised Code, the transfer is deemed made immediately before the commencement of the action.

(b) If applicable law does not permit the transfer to be perfected as provided in division (A) of this section, the transfer is made when it becomes effective between the debtor and the transferee.

(3) A transfer is not made until the debtor has acquired rights in the asset transferred.

(B) An obligation is incurred as follows:

(1) If oral, when it becomes effective between the parties;

(2) If evidenced by a writing, when the writing executed by the obligor is delivered to or for the benefit of the obligee.

(1990 H 506, eff. 9–28–90)

Historical and Statutory Notes

Ed. Note: Former 1336.06 repealed by 1990 H 506, eff. 9–28–90; 129 v 1006.

Library References

Fraudulent Conveyances ⚖23.
Westlaw Topic No. 186.

1336.07 Remedies

(A) In an action for relief arising out of a transfer or an obligation that is fraudulent under section 1336.04 or 1336.05 of the Revised Code, a creditor or a child support enforcement agency on behalf of a support creditor, subject to the limitations in section 1336.08 of the Revised Code, may obtain one of the following:

(1) Avoidance of the transfer or obligation to the extent necessary to satisfy the claim of the creditor;

(2) An attachment or garnishment against the asset transferred or other property of the transferee in accordance with Chapters 2715. and 2716. of the Revised Code;

(3) Subject to the applicable principles of equity and in accordance with the Rules of Civil Procedure, any of the following:

(a) An injunction against further disposition by the debtor or a transferee, or both, of the asset transferred or of other property;

(b) Appointment of a receiver to take charge of the asset transferred or of other property of the transferee;

(c) Any other relief that the circumstances may require.

(B) If a creditor or child support enforcement agency has obtained a judgment on a claim against the debtor, the creditor or agency, if the court so orders, may levy execution on the asset transferred or its proceeds in accordance with Chapter 2329. of the Revised Code.

(1997 H 352, eff. 1-1-98; 1990 H 506, eff. 9-28-90)

Historical and Statutory Notes

Ed. Note: Former 1336.07 repealed by 1990 H 506, eff. 9-28-90; 129 v 1006.

Amendment Note: 1997 H 352 inserted "or a child support enforcement agency on behalf of a support creditor" in the first paragraph in division (A); and inserted "or child support enforcement agency" and "or agency" in division (B).

Library References

Fraudulent Conveyances ⚖=226 to 230.
Westlaw Topic No. 186.

1336.08 Defenses; recovery by creditors; rights of good faith transferees and obligees

(A) A transfer or an obligation is not fraudulent under division (A)(1) of section 1336.04 of the Revised Code against a person who took in good faith and for a reasonably equivalent value or against any subsequent transferee or obligee.

(B)(1) Except as otherwise provided in this section, to the extent a transfer is voidable in an action by a creditor or a child support enforcement agency under division (A)(1) of section 1336.07 of the Revised Code, the creditor or agency may recover a judgment for the value of the asset transferred, as adjusted under division (B)(2) of this section, or the amount necessary to satisfy the claim of the creditor or agency, whichever is less. The judgment may be entered against either of the following:

(a) The first transferee of the asset or the person for whose benefit the transfer was made;

(b) Any subsequent transferee other than a good faith transferee who took for value or from any subsequent transferee.

(2) If the judgment under division (B)(1) of this section is based upon the value of the asset transferred, the judgment shall be in an amount equal to the value of the asset at the time of the transfer, subject to adjustment as the equities may require.

(C) Notwithstanding the voidability of a transfer or an obligation under division (A)(1) of section 1336.07 of the Revised Code, a good faith transferee or obligee is entitled, to the extent of the value given to the debtor for the transfer or obligation, to any of the following:

(1) A lien on or a right to retain any interest in the asset transferred;

(2) Enforcement of any obligation incurred;

(3) A reduction in the amount of the liability on the judgment.

(D) A transfer is not fraudulent under division (A)(2) of section 1336.04 or section 1336.05 of the Revised Code if the transfer results from either of the following:

(1) Termination of a lease upon default by the debtor when the termination is pursuant to the lease and applicable law;

(2) Enforcement of a security interest in compliance with section sections [1] 1309.601 to 1309.604 of the Revised Code.

(E) A transfer is not fraudulent under division (B) of section 1336.05 of the Revised Code as follows:

(1) To the extent the insider gave new value to or for the benefit of the debtor after the transfer was made, unless the new value was secured by a valid lien;

(2) If made in the ordinary course of business or financial affairs of the debtor and the insider;

(3) If made pursuant to a good faith effort to rehabilitate the debtor and the transfer secured present value given for that purpose as well as an antecedent debt of the debtor.

(2001 S 74, eff. 7-1-01; 1997 H 352, eff. 1-1-98; 1990 H 506, eff. 9-28-90)

[1] So in original; 2001 S 74.

Historical and Statutory Notes

Ed. Note: Former 1336.08 repealed by 1990 H 506, eff. 9-28-90; 129 v 1006.

Amendment Note: 2001 S 74 substituted "sections 1309.601 to 1309.604" for "1309.44" in division (D)(2).

Amendment Note: 1997 H 352 inserted "or a child support enforcement agency" and "or agency" in the first paragraph in division (B)(1).

Library References

Fraudulent Conveyances ⚖=174, 184(1), 313(1).
Westlaw Topic No. 186.

1336.09 Limitation of actions

A claim for relief with respect to a transfer or an obligation that is fraudulent under section 1336.04 or 1336.05 of the Revised Code is extinguished unless an action is brought in accordance with one of the following:

(A) If the transfer or obligation is fraudulent under division (A)(1) of section 1336.04 of the Revised Code, within four years after the transfer was made or the obligation was incurred or, if later, within one year after the transfer or obligation was or reasonably could have been discovered by the claimant;

(B) If the transfer or obligation is fraudulent under division (A)(2) of section 1336.04 or division (A) of section 1336.05 of the Revised Code, within four years after the transfer was made or the obligation was incurred;

(C) If the transfer or obligation is fraudulent under division (B) of section 1336.05 of the Revised Code, within one year after the transfer was made or the obligation was incurred.

(1990 H 506, eff. 9-28-90)

Historical and Statutory Notes

Ed. Note: Former 1336.09 repealed by 1990 H 506, eff. 9-28-90; 129 v 1006.

Library References

Fraudulent Conveyances ⚖=248.
Limitation of Actions ⚖=37(1).
Westlaw Topic Nos. 186, 241.

C.J.S. Limitations of Actions § 34.

1336.10 Effect of other laws

Unless displaced by this chapter, the principles of law and equity, including, but not limited to, the law merchant and the law relating to principal and agent, estoppel, laches, fraud, misrepresentation, duress, coercion, mistake, insolvency, or other validating or invalidating cause, supplement the provisions of this chapter.

(1990 H 506, eff. 9–28–90)

Historical and Statutory Notes

Ed. Note: Former 1336.10 repealed by 1990 H 506, eff. 9–28–90; 129 v 1006.

Library References

Fraudulent Conveyances ⇐237(1) to 237(3).
Westlaw Topic No. 186.

1336.11 Short title

This chapter may be cited as the Ohio uniform fraudulent transfer act.

(1990 H 506, eff. 9–28–90)

Historical and Statutory Notes

Ed. Note: Former 1336.11 repealed by 1990 H 506, eff. 9–28–90; 129 v 1006.

CHAPTER 1337

POWER OF ATTORNEY

MISCELLANEOUS PROVISIONS

Section
1337.01   Power of attorney
1337.02   Form and effect of power of attorney
1337.03   Validity of certain acts of attorney in fact
1337.04   Recording of powers of attorney
1337.05   Revocation of power of attorney must be recorded
1337.06   Execution and evidence of power of attorney
1337.07   Admission of power of attorney to record
1337.08   Record of power of attorney authorizing transfer of personal property
1337.09   Power of attorney may survive disability of principal; nomination of attorney as guardian of person or estate
1337.091   Action without knowledge of death or disability
1337.092   Contracts entered into in representative capacity; personal liability for principal's debt
1337.093   Applicability of "powers of attorney" and "attorney in fact"
1337.10   Fees of recorder; use of separate instrument

DURABLE POWER OF ATTORNEY FOR HEALTH CARE

1337.11   Definitions
1337.12   Creation; witness; acknowledgment; effect of living will
1337.13   Health care decisions by attorney in fact
1337.14   Revocation by principal
1337.15   Immunities
1337.16   Power of attorney may not be required or prohibited; refusal to comply with instructions of attorney in fact; transfer of principal to complying physician or health care facility; records; notice requirements; objections; complaints; comfort care
1337.17   Form
1337.18   Form to create power of attorney
1337.19   Powers of attorney in fact
1337.20   Construction of powers of attorney in fact

Comparative Laws

Conn.—C.G.S.A. § 47-5.
Ky.—Baldwin's KRS 382.370.
Mass.—M.G.L.A. c. 185, § 110.
Mo.—V.A.M.S. § 442.360.

MISCELLANEOUS PROVISIONS

1337.01 Power of attorney

A power of attorney for the conveyance, mortgage, or lease of any interest in real property shall be signed, acknowledged, and certified as provided in section 5301.01 of the Revised Code.

(2001 H 279, eff. 2–1–02; 1953 H 1, eff. 10–1–53; GC 8512)

Historical and Statutory Notes

Pre-1953 H 1 Amendments: RS 4108

Amendment Note: 2001 H 279 substituted "shall" for "must" and deleted "attested" after "signed" in the section.

Library References

Principal and Agent ⇐8 to 12.
Westlaw Topic No. 308.
C.J.S. Agency §§ 36 to 42.

1337.02 Form and effect of power of attorney

A deed, mortgage, or lease of any interest in real property, made by virtue of a power of attorney, must contain the name of the grantor, mortgagor, or lessor, and shall convey, mortgage, or lease the interest of such grantor, mortgagor, or lessor as fully as if such deed, mortgage, or lease were executed by such grantor, mortgagor, or lessor, in person. At any time previous to the conveyance, mortgage, or lease, the grantor, mortgagor, or lessor may revoke such power of attorney.

(1953 H 1, eff. 10–1–53; GC 8513)

Historical and Statutory Notes

Pre-1953 H 1 Amendments: RS 4109

Library References

Principal and Agent ⇐9, 37.
Westlaw Topic No. 308.
C.J.S. Agency §§ 41 to 42, 126.

1337.03 Validity of certain acts of attorney in fact

No deed executed by a person acting for another, under a power of attorney, acknowledged, and recorded, is invalid or defective because he, instead of his principal, is named in such deed as such attorney, as grantor; nor because his name, as such attorney, is subscribed to such deed, instead of the name of his principal; nor because the certificate of acknowledgment, instead of setting forth that the deed was acknowledged by the principal, by his attorney, sets forth that it was acknowledged by the person who executed it, as such attorney. All such deeds shall be as valid and effectual, in all respects, within the authority conferred by such powers of attorney, as if they had been executed by the principals of such attorneys, in person.

(1953 H 1, eff. 10–1–53; GC 8514)

Historical and Statutory Notes

Pre–1953 H 1 Amendments: RS 4110

Library References

Principal and Agent ⚖︎126(4).
Westlaw Topic No. 308.
C.J.S. Agency §§ 248 to 255.

1337.04 Recording of powers of attorney

A power of attorney for the conveyance, mortgage, or lease of an interest in real property must be recorded in the office of the county recorder of the county in which such property is situated, previous to the recording of a deed, mortgage, or lease by virtue of such power of attorney.

(1953 H 1, eff. 10–1–53; GC 8536)

Historical and Statutory Notes

Pre–1953 H 1 Amendments: 120 v 226; RS 4131

Comparative Laws

W.Va.—Code, 39–1–1.

Library References

Principal and Agent ⚖︎10(2).
Westlaw Topic No. 308.
C.J.S. Agency §§ 41 to 42.

1337.05 Revocation of power of attorney must be recorded

No instrument containing a power of attorney for the conveyance, mortgage, or lease of an interest in real property, which has been recorded, will be revoked by any act of the person by whom it was executed, unless the instrument containing such revocation is also recorded in the same office in which the instrument containing the power of attorney was recorded.

(1953 H 1, eff. 10–1–53; GC 8537)

Historical and Statutory Notes

Pre–1953 H 1 Amendments: RS 4132

Library References

Principal and Agent ⚖︎37.
Westlaw Topic No. 308.
C.J.S. Agency § 126.

1337.06 Execution and evidence of power of attorney

A power of attorney for the transfer of personal property or the transaction of business relating to the transfer of personal property, in order to be admitted to record as provided in section 1337.07 of the Revised Code, shall be signed and acknowledged in the same manner as deeds and mortgages under section 5301.01 of the Revised Code. When so executed, acknowledged, and recorded, a copy of the record, certified by the county recorder, with the recorder's official seal affixed to it, shall be received in all courts and places within this state as prima-facie evidence of the existence of that instrument and as conclusive evidence of the existence of that record.

(2001 H 279, eff. 2–1–02; 126 v 392, eff. 3–17–55; 1953 H 1; GC 8540)

Historical and Statutory Notes

Pre–1953 H 1 Amendments: 90 v 356, § 2

Amendment Note: 2001 H 279 substituted "shall" for "must" and deleted ", witnessed," after "signed" in the first sentence of the section; made changes to reflect gender neutral language, and made other nonsubstantive changes.

Library References

Principal and Agent ⚖︎10(2).
Westlaw Topic No. 308.
C.J.S. Agency §§ 41 to 42.

1337.07 Admission of power of attorney to record

Any person interested may have a power of attorney authorizing the transfer of personal property or the transaction of any business relating thereto admitted to record in the office of the county recorder of the county in which such property is situated, or in which any of such business is to be transacted.

(1953 H 1, eff. 10–1–53; GC 8539)

Historical and Statutory Notes

Pre–1953 H 1 Amendments: 90 v 356, § 2

Library References

Principal and Agent ⚖︎10(2).
Westlaw Topic No. 308.
C.J.S. Agency §§ 41 to 42.

1337.08 Record of power of attorney authorizing transfer of personal property

The county recorder shall keep a record, in which shall be recorded powers of attorney authorizing the transfer of personal property or the transaction of any business relating thereto. Upon presentation of such a power of attorney the recorder shall endorse thereon the date of its presentation, and after it is recorded endorse thereon the time at which the instrument was recorded, and the number or letter and page of the book in which it is recorded. He also shall keep an alphabetical index of each power of attorney so recorded.

(1981 S 114, eff. 10–27–81; 1953 H 1; GC 8538)

Historical and Statutory Notes

Pre–1953 H 1 Amendments: 90 v 355, § 1

Library References

Principal and Agent ⚖10(2).
Westlaw Topic No. 308.
C.J.S. Agency §§ 41 to 42.

1337.09 Power of attorney may survive disability of principal; nomination of attorney as guardian of person or estate

(A) Whenever a principal designates another as attorney in fact by a power of attorney in writing and the writing contains the words "This power of attorney shall not be affected by disability of the principal," "this power of attorney shall not be affected by disability of the principal or lapse of time," or words of similar import, the authority of the attorney in fact is exercisable by the attorney in fact as provided in the written instrument notwithstanding the later disability, incapacity, or adjudged incompetency of the principal and, unless it states a time of termination, notwithstanding the lapse of time since the execution of the instrument.

(B) Whenever a principal designates another the principal's attorney in fact by a power of attorney in writing and the writing expressly states that the power of attorney shall become effective at a later time or upon the occurrence of a specified event, including, but not limited to, the disability, incapacity, or adjudged incompetency of the principal, the attorney in fact may exercise the authority provided to the attorney in fact in the written instrument at the later time or upon the occurrence of the specified event notwithstanding the later disability, incapacity, or adjudged incompetency of the principal and, unless the instrument states a time of termination, notwithstanding the lapse of time since its execution.

(C) All acts done by an attorney in fact pursuant to an instrument as described in division (A) or (B) of this section during any period of disability, incapacity, or adjudged incompetency of the principal shall have the same effect and inure to the benefit of and bind the principal or the principal's heirs, devisees, and personal representatives as if the principal were competent and not disabled or incapacitated. If a guardian thereafter is appointed for the principal and the guardian is not the attorney in fact, the attorney in fact, during the continuance of the appointment, shall account to the guardian rather than the principal. The guardian has the same power the principal would have had if not incompetent, to revoke all or any part of the power and authority of the attorney in fact.

(D) In a durable power of attorney as described in division (A) or (B) of this section, a principal may nominate the attorney in fact or any other person to be the guardian of the principal's person, estate, or both and may nominate the attorney in fact or any other person to be the guardian of the person, the estate, or both of one or more of the principal's minor children, whether born at the time of the execution of the durable power of attorney or afterward. The nomination is for consideration by a court if proceedings for the appointment of a guardian for the principal's person, estate, or both or if proceedings for the appointment of a guardian of the person, the estate, or both of one or more of the principal's minor children are commenced at a later time. The principal may authorize in a power of attorney of that nature the person nominated as guardian or the attorney in fact to nominate a successor guardian for consideration by a court.

The principal may direct, in a power of attorney of that nature, that bond be waived for a person nominated as guardian in it or nominated as a successor guardian in accordance with an authorization in it.

Nomination of a person as a guardian or successor guardian of the person, the estate, or both of one or more of the principal's minor children under this division, and any subsequent appointment of the guardian or successor guardian as guardian under section 2111.02 of the Revised Code, does not vacate the jurisdiction of any other court that previously may have exercised jurisdiction over the person of the minor.

The durable power of attorney as described in division (A) or (B) of this section that contains the nomination of a person to be the guardian of the person, the estate, or both of one or more of the principal's minor children under this division may be filed with the probate court for safekeeping, and the probate court shall designate the nomination as the nomination of a standby guardian.

(1996 H 288, eff. 1–14–97; 1988 S 228, eff. 3–22–89; 1983 S 115; 1976 S 165)

Historical and Statutory Notes

Ed. Note: Former section 1337.09 repealed by 1976 S 165, eff. 7–12–76; 1953 H 1; GC 8541–1.

Pre–1953 H 1 Amendments: 124 v S 54

Amendment Note: 1996 H 288 inserted "and may nominate the attorney in fact or any other person to be the guardian of the person, the estate, or both of one or more of the principal's minor children, whether born at the time of the execution of the durable power of attorney or afterward" and "or if proceedings for the appointment of a guardian of the person, the estate, or both of one or more of the principal's minor children" in the first paragraph in division (D); added the third and fourth paragraphs in division (D); and made changes to reflect gender neutral language and other nonsubstantive changes.

Library References

Principal and Agent ⚖42, 51.
Westlaw Topic No. 308.
C.J.S. Agency §§ 133, 145 to 146.

Baldwin's Ohio Legislative Service, 1988 Laws of Ohio, S 228—LSC Analysis, p 5–968

1337.091 Action without knowledge of death or disability

(A) The death or adjudged incompetency of any principal who has executed a power of attorney in writing does not revoke the power and authority of the attorney in fact who, without actual knowledge of the death or adjudged incompetency of the principal, acts in good faith under the power of attorney. Any action so taken, unless otherwise invalid or unenforceable, inures to the benefit of and binds the principal and the principal's heirs, devisees, and personal representatives.

(B)(1) An affidavit that is executed by the attorney in fact is, in the absence of fraud, conclusive proof of the nonrevocation of the power of attorney at the time of the attorney in fact doing an act pursuant to the power of attorney if the affadavit [1] contains the following:

(a) A statement that the attorney in fact, at the time of doing an act pursuant to the power of attorney, had no actual knowledge of the revocation of the power of attorney by the principal;

(b) A statement that the attorney in fact, at the time of doing an act pursuant to the power of attorney, had no actual knowledge of the revocation of the power of attorney by death or adjudged incompetency of the principal;

(c) One of the following statements, whichever is applicable:

(i) The attorney in fact was never married to the principal.

(ii) The attorney in fact was married to the principal, the marriage has been terminated, and the power of attorney states that the power of attorney is not revoked by reason of law due to the termination of the marriage between the principal and the attorney in fact.

(iii) The attorney in fact is married to the principal, a separation agreement has been entered into between the principal and the attorney in fact in which they intend to fully and finally settle each spouse's prospective property rights in the property of the other, and the power of attorney states that the power of attorney is not revoked by reason of law due to the existence of a separation agreement of that nature entered into between the principal and the attorney in fact.

(2) If the exercise of the power of attorney requires the execution and delivery of any instrument that is recordable, the affidavit that is executed under division (B)(1) of this section, if acknowledged before a notary public in the same manner as a deed, is likewise recordable.

(C) This section shall not be construed to alter or affect any provision for revocation contained in any power of attorney. This section shall not be construed to affect any provision of a power of attorney that indicates, consistent with section 1337.09 of the Revised Code, that the authority of the attorney in fact is exercisable by the attorney in fact as provided in the power of attorney notwithstanding the later disability, incapacity, or adjudged incompetency of the principal.

(2003 S 64, eff. 10-21-03; 2001 H 279, eff. 2-1-02; 1980 S 317, eff. 3-23-81; 1976 S 165)

[1] So in original; 2003 S 64.

Historical and Statutory Notes

Amendment Note: 2003 S 64 rewrote division (B), which prior thereto read:

"(B) An affidavit, executed by the attorney in fact stating that the attorney in fact did not have, at the time of doing an act pursuant to the power of attorney, actual knowledge of the revocation of the power of attorney by the principal, or the revocation of the power of attorney by death or adjudged incompetency of the principal is, in the absence of fraud, conclusive proof of the nonrevocation of the power at that time. If the exercise of the power requires the execution and delivery of any instrument that is recordable, the affidavit when acknowledged before a notary public in the same manner as a deed, is likewise recordable."

Amendment Note: 2001 H 279 deleted "witnessed and" before "acknowledged" in the last sentence of division (B); and made changes to reflect gender neutral language.

Library References

Principal and Agent ⚖136(2).
Westlaw Topic No. 308.
C.J.S. Agency § 121.

1337.092 Contracts entered into in representative capacity; personal liability for principal's debt

(A) If an attorney in fact enters into a contract in the representative capacity of the attorney in fact, if the contract is within the authority of the attorney in fact, and if the attorney in fact discloses in the contract that it is being entered into in the representative capacity of the attorney in fact, the attorney in fact is not personally liable on the contract, unless the contract otherwise specifies. If the words or initialism "attorney in fact," "as attorney in fact," "AIF," "power of attorney," "POA," or any other word or words or initialism indicating representative capacity as an attorney in fact are included in a contract following the name or signature of an attorney in fact, the inclusion is sufficient disclosure for purposes of this division that the contract is being entered into in the attorney in fact's representative capacity as attorney in fact.

(B) An attorney in fact is not personally liable for a debt of the attorney in fact's principal, unless one or more of the following applies:

(1) The attorney in fact agrees to be personally responsible for the debt.

(2) The debt was incurred for the support of the principal, and the attorney in fact is liable for that debt because of another legal relationship that gives rise to or results in a duty of support relative to the principal.

(3) The negligence of the attorney in fact gave rise to or resulted in the debt.

(4) An act of the attorney in fact that was beyond the attorney in fact's authority gave rise to or resulted in the debt.

(5) An agreement to assist in the recovery of funds under section 169.13 of the Revised Code was the subject of the power of attorney that gave rise to or resulted in the debt.

(1996 H 391, eff. 10-1-96)

Uncodified Law

1996 H 391, § 3, eff. 10-1-96, reads: New section 1337.092 of the Revised Code, as enacted by this act, and the amendments to section 2111.151 of the Revised Code made in this act shall apply only to contracts entered into or debts incurred on or after the effective date of this act. The personal liability of or defenses to or immunity from personal liability of an attorney in fact in connection with contracts that were entered into prior to the effective date of this act and that pertain to the attorney in fact's principal and in connection with debts of an attorney in fact's principal, a guardian's ward, or a conservator's physically infirm, competent adult that were incurred prior to the effective date of this act shall be determined in accordance with the common law of this state and any applicable sections of the Revised Code in effect on the day immediately prior to the effective date of this act.

Historical and Statutory Notes

Ed. Note: Former 1337.092 amended and recodified as 1337.093 by 1996 H 391, eff. 10-1-96; 1980 S 317, eff. 3-23-81.

Library References

Principal and Agent ⚖136(2).
Westlaw Topic No. 308.
C.J.S. Agency §§ 361, 365, 390, 394.

1337.093 Applicability of "powers of attorney" and "attorney in fact"

Sections 1337.09 to 1337.092 of the Revised Code, and the terms "power of attorney" and "attorney in fact" used in those sections include, but are not limited to, an agency agreement and an agent under an agency agreement.

(1996 H 391, eff. 10-1-96)

Historical and Statutory Notes

Ed. Note: 1337.093 is former 1337.092, amended and recodified by 1996 H 391, eff. 10-1-96; 1980 S 317, eff. 3-23-81.

Amendment Note: 1996 H 391 substituted "to 1337.092" for "and 1337.091" and "but are not limited to" for "without limitation".

Library References

Principal and Agent ⚖1.
Westlaw Topic No. 308.
C.J.S. Agency §§ 2, 4 to 5, 23, 25 to 27, 33, 38 to 40, 58.
C.J.S. Architects § 21.

1337.10 Fees of recorder; use of separate instrument

The county recorder shall charge the same fee for the recording of a power of attorney authorizing the transfer of personal property or the transaction of business relating to the transfer of personal property, the indexing of that instrument, and for making a certified copy of the record of the instrument, that the recorder is allowed by section 317.32 of the Revised Code to charge for similar services in regard to other instruments.

In a county in which the county recorder has determined to use the microfilm process as provided by section 9.01 of the Revised Code, the recorder may require that all cancellations, releases, or other actions affecting recorded powers of attorney be by separate instrument, signed and acknowledged as provided by section 5301.01 of the Revised Code. The original instrument bearing the proper endorsement may be used as that separate instrument. Any cancellations, releases, or other actions described in this section shall be recorded in the books in which the powers of attorney were recorded. The fee for recordation shall be as set forth in this section.

(2001 H 279, eff. 2–1–02; 1993 H 152, eff. 7–1–93; 1973 S 341; 1953 H 1; GC 8541)

Historical and Statutory Notes

Pre–1953 H 1 Amendments: 90 v 356, § 3

Amendment Note: 2001 H 279 substituted "similar" for "like" in the last sentence of the first paragraph; deleted ", witnessed," after "signed" in the second paragraph; made changes to reflect gender neutral language; and made other nonsubstantive changes to the section.

Amendment Note: 1993 H 152 deleted "divisions (A)(1) to (A)(6)" from the reference to section 317.32 in, and substituted "other instruments" for "mortgages and deeds of conveyances" in, the first paragraph.

Library References

Principal and Agent ⚖10(2).
Westlaw Topic No. 308.
C.J.S. Agency §§ 41 to 42.

DURABLE POWER OF ATTORNEY FOR HEALTH CARE

Uncodified Law

1991 S 1, §§ 4 and 5, eff. 10–10–91, read:

Section 4. The amendments made to sections 1337.11 to 1337.17 of the Revised Code by Section 1 of this act do not affect, and shall not be construed as affecting, the continued validity of a durable power of attorney for health care that was created on or after September 27, 1989, and prior to the effective date of this act. The principal of such a durable power of attorney for health care, in his discretion, may allow the instrument to operate in accordance with its terms and the provisions of former sections 1337.11 to 1337.17 of the Revised Code, or create a new durable power of attorney for health care in accordance with the provisions of those sections as amended by this act.

Section 5. The General Assembly declares that its several intents in enacting Amended Substitute Senate Bill No. 13 of the 118th General Assembly did not include any intent to affect the ability of competent adults or the guardians of incompetents or minors to make informed health care decisions for themselves or their wards.

1337.11 Definitions

As used in sections 1337.11 to 1337.17 of the Revised Code:

(A) "Adult" means a person who is eighteen years of age or older.

(B) "Attending physician" means the physician to whom a principal or the family of a principal has assigned primary responsibility for the treatment or care of the principal or, if the responsibility has not been assigned, the physician who has accepted that responsibility.

(C) "Comfort care" means any of the following:

(1) Nutrition when administered to diminish the pain or discomfort of a principal, but not to postpone death;

(2) Hydration when administered to diminish the pain or discomfort of a principal, but not to postpone death;

(3) Any other medical or nursing procedure, treatment, intervention, or other measure that is taken to diminish the pain or discomfort of a principal, but not to postpone death.

(D) "Consulting physician" means a physician who, in conjunction with the attending physician of a principal, makes one or more determinations that are required to be made by the attending physician, or to be made by the attending physician and one other physician, by an applicable provision of sections 1337.11 to 1337.17 of the Revised Code, to a reasonable degree of medical certainty and in accordance with reasonable medical standards.

(E) "Declaration for mental health treatment" has the same meaning as in section 2135.01 of the Revised Code.

(F) "Guardian" means a person appointed by a probate court pursuant to Chapter 2111. of the Revised Code to have the care and management of the person of an incompetent.

(G) "Health care" means any care, treatment, service, or procedure to maintain, diagnose, or treat an individual's physical or mental condition or physical or mental health.

(H) "Health care decision" means informed consent, refusal to give informed consent, or withdrawal of informed consent to health care.

(I) "Health care facility" means any of the following:

(1) A hospital;

(2) A hospice care program or other institution that specializes in comfort care of patients in a terminal condition or in a permanently unconscious state;

(3) A nursing home;

(4) A home health agency;

(5) An intermediate care facility for the mentally retarded;

(6) A regulated community mental health organization.

(J) "Health care personnel" means physicians, nurses, physician assistants, emergency medical technicians-basic, emergency medical technicians-intermediate, emergency medical technicians-paramedic, medical technicians, dietitians, other authorized persons acting under the direction of an attending physician, and administrators of health care facilities.

(K) "Home health agency" has the same meaning as in section 3701.881 5101.61 [1] of the Revised Code.

(L) "Hospice care program" has the same meaning as in section 3712.01 of the Revised Code.

(M) "Hospital" has the same meanings as in sections 2108.01, 3701.01, and 5122.01 of the Revised Code.

(N) "Hydration" means fluids that are artificially or technologically administered.

(O) "Incompetent" has the same meaning as in section 2111.01 of the Revised Code.

(P) "Intermediate care facility for the mentally retarded" has the same meaning as in section 5111.20 of the Revised Code.

(Q) "Life–sustaining treatment" means any medical procedure, treatment, intervention, or other measure that, when administered to a principal, will serve principally to prolong the process of dying.

(R) "Medical claim" has the same meaning as in section 2305.113 of the Revised Code.

(S) "Mental health treatment" has the same meaning as in section 2135.01 of the Revised Code.

(T) "Nursing home" has the same meaning as in section 3721.01 of the Revised Code.

(U) "Nutrition" means sustenance that is artificially or technologically administered.

(V) "Permanently unconscious state" means a state of permanent unconsciousness in a principal that, to a reasonable degree of medical certainty as determined in accordance with reasonable medical standards by the principal's attending physician and one other physician who has examined the principal, is characterized by both of the following:

(1) Irreversible unawareness of one's being and environment.

(2) Total loss of cerebral cortical functioning, resulting in the principal having no capacity to experience pain or suffering.

(W) "Person" has the same meaning as in section 1.59 of the Revised Code and additionally includes political subdivisions and governmental agencies, boards, commissions, departments, institutions, offices, and other instrumentalities.

(X) "Physician" means a person who is authorized under Chapter 4731. of the Revised Code to practice medicine and surgery or osteopathic medicine and surgery.

(Y) "Political subdivision" and "state" have the same meanings as in section 2744.01 of the Revised Code.

(Z) "Professional disciplinary action" means action taken by the board or other entity that regulates the professional conduct of health care personnel, including the state medical board and the board of nursing.

(AA) "Regulated community mental health organization" means a residential facility as defined and licensed under section 5119.22 of the Revised Code or a community mental health agency as defined in section 5122.01 of the Revised Code.

(BB) "Terminal condition" means an irreversible, incurable, and untreatable condition caused by disease, illness, or injury from which, to a reasonable degree of medical certainty as determined in accordance with reasonable medical standards by a principal's attending physician and one other physician who has examined the principal, both of the following apply:

(1) There can be no recovery.

(2) Death is likely to occur within a relatively short time if life-sustaining treatment is not administered.

(CC) "Tort action" means a civil action for damages for injury, death, or loss to person or property, other than a civil action for damages for a breach of contract or another agreement between persons.

(2003 H 72, eff. 10–29–03; 2003 H 95, eff. 9–26–03; 1995 S 143, eff. 3–5–96; 1995 S 150, eff. 11–24–95; 1991 S 1, eff. 10–10–91; 1989 S 13)

[1] So in original; language appears as the result of the harmonization of 2003 H 72 and 2003 H 95.

Uncodified Law

1991 S 1, §§ 4 and 5: See Uncodified Law under 1337.12.

Historical and Statutory Notes

Ed. Note: Comparison of these amendments [2003 H 72, eff. 10–29–03 and 2003 H 95, eff. 9–26–03] in pursuance of section 1.52 of the Revised Code discloses that they are not substantively irreconcilable so that they are required by that section to be harmonized to give effect to each amendment. In recognition of this rule of construction, changes made by 2003 H 72, eff. 10–29–03, and 2003 H 95, eff. 9–26–03, have been incorporated in the above amendment. See *Baldwin's Ohio Legislative Service Annotated*, 2003, pages 7/L–1854 and 6/L–433, or the OH–LEGIS or OH–LEGIS–OLD database on Westlaw, for original versions of these Acts.

Amendment Note: 2003 H 72 created new division (E); redesignated former divisions (E) through (Q) as new divisions (F) through (R) respectively; created new division (S); redesignated former divisions (R) through (X) as new divisions (T) through (Z) respectively; added new division (AA); redesignated former division (Y) as new division (BB); redesignated former division (Z) as new division (CC); added "or physical or mental health" to new division (G); added new division (I)(6); substituted "5101.61" for "3701.88" in new division (K); and substituted "2305.113" for "2305.11" in new division (R).

Amendment Note: 2003 H 95 substituted "3701.881" for "3701.88" in division (J).

Amendment Note: 1995 S 143 substituted "physician assistants" for "physician's assistants" in division (I).

Amendment Note: 1995 S 150 substituted "technicians-basic" for "technicians-ambulance" and "emergency medical technicians-intermediate" for "advanced emergency medical technicians-ambulance" in division (I); substituted "authorized" for "licensed" and "and" for "or" in division (V); deleted ", or a person who otherwise is authorized to practice medicine or surgery or osteopathic medicine and surgery in this state" from the end of, division (V); and made changes to reflect gender neutral language and other nonsubstantive changes.

Library References

Baldwin's Ohio Legislative Service, 1991 Laws of Ohio, S 1—LSC Analysis, p 5–250

1337.12 Creation; witness; acknowledgment; effect of living will

(A)(1) An adult who is of sound mind voluntarily may create a valid durable power of attorney for health care by executing a durable power of attorney, in accordance with division (B) of section 1337.09 of the Revised Code, that authorizes an attorney in fact as described in division (A)(2) of this section to make health care decisions for the principal at any time that the attending physician of the principal determines that the principal has lost the capacity to make informed health care decisions for the principal. Except as otherwise provided in divisions (B) to (F) of section 1337.13 of the Revised Code, the authorization may include the right to give informed consent, to refuse to give informed consent, or to withdraw informed consent to any health care that is being or could be provided to the principal. Additionally, to be valid, a durable power of attorney for health care shall satisfy both of the following:

(a) It shall be signed at the end of the instrument by the principal and shall state the date of its execution.

(b) It shall be witnessed in accordance with division (B) of this section or be acknowledged by the principal in accordance with division (C) of this section.

(2) Except as otherwise provided in this division, a durable power of attorney for health care may designate any competent adult as the attorney in fact. The attending physician of the principal and an administrator of any nursing home in which the principal is receiving care shall not be designated as an attorney in fact in, or act as an attorney in fact pursuant to, a durable power of attorney for health care. An employee or agent of the attending physician of the principal and an employee or agent of any health care facility in which the principal is being treated shall not be designated as an attorney in fact in, or act as an attorney in fact pursuant to, a durable power of attorney for health care, except that these limitations do not preclude a principal from designating either type of employee or agent as the principal's attorney in fact if the individual is a competent adult and related to the principal by blood, marriage, or adoption, or if the individual is a competent adult and the principal and the individual are members of the same religious order.

(3) A durable power of attorney for health care shall not expire, unless the principal specifies an expiration date in the instrument. However, when a durable power of attorney contains an expiration date, if the principal lacks the capacity to make informed health care decisions for the principal on the expiration date, the instrument shall continue in effect until the principal regains the capacity to make informed health care decisions for the principal.

(B) If witnessed for purposes of division (A)(1)(b) of this section, a durable power of attorney for health care shall be witnessed by at least two individuals who are adults and who are not ineligible to be witnesses under this division. Any person who is related to the principal by blood, marriage, or adoption, any person who is designated as the attorney in fact in the instrument, the attending physician of the principal, and the administrator of any nursing home in which the principal is receiving care are ineligible to be witnesses.

The witnessing of a durable power of attorney for health care shall involve the principal signing, or acknowledging the principal's signature, at the end of the instrument in the presence of each witness. Then, each witness shall subscribe the witness's signature after the signature of the principal and, by doing so, attest to the witness's belief that the principal appears to be of sound mind and not under or subject to duress, fraud, or undue influence. The signatures of the principal and the witnesses under this division are not required to appear on the same page of the instrument.

(C) If acknowledged for purposes of division (A)(1)(b) of this section, a durable power of attorney for health care shall be acknowledged before a notary public, who shall make the certification described in section 147.53 of the Revised Code and also shall attest that the principal appears to be of sound mind and not under or subject to duress, fraud, or undue influence.

(D)(1) If a principal has both a valid durable power of attorney for health care and a valid declaration, division (B) of section 2133.03 of the Revised Code applies. If a principal has both a valid durable power of attorney for health care and a DNR identification that is based upon a valid declaration and if the declaration supersedes the durable power of attorney for health care under division (B) of section 2133.03 of the Revised Code, the DNR identification supersedes the durable power of attorney for health care to the extent of any conflict between the two. A valid durable power of attorney for health care supersedes any DNR identification that is based upon a do-not-resuscitate order that a physician issued for the principal which is inconsistent with the durable power of attorney for health care or a valid decision by the attorney in fact under a durable power of attorney.

(2) As used in division (D) of this section:

(a) "Declaration" has the same meaning as in section 2133.01 of the Revised Code.

(b) "Do–not–resuscitate order" and "DNR identification" have the same meanings as in section 2133.21 of the Revised Code.

(2000 H 494, eff. 3-15-01; 1998 H 354, eff. 7-9-98; 1991 S 1, eff. 10-10-91; 1989 S 13)

Uncodified Law

1991 S 1, §§ 4 and 5, eff. 10-10-91, read:

Section 4. The amendments made to sections 1337.11 to 1337.17 of the Revised Code by Section 1 of this act do not affect, and shall not be construed as affecting, the continued validity of a durable power of attorney for health care that was created on or after September 27, 1989, and prior to the effective date of this act. The principal of such a durable power of attorney for health care, in his discretion, may allow the instrument to operate in accordance with its terms and the provisions of former sections 1337.11 to 1337.17 of the Revised Code, or create a new durable power of attorney for health care in accordance with the provisions of those sections as amended by this act.

Section 5. The General Assembly declares that its several intents in enacting Amended Substitute Senate Bill No. 13 of the 118th General Assembly did not include any intent to affect the ability of competent adults or the guardians of incompetents or minors to make informed health care decisions for themselves or their wards.

Historical and Statutory Notes

Amendment Note: 2000 H 494 inserted "at the end of the instrument" and "shall" in division (A)(1)(a); and substituted "at the end of" for "on" and "after the signature of the principal" for "on the durable power of attorney for health care", and added the second sentence, in the second paragraph in division (B).

Amendment Note: 1998 H 354 added division (D); and made changes to reflect gender neutral language.

Library References

Health ⟸910, 913.
Principal and Agent ⟸10.
Westlaw Topic Nos. 198H, 308.
C.J.S. Agency §§ 41 to 42.
Baldwin's Ohio Legislative Service, 1991 Laws of Ohio, S 1—LSC Analysis, p 5–250

1337.13 Health care decisions by attorney in fact

(A)(1) An attorney in fact under a durable power of attorney for health care shall make health care decisions for the principal only if the instrument substantially complies with section 1337.12 of the Revised Code and specifically authorizes the attorney in fact to make health care decisions for the principal, and only if the attending physician of the principal determines that the principal has lost the capacity to make informed health care decisions for the principal. Except as otherwise provided in divisions (B) to (F) of this section and subject to any specific limitations in the instrument, the attorney in fact may make health care decisions for the principal to the same extent as the principal could make those decisions for the principal if the principal had the capacity to do so. Except as otherwise provided in divisions (B) to (F) of this section, in exercising that authority, the attorney in fact shall act consistently with the desires of the principal or, if the desires of the principal are unknown, shall act in the best interest of the principal.

(2) This section does not affect, and shall not be construed as affecting, any right that the person designated as attorney in fact in a durable power of attorney for health care may have, apart from the instrument, to make or participate in the making of health care decisions on behalf of the principal.

(3) Unless the right is limited in a durable power of attorney for health care, when acting pursuant to the instrument, the attorney in fact has the same right as the principal to receive information about proposed health care, to review health care records, and to consent to the disclosure of health care records.

(B)(1) An attorney in fact under a durable power of attorney for health care does not have authority, on behalf of the principal, to refuse or withdraw informed consent to life-sustaining treatment, unless the principal is in a terminal condition or in a permanently unconscious state and unless the applicable requirements of divisions (B)(2) and (3) of this section are satisfied.

(2) In order for an attorney in fact to refuse or withdraw informed consent to life-sustaining treatment for a principal who is in a permanently unconscious state, the consulting physician associated with the determination that the principal is in the permanently unconscious state shall be a physician who, by virtue of advanced education or training, of a practice limited to particular diseases, illnesses, injuries, therapies, or branches of medicine and surgery or osteopathic medicine and surgery, of certification as a specialist in a particular branch of medicine or surgery or osteopathic medicine and surgery, or of experience acquired in the practice of medicine and surgery or osteopathic medicine and surgery, is qualified to determine whether the principal is in a permanently unconscious state.

(3) In order for an attorney in fact to refuse or withdraw informed consent to life-sustaining treatment for a principal who is in a terminal condition or in a permanently unconscious state,

the attending physician of the principal shall determine, in good faith, to a reasonable degree of medical certainty, and in accordance with reasonable medical standards, that there is no reasonable possibility that the principal will regain the capacity to make informed health care decisions for the principal.

(C) Except as otherwise provided in this division, an attorney in fact under a durable power of attorney for health care does not have authority, on behalf of the principal, to refuse or withdraw informed consent to health care necessary to provide comfort care. This division does not preclude, and shall not be construed as precluding, an attorney in fact under a durable power of attorney for health care from refusing or withdrawing informed consent to the provision of nutrition or hydration to the principal if, under the circumstances described in division (E) of this section, the attorney in fact would not be prohibited from refusing or withdrawing informed consent to the provision of nutrition or hydration to the principal.

(D) An attorney in fact under a durable power of attorney for health care does not have authority to refuse or withdraw informed consent to health care for a principal who is pregnant if the refusal or withdrawal of the health care would terminate the pregnancy, unless the pregnancy or the health care would pose a substantial risk to the life of the principal, or unless the principal's attending physician and at least one other physician who has examined the principal determine, to a reasonable degree of medical certainty and in accordance with reasonable medical standards, that the fetus would not be born alive.

(E) An attorney in fact under a durable power of attorney for health care does not have authority to refuse or withdraw informed consent to the provision of nutrition or hydration to the principal, unless the principal is in a terminal condition or in a permanently unconscious state and unless the following apply:

(1) The principal's attending physician and at least one other physician who has examined the principal determine, to a reasonable degree of medical certainty and in accordance with reasonable medical standards, that nutrition or hydration will not or no longer will serve to provide comfort to, or alleviate pain of, the principal.

(2) If the principal is in a permanently unconscious state, the principal has authorized the attorney in fact to refuse or withdraw informed consent to the provision of nutrition or hydration to the principal when the principal is in a permanently unconscious state by doing both of the following in the durable power of attorney for health care:

(a) Including a statement in capital letters or other conspicuous type, including, but not limited to, a different font, bigger type, or boldface type, that the attorney in fact may refuse or withdraw informed consent to the provision of nutrition or hydration to the principal if the principal is in a permanently unconscious state and if the determination described in division (E)(1) of this section is made, or checking or otherwise marking a box or line that is adjacent to a similar statement on a printed form of a durable power of attorney for health care;

(b) Placing the principal's initials or signature underneath or adjacent to the statement, check, or other mark described in division (E)(2)(a) of this section.

(3) If the principal is in a permanently unconscious state, the principal's attending physician determines, in good faith, that the principal authorized the attorney in fact to refuse or withdraw informed consent to the provision of nutrition or hydration to the principal when the principal is in a permanently unconscious state by complying with the requirements of divisions (E)(2)(a) and (b) of this section.

(F) An attorney in fact under a durable power of attorney for health care does not have authority to withdraw informed consent to any health care to which the principal previously consented, unless at least one of the following applies:

(1) A change in the physical condition of the principal has significantly decreased the benefit of that health care to the principal.

(2) The health care is not, or is no longer, significantly effective in achieving the purposes for which the principal consented to its use.

(2000 H 494, eff. 3–15–01; 1991 S 1, eff. 10–10–91; 1989 S 13)

Uncodified Law

1991 S 1, §§ 4 and 5: See Uncodified Law under 1337.12.

Historical and Statutory Notes

Amendment Note: 2000 H 494 inserted "or other conspicuous type, including, but not limited to, a different font, bigger type, or boldface type," in division (E)(2)(a); and made changes to reflect gender neutral language.

Library References

Health ⚖910, 913.
Westlaw Topic No. 198H.
Baldwin's Ohio Legislative Service, 1991 Laws of Ohio, S 1—LSC Analysis, p 5–250

1337.14 Revocation by principal

(A) A principal who creates a valid durable power of attorney for health care may revoke that instrument or the designation of the attorney in fact under it.

The principal may so revoke at any time and in any manner. The revocation shall be effective when the principal expresses an intention to so revoke, except that, if the principal made the principal's attending physician aware of the durable power of attorney for health care, the revocation shall be effective upon its communication to the attending physician by the principal, a witness to the revocation, or other health care personnel to whom the revocation is communicated by such a witness. Absent actual knowledge to the contrary, the attending physician of the principal and other health care personnel who are informed of the revocation of a durable power of attorney for health care by an alleged witness may rely on the information and act in accordance with the revocation.

(B) Upon the communication as described in division (A) of this section to the attending physician of a principal of the fact that the principal's durable power of attorney for health care has been revoked, the attending physician or other health care personnel acting under the direction of the attending physician shall make the fact a part of the principal's medical record.

(C) Unless the instrument provides otherwise, a valid durable power of attorney for health care revokes a prior, valid durable power of attorney for health care.

(D) Regardless of when the declaration is drafted, the execution of a declaration for mental health treatment does not revoke a valid durable power of attorney for health care. A declaration for mental health treatment executed in accordance with Chapter 2135. of the Revised Code supersedes a valid durable power of attorney for health care with regard to mental health treatment and the designation of a proxy to make decisions regarding mental health treatment.

(2003 H 72, eff. 10–29–03; 1991 S 1, eff. 10–10–91; 1989 S 13)

Uncodified Law

1991 S 1, §§ 4 and 5: See Uncodified Law under 1337.12.

Historical and Statutory Notes

Amendment Note: 2003 H 72 added new division (D) and made changes to reflect gender neutral language.

Library References

Health ⇐910.
Principal and Agent ⇐37.
Westlaw Topic Nos. 198H, 308.
C.J.S. Agency § 126.
Baldwin's Ohio Legislative Service, 1991 Laws of Ohio, S 1—LSC Analysis, p 5–250

1337.15 Immunities

(A) Subject to division (H) of this section, an attending physician of a principal is not subject to criminal prosecution or professional disciplinary action and is not liable in damages in a tort or other civil action for actions taken in good faith and in reliance on a health care decision when all of the following are satisfied:

(1) The decision is made by an attorney in fact under a durable power of attorney for health care after the attorney in fact receives information sufficient to satisfy the requirements of informed consent or refusal or withdrawal of informed consent, and the attending physician, in good faith, believes that the attorney in fact is authorized to make the decision.

(2) The attending physician, in good faith, believes that the decision is consistent with the desires of the principal, or the attorney in fact informs the attending physician that the desires of the principal are unknown and the attending physician, in good faith, believes that the desires of the principal are unknown and that the decision is in the best interest of the principal.

(3) The attending physician determines, in good faith, to a reasonable degree of medical certainty, and in accordance with reasonable medical standards, that the principal has lost the capacity to make informed health care decisions for the principal.

(4) If the decision is to withhold or withdraw life-sustaining treatment, the attending physician attempts, in good faith, to determine the desires of the principal to the extent that the principal is able to convey them and places a report of the attempt in the health care records of the principal.

(5) If the decision is to withhold or withdraw life-sustaining treatment, the attending physician determines, in good faith, to a reasonable degree of medical certainty, and in accordance with reasonable medical standards, that both of the following apply:

(a) The principal is in a terminal condition or in a permanently unconscious state.

(b) There is no reasonable possibility that the principal will regain the capacity to make informed health care decisions for the principal.

(6) If the decision pertains to a principal who is pregnant and if the withholding or withdrawal of health care would terminate the pregnancy, the attending physician makes, in good faith, to a reasonable degree of medical certainty, and in accordance with reasonable medical standards, a determination whether or not the pregnancy or health care involved would pose a substantial risk to the life of the principal or a determination whether or not the fetus would be born alive.

(7) If the decision pertains to the provision of nutrition or hydration to a principal who is in a terminal condition or in a permanently unconscious state, the attending physician determines, in good faith, to a reasonable degree of medical certainty, and in accordance with reasonable medical standards, that nutrition or hydration will not or no longer will serve to provide comfort to, or alleviate pain of, the principal.

(8) If the decision pertains to the provision of nutrition or hydration to a principal who is in a permanently unconscious state, the attending physician determines, in good faith, that the principal authorized the attorney in fact to refuse or withdraw informed consent to the provision of nutrition or hydration to the principal when the principal is in a permanently unconscious state by complying with the requirements of divisions (E)(2)(a) and (b) of section 1337.13 of the Revised Code.

(B)(1) Notwithstanding the health care decision of the attorney in fact, subject to division (H) of this section, an attending physician of a principal is not subject to criminal prosecution or professional disciplinary action and is not liable in damages in a tort or other civil action for providing or for failing to withdraw life-sustaining treatment.

(2) Subject to division (H) of this section, an attending physician who is carrying out in good faith and in a manner consistent with divisions (C) and (E) of section 1337.13 of the Revised Code the responsibility to provide comfort care to a principal in a terminal condition or in a permanently unconscious state is not subject to criminal prosecution or professional disciplinary action and is not liable in damages in a tort or other civil action for prescribing, dispensing, administering, or causing to be administered any particular medical procedure, treatment, intervention, or other measure to the principal, including, but not limited to, prescribing, personally furnishing, administering, or causing to be administered by judicious titration or in another manner any form of medication, for the purpose of diminishing the principal's pain or discomfort and not for the purpose of postponing or causing the principal's death, even though the medical procedure, treatment, intervention, or other measure may appear to hasten or increase the risk of the principal's death.

(C) Subject to division (H) of this section, a consulting physician is not subject to criminal prosecution or professional disciplinary action and is not liable in damages in a tort or other civil action as follows:

(1) If the health care decision involved is one other than the health care decision described in division (C)(2), (3), or (4) of this section, the consulting physician made a determination, in good faith, to a reasonable degree of medical certainty, and in accordance with reasonable medical standards, in conjunction with the attending physician of a principal.

(2) If the decision is to withhold or withdraw life-sustaining treatment, the consulting physician determines, in good faith, to a reasonable degree of medical certainty, and in accordance with reasonable medical standards, after examining the principal, that the principal is in a terminal condition or in a permanently unconscious state.

(3) If the health care decision involved pertains to a principal who is pregnant and if the withholding or withdrawal of health care would terminate the pregnancy, the consulting physician makes, in good faith, to a reasonable degree of medical certainty, and in accordance with reasonable medical standards, a determination whether or not the pregnancy or health care involved would pose a substantial risk to the life of the principal or a determination whether or not the fetus would be born alive.

(4) If the decision pertains to the provision of nutrition or hydration to a principal who is in a terminal condition or in a permanently unconscious state, the consulting physician determines, in good faith, to a reasonable degree of medical certainty, and in accordance with reasonable medical standards, that nutrition or hydration will not or no longer will serve to provide comfort to, or alleviate pain of, the principal.

(D) Subject to division (H) of this section, a person is not subject to criminal prosecution or professional disciplinary action and is not liable in damages in a tort or other civil action for actions taken, in good faith, while relying on a durable power of attorney for health care if the person does not have actual knowledge of either of the following facts:

(1) The durable power of attorney has been revoked pursuant to section 1337.14 of the Revised Code.

(2) The durable power of attorney does not substantially comply with sections 1337.11 to 1337.17 of the Revised Code.

(E)(1) Subject to division (H) of this section, a consulting physician, an employee or agent of any health care facility or the attending physician of a principal, and health care personnel acting under the direction of the attending physician of a principal are not subject to criminal prosecution or professional disciplinary action and are not liable in damages in a tort or other civil action for any action described in division (A), (B), (C), or (D) of this section that was undertaken, in good faith, pursuant to the direction of the attending physician of the principal.

(2) Subject to division (H) of this section, health care personnel who are acting under the direction of the principal's attending physician and who carry out the responsibility to provide comfort care to a principal in a terminal condition or in a permanently unconscious state in good faith and in a manner consistent with divisions (C) and (E) of section 1337.13 of the Revised Code are not subject to criminal prosecution or professional disciplinary action and are not liable in damages in a tort or other civil action for dispensing, administering, or causing to be administered any particular medical procedure, treatment, intervention, or other measure to the principal, including, but not limited to, personally furnishing, administering, or causing to be administered by judicious titration or in another manner any form of medication, for the purpose of diminishing the principal's pain or discomfort and not for the purpose of postponing or causing the principal's death, even though the medical procedure, treatment, intervention, or other measure may appear to hasten or increase the risk of the principal's death.

(F) Subject to division (H) of this section, a health care facility is not subject to criminal prosecution or professional disciplinary action and is not liable in damages in a tort or other civil action for any action that properly was undertaken pursuant to division (A), (B), (C), (D), or (E) of this section.

(G) Subject to division (H) of this section, an attorney in fact is not subject to criminal prosecution or professional disciplinary action and is not liable in damages in a tort or other civil action for health care decisions made in good faith while acting pursuant to the attorney in fact's authority under a durable power of attorney for health care.

(H)(1) Sections 1337.11 to 1337.17 of the Revised Code and a durable power of attorney for health care do not affect or limit any potential tort or other civil liability of an attending or consulting physician, an employee or agent of a health care facility or an attending physician, health care personnel acting under the direction of an attending physician, a health care facility, an attorney in fact, or any other person, including, but not limited to, liability associated with a medical claim, that satisfies both of the following:

(a) The liability arises out of a negligent action or omission in connection with the medical diagnosis, care, or treatment of a principal under a durable power of attorney for health care or arises out of any deviation from reasonable medical standards.

(b) The liability is based on the fact that the negligent action or omission, or the deviation, as described in division (H)(1)(a) of this section caused or contributed to the principal under the durable power of attorney for health care having a terminal condition or being in a permanently unconscious state, or otherwise caused or contributed to any injury to or the wrongful death of the principal.

(2) Sections 1337.11 to 1337.17 of the Revised Code and a durable power of attorney for health care do not grant an immunity from criminal or civil liability or from professional disciplinary action to health care personnel for actions that are outside the scope of their authority.

(1998 S 66, eff. 7–22–98; 1994 H 343, eff. 7–22–94; 1991 S 1, eff. 10–10–91; 1989 S 13)

Uncodified Law

1991 S 1, §§ 4 and 5: See Uncodified Law under 1337.12.

Historical and Statutory Notes

Amendment Note: 1998 S 66 substituted "personally furnishing" for "dispensing" in divisions (B)(2) and (E)(2); and made changes to reflect gender neutral language.

Amendment Note: 1994 H 343 designated division (B)(1); added division (B)(2); designated division (E)(1); and added division (E)(2).

Library References

Health ⟴921.
Westlaw Topic No. 198H.
Baldwin's Ohio Legislative Service, 1991 Laws of Ohio, S 1—LSC Analysis, p 5–250

1337.16 Power of attorney may not be required or prohibited; refusal to comply with instructions of attorney in fact; transfer of principal to complying physician or health care facility; records; notice requirements; objections; complaints; comfort care

(A) No physician, health care facility, other health care provider, person authorized to engage in the business of insurance in this state under Title XXXIX of the Revised Code, health insuring corporation, other health care plan, or legal entity that is self-insured and provides benefits to its employees or members shall require an individual to create or refrain from creating a durable power of attorney for health care, or shall require an individual to revoke or refrain from revoking a durable power of attorney for health care, as a condition of being admitted to a health care facility, being provided health care, being insured, or being the recipient of benefits.

(B)(1) Subject to division (B)(2) of this section, an attending physician of a principal or a health care facility in which a principal is confined may refuse to comply or allow compliance with the instructions of an attorney in fact under a durable power of attorney for health care on the basis of a matter of conscience or on another basis. An employee or agent of an attending physician of a principal or of a health care facility in which a principal is confined may refuse to comply with the instructions of an attorney in fact under a durable power of attorney for health care on the basis of a matter of conscience.

(2)(a) An attending physician of a principal who, or health care facility in which a principal is confined that, is not willing or not able to comply or allow compliance with the instructions of an attorney in fact under a durable power of attorney for health care to use or continue, or to withhold or withdraw, health care that were [sic.] given under division (A) of section 1337.13 of the Revised Code, or with any probate court reevaluation order issued pursuant to division (D)(6) of this section, shall not prevent or attempt to prevent, or unreasonably delay or attempt to unreasonably delay, the transfer of the principal to the care of a physician who, or a health care facility that, is willing and able to so comply or allow compliance.

(b) If the instruction of an attorney in fact under a durable power of attorney for health care that is given under division (A) of section 1337.13 of the Revised Code is to use or continue life-sustaining treatment in connection with a principal who is in a terminal condition or in a permanently unconscious state, the attending physician of the principal who, or the health care facility in which the principal is confined that, is not willing or not able to comply or allow compliance with that instruction shall use or continue the life-sustaining treatment or cause it to be used or continued until a transfer as described in division (B)(2)(a) of this section is made.

(C) Sections 1337.11 to 1337.17 of the Revised Code and a durable power of attorney for health care created under section 1337.12 of the Revised Code do not affect or limit the authority of a physician or a health care facility to provide or not to provide health care to a person in accordance with reasonable medical standards applicable in an emergency situation.

(D)(1) If the attending physician of a principal and one other physician who examines the principal determine that the principal is in a terminal condition or in a permanently unconscious state, if the attending physician additionally determines that the principal has lost the capacity to make informed health care decisions for the principal and that there is no reasonable possibility that the principal will regain the capacity to make informed health care decisions for the principal, and if the attorney in fact under the principal's durable power of attorney for health care makes a health care decision pertaining to the use or continuation, or the withholding or withdrawal, of life-sustaining treatment, the attending physician shall do all of the following:

(a) Record the determinations and health care decision in the principal's medical record;

(b) Make a good faith effort, and use reasonable diligence, to notify the appropriate individual or individuals, in accordance with the following descending order of priority, of the determinations and health care decision:

(i) If any, the guardian of the principal. This division does not permit or require the appointment of a guardian for the principal.

(ii) The principal's spouse;

(iii) The principal's adult children who are available within a reasonable period of time for consultation with the principal's attending physician;

(iv) The principal's parents;

(v) An adult sibling of the principal or, if there is more than one adult sibling, a majority of the principal's adult siblings who are available within a reasonable period of time for such consultation.

(c) Record in the principal's medical record the names of the individual or individuals notified pursuant to division (D)(1)(b) of this section and the manner of notification;

(d) Afford time for the individual or individuals notified pursuant to division (D)(1)(b) of this section to object in the manner described in division (D)(3)(a) of this section.

(2)(a) If, despite making a good faith effort, and despite using reasonable diligence, to notify the appropriate individual or individuals described in division (D)(1)(b) of this section, the attending physician cannot notify the individual or individuals of the determinations and health care decision because the individual or individuals are deceased, cannot be located, or cannot be notified for some other reason, the requirements of divisions (D)(1)(b), (c), and (d) of this section and, except as provided in division (D)(3)(b) of this section, the provisions of divisions (D)(3) to (6) of this section shall not apply in connection with the principal. However, the attending physician shall record in the principal's medical record information pertaining to the reason for the failure to provide the requisite notices and information pertaining to the nature of the good faith effort and reasonable diligence used.

(b) The requirements of divisions (D)(1)(b), (c), and (d) of this section and, except as provided in division (D)(3)(b) of this section, the provisions of divisions (D)(3) to (6) of this section shall not apply in connection with the principal if only one individual would have to be notified pursuant to division (D)(1)(b) of this section and that individual is the attorney in fact under the durable power of attorney for health care. However, the attending physician of the principal shall record in the principal's medical record information indicating that no notice was given pursuant to division (D)(1)(b) of this section because of the provisions of division (D)(2)(b) of this section.

(3)(a) Within forty-eight hours after receipt of a notice pursuant to division (D)(1) of this section, any individual so notified shall advise the attending physician of the principal whether the individual objects on a basis specified in division (D)(4)(c) of this section. If an objection as described in that division is communicated to the attending physician, then, within two business days after the communication, the individual shall file a complaint as described in division (D)(4) of this section in the probate court of the county in which the principal is located. If the individual fails to so file a complaint, the individual's objections as described in division (D)(4)(c) of this section shall be considered to be void.

(b) Within forty-eight hours after the priority individual or any member of a priority class of individuals receives a notice pursuant to division (D)(1) of this section or within forty-eight hours after information pertaining to an unnotified priority individual or unnotified priority class of individuals is recorded in a principal's medical record pursuant to division (D)(2)(a) or (b) of this section, the individual or a majority of the individuals in the next class of individuals that pertains to the principal in the descending order of priority set forth in divisions (D)(1)(b)(i) to (v) of this section shall advise the attending physician of the principal whether the individual or majority object on a basis specified in division (D)(4)(c) of this section. If an objection as described in that division is communicated to the attending physician, then, within two business days after the communication, the objecting individual or majority shall file a complaint as described in division (D)(4) of this section in the probate court of the county in which the principal is located. If the objecting individual or majority fails to file a complaint, the objections as described in division (D)(4)(c) of this section shall be considered to be void.

(4) A complaint of an individual that is filed in accordance with division (D)(3)(a) of this section or of an individual or majority of individuals that is filed in accordance with division (D)(3)(b) of this section shall satisfy all of the following:

(a) Name any health care facility in which the principal is confined;

(b) Name the principal, the principal's attending physician, and the consulting physician associated with the determination that the principal is in a terminal condition or in a permanently unconscious state;

(c) Indicate whether the plaintiff or plaintiffs object on one or more of the following bases:

(i) To the attending physician's determination that the principal has lost the capacity to make informed health care decisions for the principal;

(ii) To the attending physician's determination that there is no reasonable possibility that the principal will regain the capacity to make informed health care decisions for the principal;

(iii) That, in exercising the attorney in fact's authority, the attorney in fact is not acting consistently with the desires of the principal or, if the desires of the principal are unknown, in the best interest of the principal;

(iv) That the durable power of attorney for health care has expired or otherwise is no longer effective;

(v) To the attending physician's and consulting physician's determinations that the principal is in a terminal condition or in a permanently unconscious state;

(vi) That the attorney in fact's health care decision pertaining to the use or continuation, or the withholding or withdrawal, of life-sustaining treatment is not authorized by the durable power of attorney for health care or is prohibited under section 1337.13 of the Revised Code;

(vii) That the durable power of attorney for health care was executed when the principal was not of sound mind or was under or subject to duress, fraud, or undue influence;

(viii) That the durable power of attorney for health care otherwise does not substantially comply with section 1337.12 of the Revised Code.

(d) Request the probate court to issue one or more of the following types of orders:

(i) An order to the attending physician to reevaluate, in light of the court proceedings, the determination that the principal has lost the capacity to make informed health care decisions for the principal, the determination that the principal is in a terminal condition or in a permanently unconscious state, or the determination that there is no reasonable possibility that the principal will regain the capacity to make informed health care decisions for the principal;

(ii) An order to the attorney in fact to act consistently with the desires of the principal or, if the desires of the principal are unknown, in the best interest of the principal in exercising the attorney in fact's authority, or to make only health care decisions pertaining to life-sustaining treatment that are authorized by the durable power of attorney for health care and that are not prohibited under section 1337.13 of the Revised Code;

(iii) An order invalidating the durable power of attorney for health care because it has expired or otherwise is no longer effective, it was executed when the principal was not of sound mind or was under or subject to duress, fraud, or undue influence, or it otherwise does not substantially comply with section 1337.12 of the Revised Code.

(e) Be accompanied by an affidavit of the plaintiff or plaintiffs that includes averments relative to whether the plaintiff is an individual or the plaintiffs are individuals as described in division (D)(1)(b)(i), (ii), (iii), (iv), or (v) of this section and to the factual basis for the plaintiff's or the plaintiffs' objections;

(f) Name any individuals who were notified by the attending physician in accordance with division (D)(1)(b) of this section and who are not joining in the complaint as plaintiffs;

(g) Name, in the caption of the complaint, as defendants the attending physician of the principal, the attorney in fact under the durable power of attorney for health care, the consulting physician associated with the determination that the principal is in a terminal condition or in a permanently unconscious state, any health care facility in which the principal is confined, and any individuals who were notified by the attending physician in accordance with division (D)(1)(b) of this section and who are not joining in the complaint as plaintiffs.

(5) Notwithstanding any contrary provision of the Revised Code or of the Rules of Civil Procedure, the state and persons other than an objecting individual as described in division (D)(3)(a) of this section, other than an objecting individual or majority of individuals as described in division (D)(3)(b) of this section, and other than persons described in division (D)(4)(g) of this section are prohibited from commencing a civil action under division (D) of this section and from joining or being joined as parties to an action commenced under division (D) of this section, including joining by way of intervention.

(6)(a) A probate court in which a complaint as described in division (D)(4) of this section is filed within the period specified in division (D)(3)(a) or (b) of this section shall conduct a hearing on the complaint after a copy of it and a notice of the hearing have been served upon the defendants. The clerk of the probate court in which the complaint is filed shall cause the complaint and the notice of the hearing to be so served in accordance with the Rules of Civil Procedure, which service shall be made, if possible, within three days after the filing of the complaint. The hearing shall be conducted at the earliest possible time, but no later than the third business day after such service has been completed. Immediately following the hearing, the court shall enter on its journal its determination whether a requested order will be issued.

(b) If the health care decision of the attorney in fact authorized the use or continuation of life-sustaining treatment and if the plaintiff or plaintiffs requested a reevaluation order to the attending physician of the principal or an order to the attorney in fact as described in division (D)(4)(d)(i) or (ii) of this section, the court shall issue the requested order only if it finds that the plaintiff or plaintiffs have established a factual basis for the objection or objections involved by clear and convincing evidence and, if applicable, to a reasonable degree of medical certainty and in accordance with reasonable medical standards.

(c) If the health care decision of the attorney in fact authorized the withholding or withdrawal of life-sustaining treatment and if the plaintiff or plaintiffs requested a reevaluation order to the attending physician of the principal or an order to the attorney in fact as described in division (D)(4)(d)(i) or (ii) of this section, the court shall issue the requested order only if it finds that the plaintiff or plaintiffs have established a factual basis for the objection or objections involved by a preponderance of the evidence and, if applicable, to a reasonable degree of medical certainty and in accordance with reasonable medical standards.

(d) If the plaintiff or plaintiffs requested an invalidation order as described in division (D)(4)(d)(iii) of this section, the court shall issue the order only if it finds that the plaintiff or plaintiffs have established a factual basis for the objection or objections involved by clear and convincing evidence.

(e) If the court issues a reevaluation order to the principal's attending physician pursuant to division (D)(6)(b) or (c) of this section, the attending physician shall make the requisite reevaluation. If, after doing so, the attending physician again determines that the principal has lost the capacity to make informed health care decisions for the principal, that the principal is in a terminal condition or in a permanently unconscious state, or that there is no reasonable possibility that the principal will regain the capacity to make informed health care decisions for the principal, the attending physician shall notify the court in writing of the determination and comply with division (B)(2) of this section.

(E)(1) In connection with the provision of comfort care in a manner consistent with divisions (C) and (E) of section 1337.13 of the Revised Code to a principal who is in a terminal condition or in a permanently unconscious state, nothing in sections 1337.11 to 1337.17 of the Revised Code precludes the attending physician of the principal who carries out the responsibility to provide comfort care to the principal in good faith and while acting within the scope of the attending physician's authority from prescribing, dispensing, administering, or causing to be administered any particular medical procedure, treatment, intervention, or other measure to the principal, including, but not limited to, prescribing, personally furnishing, administering, or causing to be administered by judicious titration or in another manner any form of medication, for the purpose of diminishing the principal's pain or discomfort and not for the purpose of postponing or causing the principal's death, even though the medical procedure, treatment, intervention, or other measure may appear to hasten or increase the risk of the principal's death. In connection with the provision of comfort care in a manner consistent with divisions (C) and (E) of section 1337.13 of the Revised Code to a principal who is in a terminal condition or in a permanently unconscious state, nothing in sections 1337.11 to 1337.17 of the Revised Code precludes health care personnel acting under the direction of the principal's attending physician who carry out the responsibility to provide comfort care to the principal in good faith and while acting within the scope of their authority from dispensing, administering, or causing to be administered any particular medical procedure, treatment, intervention, or other measure to the principal, including, but not limited to, personally furnishing, administering, or causing to be administered by judicious titration or in another manner any form of medication, for the purpose of diminishing the principal's pain or discomfort and not for the purpose of postponing or causing the principal's death, even though the medical procedure, treatment, intervention, or other measure may appear to hasten or increase the risk of the principal's death.

(2) If, at any time, a priority individual or any member of a priority class of individuals under division (D)(1)(b) of this section or if, at any time, the individual or a majority of the individuals in the next class of individuals that pertains to the principal in the descending order of priority set forth in that division, believes in good faith that both of the following circumstances apply, the priority individual, the member of the priority class of individuals, or the individual or majority of individuals in the next class of individuals that pertains to the principal may commence an action in the probate court of the county in which a principal who is in a terminal condition or permanently unconscious state is located for the issuance of an order mandating the use or continuation of comfort care in connection with the principal in a manner that is consistent with sections 1337.11 to 1337.17 of the Revised Code:

(a) Comfort care is not being used or continued in connection with the principal.

(b) The withholding or withdrawal of the comfort care is contrary to sections 1337.11 to 1337.17 of the Revised Code.

(F) Except as provided in divisions (D) and (E) of this section in connection with principals who are in a terminal condition or in a permanently unconscious state, sections 1337.11 to 1337.17 of the Revised Code do not authorize the commencement of any civil action in a probate court or court of common pleas for the purpose of obtaining an order relative to a health care decision made by an attorney in fact under a durable power of attorney for health care.

(G) A durable power of attorney for health care, or other document, that is similar to a durable power of attorney for health care authorized by sections 1337.11 to 1337.17 of the Revised Code, that is or has been executed under the law of another state prior to, on, or after October 10, 1991, and that substantially complies with that law or with sections 1337.11 to 1337.17 of the Revised Code shall be considered to be valid for purposes of those sections.

(1998 S 66, eff. 7-22-98; 1997 S 67, eff. 6-4-97; 1994 H 343, eff. 7-22-94; 1991 S 1, eff. 10-10-91; 1989 S 13)

Uncodified Law

1991 S 1, §§ 4 and 5: See Uncodified Law under 1337.12.

Historical and Statutory Notes

Amendment Note: 1998 S 66 substituted "personally furnishing" for "dispensing" twice in division (E)(1).

Amendment Note: 1997 S 67 replaced references to medical care corporations, health care corporations and health maintenance organizations with language pertaining to health insuring corporations in division (A); and made changes to reflect gender neutral language.

Amendment Note: 1994 H 343 added division (E)(1); designated division (E)(2) and redesignated former divisions (E)(1) and (E)(2) as divisions (E)(2)(a) and (E)(2)(b); and substituted "October 10, 1991" for "the effective date of this amendment" in division (G).

Library References

Health ⇔910, 914 to 916, 923.
Westlaw Topic No. 198H.
  Baldwin's Ohio Legislative Service, 1991 Laws of Ohio, S 1—LSC Analysis, p 5–250

1337.17 Form

A printed form of durable power of attorney for health care may be sold or otherwise distributed in this state for use by adults who are not advised by an attorney. By use of such a printed form, a principal may authorize an attorney in fact to make health care decisions on the principal's behalf, but the printed form shall not be used as an instrument for granting authority for any other decisions. Any printed form that is sold or otherwise distributed in this state for the purpose described in this section shall include the following notice:

"Notice to Adult Executing This Document

This is an important legal document. Before executing this document, you should know these facts:

This document gives the person you designate (the attorney in fact) the power to make most* health care decisions for you if you lose the capacity to make informed health care decisions for yourself. This power is effective only when your attending physician determines that you have lost the capacity to make informed health care decisions for yourself and, notwithstanding this document, as long as you have the capacity to make informed health care decisions for yourself, you retain the right to make all medical and other health care decisions for yourself.

You may include specific limitations in this document on the authority of the attorney in fact to make health care decisions for you.

Subject to any specific limitations you include in this document, if your attending physician determines that you have lost the capacity to make an informed decision on a health care matter, the attorney in fact generally* will be authorized by this document to make health care decisions for you to the same extent as you could make those decisions yourself, if you had the capacity to do so. The authority of the attorney in fact to make health care decisions for you generally* will include the authority to give informed consent, to refuse to give informed consent, or to withdraw informed consent to any care, treatment, service, or procedure to maintain, diagnose, or treat a physical or mental condition.

However*, even if the attorney in fact has general authority to make health care decisions for you under this document, the attorney in fact never* will be authorized to do any of the following:

(1) Refuse or withdraw informed consent to life-sustaining treatment (unless your attending physician and one other physician who examines you determine, to a reasonable degree of medical certainty and in accordance with reasonable medical standards, that either of the following applies:

(a) You are suffering from an irreversible, incurable, and untreatable condition caused by disease, illness, or injury from which (i) there can be no recovery and (ii) your death is likely to occur within a relatively short time if life-sustaining treatment is not administered, and your attending physician additionally determines, to a reasonable degree of medical certainty and in accordance with reasonable medical standards, that there is no reasonable possibility that you will regain the capacity to make informed health care decisions for yourself.

(b) You are in a state of permanent unconsciousness that is characterized by you being irreversibly unaware of yourself and your environment and by a total loss of cerebral cortical functioning, resulting in you having no capacity to experience pain or suffering, and your attending physician additionally determines, to a reasonable degree of medical certainty and in accordance with reasonable medical standards, that there is no reasonable possibility that you will regain the capacity to make informed health care decisions for yourself);

(2) Refuse or withdraw informed consent to health care necessary to provide you with comfort care (except that, if the attorney in fact is not prohibited from doing so under (4) below, the attorney in fact could refuse or withdraw informed consent to the provision of nutrition or hydration to you as described under (4) below). (You should understand that comfort care is defined in Ohio law to mean artificially or technologically administered sustenance (nutrition) or fluids (hydration) when administered to

diminish your pain or discomfort, not to postpone your death, and any other medical or nursing procedure, treatment, intervention, or other measure that would be taken to diminish your pain or discomfort, not to postpone your death. Consequently, if your attending physician were to determine that a previously described medical or nursing procedure, treatment, intervention, or other measure will not or no longer will serve to provide comfort to you or alleviate your pain, then, subject to (4) below, your attorney in fact would be authorized to refuse or withdraw informed consent to the procedure, treatment, intervention, or other measure.*);

(3) Refuse or withdraw informed consent to health care for you if you are pregnant and if the refusal or withdrawal would terminate the pregnancy (unless the pregnancy or health care would pose a substantial risk to your life, or unless your attending physician and at least one other physician who examines you determine, to a reasonable degree of medical certainty and in accordance with reasonable medical standards, that the fetus would not be born alive);

(4) Refuse or withdraw informed consent to the provision of artificially or technologically administered sustenance (nutrition) or fluids (hydration) to you, unless:

(a) You are in a terminal condition or in a permanently unconscious state.

(b) Your attending physician and at least one other physician who has examined you determine, to a reasonable degree of medical certainty and in accordance with reasonable medical standards, that nutrition or hydration will not or no longer will serve to provide comfort to you or alleviate your pain.

(c) If, but only if, you are in a permanently unconscious state, you authorize the attorney in fact to refuse or withdraw informed consent to the provision of nutrition or hydration to you by doing both of the following in this document:

(i) Including a statement in capital letters or other conspicuous type, including, but not limited to, a different font, bigger type, or boldface type, that the attorney in fact may refuse or withdraw informed consent to the provision of nutrition or hydration to you if you are in a permanently unconscious state and if the determination that nutrition or hydration will not or no longer will serve to provide comfort to you or alleviate your pain is made, or checking or otherwise marking a box or line (if any) that is adjacent to a similar statement on this document;

(ii) Placing your initials or signature underneath or adjacent to the statement, check, or other mark previously described.

(d) Your attending physician determines, in good faith, that you authorized the attorney in fact to refuse or withdraw informed consent to the provision of nutrition or hydration to you if you are in a permanently unconscious state by complying with the requirements of (4)(c)(i) and (ii) above.

(5) Withdraw informed consent to any health care to which you previously consented, unless a change in your physical condition has significantly decreased the benefit of that health care to you, or unless the health care is not, or is no longer, significantly effective in achieving the purposes for which you consented to its use.

Additionally, when exercising authority to make health care decisions for you, the attorney in fact will have to act consistently with your desires or, if your desires are unknown, to act in your best interest. You may express your desires to the attorney in fact by including them in this document or by making them known to the attorney in fact in another manner.

When acting pursuant to this document, the attorney in fact generally* will have the same rights that you have to receive information about proposed health care, to review health care records, and to consent to the disclosure of health care records. You can limit that right in this document if you so choose.

Generally, you may designate any competent adult as the attorney in fact under this document. However, you cannot* designate your attending physician or the administrator of any nursing home in which you are receiving care as the attorney in fact under this document. Additionally, you cannot* designate an employee or agent of your attending physician, or an employee or agent of a health care facility at which you are being treated, as the attorney in fact under this document, unless either type of employee or agent is a competent adult and related to you by blood, marriage, or adoption, or unless either type of employee or agent is a competent adult and you and the employee or agent are members of the same religious order.

This document has no expiration date under Ohio law, but you may choose to specify a date upon which your durable power of attorney for health care generally will expire. However, if you specify an expiration date and then lack the capacity to make informed health care decisions for yourself on that date, the document and the power it grants to your attorney in fact will continue in effect until you regain the capacity to make informed health care decisions for yourself.

You have the right to revoke the designation of the attorney in fact and the right to revoke this entire document at any time and in any manner. Any such revocation generally will be effective when you express your intention to make the revocation. However, if you made your attending physician aware of this document, any such revocation will be effective only when you communicate it to your attending physician, or when a witness to the revocation or other health care personnel to whom the revocation is communicated by such a witness communicate it to your attending physician.

If you execute this document and create a valid durable power of attorney for health care with it, it will revoke any prior, valid durable power of attorney for health care that you created, unless you indicate otherwise in this document.

This document is not valid as a durable power of attorney for health care unless it is acknowledged before a notary public or is signed by at least two adult witnesses who are present when you sign or acknowledge your signature. No person who is related to you by blood, marriage, or adoption may be a witness. The attorney in fact, your attending physician, and the administrator of any nursing home in which you are receiving care also are ineligible to be witnesses.

If there is anything in this document that you do not understand, you should ask your lawyer to explain it to you."

In the preceding notice, the single words, and the two sentences in the second set of parentheses in paragraph (2), followed by an asterisk and all of paragraph (4) shall appear in the printed form in capital letters or other conspicuous type, including, but not limited to, a different font, bigger type, or boldface type.

(2000 H 494, eff. 3–15–01; 1991 S 1, eff. 10–10–91; 1989 S 13)

Uncodified Law

1991 S 1, §§ 4 and 5: See Uncodified Law under 1337.12.

Historical and Statutory Notes

Amendment Note: 2000 H 494 inserted "or other conspicuous type, including, but not limited to, a different font, bigger type, or boldface type" in division (4)(c)(i) and in the final paragraph; and made changes to reflect gender neutral language and other nonsubstantive changes.

Library References

Health ⇨910.
Westlaw Topic No. 198H.

Baldwin's Ohio Legislative Service, 1991 Laws of Ohio, S 1—LSC Analysis, p 5–250

1337.18 Form to create power of attorney

(A) The following form may be used to create a power of attorney:

Power of Attorney

[The powers granted by this document are broad and sweeping. They are explained in Ohio Revised Code section 1337.20. If you have any questions about these powers, obtain legal advice. You can use any different form of power of attorney you may desire. This document does not authorize anyone to make health-care decisions for you. You can revoke this power of attorney at any time.]

Principal (Person Granting the Power)

Name:

....

Address:

....

....

Telephone:

....

1. Notice to Principal.

As the principal, you are using this document to give authority to another person, known as your agent or attorney-in-fact, to make decisions regarding your money and property. Your agent will have the powers that you indicate below to make decisions about your money and property without advance notice to you or approval by you.

Unless expressly authorized in the power of attorney, a power of attorney does not grant authority to an agent to do any of the following:

(a) Create, modify, or revoke a trust;

(b) Fund with your property a trust not created by you or a person authorized to create a trust for your benefit;

(c) Make or revoke a gift of your property in trust or otherwise;

(d) Create or change rights of survivorship in your property or in property in which you may have an interest;

(e) Designate or change the designation of a beneficiary to receive any property, benefit, or contractual right on your death, such as insurance benefits and retirement benefits;

(f) Create in the agent or a person to whom the agent owes a legal duty of support the right to receive property, a benefit, or a contractual right in which you have an interest;

(g) Delegate the powers granted under the power of attorney to another person.

(h) Elect or change a retirement allowance plan of payment on your behalf under Ohio Revised Code Chapter 145., 742., 3305., 3307., 3309., or 5505., other than a joint and survivor annuity leaving one-half to your spouse if you are married, a single life annuity if you are single, or any plan that includes a partial lump sum option; except that no express authority is necessary to elect a plan that meets the minimum requirements of a court order to elect a plan that will pay a lifetime benefit to a former spouse.

(i) If authorized under Ohio Revised Code section 145.814, change an election made under Ohio Revised Code section 145.19 or 145.191.

(j) Terminate your membership in the public employees retirement system, state teachers retirement system, school employees retirement system, Ohio police and fire pension fund, or state highway patrol retirement system by withdrawing your accumulated employee contributions.

The powers that you give to your agent are explained more fully in Ohio Revised Code sections 1337.19 and 1337.20. If you have any questions about this document or the powers that you are giving to your agent, you should obtain legal advice.

2. Notice to Agent.

Once you accept designation as the agent under this document or exercise authority granted to you by the principal, a fiduciary relationship is created between you and the principal. Unless otherwise modified in this power of attorney, your duties include the duty to do all of the following:

(a) Act in good faith, with reasonable care for the best interests of the principal;

(b) Take no action beyond the scope of the authority given to you in this document;

(c) Keep complete record of all receipts, disbursements, and transactions conducted for the principal.

If you violate the terms of this document or the fiduciary duties created by this relationship, you will be liable to the principal or the principal's successors for loss or damage caused by your violation.

If there is anything about this document or your duties that you do not understand, you should obtain legal advice.

3. Designation of Agent(s).

I, the above-named principal, hereby appoint and designate the following as my Attorney(s)–in–Fact. (Insert the name(s), address(es), and telephone number(s) of your agent(s) below. If more space is needed, you may attach additional sheets.)

Name: Name:

....

Address: Address:

....

Telephone: Telephone:

....

4. Designation of Successor Agent(s).

(Optional: acts if any named Agent dies, resigns, or is otherwise unable to act or serve.)

I, the above-named principal, hereby appoint and designate the following as my successor Agent(s).

First Successor: Second Successor:
Name: Name:

....

Address: Address:

....

....

Telephone: Telephone:

....

[If more than one Agent is designated, check the box in front of one of the following statements.]

[ ] Each Agent may independently exercise the powers granted.

[ ] All Agents must jointly exercise the powers granted.

[ ] A majority in number of Agents must jointly exercise the powers granted.

Any person can rely on a statement by a successor Agent that he or she is properly acting under this document and may rely conclusively on any action or decision made by that successor Agent. That person does not have to make any further investigation or inquiry.

5. Grant of Power.

I, the above-named Principal hereby appoint the above named Agent(s) to act as my agent(s) in any way that I could act with respect to the following matters, as each of them is defined in Ohio Revised Code section 1337.20:

[To grant all of the following powers, initial the line in front of (W) and ignore the lines in front of the other powers. To grant one or more, but fewer than all, of the following powers, initial the line in front of each power you are granting. To withhold a power, do not initial the line in front of it. You may, but need not, cross out each power withheld.]

Initial

.... (A) Real property transactions
.... (B) Tangible personal property transactions
.... (C) Stock and bond transactions
.... (D) Commodity and option transactions
.... (E) Banking and other financial institution transactions
.... (F) Business operating transactions
.... (G) Proprietary interests and materials transactions
.... (H) Insurance and annuity transactions
.... (I) Retirement plan transactions
.... (J) Safe deposit box transactions
.... (K) Estate, trust, and other beneficiary transactions
.... (L) Borrowing transactions
.... (M) Fiduciary transactions
.... (N) Personal relationships and affairs
.... (O) Benefits from Social Security, Medicare, Medicaid, and other governmental programs, or military service
.... (P) Records, reports, and statements
.... (Q) Tax matters
.... (R) Licenses
.... (S) Access to documents
.... (T) Employment of agents
.... (U) Power to delegate
.... (V) Claims and litigation
.... (W) All powers listed above

Special Instructions:

[On the following lines or on additional pages you may give special instructions limiting or extending the powers granted to your Agent.]

....
....
....
....
....

6. Commencement and Duration of Power.

This power of attorney is effective:

[Check the appropriate box below to the left of your choice. If you do not check any box, this power of attorney will become effective when you sign it.]

[ ] Immediately.

[ ] Upon my incapacity as determined by the following person or persons and set forth in an affidavit:

....

....

[ ] Upon my incapacity as determined by two physicians and set forth in an affidavit.

[ ] Upon the following future date or event:

....

....

This power of attorney shall terminate:

[Check the appropriate box below to the left of your choice. If you do not check any box, this power of attorney will terminate upon your death.]

[ ] Upon my death.

[ ] Upon my incapacity as determined by the following person or persons and set forth in an affidavit:

....

....

[ ] Upon my incapacity as determined by two physicians and set forth in an affidavit.

[ ] Upon the following future date or event:

....

....

7. Durability of Power.

[The authority granted in this power of attorney can be effective even during a period of disability. Check the appropriate box below if you want this power of attorney to be effective or to not be effective during any period of disability.]

[ ] This power of attorney will continue in force and effect even during any period in which I am disabled.

[ ] This power of attorney will not be in force and will have no effect during any period in which I am disabled.

8. Obtaining Personal Health Information.

[ ] My Agent shall be treated as my personal representative for all purposes relating to my Personal Health Information as provided in 45 CFR 164.502(g)(2) and for the Health Insurance Portability and Accountability Act of 1996.

[ ] My Agent shall not be treated as my personal representative for any purposes relating to my Personal Health Information as provided in 45 CFR 164.502(g)(2) and for the Health Insurance Portability and Accountability Act of 1996.

9. Compensation of Agent.

[Your Agent will be reimbursed for all reasonable expenses incurred in acting under this power of attorney. Check the appropriate box below to indicate whether you want your Agent also to be reasonably paid or not to be paid for services rendered as Agent.]

[ ] My Agent is entitled to reasonable compensation for services rendered as Agent under this power of attorney.

[ ] My Agent shall not receive any compensation for services rendered as Agent under this power of attorney.

10. Exoneration of Agent(s).

My Agent is released from any liability to me and my estate arising out of the acts or failures to act of my Agent, except for willful misconduct or gross negligence. I agree to indemnify and hold my Agent harmless against any liability or expense, including attorney's fees, that my Agent may incur as the result of acting or failing to act under this instrument, except for liability and expense resulting from willful misconduct or gross negligence.

11. Exoneration of Third Parties.

I agree that any third party who receives a copy of this document may act under it. Revocation of the power of attorney is not effective as to a third party until the third party learns of the revocation. I agree to indemnify the third party for any claims that arise against the third party because of reliance on this power of attorney.

12. Self–Dealing.

[With respect to the Agent's right to or not to enter into transactions with you, check the box in front of one of the following statements.]

[ ] My Agent can enter into transactions with me or in my behalf in which my Agent is personally interested as long as the terms of the transaction are fair to me, notwithstanding any law prohibiting acts of self-dealing.

[ ] My Agent cannot enter into transactions with me or in my behalf in which my Agent is personally interested.

13. Property to Which this Instrument Applies.

[Your Agent will have authority over some or all of your property. Check the appropriate box below to indicate whether your Agent's authority is over all of your property or over only some of your property. If your Agent's authority is over only some of your property, identify the property not subject to this power of attorney.]

[ ] This instrument will apply to all of my property, real or personal, wherever located.

[ ] This instrument will apply to all of my property, real or personal, wherever located except for the following:

[On the following lines or on additional pages you may list property not subject to this power of attorney.]

....
....
....
....
....

14. Amending and Revocation.

I may amend or revoke this power of attorney at any time by a signed instrument delivered to my Agent. If this instrument has been filed or recorded in public records, then any amendment or revocation also will be similarly filed or recorded, but a similar filing or recording of the amendment or revocation will not be necessary to effectuate the amendment or revocation with respect to my Agent and to all persons who have actual knowledge of the amendment or revocation.

15. Nomination of Guardian.

[With respect to your right to nominate a guardian of your person or estate, or both, check the box in front of one of the following statements.]

[ ] If a guardian or conservator is ever needed for my estate, I nominate my Agent or any other person that my Agent nominates as my guardian or conservator. This nomination revokes any other nomination I may have made in any other document dated prior to the date of this power of attorney, including any nomination set forth in a Health Care Durable Power of Attorney.

[ ] If a guardian or conservator is ever needed for my estate, I nominate .... as my guardian or conservator. This nomination revokes any other nomination I may have made in any other document dated prior to the date of this power of attorney, including any nomination set forth in a Health Care Durable Power of Attorney.

[ ] I do not nominate any person as the guardian or conservator of my estate under this instrument.

16. Governing Law.

The laws of the State of Ohio will govern all questions pertaining to the validity and construction of this power of attorney.

IN WITNESS WHEREOF, I have signed this Power of Attorney on [Date] ....

....
(Principal's Signature)

[This instrument should be notarized or witnessed, or both, as applicable law may require or as may be desired.]

On .... [Date], this instrument was signed by .... [Name of Principal] in our presence and was acknowledged and declared by the Principal to be the Principal's Power of Attorney. Immediately thereafter, at the Principal's request, in the Principal's presence, and in the presence of each other, we signed this instrument as subscribing witnesses.

....
(Witness)   (Witness)

This document was acknowledged before me .... [Date] by .... [Name of Principal] who is known to me or from whom I have obtained adequate proof of identity.

....
(Signature of notarial officer)
(Seal, if any)
....
                (Title and Rank)

[My commission expires:
....

(B) Except as otherwise required by the Revised Code, a person may create a power of attorney using the form set forth in division (A) of this section or any other form that is valid under the common law of this state.

(C) A power of attorney may incorporate by reference any one or more powers set forth in section 1337.20 of the Revised Code by referencing the appropriate division of that section and the power or powers to be incorporated.

(2005 H 246, eff. 3–29–06)

1337.19 Powers of attorney in fact

By executing a power of attorney in the form set forth in division (A) of section 1337.18 of the Revised Code or any other power of attorney that incorporates by reference a power set forth in section 1337.20 of the Revised Code, the principal, except as modified in the power of attorney, authorizes the attorney in fact with respect to that power to do all of the following:

(A) Demand, receive, and obtain by litigation or otherwise money or any other thing of value to which the principal is, may become, or claims to be entitled and conserve, invest, disburse, or use anything so received for the purposes intended;

(B) Contract in any manner with any person, on terms agreeable to the attorney in fact, to accomplish a purpose of a transaction, and perform, rescind, reform, release, or modify the contract or another contract made by or for the principal;

(C) Execute, acknowledge, seal, and deliver a deed, revocation, mortgage, security interest, lease, notice, check, promissory note, electronic funds transfer, release, or other instrument or communication the attorney in fact considers desirable to accomplish a purpose of a transaction;

(D) Prosecute, defend, submit to arbitration, settle, or propose or accept a compromise with respect to a claim existing in favor of or against the principal or intervene in litigation relating to the claim;

(E) Seek on the principal's behalf the assistance of a court to carry out an act authorized by the power of attorney;

(F) Engage, compensate, and discharge an attorney, accountant, expert witness, or other assistant;

(G) Keep appropriate records of each transaction, including an accounting of receipts and disbursements;

(H) Prepare, execute, and file a record, report, or other document the attorney in fact considers desirable to safeguard or promote the principal's interest under a statute or governmental regulation;

(I) Reimburse the attorney in fact for expenditures properly made by the attorney in fact in exercising the powers granted by the power of attorney;

(J) Do any other lawful act with respect to the power of attorney.

(2005 H 246, eff. 3–29–06)

1337.20 Construction of powers of attorney in fact

Except as modified by the principal, a power of attorney created by use of the form set forth in section 1337.18 of the Revised Code or any other power of attorney that incorporates by reference any of the powers set forth below shall be construed as follows:

(A) Language in a power of attorney that grants power with respect to transactions concerning real property authorizes the attorney in fact to do all of the following:

(1) Accept as a gift or as security for a loan, reject, demand, buy, lease, receive, or otherwise acquire an interest in real property, a right incident to real property, or real property held in an undisclosed trust;

(2) Sell, exchange, convey with or without covenants, quitclaim, release, surrender, mortgage, encumber, partition, consent to partitioning, subdivide, apply for zoning, rezoning, or other governmental permits, plat or consent to platting, develop, grant options concerning, lease, sublease, or otherwise dispose of an interest in real property or a right incident to real property;

(3) Release, assign, satisfy, and enforce by litigation or otherwise a mortgage, deed of trust, encumbrance, lien, or other claim to real property that exists or is asserted;

(4) Do any act of management or of conservation with respect to an interest in real property, or a right incident to real property, owned or claimed to be owned by the principal, including, but not limited to, all of the following:

(a) Insure against a casualty, liability, or loss;

(b) Obtain or regain possession or protect, by litigation or otherwise;

(c) Pay, compromise, or contest taxes or assessments or apply for and receive refunds in connection with taxes or assessments;

(d) Purchase supplies, hire assistance or labor, and make repairs or alterations;

(e) Use, develop, alter, replace, remove, erect, or install structures or other improvements upon real property in or incident to which the principal has, or claims to have, an interest or right;

(6) Participate in a reorganization with respect to real property or a legal entity that owns an interest in or right incident to real property and receive and hold, directly or indirectly, shares of stock or obligations received in a plan of reorganization, and act with respect to them, including, but not limited to, all of the following:

(a) Sell or otherwise dispose of the shares or obligations;

(b) Exercise or sell an option, conversion, or similar right with respect to the shares or obligations;

(c) Vote shares in person or by proxy;

(7) If specifically authorized in the power of attorney, change the form of title of an interest in or right incident to real property;

(8) Dedicate to public use, with or without consideration, easements or other real property in which the principal has, or claims to have, an interest.

(B) Language in a power of attorney granting power with respect to transactions concerning tangible personal property authorizes the attorney in fact to do all of the following:

(1) Accept as a gift or as security for a loan, reject, demand, buy, receive, or otherwise acquire ownership or possession of tangible personal property or an interest in tangible personal property;

(2) Sell, exchange, convey with or without covenants, release, surrender, create a security interest in, grant options concerning, lease, sublease to others, or otherwise dispose of tangible personal property or an interest in tangible personal property;

(3) Release, assign, satisfy, or enforce, by litigation or otherwise, a security interest, lien, or other claim with respect to tangible personal property or an interest in tangible personal property;

(4) Do an act of management or conservation with respect to tangible personal property or an interest in tangible personal property, including, but not limited to, all of the following:

(a) Insure against casualty, liability, or loss;

(b) Obtain or regain possession, or protect, by litigation or otherwise;

(c) Pay, compromise, or contest taxes or assessments or apply for and receive refunds in connection with taxes or assessments;

(d) Move from place to place;

(e) Store for hire or on a gratuitous bailment;

(f) Use, alter, and make repairs or alterations;

(5) If specifically authorized in the power of attorney, change the form of title of an interest in or right incident to tangible personal property.

(C) Language in a power of attorney granting power with respect to transactions concerning stocks and bonds authorizes the attorney in fact to do all of the following:

(1) Buy, sell, and exchange stocks, bonds, mutual funds, and all other types of securities and financial instruments, whether held directly or indirectly, except commodity futures contracts and call and put options on stocks and stock indexes;

(2) Receive certificates and other evidences of ownership with respect to securities;

(3) Exercise voting rights with respect to securities in person, in writing, or by proxy;

(4) Enter into voting trusts;

(5) Consent to limitations on the right to vote.

(D) Language in a power of attorney granting power with respect to transactions concerning commodities and options authorizes the attorney in fact to do all of the following:

(1) Buy, sell, exchange, assign, settle, and exercise commodity futures contracts and call and put options on stocks and stock indexes traded on a regulated option exchange;

(2) Establish, continue, modify, and terminate option accounts with a broker.

(E) Language granting power with respect to transactions concerning banks and other financial institutions authorizes the attorney in fact to do all of the following:

(1) Continue, modify, and terminate an account or other banking arrangement made by or for the principal;

(2) Establish, modify, and terminate an account or other banking arrangement with a bank, trust company, savings and loan association, credit union, thrift company, brokerage firm, or other financial institution selected by the attorney in fact;

(3) Contract to procure other services available from a financial institution as the attorney in fact considers desirable;

(4) Withdraw by check, order, or otherwise money or property of the principal deposited with or left in the custody of a financial institution;

(5) Receive bank statements, vouchers, notices, and similar documents from a financial institution and act with respect to them;

(6) Borrow money at an interest rate agreeable to the attorney in fact and pledge as security personal property of the principal necessary in order to borrow, pay, renew, or extend the time of payment of a debt of the principal;

(7) Make, assign, draw, endorse, discount, guarantee, and negotiate promissory notes, checks, drafts, and other negotiable or nonnegotiable paper of the principal, or payable to the principal or the principal's order, make funds transfers, receive the cash or other proceeds of those transactions, and accept and pay when due a draft drawn by a person upon the principal;

(8) Receive and act upon a sight draft, warehouse receipt, or other negotiable or nonnegotiable instrument;

(9) Apply for and receive letters of credit, credit and debit cards, and traveler's checks from a financial institution, and give an indemnity or other agreement in connection with letters of credit;

(10) Consent to an extension of the time of payment with respect to commercial paper or a financial transaction with a financial institution.

(F) Language in a power of attorney granting power with respect to operating a business authorizes the attorney in fact to do all of the following:

(1) Operate, buy, sell, enlarge, reduce, or terminate a business interest;

(2) Subject to the terms of a partnership agreement or operating agreement, do all of the following:

(a) Perform a duty or discharge a liability and exercise a right, power, privilege, or option that the principal has, may have, or claims to have, under the partnership agreement or operating agreement;

(b) Enforce the terms of the partnership agreement or operating agreement by litigation or otherwise;

(c) Defend, submit to arbitration, settle, or compromise litigation to which the principal is a party because of membership in a partnership or limited liability company;

(3) Exercise in person or by proxy, or enforce by litigation or otherwise, a right, power, privilege, or option the principal has or claims to have as the holder of a bond, share, or other instrument of similar character and defend, submit to arbitration, settle, or compromise litigation to which the principal is a party because of a bond, share, or similar instrument;

(4) With respect to a business controlled by the principal, do all of the following:

(a) Continue, modify, renegotiate, extend, and terminate a contract made with an individual or a legal entity by or for the principal with respect to the business before execution of the power of attorney;

(b) Determine all of the following:

(i) The location of its operation;

(ii) The nature and extent of its business;

(iii) The methods of manufacturing, selling, merchandising, financing, accounting, and advertising employed in its operation;

(iv) The amount and types of insurance carried;

(v) The mode of engaging, compensating, and dealing with its accountants, attorneys, and other attorneys in fact and employees;

(c) Change the name or form of organization under which the business is operated and enter into a partnership agreement or operating agreement with other persons or organize a corporation or other business entity to take over all or part of the operation of the business;

(d) Demand and receive money due or claimed by the principal or on the principal's behalf in the operation of the business, and control and disburse the money in the operation of the business;

(5) Put additional capital into a business in which the principal has an interest;

(6) Join in a plan of reorganization, consolidation, or merger of the business;

(7) Sell or liquidate a business or part of it at the time and upon the terms the attorney in fact considers desirable;

(8) Establish the value of a business under a buy-out agreement to which the principal is a party;

(9) Prepare, sign, file, and deliver reports, compilations of information, returns, or other papers with respect to a business that are required by a governmental agency or instrumentality or that the attorney in fact considers desirable and make related payments;

(10) Pay, compromise, or contest taxes or assessments and do any other act that the attorney in fact considers desirable to protect the principal from illegal or unnecessary taxation, fines, penalties, or assessments with respect to a business, including attempts to recover, in any manner permitted by law, money paid before or after the execution of the power of attorney.

(G) Language in a power of attorney granting power with respect to proprietary interests and materials transactions authorizes the attorney in fact in connection with or with respect to any artistic, domestic, intellectual, literary, mechanical, scientific, or other proprietary interest or material to do all of the following:

(1) Abandon, apply for, extend, maintain, modify, receive, renew, secure, or terminate any protection by copyright, patent, registration, or other mechanism for any composition, design, device, discovery, formula, invention, mark, name, process, program, recipe, service mark, trademark, trade name, or other protectable intangible or tangible endeavor or work;

(2) Appeal from, compromise, conduct, defend, intervene in, participate in, prosecute, settle, or terminate any proceeding before any administrative, judicial, or other agency, board, body, commission, court, examiner, judge, magistrate, officer, or other official or tribunal with jurisdiction of any proprietary interest or material;

(3) Arrange or contract for payment or receipt of any charges, fees, royalties, or other payments for assignment, license, sale, transfer, use, or other exploitation of any proprietary interest or material;

(4) Deal in and with any business data, business or trade secret, business method, client or customer list, dealership, franchise, license, manufacturing process, or other proprietary interest or material.

(H) Language in a power of attorney granting power with respect to insurance and annuities authorizes the attorney in fact to do all of the following:

(1) Continue, pay the premium or assessment on, modify, rescind, release, or terminate a contract procured by or for the principal that insures or provides an annuity to either the principal or another person, whether or not the principal is a beneficiary under the contract;

(2) Procure new, different, or additional contracts of insurance or annuities for the principal or the principal's spouse, children, or other dependents and select the amount, type of insurance or annuity, and mode of payment;

(3) Pay the premium or assessment on, modify, rescind, release, or terminate a contract of insurance or annuity procured by the attorney in fact;

(4) Apply for and receive a loan on the security of a contract of insurance or annuity;

(5) Surrender and receive the cash surrender value;

(6) Exercise an election that is not specifically prohibited;

(7) Change the manner of paying premiums;

(8) Change or convert the type of insurance or annuity, with respect to which the principal has or claims to have a power described in this section;

(9) If specifically authorized in the power of attorney, change the beneficiary of a contract of insurance or annuity designated by the principal;

(10) Apply for and procure government aid to guarantee or pay premiums of a contract of insurance on the life of the principal;

(11) Collect, sell, assign, hypothecate, borrow upon, or pledge the interest of the principal in a contract of insurance or annuity;

(12) Pay from proceeds or otherwise, compromise or contest, and apply for refunds in connection with, a tax or assessment levied by a taxing authority with respect to a contract of insurance or annuity or its proceeds or liability accruing by reason of the tax or assessment.

(I)(1) Except for the restrictions set forth in division (I)(2) of this section, language in a power of attorney granting power with respect to retirement plan transactions authorizes the attorney in fact to do all of the following:

(a) Contribute to, withdraw from, and deposit funds in any type of retirement plan, including, but not limited to, any tax qualified or nonqualified pension, profit sharing, stock bonus, employee savings and other retirement plan, individual retirement account, deferred compensation plan, or other type of employee benefit plan;

(b) Select and change payment options for the principal under any retirement plan;

(c) Make rollover contributions from any retirement plan to other retirement plans or individual retirement accounts;

(d) Exercise all investment powers available under any type of self-directed retirement plan.

(2) Unless specifically authorized in a power of attorney, language in a power of attorney granting power with respect to retirement plan transactions does not authorize the attorney in fact to do any of the following:

(a) Elect or change a retirement allowance plan of payment on the principal's behalf under Chapter 145., 742., 3305., 3307., 3309., or 5505. of the Revised Code, other than a joint and survivor annuity leaving one-half to the spouse if the principal is married, a single life annuity if the principal is single, or any plan that includes a partial lump sum option; except that no express authority is necessary to elect a plan that meets the minimum requirements of a court order to elect a plan that will pay a lifetime benefit to a former spouse.

(b) If authorized under section 145.814 of the Revised Code, change an election made under section 145.19 or 145.191 of the Revised Code;

(c) Terminate the principal's membership in the public employees retirement system, state teachers retirement system, school employees retirement system, Ohio police and fire pension fund, or state highway patrol retirement system by withdrawing the principal's accumulated employee contributions.

(J) Language in a power of attorney granting power with respect to safe deposit transactions authorizes the attorney in fact to do all of the following:

(1) Open, continue, and have access to all safe deposit boxes;

(2) Sign, renew, release, or terminate any safe deposit contract;

(3) Drill or surrender any safe deposit box.

(K)(1) Language in a power of attorney granting power with respect to estates, trusts, and other relationships in which the principal is a beneficiary authorizes the attorney in fact to act for the principal in all matters that affect a trust, probate estate, guardianship, conservatorship, escrow, custodianship, or other fund from which the principal is, may become, or claims to be entitled as a beneficiary to a share or payment, including all of the following:

(a) Accept, reject, disclaim, receive, receipt for, sell, assign, release, pledge, exchange, or consent to a reduction in or modification of a share in or payment from the fund;

(b) Demand or obtain by litigation or otherwise money or any other thing of value to which the principal is, may become, or claims to be entitled by reason of the fund;

(c) Initiate, participate in, and oppose litigation to ascertain the meaning, validity, or effect of a deed, will, declaration of trust, or other instrument or transaction affecting the interest of the principal;

(d) Initiate, participate in, and oppose litigation to remove, substitute, or surcharge a fiduciary;

(e) Conserve, invest, disburse, and use anything received for an authorized purpose;

(f) Transfer an interest of the principal in real property, stocks, bonds, accounts with financial institutions, insurance, and other property to the trustee of a revocable trust created by the principal as settlor;

(g) Transfer an interest of the principal in real property to any trustee or trustees of an undisclosed trust for the benefit of the principal;

(h) If specifically authorized in the power of attorney, designate or change the designation of a beneficiary to receive any property, benefit, or contractual right on the principal's death.

(2) Unless expressly authorized in the power of attorney, language granting power with respect to estates, trusts, and other relationships in which the principal is a beneficiary does not include authority to create, modify, or revoke a trust or authority to fund with the principal's property a trust not created by the principal or a person authorized to create a trust for the principal.

(L) Language in a power of attorney granting power with respect to borrowing transactions authorizes the attorney in fact to do all of the following:

(1) Borrow money;

(2) Mortgage or pledge any real estate, tangible personal property, or intangible personal property as security for any borrowing transactions;

(3) Sign, renew, extend, pay, and satisfy any notes or other forms of obligations.

(M)(1) Language in a power of attorney granting power with respect to fiduciary transactions authorizes the attorney in fact to do all of the following:

(a) Represent and act for the principal in all ways and in all matters affecting any fund with respect to which the principal is a fiduciary;

(b) Initiate, participate in, and oppose any judicial or other proceeding for the removal, substitution, or surcharge of a fiduciary, conserve, invest, or disburse anything received for the purposes of the fund for which it is received, and reimburse the attorney in fact for any expenditures properly made by the attorney in fact in the execution of the powers conferred on the attorney in fact by the power of attorney;

(c) Agree and contract in any manner, with any person, and on any terms that the attorney in fact selects for the accomplishment of the purposes set forth in division (M) of this section and perform, rescind, reform, release, or modify the agreement or contract or any other similar agreement or contract made by or for the principal;

(d) Execute, acknowledge, verify, seal, file, and deliver any consent, designation, pleading, notice, demand, election, conveyance, release, assignment, check, pledge, waiver, admission of service, notice of appearance, or other instrument that the attorney in fact determines is useful for the accomplishment of any of the purposes set forth in division (M) of this section;

(e) Hire, discharge, and compensate any attorney, accountant, expert witness, or other assistants when the attorney in fact determines that action to be desirable for the proper execution by the attorney in fact of any of the powers described in division (M) of this section and for the keeping of needed records;

(f) Perform any other acts with respect to a fund of which the principal is a fiduciary.

(2) Division (M) of this section does not authorize a fiduciary to delegate any power of a fiduciary unless the power is one the fiduciary is authorized to delegate under the terms of the trust agreement or other instrument governing the exercise of the power or under the law of the jurisdiction that governs that trust agreement or other instrument.

(3) As used in division (M) of this section, "fund" means any trust, probate estate, guardianship, conservatorship, escrow, custodianship, or other fund in which the principal has, or claims to have, an interest as a fiduciary.

(4) All powers described in division (M) of this section may be exercised equally with respect to any fund of which the principal is a fiduciary as of the date of the power of attorney or becomes a fiduciary after that date, and regardless of whether the fund is located in the state of Ohio or elsewhere.

(N) Language in a power of attorney granting power with respect to personal and family maintenance authorizes the attorney in fact to do all of the following:

(1) Do the acts necessary to maintain the customary standard of living of the principal, the principal's spouse, children, and other individuals customarily or legally entitled to be supported by the principal, including providing living quarters by purchase, lease, or other contract or paying the operating costs, including interest, amortization payments, repairs, and taxes, on premises owned by the principal and occupied by those individuals;

(2) For the individuals described in division (N)(1) of this section, provide normal domestic help, usual vacations and travel expenses, and funds for shelter, clothing, food, appropriate education, and other current living costs;

(3) For the individuals described in division (N)(1) of this section, pay expenses for necessary medical, dental, and surgical care, hospitalization, and custodial care;

(4) For the individuals described in division (N)(1) of this section, continue any provision made by the principal for automobiles or other means of transportation, including registering, licensing, insuring, and replacing them;

(5) Maintain or open charge accounts for the convenience of the individuals described in division (N)(1) of this section and open new accounts the attorney in fact considers desirable to accomplish a lawful purpose;

(6) Continue payments incidental to the membership or affiliation of the principal in a church, club, society, order, or other organization or continue contributions to those organizations.

(O) Language in a power of attorney granting power with respect to benefits from social security, medicare, medicaid, other governmental programs, or civil or military service authorizes the attorney in fact to do all of the following:

(1) Execute vouchers in the name of the principal for allowances and reimbursements payable by the United States or a foreign government or by a state or political subdivision of a state to the principal, including allowances and reimbursements for transportation of the principal's spouse, children, and other individuals customarily or legally entitled to be supported by the principal, and for shipment of their household effects;

(2) Take possession and order the removal and shipment of property of the principal from a governmental or private post, warehouse, depot, dock, or other place of storage or safekeeping and execute and deliver a release, voucher, receipt, bill of lading, shipping ticket, certificate, or other instrument for that purpose;

(3) Prepare, file, and prosecute a claim of the principal to a benefit or assistance, financial or otherwise, to which the principal claims to be entitled under a statute or governmental regulation;

(4) Prosecute, defend, submit to arbitration, settle, and propose or accept a compromise with respect to any benefits the principal may be entitled to receive;

(5) Receive the financial proceeds of a claim of the type described in division (O) of this section and conserve, invest, disburse, or use anything so received for a lawful purpose.

(P)(1) Language in a power of attorney granting power with respect to records, reports, and statements authorizes the attorney in fact to do all of the following:

(a) Keep records of all cash received and disbursed for or on account of the principal, of all credits and debits to the account of the principal, and of all transactions affecting in any way the assets and liabilities of the principal;

(b) Prepare, execute, and file all tax, social security, unemployment insurance, and information returns required by the laws of the United States, of any state or political subdivision of any state, or of any foreign government and to prepare, execute, and file all other papers and instruments that the attorney in fact determines is desirable or necessary for the safeguarding of the principal against excess or illegal taxation or against penalties imposed for a claimed violation of any law or other governmental regulation;

(c) Prepare, execute, and file any record, report, or statement with respect to price, rent, wage, or rationing control or other governmental activity that the attorney in fact determines is desirable or necessary for the safeguarding or maintenance of the principal's interest;

(d) Hire, discharge, and compensate any attorney, accountant, or other assistant when the attorney in fact determines that action to be desirable for the proper execution by the attorney in fact of any of the powers described in this section;

(e) Do any other act, in connection with the preparation, execution, filing, storage, or other utilization of any records, reports, or statements of or concerning the principal's affairs that the principal can do through an attorney in fact.

(2) An attorney in fact may exercise all powers described in division (P)(1) of this section equally with respect to any records, reports, or statements of or concerning the affairs of the principal as they exist at the time the principal gives the power of attorney or after the principal gives the power of attorney, in the state of Ohio or elsewhere.

(Q) Language in a power of attorney granting power with respect to tax matters authorizes the attorney in fact to do all of the following:

(1) Prepare, sign, and file federal, state, local, and foreign income, gift, payroll, and other tax returns, claims for refunds, requests for extensions of time, petitions regarding tax matters, and any other tax-related documents, including receipts, offers, waivers, consents (including consents and agreements under section 2032A of the "Internal Revenue Code of 1986," Pub. L. No. 94–455, 26 U.S.C. 2032A, as amended), closing agreements, and any power of attorney required by any tax collection or enforcement agency with respect to a tax year upon which the statute of limitations has not run and the following twenty-five tax years;

(2) Pay taxes due, collect refunds, post bonds, receive confidential information, and contest deficiencies determined by any tax collection or enforcement agency;

(3) Exercise any election available to the principal under federal, state, local, or foreign tax law;

(4) Act for the principal in all tax matters for all periods before any tax collection or enforcement agency.

(R) Language in a power of attorney granting power with respect to licenses authorizes the attorney in fact to obtain, renew, or transfer all of the following:

(1) Automobile, truck, boat, and other vehicle licenses;

(2) Business licenses of any type.

(S) Language in a power of attorney granting power with respect to access to documents authorizes the attorney in fact to do all of the following:

(1) Have access to and possession of the principal's will, trusts, instruments, deeds, life insurance policies, contracts, employee benefit records, and other documents, including, but not limited to, documents protected under the "Financial Services Modernization Act of 1999," Pub. L. No. 106–102, 15 U.S.C. 6801, as amended, and the "Health Insurance Portability and Accountability Act of 1996," Pub. L. No. 104–191, 42 U.S.C. 300gg, as amended;

(2) Have access to mail and redirect mail.

(T) Language in a power of attorney granting power with respect to employment of agents authorizes the attorney in fact to do all of the following:

(1) Employ attorneys, accountants, investment advisors, expert witnesses, realtors, or other professionals when the attorney in fact believes the employment of the professional to be desirable;

(2) Pay any agents reasonable compensation.

(U) Language in a power of attorney with respect to delegation authorizes the attorney in fact to delegate any or all of the powers granted by the principal to any person or persons whom the attorney in fact selects.

(V) Language in a power of attorney granting power with respect to claims and litigation authorizes the attorney in fact to do all of the following:

(1) Assert and prosecute before a court or administrative agency a claim, claim for relief, cause of action, counterclaim, offset, or defense against an individual, organization, or government, including an action to recover property or any other thing of value, to recover damages sustained by the principal, to eliminate or modify tax liability, or to seek an injunction, specific performance, or other relief;

(2) Bring an action to determine adverse claims, intervene in litigation, and act as amicus curiae;

(3) In connection with litigation, procure an attachment, garnishment, libel, order of arrest, or other preliminary, provisional, or intermediate relief and use any available procedure to effect or satisfy a judgment, order, or decree;

(4) In connection with litigation, perform any lawful act, including acceptance of tender, offer of judgment, admission of facts, submission of a controversy on an agreed statement of facts, consent to examination before trial, and bind the principal in litigation;

(5) Submit to arbitration, settle, and propose or accept a compromise with respect to a claim or litigation;

(6) Waive the issuance and service of process upon the principal, accept service of process, appear for the principal, designate persons upon whom process directed to the principal may be served, execute and file or deliver stipulations on the principal's behalf, verify pleadings, seek appellate review, procure and give surety and indemnity bonds, contract and pay for the preparation and printing of records and briefs, and receive and execute and file or deliver a consent, waiver, release, confession of judgment, satisfaction of judgment, notice, agreement, or other instrument in connection with the prosecution, settlement, or defense of a claim or litigation;

(7) Act for the principal with respect to a voluntary or involuntary bankruptcy or insolvency proceeding concerning the principal or another person, a reorganization proceeding, or a receivership or application for the appointment of a receiver or trustee that affects an interest of the principal in property or any other thing of value;

(8) Pay a judgment against the principal or a settlement made in connection with litigation and receive and conserve money or any other thing of value paid in settlement of or as proceeds of a claim or litigation.

(2005 H 246, eff. 3–29–06)

CHAPTER 1339

FIDUCIARY LAW

ISSUE OF SECURITIES

Section
1339.01 Issuers of securities and holders of record—Repealed

FIDUCIARY BANK ACCOUNTS (UNIFORM FIDUCIARY ACT)

1339.03 Definitions—Repealed
1339.031 Interpretation of terms—Repealed
1339.18 Fiduciary duties of attorney of fiduciary—Repealed

Section

OHIO TRANSFERS TO MINORS ACT

1339.34 Powers and duties of custodian—Repealed

INTER VIVOS OR TESTAMENTARY TRUSTS

1339.411 Spendthrift provision not causing forfeiture or postponement of interest in property—Repealed
1339.412 Accumulation for more than one year of income of property—Repealed

Section

1339.45 Provision for generation skipping transfer tax—Repealed
1339.51 Trusts for supplemental services for disabled individuals—Repealed

UNIFORM PRUDENT INVESTOR ACT

1339.52 Prudent investor rule—Repealed
1339.53 Standard of care; portfolio strategy; risk and return objectives—Repealed
1339.54 Diversification—Repealed
1339.55 Loyalty; impartiality—Repealed
1339.56 Duties at inception of trusteeship—Repealed
1339.57 Investment costs—Repealed
1339.58 Reviewing compliance—Repealed
1339.59 Delegation of investment and management functions—Repealed
1339.60 Language invoking standard of act—Repealed
1339.61 Uniformity of application and construction; application to existing trusts—Repealed

MISCELLANEOUS PROVISIONS

1339.621 Revocation of spouse's power of attorney upon divorce, dissolution, or separation—Repealed
1339.63 Spouse designated as beneficiary of death benefits; effect of termination of marriage—Repealed
1339.64 Personal property held jointly by spouses; effect of termination of marriage—Repealed
1339.65 Liability when acting as general partner; disclosures—Repealed
1339.66 Termination of trust; distribution—Repealed
1339.67 Consolidation or division of trusts—Repealed
1339.68 Disclaimers of successions to property—Repealed
1339.69 Reports of inter vivos trustees—Repealed

Law Review and Journal Commentaries

Fiduciary preludes: Likely issues for LLCs, Deborah A. DeMott. 66 U Colo L Rev 1043 (1995).

Gifts to Improve the Family's Over-all Tax Situation, Sterling Newell, Jr. 13 W Reserve U L Rev 291 (March 1962).

New Rules for Providers: The Rise of Fiduciary Law, Maxwell J. Mehlman. 2 Health L J Ohio 83 (January/February 1991).

Planning the Form of the Gifts, Edward J. Hawkins, Jr. 13 W Reserve U L Rev 300 (March 1962).

The Uniform Trust Code (2000) and its application to Ohio. David M. English, 30 Cap U L Rev 1 (2002).

ISSUE OF SECURITIES

1339.01 Issuers of securities and holders of record—Repealed

(2006 H 416, eff. 1–1–07; 1953 H 1, eff. 10–1–53; GC 8509–2)

Historical and Statutory Notes

Ed. Note: Former RC 1339.01 amended and recodified as RC 5815.02 by 2006 H 416, eff. 1–1–07.

Pre–1953 H 1 Amendments: 119 v 449, § 2

FIDUCIARY BANK ACCOUNTS (UNIFORM FIDUCIARY ACT)

Comparative Laws
Uniform Fiduciaries Act
Table of Jurisdictions Wherein Act Has Been Adopted.

For text of Uniform Act, and variation notes and annotation materials for adopting jurisdictions, see Uniform Laws Annotated, Master Edition, Volume 7A.

Jurisdiction	Statutory Citation
Alabama	Code 1975, § 19–1–1 to 19–1–13.
Arizona	A.R.S. § 14–7501 to 14–7512.
Colorado	West's C.R.S.A. § 15–1–101 to 15–1–113.
District of Columbia	D.C. Official Code, 2001 Ed. § 21–1701 to 21–1712.
Hawaii	HRS § 556–1 to 556–10.
Idaho	I.C. § 68–301 to 68–315.
Illinois	S.H.A. 760 ILCS 65/0.01 to 65/12.
Indiana	West's A.I.C. 30–2–4–1 to 30–2–4–14.
Louisiana	LSA–R.S. 9:3801 to 9:3814.
Maryland	Code, Estates and Trusts, § 15–201 to 15–211.
Minnesota	M.S.A. § 520.01 to 520.13.
Missouri	V.A.M.S. § 456.240 to 456.350.
Nevada	N.R.S. 162.010 to 162.140.
New Jersey	N.J.S.A. 3B:14–52 to 3B:14–61.
New Mexico	NMSA 1978, § 46–1–1 to 46–1–11.
New York	McKinney's General Business Law § 359–i, 359–l.
North Carolina	G.S. § 32–1 to 32–13.
Pennsylvania	7 P.S. § 6351 to 6404.
Rhode Island	Gen.Laws 1956, § 18–4–15 to 18–4–21.
South Dakota	SDCL 55–7–2 to 55–7–15.
Tennessee	T.C.A. § 35–2–101 to 35–2–112.
Utah	U.C.A.1953, 22–1–1 to 22–1–11.
Virgin Islands	15 V.I.C. § 1041 to 1053.
Wisconsin	W.S.A. 112.01 (1 to 16).
Wyoming	Wyo.Stat.Ann., § 2–3–201 to 2–3–211.

1339.03 Definitions—Repealed

(2006 H 416, eff. 1–1–07; 1953 H 1, eff. 10–1–53; GC 8509–7)

Historical and Statutory Notes

Ed. Note: Former RC 1339.03 amended and recodified as RC 5815.04 by 2006 H 416, eff. 1–1–07.

Pre–1953 H 1 Amendments: 120 v 343, § 1

1339.031 Interpretation of terms—Repealed

(2006 H 416, eff. 1–1–07; 1994 H 208, eff. 6–23–94)

Historical and Statutory Notes

Ed. Note: Former RC 1339.031 recodified as RC 5815.01 by 2006 H 416, eff. 1–1–07.

1339.18 Fiduciary duties of attorney of fiduciary—Repealed

(2006 H 416, eff. 1–1–07; 1998 H 701, eff. 3–22–99)

Historical and Statutory Notes

Ed. Note: Former RC 1339.18 recodified as RC 5815.16 by 2006 H 416, eff. 1–1–07.

Ed. Note: Prior 1339.18 repealed by 1987 S 146, eff. 10–20–87; 1953 H 1; GC 8509–20.

Pre–1953 H 1 Amendments: 120 v 354

1339.34 Repealed

OHIO TRANSFERS TO MINORS ACT
Comparative Laws
Uniform Transfers to Minors Act
Table of Jurisdictions Wherein Act Has Been Adopted.

For text of Uniform Act, and variation notes and annotation materials for adopting jurisdictions, see Uniform Laws Annotated, Master Edition, Volume 8B.

Jurisdiction	Statutory Citation
Alabama	Code 1975, § 35–5A–1 to 35–5A–24.
Alaska	AS 13.46.010 to 13.46.999.
Arizona	A.R.S. § 14–7651 to 14–7671.
Arkansas	A.C.A. § 9–26–201 to 9–26–227.
California	West's Ann.Cal.Prob. Code, § 3900 to 3925.
Colorado	West's C.R.S.A. § 11–50–101 to 11–50–126.
Connecticut	C.G.S.A. § 45a–557 to 45a–560b.
Delaware	12 Del.C. § 4501 to 4523.
District of Columbia	D.C. Official Code 2001 Ed., § 21–301 to 21–324.
Florida	West's F.S.A. § 710.101 to 710.126.
Georgia	O.C.G.A. § 44–5–110 to 44–5–134.
Hawaii	HRS § 553A–1 to 553A–24.
Idaho	I.C. § 68–801 to 68–825.
Illinois	S.H.A., 760 ILCS 20/1 to 20/24.
Indiana	West's A.I.C. 30-2-8.5–1 to 30-2-8.5–40.
Iowa	I.C.A. § 565B.1 to 565B.25.
Kansas	K.S.A. 38–1701 to 38–1726.
Kentucky	KRS 385.012 to 385.252.
Louisiana	LSA–R.S. 9:751 to 9:773.
Maine	33 M.R.S.A. § 1651 to 1674.
Maryland	Code, Estates and Trusts, § 13–301 to 13–324.
Massachusetts	M.G.L.A. c. 201A, § 1 to 24.
Michigan	M.C.L.A. § 554.521 to 554.552.
Minnesota	M.S.A. § 527.21 to 527.44.
Mississippi	Code 1972, § 91–20–1 to 91–20–49.
Missouri	V.A.M.S. § 404.005 to 404.094.
Montana	MCA 72–26–501 to 72–26–803.
Nebraska	R.R.S.1943, § 43–2701 to 43–2724.
Nevada	N.R.S. 167.010 to 167.100.
New Hampshire	RSA 463–A:1 to 463–A:26.
New Jersey	N.J.S.A. 46:38A–1 to 46:38A–57.
New Mexico	NMSA 1978, § 46–7–11 to 46–7–34.
New York	McKinney's EPTL, 7–6.1 to 7–6.26.
North Carolina	G.S. § 33A–1 to 33A–24.
North Dakota	NDCC 47–24.1–01 to 47–24.1–22.
Oklahoma	58 Okl.St.Ann. § 1201 to 1225.
Oregon	ORS 126.805 to 126.886.
Pennsylvania	20 Pa.C.S.A., § 5301 to 5321.
Rhode Island	Gen.Laws 1956, § 18–7–1 to 18–7–26.
South Dakota	SDCL 55–10A–1 to 55–10A–26.
Tennessee	T.C.A. § 35–7–201 to 35–7–226.
Texas	V.T.C.A. Property Code, § 141.001 to 141.025.
Utah	U.C.A. 1953, 75–5a–101 to 75–5a–123.
Virginia	Code 1950, § 31–37 to 31–59.
Virgin Islands	15 V.I.C. § 1251a to 1251x.
Washington	West's RCWA 11.114.010 to 11.114.904.
West Virginia	Code, 36–7–1 to 36–7–24.

Jurisdiction	Statutory Citation
Wisconsin	W.S.A. 880.61 to 880.72.
Wyoming	Wyo.Stat.Ann., § 34–13–114 to 34–13–137.

1339.34 Powers and duties of custodian—Repealed

(2006 H 416, eff. 1–1–07; 1993 H 62, eff. 10–1–93; 1986 H 297; 1980 H 1007; 1977 H 1; 1976 S 166; 1973 S 1; 129 v 1550)

Historical and Statutory Notes

Ed. Note: Former RC 1339.34 amended and recodified as RC 5814.04 by 2006 H 416, eff. 1–1–07.

Ed. Note: 1339.34 is analogous to former 1339.21, repealed by 129 v 1550, eff. 1–1–62.

INTER VIVOS OR TESTAMENTARY TRUSTS

1339.411 Spendthrift provision not causing forfeiture or postponement of interest in property—Repealed

(2006 H 416, eff. 1–1–07; 2003 S 64, eff. 10–21–03; 2000 H 313, eff. 8–29–00; 1996 H 391, eff. 10–1–96; 1992 H 427, eff. 10–8–92)

Historical and Statutory Notes

Ed. Note: Former RC 1339.411 recodified as RC 5815.22 by 2006 H 416, eff. 1–1–07.

1339.412 Accumulation for more than one year of income of property—Repealed

(2006 H 416, eff. 1–1–07; 2003 S 64, eff. 10–21–03; 2000 S 108, eff. 9–29–00; 1996 H 391, eff. 10–1–96)

Historical and Statutory Notes

Ed. Note: Former RC 1339.412 recodified as RC 5815.23 by 2006 H 416, eff. 1–1–07.

1339.45 Provision for generation skipping transfer tax—Repealed

(2006 H 416, eff. 1–1–07; 1990 H 286, eff. 11–8–90; 1978 H 1127)

Historical and Statutory Notes

Ed. Note: Former RC 1339.45 recodified as RC 5815.27 by 2006 H 416, eff. 1–1–07.

1339.51 Trusts for supplemental services for disabled individuals—Repealed

(2006 H 416, eff. 1–1–07; 2001 H 178, eff. 10–26–01; 1994 H 694, eff. 11–11–94; 1992 S 124, eff. 4–16–93)

Historical and Statutory Notes

Ed. Note: Former RC 1339.51 recodified as RC 5815.28 by 2006 H 416, eff. 1–1–07.

Ed. Note: Prior 1339.51 repealed by 1987 S 146, eff. 10–20–87; 1969 H 738; see now Ch 1340 for provisions analogous to prior 1339.51.

UNIFORM PRUDENT INVESTOR ACT

Comparative Laws

Uniform Prudent Investor Act

Table of Jurisdictions Wherein Act Has Been Adopted.

For text of Uniform Act, and variation notes and annotation materials for adopting jurisdictions, see Uniform Laws Annotated, Master Edition, Volume 7B.

Jurisdiction	Statutory Citation
Alaska	AS 13.36.200 to 13.36.275.
Arizona	A.R.S. § 14–7601 to 14–7611.
Arkansas	A.C.A. § 24–2–610 to 24–2–619.
California	West's Ann. Cal. Probate Code, § 16045 to 16054.
Colorado	West's C.R.S.A. § 15–1.1–101 to 15–1.1–115.
Connecticut	C.G.S.A. § 45a–541 to 45a–541l.
District of Columbia	D.C. Official Code, 2001 Ed. § 28–4701 to 28–4712.
Florida	West's F.S.A. § 518.11, 518.112.
Hawaii	H.R.S. § 554C–1 to 554C–12.
Idaho	I.C. § 68–501 to 68–514.
Illinois	S.H.A. 760 ILCS 5/5, 5/5.1.
Indiana	West's A.I.C. 30–4–3.5–1 to 30–4–3.5–13.
Iowa	I.C.A. § 633.4301 to 633.4310.
Kansas	K.S.A. 58–24a01 to 58–24a19.
Maine	18–A M.R.S.A. § 7–302, 7–302 note.
Massachusetts	M.G.L.A. c. 203C, § 1 to 11.
Michigan	M.C.L.A. § 700.1501 to 700.1512.
Minnesota	M.S.A. § 501B.151, 501B.152.
Missouri	V.A.M.S. § 456.900 to 456.913.
Montana	M.C.A. 72–34–601 to 72–34–610.
Nebraska	R.R.S.1943, § 8–2201 to 8–2213.
New Jersey	N.J.S.A. 3B:20–11.1 to 3B:20–11.12.
New Mexico	NMSA 1978, § 45–7–601 to 45–7–612.
New York	McKinney's EPTL 11–2.3.
North Carolina	G.S. § 36A–161 to 36A–173.
North Dakota	NDCC 59–02–08.1 to 59–02–08.11.
Oklahoma	60 Okl.St.Ann. § 175.60 to 175.72.
Oregon	ORS 128.192 to 128.218.
Pennsylvania	20 Pa.C.S.A. § 7201 to 7214.
Rhode Island	Gen. Laws 1956, § 18–15–1 to 18–15–13.
Tennessee	T.C.A. § 35–14–101 to 35–14–114.
Texas	V.T.C.A. Property Code § 117.001 to 117.012.
Utah	U.C.A.1953, 75–7–302.
Vermont	9 V.S.A. § 4651 to 4662.
Virginia	Code 1950, § 26–45.3 to 26–45.14.
Washington	West's RCWA 11.100.010 to 11.100.140.
West Virginia	Code, 44–6C–1 to 44–6C–15.
Wyoming	Wyo.Stat.Ann. § 4–10–901 to 4–10–913.

1339.52   Prudent investor rule—Repealed

(2006 H 416, eff. 1–1–07; 1998 H 701, eff. 3–22–99)

Historical and Statutory Notes

Ed. Note: Former RC 1339.52 amended and recodified as RC 5809.01 by 2006 H 416, eff. 1–1–07.

Notes of Decisions

Trustee, powers and duties 1

1. Trustee, powers and duties

Trust document provision did not clearly indicate an intention to abrogate the duty of the trustee to diversify from the stock that was used to establish charitable trust, and therefore, did not allow trustee to avoid liability for breaching the duty to diversify, which language stated that the trustee's powers included the power to "retain, without liability for loss or depreciation resulting from such retention, original property, real or personal, received from grantor or from any other source, although it may represent a disproportionate part of the trust." Fifth Third Bank v. Firstar Bank, N.A. (Ohio App. 1 Dist., Hamilton, 09-01-2006) No. C-050518, 2006-Ohio-4506, 2006 WL 2520329, Unreported. Charities ⚖ 48(1)

1339.53   Standard of care; portfolio strategy; risk and return objectives—Repealed

(2006 H 416, eff. 1–1–07; 1998 H 701, eff. 3–22–99)

Historical and Statutory Notes

Ed. Note: Former RC 1339.53 amended and recodified as RC 5809.02 by 2006 H 416, eff. 1–1–07.

Notes of Decisions

Breach of fiduciary duty action 1

1. Breach of fiduciary duty action

Evidence demonstrating that former trustee of charitable trust failed to verify facts relevant to the investment and management of the trust, as required by statute, and that trustee did not take into consideration economic conditions, tax consequences, and need for liquidity in deciding when to sell the stock that established the trust, created an issue for the jury in breach of fiduciary duty action brought by creator of trust and the new trustee. Fifth Third Bank v. Firstar Bank, N.A. (Ohio App. 1 Dist., Hamilton, 09-01-2006) No. C-050518, 2006-Ohio-4506, 2006 WL 2520329, Unreported. Charities ⚖ 50

Trial court's decision to admit testimony explaining the terms of a charitable trust document was warranted, in breach of fiduciary duty action brought against the former trustee of the trust, despite former trustee's contentions that such testimony constituted parol evidence or impermissibly stated the law; the testimony was not offered to vary the clear terms of the trust document, and the trial judge repeatedly informed the jury that the judge would instruct the jury on the applicable law. Fifth Third Bank v. Firstar Bank, N.A. (Ohio App. 1 Dist., Hamilton, 09-01-2006) No. C-050518, 2006-Ohio-4506, 2006 WL 2520329, Unreported. Charities ⚖ 50

1339.54   Diversification—Repealed

(2006 H 416, eff. 1–1–07; 1998 H 701, eff. 3–22–99)

Historical and Statutory Notes

Ed. Note: Former RC 1339.54 amended and recodified as RC 5809.03 by 2006 H 416, eff. 1–1–07.

1339.55   Loyalty; impartiality—Repealed

(2006 H 416, eff. 1–1–07; 1998 H 701, eff. 3–22–99)

Historical and Statutory Notes

Ed. Note: Former RC 1339.55 amended and recodified as RC 5808.03 by 2006 H 416, eff. 1–1–07.

1339.56   Duties at inception of trusteeship—Repealed

(2006 H 416, eff. 1–1–07; 1998 H 701, eff. 3–22–99)

1339.56 Repealed

Historical and Statutory Notes

Ed. Note: Former RC 1339.56 amended and recodified as RC 5809.04 by 2006 H 416, eff. 1–1–07.

1339.57 Investment costs—Repealed

(2006 H 416, eff. 1–1–07; 1998 H 701, eff. 3–22–99)

Historical and Statutory Notes

Ed. Note: Former RC 1339.57 amended and recodified as RC 5808.05 by 2006 H 416, eff. 1–1–07.

1339.58 Reviewing compliance—Repealed

(2006 H 416, eff. 1–1–07; 1998 H 701, eff. 3–22–99)

Historical and Statutory Notes

Ed. Note: Former RC 1339.58 amended and recodified as RC 5809.05 by 2006 H 416, eff. 1–1–07.

1339.59 Delegation of investment and management functions—Repealed

(2006 H 416, eff. 1–1–07; 1998 H 701, eff. 3–22–99)

Historical and Statutory Notes

Ed. Note: Former RC 1339.59 amended and recodified as RC 5808.07 by 2006 H 416, eff. 1–1–07.

1339.60 Language invoking standard of act—Repealed

(2006 H 416, eff. 1–1–07; 1998 H 701, eff. 3–22–99)

Historical and Statutory Notes

Ed. Note: Former RC 1339.60 amended and recodified as RC 5809.07 by 2006 H 416, eff. 1–1–07.

Ed. Note: Former 1339.60 amended and recodified as 1339.68 by 1998 H 701, eff. 3–22–99; 1986 S 248, eff. 12–17–86; 1984 S 201; 1980 S 317; 1976 S 168.

1339.61 Uniformity of application and construction; application to existing trusts—Repealed

(2006 H 416, eff. 1–1–07; 1998 H 701, eff. 3–22–99)

Historical and Statutory Notes

Ed. Note: Former RC 1339.61 amended and recodified as RC 5809.08 by 2006 H 416, eff. 1–1–07.

MISCELLANEOUS PROVISIONS

1339.621 Revocation of spouse's power of attorney upon divorce, dissolution, or separation—Repealed

(2006 H 416, eff. 1–1–07; 2003 S 64, eff. 10–21–03)

Historical and Statutory Notes

Ed. Note: Former RC 1339.621 recodified as RC 5815.32 by 2006 H 416, eff. 1–1–07.

1339.63 Spouse designated as beneficiary of death benefits; effect of termination of marriage—Repealed

(2006 H 416, eff. 1–1–07; 1990 H 346, eff. 5–31–90)

Historical and Statutory Notes

Ed. Note: Former RC 1339.63 recodified as RC 5815.33 by 2006 H 416, eff. 1–1–07.

1339.64 Personal property held jointly by spouses; effect of termination of marriage—Repealed

(2006 H 416, eff. 1–1–07; 1990 H 346, eff. 5–31–90)

Historical and Statutory Notes

Ed. Note: Former RC 1339.64 amended and recodified as RC 5815.34 by 2006 H 416, eff. 1–1–07.

1339.65 Liability when acting as general partner; disclosures—Repealed

(2006 H 416, eff. 1–1–07; 1989 S 46, eff. 1–1–90; 1983 H 288)

Historical and Statutory Notes

Ed. Note: Former RC 1339.65 amended and recodified as RC 5815.35 by 2006 H 416, eff. 1–1–07.

1339.66 Termination of trust; distribution—Repealed

(2006 H 416, eff. 1–1–07; 2003 S 64, eff. 10–21–03; 2002 H 345, eff. 7–23–02; 1986 H 139, eff. 7–24–86)

Historical and Statutory Notes

Amendment Note: 2003 S 64 added new divisions (C) and (D).

Amendment Note: 2002 H 345 substituted "one hundred" for "fifty" in division (A)(1)(d); and made other nonsubstantive changes.

1339.67 Consolidation or division of trusts—Repealed

(2006 H 416, eff. 1–1–07; 1992 H 427, eff. 10–8–92)

1339.68 Disclaimers of successions to property—Repealed

(2006 H 416, eff. 1–1–07; 2002 H 345, eff. 7–23–02; 2000 H 313, eff. 8–29–00; 1998 H 701, eff. 3–22–99)

Historical and Statutory Notes

Ed. Note: Former RC 1339.68 recodified as RC 5815.36 by 2006 H 416, eff. 1–1–07.

Ed. Note: 1339.68 was former 1339.60, amended and recodified by 1998 H 701, eff. 3–22–99; 1986 S 248, eff. 12–17–86; 1984 S 201; 1980 S 317; 1976 S 168.

1339.69 Reports of inter vivos trustees—Repealed

(2006 H 416, eff. 1–1–07; 2002 H 522, eff. 1–1–03)

Historical and Statutory Notes

Ed. Note: 1339.69 is former 1340.031, amended and recodified by 2002 H 522, eff. 1–1–03; 1999 H 59, eff. 10–29–99.

Amendment Note: 2002 H 522 added new division (A); redesignated former division (A) as new division (B) and designated subdivisions (1), (2), and (3); redesignated former division (B) as new division (C); and redesignated former division (C) as new division (D).

Notes of Decisions

Evidence 1

---

1. Evidence

Trust beneficiary was afforded relief under statute that entitled beneficiary to trustee's report regarding administration of trust for past two years, and beneficiary failed to show good cause for full accounting, and thus, trial court did not abuse its discretion in denying beneficiary equitable relief; beneficiary failed to show any absolute right to equitable remedy, beneficiary did not allege any facts to substantiate good cause for ordering trustees to render account, and other remedies available to court were redundant with legal remedy provided by statute. Stavick v. Coyne (Ohio App. 7 Dist., Mahoning, 12-17-2003) No. 02 CA 24, 2003-Ohio-6999, 2003 WL 22997262, Unreported. Trusts ⇐ 305

Trustee's counterclaim and request for sanctions, in beneficiary's action for accounting, was not frivolous so as to warrant sanctions; accounting was adequate, and no evidence indicted that motions were frivolous. Diemert v. Diemert (Ohio App. 8 Dist., Cuyahoga, 12-04-2003) No. 82597, 2003-Ohio-6496, 2003 WL 22862810, Unreported, appeal not allowed 102 Ohio St.3d 1446, 808 N.E.2d 397, 2004-Ohio-2263. Trusts ⇐ 330

Evidence supported trial court's determination that beneficiary was provided with a full and complete accounting of family trusts; attorney testified that accounting provided was complete and complied with all appropriate accounting requirements, and trustee provided ledger sheets and bank statements from trust's only bank account. Diemert v. Diemert (Ohio App. 8 Dist., Cuyahoga, 12-04-2003) No. 82597, 2003-Ohio-6496, 2003 WL 22862810, Unreported, appeal not allowed 102 Ohio St.3d 1446, 808 N.E.2d 397, 2004-Ohio-2263. Trusts ⇐ 325

CHAPTER 1340

FIDUCIARY LAW

DISCRETIONARY DISTRIBUTIONS BY FIDUCIARIES

Section	
1340.21	Definitions—Repealed
1340.22	Discretionary distributions by fiduciaries—Repealed
1340.23	Interpretation of governing instruments—Repealed

INSTITUTIONAL TRUST FUNDS ACT

Section	
1340.31	Definitions—Repealed
1340.32	Income defined—Repealed
1340.33	Application of statutory definition of income when settlor expressly indicates intent—Repealed
1340.34	Standard of care—Repealed
1340.35	Restrictions on definition of income or on distributions—Repealed
1340.36	Effect on Uniform Management of Institutional Funds Act—Repealed
1340.37	Citation of Act—Repealed

UNIFORM PRINCIPAL AND INCOME ACT (1997)

Section	
1340.40	Definitions—Repealed
1340.41	Fiduciary duties; general principles—Repealed
1340.42	Trustee's power to adjust—Repealed
1340.46	Determination and distribution of net income—Repealed
1340.47	Distribution to residuary and remainder beneficiaries—Repealed
1340.51	When right to income begins and ends—Repealed
1340.52	Apportionment of receipts and disbursements when decedent dies or income interest begins—Repealed
1340.53	Apportionment when income interest ends—Repealed
1340.57	Character of receipts—Repealed
1340.58	Distribution from trust or estate—Repealed
1340.59	Business and other activities conducted by trustee—Repealed
1340.63	Principal receipts—Repealed
1340.64	Rental property—Repealed
1340.65	Obligation to pay money—Repealed
1340.66	Insurance policies and similar contracts—Repealed
1340.70	Insubstantial allocations not required—Repealed
1340.71	Deferred compensation, annuities, and similar payments—Repealed
1340.72	Liquidating asset—Repealed
1340.73	Minerals, water, and other natural resources—Repealed
1340.74	Timber—Repealed
1340.75	Property not productive of income—Repealed
1340.76	Derivatives and options—Repealed
1340.77	Asset–backed securities—Repealed
1340.81	Disbursements from income—Repealed
1340.82	Disbursements from principal—Repealed
1340.83	Transfers from income to principal for depreciation—Repealed
1340.84	Transfers from income to reimburse principal—Repealed
1340.85	Income taxes—Repealed
1340.86	Adjustments between principal and income because of taxes—Repealed
1340.90	Uniformity of application and construction—Repealed
1340.91	Application to existing trust or decedent's estate—Repealed

Comparative Laws

Uniform Principal and Income Act

Table of Jurisdictions Wherein Act Has Been Adopted.

For text of Uniform Act, and variation notes and annotation materials for adopting jurisdictions, see Uniform Laws Annotated, Master Edition, Volume 7B.

Jurisdiction	Statutory Citation
Alaska	AS 13.38.010 to 13.38.140.
Arizona	A.R.S. § 14–7401 to 14–7413.
Florida	West's F.S.A. § 738.01 to 738.15.
Georgia	O.C.G.A. § 53–12–210 to 53–12–219.
Idaho	I.C. § 68–1001 to 68–1016.
Illinois	760 ILCS 15/1 to 15/17.
Indiana	West's A.I.C. 30-4-5-1 to 30-4-5-11.
Kentucky	KRS 386.191 to 386.349.
Michigan	M.C.L.A. § 555.51 to 555.68.
Minnesota	M.S.A. § 501B.59 to 501B.76.
Mississippi	Code 1972, § 91–17–1 to 91–17–31.
Missouri	V.A.M.S. § 456.700 to 456.820.
Montana	MCA 72–34–401 to 72–34–416.
Nebraska	R.R.S.1943, § 30–3101 to 30–3115.
Nevada	N.R.S. 164.140 to 164.370.
New Jersey	N.J.S.A. 3B:19A–1 to 3B:19A–35.
New Mexico	NMSA 1978, § 46–3–1 to 46–3–15.
New York	McKinney's EPTL 11–2.1.

Jurisdiction	Statutory Citation
North Carolina	G.S. § 37–16 to 37–40.
Oregon	ORS 129.005 to 129.125.
South Carolina	Code 1976, § 62–7–401 to 62–7–421.
South Dakota	SDCL 55–13–1 to 55–13–17.
Texas	V.T.C.A., Property Code § 113.101 to 113.111.
Utah	U.C.A.1953, 22–3–1 to 22–3–16.
Washington	West's RCWA 11.104.010 to 11.104.940.
Wisconsin	W.S.A. 701.20.
Wyoming	Wyo.Stat.Ann., § 2–3–601 to 2–3–614.

Law Review and Journal Commentaries

Administering Trusts Pursuant to Ohio's New Uniform Principal and Income Act, Michael Thacker. 13 Prob L J Ohio 45 (January/February 2003).

The New Uniform Principal and Income Act, Richard V. Wellman. 10 Prob L J Ohio 19 (November/December 1999).

Ohio's New Uniform Principal & Income Act, William F. Bates. 13 Prob L J Ohio 42 (January/February 2003).

Perspectives on Modernization of the Principal and Income Act, Charles M. Aulino. 13 Prob L J Ohio 48 (January/February 2003).

Should Everyone Trust a Living Trust?, (Revisited), William A. Fields. 9 Prob L J Ohio 106 (July/August 1999).

The Uniform Trust Code (2000) and its application to Ohio. David M. English, 30 Cap U L Rev 1 (2002).

DISCRETIONARY DISTRIBUTIONS BY FIDUCIARIES

1340.21   Definitions—Repealed

(2006 H 416, eff. 1–1–07; 1992 H 427, eff. 10–8–92)

Uncodified Law

1992 H 427, § 6, eff. 10–8–92 reads: In enacting sections 1340.21, 1340.22, and 1340.23 of the Revised Code in Section 1 of this act, the General Assembly hereby declares its intent to codify certain fiduciary and trust law principles relating to a fiduciary's conflict of interests and, in general, to provide for the exercise of certain discretionary powers to distribute either principal or income to a beneficiary by a beneficially interested fiduciary for his own benefit to the extent of an ascertainable standard.

1340.22   Discretionary distributions by fiduciaries—Repealed

(2006 H 416, eff. 1–1–07; 2002 H 345, eff. 7–23–02; 1996 S 158, eff. 5–8–96; 1992 H 427, eff. 10–8–92)

Uncodified Law

1992 H 427, § 6: See Uncodified Law under 1340.21.

Historical and Statutory Notes

Amendment Note: 2002 H 345 inserted "that may include but is not limited to the beneficiary, any of the beneficiaries, or any related or subordinate person, within the meaning of section 672(c) of the 'Internal Revenue Code of 1986,' 100 Stat. 2085, 26 U.S.C. 672(c), with respect to the beneficiary or any of the beneficiaries"; and added new divisions (E)(3), (E)(4), and (E)(5).

Amendment Note: 1996 S 158 substituted "by the governing instrument" for "upon him" in division (B)(1); inserted ", other than a beneficiary who is also a fiduciary," in division (E)(1); and made changes to reflect gender neutral language and other nonsubstantive changes.

Notes of Decisions

Arbitration provision effect   1

---

1. Arbitration provision effect

Claim, that lack of consideration invalidated pledge of security by trust beneficiary given in exchange for trustee's promise to make discretionary disbursements of principal, was subject to arbitration under broad arbitration provision contained in challenged agreement; alleged lack of consideration was not an attack upon making of the arbitration agreement itself. Roberts v. Bank of Am. NT & SA (Ohio App. 10 Dist., 11-07-1995) 107 Ohio App.3d 301, 668 N.E.2d 942. Arbitration ⚖ 7.5

Fact that trust beneficiary voluntarily signed contract containing arbitration clause, when trust beneficiary gave security interest in her estate in exchange for trustee's promise to make discretionary principal distributions, gave rise to presumption that parties intended to submit all disputes to arbitration, including those regarding validity of the contract in general. Roberts v. Bank of Am. NT & SA (Ohio App. 10 Dist., 11-07-1995) 107 Ohio App.3d 301, 668 N.E.2d 942. Arbitration ⚖ 23.10

1340.23   Interpretation of governing instruments—Repealed

(2006 H 416, eff. 1–1–07; 1992 H 427, eff. 10–8–92)

Uncodified Law

1992 H 427, § 6: See Uncodified Law under 1340.21.

INSTITUTIONAL TRUST FUNDS ACT

1340.31   Definitions—Repealed

(2006 H 416, eff. 1–1–07; 1999 H 161, eff. 9–15–99)

Historical and Statutory Notes

Ed. Note: Former RC 1340.31 amended and recodified as RC 5813.01 by 2006 H 416, eff. 1–1–07.

1340.32   Income defined—Repealed

(2006 H 416, eff. 1–1–07; 1999 H 161, eff. 9–15–99)

Historical and Statutory Notes

Ed. Note: Former RC 1340.32 amended and recodified as RC 5813.02 by 2006 H 416, eff. 1–1–07.

1340.33   Application of statutory definition of income when settlor expressly indicates intent—Repealed

(2006 H 416, eff. 1–1–07; 1999 H 161, eff. 9–15–99)

Historical and Statutory Notes

Ed. Note: Former RC 1340.33 amended and recodified as RC 5813.03 by 2006 H 416, eff. 1–1–07.

1340.34   Standard of care—Repealed

(2006 H 416, eff. 1–1–07; 1999 H 161, eff. 9–15–99)

Historical and Statutory Notes

Ed. Note: Former RC 1340.34 amended and recodified as RC 5813.04 by 2006 H 416, eff. 1–1–07.

1340.35 Restrictions on definition of income or on distributions—Repealed

(2006 H 416, eff. 1–1–07; 2002 H 522, eff. 1–1–03; 1999 H 161, eff. 9–15–99)

Historical and Statutory Notes

Ed. Note: Former RC 1340.35 amended and recodified as RC 5813.05 by 2006 H 416, eff. 1–1–07.

1340.36 Effect on Uniform Management of Institutional Funds Act—Repealed

(2006 H 416, eff. 1–1–07; 1999 H 161, eff. 9–15–99)

Historical and Statutory Notes

Ed. Note: Former RC 1340.36 amended and recodified as RC 5813.06 by 2006 H 416, eff. 1–1–07.

1340.37 Citation of Act—Repealed

(2006 H 416, eff. 1–1–07; 1999 H 161, eff. 9–15–99)

Historical and Statutory Notes

Ed. Note: Former RC 1340.37 amended and recodified as RC 5813.07 by 2006 H 416, eff. 1–1–07.

UNIFORM PRINCIPAL AND INCOME ACT (1997)

Comparative Laws

Uniform Principal and Income Act (1997 Act)
Table of Jurisdictions Wherein Act Has Been Adopted.

For text of Uniform Act, and variation notes and annotation materials for adopting jurisdictions, see Uniform Laws Annotated, Master Edition, Volume 7b.

Jurisdiction	Statutory Citation
Alabama	Code 1975, § 19–3A–101 to 19–3A–605.
Alaska	AS § 13.38.200 to 13.38.990.
Arizona	A.R.S. § 14–7401 to 14–7431.
Arkansas	A.C.A. § 28–70–101 to 28–70–605.
California	West's Ann.Cal.Probate Code § 16320 to 16375.
Colorado	West's C.R.S.A. § 15–1–401 to 15–1–434.
Connecticut	C.G.S.A. § 45a–542 to 45a–542ff.
District of Columbia	D.C. Official Code, 2001 Ed. § 28–4801.1 to 28–4806.2.
Florida	West's F.S.A. § 738.101 to 738.804.
Hawaii	HRS § 557A–101 to 557A–506.
Idaho	I.C. § 68–10–101 to 68–10–605.
Iowa	I.C.A. § 637.101 to 637.701.
Kansas	K.S.A. § 58–9–101 to 58–9–603.
Maine	18–A M.R.S.A. § 7–701 to 7–773.
Maryland	Code, Estates and Trusts, § 15–501 to 15–530.
Minnesota[1]	M.S.A. § 501B.59 to 501B.76.
Missouri	V.A.M.S. § 469.401 to 469.467.
Montana	MCA § 72–34–421 to 72–34–453.
Nebraska	R.R.S.1943, § 30–3116 to 30–3149.
Nevada	NRS 164.700, 164.780 to 164.925.
New Jersey	N.J.S.A. 3B:19B–1 to 3B:19B–31.
New Mexico	NMSA 1978, § 46–3A–101 to 46–3A–603.
New York	McKinney's EPTL 11–A–1.1 to 11–A–6.4.
North Carolina	G.S. § 37A–1–101 to 37A–6–602.
North Dakota	NDCC 59–04.2–01 to 59–04.2–30.
Oklahoma	60 Okl.St.Ann. § 175.101 to 175.602.
Oregon	ORS 116.007.
Pennsylvania	20 Pa.C.S.A. § 8101 to 8191.
South Carolina	Code 1976, § 62–7–401 to 62–7–432.
Tennessee	T.C.A. § 35–6–101 to 35–6–602.
Texas	V.T.C.A. Property Code § 116.001 to 116.206.
Virginia	Code 1950, § 55–277.1 to 55–277.33.
Washington	West's RCWA 11.104A.001 to 11.104A.905.
West Virginia	Code, 44B–1–101 to 44B–6–604.
Wyoming	Wyo.Stat.Ann. § 2–3–801 to 2–3–834.

[1] Minnesota's act remains a substantial adoption of the provisions of the 1962 Uniform Principal and Income Act, but various amendments and newly enacted sections have adopted several provisions of the 1997 Uniform Principal and Income Act. Therefore, Minnesota will be carried in the Table of Adopting Jurisdictions for both acts.

1340.40 Definitions—Repealed

(2006 H 416, eff. 1–1–07; 2002 H 522, eff. 1–1–03)

Historical and Statutory Notes

Ed. Note: Former RC 1340.40 amended and recodified as RC 5812.01 by 2006 H 416, eff. 1–1–07.

1340.41 Fiduciary duties; general principles—Repealed

(2006 H 416, eff. 1–1–07; 2002 H 522, eff. 1–1–03)

Historical and Statutory Notes

Ed. Note: Former RC 1340.41 amended and recodified as RC 5812.02 by 2006 H 416, eff. 1–1–07.

1340.42 Trustee's power to adjust—Repealed

(2006 H 416, eff. 1–1–07; 2002 H 522, eff. 1–1–03)

Historical and Statutory Notes

Ed. Note: Former RC 1340.42 amended and recodified as RC 5812.03 by 2006 H 416, eff. 1–1–07.

1340.46 Determination and distribution of net income—Repealed

(2006 H 416, eff. 1–1–07; 2002 H 522, eff. 1–1–03)

Historical and Statutory Notes

Ed. Note: Former RC 1340.46 amended and recodified as RC 5812.07 by 2006 H 416, eff. 1–1–07.

1340.47 Distribution to residuary and remainder beneficiaries—Repealed

(2006 H 416, eff. 1–1–07; 2002 H 522, eff. 1–1–03)

1340.51 When right to income begins and ends—Repealed

(2006 H 416, eff. 1–1–07; 2002 H 522, eff. 1–1–03)

Historical and Statutory Notes

Ed. Note: Former RC 1340.51 recodified as RC 5812.12 by 2006 H 416, eff. 1–1–07.

1340.52 Apportionment of receipts and disbursements when decedent dies or income interest begins—Repealed

(2006 H 416, eff. 1–1–07; 2002 H 522, eff. 1–1–03)

Historical and Statutory Notes

Ed. Note: Former RC 1340.52 amended and recodified as RC 5812.13 by 2006 H 416, eff. 1–1–07.

1340.53 Apportionment when income interest ends—Repealed

(2006 H 416, eff. 1–1–07; 2002 H 522, eff. 1–1–03)

Historical and Statutory Notes

Ed. Note: Former RC 1340.53 recodified as RC 5812.14 by 2006 H 416, eff. 1–1–07.

1340.57 Character of receipts—Repealed

(2006 H 416, eff. 1–1–07; 2002 H 522, eff. 1–1–03)

Historical and Statutory Notes

Ed. Note: Former RC 1340.57 amended and recodified as RC 5812.18 by 2006 H 416, eff. 1–1–07.

1340.58 Distribution from trust or estate—Repealed

(2006 H 416, eff. 1–1–07; 2002 H 522, eff. 1–1–03)

Historical and Statutory Notes

Ed. Note: Former RC 1340.58 amended and recodified as RC 5812.19 by 2006 H 416, eff. 1–1–07.

1340.59 Business and other activities conducted by trustee—Repealed

(2006 H 416, eff. 1–1–07; 2002 H 522, eff. 1–1–03)

Historical and Statutory Notes

Ed. Note: Former RC 1340.59 amended and recodified as RC 5812.20 by 2006 H 416, eff. 1–1–07.

1340.63 Principal receipts—Repealed

(2006 H 416, eff. 1–1–07; 2002 H 522, eff. 1–1–03)

Historical and Statutory Notes

Ed. Note: Former RC 1340.63 amended and recodified as RC 5812.24 by 2006 H 416, eff. 1–1–07.

1340.64 Rental property—Repealed

(2006 H 416, eff. 1–1–07; 2002 H 522, eff. 1–1–03)

Historical and Statutory Notes

Ed. Note: Former RC 1340.64 recodified as RC 5812.25 by 2006 H 416, eff. 1–1–07.

1340.65 Obligation to pay money—Repealed

(2006 H 416, eff. 1–1–07; 2002 H 522, eff. 1–1–03)

Historical and Statutory Notes

Ed. Note: Former RC 1340.65 amended and recodified as RC 5812.26 by 2006 H 416, eff. 1–1–07.

1340.66 Insurance policies and similar contracts—Repealed

(2006 H 416, eff. 1–1–07; 2002 H 522, eff. 1–1–03)

Historical and Statutory Notes

Ed. Note: Former RC 1340.66 amended and recodified as RC 5812.27 by 2006 H 416, eff. 1–1–07.

1340.70 Insubstantial allocations not required—Repealed

(2006 H 416, eff. 1–1–07; 2002 H 522, eff. 1–1–03)

Historical and Statutory Notes

Ed. Note: Former RC 1340.70 amended and recodified as RC 5812.31 by 2006 H 416, eff. 1–1–07.

1340.71 Deferred compensation, annuities, and similar payments—Repealed

(2006 H 416, eff. 1–1–07; 2002 H 522, eff. 1–1–03)

Historical and Statutory Notes

Ed. Note: Former RC 1340.71 amended and recodified as RC 5812.32 by 2006 H 416, eff. 1–1–07.

1340.72 Liquidating asset—Repealed

(2006 H 416, eff. 1–1–07; 2002 H 522, eff. 1–1–03)

Historical and Statutory Notes

Ed. Note: Former RC 1340.72 amended and recodified as RC 5812.33 by 2006 H 416, eff. 1–1–07.

1340.73 Minerals, water, and other natural resources—Repealed

(2006 H 416, eff. 1–1–07; 2002 H 522, eff. 1–1–03)

Historical and Statutory Notes

Ed. Note: Former RC 1340.73 amended and recodified as RC 5812.34 by 2006 H 416, eff. 1–1–07.

1340.74 Timber—Repealed

(2006 H 416, eff. 1–1–07; 2002 H 522, eff. 1–1–03)

Historical and Statutory Notes

Ed. Note: Former RC 1340.74 amended and recodified as RC 5812.35 by 2006 H 416, eff. 1–1–07.

1340.75 Property not productive of income—Repealed

(2006 H 416, eff. 1–1–07; 2002 H 522, eff. 1–1–03)

Historical and Statutory Notes

Ed. Note: Former RC 1340.75 amended and recodified as RC 5812.36 by 2006 H 416, eff. 1–1–07.

1340.76 Derivatives and options—Repealed

(2006 H 416, eff. 1–1–07; 2002 H 522, eff. 1–1–03)

Historical and Statutory Notes

Ed. Note: Former RC 1340.76 amended and recodified as RC 5812.37 by 2006 H 416, eff. 1–1–07.

1340.77 Asset–backed securities—Repealed

(2006 H 416, eff. 1–1–07; 2002 H 522, eff. 1–1–03)

Historical and Statutory Notes

Ed. Note: Former RC 1340.77 amended and recodified as RC 5812.38 by 2006 H 416, eff. 1–1–07.

1340.81 Disbursements from income—Repealed

(2006 H 416, eff. 1–1–07; 2002 H 522, eff. 1–1–03)

Historical and Statutory Notes

Ed. Note: Former RC 1340.81 amended and recodified as RC 5812.42 by 2006 H 416, eff. 1–1–07.

1340.82 Disbursements from principal—Repealed

(2006 H 416, eff. 1–1–07; 2002 H 522, eff. 1–1–03)

Historical and Statutory Notes

Ed. Note: Former RC 1340.82 amended and recodified as RC 5812.43 by 2006 H 416, eff. 1–1–07.

1340.83 Transfers from income to principal for depreciation—Repealed

(2006 H 416, eff. 1–1–07; 2002 H 522, eff. 1–1–03)

Historical and Statutory Notes

Ed. Note: Former RC 1340.83 amended and recodified as RC 5812.44 by 2006 H 416, eff. 1–1–07.

1340.84 Transfers from income to reimburse principal—Repealed

(2006 H 416, eff. 1–1–07; 2002 H 522, eff. 1–1–03)

Historical and Statutory Notes

Ed. Note: Former RC 1340.84 amended and recodified as RC 5812.45 by 2006 H 416, eff. 1–1–07.

1340.85 Income taxes—Repealed

(2006 H 416, eff. 1–1–07; 2002 H 522, eff. 1–1–03)

Historical and Statutory Notes

Ed. Note: Former RC 1340.85 recodified as RC 5812.46 by 2006 H 416, eff. 1–1–07.

1340.86 Adjustments between principal and income because of taxes—Repealed

(2006 H 416, eff. 1–1–07; 2002 H 522, eff. 1–1–03)

Historical and Statutory Notes

Ed. Note: Former RC 1340.86 recodified as RC 5812.47 by 2006 H 416, eff. 1–1–07.

1340.90 Uniformity of application and construction—Repealed

(2006 H 416, eff. 1–1–07; 2002 H 522, eff. 1–1–03)

Historical and Statutory Notes

Ed. Note: Former RC 1340.90 amended and recodified as RC 5812.51 by 2006 H 416, eff. 1–1–07.

1340.91 Application to existing trust or decedent's estate—Repealed

(2006 H 416, eff. 1–1–07; 2002 H 522, eff. 1–1–03)

Historical and Statutory Notes

Ed. Note: Former RC 1340.91 amended and recodified as RC 5812.52 by 2006 H 416, eff. 1–1–07.

CHAPTER 1548

WATERCRAFT CERTIFICATES OF TITLE

Section
1548.072 Designation of transfer-on-death beneficiary

1548.072 Designation of transfer-on-death beneficiary

Any person who owns a watercraft or outboard motor for which a certificate of title is required under this chapter may establish ownership of the watercraft or outboard motor that is transferable on death by designating the watercraft or outboard motor in beneficiary form in accordance with section 2131.13 of the Revised Code. Any person who establishes ownership of a watercraft or outboard motor that is transferable on death in accordance with section 2131.13 of the Revised Code may terminate that type of ownership or change the designation of the transfer-on-death beneficiary or beneficiaries by applying for a certificate of title in accordance with this chapter.

(2002 H 345, eff. 7-23-02)

CHAPTER 1709

UNIFORM TRANSFER–ON–DEATH SECURITY REGISTRATION ACT

Section
1709.01 Definitions
1709.02 Tenancy in common precluded

Comparative Laws
Uniform TOD Security Registration Act
Table of Jurisdictions Wherein Act Has Been Adopted.

For text of Uniform Act, and variation notes and annotation materials for adopting jurisdictions, see Uniform Laws Annotated, Master Edition, Volume 8B.

Jurisdiction	Statutory Citation
Alabama	Code 1975, 8-6-140 to 8-6-151.
Alaska	AS 13.06.050, 13.33.101 to 13.33.310.
Arizona	A.R.S. § 14-1201, 14-6301 to 14-6311.
Arkansas	A.C.A. § 28-14-101 to 28-14-112.
California	West's Ann.Cal.Probate Code, § 5500 to 5512.
Colorado	West's C.R.S.A. § 15-10-201, 15-15-301 to 15-15-311.
Connecticut	C.G.S.A. § 45a-468 to 45a-468m.
Delaware	12 Del.C. § 801 to 812.
District of Columbia	D.C. Official Code, 2001 Ed. § 19-603.1 to 19-603.11.
Florida	West's F.S.A. § 711.50 to 711.512.
Georgia	O.C.G.A. § 53-5-60 to 53-5-71.
Hawaii	HRS § 539-1 to 539-12.
Idaho	I.C. § 15-6-301 to 15-6-312.
Illinois	S.H.A. 815 ILCS 10/0.01 to 10/12.
Indiana	West's A.I.C. 32-17-9-1 to 32-17-9-15.
Iowa	I.C.A. § 633.800 to 633.811.
Kansas	K.S.A. 17-49a 01 to 17-49a 12.
Kentucky	KRS 292.6501 to 292.6512.
Maine	18-A M.R.S.A. § 6-301 to 6-312.
Maryland	Code, Estates and Trusts, § 16-101 to 16-112.
Massachusetts	M.G.L.A. c. 201E, § 101 to 402.
Michigan	M.C.L.A. § 700.6301 to 700.6310.
Minnesota	M.S.A. § 524.1-201, 524.6-301 to 524.6-311.
Mississippi	Code 1972, § 91-21-1 to 91-21-25.
Montana	MCA § 72-1-103, 72-6-301 to 72-6-311.
Nebraska	R.R.S.1943, § 30-2209, 30-2734 to 30-2746.
Nevada	N.R.S. 111.480 to 111.650.
New Hampshire	RSA 563-C:1 to 563-C:12.
New Jersey	N.J.S.A. 3B:30-1 to 3B:30-12.
New Mexico	NMSA 1978, § 45-1-201, 45-6-301 to 45-6-311.
North Dakota	NDCC 30.1-01-06, 30.1-31-21 to 30.1-31-30.
Oklahoma	71 Okl.St.Ann. § 901 to 913.
Oregon	ORS 59.535 to 59.585.
Pennsylvania	20 Pa.C.S.A. § 6401 to 6413.
Rhode Island	Gen. Laws 1956, § 7-11.1-1 to 7-11.1-12.
South Carolina	Code 1976, § 35-6-10 to 35-6-100.
South Dakota	SDCL 29A-6-301 to 29A-6-311.
Tennessee	T.C.A. § 35-12-101 to 35-12-113.
Utah	U.C.A. 1953, 75-6-301 to 75-6-313.
Vermont	9 V.S.A. § 4351 to 4360.
Virginia	Code 1950, § 64.1-206.1 to 64.1-206.8.
Washington	West's RCWA 21.35.005 to 21.35.901.
West Virginia	Code, 36-10-1 to 36-10-12.
Wisconsin	W.S.A. 705.21 to 705.30.
Wyoming	Wyo.Stat.Ann., § 2-16-101 to 2-16-112.

1709.01 Definitions

As used in sections 1709.01 to 1709.11 of the Revised Code, unless the context otherwise requires:

(A) "Beneficiary form" means a registration of a security that indicates the present owner of the security and the intention of the present owner regarding the person who will become the owner of the security upon the death of the present owner.

(B) "Devisee" means any person designated in a will to receive a disposition of real or personal property.

(C) "Heirs" means those persons, including the surviving spouse of a decedent, who are entitled under the statutes of intestate succession to the property of an intestate decedent, including, when applicable, section 2105.06 of the Revised Code.

(D) "Person" means an individual, a corporation, an organization, or other legal entity.

(E) "Personal representative" includes an executor, administrator, successor personal representative, special administrator, and persons who perform substantially the same function under the law governing their status.

(F) "Property" means anything that may be the subject of ownership, including, but not limited to, real and personal property and any interest in real or personal property.

(G) "Register," including its derivatives, means to issue a certificate showing the ownership of a certificated security or, in the case of an uncertificated security, to initiate or transfer an account showing ownership of that security.

(H) "Registering entity" means a person who originates or transfers a security title by registration and includes, but is not limited to, a financial institution maintaining security accounts for customers, a securities dealer or broker maintaining security accounts for customers, and a transfer agent or other person acting for or as an issuer of securities.

(I) "Security" has the same meaning as in division (B) of section 1707.01 of the Revised Code and includes, but is not limited to, a certificated security, an uncertificated security, and a security account.

(J) "Security account" means either of the following:

(1) A reinvestment account associated with a security; a securities account with a financial institution or a securities dealer or broker and any cash balance in a brokerage account with a financial institution or a securities dealer or broker; or cash, interest, earnings, or dividends earned or declared on a security in an account, a reinvestment account, or a brokerage account, whether or not credited to the account before the owner's death;

(2) A cash balance or other property held for or due to the owner of a security as a replacement for or product of an account security, whether or not credited to the account before the owner's death.

(1994 H 208, eff. 6–23–94; 1993 H 62, eff. 10–1–93)

Uncodified Law

2002 H 509, § 3, eff. 3–14–03, reads:

No liability shall arise against any one of the following that, prior to the effective date of this section, authorized or was otherwise responsible for a distribution or other payment or a transfer of property that is inconsistent with division (A)(3) of section 3107.15 of the Revised Code, as amended by this act:

(1) A fiduciary under a trust instrument, will, or other document;

(2) A bank, savings and loan association, credit union, or society for savings, in connection with written contracts described in sections 2131.10 and 2131.11 of the Revised Code;

(3) A registering entity, as defined in division (H) of section 1709.01 of the Revised Code, for a transfer-on-death made pursuant to Chapter 1709. of the Revised Code.

Historical and Statutory Notes

Ed. Note: Former 1709.01 repealed by 1975 H 338, eff. 1–9–76; 126 v 432; 1953 H 1; GC 9873.

Pre–1953 H 1 Amendments: 95 v 324, § 1

1709.02 Tenancy in common precluded

Only individuals whose registration of a security shows sole ownership by one individual or multiple ownership by two or more individuals with a right of survivorship, rather than ownership as tenants in common, may obtain registration in beneficiary form. Multiple owners of a security registered in beneficiary form hold as joint tenants with a right of survivorship and not as tenants in common.

(1993 H 62, eff. 10–1–93)

Historical and Statutory Notes

Ed. Note: Former 1709.02 repealed by 1975 H 338, eff. 1–9–76; 1953 H 1; GC 9873.

Pre–1953 H 1 Amendments: 95 v 324, § 1

OHIO REVISED CODE
TITLE 21
COURTS—PROBATE—JUVENILE

Complete to February 28, 2007

CHAPTER		CHAPTER	
2101	Probate Court—Jurisdiction; Procedure	2127	Sale of Lands
2103	Dower	2129	Ancillary Administration
2105	Descent and Distribution	2131	Miscellaneous
2106	Rights of Surviving Spouses	2133	Modified Uniform Rights of the Terminally Ill Act and the DNR Identification and Do–Not–Resuscitate Order Law
2107	Wills		
2108	Human Bodies or Parts Thereof	2135	Declarations for Mental Health Treatment
2109	Fiduciaries	2151	Juvenile Courts—General Provisions
2111	Guardians; Conservatorships	2152	Juvenile Courts—Criminal Provisions
2113	Executors and Administrators—Appointment; Powers; Duties	2153	Cuyahoga County Juvenile Court
2115	Executors and Administrators—Inventory		
2117	Presentment of Claims Against Estate		
2119	Trustee for Absentee		
2121	Presumed Decedents' Law		
2123	Determination of Heirship		
2125	Action for Wrongful Death		

Publisher's Note: Comments of the Probate and Trust Law Committee/Section of the Ohio State Bar Association, and excerpts from the Legislative Service Commission's analysis of the 1975 Probate Reform Act, are printed following applicable sections. These comments and excerpts should be read in light of the language of the statute as it existed at the time of the amendment or enactment.

CHAPTER 2101

PROBATE COURT—JURISDICTION; PROCEDURE

ADMINISTRATION AND OFFICIALS

Section	
2101.01	Probate division; location; records; equipment; employees; investigators and assessors
2101.02	Judge of probate division; election; qualification; term
2101.021	Additional probate judge in Cuyahoga County
2101.022	Powers of judge of probate division of Marion county common pleas court on and after 2–9–03
2101.023	Additional judge in Erie county; jurisdictional responsibilities
2101.024	Powers and jurisdiction of probate judge of Logan county
2101.03	Bond of probate judge
2101.04	Rules of practice submitted to supreme court
2101.05	Oaths and depositions
2101.06	Master commissioners; appointment and bond; duties
2101.07	Master commissioners; powers; fees
2101.08	Stenographic reporter
2101.09	Liability of sheriffs, coroners, and constables for failure to serve and return process
2101.10	Liability of sheriffs, coroners, and constables for failure to pay over moneys

FILES AND RECORDS; COURT INVESTIGATORS

Section	
2101.11	Custody of files; investigators; clerks and appointees; appropriation; action in court of appeals; limitation of contempt power
2101.12	Records to be kept by probate court
2101.121	Record–keeping methods; equipment for examination; indices
2101.13	Probate judge shall make entries omitted by his predecessor
2101.14	Care and preservation of papers; time stamp
2101.141	Disposition of obsolete papers

FEES AND COSTS

Section	
2101.15	Probate judge to file itemized account of fees with county auditor
2101.16	Fees; cost of investigations; advance deposit
2101.161	Deposit of prepaid and unearned costs; interest
2101.162	Additional fees for computer services
2101.163	Fee for dispute resolution procedures
2101.17	Fees from county treasury
2101.18	Fees for other services
2101.19	Limitation of charges by probate judge; probate court conduct of business fund
2101.20	Reduction of fees
2101.21	Fiduciary; payment of costs in advance

PRACTICE AND PROCEDURE; JURISDICTION

Section	
2101.22	Process
2101.23	Contempt
2101.24	Jurisdiction of probate court
2101.25	Optional jurisdiction of probate judge
2101.26	Abuse of elderly or wards or theft from estates; referral of information to law enforcement agency
2101.27	Solemnization of marriages
2101.30	Jury; drawing
2101.31	Determination of questions of fact
2101.32	Rules and procedure of court of common pleas to govern; power to award and tax costs
2101.33	Vacation and modification of judgments
2101.34	Judgments by confession
2101.35	Execution

Section	
2101.36	"Probate judge" includes court of common pleas in lunacy proceedings
2101.37	Judge of court of common pleas to act as probate judge; compensation
2101.38	Administration when the probate judge is interested; certification to common pleas court
2101.39	Affidavit of disqualification of probate judge for prejudice
2101.40	Dealing in assets of estate
2101.41	Limits on practice of law by judges, deputy clerks, and referees
2101.42	Cases appealable from probate court

COMBINING PROBATE AND COMMON PLEAS COURTS

2101.43	Petition for submission of question of combining probate court and court of common pleas
2101.44	Conduct of election; form of ballot; returns and canvass
2101.45	Probate division established; appeals
2101.46	Re-establishment of the probate court

PENALTIES

2101.99	Penalties

Publisher's Note: Until 1968, when the Modern Courts Amendment to the Ohio Constitution was adopted, Ohio court procedure was governed entirely by statute and case law. The Modern Courts Amendment required the Supreme Court of Ohio, subject to the approval of the General Assembly, to "prescribe rules governing practice and procedure in all courts of the state." Rules of practice and procedure are the Civil, Criminal, Appellate, and Juvenile Rules, Rules of the Court of Claims, and the Ohio Rules of Evidence. Pursuant to Ohio Constitution Article IV, Section 5(B), such rules "shall not abridge, enlarge, or modify any substantive right," and " [a]ll laws in conflict with such rules shall be of no further force or effect." Provisions of Chapter 2101 should be read with this in mind.

Cross References

Assignment for benefit of creditors; duties of probate judge, Ch 1313
Common pleas courts; probate and other divisions; jurisdiction, O Const Art IV §4
Courts of record, premature judgment deemed clerical error, 2701.18
Definitions of guardians, 2111.01
Dower, defined, 2103.02
Fiduciaries, rights as to shares in corporation, 2109.29
Fiduciary, defined, 2109.01
Foreign wards and guardians, 2111.43
Judicial power vested in courts, O Const Art IV §1
Legal disability, defined, 2131.02
Marion county common pleas judges, concurrent jurisdiction, 2301.03
Powers of guardian of person and estate, 2111.07
Probate judge to notify elections board monthly of individuals adjudged incompetent to vote, 3503.18
Will, defined, 2107.01

Law Review and Journal Commentaries

A Beginner's Guide to (RE)Probate Court, Richard A. Hennig. 12 Lake Legal Views 11 (February 1989).

The Conflict of Laws Relating to Wills, Probate Decrees and Estates, Robert M. Bozeman. 49 A B A J 670 (July 1963).

Don't Do to the Ohio Probate System What was Done to the Savings and Loan Industry, Hon. John J. Donnelly. 3 Prob L J Ohio 1 (September/October 1992).

The Future of Probate and the Merger of Probate and Nonprobate Transfer Systems, David F. Allen. 7 Prob L J Ohio 13 (November/December 1996).

The New Uniform Probate Code, Richard V. Wellman. 56 A B A J 636 (July 1970).

Ohio's 1975 Probate Reform Act: Analysis of Major Changes in Ohio's Probate Code, Note. 45 U Cin L Rev 429 (1976).

Quo TOD; Quo Probate Reform, William A. Fields. 3 Prob L J Ohio 32 (January/February 1993).

Seven Questions (Answered) About Probate Reform, Robert M. Brucken. 2 Prob L J Ohio 73 (March/April 1992).

Should Everyone Trust a Living Trust?, William A. Fields. 2 Prob L J of Ohio 5 (September/October 1991).

The Uniform Probate Code and the Veterans' Administration, William Fratcher. 24 Case W Res L Rev 261 (Winter 1973).

ADMINISTRATION AND OFFICIALS

2101.01 Probate division; location; records; equipment; employees; investigators and assessors

(A) A probate division of the court of common pleas shall be held at the county seat in each county in an office furnished by the board of county commissioners, in which the books, records, and papers pertaining to the probate division shall be deposited and safely kept by the probate judge. The board shall provide suitable cases or other necessary items for the safekeeping and preservation of the books, records, and papers of the court and shall furnish any blankbooks, blanks, and stationery, and any machines, equipment, and materials for the keeping or examining of records, that the probate judge requires in the discharge of official duties. The board also shall authorize expenditures for accountants, financial consultants, and other agents required for auditing or financial consulting by the probate division whenever the probate judge considers these services and expenditures necessary for the efficient performance of the division's duties. The probate judge shall employ and supervise all clerks, deputies, magistrates, and other employees of the probate division. The probate judge shall supervise all probate court investigators and assessors in the performance of their duties as investigators and assessors and shall employ, appoint, or designate all probate court investigators and assessors in the manner described in divisions (A)(2) and (3) of section 2101.11 of the Revised Code.

(B) As used in the Revised Code:

(1) Except as provided in division (B)(2) of this section, "probate court" means the probate division of the court of common pleas, and "probate judge" means the judge of the court of common pleas who is judge of the probate division.

(2) With respect to Lorain county:

(a) From January 1, 2006, through February 8, 2009, "probate court" means both the probate division and the domestic relations division of the court of common pleas, and "probate judge" means both the judge of the court of common pleas who is judge of the probate division and each of the judges of the court of common pleas who are judges of the domestic relations division.

(b) On and after February 9, 2009, "probate court" means the domestic relations division of the court of common pleas, and "probate judge" means each of the judges of the court of common pleas who are judges of the domestic relations division.

(C) Except as otherwise provided in this division, all pleadings, forms, journals, and other records filed or used in the probate division shall be entitled "In the Court of Common Pleas, Probate Division," but are not defective if entitled "In the Probate Court." In Lorain county, on and after February 9, 2009, all pleadings, forms, journals, and other records filed or used in probate matters shall be entitled "In the Court of Common Pleas, Domestic Relations Division," but are not defective if entitled "In the Probate Division" or "In the Probate Court."

(2005 S 128, eff. 12–20–05; 1998 H 446, eff. 8–5–98; 1996 H 377, eff. 10–17–96; 1989 S 46, eff. 1–1–90; 1985 H 419; 1975 S 145; 1969 H 7; 1953 H 1; GC 10501–4)

Historical and Statutory Notes

Pre–1953 H 1 Amendments: 114 v 321

Amendment Note: 2005 S 128 designated division (A); designated division (B) and (B)(1); inserted "Except as provided in division (B)(2) of this section," at the beginning of the first sentence and deleted "All" in division (B)(1); added division (B)(2); designated division (C) and inserted "Except as otherwise provided in this division, all" in the beginning of the first sentence of division (C); added the last sentence in division (C); and made other nonsubstantive changes.

Amendment Note: 1998 H 446 inserted "and assessors" three times and substituted "divisions (A)(2) and (A)(3)" for "division (A)(2)" in the first paragraph.

Amendment Note: 1996 H 377 substituted "magistrates" for "referees."

Cross References

Compensation of probate judge, 141.04 to 141.07
Probate court may require sheriff to attend upon it, 311.07
Probate judge ineligible for certain other offices, 3.11, 319.07
Securing writings by deception, 2913.43
Tampering with records, 2913.42
Vacancy in office of judge, 107.08

Library References

Counties ⚖138.
Courts ⚖50.
Westlaw Topic Nos. 104, 106.
C.J.S. Counties § 175.
C.J.S. Courts § 106.

Research References

Encyclopedias
OH Jur. 3d Abstracts & Land Titles § 8, Overview of Land Registration Statutes.
OH Jur. 3d Counties, Townships, & Municipal Corp. § 221, Courthouses.
OH Jur. 3d Courts & Judges § 3, Judge.
OH Jur. 3d Courts & Judges § 19, Courts of Common Pleas—Probate Division.
OH Jur. 3d Courts & Judges § 66, Employment of Clerks and Other Employees of Probate Division; Care and Custody of Papers and Records.
OH Jur. 3d Courts & Judges § 80, Generally; Rights, Privileges.
OH Jur. 3d Courts & Judges § 211, Custody of Papers.
OH Jur. 3d Courts & Judges § 215, Office Equipment and Supplies.
OH Jur. 3d Decedents' Estates § 1370, Personal Liability of Representative for Attorneys' Fees—Whether Charged to General Estate or Apportioned.
OH Jur. 3d Eminent Domain § 220, Generally; Jurisdiction of State Courts.
OH Jur. 3d Fiduciaries § 127, Hearing and Judgment—Transfer to Another Division of Court of Common Pleas.
OH Jur. 3d Guardian & Ward § 1, Generally; Jurisdiction Over Guardianship Matters.
OH Jur. 3d Jury § 38, Probate Division of Common Pleas Court.
OH Jur. 3d Jury § 86, Drawing Jurors in Probate Division of Common Pleas Court.

Forms
Ohio Jurisprudence Pleading and Practice Forms § 2:6, Courts of Common Pleas—Probate Division.
Ohio Jurisprudence Pleading and Practice Forms § 2:24, Powers and Duties Via Particular Courts—Probate Division.

Treatises and Practice Aids
Carlin, Baldwin's Ohio Practice, Merrick-Rippner Probate Law § 62:19, Appointment of Guardian—Application—Investigations by Court.
Carlin, Baldwin's Ohio Practice, Merrick-Rippner Probate Law § 98:12, Adoption—Suitability of Adoptive Parents—Regulation of Persons With Criminal Record.
Carlin, Baldwin's Ohio Practice, Merrick-Rippner Probate Law § 3:2.50, Jurisdiction of Probate Court—Statutory—Exceptions—Lorain County.

Law Review and Journal Commentaries

A Beginner's Guide to (RE)Probate Court, Richard A. Hennig. 12 Lake Legal Views 11 (February 1989).

The Probate Courts of Ohio, John F. Winkler. 28 U Tol L Rev 563 (Spring 1997).

Notes of Decisions

Compensation 3
Court, defined 2
Employees 5
Jurisdiction 4
Necessary facilities and supplies 1

---

1. Necessary facilities and supplies

A court of general jurisdiction located in a courthouse has a paramount right to space therein which is essential for the proper and efficient operation of such court, but the necessity for such space constitutes a question of fact and a court is entitled to additional space as against other branches of government only where it is shown that such space is reasonably necessary for its operation as distinguished from being merely desirable. State ex rel. Finley v. Pfeiffer (Ohio 1955) 163 Ohio St. 149, 126 N.E.2d 57, 56 O.O. 190.

Book in which cost bills are recorded must be furnished by county commissioners. Lucas County Bd of Commrs v Millard, 4 NP 53, 4 D 419 (CP, Lucas 1896), affirmed by 13 CC 518, 7 CD 115 (Lucas 1897).

A probate court has inherent power to acquire and control the ordinary facilities necessary and essential for its proper and efficient operation, but such power may be exercised only to acquire necessary as distinguished from desirable, quarters, space and facilities. OAG 76–064.

Under the terms of RC 307.01, the power to determine size, style and expense of a courthouse is vested in the board of county commissioners, and so the exercise of inherent judicial powers by a court relative to such matters is permissible only where essential to the proper and efficient operation of the court. OAG 76–064.

2. Court, defined

A "court" is an incorporeal, political being, composed of one or more judges who sit at fixed times and places attended by proper officers under lawful authority to administer justice; the word "court" in a statute is not always synonymous with the word "judge" but in a broad sense also includes the jury or may even be taken to mean "jury" alone in a particular instance when the jury is trier of fact. Hubner v. Sigall (Franklin 1988) 47 Ohio App.3d 15, 546 N.E.2d 1337, motion overruled 38 Ohio St.3d 710, 533 N.E.2d 363.

3. Compensation

A county which has one judge of the court of common pleas and one judge of the probate division of that same court does have two judges of the court of common pleas, and the compensation of the county's law librarian is, therefore, not limited under RC 3375.48 to $500 per annum. OAG 75–057.

4. Jurisdiction

Jurisdiction in probate and testamentary matters is special and not general. (See also Jones v Standard Home & Savings Assn, 18 CC 189, 10 CD 41 (Belmont 1899); affirmed by 64 OS 147, 59 NE 885 (1901).) Davis v. Davis (Ohio 1860) 11 Ohio St. 386.

5. Employees

Magistrate for Ohio Probate Court was exempt from Title VII definition of "employee" as "appointee on the policymaking level"; presiding judge had authority to appoint magistrates, who were exempt from civil service laws, and magistrate effectively made policy for court by resolving disputes and recommending dispositions to presiding judge. Birch v. Cuyahoga County Probate Court (C.A.6 (Ohio), 12-01-2004) 392 F.3d 151. Civil Rights ⚖ 1116(3)

Neither the summit county charter nor rules adopted thereunder, may vest the county executive, through a human resource commission, with the authority to establish personnel policy or make personnel decisions for the summit county court of common pleas, probate division. OAG 96–043.

2101.02 Judge of probate division; election; qualification; term

Every six years, in each county having a separate judge of the probate division of the court of common pleas, one probate judge shall be elected who is qualified as required by section 2301.01 of the Revised Code. He shall hold office for six years, commencing on the ninth day of February next following his election.

(1969 H 7, eff. 11–19–69; 125 v 107; 1953 H 1; GC 10501–1)

Historical and Statutory Notes

Pre–1953 H 1 Amendments: 123 v 467; 116 v 481; 114 v 320

Cross References

Compensation of probate judge, 141.04 to 141.07
Courts of common pleas, probate division, O Const Art IV §4
Election, term, and compensation of judges; assignment of retired judges, O Const Art IV §6
Number of judges for each county; terms of office, 2301.02
Time for holding elections for state and local officers; terms of office, O Const Art XVII §1
Vacancies, how filled, O Const Art IV §13, O Const Art XVII §2

Library References

Judges ⊂⊃3, 7.
Westlaw Topic No. 227.
C.J.S. Judges §§ 12 to 13, 21 to 24, 27 to 29.

Research References

Encyclopedias
OH Jur. 3d Courts & Judges § 29, Generally; Elective Nature of Office.
OH Jur. 3d Courts & Judges § 30, Time of Election; Additional Judges.
OH Jur. 3d Courts & Judges § 32, Term of Office.
OH Jur. 3d Courts & Judges § 33, Commencement of Term.
OH Jur. 3d Courts & Judges § 35, Generally; Admission to Practice as Attorney.

Forms
Ohio Jurisprudence Pleading and Practice Forms § 2:20, Qualifications and Selection in General.

Notes of Decisions

Compatibility of offices   4
Court of record   3
Immunity   1
Liability   5
Vacancies   2

1. Immunity

Absolute immunity is determined by a functional analysis that looks to the nature of the function performed, not the identity of the actor who performed it. Holloway v. Brush (C.A.6 (Ohio), 07-31-2000) 220 F.3d 767. Officers And Public Employees ⊂⊃ 114

The official seeking absolute immunity bears the burden of showing that immunity is justified in light of the function she was performing. Holloway v. Brush (C.A.6 (Ohio), 07-31-2000) 220 F.3d 767. Officers And Public Employees ⊂⊃ 114

A court is not a "person" within the meaning of 42 USC 1983 and consequently cannot be sued under that law; such an attempt at a suit is to be distinguished from a suit against an individual judge performing unconstitutional acts. Foster v. Walsh (C.A.6 (Ohio) 1988) 864 F.2d 416.

2. Vacancies

A person elected to fill a vacancy in the office of judge of a county probate court is elected for the unexpired term only. 1930 OAG 2639.

A person elected to fill a vacancy in the office of judge of a county probate court takes office when he has received his certificate of election from the county board of elections, obtained his commission from the governor, given bond to the state of Ohio and taken the oath of office. 1930 OAG 2639.

When the office of probate judge becomes vacant by reason of the expiration of the term of the incumbent, and a failure to provide therefor at the preceding election, such vacancy shall be filled by appointment by the governor; the person so appointed shall hold the office until a successor is elected and qualified. 1929 OAG 026.

3. Court of record

Probate courts are courts of record in the fullest sense; their records import absolute verity; they are competent to pass upon their own jurisdiction and to exercise it to final judgment without setting forth the facts and evidence on which it is rendered. Shroyer v. Richmond (Ohio 1866) 16 Ohio St. 455. Courts ⊂⊃ 33

4. Compatibility of offices

O Const Art IV §6(B) and RC 141.04(D) prohibit the same person from simultaneously serving in the positions of judge of the court of common pleas under RC 2301.01 to 2301.02 and judge of the probate division of the court of common pleas under RC 2101.02 to 2101.021, except in circumstances authorized under the provisions of O Const Art IV §5(A)(3) and O Const Art IV §23. OAG 96–031.

5. Liability

Even if judge exceeded his jurisdiction, judge did not act in clear absence of all jurisdiction when, instead of merely reporting conduct to prosecutors for possible action, he swore out criminal complaint against person who had fraudulently obtained marriage license from probate court office, and thus judge did not lose judicial immunity for his actions; judge had jurisdiction over subject matter, in that he had authority to issue or deny marriage licenses, and had obligation to report potentially obstructive conduct to proper authorities. Brookings v. Clunk (C.A.6 (Ohio), 11-18-2004) 389 F.3d 614. Judges ⊂⊃ 36

Any malice or ill motive on part of probate judge in swearing out complaint against person who had fraudulently obtained marriage license from probate court office did not alter judicial nature of judge's act, for purposes of determining judge's entitlement to immunity. Brookings v. Clunk (C.A.6 (Ohio), 11-18-2004) 389 F.3d 614. Judges ⊂⊃ 36

Probate judge was entitled to absolute judicial immunity from civil rights liability for swearing out criminal complaint against person who had falsified information about his legal gender on his marriage license application in probate court office; judge's initiation of proceedings constituted judicial act, as judge had obligation to report that crime had been committed in his court, and his efforts to stop person's repeated attempts to fraudulently obtain marriage licenses protected integrity of judicial system, judge's action arose directly from information provided to him in his judicial capacity, and action was not performed without any jurisdiction to do so. Brookings v. Clunk (C.A.6 (Ohio), 11-18-2004) 389 F.3d 614. Civil Rights ⊂⊃ 1376(8)

2101.021 Additional probate judge in Cuyahoga County

There shall be one additional probate judge for the probate court of Cuyahoga County.

Such additional judge shall be elected at the general election to be held in 1954 and every six years thereafter, for a term of six years commencing on the first day of January next following his election.

The judge elected pursuant to this section shall comply with the qualifications provided for in section 2101.02 of the Revised Code.

The probate judge who is senior in point of service shall be the presiding judge and shall have the care and custody of the files, papers, books and records belonging to the probate court of Cuyahoga county and shall have all the other powers and duties of the judge as provided in section 2101.11 of the Revised Code.

(125 v 161, eff. 10–2–53)

Cross References

Election, term, and compensation of judges; assignment of retired judges, O Const Art IV §6
Filling vacancy in judgeship, O Const Art IV §13
Number of judges for each county; terms of office, 2301.02
Time for holding elections for state and local officers; terms of office, O Const Art XVII §1

Library References

Judges ⚖3, 7, 34.
Westlaw Topic No. 227.
C.J.S. Judges §§ 12 to 13, 21 to 24, 27 to 29, 56.

Research References

Encyclopedias

OH Jur. 3d Courts & Judges § 29, Generally; Elective Nature of Office.
OH Jur. 3d Courts & Judges § 33, Commencement of Term.

Forms

Ohio Jurisprudence Pleading and Practice Forms § 2:20, Qualifications and Selection in General.
Ohio Jurisprudence Pleading and Practice Forms § 2:24, Powers and Duties Via Particular Courts—Probate Division.

2101.022 Powers of judge of probate division of Marion county common pleas court on and after 2-9-03

(A) Except as provided in division (B) of this section and notwithstanding any provision of this chapter or of any other provision of the Revised Code, on and after February 9, 2003, the judge of the probate division of the court of common pleas of Marion county who is elected in 2002 pursuant to section 2101.02 of the Revised Code to fill the office of the judge of the probate division of the court of common pleas of Marion county whose term expires on February 8, 2003, and successors to that judge, shall have all the powers relating to the domestic relations-juvenile-probate division of the court of common pleas of Marion county, as established pursuant to division (Z)(1) of section 2301.03 of the Revised Code, in addition to the powers relating to the probate division of that court, and shall exercise concurrent jurisdiction with the judge of the domestic relations-juvenile-probate division of the court of common pleas of Marion county over all matters that are within the jurisdiction of the probate division of that court under Chapter 2101., and other provisions, of the Revised Code and all matters that are within the jurisdiction of the domestic relations-juvenile-probate division of that court, as set forth in division (Z)(1) of section 2301.03 of the Revised Code.

(B) On and after February 9, 2003, the judge of the court of common pleas of Marion county who is to serve as the clerk of the probate division of the court of common pleas of Marion county shall be determined as provided in division (Z)(2) of section 2301.03 of the Revised Code.

(1998 H 444, eff. 1–15–98)

Cross References

Action for child support order, 2151.231
Action for child support order before acknowledgment becomes final, 2151.232
Communication between enforcing and modifying court, effect of out-of-state pending modification order on enforcement order, 3127.37
Enforcement of order relating to abducted child, 3127.32
Enforcement of out-of-state registered child custody determination, 3127.36
Registration of out-of-state child custody determination, contest of determination, 3127.35

Ohio Administrative Code References

Objecting to the administrative support order, OAC 5101:12–45–05.4

Library References

Judges ⚖24.
Westlaw Topic No. 227.
C.J.S. Judges §§ 35, 53 to 63.

Research References

Encyclopedias

OH Jur. 3d Courts & Judges § 29, Generally; Elective Nature of Office.
OH Jur. 3d Family Law § 973, Jurisdiction.
OH Jur. 3d Family Law § 1039, Request for Administrative Order.
OH Jur. 3d Family Law § 1031.1, Rescission of Acknowledgment of Paternity.

Forms

Ohio Jurisprudence Pleading and Practice Forms § 2:25, Powers and Duties Via Particular Courts—Juvenile Division.
Ohio Jurisprudence Pleading and Practice Forms § 111:4, Jurisdiction.

Treatises and Practice Aids

Sowald & Morganstern, Baldwin's Ohio Practice Domestic Relations Law § 3:31, Relief from Judgment Under 2000 S.B. 180 or RC 3119.961.
Carlin, Baldwin's Ohio Practice, Merrick-Rippner Probate Law § 19:2, Legitimation—Procedure—Acknowledgment of Paternity.
Carlin, Baldwin's Ohio Practice, Merrick-Rippner Probate Law § 19:6, Uniform Parentage Act—Jurisdiction of Action to Determine Father-Child Relationship.
Carlin, Baldwin's Ohio Practice, Merrick-Rippner Probate Law § 19:8, Uniform Parentage Act—Support Order.
Carlin, Baldwin's Ohio Practice, Merrick-Rippner Probate Law § 19:10, Uniform Parentage Act—Procedure in Action to Determine Father-Child Relationship.
Carlin, Baldwin's Ohio Practice, Merrick-Rippner Probate Law § 108:13, Juvenile Court—Jurisdiction Over Child Custody Matters—Determination of Custody.
Carlin, Baldwin's Ohio Practice, Merrick-Rippner Probate Law § 108:20, Juvenile Court—Parentage Act—Jurisdiction and Venue.
Carlin, Baldwin's Ohio Practice, Merrick-Rippner Probate Law § 108:22, Juvenile Court—Parentage Act—Presumption of Paternity.
Carlin, Baldwin's Ohio Practice, Merrick-Rippner Probate Law § 108:28, Juvenile Court—Parentage Act—Trial of Parentage Action.

2101.023 Additional judge in Erie county; jurisdictional responsibilities

The judge of the court of common pleas of Erie county who is elected in 2008, and successors, is the successor to the judge of the probate division of that court whose term expires on February 8, 2009, shall be designated as a judge of the court of common pleas, general division, shall have all the powers relating to the general division of the court of common pleas of Erie county, shall be the clerk of the probate court, and shall exercise concurrent jurisdiction with the other judges of the general division of the court of common pleas of Erie county over matters that are within the jurisdiction of the probate division of that court under Chapter 2101., and other provisions, of the Revised Code and all matters that are within the jurisdiction of the general division of that court, as set forth in division (N)(2) of section 2301.03 of the Revised Code.

(2003 H 86, eff. 11–13–03)

Library References

Judges ⚖24.
Westlaw Topic No. 227.
C.J.S. Judges §§ 35, 53 to 63.

Research References

Encyclopedias

OH Jur. 3d Courts & Judges § 15, Courts of Common Pleas—More Than One Judge; Districts.

2101.024 Powers and jurisdiction of probate judge of Logan county

Effective January 2, 2005, the probate judge of the court of common pleas of Logan county shall have all the powers relating to the domestic relations-juvenile-probate division of the court of common pleas of Logan county, as established pursuant to division (CC)(1) of section 2301.03 of the Revised Code, and shall exercise concurrent jurisdiction with the judge of the domestic relations-juvenile-probate division of the court of common pleas of Logan county over matters that are within the jurisdiction of the domestic relations-juvenile-probate division, as set forth in division (CC)(1) of section 2301.03 of the Revised Code.

(2003 H 86, eff. 11–13–03)

Library References

Judges ⚖24.
Westlaw Topic No. 227.
C.J.S. Judges §§ 35, 53 to 63.

2101.03 Bond of probate judge

Before entering upon the discharge of his duties, the probate judge shall give a bond to the state in a sum not less than five thousand dollars. Such bond shall have sufficient surety, approved by the board of county commissioners, or by the county auditor and county recorder in the absence from the county of two of the members of the board, and shall be conditioned that such judge will faithfully pay over all moneys received by him in his official capacity, enter and record the orders, judgments, and proceedings of the court, and faithfully and impartially perform all the duties of his office. Such bond, with the oath of office required by sections 3.22 and 3.23 of the Revised Code indorsed thereon, shall be deposited with the county treasurer and kept in his office. As the state of business in his office renders it necessary, the board may require the probate judge to give additional bond.

(1953 H 1, eff. 10–1–53; GC 10501–2)

Historical and Statutory Notes

Pre–1953 H 1 Amendments: 114 v 320

Cross References

Official bonds, 3.30 to 3.34

Library References

Judges ⚖5.
Westlaw Topic No. 227.
C.J.S. Judges §§ 15 to 19.

Research References

Encyclopedias

OH Jur. 3d Courts & Judges § 38, Official Bond.

Forms

Ohio Jurisprudence Pleading and Practice Forms § 2:24, Powers and Duties Via Particular Courts—Probate Division.

Treatises and Practice Aids

Carlin, Baldwin's Ohio Practice, Merrick-Rippner Probate Law § 3:36, Bond of Probate Judge—Form.

Carlin, Baldwin's Ohio Practice, Merrick-Rippner Probate Law § 3:37, Oath of Office of Probate Judge—Form.

Notes of Decisions

Blanket bond 2
Liability; judicial immunity 1

---

1. Liability; judicial immunity

Probate judge is not liable on his bond for acts clearly judicial in character, as distinguished from ministerial or clerical acts. Place v. Taylor (Ohio 1872) 22 Ohio St. 317.

A surety may assert the defense of judicial immunity in an action to enforce a surety bond posted to insure a probate judge's faithful performance of all his official duties. Hopkins v. INA Underwriters Ins. Co. (Pickaway 1988) 44 Ohio App.3d 186, 542 N.E.2d 679. Principal And Surety ⚖ 143

Probate judge is liable on his official bond for funds received by him by virtue of his office and lost through failure of the bank in which he deposited them. State ex rel. Struble v. Ferris (Ohio Com.Pl. 1911) 23 Ohio Dec. 328, 12 Ohio NP(NS) 171.

Probate judge is duty bound to require an inventory and, perhaps, is liable for failure. In re Pickands' Estate (Ohio Prob. 1898) 7 Ohio Dec. 476, 5 Ohio N.P. 493.

Even if judge exceeded his jurisdiction, judge did not act in clear absence of all jurisdiction when, instead of merely reporting conduct to prosecutors for possible action, he swore out criminal complaint against person who had fraudulently obtained marriage license from probate court office, and thus judge did not lose judicial immunity for his actions; judge had jurisdiction over subject matter, in that he had authority to issue or deny marriage licenses, and had obligation to report potentially obstructive conduct to proper authorities. Brookings v. Clunk (C.A.6 (Ohio), 11-18-2004) 389 F.3d 614. Judges ⚖ 36

Judge acts in the clear absence of all jurisdiction, so as to lose judicial immunity, only when the matter upon which he acts is clearly outside the subject matter of the court over which he presides; immunity is not lost for those actions merely in excess of jurisdiction. Brookings v. Clunk (C.A.6 (Ohio), 11-18-2004) 389 F.3d 614. Judges ⚖ 36

Any malice or ill motive on part of probate judge in swearing out complaint against person who had fraudulently obtained marriage license from probate court office did not alter judicial nature of judge's act, for purposes of determining judge's entitlement to immunity. Brookings v. Clunk (C.A.6 (Ohio), 11-18-2004) 389 F.3d 614. Judges ⚖ 36

Even if the particular act is not a function normally performed by a judge, it may constitute a judicial act for which judge is entitled to judicial immunity if it relates to a general function normally performed by a judge. Brookings v. Clunk (C.A.6 (Ohio), 11-18-2004) 389 F.3d 614. Judges ⚖ 36

Probate judge was entitled to absolute judicial immunity from civil rights liability for swearing out criminal complaint against person who had falsified information about his legal gender on his marriage license application in probate court office; judge's initiation of proceedings constituted judicial act, as judge had obligation to report that crime had been committed in his court, and his efforts to stop person's repeated attempts to fraudulently obtain marriage licenses protected integrity of judicial system, judge's action arose directly from information provided to him in his judicial capacity, and action was not performed without any jurisdiction to do so. Brookings v. Clunk (C.A.6 (Ohio), 11-18-2004) 389 F.3d 614. Civil Rights ⚖ 1376(8)

2. Blanket bond

Assuming that the requirement can be fulfilled which calls for a bond to be filed with a certain official, all officers, deputies, clerks, assistants, bookkeepers and employees of the offices of a political subdivision who are required to file a bond, and who may be properly covered by a blanket bond, may be covered under the same blanket bond. OAG 65–087.

2101.04 Rules of practice submitted to supreme court

The several judges of the probate court shall make rules regulating the practice and conducting the business of the court, which they shall submit to the supreme court. In order to maintain regularity and uniformity in the proceedings of all the probate courts, the supreme court may alter and amend such rules and make other rules.

(125 v 903, eff. 10–1–53; 1953 H 1; GC 10501–13)

Historical and Statutory Notes

Pre–1953 H 1 Amendments: 114 v 323

Cross References

Powers and duties of supreme court, conflict of rules with statutes, O Const Art IV §5
Procedure in probate court, Civ R 73

Library References

Courts ⚖81.
Westlaw Topic No. 106.
C.J.S. Courts § 129.

Research References

Encyclopedias

OH Jur. 3d Courts & Judges § 363, Statutory Authority for Rulemaking.

Law Review and Journal Commentaries

Pretrial practice and procedure. 10 Clev B J 167 (August 1939).

Notes of Decisions

Approval of rules 2
Authority and binding effect of court judgments 1

---

1. Authority and binding effect of court judgments

Where the rules of a probate court prescribe the time within which a petition shall be filed to secure a review of a widow's allowance, the court does not have authority to diminish such allowance upon a petition filed after such time has expired. In re Johnson's Estate (Cuyahoga 1958) 150 N.E.2d 501, 80 Ohio Law Abs. 180.

The probate court, as to matters that come within its jurisdiction, is a court of record, and its judgments are of the same binding effect as those in any other court, and such judgments can only be impeached for fraud. Woodward v. Curtis (Ohio Cir. 1899) 10 Ohio C.D. 400. Judgment ⚖ 443(1)

2. Approval of rules

Rule 27 of the uniform rules of practice in the probate courts of Ohio, adopted pursuant to this section, and providing that "in applications for the appointment of guardians for... incompetents,... the notice to the proposed ward must be served by the sheriff or some other disinterested person," is reasonable and salutary, supplements GC 10507–4 (RC 2111.04), and does not contravene GC 10501–21 (RC 2101.26 and RC 2101.27). In re Irvine's Guardianship (Knox 1943) 72 Ohio App. 405, 52 N.E.2d 536, 27 O.O. 332.

Uniform rules of practice in probate courts of Ohio, approved by Supreme Court, February 24, 1932. Uniform Rules of Practice in Probate Courts of Ohio, 11 Abs 385 (1932).

2101.05 Oaths and depositions

A probate judge may administer oaths, take acknowledgment of instruments in writing required to be acknowledged, and take depositions.

Depositions taken according to sections 2319.05 to 2319.31, inclusive, of the Revised Code, to be used on the trial of civil cases, may be taken and used on the trial of any question before the probate court.

(1953 H 1, eff. 10–1–53; GC 10501–3, 10501–19)

Historical and Statutory Notes

Pre–1953 H 1 Amendments: 114 v 321, 325

Cross References

Depositions, Civ R 27, 28, 30, 31, 32

Library References

Acknowledgment ⚖16.
Judges ⚖24.
Oath ⚖2.
Pretrial Procedure ⚖67, 138.
Westlaw Topic Nos. 12, 227, 280, 307A.
C.J.S. Acknowledgments §§ 30, 33.
C.J.S. Depositions §§ 21 to 27.
C.J.S. Discovery §§ 30, 39, 51 to 53.
C.J.S. Judges §§ 35, 53 to 63.
C.J.S. Oaths and Affirmations §§ 5 to 6.

Research References

Encyclopedias

OH Jur. 3d Acknowledgmts, Affid., Oaths, & Notar. § 50, Administration of Oath or Affirmation.
OH Jur. 3d Courts & Judges § 67, Miscellaneous Powers and Functions of Probate Judge.
OH Jur. 3d Discovery & Depositions § 50, Persons Before Whom Depositions May be Taken, Generally.

Forms

Ohio Forms Legal and Business § 2:131, General Background.
Ohio Forms and Transactions KP 22.02, Notarial Acts.
Ohio Jurisprudence Pleading and Practice Forms § 2:24, Powers and Duties Via Particular Courts—Probate Division.

2101.06 Master commissioners; appointment and bond; duties

The probate judge, upon motion of a party or his own motion, may appoint a special master commissioner in any matter pending before such judge. Such commissioner shall be an attorney at law, and shall be sworn faithfully to discharge his duties. When requested by the probate judge, such commissioner shall execute a bond to the state in such sum as the court directs, with surety approved by the court, and conditioned that such commissioner will faithfully discharge his duties and pay over all money received by him in that capacity. Such bond shall be for the benefit of anyone aggrieved and shall be filed in the probate court.

Such commissioner shall take the testimony and report such testimony to the court with his conclusions on the law and the facts involved therein, which report may be excepted to by the parties, and confirmed, modified, or set aside by the court.

(1953 H 1, eff. 10–1–53; GC 10501–33, 10501–36)

Historical and Statutory Notes

Pre–1953 H 1 Amendments: 114 v 328, 329

Comparative Laws

Ind.—West's A.I.C. 29–2–2–1.
Pa.—20 Pa.C.S.A. § 751.

Cross References

Powers and duties of supreme court, conflict of rules with statutes, O Const Art IV, § 5
Procedure in probate court, Civ R 73
Referees, Civ R 53

Library References

Reference ⚖35, 37.
Westlaw Topic No. 327.
C.J.S. References §§ 40 to 41.

Research References

Encyclopedias

OH Jur. 3d Courts & Judges § 67, Miscellaneous Powers and Functions of Probate Judge.

OH Jur. 3d Declar. Judgments & Related Proceedings § 39, Determination of Issues of Fact—Determination in Probate Court.
OH Jur. 3d Jury § 38, Probate Division of Common Pleas Court.

Forms

Ohio Jurisprudence Pleading and Practice Forms § 2:24, Powers and Duties Via Particular Courts—Probate Division.

Treatises and Practice Aids

Klein, Darling, & Terez, Baldwin's Ohio Practice Civil Practice § 73:6, Probate Division--Service of Notice.

Carlin, Baldwin's Ohio Practice, Merrick-Rippner Probate Law § 6:5, Declaratory Judgments—Action—Jury.

Carlin, Baldwin's Ohio Practice, Merrick-Rippner Probate Law § 3:42, Motion for Reference to Master Commissioner—Form.

Carlin, Baldwin's Ohio Practice, Merrick-Rippner Probate Law § 3:43, Entry of Reference to Master Commissioner—Form.

Carlin, Baldwin's Ohio Practice, Merrick-Rippner Probate Law § 3:44, Bond of Master Commissioner—Form.

Carlin, Baldwin's Ohio Practice, Merrick-Rippner Probate Law § 3:45, Oath of Master Commissioner—Form.

Notes of Decisions

Non–jury trial 1

---

1. Non–jury trial

Probate court judge was authorized to appoint special master commissioner to resolve attorney fee dispute in guardianship case, to remove guardian, and to appoint successor guardian. State ex rel. Estate of Hards v. Klammer (Ohio, 08-02-2006) 110 Ohio St.3d 104, 850 N.E.2d 1197, 2006-Ohio-3670. Guardian And Ward ⇐ 158

Action brought under GC 10506–67 (RC 2109.50) for discovery of concealed assets was properly referred to a master commissioner where no jury trial was requested. In re Leiby's Estate (Franklin 1951) 101 N.E.2d 214, 60 Ohio Law Abs. 245, appeal dismissed 156 Ohio St. 254, 101 N.E.2d 906, 46 O.O. 121, reversed 157 Ohio St. 374, 105 N.E.2d 583, 47 O.O. 265.

2101.07 Master commissioners; powers; fees

A special master commissioner of the probate court may administer all oaths required in the discharge of his duties, may summon and enforce the attendance of witnesses, compel the production of books and papers, grant adjournments the same as the court, and, when the court directs, such commissioner shall require the witnesses severally to subscribe their testimony.

All process and orders issued by such commissioner, shall be directed to the sheriff and shall be served and return thereof made, as if issued by the probate judge.

The court shall allow such commissioner such fees as are allowed to other officers for similar services, which fees shall be taxed with the costs.

(1953 H 1, eff. 10–1–53; GC 10501–34, 10501–35, 10501–37)

Historical and Statutory Notes

Pre–1953 H 1 Amendments: 114 v 329

Cross References

Powers and duties of supreme court, conflict of rules with statutes, O Const Art IV, § 5
Procedure in probate court, Civ R 73
Referees, Civ R 53

Library References

Reference ⇐47.
Westlaw Topic No. 327.
C.J.S. References §§ 51, 53, 59.

Research References

Encyclopedias

OH Jur. 3d Costs in Civil Actions § 11, Fees and Expenses of Officers and Court Personnel or Appointees.
OH Jur. 3d Declar. Judgments & Related Proceedings § 39, Determination of Issues of Fact—Determination in Probate Court.
OH Jur. 3d Evidence & Witnesses § 691, Authority of the Court—Particular Judicial Body or Officer.
OH Jur. 3d Evidence & Witnesses § 694, Subpoenas—Subpoena Duces Tecum.
OH Jur. 3d Jury § 38, Probate Division of Common Pleas Court.
OH Jur. 3d References § 27, Compelling Production of Evidence.

Treatises and Practice Aids

Baldwin's Ohio Handbook Series—Trial Handbook § 11:4, Subpoena and Subpoena Duces Tecum.
Carlin, Baldwin's Ohio Practice, Merrick-Rippner Probate Law § 6:5, Declaratory Judgments—Action—Jury.

Notes of Decisions

Guardianships 1

---

1. Guardianships

Rule stating that costs would be allowed to the prevailing party unless court otherwise directed did not require that judge assess against law firm, which had been hired to represent guardianship in civil suit, costs associated with appointment of special master commissioner to resolve motions and applications filed in fee dispute with guardianship subsequent to fee judgment in favor of law firm, even though, on guardian's motion for relief from judgment, probate court adopted master commissioner's report and denied law firm's request for fees. State ex rel. Estate of Hards v. Klammer (Ohio, 08-02-2006) 110 Ohio St.3d 104, 850 N.E.2d 1197, 2006-Ohio-3670. Guardian And Ward ⇐ 136

Probate court judge was authorized to appoint special master commissioner to resolve attorney fee dispute in guardianship case, to remove guardian, and to appoint successor guardian. State ex rel. Estate of Hards v. Klammer (Ohio, 08-02-2006) 110 Ohio St.3d 104, 850 N.E.2d 1197, 2006-Ohio-3670. Guardian And Ward ⇐ 158

2101.08 Stenographic reporter

The probate judge may appoint a stenographic reporter and fix his compensation in the manner provided for the court of common pleas in sections 2301.18 to 2301.26, inclusive, of the Revised Code.

(1953 H 1, eff. 10–1–53; GC 10501–63)

Historical and Statutory Notes

Pre–1953 H 1 Amendments: 118 v 78, § 3

Cross References

Probate court employees, power invested in judge to appoint and control, O Const Art IV §4

Library References

Courts ⇐57(1), 57(2).
Westlaw Topic No. 106.
C.J.S. Stenographers §§ 4 to 6, 10, 13, 16 to 19.

Research References

Encyclopedias

OH Jur. 3d Courts & Judges § 66, Employment of Clerks and Other Employees of Probate Division; Care and Custody of Papers and Records.
OH Jur. 3d Courts & Judges § 168, Probate Divisions of the Common Pleas Court.

Notes of Decisions

Compelling appointment 1

Private reporter 2

1. Compelling appointment

In an action to compel probate judge to appoint a reporter to his court and to compel presiding judge of common pleas court to supply such reporter until one was furnished, presiding judge was properly dismissed from action. State ex rel. Bartlett v. Ludeman (Ohio 1970) 24 Ohio St.2d 156, 265 N.E.2d 293, 53 O.O.2d 353.

2. Private reporter

Where the oral testimony, objections of counsel and rulings of the court thereon at a probate court hearing are taken down in shorthand by a privately employed reporter, and a typewritten transcript thereof is made but is not filed with or delivered to the probate court, but a copy thereof is sold to the opposing counsel, a record has been taken in such probate court hearing, and the only appeal therefrom is to the court of appeals. In re Todd's Estate (Crawford 1957) 104 Ohio App. 284, 148 N.E.2d 261, 4 O.O.2d 421, appeal dismissed 167 Ohio St. 148, 146 N.E.2d 598, 4 O.O.2d 140.

2101.09 Liability of sheriffs, coroners, and constables for failure to serve and return process

When required by the probate judge, sheriffs, coroners, and constables shall attend his court and serve and return process directed and delivered to them by such judge. No such officer shall neglect or refuse to serve and return such process. If such officer does neglect or refuse to serve and return such process, the judge shall issue a summons specifying the cause for amercement, directed to the officer, therein named, commanding him to summon the officer guilty of such misconduct to appear within two days after the service of summons and show cause why he should not be amerced. In addition to a fine, as provided by section 2101.99 of the Revised Code, to be paid into the county treasury, such officer and his sureties shall be liable upon his official bond for damages sustained by any person by reason of such officer's misconduct.

(1953 H 1, eff. 10–1–53; GC 10501–26)

Historical and Statutory Notes

Pre–1953 H 1 Amendments: 114 v 327

Cross References

Penalty: 2101.99(A)
Amercing officer for neglect or refusal to perform duties, Ch 2707
Procedure in probate court, Civ R 73

Library References

Coroners ⚖8, 23.
Sheriffs and Constables ⚖87, 125(1).
Westlaw Topic Nos. 100, 353.
C.J.S. Coroners and Medical Examiners §§ 8 to 9, 31.
C.J.S. Sheriffs and Constables §§ 80 to 88, 335 to 344, 359 to 375.

Research References

Encyclopedias
 OH Jur. 3d Cvl. Servants & Pub. Officers & Employ. § 535, Official Bond.
 OH Jur. 3d Cvl. Servants & Pub. Officers & Employ. § 543, Duty to Act in Capacity of Sheriff or Constable.
 OH Jur. 3d Police, Sheriffs, & Related Officers § 4, Status of Police as Public Officers—Sheriffs and Constables.
 OH Jur. 3d Police, Sheriffs, & Related Officers § 52, Sheriff as Court Officer; Attendance Upon, and Adjournment Of, Courts.
 OH Jur. 3d Police, Sheriffs, & Related Officers § 70, Particular Breaches of Conditions of Bonds—Service or Execution of Process.
 OH Jur. 3d Police, Sheriffs, & Related Officers § 112, Special Provisions as to Probate Courts and Constables.

Forms
 Ohio Jurisprudence Pleading and Practice Forms § 9:21, Special Statutory Provisions.

Treatises and Practice Aids
 Carlin, Baldwin's Ohio Practice, Merrick-Rippner Probate Law § 3:46, Entry to Summon Officer to Show Cause Why He or She Should Not Be Amerced—Form.

2101.10 Liability of sheriffs, coroners, and constables for failure to pay over moneys

No sheriff, coroner, or constable shall refuse to pay moneys, collected by him, to the probate judge or other person, when so directed by the judge. For refusal to pay over moneys collected, such officer shall be summoned as provided in section 2101.09 of the Revised Code and amerced for the use of the parties interested, in the amount required to be collected by such process, with ten per cent thereon. The judge may enforce the collection of such amercement by execution or other process, by imprisonment as for contempt of court, or both. The delinquent officer and his sureties shall also be liable on his official bond for the amount of the amercement at the suit of the person interested.

(1953 H 1, eff. 10–1–53; GC 10501–27)

Historical and Statutory Notes

Pre–1953 H 1 Amendments: 114 v 327

Cross References

Amercing officer for neglect or refusal to perform duties, Ch 2707

Library References

Coroners ⚖23.
Sheriffs and Constables ⚖125(1).
Westlaw Topic Nos. 100, 353.
C.J.S. Coroners and Medical Examiners § 31.
C.J.S. Sheriffs and Constables §§ 335 to 344, 359 to 375.

Research References

Encyclopedias
 OH Jur. 3d Cvl. Servants & Pub. Officers & Employ. § 535, Official Bond.
 OH Jur. 3d Police, Sheriffs, & Related Officers § 4, Status of Police as Public Officers—Sheriffs and Constables.
 OH Jur. 3d Police, Sheriffs, & Related Officers § 71, Particular Breaches of Conditions of Bonds—Failure to Pay Over or Account for Moneys Received.
 OH Jur. 3d Police, Sheriffs, & Related Officers § 112, Special Provisions as to Probate Courts and Constables.

Treatises and Practice Aids
 Carlin, Baldwin's Ohio Practice, Merrick-Rippner Probate Law § 3:46, Entry to Summon Officer to Show Cause Why He or She Should Not Be Amerced—Form.

FILES AND RECORDS; COURT INVESTIGATORS

2101.11 Custody of files; investigators; clerks and appointees; appropriation; action in court of appeals; limitation of contempt power

(A)(1) The probate judge shall have the care and custody of the files, papers, books, and records belonging to the probate court. The probate judge is authorized to perform the duties of clerk of the judge's court. The probate judge may appoint deputy clerks, stenographers, a bailiff, and any other necessary employees, each of whom shall take an oath of office before entering upon the duties of the employee's appointment and, when so qualified, may perform the duties appertaining to the office of clerk of the court.

(2)(a) The probate judge shall provide for one or more probate court investigators to perform the duties that are established for a probate court investigator by the Revised Code or the probate judge. The probate judge may provide for an investigator in any of the following manners, as the court determines is appropriate:

(i) By appointing a person as a full-time or part-time employee of the probate court to serve as investigator, or by designating a current full-time or part-time employee of the probate court to serve as investigator;

(ii) By contracting with a person to serve and be compensated as investigator only when needed by the probate court, as determined by the court, and by designating that person as a probate court investigator during the times when the person is performing the duties of an investigator for the court;

(iii) By entering into an agreement with another department or agency of the county, including, but not limited to, the sheriff's department or the county department of job and family services, pursuant to which an employee of the other department or agency will serve and perform the duties of investigator for the court, upon request of the probate judge, and designating that employee as a probate court investigator during the times when the person is performing the duties of an investigator for the court.

(b) Each person appointed or otherwise designated as a probate court investigator shall take an oath of office before entering upon the duties of the person's appointment. When so qualified, an investigator may perform the duties that are established for a probate court investigator by the Revised Code or the probate judge.

(c) Except as otherwise provided in this division, a probate court investigator shall hold at least a bachelor's degree in social work, psychology, education, special education, or a related human services field. A probate judge may waive the education requirement of this division for a person the judge appoints or otherwise designates as a probate court investigator if the judge determines that the person has experience in family services work that is equivalent to the required education.

(d) Within one year after appointment or designation, a probate court investigator shall attend an orientation course of at least six hours, and each calendar year after the calendar year of appointment or designation, a probate court investigator shall satisfactorily complete at least six hours of continuing education.

(e) For purposes of divisions (A)(4), (B), and (C) of this section, a person designated as a probate court investigator under division (A)(2)(a)(ii) or (iii) of this section shall be considered an appointee of the probate court at any time that the person is performing the duties established under the Revised Code or by the probate judge for a probate court investigator.

(3)(a) The probate judge may provide for one or more persons to perform the duties of an assessor under sections 3107.031, 3107.032, 3107.082, 3107.09, 3107.101, and 3107.12 of the Revised Code or may enter into agreements with public children services agencies, private child placing agencies, or private noncustodial agencies under which the agency provides for one or more persons to perform the duties of an assessor. A probate judge who provides for an assessor shall do so in either of the following manners, as the judge considers appropriate:

(i) By appointing a person as a full-time or part-time employee of the probate court to serve as assessor, or by designating a current full-time or part-time employee of the probate court to serve as assessor;

(ii) By contracting with a person to serve and be compensated as assessor only when needed by the probate court, as determined by the court, and by designating that person as an assessor during the times when the person is performing the duties of an assessor for the court.

(b) Each person appointed or designated as a probate court assessor shall take an oath of office before entering on the duties of the person's appointment.

(c) A probate court assessor must meet the qualifications for an assessor established by section 3107.014 of the Revised Code.

(d) A probate court assessor shall perform additional duties, including duties of an investigator under division (A)(2) of this section, when the probate judge assigns additional duties to the assessor.

(e) For purposes of divisions (A)(4), (B), and (C) of this section, a person designated as a probate court assessor shall be considered an appointee of the probate court at any time that the person is performing assessor duties.

(4) Each appointee of the probate judge may administer oaths in all cases when necessary, in the discharge of official duties.

(B)(1)(a) Subject to the appropriation made by the board of county commissioners pursuant to this division, each appointee of a probate judge under division (A) of this section shall receive such compensation and expenses as the judge determines and shall serve during the pleasure of the judge. The compensation of each appointee shall be paid in semimonthly installments by the county treasurer from the county treasury, upon the warrants of the county auditor, certified to by the judge.

(b) Except as otherwise provided in the Revised Code, the total compensation paid to all appointees of the probate judge in any calendar year shall not exceed the total fees earned by the probate court during the preceding calendar year, unless the board of county commissioners approves otherwise.

(2) The probate judge annually shall submit a written request for an appropriation to the board of county commissioners that shall set forth estimated administrative expenses of the court, including the salaries of appointees as determined by the judge and any other costs, fees, and expenses, including, but not limited to, those enumerated in section 5123.96 of the Revised Code, that the judge considers reasonably necessary for the operation of the court. The board shall conduct a public hearing with respect to the written request submitted by the judge and shall appropriate such sum of money each year as it determines, after conducting the public hearing and considering the written request of the judge, is reasonably necessary to meet all the administrative expenses of the court, including the salaries of appointees as determined by the judge and any other costs, fees, and expenses, including, but not limited to, the costs, fees, and expenses enumerated in section 5123.96 of the Revised Code.

If the judge considers the appropriation made by the board pursuant to this division insufficient to meet all the administrative expenses of the court, the judge shall commence an action under Chapter 2731. of the Revised Code in the court of appeals for the judicial district for a determination of the duty of the board of county commissioners to appropriate the amount of money in dispute. The court of appeals shall give priority to the action filed by the probate judge over all cases pending on its docket. The burden shall be on the probate judge to prove that the appropriation requested is reasonably necessary to meet all administrative expenses of the court. If, prior to the filing of an action under Chapter 2731. of the Revised Code or during the pendency of the action, the judge exercises the judge's contempt power in order to obtain the sum of money in dispute, the judge shall not order the imprisonment of any member of the board of county commissioners notwithstanding sections 2705.02 to 2705.06 of the Revised Code.

(C) The probate judge may require any of the judge's appointees to give bond in the sum of not less than one thousand dollars, conditioned for the honest and faithful performance of the appointee's duties. The sureties on the bonds shall be approved in the manner provided in section 2101.03 of the Revised Code.

PROBATE COURT—JURISDICTION; PROCEDURE
2101.11
Note 1

The judge is personally liable for the default, malfeasance, or nonfeasance of any such appointee, but, if a bond is required of the appointee, the liability of the judge is limited to the amount by which the loss resulting from the default, malfeasance, or nonfeasance exceeds the amount of the bond.

All bonds required to be given in the probate court, on being accepted and approved by the probate judge, shall be filed in the judge's office.

(2006 S 238, eff. 9–21–06; 2000 H 448, eff. 10–5–00; 1999 H 471, eff. 7–1–00; 1998 H 446, eff. 8–5–98; 1989 S 46, eff. 1–1–90; 1979 S 63; 1977 H 164; 125 v 903; 1953 H 1; GC 10501–5, 10501–7)

Historical and Statutory Notes

Pre–1953 H 1 Amendments: 119 v 394, § 1; 114 v 321, 322

Amendment Note: 2006 S 238 inserted ", 3107.032" and "3107.101," in the first sentence of division (A)(3)(a).

Amendment Note: 2000 H 448 substituted "3107.014" for "3107.012" in division (A)(3)(c).

Amendment Note: 1999 H 471 substituted "family" for "human" in division (A)(2)(c).

Amendment Note: 1998 H 446 substituted "(A)(4)" for "(A)(3)" in division (A)(2)(e); added new division (A)(3); redesignated former division (A)(3) as new division (A)(4); and made changes to reflect gender neutral language.

Cross References

County auditor, warrants on treasury, 319.16
County commissioners' appropriation for common pleas court, procedure, action for writ of mandamus by dissatisfied court, 307.10
Investigator, appointment, 2111.042
Investigator making personal service of notice of appointment of guardian, 2111.04
Judicial and court fund, tax levy, 5707.02
Oath of office, 3.20 to 3.24
Official bonds, 3.30 to 3.34

Library References

Clerks of Courts ⚖6.
Courts ⚖55 to 58, 113.
Judges ⚖23, 34.
Westlaw Topic Nos. 106, 227, 79.
C.J.S. Courts §§ 107 to 110, 179, 181, 260 to 265.
C.J.S. Judges §§ 53 to 56, 61 to 62.
C.J.S. Stenographers §§ 2 to 21.

Research References

Encyclopedias
OH Jur. 3d Acknowledgmts, Affid., Oaths, & Notar. § 50, Administration of Oath or Affirmation.
OH Jur. 3d Courts & Judges § 19, Courts of Common Pleas—Probate Division.
OH Jur. 3d Courts & Judges § 66, Employment of Clerks and Other Employees of Probate Division; Care and Custody of Papers and Records.
OH Jur. 3d Courts & Judges § 112, Insurance; Liability for Acts of Subordinates.
OH Jur. 3d Courts & Judges § 168, Probate Divisions of the Common Pleas Court.
OH Jur. 3d Courts & Judges § 182, Appointment or Election, in General—Probate Division.
OH Jur. 3d Courts & Judges § 188, Official Bonds.
OH Jur. 3d Courts & Judges § 189, Oath of Office.
OH Jur. 3d Courts & Judges § 192, Term of Office.
OH Jur. 3d Courts & Judges § 199, Salaries.
OH Jur. 3d Courts & Judges § 211, Custody of Papers.
OH Jur. 3d Courts & Judges § 216, Powers and Duties of Deputies and Assistants.
OH Jur. 3d Courts & Judges § 217, Civil Action, Generally; Defenses.
OH Jur. 3d Guardian & Ward § 53, Application for Guardian for Incompetent—Investigation of Circumstances of an Alleged Incompetent.

Forms
Ohio Jurisprudence Pleading and Practice Forms § 2:24, Powers and Duties Via Particular Courts—Probate Division.

Treatises and Practice Aids
Carlin, Baldwin's Ohio Practice, Merrick-Rippner Probate Law § 3:1, Jurisdiction of Probate Court—Constitutional Grant of Power.
Carlin, Baldwin's Ohio Practice, Merrick-Rippner Probate Law § 3:3, Jurisdiction of Probate Court—Subject Matter—in General.
Carlin, Baldwin's Ohio Practice, Merrick-Rippner Probate Law § 3:5, Jurisdiction of Probate Court—Subject Matter—Specific Areas—Fiduciaries.
Carlin, Baldwin's Ohio Practice, Merrick-Rippner Probate Law § 3:40, Appointment of Magistrate—Form.
Carlin, Baldwin's Ohio Practice, Merrick-Rippner Probate Law § 3:47, Bond of Deputy Clerk—Form.
Carlin, Baldwin's Ohio Practice, Merrick-Rippner Probate Law § 3:48, Oath of Deputy Clerk—Form.
Carlin, Baldwin's Ohio Practice, Merrick-Rippner Probate Law § 63:3, Notice of Guardianship Hearing—Service—Guardianship of Incompetent.
Carlin, Baldwin's Ohio Practice, Merrick-Rippner Probate Law § 62:19, Appointment of Guardian—Application—Investigations by Court.
Carlin, Baldwin's Ohio Practice, Merrick-Rippner Probate Law § 62:45, Guardianship Proceedings—Role of Physician or Investigators.
Carlin, Baldwin's Ohio Practice, Merrick-Rippner Probate Law § 62:51, Appointment of Guardian of a Minor—Investigations.
Carlin, Baldwin's Ohio Practice, Merrick-Rippner Probate Law § 65:23, Settlement of Suits—Attorney Fees in Cases Where Court Approval is Required.
Carlin, Baldwin's Ohio Practice, Merrick-Rippner Probate Law § 98:12, Adoption—Suitability of Adoptive Parents—Regulation of Persons With Criminal Record.

Notes of Decisions

Administrative expenses 7
Appeal 10
Appropriations 4
Authority of court 3
Clerk of court 2
Compensation 6
Constitutional issues 1
Deputies 8
Docketing 9
Fees 5

---

1. Constitutional issues

Statute requiring a probate court judge who disagreed with the amount appropriated by county board of commissioners to file a mandamus action in the Court of Appeals to resolve the dispute was unconstitutional; statute prevented a probate court judge dissatisfied with the amount appropriated for the probate court from invoking the original jurisdiction of the Supreme Court in mandamus, instead, relegating an aggrieved probate court judge to a mandamus action in the Court of Appeals. State ex rel. Wilke v. Hamilton Cty. Bd. of Commrs. (Ohio, 09-20-2000) 90 Ohio St.3d 55, 734 N.E.2d 811, 2000-Ohio-13. Constitutional Law ⚖ 56; Mandamus ⚖ 2

Unconstitutional statute establishing budget process whereby probate court judge who disagreed with the amount appropriated by county board of commissioners was required to file a mandamus action in the Court of Appeals to resolve the dispute did not provide an adequate legal remedy that precluded probate court's request for extraordinary relief in mandamus; statute would have permitted board to substitute its judgment for that of the court regarding the propriety of funding requested by the court and placed the burden on the probate court to prove that its request was reasonably necessary. State ex rel. Wilke v. Hamilton Cty. Bd. of Commrs. (Ohio, 09-20-2000) 90 Ohio St.3d 55, 734 N.E.2d 811, 2000-Ohio-13. Mandamus ⚖ 3(8)

That portion of RC 2101.11(B) containing language substantially identical to that in RC 2151.10 is unconstitutional. State ex rel. Slaby v. Summit County Council (Summit 1983) 7 Ohio App.3d 199, 454 N.E.2d 1379, 7 O.B.R. 258.

2. Clerk of court

Probate judge is his own clerk, and in acts done as clerk is responsible the same as a ministerial officer. State ex rel. v. Craig (Ohio Com.Pl. 1900) 10 Ohio Dec. 577, 8 Ohio N.P. 148.

A probate judge is authorized and empowered to perform the duties of clerk of his own court, and the probate court is a court of record, so such probate judge must keep the same records as other clerks. (See also Lucas Bd of Commrs v Millard, 4 NP 53, 4 D 419 (CP, Lucas 1896), affirmed by 13 CC 518, 7 CD 115 (Lucas 1897).) Millard v Lucas County Bd of Commrs, 13 CC 518, 7 CD 115 (Lucas 1897).

The words "clerks" and "deputies," as used in § 4(C) of 132 v HR 42, refer to persons employed in such capacities in the probate division of the court of common pleas. OAG 68–126.

No provision of any amendment proposed in 132 v HR 42 requires the assumption by the clerk of the court of common pleas, of any duties, functions or responsibilities over the operations of the probate division of the court of common pleas. OAG 68–126.

The amendments contained in 132 v HR 42 do not affect RC 2101.11, and the judge of the probate division of the common pleas court is still the clerk of his own court as prescribed in said section. OAG 68–126.

The amendments contained in 132 v HR 42 repeal Title XXI of the Revised Code only to the extent that any provision thereof is inconsistent with the constitutional amendments proposed in said resolution. OAG 68–126.

3. Authority of court

Probate court abused its discretion by conducting its own investigation in guardianship proceeding, rather than appointing court investigators. In re Guardianship of Lauder (Ohio App. 10 Dist., 11-12-2002) 150 Ohio App.3d 277, 780 N.E.2d 1025, 2002-Ohio-6102, entered nunc pro tunc 2003-Ohio-406, 2003 WL 194760. Mental Health 137.1

Board of county commissioners failed to sustain their burden of proving that budget requests submitted by common pleas courts were both unreasonable and unnecessary and, hence, the board abused its discretion in appropriating lesser amounts; courts must not be held hostage to competing interests when, in their discretionary power, they have submitted budgetary requests that are reasonable and necessary. State ex rel. Rudes v. Rofkar (Ohio 1984) 15 Ohio St.3d 69, 472 N.E.2d 354, 15 O.B.R. 163. Counties 162

Court's modification of budget was within its discretion, and county's claim of governmental hardship, while relevant to a determination of reasonableness and necessity, was not solely determinative of the issue. State ex rel. Arbaugh v. Richland County Bd. of Com'rs (Ohio 1984) 14 Ohio St.3d 5, 470 N.E.2d 880, 14 O.B.R. 311. Counties 137

Where a probate court, by its judgment and entry, orders letters of guardianship issued to a guardian of an estate, but, through error and clerical inadvertency, letters of guardianship are subsequently issued authorizing guardianship of the person and estate of the ward, such probate court has full authority to correct such error. In re Guardianship of Lohman (Hamilton 1967) 13 Ohio App.2d 106, 234 N.E.2d 512, 42 O.O.2d 214. Guardian And Ward 13(7)

Deputy clerk of the probate court has no authority to receive the election of a widow to take under the will of her deceased husband, and such an election may be vacated and set aside by a court of equity on application of the party making it. Mellinger v. Mellinger (Ohio Cir. 1904) 16 Ohio C.D. 683, 5 Ohio C.C.(N.S.) 435, affirmed 73 Ohio St. 221, 76 N.E. 615, 3 Ohio Law Rep. 536.

4. Appropriations

County commissioners had exclusive authority to conduct a budget hearing on a probate judge's appropriation request; thus, the probate judge had no authority to conduct such a hearing. State ex rel. Mahoning Cty. Commrs. v. Maloney (Ohio, 11-12-2003) 100 Ohio St.3d 248, 797 N.E.2d 1284, 2003-Ohio-5770. Counties 159

Where the basic function of a court, whether named in the constitution or established in pursuance of provisions of the constitution, is impeded by a failure or refusal of the body responsible to provide a necessary appropriation, that court possesses the inherent power to order such appropriation and to enforce its order by contempt proceedings. State ex rel. Edwards v. Murray (Ohio 1976) 48 Ohio St.2d 303, 358 N.E.2d 577, 2 O.O.3d 446. Mandamus 141; Mandamus 185

The provisions of this section regarding appropriations by county commissioners are mandatory and it is their duty to make appropriations for such purposes accordingly. State ex rel. Motter v. Atkinson (Ohio 1945) 146 Ohio St. 11, 63 N.E.2d 440, 31 O.O. 472.

RC 2101.11 permits but does not require the board of county commissioners to approve a budget for the probate court which exceeds the amount collected in the preceding year by that court. OAG 68–094.

5. Fees

Trial court abused its discretion when it ordered that special master appointed to settle fee dispute in guardianship matter be paid $11,855 for his fees and expenses, when there was no evidence in record to demonstrate such an amount was reasonable; while special master submitted exhibit listing dates and a brief statement of what was performed, services were itemized in too little detail to determine what these services entailed. In re Guardianship of Hards (Ohio App. 11 Dist., Lake, 08-08-2003) No. 2002-L-054, 2003-Ohio-4224, 2003 WL 21892925, Unreported, on subsequent appeal 2004-Ohio-4866, 2004 WL 2047486. Guardian And Ward 58

The words "fees earned," as used in RC 2101.11, mean fees collected by the probate court. State ex rel. Ray v. South (Ohio 1964) 176 Ohio St. 241, 198 N.E.2d 919, 27 O.O.2d 133.

Term "total fees earned by the probate court," refers to total fees charged by probate court for services rendered during calendar year, whether collected or not. 1948 OAG 2648.

6. Compensation

Although some measured increases in salaries in all categories of court personnel would have been reasonable and were necessary to retain quality of employees currently in county court of common pleas, overall budget submitted by court of common pleas relative to court personnel was unreasonable and unnecessary in that, in many categories, level of increases was at, or greater than, highest level of compensation provided in other counties, and increases were attempted to be accomplished in one year. State ex rel. Britt v. Board of County Com'rs, Franklin County (Ohio 1985) 18 Ohio St.3d 1, 480 N.E.2d 77, 18 O.B.R. 1. Counties 137

The statutory limitation on appointee compensation may not validly be applied when there is no showing that the judge has abused his discretion in establishing either the size or compensation ranges of his staff. State ex rel. Slaby v. Summit County Council (Summit 1983) 7 Ohio App.3d 199, 454 N.E.2d 1379, 7 O.B.R. 258. Constitutional Law 52; Officers And Public Employees 99

The mandatory duty of county commissioners under RC 2101.11, to appropriate annually such sum of money as will meet all the administrative expenses of the court, including the salaries of such appointees as the judge determines, provided that the total compensation paid to appointees in any calendar year shall not exceed the total fees earned by the court during the preceding calendar year unless approved by the board, is not enforceable by an action for contempt of court. In re Contempt of Common Pleas Court (Ohio 1972) 30 Ohio St.2d 182, 283 N.E.2d 126, 59 O.O.2d 188.

In the absence of an abuse of discretion on the part of the judge of the probate court in making up the annual budget, the board of county commissioners is obligated to appropriate annually such sum of money as will meet all the administrative expenses of such court which the judge thereof deems necessary, including such salaries of court appointees as the judge shall fix and determine, provided, however, that the total compensation of such appointees in any calendar year shall not exceed the total fees earned by the court during the preceding calendar year. State ex rel. Ray v. South (Ohio 1964) 176 Ohio St. 241, 198 N.E.2d 919, 27 O.O.2d 133.

A board of county commissioners acting to fix the compensation of deputies, assistants and other employees of a probate court must appropriate the amount deemed necessary by the judge of such court, subject to the limitation set by such section, in the absence of an abuse of discretion by such judge. OAG 65–032.

7. Administrative expenses

Regardless of statutory authorization, the judges of the courts of common pleas and their divisions have the inherent authority to determine in the first instance, in the exercise of sound discretion, the sum of money reasonable for the efficient operation of the court, and absent an abuse of discretion in the determination of such sum, may proceed either in contempt or mandamus to receive the necessary funding from their respective counties. State ex rel. Slaby v. Summit County Council

(Summit 1983) 7 Ohio App.3d 199, 454 N.E.2d 1379, 7 O.B.R. 258. Contempt ⊕ 2; Counties ⊕ 137; Mandamus ⊕ 100

As used in RC 2101.11 and RC 2151.10, "administrative expenses" of the juvenile and probate courts, respectively, include expenses of office equipment, stationery and supplies. State ex rel. Ray v. South (Ohio 1964) 176 Ohio St. 241, 198 N.E.2d 919, 27 O.O.2d 133.

8. Deputies

Perjury cannot be based on oath administered by deputy holding over his time. Staight v. State (Ohio 1883) 39 Ohio St. 496, 10 W.L.B. 424.

Deputy has authority to administer oaths. Warwick v. State (Ohio 1874) 25 Ohio St. 21.

Deputy may be a female. Warwick v. State (Ohio 1874) 25 Ohio St. 21.

9. Docketing

Where an action to contest a will is mistakenly docketed in the general division of the court of common pleas rather than the probate division of that court, prejudicial error is committed if the court dismisses the complaint instead of transferring the action to the docket of the probate division, pursuant to a motion of the complainant. Siebenthal v. Summers (Franklin 1978) 56 Ohio App.2d 168, 381 N.E.2d 1344, 10 O.O.3d 186. Courts ⊕ 50; Wills ⊕ 400

10. Appeal

A coexecutor dissatisfied with the finding and allowance of a personal claim by the probate court in favor of his coexecutor and desiring to appeal the same must file the undertaking required by this section. Downing v Downing, 3 CC(NS) 623, 13 CD 389 (Trumbull 1902).

2101.12 Records to be kept by probate court

The following records shall be kept by the probate court:

(A) An administration docket, showing the grant of letters of administration or letters testamentary, the name of the decedent, the amount of bond and names of sureties in the bond, and the date of filing and a brief note of each order or proceeding relating to the estate with reference to the journal or other record in which the order or proceeding is found;

(B) A guardian's docket, showing the name of each ward and, if the ward is an infant, the infant's age and the name of the infant's parents, the amount of bond and names of sureties in any bond, any limited powers or limited duration of powers, and the date of filing and a brief note of the orders and proceedings as described in division (A) of this section;

(C) A civil docket, in which shall be noted the names of parties to actions and proceedings, the date of the commencement of the actions and proceedings and of the filing of the papers relating to the actions and proceedings, a brief note of the orders made in the actions and proceedings, and the date of entering the orders;

(D) A journal, in which shall be kept minutes of official business transacted in the probate court, or by the probate judge, in civil actions and proceedings;

(E) A record of wills, in which the wills proved in the court shall be recorded with a certificate of the probate of the will, and wills proved elsewhere with the certificate of probate, authenticated copies of which have been admitted to record by the court;

(F) A final record that shall contain a complete record of each cause or matter and shall be completed within ninety days after the final order or judgment has been made in the cause or matter;

(G) An execution docket, in which shall be entered a memorandum of executions issued by the probate judge stating the names of the parties, the name of the person to whom the execution is delivered, the person's return on the execution, the date of issuing the execution, the amount ordered to be collected, stating the costs separately from the fine or damages, the payments on the execution, and the satisfaction of the execution when it is satisfied;

(H) A marriage record, in which shall be entered licenses, the names of the parties to whom a license is issued, the names of the persons applying for a license, a brief statement of the facts sworn to by persons applying for a license, and the returns of the person solemnizing the marriage;

(I) A naturalization record, in which shall be entered the declaration of intention of the person seeking to be naturalized, the oath of the person naturalized, and the affidavit or oath of witnesses who testify in the person's behalf, in which affidavit shall be stated the place of residence of the witnesses;

(J) A permanent record of all births and deaths occurring within the county, reported as provided by law, which record shall be kept in the form and manner that may be designated by the director of health;

(K) A separate record and index of adoptions, in accordance with section 3107.17 of the Revised Code;

(L) A summary release from administration docket, showing the date of the filing of the application for a summary release from administration pursuant to section 2113.031 of the Revised Code, the decedent's name, the applicant's name, whether the applicant is the decedent's surviving spouse or a person described in division (B)(1) of that section, and a brief note of the grant of the order of summary release from administration and of any other order or proceeding relating to the decedent's estate, with reference to the journal or other record in which the order or proceeding is found.

For each record required by this section, an index shall be maintained. Each index shall be kept current with the entries in the record and shall refer to the entries alphabetically by the names of the persons as they were originally entered, indexing the page of the record where the entry is made. On the order of the probate judge, blankbooks, other record forms, or other record-keeping materials approved by the judge for the records and indexes shall be furnished by the board of county commissioners at the expense of the county.

(2000 H 313, eff. 8–29–00; 1989 S 46, eff. 1–1–90; 1985 H 419; 1978 H 817; 1976 H 156; 1975 S 145; 129 v 1448, 1484; 125 v 903; 1953 H 1; GC 10501–15, 10501–16)

Historical and Statutory Notes

Pre–1953 H 1 Amendments: 114 v 324, 325

Amendment Note: 2000 H 313 added new division (L); inserted "probate" before "judge" in the last paragraph of the section; made changes to reflect gender neutral language; and made other nonsubstantive changes.

Cross References

Lost and destroyed probate court records, restoration, Ch 2729
Minister or official to certify each marriage to probate court, 3101.13
Public records, availability, 149.43
Will admitted to probate, filing and recording, 2107.20
Wills proved elsewhere, filing and recording in county of testator's real estate, 2107.21

Library References

Courts ⊕110.
Westlaw Topic No. 106.
C.J.S. Courts § 178.

Research References

Encyclopedias

OH Jur. 3d Aliens & Citizens § 17, Generally; Naturalization Proceedings.
OH Jur. 3d Courts & Judges § 66, Employment of Clerks and Other Employees of Probate Division; Care and Custody of Papers and Records.
OH Jur. 3d Courts & Judges § 205, Records of Court Judgments and Proceedings, and Miscellaneous Records Prescribed by Statute.
OH Jur. 3d Courts & Judges § 207, Dockets.

OH Jur. 3d Enforcement & Execution of Judgments § 381, Execution Docket and Index.
OH Jur. 3d Family Law § 32, Record and Certificate of Marriage.
OH Jur. 3d Fiduciaries § 176, Record that Bonds Were Approved.
OH Jur. 3d Health & Sanitation § 54, Generally; Administrative Provisions.
OH Jur. 3d Judgments § 62, Indexing.

Treatises and Practice Aids

Sowald & Morganstern, Baldwin's Ohio Practice Domestic Relations Law § 2:13, Ceremonial Marriage—Recording the License.

Notes of Decisions

Adoption 6
Births and deaths 5
Divorces 3
Duplication 7
Index 2
Inheritance tax 9
Journalization 1
Naturalization 8
Wills 4

---

1. Journalization

There is no requirement of journalization of appointment to statutorily created public offices by the probate court. State ex rel. Crance v. Kennedy (Ohio 1978) 53 Ohio St.2d 166, 373 N.E.2d 383, 7 O.O.3d 316.

Where the former judge of a juvenile-probate court found a minor child to be dependent and neglected but failed to journalize the entry, a successor judge may enter a nunc pro tunc entry in conformity therewith. In re Howell (Ohio Juv. 1956) 140 N.E.2d 347, 74 Ohio Law Abs. 217.

Neither this section nor GC 11604 (RC 2323.22) requires probate judge to sign journal entry of probate court. Rowe v. AEtna Cas. & Sur. Co. (Franklin 1941) 69 Ohio App. 291, 42 N.E.2d 706, 36 Ohio Law Abs. 36, 24 O.O. 74.

2. Index

Where probate court maintains in addition to records and indexes required by GC 10501-15 and 10501-16 (RC 2101.12) a coded card index, information from which is available to relator through court's clerks, mandamus will not lie to make such index available for inspection and use by relator abstract company and its employees, as respondent had not failed to perform act which law specially enjoins. State ex rel. Louisville Title Ins. Co. v. Brewer (Ohio 1946) 147 Ohio St. 161, 70 N.E.2d 265, 34 O.O. 36.

The probate court is required to keep books incorporating the records and data mentioned in RC 2101.12(A) to RC 2101.12(O) and may properly include in one book, provided the same is properly indexed, the dockets mentioned in RC 2101.12(B) to RC 2101.12(J) and RC 2101.12(L) of such section. OAG 67–060.

Probate court, by order duly entered, may include in one book, provided the same is properly indexed, the dockets mentioned in subsections two, three, four and nine of this section. 1948 OAG 3489.

3. Divorces

A nunc pro tunc decree of divorce entered on evidence of the probate judge's memorandum on his court calendar, which is not a public record as required by GC 1594 (RC 2101.12), is not sustained by legal evidence and should be reversed. Stark v. Stark (Ohio Cir. 1913) 24 Ohio C.D. 135, 17 Ohio C.C.(N.S.) 398, affirmed 88 Ohio St. 586, 106 N.E. 1078, 11 Ohio Law Rep. 62.

4. Wills

The court of common pleas has jurisdiction to set aside its order admitting a copy of a foreign will into record for misrepresentations by a party, and to order a new trial for irregularities in the proceedings. Lucas County Bd of Commrs v Millard, 4 NP 53, 4 D 419 (CP, Lucas 1896), affirmed by 13 CC 518, 7 CD 115 (Lucas 1897).

5. Births and deaths

Birth and death records kept by a probate court pursuant to RC 2101.12 are public records which must be made available to any member of the general public as required by RC 149.43, regardless of the motive which such member of the public has for inspecting such records. OAG 82–104.

A probate judge, after having accurately recorded a birth or death certificate, is without authority to change his records, but when an instrument has been erroneously recorded by a probate judge or his predecessor, he may, by amendment showing the purpose of such correction, correct his records to conform to the facts contained in the original instrument. 1940 OAG 1744.

The probate judge must keep a record of all births and deaths reported by local registrar of vital statistics. 1940 OAG 1744.

Probate judge can record only such information as has been duly transmitted to him according to law, and has no authority or duty to supply a missing birth or death certificate or to supply supplemental information to an incomplete certificate. 1940 OAG 1744.

6. Adoption

Proceedings in adoption cases should be separately recorded in a book kept for that purpose and separately indexed and should not be journalized or generally recorded. 1959 OAG 652.

7. Duplication

A probate court may make up the record required by RC 2101.12, RC 3107.14, RC 5123.37, RC 5123.38, and RC 5731.48 by microfilming or other duplication process authorized by RC 9.01, provided the originals are maintained on file until they are eventually destroyed, in accordance with RC 149.38. 1955 OAG 5667.

8. Naturalization

The records held by clerks of courts dealing with naturalization proceedings had prior to the Federal Naturalization Act of June 29, 1906, are not federal records and are subject to destruction pursuant to RC 149.38 and related sections. 1962 OAG 2986.

9. Inheritance tax

Probate court is required to keep books wherein shall be incorporated the records and data mentioned in this section; therefore said probate court, by order duly entered, may include in one book, provided same is as required by GC 10501–16 (RC 2101.12), the records and data mentioned in subsections five, six, seven, eight and eleven of this section; however, inheritance tax proceedings should be kept in a separate book in view of the terms of GC 5348–7 (RC 5731.48). 1948 OAG 3489.

2101.121 Record–keeping methods; equipment for examination; indices

(A) A probate court may keep and maintain records that are required by section 2101.12 or another section of the Revised Code by record-keeping methods other than bound volumes of paper pages. These record-keeping methods include, but are not limited to, photography, microphotography, photostatic process, electrostatic process, facsimile reproduction, perforated tape, magnetic tape or other electromagnetic methods, electronic data processing, machine-readable media, and graphic or video display.

(B) If a probate court keeps records by record-keeping methods other than bound volumes of paper pages, it shall possess, and make readily available to the public, machines or equipment necessary for an examination of the records. The machines or equipment shall present the records in a format that is readable without difficulty.

(C) If a probate court keeps records by record-keeping methods other than bound volumes of paper pages, it shall keep and maintain indices to the records that permit the records to be retrieved readily.

(1985 H 419, eff. 3–13–86)

Cross References

Probate division records, 2101.01
Public records, availability, 149.43

Library References

Courts ⇐113.
Westlaw Topic No. 106.
C.J.S. Courts §§ 179, 181.

Research References

Encyclopedias

OH Jur. 3d Courts & Judges § 205, Records of Court Judgments and Proceedings, and Miscellaneous Records Prescribed by Statute.

2101.13 Probate judge shall make entries omitted by his predecessor

When a probate judge, whether elected or appointed, enters upon the discharge of his duties, he shall make, in the books and other record-keeping materials of his office, the proper records, entries, and indexes omitted by his predecessors in office. When made, the entries shall have the same validity and effect as though they had been made at the proper time and by the officer whose duty it was to make them, and the judge shall sign all entries and records made by him as though the entries, proceedings, and records had been commenced, prosecuted, determined, and made by or before him.

(1985 H 419, eff. 3-13-86; 125 v 903; 1953 H 1; GC 10501-8)

Historical and Statutory Notes

Pre-1953 H 1 Amendments: 114 v 322

Library References

Judges ⇐32.
Westlaw Topic No. 227.
C.J.S. Judges § 63.

Research References

Encyclopedias

OH Jur. 3d Courts & Judges § 47, Successor Judges; Power as to Unfinished Business of Another Judge.
OH Jur. 3d Judgments § 85, Absence of Entry of Rendered Judgment.
OH Jur. 3d Records & Recording § 41, Nunc Pro Tunc Entries After Term of Court.

Notes of Decisions

Corrections 3
Discretionary acts 1
Juvenile proceedings 2

---

1. Discretionary acts

This section places upon successor judge duty to perform non-discretionary acts omitted by his predecessor, but does not place upon him duty to make journal entry allowing attorney fees, which involves the exercise of discretion. State ex rel. Egbert v. Leiser (Butler 1941) 67 Ohio App. 350, 36 N.E.2d 874, 34 Ohio Law Abs. 213, 21 O.O. 303.

2. Juvenile proceedings

This section applies to juvenile proceedings in a combined probate-juvenile court, and where the former judge of a juvenile-probate court found a minor child to be dependent and neglected but failed to journalize the entry, a successor judge may enter a nunc pro tunc entry in conformity therewith. In re Howell (Ohio Juv. 1956) 140 N.E.2d 347, 74 Ohio Law Abs. 217.

3. Corrections

A probate judge, after having accurately recorded a birth or death certificate, is without authority to change his records, but when an instrument has been erroneously recorded by a probate judge or his predecessor, he may, by amendment showing the purpose of such correction, correct his records to conform to the facts contained in the original instrument. 1940 OAG 1744.

2101.14 Care and preservation of papers; time stamp

All pleadings, accounts, vouchers, and other papers in each estate, trust, assignment, guardianship, or other proceeding, ex parte or adversary, which are filed in the probate court shall be kept together, and upon the final termination or settlement of the case, cause, or proceeding shall be preserved for future reference and examination. The papers shall be properly jacketed, and otherwise tied, fastened, or held together, numbered, lettered, or otherwise marked in such manner that they may be readily found by reference to proper memoranda upon the docket, record, or index entries thereof, which memoranda shall be made by the probate judge, or the papers may be kept, maintained, and indexed as described in section 2101.121 of the Revised Code. Certificates of marriage, reports of births and deaths, and similar papers not part of a case or proceeding, shall be arranged and preserved separately in the order of their dates or in which they were filed. As used in this section "case" or "cause" includes all proceedings in the settlement of any estate, guardianship, or assignment, except as provided in section 2101.141 of the Revised Code.

The probate court shall provide a time stamp and shall stamp on all papers filed in that court the day, month, and year of the filing.

(1985 H 419, eff. 3-13-86; 125 v 245; 1953 H 1; GC 10501-6, 10501-38)

Historical and Statutory Notes

Pre-1953 H 1 Amendments: 114 v 321, 329

Library References

Courts ⇐113.
Records ⇐8.
Westlaw Topic Nos. 106, 326.
C.J.S. Courts §§ 179, 181.
C.J.S. Records § 15.

Research References

Encyclopedias

OH Jur. 3d Courts & Judges § 66, Employment of Clerks and Other Employees of Probate Division; Care and Custody of Papers and Records.
OH Jur. 3d Records & Recording § 34, Preservation and Disposal—Probate Courts.

Forms

Ohio Jurisprudence Pleading and Practice Forms § 6:19, Cause.

2101.141 Disposition of obsolete papers

The vouchers, proof, or other evidence filed in support of the expenditures or distribution stated in an account, which has been filed in the probate court, may be ordered destroyed or otherwise disposed of five years after the account with which it was filed has been approved or settled and recorded and after there has been a compliance with section 149.38 of the Revised Code.

When the vouchers, proof, or other evidence filed in support of expenditures or distribution stated in an account are microfilmed, they may be ordered destroyed immediately after such record is made and, if required by law, after the approval and settlement of the account.

The inventories, schedules of debts, accounts, pleadings, wills, trusts, bonds, and other papers, excluding vouchers or other evidence of expenditures and distributions, filed in the probate courts by fiduciaries appointed by the probate courts, and all pleadings filed and court entries for the determination of inheritance tax under former sections 5731.01 to 5731.56 of the Revised Code, and estate tax under sections 5731.01 to 5731.51 of the Revised Code, and all documents filed or received and entries made by the court in conjunction with the instruments referred to in this section, after having been recorded, if required by law to be recorded, may be ordered microfilmed and destroyed after being microfilmed. All instruments referred to in this paragraph that are not microfilmed may be ordered destroyed or otherwise disposed of without microfilming after a period of twenty-one years has elapsed from the closing or termination of the administration of the estate, trust, or other fiduciary relationship and after there has been a compliance with section 149.38 of the Revised Code.

Nothing in this section shall apply to records pertaining to estates on which inheritance tax temporary orders are pending.

Prior to the order of the court directing the destruction or disposition of the vouchers, proof, or other evidence of expenditures or distribution, any party in interest, upon application filed, may have the vouchers, proof, or other evidence of expenditures or distribution recorded, upon payment of the costs incident to doing so.

An estate, trust, or other fiduciary relationship shall be deemed to be closed or terminated when a final accounting has been filed, and if required by law at the time of filing, the account has been approved and settled.

(1990 H 580, eff. 9–26–90; 1973 H 75; 1969 H 363; 131 v S 83; 125 v 245)

Library References

Records ⚖22.
Westlaw Topic No. 326.
C.J.S. Records §§ 32, 57 to 59.

Research References

Encyclopedias

OH Jur. 3d Courts & Judges § 66, Employment of Clerks and Other Employees of Probate Division; Care and Custody of Papers and Records.

OH Jur. 3d Decedents' Estates § 1668, Hearing on Account; Notice; Exceptions to Account.

OH Jur. 3d Records & Recording § 34, Preservation and Disposal—Probate Courts.

FEES AND COSTS

2101.15 Probate judge to file itemized account of fees with county auditor

In each case, examination, or proceeding, the probate judge shall file an itemized account of fees received or charged by him. On the first day of January, in each year, he shall file with the county auditor an account, certified by such judge, of all fees received by him during the preceding year. No judge shall fail to perform the duties imposed in this section. At the instance of any person, an action shall be instituted and prosecuted by the prosecuting attorney against any such defaulting judge.

(125 v 903, eff. 10–1–53; 1953 H 1; GC 10501–41)

Historical and Statutory Notes

Pre–1953 H 1 Amendments: 114 v 330

Cross References

Penalty: 2101.99(B)

Library References

Judges ⚖22(12).
Westlaw Topic No. 227.
C.J.S. Judges §§ 75, 82.

Notes of Decisions

Journalized orders 1

1. **Journalized orders**

A record book for cost bills must be furnished by the county. Lucas County Bd of Commrs v Millard, 4 NP 53, 4 D 419 (CP, Lucas 1896), affirmed by 13 CC 518, 7 CD 115 (Lucas 1897).

Probate judges are entitled to six cents per hundred words for orders entered on journal. State ex rel Martin v Adams, 8 CC(NS) 513, 18 CD 643 (Columbiana 1906).

2101.16 Fees; cost of investigations; advance deposit

(A) The fees enumerated in this division shall be charged and collected, if possible, by the probate judge and shall be in full for all services rendered in the respective proceedings:

(1) Account, in addition to advertising charges $12.00
    Waivers and proof of notice of hearing on account, per page, minimum one dollar .... $ 1.00
(2) Account of distribution, in addition to advertising charges .... $ 7.00
(3) Adoption of child, petition for $50.00
(4) Alter or cancel contract for sale or purchase of real estate, petition to $20.00
(5) Application and order not otherwise provided for in this section or by rule adopted pursuant to division (E) of this section .... $ 5.00
(6) Appropriation suit, per day, hearing in $20.00
(7) Birth, application for registration of .... $ 7.00
(8) Birth record, application to correct .... $ 5.00
(9) Bond, application for new or additional ..... $ 5.00
(10) Bond, application for release of surety or reduction of .... $ 5.00
(11) Bond, receipt for securities deposited in lieu of .... $ 5.00
(12) Certified copy of journal entry, record, or proceeding, per page, minimum fee one dollar .... $ 1.00
(13) Citation and issuing citation, application for .... $ 5.00
(14) Change of name, petition for $20.00
(15) Claim, application of administrator or executor for allowance of administrator's or executor's own $10.00
(16) Claim, application to compromise or settle $10.00
(17) Claim, authority to present $10.00
(18) Commissioner, appointment of .... $ 5.00
(19) Compensation for extraordinary services and attorney's fees for fiduciary, application for .... $ 5.00

(20) Competency, application to procure adjudication of $20.00
(21) Complete contract, application to $10.00
(22) Concealment of assets, citation for $10.00
(23) Construction of will, petition for $20.00
(24) Continue decedent's business, application to $10.00
Monthly reports of operation .... $ 5.00
(25) Declaratory judgment, petition for $20.00
(26) Deposit of will .... $ 5.00
(27) Designation of heir $20.00
(28) Distribution in kind, application, assent, and order for .... $ 5.00
(29) Distribution under section 2109.36 of the Revised Code, application for an order of .... $ 7.00
(30) Docketing and indexing proceedings, including the filing and noting of all necessary documents, maximum fee, fifteen dollars $15.00
(31) Exceptions to any proceeding named in this section, contest of appointment or ... $10.00
(32) Election of surviving partner to purchase assets of partnership, proceedings relating to $10.00
(33) Election of surviving spouse under will ...... $ 5.00
(34) Fiduciary, including an assignee or trustee of an insolvent debtor or any guardian or conservator accountable to the probate court, appointment of $35.00
(35) Foreign will, application to record $10.00
Record of foreign will, additional, per page .... $ 1.00
(36) Forms when supplied by the probate court, not to exceed $10.00
(37) Heirship, petition to determine $20.00
(38) Injunction proceedings $20.00
(39) Improve real estate, petition to $20.00
(40) Inventory with appraisement $10.00
(41) Inventory without appraisement .... $ 7.00
(42) Investment or expenditure of funds, application for $10.00
(43) Invest in real estate, application to $10.00
(44) Lease for oil, gas, coal, or other mineral, petition to $20.00
(45) Lease or lease and improve real estate, petition to $20.00
(46) Marriage license $10.00
Certified abstract of each marriage .... $ 2.00
(47) Minor or mentally ill person, etc., disposal of estate under ten thousand dollars of $10.00
(48) Mortgage or mortgage and repair or improve real estate, petition to $20.00
(49) Newly discovered assets, report of .... $ 7.00
(50) Nonresident executor or administrator to bar creditors' claims, proceedings by $20.00
(51) Power of attorney or revocation of power, bonding company $10.00
(52) Presumption of death, petition to establish $20.00
(53) Probating will $15.00
Proof of notice to beneficiaries .... $ 5.00
(54) Purchase personal property, application of surviving spouse to $10.00
(55) Purchase real estate at appraised value, petition of surviving spouse to $20.00
(56) Receipts in addition to advertising charges, application and order to record .... $ 5.00
Record of those receipts, additional, per page .... $ 1.00
(57) Record in excess of fifteen hundred words in any proceeding in the probate court, per page .... $ 1.00
(58) Release of estate by mortgagee or other lienholder .... $ 5.00
(59) Relieving an estate from administration under section 2113.03 of the Revised Code or granting an order for a summary release from administration under section 2113.031 of the Revised Code $60.00
(60) Removal of fiduciary, application for $10.00
(61) Requalification of executor or administrator $10.00
(62) Resignation of fiduciary .... $ 5.00
(63) Sale bill, public sale of personal property $10.00
(64) Sale of personal property and report, application for $10.00
(65) Sale of real estate, petition for $25.00
(66) Terminate guardianship, petition to $10.00
(67) Transfer of real estate, application, entry, and certificate for .... $ 7.00
(68) Unclaimed money, application to invest ..... $ 7.00
(69) Vacate approval of account or order of distribution, motion to $10.00
(70) Writ of execution .... $ 5.00
(71) Writ of possession .... $ 5.00
(72) Wrongful death, application and settlement of claim for $20.00
(73) Year's allowance, petition to review .... $ 7.00
(74) Guardian's report, filing and review of ...... $ 5.00

(B)(1) In relation to an application for the appointment of a guardian or the review of a report of a guardian under section 2111.49 of the Revised Code, the probate court, pursuant to court order or in accordance with a court rule, may direct that the applicant or the estate pay any or all of the expenses of an investigation conducted pursuant to section 2111.041 or division (A)(2) of section 2111.49 of the Revised Code. If the investigation is conducted by a public employee or investigator who is paid by the county, the fees for the investigation shall be paid into the county treasury. If the court finds that an alleged incompetent or a ward is indigent, the court may waive the costs, fees, and expenses of an investigation.

(2) In relation to the appointment or functioning of a guardian for a minor or the guardianship of a minor, the probate court may direct that the applicant or the estate pay any or all of the expenses of an investigation conducted pursuant to section 2111.042 of the Revised Code. If the investigation is conducted by a public employee or investigator who is paid by the county, the fees for the investigation shall be paid into the county treasury. If the court finds that the guardian or applicant is indigent, the court may waive the costs, fees, and expenses of an investigation.

(C) Thirty dollars of the thirty-five-dollar fee collected pursuant to division (A)(34) of this section and twenty dollars of the sixty-dollar fee collected pursuant to division (A)(59) of this section shall be deposited by the county treasurer in the indigent guardianship fund created pursuant to section 2111.51 of the Revised Code.

(D) The fees of witnesses, jurors, sheriffs, coroners, and constables for services rendered in the probate court or by order of the probate judge shall be the same as provided for like services in the court of common pleas.

(E) The probate court, by rule, may require an advance deposit for costs, not to exceed one hundred twenty-five dollars, at the time application is made for an appointment as executor or administrator or at the time a will is presented for probate.

(F) The probate court, by rule, shall establish a reasonable fee, not to exceed fifty dollars, for the filing of a petition for the release of information regarding an adopted person's name by birth and the identity of the adopted person's biological parents and biological siblings pursuant to section 3107.41 of the Revised Code, all proceedings relative to the petition, the entry of an order relative to the petition, and all services required to be performed in connection with the petition. The probate court may use a reasonable portion of a fee charged under authority of this division to reimburse any agency, as defined in section 3107.39 of the Revised Code, for any services it renders in performing a task described in section 3107.41 of the Revised Code relative to or in connection with the petition for which the fee was charged.

(G)(1) Thirty dollars of the fifty-dollar fee collected pursuant to division (A)(3) of this section shall be deposited into the "putative father registry fund," which is hereby created in the state treasury. The department of job and family services shall use the money in the fund to fund the department's costs of performing its duties related to the putative father registry established under section 3107.062 of the Revised Code.

(2) If the department determines that money in the putative father registry fund is more than is needed for its duties related to the putative father registry, the department may use the surplus moneys in the fund as permitted in division (C) of section 2151.3529, division (B) of section 2151.3530, or section 5103.155 of the Revised Code.

(2003 H 95, eff. 6-26-03; 2000 H 313, eff. 8-29-00; 1999 H 471, eff. 7-1-00; 1996 H 419, eff. 9-18-96; 1994 H 457, eff. 11-9-94; 1993 H 9, eff. 9-14-93; 1992 H 89; 1989 S 46; 1985 H 419; 1984 H 84; 1982 H 317; 1977 H 1; 1976 S 466, H 740; 1975 S 145, H 1; 126 v 607; 1953 H 1; GC 10501-20, 10501-42)

Uncodified Law

1994 H 457, § 3, eff. 11-9-94, reads: Sections 2101.16, 2111.51, and 2113.03 of the Revised Code, as amended by this act, and section 2111.042 of the Revised Code, as enacted by this act, apply to the estates of decedents who die on or after the effective date of this act.

1993 H 9, § 3, eff. 9-14-93, reads: Sections 2101.16, 2111.51, and 2113.03 of the Revised Code, as amended by this act, shall apply to the estates of decedents who die on or after the effective date of this act.

1992 H 89, § 3, eff. 4-16-93, reads: Sections 2101.16 and 2113.03 of the Revised Code, as amended by this act, shall apply only to the estates of decedents who die on or after the effective date of this act.

Historical and Statutory Notes

Pre-1953 H 1 Amendments: 119 v 297; 115 v 393; 114 v 326, 330

Amendment Note: 2003 H 95 redesignated former division (G) as (G)(1); and added (G)(2).

Amendment Note: 2000 H 313 rewrote this section. See *Baldwin's Ohio Legislative Service Annotated*, 2000, p 4/L–798, or the OH–LEGIS or OH–LEGIS–OLD database on Westlaw, for prior version of this section.

Amendment Note: 1999 H 471 substituted "job and family" for "human" in division (G).

Amendment Note: 1996 H 419 substituted "$50.00" for "$20.00" in division (A)(3), "administrator's or executor's" for "his" in division (A)(15), and "writ" for "write" in divisions (A)(70) and (71); substituted "the adopted person's" for "his" in division (F); added division (G); and made a nonsubstantive change.

Amendment Note: 1994 H 457 rewrote division (A)(59); designated division (B)(1); added division (B)(2); and substituted "sixty" for "seventy" and deleted "(b)" after "(A)(59)" in division (C). Prior to amendment, division (A)(59) read:

"(59) Relieving estate from administration:

"(a) Value of the estate is twenty-five thousand dollars or less $30.00
"(b) Value of the estate is eighty-five thousand dollars or less and division (A)(2) of section 2113.03 of the Revised Code applies .... $70.00"

Amendment Note: 1993 H 9 substituted "$70.00" for "$50.00" in division (A)(59)(b); and inserted "and twenty dollars of the seventy-dollar fee collected pursuant to division (A)(59)(b) of this section" in division (C).

Cross References

Additional marriage license fee for domestic violence shelters, 3113.34
Court costs, Sup R 58
Distribution of forms and materials by job and family services department, 2151.3530.
Executors and administrators, fees, 2113.63
Fees, costs, and percentages shall be for use of county, 325.27
Fees of probate judge relating to assignment for benefit of creditors, 1313.52
Guardian, one bond and application for letters for two or more wards, 2109.16
Receipt for fees, 325.28
Rights of an adult who believes he is an adopted person to petition for information, fees, 3107.41
Summary release from administration by person obligated to pay decedent's funeral and burial expenses, application, 2113.031

Library References

Clerks of Courts ⚖17.
Judges ⚖22(1), 22(5).
Westlaw Topic Nos. 227, 79.
C.J.S. Courts §§ 242 to 243.
C.J.S. Judges §§ 75 to 77, 84.

Research References

Encyclopedias

OH Jur. 3d Courts & Judges § 197, Statutory Authorization of Filing Fees; Fees of Particular Clerks or for Particular Services.
OH Jur. 3d Enforcement & Execution of Judgments § 52, Probate Court.
OH Jur. 3d Family Law § 27, Issuance of Marriage License; License Requirements and Fees.
OH Jur. 3d Fiduciaries § 8, Fees or Costs.
OH Jur. 3d Jury § 233, Compensation of Trial Jurors.
OH Jur. 3d Police, Sheriffs, & Related Officers § 47, Other Sheriff's Fees.

Forms

Ohio Jurisprudence Pleading and Practice Forms § 96:36, Adult Adopted Person's Petition for Information.

Treatises and Practice Aids

Baldwin's Ohio Handbook Series—Trial Handbook § 11:5, Compensation.
Klein, Darling, & Terez, Baldwin's Ohio Practice Civil Practice § 73:6, Probate Division--Service of Notice.
Carlin, Baldwin's Ohio Practice, Merrick-Rippner Probate Law § 6:6, Declaratory Judgments—Probate Court Proceedings.
Carlin, Baldwin's Ohio Practice, Merrick-Rippner Probate Law § 3:16, Dispute Resolution Procedure in Probate Court.
Carlin, Baldwin's Ohio Practice, Merrick-Rippner Probate Law § 38:2, Will Contests—Statutory Provisions.
Carlin, Baldwin's Ohio Practice, Merrick-Rippner Probate Law § 43:4, Construing a Will—Action for Construction—Function of the Court.
Carlin, Baldwin's Ohio Practice, Merrick-Rippner Probate Law § 65:1, Litigation Involving Guardians—Guardian May Sue or be Sued; Intervenor—Dispute Resolution Procedure.
Carlin, Baldwin's Ohio Practice, Merrick-Rippner Probate Law § 38:12, Will Contests—Pretrial Procedure.

Carlin, Baldwin's Ohio Practice, Merrick-Rippner Probate Law § 38:15, Will Contests—Trial—Juries.

Carlin, Baldwin's Ohio Practice, Merrick-Rippner Probate Law § 56:15, Concealed or Embezzled Assets—Right to Trial by Jury—Dispute Resolution Procedure.

Carlin, Baldwin's Ohio Practice, Merrick-Rippner Probate Law § 62:46, Guardianship Proceedings—Costs.

Carlin, Baldwin's Ohio Practice, Merrick-Rippner Probate Law § 62:49, Guardianship Proceedings—Advance Deposit of Costs.

Notes of Decisions

Affidavits 10
Compensation not required 1
Complete record 6
Copies 9
Court calendar 7
Entertainment permit 8
Estates 2
Lunacy inquests 5
Proceedings under seal 4
Rules of practice 3

1. Compensation not required

A probate judge is required to record cost bills but is not entitled to compensation therefor. Millard v Lucas County Bd of Commrs, 4 NP 53, 4 D 419 (CP, Lucas 1896), affirmed by 13 CC 518, 7 CD 115 (Lucas 1897).

A probate judge is not entitled to fees for making out report of social statistics. Swartz v Wayne County Bd of Commrs, OS Unrep 428, 35 B 275 (1896).

As a public officer, a probate judge is not entitled to compensation for any service which is part of his official duties, unless the fee therefor is fixed by statute. Millard v Lucas County Bd of Commrs, 13 CC 518, 7 CD 115 (Lucas 1897).

2. Estates

Where testator executed a will which provided that charitable beneficiaries receive the residual portion of the estate, and such bequest is limited to twenty-five per cent of the estate because of the mortmain statute, the statutorily created residuary share is chargeable with estate taxes, fees and costs of administration. Woods v. Neissen (Summit 1983) 11 Ohio App.3d 62, 463 N.E.2d 92, 11 O.B.R. 96.

A probate court has power to requalify a discharged fiduciary and reopen an estate for proper cause, as indicated by the provision of a fee therefor by RC 2101.16(A)(63). In re McDonald's Estate (Ohio Prob. 1966) 15 Ohio Misc. 74, 239 N.E.2d 277, 44 O.O.2d 262.

The limitation of a maximum of $10 in probate court fees chargeable in an estate, the assets of which do not exceed $500, as provided for in this section, does not apply to a proceeding for settling a claim for wrongful injury; such limitation only applies to proceedings in an estate listed in said section where the costs are taxed against the fiduciary in his fiduciary capacity, and not to proceedings where the costs are taxed to other persons, or to proceedings not listed therein. (Ed. note: See also RC 2113.03 as to present limitations in relieving an estate from administration.) In re Crum, 31 NP(NS) 105 (Prob, Tuscarawas 1933).

Each step in an estate of guardianship is considered a separate proceeding under Rule 39 of the Uniform Rules of Practice in Probate Courts of Ohio, 11 Abs 385. As to each such proceeding costs must be taxed under the fee schedule in effect when the proceeding is made, and not under the fee schedule in effect on the date of decedent's death or the date the estate is opened in probate court. In re Murphy's Estate (Ohio Prob. 1932) 29 Ohio NP(NS) 183.

The term "assets" as used in paragraph 48 (now (76)) of this section, in connection with the word "estates," includes real estate which is available for or may be appropriated to the payment of the debts of an estate. 1935 OAG 3977.

3. Rules of practice

Uniform rules of practice in probate courts of Ohio, approved by Supreme Court, February 24, 1932. Uniform Rules of Practice in Probate Courts of Ohio, 11 Abs 385 (1932).

4. Proceedings under seal

A probate judge is entitled to eight cents per hundred words fee for copies of records of proceedings under seal, and since the certificate of the medical witness and his findings are part of the record in the proceedings, the judge is not entitled to an additional thirty-five cents for such a certificate. State ex rel Martin v Adams, 8 CC(NS) 513, 18 CD 643 (Columbiana 1906).

5. Lunacy inquests

Costs and fees of the probate court are compensation authorized in lunacy inquests. Millard v Conradi, 5 CC(NS) 145, 16 CD 445 (Lucas 1904), appeal dismissed by 51 B 234 (OS 1906).

6. Complete record

A complete record shall not be made by a probate judge in any case except when the title to real estate is drawn in question, or when the court may order it, or when either party may require it at his own cost. Millard v Lucas County Bd of Commrs, 13 CC 518, 7 CD 115 (Lucas 1897).

7. Court calendar

There is no law requiring or authorizing a probate judge to keep the book which is called the court calendar. Millard v Lucas County Bd of Commrs, 4 NP 53, 4 D 419 (CP, Lucas 1896), affirmed by 13 CC 518, 7 CD 115 (Lucas 1897).

8. Entertainment permit

Charge to be made by a probate judge for a permit for public dancing, roller skating or like entertainment, under GC 13393 (RC 3773.19), shall, by provisions of this section, be five dollars. 1940 OAG 2159.

9. Copies

Charge for certification by a probate judge of the correctness of a copy of an original journal entry or proceeding is governed by GC 2901 (RC 2303.20). 1939 OAG 1454.

Charges for typing of a copy of journal entry, record or proceeding made by deputy of the probate court, working after office hours, are matters of personal concern between the deputy and the person requesting the copy and are not made the subject of statutory regulation. 1939 OAG 1454.

10. Affidavits

A probate judge should charge the sums provided by GC 2900 and GC 2901 (RC 2303.20) for taking affidavits and acknowledgments in cases docketed in the probate court. 1936 OAG 5092.

2101.161 Deposit of prepaid and unearned costs; interest

The probate court may order that prepaid and unearned costs be deposited with a bank, savings bank, savings and loan association, credit union, or trust company incorporated under the laws of this state or of the United States. The order shall be entered on the journal of the court and may specify that deposited costs are to be held in an account, or invested in an investment, supervised by the bank, savings bank, association, credit union, or company. Interest earned on deposited costs shall be paid into the county treasury by the end of the calendar year in which it is received.

(2005 H 81, eff. 4–14–06; 1985 H 419, eff. 3–13–86)

Historical and Statutory Notes

Amendment Note: 2005 H 81 inserted "savings bank, " and "credit union," in the first and second sentence.

Library References

Deposits and Escrows ⚖31.
Westlaw Topic No. 122A.
C.J.S. Depositaries §§ 54 to 61.

Research References

Encyclopedias

OH Jur. 3d Courts & Judges § 198, Prepayment of Fees.

2101.162   Additional fees for computer services

(A)(1) The probate judge may determine that, for the efficient operation of the probate court, additional funds are required to computerize the court, make available computerized legal research services, or to do both. Upon making a determination that additional funds are required for either or both of those purposes, the probate judge shall charge a fee not to exceed three dollars or authorize and direct a deputy clerk of his court to charge a fee not to exceed three dollars, in addition to the fees specified in divisions (A)(1), (3), (4), (6), (14) to (17), (20) to (25), (27), (30) to (32), (34), (35), (37) to (48), (50) to (55), (59) to (61), (63) to (66), (69), and (72) of section 2101.16 of the Revised Code, the fee adopted pursuant to division (F) of that section, and the fee charged in connection with the docketing and indexing of an appeal.

(2) All moneys collected under division (A)(1) of this section shall be paid to the county treasurer. The treasurer shall place the moneys from the fees in a separate fund to be disbursed, upon an order of the probate judge, in an amount no greater than the actual cost to the court of procuring and maintaining computerization of the court, computerized legal research services, or both.

(3) If the court determines that the funds in the fund described in division (A)(2) of this section are more than sufficient to satisfy the purpose for which the additional fee described in division (A)(1) of this section was imposed, the court may declare a surplus in the fund and expend those surplus funds for other appropriate technological expenses of the court.

(B)(1) The probate judge may determine that, for the efficient operation of his court, additional funds are required to computerize the office of the clerk of the court and, upon that determination, may charge a fee, not to exceed ten dollars, or authorize and direct a deputy clerk of the probate court to charge a fee, not to exceed ten dollars, in addition to the fees specified in divisions (A)(1), (3), (4), (6), (14) to (17), (20) to (25), (27), (30) to (32), (34), (35), (37) to (48), (50) to (55), (59) to (61), (63) to (66), (69), and (72) of section 2101.16 of the Revised Code, the fee adopted pursuant to division (F) of that section, and the fee charged in connection with the docketing and indexing of an appeal. Subject to division (B)(2) of this section, all moneys collected under this division shall be paid to the county treasurer to be disbursed, upon an order of the probate judge and subject to appropriation by the board of county commissioners, in an amount no greater than the actual cost to the probate court of procuring and maintaining computer systems for the office of the clerk of the court.

(2) If the probate judge makes the determination described in division (B)(1) of this section, the board of county commissioners may issue one or more general obligation bonds for the purpose of procuring and maintaining the computer systems for the office of the clerk of the probate court. In addition to the purposes stated in division (B)(1) of this section for which the moneys collected under that division may be expended, the moneys additionally may be expended to pay debt charges on and financing costs related to any general obligation bonds issued pursuant to this division as they become due. General obligation bonds issued pursuant to this division are Chapter 133. securities.

(1992 S 246, eff. 3-24-93; 1992 H 405)

Cross References

Net indebtedness of county, securities not considered in calculation of, 133.07

Library References

Clerks of Courts ⚖=17.
Judges ⚖=22(0.5).
Westlaw Topic Nos. 227, 79.
C.J.S. Courts §§ 242 to 243.
C.J.S. Judges § 75.

2101.163   Fee for dispute resolution procedures

(A) A probate judge may establish by rule procedures for the resolution of disputes between parties to any civil action or proceeding that is within the jurisdiction of the probate court. Any procedures so adopted shall include, but are not limited to, mediation. If the probate judge establishes any procedures under this division, the probate judge may charge, in addition to the fees and costs authorized under section 2101.16 of the Revised Code, a reasonable fee, not to exceed fifteen dollars, that is to be collected on the filing of each action or proceeding and that is to be used to implement the procedures.

(B) The probate court shall pay to the county treasurer of the county in which the court is located all fees collected under division (A) of this section. The treasurer shall place the funds from the fees in a separate fund to be disbursed upon an order of the probate judge.

(C) If the probate judge determines that the amount of the moneys in the fund described in division (B) of this section is more than the amount that is sufficient to satisfy the purpose for which the additional fee described in division (A) of this section was imposed, the probate judge may declare a surplus in the fund and expend the surplus moneys for other appropriate judicial expenses of the probate court.

(2003 H 51, eff. 4-8-04)

Uncodified Law

2004 H 161, § 3, eff. 4-8-04 reads, in part:

(B) Section 2101.163 of the Revised Code, as enacted by Am. Sub. H.B. 51 of the 125th General Assembly, applies to civil actions and proceedings that are pending in or brought before the probate court on or after April 8, 2004.

Historical and Statutory Notes

Ed. Note: Former 2101.163 repealed by 2001 S 108, eff. 7-6-01; 1996 H 350, eff. 1-27-97 [1].

[1] See Notes of Decisions, *State ex rel. Ohio Academy of Trial Lawyers v. Sheward* (Ohio 1999), 86 Ohio St.3d 451, 715 N.E.2d 1062.

Library References

Courts ⚖=80(5).
Judges ⚖=22(0.5).
Westlaw Topic Nos. 106, 227.
C.J.S. Courts § 128.
C.J.S. Judges § 75.

Research References

Encyclopedias

OH Jur. 3d Alternative Dispute Resolution § 14, Court-Annexed Adr, Generally.

OH Jur. 3d Alternative Dispute Resolution § 188, Court-Annexed Mediation Programs.

OH Jur. 3d Courts & Judges § 67, Miscellaneous Powers and Functions of Probate Judge.

Treatises and Practice Aids

Carlin, Baldwin's Ohio Practice, Merrick-Rippner Probate Law § 3:2, Jurisdiction of Probate Court—Statutory.

Carlin, Baldwin's Ohio Practice, Merrick-Rippner Probate Law § 3:3, Jurisdiction of Probate Court—Subject Matter—in General.

Carlin, Baldwin's Ohio Practice, Merrick-Rippner Probate Law § 6:6, Declaratory Judgments—Probate Court Proceedings.

Carlin, Baldwin's Ohio Practice, Merrick-Rippner Probate Law § 3:16, Dispute Resolution Procedure in Probate Court.

Carlin, Baldwin's Ohio Practice, Merrick-Rippner Probate Law § 38:2, Will Contests—Statutory Provisions.

Carlin, Baldwin's Ohio Practice, Merrick-Rippner Probate Law § 43:4, Construing a Will—Action for Construction—Function of the Court.

Carlin, Baldwin's Ohio Practice, Merrick-Rippner Probate Law § 65:1, Litigation Involving Guardians—Guardian May Sue or be Sued; Intervenor—Dispute Resolution Procedure.

Carlin, Baldwin's Ohio Practice, Merrick-Rippner Probate Law § 38:12, Will Contests—Pretrial Procedure.

Carlin, Baldwin's Ohio Practice, Merrick-Rippner Probate Law § 38:15, Will Contests—Trial—Juries.

Carlin, Baldwin's Ohio Practice, Merrick-Rippner Probate Law § 56:15, Concealed or Embezzled Assets—Right to Trial by Jury—Dispute Resolution Procedure.

Ohio Personal Injury Practice App. C, Appendix C. Ohio Academy of Trial Lawyers v. Sheward.

Notes of Decisions

Constitutional issues   1

1. Constitutional issues

1996 H 350, which amended more than 100 statutes and a variety of rules relating to tort and other civil actions, and which was an attempt to reenact provisions of law previously held unconstitutional by the Supreme Court of Ohio, is an act of usurpation of judicial power in violation of the doctrine of separation of powers; for that reason, and because of violation of the one-subject rule of the Ohio Constitution, 1996 H 350 is unconstitutional. State ex rel. Ohio Academy of Trial Lawyers v. Sheward (Ohio, 08-16-1999) 86 Ohio St.3d 451, 715 N.E.2d 1062, 1999-Ohio-123, reconsideration denied 87 Ohio St.3d 1409, 716 N.E.2d 1170.

2101.17   Fees from county treasury

The fees enumerated in this section shall be paid to the probate court from the county treasury upon the warrant of the county auditor which shall issue upon the certificate of the probate judge and shall be in full for all services rendered in the respective proceedings as follows:

(A) For each hearing to determine if a person is a mentally ill individual subject to hospitalization when the person is committed to a state hospital or to relatives $12.00;

(B) When the person is discharged 7.00;

(C) For order of return of a mentally ill person to a state hospital or removal therefrom 2.00;

(D) For proceedings for committing a person to an institution for the mentally retarded 10.00;

(E) For habeas corpus proceedings when a person is confined under color of proceedings in a criminal case and is discharged 10.00;

(F) When acting as a juvenile judge, for each case filed against a delinquency, dependent, unruly, or neglected child, or a juvenile traffic offender 5.00;

(G) For proceedings to take a child from parents or other persons having control thereof .... 5.00.

(1975 S 145, eff. 1-1-76; 1953 H 1; GC 10501-43)

Historical and Statutory Notes

Pre–1953 H 1 Amendments: 114 v 332

Library References

Counties ⇌138.
Westlaw Topic No. 104.
C.J.S. Counties § 175.

Research References

Encyclopedias

OH Jur. 3d Courts & Judges § 197, Statutory Authorization of Filing Fees; Fees of Particular Clerks or for Particular Services.

2101.18   Fees for other services

For services for which compensation is not provided but subject to section 2101.27 of the Revised Code insofar as the probate judge solemnizes marriages, the probate judge shall be allowed the same fees as are allowed the clerk of the court of common pleas for similar services.

The probate judge shall administer oaths and make certificates in pension and bounty cases without compensation.

(1990 H 211, eff. 4-11-91; 1953 H 1; GC 10501-44, 10501-46)

Historical and Statutory Notes

Pre–1953 H 1 Amendments: 114 v 332, 333

Cross References

Fees of clerk of common pleas court, 2303.20
Fees of probate judge relating to assignment for benefit of creditors, 1313.52

Library References

Judges ⇌22(1).
Westlaw Topic No. 227.
C.J.S. Judges §§ 75 to 76, 84.

Research References

Encyclopedias

OH Jur. 3d Courts & Judges § 197, Statutory Authorization of Filing Fees; Fees of Particular Clerks or for Particular Services.

Notes of Decisions

Compensation not required   2
Notices   3
Pensions and bounties   1

1. Pensions and bounties

The provision as to oaths and certificates in pension and bounty cases applies to all oaths and certificates required under the laws of the United States in the procurement of pensions and bounties. Fees for Certificates as to Death, Marriage and Birth Records and Administering Oaths, 6 LR 341 (OAG 1908).

2. Compensation not required

No fees will be allowed for record of cost bills. Millard v Lucas County Bd of Commrs, 4 NP 53, 4 D 419 (CP, Lucas 1896), affirmed by 13 CC 518, 7 CD 115 (Lucas 1897).

A probate judge is not entitled to compensation for appointment of county treasury examiners. Millard v Conradi, 5 CC(NS) 145, 16 CD 445 (Lucas 1904), appeal dismissed by 51 B 234 (OS 1906).

3. Notices

Costs of legal advertising or printer's fees for the publication of notice of appointment and other notices necessary to be made or published in the probate court are not such costs as referred to in paragraph 48 (now (76)) of GC 10501-42 (RC 2101.16), and are properly chargeable by the probate judge in addition to the $10.00 minimum fee in estates not exceeding $500.00 in total value. 1937 OAG 441.

2101.19 Limitation of charges by probate judge; probate court conduct of business fund

(A) No probate judge or his deputy clerk shall sell or offer for sale for more than one dollar any merchandise to be used in connection with any license, order, or document issued by the probate court, or make any charge in connection with the issuance of any license, order, or document except that specifically provided by law.

(B) All moneys obtained from the sale of merchandise to be used in connection with any license, order, or document issued by a probate court shall be paid by the probate judge or the deputy clerk of the court into the county treasury. The moneys shall be credited to a fund to be known as the probate court conduct of business fund. The moneys so credited shall be used solely for the conduct of the business of the probate court.

Upon receipt of an order of the probate judge for the payment of moneys from the fund for the conduct of the business of the court, the county auditor shall draw a warrant on the county treasurer for the amount of money specified in the order, but not exceeding the balance of the moneys in the fund, which warrant shall be made payable to the probate judge or another person designated in the order.

(1985 H 419, eff. 3-13-86; 1953 H 1; GC 10501-64)

Historical and Statutory Notes

Pre-1953 H 1 Amendments: 120 v 330, § 2

Library References

Clerks of Courts ⇌11.
Judges ⇌22(5).
Westlaw Topic Nos. 227, 79.
C.J.S. Courts §§ 242, 244.
C.J.S. Judges §§ 75, 77.

Notes of Decisions

Marriage certificates 1

---

1. Marriage certificates

Although RC 2101.19 impliedly authorizes a probate court judge to sell marriage certificates providing the cost does not exceed one dollar, O Const Art IV, § 6(B), prohibits the judge from retaining the proceeds personally; such proceeds must be paid over to the county pursuant to RC 325.27. OAG 82-022.

2101.20 Reduction of fees

When the aggregate amount of fees and allowances collected by the probate judge in any calendar year exceeds by more than ten per cent the amount necessary to pay the salaries of said judge and the employees of the probate court, including court constables, for the same calendar year, such judge may, by an order entered on his journal, provide for a discount of all the fees and allowances he is required to charge and collect for the use of the county by fixing a per cent of discount which shall be applied to all the earnings of said office for the ensuing year and shall constitute the legal fees of said office for said year.

(1953 H 1, eff. 10-1-53; GC 10501-45)

Historical and Statutory Notes

Pre-1953 H 1 Amendments: 114 v 332

Library References

Judges ⇌22(5).
Westlaw Topic No. 227.
C.J.S. Judges §§ 75, 77.

Research References

Encyclopedias
OH Jur. 3d Courts & Judges § 197, Statutory Authorization of Filing Fees; Fees of Particular Clerks or for Particular Services.

Notes of Decisions

Salaries 1

---

1. Salaries

Probation officers are not to be considered employees of the office of the probate judge, in determining whether the fees collected during any calendar year exceed by more than ten per centum the amount necessary to pay the salaries and other employees of the office of the probate judge for the same calendar year. Funk v Lamneck, 30 NP(NS) 174 (CP, Tuscarawas 1933).

2101.21 Fiduciary; payment of costs in advance

Before appointing any person as a fiduciary, the probate court may require payment of the costs incident to such appointment.

(1953 H 1, eff. 10-1-53; GC 10501-39)

Historical and Statutory Notes

Pre-1953 H 1 Amendments: 114 v 329

Cross References

Fiduciaries, appointment, 2109.02

Library References

Judges ⇌22(0.5).
Westlaw Topic No. 227.
C.J.S. Judges § 75.

Research References

Encyclopedias
OH Jur. 3d Fiduciaries § 8, Fees or Costs.

PRACTICE AND PROCEDURE; JURISDICTION

2101.22 Process

The probate judge shall issue any process, notices, commissions, rules, and orders that are necessary to carry into effect the powers granted to him.

(1953 H 1, eff. 10-1-53; GC 10501-23)

Historical and Statutory Notes

Pre-1953 H 1 Amendments: 114 v 326

Cross References

Procedure in probate court, Civ R 73

Library References

Courts ⚖198.
Judges ⚖24.
Westlaw Topic Nos. 106, 227.
C.J.S. Judges §§ 35, 53 to 63.

Research References

Encyclopedias

OH Jur. 3d Courts & Judges § 18, Courts of Common Pleas—Juvenile Division and Juvenile Courts.
OH Jur. 3d Courts & Judges § 208, Writs and Process.
OH Jur. 3d Family Law § 1535, Definitions.

Forms

Ohio Jurisprudence Pleading and Practice Forms § 9:2, Issuance at Commencement of Action.

Treatises and Practice Aids

Carlin, Baldwin's Ohio Practice, Merrick-Rippner Probate Law § 18:2, Inheritance Rights of Illegitimate Child—Statutory Provisions.

2101.23 Contempt

The probate judge may keep order in his court and has authority throughout the state to compel performance of any duty incumbent upon any fiduciary appointed by or accounting to him. The probate judge may punish any contempt of his authority as such contempt might be punished in the court of common pleas.

If a person neglects or refuses to perform an order or judgment of a probate court, other than for the payment of money, he shall be guilty of a contempt of court and the judge shall issue a summons directing such person to appear before the court, within two days from the service thereof, and show cause why he should not be punished for contempt. If it appears to the judge that such person is secreting himself to avoid the process of the court, or is about to leave the county for that purpose, the judge may issue an attachment instead of the summons, commanding the officer, to whom it is directed, to bring such person before such judge to answer for contempt. If no sufficient excuse is shown, such person shall be punished for contempt.

(1953 H 1, eff. 10–1–53; GC 10501–28)

Historical and Statutory Notes

Pre–1953 H 1 Amendments: 114 v 327

Cross References

Contempt of court, powers, procedure, penalties, Ch 2705

Library References

Contempt ⚖35, 51.
Westlaw Topic No. 93.
C.J.S. Contempt §§ 51, 59, 63, 74 to 77.

Research References

Encyclopedias

OH Jur. 3d Contempt § 48, Courts of General Jurisdiction—Probate Division.
OH Jur. 3d Trusts § 530, Enforcement by Contempt Process.

Treatises and Practice Aids

Carlin, Baldwin's Ohio Practice, Merrick-Rippner Probate Law § 1:5, Constitutional and Legislative Provisions.
Carlin, Baldwin's Ohio Practice, Merrick-Rippner Probate Law § 95:10, Purchaser—Limitations Upon.

Notes of Decisions

Constitutional issues 1
Enforcement of judgments 4
Jury trials 3
Limitations on power of court 5
Payment of money 2

---

1. Constitutional issues

In guardianship proceeding, probate court followed applicable statutory guidelines in contempt proceedings against attorney for refusing to comply with orders requiring him to return improperly disbursed attorney fees, and court did not act in violation of attorney's rights to due process. In re Guardianship of Brisboy (Ohio App. 6 Dist., 04-15-1994) 94 Ohio App.3d 361, 640 N.E.2d 908. Constitutional Law ⚖ 273

The automatic stay provision provided in 11 USC 362 is not violative of US Const Am 10 insofar as it stays a state court contempt action to enforce a divorce decree dividing marital property. Barnett v. Barnett (Ohio 1984) 9 Ohio St.3d 47, 458 N.E.2d 834, 9 O.B.R. 165. Bankruptcy ⚖ 2013.1; States ⚖ 4.16(1)

Where the basic function of a court, whether named in the constitution or established in pursuance of provisions of the constitution, is impeded by a failure or refusal of the body responsible to provide a necessary appropriation, that court possesses the inherent power to order such appropriation and to enforce its order by contempt proceedings. State ex rel. Edwards v. Murray (Ohio 1976) 48 Ohio St.2d 303, 358 N.E.2d 577, 2 O.O.3d 446. Mandamus ⚖ 141; Mandamus ⚖ 185

2. Payment of money

Probate court which had previously denied application in guardianship proceeding for approval of settlement of child's personal injury claims had subject matter jurisdiction to hold attorney in contempt for failing to comply with court orders requiring attorney to return fees improperly disbursed pursuant to subsequent order of another probate court, notwithstanding attorney's contention that statutory contempt authority specifically excluded power to find him in contempt for refusing to pay money to guardian; order in question was not order for payment of money, but order to return funds improperly disbursed. In re Guardianship of Brisboy (Ohio App. 6 Dist., 04-15-1994) 94 Ohio App.3d 361, 640 N.E.2d 908. Contempt ⚖ 44

Under RC 2101.23, an order of the probate judge, seeking to compel the payment of money in the form of increased salaries by the members of the board of county commissioners to probate court employees, is not enforceable by contempt of court proceedings. In re Contempt of Common Pleas Court (Ohio 1972) 30 Ohio St.2d 182, 283 N.E.2d 126, 59 O.O.2d 188.

Probate cannot punish for contempt, failure to obey order for the payment of money. In re Rowekamp, 11 D Repr 539, 27 B 289 (Prob, Clark 1892).

3. Jury trials

When the nature of the issues renders it appropriate, the probate court has jurisdiction to afford the parties a jury trial. (See also Lawrence RR Co v O'Harra, 48 OS 343, 28 NE 175 (1891); In re Rowekamp, 11 D Repr 539, 27 B 289 (Prob, Clark 1892).) Doan v. Biteley (Ohio 1892) 49 Ohio St. 588, 32 N.E. 600.

Any order necessary for the common pleas court to make in impaneling a struck jury, the probate court may make. Wiler v. Logan Nat. Gas & Fuel Co. (Ohio Cir. 1904) 17 Ohio C.D. 257, 6 Ohio C.C.(N.S.) 206, affirmed 72 Ohio St. 628, 76 N.E. 1128, 2 Ohio Law Rep. 536.

4. Enforcement of judgments

The probate court has general power to issue executions on its judgments, subject to special and exclusive methods of enforcing its judgments that may be provided by statute. 1920 OAG 700.

5. Limitations on power of court

The probate court has no power to imprison for refusal to obey its order. (See also In re Rowekamp, 11 D Repr 539, 27 B 289 (Prob, Clark 1892).) White v. Gates (Ohio 1884) 42 Ohio St. 109.

Statute providing that probate judge may punish contempt as it might be punished in the court of common pleas did not necessitate that the procedural requirements of general contempt statutes apply and supersede the specific procedural requirements of statute governing contempt in probate court. In re Estate of Orville (Ohio App. 7 Dist., Mahoning, 12-03-2004) No. 04 MA 97, No. 04 MA 100, 2004-Ohio-6510, 2004 WL 2808392, Unreported. Contempt ⚖ 40

Probate court has no jurisdiction to order an administrator to perform an agreement made by his intestate. Jones v. Green (Ohio Cir. 1901) 11 Ohio C.D. 548.

The probate court has no power to punish in contempt an assignee for failure to perform its order. (See also Israel v Zanesville & Ohio Railway Co, 10 D Repr 225, 19 B 258 (CP, Washington 1888).) In re Rowekamp, 11 D Repr 539, 27 B 289 (Prob, Clark 1892).

2101.24 Jurisdiction of probate court

(A)(1) Except as otherwise provided by law, the probate court has exclusive jurisdiction:

(a) To take the proof of wills and to admit to record authenticated copies of wills executed, proved, and allowed in the courts of any other state, territory, or country. If the probate judge is unavoidably absent, any judge of the court of common pleas may take proof of wills and approve bonds to be given, but the record of these acts shall be preserved in the usual records of the probate court.

(b) To grant and revoke letters testamentary and of administration;

(c) To direct and control the conduct and settle the accounts of executors and administrators and order the distribution of estates;

(d) To appoint the attorney general to serve as the administrator of an estate pursuant to section 2113.06 of the Revised Code;

(e) To appoint and remove guardians, conservators, and testamentary trustees, direct and control their conduct, and settle their accounts;

(f) To grant marriage licenses;

(g) To make inquests respecting persons who are so mentally impaired as a result of a mental or physical illness or disability, or mental retardation, or as a result of chronic substance abuse, that they are unable to manage their property and affairs effectively, subject to guardianship;

(h) To qualify assignees, appoint and qualify trustees and commissioners of insolvents, control their conduct, and settle their accounts;

(i) To authorize the sale of lands, equitable estates, or interests in lands or equitable estates, and the assignments of inchoate dower in such cases of sale, on petition by executors, administrators, and guardians;

(j) To authorize the completion of real estate contracts on petition of executors and administrators;

(k) To construe wills;

(*l*) To render declaratory judgments, including, but not limited to, those rendered pursuant to section 2107.084 of the Revised Code;

(m) To direct and control the conduct of fiduciaries and settle their accounts;

(n) To authorize the sale or lease of any estate created by will if the estate is held in trust, on petition by the trustee;

(o) To terminate a testamentary trust in any case in which a court of equity may do so;

(p) To hear and determine actions to contest the validity of wills;

(q) To make a determination of the presumption of death of missing persons and to adjudicate the property rights and obligations of all parties affected by the presumption;

(r) To hear and determine an action commenced pursuant to section 3107.41 of the Revised Code to obtain the release of information pertaining to the birth name of the adopted person and the identity of the adopted person's biological parents and biological siblings;

(s) To act for and issue orders regarding wards pursuant to section 2111.50 of the Revised Code;

(t) To hear and determine actions against sureties on the bonds of fiduciaries appointed by the probate court;

(u) To hear and determine actions involving informed consent for medication of persons hospitalized pursuant to section 5122.141 or 5122.15 of the Revised Code;

(v) To hear and determine actions relating to durable powers of attorney for health care as described in division (D) of section 1337.16 of the Revised Code;

(w) To hear and determine actions commenced by objecting individuals, in accordance with section 2133.05 of the Revised Code;

(x) To hear and determine complaints that pertain to the use or continuation, or the withholding or withdrawal, of life-sustaining treatment in connection with certain patients allegedly in a terminal condition or in a permanently unconscious state pursuant to division (E) of section 2133.08 of the Revised Code, in accordance with that division;

(y) To hear and determine applications that pertain to the withholding or withdrawal of nutrition and hydration from certain patients allegedly in a permanently unconscious state pursuant to section 2133.09 of the Revised Code, in accordance with that section;

(z) To hear and determine applications of attending physicians in accordance with division (B) of section 2133.15 of the Revised Code;

(aa) To hear and determine actions relative to the use or continuation of comfort care in connection with certain principals under durable powers of attorney for health care, declarants under declarations, or patients in accordance with division (E) of either section 1337.16 or 2133.12 of the Revised Code;

(bb) To hear and determine applications for an order relieving an estate from administration under section 2113.03 of the Revised Code;

(cc) To hear and determine applications for an order granting a summary release from administration under section 2113.031 of the Revised Code ;

(dd) To hear and determine actions relating to the exercise of the right of disposition, in accordance with section 2108.90 of the Revised Code;

(ee) To hear and determine actions relating to the disinterment and reinterment of human remains under section 517.23 of the Revised Code.

(2) In addition to the exclusive jurisdiction conferred upon the probate court by division (A)(1) of this section, the probate court shall have exclusive jurisdiction over a particular subject matter if both of the following apply:

(a) Another section of the Revised Code expressly confers jurisdiction over that subject matter upon the probate court.

(b) No section of the Revised Code expressly confers jurisdiction over that subject matter upon any other court or agency.

(B)(1) The probate court has concurrent jurisdiction with, and the same powers at law and in equity as, the general division of the court of common pleas to issue writs and orders, and to hear and determine actions as follows:

(a) If jurisdiction relative to a particular subject matter is stated to be concurrent in a section of the Revised Code or has been construed by judicial decision to be concurrent, any action that involves that subject matter;

(b) Any action that involves an inter vivos trust; a trust created pursuant to section 5815.28 of the Revised Code; a charitable trust or foundation; subject to divisions (A)(1)(u) and (z) of this section, a power of attorney, including, but not limited to, a durable power of attorney; the medical treatment of a competent adult; or a writ of habeas corpus.

(2) Any action that involves a concurrent jurisdiction subject matter and that is before the probate court may be transferred by the probate court, on its order, to the general division of the court of common pleas.

(C) The probate court has plenary power at law and in equity to dispose fully of any matter that is properly before the court, unless the power is expressly otherwise limited or denied by a section of the Revised Code.

(D) The jurisdiction acquired by a probate court over a matter or proceeding is exclusive of that of any other probate court, except when otherwise provided by law.

(2006 H 426, eff. 10–12–06; 2006 H 416, eff. 1–1–07; 2000 H 313, eff. 8–29–00; 1995 H 167, eff. 11–15–95; 1992 S 124, eff. 4–16–93; 1991 S 1; 1990 H 764; 1989 S 46; 1985 S 135; 1984 H 84; 1978 H 505; 1977 S 112, H 1; 1976 S 466; 1975 S 145; 130 v H 804; 129 v 7; 127 v 27; 125 v 903; 1953 H 1; GC 10501–53, 10501–55)

Uncodified Law

1992 S 124, § 8, eff. 4–16–93, reads: In enacting sections 1339.51 and 5111.15 and in amending sections 2101.24, 5119.01, 5121.04, 5121.10, 5123,04, 5123.18, and 5123.28 of the Revised Code, the General Assembly hereby declares its intent to supersede the effect of the holding of the Ohio Supreme Court in the December 31, 1968, decision in *Bureau of Support v. Kreitzer* (1968), 16 Ohio St. 2d 147.

1975 S 145, § 3, eff. 11–28–75 reads: Sections 1 and 2 of this act shall take effect on January 1, 1976, and apply only to estates resulting from deaths that occur on and after that date.

Historical and Statutory Notes

Ed. Note: The legal review and technical services staff of the Legislative Service Commission has issued an opinion regarding the treatment of multiple amendments. The opinion is neither legally authoritative nor binding, but is provided as a general indication that the amendments of the several acts [2006 H 426, eff. 10–12–06 and 2006 H 416, eff. 1–1–07] may be harmonized pursuant to the rule of construction contained in R.C. 1.52(B) requiring all amendments be given effect if they can reasonably be put into simultaneous operation. See *Baldwin's Ohio Legislative Service Annotated*, 2006, pages 4/L–2119 and 3/L–1782, or the OH-LEGIS or OH-LEGIS-OLD database on Westlaw, for original versions of these Acts.

Pre–1953 H 1 Amendments: 114 v 335, 336

Amendment Note: 2006 H 416 substituted "5815.28" for "1339.51" in division (B)(1)(b).

Amendment Note: 2006 H 426 added division (A)(1)(dd) and (A)(1)(ee); and made other nonsubstantive changes.

Amendment Note: 2000 H 313 added new divisions (A)(1)(bb) and (A)(1)(cc).

Amendment Note: 1995 H 167 added division (A)(1)(d); redesignated former divisions (A)(1)(d) through (A)(1)(z) as division (A)(1)(e) through (A)(1)(aa), respectively; and made other changes to reflect gender neutral language.

OSBA Probate and Trust Law Section

1961:

The committee is of the opinion that probate courts do not now have jurisdiction to terminate trusts as a result of the acts of the parties or in those situations where the trust purposes have failed.

Article IV, Section 8, of the Ohio Constitution is silent on the question of the jurisdiction of the probate court with regard to testamentary trusts but does empower the Legislature to clothe the probate court with jurisdiction "as may be provided by law."

Furthermore, Section 2101.24, which defines the areas in which the probate court has jurisdiction, limits the authority of the court as follows:

"(D) To appoint and remove guardians and testamentary trustees, direct and control their conduct, and settle their accounts;

"...

"(M) To direct and control the conduct of fiduciaries and settle their accounts."

While plenary power in law and equity is given the court in this Section to dispose of any matter properly before it, there is no reference to the termination of testamentary trusts. Furthermore, the declaratory judgment section (2721.09, R. C. O.) does not extend the jurisdiction of the court.

The committee sees no reason why parties who have issues to be resolved involving the possible termination of a testamentary trust must necessarily go into common pleas court when all other matters incident to such a trust are under the jurisdiction of the probate court. It is, therefore, recommended that Section 2101.24 be amended by the addition of a new subparagraph as follows:

"(N) To authorize the sale or lease of any estate created by will if the estate is held in trust on petition by trustee;

"*(O) To terminate a testamentary trust in any case in which a court of equity may do so.*

"...."

1957:

The proposed amendment to section 2101.24 of the probate chapter extends the jurisdiction of the probate court to authorize the sale or lease of any estate in an action by the trustee if the estate is one created by will and is held in trust.

Cross References

Application to probate court to complete sale of land by decedent, hearing, 2113.48 to 2113.51
Assignment for benefit of creditors; duties of probate judge, Ch 1313
Estate tax administration, probate court jurisdiction of, 5731.31
Habeas corpus proceedings, Ch 2725
Judicial hospitalization of mentally ill, 5122.11
Jurisdiction in intestate estate, 2113.01
Jurisdiction of common pleas and probate courts, O Const Art IV §4
Jurisdiction to probate a will, 2107.11
Liability for cost of goods and services relating to exercise of right of disposition, 2108.90
Marriage, Ch 3101
Metropolitan housing authority, probate court to appoint one member, 3735.27
Park districts, application to probate judge to create, 1545.02
Powers and jurisdiction of judges, O Const Art IV §18
Will contest, 2107.71 to 2107.77

Library References

Courts ⚖198, 472.4.
Westlaw Topic No. 106.
C.J.S. Courts § 186.
Baldwin's Ohio Legislative Service Annotated, 2006 H 416 LSC Analysis, p 3/L–1709

Research References

Encyclopedias

OH Jur. 3d Cancellation & Reform. of Instruments § 44, Generally; Jurisdiction.
OH Jur. 3d Charities § 26, Jurisdiction of Courts.
OH Jur. 3d Conversion in Equity § 10, Conversion Resulting from Contract to Sell Realty.
OH Jur. 3d Courts & Judges § 17, Courts of Common Pleas—Domestic Relations Division.
OH Jur. 3d Courts & Judges § 18, Courts of Common Pleas—Juvenile Division and Juvenile Courts.
OH Jur. 3d Courts & Judges § 19, Courts of Common Pleas—Probate Division.
OH Jur. 3d Courts & Judges § 284, Jurisdiction Granted by Statute.
OH Jur. 3d Courts & Judges § 285, Jurisdiction Granted by Statute—Jurisdiction to Award Monetary Damages.
OH Jur. 3d Courts & Judges § 286, Concurrent Jurisdiction.
OH Jur. 3d Creditors' Rights & Remedies § 150, Sale of Real Property—Where Property is Subject to Mortgage, Lien, Encumbrance, or Dower.
OH Jur. 3d Creditors' Rights & Remedies § 219, Generally; "Exclusive" Jurisdiction.
OH Jur. 3d Criminal Law § 2015, Probate Courts.
OH Jur. 3d Death § 16, Proceedings; Complaint.
OH Jur. 3d Decedents' Estates § 199, Jurisdiction and Venue.

OH Jur. 3d Decedents' Estates § 653, Probate Court; Applicability of the Declaratory Judgment Act.
OH Jur. 3d Decedents' Estates § 655, Court of Common Pleas.
OH Jur. 3d Decedents' Estates § 663, Answer.
OH Jur. 3d Decedents' Estates § 868, Jurisdiction of Probate Court.
OH Jur. 3d Decedents' Estates § 872, Jurisdiction of Common Pleas Court.
OH Jur. 3d Decedents' Estates § 877, Equity Jurisdiction of Probate Court.
OH Jur. 3d Decedents' Estates § 892, Venue.
OH Jur. 3d Decedents' Estates § 964, Judicial Supervision of Representatives.
OH Jur. 3d Decedents' Estates § 1078, Scope of Inquiry and Action.
OH Jur. 3d Decedents' Estates § 1268, Nature and Scope of Hearing on Exceptions.
OH Jur. 3d Decedents' Estates § 1406, Contracts Relating to Realty.
OH Jur. 3d Decedents' Estates § 1524, Jurisdiction and Powers of the Probate Court.
OH Jur. 3d Decedents' Estates § 1527, Jurisdiction and Powers of the Probate Court—Exclusive Jurisdiction of One Court.
OH Jur. 3d Decedents' Estates § 1658, Probate Court's Jurisdiction Over Order of Distribution.
OH Jur. 3d Decedents' Estates § 1796, Exclusive Jurisdiction of Probate Court.
OH Jur. 3d Decedents' Estates § 1797, Concurrent Jurisdiction of Probate Court and Other Courts.
OH Jur. 3d Declar. Judgments & Related Proceedings § 37, Jurisdiction, Generally—Probate Matters.
OH Jur. 3d Family Law § 25, Application for Marriage License.
OH Jur. 3d Fiduciaries § 10, Issuance of Letters of Appointment; Acceptance by Fiduciary.
OH Jur. 3d Fiduciaries § 88, Generally; Failure to Invest or Negligence—Procedure; Findings and Evidence of Negligence.
OH Jur. 3d Fiduciaries § 129, Jurisdiction of Probate Division of the Court of Common Pleas.
OH Jur. 3d Fiduciaries § 130, Jurisdiction of Probate Division of the Court of Common Pleas—Concurrent Jurisdiction.
OH Jur. 3d Fiduciaries § 152, Jurisdiction and Venue.
OH Jur. 3d Fiduciaries § 158, Citation, Attachment, or Warrant of Suspected Person or Persons Interested in Assets—Prejudgment Attachment; Limitations and Prerequisites.
OH Jur. 3d Fiduciaries § 163, Hearing; Submission to Jury or Referee—Determination of Questions of Title.
OH Jur. 3d Fiduciaries § 175, Authority to Approve Bonds.
OH Jur. 3d Fiduciaries § 176, Record that Bonds Were Approved.
OH Jur. 3d Fiduciaries § 217, Jurisdiction.
OH Jur. 3d Fiduciaries § 259, Jurisdiction of Probate Court.
OH Jur. 3d Fiduciaries § 314, Generally; Jurisdiction.
OH Jur. 3d Guardian & Ward § 1, Generally; Jurisdiction Over Guardianship Matters.
OH Jur. 3d Guardian & Ward § 79, Judicial Control.
OH Jur. 3d Habeas Corpus & Post Convict. Remedies § 40, Jurisdiction, Generally.
OH Jur. 3d Incompetent Persons § 42, Jurisdiction and Venue.
OH Jur. 3d Incompetent Persons § 53, Disposition—Commitment to Facility at Public Expense.
OH Jur. 3d Incompetent Persons § 68, Consent to Treatment.
OH Jur. 3d Mandamus, Procedendo, & Prohibition § 183, Effect of Patent and Unambiguous Lack of Jurisdiction.
OH Jur. 3d Real Property Sales & Exchanges § 228, Claimants Under Deceased Vendor.
OH Jur. 3d Trusts § 155, Jurisdiction.
OH Jur. 3d Trusts § 186, Removal—Proceedings.
OH Jur. 3d Trusts § 346, Probate Court.
OH Jur. 3d Trusts § 371, Statutory Basis.
OH Jur. 3d Trusts § 388, Judicial Control—Statutory Provisions.
OH Jur. 3d Trusts § 401, Judicial Authorization.
OH Jur. 3d Trusts § 480, Jurisdiction of Probate Court.
OH Jur. 3d Trusts § 517, Jurisdiction—Probate Court.
OH Jur. 3d Trusts § 544, Lis Pendens.

Forms

Ohio Jurisprudence Pleading and Practice Forms § 2:6, Courts of Common Pleas—Probate Division.
Ohio Jurisprudence Pleading and Practice Forms § 5:41, Divisions of the Common Pleas Courts—Probate Division.

Treatises and Practice Aids

Sowald & Morganstern, Baldwin's Ohio Practice Domestic Relations Law § 2:27, Capacity to Marry—Consent of Parties.
Carlin, Baldwin's Ohio Practice, Merrick-Rippner Probate Law § 1:5, Constitutional and Legislative Provisions.
Carlin, Baldwin's Ohio Practice, Merrick-Rippner Probate Law § 3:2, Jurisdiction of Probate Court—Statutory.
Carlin, Baldwin's Ohio Practice, Merrick-Rippner Probate Law § 3:3, Jurisdiction of Probate Court—Subject Matter—in General.
Carlin, Baldwin's Ohio Practice, Merrick-Rippner Probate Law § 3:4, Jurisdiction of Probate Court—Subject Matter—Specific Areas—Inter Vivos Trusts.
Carlin, Baldwin's Ohio Practice, Merrick-Rippner Probate Law § 3:5, Jurisdiction of Probate Court—Subject Matter—Specific Areas—Fiduciaries.
Carlin, Baldwin's Ohio Practice, Merrick-Rippner Probate Law § 3:6, Jurisdiction of Probate Court—Subject Matter—Specific Areas—Testamentary Trusts.
Carlin, Baldwin's Ohio Practice, Merrick-Rippner Probate Law § 3:8, Jurisdiction of Probate Court—Subject Matter—Specific Areas—Will Contests.
Carlin, Baldwin's Ohio Practice, Merrick-Rippner Probate Law § 6:6, Declaratory Judgments—Probate Court Proceedings.
Carlin, Baldwin's Ohio Practice, Merrick-Rippner Probate Law § 7:1, Power of Probate Court to Vacate or Modify Judgments—in General.
Carlin, Baldwin's Ohio Practice, Merrick-Rippner Probate Law § 12:3, Wrongful Death—Jurisdiction of Probate Court.
Carlin, Baldwin's Ohio Practice, Merrick-Rippner Probate Law § 19:2, Legitimation—Procedure—Acknowledgment of Paternity.
Carlin, Baldwin's Ohio Practice, Merrick-Rippner Probate Law § 22:4, Effect of Prohibition to Benefit—Joint Accounts.
Carlin, Baldwin's Ohio Practice, Merrick-Rippner Probate Law § 3:11, Jurisdiction of Probate Court—Subject Matter—Specific Areas—Removal of Life Support.
Carlin, Baldwin's Ohio Practice, Merrick-Rippner Probate Law § 3:12, Jurisdiction of Probate Court—Subject Matter—Specific Areas—Medication of Hospitalized Persons.
Carlin, Baldwin's Ohio Practice, Merrick-Rippner Probate Law § 3:13, Jurisdiction of Probate Court—Scope—Exclusive and Concurrent Jurisdiction.
Carlin, Baldwin's Ohio Practice, Merrick-Rippner Probate Law § 3:14, Jurisdiction of Probate Court—Scope—as Between Probate Courts.
Carlin, Baldwin's Ohio Practice, Merrick-Rippner Probate Law § 34:1, Declaring the Validity of a Will—Introduction.
Carlin, Baldwin's Ohio Practice, Merrick-Rippner Probate Law § 38:1, Will Contests.
Carlin, Baldwin's Ohio Practice, Merrick-Rippner Probate Law § 43:1, Construing a Will—Action for Instructions—Scope.
Carlin, Baldwin's Ohio Practice, Merrick-Rippner Probate Law § 56:2, Concealed or Embezzled Assets—Jurisdiction Over Complaint.
Carlin, Baldwin's Ohio Practice, Merrick-Rippner Probate Law § 57:3, Removal of Fiduciary—Trustee.
Carlin, Baldwin's Ohio Practice, Merrick-Rippner Probate Law § 64:2, Powers and Duties of Guardian—Probate Court is the Superior Guardian.
Carlin, Baldwin's Ohio Practice, Merrick-Rippner Probate Law § 68:1, Letters—in General—Jurisdiction.
Carlin, Baldwin's Ohio Practice, Merrick-Rippner Probate Law § 83:7, Fiduciary Claims—Jurisdiction to Allow.
Carlin, Baldwin's Ohio Practice, Merrick-Rippner Probate Law § 90:3, Persons Entitled to Bring Land Sale Actions—Testamentary Trustee.
Carlin, Baldwin's Ohio Practice, Merrick-Rippner Probate Law § 110:3, Reapportionment of Tax on Interest Not Part of Residuary Estate.
Carlin, Baldwin's Ohio Practice, Merrick-Rippner Probate Law § 12:10, Wrongful Death—Damages—Loss of Chance Doctrine.
Carlin, Baldwin's Ohio Practice, Merrick-Rippner Probate Law § 19:10, Uniform Parentage Act—Procedure in Action to Determine Father-Child Relationship.
Carlin, Baldwin's Ohio Practice, Merrick-Rippner Probate Law § 43:10, Construing a Will—Rules of Construction—Guides to Ascertain Testator's Intent.
Carlin, Baldwin's Ohio Practice, Merrick-Rippner Probate Law § 43:15, Construing a Will—Liberal Construction—Charitable Bequests; or Construction Problems.

Carlin, Baldwin's Ohio Practice, Merrick-Rippner Probate Law § 43:20, Construing a Will—Language—Ambiguous.

Carlin, Baldwin's Ohio Practice, Merrick-Rippner Probate Law § 43:34, Construing a Will—Words and Phrases—Stocks and Stock Dividends.

Carlin, Baldwin's Ohio Practice, Merrick-Rippner Probate Law § 60:27, Power of Attorney for Health Care—Decision in Absence of Valid Health Care Instrument; Probate Court Proceedings.

Carlin, Baldwin's Ohio Practice, Merrick-Rippner Probate Law § 62:10, Appointment of Guardian—Definitions—Legal Settlement.

Carlin, Baldwin's Ohio Practice, Merrick-Rippner Probate Law § 62:11, Appointment of Guardian—Definitions—Domicile.

Carlin, Baldwin's Ohio Practice, Merrick-Rippner Probate Law § 62:12, Appointment of Guardian—Definitions—Residence.

Carlin, Baldwin's Ohio Practice, Merrick-Rippner Probate Law § 62:14, Appointment of Guardian—Application—Jurisdiction.

Carlin, Baldwin's Ohio Practice, Merrick-Rippner Probate Law § 62:31, Appointment of Guardian—Miscellaneous—Veteran's Guardianships.

Carlin, Baldwin's Ohio Practice, Merrick-Rippner Probate Law § 62:33, Guardianship Proceedings—Court's Jurisdiction.

Carlin, Baldwin's Ohio Practice, Merrick-Rippner Probate Law § 62:43, Guardianship Proceedings—Who May Serve—Life Support Cases.

Carlin, Baldwin's Ohio Practice, Merrick-Rippner Probate Law § 64:24, Powers and Duties of Guardian—Ward's Estate—Acts of the Ward—Trusts.

Carlin, Baldwin's Ohio Practice, Merrick-Rippner Probate Law § 79:20, Inventory—Exceptions—Hearing.

Carlin, Baldwin's Ohio Practice, Merrick-Rippner Probate Law § 90:13, Land Sale Action—Jurisdiction of Probate Court.

Carlin, Baldwin's Ohio Practice, Merrick-Rippner Probate Law § 96:10, Expenses of Sale—Jurisdiction to Determine Costs and Expenses.

Carlin, Baldwin's Ohio Practice, Merrick-Rippner Probate Law § 98:29, Adoption—Papers and Records—Confidentiality.

Carlin, Baldwin's Ohio Practice, Merrick-Rippner Probate Law § 101:58, Consent to Treatment (RC 5122.271)—Psychotropic Medication.

Carlin, Baldwin's Ohio Practice, Merrick-Rippner Probate Law § 110:16, Objection to Apportionment and Determination of Apportionment by Probate Court.

Bogert - the Law of Trusts and Trustees § 292, Judicial Jurisdiction.

Bogert - the Law of Trusts and Trustees § 870, Jurisdiction to Enforce Trust—Actions Available.

Bogert - the Law of Trusts and Trustees § 963, Duty to Render Formal Account in Court of Equity.

Kuehnle and Levey, Ohio Real Estate Law and Practice § 52:3, Statutory Fiduciary Sales—21 Statutory Proceedings.

Kuehnle and Levey, Ohio Real Estate Law and Practice § 52:21, Statutory Fiduciary Sales—Action by Trustee to Sell Trust Property.

Kuehnle and Levey, Ohio Real Estate Law and Practice § 53:12, Land Sales—Parties Defendant—Determination of Heirship Prior to Action to Sell.

Law Review and Journal Commentaries

The Constructive Trust: a Neglected Remedy in Ohio, Harry W. Vanneman. 10 U Cin L Rev 366 (November 1936).

The Future of Probate and the Merger of Probate and Nonprobate Transfer Systems, David F. Allen. 7 Prob L J Ohio 13 (November/December 1996).

Informed Consent for Medication in Persons with Mental Retardation and Mental Illness. Joan L. O'Sullivan and Breck G. Borcherding, 12 Health Matrix: J Law-Medicine 63 (Winter 2002).

Investments By Fiduciaries Under the New Ohio Probate Code, Samuel Freifeld. 5 U Cin L Rev 429 (November 1931).

Joint and Survivorship Accounts: A New Approach to an Old Problem, William B. McNeil. 13 Prob L J Ohio 26 (November/December 2002).

The Lombardo Case, Michael Stark. (Ed. Note: Whether an irrevocable trust by an individual who is now incompetent may be revoked at the behest of the guardian is the subject of the article.) 9 Prob L J Ohio 104 (July/August 1999).

The Probate Courts of Ohio, John F. Winkler. 28 U Tol L Rev 563 (Spring 1997).

Probate Malpractice, Hon. Fred V. Skok. 14 Lake Legal Views 1 (February 1991).

Sale of Real Estate, Construction of Wills, and Inheritance Taxes Are Discussed, Hon. Nelson J. Brewer. 11 Clev B J 121 (May 1940).

Should Everyone Trust a Living Trust?, William A. Fields. 2 Prob L J Ohio 5 (September/October 1991).

The Uniform Trusts Act, Frank S. Rowley and Harry W. Vanneman. 5 Ohio St L J 145 (March 1939).

The Uniform Trusts Act, Frank S. Rowley and Harry W. Vanneman. 13 U Cin L Rev 157 (March 1939).

Notes of Decisions

Adoption, paternity, sterility 2
Attorney fees 3
Constitutional issues 1
Equity powers 4
Estates 5-10
    Debts, expenses and claims 5
    Distribution and inventory 6
    Domicile of decedent 7
    Intestate 8
    Real estate 9
    Surviving spouse 10
Executors and administrators 11, 12
    Appointment 11
    Removal and other actions 12
Foreclosures 13
Fraud 14
Guardianships 15
Inheritance taxes 16
Insolvency 17
Jury trial 18
Mental impairment, confinement costs 19
Statutory jurisdiction 20
Testamentary trusts and trustees 21
Wills 22

---

1. Constitutional issues

The act of 1853 vested in a probate court only such jurisdiction in regard to ordering sales as was possessed by the courts of common pleas. Foresman v. Haag (Ohio 1880) 36 Ohio St. 102, supplemented 37 Ohio St. 143.

Probate courts are courts of record. Shroyer v. Richmond (Ohio 1866) 16 Ohio St. 455.

A preliminary hearing before a magistrate is necessary to confer jurisdiction in probate court. Gates v. State (Ohio 1854) 3 Ohio St. 293.

Ward waived her appellate arguments that alleged the trial court lacked in personam jurisdiction over ward and that the trial court's failure to dismiss the action violated due process, where ward failed to appeal from order appointing guardian for ward. In re Helen Riva Guardianship (Ohio App. 5 Dist., Richland, 10-19-2006) No. 2006-CA-0067, 2006-Ohio-5547, 2006 WL 3020316, Unreported. Mental Health ☞ 148.1

Former trustee received adequate notice and had an opportunity to be heard on current trustee's motion to surcharge former trustee due to his alleged negligent administration of trust, and thus, probate court had personal jurisdiction over former trustee, where former trustee appeared at all hearings related to motion and received two continuances that he requested. In re Testamentary Trusteeship of Cheek (Ohio App. 2 Dist., Montgomery, 05-16-2003) No. 19513, 2003-Ohio-2515, 2003 WL 21122663, Unreported. Trusts ☞ 298

As a court of limited jurisdiction, the probate division of the court of common pleas may exercise only such jurisdiction as is expressly granted to it by the Ohio Constitution or a statute. In re Petition of Stratcap Investments, Inc. (Ohio App. 2 Dist., 08-29-2003) 154 Ohio App.3d 89, 796 N.E.2d 73, 2003-Ohio-4589. Courts ☞ 50

A probate court is without jurisdiction to entertain an original action wherein plaintiff seeks to obtain a declaratory judgment by that court that an ordinance of a municipality is unconstitutional as it relates to plaintiff's property, together with injunctive and equitable relief; a declaratory judgment rendered by such court, without jurisdiction, is void and of no effect. State ex rel. City of Mayfield Heights v. Bartunek (Cuyahoga 1967) 12 Ohio App.2d 141, 231 N.E.2d 326, 41 O.O.2d 222.

Under O Const Art IV, § 8 and GC 10501–53 (RC 2101.24) and 10506–39 (RC 2109.32), probate court has plenary power at law and in equity to hear, determine and finally dispose of all matters relative to manner in which guardian has executed his trust and to require such guardian to account not only for estate of his ward which came into the guardian's hands but for estate of his ward which should have come into his hands through exercise of reasonable diligence and that care which a reasonable man would have used in conduct of his own affairs as well. Guardianship of Zimmerman (Ohio 1943) 141 Ohio St. 207, 47 N.E.2d 782, 25 O.O. 326. Guardian And Ward ⇨ 144

Under O Const Art IV, § 8 and GC 10492 (RC 2101.24), claim for attorney fees expended by an heir in contesting with partial success a claim against the estate by filing requisition for rejection in the probate court should be presented to the probate court for allowance and may not be allowed by the common pleas court. Koelble v. Runyan (Brown 1927) 25 Ohio App. 426, 158 N.E. 279, 6 Ohio Law Abs. 41.

Under GC 10492 and O Const Art IV, § 8, the common pleas court cannot make an order controlling the distribution of funds of an estate which are in the custody of the probate court. Koelble v. Runyan (Brown 1927) 25 Ohio App. 426, 158 N.E. 279, 6 Ohio Law Abs. 41. Courts ⇨ 478

Probate courts are courts of record. Cincinnati, S. & C.R. Co. v. Village of Belle Centre (Ohio 1891) 48 Ohio St. 273, 25 W.L.B. 298, 27 N.E. 464.

Probate is a court of record within its jurisdiction and its judgments can only be impeached for fraud. Woodward v. Curtis (Ohio Cir. 1899) 10 Ohio C.D. 400.

GC 10501–53 (RC 2101.24) and 10510–10 (RC 2127.08) are not unconstitutional as violative of O Const Art IV, § 8. Hatch v. Buckeye State Bldg. & Loan Co. (Ohio Prob. 1934) 32 Ohio N.P.N.S. 297, 16 Ohio Law Abs. 661.

2. Adoption, paternity, sterility

Continuing jurisdiction of juvenile court is not jurisdictional bar to adoption proceedings in probate court; probate court may exercise its jurisdiction in adoption proceedings while juvenile court has continuing jurisdiction over custody, and adoption hearing can go forth in probate court even if juvenile court may not agree with specific adoption. In re Hitchcock (Ohio App. 8 Dist., 11-21-1996) 120 Ohio App.3d 88, 696 N.E.2d 1090, stay granted 77 Ohio St.3d 1462, 672 N.E.2d 1119, stay denied 77 Ohio St.3d 1502, 673 N.E.2d 921, motion to vacate stay denied 77 Ohio St.3d 1521, 674 N.E.2d 373, appeal allowed 78 Ohio St.3d 1455, 677 N.E.2d 815, appeal dismissed as improvidently allowed 81 Ohio St.3d 1222, 689 N.E.2d 43, 1998-Ohio-653, stay denied 81 Ohio St.3d 1469, 690 N.E.2d 1288, stay denied 81 Ohio St.3d 1476, 691 N.E.2d 294. Adoption ⇨ 10; Infants ⇨ 230.1

Continuing jurisdiction of juvenile court over child does not present jurisdictional bar to adoption proceedings in probate court, as probate court has exclusive jurisdiction over adoption proceedings. State ex rel. Hitchcock v. Cuyahoga Cty. Court of Common Pleas, Probate Div. (Ohio App. 8 Dist., 10-07-1994) 97 Ohio App.3d 600, 647 N.E.2d 208. Courts ⇨ 472.4(8)

On the evidence probate court had authority to order feeble minded young woman sterilized. (See also Wade v Bethesda Hospital, 337 FSupp 671 (SD Ohio 1971).) In re Simpson (Ohio Prob. 1962) 180 N.E.2d 206, 88 Ohio Law Abs. 193.

Where in an action to vacate an adoption decree upon the ground that the next friend of the child fraudulently concealed the fact that the child was mentally defective, the court sustained a motion to quash service upon the next friend, the action to vacate was not terminated in its entirety, and hence the order was not final. In re Adoption of Sladky (Franklin 1958) 109 Ohio App. 120, 161 N.E.2d 554, 81 Ohio Law Abs. 264, 10 O.O.2d 304.

The sustaining of a motion by an adoption agency to quash the service of summons on a petition filed by adopting parents seeking to have a decree of adoption vacated and set aside on the ground that such agency knowingly made untrue and misleading reports to the court prior to the final decree in the adoption proceeding is not a final order. In re Adoption of Sladky (Franklin 1958) 109 Ohio App. 120, 161 N.E.2d 554, 81 Ohio Law Abs. 264, 10 O.O.2d 304.

Where there is no set of circumstances under Ohio law which would permit a probate court judge to order an individual to submit to sterilization, in making such an order the judge acts wholly without jurisdiction and, thus, is not protected by the doctrine of judicial immunity. Wade v. Bethesda Hospital (S.D.Ohio 1971) 337 F.Supp. 671, 61 O.O.2d 147, motion denied 356 F.Supp. 380, 70 O.O.2d 218.

Defendant probate judge in ordering plaintiff sterilized acted outside the scope of his jurisdiction and was not immune from liability therefor, there being no statute in Ohio which authorizes a judge to order sterilization for any purpose. Wade v. Bethesda Hospital (S.D.Ohio 1971) 337 F.Supp. 671, 61 O.O.2d 147, motion denied 356 F.Supp. 380, 70 O.O.2d 218.

RC 3107.06(D) may not operate to divest the probate court of its necessary judicial power to fully hear and determine an adoption proceeding. State ex rel. Portage County Welfare Dept. v. Summers (Ohio 1974) 38 Ohio St.2d 144, 311 N.E.2d 6, 67 O.O.2d 151.

Original and exclusive jurisdiction over adoption proceedings is vested specifically in the probate court pursuant to RC Ch 3107. State ex rel. Portage County Welfare Dept. v. Summers (Ohio 1974) 38 Ohio St.2d 144, 311 N.E.2d 6, 67 O.O.2d 151.

Where jurisdiction over custody matters concerning a minor child was certified to the juvenile court, the probate court has jurisdiction to hear adoption proceedings where such minor child was not placed in custody of the juvenile court and there were no pending proceedings in said court concerning custody. In re Adoption of Bailey, No. L–82–358 (6th Dist Ct App, Lucas, 4–15–83).

3. Attorney fees

Probate court patently and unambiguously lacked jurisdiction to appoint counsel on estate's behalf to appeal a decision of Court of Appeals reversing a judgment of probate court which reduced by $1,324.61 expenses requested by law firm retained to pursue wrongful death claims, and thus writ of prohibition would issue, where estate had been settled except for this issue, and executrix and sole beneficiary of estate objected to probate court's order; matter did not directly pertain to administration of estate, and, given fees and expenses associated with appeal, estate could lose more money on appeal than it stood to gain. State ex rel. Marsteller v. Maloney (Ohio App. 7 Dist., Mahoning, 04-14-2005) No. 04-MA-279, 2005-Ohio-1836, 2005 WL 911140, Unreported. Prohibition ⇨ 10(2)

Trial court had discretion to order trust to pay all attorney fees it had incurred during course of will contest under statute, providing court with such jurisdiction in any action that involved an inter vivos trust. Miller v. Harrison ex rel. Roxanne Sparr Harrison Revocable Living Trust (Ohio App. 2 Dist., Greene, 01-16-2004) No. 2003 CA 6, 2004-Ohio-173, 2004 WL 68773, Unreported. Wills ⇨ 413

Trial court acted within its discretion when it solicited attorney's testimony about legal fees that had been billed to trustee, for purposes of determining whether fees and costs should be paid out of trust for fees incurred in will contest; attorney was in best position to support those fees. Miller v. Harrison ex rel. Roxanne Sparr Harrison Revocable Living Trust (Ohio App. 2 Dist., Greene, 01-16-2004) No. 2003 CA 6, 2004-Ohio-173, 2004 WL 68773, Unreported. Wills ⇨ 416

A probate court's finding that a contingent fee agreement regarding a personal injury claim of a minor ward under which an attorney would have received one-third of a $90,000 settlement, was not an enforceable contract because (1) it was signed only by the parents, (2) it was signed when the parents were under great mental stress, and (3) it was not approved by the court prior to the agreement being entered into by the guardian as required by statute, and in the place of the agreement, awarding the attorney $9,142.50, the reasonable value of his services (60.95 hours X $150 per hour), plus costs and expenses advanced of $423.50, does not constitute an abuse of discretion. In re Guardianship of Patrick (Huron 1991) 66 Ohio App.3d 415, 584 N.E.2d 86.

The failure to pay attorney's fees found due and ordered paid by the court is a breach of the administration bond for which the surety is liable. Smith v. Rhodes (Ohio 1903) 68 Ohio St. 500, 48 W.L.B. 682, 68 N.E. 7, 1 Ohio Law Rep. 89, 1 Ohio Law Rep. 135, 1 Ohio Law Rep. 493.

4. Equity powers

Probate court correctly ignored testimony provided by decedent's son, in proceeding interpreting settlement agreement entered into by decedent's spouse and son regarding funeral arrangements for decedent, where agreement, providing that spouse would make all funeral arrangements "necessary to properly lay the ward to rest," was clear on its face. In re Guardianship of Napier (Ohio App. 10 Dist., Franklin, 10-07-2005) No. 05AP-405, 2005-Ohio-5355, 2005 WL 2472055, Unreported. Dead Bodies ⇨ 1

Probate court's judgment determining that decedent's spouse had sole authority to make funeral arrangements for decedent, in accordance with previous agreement between parties, was not against the manifest weight of the evidence; agreement entered into by decedent's son and spouse, providing that spouse would make all funeral arrangements "necessary to properly lay the ward to rest" was valid and clear on its face, and phrase "lay the ward to rest" could include both full body burial and cremation. In re Guardianship of Napier (Ohio App. 10 Dist., Franklin, 10-07-2005) No. 05AP-405, 2005-Ohio-5355, 2005 WL 2472055, Unreported. Dead Bodies ⇐ 1

Even assuming that attorney did not appear as an attorney of record in any of the underlying cases, he placed himself under the de facto authority of the probate court by representing client in matters that were governed by probate court, including court's authority to impose sanctions, and, thus, attorney's challenge to sanctions should have been dealt with in a direct appeal, rather than mandamus proceeding. State ex rel. Buck v. Maloney (Ohio App. 7 Dist., Mahoning, 10-02-2003) No. 02CA237, 2003-Ohio-5309, 2003 WL 22284078, Unreported, reversed 102 Ohio St.3d 250, 809 N.E.2d 20, 2004-Ohio-2590. Prohibition ⇐ 3(3)

Where court could not determine which of three charitable organizations was intended beneficiary of individual retirement account (IRA) whose designated beneficiary was "Alzheimer's Research Center," court properly exercised its statutory equitable powers to divide contested funds equally among those three organizations, each of which promoted settlor's general charitable intent of benefiting patients with Alzheimer's Disease. McDonald & Co. Sec., Inc., Gradison Div. v. Alzheimer's Disease & Related Disorders Assn., Inc. (Ohio App. 1 Dist., 07-21-2000) 140 Ohio App.3d 358, 747 N.E.2d 843. Charities ⇐ 48(1)

Record supported finding that settlor's intent in designating "Alzheimer's Research Center" as beneficiary of individual retirement account (IRA) was to help patients with Alzheimer's Disease, for purposes of determining whether university medical center, or one of two private charitable medical foundations, should receive money in that IRA; while university argued that it should receive money because it was only organization before court that actually operated Alzheimer's research center, settlor's friend testified that settlor merely said that he wanted money to go to "Alzheimer's" and that he never spoke words "research" and "center," and during his life settlor gave some monies, however meager, to the private organizations, but none to university. McDonald & Co. Sec., Inc., Gradison Div. v. Alzheimer's Disease & Related Disorders Assn., Inc. (Ohio App. 1 Dist., 07-21-2000) 140 Ohio App.3d 358, 747 N.E.2d 843. Charities ⇐ 50

Phrase "Alzheimer's Research Center" was ambiguous, and thus, extrinsic evidence was admissible for purposes of determining which charitable organization should receive money in individual retirement account (IRA) whose designated beneficiary was Alzheimer's Research Center; that phrase did not, standing alone, identify any particular entity, as no organization solely used that phrase as its name, and that particular designation could reasonably apply to any one of numerous organizations. McDonald & Co. Sec., Inc., Gradison Div. v. Alzheimer's Disease & Related Disorders Assn., Inc. (Ohio App. 1 Dist., 07-21-2000) 140 Ohio App.3d 358, 747 N.E.2d 843. Evidence ⇐ 450(1)

Probate court has plenary power at law and in equity to fully dispose of any matter properly before the court. Rinehart v. Bank One, Columbus, N.A. (Ohio App. 10 Dist., 03-31-1998) 125 Ohio App.3d 719, 709 N.E.2d 559, dismissed, appeal not allowed 82 Ohio St.3d 1480, 696 N.E.2d 1087. Courts ⇐ 198

Predominantly equitable relief was being sought when the executor of a testator's estate sued, and the heirs countersued, for a declaration of whether a charitable testamentary trust to promote cross-cultural understanding with "the peoples of . . . the Union of Soviet Socialist Republics " (USSR) remained valid after the USSR dissolved; accordingly, the heirs did not have a statutory right to a jury trial. First Nat. Bank of Southwestern Ohio v. Miami University (Ohio App. 12 Dist., 06-02-1997) 121 Ohio App.3d 170, 699 N.E.2d 523, dismissed, appeal not allowed 80 Ohio St.3d 1411, 684 N.E.2d 704, reconsideration denied 80 Ohio St.3d 1450, 686 N.E.2d 276, certiorari denied 119 S.Ct. 70, 525 U.S. 825, 142 L.Ed.2d 55. Jury ⇐ 14(12.5)

A hearing by a probate court for the purpose of settling the "final and distributive account" of a receiver is not one of the equitable actions encompassed by RC 2501.02. In re Wisser and Gabler (Ohio 1966) 5 Ohio St.2d 89, 214 N.E.2d 92, 34 O.O.2d 217. Appeal And Error ⇐ 15

Probate court, sitting as court of equity, had inherent power, independent of statute, to intervene and permit guardian of incompetent surviving spouse to exercise for her, the election to purchase mansion-house from estate at appraised value, in view of fact that failure to exercise such power would cause to be lost to incompetent surviving spouse such right, there being no statute which gives an incompetent surviving spouse an adequate remedy at law. Dorfmeier v. Dorfmeier (Ohio Prob. 1954) 123 N.E.2d 681, 69 Ohio Law Abs. 15. Mental Health ⇐ 214; Mental Health ⇐ 236

GC 10501–53 (RC 2101.24) adds nothing to the equity power of the probate court. Foerster v. Foerster (Ohio Prob. 1954) 122 N.E.2d 314, 71 Ohio Law Abs. 129, 54 O.O. 441.

Petition raising question whether plaintiff allegedly entering into ceremonial marriage with woman without knowledge that woman was married and placing title to his house and lot in her name without intending to relinquish ownership and depositing his savings in her name was entitled to return of his property stated cause of action coming within equity power of common pleas court, and fact that woman was dead, and that defendant was administrator of her estate did not oust court of its jurisdiction. Carter v. Birnbaum (Cuyahoga 1953) 113 N.E.2d 102, 68 Ohio Law Abs. 97. Executors And Administrators ⇐ 435

General equity powers are not conferred on the probate court under this section. In re Dickey's Estate (Montgomery 1949) 87 Ohio App. 255, 94 N.E.2d 223, 20 A.L.R.2d 1220, 57 Ohio Law Abs. 346, 42 O.O. 474.

This section gives the probate court, in matters within its jurisdiction, the authority to exercise equity powers in disposing of matters where there is no legal remedy or where the legal remedy is inadequate. In re Dickey's Estate (Montgomery 1949) 87 Ohio App. 255, 94 N.E.2d 223, 20 A.L.R.2d 1220, 57 Ohio Law Abs. 346, 42 O.O. 474. Courts ⇐ 200.5

Grant of a limited equity jurisdiction to probate court, under provisions of GC 10501–53 (RC 2101.24) and GC 10501–17 (RC 2101.33), does not oust court of common pleas from its original equity jurisdiction to declare void the judgments and orders of probate court for lack of jurisdiction. Young v. Guella (Summit 1941) 67 Ohio App. 11, 35 N.E.2d 997, 21 O.O. 66.

Specific grant of power to a probate court as contained in GC 10501–53 (RC 2101.24) and GC 10501–17 (RC 2101.33), does not confer upon such court general equity jurisdiction. Hooffstetter v. Adams (Summit 1941) 67 Ohio App. 21, 35 N.E.2d 896, 21 O.O. 70.

Probate court has the same jurisdiction, at law and in equity, to vacate or modify its own orders and judgments as has a court of common pleas. Hooffstetter v. Adams (Summit 1941) 67 Ohio App. 21, 35 N.E.2d 896, 21 O.O. 70.

Where the probate court erroneously rendered personal judgment against a legatee in a proceeding to sell real estate to pay assets and execution is levied on stock devised to the legatee, notwithstanding the stock was subsequently attached in a proceeding in another court, the probate court will be compelled by mandamus to enter on its journal an order sustaining an application to set aside the writ of execution, for the probate court speaks through its journal. State ex rel. Voight v. Lueders (Ohio 1920) 101 Ohio St. 256, 128 N.E. 72, 18 Ohio Law Rep. 66. Courts ⇐ 202(4); Mandamus ⇐ 55

5. Estates—Debts, expenses and claims

Determination made by probate court in interpleader claim, which was filed by insurer in connection with settling of estate of motorist who was killed in accident, as to insurer's limits of liability under motorist's automobile policy applied under doctrine of res judicata to subsequent action arising from accident which was brought against Ohio Department of Transportation (ODOT), county, and township. Kniskern v. Somerford Twp. (Ohio App. 10 Dist., 06-28-1996) 112 Ohio App.3d 189, 678 N.E.2d 273, dismissed, appeal not allowed 77 Ohio St.3d 1485, 673 N.E.2d 145, reconsideration denied 77 Ohio St.3d 1549, 674 N.E.2d 1187, certiorari denied 117 S.Ct. 2513, 521 U.S. 1120, 138 L.Ed.2d 1015. Judgment ⇐ 545

Probate court lacks subject matter jurisdiction to enter order adjudicating claim against estate when claim was been rejected by estate; only remedy for claimant is action in court of general jurisdiction. In re Estate of Vitelli (Ohio App. 2 Dist., 03-29-1996) 110 Ohio App.3d 181, 673 N.E.2d 948. Executors And Administrators ⇐ 236

Probate court order, directing estate to pay one half of balances due on promissory notes secured by mortgages at death of co-obligor, was coram non judice and void ab initio when made after claim had been rejected by estate. In re Estate of Vitelli (Ohio App. 2 Dist., 03-29-1996) 110 Ohio App.3d 181, 673 N.E.2d 948. Executors And Administrators ⇐ 237

Claim that order of probate court, directing estate to pay claim, was void ab initio when made after estate rejected claim, could be raised in otherwise untimely appeal, even though proper course of action would have been to file motion in probate court to vacate its void judgment. In re Estate of Vitelli (Ohio App. 2 Dist., 03-29-1996) 110 Ohio App.3d 181,

673 N.E.2d 948. Executors And Administrators ⇔ 238; Executors And Administrators ⇔ 239

Court of Common Pleas, Division of Domestic Relations, had no jurisdiction to require husband to pay expenses incurred by wife's guardian in divorce action, where court itself noted that guardian's expenses had not been submitted or approved by probate court. Caudill v. Caudill (Franklin 1986) 29 Ohio App.3d 51, 502 N.E.2d 703, 29 O.B.R. 53. Mental Health ⇔ 518

A probate court has no jurisdiction to consider the validity or effect of a contract between the distributees of a decedent's estate and one who contracted to collect their share of the estate for a percentage thereof, where the purported contract has no bearing on the assets of the estate, the duties of the administrator or the court's supervision of his administration. In re Porter's Estate (Ohio Prob. 1969) 17 Ohio Misc. 136, 243 N.E.2d 794, 46 O.O.2d 180.

A probate court cannot assert jurisdiction over an action on a rejected claim through the device of a declaratory judgment or an action for specific performance. Mainline Const. Co. v. Warren (Ohio Prob. 1967) 11 Ohio Misc. 233, 227 N.E.2d 432, 40 O.O.2d 509.

A probate court has jurisdiction to pass upon a claim against an estate filed individually by one of the co-administrators of such estate, but such court has no jurisdiction in such proceeding to examine into a claim of such estate against such co-administrator and her husband for moneys allegedly owing the estate on promissory notes. In re Stutz's Estate (Darke 1964) 1 Ohio App.2d 188, 204 N.E.2d 248, 30 O.O.2d 212. Courts ⇔ 201; Executors And Administrators ⇔ 250

The issue whether a release of a negligence claim executed in the probate court is void may be determined by a common pleas court in an action therein to recover for personal injury damages caused by such negligence. Carpenter v. Pontius (Stark 1963) 119 Ohio App. 383, 200 N.E.2d 682, 28 O.O.2d 12. Courts ⇔ 472.4(1)

The giving of the key to a box taken from a closet, together with a key to a safe deposit box in a bank, with the direction that the donee is to "have everything in this box" and in the safe deposit box in the bank, is not sufficient to establish a gift causa mortis, where such box was still in the donor's room at the time of his death and the donee's residence was different from that of the donor, and in an action for a declaratory judgment brought by a person in possession of personal property claimed by the executor of decedent's estate and which the party in possession claims by virtue of a gift inter vivos, a probate court has jurisdiction to determine the title to such personal property. Renee v. Sanders (Cuyahoga 1956) 102 Ohio App. 21, 131 N.E.2d 846, 73 Ohio Law Abs. 449, 2 O.O.2d 7.

Where in an action against the executor and heirs at law of a decedent the plaintiff claims that certain property in her hands was given to her by the decedent prior to his death and seeks a declaratory judgment setting forth her rights therein as opposed to the executor's claim thereto, the probate court has jurisdiction of such action. Renee v. Sanders (Cuyahoga 1956) 102 Ohio App. 21, 131 N.E.2d 846, 73 Ohio Law Abs. 449, 2 O.O.2d 7.

Under statute giving probate court full power to hear and determine any matter properly before it, if administrator and his wife had separable interests in an agreement to serve and the services performed for his decedent during her lifetime, and in obtaining payment for the services, probate court had concurrent jurisdiction with Common Pleas Court as to claim of administrator's wife, and decision of probate court would be res judicata in subsequent action brought on same claim in Common Pleas Court. In re Smith's Estate (Ohio Prob. 1952) 120 N.E.2d 632, 67 Ohio Law Abs. 409. Courts ⇔ 472.4(4); Judgment ⇔ 545

Where a co-administrator and his wife hold a joint claim against an estate for services rendered, the probate court has jurisdiction to pass on the claim. In re Smith's Estate (Ohio Prob. 1952) 120 N.E.2d 632, 67 Ohio Law Abs. 409.

When in an action to subject a decedent's property to sale in order to pay debts it is determined that title is not in the decedent, the action should be dismissed. Piatt v. Piatt (Darke 1952) 114 N.E.2d 441, 65 Ohio Law Abs. 284.

The common pleas court has jurisdiction of an action in which the plaintiff seeks the return of property placed in the name of a decedent under the mistaken impression she was his wife against the administrator of her estate. Carter v. Birnbaum (Cuyahoga 1953) 113 N.E.2d 102, 68 Ohio Law Abs. 97.

A person claiming ownership of certain chattles may bring a replevin action in common pleas court to recover possession of such property from the administrator of an estate who is wrongfully detaining it, for the reason that such owner is not interested in the inventory and has no claim against the estate. Service Transport Co. v. Matyas (Ohio 1953) 159 Ohio St. 300, 112 N.E.2d 20, 42 A.L.R.2d 413, 50 O.O. 298.

The probate court is invested with the power and jurisdiction to adjudicate a matter relating to the title to and status of personal property, where during the administration of a decedent's estate in such court a decedent's widow files her petition asking for a declaration that certain personal property is an asset of the estate and must be administered as such, as against the claim that such property was effectually disposed of by the decedent during his lifetime through a written declaration of trust. In re Morrison's Estate (Ohio 1953) 159 Ohio St. 285, 112 N.E.2d 13, 50 O.O. 291. Declaratory Judgment ⇔ 273

An alleged owner cannot ordinarily bring a replevin action in common pleas court against an executor or administrator of an estate in the course of administration in probate court. Service Transport Co. v. Matyas (Cuyahoga 1952) 108 N.E.2d 741, 63 Ohio Law Abs. 236, 63 Ohio Law Abs. 244, reversed 159 Ohio St. 300, 112 N.E.2d 20, 42 A.L.R.2d 413, 50 O.O. 298.

Claim for attorney's fees of requisitor who contested claim against estate with partial success should be presented to probate court for allowance. Koelble v. Runyan (Brown 1927) 25 Ohio App. 426, 158 N.E. 279, 6 Ohio Law Abs. 41. Executors And Administrators ⇔ 224

RS 6185 (See GC 10509-178) authorized the probate court to allow an administrator any reasonable sum for a tombstone for decedent. Held, that the court is without jurisdiction, in advance of the settlement of the estate, to entertain an application to fix a sum for that purpose and order the administrator, if the monument is not procured by the widow or next of kin, to erect such monument and charge the expense to the estate. In re Ferguson's Estate (Ohio 1909) 81 Ohio St. 58, 89 N.E. 1070, 7 Ohio Law Rep. 407. Courts ⇔ 199

A probate court is without jurisdiction to fix the maximum sum to be expended for a tombstone. In re Ferguson's Estate (Ohio 1909) 81 Ohio St. 58, 89 N.E. 1070, 7 Ohio Law Rep. 407.

Where an administrator is required to file an account of the expenses of his administration, and such account includes an amount due his attorney for services and expenses, and said account is allowed, and the administrator ordered to pay to such attorney the sum so found due, a failure to comply with such order is a breach of the administration bond. Smith v. Rhodes (Ohio 1903) 68 Ohio St. 500, 48 W.L.B. 682, 68 N.E. 7, 1 Ohio Law Rep. 89, 1 Ohio Law Rep. 135, 1 Ohio Law Rep. 493. Executors And Administrators ⇔ 532

Probate court has exclusive jurisdiction as to credits and payment of unsecured claims. Tidd v. Bloch (Ohio Cir. 1904) 16 Ohio C.D. 113, 4 Ohio C.C.N.S. 216.

A probate court does not have jurisdiction to order an administrator, against his objection, to pay a claim made against the estate by a claimant other than the administrator; a suit on a rejected claim must be commenced in a court having general jurisdiction of suits or actions. Jones v. Green (Ohio Cir. 1901) 11 Ohio C.D. 548.

The probate court, in the administration of estates, has the power to order the payment of a particular claim out of a particular fund. Brown v. Trottner (Ohio Cir. 1896) 5 Ohio C.D. 222.

An order of the probate court allowing claims against an estate which substantially and adversely affect the property rights of three beneficiaries of the estate is a binding determination that the claims are valid for federal estate tax purposes. Goodwin's Estate v. C.I.R. (C.A.6 (Ohio) 1953) 201 F.2d 576, 67 Ohio Law Abs. 233, 51 O.O. 73.

Municipal court, rather than probate court, had subject matter jurisdiction over action by decedents' son against his sisters for recovery of boat motor that had been in his parents' possession prior to their deaths; sisters did not claim ownership of motor, motor did not pass through estates as the property of either decedent, and son sought possession on basis that he owned motor pursuant to certificate of title, not through estates. Hugo v. Mulica (Ohio App. 8 Dist., Cuyahoga, 09-19-2002) No. 80798, 2002-Ohio-4918, 2002 WL 31087427, Unreported. Courts ⇔ 472.4(1); Courts ⇔ 472.6

Where plaintiff brings a cause of action in malpractice for money damages against the attorney-executor of decedent's estate, such action is properly brought in the common pleas court since the probate court lacks jurisdiction. Elden v Sylvania Savings Bank Co, No. L-83-211 (6th Dist Ct App, Lucas, 10-21-83).

Where the probate court determines from conflicting testimony that the decedent at the time of the creation of joint and survivorship accounts had the present intent that such accounts should belong to the surviving party, the appellate court will not reverse the judgment as being against the manifest weight of the evidence. Sutton v Tincombe, No. L–83–183 (6th Dist Ct App, Lucas, 10–7–83).

The probate court has jurisdiction on exceptions being filed to the schedule of debts to allow, reject or reduce any claim previously presented to an executor or administrator without the intervention of a jury. In re Czatt's Estate (Ohio Prob. 1933) 30 Ohio NP(NS) 355.

6. —— Distribution and inventory, estates

A probate court may issue only a general order of distribution, and has no authority to designate by name or otherwise the persons entitled to receive the funds to be distributed; such designation, if made, is void and of no effect. Armstrong v. Grandin (Ohio 1883) 39 Ohio St. 368, 10 W.L.B. 300. Executors And Administrators 314(2)

In action by estate executrix alleging that testator's agent by power of attorney concealed, embezzled, or conveyed assets of estate, probate court had subject matter jurisdiction to consider inter vivos transfers by power of attorney, transfers based upon contracts for services, and funds in a joint and survivorship account of testator and agent; the validity of the underlying transfers was challenged. Burwell v. Rains (Ohio App. 11 Dist., Trumbull, 04-22-2005) No. 2004-T-0042, 2005-Ohio-1893, 2005 WL 940580, Unreported. Executors And Administrators 435

Probate court had jurisdiction to offset niece's distributive share of her aunt's estate by amount of deficiency balance owed on car loan obtained by aunt for benefit of niece; statute governing powers of probate court authorized court to exercise plenary power to require niece to save estate harmless as to the deficiency balance by charge against her distributive share of estate. Estate of Shively v. Peterman (Ohio App. 5 Dist., Delaware, 07-07-2004) No. 03-CA-F10-053, 2004-Ohio-3644, 2004 WL 1535653, Unreported. Courts 198; Executors And Administrators 294

Probate division had subject matter jurisdiction over action for restoration of estate assets which were allegedly taken in a manner inconsistent with power of attorney granted to defendants, since probate division of the court of common pleas had concurrent jurisdiction with general division of the court of common pleas over any action involving "a power of attorney." Guardianship of Vasko v. Brown (Ohio App. 8 Dist., Cuyahoga, 12-18-2003) No. 82433, No. 82560, No. 82780, 2003-Ohio-6858, 2003 WL 22966198, Unreported. Courts 50

Common pleas court, rather than probate court, had exclusive jurisdiction over client's legal malpractice and breach of contract claims against attorney, relating to settlement of client's underlying action for wrongful death of her husband, though probate court had held exclusive jurisdiction over the settlement of the underlying wrongful death action. Buckman-Peirson v. Brannon (Ohio App. 2 Dist., 11-05-2004) 159 Ohio App.3d 12, 822 N.E.2d 830, 2004-Ohio-6074, appeal allowed 105 Ohio St.3d 1463, 824 N.E.2d 91, 2005-Ohio-1024, cause dismissed 106 Ohio St.3d 1520, 834 N.E.2d 824, 2005-Ohio-4949. Courts 472.4(1)

Probate court in which decedent's grandson had opened estate had jurisdiction over action in which grandson asked for declaratory judgment that certain assets, which had been transferred to individual who had held power of attorney over decedent, should be included in estate; validity of transfers was related to administration of estate, since property at issue would revert to estate if transfers were found invalid. Sayer v. Epler (Ohio App. 5 Dist., 07-21-1997) 121 Ohio App.3d 329, 699 N.E.2d 1000, on subsequent appeal 2001 WL 815507, appeal allowed 93 Ohio St.3d 1496, 758 N.E.2d 1148, cause dismissed 95 Ohio St.3d 1433, 766 N.E.2d 999, 2002-Ohio-2020. Courts 198

Once asset is properly distributed from estate, estate can no longer be responsible for its maintenance and probate court loses jurisdiction over it. Whitaker v. Estate of Whitaker (Ohio App. 4 Dist., 06-26-1995) 105 Ohio App.3d 46, 663 N.E.2d 681. Executors And Administrators 132

Whether personal injury settlement funds should be expended by guardian to care for ward was matter properly left to sound discretion of probate court. Gorenflo v. Ohio Dept. of Human Serv. (Marion 1992) 81 Ohio App.3d 500, 611 N.E.2d 425. Mental Health 232

The jurisdiction of probate court under RC 2101.24 includes jurisdiction over declaratory judgment actions involving the administration of an estate. Bobko v. Sagen (Cuyahoga 1989) 61 Ohio App.3d 397, 572 N.E.2d 823, dismissed 45 Ohio St.3d 716, 545 N.E.2d 901.

A probate court exercising jurisdiction granted by RC 2125.02(C) to approve a wrongful death settlement by the personal representative of the decedent has limited plenary jurisdiction under RC 2101.24 to construe a policy of liability insurance for the purpose of determining the amount of insurance coverage available to settle the wrongful death claim. Burris v. Grange Mut. Companies (Ohio 1989) 46 Ohio St.3d 84, 545 N.E.2d 83, rehearing denied 46 Ohio St.3d 717, 546 N.E.2d 1335, rehearing denied 53 Ohio St.3d 718, 560 N.E.2d 779. Courts 198

In a hearing on exceptions to inventory where decedent's nieces and nephews asserted that savings bonds co-owned by the decedent and the nieces and nephews should not be included in the inventory, the probate court was without jurisdiction to impose a constructive trust on one-half of the savings bonds for the benefit of decedent's surviving spouse. Etzensperger v Hurst, No. OT-82-18 (6th Dist Ct App, Ottawa, 12-3-82), affirmed by 9 OS(3d) 19, 9 OBR 112, 457 NE(2d) 1161 (1984).

Probate court has exclusive jurisdiction to direct and control conduct and settle accounts of executors and administrators and order distribution of estates. Border v. Ohio Sav. & Trust Co. (Ohio Com.Pl. 1970) 26 Ohio Misc. 273, 267 N.E.2d 120, 55 O.O.2d 410, 55 O.O.2d 433.

The determination by the probate court, in the summary proceeding provided for by RC 2115.16, that assets should be included in an estate makes the question of title res judicata as between all parties to the proceeding, but the judgment of the probate court may be attacked in a subsequent action by other interested persons who were not parties to the proceeding in probate court. Cole v. Ottawa Home & Sav. Ass'n (Ohio 1969) 18 Ohio St.2d 1, 246 N.E.2d 542, 47 O.O.2d 1. Judgment 475; Judgment 640

The only parties to a hearing on exceptions to an inventory filed in the probate court pursuant to RC 2115.16 are the exceptor and the executor, unless other persons voluntarily appear and are allowed by the court to be made parties to the proceeding. Cole v. Ottawa Home & Sav. Ass'n (Ohio 1969) 18 Ohio St.2d 1, 246 N.E.2d 542, 47 O.O.2d 1. Executors And Administrators 69

As an incident to a hearing upon exceptions to an inventory, the probate court has jurisdiction to determine the issue of a common-law marriage. In re Soeder's Estate (Cuyahoga 1966) 7 Ohio App.2d 271, 220 N.E.2d 547, 36 O.O.2d 404.

No authority exists for ordering a partial distribution of personal estate without formal administration where the estate exceeds $1000 in value. In re McKenzie's Estate (Ohio Prob. 1956) 139 N.E.2d 505, 74 Ohio Law Abs. 106, 1 O.O.2d 485.

No relief for a probate court estate, upon a complaint to the probate court pursuant to GC 10506–67 (RC 2109.50) can be given except with respect to property of such estate. In re Sexton's Estate (Ohio 1955) 163 Ohio St. 124, 126 N.E.2d 129, 56 O.O. 178, certiorari denied 76 S.Ct. 75, 350 U.S. 838, 100 L.Ed. 747.

In action for declaratory judgment, common pleas court has no power to make order of distribution of estate as that matter is within exclusive jurisdiction of probate court. Mally v. Kekich (Cuyahoga 1946) 71 N.E.2d 305, 47 Ohio Law Abs. 120.

Probate court has jurisdiction to adjudicate rights of parties in specific items of property upon filing in such court of a pleading captioned "Petition to determine heirship," under authority conferred by GC 10509–95 (RC 2123.01) et seq. and under this section, conferring plenary power upon probate court to dispose of any matter properly before it which power is exclusive "unless otherwise provided by law;" and such court has exclusive jurisdiction to make such an adjudication irrespective of such captioned pleading, when prayer therein asks for determination not only of names of heirs but also of interest each inherits. Speidel v. Schaller (Clermont 1943) 73 Ohio App. 141, 55 N.E.2d 346, 40 Ohio Law Abs. 190, 28 O.O. 252.

Where no order of distribution has been made by probate court, that court has exclusive jurisdiction, under this section, of action against executor for refusal to pay interested person his share of estate, GC 10509–206 (Repealed) giving common pleas court concurrent jurisdiction only where probate court order of distribution has been made. Heater v. Mittendorf (Hamilton 1943) 72 Ohio App. 4, 50 N.E.2d 559, 38 Ohio Law Abs. 323, 26 O.O. 508.

By GC 10501–53 (RC 2101.24), probate court is given, inter alia, exclusive jurisdiction over administration of decedents estates. Saluppo v. Santangelo (Hamilton 1942) 71 Ohio App. 185, 48 N.E.2d 903, 39 Ohio Law Abs. 169, 26 O.O. 10.

Claimants of stock inventoried as assets of intestate's estate may raise question of ownership by direct proceeding in probate court, though they failed to file exceptions to inventory; "persons interested in estate." Brown v. Southern Ohio Sav. Bank & Trust Co. (Hamilton 1926) 22 Ohio App. 324, 153 N.E. 864. Executors And Administrators 69

The probate court's power is exhausted upon final settlement of the account of the executor or administrator when it enters a general order of distribution, and it has no jurisdiction to determine the persons to whom distribution is to be made or the amount going to each. First Nat. Bank of

2101.24
Note 6

Cadiz v. Beebe (Ohio 1900) 62 Ohio St. 41, 43 W.L.B. 191, 56 N.E. 485. Courts ⚖ 198; Executors And Administrators ⚖ 314(2)

A final settlement may be attacked in common pleas court. Rote v. Stratton (Ohio Com.Pl. 1895) 3 Ohio Dec. 156, 2 Ohio N.P. 27.

The probate court is without jurisdiction to determine to whom the estate of a decedent shall be distributed, but is limited in its jurisdiction to disputes as to the amount which a particular heir or heirs shall receive. Skardon v. Robinson (Ohio Prob. 1910) 55 W.L.B. 373, 8 Ohio Law Rep. 412.

In Ohio, the power of a probate court is exhausted in making an order of distribution, and the court has no authority to determine the persons who will receive the assets or the amount to be paid to each. Brown v. Routzahn (N.D.Ohio 1931) 58 F.2d 329, reversed 63 F.2d 914, certiorari denied 54 S.Ct. 60, 290 U.S. 641, 78 L.Ed. 557.

Where the assets of an estate have been distributed in accordance with a will to life tenants, the estate has been closed, the final account has been settled and determined, and the life tenants die, in the absence of a motion filed in accordance with RC 2109.35 to vacate the order of the probate court, such court lacks jurisdiction to entertain an application by the remaindermen to commit securities formerly in the estate to a trustee. State ex rel. Beedle v. Kiracofe (Ohio 1964) 176 Ohio St. 149, 198 N.E.2d 61, 27 O.O.2d 25.

Where bonds are stricken from an inventory of estate assets because the name of a survivor as well as the name of the decedent appears on the face of each bond, the probate court is without authority to determine ownership of the bonds or to order their delivery to the survivors by the executor. Etzensperger v Hurst, No. OT–84–21 (6th Dist Ct App, Ottawa, 12–14–84).

7. —— Domicile of decedent, estates

Ward's nephew waived, for purposes of appeal, his arguments that intrusion into ward's home by Adult Protective Services (APS) was unlawful, that ward was prohibited from attending competency hearing, that attorneys for ward engaged in fraud, that guardian financially benefited by becoming guardian, and that guardian and attorney for ward colluded, where nephew did not raise these arguments at competency hearing before magistrate, or in objections to magistrate's report, and did not submit transcript of magistrate's hearing or an affidavit to trial court to support the objections nephew did raise. In re Kupchik (Ohio App. 8 Dist., Cuyahoga, 01-06-2005) No. 84493, 2005-Ohio-23, 2005 WL 23321, Unreported, appeal not allowed 106 Ohio St.3d 1413, 830 N.E.2d 346, 2005-Ohio-3154, reconsideration denied 106 Ohio St.3d 1510, 833 N.E.2d 1251, 2005-Ohio-4605. Mental Health ⚖ 148.1

Federal court lacked jurisdiction over declaratory judgment suit seeking determination of decedent's domicile at death, in order to determine which of two states has proper jurisdiction over decedent's estate; determination would directly interfere with state probate proceedings, and declaratory judgment would not clarify issues in decedent's estate and could not terminate the controversy. Bortz v. DeGolyer (S.D.Ohio, 11-07-1995) 904 F.Supp. 680. Declaratory Judgment ⚖ 45; Federal Courts ⚖ 51

8. —— Intestate, estates

RS 6195 to RS 6201 furnishes a complete remedy to the next of kin to recover distributive shares in a portion of an estate as to which the testator died intestate by an action in the probate or common pleas court; these courts are empowered by said statutes to bring in all interested parties, settle finally all matters in controversy, render judgment, and award execution where the amount coming to any heir, legatee, widow, or other distributee is uncertain or in dispute, depending on the construction given any devise or bequest, or any other question; a suit in equity against executors to impose a trust on the portion before final settlement will be unsuccessful where it is not proved that the executors are insolvent, their bond is insufficient, or the plaintiffs are in danger of losing their rights. Bowen v. Bowen (Ohio 1882) 38 Ohio St. 426, 8 W.L.B. 251.

The courts of probate in this state are invested with the power to order distribution of moneys remaining upon final settlement of an intestate estate to the persons entitled thereto; but upon such distribution, its powers are exhausted and it has no jurisdiction to entertain a petition brought to enforce the collection of the amount awarded to a distributee as a debt against the administrator. (See also Doan v Biteley, 49 OS 588, 32 NE 600 (1892); Davis v Davis, 11 OS 386 (1860); Brown v Burdick, 25 OS 260 (1874); Mosier v Harmon, 29 OS 220 (1876); Newton v Hammond, 38 OS 430 (1882); Gorman v Taylor, 43 OS 86, 1 NE 227 (1885).) McLaughlin v. McLaughlin (Ohio 1855) 4 Ohio St. 508, 64 Am.Dec. 603.

The probate court has exclusive jurisdiction of an action to rescind a renunciation of intestate succession properly filed with it. Wolfrum v. Wolfrum (Ohio 1965) 2 Ohio St.2d 237, 208 N.E.2d 537, 31 O.O.2d 501. Courts ⚖ 472.4(2.1)

Probate has no jurisdiction to order an administrator to perform an agreement made by his intestate. Jones v. Green (Ohio Cir. 1901) 11 Ohio C.D. 548.

9. —— Real estate, estates

Executrix did not need to seek probate court approval of real estate transfers between some of decedent's children, as only note as secured by mortgage were estate assets within the jurisdiction of the court. In re Mizer (Ohio App. 5 Dist., Tuscarawas, 02-24-2005) No. 2004 AP 04 0035, 2005-Ohio-862, 2005 WL 469268, Unreported. Executors And Administrators ⚖ 137

Trial court had authority to reopen probate case and to clarify prior judgment in order to resolve ambiguity in will as to when valuation of farm, which was part of residue of estate, would arise for purposes of will provisions requiring residue of estate to be divided equally and son to receive farm. In re Estate of Smith (Ohio App. 3 Dist., Seneca, 04-16-2003) No. 13-02-37, 2003-Ohio-1910, 2003 WL 1877624, Unreported. Wills ⚖ 705

By mere probating of will and appointment of executor, jurisdiction of probate court over sale of real estate of decedent is not acquired, and such jurisdiction is not acquired until executor has filed a petition in that court to sell real estate to pay debts, and interested parties have entered their appearance therein, or process has been issued upon said petition which is later served according to law. Home Owners' Loan Corp. v. Roth (Lorain 1937) 24 Ohio Law Abs. 693. Executors And Administrators ⚖ 333

Determination that guardian was liable for damages in failing to rent or sell residence of ward who was in nursing home without any reasonable prospect of returning to her home even though guardian relied upon advice of attorney who told guardian that he could not sell or rent home as long as money that would be realized therefrom was not needed to pay ward's expenses was not contrary to law or weight of evidence. In re Guardianship of McPheter (Ohio App. 6 Dist., 08-05-1994) 95 Ohio App.3d 440, 642 N.E.2d 690. Mental Health ⚖ 258.1; Mental Health ⚖ 274

While the powers of the probate division of the court of common pleas are plenary, they are so only with respect to matters "properly before the court," and so the probate division of the court of common pleas is without jurisdiction either to reform a deed executed prior to an owner's death or to order a series of conveyances to correct alleged defects in that deed. Oncu v. Bell (Medina 1976) 49 Ohio App.2d 109, 359 N.E.2d 712, 3 O.O.3d 175. Courts ⚖ 198

That decedent's estate was under administration in probate court, and that probate court was considering action to sell realty, did not deprive court of common pleas of jurisdiction of purchaser's action for specific performance of contract with decedent. Fellers v. Belau (Ohio Com.Pl. 1961) 178 N.E.2d 530, 87 Ohio Law Abs. 54. Courts ⚖ 475(2)

Either the probate court of the county in which a decedent's estate is being administered or the common pleas court of the county in which land is located may have jurisdiction of an action for specific performance of a contract to sell the land, depending upon which first acquires jurisdiction of all necessary parties. Fellers v. Belau (Ohio Com.Pl. 1961) 178 N.E.2d 530, 87 Ohio Law Abs. 54.

The language of RC 2101.24 and RC 5303.03 does not subtract from or limit the full jurisdiction of the common pleas court in an action of ejectment to determine the legal title to land, be it by will, deed or otherwise, upon which to award possession of land. Avery v. Avery (Wood 1958) 107 Ohio App. 199, 157 N.E.2d 917, 8 O.O.2d 91.

A probate court, in which estate of deceased lessee was being administered, had jurisdiction to determine what rights, if any, the administratrix of the lessee's estate had in purported oral lease. In re Logan's Estate (Ohio Prob. 1955) 131 N.E.2d 454, 71 Ohio Law Abs. 391. Courts ⚖ 201

In a proceeding in the probate court by a village against a township for division of property the issue is the division of funds and assets, and where the court makes its order of division its jurisdiction is exhausted and it has no continuing jurisdiction over the divided property, and may not entertain a proceeding instituted by the attorney who represented the village to impress a lien on such fund. Village of Eastlake v. Davis (Lake 1952) 94 Ohio App. 71, 114 N.E.2d 627, 51 O.O. 279.

Where executor petitioned for sale of decedent's realty to pay debts, and Probate Court found that decedent's deed to grandson conveyed good title and that realty was not asset of estate, Probate Court did not have jurisdiction to determine only remaining issue whether State of Ohio had waived its priority under trust mortgage which decedent had executed on receiving aid for aged and whether State had released its lien to extent of value of services rendered to decedent by decedent's grandson and latter's wife. Piatt v. Piatt (Darke 1952) 114 N.E.2d 441, 65 Ohio Law Abs. 284. Courts ⇐ 198

The probate court has authority to authorize a trustee for a missing person to bring an action for equitable partition of lands in which the missing person owned a fractional interest. In re Parrett (Franklin 1949) 86 Ohio App. 162, 90 N.E.2d 425, 41 O.O. 20. Absentees ⇐ 7

A probate court does not have jurisdiction, in a proceeding upon exceptions to the inventory filed in a decedent's estate, to determine the title to real or personal property that had been duly transferred, and possession thereof delivered, by the decedent before death. (But see In re Estate of Brady, 34 Abs 410, 6 OSupp 284 (Prob, Cuyahoga 1941).) In re Brunskill's Estate (Summit 1940) 63 Ohio App. 529, 27 N.E.2d 492, 17 O.O. 265. Courts ⇐ 200.7

Probate court has concurrent jurisdiction with common pleas in proceedings to sell realty to pay debts. Helmbold v. Helmbold (Lucas 1926) 25 Ohio App. 32, 158 N.E. 499, 4 Ohio Law Abs. 532. Courts ⇐ 472.4(2.1); Executors And Administrators ⇐ 333

Probate in a proceeding to sell land can adjudicate on the title and holders of outside titles can properly be made parties. Bitely v. Doan (Ohio Cir. 1889) 2 Ohio C.D. 388, affirmed 49 Ohio St. 588, 32 N.E. 600.

Probate court has jurisdiction to adjudicate on title and its decrees to sell land will be sustained. Brigel v Kittredge, 2 NP 329, (Super, Cincinnati 1895).

Probate court can determine title to property on exceptions to an inventory, but it is discretionary whether a summary proceeding should be employed or the exceptors ordered to pursue other remedies. (But see In re Estate of Brunskill, 63 App 529, 27 NE(2d) 492 (1940).) In re Brady's Estate (Ohio Prob. 1941) 6 Ohio Supp. 284, 34 Ohio Law Abs. 410, 21 O.O. 374.

The fact that a complaint is denominated as a complaint to quiet title does not deprive the probate court of jurisdiction or power to dispose of any issue flowing from a case which is properly transferred to the court. Bachman v Swearingen, No. 82–CA–24 (5th Dist Ct App, Delaware, 2–8–83).

10. —— Surviving spouse, estates

General division of Court of Common Pleas, rather than probate division, had jurisdiction over widow's action against husband's estate; widow did not contest validity of will or challenge inventory of his probate estate, but, rather, alleged that husband fraudulently transferred assets to inter vivos trust and did so with intent to deprive widow of her elective share in his probate estate, even though widow sought order to rescind transfer and return property to her which, if granted, might affect administration of husband's estate. Dumas v. Estate of Dumas (Ohio, 03-09-1994) 68 Ohio St.3d 405, 627 N.E.2d 978, 1994-Ohio-312. Executors And Administrators ⇐ 435

The right of a widow to a year's allowance in the estate of her deceased husband vests immediately upon death, becomes a preferred and secured debt of his estate, and, when it has not been paid to the widow during her lifetime, such allowance survives as an asset of her estate and is includable in the inventory of her estate as a debt due from the estate of her deceased husband, but if an exception to the inventory, based on the running of the statute of limitations against such debt, is filed by several of such children, upon a hearing on exceptions to the inventory the probate court may summarily determine only whether such year's allowance is includable in the inventory as a debt but has no power to determine whether the debt is uncollectible by reason of the statute of limitations. In re Wreede's Estate (Van Wert 1958) 106 Ohio App. 324, 154 N.E.2d 756, 7 O.O.2d 75.

Where services are rendered by an attorney for a widow in effecting a settlement of all her rights and claims in and to the estate of her deceased husband, the probate court has jurisdiction to hear and determine an application by the attorney for the allowance of compensation out of the estate; but, although it may have been fortuitous for the estate that a settlement of many problems may have been effected, such circumstances do not justify payment of attorney fees by the estate. In re Colosimo's Estate (Montgomery 1957) 104 Ohio App. 342, 149 N.E.2d 31, 5 O.O.2d 24.

Probate court has jurisdiction under the provisions of this section, to determine whether a surviving spouse is estopped by a contract from electing to take the mansion house at the appraised value as fixed by the appraisers in a proceeding instituted under GC 10509–89 (RC 2113.38).

Passoni v. Breehl (Ohio Prob. 1944) 14 Ohio Supp. 100, 41 Ohio Law Abs. 315, 29 O.O. 220.

In hearing on exceptions by surviving spouse to executor's inventory and appraisement which made no provision for allowance of property not deemed assets under GC 10509–54 (RC 2115.13) or for a year's support under GC 10509–74 (RC 2117.20), probate court had power, under this section, to construe post-nuptial contract whereby allowances were allegedly barred. In re Crabtree's Estate (Ohio Prob. 1938) 1 Ohio Supp. 332, 30 Ohio Law Abs. 176, 15 O.O. 487.

Relief to which widow would otherwise be entitled under GC 10501–53 (RC 2101.24), GC 10503–4 (RC 2105.06) and GC 10509–89 (RC 2113.38), will not be decreed where by contract she has agreed not to claim any other part of the estate than that given her by the contract. In re Schubert's Estate (Ohio Prob. 1934) 32 Ohio NP(NS) 169.

Contract of settlement and execution of deed and mortgage in pursuance thereof, held to estop widow from setting up further claim against the estate or having any standing in probate court. In re Schubert's Estate (Ohio Prob. 1934) 32 Ohio NP(NS) 169.

11. Executors and administrators—Appointment

Administrator was not acting as daughter's attorney, but as administrator of mother's estate, and therefore, owed daughter no duty as her attorney, precluding daughter's claim of legal malpractice; administrator only owed daughter a duty as beneficiary of the estate. Holik v. Lafferty (Ohio App. 11 Dist., Ashtabula, 05-26-2006) No. 2005-A-0005, 2006-Ohio-2652, 2006 WL 1459751, Unreported. Executors And Administrators ⇐ 75

Probate court abused its discretion in appointing successor trustee for family trust after trustee filed declaratory judgment action and resigned his position; trust instrument gave authority to appoint successor trustee to beneficiaries, and court did not give beneficiaries sufficient time to choose their own successor trustee inasmuch as beneficiaries lived throughout United States and court gave them only approximately one month to reach consensus and find trustee who was willing and qualified to serve. Galbreath v. del Valle (Ohio App. 10 Dist., 11-24-1993) 91 Ohio App.3d 829, 633 N.E.2d 1185, dismissed, jurisdictional motion overruled 69 Ohio St.3d 1414, 630 N.E.2d 376. Trusts ⇐ 169(1)

Jurisdiction of court, once acquired over estate, is exclusive, and writ of prohibition lies against second court appointing administrator. State ex rel. Taylor v. Gregory (Ohio 1930) 122 Ohio St. 512, 172 N.E. 365.

The court of common pleas has jurisdiction to review an order of the probate court, denying the right to administer the estate of a decedent, conferred by RS 6005 (See GC 10506–65, 10509–3, 10509–4) on the next of kin if a suitable person. Schumacher v. McCallip (Ohio 1904) 69 Ohio St. 500, 69 N.E. 986, 1 Ohio Law Rep. 789, 1 Ohio Law Rep. 945. Courts ⇐ 202(5); Executors And Administrators ⇐ 20(10)

This section and GC 10617 do not permit trust companies to act as administrators nor make an act giving them such power of uniform operation. Schumacher v. McCallip (Ohio 1904) 69 Ohio St. 500, 69 N.E. 986, 1 Ohio Law Rep. 789, 1 Ohio Law Rep. 945.

In an action on the bond of one appointed executor by the probate court, it appeared that the bond had been approved by said court and contained a recital that the principal had been appointed executor of the will of the testatrix, and also contained a condition that the principal, as executor, would administer all the goods, chattels, and credits, and proceeds of the real estate that may be sold for the payment of debts and legacies, which, upon appointment and giving of such bond, shall pass as assets into the hands of the principal as such executor. Held, that the sureties on the bond were estopped from showing as a defense that the principal was not duly appointed as executor, or that the will was not duly probated. Hoffman v. Fleming (Ohio 1902) 66 Ohio St. 143, 47 W.L.B. 430, 64 N.E. 63. Executors And Administrators ⇐ 537(3)

Sureties on the bond of an executor are estopped from questioning his appointment by the probate court. Hoffman v. Fleming (Ohio 1902) 66 Ohio St. 143, 47 W.L.B. 430, 64 N.E. 63.

The omission to give a bond with the requisite number of sureties upon it cannot defeat an administrator's right to recover in an action upon such bond, so long as the title conferred by his letters from the probate court remains unrevoked. Slagle v. Entrekin (Ohio 1887) 44 Ohio St. 637, 17 W.L.B. 211, 10 N.E. 675. Executors And Administrators ⇐ 26(2); Executors And Administrators ⇐ 29(4)

Probate may apportion commissions between coexecutors when their accounts are not settled. Meyers v. Hopkins (Ohio Cir. 1905) 18 Ohio C.D. 208, 7 Ohio C.C.N.S. 240.

2101.24
Note 11

This section confers exclusive, original and final jurisdiction on probate court in granting and revoking letters testamentary and of administration. Stafford v. American Missionary Ass'n (Ohio Cir. 1901) 12 Ohio C.D. 442.

The conduct of an administrator in management of an estate is in the control of the probate court unless otherwise provided by statute. Jones v. Green (Ohio Cir. 1901) 11 Ohio C.D. 548.

The right of appeal to the common pleas from an order of the probate court removing an executor is not in conflict with the provision of GC 10492, which gives the probate court exclusive jurisdiction to grant and revoke letters testamentary. In re Sells' Estate (Ohio Com.Pl. 1909) 19 Ohio Dec. 567, 8 Ohio NP(NS) 175.

The giving of a bond by an administratrix is not a jurisdictional requirement, and the failure to give such bond renders the appointment merely voidable and not subject to collateral attack. Mitchell v. Albright (Ohio Com.Pl. 1888) 20 W.L.B. 101.

Ohio probate court had exclusive jurisdiction to appoint an administrator of the debtor's estate and had exclusive jurisdiction over the rem of the estate. U.S. v. First Nat. Bank (N.D.Ohio 1943) 54 F.Supp. 351, 28 O.O. 445. Courts ⇔ 472.4(2.1)

12. —— Removal and other actions, executors and administrators

Trial court did not abuse its discretion, on consideration of objections to magistrate's report in competency proceeding, by finding that ward was incompetent and appointing a guardian; magistrate's report indicated that social worker testified that ward was unable to give detailed information regarding her finances, was unable to prepare food, was unable to recognize her physical and mental impairments, and was unaware of her surroundings, and report also indicated that physician evaluated ward, concluded she suffered from dementia, and recommended appointment of guardian. In re Kupchik (Ohio App. 8 Dist., Cuyahoga, 01-06-2005) No. 84493, 2005-Ohio-23, 2005 WL 23321, Unreported, appeal not allowed 106 Ohio St.3d 1413, 830 N.E.2d 346, 2005-Ohio-3154, reconsideration denied 106 Ohio St.3d 1510, 833 N.E.2d 1251, 2005-Ohio-4605. Mental Health ⇔ 107

Trial court did not have jurisdiction to file judgment entry vacating order removing former administratrix and order appointing successor administrator while former administratrix's appeal of order appointing successor administrator was pending; trial court's actions were inconsistent with jurisdiction of Court of Appeals to affirm, reverse, or modify trial court's decision. In re Estate of Staib (Ohio App. 7 Dist., Columbiana, 11-17-2003) No. 02 CO 59, 2003-Ohio-6280, 2003 WL 22765110, Unreported. Executors And Administrators ⇔ 35(19)

Probate court had plenary power to surcharge former trustee to rectify trustee's mismanagement of trust assets, even if probate statute only allowed for surcharge when a trustee failed to invest funds within a reasonable time, where former trustee's poor decision making, negligence, and mismanagement caused numerous trust expenses to be disallowed and funds to be dissipated. In re Testamentary Trusteeship of Cheek (Ohio App. 2 Dist., Montgomery, 05-16-2003) No. 19513, 2003-Ohio-2515, 2003 WL 21122663, Unreported. Trusts ⇔ 308

Once administrator of estate was replaced, his claim against the estate took on status of any other creditor's claim, and probate court retained jurisdiction over claim through its plenary power to dispose of the matter which was already properly before the court. Talbott v. Fisk (Ohio App. 10 Dist., Franklin, 12-17-2002) No. 02AP-427, No. 02AP-428, 2002-Ohio-6960, 2002 WL 31819671, Unreported. Executors And Administrators ⇔ 219; Executors And Administrators ⇔ 250

Probate court has exclusive jurisdiction of action against an executor for conduct in relation to settlement of his accounts where no fraud or collusion is alleged except in general terms and by way of legal conclusions. Truss v. Clouse (Miami 1937) 23 Ohio Law Abs. 610.

Probate court had exclusive subject matter jurisdiction over suit for conversion of estate assets brought against executor of estate and for breach of fiduciary duties brought against guardian of decedent's minor child and, thus, common pleas court properly dismissed complaint. Johnson v. Allen (Ohio App. 8 Dist., 02-13-1995) 101 Ohio App.3d 181, 655 N.E.2d 240. Courts ⇔ 472.4(4); Courts ⇔ 472.4(8); Pretrial Procedure ⇔ 554

Prior rulings of probate court, finding that decedent's mother was neither heir of estate nor guardian of heir, had res judicata effect and precluded decedent's mother from having standing to bring suit against executor of estate for conversion of estate assets and against guardian of decedent's minor child for breach of fiduciary duties. Johnson v. Allen (Ohio App. 8 Dist., 02-13-1995) 101 Ohio App.3d 181, 655 N.E.2d 240. Judgment ⇔ 639

The probate court has jurisdiction to determine an executor's right to crops planted by decedent and decedent's obligations under an oral lease. In re Logan's Estate (Ohio Prob. 1955) 131 N.E.2d 454, 71 Ohio Law Abs. 391.

An action in the probate court for the removal of a testamentary trustee is one in chancery and hence appealable on questions of law and fact. In re Yost's Estate (Ohio 1955) 163 Ohio St. 593, 128 N.E.2d 12, 57 O.O. 24. Trusts ⇔ 167

Probate court has jurisdiction to order administrator to pay debt incurred by him in administration of estate even where there is issue of fact, and the administrator has no right to trial by jury under such circumstances. In re Kaffenberger's Estate (Butler 1942) 71 Ohio App. 201, 48 N.E.2d 885, 26 O.O. 17.

Under statute providing that the probate court shall have plenary power at law and in equity fully to dispose of any matter before the court, unless the power is expressly otherwise limited or denied by statute, the probate court has exclusive jurisdiction as to the allowance of fees to attorneys for services in the unsuccessful prosecution of an application for the removal of a guardian of an incompetent. Unger v. Wolfe (Ohio 1938) 134 Ohio St. 69, 15 N.E.2d 955, 11 O.O. 483. Courts ⇔ 472.4(8)

Under Const Art IV, §8 and GC 10492 (repealed 1932. See §10501–53) plenary jurisdiction is conferred on probate court to direct and control conduct of executors and administrators. Trumpler v. Royer (Ohio 1917) 95 Ohio St. 194, 115 N.E. 1018, 14 Ohio Law Rep. 551. Courts ⇔ 199

Exclusive jurisdiction to remove a guardian being vested in the probate court under RS 1906, § 524 (repealed 1932. See GC 10501–53), the court of common pleas is without original jurisdiction to entertain an application to remove a guardian. In re Oliver's Guardianship (Ohio 1908) 77 Ohio St. 474, 83 N.E. 795, 5 Ohio Law Rep. 586. Mental Health ⇔ 174.1

By accepting the resignation of an administrator pending the settlement of his accounts, the probate court does not thereby lose its jurisdiction over his person or the settlement of his accounts, and may proceed to hear and determine exceptions thereto, and ascertain the amount due from him to the estate in like manner as if he had continued in the execution of his trust, and the amount so found will be conclusive not only upon him but upon his sureties. Slagle v. Entrekin (Ohio 1887) 44 Ohio St. 637, 17 W.L.B. 211, 10 N.E. 675. Courts ⇔ 30; Executors And Administrators ⇔ 469(2)

Probate court has exclusive jurisdiction of the accounts of executors and administrators. Jones v. Green (Ohio Cir. 1901) 11 Ohio C.D. 548.

Probate court cannot order an administrator to perform an agreement made by his intestate. Jones v. Green (Ohio Cir. 1901) 11 Ohio C.D. 548.

The statutory right conferred by GC 11206 to appeal to common pleas from an order of probate removing executor does not conflict with this section. In re Sells' Estate (Ohio Com.Pl. 1909) 19 Ohio Dec. 567, 8 Ohio NP(NS) 175.

The jurisdiction of probate court in removing executors and administrators is exclusive and can only be reviewed for fraud or abuse of power and when substantial rights are affected. Munger v. Jeffries (Ohio Com.Pl. 1900) 10 Ohio Dec. 12, 7 Ohio N.P. 55.

The probate court has jurisdiction in an action by a legatee to compel the executor to show cause why the balance of legacy should not be paid to such legatee. In re Isherwood's Estate (Ohio Prob. 1894) 5 Ohio Dec. 143, 7 Ohio N.P. 332, 1 Ohio Leg. N. 19. Executors And Administrators ⇔ 314(2)

There is no federal diversity jurisdiction over probate matters; thus an action by heirs against an executrix seeking damages for alleged irregularities is properly dismissed from a district court. Bedo v. McGuire (C.A.6 (Ohio) 1985) 767 F.2d 305.

Federal court does not have jurisdiction of an action against an executor or administrator involving an alleged breach of fiduciary duties. Starr v. Rupp (C.A.6 (Ohio) 1970) 25 Ohio Misc. 224, 421 F.2d 999, 12 A.L.R. Fed. 279, 53 O.O.2d 169, 54 O.O.2d 343.

A complaint attacking action of probate court in removing for neglect and incompetency an executor under a will during pendency of action to contest will, such complaint filed in federal court upon ground of diversity of citizenship and the matter in controversy not exceeding sum of $3,000, was properly dismissed by district court for action of probate court in exercise of its exclusive and plenary jurisdiction to direct and control the conduct and settle accounts of executors and administrators is not subject to review by federal court, and no substantial constitutional or federal question is involved. Pettiford v. George (C.C.A.6 (Ohio) 1942) 125 F.2d 144, 22 O.O. 460. Federal Courts ⇔ 927

While the probate court has power to control the conduct of fiduciaries in the administration of estates, the thing complained of must be the result of an act committed or omitted by the fiduciary, and not of an act done by the complaining party or in which she participated of her own free will. In re Schubert's Estate (Ohio Prob. 1934) 32 Ohio NP(NS) 169.

13. Foreclosures

Probate court and court of common pleas have concurrent jurisdiction of an action to foreclose a mortgage on real estate of deceased mortgagor of whose estate an administratrix has been appointed and qualified, when it is necessary to sell real estate to pay decedent's debts, and court which first acquires jurisdiction thereof retains it to the exclusion of the other. Government Nat. Mortg. Ass'n v. Smith (Hamilton 1971) 28 Ohio App.2d 300, 277 N.E.2d 233, 57 O.O.2d 453.   Courts ⇔ 475(2)

Where probate court has acquired jurisdiction of subject-matter of proceeding brought by an administrator to sell real estate of a decedent to pay the debts of the estate, common pleas court is without jurisdiction in an action subsequently brought by a mortgagee to foreclose a mortgage on the same property. (See also Peoples Savings Assn v Sanford, 59 App 294, 18 NE(2d) 126 (1938).) Home Bldg. & Sav. Co. v. Sanford (Lucas 1938) 59 Ohio App. 302, 18 N.E.2d 127, 13 O.O. 90.   Courts ⇔ 472.4(3); Courts ⇔ 475(2)

Both the probate and the common pleas court have jurisdiction of an action to foreclose a mortgage on the real estate of a deceased mortgagor of whose estate an administrator or executor has been appointed and qualified, and therefore the court which first acquires jurisdiction thereof retains it to the exclusion of the other. Peoples Sav. Ass'n v. Sanford (Lucas 1938) 59 Ohio App. 294, 18 N.E.2d 126, 13 O.O. 86.   Courts ⇔ 472.4(1); Courts ⇔ 475(2)

The probate court has jurisdiction to give full relief in assignment proceedings, including the sale of mortgaged premises free from the inchoate dower interest of the husband who did not sign the assignment agreement made by his wife; and such jurisdiction cannot be defeated by the mortgagee instituting foreclosure proceedings in the common pleas court under a mortgage signed by both husband and wife. Madigan v. Dollar Bldg. & Loan Co. (Franklin 1935) 52 Ohio App. 553, 4 N.E.2d 68, 20 Ohio Law Abs. 132, 6 O.O. 478.

Unless the administrator of a deceased person's estate is made a party to an action in common pleas court brought by a mortgagee to foreclose on the deceased's real estate, the administrator is not prevented from bringing an action in the probate court to sell the same property to pay debts of the deceased. Bateman v Morris, 4 NP 397, 7 D 287 (Prob, Clark 1897).   Courts ⇔ 475(2)

Where a summons has been served or publication made, the action is pending so as to charge third persons with notice of its pendency, and where a foreclosure action is pending in common pleas, an assignment will not transfer jurisdiction to the court of insolvency. Omwake v Jackson, 15 CC 615, 8 CD 235 (Hamilton 1898).

Jurisdiction of a probate court is limited to the powers given it by the constitution and legislative enactment, and having received no authority to hear and determine actions for the foreclosure of mortgages and marshalling of liens other than in land sale proceedings, it has no jurisdiction of actions to foreclose delinquent tax liens as provided in GC 5718–3 (RC 5721.18) and GC 5719 (RC 5721.19). 1940 OAG 2457.

14. Fraud

Probate court, at hearing on exceptions to inventory of decedent's estate, was not empowered to impress constructive trust upon savings bonds, which had been issued in names of decedent and one of her relatives as co-owners, on ground that decedent fraudulently used her husband's funds to purchase the bonds. In re Estate of Etzensperger (Ohio 1984) 9 Ohio St.3d 19, 457 N.E.2d 1161, 9 O.B.R. 112.   Executors And Administrators ⇔ 85(8)

Notwithstanding RC 2101.24, the probate court does not have the authority under RC 2115.16 to impress a constructive trust on savings bonds at a hearing on exceptions, since such a hearing is a summary proceeding conducted by the probate court solely to determine whether all of the proper assets and liabilities have been included in a decedent's estate; the issue of the fraudulent appropriation of the purchase money for the bonds should be brought pursuant to RC 2117.02. In re Estate of Etzensperger (Ohio 1984) 9 Ohio St.3d 19, 457 N.E.2d 1161, 9 O.B.R. 112.

Probate courts have no jurisdiction over claims for money damages resulting from fraud. Alexander v. Compton (Clinton 1978) 57 Ohio App.2d 89, 385 N.E.2d 638, 11 O.O.3d 81.

A probate court has inherent power to vacate, after term, a judgment procured by fraud. In re Adoption of Sladky (Franklin 1958) 109 Ohio App. 120, 161 N.E.2d 554, 81 Ohio Law Abs. 264, 10 O.O.2d 304.

In action in Probate Court for declaratory judgment determining widow's rights in estate of deceased husband and that conveyance of certain shares of stock made by husband during his lifetime be set aside on grounds of fraud, only question properly before Probate Court was one of law since Probate Court does not have general equitable power, and hence appeal from decision of Probate Court on questions of law and fact could not be maintained. MacLean v. J.S. MacLean Co. (Franklin 1955) 133 N.E.2d 198, 71 Ohio Law Abs. 589, 71 Ohio Law Abs. 590.   Courts ⇔ 202(5)

Dishonest and collusive judgment is open to attack when it affects creditors, and fraud in such cases is regarded as perpetrated not only upon the person aggrieved but likewise upon the court. Hooffstetter v. Adams (Summit 1941) 67 Ohio App. 21, 35 N.E.2d 896, 21 O.O. 70.

Judgment creditor of a person who has fraudulently transferred his assets to an estate in pursuance of a conspiracy between such judgment debtor and the administrator of the estate, may maintain an action in a probate court to set aside and vacate a judgment of the probate court, entered as a result of such fraudulent conspiracy. Hooffstetter v. Adams (Summit 1941) 67 Ohio App. 21, 35 N.E.2d 896, 21 O.O. 70.

Where matters covered by the ninth account were not "in dispute" nor determined by the court as such at the time of its approval, the probate court was authorized to open the account and to vacate its order of settlement which had been secured by fraud. Massachusetts Bonding & Ins. Co. v. Winters Nat. Bank & Trust Co. of Dayton, Ohio (C.C.A.6 (Ohio) 1942) 130 F.2d 5, 24 O.O. 225, certiorari denied 63 S.Ct. 526, 317 U.S. 700, 87 L.Ed. 560.

15. Guardianships

Guardians of minors appointed in one county cannot institute proceedings in the probate court of another county to sell real estate of their wards situated in the latter county. Foresman v. Haag (Ohio 1880) 36 Ohio St. 102, supplemented 37 Ohio St. 143.

In proceedings for the appointment of guardians, plenary and exclusive jurisdiction of the subject matter has been conferred by statute upon the probate court, and that jurisdiction attaches whenever application is made to the court for its exercise in a given case. (See also Kittredge v Miller, 12 CC 128, 5 CD 391 (Hamilton 1896), affirmed by 56 OS 779, 49 NE 1113 (1897); Keifer v Spence, 5 NP 522, 5 D 609 (Prob, Clark 1898); Fox v Keister, 6 NP 216, 8 D 636 (CP, Darke 1899).) Shroyer v. Richmond (Ohio 1866) 16 Ohio St. 455.

A probate court is without jurisdiction to hear and determine an application for an allowance to applicants' counsel for services rendered in a prior action to construe a will, brought in the common pleas court of the county and carried through to the supreme court, to which prior action applicants were parties. Union Sav. Bank & Trust Co. v. Alter (Ohio App. 1 Dist. 1922) 17 Ohio App. 29.

The trial court's denial of ward's motion to relocate to the State of Pennsylvania was not an abuse of discretion, even though ward preferred to relocate; two experts opined that ward needed constant assistance, and ward conceded that she needed assistance with daily life. In re Helen Riva Guardianship (Ohio App. 5 Dist., Richland, 10-19-2006) No. 2006-CA-0067, 2006-Ohio-5547, 2006 WL 3020316, Unreported.   Mental Health ⇔ 35

Probate court did not have jurisdiction to consider mother's application for guardianship over the person of her eighteen-year-old autistic son due to previous order from domestic relations court concerning terms of the shared parenting agreement, even though the terms of such agreement were not a part of the probate court record; regardless of the terms of the agreement, the existence of the prior parenting agreement concerning the autistic son required the probate court to defer jurisdiction. In re Campbell (Ohio App. 7 Dist., Mahoning, 03-31-2006) No. 05 MA 10, 2006-Ohio-1764, 2006 WL 890999, Unreported.   Mental Health ⇔ 109

Court of Common Pleas lacked subject matter jurisdiction over action by ward's son against guardian, asserting various causes of action arising out of guardian's fiduciary relationship with ward, despite son's contention that probate court could not award monetary damages; probate court had exclusive jurisdiction over matters touching upon a guardianship, and had plenary power to dispose of cases properly before it, including awarding monetary damages. Rowan v. McLaughlin (Ohio App. 8 Dist., Cuyahoga,

Note 15

07-07-2005) No. 85665, 2005-Ohio-3473, 2005 WL 1581109, Unreported. Guardian And Ward ⇒ 123

Evidence supported probate court's decision to appoint guardian of the person and the estate, although ward allegedly was medication compliant at time of hearing; evidence indicated that ward had history of substance abuse, ward had been diagnosed as having bi-polar disorder and borderline personality disorder, ward could not appropriately handle her finances on her own, and ward's case worker believed that ward may have only been attempting compliance with medication because court had become involved. In re Guardianship of Slone (Ohio App. 3 Dist., Crawford, 11-15-2004) No. 3-04-13, 2004-Ohio-6041, 2004 WL 2581081, Unreported. Guardian And Ward ⇒ 13(4)

Evidence was insufficient to support finding that mother waived notice of guardianship hearing at which she failed to appear, so as to support probate court's denial of mother's motion for new trial; while mother initially signed a waiver of notice and consent, which was filed with guardianship application, mother appeared at the initial guardianship hearing at which she withdrew her consent and she objected to appointment of applicants as guardians, and trial court granted a continuance so that mother could retain counsel to represent her at the guardianship hearing. In re Guardianship of Pierce (Ohio App. 4 Dist., Ross, 07-22-2003) No. 03CA2712, 2003-Ohio-3997, 2003 WL 21715997, Unreported. Judgment ⇒ 162(4)

Denial of mother's motion for new trial following probate court's creation of a guardianship over her son in favor of grandparents who applied for guardianship was abuse of discretion, which denial was based on trial court's conclusion that mother had actual notice of guardianship hearing at which she failed to appear, where mother testified that she did not receive notice, while applicants testified that they provided notice, there was confusion over which notice was given, as there was also a juvenile court proceeding involving same issues scheduled for one hour after guardianship hearing on same day, and fact that mother appeared for juvenile court proceeding but not guardianship hearing logically indicated that mother did not receive notice of the guardianship hearing. In re Guardianship of Pierce (Ohio App. 4 Dist., Ross, 07-22-2003) No. 03CA2712, 2003-Ohio-3997, 2003 WL 21715997, Unreported. Judgment ⇒ 162(4)

Filing of juvenile court complaint alleging child was neglected or dependent child did not divest probate court of jurisdiction to issue letters of guardianship over child but, rather, probate court and juvenile court retained concurrent jurisdiction as to child, where guardianship application was filed first-in-time, and the juvenile court had yet to adjudicate child neglected or dependent or enter dispositional order at time guardianship letters issued. In re Guardianship of Pierce (Ohio App. 4 Dist., Ross, 07-22-2003) No. 03CA2712, 2003-Ohio-3997, 2003 WL 21715997, Unreported. Courts ⇒ 472.1; Infants ⇒ 196

Issues raised in action by which creditors that had provided goods and services to ward sought removal of guardian and payment of debts incurred "touched" the guardianship and, thus, probate court was the proper court to adjudicate debts, which guardian never contested. In re Ewanicky (Ohio App. 8 Dist., Cuyahoga, 06-26-2003) No. 81742, 2003-Ohio-3351, 2003 WL 21469181, Unreported, stay denied 99 Ohio St.3d 1534, 795 N.E.2d 55, 2003-Ohio-4677, appeal not allowed 100 Ohio St.3d 1506, 799 N.E.2d 186, 2003-Ohio-6161, reconsideration denied 101 Ohio St.3d 1425, 802 N.E.2d 155, 2004-Ohio-123. Guardian And Ward ⇒ 25; Guardian And Ward ⇒ 123

Probate Court had jurisdiction to appoint maternal grandparents as guardian of minor child whose father was incarcerated for killing his mother. In re Hoke (Ohio App. 10 Dist., Franklin, 05-08-2003) No. 02AP-1159, 2003-Ohio-2329, 2003 WL 21028323, Unreported. Guardian And Ward ⇒ 8

Trial court acted within its discretion, and in best interest of child, when court decided that monetary conflict of interest regarding settlement of father's insurance claims rendered mother unsuitable to become guardian of child's estate, where amount child would receive from settlement was inversely proportional to amount mother would receive. In re Guardianship of Muehrcke (Ohio App. 8 Dist., Cuyahoga, 01-16-2003) No. 81353, 2003-Ohio-176, 2003 WL 132422, Unreported, appeal not allowed 99 Ohio St.3d 1412, 788 N.E.2d 648, 2003-Ohio-2454. Guardian And Ward ⇒ 10

A mother is removed as co-guardian of her adult son, an incompetent, and sole guardianship granted to Advocacy and Protective Services based upon the mother's failure to act on behalf of her son's best interest as demonstrated by her abusive and disruptive behavior toward the agency and her lack of insight and paranoia which (1) completely thwart the agency's efforts to act in the ward's best interest, (2) delays services, and (3) challenges the agency's motivation and destroys its credibility with her son. In re Briggs (Ohio App. 9 Dist., Summit, 07-09-1997) No. 18117, 1997 WL 416331, Unreported.

A trial court acts reasonably in maintaining as guardian an individual who is not a family member where the guardian has not wasted assets or been negligent in the care of the ward's person and estate. In Matter of Guardianship of Volkert (Ohio App. 10 Dist., Franklin, 09-21-1995) No. 95APF03-265, 1995 WL 559943, Unreported.

Administrator of ward's estate was not entitled to writ of prohibition to prevent probate court judge from ordering payment of special master commissioner and successor guardian from guardianship estate; the judge did not patently and unambiguously lack jurisdiction to resolve right of commissioner and successor guardian to attorney fees from the guardianship estate, and administrator had an adequate legal remedy by appeal. State ex rel. Estate of Hards v. Klammer (Ohio, 08-02-2006) 110 Ohio St.3d 104, 850 N.E.2d 1197, 2006-Ohio-3670. Prohibition ⇒ 3(3)

Probate court judge was authorized to appoint special master commissioner to resolve attorney fee dispute in guardianship case, to remove guardian, and to appoint successor guardian. State ex rel. Estate of Hards v. Klammer (Ohio, 08-02-2006) 110 Ohio St.3d 104, 850 N.E.2d 1197, 2006-Ohio-3670. Guardian And Ward ⇒ 158

Mother, whose sons applied for appointment of guardian for her, was not entitled to writ of prohibition to prevent probate judge from appointing guardian ad litem (GAL) for her in guardianship proceeding; given evidence that mother was confused and might not have intended to leave her home and probate court's interest in determining veracity of conflicting allegations of mother's children, that mother was incompetent and that son removed mother from her home despite her desire to remain there, judge did not patently and unambiguously lack jurisdiction to appoint GAL for mother. State ex rel. Florence v. Zitter (Ohio, 08-10-2005) 106 Ohio St.3d 87, 831 N.E.2d 1003, 2005-Ohio-3804. Prohibition ⇒ 10(2)

Trial court, as part of its authority in matters involving guardianship of woman, could revoke power of attorney granted to woman's new husband; court found woman incompetent, and court assumed no greater right than woman would have been able to exercise if she had been competent. In re Guardianship of Thomas (Ohio App. 10 Dist., 03-12-2002) 148 Ohio App.3d 11, 771 N.E.2d 882, 2002-Ohio-1037. Mental Health ⇒ 139

Voting trust is an inter vivos trust over which probate court has concurrent jurisdiction with the general division of the court of common pleas. In re Guardianship of Lombardo (Ohio, 09-29-1999) 86 Ohio St.3d 600, 716 N.E.2d 189, 1999-Ohio-132. Courts ⇒ 472.4(7)

Probate court's overruling of guardian's application to disburse funds from guardianship estate in lump sum after domestic relations court determined that father owed child support arrearage was not collateral attack on domestic relations court's judgment. In re Guardianship of Derakhshan (Ohio App. 11 Dist., 04-01-1996) 110 Ohio App.3d 190, 673 N.E.2d 954. Child Support ⇒ 498

Jurisdiction of probate court extends to all matters which touch guardianship. In re Guardianship of Derakhshan (Ohio App. 11 Dist., 04-01-1996) 110 Ohio App.3d 190, 673 N.E.2d 954. Guardian And Ward ⇒ 8

Probate court acted within limitations of its authority as superior guardian when it denied mother's request to distribute funds in guardianship estate in lump sum after domestic relations court determined that father owed child support arrearage, although funds in estate represented prepaid child support; probate court's decision to deny lump-sum disbursement was reasonable attempt to balance competing concerns of guardian while at same time adhering to best interests of child standard. In re Guardianship of Derakhshan (Ohio App. 11 Dist., 04-01-1996) 110 Ohio App.3d 190, 673 N.E.2d 954. Guardian And Ward ⇒ 58

Probate court has continuing and exclusive jurisdiction over all matters pertaining to relationship between guardian and ward. Ohio Dept. of Mental Health v. Baldauf (Ohio App. 11 Dist., 11-20-1995) 107 Ohio App.3d 467, 669 N.E.2d 39. Courts ⇒ 472.4(8); Mental Health ⇒ 109

Once state obtained judgment in common pleas court for sums that it expended for mentally ill criminal defendant committed to state mental institution, it had to look to probate court for order requiring guardian to pay judgment, since granting permission or requiring guardian to pay such an award was within exclusive jurisdiction of probate court. Ohio Dept. of Mental Health v. Baldauf (Ohio App. 11 Dist., 11-20-1995) 107 Ohio App.3d 467, 669 N.E.2d 39. Courts ⇒ 472.4(8); Mental Health ⇒ 451

Probate courts have primarily been responsible for preservation and correct administration of property belonging to ward's estate, but are not primarily concerned with litigation of serious and ofttimes acrimonious disputes involving ward. Ohio Dept. of Mental Health v. Baldauf (Ohio App. 11 Dist., 11-20-1995) 107 Ohio App.3d 467, 669 N.E.2d 39. Mental Health ⇒ 214

No trust, express or otherwise, was ever created to hold semicomatose person's share of proceeds of personal injury settlement, despite probate court's continuing jurisdiction over that person, her funds and her guardian. Gorenflo v. Ohio Dept. of Human Serv. (Marion 1992) 81 Ohio App.3d 500, 611 N.E.2d 425. Trusts ⇐ 30.5(1)

A probate court has the jurisdiction and power to authorize the guardian of a minor or incompetent to refuse or terminate life-sustaining care of the ward who is in a chronic vegetative state; RC 1337.13 shows the express intent of the legislature to allow the guardian of a minor to be empowered to make health care decisions regarding the care of the ward. In re Guardianship of Crum (Ohio Prob. 1991) 61 Ohio Misc.2d 596, 580 N.E.2d 876.

Once a probate court terminates a guardianship, the subject of the terminated guardianship ceases to be a ward of the court and the juvenile court then has exclusive jurisdiction to determine custody of the minor. In re Guardianship of Harrison (Hamilton 1989) 60 Ohio App.3d 19, 572 N.E.2d 855, motion overruled 47 Ohio St.3d 708, 547 N.E.2d 992. Courts ⇐ 472.1; Guardian And Ward ⇐ 25

The probate division of a court of common pleas has no subject matter jurisdiction in paternity actions. Martin v. Davidson (Ohio 1990) 53 Ohio St.3d 240, 559 N.E.2d 1348.

In the making of health care decisions by guardians, the "best interest of the ward" standard must be construed in light of RC 1337.13, Ohio's durable power of attorney for health care statute. Couture v. Couture (Montgomery 1989) 48 Ohio App.3d 208, 549 N.E.2d 571.

Probate court has subject matter jurisdiction over all matters concerning guardian's expenditure of ward's funds, including proposed expenditure of ward's funds to pay medical expenses of ward's wife. In re Rauscher (Cuyahoga 1987) 40 Ohio App.3d 106, 531 N.E.2d 745. Guardian And Ward ⇐ 58

The probate court has subject matter jurisdiction over all matters touching the guardianship pursuant to RC 2101.24 and 2111.13(A)(4), including all expenditures of a ward's funds and the proposed expenditure of a ward's funds to pay for the medical expenses of the ward's wife. In re Rauscher (Cuyahoga 1987) 40 Ohio App.3d 106, 531 N.E.2d 745. Guardian And Ward ⇐ 58

While juvenile court entered order granting temporary custody of minor child to county welfare department of social services upon adjudging minor child to be dependent child, when juvenile court terminated order and returned minor child to mother, jurisdiction of juvenile court ceased, so that when grandmother of minor child applied to probate court to become child's guardian, probate court acquired exclusive jurisdiction over ward and guardian, and juvenile court was without jurisdiction to grant custody over ward to another person until guardianship had been terminated. In re Miller (Cuyahoga 1986) 33 Ohio App.3d 224, 515 N.E.2d 635. Courts ⇐ 475(6)

Where a probate court appoints a guardian for a minor child, the probate court retains continuing and exclusive jurisdiction over the ward and the guardian; thus, a juvenile court is without jurisdiction to grant custody of the ward to another person until the guardianship has been terminated. In re Miller (Cuyahoga 1986) 33 Ohio App.3d 224, 515 N.E.2d 635.

In a divorce proceeding involving a spouse for whom a guardian has been appointed by a probate court, the domestic relations court should not order one party to pay the expenses of the guardian as part of its divorce decree, since the guardianship is an issue before the probate court. Caudill v. Caudill (Franklin 1986) 29 Ohio App.3d 51, 502 N.E.2d 703, 29 O.B.R. 53.

Under guardianship statutes, probate court has jurisdiction in appointment and control of guardians which extends to all matters touching guardianship, including custody of minor and visitation rights of third parties. In re Zahoransky (Cuyahoga 1985) 22 Ohio App.3d 75, 488 N.E.2d 944, 22 O.B.R. 173. Guardian And Ward ⇐ 8

A probate court has jurisdiction to order a guardian to allow a third party to visit the ward, inasmuch as the order is one "touching the guardianship" within the meaning of RC 2111.13. In re Zahoransky (Cuyahoga 1985) 22 Ohio App.3d 75, 488 N.E.2d 944, 22 O.B.R. 173.

Probate courts have only such equitable powers as have been delegated to them. City of Brook Park v. Columbia Road Inv., Inc. (Ohio Prob. 1970) 23 Ohio Misc. 363, 256 N.E.2d 284, 51 O.O.2d 247, 52 O.O.2d 361. Courts ⇐ 200.5

Where a person, now deceased, created during her lifetime a joint and survivorship bank account for the benefit of the survivor, and the trial court finds that the deceased intended to create a joint and survivorship account, and the evidence and the record support that finding, the fact that the decedent, after she had created the account, was declared to be an incompetent and a guardian was properly appointed for her, does not, as a matter of law, terminate the joint and survivorship nature of the account. Miller v. Yocum (Ohio 1970) 21 Ohio St.2d 162, 256 N.E.2d 208, 50 O.O.2d 372.

The jurisdiction of the probate court under RC 2101.24(F) to make inquests respecting insane persons subject to guardianships is, by the terms of that section, exclusive unless otherwise provided by law. In re Moser (Ohio Com.Pl. 1967) 19 Ohio Misc. 81, 246 N.E.2d 626, 47 O.O.2d 420, 48 O.O.2d 253.

A probate court has authority to appoint a guardian for one incompetent by reason of physical disability even though prior to such appointment said incompetent was sued by his wife for divorce and restrained from disposing of his property. In re Guardianship of Stephens (Ohio Prob. 1964) 2 Ohio Misc. 47, 202 N.E.2d 458, 30 O.O.2d 325.

A guardian of an incompetent surviving spouse may obtain approval for the purchase of the mansion house of the decedent. Dorfmeier v. Dorfmeier (Ohio Prob. 1954) 123 N.E.2d 681, 69 Ohio Law Abs. 15.

Where a guardian has been validly appointed by the probate court of one county, the probate court of another county is without authority to entertain an application for a change of guardian. Guardianship of Kollmeyer (Darke 1952) 113 N.E.2d 122, 64 Ohio Law Abs. 577, 64 Ohio Law Abs. 578.

The probate court had jurisdiction to entertain guardian's application to enter into trust agreement relative to operation of land owned by guardian's wards and others as tenants in common and to exercise that jurisdiction to extent authorized by statutes, notwithstanding irregularities in proceedings as to manner of service of process on wards, as to appointment of guardian ad litem and filing of answer on behalf of minors. Pence v. Pence (Shelby 1942) 43 N.E.2d 924, 36 Ohio Law Abs. 369. Guardian And Ward ⇐ 48

Probate court has exclusive jurisdiction as to allowance of fees to attorney for his services in unsuccessful prosecution of application for removal of guardian of incompetent. Unger v. Wolfe (Ohio 1938) 134 Ohio St. 69, 15 N.E.2d 955, 11 O.O. 483.

Exclusive original jurisdiction to remove a guardian being, by this section, vested in probate court, common pleas is without original jurisdiction to entertain application to remove guardian. In re Oliver's Guardianship (Ohio 1908) 77 Ohio St. 474, 83 N.E. 795, 5 Ohio Law Rep. 586. Mental Health ⇐ 174.1

Where a probate court appoints a guardian for the person and estate of a minor, it does not lose jurisdiction of such guardianship by the removal of the guardian from the state; the probate court may compel the foreign administratrix of such guardian, after his decease, to account to such ward. Netting v. Strickland (Ohio Cir. 1899) 9 Ohio C.D. 841. Guardian And Ward ⇐ 144; Guardian And Ward ⇐ 146

Where a probate court appoints an aunt the guardian of a minor child, such appointment is a final order affecting a substantial right of the child's father, and is reviewable on error. Hare v. Sears (Ohio Com.Pl. 1906) 17 Ohio Dec. 590, 4 Ohio N.P.N.S. 566.

Under GC 10915, probate court has exclusive original jurisdiction to appoint and remove guardians, and the orders of that court in such proceedings are not subject to collateral attack. State ex rel. Fisher v. Madden (Ohio Com.Pl. 1901) 12 Ohio Dec. 83.

When a minor reaches her majority and the probate court grants the request to terminate her guardianship the probate court loses jurisdiction over any matter pertaining to her including a personal injury claim from an automobile accident which occurs during minority. In re Layshock (Ohio App. 7 Dist., Mahoning, 12-28-2001) No. 00-C.A.-198, 2001-Ohio-3381, 2001 WL 1667872, Unreported.

The probate court may terminate a guardianship upon adjudication that a person is no longer incompetent pursuant to RC 2101.24(A)(4), 2101.24(A)(6) and 2111.47; such person then regains full control over his property and may validly revoke an inter vivos trust. Old Phoenix Natl Bank of Medina v Oenslager, No. 1586 (9th Dist Ct App, Medina, 10–14–87).

Where the accounting required of a guardian by RC 2109.30 is impracticable or impossible, the probate court has plenary power under RC 2101.24 to substitute an alternative means of accounting such as a hearing upon statements offered in lien of a formal account; such a hearing, provided for by RC 2109.32, requires formal notice to all interested parties, so that an order closing a guardianship after a hearing held without notice to a ward must be reversed. In re Guardianship of Flesh, No. 84–CA–6 (2d Dist Ct App, Miami, 7–20–84).

Note 15

The common pleas court can acquire no jurisdiction in the matter of the settlement of a guardian's account so long as any item of the account remains undetermined. Gregg v Klein, 12 CC(NS) 264, 22 CD 698 (Hamilton 1908).

The death of a guardian without filing an account does not give common pleas jurisdiction of action on guardian's bond to compel an accounting. Wegner v Wiltsie, 3 CC(NS) 410, 13 CD 302 (Lucas 1902).

The court of common pleas does not get jurisdiction of an action on a guardian's bond for an accounting. Wegner v Wiltsie, 3 CC(NS) 410, 13 CD 302 (Lucas 1902).

16. Inheritance taxes

Where an order is entered determining the inheritance tax due and the department of taxation files exceptions thereto, the court's order on the exceptions is the final order from which an appeal may be taken. In re Linton's Estate (Guernsey 1961) 181 N.E.2d 48, 86 Ohio Law Abs. 409.

An executor does not lose his right to have a final order determining inheritance taxes modified for a mistake of fact in erroneously listing assets for taxation by a failure to file exceptions to the interlocutory order determining inheritance taxes. In re Beckman's Estate (Mercer 1951) 91 Ohio App. 42, 107 N.E.2d 538, 48 O.O. 236.

In a proceeding in the probate court to fix inheritance tax the executor of one of two joint and several obligors listed the obligation at one-half of the debt and the court fixed the tax on the balance of the estate after deducting one-half of the debt; about ten years thereafter, upon discovering the error, the executor filed an application to modify the finding of the amount of the tax held: jurisdiction of probate court to redetermine its finding or modify its order or instruct its fiduciary is not limited by the power conferred by GC 5339 (RC 5731.20), but includes the broad powers conferred by this section. In re Shafer's Estate (Butler 1943) 74 Ohio App. 33, 56 N.E.2d 926, 40 Ohio Law Abs. 496, 29 O.O. 233.

17. Insolvency

The probate court has exclusive jurisdiction over an assignee for the benefit of creditors of an insolvent debtor. Kerr Hardware Co. v. Cherrington (Gallia 1930) 37 Ohio App. 395, 174 N.E. 787, 9 Ohio Law Abs. 505.

The judge of the probate court is authorized to transfer to the court of insolvency any and all cases pending in the probate court arising under the act regulating the mode of administering assignments in trust for the benefit of creditors, and all laws now in force or that may be enacted regulating the mode and manner of proceedings in such cases by the probate court shall be held and deemed to extend to the court of insolvency. State ex rel. Fay v. Archibald (Ohio 1894) 52 Ohio St. 1, 32 W.L.B. 307, 38 N.E. 314, 2 Ohio Leg. N. 25.

18. Jury trial

Where defendant in a will contest action requested a trial by jury and at no time before or during trial did such defendant object to a jury trial, the defendant may not later collaterally attack the trial court's judgment on the basis the trial court abused its discretion in impanelling a jury. Weissberg v Rager, No. 44602 (8th Dist Ct App, Cuyahoga, 11–4–82).

19. Mental impairment, confinement costs

Action brought by state to recover sums expended for medical treatment and support of defendant committed to state mental institution after he was found not guilty by reason of insanity on charge of aggravated murder did not directly affect guardian and ward relationship, and was not action committed to exclusive jurisdiction of probate court; rather, general division of common pleas court could assume jurisdiction. Ohio Dept. of Mental Health v. Baldauf (Ohio App. 11 Dist., 11-20-1995) 107 Ohio App.3d 467, 669 N.E.2d 39. Courts ⇨ 472.4(8); Mental Health ⇨ 451

20. Statutory jurisdiction

The probate court has chancery jurisdiction. Gilliland v. Sellers' Adm'rs (Ohio 1853) 2 Ohio St. 223.

Probate court's decision to compel administrator of decedent's estate to authorize release of decedent's medical, school, and employment records so that attorney representing the father of decedent's children, as next friend of children, could prepare prosecution in federal wrongful death action, was warranted, regardless of whether the father was the proper party in the wrongful death action given that a different person was appointed as the children's' guardian; release of the information was in the best interest of the children, who were the beneficiaries of decedent's estate, and any issue concerning proper party was for the federal court. In re Estate of Sarantino (Ohio App. 11 Dist., Trumbull, 07-14-2006) No. 2005-T-0071, 2006-Ohio-3641, 2006 WL 1976753, Unreported. Executors And Administrators ⇨ 82

Daughter's claims regarding the administration of her mother's estate, which claims included assertions that administrator sold her mother's house below market value, unilaterally raised his hourly rate, improperly charged daughter rent to live in mother's house, and charged an unreasonable fee, were within the exclusive jurisdiction of the probate court, and thus Court of Common Pleas lacked jurisdiction to hear the claims. Holik v. Lafferty (Ohio App. 11 Dist., Ashtabula, 05-26-2006) No. 2005-A-0005, 2006-Ohio-2652, 2006 WL 1459751, Unreported. Courts ⇨ 472.4(4)

Due to previous order from domestic relations court concerning parents' divorce and shared parenting agreement, the domestic relations court retained exclusive jurisdiction over the custody, care, and support of parents' autistic son even after son turned eighteen, precluding probate court from considering mother's application for guardianship over the person of her son, despite probate court's exclusive statutory jurisdiction over guardianships; due to son's legal disability, son did not automatically reach age of majority at eighteen, and domestic relations court did not have opportunity to exercise or reject continuing jurisdiction. In re Campbell (Ohio App. 7 Dist., Mahoning, 03-31-2006) No. 05 MA 10, 2006-Ohio-1764, 2006 WL 890999, Unreported. Courts ⇨ 472.4(8)

Provisions of trust instrument granting trustee authority to "settle and adjust all claims and demands in favor of or against the estate" did not give trustee discretion to determine whether estate of deceased trust beneficiary was entitled to beneficiary's share of trust assets upon distribution of those assets, and thus trial court had jurisdiction to determine estate's entitlement; trustee's powers related to management of the trust, and interpretation of trust provision defining beneficiaries was an issue within the province of the court. McCoy v. Witzleb (Ohio App. 2 Dist., Greene, 12-16-2005) No. 2005 CA 25, 2005-Ohio-6678, 2005 WL 3454689, Unreported. Trusts ⇨ 363

Probate court has subject matter jurisdiction in proceeding in which trust beneficiary seeks to have inter vivos trustee removed and trust terminated. Martin v. Wayne County Nat. Bank Trust (Ohio App. 9 Dist., Wayne, 08-11-2004) No. 03CA0079, 2004-Ohio-4194, 2004 WL 1778822, Unreported, appeal not allowed 104 Ohio St.3d 1409, 818 N.E.2d 710, 2004-Ohio-6364. Trusts ⇨ 167

Probate division lacked jurisdiction over bank's legal malpractice claims against estate's attorney, as neither constitution nor jurisdiction statute granted probate division jurisdiction over legal malpractice claims; actions alleging legal malpractice were within the jurisdiction of the general division of the common pleas court, not within the jurisdiction of the probate court. Gilpin v. Bank One Corp. (Ohio App. 12 Dist., Clermont, 06-14-2004) No. CA2003-09-073, 2004-Ohio-3012, 2004 WL 1301304, Unreported. Courts ⇨ 50

Juvenile court lacked subject matter jurisdiction to determine whether child support arrearages were asset of mother's estate, as request for such a determination was within probate court's exclusive jurisdiction to decide questions of title to claimed assets of an estate. Miller ex rel. Lafountain v. McMichael (Ohio App. 3 Dist., Paulding, 12-15-2003) No. 11-03-08, 2003-Ohio-6713, 2003 WL 22939494, Unreported. Courts ⇨ 472.4(3)

Joint and survivorship bank accounts were not probate assets, and thus probate court lacked subject matter jurisdiction to consider complaint for concealment of assets by joint owner against attorney-in-fact who removed funds from account; any cause of action concerning joint and survivorship accounts lay individually with joint owner against attorney-in-fact in Common Pleas Court. In re Estate of Jaric (Ohio App. 7 Dist., Mahoning, 09-18-2002) No. 00 CA 243, 2002-Ohio-5016, 2002 WL 31116088, Unreported, appeal not allowed 98 Ohio St.3d 1461, 783 N.E.2d 520, 2003-Ohio-644. Joint Tenancy ⇨ 14

A probate court (1) has subject matter jurisdiction over plaintiff's claim of legal malpractice which attacks distribution of his mother's estate, (2) properly denies transfer to the general division, and (3) dismisses the complaint on the basis that defendant attorney handles the mother's estate as administrator and does not represent plaintiff as beneficiary; in addition, the complaint is properly dismissed because it fails to set forth facts regarding an attorney-client relationship as well as any facts on which a negligence claim is based. Zeigler v. Bove (Ohio App. 5 Dist., Richland, 12-23-1998) No. 98 CA 65, 1999 WL 4080, Unreported.

The Michigan probate court has jurisdiction to administer an estate that is admitted to probate in Michigan and where the proceedings are not challenged and are concluded before a claim is filed in an Ohio court: (1) the certificate of completion issued by the Michigan probate court does not divest the trial court of subject matter jurisdiction; (2) such a judgment is however entitled to full faith and credit in Ohio of issues that were or could have been raised in the Michigan probate proceeding; and (3) res judicata is an affirmative defense which may not be raised in a motion to dismiss. Holzemer v. Urbanski (Ohio App. 6 Dist., Lucas, 04-18-1997) No. L-96-261, 1997 WL 195455, Unreported.

Statute granting probate court exclusive jurisdiction over a particular subject matter when no other statute expressly conferred jurisdiction over that subject matter upon any other court or agency did not authorize probate court or its judge to issue prejudgment attachment orders in concealment proceeding; no statutory section expressly conferred jurisdiction on probate courts to provide for prejudgment attachment of personal property in any context, and probate courts were specifically divested of authority to issue prejudgment attachment orders in concealment actions. State ex rel. Goldberg v. Mahoning Cty. Probate Court (Ohio, 09-05-2001) 93 Ohio St.3d 160, 753 N.E.2d 192, 2001-Ohio-1297, reconsideration denied 93 Ohio St.3d 1464, 756 N.E.2d 1239. Attachment ⚖ 67; Attachment ⚖ 70

Probate Court's statutory jurisdiction to distribute among the beneficiaries the amount received by a personal representative in an action for wrongful death does not empower the probate court to determine collateral-source deductions in actions brought against a state university, and that function remains exclusively with the Court of Claims. McMullen v. Ohio State Univ. Hosp. (Ohio, 04-12-2000) 88 Ohio St.3d 332, 725 N.E.2d 1117, 2000-Ohio-342. States ⚖ 184.32

Statutes granting probate courts general, exclusive jurisdiction to grant and revoke letters testamentary and of administration and to direct and control the conduct and settle the accounts of executors and administrators and order the distribution of estates did not give a probate court jurisdiction to administer an intestate nonresident decedent's non-Ohio property. State ex rel. Lee v. Trumbull County Probate Court (Ohio, 10-14-1998) 83 Ohio St.3d 369, 700 N.E.2d 4, 1998-Ohio-51, on remand 1999 WL 744032. Courts ⚖ 198; Courts ⚖ 200.7

Probate court had jurisdiction over income beneficiary's counterclaim for money damages in trustee's declaratory judgment action seeking judicial determination regarding its obligation to obtain trust income of at least eight percent for income beneficiary. Bank One Trust Co., N.A. v. Nye (Ohio Prob., 02-13-1998) 91 Ohio Misc.2d 204, 698 N.E.2d 519. Declaratory Judgment ⚖ 273

Probate courts have plenary power at law and in equity to dispose fully of any matter that is properly before court, unless power is expressly otherwise limited or denied by Revised Code. In re Mantia-Allen (Ohio App. 2 Dist., 01-12-1996) 108 Ohio App.3d 302, 670 N.E.2d 570. Courts ⚖ 198; Courts ⚖ 200.5

Since probate court is a court of limited jurisdiction, probate proceedings are restricted to those actions permitted by statute and by the Constitution. State ex rel. Lipinski v. Cuyahoga Cty. Court of Common Pleas, Probate Div. (Ohio, 11-01-1995) 74 Ohio St.3d 19, 655 N.E.2d 1303, 1995-Ohio-96. Courts ⚖ 198

Statutes vest probate courts with jurisdiction over declaratory judgment actions upon questions relating to administration of estate. State ex rel. Lipinski v. Cuyahoga Cty. Court of Common Pleas, Probate Div. (Ohio, 11-01-1995) 74 Ohio St.3d 19, 655 N.E.2d 1303, 1995-Ohio-96. Declaratory Judgment ⚖ 273

Following wife's death after she filed divorce petition, enforcement of antenuptial agreement fell within jurisdiction of probate division, not domestic relations division, as interpretation and enforcement of the agreement was not a "matter." Diemer v. Diemer (Ohio App. 8 Dist., 12-08-1994) 99 Ohio App.3d 54, 649 N.E.2d 1285. Courts ⚖ 50

Legatee was not entitled to writ of mandamus to require court of common pleas to reverse its earlier decision transferring case against executor to probate court, and assume jurisdiction over legatee's claim that executor improperly sold family paintings rather than turning them over to her and misallocated tax benefit; transfer order was not a final decision and legatee had adequate legal remedy in form of appeal. State ex rel. Lewis v. Moser (Ohio, 04-12-1995) 72 Ohio St.3d 25, 647 N.E.2d 155. Mandamus ⚖ 4(4); Mandamus ⚖ 44

Probate court had jurisdiction to award money damages for failure of guardian to rent or sell ward's residence while ward was in nursing home without reasonable prospect that she would ever return to her home. In re Guardianship of McPheter (Ohio App. 6 Dist., 08-05-1994) 95 Ohio App.3d 440, 642 N.E.2d 690. Mental Health ⚖ 258.1; Mental Health ⚖ 274

County probate court possesses jurisdiction to issue order of involuntary commitment for mental health treatment pursuant to statutes governing involuntary confinement proceedings and jurisdiction of probate court. In re Hays (Ohio, 10-05-1994) 70 Ohio St.3d 471, 639 N.E.2d 433, 1995-Ohio-46. Mental Health ⚖ 33

Probate court possesses statutory authority and duty to place mentally ill individual in least restrictive alternative available. In re Hays (Ohio, 10-05-1994) 70 Ohio St.3d 471, 639 N.E.2d 433, 1995-Ohio-46. Mental Health ⚖ 51.10

Juvenile courts do not possess jurisdiction to issue order of involuntary commitment for mental health treatment. In re Hays (Ohio, 10-05-1994) 70 Ohio St.3d 471, 639 N.E.2d 433, 1995-Ohio-46. Mental Health ⚖ 227

Probate court had subject matter jurisdiction over declaratory judgment action brought by trustee of family trust, in which court ultimately appointed successor trustee. Galbreath v. del Valle (Ohio App. 10 Dist., 11-24-1993) 91 Ohio App.3d 829, 633 N.E.2d 1185, dismissed, jurisdictional motion overruled 69 Ohio St.3d 1414, 630 N.E.2d 376. Trusts ⚖ 169(3)

In determining whether declaratory judgment action may be brought in probate court, underlying question is whether assets at issue are related to administration of estate. Wozniak v. Wozniak (Ohio App. 9 Dist., 09-22-1993) 90 Ohio App.3d 400, 629 N.E.2d 500, cause dismissed 68 Ohio St.3d 1440, 626 N.E.2d 124. Declaratory Judgment ⚖ 273

Probate court had jurisdiction, in declaratory judgment action, to determine title to automobile and to determine whether estate or heir was liable on three mortgages secured by estate property; resolution of issues was necessary to determine extent and ultimate distribution of estate assets, and thus issues were directly related to administration of estate. Wozniak v. Wozniak (Ohio App. 9 Dist., 09-22-1993) 90 Ohio App.3d 400, 629 N.E.2d 500, cause dismissed 68 Ohio St.3d 1440, 626 N.E.2d 124. Declaratory Judgment ⚖ 273

Plaintiff personally interested in estate may bring declaratory judgment action in probate court to determine title to estate assets and to adjudicate questions directly affecting administration of estate. Wozniak v. Wozniak (Ohio App. 9 Dist., 09-22-1993) 90 Ohio App.3d 400, 629 N.E.2d 500, cause dismissed 68 Ohio St.3d 1440, 626 N.E.2d 124. Declaratory Judgment ⚖ 300

Probate court has jurisdiction to entertain declaratory judgment action on probate matters against state without violating Court of Claims Act, which gives Court of Claims jurisdiction over actions against state for money damages. Oakar v. Ohio Dept. of Mental Retardation (Cuyahoga 1993) 88 Ohio App.3d 332, 623 N.E.2d 1296, motion overruled 67 Ohio St.3d 1489, 621 N.E.2d 410. States ⚖ 184.2(2)

Probate court does not have authority to order Department of Mental Health or county board of health to pay cost of care of mentally ill person placed in private facility; code section which grants probate court jurisdiction to determine whether individual is mentally ill person subject to hospitalization does not bestow on probate court authority to order Department of Mental Health to pay for person's care in private nursing home. Berger v. Clermont Cty. Alcohol, Drug Addiction & Mental Health Serv. Bd. (Clermont 1993) 86 Ohio App.3d 349, 620 N.E.2d 1027, dismissed, jurisdictional motion overruled 67 Ohio St.3d 1421, 616 N.E.2d 504, rehearing denied 67 Ohio St.3d 1457, 619 N.E.2d 425. Mental Health ⚖ 79

Statutory change vesting probate court with exclusive jurisdiction over cases involving informed consent hearings for medication of hospital patients was significant, and, thus, injunction issued by court of common pleas could no longer equitably remain in force. Cleveland v. Ohio Dept. of Mental Health (Franklin 1992) 84 Ohio App.3d 769, 618 N.E.2d 244, motion overruled 66 Ohio St.3d 1497, 613 N.E.2d 239. Injunction ⚖ 210

Probate court had personal jurisdiction over attorney engaged to prosecute wrongful death action on behalf of estate, and had inherent power to issue order to attorney to account for settlement funds distributed to him; moreover, attorney was subpoenaed and attended certain hearings before trial court, and testified at hearing that generated court's order, of which he was thereafter found in contempt. In re Kinross (Hamilton 1992) 84 Ohio App.3d 335, 616 N.E.2d 1128, dismissed, jurisdictional motion overruled 66 Ohio St.3d 1484, 612 N.E.2d 1241. Executors And Administrators ⚖ 469(1)

Probate court is court of limited jurisdiction, and its proceedings are restricted to those permitted by statute and Constitution. In re Elmore (Franklin 1992) 83 Ohio App.3d 348, 614 N.E.2d 1116, dismissed, jurisdictional motion overruled 66 Ohio St.3d 1421, 607 N.E.2d 843. Courts ⚖ 198

The fact that defendants in an action to have a body exhumed appeal the order of the probate court does not deprive the probate court of jurisdiction to dismiss the action pursuant to the plaintiff's stipulation of dismissal under Civ R 41(A)(1). Alexander v. Alexander (Franklin 1989) 54 Ohio App.3d 77, 560 N.E.2d 1337. Dead Bodies ⚖ 5

Note 20

Probate court exercising jurisdiction granted by statute to approve wrongful death settlement by personal representative of decedent has limited plenary jurisdiction to construe policy of liability insurance for purpose of determining amount of insurance coverage available to settle the wrongful death claim. Burris v. Grange Mut. Companies (Ohio 1989) 46 Ohio St.3d 84, 545 N.E.2d 83, rehearing denied 46 Ohio St.3d 717, 546 N.E.2d 1335, rehearing denied 53 Ohio St.3d 718, 560 N.E.2d 779. Courts ⇐ 198

Claim that testator was incompetent and lacked capacity to execute valid inter vivos transfer or contract was not proper matter for determination by probate court, in that no justiciable controversy existed among interested parties as to includability of disputed property in testator's estate; court of common pleas was appropriate forum for claim alleging incapacity to execute contract. Corron v. Corron (Ohio 1988) 40 Ohio St.3d 75, 531 N.E.2d 708. Wills ⇐ 257

Proceedings in probate court are restricted to those actions permitted by statute and by the constitution since the probate court is a court of limited jurisdiction. Corron v. Corron (Ohio 1988) 40 Ohio St.3d 75, 531 N.E.2d 708. Courts ⇐ 198

Rule of civil procedure clearly authorizes a court other than a probate court to appoint a guardian ad litem for protection of an individual the court believes to be an incompetent; probate courts do not possess exclusive jurisdiction in such matters. Dailey v. Dailey (Montgomery 1983) 11 Ohio App.3d 121, 463 N.E.2d 427, 11 O.B.R. 176. Courts ⇐ 472.4(8)

The juvenile court acts beyond the scope of its jurisdiction when it orders the Ohio department of mental health to pay the cost of care of a child placed in a private, non-public psychiatric hospital. In re Hamil (Ohio 1982) 69 Ohio St.2d 97, 431 N.E.2d 317, 23 O.O.3d 151. Infants ⇐ 228(1)

The authority of the common pleas court in a criminal prosecution to determine that the defendant is then insane under RC 2945.37 et seq. is an exception to the exclusiveness of the jurisdiction of the probate court over determinations concerning mental capacity. In re Moser (Ohio Com.Pl. 1967) 19 Ohio Misc. 81, 246 N.E.2d 626, 47 O.O.2d 420, 48 O.O.2d 253.

Unless a matter is within the jurisdiction of the probate court, it has no power to render a declaratory judgment relating to it. Mainline Const. Co. v. Warren (Ohio Prob. 1967) 11 Ohio Misc. 233, 227 N.E.2d 432, 40 O.O.2d 509. Declaratory Judgment ⇐ 273

The probate court has exclusive jurisdiction, unless otherwise provided by law, as to all matters set forth in RC 2101.24, and as to all matters pertaining directly to the administration of estates. Wolfrum v. Wolfrum (Ohio 1965) 2 Ohio St.2d 237, 208 N.E.2d 537, 31 O.O.2d 501. Courts ⇐ 472.4(2.1)

The common pleas court has jurisdiction to declare void judgments and orders of the probate court for lack of jurisdiction. Armstrong v. Brufach (Ohio Com.Pl. 1950) 136 N.E.2d 463, 74 Ohio Law Abs. 370, 59 O.O. 352.

When an action for declaratory judgment is properly instituted in the probate court, questions of fact arising in the trial of the issues shall be determined by the probate judge unless upon his own initiative or upon request of either party he shall in his discretion order such questions of fact to be tried by a jury or referred as otherwise authorized in the statutes. Renee v. Sanders (Ohio 1953) 160 Ohio St. 279, 116 N.E.2d 420, 52 O.O. 175. Jury ⇐ 14(12.5)

The grant of exclusive jurisdiction to the probate court is subject to the general limitation that "such jurisdiction shall be exclusive in the probate court unless otherwise provided by law." Haag v. Meffley (Lucas 1951) 89 Ohio App. 471, 103 N.E.2d 37, 46 O.O. 274.

Exclusive jurisdiction of probate court referred to in this section does not apply when otherwise provided by law. State ex rel. Overlander v. Brewer (Ohio 1947) 147 Ohio St. 386, 72 N.E.2d 84, 34 O.O. 338.

Power of court to render declaratory judgment by virtue of uniform declaratory judgments act does not empower court to expand its jurisdiction over subject matter. Sherrets v. Tuscarawas Sav. & Loan Co. (Tuscarawas 1945) 78 Ohio App. 307, 70 N.E.2d 127, 34 O.O. 21. Declaratory Judgment ⇐ 272

Where the administration of an estate has been lawfully committed to the probate court of a particular county, the jurisdiction of such court to settle such estate is exclusive. State ex rel. Black v. White (Ohio 1936) 132 Ohio St. 58, 5 N.E.2d 163, 7 O.O. 165.

Probate court of county of decedent's residence first appointing administrator acquired jurisdiction exclusive of any other probate court. State ex rel. Taylor v. Gregory (Ohio 1930) 122 Ohio St. 512, 172 N.E. 365. Courts ⇐ 475(2); Executors And Administrators ⇐ 9

The probate court has jurisdiction to determine conclusively as against collateral attack all questions involved in the application, including that of testator's domicile. Wilberding v. Miller (Ohio 1913) 88 Ohio St. 609, 90 Ohio St. 28, 106 N.E. 665, 11 Ohio Law Rep. 96, 11 Ohio Law Rep. 262, 11 Ohio Law Rep. 447. Wills ⇐ 309

An order of the probate court, appointing an executor, if made without jurisdiction, is void, and may be disregarded in any other court; but, if made in the exercise of proper jurisdiction over the subject-matter and estate, though based on erroneous conclusions of law or fact, it cannot be collaterally attacked. Union Sav. Bank & Trust Co. v. Western Union Tel. Co. (Ohio 1908) 79 Ohio St. 89, 86 N.E. 478, 128 Am.St.Rep. 675, 6 Ohio Law Rep. 554. Courts ⇐ 202(4); Executors And Administrators ⇐ 29(3); Judgment ⇐ 475

Probate court cannot set aside or vacate a deed of assignment. Standard Home & Savings Ass'n Co. v. Jones (Ohio 1901) 64 Ohio St. 147, 59 N.E. 885.

The probate court has jurisdiction to try any question of fact arising in such action therein prosecuted, or afford the parties a trial by jury when the nature of the issues entitle them to a jury trial, or render it appropriate. Doan v. Biteley (Ohio 1892) 49 Ohio St. 588, 32 N.E. 600.

The probate court has the capacity to receive any jurisdiction which the legislature may give it, providing it is within the constitutional limits. Hatch v. Buckeye State Bldg. & Loan Co. (Ohio Prob. 1934) 32 Ohio N.P.N.S. 297, 16 Ohio Law Abs. 661. Courts ⇐ 198

Application to one probate court for administration excludes other probate courts in the state. In re Worthington's Estate (Ohio Prob. 1896) 4 Ohio Dec. 381.

Under Ohio doctrine of claim preclusion, probate court judgment ordering return of ward's property did not preclude federal suit by person who allegedly acquired property by gift from ward based on allegations that guardian and attorneys in probate matter converted his property; probate court had not issued final judgment on factual issues relating to ward's competency and capacity to make gifts. Worrall v. Irwin (S.D.Ohio, 07-01-1994) 890 F.Supp. 696. Judgment ⇐ 828.16(4)

Financial services company was entitled to rely on facial validity of probate court order requiring it to transfer securities to guardian's account from person who allegedly obtained securities by gift from ward, despite contention that probate court did not have personal jurisdiction and did not contact account holder before making transfer. Worrall v. Irwin (S.D.Ohio, 07-01-1994) 890 F.Supp. 696. Trover And Conversion ⇐ 10

Jurisdiction of probate court is one of special limited and delegated jurisdiction, and is created by statute as provided for in this section. In re Rich's Will (Ohio Prob. 1935) 1 Ohio Supp. 159, 19 Ohio Law Abs. 402, 3 O.O. 315. Courts ⇐ 198

RC 2101.24 does not indicate that the probate court has authority to determine issues regarding immigration and naturalization and a determination that a marriage is for hire, and intended to circumvent the immigration and naturalization laws, is improper; however, the court has jurisdiction to determine the validity of a marriage where there is no consent by a minor's parent or guardian and no consummation of the marriage. In re Ababseh, No. 95–CA–179, 1996 WL 116148 (7th Dist Ct App, Mahoning, 3–12–96).

21. Testamentary trusts and trustees

Whether the present members of an open class of remaindermen desired a portion of testamentary trust realty to be severed from the trust was immaterial to application of settlor's son to acquire entire interest in the realty. In re Testamentary Trust of Hasch (Ohio App. 3 Dist., 02-24-1999) 131 Ohio App.3d 143, 721 N.E.2d 1111. Wills ⇐ 681(2)

Doctrine of merger did not warrant termination of testamentary trust with respect to certain parcel of real estate, though settlor's wife, who had right to receive income produced by trust property during her life, and children of settlor's son, who had vested remainder interest in parcel, purported to grant parcel to son, and trustee did not contest son's ownership of parcel, as trustee had not transferred to son any interest in parcel, and class of remaindermen composed of all of son's children would remain open so long as son lived; there had been no merger of all the legal and beneficial interests in and to the parcel. In re Testamentary Trust of Hasch (Ohio App. 3 Dist., 02-24-1999) 131 Ohio App.3d 143, 721 N.E.2d 1111. Wills ⇐ 686(1)

Complaint brought by beneficiaries of inter vivos trust to enjoin trustee from exercising voting rights in certain manner was not request for order to direct and control conduct of testamentary trustee, so as to vest jurisdiction exclusively in probate courts. Sherman v. Fifth Third Bank (Ohio App. 2

Dist., 02-24-1992) 93 Ohio App.3d 57, 637 N.E.2d 929, motion overruled 64 Ohio St.3d 1442, 596 N.E.2d 472. Courts ⚯ 472.4(7)

Probate Division of Court of Common Pleas was precluded from considering issues raised in trustee's action seeking declaration of validity and reformation of trust; issues raised by parties were same issues raised in previously initiated action in General Division of Court of Common Pleas, which first obtained jurisdiction over parties and subject matter, and General Division retained jurisdiction to determine all matters properly before it. DeMar v. Mosley (Ohio Com.Pl. 1993) 63 Ohio Misc.2d 102, 619 N.E.2d 1239. Courts ⚯ 475(4)

A probate court lacks jurisdiction to order the trustee of an estate to retain estate funds to pay a fine imposed upon the husband of the decedent as a result of his conviction of her murder. In re Estate of Wolfe (Wood 1991) 71 Ohio App.3d 501, 594 N.E.2d 1055.

Jurisdiction over action alleging fraud, self-dealing, conflicts of interest and other breaches of duties against trustees of certain inter vivos trusts was in general division of the court of common pleas, rather than in the probate division. Schucker v. Metcalf (Ohio 1986) 22 Ohio St.3d 33, 488 N.E.2d 210, 22 O.B.R. 27. Courts ⚯ 50

Though the jurisdiction of the probate court in Ohio is limited to testamentary trustees, it does not preclude the court from following the assets of a testamentary trust into an inter vivos trust, in furtherance of its jurisdiction of the testamentary trust, in order to fully dispose of the issues properly before it. Dollar Sav. & Trust Co. v. First Nat. Bank of Boston (Ohio Com.Pl. 1972) 32 Ohio Misc. 81, 285 N.E.2d 768, 61 O.O.2d 134.

Where there is no repugnancy in a will creating a trust and it is not against public policy, such trust cannot be judicially terminated before the objects of the trust have been fully accomplished, and generally a change in circumstances and the needs of beneficiaries do not justify a court termination of such a trust. Collins v. First Natl. Bank of Cincinnati (Hamilton 1969) 20 Ohio App.2d 1, 251 N.E.2d 610, 49 O.O.2d 1.

The probate court has jurisdiction to entertain an application by the beneficiary of a testamentary trust to direct and control the conduct of testamentary trustees in the payment, or the withholding of payment, of trust income which is payable to such beneficiary under the will of the decedent. In re Gallagher's Trust (Mahoning 1963) 118 Ohio App. 477, 195 N.E.2d 601, 25 O.O.2d 394. Trusts ⚯ 280

One who as a testamentary trustee and as an individual is interested in a provision of the will authorizing the removal of certain real estate from the trust and the substitution of a sum of money therefor may bring a declaratory judgment action in the probate court to secure a determination and declaration of his rights as trustee and as an individual. Sessions v. Skelton (Ohio 1955) 163 Ohio St. 409, 127 N.E.2d 378, 56 O.O. 370.

Even though the probate court has the power to control the conduct of trustees, under this section, ex parte orders of the court (without notice to life tenant) issued upon application of the trustee for authority to do certain things in the conduct of the trust, are not binding upon the life tenant. Holmes v. Hrobon (Franklin 1951) 93 Ohio App. 1, 103 N.E.2d 845, 61 Ohio Law Abs. 113, 64 Ohio Law Abs. 241, 50 O.O. 178, affirmed in part, reversed in part 158 Ohio St. 508, 110 N.E.2d 574, 49 O.O. 450.

In controlling administration of testamentary trust, probate court has power to determine validity of deed obtained from beneficiary of trust, where validity of such conveyance is challenged on ground of undue influence, mental incapacity or fraud. In re Stuckey's Will (Madison 1947) 80 Ohio App. 421, 73 N.E.2d 208, 36 O.O. 117.

Probate court has jurisdiction to hear exceptions to the account of the superintendent of banks in charge of liquidation of an Ohio bank as to a trust for which such bank, before its liquidation, was trustee through appointment by that court, to settle such account, to surcharge the bank as such trustee, and to direct the superintendent of banks to issue a certificate of claim against the assets of such bank to and in favor of a successor trustee; such court does not have jurisdiction to render a money judgment against the bank or superintendent of banks, or to determine the character of the claim as to preferences, or to impress a lien upon property held by the bank as trustee in favor of the successor trustee. In re Binder's Estate (Ohio 1940) 137 Ohio St. 26, 27 N.E.2d 939, 129 A.L.R. 130, 17 O.O. 364. Courts ⚯ 472.4(7)

Where once the probate court acquires jurisdiction over testamentary trustees by virtue of this section, it has exclusive jurisdiction, both on general principles of comity and by virtue of such section. Morehead v. Central Trust Co. (Hamilton 1935) 54 Ohio App. 9, 5 N.E.2d 932, 20 Ohio Law Abs. 321, 7 O.O. 372.

Where a probate court has taken jurisdiction of a certain testamentary trust which is being administered under the orders of that court, a common pleas court, in a suit by the executor and trustee to construe the terms of such trust, does not have jurisdiction of a cause of action stated in a cross-petition filed in such suit by a beneficiary under the will, alleging maladministration of the trust and asking for injunctive relief against the trustee. Morehead v. Central Trust Co. (Hamilton 1935) 54 Ohio App. 9, 5 N.E.2d 932, 20 Ohio Law Abs. 321, 7 O.O. 372.

Where trust property has been set off but managed by a trustee for twenty years, the trustee can only be called to account in a court of general jurisdiction and not in probate court. Culver v. Culver (Ohio 1898) 58 Ohio St. 172, 39 W.L.B. 371, 50 N.E. 505.

Probate court has plenary power in law and in equity in matters over which it has specific jurisdiction as set forth in statute, and conversely if authority is not specifically given probate court has no such authority; there is not specific authority to terminate a testamentary trust, and had legislature so intended it would have so worded statute that specific authority would have been given. In re Rich's Will (Ohio Prob. 1935) 1 Ohio Supp. 159, 19 Ohio Law Abs. 402, 3 O.O. 315.

Probate court had jurisdiction to entertain action against attorney in fact for concealed or embezzled assets, as assets were withdrawn with a power of attorney and partly withdrawn from intervivos trust funds. Fox v. Stockmaster (Ohio App. 3 Dist., Seneca, 06-05-2002) No. 13-01-34, No. 13-01-35, 2002-Ohio-2824, 2002 WL 1299985, Unreported, appeal not allowed 96 Ohio St.3d 1525, 775 N.E.2d 864, 2002-Ohio-5099. Trusts ⚯ 360

Jurisdiction of probate court to authorize sale of real property held in testamentary trust is not exclusive by reason of GC 11925 (RC 5303.21) et seq. which confer jurisdiction upon court of common pleas. State ex rel. Ehmann v. Schneider (Hamilton 1946) 78 Ohio App. 27, 67 N.E.2d 117, 45 Ohio Law Abs. 239, 33 O.O. 391.

Where the terms of a testamentary trust provide for termination of the trust fifteen years after execution of the will and for distribution of the corpus to a beneficiary's lineal descendants if such beneficiary dies before the age of thirty-five, the trial court may not order the trust terminated and the corpus paid over to each beneficiary as he reaches age thirty-five absent an express provision in the trust instrument. Harter Bank & Trust Co v Stanfield, No. CA–5899 (5th Dist Ct App, Stark, 11–23–82).

22. Wills

The power to sell land given by will cannot be executed by administrator. Wills v. Cowper (Ohio 1825) 2 Ohio 124, adhered to 3 Ohio 486.

Testator's son was implicitly disinherited by testator, and thus he was not entitled to the remainder of testator's estate, where testator's will completely disposed of all his real and personal property, and the will provided the remainder of testator's estate, if his girlfriend should predecease him, would go to the executrix of his estate. Estate of Snell v. Kilburn (Ohio App. 7 Dist., 12-23-2005) 165 Ohio App.3d 352, 846 N.E.2d 572, 2005-Ohio-7076. Wills ⚯ 587(1)

Objections filed by testator's son to final accounting of estate, which asked for an accounting and declaratory judgment to construe testator's will, were barred by res judicata, where testator's son had previously filed a will contest action, in that action the court determined that testator's son was implicitly disinherited, and the parties and the claims were the same in both actions. Estate of Snell v. Kilburn (Ohio App. 7 Dist., 12-23-2005) 165 Ohio App.3d 352, 846 N.E.2d 572, 2005-Ohio-7076. Wills ⚯ 423

Probate court could rule on issues of will construction during will contest action; statute provided that whenever a probate court had a case it also had plenary power at law and in equity to dispose of any matter that was properly before the court, unless the power was expressly limited or denied by statute. Estate of Snell v. Kilburn (Ohio App. 7 Dist., 12-23-2005) 165 Ohio App.3d 352, 846 N.E.2d 572, 2005-Ohio-7076. Wills ⚯ 215

By filing exceptions to inventory of probate assets, and objections to sale of probate assets, and a motion to remove executrix, testator's daughter was in effect asking probate court to exercise its power of review, and thus, such acts did not invoke no-contest clause in will and did not thereby bar daughter from taking under the will. Modie v. Andrews (Ohio App. 9 Dist., Summit, 10-23-2002) No. C.A. 21029, 2002-Ohio-5765, 2002 WL 31386482, Unreported, appeal not allowed 98 Ohio St.3d 1480, 784 N.E.2d 712, 2003-Ohio-974. Wills ⚯ 665

Probate court could rule on issues of will construction during will contest action; statute provided that whenever a probate court had a case it also had plenary power at law and in equity to dispose of any matter that was properly before the court, unless the power was expressly limited or denied by statute. Estate of Snell v. Kilburn (Ohio App. 7 Dist., 12-23-2005) 165 Ohio App.3d 352, 846 N.E.2d 572, 2005-Ohio-7076. Wills ⚯ 215

Probate court, in a declaratory judgment action, is authorized to construe a will and to declare the rights and legal relations of persons

2101.24 Note 22

interested in the administration of an estate or a trust. First Nat. Bank of Southwestern Ohio v. Miami University (Ohio App. 12 Dist., 06-02-1997) 121 Ohio App.3d 170, 699 N.E.2d 523, dismissed, appeal not allowed 80 Ohio St.3d 1411, 684 N.E.2d 704, reconsideration denied 80 Ohio St.3d 1450, 686 N.E.2d 276, certiorari denied 119 S.Ct. 70, 525 U.S. 825, 142 L.Ed.2d 55. Declaratory Judgment ⚖ 241; Declaratory Judgment ⚖ 242

In construction of will, sole purpose of probate court should be to ascertain and carry out intention of testator, and that intention must be ascertained from words contained in will. Bank One Ohio Trust Co., N.A. v. Hiram College (Ohio App. 7 Dist., 10-31-1996) 115 Ohio App.3d 159, 684 N.E.2d 1275. Wills ⚖ 439; Wills ⚖ 440

When a probate court is required to interpret a will, the court must determine and carry out the intentions of the testator as determined by reading the entire document. Varns v. Varns (Wayne 1991) 81 Ohio App.3d 26, 610 N.E.2d 440, motion overruled 62 Ohio St.3d 1447, 579 N.E.2d 491.

In ascertaining the intentions of a testator, the words in his will must be taken in their primary or ordinary sense unless it is evidenced by the entire will or subject matter that he intended the words to mean something different. Varns v. Varns (Wayne 1991) 81 Ohio App.3d 26, 610 N.E.2d 440, motion overruled 62 Ohio St.3d 1447, 579 N.E.2d 491. Wills ⚖ 456

A declaratory judgment action cannot be brought in probate court under RC 2101.24 to determine the validity or enforceability of a contract or agreement between the executor of an estate, who is also a beneficiary, and two other beneficiaries providing for a division of the testator's estate different from that provided in the will; such contract or agreement is not directly related to the administration of the estate and has nothing to do with the executor's duties or construction of the will but is merely an attempt by the beneficiaries to contractually provide for a different division of the estate. Zuendel v. Zuendel (Ohio 1992) 63 Ohio St.3d 733, 590 N.E.2d 1260.

Probate court had no jurisdiction to decide validity of will that had not been admitted to probate and to decide validity of testator's inter vivos transfers unrelated to administration of estate; only question properly before court was validity of will admitted for probate. Corron v. Corron (Ohio 1988) 40 Ohio St.3d 75, 531 N.E.2d 708. Wills ⚖ 255

Where an action to contest a will is mistakenly docketed in the general division of the court of common pleas rather than the probate division of that court, prejudicial error is committed if the court dismisses the complaint instead of transferring the action to the docket of the probate division, pursuant to a motion of the complainant. Siebenthal v. Summers (Franklin 1978) 56 Ohio App.2d 168, 381 N.E.2d 1344, 10 O.O.3d 186. Courts ⚖ 50; Wills ⚖ 400

An action for money damages is not within jurisdiction of probate division of common pleas court, although filed as counterclaim to an action within jurisdiction of that division by trust adviser named in a will being administered under its authority. Kindt v. Cleveland Trust Co. (Ohio Com.Pl. 1971) 26 Ohio Misc. 1, 266 N.E.2d 84, 55 O.O.2d 53.

The probate court is without jurisdiction, in a declaratory judgment action by an executor, to declare the validity of a purported contract among the heirs and devisees under the will of a decedent, where the purported contract has no bearing upon the assets of the estate, the duties of the executor or the court's supervision of the administration of the estate. In re Martin's Estate (Fayette 1962) 115 Ohio App. 515, 185 N.E.2d 785, 21 O.O.2d 166.

Attorney fees may be allowed to counsel successfully obtaining the probate of a will and defending it against contest for services rendered prior to the date of probate as well as thereafter. In re Woods' Estate (Ohio Prob. 1957) 159 N.E.2d 638, 80 Ohio Law Abs. 336.

Whether the probate court has jurisdiction or not, the common pleas court may afford relief to parties damaged by a fraudulently procured or forged will. Jacobsen v. Jacobsen (Ohio 1956) 164 Ohio St. 413, 131 N.E.2d 833, 58 O.O. 239. Courts ⚖ 475(2)

Where a will expresses an intention that possession of the residue of the testator's personal estate should be delivered to those to whom he has given only life interest therein and does not provide for the taking of security therefor, such expressed intention may be given effect, and the executor under such will may lawfully distribute such residue to those having such life interests therein without requiring any security from them; such personal property or its proceeds will not thereafter be, or on the death of the life tenant will it again become, property of such estate. In re Sexton's Estate (Ohio 1955) 163 Ohio St. 124, 126 N.E.2d 129, 56 O.O. 178, certiorari denied 76 S.Ct. 75, 350 U.S. 838, 100 L.Ed. 747.

Where personal property is bequeathed to a life tenant, with a remainder to her children, and such life tenant is shown to be financially irresponsible, a probate court may direct that the property be held by a trustee, even though the will expressly directs otherwise. In re Miller's Estate (Franklin 1953) 95 Ohio App. 457, 121 N.E.2d 26, 54 O.O. 98, affirmed 160 Ohio St. 529, 117 N.E.2d 598, 46 A.L.R.2d 493, 52 O.O. 437.

In an action to impress and declare a trust in which it is necessary to construe the wills involved, the probate court has exclusive jurisdiction. Van Stone v. Van Stone (Lucas 1952) 95 Ohio App. 406, 120 N.E.2d 154, 53 O.O. 438.

Common pleas judges may take proof of wills and approve bonds. State ex rel. Fay v. Archibald (Ohio 1894) 52 Ohio St. 1, 32 W.L.B. 307, 38 N.E. 314, 2 Ohio Leg. N. 25.

Probate exception to federal courts' subject matter jurisdiction did not apply in action to approve settlement of minors' personal-injury claims, so as to preclude removal, even though action was brought in state probate court, since action did not involve probate of will or proceedings concerning decedent's estate, and removal was sought on federal-question rather than diversity grounds. Community Ins. Co. v. Rowe (S.D.Ohio, 08-12-1999) 85 F.Supp.2d 800. Federal Courts ⚖ 9; Removal Of Cases ⚖ 19(1)

Under probate exception, federal courts lack subject matter jurisdiction to probate a will or to administer a decedent's estate. Community Ins. Co. v. Rowe (S.D.Ohio, 08-12-1999) 85 F.Supp.2d 800. Federal Courts ⚖ 9

Where a clause in decedent's will provided for a disposition to decedent's brother only if such brother was not married, such restraint against marriage or inducement to divorce is not void as a matter of public policy where the brother was married thirty years before decedent's death and did not know of the will's provision. McCarthy v Donnellon, No. C–820946 (1st Dist Ct App, Hamilton, 10–26–83).

Where beneficiaries of a will enter into an agreement concerning the proceeds of decedent's estate, the common pleas court has jurisdiction in a declaratory judgment action concerning the construction of such agreement. Hall v Peck, No. 45656 (8th Dist Ct App, Cuyahoga, 8–25–83).

2101.25 Optional jurisdiction of probate judge

When any action for the appropriation of property or any appeal in a road case, in a sewer district case, or in any county water supply system case is filed in the probate court, the judge may certify such cause to the court of common pleas of the county, together with all the papers filed therein, whereupon the clerk of court of common pleas shall file said papers and enter said cause on the docket. Thereupon the court of common pleas shall have jurisdiction to hear, determine, and make a record of said cause, as if commenced in such court. The court of common pleas, upon said case being docketed in that court, shall advance the same for trial at the earliest date permitted, on application by any party to said case.

(127 v 36, eff. 9–4–57; 1953 H 1; GC 10501–54)

Historical and Statutory Notes

Pre–1953 H 1 Amendments: 114 v 335

OSBA Probate and Trust Law Section

1957:

The probate court is given appellate jurisdiction by Section 6117.09 of the Revised Code in sewer district cases or county water supply system cases. In a number of counties, the volume of such cases has been, and will continue to be, such as to seriously interfere with the hearing and determination of normal probate matters.

The Committee does not believe that the probate court should be deprived of the jurisdiction granted it by statute, but recommends that Section 2101.25 should be amended to permit the probate judges to certify appeals in sewer district and water supply cases to the common pleas court, as well as appropriation and road cases which may now be so certified.

Cross References

Appeals in county road cases, Ch 5563
Powers and jurisdiction of judges, O Const Art IV §18

Library References

Courts ⟐485.
Westlaw Topic No. 106.
C.J.S. Courts § 194.

Research References

Encyclopedias

OH Jur. 3d Decedents' Estates § 892, Venue.
OH Jur. 3d Eminent Domain § 220, Generally; Jurisdiction of State Courts.

Treatises and Practice Aids

Carlin, Baldwin's Ohio Practice, Merrick-Rippner Probate Law § 1:5, Constitutional and Legislative Provisions.
Carlin, Baldwin's Ohio Practice, Merrick-Rippner Probate Law § 3:7, Jurisdiction of Probate Court—Subject Matter—Specific Areas—Specific Performance of Contract.

Notes of Decisions

Specific performance contract 1

1. Specific performance contract

Either the probate court of the county in which a decedent's estate is being administered or the common pleas court of the county in which land is located may have jurisdiction of an action for specific performance of a contract to sell the land, depending upon which first acquires jurisdiction of all necessary parties. Fellers v. Belau (Ohio Com.Pl. 1961) 178 N.E.2d 530, 87 Ohio Law Abs. 54.

2101.26 Abuse of elderly or wards or theft from estates; referral of information to law enforcement agency

If the probate judge receives information of the alleged abuse or financial exploitation of a person of advanced age or of an incompetent or minor under guardianship, or receives information of an alleged theft from the estate of a decedent, the judge may refer the information to the appropriate law enforcement agency of the political subdivision in which the abuse, exploitation, or theft allegedly occurred, which agency shall conduct an investigation to determine whether there is probable cause to believe that a violation of any section of the Revised Code that sets forth a criminal offense, or of any ordinance, resolution, or regulation of a municipal corporation or other political subdivision of the state that sets forth a criminal offense, has occurred. Upon completion of the investigation, the law enforcement agency involved shall file with the judge a report that summarizes its findings and indicates whether an indictment will be sought or charges will be filed as a result of the investigation.

(1989 S 46, eff. 1–1–90)

Historical and Statutory Notes

Ed. Note: Former 2101.26 repealed by 1975 S 145, eff. 1–1–76; 125 v 903; 1953 H 1; GC 10501–21; see now Civ R 73 for provisions analogous to former 2101.26.

Pre–1953 H 1 Amendments: 121 v 270; 120 v 649; 119 v 394; 114 v 326

Library References

Guardian and Ward ⟐123.
Infants ⟐20.
Mental Health ⟐179.
Westlaw Topic Nos. 196, 211, 257A.
C.J.S. Infants §§ 93 to 100.
C.J.S. Mental Health §§ 158 to 159.
C.J.S. Right to Die §§ 5, 8.

Research References

Encyclopedias

OH Jur. 3d Decedents' Estates § 896, Service of Notice—Proof of Service; When Complete.
OH Jur. 3d Fiduciaries § 50, Generally; Criminal Liability.

Treatises and Practice Aids

Klein, Darling, & Terez, Baldwin's Ohio Practice Civil Practice § 73:6, Probate Division--Service of Notice.
Klein, Darling, & Terez, Baldwin's Ohio Practice Civil Practice § 73:7, Probate Division--Proof of Service of Notice; When Service of Notice is Complete.
Carlin, Baldwin's Ohio Practice, Merrick-Rippner Probate Law § 64:28, Evidence of Abuse or Exploitation.

2101.27 Solemnization of marriages

(A) A probate judge has jurisdiction and authority to solemnize marriages within the county and may charge a fee for providing the service in accordance with division (B) of this section. The fee charged is subject to disposition in accordance with division (C) of this section.

(B)(1) If a probate judge intends to charge a fee for solemnizing any marriage in accordance with division (A) of this section, prior to doing so, the probate judge, by rule, shall establish a reasonable fee for providing the service.

(2) Division (B)(1) of this section does not do either of the following:

(a) Require a probate judge who, by rule, has established a reasonable fee for solemnizing marriages to charge that fee for every marriage that he solemnizes;

(b) Affect specific fees to which the probate judge is entitled under section 2101.16 or any other section of the Revised Code for issuing marriage licenses, recording returns of solemnized marriages, providing certified abstracts of marriages, or performing any other task related to a marriage other than its solemnization.

(C) If, in accordance with division (B) of this section, a reasonable fee is charged by a probate judge for solemnizing any marriage, the probate judge shall not retain any portion of that fee and instead shall pay the entire fee into the county treasury. The county treasurer shall credit the fee to the general fund of the county.

(1990 H 211, eff. 4–11–91)

Historical and Statutory Notes

Ed. Note: Former 2101.27 repealed by 1975 S 145, eff. 1–1–76; 1953 H 1; GC 10501–21; see now Civ R 73 for provisions analogous to former 2101.27.

Pre–1953 H 1 Amendments: 121 v 270; 120 v 649; 119 v 394; 114 v 326

Cross References

Notice on license of penalty for failure to return certificate, 3101.14
Power to solemnize marriages, 3101.08
Record of marriage, 3101.13

Library References

Marriage ⟐27.
Westlaw Topic No. 253.
C.J.S. Marriage § 30.

Research References

Encyclopedias

OH Jur. 3d Courts & Judges § 67, Miscellaneous Powers and Functions of Probate Judge.
OH Jur. 3d Decedents' Estates § 896, Service of Notice—Proof of Service; When Complete.
OH Jur. 3d Family Law § 30, Who May Solemnize Marriage.

OH Jur. 3d Family Law § 32, Record and Certificate of Marriage.

Forms

Ohio Jurisprudence Pleading and Practice Forms § 2:24, Powers and Duties Via Particular Courts—Probate Division.

Treatises and Practice Aids

Klein, Darling, & Terez, Baldwin's Ohio Practice Civil Practice § 73:6, Probate Division--Service of Notice.

Klein, Darling, & Terez, Baldwin's Ohio Practice Civil Practice § 73:7, Probate Division--Proof of Service of Notice; When Service of Notice is Complete.

Sowald & Morganstern, Baldwin's Ohio Practice Domestic Relations Law § 2:9, Ceremonial Marriage—Solemnization.

2101.30 Jury; drawing

Whenever a jury is required in the probate court, the probate judge shall forthwith notify the commissioners of jurors, who shall cause to be drawn from the jury wheel, or to be drawn by use of the automation data processing equipment and procedures described in section 2313.07 of the Revised Code, the names of sixteen persons as jurymen. Additional names may be drawn if required. The clerk of the court of common pleas or one of his deputies shall make a list of such names in the order drawn and certify it to the probate court, and such court shall issue a venire commanding the persons whose names were drawn to appear on the day and at the hour set for trial. The probate court shall deliver the venire to the sheriff, who shall serve it within five days thereafter and make prompt return of such service.

(1969 H 424, eff. 11–25–69; 131 v S 20; 1953 H 1; GC 10501–30)

Historical and Statutory Notes

Pre–1953 H 1 Amendments: 115 v 391; 114 v 328

Comparative Laws

Ill.—ILCS 705 305/2.
Mich.—M.C.L.A. § 600.1304.
N.Y.—McKinney's Judiciary Law § 500 et seq.

Cross References

Jury trial, Civ R 38, 39
Protracted civil trials, alternate jurors, 2313.37
Trial by jury, O Const Art I, § 5

Library References

Jury ⚖65 to 68.
Westlaw Topic No. 230.
C.J.S. Juries §§ 271, 309, 312 to 323.

Research References

Encyclopedias

OH Jur. 3d Jury § 86, Drawing Jurors in Probate Division of Common Pleas Court.
OH Jur. 3d Jury § 87, Generally; Delivery of Venires to Sheriff.
OH Jur. 3d Jury § 90, Service and Return of Venires—Where Venire Issued by Probate Division of Common Pleas Court.

Treatises and Practice Aids

Carlin, Baldwin's Ohio Practice, Merrick-Rippner Probate Law § 3:49, Demand for Jury—Form.
Carlin, Baldwin's Ohio Practice, Merrick-Rippner Probate Law § 3:50, Entry to Draw Jury—Form.
Carlin, Baldwin's Ohio Practice, Merrick-Rippner Probate Law § 3:51, Notice of Jury Trial, to Clerk of Courts—Form.
Carlin, Baldwin's Ohio Practice, Merrick-Rippner Probate Law § 3:52, Certificate of Clerk of Courts—Form.
Carlin, Baldwin's Ohio Practice, Merrick-Rippner Probate Law § 3:53, Venire for Jury—Form.
Carlin, Baldwin's Ohio Practice, Merrick-Rippner Probate Law § 3:54, Notice to Jurors—Form.

Carlin, Baldwin's Ohio Practice, Merrick-Rippner Probate Law § 3:55, Return of Sheriff—Form.

2101.31 Determination of questions of fact

All questions of fact shall be determined by the probate judge, unless the judge orders those questions of fact to be tried before a jury or refers those questions of fact to a special master commissioner as provided in sections 2101.06 and 2101.07 of the Revised Code.

(2001 S 108, eff. 7–6–01; 125 v 903, eff. 10–1–53; 1953 H 1; GC 10501–32)

Uncodified Law

2001 S 108, § 1, eff. 7–6–01, reads:

It is the intent of this act (1) to repeal the Tort Reform Act, Am. Sub. H.B. 350 of the 121st General Assembly, 146 Ohio Laws 3867, in conformity with the Supreme Court of Ohio's decision in *State, ex rel. Ohio Academy of Trial Lawyers, v. Sheward* (1999), 86 Ohio St.3d 451; (2) to clarify the status of the law; and (3) to revive the law as it existed prior to the Tort Reform Act.

Historical and Statutory Notes

Pre–1953 H 1 Amendments: 114 v 328

Cross References

Jury trial, Civ R 38, 39
Referees, Civ R 53
Trial by jury, O Const Art I, § 5

Library References

Courts ⚖202(3).
Jury ⚖19(7.5).
Westlaw Topic Nos. 106, 230.
C.J.S. Juries §§ 22, 45, 60, 63, 65, 73, 83, 99, 107, 126.

Research References

Encyclopedias

OH Jur. 3d Declar. Judgments & Related Proceedings § 39, Determination of Issues of Fact—Determination in Probate Court.
OH Jur. 3d Jury § 38, Probate Division of Common Pleas Court.

Treatises and Practice Aids

Klein, Darling, & Terez, Baldwin's Ohio Practice Civil Practice § 38:12, Right to Jury Trial Under Ohio Statutes--RC 2311.04--In General.
Carlin, Baldwin's Ohio Practice, Merrick-Rippner Probate Law § 6:5, Declaratory Judgments—Action—Jury.
Carlin, Baldwin's Ohio Practice, Merrick-Rippner Probate Law § 6:6, Declaratory Judgments—Probate Court Proceedings.
Carlin, Baldwin's Ohio Practice, Merrick-Rippner Probate Law § 14:18, Payable on Death Accounts.
Carlin, Baldwin's Ohio Practice, Merrick-Rippner Probate Law § 38:15, Will Contests—Trial—Juries.
Carlin, Baldwin's Ohio Practice, Merrick-Rippner Probate Law § 43:10, Construing a Will—Rules of Construction—Guides to Ascertain Testator's Intent.
Carlin, Baldwin's Ohio Practice, Merrick-Rippner Probate Law § 43:15, Construing a Will—Liberal Construction—Charitable Bequests; or Construction Problems.
Bogert - the Law of Trusts and Trustees § 870, Jurisdiction to Enforce Trust—Actions Available.

Notes of Decisions

Constitutional issues 1
Discretion of court 2
Property disputes 3

View by jury 4

1. Constitutional issues

Statutory provisions as to hearing without intervention of a jury on schedule of debts and exceptions, if any thereto, does not deny to any one his constitutional right to trial by jury since the constitution preserves the right to trial by jury in those cases only where it existed prior to its adoption. In re Blue's Estate (Union 1939) 67 Ohio App. 37, 32 N.E.2d 499, 29 Ohio Law Abs. 161, 14 O.O. 447.

Summary determination of exceptions to an executor's account does not deny the constitutional right to a jury. Brown v. Reed (Ohio 1897) 56 Ohio St. 264, 37 W.L.B. 324, 46 N.E. 982.

2. Discretion of court

A party to a will contest action does not have the right to a jury trial; instead, a probate court has discretion to determine whether to sit as the trier of fact in a will contest action or to impanel a jury. State ex rel. Kear v. Court of Common Pleas of Lucas County, Probate Division (Ohio 1981) 67 Ohio St.2d 189, 423 N.E.2d 427, 21 O.O.3d 118. Jury ☞ 19(7.5)

When an action for declaratory judgment is properly instituted in the probate court, questions of fact arising in the trial of the issues shall be determined by the probate judge unless upon his own initiative or upon request of either party he shall in his discretion order such questions of fact to be tried by a jury or referred as otherwise authorized in the statutes. Renee v. Sanders (Ohio 1953) 160 Ohio St. 279, 116 N.E.2d 420, 52 O.O. 175. Jury ☞ 14(12.5)

3. Property disputes

Under RC 2101.31 a probate judge has discretion as to whether to impanel a jury, and this provision shall prevail in a declaratory judgment action to determine the validity of inter vivos property transfers, notwithstanding the provisions of RC 2311.04. Bobko v. Sagen (Cuyahoga 1989) 61 Ohio App.3d 397, 572 N.E.2d 823, dismissed 45 Ohio St.3d 716, 545 N.E.2d 901.

In a proceeding by an administrator to sell real estate, the probate court has jurisdiction to try any question of fact therein, or grant jury trial. Doan v. Biteley (Ohio 1892) 49 Ohio St. 588, 32 N.E. 600.

In an appropriation proceeding the court may, on demand of either party, impanel a jury in any of the modes of common pleas. Lawrence R. Co. v. O'Harra (Ohio 1891) 48 Ohio St. 343, 26 W.L.B. 25, 28 N.E. 175.

4. View by jury

GC 11448, concerning a view by the jury of property, the subject of litigation, or the place where a material fact occurred, applies to probate practice. Israel v. Zanesville & O. R. Co. (Ohio Com.Pl. 1888) 19 W.L.B. 258.

2101.32 Rules and procedure of court of common pleas to govern; power to award and tax costs

The probate judge shall have the powers and perform the duties provided for, and shall be governed by the sections of the Revised Code and rules that apply to, the courts of common pleas and the judges of those courts. The Rules of Civil Procedure shall govern actions and proceedings in the probate court as provided in Civil Rule 73.

In all actions or proceedings in the probate court, whether ex parte or adversary, costs may be awarded to, taxed against, and apportioned between the parties, whether on the same or adverse sides, including, but not limited to, costs covered by division (B) of section 2101.16 of the Revised Code.

(1989 S 46, eff. 1–1–90; 1953 H 1; GC 10501–22)

Historical and Statutory Notes

Pre–1953 H 1 Amendments: 119 v 394, § 1; 114 v 326

Cross References

Procedure in probate court, Civ R 73
Rules of civil procedure; scope, applicability, construction, exceptions, Civ R 1

Library References

Costs ☞169.
Courts ☞202(1).
Judges ☞24.
Westlaw Topic Nos. 102, 106, 227.
C.J.S. Costs § 100.
C.J.S. Judges §§ 35, 53 to 63.
C.J.S. Summary Proceedings §§ 7, 9.

Research References

Encyclopedias
OH Jur. 3d Courts & Judges § 67, Miscellaneous Powers and Functions of Probate Judge.
OH Jur. 3d Courts & Judges § 332, in Probate Divisions Court of Common Pleas.
OH Jur. 3d Decedents' Estates § 1801, Joinder of Parties.
OH Jur. 3d Decedents' Estates § 1803, Pleading, Generally.
OH Jur. 3d Fiduciaries § 151, Generally; Application of Statute of Limitations.

Forms
Ohio Jurisprudence Pleading and Practice Forms § 2:24, Powers and Duties Via Particular Courts—Probate Division.

Notes of Decisions

Attorney fees 5
Court costs 2
Jury trials 1
Procedure 3
Res judicata 4

1. Jury trials

When the nature of the issues entitle them to a jury trial or render it appropriate, the probate court has jurisdiction to try any question of fact arising in such action therein prosecuted or afford the parties a trial by jury. (See also Lawrence RR Co v O'Harra, 48 OS 343, 28 NE 175 (1891); Rote v Stratton, 2 NP 27, 3 D 156 (CP, Lake 1895); Champion v Williams, 2 NP 329, 2 D 388 (CP, Hamilton 1893); Israel v Zanesville & Ohio Railway Co, 10 D Repr 219, 19 B 258 (CP, Washington 1888); Woodward v Curtis, 19 CC 15, 10 CD 400 (Knox 1899); affirmed by 63 OS 575, 60 NE 1135 (1900); T, AA & NM Railway v Toledo & Michigan Belt Railway Co, 6 CC 521, 3 CD 566 (Lucas 1892).) Doan v. Biteley (Ohio 1892) 49 Ohio St. 588, 32 N.E. 600.

Under GC 11212 (RC 2101.32), the law governing civil proceedings in the common pleas shall govern the probate court, and the three-fourths jury law applies. Smith v. Craig (Ohio App. 1918) 30 Ohio C.D. 544, 9 Ohio App. 316, 29 Ohio C.A. 236.

The probate court has the same power and authority as the common pleas in regard to struck juries. Wiler v. Logan Nat. Gas & Fuel Co. (Ohio Cir. 1904) 17 Ohio C.D. 257, 6 Ohio C.C.(N.S.) 206, affirmed 72 Ohio St. 628, 76 N.E. 1128, 2 Ohio Law Rep. 536.

2. Court costs

Under testatrix's will expenses of defending a will contest and of defending title to specifically bequeathed securities were properly a charge upon the residue of the estate. In re Jacoby's Estate (Ohio Prob. 1957) 155 N.E.2d 275, 79 Ohio Law Abs. 239.

The probate court has the same power to award and tax costs and apportion them between the parties as the courts of common pleas. The term, "costs," as used in this section includes not only court costs, but also other expenses incident to litigation with respect to which the court may make an award and finding. (See also Holmes v Hrobon, 116 App 363, 188 NE(2d) 187 (1961) and Holmes v Hrobon, 116 App 366, 188 NE(2d) 189 (1961).) Holmes v. Hrobon (Franklin 1951) 93 Ohio App. 1, 103 N.E.2d 845, 61 Ohio Law Abs. 113, 61 Ohio Law Abs. 241, 50 O.O. 178,

Note 2

affirmed in part, reversed in part 158 Ohio St. 508, 110 N.E.2d 574, 49 O.O. 450. Costs ⚖ 169

Where judgment was found against plaintiffs who filed a declaratory action seeking the termination of a trust on the grounds of invalid exercise of power of appointment after the trustee refused to institute a court action, such plaintiffs are not entitled to an award of attorneys fees under the "common fund" doctrine where such plaintiffs are not among the class of designated beneficiaries nor are such plaintiffs entitled to the recovery of court costs or expenses under the Declaratory Judgment Act. Wills v Union Savings & Trust Co, No. 3155 (11th Dist Ct App, Trumbull, 6–24–83).

3. Procedure

A proceeding to admit a lost, spoliated, or destroyed will is a special statutory proceeding in which hearsay rule is inapplicable. In re Estate of Haynes (Ohio 1986) 25 Ohio St.3d 101, 495 N.E.2d 23, 25 O.B.R. 150. Wills ⚖ 293(4)

Petition for authority to present claim of a minor for damages against an estate to the executor thereof after expiration of the time for presentment of claims was properly brought by minor through her father and next friend. In re Noie's Estate (Franklin 1960) 179 N.E.2d 536, 87 Ohio Law Abs. 276.

Where juvenile court ordered, adjudged and decreed that minor child be committed to the permanent custody of County Child Welfare Board as a dependent and neglected child, and the judgment was signed at the end by the juvenile judge, but was not journalized, entry of such judgment on the journal by subsequent juvenile judge nunc pro tunc was mandatory. In re Howell (Ohio Juv. 1956) 140 N.E.2d 347, 74 Ohio Law Abs. 217. Judges ⚖ 32

Where a guardian is appointed, the journal entry reciting that the notice was given and the consent of the ward obtained, the probate court cannot four years later vacate such order nunc pro tunc upon the ground that such consent was not obtained. In re Gerstenek (Cuyahoga 1956) 139 N.E.2d 64, 76 Ohio Law Abs. 280.

For purpose of determining whether probate court had jurisdiction of proceeding by administrator and his wife for allowance of their joint claim against decedent's estate, the action was a "like proceeding" within statute providing that provisions of law governing civil proceedings in Common Pleas Court shall govern like proceedings in probate court. In re Smith's Estate (Ohio Prob. 1952) 120 N.E.2d 632, 67 Ohio Law Abs. 409. Executors And Administrators ⚖ 250

Where a co-administrator and his wife hold a joint claim against an estate for services rendered, the probate court has jurisdiction to pass on the claim. In re Smith's Estate (Ohio Prob. 1952) 120 N.E.2d 632, 67 Ohio Law Abs. 409.

Exceptions to the accounts of a testamentary trustee having been sustained, and money judgment having been rendered against him by the probate court, the judgment remaining unpaid and not collectible, the surety on his official bond may be made a party and judgment may be rendered against it by the probate court in the same action. In re Johnson's Estate (Cuyahoga 1941) 66 Ohio App. 433, 34 N.E.2d 1017, 20 O.O. 392, appeal dismissed 138 Ohio St. 124, 33 N.E.2d 3, 20 O.O. 162.

Pleadings other than the petition may be filed in appropriation proceedings under the provisions of this section. Union Sav. Bank & Trust Co. v. Baltimore & O.S.W.R. Co. (Ohio Insolv. 1908) 7 Ohio NP(NS) 497, 53 W.L.B. 450.

No legal claim for expenses and fees will be allowed when the probate court makes reference without consent of the parties. In re Guardianship of Gorman, 2 NP(NS) 667, 15 D 204 (CP, Franklin 1904).

A county which has one judge of the court of common pleas and one judge of the probate division of that same court does have two judges of the court of common pleas, and the compensation of the county's law librarian is, therefore, not limited under RC 3375.48 to $500 per annum. OAG 75-057.

4. Res judicata

Under statute giving probate court full power to hear and determine any matter properly before it, if administrator and his wife had separable interests in an agreement to serve and the services performed for his decedent during her lifetime, and in obtaining payment for the services, probate court had concurrent jurisdiction with Common Pleas Court as to claim of administrator's wife, and decision of probate court would be res judicata in subsequent action brought on same claim in Common Pleas Court. In re Smith's Estate (Ohio Prob. 1952) 120 N.E.2d 632, 67 Ohio Law Abs. 409. Courts ⚖ 472.4(4); Judgment ⚖ 545

5. Attorney fees

Counsel for next-of-kin was not entitled to attorney fee award out of assets of estate in litigation over entitlement to settlement proceeds arising out of decedent's death absent evidence that counsel participated in obtaining tort settlement or otherwise acted to benefit estate. Hooks v. Owen (Ohio App. 7 Dist., 09-23-1998) 130 Ohio App.3d 38, 719 N.E.2d 581, dismissed, appeal not allowed 85 Ohio St.3d 1405, 706 N.E.2d 787. Executors And Administrators ⚖ 216(2)

2101.33 Vacation and modification of judgments

The probate court has the same power as the court of common pleas to vacate or modify its orders or judgments.

(1976 H 390, eff. 8–6–76; 125 v 903; 1953 H 1; GC 10501–17, 10501–18)

Historical and Statutory Notes

Pre–1953 H 1 Amendments: 114 v 325

Cross References

Common pleas court, new trial, exceptions, Ch 2321
Powers and duties of supreme court, conflict of rules with statutes, O Const Art IV, § 5
Relief from judgment, Civ R 60

Library References

Courts ⚖ 202(4), 202(5).
Westlaw Topic No. 106.

Research References

Encyclopedias

OH Jur. 3d Decedents' Estates § 1025, Relief by Vacation or Modification of Order Admitting Will to Probate.
OH Jur. 3d Family Law § 1706, Modification or Vacation of Order.

Forms

Ohio Jurisprudence Pleading and Practice Forms § 9:2, Issuance at Commencement of Action.
Ohio Jurisprudence Pleading and Practice Forms § 5:41, Divisions of the Common Pleas Courts—Probate Division.

Treatises and Practice Aids

Carlin, Baldwin's Ohio Practice, Merrick-Rippner Probate Law § 3:3, Jurisdiction of Probate Court—Subject Matter—in General.
Carlin, Baldwin's Ohio Practice, Merrick-Rippner Probate Law § 7:1, Power of Probate Court to Vacate or Modify Judgments—in General.
Carlin, Baldwin's Ohio Practice, Merrick-Rippner Probate Law § 19:2, Legitimation—Procedure—Acknowledgment of Paternity.

Notes of Decisions

Equitable grounds 3
Errors, fraud, mistake 4
Procedural issues 2
Vacation of order 1

---

1. Vacation of order

An order of a probate court making an election for an incompetent surviving spouse under RC 2107.45 is subject to the control of the court and may be vacated under RC 2101.33 within term time. (Ed. note: See Civil Rule 6(C).) In re Strauch's Estate (Franklin 1967) 11 Ohio App.2d 173, 229 N.E.2d 95, 40 O.O.2d 331, affirmed 15 Ohio St.2d 192, 239 N.E.2d 43, 44 O.O.2d 158. Wills ⚖ 788

An order modifying the year's allowance does not constitute a vacation of the previous order approving the inventory so as to reinstate in such surviving spouse the right of election to purchase the mansion house for the one-month period from the date of such order of modification. In re Hrabnicky's Estate (Ohio 1958) 167 Ohio St. 507, 149 N.E.2d 909, 5 O.O.2d 181.

Where a guardian is appointed, the journal entry reciting that the notice was given and the consent of the ward obtained, the probate court cannot four years later vacate such order nunc pro tunc upon the ground that such consent was not obtained. In re Gerstenek (Cuyahoga 1956) 139 N.E.2d 64, 76 Ohio Law Abs. 280.

The common pleas court has jurisdiction to declare void judgments and orders of the probate court for lack of jurisdiction. Armstrong v. Brufach (Ohio Com.Pl. 1950) 136 N.E.2d 463, 74 Ohio Law Abs. 370, 59 O.O. 352.

This section giving to probate court same power as common pleas court to vacate or modify its orders or judgments, confers on probate court jurisdiction to vacate confirmation of final account in decedent's estate. Pengelly v. Thomas (Franklin 1946) 79 Ohio App. 53, 65 N.E.2d 897, 46 Ohio Law Abs. 481, 34 O.O. 449, appeal dismissed 146 Ohio St. 693, 67 N.E.2d 714, 33 O.O. 169. Executors And Administrators ⚖ 509(1)

The probate court has the same powers as the common pleas court to vacate or modify its judgments during the same term of court in which the judgment is rendered. (Ed. note: But see Civil Rule 6(C).) In re Kleinhen's Estate (Hancock 1944) 76 Ohio App. 122, 63 N.E.2d 315, 31 O.O. 429. Courts ⚖ 202(4)

2. Procedural issues

The probate court has the same power at law and in equity to vacate or modify its orders and judgments after term as the court of common pleas. (See also Hoofstetter v Adams, 67 App 21, 35 NE(2d) 869 (1941).) In re Gray's Estate (Ohio 1954) 162 Ohio St. 384, 123 N.E.2d 408, 55 O.O. 224. Courts ⚖ 202(4)

The power granted the probate court in this section is not limited to the grounds set forth by GC 11631 (RC 2325.01) but is the same power as that granted to the common pleas court, and is not exclusive, but cumulative. In re Beckman's Estate (Mercer 1951) 91 Ohio App. 42, 107 N.E.2d 538, 48 O.O. 236.

This section is remedial, is not affected by GC 26 (RC 1.58), is not violative of any provision of the constitution and applies to proceeding to vacate confirmation of final account in decedent's estate, even though confirmation was made prior to effective date of section. Pengelly v. Thomas (Franklin 1946) 79 Ohio App. 53, 65 N.E.2d 897, 46 Ohio Law Abs. 481, 34 O.O. 449, appeal dismissed 146 Ohio St. 693, 67 N.E.2d 714, 33 O.O. 169.

The jurisdiction of probate court to modify or vacate its orders or judgments is limited by same rules that govern courts of common pleas; and by GC 10501–18 (RC 2101.33), the year is divided into three terms of four months each, for purpose of modifying or vacating its orders or judgments. (Ed. note: But see Civil Rule 6(C).) In re Shafer's Estate (Butler 1943) 74 Ohio App. 33, 56 N.E.2d 926, 40 Ohio Law Abs. 496, 29 O.O. 233.

Under GC 10509–119 (RC 2117.17), a probate court's approval of a claim against an estate, on a hearing of a schedule of debts and exceptions filed thereto, is final as to all persons interested in the estate, subject to a right of review and to be vacated or set aside under this section, or to be opened up for fraud, collusion or mistake. In re Blue's Estate (Union 1939) 67 Ohio App. 37, 32 N.E.2d 499, 29 Ohio Law Abs. 161, 14 O.O. 447.

3. Equitable grounds

The probate court has the power to modify a previously rendered order, after term, on equitable grounds as well as those grounds enumerated by statute. (Ed. note: See Civil Rules 6(C) and 60(B).) McCallister v. Craig (Clinton 1965) 5 Ohio App.2d 137, 214 N.E.2d 122, 34 O.O.2d 245.

Grant of a limited equity jurisdiction to probate court, under provisions of GC 10501–53 (RC 2101.24) and this section, does not oust court of common pleas from its original equity jurisdiction to declare void the judgments and orders of probate court for lack of jurisdiction. Young v. Guella (Summit 1941) 67 Ohio App. 11, 35 N.E.2d 997, 21 O.O. 66.

Specific grant of power to a probate court as contained in GC 10501–53 (RC 2101.24) and this section, does not confer upon such court general equity jurisdiction. Hooffstetter v. Adams (Summit 1941) 67 Ohio App. 21, 35 N.E.2d 896, 21 O.O. 70.

A probate court can vacate or modify its orders and judgments the same as a common pleas court, and as its jurisdiction in that respect is not limited either by the constitution or legislative enactment to statutory grounds only, such jurisdiction includes equitable grounds as well. Abicht v. O'Donnell (Franklin 1936) 52 Ohio App. 513, 3 N.E.2d 993, 22 Ohio Law Abs. 82, 6 O.O. 462.

4. Errors, fraud, mistake

Probate courts have no jurisdiction over claims for money damages resulting from fraud. Alexander v. Compton (Clinton 1978) 57 Ohio App.2d 89, 385 N.E.2d 638, 11 O.O.3d 81.

Error in the application of the law to the facts in the rendition of a judgment is judicial error, is a matter which must be raised by appeal, and is not an irregularity in obtaining the judgment within the meaning of RC 2325.01. Bartlett v. Bartlett (Ohio 1964) 176 Ohio St. 299, 199 N.E.2d 586, 27 O.O.2d 206. Descent And Distribution ⚖ 71(7)

A probate court has inherent power to vacate, after term, a judgment procured by fraud. In re Adoption of Sladky (Franklin 1958) 109 Ohio App. 120, 161 N.E.2d 554, 81 Ohio Law Abs. 264, 10 O.O.2d 304.

An executor does not lose his right to have a final order determining inheritance taxes modified for a mistake of fact in erroneously listing assets for taxation by a failure to file exceptions to the interlocutory order determining inheritance taxes. In re Beckman's Estate (Mercer 1951) 91 Ohio App. 42, 107 N.E.2d 538, 48 O.O. 236.

The probate court has the power during term to modify its order determining inheritance tax on the ground of a mistake of fact when the tax has been paid and no exceptions have been filed to the determination of such tax. (Ed. note: But see Civil Rule 6(C).) In re Wampler's Estate (Montgomery 1950) 103 Ohio App. 303, 60 Ohio Law Abs. 593.

Probate court, in determining the amount of inheritance tax, acts in a judicial as well as an administrative capacity, has the same power in respect thereto that it has in respect to other matters rightfully lodged with it, and may, in accordance with such power, set aside its determination based upon a mistaken appraisal and make a second determination based upon the true appraisal. In re Seidensticker's Estate (Franklin 1944) 75 Ohio App. 73, 60 N.E.2d 74, 42 Ohio Law Abs. 161, 30 O.O. 381.

Judgment creditor of a person who has fraudulently transferred his assets to an estate in pursuance of a conspiracy between such judgment debtor and the administrator of the estate, may maintain an action in a probate court to set aside and vacate a judgment of the probate court, entered as a result of such fraudulent conspiracy. Hooffstetter v. Adams (Summit 1941) 67 Ohio App. 21, 35 N.E.2d 896, 21 O.O. 70.

2101.34 Judgments by confession

If the judges of the court of common pleas are absent from the county or are under a disability, the probate judge of the county may enter judgments by confession in cases pending in the court of common pleas of his county.

(1953 H 1, eff. 10–1–53; GC 10501–31)

Historical and Statutory Notes

Pre–1953 H 1 Amendments: 114 v 328

Cross References

Judgment by confession, 2323.12 to 2323.14

Library References

Courts ⚖202(4).
Westlaw Topic No. 106.

Research References

Encyclopedias

OH Jur. 3d Courts & Judges § 67, Miscellaneous Powers and Functions of Probate Judge.
OH Jur. 3d Judgments § 256, Jurisdiction; of Particular Courts.

Forms

Ohio Jurisprudence Pleading and Practice Forms § 2:24, Powers and Duties Via Particular Courts—Probate Division.

Notes of Decisions

Attorney fees 2

Original jurisdiction 1

1. Original jurisdiction

Since the Ohio Constitution provides that the probate court shall have "such other jurisdiction in any county or counties as may be provided by law," the legislature can confer upon the probate court original jurisdiction which it cannot confer upon either the supreme court or the appeals court. Phelon v. Pittsburg, A. & W.R. Co. (Ohio Cir. 1891) 3 Ohio C.D. 267.

2. Attorney fees

Under Ohio law, stipulations incorporated in promissory notes for payment of attorney fees, if principal and interest are not paid at maturity, are contrary to public policy and void. Clarklift of Northwest Ohio, Inc. v. Clark Equipment Co. (N.D.Ohio, 11-15-1994) 869 F.Supp. 533, affirmed 117 F.3d 1420. Bills And Notes ⚖ 534

2101.35 Execution

Orders for the payment of money may be enforced as judgments in the court of common pleas. Such execution shall be directed to the sheriff, or, in the sheriff's absence or disability, to the coroner.

(1953 H 1, eff. 10–1–53; GC 10501–29)

Historical and Statutory Notes

Pre–1953 H 1 Amendments: 114 v 328

Cross References

Execution, Civ R 69
Powers and duties of supreme court, conflict of rules with statutes, O Const Art IV §5

Library References

Execution ⚖ 60.
Westlaw Topic No. 161.
C.J.S. Executions § 57.

Research References

Encyclopedias

OH Jur. 3d Decedents' Estates § 1812, Enforcement of Judgment; Execution.
OH Jur. 3d Decedents' Estates § 1814, Proceedings in Aid of Execution.
OH Jur. 3d Enforcement & Execution of Judgments § 52, Probate Court.
OH Jur. 3d Enforcement & Execution of Judgments § 67, to Whom Directed.
OH Jur. 3d Enforcement & Execution of Judgments § 143, Particular Officers.
OH Jur. 3d Enforcement & Execution of Judgments § 403, Recovery of Judgment—Particular Orders and Decrees as Judgments.

Notes of Decisions

Administrator's account 1

1. Administrator's account

Action in the nature of a creditor's bill is properly based on an order of the probate court, upon settlement of the administrator's accounts, to the administrator for payment of money. Warner v. York (Ohio Cir. 1903) 15 Ohio C.D. 310, 1 Ohio C.C.N.S. 73.

2101.36 "Probate judge" includes court of common pleas in lunacy proceedings

"Probate judge" in the statutes relating to lunacy matters includes the court of common pleas of such county, when it is made to appear to the judge thereof that the probate judge is incapacitated from sitting in such case.

(1953 H 1, eff. 10–1–53; GC 10501–14)

Historical and Statutory Notes

Pre–1953 H 1 Amendments: 114 v 328

Cross References

Assignment of judges, O Const Art IV §5
Judges of the court of common pleas, divisions, O Const Art IV §4

Library References

Judges ⚖ 29.
Westlaw Topic No. 227.
C.J.S. Judges § 69.

Research References

Encyclopedias

OH Jur. 3d Courts & Judges § 128, Probate Judge; Certification to General Court of Common Pleas.

2101.37 Judge of court of common pleas to act as probate judge; compensation

When the probate judge of any county is absent, or is unable to attend court, or the volume of work in his office necessitates it, he may call upon a judge of the court of common pleas having jurisdiction in said county to act in his place, or in conjunction with him, or he may call upon the chief justice of the supreme court, who shall designate a judge of the court of common pleas or a probate judge to act in the place of such absent or incapacitated probate judge, or in conjunction with him. If the probate judge of any county dies or resigns during his term of office, a judge of the court of common pleas of said county shall act in the place of said probate judge until his successor is appointed and qualified. When a judge of the court of common pleas or a probate judge so designated resides outside the county in which he is called upon to act, he shall receive such compensation as is provided for judges of the court of common pleas designated by the chief justice to hold court outside their respective counties. The record of such cases shall be made and preserved in the proper records of the probate court by the deputy clerk thereof.

(1953 H 1, eff. 10–1–53; GC 10501–12)

Historical and Statutory Notes

Pre–1953 H 1 Amendments: 123 v 504; 116 v 558; 114 v 323

Cross References

Assignment of judges, O Const Art IV §5
Compensation and expenses of judges holding court outside county of residence, 141.07
Judges of the court of common pleas, divisions, O Const Art IV §4

Library References

Judges ⚖ 29.
Westlaw Topic No. 227.
C.J.S. Judges § 69.

Research References

Encyclopedias

OH Jur. 3d Courts & Judges § 68, Assignment of Judges.
OH Jur. 3d Courts & Judges § 104, Courts of Common Pleas and Divisions.

Forms

Ohio Jurisprudence Pleading and Practice Forms § 2:21, Powers and Duties Via Particular Courts—Supreme Court of Ohio.

Notes of Decisions

Constitutional issues 1
Request for transfer 2

---

1. Constitutional issues

The general assembly has constitutional authority to assign a probate judge to perform the duties of a judge of the court of common pleas. (Ed. note: But see O Const Art IV, § 5(A)(3).) In re Ely's Trust Estate (Ohio 1964) 176 Ohio St. 311, 199 N.E.2d 746, 27 O.O.2d 236.

2. Request for transfer

A probate court may not certify a cause to the common pleas court for hearing and determination upon exceptions to inventory and appraisement where no request is made for the transfer and no finding is made which brings the matter within the terms of RC 2101.37 and RC 2101.38. In re Byerly's Estate (Madison 1956) 141 N.E.2d 771, 74 Ohio Law Abs. 586.

2101.38 Administration when the probate judge is interested; certification to common pleas court

Letters testamentary, of administration, or of guardianship shall not be issued to a person after his election to the office of probate judge and before the expiration of his term. If a probate judge is interested, as heir, legatee, devisee, or other manner in an estate which would otherwise be settled in the probate court of the county where he resides, such estate, and all of the accounts of guardians in which the judge is interested, shall be settled by the court of common pleas of the county. In such matters and cases in which the judge is interested, the original papers shall be by him forthwith certified to the court of common pleas. In other matters and proceedings in a probate court in which the judge thereof is interested or in which he is required to be a witness to a will, such judge shall, upon the motion of a party interested in the proceedings, or upon his own motion, certify the matters and proceedings to the court of common pleas and forthwith file with the clerk of the court of common pleas all original papers connected therewith.

When a matter or proceeding is so certified, the court of common pleas, at chambers, by a judge thereof, or in open court shall hear and determine it as though such court had original jurisdiction of the subject matter. Upon final decision of the questions involved in such proceedings, the final settlement of the estate in which the judge is interested as executor, administrator, or guardian, or when his interest therein ceases, the clerk shall deliver to the probate court from which they came the original papers and make and file therein an authenticated transcript of the orders, judgments, and proceedings of the court of common pleas. Thereupon the probate judge shall record such orders, judgments, and proceedings in the proper records.

(1953 H 1, eff. 10–1–53; GC 10501–9, 10501–10)

Historical and Statutory Notes

Pre–1953 H 1 Amendments: 114 v 322

Cross References

Election, term, and compensation of judges; assignment of retired judges, O Const Art IV §6

Library References

Courts ☞486.
Judges ☞42.
Westlaw Topic Nos. 106, 227.
C.J.S. Courts § 194.
C.J.S. Judges § 119.

Research References

Encyclopedias

OH Jur. 3d Courts & Judges § 44, Powers at Chambers.
OH Jur. 3d Courts & Judges § 117, Interest of Judge.
OH Jur. 3d Courts & Judges § 128, Probate Judge; Certification to General Court of Common Pleas.
OH Jur. 3d Courts & Judges § 132, Affidavit as to Particular Judge: Judge of Court of Appeals—Judge of Probate Division.
OH Jur. 3d Courts & Judges § 209, Filing of Papers Connected With Litigation.
OH Jur. 3d Courts & Judges § 287, Administration When Probate Judge Interested in Estate.
OH Jur. 3d Decedents' Estates § 911, Meaning of "Suitable" and "Competent", Generally.
OH Jur. 3d Decedents' Estates § 938, Meaning of "Competent" and "Suitable", Generally; Discretion of Court.
OH Jur. 3d Family Law § 25, Application for Marriage License.
OH Jur. 3d Fiduciaries § 152, Jurisdiction and Venue.

Forms

Ohio Jurisprudence Pleading and Practice Forms § 2:30, Disqualification—Grounds.

Treatises and Practice Aids

Carlin, Baldwin's Ohio Practice, Merrick-Rippner Probate Law § 3:58, Entry Certifying to Common Pleas Court—Form.
Carlin, Baldwin's Ohio Practice, Merrick-Rippner Probate Law § 68:18, Letters Testamentary—Letters of Administration With the Will Annexed.

Notes of Decisions

Certification 4
Constitutional issues 1
Limited and special jurisdiction 3
Procedural issues 2

---

1. Constitutional issues

O Const Art IV, § 8, does not confer conclusive jurisdiction in all probate and guardianship matters, as matters in which probate judge is interested are conferred upon common pleas. State ex rel. Fay v. Archibald (Ohio 1894) 52 Ohio St. 1, 32 W.L.B. 307, 38 N.E. 314, 2 Ohio Leg. N. 25.

2. Procedural issues

Denial of request by financial institution charged with wrongful conveyance under statute prohibiting wrongful or culpable withholding or concealing of estate assets to transfer action to court of common pleas and, instead, transfer of case to another probate court was proper, where probate court was not shown to be interested party as contemplated by statute. In re Estate of Popp (Ohio App. 8 Dist., 04-18-1994) 94 Ohio App.3d 640, 641 N.E.2d 739, dismissed 70 Ohio St.3d 1446, 639 N.E.2d 114, certiorari denied 115 S.Ct. 1256, 513 U.S. 1192, 131 L.Ed.2d 136. Courts ☞ 484

A probate court may not certify a cause to the common pleas court for hearing and determination upon exceptions to inventory and appraisement where no request is made for the transfer and no finding is made which brings the matter within the terms of RC 2101.37 and RC 2101.38. In re Byerly's Estate (Madison 1956) 141 N.E.2d 771, 74 Ohio Law Abs. 586.

Federal courts do not follow the state practice in equity suits. McClaskey v. Barr (C.C.S.D.Ohio 1891) 48 F. 130.

Where the court fails to send up all the papers, a case will not be dismissed. Barr v Closterman, 7 CC 363, 4 CD 637 (Hamilton 1892).

3. Limited and special jurisdiction

The probate court has only such jurisdiction to sell property on the petition of executors, administrators, and guardians as is possessed by the common pleas court. Hence, if at the time of the passage of the act conferring such jurisdiction on the probate court, the common pleas court has not jurisdiction to order the sale of the lands of a ward, on the application of his guardian, the probate court could not order such a sale.

Note 3

Foresman v. Haag (Ohio 1880) 36 Ohio St. 102, supplemented 37 Ohio St. 143.

Common pleas court has jurisdiction in probate matters whenever the probate court's jurisdiction is inadequate, as where a trustee's settlement was obtained by fraud. Rote v. Stratton (Ohio Com.Pl. 1895) 3 Ohio Dec. 156, 2 Ohio N.P. 27.

This section gives to common pleas court, under certificate of probate judge, a limited and special jurisdiction to do what is prescribed by statute. McClaskey v. Barr (C.C.S.D.Ohio 1891) 48 F. 130.

Jurisdiction of common pleas court continues until it acts and certifies its action back to probate court and no longer. McClaskey v. Barr (C.C.S.D.Ohio 1891) 48 F. 130.

4. Certification

Where a matter is certified from the probate court to the common pleas court, the latter has the same power to hear and determine exceptions to an inventory as the former would have. In re Barnes' Estate (Ohio Com.Pl. 1950) 108 N.E.2d 88, 64 Ohio Law Abs. 6, affirmed 108 N.E.2d 101, 64 Ohio Law Abs. 28.

Where a probate judge has any interest whatever in a controversy, whether financial or otherwise, he is authorized under GC 1589 and GC 1590 to certify the case to the common pleas court, either on motion of the party interested or acting sua sponte. In re Ullman (Ohio Cir. 1909) 21 Ohio C.D. 370, 12 Ohio C.C.(N.S.) 340. Judges ⇔ 42; Judges ⇔ 50

2101.39 Affidavit of disqualification of probate judge for prejudice

If a probate judge allegedly has a bias or prejudice for or against a party or a party's counsel in a proceeding pending before the judge, allegedly otherwise is interested in a proceeding pending before the judge, or allegedly is disqualified to preside in the proceeding and if the bias, prejudice, interest, or disqualification does not permit or require certification of the proceeding to the court of common pleas as provided by section 2101.38 of the Revised Code, any party to the proceeding or the party's counsel may file an affidavit of disqualification with the clerk of the supreme court. The affidavit of disqualification shall be filed and decided in accordance with divisions (B) to (E) of section 2701.03 of the Revised Code, and, upon the filing of the affidavit, the provisions of those divisions apply to the affidavit, the proceeding, the judge, and the parties to the proceeding.

(1996 S 263, eff. 11–20–96; 1984 H 426, eff. 4–4–85; 126 v 36; 1953 H 1; GC 10501–11)

Uncodified Law

1996 S 263, § 3, eff. 11–20–96, reads: The amendments to sections 2101.39, 2501.13, 2701.03, and 2937.20 (2701.031) of the Revised Code that are made by this act shall apply to each affidavit of disqualification that is filed on or after the effective date of this act regarding a judge of a court of appeals, court of common pleas, probate court, municipal court, or county court.

Historical and Statutory Notes

Ed. Note: Guidelines for Assignment of Judges were announced by the Chief Justice of the Ohio Supreme Court on 5-24-88, and revised 2-25-94 and 3-25-94, but not adopted as rules pursuant to O Const Art IV §5. For the full text, see 37 OS(3d) xxxix, 61 OBar A-2 (6-13-88) and 69 OS(3d) XCIX, 67 OBar xiii (4-18-94).

Pre–1953 H 1 Amendments: 114 v 323

Amendment Note: 1996 S 263 rewrote this section, which prior thereto read:

"When a probate judge has a prejudice, either for or against a party or his counsel in a matter or cause pending before him, or is otherwise interested in such a cause or matter, or disqualified to sit in the cause or matter, but the prejudice, interest, or disqualification is not such as to permit or require certification of the proceedings to the court of common pleas as provided by section 2101.38 of the Revised Code, any party to the cause or matter, or the counsel of any such party, may file an affidavit with the clerk of the supreme court setting forth the prejudice, interest, or disqualification. The clerk of the supreme court forthwith shall notify the probate court of the filing of such an affidavit, and the fact of the filing of the affidavit shall be entered upon the record of the probate court. The judge may upon his own motion make an entry setting forth the prejudice, interest, or disqualification, a copy of which shall be filed with the clerk of the supreme court.

"Forthwith upon the filing of such an affidavit or entry, the clerk of the supreme court shall forward the affidavit or entry to the chief justice of the supreme court who, if satisfied that the prejudice, interest, or disqualification exists, shall assign a probate judge or a judge of the court of common pleas to hear the cause or matter in place of such probate judge. The judge assigned shall proceed and try the cause or matter. The affidavit referred to in this section shall be filed not less than three days prior to the time set for the hearing of the cause or matter."

Cross References

Disqualification of judge, assignment of judge, 2701.03
Election, term, and compensation of judges; assignment of retired judges, O Const Art IV §6

Library References

Judges ⇔51(1).
Westlaw Topic No. 227.
C.J.S. Judges §§ 130, 133, 152.

Research References

Encyclopedias

OH Jur. 3d Courts & Judges § 117, Interest of Judge.
OH Jur. 3d Courts & Judges § 125, Bias or Prejudice.
OH Jur. 3d Courts & Judges § 128, Probate Judge; Certification to General Court of Common Pleas.
OH Jur. 3d Courts & Judges § 132, Affidavit as to Particular Judge: Judge of Court of Appeals—Judge of Probate Division.
OH Jur. 3d Courts & Judges § 138, Determination of Disqualification; Substitution of Judge—Probate Judge.
OH Jur. 3d Courts & Judges § 287, Administration When Probate Judge Interested in Estate.
OH Jur. 3d Decedents' Estates § 871, Jurisdiction of Probate Court—Contesting Jurisdiction.

Forms

Ohio Jurisprudence Pleading and Practice Forms § 2:30, Disqualification—Grounds.
Ohio Jurisprudence Pleading and Practice Forms § 2:31, Disqualification—Procedure and Remedies.

Treatises and Practice Aids

Carlin, Baldwin's Ohio Practice, Merrick-Rippner Probate Law § 3:15, Jurisdiction of Probate Court—Scope—Migratory Jurisdiction of Probate Judge.
Carlin, Baldwin's Ohio Practice, Merrick-Rippner Probate Law § 3:59, Affidavit of Prejudice—Form.
Carlin, Baldwin's Ohio Practice, Merrick-Rippner Probate Law § 104:20, Affidavit for Disqualification of Judge—Form.

Law Review and Journal Commentaries

New provisions for affidavits of disqualification, Richard A. Dove. 10 Ohio Law 14 (November/December 1996).

Notes of Decisions

Authority to reassign 3
Constitutional issues 1
Standing 2

---

1. Constitutional issues

The general assembly has constitutional authority to assign a probate judge to perform the duties of a judge of the court of common pleas. (Ed. note: But see O Const Art IV §5(A)(3).) In re Ely's Trust Estate (Ohio 1964) 176 Ohio St. 311, 199 N.E.2d 746, 27 O.O.2d 236.

2. Standing

A party seeking appointment as successor guardian of an incompetent does not have standing to file an affidavit of bias and prejudice against a probate judge. In re Guardianship of Hill (Ohio Prob. 1963) 196 N.E.2d 816, 93 Ohio Law Abs. 237, 29 O.O.2d 60.

3. Authority to reassign

Only chief justice or acting chief justice of Supreme Court has any authority to assign a judge from one court to another, or from one division of the same court to another, other than in specified instances, thus precluding an administrative judge from reassigning a judge of probate division of court of common pleas to hear a case in the general division. Schucker v. Metcalf (Ohio 1986) 22 Ohio St.3d 33, 488 N.E.2d 210, 22 O.B.R. 27. Courts ⇐ 70

2101.40 Dealing in assets of estate

A probate judge shall not in any way deal in property or securities involved in probate court cases. This section applies to all appointees of the probate court.

(1953 H 1, eff. 10–1–53; GC 10501–40)

Historical and Statutory Notes

Pre–1953 H 1 Amendments: 114 v 329

Cross References

Conflict of interest, 102.03

Library References

Judges ⇐ 21.
Westlaw Topic No. 227.
C.J.S. Judges §§ 35 to 36.

2101.41 Limits on practice of law by judges, deputy clerks, and referees

No probate judge shall practice law, be associated with another as partner in the practice of law in a court or tribunal of this state, prepare a complaint or answer, make out an account required for the settlement of an estate committed to the care or management of another, or appear as attorney before a court or judicial tribunal. Whoever violates this section shall forfeit his office.

The deputy clerk of a probate court may engage in the practice of law if his practice is not related in any way to probate law or practice. The deputy may engage in the practice of law only with the continued consent and approval of all of the judges of the probate court.

A referee appointed solely to conduct hearings under Chapters 5122. and 5123. of the Revised Code may engage in the practice of law, including probate law, except that he shall not practice law under these chapters other than as a referee and shall not knowingly accept any business arising out of or otherwise connected with a proceeding in which he served as a referee under these chapters.

The prosecuting attorney shall file his information against a judge or deputy clerk who practices law in violation of this section in the court of common pleas, and proceed as upon indictment.

This section does not prevent a probate judge or deputy clerk from finishing business commenced by him prior to his election or appointment, provided it is not connected with his official duty.

(1977 H 725, eff. 3–16–78; 1975 S 145; 129 v 582; 1953 H 1; GC 12854 to 12856)

Historical and Statutory Notes

Pre–1953 H 1 Amendments: RS 534

Cross References

Penalty: 2101.99(C)
Conflict of interest, 102.03
Judges not to practice law, Code of Jud Cond Canon 5
Practice of law, prohibitions, 4705.01

Library References

Clerks of Courts ⇐ 64.1.
Judges ⇐ 21.
Reference ⇐ 44.
Westlaw Topic Nos. 227, 327, 79.
C.J.S. Courts §§ 249, 254.
C.J.S. Judges §§ 35 to 36.
C.J.S. References §§ 46 to 47.

Research References

Encyclopedias

OH Jur. 3d Courts & Judges § 98, Practicing Law.

Notes of Decisions

Judge elect 1

---

1. Judge elect

GC 1706, now provided for in this section, prohibiting one holding a commission as judge from practicing as an attorney at law, does not apply to a judge elect whose term has not yet begun. State ex rel. Savage v. Hidy (Ohio 1900) 61 Ohio St. 549, 43 W.L.B. 145, 56 N.E. 469.

A probate judge may finish business commenced by him prior to his election provided it is not connected with his official duty. OAG 67–034.

2101.42 Cases appealable from probate court

From any final order, judgment, or decree of the probate court, an appeal on a question of law may be prosecuted to the court of appeals in the manner and within the time provided for the prosecution of such appeals from the court of common pleas to the court of appeals. For the purpose of prosecuting appeals on questions of law from the probate court, the probate court shall exercise judicial functions inferior only to the court of appeals and the supreme court.

(1975 S 145, eff. 1–1–76; 1953 H 1; GC 10501–56)

Uncodified Law

1975 S 145, § 3: See Uncodified Law under 2101.24.

Historical and Statutory Notes

Pre–1953 H 1 Amendments: 119 v 394, § 1; 118 v 78, § 1; 114 v 336

Legislative Service Commission

1975:

This section would be amended to conform with the "Modern Courts Amendment" to the Ohio Constitution and with Rule 2 of the Ohio Rules of Appellate Procedure. The provision that allows an appeal to be taken from probate court to the court of common pleas would be deleted. Also, references to appeals on questions of law and fact would be removed, since they are prohibited by the Rules of Appellate Procedure.

Cross References

Affidavit before private sale confirmed, 2109.45
Final order defined, 2505.02
Law and fact appeals abolished, App R 2
Probate court estate tax determination, appeal from, 5731.22

Library References

Courts ⇐ 202(5).
Westlaw Topic No. 106.

Research References

Encyclopedias

OH Jur. 3d Appellate Review § 7, Nature of Pre-1971 Appeal De Novo, Appeal on Questions of Law and Fact.

OH Jur. 3d Appellate Review § 29, Appeals from Probate Division of Common Pleas Court.

OH Jur. 3d Decedents' Estates § 1023, Appeal from Probate Proceedings.

OH Jur. 3d Decedents' Estates § 1033, Appeal.

OH Jur. 3d Decedents' Estates § 1056, Appeal from Denial of Probate.

OH Jur. 3d Decedents' Estates § 1067, Wills Admitted in Another State or Territory—Appeal from Order Refusing to Admit to Record.

OH Jur. 3d Decedents' Estates § 1072, Contest of Authenticity of Record; Appeals.

OH Jur. 3d Decedents' Estates § 1242, Final Order.

Forms

Ohio Jurisprudence Pleading and Practice Forms § 5:37, Appeals from Probate Division of Common Pleas Courts.

Ohio Jurisprudence Pleading and Practice Forms § 84:12, Generally—Inferior Courts of Record Within District.

Treatises and Practice Aids

Carlin, Baldwin's Ohio Practice, Merrick-Rippner Probate Law § 8:1, Appeal—Statutory Provisions.

Carlin, Baldwin's Ohio Practice, Merrick-Rippner Probate Law § 52:35, Fiduciary's Bond—Appeal.

Carlin, Baldwin's Ohio Practice, Merrick-Rippner Probate Law § 57:12, Removal of Fiduciary—Appeal.

Carlin, Baldwin's Ohio Practice, Merrick-Rippner Probate Law § 62:64, Appeal of Appointment of Guardian.

Carlin, Baldwin's Ohio Practice, Merrick-Rippner Probate Law § 80:21, Attorney Fees—Dispute—Appeal.

Carlin, Baldwin's Ohio Practice, Merrick-Rippner Probate Law § 103:47, Appropriation of Property—Appeal.

Painter & Dennis, Ohio Appellate Practice § 1:23, Right to Appeal-Appeal from Lower to Higher Court.

Notes of Decisions

Administrators 2-4
    Accounts 2
    Ancillary 3
    Removal 4
Constitutional issues 1
Creditors 5
Final order affecting property rights 6
Guardianship 7
Procedural issues 8
Sale of real estate 9
Standing 10
Wills and trusts 11

---

1. Constitutional issues

By virtue of O Const Art IV, § 4, a court of common pleas has no jurisdiction to hear an appeal from a probate court. In re Guardianship of Derr (Scioto 1970) 24 Ohio App.2d 91, 263 N.E.2d 911, 53 O.O.2d 229. Courts ⇐ 42(3)

2. Administrators—Accounts

Statute permitting appeal from judgment of probate court in settling accounts of executor or trustee is remedial and must be liberally construed; surety of trustee could appeal from finding of probate court that error had been made in previous account approved by court; surety could not contend that it was surety for principal as trustee and not as executor, where surety knew that executor without further appointment and without giving new bond assumed trustee's duties. U.S. Fidelity & Guaranty Co. of Baltimore, Md. v. Wood (Morrow 1929) 35 Ohio App. 224, 172 N.E. 383.

Cited as to the special provision for appeal to the court of common pleas from any order, decision or judgment of the probate court in settling the accounts of administrators. McMahon v. Ambach & Co. (Ohio 1908) 79 Ohio St. 103, 86 N.E. 512, 6 Ohio Law Rep. 554.

An executor having rejected a claim of attorneys for successfully resisting a contest of the will, and the attorneys having by petition to the probate court with notice to all parties interested procured an order of the court that part of the claim be allowed and part rejected, this order amounts to a judgment in settling the executor's accounts within former GC 11206 (RC 2101.42), and is therefore appealable by the attorneys. Royer v. Trumpler (Seneca 1916) 28 Ohio C.D. 186, 7 Ohio App. 312, 27 Ohio C.A. 117, affirmed 95 Ohio St. 194, 115 N.E. 1018, 14 Ohio Law Rep. 551.

3. —— Ancillary, administrators

Ancillary administrator of estate may appeal from order of probate court prescribing that he reject claims of domiciliary executor set forth in schedule of debts, which claims were presented to and allowed by proper court of state of domiciliary executor, prescribing that ancillary administrator require domiciliary executor to perfect his claims under GC 10509–112 (RC 2117.06) et seq., and prescribing that, after proper adjudication of rejection or allowance of domiciliary executor's claims, ancillary administrator distribute entire funds in his hands to beneficiaries named in will of decedent. In re Kelley's Estate (Hancock 1940) 68 Ohio App. 51, 34 N.E.2d 34, 33 Ohio Law Abs. 258, 22 O.O. 158.

4. —— Removal, administrators

An order of the probate court removing an administrator is not appealable to the court of common pleas. In re Still's Estate (Ohio 1864) 15 Ohio St. 484. Executors And Administrators ⇐ 35(19)

Refusal to remove an administrator is not appealable. Ebersole v. Schiller (Ohio 1893) 50 Ohio St. 701, 30 W.L.B. 389, 35 N.E. 793.

The right of appeal to the common pleas court from an order of the probate court removing an executor, is not in conflict with the provision of GC 10492, giving the probate court exclusive jurisdiction to grant and revoke letters testamentary. In re Sells' Estate (Ohio Com.Pl. 1909) 19 Ohio Dec. 567, 8 Ohio NP(NS) 175.

Error does not lie to order removing executor. In re Ferguson's Estate (Ohio Com.Pl. 1904) 16 Ohio Dec. 486, 3 Ohio NP(NS) 549.

5. Creditors

The jurisdiction of the probate court to determine the question of priorities as between creditors of a partnership and of its individual members may be maintained on the ground that it is a necessary step to the making of a final order, and if such jurisdiction exists in the probate court, it also exists in the common pleas on appeal. Clapp v. Huron County Banking Co. (Ohio 1893) 50 Ohio St. 528, 30 W.L.B. 359, 35 N.E. 308.

The decree of probate court upon the final account of an assignee for benefit of creditors concludes his sureties unless an appeal has been taken. Garver v. Tisinger (Ohio 1888) 46 Ohio St. 56, 20 W.L.B. 406, 18 N.E. 491.

A creditor desiring to remove an administrator and proceed against him for concealing assets may unite same in one complaint and such a proceeding is appealable. Harris v. Westervelt (Ohio Cir. 1898) 8 Ohio C.D. 367.

In a proceeding instituted in the probate court by an assignee for the benefit of creditors to sell land and determine priority of liens, the costs of an appeal to the court of common pleas by a lienholder should be adjudged against such lienholder and not against the fund constituting the proceeds of the sale. Mutual Aid Building & Loan Co. v. Gashe (Ohio Cir. 1895) 6 Ohio C.D. 779, 3 Ohio Dec. 647, modified 56 Ohio St. 273, 37 W.L.B. 315, 46 N.E. 985.

On appeal by a creditor of a decedent estate, the common pleas court may inquire whether or not the appellant is a creditor or not and entitled to appeal. In re Dunham's Estate (Ohio Cir. 1894) 4 Ohio C.D. 325, 1 Ohio Dec. 329.

A creditor of an insolvent estate may appeal from the order of the probate court, making allowance to a widow for a year's support. In re Rahe's Estate (Ohio Com.Pl. 1902) 12 Ohio Dec. 590.

6. Final order affecting property rights

Orders must be final and affect property rights, and not merely the administration of the trust. Brigel v. Starbuck (Ohio 1877) 34 Ohio St. 280.

The approval by the probate court of the election of an assignee by the creditors in a proceeding under the statutes in relation to assignments for the benefit of creditors is not a definite final order affecting property rights, and is not appealable to the court of common pleas. Brigel v. Starbuck (Ohio 1877) 34 Ohio St. 280. Debtor And Creditor ⇒ 4

The refusal to confirm, or the setting aside of, a sale leaves the property undisposed of, and concludes no rights of property; thus, it is not a final order, and an appeal may not be taken from such refusal. Aultman, Miller & Co. v. J.F. Seiberling Co. (Ohio 1877) 31 Ohio St. 201.

Attempted appeal from refusal of probate court to entertain application and exceptions, presented approximately a year after an account had been settled is properly dismissed since it is not a final order, decision or judgment. In re French's Estate (Montgomery 1937) 23 Ohio Law Abs. 702.

Although no provision is made for the filing of exceptions by a township or municipality to a determination by the probate court of the place of origin of inheritance tax, such determination is a final order from which an appeal may be taken. (See also Amelia v Bethel, 165 OS 115, 133 NE(2d) 347 (1956).) In re Hutson's Estate (Clermont 1953) 100 Ohio App. 473, 137 N.E.2d 407, 60 O.O. 377.

Words "order, decision, or judgment" in this section, are used in their usual and ordinary sense, and comprehend only such orders, decisions and judgments as are final in their nature. In re Hamilton's Estate (Marion 1940) 67 Ohio App. 242, 36 N.E.2d 439, 32 Ohio Law Abs. 414, 21 O.O. 228. Courts ⇒ 202(5)

An order of a probate court setting aside a former order permitting an answer to be withdrawn is not a final order. Hawke v. Noyes (Hamilton 1939) 62 Ohio App. 186, 23 N.E.2d 508, 29 Ohio Law Abs. 683, 15 O.O. 458. Appeal And Error ⇒ 82(3)

An order for sale defining and determining the amount and terms of the sale and rights of the parties is appealable. Assignment of Norwood Park Co. (Ohio Com.Pl. 1897) 6 Ohio Dec. 341, 4 Ohio N.P. 240.

No appeal from part of an inadmissible order of distribution can be made. Keck v Douglass, 6 CC 649, 3 CD 629 (Hamilton 1892).

7. Guardianship

A guardian of a mentally incompetent ward does not have a right of appeal under RC 2101.42 from an order of the probate court terminating the guardianship pursuant to RC 2111.47 upon satisfactory proof that the ward has regained his mental competency and the necessity for the guardianship has ceased to exist, where the record does not reflect any interest of the guardian adverse to the ward in such order of termination, or show that the guardian has been aggrieved in any manner by the order of termination. In re Guardianship of Love (Ohio 1969) 19 Ohio St.2d 111, 249 N.E.2d 794, 48 O.O.2d 107.

An order appointing a guardian of an incompetent cannot be collaterally attacked. In re Guardianship of Titington (Ohio Prob. 1958) 162 N.E.2d 628, 82 Ohio Law Abs. 563.

An adjudication by the probate court that a person is incompetent and appointing a resident guardian for such person's property in Ohio is an order affecting such person from which an appeal may be taken on his behalf. In re Guardianship of Reynolds (Lucas 1957) 106 Ohio App. 488, 155 N.E.2d 686, 7 O.O.2d 222.

Order of probate court refusing to remove guardian upon application of ward, being an order "affecting a substantial right made in a special proceeding" within meaning of GC 12223-2 (RC 2505.02), is a "final order" from which the ward may appeal to the court of appeals on questions of law. In re Irvine's Guardianship (Knox 1943) 72 Ohio App. 329, 51 N.E.2d 907, 27 O.O. 255. Appeal And Error ⇒ 77(2); Appeal And Error ⇒ 91(3)

Mother of a minor child for whom a guardian has been appointed over her objection may appeal from such order. In re Guardianship of Moyer (Lucas 1941) 68 Ohio App. 319, 40 N.E.2d 695, 22 O.O. 483.

Common pleas court may appoint a guardian for an imbecile upon appeal from probate court refusing to do so. In re Oliver's Guardianship (Ohio 1908) 77 Ohio St. 474, 83 N.E. 795, 5 Ohio Law Rep. 586.

The circuit court has no jurisdiction to review on error an order of common pleas made on appeal from probate removing a guardian for cause. North v. Smith (Ohio 1906) 73 Ohio St. 247, 76 N.E. 619, 3 Ohio Law Rep. 537. Courts ⇒ 240; Guardian And Ward ⇒ 25

Since the probate court may at any time remove any executor or administrator for any cause which, in the opinion of the court, renders it for the interest of the estate that such executor or administrator be removed, the guardian and administrator cannot appeal from a decision of the probate court terminating the guardianship of a drunkard. Martin v. Dershem (Ohio 1901) 65 Ohio St. 556, 46 W.L.B. 172, 63 N.E. 1130.

Where letters of guardianship were improperly issued, an appeal will lie from an order of a probate court overruling the motion of an imbecile ward to terminate the guardianship on the ground that the imbecile has since the time the letters were issued been fully restored to reason. Hiett v. Nebergall (Ohio 1888) 45 Ohio St. 702, 17 N.E. 558. Courts ⇒ 202(5); Mental Health ⇒ 45; Mental Health ⇒ 167

Sureties of guardian who removed from state, and upon whom probate court secured service by publication, may appeal. Netting v. Strickland (Ohio Cir. 1899) 9 Ohio C.D. 841.

An appeal may be taken by the guardian of an imbecile in the interest of the trust from an order of the probate court, made upon the application of the alleged imbecile himself, terminating the guardianship. Kraner, Guardianship of (Ohio Com.Pl. 1909) 19 Ohio Dec. 444, 8 Ohio N.P.N.S. 217.

An order of the probate court finding the necessity for appointment of a guardian for an alleged imbecile is not a final order affecting property rights prior to the appointment of a guardian, and the alleged imbecile is not entitled to an appeal from such finding. In re Breitenstein (Ohio Com.Pl. 1906) 17 Ohio Dec. 71, 4 Ohio NP(NS) 358.

An order of a probate court striking exceptions to the account of a guardian from the files is a final order and the time to appeal it cannot be prolonged by a later motion to set aside such order. In re Streit's Estate (Ohio Com.Pl. 1901) 12 Ohio Dec. 158. Appeal And Error ⇒ 346.1; Guardian And Ward ⇒ 161

No appeal can be taken in the matter of the settlement of a guardian's account so long as any item of the account remains undetermined. Gregg v Klein, 12 CC(NS) 264, 22 CD 698 (Hamilton 1908).

The common pleas court can acquire no jurisdiction in the matter of the settlement of a guardian's account so long as any item of the account remains undetermined. Gregg v Klein, 12 CC(NS) 264, 22 CD 698 (Hamilton 1908).

An uncle of a minor may appeal from an order overruling a motion for removal of a guardian. In re Guardianship of Murray, 8 CC(NS) 498, 18 CD 652 (Lorain 1906).

Circuit court has no jurisdiction to review order of common pleas court removing or refusing to remove guardian. North v Smith, 5 CC(NS) 495, 17 CD 367 (Darke 1904), vacated by 73 OS 247, 76 NE 619 (1906).

This section authorizes an appeal to common pleas court from allowance of costs for guardian by probate court. In re Guardianship of Gorman, 2 NP(NS) 667, 15 D 204 (CP, Franklin 1904).

8. Procedural issues

Right of appeal here given relates to judgments when the probate court had jurisdiction to hear and determine complaints under RS 6053 to RS 6059. Meinzer v. Bevington (Ohio 1884) 42 Ohio St. 325.

Either party may appeal from probate court and bills of exceptions may be taken. Shroyer v. Richmond (Ohio 1866) 16 Ohio St. 455.

Upon an appeal, the judgment appealed from is not vacated but only superseded or stayed pending a final determination, so that where the appellate court renders a judgment to replace the judgment appealed from, the appellate court judgment replaces the judgment appealed from except where otherwise ordered by a superior court, and if its judgment is reversed for reasons which indicate that the original judgment was valid, that original judgment will be regarded as a valid judgment from the time of its entry. In re Witteman's Estate (Ohio 1969) 21 Ohio St.2d 3, 254 N.E.2d 345, 50 O.O.2d 2.

This section is operative as to appeals from probate court, and the general provisions relating to appeal in GC 12223-3 (RC 2505.03) affect only such cases within those general provisions as are not within the provisions of this section. In re Hamilton's Estate (Marion 1940) 67 Ohio App. 242, 36 N.E.2d 439, 32 Ohio Law Abs. 414, 21 O.O. 228. Courts ⇒ 202(5)

In an appeal from the probate court to the common pleas, the cause shall be tried, heard and decided the same as though the common pleas had original jurisdiction thereof. James v. West (Ohio 1902) 67 Ohio St. 28, 47 W.L.B. 857, 65 N.E. 156.

Error as well as appeal may be prosecuted from judgments of probate court. Kittredge v. Miller (Ohio Cir. 1896) 5 Ohio C.D. 391.

Given notice of intention to appeal by an entry upon the journal is sufficient. Hirsh v Kilsheimer, 12 CC 291, 5 CD 551 (Hamilton 1896).

No jury can be demanded in a suit to compel the allowance of a claim by an assignee of an insolvent estate, since it is an equitable action, though such an action is appealable. Meader v Root, 5 CD 61 (Cir. 1895).

Where the applicants for an order by the probate court are numerous, a properly perfected appeal by a number of them "and others" is effectual as to all; the appeal may be from the whole or a part of the order or judgment complained of, and notice of intention to appeal is not necessary. In re Assignment of Fairview Glass Co, 9 NP(NS) 157, 21 D 822 (CP, Knox 1909).

9. Sale of real estate

An Ohio probate court, although it has admitted to probate an Ohio will, has no power to review accounts of the executor respecting property situate in the state of Michigan for which he has duly accounted to the proper court of that state. In re Crawford (Ohio 1903) 68 Ohio St. 58, 48 W.L.B. 492, 67 N.E. 156, 96 Am.St.Rep. 648, 1 Ohio Law Rep. 91.

The judgment of a probate court confirming a sale of real estate by an assignee, at private sale, may be appealed. Browne v. Wallace (Ohio 1899) 60 Ohio St. 177, 41 W.L.B. 359, 53 N.E. 957. Debtor And Creditor ⇨ 5; Courts ⇨ 185; Courts ⇨ 202(5)

Judgment of a probate court upon the priority and validity of liens on property of an insolvent estate may be appealed. Sayler v. Simpson (Ohio 1887) 45 Ohio St. 141, 17 W.L.B. 379, 12 N.E. 181.

Where no appeal is taken on allowances to a widow made in a proceeding to sell real estate belonging to her husband to pay debts, such allowances cannot be collaterally attacked by exception to her account as administratrix of the said estate. In re Hess' Estate (Ohio Cir. 1911) 23 Ohio C.D. 449, 14 Ohio C.C.(N.S.) 463. Executors And Administrators ⇨ 194(6); Homestead ⇨ 150(2)

An order by the court of insolvency confirming a sale is not an appealable order under this section. Assignment of Norwood Park Co. (Ohio Com.Pl. 1897) 6 Ohio Dec. 341, 4 Ohio N.P. 240. Debtor And Creditor ⇨ 12

An order confirming a defective sale and overruling a motion to set aside the sale of property by an assignee in insolvency is appealable. Assignment of Schumacher (Ohio Com.Pl. 1897) 5 Ohio Dec. 386, 5 Ohio N.P. 145.

10. Standing

A person who is not included in any of the classes of persons to whom notice of the filing of an inventory, the hearing thereon, the filing of exceptions, or the hearing thereon, is required to be given and who was never served with such notice but merely appeared as a witness at the hearing on exceptions to the inventory, claiming ownership of certain items of personal property claimed by the exceptor to belong to the estate, cannot appeal from a judgment of the probate court ordering such property included in the inventory. In re Apger's Estate (Van Wert 1960) 111 Ohio App. 164, 171 N.E.2d 347, 14 O.O.2d 54.

Where upon sustaining exceptions to an inventory the court orders the executor to include certain property in the inventory which the executor claims he cannot locate, the executor is an interested party and may appeal therefrom. In re Byerly's Estate (Madison 1956) 141 N.E.2d 771, 74 Ohio Law Abs. 586.

An executrix is not qualified to appeal a decision deciding which of several claimants is entitled to receive rents accruing after the death of the testatrix. (See also In re Estate of Anderson, 74 Abs 549, 141 NE(2d) 478 (1956).) In re Anderson's Estate (Franklin 1955) 130 N.E.2d 250, 71 Ohio Law Abs. 126.

A party who is competent to file exceptions to an account has capacity to appeal from an adverse ruling thereon. Burke v. McKee (Hocking 1928) 30 Ohio App. 236, 164 N.E. 776. Executors And Administrators ⇨ 510(3)

Refusal either to increase or diminish a widow's year's allowance did not warrant appeal under original GC 11206. Reidermann v. Tafel (Ohio Dist. 1883) 12 W.L.B. 284.

Right of appeal in divorce proceedings is permitted in certain counties. Pierson v Pierson, 5 NP(NS) 235, 18 D 822 (CP, Licking 1907).

11. Wills and trusts

An executor may appeal from a judgment which establishes a vested interest in the remainder of the estate in a designated beneficiary under a trust created in the will, which judgment terminates the trust upon the expiration of a designated life interest; all of which is in conflict with provisions of the will to terminate the trust at a different time, under different conditions, and with gifts of the remainder to other beneficiaries, if designated events occurred. Fineman v. Central Nat. Bank of Cleveland (Cuyahoga 1961) 175 N.E.2d 837, 87 Ohio Law Abs. 236, 18 O.O.2d 33. Appeal And Error ⇨ 150(3)

An order of the probate court admitting a lost will to probate is not a final order and an appeal may not be taken therefrom. In re Brown's Estate (Montgomery 1954) 97 Ohio App. 499, 127 N.E.2d 226, 56 O.O. 454. Appeal And Error ⇨ 77(2)

Award of allowance to a testamentary trustee is not a final order and an appeal will not lie therefrom. In re Thomas' Will (Franklin 1948) 84 Ohio App. 30, 84 N.E.2d 294, 53 Ohio Law Abs. 21, 39 O.O. 46.

Order of probate court admitting instrument to probate as a last will is not reviewable on appeal. In re Frey's Estate (Ohio 1942) 139 Ohio St. 354, 40 N.E.2d 145, 22 O.O. 411. Appeal And Error ⇨ 77(2)

The probate court has complete and exclusive jurisdiction to remove a trustee appointed by it under a will, and an appeal from such a removal order will not lie. Stafford v. American Missionary Ass'n (Ohio Cir. 1901) 12 Ohio C.D. 442. Trusts ⇨ 167

From proceedings under GC 10535 and GC 10536, to admit a foreign will to probate, appeal cannot be had to common pleas court. Barr v. Closterman (Ohio Cir. 1887) 1 Ohio C.D. 546, affirmed.

COMBINING PROBATE AND COMMON PLEAS COURTS

2101.43 Petition for submission of question of combining probate court and court of common pleas

Whenever ten per cent of the number of electors voting for governor at the most recent election in any county having less than sixty thousand population, as determined by the most recent federal census, petition a judge of the court of common pleas of such county, not less than seventy-five days before any general election for county officers, for the submission to the electors of such county the question of combining the probate court with the court of common pleas, such judge shall place upon the journal of said court an order requiring the sheriff to make proclamation that at the next general election there will be submitted to the electors the question of combining the probate court with the court of common pleas. The clerk of the court of common pleas shall, thereupon, make and deliver a certified copy of such order to the sheriff, and the sheriff shall include notice of the submission of such question in his proclamation of election for the next general election.

Each elector joining in a petition for the submission of said question shall sign such petition in the elector's own handwriting, unless the elector cannot write and the elector's signature is made by mark, and shall add thereto the township, precinct, or ward of which the elector is a resident. Such petition may consist of as many parts as are convenient. One of the signers to each separate paper shall swear before some officer qualified to administer the oath that the petition is bona fide to the best of the signer's knowledge and belief. Such oath shall be a part of or attached to such paper. The judge upon receipt of such petition shall deposit it with the clerk of the court of common pleas.

No signature shall be taken from or added to such petition after it has been filed with the judge. When deposited such petition shall be preserved and open to public inspection, and if it is in conformity with this section, it shall be valid, unless objection thereto is made in writing by an elector of the county within five days after the filing thereof. Such objections, or any other questions arising in the course of the submission of the question of combining said courts, shall be considered and determined by the judge, and his decision shall be final.

(1995 H 99, eff. 8–22–95; 1980 H 1062, eff. 3–23–81; 1953 H 1; GC 10501–47, 10501–48)

Historical and Statutory Notes

Pre–1953 H 1 Amendments: 114 v 333

Amendment Note: 1995 H 99 substituted "most recent" for "next preceding" twice in the first paragraph; substituted "next" for "ensuing" before "general election" throughout the first paragraph; and made other changes to reflect gender neutral language.

Cross References

Notary public may administer oaths, 147.07
Number of judges for each county; terms of office, 2301.02
Oath defined, 1.59
Oath includes affirmation, form of oath, 3.20, 3.21
Single judge may serve several courts in small counties, O Const Art IV §23

Library References

Courts ⚖54.
Elections ⚖33.
Westlaw Topic Nos. 106, 144.
C.J.S. Courts § 103.

2101.44 Conduct of election; form of ballot; returns and canvass

The election upon the question of combining the probate court and the court of common pleas shall be conducted as provided for the election of county officers.

The board of election shall provide separate ballots, ballot boxes, tally sheets, blanks, stationery, and all such other supplies as may be necessary in the conduct of such election.

Ballots shall be printed with an affirmative and negative statement thereon, as follows:

The probate court and the court of common pleas shall be combined.
The probate court and the court of common pleas shall not be combined.

Returns of said election shall be made and canvassed at the same time and in the same manner as an election for county officers. The board shall certify the result of said election to the secretary of state, to the probate judge of said county, and to the judge of the court of common pleas, and such result shall be spread upon the journal of the probate court and of the court of common pleas.

If a majority of the votes cast at such an election are in favor of combining said courts, such courts shall stand combined upon determination of the fact that a majority of the persons voting upon the question of the combination of such courts voted in favor of such combination.

(1953 H 1, eff. 10–1–53; GC 10501–49)

Historical and Statutory Notes

Pre–1953 H 1 Amendments: 116 v 385; 114 v 333

Cross References

Single judge may serve several courts in small counties, O Const Art IV §23

Library References

Courts ⚖54.
Elections ⚖164, 198, 235.
Westlaw Topic Nos. 106, 144.
C.J.S. Courts § 103.
C.J.S. Elections §§ 191(1), 221, 235, 243.

Notes of Decisions

Contest 1
Term 2

1. Contest

Common pleas judge has jurisdiction of contest of election where court combined with probate court. State ex rel. Sattler v. Cahill (Ohio 1930) 122 Ohio St. 354, 171 N.E. 595.

2. Term

Pursuant to the provisions of former GC 1604–3 (RC 2101.44), when a majority of the votes cast at an election shall be in favor of combining the probate court with the court of common pleas of a given county, such courts shall stand combined and consolidated at the expiration of the term for which the probate judge, then serving, has been elected. 1924 OAG p 670.

2101.45 Probate division established; appeals

When the probate court and the court of common pleas have been combined as provided in sections 2101.43 and 2101.44 of the Revised Code, there shall be established in the court of common pleas a probate division and all matters of which the probate court has jurisdiction shall be filed and separately docketed in that division. The resident judge of the court of common pleas shall appoint the necessary deputies, clerks, and assistants to have charge of and perform the work incident to the division. An appeal on questions of law may be prosecuted from that division to the court of appeals.

(1986 H 412, eff. 3–17–87; 1953 H 1; GC 10501–50)

Historical and Statutory Notes

Pre–1953 H 1 Amendments: 116 v 385; 114 v 334

Cross References

Appeals on law and fact abolished, App R 2
Single judge may serve several courts in small counties, O Const Art IV §23

Library References

Courts ⚖50.
Westlaw Topic No. 106.
C.J.S. Courts § 106.

Research References

Encyclopedias

OH Jur. 3d Courts & Judges § 181, Appointment or Election, in General—Court of Common Pleas.
OH Jur. 3d Guardian & Ward § 205, Appeal from Order.

Treatises and Practice Aids

Painter & Dennis, Ohio Appellate Practice § 1:23, Right to Appeal-Appeal from Lower to Higher Court.

Law Review and Journal Commentaries

The Probate Courts of Ohio, John F. Winkler. 28 U Tol L Rev 563 (Spring 1997).

Notes of Decisions

Appeals 1

1. Appeals

An order of the probate court in a proceeding to remove a fiduciary is reviewable under RC 2101.45. In re Guardianship of Escola (Stark 1987) 41 Ohio App.3d 42, 534 N.E.2d 866. Guardian And Ward ⇐ 25

2101.46 Re–establishment of the probate court

After three years from the date of an election held under sections 2101.43 to 2101.45, inclusive, of the Revised Code, another election may be petitioned for and shall be ordered by the judge of the court of common pleas as provided in such sections either to perfect a combination of said court or to dissolve said combination and re-establish the probate court.

Whenever in any county where such courts have been combined a decennial federal census shows that such county has a population of sixty thousand or more, and such fact is certified by the secretary of state to said court of common pleas and entered upon its journal, the probate court shall be re-established in such county. A probate judge shall be elected for the regular term at the next election ensuing in an even-numbered year, and the records of the probate division of the court of common pleas shall be delivered to such re-established probate court upon the entry into office of an elected probate judge.

(1953 H 1, eff. 10–1–53; GC 10501–51, 10501–52)

Historical and Statutory Notes

Pre–1953 H 1 Amendments: 114 v 334

Cross References

Single judge may serve several courts in smaller counties, O Const Art IV §23

Library References

Courts ⇐ 53, 54.
Elections ⇐ 33.
Westlaw Topic Nos. 106, 144.
C.J.S. Courts § 103.

Notes of Decisions

Judges 1

1. Judges

A judge of a probate court which has been combined with the common pleas court, upon the determination of the due separation of said probate court from the court of common pleas within the four years for which said person had been qualified as probate judge, is entitled to perform the duties of probate judge in the re-established probate court. 1928 OAG 2885.

PENALTIES

2101.99 Penalties

(A) Whoever violates section 2101.09 of the Revised Code shall be fined not more than one hundred dollars.

(B) Whoever violates section 2101.15 of the Revised Code shall be fined not less than ten nor more than two hundred dollars.

(C) Whoever violates section 2101.41 of the Revised Code shall be fined not more than fifty dollars.

(1953 H 1, eff. 10–1–53)

Cross References

Classification of offenses, 2901.02

Library References

Coroners ⇐ 23.
Fines ⇐ 1.5.
Judges ⇐ 36.
Sheriffs and Constables ⇐ 152.
Westlaw Topic Nos. 100, 174, 227, 353.
C.J.S. Coroners and Medical Examiners § 31.
C.J.S. Judges §§ 86 to 89, 94 to 96.

Research References

Encyclopedias
OH Jur. 3d Courts & Judges § 98, Practicing Law.
OH Jur. 3d Police, Sheriffs, & Related Officers § 112, Special Provisions as to Probate Courts and Constables.

CHAPTER 2103

DOWER

Section	
2103.01	"Property" construed
2103.02	Dower
2103.021	Trustee as grantee in instrument; affidavit for dower interest required
2103.03	Conveyance in lieu of dower
2103.04	Eviction from premises conveyed in lieu of dower
2103.041	Subjection of dower interest to judicial sale
2103.05	Adultery a bar to dower
2103.06	Lands given up by fraud
2103.07	Dower is forfeited by waste
2103.08	Assignment of dower
2103.09	Estate by curtesy abolished

Cross References

Surviving spouses, rights to dower, 2106.24

Law Review and Journal Commentaries

Disinheritance and the Modern Family, Ralph C. Brashier. 45 Case W Res L Rev 83 (Fall 1994).

Is There Any Constitutional Prohibition Against a Statute That Would Abolish Existing Inchoate Right of Dower?, James P. McAndrews. 55 Title Topics 4 (March 1988).

2103.01 "Property" construed

In sections 2103.01 to 2103.09, inclusive, of the Revised Code, unless the context shows that another sense was intended, "property" includes lands, tenements, hereditaments, money, chattels, choses in action, and evidences of debt.

(1953 H 1, eff. 10–1–53; GC 10502–9)

Historical and Statutory Notes

Pre–1953 H 1 Amendments: 114 v 339

Cross References

Anything of value, defined, 1.03
Property, defined, 2901.01

Library References

Dower and Curtesy ⚖10.
Westlaw Topic No. 136.
C.J.S. Dower and Curtesy §§ 8 to 17, 140.

Research References

Encyclopedias

OH Jur. 3d Decedents' Estates § 9, Spouse's Right.
OH Jur. 3d Family Law § 74, Statutory Dower.

Forms

Ohio Forms Legal and Business § 1:4, Necessity for Written Instrument; Basic Elements.
Ohio Forms Legal and Business § 3:60, Release of Dower Rights.

2103.02 Dower

A spouse who has not relinquished or been barred from it shall be endowed of an estate for life in one third of the real property of which the consort was seized as an estate of inheritance at any time during the marriage. Such dower interest shall terminate upon the death of the consort except:

(A) To the extent that any such real property was conveyed by the deceased consort during the marriage, the surviving spouse not having relinquished or been barred from dower therein;

(B) To the extent that any such real property during the marriage was encumbered by the deceased consort by mortgage, judgment, lien except tax lien, or otherwise, or aliened by involuntary sale, the surviving spouse not having relinquished or been barred from dower therein. If such real property was encumbered or aliened prior to decease, the dower interest of the surviving spouse therein shall be computed on the basis of the amount of the encumbrance at the time of the death of such consort or at the time of such alienation, but not upon an amount exceeding the sale price of such property.

In lieu of such dower interest which terminates pursuant to this section, a surviving spouse shall be entitled to the distributive share provided by section 2105.06 of the Revised Code.

Dower interest shall terminate upon the granting of an absolute divorce in favor of or against such spouse by a court of competent jurisdiction within or without this state.

Wherever dower is referred to in Chapters 2101. to 2131., inclusive, of the Revised Code, it means the dower to which a spouse is entitled by this section.

(125 v 903, eff. 10–1–53; 1953 H 1; GC 10502–1)

Historical and Statutory Notes

Pre–1953 H 1 Amendments: 116 v 385; 114 v 337

Cross References

Dower, Ch 5305
Dower not abated by death, 2311.22
Election by surviving spouse, 2106.01
Partnership property not subject to dower or statutory share, 1775.24
Power to dissolve marriage contract, defenses barred, effect on dower, 3105.10

Library References

Dower and Curtesy ⚖5, 11.
Westlaw Topic No. 136.
C.J.S. Dower and Curtesy §§ 8, 18 to 29, 141 to 152.

Research References

Encyclopedias

OH Jur. 3d Cotenancy & Partition § 97, Husband and Wife.
OH Jur. 3d Decedents' Estates § 18, Distributive Share.
OH Jur. 3d Decedents' Estates § 58, Failure to Provide for Surviving Spouse.
OH Jur. 3d Decedents' Estates § 767, Right to Dower; Right to Remain in Mansion House.
OH Jur. 3d Estates, Pwrs., & Restrnts. on Alienat. § 41, Definition and Classification.
OH Jur. 3d Family Law § 71, Generally; Definitions.
OH Jur. 3d Family Law § 74, Statutory Dower.
OH Jur. 3d Family Law § 84, Death.
OH Jur. 3d Family Law § 95, Nature—as an "Estate".
OH Jur. 3d Family Law § 96, Value.
OH Jur. 3d Family Law § 103, Reversions and Remainders.
OH Jur. 3d Family Law § 122, Rights of Heirs, Devisees, and Legatees.
OH Jur. 3d Family Law § 128, Multiple Parcels of Land.
OH Jur. 3d Family Law § 131, Purchase-Money Mortgages; Prior to Marriage—After Marriage.
OH Jur. 3d Specific Performance § 61, Partial Impossibility; Waiver by Plaintiff—Title Subject to Dower Interest.

Forms

Ohio Forms Legal and Business § 2:2, Effect of Dower—Rights of Married Women.
Ohio Forms Legal and Business § 1C:5, Execution and Recordation.
Ohio Forms Legal and Business § 25:26, Deed of Real Property in Trust.
Ohio Forms Legal and Business § 25:41, Revocable Trusts—General Form.
Ohio Forms Legal and Business § 25:53, Irrevocable Trusts—Husband and Wife as Grantors—Income to Children for Life—Remainder to Descendants.
Ohio Forms Legal and Business § 25:61, Trust for Minor Qualifying for Annual Gift Tax Exclusion—General Form.
Ohio Forms Legal and Business § 24:143, Drafting Will.
Ohio Forms Legal and Business § 24:169, Bequests and Devises to Spouse in Lieu of Dower or Curtesy—Residuary Estate to Children—Life Estate of Real Property to Parents—Remainder Over to Specified Person.
Ohio Forms Legal and Business § 24:891, Bequest in Lieu of Dower.
Ohio Forms Legal and Business § 25:384, Approval of Trust Instrument by Spouse With Inchoate Right of Dower.

Treatises and Practice Aids

Sowald & Morganstern, Baldwin's Ohio Practice Domestic Relations Law § 1:5, Terms.
Sowald & Morganstern, Baldwin's Ohio Practice Domestic Relations Law § 4:5, Property Rights During Marriage—Individual Ownership—Dower.
Sowald & Morganstern, Baldwin's Ohio Practice Domestic Relations Law § 4:6, Property Rights During Marriage—Individual Ownership—Descent and Distribution.
Carlin, Baldwin's Ohio Practice, Merrick-Rippner Probate Law § 2:121, Administration of Decedent's Estate—Checklist.
Carlin, Baldwin's Ohio Practice, Merrick-Rippner Probate Law § 91:25, Land Sale—Necessary Parties Defendant—Person With Dower Interest.
Carlin, Baldwin's Ohio Practice, Merrick-Rippner Probate Law § 92:14, Dower—Nature of Interest.
Carlin, Baldwin's Ohio Practice, Merrick-Rippner Probate Law § 92:15, Dower—Termination of Interest.
Carlin, Baldwin's Ohio Practice, Merrick-Rippner Probate Law § 92:16, Dower—Computation of Interest.
Carlin, Baldwin's Ohio Practice, Merrick-Rippner Probate Law § 92:17, Dower—Interest Subject to Debts.
Carlin, Baldwin's Ohio Practice, Merrick-Rippner Probate Law § 92:19, Dower—Sale of Land Subject to Interest.
Kuehnle and Levey, Ohio Real Estate Law and Practice § 41:9, Sales—Remedies—Caveat Emptor—Constructive Fraud.

Law Review and Journal Commentaries

The Antenuptial Contract in Ohio, Note. 28 Case W Res L Rev 1040 (Summer 1978).

Does Dower Still Lurk in Elections to Take Under the Will, Charles E. Stevenson. 30 U Cin L Rev 172 (Spring 1961).

Is There Any Constitutional Prohibition Against a Statute That Would Abolish Existing Inchoate Right of Dower?, James P. McAndrews. 55 Title Topics 4 (March 1988).

Trusts and the Young Case: Planning for disabled beneficiaries, William J. Browning. 11 Ohio Law 6 (November/December 1997).

Notes of Decisions

Distributive share in lieu of dower   1
Inchoate dower   2-10
   In general   2
   Antenuptial agreements   3
   Bankruptcy   4
   Divorce; remarriage   5
   Fee tail, inchoate dower   6
   Liens   7
   Mortgaged property   8
   Rights of creditors   9
   Sale or partitioning of land   10
Nature and computation of interest; subject to debts   11-21
   In general   11
   Bankruptcy and insolvency   12
   Creditors' rights   13
   Dower interest in forfeited property   14
   Dower interest in leased property   15
   Dower interest in mortgaged property   16
   Dower interest in partnership property   17
   Dower interest in property given for public use   18
   Dower interest in trust property   19
   Dower interest versus mechanic's lien   20
   Husband's rights   21
Procedural issues   22
Release, bar and election   23

---

1. Distributive share in lieu of dower

Where widow insured premises which were subject to her dower interest and policy was made payable to heirs, though conditioned that premises were not incumbered, in case of loss, heirs can recover. Ohio Farmers' Ins. Co. v. Britton (Ohio 1877) 31 Ohio St. 488.

In this section "distributive share" is employed as meaning that share which surviving spouse may take by statute of descent and distribution, clearly relating to real and personal property. Seman v. Seman (Darke 1935) 19 Ohio Law Abs. 600.

Either spouse is entitled to a one-third dower interest in real property unless it has been relinquished or barred. Std. Fed. Bank v. Staff (Ohio App. 1 Dist., 07-14-2006) 2006-Ohio-3601, 2006 WL 1933729. Dower And Curtesy 22

Surviving wife who had been omitted from her deceased husband's will, and who elected to take statutory distributive share of husband's estate, was also entitled to her dower interest in husband's one-half interest in marital residence, and was not required to make election between the two, where husband had prior to his death quitclaimed his interest in marital residence, and wife had not consented to transfer or waived her dower interest in property. Armstrong v. Armstrong (Ohio App. 9 Dist., 06-17-1998) 128 Ohio App.3d 393, 715 N.E.2d 207. Descent And Distribution 64.1; Dower And Curtesy 54

Widow of son who predeceased his father, the first donee in fee tail, is not entitled to her distributive share in proceeds from sale of land entailed, in lieu of dower under GC 10502–1 (RC 2103.02), as surviving spouse of such issue. Mays v. Mays (Montgomery 1942) 42 N.E.2d 446, 37 Ohio Law Abs. 102.

Where a testator gave to his wife all that part and interest in his estate, real, personal, and mixed, which is secured to her as his widow by the laws of distribution of estates of the state of Ohio, in the cases where wives survive husbands who die intestate, and gave, absolutely, the remainder of his property, real, personal, and mixed, to his brother, under the will the widow took (1) her dower interest in the testator's real estate situated in Ohio, (2) one-half of the first $400, (3) one-third of the remainder of the personal property subject to distribution, (4) the use of the mansion house, and (5) a year's allowance; the remainder of the estate, real, personal, and mixed, went to the brother. Foster v. Clifford (Ohio 1913) 87 Ohio St. 294, 101 N.E. 269, 10 Ohio Law Rep. 600, Am.Ann.Cas. 1915B, 65.

When widow elects not to take under will, her dower and distributive share are measured as if husband had died intestate, leaving children, and can be neither increased nor diminished by will. Geiger v. Bitzer (Ohio 1909) 80 Ohio St. 65, 88 N.E. 134, 6 Ohio Law Rep. 661, 17 Am.Ann.Cas. 151.

A widow for whom no provision is made in her husband's will and who has been paid the value of her dower in money from the proceeds of the sale of real estate, converted into personal property, pursuant to a direction in the will, is not thereby precluded from asserting and receiving the widow's distributive share in such proceeds, as well as in the other personal property of the testator. Hutchings v. Davis (Ohio 1903) 68 Ohio St. 160, 48 W.L.B. 526, 67 N.E. 251, 1 Ohio Law Rep. 203. Conversion 21(2)

Contingent right of dower is property having a substantial value that may be ascertained with reasonable certainty. Mandel v. McClave (Ohio 1889) 46 Ohio St. 407, 22 W.L.B. 267, 22 N.E. 290, 15 Am.St.Rep. 627.

Release in mortgage of wife's contingent right of dower does not inure to her husband's subsequent creditors and she can have her dower paid before their claims are paid. Mandel v. McClave (Ohio 1889) 46 Ohio St. 407, 22 W.L.B. 267, 22 N.E. 290, 15 Am.St.Rep. 627. Dower And Curtesy 49

Where wife has joined in a mortgage of the husband's lands to secure his debt, upon a judicial sale thereof, she may have value of her contingent right of dower ascertained and husband's interest exhausted first before resorting to her interest. Mandel v. McClave (Ohio 1889) 46 Ohio St. 407, 22 W.L.B. 267, 22 N.E. 290, 15 Am.St.Rep. 627.

A devise to a wife "of that part and interest in my estate, which is secured to her as my widow by the laws of distribution of estates of the state of Ohio in cases where wives survive husbands who die intestate" is an incorporation into the will of such laws. Clifford v. Foster (Ohio Com.Pl. 1910) 25 Ohio Dec. 657, 10 Ohio N.P.(N.S.) 446, affirmed 23 Ohio C.D. 429, 14 Ohio C.C.(N.S.) 391, reversed 87 Ohio St. 294, 101 N.E. 269, 10 Ohio Law Rep. 600, Am.Ann.Cas. 1915B, 65. Wills 488; Wills 525

Where widow makes agreement with heir reciting that it is in lieu of dower, she is barred of dower. Shotwell v Sedam, 3 O 1 (1827).

2. Inchoate dower—In general

Where a grantor makes an absolute delivery of a deed to the officer taking the acknowledgment, who brings the knowledge of such delivery to the grantee the next day, notwithstanding that the grantee doesn't take possession of the realty before the grantor marries, the grantor's wife has no inchoate right of dower in the premises. Black v. Hoyt (Ohio 1877) 33 Ohio St. 203. Dower And Curtesy 5

The inchoate right of dower is something more than the mere naked possibility of an heir apparent; it is a present vested right of value, contingent on the wife's survivorship. Rosenthal v. Mayhugh (Ohio 1877) 33 Ohio St. 155.

Where husband holding title to land in trust for his wife, at her request sells same to a stranger, she can have no dower in the same. Rostetter v. Grant (Ohio 1868) 18 Ohio St. 126, 98 Am.Dec. 93.

Dower inchoate is not an estate; nevertheless, it is a right or interest in the land created by the law for the wife's benefit and vested in her. McArthur v. Franklin (Ohio 1865) 16 Ohio St. 193. Dower And Curtesy 29

Where husband and wife join in signing, sealing and acknowledging blank deed intended to convey small piece of land, and husband secretly fills out such blank for large tract of land, wife is not thereby barred of her dower therein. Conover v. Porter (Ohio 1863) 14 Ohio St. 450.

Dower takes effect upon the decease of the consort, subject only to the expenses of administration. (See also Hickle v Hickle, 6 CC 490, 3 CD 552 (Pike 1892), appeal dismissed by 33 B 107 (1895).) Conger v. Barker's Adm'r (Ohio 1860) 11 Ohio St. 1.

A conveyance and release of dower to a third person does not inure to benefit of purchaser at sheriff's sale to bar dower. Kitzmille v. Van Rensselaer (Ohio 1859) 10 Ohio St. 63.

On petition for dower, the grantee of a deceased husband, and those holding under him, are not estopped to deny that their grantor had title. Coakley v. Perry (Ohio 1854) 3 Ohio St. 344.

Widow is entitled to dower in both legal and equitable interests. Miller v. Wilson (Ohio 1846) 15 Ohio 108.

A married woman can only be divested during coverture of her interest in her husband's estate in the manner pointed out by statute. Silliman v. Cummins (Ohio 1844) 13 Ohio 116.

Where widow is beyond the seas, and so within the saving clause of the statute of limitations, staleness of claim will not bar her dower. Larrowe v. Beam (Ohio 1841) 10 Ohio 498.

Deed by infant wife does not bar dower. Hughes v. Watson (Ohio 1840) 10 Ohio 127.

Wild, uncultivated lands are subject to dower. Allen v. McCoy (Ohio 1838) 8 Ohio 418.

Right of dower does not accrue to wife in any form until death of husband. Liberty Folder Co. v. Anderson (Shelby 1949) 86 Ohio App. 399, 90 N.E.2d 409, 55 Ohio Law Abs. 389, 41 O.O. 521.

This section provides for inchoate but not vested dower, thereby abolishing the latter. Geiselman v. Wise (Ohio 1940) 137 Ohio St. 93, 28 N.E.2d 199, 17 O.O. 430. Dower And Curtesy 3

Contingent right of wife to dower during husband's life, in his real estate, is property having substantial value. Smith v. McKelvey (Lucas 1928) 28 Ohio App. 361, 162 N.E. 722, 6 Ohio Law Abs. 677. Dower And Curtesy 29; Debtor And Creditor 12

Dower is a legal estate and not a secret equity, and until assigned and set off is a recognized encumbrance upon the land. Arnold v. Donaldson (Ohio 1888) 46 Ohio St. 73, 20 W.L.B. 431, 18 N.E. 540.

Dower, unassigned, does not constitute an estate in land, and the words "an estate for life" in this section were intended to indicate merely the duration of the dower right. Lape v. Lape (Ohio Com.Pl. 1920) 31 Ohio Dec. 188, 22 Ohio N.P.N.S. 392.

Inchoate dower is not an estate, but a mere right of action, and the words "estate for life" in GC 8606 (RC 2103.02), were inserted to indicate duration and not establish dower as an estate. Lape v. Lape (Ohio Com.Pl. 1920) 31 Ohio Dec. 188, 22 Ohio N.P.N.S. 392.

As to heirs of husband, widow is not estopped from claiming dower by conduct during life of husband amounting to a denial that she was his wife. Brown v. Kerns (Ohio Com.Pl. 1899) 9 Ohio Dec. 112, 6 Ohio N.P. 68.

That different pieces of land were purchased successively, one with proceeds of the other, does not bar wife's right of dower in each piece of which her husband was seized during coverture. Brown v. Kerns (Ohio Com.Pl. 1899) 9 Ohio Dec. 112, 6 Ohio N.P. 68.

Under Ohio law, wife had inchoate dower interest in real property that was titled in her husband's name only. In re Miller (Bkrtcy.N.D.Ohio 1992) 151 B.R. 800. Dower And Curtesy 29

Property defined in Ohio's dower statute as "seized of inheritance" must be the full value of property. In re Miller (Bkrtcy.N.D.Ohio 1992) 151 B.R. 800. Dower And Curtesy 32

Under Ohio statute, wife's inchoate dower interest in real property titled in her husband's name only constituted "interest" in real property for which wife could claim homestead exemption. In re Miller (Bkrtcy. N.D.Ohio 1992) 151 B.R. 800. Homestead 81

3. —— Antenuptial agreements, inchoate dower

A reasonable antenuptial agreement will bar dower. Murphy v. Murphy (Ohio 1861) 12 Ohio St. 407.

4. —— Bankruptcy, inchoate dower

Despite husband's defense in foreclosure proceedings that his dower interest in mortgaged real property had been part of bankruptcy estate and not subject to transfer at time of mortgage, whether husband's dower interest was released upon settlement with bankruptcy trustee, or whether dower interest was abandoned to husband upon the termination of bankruptcy proceedings, husband's dower interest reverted to him when bankruptcy case was terminated as if no bankruptcy had ever been filed, and thus husband's conveyance of the dower rights through signing the mortgage became effective with the close of the bankruptcy case. Std. Fed. Bank v. Staff (Ohio App. 1 Dist., 07-14-2006) 2006-Ohio-3601, 2006 WL 1933729. Bankruptcy 3445

When the spouse alleged to have an inchoate dower is the debtor, the dower interest becomes the property of the bankruptcy estate. Std. Fed. Bank v. Staff (Ohio App. 1 Dist., 07-14-2006) 2006-Ohio-3601, 2006 WL 1933729. Bankruptcy 2535(4)

A dower interest can be measured and included in a bankruptcy estate. Std. Fed. Bank v. Staff (Ohio App. 1 Dist., 07-14-2006) 2006-Ohio-3601, 2006 WL 1933729. Bankruptcy 2535(4)

All interests of debtor in property come into "property of the estate" upon commencement of bankruptcy case, regardless of whether they are transferable, or whether creditors could have reached them. In re Bowling (Bkrtcy.S.D.Ohio, 06-10-2004) 314 B.R. 127. Bankruptcy 2532

Inchoate and vested rights which one spouse possesses, as of commencement of his or her bankruptcy case, in legal and equitable estates possessed by the other spouse during marriage or at time of death are included in "property of the estate." In re Bowling (Bkrtcy.S.D.Ohio, 06-10-2004) 314 B.R. 127. Bankruptcy 2535(1)

Under Ohio law, wife was entitled to homestead exemption in real property titled solely in her husband's name in amount no more than present value of her inchoate dower interest. In re Miller (Bkrtcy. N.D.Ohio 1992) 151 B.R. 800. Homestead 66

"American Experience Table," expressly made applicable to cases involving judicial sale by Ohio statute, is better choice than "Bowditch Table" in determining present value of wife's inchoate dower interest in real property titled in her husband's name only, and, thus, in determining wife's entitlement to homestead exemption. In re Miller (Bkrtcy. N.D.Ohio 1992) 151 B.R. 800. Homestead 66

Wife's inchoate dower interest in real property titled in her husband's name only was $10,063 under Ohio law, and, thus, wife was entitled in Chapter 7 proceeding to claim a full $5,000 homestead exemption when there was $14,000 in equity on property; property was scheduled at $44,000, wife's dower interest equal to one third of that amount was $14,666.67, wife's yearly allocation based upon 6% present value rate was $880, wife's assigned age of 51 years resulted in present value multiplier of 11.436, and that multiplier when applied to yearly allocation of $880 equaled $10,063. In re Miller (Bkrtcy.N.D.Ohio 1992) 151 B.R. 800. Homestead 66; Homestead 86

The inchoate dower right in a wife's real estate of a husband who is a joint debtor in bankruptcy with his wife is an "asset" of the bankruptcy estate within the meaning of 11 USC 541 and is exempt in an amount up to $5000 under RC 2329.66(A)(1); the amount is payable, however, only from funds left after the proceeds of the sale of the property have been used to pay the mortgage, taxes, and expenses of sale. In re Castor (Bkrtcy.S.D.Ohio 1989) 99 B.R. 807.

A husband's dower interest, under Ohio law, in real property owned by his wife is an interest recognized as part of the husband's bankruptcy estate. In re Lambert (Bkrtcy.N.D.Ohio 1986) 57 B.R. 710.

5. —— Divorce; remarriage, inchoate dower

Where wife deserted her husband and went to parts unknown and returned after three years, claiming she had secured a divorce, and on marriage of deserted husband and his death, a finding by a court that she was barred of dower in his estate may be supported by her statements as to obtaining divorce. Edgar v. Richardson (Ohio 1878) 33 Ohio St. 581, 31 Am.Rep. 571.

Under act of 1840, a divorced wife could remarry and not bar her right of dower in property of first husband. Lamkin v. Knapp (Ohio 1870) 20 Ohio St. 454.

Where testator left life use of all his property to his widow in case she did not remarry and widow elected to take under will, after remarrying she cannot claim dower in testator's property. Hawkins v. Jones (Ohio 1869) 19 Ohio St. 22.

A divorced wife by remarrying is barred of dower in property of first husband. Rice v. Lumley (Ohio 1857) 10 Ohio St. 596.

An undivorced wife whose husband is living at the time of an attempted second marriage is not entitled to dower in second husband's property. Smith v. Smith (Ohio 1855) 5 Ohio St. 32.

Kentucky divorce does not bar dower in Ohio land. Mansfield v. McIntyre (Ohio 1840) 10 Ohio 27.

A conveyance of realty to children of a former marriage, without consideration other than love and affection, by a man engaged to be married, without disclosure of the conveyance to his intended wife whom he later marries, does not defraud her of her right of dower, provided for in RC 2103.02. Perlberg v. Perlberg (Ohio 1969) 18 Ohio St.2d 55, 247 N.E.2d 306, 47 O.O.2d 167. Dower And Curtesy ⇨ 20

A divorced wife who had an inchoate right of dower prior to amendment of the pertinent statutes in 1932 lost such right as a result thereof, and such legislation was valid and any injustice done her thereby could be remedied by a modification of the alimony award; GC 26 (RC 1.20) has no application to a pending divorce or alimony action where the statute involved relates to inchoate right of dower. Goodman v. Gerstle (Ohio 1952) 158 Ohio St. 353, 109 N.E.2d 489, 49 O.O. 235.

Under statute, divorce held to extinguish all dower rights so that words in decree granting husband divorce which barred dower were mere surplusage. Ball v. Ball (Stark 1933) 47 Ohio App. 547, 192 N.E. 364, 17 Ohio Law Abs. 592, 40 Ohio Law Rep. 407. Dower And Curtesy ⇨ 52

A woman divorced a vinculo by reason of aggression of husband, under act passed March 11, 1853, who subsequently marries another man during life of her first husband, is entitled to dower in land of first husband. McGill v. Deming (Ohio 1887) 44 Ohio St. 645, 17 W.L.B. 213, 11 N.E. 118.

Where in a decree for alimony wife's dower in husband's lands is released, but does not appear to be with wife's consent, such decree is no bar to her dower. King v. King (Ohio Cir. 1893) 4 Ohio C.D. 1, 1 Ohio Leg. N. 13.

Where woman innocently marries a man having a living undivorced wife, second wife does not acquire any dower interest in his property. Kennelly v. Cowle (Ohio Com.Pl. 1897) 6 Ohio Dec. 170, 4 Ohio N.P. 105.

Allowable extent of wife's homestead exemption in real property titled in her husband's name only, due to wife's inchoate dower interest in that property, was limited under Ohio law by equity held in property. In re Miller (Bkrtcy.N.D.Ohio 1992) 151 B.R. 800. Homestead ⇨ 88

6. —— Fee tail, inchoate dower

A will devising land to testator's son and to heirs of son's body, or, if son should die without issue or heirs of his body surviving, then to other persons, created a "fee tail estate," and during son's lifetime his issue had no interest and when issue predeceased son or donee in tail, issue's surviving spouse had no dower or analogous interest. Mays v. Mays (Montgomery 1942) 42 N.E.2d 446, 37 Ohio Law Abs. 102. Dower And Curtesy ⇨ 11; Wills ⇨ 605

7. —— Liens, inchoate dower

Sale under vendor's lien does not bar widow from claiming dower after lien paid. McArthur v. Porter (Ohio 1823) 1 Ohio 99.

8. —— Mortgaged property, inchoate dower

In suit of foreclosure of sundry mortgages where wife had signed only one of them, the mortgagee holding such mortgage is entitled on distribution to receive the proportionate value of such released dower though proceeds of sale insufficient to satisfy prior mortgages. Black's Adm'r v. Kuhlman (Ohio 1876) 30 Ohio St. 196.

Widow by joining with husband in mortgage thereby bars her dower until mortgage is paid. Baker v. Fetters (Ohio 1866) 16 Ohio St. 596.

A foreclosure in the lifetime of the husband to which the widow is not a party does not bar her equity of redemption; she can pay mortgage and have dower. McArthur v. Franklin (Ohio 1864) 15 Ohio St. 485. Dower And Curtesy ⇨ 46; Mortgages ⇨ 497(2)

Where in proceedings by administrator to sell real estate, mortgagee is made a party and dower is assigned in all the land without his objection, he is thereby concluded as to dower assigned widow. Affleck's Adm'r v. Snodgrass's Adm'r (Ohio 1858) 8 Ohio St. 234.

Widow is entitled to dower in mortgaged premises except as to mortgagee, where same are in his possession. Carter v. Goodin (Ohio 1853) 3 Ohio St. 75.

Where husband mortgages land and wife does not sign, and later husband and wife join in deed of same land and mortgagor forecloses, making grantee in deed a party, a purchaser at foreclosure takes premises free of wife's dower. Carter v. Walker (Ohio 1853) 2 Ohio St. 339.

Where lands are mortgaged and condition broken before marriage and equity of redemption released after marriage, dower is barred. Rands v. Kendall (Ohio 1846) 15 Ohio 671.

When the owner of property mortgages the same and thereafter marries before the condition of the mortgage is broken, and the property is subsequently sold on foreclosure, the wife is entitled, out of the surplus, to the value of her inchoate dower calculated on the entire proceeds of sale, unless the mortgage was for purchase money. Canan v. Heffey (Hocking 1927) 27 Ohio App. 430, 161 N.E. 235, 6 Ohio Law Abs. 401.

Inchoate dower of wife is not a lien upon the land of the husband but is an interest in it. Jewett v. Feldheiser (Ohio 1903) 68 Ohio St. 523, 48 W.L.B. 688, 67 N.E. 1072, 1 Ohio Law Rep. 136, 1 Ohio Law Rep. 509. Dower And Curtesy ⇨ 29

Where husband and wife join in a mortgage but notary omits to certify acknowledgment of husband and mortgage is reformed, the wife's dower is barred. Straman v. Rechtine (Ohio 1898) 58 Ohio St. 443, 40 W.L.B. 74, 51 N.E. 44.

There can be no dower interest or homestead exemption as against a mortgage which the claimants to dower or homestead have joined in executing. Stoehr v. Moerlein Brewing Co. (Ohio Cir. 1905) 17 Ohio C.D. 330, 2 Ohio Law Rep. 449.

A mortgage and deed of same date between same parties for same land raises presumption that mortgage was for purchase money and widow of grantee not entitled to dower. Ruffner v. Evans (Ohio Cir. 1887) 1 Ohio C.D. 368.

Chapter 7 debtor-wife's inchoate dower interest in real property that was titled solely in name of her husband was included in "property of the estate," notwithstanding that these dower rights may not have been transferable under Ohio law. In re Bowling (Bkrtcy.S.D.Ohio, 06-10-2004) 314 B.R. 127. Bankruptcy ⇨ 2535(4)

Under Ohio law, wife's inchoate dower interest in real property titled in her husband's name only was subordinated to claim of mortgagee; both husband and wife executed original mortgage. In re Miller (Bkrtcy. N.D.Ohio 1992) 151 B.R. 800. Dower And Curtesy ⇨ 49

In determining value of wife's inchoate dower interest in real property titled in her husband's name only, and, thus, in determining amount of wife's homestead exemption under Ohio law, distinction will not be made between purchase money mortgages and other liens on real property debts. In re Miller (Bkrtcy.N.D.Ohio 1992) 151 B.R. 800. Homestead ⇨ 66

Under Ohio law, wife's inchoate dower interest in real property titled in her husband's name only had to be calculated on full fair market value of real estate regardless of amount of any mortgages which mortgagees had not foreclosed upon, for purpose of determining wife's homestead exemption. In re Miller (Bkrtcy.N.D.Ohio 1992) 151 B.R. 800. Homestead ⇨ 66

9. —— Rights of creditors, inchoate dower

Where land was devised to husband charged with the payment of legacies, and is sold in suit by creditor of husband, wife can claim dower in remainder of proceeds after legacies paid. Dingman v. Dingman (Ohio 1883) 39 Ohio St. 172, 9 W.L.B. 342.

Where a wife releases her dower in consideration of a reduction of the claims of certain of her husband's creditors, and an extension of time on such amounts, such a release is operative as to the named creditors but not to other general creditors. Case v. Hewitt (Ohio Cir. 1901) 11 Ohio C.D. 823, affirmed 67 Ohio St. 553, 67 N.E. 1098.

Widower's dower before assignment is not subject to lien of judgment nor to levy and execution, but can be reached in equity. Maclaren v. Stone (Ohio Cir. 1899) 9 Ohio C.D. 794.

A release of dower in deed executed by husband and wife without consideration to defraud creditors will not estop her claim to dower. Woodworth v Paige, 5 OS 70 (1855).

10. —— Sale or partitioning of land, inchoate dower

In proceeding for partition under the statute, court may assign dower in special manner and may assign in form of life annuity and make it a charge upon realty. Miller v. Peters (Ohio 1874) 25 Ohio St. 270.

A codevisee of an estate who had an inchoate dower right in premises set off to another by a partition is not estopped to claim dower against her copartitioners when the inchoate right becomes perfect by the death of her husband; equity, in sustaining the dower claim, will enforce a contribution by all copartitioners to make whole the codevisees in whose share the dower is assigned. Walker v. Hall (Ohio 1864) 15 Ohio St. 355, 86 Am.Dec. 482. Partition ⇨ 116(1)

Where a sale in partition is compelled under statute because the estate is incapable of actual partition without harm, the wife is divested of her inchoate dower in the land and instead is remitted to her inchoate right to a distributive share of the personalty into which it has been transmitted, notwithstanding that she was not a party to the proceedings. Weaver v. Gregg (Ohio 1856) 6 Ohio St. 547, 67 Am.Dec. 355.

Spouses of cotenants are not essential parties to a partition action by one cotenant against another. Dunkle v. Dunkle (Ohio Com.Pl. 1956) 137 N.E.2d 170, 73 Ohio Law Abs. 477, 2 O.O.2d 399.

Where a vendor's warranty deed does not contain a covenant against encumbrances and his wife has not released her inchoate right of dower in the land, the vendee who is aware of these facts must take the property subject to such dower without abatement. People's Sav. Bank Co. v. Parisette (Ohio 1903) 68 Ohio St. 450, 48 W.L.B. 667, 67 N.E. 896, 96 Am.St.Rep. 672, 1 Ohio Law Rep. 88, 1 Ohio Law Rep. 458.

Where land is amicably partitioned into a larger and a smaller part, a mortgage given by one tenant in common, in which his wife does not join, to equalize the allotments, is subordinate to the wife's inchoate dower right in the undivided interest acquired by descent of such mortgagor, but is superior to dower in the share acquired by purchase from the mortgagee. Fleming v. Morningstar (Ohio Com.Pl. 1904) 17 Ohio Dec. 430, 4 Ohio N.P.(N.S.) 405, affirmed 72 Ohio St. 647, 76 N.E. 1124, 3 Ohio Law Rep. 21.

11. Nature and computation of interest; subject to debts—In general

Widow's dower may be subjected in equity to payment of claims created by her after her husband's death. Boltz v. Stolz (Ohio 1885) 41 Ohio St. 540.

A widow may claim dower in premises sold in judicial proceedings to which she is not a party, or may have dower from the proceeds of the sale, but cannot claim both ways. (See also Ketchum v Shaw, 28 OS 503 (1876).) Sweesey v. Shady (Ohio 1872) 22 Ohio St. 333.

Dower always attaches subject to all equities that exist against the title of the husband. Firestone v. Firestone (Ohio 1853) 2 Ohio St. 415.

Widow not entitled to dower in shares in a railroad company, as they are personal property. Johns v. Johns (Ohio 1853) 1 Ohio St. 350.

Where husband during coverture was seized of several tracts of land which after his death passed into various hands, a claim for dower should be made against each separate holder. Allen v. McCoy (Ohio 1838) 8 Ohio 418.

Widow is endowed according to value of ground at the time of assignment of dower. Dunseth v. Bank of U. S. (Ohio 1833) 6 Ohio 76.

A vendee from judgment debtor, having relinquishment of dower, cannot set up that dower as a separate independent estate, against preferable purchase under judgment. Douglass v. McCoy (Ohio 1832) 5 Ohio 522.

A widow is not entitled to dower in land sold by her husband by a parol agreement before marriage and conveyed by him without her signature after marriage. Rohn v. Leach (Ohio Com.Pl. 1922) 24 Ohio N.P.(N.S.) 459, affirmed 1 Ohio Law Abs. 700.

During the lifetime of both spouses, "dower" is a contingent inchoate right that becomes vested in the surviving spouse only upon the death of the other spouse. Ogan v. Ogan (Ohio App. 12 Dist., 09-08-1997) 122 Ohio App.3d 580, 702 N.E.2d 472. Dower And Curtesy ⚖ 29

The surviving spouse is an heir for the purposes of inheritance, is subject to and has all the rights of an heir, and the special relationship of wife or husband neither enlarges nor detracts from this status as an heir or gives special preference by virtue of being a surviving spouse. In re Morgan's Estate (Ohio Prob. 1962) 185 N.E.2d 822, 89 Ohio Law Abs. 225.

A vested dower interest in real estate is a personal right which must be asserted during life of owner, and no right thereto survives unless an action to have it assigned is commenced during that life. Dick v. Bauman (Sandusky 1943) 73 Ohio App. 107, 55 N.E.2d 137, 28 O.O. 176. Dower And Curtesy ⚖ 54

Under this section, legislature intended generally to terminate dower interests as such and such interest was retained only under exceptions in dower statute. Disher v. Disher (Darke 1936) 35 N.E.2d 582, 21 Ohio Law Abs. 610, 8 O.O. 203.

In computing the amount of dower to which a widow is entitled, computation must be made separately on each tract of land owned by the deceased consort, and must be limited to the proceeds of sale of such tract where the aggregate of the judgment liens on the tract exceeds the sale price. Dillman v. Warner (Allen 1935) 54 Ohio App. 170, 6 N.E.2d 757, 20 Ohio Law Abs. 459, 7 O.O. 492. Dower And Curtesy ⚖ 83

Where a married woman became seized of property before passage of the act of April 3, 1861 "concerning the rights and liabilities of married women," her husband's interest is vested in such lands, and a right of action to recover possession thereof from one who during coverture had taken it without right does not accrue until the husband's death. Westlake v. City of Youngstown (Ohio 1900) 62 Ohio St. 249, 43 W.L.B. 261, 56 N.E. 873. Husband And Wife ⚖ 11(1); Husband And Wife ⚖ 68; Husband And Wife ⚖ 136; Husband And Wife ⚖ 210(3)

Where a husband conveys his equitable interest in real estate during coverture without consideration or the consent or knowledge of his wife, such transfer is a fraud on her rights, and she is entitled to dower in the land as against all except a subsequent bona fide purchaser for value and without knowledge of her rights. Fast v. Umbaugh (Ohio Cir. 1901) 12 Ohio C.D. 434.

Vested dower is a chose in action which may be conveyed by the widow to anyone, stranger or other, who is willing to purchase it, even before assignment. (See also Fletcher v Huntington, 8 NP 333, 11 D 338 (Super, Cincinnati 1901).) Weyer v. Sager (Ohio Cir. 1901) 12 Ohio C.D. 193.

Widow not dowable under statute of 1848 in lands in which her husband had but a vested remainder. Wood v. Phillips (Ohio Cir. 1887) 1 Ohio C.D. 406.

Where one dies seized of land in fee simple subject to a condition subsequent that the land will pass to his brother if he is the first to die, such decedent's widow is not entitled to dower in the land. Myers v. Moore (Ohio Super. 1884) 12 Ohio Dec. 812, 12 W.L.B. 90.

Widow is interested in will within meaning of GC 12079, and may maintain action to contest it. Moyses v. Neilson (Ohio Com.Pl. 1900) 9 Ohio Dec. 623, 7 Ohio N.P. 607.

Unassigned dower is not subject to levy by execution. Moore's Adm'r v. Moore (Ohio Com.Pl. 1897) 6 Ohio Dec. 154, 7 Ohio N.P. 320.

A deed in which a husband and wife join to convey her estate is good against the husband to convey his estate by the curtesy even though it is defective as to the wife's interest. Newcomb's Lessee v Smith, W 208 (Hamilton 1833).

12. —— Bankruptcy and insolvency, nature and computation of interest; subject to debts

Since the Bankruptcy Act has superseded the state insolvency and assignment laws, the bankruptcy court should determine the dowable interest of a husband in his bankrupt wife's realty in accordance with the laws of the state relating thereto. In re Rosing (D.C.Ohio 1931) 56 F.2d 1049.

The jurisdiction of a court of bankruptcy to determine the dowable interest of the husband in his bankrupt wife's estate may not be impaired or defeated by failure to respond to referee's order to show cause. In re Rosing (D.C.Ohio 1931) 56 F.2d 1049. Bankruptcy ⚖ 2744.1

A wife's inchoate dower in her husband's real estate does not pass to her trustee when she is adjudged bankrupt, and when the husband's property is sold by his trustee in bankruptcy the value of her dower, as fixed under the Ohio statutes, should be paid to her. In re Kiehl (N.D.Ohio 1932) 36 Ohio Law Rep. 633. Bankruptcy ⚖ 2535(1)

Wife is entitled to present worth of her dower interest in real estate inherited by her husband while insolvent. Smith v Smith, 12 CC 528, 5 CD 588 (Hamilton 1893).

13. —— Creditors' rights, nature and computation of interest; subject to debts

The value of a wife's inchoate right of dower is not affected by an assignment made by her husband for the benefit of creditors. Second Nat. Bank v. Renick (Pickaway 1924) 19 Ohio App. 278, 3 Ohio Law Abs. 86.

Spouse of man whose real estate was sold in proceeding to marshal liens under provisions of this section had estate for and during life of her husband in one third of real estate in question, and she is entitled to have this paid out of said proceeds prior to judgment creditors. Welbaum v. Baker (Darke 1935) 19 Ohio Law Abs. 23.

Unsecured claim cannot, in any interpretation thereof, be classified as encumbrance upon real property during lifetime of debtor though upon his death it is lien upon real estate which descends to his heirs at law. Disher v. Disher (Darke 1936) 35 N.E.2d 582, 21 Ohio Law Abs. 610, 8 O.O. 203.

Those who share under statute of descent and distribution take subject to decedent's debts, and surviving spouse stands in relation of heir at law, so classified with others in statute, and taking thereunder must be subjected to same priority in unsecured creditors as would obtain against any other heir at law. Disher v. Disher (Darke 1936) 35 N.E.2d 582, 21 Ohio Law Abs. 610, 8 O.O. 203.

Inchoate right of dower cannot be reached by a creditor's bill. Geiselman v. Wise (Ohio 1940) 137 Ohio St. 93, 28 N.E.2d 199, 17 O.O. 430. Debtor And Creditor ⚖ 11

Where a husband mortgaged his property before marriage, and hence only had an equity or redemption at death, his widow is dowable only in the surplus, as against judgment creditors. King v. Alt (Ohio Com.Pl. 1911) 22 Ohio Dec. 183, 11 Ohio N.P.N.S. 433.

Presumption is that a wife's portion is not charged with debts. Smith v. McIntire (C.C.N.D.Ohio 1897) 83 F. 456.

Wife is not entitled to dower where there are superior liens. Phillips v Keels, 2 CD 568 (Cir. 1890).

14. —— Dower interest in forfeited property, nature and computation of interest; subject to debts

The wife of a man convicted for violating the Ohio racketeer influenced and corrupt organizations statute has no dower rights in property forfeited to the state under RICO. State v. Thrower (Summit 1991) 81 Ohio App.3d 15, 610 N.E.2d 433, motion overruled 62 Ohio St.3d 1434, 578 N.E.2d 826.

15. —— Dower interest in leased property, nature and computation of interest; subject to debts

A ninety-nine year lease signed by only one witness creates only an equitable title and husband must own same at time of his decease to entitle his widow to dower therein. Abbott v. Bosworth (Ohio 1881) 36 Ohio St. 605.

Widow can recover dower in premises leased by her deceased husband for ninety-nine years renewable forever. McAlpin v. Woodruff (Ohio 1860) 11 Ohio St. 120.

Widow taking life estate on one-third of decedent's one-sixth interest in land, subsequently leased, with her consent, by owners of remaining interest to parties taking and selling oil therefrom, entitled only to income from one-third of such interest, though her dower or life interest has not been set apart to her. Fourth & Central Trust Co. v. Woolley (Ohio App. 1928) 31 Ohio App. 259, 165 N.E. 742, 28 Ohio Law Rep. 497. Life Estates ⚖ 12; Waste ⚖ 8

Where a husband's estate as lessee, under a ninety-nine year lease, renewable forever, is subject to forfeiture by reason of his failure to comply with the terms of the lease, and he agrees to a forfeiture of his estate, and surrenders the same in consideration of being relieved of the burdens of the lease, and the transaction is free from fraud or collusion, his wife's inchoate right of dower in said estate is thereby terminated. National Holding Co. v. Oram (Summit 1928) 29 Ohio App. 138, 162 N.E. 704, 6 Ohio Law Abs. 415.

Where the owner of real estate leases it to another and his heirs and assigns for a term of ninety-nine years, renewable forever, the estate created by such instrument becomes a freehold estate in real property and subject to dower. Ralston Steel Car Co. v. Ralston (Ohio 1925) 112 Ohio St. 306, 147 N.E. 513, 39 A.L.R. 334, 3 Ohio Law Abs. 200, 23 Ohio Law Rep. 125, 23 Ohio Law Rep. 126.

Perpetual leaseholds are not subject to dower. (See also Kampman v Schaaf, 8 D Repr 351, 7 B 159 (D, Hamilton 1882); Abbott v Bosworth, 7 D Repr 300, 2 B 92 (Super, Cincinnati 1877), affirmed by 36 OS 605 (1881).) Oliver v. Jones (Ohio Com.Pl. 1895) 6 Ohio Dec. 194, 3 Ohio N.P. 129.

Widow is not entitled to dower in leasehold estates unless the husband was the owner of the same at the time of his death. Kampmann v. Schaaf (Ohio Dist. 1882) 7 W.L.B. 159.

16. —— Dower interest in mortgaged property, nature and computation of interest; subject to debts

Where husband died testate leaving land incumbered by a mortgage for his debt made by himself and wife, and she elected to take under the law and there was sufficient property to pay all claims against estate, the wife is entitled to be dowered in the entire proceeds of the land. Kling v. Ballentine (Ohio 1883) 40 Ohio St. 391.

In suit to enforce vendor's lien on land on which vendee alone has executed mortgage, after payment of vendor's lien, wife can have dower before mortgagee is paid. Unger v. Leiter (Ohio 1877) 32 Ohio St. 210.

Where wife joins husband in a mortgage and husband's assignee for benefit of creditors pays same out of general funds, she as widow can claim dower in all the land. Ketchum v. Shaw (Ohio 1876) 28 Ohio St. 503.

In action to foreclose mortgages where prior ones had not been signed by wife and she is only made a party by a supplemental petition which fails to state any claim against her, she, by payment of mortgage which she signed, can have dower assigned in premises. Parmenter v. Binkley (Ohio 1875) 28 Ohio St. 32.

Where widow has had dower fully assigned and afterward heirs pay purchase money mortgage, widow is not entitled to further dower. Fox v. Pratt (Ohio 1875) 27 Ohio St. 512.

A widow is dowable of the surplus remaining after payment of a purchase money mortgage, not of the entire proceeds. (See also Fox v Pratt, 27 OS 512 (1875); Hayes v Hayes, 16 OFD 436, 181 F 674, 8 LR 155 (ND Ohio 1910).) Culver v. Harper (Ohio 1875) 27 Ohio St. 464.

Widow is not entitled to dower or to redeem land sold to pay a purchase money mortgage. Folsom v. Rhodes (Ohio 1872) 22 Ohio St. 435.

A widow joining with her husband in a mortgage during coverture thereby extinguishes her right of dower in the proceeds of a sale in foreclosure to the extent that such proceeds are applied in satisfaction of the mortgage. (See also Stoehr v Moerlein Brewing Co, 17 CD 330, 2 LR 449 (Hamilton 1905).) State Bank of Ohio v. Hinton (Ohio 1871) 21 Ohio St. 509.

Where husband sells land subject to a purchase money mortgage and vendee pays same, wife of vendor can claim dower in premises. Carter v. Goodin (Ohio 1853) 3 Ohio St. 75.

Wife can claim dower in land sold by judgment creditor though she has joined with husband in mortgage. Taylor v. Fowler (Ohio 1849) 18 Ohio 567, 51 Am.Dec. 469.

Whenever a married person buys real estate in Ohio, the married person's spouse automatically receives a dower interest; thus, any document that intends to convey or mortgage an interest in the property is not effective as to the nontitle-holding spouse's dower interest unless that spouse has also signed the document. Std. Fed. Bank v. Staff (Ohio App. 1 Dist., 07-14-2006) 2006-Ohio-3601, 2006 WL 1933729. Dower And Curtesy ⚖ 45

Dower interest arises when property is purchased during a marriage and continues unless the interest is specifically released, and such a release must be done in writing and recorded. Ogan v. Ogan (Ohio App. 12 Dist., 09-08-1997) 122 Ohio App.3d 580, 702 N.E.2d 472. Dower And Curtesy ⚖ 31; Dower And Curtesy ⚖ 49

Dower interest of property owner's wife regarding mortgaged property would be determined from entire fair market value of property, not fair market value of property minus mortgage interest; owner was seised of entire property during marriage. Stand Energy Corp. v. Epler (Ohio App. 10 Dist., 09-15-2005) 163 Ohio App.3d 354, 837 N.E.2d 1229, 2005-Ohio-4820. Dower And Curtesy ⚖ 32

Where a husband and wife purchase real property subject to a mortgage which they assume and agree to pay, such mortgage is to be considered as a purchase-money mortgage, and upon the death of the husband his wife is entitled to dower out of the surplus only after payment of the mortgage obligation. George v. George (Cuyahoga 1924) 51 Ohio App. 174, 200 N.E. 145, 20 Ohio Law Abs. 448, 4 O.O. 260.

Where marriage of parties has been effected after husband has mortgaged his property and after conditions of mortgage have been broken, wife is dowable only in surplus arising after foreclosure sale. Canan v. Heffey (Hocking 1927) 27 Ohio App. 430, 161 N.E. 235, 6 Ohio Law Abs. 401. Dower And Curtesy ⚖ 23

In action to foreclose mechanic's lien, in which mortgagees intervened, and their claims were found superior to dower estate, and sale pursuant thereto was required to be made free of dower estate, so that wife was divested of her dower by sale, it was duty of court to ascertain value thereof and pay same out of proceeds of sale. Canan v. Heffey (Hocking 1927) 27 Ohio App. 430, 161 N.E. 235, 6 Ohio Law Abs. 401.

Where mortgage was executed after marriage of parties and wife's dower was pledged as security for husband's debt, wife was entitled to have her dower calculated on basis of whole value of property as regards such mortgage. Canan v. Heffey (Hocking 1927) 27 Ohio App. 430, 161 N.E. 235, 6 Ohio Law Abs. 401. Dower And Curtesy ⚖ 49

A simultaneous conveyance and mortgage back to secure the purchase price gives the wife of the mortgagor no inchoate dower interest superior to the mortgagee's equitable lien on the property. (See also Welch v Buckins, 9 OS 331 (1859).) Elliott v. Plattor (Ohio 1885) 43 Ohio St. 198, 13 W.L.B. 623, 1 N.E. 222.

Dower is based on the entire proceeds from the sale of the consort's land, though it is payable only from the residue after satisfying a purchase money mortgage. Hickey v. Conine (Ohio Cir. 1904) 17 Ohio C.D. 369, 6 Ohio C.C.(N.S.) 321, affirmed 71 Ohio St. 548, 74 N.E. 1137, 2 Ohio Law Rep. 451.

Where a husband mortgaged his property before marriage, and hence only had an equity or redemption at death, his widow is dowable only in the surplus, as against judgment creditors. King v. Alt (Ohio Com.Pl. 1911) 22 Ohio Dec. 183, 11 Ohio N.P.N.S. 433.

Where husband has only dower interest in lands of deceased wife and lands are mortgaged to secure joint note of husband and wife, husband cannot force mortgagee to have dower assigned. Winship v West, 4 NP 84, 6 D 93 (CP, Cuyahoga 1896).

Under Ohio law, expressed for example in Culver v Harper, 27 OS 464 (1875), a buyer of real property who makes a purchase-money mortgage is seized of the land in a technical sense only, and if buying before married does not have an estate in the land to which dower attaches because the seizin, whatever it amounted to, instantaneous or otherwise, is conveyed away by the mortgage; the practical consequence of this circumstance is that the dower interest of the spouse relates only to the residue from the proceeds of sale of the property after the mortgage has been paid; where mortgages are made during marriage or coverture, however, the dower right relates to the entire fair market value of the property, subordinated to the mortgage. In re Castor (Bkrtcy.S.D.Ohio 1989) 99 B.R. 807.

This section does not change in favor of a surviving spouse, or at least does not enlarge upon the surviving spouse's interest, and where it appeared that a mortgage was executed by a wife before her marriage, and that after her marriage upon foreclosure and sale at no time was there any excess over the mortgage, liens, costs of sale, taxes, etc., the husband during coverture was not dowable in any part of said real estate. Home Owners' Loan Corp. v. Grant (Ohio Com.Pl. 1938) 3 Ohio Supp. 24, 33 Ohio Law Abs. 662, 20 O.O. 116.

17. —— Dower interest in partnership property, nature and computation of interest; subject to debts

Lands held and sold as partnership property are not subject to dower to the prejudice of partnership creditors. (See also Greene v Greene, 1 O 535 (1824).) Sumner v. Hampson (Ohio 1838) 8 Ohio 328, 32 Am.Dec. 722.

18. —— Dower interest in property given for public use, nature and computation of interest; subject to debts

A widow is not entitled to dower in land given for a market house or other public purpose, since all private rights must be abrogated as inconsistent with a public use. (See also Steel v Board of Education, 1 D 277, 31 B 85 (CP, Richland 1893).) Gwynne v. City of Cincinnati (Ohio 1827) 3 Ohio 24, 17 Am.Dec. 576.

19. —— Dower interest in trust property, nature and computation of interest; subject to debts

Widow has no dower interest in lands held in trust by husband. Derush v. Brown (Ohio 1838) 8 Ohio 412.

20. —— Dower interest versus mechanic's lien, nature and computation of interest; subject to debts

Wife was not estopped to claim that her dower rights were superior to rights of plaintiff in suit to foreclose mechanic's lien for placing improvement on property under contract with husband because she stood by while plaintiff was placing improvement on property, since she had no duty to speak. Canan v. Heffey (Hocking 1927) 27 Ohio App. 430, 161 N.E. 235, 6 Ohio Law Abs. 401. Dower And Curtesy ⚖ 50; Estoppel ⚖ 95

Where a mechanic or materialman furnishes labor and material under a contract with the husband alone, adding labor and materials to his separate realty improvement and the wife is not a party to the contract and has not given any release, her inchoate dower right is paramount to the right of the mechanic's lien. Glassmeyer v. Michelson (Ohio Super. 1921) 23 Ohio N.P.N.S. 537.

21. —— Husband's rights, nature and computation of interest; subject to debts

Act of March 14, 1853, did not affect or modify the rights or interests of a husband in the lands of his wife during her life. Denny v. McCabe (Ohio 1880) 35 Ohio St. 576.

Freehold of a husband in his wife's lands may be sold on execution. Canby's Lessee v. Porter (Ohio 1843) 12 Ohio 79. Execution ⚖ 33; Husband And Wife ⚖ 9

Where a husband has a freehold in his wife's land for their joint lives and a contingent tenancy by curtesy, the nonjoinder of the husband in a partition proceeding leaves his rights unimpaired; however, his decease ends his estate, and the wife is bound by a decree against her until reversed. Pillsbury's Lessee v. Dugan's Adm'r (Ohio 1839) 9 Ohio 117, 34 Am.Dec. 427.

Surviving spouse had valid cause of action against executor of decedent's estate to obtain reimbursement of full amount she paid to bank to satisfy decedent's debt under a note; decedent had obligation to pay bank the amount owed on the note, executor of estate accepted duty to pay decedent's debts upon decedent's death, and surviving spouse took place of bank and became creditor of estate by paying the debt under the note. Ogan v. Ogan (Ohio App. 12 Dist., 09-08-1997) 122 Ohio App.3d 580, 702 N.E.2d 472. Executors And Administrators ⚖ 202.10

A conveyance of realty to children of a former marriage, without consideration other than love and affection, by a man engaged to be married, without disclosure of the conveyance to his intended wife whom he later marries, does not defraud her of her right of dower, provided for in RC 2103.02. Perlberg v. Perlberg (Ohio 1969) 18 Ohio St.2d 55, 247 N.E.2d 306, 47 O.O.2d 167. Dower And Curtesy ⚖ 20

Subject to limitations contained in GC 10502-1 (RC 2103.02) and 10502-6 (RC 2103.06), a husband may dispose of his real property during his lifetime without consent of his wife. Neville v. Sawicki (Ohio 1946) 146 Ohio St. 539, 67 N.E.2d 323, 33 O.O. 19. Husband And Wife ⚖ 6(2)

Widow's rights to her distributive share, to that portion of estate exempt from administration and to a year's allowance, do not come into existence until death of husband, and, therefore, any transfer of property of husband during his lifetime will be free of such claims. Neville v. Sawicki (Cuyahoga 1945) 64 N.E.2d 685, 44 Ohio Law Abs. 408, affirmed 146 Ohio St. 539, 67 N.E.2d 323, 33 O.O. 19. Executors And Administrators ⚖ 182

A wife is not a "creditor" of her husband during his lifetime with regard to what may become her year's allowance in the estate of her husband upon his death so as to be entitled to set aside a transfer of such portion of husband's estate during his lifetime. Neville v. Sawicki (Cuyahoga 1945) 64 N.E.2d 685, 44 Ohio Law Abs. 408, affirmed 146 Ohio St. 539, 67 N.E.2d 323, 33 O.O. 19. Descent And Distribution ⚖ 90(1)

Where a man who has entered into a contract of marriage conveys a portion of his lands to his sons from a former marriage without consideration other than love and affection, and does not obtain his future wife's consent, such a conveyance is a fraud on her marital rights, and she is entitled to dower in those lands upon her husband's death. Ward v. Ward (Ohio 1900) 63 Ohio St. 125, 44 W.L.B. 205, 57 N.E. 1095, 81 Am.St.Rep. 621. Dower And Curtesy ⚖ 20; Husband And Wife ⚖ 70

Husband as heir of wife takes her estate encumbered with all her debts and his interest is amount remaining for distribution. Moore's Adm'r v. Moore (Ohio Com.Pl. 1897) 6 Ohio Dec. 154, 7 Ohio N.P. 320.

Husband's dower will merge in his inherited title only when justice will be promoted thereby and not when an equity would be thereby extinguished. Moore's Adm'r v. Moore (Ohio Com.Pl. 1897) 6 Ohio Dec. 154, 7 Ohio N.P. 320.

22. Procedural issues

Where statute requires that the contents of a deed should be made known to married woman, she is not barred of dower unless magistrate's certificate shows that this was done. Silliman v. Cummins (Ohio 1844) 13 Ohio 116.

The costs in assignment of dower are to be paid, one-third by petitioner and two-thirds by owner of the inheritance. Bank of U. S. v. Dunseth (Ohio 1840) 10 Ohio 18.

Declarations of husband seized in fee cannot be given in evidence to effect widow's claim for dower. Derush v. Brown (Ohio 1838) 8 Ohio 412. Dower And Curtesy ⚖ 79; Evidence ⚖ 229

2103.02
Note 22

Certificate of relinquishment of dower is sufficient if it contains a substantial enumeration of acts required by statute. Brown v. Farran (Ohio 1827) 3 Ohio 140. Dower And Curtesy ⚖ 49

Dower is regulated by statute. In re Russell, 14 OFD 364, 50 B 19 (ND Ohio 1904).

Property owner's wife preserved for appellate review her claim that her dower interest in property was required to be determined by use of Internal Revenue Service (IRS) table in judgment creditor's action to foreclose judgment lien, although wife originally advocated using a different IRS table, where wife argued in trial court that state law mandated use of an IRS table, not dower table that was used by trial court. Stand Energy Corp. v. Epler (Ohio App. 10 Dist., 09-15-2005) 163 Ohio App.3d 354, 837 N.E.2d 1229, 2005-Ohio-4820. Dower And Curtesy ⚖ 110

Under Ohio law, right of dower does not come into existence until time of marriage, and there exists no right of dower in absence of valid marriage. In re Wycuff (Bkrtcy.N.D.Ohio, 08-23-2005) 332 B.R. 297. Dower And Curtesy ⚖ 5

Under Ohio law, one spouse's right to dower confers upon that spouse a cognizable interest in real property owned by the other spouse. In re Martz (Bkrtcy.N.D.Ohio, 10-17-2002) 293 B.R. 409. Dower And Curtesy ⚖ 10

Dower, a means to protect wives by recognizing their right to a livelihood from their consorts' estates, is as old as the common law, and Ohio provided for vested dower by statute until 1932 when a drive to abolish dower reached its zenith; because of strong resistance to abolition at local and regional hearings, however, the general assembly decided to preserve inchoate dower and some aspects of vested dower in GC 10502-1 (RC 2103.02). In re Castor (Bkrtcy.S.D.Ohio 1989) 99 B.R. 807.

Widow cannot treat real estate as equitably converted for one purpose and not for another purpose. In re Hutchins, 12 CD 29 (Cuyahoga 1901), modified sub nom Hutchins v Davis, 68 OS 160, 67 NE 251 (1903).

23. Release, bar and election

Where widow elects not to take under will she cannot have bequests in lieu of dower. Jones v. Lloyd (Ohio 1878) 33 Ohio St. 572.

A release of dower in a deed to defraud purchasers is binding only as against the releasee and his privies. Ridgway v. Masting (Ohio 1872) 23 Ohio St. 294, 13 Am.Rep. 251. Dower And Curtesy ⚖ 49

Where husband conveyed by deed but wife's release of dower was defective, the possession of grantee is prima facie evidence of seisin in fee simple by husband. Ward's Heirs v. McIntosh (Ohio 1861) 12 Ohio St. 231.

Grantee as against claim of grantor's widow for dower cannot show title in stranger. Ward's Heirs v. McIntosh (Ohio 1861) 12 Ohio St. 231.

Tax sale bars dower. Jones v. Devore (Ohio 1858) 8 Ohio St. 430.

A wife who unites with her husband in the granting clause of a deed is barred of dower in that land as against all those who claim under such deed. (See also St. Clair v Morris, 9 O 15 (1839).) Smith v. Handy (Ohio 1847) 16 Ohio 191.

Election to take under the will to bar dower must be made in court within six months after probate of the will. Stilley v. Folger (Ohio 1846) 14 Ohio 610.

Where a wife joins her husband in a power of attorney to convey, she precludes herself from demanding dower in those lands. Glenn v. Bank of U. S. (Ohio 1837) 8 Ohio 72, 31 Am.Dec. 429.

Where widow entitled to dower consents to judicial sale free of dower, she is thereby barred though purchaser knew of her title. Smiley v. Wright (Ohio 1826) 2 Ohio 506.

Surviving spouse had no obligation under a note signed by decedent to pay debt the decedent owed to bank, and thus she had no right of contribution from decedent's estate, though surviving spouse signed security instrument which secured the note, where terms of security instrument provided that surviving spouse could convey only the interest she had in property at time she signed the instrument, only interest surviving spouse had in property at that time was her dower interest, and there was no specific release of surviving spouse's dower interest in the security instrument or the record. Ogan v. Ogan (Ohio App. 12 Dist., 09-08-1997) 122 Ohio App.3d 580, 702 N.E.2d 472. Executors And Administrators ⚖ 202.10

Release of dower interest by property owner's wife with respect to mortgage did not constitute an absolute release of dower interest, and thus release was relevant in judgment creditor's action to foreclose judgment lien only in that it subordinated wife's dower interest to mortgagee's interest. Stand Energy Corp. v. Epler (Ohio App. 10 Dist., 09-15-2005) 163 Ohio App.3d 354, 837 N.E.2d 1229, 2005-Ohio-4820. Judgment ⚖ 801

This section by its wording bars a surviving spouse of any dower interest in an estate in fee tail of which the deceased spouse was endowed. Miller v. Miller (Ohio Com.Pl. 1948) 83 N.E.2d 254, 52 Ohio Law Abs. 121, 41 O.O. 233.

Probate code act of 1932 placed no new restraints upon rights of one in life to dispose of his property, and preserved to surviving spouse only a vested dower estate in any lands conveyed during marriage in which such survivor had not relinquished or been barred of dower. Dick v. Bauman (Sandusky 1943) 73 Ohio App. 107, 55 N.E.2d 137, 28 O.O. 176. Dower And Curtesy ⚖ 44

Divorce extinguishes all dower rights so that words in decree granting husband divorce which barred dower were mere surplusage. Ball v. Ball (Stark 1933) 47 Ohio App. 547, 192 N.E. 364, 17 Ohio Law Abs. 592, 40 Ohio Law Rep. 407. Dower And Curtesy ⚖ 52

A widow who, during the lifetime of her husband, entered into a separation agreement with him, by the terms of which she agreed to be barred of dower in his real estate and to release the same upon his demand, will not be permitted to have dower as against one who loaned money to him and took a mortgage upon his real estate to secure the same in reliance upon the terms of said agreement. Kneiley v. Kneiley (Summit 1931) 38 Ohio App. 467, 176 N.E. 476, 9 Ohio Law Abs. 556.

Husband electing to take under will waives right to dower in wife's realty. Barrett v. W. P. Southworth Co. (Ohio App. 1930) 35 Ohio App. 452, 172 N.E. 563, 33 Ohio Law Rep. 24. Wills ⚖ 778

Where a widow, in a proceeding to sell real estate according to a direction in her husband's will in which the testator makes a disposition of his whole estate without making any provision for her, elects to receive and is paid the value of her dower in money, she does not thereby elect to take either under or against the will. She stands solely on her statutory right of dower. Hutchings v. Davis (Ohio 1903) 68 Ohio St. 160, 48 W.L.B. 526, 67 N.E. 251, 1 Ohio Law Rep. 203. Wills ⚖ 782(8)

Electing to take under will bars dower. Corry v. Lamb (Ohio 1887) 45 Ohio St. 203, 18 W.L.B. 22, 12 N.E. 660.

Widow electing to take under will is barred of dower in land sold on foreclosure of a mortgage in which she did not join, unless it plainly appears by will that she should have such provision in addition to her dower. Corry v. Lamb (Ohio 1887) 45 Ohio St. 203, 18 W.L.B. 22, 12 N.E. 660.

Where a wife is not named as a party in a suit by her husband's judgment creditor to marshall liens and sell the real estate of the husband, the mortgage of which was signed by the wife, and the wife does not appear or participate in the proceedings, her right of dower in the property is not extinguished by a decree ordering the sale of the property. Kaufman v. Heckman (Ohio Cir. 1908) 22 Ohio C.D. 277, 13 Ohio C.C.N.S. 309.

Where widow dies before she elects to take under a will her heirs inherit all her rights thereunder. Hawkins v. Barrow (Ohio Cir. 1897) 8 Ohio C.D. 251.

If there are no children and husband declines to take under the will, he only takes as if there were children. Wilson v. Hall (Ohio Cir. 1892) 3 Ohio C.D. 589, affirmed 53 Ohio St. 679, 44 N.E. 1137.

Electing to take under will by widow is release of dower only to heirs and not as to strangers. Hessenmueller v Mulrooney, 6 D 123, 4 NP 50 (CP 1896).

Where a deed containing no terms applicable to her estate in dower is executed by a wife who believes that the deed is inoperative to convey her rights, her silence as to this defect does not estop her from taking advantage of it. McFarland v. Febiger (Ohio 1835) 7 Ohio 194, PT. I.

A widow having elected to be endowed in real estate cannot claim as for personalty out of the avails. In Re Hutchins, 12 CD 29 (Cir. 1901).

2103.021 Trustee as grantee in instrument; affidavit for dower interest required

Whenever "trustee," "as trustee," or "agent" follows the name of the grantee in any deed of conveyance of land recorded in this state and no other instrument containing a description of such land has been recorded in the office of the recorder of the county in which such land is situated which puts upon inquiry any person dealing with such land that a spouse of such grantee would have a dower interest in such land, a conveyance of such land by such grantee to a bona fide purchaser conveys a title free from the claims of any spouse of such grantee in such land, for dower, inchoate, or otherwise, unless such spouse, prior to the recording of such conveyance by such grantee to said purchaser, has recorded in the office of the recorder of the county in which the land is situated an affidavit describing such land and setting forth the nature of such spouse's interest in such land.

(129 v 339, eff. 10–17–61)

Library References

Dower and Curtesy ⚖22.
Westlaw Topic No. 136.
C.J.S. Dower and Curtesy § 5.

Research References

Encyclopedias

OH Jur. 3d Family Law § 150, Acts or Instruments of One Spouse—Deed in Fiduciary or Agency Form.

Treatises and Practice Aids

Carlin, Baldwin's Ohio Practice, Merrick-Rippner Probate Law § 92:19, Dower—Sale of Land Subject to Interest.

Kuehnle and Levey, Ohio Real Estate Law and Practice § 18:1, Ohio State Bar Association Standards of Title Examination.

Kuehnle and Levey, Ohio Real Estate Law and Practice § 2:11, Estates—Fee Simple Absolute—Use of "Trustee" or "As Trustee" or "Agent"; Notice of Dower.

Kuehnle and Levey, Ohio Real Estate Law and Practice § 20:26, Conveyancing—Grantors—Trustees—Dower.

Kuehnle and Levey, Ohio Real Estate Law and Practice § 21:13, Execution—Dower—Preservation of Dower in Spouse of "Trustee".

Kuehnle and Levey, Ohio Real Estate Law and Practice § 56:87, Conveyances—Affidavit to Preserve Dower.

2103.03 Conveyance in lieu of dower

If accepted by the grantee, the conveyance of an estate or interest in real property in lieu of dower, to take effect on the death of the grantor, will bar such grantee's right of dower in the real property of the grantor. If the conveyance was made when the grantee was a minor or during the marriage, the grantee may waive title to such real property and demand dower.

When a conveyance which is intended to be in lieu of dower fails through any defect to be a bar thereto, and the widow or widower availing of such defect demands dower, the estate or interest conveyed to such widow or widower shall cease.

(1953 H 1, eff. 10–1–53; GC 10502–2; Source—GC 10502–3)

Historical and Statutory Notes

Pre–1953 H 1 Amendments: 114 v 338

Library References

Dower and Curtesy ⚖49.
Westlaw Topic No. 136.
C.J.S. Dower and Curtesy §§ 61, 155.

Research References

Encyclopedias

OH Jur. 3d Family Law § 162, Jointure.

Forms

Ohio Forms Legal and Business § 24:891, Bequest in Lieu of Dower.

Notes of Decisions

Antenuptial contract   1
Dower not barred   3

Estate   2

---

1. Antenuptial contract

Antenuptial verbal contract where woman promised in consideration that man would marry her and put certain improvements on her real estate she would give him fee simple title, though fully performed by man, is void under statute. Henry v. Henry (Ohio 1875) 27 Ohio St. 121.

Verbal agreement is within statute of frauds and wife's use of property with husband's consent does not take case out of statute. Finch v. Finch (Ohio 1860) 10 Ohio St. 501.

Antenuptial contract in Germany for valuable consideration will be enforced here, and creditor will be enjoined from selling such property. Scheferling v. Huffman (Ohio 1854) 4 Ohio St. 241, 62 Am.Dec. 281.

A reasonable antenuptial agreement will bar dower. (See also Mintier v Mintier, 28 OS 307 (1876); Murphy v Murphy, 12 OS 407 (1861).) Stilley v. Folger (Ohio 1846) 14 Ohio 610.

A widow may elect between jointure and dower but cannot claim both. (See also Spangler v Dukes, 39 OS 642 (1884).) Broadstone v. Baldwin (Ohio Com.Pl. 1898) 8 Ohio Dec. 236, 5 Ohio N.P. 39.

Antenuptial contracts intended to operate as an equitable jointure, must be fair and entered into with full knowledge of each other's property and resources. Duttenhofer v. Duttenhofer (Ohio Super. 1902) 12 Ohio Dec. 741.

2. Estate

Where estate conveyed is less than one-third of husband's lands, it is prima facie not good jointure. Grogan v. Garrison (Ohio 1875) 27 Ohio St. 50.

An estate conveyed as jointure, in order to be a statutory bar to dower, must be an estate in severalty, not in common with others. Grogan v. Garrison (Ohio 1875) 27 Ohio St. 50.

Whether estate in common would constitute good equitable jointure depends on facts and circumstances of each case. Grogan v. Garrison (Ohio 1875) 27 Ohio St. 50.

3. Dower not barred

Antenuptial covenant not to claim dower is no bar. Grogan v. Garrison (Ohio 1875) 27 Ohio St. 50.

If contract is not performed it does not bar dower. Lowe v. Phillips (Ohio 1863) 14 Ohio St. 308.

Agreement to marry man seventy-seven years of age with nine children, owning 366 acres of no great value, for $700 in lieu of dower does not bar her dower. Johnson v. Johnson (Ohio Cir. 1886) 1 Ohio C.D. 291, dismissed.

2103.04 Eviction from premises conveyed in lieu of dower

A widow or widower lawfully evicted from real property conveyed in lieu of dower, or any part thereof, shall be endowed with as much of the residue of the real property of the deceased consort as will equal that from which such widow or widower is evicted.

(1953 H 1, eff. 10–1–53; GC 10502–4)

Historical and Statutory Notes

Pre–1953 H 1 Amendments: 114 v 338

Research References

Encyclopedias

OH Jur. 3d Family Law § 162, Jointure.

Notes of Decisions

Defects 1

1. Defects

A party avoiding a conveyance in lieu of dower on account of a defect must restore the consideration received. Duttenhofer v. Duttenhofer (Ohio Super. 1902) 12 Ohio Dec. 741.

2103.041 Subjection of dower interest to judicial sale

In any action involving the judicial sale of real property for the purpose of satisfying the claims of creditors of an owner of an interest in the property, the spouse of the owner may be made a party to the action, and the dower interest of the spouse, whether inchoate or otherwise, may be subjected to the sale without the consent of the spouse. The court shall determine the present value and priority of the dower interest in accordance with section 2131.01 of the Revised Code and shall award the spouse a sum of money equal to the present value of the dower interest, to be paid out of the proceeds of the sale according to the priority of the interest. To the extent that the owner and the owner's spouse are both liable for the indebtedness, the dower interest of the spouse is subordinate to the claims of their common creditors.

(1999 H 59, eff. 10–29–99; 1977 S 161, eff. 11–16–77)

Historical and Statutory Notes

Amendment Note: 1999 H 59 substituted "in accordance with section 2131.01 of the Revised Code" for ", using the American experience table of mortality as the basis for determining the value,"; and made changes to reflect gender neutral language and other nonsubstantive changes.

Cross References

Dower right of spouse in property assigned for benefit of creditors, 1313.29, 1313.33

Library References

Dower and Curtesy ⬀46.
Westlaw Topic No. 136.
C.J.S. Dower and Curtesy § 57.

Research References

Encyclopedias

OH Jur. 3d Family Law § 84, Death.
OH Jur. 3d Family Law § 131, Purchase-Money Mortgages; Prior to Marriage—After Marriage.
OH Jur. 3d Family Law § 153, Statutory Provisions.

Treatises and Practice Aids

Carlin, Baldwin's Ohio Practice, Merrick-Rippner Probate Law § 64:78, Application of Guardian for Sale of Dower Interest—Form.
Carlin, Baldwin's Ohio Practice, Merrick-Rippner Probate Law § 91:47, Complaint of Guardian for Authority to Sell Real Estate—Form.
Carlin, Baldwin's Ohio Practice, Merrick-Rippner Probate Law § 91:48, Entry Authorizing Sale of Real Estate and Appraisal—Form.
Carlin, Baldwin's Ohio Practice, Merrick-Rippner Probate Law § 91:49, Complaint for Authority to Sell Entire Interest in Real Estate—Form.
Carlin, Baldwin's Ohio Practice, Merrick-Rippner Probate Law § 91:51, Entry Granting Complaint and Ordering Appraisal of Entire Interest—Form.
Carlin, Baldwin's Ohio Practice, Merrick-Rippner Probate Law § 92:17, Dower—Interest Subject to Debts.
Carlin, Baldwin's Ohio Practice, Merrick-Rippner Probate Law § 92:19, Dower—Sale of Land Subject to Interest.
Carlin, Baldwin's Ohio Practice, Merrick-Rippner Probate Law § 92:23, Answer of Spouse—Form.
Carlin, Baldwin's Ohio Practice, Merrick-Rippner Probate Law § 95:21, Entry Authorizing Sale of Real Estate at Private Sale—Form.
Carlin, Baldwin's Ohio Practice, Merrick-Rippner Probate Law § 96:16, Entry Confirming Sale, Ordering Deed and Distribution—Form.
Carlin, Baldwin's Ohio Practice, Merrick-Rippner Probate Law § 96:17, Entry Confirming Sale, Ordering Deed and Distribution Where Entire Interest in Real Estate Sold—Form.
Kuehnle and Levey, Ohio Real Estate Law and Practice § 9:4, Inchoate Right of Dower of Person Not a Party to Contract of Sale.
Kuehnle and Levey, Ohio Real Estate Law and Practice § 51:6, Partition—Spouse of Co-Tenant as Necessary Party.
Kuehnle and Levey, Ohio Real Estate Law and Practice § 36:24, Foreclosure—Parties—Defendants—Parties Required to Pass Good Title to Purchasers—Owners.
Kuehnle and Levey, Ohio Real Estate Law and Practice § 38:15, Foreclosure—Sheriff's Sales—Distribution—Dower.

Notes of Decisions

Calculation of value 1
Priority of dower interest 2

1. Calculation of value

Property owner's wife preserved for appellate review her claim that her dower interest in property was required to be determined by use of Internal Revenue Service (IRS) table in judgment creditor's action to foreclose judgment lien, although wife originally advocated using a different IRS table, where wife argued in trial court that state law mandated use of an IRS table, not dower table that was used by trial court. Stand Energy Corp. v. Epler (Ohio App. 10 Dist., 09-15-2005) 163 Ohio App.3d 354, 2005-Ohio-4820. Dower And Curtesy ⬀ 110

Dower interest of property owner's wife regarding mortgaged property would be determined from entire fair market value of property, not fair market value of property minus mortgage interest; owner was seised of entire property during marriage. Stand Energy Corp. v. Epler (Ohio App. 10 Dist., 09-15-2005) 163 Ohio App.3d 354, 2005-Ohio-4820. Dower And Curtesy ⬀ 32

"American Experience Table," expressly made applicable to cases involving judicial sale by Ohio statute, is better choice than "Bowditch Table" in determining present value of wife's inchoate dower interest in real property titled in her husband's name only, and, thus, in determining wife's entitlement to homestead exemption. In re Miller (Bkrtcy. N.D.Ohio 1992) 151 B.R. 800. Homestead ⬀ 66

Wife's inchoate dower interest in real property titled in her husband's name only was $10,063 under Ohio law, and, thus, wife was entitled in Chapter 7 proceeding to claim a full $5,000 homestead exemption when there was $14,000 in equity on property; property was scheduled at $44,000, wife's dower interest equal to one third of that amount was $14,666.67, wife's yearly allocation based upon 6% present value rate was $880, wife's assigned age of 51 years resulted in present value multiplier of 11.436, and that multiplier when applied to yearly allocation of $880 equaled $10,063. In re Miller (Bkrtcy.N.D.Ohio 1992) 151 B.R. 800. Homestead ⬀ 66; Homestead ⬀ 86

2. Priority of dower interest

Generally, in judicial foreclosure sale conducted under Ohio law, spouse's dower interest takes priority over judgment lien filed only with respect to the other spouse. In re Rudicil (Bkrtcy.S.D.Ohio, 06-07-2006) 343 B.R. 181. Dower And Curtesy ⬀ 34

2103.05 Adultery a bar to dower

A husband or wife who leaves the other and dwells in adultery will be barred from dower in the real property of the other, unless the offense is condoned by the injured consort.

(1953 H 1, eff. 10–1–53; GC 10502–5)

Historical and Statutory Notes

Pre–1953 H 1 Amendments: 114 v 338

Library References

Dower and Curtesy ☞51.
Westlaw Topic No. 136.
C.J.S. Dower and Curtesy §§ 50, 160.

Research References

Encyclopedias

OH Jur. 3d Family Law § 171, Marital Misconduct.

Treatises and Practice Aids

Sowald & Morganstern, Baldwin's Ohio Practice Domestic Relations Law § 4:5, Property Rights During Marriage—Individual Ownership—Dower.

Notes of Decisions

Excuse 2
Forfeiture 1

---

1. Forfeiture

Dower is forfeited by adultery. (See also Brown v Kerns, 1 NP 332, 3 D 392 (CP, Darke 1898).) Brenneman v Brenneman, 6 NP 73, 9 D 119 (CP, Allen 1895).

2. Excuse

Husband's adultery does not condone adultery of wife and believing that she was divorced is no excuse for his adultery. Brown v. Kerns (Ohio Com.Pl. 1899) 9 Ohio Dec. 112, 6 Ohio N.P. 68.

2103.06 Lands given up by fraud

If a husband or wife gives up real property by collusion or fraud, or loses it by default, the widow or widower may recover dower therein.

(1953 H 1, eff. 10–1–53; GC 10502–6)

Historical and Statutory Notes

Pre–1953 H 1 Amendments: 114 v 338

Research References

Encyclopedias

OH Jur. 3d Family Law § 92, Immunity from Impairment by Spouse.
OH Jur. 3d Family Law § 148, Grounds for Avoidance.

Treatises and Practice Aids

Sowald & Morganstern, Baldwin's Ohio Practice Domestic Relations Law § 4:5, Property Rights During Marriage—Individual Ownership—Dower.
Carlin, Baldwin's Ohio Practice, Merrick-Rippner Probate Law § 92:14, Dower—Nature of Interest.

Notes of Decisions

Consent 2
Disclosure 1

---

1. Disclosure

A conveyance of realty to children of a former marriage, without consideration other than love and affection, by a man engaged to be married, without disclosure of the conveyance to his intended wife whom he later marries, does not defraud her of her right of dower, provided for in RC 2103.02. Perlberg v. Perlberg (Ohio 1969) 18 Ohio St.2d 55, 247 N.E.2d 306, 47 O.O.2d 167. Dower And Curtesy ☞ 20

2. Consent

Subject to limitations contained in GC 10502–1 (RC 2103.02) and 10502–6 (RC 2103.06), a husband may dispose of his real property during his lifetime without consent of his wife. Neville v. Sawicki (Ohio 1946) 146 Ohio St. 539, 67 N.E.2d 323, 33 O.O. 19. Husband And Wife ☞ 6(2)

Where a man who has entered into a contract of marriage conveys a portion of his lands to his sons from a former marriage without consideration other than love and affection, and does not obtain his future wife's consent, such a conveyance is a fraud on her marital rights, and she is entitled to dower in those lands upon her husband's death. Ward v. Ward (Ohio 1900) 63 Ohio St. 125, 44 W.L.B. 205, 57 N.E. 1095, 81 Am.St.Rep. 621. Dower And Curtesy ☞ 20; Husband And Wife ☞ 70

2103.07 Dower is forfeited by waste

A tenant in dower in real property who commits or suffers waste thereto will forfeit that part of the property to which such waste is committed or suffered to the person having the immediate estate in reversion or remainder and will be liable in damages to such person for the waste committed or suffered thereto.

(1953 H 1, eff. 10–1–53; GC 10502–7)

Historical and Statutory Notes

Pre–1953 H 1 Amendments: 114 v 338

Cross References

Waste by tenant for life, 2105.20

Library References

Dower and Curtesy ☞38.
Westlaw Topic No. 136.
C.J.S. Dower and Curtesy §§ 47, 55, 153 to 154, 161.

Research References

Encyclopedias

OH Jur. 3d Family Law § 199, Waste.
OH Jur. 3d Waste § 1, Waste Defined.
OH Jur. 3d Waste § 13, Damages.
OH Jur. 3d Waste § 15, Forfeiture.
OH Jur. 3d Waste § 18, Generally; Reversioner, Remainderman, or Tenants in Common.
OH Jur. 3d Waste § 23, Generally; Tenants in Possession or in Common.

Law Review and Journal Commentaries

Remedies for Waste in Ohio, Comment. 17 Ohio St L J 326 (Summer 1956).

Notes of Decisions

Actions not considered waste 4
Appeal 2
Common–law rule 3
Forfeiture 1

---

1. Forfeiture

Conveying life estate does not work forfeiture of same to reversioner or remainderman. Carpenter v. Denoon (Ohio 1876) 29 Ohio St. 379.

Where a testatrix executed mortgages only to save her husband from having to pay building association dues, and the right of forfeiture is based on a provision in her will relating to default on her husband's part in meeting the charges for maintenance and taxes on the property, a forfeiture of the husband's life estate will not be decreed for failure to pay off the mortgages, where the mortgagees have not sued in foreclosure. Bonham v. Lucas (Ohio Com.Pl. 1909) 7 Ohio Law Rep. 301.

2103.07
Note 2

2. Appeal

One cannot appeal action to enjoin waste. Jenks v. Langdon (Ohio 1871) 21 Ohio St. 362.

3. Common–law rule

Strict common law rule as to waste is not followed in Ohio. Crockett v. Crockett (Ohio 1853) 2 Ohio St. 180. Waste ⚖ 1

4. Actions not considered waste

Widow dowered of unproductive town lots and tract of woodland may sell growing timber to pay taxes. Crockett v. Crockett (Ohio 1853) 2 Ohio St. 180.

2103.08 Assignment of dower

Sections 5305.01 to 5305.22, inclusive, of the Revised Code apply to the assignment of the dower of a husband.

(1953 H 1, eff. 10–1–53; GC 10502–10)

Historical and Statutory Notes

Pre–1953 H 1 Amendments: 114 v 339

Library References

Dower and Curtesy ⚖65.
Westlaw Topic No. 136.
C.J.S. Dower and Curtesy §§ 85 to 86.

Research References

Encyclopedias

OH Jur. 3d Family Law § 90, Rights of Creditors.
OH Jur. 3d Family Law § 110, Timberlands or Other Unimproved Lands.
OH Jur. 3d Family Law § 133, Partition Sale.
OH Jur. 3d Family Law § 153, Statutory Provisions.
OH Jur. 3d Family Law § 156, Insane and Other Incompetent Persons.
OH Jur. 3d Family Law § 180, Lands Lying in Different Counties.

Notes of Decisions

Application 1

1. Application

All provisions of dower for wife apply to husband. Brenneman v. Brenneman (Ohio Com.Pl. 1895) 3 Ohio Dec. 392, 1 Ohio N.P. 332.

2103.09 Estate by curtesy abolished

The estate by the curtesy is abolished; but sections 2103.01 to 2103.09, inclusive, of the Revised Code shall not affect vested rights nor any section of the Revised Code.

(1953 H 1, eff. 10–1–53; GC 10502–8)

Historical and Statutory Notes

Pre–1953 H 1 Amendments: 114 v 339

Library References

Dower and Curtesy ⚖3.
Westlaw Topic No. 136.
C.J.S. Dower and Curtesy §§ 3 to 4, 139.

Research References

Encyclopedias

OH Jur. 3d Family Law § 71, Generally; Definitions.

Forms

Ohio Forms Legal and Business § 24:169, Bequests and Devises to Spouse in Lieu of Dower or Curtesy—Residuary Estate to Children—Life Estate of Real Property to Parents—Remainder Over to Specified Person.

Ohio Forms Legal and Business § 24:891, Bequest in Lieu of Dower.

Treatises and Practice Aids

Kuehnle and Levey, Ohio Real Estate Law and Practice § 9:4, Incohate Right of Dower of Person Not a Party to Contract of Sale.

Notes of Decisions

Remainder 1

1. Remainder

A vested right of the children to the remainder estate subject to the husband's curtesy cannot be affected by the subsequent repeal of the estate by curtesy. Cameron v. Goebel & Bettinger (Ohio Cir. 1900) 11 Ohio C.D. 118.

CHAPTER 2105

DESCENT AND DISTRIBUTION

GENERAL PROVISIONS

Section	
2105.01	No distinction between ancestral and nonancestral or real and personal property
2105.02	Construction of "living" and "died"
2105.03	Determination of next of kin
2105.04	Permanent leases to descend same as estates in fee

ADVANCEMENTS

2105.051	Advancement of inheritance; time of valuation
2105.052	Debt owed decedent not chargeable against intestate shares

DESCENT AND DISTRIBUTION; RIGHTS OF SURVIVING SPOUSE

2105.06	Statute of descent and distribution
2105.061	Descent and distribution of title to real property

ESCHEAT

2105.07	Escheat of personal estate
2105.08	Application of provisions relating to escheating estates
2105.09	Disposition of escheated lands; alternate method of sale

INHERITANCE BY DESCENDANTS

2105.10	Inheritance by parent of deceased abandoned child prohibited
2105.11	Estate to descend equally to children of intestate
2105.12	Descent when all descendants of equal degree of consanguinity
2105.13	Descent when children and heirs of deceased children are living
2105.14	Posthumous child to inherit

DESIGNATED HEIR; ALIENS

2105.15	Designation of heir at law
2105.16	Heirs of aliens may inherit; aliens may hold lands

Section

ILLEGITIMATE CHILDREN

2105.17 Capability of children born out of wedlock as to inheritance

MISCELLANEOUS PROVISIONS

2105.19 Certain persons not to benefit; complaint to restore rights
2105.20 Waste by tenant for life
2105.25 Declaration of fatherhood of adult child
2105.26 Order declaring man alleging himself to be father of adult child as adult child's father

SURVIVORSHIP

2105.31 Definitions
2105.32 Determination of survivorship with respect to specified person
2105.33 Determination of survivorship with respect to specified event
2105.34 Co-owners with right of survivorship
2105.35 Establishment of death
2105.36 Determination of survivorship; exceptions
2105.37 Liability of payor or other third party
2105.38 Protected purchasers
2105.39 Applicability; severability

Cross References

Afterborn or pretermitted heirs, effect on will, 2107.34
Commission issued to take election of surviving spouse, 2106.07
Death, complaint to establish presumption, 2121.02
Determination of heirship, Ch 2123
Disclaimer of succession to interest in property; procedure; distributor unaware of disclaimer not liable, 1339.60
Disinterment, application for court order, 517.24
Dower, defined, 2103.02
Election made by spouse under legal disability, 2106.08
Fiduciary, defined, 2109.01
Foreign wards and guardians, 2111.43
Guardians, next of kin defined, 2111.01
Heirs; afterborn or pretermitted, effect on will, 2107.34
Notice of admission of will to probate, 2107.19
Paternity proceedings, action to determine father and child relationship, effect on inheritance or succession, 3111.05
Powers of guardian of person and estate, 2111.07
Presumed decedent law, Ch 2121
Probate, application to admit lost, spoliated, or destroyed will, 2107.27
Title to real estate of presumed decedent, 2121.06
Wills, definitions, 2107.01

Law Review and Journal Commentaries

How a Will Is Admitted to Probate in Ohio. 50 Title Topics 6 (June 1983).

Kass v. Kass, Blazing Legal Trails in the Field of Human Reproductive Technology, Kelly Summers. 48 Clev St L Rev 637 (2000).

Multiplication and Division—New Math for the Courts: New Reproductive Technologies Create Potential Legal Time Bombs, Comment. 95 Dick L Rev 155 (Fall 1990).

Ohio's 1975 Probate Reform Act: Analysis of Major Changes in Ohio's Probate Code, Note. 45 U Cin L Rev 429 (1976).

Should Everyone Trust a Living Trust?, William A. Fields. 2 Prob L J Ohio 5 (September/October 1991).

Uniform Probate Code: Article II—Intestacy, Wills, and Donative Transfers, Richard V. Wellman. 2 Prob L J Ohio 15 (September/October 1991).

GENERAL PROVISIONS

2105.01 No distinction between ancestral and nonancestral or real and personal property

In intestate succession, there shall be no difference between ancestral and nonancestral property or between real and personal property.

(1953 H 1, eff. 10–1–53; GC 10503–1)

Historical and Statutory Notes

Pre–1953 H 1 Amendments: 114 v 339

Baldwin's Ohio Legislative Service, 1996 H 350—LSC Analysis, p 10/L-3476

Library References

Descent and Distribution ⚖9, 11.
Westlaw Topic No. 124.
C.J.S. Descent and Distribution §§ 13 to 15, 18 to 19.

Research References

Encyclopedias

OH Jur. 3d Abandoned, Lost, & Escheated Property § 29, Generally; Release of State's Right of Escheat.
OH Jur. 3d Death § 20, Effect of Decree.
OH Jur. 3d Decedents' Estates § 15, Descent and Distribution.
OH Jur. 3d Decedents' Estates § 30, Other Terms.
OH Jur. 3d Decedents' Estates § 33, Ohio Laws; Territorial Legislation—Ohio Acts.
OH Jur. 3d Decedents' Estates § 48, No Distinction Between Real and Personal Property.
OH Jur. 3d Decedents' Estates § 50, Effect of Source of Title; Ancestral Property.
OH Jur. 3d Decedents' Estates § 70, Rents; Ground Rents; Leaseholds.
OH Jur. 3d Decedents' Estates § 640, Effect of Reference to Statute of Descent and Distribution.
OH Jur. 3d Decedents' Estates § 1299, Leaseholds.

Forms

Ohio Forms Legal and Business § 24:304, Devise of Estate According to Laws of Descent and Distribution.

Treatises and Practice Aids

Carlin, Baldwin's Ohio Practice, Merrick-Rippner Probate Law § 9:1, Presumption of Death—Statutory.
Carlin, Baldwin's Ohio Practice, Merrick-Rippner Probate Law § 9:2, Presumption of Death—Procedure for Establishing—Jurisdiction.
Carlin, Baldwin's Ohio Practice, Merrick-Rippner Probate Law § 9:5, Presumption of Death—Procedure for Establishing—Filing Complaint.
Carlin, Baldwin's Ohio Practice, Merrick-Rippner Probate Law § 9:7, Presumption of Death—Effect of Decree.
Carlin, Baldwin's Ohio Practice, Merrick-Rippner Probate Law § 9:9, Presumption of Death—Complaint—Form.
Carlin, Baldwin's Ohio Practice, Merrick-Rippner Probate Law § 15:1, Descent and Distribution—Scope of Statutes.
Carlin, Baldwin's Ohio Practice, Merrick-Rippner Probate Law § 15:2, Descent and Distribution—Definitions.
Carlin, Baldwin's Ohio Practice, Merrick-Rippner Probate Law § 17:2, Designation—Effect.
Carlin, Baldwin's Ohio Practice, Merrick-Rippner Probate Law § 20:5, Advancement—Rights of a Pretermitted Child.
Carlin, Baldwin's Ohio Practice, Merrick-Rippner Probate Law § 21:5, Rights of Surviving Spouse to Make Election—Statutory Provisions—Effect.
Carlin, Baldwin's Ohio Practice, Merrick-Rippner Probate Law § 24:2, Escheat—Scope of Statutes.
Carlin, Baldwin's Ohio Practice, Merrick-Rippner Probate Law § 24:3, Escheat—Operation.
Carlin, Baldwin's Ohio Practice, Merrick-Rippner Probate Law § 46:1, Anti-Lapse Statute.

Carlin, Baldwin's Ohio Practice, Merrick-Rippner Probate Law § 47:1, Afterborn or Pretermitted Heirs—Definitions.

Carlin, Baldwin's Ohio Practice, Merrick-Rippner Probate Law § 47:2, Afterborn or Pretermitted Heirs—Statutory Provisions.

Carlin, Baldwin's Ohio Practice, Merrick-Rippner Probate Law § 47:3, Afterborn or Pretermitted Heirs—Explanatory Chart 1.

Carlin, Baldwin's Ohio Practice, Merrick-Rippner Probate Law § 47:4, Afterborn or Pretermitted Heirs—Explanatory Chart 2.

Carlin, Baldwin's Ohio Practice, Merrick-Rippner Probate Law § 47:5, Afterborn or Pretermitted Heirs—Intent to Disinherit.

Carlin, Baldwin's Ohio Practice, Merrick-Rippner Probate Law § 77:3, Unclaimed Money—Escheat Distinguished.

Carlin, Baldwin's Ohio Practice, Merrick-Rippner Probate Law § 9:10, Presumption of Death—Entry Setting for Hearing, Ordering Notice, and Service of Summons—Form.

Carlin, Baldwin's Ohio Practice, Merrick-Rippner Probate Law § 15:43, Descent and Distribution—Escheat.

Carlin, Baldwin's Ohio Practice, Merrick-Rippner Probate Law § 19:10, Uniform Parentage Act—Procedure in Action to Determine Father-Child Relationship.

Carlin, Baldwin's Ohio Practice, Merrick-Rippner Probate Law § 21:15, Rights of Surviving Spouse to Make Election—Proceedings for Advice or Declaratory Judgment.

Carlin, Baldwin's Ohio Practice, Merrick-Rippner Probate Law § 21:30, Rights of Surviving Spouse to Make Election—Right to Use of Mansion House and Family Allowance.

Carlin, Baldwin's Ohio Practice, Merrick-Rippner Probate Law § 21:39, Rights of Surviving Spouse to Make Election—Failure to Make Election—Scope of RC 2106.04.

Carlin, Baldwin's Ohio Practice, Merrick-Rippner Probate Law § 21:41, Rights of Surviving Spouse to Make Election—Failure to Make Election—Conclusive Presumption.

Carlin, Baldwin's Ohio Practice, Merrick-Rippner Probate Law § 21:56, Rights of Surviving Spouse—Family Allowance—Time Limitations.

Carlin, Baldwin's Ohio Practice, Merrick-Rippner Probate Law § 30:21, Drafting a Will—Beneficiary Clauses—Disinheritance of Afterborn or Pretermitted Heirs.

Carlin, Baldwin's Ohio Practice, Merrick-Rippner Probate Law § 30:120, Distribution to a Custodian Under the Transfers to Minors Act of Ohio When a Devisee Shall be Under 18 Years of Age—Form.

Carlin, Baldwin's Ohio Practice, Merrick-Rippner Probate Law § 30:131, Legacy to Two Persons or the Survivor; or as Part of Residue—Form.

Carlin, Baldwin's Ohio Practice, Merrick-Rippner Probate Law App B SPF 8.2, Election of Surviving Spouse to Take Against Will.

Kuehnle and Levey, Ohio Real Estate Law and Practice § 5:2, Descent and Distribution.

Kuehnle and Levey, Ohio Real Estate Law and Practice § 5:3, The Half-And-Half Statute.

Restatement (3d) Property (Wills & Don. Trans.) § 2.4, Intestate Share of Surviving Ancestors and Collateral Relatives.

Law Review and Journal Commentaries

Ancestral and Non–Ancestral Realty Under the Ohio Statutes of Descent, Lewis M. Simes. 2 U Cin L Rev 387 (November 1928).

Notes of Decisions

Estates 1-3
   By devise or gift 1
   By purchase 2
   Subject to divestiture 3
Heirs at law, next of kin 6
Partition 5
Personalty 7
Siblings' interest 4
Title 8

1. Estates—By devise or gift

The statute of descents as amended March 4, 1865, provides for the descent of such estates only as descend to the intestate in right of blood or which came to him by devise or deed of gift from one from whom he might have inherited the same. Lathrop v. Young (Ohio 1874) 25 Ohio St. 451.

"Ancestor from whom the estate came" is he from whom an estate was immediately inherited. (See also Clayton v Drake, 17 OS 367 (1867).) Prickett's Lessee v. Parker (Ohio 1854) 3 Ohio St. 394.

Effect of this section is to cause all property to pass according to one common rule, whatever its character and from whatever source derived; reasons for distinction between ancestral and nonancestral property and between real and personal property, in intestate succession, have long since disappeared, these differences being at present time purely arbitrary and productive of artificial inequality. Seman v. Seman (Darke 1935) 19 Ohio Law Abs. 600.

If the land came to the husband by purchase, his widow took it in fee, but if by deed of gift, she took it for life only, with remainder to his brothers and sisters. Groves v. Groves (Ohio 1902) 65 Ohio St. 442, 47 W.L.B. 207, 62 N.E. 1044.

2. —— By purchase, estates

Deed in consideration of love and affection, faithful service, and one dollar is not a deed of gift but of purchase. Brown v. Whaley (Ohio 1898) 58 Ohio St. 654, 39 W.L.B. 129, 40 W.L.B. 130, 49 N.E. 479, 65 Am.St. Rep. 793.

Where deed recites valuable consideration, the estate is by purchase and not by deed of gift from an ancestor. Patterson v. Lamson (Ohio 1887) 45 Ohio St. 77, 17 W.L.B. 255, 12 N.E. 531.

An ancestral estate is not changed to an estate by purchase by the owner conveying away and immediately receiving back title though done for the sole purpose of breaking descent. Helfinger v Wolfee, 11 D Repr 906, 30 B 383 (CP, Hamilton 1893).

Widow by converting personalty into realty is seized of latter by purchase. Ellis v Ellis, 3 CC 186, 2 CD 105 (Logan 1888).

3. —— Subject to divestiture, estates

Where there is a devise of lands to a daughter for life and remainder to her children then unborn, reversion in fee descends to and vests in the heirs of the testator subject to be divested to any children of the daughter subsequently born. Gilpin v. Williams (Ohio 1874) 25 Ohio St. 283. Wills ⇨ 866

Ancestral property ceases to be such when change of title or form occurs. Digby v. Digby (Ohio Cir. 1903) 16 Ohio C.D. 417, 5 Ohio C.C.N.S. 130.

Land descending to an heir may be divested by birth of a near heir. Dunn v. Evans (Ohio 1835) 7 Ohio 169, PT. I.

In determining whether land is ancestral or nonancestral, court will be governed by the legal title under which the intestate held. Olmstead v Douglass, 16 CC 171, 8 CD 465 (Cuyahoga 1898).

Where heir inherits equitable title and later forces conveyance of legal title in action for specific performance, the whole estate is ancestral. Higgins v Higgins, 11 CC 131, 5 CD 349 (Wyandot 1895), reversed by 57 OS 239, 48 NE 943 (1897).

4. Siblings' interest

Where a person without brothers or sisters, lineal descendants or wife, dies, leaving an inherited ancestral estate from his father, the father's brothers and sisters will inherit the same. Stannard v. Case (Ohio 1883) 40 Ohio St. 211, 10 W.L.B. 264.

Under the act of March 14, 1853, nonancestral lands of an intestate who died leaving no children but leaving a wife and brothers, vests life estate in the wife and fee in the brothers subject to life estate. Jenks v. Langdon (Ohio 1871) 21 Ohio St. 362.

Where an intestate died seized of land which had descended from her grandfather to her father and from her father to her, the land under the act of April 17, 1857, passed to the half brother and sister of her father. White v. White (Ohio 1869) 19 Ohio St. 531.

Under the act of 1881, lands of an intestate inherited from his father, if intestate left no descendants, or brothers or sisters, passed to the brothers and sisters of the father and not to the grandfather of the intestate, though the estate came by deed of gift from the grandfather to the father. Curren v. Taylor (Ohio 1850) 19 Ohio 36.

Where owner of ancestral land conveys and dies and grantee reconveys to grantee's widow, brothers and sisters of reconveying grantee have no rights in the land. Kihlken v. Kihlken (Ohio 1898) 59 Ohio St. 106, 40 W.L.B. 361, 51 N.E. 969.

5. Partition

In partition, where one of the heirs elects to take the land, the part he inherited remains ancestral and the parts he receives from others become estates by purchase. Freeman v. Allen (Ohio 1867) 17 Ohio St. 527.

In a wrongful death action against a truck driver and driver's employer involving a collision between the truck driver and a motorist, dismissal is proper on the basis that the plaintiff could not maintain a wrongful death suit on behalf of an alleged minor child of the motorist where the plaintiff and the motorist were not married, the motorist did not in probate court formally acknowledge the child as his with consent of the mother, and the motorist did not designate the child as his heir-at-law, adopt the child, or make provision for the child in his will, and, although a parentage action was brought by the plaintiff and her son, the action was brought after the death of the motorist; thus, as a matter of law, the child cannot inherit from the decedent's estate, including any recovery from the wrongful death action. Hunter–Martin v. Winchester Transp., Inc. (Shelby 1991) 71 Ohio App.3d 273, 593 N.E.2d 383, motion overruled 62 Ohio St.3d 1408, 577 N.E.2d 361.

The ancestral character of property is not changed by partition by mutual deeds. (See also King v Anderson, 7 NP(NS) 333, 19 D 106 (CP, Licking 1908); but see Wilson v Hall, 6 CC 570, 3 CD 589 (Franklin 1892), affirmed by 53 OS 679, 44 NE 1137 (1895).) Carter v. Day (Ohio 1898) 59 Ohio St. 96, 40 W.L.B. 365, 51 N.E. 967, 69 Am.St.Rep. 757.

Where the estate in common came by descent, devise or gift, the parcel allotted to each on partition descends according to this section. Carter v. Day (Ohio 1898) 59 Ohio St. 96, 40 W.L.B. 365, 51 N.E. 967, 69 Am.St.Rep. 757.

Under a devise of the remainder to the "legal heirs" of the life tenant, nonancestral property passes to the half sister of the life tenant. Reif v. Ulmer (Ohio Super. 1909) 20 Ohio Dec. 342, 9 Ohio N.P.N.S. 234.

6. Heirs at law, next of kin

Where a nonancestral estate left in trust for the benefit of the sole heir and directed in case of such heir's death without surviving issue, then to the heirs at law, upon the death of such child without issue, the widow of the testator takes the property. Weston v. Weston (Ohio 1882) 38 Ohio St. 473, 8 W.L.B. 301.

Where a person died seized of lands leaving a widow and only one child to whom the land descended, and the child died without issue or brothers or sisters, the land descends to the father's next of kin. Drake v. Rogers (Ohio 1861) 13 Ohio St. 21.

Ancestral estates, though received by devise or deed of gift, descend to the heirs who are of the blood of the ancestor from whom they came, whether such ancestor be lineal or not. (See also Penn v Cox, 16 O 30 (1849); Prickett v Parker, 3 OS 394 (1854).) Brewster v. Benedict (Ohio 1846) 14 Ohio 368.

Equitable title passes by descent. (See also Bolton v Bank, 50 OS 290, 33 NE 1115 (1893).) Avery's Lessee v. Dufrees (Ohio 1839) 9 Ohio 145.

A certificate of tax sale held by an ancestor descends at his death to his heir. Rice's Lessee v. White (Ohio 1837) 8 Ohio 216.

When one dies seized of an ancestral estate leaving neither father, brother, sister nor descendants but leaving a mother, the estate passes to the next of kin of the blood from which the estate came. Dunn v. Evans (Ohio 1835) 7 Ohio 169, PT. I.

Under act of 1806, if an infant died seized of an estate from his father and left neither brothers, sisters nor children, his mother would inherit to the exclusion of father's sister. Doe ex dem. McCullough v. Lee (Ohio 1835) 7 Ohio 15, PT. I.

7. Personalty

Where a testator directs that land named in his will be converted into money and distributed among his heirs in that form, such land is treated as personal rather than real property. Ferguson v. Stuart's Ex'rs (Ohio 1846) 14 Ohio 140.

Where land inherited by an infant from his father is sold and converted into money for his support, upon the death of such infant his half brothers and sisters, children of his mother by a second marriage, inherit the money remaining unexpended. Armstrong v. Miller (Ohio 1833) 6 Ohio 118.

Real estate devised in trust loses its ancestral property upon sale and reinvestment as other realty. Renick v Renick, 6 NP(NS) 304, 18 D 308 (CP, Franklin 1907).

8. Title

In determining questions as to the descent of real property, regard is had to the legal title only; and where the legal title is acquired by purchase, and an equity in the property by inheritance, the legal title and equitable interest at once unite, and upon the death of the owner, the descent of the property will be cast as an estate which came by purchase. Higgins v. Higgins (Ohio 1897) 57 Ohio St. 239, 39 W.L.B. 40, 48 N.E. 943. Descent And Distribution ⚖ 12

The course of descent of real estate is controlled by the legal title. (See also Higgins v Higgins, 57 OS 239, 48 NE 943 (1897); Patterson v Lamson, 45 OS 77, 12 NE 531 (1887); Richardson v Michener, 11 D Repr 830, 30 B 120 (CP, Stark 1893).) Stembel v Martin, 50 OS 495, 35 NE 208 (1893).

2105.02   Construction of "living" and "died"

When, in Chapter 2105. of the Revised Code, a person is described as living, it means that the person was living at the time of the death of the intestate from whom the estate came, and when a person is described as having died, it means that the person died before such intestate.

(2002 H 242, eff. 5–16–02; 1953 H 1, eff. 10–1–53; GC 10503–3)

Historical and Statutory Notes

Pre–1953 H 1 Amendments: 114 v 339

Amendment Note: 2002 H 242 substituted "Chapter 2105." for "sections 2105.01 to 2105.21, inclusive,"; and made changes to reflect gender neutral language.

Baldwin's Ohio Legislative Service, 1996 H 350—LSC Analysis, p 10/L–3476

Library References

Descent and Distribution ⚖6.

Westlaw Topic No. 124.

C.J.S. Descent and Distribution § 8.

Research References

Encyclopedias

OH Jur. 3d Decedents' Estates § 30, Other Terms.

Notes of Decisions

Election against will   2
Estate by purchase   1

---

1.   Estate by purchase

Where the legal title is acquired by purchase and an equitable interest is acquired by inheritance, on the death of the owner, the property will descend as an estate acquired by purchase. (See also Higgins v Higgins, 57 OS 289, 48 NE 1097 (1897).) Stembel v Martin, 50 OS 495, 35 NE 208 (1893).

2.   Election against will

A widow with no children whose husband dies testate, who elects to take under the law instead of his will will receive the interest in his estate as she would if he had died leaving children; if her husband dies intestate with no children, she will receive a life estate in all his property or the entire estate, depending on the source from which the property came to the husband. Moyses v. Neilson (Ohio Com.Pl. 1900) 9 Ohio Dec. 623, 7 Ohio N.P. 607.

2105.03 Determination of next of kin

In the determination of intestate succession, next of kin shall be determined by degrees of relationship computed by the rules of civil law.

(1953 H 1, eff. 10–1–53; GC 10503–2)

Historical and Statutory Notes

Pre–1953 H 1 Amendments: 114 v 339

Cross References

Transfer and indorsement by auditor before recording deed, 317.22

Library References

Descent and Distribution ⇔20.1.
Westlaw Topic No. 124.
C.J.S. Descent and Distribution § 23.

Research References

Encyclopedias

OH Jur. 3d Decedents' Estates § 90, Method of Computation.
OH Jur. 3d Decedents' Estates § 92, Particular Degrees—Preferences Within Degrees.

Treatises and Practice Aids

Carlin, Baldwin's Ohio Practice, Merrick-Rippner Probate Law § 15:7, Descent and Distribution—Spouse as Heir at Law and Next of Kin.
Carlin, Baldwin's Ohio Practice, Merrick-Rippner Probate Law § 12:21, Wrongful Death—Denial of Damages to Parent Who Abandoned Child—Hearing; Burden of Proof; Order; Effect.
Carlin, Baldwin's Ohio Practice, Merrick-Rippner Probate Law § 15:39, Descent and Distribution—No Grandparents or Their Lineal Descendants.
Restatement (3d) Property (Wills & Don. Trans.) § 2.4, Intestate Share of Surviving Ancestors and Collateral Relatives.

Notes of Decisions

Blood of ancestor 2
Computation 1
Not next of kin 3

---

1. Computation

Next of kin means persons related to the intestate in equal degree excluding remote kindred and the principle of representation. Clayton v. Drake (Ohio 1867) 17 Ohio St. 367.

The rule of the civil law is the common law of this county in the computation of the degrees of kindred; the canon law method of computing kindred grew out of the feudal system of tenures and the state policy to perpetuate that system in England, both of which are foreign to the spirit of republican institutions, and such laws have never been the law of this state. Clayton v. Drake (Ohio 1867) 17 Ohio St. 367.

First cousin held next of kin and entitled to inherit within statute, where only other relatives were children of deceased great-aunt. Weisflock v. Sigling (Ohio 1927) 116 Ohio St. 435, 156 N.E. 905, 25 Ohio Law Rep. 331. Descent And Distribution ⇔ 40

Where a will provided that on death of testator's widow all his estate then in existence should be equally divided between his and his wife's nearest of kin, "they sharing like and like," and where the next of kin of testator and of his own nearest of kin and one-half to her nearest of kin; the expression "they sharing like and like" referring to the proportionate share that each one of the two classes should take. Godfrey v. Epple (Ohio 1919) 100 Ohio St. 447, 126 N.E. 886, 11 A.L.R. 317, 17 Ohio Law Rep. 379, 17 Ohio Law Rep. 482. Wills ⇔ 531(3)

2. Blood of ancestor

Under act of 1835, half brothers and sisters of the ancestor are included in the words "brothers and sisters of such ancestor," and are preferred to the brothers and sisters of the intestate of the half blood who are not of the blood of the ancestor from whom the estate came. Cliver v. Sanders (Ohio 1858) 8 Ohio St. 501.

The half brothers and half sisters of the ancestor are included in the words "brothers and sisters of such ancestors," in the fifth subdivision of GC 8573, prescribing the order of descent of ancestral real estate. Stockton v. Frazier (Ohio 1909) 81 Ohio St. 227, 90 N.E. 168, 7 Ohio Law Rep. 507. Descent And Distribution ⇔ 35

A designated heir takes ahead of "ancestors," ahead of "brothers and sisters," and with "children born in lawful wedlock." Fugmann v Theobald, 4 D 65, 3 NP 65 (CP 1895).

Averment that there is no one of the blood of the particular ancestors to inherit is sufficient. Rhino v. Emery (C.C.A.6 (Ohio) 1895) 35 W.L.B. 368, 72 F. 382, 18 C.C.A. 600.

Under the doctrine of ancestral property, the next of kin to the intestate of blood that differs from that of the ancestors from whom the estate came may take the estate only by averring and proving the blood of that line extinct, and lack of a relict husband or wife as heir. Rhino v. Emery (C.C.A.6 (Ohio) 1895) 35 W.L.B. 368, 72 F. 382, 18 C.C.A. 600.

3. Not next of kin

Next of kin as provided in GC 10509–3 (RC 2113.06), means those who would inherit in case of intestacy, and the provisions of this section have no application for determining the right of appointment as administrator. In re Applegate's Estate (Ohio Prob. 1951) 100 N.E.2d 322, 61 Ohio Law Abs. 277, 45 O.O. 24.

A widow is not the next of kin of an adopted child. In re Raspold, 6 NP(NS) 172, 18 D 396 (CP, Cuyahoga 1907).

2105.04 Permanent leases to descend same as estates in fee

Permanent leasehold estates, renewable forever, are subject to Chapter 2105. of the Revised Code.

(2002 H 242, eff. 5–16–02; 1953 H 1, eff. 10–1–53; GC 10503–11)

Historical and Statutory Notes

Pre–1953 H 1 Amendments: 114 v 341

Amendment Note: 2002 H 242 substituted "Chapter 2105." for "sections 2105.01 to 2105.21, inclusive,".

Library References

Descent and Distribution ⇔8.
Westlaw Topic No. 124.
C.J.S. Descent and Distribution §§ 9 to 12.
C.J.S. Right of Privacy and Publicity § 41.

Research References

Encyclopedias

OH Jur. 3d Decedents' Estates § 70, Rents; Ground Rents; Leaseholds.
OH Jur. 3d Decedents' Estates § 1299, Leaseholds.
OH Jur. 3d Family Law § 104, Leaseholds.
OH Jur. 3d Landlord & Tenant § 4, Character of Leasehold as Personalty or Realty.
OH Jur. 3d Landlord & Tenant § 10, Permanent Leasehold.

Forms

Ohio Forms Legal and Business § 4C:1, Definitions and Distinctions.

Treatises and Practice Aids

Restatement (2d) of Property, Land. & Ten. § 1.4, Lease for a Fixed or Computable Period of Time.

Notes of Decisions

Dower 2
Owner 3
Renewable forever 4
Taxes 6
Term of lease 5

Transformation into freehold estate 1

---

1. Transformation into freehold estate

A permanent leasehold estate is not a chattel, but land carrying the fee, and as such is subject to all the rules and laws which attach to lands for all purposes. (See also McLean v Rocky, 2 OFD 270 (6th Cir Ohio 1843).) Loring v. Melendy (Ohio 1842) 11 Ohio 355.

A permanent leasehold becomes a freehold estate, subject to the laws of descent as an estate in fee. Ralston Steel Car Co. v. Ralston (Ohio 1925) 112 Ohio St. 306, 147 N.E. 513, 39 A.L.R. 334, 3 Ohio Law Abs. 200, 23 Ohio Law Rep. 125, 23 Ohio Law Rep. 126. Descent And Distribution ⚖ 9

2. Dower

To entitle a widow to dower in an equitable estate of her husband, he must have owned said estate at the time of his decease. Abbott v. Bosworth (Ohio 1881) 36 Ohio St. 605. Dower And Curtesy ⚖ 11

Perpetual leaseholds are not estates of inheritance, within the meaning of the Dower Act. Oliver v. Jones (Ohio Com.Pl. 1895) 6 Ohio Dec. 194, 3 Ohio N.P. 129.

3. Owner

"Owner," for assessment purposes, does not include a lessee for a term of ten years. Davis v. City of Cincinnati (Ohio 1880) 36 Ohio St. 24.

The holder of a perpetual lease with privilege of purchase is an owner within the meaning of the street assessment statutes. Clements v Norwood, 2 NP 274, 1 D 193 (CP, Hamilton 1895). Landlord And Tenant ⚖ 149; Municipal Corporations ⚖ 422

4. Renewable forever

This section does not have the effect of transforming a permanent leasehold estate renewable forever into a fee simple, and the fee remains in the lessor, his heirs and assigns. (But see Ralston Steel Car Co v Ralston, 112 OS 306, 147 NE 513 (1925).) Rawson v. Brown (Ohio 1922) 104 Ohio St. 537, 136 N.E. 209, 20 Ohio Law Rep. 44, 20 Ohio Law Rep. 45.

A lease for three and one-half years, renewable forever, is a perpetual lease within this statute. Ellison v. Foster (Ohio Com.Pl. 1909) 19 Ohio Dec. 849, 6 Ohio Law Rep. 666, affirmed 21 Ohio C.D. 513, 12 Ohio C.C.(N.S.) 399.

5. Term of lease

Father demonstrated lack of commitment to children, as basis for adjudication that children were either neglected or dependent, for purposes of granting County Job and Family Services custody of children; father was perpetrator of violence against one of children, he utilized corporal punishment, and he refused to address his anger management issues and lack of parenting skills. In re Green (Ohio App. 5 Dist., Tuscarawas, 06-23-2005) No. 2005AP010007, No. 2005AP020008, 2005-Ohio-3308, 2005 WL 1523855, Unreported. Infants ⚖ 156

Agreement between coliseum owner and city did not give rise to exclusivity of possession, and thus coliseum owner's interest in parking and staging on city's stadium parking facilities was not a leasehold estate, even though agreement referred to parties as landlord and tenant, where coliseum owner was granted possession of parking areas only for the limited time of certain coliseum events, full control of the physical facilities was reserved to city, and, in the case of simultaneous stadium and coliseum events, both sets of patrons would share parking facility. Cincinnati Entertainment Assoc., Ltd. v. Hamilton Cty. Bd. of Commrs. (Ohio App. 1 Dist., 03-09-2001) 141 Ohio App.3d 803, 753 N.E.2d 884, dismissed, appeal not allowed 92 Ohio St.3d 1441, 751 N.E.2d 481. Landlord And Tenant ⚖ 20

Ninety-nine year leases are subject to the same law of descent as estates in fee simple. Village of St. Bernard v. Kemper (Ohio 1899) 60 Ohio St. 244, 42 W.L.B. 41, 54 N.E. 267.

6. Taxes

Upon a perpetual lease, although without covenant by lessee to pay taxes, so much of the taxes as are on account of improvements put upon the lot by lessee, are chargeable to him. Joslyn v Spellman, 9 D Repr 258, 12 B 7 (Super, Cincinnati 1884). Landlord And Tenant ⚖ 149

ADVANCEMENTS

2105.051 Advancement of inheritance; time of valuation

When a person dies, property that he gave during his lifetime to an heir shall be treated as an advancement against the heir's share of the estate only if declared in a contemporaneous writing by the decedent, or acknowledged in writing by the heir to be an advancement. For this purpose, property advanced is valued as of the time the heir came into possession or enjoyment of the property, or as of the time of death of the decedent, whichever occurs first. If the heir does not survive the decedent, the property shall not be taken into account in computing the intestate share to be received by the heir's issue, unless the declaration or acknowledgment provides otherwise.

(1975 S 145, eff. 1–1–76)

Uncodified Law

1975 S 145, § 3: See Uncodified Law under 2105.06.

Legislative Service Commission

1975:

In current Ohio law, if an intestate makes a gift to one of his children before his death, the gift could be *considered* to be an advancement and the value of the gift would then be deducted from the share the child receives under the statute of descent and distribution. Whether or not the gift to the child is an advancement depends upon the intent of the donor at the time the gift is made.

The bill would provide that the gift given to an heir would be an advancement only if a contemporaneous writing by the decedent or a written acknowledgement by the heir declares that the gift is an advancement. The section would stipulate that property advanced is valued as of the time the heir came into possession or the date of death, whichever is first. If the heir doesn't survive, the property would not be used to compute the intestate share of the heir's issue, unless specifically provided otherwise.

Library References

Descent and Distribution ⚖93 to 104.
Westlaw Topic No. 124.
C.J.S. Descent and Distribution §§ 95 to 103, 116.

Research References

Encyclopedias

83 Am. Jur. Proof of Facts 3d 295, Proof of Decedent's Intent that Inter Vivos Gift to Heir Constitutes Advancement.
OH Jur. 3d Decedents' Estates § 162, Generally; Donor's Intention.
OH Jur. 3d Decedents' Estates § 163, Donor's Intestacy.
OH Jur. 3d Decedents' Estates § 165, Mode of Making Advancement.
OH Jur. 3d Decedents' Estates § 166, Donee's Acceptance.
OH Jur. 3d Decedents' Estates § 168, Property Affected.
OH Jur. 3d Decedents' Estates § 169, Persons as to Whom Doctrine Applies.
OH Jur. 3d Decedents' Estates § 170, Generally; Time of Taking Effect.
OH Jur. 3d Decedents' Estates § 172, Valuation of Advancement; Interest on Advancements.
OH Jur. 3d Decedents' Estates § 174, Effect on Donee's Heirs.
OH Jur. 3d Decedents' Estates § 816, Relationship Between Ademption by Satisfaction and Advancements.
OH Jur. 3d Decedents' Estates § 1652, Advancements.

Forms

Ohio Forms Legal and Business § 26:27, Declaration of Advancement—by Donor.
Ohio Forms and Transactions F 30.08, Advancements.
Ohio Forms and Transactions KP 30.05, Advancements.

Treatises and Practice Aids

Carlin, Baldwin's Ohio Practice, Merrick-Rippner Probate Law § 20:1, Advancement—Definition.

Carlin, Baldwin's Ohio Practice, Merrick-Rippner Probate Law § 20:2, Advancement—Valuation.

Carlin, Baldwin's Ohio Practice, Merrick-Rippner Probate Law § 20:4, Advancement—Effect on Issue of Heir.

Carlin, Baldwin's Ohio Practice, Merrick-Rippner Probate Law § 21:19, Rights of Surviving Spouse to Make Election—Effect of Election—Generally.

Restatement (3d) Property (Wills & Don. Trans.) § 2.6, Advancements.

Notes of Decisions

Deduction 2
Statutory requirements 1

---

1. Statutory requirements

Children who challenged certain lifetime transfers made by deceased mother failed to establish that use of mother's funds to pay tuition for children of one son was against mother's wishes, even though mother had never paid tuition for other grandchildren; son whose children benefited from the tuition payment never testified at the probate proceeding. Hillis v. Humphrey (Ohio App. 5 Dist., Perry, 06-30-2005) No. 05CA6, 2005-Ohio-3459, 2005 WL 1579392, Unreported. Gifts ⚖ 49(5)

Valid inter vivos gift will be recognized where it is shown by clear and convincing evidence that owner intended to transfer property to donee then and there and that, pursuant to such intention, donor made delivery to donee while relinquishing ownership, dominion, and control. Neel v. Neel (Ohio App. 8 Dist., 07-25-1996) 113 Ohio App.3d 24, 680 N.E.2d 207, dismissed, appeal not allowed 77 Ohio St.3d 1514, 674 N.E.2d 369. Gifts ⚖ 4; Gifts ⚖ 49(1)

The inter vivos gift of "Blackacre" by a decedent to his spouse without any writing indicating that it was an advancement will not be considered as such; there is no similar equitable remedy available when the statutory requirements of RC 2105.051 are not fulfilled. King v. King (Montgomery 1992) 82 Ohio App.3d 747, 613 N.E.2d 251.

A deed which does not satisfy the requirements of RC 2105.051 will not constitute an advancement. King v. King (Montgomery 1992) 82 Ohio App.3d 747, 613 N.E.2d 251.

The operation of the statute regulating advancements can only apply where the decedent died intestate as to his property. In re Bullock's Estate (Ohio Com.Pl. 1905) 15 Ohio Dec. 783, 3 Ohio NP(NS) 190. Descent And Distribution ⚖ 93

It is error to consider checks from a decedent to a legatee as advancements where the only evidence that they were intended as such consists of undated notes of the decedent pertaining to such checks and an acknowledgment by the legatee of financial assistance received. In re Estate of March, No. WD-84-29 (6th Dist Ct App, Wood, 8-24-84).

2. Deduction

Where a testator's intent that any claims against his estate by his children should be rejected as the testator was not in debt to any of them, the amount of any judgment and costs recovered on a claim against the estate by a child should be deducted from that child's share under the will, or from the share of his assignee if such assignee had recovered a judgment against the estate. Scheets v. Hunter (Ohio 1897) 56 Ohio St. 761, 37 W.L.B. 283, 49 N.E. 1116.

2105.052 Debt owed decedent not chargeable against intestate shares

Any debt owed to a decedent shall not be charged against the intestate share of any person except the debtor. If the debtor fails to survive decedent, the debt shall not be taken into account in computing the intestate share of the debtor's issue.

(1975 S 145, eff. 1-1-76)

Uncodified Law

1975 S 145, § 3: See Uncodified Law under 2105.06.

Library References

Descent and Distribution ⚖ 80.
Westlaw Topic No. 124.
C.J.S. Descent and Distribution § 70.

Research References

Encyclopedias

OH Jur. 3d Decedents' Estates § 186, Liability of Heir's Share for Heir's Indebtedness to Intestate.

OH Jur. 3d Decedents' Estates § 1280, Debts of Heirs, Legatees, or Distributees.

Treatises and Practice Aids

Carlin, Baldwin's Ohio Practice, Merrick-Rippner Probate Law § 76:2, Issue of Debtor Not Liable.

Notes of Decisions

Interest of debtor's issue 1
Priority of debts 3
Vesting 2

---

1. Interest of debtor's issue

Where a devisee named in a will dies during the testator's lifetime leaving issue and is indebted to the estate of the testator, his issue takes the estate devised to his parent subject to the parent/primary legatee's debt. Baker v. Carpenter (Ohio 1903) 69 Ohio St. 15, 48 W.L.B. 907, 68 N.E. 577, 1 Ohio Law Rep. 489, 1 Ohio Law Rep. 589.

2. Vesting

An heir takes lands immediately upon the death of the ancestor intestate, and legal title vests in him subject to the right of the administrator to sell such lands for the payment of debts of the ancestor. (See also Piatt v St. Clair, 6 O 227 (1833); Ramsdall v Craighill, 9 O 197 (1839); Overturf v Dugan, 29 OS 230 (1876); Faran v Robinson, 17 OS 242 (1867).) Douglass' Lessee v. Massie (Ohio 1847) 16 Ohio 271, 47 Am.Dec. 375.

3. Priority of debts

A debt owed by a son to his father's estate has priority over a mortgage or judgment lien against him on real estate coming to him from his father by way of general devise, so that the son must pay his debt to the estate before he or his creditors may share in the devised estate. Woodruff v. Woodruff (Ohio Cir. 1902) 13 Ohio C.D. 408, 3 Ohio C.C.N.S. 616.

DESCENT AND DISTRIBUTION; RIGHTS OF SURVIVING SPOUSE

2105.06 Statute of descent and distribution

When a person dies intestate having title or right to any personal property, or to any real estate or inheritance, in this state, the personal property shall be distributed, and the real estate or inheritance shall descend and pass in parcenary, except as otherwise provided by law, in the following course:

(A) If there is no surviving spouse, to the children of the intestate or their lineal descendants, per stirpes;

(B) If there is a spouse and one or more children of the decedent or their lineal descendants surviving, and all of the decedent's children who survive or have lineal descendants surviving also are children of the surviving spouse, then the whole to the surviving spouse;

(C) If there is a spouse and one child of the decedent or the child's lineal descendants surviving and the surviving spouse is not the natural or adoptive parent of the decedent's child, the first twenty thousand dollars plus one-half of the balance of the intestate estate to the spouse and the remainder to the child or the child's lineal descendants, per stirpes;

(D) If there is a spouse and more than one child or their lineal descendants surviving, the first sixty thousand dollars if the spouse is the natural or adoptive parent of one, but not all, of the children, or the first twenty thousand dollars if the spouse is the natural or adoptive parent of none of the children, plus one-third of the balance of the intestate estate to the spouse and the remainder to the children equally, or to the lineal descendants of any deceased child, per stirpes;

(E) If there are no children or their lineal descendants, then the whole to the surviving spouse;

(F) If there is no spouse and no children or their lineal descendants, to the parents of the intestate equally, or to the surviving parent;

(G) If there is no spouse, no children or their lineal descendants, and no parent surviving, to the brothers and sisters, whether of the whole or of the half blood of the intestate, or their lineal descendants, per stirpes;

(H) If there are no brothers or sisters or their lineal descendants, one-half to the paternal grandparents of the intestate equally, or to the survivor of them, and one-half to the maternal grandparents of the intestate equally, or to the survivor of them;

(I) If there is no paternal grandparent or no maternal grandparent, one-half to the lineal descendants of the deceased grandparents, per stirpes; if there are no such lineal descendants, then to the surviving grandparents or their lineal descendants, per stirpes; if there are no surviving grandparents or their lineal descendants, then to the next of kin of the intestate, provided there shall be no representation among such next of kin;

(J) If there are no next of kin, to stepchildren or their lineal descendants, per stirpes;

(K) If there are no stepchildren or their lineal descendants, escheat to the state.

(2000 S 152, eff. 3–22–01; 1986 S 248, eff. 12–17–86; 1976 S 466; 1975 S 145; 128 v 155; 1953 H 1; GC 10503–4)

Uncodified Law

1975 S 145, § 3, eff. 11–28–75, reads: Sections 1 and 2 of this act shall take effect on January 1, 1976, and apply only to estates resulting from deaths that occur on and after that date.

Historical and Statutory Notes

Pre–1953 H 1 Amendments: 116 v 385; 114 v 339

Amendment Note: 2000 S 152 added new division (B); redesignated former divisions (B) through (J) as new divisions (C) through (K); rewrote new division (C); inserted ", but not all," in new division (D). Prior to amendment new division (C), as former division (B) read:

"(B) If there is a spouse and one child or its lineal descendants surviving, the first sixty thousand dollars if the spouse is the natural or adoptive parent of the child, or the first twenty thousand dollars if the spouse is not the natural or adoptive parent of the child, plus one-half of the balance of the intestate estate to the spouse and the remainder to the child or his lineal descendants, per stirpes;"

OSBA Probate and Trust Law Section

1986:

The Probate and Trust Law Section of the Ohio State Bar Association is recommending that Divisions (B) and (C) of Section 2105.06 of the Ohio Revised Code be changed to increase the initial dollar amount to be given to the surviving spouse of a decedent who dies intestate with children or lineal descendants surviving.

Under the current Code, the surviving spouse who is the natural or adoptive parent of one or more of the decedent's surviving children receives the first $30,000 of the estate. This amount is reduced to $10,000 if the surviving spouse is not the natural or adoptive parent of any of the children. It is proposed to change these amounts to $60,000 and $20,000, respectively.

Section 2105.06 was last amended in 1976, and it is believed that the increase is necessary in light of the inflation of the past decade.

Cross References

Antemortem cremation authorizations, authorizing agents, 4717.22
Complaint to establish presumption of death, parties, notice, 2121.02
Election by surviving spouse, 2106.01
Election made by one under disability, 2106.08
Election of surviving spouse to receive mansion house, 2106.10
Election of surviving spouse to take under statute to be made in person, 2106.06
Estate tax, apportionment among interested persons, 2113.86
Estates, release from administration, 2113.03
Method of payment of specific monetary share of surviving spouse, 2106.11
Persons not to benefit from death, complaint to restore rights, 2105.19
Priority of assignment of right of disposition, 2108.81
Probate court's power as guardian, notice to prospective heirs, 2111.50
Public officers and employees, disclosure of sources of income and gifts, 102.022
Transfer of realty by laws of descent, affidavit necessary, 317.22
Uniform Transfer-on-Death Security Registration Act, heirs defined, 1709.01
Will contest, heirs are necessary parties, 2107.73

Library References

Descent and Distribution ⇐20.1, 52 to 67.
Escheat ⇐3.
Westlaw Topic Nos. 124, 152.
C.J.S. Descent and Distribution §§ 23, 60 to 67.
C.J.S. Escheat § 4.

Research References

Encyclopedias

OH Jur. 3d Abandoned, Lost, & Escheated Property § 23, Generally; "Escheat" Defined.
OH Jur. 3d Abandoned, Lost, & Escheated Property § 24, Requirement of Failure or Absence of Persons Legally Entitled to Inherit; State's Interest in Estate.
OH Jur. 3d Abandoned, Lost, & Escheated Property § 25, Property Subject to Escheat.
OH Jur. 3d Conflict of Laws § 44, Rights of Surviving Spouse; Election.
OH Jur. 3d Death § 16, Proceedings; Complaint.
OH Jur. 3d Death § 17, Proceedings; Complaint—Parties.
OH Jur. 3d Decedents' Estates § 11, Descent.
OH Jur. 3d Decedents' Estates § 13, Inheritance.
OH Jur. 3d Decedents' Estates § 15, Descent and Distribution.
OH Jur. 3d Decedents' Estates § 18, Distributive Share.
OH Jur. 3d Decedents' Estates § 24, Next of Kin—as Permitting Representation.
OH Jur. 3d Decedents' Estates § 34, Ohio Laws; Territorial Legislation—the Probate and Revised Codes.
OH Jur. 3d Decedents' Estates § 35, Ohio Laws; Territorial Legislation—Half-And-Half Statute Governing Property of Spouse Which Came from Former Spouse.
OH Jur. 3d Decedents' Estates § 41, Intestacy.
OH Jur. 3d Decedents' Estates § 48, No Distinction Between Real and Personal Property.
OH Jur. 3d Decedents' Estates § 49, Title to Property, and Not Seisin, as Determinative.
OH Jur. 3d Decedents' Estates § 78, Statute of Descent and Distribution and Its Relation to Other Statutes.
OH Jur. 3d Decedents' Estates § 79, Heirs and Next of Kin as Successors Under the Statute of Descent and Distribution.
OH Jur. 3d Decedents' Estates § 82, General Order of Succession; Escheat.
OH Jur. 3d Decedents' Estates § 83, General Order of Succession; Escheat—When Property Escheats.
OH Jur. 3d Decedents' Estates § 85, Effect of Consanguinity or Blood Ties.
OH Jur. 3d Decedents' Estates § 87, Illegitimate Blood Relationship—Ohio Parentage Act.
OH Jur. 3d Decedents' Estates § 88, Distinctions Based Whole and Half Blood.
OH Jur. 3d Decedents' Estates § 89, Importance of Degrees of Kindred, Generally.
OH Jur. 3d Decedents' Estates § 93, Taking by "Representation" Defined.
OH Jur. 3d Decedents' Estates § 96, Taking Per Stirpes and Per Capita Under the Statutes of Descent and Distribution.

OH Jur. 3d Decedents' Estates § 97, Descent When All Descendants Are Equal in Degree of Consanguinity.
OH Jur. 3d Decedents' Estates § 98, Descent When Descendants Are of an Unequal Degree of Consanguinity.
OH Jur. 3d Decedents' Estates § 100, Children of Intestate and Their Descendants; Adopted Children.
OH Jur. 3d Decedents' Estates § 102, Children of Intestate and Their Descendants; Adopted Children—Representation; Taking Per Capita or Per Stirpes.
OH Jur. 3d Decedents' Estates § 103, Parents of Intestate.
OH Jur. 3d Decedents' Estates § 104, Brothers and Sisters of Intestate and Their Descendants.
OH Jur. 3d Decedents' Estates § 105, Nephews and Nieces of Intestate and Their Descendants.
OH Jur. 3d Decedents' Estates § 106, Grandparents of Intestate and Their Descendants.
OH Jur. 3d Decedents' Estates § 107, Grandparents of Intestate and Their Descendants—Rule of Equal Division.
OH Jur. 3d Decedents' Estates § 109, Next of Kin.
OH Jur. 3d Decedents' Estates § 110, Stepchildren of Intestate and Their Descendants.
OH Jur. 3d Decedents' Estates § 116, Under the Statute of Descent and Distribution.
OH Jur. 3d Decedents' Estates § 117, Under the Statute of Descent and Distribution—Rights in Mansion House.
OH Jur. 3d Decedents' Estates § 121, Surviving Spouse as Decedent's Heir; Decedent as Ancestor.
OH Jur. 3d Decedents' Estates § 125, Acts that Will Bar Succession, Generally—Surviving Spouse's Rights.
OH Jur. 3d Decedents' Estates § 138, Nature of Heir's Title; Parcenary.
OH Jur. 3d Decedents' Estates § 142, Title as Complete.
OH Jur. 3d Decedents' Estates § 542, "Next or Nearest of Kin".
OH Jur. 3d Decedents' Estates § 543, "Next or Nearest of Kin"—Surviving Spouse as "Next of Kin".
OH Jur. 3d Decedents' Estates § 613, Shares Taken by Beneficiaries—Gift to Surviving Spouse of Share Provided by Law.
OH Jur. 3d Decedents' Estates § 747, Citation Notice to Surviving Spouse of Right to Election.
OH Jur. 3d Decedents' Estates § 769, Percentage of the Estate Taken.
OH Jur. 3d Decedents' Estates § 770, Percentage of the Estate Taken—Meaning of "Net Estate".
OH Jur. 3d Decedents' Estates § 773, Property in Inter Vivos Trust.
OH Jur. 3d Decedents' Estates § 1519, Purposes Demanded, or Consented To, by Beneficiaries.
OH Jur. 3d Decedents' Estates § 1640, Distribution in Kind—Distribution to Surviving Spouse of Appraised Personal Property in Cases of Intestacy.
OH Jur. 3d Decedents' Estates § 1676, Right to Receive Mansion House as Part of Intestate Share.
OH Jur. 3d Decedents' Estates § 1831, When Administration May be Dispensed With.
OH Jur. 3d Estates, Pwrs., & Restrnts. on Alienat. § 120, Election by Surviving Spouse.
OH Jur. 3d Taxation § 983, Exemption of Spouse's Share.

Forms

Ohio Forms Legal and Business § 24:1, Introduction.
Ohio Forms Legal and Business § 24:4, Wills and Estate Planning.
Ohio Forms Legal and Business § 24:5, Intestate Succession.
Ohio Forms Legal and Business § 28:2, Definitions.
Ohio Forms Legal and Business § 25:53, Irrevocable Trusts—Husband and Wife as Grantors—Income to Children for Life—Remainder to Descendants.
Ohio Forms Legal and Business § 25:62, Trust for Minor Qualifying for Annual Gift Tax Exclusion—Parents as Trustors—"Crummey" Withdrawal Provisions for Benefit of Child.
Ohio Forms Legal and Business § 25:97, Trust Provision for Spouse—Minimum Bequest.
Ohio Forms Legal and Business § 17A:22, General Background.
Ohio Forms Legal and Business § 24:143, Drafting Will.
Ohio Forms Legal and Business § 24:205, Residue to Trust for Spouse and Children.
Ohio Forms Legal and Business § 25:154, Duration of Trust—Life of Trustor.
Ohio Forms and Transactions F 30.21, Alternate or Additional Trust Clauses.
Ohio Forms and Transactions KP 30.02, Bequests and Devises in Will; Disposition of Remainder.
Ohio Forms and Transactions KP 30.04, Common Disaster and Presumed Order of Death.
Ohio Forms and Transactions KP 30.06, Rights of Surviving Spouse.

Treatises and Practice Aids

Sowald & Morganstern, Baldwin's Ohio Practice Domestic Relations Law § 1:5, Terms.
Sowald & Morganstern, Baldwin's Ohio Practice Domestic Relations Law § 4:4, Property Rights During Marriage—Individual Ownership—in General.
Sowald & Morganstern, Baldwin's Ohio Practice Domestic Relations Law § 4:6, Property Rights During Marriage—Individual Ownership—Descent and Distribution.
Sowald & Morganstern, Baldwin's Ohio Practice Domestic Relations Law § 2:73, Cohabitation Agreements—Limitations.
Sowald & Morganstern, Baldwin's Ohio Practice Domestic Relations Law § 3:45, Effect of Judgment—Inheritance.
Sowald & Morganstern, Baldwin's Ohio Practice Domestic Relations Law § 3:38.50, Effect of Judgment--Child Support--Past Care--Claim Brought After Child is Emancipated.
Carlin, Baldwin's Ohio Practice, Merrick-Rippner Probate Law § 2:3, Time for Administration of Decedent's Estate and Payment of Estate Taxes.
Carlin, Baldwin's Ohio Practice, Merrick-Rippner Probate Law § 2:4, Identification of Heirs.
Carlin, Baldwin's Ohio Practice, Merrick-Rippner Probate Law § 9:1, Presumption of Death—Statutory.
Carlin, Baldwin's Ohio Practice, Merrick-Rippner Probate Law § 9:2, Presumption of Death—Procedure for Establishing—Jurisdiction.
Carlin, Baldwin's Ohio Practice, Merrick-Rippner Probate Law § 9:3, Presumption of Death—Procedure for Establishing—Necessary Parties Defendant.
Carlin, Baldwin's Ohio Practice, Merrick-Rippner Probate Law § 9:4, Presumption of Death—Procedure for Establishing—Notice.
Carlin, Baldwin's Ohio Practice, Merrick-Rippner Probate Law § 9:5, Presumption of Death—Procedure for Establishing—Filing Complaint.
Carlin, Baldwin's Ohio Practice, Merrick-Rippner Probate Law § 9:7, Presumption of Death—Effect of Decree.
Carlin, Baldwin's Ohio Practice, Merrick-Rippner Probate Law § 12:7, Wrongful Death—Status of Beneficiaries Fixed at Death of Decedent.
Carlin, Baldwin's Ohio Practice, Merrick-Rippner Probate Law § 12:8, Wrongful Death—Afterborn Beneficiary; Next of Kin.
Carlin, Baldwin's Ohio Practice, Merrick-Rippner Probate Law § 15:2, Descent and Distribution—Definitions.
Carlin, Baldwin's Ohio Practice, Merrick-Rippner Probate Law § 15:6, Descent and Distribution—Surviving Spouse—in General.
Carlin, Baldwin's Ohio Practice, Merrick-Rippner Probate Law § 15:8, Descent and Distribution—Satisfaction of Monetary Share.
Carlin, Baldwin's Ohio Practice, Merrick-Rippner Probate Law § 16:1, Statutory Provisions.
Carlin, Baldwin's Ohio Practice, Merrick-Rippner Probate Law § 18:2, Inheritance Rights of Illegitimate Child—Statutory Provisions.
Carlin, Baldwin's Ohio Practice, Merrick-Rippner Probate Law § 18:3, Inheritance Rights of Illegitimate Child—Case Law Affecting Rules of Inheritance Generally.
Carlin, Baldwin's Ohio Practice, Merrick-Rippner Probate Law § 18:4, Inheritance Rights of Illegitimate Child—Affinity.
Carlin, Baldwin's Ohio Practice, Merrick-Rippner Probate Law § 18:6, Inheritance Rights of Illegitimate Child—Will.
Carlin, Baldwin's Ohio Practice, Merrick-Rippner Probate Law § 19:2, Legitimation—Procedure—Acknowledgment of Paternity.
Carlin, Baldwin's Ohio Practice, Merrick-Rippner Probate Law § 19:3, Legitimation—Constitutional Issues.
Carlin, Baldwin's Ohio Practice, Merrick-Rippner Probate Law § 19:6, Uniform Parentage Act—Jurisdiction of Action to Determine Father-Child Relationship.
Carlin, Baldwin's Ohio Practice, Merrick-Rippner Probate Law § 2:35, Elective Rights of Surviving Spouse—Election to Take Under Law or Under the Will—Issuance of Citation.
Carlin, Baldwin's Ohio Practice, Merrick-Rippner Probate Law § 2:36, Elective Rights of Surviving Spouse—Election to Take Under Law or Under the Will—Time for Making Election.

Carlin, Baldwin's Ohio Practice, Merrick-Rippner Probate Law § 2:37, Elective Rights of Surviving Spouse—Election to Take Under Law or Under the Will—Procedure for Making Election.

Carlin, Baldwin's Ohio Practice, Merrick-Rippner Probate Law § 2:39, Elective Rights of Surviving Spouse—Election to Take Under Law or Under the Will—Failure to Make Election Against the Will.

Carlin, Baldwin's Ohio Practice, Merrick-Rippner Probate Law § 2:45, Elective Rights of Surviving Spouse—Election of Surviving Spouse to Receive Property as Part of Intestate Share and Allowance for Support.

Carlin, Baldwin's Ohio Practice, Merrick-Rippner Probate Law § 2:46, Elective Rights of Surviving Spouse—Election of Surviving Spouse to Receive Property—Payment of Specific Monetary Share.

Carlin, Baldwin's Ohio Practice, Merrick-Rippner Probate Law § 20:1, Advancement—Definition.

Carlin, Baldwin's Ohio Practice, Merrick-Rippner Probate Law § 21:2, Rights of Surviving Spouse to Make Election—Statutory Provisions—Generally.

Carlin, Baldwin's Ohio Practice, Merrick-Rippner Probate Law § 21:3, Rights of Surviving Spouse to Make Election—Statutory Provisions—Citation—Issuance—Waiver of Citation.

Carlin, Baldwin's Ohio Practice, Merrick-Rippner Probate Law § 21:4, Rights of Surviving Spouse to Make Election—Statutory Provisions—Citation—Service.

Carlin, Baldwin's Ohio Practice, Merrick-Rippner Probate Law § 21:5, Rights of Surviving Spouse to Make Election—Statutory Provisions—Effect.

Carlin, Baldwin's Ohio Practice, Merrick-Rippner Probate Law § 21:6, Rights of Surviving Spouse to Make Election—Statutory Provisions—Acceleration of Remainder.

Carlin, Baldwin's Ohio Practice, Merrick-Rippner Probate Law § 21:8, Rights of Surviving Spouse to Make Election—Statutory Provisions—Manner and Time—Time Within Which to Make Election.

Carlin, Baldwin's Ohio Practice, Merrick-Rippner Probate Law § 21:9, Rights of Surviving Spouse to Make Election—Statutory Provisions—Manner and Time—Extension of Time for Election.

Carlin, Baldwin's Ohio Practice, Merrick-Rippner Probate Law § 22:5, Necessity for Conviction; Common Law Forfeiture.

Carlin, Baldwin's Ohio Practice, Merrick-Rippner Probate Law § 24:2, Escheat—Scope of Statutes.

Carlin, Baldwin's Ohio Practice, Merrick-Rippner Probate Law § 24:3, Escheat—Operation.

Carlin, Baldwin's Ohio Practice, Merrick-Rippner Probate Law § 24:4, Escheat—Interest of State.

Carlin, Baldwin's Ohio Practice, Merrick-Rippner Probate Law § 30:2, Drafting a Will—General Recommendations—Clarity and Brevity.

Carlin, Baldwin's Ohio Practice, Merrick-Rippner Probate Law § 38:4, Will Contests—Interested Persons.

Carlin, Baldwin's Ohio Practice, Merrick-Rippner Probate Law § 38:6, Will Contests—Capacity to Contest a Will.

Carlin, Baldwin's Ohio Practice, Merrick-Rippner Probate Law § 38:8, Will Contests—Parties to Action—Necessary Parties.

Carlin, Baldwin's Ohio Practice, Merrick-Rippner Probate Law § 46:2, Anti-Lapse Statute—"Relative" as Beneficiary.

Carlin, Baldwin's Ohio Practice, Merrick-Rippner Probate Law § 46:5, Anti-Lapse Statute—Putative Child as Beneficiary.

Carlin, Baldwin's Ohio Practice, Merrick-Rippner Probate Law § 48:8, Property Liable for Payment of Debts—Personal Property—Effect of Spousal Election.

Carlin, Baldwin's Ohio Practice, Merrick-Rippner Probate Law § 77:3, Unclaimed Money—Escheat Distinguished.

Carlin, Baldwin's Ohio Practice, Merrick-Rippner Probate Law § 9:10, Presumption of Death—Entry Setting for Hearing, Ordering Notice, and Service of Summons—Form.

Carlin, Baldwin's Ohio Practice, Merrick-Rippner Probate Law § 90:7, Authority for Land Sale Action—Consent or Demand of Beneficiaries.

Carlin, Baldwin's Ohio Practice, Merrick-Rippner Probate Law § 11:24, Disclaimer With Certificate of Filing—Form.

Carlin, Baldwin's Ohio Practice, Merrick-Rippner Probate Law § 110:6, Elective Share or Intestate Share of Surviving Spouse.

Carlin, Baldwin's Ohio Practice, Merrick-Rippner Probate Law § 12:11, Wrongful Death—Damages—Compensatory.

Carlin, Baldwin's Ohio Practice, Merrick-Rippner Probate Law § 15:10, Descent and Distribution—Rights of Surviving Spouse—Example 1.

Carlin, Baldwin's Ohio Practice, Merrick-Rippner Probate Law § 15:12, Descent and Distribution—Rights of Surviving Spouse—Example 2.

Carlin, Baldwin's Ohio Practice, Merrick-Rippner Probate Law § 15:14, Descent and Distribution—Rights of Surviving Spouse—Example 3.

Carlin, Baldwin's Ohio Practice, Merrick-Rippner Probate Law § 15:16, Descent and Distribution—Rights of Surviving Spouse—Example 4.

Carlin, Baldwin's Ohio Practice, Merrick-Rippner Probate Law § 15:18, Descent and Distribution—Rights of Surviving Spouse—Example 5.

Carlin, Baldwin's Ohio Practice, Merrick-Rippner Probate Law § 15:20, Descent and Distribution—Children or Lineal Descendants—in General.

Carlin, Baldwin's Ohio Practice, Merrick-Rippner Probate Law § 15:23, Descent and Distribution—Children or Lineal Descendants—Per Stirpes—Example 1—Chart.

Carlin, Baldwin's Ohio Practice, Merrick-Rippner Probate Law § 15:27, Descent and Distribution—Child Without Issue Predeceasing Parent.

Carlin, Baldwin's Ohio Practice, Merrick-Rippner Probate Law § 15:30, Descent and Distribution—Child Born Out of Wedlock.

Carlin, Baldwin's Ohio Practice, Merrick-Rippner Probate Law § 15:31, Descent and Distribution—Parents.

Carlin, Baldwin's Ohio Practice, Merrick-Rippner Probate Law § 15:32, Descent and Distribution—Siblings or Their Lineal Descendants.

Carlin, Baldwin's Ohio Practice, Merrick-Rippner Probate Law § 15:33, Descent and Distribution—Grandparents or Their Lineal Descendants.

Carlin, Baldwin's Ohio Practice, Merrick-Rippner Probate Law § 15:39, Descent and Distribution—No Grandparents or Their Lineal Descendants.

Carlin, Baldwin's Ohio Practice, Merrick-Rippner Probate Law § 15:40, Descent and Distribution—No Grandparents or Their Lineal Descendants—Example.

Carlin, Baldwin's Ohio Practice, Merrick-Rippner Probate Law § 15:42, Descent and Distribution—Stepchild.

Carlin, Baldwin's Ohio Practice, Merrick-Rippner Probate Law § 15:43, Descent and Distribution—Escheat.

Carlin, Baldwin's Ohio Practice, Merrick-Rippner Probate Law § 15:44, Descent and Distribution—Equal Degree of Consanguinity.

Carlin, Baldwin's Ohio Practice, Merrick-Rippner Probate Law § 15:45, Descent and Distribution—Equal Degree of Consanguinity—Example 1.

Carlin, Baldwin's Ohio Practice, Merrick-Rippner Probate Law § 15:55, Descent and Distribution—Denial of Inheritance to Parent Who Abandons Minor—Finding of the Court.

Carlin, Baldwin's Ohio Practice, Merrick-Rippner Probate Law § 15:56, Descent and Distribution—Denial of Inheritance to Parent Who Abandons Minor—Statute of Limitations.

Carlin, Baldwin's Ohio Practice, Merrick-Rippner Probate Law § 19:10, Uniform Parentage Act—Procedure in Action to Determine Father-Child Relationship.

Carlin, Baldwin's Ohio Practice, Merrick-Rippner Probate Law § 2:102, Distribution of Assets—to Surviving Spouse Under Intestate succession.

Carlin, Baldwin's Ohio Practice, Merrick-Rippner Probate Law § 2:106, Distribution of Assets—Transfer of Real Estate.

Carlin, Baldwin's Ohio Practice, Merrick-Rippner Probate Law § 2:111, Release from Administration—Election of Surviving Spouse to Receive Mansion House.

Carlin, Baldwin's Ohio Practice, Merrick-Rippner Probate Law § 2:121, Administration of Decedent's Estate—Checklist.

Carlin, Baldwin's Ohio Practice, Merrick-Rippner Probate Law § 2:122, Administration of Decedent's Estate—Release—Checklist.

Carlin, Baldwin's Ohio Practice, Merrick-Rippner Probate Law § 2:123, Client Interview—Checklist.

Carlin, Baldwin's Ohio Practice, Merrick-Rippner Probate Law § 21:17, Rights of Surviving Spouse to Make Election—Commissioner Appointed to Take Election of Spouse.

Carlin, Baldwin's Ohio Practice, Merrick-Rippner Probate Law § 21:18, Rights of Surviving Spouse to Make Election—Duty of Probate Judge.

Carlin, Baldwin's Ohio Practice, Merrick-Rippner Probate Law § 21:19, Rights of Surviving Spouse to Make Election—Effect of Election—Generally.

Carlin, Baldwin's Ohio Practice, Merrick-Rippner Probate Law § 21:20, Rights of Surviving Spouse to Make Election—Acceleration of Remainder.

Carlin, Baldwin's Ohio Practice, Merrick-Rippner Probate Law § 21:22, Rights of Surviving Spouse to Make Election—Share as Intestate Property.

Carlin, Baldwin's Ohio Practice, Merrick-Rippner Probate Law § 21:23, Rights of Surviving Spouse to Make Election—Distribution of Estate.

Carlin, Baldwin's Ohio Practice, Merrick-Rippner Probate Law § 21:25, Rights of Surviving Spouse to Make Election—Effect on Inter Vivos Trust of Election.

Carlin, Baldwin's Ohio Practice, Merrick-Rippner Probate Law § 21:27, Rights of Surviving Spouse to Make Election—Effect of Ancillary Administration on Right of Election.

Carlin, Baldwin's Ohio Practice, Merrick-Rippner Probate Law § 21:32, Rights of Surviving Spouse to Make Election—Election to be Made in Person—Scope of RC 2106.06.

Carlin, Baldwin's Ohio Practice, Merrick-Rippner Probate Law § 21:35, Rights of Surviving Spouse to Make Election—One Under Legal Disability—Scope of RC 2106.08.

Carlin, Baldwin's Ohio Practice, Merrick-Rippner Probate Law § 21:43, Rights of Surviving Spouse to Make All Elections Under RC Chap. 2106—Time Limit.

Carlin, Baldwin's Ohio Practice, Merrick-Rippner Probate Law § 21:44, Rights of Surviving Spouse to Elect to Receive Mansion House—Statutory Right.

Carlin, Baldwin's Ohio Practice, Merrick-Rippner Probate Law § 21:46, Rights of Surviving Spouse to Elect to Receive Mansion House—Procedure—Application for Certificate of Transfer.

Carlin, Baldwin's Ohio Practice, Merrick-Rippner Probate Law § 21:48, Rights of Surviving Spouse to Payment of Specific Monetary Share—Valuation of Monetary Share.

Carlin, Baldwin's Ohio Practice, Merrick-Rippner Probate Law § 21:50, Rights of Surviving Spouse to Payment of Specific Monetary Share—Monetary Share as Charge on Real Estate.

Carlin, Baldwin's Ohio Practice, Merrick-Rippner Probate Law § 21:77, Rights of Surviving Spouse—Right to Receive Motor Vehicles, Boat or Outboard Motor—Automobile or Truck Owned by Decedent.

Carlin, Baldwin's Ohio Practice, Merrick-Rippner Probate Law § 30:17, Drafting a Will—Beneficiary Clauses—Alternate Beneficiary.

Carlin, Baldwin's Ohio Practice, Merrick-Rippner Probate Law § 30:24, Drafting a Will—Surviving Spouse—Election to Take Against the Will.

Carlin, Baldwin's Ohio Practice, Merrick-Rippner Probate Law § 30:30, Drafting a Will—Clauses to Discourage a Will Contest Action—Designation of Heir.

Carlin, Baldwin's Ohio Practice, Merrick-Rippner Probate Law § 30:57, Simple Will—Form.

Carlin, Baldwin's Ohio Practice, Merrick-Rippner Probate Law § 43:10, Construing a Will—Rules of Construction—Guides to Ascertain Testator's Intent.

Carlin, Baldwin's Ohio Practice, Merrick-Rippner Probate Law § 43:15, Construing a Will—Liberal Construction—Charitable Bequests; or Construction Problems.

Carlin, Baldwin's Ohio Practice, Merrick-Rippner Probate Law § 43:40, Construing a Will—Admissibility of Parol Evidence—Inadmissible Parol Evidence.

Carlin, Baldwin's Ohio Practice, Merrick-Rippner Probate Law § 75:14, Transfer of Automobiles to Surviving Spouse.

Carlin, Baldwin's Ohio Practice, Merrick-Rippner Probate Law § 91:28, Land Sale—Necessary Parties Defendant—Escheated Property.

Carlin, Baldwin's Ohio Practice, Merrick-Rippner Probate Law § 91:46, Complaint for Authority to Sell Real Estate With Consent of Less Than All Interested Persons—Form.

Carlin, Baldwin's Ohio Practice, Merrick-Rippner Probate Law § 91:52, Complaint for Sale of Decedent's Real Estate—Alternate Circumstances—Form.

Carlin, Baldwin's Ohio Practice, Merrick-Rippner Probate Law § 92:18, Dower—Distributive Share in Lieu of Interest.

Carlin, Baldwin's Ohio Practice, Merrick-Rippner Probate Law § 108:20, Juvenile Court—Parentage Act—Jurisdiction and Venue.

Carlin, Baldwin's Ohio Practice, Merrick-Rippner Probate Law § 111:19, Federal Estate Tax—Liability of Fiduciary for Payment.

Carlin, Baldwin's Ohio Practice, Merrick-Rippner Probate Law App B SPF 1.0, Surviving Spouse, Children, Next of Kin, Legatees and Devisees.

Carlin, Baldwin's Ohio Practice, Merrick-Rippner Probate Law App B SPF 4.0, Application for Authority to Administer Estate.

Carlin, Baldwin's Ohio Practice, Merrick-Rippner Probate Law App B SPF 8.0, Citation to Surviving Spouse to Elect Exercise Elective Rights.

Carlin, Baldwin's Ohio Practice, Merrick-Rippner Probate Law App B SPF 1.0A, Surviving Spouse, Next of Kin, Legatees and Devisees (Decedent Dying on or After 5-31-90).

Bogert - the Law of Trusts and Trustees § 171, Disclaimer Statutes.

Ohio Personal Injury Practice § 4:8, Wrongful Death and Survival Claims—Wrongful Death—Damages Available Under the Wrongful Death Statute.

Kuehnle and Levey, Ohio Real Estate Law and Practice § 5:1, General Rules Affecting Intestate Succession.

Kuehnle and Levey, Ohio Real Estate Law and Practice § 5:2, Descent and Distribution.

Kuehnle and Levey, Ohio Real Estate Law and Practice § 6:2, Cotenancies—Coparceny Same as Tenancy in Common.

Kuehnle and Levey, Ohio Real Estate Law and Practice § 6:4, Cotenancies—Tenancy in Common—Favored in Ohio.

Kuehnle and Levey, Ohio Real Estate Law and Practice § 52:3, Statutory Fiduciary Sales—21 Statutory Proceedings.

Kuehnle and Levey, Ohio Real Estate Law and Practice § 52:5, Statutory Fiduciary Sales—Sales With Consent of 50% of All Interested Parties; Where No Person's Interest Exceeds 10%; or When Property Escheats.

Kuehnle and Levey, Ohio Real Estate Law and Practice § 52:12, Statutory Fiduciary Sales—Enjoining Creditors from Levying After Owner's Death.

Hastings, Manoloff, Sheeran, & Stype, Ohio School Law § 39:22, Estate and Inheritance Taxes.

Restatement (2d) of Property, Don. Trans. § 28.2, Class Gift to "Issue" or "Descendants".

Restatement (3d) Property (Wills & Don. Trans.) § 2.2, Intestate Share of Surviving Spouse.

Restatement (3d) Property (Wills & Don. Trans.) § 2.3, Intestate Share of Surviving Descendants.

Law Review and Journal Commentaries

Choice of Law, Jurisdiction, and Judgment Issues in Interstate Adoption Cases, Ralph U. Whitten. 31 Cap U L Rev 803 (2003).

Descent and Distribution: Right of Adopted Child to Inherit Through Its Adoptive Parents, Comment. 7 Ohio St L J 441 (June 1941).

Does Ohio Need Uniform Probate Code Solutions for the Surviving Spouse's Intestate and Forced Share Rights?, David F. Allen. 3 Prob L J Ohio 8 (September/October 1992).

Ghosts from the Grave-Inheriting Through the Predeceased Under Ohio Law. Kevin Purcell, 50 Clev St L Rev 189 (2002-03).

How the Family Fares: A Comparison of the Uniform Probate Code and the Ohio Probate Reform Act, Donald L. Robertson. 37 Ohio St L J 321 (1976).

Illegitimacy and Intestate Succession: White v Randolph, Comment. 41 Ohio St L J 1037 (1980).

The Inheritance Rights (or Lack Thereof) of Legitimated Children in Ohio. Angela G. Carlin, 11 Prob L J Ohio 109 (July/August 2001).

Intestate Succession and Wills: A Comparative Analysis of Article II of the Uniform Probate Code and the Law of Ohio, Earl Curry, Jr. 34 Ohio St L J 114 (1973).

Methods of intestate succession, Herbert E. Ritchie. 14 U Cin L Rev 508 (November 1940).

The Ohio Designated Heir Statute, Albert H. Leyerle. 21 Akron L Rev 391 (Spring 1988).

"Per Stirpes or Per Capita", Charles C. White. 13 U Cin L Rev 298 (March 1939).

Revised Spousal Rights Under Ohio S.B. 95 and Where Is My Grandfather?, James R. Bright and Jeffry L. Weiler. 8 Prob L J Ohio 3 (September/October 1997).

Rights of the Surviving Spouse, Patricia D. Consolo and Jeffrey P. Consolo. 56 Clev B J 52 (December 1984).

Should The Surviving Spouse's Forced Share Be Retained?, J. Thomas Oldham. 38 Case W Res L Rev 223 (1987–88).

Spousal Rights On Death, David F. Allen. 6 Prob L J Ohio 1 (September/October 1995).

Spouse's Intestate Share Increased. David F. Allen, 11 Prob L J Ohio 73 (May/June 2001).

The Use of Will Substitutes to Disinherit the Surviving Spouse, William A. Polster. 13 W Reserve U L Rev 674 (1962).

Notes of Decisions

Changing line of descent 1
Children 2-6
    In general 2
    Adoption 3
    Legitimacy or illegitimacy 4
    Stepchildren 5
    Termination of parental rights, effect 6
Escheat 7
Heirship 8
Legislative intent of section 9
Life estates and remainders 10
Next of kin 11-14
    In general 11
    Paternal and maternal branches 12
    Siblings 13
    Whole and half blood 14
Per stirpes and per capita 15
Property subject to statute of descent and distribution 16
Residue 17
Setoffs 18
Surviving spouse 19-24
    Antenuptial agreements 19
    As intestate 20
    Computation of share 21
    Election to take against will 22
    General rights of surviving spouse 23
    Separation agreements 24
Taxation 25
Title 26

---

1. Changing line of descent

The legislature may change the course of descent during the lifetime of the owner. (See also Pollock v Speidel, 27 OS 86 (1875); Tarrin v Broughton, 8 D Repr 451, 8 B 21 (Hamilton 1882), affirmed by 12 B 264 (1884).) Gilpin v. Williams (Ohio 1874) 25 Ohio St. 283.

The recital of a pecuniary consideration in a deed from an ancestor to an heir cannot be varied or explained for the purpose of changing the line of descent of the property conveyed. Lee v. Fike (Medina 1928) 28 Ohio App. 283, 162 N.E. 682, 6 Ohio Law Abs. 151. Evidence 419(2)

A distributive share cannot be increased or diminished by will. Geiger v. Bitzer (Ohio 1909) 80 Ohio St. 65, 88 N.E. 134, 6 Ohio Law Rep. 661, 17 Am.Ann.Cas. 151.

Statutes of descents operate on all intestate property and the course which it indicates can be changed only by a testamentary disposition. Mathews v. Krisher (Ohio 1899) 59 Ohio St. 562, 41 W.L.B. 202, 53 N.E. 52.

Statutes of descent operate upon all intestate property and the course which they indicate can only be changed by will. Mathews v. Krisher (Ohio 1899) 59 Ohio St. 562, 41 W.L.B. 202, 53 N.E. 52.

The line of descent is not broken by partition. Carter v. Day (Ohio 1898) 59 Ohio St. 96, 40 W.L.B. 365, 51 N.E. 967, 69 Am.St.Rep. 757.

2. Children—In general

Where a child dies before its parent, a husband or wife relict of such child does not inherit from the parent. Lane v. McKinstry (Ohio 1877) 31 Ohio St. 640.

The child's estate, as between the brothers and sisters of its father and mother, belonged to the mother and legal representatives of the child. Pence v. Pence's Adm'r (Ohio 1860) 11 Ohio St. 290.

As joint tenancies with the common law incidents do not exist in Ohio, and as there is no substantial difference between coparceners and tenants in common, where lands descend to all children of a deceased equally, even the technical distinction between them may be considered abolished. Tabler v. Wiseman (Ohio 1853) 2 Ohio St. 207.

Children of intestate waived claim that trial court erred in admitting testimony of intestate's putative wife regarding settlement discussions with children, where objection to testimony at trial related to relevancy to issue of existence of common-law marriage. Polly v. Coffey (Ohio App. 12 Dist., Clermont, 02-03-2003) No. CA2002-06-047, 2003-Ohio-509, 2003 WL 231293, Unreported. Descent And Distribution 151

The words "child" or "children" appearing in RC 2105.06, the statute of descent and distribution, means all children, both legitimate and illegitimate. Green v. Woodard (Cuyahoga 1974) 40 Ohio App.2d 101, 318 N.E.2d 397, 69 O.O.2d 130.

The word "children," as it appears in the substitute beneficiary clause of a group life insurance policy, is to be construed to mean all offspring, regardless of whether they are born in or out of wedlock. Butcher v. Pollard (Cuyahoga 1972) 32 Ohio App.2d 1, 288 N.E.2d 204, 62 A.L.R.3d 1316, 61 O.O.2d 1. Insurance 3480

A stepbrother's claim is clearly not superior to that of a parent of the decedent under RC 2105.06. Mancino v. Smith (Ohio Prob. 1964) 201 N.E.2d 93, 95 Ohio Law Abs. 51, 30 O.O.2d 282.

The act relating to descents applies to children of a former marriage between the same parties. Blum v. Blum (Ohio 1899) 60 Ohio St. 41, 41 W.L.B. 276, 53 N.E. 493.

Issue of the body includes all whom the law classes an issue of the body. Fugmann v Theobald, 4 D 65, 3 NP 65 (CP 1895).

3. —— Adoption, children

The personal estate of an adopted child, dying intestate, and leaving its natural mother, its adopting parents, and children of the adopting parents surviving it, passes to the natural mother to the exclusion of the adopting parents and their children born in lawful wedlock. Upson v. Noble (Ohio 1880) 35 Ohio St. 655. Adoption 22

The act of April 20, 1854, and of March 29, 1859, gave an adopted heir the legal status of a child of the adopter as to inheriting and tracing descent to or from him. Lathrop v. Young (Ohio 1874) 25 Ohio St. 451.

Twin sisters who live as foster children with a testatrix twenty-eight years and are not related to the testatrix by law through formal adoption or consanguinity are not "interested persons" with standing to contest the will; the very limited and narrow doctrine of "equitable adoption" will not be expanded to encompass the law of inheritance. York v. Nunley (Cuyahoga 1992) 80 Ohio App.3d 697, 610 N.E.2d 576.

The provisions of RC 3107.13 preclude an adopted child who has again been adopted subsequent to the deaths of both the first adopting parents and prior to the death of an ancestor of a first adopting parent from inheriting under the statute of descent and distribution through the first adopting parent from the first adopting parent's ancestor who died subsequent to the second adoption. Evans v. Freter (Tuscarawas 1969) 20 Ohio App.2d 8, 251 N.E.2d 513, 49 O.O.2d 4.

The natural mother and adoptive father of a decedent are entitled to share equally in his estate. Mancino v. Smith (Ohio Prob. 1964) 201 N.E.2d 93, 95 Ohio Law Abs. 51, 30 O.O.2d 282.

Even if it were shown that adopting mother had perpetrated a fraud by adopting child and using such child's estate for child's support, thus neglecting principal duty of a parent to support his child, such situation would not be enough to invalidate an otherwise legal adoption or change the plan provided under the laws of descent and distribution for the descent and distribution of adopted child's property. Vodrey v. Quigley (Ohio Prob. 1956) 139 N.E.2d 108, 74 Ohio Law Abs. 29, affirmed 143 N.E.2d 162, 75 Ohio Law Abs. 65. Adoption 14; Adoption 23

That an adopting parent perpetrated a fraud by adopting a child, and then using such child's estate for its support, even if true, would not invalidate the adoption or change the application of the laws of descent and distribution. Vodrey v. Quigley (Ohio Prob. 1956) 139 N.E.2d 108, 74 Ohio Law Abs. 29, affirmed 143 N.E.2d 162, 75 Ohio Law Abs. 65. Adoption 14; Adoption 23

Where a child has been validly adopted, a blood relative is deprived of all rights of intestate succession, regardless of whether the natural parents were alive at the time of such adoption. Vodrey v. Quigley (Ohio Prob. 1956) 139 N.E.2d 108, 74 Ohio Law Abs. 29, affirmed 143 N.E.2d 162, 75 Ohio Law Abs. 65.

RC 3107.13 precludes a legally adopted child from inheriting from her intestate natural parent. In re Millward's Estate (Cuyahoga 1956) 102 Ohio App. 469, 136 N.E.2d 649, 3 O.O.2d 22, appeal dismissed 166 Ohio St. 112, 139 N.E.2d 47, 1 O.O.2d 228, affirmed 166 Ohio St. 243, 141 N.E.2d 462, 2 O.O.2d 61.

Under statute providing that for purposes of inheritance, an adopted child is as if he were natural child of adopting parents and ceases to be treated as child of natural parents for purposes of intestate succession, adopted child ceases to be child of natural parents for every possibility of inheritance, the blood-line is completely severed, and where, after his natural father died and his mother remarried, child was adopted by his step-father, he could not take by intestate succession the property from estate of his natural paternal grandfather. Frantz v. Florence (Ohio Com.Pl. 1954) 131 N.E.2d 630, 72 Ohio Law Abs. 222. Adoption ⇔ 21

An adopted child cannot take under the statute of descent and distribution from a parent of his natural parent. Frantz v. Florence (Ohio Com.Pl. 1954) 131 N.E.2d 630, 72 Ohio Law Abs. 222.

Under this section and GC 10512–19 (Repealed), an adopted child is entitled to inherit not only from an adopting parent, but also through such adopting parent from a deceased sister of the adopting parent. White v. Meyer (Cuyahoga 1940) 66 Ohio App. 549, 37 N.E.2d 546, 33 Ohio Law Abs. 151, 21 O.O. 38.

Where children of a deceased mother have been adopted by their natural grandparents and one of the grandparents dies, such children cannot inherit from their grandmother and adopted mother in a two-fold capacity but take only as children of the adopting grandmother, because in such a situation the smaller interest receivable by them will be merged in the larger, so that the most they can receive is the larger of the two interests. Paul v. Paul (Ohio Prob. 1940) 2 Ohio Supp. 349, 31 Ohio Law Abs. 453, 17 O.O. 392. Adoption ⇔ 21

A grandchild adopted by its grandfather inherits as a child of the grandparents and not as a grandchild. Smith v Carver, OS Unrep 489, 36 B 189 (1896).

A widow is not the next of kin of an adopted child. In re Raspold, 6 NP(NS) 172, 18 D 396 (CP, Cuyahoga 1907).

4. —— Legitimacy or illegitimacy, children

Where a bastard dies before the passage of the act of 1853 "regulating descents and the distribution of estates," but the act takes effect while the estate is in the course of settlement and before any order of distribution is made, such act operates upon the distribution of the bastard's estate, prevents escheat, and entitles the surviving children of the bastard's mother to his estate. Lewis v. Eutsler (Ohio 1854) 4 Ohio St. 354.

Child born out of wedlock was an heir-at-law of deceased father, where parent-child relationship was established under the Parentage Act prior to father's death. Stima v. Armatrout (Ohio App. 3 Dist., Seneca, 10-11-2002) No. 13-02-26, 2002-Ohio-5493, 2002 WL 31268408, Unreported. Children Out-of-wedlock ⇔ 86

Parentage must be determined prior to death of putative father to the extent that parent-child relationship is being established under chapter governing descent and distribution; however, parent-child relationship may be established after death of putative father under chapter governing paternity actions. In re Estate of Hicks (Ohio App. 6 Dist., 09-30-1993) 90 Ohio App.3d 483, 629 N.E.2d 1086. Children Out-of-wedlock ⇔ 33; Children Out-of-wedlock ⇔ 86

Assuming that probate court's finding that woman was intestate's biological child was supported by competent, credible evidence, woman failed to establish that she was "legitimized" in one of recognized manners and thus had no right to intestate's estate; only method by which woman could affirmatively seek relief would have been under Parentage Act which required that parentage action be brought in juvenile court which woman had failed to do. In re Estate of Hicks (Ohio App. 6 Dist., 09-30-1993) 90 Ohio App.3d 483, 629 N.E.2d 1086. Children Out-of-wedlock ⇔ 86

In a wrongful death action against a truck driver and driver's employer involving a collision between the truck driver and a motorist, dismissal is proper on the basis that the plaintiff could not maintain a wrongful death suit on behalf of an alleged minor child of the motorist where the plaintiff and the motorist were not married, the motorist did not in probate court formally acknowledge the child as his with consent of the mother, and the motorist did not designate the child as his heir-at-law, adopt the child, or make provision for the child in his will, and, although a parentage action was brought by the plaintiff and her son, the action was brought after the death of the motorist; thus, as a matter of law, the child cannot inherit from the decedent's estate, including any recovery from the wrongful death action. Hunter–Martin v. Winchester Transp., Inc. (Shelby 1991) 71 Ohio App.3d 273, 593 N.E.2d 383, motion overruled 62 Ohio St.3d 1408, 577 N.E.2d 361.

A child born out of wedlock may establish paternity for purposes of descent and distribution through genetic testing and the probate court may permit disinterment in order to effect such testing. Alexander v. Alexander (Ohio Prob. 1988) 42 Ohio Misc.2d 30, 537 N.E.2d 1310. Children Out-of-wedlock ⇔ 86; Dead Bodies ⇔ 5

Proceedings under former parentage statute R.C. §3111.17, resulting in determination that decedent was "reputed" father of child, were sufficient to establish father-child relationship for purposes of descent and distribution statute R.C. §2105.06, and thus, child had standing to contest will of decedent. Beck v. Jolliff (Knox 1984) 22 Ohio App.3d 84, 489 N.E.2d 825, 22 O.B.R. 237. Children Out-of-wedlock ⇔ 86; Wills ⇔ 229

The children who are entitled to inherit under RC 2105.06 include children born out of wedlock if parentage has been established pursuant to RC Ch 3111. Beck v. Jolliff (Knox 1984) 22 Ohio App.3d 84, 489 N.E.2d 825, 22 O.B.R. 237.

An illegitimate child cannot inherit from or through his natural father unless the father takes some steps during his lifetime to permit such inheritance, such as acknowledgment pursuant to RC 2105.18, designating the illegitimate as an heir pursuant to RC 2105.15, adopting the illegitimate, or providing for the illegitimate in his will. Moore v. Dague (Franklin 1975) 46 Ohio App.2d 75, 345 N.E.2d 449, 75 O.O.2d 68. Children Out-of-wedlock ⇔ 86; Children Out-of-wedlock ⇔ 90

There is no invidious discrimination constituting an unconstitutional denial of the equal protection of the law in the application of Ohio law denying to one who is illegitimate any right to inherit from the natural father unless the father has provided for such inheritance. Moore v. Dague (Franklin 1975) 46 Ohio App.2d 75, 345 N.E.2d 449, 75 O.O.2d 68. Children Out-of-wedlock ⇔ 82; Constitutional Law ⇔ 225.5

The word "marriage" in the phrase, "whose marriage is null in law," in RC 2105.18, must be interpreted to mean a de facto marriage, a purported marriage, a marital statute, or an informal marriage, and where such a marriage is entered into in good faith by at least one of the parties and children are afterwards born of that marriage, such children are legitimate, regardless of the reasons for the nullity of the marriage. Santill v. Rossetti (Ohio Com.Pl. 1961) 178 N.E.2d 633, 87 Ohio Law Abs. 400, 18 O.O.2d 109.

An illegitimate child whose mother subsequently marries a man not the child's father is a stepchild of such man for the purpose of determining the descent and distribution of property. Kest v. Lewis (Ohio 1959) 169 Ohio St. 317, 159 N.E.2d 449, 8 O.O.2d 317. Descent And Distribution ⇔ 31

An illegitimate child is considered the stepchild of the husband whom the mother subsequently marries and who is not the father of the child, and such child may inherit from such husband. Kest v. State (Ohio Prob. 1957) 146 N.E.2d 755, 77 Ohio Law Abs. 193, 4 O.O.2d 250. Children Out-of-wedlock ⇔ 1

Presumption that children born during lawful wedlock are legitimate holds good, notwithstanding question of heirship is involved. Harris v. Seabury (Fayette 1928) 30 Ohio App. 42, 164 N.E. 121. Children Out-of-wedlock ⇔ 3; Descent And Distribution ⇔ 71(4)

Although a child may be the biological offspring of a deceased, unless the child is legitimized by one of the methods allowed: intermarriage of father to mother, will, adoption, acknowledgement of paternity (RC 2105.18), designation of heir at law (RC 2105.15), or by a parentage action to determine the father and child relationship (RC 3111.04), the child has no right to inherit from the father under RC 2105.06. In re Estate of Hicks, No. E–92–73, 1993 WL 381571 (6th Dist Ct App, Erie, 9–30–93).

5. —— Stepchildren, children

A person who does not have a direct pecuniary interest in a ward's estate, although he is the ward's stepson, is not an "interested person" within the meaning of RC 2109.33 and as such has no standing to except to an accounting where the ward's will specifically excludes the "exceptor" from participation in her testamentary estate. In re Guardianship of Dougherty (Montgomery 1989) 63 Ohio App.3d 289, 578 N.E.2d 832, dismissed, jurisdictional motion overruled 45 Ohio St.3d 713, 545 N.E.2d 901.

By the repeal of GC 8576 and the enactment of this section in its place, the legislature intended that stepchildren shall inherit irrespective of the dissolution of the marriage by divorce, and such stepchildren are entitled to notice of probate of will. In re McGraff's Estate (Ohio Prob. 1948) 83 N.E.2d 427, 54 Ohio Law Abs. 336, 38 O.O. 187.

6. —— Termination of parental rights, effect, children

Termination of parental rights does not divest children of rights to inheritance from their mother until such time as the children have been legally adopted where (1) the mother loses custody of her children after an auto accident which leaves her mentally and physically disabled, (2) the mother dies while the appeal of custody is pending, (3) a lawsuit arising out of the accident is settled leaving a substantial sum of money with the estate, and (4) the administratrix files a complaint in probate court to determine heirship pursuant to RC 2123.02. Pledgure v. Goutras (Ohio App. 5 Dist., Stark, 04-03-2000) No. 2000CA00035, 2000 WL 492578, Unreported.

7. Escheat

The 1862 amendment of section three of the act regulating descents enlarges the class of persons entitled to the estate before it can escheat. Lathrop v. Young (Ohio 1874) 25 Ohio St. 451.

Law of escheat must not be applied cavalierly but must be the last resort in the construction of a will based on an unquestionable determination that there are no next of kin. Estate of Parks v. Hodge (Cuyahoga 1993) 87 Ohio App.3d 831, 623 N.E.2d 227. Escheat ⇐ 4

The specific mandate of RC 2105.06 et seq., governing escheats of property to the state, must be strictly followed to create a valid finding and judgment by the probate court of the escheat of property to the state where a decedent leaves no heirs, and to be valid, such judgment of escheat must be that there are no heirs, not that "to the knowledge of plaintiff there are no known next of kin." Borovskaya v. State (Wood 1977) 54 Ohio App.2d 79, 375 N.E.2d 57, 8 O.O.3d 132.

Where there is a living heir of a decedent, even though he may be unknown to the administrator at the time of administration of the estate, the state takes no title to the personal property of the estate by escheat. Borovskaya v. State (Wood 1977) 54 Ohio App.2d 79, 375 N.E.2d 57, 8 O.O.3d 132. Escheat ⇐ 4

There is no authority for escheating property to the state, where there is no finding of an absence of heirs. Maurer v. Mihalyne (Stark 1957) 105 Ohio App. 83, 151 N.E.2d 383, 5 O.O.2d 367.

Where United States war savings bonds, purchased by a husband out of his separate funds, are issued to the purchaser and his wife as co-owners and upon the death of the husband pass to the wife as surviving co-owner under the provisions of the bonds and the regulations of the United States treasury department, the descent of such bonds upon the death of the wife is not governed by the so-called half-and-half statute, but such bonds descend in accordance with the statute of descent and distribution, and where the wife dies intestate leaving no heirs or next of kin, such bonds escheat to the state of Ohio. Lambert v. Lambert (Montgomery 1953) 95 Ohio App. 187, 118 N.E.2d 545, 53 O.O. 128.

8. Heirship

If a husband leaves no descendants, his surviving widow is heir of the nonancestral property. Weston v. Weston (Ohio 1882) 38 Ohio St. 473, 8 W.L.B. 301.

Under the law of 1853 the relation of ancestor and heir could not arise between husband and wife. Birney v. Wilson (Ohio 1860) 11 Ohio St. 426.

Admission of putative common-law wife's testimony regarding settlement discussions with children of husband after he died intestate was not plain error, in action by wife to determine heirship, where outcome of trial would not clearly have been otherwise had testimony been excluded. Polly v. Coffey (Ohio App. 12 Dist., Clermont, 02-03-2003) No. CA2002-06-047, 2003-Ohio-509, 2003 WL 231293, Unreported. Descent And Distribution ⇐ 151

Wrongful death statute does not incorporate "heirship" into its provisions; in fact, beneficiaries may include relatives who would not be eligible to inherit under statute of descent and distribution. Brookbank v. Gray (Ohio, 01-17-1996) 74 Ohio St.3d 279, 658 N.E.2d 724, 1996-Ohio-135. Death ⇐ 32

While the term "heirs," as used in a will, is flexible, the technical meaning of an heir is any person who would "take the estate of an intestate under the statute of descent and distribution." Varns v. Varns (Wayne 1991) 81 Ohio App.3d 26, 610 N.E.2d 440, motion overruled 62 Ohio St.3d 1447, 579 N.E.2d 491. Wills ⇐ 506(2)

The term "heir" may be used in a will to include only blood relatives or children. Varns v. Varns (Wayne 1991) 81 Ohio App.3d 26, 610 N.E.2d 440, motion overruled 62 Ohio St.3d 1447, 579 N.E.2d 491.

The surviving spouse is an heir for the purposes of inheritance, is subject to and has all the rights of an heir, and the special relationship of wife or husband neither enlarges nor detracts from this status as an heir or gives special preference by virtue of being a surviving spouse. In re Morgan's Estate (Ohio Prob. 1962) 185 N.E.2d 822, 89 Ohio Law Abs. 225.

In an action in the probate court for a determination of heirship where the state of the record makes it impossible to intelligently determine the heirs entitled to the estate, time should be given for additional testimony and evidence pertinent to the issue of relationship, and "letters rogatory" should be issued accordingly; and an application therefore should be allowed, even where the trial court has already rendered an opinion adverse to the applicant, but on which no judgment has been entered. Maurer v. Mihalyne (Stark 1957) 105 Ohio App. 83, 151 N.E.2d 383, 5 O.O.2d 367. Pretrial Procedure ⇐ 122; Descent And Distribution ⇐ 71(7)

In its technical sense the term "heirs" embraces those who take estate of intestate under statute of descent and distribution, and in event such statute designates widow, she takes as heir. Holt v. Miller (Ohio 1938) 133 Ohio St. 418, 14 N.E.2d 409, 11 O.O. 85.

Where lands are inherited by a minor and sold by order of the court and proceeds are invested in various enterprises and finally in ground rent, on the death of the minor, the estate passes to the next of kin of the deceased and not to the heirs at law of the ancestor. McCammon v. Cooper (Ohio 1904) 69 Ohio St. 366, 69 N.E. 658, 1 Ohio Law Rep. 753, 1 Ohio Law Rep. 869.

The word heir, in its technical signification, includes a widow, as a widow may inherit property. Todd v. Todd (Ohio Cir. 1905) 17 Ohio C.D. 224, 6 Ohio C.C.N.S. 105.

A widow is a beneficiary of insurance "to heirs" when her husband leaves brothers and sisters but no children. Jamieson v Knights Templar, 9 D Repr 388, 12 B 272 (Super, Cincinnati 1883).

RC 2105.06 does not apply to a person who dies testate; therefore someone born out of wedlock who contests the will and seeks a petition to determine heirship may not utilize RC Ch 3111 to establish paternity post mortem in order to inherit from the deceased who dies testate without taking any affirmative measures at his disposal to leave an inheritance to the child born out of wedlock. Rushford v Caines, No. 00AP–1072, 2001 WL 310006 (10th Dist Ct App, Franklin, 3–30–01).

"Heirs" is construed to mean distributees of personal property. Young Men's Mutual Life Assn v Pollard, 3 CC 577, 2 CD 333 (Hamilton 1888).

"Heirs" is construed to mean distributees of the decedent's personal estate according to the statute of descent and distribution, and thus the widow is deemed an heir as to the proceeds of her husband's insurance policy. (See also Simpson v Hook, 6 CC 27, 3 CD 333 (Morgan 1891), appeal dismissed by 28 B 207 (1892).) Young Men's Mutual Life Assn v Pollard, 3 CC 577, 2 CD 333 (Hamilton 1888).

9. Legislative intent of section

RS 6195 to RS 6201 furnishes a complete remedy to the next of kin to recover distributive shares in a portion of an estate as to which the testator died intestate by an action in the probate or common pleas court; these courts are empowered by said statutes to bring in all interested parties, settle finally all matters in controversy, render judgment, and award execution where the amount coming to any heir, legatee, widow, or other distributee is uncertain or in dispute, depending on the construction given any devise or bequest, or any other question; a suit in equity against executors to impose a trust on the portion before final settlement will be unsuccessful where it is not proved that the executors are insolvent, their bond is insufficient, or the plaintiffs are in danger of losing their rights. Bowen v. Bowen (Ohio 1882) 38 Ohio St. 426, 8 W.L.B. 251.

A contingent interest of a person not ascertained, or a mere possibility as distinguished from a contingent interest, or the mere expectancy of an heir apparent, cannot be released for the reason that a release must be founded on a right in being, either vested or contingent. (See also Hart v Gregs, 32 OS 502 (1877).) Needles v. Needles (Ohio 1857) 7 Ohio St. 432, 70 Am.Dec. 85.

Debtor on cognovit note held by creditor's estate had no standing to contest the intestate distribution of estate, including the note; debtor was not a beneficiary or creditor of the estate. In re Smart (Ohio App. 9 Dist., Summit, 03-23-2005) No. 22288, 2005-Ohio-1267, 2005 WL 662709, Unreported. Descent And Distribution ⇐ 91(1)

2105.06
Note 9

This section establishes that no distinction is made between descent of real estate and distribution of personal property as to share which those designated in section are to take. Seman v. Seman (Darke 1935) 19 Ohio Law Abs. 600.

While the law disfavors intestate disposition, the law does not prohibit it. Polen v. Baker (Ohio, 08-22-2001) 92 Ohio St.3d 563, 752 N.E.2d 258, 2001-Ohio-1286. Descent And Distribution ⇌ 1

RC 2105.12 is in pari materia with RC 2105.06 and operates as an exception to the general rules of descent and distribution. Washburn v. Scurlock (Jackson 1982) 5 Ohio App.3d 125, 449 N.E.2d 797, 5 O.B.R. 284.

Intestate succession to personal property is governed by the law of deceased owner's domicile. Howard v. Reynolds (Ohio 1972) 30 Ohio St.2d 214, 283 N.E.2d 629, 59 O.O.2d 228.

A legislative enactment repealing, modifying or changing the course of descent and distribution of property and the right to inherit or transmit property is not an unlawful interference with or deprivation of vested rights, and, unless expressly inhibited by constitutional provision, is to be deemed valid. Ostrander v. Preece (Ohio 1935) 129 Ohio St. 625, 196 N.E. 670, 103 A.L.R. 218, 3 O.O. 24, appeal dismissed 56 S.Ct. 151, 296 U.S. 543, 80 L.Ed. 386. Descent And Distribution ⇌ 6

The word "descendant" should be construed to include all those to whom an estate descends, whether in a direct or collateral line from the intestate. Oakley v. Davey (Cuyahoga 1934) 49 Ohio App. 113, 195 N.E. 406, 18 Ohio Law Abs. 524, 1 O.O. 144. Descent And Distribution ⇌ 43

The theory that the word "devise" as used in the statute means only and is limited to gratuitous devise or unconditional devise finds no support in Ohio cases. Drake v. Knouff (Ohio 1930) 121 Ohio St. 535, 170 N.E. 170, 67 A.L.R. 1160.

Former GC 8578 (RC 2105.06), as it existed prior to the amendment of March 12, 1925 (111 v 32), relative to the distribution of funds in the hands of an administrator arising from sale of realty, held not applicable to funds derived from a foreign state which, though vested prior to the amendment, did not reach the administrator's hands in this state until after its passage. Planson v. Scott (Williams 1927) 26 Ohio App. 122, 158 N.E. 588, 5 Ohio Law Abs. 388.

Former GC 8578 (RC 2105.06), as it existed prior to the amendment of March 12, 1925 (111 v 32), relative to the distribution of funds in the hands of an administrator arising from sale of real estate, held not applicable where fund had been declared penalnty by foreign court from which the fund came. Planson v. Scott (Williams 1927) 26 Ohio App. 122, 158 N.E. 588, 5 Ohio Law Abs. 388. Descent And Distribution ⇌ 5

Former GC 8576 did not relate to personal property. Center v. Kramer (Ohio 1925) 112 Ohio St. 269, 147 N.E. 602, 3 Ohio Law Abs. 200, 23 Ohio Law Rep. 126.

The provisions of this section are controlling only "except as otherwise provided by law." Stocker v. Tranter (Ohio Prob. 1934) 31 Ohio N.P.N.S. 467.

The provisions of this section control over the provisions of GC 10503–9 (RC 2105.13), which was found in the old probate code and reenacted into the new probate code. Davey v. Climo (Ohio Com.Pl. 1933) 30 Ohio N.P.N.S. 457.

The term "legal representatives" means lineal descendants. Thomas v Lett, 4 NP 393, 6 D 429 (CP, Delaware 1897).

Amendment operates as an implied repeal of GC 10503–7 (RC 2105.12) to the extent of any irreconcilable inconsistency where the amendment of this section (116 v 385) is so irreconcilably in conflict with GC 10503–7 (RC 2105.12) that the two sections cannot be harmonized in order to effect the purpose of the amendment. Ryan v. Dixon (Ohio Prob. 1938) 2 Ohio Supp. 248, 26 Ohio Law Abs. 450, 12 O.O. 185.

Former GC 8592 (RC 2105.06) is an intestate law, notwithstanding it was enacted as part of the husband and wife act of 1887 (84 v 132); nor is it any the less an intestate law because in certain cases it is dependent for its operation on former GC 10571 (RC 2107.39, RC 2107.41, RC 2107.43), which allows the widow to make an election. In re Lackman's Estate (Ohio Com.Pl. 1927) 26 Ohio NP(NS) 387.

The object of the statute is to change the distribution of moneys remaining in the hands of the guardian which arose from the sale of ancestral real estate. McCammon v Cooper, 1 NP(NS) 154, 12 D 679 (CP, Hamilton 1902).

10. Life estates and remainders

Where a testator makes a devise to his son "for his natural life and then to his heirs" and in another part of the will used the word "heirs" to mean "children," the context shows that "heirs" means children, so that the son takes a life estate with remainder to his children, and not to his heirs generally. Bunnell v. Evans (Ohio 1875) 26 Ohio St. 409. Reversions ⇌ 1; Wills ⇌ 614(6.1)

Nonancestral lands of an intestate who died leaving no descendants, but left a wife and brothers, go to the wife for life and at her death to the brothers. Jenks v. Langdon (Ohio 1871) 21 Ohio St. 362.

Where a testator devised to his son for life with a remainder to his grandchildren, the grandchildren's interest vested on the death of the testator, and the interest of a grandchild who died intestate during the life of the life tenant passed under the law of descent and distribution. Hoppes v. American Nat. Red Cross (Ohio Com.Pl. 1955) 128 N.E.2d 851, 71 Ohio Law Abs. 259.

Where testator wills part of his estate to another, directing that she shall receive therefrom stipulated sum annually for and during her natural life and further provides that after her death the unconsumed portion shall be paid to "my heirs, share and share alike," the remainder in such portion of estate as may be unconsumed by life beneficiary vests at testator's death in such person or persons as then answer description of testator's heirs under the statute of descent and distribution in force at such time, unless a contrary design on the part of the testator is plainly apparent. Ohio Nat. Bank of Columbus v. Boone (Ohio 1942) 139 Ohio St. 361, 40 N.E.2d 149, 144 A.L.R. 1150, 22 O.O. 414.

Remainder, where only a life estate is devised, passes as a vested estate and upon the death of a daughter intestate and without issue that share would pass to her husband for life with remainder in the heirs of the deceased ancestor. Groppengeiser v. Walter (Ohio Cir. 1900) 10 Ohio C.D. 673.

Where a testator devises a life estate in land and makes no provision for the remainder, such remainder passes to his heirs under the statute of descent as a vested estate and not as a mere expectancy or as contingent upon them outliving the life tenant. Groppengeiser v. Walter (Ohio Cir. 1900) 10 Ohio C.D. 673.

11. Next of kin—In general

Trial court's determination in probate proceeding that there were no next of kin and that the residual estate escheated to the state was arbitrary and capricious; rejection of birth and death certificates on ground that it was "entirely possible" that individuals in question were only relatives by marriage and not blood relatives had no basis, but was based on speculation or conjecture; moreover, court could not find that affidavit was insufficient to establish relationship to decedent without stating its reason for rejecting affidavit. Estate of Parks v. Hodge (Cuyahoga 1993) 87 Ohio App.3d 831, 623 N.E.2d 227. Escheat ⇌ 4

A paternity adjudication under RC Ch 3111 has the effect of res judicata on the determination of next of kin under the descent and distribution statute, RC 2105.06. In re Estate of River, No. 1386 (4th Dist Ct App, Ross, 12–23–87).

12. —— Paternal and maternal branches, next of kin

Property left to an individual who thereafter dies intestate, unmarried, and without issue ascends to the parents of the individual. Baker v. McGrew (Ohio 1884) 41 Ohio St. 113.

Where a first will is determined to be invalid as to disposition or in toto descendents of the deceased's maternal and paternal grandparents who may be able to inherit as lineal descendents pursuant to RC 2105.06(H) have an interest in and are necessary parties to a will contest action. In re Peachley (Ohio App. 9 Dist., Summit, 04-26-2000) No. 19697, No. 19788, 2000 WL 487732, Unreported.

Before it is required that an estate be divided into equal halves and descend to the heirs of both branches of the family, at least one grandparent must survive, or not surviving must leave lineal descendants; where both do not survive and both do not leave lineal descendants there is no division of the estate and the entire estate goes to the next of kin without representation. Vodrey v. Quigley (Ohio Prob. 1956) 139 N.E.2d 108, 74 Ohio Law Abs. 29, affirmed 143 N.E.2d 162, 75 Ohio Law Abs. 65.

Under the statute of descent and distribution uncles and aunt on the maternal side take the entire estate as lineal descendants of the maternal grandparents in preference to first cousins once removed on the paternal side who are not descendants of the paternal grandparents, but of the paternal great-grandparents, rather than there being an even distribution between both lines. (See also Hunziker v Micklethwaite, 102 App 518, 144 NE(2d) 130 (1956).) In re Kelly's Estate (Ohio 1956) 165 Ohio St. 259, 135 N.E.2d 378, 59 O.O. 354.

Where the heirs of a decedent take under paragraph (H) of this section, half of the estate goes to descendants of the maternal grandparents and half to descendants of the paternal grandparents. Sheeler v. Burkhart (Ohio Prob. 1951) 101 N.E.2d 401, 62 Ohio Law Abs. 356, 45 O.O. 415.

Examination of the seventh and eighth paragraphs of this section shows a manifest intention that an estate should be equally divided in halves and that the half portions are to be distributed or descend separately according to law. Snodgrass v. Bedell (Ohio 1938) 134 Ohio St. 311, 16 N.E.2d 463, 12 O.O. 103.

There is nothing in either section 7 or 8 of this section indicating an intention that an estate should be divided equally between the paternal and maternal branches. (See also Snodgrass v Bedell, 134 OS 311, 16 NE(2d) 463 (1938).) Oakley v. Davey (Cuyahoga 1934) 49 Ohio App. 113, 195 N.E. 406, 18 Ohio Law Abs. 524, 1 O.O. 144.

Words "such one-half" employed by legislature in this section are clear, and section divides the estate in halves, one-half going to the paternal side and one-half going to the maternal side. Ryan v. Dixon (Ohio Prob. 1938) 2 Ohio Supp. 248, 26 Ohio Law Abs. 450, 12 O.O. 185.

Former GC 8574 (RC 2105.06), paragraph 6, is not confined to issue or parents or the issue of parents, and the next of kin, where the decedent left no issue nor parents nor issue of parents, are the descendants of grandparents or great-grandparents as far back as may be necessary to find one of decedent's blood. Champlin v Walsh, 26 CC(NS) 460, 27 CD 534 (Hamilton 1916).

As between the uncles and aunts and the grandmother of an intestate, the uncles and aunts are next of kin, and the grandmother takes nothing. Gildehaus v Schildman, 10 NP(NS) 241, 24 D 626 (CP, Hamilton 1910).

13. —— Siblings, next of kin

Where A devises land to B, his brother, and to C, the wife of B, and C dies without issue during the life of B, her interest in the land will descend to her brothers and sisters, though not of A and not of her husband. Penn v. Cox (Ohio 1847) 16 Ohio 30. Descent And Distribution ⊜ 33

Where land inherited by an infant from his father is sold and converted into money by order of court, upon the death of such infant without issue, the remaining money goes to his half brother's and half sister's, children of his mother by a second marriage. Armstrong v. Miller (Ohio 1833) 6 Ohio 118.

The personal property of an intestate who leaves neither wife nor child passes to his brothers and sisters who survive him and to the legal representatives of those who die before him. Martin v. Martin (Ohio 1897) 56 Ohio St. 333, 37 W.L.B. 326, 46 N.E. 981.

Where the evidence shows that certain persons are brothers and sisters, it will be presumed that they are brothers and sisters of the full blood and legitimate. Ossman v. Schmitz (Ohio Cir. 1903) 14 Ohio C.D. 709, 4 Ohio C.C.N.S. 502. Children Out-of-wedlock ⊜ 3

Brothers and sisters include those of the whole and half blood. Stone v. Doster (Ohio Cir. 1892) 3 Ohio C.D. 637, affirmed in part, reversed in part 50 Ohio St. 495, 30 W.L.B. 344, 35 N.E. 208.

The course of the moiety which passes to the brothers and sisters of a husband or wife is controlled by GC 8574 (RC 2105.06) and passes to the brothers and sisters of the whole blood and, if there are none, then to the brothers and sisters of the half blood. Martin v Falconer, 5 CC 584, 3 CD 286 (Franklin 1891), affirmed sub nom Stembel v Martin, 50 OS 495, 35 NE 208 (1893).

Where the federal government, after paying installments on the proceeds of the war risk insurance of a deceased soldier to the designated beneficiary (mother) until her death, elects to pay the balance to the administrator of the soldier's estate, and where it appears that the soldier died without wife or issue and his father died prior to his mother, the fund in the administrator's hands descends, under the Ohio statutes of descent and distribution in effect at the time, to the brothers and sisters of the whole blood. In re Estate of Lewis, 28 NP(NS) 384 (Prob, Auglaize 1930).

14. —— Whole and half blood, next of kin

Where land inherited by an infant from his father is sold and converted into money by order of court, upon the death of such infant without issue, the remaining money goes to his half brothers and half sisters, children of his mother by a second marriage. Armstrong v. Miller (Ohio 1833) 6 Ohio 118.

Where testator, who died in 1934, provided a life estate for his wife, and that "all of my full blood and all of the half blood relations shall share alike in the remainder, if any," the 1934 law governs, the lineal descendants of the testator's deceased grandparents succeed to the title of the devised real property per stirpes, and not by equal distribution between the paternal and maternal branches, and the terms, "full blood" and "half blood," refer to a common single or couple of ancestors rather than a parent or parents, and the term, "shall share alike," means the full-blood relations of testator share alike with the half-blood relations. Parrett v. Paul (Paulding 1962) 115 Ohio App. 488, 185 N.E.2d 798, 21 O.O.2d 134.

Where an intestate's heirs include first cousins of the whole blood and of the half blood, no distinction is to be made between them for purposes of descent and distribution. Sheeler v. Burkhart (Ohio Prob. 1951) 101 N.E.2d 401, 62 Ohio Law Abs. 356, 45 O.O. 415.

Where decedent's paternal grandmother had been married three times and had left lineal descendants from each marriage, and there are no kin more closely related to decedent, these lineal descendants of all three marriages are entitled to share in estate of decedent since there is no distinction between the blood of the whole and the half blood. Shepard v. Wilson (Hamilton 1938) 61 Ohio App. 191, 22 N.E.2d 568, 28 Ohio Law Abs. 448, 14 O.O. 282. Descent And Distribution ⊜ 41

Brothers and sisters include both those of the half blood and those of the whole blood. (See also Clivers v Sanders, 8 OS 501 (1858); Burdick v Shaw, 8 NP 22, 10 D 533 (CP, Lucas 1899); Stone v Doster, 7 CC 8, 3 CD 637 (Cuyahoga 1892), modified by 50 OS 495, 35 NE 208 (1893).) Stockton v. Frazier (Ohio 1909) 81 Ohio St. 227, 90 N.E. 168, 7 Ohio Law Rep. 507.

Where the evidence shows that certain persons are brothers and sisters, it will be presumed that they are brothers and sisters of the full blood and legitimate. Ossman v. Schmitz (Ohio Cir. 1903) 14 Ohio C.D. 709, 4 Ohio C.C.N.S. 502. Children Out-of-wedlock ⊜ 3

Brothers and sisters include those of the whole and of the half blood. Stone v. Doster (Ohio Cir. 1892) 3 Ohio C.D. 637, affirmed in part, reversed in part 50 Ohio St. 495, 30 W.L.B. 344, 35 N.E. 208.

Next of kin, as used in the sixth paragraph of this section, excludes the half blood. Lyon v Lyon, 1 CC(NS) 246, 14 CD 498 (Morrow 1902).

The course of the moiety which passes to the brothers and sisters of a husband or wife is controlled by GC 8574 (RC 2105.06) and passes to the brothers and sisters of the whole blood and, if there are none, then to the brothers and sisters of the half blood. Martin v Falconer, 5 CC 584, 3 CD 286 (Franklin 1891), affirmed sub nom Stembel v Martin, 50 OS 495, 35 NE 208 (1893).

15. Per stirpes and per capita

As there are no words providing for the principle of representation in the clause giving the estate to the next of kin, the doctrine does apply, and the children of members of a class who have died prior to the death of the ancestor do not take as representatives of such next of kin. Clayton v. Drake (Ohio 1867) 17 Ohio St. 367.

Inheritance per stirpes prevails in Ohio, not per capita. Ewers v. Follin (Ohio 1859) 9 Ohio St. 327.

Words "except as otherwise provided by law," have reference to other legislative enactments, and in GC 10503-7 (RC 2105.12) contrary provision for distribution is given, which under this set of facts passes property to heirs per capita and not per stirpes. Morrow v. Morrow (Shelby 1934) 18 Ohio Law Abs. 235.

Where a testator in his will makes a bequest to his daughter or her heirs per stirpes, the term "heirs" refers only to the daughter's children and not her surviving spouse where the testator specifically includes a bequest to another son-in-law and was aware of his daughter's death when he executed two separate codicils but did not specifically provide for her surviving spouse. Varns v. Varns (Wayne 1991) 81 Ohio App.3d 26, 610 N.E.2d 440, motion overruled 62 Ohio St.3d 1447, 579 N.E.2d 491.

The legal term "per stirpes" does not designate who will share in an estate but expresses the manner in which the estate will be divided among those who do share. Varns v. Varns (Wayne 1991) 81 Ohio App.3d 26, 610 N.E.2d 440, motion overruled 62 Ohio St.3d 1447, 579 N.E.2d 491. Wills ⊜ 531(1)

Where intestate died leaving no spouse, no children or their lineal descendants, and no surviving parent and was preceded in death by two brothers, one of whom left one child and one of whom left two children surviving at time of death of intestate, children of such deceased brothers,

Note 15

being in equal degree of consanguinity to intestate, inherited per capita. Washburn v. Scurlock (Jackson 1982) 5 Ohio App.3d 125, 449 N.E.2d 797, 5 O.B.R. 284. Descent And Distribution ⇔ 43

Where testator, who died in 1934, provided a life estate for his wife, and that "all of my full blood and all of the half blood relations shall share alike in the remainder, if any," the 1934 law governs, the lineal descendants of the testator's deceased grandparents succeed to the title of the devised real property per stirpes, and not by equal distribution between the paternal and maternal branches, and the terms, "full blood" and "half blood," refer to a common single or couple of ancestors rather than a parent or parents, and the term, "shall share alike," means the full-blood relations of testator share alike with the half-blood relations. Parrett v. Paul (Paulding 1962) 115 Ohio App. 488, 185 N.E.2d 798, 21 O.O.2d 134.

Where a testator leaves all or a part of his estate "per stirpes among my heirs at law" and expresses an intent that such heirs are to be determined as of the time of the termination of a testamentary trust and by the statutes of descent and distribution in effect at the time of the execution of the will, and where, at the time of the termination of the trust, such statutes identify testator's nieces and nephews as composing the nearest generation of the testator's heirs at law having living members, that generation is to be considered the roots or stirpes of the per stirpes gift. Kraemer v. Hook (Ohio 1958) 168 Ohio St. 221, 152 N.E.2d 430, 6 O.O.2d 11.

Under GC 10503–5 (RC 2105.10) cousins of a decedent are entitled, by provisions of this section, to take the share their parents would have taken had they survived, although uncles and aunts of intestate are also living. Ritter v. Ritter (Hamilton 1939) 62 Ohio App. 488, 24 N.E.2d 603, 28 Ohio Law Abs. 393, 14 O.O. 375.

Where those entitled to share in an estate are nieces, nephews, grandnieces and grandnephews of the intestate, the nieces and nephews take equally, per capita, according to the total number of nieces and nephews whether surviving or not, and the grandnieces and grandnephews take per stirpes or by representation the shares of their deceased parents. Kincaid v. Cronin (Hamilton 1939) 61 Ohio App. 300, 22 N.E.2d 576, 28 Ohio Law Abs. 475, 15 O.O. 198.

The words "per stirpes," as used in paragraph 8 of this section, modify the word "descendants" and not the words "grandparent or grandparents;" and in construing bequests to the "descendants" of named persons who are dead, the roots are not the named persons, but the descendants, then in being, nearest in consanguinity to the named persons; thus this section designates the descendants as the roots, the term "of such grandparent or grandparents" being descriptive only, and passes the estate not to the grandparents, but to their lineal descendants, as a class, with the right of representation. Oakley v. Davey (Cuyahoga 1934) 49 Ohio App. 113, 195 N.E. 406, 18 Ohio Law Abs. 524, 1 O.O. 144.

According to the general rules of interpreting statutes of descent and distribution, descendants of the nearest degree of consanguinity, however remote, take in their own right such shares as would come to them if all the descendants of the same degree with the testator were living, and those of a more remote degree take per stirpes, or by representation, the shares of their deceased ancestors of the degree of consanguinity represented by living members. Oakley v. Davey (Cuyahoga 1934) 49 Ohio App. 113, 195 N.E. 406, 18 Ohio Law Abs. 524, 1 O.O. 144.

Children of a predeceased brother take in a representative character and subject to the indebtedness of their principal to the intestate. Martin v. Martin (Ohio 1897) 56 Ohio St. 333, 37 W.L.B. 326, 46 N.E. 981.

Under the provisions of GC 10503–4 (RC 2105.06), 10503–7 (RC 2105.12), 10503–8 (RC 2105.13) and 10503–9 (RC 2105.13), which must be read in pari materia, nephews and nieces of a decedent who left no other next nearer of kin surviving, take per capita, and the descendants of deceased nephews and nieces take per stirpes. Stocker v. Tranter (Ohio Prob. 1934) 31 Ohio N.P.N.S. 467.

D died on January 18, 1932, leaving no surviving spouse nor children, he never having married, and never having had any brothers or sisters, his parents having predeceased him, and all of his paternal and maternal grandparents having predeceased him; he had had seven uncles and aunts on the maternal side, six of whom predeceased him, but who left issue, and he had one uncle on the paternal side who predeceased him but left issue; decedent's will contained the following language: "All the residue of my estate shall be distributed to the persons entitled thereto under the laws of descent and distribution of the state of Ohio in effect at the time of my decease;" held: the paternal grandparents on the one side, the maternal grandparents on the other, are the stirpes or root, and that one-half of decedent's estate goes to the lineal descendants of the paternal grandparents and the other one-half goes to the lineal descendants of the maternal grandparents, all of whom take per stirpes. Davey v. Climo (Ohio Com.Pl. 1933) 30 Ohio N.P.N.S. 457.

A will directing that "all the residue of my estate shall be equally divided share and share alike among my legal heirs according to law" requires a per capita distribution among all the testator's heirs, regardless of the degree of kinship. Jameson v. Glenny (Ohio Com.Pl. 1910) 20 Ohio Dec. 353, 10 Ohio N.P.N.S. 168. Wills ⇔ 531(2)

Where a decedent's only surviving lineal descendants are nephews and nieces together with a grandnephew, son of a deceased nephew, a court errs in ordering a per stirpes distribution based on the decedent's brothers and sisters, the nephews' and nieces', as all are of equal consanguinity with the exception of the grandnephew who takes per stirpes as representative of his deceased father. In re Estate of Huffman, No. 1844 (4th Dist Ct App, Scioto, 10–19–90).

GC 10503–7 (RC 2105.12) and the case law thereunder is controlled by the special provisions contained in this section; hence, where there are no grandparents, the lineal descendants of such grandparents take per stirpes and not per capita, the grandparents being the stock or root. Shearer v Gasstman, 31 NP(NS) 219, 15 Abs 103 (Prob, Franklin 1933).

16. Property subject to statute of descent and distribution

This section governs the distribution of personal property on failure of a charitable bequest because it was not made a year before the decease. Patton v. Patton (Ohio 1883) 39 Ohio St. 590.

Acquisition of real property whether by descent or devise is governed by the law of the place where the property is situated. Jones v. Robinson (Ohio 1867) 17 Ohio St. 171.

Where a husband died leaving lands which descended to his posthumous child, leaving a widow and surviving brothers and sisters, and the lands are sold by order of the court to pay debts and dower is assigned and before distribution the child died without lineal heir, the father's estate is, under the act of 1840, realty, but the child's estate is personalty. Pence v. Pence's Adm'r (Ohio 1860) 11 Ohio St. 290.

Distributees of the personal estate of an intestate cannot join in an action against the administrators for their distributive share. Waldsmith's Heirs v. Waldsmith's Adm'rs (Ohio 1825) 2 Ohio 156. Executors And Administrators ⇔ 438(1); Parties ⇔ 14

The claims of distributees of a personal estate are separate and not joint. Waldsmith's Heirs v. Waldsmith's Adm'rs (Ohio 1825) 2 Ohio 156.

Where, during her lifetime, a widow transferred title to bonds, received from her deceased husband, to treasurer of political subdivision issuing them, agreeing to accept refunding bonds therefor, such refunding bonds having been delivered after her death to administrator of her estate, pass to her next of kin, under provisions of this section, the contract right to refunding bonds not being the "identical" property coming from deceased husband within meaning of GC 10503–5 (RC 2105.10). Speidel v. Schaller (Clermont 1943) 73 Ohio App. 141, 55 N.E.2d 346, 40 Ohio Law Abs. 190, 28 O.O. 252.

An accommodation note, held by a privately and solely owned bank, does not devolve upon the heirs of the owner of such bank by descent upon the death of such owner; such heirs do not have even a beneficial interest in such note or its proceeds and a transfer of such note by the heirs does not invest the transferee with any title to such note. Charpiot v. State ex rel. Scott (Ohio 1928) 119 Ohio St. 66, 162 N.E. 277, 6 Ohio Law Abs. 384, 26 Ohio Law Rep. 519.

Under section 303 of the World War Veterans Act, approved March 4, 1925, if the designated beneficiary survives the insured and dies prior to receiving all the installments of war risk insurance payable, the present value of the insurance thereafter payable must be paid to the estate of the insured soldier and, in case of his intestacy, distributed according to the law of descent and distribution in force at the date of the soldier's death. Palmer v. Mitchell (Ohio 1927) 117 Ohio St. 87, 158 N.E. 187, 55 A.L.R. 566, 5 Ohio Law Abs. 401, 25 Ohio Law Rep. 378.

When a mortgagor dies in possession of goods, interest of the mortgagee is transferred to a fund arising from a sale by the administrator. Lingler v. Wesco (Ohio 1908) 79 Ohio St. 225, 86 N.E. 1004, 128 Am.St.Rep. 714, 6 Ohio Law Rep. 572.

Ground rent will descend according to this section. McCammon v. Cooper (Ohio 1904) 69 Ohio St. 366, 69 N.E. 658, 1 Ohio Law Rep. 753, 1 Ohio Law Rep. 869.

Ground rent is not within the purview of this section. McCammon v. Cooper (Ohio 1904) 69 Ohio St. 366, 69 N.E. 658, 1 Ohio Law Rep. 753, 1 Ohio Law Rep. 869.

The rule that the course of descent of real estate follows legal title does not apply to personal property. Bruer v. Johnson (Ohio 1901) 64 Ohio St. 7, 45 W.L.B. 153, 59 N.E. 741.

Where an owner of ancestral lands conveys them to a third person to hinder and delay a creditor, and the third person conveys them to his widow after the grantor's death without issue, the brother and sister of the grantor cannot maintain an action against the grantee's widow to compel a conveyance of the lands to them; they stand in the shoes of the grantor who had no rights in the land because of his fraud. Kihlken v. Kihlken (Ohio 1898) 59 Ohio St. 106, 40 W.L.B. 361, 51 N.E. 969. Descent And Distribution ⇨ 90(1); Fraudulent Conveyances ⇨ 174(3)

The wrongful taking of land by a railroad company for a right of way does not divest the title of the owner and reduce his remedy to a mere claim for compensation and damages; at the owner's death, the title to the land with the right of recovery descends to his heirs and not to his administrator. Lawrence R. Co. v. O'Harra (Ohio 1893) 50 Ohio St. 667, 36 N.E. 14.

Money received from oil during the lifetime of decedent is not identical with the land from which it came and is to be distributed after her death. Digby v. Digby (Ohio Cir. 1903) 16 Ohio C.D. 417, 5 Ohio C.C.N.S. 130.

Real property purchased with partnership funds and used for partnership purposes is thereby converted into personalty and so continues after the death of one of the partners until a complete settlement of partnership business. Fisher v Lang, 10 D Repr 178, 19 B 139 (Super, Cincinnati 1887). Conversion ⇨ 3; Partnership ⇨ 246

Where a husband and wife die intestate and without issue seized of nonancestral estate, it descends under this section. Stembel v Martin, 50 OS 495, 35 NE 208 (1893).

Real estate devised in trust loses its ancestral quality upon sale and reinvestment in other realty, and upon the death of the trustee's son, the cestui que trust, the legal and equitable estate merges in and descends as nonancestral estate to the trustee. Renick v Renick, 6 NP(NS) 304, 18 D 308 (CP, Franklin 1907).

17. Residue

A residuary bequest, invalid under the mortmain statute, will be distributed as intestate property. Newman v. Newman (Ohio Prob. 1964) 199 N.E.2d 904, 94 Ohio Law Abs. 321, 28 O.O.2d 154.

In the absence of a residuary clause, the residue descends as intestate property. Wilson v. Hall (Ohio Cir. 1892) 3 Ohio C.D. 589, affirmed 53 Ohio St. 679, 44 N.E. 1137.

18. Setoffs

Nieces and nephews of an intestate decedent are subject to having a debt of their father, who predeceased the decedent, set off against their distributive share, when decedent has a brother and sister still living. Gruhler v. Hossapaus (Ohio Prob. 1963) 195 N.E.2d 387, 93 Ohio Law Abs. 71, 28 O.O.2d 477.

Payments made by an insured decedent on policy assigned by him to the payee of the note, but which under this section inured to the benefit of insured's estate, cannot be set off against the note. Claypool v. Claypool (Ohio Cir. 1903) 15 Ohio C.D. 327, 4 Ohio C.C.(N.S.) 577, affirmed 75 Ohio St. 578, 80 N.E. 1125, 4 Ohio Law Rep. 479.

19. Surviving spouse—Antenuptial agreements

An antenuptial agreement voluntarily signed by a party after disclosure of the value of assets brought to the marriage is enforceable upon the death of the spouse although the agreement provides that the spouse expressly waives any right to share in the decedent's estate where the provisions provide that each party retains its premarital assets and waives rights to share in the other's estate. Sasarak v. Sasarak (Cuyahoga 1990) 66 Ohio App.3d 744, 586 N.E.2d 172.

An antenuptial contract must be voluntarily entered into and the provisions for the wife must be fair and reasonable under all the surrounding facts and circumstances; and an adult man and woman, each owning a substantial amount of property and each having grown children by prior marriages, may lawfully enter a pre-nuptial agreement whereby each relinquishes every and all rights in the property of the other. Osborn v. Osborn (Ohio Com.Pl. 1966) 10 Ohio Misc. 171, 226 N.E.2d 814, 39 O.O.2d 275, affirmed 18 Ohio St.2d 144, 248 N.E.2d 191, 47 O.O.2d 310.

Where an antenuptial agreement is silent as to the right of the spouse to take against the will, such antenuptial agreement does not bar the surviving spouse from electing to take against the will of the deceased spouse. In re Estate of Mowery, No. 10813 (9th Dist Ct App, Summit, 12–8–82).

20. —— As intestate, surviving spouse

Where a will provides for a gift over to "my heirs-at-law," the ordinary and legal meaning of the request is that the property pass as if the testator had died intestate; such being the case, the testator's wife takes the property rather than his brothers and sisters. Weston v. Weston (Ohio 1882) 38 Ohio St. 473, 8 W.L.B. 301.

An estate which came to the intestate from her deceased husband does not pass to those of the blood of the husband who are not of kin of the intestate. Brower v. Hunt (Ohio 1868) 18 Ohio St. 311.

Election for incompetent surviving spouse to take against deceased spouse's will, under which surviving spouse took nothing, and receive intestate share was necessary for surviving spouse's future support, as statutorily required for election against will, and thus was not abuse of discretion, inasmuch as surviving spouse, who relied solely on Medicaid benefits for care and support, had legal interest in and ability to use or dispose of her intestate share of deceased spouse's estate under right to take against will, and failure to avail herself of such potential income would render her ineligible for benefits under state Medicaid eligibility requirements. In re Estate of Cross (Ohio, 06-05-1996) 75 Ohio St.3d 530, 664 N.E.2d 905, 1996-Ohio-196. Wills ⇨ 788

Where, during her lifetime, a widow transferred title to bonds, received from her deceased husband, to treasurer of political subdivision issuing them, agreeing to accept refunding bonds therefor, such refunding bonds having been delivered after her death to administrator of her estate, pass to her next of kin, under provisions of this section, the contract right to refunding bonds not being the "identical" property coming from deceased husband within meaning of GC 10503–5 (RC 2105.10). Speidel v. Schaller (Clermont 1943) 73 Ohio App. 141, 55 N.E.2d 346, 40 Ohio Law Abs. 190, 28 O.O. 252.

Real estate which has been purchased and paid for solely by a wife, and title thereto taken jointly with her husband but he having thereafter immediately conveyed his interest to her, passes, upon wife's death intestate after her husband's decease, to her next of kin, under this section. Speidel v. Schaller (Clermont 1943) 73 Ohio App. 141, 55 N.E.2d 346, 40 Ohio Law Abs. 190, 28 O.O. 252.

Property exempt from administration of husband's estate and the year's allowance to the widow constitute a debt against the deceased's estate and on the widow's dying intestate such assets pass according to this section and are not affected by GC 10503–5 (RC 2105.10). Russell v. Roberts (Athens 1936) 54 Ohio App. 441, 7 N.E.2d 811, 23 Ohio Law Abs. 435, 8 O.O. 196.

Upon the death of a relict seized of nonancestral property, it descends one-half to brothers and sisters of the whole blood of the deceased husband or wife or their representatives; if not, then to those of the half blood and their representatives and the other half to the brothers and sisters of the deceased relict. Stembel v Martin, 50 OS 495, 35 NE 208 (1893).

Estate descends to the heirs of a wife relict. Ellis v Ellis, 3 CC 186, 2 CD 105 (Logan 1888).

Where a husband dies without issue, or brothers and sisters, but leaving uncles and cousins, on his wife's death intestate without issue leaving brothers or sisters, the estate of the husband which passed to the wife goes to her brothers and sisters. Ellis v Ellis, 3 CC 186, 2 CD 105 (Logan 1888).

21. —— Computation of share, surviving spouse

Where testator died leaving no children or their lineal descendants and no surviving parent or parents and testator's wife elected to take under the statute instead of under the will, by virtue of such election under GC 10504–55 (RC 2107.39), wife was entitled to one-half of testator's estate and by virtue of this section she was entitled to the whole of the remaining one-half of said estate as surviving spouse. (See also Shearn v Shearn, 60 App 317, 21 NE(2d) 133 (1937).) Goodfellow v. Wilson (Clark 1940) 32 Ohio Law Abs. 569.

Probate court or any other court cannot determine distributive share of widow until final distribution, share of widow must be based on this section as construed by GC 10504–55 (RC 2107.39). In re Balliett's Estate (Richland 1934) 18 Ohio Law Abs. 41.

The first $30,000 which a surviving spouse is to receive pursuant to statute of descent and distribution is a distribution which is to be made from the net estate rather than a charge against and deduction from the gross estate. Winkelfoos v. Mann (Huron 1984) 16 Ohio App.3d 266, 475 N.E.2d 509, 16 O.B.R. 291. Wills ⟵ 801(5.1)

In computing the share of a surviving spouse who elects to take against the will of the deceased spouse, the "first $30,000" referred to in RC 2105.06(C) is a deduction from the net estate and is therefore charged against the maximum one-third of the net estate which the surviving spouse can receive. Winkelfoos v. Mann (Huron 1984) 16 Ohio App.3d 266, 475 N.E.2d 509, 16 O.B.R. 291.

The value of an automobile taken under RC 2113.532 shall not be considered an asset of the estate in computing a surviving spouse's interest under RC 2105.06. In re Green's Estate (Ohio Com.Pl. 1980) 63 Ohio Misc. 44, 410 N.E.2d 812, 17 O.O.3d 388.

The value of the statutory allowance taken under RC 2117.20 shall be deducted from the gross estate prior to computing a surviving spouse's interest under RC 2105.06. In re Green's Estate (Ohio Com.Pl. 1980) 63 Ohio Misc. 44, 410 N.E.2d 812, 17 O.O.3d 388. Wills ⟵ 801(4)

Under will which devises "to my husband... amount that he is allowed under laws of Ohio in my estate," and then bequeaths all residue to testatrix' sisters and nieces, husband, upon electing to take thereunder, would take that part allowed by law alone and not dependent in any way upon testatrix' bounty, i.e., twenty per cent of estate, not less than $500 and not exceeding $2500, and right to reside in mansion house for one year free of charge; should husband elect to take under law he would be entitled to one-half of estate in addition to above. Schardt v. Prexler (Hamilton 1946) 67 N.E.2d 549, 45 Ohio Law Abs. 119. Wills ⟵ 800

Where a will devises realty to a child of testator on condition the devisee pay certain expenses, directs that all other debts be paid out of remaining assets, that executor convert into money remainder of estate, and that upon payment of debts executor "shall out of said fund first pay to my wife... what law allows her as my wife," and that other children shall take residue, the one-third interest of widow, under this section, is to be computed by adding appraised value of specifically devised realty to amount of cash remaining after having converted remainder of estate into money and after having deducted therefrom the debts, funeral expenses, costs of administration, allowance to widow for a year's support and the twenty per cent allowance under GC 10509-54 (RC 2115.13). In re Thoroman's Estate (Montgomery 1945) 76 Ohio App. 309, 62 N.E.2d 530, 43 Ohio Law Abs. 259, 32 O.O. 16.

Where testatrix by will devises one-half of her real estate to her spouse for life, remainder to be sold and proceeds divided among devisees, and other half to a devisee in fee, surviving spouse, electing not to take under the will and there being no surviving children or parents of deceased, does not take the whole estate under provisions of this section, but is limited to one-half the net estate under terms of GC 10504-55 (RC 2107.39). (See also Goodfellow v Wilson, 32 Abs 569 (1940).) Shearn v. Shearn (Coshocton 1937) 60 Ohio App. 317, 21 N.E.2d 133, 14 O.O. 262. Wills ⟵ 801(3)

A widow or widower is not entitled to interest on the distributive share in the personalty. Hutchings v. Davis (Ohio 1903) 68 Ohio St. 160, 48 W.L.B. 526, 67 N.E. 251, 1 Ohio Law Rep. 203.

22. —— Election to take against will, surviving spouse

RC 2106.08 provides guidelines for use by the suitable person and the court in determining adequate support needs of a surviving spouse, taking into consideration other available resources, age, probable life expectancy, physical and mental condition, and present and reasonably anticipated future needs of the surviving spouse who is under legal disability so that the end result of the court's judgment should be identical to that of the surviving spouse had she been competent to do her own reasoning; where a surviving spouse is seventy-nine years of age with Alzheimer's disease, unable to conduct her own affairs, and in a nursing home where all expenses are paid by medicaid, a probate court has before it the basis to consider the statutory guidelines under RC 2106.08, and properly determines that such surviving spouse would have chosen to take under the will as the cost of her care in the nursing home was covered, rendering it unnecessary and not in her interest to take against her husband's will. In re Estate of Cross (Ohio App. 8 Dist., Cuyahoga, 02-23-1995) No. 66503, 1995 WL 79792, Unreported, appeal allowed 73 Ohio St.3d 1413, 651 N.E.2d 1310, reversed 75 Ohio St.3d 530, 664 N.E.2d 905, 1996-Ohio-196.

Contestants in a will contest action who reach agreement with fewer than all the legatees do not necessarily hold both under and against a will. Krischbaum v. Dillon (Ohio 1991) 58 Ohio St.3d 58, 567 N.E.2d 1291.

Where a widow elects to take under the Ohio statute of descent and distribution, the amount of the federal estate tax on the decedent's estate should be deducted therefrom before computing the widow's share thereof.

Weeks v. Vandeveer (Ohio 1968) 13 Ohio St.2d 15, 233 N.E.2d 502, 42 O.O.2d 25. Wills ⟵ 801(7)

The presence or absence of a tax provision in the will of a testator does not alter the statutory share of a surviving spouse electing to take against the will. Weeks v. Vandeveer (Ohio 1968) 13 Ohio St.2d 15, 233 N.E.2d 502, 42 O.O.2d 25. Wills ⟵ 801(7)

Where an authenticated copy of a will, executed and proved according to the laws of the state of the decedent's domicile, has been admitted to record pursuant to RC 2129.05, and where it is not established that the widow who was domiciled in that state had claimed anything under that will or otherwise elected to take thereunder and where the testator owned real estate in Ohio at his death, such widow has the right, with respect to that Ohio real estate, to elect not to take under the testator's will but to take under the Ohio statute of descent and distribution, even though no such election is permitted by the law of the state of the testator's domicile at death. Pfau v. Moseley (Ohio 1966) 9 Ohio St.2d 13, 222 N.E.2d 639, 38 O.O.2d 8. Wills ⟵ 778

If a surviving spouse remains alive and competent and, within nine months after the appointment of the first fiduciary charged with the administration of the estate under the will of the deceased spouse, no citation is issued and served upon him to elect whether to take under the will or under RC 2105.06, and within such nine-month period he also fails voluntarily so to elect, he will be conclusively presumed to have elected to take under the will, regardless of whether or not the inventory, appraisement and schedule of debts are filed. (Ed. note: But see RC 2107.39, which under amendment 1975 S 145, eff. 1-1-76, requires the probate court to send citation to elect, suggesting that the basis for this decision may now be eroded.) In re Witteman's Estate (Ohio 1965) 3 Ohio St.2d 66, 209 N.E.2d 427, 32 O.O.2d 49.

Where a deceased husband, by his will, made a specific bequest of a certain number of shares of stock in a corporation for the creation of a trust for the benefit of one of his employees, and where the remaining portion of his estate is sufficient, after the payment of all debts and other obligations, to provide his relict, who elected not to take under the will, with the share of his net estate to which she is entitled under RC 2105.06, the relict's share of the net estate is an undivided fractional interest in the real estate plus such additional amount of personal property not specifically bequeathed under the will, either in kind or in money, as shall make her total share of the net estate that amount to which she is entitled under the provisions of the statute. Winters Nat. Bank & Trust Co. v. Riffe (Ohio 1965) 2 Ohio St.2d 72, 206 N.E.2d 212, 31 O.O.2d 56.

A surviving spouse may file her election prior to filing of the inventory and appraisement if she waives her right not to elect until said inventory is filed. (Ed. note: But compare share under this section and RC 2107.39, both as amended 1975 S 145, eff. 1-1-76.) In re Rogers' Estate (Ohio Prob. 1959) 160 N.E.2d 442, 81 Ohio Law Abs. 10, 10 O.O.2d 205.

In the absence of a showing that the testator intended that the effect of an election of a surviving spouse to take against the will should be borne to the contrary, when the election results in the executor being deprived of property, or interests in property, to such extent and in such manner that the property, or interests in property, remaining available for distribution to different classes of legatees named in different items of the will would, if so distributed, cause the reduction resulting from said election to be borne equitably, but not necessarily equally or proportionately, between said classes, distribution shall be made accordingly without further adjustment or contribution between the classes. Blackford v. Vermillion (Hancock 1958) 107 Ohio App. 26, 156 N.E.2d 339, 7 O.O.2d 350. Wills ⟵ 802(6)

Where a widow elects to take under the statute of descent and distribution, the amount of the federal estate tax should be deducted before computing the widow's share thereof. (See also Hall v Ball, 162 OS 299, 123 NE(2d) 259 (1954).) Campbell v. Lloyd (Ohio 1954) 162 Ohio St. 203, 122 N.E.2d 695, 55 O.O. 102, certiorari denied 75 S.Ct. 600, 349 U.S. 911, 99 L.Ed. 1246, rehearing denied 75 S.Ct. 870, 349 U.S. 948, 99 L.Ed. 1274.

Where a widow elects to take under the will, a proportionate amount of the federal estate tax must be deducted from the residue before she reserves her specified one half thereof, and the residue must also bear the burden of the tax on a specific legacy to her. Foerster v. Foerster (Ohio Prob. 1954) 122 N.E.2d 314, 71 Ohio Law Abs. 129, 54 O.O. 441.

Where the relict of a deceased husband elects not to take under his will, she takes her share not by way of a distributive share in money, but by way of inheritance as though it came to her from her deceased husband as an intestate under this section, limited by the provision of GC 10504-55 (RC 2107.38). Barlow v. Winters Nat. Bank & Trust Co. (Ohio 1945) 145 Ohio St. 270, 61 N.E.2d 603, 160 A.L.R. 423, 30 O.O. 484. Wills ⟵ 801(3)

Where widow died within time limited for filing election without having made election to take under laws of descent and conclusive presumption that she so elected arose, her estate took only one-half husband's estate. Davis v. Warner (Morrow 1933) 47 Ohio App. 495, 192 N.E. 270, 18 Ohio Law Abs. 26, 40 Ohio Law Rep. 384, error dismissed 127 Ohio St. 597, 190 N.E. 386, 39 Ohio Law Rep. 655. Wills ⬥ 801(3)

Under the equitable doctrine of election, a donee who claims both under and against the will does not thereby either make the election or waive his right to make it. Where a devise of land is rejected by a donee electing to enforce his proprietary right, such devise passes to the disappointed donee to the extent necessary for his compensation. Bebout v. Quick (Ohio 1909) 81 Ohio St. 196, 90 N.E. 162, 7 Ohio Law Rep. 506. Wills ⬥ 792(1)

It is not the policy of the law to permit a widow to make her election to take as heir at law or devisee; she must elect to take as widow or devisee, and she cannot defeat her husband's will by claiming dower in all his real estate and her rights as widow in all his personal property and then claim that she takes as heir the property that her husband devised to her in lieu of dower and her distributive share while neglecting to make a gift over in the event she did not elect to take under the will. Armstrong v. Armstrong (Ohio Cir. 1907) 21 Ohio C.D. 261, 11 Ohio C.C.N.S. 474.

Failure of a widow to take under a will does not make the property intestate. Armstrong v. Armstrong (Ohio Cir. 1907) 21 Ohio C.D. 261, 11 Ohio C.C.N.S. 474.

This section does not permit a widow to elect to take as heir at law or devisee, but only as widow or devisee. Armstrong v. Armstrong (Ohio Cir. 1907) 21 Ohio C.D. 261, 11 Ohio C.C.N.S. 474.

If there are no children, a husband who declines to take under a will takes only as if there were children. Wilson v. Hall (Ohio Cir. 1892) 3 Ohio C.D. 589, affirmed 53 Ohio St. 679, 44 N.E. 1137.

A will is affected only as to the consort refusing to take under it. Wilson v. Hall (Ohio Cir. 1892) 3 Ohio C.D. 589, affirmed 53 Ohio St. 679, 44 N.E. 1137.

If a husband dies without a will, his widow will get a much larger portion of his estate than if he died testate and she elects to take under the law. Moyses v. Neilson (Ohio Com.Pl. 1900) 9 Ohio Dec. 623, 7 Ohio N.P. 607.

A wife's election to take under a will does not bar her claim as heir at law of a part of the husband's estate undisposed of by the will. Alexander v. Mendenhall (Ohio Com.Pl. 1894) 1 Ohio Dec. 655, 32 W.L.B. 173.

Where an antenuptial agreement is silent as to the right of the spouse to take against the will, such antenuptial agreement does not bar the surviving spouse from electing to take against the will of the deceased spouse. In re Estate of Mowery, No. 10813 (9th Dist Ct App, Summit, 12–8–82).

23. —— General rights of surviving spouse, surviving spouse

An order by a probate court that certain funds remaining in the hands of an administratrix "be distributed and paid over to the next of kin and representatives of said intestate according to the provisions of the statute, in that behalf in force at the time of his decease," where the statute referred to gives the whole fund to the widow of the intestate, cannot be construed or held to bar the widow of her right under the statute, although in the same order the heirs and legal representatives of the deceased are described as "the next of kin and distributees." Armstrong v. Grandin (Ohio 1883) 39 Ohio St. 368, 10 W.L.B. 300. Executors And Administrators ⬥ 315.5

Damages recovered for causing death is for the benefit of the widow and next of kin and is distributed as personal property. Weidner v. Rankin (Ohio 1875) 26 Ohio St. 522.

Nonancestral lands of an intestate who died leaving no descendants, but left a wife and brothers, go to the wife for life and at her death to the brothers. Jenks v. Langdon (Ohio 1871) 21 Ohio St. 362.

Where a testator died without issue and willed his estate to his widow and the widow before electing to take under the will died leaving a will, the widow was entitled to the personal estate as next of kin. Gardner v. Gardner's Ex'r (Ohio 1862) 13 Ohio St. 426.

Where a husband took an estate by purchase previous to 1856 and died the same year without descendants, the character in which his wife takes same is determined by the statutes of 1853 and not by the act of 1857. Birney v. Wilson (Ohio 1860) 11 Ohio St. 426.

When an equitable estate is conveyed to a husband and wife, they hold as tenants in common; if either dies, the other takes only a moiety. Wilson v. Fleming (Ohio 1844) 13 Ohio 68.

Medicaid eligibility provisions related to determining eligibility for benefits when one spouse is institutionalized and other spouse is community spouse did not apply when "other spouse" was deceased, for purposes of determining whether institutionalized spouse should elect to take against deceased spouse's will. In re Estate of Cross (Ohio, 06-05-1996) 75 Ohio St.3d 530, 664 N.E.2d 905, 1996-Ohio-196. Health ⬥ 471(5); Wills ⬥ 788

Conviction of surviving spouse of manslaughter in the first degree in connection with his wife's death does not affect his right to inherit his statutory share in her estate under RC 2105.06. Wadsworth v. Siek (Ohio Prob. 1970) 23 Ohio Misc. 112, 254 N.E.2d 738, 50 O.O.2d 507, 52 O.O.2d 147.

On the evidence, settlor retained such control over trust as to render it a mere agency account, and hence wife was entitled to her statutory share thereof on testator's death. Osborn v. Osborn (Ohio Com.Pl. 1966) 10 Ohio Misc. 171, 226 N.E.2d 814, 39 O.O.2d 275, affirmed 18 Ohio St.2d 144, 248 N.E.2d 191, 47 O.O.2d 310.

Where a widow elects to take under the statute of descent and distribution and the applicable portions of that statute provide that "personal property shall be distributed" and any "real estate or inheritance shall descend and pass in parcenary" in part to the surviving spouse, the amount of the federal estate tax on the decedent's estate should be deducted therefrom before computing the widow's share thereof. Campbell v. Lloyd (Ohio 1954) 162 Ohio St. 203, 122 N.E.2d 695, 55 O.O. 102, certiorari denied 75 S.Ct. 600, 349 U.S. 911, 99 L.Ed. 1246, rehearing denied 75 S.Ct. 870, 349 U.S. 948, 99 L.Ed. 1274.

The marital deduction must be deducted from the gross estate before the federal estate tax may be determined, and, after the tax is paid, the widow is entitled on distribution to one-third of the net balance of the estate, which means that the widow must bear her proportionate share of the burden of the whole of the estate tax. (156 OS 475 overruled by Campbell v Lloyd, 162 OS 203, 122 NE(2d) 695 (1954); cert denied 349 US 911, 75 SCt 600, 99 LEd 1246 (1955). See also Foerster v Foerster, 71 Abs 129, 122 NE(2d) 514 (Prob, Franklin 1954).) In re Miller's Estate (Ohio Prob. 1950) 94 N.E.2d 67, 81 Ohio Law Abs. 553, 42 O.O. 325.

Where plaintiff seeks to bring himself within this section, the mere allegation of petition that there was no spouse cannot establish this material fact when a named defendant files answer averring that she is a surviving spouse. Rea v. Fornan (Franklin 1942) 46 N.E.2d 649, 37 Ohio Law Abs. 135, 26 O.O. 485, rehearing denied 46 N.E.2d 664, motion overruled 46 N.E.2d 667, 37 Ohio Law Abs. 407, appeal dismissed 140 Ohio St. 546, 45 N.E.2d 600, 25 O.O. 568, appeal dismissed 141 Ohio St. 476, 48 N.E.2d 1009, 26 O.O. 74, certiorari denied 64 S.Ct. 75, 320 U.S. 774, 88 L.Ed. 464.

A widow is, under the law, entitled to dower in the real estate of her deceased husband and a share of his personal property subject to distribution when he dies intestate or without making provisions for her by will; when provision is made for her by his will she may elect to retain her dower and distributive share and not to take under the will, and when she retains her dower and distributive share, either by election or because no provision is made for her by will, such share is to be ascertained by regarding the husband's estate as if he had died intestate, leaving children, and can be neither increased nor diminished by any of the provisions of the will. The doctrine of equitable conversion in such case can have no application in ascertaining the widow's share. Geiger v. Bitzer (Ohio 1909) 80 Ohio St. 65, 88 N.E. 134, 6 Ohio Law Rep. 661, 17 Am.Ann.Cas. 151. Conversion ⬥ 21(2)

Where a testator directed that all his property should be reduced to realty before distribution, it becomes subject to his widow's distributive share under this section. Hutchings v. Davis (Ohio 1903) 68 Ohio St. 160, 48 W.L.B. 526, 67 N.E. 251, 1 Ohio Law Rep. 203.

Property coming to the husband by purchase is inherited by the wife in fee under this statute. Groves v. Groves (Ohio 1902) 65 Ohio St. 442, 47 W.L.B. 207, 62 N.E. 1044.

A husband and wife living separately under an agreement that neither should claim any interest in the property of the other does not affect their right to inherit from each other. Smith v. Smith (Ohio 1897) 57 Ohio St. 27, 38 W.L.B. 256, 48 N.E. 28.

Where a husband leaves a will in which he disposes of all of his personal estate to others without making any provision for his wife, the widow is not deprived of a distributive share in such property of her deceased husband; he is regarded as dying intestate as to her in that case. Doyle v. Doyle (Ohio 1893) 50 Ohio St. 330, 29 W.L.B. 371, 34 N.E. 166.

Where real estate is devised to a wife for life with no gift over, the reversion of the fee descends to the heirs of the testator; where the wife has not elected to take under the will, she will take the reversion as her husband's heir at law under RS 4159, as well as dower in the lands.

2105.06
Note 23

Armstrong v. Armstrong (Ohio Cir. 1907) 21 Ohio C.D. 261, 11 Ohio C.C.N.S. 474.

With reference to the fee of property devised to a widow for life with a power to sell which has not been exercised, the husband will be held to have died intestate. Armstrong v. Armstrong (Ohio Cir. 1907) 21 Ohio C.D. 261, 11 Ohio C.C.N.S. 474.

Where a contract is entered into by a wife, her husband joining and agreeing to release his contingent right of dower upon execution of deed, and the death of the wife occurs before the contract is carried out, the husband has an interest in the proceeds of the sale as an interest in the personal estate of his deceased wife, and not a dower interest in the property as realty. Swartzel v. Snyder (Ohio Com.Pl. 1927) 26 Ohio N.P.N.S. 449.

A devise to a wife "of that part and interest in my estate, real, personal and mixed which is secured to her as my widow by the laws of distribution of estates of the state of Ohio in cases where wives survive husbands who die intestate," is an incorporation into the will of such laws. Clifford v. Foster (Ohio Com.Pl. 1910) 25 Ohio Dec. 657, 10 Ohio N.P.(N.S.) 446, affirmed 23 Ohio C.D. 429, 14 Ohio C.C.(N.S.) 391, reversed 87 Ohio St. 294, 101 N.E. 269, 10 Ohio Law Rep. 600, Am.Ann.Cas. 1915B, 65. Wills ⟹ 488; Wills ⟹ 525

Land conveyed to a wife by her husband through a trustee descends as land coming by purchase. Sullivan v. Corrigan (Ohio Com.Pl. 1908) 18 Ohio Dec. 832, 6 Ohio N.P.N.S. 606.

Property which came to a relict under this section is nonancestral. Burdick v Shaw, 8 NP 22, 10 D 533 (CP, Lucas 1899).

Husband can give away all his personal estate during his lifetime though done to defeat his wife of any share in his estate. Brodt v. Rannells (Ohio Com.Pl. 1899) 9 Ohio Dec. 503, 7 Ohio N.P. 79.

Where a husband willed a nonancestral estate to his wife on the condition that she did not remarry and that if she did, the estate was to go to his brothers and sisters, the wife takes the life estate provided in the will and the remainder of the estate as sole heir at law. Alexander v. Mendenhall (Ohio Com.Pl. 1894) 1 Ohio Dec. 655, 32 W.L.B. 173.

Where a husband or wife dies intestate and without issue, seized of nonancestral realty or personalty, it descends to the relict of such husband or wife. Stembel v Martin, 50 OS 495, 35 NE 208 (1893).

A widow has no blood relationship to a brother of her husband, and where her husband predeceased such brother she does not share in the estate which he left, which goes to his lineal descendants. Nieding v Buckley, 27 LR 320, 6 Abs 607 (App, Cuyahoga 1928).

When a wife dies leaving a will in which no provision is made for her surviving husband, the estate will be treated to him as if she had died intestate. Coon v DeMoore, 2 CC(NS) 444, 15 CD 776 (Cuyahoga 1903), affirmed sub nom Coon v Coon, 71 OS 537, 74 NE 1134 (1905).

A widow converting personalty inherited from her husband into real estate is seized of the latter as by purchase. Ellis v Ellis, 3 CC 186, 2 CD 105 (Logan 1888).

24. —— Separation agreements, surviving spouse

A divorce obtained in Mexico by a husband who has not acquired a bona fide residence there and without the wife's presence or cooperation cannot be given comity in Ohio and is void ab initio; thus, when the husband dies, the wife is still his surviving spouse for purposes of intestate succession, although the wife has acquiesced in the divorce for twenty-five years by living apart from the husband and countenancing his subsequent remarriage. In re Estate of Newton (Muskingum 1989) 65 Ohio App.3d 286, 583 N.E.2d 1026.

Separation agreement executed by parties prior to husband's death was enforceable against wife, though husband's death had resulted in dismissal of wife's dissolution action, where agreement provided that it was not executed in consideration of divorce and was intended to be binding on parties independently of any dissolution proceeding. In re Estate of Hogrefe (Henry 1986) 30 Ohio App.3d 238, 507 N.E.2d 414, 30 O.B.R. 397. Husband And Wife ⟹ 279(1)

A separation agreement, which includes a specific provision requiring disclosure of the agreement to a court in the event either party initiates an action for divorce, dissolution of marriage, or for alimony only, will be held to survive the death of one of the parties to the agreement and the resulting dismissal of a pending dissolution proceeding; consequently, a covenant within the separation agreement providing that the agreement is a full settlement of the rights of each party in the estate of the other is binding and extinguishes all statutory rights of the surviving spouse where

PROBATE LAWS & RULES ANNOTATED 154

decedent dies intestate. In re Estate of Hogrefe (Henry 1986) 30 Ohio App.3d 238, 507 N.E.2d 414, 30 O.B.R. 397.

25. Taxation

Where a widow elects to take under the Ohio statute of descent and distribution, the amount of the federal estate tax on the decedent's estate should be deducted therefrom before computing the widow's share thereof. Weeks v. Vandeveer (Ohio 1968) 13 Ohio St.2d 15, 233 N.E.2d 502, 42 O.O.2d 25. Wills ⟹ 801(7)

A testator who wants to take advantage of the marital deduction in order to preserve a greater portion of his estate for his family should be permitted to do so, and where he employs a tax clause to accomplish this purpose, it should be held effective even though his widow elects to take against the will, provided, of course, that the language of the tax clause is sufficiently broad to warrant such a construction. Weeks v. Vandeveer (Ohio Prob. 1966) 7 Ohio Misc. 51, 216 N.E.2d 78, 36 O.O.2d 127, reversed 13 Ohio St.2d 15, 233 N.E.2d 502, 42 O.O.2d 25. Internal Revenue ⟹ 4169(3)

Relationship of devisee to decedent is immaterial insofar as it relates to taxability of good will, and mere fact that devisee is widow does not give her exemption from inheritance tax on good will. In re Morgan's Estate (Ohio Prob. 1962) 185 N.E.2d 822, 89 Ohio Law Abs. 225. Taxation ⟹ 3327(1)

Where a widow elects to take under the statute of descent and distribution, the amount of the federal estate tax should be deducted before computing the widow's share thereof. (See also Hall v Ball, 162 OS 299, 123 NE(2d) 259 (1954).) Campbell v. Lloyd (Ohio 1954) 162 Ohio St. 203, 122 N.E.2d 695, 55 O.O. 102, certiorari denied 75 S.Ct. 600, 349 U.S. 911, 99 L.Ed. 1246, rehearing denied 75 S.Ct. 870, 349 U.S. 948, 99 L.Ed. 1274.

Where a widow elects to take under the will, a proportionate amount of the federal estate tax must be deducted from the residue before she reserves her specified one half thereof, and the residue must also bear the burden of the tax on a specific legacy to her. Foerster v. Foerster (Ohio Prob. 1954) 122 N.E.2d 314, 71 Ohio Law Abs. 129, 54 O.O. 441.

The marital deduction must be deducted from the gross estate before the federal estate tax may be determined, and, after the tax is paid, the widow is entitled on distribution to one-third of the net balance of the estate, which means that the widow must bear her proportionate share of the burden of the whole of the estate tax. (156 OS 475 overruled by Campbell v Lloyd, 162 OS 203, 122 NE(2d) 695 (1954); cert denied 349 US 911, 75 SCt 600, 99 LEd 1246 (1955). See also Foerster v Foerster, 71 Abs 129, 122 NE(2d) 514 (Prob, Franklin 1954).) In re Miller's Estate (Ohio Prob. 1950) 94 N.E.2d 67, 81 Ohio Law Abs. 553, 42 O.O. 325.

A renunciation by a surviving wife of her joint interest in bank accounts and stocks held jointly was ineffective where she had signed bank signature cards and indorsed dividend checks, and consequently where she purported to renounce so that two-thirds of the property passed to the children, a gift tax was properly imposed thereon. (See also Krakoff v United States, 431 F(2d) 847, 31 Misc 252 (1970).) Krakoff v. U. S. (C.A.6 (Ohio) 1971) 439 F.2d 1023, 58 O.O.2d 381, 60 O.O.2d 417.

Where a widow has elected, under former GC 10571 (RC 2107.39, RC 2107.41, RC 2107.43), not to take under the will of her husband, she succeeds by virtue of the intestate laws to her distributive share in her husband's personal property, and such succession is taxable under GC 5332 (RC 5731.02). (Ed. note: But compare share under this section and 2107.39, both as amended 1975 S 145, eff. 1–1–76.) In re Lackman's Estate (Ohio Com.Pl. 1927) 26 Ohio NP(NS) 387.

26. Title

The course of descent of real estate is controlled by legal title. (See also Russell v Bruer, 64 OS 1, 59 NE 740 (1901).) Patterson v. Lamson (Ohio 1887) 45 Ohio St. 77, 17 W.L.B. 255, 12 N.E. 531. Descent And Distribution ⟹ 11

The legal title and the legal status determine the rights of the parties when it comes to the matter of descent of property. GC 8577 construed. Digby v. Digby (Ohio Cir. 1903) 16 Ohio C.D. 417, 5 Ohio C.C.N.S. 130.

Descent of real estate is controlled by the legal title. Richardson v Michener, 11 D Repr 830, 30 B 120 (CP, Stark 1893).

2105.061 Descent and distribution of title to real property

Except any real property that a surviving spouse elects to receive under section 2106.10 of the Revised Code, the title to real property in an intestate estate shall descend and pass in parcenary to those persons entitled to it under division (B), (C), or (D) of section 2105.06 of the Revised Code, subject to the monetary charge of the surviving spouse. The administrator or executor shall file an application for a certificate of transfer as provided in section 2113.61 of the Revised Code, and the application shall include a statement of the amount of money that remains due and payable to the surviving spouse as found by the probate court. The certificate of transfer ordered by the probate court shall recite that the title to the real property described in the certificate is subject to the monetary charge in favor of the surviving spouse and shall recite the value in dollars of the charge on the title to the real property included in the certificate.

(2000 S 152, eff. 3–22–01; 1990 H 346, eff. 5–31–90)

Uncodified Law

1990 H 346, § 3, eff. 5–31–90, reads, in part: (A) Sections 1 and 2 of this act shall apply only to the estates of decedents who die on or after the effective date of this act.

Historical and Statutory Notes

Ed. Note: Former 2105.061 repealed by 1980 S 317, eff. 3-23-81; 129 v 545.

Amendment Note: 2000 S 152 inserted "or (D)" in the first sentence; substituted "and the application" for "which"; and made other nonsubstantive changes.

Baldwin's Ohio Legislative Service, 1990 Laws of Ohio, H 346—LSC Analysis, p 5–87

Library References

Descent and Distribution ⚖20.1, 52(1).
Westlaw Topic No. 124.
C.J.S. Descent and Distribution §§ 23, 60 to 62, 64.

Research References

Encyclopedias

OH Jur. 3d Decedents' Estates § 44, Statutory Nonsurvivorship; Simultaneous Death Statute—Present and Former Simultaneous Death Statute Distinguished.
OH Jur. 3d Decedents' Estates § 138, Nature of Heir's Title; Parcenary.
OH Jur. 3d Decedents' Estates § 139, Extent of Heir's Title.
OH Jur. 3d Decedents' Estates § 142, Title as Complete.
OH Jur. 3d Decedents' Estates § 146, Record of Transfer.
OH Jur. 3d Decedents' Estates § 192, Disclaiming or Renouncing Succession to Property—Rescission of Renunciation.
OH Jur. 3d Decedents' Estates § 1640, Distribution in Kind—Distribution to Surviving Spouse of Appraised Personal Property in Cases of Intestacy.

Treatises and Practice Aids

Carlin, Baldwin's Ohio Practice, Merrick-Rippner Probate Law § 15:6, Descent and Distribution—Surviving Spouse—in General.
Carlin, Baldwin's Ohio Practice, Merrick-Rippner Probate Law § 15:8, Descent and Distribution—Satisfaction of Monetary Share.
Carlin, Baldwin's Ohio Practice, Merrick-Rippner Probate Law § 2:102, Distribution of Assets—to Surviving Spouse Under Intestate succession.
Carlin, Baldwin's Ohio Practice, Merrick-Rippner Probate Law § 2:106, Distribution of Assets—Transfer of Real Estate.
Carlin, Baldwin's Ohio Practice, Merrick-Rippner Probate Law § 21:50, Rights of Surviving Spouse to Payment of Specific Monetary Share—Monetary Share as Charge on Real Estate.
Kuehnle and Levey, Ohio Real Estate Law and Practice § 5:2, Descent and Distribution.

ESCHEAT

2105.07 Escheat of personal estate

When, under Chapter 2105. of the Revised Code, personal property escheats to the state, the prosecuting attorney of the county in which letters of administration are granted upon such estate shall collect and pay it over to the county treasurer. Such estate shall be applied exclusively to the support of the common schools of the county in which collected.

(2002 H 242, eff. 5–16–02; 1953 H 1, eff. 10–1–53; GC 10503–24)

Historical and Statutory Notes

Pre–1953 H 1 Amendments: 114 v 344

Amendment Note: 2002 H 242 substituted "Chapter 2105." for "sections 2105.01 to 2105.21, inclusive," in the first sentence.

Cross References

Complaint to establish presumption, parties, notice, 2121.02
County commissioners empowered to receive bequests for education, 307.22

Library References

Escheat ⚖8(1).
Westlaw Topic No. 152.
C.J.S. Escheat §§ 7, 22 to 23.

Research References

Encyclopedias

OH Jur. 3d Abandoned, Lost, & Escheated Property § 27, Personal Property.
OH Jur. 3d Abandoned, Lost, & Escheated Property § 29, Generally; Release of State's Right of Escheat.
OH Jur. 3d Cvl. Servants & Pub. Officers & Employ. § 466, Duties, Generally; Financial Matters.
OH Jur. 3d Decedents' Estates § 83, General Order of Succession; Escheat—When Property Escheats.

Forms

Ohio Forms Legal and Business § 17A:1, Definitions and Distinctions.
Ohio Forms Legal and Business § 17A:22, General Background.

Treatises and Practice Aids

Carlin, Baldwin's Ohio Practice, Merrick-Rippner Probate Law § 24:2, Escheat—Scope of Statutes.
Carlin, Baldwin's Ohio Practice, Merrick-Rippner Probate Law § 24:3, Escheat—Operation.
Carlin, Baldwin's Ohio Practice, Merrick-Rippner Probate Law § 77:3, Unclaimed Money—Escheat Distinguished.
Carlin, Baldwin's Ohio Practice, Merrick-Rippner Probate Law § 15:43, Descent and Distribution—Escheat.
Bogert - the Law of Trusts and Trustees § 529, Death of Sole or Surviving Trustee.
Hastings, Manoloff, Sheeran, & Stype, Ohio School Law § 39:22, Estate and Inheritance Taxes.

Law Review and Journal Commentaries

Escheat, Unclaimed Property, and the Supreme Court, R. Perry Sentell, Jr. 17 W Reserve U L Rev 50 (October 1965).

Notes of Decisions

Collection and distribution of funds   1
Existence of living heirs   3
Recovery by heirs   2

Sovereignty 4

1. Collection and distribution of funds

Escheated property may by legislative act be transferred from one public fund to another or from one to another better entitled to it. Lewis v. Eutsler (Ohio 1854) 4 Ohio St. 354.

The specific mandate of RC 2105.06 et seq., governing escheats of property to the state, must be strictly followed to create a valid finding and judgment by the probate court of the escheat of property to the state where a decedent leaves no heirs, and to be valid, such judgment of escheat must be that there are no heirs, not that "to the knowledge of plaintiff there are no known next of kin." Borovskaya v. State (Wood 1977) 54 Ohio App.2d 79, 375 N.E.2d 57, 8 O.O.3d 132.

Escheat, unclaimed securities distributions, interstate disputes, secondary rule, state of intermediary's incorporation. Delaware v. New York (U.S. 1993) 113 S.Ct. 1550, 507 U.S. 490, 123 L.Ed.2d 211.

Only when property is held in the hands of an administrator of an estate of a person who dies leaving no heirs or next of kin and leaving no stepchildren or their lineal descendants, that the prosecuting attorney of a county is authorized to collect said person's property, on behalf of the state. State ex rel. Rich v. Page (Ohio Com.Pl. 1941) 6 Ohio Supp. 104, 33 Ohio Law Abs. 647, 20 O.O. 155. Escheat ⇐ 4

RC 2105.07 does not indicate which entities should be included as common schools for purposes of distributing escheated funds. Therefore, any reasonable definition of "common schools" may be adopted. OAG 95–031.

In the absence of statutory direction, the county may distribute funds under RC 2105.07 to the support of the common schools of the county in any manner that it determines to be fair and equitable. OAG 95–031.

The provisions of RC 3315.32, repealed by 1985–1986 Ohio Laws, Part I, 1760, 2640, might provide some guidance as to an interpretation of RC 2105.07 that could be considered reasonable. OAG 95–031.

Personal property which, by virtue of former GC 8579 (RC 2105.07), escheats to the state and may be collected by the prosecuting attorney of the county, whether the same be in money or other form; it is the duty of the prosecuting attorney to reduce such property to money and pay over the proceeds to the county treasurer. 1928 OAG 2007.

Moneys paid into the county treasury under former GC 8579 (RC 2105.07) should be apportioned and distributed to the various school districts and parts of districts in the county at the times and in the manner provided for the apportionment and distribution of the levy of two and sixty-five hundredths mills, as provided in GC 7575 (Repealed). 1928 OAG 2007.

2. Recovery by heirs

No statutory or case law exists in Ohio which authorizes a rightful heir to recover escheated funds subsequent to their distribution. Illes v. State (Franklin 1983) 10 Ohio App.3d 111, 460 N.E.2d 707, 10 O.B.R. 135. Escheat ⇐ 8(2)

Where escheated funds were paid directly by an estate's administrator to the county treasurer, who is not proved to be an agent of the state, the court of claims properly dismissed an action against the state to recover such escheated funds for failure to state a claim for which relief can be granted. Illes v. State (Franklin 1983) 10 Ohio App.3d 111, 460 N.E.2d 707, 10 O.B.R. 135.

The court of common pleas has jurisdiction to engraft a trust upon the undistributed proceeds of a soldier's war-risk insurance policy, notwithstanding failure to comply with government regulation in designation of beneficiaries. Duncan v Linton, 27 NP(NS) 244 (CP, Franklin 1928).

3. Existence of living heirs

Where there is a living heir of a decedent, even though he may be unknown to the administrator at the time of administration of the estate, the state takes no title to the personal property of the estate by escheat. Borovskaya v. State (Wood 1977) 54 Ohio App.2d 79, 375 N.E.2d 57, 8 O.O.3d 132. Escheat ⇐ 4

Where a person dies intestate, leaving personal property only, and leaving no spouse relict and no heirs at law or next of kin, but survived by children of the deceased wife of the intestate by a prior marriage of the wife with a husband not the intestate, such personal estate does not pass to such children of the deceased wife under former GC 8576 (RC 2105.06), but passes to and is vested in the state under former GC 8579 (RC 2105.07). Center v. Kramer (Ohio 1925) 112 Ohio St. 269, 147 N.E. 602, 3 Ohio Law Abs. 200, 23 Ohio Law Rep. 126.

4. Sovereignty

The right of the state to escheated funds is an attribute or incident of the state's sovereignty, which, by virtue of RC 2105.07, has been relinquished to the counties. Illes v. State (Franklin 1983) 10 Ohio App.3d 111, 460 N.E.2d 707, 10 O.B.R. 135.

To "escheat" means to revert to the crown or government because of the nonexistence of legal heirs. State ex rel. Rich v. Page (Ohio Com.Pl. 1941) 6 Ohio Supp. 104, 33 Ohio Law Abs. 647, 20 O.O. 155.

2105.08 Application of provisions relating to escheating estates

Chapter 2105. of the Revised Code applies to any escheating estate of which possession has not been taken, or which has not been collected by the proper officers of the state or those acting under their authority. Right or claim of the state thereto is hereby relinquished to the person who would have been entitled thereto had such sections been in force when the intestate died.

(2002 H 242, eff. 5–16–02; 1953 H 1, eff. 10–1–53; GC 10503–25)

Historical and Statutory Notes

Pre–1953 H 1 Amendments: 114 v 344

Amendment Note: 2002 H 242 substituted "Chapter 2105." for "sections 2105.01 to 2105.21, inclusive," and "applies" for "apply" in the first sentence.

Library References

Escheat ⇐1 to 8.
Westlaw Topic No. 152.
C.J.S. Escheat §§ 2 to 23.

Research References

Encyclopedias

OH Jur. 3d Abandoned, Lost, & Escheated Property § 29, Generally; Release of State's Right of Escheat.

Notes of Decisions

Recovery of funds 1
Unknown heir 2

1. Recovery of funds

When an administrator has filed his final account and has made a final distribution of the assets of a decedent's estate by paying the residue of the funds in his hands to the prosecuting attorney as escheated to the state, which funds have been paid into the general fund of the county where they still remain, if it be made to appear to the satisfaction of the probate court that there is a living heir of the decedent, the court may vacate the former order of the court and order the funds paid to the heir. 1934 OAG 2257.

There is no provision of law authorizing the payment of interest by the county treasurer on funds paid to him as escheated but subsequently claimed by an heir. 1934 OAG 2257.

2. Unknown heir

The provisions of former GC 8579 (RC 2105.07) did not cause the title to a decedent's personal property to escheat to the state when there was a living heir at the time of the demise even though he may be unknown to the administrator at the time of the closing of the administration proceedings. 1934 OAG 2257.

2105.09 Disposition of escheated lands; alternate method of sale

(A) The county auditor, unless he acts pursuant to division (C) of this section, shall take possession of real property escheated to the state that is located in his county and outside the incorporated area of a city. The auditor shall take possession in the name of the state and sell the property at public auction, at the county seat of the county, to the highest bidder, after having given thirty days' notice of the intended sale in a newspaper published within the county.

On the application of the auditor, the court of common pleas shall appoint three disinterested freeholders of the county to appraise the real property. The freeholders shall be governed by the same rule as appraisers in sheriffs' or administrators' sales. The auditor shall sell the property at not less than two thirds of its appraised value and may sell it for cash, or for one-third cash and the balance in equal annual payments, the deferred payments to be amply secured. Upon payment of the whole consideration, the auditor shall execute a deed to the purchaser, in the name and on behalf of the state. The proceeds of the sale shall be paid by the auditor to the county treasurer.

If there is a regularly organized agricultural society within the county, the treasurer shall pay the greater of six hundred dollars or five per cent of the proceeds, in any case, to the society. The excess of the proceeds, or the whole thereof if there is no regularly organized agricultural society within the county, shall be distributed as follows:

(1) Twenty-five per cent shall be paid equally to the townships of the county;

(2) Seventy per cent shall be paid into the state treasury to the credit of the agro Ohio fund created under section 901.04 of the Revised Code;

(3) Five per cent shall be credited to the county general fund for such lawful purposes as the board of county commissioners provides.

(B) The legislative authority of a city within which are lands escheated to the state, unless it acts pursuant to division (C) of this section, shall take possession of the lands for the city, and the title to the lands shall vest in the city. The city shall use the premises primarily for health, welfare, or recreational purposes, or may lease them at such prices and for such purposes as it considers proper. With the approval of the tax commissioner, the city may sell the lands or any undivided interest in the lands, in the same manner as is provided in the sale of land not needed for any municipal purposes; provided, that the net proceeds from the rent or sale of the premises shall be devoted to health, welfare, or recreational purposes.

(C) As an alternative to the procedure prescribed in divisions (A) and (B) of this section, the county auditor, or if the real property is located within the incorporated area of a city, the legislative authority of that city by an affirmative vote of at least a majority of its members, may request the probate court to direct the administrator or executor of the estate that contains the escheated property to commence an action in the probate court for authority to sell the real property in the manner provided in Chapter 2127. of the Revised Code. The proceeds from the sale of real property that is located outside the incorporated area of a city shall be distributed by the court in the same manner as the proceeds are distributed under division (A) of this section. The proceeds from the sale of real property that is located within the incorporated area of a city shall be distributed by the court in the same manner as the proceeds are distributed under division (B) of this section.

(1986 H 751, eff. 9–8–86; 1985 H 201; 1983 H 260; 1977 H 42; 1976 H 920, H 1098; 1953 H 1; GC 10503–26 to 10503–29)

Historical and Statutory Notes

Pre–1953 H 1 Amendments: 122 v S 166; 114 v 344, 345

Cross References

Agro Ohio fund, 901.04

Library References

Escheat ⚖8(1).
Westlaw Topic No. 152.
C.J.S. Escheat §§ 7, 22 to 23.

Research References

Encyclopedias

OH Jur. 3d Abandoned, Lost, & Escheated Property § 28, Real Property.

OH Jur. 3d Decedents' Estates § 83, General Order of Succession; Escheat—When Property Escheats.

Treatises and Practice Aids

Carlin, Baldwin's Ohio Practice, Merrick-Rippner Probate Law § 24:2, Escheat—Scope of Statutes.

Carlin, Baldwin's Ohio Practice, Merrick-Rippner Probate Law § 15:43, Descent and Distribution—Escheat.

Carlin, Baldwin's Ohio Practice, Merrick-Rippner Probate Law § 91:28, Land Sale—Necessary Parties Defendant—Escheated Property.

Bogert - the Law of Trusts and Trustees § 529, Death of Sole or Surviving Trustee.

Notes of Decisions

Bastard's estate 1

---

1. Bastard's estate

Where the act of 1853 "regulating descents and distribution of personal estates" was passed during the course of settlement of a bastard's estate, but before distribution, the previous enactment operates upon the distribution of the estate, preventing escheat and entitling the surviving children of the bastard's mother to his estate. Lewis v. Eutsler (Ohio 1854) 4 Ohio St. 354.

INHERITANCE BY DESCENDANTS

2105.10 Inheritance by parent of deceased abandoned child prohibited

(A) As used in this section:

(1) "Abandoned" means that a parent of a minor failed without justifiable cause to communicate with the minor, care for him, and provide for his maintenance or support as required by law or judicial decree for a period of at least one year immediately prior to the date of the death of the minor.

(2) "Minor" means a person who is less than eighteen years of age.

(B) Subject to divisions (C), (D), and (E) of this section, a parent who has abandoned his minor child who subsequently dies intestate as a minor shall not inherit the real or personal property of the deceased child pursuant to section 2105.06 of the Revised Code. If a parent is prohibited by this division from inheriting from his deceased child, the real or personal property of the deceased child shall be distributed, or shall descend and pass in parcenary, pursuant to section 2105.06 of the Revised Code as if the parent had predeceased the deceased child.

(C) Subject to divisions (D) and (E) of this section, a parent who is alleged to have abandoned a child who died as an intestate minor shall be considered as a next of kin or an heir at law of the deceased child only for the following purposes:

(1) To receive any notice required to be given to the heirs at law of a decedent in connection with an application for release of an estate from administration under section 2113.03 of the Revised Code;

(2) To be named as a next of kin in an application for the appointment of a person as the administrator of the estate of the deceased child, if the parent is known to the person filing the application pursuant to section 2113.07 of the Revised Code, and to receive a citation issued by the probate court pursuant to that section.

(D)(1) The prohibition against inheritance set forth in division (B) of this section shall be enforceable only in accordance with a probate court adjudication rendered pursuant to this division.

(2) If the administrator of the estate of an intestate minor has actual knowledge, or reasonable cause to believe, that the minor was abandoned by a parent, the administrator shall file a petition pursuant to section 2123.02 of the Revised Code to obtain an adjudication that the parent abandoned the child and that, because of the prohibition against inheritance set forth in division (B) of this section, the parent shall not be considered to be an heir at law of, and shall not be entitled to inherit the real and personal property of, the deceased child pursuant to section 2105.06 of the Revised Code. That parent shall be named as a defendant in the petition and, whether or not that parent is a resident of this state, shall be served with a summons and a copy of the petition in accordance with the Rules of Civil Procedure. In the heirship determination proceeding, the administrator has the burden of proving, by a preponderance of the evidence, that the parent abandoned the child. If, after the hearing, the probate court finds that the administrator has sustained that burden of proof, the probate court shall include in its adjudication described in section 2123.05 of the Revised Code its findings that the parent abandoned the child and, because of the prohibition against inheritance set forth in division (B) of this section, the parent shall not be considered to be an heir at law of, and shall not be entitled to inherit the real and personal property of, the deceased child pursuant to section 2105.06 of the Revised Code. If the probate court so finds, then, upon the entry of its adjudication on its journal, the administrator may make a final distribution of the estate of the deceased child in accordance with division (B) of this section.

(3) An heirship determination proceeding resulting from the filing of a petition pursuant to this division shall be conducted in accordance with Chapter 2123. of the Revised Code, except to the extent that a provision of this section conflicts with a provision of that chapter, in which case the provision of this section shall control.

(E) If the administrator of the estate of an intestate minor has not commenced an heirship determination proceeding as described in division (D) of this section within four months from the date that he receives his letters of administration, then such a proceeding may not be commenced subsequently, no parent of the deceased child shall be prohibited from inheriting the real or personal property of the deceased child pursuant to division (B) of this section, and the probate of the estate of the deceased child in accordance with section 2105.06 and other relevant sections of the Revised Code shall be forever binding.

(1992 H 166, eff. 8–3–92)

Uncodified Law

1992 H 166, § 3, eff. 8–3–92, reads, in part: The provisions of section 2105.10 of the Revised Code, as enacted by this act, shall apply to all parents of minors who die intestate on or after the effective date of this act, whether or not the abandonment described in that section commenced prior to, on, or after the effective date of this act.

Historical and Statutory Notes

Ed. Note: Former 2105.10 repealed by 1975 S 145, eff. 1–1–76; 1953 H 1; GC 10503–5.

Pre–1953 H 1 Amendments: 119 v 394, § 1; 116 v 385; 114 v 340

Library References

Descent and Distribution ⚖ 30, 49.1.
Westlaw Topic No. 124.
C.J.S. Descent and Distribution §§ 37, 56 to 59.

Research References

Encyclopedias

OH Jur. 3d Decedents' Estates § 11, Descent.
OH Jur. 3d Decedents' Estates § 35, Ohio Laws; Territorial Legislation—Half-And-Half Statute Governing Property of Spouse Which Came from Former Spouse.
OH Jur. 3d Decedents' Estates § 79, Heirs and Next of Kin as Successors Under the Statute of Descent and Distribution.
OH Jur. 3d Decedents' Estates § 136, Abandoning a Minor Child.

Forms

Ohio Forms Legal and Business § 28:81, Introduction.

Treatises and Practice Aids

Carlin, Baldwin's Ohio Practice, Merrick-Rippner Probate Law § 15:51, Descent and Distribution—Denial of Inheritance to Parent Who Abandons Minor—Scope of RC 2105.10.
Carlin, Baldwin's Ohio Practice, Merrick-Rippner Probate Law § 15:52, Descent and Distribution—Denial of Inheritance to Parent Who Abandons Minor—Filing of Petition in Probate Court.
Carlin, Baldwin's Ohio Practice, Merrick-Rippner Probate Law § 15:53, Descent and Distribution—Denial of Inheritance to Parent Who Abandons Minor—Service of Summons.
Carlin, Baldwin's Ohio Practice, Merrick-Rippner Probate Law § 15:54, Descent and Distribution—Denial of Inheritance to Parent Who Abandons Minor—Burden of Proof.
Carlin, Baldwin's Ohio Practice, Merrick-Rippner Probate Law § 15:55, Descent and Distribution—Denial of Inheritance to Parent Who Abandons Minor—Finding of the Court.
Carlin, Baldwin's Ohio Practice, Merrick-Rippner Probate Law § 15:56, Descent and Distribution—Denial of Inheritance to Parent Who Abandons Minor—Statute of Limitations.
Carlin, Baldwin's Ohio Practice, Merrick-Rippner Probate Law § 21:44, Rights of Surviving Spouse to Elect to Receive Mansion House—Statutory Right.
Kuehnle and Levey, Ohio Real Estate Law and Practice § 5:2, Descent and Distribution.
Kuehnle and Levey, Ohio Real Estate Law and Practice § 5:3, The Half-And-Half Statute.
Restatement (3d) Property (Wills & Don. Trans.) § 2.5, Parent and Child Relationship.

Law Review and Journal Commentaries

Ghosts from the Grave-Inheriting Through the Predeceased Under Ohio Law. Kevin Purcell, 50 Clev St L Rev 189 (2002-03).

2105.11 Estate to descend equally to children of intestate

When a person dies intestate leaving children and none of the children of such intestate have died leaving children or their lineal descendants, such estate shall descend to the children of such intestate, living at the time of his death, in equal proportions.

(1953 H 1, eff. 10–1–53; GC 10503–6)

Historical and Statutory Notes

Pre–1953 H 1 Amendments: 114 v 340

Library References

Descent and Distribution ⟲43.
Westlaw Topic No. 124.
C.J.S. Descent and Distribution §§ 27 to 28.

Research References

Encyclopedias

OH Jur. 3d Decedents' Estates § 96, Taking Per Stirpes and Per Capita Under the Statutes of Descent and Distribution.
OH Jur. 3d Decedents' Estates § 100, Children of Intestate and Their Descendants; Adopted Children.
OH Jur. 3d Decedents' Estates § 102, Children of Intestate and Their Descendants; Adopted Children—Representation; Taking Per Capita or Per Stirpes.

Treatises and Practice Aids

Carlin, Baldwin's Ohio Practice, Merrick-Rippner Probate Law § 15:2, Descent and Distribution—Definitions.
Carlin, Baldwin's Ohio Practice, Merrick-Rippner Probate Law § 15:21, Descent and Distribution—Children or Lineal Descendants—Per Stirpes.
Bogert - the Law of Trusts and Trustees § 478, Property Acquired by Killing Relative or Testator.

Law Review and Journal Commentaries

"Per Stirpes or Per Capita", Charles C. White. 13 U Cin L Rev 298 (March 1939).

Notes of Decisions

Adopted children 3
Heirs 1
Per capita 2

---

1. Heirs

"Heirs" means "all those persons named in a will who might, under some circumstances, have stood in the relation of heirs to the testatrix." Townsend's Ex'rs v. Townsend (Ohio 1874) 25 Ohio St. 477.

2. Per capita

When no brother or sister survives an intestate and the property goes to nephews and nieces, they take per capita, or if any of them have died, their children take per stirpes. Ewers v. Follin (Ohio 1859) 9 Ohio St. 327.

3. Adopted children

RC 3107.13 precludes a legally adopted child from inheriting from her intestate natural parent. In re Millward's Estate (Cuyahoga 1956) 102 Ohio App. 469, 136 N.E.2d 649, 3 O.O.2d 22, appeal dismissed 166 Ohio St. 112, 139 N.E.2d 47, 1 O.O.2d 228, affirmed 166 Ohio St. 243, 141 N.E.2d 462, 2 O.O.2d 61.

2105.12 Descent when all descendants of equal degree of consanguinity

When all the descendants of an intestate, in a direct line of descent, are on an equal degree of consanguinity to the intestate, the estate shall pass to such persons in equal parts, however remote from the intestate such equal and common degree of consanguinity may be.

(1953 H 1, eff. 10–1–53; GC 10503–7)

Historical and Statutory Notes

Pre–1953 H 1 Amendments: 114 v 341

Library References

Descent and Distribution ⟲43.
Westlaw Topic No. 124.
C.J.S. Descent and Distribution §§ 27 to 28.

Research References

Encyclopedias

OH Jur. 3d Decedents' Estates § 27, Descendant.
OH Jur. 3d Decedents' Estates § 89, Importance of Degrees of Kindred, Generally.
OH Jur. 3d Decedents' Estates § 96, Taking Per Stirpes and Per Capita Under the Statutes of Descent and Distribution.
OH Jur. 3d Decedents' Estates § 97, Descent When All Descendants Are Equal in Degree of Consanguinity.
OH Jur. 3d Decedents' Estates § 104, Brothers and Sisters of Intestate and Their Descendants.
OH Jur. 3d Decedents' Estates § 105, Nephews and Nieces of Intestate and Their Descendants.
OH Jur. 3d Decedents' Estates § 107, Grandparents of Intestate and Their Descendants—Rule of Equal Division.
OH Jur. 3d Decedents' Estates § 640, Effect of Reference to Statute of Descent and Distribution.

Treatises and Practice Aids

Carlin, Baldwin's Ohio Practice, Merrick-Rippner Probate Law § 15:23, Descent and Distribution—Children or Lineal Descendants—Per Stirpes—Example 1—Chart.
Carlin, Baldwin's Ohio Practice, Merrick-Rippner Probate Law § 15:24, Descent and Distribution—Children or Lineal Descendants—Per Stirpes—Example 2.
Carlin, Baldwin's Ohio Practice, Merrick-Rippner Probate Law § 15:32, Descent and Distribution—Siblings or Their Lineal Descendants.
Carlin, Baldwin's Ohio Practice, Merrick-Rippner Probate Law § 15:44, Descent and Distribution—Equal Degree of Consanguinity.
Carlin, Baldwin's Ohio Practice, Merrick-Rippner Probate Law § 15:45, Descent and Distribution—Equal Degree of Consanguinity—Example 1.
Restatement (2d) of Property, Don. Trans. § 28.2, Class Gift to "Issue" or "Descendants".
Restatement (3d) Property (Wills & Don. Trans.) § 2.3, Intestate Share of Surviving Descendants.

Law Review and Journal Commentaries

Ghosts from the Grave-Inheriting Through the Predeceased Under Ohio Law. Kevin Purcell, 50 Clev St L Rev 189 (2002-03).

"Per Stirpes or Per Capita", Charles C. White. 13 U Cin L Rev 298 (March 1939).

Notes of Decisions

Per capita 1
Per stirpes 2
Statutory method of descent 3

---

1. Per capita

Where a testator gives certain children and grandchildren a specific legacy in his will, and by a residuary clause directs that the proceeds of certain personal property should be "divided equally share and share alike between all my aforesaid heirs," a distribution per capita is required. (See also McKelvey v McKelvey, 43 OS 213, 1 NE 594 (1885); Mooney v Purpus, 70 OS 57, 70 NE 894 (1904).) Huston v. Crook (Ohio 1882) 38 Ohio St. 328.

A will's use of the phrase "equally share and share alike" designates the manner in which beneficiaries are to take; such language presumptively indicates an intent for the beneficiaries to take per capita and not per stirpes. Polen v. Baker (Ohio, 08-22-2001) 92 Ohio St.3d 563, 752 N.E.2d 258, 2001-Ohio-1286. Wills ⟲ 531(1)

Use of the phrase "equally share and share alike, the same to be theirs absolutely" in residuary clause mandated a per capita distribution, with each surviving beneficiary to take an absolute, or unencumbered, respective share, and did not create bequest to named individuals that entitled their issue to per stirpes distribution. Polen v. Baker (Ohio, 08-22-2001) 92 Ohio St.3d 563, 752 N.E.2d 258, 2001-Ohio-1286. Wills ⟲ 587(5)

When an intestate dies survived only by the daughter and son of one predeceased brother of the intestate and the daughter of another predeceased brother, the two nieces and nephew, being in equal degree of consanguinity, inherit per capita and not per stirpes. Washburn v. Scurlock (Jackson 1982) 5 Ohio App.3d 125, 449 N.E.2d 797, 5 O.B.R. 284.

Under RC 2105.12, when all the descendants, whether lineal or collateral, are of an equal degree of consanguinity, they take per capita and not per stirpes. Washburn v. Scurlock (Jackson 1982) 5 Ohio App.3d 125, 449 N.E.2d 797, 5 O.B.R. 284.

Where those entitled to share in an estate are nieces, nephews, grandnieces and grandnephews of the intestate, the nieces and nephews take equally, per capita, according to the total number of nieces and nephews whether surviving or not, and the grandnieces and grandnephews take per stirpes or by representation the shares of their deceased parents. Kincaid v. Cronin (Hamilton 1939) 61 Ohio App. 300, 22 N.E.2d 576, 28 Ohio Law Abs. 475, 15 O.O. 198.

Testator bequeathed his residuary estate to his lawful heirs, without other designation as to who were intended as his beneficiaries, and directed that the residuum should be equally divided "among my lawful heirs, share and share alike." Held, that all persons who at the time of testator's death were his lawful heirs were entitled to share in his residuary estate, regardless of their relationship to the testator, per capita. Mooney v. Purpus (Ohio 1904) 70 Ohio St. 57, 70 N.E. 894, 2 Ohio Law Rep. 3. Wills ⚖ 531(2)

Devise of remainder to heirs descends per stirpes. Eichenlaub v. Heschong (Ohio Com.Pl. 1907) 18 Ohio Dec. 47, 5 Ohio N.P.N.S. 367.

Under former GC 8581 (RC 2105.12), when devise with possibility of reverter was enlarged into estate of inheritance by reversion on determination of trust estate, title vested in deceased's then heirs as her representatives, and not as representatives of heirs living at time of her death, and, being of equal consanguinity, they take per capita and not per stirpes. President and Fellows of Harvard College v. Jewett (C.C.A.6 (Ohio) 1925) 11 F.2d 119. Descent And Distribution ⚖ 43

Where an intestate leaves property acquired by purchase and has only nieces and nephews, children of different brothers and sisters, as heirs, the property descends to such nieces and nephews per capita since they are in the same degree of consanguinity. Goff v Disbennet, 14 CC(NS) 557, 23 CD 234 (Licking 1911).

2. Per stirpes

Will devising land to testator's daughter for her natural life "and at her death to the issue of her body then living" held to require distribution per stirpes among living children of life tenant and grandchildren, the children of a deceased child, where no intention to make per capita distribution appeared, in view of policy of law in favor of per stirpes distribution as expressed in former GC 8581 (RC 2105.12) et seq. Watson v. Watson (Pickaway 1929) 34 Ohio App. 311, 171 N.E. 257.

This section and the case law thereunder is controlled by the special provisions contained in GC 10503-4 (RC 2105.06); hence, where there are no grandparents, the lineal descendants of such grandparents take per stirpes and not per capita, the grandparents being the stock or root. Shearer v Gasstman, 31 NP(NS) 219, 15 Abs 103 (Prob, Franklin 1933).

3. Statutory method of descent

The legislature intended that the rule in the act of 1853, providing for per stirpes and per capita representation, be extended and applied to every case in which an estate was to be divided among a class of descendants, whether their consanguinity to the intestate be lineal or collateral. (See also Goff v Disbennet, 14 CC(NS) 557, 23 CD 234 (Licking 1911).) Ewers v. Follin (Ohio 1859) 9 Ohio St. 327.

The effect of the present act regulating descents is to extend, not to limit, the rule regarding distribution per capita and per stirpes which obtained in Ohio at common law. (See also Dutoit v Doyle, 16 OS 400 (1865); Parsons v Parsons, 52 OS 470, 40 NE 165 (1895).) Ewers v. Follin (Ohio 1859) 9 Ohio St. 327.

RC 2105.12 is in pari materia with RC 2105.06 and operates as an exception to the general rules of descent and distribution. Washburn v. Scurlock (Jackson 1982) 5 Ohio App.3d 125, 449 N.E.2d 797, 5 O.B.R. 284.

With reference to lineal descendants this section provides for a per capita distribution or descent where all are of equal degree of consanguinity, and by GC 10503-8 (RC 2105.13), a method of descent is provided where the lineal descendants are of unequal degree of consanguinity. Snodgrass v. Bedell (Ohio 1938) 134 Ohio St. 311, 16 N.E.2d 463, 12 O.O. 103.

This section has a direct connection with GC 10503-4 (RC 2105.06) and makes the course of descent only when the lineal descendants are on equal degree of consanguinity to the intestate. Schwaigert v. Vitzhum (Ohio Prob. 1938) 2 Ohio Supp. 241, 26 Ohio Law Abs. 442, 12 O.O. 114.

2105.13 Descent when children and heirs of deceased children are living

If some of the children of an intestate are living and others are dead, the estate shall descend to the children who are living and to the lineal descendants of such children as are dead, so that each child who is living will inherit the share to which he would have been entitled if all the children of the intestate were living, and the lineal descendants of the deceased child will inherit equal parts of that portion of the estate to which such deceased child would be entitled if he were living.

This section shall apply in all cases in which the descendants of the intestate, not more remote than lineal descendants of grandparents, entitled to share in the estate, are of unequal degree of consanguinity to the intestate, so that those who are of the nearest degree of consanguinity will take the share to which they would have been entitled, had all the descendants in the same degree of consanguinity with them who died leaving issue, been living.

(1953 H 1, eff. 10–1–53; GC 10503–8, 10503–9)

Historical and Statutory Notes

Pre–1953 H 1 Amendments: 116 v 385; 114 v 341

Library References

Descent and Distribution ⚖43.
Westlaw Topic No. 124.
C.J.S. Descent and Distribution §§ 27 to 28.

Research References

Encyclopedias

OH Jur. 3d Decedents' Estates § 11, Descent.
OH Jur. 3d Decedents' Estates § 27, Descendant.
OH Jur. 3d Decedents' Estates § 96, Taking Per Stirpes and Per Capita Under the Statutes of Descent and Distribution.
OH Jur. 3d Decedents' Estates § 98, Descent When Descendants Are of an Unequal Degree of Consanguinity.
OH Jur. 3d Decedents' Estates § 100, Children of Intestate and Their Descendants; Adopted Children.
OH Jur. 3d Decedents' Estates § 102, Children of Intestate and Their Descendants; Adopted Children—Representation; Taking Per Capita or Per Stirpes.
OH Jur. 3d Decedents' Estates § 107, Grandparents of Intestate and Their Descendants—Rule of Equal Division.

Treatises and Practice Aids

Carlin, Baldwin's Ohio Practice, Merrick-Rippner Probate Law § 15:2, Descent and Distribution—Definitions.
Carlin, Baldwin's Ohio Practice, Merrick-Rippner Probate Law § 15:21, Descent and Distribution—Children or Lineal Descendants—Per Stirpes.
Carlin, Baldwin's Ohio Practice, Merrick-Rippner Probate Law § 15:22, Descent and Distribution—Children or Lineal Descendants—Per Stirpes—Example 1.
Carlin, Baldwin's Ohio Practice, Merrick-Rippner Probate Law § 15:45, Descent and Distribution—Equal Degree of Consanguinity—Example 1.
Carlin, Baldwin's Ohio Practice, Merrick-Rippner Probate Law § 15:47, Descent and Distribution—Equal Degree of Consanguinity—Example 2.
Carlin, Baldwin's Ohio Practice, Merrick-Rippner Probate Law § 15:49, Descent and Distribution—Equal Degree of Consanguinity—Example 3.

Law Review and Journal Commentaries

Ghosts from the Grave-Inheriting Through the Predeceased Under Ohio Law. Kevin Purcell, 50 Clev St L Rev 189 (2002-03).

"Per Stirpes or Per Capita", Charles C. White. 13 U Cin L Rev 298 (March 1939).

Spouse's Intestate Share Increased. David F. Allen, 11 Prob L J Ohio 73 (May/June 2001).

Notes of Decisions

Advancement effect 5
Amendments to statute 3
Intent of testator 1
Per stirpes 2
Whole and half blood 4

---

1. Intent of testator

Where a will devises one-half of an estate to testator's lawful heirs and one-half to the lawful heirs of his wife, and provides for the disposition of stock bequeathed to his sister, and to the sister and brother of his wife, the persons included in the designation "lawful heirs" are to be ascertained as of the date of the death of testator or his wife, respectively. Wilberding v. Miller (Ohio 1913) 88 Ohio St. 609, 90 Ohio St. 28, 106 N.E. 665, 11 Ohio Law Rep. 96, 11 Ohio Law Rep. 262, 11 Ohio Law Rep. 447. Wills ⇨ 524(1)

Where a testator directs that his residuary estate "shall be equally divided amongst my lawful heirs, share and share alike," without further designation as to who the intended beneficiaries are, all "lawful" heirs at the time of his death, regardless of degree of consanguinity, are entitled to share in the distribution of the estate per capita and not per stirpes. Mooney v. Purpus (Ohio 1904) 70 Ohio St. 57, 70 N.E. 894, 2 Ohio Law Rep. 3.

A testator who requires the remainder of his estate (all personalty in this case) to descend according to the laws of inheritance, thereby intends distribution of the same as intestate property; and where he left three nephews and nieces and the children of two deceased nieces, each living nephew and niece will receive one-fifth and each set of children of deceased nieces will take the fifth of the deceased parent. Elliott v. Shaw (Ohio Com.Pl. 1913) 23 Ohio Dec. 662, 15 Ohio N.P.N.S. 81.

2. Per stirpes

Section 7 of the act of March 14, 1853, regulating descents, now this section, did not change the rule of descent by representation or per stirpes, which has always prevailed in Ohio. (See also Parsons v Parsons, 52 OS 470, 40 NE 165 (1895).) Dutoit v. Doyle (Ohio 1865) 16 Ohio St. 400.

Where a decedent's only surviving lineal descendants are nephews and nieces together with a grandnephew, son of a deceased nephew, a court errs in ordering a per stirpes distribution based on the decedent's brothers and sisters, the nephews' and nieces' parents, as all are of equal consanguinity with the exception of the grandnephew who takes per stirpes as representative of his deceased father. In re Estate of Huffman, No. 1844 (4th Dist Ct App, Scioto, 10–19–90).

3. Amendments to statute

GC 10503–4 (RC 2105.06) being a new provision in the probate code which became effective January 1, 1932, the provisions of said new section control over the provisions of GC 10503–9 (RC 2105.13), which was found in the old probate code and reenacted into the new probate code. Davey v. Climo (Ohio Com.Pl. 1933) 30 Ohio N.P.N.S. 457.

There is nothing in the portion of GC 10503–9 (RC 2105.13) amended by 116 v 385, which affects descent to lineal descendants of grandparents. Ryan v. Dixon (Ohio Prob. 1938) 2 Ohio Supp. 248, 26 Ohio Law Abs. 450, 12 O.O. 185.

Purpose of amendment to GC 10503–9 (RC 2105.13) (116 v 385) was to correct an inconsistency between this section and GC 10503–4 (RC 2105.06) as they were originally enacted in the 1932 probate code. Ryan v. Dixon (Ohio Prob. 1938) 2 Ohio Supp. 248, 26 Ohio Law Abs. 450, 12 O.O. 185.

4. Whole and half blood

Brothers and sisters include those of the whole and the half blood. Stone v. Doster (Ohio Cir. 1892) 3 Ohio C.D. 637, affirmed in part, reversed in part 50 Ohio St. 495, 30 W.L.B. 344, 35 N.E. 208.

Children of a brother of the whole blood stand in place of their father. Stone v. Doster (Ohio Cir. 1892) 3 Ohio C.D. 637, affirmed in part, reversed in part 50 Ohio St. 495, 30 W.L.B. 344, 35 N.E. 208.

5. Advancement effect

In a partition of land of an intestate among his children and the children of a deceased son, latter's portion should be charged with an advancement made to such deceased son. Parsons v. Parsons (Ohio 1895) 52 Ohio St. 470, 33 W.L.B. 192, 40 N.E. 165, 2 Ohio Leg. N. 437. Descent And Distribution ⇨ 105; Partition ⇨ 83; Partition ⇨ 87

2105.14 Posthumous child to inherit

Descendants of an intestate begotten before his death, but born thereafter, in all cases will inherit as if born in the lifetime of the intestate and surviving him; but in no other case can a person inherit unless living at the time of the death of the intestate.

(1953 H 1, eff. 10–1–53; GC 10503–16)

Historical and Statutory Notes

Pre–1953 H 1 Amendments: 114 v 342

Library References

Descent and Distribution ⇨27.
Westlaw Topic No. 124.
C.J.S. Descent and Distribution §§ 32, 34.

Research References

Encyclopedias
OH Jur. 3d Decedents' Estates § 11, Descent.
OH Jur. 3d Decedents' Estates § 39, List of Prerequisites.
OH Jur. 3d Decedents' Estates § 42, Survivorship.
OH Jur. 3d Decedents' Estates § 80, Heirs and Next of Kin as Successors Under the Statute of Descent and Distribution—Status Fixed at Ancestor's Death; No Rule of Shifting Descents.
OH Jur. 3d Decedents' Estates § 101, Children of Intestate and Their Descendants; Adopted Children—After-Born Children; Pretermitted Children.

Treatises and Practice Aids
Carlin, Baldwin's Ohio Practice, Merrick-Rippner Probate Law § 15:26, Descent and Distribution—Afterborn or Posthumous Child.
Restatement (2d) of Property, Don. Trans. § 26.1, Gifts Immediate in Form to Class-When Class Closes to After-Conceived and After-Adopted Persons.

Notes of Decisions

Unborn child 1

---

1. Unborn child

A bequest to a class of persons "living at the time of my death" includes in such class a child en ventre sa mere who is a viable unborn child capable of sustaining life outside the mother's womb even though not born until three days after the time of the death of testatrix. Ebbs v. Smith (Ohio Com.Pl. 1979) 59 Ohio Misc. 133, 394 N.E.2d 1034, 11 O.O.3d 356, 13 O.O.3d 345.

DESIGNATED HEIR; ALIENS

2105.15 Designation of heir at law

A person of sound mind and memory may appear before the probate judge of his county and in the presence of such judge and two disinterested persons of such person's acquaintance, file a written declaration declaring that, as his free and voluntary act, he did designate and appoint another, stating the name and place of resident of such person specifically, to stand toward him in the relation of an heir at law in the event of his death. Such declaration must be attested by the two disinterested persons and subscribed by the declarant. If satisfied that such declarant is of sound mind and memory and free from restraint, the judge thereupon shall enter that fact upon his journal and make a complete record of such proceedings. Thenceforward the person designated will stand in the same relation, for all purposes, to such declarant as he could if a child born in lawful wedlock. The rules of inheritance will be the same between him and the relations by blood of the declarant, as if so born. A certified copy of such record will be prima-facie evidence of the fact stated therein, and conclusive evidence, unless impeached for actual fraud or undue influence. After a lapse of one year from the date of such designation, such declarant may have such designation vacated or changed by filing in said probate court an application to vacate or change such designation of heir; provided, that there is compliance with the procedure, conditions, and prerequisites required in the making of the original declaration.

(1953 H 1, eff. 10–1–53; GC 10503–12)

Historical and Statutory Notes

Pre–1953 H 1 Amendments: 118 v 406, § 1; 114 v 341

Cross References

Death of devisee or legatee, relative defined, 2107.52
Designated heir as necessary party in will contest, 2107.73

Library References

Adoption ⇌21.
Descent and Distribution ⇌25.1.
Westlaw Topic Nos. 124, 17.
C.J.S. Adoption of Persons §§ 146 to 150.
C.J.S. Descent and Distribution § 32.

Research References

Encyclopedias

OH Jur. 3d Decedents' Estates § 15, Descent and Distribution.
OH Jur. 3d Decedents' Estates § 86, Illegitimate Blood Relationship.
OH Jur. 3d Decedents' Estates § 111, Designated Heirs.
OH Jur. 3d Decedents' Estates § 209, Who May Designate or be Designated.
OH Jur. 3d Decedents' Estates § 210, Procedure.
OH Jur. 3d Decedents' Estates § 211, Operation and Effect of Declaration.
OH Jur. 3d Decedents' Estates § 212, Vacation or Change of Declaration.
OH Jur. 3d Decedents' Estates § 392, Designation of an Heir; Return of Child or Designated Heir Absent and Reported Dead.
OH Jur. 3d Decedents' Estates § 792, Who is a "Relative" Within Statute.
OH Jur. 3d Decedents' Estates § 1093, Heirs and Next of Kin—Designated Heirs.
OH Jur. 3d Family Law § 891, Existence and Proof of Relationship.
OH Jur. 3d Family Law § 1013, Effect of Designating Illegitimate Child as Heir at Law.

Forms

Ohio Forms Legal and Business § 24:161, Entire Estate to Spouse—Alternatively to Children—Guardianship of Minors.
Ohio Forms Legal and Business § 24:201, Entire Estate to Specified Relatives or Issue—Provision for Future Spouse—Anatomical Dispositions—No Funeral Services.
Ohio Forms Legal and Business § 24:801, Bequest Not to Lapse on Death of Beneficiary Before Death of Testator.

Treatises and Practice Aids

Carlin, Baldwin's Ohio Practice, Merrick-Rippner Probate Law § 12:7, Wrongful Death—Status of Beneficiaries Fixed at Death of Decedent.
Carlin, Baldwin's Ohio Practice, Merrick-Rippner Probate Law § 17:1, Designation—Procedure for Making.
Carlin, Baldwin's Ohio Practice, Merrick-Rippner Probate Law § 17:2, Designation—Effect.
Carlin, Baldwin's Ohio Practice, Merrick-Rippner Probate Law § 17:3, Designation—Contrast With Adoption.
Carlin, Baldwin's Ohio Practice, Merrick-Rippner Probate Law § 17:4, Designation—Vacation.
Carlin, Baldwin's Ohio Practice, Merrick-Rippner Probate Law § 17:5, Designation of Heir-At-Law—Form.
Carlin, Baldwin's Ohio Practice, Merrick-Rippner Probate Law § 17:6, Entry Approving Designation of Heir—Form.
Carlin, Baldwin's Ohio Practice, Merrick-Rippner Probate Law § 17:7, Application for Revocation, or Change, of Designation of Heir-At-Law—Form.
Carlin, Baldwin's Ohio Practice, Merrick-Rippner Probate Law § 18:2, Inheritance Rights of Illegitimate Child—Statutory Provisions.
Carlin, Baldwin's Ohio Practice, Merrick-Rippner Probate Law § 19:2, Legitimation—Procedure—Acknowledgment of Paternity.
Carlin, Baldwin's Ohio Practice, Merrick-Rippner Probate Law § 19:3, Legitimation—Constitutional Issues.
Carlin, Baldwin's Ohio Practice, Merrick-Rippner Probate Law § 19:6, Uniform Parentage Act—Jurisdiction of Action to Determine Father-Child Relationship.
Carlin, Baldwin's Ohio Practice, Merrick-Rippner Probate Law § 46:1, Anti-Lapse Statute.
Carlin, Baldwin's Ohio Practice, Merrick-Rippner Probate Law § 46:2, Anti-Lapse Statute—"Relative" as Beneficiary.
Carlin, Baldwin's Ohio Practice, Merrick-Rippner Probate Law § 46:3, Anti-Lapse Statute—"Issue" as Beneficiary.
Carlin, Baldwin's Ohio Practice, Merrick-Rippner Probate Law § 46:5, Anti-Lapse Statute—Putative Child as Beneficiary.
Carlin, Baldwin's Ohio Practice, Merrick-Rippner Probate Law § 98:5, Adoption—Parties—Who May be Adopted—Statutory Provisions.
Carlin, Baldwin's Ohio Practice, Merrick-Rippner Probate Law § 15:20, Descent and Distribution—Children or Lineal Descendants—in General.
Carlin, Baldwin's Ohio Practice, Merrick-Rippner Probate Law § 15:27, Descent and Distribution—Child Without Issue Predeceasing Parent.
Carlin, Baldwin's Ohio Practice, Merrick-Rippner Probate Law § 15:29, Descent and Distribution—Designated Heir.
Carlin, Baldwin's Ohio Practice, Merrick-Rippner Probate Law § 15:30, Descent and Distribution—Child Born Out of Wedlock.
Carlin, Baldwin's Ohio Practice, Merrick-Rippner Probate Law § 19:10, Uniform Parentage Act—Procedure in Action to Determine Father-Child Relationship.
Carlin, Baldwin's Ohio Practice, Merrick-Rippner Probate Law § 30:30, Drafting a Will—Clauses to Discourage a Will Contest Action—Designation of Heir.
Carlin, Baldwin's Ohio Practice, Merrick-Rippner Probate Law § 108:20, Juvenile Court—Parentage Act—Jurisdiction and Venue.

Law Review and Journal Commentaries

Descent and Distribution—Designated Heir Statute—Statutory Construction, Note. 15 U Cin L Rev 347 (May 1941).

Estate planning techniques for nontraditional couples. Susan L. Racey, 14 Prob L J Ohio 57 (January/February 2004).

Ghosts from the Grave-Inheriting Through the Predeceased Under Ohio Law. Kevin Purcell, 50 Clev St L Rev 189 (2002-03).

The Law of Adoption in Ohio, Beverly E. Sylvester. 2 Cap U L Rev 23 (1973).

The Ohio Designated Heir Statute, Albert H. Leyerle. 21 Akron L Rev 391 (Spring 1988).

Wills Can Be Made "Unbreakable," Ellis V. Rippner. 6 Clev–Marshall L Rev 336 (May 1957).

Notes of Decisions

Adopted child 2
Constitutional issues 1
Designation as heir 8
Illegitimate child 3
Inheritance from, not through 5
Issue 6
Procedural issues 4

Taxation 7

1. Constitutional issues

The act of April 25, 1904, 97 v 398, imposing a direct inheritance tax, is constitutional. State ex rel. Taylor v. Guilbert (Ohio 1904) 70 Ohio St. 229, 71 N.E. 636, 2 Ohio Law Rep. 56, 1 Am.Ann.Cas. 25.

Collateral inheritance tax is constitutional. Hagerty v. State, ex rel. Dyer (Ohio 1897) 55 Ohio St. 613, 37 W.L.B. 99, 45 N.E. 1046.

The act of April 20, 1894, 91 v 166, imposing a direct inheritance tax, is unconstitutional. State ex rel. Schwartz v. Ferris (Ohio 1895) 53 Ohio St. 314, 34 W.L.B. 203, 41 N.E. 579.

2. Adopted child

The personal estate of an adopted child dying intestate and leaving its natural born mother, its adopting parents, and children of adopting parents surviving it, passes to the natural mother to the exclusion of the adopting parents and their children born in lawful wedlock. Upson v. Noble (Ohio 1880) 35 Ohio St. 655. Adoption ⇐ 22

The act of April 20, 1854, and of March 29, 1859, gave an adopted heir the legal status of a child of the adopter and required him to be regarded as such child in tracing descent to or from him. Dawson v. Dawson (Ohio 1874) 25 Ohio St. 443.

A child, surrendered by its parents into the permanent custody of an institution established for the purpose of aiding, caring for and placing children in homes, under a written agreement pursuant to RC 5103.15, which agreement provides that the institution may appear in any legal proceeding for the adoption of such child and consent to the child's adoption, continues as an heir of its parents, either natural or adoptive, until such time as the child has been legally adopted pursuant to RC Ch 3107. Maurer v. Becker (Ohio 1971) 26 Ohio St.2d 254, 271 N.E.2d 255, 55 O.O.2d 486. Adoption ⇐ 21

A person, who was designated as an heir by a decedent pursuant to RC 2105.15, is, within the meaning of RC 5731.09, a "person recognized by the decedent as an adopted child and designated by such decedent as an heir under a statute of this... state," even where there is no other showing, apart from such designation, that the decedent recognized the designee as an adopted child. In re Gompf's Estate (Ohio 1964) 175 Ohio St. 400, 195 N.E.2d 806, 25 O.O.2d 388.

This section authorizes an adopter to say who shall be his heir, but not otherwise to change the course of descents. Richardson v. Cincinnati Union Stockyard Co. (Ohio Super. 1901) 11 Ohio Dec. 367, 8 Ohio N.P. 213.

Where a bequest is made to the wife of an adopted son who was made the legal heir of the testatrix, such adopted son is not in the class of a "son," and such a bequest is subject to the collateral inheritance tax. In re Hunnewell, 3 LR 52 (Prob, Hamilton 1905).

3. Illegitimate child

Assuming that probate court's finding that woman was intestate's biological child was supported by competent, credible evidence, woman failed to establish that she was "legitimized" in one of recognized manners and thus had no right to intestate's estate; only method by which woman could affirmatively seek relief would have been under Parentage Act which required that parentage action be brought in juvenile court which woman had failed to do. In re Estate of Hicks (Ohio App. 6 Dist., 09-30-1993) 90 Ohio App.3d 483, 629 N.E.2d 1086. Children Out-of-wedlock ⇐ 86

In a wrongful death action against a truck driver and driver's employer involving a collision between the truck driver and a motorist, dismissal is proper on the basis that the plaintiff could not maintain a wrongful death suit on behalf of an alleged minor child of the motorist where the plaintiff and the motorist were not married, the motorist did not in probate court formally acknowledge the child as his with consent of the mother, and the motorist did not designate the child as his heir-at-law, adopt the child, or make provision for the child in his will, and, although a parentage action was brought by the plaintiff and her son, the action was brought after the death of the motorist; thus, as a matter of law, the child cannot inherit from the decedent's estate, including any recovery from the wrongful death action. Hunter–Martin v. Winchester Transp., Inc. (Shelby 1991) 71 Ohio App.3d 273, 593 N.E.2d 383, motion overruled 62 Ohio St.3d 1408, 577 N.E.2d 361.

The Ohio laws of descent and distribution denying a right of an illegitimate child to inherit from a natural father unless the father has taken certain steps such as marrying the mother, acknowledging the child, designating the child as an heir-at-law, adoption, or making a provision in a will, are valid. White v. Randolph (Ohio 1979) 59 Ohio St.2d 6, 391 N.E.2d 333, 13 O.O.3d 3, appeal dismissed 100 S.Ct. 1000, 444 U.S. 1061, 62 L.Ed.2d 743. Children Out-of-wedlock ⇐ 82; Constitutional Law ⇐ 225.5

An illegitimate child cannot inherit from or through his natural father unless the father takes some steps during his lifetime to permit such inheritance, such as acknowledgment pursuant to RC 2105.18, designating the illegitimate as an heir pursuant to RC 2105.15, adopting the illegitimate, or providing for the illegitimate in his will. Moore v. Dague (Franklin 1975) 46 Ohio App.2d 75, 345 N.E.2d 449, 75 O.O.2d 68. Children Out-of-wedlock ⇐ 86; Children Out-of-wedlock ⇐ 90

An illegitimate son, designated as heir at law by his natural father pursuant to the provisions of this section, is not authorized under GC 12079 (RC 2741.01) to bring an action to contest the will of the brother of the natural father, which brother died subsequent to the decease of the natural father. Blackwell v. Bowman (Ohio 1948) 150 Ohio St. 34, 80 N.E.2d 493, 37 O.O. 323. Wills ⇐ 229

4. Procedural issues

Declaration need not be made in open court, but may be made any place. Bird v. Young (Ohio 1897) 56 Ohio St. 210, 37 W.L.B. 286, 46 N.E. 819.

The entry is not a judgment in the general sense and it is not essential to the validity of the proceedings that the order for such entry be made by the court; it is sufficient if made by the judge. Bird v. Young (Ohio 1897) 56 Ohio St. 210, 37 W.L.B. 286, 46 N.E. 819.

Designation in a will of a person as a daughter is not sufficient to make her an heir at law. In re Williamson's Will (Ohio Prob. 1897) 6 Ohio Dec. 507, 5 Ohio N.P. 1, reversed 8 Ohio Dec. 47, 6 Ohio N.P. 79.

To qualify as a designated heir under RC 5731.09 the successor must establish that during his minority his relationship to the decedent was similar to that of a parent and child and that he was designated as an heir by the decedent according to law, although such designation need not necessarily have occurred during the minority of said successor. (See also In re Estate of Gompf, 175 OS 400, 195 NE(2d) 806 (1964).) In re Estate of George, 82 Abs 452 (Prob, Cuyahoga 1959).

Proceeding in probate court for designation of heir under this section is purely ex parte; it bears resemblance to proceedings in rem which fixes status of a person as in lunacy or insolvency proceedings. Horine v Horine, 16 Abs 155 (App, Darke 1934).

Action of probate court under this section is quasi judicial insofar as court is required to determine that declarant is of sound mind and memory and free from any restraint. Horine v Horine, 16 Abs 155 (App, Darke 1934).

5. Inheritance from, not through

When court is dealing with designated heir, whether in will, trust or intestacy situation, judicial rule that limits designated heir only to taking from, but not through, designator applies. PNC Bank, Ohio, N.A. v. Stanton (Ohio App. 1 Dist., 06-14-1995) 104 Ohio App.3d 558, 662 N.E.2d 875, appeal not allowed 74 Ohio St.3d 1446, 656 N.E.2d 347. Descent And Distribution ⇐ 25.1; Trusts ⇐ 124; Wills ⇐ 506(1)

Designated heir of deceased son of trust's grantor could not take trust principal upon trust's life income beneficiary's death, even though trust provided for payment of principal following life income beneficiary's death to grantor's son's heirs at law if son predeceased life beneficiary, given judicial rule limiting designated heir to taking from, but not through, designator. PNC Bank, Ohio, N.A. v. Stanton (Ohio App. 1 Dist., 06-14-1995) 104 Ohio App.3d 558, 662 N.E.2d 875, appeal not allowed 74 Ohio St.3d 1446, 656 N.E.2d 347. Trusts ⇐ 124

If individual who creates a legal document is presumed to know law in effect at document's creation, trust grantor was entitled to rely, in creating trust, upon limitations case law placed upon inheritance rights of designated heirs, under which a designated heir of grantor's son could inherit only from and not through son, and therefore designated heir of grantor's son could not rely on this principle to take trust principal under trust provision requiring that principal be paid to grantor's son's heirs at law if son predeceased trust's life income beneficiary. PNC Bank, Ohio, N.A. v. Stanton (Ohio App. 1 Dist., 06-14-1995) 104 Ohio App.3d 558, 662 N.E.2d 875, appeal not allowed 74 Ohio St.3d 1446, 656 N.E.2d 347. Trusts ⇐ 124

2105.15
Note 5

One who has been designated and appointed by another by virtue of RC 2105.15 as an heir at law inherits from, but not through his designator. Witten v. Landrum (Van Wert 1974) 41 Ohio App.2d 65, 322 N.E.2d 146, 70 O.O.2d 61. Wills ⚖═ 506(2)

An heir designated by virtue of RC 2105.15 is an heir under the statute of descent and distribution. Witten v. Landrum (Van Wert 1974) 41 Ohio App.2d 65, 322 N.E.2d 146, 70 O.O.2d 61.

A designated heir can inherit from but not through the designator. Uhl v. Armstrong (Cuyahoga 1957) 140 N.E.2d 60, 78 Ohio Law Abs. 592. Descent And Distribution ⚖═ 45

This section, authorizing the designation of an heir, creates upon such designation contingent rights of inheritance under the statute of descent and distribution, and if the designated heir survives his intestate designator he becomes entitled to the same right of property in the estate of his designator as if he were a child of such designator born in lawful wedlock. Kirsheman v. Paulin (Ohio 1951) 155 Ohio St. 137, 98 N.E.2d 26, 44 O.O. 134. Descent And Distribution ⚖═ 23

Under the statutes of descent and distribution, a person who has been designated and appointed by another as an heir at law inherits from but not through his designator. Blackwell v. Bowman (Ohio 1948) 150 Ohio St. 34, 80 N.E.2d 493, 37 O.O. 323.

Rights by inheritance of a person designated as heir under provisions of this section, are limited to the estate descending from the declarant, and such proceeding confers no right in the estate of any other person upon the designated person. Southern Ohio Sav. Bank & Trust Co. v. Boyer (Hamilton 1940) 66 Ohio App. 136, 31 N.E.2d 161, 32 Ohio Law Abs. 626, 19 O.O. 398.

Designated heir of a brother of an intestate is not an heir of such intestate, and the intestate's niece, being the nearest of kin under the statutes of descent and distribution, inherits the estate. Southern Ohio Sav. Bank & Trust Co. v. Boyer (Hamilton 1940) 66 Ohio App. 136, 31 N.E.2d 161, 32 Ohio Law Abs. 626, 19 O.O. 398.

Provision in will devising property to daughter, to be held by her during her natural life, and at her death to her heirs at law in fee, held not to exclude heir at law designated as such by daughter. Laws v. Davis (Ohio App. 1929) 34 Ohio App. 157, 170 N.E. 601, 31 Ohio Law Rep. 419, error dismissed 121 Ohio St. 621, 172 N.E. 380.

6. Issue

Former GC 8598 (RC 2105.15) creates rights of inheritance under the statutes of descent and distribution, and the designated heir becomes entitled to the same right of property as if he were a child born in lawful wedlock, and is to be regarded as "issue" of the person so designating under the statutes of descent and distribution. Cochrel v. Robinson (Ohio 1925) 113 Ohio St. 526, 149 N.E. 871, 3 Ohio Law Abs. 740, 23 Ohio Law Rep. 607.

A person not of the blood of the testator who is designated as an heir-at-law under RS 4182 is not issue of the body within the meaning of RS 5915 so as to render invalid a charitable bequest in a will executed within one year of the death of the testator. Theobald v. Fugman (Ohio 1901) 64 Ohio St. 473, 45 W.L.B. 382, 60 N.E. 606.

A designated heir is not an issue of the body within the meaning of GC 10504 (RC 2105.15), making void a charitable bequest executed within one year of testator's death. Theobald v. Fugman (Ohio 1901) 64 Ohio St. 473, 45 W.L.B. 382, 60 N.E. 606.

7. Taxation

A person who receives farm property as a result of a devise cannot be considered a foster child of the decedent for special tax valuation purposes where the person claiming to be the foster child never resided with the decedent, was not adopted by the decedent, and where the decedent had no control over the purported foster child but the child received gifts and affection from the decedent and provided assistance to the decedent and was very close to the decedent for over fifty years. In re Estate of Cummins (Ohio Com.Pl. 1991) 61 Ohio Misc.2d 579, 580 N.E.2d 866.

Where a testator designated his wife's daughter by a former marriage and her daughter as his designated heirs, to stand toward him in the relation of daughters, such designated heirs were entitled to the inheritance tax exemption set forth in RC 5731.09(B). (See also In re Estate of Gompf, 175 OS 400, 195 NE(2d) 806 (1964).) In re Powell's Estate (Ohio Prob. 1959) 168 N.E.2d 27, 82 Ohio Law Abs. 549.

8. Designation as heir

Trust's grantor could not have knowingly intended to include designated heir of his son in his estate plan, inasmuch as son did not designate heir until after grantor's death, and thus designated heir could not take trust principal, even though trust provided for payment of principal to son's heirs at law upon death of trust's surviving life income beneficiary in event son predeceased surviving life income beneficiary, based upon maxim that grantor's intent should be ascertained and given effect whenever possible. PNC Bank, Ohio, N.A. v. Stanton (Ohio App. 1 Dist., 06-14-1995) 104 Ohio App.3d 558, 662 N.E.2d 875, appeal not allowed 74 Ohio St.3d 1446, 656 N.E.2d 347. Trusts ⚖═ 124

An instrument, executed in compliance with the statute of wills, appointing an executor to settle up all property, both personal and real, and making the grand-daughters of testatrix equal "heirs" with her own children, is dispositive, and devised to the granddaughters each an equal share with the children of testatrix. Moon v. Stewart (Ohio 1913) 87 Ohio St. 349, 101 N.E. 344, 10 Ohio Law Rep. 601, Am.Ann.Cas. 1914A, 104. Wills ⚖═ 525

2105.16 Heirs of aliens may inherit; aliens may hold lands

No person who is capable of inheriting shall be deprived of the inheritance by reason of any of his ancestors having been aliens. Aliens may hold, possess, and enjoy lands, tenements, and hereditaments within this state, either by descent, devise, gift, or purchase, as fully as any citizen of the United States or of this state may do.

(1953 H 1, eff. 10–1–53; GC 10503–13)

Historical and Statutory Notes

Pre–1953 H 1 Amendments: 114 v 342

Comparative Laws

Ky.—Baldwin's KRS 381.290.
Mass.—M.G.L.A. c. 184, § 1.
Mich.—M.C.L.A. § 554.135.
Mo.—V.A.M.S. § 442.560.
Okl.—60 Okl.St.Ann. § 121 et seq.
Pa.—68 P.S. § 22 et seq.
W.Va.—Code, 42–1–4.

Cross References

Money and property to be held in trust for safekeeping for nonresident of the United States, 2113.81

Library References

Aliens ⚖═9.
Westlaw Topic No. 24.
C.J.S. Aliens §§ 33 to 38, 45.

Research References

Encyclopedias

OH Jur. 3d Aliens & Citizens § 13, Rights in Real and Personal Property.
OH Jur. 3d Aliens & Citizens § 15, Rights in Estates of Deceased Persons.
OH Jur. 3d Decedents' Estates § 26, Ancestor.
OH Jur. 3d Decedents' Estates § 226, Aliens.

Forms

Ohio Forms Legal and Business § 24:873, Devises—to Aliens.

Treatises and Practice Aids

Carlin, Baldwin's Ohio Practice, Merrick-Rippner Probate Law § 26:3, Testamentary Capacity—Who May Make a Will—"A Person".
Carlin, Baldwin's Ohio Practice, Merrick-Rippner Probate Law § 21:101, Application to Fix Rental Value of Mansion House—Form.
Bogert - the Law of Trusts and Trustees § 126, Trustee Capable of Taking But Not Holding Title.

Bogert - the Law of Trusts and Trustees § 168, Capacity to be a Beneficiary—Special Cases.

Restatement (3d) Property (Wills & Don. Trans.) § 1.3, Noncitizens.

Law Review and Journal Commentaries

Legatees Behind The Iron Curtain, Carl H. Fulda. 16 Ohio St L J 496 (Autumn 1956).

Notes of Decisions

Aliens 1
Foreign nation 2

1. Aliens

Former GC 8589 (RC 2105.16) authorizes aliens to hold and enjoy estates by way of dower in lands in Ohio. Falkoff v. Sugerman (Ohio Com.Pl. 1925) 26 Ohio N.P.N.S. 81.

By reason of former GC 8589 (RC 2105.16), aliens stand on the same footing with citizens of the United States, as far as the right under the laws of Ohio to inherit property is concerned. 1920 OAG p 1038.

2. Foreign nation

A foreign nation, in the absence of a treaty with the United States, may not hold title to real estate located in the state of Ohio without the express consent of the state. 1949 OAG 998.

ILLEGITIMATE CHILDREN

Cross References

Paternity proceedings, Ch 3111

2105.17 Capability of children born out of wedlock as to inheritance

Children born out of wedlock shall be capable of inheriting or transmitting inheritance from and to their mother, and from and to those from whom she may inherit, or to whom she may transmit inheritance, as if born in lawful wedlock.

(1975 S 145, eff. 1–1–76; 1953 H 1; GC 10503–14)

Uncodified Law

1975 S 145, § 3: See Uncodified Law under 2105.06.

Historical and Statutory Notes

Pre–1953 H 1 Amendments: 114 v 342

Cross References

Paternity proceedings, Ch 3111

Library References

Children Out-of-Wedlock ⚖=87, 89.
Westlaw Topic No. 76H.
C.J.S. Children Out-of-Wedlock §§ 63 to 65, 69.

Research References

Encyclopedias

OH Jur. 3d Decedents' Estates § 86, Illegitimate Blood Relationship.
OH Jur. 3d Decedents' Estates § 110, Stepchildren of Intestate and Their Descendants.
OH Jur. 3d Decedents' Estates § 527, "Heirs"—as Including Illegitimate Children.
OH Jur. 3d Decedents' Estates § 534, "Children," "Sons" and "Daughters"—Illegitimate Children.
OH Jur. 3d Decedents' Estates § 1092, Heirs and Next of Kin.
OH Jur. 3d Family Law § 1010, Inheritance from or Through Mother.
OH Jur. 3d Family Law § 1012, Inheritance from or Through Child Born Out of Wedlock.

Treatises and Practice Aids

Sowald & Morganstern, Baldwin's Ohio Practice Domestic Relations Law § 3:45, Effect of Judgment—Inheritance.
Carlin, Baldwin's Ohio Practice, Merrick-Rippner Probate Law § 18:1, Inheritance Rights of Illegitimate Child—History in Ohio.
Carlin, Baldwin's Ohio Practice, Merrick-Rippner Probate Law § 18:2, Inheritance Rights of Illegitimate Child—Statutory Provisions.
Carlin, Baldwin's Ohio Practice, Merrick-Rippner Probate Law § 18:3, Inheritance Rights of Illegitimate Child—Case Law Affecting Rules of Inheritance Generally.
Carlin, Baldwin's Ohio Practice, Merrick-Rippner Probate Law § 18:6, Inheritance Rights of Illegitimate Child—Will.
Carlin, Baldwin's Ohio Practice, Merrick-Rippner Probate Law § 19:6, Uniform Parentage Act—Jurisdiction of Action to Determine Father-Child Relationship.
Carlin, Baldwin's Ohio Practice, Merrick-Rippner Probate Law § 15:20, Descent and Distribution—Children or Lineal Descendants—in General.
Carlin, Baldwin's Ohio Practice, Merrick-Rippner Probate Law § 15:30, Descent and Distribution—Child Born Out of Wedlock.
Ohio Consumer Law § 6:8, Ohio's Odometer Rollback and Disclosure Act—Disclosures.
Restatement (2d) of Property, Don. Trans. § 25.2, Gifts to "Children"-Children Born Out of Wedlock.

Law Review and Journal Commentaries

Acknowledgement of Paternity—Changes in Statutes and Forms, Angela G. Carlin. 10 Prob L J Ohio 10 (September/October 1999).

Illegitimacy and Intestate Succession: White v Randolph, Comment. 41 Ohio St L J 1037 (1980).

The Inheritance Rights (or Lack Thereof) of Legitimated Children in Ohio. Angela G. Carlin, 11 Prob L J Ohio 109 (July/August 2001).

Notes of Decisions

Adopted child's estate 2
Children and issue 7
Constitutional issues 1
Father's estate 5
Illegitimate child's estate 3
Mother's estate 6
Wills, bequests and devises 4

1. Constitutional issues

To withstand intermediate level of scrutiny applied to discriminatory classifications based on illegitimacy, statutory classification must be substantially related to important governmental objective. Brookbank v. Gray (Ohio, 01-17-1996) 74 Ohio St.3d 279, 658 N.E.2d 724, 1996-Ohio-135. Constitutional Law ⚖= 213.1(2)

Where a decedent died intestate before statutes excluding illegitimate children from intestates' estates were declared unconstitutional, and where the decedent's illegitimate offspring filed a claim to share in the still-open estate after the declaration of unconstitutionality, the claim cannot be rejected. Reed v. Campbell (U.S.Tex. 1986) 106 S.Ct. 2234, 476 U.S. 852, 90 L.Ed.2d 858, rehearing denied 107 S.Ct. 11, 478 U.S. 1031, 92 L.Ed.2d 766, on remand 719 S.W.2d 655.

Ohio's intestate succession statute, RC Ch 2105, does not unconstitutionally deprive illegitimate children of equal protection of the laws. Young v. Secretary of Health and Human Services (C.A.6 (Ohio) 1986) 787 F.2d 1064, certiorari denied 107 S.Ct. 585, 479 U.S. 990, 93 L.Ed.2d 587.

2. Adopted child's estate

Under the act of March 29, 1859, construed in connection with statutes of descent, the personal estate of an adopted child dying intestate passes to the child's natural mother to the exclusion of adoptive parents and their children. Upson v. Noble (Ohio 1880) 35 Ohio St. 655.

3. Illegitimate child's estate

Where a bastard purchased land and survived his mother, the estate did not, at his death intestate, and without issue, pass to the illegitimate children of his mother, but went to the bastard's widow. Hawkins v. Jones (Ohio 1869) 19 Ohio St. 22.

A bastard, unmarried and intestate, died in 1852 without issue, but survived his mother, who left other children by a marriage which was contracted subsequent to the birth of the bastard; such children were entitled to the bastard's estate. Lewis v. Eutsler (Ohio 1854) 4 Ohio St. 354.

In 1838, the estate of an illegitimate surviving its mother does not, in the case of intestacy without issue, pass to the maternal line. Little's Lessee v. Lake (Ohio 1838) 8 Ohio 289.

The illegitimate brothers of a decedent are incapable of inheriting from him because in contemplation of the law, they are not his brothers, and the statute allowing a bastard to inherit through its mother has no operation where such decedent's estate never vested in or passed through the mother. Stevenson's Heirs v Sullivant, 18 US 207, 5 LEd 70 (1820).

4. Wills, bequests and devises

Children, legitimate or not, can be completely disinherited by implication if a testator completely disposes of all his property by will; such disposition of property overcomes the presumption against disinheritance. Estate of Snell v. Kilburn (Ohio App. 7 Dist., 12-23-2005) 165 Ohio App.3d 352, 846 N.E.2d 572, 2005-Ohio-7076. Wills ⇐ 535

A testator is presumed to disinherit an illegitimate child whose existence he is aware of when he makes specific bequests to his other children but makes no mention of the illegitimate one. Birman v. Sproat (Miami 1988) 47 Ohio App.3d 65, 546 N.E.2d 1354.

An intention to include illegitimate issue must be deduced from the language of a will itself. Flora v. Anderson (C.C.S.D.Ohio 1896) 36 W.L.B. 250, 75 F. 217.

5. Father's estate

An illegitimate child cannot inherit from or through his natural father unless the father takes some steps during his lifetime to permit such inheritance, such as acknowledgment pursuant to RC 2105.18, designating the illegitimate as an heir pursuant to RC 2105.15, adopting the illegitimate, or providing for the illegitimate in his will. Moore v. Dague (Franklin 1975) 46 Ohio App.2d 75, 345 N.E.2d 449, 75 O.O.2d 68. Children Out-of-wedlock ⇐ 86; Children Out-of-wedlock ⇐ 90

An illegitimate child whose paternity has been established during the lifetime of the natural father is entitled to a year's allowance for support from the father's estate. In re Estate of Holley (Ohio Com.Pl. 1975) 44 Ohio Misc. 78, 337 N.E.2d 675, 73 O.O.2d 265. Children Out-of-wedlock ⇐ 90

An illegitimate child is considered the stepchild of the husband whom the mother subsequently marries and who is not the father of the child, and such child may inherit from such husband. Kest v. State (Ohio Prob. 1957) 146 N.E.2d 755, 77 Ohio Law Abs. 193, 4 O.O.2d 250. Children Out-of-wedlock ⇐ 1

6. Mother's estate

An illegitimate daughter could not, in 1847, take under a will as the "issue" of her mother, nor could she inherit collaterally from her mother's niece. Gibson v. McNeely (Ohio 1860) 11 Ohio St. 131.

7. Children and issue

The word "children" appearing in RC 2105.10 (Repealed), the half and half statute, means all children, both legitimate and illegitimate. Green v. Woodard (Cuyahoga 1974) 40 Ohio App.2d 101, 318 N.E.2d 397, 69 O.O.2d 130.

A devise to "issue of her body" means prima facie legitimate issue. Flora v. Anderson (C.C.S.D.Ohio 1896) 36 W.L.B. 250, 75 F. 217.

MISCELLANEOUS PROVISIONS

2105.19 Certain persons not to benefit; complaint to restore rights

(A) Except as provided in division (C) of this section, no person who is convicted of, pleads guilty to, or is found not guilty by reason of insanity of a violation of or complicity in the violation of section 2903.01, 2903.02, or 2903.03 of the Revised Code or of an existing or former law of any other state, the United States, or a foreign nation, substantially equivalent to a violation of or complicity in the violation of any of these sections, no person who is indicted for a violation of or complicity in the violation of any of those sections or laws and subsequently is adjudicated incompetent to stand trial on that charge, and no juvenile who is found to be a delinquent child by reason of committing an act that, if committed by an adult, would be a violation of or complicity in the violation of any of those sections or laws, shall in any way benefit by the death. All property of the decedent, and all money, insurance proceeds, or other property or benefits payable or distributable in respect of the decedent's death, shall pass or be paid or distributed as if the person who caused the death of the decedent had predeceased the decedent.

(B) A person prohibited by division (A) of this section from benefiting by the death of another is a constructive trustee for the benefit of those entitled to any property or benefit that the person has obtained, or over which he has exerted control, because of the decedent's death. A person who purchases any such property or benefit from the constructive trustee, for value, in good faith, and without notice of the constructive trustee's disability under division (A) of this section, acquires good title, but the constructive trustee is accountable to the beneficiaries for the proceeds or value of the property or benefit.

(C) A person who is prohibited from benefiting from a death pursuant to division (A) of this section either because he was adjudicated incompetent to stand trial or was found not guilty by reason of insanity, or his guardian appointed pursuant to Chapter 2111. of the Revised Code or other legal representative, may file a complaint to declare his right to benefit from the death in the probate court in which the decedent's estate is being administered or which released the estate from administration. The complaint shall be filed no later than sixty days after the person is adjudicated incompetent to stand trial or found not guilty by reason of insanity. The court shall notify each person who is a devisee or legatee under the decedent's will, or if there is no will, each person who is an heir of the decedent pursuant to section 2105.06 of the Revised Code that such a complaint has been filed within ten days after the filing of such a complaint. The person who files the motion, and each person who is required to be notified of the filing of the motion under this division is entitled to a jury trial in the action. To assert the right, the person desiring a jury trial shall demand a jury in the manner prescribed in the Civil Rules.

A person who files a complaint pursuant to this division shall be restored to his right to benefit from the death unless the court determines, by a preponderance of the evidence, that the person would have been convicted of a violation of, or complicity in the violation of, section 2903.01, 2903.02, or 2903.03 of the Revised Code, or of a law of another state, the United States, or a foreign nation that is substantially similar to any of those sections, if he had been brought to trial in the case in which he was adjudicated incompetent or if he were not insane at the time of the commission of the offense.

(1985 S 102, eff. 10–17–85; 1982 S 176; 1975 S 145, H 490)

Uncodified Law

1975 S 145, § 3: See Uncodified Law under 2105.06.

Historical and Statutory Notes

Ed. Note: Former 2105.19 repealed by 1975 H 490, eff. 11-20-75; 1953 H 1; GC 10503–17.

Pre–1953 H 1 Amendments: 114 v 342

Legislative Service Commission

1975:

Current law provides that a murderer cannot benefit by inheritance from the one he murders. This new section would expand the coverage of the section to include voluntary manslaughter and conform language to Ohio's new criminal code by defining such a person as one who is convicted of or pleads guilty to a violation or complicity in the violation of the sections that deal with aggravated murder, murder, or voluntary manslaughter. Anything distributable to the wrongdoer—property, money or insurance proceeds—would pass as if the wrongdoer predeceased the decedent. This section would also make the wrongdoer a constructive trustee for the benefit of those entitled to the property or proceeds that he obtained because of the decedent's death. A good faith purchaser of the property would acquire good title but the constructive trustee would be "accountable" for the proceeds to the beneficiaries.

Library References

Descent and Distribution ⚖=51, 90(0.5).
Wills ⚖=711.
Westlaw Topic Nos. 124, 409.
C.J.S. Descent and Distribution §§ 56 to 59, 89 to 90.
C.J.S. Wills §§ 99 to 100.

Research References

Encyclopedias

OH Jur. 3d Decedents' Estates § 15, Descent and Distribution.
OH Jur. 3d Decedents' Estates § 130, Killing of Intestate; Murderer as Constructive Trustee.
OH Jur. 3d Decedents' Estates § 131, Killing of Intestate; Murderer as Constructive Trustee—Right to Insurance Proceeds.
OH Jur. 3d Decedents' Estates § 132, Killing of Intestate; Murderer as Constructive Trustee—Constitutionality.
OH Jur. 3d Decedents' Estates § 264, Person Who Feloniously Kills Testator.
OH Jur. 3d Insurance § 1207, Right of Assignee, Alternative Beneficiary and Estate of Insured.

Forms

Ohio Jurisprudence Pleading and Practice Forms § 108:15, for Peremptory Writ—Compel Lower Court to Journalize Entry.

Treatises and Practice Aids

Klein, Darling, & Terez, Baldwin's Ohio Practice Civil Practice § 38:15, Right to Jury Trial Under Ohio Statutes--Other Statutes.
Carlin, Baldwin's Ohio Practice, Merrick-Rippner Probate Law § 3:3, Jurisdiction of Probate Court—Subject Matter—in General.
Carlin, Baldwin's Ohio Practice, Merrick-Rippner Probate Law § 16:2, Statutory Presumption—Scope.
Carlin, Baldwin's Ohio Practice, Merrick-Rippner Probate Law § 22:1, Statutory Provisions Prohibiting Specified Persons from Benefiting Under Will.
Carlin, Baldwin's Ohio Practice, Merrick-Rippner Probate Law § 22:2, Action to Determine Right to Benefit from Death.
Carlin, Baldwin's Ohio Practice, Merrick-Rippner Probate Law § 22:3, Effect of Prohibition to Benefit.
Carlin, Baldwin's Ohio Practice, Merrick-Rippner Probate Law § 22:4, Effect of Prohibition to Benefit—Joint Accounts.
Carlin, Baldwin's Ohio Practice, Merrick-Rippner Probate Law § 22:5, Necessity for Conviction; Common Law Forfeiture.
Carlin, Baldwin's Ohio Practice, Merrick-Rippner Probate Law § 106:4, Juvenile Court Jurisdiction—Delinquent Child—Non-Criminal Nature of Delinquency Proceedings.
Bogert - the Law of Trusts and Trustees § 478, Property Acquired by Killing Relative or Testator.
Kuehnle and Levey, Ohio Real Estate Law and Practice § 6:27, Cotenancies—Survivorship Tenancies—Succession by Murder.
Restatement (2d) of Property, Don. Trans. § 34.8, Donee Criminally Causes the Death of the Donor.
Restatement (3d) Property (Wills & Don. Trans.) § 8.4, Homicide-The Slayer Rule.

Law Review and Journal Commentaries

Civil Murder Trials: Macabre Reflections Of Our Violent Society, Addison E. Dewey. 19 Cap U L Rev 897 (Fall 1990).

The Constructive Trust: a Neglected Remedy in Ohio, Harry W. Vanneman. 3 Ohio St L J 1 (December 1936).

Mercy Killing and The Right to Inherit, Jeffrey G. Sherman. 61 U Cin L Rev 803 (1993).

Thou Shalt Not Kill (Thy Spouse): A Recent Exception To The ERISA Preemption Doctrine, Note. 29 J Fam L 129 (1990–91).

Notes of Decisions

Ed. Note: This section contains annotations from former RC 2105.19.

Common law 7
Constitutional issues 1
Conviction for less than murder 3
Insurance 5
Joint and survivor property 8
Minors 6
Procedure and evidence 2
Scope of bar 4

---

1. Constitutional issues

RC 2105.19 does not violate O Const Art I, § 12, US Const Art I, § 10, or O Const Art II, § 28. In re Estate of Fiore (Cuyahoga 1984) 16 Ohio App.3d 473, 476 N.E.2d 1093, 16 O.B.R. 555.

Res judicata barred consideration of widower's argument that he did not receive a fair trial during a state wrongful death action, in action by insurer seeking declaratory judgment as to proper recipients of deceased wife's death benefits; a state court found that widower had intentionally and feloniously killed his wife, and a second court had determined that the judgment was sufficient to prohibit widower from receiving the proceeds of the life insurance policy. Metropolitan Life Ins. Co. v. Brown (C.A.6 (Ohio), 03-06-2002) No. 01-3242, 31 Fed.Appx. 166, 2002 WL 370011, Unreported. Insurance ⚖=3557

This section, which does not permit one guilty of murder in the first or second degree to inherit from the person killed, does not violate O Const Art I, § 12. Egelhoff v. Presler (Ohio Prob. 1945) 16 Ohio Supp. 195, 44 Ohio Law Abs. 376, 32 O.O. 252.

Defendant's claims of ineffectiveness of counsel were without merit, in action by administrator to disinherit testator's husband; civil litigants did not have a constitutional right to effective assistance of counsel. In re Estate of Ahmed (Ohio App. 7 Dist., Belmont, 06-20-2002) No. 01-BA-16, 2002-Ohio-3175, 2002 WL 1396794, Unreported, appeal not allowed 96 Ohio St.3d 1516, 775 N.E.2d 857, 2002-Ohio-4950. Trial ⚖= 107

2. Procedure and evidence

The fact that a murder conviction was based on a plea of no contest is irrelevant to the application of RC 2105.19. In re Estate of Fiore (Cuyahoga 1984) 16 Ohio App.3d 473, 476 N.E.2d 1093, 16 O.B.R. 555.

Where RC 2105.19 is inapplicable, the person challenging the claim of the beneficiary has the burden of proving the malicious and intentional killing. Huff v. Union Fidelity Life Ins. Co. (Cuyahoga 1984) 14 Ohio App.3d 135, 470 N.E.2d 236, 14 O.B.R. 151.

RC 2105.19 does not supersede the common-law prohibition against benefiting from a death caused by one's intentional and felonious act; rather, the statute simply eliminates the need to prove that the beneficiary caused a decedent's death by his intentional and felonious act when the beneficiary has been convicted of a designated homicide offense. Huff v. Union Fidelity Life Ins. Co. (Cuyahoga 1984) 14 Ohio App.3d 135, 470 N.E.2d 236, 14 O.B.R. 151.

Where plaintiff's evidence to support a petition by plaintiff as guardian of a minor ward to sell real property of such ward shows that the parents of the ward each owned an undivided one-half interest in real property, that the wife was convicted of murdering her husband but that no attempt was made under RC 2105.19 to deprive her of a share in the estate of her husband who died intestate, and that, thereafter, the wife executed a quit-claim deed in which the grantee, her minor son, was designated as "Estate of..., Ward," such deed effectively divests the wife of all her right, title and interest in the real property and plaintiff has made a prima facie case. Alston v. Alston (Franklin 1964) 4 Ohio App.2d 270, 212 N.E.2d 65, 33 O.O.2d 311. Guardian And Ward ⚖= 88

The stay of execution in testator's husband's criminal case for murdering testator did not bar the probate court from disinheriting testator's husband; statute which prevented a person convicted of murder from benefiting from the death of their victim did not prevent the probate court from disinheriting testator's husband by virtue of him having filed an appeal and obtained a stay of execution. In re Estate of Ahmed (Ohio App. 7 Dist., Belmont, 06-20-2002) No. 01-BA-16, 2002-Ohio-3175, 2002 WL 1396794,

Unreported, appeal not allowed 96 Ohio St.3d 1516, 775 N.E.2d 857, 2002-Ohio-4950. Descent And Distribution 🔑 51

In an action for proceeds of a life insurance policy where the identity of the killer of the insured has not been established in any criminal proceeding, the insurer may not seek to prove that the beneficiary committed the crime; RC 2105.19 states the exclusive method for disqualifying a beneficiary who is claimed to have caused the insured's death by murder or voluntary manslaughter, at least where the identity of the killer is factually in issue and criminal process is available for that determination. Shrader v Equitable Life Assurance Society of the United States, No. 83AP–868 (10th Dist Ct App, Franklin, 12–6–84), reversed by 20 OS(3d) 41, 20 OBR 343, 485 NE(2d) 1031 (1985).

3. Conviction for less than murder

This section could not affect the right to inherit of a defendant who was not convicted of murder in the first or second degree. Demos v. Freemas (Franklin 1938) 26 Ohio Law Abs. 601.

A justifiable killing in defense of oneself or another will not disqualify a beneficiary from recovering benefits resulting from that death. Huff v. Union Fidelity Life Ins. Co. (Cuyahoga 1984) 14 Ohio App.3d 135, 470 N.E.2d 236, 14 O.B.R. 151. Insurance 🔑 3484

The fact that the beneficiary of a life insurance policy pleads guilty to first degree manslaughter of the insured does not preclude her collecting insurance proceeds on his life. Travelers Ins. Co. v. Gray (Ohio Com.Pl. 1973) 37 Ohio Misc. 27, 306 N.E.2d 189, 66 O.O.2d 64.

Conviction of surviving spouse of manslaughter in the first degree in connection with his wife's death does not affect his right to inherit his statutory share in her estate under RC 2105.06. Wadsworth v. Siek (Ohio Prob. 1970) 23 Ohio Misc. 112, 254 N.E.2d 738, 50 O.O.2d 507, 52 O.O.2d 147.

Guardian of a widow who killed her husband and is being held in hospital as insane is entitled to receive the sum of money allowed to her in lieu of property not deemed assets of said estate under GC 10509–54 (RC 2115.13), and her portion of the year's allowance under GC 10509–74 (RC 2117.20), together with her distributive share in the net estate, and, also, is entitled to a certificate of transfer of her interest in the real estate, if any remains unsold. Winters Nat. Bank & Trust Co. v. Shields (Ohio Prob. 1939) 3 Ohio Supp. 134, 29 Ohio Law Abs. 193, 14 O.O. 438.

This section does not apply when murderer commits suicide prior to conviction of first or second degree murder, or where a conviction was of a lesser degree than first or second degree murder. Harrison v. Hillegas (Ohio Prob. 1939) 1 Ohio Supp. 160, 28 Ohio Law Abs. 404, 13 O.O. 523.

4. Scope of bar

Husband who intentionally and feloniously killed his wife forfeited, under common law, right to inherit under wife's will, even though husband was not convicted of offense listed in disqualification statute. In re Estate of Cotton (Ohio App. 10 Dist., 06-06-1995) 104 Ohio App.3d 368, 662 N.E.2d 63. Wills 🔑 711

Neither estate nor parents of wife murdered by husband were entitled to death benefits payable under group life policy obtained through husband's employer, which named husband as sole beneficiary; only husband was entitled to payment and, upon his disqualification, neither wife's estate nor her parents had any right to claim death benefit. Caliman v. Am. Gen. Fire & Cas. Co. (Hamilton 1994) 94 Ohio App.3d 572, 641 N.E.2d 261. Insurance 🔑 3484

The payment of a criminal fine imposed following conviction of the husband of his wife's murder from the proceeds of the wife's estate is a prohibited benefit to the decedent's murderer. In re Estate of Wolfe (Wood 1991) 71 Ohio App.3d 501, 594 N.E.2d 1055.

A probate court lacks jurisdiction to order the trustee of an estate to retain estate funds to pay a fine imposed upon the husband of the decedent as a result of his conviction of her murder. In re Estate of Wolfe (Wood 1991) 71 Ohio App.3d 501, 594 N.E.2d 1055.

A husband finally adjudged guilty of murdering his wife cannot receive or take anything as a surviving spouse. Bauman v. Hogue (Ohio 1953) 160 Ohio St. 296, 116 N.E.2d 439, 52 O.O. 183.

GC 10503–17 (RC 2105.19) does not completely bar a convicted murderer from sharing any benefit from any property, real or personal, owned by the deceased person at his death. (But see Bauman v Hogue, 160 OS 296, 116 NE(2d) 439 (1953).) Tyack v. Tipton (Franklin 1951) 115 N.E.2d 29, 65 Ohio Law Abs. 397.

Murder of a parent in order to inherit will not defeat such inheritance. Zumstein v Consolidated Coal & Mining Co, 11 D Repr 156, 25 B 95 (CP, Hamilton 1891).

This section, which forbids the murderer from benefiting from estate of his victim, clearly manifests an intention of legislature that the estate should vest, that title should pass, and that estate may be possessed and fully enjoyed by the heir before conviction. Winters Nat. Bank & Trust Co. v. Shields (Ohio Prob. 1939) 3 Ohio Supp. 134, 29 Ohio Law Abs. 193, 14 O.O. 438.

One who murders his ancestor is not thereby prevented from inheriting. Deem v Millikin, 6 CC 357, 3 CD 491 (Preble 1892), affirmed by 53 OS 668, 44 NE 1134 (1895).

5. Insurance

This section is not relevant to an action by administrator of estate of deceased woman to recover from husband who killed her the proceeds of an insurance policy of which husband was the beneficiary and which husband had collected, since the money was never part of wife's estate. (See also Cook v Western & Southern Life Insurance Co, 30 NP(NS) 247 (1932).) Hennigh v. Neff (Franklin 1938) 27 Ohio Law Abs. 364.

No credible, probative, or substantial evidence existed to prove, directly or inferentially, that when insured applied for life insurance policy she was acting as unwitting or unknowing instrumentality or agent for husband/primary beneficiary to perform unlawful act that stemmed from husband's present intent to murder insured for money, such as might have established insurer's defense that policy was void ab initio as having been obtained for unlawful purpose, in contingent beneficiary's action to recover policy proceeds after husband was convicted of murdering insured. Bradley v. Farmers New World Life Ins. Co. (Ohio App. 1 Dist., 07-24-1996) 112 Ohio App.3d 696, 679 N.E.2d 1178, cause dismissed 77 Ohio St.3d 1409, 670 N.E.2d 999. Insurance 🔑 1656; Insurance 🔑 3017

No one can be unknowing agent to perform unlawful act by persuading life insurer to issue policy at behest, instruction, or command of principal whose purpose is to murder insured who is his agent. Bradley v. Farmers New World Life Ins. Co. (Ohio App. 1 Dist., 07-24-1996) 112 Ohio App.3d 696, 679 N.E.2d 1178, cause dismissed 77 Ohio St.3d 1409, 670 N.E.2d 999. Insurance 🔑 1656

Evidence did not support life insurer's claim that insured, in completing policy application, had, by not mentioning that she had applied for policy from another life insurer on previous day, submitted willfully false information in response to question asking whether "any life insurance" was "pending," which claim insurer made in connection with its defense that policy was voidable, in contingent beneficiary's action to recover policy proceeds after insured's husband, who was primary beneficiary, was convicted of murdering insured. Bradley v. Farmers New World Life Ins. Co. (Ohio App. 1 Dist., 07-24-1996) 112 Ohio App.3d 696, 679 N.E.2d 1178, cause dismissed 77 Ohio St.3d 1409, 670 N.E.2d 999. Insurance 🔑 3024

Where a murder victim would have held a house as sole owner if surviving the killer and where the house burns after the killing, the victim is deemed entitled to the insurance proceeds less any outstanding encumbrances; where the house is rebuilt with the proceeds and with money supplied by innocent third parties but then sold on foreclosure for a sum less than that invested, the victim's claim takes precedence over the claims of the third parties. Home Sav. & Loan Ass'n v. Potter (Ohio Com.Pl. 1984) 21 Ohio Misc.2d 1, 487 N.E.2d 927, 21 O.B.R. 312.

The identity of a person who intentionally and feloniously causes the death of another can be established in a civil proceeding in order to prevent the wrongdoer from receiving the proceeds of the deceased's life insurance policy. Shrader v. Equitable Life Assur. Soc. of U.S. (Ohio 1985) 20 Ohio St.3d 41, 485 N.E.2d 1031, 20 O.B.R. 343. Insurance 🔑 3557

The permitting of a beneficiary who intentionally and feloniously takes an insured's life to recover on the proceeds of a life insurance policy is contrary to public policy. Travelers Ins. Co. v. Gray (Ohio Com.Pl. 1973) 37 Ohio Misc. 27, 306 N.E.2d 189, 66 O.O.2d 64. Insurance 🔑 3484

Under the common law rule that no one may be allowed to reap a benefit from his own wrong, a beneficiary of a life insurance policy who has murdered the insured acquires no right or title to the proceeds of the policy; further, the same rule applies to prevent one claiming through or under the beneficiary from taking under the policy, so that the administrator as representative of the beneficiary's estate cannot recover in such a case. Cook v. Western & Southern Life Ins. Co. (Ohio Com.Pl. 1932) 30 Ohio N.P.N.S. 247.

RC 2105.19 does not reach a case in which an insurance company seeks to void a policy altogether on the ground that it was purchased for the purpose of defrauding the insuror; neither the statutory nor common law of Ohio comprehends such a case. Henkel v. Stratton (N.D.Ohio 1985) 612 F.Supp. 190.

Person who as beneficiary is denied the right to recover the proceeds of an insurance policy by reason of having feloniously killed the insured, is not precluded as widow and heir of the estate of the insured from participating as such in the insurance proceeds after such proceeds become a part of the general assets of said estate, where she is not the sole distributee. Winters Nat. Bank & Trust Co. v. Shields (Ohio Prob. 1939) 3 Ohio Supp. 134, 29 Ohio Law Abs. 193, 14 O.O. 438. Descent And Distribution ⊕ 63

6. Minors

A juvenile who is found to be delinquent by reason of having committed acts which if committed by an adult would constitute aggravated murder is "convicted" of aggravated murder as that term is used in RC 2105.19 and is therefore barred from benefiting from the death. Bosley v. Hawkins (Ohio Com.Pl. 1985) 24 Ohio Misc.2d 11, 494 N.E.2d 460, 24 O.B.R. 332.

The allowance for surviving minors provided by RC 2117.20 is a benefit within the meaning of RC 2105.19 and is therefore forbidden to the murderer of the decedent. Bosley v. Hawkins (Ohio Com.Pl. 1985) 24 Ohio Misc.2d 11, 494 N.E.2d 460, 24 O.B.R. 332.

Because RC 2151.358(H) declares that a judgment of delinquency neither imposes any of the civil disabilities imposed by a conviction nor renders the child a criminal, a child found delinquent by reason of having purposely killed his father is not disqualified by RC 2105.19 from taking under his father's will. In re Estate of Birt (Ohio Com.Pl. 1983) 18 Ohio Misc.2d 7, 481 N.E.2d 1387, 18 O.B.R. 407.

A minor son, on conviction of murder of his father in second degree, is not entitled to inherit from his father, but this section being a penal statute, and therefore to be strictly construed, does not prevent the son from taking the allowance provided by GC 10509–54 (RC 2115.13). (But see Bauman v Hogue, 160 OS 296, 116 NE(2d) 439 (1953).) Egelhoff v. Presler (Ohio Prob. 1945) 16 Ohio Supp. 195, 44 Ohio Law Abs. 376, 32 O.O. 252.

7. Common law

Determination of who was a beneficiary of life insurance policy bought by employer for employee who was murdered by the designated primary beneficiary of the policy was a question of federal law that had to be determined using federal common law; Employee Retirement Income Security Act of 1974 (ERISA) preempted state slayer statute that barred primary beneficiary from recovering proceeds of policy. Ahmed v. Ahmed (Ohio App. 7 Dist., 09-24-2004) 158 Ohio App.3d 527, 817 N.E.2d 424, 2004-Ohio-5120. Courts ⊕ 97(1); Insurance ⊕ 1117(1); States ⊕ 18.41

Disqualification statute, which prohibits persons who commit specified offenses from benefiting from victim's death, is not exclusive means for disqualifying wrongdoer from inheriting from decedent; common law bars one who intentionally and feloniously killed decedent from receiving property under decedent's last will and testament. In re Estate of Cotton (Ohio App. 10 Dist., 06-06-1995) 104 Ohio App.3d 368, 662 N.E.2d 63. Wills ⊕ 711

RC 2105.19 does not purport to allow recovery by persons whose rights are curtailed by the common law. Huff v. Union Fidelity Life Ins. Co. (Cuyahoga 1984) 14 Ohio App.3d 135, 470 N.E.2d 236, 14 O.B.R. 151.

A minor whose age precludes a conviction that would statutorily bar the receipt of benefit from a decedent's estate can still forfeit beneficial rights under the common law. Huff v. Union Fidelity Life Ins. Co. (Cuyahoga 1984) 14 Ohio App.3d 135, 470 N.E.2d 236, 14 O.B.R. 151. Insurance ⊕ 3484

Under the common law principle that no one may be allowed to reap a benefit from his own wrong, a beneficiary of a life insurance policy who murdered the insured acquires no right or title to the proceeds of the policy; and the same rule applies to prevent one claiming through or under the beneficiary from taking under the policy; hence, the administrator as representative of the beneficiary's estate cannot recover in such case; this section is not intended to abrogate or delimit the common law rule, but to establish by the fact of conviction for murder the legal status of a person so convicted with respect to receiving any benefit from the death of the person unlawfully killed. (See also Hennigh v Neff, 27 Abs 364 (App, Franklin 1938).) Cook v. Western & Southern Life Ins. Co. (Ohio Com.Pl. 1932) 30 Ohio N.P.N.S. 247.

8. Joint and survivor property

Mortgages executed to defense attorneys by a spouse accused of murdering the other spouse are defeatable on the mortgagor's conviction for murder where the property was held jointly at the time of the crime and would have passed to the victim had the victim survived the murderer; the attorneys are presumed to have been aware of RC 2105.19. Home Sav. & Loan Ass'n v. Potter (Ohio Com.Pl. 1984) 21 Ohio Misc.2d 1, 487 N.E.2d 927, 21 O.B.R. 312.

Where two parties contribute funds to, and have an equal right to the proceeds of, a joint and survivorship account, and one murders the other, RC 2105.19 treats the murderer as though he had predeceased the decedent, thereby making the decedent the survivor entitled to the whole account. In re Estate of Fiore (Cuyahoga 1984) 16 Ohio App.3d 473, 476 N.E.2d 1093, 16 O.B.R. 555.

In the absence of a controlling statute, the fact that one of the owners of a joint and survivor bank account murders another such owner does not divest the murderer of his right in such account. Shuman v. Schick (Meigs 1953) 95 Ohio App. 413, 120 N.E.2d 330, 53 O.O. 441. Joint Tenancy ⊕ 6

2105.20 Waste by tenant for life

A tenant for life in real property who commits or suffers waste thereto shall forfeit that part of the property, to which such waste is committed or suffered, to the person having the immediate estate in reversion or remainder and such tenant will be liable in damages to such person for the waste committed or suffered thereto.

(1953 H 1, eff. 10–1–53; GC 10503–23)

Historical and Statutory Notes

Pre–1953 H 1 Amendments: 114 v 344

Comparative Laws

Cal.—West's Ann.Cal.Civ.Proc.Code § 732.
Ky.—Baldwin's KRS 381.350.
Mich.—M.C.L.A. § 600.2919.

Cross References

Actions by one coparcener against another, 5307.21
Dower is forfeited by waste, 2103.07

Library References

Life Estates ⊕5.
Westlaw Topic No. 240.
C.J.S. Estates §§ 32, 35.

Research References

Encyclopedias

OH Jur. 3d Estates, Pwrs., & Restrnts. on Alienat. § 66, Waste.
OH Jur. 3d Estates, Pwrs., & Restrnts. on Alienat. § 76, Waste.
OH Jur. 3d Waste § 1, Waste Defined.
OH Jur. 3d Waste § 13, Damages.
OH Jur. 3d Waste § 15, Forfeiture.
OH Jur. 3d Waste § 18, Generally; Reversioner, Remainderman, or Tenants in Common.
OH Jur. 3d Waste § 23, Generally; Tenants in Possession or in Common.
OH Jur. 3d Waste § 30, Limitation of Actions.

Forms

Am. Jur. Pl. & Pr. Forms Estates § 2, 2.

Treatises and Practice Aids

Carlin, Baldwin's Ohio Practice, Merrick-Rippner Probate Law § 23:1, Actionable Waste.
Carlin, Baldwin's Ohio Practice, Merrick-Rippner Probate Law § 23:3, Who May Bring an Action for Waste.
Carlin, Baldwin's Ohio Practice, Merrick-Rippner Probate Law § 23:4, Relief Available in an Action for Waste.

Carlin, Baldwin's Ohio Practice, Merrick-Rippner Probate Law § 30:21, Drafting a Will—Beneficiary Clauses—Disinheritance of Afterborn or Pretermitted Heirs.

Restatement (2d) of Property, Land. & Ten. § 12.2, Tenant's Rights and Obligations as to Changes in the Physical Condition of the Leased Property.

Law Review and Journal Commentaries

Remedies for Waste In Ohio, Comment. 17 Ohio St L J 326 (Summer 1956).

Notes of Decisions

Common law 4
Evidence and damages 2
Procedural issues 1
Reversion or remainder 5
Waste 3

---

1. Procedural issues

Forfeiture was not available remedy in property owner's action against life tenant for intentional waste on property, where lease did not contain provision for forfeiture as remedy for breach of lease terms. Barkacs v. Perkins (Ohio App. 6 Dist., 02-03-2006) 165 Ohio App.3d 576, 847 N.E.2d 481, 2006-Ohio-469. Waste ⚖ 22

Where as part of a separation agreement a husband conveyed property to his wife for life, and upon her death and upon his to a third person in fee simple, he had standing to bring an action under RC 2105.20. Folden v. Folden (Meigs 1962) 188 N.E.2d 193, 90 Ohio Law Abs. 218, 26 O.O.2d 240.

Provisions of this section, relating to relief against waste committed by tenant for life in real property, are to be construed strictly, the action contemplated being a special proceeding at law. Cook v. Hardin County Bank Co. (Hancock 1945) 76 Ohio App. 203, 63 N.E.2d 686, 31 O.O. 498.

Executor's action to forfeit life estate created by will and obtain possession of realty for sale and distribution of proceeds *held* not "chancery case," and therefore not appealable (GC § 8593; Const Art IV, §6). Oglesbee v. Miller (Ohio 1932) 125 Ohio St. 223, 181 N.E. 26, 36 Ohio Law Rep. 308. Appeal And Error ⚖ 4; Courts ⚖ 240

If there is an estate of freehold in esse interposed between an estate and a tenant for life who commits waste and the subsequent estate of inheritance, then, during continuance of the interposed estate, the action of waste is suspended. Hatch v. Hatch (Ohio Com.Pl. 1893) 1 Ohio Dec. 270, 31 W.L.B. 57.

2. Evidence and damages

In an action to enjoin waste and forfeit life estate in which a final decree has been taken to enjoin and for an accounting, but no judgment has been taken for recovery of the land, parties can appeal, but cannot have a second trial. Jenks v. Langdon (Ohio 1871) 21 Ohio St. 362.

Even if owner of real property could seek remedy of forfeiture in action against life tenant for intentional waste on property, owner failed to establish that damages would not be adequate remedy, where only evidence present by owner on issue was owner's bald assertions that seeking damages would be impractical. Barkacs v. Perkins (Ohio App. 6 Dist., 02-03-2006) 165 Ohio App.3d 576, 847 N.E.2d 481, 2006-Ohio-469. Waste ⚖ 22

Evidence did not warrant a forfeiture of a life estate under RC 2105.20. Folden v. Folden (Meigs 1962) 188 N.E.2d 193, 90 Ohio Law Abs. 218, 26 O.O.2d 240.

A cause of action for damages for waste accrues at the time such waste is committed or suffered and is barred in four years thereafter. Reams v. Henney (Franklin 1950) 88 Ohio App. 409, 97 N.E.2d 37, 58 Ohio Law Abs. 507, 44 O.O. 196.

In an action by remaindermen against the administrator of the estate of a life tenant to recover damages for permissive waste, evidence of waste suffered prior to the four-year period immediately preceding the institution of the action is not admissible. Reams v. Henney (Franklin 1950) 88 Ohio App. 409, 97 N.E.2d 37, 58 Ohio Law Abs. 507, 44 O.O. 196. Limitation Of Actions ⚖ 199(1)

Rule of damages is the diminished value of the estate in remainder by reason of waste. Kent v. Bentley (Ohio Cir. 1895) 6 Ohio C.D. 457, 3 Ohio Dec. 173. Damages ⚖ 108; Life Estates ⚖ 28; Waste ⚖ 18

3. Waste

Where dower consists of unimproved town lots and unimproved woodland, a widow may sell growing timber to pay taxes and an agent's compensation for selling. Crockett v. Crockett (Ohio 1853) 2 Ohio St. 180.

Timber cut in improving the land belongs to the tenant for life and not to the reversioner. Crockett v. Crockett (Ohio 1853) 2 Ohio St. 180. Life Estates ⚖ 13; Logs And Logging ⚖ 5; Reversions ⚖ 5

The tenant for life of a conventional life estate who assigns all of his interest in such premises and surrenders possession to his assignee cannot be held liable for waste suffered subsequent to such assignment and surrender of possession. Howell v. Howell (Ohio 1930) 122 Ohio St. 543, 172 N.E. 528, 71 A.L.R. 1182, 8 Ohio Law Abs. 337, 32 Ohio Law Rep. 76.

One acquiring a life estate in land before commencement of mining operations cannot operate for oil, or make oil lease thereon, without committing enjoinable waste. Fourth & Central Trust Co. v. Woolley (Ohio App. 1928) 31 Ohio App. 259, 165 N.E. 742, 28 Ohio Law Rep. 497. Life Estates ⚖ 12; Waste ⚖ 8

Originally, this section provided that a widow should not commit waste; the amendment provides that a tenant for life shall not commit waste. Brenneman v. Brenneman (Ohio Com.Pl. 1895) 3 Ohio Dec. 392, 1 Ohio N.P. 332.

Under Ohio law, there is no common or joint right of possession as between life tenant and remainderman, and life tenant may, subject to doctrine of waste, exclude remainderman from possession and use of property. In re Sargent (Bkrtcy.N.D.Ohio, 01-04-2006) 337 B.R. 661. Life Estates ⚖ 11

4. Common law

The strict common law rule as to waste has never prevailed in Ohio and many things may be done by a tenant for life here that in England would be waste. Crockett v. Crockett (Ohio 1853) 2 Ohio St. 180.

Common-law waste as to life estates is not recognized in Ohio and is not substantive ground for equitable relief. Gard v. Beard (Butler 1929) 36 Ohio App. 105, 172 N.E. 673, 9 Ohio Law Abs. 298. Life Estates ⚖ 11; Waste ⚖ 15

Prior to March 19, 1887, in Ohio, estates for life other than dower of curtesy, were not forfeitable for waste committed or suffered by life tenant. Kent v. Bentley (Ohio Cir. 1895) 6 Ohio C.D. 457, 3 Ohio Dec. 173.

This section does not affect life estates vested before its passage. Kent v. Bentley (Ohio Cir. 1895) 6 Ohio C.D. 457, 3 Ohio Dec. 173.

5. Reversion or remainder

This section authorizes action for damages by the person having the immediate estate in reversion against a tenant for life in real property for waste either committed or suffered by such life tenant. Reams v. Henney (Franklin 1950) 88 Ohio App. 409, 97 N.E.2d 37, 58 Ohio Law Abs. 507, 44 O.O. 196.

An estate tail in expectancy in real estate is not an "immediate estate in reversion or remainder" within meaning of that phrase as used in this section. Cook v. Hardin County Bank Co. (Hancock 1945) 76 Ohio App. 203, 63 N.E.2d 686, 31 O.O. 498. Waste ⚖ 22

Will devised either an estate tail or a life estate to a named person and either an estate tail in expectancy or an estate in remainder to his children, in the same real estate; children gave quitclaim deeds of their interest to the named person; interest devised to the named person was purchased by bank at sheriff's sale pursuant to a judgment in a foreclosure action; some years later children commenced an action against bank praying for forfeiture of its interest and for damages for waste, which action was based upon provisions of this section; held: children do not have required "immediate estate in reversion or remainder" in property to maintain action. Cook v. Hardin County Bank Co. (Hancock 1945) 76 Ohio App. 203, 63 N.E.2d 686, 31 O.O. 498. Waste ⚖ 22

An action predicated upon this section may be maintained only by person or persons having the immediate estate in reversion or remainder in the real property. Cook v. Hardin County Bank Co. (Hancock 1945) 76 Ohio App. 203, 63 N.E.2d 686, 31 O.O. 498. Waste ⚖ 22

2105.25 Declaration of fatherhood of adult child

(A) As used in this section and section 2105.26 of the Revised Code:

(1) "Adult child" means a person born in this state who is twenty-three years old or older.

(2) "Genetic test" has the same meaning as in section 3111.09 of the Revised Code.

(B) A man alleging himself to be the father of an adult child, the adult child's mother, and the adult child may appear together before the probate judge of the county in which the man resides and jointly file a declaration stating that the man is the adult child's father and requesting that the court issue an order declaring the man to be the adult child's father. The declaration must state that the adult child's birth certificate does not designate anyone as the adult child's father, the request for the order is made freely and voluntarily by all parties appearing before the court, and genetic test results show the man is the adult child's father. A copy of the birth certificate and the genetic test results must be attached to the declaration.

(C) The man alleging himself to be the adult child's father and the adult child may appear before the court without the adult child's mother and file the declaration if the mother is deceased or has been adjudicated incompetent. If the man alleging himself to be the adult child's father is not a resident of this state, appearance under this section may be made before a probate judge of any county of this state.

(2001 H 85, eff. 10–31–01)

Library References

Children Out-of-Wedlock ⚖12, 90.
Westlaw Topic No. 76H.
C.J.S. Children Out-of-Wedlock §§ 23, 25, 29.

Research References

Encyclopedias

OH Jur. 3d Decedents' Estates § 86, Illegitimate Blood Relationship.

Law Review and Journal Commentaries

Practical Application of House Bill 85 (Probate Reform 2001), Marilyn J. Maag. 13 Prob L J Ohio 19 (November/December 2002).

2105.26 Order declaring man alleging himself to be father of adult child as adult child's father

(A) If the probate court determines the following, it shall issue the order requested under section 2105.25 of the Revised Code declaring the man alleging himself to be the father of the adult child to be the adult child's father:

(1) The order was freely and voluntarily requested.

(2) No person is designated as the father on the birth certificate of the adult child.

(3) Genetic test results show that the man is the father of the adult child.

(4) It is in the best interests of the man and adult child that the order be issued.

(B) As part of the order, the court shall order the adult child's birth certificate to be changed to designate the man as the adult child's father.

(C) After issuance of an order under this section, the adult child shall be considered the child of the man declared to be the father as if born to him in lawful wedlock, except that the adult child and the adult child's mother shall not be awarded child support from the man for the time the adult child was a minor.

(2001 H 85, eff. 10–31–01)

Library References

Children Out-of-Wedlock ⚖12, 13, 90.
Westlaw Topic No. 76H.
C.J.S. Children Out-of-Wedlock §§ 23, 25, 28 to 29.

Research References

Encyclopedias

OH Jur. 3d Decedents' Estates § 86, Illegitimate Blood Relationship.

SURVIVORSHIP

2105.31 Definitions

As used in sections 2105.31 to 2105.39 of the Revised Code:

(A) "Co–owners with right of survivorship" includes joint tenants, tenants by the entireties, and other co-owners of real or personal property; insurance or other policies; or bank, savings bank, credit union, or other accounts, held under circumstances that entitle one or more persons to the whole of the property or account on the death of the other person or persons.

(B) "Governing instrument" means a deed, will, trust, insurance or annuity policy, account with a transfer-on-death designation or the abbreviation TOD, account with a payable-on-death designation or the abbreviation POD, pension, profit-sharing, retirement, or similar benefit plan, instrument creating or exercising a power of appointment or a power of attorney, or a dispositive, appointive, or nominative instrument of any similar type.

(C) "Payor" means a trustee, insurer, business entity, employer, governmental agency, political subdivision, or any other person authorized or obligated by law or a governing instrument to make payments or transfers.

(D) "Event" includes the death of another person.

(2005 H 81, eff. 4–14–06; 2002 H 242, eff. 5–16–02)

Historical and Statutory Notes

Amendment Note: 2005 H 81 inserted ", savings bank, credit union," in division (A); and made other nonsubstantive changes.

Cross References

Wills, failure to make election, 2106.04

Research References

Encyclopedias

OH Jur. 3d Decedents' Estates § 15, Descent and Distribution.
OH Jur. 3d Decedents' Estates § 43, Statutory Nonsurvivorship; Simultaneous Death Statute.
OH Jur. 3d Decedents' Estates § 44, Statutory Nonsurvivorship; Simultaneous Death Statute—Present and Former Simultaneous Death Statute Distinguished.
OH Jur. 3d Decedents' Estates § 45, Statutory Nonsurvivorship; Simultaneous Death Statute—Purpose and Effect of the Simultaneous Death Statute.
OH Jur. 3d Decedents' Estates § 46, Statutory Nonsurvivorship; Simultaneous Death Statute—Application of the Simultaneous Death Statute.
OH Jur. 3d Decedents' Estates § 116, Under the Statute of Descent and Distribution.
OH Jur. 3d Decedents' Estates § 263, Deceased Person or Person Dying Within 30 Days of Testator's Death.
OH Jur. 3d Decedents' Estates § 746, Election as Affected by Simultaneous Death or Death Within 30 Days.
OH Jur. 3d Decedents' Estates § 750, Effect of Failure to Make Election or Seek Extension.

OH Jur. 3d Decedents' Estates § 751, Effect of Failure to Make Election or Seek Extension—Death Before Expiration of Time for Election.

OH Jur. 3d Decedents' Estates § 779, Constructive Death.

Forms

Ohio Forms and Transactions KP 30.04, Common Disaster and Presumed Order of Death.

Treatises and Practice Aids

Carlin, Baldwin's Ohio Practice, Merrick-Rippner Probate Law § 9:1, Presumption of Death—Statutory.

Carlin, Baldwin's Ohio Practice, Merrick-Rippner Probate Law § 9:2, Presumption of Death—Procedure for Establishing—Jurisdiction.

Carlin, Baldwin's Ohio Practice, Merrick-Rippner Probate Law § 9:3, Presumption of Death—Procedure for Establishing—Necessary Parties Defendant.

Carlin, Baldwin's Ohio Practice, Merrick-Rippner Probate Law § 9:4, Presumption of Death—Procedure for Establishing—Notice.

Carlin, Baldwin's Ohio Practice, Merrick-Rippner Probate Law § 9:5, Presumption of Death—Procedure for Establishing—Filing Complaint.

Carlin, Baldwin's Ohio Practice, Merrick-Rippner Probate Law § 9:7, Presumption of Death—Effect of Decree.

Carlin, Baldwin's Ohio Practice, Merrick-Rippner Probate Law § 9:9, Presumption of Death—Complaint—Form.

Carlin, Baldwin's Ohio Practice, Merrick-Rippner Probate Law § 15:1, Descent and Distribution—Scope of Statutes.

Carlin, Baldwin's Ohio Practice, Merrick-Rippner Probate Law § 15:2, Descent and Distribution—Definitions.

Carlin, Baldwin's Ohio Practice, Merrick-Rippner Probate Law § 16:1, Statutory Provisions.

Carlin, Baldwin's Ohio Practice, Merrick-Rippner Probate Law § 17:2, Designation—Effect.

Carlin, Baldwin's Ohio Practice, Merrick-Rippner Probate Law § 2:39, Elective Rights of Surviving Spouse—Election to Take Under Law or Under the Will—Failure to Make Election Against the Will.

Carlin, Baldwin's Ohio Practice, Merrick-Rippner Probate Law § 20:5, Advancement—Rights of a Pretermitted Child.

Carlin, Baldwin's Ohio Practice, Merrick-Rippner Probate Law § 21:5, Rights of Surviving Spouse to Make Election—Statutory Provisions—Effect.

Carlin, Baldwin's Ohio Practice, Merrick-Rippner Probate Law § 24:2, Escheat—Scope of Statutes.

Carlin, Baldwin's Ohio Practice, Merrick-Rippner Probate Law § 24:3, Escheat—Operation.

Carlin, Baldwin's Ohio Practice, Merrick-Rippner Probate Law § 46:1, Anti-Lapse Statute.

Carlin, Baldwin's Ohio Practice, Merrick-Rippner Probate Law § 47:1, Afterborn or Pretermitted Heirs—Definitions.

Carlin, Baldwin's Ohio Practice, Merrick-Rippner Probate Law § 47:2, Afterborn or Pretermitted Heirs—Statutory Provisions.

Carlin, Baldwin's Ohio Practice, Merrick-Rippner Probate Law § 47:3, Afterborn or Pretermitted Heirs—Explanatory Chart 1.

Carlin, Baldwin's Ohio Practice, Merrick-Rippner Probate Law § 47:4, Afterborn or Pretermitted Heirs—Explanatory Chart 2.

Carlin, Baldwin's Ohio Practice, Merrick-Rippner Probate Law § 47:5, Afterborn or Pretermitted Heirs—Intent to Disinherit.

Carlin, Baldwin's Ohio Practice, Merrick-Rippner Probate Law § 77:3, Unclaimed Money—Escheat Distinguished.

Carlin, Baldwin's Ohio Practice, Merrick-Rippner Probate Law § 9:10, Presumption of Death—Entry Setting for Hearing, Ordering Notice, and Service of Summons—Form.

Carlin, Baldwin's Ohio Practice, Merrick-Rippner Probate Law § 15:43, Descent and Distribution—Escheat.

Carlin, Baldwin's Ohio Practice, Merrick-Rippner Probate Law § 19:10, Uniform Parentage Act—Procedure in Action to Determine Father-Child Relationship.

Carlin, Baldwin's Ohio Practice, Merrick-Rippner Probate Law § 21:15, Rights of Surviving Spouse to Make Election—Proceedings for Advice or Declaratory Judgment.

Carlin, Baldwin's Ohio Practice, Merrick-Rippner Probate Law § 21:30, Rights of Surviving Spouse to Make Election—Right to Use of Mansion House and Family Allowance.

Carlin, Baldwin's Ohio Practice, Merrick-Rippner Probate Law § 21:39, Rights of Surviving Spouse to Make Election—Failure to Make Election—Scope of RC 2106.04.

Carlin, Baldwin's Ohio Practice, Merrick-Rippner Probate Law § 21:41, Rights of Surviving Spouse to Make Election—Failure to Make Election—Conclusive Presumption.

Carlin, Baldwin's Ohio Practice, Merrick-Rippner Probate Law § 21:56, Rights of Surviving Spouse—Family Allowance—Time Limitations.

Carlin, Baldwin's Ohio Practice, Merrick-Rippner Probate Law § 30:17, Drafting a Will—Beneficiary Clauses—Alternate Beneficiary.

Carlin, Baldwin's Ohio Practice, Merrick-Rippner Probate Law § 30:21, Drafting a Will—Beneficiary Clauses—Disinheritance of Afterborn or Pretermitted Heirs.

Carlin, Baldwin's Ohio Practice, Merrick-Rippner Probate Law § 30:57, Simple Will—Form.

Carlin, Baldwin's Ohio Practice, Merrick-Rippner Probate Law § 30:120, Distribution to a Custodian Under the Transfers to Minors Act of Ohio When a Devisee Shall be Under 18 Years of Age—Form.

Carlin, Baldwin's Ohio Practice, Merrick-Rippner Probate Law § 30:131, Legacy to Two Persons or the Survivor; or as Part of Residue—Form.

Carlin, Baldwin's Ohio Practice, Merrick-Rippner Probate Law § 30:132, Simultaneous Death—Form.

Law Review and Journal Commentaries

Ohio Enacts the Uniform Simultaneous Death Act. Richard E. Davis, 12 Prob L J Ohio 54 (March/April 2002).

2105.32 Determination of survivorship with respect to specified person

(A) Except as provided in section 2105.36 of the Revised Code, a person who is not established by clear and convincing evidence to have survived another specified person by one hundred twenty hours is deemed to have predeceased the other person for the following purposes:

(1) When the title to real or personal property or the devolution of real or personal property depends upon a person's survivorship of the death of another person;

(2) When the right to elect an interest in or exempt a surviving spouse's share of an intestate estate under section 2105.06 of the Revised Code depends upon a person's survivorship of the death of another person;

(3) When the right to elect an interest in or exempt an interest of the decedent in the mansion house pursuant to section 2106.10 of the Revised Code depends upon a person's survivorship of the death of another person;

(4) When the right to elect an interest in or exempt an allowance for support pursuant to section 2106.13 of the Revised Code depends upon a person's survivorship of the death of another person.

(B) This section does not apply if its application would result in a taking of an intestate estate by the state.

(2002 H 242, eff. 5–16–02)

Library References

Joint Tenancy ⚖6.
Westlaw Topic No. 226.
C.J.S. Joint Tenancy §§ 3 to 5, 7, 10, 19 to 20, 36.

Research References

Forms

Ohio Forms and Transactions KP 30.04, Common Disaster and Presumed Order of Death.

Treatises and Practice Aids

Carlin, Baldwin's Ohio Practice, Merrick-Rippner Probate Law § 16:1, Statutory Provisions.

Carlin, Baldwin's Ohio Practice, Merrick-Rippner Probate Law § 2:39, Elective Rights of Surviving Spouse—Election to Take Under Law or Under the Will—Failure to Make Election Against the Will.

2105.33 Determination of survivorship with respect to specified event

Except as provided in section 2105.36 of the Revised Code, a person who is not established by clear and convincing evidence to have survived a specified event by one hundred twenty hours is deemed to have predeceased the event for purposes of a provision of a governing instrument that relates to the person surviving an event.

(2002 H 242, eff. 5–16–02)

Library References

Joint Tenancy ⚖6.
Westlaw Topic No. 226.
C.J.S. Joint Tenancy §§ 3 to 5, 7, 10, 19 to 20, 36.

Research References

Treatises and Practice Aids
Carlin, Baldwin's Ohio Practice, Merrick-Rippner Probate Law § 16:1, Statutory Provisions.

2105.34 Co–owners with right of survivorship

Except as provided in section 2105.36 of the Revised Code:

(A) If it is not established by clear and convincing evidence that one of two co-owners with right of survivorship in specified real or personal property survived the other co-owner by one hundred twenty hours, that property shall pass as if each person had survived the other person by one hundred twenty hours.

(B) If there are more than two co-owners with right of survivorship in specified real or personal property and it is not established by clear and convincing evidence that at least one of the co-owners survived the others by one hundred twenty hours, that property shall pass in the proportion that each person owns.

(2002 H 242, eff. 5–16–02)

Library References

Joint Tenancy ⚖6.
Westlaw Topic No. 226.
C.J.S. Joint Tenancy §§ 3 to 5, 7, 10, 19 to 20, 36.

Research References

Treatises and Practice Aids
Carlin, Baldwin's Ohio Practice, Merrick-Rippner Probate Law § 16:1, Statutory Provisions.

2105.35 Establishment of death

(A)(1) A person is dead if the person has been determined to be dead pursuant to standards established under section 2108.30 of the Revised Code.

(2) A physician who makes a determination of death in accordance with section 2108.30 of the Revised Code and any person who acts in good faith in reliance on a determination of death made by a physician in accordance with that section is entitled to the immunity conveyed by that section.

(B) A certified or authenticated copy of a death certificate purporting to be issued by an official or agency of the place where the death of a person purportedly occurred is prima-facie evidence of the fact, place, date, and time of the person's death and the identity of the decedent.

(C) A certified or authenticated copy of any record or report of a domestic or foreign governmental agency that a person is missing, detained, dead, or alive is prima-facie evidence of the status and of the dates, circumstances, and places disclosed by the record or report.

(D) In the absence of prima-facie evidence of death under division (B) or (C) of this section, the fact of death may be established by clear and convincing evidence, including circumstantial evidence.

(E) Except as provided in division (F) of this section, a presumption of the death of a person arises:

(1) When the person has disappeared and been continuously absent from the person's place of last domicile for a five-year period without being heard from during the period;

(2) When the person has disappeared and been continuously absent from the person's place of last domicile without being heard from and was at the beginning of the person's absence exposed to a specific peril of death, even though the absence has continued for less than a five-year period.

(F) When a person who is on active duty in the armed services of the United States has been officially determined to be absent in a status of "missing" or "missing in action," a presumption of death arises when the head of the federal department concerned has made a finding of death pursuant to the "Federal Missing Persons Act," 80 Stat. 625 (1966), 37 U.S.C.A. 551, as amended.

(G) In the absence of evidence disputing the time of death stipulated on a document described in division (B) or (C) of this section, a document described in either of those divisions that stipulates a time of death one hundred twenty hours or more after the time of death of another person, however the time of death of the other person is determined, establishes by clear and convincing evidence that the person survived the other person by one hundred twenty hours.

(H) The provisions of divisions (A) to (G) of this section are in addition to any other provisions of the Revised Code, the Rules of Criminal Procedure, or the Rules of Evidence that pertain to the determination of death and status of a person.

(2002 H 242, eff. 5–16–02)

Library References

Descent and Distribution ⚖18.
Joint Tenancy ⚖6.
Westlaw Topic Nos. 124, 226.
C.J.S. Joint Tenancy §§ 3 to 5, 7, 10, 19 to 20, 36.

Research References

Encyclopedias
OH Jur. 3d Insurance § 1462, Public or Official Records—Death Certificates.

Treatises and Practice Aids
Carlin, Baldwin's Ohio Practice, Merrick-Rippner Probate Law § 16:1, Statutory Provisions.

2105.36 Determination of survivorship; exceptions

A person who is not established by clear and convincing evidence to have survived another specified person by one hundred twenty hours shall not be deemed to have predeceased the other person if any of the following apply:

(A) The governing instrument contains language dealing explicitly with simultaneous deaths or deaths in a common disaster, and that language is operative under the situation in question.

(B) The governing instrument expressly indicates that a person is not required to survive an event by any specified period in order for any right or interest governed by the instrument to properly vest or transfer.

(C) The governing instrument expressly requires the person to survive the event for a specified period in order for any right or interest governed by the instrument to properly vest or transfer, and the survival of the event by the person or survival of the event by the person for the specified period is established by clear and convincing evidence.

(D) The imposition of a one-hundred-twenty-hour requirement of the person's survival of the other specified person causes a nonvested property interest or a power of appointment to be invalid under section 2131.08 of the Revised Code, and the person's survival of the other specified person is established by clear and convincing evidence.

(E) The application of a one-hundred-twenty-hour requirement of survival to multiple governing instruments would result in an unintended failure or duplication of a disposition, and the person's survival of the other specified person is established by clear and convincing evidence.

(2002 H 242, eff. 5–16–02)

Library References

Joint Tenancy ⚖6.
Westlaw Topic No. 226.
C.J.S. Joint Tenancy §§ 3 to 5, 7, 10, 19 to 20, 36.

Research References

Forms

Ohio Forms and Transactions KP 30.04, Common Disaster and Presumed Order of Death.

Treatises and Practice Aids

Carlin, Baldwin's Ohio Practice, Merrick-Rippner Probate Law § 16:1, Statutory Provisions.

Carlin, Baldwin's Ohio Practice, Merrick-Rippner Probate Law § 2:39, Elective Rights of Surviving Spouse—Election to Take Under Law or Under the Will—Failure to Make Election Against the Will.

2105.37 Liability of payor or other third party

(A) A payor or other third party is not liable for any of the following:

(1) Making a payment, transferring an item of real or personal property, or otherwise transferring any other benefit to a person designated in a governing instrument who, under sections 2105.31 to 2105.39 of the Revised Code, is not entitled to the payment or item of property, if the payment or transfer was made before the payor or other third party received written notice of a claimed lack of entitlement pursuant to sections 2105.31 to 2105.39 of the Revised Code;

(2) Taking any other action not specified in division (A)(1) of this section in good faith reliance on the person's apparent entitlement under the terms of the governing instrument before the payor or other third party received written notice of a claimed lack of entitlement pursuant to sections 2105.31 to 2105.39 of the Revised Code.

(B) A payor or other third party is liable for a payment, transfer, or other action taken after the payor or other third party receives written notice of a claimed lack of entitlement pursuant to sections 2105.31 to 2105.39 of the Revised Code.

(C) Written notice of a claimed lack of entitlement under divisions (A) or (B) of this section must be mailed to the payor's or other third party's main office or home by registered or certified mail, return receipt requested, or served upon the payor or other third party in the same manner as a summons in a civil action. Upon receipt of written notice of a claimed lack of entitlement pursuant to sections 2105.31 to 2105.39 of the Revised Code, a payor or other third party may pay any amount owed or transfer or deposit any item of real or personal property held by it to or with the probate court that has jurisdiction over the decedent's estate. If no probate proceedings have been commenced, upon receipt of written notice of a claimed lack of entitlement pursuant to sections 2105.31 to 2105.39 of the Revised Code, a payor or other third party may pay any amount owed or transfer or deposit any item of real or personal property held by it to or with the probate court located in the county of the decedent's residence. The court shall hold the funds or real or personal property until it is determined pursuant to sections 2105.31 to 2105.39 of the Revised Code to whom the funds or real or personal property should be disbursed. The court then shall order disbursement of the funds or real or personal property in accordance with that determination. Payments, transfers, or deposits made to or with the court discharge the payor or other third party from all claims for the value of amounts paid to or items of property transferred to or deposited with the court.

(2002 H 242, eff. 5–16–02)

Library References

Joint Tenancy ⚖12.
Westlaw Topic No. 226.
C.J.S. Joint Tenancy §§ 31 to 34.

Research References

Treatises and Practice Aids

Carlin, Baldwin's Ohio Practice, Merrick-Rippner Probate Law § 16:1, Statutory Provisions.

Law Review and Journal Commentaries

Ohio Enacts the Uniform Simultaneous Death Act. Richard E. Davis, 12 Prob L J Ohio 54 (March/April 2002).

2105.38 Protected purchasers

(A) A person who purchases real or personal property that would otherwise be subject to sections 2105.31 to 2105.39 of the Revised Code for value and without notice that the person selling or otherwise transferring the real or personal property is not entitled to the real or personal property pursuant to sections 2105.31 to 2105.39 of the Revised Code is neither obligated under sections 2105.31 to 2105.39 of the Revised Code to return the payment, item of property, or benefit nor liable under sections 2105.31 to 2105.39 of the Revised Code for the amount of the payment or the value of the item of property or benefit.

A person who receives a payment or other item of real or personal property in partial or full satisfaction of a legally enforceable obligation without notice that the person making the payment or otherwise transferring the real or personal property is not entitled to the real or personal property pursuant to sections 2105.31 to 2105.39 of the Revised Code is neither obligated under sections 2105.31 to 2105.39 of the Revised Code to return the payment, item of property, or benefit nor liable under sections 2105.31 to 2105.39 of the Revised Code for the amount of the payment or the value of the item of property or benefit.

(B) A person who, not for value, receives a payment, item of real or personal property, or any other benefit to which the person is not entitled under sections 2105.31 to 2105.39 of the Revised Code is obligated to return the payment, item of real or personal property, or benefit, and is personally liable for the amount of the payment or the value of the item of property or benefit, to the person who is entitled to it under sections 2105.31 to 2105.39 of the Revised Code.

(C) If sections 2105.31 to 2105.39 of the Revised Code or any provision of sections 2105.31 to 2105.39 of the Revised Code are preempted by federal law with respect to a payment, an item of real or personal property, or any other benefit covered by sections 2105.31 to 2105.39 of the Revised Code, a person who, not for value, receives the payment, item of property, or any other benefit to which the person is not entitled under sections 2105.31 to 2105.39 of the Revised Code is obligated to return the payment, item of property, or benefit, and is personally liable for the amount of the payment or the value of the item of property or benefit, to the person who would have been entitled to it were sections 2105.31 to 2105.39 of the Revised Code or any provision of sections 2105.31 to 2105.39 of the Revised Code not preempted.

(2002 H 242, eff. 5-16-02)

Library References

Joint Tenancy ⚖︎12.
Westlaw Topic No. 226.
C.J.S. Joint Tenancy §§ 31 to 34.

Research References

Treatises and Practice Aids

Carlin, Baldwin's Ohio Practice, Merrick-Rippner Probate Law § 16:1, Statutory Provisions.

Law Review and Journal Commentaries

Ohio Enacts the Uniform Simultaneous Death Act. Richard E. Davis, 12 Prob L J Ohio 54 (March/April 2002).

2105.39 Applicability; severability

(A) Sections 2105.31 to 2105.39 of the Revised Code do not impair any act done in any proceeding, or any right that accrued, before May 16, 2002. If a right is acquired, extinguished, or barred upon the expiration of a prescribed period of time that has commenced to run prior to May 16, 2002, under any provision of the Revised Code, the provision of the applicable section of the Revised Code applies with respect to that right.

(B) Any rule of construction or presumption that is provided in sections 2105.31 to 2105.39 of the Revised Code applies to any governing instrument that is executed, or any multiple-party account that is opened, prior to May 16, 2002, unless there is a clear indication of a contrary intent in the governing instrument or multiple-party account.

(C) If any provision of sections 2105.31 to 2105.39 of the Revised Code or the application of those sections to any persons or circumstance is held invalid, the invalidity does not affect other provisions or applications of sections 2105.31 to 2105.39 of the Revised Code that can be given effect without the invalid provision or application.

(2002 H 345, § 3, eff. 5-16-02; 2002 H 242, eff. 5-16-02)

Historical and Statutory Notes

Amendment Note: 2002 H 345 substituted "May 16" for "January 1" in divisions (A) and (B).

Library References

Statutes ⚖︎64.
Westlaw Topic No. 361.
C.J.S. Statutes §§ 83 to 107.

Research References

Encyclopedias

OH Jur. 3d Decedents' Estates § 15, Descent and Distribution.
OH Jur. 3d Decedents' Estates § 43, Statutory Nonsurvivorship; Simultaneous Death Statute.
OH Jur. 3d Decedents' Estates § 44, Statutory Nonsurvivorship; Simultaneous Death Statute—Present and Former Simultaneous Death Statute Distinguished.
OH Jur. 3d Decedents' Estates § 45, Statutory Nonsurvivorship; Simultaneous Death Statute—Purpose and Effect of the Simultaneous Death Statute.
OH Jur. 3d Decedents' Estates § 46, Statutory Nonsurvivorship; Simultaneous Death Statute—Application of the Simultaneous Death Statute.
OH Jur. 3d Decedents' Estates § 116, Under the Statute of Descent and Distribution.
OH Jur. 3d Decedents' Estates § 263, Deceased Person or Person Dying Within 30 Days of Testator's Death.
OH Jur. 3d Decedents' Estates § 746, Election as Affected by Simultaneous Death or Death Within 30 Days.
OH Jur. 3d Decedents' Estates § 750, Effect of Failure to Make Election or Seek Extension.
OH Jur. 3d Decedents' Estates § 751, Effect of Failure to Make Election or Seek Extension—Death Before Expiration of Time for Election.
OH Jur. 3d Decedents' Estates § 779, Constructive Death.

Forms

Ohio Forms and Transactions KP 30.04, Common Disaster and Presumed Order of Death.

Treatises and Practice Aids

Carlin, Baldwin's Ohio Practice, Merrick-Rippner Probate Law § 9:1, Presumption of Death—Statutory.
Carlin, Baldwin's Ohio Practice, Merrick-Rippner Probate Law § 9:2, Presumption of Death—Procedure for Establishing—Jurisdiction.
Carlin, Baldwin's Ohio Practice, Merrick-Rippner Probate Law § 9:3, Presumption of Death—Procedure for Establishing—Necessary Parties Defendant.
Carlin, Baldwin's Ohio Practice, Merrick-Rippner Probate Law § 9:4, Presumption of Death—Procedure for Establishing—Notice.
Carlin, Baldwin's Ohio Practice, Merrick-Rippner Probate Law § 9:5, Presumption of Death—Procedure for Establishing—Filing Complaint.
Carlin, Baldwin's Ohio Practice, Merrick-Rippner Probate Law § 9:7, Presumption of Death—Effect of Decree.
Carlin, Baldwin's Ohio Practice, Merrick-Rippner Probate Law § 9:9, Presumption of Death—Complaint—Form.
Carlin, Baldwin's Ohio Practice, Merrick-Rippner Probate Law § 15:1, Descent and Distribution—Scope of Statutes.
Carlin, Baldwin's Ohio Practice, Merrick-Rippner Probate Law § 15:2, Descent and Distribution—Definitions.
Carlin, Baldwin's Ohio Practice, Merrick-Rippner Probate Law § 16:1, Statutory Provisions.
Carlin, Baldwin's Ohio Practice, Merrick-Rippner Probate Law § 17:2, Designation—Effect.
Carlin, Baldwin's Ohio Practice, Merrick-Rippner Probate Law § 2:39, Elective Rights of Surviving Spouse—Election to Take Under Law or Under the Will—Failure to Make Election Against the Will.
Carlin, Baldwin's Ohio Practice, Merrick-Rippner Probate Law § 20:5, Advancement—Rights of a Pretermitted Child.
Carlin, Baldwin's Ohio Practice, Merrick-Rippner Probate Law § 21:5, Rights of Surviving Spouse to Make Election—Statutory Provisions—Effect.
Carlin, Baldwin's Ohio Practice, Merrick-Rippner Probate Law § 24:2, Escheat—Scope of Statutes.
Carlin, Baldwin's Ohio Practice, Merrick-Rippner Probate Law § 24:3, Escheat—Operation.
Carlin, Baldwin's Ohio Practice, Merrick-Rippner Probate Law § 46:1, Anti-Lapse Statute.
Carlin, Baldwin's Ohio Practice, Merrick-Rippner Probate Law § 47:1, Afterborn or Pretermitted Heirs—Definitions.
Carlin, Baldwin's Ohio Practice, Merrick-Rippner Probate Law § 47:2, Afterborn or Pretermitted Heirs—Statutory Provisions.
Carlin, Baldwin's Ohio Practice, Merrick-Rippner Probate Law § 47:3, Afterborn or Pretermitted Heirs—Explanatory Chart 1.
Carlin, Baldwin's Ohio Practice, Merrick-Rippner Probate Law § 47:4, Afterborn or Pretermitted Heirs—Explanatory Chart 2.
Carlin, Baldwin's Ohio Practice, Merrick-Rippner Probate Law § 47:5, Afterborn or Pretermitted Heirs—Intent to Disinherit.
Carlin, Baldwin's Ohio Practice, Merrick-Rippner Probate Law § 77:3, Unclaimed Money—Escheat Distinguished.
Carlin, Baldwin's Ohio Practice, Merrick-Rippner Probate Law § 9:10, Presumption of Death—Entry Setting for Hearing, Ordering Notice, and Service of Summons—Form.
Carlin, Baldwin's Ohio Practice, Merrick-Rippner Probate Law § 15:43, Descent and Distribution—Escheat.
Carlin, Baldwin's Ohio Practice, Merrick-Rippner Probate Law § 19:10, Uniform Parentage Act—Procedure in Action to Determine Father-Child Relationship.
Carlin, Baldwin's Ohio Practice, Merrick-Rippner Probate Law § 21:15, Rights of Surviving Spouse to Make Election—Proceedings for Advice or Declaratory Judgment.

Carlin, Baldwin's Ohio Practice, Merrick-Rippner Probate Law § 21:30, Rights of Surviving Spouse to Make Election—Right to Use of Mansion House and Family Allowance.

Carlin, Baldwin's Ohio Practice, Merrick-Rippner Probate Law § 21:39, Rights of Surviving Spouse to Make Election—Failure to Make Election—Scope of RC 2106.04.

Carlin, Baldwin's Ohio Practice, Merrick-Rippner Probate Law § 21:41, Rights of Surviving Spouse to Make Election—Failure to Make Election—Conclusive Presumption.

Carlin, Baldwin's Ohio Practice, Merrick-Rippner Probate Law § 21:56, Rights of Surviving Spouse—Family Allowance—Time Limitations.

Carlin, Baldwin's Ohio Practice, Merrick-Rippner Probate Law § 30:17, Drafting a Will—Beneficiary Clauses—Alternate Beneficiary.

Carlin, Baldwin's Ohio Practice, Merrick-Rippner Probate Law § 30:21, Drafting a Will—Beneficiary Clauses—Disinheritance of Afterborn or Pretermitted Heirs.

Carlin, Baldwin's Ohio Practice, Merrick-Rippner Probate Law § 30:57, Simple Will—Form.

Carlin, Baldwin's Ohio Practice, Merrick-Rippner Probate Law § 30:120, Distribution to a Custodian Under the Transfers to Minors Act of Ohio When a Devisee Shall be Under 18 Years of Age—Form.

Carlin, Baldwin's Ohio Practice, Merrick-Rippner Probate Law § 30:131, Legacy to Two Persons or the Survivor; or as Part of Residue—Form.

Carlin, Baldwin's Ohio Practice, Merrick-Rippner Probate Law § 30:132, Simultaneous Death—Form.

Law Review and Journal Commentaries

Ohio Enacts the Uniform Simultaneous Death Act. Richard E. Davis, 12 Prob L J Ohio 54 (March/April 2002).

CHAPTER 2106

RIGHTS OF SURVIVING SPOUSES

Section
2106.01 Election by surviving spouse
2106.02 Citation to surviving spouse to make election
2106.03 Complaint for construction of will
2106.04 Failure to make election; presumption
2106.05 Election to take under the will; effect
2106.06 Election to take under statute to be made in person
2106.07 Commission issued to take election of surviving spouse
2106.08 Election made by one under legal disability
2106.10 Election of surviving spouse to receive mansion house
2106.11 Method of payment of specific monetary share of surviving spouse
2106.13 Allowance for support of surviving spouse and minor children
2106.15 Mansion house
2106.16 Surviving spouse may purchase property
2106.18 Right of surviving spouse to automobiles of decedent
2106.19 Right of surviving spouse to one watercraft or outboard motor of decedent
2106.20 Reimbursement of funeral expenses to surviving spouse or person with right of disposition
2106.22 Action to set aside antenuptial or separation agreement
2106.24 Other rights of surviving spouse
2106.25 Exercising of rights under Chapter 2106 by surviving spouse

Law Review and Journal Commentaries

Disinheritance and the Modern Family, Ralph C. Brashier. 45 Case W Res L Rev 83 (Fall 1994).

Rights of Surviving Spouses, Robert G. Dykes. 1 Prob L J Ohio 7 (September/October 1990).

2106.01 Election by surviving spouse

(A) After the initial appointment of an administrator or executor of the estate, the probate court shall issue a citation to the surviving spouse, if any is living at the time of the issuance of the citation, to elect whether to exercise the surviving spouse's rights under Chapter 2106. of the Revised Code, including, after the probate of a will, the right to elect to take under the will or under section 2105.06 of the Revised Code.

A surviving spouse may waive the service of the citation required under this division by filing in the probate court a written waiver of the citation. The waiver shall include an acknowledgment of receipt of the description of the general rights of the surviving spouse required by division (B) of section 2106.02 of the Revised Code.

(B) If the surviving spouse elects to take under section 2105.06 of the Revised Code and if the value of the property that the surviving spouse is entitled to receive is equal to or greater than the value of the decedent's interest in the mansion house as determined under section 2106.10 of the Revised Code, the surviving spouse also is entitled to make an election pursuant to division (A) of section 2106.10 of the Revised Code.

(C) If the surviving spouse elects to take under section 2105.06 of the Revised Code, the surviving spouse shall take not to exceed one-half of the net estate, unless two or more of the decedent's children or their lineal descendants survive, in which case the surviving spouse shall take not to exceed one-third of the net estate.

For purposes of this division, the net estate shall be determined before payment of federal estate tax, estate taxes under Chapter 5731. of the Revised Code, or any other tax that is subject to apportionment under section 2113.86 or 2113.861 of the Revised Code.

(D) Unless the will expressly provides that in case of an election under division (A) of this section there shall be no acceleration of remainder or other interests bequeathed or devised by the will, the balance of the net estate shall be disposed of as though the surviving spouse had predeceased the testator. If there is a disposition by a will to an inter vivos trust that was created by the testator, if under the terms of the trust the surviving spouse is entitled to any interest in the trust or is granted any power or nomination with respect to the trust, and if the surviving spouse makes an election to take under section 2105.06 of the Revised Code, then, unless the trust instrument provides otherwise, the surviving spouse is deemed for purposes of the trust to have predeceased the testator, and there shall be an acceleration of remainder or other interests in all property bequeathed or devised to the trust by the will, in all property held by the trustee at the time of the death of the decedent, and in all property that comes into the hands of the trustee by reason of the death of the decedent.

(E) The election of a surviving spouse to take under a will or under section 2105.06 of the Revised Code may be made at any time after the death of the decedent, but the surviving spouse shall not make the election later than five months from the date of the initial appointment of an administrator or executor of the estate. On a motion filed before the expiration of the five-month period, and for good cause shown, the court may allow further time for the making of the election. If no action is taken by the surviving spouse before the expiration of the five-month period, it is conclusively presumed that the surviving spouse elects to take under the will. The election shall be entered on the journal of the court.

When proceedings for advice or to contest the validity of a will are begun within the time allowed by this division for making the election, the election may be made within three months after the final disposition of the proceedings, if the will is not set aside.

(F) When a surviving spouse succeeds to the entire estate of the testator, having been named the sole devisee and legatee, it shall be presumed that the spouse elects to take under the will of the testator, unless the surviving spouse manifests a contrary intention.

(2003 H 51, eff. 4–8–04; 2001 H 85, eff. 10–31–01; 1990 H 346, eff. 5–31–90)

Uncodified Law

2004 H 161, § 3, eff. 4–8–04 reads, in part:

(A) Sections 2106.01, 2106.02, and 2109.32 of the Revised Code, as amended by Am. Sub. H.B. 51 of the 125th General Assembly, apply to estates that are in existence or are initiated on or after April 8, 2004.

1990 H 346, § 3, eff. 5–31–90, reads, in part: (A) Sections 1 and 2 of this act shall apply only to the estates of decedents who die on or after the effective date of this act.

1988 S 228, § 4, eff. 3–22–89, reads: The amendments to sections 2107.39 [recodified as 2106.01], 2115.02, and 2117.06 of the Revised Code contained in this act shall apply only with respect to the estates of decedents whose deaths occur on or after the effective date of this act.

1986 H 139, § 3 and 6, eff. 7–24–86, read, in part:

Section 3. Except as provided in Sections... 6 of this act..., Sections 1 and 2 of this act shall apply only to the estates of decedents whose death occurs on or after the effective date of this act.

Section 6. The amendments made to division (C) of section 2107.39 [recodified as 2106.01] and to former sections 2113.86 and 2113.87 of the Revised Code as they existed prior to the effective date of this act, the enactment of new section 2113.86 except for its division (I), and the enactment of section 2113.861 of the Revised Code, by Section 1 of this act, are clarifying amendments or enactments and generally are declaratory of the law of this state prior to the effective date of this act. The provisions of new section 2113.86 and section 2113.861 of the Revised Code as enacted by Section 1 of this act, the provisions of division (C) of section 2107.39 of the Revised Code as amended by Section 1 of this act, and the provisions of former sections 2113.86 and 2113.87 of the Revised Code as amended by Section 1 of this act, shall apply to the estates of decedents who died on or after March 23, 1981.

Historical and Statutory Notes

Ed. Note: 2106.01 is former RC 2107.39, amended and recodified by 1990 H 346, eff. 5–31–90; 1988 S 228; 1986 S 248, H 139; 1980 S 317; 1975 S 145; 1973 H 374; 1970 S 185; 125 v 411; 1953 H 1; GC 10504–55, 10504–58.

Amendment Note: 2003 H 51 added the second paragraph of division (A).

Amendment Note: 2001 H 85 rewrote divisions (A), (E), and (F) which prior thereto read:

"(A) After the probate of a will and the filing of the inventory and the appraisement, the probate court shall issue a citation to the surviving spouse, if any is living at the time of the issuance of the citation, to elect whether to take under the will or under section 2105.06 of the Revised Code.

"(E) The election of a surviving spouse to take under a will or under section 2105.06 of the Revised Code may be made at any time after the death of the decedent, but shall be made not later than one month from the service of the citation to elect. On a motion filed before the expiration of the one-month period, and for good cause shown, the court may allow further time for the making of the election. If no action is taken by the surviving spouse before the expiration of the one-month period, it is conclusively presumed that the surviving spouse elects to take under the will. The election shall be entered on the journal of the court.

"When proceedings for advice or to contest the validity of a will are begun within the time allowed by this division for making the election, the election may be made within three months after the final disposition of the proceedings, if the will is not set aside.

"(F) When a surviving spouse succeeds to the entire estate of the testator, having been named the sole devisee and legatee, it shall be presumed that the spouse elects to take under the will of the testator. No citation shall be issued to the surviving spouse as provided in division (A) of this section, and no election shall be required, unless the surviving spouse manifests a contrary intention."

OSBA Probate and Trust Law Section

1988:

The purpose of the change to Paragraph "D" is to make it clear that if a surviving spouse elects to take against the will of the decedent, and if the decedent's will pours his estate over into an inter-vivos trust created by the decedent, the surviving spouse loses all interest in the trust. (Commentary from former RC 2107.39.)

1980:

First, the present Sec. 2107.39 (which grants a surviving spouse the election to take under the will or under the law) is clear as to the deadline for exercise of the election. However, the section is not at all clear as to when the election may first be exercised; that is, when it arises and can be availed of at the earliest possible date.

The Ohio Supreme Court has suggested in the recent case of *In Re Estate of LaSpina*, 60 Ohio St. 2d 101 (1979), that "there is nothing in the statute to prohibit the relict from making his or her election prior to the issuance of a citation".

Unfortunately, this fairly strong indication that the surviving spouse can make his or her election under this section at an early date was contained in obiter dicta. The specific issue has not been before the court, and many Ohio lawyers are of the opinion that no election can be made until sometime after a number of steps in the probate process have been completed. This understanding is based upon the present language of Sec. 2107.39 which provides: "After the probate of a will and the filing of the inventory, appraisement, and a schedule of debts where ordered, the probate court shall issue a citation to the surviving spouse, if any be living at the time of the issuance of the citation, to elect".

The purpose of the proposed amendment to Sec. 2107.39 is to provide specifically that the surviving spouse has a right to make the election as soon as the will is admitted to probate, without waiting for the completion of all the steps prerequisite to the issuance of the citation.

Obviously, an executor who is not diligent in pursuing the administration of the estate might prevent the exercise under this section if the spouse should die before all of the steps possibly required are completed.

Moreover, if there is a conflict in interest between a beneficiary-executor and a surviving spouse who intends to take against the will, the fiduciary should not be able to benefit from his own intentional delay in taking certain steps which only he can take, thus preventing the surviving spouse from making the election.

The proposed amendment therefore provides that the spouse must still personally make the election "not later than" the same period now specified, which is "one month after service of the citation to elect". But, more specifically, the section, as amended, provides that the election can be made "at any time after the probate of the will".

Second, if the surviving spouse exercises the election available to him or her under Sec. 2107.39 so that he or she is entitled to take under the law, that is, under the statutes of descent and distribution contained in Sec. 2105.06 *et. seq.*, it should be made clear that among the rights of the surviving spouse who takes under the statutes of descent and distribution after an election not to take under a will, is the right provided by Sec. 2105.062 to elect "to receive, as part of his share of the intestate estate under Sec. 2105.06 of the Revised Code, the entire interest of the decedent spouse in the mansion house". Since this right is available to every other surviving spouse taking under the statute of descent and distribution, the right should be equally available to a surviving spouse taking under such statute by reason of an election not to take under a will pursuant to Sec. 2107.39. (Commentary from former RC 2107.39.)

Cross References

Addition to trust estate, 2107.63
Distribution of assets, liability of beneficiary or heir to surviving spouse, 2113.53
Distribution of assets to legatees and distributees, 2113.54
Estate tax, apportionment among interested persons, 2113.86
Partnership property not subject to dower or statutory share, 1775.24
Presumption of order of death, 2105.21
Proceedings to admit foreign will to record, election period, 2129.07

Library References

Descent and Distribution ⚖64.1 to 67.
Wills ⚖781, 799.
Westlaw Topic Nos. 124, 409.
C.J.S. Wills §§ 1841, 1866 to 1868.
Baldwin's Ohio Legislative Service, 1988 Laws of Ohio, S 228—LSC Analysis, p 5–968; 1990 Laws of Ohio, H 346—LSC Analysis, p 5–87

Research References

Encyclopedias

OH Jur. 3d Decedents' Estates § 14, Succession.
OH Jur. 3d Decedents' Estates § 58, Failure to Provide for Surviving Spouse.
OH Jur. 3d Decedents' Estates § 125, Acts that Will Bar Succession, Generally—Surviving Spouse's Rights.
OH Jur. 3d Decedents' Estates § 225, Nature of Power; Legislative Control.
OH Jur. 3d Decedents' Estates § 235, Restrictions as to Surviving Spouse.
OH Jur. 3d Decedents' Estates § 501, Testator's Knowledge of Law; Changes in Laws of Descent.
OH Jur. 3d Decedents' Estates § 613, Shares Taken by Beneficiaries—Gift to Surviving Spouse of Share Provided by Law.
OH Jur. 3d Decedents' Estates § 747, Citation Notice to Surviving Spouse of Right to Election.
OH Jur. 3d Decedents' Estates § 748, Time of Making Election; Extension of Time.
OH Jur. 3d Decedents' Estates § 749, Time of Making Election; Extension of Time—Effect of Contest or Proceeding for Advice.
OH Jur. 3d Decedents' Estates § 750, Effect of Failure to Make Election or Seek Extension.
OH Jur. 3d Decedents' Estates § 755, Record of Election.
OH Jur. 3d Decedents' Estates § 756, Election by Spouse Under a Legal Disability.
OH Jur. 3d Decedents' Estates § 769, Percentage of the Estate Taken.
OH Jur. 3d Decedents' Estates § 770, Percentage of the Estate Taken—Meaning of "Net Estate".
OH Jur. 3d Decedents' Estates § 771, Percentage of the Estate Taken—as Affected by Estate Taxes and Tax Provision in Will.
OH Jur. 3d Decedents' Estates § 773, Property in Inter Vivos Trust.
OH Jur. 3d Decedents' Estates § 774, Acceleration of Remainders.
OH Jur. 3d Decedents' Estates § 776, Compensation to Disappointed Legatees—Relation to Acceleration of Remainders.
OH Jur. 3d Decedents' Estates § 1637, Time When Legatee or Distributee May Apply for Distribution.
OH Jur. 3d Decedents' Estates § 1676, Right to Receive Mansion House as Part of Intestate Share.
OH Jur. 3d Estates, Pwrs., & Restrnts. on Alienat. § 120, Election by Surviving Spouse.
OH Jur. 3d Estates, Pwrs., & Restrnts. on Alienat. § 121, Acceleration of Contingent Remainders.
OH Jur. 3d Taxation § 983, Exemption of Spouse's Share.
OH Jur. 3d Trusts § 73, Application of Statute of Wills.

Forms

Ohio Forms Legal and Business § 24:143, Drafting Will.
Ohio Forms Legal and Business § 24:161, Entire Estate to Spouse—Alternatively to Children—Guardianship of Minors.
Ohio Forms Legal and Business § 24:421, General Clause.
Ohio Forms Legal and Business § 24:971, Spouse's Election to Take Under Will.

Treatises and Practice Aids

Carlin, Baldwin's Ohio Practice, Merrick-Rippner Probate Law § 2:3, Time for Administration of Decedent's Estate and Payment of Estate Taxes.
Carlin, Baldwin's Ohio Practice, Merrick-Rippner Probate Law § 15:6, Descent and Distribution—Surviving Spouse—in General.
Carlin, Baldwin's Ohio Practice, Merrick-Rippner Probate Law § 2:35, Elective Rights of Surviving Spouse—Election to Take Under Law or Under the Will—Issuance of Citation.
Carlin, Baldwin's Ohio Practice, Merrick-Rippner Probate Law § 2:36, Elective Rights of Surviving Spouse—Election to Take Under Law or Under the Will—Time for Making Election.
Carlin, Baldwin's Ohio Practice, Merrick-Rippner Probate Law § 2:38, Elective Rights of Surviving Spouse—Election to Take Under Law or Under the Will—Elective Share of Surviving Spouse Against the Will.
Carlin, Baldwin's Ohio Practice, Merrick-Rippner Probate Law § 21:2, Rights of Surviving Spouse to Make Election—Statutory Provisions—Generally.
Carlin, Baldwin's Ohio Practice, Merrick-Rippner Probate Law § 21:3, Rights of Surviving Spouse to Make Election—Statutory Provisions—Citation—Issuance—Waiver of Citation.
Carlin, Baldwin's Ohio Practice, Merrick-Rippner Probate Law § 21:4, Rights of Surviving Spouse to Make Election—Statutory Provisions—Citation—Service.
Carlin, Baldwin's Ohio Practice, Merrick-Rippner Probate Law § 21:5, Rights of Surviving Spouse to Make Election—Statutory Provisions—Effect.
Carlin, Baldwin's Ohio Practice, Merrick-Rippner Probate Law § 21:6, Rights of Surviving Spouse to Make Election—Statutory Provisions—Acceleration of Remainder.
Carlin, Baldwin's Ohio Practice, Merrick-Rippner Probate Law § 21:8, Rights of Surviving Spouse to Make Election—Statutory Provisions—Manner and Time—Time Within Which to Make Election.
Carlin, Baldwin's Ohio Practice, Merrick-Rippner Probate Law § 21:9, Rights of Surviving Spouse to Make Election—Statutory Provisions—Manner and Time—Extension of Time for Election.
Carlin, Baldwin's Ohio Practice, Merrick-Rippner Probate Law § 22:5, Necessity for Conviction; Common Law Forfeiture.
Carlin, Baldwin's Ohio Practice, Merrick-Rippner Probate Law § 33:1, Trusts—Testamentary Addition to Existing Trust—Statutory Provisions for Pour-Over.
Carlin, Baldwin's Ohio Practice, Merrick-Rippner Probate Law § 33:2, Trusts—Testamentary Addition to Existing Trust—Purpose of Pour-Over Statute.
Carlin, Baldwin's Ohio Practice, Merrick-Rippner Probate Law § 38:6, Will Contests—Capacity to Contest a Will.
Carlin, Baldwin's Ohio Practice, Merrick-Rippner Probate Law § 48:8, Property Liable for Payment of Debts—Personal Property—Effect of Spousal Election.
Carlin, Baldwin's Ohio Practice, Merrick-Rippner Probate Law § 75:2, Distribution—Voluntary—Required Notice to Distributee.
Carlin, Baldwin's Ohio Practice, Merrick-Rippner Probate Law § 75:3, Distribution—Voluntary—Liability—Beneficiaries or Heirs.
Carlin, Baldwin's Ohio Practice, Merrick-Rippner Probate Law § 75:4, Distribution—Voluntary—Liability—Executor or Administrator.
Carlin, Baldwin's Ohio Practice, Merrick-Rippner Probate Law § 75:8, Distribution—Upon Application—Five-Month Time Limit.
Carlin, Baldwin's Ohio Practice, Merrick-Rippner Probate Law § 100:4, Antenuptial or Separation Agreement—Consideration.
Carlin, Baldwin's Ohio Practice, Merrick-Rippner Probate Law § 110:1, Apportionment Law—Overview.
Carlin, Baldwin's Ohio Practice, Merrick-Rippner Probate Law § 110:6, Elective Share or Intestate Share of Surviving Spouse.
Carlin, Baldwin's Ohio Practice, Merrick-Rippner Probate Law § 2:101, Distribution of Assets—Legacies and Distributions.
Carlin, Baldwin's Ohio Practice, Merrick-Rippner Probate Law § 2:121, Administration of Decedent's Estate—Checklist.
Carlin, Baldwin's Ohio Practice, Merrick-Rippner Probate Law § 21:10, Rights of Surviving Spouse to Make Election—Statutory Provisions—Presumption of Election.
Carlin, Baldwin's Ohio Practice, Merrick-Rippner Probate Law § 21:12, Rights of Surviving Spouse to Make Election—Statutory Provisions—Purpose of RC 2106.01.
Carlin, Baldwin's Ohio Practice, Merrick-Rippner Probate Law § 21:13, Rights of Surviving Spouse to Make Election—Ineffective Action to Extend Time of Election.
Carlin, Baldwin's Ohio Practice, Merrick-Rippner Probate Law § 21:14, Rights of Surviving Spouse to Make Election—Effect of Election on Will Contest.
Carlin, Baldwin's Ohio Practice, Merrick-Rippner Probate Law § 21:15, Rights of Surviving Spouse to Make Election—Proceedings for Advice or Declaratory Judgment.
Carlin, Baldwin's Ohio Practice, Merrick-Rippner Probate Law § 21:16, Rights of Surviving Spouse to Make Election—Personal Right.
Carlin, Baldwin's Ohio Practice, Merrick-Rippner Probate Law § 21:17, Rights of Surviving Spouse to Make Election—Commissioner Appointed to Take Election of Spouse.

Carlin, Baldwin's Ohio Practice, Merrick-Rippner Probate Law § 21:19, Rights of Surviving Spouse to Make Election—Effect of Election—Generally.

Carlin, Baldwin's Ohio Practice, Merrick-Rippner Probate Law § 21:20, Rights of Surviving Spouse to Make Election—Acceleration of Remainder.

Carlin, Baldwin's Ohio Practice, Merrick-Rippner Probate Law § 21:24, Rights of Surviving Spouse to Make Election—Effect of Taxes on Election.

Carlin, Baldwin's Ohio Practice, Merrick-Rippner Probate Law § 21:25, Rights of Surviving Spouse to Make Election—Effect on Inter Vivos Trust of Election.

Carlin, Baldwin's Ohio Practice, Merrick-Rippner Probate Law § 21:30, Rights of Surviving Spouse to Make Election—Right to Use of Mansion House and Family Allowance.

Carlin, Baldwin's Ohio Practice, Merrick-Rippner Probate Law § 21:35, Rights of Surviving Spouse to Make Election—One Under Legal Disability—Scope of RC 2106.08.

Carlin, Baldwin's Ohio Practice, Merrick-Rippner Probate Law § 21:37, Rights of Surviving Spouse to Make Election—One Under Legal Disability—Time Limit for Election.

Carlin, Baldwin's Ohio Practice, Merrick-Rippner Probate Law § 21:39, Rights of Surviving Spouse to Make Election—Failure to Make Election—Scope of RC 2106.04.

Carlin, Baldwin's Ohio Practice, Merrick-Rippner Probate Law § 21:51, Rights of Surviving Spouse—Family Allowance—Distribution.

Carlin, Baldwin's Ohio Practice, Merrick-Rippner Probate Law § 21:58, Rights of Surviving Spouse—Mansion House—Right to Remain in House for One Year.

Carlin, Baldwin's Ohio Practice, Merrick-Rippner Probate Law § 21:87, Motion of Surviving Spouse for Extension of Time to Make Election—Form.

Carlin, Baldwin's Ohio Practice, Merrick-Rippner Probate Law § 21:88, Entry Extending Time for Surviving Spouse to Make Election—Form.

Carlin, Baldwin's Ohio Practice, Merrick-Rippner Probate Law § 21:89, Citation to Surviving Spouse to Elect to Take Under or Against Will—Form.

Carlin, Baldwin's Ohio Practice, Merrick-Rippner Probate Law § 30:24, Drafting a Will—Surviving Spouse—Election to Take Against the Will.

Carlin, Baldwin's Ohio Practice, Merrick-Rippner Probate Law § 30:25, Drafting a Will—Surviving Spouse—Disinheritance of Spouse.

Carlin, Baldwin's Ohio Practice, Merrick-Rippner Probate Law § 89:12, Payment of Debts—Allowance for Support of Surviving Spouse and Minor Children—Distribution.

Carlin, Baldwin's Ohio Practice, Merrick-Rippner Probate Law § 89:17, Payment of Debts—Allowance for Support of Surviving Spouse and Minor Children—Preference Under Federal Law.

Carlin, Baldwin's Ohio Practice, Merrick-Rippner Probate Law § 96:21, Entry Referring Action to Torrens Examiner—Form.

Carlin, Baldwin's Ohio Practice, Merrick-Rippner Probate Law § 96:22, Entry Approving Report of Torrens Examiner—Form.

Carlin, Baldwin's Ohio Practice, Merrick-Rippner Probate Law § 111:19, Federal Estate Tax—Liability of Fiduciary for Payment.

Carlin, Baldwin's Ohio Practice, Merrick-Rippner Probate Law App B SPF 8.0, Citation to Surviving Spouse to Elect Exercise Elective Rights.

Carlin, Baldwin's Ohio Practice, Merrick-Rippner Probate Law App B SPF 8.2, Election of Surviving Spouse to Take Against Will.

Carlin, Baldwin's Ohio Practice, Merrick-Rippner Probate Law App B SPF 8.6, Waiver of Service to Surviving Spouse of the Citation to Elect—Form.

Bogert - the Law of Trusts and Trustees § 211, Trusts for Unlawful Purposes.

Kuehnle and Levey, Ohio Real Estate Law and Practice § 5:4, Elect Surviving Spouse to Take Under or Against Will.

Restatement (2d) of Property, Don. Trans. § 34.1, Effect of Donative Transfer on Spouse of Donor.

Restatement (3d) Property (Wills & Don. Trans.) § 9.4, Premarital or Marital Agreement.

Law Review and Journal Commentaries

Does Dower Still Lurk in Elections to Take Under the Will, Charles E. Stevenson. 30 U Cin L Rev 172 (Spring 1961).

Dumas v Estate of Dumas: The Ohio Supreme Court's Continued Endorsement Of Spousal Disinheritance, Note. 25 U Tol L Rev 847 (1994).

Election Rights of a Surviving Spouse in Ohio, Robert C. Bensing. 2 W Reserve U L Rev 123 (1950).

Entitlement of a Surviving Spouse: A Quandary, B. Redman. 27 Cap U L Rev 573 (1999).

Error in Omitting "or Die" after a Testamentary Gift of Income to Widow, Anthony A. Morano. 17 Clev–Marshall L Rev 567 (September 1968).

Estate planning techniques for nontraditional couples. Susan L. Racey, 14 Prob L J Ohio 57 (January/February 2004).

House Bill 85, Probate Reform Bill 2001: A Noble Experiment. Marilyn J. Maag, 12 Prob L J Ohio 21 (November/December 2001).

How the Family Fares: A Comparison of the Uniform Probate Code and the Ohio Probate Reform Act, Donald L. Robertson. 37 Ohio St L J 321 (1976).

Native American Restricted Allotments: A Surviving Spouse's Elective Share Rights, Jeffrey S. Kinsler. 20 Ohio N U L Rev 263 (1993).

Practical Application of House Bill 85 (Probate Reform 2001), Marilyn J. Maag. 13 Prob L J Ohio 19 (November/December 2002).

A Proposed Solution to Spousal Disinheritance in Ohio: The Uniform Probate Code's Elective Share Revision, Comment. 19 Ohio N U L Rev 951 (1993).

Rights of the Surviving Spouse, Patricia D. Consolo and Jeffrey P. Consolo. 56 Clev B J 52 (December 1984).

The Surviving Spouse's Sacred Right To Elect Against The Will: Is It A Pyrrhic Victory?, Comment. 19 Cap U L Rev 553 (Spring 1990).

Trusts and the Young Case: Planning for disabled beneficiaries, William J. Browning. 11 Ohio Law 6 (November/December 1997).

The Ultimate Penalty For Having Elected Against Will—When Deceased Spouse Had Inter Vivos Trust and Pours Over Any Part of the Probate Estate to the Trust. [R.C. § 2107.39, amended effective March 22, 1989], Robert L. Hausser. 56 Title Topics 9 (April 1989).

The Widow, the Family Attorney, The Eldest Son–Executor, The Reappearance of The Old College Boy Friend. (Ed. note: The form and substance of a letter from the family lawyer to a surviving spouse advising of her rights under, against, and outside the will are suggested.) 54 Title Topics 6 (January 1987).

Notes of Decisions

Ed. Note: This section contains annotations from former RC 2107.39 and RC 2115.13.

Antenuptial and other contracts 1
Election 2-4
    Effect of election under law 2
    Effect on other interests 3
    Right of election 4
Marital deduction; taxation 5
Objection to or action to set aside election 6
Presumptions, waiver and release 7
Procedural issues 8
Property subject to right of election 9
Time for election 10

---

1. Antenuptial and other contracts

Provisions of an antenuptial agreement which cut the parties off entirely from any participation in the estate of the other upon the death of either will be upheld upon a showing that the parties entered into the contract after full disclosure or with full knowledge of the effects of the agreement. Hook v. Hook (Ohio 1982) 69 Ohio St.2d 234, 431 N.E.2d 667, 23 O.O.3d 239.

An antenuptial contract must be voluntarily entered into and the provisions for the wife must be fair and reasonable under all the surrounding facts and circumstances, and an adult man and woman, each owning a substantial amount of property and each having grown children by prior marriages, may lawfully enter a prenuptial agreement whereby each relinquishes every and all rights in the property of the other. Osborn v.

Osborn (Ohio Com.Pl. 1966) 10 Ohio Misc. 171, 226 N.E.2d 814, 39 O.O.2d 275, affirmed 18 Ohio St.2d 144, 248 N.E.2d 191, 47 O.O.2d 310.

A widow who, freely and with equal knowledge of the facts and law, entered into a contract with the other beneficiaries under the will of her deceased husband, before an inventory of the estate was made, thereby releasing her claims against the estate in consideration of immediate payment by such beneficiaries to her of what the will provided for her and a specified sum for her year's support, is not, after performance of the contract, and discovery that her rights under the law far exceeded the amount she received under the settlement, entitled to rescission of the contract for mistake merely because of a disproportion between the amount which she got under the agreement and the amount she would have received under the law. Carnahan v. Carnahan (Clinton 1959) 109 Ohio App. 350, 159 N.E.2d 795, 11 O.O.2d 142.

Where an antenuptial agreement is silent as to the right of the spouse to take against the will, such antenuptial agreement does not bar the surviving spouse from electing to take against the will of the deceased spouse. In re Estate of Mowery, No. 10813 (9th Dist Ct App, Summit, 12-8-82).

2. Election—Effect of election under law

The right of a widow to a year's support is not barred by accepting a provision in lieu of all claims against the estate before her husband's death. Spangler v. Dukes (Ohio 1884) 39 Ohio St. 642.

Where a widow elects not to take under the will, she can take nothing in virtue of the bequests, made to her by the will in lieu of dower. Jones v. Lloyd (Ohio 1878) 33 Ohio St. 572.

A widower, electing not to take under the will of his wife who died leaving no children or their legal representatives, is entitled to one-half of the first four hundred dollars and one-third of the remainder of the personal property. Whyde v. Lunn (Ohio App. 5 Dist. 1921) 15 Ohio App. 297, 32 Ohio C.A. 183. Wills ⇒ 801(3)

Trust invoked statutory exception to rule that surviving spouse's election against will would defeat her right to benefit from inter vivos trust, even though statute had not been adopted at time grantor settled the trust, and trust did not make specific mention of statutory exception, where trust stated that distributions to surviving spouse should not lapse on account of "any other law or rule of law treating my wife as though she had predeceased me." Gottesman v. Estate of Gottesman (Ohio App. 8 Dist., Cuyahoga, 11-07-2002) No. 81265, 2002-Ohio-6058, 2002 WL 31479037, Unreported, appeal allowed 786 N.E.2d 61, 2003-Ohio-1572, appeal dismissed as improvidently allowed 101 Ohio St.3d 60, 800 N.E.2d 1160, 2004-Ohio-4. Trusts ⇒ 124

Where testator died leaving no children or their lineal descendants and no surviving parent or parents, and testator's wife elected to take under the statute, under this section, wife was entitled to one-half of testator's estate and by virtue of GC 10503-4 (RC 2103.04) par 4, she was entitled to the whole of the remaining one-half of said estate as surviving spouse. Goodfellow v. Wilson (Clark 1940) 32 Ohio Law Abs. 569.

A surviving spouse with a one-sixth interest in real property as a result of an election to take against the will is a cotenant with a right to enter upon the common estate and take possession of the property, subject to the right of her cotenants to take possession; thus, a forcible entry and detainer action by cotenants holding the remaining five-sixths interest in the property must fail as one tenant cannot recover sole possession from another cotenant, but can only share possession. Collins v. Jackson (Cuyahoga 1986) 34 Ohio App.3d 101, 517 N.E.2d 269.

A surviving spouse taking against a will of a deceased spouse under RC 2107.39 is entitled to the $5,000 statutory allowance under RC 2117.20 unless specifically barred by the will. In re Green's Estate (Ohio Com.Pl. 1980) 63 Ohio Misc. 44, 410 N.E.2d 812, 17 O.O.3d 388.

Conviction of surviving spouse of manslaughter in the first degree in connection with his wife's death does not affect his right to inherit his statutory share in her estate under RC 2105.06. Wadsworth v. Siek (Ohio Prob. 1970) 23 Ohio Misc. 112, 254 N.E.2d 738, 50 O.O.2d 507, 52 O.O.2d 147.

Where a deceased husband, by his will, made a specific bequest of a certain number of shares of stock in a corporation for the creation of a trust for the benefit of one of his employees, and where the remaining portion of his estate is sufficient, after the payment of all debts and other obligations, to provide his relict, who elected not to take under the will, with the share of his net estate to which she is entitled under 2105.06, the relict's share of the net estate is an undivided fractional interest in the real estate plus such additional amount of personal property not specifically bequeathed under the will, either in kind or in money, as shall make her total share of the net estate that amount to which she is entitled under the provisions of the statute. Winters Nat. Bank & Trust Co. v. Riffe (Ohio 1965) 2 Ohio St.2d 72, 206 N.E.2d 212, 31 O.O.2d 56.

Where the relict of a deceased husband elects not to take under his will, she takes her share by way of inheritance as though it came to her from her deceased husband as an intestate. Winters Nat. Bank & Trust Co. v. Riffe (Ohio 1965) 2 Ohio St.2d 72, 206 N.E.2d 212, 31 O.O.2d 56. Wills ⇒ 801(1)

A provision in a will "that all estate, inheritance and succession taxes... which may be payable... with respect to any property, whether passing under this will or otherwise,... be paid by my executors out of my residuary estate... and no beneficiary of any such property shall be required to reimburse my residuary estate for any taxes so paid" is not affected by the surviving spouse's election to take under the law instead of under the will, and is effective and binding on the executor. Union Commerce Bank v. Roth (Cuyahoga 1964) 120 Ohio App. 349, 197 N.E.2d 216, 94 Ohio Law Abs. 408, 29 O.O.2d 199.

The surviving spouse of a testatrix, both of whom were American citizens, domiciled in a foreign country at the time of her death, at which time she owned personal property located in Ohio, where the sole original administration of her estate was being administered in a probate court, is entitled to elect to take under the law rather than under her will. In re Gould's Estate (Ohio Prob. 1956) 140 N.E.2d 793, 75 Ohio Law Abs. 289, 1 O.O.2d 366, affirmed 140 N.E.2d 801, 75 Ohio Law Abs. 298, 1 O.O.2d 372.

A devise by a testatrix of all real estate in a specific town is a specific devise, and the surviving spouse has no right to purchase the real estate at the appraised value, whether he takes under or against the will, since the rejection of a will does not nullify and invalidate the plain intent of the testatrix. In re Reed's Estate (Ohio Prob. 1952) 114 N.E.2d 314, 65 Ohio Law Abs. 129.

Under will which devises "to my husband... amount that he is allowed under laws of Ohio in my estate. I leave him no more than this amount because of his indifferent and careless treatment of me," and then devises all residue to testatrix' sisters and nieces, husband, upon electing to take thereunder, would take that part allowed by law alone and not dependent in any way upon testatrix' bounty; twenty per cent of estate, not less than $500 and not exceeding $2500 and right to reside in mansion house for one year free of charge; should husband elect to take under law he would be entitled to one-half of estate in addition to above. Schardt v. Prexler (Hamilton 1946) 67 N.E.2d 549, 45 Ohio Law Abs. 119.

If an estate of deceased husband consists of real estate and his widow elects to take under the statute of descent and distribution, she takes her quantitive share in such real estate as an estate of inheritance, subject to sale to pay the debts of the estate, and in such case, she is entitled to the rentals from her share of such real estate from the date of the death of her husband. Barlow v. Winters Nat. Bank & Trust Co. (Ohio 1945) 145 Ohio St. 270, 61 N.E.2d 603, 160 A.L.R. 423, 30 O.O. 484. Wills ⇒ 801(8.1)

Where widow elects not to take under his will, she takes her share by way of inheritance as though it came to her from her deceased husband as an intestate under GC 10503-4 (RC 2105.06), limited by this section. Barlow v. Winters Nat. Bank & Trust Co. (Ohio 1945) 145 Ohio St. 270, 61 N.E.2d 603, 160 A.L.R. 423, 30 O.O. 484. Wills ⇒ 801(3)

Where widow elects not to take under a will she takes as if the testator had died intestate, leaving children, and her share can be neither increased nor decreased by the will; the doctrine of equitable conversion has no application in ascertaining her share. Geiger v. Bitzer (Ohio 1909) 80 Ohio St. 65, 88 N.E. 134, 6 Ohio Law Rep. 661, 17 Am.Ann.Cas. 151.

A widow electing not to take under the will is entitled to the share of personalty which she would have received in case of intestacy. Harbeson v. Mellinger (Ohio App. 1913) 25 Ohio C.D. 195, 18 Ohio C.C.(N.S.) 504, 2 Ohio App. 75.

Where a husband possessed of real estate acquired by purchase dies testate but without issue, property devised to his widow in fee, with no devise over in the event that she elected not to take or failed to take under the will, does not become intestate property as to her and she cannot take as heir at law the property thus devised to her in lieu of dower and distributive share. Armstrong v. Armstrong (Ohio Cir. 1907) 21 Ohio C.D. 261, 11 Ohio C.C.N.S. 474.

This section measures the share of the estate passing to surviving spouse who elects not to take under the will, and legal title thereto does not pass by "descent" within the meaning of GC 10503-5 (RC 2105.10). (See also Barlow v Winters Natl Bank & Trust Co, 145 OS 270, 61 NE(2d) 603 (1945).) Fee v. Linthicum (Ohio Com.Pl. 1938) 2 Ohio Supp. 393, 26 Ohio Law Abs. 590, 11 O.O. 568.

3. —— Effect on other interests, election

Where a widow dies before electing to take under her husband's will and leaves her own will which disposes of the personal estate devised to her under her husband's will, an action by the heirs of the husband to recover his personal estate will not deprive the wife's heirs from taking all personal estate as her husband's "next of kin," as he died intestate as to that property. Gardner v. Gardner's Ex'r (Ohio 1862) 13 Ohio St. 426.

An election to take against the will by a surviving spouse under RC 2107.39 has no effect on a surviving spouse's beneficial life income interest in the assets of an inter vivos trust even where some assets are added to the trust through a residuary clause in the decedent spouse's will. Carnahan v. Stallman (Franklin 1986) 29 Ohio App.3d 293, 504 N.E.2d 1218, 29 O.B.R. 359.

Parties desiring to determine their rights in the event they renounce legacies, and a surviving spouse desiring to determine her rights should she elect under the will of the decedent, may obtain declaratory relief. Abram v. Wilson (Ohio Prob. 1966) 8 Ohio Misc. 420, 220 N.E.2d 739, 37 O.O.2d 288, 37 O.O.2d 394.

Property in a revocable inter vivos trust created by the deceased spouse cannot be reached by a surviving spouse who rejects his deceased spouse's will, and the only rights he has are those specifically given to him by the trust agreement. Purcell v. Cleveland Trust Co. (Cuyahoga 1965) 6 Ohio App.2d 235, 217 N.E.2d 876, 35 O.O.2d 426. Wills ⚖ 801(6)

Creation of a contingent remainder does not constitute an express provision against acceleration under RC 2107.39. Funkhouser v. Dorfmeier (Ohio Prob. 1963) 202 N.E.2d 226, 95 Ohio Law Abs. 140, 31 O.O.2d 42.

In order to prevent the application of an acceleration of the remainder or other interest, the testator must use words which anticipate the situation in which the spouse would elect to take against the will or at least must use words which prohibit the acceleration in any event. Funkhouser v. Dorfmeier (Ohio Prob. 1963) 202 N.E.2d 226, 95 Ohio Law Abs. 140, 31 O.O.2d 42.

In the 1953 amendment of RC 2107.39 the legislature clearly placed the burden upon the testator to expressly prevent the acceleration of remainders and other interests in the event that his or her spouse elects to take against the will. Funkhouser v. Dorfmeier (Ohio Prob. 1963) 202 N.E.2d 226, 95 Ohio Law Abs. 140, 31 O.O.2d 42.

A surviving spouse who elects to take against the will is entitled to a share of property held in a revocable inter vivos trust created by the deceased spouse. Purcell v. Cleveland Trust Co. (Ohio Prob. 1964) 200 N.E.2d 602, 94 Ohio Law Abs. 455, 28 O.O.2d 262, reversed 6 Ohio App.2d 235, 217 N.E.2d 876, 35 O.O.2d 426. Wills ⚖ 801(6)

In the absence of a showing that the testator intended that the effect of an election of a surviving spouse to take against the will should be borne to the contrary, when the election results in the executor being deprived of property, or interests in property, to such extent and in such manner that the property, or interests in property, remaining available for distribution to different classes of legatees named in different items of the will would, if so distributed, cause the reduction resulting from said election to be borne equitably, but not necessarily equally or proportionately, between said classes, distribution shall be made accordingly without further adjustment or contribution between the classes. Blackford v. Vermillion (Hancock 1958) 107 Ohio App. 26, 156 N.E.2d 339, 7 O.O.2d 350. Wills ⚖ 802(6)

A probate court, in determining that the best interest of an eighty-three year old incompetent widow would be served by the court's exercising, in such widow's behalf, the widow's election to take against the will and under the laws of intestacy, is not, under such circumstances, abusing its discretion, where the value of the widow's interest under the law was $267,736, as against $83,900 under will, though such election defeated the joint testamentary plan of both testator and spouse. In re Callan's Estate (Cuyahoga 1956) 101 Ohio App. 114, 135 N.E.2d 464, 1 O.O.2d 64. Wills ⚖ 786

Election by a surviving spouse to take under the law under this section, does not destroy the efficacy of the testator's last will and testament as to other provisions, and the surviving spouse is not entitled to have her one-half of the net estate administered as though there were no will. In re Ellis' Estate (Lake 1940) 66 Ohio App. 121, 32 N.E.2d 23, 19 O.O. 392.

Election by a surviving spouse not to take under a will does not destroy the efficacy of that instrument. Shearn v. Shearn (Coshocton 1937) 60 Ohio App. 317, 21 N.E.2d 133, 14 O.O. 262.

A made his last will and testament in which he directed that his estate be placed in perpetual trust, one-half of the income to his brother, B, for life and then to a church; the other half to his friend, C, for life and then to a hospital association; thereafter, A married C, and testator died in four days; C elected to reject the will and take under the law, thereby receiving one-half of the estate absolutely. The widow's election is equivalent to her death so far as the will is concerned; the trust is operative as to the remaining half of the estate, one-half of the income therefrom being payable to B for life and then to the church, and the other half being payable to the hospital association, the election of C having accelerated the time of its enjoyment. Davidson v. Miners' & Mechanics' Sav. & Trust Co. (Ohio 1935) 129 Ohio St. 418, 195 N.E. 845, 98 A.L.R. 1318, 2 O.O. 404.

A direction by a testator in his will to sell real estate and to divide the proceeds among his children does not transmute the real estate into money, and the widow cannot, after electing to take under the law, claim the proceeds of the real estate as her distributive share since that would be claiming a benefit under the will. Geiger v. Bitzer (Ohio 1909) 80 Ohio St. 65, 88 N.E. 134, 6 Ohio Law Rep. 661, 17 Am.Ann.Cas. 151.

Where a widow elects to take under the law, and the value of her statutory share exceeds the life estate under the will, the life estate she would have taken under the will will be sequestered to compensate the disappointed devisees. Holdren v. Holdren (Ohio 1908) 78 Ohio St. 276, 85 N.E. 537, 6 Ohio Law Rep. 109.

There is no such inconsistency between the right of dower and the distributive share in personalty, as to make the taking of one an exclusion of the other. Hutchings v. Davis (Ohio 1903) 68 Ohio St. 160, 48 W.L.B. 526, 67 N.E. 251, 1 Ohio Law Rep. 203.

Refusal of the widow to take under the will which created a trust for her for life terminates the trust and accelerates the remainders by passing them as intestate property but does not destroy an independent trust in one of the remainders. Blocher v. Trick (Ohio App. 1917) 30 Ohio C.D. 98, 8 Ohio App. 222, 28 Ohio C.A. 46.

It is not the policy of the law to permit a widow to make her election to take as heir at law or devisee; she must elect to take as widow or devisee, and she cannot defeat her husband's will by claiming dower in all his real estate and her rights as widow in all his personal property and then claim that she takes as heir the property that her husband devised to her in lieu of dower and her distributive share while neglecting to make a gift over in the event she did not elect to take under the will. Armstrong v. Armstrong (Ohio Cir. 1907) 21 Ohio C.D. 261, 11 Ohio C.C.N.S. 474.

Where testator's estate consisted of insurance and stocks, the insurance being partly payable to his widow with the power of changing beneficiary reserved, and partly payable to the corporation of which he was president, and the stock being held in trust by a trustee having power to vote, but no power to sell without the consent of the testator's widow to whom specified sum was to be paid during her lifetime from the income of the estate, and there being conflicting provisions of the will that debts be paid (1) out of the estate, and (2) out of the insurance: if the widow elects to take under the will, she receives the insurance subject to the testamentary condition that the debts be paid therefrom, but if she elects to take under the law, she takes the insurance free from any claims and debts must be paid from the property of the estate; if she elects to take under the law, the stock will go immediately to the trustee absolutely, subject to the payment of the estate's debts and the distributive share of the widow, if it be found necessary; only when the stock becomes the absolute property of the trustee may he sell and dispose of the same without the consent of the widow; if the widow elects to take under the law rather than under the will, she takes one-half of the estate after the debts and cost of administration have been paid, and accordingly there is no contribution. Weller v. Weller (Ohio Com.Pl. 1934) 32 Ohio N.P.N.S. 329.

Where S died intestate without issue, leaving brothers and sisters and a widow, who elected not to take under the will, and later died intestate, without either issue or brothers and sisters, she took her distributive share of her husband's personal estate under former GC 10571 (RC 2107.39, RC 2107.41, RC 2107.43), 8592 (RC 2105.06), and not under former GC 8574 (RC 2105.06) paragraph 2; hence former GC 8577 (RC 2105.10) does not apply, and her heirs take what she leaves, to the exclusion of her husband's brothers and sisters. Seney v Schroth, 25 CC(NS) 185, 35 CD 239 (Seneca 1916).

4. —— Right of election, election

A divorced wife, on the death of her former husband, not being his widow, has no right of election between the provisions of his will and dower, but must take the provisions made for her under the will. Charlton v. Miller (Ohio 1875) 27 Ohio St. 298, 22 Am.Rep. 307.

Where a testator makes a bequest to his "intended wife" in his will, divorces such wife, and dies without revoking his will, the procuring of a divorce does not necessarily imply a revocation of the will, for it is

Note 4

consistent with an intent to annul her right of dower only and the consequent right of election. Charlton v. Miller (Ohio 1875) 27 Ohio St. 298, 22 Am.Rep. 307.

Probate court exceeded limited statutory purposes in decedent's son's will contest action, where court did not explain reasons for granting summary judgment to decedent's wife on basis that net value of assets of estate was less than statutory allowance she was entitled to received as surviving spouse if will were declared invalid, and inventory had not been filed, and neither content nor value of estate had been determined; it was not probate court's function to determine content and value of estate's inventory. Dunaway v. Dunaway (Ohio App. 12 Dist., Brown, 02-18-2003) No. CA2002-07012, 2003-Ohio-706, 2003 WL 355719, Unreported. Wills ⟹ 351

The right of a surviving spouse to elect against the will, granted pursuant to RC 2107.39, is personal to such surviving spouse and does not survive his or her death, and that right may not be exercised in favor of the surviving spouse's estate. In re LaSpina's Estate (Ohio 1979) 60 Ohio St.2d 101, 397 N.E.2d 1196, 14 O.O.3d 336. Wills ⟹ 785(2)

A surviving spouse may not contest a will when the same result may be achieved by electing to take against the will. Klicke v. Uhlenbrock (Ohio Com.Pl. 1964) 200 N.E.2d 497, 94 Ohio Law Abs. 402, 27 O.O.2d 290. Wills ⟹ 229

When the probate judge has made election in behalf of an incompetent widow to take either under the will or under the law of intestacy, the election so made has the same effect as if made by one not under disability, and the widow's right thereby becomes absolute; and third parties are without right to complain. In re Callan's Estate (Cuyahoga 1956) 101 Ohio App. 114, 135 N.E.2d 464, 1 O.O.2d 64. Wills ⟹ 800; Wills ⟹ 801(1)

There is no such inconsistency between the right of dower and the distributive share in personalty, as to make the taking of one an exclusion of the other. Hutchings v. Davis (Ohio 1903) 68 Ohio St. 160, 48 W.L.B. 526, 67 N.E. 251, 1 Ohio Law Rep. 203.

Where provisions are made in a will for a surviving husband, and he declines to take under the will, he is entitled to his dower in the lands of his wife, and such portion of her personal estate as he would be entitled to had his wife died intestate leaving children. Wilson v. Hall (Ohio Cir. 1892) 3 Ohio C.D. 589, affirmed 53 Ohio St. 679, 44 N.E. 1137.

Where surviving spouse appeared in court and timely elected to take against decedent's will pursuant to RC 2107.39 but such election was not journalized through no fault of the spouse, probate court may subsequently file a nunc pro tunc order authorizing the election. In re Estate of Courtney, No. CA80–09–0097 (12th Dist Ct App, Butler, 3–31–82).

A widow for whom no provision is made in the will of her deceased husband has the same rights in his personal estate as she would have had if provision had been made for her and she had rejected it. In re Hutchins' Estate, 21 CC 720, 12 CD 29 (Cuyahoga 1901), modified by Hutchings v Davis, 68 OS 160, 67 NE 251 (1903).

5. Marital deduction; taxation

The interest of a surviving spouse electing to take against the will under RC 2107.39 is determined after deducting federal estate taxes from the estate, notwithstanding RC 2113.88, which exempts from apportionment of federal taxes only the share of a spouse whose interest is created by the will, as indicated by use of the words "legatee, devisee, or donee." In re Estate of McVicker (Ohio Com.Pl. 1985) 23 Ohio Misc.2d 43, 492 N.E.2d 491, 23 O.B.R. 437.

The presence or absence of a tax provision in the will of a testator does not alter the statutory share of a surviving spouse electing to take against the will. Weeks v. Vandeveer (Ohio 1968) 13 Ohio St.2d 15, 233 N.E.2d 502, 42 O.O.2d 25. Wills ⟹ 801(7)

Where a widow elects to take under the Ohio statute of descent and distribution, the amount of the federal estate tax on the decedent's estate should be deducted therefrom before computing the widow's share thereof. (See also Campbell v Lloyd, 162 OS 203, 122 NE(2d) 695 (1954), cert denied 349 US 911, 75 SCt 600, 99 LEd 1246 (1955); Hall v Ball, 162 OS 299, 123 NE(2d) 259 (1954).) Weeks v. Vandeveer (Ohio 1968) 13 Ohio St.2d 15, 233 N.E.2d 502, 42 O.O.2d 25. Wills ⟹ 801(7)

A testator who wants to take advantage of the marital deduction in order to preserve a greater portion of his estate for his family should be permitted to do so, and where he employs a tax clause to accomplish this purpose, it should be held effective even though his widow elects to take against the will, provided, of course, that the language of the tax clause is sufficiently broad to warrant such a construction. Weeks v. Vandeveer (Ohio Prob. 1966) 7 Ohio Misc. 51, 216 N.E.2d 78, 36 O.O.2d 127, reversed 13 Ohio St.2d 15, 233 N.E.2d 502, 42 O.O.2d 25. Internal Revenue ⟹ 4169(3)

If a settlor reserves to himself the income of a trust during his life with the right to amend or revoke the trust or any part thereof, such reserved rights and powers do not defeat the parting with dominion over the trust property and the surviving spouse upon the death of the settlor is bound from claiming a distributive share of the trust property upon her election to take against the will. Smyth v. Cleveland Trust Co. (Ohio 1961) 172 Ohio St. 489, 179 N.E.2d 60, 18 O.O.2d 42.

Whether the surviving spouse takes under the will or under the statute of descent and distribution, the federal estate tax is considered a debt against the entire estate and shall be deducted before a distribution. Ginder v. Ginder (Ohio Prob. 1954) 134 N.E.2d 603, 72 Ohio Law Abs. 277, 82 Ohio Law Abs. 129, 59 O.O. 320. Wills ⟹ 799

Where, under the terms of a declaration of trust in personal property, a present interest passes to another and the trust is by its terms irrevocable, the trust, so declared, is not testamentary in character, and the trust is valid as against the election of a surviving spouse of the settlor. (But see Smyth v Cleveland Trust Co, 172 OS 489, 179 NE(2d) 60 (1961).) Morrison v. Morrison (Lucas 1955) 99 Ohio App. 203, 132 N.E.2d 233, 58 O.O. 361.

Where a widow elects to take under the statute of descent and distribution which provides that "personal property shall be distributed" and any "real estate or inheritance shall descend and pass in parcenary" in part to the surviving spouse, the amount of the federal estate tax on the decedent's estate should be deducted therefrom before computing the widow's share thereof. Campbell v. Lloyd (Ohio 1954) 162 Ohio St. 203, 122 N.E.2d 695, 55 O.O. 102, certiorari denied 75 S.Ct. 600, 349 U.S. 911, 99 L.Ed. 1246, rehearing denied 75 S.Ct. 870, 349 U.S. 948, 99 L.Ed. 1274.

Where a widow elects to take under the will, a proportionate amount of the federal estate tax must be deducted from the residue before she reserves her specified one half thereof, and the residue must also bear the burden of the tax on a specific legacy to her. (Distinguished in Miller v Hammond, 156 OS 475, 104 NE(2d) 9 (1952); overruled by Campbell v Lloyd, 162 OS 203, 122 NE(2d) 695 (1954).) Foerster v. Foerster (Ohio Prob. 1954) 122 N.E.2d 314, 71 Ohio Law Abs. 129, 54 O.O. 441.

The marital deduction must be deducted from the gross estate before the federal estate tax may be determined, and, after the tax is paid, the widow is entitled on distribution to one-third of the net balance of the estate, which means that the widow must bear her proportionate share of the burden of the whole of the estate tax. (See also Foerster v Foerster, 71 Abs 129, 122 NE(2d) 514 (Prob, Franklin 1954).) In re Miller's Estate (Ohio Prob. 1950) 94 N.E.2d 67, 81 Ohio Law Abs. 553, 42 O.O. 325.

To the extent that transfers of nonprobate assets did not generate tax, Ohio law does not charge them with tax liability, and the entire federal estate tax burden attributable to the probate estate should fall upon the residuary legatees. Estate of Penney (C.A.6 1974) 504 F.2d 37.

Where a widow has elected, under former GC 10571 (RC 2107.39, RC 2107.41, RC 2107.43), not to take under the will of her husband, she succeeds to her distributive share in her husband's personal property, and such succession is taxable under GC 5332 (RC 5731.02). In re Lackman's Estate (Ohio Com.Pl. 1927) 26 Ohio NP(NS) 387.

6. Objection to or action to set aside election

The year within which an election must be made begins to run from the time of the service of the citation, and where the widow appears in open court, without service of citation, and declines to make her election, she does not thereby waive the issuing and service of citation, or estop herself from denying that a citation had been served. Bowen v. Bowen (Ohio 1877) 34 Ohio St. 164. Wills ⟹ 790

A probate judge has no right to cancel an election previously made and entered upon his journal, at her instance, for an alleged misapprehension on her part as to the provisions and effect of such will. Davis v. Davis (Ohio 1860) 11 Ohio St. 386. Wills ⟹ 796

On appeal from trial court's determination that election by decedent's surviving spouse to take under will would not be set aside, Court of Appeals would not address claim that executor of will owed fiduciary duty to surviving spouse and that this duty was breached, where claim was not presented to trial court. Martin v. Estate of Martin (Ohio App. 3 Dist., Allen, 03-22-2004) No. 1-03-55, 2004-Ohio-1397, 2004 WL 549474, Unreported, appeal not allowed 103 Ohio St.3d 1406, 812 N.E.2d 1288, 2004-Ohio-3980. Wills ⟹ 396

Some competent, credible evidence supported trial court's finding that decedent's surviving spouse did not sustain burden of proof to set aside her election to take under will; probate court was not required to explain rights under will and rights by law in event of refusal to take under will given that spouse's election to take under will was not made in court, spouse expressed several times that she did not want to go against decedent's wishes, there was at least opportunity for spouse to become knowledgeable as to estate's value, and spouse was advised as to legal rights under will and under law before she signed election to take under will. Martin v. Estate of Martin (Ohio App. 3 Dist., Allen, 03-22-2004) No. 1-03-55, 2004-Ohio-1397, 2004 WL 549474, Unreported, appeal not allowed 103 Ohio St.3d 1406, 812 N.E.2d 1288, 2004-Ohio-3980. Wills ⇐ 788

Vacation by probate court of an election by surviving spouse to take under statute of descent and distribution, when ordered upon motion filed by interested relative other than surviving spouse, is void for lack of jurisdiction, and such election may be vacated only upon filing of petition therefor by surviving spouse. Baker v. Hutyera (Ohio Com.Pl. 1971) 27 Ohio Misc. 19, 267 N.E.2d 604, 56 O.O.2d 230.

Inasmuch as the executor and testamentary trustee under a deceased husband's will, as well as a legatee under the will, have interests which conflict with what is "better" for the incompetent widow, they have no standing to contest the court's election on behalf of the spouse, which can be questioned only by the guardian of such spouse or by some other party acting on behalf of such spouse. In re Cook's Estate (Ohio 1969) 19 Ohio St.2d 121, 249 N.E.2d 799, 48 O.O.2d 113. Wills ⇐ 786

Legatees under a will have no right to contest an election not to take under a will made by the probate court on behalf of a surviving spouse who, because of legal disability, is unable to make such election on his own behalf. In re Strauch's Estate (Ohio 1968) 15 Ohio St.2d 192, 239 N.E.2d 43, 44 O.O.2d 158. Wills ⇐ 797

The period of time prescribed by RC 2107.39, within which a surviving spouse may make an election to take under the will of a decedent or under the statute of descent and distribution, is not extended by the filing after the termination of such period of an action alleging that an election made during the period is void and praying that it be held void, so that the making and filing of a purported election after the expiration of the period is a nullity and the same should be stricken from the files. In re Wolfel's Estate (Marion 1965) 3 Ohio App.2d 11, 209 N.E.2d 594, 32 O.O.2d 75.

For the purpose of determining if distribution should be made under the terms of a will or under the provisions of law when a surviving spouse has elected to take against a will, an executor or a testamentary trustee has the right to object to the making of an election by such spouse. In re Gould's Estate (Ohio Prob. 1956) 140 N.E.2d 793, 75 Ohio Law Abs. 289, 1 O.O.2d 366, affirmed 140 N.E.2d 801, 75 Ohio Law Abs. 298, 1 O.O.2d 372.

Where a surviving widow not mentioned in the will of her deceased husband elected to take under the statute of descent and distribution twenty-five days after the inventory and appraisement was filed, which was more than nine months after the probate of the will and the appointment of the executor, and no extension of time had been granted for filing such inventory beyond the statutory period, nor for making the election, but no citation to make an election had been served on the widow, and no explanation had been given to her by the probate court as to her rights under the law and under the will, and the inventory and appraisement was given final approval on the day when the election was filed, and at the time the election was so filed there had been no administration of the estate and the rights of third persons had not intervened, it was error prejudicial to the surviving widow for the probate court to strike the written election from the files. In re Bersin's Estate (Medina 1955) 98 Ohio App. 432, 129 N.E.2d 868, 57 O.O. 475.

A widow may rescind her election to take against the husband's will where such election was made in reliance upon erroneous advice of her attorney and the probate judge did not explain the provisions of the will. Smith v. First Nat. Bank of Akron (Ohio Com.Pl. 1954) 124 N.E.2d 851, 69 Ohio Law Abs. 102.

Where the granddaughters of a testator bring an action against his widow claiming she was appropriating property which did not pass to her because she had not taken under the will, and their petition does not allege that she was cited and had elected not to take under the will, such petition does not state a good cause of action against the widow. Spreen v. Sandman (Ohio Cir. 1887) 1 Ohio C.D. 577, dismissed.

7. Presumptions, waiver and release

A provision in lieu of dower made for a wife by the husband before his death may be waived by the wife on the death of the husband and an election of her dower rights in his property made. Spangler v. Dukes (Ohio 1884) 39 Ohio St. 642.

Will bequest of $1 in lieu of statutory support precluded testator's surviving spouse from support after time for spouse to elect against the will had expired; spouse was conclusively presumed to have elected to take under will. In re Estate of Reddick (Ohio App. 3 Dist., 04-11-1995) 102 Ohio App.3d 488, 657 N.E.2d 531. Executors And Administrators ⇐ 186

GC 10504–60 (RC 2107.41), providing for a conclusive presumption of election, is not violative of due process, where the surviving spouse fails to elect by reason of continued insanity and his guardian fails to make application for a commission to elect, within the time provided by this section. In re Iwinski's Estate (Cuyahoga 1947) 83 Ohio App. 463, 77 N.E.2d 375, 49 Ohio Law Abs. 609, 38 O.O. 491.

Where there is no direct evidence that a widow was cited to elect or made any election to take under her deceased husband's will, and where all the records of the probate court were destroyed by fire subsequent to the probate of such will and the settlement of the estate, a court will presume that the required citation was issued and that the widow elected to take the more valuable estate. Weaver v. King (Ohio Cir. 1907) 21 Ohio C.D. 199, 12 Ohio C.C.(N.S.) 129, affirmed 80 Ohio St. 717, 89 N.E. 1127, 7 Ohio Law Rep. 13.

Where a widow fails to make a proper election under her late husband's will and there is no proof or record that she ever received any consideration by order of the court or otherwise in lieu of her dower, her sale of her husband's real estate to satisfy his debts is not a release of her vested right of dower in such real estate, and her creditor is entitled to have it subjected to the payment of his judgment. Hessenmueller v Mulrooney, 6 D 123, 4 NP 50 (CP 1896).

The release of dower by election to take under the will is intended to be a release of the dower interest to the heirs at law or those entitled to inherit, and not as a means of conveyance to strangers. Hessenmueller v Mulrooney, 6 D 123, 4 NP 50 (CP 1896).

A separation agreement incorporated into an "Agreed Final Judgment for Alimony Only" that is silent regarding any claims one party may make on the estate of the other is not a waiver of the right conferred by RC 2107.39. In re Estate of Robinson, No. 85 CA 16 (2d Dist Ct App, Green, 9–19–85).

8. Procedural issues

Probate court's failure to maintain an appearance docket at time testator's surviving spouse received notice of her right to elect against the will did not entitle surviving spouse to file election after expiration of the five-month limitations period, even though general rule governing service required the fact of mailing of the notice and the receipt of a certified mail receipt to be reflected in an appearance docket; special rule governing service in probate proceedings contained no such requirement, and any defect did not prejudice spouse in light of the fact that notice was actually delivered to her residence. In re Estate of Riley (Ohio App. 4 Dist., 02-09-2006) 165 Ohio App.3d 471, 847 N.E.2d 22, 2006-Ohio-956. Wills ⇐ 790

Sufficient evidence established that testator's surviving spouse was served by certified mail with notice of her right to elect against testator's will, so as to trigger five-month limitations period within which she was required to file any election, even though certified mail receipt card was not signed; surviving spouse's son signed a delivery receipt that contained the same tracking number as the certified mail receipt card, and son testified that he helped surviving spouse with odd jobs including retrieving her mail, such that receipt of the service by son satisfied due process and applicable rules as to service. In re Estate of Riley (Ohio App. 4 Dist., 02-09-2006) 165 Ohio App.3d 471, 847 N.E.2d 22, 2006-Ohio-956. Wills ⇐ 790

The election provided by statute for a surviving spouse to choose whether she desires to take under her husband's will or under the statute of descent and distribution is solely for the benefit of the surviving spouse, and where that spouse is under a legal disability the probate court must elect on her behalf the provision which is better for her, considering only her interests. In re Cook's Estate (Ohio 1969) 19 Ohio St.2d 121, 249 N.E.2d 799, 48 O.O.2d 113.

Where an authenticated copy of a will, executed and proved according to the laws of the state of the decedent's domicile, has been admitted to record pursuant to RC 2129.05, and where it is not established that the widow who was domiciled in that state had claimed anything under the will or otherwise elected to take thereunder and where the testator owned real estate in Ohio at his death, such widow has the right, with respect to that Ohio real estate, to elect not to take under the testator's will but to take under the Ohio statute of descent and distribution, even though no such election is permitted by the law of the state of the testator's domicile at death. Pfau v. Moseley (Ohio 1966) 9 Ohio St.2d 13, 222 N.E.2d 639, 38 O.O.2d 8. Wills ⇐ 778

2106.01
Note 8

A general legacy bears interest at the legal rate from the end of nine months from the date of the issuance of letters of appointment from the probate court to the executor, unless it be clearly apparent that the testator did not so intend, and a legatee is entitled to such interest from said date, unless the will provides otherwise, regardless of the pendency of a contest delaying the settlement of an estate and the participation in that contest by the legatees claiming interest; interest upon arrearages of annuities is recoverable from the time the installment of annuities became due and payable, which time shall be determined from the intent of the testator as shown by the terms of the will which created the annuity. In re Rothschild's Estate (Ohio Prob. 1948) 114 N.E.2d 143, 66 Ohio Law Abs. 237, 51 O.O. 110. Wills ⇨ 734(4); Wills ⇨ 734(8)

In an action for construction of a will giving to testator's widow the part of the estate secured to her by the laws of distribution and to testator's brother the remainder, evidence of the circumstances of the testator, his character, the objects of his bounty, his ties of affection and the instruction to the scrivener, was properly excluded. Foster v. Clifford (Ohio 1913) 87 Ohio St. 294, 101 N.E. 269, 10 Ohio Law Rep. 600, Am.Ann.Cas. 1915B, 65. Wills ⇨ 487(2)

An election must be a matter of record in a proper court, or such actual election as would create an estoppel in order to bar the widow of her dower right and share of her husband's personal estate. Millikin v Welliver, 3 OS 460 (1882).

The probate judge having judicially determined that a widow has elected to take, the duty to make an entry of the fact under former GC 10571 (RC 2107.39, RC 2107.41, RC 2107.43), is ministerial, and mandamus lies to compel its performance; the executor is not the proper party to bring such mandamus, but proper party may be substituted. State ex rel. Zollinger v. Sloane (Ohio Com.Pl. 1912) 24 Ohio Dec. 119.

9. Property subject to right of election

Where land is being sold under a direction in the will to pay debts, all of which were paid, the widow as against devisees is entitled to dower in the entire proceeds of the land, she having elected to take dower instead of the testamentary provision. Kling v. Ballentine (Ohio 1883) 40 Ohio St. 391.

When the widow elects to be endowed of the lands of her husband instead of under the will, the devisees who are prejudiced by such election are equitably entitled to compensation out of the rejected provisions made for her in the will. Jennings v. Jennings (Ohio 1871) 21 Ohio St. 56.

This section relates to testamentary disposition of estates, its purpose being to limit a widow who declines to take under will of husband to not more than one-half of the estate in lieu of the provision made for her in the rejected will, as against the other devisees and legatees named in the will who may be children of herself and her deceased husband or other designated beneficiaries. Goodfellow v. Wilson (Clark 1940) 32 Ohio Law Abs. 569.

In computing the share of a surviving spouse who elects to take against the will of the deceased spouse, the "first $30,000" referred to in RC 2105.06(C) is a deduction from the net estate and is therefore charged against the maximum one-third of the net estate which the surviving spouse can receive. Winkelfoos v. Mann (Huron 1984) 16 Ohio App.3d 266, 475 N.E.2d 509, 16 O.B.R. 291.

A surviving spouse taking against a will of a deceased spouse is entitled to an automobile under RC 2113.532 if the will does not specifically dispose of said vehicle. In re Green's Estate (Ohio Com.Pl. 1980) 63 Ohio Misc. 44, 410 N.E.2d 812, 17 O.O.3d 388. Wills ⇨ 801(1)

On the evidence settlor retained such control over trust as to render it a mere agency account, and hence wife was entitled to her statutory share thereof on testator's death. Osborn v. Osborn (Ohio Com.Pl. 1966) 10 Ohio Misc. 171, 226 N.E.2d 814, 39 O.O.2d 275, affirmed 18 Ohio St.2d 144, 248 N.E.2d 191, 47 O.O.2d 310.

A probate court does not have jurisdiction of an action in which plaintiff seeks an order that a trustee (not appointed by such court) of an inter vivos trust turn over to plaintiff, the surviving spouse of the deceased settlor, property delivered by the settlor, prior to her death, to, and held by, such trustee. (See also Roesch v Cleveland Trust Co, 12 Misc 239, 230 NE(2d) 746 (CP, Cuyahoga 1967).) Purcell v. Cleveland Trust Co. (Cuyahoga 1965) 6 Ohio App.2d 235, 217 N.E.2d 876, 35 O.O.2d 426.

Where a surviving spouse elects to take against the will, she takes her distributive share in the real property and in the personal property. Winters Nat. Bank & Trust Co. v. Riffe (Ohio Prob. 1963) 194 N.E.2d 921, 93 Ohio Law Abs. 171, 27 O.O.2d 261, reversed 2 Ohio St.2d 72, 206 N.E.2d 212, 31 O.O.2d 56.

Uncompensated loss resulting from an election to take against the will falls upon all legatees equally rather than upon the residuary estate. Winters Nat. Bank & Trust Co. v. Riffe (Ohio Prob. 1963) 194 N.E.2d 921, 93 Ohio Law Abs. 171, 27 O.O.2d 261, reversed 2 Ohio St.2d 72, 206 N.E.2d 212, 31 O.O.2d 56.

A valid voluntary trust in praesenti, formally executed by a husband and existing at the time of his death, and in which he reserved to himself the income therefrom during life, coupled with an absolute power to revoke the trust in whole or in part, as well as the right to modify the terms of the settlement and to control investments, bars the wife, upon the death of the settlor, from a claimed right to a distributive share of the property in the trust upon her election to take under the statute of descent and distribution. Smyth v. Cleveland Trust Co. (Ohio 1961) 172 Ohio St. 489, 179 N.E.2d 60, 18 O.O.2d 42.

Widow may enforce her right to distributive share of property transferred by her husband in his lifetime to a trustee under terms of an indenture, in which settlor husband reserves to himself income during his life, with right to amend and revoke settlement, and wherein he does not part with dominion and control over trust property. Harris v. Harris (Summit 1945) 79 Ohio App. 443, 74 N.E.2d 407, 35 O.O. 254, affirmed 147 Ohio St. 437, 72 N.E.2d 378, 34 O.O. 371. Descent And Distribution ⇨ 69

Under GC 8617 (RC 1335.01), transfer of property to trustee is valid under agreement whereby settlor reserves to himself income during his life with right to amend or revoke, but when settlor does not part with dominion and control over trust property his widow may elect to take under statutes of descent and distribution. Harris v. Harris (Ohio 1947) 147 Ohio St. 437, 72 N.E.2d 378, 34 O.O. 371. Wills ⇨ 801(6)

The term "net estate" in this section, has no limitation which would restrict the widow to the distributive share in money, and upon her election to take under statute of descent and distribution rather than under the will she has a vested interest in fee in the real estate as well as the personalty. Barlow v. Winters Nat. Bank & Trust Co. (Montgomery 1944) 59 N.E.2d 212, 41 Ohio Law Abs. 457, motion granted 75 Ohio App. 392, 62 N.E.2d 351, 31 O.O. 150, affirmed 145 Ohio St. 270, 61 N.E.2d 603, 160 A.L.R. 423, 30 O.O. 484.

Where the property to which a widow is entitled under her election to take under statute of descent and distribution has been placed in a testamentary trust with rest of decedent's estate for benefit of certain beneficiaries, widow is entitled to the income from the trust in the proportion that her share of the corpus bears to the entire corpus. Barlow v. Winters Nat. Bank & Trust Co. (Montgomery 1944) 59 N.E.2d 212, 41 Ohio Law Abs. 457, motion granted 75 Ohio App. 392, 62 N.E.2d 351, 31 O.O. 150, affirmed 145 Ohio St. 270, 61 N.E.2d 603, 160 A.L.R. 423, 30 O.O. 484.

Case decided against widow who claimed an inter vivos gift of securities from her husband was held to be res judicata of later action brought by her as the beneficiary of a trust of which the same securities were the res, but such widow is not thereby estopped from asserting her right to a distributive share of such property under this section. Bolles v. Toledo Trust Co. (Ohio 1944) 144 Ohio St. 195, 58 N.E.2d 381, 157 A.L.R. 1164, 29 O.O. 376. Judgment ⇨ 585(3)

Where a husband, concurrently with the execution of his will, established a revocable, amendable living trust in which he deposited res inadequate for declared purpose of creating an annuity for his widow, and, by another later revocable, amendable, living trust the res remaining in the trust was to be transferred at his death to the first trust, provided sufficient res to carry out the declared purpose of the first trust and which provision by the terms of the husband's will was to be in lieu of all rights given the widow by law, the widow if she elects to take under the statute of descent and distribution may assert her right to a distributive share of the property already in, as well as the property coming to, such trust under the will. Bolles v. Toledo Trust Co. (Ohio 1944) 144 Ohio St. 195, 58 N.E.2d 381, 157 A.L.R. 1164, 29 O.O. 376. Wills ⇨ 801(6)

Where testatrix devises one-half of her real estate to spouse for life, remainder to devisees, and other half to a devisee in fee, surviving spouse, electing not to take under the will and there being no surviving children or parents of deceased, does not take the whole estate under provisions of GC 10503-4 (RC 2103.04), but is limited to one-half the net estate under this section; in such case, the personal estate of the deceased being inconsequential, spouse is not entitled to maintain an action for partition of real estate, but estate should be ordered sold for purpose of making an equitable distribution among disappointed devisees, after paying one-half to surviving spouse. Shearn v. Shearn (Coshocton 1937) 60 Ohio App. 317, 21 N.E.2d 133, 14 O.O. 262.

Where it appears that there is land enough to set off the dower of a widow who elects to take against the will without interfering with land specifically devised for life, it should be so done; otherwise, the disappointed devisees are equitably entitled to compensation out of the rejected provisions for the widow, and if they do not fully compensate such devisees, the resulting uncompensated loss should fall upon the residuary estate in preference to the specific devises, unless a contrary intention appears from the will. Dunlap v. McCloud (Ohio 1911) 84 Ohio St. 272, 95 N.E. 774, 9 Ohio Law Rep. 94. Wills ⚖ 802(5)

Where a widow elects to take under the law, and the value of her statutory share exceeds the life estate under the will, the life estate she would have taken under the will will be sequestered to compensate the disappointed devisees. Holdren v. Holdren (Ohio 1908) 78 Ohio St. 276, 85 N.E. 537, 6 Ohio Law Rep. 109.

A widow is entitled to a distributive share of personalty even though her deceased husband makes no provision for her in his will, inasmuch as the spirit of RS 5964 extends to such cases. Doyle v. Doyle (Ohio 1893) 50 Ohio St. 330, 29 W.L.B. 371, 34 N.E. 166.

A renunciation by a surviving wife of her joint interest in bank accounts and stocks held jointly was ineffective where she had signed bank signature cards and indorsed dividend checks, and consequently where she purported to renounce so that two-thirds of the property passed to the children, a gift tax was properly imposed thereon. (See also Krakoff v United States, 431 F(2d) 847, 31 Misc 252 (6th Cir Ohio 1970).) Krakoff v. U. S. (C.A.6 (Ohio) 1971) 439 F.2d 1023, 58 O.O.2d 381, 60 O.O.2d 417.

A husband not provided for in his wife's will is entitled to the same distributive share of her personal estate as if she had died intestate. Coon v DeMoore, 2 CC(NS) 444, 15 CD 776 (Cuyahoga 1903), affirmed sub nom Coon v Coon, 71 OS 537, 74 NE 1134 (1905).

10. Time for election

The rules of the wills act, prescribing the time and the manner of election by widows, are not applicable to foreign wills, but whenever a foreign will, properly construed, creates a case for election at common law, such election must be made whenever the protection of the rights of other interested parties makes it necessary, and in such manner as will be binding upon the widow. Jennings v. Jennings (Ohio 1871) 21 Ohio St. 56.

Where, by reason of oversight no citation was issued by probate court to widow as provided by former GC 10566 (RC 2107.39), even though she did not file written instrument under former GC 10571 (RC 2107.39, RC 2107.41, RC 2107.43) and did not make election under former GC 10570 (RC 2107.43), citation to widow to appear and elect will issue where probate judge thoroughly understood that widow did not intend to take under will, but intended to insist upon her rights at law. Adams v. Taylor (Franklin 1932) 13 Ohio Law Abs. 278, 37 Ohio Law Rep. 496.

Where, due to an oversight, no citation has been issued to a widow to appear and elect whether she will take under her husband's will or at law, she is, despite lapse of time and the presumption arising therefrom according to GC 10504–60 (RC 2107.41), entitled to a citation and opportunity to make an election. Adams v. Taylor (Franklin 1932) 13 Ohio Law Abs. 278, 37 Ohio Law Rep. 496.

Probate court's order concluding that testator's surviving spouse failed to file a timely election against testator's will was a final order affecting a substantial right in a special proceeding and, thus, was appealable; surviving spouse would be denied effective future relief in the absence of immediate review, since property to which she might be entitled could be sold during the remainder of the probate proceedings. In re Estate of Riley (Ohio App. 4 Dist., 02-09-2006) 165 Ohio App.3d 471, 847 N.E.2d 22, 2006-Ohio-956. Wills ⚖ 788

Spouse must make an election either under will or against will within one month after service of citation to elect, or spouse may file motion for extension of time within one-month period and court may allow additional time for making election for good cause shown. In re Estate of Reddick (Ohio App. 3 Dist., 04-11-1995) 102 Ohio App.3d 488, 657 N.E.2d 531. Wills ⚖ 790

Where the probate court sends a citation to the residence of the surviving spouse, by certified mail, so that the surviving spouse may make an election pursuant to RC 2107.39, and where the facts show, inter alia, that the son of the surviving spouse, who did not live at his father's home and who was not authorized to sign for certified mail for his father, signed his father's name on the receipt for the citation, it is error for the probate court, upon motion of the surviving spouse, to fail to set aside the father's "waiver" to take under the statute, even though the one-month period for response to the citation had expired. In re Jone's Estate (Hamilton 1981) 1 Ohio App.3d 70, 439 N.E.2d 458, 1 O.B.R. 350.

Where antenuptial agreement places restraints upon testator and where such testator neglects to comply properly with such provisions in his will, and widow, within nine months following the appointment of the executor, brings action in declaratory judgment proceeding to determine validity of such antenuptial agreement and seeks advice of court, such declaratory judgment action is "proceedings for advice" as is contemplated in RC 2107.39, and widow has three months after final disposition of such declaratory judgment proceedings within which to make her election as to whether she will take under statute of descent and distribution or whether she will take under will. Barlup v. Holloway (Logan 1971) 25 Ohio App.2d 44, 266 N.E.2d 241, 54 O.O.2d 77.

A void election, as contrasted with a voidable one, is void ab initio, and if no valid election is made thereafter within the time allowed and nothing has occurred or failed to occur which would operate to extend such period, the surviving spouse shall be conclusively presumed to have elected to take under the will of the decedent. In re Wolfel's Estate (Marion 1965) 3 Ohio App.2d 11, 209 N.E.2d 594, 32 O.O.2d 75.

After the time has elapsed for making the election, a surviving spouse, who remains alive and competent, is precluded by RC 2107.39 from making a valid election to take against the will of his deceased spouse, unless, before the expiration of the time period, he requests and is allowed further time for making the election. In re Witteman's Estate (Ohio 1965) 3 Ohio St.2d 66, 209 N.E.2d 427, 32 O.O.2d 49.

A surviving spouse may file her election prior to filing of the inventory and appraisement if she waives her right not to elect until said inventory is filed. (Ed. note: This case may have been overruled by revision of requirements for citation to elect.) In re Rogers' Estate (Ohio Prob. 1959) 160 N.E.2d 442, 81 Ohio Law Abs. 10, 10 O.O.2d 205.

The entry of a probate court granting the spouse sixty additional days in which to make his election was not expected to be, and was not, a judgment rendered upon the merits of the question of the spouse's right, or lack of right, to make an election to take against his wife's will. In re Gould's Estate (Ohio Prob. 1956) 140 N.E.2d 793, 75 Ohio Law Abs. 289, 1 O.O.2d 366, affirmed 140 N.E.2d 801, 75 Ohio Law Abs. 298, 1 O.O.2d 372. Judgment ⚖ 563(2)

Under this section a surviving spouse cannot elect to take under will or under statute of descent and distribution until after the probate of the will. Raleigh v. Raleigh (Ohio 1950) 153 Ohio St. 160, 91 N.E.2d 241, 41 O.O. 209. Wills ⚖ 790

By virtue of GC 1504–63 (RC 2107.45), 10504–55 (RC 2107.39) and 10504–60 (RC 2107.41), which are in pari materia, a surviving spouse may not elect after the expiration of the time allowed for the election; after the expiration of such time, such spouse shall be conclusively presumed to have elected to take under the will. In re Iwinski's Estate (Cuyahoga 1947) 83 Ohio App. 463, 77 N.E.2d 375, 49 Ohio Law Abs. 609, 38 O.O. 491.

Surviving spouse may make election at and after admittance of will to probate, within time limited, and need not wait until schedule of debts is filed and citation issued. (Ed. note: This case may have been overruled by revision of requirements for citation to elect.) Davis v. Warner (Morrow 1933) 47 Ohio App. 495, 192 N.E. 270, 18 Ohio Law Abs. 26, 40 Ohio Law Rep. 384, error dismissed 127 Ohio St. 597, 190 N.E. 386, 39 Ohio Law Rep. 655. Wills ⚖ 790

GC 10504–58 (RC 2107.39), which allows an extension of time for election, applies both to competent and incompetent spouses. In re Jones Estate (Ohio Com.Pl. 1939) 1 Ohio Supp. 32, 29 Ohio Law Abs. 148, 15 O.O. 250.

2106.02 Citation to surviving spouse to make election

(A) The citation to make the election referred to in section 2106.01 of the Revised Code shall be served on the surviving spouse pursuant to Civil Rule 73. Notice that the citation has been issued by the court shall be given to the administrator or executor of the estate of the deceased spouse.

(B) The citation shall be accompanied by a general description of the effect of the election to take under the will or under section 2105.06 of the Revised Code and the general rights of the surviving spouse under Chapter 2106. of the Revised Code. The description shall include a specific reference to the procedures available to the surviving spouse under section 2106.03 of the Revised Code and to the presumption that arises if the surviving spouse does not make the election in accordance with division (E) of section 2106.01 of the Revised Code. The description of the general rights of the surviving spouse under Chapter 2106. of the Revised Code shall include a specific reference to the presumption that arises if the surviving spouse does not exercise the rights under Chapter 2106. of the Revised Code within the time period specified by section 2106.25 of the Revised Code. The description of the effect of the election and of the general rights of the surviving spouse need not relate to the nature of any particular estate.

(C) A surviving spouse electing to take under the will may manifest the election in writing within the times described in division (E) of section 2106.01 of the Revised Code.

(2003 H 51, eff. 4–8–04; 2001 H 85, eff. 10–31–01; 1990 H 346, eff. 5–31–90)

Uncodified Law

2004 H 161, § 3. See Uncodified Law under 2106.01.

1990 H 346, § 3, eff. 5–31–90, reads, in part: (A) Sections 1 and 2 of this act shall apply only to the estates of decedents who die on or after the effective date of this act.

Historical and Statutory Notes

Ed. Note: 2106.02 is former RC 2107.391, amended and recodified by 1990 H 346, eff. 5–31–90; 1976 S 466; 1975 S 145.

Amendment Note: 2003 H 51 substituted "served on" for "sent to" and substituted "pursuant to Civil Rule 73" for "by certified mail" in division (A); and substituted "exercise" for "make" following "surviving spouse does not" and substituted "rights under Chapter 2106. of the Revised Code" for "election" in division (B).

Amendment Note: 2001 H 85 rewrote division (B) which prior thereto read:

"(B) The citation shall be accompanied by a general description of the effect of the election and the general rights of the surviving spouse. The description shall include a specific reference to the procedures available to the surviving spouse under section 2106.03 of the Revised Code and to the presumption that arises if the surviving spouse does not make the election in accordance with division (E) of section 2106.01 of the Revised Code. The description of the effect of the election and of the rights of the surviving spouse need not relate to the nature of any particular estate."

Legislative Service Commission

1975:

This new section would provide that the citation to elect must be sent to the surviving spouse by certified mail with notice that the citation has been issued being given to the administrator or executor.

The new section would also require that the citation to elect sent to the surviving spouse be accompanied by an explanation in general terms of the rights of the surviving spouse with respect to the election and the consequences if no election is made.

The surviving spouse would be permitted to elect to take under the will by filling out the citation, signing it, having it notarized, and delivering it to the administrator or executor. The administrator or executor would then sign the election and file it with the probate court. If the executor refused to sign it, the spouse could indicate such on the citation and return it to the court and the election would be valid. (Commentary from former RC 2107.391.)

Baldwin's Ohio Legislative Service, 1990 Laws of Ohio, H 346—LSC Analysis, p 5–87

Library References

Descent and Distribution ⚖64.1.
Wills ⚖788.
Westlaw Topic Nos. 124, 409.
C.J.S. Wills §§ 1841, 1863 to 1865.

Research References

Encyclopedias

OH Jur. 3d Decedents' Estates § 747, Citation Notice to Surviving Spouse of Right to Election.
OH Jur. 3d Decedents' Estates § 748, Time of Making Election; Extension of Time.
OH Jur. 3d Decedents' Estates § 753, Surviving Spouse's Right to Explanation of Election Rights.

Forms

Ohio Forms Legal and Business § 24:143, Drafting Will.

Treatises and Practice Aids

Carlin, Baldwin's Ohio Practice, Merrick-Rippner Probate Law § 2:35, Elective Rights of Surviving Spouse—Election to Take Under Law or Under the Will—Issuance of Citation.

Carlin, Baldwin's Ohio Practice, Merrick-Rippner Probate Law § 2:36, Elective Rights of Surviving Spouse—Election to Take Under Law or Under the Will—Time for Making Election.

Carlin, Baldwin's Ohio Practice, Merrick-Rippner Probate Law § 2:37, Elective Rights of Surviving Spouse—Election to Take Under Law or Under the Will—Procedure for Making Election.

Carlin, Baldwin's Ohio Practice, Merrick-Rippner Probate Law § 21:2, Rights of Surviving Spouse to Make Election—Statutory Provisions—Generally.

Carlin, Baldwin's Ohio Practice, Merrick-Rippner Probate Law § 21:3, Rights of Surviving Spouse to Make Election—Statutory Provisions—Citation—Issuance—Waiver of Citation.

Carlin, Baldwin's Ohio Practice, Merrick-Rippner Probate Law § 21:4, Rights of Surviving Spouse to Make Election—Statutory Provisions—Citation—Service.

Carlin, Baldwin's Ohio Practice, Merrick-Rippner Probate Law § 21:7, Rights of Surviving Spouse to Make Election—Statutory Provisions—Manner and Time—Election in Writing.

Carlin, Baldwin's Ohio Practice, Merrick-Rippner Probate Law § 2:121, Administration of Decedent's Estate—Checklist.

Carlin, Baldwin's Ohio Practice, Merrick-Rippner Probate Law § 21:34, Rights of Surviving Spouse to Make Election—Constitutionality of "In Person" Requirement.

Carlin, Baldwin's Ohio Practice, Merrick-Rippner Probate Law § 21:41, Rights of Surviving Spouse to Make Election—Failure to Make Election—Conclusive Presumption.

Carlin, Baldwin's Ohio Practice, Merrick-Rippner Probate Law § 21:43, Rights of Surviving Spouse to Make All Elections Under RC Chap. 2106—Time Limit.

Carlin, Baldwin's Ohio Practice, Merrick-Rippner Probate Law § 21:89, Citation to Surviving Spouse to Elect to Take Under or Against Will—Form.

Carlin, Baldwin's Ohio Practice, Merrick-Rippner Probate Law § 30:24, Drafting a Will—Surviving Spouse—Election to Take Against the Will.

Carlin, Baldwin's Ohio Practice, Merrick-Rippner Probate Law App B SPF 6.0, Inventory and Appraisal—Form.

Carlin, Baldwin's Ohio Practice, Merrick-Rippner Probate Law App B SPF 8.0, Citation to Surviving Spouse to Elect Exercise Elective Rights.

Carlin, Baldwin's Ohio Practice, Merrick-Rippner Probate Law App B SPF 8.1, Election of Surviving Spouse to Take Under Will.

Carlin, Baldwin's Ohio Practice, Merrick-Rippner Probate Law App B SPF 8.3, Summary of General Rights of Surviving Spouses.

Carlin, Baldwin's Ohio Practice, Merrick-Rippner Probate Law App B SPF 8.4, Certificate of Service and Notice of Citation to Surviving Spouse to Exercise Elective Rights.

Carlin, Baldwin's Ohio Practice, Merrick-Rippner Probate Law App B SPF 8.5, Return for Certificate of Service of Citation to Surviving Spouse to Exercise Elective Rights.

Law Review and Journal Commentaries

House Bill 85, Probate Reform Bill 2001: A Noble Experiment. Marilyn J. Maag. 12 Prob L J Ohio 21 (November/December 2001).

Practical Application of House Bill 85 (Probate Reform 2001), Marilyn J. Maag. 13 Prob L J Ohio 19 (November/December 2002).

Notes of Decisions

Ed. Note: *This section contains annotations from former RC 2107.391 and RC 2107.39.*

Entitlement to citation 3
Judicial advice 2
Service of citation 4

Time for election 1

1. Time for election

The year within which an election must be made begins to run from the time of the service of the citation, and where the widow appears in open court, without service of citation, and declines to make her election, she does not thereby waive the issuing and service of citation, or estop herself from denying that a citation had been served. Bowen v. Bowen (Ohio 1877) 34 Ohio St. 164. Wills ⚖ 790

Evidence supported probate court's order that surviving spouse take under will, despite her contention that, although citation to make election was issued, form mailing book for certified mail listed her mailing address as "Pearl River" rather than "Crystal River" and that no return card stating election was received by probate court; after citation was issued, spouse filed requests for extension of time within statutory 30–day election period, and there was no evidence that she was unaware of probate proceeding or of her opportunity to elect. Hutton v. Rygalski (Lucas 1989) 62 Ohio App.3d 125, 574 N.E.2d 1128. Wills ⚖ 788

If a surviving spouse remains alive and competent and, within nine months after the appointment of the first fiduciary charged with the administration of the estate under the will of the deceased spouse, no citation is issued and served upon him to elect whether to take under the will or under RC 2105.06, and within such nine-month period he also fails voluntarily so to elect, he will be conclusively presumed to have elected to take under the will, regardless of whether or not the inventory, appraisement and schedule of debts are filed. In re Witteman's Estate (Ohio 1965) 3 Ohio St.2d 66, 209 N.E.2d 427, 32 O.O.2d 49.

Where a surviving widow not mentioned in the will of her deceased husband elected to take under the statute of descent and distribution twenty-five days after the inventory and appraisement was filed, which was more than nine months after the probate of the will and the appointment of the executor, and no extension of time had been granted for filing such inventory beyond the statutory period, nor for making the election, but no citation to make an election had been served on the widow, and no explanation had been given to her by the probate court as to her rights under the law and under the will, and the inventory and appraisement was given final approval on the day when the election was filed, and at the time the election was so filed there had been no administration of the estate and the rights of third persons had not intervened, it was error prejudicial to the surviving widow for the probate court to strike the written election from the files. In re Bersin's Estate (Medina 1955) 98 Ohio App. 432, 129 N.E.2d 868, 57 O.O. 475.

2. Judicial advice

A widow may rescind her election to take against the husband's will where such election was made in reliance upon erroneous advice of her attorney and the probate judge did not explain the provisions of the will. Smith v. First Nat. Bank of Akron (Ohio Com.Pl. 1954) 124 N.E.2d 851, 69 Ohio Law Abs. 102.

When a widow is cited to elect, and it appears property specifically devised is required to pay debts, she is entitled to be judicially advised whether if she accepts she will be required to contribute to the person from whom the special legacy is taken. Allen v. Tressenrider (Ohio 1905) 72 Ohio St. 77, 73 N.E. 1015, 2 Ohio Law Rep. 495, 2 Am.Ann.Cas. 974.

3. Entitlement to citation

Where, by reason of oversight no citation was issued by probate court to widow as provided by GC 10566 (RC 2107.39), even though she did not file written instrument under GC 10571 (RC 2107.39, RC 2107.41, RC 2107.43) and did not make election under GC 10570 (RC 2107.43), citation to widow to appear and elect will issue where probate judge thoroughly understood that widow did not intend to take under will, but intended to insist upon her rights at law. Adams v. Taylor (Franklin 1932) 13 Ohio Law Abs. 278, 37 Ohio Law Rep. 496.

Where, due to an oversight, no citation has been issued to a widow to appear and elect whether she will take under her husband's will or at law, she is, despite lapse of time and the presumption arising therefrom according to GC 10504–60 (RC 2107.41) entitled to a citation and opportunity to make an election. Adams v. Taylor (Franklin 1932) 13 Ohio Law Abs. 278, 37 Ohio Law Rep. 496.

4. Service of citation

Sufficient evidence established that testator's surviving spouse was served by certified mail with notice of her right to elect against testator's will, so as to trigger five-month limitations period within which she was required to file any election, even though certified mail receipt card was not signed; surviving spouse's son signed a delivery receipt that contained the same tracking number as the certified mail receipt card, and son testified that he helped surviving spouse with odd jobs including retrieving her mail, such that receipt of the service by son satisfied due process and applicable rules as to service. In re Estate of Riley (Ohio App. 4 Dist., 02-09-2006) 165 Ohio App.3d 471, 847 N.E.2d 22, 2006-Ohio-956. Wills ⚖ 790

Where delivery of service of citation informing surviving spouse of right to elective share in deceased wife's estate never took place at husband's residence but, instead, notice of attempted delivery was placed in his mail box and later acted upon by his son who neither lived at residence nor possessed any authority, actual or implied, to act on surviving spouse's behalf for purposes of delivery and acceptance of posted materials, service against surviving spouse was invalid and it was error to fail to set aside his "waiver" to take under statute, even though one-month period for response to citation had expired. In re Jone's Estate (Hamilton 1981) 1 Ohio App.3d 70, 439 N.E.2d 458, 1 O.B.R. 350. Wills ⚖ 788; Wills ⚖ 790

2106.03 Complaint for construction of will

Within the times described in division (E) of section 2106.01 of the Revised Code for making an election, the surviving spouse may file a complaint in the probate court, making all persons interested in the will defendants, that requests a construction of the will in favor of the surviving spouse and for the court to render a judgment to that effect.

(1990 H 346, eff. 5–31–90)

Uncodified Law

1990 H 346, § 3, eff. 5–31–90, reads, in part: (A) Sections 1 and 2 of this act shall apply only to the estates of decedents who die on or after the effective date of this act.

Historical and Statutory Notes

Ed. Note: 2106.03 is former 2107.40, amended and recodified by 1990 H 346, eff. 5–31–90; 1975 S 145; 1953 H 1; GC 10504–57.

Cross References

Appeal, 2101.42
Computation of time, 1.14

Library References

Wills ⚖ 697(2), 788.
Westlaw Topic No. 409.
C.J.S. Wills §§ 1568, 1571 to 1572, 1841, 1863 to 1865.
  Baldwin's Ohio Legislative Service, 1990 Laws of Ohio, H 346—LSC Analysis, p 5–87

Research References

Encyclopedias
  OH Jur. 3d Decedents' Estates § 754, Surviving Spouse's Right to Explanation of Election Rights—Right to Formal Construction of Will Before Expiration of Time for Election.

Treatises and Practice Aids
Klein, Darling, & Terez, Baldwin's Ohio Practice Civil Practice § 73:1, Probate Division--In General.
Klein, Darling, & Terez, Baldwin's Ohio Practice Civil Practice § 73:3, Probate Division--Venue.
Carlin, Baldwin's Ohio Practice, Merrick-Rippner Probate Law § 4:53, Summons in Adversary Action—Form.
Carlin, Baldwin's Ohio Practice, Merrick-Rippner Probate Law § 43:2, Construing a Will—Action for Instructions—Preferability of Declaratory Judgment Action.
Carlin, Baldwin's Ohio Practice, Merrick-Rippner Probate Law § 21:86, Complaint by Surviving Spouse for Construction of Will—Form.

Carlin, Baldwin's Ohio Practice, Merrick-Rippner Probate Law § 30:24, Drafting a Will—Surviving Spouse—Election to Take Against the Will.

Notes of Decisions

Ed. Note: This section contains annotations from former RC 2107.40.

Parties 1
Procedural issues 2

---

1. Parties

The state of Ohio is not a necessary party in an action to construe a will where there has been no prior judicial determination of escheat to the state. Boulger v. Evans (Ohio 1978) 54 Ohio St.2d 371, 377 N.E.2d 753, 8 O.O.3d 388.

A widow whose husband dies intestate without children gets a much larger portion of his estate than she would get if she took against a will and under the law; she is therefore interested in having her husband's will set aside, and may maintain such an action. Moyses v. Neilson (Ohio Com.Pl. 1900) 9 Ohio Dec. 623, 7 Ohio N.P. 607.

Legatees and distributees are necessary parties in a federal court suit by an heir at law to obtain construction of a will. Stevens v. Smith (C.C.A.6 (Ohio) 1903) 126 F. 706, 61 C.C.A. 624, certiorari denied 24 S.Ct. 853, 193 U.S. 671, 48 L.Ed. 841.

2. Procedural issues

At common law, a provision in a testator's will made for his widow was regarded as having been given in addition to dower, but the laws of Ohio reversed this rule so that a widow shall not be entitled to both, unless it plainly appears by the will that the testator intended her to have both; since the construction of wills must be governed by the law of the place where the property is situated, a testator's Ohio property must come under the latter rule, not the former, which is the law of his domicile. Jennings v. Jennings (Ohio 1871) 21 Ohio St. 56.

Where antenuptial agreement places restraints upon testator and where such testator neglects to comply properly with such provisions in his will, and widow, within nine months following the appointment of the executor, brings action in declaratory judgment proceeding to determine validity of such antenuptial agreement and seeks advice of court, such declaratory judgment action is "proceedings for advice" as is contemplated in RC 2107.39, and widow has three months after final disposition of such declaratory judgment proceedings within which to make her election as to whether she will take under statute of descent and distribution or whether she will take under will. Barlup v. Holloway (Logan 1971) 25 Ohio App.2d 44, 266 N.E.2d 241, 54 O.O.2d 77.

A petition, in a cause brought under RS 6202 to obtain a construction of one item only of a will, which does not set forth the entire will, is bad on general demurrer. Devenney v. Devenney (Ohio 1906) 74 Ohio St. 96, 77 N.E. 688, 3 Ohio Law Rep. 674, 4 Ohio Law Rep. 9. Declaratory Judgment ⇔ 316; Wills ⇔ 702

Under RS 5963, an error in judgment of the circuit court in reversing construction placed upon a will by the common pleas court at the suit of a widow may be prosecuted to the supreme court. Davis v. Coffman (Ohio 1897) 55 Ohio St. 556, 37 W.L.B. 53, 45 N.E. 707.

If all parties in interest are before court and all concur in asking court for construction of will, court can do so, but if court sees fit not to, it would not be error to refuse to make finding and construction of will in proceeding to set aside will. Heron v. Spitzer-Rorick Trust & Savings Bank (Lucas 1934) 18 Ohio Law Abs. 289.

2106.04 Failure to make election; presumption

If the surviving spouse dies before probate of the will, or, having survived the probate, thereafter either fails to make the election provided by section 2106.01 of the Revised Code or dies without having made an election within the times described in division (E) of that section, the surviving spouse shall be conclusively presumed to have elected to take under the will, and the surviving spouse and the heirs, devisees, and legatees of the surviving spouse, and those claiming through or under them, shall be bound by the conclusive presumption, and persons may deal with the property of the decedent accordingly; provided that, if applicable, the provisions of sections 2105.31 to 2105.39 of the Revised Code shall prevail over the provisions relating to the right of election of a surviving spouse.

(2002 H 242, eff. 5–16–02; 1990 H 346, eff. 5–31–90)

Uncodified Law

1990 H 346, § 3, eff. 5–31–90, reads, in part: (A) Sections 1 and 2 of this act shall apply only to the estates of decedents who die on or after the effective date of this act.

Historical and Statutory Notes

Ed. Note: 2106.04 is former 2107.41, amended and recodified by 1990 H 346, eff. 5–31–90; 125 v 411; 1953 H 1; GC 10504–60.

Amendment Note: 2002 H 242 substituted "sections 2105.31 to 2105.39" for "section 2105.21".

Baldwin's Ohio Legislative Service, 1990 Laws of Ohio, H 346—LSC Analysis, p 5–87

Library References

Descent and Distribution ⇔ 64.1.
Wills ⇔ 785(2).
Westlaw Topic Nos. 124, 409.
C.J.S. Wills §§ 1841, 1845, 1847, 1849 to 1851.

Research References

Encyclopedias

OH Jur. 3d Decedents' Estates § 750, Effect of Failure to Make Election or Seek Extension.

OH Jur. 3d Decedents' Estates § 751, Effect of Failure to Make Election or Seek Extension—Death Before Expiration of Time for Election.

Forms

Ohio Forms Legal and Business § 24:971, Spouse's Election to Take Under Will.

Treatises and Practice Aids

Carlin, Baldwin's Ohio Practice, Merrick-Rippner Probate Law § 2:39, Elective Rights of Surviving Spouse—Election to Take Under Law or Under the Will—Failure to Make Election Against the Will.

Carlin, Baldwin's Ohio Practice, Merrick-Rippner Probate Law § 2:121, Administration of Decedent's Estate—Checklist.

Carlin, Baldwin's Ohio Practice, Merrick-Rippner Probate Law § 21:11, Rights of Surviving Spouse to Make Election—Statutory Provisions—Personal Nature of Right of Election.

Carlin, Baldwin's Ohio Practice, Merrick-Rippner Probate Law § 21:15, Rights of Surviving Spouse to Make Election—Proceedings for Advice or Declaratory Judgment.

Carlin, Baldwin's Ohio Practice, Merrick-Rippner Probate Law § 21:30, Rights of Surviving Spouse to Make Election—Right to Use of Mansion House and Family Allowance.

Carlin, Baldwin's Ohio Practice, Merrick-Rippner Probate Law § 21:34, Rights of Surviving Spouse to Make Election—Constitutionality of "In Person" Requirement.

Carlin, Baldwin's Ohio Practice, Merrick-Rippner Probate Law § 21:39, Rights of Surviving Spouse to Make Election—Failure to Make Election—Scope of RC 2106.04.

Carlin, Baldwin's Ohio Practice, Merrick-Rippner Probate Law § 21:41, Rights of Surviving Spouse to Make Election—Failure to Make Election—Conclusive Presumption.

Carlin, Baldwin's Ohio Practice, Merrick-Rippner Probate Law § 21:58, Rights of Surviving Spouse—Mansion House—Right to Remain in House for One Year.

Law Review and Journal Commentaries

Ohio Enacts the Uniform Simultaneous Death Act. Richard E. Davis, 12 Prob L J Ohio 54 (March/April 2002).

Notes of Decisions

Ed. Note: This section contains annotations from former RC 2107.41.

Constitutional issues 1

Court election for estate 2
Descent and distribution statute 5
Incompetence 3
Possession and sale of property 6
Time for election 7
Will 4

---

1. Constitutional issues

This section is not violative of due process, where the surviving spouse fails to elect by reason of continued insanity and his guardian fails to make application for a commission to elect, within the time provided by GC 10504–55 (RC 2107.39). In re Iwinski's Estate (Cuyahoga 1947) 83 Ohio App. 463, 77 N.E.2d 375, 49 Ohio Law Abs. 609, 38 O.O. 491.

This section does not deny due process of law and is constitutional. In re Knofler's Estate (Ohio 1944) 143 Ohio St. 294, 55 N.E.2d 262, 28 O.O. 203.

This section does not violate constitutional provision prohibiting retroactive laws. Davis v. Warner (Morrow 1933) 47 Ohio App. 495, 192 N.E. 270, 18 Ohio Law Abs. 26, 40 Ohio Law Rep. 384, error dismissed 127 Ohio St. 597, 190 N.E. 386, 39 Ohio Law Rep. 655.

2. Court election for estate

Death is not a "legal disability" within the meaning of RC 2107.45, which would require the probate court to make an election for the estate of a surviving spouse who dies having failed to elect against the will. In re LaSpina's Estate (Ohio 1979) 60 Ohio St.2d 101, 397 N.E.2d 1196, 14 O.O.3d 336. Wills ⊕ 785(2)

The right of a surviving spouse to elect against the will, granted pursuant to RC 2107.39, is personal to such surviving spouse and does not survive his or her death, and that right may not be exercised in favor of the surviving spouse's estate. In re LaSpina's Estate (Ohio 1979) 60 Ohio St.2d 101, 397 N.E.2d 1196, 14 O.O.3d 336. Wills ⊕ 785(2)

This section not applicable if the surviving spouse referred to therein dies before the probate of the will of his spouse, and, in such case, the probate court is authorized to make the election for the estate of the deceased surviving spouse that will be most advantageous to that estate. Raleigh v. Raleigh (Ohio 1950) 153 Ohio St. 160, 91 N.E.2d 241, 41 O.O. 209.

3. Incompetence

When surviving spouse dies before expiration of time for making election, she shall be conclusively presumed to have elected to take under will notwithstanding that during period between testator's death and her death she was continuously insane and incapable of making an election. In re Knofler's Estate (Ohio 1944) 143 Ohio St. 294, 55 N.E.2d 262, 28 O.O. 203. Wills ⊕ 786

The provisions of former GC 10571 (RC 2107.41) that if spouse fails to make an election within the time specified, it shall be deemed that she or he has elected to take under the will have no application where the widow was mentally incompetent at time of testator's death, and continued so until her death two months later, during which period no action was taken by the probate court pursuant to the provisions of former GC 10574 and 10575 (RC 2107.45). Ambrose v. Rugg (Ohio 1931) 123 Ohio St. 433, 175 N.E. 691, 74 A.L.R. 449, 9 Ohio Law Abs. 477, 34 Ohio Law Rep. 226.

This section, as to presumption of election to take under the will in event of failure to make election, applies solely to a competent surviving spouse. In re Jones Estate (Ohio Com.Pl. 1939) 1 Ohio Supp. 32, 29 Ohio Law Abs. 148, 15 O.O. 250.

Court must make an election for an incompetent spouse even after her death since her rights are still protected by GC 10504–63 (RC 2107.45), and since this section is inapplicable when spouse is an incompetent and time for election has not elapsed. In re Jones Estate (Ohio Com.Pl. 1939) 1 Ohio Supp. 32, 29 Ohio Law Abs. 148, 15 O.O. 250.

4. Will

Where the provisions in the will include dower, if the widow actually accepts the provisions made for her and then dies without making the statutory election in court and without being cited to appear in court for that purpose, but within the time allowed for such citation, she will be held to have taken under the will, and her representative will be entitled to no part of the personal estate except that given to her in the will. Baxter v. Bowyer (Ohio 1869) 19 Ohio St. 490. Wills ⊕ 793

The surviving spouse is entitled to her year's allowance, use of the mansion house and exemptions under RC 2117.20 and RC 2115.13 even though she takes under the will, whether by her voluntary election or by operation of law. Jacobsen v. Cleveland Trust Co. (Ohio Com.Pl. 1965) 6 Ohio Misc. 173, 217 N.E.2d 262, 35 O.O.2d 366. Wills ⊕ 800

A void election, as contrasted with a voidable one, is void ab initio, and if no valid election is made thereafter within the time allowed and nothing has occurred or failed to occur which would operate to extend such period, the surviving spouse shall be conclusively presumed to have elected to take under the will of the decedent. In re Wolfel's Estate (Marion 1965) 3 Ohio App.2d 11, 209 N.E.2d 594, 32 O.O.2d 75.

Where a widow selected as property exempt from administration property which was specifically bequeathed to her, and then by inaction and operation of law elected to take under the will, she was entitled to have vacated the election to take such property as part of the statutory exemption. In re Fetzer's Estate (Medina 1954) 130 N.E.2d 732, 71 Ohio Law Abs. 275.

The statute creates a presumption that the testamentary gift is in lieu of dower unless the will plainly shows a contrary intention. Schuette v. Bowers (C.C.A.2 (N.Y.) 1930) 40 F.2d 208.

Testator provides in his will that the interest given to widow "shall be in lieu of her statutory allowances, as provided by law"; widow fails to make election within time, and is conclusively presumed to have taken under the will; she will be barred of her right to the year's allowance, but not of her right to the setoff, the statute on election not having given testator power to bar the right of the surviving spouse to setoff by expressly making provisions in lieu thereof in the will. In re Felman's Estate (Ohio Prob. 1933) 32 Ohio NP(NS) 73.

5. Descent and distribution statute

When a surviving spouse dies within the time limit for election, without having made any election, the conclusive presumption of this section is equivalent to election to take under statute of descent and distribution, and GC 10504–55 (RC 2107.39), applies to ascertain the limit of the share of the estate to which the surviving spouse may be entitled. Miller v. Miller (Ohio 1935) 129 Ohio St. 230, 194 N.E. 450, 2 O.O. 45.

The phrase "under the statute of descent and distribution," as used in GC 10504–55 (RC 2107.39) and 10504–60 (RC 2107.41), does not mean that the surviving spouse is actually placed within the operation of the statute of descent and distribution, but such phrase is used as merely definitive or descriptive of the share to be taken by the surviving spouse within a limitation of not to exceed one-half of the estate. Miller v. Miller (Ohio 1935) 129 Ohio St. 230, 194 N.E. 450, 2 O.O. 45.

Where widow died before filing of schedule of debts without having made election to take under deceased husband's will, she was conclusively presumed to have elected to take under statute of descent and distribution. Davis v. Warner (Morrow 1933) 47 Ohio App. 495, 192 N.E. 270, 18 Ohio Law Abs. 26, 40 Ohio Law Rep. 384, error dismissed 127 Ohio St. 597, 190 N.E. 386, 39 Ohio Law Rep. 655. Wills ⊕ 790

Word "election" in this section has the same meaning as in GC 10504–55 (RC 2107.39); effect of the presumed election is to pass to the widow not to exceed one-half of the estate rather than the entire estate as upon intestate descent under GC 10503–4 (RC 2105.06). Miller v. United Brethren Church (Ohio Com.Pl. 1933) 31 Ohio N.P.N.S. 43.

6. Possession and sale of property

Where it does not appear that a widow has acted with full knowledge of the condition of her husband's estate and of her rights under the will and the law, her acts in paying her husband out of his money and having possession and control of the real and personal estate for five months after her husband's death do not constitute such an election to take under the will as estops her from claiming under the law within the time allowed. Millikin v. Welliver (Ohio 1882) 37 Ohio St. 460. Estoppel ⊕ 92(1); Wills ⊕ 792(3)

A widow who takes possession of real estate devised to her by her late husband for her life or while she remains unmarried, and occupies the land with the knowledge of the heirs at law for a series of years after the time in which she is required to make her election, in the absence of a contrary showing, will be presumed to have made her election in fact. Nimmons v. Westfall (Ohio 1877) 33 Ohio St. 213.

Where the widow, with the full knowledge and acquiescence of the heirs and devisees of the testator, sets up no claim for dower but actually takes

2106.04 Note 6

possession and has the use and occupancy of the property devised to her under the will for a series of years after the probate of the will, the heirs or devisees are estopped to deny the election of the widow to take under the will. Stockton v. Wooley (Ohio 1870) 20 Ohio St. 184. Dower And Curtesy ⚖ 50; Wills ⚖ 794

Where a widow, without following the forms prescribed by law for making her election to take under the will, sets up no claim for dower, but actually and in fact takes under the will, and for a series of years has the use and occupancy of the property devised, she is barred of her dower and estopped to deny her election to take under the will. Thompson's Lessee v. Hoop (Ohio 1856) 6 Ohio St. 480. Dower And Curtesy ⚖ 50; Wills ⚖ 794

Where a widow fails to make a proper election under her late husband's will and there is no proof or record that she ever received any consideration by order of the court or otherwise in lieu of her dower, her sale of her husband's real estate to satisfy his debts is not a release of her vested right of dower in such real estate, and her creditor is entitled to have it subjected to the payment of his judgment. Hessenmueller v Mulrooney, 6 D 123, 4 NP 50 (CP 1896).

A widow who did not formally elect to take under the will may be considered to have made the election where she did nothing to indicate an intention to claim as heir at law, remained in possession of the whole estate, and carried out the husband's wishes by paying debts and legacies. Alexander v. Mendenhall (Ohio Com.Pl. 1894) 1 Ohio Dec. 655, 32 W.L.B. 173.

7. Time for election

Will bequest of $1 in lieu of statutory support precluded testator's surviving spouse from support after time for spouse to elect against the will had expired; spouse was conclusively presumed to have elected to take under will. In re Estate of Reddick (Ohio App. 3 Dist., 04-11-1995) 102 Ohio App.3d 488, 657 N.E.2d 531. Executors And Administrators ⚖ 186

Spouse who fails to timely make election either under will or against will is conclusively presumed to have elected to take under will. In re Estate of Reddick (Ohio App. 3 Dist., 04-11-1995) 102 Ohio App.3d 488, 657 N.E.2d 531. Wills ⚖ 790

The period of time prescribed by RC 2107.39, within which a surviving spouse may make an election to take under the will of a decedent or under the statute of descent and distribution, is not extended by the filing after the termination of such period of an action alleging that an election made during the period is void and praying that it be held void, so that the making and filing of a purported election after the expiration of the period is a nullity and the same should be stricken from the files. In re Wolfel's Estate (Marion 1965) 3 Ohio App.2d 11, 209 N.E.2d 594, 32 O.O.2d 75.

Where a surviving widow not mentioned in the will of her deceased husband elected to take under the statute of descent and distribution twenty-five days after the inventory and appraisement was filed, which was more than nine months after the probate of the will and the appointment of the executor, and no extension of time had been granted for filing such inventory beyond the statutory period, nor for making the election, but no citation to make an election had been served on the widow, and no explanation had been given to her by the probate court as to her rights under the law and under the will, and the inventory and appraisement was given final approval on the day when the election was filed, and at the time the election was so filed there had been no administration of the estate and the rights of third persons had not intervened, it was error prejudicial to the surviving widow for the probate court to strike the written election from the files. In re Bersin's Estate (Medina 1955) 98 Ohio App. 432, 129 N.E.2d 868, 57 O.O. 475.

A surviving spouse may not elect after time has expired, and, after such time, spouse shall be conclusively presumed to have elected to take under the will. In re Iwinski's Estate (Cuyahoga 1947) 83 Ohio App. 463, 77 N.E.2d 375, 49 Ohio Law Abs. 609, 38 O.O. 491.

Under present section, where death occurs at any time before time limit of election, spouse is conclusively presumed to take under the will. Price v. Herbert (Delaware 1937) 33 N.E.2d 398, 26 Ohio Law Abs. 330, 11 O.O. 138.

Where a husband dies testate, without issue but leaving a widow, and the widow dies within five days thereafter without having made an election, it is conclusively presumed, under this section, that the widow elected to take under the law. Miller v. United Brethren Church (Ohio Com.Pl. 1933) 31 Ohio N.P.N.S. 43.

2106.05 Election to take under the will; effect

If a surviving spouse elects to take under the will, the surviving spouse shall be barred of all right to an intestate share of the property passing under the will and shall take under the will alone, unless it plainly appears from the will that the provision for the surviving spouse was intended to be in addition to an intestate share. An election to take under the will does not bar the right of the surviving spouse to an intestate share of that portion of the estate as to which the decedent dies intestate. Unless the will expressly otherwise directs, an election to take under the will does not bar the right of the surviving spouse to remain in the mansion house, and does not bar the right of the surviving spouse to receive the allowance for the support provided by section 2106.13 of the Revised Code.

(1990 H 346, eff. 5–31–90)

Uncodified Law

1990 H 346, § 3, eff. 5–31–90, reads, in part: (A) Sections 1 and 2 of this act shall apply only to the estates of decedents who die on or after the effective date of this act.

Historical and Statutory Notes

Ed. Note: 2106.05 is former 2107.42, amended and recodified by 1990 H 346, eff. 5–31–90; 1975 S 145; 1953 H 1; GC 10504–61.

Cross References

Intestate share, 2105.06

Library References

Wills ⚖800.
Westlaw Topic No. 409.
C.J.S. Wills §§ 1841, 1866 to 1868.
Baldwin's Ohio Legislative Service, 1990 Laws of Ohio, H 346—LSC Analysis, p 5–87

Research References

Encyclopedias

OH Jur. 3d Decedents' Estates § 57, Renounced Legacies or Devises.
OH Jur. 3d Decedents' Estates § 765, Right to Share in Intestate Property.
OH Jur. 3d Decedents' Estates § 766, Right to Allowance for Support.
OH Jur. 3d Decedents' Estates § 767, Right to Dower; Right to Remain in Mansion House.
OH Jur. 3d Decedents' Estates § 1675, Right to Remain in Mansion House.
OH Jur. 3d Decedents' Estates § 1685, Right to Allowance.

Forms

Ohio Forms Legal and Business § 24:143, Drafting Will.
Ohio Forms Legal and Business § 24:637, Bequests—in Lieu of Statutory Family Maintenance Allowance.
Ohio Forms Legal and Business § 24:891, Bequest in Lieu of Dower.
Ohio Forms Legal and Business § 24:956, Settlement Among Testator's Legatees and Heirs—Family Home to be Set Aside for Surviving Spouse.
Ohio Forms Legal and Business § 24:971, Spouse's Election to Take Under Will.

Treatises and Practice Aids

Carlin, Baldwin's Ohio Practice, Merrick-Rippner Probate Law § 2:40, Elective Rights of Surviving Spouse—Election to Take Under Law or Under the Will—Election of Surviving Spouse to Take Under the Will.
Carlin, Baldwin's Ohio Practice, Merrick-Rippner Probate Law § 20:1, Advancement—Definition.
Carlin, Baldwin's Ohio Practice, Merrick-Rippner Probate Law § 21:29, Rights of Surviving Spouse to Make Election—Property Not Passing Under the Will.

Carlin, Baldwin's Ohio Practice, Merrick-Rippner Probate Law § 21:30, Rights of Surviving Spouse to Make Election—Right to Use of Mansion House and Family Allowance.

Carlin, Baldwin's Ohio Practice, Merrick-Rippner Probate Law § 21:90, Election of Surviving Spouse to Take Under Will—Form.

Carlin, Baldwin's Ohio Practice, Merrick-Rippner Probate Law § 30:23, Drafting a Will—Surviving Spouse—Bequest in Lieu of Statutory Rights.

Carlin, Baldwin's Ohio Practice, Merrick-Rippner Probate Law App B SPF 8.1, Election of Surviving Spouse to Take Under Will.

Carlin, Baldwin's Ohio Practice, Merrick-Rippner Probate Law App B SPF 8.3, Summary of General Rights of Surviving Spouses.

Law Review and Journal Commentaries

Error in Omitting "or Die" After a Testamentary Gift of Income to Widow, Anthony A. Morano. 17 Clev–Marshall L Rev 567 (September 1968).

Rights of the Surviving Spouse, Patricia D. Consolo and Jeffrey P. Consolo. 56 Clev B J 52 (December 1984).

Notes of Decisions

Ed. Note: This section contains annotations from former RC 2107.42.

Allowance and mansion house 3
Debts 8
Disclaimer of gifts 7
Dower rights 6
Estate and inheritance tax 1
Intent that will provisions be in addition to dower 4
Intestate share 2
Procedure 5

---

1. Estate and inheritance tax

Where a widow elects to take under the statute of descent and distribution which provides that "personal property shall be distributed" and any "real estate or inheritance shall descend and pass in parcenary" in part to the surviving spouse, the amount of the federal estate tax on the decedent's estate should be deducted therefrom before computing the widow's share thereof. Campbell v. Lloyd (Ohio 1954) 162 Ohio St. 203, 122 N.E.2d 695, 55 O.O. 102, certiorari denied 75 S.Ct. 600, 349 U.S. 911, 99 L.Ed. 1246, rehearing denied 75 S.Ct. 870, 349 U.S. 948, 99 L.Ed. 1274.

Where a widow elects to take under the will, a proportionate amount of the federal estate tax must be deducted from the residue before she reserves her specified one half thereof, and the residue must also bear the burden of the tax on a specific legacy to her. (Distinguished in Miller v Hammond, 156 OS 475, 104 NE(2d) 9 (1952); overruled by Campbell v Lloyd, 162 OS 203, 122 NE(2d) 695 (1954).) Foerster v. Foerster (Ohio Prob. 1954) 122 N.E.2d 314, 71 Ohio Law Abs. 129, 54 O.O. 441.

In the event of testate successions, where a case for an election arises and the widow elects to take under the will, no deduction is to be made for inheritance tax purposes from the value of the estate which she takes under the will on account of the dower interest of which she has thus barred herself. 1920 OAG p 834.

2. Intestate share

An election on her part to take under the will does not bar a widow of her right to the distributive share of personal estate not disposed of in the will. Bane v. Wick (Ohio 1863) 14 Ohio St. 505.

When a widow elects to take under a will which divides the real and personal estate of the testator between her and two children, giving to the widow and her heirs one-third of the real estate and more than one-third of the personalty, she is not entitled to a distributive share of the personal property, under the statute, for the reason that the personal property is not intestate, although a subsequent clause of the will recites that the devises and bequests to his wife were not intended to be in lieu of her dower, either in his real or personal estate. Parker v. Parker's Adm'r (Ohio 1861) 13 Ohio St. 95.

Where surviving spouse elected to take under her husband's will in 1940, she and her heirs are barred from sharing in decedent's intestate property. Johnson v First Natl Bank of Dayton, No. 92-CA-40, 1993 WL 102054 (2d Dist Ct App, Miami, 3-29-93).

This section applies to all intestate personalty and realty in testator's estate. Jones v. Webster (Ohio 1938) 133 Ohio St. 492, 14 N.E.2d 928, 11 O.O. 184.

A widow's rights when she is not mentioned in husband's will are the same as if he had died intestate. Doyle v. Doyle (Ohio 1893) 50 Ohio St. 330, 29 W.L.B. 371, 34 N.E. 166.

After election to take under the will of her husband, a widow cannot claim dower in his real estate not disposed of in the will. Swihart v. Swihart (Ohio Cir. 1893) 4 Ohio C.D. 624.

Election of a widow to take under a will does not preclude her from inheriting lands as to which her husband died intestate and to which no reference was made in the will. Bowers v. McGill (Ohio Com.Pl. 1911) 22 Ohio Dec. 407, 12 Ohio NP(NS) 124. Wills ⇐ 800

A widow whose husband dies intestate without children gets a much larger portion of his estate than she would get if she took against a will and under the law; she is therefore interested in having her husband's will set aside, and may maintain such an action. Moyses v. Neilson (Ohio Com.Pl. 1900) 9 Ohio Dec. 623, 7 Ohio N.P. 607.

Where a testator leaves his wife the interest for life from a sum invested in bonds but does not dispose of the principal, and where the will designates no residuary legatee, the testator died intestate as to this principal sum and it passes under the statute of descent and distribution. Hollister v. Howe (Ohio Com.Pl. 1897) 6 Ohio Dec. 157, 4 Ohio N.P. 168.

3. Allowance and mansion house

An election to take under a will which provides in lieu of dower does not bar a widow's year's support provided by law. Collier v. Collier's Ex'rs (Ohio 1854) 3 Ohio St. 369.

Surviving spouse who did not elect against decedent's will, and who sought to establish her entitlement to purchase marital residence with offset for her statutory support allowance, failed to establish that will did not expressly bar her from receiving support allowance, where spouse did not provide copy of decedent's will to trial court. Frinkley v. Meeker (Ohio App. 11 Dist., Portage, 12-10-2004) No. 2004-P-0022, 2004-Ohio-6696, 2004 WL 2860402, Unreported, appeal not allowed 105 Ohio St.3d 1518, 826 N.E.2d 315, 2005-Ohio-1880. Executors And Administrators ⇐ 186

Trial court in surviving spouse's declaratory judgment action seeking to establish her right to purchase marital residence with offset for her statutory support allowance could not take judicial notice of probate court proceedings involving probate of decedent's will; consideration of material outside the record prevented Court of Appeals from reviewing whether trial court properly interpreted the material. Frinkley v. Meeker (Ohio App. 11 Dist., Portage, 12-10-2004) No. 2004-P-0022, 2004-Ohio-6696, 2004 WL 2860402, Unreported, appeal not allowed 105 Ohio St.3d 1518, 826 N.E.2d 315, 2005-Ohio-1880. Evidence ⇐ 43(4)

The surviving spouse is entitled to her year's allowance, use of the mansion house and exemptions under RC 2117.20 and RC 2115.13 even though she takes under the will, whether by her voluntary election or by operation of law. Jacobsen v. Cleveland Trust Co. (Ohio Com.Pl. 1965) 6 Ohio Misc. 173, 217 N.E.2d 262, 35 O.O.2d 366. Wills ⇐ 800

Under this section as enacted in 114 v 357, a testator may, by express direction in his will, bar the right of his widow to receive one year's allowance for the support of herself and children if she elects to take under the will. Bolles v. Toledo Trust Co. (Ohio 1944) 144 Ohio St. 195, 58 N.E.2d 381, 157 A.L.R. 1164, 29 O.O. 376. Executors And Administrators ⇐ 186

Where by the language of a will it is plainly shown to be the intention of the testator to bar his widow of a first year's support and a provision is made for her in lieu thereof, if she elects to take under such a will she is not entitled to a year's support. In re Witner's Estate (Ohio Prob. 1900) 10 Ohio Dec. 30, 7 Ohio N.P. 143. Wills ⇐ 800

It is the duty of an administrator to make an inventory and of the appraisers to set apart the widow's year's allowance; the widow who accepts the terms of her husband's will is not required to demand such allowance, and where no appraisement has been made, the lapse of time will not be considered a waiver or relinquishment of such right to an allowance. In re Rierdon's Estate (Ohio Prob. 1898) 5 Ohio Dec. 606, 5 Ohio N.P. 516.

4. Intent that will provisions be in addition to dower

At common law, a provision in a testator's will made for his widow was regarded as having been given in addition to dower, but the laws of Ohio

2106.05
Note 4

reversed this rule so that a widow shall not be entitled to both, unless it plainly appears by the will that the testator intended her to have both; since the construction of wills must be governed by the law of the place where the property is situated, a testator's Ohio property must come under the latter rule, not the former, which is the law of his domicile. Jennings v. Jennings (Ohio 1871) 21 Ohio St. 56.

Where there is a devise to a wife of all of the testator's estate for life, provided she so long remain his widow with remainder to his children, upon her election to take under the will she is barred of dower and loses all her estate upon marrying again. Luigart v. Ripley (Ohio 1869) 19 Ohio St. 24.

Under this section, if surviving spouse elects to take under will, such spouse shall be barred of all rights to intestate share of estate, unless it plainly appears from will that provision therein for spouse was intended to be in addition to intestate share. Jones v. Webster (Ohio 1938) 133 Ohio St. 492, 14 N.E.2d 928, 11 O.O. 184. Wills ⟐ 800

Where a widow elects to take under her husband's will, she will be barred of dower in land of which he was seized as an estate of inheritance during coverture and which was sold and conveyed on foreclosure of a mortgage executed by him in which she did not join, unless the will plainly states that she is to have such provision in addition to her dower. Corry v. Lamb (Ohio 1887) 45 Ohio St. 203, 18 W.L.B. 22, 12 N.E. 660.

Where a widow elects to take under the will of her deceased husband, she is not barred of dower in lands undevised by will unless the will expressly provides that the provision made therein for the widow shall be in lieu of dower in all the lands of which her husband died seized, including those undevised as well as lands devised. In re McDonald's Estate (Ohio Prob. 1895) 4 Ohio Dec. 396, 2 Ohio N.P. 232.

5. Procedure

The election of the widow to take under the will does not estop her from setting up her right as heir to the estate, from contesting the validity of the will, nor from controverting the validity of devises therein made. Carder v. Board of Com'rs of Fayette County (Ohio 1865) 16 Ohio St. 354. Estoppel ⟐ 92(1); Wills ⟐ 782(10)

An election, formally made and entered upon the journal at the instance of the widow, cannot afterward, even within a year from the service of a citation, be set aside at her pleasure. Davis v. Davis (Ohio 1860) 11 Ohio St. 386.

An election to take under the will, when made and recorded, can be vacated only on petition to common pleas court or another court having general equity jurisdiction. Davis v. Davis (Ohio 1860) 11 Ohio St. 386. Wills ⟐ 797

A will, by which testator devises and bequeathes the residue of his estate to his wife and son to share according to law, gives to the wife and son the same interests which they would have received had the testator died intestate; she, having elected to take under the will as authorized by former GC 10572 (RC 2107.42), as in force at the time of testator's death, providing that the widow has the election of taking under the will or enforcing her dower rights, is a devisee, and is entitled to a partition of the real estate. Bunnell v. Bunnell (Warren 1936) 53 Ohio App. 235, 4 N.E.2d 698, 22 Ohio Law Abs. 113, 6 O.O. 488.

Under Ohio law, the only effect of the formal election of a decedent to take under the will is to bar his right of curtesy; it is still open to him to accept or reject the gift, and where separate gifts are made, acceptance of one part does not preclude renunciation of another part of the legacy. Brown v. Routzahn (C.C.A.6 (Ohio) 1933) 63 F.2d 914, certiorari denied 54 S.Ct. 60, 290 U.S. 641, 78 L.Ed. 557.

A specific legacy or a general legacy carries with it the profits or income arising after testator's death in the absence of other disposition; consequently, acceptance of this income was acceptance of a part of the legacy, and thereafter there could be no renunciation. This prima-facie rule can only be rebutted if the will manifests a sufficient intention of the testator to the contrary. Brown v. Routzahn (N.D.Ohio 1931) 58 F.2d 329, reversed 63 F.2d 914, certiorari denied 54 S.Ct. 60, 290 U.S. 641, 78 L.Ed. 557.

Assuming that a mere declaration of renunciation of the legatee is sufficient, the rule still requires that the act or declaration relied on be unequivocal and consistent with his other conduct. Brown v. Routzahn (N.D.Ohio 1931) 58 F.2d 329, reversed 63 F.2d 914, certiorari denied 54 S.Ct. 60, 290 U.S. 641, 78 L.Ed. 557.

The fact that the executors had averred that the beneficiary had renounced certain portions of a will and that the court, under former GC 10839 (RC 2113.53), approved the proceeding, did not judicially establish the renunciation. Brown v. Routzahn (N.D.Ohio 1931) 58 F.2d 329, reversed 63 F.2d 914, certiorari denied 54 S.Ct. 60, 290 U.S. 641, 78 L.Ed. 557.

6. Dower rights

Where dower is barred by a legal jointure, an election is not necessary to entitle a widow to take the provisions made for her in her husband's will. Bowen v. Bowen (Ohio 1877) 34 Ohio St. 164. Wills ⟐ 782(1)

Election to take under will waives dower or rights under law. Barrett v. W. P. Southworth Co. (Ohio App. 1930) 35 Ohio App. 452, 172 N.E. 563, 33 Ohio Law Rep. 24.

By electing to take under the will, a widow takes the estate there created; it being a life estate she may alien it at once, which is not true of her dower right. Dukes v. Dukes (Ohio Cir. 1890) 2 Ohio C.D. 676.

Where a widow received all her husband's estate through his will and there was no admeasurement of dower, but the widow, taking all the real property, had sold some of it, she thereby elected to take under the will and waived her dower rights. Schuette v. Bowers (S.D.N.Y. 1929) 32 F.2d 817, affirmed 40 F.2d 408.

7. Disclaimer of gifts

Will bequest of $1 in lieu of statutory support precluded testator's surviving spouse from support after time for spouse to elect against the will had expired; spouse was conclusively presumed to have elected to take under will. In re Estate of Reddick (Ohio App. 3 Dist., 04-11-1995) 102 Ohio App.3d 488, 657 N.E.2d 531. Executors And Administrators ⟐ 186

Even though a surviving spouse elected to take under the will he still had a right to say what of its separate gifts he would accept and what he would decline; he is at liberty to refuse or disclaim them and his disclaimer may be express or implied. An election, like disclaimer, may be inferred from the conduct of the party and if onerous and beneficial property are included in the same gift as an aggregate, unless a contrary intention appears by the will, the donee cannot disclaim the onerous property and accept that which is beneficial but he must take the whole gift or nothing. If two distinct gifts are made by the same will, one of them being onerous and the other beneficial, the donee may reject the former and take the latter. Brown v. Routzahn (N.D.Ohio 1931) 58 F.2d 329, reversed 63 F.2d 914, certiorari denied 54 S.Ct. 60, 290 U.S. 641, 78 L.Ed. 557.

8. Debts

A widow who elects to take under the will does not become personally liable for the debts of her deceased husband beyond the assets which came to her hands applicable, in her discretion, to their payment. Watts v. Watts (Ohio 1882) 38 Ohio St. 480, 8 W.L.B. 287.

2106.06 Election to take under statute to be made in person

The election of a surviving spouse to take under section 2105.06 of the Revised Code and thereby refusing to take under the will shall be made in person before the probate judge, or a deputy clerk who has been appointed to act as a referee, except as provided in sections 2106.07 and 2106.08 of the Revised Code.

When the election is made in person before the judge or referee, the judge or referee shall explain the will, the rights under the will, and the rights, by law, in the event of a refusal to take under the will.

(1990 H 346, eff. 5-31-90)

Uncodified Law

1990 H 346, § 3, eff. 5-31-90, reads, in part: (A) Sections 1 and 2 of this act shall apply only to the estates of decedents who die on or after the effective date of this act.

Historical and Statutory Notes

Ed. Note: 2106.06 is former 2107.43, amended and recodified by 1990 H 346, eff. 5-31-90; 1976 S 466; 1975 S 145; 125 v 411; 1953 H 1; GC 10504-56, 10504-59.

Legislative Service Commission

1975:

This section currently provides that the election of the surviving spouse must be made in person before the probate court. It would be amended to provide that only if the spouse elects to take against the provisions of the will, must the election be made in person. (Commentary from former RC 2107.43.)

Baldwin's Ohio Legislative Service, 1990 Laws of Ohio, H 346—LSC Analysis, p 5–87

Library References

Wills ⚖︎801(1).
Westlaw Topic No. 409.
C.J.S. Wills §§ 1841, 1866 to 1868.

Research References

Encyclopedias

OH Jur. 3d Decedents' Estates § 125, Acts that Will Bar Succession, Generally—Surviving Spouse's Rights.

OH Jur. 3d Decedents' Estates § 752, How Election Made.

OH Jur. 3d Decedents' Estates § 753, Surviving Spouse's Right to Explanation of Election Rights.

Treatises and Practice Aids

Carlin, Baldwin's Ohio Practice, Merrick-Rippner Probate Law § 2:37, Elective Rights of Surviving Spouse—Election to Take Under Law or Under the Will—Procedure for Making Election.

Carlin, Baldwin's Ohio Practice, Merrick-Rippner Probate Law § 21:5, Rights of Surviving Spouse to Make Election—Statutory Provisions—Effect.

Carlin, Baldwin's Ohio Practice, Merrick-Rippner Probate Law § 2:121, Administration of Decedent's Estate—Checklist.

Carlin, Baldwin's Ohio Practice, Merrick-Rippner Probate Law § 21:32, Rights of Surviving Spouse to Make Election—Election to be Made in Person—Scope of RC 2106.06.

Carlin, Baldwin's Ohio Practice, Merrick-Rippner Probate Law § 21:34, Rights of Surviving Spouse to Make Election—Constitutionality of "In Person" Requirement.

Carlin, Baldwin's Ohio Practice, Merrick-Rippner Probate Law § 21:36, Rights of Surviving Spouse to Make Election—One Under Legal Disability—Discretion of Probate Court in Making Election.

Carlin, Baldwin's Ohio Practice, Merrick-Rippner Probate Law § 21:91, Election of Surviving Spouse to Take Against Will—Form.

Carlin, Baldwin's Ohio Practice, Merrick-Rippner Probate Law § 30:24, Drafting a Will—Surviving Spouse—Election to Take Against the Will.

Carlin, Baldwin's Ohio Practice, Merrick-Rippner Probate Law App B SPF 8.2, Election of Surviving Spouse to Take Against Will.

Notes of Decisions

Ed. Note: This section contains annotations from former RC 2107.43.

Court election   2
Explanation by court   3
Method of election   5
Personal appearance   4
Time for election   1

1. Time for election

Where, in a will, a testator gives to his wife one-half of his net estate, with provision that she "shall" make selection of such property as she desires within one month from a fixed date, the word, "shall," will be construed as directory and not mandatory; the time limit placed on her selection is not a condition precedent to her right to take under the will; and an inconsequential delay beyond the period of one month does not bar her from her full rights under the will. Poe v. Sheehan (Cuyahoga 1958) 106 Ohio App. 413, 151 N.E.2d 660, 79 Ohio Law Abs. 175, 7 O.O.2d 166.

Where a surviving widow not mentioned in the will of her deceased husband elected to take under the statute of descent and distribution twenty-five days after the inventory and appraisement was filed, which was more than nine months after the probate of the will and the appointment of the executor, and no extension of time had been granted for filing such inventory beyond the statutory period, nor for making the election, but no citation to make an election had been served on the widow, and no explanation had been given to her by the probate court as to her rights under the law and under the will, and the inventory and appraisement was given final approval on the day when the election was filed, and at the time the election was so filed there had been no administration of the estate and the rights of third persons had not intervened, it was error prejudicial to the surviving widow for the probate court to strike the written election from the files. In re Bersin's Estate (Medina 1955) 98 Ohio App. 432, 129 N.E.2d 868, 57 O.O. 475.

RS 5964 applies only to domestic wills so far as it relates to the time and manner of making an election. Waterfield v. Rice (C.C.A.6 (Ohio) 1901) 111 F. 625, 49 C.C.A. 504.

2. Court election

Death is not a "legal disability" within the meaning of RC 2107.45, which would require the probate court to make an election for the estate of a surviving spouse who dies having failed to elect against the will. In re LaSpina's Estate (Ohio 1979) 60 Ohio St.2d 101, 397 N.E.2d 1196, 14 O.O.3d 336. Wills ⚖︎ 785(2)

When the probate judge has made election in behalf of an incompetent widow to take either under the will or under the law of intestacy, the election so made has the same effect as if made by one not under disability, and the widow's right thereby becomes absolute; and third parties are without right to complain. In re Callan's Estate (Cuyahoga 1956) 101 Ohio App. 114, 135 N.E.2d 464, 1 O.O.2d 64. Wills ⚖︎ 800; Wills ⚖︎ 801(1)

Failure of mental strength and alertness in an aged person which impairs memory, and causes forgetfulness to some extent, and at times prevents the recognition of acquaintances, does not alone indicate incapacity to transact business or to execute a paper writing. Bell v. Henry (Ohio App. 5 Dist. 1929) 28 Ohio Law Rep. 528, affirmed 121 Ohio St. 241, 167 N.E. 880, 7 Ohio Law Abs. 378, 29 Ohio Law Rep. 365.

3. Explanation by court

It is not the duty of the probate judge to explain to a widow her rights as an heir at the time of the election. He is to advise her as to the effects of the election on her rights as a widow. Carder v. Board of Com'rs of Fayette County (Ohio 1865) 16 Ohio St. 354.

The entry of an election by a widow to take under the will of her husband in the probate court need not show affirmatively that the judge had explained to her the provisions of the will, etc., for, in the absence of an averment or proof to the contrary, such explanation will be presumed. Davis v. Davis (Ohio 1860) 11 Ohio St. 386. Evidence ⚖︎ 82; Wills ⚖︎ 793

4. Personal appearance

An election to take against a will must be exercised in person. (See also Gardner v Gardner's Executor, 13 OS 426 (1862).) Millikin v. Welliver (Ohio 1882) 37 Ohio St. 460.

Requiring a surviving spouse to personally appear in court in order to take against a will while a surviving spouse who elects to take under a will may manifest his intention in writing does not violate equal protection, as the requirement that a spouse taking against a will appear in court seeks to protect the personal nature of the election and to enable the court to explain the available options. Hutton v. Rygalski (Lucas 1989) 62 Ohio App.3d 125, 574 N.E.2d 1128.

5. Method of election

A probate judge has no right to cancel an election previously made and entered upon his journal, at her instance, for an alleged misapprehension on her part as to the provisions and effect of such will. Davis v. Davis (Ohio 1860) 11 Ohio St. 386. Wills ⚖︎ 796

Where a widow selected as property exempt from administration property which was specifically bequeathed to her, and then by inaction and operation by law elected to take under the will, she was entitled to have vacated the election to take such property as part of the statutory exemption. In re Fetzer's Estate (Medina 1954) 130 N.E.2d 732, 71 Ohio Law Abs. 275.

A widow may rescind her election to take against the husband's will where such election was made in reliance upon erroneous advice of her attorney, and the probate judge did not explain the provisions of the will. Smith v. First Nat. Bank of Akron (Ohio Com.Pl. 1954) 124 N.E.2d 851, 69 Ohio Law Abs. 102.

Execution by widow of papers prepared by attorneys for administrator, who were also acting as widow's attorneys, without knowledge of their effect, held not election by conduct to take under will. Ohio Merchants' Trust Co. v. Conrad (Stark 1931) 42 Ohio App. 150, 181 N.E. 274, 12 Ohio Law Abs. 166. Wills ⚖ 793

A deputy clerk of a probate court is without authority to receive the election of a widow or widower to take under a will; an election so made may, on application of the party, be vacated. Mellinger v. Mellinger (Ohio 1906) 73 Ohio St. 221, 76 N.E. 615, 3 Ohio Law Rep. 536. Wills ⚖ 797

2106.07 Commission issued to take election of surviving spouse

Upon the filing of an application on behalf of a surviving spouse, the probate court may issue a commission, with a copy of the will annexed, directed to any suitable person, to take the election of the surviving spouse as described in section 2106.01 of the Revised Code. In the commission, the court shall direct the suitable person to explain the rights of the surviving spouse under the will and under Chapter 2105. of the Revised Code.

(1990 H 346, eff. 5-31-90)

Uncodified Law

1990 H 346, § 3, eff. 5-31-90, reads, in part: (A) Sections 1 and 2 of this act shall apply only to the estates of decedents who die on or after the effective date of this act.

Historical and Statutory Notes

Ed. Note: 2106.07 is former 2107.44, amended and recodified by 1990 H 346, eff. 5-31-90; 1953 H 1; GC 10504-62.

Library References

Wills ⚖ 785(1).
Westlaw Topic No. 409.
C.J.S. Wills §§ 1841, 1845 to 1846, 1848.
Baldwin's Ohio Legislative Service, 1990 Laws of Ohio, H 346—LSC Analysis, p 5-87

Research References

Encyclopedias
OH Jur. 3d Decedents' Estates § 752, How Election Made.
OH Jur. 3d Decedents' Estates § 753, Surviving Spouse's Right to Explanation of Election Rights.
OH Jur. 3d Decedents' Estates § 757, Election Taken by Commissioner.

Treatises and Practice Aids
Carlin, Baldwin's Ohio Practice, Merrick-Rippner Probate Law § 2:37, Elective Rights of Surviving Spouse—Election to Take Under Law or Under the Will—Procedure for Making Election.
Carlin, Baldwin's Ohio Practice, Merrick-Rippner Probate Law § 2:121, Administration of Decedent's Estate—Checklist.
Carlin, Baldwin's Ohio Practice, Merrick-Rippner Probate Law § 21:17, Rights of Surviving Spouse to Make Election—Commissioner Appointed to Take Election of Spouse.
Carlin, Baldwin's Ohio Practice, Merrick-Rippner Probate Law § 21:18, Rights of Surviving Spouse to Make Election—Duty of Probate Judge.
Carlin, Baldwin's Ohio Practice, Merrick-Rippner Probate Law § 21:32, Rights of Surviving Spouse to Make Election—Election to be Made in Person—Scope of RC 2106.06.
Carlin, Baldwin's Ohio Practice, Merrick-Rippner Probate Law § 21:92, Application for Appointment of Commissioner to Take Election of Surviving Spouse Unable to Appear in Court—Form.
Carlin, Baldwin's Ohio Practice, Merrick-Rippner Probate Law § 21:93, Entry Appointing Commissioner—Form.
Carlin, Baldwin's Ohio Practice, Merrick-Rippner Probate Law § 21:94, Commission—Form.
Carlin, Baldwin's Ohio Practice, Merrick-Rippner Probate Law § 21:95, Report of Commissioner—Form.
Carlin, Baldwin's Ohio Practice, Merrick-Rippner Probate Law § 21:96, Entry Confirming Election of Surviving Spouse—Form.
Carlin, Baldwin's Ohio Practice, Merrick-Rippner Probate Law App B SPF 8.2, Election of Surviving Spouse to Take Against Will.

Notes of Decisions

Ed. Note: This section contains annotations from former RC 2107.44.

Vacation 1

---

1. **Vacation**

Vacation by probate court of an election by surviving spouse to take under statute of descent and distribution, when ordered upon motion filed by interested relative other than surviving spouse, is void for lack of jurisdiction, and such election may be vacated only upon filing of petition therefor by surviving spouse. Baker v. Hutyera (Ohio Com.Pl. 1971) 27 Ohio Misc. 19, 267 N.E.2d 604, 56 O.O.2d 230.

2106.08 Election made by one under legal disability

If, because of a legal disability, a surviving spouse is unable to make an election as provided by section 2106.01 of the Revised Code, as soon as the facts come to the knowledge of the probate court, the probate court shall appoint some suitable person to ascertain the value of the provision made for the surviving spouse by the testator, the value of the rights of the surviving spouse in the estate of the testator under Chapter 2105. of the Revised Code, and the adequate support needs of the surviving spouse after taking into consideration the other available resources and the age, probable life expectancy, physical and mental condition, and present and reasonably anticipated future needs of the surviving spouse. The appointment by the court shall be made at any time within the times described in division (E) of section 2106.01 of the Revised Code for making an election under that section.

When the person so appointed returns the report of his investigation, the court may elect for the surviving spouse to take under section 2105.06 of the Revised Code only if it finds, after taking into consideration the other available resources and the age, probable life expectancy, physical and mental condition, and present and reasonably anticipated future needs of the surviving spouse, that the election to take under section 2105.06 of the Revised Code is necessary to provide adequate support for the surviving spouse during his life expectancy.

After making its determination under this section, the court shall record upon its journal the election made for the surviving spouse. The election, when so entered, shall have the same effect as an election made by one not under legal disability.

(1990 H 346, eff. 5-31-90)

Uncodified Law

1990 H 346, § 3, eff. 5-31-90, reads, in part: (A) Sections 1 and 2 of this act shall apply only to the estates of decedents who die on or after the effective date of this act.

Historical and Statutory Notes

Ed. Note: 2106.08 is former 2107.45, amended and recodified by 1990 H 346, eff. 5-31-90; 1986 S 248; 125 v 903; 1953 H 1; GC 10504-63, 10504-64.

OSBA Probate and Trust Law Section

1986:

Under existing Section 2107.45 an election on behalf of a surviving spouse under a legal disability must be made only on the basis of what is "better for such spouse", which the Ohio Supreme Court has interpreted in *In re: Cook*, 19 Ohio St. 2d 121 to mean in which the surviving spouse will receive a greater benefit. There are instances where more may not be equated with better. For example, a surviving spouse may have sufficient wealth so that more wealth will only increase the tax burdens of the surviving spouse and his or her survivors. Therefore, the purpose of the amendment is to overrule the *In re: Cook* case and to permit the court to take into consideration factors other than simple mathematics. (Commentary from former RC 2107.45.)

Cross References

Appeal from probate court, 2101.42
Fiduciary defined, 2109.01
Probate court's power as guardian to exercise right to elective share in estate of deceased spouse, 2111.50

Library References

Wills ⟲786.
Westlaw Topic No. 409.
C.J.S. Wills § 1841.

 Baldwin's Ohio Legislative Service, 1990 Laws of Ohio, H 346—LSC Analysis, p 5–87

Research References

Encyclopedias

 OH Jur. 3d Appellate Review § 98, Orders of the Probate Division of the Court of Common Pleas.

 OH Jur. 3d Constitutional Law § 487, What Legislation Specifically Relates to the Remedy.

 OH Jur. 3d Decedents' Estates § 125, Acts that Will Bar Succession, Generally—Surviving Spouse's Rights.

 OH Jur. 3d Decedents' Estates § 756, Election by Spouse Under a Legal Disability.

Treatises and Practice Aids

Carlin, Baldwin's Ohio Practice, Merrick-Rippner Probate Law § 2:37, Elective Rights of Surviving Spouse—Election to Take Under Law or Under the Will—Procedure for Making Election.

Carlin, Baldwin's Ohio Practice, Merrick-Rippner Probate Law § 2:121, Administration of Decedent's Estate—Checklist.

Carlin, Baldwin's Ohio Practice, Merrick-Rippner Probate Law § 21:18, Rights of Surviving Spouse to Make Election—Duty of Probate Judge.

Carlin, Baldwin's Ohio Practice, Merrick-Rippner Probate Law § 21:32, Rights of Surviving Spouse to Make Election—Election to be Made in Person—Scope of RC 2106.06.

Carlin, Baldwin's Ohio Practice, Merrick-Rippner Probate Law § 21:35, Rights of Surviving Spouse to Make Election—One Under Legal Disability—Scope of RC 2106.08.

Carlin, Baldwin's Ohio Practice, Merrick-Rippner Probate Law § 21:36, Rights of Surviving Spouse to Make Election—One Under Legal Disability—Discretion of Probate Court in Making Election.

Carlin, Baldwin's Ohio Practice, Merrick-Rippner Probate Law § 21:97, Application for Appointment of Commissioner to Ascertain Value of Rights of Surviving Spouse Under Legal Disability—Form.

Carlin, Baldwin's Ohio Practice, Merrick-Rippner Probate Law § 21:98, Entry Appointing Commissioner to Take Election of Surviving Spouse Under Legal Disability—Form.

Carlin, Baldwin's Ohio Practice, Merrick-Rippner Probate Law § 21:99, Appointment of Commissioner—Spouse Under Disability—Form.

Carlin, Baldwin's Ohio Practice, Merrick-Rippner Probate Law § 21:100, Entry on Election of Surviving Spouse Under Disability—Form.

Bogert - the Law of Trusts and Trustees § 211, Trusts for Unlawful Purposes.

Kuehnle and Levey, Ohio Real Estate Law and Practice § 5:4, Elect Surviving Spouse to Take Under or Against Will.

Notes of Decisions

 Ed. Note: This section contains annotations from former RC 2107.45.

Abuse of court's discretion   5
Construction and application   6
Court election standards   1
Death, effect   4
Procedural issues   2

Third party rights   3

---

1. Court election standards

 Changes in probate statute were remedial, rather than substantive, and thus probate court properly applied amended statute in order to make its election for the testator's disabled surviving spouse; the same duty to elect for the disabled surviving spouse existed under both versions of the statute, and the only thing the assembly changed was the number of factors that the probate court had to consider before carrying out its duty. In re Estate of Pendleton (Ohio App. 4 Dist., 03-09-2001) 141 Ohio App.3d 708, 753 N.E.2d 237, 2001-Ohio-2413. Wills ⟲ 779

 In determining whether to elect for incompetent surviving spouse to take under or against deceased spouse's will, probate court must ascertain what surviving spouse would have done for her financial benefit had she been competent to make decision for herself. In re Estate of Cross (Ohio, 06-05-1996) 75 Ohio St.3d 530, 664 N.E.2d 905, 1996-Ohio-196. Wills ⟲ 788

 Where the surviving spouse is under a disability and the probate court must make an election to take under or against the will, the probate court's discretion in making the election is limited to considering only the incompetent's interests. In re Estate of Cromley (Pickaway 1981) 2 Ohio App.3d 27, 440 N.E.2d 588, 2 O.B.R. 30.

 The election provided by statute for a surviving spouse to choose whether she desires to take under her husband's will or under the statute of descent and distribution is solely for the benefit of the surviving spouse, and where that spouse is under a legal disability the probate court must elect on her behalf the provision which is better for her, considering only her interests. In re Cook's Estate (Ohio 1969) 19 Ohio St.2d 121, 249 N.E.2d 799, 48 O.O.2d 113.

 Inasmuch as the executor and testamentary trustee under a deceased husband's will, as well as a legatee under the will, have interests which conflict with what is "better" for the incompetent widow, they have no standing to contest the court's election on behalf of the spouse, which can be questioned only by the guardian of such spouse or by some other party acting on behalf of such spouse. In re Cook's Estate (Ohio 1969) 19 Ohio St.2d 121, 249 N.E.2d 799, 48 O.O.2d 113. Wills ⟲ 786

 In making an election for a surviving spouse under RC 2107.45, a probate court is to determine which is better as between the provision "in the will" and the provision under the statutes, and may not consider provisions by the decedent or others outside the will and cannot consider the effect of an election upon legatees, heirs, next of kin or the tax collector. In re Strauch's Estate (Franklin 1967) 11 Ohio App.2d 173, 229 N.E.2d 95, 40 O.O.2d 331, affirmed 15 Ohio St.2d 192, 239 N.E.2d 43, 44 O.O.2d 158. Wills ⟲ 786

 An incompetent surviving spouse's lack of financial need, her probable intent to honor the testator's intent, and the existence of a plan of disposition of assets are not permissible standards for making an election under RC 2107.45. In re Strauch's Estate (Franklin 1967) 11 Ohio App.2d 173, 229 N.E.2d 95, 40 O.O.2d 331, affirmed 15 Ohio St.2d 192, 239 N.E.2d 43, 44 O.O.2d 158. Wills ⟲ 786

 Where an election is made for an incompetent surviving spouse under RC 2107.45, the court is not required to be guided solely by which choice will produce the greatest amount for the survivor, but may also consider the needs of the surviving spouse and the extent to which they are met from his or her own estate and the tax benefits resulting from the choice made. In re Rieley's Estate (Ohio Prob. 1963) 194 N.E.2d 918, 92 Ohio Law Abs. 296, 28 O.O.2d 122.

 The election by the probate judge made in behalf of an incompetent widow to take either under the law or under the will is made solely for the benefit of the incompetent spouse and not for the benefit of third parties. In re Callan's Estate (Cuyahoga 1956) 101 Ohio App. 114, 135 N.E.2d 464, 1 O.O.2d 64. Wills ⟲ 786

 Probate court in making election for incompetent spouse has plenary power, fully to dispose of matter, and may take into consideration equities of situation as well as requirements of statute. In re Morton's Estate (Ohio Prob. 1936) 2 Ohio Supp. 361, 21 Ohio Law Abs. 438, 6 O.O. 343. Wills ⟲ 786

2. Procedural issues

 An order of a probate court making an election for an incompetent surviving spouse under RC 2107.45 is subject to the control of the court and may be vacated under RC 2101.33 within term time. (Ed. note: See Civ R 6(C).) In re Strauch's Estate (Franklin 1967) 11 Ohio App.2d 173,

229 N.E.2d 95, 40 O.O.2d 331, affirmed 15 Ohio St.2d 192, 239 N.E.2d 43, 44 O.O.2d 158. Wills ⇐ 788

GC 11397 (RC 2311.21), prescribing that no action or pending proceeding shall abate by death of either or both parties thereto, applies only to actions or proceedings of an adversary character, and not to a special proceeding under GC 10504–63, 10504–64 (RC 2107.45) relative to election of surviving spouse to take under a will. In re Knofler's Estate (Marion 1943) 73 Ohio App. 383, 52 N.E.2d 667, 39 Ohio Law Abs. 263, 29 O.O. 93, affirmed 143 Ohio St. 294, 55 N.E.2d 262, 28 O.O. 203. Abatement And Revival ⇐ 58(.5)

An order made by probate court in special proceeding under GC 10504–63, 10504–64 (RC 2107.45), relative to the election by surviving spouse under legal disability, is a final order affecting a substantial right in a special proceeding, and appealable under GC 12223–2 (RC 2505.02), and where, in such case, the election was not made by court until after death of surviving spouse, the residuary legatee, the only person to benefit from an appeal from such order, is a proper, but not necessary, party to the appeal. In re Knofler's Estate (Marion 1943) 73 Ohio App. 383, 52 N.E.2d 667, 39 Ohio Law Abs. 263, 29 O.O. 93, affirmed 143 Ohio St. 294, 55 N.E.2d 262, 28 O.O. 203.

3. Third party rights

A general power of appointment established in a beneficiary under a trust instrument may not be exercised by a guardian appointed after the beneficiary becomes incompetent, where such exercise is not to provide care, maintenance and support, but is to effect a testamentary disposition of property. Toledo Trust Co. v. National Bank of Detroit (Lucas 1976) 50 Ohio App.2d 147, 362 N.E.2d 273, 4 O.O.3d 125. Mental Health ⇐ 236

Legatees under a will have no right to contest an election not to take under a will made by the probate court on behalf of a surviving spouse who, because of legal disability, is unable to make such election on his own behalf. In re Strauch's Estate (Ohio 1968) 15 Ohio St.2d 192, 239 N.E.2d 43, 44 O.O.2d 158. Wills ⇐ 797

Legatees under the will of a decedent have no legal interest in or right to contest an election of a surviving spouse under RC 2107.45 and are not properly appellees in an appeal by the guardian of the surviving spouse. In re Strauch's Estate (Franklin 1967) 11 Ohio App.2d 173, 229 N.E.2d 95, 40 O.O.2d 331, affirmed 15 Ohio St.2d 192, 239 N.E.2d 43, 44 O.O.2d 158.

When the probate judge has made election in behalf of an incompetent widow to take either under the will or under the law of intestacy, the election so made has the same effect as if made by one not under disability, and the widow's right thereby becomes absolute; and third parties are without right to complain. In re Callan's Estate (Cuyahoga 1956) 101 Ohio App. 114, 135 N.E.2d 464, 1 O.O.2d 64. Wills ⇐ 800; Wills ⇐ 801(1)

When the probate court has made an election in behalf of an incompetent widow and provided for in the probate code and journalized it, the rights of all parties become fixed and the court has no right to set aside that election except upon a proper showing that the surviving spouse has been deceived, defrauded or in some way precluded from exercising her free will in such election. In re Miller's Estate (Ohio Prob. 1943) 12 Ohio Supp. 108, 38 Ohio Law Abs. 566, 27 O.O. 10.

4. Death, effect

Medicaid eligibility provisions related to determining eligibility for benefits when one spouse is institutionalized and other spouse is community spouse did not apply when "other spouse" was deceased, for purposes of determining whether institutionalized spouse should elect to take against deceased spouse's will. In re Estate of Cross (Ohio, 06-05-1996) 75 Ohio St.3d 530, 664 N.E.2d 905, 1996-Ohio-196. Health ⇐ 471(5); Wills ⇐ 788

Death is not a "legal disability" within the meaning of RC 2107.45, which would require the probate court to make an election for the estate of a surviving spouse who dies having failed to elect against the will. In re LaSpina's Estate (Ohio 1979) 60 Ohio St.2d 101, 397 N.E.2d 1196, 14 O.O.3d 336. Wills ⇐ 785(2)

Court must make an election for an incompetent spouse even after her death since her rights are still protected by this section, and since GC 10504–60 (RC 2107.41), setting forth a presumption in event of failure to elect is inapplicable when spouse is an incompetent and when time for election has not elapsed. In re Jones Estate (Ohio Com.Pl. 1939) 1 Ohio Supp. 32, 29 Ohio Law Abs. 148, 15 O.O. 250.

Death of an incompetent spouse does not extinguish the agency of the person appointed by the court to make an election for her. In re Jones Estate (Ohio Com.Pl. 1939) 1 Ohio Supp. 32, 29 Ohio Law Abs. 148, 15 O.O. 250.

5. Abuse of court's discretion

The amendments to RC 2107.45, effective 12–17–86, are purely procedural and must be applied to actions pending on the effective date; a court's failure to appoint a suitable person to ascertain the value of the provisions under the will and those provided by law and present a report to the court requires reversal of a trial court's judgment permitting an election to take under the will where hearings held in lieu of the investigation and report do not reveal all pertinent facts to the court. In re Estate of Hinklin (Marion 1989) 66 Ohio App.3d 676, 586 N.E.2d 130.

Where the provision in a will is a simple bequest worth $8,820.50, and the statutory share is $44,102.50, it is an abuse of discretion for a probate court to elect on behalf of the incompetent spouse to take under the will and against the statutory right. In re Strauch's Estate (Franklin 1967) 11 Ohio App.2d 173, 229 N.E.2d 95, 40 O.O.2d 331, affirmed 15 Ohio St.2d 192, 239 N.E.2d 43, 44 O.O.2d 158.

A probate court, in determining that the best interest of an eighty-three year old incompetent widow would be served by the court's exercising, in such widow's behalf, the widow's election to take against the will and under the laws of intestacy, is not, under such circumstances, abusing its discretion, where the value of the widow's interest under the law was $267,736, as against $83,900 under will, though such election defeated the joint testamentary plan of both testator and spouse. In re Callan's Estate (Cuyahoga 1956) 101 Ohio App. 114, 135 N.E.2d 464, 1 O.O.2d 64. Wills ⇐ 786

6. Construction and application

RC 2106.08 provides guidelines for use by the suitable person and the court in determining adequate support needs of a surviving spouse, taking into consideration other available resources, age, probable life expectancy, physical and mental condition, and present and reasonably anticipated future needs of the surviving spouse who is under legal disability so that the end result of the court's judgment should be identical to that of the surviving spouse had she been competent to do her own reasoning; where a surviving spouse is seventy-nine years of age with Alzheimer's disease, unable to conduct her own affairs, and in a nursing home where all expenses are paid by medicaid, a probate court has before it the basis to consider the statutory guidelines under RC 2106.08, and properly determines that such surviving spouse would have chosen to take under the will as the cost of her care in the nursing home was covered, rendering it unnecessary and not in her interest to take against her husband's will. In re Estate of Cross (Ohio App. 8 Dist., Cuyahoga, 02-23-1995) No. 66503, 1995 WL 79792, Unreported, appeal allowed 73 Ohio St.3d 1413, 651 N.E.2d 1310, reversed 75 Ohio St.3d 530, 664 N.E.2d 905, 1996-Ohio-196.

Election for incompetent surviving spouse to take against deceased spouse's will, under which surviving spouse took nothing, and receive intestate share was necessary for surviving spouse's future support, as statutorily required for election against will, and thus was not abuse of discretion, inasmuch as surviving spouse, who relied solely on Medicaid benefits for care and support, had legal interest in and ability to use or dispose of her intestate share of deceased spouse's estate under right to take against will, and failure to avail herself of such potential income would render her ineligible for benefits under state Medicaid eligibility requirements. In re Estate of Cross (Ohio, 06-05-1996) 75 Ohio St.3d 530, 664 N.E.2d 905, 1996-Ohio-196. Wills ⇐ 788

This section cannot be construed to preserve right of surviving spouse, an incompetent, to elect to take under the will or by law until such time as the facts of his incapacity come to the knowledge of the probate court. In re Iwinski's Estate (Cuyahoga 1947) 83 Ohio App. 463, 77 N.E.2d 375, 49 Ohio Law Abs. 609, 38 O.O. 491.

This section, as to election by one under legal disability, applies solely to an incompetent spouse. In re Jones Estate (Ohio Com.Pl. 1939) 1 Ohio Supp. 32, 29 Ohio Law Abs. 148, 15 O.O. 250.

2106.10 Election of surviving spouse to receive mansion house

(A) A surviving spouse may elect to receive, as part of the surviving spouse's share of an intestate estate under section 2105.06 of the Revised Code and the allowance for support under section 2106.13 of the Revised Code, the entire interest of the decedent spouse in the mansion house. The interest of the decedent spouse in the mansion house shall be valued at the appraised value with the deduction of that portion of all liens on the mansion house existing at the time of death and attributable to the decedent's interest in the mansion house.

(B) The election pursuant to division (A) of this section shall be made at or before the time a final account is rendered.

(C) If the spouse makes an election pursuant to division (A) of this section, the administrator or executor shall file, unless the election is one made under division (D) of this section, an application for a certificate of transfer as provided for in section 2113.61 of the Revised Code. The application also shall contain an inventory of the property and the allowance for support that the spouse is entitled to receive under sections 2105.06 and 2106.13 of the Revised Code. If the value of the property and the allowance for support that the spouse is entitled to receive is equal to or greater than the value of the decedent's interest in the mansion house, the court shall issue the certificate of transfer.

(D) The surviving spouse may make an election pursuant to division (A) of this section in an estate relieved from administration under section 2113.03 of the Revised Code or in an estate that is subject to an order granting a summary release from administration under section 2113.031 of the Revised Code. The election shall be made at the time of or prior to the entry of the order relieving the estate from administration or the order granting a summary release from administration. Either the surviving spouse or the applicant for the order shall file the application for the certificate of transfer under division (C) of this section.

(E) If the surviving spouse dies prior to making an election pursuant to division (A) of this section, the surviving spouse shall be conclusively presumed not to have made an election pursuant to that division. After the surviving spouse's death, no other person is authorized to make an election pursuant to that division on behalf of the estate of the surviving spouse.

(F) As used in this section, the mansion house includes the decedent's title in the parcel of land on which the house is situated and, at the option of the surviving spouse, the decedent's title in the household goods contained within the house and the lots or farmland adjacent to the house and used in conjunction with it as the home of the decedent.

(2000 H 313, eff. 8–29–00; 1996 H 391, eff. 10–1–96; 1990 H 346, eff. 5–31–90)

Uncodified Law

1990 H 346, § 3, eff. 5–31–90, reads, in part: (A) Sections 1 and 2 of this act shall apply only to the estates of decedents who die on or after the effective date of this act.

Historical and Statutory Notes

Ed. Note: 2106.10 is former 2105.062, amended and recodified by 1990 H 346, eff. 5–31–90; 1986 S 248; 1980 S 317; 1978 H 1003; 1976 S 466; 1975 S 145.

Amendment Note: 2000 H 313 rewrote division (D); and substituted "farmland" for "farm-land" in division (F). Prior to amendment, division (D) read:

"(D) The surviving spouse may make an election pursuant to division (A) of this section in an estate relieved from administration under section 2113.03 of the Revised Code. The election shall be made at the time of or prior to the entry of the order relieving the estate from administration. Either the spouse or the applicant for the order relieving the estate from administration shall file the application for certificate of transfer under division (C) of this section."

Amendment Note: 1996 H 391 inserted "and the allowance for support under section 2106.13 of the Revised Code" in division (A) and substituted "and the allowance for support that the spouse is entitled to receive under sections 2105.06 and 2106.13 of the Revised Code. If the value of the property and the allowance for support that the spouse is entitled to receive" for "that the spouse is entitled to receive under section 2105.06 of the Revised Code. If the value of the property the spouse is entitled to receive" in division (C).

Legislative Service Commission

1975:

Under existing law, if a person dies and part or all of his property passes through intestacy, his surviving spouse and other heirs take in parcenary (together), as co-tenants. If the deceased spouse's interest in the mansion home passes through intestacy and the surviving spouse desires to retain the mansion house free of interests of the other heirs, he must make application to the probate court to purchase it.

The bill would provide an alternative method for a surviving spouse to retain the mansion house free of interests of the other heirs. If the value of the property the surviving spouse is entitled to receive through intestacy is equal to or greater than the appraised value of the mansion house will all liens deducted, the surviving spouse could elect at or before the time a final account is rendered to receive the mansion house free of other heirs. The election would be made by filing for a certificate of transfer with an inventory of property. If all conditions are met, the court would have to issue the certificate.

The bill would define mansion house to include the parcel of land on which the house sits and the household goods, and at the option of the surviving spouse, lots or farm land adjacent to the mansion house and used in connection with the mansion house as the home of the decedent. (Commentary from former RC 2105.062.)

OSBA Probate and Trust Law Section

1980:

When Sec. 2105.062 was added to the Revised Code as new legislation in 1976, the section as originally drafted did not make clear whether the election contained in it for the benefit of the surviving spouse could only be exercised personally by the surviving spouse during his or her lifetime, or whether such election might be exercised by the fiduciary of the estate of a surviving spouse who died before the administration of the estate of the first spouse was completed on behalf of the estate of the second spouse to die.

The Board is strongly of the belief that the right to the election under Sec. 2105.062 should only be available to a surviving spouse during his or her lifetime, that it should be treated as an election which is personal to the surviving spouse, and that it should not be available to the estate of a surviving spouse who dies without having made the election, even though the administration of the estate of the first spouse to die is not yet completed.

Restricting the election available to the surviving spouse under Sec. 2105.062 to the lifetime of the surviving spouse as a personal right is similar to the treatment accorded the election of the surviving spouse to take under the will or under law which is granted by Sec. 2107.39. Such election to take against the will is also restricted to exercise during the lifetime of the surviving spouse by Sec. 2107.41. (Commentary from former RC 2105.062.)

Cross References

Application for certificate of realty transfer, 2113.61
Descent and distribution of title to real property, applicability, 2105.061
Right to purchase mansion house at appraised value, 2106.16

Library References

Wills ⚖︎784, 785(2).
Westlaw Topic No. 409.
C.J.S. Wills §§ 1841, 1845, 1847, 1849 to 1851.
  Baldwin's Ohio Legislative Service, 1990 Laws of Ohio, H 346—LSC Analysis, p 5–87

Research References

Encyclopedias

OH Jur. 3d Decedents' Estates § 116, Under the Statute of Descent and Distribution.
OH Jur. 3d Decedents' Estates § 117, Under the Statute of Descent and Distribution—Rights in Mansion House.
OH Jur. 3d Decedents' Estates § 138, Nature of Heir's Title; Parcenary.
OH Jur. 3d Decedents' Estates § 142, Title as Complete.
OH Jur. 3d Decedents' Estates § 235, Restrictions as to Surviving Spouse.
OH Jur. 3d Decedents' Estates § 1676, Right to Receive Mansion House as Part of Intestate Share.

Forms

Ohio Forms and Transactions KP 30.04, Common Disaster and Presumed Order of Death.

Treatises and Practice Aids

Carlin, Baldwin's Ohio Practice, Merrick-Rippner Probate Law § 15:8, Descent and Distribution—Satisfaction of Monetary Share.

Carlin, Baldwin's Ohio Practice, Merrick-Rippner Probate Law § 16:1, Statutory Provisions.

Carlin, Baldwin's Ohio Practice, Merrick-Rippner Probate Law § 2:22, Inventory and Appraisal—Family Allowance.

Carlin, Baldwin's Ohio Practice, Merrick-Rippner Probate Law § 2:38, Elective Rights of Surviving Spouse—Election to Take Under Law or Under the Will—Elective Share of Surviving Spouse Against the Will.

Carlin, Baldwin's Ohio Practice, Merrick-Rippner Probate Law § 2:39, Elective Rights of Surviving Spouse—Election to Take Under Law or Under the Will—Failure to Make Election Against the Will.

Carlin, Baldwin's Ohio Practice, Merrick-Rippner Probate Law § 2:45, Elective Rights of Surviving Spouse—Election of Surviving Spouse to Receive Property as Part of Intestate Share and Allowance for Support.

Carlin, Baldwin's Ohio Practice, Merrick-Rippner Probate Law § 21:5, Rights of Surviving Spouse to Make Election—Statutory Provisions—Effect.

Carlin, Baldwin's Ohio Practice, Merrick-Rippner Probate Law § 48:8, Property Liable for Payment of Debts—Personal Property—Effect of Spousal Election.

Carlin, Baldwin's Ohio Practice, Merrick-Rippner Probate Law § 90:9, Authority for Land Sale Action—Overriding Rights of Surviving Spouse.

Carlin, Baldwin's Ohio Practice, Merrick-Rippner Probate Law § 2:102, Distribution of Assets—to Surviving Spouse Under Intestate succession.

Carlin, Baldwin's Ohio Practice, Merrick-Rippner Probate Law § 2:111, Release from Administration—Election of Surviving Spouse to Receive Mansion House.

Carlin, Baldwin's Ohio Practice, Merrick-Rippner Probate Law § 2:117, Election of Surviving Spouse to Receive Mansion House.

Carlin, Baldwin's Ohio Practice, Merrick-Rippner Probate Law § 2:121, Administration of Decedent's Estate—Checklist.

Carlin, Baldwin's Ohio Practice, Merrick-Rippner Probate Law § 21:30, Rights of Surviving Spouse to Make Election—Right to Use of Mansion House and Family Allowance.

Carlin, Baldwin's Ohio Practice, Merrick-Rippner Probate Law § 21:44, Rights of Surviving Spouse to Elect to Receive Mansion House—Statutory Right.

Carlin, Baldwin's Ohio Practice, Merrick-Rippner Probate Law § 21:45, Rights of Surviving Spouse to Elect to Receive Mansion House—Procedure—Time of Election.

Carlin, Baldwin's Ohio Practice, Merrick-Rippner Probate Law § 21:46, Rights of Surviving Spouse to Elect to Receive Mansion House—Procedure—Application for Certificate of Transfer.

Carlin, Baldwin's Ohio Practice, Merrick-Rippner Probate Law § 21:47, Rights of Surviving Spouse to Elect to Receive Mansion House—Procedure—Election Where Estate Relieved from Administration.

Carlin, Baldwin's Ohio Practice, Merrick-Rippner Probate Law § 21:48, Rights of Surviving Spouse to Payment of Specific Monetary Share—Valuation of Monetary Share.

Carlin, Baldwin's Ohio Practice, Merrick-Rippner Probate Law § 21:50, Rights of Surviving Spouse to Payment of Specific Monetary Share—Monetary Share as Charge on Real Estate.

Carlin, Baldwin's Ohio Practice, Merrick-Rippner Probate Law § 91:51, Entry Granting Complaint and Ordering Appraisal of Entire Interest—Form.

Carlin, Baldwin's Ohio Practice, Merrick-Rippner Probate Law App B SPF 12.0, Application for Certificate of Transfer.

Carlin, Baldwin's Ohio Practice, Merrick-Rippner Probate Law App B SPF 12.1, Certificate of Transfer.

Law Review and Journal Commentaries

Entitlement of a Surviving Spouse: A Quandary, B. Redman. 27 Cap U L Rev 573 (1999).

Substitute House Bill 391—Omnibus Probate Bill, William B. McNeil. 7 Prob L J Ohio 2 (September/October 1996).

Notes of Decisions

Ed. Note: This section contains annotations from former RC 2105.062.

Purchase of house 1

1. Purchase of house

Surviving spouse's declaratory judgment action seeking to establish her right to purchase marital residence with offset for her statutory support allowance was untimely, where it was filed several years after decedent's death and the resolution of decedent's estate. Frinkley v. Meeker (Ohio App. 11 Dist., Portage, 12-10-2004) No. 2004-P-0022, 2004-Ohio-6696, 2004 WL 2860402, Unreported, appeal not allowed 105 Ohio St.3d 1518, 826 N.E.2d 315, 2005-Ohio-1880. Executors And Administrators ⚖ 136.1

Surviving spouse who did not elect against decedent's will, and who sought to establish her entitlement to purchase marital residence with offset for her statutory support allowance, failed to establish that will did not expressly bar her from receiving support allowance, where spouse did not provide copy of decedent's will to trial court. Frinkley v. Meeker (Ohio App. 11 Dist., Portage, 12-10-2004) No. 2004-P-0022, 2004-Ohio-6696, 2004 WL 2860402, Unreported, appeal not allowed 105 Ohio St.3d 1518, 826 N.E.2d 315, 2005-Ohio-1880. Executors And Administrators ⚖ 186

Trial court in surviving spouse's declaratory judgment action seeking to establish her right to purchase marital residence with offset for her statutory support allowance could not take judicial notice of probate court proceedings involving probate of decedent's will; consideration of material outside the record prevented Court of Appeals from reviewing whether trial court properly interpreted the material. Frinkley v. Meeker (Ohio App. 11 Dist., Portage, 12-10-2004) No. 2004-P-0022, 2004-Ohio-6696, 2004 WL 2860402, Unreported, appeal not allowed 105 Ohio St.3d 1518, 826 N.E.2d 315, 2005-Ohio-1880. Evidence ⚖ 43(4)

An election of a surviving spouse to receive a mansion house as part of the spouse's distributive share under RC 2105.062, does not require an additional proceeding to purchase under RC 2113.38. In re Estate of Reynolds, No. 985 (4th Dist Ct App, Ross, 7–1–83).

2106.11 Method of payment of specific monetary share of surviving spouse

Subject to the right of the surviving spouse to elect to receive the decedent's interest in the mansion house pursuant to section 2106.10 of the Revised Code, the specific monetary share payable to a surviving spouse under division (B), (C), or (D) of section 2105.06 of the Revised Code shall be paid out of the tangible and intangible personal property in the intestate estate to the extent that the personal property is available for distribution. The personal property distributed to the surviving spouse, other than cash, shall be valued at the appraised value.

Before tangible and intangible personal property is transferred to the surviving spouse in payment or part payment of the specific monetary share, the administrator or executor shall file an application that includes an inventory of the personal property intended to be distributed in kind to the surviving spouse, together with a statement of the appraised value of each item of personal property included. The court shall examine the application and make a finding of the amount of personal property to be distributed to the surviving spouse, and shall order that the personal property be distributed to the surviving spouse. The court concurrently shall make a finding of the amount of money that remains due and payable to the surviving spouse in satisfaction of the specific monetary share to which the surviving spouse is entitled under division (B), (C), or (D) of section 2105.06 of the Revised Code. Any amount that remains due and payable shall be a charge on the title to any real property in the estate but the charge does not bear interest. This charge may be conveyed or released in the same manner as any other interest in real estate and may be enforced by foreclosure or any other appropriate remedy.

(2000 S 152, eff. 3-22-01; 1990 H 346, eff. 5-31-90)

Uncodified Law

1990 H 346, § 3, eff. 5–31–90, reads, in part: (A) Sections 1 and 2 of this act shall apply only to the estates of decedents who die on or after the effective date of this act.

Historical and Statutory Notes

Ed. Note: 2106.11 is former 2105.063, amended and recodified by 1990 H 346, eff. 5–31–90; 1986 S 248; 1976 S 466.

Amendment Note: 2000 S 152 inserted "or (D)" twice; and made other nonsubstantive changes.

Cross References

Application for certificate of realty transfer, 2113.61
Distribution in kind, 2113.55

Library References

Wills ⇐801(8.1).
Westlaw Topic No. 409.
C.J.S. Wills §§ 1841, 1866 to 1868.
Baldwin's Ohio Legislative Service, 1990 Laws of Ohio, H 346—LSC Analysis, p 5–87

Research References

Encyclopedias
OH Jur. 3d Decedents' Estates § 116, Under the Statute of Descent and Distribution.
OH Jur. 3d Decedents' Estates § 146, Record of Transfer.
OH Jur. 3d Decedents' Estates § 1640, Distribution in Kind—Distribution to Surviving Spouse of Appraised Personal Property in Cases of Intestacy.

Treatises and Practice Aids
Carlin, Baldwin's Ohio Practice, Merrick-Rippner Probate Law § 15:6, Descent and Distribution—Surviving Spouse—in General.
Carlin, Baldwin's Ohio Practice, Merrick-Rippner Probate Law § 15:8, Descent and Distribution—Satisfaction of Monetary Share.
Carlin, Baldwin's Ohio Practice, Merrick-Rippner Probate Law § 2:102, Distribution of Assets—to Surviving Spouse Under Intestate succession.
Carlin, Baldwin's Ohio Practice, Merrick-Rippner Probate Law § 2:106, Distribution of Assets—Transfer of Real Estate.
Carlin, Baldwin's Ohio Practice, Merrick-Rippner Probate Law § 2:121, Administration of Decedent's Estate—Checklist.
Carlin, Baldwin's Ohio Practice, Merrick-Rippner Probate Law § 21:48, Rights of Surviving Spouse to Payment of Specific Monetary Share—Valuation of Monetary Share.
Carlin, Baldwin's Ohio Practice, Merrick-Rippner Probate Law § 21:49, Rights of Surviving Spouse to Payment of Specific Monetary Share—Distribution in Kind of Personal Property.
Carlin, Baldwin's Ohio Practice, Merrick-Rippner Probate Law § 21:50, Rights of Surviving Spouse to Payment of Specific Monetary Share—Monetary Share as Charge on Real Estate.
Carlin, Baldwin's Ohio Practice, Merrick-Rippner Probate Law § 75:20, Application to Distribute in Kind—Form.
Carlin, Baldwin's Ohio Practice, Merrick-Rippner Probate Law § 91:34, Application for Certificate of Transfer—Form.
Carlin, Baldwin's Ohio Practice, Merrick-Rippner Probate Law § 91:36, Certificate of Transfer—Form.
Carlin, Baldwin's Ohio Practice, Merrick-Rippner Probate Law App B SPF 10.0, Application to Distribute in Kind—Form.
Carlin, Baldwin's Ohio Practice, Merrick-Rippner Probate Law App B SPF 12.0, Application for Certificate of Transfer.
Carlin, Baldwin's Ohio Practice, Merrick-Rippner Probate Law App B SPF 12.1, Certificate of Transfer.

2106.13 Allowance for support of surviving spouse and minor children

(A) If a person dies leaving a surviving spouse and no minor children, leaving a surviving spouse and minor children, or leaving minor children and no surviving spouse, the surviving spouse, minor children, or both shall be entitled to receive, subject to division (B) of this section, in money or property the sum of forty thousand dollars as an allowance for support. If the surviving spouse selected two automobiles under section 2106.18 of the Revised Code, the allowance for support prescribed by this section shall be reduced by the value of the automobile having the lower value of the two automobiles so selected. The money or property set off as an allowance for support shall be considered estate assets.

(B) The probate court shall order the distribution of the allowance for support described in division (A) of this section as follows:

(1) If the person died leaving a surviving spouse and no minor children, one hundred per cent to the surviving spouse;

(2) If the person died leaving a surviving spouse and minor children, and if all of the minor children are the children of the surviving spouse, one hundred per cent to the surviving spouse;

(3) If the person died leaving a surviving spouse and minor children, and if not all of the minor children are children of the surviving spouse, in equitable shares, as fixed by the probate court in accordance with this division, to the surviving spouse and the minor children who are not the children of the surviving spouse. In determining equitable shares under this division, the probate court shall do all of the following:

(a) Consider the respective needs of the surviving spouse, the minor children who are children of the surviving spouse, and the minor children who are not children of the surviving spouse;

(b) Allocate to the surviving spouse, the share that is equitable in light of the needs of the surviving spouse and the minor children who are children of the surviving spouse;

(c) Allocate to the minor children who are not children of the surviving spouse, the share that is equitable in light of the needs of those minor children.

(4) If the person died leaving minor children and no surviving spouse, in equitable shares, as fixed by the probate court in accordance with this division, to the minor children. In determining equitable shares under this division, the probate court shall consider the respective needs of the minor children and allocate to each minor child the share that is equitable in light of the child's needs.

(C) If the surviving spouse selected two automobiles under section 2106.18 of the Revised Code, the probate court, in considering the respective needs of the surviving spouse and the minor children when allocating an allowance for support under division (B)(3) of this section, shall consider the benefit derived by the surviving spouse from the transfer of the automobile having the lower value of the two automobiles so selected.

(D) If, pursuant to this section, the probate court must allocate the allowance for support, the administrator or executor, within five months of the initial appointment of an administrator or executor, shall file with the probate court an application to allocate the allowance for support.

(E) The administrator or executor shall pay the allowance for support unless a competent adult or a guardian with the consent of the court having jurisdiction over the guardianship waives the allowance for support to which the adult or the ward represented by the guardian is entitled.

(F) For the purposes of this section, the value of an automobile that a surviving spouse selects pursuant to section 2106.18 of the Revised Code is the value that the surviving spouse specifies for the automobile in the affidavit executed pursuant to division (B) of section 4505.10 of the Revised Code.

(2001 H 85, eff. 10–31–01; 2000 H 313, eff. 8–29–00; 1998 H 366, eff. 3–18–99; 1995 H 156, eff. 3–11–96; 1990 H 346, eff. 5–31–90)

Uncodified Law

1998 H 366, § 3, eff. 3–18–99, reads:

Sections 2106.13 and 2113.03 of the Revised Code, as amended by this act, apply to the estates of decedents who die on or after the effective date of this act.

1990 H 346, § 3, eff. 5–31–90, reads, in part: (A) Sections 1 and 2 of this act shall apply only to the estates of decedents who die on or after the effective date of this act.

Historical and Statutory Notes

Ed. Note: 2106.13 is former 2117.20, amended and recodified by 1990 H 346, eff. 5–31–90; 1975 S 145.

Amendment Note: 2001 H 85 added new divisions (D) and (E); and redesignated former division (D) as new division (F).

Amendment Note: 2000 H 313 deleted "appraised" before "value" twice in division (A) and once in division (C); and added new division (D).

Amendment Note: 1998 H 366 increased the allowance for support to forty thousand dollars from twenty-five thousand dollars.

Amendment Note: 1995 H 156 added the second sentence in division (A); substituted "the child's" for "his" in division (B)(4); and added division (C).

Legislative Service Commission

1975:

Existing section 2117.20 provides a widow's allowance for one year's support, which is set by the administrator or court. It has no maximum amount. This claim has a high priority with respect to estate debts. Section 2117.21 provides for making up any balance of this allowance whenever, initially, there is not enough suitable property to do so, and section 2117.22 permits the court, on motion, to increase or diminish the allowance.

The bill would enact a new section 2117.20, entitling the surviving spouse, or if there is no spouse, then the minor children, to receive $5,000 worth of property or money as an allowance for support. This allowance would be considered to be an estate asset. Sections 2117.21 and 2117.22 would be repealed. (Commentary from former RC 2117.20.)

Cross References

Action for sale to pay debts, legacy, 2127.02, 2127.03
Bond to prevent sale of property of decedent, 2127.31
Estate tax lien, discharge of, 5731.37
Estates, release from administration, 2113.03
Exceptions to allowance for support, 2115.16
Inheritance tax, marital deduction, 5731.15
Order of payment of debts, 2117.25
Principal of estate, expenses charged to, 2109.67
Proceeds from partition of real estate, 2127.41
Specific partnership property not subject to, 1775.24
Summary release from administration by person obligated to pay decedent's funeral and burial expenses, application, 2113.031
Survivorship, determination with respect to specified person, 2105.32
Tax deductions for funeral and administration expenses, debts, and mortgage debts, 5731.16

Library References

Executors and Administrators ⚖176.
Wills ⚖800.
Westlaw Topic Nos. 162, 409.
C.J.S. Executors and Administrators § 353.
C.J.S. Wills §§ 1841, 1866 to 1868.

Baldwin's Ohio Legislative Service, 1990 Laws of Ohio, H 346—LSC Analysis, p 5–87

Research References

Encyclopedias

OH Jur. 3d Decedents' Estates § 117, Under the Statute of Descent and Distribution—Rights in Mansion House.
OH Jur. 3d Decedents' Estates § 118, Under the Statute of Descent and Distribution—Support Allowance.
OH Jur. 3d Decedents' Estates § 119, Under the Statute of Descent and Distribution—Motor Vehicles and Boats.
OH Jur. 3d Decedents' Estates § 150, Computation of Distributive Shares.
OH Jur. 3d Decedents' Estates § 235, Restrictions as to Surviving Spouse.
OH Jur. 3d Decedents' Estates § 770, Percentage of the Estate Taken—Meaning of "Net Estate".
OH Jur. 3d Decedents' Estates § 1677, Right to Automobiles and Boats.
OH Jur. 3d Decedents' Estates § 1685, Right to Allowance.
OH Jur. 3d Decedents' Estates § 1688, Allowance to Children.
OH Jur. 3d Decedents' Estates § 1689, Property Out of Which Allowance May be Made.
OH Jur. 3d Decedents' Estates § 1831, When Administration May be Dispensed With.
OH Jur. 3d Decedents' Estates § 1832, Application to Release, and Order Releasing, Estate from Administration.

Forms

Ohio Forms Legal and Business § 20:10, General Partnership Agreement.
Ohio Forms Legal and Business § 25:88, Surviving Spouse's Trust Income Withheld to Extent of Family Allowance.
Ohio Forms Legal and Business § 24:143, Drafting Will.
Ohio Forms Legal and Business § 24:161, Entire Estate to Spouse—Alternatively to Children—Guardianship of Minors.
Ohio Forms Legal and Business § 24:637, Bequests—in Lieu of Statutory Family Maintenance Allowance.
Ohio Forms Legal and Business § 24:956, Settlement Among Testator's Legatees and Heirs—Family Home to be Set Aside for Surviving Spouse.
Ohio Forms Legal and Business § 24:971, Spouse's Election to Take Under Will.
Ohio Forms Legal and Business § 25:301, Authorization and Direction to Trustee to Maintain or Sell, and to Purchase or Build Family Residence.
Ohio Forms and Transactions KP 30.04, Common Disaster and Presumed Order of Death.

Treatises and Practice Aids

Sowald & Morgastern, Baldwin's Ohio Practice Domestic Relations Law § 1:5, Terms.
Sowald & Morgastern, Baldwin's Ohio Practice Domestic Relations Law § 8:7, Effect of Decree.
Carlin, Baldwin's Ohio Practice, Merrick-Rippner Probate Law § 2:3, Time for Administration of Decedent's Estate and Payment of Estate Taxes.
Carlin, Baldwin's Ohio Practice, Merrick-Rippner Probate Law § 15:6, Descent and Distribution—Surviving Spouse—in General.
Carlin, Baldwin's Ohio Practice, Merrick-Rippner Probate Law § 15:8, Descent and Distribution—Satisfaction of Monetary Share.
Carlin, Baldwin's Ohio Practice, Merrick-Rippner Probate Law § 16:1, Statutory Provisions.
Carlin, Baldwin's Ohio Practice, Merrick-Rippner Probate Law § 2:22, Inventory and Appraisal—Family Allowance.
Carlin, Baldwin's Ohio Practice, Merrick-Rippner Probate Law § 2:38, Elective Rights of Surviving Spouse—Election to Take Under Law or Under the Will—Elective Share of Surviving Spouse Against the Will.
Carlin, Baldwin's Ohio Practice, Merrick-Rippner Probate Law § 2:39, Elective Rights of Surviving Spouse—Election to Take Under Law or Under the Will—Failure to Make Election Against the Will.
Carlin, Baldwin's Ohio Practice, Merrick-Rippner Probate Law § 2:40, Elective Rights of Surviving Spouse—Election to Take Under Law or Under the Will—Election of Surviving Spouse to Take Under the Will.
Carlin, Baldwin's Ohio Practice, Merrick-Rippner Probate Law § 2:45, Elective Rights of Surviving Spouse—Election of Surviving Spouse to Receive Property as Part of Intestate Share and Allowance for Support.
Carlin, Baldwin's Ohio Practice, Merrick-Rippner Probate Law § 2:46, Elective Rights of Surviving Spouse—Election of Surviving Spouse to Receive Property—Payment of Specific Monetary Share.
Carlin, Baldwin's Ohio Practice, Merrick-Rippner Probate Law § 2:78, Ohio Estate Tax—Determining the Gross Estate—Deductions.
Carlin, Baldwin's Ohio Practice, Merrick-Rippner Probate Law § 21:5, Rights of Surviving Spouse to Make Election—Statutory Provisions—Effect.

Carlin, Baldwin's Ohio Practice, Merrick-Rippner Probate Law § 22:3, Effect of Prohibition to Benefit.

Carlin, Baldwin's Ohio Practice, Merrick-Rippner Probate Law § 84:1, Creditor's Claims—Introduction.

Carlin, Baldwin's Ohio Practice, Merrick-Rippner Probate Law § 89:4, Payment of Debts—Order of Payment.

Carlin, Baldwin's Ohio Practice, Merrick-Rippner Probate Law § 90:8, Authority for Land Sale Action—Insufficient Personal Property to Pay Debts.

Carlin, Baldwin's Ohio Practice, Merrick-Rippner Probate Law § 91:9, Land Sale—to Pay Family Allowance.

Carlin, Baldwin's Ohio Practice, Merrick-Rippner Probate Law § 92:7, Sale of Land Fraudulently Conveyed.

Carlin, Baldwin's Ohio Practice, Merrick-Rippner Probate Law § 94:2, Bond of Interested Person to Prevent Sale.

Carlin, Baldwin's Ohio Practice, Merrick-Rippner Probate Law § 2:111, Release from Administration—Election of Surviving Spouse to Receive Mansion House.

Carlin, Baldwin's Ohio Practice, Merrick-Rippner Probate Law § 2:113, Value of Decedent's Assets Which May be Transferred.

Carlin, Baldwin's Ohio Practice, Merrick-Rippner Probate Law § 2:121, Administration of Decedent's Estate—Checklist.

Carlin, Baldwin's Ohio Practice, Merrick-Rippner Probate Law § 2:122, Administration of Decedent's Estate—Release—Checklist.

Carlin, Baldwin's Ohio Practice, Merrick-Rippner Probate Law § 21:19, Rights of Surviving Spouse to Make Election—Effect of Election—Generally.

Carlin, Baldwin's Ohio Practice, Merrick-Rippner Probate Law § 21:30, Rights of Surviving Spouse to Make Election—Right to Use of Mansion House and Family Allowance.

Carlin, Baldwin's Ohio Practice, Merrick-Rippner Probate Law § 21:44, Rights of Surviving Spouse to Elect to Receive Mansion House—Statutory Right.

Carlin, Baldwin's Ohio Practice, Merrick-Rippner Probate Law § 21:46, Rights of Surviving Spouse to Elect to Receive Mansion House—Procedure—Application for Certificate of Transfer.

Carlin, Baldwin's Ohio Practice, Merrick-Rippner Probate Law § 21:48, Rights of Surviving Spouse to Payment of Specific Monetary Share—Valuation of Monetary Share.

Carlin, Baldwin's Ohio Practice, Merrick-Rippner Probate Law § 21:51, Rights of Surviving Spouse—Family Allowance—Distribution.

Carlin, Baldwin's Ohio Practice, Merrick-Rippner Probate Law § 21:52, Rights of Surviving Spouse—Family Allowance—Reduction.

Carlin, Baldwin's Ohio Practice, Merrick-Rippner Probate Law § 21:55, Rights of Surviving Spouse—Family Allowance—Estate of Nonresident Decedent.

Carlin, Baldwin's Ohio Practice, Merrick-Rippner Probate Law § 21:58, Rights of Surviving Spouse—Mansion House—Right to Remain in House for One Year.

Carlin, Baldwin's Ohio Practice, Merrick-Rippner Probate Law § 21:77, Rights of Surviving Spouse—Right to Receive Motor Vehicles, Boat or Outboard Motor—Automobile or Truck Owned by Decedent.

Carlin, Baldwin's Ohio Practice, Merrick-Rippner Probate Law § 30:23, Drafting a Will—Surviving Spouse—Bequest in Lieu of Statutory Rights.

Carlin, Baldwin's Ohio Practice, Merrick-Rippner Probate Law § 30:25, Drafting a Will—Surviving Spouse—Disinheritance of Spouse.

Carlin, Baldwin's Ohio Practice, Merrick-Rippner Probate Law § 89:12, Payment of Debts—Allowance for Support of Surviving Spouse and Minor Children—Distribution.

Carlin, Baldwin's Ohio Practice, Merrick-Rippner Probate Law § 89:15, Payment of Debts—Allowance for Support of Surviving Spouse and Minor Children—Estate of Nonresident Decedent.

Carlin, Baldwin's Ohio Practice, Merrick-Rippner Probate Law § 91:13, Land Sale—Not to Pay for Claims of Surviving Spouse.

Carlin, Baldwin's Ohio Practice, Merrick-Rippner Probate Law § 92:14, Dower—Nature of Interest.

Carlin, Baldwin's Ohio Practice, Merrick-Rippner Probate Law § 96:15, Mortgages, Judgments, and Liens.

Carlin, Baldwin's Ohio Practice, Merrick-Rippner Probate Law § 100:10, Antenuptial or Separation Agreement—Effect on Probate Formalities.

Carlin, Baldwin's Ohio Practice, Merrick-Rippner Probate Law § 30:126, Barring Spouse from Some Rights in Estate, But Not All—Form.

Carlin, Baldwin's Ohio Practice, Merrick-Rippner Probate Law App B SPF 1.0, Surviving Spouse, Children, Next of Kin, Legatees and Devisees.

Carlin, Baldwin's Ohio Practice, Merrick-Rippner Probate Law App B SPF 5.1, Assets and Liabilities of Estate to be Relieved from Administration—Form.

Carlin, Baldwin's Ohio Practice, Merrick-Rippner Probate Law App B SPF 6.0, Inventory and Appraisal—Form.

Carlin, Baldwin's Ohio Practice, Merrick-Rippner Probate Law App B SPF 7.1, Application for Family Allowance—Form.

Carlin, Baldwin's Ohio Practice, Merrick-Rippner Probate Law App B SPF 7.2, Application for Apportionment of Family Allowance—Form.

Carlin, Baldwin's Ohio Practice, Merrick-Rippner Probate Law App B SPF 1.0A, Surviving Spouse, Next of Kin, Legatees and Devisees (Decedent Dying on or After 5-31-90).

Kuehnle and Levey, Ohio Real Estate Law and Practice § 52:7, Statutory Fiduciary Sales—Grounds for Judicial Sale—Payment of Debts.

Kuehnle and Levey, Ohio Real Estate Law and Practice § 52:8, Statutory Fiduciary Sales—Grounds for Judicial Sale—Payment of Legacies.

Law Review and Journal Commentaries

House Bill 85, Probate Reform Bill 2001: A Noble Experiment. Marilyn J. Maag, 12 Prob L J Ohio 21 (November/December 2001).

How the Family Fares: A Comparison of the Uniform Probate Code and the Ohio Probate Reform Act, Donald L. Robertson. 37 Ohio St L J 321 (1976).

The Impact of H.B. 85 Upon the Allowance of Support to a Surviving Spouse: Must a spouse affirmatively claim it? Is there a time limit to its payment, with or without a claim?, C. Terry Johnson. 13 Prob L J Ohio 80 (March/April 2003).

The Surviving Spouse and the Family Truck, David A. Allen. 10 Prob L J Ohio 71 (May/June 2000).

Trusts and the Young Case: Planning for disabled beneficiaries, William J. Browning. 11 Ohio Law 6 (November/December 1997).

Notes of Decisions

Ed. Note: This section contains annotations from former RC 2117.20 and RC 2115.13.

Allowance as debt of estate 3
Bankruptcy effect 4
Claim for allowance barred 1
Claim for allowance not barred 2

---

1. Claim for allowance barred

Implicit in the grant of the legal separation was the termination of the rights of the surviving spouse, and thus, after wife's death, husband was not entitled to "allowance for support" or "a family allowance" as surviving spouse; legal separation decree extensively addressed the property and support rights of the separating parties. In re Estate of Ramminger (Ohio App. 12 Dist., Butler, 07-14-2003) No. CA2002-08-189, 2003-Ohio-3697, 2003 WL 21637943, Unreported, appeal not allowed 100 Ohio St.3d 1486, 798 N.E.2d 1093, 2003-Ohio-5992. Divorce ⇐ 314

Will bequest of $1 in lieu of statutory support precluded testator's surviving spouse from support after time for spouse to elect against the will had expired; spouse was conclusively presumed to have elected to take under will. In re Estate of Reddick (Ohio App. 3 Dist., 04-11-1995) 102 Ohio App.3d 488, 657 N.E.2d 531. Executors And Administrators ⇐ 186

The allowance for surviving minors provided by RC 2117.20 is a benefit within the meaning of RC 2105.19 and is therefore forbidden to the murderer of the decedent. Bosley v. Hawkins (Ohio Com.Pl. 1985) 24 Ohio Misc.2d 11, 494 N.E.2d 460, 24 O.B.R. 332.

A common-law marriage entered into in Ohio between an uncle and his niece is incestuous and void ab initio and thus the niece is not entitled to the statutory widow's allowance upon the death of her uncle whom she claims was her common-law husband. In re Stiles Estate (Ohio 1979) 59 Ohio St.2d 73, 391 N.E.2d 1026, 13 O.O.3d 62.

When the evidence relating to exceptions to an inventory and final account shows that the surviving spouse has, on numerous occasions, counseled and directed the administratrix of her husband's estate to pay the bills of the estate, even if such payment would result in no money being left for distribution to the surviving spouse, stating as her reason that her husband never had any bills that were not paid, and the surviving spouse has offered no evidence of probative value to the contrary, it is clearly apparent that she has waived the determination and payment or allowance to her of the year's allowance and the property exempt from administration. In re Burchett's Estate (Marion 1968) 16 Ohio App.2d 45, 241 N.E.2d 787, 45 O.O.2d 133. Executors And Administrators ⇔ 189

By delaying eight years after her husband's death in seeking her year's allowance a widow loses her right thereto, as well as her right to exempt property. In re Gardner's Estate (Ohio Com.Pl. 1959) 160 N.E.2d 20, 81 Ohio Law Abs. 250, 13 O.O.2d 293, affirmed 112 Ohio App. 462, 176 N.E.2d 316, 16 O.O.2d 349.

An adult man and woman, each owning a substantial amount of property and each having grown children by prior marriages, may lawfully enter into a prenuptial agreement whereby each relinquishes every and all rights in the property of the other, and, where such an agreement is duly executed, the parties subsequently marry and thereafter the husband dies, the widow is barred from any part of his estate, including the special benefits conferred on the widow by statute and the privilege of administering the estate, where the agreement by its clear wording shows that such a result was intended. Troha v. Sneller (Ohio 1959) 169 Ohio St. 397, 159 N.E.2d 899, 8 O.O.2d 435. Descent And Distribution ⇔ 62; Executors And Administrators ⇔ 19; Executors And Administrators ⇔ 185

A widow who, freely and with equal knowledge of the facts and law, entered into a contract with the other beneficiaries under the will of her deceased husband, before an inventory of the estate was made, thereby releasing her claims against the estate in consideration of immediate payment by such beneficiaries to her of what the will provided for her and a specified sum for her year's support, is not, after performance of the contract, and discovery that her rights under the law far exceeded the amount she received under the settlement, entitled to rescission of the contract for mistake merely because of a disproportion between the amount which she got under the agreement and the amount she would have received under the law. Carnahan v. Carnahan (Clinton 1959) 109 Ohio App. 350, 159 N.E.2d 795, 11 O.O.2d 142.

Where a man and woman enter into a prenuptial agreement whereby each relinquishes all rights in the property of the other, the parties thereafter marry, and, subsequently, while they are on a trip to Europe, the husband dies, but the widow does not accompany his body on its return home but continues on the European trip for a period of three months without evincing any interest in the affairs of her deceased husband, she is barred from all rights in his estate, including statutory benefits and the priority in the right to administer the estate. Troha v. Sneller (Cuyahoga 1958) 108 Ohio App. 153, 151 N.E.2d 595, 79 Ohio Law Abs. 74, 9 O.O.2d 195, affirmed 169 Ohio St. 397, 159 N.E.2d 899, 8 O.O.2d 435.

On the record an antenuptial contract signed by decedent's surviving spouse barred her from her exempt property allowance, year's allowance, and right to occupy the mansion house. Troha v. Sneller (Cuyahoga 1958) 108 Ohio App. 153, 151 N.E.2d 595, 79 Ohio Law Abs. 74, 9 O.O.2d 195, affirmed 169 Ohio St. 397, 159 N.E.2d 899, 8 O.O.2d 435.

A surviving spouse may have waived any right to her husband's estate set off to her by statute by virtue of a separation agreement. Burlovic v. Farmer (Cuyahoga 1953) 96 Ohio App. 403, 115 N.E.2d 411, 54 O.O. 399, affirmed 162 Ohio St. 46, 120 N.E.2d 705, 54 O.O. 5.

Appraisers were without authority to set off a year's allowance to widow of testator who though maintaining a residence in Ohio was domiciled in another state at time of his death, and probate court was without jurisdiction to approve inventory and appraisement with the year's allowance fixed by the appraisers. In re McCombs' Estate (Ohio Prob. 1948) 80 N.E.2d 573, 52 Ohio Law Abs. 353. Executors And Administrators ⇔ 193

Where no claim by a widow for her year's support was asserted at the time her husband's estate was being settled, the settlement made by an administrator will not be opened up forty years after the estate was closed in order to let in the widow's claim for the first year's support. Evans v. Evans (Ohio Cir. 1909) 21 Ohio C.D. 635, 13 Ohio C.C.(N.S.) 62, affirmed 83 Ohio St. 482, 94 N.E. 1106, 8 Ohio Law Rep. 525.

Where by the language of a will it is plainly shown to be the intention of the testator that to bar his widow of a first year's support, and a provision is made for her in lieu thereof, if she elects to take under the will she is not entitled to a year's support. In re Witner's Estate (Ohio Prob. 1900) 10 Ohio Dec. 30, 7 Ohio N.P. 143. Wills ⇔ 800

2. Claim for allowance not barred

Where a husband makes a post-nuptial provision for his wife in lieu of dower and all claims against his estate which she accepts, and he dies intestate, she is not thereby barred of her right to the year's support provided by law out of his estate. Spangler v. Dukes (Ohio 1884) 39 Ohio St. 642.

Where a widow dies without waiving or relinquishing her right to a year's allowance for support as required by statute, and the appraisers neglected to set off and allow to such widow her year's allowance, the right to the allowance survives to her personal representative notwithstanding that the widow's death came after the year's time. Bane v. Wick (Ohio 1863) 14 Ohio St. 505.

An antenuptial contract which makes provision for the wife in case of her survivorship and is expressed to be "in bar and full satisfaction of all such part or share of the personal estate" of her husband which she is entitled to by law will not so operate unless the provisions of the contract in favor of the wife have been fairly performed, and an averment that such contract is valid and binding is not a sufficient averment of such performance. Lowe v. Phillips (Ohio 1863) 14 Ohio St. 308. Dower And Curtesy ⇔ 41; Husband And Wife ⇔ 29(5)

The death of a widow to whom a statutory allowance has been made before the end of a year and before the allowance had been expended in her support does not bar the right of her executor to recover the amount unpaid from her husband's executor, as such allowance confers a vested right of property. Dorah's Adm'r v. Dorah's Ex'r (Ohio 1854) 4 Ohio St. 292.

Where a widow elects to take under her husband's will which contained provisions for her in lieu of dower, she is not thereby barred of her right to the year's support provided by law. Collier v. Collier's Ex'rs (Ohio 1854) 3 Ohio St. 369.

Where difficulties generated by a missing will are not due to any action by the surviving spouse, equity requires that the surviving spouse be given credit for tax payments unknowingly made with respect to the devisee's interest in real property, and a probate court has authority to assess costs as it deems appropriate given an unusual sequence of events. In re Estate of Hudson (Licking 1993) 82 Ohio App.3d 422, 612 N.E.2d 506.

Admission of a will to probate one and one-half years after final administration is approved does not restart the time for presentation of charges against the estate, and it is not error for a probate court to apply the will to real estate which is the only identifiable asset of the estate by the time the will is admitted to probate, finding that the estate should not be reopened and that the will acted only to dispose of the issue of heirship. In re Estate of Hudson (Licking 1993) 82 Ohio App.3d 422, 612 N.E.2d 506.

A surviving spouse taking against a will of a deceased spouse under RC 2107.39 is entitled to the $5,000 statutory allowance under RC 2117.20 unless specifically barred by the will. In re Green's Estate (Ohio Com.Pl. 1980) 63 Ohio Misc. 44, 410 N.E.2d 812, 17 O.O.3d 388.

An illegitimate child whose paternity has been established during the lifetime of the natural father is entitled to a year's allowance for support from the father's estate. In re Estate of Holley (Ohio Com.Pl. 1975) 44 Ohio Misc. 78, 337 N.E.2d 675, 73 O.O.2d 265. Children Out-of-wedlock ⇔ 90

The surviving spouse is entitled to her year's allowance, use of the mansion house and exemptions under RC 2117.20 and RC 2115.13 even though she takes under the will, whether by her voluntary election or by operation of law. Jacobsen v. Cleveland Trust Co. (Ohio Com.Pl. 1965) 6 Ohio Misc. 173, 217 N.E.2d 262, 35 O.O.2d 366. Wills ⇔ 800

Under will which devises "to my husband... amount that he is allowed under laws of Ohio in my estate. I leave him no more than this amount because of his indifferent and careless treatment of me," and then devises all residue to testatrix' sisters and nieces, husband, upon electing to take thereunder, would take that part allowed by law alone and not dependent in any way upon testatrix' bounty; twenty per cent of estate, not less than $500 and not exceeding $2500 and right to reside in mansion house for one year free of charge; should husband elect to take under law he would be entitled to one-half of estate in addition to above. Schardt v. Prexler (Hamilton 1946) 67 N.E.2d 549, 45 Ohio Law Abs. 119.

Although a husband may, by conveyance and trust agreement made during his lifetime, defeat his widow's interest as statutory heir and distributee, yet such conveyance and trust agreement will be constructively fraudulent to extent of wife's statutory right to an allowance for a year's support from estate of husband, and a lien for amount of such allowance will be impressed on real estate conveyed in proportion that value of such real estate bears to total value of such real estate plus value of real estate of which husband died seized. Routson v. Hovis (Hancock 1938) 60 Ohio App. 536, 22 N.E.2d 209, 15 O.O. 38. Executors And Administrators ⇔ 184

Where deceased's estate had not been closed, claim for widow's allowance, made over three years after it could have been made, held not stale. In re Crouse's Estate (Columbiana 1932) 44 Ohio App. 31, 184 N.E. 253, 13 Ohio Law Abs. 652. Executors And Administrators ⇐ 190

Until a husband and wife are divorced, the wife at his death is entitled to a year's support and the articles of personal property mentioned in the statute, notwithstanding that they have lived separate and apart for many years. In re McMillan's Estate (Ohio Cir. 1906) 18 Ohio C.D. 645, 8 Ohio C.C.(N.S.) 294.

A widow, in order to be entitled to her year's allowance upon her husband's death, must establish not only that the marriage relation once existed and was never legally severed, but also that the relation actually existed at the time of the decedent's death, or if it did not exist, that it was against the wishes of the widow and without her fault. In re Roth's Estate (Ohio Prob. 1899) 9 Ohio Dec. 429, 6 Ohio N.P. 498.

The private life of an individual can have no effect upon the widow's right to a year's maintenance so long as the contractual relationship between husband and wife is not dissolved; her right to the year's allowance is a statutory right and is in no wise affected except by divorce. In re Diller (Ohio Prob. 1896) 6 Ohio Dec. 182, 5 Ohio N.P. 255.

Mere lapse of time will not be considered a waiver or relinquishment of the widow and minor children's right to a year's allowance, since they are not required to make a demand to secure it. In re Rierdon's Estate (Ohio Prob. 1898) 5 Ohio Dec. 606, 5 Ohio N.P. 516.

The widow of a bankrupt residing in Ohio is entitled to reside a year in the mansion house of her deceased husband and to an allowance for a year's support for herself and minor children under the Bankruptcy Act of 1898 and the laws of Ohio. In re Parschen (C.C.N.D.Ohio 1902) 119 F. 976.

A widow has no power by any form of ante-nuptial or post-nuptial contract to deprive herself of the statutory year's allowance given to her as widow by statute. Baldwin v Broadstone, 35 B 161 (OS Unrep 1896).

3. Allowance as debt of estate

The statutory allowance of $250 to the widow for herself and the same sum for each minor child is a debt of the estate, to be paid out of estate assets as other debts. Watts v. Watts (Ohio 1882) 38 Ohio St. 480, 8 W.L.B. 287.

The year's allowance to a widow and minor children is a debt of the estate, and payment of such allowance by the executrix is a proper credit on her account. Watts v. Watts (Ohio 1882) 38 Ohio St. 480, 8 W.L.B. 287. Executors And Administrators ⇐ 192

An executor or administrator of an estate should have notice of the proceedings to appoint a new appraiser to make the widow's year's allowance where the appraisers first appointed failed to make such allowance. Heck v. Heck (Ohio 1878) 34 Ohio St. 369, 3 W.L.B. 363.

The probate court is empowered to review and increase the allowance made to the widow's year's support if the action is invoked by a "person interested" other than the widow, such as a creditor of the widow's estate for services and expenses in supporting and taking care of her during the year and up to her death, and such action can be had after the widow's death. Sherman's Ex'r v. Sherman (Ohio 1871) 21 Ohio St. 631.

A year's allowance for the support of the widow and her child is a debt for which real estate may be ordered sold by the court. Allen v. Allen's Adm'r (Ohio 1868) 18 Ohio St. 234.

The value of the statutory allowance taken under RC 2117.20 shall be deducted from the gross estate prior to computing a surviving spouse's interest under RC 2105.06. In re Green's Estate (Ohio Com.Pl. 1980) 63 Ohio Misc. 44, 410 N.E.2d 812, 17 O.O.3d 388. Wills ⇐ 801(4)

Under the provisions of section, the right of a widow to an allowance for support vests immediately upon her husband's death, and becomes a preferred and secured debt of the estate; even though such widow dies within the period of twelve months after the death of her husband and such allowance has not been set off to her during her lifetime, the allowance must be awarded, and such allowance or any unpaid balance thereof survives as an asset of her estate. In re Croke's Estate (Ohio 1951) 155 Ohio St. 434, 99 N.E.2d 483, 44 O.O. 411.

The year's allowance given to a widow by section, is governed by GC 10510–46 (RC 2127.38), so that the widow's claim is subject and subordinate to the claims of judgment lien creditors to the proceeds of the sale of real estate. Dillman v. Warner (Allen 1935) 54 Ohio App. 170, 6 N.E.2d 757, 20 Ohio Law Abs. 459, 7 O.O. 492.

Children under fifteen years of age are entitled to a year's support out of the estate of their mother, the same as such children are entitled to such support out of the estate of their father. (See also In re Glenn, 3 CC(NS) 608, 13 CD 397 (Hamilton 1902).) In re Hinton's Estate (Ohio 1901) 64 Ohio St. 485, 45 W.L.B. 423, 60 N.E. 621.

Where no error was prosecuted nor an appeal taken from a proceeding to sell real estate belonging to a widow's deceased husband to pay debts, allowances made to the widow in such proceeding cannot be collaterally attacked by exception to her account as administratrix of the said estate. In re Hess' Estate (Ohio Cir. 1911) 23 Ohio C.D. 449, 14 Ohio C.C.(N.S.) 463. Executors And Administrators ⇐ 194(6); Homestead ⇐ 150(2)

A child under fifteen is entitled to a year's support out of the estate of her father in addition to the distributive share to which she may be entitled, although such child was never a resident of Ohio. Banse v. Muhme (Ohio Cir. 1897) 7 Ohio C.D. 224. Executors And Administrators ⇐ 180

Where the property consumed by the widow is greater than the allowance to her, which was made after her death, the allowance will be held to have been paid. In re McDermott's Estate (Ohio Com.Pl. 1902) 13 Ohio Dec. 390.

4. Bankruptcy effect

Bankruptcy court could not conclude that widow's allowance to which Chapter 7 debtor was entitled from her deceased husband's probate estate was reasonably necessary for support of debtor or debtor's dependents merely from fact that Ohio legislature had already determined that widows were entitled to $40,000 allowance; rather, whether allowance was reasonably necessary for support was question of fact, which bankruptcy court would have to determine after parties had full and fair opportunity to consider their respective positions. In re Jackson (Bkrtcy.S.D.Ohio, 07-18-2006) 348 B.R. 771. Bankruptcy ⇐ 2802

Chapter 7 debtor could not utilize Ohio probate statutes, which protected her widow's allowance of up to $25,000.00 from claims of her late husband's creditors, in order to exempt, from claims of her own creditors, her interest in insurance renewal commissions earned by her late husband prior to his death; probate statutes did not apply in bankruptcy, and served to protect widow's allowance only from claims of the creditors of debtor's late husband, not from the claims of debtor's own creditors. In re Wicheff (6th Cir.BAP (Ohio), 01-29-1998) 215 B.R. 839. Bankruptcy ⇐ 2762.1; Exemptions ⇐ 37

2106.15 Mansion house

A surviving spouse may remain in the mansion house free of charge for one year, except that such real property may be sold within that time for the payment of debts of the decedent. If the real property is so sold, the surviving spouse shall be compensated from the estate to the extent of the fair rental value for the unexpired term, such compensation to have the same priority in payment of debts of estates as the allowance for support made to the surviving spouse, minor children, or surviving spouse and minor children of the decedent under section 2106.13 of the Revised Code.

(1990 H 346, eff. 5–31–90)

Uncodified Law

1990 H 346, § 3, eff. 5–31–90, reads, in part: (A) Sections 1 and 2 of this act shall apply only to the estates of decedents who die on or after the effective date of this act.

Historical and Statutory Notes

Ed. Note: 2106.15 is former 2117.24, amended and recodified by 1990 H 346, eff. 5–31–90; 1976 S 466; 1953 H 1; GC 10509–79.

Cross References

Right of surviving spouse to remain in mansion house not affected, 2329.83

Library References

Executors and Administrators ⇐175.
Westlaw Topic No. 162.
C.J.S. Executors and Administrators §§ 348 to 352.

Research References

Encyclopedias

OH Jur. 3d Appellate Review § 139, Plain Error.

OH Jur. 3d Decedents' Estates § 117, Under the Statute of Descent and Distribution—Rights in Mansion House.

OH Jur. 3d Decedents' Estates § 235, Restrictions as to Surviving Spouse.

OH Jur. 3d Decedents' Estates § 1304, Rents and Profits—Special Rights of Surviving Spouse.

OH Jur. 3d Decedents' Estates § 1590, Generally; Statutory Order.

OH Jur. 3d Decedents' Estates § 1675, Right to Remain in Mansion House.

Forms

Ohio Forms Legal and Business § 4A:1, Introduction.

Ohio Forms Legal and Business § 24:956, Settlement Among Testator's Legatees and Heirs—Family Home to be Set Aside for Surviving Spouse.

Ohio Forms Legal and Business § 25:301, Authorization and Direction to Trustee to Maintain or Sell, and to Purchase or Build Family Residence.

Ohio Forms and Transactions KP 30.06, Rights of Surviving Spouse.

Treatises and Practice Aids

Sowald & Morganstern, Baldwin's Ohio Practice Domestic Relations Law § 1:5, Terms.

Sowald & Morganstern, Baldwin's Ohio Practice Domestic Relations Law § 4:4, Property Rights During Marriage—Individual Ownership—in General.

Carlin, Baldwin's Ohio Practice, Merrick-Rippner Probate Law § 15:6, Descent and Distribution—Surviving Spouse—in General.

Carlin, Baldwin's Ohio Practice, Merrick-Rippner Probate Law § 2:40, Elective Rights of Surviving Spouse—Election to Take Under Law or Under the Will—Election of Surviving Spouse to Take Under the Will.

Carlin, Baldwin's Ohio Practice, Merrick-Rippner Probate Law § 2:121, Administration of Decedent's Estate—Checklist.

Carlin, Baldwin's Ohio Practice, Merrick-Rippner Probate Law § 21:30, Rights of Surviving Spouse to Make Election—Right to Use of Mansion House and Family Allowance.

Carlin, Baldwin's Ohio Practice, Merrick-Rippner Probate Law § 21:57, Rights of Surviving Spouse—Mansion House—"Mansion House" Defined.

Carlin, Baldwin's Ohio Practice, Merrick-Rippner Probate Law § 21:58, Rights of Surviving Spouse—Mansion House—Right to Remain in House for One Year.

Carlin, Baldwin's Ohio Practice, Merrick-Rippner Probate Law § 30:23, Drafting a Will—Surviving Spouse—Bequest in Lieu of Statutory Rights.

Carlin, Baldwin's Ohio Practice, Merrick-Rippner Probate Law § 89:16, Payment of Debts—Allowance for Support of Surviving Spouse and Minor Children—Mansion House.

Carlin, Baldwin's Ohio Practice, Merrick-Rippner Probate Law § 96:16, Entry Confirming Sale, Ordering Deed and Distribution—Form.

Carlin, Baldwin's Ohio Practice, Merrick-Rippner Probate Law § 96:17, Entry Confirming Sale, Ordering Deed and Distribution Where Entire Interest in Real Estate Sold—Form.

Carlin, Baldwin's Ohio Practice, Merrick-Rippner Probate Law § 21:102, Entry Fixing Value of Mansion House—Form.

Carlin, Baldwin's Ohio Practice, Merrick-Rippner Probate Law § 30:126, Barring Spouse from Some Rights in Estate, But Not All—Form.

Law Review and Journal Commentaries

How the Family Fares: A Comparison of the Uniform Probate Code and the Ohio Probate Reform Act, Donald L. Robertson. 37 Ohio St L J 321 (1976).

Is There Any Constitutional Prohibition Against a Statute That Would Abolish Existing Inchoate Right of Dower?, James P. McAndrews. 55 Title Topics 4 (March 1988).

Notes of Decisions

Ed. Note: This section contains annotations from former RC 2117.24, RC 2115.13, and RC 2117.23.

Antenuptial agreements 1
Effect of other laws 3
Nonresident survivor 6
Purchase 5
Rights retained 4
Use of house 2

---

1. Antenuptial agreements

A prenuptial agreement made by two adult persons who each have a substantial amount of property and grown children from prior marriages which contains strong and unmistakable language designed and intended to deprive the surviving spouse of the special benefits conferred by statute will operate to bar the widow from any part of her deceased husband's estate including the privilege of administering his estate. Troha v. Sneller (Ohio 1959) 169 Ohio St. 397, 159 N.E.2d 899, 8 O.O.2d 435.

Where a man and woman enter into a prenuptial agreement whereby each relinquishes all rights in the property of the other, the parties thereafter marry, and, subsequently, while they are on a trip to Europe, the husband dies, but the widow does not accompany his body on its return home but continues on the European trip for a period of three months without evincing any interest in the affairs of her deceased husband, she is barred from all rights in his estate, including statutory benefits and the priority in the right to administer the estate. Troha v. Sneller (Cuyahoga 1958) 108 Ohio App. 153, 151 N.E.2d 595, 79 Ohio Law Abs. 74, 9 O.O.2d 195, affirmed 169 Ohio St. 397, 159 N.E.2d 899, 8 O.O.2d 435.

On the record an antenuptial contract signed by decedent's surviving spouse barred her from her exempt property allowance, her year's allowance, and her right to occupy the mansion house. Troha v. Sneller (Cuyahoga 1958) 108 Ohio App. 153, 151 N.E.2d 595, 79 Ohio Law Abs. 74, 9 O.O.2d 195, affirmed 169 Ohio St. 397, 159 N.E.2d 899, 8 O.O.2d 435.

2. Use of house

A widow has exclusive possession of the mansion house of her deceased husband for a year, and she is entitled to a reasonable enjoyment of the premises and may personally occupy them or rent them as she deems best. Conger v. Atwood (Ohio 1875) 28 Ohio St. 134, 22 Am.Rep. 462. Executors And Administrators ⇐ 175

Wife was on notice when she endorsed waiver of her marital rights that real estate, i.e., marital home, was being transferred to husband's trust, even though first page of husband's trust declaration stated that he desired to create revocable trust "of the property described in Schedule A hereto annexed," whereas no "Schedule A" was attached; under trust's "Schedule of Beneficiaries and Distributive Shares," residence and its furniture and fixtures were identified with wife as beneficiary, being given right to live there during her lifetime, husband's then-living sons, as beneficiaries, were to evenly divide proceeds from sale of residence after wife's death, and wife also endorsed quitclaim deed transferring residence to trust. Miller v. Miller (Ohio App. 8 Dist., 10-03-2000) 139 Ohio App.3d 512, 744 N.E.2d 778, dismissed, appeal not allowed 91 Ohio St.3d 1445, 742 N.E.2d 143. Trusts ⇐ 25(1)

Surviving spouse is not entitled, within meaning of section providing that a surviving spouse may remain in mansion house of deceased consort free for one year, to money received from rental of an apartment inside mansion house but not a part thereof. Scobey v. Fair (Ashland 1942) 70 Ohio App. 51, 45 N.E.2d 139, 24 O.O. 371. Executors And Administrators ⇐ 175

Section, granting to the surviving spouse of a deceased consort the right to remain in the mansion house for one year free of charge does not entitle a husband living separate and apart from his wife for twenty-five years to the occupancy of the mansion house for one year after the wife's death, where the husband never occupied the property after his separation from his wife and she continued to remain therein until her death. Lonz' Estate v. Glann (Lucas 1940) 66 Ohio App. 467, 35 N.E.2d 153, 20 O.O. 430. Executors And Administrators ⇐ 188

3. Effect of other laws

If the homestead is charged with liens which preclude the assignment of a homestead in the manner prescribed by RS 5437 and RS 5438, the widow is not entitled to anything in lieu of it. In re Martin, 3 D Repr 542 (Prob, Erie 1882).

Husband's transfer of his individually-owned automobile to his trust did not have to be enumerated in trust declaration; as with any other property owned by husband individually, wife would have no claim to automobile during coverture. Miller v. Miller (Ohio App. 8 Dist., 10-03-2000) 139 Ohio App.3d 512, 744 N.E.2d 778, dismissed, appeal not allowed 91 Ohio St.3d 1445, 742 N.E.2d 143. Trusts ⇐ 25(1)

A surviving spouse who has been absent eight months from the mansion house of her husband at the time of his decease, and who is barred by restraining order from being at the marital residence, retains the rights granted by RC 2117.24. Matter of Estate of Johnson (Hancock 1984) 14 Ohio App.3d 235, 470 N.E.2d 492, 14 O.B.R. 264.

The widow of a bankrupt residing in Ohio is entitled to reside a year in the mansion house of her deceased husband and to an allowance for a year's support for herself and minor children under the Bankruptcy Act of 1898 and the laws of Ohio. In re Parschen (C.C.N.D.Ohio 1902) 119 F. 976.

4. Rights retained

Magistrate's unobjected-to failure to rule on whether wife had life interest in marital home after husband's death, and trial judge's unobjected-to failure to recognize this oversight, were plain error, thus requiring remand to address that issue in wife's action alleging, inter alia, that husband's inter vivos trust, as well as statute governing rights of surviving spouse, granted her either unconditional right to live in marital residence, or, if home were occupied by someone else, fair market rental value during that time period. Miller v. Miller (Ohio App. 8 Dist., 10-03-2000) 139 Ohio App.3d 512, 744 N.E.2d 778, dismissed, appeal not allowed 91 Ohio St.3d 1445, 742 N.E.2d 143. Husband And Wife ⇐ 243

The surviving spouse is entitled to her year's allowance, use of the mansion house and exemptions under RC 2117.20 and RC 2115.13 even though she takes under the will, whether by her voluntary election or by operation of law. Jacobsen v. Cleveland Trust Co. (Ohio Com.Pl. 1965) 6 Ohio Misc. 173, 217 N.E.2d 262, 35 O.O.2d 366. Wills ⇐ 800

Under will which devises "to my husband... amount that he is allowed under laws of Ohio in my estate. I leave him no more than this amount because of his indifferent and careless treatment of me," and then devises all residue to testatrix' sisters and nieces, husband, upon electing to take thereunder, would take that part allowed by law alone and not dependent in any way upon testatrix' bounty; twenty per cent of estate, not less than $500 and not exceeding $2500 and right to reside in mansion house for one year free of charge; should husband elect to take under law he would be entitled to one-half of estate in addition to above. Schardt v. Prexler (Hamilton 1946) 67 N.E.2d 549, 45 Ohio Law Abs. 119.

5. Purchase

The entire premises of a double house constitute a mansion house which the surviving spouse may purchase at the appraised value. Dorfmeier v. Dorfmeier (Ohio Prob. 1954) 123 N.E.2d 681, 69 Ohio Law Abs. 15.

6. Nonresident survivor

A year's allowance should be set off to a nonresident surviving spouse in the local estate of a nonresident decedent where the state of her residence does not make provision for widows and children. In re Weatherhead's Estate (Ohio Prob. 1956) 137 N.E.2d 315, 73 Ohio Law Abs. 524. Executors And Administrators ⇐ 181

A surviving spouse though a nonresident is entitled to have set off to her the property deemed exempt from administration provided for by statute in effect at the time her husband died. In re Weatherhead's Estate (Ohio Prob. 1956) 137 N.E.2d 315, 73 Ohio Law Abs. 524.

An allowance for property exempt from administration must be set off to a nonresident surviving spouse in the local estate of a nonresident decedent. In re Mitchell's Estate (Lorain 1954) 97 Ohio App. 443, 127 N.E.2d 39, 51 A.L.R.2d 1020, 56 O.O. 357. Executors And Administrators ⇐ 181

Rights of widow of nonresident decedent in Ohio property owned by decedent, discussed. In re McCombs' Estate (Ohio Prob. 1948) 80 N.E.2d 573, 52 Ohio Law Abs. 353.

2106.16 Surviving spouse may purchase property

A surviving spouse, even though acting as executor or administrator, may purchase the following property, if left by the decedent, and if not specifically devised or bequeathed:

(A) The decedent's interest in the mansion house, including the decedent's title in the parcel of land on which the mansion house is situated and lots or farm land adjacent to the mansion house and used in conjunction with it as the home of the decedent, and the decedent's title in the household goods contained in the mansion house, at the appraised value as fixed by the appraisers;

(B) Except for any automobile that passes to the surviving spouse of the decedent under division (A) of section 2106.18 of the Revised Code, any other real or personal property of the decedent not exceeding, with the decedent's interest in the mansion house and the decedent's title in the land used in conjunction with it, and the decedent's title in the household goods the spouse elects to purchase, one-third of the gross appraised value of the estate, at the appraised value as fixed by the appraisers.

A spouse desiring to exercise this right of purchase with respect to personal property shall file in the probate court an application setting forth an accurate description of the personal property and the election of the spouse to purchase it at the appraised value. No notice is required for the court to hear the application insofar as it pertains to household goods contained in the mansion house. If the application includes other personal property, the court shall cause a notice of the time and place of the hearing of the application with respect to the other personal property to be given to the executor or administrator, the heirs or beneficiaries interested in the estate, and to any other interested persons as the court determines.

A spouse desiring to exercise this right of purchase with respect to an interest in real property shall file in the court a petition containing an accurate description of the real property and naming as defendants the executor or administrator, the persons to whom the real property passes by inheritance or residuary devise, and all mortgagees and other lienholders whose claims affect the real property or any part of it. Spouses of defendants need not be made defendants. The petition shall set forth the election of the surviving spouse to purchase the interest in real property at the appraised value and shall contain a prayer accordingly. A summons upon that petition shall be issued and served on the defendants in the same manner as provided for service of summons in actions to sell real property to pay debts.

No hearing on the application or petition shall be held until the inventory is approved. On the hearing of the application or petition, the finding of the court shall be in favor of the surviving spouse, unless it appears that the appraisement was made as a result of collusion or fraud or that it is so manifestly inadequate that a sale at that price would unconscionably prejudice the rights of the parties in interest or creditors. The action of the court shall not be held to prejudice the rights of lienholders.

Upon a finding in favor of the surviving spouse, the court shall make an entry fixing the terms of payment to the executor or administrator for the property, having regard for the rights of creditors of the estate, and ordering the executor or administrator, or a commissioner who may be appointed and authorized for the purpose, to transfer and convey the property to the spouse upon compliance with the terms fixed by the court. If the court, having regard for the amount of property to be purchased, its appraised value, and the distribution to be made of the proceeds arising from the sale, finds that the original bond given by the executor or administrator is sufficient, the court may dispense with the giving of additional bonds. If the court finds that the original bond is insufficient, as a condition to transfer and conveyance, the court shall require the executor or administrator to execute an additional bond in an amount as the court may fix, with proper surety, conditioned and payable as provided in section 2127.27 of the Revised Code. This section does not prevent the court from ordering transfer and conveyance without bond in cases where the will of a testator provides that the executor need not give bond. The executor or administrator, or a commissioner, then shall execute and deliver to the surviving spouse a proper bill of sale or deed, as the case may be, for the property, and shall make a return to the court.

The death of the surviving spouse prior to the filing of the court's entry fixing the terms of payment for property elected to be purchased shall nullify the election. The real or personal property then shall be free of the right granted in this section.

The application or petition provided for in this section shall not be filed prior to filing the inventory required by section 2115.02 of the Revised Code or later than one month after the approval of that inventory. Failure to file an application or petition within that time nullifies the election with respect to the property required to be included, and the real or personal property then shall be free of the right granted in this section.

(1995 H 156, eff. 3–11–96; 1990 H 346, eff. 5–31–90)

Uncodified Law

1990 H 346, § 3, eff. 5–31–90, reads, in part: (A) Sections 1 and 2 of this act shall apply only to the estates of decedents who die on or after the effective date of this act.

Historical and Statutory Notes

Ed. Note: 2106.16 is former 2113.38, amended and recodified by 1990 H 346, eff. 5–31–90; 1986 S 248; 1975 S 145; 132 v S 398; 125 v 903; 1953 H 1; GC 10509–89.

Amendment Note: 1995 H 156 inserted "Except for any automobile that passes to the surviving spouse of the decedent under division (A) of section 2106.18 of the Revised Code," at the beginning of division (B); and made other nonsubstantive changes.

Cross References

County auditor, compensation for services, 319.54
Service of process, Civ R 73
Transfer of automobile title, 2106.18

Library References

Executors and Administrators ⚖191.
Wills ⚖725.
Westlaw Topic Nos. 162, 409.
C.J.S. Executors and Administrators § 375.
C.J.S. Wills §§ 1619 to 1620.

Baldwin's Ohio Legislative Service, 1990 Laws of Ohio, H 346—LSC Analysis, p 5–87

Research References

Encyclopedias

OH Jur. 3d Actions § 136, Special Proceedings; Statutory Actions.
OH Jur. 3d Cotenancy & Partition § 48, Effect of Surviving Spouse's Election to Purchase.
OH Jur. 3d Cotenancy & Partition § 90, Effect of Decedent's Estates Issues on Jurisdiction.
OH Jur. 3d Decedents' Estates § 120, Under the Statute of Descent and Distribution—Purchase Rights.
OH Jur. 3d Decedents' Estates § 1483, Property Subject to Sale.
OH Jur. 3d Decedents' Estates § 1679, Mansion House, Adjacent Land, and Household Goods.
OH Jur. 3d Decedents' Estates § 1680, Other Property Up to One Third of the Gross Value of the Estate.
OH Jur. 3d Decedents' Estates § 1681, Proceedings for Purchase.

Treatises and Practice Aids

Klein, Darling, & Terez, Baldwin's Ohio Practice Civil Practice § 73:5, Probate Division--Service and Filing of Pleadings and Papers Subsequent to the Original Complaint.
Sowald & Morganstern, Baldwin's Ohio Practice Domestic Relations Law § 1:5, Terms.
Sowald & Morganstern, Baldwin's Ohio Practice Domestic Relations Law § 4:6, Property Rights During Marriage—Individual Ownership—Descent and Distribution.
Carlin, Baldwin's Ohio Practice, Merrick-Rippner Probate Law § 2:42, Elective Rights of Surviving Spouse—Election of Surviving Spouse to Purchase Property—Property Spouse Can Purchase.
Carlin, Baldwin's Ohio Practice, Merrick-Rippner Probate Law § 2:43, Elective Rights of Surviving Spouse—Election of Surviving Spouse to Purchase Property—Time of Election.
Carlin, Baldwin's Ohio Practice, Merrick-Rippner Probate Law § 2:44, Elective Rights of Surviving Spouse—Election of Surviving Spouse to Purchase Property—Application or Complaint to Purchase, Notice and Hearing.
Carlin, Baldwin's Ohio Practice, Merrick-Rippner Probate Law § 2:51, Sale of Decedent's Personal Property.
Carlin, Baldwin's Ohio Practice, Merrick-Rippner Probate Law § 48:2, Property Chargeable With Payment of Debts—Legacies Defined.
Carlin, Baldwin's Ohio Practice, Merrick-Rippner Probate Law § 90:2, Persons Entitled to Bring Land Sale Actions—Other Parties.
Carlin, Baldwin's Ohio Practice, Merrick-Rippner Probate Law § 90:9, Authority for Land Sale Action—Overriding Rights of Surviving Spouse.
Carlin, Baldwin's Ohio Practice, Merrick-Rippner Probate Law § 2:121, Administration of Decedent's Estate—Checklist.
Carlin, Baldwin's Ohio Practice, Merrick-Rippner Probate Law § 21:20, Rights of Surviving Spouse to Make Election—Acceleration of Remainder.
Carlin, Baldwin's Ohio Practice, Merrick-Rippner Probate Law § 21:60, Rights of Surviving Spouse—Purchase of Property.
Carlin, Baldwin's Ohio Practice, Merrick-Rippner Probate Law § 21:62, Rights of Surviving Spouse—Purchase of Other Property at Appraised Value.
Carlin, Baldwin's Ohio Practice, Merrick-Rippner Probate Law § 21:63, Rights of Surviving Spouse—Purchase of Securities.
Carlin, Baldwin's Ohio Practice, Merrick-Rippner Probate Law § 21:64, Rights of Surviving Spouse—Procedure for Purchase—Limitation on Time to Elect.
Carlin, Baldwin's Ohio Practice, Merrick-Rippner Probate Law § 21:67, Rights of Surviving Spouse—Procedure for Purchase—Hearing of Application or Complaint.
Carlin, Baldwin's Ohio Practice, Merrick-Rippner Probate Law § 21:68, Rights of Surviving Spouse—Procedure for Purchase—Objections to Appraised Value.
Carlin, Baldwin's Ohio Practice, Merrick-Rippner Probate Law § 21:69, Rights of Surviving Spouse—Procedure for Purchase—Finding in Favor of Surviving Spouse.
Carlin, Baldwin's Ohio Practice, Merrick-Rippner Probate Law § 21:70, Rights of Surviving Spouse—Procedure for Purchase—Death of Surviving Spouse.
Carlin, Baldwin's Ohio Practice, Merrick-Rippner Probate Law § 21:72, Rights of Surviving Spouse—Procedure for Purchase—Limitations on Purchase—Property Specifically Devised or Bequeathed.
Carlin, Baldwin's Ohio Practice, Merrick-Rippner Probate Law § 21:73, Rights of Surviving Spouse—Procedure for Purchase—Limitations on Purchase—Farm Land Adjacent to Mansion House and Used in Conjunction With It.
Carlin, Baldwin's Ohio Practice, Merrick-Rippner Probate Law § 21:74, Rights of Surviving Spouse—Procedure for Purchase—Limitations on Purchase—Jurisdiction of Court to Estop Election.
Carlin, Baldwin's Ohio Practice, Merrick-Rippner Probate Law § 21:75, Rights of Surviving Spouse—Procedure for Purchase—Limitations on Purchase—Lienholders.
Carlin, Baldwin's Ohio Practice, Merrick-Rippner Probate Law § 21:80, Rights of Surviving Spouse—Right to Receive Motor Vehicles, Boat or Outboard Motor—Transfer With Approval of Probate Court.
Carlin, Baldwin's Ohio Practice, Merrick-Rippner Probate Law § 75:17, Other Transfers of Automobiles, Watercraft and Outboard Motor.
Carlin, Baldwin's Ohio Practice, Merrick-Rippner Probate Law § 79:20, Inventory—Exceptions—Hearing.
Carlin, Baldwin's Ohio Practice, Merrick-Rippner Probate Law § 21:103, Application by Surviving Spouse to Purchase Personal Property at Appraised Value—Form.
Carlin, Baldwin's Ohio Practice, Merrick-Rippner Probate Law § 21:104, Entry Granting Application to Purchase at Appraised Value—Form.
Carlin, Baldwin's Ohio Practice, Merrick-Rippner Probate Law § 21:105, Complaint of Surviving Spouse to Purchase Real Property at Appraised Value—Form.
Carlin, Baldwin's Ohio Practice, Merrick-Rippner Probate Law § 21:106, Entry Granting Complaint to Purchase Real Property at Appraised Value—Form.

Carlin, Baldwin's Ohio Practice, Merrick-Rippner Probate Law § 21:107, Commissioner's Deed—Form.

Carlin, Baldwin's Ohio Practice, Merrick-Rippner Probate Law § 21:108, Entry Confirming Sale of Real Property to Surviving Spouse—Form.

Carlin, Baldwin's Ohio Practice, Merrick-Rippner Probate Law § 21:109, Return of Administrator on Transfer of Property to Surviving Spouse—Form.

Carlin, Baldwin's Ohio Practice, Merrick-Rippner Probate Law § 21:110, Return of Commissioner on Transfer of Property—Form.

Carlin, Baldwin's Ohio Practice, Merrick-Rippner Probate Law § 30:126, Barring Spouse from Some Rights in Estate, But Not All—Form.

Kuehnle and Levey, Ohio Real Estate Law and Practice § 18:1, Ohio State Bar Association Standards of Title Examination.

Kuehnle and Levey, Ohio Real Estate Law and Practice § 52:3, Statutory Fiduciary Sales—21 Statutory Proceedings.

Kuehnle and Levey, Ohio Real Estate Law and Practice § 21:27, Execution—Ohio State Conveyance Fee—RC 319.54(F)(3).

Law Review and Journal Commentaries

How the Family Fares: A Comparison of the Uniform Probate Code and the Ohio Probate Reform Act, Donald L. Robertson. 37 Ohio St L J 321 (1976).

Substitute House Bill 391—Omnibus Probate Bill, William B. McNeil. 7 Prob L J Ohio 2 (September/October 1996).

Notes of Decisions

Ed. Note: This section contains annotations from former RC 2113.38.

Common law curtilage right 7
Incompetence 6
Inventory and appraisement 3
Legacy types 5
Procedural issues 1
Residuary devise 2
Use of property for business 4

---

1. Procedural issues

Surviving spouse who did not elect against decedent's will, and who sought to establish her entitlement to purchase marital residence with offset for her statutory support allowance, failed to establish that will did not expressly bar her from receiving support allowance, where spouse did not provide copy of decedent's will to trial court. Frinkley v. Meeker (Ohio App. 11 Dist., Portage, 12-10-2004) No. 2004-P-0022, 2004-Ohio-6696, 2004 WL 2860402, Unreported, appeal not allowed 105 Ohio St.3d 1518, 826 N.E.2d 315, 2005-Ohio-1880. Executors And Administrators ⚖ 186

Trial court in surviving spouse's declaratory judgment action seeking to establish her right to purchase marital residence with offset for her statutory support allowance could not take judicial notice of probate court proceedings involving probate of decedent's will; consideration of material outside the record prevented Court of Appeals from reviewing whether trial court properly interpreted the material. Frinkley v. Meeker (Ohio App. 11 Dist., Portage, 12-10-2004) No. 2004-P-0022, 2004-Ohio-6696, 2004 WL 2860402, Unreported, appeal not allowed 105 Ohio St.3d 1518, 826 N.E.2d 315, 2005-Ohio-1880. Evidence ⚖ 43(4)

It is mandatory that widow's application to purchase be filed within one month after approval of inventory. Palmer v. Smith (Cuyahoga 1939) 28 Ohio Law Abs. 673.

The adversary proceeding contemplated by RC 2113.38 should permit a defendant the opportunity to have pretrial discovery in the form of an independent appraisal. Bratanov v. Riemenschneider (Summit 1980) 1 Ohio App.3d 42, 439 N.E.2d 434, 1 O.B.R. 251. Executors And Administrators ⚖ 194(1)

Where a valid judgment entry has been made in favor of the petition of a surviving spouse to purchase an interest in real estate pursuant to RC 2113.38, and fixing the terms of payment therefor, the subsequent death of that spouse will not nullify the right to purchase on those terms. In re Witteman's Estate (Ohio 1969) 21 Ohio St.2d 3, 254 N.E.2d 345, 50 O.O.2d 2. Wills ⚖ 725

Exercise of the right of the surviving spouse to purchase the mansion house deprives a court of any jurisdiction in partition, even though such election was made more than sixty days after an administrator was appointed but before the inventory was filed. Strawser v. Stanton (Ohio Com.Pl. 1952) 103 N.E.2d 797, 66 Ohio Law Abs. 121, 47 O.O. 255, appeal dismissed 106 N.E.2d 672, 66 Ohio Law Abs. 124.

Probate court has jurisdiction under the provisions of GC 10501–53 (RC 2101.24), to determine whether a surviving spouse is estopped by a contract from electing to take the mansion house at the appraised value as fixed by the appraisers in a proceeding instituted under this section. Passoni v. Breehl (Ohio Prob. 1944) 14 Ohio Supp. 100, 41 Ohio Law Abs. 315, 29 O.O. 220.

An election of a surviving spouse to receive a mansion house as part of the spouse's distributive share under RC 2105.062, does not require an additional proceeding to purchase under RC 2113.38. In re Estate of Reynolds, No. 985 (4th Dist Ct App, Ross, 7-1-83).

2. Residuary devise

The fact that the testator owned only one parcel of real estate will not cause his devise of "all" his real property to be a specific devise, so that if there is no other devise of any real property, a devise of "all of my real property" constitutes a residuary devise of the testator's real property. In re Witteman's Estate (Ohio 1969) 21 Ohio St.2d 3, 254 N.E.2d 345, 50 O.O.2d 2.

A residuary bequest of stock to trustees for the purpose of constructing and maintaining a city public library building is specific even although the title may be divested subsequently by failure of the city to provide the necessary sites therefor within twenty years. In re Mellott's Estate (Ohio 1954) 162 Ohio St. 113, 121 N.E.2d 7, 54 O.O. 53.

Devise to testatrix' husband for life of "all real estate located in the Village of Donnelsville, Clark County, Ohio, that I may own at time of my decease," and at his death to testatrix' daughter in fee simple, was a "specific devise" within statute giving surviving spouse right to purchase mansion house if not specifically devised, and surviving husband who elected to renounce will and take under statute did not have right under statute to purchase at appraised value the part of such realty which was specifically devised to testatrix' daughter. In re Reed's Estate (Ohio Prob. 1952) 114 N.E.2d 314, 65 Ohio Law Abs. 129. Wills ⚖ 801(4)

A surviving spouse may purchase the decedent's interest in real property where such property was not specifically devised in the decedent's will, but passed under a residual clause. In re Estate of Lahmers, No. 91-AP-110088 (5th Dist Ct App, Tuscarawas, 8-24-92).

3. Inventory and appraisement

Under these provisions the widow electing to take property at the appraisement stands on the footing of a preferred purchaser, and the preference consists in her having the privilege of purchasing at the price fixed by the appraisement, instead of being required to buy at the price determined by competition at the sale; in other respects, she is required to conform to the conditions prescribed for other purchasers. Overturf v. Wear (Ohio 1875) 26 Ohio St. 538.

Term "distributive share" contemplates that which a widow may take at its appraised value by virtue of this section and includes both real estate and personal property. Seman v. Seman (Darke 1935) 19 Ohio Law Abs. 600.

Decedent's son, who claimed, in his answer to petition of decedent's surviving spouse to purchase the "mansion house" at appraised value pursuant to statute, that the appraisement was manifestly inadequate, should have been permitted to have independent appraisal made of the property to enable him to prove his contentions, and trial court erred in ordering sale of the property without hearing required by statute and without determining whether or not surviving spouse was legally or equitably entitled to benefits of the statute. Bratanov v. Riemenschneider (Summit 1980) 1 Ohio App.3d 42, 439 N.E.2d 434, 1 O.B.R. 251. Executors And Administrators ⚖ 194(6)

Filing an objection to the inventory and appraisement is not a condition precedent to attacking the appraisement under RC 2113.38, nor a waiver of any rights. Bratanov v. Riemenschneider (Summit 1980) 1 Ohio App.3d 42, 439 N.E.2d 434, 1 O.B.R. 251. Executors And Administrators ⚖ 194(4)

RC 2113.38 contemplates an adversary-type proceeding in which the defendants—the heirs, devisees, legatees, lienholders et al.—are given the opportunity to show the presence of fraud, collusion or the manifest inadequacy of the price fixed in the inventory, and if the evidence obtained shows fraud, collusion or the manifest inadequacy of the price, the court shall order a reappraisal as provided in RC 2115.17; if these items are not shown, the price fixed in the inventory is final. Bratanov v. Riemenschneider (Summit 1980) 1 Ohio App.3d 42, 439 N.E.2d 434, 1 O.B.R. 251.

When devisees, other than the surviving spouse, have added substantial value to the mansion house after the appraisement, the surviving spouse is not entitled to purchase the property at the appraisement price. Wobser v. Tanner (Ohio 1979) 60 Ohio St.2d 28, 396 N.E.2d 753, 14 O.O.3d 195.

Where, in the administration of an estate, a motion to vacate and set aside an order previously entered approving and confirming an inventory filed therein is timely filed by the surviving spouse, although not within one month after such order approving such inventory, and is subsequently found to be well taken and an order is thereupon entered that such previously approved inventory be modified by the deletion therefrom of certain personal property and by increasing the amount of the widow's year's allowance, such order of modification does not constitute a vacation of the previous order of approval so as to reinstate in such surviving spouse the right of election to purchase the mansion house for the one-month period from the date of such order of modification. In re Hrabnicky's Estate (Ohio 1958) 167 Ohio St. 507, 149 N.E.2d 909, 5 O.O.2d 181. Executors And Administrators ⇒ 67; Executors And Administrators ⇒ 191

RC 2113.38 does not authorize the court to require the surviving spouse to pay more than the appraised value for the property. In re Fouts' Estate (Clark 1957) 103 Ohio App. 313, 145 N.E.2d 440, 3 O.O.2d 353.

The appraisement of property of a decedent is made as of the time of such decedent's death, and a surviving spouse electing to purchase at the appraised value takes such property as evaluated as of the date of death. In re Fouts' Estate (Clark 1957) 103 Ohio App. 313, 145 N.E.2d 440, 3 O.O.2d 353. Executors And Administrators ⇒ 67; Executors And Administrators ⇒ 191

When a spouse dies possessed of a mansion house which is encumbered with a mortgage given to secure a note of the deceased spouse, and the surviving spouse elects to purchase said mansion house at the appraised value as fixed by the appraisers, such surviving spouse is not required to pay the balance due on said mortgage in addition to the value fixed by the appraisers, and the executor shall pay it even though the mortgagee did not present its claim within four months. McAdams v. Bolsinger (Ohio Prob. 1950) 129 N.E.2d 878, 71 Ohio Law Abs. 531, 57 O.O. 338.

In the administration of a decedent's estate, where, pursuant to section, surviving spouse elects to purchase mansion house at its appraised value and such election is denied by probate court on ground that lot containing mansion house also contained a business building and lot was appraised as a whole, such surviving spouse is entitled, on motion to have appraisal set aside and a reappraisement made to remove such bar to his election, even though surviving spouse, as administrator, had effected appraisal. In re Burgoon's Estate (Henry 1947) 81 Ohio App. 370, 79 N.E.2d 682, 37 O.O. 210.

Probate court must approve election of surviving spouse to purchase the mansion house of a decedent at appraised value as fixed by the appraisers, under section, unless it is affirmatively shown (1) that such spouse is estopped from making such election to purchase, or (2) that the mansion house was specifically devised, or (3) that the appraisement was the result of collusion or fraud, or (4) that the price to be paid is so inadequate as to prejudice the rights of heirs or creditors. Passoni v. Breehl (Ohio Prob. 1944) 14 Ohio Supp. 100, 41 Ohio Law Abs. 315, 29 O.O. 220.

Where decedent, a few days before his death, placed a down-payment on a car which he orally agreed to buy and after his death decedent's wife completed the purchase, said wife is not entitled to reimbursement by the estate for her payment of the balance paid for the car where the car dealer made no formal or informal claims upon the estate to complete the purchase. In re Estate of DiBlasio, No. 82 C.A. 25 (7th Dist Ct App, Mahoning, 5–19–83).

4. Use of property for business

A surviving spouse may purchase at the appraised value the interest of the decedent in a farm which had been owned in common by the spouse and the decedent, jointly operated by them as a farm, and used by them as their residence, with all the parts of the farm being combined to make up the "farm home," and not as a business or commercial enterprise so as to deprive the spouse of such right, even though both husband and wife had outside employment. Young v. Young (Madison 1958) 106 Ohio App. 206, 154 N.E.2d 19, 6 O.O.2d 458.

A surviving spouse has the right to purchase, at the appraised value, an entire farm, where such farm land and the buildings thereon were used in conjunction with the mansion house in establishing and maintaining a home for the decedent and his family. In re Clark's Estate (Ross 1956) 102 Ohio App. 200, 141 N.E.2d 890, 2 O.O.2d 185.

Where husband and wife, occupied a nondivisible urban house as a home, fact that part of house was used for rental purposes, which were not so pretentious that occupancy of the home was merely incidental to commercial use of premises, did not destroy mansion house character of premises involved within meaning of statute permitting widow to purchase mansion house at appraised price. Dorfmeier v. Dorfmeier (Ohio Prob. 1954) 123 N.E.2d 681, 69 Ohio Law Abs. 15. Executors And Administrators ⇒ 181

The entire premises of a double house constitute a mansion house which the surviving spouse may purchase at the appraised value. Dorfmeier v. Dorfmeier (Ohio Prob. 1954) 123 N.E.2d 681, 69 Ohio Law Abs. 15.

Section does not entitle a surviving spouse to purchase at appraised value entire lot on which mansion house is situated where there are located on same lot two other buildings which are rented and used for business purposes not in conjunction with mansion house, but limits spouse to purchase of only that portion of lot which is not occupied by other buildings. In re Burgoon's Estate (Henry 1946) 80 Ohio App. 465, 76 N.E.2d 310, 36 O.O. 200. Executors And Administrators ⇒ 191

Where decedent's farm was composed of three parcels separated by public roads and had been operated as a single unit for many years, decedent's spouse was entitled to purchase all such property at the appraised value, and not just the parcel upon which the residence was located. In re Estate of Clark, 74 Abs 460, 141 NE(2d) 259 (Prob, Ross 1955), affirmed by 102 App 200, 141 NE(2d) 890 (App, Ross 1956).

5. Legacy types

The authority of a surviving spouse to elect to purchase property "not specifically devised or bequeathed," as provided by RC 2113.38, applies to general, as opposed to a specific legacy, as determined by usual principles of testamentary law. In re Witteman's Estate (Franklin 1968) 15 Ohio App.2d 126, 239 N.E.2d 107, 44 O.O.2d 255, affirmed 21 Ohio St.2d 3, 254 N.E.2d 345, 50 O.O.2d 2.

A devise by a testatrix of all real estate in a specific town is a specific devise, and the surviving spouse has no right to purchase the real estate at the appraised value, whether he takes under or against the will, since the rejection of a will does not nullify and invalidate the plain intent of the testatrix. In re Reed's Estate (Ohio Prob. 1952) 114 N.E.2d 314, 65 Ohio Law Abs. 129.

Testator held to have made a specific bequest of stock under the terms of the will therein involved. In re Mellott's Estate (Ohio Prob. 1953) 113 N.E.2d 780, 65 Ohio Law Abs. 182, 50 O.O. 517, affirmed 162 Ohio St. 113, 121 N.E.2d 7, 54 O.O. 53.

It is a rule of the courts to construe legacies of a doubtful nature as general or demonstrative rather than specific. In re Mellott's Estate (Ohio Prob. 1953) 113 N.E.2d 780, 65 Ohio Law Abs. 182, 50 O.O. 517, affirmed 162 Ohio St. 113, 121 N.E.2d 7, 54 O.O. 53. Wills ⇒ 750

The distinction between specific and general legacies is that a specific legacy singles out the particular thing which the testator intends the donee to have, no regard being had to its value, while general legacies are payable out of the general assets, the chief element being the quantity or its value. In re Mellott's Estate (Ohio Prob. 1953) 113 N.E.2d 780, 65 Ohio Law Abs. 182, 50 O.O. 517, affirmed 162 Ohio St. 113, 121 N.E.2d 7, 54 O.O. 53. Wills ⇒ 753; Wills ⇒ 756

The use of the word "my" in reference to stock which is the subject of a bequest is convincing evidence of an intention to make the gift specific. In re Mellott's Estate (Ohio Prob. 1953) 113 N.E.2d 780, 65 Ohio Law Abs. 182, 50 O.O. 517, affirmed 162 Ohio St. 113, 121 N.E.2d 7, 54 O.O. 53. Wills ⇒ 754

6. Incompetence

A guardian of an incompetent surviving spouse may obtain approval for the purchase of the mansion house of the decedent. Dorfmeier v. Dorfmeier (Ohio Prob. 1954) 123 N.E.2d 681, 69 Ohio Law Abs. 15.

7. Common law curtilage right

The words and phrases describing the real property subject to purchase by the surviving spouse under RC 2113.38 may, under proper circumstances, contemplate a larger amount of property than that which would ordinarily fall within the limits of the curtilage of common law. Nagel v. Wilcox (Lorain 1957) 104 Ohio App. 534, 150 N.E.2d 667, 5 O.O.2d 267.

The rights given by RC 2113.38 extend beyond the common law right of curtilage. In re Estate of Clark, 74 Abs 460, 141 NE(2d) 259 (Prob, Ross 1955), affirmed by 102 App 200, 141 NE(2d) 890 (App, Ross 1956).

2106.18 Right of surviving spouse to automobiles of decedent

(A) Upon the death of a married resident who owned at least one automobile at the time of death, the interest of the deceased spouse in up to two automobiles that are not transferred to the surviving spouse due to joint ownership with right of survivorship established under section 2131.12 of the Revised Code, that are not transferred to a transfer-on-death beneficiary or beneficiaries designated under section 2131.13 of the Revised Code, and that are not otherwise specifically disposed of by testamentary disposition may be selected by the surviving spouse. This interest shall immediately pass to the surviving spouse upon transfer of the title or titles in accordance with section 4505.10 of the Revised Code. The sum total of the values of the automobiles selected by a surviving spouse under this division, as specified in the affidavit that the surviving spouse executes pursuant to division (B) of section 4505.10 of the Revised Code, shall not exceed forty thousand dollars. Each automobile that passes to a surviving spouse under this division shall not be considered an estate asset and shall not be included in the estate inventory.

(B) The executor or administrator, with the approval of the probate court, may transfer title to an automobile owned by the decedent to any of the following:

(1) The surviving spouse, when the automobile is purchased by the surviving spouse pursuant to section 2106.16 of the Revised Code;

(2) A distributee;

(3) A purchaser.

(C) The executor or administrator may transfer title to an automobile owned by the decedent without the approval of the probate court to any of the following:

(1) A legatee entitled to the automobile under the terms of the will;

(2) A distributee if the distribution of the automobile is made without court order pursuant to section 2113.55 of the Revised Code;

(3) A purchaser if the sale of the automobile is made pursuant to section 2113.39 of the Revised Code.

(D) As used in division (A) of this section, "automobile" includes a motorcycle and includes a truck if the truck was used as a method of conveyance by the deceased spouse or the deceased spouse's family when the deceased spouse was alive.

(2005 H 246, eff. 3–29–06; 2002 H 345, eff. 7–23–02; 2000 H 313, eff. 8–29–00; 1995 H 156, eff. 3–11–96; 1994 H 458, eff. 7–20–94; 1990 H 346, eff. 5–31–90)

Uncodified Law

1990 H 346, § 3, eff. 5–31–90, reads, in part: (A) Sections 1 and 2 of this act shall apply only to the estates of decedents who die on or after the effective date of this act.

Historical and Statutory Notes

Ed. Note: 2106.18 is former 2113.532, amended and recodified by 1990 H 346, eff. 5–31–90; 1984 S 260; 1982 H 620; 1977 S 277; 1976 S 466; 1975 S 145; 1970 S 185.

Amendment Note: 2005 H 246 inserted "a motorcycle and includes" in division (D).

Amendment Note: 2002 H 345 substituted "2131.12" for "2106.17"; inserted "that are not transferred to a transfer-on-death beneficiary or beneficiaries designated under section 2131.13 of the Revised Code,"; and made other nonsubstantive changes in division (A).

Amendment Note: 2000 H 313 deleted "appraised" after "The sum total of the" and "and stated" after "and shall not be included" and inserted "as specified in the affidavit that the surviving spouse executes pursuant to division (B) of section 4505.10 of the Revised Code" in division (A); deleted "if the deceased spouse did not own an automobile and" after "includes a truck" in division (D); and made changes to reflect gender neutral language.

Amendment Note: 1995 H 156 substituted "up to two automobiles" for "one automobile" and added the third sentence in division (A); and made other nonsubstantive changes.

Amendment Note: 1994 H 458 inserted "that is not transferred to the surviving spouse due to joint ownership with right of survivorship established under section 2106.17 of the Revised Code," in division (A).

Cross References

Application for certificate of motor vehicle title, conditions, procedures, odometer reading, 4505.06
Certificate of motor vehicle title when ownership changed by operation of law, 4505.10
Odometer Rollback and Disclosure Act, transfer defined, 4549.41

Library References

Executors and Administrators ⚖191.
Wills ⚖801(1).
Westlaw Topic Nos. 162, 409.
C.J.S. Executors and Administrators § 375.
C.J.S. Wills §§ 1841, 1866 to 1868.
Baldwin's Ohio Legislative Service, 1990 Laws of Ohio, H 346—LSC Analysis, p 5–87

Research References

Encyclopedias

OH Jur. 3d Automobiles & Other Vehicles § 67, Change of Ownership by Operation of Law.
OH Jur. 3d Decedents' Estates § 118, Under the Statute of Descent and Distribution—Support Allowance.
OH Jur. 3d Decedents' Estates § 119, Under the Statute of Descent and Distribution—Motor Vehicles and Boats.
OH Jur. 3d Decedents' Estates § 120, Under the Statute of Descent and Distribution—Purchase Rights.
OH Jur. 3d Decedents' Estates § 1483, Property Subject to Sale.
OH Jur. 3d Decedents' Estates § 1610, Necessity of Court Order.
OH Jur. 3d Decedents' Estates § 1641, Distribution in Kind—Transfer of Automobile Title.
OH Jur. 3d Decedents' Estates § 1677, Right to Automobiles and Boats.
OH Jur. 3d Decedents' Estates § 1680, Other Property Up to One Third of the Gross Value of the Estate.

Forms

Ohio Forms Legal and Business § 24:161, Entire Estate to Spouse—Alternatively to Children—Guardianship of Minors.

Treatises and Practice Aids

Carlin, Baldwin's Ohio Practice, Merrick-Rippner Probate Law § 15:6, Descent and Distribution—Surviving Spouse—in General.
Carlin, Baldwin's Ohio Practice, Merrick-Rippner Probate Law § 2:21, Inventory and Appraisal—Decedent's Automobiles to Spouse, or Motor Vehicle, Boat or Outboard Motor to Surviving Joint Owner.
Carlin, Baldwin's Ohio Practice, Merrick-Rippner Probate Law § 2:22, Inventory and Appraisal—Family Allowance.
Carlin, Baldwin's Ohio Practice, Merrick-Rippner Probate Law § 2:38, Elective Rights of Surviving Spouse—Election to Take Under Law or Under the Will—Elective Share of Surviving Spouse Against the Will.
Carlin, Baldwin's Ohio Practice, Merrick-Rippner Probate Law § 2:45, Elective Rights of Surviving Spouse—Election of Surviving Spouse to Receive Property as Part of Intestate Share and Allowance for Support.
Carlin, Baldwin's Ohio Practice, Merrick-Rippner Probate Law § 21:5, Rights of Surviving Spouse to Make Election—Statutory Provisions—Effect.
Carlin, Baldwin's Ohio Practice, Merrick-Rippner Probate Law § 89:4, Payment of Debts—Order of Payment.

Carlin, Baldwin's Ohio Practice, Merrick-Rippner Probate Law § 2:107, Distribution of Assets—Transfer of Titles to Motor Vehicles, Boat or Outboard Motor.

Carlin, Baldwin's Ohio Practice, Merrick-Rippner Probate Law § 2:121, Administration of Decedent's Estate—Checklist.

Carlin, Baldwin's Ohio Practice, Merrick-Rippner Probate Law § 2:122, Administration of Decedent's Estate—Release—Checklist.

Carlin, Baldwin's Ohio Practice, Merrick-Rippner Probate Law § 21:19, Rights of Surviving Spouse to Make Election—Effect of Election—Generally.

Carlin, Baldwin's Ohio Practice, Merrick-Rippner Probate Law § 21:51, Rights of Surviving Spouse—Family Allowance—Distribution.

Carlin, Baldwin's Ohio Practice, Merrick-Rippner Probate Law § 21:52, Rights of Surviving Spouse—Family Allowance—Reduction.

Carlin, Baldwin's Ohio Practice, Merrick-Rippner Probate Law § 21:62, Rights of Surviving Spouse—Purchase of Other Property at Appraised Value.

Carlin, Baldwin's Ohio Practice, Merrick-Rippner Probate Law § 21:77, Rights of Surviving Spouse—Right to Receive Motor Vehicles, Boat or Outboard Motor—Automobile or Truck Owned by Decedent.

Carlin, Baldwin's Ohio Practice, Merrick-Rippner Probate Law § 21:78, Rights of Surviving Spouse—Right to Receive Motor Vehicles, Boat or Outboard Motor—Motor Vehicle, Boat or Motor Owned Jointly With Right of Survivorship.

Carlin, Baldwin's Ohio Practice, Merrick-Rippner Probate Law § 21:79, Rights of Surviving Spouse—Right to Receive Motor Vehicles, Boat or Outboard Motor—Watercraft or Outboard Motor Owned by Decedent.

Carlin, Baldwin's Ohio Practice, Merrick-Rippner Probate Law § 21:80, Rights of Surviving Spouse—Right to Receive Motor Vehicles, Boat or Outboard Motor—Transfer With Approval of Probate Court.

Carlin, Baldwin's Ohio Practice, Merrick-Rippner Probate Law § 21:81, Rights of Surviving Spouse—Right to Receive Motor Vehicles, Boat or Outboard Motor—Transfer Without Approval of Probate Court.

Carlin, Baldwin's Ohio Practice, Merrick-Rippner Probate Law § 30:23, Drafting a Will—Surviving Spouse—Bequest in Lieu of Statutory Rights.

Carlin, Baldwin's Ohio Practice, Merrick-Rippner Probate Law § 30:25, Drafting a Will—Surviving Spouse—Disinheritance of Spouse.

Carlin, Baldwin's Ohio Practice, Merrick-Rippner Probate Law § 30:88, Automobile, Specific Bequest; Provision If There is More Than One—Form.

Carlin, Baldwin's Ohio Practice, Merrick-Rippner Probate Law § 68:40, Application for Transfer of Motor Vehicle, and Judgment Entry—Form.

Carlin, Baldwin's Ohio Practice, Merrick-Rippner Probate Law § 75:14, Transfer of Automobiles to Surviving Spouse.

Carlin, Baldwin's Ohio Practice, Merrick-Rippner Probate Law § 75:16, Transfer of Motor Vehicle, Watercraft or Outboard Motor to Surviving Joint Owner.

Carlin, Baldwin's Ohio Practice, Merrick-Rippner Probate Law § 75:17, Other Transfers of Automobiles, Watercraft and Outboard Motor.

Carlin, Baldwin's Ohio Practice, Merrick-Rippner Probate Law § 89:12, Payment of Debts—Allowance for Support of Surviving Spouse and Minor Children—Distribution.

Carlin, Baldwin's Ohio Practice, Merrick-Rippner Probate Law App B SPF 5.1, Assets and Liabilities of Estate to be Relieved from Administration—Form.

Ohio Consumer Law § 6:8, Ohio's Odometer Rollback and Disclosure Act—Disclosures.

Law Review and Journal Commentaries

How the Family Fares: A Comparison of the Uniform Probate Code and the Ohio Probate Reform Act, Donald L. Robertson. 37 Ohio St L J 321 (1976).

The Surviving Spouse and the Family Truck, David A. Allen. 10 Prob L J Ohio 71 (May/June 2000).

Notes of Decisions

Ed. Note: This section contains annotations from former RC 2113.532.

Asset of estate   2
Election against will   3

Vehicles included   1

---

1. Vehicles included

A truck not specifically devised in a decedent's will passes to the surviving spouse and is not to be included in the estate. In re Estate of LaMar, No. CA–2070–M (9th Dist Ct App, Medina, 6-24-92).

"Automobile" as used in RC 2113.532 means a "passenger car," except when the decedent did not own a passenger car, in which case "automobile" includes a truck, if the truck was used as a method of conveyance by the deceased spouse or his family when the deceased spouse was alive; where both an automobile i.e., a passenger car, and a truck are left by a decedent, the surviving spouse is entitled to the automobile, but may not select the truck. OAG 83–083.

Pursuant to RC 2113.532, where the decedent left an automobile, a truck, and a motor home or any other type of motor vehicle, the surviving spouse is entitled to the automobile, but may not select from among the motor vehicles. OAG 83–083.

2. Asset of estate

The value of an automobile taken under RC 2113.532 shall not be considered an asset of the estate in computing a surviving spouse's interest under RC 2105.06. In re Green's Estate (Ohio Com.Pl. 1980) 63 Ohio Misc. 44, 410 N.E.2d 812, 17 O.O.3d 388.

A motor vehicle claimed by a surviving spouse under RC 2113.532 is no longer considered an estate asset and the executrix of the estate is relieved of all duties with respect thereto. Seven Seventeen Credit Union Inc v Benner, No. 3780 (11th Dist Ct App, Trumbull, 9–30–87).

Where decedent, a few days before his death, placed a down-payment on a car which he orally agreed to buy and after his death decedent's wife completed the purchase, said wife is not entitled to reimbursement by the estate for her payment of the balance paid for the car where the car dealer made no formal or informal claims upon the estate to complete the purchase. In re Estate of DiBlasio, No. 82 C.A. 25 (7th Dist Ct App, Mahoning, 5–19–83).

3. Election against will

A surviving spouse taking against a will of a deceased spouse is entitled to an automobile under RC 2113.532 if the will does not specifically dispose of said vehicle. In re Green's Estate (Ohio Com.Pl. 1980) 63 Ohio Misc. 44, 410 N.E.2d 812, 17 O.O.3d 388. Wills ⇐ 801(1)

2106.19   Right of surviving spouse to one watercraft or outboard motor of decedent

(A) Upon the death of a married resident who owned at least one watercraft, one outboard motor, or one of each at the time of death, the interest of the deceased spouse in one watercraft, one outboard motor, or one of each that is not otherwise specifically disposed of by testamentary disposition and that is selected by the surviving spouse immediately shall pass to the surviving spouse upon receipt by the clerk of the court of common pleas of both of the following:

(1) The title executed by the surviving spouse;

(2) An affidavit sworn by the surviving spouse stating the date of the decedent's death, a description of the watercraft, outboard motor, or both, its or their approximate value, and that the watercraft, outboard motor, or both are not disposed of by testamentary disposition.

The watercraft, outboard motor, or both shall not be considered an estate asset and shall not be included and stated in the estate inventory.

Transfer of a decedent's interest under this division does not affect the existence of any lien against a watercraft or outboard motor so transferred.

(B) Except for a watercraft, outboard motor, or both transferred as provided in division (A) of this section, the executor or administrator may transfer title to a watercraft or outboard motor in the manner provided for transfer of an automobile under divisions (B) and (C) of section 2106.18 of the Revised Code.

(1994 S 182, eff. 10–20–94)

Cross References

Watercraft, certificate of title, transfer of decedent's interest, 1548.11

Library References

Executors and Administrators ⚖=191.
Wills ⚖=801(1).
Westlaw Topic Nos. 162, 409.
C.J.S. Executors and Administrators § 375.
C.J.S. Wills §§ 1841, 1866 to 1868.

Research References

Encyclopedias

OH Jur. 3d Boats, Ships, & Shipping § 9, Certificate of Title; Manufacturer's or Importer's Certificate—Assignment; Change of Ownership by Operation of Law; Surrender and Cancellation.
OH Jur. 3d Decedents' Estates § 119, Under the Statute of Descent and Distribution—Motor Vehicles and Boats.
OH Jur. 3d Decedents' Estates § 1677, Right to Automobiles and Boats.

Treatises and Practice Aids

Carlin, Baldwin's Ohio Practice, Merrick-Rippner Probate Law § 15:6, Descent and Distribution—Surviving Spouse—in General.
Carlin, Baldwin's Ohio Practice, Merrick-Rippner Probate Law § 2:21, Inventory and Appraisal—Decedent's Automobiles to Spouse, or Motor Vehicle, Boat or Outboard Motor to Surviving Joint Owner.
Carlin, Baldwin's Ohio Practice, Merrick-Rippner Probate Law § 2:38, Elective Rights of Surviving Spouse—Election to Take Under Law or Under the Will—Elective Share of Surviving Spouse Against the Will.
Carlin, Baldwin's Ohio Practice, Merrick-Rippner Probate Law § 21:5, Rights of Surviving Spouse to Make Election—Statutory Provisions—Effect.
Carlin, Baldwin's Ohio Practice, Merrick-Rippner Probate Law § 21:19, Rights of Surviving Spouse to Make Election—Effect of Election—Generally.
Carlin, Baldwin's Ohio Practice, Merrick-Rippner Probate Law § 21:79, Rights of Surviving Spouse—Right to Receive Motor Vehicles, Boat or Outboard Motor—Watercraft or Outboard Motor Owned by Decedent.
Carlin, Baldwin's Ohio Practice, Merrick-Rippner Probate Law § 30:23, Drafting a Will—Surviving Spouse—Bequest in Lieu of Statutory Rights.
Carlin, Baldwin's Ohio Practice, Merrick-Rippner Probate Law § 75:15, Transfer of Watercraft or Outboard Motor to Surviving Spouse.
Carlin, Baldwin's Ohio Practice, Merrick-Rippner Probate Law § 75:17, Other Transfers of Automobiles, Watercraft and Outboard Motor.

2106.20 Reimbursement of funeral expenses to surviving spouse or person with right of disposition

A surviving spouse or a person with the right of disposition under section 2108.70 or 2108.81 of the Revised Code is entitled to a reimbursement from the estate of the decedent for funeral and burial expenses, if paid by the surviving spouse or person with the right of disposition, to the extent that the rights of other creditors of the estate will not be prejudiced by the reimbursement.

(2006 H 426, eff. 10–12–06; 1990 H 346, eff. 5–31–90)

Uncodified Law

1990 H 346, § 3, eff. 5–31–90, reads, in part: (A) Sections 1 and 2 of this act shall apply only to the estates of decedents who die on or after the effective date of this act.

Historical and Statutory Notes

Ed. Note: 2106.20 is former 2117.26, amended and recodified by 1990 H 346, eff. 5–31–90; 129 v 1265; 1953 H 1; GC 10509–125.

Amendment Note: 2006 H 426 rewrote this section which prior thereto read:

"A surviving spouse is entitled to a reimbursement from the estate of the deceased spouse for funeral expenses, if paid by the surviving spouse, to the extent that the rights of other creditors of the estate will not be prejudiced by the reimbursement."

Library References

Wills ⚖=708.
Westlaw Topic No. 409.
C.J.S. Wills §§ 451 to 452.
Baldwin's Ohio Legislative Service, 1990 Laws of Ohio, H 346—LSC Analysis, p 5–87

Research References

Encyclopedias

OH Jur. 3d Decedents' Estates § 1344, Liability for Funeral Expenses of Spouse.
OH Jur. 3d Decedents' Estates § 1345, Liability for Funeral Expenses of Spouse—Effect of Separation.
OH Jur. 3d Decedents' Estates § 1347, Liability for Funeral Expenses of Spouse—Liability of Wife for Husband's Expenses.

Treatises and Practice Aids

Carlin, Baldwin's Ohio Practice, Merrick-Rippner Probate Law § 89:8, Payment of Debts—Funeral Expenses—Reimbursement of Surviving Spouse.
Carlin, Baldwin's Ohio Practice, Merrick-Rippner Probate Law § 91:7, Land Sale—to Pay Medical and Funeral Expenses.
Carlin, Baldwin's Ohio Practice, Merrick-Rippner Probate Law § 2:121, Administration of Decedent's Estate—Checklist.
Carlin, Baldwin's Ohio Practice, Merrick-Rippner Probate Law § 21:82, Rights of Surviving Spouse—Right to Reimbursement for Funeral Expenses.

2106.22 Action to set aside antenuptial or separation agreement

Any antenuptial or separation agreement to which a decedent was a party is valid unless an action to set it aside is commenced within four months after the appointment of the executor or administrator of the estate of the decedent, or unless, within the four-month period, the validity of the agreement otherwise is attacked.

(1990 H 346, eff. 5–31–90)

Uncodified Law

1990 H 346, § 3, eff. 5–31–90, reads, in part: (A) Sections 1 and 2 of this act shall apply only to the estates of decedents who die on or after the effective date of this act.

Historical and Statutory Notes

Ed. Note: 2106.22 is former 2131.03, amended and recodified by 1990 H 346, eff. 5–31–90; 1953 H 1; GC 10512–3.

Library References

Husband and Wife ⚖=29(9), 279(4).
Westlaw Topic No. 205.
Baldwin's Ohio Legislative Service, 1990 Laws of Ohio, H 346—LSC Analysis, p 5–87

Research References

Encyclopedias

OH Jur. 3d Decedents' Estates § 135, Contracts Between Spouses Releasing Inheritance Rights—Antenuptial Agreements.

OH Jur. 3d Decedents' Estates § 195, Enforcement of Contract Between Heirs.

OH Jur. 3d Family Law § 218, Statute of Limitations.

OH Jur. 3d Family Law § 390, Avoidance of Agreement—Limitation of Actions.

Forms

Ohio Jurisprudence Pleading and Practice Forms § 12:11, Checklist—Statutes of Limitations.

Treatises and Practice Aids

Sowald & Morganstern, Baldwin's Ohio Practice Domestic Relations Law § 1:1, Function and Nature.

Sowald & Morganstern, Baldwin's Ohio Practice Domestic Relations Law § 1:7, Enforcing or Attacking the Antenuptial Contract.

Sowald & Morganstern, Baldwin's Ohio Practice Domestic Relations Law § 1:23, Complaint to Set Aside Antenuptial Agreement—Form.

Sowald & Morganstern, Baldwin's Ohio Practice Domestic Relations Law § 9:49, Action to Set Aside Separation Agreement.

Sowald & Morganstern, Baldwin's Ohio Practice Domestic Relations Law § 9:243, Complaint to Set Aside Separation Agreement—Form.

Carlin, Baldwin's Ohio Practice, Merrick-Rippner Probate Law § 100:1, Antenuptial or Separation Agreement—Four-Month Statute of Limitations to Set Aside.

Carlin, Baldwin's Ohio Practice, Merrick-Rippner Probate Law § 100:2, Antenuptial or Separation Agreement—Nature of Attack; Survival of Action.

Law Review and Journal Commentaries

Marriage is a Damnably Serious Business—Especially the Second Time Around!, Ellis V. Rippner. 40 Ohio St B Ass'n Rep 291 (March 6, 1967).

Presentment and Enforcement of Separation Agreements, Anthony R. Fioretta. Ohio B Ass'n Serv Letter, Separation Agreements, May, 1970; June, 1970.

Notes of Decisions

Ed. Note: This section contains annotations from former RC 2131.03.

Agreement upheld 5
Disclosure 2
Effect on other laws 6
Performance of contract 3
Procedural issues 4
Time and requirements for attack 1

---

1. Time and requirements for attack

Separation agreement which has been incorporated into a decree for alimony may be attacked only by proving the voidability of such decree. Davis v. Davis (Ohio Com.Pl. 1970) 24 Ohio Misc. 17, 258 N.E.2d 277, 51 O.O.2d 388, 53 O.O.2d 48.

An attack upon an antenuptial agreement alleged to be invalid because of fraud in the inducement must be brought within six months of the appointment of the executor or administrator. Cantor v. Cantor (Ohio Prob. 1959) 174 N.E.2d 304, 86 Ohio Law Abs. 452, 15 O.O.2d 148.

The six-month period within which the validity of a separation agreement must be attacked by a surviving spouse after the appointment of the executor or administrator of the estate of her deceased spouse applies to a surviving spouse notwithstanding she was an infant at the time of her marriage, at the time the separation agreement was executed, and during the entire period of limitation. Burlovic v. Farmer (Ohio 1954) 162 Ohio St. 46, 120 N.E.2d 705, 54 O.O. 5. Limitation Of Actions ⟸ 72(5)

Where exceptions to an inventory of a decedent husband's estate states that, by a separation agreement between such decedent and his wife, latter is barred from certain allowances set off to her in inventory, and wife by reply to exceptions pleads that she is entitled to such allowances because such agreement is null and void, such reply is an attack on agreement, within purview of section which provides that such an agreement is deemed valid unless its validity is attacked within time stated in such section; in such a case upon filing of such reply to exceptions it becomes incumbent upon exceptor to prove that the agreement was fair, reasonable and just to wife under circumstances at time of its execution. In re Estate of Shafer (Hancock 1944) 77 Ohio App. 105, 65 N.E.2d 902, 32 O.O. 380.

Under section, an antenuptial agreement is deemed valid unless an action to set it aside is brought within six months after appointment of executor or administrator or unless the validity of the agreement is otherwise attacked within that period, and neither the filing of a written election to take under the law, in which is incorporated a statement that the widow repudiates "the prenuptial agreement, which was procured by fraud," nor the filing of exceptions to the inventory and appraisement on the ground that the appraisers failed to allow the statutory setoff and a year's support to the widow, constitutes an attack within the purview of the statute. Juhasz v. Juhasz (Ohio 1938) 134 Ohio St. 257, 16 N.E.2d 328, 117 A.L.R. 993, 12 O.O. 57.

2. Disclosure

An antenuptial agreement created by a husband/decedent that provides no description or listing of properties held by either party but states that "neither member of this union will be entitled to the assets or property of the other in the event of death" is invalid where the decedent's estate seeks to enforce such agreement and fails to meet its burden to show full disclosure of assets was made. In re Mize (Hamilton 1992) 82 Ohio App.3d 97, 611 N.E.2d 460.

Provisions of an antenuptial agreement which cut the parties off entirely from any participation in the estate of the other upon the death of either will be upheld upon a showing that the parties entered into the contract after full disclosure or with full knowledge of the effects of the agreement. Hook v. Hook (Ohio 1982) 69 Ohio St.2d 234, 431 N.E.2d 667, 23 O.O.3d 239.

3. Performance of contract

Where an antenuptial contract, intended to operate as an equitable jointure and to bar all rights of dower, is entered into by parties of mature age, capable of judging in regard to their interest, without any fraud or imposition, and is reasonable in its terms, and has been in good faith carried into effect by the husband during his life, full effect should be given to it, according to the intention of the parties. Mintier v. Mintier (Ohio 1876) 28 Ohio St. 307.

Unless the provisions of an antenuptial contract relinquishing a wife's claim in the estate of her husband have been fairly performed in her favor, such contract will not operate to bar her claim in equity under S & C 574–575 to an allowance for a year's support after the death of her husband. Lowe v. Phillips (Ohio 1863) 14 Ohio St. 308.

Couple's separation was not a "marital act" required to trigger husband's obligation, under antenuptial agreement, to pay a spousal support and for half of marital home and contents should the marriage terminate. Kascak v. Diemer (Ohio App. 8 Dist., 07-17-1996) 112 Ohio App.3d 635, 679 N.E.2d 1140. Husband And Wife ⟸ 279(1)

Antenuptial agreement executed in good faith, if fair and reasonable under the circumstances, is a binding contract. Diemer v. Diemer (Ohio App. 8 Dist., 12-08-1994) 99 Ohio App.3d 54, 649 N.E.2d 1285. Husband And Wife ⟸ 29(9)

Because antenuptial agreement is binding contract, action to enforce antenuptial agreement constitutes action to enforce fixed rights and liabilities of the parties to the agreement and thus survives the death of one of the parties. Diemer v. Diemer (Ohio App. 8 Dist., 12-08-1994) 99 Ohio App.3d 54, 649 N.E.2d 1285. Husband And Wife ⟸ 35

A postnuptial agreement containing provision for a division of property, both real and personal, owned by the parties, with custody of minor children given to the wife and imposing upon her the duty of maintaining them, and barring each upon death of the other from all statutory rights, which has been executed and performed by the parties thereto, is more than a mere separation agreement, and is not revoked by a mere showing of reconciliation or recohabitation, which occurs nearly twenty years later, and upon the wife's death the husband cannot claim statutory rights. In re Price's Estate (Ohio Prob. 1935) 1 Ohio Supp. 173, 22 Ohio Law Abs. 639, 1 O.O. 459.

4. Procedural issues

Former client's failure to read antenuptial agreement drafted by law firm before executing agreement precluded her claims against law firm for breach of fiduciary duty and legal malpractice; if client had read agreement before signing, she would have discovered that agreement provided no support in event of separation or divorce. Simon v. Nadler, Nadler & Burdman Co., L.P.A. (C.A.6 (Ohio), 08-03-2005) No. 04-3671, 142 Fed. Appx. 894, 2005 WL 1869518, Unreported. Attorney And Client ⟸ 129(1)

Cause of action for legal malpractice accrued, and Ohio's one-year limitations period began to run, when client read antenuptial agreement drafted by law firm, after agreement had been executed, and realized that agreement provided for no support in event of separation or divorce. Simon v. Nadler, Nadler & Burdman Co., L.P.A. (C.A.6 (Ohio), 08-03-2005) No. 04-3671, 142 Fed.Appx. 894, 2005 WL 1869518, Unreported. Limitation Of Actions ⇔ 95(11)

Doctrine of res judicata barred former husband's claim for breach of prenuptial agreement, which agreement provided that, in event of divorce, neither party would lay claim to other's pension or social security benefits, and that either party's attempt to invalidate agreement would obligate party to pay to other party $25,000; husband failed to assert prenuptial agreement as defense in prior divorce action, which proceeding fully adjudicated distribution of those assets. Calloway v. Calloway (Ohio App. 5 Dist., Stark, 01-21-2003) No. 2002CA00231, 2003-Ohio-267, 2003 WL 152850, Unreported. Divorce ⇔ 255

Remand was required on amount of attorney fees incurred by now deceased wife in proceedings on two divorce complaints to determine husband's reimbursement obligation under antenuptial agreement, even though wife died before marriage terminated; husband's attorney fee reimbursement obligation, unlike other obligations under antenuptial agreement, was not contingent upon marriage termination. Kascak v. Diemer (Ohio App. 8 Dist., 07-17-1996) 112 Ohio App.3d 635, 679 N.E.2d 1140. Husband And Wife ⇔ 281

Testimony that handwritten strikes of specific items of property made to antenuptial agreement were made after marriage supported implied conclusion of trial court that modifications were made postmarriage and did not render agreement ambiguous. Winter v. Winter (Ohio App. 12 Dist., 05-22-1995) 102 Ohio App.3d 792, 658 N.E.2d 38. Husband And Wife ⇔ 29(9)

Decree for alimony can be opened, vacated or modified only by a proceeding for that purpose in court in which it was rendered. Davis v. Davis (Ohio Com.Pl. 1970) 24 Ohio Misc. 17, 258 N.E.2d 277, 51 O.O.2d 388, 53 O.O.2d 48.

5. Agreement upheld

Existence of ambiguous provision in antenuptial agreement as to whether wife could exercise statutory right of election against husband's will did not prevent other unambiguous provisions from constituting strong and unmistakable language depriving wife of that right; ambiguous provision was adjudicated to be consistent with remainder of agreement, and did not negate the strength and certainty of the unambiguous provisions. In re Estate of Taris (Ohio App. 10 Dist., Franklin, 03-31-2005) No. 04AP-1264, 2005-Ohio-1516, 2005 WL 736627, Unreported. Wills ⇔ 785.5(2)

Statement in antenuptial agreement that neither party "shall surrender any rights as they might exist at the time of the death of the other party" did not entitle wife to exercise statutory right to elect against husband's will; statement was ambiguous in light of preceding statement, which authorized parties to "make such wills and bequests as they each determine," remainder of agreement indicated an intent to deprive wife of right to elect against will, circumstances surrounding agreement supported conclusion that parties intended to exclude each other from inheriting, and agreement would be construed against wife, who drafted it and who was only party represented by counsel. In re Estate of Taris (Ohio App. 10 Dist., Franklin, 03-31-2005) No. 04AP-1264, 2005-Ohio-1516, 2005 WL 736627, Unreported. Wills ⇔ 785.5(2)

Parties' antenuptial agreement, providing that parties' separate property prior to marriage would remain in their separate estates in the event of death or termination of the marriage, listing certain specific property deemed separate, and stating that in event of divorce, dissolution or separation each party would return to the other any gifts given to each other during marriage, was valid and enforceable. Dudich v. Dudich (Ohio App. 8 Dist., Cuyahoga, 03-03-2005) No. 84742, 2005-Ohio-889, 2005 WL 488910, Unreported. Husband And Wife ⇔ 29(9)

Antenuptial agreement was enforceable, despite surviving spouse's testimony that she only read one page of agreement, relied upon husband's representations as to impact prior to signing, and that husband crossed out certain assets while informing wife that those items would be hers if he died; wife had contact with husband's attorney during preparation of agreement and was experienced, intelligent person. Winter v. Winter (Ohio App. 12 Dist., 05-22-1995) 102 Ohio App.3d 792, 658 N.E.2d 38. Husband And Wife ⇔ 29(9)

Antenuptial contract is not invalidated merely because the spouse's share taken is small or disproportionate; after being fully informed of the property holdings of the other party and being satisfied with the terms, spouse who agrees and voluntarily signs the contract is bound. Sasarak v. Sasarak (Cuyahoga 1990) 66 Ohio App.3d 744, 586 N.E.2d 172. Husband And Wife ⇔ 29(6); Husband And Wife ⇔ 29(9)

In a proceeding to test validity of a separation agreement, such as one to determine statutory rights of a surviving spouse, evidence of a disproportionately small property provision for wife would tend to vitiate the agreement, but in proceedings to determine the rights of a divorced wife under her former husband's will, disparity between earlier provision for wife in husband's will and later provision for her in separation agreement would constitute evidence of an intent to revoke the more ample provisions for wife contained in earlier will. Davis v. Davis (Ohio Com.Pl. 1970) 24 Ohio Misc. 17, 258 N.E.2d 277, 51 O.O.2d 388, 53 O.O.2d 48. Husband And Wife ⇔ 278(1); Wills ⇔ 306

Antenuptial agreement, whereby husband aged seventy-seven waived all rights in his second wife's estate and provided she should receive $10,000 in satisfaction of her rights, was not grossly disproportionate where his estate at the time of execution was about $50,000 and the wife was an experienced businesswoman, and hence would not be set aside or cancelled. Rocker v. Rocker (Ohio Prob. 1967) 13 Ohio Misc. 199, 232 N.E.2d 445, 42 O.O.2d 184, 42 O.O.2d 241.

Under evidence including showing that husband's assets on date of execution of antenuptial agreement totaled $48,779.03, plus unlisted stocks, that wife was a bright and experienced woman who had engaged in profitable business venture for many years and who was well aware of husband's desire that their marriage would interfere as little as possible with inheritance which husband's heirs would normally receive, that she acknowledged that agreement was "her free act and deed", and that husband agreed to relinquish his interest in her estate in case of her prior death, the provision of $10,000 tax free, to the wife was not wholly disproportionate to husband's means and hence agreement was valid. Rocker v. Rocker (Ohio Prob. 1967) 13 Ohio Misc. 199, 232 N.E.2d 445, 42 O.O.2d 184, 42 O.O.2d 241. Husband And Wife ⇔ 34

On the evidence settlor retained such control over trust as to render it a mere agency account, and hence wife was entitled to her statutory share, thereof on testator's death. Osborn v. Osborn (Ohio Com.Pl. 1966) 10 Ohio Misc. 171, 226 N.E.2d 814, 39 O.O.2d 275, affirmed 18 Ohio St.2d 144, 248 N.E.2d 191, 47 O.O.2d 310.

An antenuptial contract must be voluntarily entered into and the provisions for the wife must be fair and reasonable under all the surrounding facts and circumstances; and an adult man and woman, each owning a substantial amount of property and each having grown children by prior marriages, may lawfully enter a prenuptial agreement whereby each relinquishes every and all rights in the property of the other. Osborn v. Osborn (Ohio Com.Pl. 1966) 10 Ohio Misc. 171, 226 N.E.2d 814, 39 O.O.2d 275, affirmed 18 Ohio St.2d 144, 248 N.E.2d 191, 47 O.O.2d 310.

Where testator agreed in an antenuptial agreement to leave $15,000 to his wife and that the rest of his property should pass according to the statute of descent and distribution, upon his death intestate the widow was entitled to $15,000 and the balance passed to his heirs at law as donee beneficiaries. Cantor v. Cantor (Ohio Prob. 1959) 174 N.E.2d 304, 86 Ohio Law Abs. 452, 15 O.O.2d 148.

Antenuptial contract cannot be avoided by surviving husband by proof of concealment of fact not affecting survivor's interest. Keever v. Brown (Ohio App. 1930) 36 Ohio App. 1, 172 N.E. 626, 9 Ohio Law Abs. 296. Husband And Wife ⇔ 33

Wife entered into prenuptial agreement freely and without fraud, duress, coercion, or overreaching; wife independently retained one of the foremost domestic relations attorneys at that time, the attorney participated in negotiating the agreement, wife did not sign the agreement until eight days after she received the final draft and she therefore had ample time to pursue changes, to retain new counsel, or to refuse to sign it, and wife could have postponed the wedding without undue embarrassment if she chose to further negotiate terms in the prenuptial agreement. Millstein v. Millstein (Ohio App. 8 Dist., Cuyahoga, 09-12-2002) No. 79617, No. 80185, No. 80188, No. 79754, No. 80186, No. 80963, No. 80184, No. 80187, 2002-Ohio-4783, 2002 WL 31031676, Unreported, appeal not allowed 98 Ohio St.3d 1462, 783 N.E.2d 521, 2003-Ohio-644. Husband And Wife ⇔ 29(9)

Prenuptial agreement was enforceable in divorce action, though the parties had been married for 19 years, the marriage produced two children, and the agreement granted the wife only one percent of husband's assets. Millstein v. Millstein (Ohio App. 8 Dist., Cuyahoga, 09-12-2002) No. 79617, No. 80185, No. 80188, No. 79754, No. 80186, No. 80963, No. 80184, No. 80187, 2002-Ohio-4783, 2002 WL 31031676, Unreported, appeal not allowed 98 Ohio St.3d 1462, 783 N.E.2d 521, 2003-Ohio-644. Husband And Wife ⇔ 29(6); Husband And Wife ⇔ 29(9)

2106.22
Note 6

6. Effect on other laws

RC 2131.03 does not give the parties thereto the power to change the effect of the statutes of descent and distribution. Cantor v. Cantor (Ohio Prob. 1959) 174 N.E.2d 304, 86 Ohio Law Abs. 452, 15 O.O.2d 148. Husband And Wife ⇔ 29(9)

2106.24 Other rights of surviving spouse

In addition to the rights provided in this chapter, a surviving spouse of a decedent who died testate or intestate is entitled to any other rights prescribed in other chapters of the Revised Code, including, but not limited to, any dower rights under Chapters 2103. and 5305. of the Revised Code.

(1990 H 346, eff. 5-31-90)

Uncodified Law

1990 H 346, § 3, eff. 5-31-90, reads, in part: (A) Sections 1 and 2 of this act shall apply only to the estates of decedents who die on or after the effective date of this act.

Library References

Descent and Distribution ⇔52(1).
Wills ⇔708.
Westlaw Topic Nos. 124, 409.
C.J.S. Descent and Distribution §§ 60 to 62, 64.
C.J.S. Wills §§ 451 to 452.
Baldwin's Ohio Legislative Service, 1990 Laws of Ohio, H 346—LSC Analysis, p 5-87

Research References

Encyclopedias

OH Jur. 3d Decedents' Estates § 17, Purchase Distinguished from Descent—Illustrative Applications.
OH Jur. 3d Decedents' Estates § 235, Restrictions as to Surviving Spouse.
OH Jur. 3d Decedents' Estates § 767, Right to Dower; Right to Remain in Mansion House.

Treatises and Practice Aids

Carlin, Baldwin's Ohio Practice, Merrick-Rippner Probate Law § 21:84, Rights of Surviving Spouse—Dower.

2106.25 Exercising of rights under Chapter 2106 by surviving spouse

Unless otherwise specified by a provision of the Revised Code or this section, a surviving spouse shall exercise all rights under Chapter 2106. of the Revised Code within five months of the initial appointment of an executor or administrator of the estate. It is conclusively presumed that a surviving spouse has waived any right not exercised within that five-month period or within any longer period of time allowed by the court pursuant to this section. Upon the filing of a motion to extend the time for exercising a right under Chapter 2106. of the Revised Code and for good cause shown, the court may allow further time for exercising the right that is the subject of the motion.

(2001 H 85, eff. 10-31-01)

Library References

Descent and Distribution ⇔52(1), 62.
Wills ⇔781, 785.5(1).
Westlaw Topic Nos. 124, 409.
C.J.S. Descent and Distribution §§ 60 to 62, 64 to 65.
C.J.S. Wills §§ 1841, 1858.

Research References

Treatises and Practice Aids

Carlin, Baldwin's Ohio Practice, Merrick-Rippner Probate Law § 2:35, Elective Rights of Surviving Spouse—Election to Take Under Law or Under the Will—Issuance of Citation.
Carlin, Baldwin's Ohio Practice, Merrick-Rippner Probate Law § 2:36, Elective Rights of Surviving Spouse—Election to Take Under Law or Under the Will—Time for Making Election.
Carlin, Baldwin's Ohio Practice, Merrick-Rippner Probate Law § 2:41, Election Rights of Surviving Spouse—RC Chap. 2106—Time Limitation.
Carlin, Baldwin's Ohio Practice, Merrick-Rippner Probate Law § 21:2, Rights of Surviving Spouse to Make Election—Statutory Provisions—Generally.
Carlin, Baldwin's Ohio Practice, Merrick-Rippner Probate Law § 21:3, Rights of Surviving Spouse to Make Election—Statutory Provisions—Citation—Issuance—Waiver of Citation.
Carlin, Baldwin's Ohio Practice, Merrick-Rippner Probate Law § 21:4, Rights of Surviving Spouse to Make Election—Statutory Provisions—Citation—Service.
Carlin, Baldwin's Ohio Practice, Merrick-Rippner Probate Law § 21:8, Rights of Surviving Spouse to Make Election—Statutory Provisions—Manner and Time—Time Within Which to Make Election.
Carlin, Baldwin's Ohio Practice, Merrick-Rippner Probate Law § 2:121, Administration of Decedent's Estate—Checklist.
Carlin, Baldwin's Ohio Practice, Merrick-Rippner Probate Law § 21:43, Rights of Surviving Spouse to Make All Elections Under RC Chap. 2106—Time Limit.
Carlin, Baldwin's Ohio Practice, Merrick-Rippner Probate Law § 21:45, Rights of Surviving Spouse to Elect to Receive Mansion House—Procedure—Time of Election.
Carlin, Baldwin's Ohio Practice, Merrick-Rippner Probate Law § 21:56, Rights of Surviving Spouse—Family Allowance—Time Limitations.
Carlin, Baldwin's Ohio Practice, Merrick-Rippner Probate Law § 21:59, Rights of Surviving Spouse—Mansion House—Time Limitation.
Carlin, Baldwin's Ohio Practice, Merrick-Rippner Probate Law § 21:64, Rights of Surviving Spouse—Procedure for Purchase—Limitation on Time to Elect.
Carlin, Baldwin's Ohio Practice, Merrick-Rippner Probate Law § 21:82, Rights of Surviving Spouse—Right to Reimbursement for Funeral Expenses.
Carlin, Baldwin's Ohio Practice, Merrick-Rippner Probate Law § 30:24, Drafting a Will—Surviving Spouse—Election to Take Against the Will.
Carlin, Baldwin's Ohio Practice, Merrick-Rippner Probate Law App B SPF 8.3, Summary of General Rights of Surviving Spouses.

Law Review and Journal Commentaries

The Impact of H.B. 85 Upon the Allowance of Support to a Surviving Spouse: Must a spouse affirmatively claim it? Is there a time limit to its payment, with or without a claim?, C. Terry Johnson. 13 Prob L J Ohio 80 (March/April 2003).

CHAPTER 2107

WILLS

DEFINITIONS

Section
2107.01 Definition
2107.011 Interpretation of terms

Section

EXECUTION

2107.02 Who may make will

Section		Section	
2107.03	Method of making will	2107.54	Contribution; exception
2107.04	Agreement to make a will	2107.55	Portion of pretermitted heir, or of witness, subject to contribution
2107.05	Incorporation by reference		
2107.06	Persons under eighteen prohibited from witnessing will	2107.56	Liability in case of insolvency
		2107.57	Contribution enforced

DEPOSIT

2107.07	Deposit of will	2107.58	Order of sale to pay debts
2107.08	Delivery of will	2107.59	Sale of land by executor's successor

DECLARATION OF VALIDITY OF WILL

NUNCUPATIVE WILLS

2107.081	Petition by testator for declaration of validity of will; failure to file not evidence	2107.60	Oral will

MISCELLANEOUS PROVISIONS

2107.082	Service of process	2107.61	Will ineffectual
2107.083	Validity of will, hearing	2107.62	Expenses and fees
2107.084	Declaration of validity; effects; disposition; revocation or modification of will after declaration		

TESTAMENTARY ADDITIONS TO TRUSTS

		2107.63	Addition to trust estate
2107.085	Effects in relation to other matters		

ASSORTED PROVISIONS

PRODUCTION

2107.09	Who may enforce production of a will; disposition of will previously declared valid	2107.64	Rights of testamentary trustee under life insurance or benefit plans
2107.10	Effect of withholding will; will previously declared valid in another county; knowledge of beneficiary	2107.65	Power to nominate

WILL CONTEST ACTION

PROBATE

2107.11	Jurisdiction to probate	2107.71	Venue of will contest; effects of previous declaration of validity; failure to seek
2107.12	Contest of jurisdiction		
2107.15	Witness a devisee or legatee	2107.72	Rules of Civil Procedure govern; exception; right to jury trial upon demand
2107.16	Will proved in certain cases; will previously declared valid		
		2107.73	Necessary parties
2107.17	Depositions may be taken by commission; legal effect	2107.74	Effective order of probate
2107.18	Admission to probate; will previously declared valid	2107.75	Defense of questionable will taxed as cost of administration
2107.181	Will not entitled to probate; procedure		
2107.19	Notice of admission of will to probate	2107.76	Contest of will within three months; exceptions; rights not affected
2107.20	Filing and recording of will; certified copy		
2107.21	Recorded in each county where real estate is situated	2107.77	Contest of later wills
2107.22	Probate of will of later date; will previously declared valid		
2107.24	Probate court to treat document as will despite noncompliance with statute		

Publisher's Note: Until 1968, when the Modern Courts Amendment to the Ohio Constitution was adopted, Ohio court procedure was governed entirely by statute and case law. The Modern Courts Amendment required the Supreme Court of Ohio, subject to the approval of the General Assembly, to "prescribe rules governing practice and procedure in all courts of the state." Rules of practice and procedure are the Civil, Criminal, Appellate, and Juvenile Rules, Rules of the Court of Claims, and the Ohio Rules of Evidence. Pursuant to Ohio Constitution Article IV, Section 5(B), such rules "shall not abridge, enlarge, or modify any substantive right," and " [a]ll laws in conflict with such rules shall be of no further force or effect." Provisions of Chapter 2107 should be read with this in mind.

LOST, SPOLIATED, OR DESTROYED WILLS

2107.26	Lost, spoliated, or destroyed wills may be admitted to probate
2107.27	Notice of application; testimony; probate
2107.28	Will lost, spoliated, or destroyed after admission to probate

NEW RECORD OF PROBATE

2107.29	Record of will destroyed
2107.30	Original will may again be admitted to probate
2107.31	Limitations as to contests
2107.32	Notice

REVOCATION

2107.33	Revocation of will; will previously declared valid
2107.34	Afterborn or pretermitted heirs; effect on will
2107.35	Encumbrances
2107.36	Effect of alteration of property
2107.37	Marriage does not revoke will
2107.38	Destruction of a subsequent will

CONSTRUCTION AND OPERATION

2107.46	Action by fiduciary
2107.47	Protection of purchaser against later will
2107.48	Foreign will cannot be contested here
2107.49	Rule in Shelley's case abolished
2107.50	Property acquired subsequent to will
2107.501	Rights of specific devisee or legatee on certain dispositions of subject property
2107.51	When whole estate to pass
2107.52	Death of devisee or legatee
2107.521	Only specific reference in will to testator's power of appointment effective
2107.53	Undevised real estate applied to debts

Cross References

Determination of heirship, Ch 2123
Disclaimer of succession to interest in property; procedure; distributor unaware of disclaimer not liable, 1339.60
End of trust; disposition of property meant to go to trust from an estate, 1339.66
Legal and equitable titles to corpus of trust not merging, testamentary trust not resulting, 1335.01
Paternity proceedings to determine father and child relationship not affecting time to assert heirship or succession, 3111.05

Law Review and Journal Commentaries

Avoiding Probate of Decedents' Estates, Gilbert A. Sheard. 36 U Cin L Rev 70 (Winter 1967).

The Cy Pres Doctrine—Is It State Action?, Comment. 18 Cap U L Rev 383 (Fall 1989).

Disinheritance and the Modern Family, Ralph C. Brashier. 45 Case W Res L Rev 83 (Fall 1994).

Estate Planning and Conflict of Laws, John W. Ester and Eugene F. Scoles. 24 Ohio St L J 270 (Winter 1963).

Estate Planning for Parents of Handicapped Child, Edmund W. Rothschild. 56 Clev B J 252 (July/August 1985).

Inheritance and Inconsistency, Adam J. Hirsch. 57 Ohio St L J 1058 (1996).

The Lawyer's Role When Death is Imminent—"The Dying Client Drill," C. Terry Johnson. 3 Prob L J Ohio 2 (September/October 1992).

The Negligent Drafting Of Wills And *Simon v. Zipperstein*: A Step Backward In Ohio Jurisprudence?, Note. 20 U Tol L Rev 133 (Fall 1988).

Ohio's 1975 Probate Reform Act: Analysis of Major Changes in Ohio's Probate Code, Note. 45 U Cin L Rev 429 (1976).

A Plain English Guide To Recognizing The Estate Freeze Trap, Hamlin C. King. 4 Ohio Law 11 (November/December 1990).

Should Everyone Trust a Living Trust?, William A. Fields. 2 Prob L J Ohio 5 (September/October 1991).

The Superwill Debate: Opening The Pandora's Box, Roberta Rosenthal Kwall and Anthony T. Aiello. 62 Temp L Rev 277 (1989).

There Is More to Succession Planning Than a Will, Joel Strom. 69 Clev B J 14 (June 1998).

Uniform Probate Code and Ohio in the 1990s, Richard V. Wellman. 1 Prob L J Ohio 55 (January/February 1991).

Videotaping Wills: A New Frontier in Estate Planning, William R. Buckley and Alfred W. Buckley. 11 Ohio N U L Rev 271 (1984).

DEFINITIONS

2107.01 Definition

In Chapters 2101. to 2131. of the Revised Code, "will" includes codicils to wills admitted to probate, lost, spoliated, or destroyed wills, and instruments admitted to probate under section 2107.081 of the Revised Code, but "will" does not include inter vivos trusts or other instruments that have not been admitted to probate.

(1992 H 427, eff. 10-8-92; 1953 H 1; GC 10504-1)

Uncodified Law

1992 H 427, § 3, eff. 10-8-92, reads: In amending sections 2107.01 and 2107.52 of the Revised Code, the General Assembly hereby declares its intent to supersede the effect of the holding of the Ohio Supreme Court on October 26, 1988, in *Dollar Savings & Trust Co. of Youngstown v. Turner* (1988), 39 Ohio St. 3d 182.

Historical and Statutory Notes

Pre-1953 H 1 Amendments: 114 v 346

Cross References

Foreign wills, 2129.05, 2129.06
Lost or destroyed wills, probate records; restoration, 2729.01 to 2729.08
Requirements for creation, 5804.02

Library References

Wills ⊖69.
Westlaw Topic No. 409.
C.J.S. Wills §§ 1, 166.

Research References

Encyclopedias

OH Jur. 3d Decedents' Estates § 214, Definition of Will.
OH Jur. 3d Decedents' Estates § 855, Enforcement of Contribution.
OH Jur. 3d Trusts § 53, Failure of Attempt to Create a Trust—Vesting of Title in Failed Trusts.
OH Jur. 3d Trusts § 73, Application of Statute of Wills.
OH Jur. 3d Trusts § 74, Effect of Incorporation Into Will.
OH Jur. 3d Trusts § 84, Parol Evidence—Sufficiency.
OH Jur. 3d Trusts § 96, Grantor's Reservation of Powers, Generally.

Forms

Ohio Forms Legal and Business § 24:1, Introduction.
Ohio Forms Legal and Business § 24:2, Law Governing Wills.
Ohio Forms Legal and Business § 24:161, Entire Estate to Spouse—Alternatively to Children—Guardianship of Minors.
Ohio Forms Legal and Business § 24:261, Prior Wills and Codicils.

Treatises and Practice Aids

Carlin, Baldwin's Ohio Practice, Merrick-Rippner Probate Law § 27:1, Testamentary Formalities—Definition of Will; Testamentary Intent.
Carlin, Baldwin's Ohio Practice, Merrick-Rippner Probate Law § 28:1, Codicils—Definition.
Carlin, Baldwin's Ohio Practice, Merrick-Rippner Probate Law § 40:8, Revocation of Will—Subsequent Written Instrument—Types—Wills and Codicils.
Carlin, Baldwin's Ohio Practice, Merrick-Rippner Probate Law § 30:189, Codicil—Form.
Restatement (3d) Property (Wills & Don. Trans.) § 5.5, Antilapse Statutes.
Restatement (3d) of Trusts § 25, Validity and Effect of Revocable Inter Vivos Trust.

Law Review and Journal Commentaries

The Traditional Wills Doctrine of Ademption and Its Exceptions Should be Extended to Revocable Trusts, Brian Layman. 13 Prob L J Ohio 119 (July/August 2003).

Notes of Decisions

Codicils 3
Intentional interference with expectancy of inheritance 1
Testamentary intent 2

---

1. Intentional interference with expectancy of inheritance

Ohio recognizes tort of intentional interference with expectancy of inheritance. Firestone v. Galbreath (Ohio 1993) 67 Ohio St.3d 87, 616 N.E.2d 202, answer to certified question conformed to 25 F.3d 323, on remand 895 F.Supp. 917. Torts ⊖ 289

Elements of tort of intentional interference with expectancy of inheritance are: existence of expectancy of inheritance in plaintiff; intentional interference by defendant with that expectancy of inheritance; conduct by defendant involving interference which is tortious, such as fraud, duress or undue influence, in nature; reasonable certainty that expectancy of inheritance would have been realized, but for interference by defendant; and damage resulting from interference. Firestone v. Galbreath (Ohio 1993) 67 Ohio St.3d 87, 616 N.E.2d 202, answer to certified question conformed to 25 F.3d 323, on remand 895 F.Supp. 917. Torts ⊖ 289

2. Testamentary intent

Intention of testator is to be ascertained, not by what occurred long after execution of will, but by what was apparently or presumably in his contemplation at the time he was making it. Bank One Ohio Trust Co., N.A. v. Hiram College (Ohio App. 7 Dist., 10-31-1996) 115 Ohio App.3d 159, 684 N.E.2d 1275. Wills ⊖ 441

Testator's will operated as *in praesenti* instrument that effectively amended terms of testator's revocable trust, given clear manifestation of testator's intent that it do so and thereby remove as beneficiary testator's wife, from whom he was separated several months before executing will; will specifically referred to trust, which reserved testator's right to revoke or amend trust, named trustee and noted trust's account number, and altered terms of disposition of trust assets by directing that they be distributed to different beneficiaries in different amounts than original trust terms directed. In re Estate of Davis (Ohio App. 12 Dist., 02-05-1996) 109 Ohio App.3d 181, 671 N.E.2d 1302, appeal not allowed 76 Ohio St.3d 1424, 667 N.E.2d 26. Trusts ⊖ 58

Instrument that contains language appropriate to two or more different instruments will be construed in accordance with intention of testator as deduced from instrument as a whole and from any extrinsic evidence that might be introduced. In re Estate of Davis (Ohio App. 12 Dist., 02-05-1996) 109 Ohio App.3d 181, 671 N.E.2d 1302, appeal not allowed 76 Ohio St.3d 1424, 667 N.E.2d 26. Wills ⊖ 470(1); Wills ⊖ 486

Interpretation of wills, including intent of testator, is question of law, and therefore subject to independent appellate review. In re Estate of Davis (Ohio App. 12 Dist., 02-05-1996) 109 Ohio App.3d 181, 671 N.E.2d 1302, appeal not allowed 76 Ohio St.3d 1424, 667 N.E.2d 26. Wills ⊖ 706

Under doctrine of "cy pres," which means "as near as possible," which is applied in construction of a will wherein testator attempts to create perpetuity and language used is so vague or uncertain that testator's design must be sought by construction, court must, to avoid invalidating entire provision, try to explain will in such a way as to carry out testator's general intention. Runser v. Lippi (Ohio App. 3 Dist., 08-18-1995) 105 Ohio App.3d 752, 664 N.E.2d 1355, appeal not allowed 74 Ohio St.3d 1501, 659 N.E.2d 316. Charities ☞ 37(1)

Doctrine of "cy pres" was inapplicable in will contest, where testator's intent was evident on face of his will. Runser v. Lippi (Ohio App. 3 Dist., 08-18-1995) 105 Ohio App.3d 752, 664 N.E.2d 1355, appeal not allowed 74 Ohio St.3d 1501, 659 N.E.2d 316. Charities ☞ 37(1)

In determining testator's intent in establishing educational assistance foundation in will, probate court could not use extrinsic evidence of foundation's rules and regulations, which were adopted after testator's death, as evidence of general intent to create charitable trust, since testator's intent to give first preference to his nieces and nephews regardless of geographical location or financial status was clear on face of will; consequently, probate court could not strike specific direction as to preference on ground that direction was not consistent with charitable nature of foundation. Runser v. Lippi (Ohio App. 3 Dist., 08-18-1995) 105 Ohio App.3d 752, 664 N.E.2d 1355, appeal not allowed 74 Ohio St.3d 1501, 659 N.E.2d 316. Charities ☞ 37(6); Wills ☞ 677

Intent of testator or grantor should be ascertained and given effect whenever possible. PNC Bank, Ohio, N.A. v. Stanton (Ohio App. 1 Dist., 06-14-1995) 104 Ohio App.3d 558, 662 N.E.2d 875, appeal not allowed 74 Ohio St.3d 1446, 656 N.E.2d 347. Trusts ☞ 112; Wills ☞ 439

Where a standard deed form prepared by decedent has been declared invalid to pass title due to want of delivery, the form will not be construed as a will absent some showing of testamentary intent on the face of the deed form. In re Estate of Ike (Shelby 1982) 7 Ohio App.3d 87, 454 N.E.2d 577, 7 O.B.R. 100.

A son acquired real estate under the will of his father, which provided that the son should "have the farm above described by paying" certain legacies, held that the real estate so acquired by the son was ancestral property, and upon his dying intestate descended as such under GC 8573 (repealed 1932. See §1503–4), the title thereto coming to such intestate by devise, which is a disposition of real property contained in a man's last will and testament; the provision requiring the devisee to pay legacies not converting the estate into one by purchase. Wheatcraft v. Hall (Ohio 1922) 106 Ohio St. 21, 138 N.E. 368, 1 Ohio Law Abs. 11, 20 Ohio Law Rep. 412. Descent And Distribution ☞ 14; Wills ☞ 725

An instrument, executed in compliance with the statute of wills, appointing an executor to settle up all property, both personal and real, and making the grand-daughters of testatrix equal "heirs" with her own children, is dispositive, and devised to the granddaughters each an equal share with the children of testatrix. Moon v. Stewart (Ohio 1913) 87 Ohio St. 349, 101 N.E. 344, 10 Ohio Law Rep. 601, Am.Ann.Cas. 1914A, 104. Wills ☞ 525

Every disposition of property must have a definite subject and a definite object; when the intent of the testator cannot be ascertained, either from the will, or by extraneous circumstances, the will is void and the estate must descend according to law. Cope v. Cope (Ohio 1888) 45 Ohio St. 464, 19 W.L.B. 98, 15 N.E. 206.

A will directs disposition of property and the person who is to carry this disposition into effect. Hall v. Hall (Ohio Com.Pl. 1904) 15 Ohio Dec. 161.

3. Codicils

In construing a will, to which are attached or added codicils, the whole is to be taken together as one instrument; the codicils constitute a part of the will. (See also Collier v Collier's Executors, 3 OS 369 (1854).) Negley v. Gard (Ohio 1851) 20 Ohio 310.

A codicil to a will is subject to the restrictions of RC 2107.06 invalidating charitable bequests made by a will executed within a year of the testator's death. Newman v. Newman (Ohio Prob. 1964) 199 N.E.2d 904, 94 Ohio Law Abs. 321, 28 O.O.2d 154. Wills ☞ 16

In action to set aside will and codicil, court's failure to use word "codicil" in connection with word "will" in general charge held not prejudicial error, where only general exception was taken. Adams v. Foley (Richland 1929) 36 Ohio App. 295, 173 N.E. 197, 9 Ohio Law Abs. 100. Wills ☞ 396

GC 10502 (RC 2107.01) and 12079 (RC 2741.01), construed together, indicate that as to the execution and probate of wills, the term "will" should include codicil, but that in the chapter relating to contests, the two may be regarded as separate testamentary dispositions. Trull v. Patrick (Ohio Com.Pl. 1920) 31 Ohio Dec. 319, 22 Ohio N.P.N.S. 385.

2107.011 Interpretation of terms

Except when the intent of the testator clearly is to the contrary, the following rules of construction shall apply in interpreting the terms "inheritance" and "bequest":

(A) The term "inheritance," in addition to its meaning at common law or under any other section or sections of the Revised Code, includes any change of title to real property by reason of the death of the owner of that real property, regardless of whether the owner died testate or intestate.

(B) The term "bequest," in addition to its meaning at common law or under any other section or sections of the Revised Code, includes any testamentary disposition of real property and any testamentary disposition of a vendor's interest in a land installment contract.

(C) The terms "inheritance" and "bequest," as defined in the rules of construction set forth in divisions (A) and (B) of this section, apply to the interest in, the title to, or both the interest in and the title to, any real property to which a fiduciary succeeds by reason of the death of the prior holder of that interest, title, or interest and title, regardless of whether the prior holder died testate or intestate.

(1994 H 208, eff. 6–23–94)

Library References

Wills ☞437, 439.
Westlaw Topic No. 409.
C.J.S. Wills §§ 796 to 797, 820, 831 to 832, 836 to 837.

Research References

Encyclopedias
OH Jur. 3d Decedents' Estates § 13, Inheritance.

Forms
Ohio Forms Legal and Business § 24:118, Construction of Wills.

Treatises and Practice Aids
Carlin, Baldwin's Ohio Practice, Merrick-Rippner Probate Law § 43:35, Construing a Will—Words and Phrases—Inheritance; Bequest.

Notes of Decisions

Ed. Note: This section contains annotations from former RC 2107.06.

Beneficiaries
    Ademption of bequest 2
    Board of county commissioners 3
    Unincorporated association 4
General rule of interpretation 1
Mortmain statute effect on charitable gifts before 1985 5
Power of appointment under will 6
Survivorship instruments--P.O.D. bank account 7

---

1. General rule of interpretation

Cardinal rule of interpretation of will is to ascertain meaning and intention of testator. Kretzer v. Brubaker (Ohio, 02-14-1996) 74 Ohio St.3d 519, 660 N.E.2d 446, 1996-Ohio-178. Wills ☞ 439

Language used in will should be given its ordinary meaning and natural effect if meaning is clear, and words employed are unequivocal and unambiguous. Kretzer v. Brubaker (Ohio, 02-14-1996) 74 Ohio St.3d 519, 660 N.E.2d 446, 1996-Ohio-178. Wills ☞ 456

2. Beneficiaries—Ademption of bequest

Principle of "ademption" refers to taking away of specific bequest and occurs when object of legacy ceases to exist. Church v. Morgan (Ohio App. 4 Dist., 11-01-1996) 115 Ohio App.3d 477, 685 N.E.2d 809. Wills ☞ 764; Wills ☞ 768

2107.011
Note 3

3. —— Board of county commissioners, beneficiaries

Under RS 20 the board of county commissioners of any county in Ohio may take and hold any property devised to it. Christy v. Com'rs of Ashtabula County (Ohio 1885) 41 Ohio St. 711, 13 W.L.B. 573.

A county can take real estate by devise, and where the devise is made to the county by name with no limitation on the property's use, it vests in the board of commissioners for the use of the county for any authorized county purposes. Carder v. Board of Com'rs of Fayette County (Ohio 1865) 16 Ohio St. 354.

4. —— Unincorporated association, beneficiaries

An unincorporated society is entirely capable of taking a personal bequest, though it might be different as to realty. American Tract Soc. v. Atwater (Ohio 1876) 30 Ohio St. 77, 27 Am.Rep. 422.

5. Mortmain statute effect on charitable gifts before 1985

Court presumed that testator was aware of potential effect of mortmain statute invalidating bequests to charities made less than one year before testator's death with respect to his testamentary bequests to charities and that his intent was to bequeath bulk of his estate to his family, where mortmain statute was viable rule of law on day will was executed and on day testator died so that testator's intent was formed with knowledge that his charitable gifts might lapse, testator included two classes of residuary legatees, and specific sum bequeathed for benefit of grandchildren was very near original corpus amount. Wendell v. AmeriTrust Co., N.A. (Ohio 1994) 69 Ohio St.3d 74, 630 N.E.2d 368. Wills ⚖ 486

Grandchildren's rights under grandfather's will vested prior to judicial decision declaring mortmain statute invalidating bequests to charities made less than one year prior to testator's death unconstitutional, and thus, decision would not apply retroactively and testamentary bequests by grandfather to charities made three months before death were void, where testator made specific residuary request to lawful children of his son thereby creating class of beneficiaries consisting of grandchildren and interest vested at time of testator's death but enjoyment of the bequest was delayed. Wendell v. AmeriTrust Co., N.A. (Ohio 1994) 69 Ohio St.3d 74, 630 N.E.2d 368. Courts ⚖ 100(1)

Former RC 2107.06, as applied to any action seeking construction of that statute pending on the date of this decision or to the last will of any testator whose death occurred on or after August 1, 1985, violates the Equal Protection Clauses of the Ohio and United States Constitutions. Shriners' Hosp. for Crippled Children v. Hester (Ohio 1986) 23 Ohio St.3d 198, 492 N.E.2d 153, 23 O.B.R. 359. Constitutional Law ⚖ 278(1.3); Wills ⚖ 13(1)

In applying RC 2107.06, when a surplus remains after all legacies have been discharged, the surplus is the residual estate and must be distributed to the testator's issue pursuant to RC 2107.06(C). Woods v. Neissen (Summit 1983) 11 Ohio App.3d 62, 463 N.E.2d 92, 11 O.B.R. 96.

There is a presumption that the language used by a testator in his will has a testamentary purpose which cannot be ignored; however, it is also presumed that a testator knew of the applicable statutes which would control the distribution of his estate, and such statutes are indicative of the testator's testamentary intent. Woods v. Neissen (Summit 1983) 11 Ohio App.3d 62, 463 N.E.2d 92, 11 O.B.R. 96.

Where testator executed a will which provided that charitable beneficiaries receive the residual portion of the estate, and such bequest is limited to twenty-five per cent of the estate because of the mortmain statute, the statutorily created residuary share is chargeable with estate taxes, fees and costs of administration. Woods v. Neissen (Summit 1983) 11 Ohio App.3d 62, 463 N.E.2d 92, 11 O.B.R. 96.

In determining whether the value of a particular testamentary gift exceeds twenty-five per cent of a testator's net probate estate for the purposes of RC 2107.06, a trial court must value the gift as of the date of the testator's death. In re Roberts' Estate (Wood 1980) 1 Ohio App.3d 15, 437 N.E.2d 1205, 1 O.B.R. 80. Wills ⚖ 15

Where the testamentary gift is given in the form of a remainder or other future interest, the value of the gift, for purposes of RC 2107.06, is the "present value" of the interest as of the date of the testator's death. In re Roberts' Estate (Wood 1980) 1 Ohio App.3d 15, 437 N.E.2d 1205, 1 O.B.R. 80. Wills ⚖ 15

To extent that property of decedent may not pass to charitable institution because of invalidity of bequest under RC 2107.06, and to extent that no provision is expressly made in will for bequest of such property to some other qualified beneficiary, decedent is intestate as to such property and same passes as prescribed by RC 2107.06(C), notwithstanding testator has specifically disinherited only person who could qualify as beneficiary under that division. Balyeat v. Morris (Allen 1971) 28 Ohio App.2d 191, 276 N.E.2d 258, 57 O.O.2d 301.

RC 2107.06 was designed for the protection of issue and adopted children or their lineal descendants, and inasmuch as grandchildren are not heirs at law where all the testator's children have survived him, they do not come within its protection, since it does not apply when those whom it was designed to protect have, in fact, no interest to protect. Central Nat. Bank of Cleveland v. Morris (Cuyahoga 1967) 10 Ohio App.2d 225, 227 N.E.2d 418, 39 O.O.2d 433.

Where a charitable bequest is made in a will drafted less than a year before the testator's death, and by reason of a gift over the heirs who come within the statutory classes would not be benefited even though the charitable gift was declared invalid, the reason for invoking the statute is absent and the charitable bequest is valid. Central Nat. Bank of Cleveland v. Morris (Ohio Prob. 1967) 9 Ohio Misc. 167, 222 N.E.2d 674, 38 O.O.2d 265, affirmed 10 Ohio App.2d 225, 227 N.E.2d 418, 39 O.O.2d 433.

RC 2107.06 is designed to protect only those persons in the designated categories who are the testator's heirs. Central Nat. Bank of Cleveland v. Morris (Ohio Prob. 1967) 9 Ohio Misc. 167, 222 N.E.2d 674, 38 O.O.2d 265, affirmed 10 Ohio App.2d 225, 227 N.E.2d 418, 39 O.O.2d 433.

A testamentary gift to a municipal police relief and pension fund is one for a benevolent or charitable purpose or to a municipal corporation within the meaning of RC 2107.06. Anderson v. Malone (Ohio Prob. 1963) 205 N.E.2d 131, 95 Ohio Law Abs. 211, 32 O.O.2d 407.

The doctrine of dependent relative revocation does not apply in mortmain cases. Newman v. Newman (Ohio Prob. 1964) 199 N.E.2d 904, 94 Ohio Law Abs. 321, 28 O.O.2d 154.

A codicil to a will is subject to the restrictions of RC 2107.06 invalidating charitable bequests made by a will executed within a year of the testator's death. Newman v. Newman (Ohio Prob. 1964) 199 N.E.2d 904, 94 Ohio Law Abs. 321, 28 O.O.2d 154. Wills ⚖ 16

A residuary bequest, invalid under the mortmain statute, will be distributed as intestate property. Newman v. Newman (Ohio Prob. 1964) 199 N.E.2d 904, 94 Ohio Law Abs. 321, 28 O.O.2d 154.

RC 2107.06 has no application to a general testamentary power of appointment given a wife following a provision for a life estate in another, where such wife, in pursuance thereof and by subsequent will, appoints a charitable institution as beneficiary of the residue of her husband's estate and leaves no surviving issue, adopted child or lineal descendant of either—notwithstanding the fact that the donor husband died within one year of the execution of his will, and the wife's appointment of such beneficiary is valid. In re Lowe's Estate (Cuyahoga 1963) 119 Ohio App. 303, 191 N.E.2d 196, 92 Ohio Law Abs. 369, 27 O.O.2d 319.

Gift to Berkshire music center by testator who left a daughter and who executed will less than one year prior to death was invalid. Lloyd v. Campbell (Ohio Prob. 1963) 189 N.E.2d 660, 91 Ohio Law Abs. 522, 23 O.O.2d 329, affirmed in part, reversed in part 120 Ohio App. 441, 196 N.E.2d 786, 94 Ohio Law Abs. 419, 29 O.O.2d 210.

Declaratory judgment denied where gift to charities was contingent upon event which might or might not occur. Lloyd v. Campbell (Ohio Prob. 1963) 189 N.E.2d 660, 91 Ohio Law Abs. 522, 23 O.O.2d 329, affirmed in part, reversed in part 120 Ohio App. 441, 196 N.E.2d 786, 94 Ohio Law Abs. 419, 29 O.O.2d 210.

An otherwise valid exercise of a general testamentary power of appointment in favor of a charitable corporation is not rendered invalid by reason of the fact that the donor of the power died within a year of the execution of his will, leaving a son. In re Lowe's Trust (Ohio Prob. 1962) 186 N.E.2d 648, 90 Ohio Law Abs. 399, 21 O.O.2d 444, affirmed 119 Ohio App. 303, 191 N.E.2d 196, 92 Ohio Law Abs. 369, 27 O.O.2d 319.

RC 2107.06 cannot be circumvented by indirect or conditional gifts to charity. Roenick v. Dollar Sav. & Trust Co. (Mahoning 1960) 179 N.E.2d 379, 87 Ohio Law Abs. 289, 21 O.O.2d 452.

Where in a will drawn less than a year prior to his death a testator bequeaths property to a grandson providing he make certain charitable gifts, and it is clear from the will and the amounts involved that testator's primary intent was to benefit the grandson, the condition is invalid but the gift to the grandson is not. Roenick v. Dollar Sav. & Trust Co. (Mahoning 1960) 179 N.E.2d 379, 87 Ohio Law Abs. 289, 21 O.O.2d 452.

A declaration of trust wherein the trustor, the primary trustee, and one of the beneficiaries are the same is not void because of those facts alone; death within one year will not destroy the charitable gift of such inter vivos trust. Drew v. Richards (Ohio Com.Pl. 1960) 177 N.E.2d 631, 87 Ohio

Law Abs. 308, 17 O.O.2d 90, affirmed 177 N.E.2d 633, 87 Ohio Law Abs. 312, 17 O.O.2d 92.

The invalidity of charitable bequests within one year of the testator's death may be waived by the sole heir at law. Ireland v. Cleveland Trust Co. (Ohio Prob. 1958) 157 N.E.2d 396, 80 Ohio Law Abs. 94, 11 O.O.2d 237.

Where testator's only lineal descendant was his granddaughter, who had been adopted by her stepfather who had married the testator's daughter-in-law after the death of the testator's son, the testator died without issue or the lineal descendant of issue, and charitable bequests executed within a year of testator's death are valid. Campbell v. Musart Soc. of Cleveland Museum of Art (Ohio Prob. 1956) 131 N.E.2d 279, 72 Ohio Law Abs. 46, 2 O.O.2d 517.

Where a testator devises or bequeaths property in trust, the income to be paid to his children and others for a period of time and at the expiration of such period the corpus of the trust property to be divided among certain charities, the devise or bequest to the charities is invalid under this section if the testator dies within one year after the execution of his will, leaving issue of his body; where, under such circumstances, the children of the testator take the benefits accruing to them under the will and express a determination not to waive the provisions of this section, they do not violate an in terrorem clause providing for their disinheritance if they make any effort to break, change or set aside the will or any part thereof, nor do they consent that the provision as to the charities shall be considered valid. Kirkbride v. Hickok (Ohio 1951) 155 Ohio St. 293, 98 N.E.2d 815, 44 O.O. 297.

Testatrix having died within one year of the execution of her will, the gift in remainder to charitable and educational institutions became invalid under this section, and said remainder descended as intestate property to the testatrix's sons. Morgan v. First Nat. Bank of Cincinnati (Hamilton 1948) 84 Ohio App. 345, 84 N.E.2d 612, 53 Ohio Law Abs. 129, 39 O.O. 487.

Person adopted in accordance with law of another state, which, at time of adoption, was domicile of adopting parent, is an "adopted child" under this section, even though such person had attained his majority at time of his adoption. Barrett v. Delmore (Ohio 1944) 143 Ohio St. 203, 54 N.E.2d 789, 153 A.L.R. 192, 28 O.O. 133.

Rights and benefits under this section are not restricted to persons adopted in this state or to minors, and such limitation will not be inserted by judicial construction; a child of testator, natural or adopted, though having attained his majority at time of testator's death, may avail himself of beneficial provisions of this section. Barrett v. Delmore (Ohio 1944) 143 Ohio St. 203, 54 N.E.2d 789, 153 A.L.R. 192, 28 O.O. 133.

This section is not applicable to a trust completed within the lifetime of the settlor, although such trust is referred to and incorporated as a part of his will. Cleveland Trust Co. v. White (Cuyahoga 1937) 58 Ohio App. 339, 16 N.E.2d 588, 24 Ohio Law Abs. 629, 9 O.O. 239. Wills ⚭ 13(2)

This section has no reference to a good and sufficient charitable trust in praesenti. Cleveland Trust Co. v. White (Ohio 1938) 134 Ohio St. 1, 15 N.E.2d 627, 118 A.L.R. 475, 11 O.O. 377.

Codicil executed within one year of testator's death revoking bequests, and thereby increasing residue which went to charities, held not void. Ruple v. Hiram College (Cuyahoga 1928) 35 Ohio App. 8, 171 N.E. 417. Charities ⚭ 4; Wills ⚭ 16

History of legislation reviewed by court in requiring that it be given strict construction; the purpose of this section is to prevent a testator, under the fears incident to impending death, from disposing of his estate to the prejudice of his descendants. Ruple v. Hiram College (Cuyahoga 1928) 35 Ohio App. 8, 171 N.E. 417.

Charitable trust, created by will devising residue to trustee for use pursuant to resolution incorporated therein providing that funds should be available for assisting charitable and educational institutions and other matters, was sufficiently definite to enable court to supervise trustee and compel application of funds for charitable objects only. Linney v. Cleveland Trust Co. (Ohio App. 1928) 30 Ohio App. 345, 165 N.E. 101, 28 Ohio Law Rep. 255.

Indefiniteness being a necessary characteristic of charitable trust, the fault, in case objects of trust are not sufficiently defined in the instrument, is cured by appointment of trustees with powers to select objects within classes named subject to control of court. Linney v. Cleveland Trust Co. (Ohio App. 1928) 30 Ohio App. 345, 165 N.E. 101, 28 Ohio Law Rep. 255.

Will devising residence to niece for life, and thereafter to church for parsonage, on condition that certain portraits be kept in their proper place, and residue of estate to church and children's home, did not indicate general charitable intent, in view of provision relating to family portraits.

Ward v. Worthington (Butler 1928) 28 Ohio App. 325, 162 N.E. 714, 6 Ohio Law Abs. 646.

A person not of the blood of the testator who is designated as an heir-at-law under RS 4182 is not issue of the body within the meaning of RS 5915 so as to render invalid a charitable bequest in a will executed within one year of the death of the testator. Theobald v. Fugman (Ohio 1901) 64 Ohio St. 473, 45 W.L.B. 382, 60 N.E. 606.

Where in a controversy over rights to Texas oil and gas royalties of an Ohio testator the Ohio courts considered only assets of the deceased testator in Ohio, and Texas courts had taken jurisdiction of questions over the ownership of such leases, the district court in Ohio will not take jurisdiction to determine ownership of such interests. Gulf Oil Corp. v. Eisenhour (N.D.Ohio 1958) 158 F.Supp. 663, 80 Ohio Law Abs. 421, 5 O.O.2d 488, affirmed 265 F.2d 798, 84 Ohio Law Abs. 272, 11 O.O.2d 308.

Devise to "Bishop of Diocese of Columbus" held to be one for religious purposes and to fall within provisions of this section. Hartley v. Whelan (Franklin 1924) 2 Ohio Law Abs. 363.

6. Power of appointment under will

RC 2107.06 does not apply to the testamentary grant of a power of appointment or the testamentary exercise thereof. In re Lowe's Estate (Cuyahoga 1963) 119 Ohio App. 303, 191 N.E.2d 196, 92 Ohio Law Abs. 369, 27 O.O.2d 319.

7. Survivorship instruments—P.O.D. bank account

A corporation may not be the beneficiary of a payable on death account. Powell v. City Nat. Bank & Trust Co. (Franklin 1981) 2 Ohio App.3d 1, 440 N.E.2d 560, 2 O.B.R. 1.

EXECUTION

2107.02 Who may make will

A person of the age of eighteen years, or over, sound mind and memory, and not under restraint may make a will.

(131 v S 25, eff. 8–10–65; 1953 H 1; GC 10504–2)

Historical and Statutory Notes

Pre–1953 H 1 Amendments: 114 v 346

OSBA Probate and Trust Law Section

1965:

The Committee recommends that the minimum age for making a will be reduced to 18 years and that such age be fixed as the lawful age for exercising a power of appointment, provided the power is not conditioned that it may be exercised only by a donee or holder of greater age. This follows the Model Probate Law.

At least 19 American jurisdictions have statutes under which the legal age for disposing of property under a will is 18. New York has just so voted with respect to both real and personalty, after a study by its Commission on the Law of Estates. Previously for many years in New York an 18 year old could bequeath personalty but not realty. The New York study lists only six states, including Ohio, wherein the age requirement is 21 and notes that of the remaining states the requirements vary according to marital status, sex, type of conveyance and military status. It also notes that of 16 foreign countries only two require a testator to be 21 years of age. The age is 18 or under in the remaining countries.

There have been widespread social and economic changes in our state and country. A man of 18 is subject to service in the Armed Forces with all the attendant responsibility and the risk of his life. Persons 16 may drive automobiles in Ohio. Many marry under 21 and have children. But, a young husband or wife may not now execute a will leaving his or her property to the survivor to avoid the complications and expense of fractional interests passing to young children, with attendant guardianships, or if there be no children, to assure that the family possessions do not have to be divided with parents.

The Committee recognizes that 21 is a more mature age but feels the equities lie strongly on the side of the recommendation. The reduced age limit for the exercise of powers of appointment being made subject to the provision that it shall not apply of [sic.] the creator of the power has seen fit to provide otherwise, this change is permissive only, and not mandatory.

Cross References

Age of majority, 3109.01

Library References

Wills ⚖21.
Westlaw Topic No. 409.
C.J.S. Wills §§ 4, 7 to 8.

Research References

Encyclopedias

38 Am. Jur. Proof of Facts 3d 227, Proof of Testamentary Incapacity of Mentally Retarded Person.

OH Jur. 3d Decedents' Estates § 224, Distinction Between Testamentary Power and Testamentary Capacity.

OH Jur. 3d Decedents' Estates § 229, Minors.

OH Jur. 3d Decedents' Estates § 230, Persons Owning No Property.

OH Jur. 3d Decedents' Estates § 240, Generally; Time as of Which Capacity is Determined.

OH Jur. 3d Decedents' Estates § 252, Generally; Mental Soundness and Testamentary Capacity.

OH Jur. 3d Decedents' Estates § 277, Testator's Body; Uniform Anatomical Gift Act.

OH Jur. 3d Decedents' Estates § 1001, Prima Facie Case of Validity Required.

OH Jur. 3d Decedents' Estates § 1177, Evidence Relating to Testamentary Capacity; Ability to Transact Business—Mental Incompetency and Disability.

Forms

Ohio Forms Legal and Business § 24:112, Who May Make a Will.
Ohio Forms Legal and Business § 24:116, Testamentary Capacity.
Ohio Forms and Transactions F 30.01, General Form of Will.
Ohio Forms and Transactions KP 30.01, Validity and Form of Will.

Treatises and Practice Aids

Carlin, Baldwin's Ohio Practice, Merrick-Rippner Probate Law § 26:2, Testamentary Capacity—Who May Make a Will—in General.

Carlin, Baldwin's Ohio Practice, Merrick-Rippner Probate Law § 26:4, Testamentary Capacity—Who May Make a Will—Lawful Age.

Carlin, Baldwin's Ohio Practice, Merrick-Rippner Probate Law § 28:1, Codicils—Definition.

Carlin, Baldwin's Ohio Practice, Merrick-Rippner Probate Law § 28:2, Codicils—Requirements.

Carlin, Baldwin's Ohio Practice, Merrick-Rippner Probate Law § 30:6, Drafting a Will—Introductory Clause—Assertion of Testamentary Capacity.

Carlin, Baldwin's Ohio Practice, Merrick-Rippner Probate Law § 34:2, Declaring the Validity of a Will—Procedure for Obtaining a Judgment—Petitioner in Action.

Carlin, Baldwin's Ohio Practice, Merrick-Rippner Probate Law § 34:5, Declaring the Validity of a Will—Procedure for Obtaining a Judgment—Judgment.

Carlin, Baldwin's Ohio Practice, Merrick-Rippner Probate Law § 34:6, Declaring the Validity of a Will—Post-Judgment Revocation or Modification.

Carlin, Baldwin's Ohio Practice, Merrick-Rippner Probate Law § 36:1, Admission to Probate—Criteria.

Carlin, Baldwin's Ohio Practice, Merrick-Rippner Probate Law § 26:10, Testamentary Capacity—Defining Capacity—Factors Bearing on Capacity—Undue Influence.

Carlin, Baldwin's Ohio Practice, Merrick-Rippner Probate Law § 30:57, Simple Will—Form.

Carlin, Baldwin's Ohio Practice, Merrick-Rippner Probate Law § 30:58, Publishing Clause—Form.

Restatement (2d) of Property, Don. Trans. § 34.4, Capacity of a Minor to Make a Donative Transfer.

Restatement (2d) of Property, Don. Trans. § 34.5, Donor Mentally Incompetent.

Law Review and Journal Commentaries

Contractual And Donative Capacity, Alexander M. Meiklejohn. 39 Case W Res L Rev 307 (1988–89).

Crisis of Competence—Capacity to execute wills is tenuous for victims of Alzheimer's disease, Robert P. Friedland and James J. McMonagle. (Ed. note: Cleveland hospital neurogeriatrics head and hospital general counsel discuss legal capacity.) 82 A B A J 80 (May 1996).

The Senile Testator: Medicolegal Aspects of Competency, Robert Gene Smith and Laurence M. Hager. 13 Clev–Marshall L Rev 397 (September 1964).

Notes of Decisions

Attorney misconduct 6
Joint will 4
Requirements 5
Testamentary capacity 1-3
    Evidence 1
    Illness or incapacity, effect 2
    Undue influence 3

---

1. Testamentary capacity—Evidence

The opinion of a witness as to the testator's capacity to make a will is not admissible as involving a question of law and fact to be determined by the jury; the witness's opinion as to the testator's sanity must relate to the time of his examination, not to the time of the making of the will, to be admissible in a will contest action. Runyan v. Price (Ohio 1864) 15 Ohio St. 1, 86 Am.Dec. 459.

Trial court did not commit prejudicial error when it sustained objection to hypothetical question posed to expert witness in will contest, regarding whether expert could form opinion as to whether or not it was probable testator suffered from extreme fatigue on date that she executed will; jurors were already aware that decedent was taking drugs that made her sleepy and tired before counsel asked hypothetical question about extreme fatigue. Roll v. Edwards (Ohio App. 4 Dist., Ross, 02-21-2006) No. 05CA2833, 2006-Ohio-830, 2006 WL 439423, Unreported. Wills ⚖ 400

Trial court's finding that mother had testamentary capacity on date she executed new will was not inconsistent with trial court's order that children return certain money taken from mother's accounts to her estate; money was taken before mother executed new will, and was not used for mother's care or maintenance. Hillis v. Humphrey (Ohio App. 5 Dist., Perry, 06-30-2005) No. 05CA6, 2005-Ohio-3459, 2005 WL 1579392, Unreported, appeal not allowed 107 Ohio St.3d 1410, 836 N.E.2d 1230, 2005-Ohio-5859, reconsideration denied 107 Ohio St.3d 1701, 840 N.E.2d 205, 2005-Ohio-6763. Wills ⚖ 21

There was no specific evidence to support nieces contention that decedent lacked the testamentary capacity to change her will, and thus nieces could not prevail in action against estate and devisees on claims of undue influence and lack of capacity; nieces cited generally to decedent's medical records, which depicted an elderly, ill, forgetful, and confused person, but which did not demonstrate a lack of capacity. Woods v. Wright (Ohio App. 5 Dist., Tuscarawas, 08-24-2004) No. 2003AP110086, 2004-Ohio-4547, 2004 WL 1925434, Unreported. Wills ⚖ 31; Wills ⚖ 156

Testator's cousin, who filed will contest, failed to establish that testator lacked testamentary capacity when she executed will, where attorney who drafted will indicated that testator knew what she was doing, individual who was present when testator signed will indicated testator was fully aware of nature and consequences of executing will, attorney stated that he include boilerplate language referencing interests in account "held jointly in my name and that of my spouse" in all wills even though testator was widow, and, although death certificate listed senile dementia as significant condition contributing to testator's death, there was no evidence as to how this condition may have affected testator's mental capacity approximately ten months earlier when she executed will. Martin v. Dew (Ohio App. 10 Dist., Franklin, 05-13-2004) No. 03AP-734, 2004-Ohio-2520, 2004 WL 1109562, Unreported. Wills ⚖ 55(7)

Evidence that testator believed she had visits from deceased relatives, and that she forgot who had brought her food, together with probate expert's affidavit that he believed testator was not of sound mind and memory when she executed will, without more, was insufficient to show that testator lacked testamentary capacity to execute will; expert never had any contact with testator, incidents regarding visits by deceased relatives and testator's forgetfulness occurred during year prior to execution of will, and attorney and secretary who assisted testator in preparing and executing will both asserted that testator was of sound mind and understood the contents of will when it was executed. Boley v. Kennedy (Ohio App. 3 Dist., Crawford, 04-01-2003) No. 3-02-35, 2003-Ohio-1663, 2003 WL

1699844, Unreported, appeal not allowed 99 Ohio St.3d 1513, 792 N.E.2d 200, 2003-Ohio-3957. Wills ⚖ 55(1)

Vague assertions and "feelings" that the testator's mental capacity was deteriorating do not establish a genuine issue of material fact to indicate a lack of testamentary capacity where the assertions are made by persons who (1) were not present at the time the will was discussed or executed in the presence of the testator's attorney, (2) offer no evidence to controvert the attorney's conclusion that the testator was competent to execute her will on the date in question, and (3) cannot specify dates and times when they observed the odd behavior and deteriorating mental and physical condition. Windsor v. Estate of Noldge (Ohio App. 3 Dist., Seneca, 08-22-1996) No. 13-96-11, 1996 WL 476867, Unreported.

Testimony that a testator told his attorney that he had no children when in fact he had several creates a genuine issue of material fact as to whether he had testamentary capacity. Springer v. Lee (Ohio App. 3 Dist., Hancock, 05-02-1996) No. 5-95-42, 1996 WL 223699, Unreported.

A jury is correctly instructed when told that testamentary capacity is shown when the person making the will is able to hold in mind the names and identity of those having natural claims on his bounty, and to appreciate his relation to his family. (See also Monroe v Barclay, 17 OS 302, 269 NE 50 (1867).) Fulkerson v. Fulkerson (Fairfield 1932) 12 Ohio Law Abs. 324, 35 Ohio Law Rep. 478. Wills ⚖ 50; Wills ⚖ 330(1)

Testator had testamentary capacity when he executed will disinheriting his son, even though testator did not mention his son while drafting and executing his will; testator's failure to mention his son was intentional, since he had executed four wills over almost 22 years without ever mentioning his son. Estate of Snell v. Kilburn (Ohio App. 7 Dist., 12-23-2005) 165 Ohio App.3d 352, 846 N.E.2d 572, 2005-Ohio-7076. Wills ⚖ 55(10)

Professor did not lack capacity at time he made his best friend the beneficiary of his life insurance policy; testimony was that he was lucid, independent, strong-willed, and recording made by professor did not demonstrate that he was suicidal. Wallbrown v. Kent State Univ. (Ohio App. 11 Dist., 06-04-2001) 143 Ohio App.3d 762, 758 N.E.2d 1213. Insurance ⚖ 3476(2)

In the absence of undue influence or lack of capacity of deceased professor in changing beneficiary of his life insurance policy to his best friend of many years, professor's wife failed to present sufficient evidence to justify application of equitable principles to allocate some of the policy proceeds to her, even though, after professor's death, she had expended money to satisfy certain outstanding financial matters, bills, and funeral expenses before discovering that she was no longer the policy beneficiary. Wallbrown v. Kent State Univ. (Ohio App. 11 Dist., 06-04-2001) 143 Ohio App.3d 762, 758 N.E.2d 1213. Insurance ⚖ 3479

Genuine issue of material fact as to whether decedent had testamentary capacity to execute valid will precluded summary judgment in action brought by his children to contest will, which named decedent's girlfriend as sole beneficiary of estate. Swihart v. Dozier (Ohio App. 3 Dist., 05-13-1998) 127 Ohio App.3d 552, 713 N.E.2d 482. Judgment ⚖ 181(15.1)

If the uncontradicted evidence adduced from the face of a will and/or from the testimony of the will's witnesses establishes as a matter of law that the testator was under restraint, the will's proponents fail to make a prima facie showing of the will's validity and the probate court may properly deny application to probate. In re Estate of Smith (Ohio App. 4 Dist., 06-02-1997) 120 Ohio App.3d 480, 698 N.E.2d 455. Wills ⚖ 288(1)

Will proponent was entitled to summary judgment on contestant's claim that will was product of testator's son's undue influence, where contestant failed to submit any evidence that testator was susceptible to influence, that son exerted or attempted to exert improper influence over testator, or that some result from the alleged improper influence occurred. Hamilton v. Hector (Ohio App. 3 Dist., 01-27-1997) 117 Ohio App.3d 816, 691 N.E.2d 745. Judgment ⚖ 185.3(1)

In determining whether testator had sufficient mental capacity to recognize those relatives with natural claim to his estate, fact finder should consider nature of relationship between testator and his distant relatives, since testator is not required to first identify and then specifically disinherit distant relatives of whose existence he is not aware. Bland v. Graves (Summit 1993) 85 Ohio App.3d 644, 620 N.E.2d 920, motion to certify overruled 67 Ohio St.3d 1464, 619 N.E.2d 698, rehearing denied 67 Ohio St.3d 1507, 622 N.E.2d 654, appeal after new trial 99 Ohio App.3d 123, 650 N.E.2d 117, dismissed, appeal not allowed 72 Ohio St.3d 1405, 647 N.E.2d 494. Wills ⚖ 50

Court in granting new trial did not impermissibly pass upon credibility of witnesses who testified that testatrix had testamentary capacity; in crediting testimony of numerous witnesses who had frequent contact with testatrix at time of signing will and who stated that testatrix was of sound mind over testimony of three persons who had no contact with testatrix at that time, court was not passing generally on credibility of witnesses but was considering whether evidence was direct or circumstantial and the amount of weight that thus should be afforded it. Bland v. Graves (Summit 1993) 85 Ohio App.3d 644, 620 N.E.2d 920, motion to certify overruled 67 Ohio St.3d 1464, 619 N.E.2d 698, rehearing denied 67 Ohio St.3d 1507, 622 N.E.2d 654, appeal after new trial 99 Ohio App.3d 123, 650 N.E.2d 117, dismissed, appeal not allowed 72 Ohio St.3d 1405, 647 N.E.2d 494. Wills ⚖ 337

Neither a finding of incompetence by the court nor a failure to find incompetence in a guardianship proceeding is to be used in a later will contest on the issue of the deceased ward's competence, which must be resolved de novo on the law and evidence in the will contest, even though some of the same evidence submitted in the guardianship proceeding may be used. In re Guardianship of Rudy (Ohio 1992) 65 Ohio St.3d 394, 604 N.E.2d 736, rehearing denied 65 Ohio St.3d 1482, 604 N.E.2d 759.

To determine whether testamentary capacity exists, it must be ascertained whether a testator has sufficient mind and memory to (1) understand the nature of the business in which he was engaged, (2) comprehend generally the nature and extent of his property, (3) know the identity of those who had natural claims upon his bounty, and (4) appreciate his relation to members of his family. Doyle v. Schott (Hamilton 1989) 65 Ohio App.3d 92, 582 N.E.2d 1057, motion overruled 49 Ohio St.3d 708, 551 N.E.2d 1304. Wills ⚖ 50

Evidence of alcohol abuse by a testatrix does not by itself create an inference of testamentary incapacity. Doyle v. Schott (Hamilton 1989) 65 Ohio App.3d 92, 582 N.E.2d 1057, motion overruled 49 Ohio St.3d 708, 551 N.E.2d 1304. Wills ⚖ 52(1)

Assertion of the invalidity of a will on the basis of undue influence by a sister-in-law against the testatrix is not sustained where the only evidence suggesting undue influence was that the will was presented to the testatrix at a party, and a brother-in-law of the testatrix speculated that the testatrix did not read the will because he could not imagine that she would sign it, and where there was no evidence that the testatrix was incapacitated or that she lacked knowledge of its contents. Doyle v. Schott (Hamilton 1989) 65 Ohio App.3d 92, 582 N.E.2d 1057, motion overruled 49 Ohio St.3d 708, 551 N.E.2d 1304. Wills ⚖ 157; Wills ⚖ 166(2)

To invalidate a will on the basis of undue influence, the person challenging the will must prove (1) susceptibility of the testator, (2) an opportunity for another to exert influence, (3) the fact of influence, and (4) an improper result of such influence. Doyle v. Schott (Hamilton 1989) 65 Ohio App.3d 92, 582 N.E.2d 1057, motion overruled 49 Ohio St.3d 708, 551 N.E.2d 1304. Wills ⚖ 155.1

A declaration of incompetency by a probate court results in a presumption of a lack of testamentary capacity, which may be rebutted by evidence which establishes that, at the time of the execution of the will, the testator had sufficient mind and memory (1) to understand the nature of the business in which he was engaged, (2) to comprehend generally the nature and extent of his property, (3) to hold in his mind the names and identity of those who had natural claims upon his bounty, and (4) to be able to appreciate his relation to members of his family; a "high degree of proof" to demonstrate testamentary capacity is not required. Taylor v. Garinger (Fayette 1986) 30 Ohio App.3d 184, 507 N.E.2d 406, 30 O.B.R. 326. Wills ⚖ 52(4)

In proceeding attacking will on grounds of undue influence, it is error for trial court to grant motion in limine limiting presentation of evidence to those events which occurred within specified time period before and after execution of contested will. Rich v. Quinn (Warren 1983) 13 Ohio App.3d 102, 468 N.E.2d 365, 13 O.B.R. 119. Wills ⚖ 319

A testator's treating physician is competent to give expert opinion on the testator's mental condition. Gannett v. Booher (Huron 1983) 12 Ohio App.3d 49, 465 N.E.2d 1326, 12 O.B.R. 190.

In will contest, trial court did not err in admitting opinion of expert that testatrix was of sound mind and was capable of making a will even though the opinion embraced ultimate issue to be decided by trier of fact since the witness' observations and analysis would provide information beyond that which a common man could provide. In re Seelig's Estate (Lucas 1981) 2 Ohio App.3d 223, 441 N.E.2d 598, 2 O.B.R. 243. Evidence ⚖ 506

In a will contest, evidence that the executor named in the will had resided with testator up to the time of his death, and had received a devise of 160 acres, and that the executor had been in intimate relation with the attorney who drew the will, held sufficient, in connection with evidence as to testator's mental capacity, due to his age of 82 years, and of his habits of life and conversations, and the provisions of the will itself, to take to the jury the issue of undue influence. Board of Education of Pickaway Tp.

Rural School Dist. v. Phillips (Ohio 1921) 103 Ohio St. 622, 134 N.E. 646, 19 Ohio Law Rep. 516. Wills ⇐ 324(3)

Under GC 11494, disqualifying an attorney from testifying concerning a communication made to him by his client except by the client's express consent, an attorney, who acted as subscribing witness to client's will, could testify as to testamentary capacity or as to any other fact affecting validity of will, since client by procuring attorney as a subscribing witness consented that he might so testify. Knepper v. Knepper (Ohio 1921) 103 Ohio St. 529, 134 N.E. 476, 19 Ohio Law Rep. 462. Attorney And Client ⇐ 22; Witnesses ⇐ 219(3)

Testamentary capacity exists where the testator has sufficient mind and memory (1) to understand the nature of the business in which he is engaged, (2) to comprehend generally the nature and extent of his property, (3) to hold in his mind the names and identity of those who have natural claim upon his bounty, and (4) to be able to appreciate his relation to the members of his family. Niemes v. Niemes (Ohio 1917) 97 Ohio St. 145, 119 N.E. 503, 15 Ohio Law Rep. 484, 15 Ohio Law Rep. 565. Wills ⇐ 50

Physician of a testator can express an opinion as to the actual condition of his patient's mind, founded on his study of testator while in attendance at the time and prior to the date of the will. Bahl v. Byal (Ohio 1914) 90 Ohio St. 129, 106 N.E. 766, 11 Ohio Law Rep. 519. Evidence ⇐ 548

An attack on a will cannot be maintained just because the testator did not make the will the witnesses liked or thought he should have made. Wilson v. Wilson (Ohio Cir. 1909) 22 Ohio C.D. 498, 14 Ohio C.C.N.S. 241.

Since a person may lack in capacity for the transaction of ordinary business and lack in contractual capacity and yet have testamentary capacity, a charge to the jury requiring "capacity enough to attend to ordinary business and to know and understand the business he was engaged in" lacks the essential requirements of testamentary capacity to make a will, and is thus misleading and prejudicial. Wadsworth v. Purdy (Ohio Cir. 1908) 21 Ohio C.D. 110, 12 Ohio C.C.N.S. 8.

The subject of delusions of a testator is of no importance to court or jury; the only question is whether the delusions were carried to such an extent that they affected either the natural or selected objects of his bounty, distorting his judgment and preventing him from making a rational disposition of his property. Wadsworth v. Purdy (Ohio Cir. 1908) 21 Ohio C.D. 110, 12 Ohio C.C.N.S. 8.

A jury charge which states that in order to make a valid will "it is necessary that a person shall have sufficient mental capacity for the transactions of the ordinary affairs of life," when followed by the charge that "he need not have sufficient capacity to make a contract but must understand substantially what he or she is doing and the nature of the act in which he or she is engaged" is a correct statement of law and not error. Welsh Hills Baptist Church v. Wilson (Ohio Cir. 1905) 19 Ohio C.D. 391, 9 Ohio C.C.(N.S.) 611, affirmed 75 Ohio St. 636, 80 N.E. 1135, 4 Ohio Law Rep. 664.

A person desiring to make a will must have sufficient mental capacity to remember his property and the proper objects of his bounty, and, without suggestion, to make a testamentary disposition of it. Moore v. Caldwell (Ohio Cir. 1904) 17 Ohio C.D. 449, 6 Ohio C.C.N.S. 484.

A delusion of a testator does not constitute mental incapacity to make a will unless it is an insane delusion, and in determining whether a testator was suffering from such a delusion at the time he made his will, the testimony offered on the subject should be considered by the jury. Moore v. Caldwell (Ohio Cir. 1904) 17 Ohio C.D. 449, 6 Ohio C.C.N.S. 484.

It does not require the highest degree of mental capacity to make a will; a person who, at the time of making his will, has an understanding of the nature of the business in which he is engaged, a recollection of the property he means to dispose of, the persons who have a claim upon his bounty and the manner in which it is to be distributed, has sufficient mental capacity to execute a will. Kettemann v. Metzger (Ohio Cir. 1901) 13 Ohio C.D. 61, 3 Ohio C.C.N.S. 224.

Where a will is contested on the ground that the testator lacked the mental capacity to make it, deeds executed by the testator at about the same time may be admitted in evidence to show his method of doing business and the nature of the business transacted by him since this may throw light on his mental capacity. Wilson v. Wilson (Ohio Com.Pl. 1908) 19 Ohio Dec. 188, 7 Ohio NP(NS) 435, reversed 22 Ohio C.D. 498, 14 Ohio C.C.(N.S.) 241.

Where a will is alleged to be invalid on the ground the testator lacked the necessary mental capacity to make it, a legatee or devisee who is a party to the proceeding is a competent witness to testify to acts of the testator, and as to his mental capacity based on those acts. Wilson v. Wilson (Ohio Com.Pl. 1908) 19 Ohio Dec. 188, 7 Ohio NP(NS) 435, reversed 22 Ohio C.D. 498, 14 Ohio C.C.(N.S.) 241.

The capacity requisite to revoke a will is the capacity requisite to make a will, and there is a clear distinction between intelligence enough to destroy and capacity to revoke; the destruction of a will does not revoke it, unless done with the intention to revoke. In re Jones' Estate (Ohio Prob. 1895) 2 Ohio Dec. 409, 2 Ohio N.P. 190, 2 Ohio N.P. 194, 2 Ohio N.P. 209.

2. —— Illness or incapacity, effect, testamentary capacity

A person is not incapacitated to make and execute a will merely by reason of advanced years or illiteracy. Barlion v. Connor (Ohio App. 1 Dist. 1917) 9 Ohio App. 72, 31 Ohio C.A. 463.

The requirement that a testator shall be of sound mind and memory at the time of executing his will, does not mean that one weakened by sickness is incapable of making a will, but only that he shall have sufficient memory and mental capacity to understand fully what he is doing, and testimony of a number of reputable witnesses in support of a will is not shaken by that of others who told of his weakened physical condition as shown by shuffling of the feet, failure to recognize some former acquaintances and halting conversations. (See also Monroe v Barclay, 17 OS 302, 269 NE 50 (1867).) Fulkerson v. Fulkerson (Fairfield 1932) 12 Ohio Law Abs. 324, 35 Ohio Law Rep. 478. Wills ⇐ 24

There was a confidential relationship between professor and his best friend that created presumption that professor changed the beneficiary of his life insurance policy to his best friend as a result of undue influence, where the relationship spanned thirty years from time both men were graduate students; professor turned to his friend when his wife failed to make arrangements to transport him from the hospital, professor made a recording that made evident their close relationship. Wallbrown v. Kent State Univ. (Ohio App. 11 Dist., 06-04-2001) 143 Ohio App.3d 762, 758 N.E.2d 1213. Insurance ⇐ 3492

Evidence that testator was in poor health and confined to a wheelchair at time she executed will and died two weeks later was insufficient to establish that testator was under restraint; evidence did not show that testator was in a weakened or susceptible mental state, and instead indicated that she directed inclusion of a provision for her deceased son's heirs after reviewing will. In re Estate of Smith (Ohio App. 4 Dist., 06-02-1997) 120 Ohio App.3d 480, 698 N.E.2d 455. Wills ⇐ 166(8)

Psychiatric testimony of lack of testamentary capacity to execute a will, despite a diagnosis of the testatrix as having a personality disorder with chronic alcoholism, is insufficient to satisfy the conclusion of testamentary capacity where a psychiatrist concluded that the testatrix was not mentally ill, was above average in intelligence, possessed a good memory other than short term memory loss caused by alcohol, and managed her daily affairs. Doyle v. Schott (Hamilton 1989) 65 Ohio App.3d 92, 582 N.E.2d 1057, motion overruled 49 Ohio St.3d 708, 551 N.E.2d 1304. Wills ⇐ 55(6)

It is presumed that a ward for whom a guardian has been appointed upon grounds of physical incompetency is mentally competent and has testamentary power. Roderick v. Fisher (Franklin 1954) 97 Ohio App. 95, 122 N.E.2d 475, 51 A.L.R.2d 762, 54 O.O. 264.

In the contest of a will, the admission of an answer to the question to a witness whether the testator had capacity to form an intent to dispose of his property is not error justifying the setting aside of a verdict sustaining the will. Dunlap v. Dunlap (Ohio 1913) 89 Ohio St. 28, 104 N.E. 1006, 11 Ohio Law Rep. 294, 11 Ohio Law Rep. 318. Wills ⇐ 400

Where there is no evidence that a testator's will was made under the influence of liquor, the fact that the testator was intoxicated during the night after he returned home from making his will does not mean that he lacked mental capacity earlier while making it. Gregg v. Moore (Ohio Cir. 1911) 23 Ohio C.D. 534, 14 Ohio C.C.N.S. 570.

A will may not be set aside due to the fact that the testator was afflicted with progressive locomotor ataxia and partially paralyzed, where during that time he directed the operation and management of a large farm business and did all that could have been done by a person of a sound and active mind, and the only testimony which went to the question of mental capacity was the testator's forgetfulness on certain occasions. Gregg v. Moore (Ohio Cir. 1911) 23 Ohio C.D. 534, 14 Ohio C.C.N.S. 570.

A testator is not required to make an equitable will, and because he makes one with which the witnesses for the contestants do not agree does not mean he lacks testamentary capacity, even though the evidence shows some physical weakness, failure of memory, or a mistake of an unimportant character in connection with business affairs of the testator. Wilson v. Wilson (Ohio Cir. 1909) 22 Ohio C.D. 498, 14 Ohio C.C.N.S. 241.

The question of the mental capacity of a testator when making his will is one of whether he had a disposing memory capable of recollecting his property, the manner of distributing it, and the objects of his bounty; the fact that the testator was eighty-four years of age and forgetful as to minor matters is not evidence of lack of testamentary capacity. Rewell v. Warden (Ohio Cir. 1903) 14 Ohio C.D. 344, 4 Ohio C.C.N.S. 545.

A person ill and dying is not of "sound mind and memory." In re Burrows' Estate (Ohio Prob. 1900) 11 Ohio Dec. 229, 8 Ohio N.P. 358.

3. —— Undue influence, testamentary capacity

Evidence supported trial court's finding that youngest son did not exert undue influence over creation of deed transferring mother's interest in farm to son; attorney who drafted mother's will and the deed transferring farm to son was mother's attorney, and when attorney met with mother he had discussions with her outside the presence of son and verified her intentions. Patterson v. Patterson (Ohio App. 3 Dist., Shelby, 05-09-2005) No. 17-04-07, 2005-Ohio-2254, 2005 WL 1074809, Unreported. Deeds ⟳ 211(4)

Testator's cousin, who filed will contest, failed to establish undue influence by beneficiary named in will; although beneficiary was present when attorney and testator discussed will changes and during execution of will, attorney indicated that testator knew what she was doing, affidavits submitted by beneficiaries indicated that testator made bequests out of desire to give to her friends, and cousin acknowledged that she never met testator. Martin v. Dew (Ohio App. 10 Dist., Franklin, 05-13-2004) No. 03AP-734, 2004-Ohio-2520, 2004 WL 1109562, Unreported. Wills ⟳ 166(2)

Testator's alleged oral statements to half-sister regarding alleged undue influence exerted upon her by niece did not come within exception to rule against hearsay for statements by deceased, in will contest; statements were not offered to rebut testimony by executor of estate as adverse party, but comprised evidence supporting half-sister's case in chief. Boley v. Kennedy (Ohio App. 3 Dist., Crawford, 04-01-2003) No. 3-02-35, 2003-Ohio-1663, 2003 WL 1699844, Unreported, appeal not allowed 99 Ohio St.3d 1513, 792 N.E.2d 200, 2003-Ohio-3957. Evidence ⟳ 317(18)

That testator's niece may have encouraged testator to purchase a vehicle, and that testator purchased vehicle but hardly ever used it, without more, was insufficient to show that niece exerted undue influence over testator at time testator executed will. Boley v. Kennedy (Ohio App. 3 Dist., Crawford, 04-01-2003) No. 3-02-35, 2003-Ohio-1663, 2003 WL 1699844, Unreported, appeal not allowed 99 Ohio St.3d 1513, 792 N.E.2d 200, 2003-Ohio-3957. Wills ⟳ 166(1)

Hearsay deposition testimony of testator's caretaker, that sole beneficiary and beneficiary's husband physically abused testator, that they removed telephones from his home, that they disconnected alarm system and terrorized him, without any competent evidence, did not show that testator was subject to undue duress such that it rendered him mentally incapacitated from creating and executing will that disinherited adopted daughter. Lakes v. Ryan (Ohio App. 12 Dist., Butler, 02-03-2003) No. CA2002-05-118, 2003-Ohio-504, 2003 WL 231272, Unreported. Wills ⟳ 166(8)

Testator was not tricked into thinking he was signing a power of attorney when he executed warranty deed conveying real property to oldest daughter, so as to render transfer void, in will contest brought by adopted daughter; testator executed deed in presence of attorney, attorney was not aware of any undue influence or duress exerted by daughter on testator during execution of transfer, and employee of law office who witnessed testator sign deed did not observe daughter exert any undue influence over testator. Lakes v. Ryan (Ohio App. 12 Dist., Butler, 02-03-2003) No. CA2002-05-118, 2003-Ohio-504, 2003 WL 231272, Unreported. Deeds ⟳ 72(7)

Father's surrender of annuities, to which adopted daughter was secondary beneficiary, was not result of undue influence by older daughter; father executed request to surrender annuities in order to pay for nursing home expenses, and there was no evidence that proceeds from surrender were used for anything other than father's expenses. Lakes v. Ryan (Ohio App. 12 Dist., Butler, 02-03-2003) No. CA2002-05-118, 2003-Ohio-504, 2003 WL 231272, Unreported. Annuities ⟳ 1

By undue influence the law means an influence which substitutes the wishes of another for the judgment of a testator; a will cannot be impeached for undue influence unless the influence under which it is made imposes some restraint upon the testator in the disposition of his property in accordance with his own independent wishes and judgment. (See also Monroe v Barclay, 17 OS 302, 269 NE 50 (1867).) Fulkerson v. Fulkerson (Fairfield 1932) 12 Ohio Law Abs. 324, 35 Ohio Law Rep. 478.

Evidence that deceased professor was not motivated by undue influence of his best friend when he made his best friend the beneficiary of his life insurance policy was sufficient to overcome presumption of undue influence arising from confidential relationship between professor and best friend in declaratory judgment action for proceeds of the policy; best friend assisted professor at professor's request, testimony showed professor to be competent, lucid, independent, and not susceptible to influence of others, professor had nearly 18 months to change his mind regarding beneficiary. Wallbrown v. Kent State Univ. (Ohio App. 11 Dist., 06-04-2001) 143 Ohio App.3d 762, 758 N.E.2d 1213. Insurance ⟳ 3492

Genuine issues of material fact as to whether decedent's girlfriend had exerted undue influence on decedent, causing him to change his will to her favor five days before he died, precluded summary judgment in action brought by decedent's children to contest will. Swihart v. Dozier (Ohio App. 3 Dist., 05-13-1998) 127 Ohio App.3d 552, 713 N.E.2d 482. Judgment ⟳ 181(15.1)

Rebuttable presumption of undue influence does not arise when attorney, who is related to testator by blood or marriage, prepares will or trust in which he or she is named as beneficiary. Lah v. Rogers (Ohio App. 11 Dist., 01-02-1998) 125 Ohio App.3d 164, 707 N.E.2d 1208. Wills ⟳ 163(4)

Undue influence must be present or operative at time of execution of will resulting in dispositions which testator would not otherwise have made. Hamilton v. Hector (Ohio App. 3 Dist., 01-27-1997) 117 Ohio App.3d 816, 691 N.E.2d 745. Wills ⟳ 159

Will contestant claiming undue influence bears burden of demonstrating: (1) susceptible testator, (2) another's opportunity to exert influence on testator, (3) fact that improper influence was exerted or attempted, and (4) result showing effect of improper influence. Hamilton v. Hector (Ohio App. 3 Dist., 01-27-1997) 117 Ohio App.3d 816, 691 N.E.2d 745. Wills ⟳ 163(1)

Trial court did not abuse its discretion in excluding testimony purporting to show that beneficiary of will wielded undue influence over testatrix; beneficiary was in testatrix' room while terms of will were discussed at testatrix' request, and, although testimony purportedly would have established that beneficiary was deeded property from another elderly person to whom she had provided care, the series of inferences that would have to be made to conclude that undue influence was wielded over testatrix were too tenuous. Bland v. Graves (Summit 1993) 85 Ohio App.3d 644, 620 N.E.2d 920, motion to certify overruled 67 Ohio St.3d 1464, 619 N.E.2d 698, rehearing denied 67 Ohio St.3d 1507, 622 N.E.2d 654, appeal after new trial 99 Ohio App.3d 123, 650 N.E.2d 117, dismissed, appeal not allowed 72 Ohio St.3d 1405, 647 N.E.2d 494. Wills ⟳ 164(1)

Trial court did not abuse its discretion in refusing to compel discovery of mortgage loan application by beneficiary of will, which application purported to support allegation of undue influence over testatrix by beneficiary; no direct evidence of undue influence was presented to court, and allegations were based solely upon innuendo. Bland v. Graves (Summit 1993) 85 Ohio App.3d 644, 620 N.E.2d 920, motion to certify overruled 67 Ohio St.3d 1464, 619 N.E.2d 698, rehearing denied 67 Ohio St.3d 1507, 622 N.E.2d 654, appeal after new trial 99 Ohio App.3d 123, 650 N.E.2d 117, dismissed, appeal not allowed 72 Ohio St.3d 1405, 647 N.E.2d 494. Wills ⟳ 314

Fact that interrogatory to jury asked only whether will, but not whether codicil, was product of undue influence did not entitle plaintiffs to retrial on issue of whether codicil was product of undue influence after jury found that will was not product of undue influence; plaintiffs could prevail only if will was found invalid. Bland v. Graves (Summit 1993) 85 Ohio App.3d 644, 620 N.E.2d 920, motion to certify overruled 67 Ohio St.3d 1464, 619 N.E.2d 698, rehearing denied 67 Ohio St.3d 1507, 622 N.E.2d 654, appeal after new trial 99 Ohio App.3d 123, 650 N.E.2d 117, dismissed, appeal not allowed 72 Ohio St.3d 1405, 647 N.E.2d 494. Wills ⟳ 337

Trial court did not abuse its discretion in ordering new trial on issue of testamentary capacity after jury returned verdict that testatrix, who failed to name as legatees her second cousins, who were her nearest living relatives, lacked capacity in that she was unaware of which persons had "natural claims" to her estate; trial court could have concluded that jury was confused from jury's questions to court, as to whether attorney drafting will is responsible for informing testatrix of her family tree, and whether testatrix is responsible for knowing names of her relatives whether or not she knows of their existence. Bland v. Graves (Summit 1993) 85 Ohio App.3d 644, 620 N.E.2d 920, motion to certify overruled 67 Ohio St.3d 1464, 619 N.E.2d 698, rehearing denied 67 Ohio St.3d 1507, 622 N.E.2d 654, appeal after new trial 99 Ohio App.3d 123, 650 N.E.2d 117, dismissed, appeal not allowed 72 Ohio St.3d 1405, 647 N.E.2d 494. Wills ⟳ 337

New trial was properly limited to issue of testamentary capacity after trial court set aside jury finding that testatrix lacked capacity but allowed jury finding that no undue influence was wielded over testatrix to stand; issues were sufficiently distinct to allow retrial of one without the other. Bland v. Graves (Summit 1993) 85 Ohio App.3d 644, 620 N.E.2d 920, motion to certify overruled 67 Ohio St.3d 1464, 619 N.E.2d 698, rehearing denied 67 Ohio St.3d 1507, 622 N.E.2d 654, appeal after new trial 99 Ohio App.3d 123, 650 N.E.2d 117, dismissed, appeal not allowed 72 Ohio St.3d 1405, 647 N.E.2d 494. Wills ⚬→ 337

A presumption of undue influence, rebuttable by a preponderance of the evidence, arises when (1) the relationship of attorney and client exists between a testator and an attorney, (2) the attorney is named as a beneficiary in the will, (3) the attorney/beneficiary is not related by blood or marriage to the testator, and (4) the attorney/beneficiary actively participates in the preparation of the will. Krischbaum v. Dillon (Ohio 1991) 58 Ohio St.3d 58, 567 N.E.2d 1291. Wills ⚬→ 163(4)

Norms of behavior prescribed in the Code of Professional Responsibility are relevant to the issue of whether an attorney has brought undue influence to bear upon a testator. Krischbaum v. Dillon (Ohio 1991) 58 Ohio St.3d 58, 567 N.E.2d 1291. Wills ⚬→ 164(1)

Undue influence by an attorney drafting a will is not established merely by the naming of the attorney as executor and the inclusion of an in terrorem clause. Gannett v. Booher (Huron 1983) 12 Ohio App.3d 49, 465 N.E.2d 1326, 12 O.B.R. 190.

The mere existence of undue influence or an opportunity to exercise it, although coupled with an interest or motive to do so, is not sufficient to invalidate a will, but such influence must be actually exerted on the mind of the testator with respect to the execution of the will in question, and, in order to invalidate the will, it must be shown that the undue influence resulted in the making of testamentary dispositions which the testator would not otherwise have made. West v. Henry (Ohio 1962) 173 Ohio St. 498, 184 N.E.2d 200, 20 O.O.2d 119. Wills ⚬→ 158

A daughter may legally seek her mother's preference to the exclusion of her sisters, so long as she does not go to the extent of making her mother do something she does not want to do, and such conduct does not amount to undue influence. Meyer v. Geiger (Hamilton 1938) 34 N.E.2d 581, 34 Ohio Law Abs. 1. Wills ⚬→ 155.3; Wills ⚬→ 159

Exercise of undue influence in execution of will need not be shown by direct proof, but it may be inferred from circumstances. Raymond v. Hearon (Hamilton 1928) 30 Ohio App. 184, 164 N.E. 644, 6 Ohio Law Abs. 548.

To amount to "undue influence" it must appear that free agency of testator is destroyed, and this may be done by importunity, overpersuasion, or moral coercion of any kind which would constrain a person to do an act against his will. Raymond v. Hearon (Hamilton 1928) 30 Ohio App. 184, 164 N.E. 644, 6 Ohio Law Abs. 548.

"Undue influence," which will invalidate a deed or will, must be such as to control mental operations of grantor, overcome his power of resistance, and oblige him to adopt the will of another, thus producing disposition of property which he would not have made freely; the means of control may consist of force or coercion, violence or threatened violence, or moral coercion; the extent or degree of undue influence is wholly immaterial, if it is sufficient to make act alleged the act of another rather than the expression of the mind of grantor. Finney v. Morehouse (Wood 1927) 27 Ohio App. 499, 161 N.E. 293, 6 Ohio Law Abs. 419.

Where a woman after long deliberations executes a will in which she follows the written instructions of her deceased husband regarding the disposition of property received by her from him instead of giving all the property to her children as she had desired, she has executed her will freely and willingly and not under undue influence. Wilder v. Taylor (Ohio Cir. 1911) 23 Ohio C.D. 643, 14 Ohio C.C.(N.S.) 255, reversed 87 Ohio St. 520, 102 N.E. 1135, 10 Ohio Law Rep. 602.

Courts of equity will not vacate a deed or set aside a will on the ground of influence or importunity, unless it has been unduly or improperly exercised; fair argument and persuasion, or appeals to the conscience or sense of duty of the testator, if fairly made, lay no foundation for setting aside a will. Gregg v. Moore (Ohio Cir. 1911) 23 Ohio C.D. 534, 14 Ohio C.C.N.S. 570.

That a testator changed his will in a manner believed by some to prevent a fair and reasonable distribution of his property is not alone reason to set the instrument aside on the ground of undue influence, where there is cause to believe the testator did so for reasons he found satisfactory. Gregg v. Moore (Ohio Cir. 1911) 23 Ohio C.D. 534, 14 Ohio C.C.N.S. 570.

A verdict setting aside a will on the ground of undue influence is not justified by the mere fact of a beneficiary's presence at the place where the will was executed, nor by the fact that he gave advice to the testator concerning the will. Wilson v. Wilson (Ohio Cir. 1909) 22 Ohio C.D. 498, 14 Ohio C.C.N.S. 241.

Actions to contest wills are inaugurated with a legal presumption in favor of the will and of the mental capacity of the testator and against undue influence. Beresford v. Stanley (Ohio Com.Pl. 1898) 9 Ohio Dec. 134, 6 Ohio N.P. 38.

Where the evidence showed that the decedent disinherited the plaintiff three weeks after making plaintiff her primary beneficiary in a proposed will that was subsequently rejected, and evidence further showed that the decedent was competent and under no undue influence when she executed her will, then the jury could properly find that decedent was of sound mind when she executed her will. Barlow v Kitts, No. 3296 (9th Dist Ct App, Lorain, 9–22–82).

A purported will may be refused admission to probate if the circumstances surrounding its execution are such as to show that the free agency of the testator was destroyed as far as the objects of his bounty are concerned, even though such circumstances when taken separately are inconclusive. In re Maurer's Will (Ohio Prob. 1933) 31 Ohio NP(NS) 247.

The sole beneficiary under a purported will who procured the scrivener to draw the instrument and her own friends to witness it and who was the testator's landlady and a nonrelative, will be presumed to have unduly influenced the maker, if the maker is an old man who signed the instrument six days before he died in the home of the sole beneficiary away from his next of kin, while in a feeble condition. In re Maurer's Will (Ohio Prob. 1933) 31 Ohio NP(NS) 247.

4. Joint will

Even though the separate wills of a husband and wife refer to the other's property and estate and the disposition in each is practically identical, a joint will is not thereby created where the wills are made at different times and are clearly separate and distinct and revocable by each maker respectively. Coghlin v. Coghlin (Ohio Cir. 1904) 16 Ohio C.D. 18, 4 Ohio C.C.N.S. 161.

5. Requirements

A married woman may make a will. Allen v. Little (Ohio 1831) 5 Ohio 65.

There is no inherent or common-law right to dispose of one's property by will; such right depends upon statute. In re Estate of Mantalis (Ohio App. 2 Dist., 01-31-1996) 109 Ohio App.3d 61, 671 N.E.2d 1062. Wills ⚬→ 1

There is no inherent right to make a will. In re Miller's Estate (Ohio 1954) 160 Ohio St. 529, 117 N.E.2d 598, 46 A.L.R.2d 493, 52 O.O. 437. Wills ⚬→ 1

Under the provisions of this section, an instrument which fulfills all other statutory requirements relative to the execution of wills, may be probated as a valid will even though it does not dispose of property. In Re Crow's Will, 4 Ohio Supp. 370, 31 Abs 35, 17 OO 8 (Prob 1940).

6. Attorney misconduct

Credible evidence supported trial court's finding that attorney acted as attorney for mother and drafted documents pursuant to her request without any undue influence from mother's youngest son, in mother's action to recover monies son allegedly took from mother; attorney testified that even though mother and youngest son came into his office together, he spoke to mother individually, outside of son's presence, and that son did not ask him to draft mother's will, power of attorney, or deed transferring farm to youngest son, mother asserted attorney-client privilege when attorney was asked to testify about his conversations with her regarding her will and the deed, and youngest son testified that he did not ask attorney to prepare the documents for mother. Patterson v. Patterson (Ohio App. 3 Dist., Shelby, 05-09-2005) No. 17-04-07, 2005-Ohio-2254, 2005 WL 1074809, Unreported. Wills ⚬→ 166(2)

Trial court was required to consider the alleged bad faith of attorney and law firm in drafting testator's will and transferring her stock shares to grandson as an element of fraud, collusion, or other malicious conduct, rather than considering it on its own, when determining whether attorney and law firm waived their immunity from legal malpractice suit brought by testator's children. LeRoy v. Allen, Yurasek & Merklin (Ohio App. 3 Dist., 08-29-2005) 162 Ohio App.3d 155, 832 N.E.2d 1246, 2005-Ohio-4452, opinion vacated and superseded on reconsideration 2005-Ohio-4452, 2005 WL 2064144, appeal allowed 108 Ohio St.3d 1411, 841 N.E.2d 317, 2006-Ohio-179, appeal allowed 108 Ohio St.3d 1435, 842 N.E.2d 61, 2006-Ohio-421. Attorney And Client ⚬→ 26

2107.03 Method of making will

Except oral wills, every last will and testament shall be in writing, but may be handwritten or typewritten. Such will shall be signed at the end by the party making it, or by some other person in such party's presence and at his express direction, and be attested and subscribed in the presence of such party, by two or more competent witnesses, who saw the testator subscribe, or heard him acknowledge his signature.

(1953 H 1, eff. 10–1–53; GC 10504–3)

Historical and Statutory Notes

Pre–1953 H 1 Amendments: 114 v 346

Cross References

Oral will, 2107.60

Library References

Wills ⚖ 108 to 123.
Westlaw Topic No. 409.
C.J.S. Wills §§ 171, 217 to 314.

Research References

Encyclopedias

OH Jur. 3d Conflict of Laws § 40, Formal Validity.
OH Jur. 3d Decedents' Estates § 68, Joint Estates; Pod Accounts.
OH Jur. 3d Decedents' Estates § 287, Copy of Original as Will.
OH Jur. 3d Decedents' Estates § 293, Reference to Existing Instruments.
OH Jur. 3d Decedents' Estates § 297, Necessity for Signature, Generally.
OH Jur. 3d Decedents' Estates § 302, Signature by Another for Testator.
OH Jur. 3d Decedents' Estates § 303, Signature at End of Will.
OH Jur. 3d Decedents' Estates § 307, Writing in Margin.
OH Jur. 3d Decedents' Estates § 308, Signature Below Attestation Clause.
OH Jur. 3d Decedents' Estates § 309, Signature Within Attestation or Testimonium Clause.
OH Jur. 3d Decedents' Estates § 310, Statutory Requirement of Attestation and Subscription.
OH Jur. 3d Decedents' Estates § 312, Attestation and Subscription Distinguished.
OH Jur. 3d Decedents' Estates § 313, Number of Witnesses.
OH Jur. 3d Decedents' Estates § 316, Attestation to Signature or Acknowledgment.
OH Jur. 3d Decedents' Estates § 318, Sufficiency of Acknowledgment—Failure of Testator to Identify Document as Will.
OH Jur. 3d Decedents' Estates § 320, Request that Witnesses Sign or Attest.
OH Jur. 3d Decedents' Estates § 321, Order of Signing as Between Testator and Witnesses.
OH Jur. 3d Decedents' Estates § 322, Signing in Presence of Testator and Other Witness.
OH Jur. 3d Decedents' Estates § 323, Place of Witness' Signature.
OH Jur. 3d Decedents' Estates § 325, Application of the Usual Evidentiary Rules for Determining Competency.
OH Jur. 3d Decedents' Estates § 329, Testator's Spouse.
OH Jur. 3d Decedents' Estates § 357, Methods of Revocation; Strict Compliance With Statute.
OH Jur. 3d Decedents' Estates § 395, Republication as Revival of Earlier Will.
OH Jur. 3d Decedents' Estates § 410, Definition; Formal Requisites.
OH Jur. 3d Decedents' Estates § 429, Statutory Requirement of a Writing.
OH Jur. 3d Decedents' Estates § 999, Requirements for Admission to Probate.
OH Jur. 3d Decedents' Estates § 1001, Prima Facie Case of Validity Required.
OH Jur. 3d Decedents' Estates § 1040, When Court May Probate Lost, Spoliated, or Destroyed Will, Generally.
OH Jur. 3d Decedents' Estates § 1050, Weight and Sufficiency of Evidence.
OH Jur. 3d Decedents' Estates § 68.5, Uniform Transfer-On-Death Security Registration Act.
OH Jur. 3d Decedents' Estates § 1039.1, Document as a Purported Will.
OH Jur. 3d Trusts § 73, Application of Statute of Wills.

Forms

Ohio Forms Legal and Business § 24:1, Introduction.
Ohio Forms Legal and Business § 25:6, Recordation.
Ohio Forms Legal and Business § 24:113, Formal Requirements—Necessity of Writing.
Ohio Forms Legal and Business § 24:114, Formal Requirements—Execution by Testator.
Ohio Forms Legal and Business § 24:115, Formal Requirements—Attestation by Witnesses.
Ohio Forms Legal and Business § 24:119, Copies of Will.
Ohio Forms Legal and Business § 24:143, Drafting Will.
Ohio Forms Legal and Business § 24:161, Entire Estate to Spouse—Alternatively to Children—Guardianship of Minors.
Ohio Forms Legal and Business § 24:213, Separate Mutual Will—by Spouse Pursuant to Agreement With Other Spouse—Entire Estate to Survivor and to Children on Death of Survivor.
Ohio Forms Legal and Business § 24:222, Form Drafting Principles.
Ohio Forms Legal and Business § 24:491, General Form.
Ohio Forms Legal and Business § 24:511, General Form.
Ohio Forms Legal and Business § 24:902, Form Drafting Guide.
Ohio Forms Legal and Business § 24:911, Codicil—General Form.
Ohio Forms Legal and Business § 24:205.10, Pour-Over Will—Residue to Trust.
Ohio Forms and Transactions F 30.01, General Form of Will.
Ohio Forms and Transactions F 30.02, Simple Will.
Ohio Forms and Transactions F 30.17, Inter Vivos Family Trust.
Ohio Forms and Transactions KP 30.01, Validity and Form of Will.
Ohio Forms and Transactions KP 30.13, Codicils or Amendments.

Treatises and Practice Aids

Sowald & Morganstern, Baldwin's Ohio Practice Domestic Relations Law § 1:5, Terms.
Carlin, Baldwin's Ohio Practice, Merrick-Rippner Probate Law § 27:2, Testamentary Formalities—Compliance With Statute.
Carlin, Baldwin's Ohio Practice, Merrick-Rippner Probate Law § 27:3, Testamentary Formalities—Necessity for a Writing.
Carlin, Baldwin's Ohio Practice, Merrick-Rippner Probate Law § 27:4, Testamentary Formalities—Signature—"At the End".
Carlin, Baldwin's Ohio Practice, Merrick-Rippner Probate Law § 27:5, Testamentary Formalities—Signature—by the Maker.
Carlin, Baldwin's Ohio Practice, Merrick-Rippner Probate Law § 27:6, Testamentary Formalities—Signature—by Another Person.
Carlin, Baldwin's Ohio Practice, Merrick-Rippner Probate Law § 27:8, Testamentary Formalities—Acknowledgment by Testator.
Carlin, Baldwin's Ohio Practice, Merrick-Rippner Probate Law § 27:9, Testamentary Formalities—Attesting Witnesses.
Carlin, Baldwin's Ohio Practice, Merrick-Rippner Probate Law § 28:1, Codicils—Definition.
Carlin, Baldwin's Ohio Practice, Merrick-Rippner Probate Law § 28:2, Codicils—Requirements.
Carlin, Baldwin's Ohio Practice, Merrick-Rippner Probate Law § 31:2, Incorporation by Reference—Pour-Over Will to a Trust.
Carlin, Baldwin's Ohio Practice, Merrick-Rippner Probate Law § 34:2, Declaring the Validity of a Will—Procedure for Obtaining a Judgment—Petitioner in Action.
Carlin, Baldwin's Ohio Practice, Merrick-Rippner Probate Law § 34:5, Declaring the Validity of a Will—Procedure for Obtaining a Judgment—Judgment.
Carlin, Baldwin's Ohio Practice, Merrick-Rippner Probate Law § 34:6, Declaring the Validity of a Will—Post-Judgment Revocation or Modification.
Carlin, Baldwin's Ohio Practice, Merrick-Rippner Probate Law § 36:1, Admission to Probate—Criteria.
Carlin, Baldwin's Ohio Practice, Merrick-Rippner Probate Law § 50:1, Agreement to Make a Will—RC 2107.04—Scope.
Carlin, Baldwin's Ohio Practice, Merrick-Rippner Probate Law § 50:3, Agreement to Make a Will—Essential Elements.

Carlin, Baldwin's Ohio Practice, Merrick-Rippner Probate Law § 50:7, Agreement to Make a Will—Part Performance And/Or Oral Contract.

Carlin, Baldwin's Ohio Practice, Merrick-Rippner Probate Law § 14:18, Payable on Death Accounts.

Carlin, Baldwin's Ohio Practice, Merrick-Rippner Probate Law § 30:42, Drafting a Will—Choosing Witnesses—in General.

Carlin, Baldwin's Ohio Practice, Merrick-Rippner Probate Law § 30:56, Malpractice Liability of Drafting Attorney; Professional Disciplinary Action.

Carlin, Baldwin's Ohio Practice, Merrick-Rippner Probate Law § 30:57, Simple Will—Form.

Carlin, Baldwin's Ohio Practice, Merrick-Rippner Probate Law § 30:181, Testimonium Clause of Testator—Form.

Carlin, Baldwin's Ohio Practice, Merrick-Rippner Probate Law § 30:182, Testator's Name Signed by Another—Form.

Carlin, Baldwin's Ohio Practice, Merrick-Rippner Probate Law § 30:184, Attestation Clause of Witnesses—Form.

Carlin, Baldwin's Ohio Practice, Merrick-Rippner Probate Law § 30:189, Codicil—Form.

Carlin, Baldwin's Ohio Practice, Merrick-Rippner Probate Law § 30:190, Codicil-Alternate—Form.

Restatement (2d) of Property, Don. Trans. § 33.1, Meaning of a Will.

Restatement (3d) Property (Wills & Don. Trans.) § 3.1, Attested Wills.

Law Review and Journal Commentaries

Collateral Attack on the Admission to Probate of a Will—Execution—Signing in the Attestation Clause as Signing at the End under General Code Sec. 10504–3, Comment. 7 Ohio St L J 105 (December 1940).

How a Will Is Admitted to Probate in Ohio. 50 Title Topics 6 (June 1983).

Inheritance and Inconsistency, Adam J. Hirsch. 57 Ohio St L J 1058 (1996).

Living Testamentary Dispositions and the Hawkins Case, Frank S. Rowley. 3 U Cin L Rev 361 (November 1929).

On Writing a "Simple" Will, Kenneth D. Troy. Cin B Ass'n Rep 7 (February 1986).

The Order of Signing in Execution of Wills, Note. 11 U Cin L Rev 390 (May 1937).

Probate Malpractice, Hon. Fred V. Skok. 14 Lake Legal Views 1 (February 1991).

Signing a Will at the End, Walter T. Dunmore. 34 Ohio L Rep 273 (April 13, 1931).

The Statutory Will: A Simple Alternative to Intestacy, Note. 35 Case W Res L Rev 307 (1984–85).

Statutory Will Methodologies—Incorporated Forms vs. Fill–In Forms: Rivalry or Peaceful Coexistence?, Gerry W. Beyer. 94 Dick L Rev 231 (Winter 1990).

There Is More to Succession Planning Than a Will, Joel Strom. 69 Clev B J 14 (June 1998).

Videotaping Wills: A New Frontier in Estate Planning, William R. Buckley and Alfred W. Buckley. 11 Ohio N U L Rev 271 (1984).

Notes of Decisions

Ed. Note: This section contains annotations from former RC 2107.14.

Acknowledgment by testator   2
Attorney misconduct in drafting will   3
Constitutional issues   1
Execution by testator   4
Payable on death account   8
Prima facie case for validity   9
Requirements   5–7
   Disposition of property   5
   Testamentary intent   6
   Writing and execution   7
Signed at end   10
Subscribing witnesses   11
Transfers on death not testamentary   12
Types of wills and devises   13

1. Constitutional issues

Dismissal of third-party negligence claims asserted against testatrix's attorney by intended beneficiaries of testatrix's will, which was denied admission to probate due to lack of statutorily required signature of one of two attesting witnesses, did not violate section of state constitution that guarantees right-to-a-remedy; state's common law did not recognize third-party claim against attorney without required "privity" with testatrix or malice on behalf of attorney. Dykes v. Gayton (Ohio App. 10 Dist., 05-23-2000) 139 Ohio App.3d 395, 744 N.E.2d 199, appeal allowed 90 Ohio St.3d 1442, 736 N.E.2d 903, cause dismissed 91 Ohio St.3d 1466, 743 N.E.2d 921. Attorney And Client ⇐ 26; Constitutional Law ⇐ 322

Application of provisions of Ohio version of Uniform Transfer–On–Death Security Registration Act which remove transfers-on-death resulting from a beneficiary form designation from decedent's testamentary estate, and also from purview of Statute of Wills, to give effect to investor's designation of his sister, rather than his wife, as pay-on-death beneficiary designation in individual retirement account (IRA) created prior to Act's effective date, was a permissible retroactive application of a remedial provision, and did not did not violate State Constitution; application of Act did not impair vested rights on part of wife, or create new right imposing burden against wife. Bielat v. Bielat (Ohio, 01-05-2000) 87 Ohio St.3d 350, 721 N.E.2d 28, 2000-Ohio-451. Constitutional Law ⇐ 191; Wills ⇐ 3

2. Acknowledgment by testator

Where a will has been signed for the testator by another, in his presence and by his express direction, in the absence of attesting witnesses, acknowledgment of the fact by the testator, in hearing of witnesses, which is requisite, is not required to be made in any particular form of words, or in any specified manner. Haynes v. Haynes (Ohio 1878) 33 Ohio St. 598, 31 Am.Rep. 579.

The fact of signing and the authority to sign, when done in the absence of the attesting witnesses may be shown by the acknowledgment to the witnesses, or by other competent testimony, or may be presumed from the facts and circumstances of the case. Haynes v. Haynes (Ohio 1878) 33 Ohio St. 598, 31 Am.Rep. 579. Wills ⇐ 293(1)

The acknowledgment need not be in express words, but may be inferred from signs, motions, conduct, or attending circumstances. Raudebaugh v. Shelley (Ohio 1856) 6 Ohio St. 307.

Proof that will was signed by testatrix and her signature was attested by two subscribing witnesses, is sufficient proof of due execution under former GC 10505 (RC 2107.03); this section only requires that subscribing witnesses see testatrix subscribe and does not require that testatrix make declaration of fact that it is her will. Glanz v. Bauer (Cuyahoga 1929) 7 Ohio Law Abs. 165.

The fact that the attestation clause of testator's will was on a separate unnumbered page of will did not negate the presumption that the will was regular or result in the will not being properly attested to as required by statute; the will was drafted by the attorney who was present at its execution, the will was regular on its face, the attestation clause was signed by two witnesses and recited compliance with statutory requirements, the witnesses signed affidavits stating that the will was properly executed, and attestation statute did not require that the signatures of the witnesses be on the same sheet as signature of the testator, that the pages be numbered, or that the attestation clause be dated. Estate of Snell v. Kilburn (Ohio App. 7 Dist., 12-23-2005) 165 Ohio App.3d 352, 846 N.E.2d 572, 2005-Ohio-7076. Wills ⇐ 123(3)

A testator need not acknowledge his signature if it is signed in the presence of the witnesses. Kemp v. Matthews (Cuyahoga 1962) 183 N.E.2d 259, 98 A.L.R.2d 837, 89 Ohio Law Abs. 524.

Where both witnesses to a will testified that the testatrix did not sign the will in their presence and that they did not see her signature on the will when they signed, there can be no probate of the will; no acknowledgment can be implied from the fact that the testatrix was a woman of some business experience. In re La Mar's Will (Ohio Prob. 1957) 146 N.E.2d 472, 77 Ohio Law Abs. 140.

Where proof of record shows that the testatrix was competent and a typewritten will is presented, signed and attested by two witnesses, one of whom is deceased and the signatures of the testatrix and witnesses are shown to be genuine, a prima-facie case in favor of validity of the will is established, which is not overcome by the fact that the surviving witness did not see the testatrix's signature nor hear her acknowledge it, and the probate court must admit such will to probate. Roosa v. Wickward (Hamilton 1950) 90 Ohio App. 213, 105 N.E.2d 454, 47 O.O. 207.

Where the witnesses to a will did not see the testatrix's signature and were not told by her that she had signed it, the presumption that she signed before them does not prevail, and the probate court did not err in refusing to admit the will to probate. In re Borgman's Estate (Franklin 1951) 105 N.E.2d 69, 61 Ohio Law Abs. 429.

When a woman asked two friends to be witnesses to her will, and said to them "This is my will," and the witnesses, at the time, saw upon the instrument some writing and the only other writing on it was the signature of the testatrix, prima-facie proof is made that she acknowledged her signature as required by GC 10504–3 (RC 2107.03). In re Fisher's Will (Lucas 1941) 67 Ohio App. 6, 35 N.E.2d 784, 21 O.O. 44. Wills ⇐ 302(1)

Where a will was signed by the testator in one room and then taken into another room where at the request of testator it was signed by two witnesses, but no express acknowledgment by the testator of his signature which was visible to the witness or of the nature of the instrument was made, the requirements of GC 10504–3 (RC 2107.03), relative to the execution of wills, have been complied with, since the production of the instrument and the request that the witnesses sign imported that the signature to be witnessed was that of the testator and that he acknowledged it to be his. Blagg v. Blagg (Montgomery 1936) 55 Ohio App. 518, 9 N.E.2d 991, 23 Ohio Law Abs. 286, 9 O.O. 180.

Essentials of a will needed to admit it to probate include that it shall have been acknowledged by the maker as his will, and his signature also shall have been acknowledged in the presence of two subscribing witnesses. Keyl v. Feuchter (Ohio 1897) 56 Ohio St. 424, 37 W.L.B. 385, 47 N.E. 140. Wills ⇐ 119

Where a son is asked to sign a paper for his father, but is not told what the paper is or why he is signing it, and only later the son is told that the paper is his father's will, such a writing is not executed in accordance with law as a will, and is therefore not a valid will. Tims v. Tims (Ohio Cir. 1911) 22 Ohio C.D. 506, 14 Ohio C.C.N.S. 273.

While it is probably necessary as the law now stands that a testator who signs his will out of the presence of the attesting witnesses shall acknowledge the signature to be his signature to his will, it is likely that when the question is presented to the supreme court it will be held that a mere acknowledgment of his signature, or an acknowledgment of the paper as an instrument signed by him is sufficient. In re Leffel's Will (Ohio Prob. 1909) 8 Ohio NP(NS) 591, 54 W.L.B. 336.

Former GC 10505 (RC 2107.03), only requires a will to be attested and subscribed by witnesses before whom the testator signed or acknowledged, and does not require the will to be published, hence the witnesses need not know that it is a will. In re Reckard's Will (Ohio Com.Pl. 1914) 24 Ohio Dec. 609, 15 Ohio NP(NS) 465.

Where a testator directs, procures, and sees a signing of his will for him by another, it is equivalent to an acknowledgement of such signature to the signer, who may also act as a witness. Trembley v. Trembley (Ohio 1884) 5 Ohio Dec. 750, 4 Ohio Law Rep. 545.

A will is properly executed if it is signed at the end by the maker in the presence of two subscribing witnesses even though the witnesses have no knowledge that the instrument signed is a will. In re Maurer's Will (Ohio Prob. 1933) 31 Ohio NP(NS) 247.

A paper writing, signed by the maker out of the presence of two subscribing witnesses, cannot be admitted to probate as a last will and testament, where it is shown that the witnesses did not know that it was a will they were attesting, and no acknowledgment of the signature thereon as his own, was made by the maker to the witnesses. In re Pittis' Will (Ohio Prob. 1930) 29 Ohio NP(NS) 41.

3. Attorney misconduct in drafting will

The maliciousness exception to the *Simon v. Zipperstein* rule, which provided than an attorney was immune from liability to third parties arising from his performance as an attorney in good faith unless such third party was in privity with the client or the attorney acted maliciously, applied to allow testator's two children to pursue a legal malpractice claim against attorney and law firm that executed testator's will; testator's children specifically alleged that there was a conflict of interest in attorney's representation of testator as well as testator's son and grandson, and children alleged that attorney and law firm committed acts in collusion with testator's son and grandson. LeRoy v. Allen Yurasek & Merklin (Ohio App. 3 Dist., Union, 08-29-2005) No. 14-04-49, 2005-Ohio-4452, 2005 WL 2064144, Unreported. Attorney And Client ⇐ 26

The privity exception to the *Simon v. Zipperstein* rule, which provided than an attorney was immune from liability to third parties arising from his performance as an attorney in good faith unless such third party was in privity with the client or the attorney acts maliciously, applied to allow testator's two children to pursue a legal malpractice claim against attorney and law firm that assisted in the transfer of all of testator's stock in closely held corporation to her grandson; testator, as the majority shareholder in closely held corporation, owed a fiduciary duty to her two children, who were minority shareholders, and attorney and law firm owed a fiduciary duty to testator, their client, and thus testator's children were in privity with testator for the purpose of the stock transfer. LeRoy v. Allen Yurasek & Merklin (Ohio App. 3 Dist., Union, 08-29-2005) No. 14-04-49, 2005-Ohio-4452, 2005 WL 2064144, Unreported.

Trial court was required to consider the alleged bad faith of attorney and law firm in drafting testator's will and transferring her stock shares to grandson as an element of fraud, collusion, or other malicious conduct, rather than considering it on its own, when determining whether attorney and law firm waived their immunity from legal malpractice suit brought by testator's children. LeRoy v. Allen, Yurasek & Merklin (Ohio App. 3 Dist., 08-29-2005) 162 Ohio App.3d 155, 832 N.E.2d 1246, 2005-Ohio-4452, opinion vacated and superseded on reconsideration 2005-Ohio-4452, 2005 WL 2064144, appeal allowed 108 Ohio St.3d 1411, 841 N.E.2d 317, 2006-Ohio-179, appeal allowed 108 Ohio St.3d 1435, 842 N.E.2d 61, 2006-Ohio-421. Attorney And Client ⇐ 26

The maliciousness exception to the *Simon v. Zipperstein* rule, which provided than an attorney was immune from liability to third parties arising from his performance as an attorney in good faith unless such third party was in privity with the client or the attorney acted maliciously, applied to allow testator's two children to pursue a legal malpractice claim against attorney and law firm that executed testator's will; testator's children specifically alleged that there was a conflict of interest in attorney's representation of testator as well as testator's son and grandson, and children alleged that attorney and law firm committed acts in collusion with testator's son and grandson. LeRoy v. Allen, Yurasek & Merklin (Ohio App. 3 Dist., 08-29-2005) 162 Ohio App.3d 155, 832 N.E.2d 1246, 2005-Ohio-4452, opinion vacated and superseded on reconsideration 2005-Ohio-4452, 2005 WL 2064144, appeal allowed 108 Ohio St.3d 1411, 841 N.E.2d 317, 2006-Ohio-179, appeal allowed 108 Ohio St.3d 1435, 842 N.E.2d 61, 2006-Ohio-421. Attorney And Client ⇐ 26

Conduct of attorney in drafting will for client in which attorney was named as beneficiary, which was reasonably affected by attorney's own interests, and later attempting to validate will six years after its execution, warranted two-year suspension from practice of law, with 18 months of suspension stayed. Disciplinary Counsel v. Bandy (Ohio, 03-25-1998) 81 Ohio St.3d 291, 690 N.E.2d 1280, 1998-Ohio-509. Attorney And Client ⇐ 58

4. Execution by testator

The due execution of a will cannot be assumed in the face of positive evidence to the contrary, or in the absence of all proof on the subject merely because it purports to be the will of the testator and the attestation is in due form; it will not, however, be defeated by the failure of memory or corruption of the attesting witnesses, if it can be established by other competent testimony. Haynes v. Haynes (Ohio 1878) 33 Ohio St. 598, 31 Am.Rep. 579.

Where a will and a codicil thereto are both legally executed, the fact that the codicil was written in the blank space between the last dispositive item and the testimonium clause of the will does not invalidate either the will or the codicil. Clark v. Carpenter (Ohio App. 5 Dist. 1921) 14 Ohio App. 278, 32 Ohio C.A. 87. Wills ⇐ 99

Issues of fact are presented and a will contest is improperly dismissed where the attorney who prepared a lost will and the secretaries who would have witnessed it at the lawyer's office give testimony that is inconclusive about whether the will was properly executed, attested to, and witnessed, since they cannot specifically recall the testator signing the will. Springer v. Lee (Ohio App. 3 Dist., Hancock, 05-02-1996) No. 5-95-42, 1996 WL 223699, Unreported.

A will made by a husband and wife in which the husband devises his property only, and signed by wife in acceptance only without disposing of any of her property, is not a joint will, but the sole will of the husband. Kunnen v Zurline, 13 D Repr 998 (Super, Cincinnati 1873).

Will speaks as of testator's time of death, not as of date of execution of the document. Church v. Morgan (Ohio App. 4 Dist., 11-01-1996) 115 Ohio App.3d 477, 685 N.E.2d 809. Wills ⇐ 481

In determining validity of will in which the signature consists of a mark, it is the duty of the court, from the face of the will and the evidence, to pass upon the question as to whether the will was lawfully executed, and submission of this question to the jury constitutes prejudicial error. Hayes v. Halle (Cuyahoga 1925) 23 Ohio App. 522, 155 N.E. 493, 4 Ohio Law Abs. 170.

Where signature to will is by mark of testatrix, it is presumed, in contest of will, in absence of contrary showing, that the signature was made by express direction of testatrix and the mark inserted by her. Aston v. Hauck (Hamilton 1926) 22 Ohio App. 430, 153 N.E. 277, 4 Ohio Law Abs. 319. Signatures ⟐ 5; Wills ⟐ 289

A signature by mark is not effective unless the testator gave express direction to some person to write the signature. This is provided for in former GC 10505 (RC 2107.03). West v. Lucas (Ohio 1922) 106 Ohio St. 255, 139 N.E. 859, 1 Ohio Law Abs. 72, 20 Ohio Law Rep. 470, 20 Ohio Law Rep. 471.

Where a will, though it leaves the property according to instructions to the scrivener, was not read to or by the testator nor acknowledged by him, and he had no knowledge of its contents, having merely scrutinized it a second or two, it is not properly executed under former GC 10505 (RC 2107.03). Koch v. Meyers (Ohio App. 1916) 30 Ohio C.D. 439, 7 Ohio App. 306, 29 Ohio C.A. 142.

Will drawn on page of one sheet blank not invalidated by six inch space between dispositive and testimonium clauses. (See also Mader v Apple, 80 OS 691, 89 NE 37 (1909).) Crafts v. Wilber (Ohio Com.Pl. 1909) 19 Ohio Dec. 421, 9 Ohio N.P.N.S. 161.

Where a testator directs, procures, and sees a signing of his will for him by another, it is equivalent to an acknowledgement of such signature to the signer, who may also act as a witness. Trembley v. Trembley (Ohio 1884) 5 Ohio Dec. 750, 4 Ohio Law Rep. 545.

Under Ohio law, the beneficiary of a life insurance policy may be changed through a will only if such a change was authorized by the policy and communicated to the insurer. In re Bunnell (Bkrtcy.N.D.Ohio, 01-25-2005) 322 B.R. 331. Insurance ⟐ 3475(7)

Will which nowhere contains name of testator but signed at end by mark before two witnesses, one of whom had been requested previously to witness testator's will, meets requirements of statute and will be admitted to probate. In re Ryan's Will (Ohio Prob. 1942) 9 Ohio Supp. 29, 36 Ohio Law Abs. 341, 23 O.O. 356.

5. Requirements—Disposition of property

Directions by an owner in respect to the disposition of his property which are to take effect after his death are of no validity, unless made through the medium of a last will and testament. Phipps v. Hope (Ohio 1866) 16 Ohio St. 586.

Writing in which former husband stated his wish that $20,000 from his inheritance from a third party's estate be directed to former wife upon his death failed as either a gift inter vivos or a gift causa mortis, as there was no present intention to transfer dominion and control of the interest in the estate to former wife; gift was to pass only upon former husband's death, and money was not to go directly to former wife, but rather to the credit union for satisfaction of former wife's loan (Per opinion of McFarland, J., with two judges concurring in the result). Bobo v. Stansberry (Ohio App. 4 Dist., 07-29-2005) 162 Ohio App.3d 565, 834 N.E.2d 373, 2005-Ohio-3928. Gifts ⟐ 60

Trust agreement providing that each settlor may transfer his interest by deed or will is not an attempt to dispose of property by will without complying with the statutory formality. Central Trust Co. v. McCarthy (Hamilton 1943) 73 Ohio App. 431, 57 N.E.2d 126, 40 Ohio Law Abs. 526, 29 O.O. 123.

Where a testatrix in her will directs that her property shall go "as the law directs, with the following modifications," she has made a testamentary disposition of the property, and her heirs take nothing by descent (See also Woodruff v Woodruff, 3 CC(NS) 616, 13 CD 408 (Hamilton 1902).) Huber v. Carew (Ohio Cir. 1904) 16 Ohio C.D. 389, 7 Ohio C.C.(N.S.) 609, affirmed 74 Ohio St. 469, 78 N.E. 1127, 3 Ohio Law Rep. 674. Wills ⟐ 713

An instrument which makes no disposition of property should be admitted to probate as the last will and testament of the decedent, where an intention by the decedent to make a disposition of his property clearly appears. In re Williamson's Will (Ohio Com.Pl. 1898) 8 Ohio Dec. 47, 6 Ohio N.P. 79.

An instrument which makes no disposition of property is not a will, even though it is called a "last will and testament." In re Williamson's Will (Ohio Prob. 1897) 6 Ohio Dec. 507, 5 Ohio N.P. 1, reversed 8 Ohio Dec. 47, 6 Ohio N.P. 79. Wills ⟐ 69; Wills ⟐ 73

Under the provisions of this section, an instrument which fulfills all other statutory requirements relative to the execution of wills, may be probated as a valid will even though it does not dispose of property. In Re Crow's Will, 4 Ohio Supp. 370, 31 Abs 35, 17 OO 8 (Prob 1940).

6. —— Testamentary intent, requirements

A written promise to pay a certain sum of money after the death of the maker, placed in the hands of a second person with injunctions to deliver it after his decease, is not good as a testamentary disposition. Hamor v. Moore's Adm'rs (Ohio 1858) 8 Ohio St. 239.

To disinherit his son, testator was not required to expressly state such intent in his will, but rather could accomplish disinheritance through implication by executing will that completely disposed of his property and made no mention of his son; testator's complete disposition of his property overcame the presumption against disinheritance. Estate of Snell v. Kilburn (Ohio App. 7 Dist., 12-23-2005) 165 Ohio App.3d 352, 846 N.E.2d 572, 2005-Ohio-7076. Wills ⟐ 535

Where a standard deed form prepared by decedent has been declared invalid to pass title due to want of delivery, the form will not be construed as a will absent some showing of testamentary intent on the face of the deed form. In re Estate of Ike (Shelby 1982) 7 Ohio App.3d 87, 454 N.E.2d 577, 7 O.B.R. 100.

Where a legatee agrees by oral contract with the testator to hold the legacy in trust for the benefit of a third party, and the legatee fails to act in accordance with the testator's instructions, such actual intentional fraud will cause a trust to be raised in equity, notwithstanding the statute of wills. Winder v. Scholey (Ohio 1910) 83 Ohio St. 204, 93 N.E. 1098, 8 Ohio Law Rep. 524, 21 Am.Ann.Cas. 1379.

Every disposition of property must have a definite subject and a definite object; when the intent of the testator cannot be ascertained, either from the will, or by extraneous circumstances, the will is void and the estate must descend according to law. Cope v. Cope (Ohio 1888) 45 Ohio St. 464, 19 W.L.B. 98, 15 N.E. 206.

7. —— Writing and execution, requirements

Writing in which former husband stated his wish that $20,000 from his inheritance from a third party's estate be directed to former wife upon his death failed as a testamentary disposition due to lack of formalities associated with a last will and testament, where writing was untitled, writing did not mention the existence of previously created last will and testament, and writing did not revoke prior will or purport to be a codicil (Per opinion of McFarland, J., with two judges concurring in the result). Bobo v. Stansberry (Ohio App. 4 Dist., 07-29-2005) 162 Ohio App.3d 565, 834 N.E.2d 373, 2005-Ohio-3928. Wills ⟐ 94

Will should be admitted to probate if it appears on its face to comply with statutory requirement for execution in effect at time of execution, unless interested person demands testimony of at least two witnesses to execution of will. In re Estate of Carmedy (Ohio App. 10 Dist., 08-18-1994) 95 Ohio App.3d 572, 642 N.E.2d 1170. Wills ⟐ 115

There can be but one original, effective, and dispositive instrument to be considered a last will and testament, and however so many copies of that original will, exact in every detail and executed by the testator and attested to by the witnesses there are, these copies remain just that: copies—copies useful to show what had existed in the case of a lost, spoliated, or destroyed will, but utterly ineffectual to be used as a substitute for the original will. In re Steel's Estate (Ohio Prob. 1966) 8 Ohio Misc. 133, 219 N.E.2d 236, 37 O.O.2d 70. Wills ⟐ 94

Where a statute governing the execution of wills prescribes the performance of certain physical acts as a condition precedent to valid execution of a will without designating the order in which such acts are to be performed, any order of performance satisfies the requirements of the statute. Bloechle v. Davis (Ohio 1937) 132 Ohio St. 415, 8 N.E.2d 247, 8 O.O. 249. Wills ⟐ 111(5); Wills ⟐ 123(4)

If this state is to be classed with the jurisdictions recognizing the power of a testator to incorporate provisions in his will by reference, the provision of former GC 10505 (RC 2107.03), "except nuncupative wills, every last will and testament must be in writing" would preclude the inclusion by reference of anything other than an existing manuscript or some other material thing which might fall within the general classification of a writing. Kurtz v. Kurtz (Ohio 1931) 123 Ohio St. 425, 175 N.E. 694, 9 Ohio Law Abs. 478, 34 Ohio Law Rep. 227.

"Codicil" is supplement to a last will and must be executed with same legal formalities as will. Foye v. Foye (Ohio App. 1928) 35 Ohio App. 283, 172 N.E. 386, 27 Ohio Law Rep. 117. Wills ⟐ 125

Revoked will may not be revived by parol declarations. Collins v. Collins (Ohio 1924) 110 Ohio St. 105, 143 N.E. 561, 38 A.L.R. 230, 2 Ohio Law Abs. 260, 22 Ohio Law Rep. 49. Evidence ☞ 439; Wills ☞ 200

The fact that a will is partly printed and partly written does not make it invalid; "writing" includes printing. (See also Sears v Sears, 77 OS 104, 82 NE 1067 (1907).) Roush v. Wensel (Ohio Cir. 1897) 8 Ohio C.D. 141.

Videotaping the reading and execution of a will is not prohibited under the Code of Professional Responsibility; however, there is no valid will without a written document properly executed and witnessed, and clients should be made aware that the videotape does not replace the written document. Bd of Commrs on Grievances & Discipline Op 88–014 (6–17–88).

8. Payable on death account

Where a natural adult person enters into a contract with his bank, depositing therein various sums of money in savings accounts payable on death to certain named individuals, such savings accounts, upon the death of the depositor, are, by such statute, expressly exempt from the statute of wills. In re Tonsic's Estate (Summit 1968) 13 Ohio App.2d 195, 235 N.E.2d 239, 42 O.O.2d 341. Wills ☞ 88(2)

A certificate of deposit made out to the owner, payable on death to another, represents an ineffectual attempt at a testamentary disposition. (Ed. note: See RC 2131.10, RC 2131.11 as to "payable on death" account.) In re Atkinson's Estate (Ohio Prob. 1961) 175 N.E.2d 548, 85 Ohio Law Abs. 540.

9. Prima facie case for validity

Testimony of will's proponent and sole beneficiary, standing alone, established prima facie case of will's validity and, thus, trial court should have probated will, absent showing that proponent was incompetent to testify. In re Estate of Wachsmann (Cuyahoga 1988) 55 Ohio App.3d 265, 563 N.E.2d 734. Wills ☞ 302(1)

10. Signed at end

Where a decedent, in his lifetime, drew a will and signed it, but did not have it witnessed, and afterwards added a clause thereto making an additional devise of the property mentioned in the will and then caused the same to be subscribed by two witnesses, but did not again sign the same "at the end thereof," the whole instrument was invalid as a last will and testament. Glancy v. Glancy (Ohio 1866) 17 Ohio St. 134.

In a proceeding to contest a paper writing alleged to be a will which is not signed at the end thereof, there is no question of fact for the jury, and it is the duty of the court, on motion, to direct a verdict setting aside the will. Schubert v. Christman (Ohio App. 1 Dist. 1922) 16 Ohio App. 432.

If a slip of paper is written and attached to a will before the will is signed, the will is not signed at the end as required by this section; but if the slip is written and attached subsequently to the execution and witnessing of the original will, it amounts to no more than an unexecuted codicil to the will. Smith v. Ellis (Ohio App. 1 Dist. 1921) 15 Ohio App. 38.

A will is not signed at the end thereof, as required by this section, where the testator's name and the words "his mark" appear in the handwriting of the scrivener, on the line where the signature of the testator is customarily inserted at the end of the testimonium clause, and the space between the words "his" and "mark" is blank, but an "X" appears between the given name and the surname of the testator on the first line of the attestation clause. Herbster v. Pincombe (Ohio App. 8 Dist. 1918) 10 Ohio App. 322, 31 Ohio C.A. 358. Wills ☞ 111(2)

Second will was not signed at the end by father, as required by statute, and thus second will was invalid; clause disinheriting daughter appeared after father's signature, the clause dispositive in nature, and father's signature was required to follow all dispositive sections of the will. In re Estate of Metz (Ohio App. 6 Dist., Huron, 09-15-2006) No. H-05-024, 2006-Ohio-4809, 2006 WL 2641862, Unreported. Wills ☞ 111(2)

The fact that the attestation clause of testator's will was on a separate unnumbered page of will did not negate the presumption that the will was regular or result in the will not being properly attested to as required by statute; the will was drafted by the attorney who was present at its execution, the will was regular on its face, the attestation clause was signed by two witnesses and recited compliance with statutory requirements, the witnesses signed affidavits stating that the will was properly executed, and attestation statute did not require that the signatures of the witnesses be on the same sheet as signature of the testator, that the pages be numbered, or that the attestation clause be dated. Estate of Snell v. Kilburn (Ohio App. 7 Dist., 12-23-2005) 165 Ohio App.3d 352, 846 N.E.2d 572, 2005-Ohio-7076. Wills ☞ 123(3)

The fact that a witness to a will is not looking over the testator's shoulder as she signs her will is insufficient to invalidate it where neither witness to the will has any interest in the testator's estate and both witnesses regularly witness documents in the course of their work. Groves v. Potocar (Ohio App. 11 Dist., Lake, 12-01-2000) No. 99-L-098, 2000 WL 1774169, Unreported.

A probate court has no jurisdiction to admit to probate, as a will, an instrument which is not signed at the end thereof by the purported maker, and an order of a probate court admitting such an instrument is a nullity and may be collaterally attacked. In re Eakins' Will (Gallia 1939) 63 Ohio App. 265, 26 N.E.2d 219, 16 O.O. 583. Wills ☞ 206; Wills ☞ 421

The leaving of a blank space between the dispositive portion of a will and the testatrix's signature will not invalidate the will so long as there is no provision as to the disposition of property or testamentary provision of any kind after her signature; such signing must be taken and held to be at the end of the will. (See also Sears v Sears, 77 OS 104, 82 NE 1067 (1907).) Mader v. Apple (Ohio 1909) 80 Ohio St. 691, 89 N.E. 37, 131 Am.St.Rep. 719, 7 Ohio Law Rep. 117.

In an action to contest a will, where the will is not signed at the end, the trial judge does not commit error in directing a verdict that the writing is not a valid will. Sears v. Sears (Ohio 1907) 77 Ohio St. 104, 82 N.E. 1067, 5 Ohio Law Rep. 495, 11 Am.Ann.Cas. 1008.

The construction or interpretation of a will, contested on the sole ground that it is not signed at the end, is not a question for court or jury. Irwin v. Jacques (Ohio 1905) 71 Ohio St. 395, 73 N.E. 683, 2 Ohio Law Rep. 442. Wills ☞ 311

A will with a clause written in the will at the margin and extending vertically below the signature and attestation clause is not "signed at the end thereof." Irwin v. Jacques (Ohio 1905) 71 Ohio St. 395, 73 N.E. 683, 2 Ohio Law Rep. 442.

Writing after the attestation clause "My sister-in-law is not required to give bond when probated," and then signing it properly before such addition is a signing at the "end" of the instrument satisfying RS 5916. Baker v. Baker (Ohio 1894) 51 Ohio St. 217, 31 W.L.B. 256, 37 N.E. 125.

A will in two sheets, fastened together in reverse order, the top sheet beginning with clause 5, appointing the executors and followed by the signature and testatum clause and the under sheets beginning as a will and proceeding with regular continuity through four clauses, is signed at the end as required by former GC 10505 (RC 2107.03). Chandler v. Dockman (Ohio App. 1917) 29 Ohio C.D. 405, 8 Ohio App. 113, 28 Ohio C.A. 297.

Under provisions of GC 10504–3 (RC 2107.03) a holographic instrument is signed at the end by party making it where following appears at end of all dispositive items: "I, Clara M. Smith, have Subscribed My Name this the 28th of August 1940. Signed and acknowledged by Clara M. Smith as and for her last Will and Testament in her presence and in presence of each other have subscribed our Names as Witnesses. John S. Leggett, Mrs. Olga M. Leggett"; and same is entitled to probate as last will and testament. In re Smith's Will (Ohio Prob. 1944) 13 Ohio Supp. 66, 39 Ohio Law Abs. 637, 27 O.O. 520.

Typewritten instrument typed on blank paper except for printed heading reading "Last Will and Testament," where maker's signature appears in ink at end of attestation clause, and it is not disputed that it is her genuine signature, and left of her signature appear names of two persons, in ink, followed by word "witnesses" in ink, and instrument can easily be identified, and there is no space in the will above decedent's signature which would permit additions to instrument after its execution is signed at the end as required by law, and also attested by two witnesses, since testimonium clause and typewritten attestation clause must be treated as mere surplusage and will is valid even if it contains neither a testimonium nor an attestation clause. In re Mazurie (Ohio Prob. 1937) 3 Ohio Supp. 63, 24 Ohio Law Abs. 622, 9 O.O. 163.

Where a testator calls witnesses to his bedside and tells them that the paper he holds is his will previously executed and acknowledged, and the witnesses sign a certificate of reacknowledgment, it is not necessary that the witnesses see the testator sign the will but it is sufficient if he acknowledges his signature to the witnesses; the will is republished as of that date and disposes of real estate acquired after the will was first made and owned by the testator at his death. Reynolds' Lessee v. Shirley (Ohio 1836) 7 Ohio 39, PT. II.

11. Subscribing witnesses

Where a foreign will executed and probated in a sister state, a copy of which has been admitted to record in this state, is attested, "signed, sealed, and published in presence," the will being signed at the end by the testator and three witnesses, in the absence of proof to the contrary, it will be presumed that the testator and the witnesses signed in presence of each other. Carpenter v. Denoon (Ohio 1876) 29 Ohio St. 379.

Subscribing witnesses need not sign their names at the same time, nor in the presence of each other. Raudebaugh v. Shelley (Ohio 1856) 6 Ohio St. 307.

Witnesses to written will were not required to interview testatrix to determine her testamentary capacity and, thus, trial court acted within its discretion in prohibiting will contestants' counsel from stating in closing argument that witnesses to a will must be satisfied that testatrix was of sound mind and memory at time will was executed, in will contest proceeding concerning last will and testament leaving entire estate to county humane society for the care of testatrix's pet cat. Waldecker v. Pfefferle (Ohio App. 6 Dist., Erie, 11-08-2002) No. E-02-002, 2002-Ohio-6187, 2002 WL 31521467, Unreported, appeal not allowed 98 Ohio St.3d 1491, 785 N.E.2d 473, 2003-Ohio-1189. Wills 323

Alleged will which was only witnessed by one person could not be admitted to probate, despite testimony that decedent intended for alleged will to govern distribution of estate; statutory requirement of two witnesses is mandatory for will to be admitted to probate. In re Estate of Carmedy (Ohio App. 10 Dist., 08-18-1994) 95 Ohio App.3d 572, 642 N.E.2d 1170. Wills 115

A will is to be admitted to probate where there is evidence to support its validity even where the witnesses to the will do not remember the circumstances of their signing. In re Estate of Wachsmann (Cuyahoga 1988) 55 Ohio App.3d 265, 563 N.E.2d 734.

Interested witnesses to a written will are competent witnesses thereto if they otherwise meet the test of competency set forth in RC 2317.01. Rogers v. Helmes (Ohio 1982) 69 Ohio St.2d 323, 432 N.E.2d 186, 23 O.O.3d 301. Wills 116

Where all signatures to the instrument are genuine, the attesting clause is in due form, and there is oral testimony by one of the witnesses that she knew it was the will of the testatrix which she was signing, and that the testatrix was of full age, of sound mind and memory, and not under any restraint, a prima-facie case is established, and it is not necessary that both attesting witnesses orally testify that all the statutory requirements regarding the execution of the will had been complied with. In re McGraw's Will (Scioto 1967) 14 Ohio App.2d 87, 236 N.E.2d 684, 43 O.O.2d 207.

Where a written will is signed by a testator and attested and subscribed by two witnesses who are attorneys and partners, one of whom prepared such will, and who are nominated in such will as executor and alternate executor, respectively, such witnesses are competent and such will, if otherwise valid, is not thereby invalidated. Blankner v. Lathrop (Ohio 1959) 169 Ohio St. 229, 159 N.E.2d 229, 74 A.L.R.2d 279, 8 O.O.2d 221. Wills 116

An executor may be a witness to a will, provided he is not a legatee or devisee. Blankner v. Lathrop (Franklin 1958) 154 N.E.2d 95, 79 Ohio Law Abs. 6, affirmed 169 Ohio St. 229, 159 N.E.2d 229, 74 A.L.R.2d 279, 8 O.O.2d 221.

A witness-executor or witness-trustee is not an incompetent subscribing witness to a will by reason of such fact. Fazekas v. Gobozy (Cuyahoga 1958) 150 N.E.2d 319, 78 Ohio Law Abs. 258.

In determining whether a will which is presented for probate and which is complete and regular in appearance and which apparently complies with all formalities should be admitted to probate, the probate court is not authorized to determine as a fact whether such will has been attested and executed according to law, but is merely required to determine whether there is substantial evidence tending to prove that fact, i.e., evidence which will enable a finding of that fact by reasonable minds, and even though all who have apparently signed an instrument as attesting witnesses affirmatively testify that the instrument was not executed according to law, such execution and attestation may be established by other competent evidence. In re Lyons' Estate (Ohio 1957) 166 Ohio St. 207, 141 N.E.2d 151, 2 O.O.2d 26. Wills 320

By virtue of GC 10504–3 (RC 2107.03), it is not necessary to the validity of a last will and testament that the attesting and subscribing witnesses thereto sign the same in the presence of each other. McFadden v. Thomas (Ohio 1951) 154 Ohio St. 405, 96 N.E.2d 254, 43 O.O. 340. Wills 123(5)

Where witnesses subscribe a will on one occasion in the presence of the testator and the testator subscribes or acknowledges it in their presence on a subsequent occasion, resubscription by attesting witnesses is not necessary where they identify the instrument and recognize but do not disaffirm their signatures thereon; failure to expressly disaffirm their signatures at the time of testator's subscription in their presence will render their prior subscription as effective as if the manual act of resubscription had been performed. Bloechle v. Davis (Ohio 1937) 132 Ohio St. 415, 8 N.E.2d 247, 8 O.O. 249.

A will, which is subscribed by witnesses in the presence of testator on one occasion and subscribed by the testator in their presence on another occasion, is deemed to have been attested by the subscribing witnesses at the time of the testator's subscription and is validly executed under the provisions of this section. Bloechle v. Davis (Ohio 1937) 132 Ohio St. 415, 8 N.E.2d 247, 8 O.O. 249. Wills 123(4)

Request in will contest to charge that every will must be in writing, and signature of testator and that of witnesses subscribed as one continuous transaction held properly refused as not correctly stating law. Scholl v. Sterkel (Richland 1933) 46 Ohio App. 389, 189 N.E. 15, 16 Ohio Law Abs. 491, 40 Ohio Law Rep. 9. Wills 331(1)

The competency of an attesting witness is not to be determined upon the state of facts existing at the time when the will is presented for probate, but upon those existing at the time of the attestation; thus, a renouncement and release of all right and interest of a legatee who was also an attesting witness made five years after the will was made is ineffective to render such legatee a competent witness. Vrooman v. Powers (Ohio 1890) 47 Ohio St. 191, 23 W.L.B. 292, 24 N.E. 267.

Two clauses written by the testatrix into her will and signed by her which direct a different distribution of two bequests are not codicils, as they were not witnessed as provided by law, nor do these clauses work a revocation of any provisions in the will. Porterfield v. Porterfield (Ohio Com.Pl. 1907) 17 Ohio Dec. 448, 4 Ohio N.P.N.S. 654. Wills 184(2)

Evidence supported finding that will was signed or acknowledged in presence of only one witness and that it was thus invalid; first witness testified that testator told witness that testator had signed will, second witness testified that testator signed will after witnesses had signed and that testator did not acknowledge his signature, and third witness testified that he did not see testator sign will and that testator did not acknowledge his signature. In re Sintic (Ohio App. 11 Dist., Lake, 06-28-2002) No. 2001-L-145, 2002-Ohio-3375, 2002 WL 1401500, Unreported. Wills 302(1)

Where a will was not signed by the testatrix in the presence of two witnesses, but was later signed by them, and one of the witnesses testified that she recognized the signature as that of the testatrix, the validity of will was not controverted, absent other sufficient evidence. Parks v Kerns, No. 82-J-32 (7th Dist Ct App, Jefferson, 1–11–84).

Where a witness to a will took part in the physical act of writing his name as a witness by holding the pencil while the name was written by another at his direction, at the testator's request and in his presence, he was an effectual subscribing witness to the will. In re Will of Gatchel, 29 NP(NS) 206 (Prob, Tuscarawas 1932).

Attestation and subscription of witnesses to a will are two separate and distinct acts, and both are necessary in the proper execution of a will. In re Pittis' Will (Ohio Prob. 1930) 29 Ohio NP(NS) 41.

A will is properly subscribed by the witnesses when they sign their names thereto in the presence of the testator, but it is not properly attested unless the witnesses see (1) the testator sign his name thereto, or (2) hear him acknowledge either the paper as his will, or his signature thereto. In re Pittis' Will (Ohio Prob. 1930) 29 Ohio NP(NS) 41.

12. Transfers on death not testamentary

Ohio version of Uniform Transfer–On–Death Security Registration Act removes transfers-on-death resulting from a registration in beneficiary form from decedent's testamentary estate, and also from the purview of Statute of Wills, which outlines the formalities that apply to testamentary dispositions. Bielat v. Bielat (Ohio, 01-05-2000) 87 Ohio St.3d 350, 721 N.E.2d 28, 2000-Ohio-451. Wills 5

13. Types of wills and devises

Tenants in common of real estate who are also owners, severally, of personal property, may dispose of the same by will by uniting in a single instrument, where the bequests are severable and the instrument is not in the nature of a compact but is, in effect, the will of each, revokable by him. Betts v. Harper (Ohio 1884) 39 Ohio St. 639, 48 Am.Rep. 477.

Devise may have a condition annexed requiring an annuity to be paid to the widow of the testator. Carder v. Board of Com'rs of Fayette County (Ohio 1865) 16 Ohio St. 354.

A joint will is unknown to the testamentary law of this state, and is inconsistent with the policy of its legislation on this subject; where a husband and wife, each being the separate owners of property, execute an instrument in the form of a will and treat the separate property as a joint fund, the instrument cannot be admitted to probate as the joint will of the parties, or as the separate will of either. Walker v. Walker (Ohio 1862) 14 Ohio St. 157, 82 Am.Dec. 474. Wills ⇐ 19

Once a will is "made" in the manner provided in RC 2107.03, it remains a will unless and until it is revoked by one of the means provided in RC 2107.33. In re Nash's Will (Ohio Com.Pl. 1976) 50 Ohio Misc. 4, 361 N.E.2d 558, 3 O.O.3d 347, 4 O.O.3d 33.

Even though the separate wills of a husband and wife refer to the other's property and estate and the disposition in each is practically identical, a joint will is not thereby created where the wills are made at different times and are clearly separate and distinct and revocable by each maker respectively. Coghlin v. Coghlin (Ohio Cir. 1904) 16 Ohio C.D. 18, 4 Ohio C.C.N.S. 161.

Where a testator devises a specific piece of real estate and other items to his wife for life and that real estate along with the residue of the estate is given to the testator's children to be equally divided among them, the devise to the children is a general and not a specific one. Woodruff v. Woodruff (Ohio Cir. 1902) 13 Ohio C.D. 408, 3 Ohio C.C.N.S. 616.

2107.04 Agreement to make a will

No agreement to make a will or to make a devise or bequest by will shall be enforceable unless it is in writing. Such agreement must be signed by the maker or by some other person at such maker's express direction. If signed by a person other than such maker, the instrument must be subscribed by two or more competent witnesses who heard such maker acknowledge that it was signed at his direction.

(1953 H 1, eff. 10–1–53; GC 10504–3a)

Historical and Statutory Notes

Pre–1953 H 1 Amendments: 116 v 385

Cross References

Testamentary trusts permitted, 1335.01

Library References

Wills ⇐58(1).
Westlaw Topic No. 409.
C.J.S. Wills §§ 133 to 134, 136.

Research References

Encyclopedias
OH Jur. 3d Decedents' Estates § 215, Distinction Between Wills and Contracts.
OH Jur. 3d Decedents' Estates § 310, Statutory Requirement of Attestation and Subscription.
OH Jur. 3d Decedents' Estates § 312, Attestation and Subscription Distinguished.
OH Jur. 3d Decedents' Estates § 313, Number of Witnesses.
OH Jur. 3d Decedents' Estates § 325, Application of the Usual Evidentiary Rules for Determining Competency.
OH Jur. 3d Decedents' Estates § 329, Testator's Spouse.
OH Jur. 3d Decedents' Estates § 410, Definition; Formal Requisites.
OH Jur. 3d Decedents' Estates § 418, Requirement of a Writing.
OH Jur. 3d Decedents' Estates § 429, Statutory Requirement of a Writing.
OH Jur. 3d Decedents' Estates § 432, Sufficiency of Writing—Will as Sufficient Writing.
OH Jur. 3d Decedents' Estates § 433, Doctrine of Part Performance as Affecting Requirement of a Writing.
OH Jur. 3d Decedents' Estates § 436, Action for Damages.
OH Jur. 3d Decedents' Estates § 439, Action on Quantum Meruit Theory.
OH Jur. 3d Decedents' Estates § 999, Requirements for Admission to Probate.
OH Jur. 3d Frauds, Statute of § 138, Rendition of Services.

Forms
Ohio Forms Legal and Business § 24:83, Form Drafting Principles.
Ohio Forms Legal and Business § 24:84, Form Drafting Principles—Checklist—Matters to be Included in Contracts Relating to Wills.
Ohio Forms Legal and Business § 24:91, Agreement—to Execute Joint or Mutual Wills—by Husband and Wife—Estate to Survivor.
Ohio Forms Legal and Business § 24:100, Agreement—to Not Revoke or Change Will.
Ohio Forms Legal and Business § 24:115, Formal Requirements—Attestation by Witnesses.
Ohio Forms Legal and Business § 24:212, Form Drafting Principles.

Treatises and Practice Aids
Carlin, Baldwin's Ohio Practice, Merrick-Rippner Probate Law § 27:2, Testamentary Formalities—Compliance With Statute.
Carlin, Baldwin's Ohio Practice, Merrick-Rippner Probate Law § 27:9, Testamentary Formalities—Attesting Witnesses.
Carlin, Baldwin's Ohio Practice, Merrick-Rippner Probate Law § 28:2, Codicils—Requirements.
Carlin, Baldwin's Ohio Practice, Merrick-Rippner Probate Law § 34:5, Declaring the Validity of a Will—Procedure for Obtaining a Judgment—Judgment.
Carlin, Baldwin's Ohio Practice, Merrick-Rippner Probate Law § 36:1, Admission to Probate—Criteria.
Carlin, Baldwin's Ohio Practice, Merrick-Rippner Probate Law § 50:1, Agreement to Make a Will—RC 2107.04—Scope.
Carlin, Baldwin's Ohio Practice, Merrick-Rippner Probate Law § 50:2, Agreement to Make a Will—RC 2107.04—Purpose.
Carlin, Baldwin's Ohio Practice, Merrick-Rippner Probate Law § 50:3, Agreement to Make a Will—Essential Elements.
Carlin, Baldwin's Ohio Practice, Merrick-Rippner Probate Law § 50:7, Agreement to Make a Will—Part Performance And/Or Oral Contract.
Carlin, Baldwin's Ohio Practice, Merrick-Rippner Probate Law § 30:42, Drafting a Will—Choosing Witnesses—in General.
Carlin, Baldwin's Ohio Practice, Merrick-Rippner Probate Law § 30:56, Malpractice Liability of Drafting Attorney; Professional Disciplinary Action.
Carlin, Baldwin's Ohio Practice, Merrick-Rippner Probate Law § 30:57, Simple Will—Form.
Carlin, Baldwin's Ohio Practice, Merrick-Rippner Probate Law § 30:184, Attestation Clause of Witnesses—Form.
Carlin, Baldwin's Ohio Practice, Merrick-Rippner Probate Law § 30:189, Codicil—Form.
Carlin, Baldwin's Ohio Practice, Merrick-Rippner Probate Law § 30:190, Codicil-Alternate—Form.
Bogert - the Law of Trusts and Trustees § 480, Breach of Contract to Bequeath, Devise, or Die Intestate in Return for Personal Services.

Law Review and Journal Commentaries

Contract to Make a Will—Statute of Frauds—Enforcement in Equity, Note. 14 U Cin L Rev 571 (November 1940).

Notes of Decisions

Consideration, oral agreements   2
Enforcement   1
Intestate shares, oral agreements   4
Oral agreements   2-5
    Consideration   2
    Intestate shares   4
    Performance   3
    Personal property   5
Performance, oral agreements   3
Personal property, oral agreements   5
Procedural issues   6
Unenforceable agreement   7

Words of agreement 8

1. Enforcement

Valid contract to make will may be specifically enforced against heirs of promissor if will is not executed. Kretzer v. Brubaker (Ohio, 02-14-1996) 74 Ohio St.3d 519, 660 N.E.2d 446, 1996-Ohio-178. Specific Performance ⚿ 86; Wills ⚿ 67

Evidence supported jury's conclusions that contract to make will and one of two probated wills entitled beneficiary to estate. Georgekopoulos v. Vasilopoulos (Summit 1984) 26 Ohio App.3d 43, 498 N.E.2d 165, 26 O.B.R. 216. Wills ⚿ 703

An agreement to make a will takes priority over any other later disposition of property made during lifetime of any of the parties to agreement. Fitch v. Oesch (Ohio Com.Pl. 1971) 30 Ohio Misc. 15, 281 N.E.2d 206, 59 O.O.2d 16.

It is not the duty of administrator of estate to recover nonprobate assets which were disposed of in violation of an agreement to make a will, but right of action is left with those parties who might be injured by not receiving their full amount under agreement and will. Fitch v. Oesch (Ohio Com.Pl. 1971) 30 Ohio Misc. 15, 281 N.E.2d 206, 59 O.O.2d 16. Executors And Administrators ⚿ 86(2)

Parties to agreement to make wills to dispose of their property in specific manner, do not then have right to give property away or place it in nonprobate assets out of reach of will and interpretation of agreement. Fitch v. Oesch (Ohio Com.Pl. 1971) 30 Ohio Misc. 15, 281 N.E.2d 206, 59 O.O.2d 16.

An agreement to convey by deed or will, effective after death, is an agreement to make a will or to make a devise by will within the meaning of this section. Sherman v. Johnson (Ohio 1953) 159 Ohio St. 209, 112 N.E.2d 326, 50 O.O. 257. Frauds, Statute Of ⚿ 75

An administrator who defends an action for specific performance of a contract, alleged to have been made by his decedent, to will the plaintiff all the residue of decedent's estate, in consideration of care and service for the rest of her life, after payment of all debts and costs, in a case in which the only heir at law is represented by counsel and actively contests the action, cannot, if unsuccessful in defending the action, charge the estate with attorney fees and expenses of litigation incurred in the contest. Foltz v. Boone (Ohio 1923) 107 Ohio St. 562, 140 N.E. 761, 1 Ohio Law Abs. 421, 1 Ohio Law Abs. 864, 21 Ohio Law Rep. 107, 21 Ohio Law Rep. 108. Executors And Administrators ⚿ 111(4)

Where decedent gave a written promise to his nephew's son to make a will in his nephew's son's favor if the son would come to the United States, the trial court properly finds that a contract to make a will was made by the decedent. Dalalau v First Natl City Bank, No. 6096 (5th Dist Ct App, Stark, 8–29–83).

2. Oral agreements—Consideration

Oral contract to make a will is unenforceable by virtue of this section and payment of consideration by one in whose favor the contract is made will not remove such a contract from the operation of the section. Snyder v. Warde (Ohio 1949) 151 Ohio St. 426, 86 N.E.2d 489, 39 O.O. 253. Frauds, Statute Of ⚿ 75; Frauds, Statute Of ⚿ 129(5); Frauds, Statute Of ⚿ 129(6)

Where an oral compact to make mutual wills is established, the consideration therefor is sufficient, and the parties have complied with other legal requirements, the wills speak for themselves; where the will of a survivor of such a compact cannot be found after her death, the provisions will be carried out if there is no question as to the content of such mutual will. Minor v. Minor (Ohio Com.Pl. 1904) 15 Ohio Dec. 264, 2 Ohio N.P.N.S. 439.

Twin wills made by a husband and wife must each be the consideration for the other, reciprocity must pervade both wills, and the contract to make such wills must be clear; if a power is reserved to one party to alter or revoke without the consent of the other, the other will cannot be upheld. Albery v. Sessions (Ohio Com.Pl. 1895) 3 Ohio Dec. 330, 2 Ohio N.P. 237.

Will could not satisfy the statute of frauds for oral contract to pay for services rendered before death where it did not indicate that bequest was being made as the return consideration for services rendered. Petitto v. Malaney (Ohio App. 11 Dist., Lake, 05-17-2002) No. 2001-L-065, 2002-Ohio-2442, 2002 WL 1012591, Unreported. Frauds, Statute Of ⚿ 108(1)

3. —— Performance, oral agreements

Fact that employee performed services as convenience store manager and turned down other employment was not that partial performance needed to remove owner's oral promise, that business would belong to employee if anything ever happened, from statute of frauds; employee's services could be adequately compensated in money and employee was paid fair wages for time worked at store. Brannan v. Fowler (Ohio App. 4 Dist., 02-01-1995) 100 Ohio App.3d 577, 654 N.E.2d 434. Frauds, Statute Of ⚿ 129(5)

Rendering of services between family members is presumptively gratuitous; however, family member may recover in quantum meruit for services he rendered to another family member, based on quasi-contract theory, where unenforceable express oral contract to leave property by will is shown to exist. Sabin v. Graves (Ottawa 1993) 86 Ohio App.3d 628, 621 N.E.2d 748, cause dismissed 66 Ohio St.3d 1503, 613 N.E.2d 648. Executors And Administrators ⚿ 206(2); Implied And Constructive Contracts ⚿ 91

Aunt and her nephew did not come to actual agreement that nephew would inherit aunt's property upon her death in exchange for his contributions to construction of addition to aunt's home, as required for nephew to recover for contributions in quantum meruit; nephew's reliance upon what he read in aunt's will, without mutual promises, amounted to no more than mere expectation of legacy or gift, and proposed written contracts that dealt with how costs of project would be shared and how costs would be recovered by nephew were not executed. Sabin v. Graves (Ottawa 1993) 86 Ohio App.3d 628, 621 N.E.2d 748, cause dismissed 66 Ohio St.3d 1503, 613 N.E.2d 648. Executors And Administrators ⚿ 206(2)

In an action against the executor or administrator of a decedent's estate to subject the estate to the payment of a claim, where the petition alleges that there is an oral contract between the plaintiff and the decedent and where the contract as alleged indicates that it created a monetary obligation of the decedent existing in his lifetime, although such obligation was not, by the terms of the contract, to be discharged until at or after the death of the decedent, such petition does not allege a contract to make a will, and states facts sufficient to show a cause of action. Moore v. Curtzweiler (Ohio 1956) 165 Ohio St. 194, 134 N.E.2d 835, 59 O.O. 263. Wills ⚿ 68

This section applies to any action instituted after its enactment, even though such action involves an oral contract entered into before its enactment and even though performance of such contract had been partially completed at the time of such enactment. Sherman v. Johnson (Ohio 1953) 159 Ohio St. 209, 112 N.E.2d 326, 50 O.O. 257.

Doctrine of partial performance may be applied to enforce provisions of an oral contract to devise real estate by will, notwithstanding GC 8621 (RC 1335.05) and 10504–3a (RC 2107.04). Emley v. Selepchak (Medina 1945) 76 Ohio App. 257, 63 N.E.2d 919, 31 O.O. 558.

Performance under this section will be given the same application as has been done under GC 8621 (RC 1335.05); neither section is applicable in an action to obtain specific performance of an agreement to make a will devising certain realty, where there is sufficient performance to take the case out of such statutes of fraud. Ayres v. Cook (Franklin 1941) 46 N.E.2d 629, 37 Ohio Law Abs. 224, affirmed 140 Ohio St. 281, 43 N.E.2d 287, 23 O.O. 491.

When an interest in a business is sold to two persons by an agreement in writing for a specified amount and one of the purchasers, as a further consideration for the sale, enters into a contemporaneous oral agreement with the vendors to devise real estate to them, a completed transfer of the business with payment of the specified amount, is such part performance of the contract as takes the case out of both the general statute of frauds, GC 8621 (RC 1335.05), which applies to a contract to devise lands and the specific statute of frauds, GC 10504–3a (RC 2107.04), which relates to agreements to make a will or to make a devise or bequest by will. Ayres v. Cook (Ohio 1942) 140 Ohio St. 281, 43 N.E.2d 287, 23 O.O. 491. Frauds, Statute Of ⚿ 129(3)

In action upon oral contract, entered into prior to effective date of this section, to make a will in consideration of performance of services as physician, plaintiff must prove that he was ready, willing, and able to perform services, to be entitled to judgment. Heyn v. Kahn (Hamilton 1941) 69 Ohio App. 274, 39 N.E.2d 866, 35 Ohio Law Abs. 217, 24 O.O. 64, appeal dismissed 140 Ohio St. 337, 43 N.E.2d 240, 23 O.O. 572.

Where a woman enters a contract to make a will devising real estate to her sister in consideration of the sister staying with her as long as she desires, and the sister performs her part of the contract but no will is ever made, the written and signed contract is valid and enforceable against the heirs of the promisor. Emery v. Darling (Ohio 1893) 50 Ohio St. 160, 29 W.L.B. 223, 33 N.E. 715.

4. —— Intestate shares, oral agreements

RC 2107.04 has no application to an oral agreement to die intestate. Frantz v. Maher (Clark 1957) 106 Ohio App. 465, 155 N.E.2d 471, 7 O.O.2d 209.

Where a divorce decree incorporates the parties' oral agreement to make wills leaving their children intestate shares, although such agreement by itself would have been unenforceable under contract law, the parties may not challenge the validity of such agreement once merged into the divorce decree. Thomas v Ferguson, Nos. 11019 and 11034 (9th Dist Ct App, Summit, 8–10–83).

5. —— Personal property, oral agreements

An action for a money judgment based on an oral agreement to not make a will but to die intestate, which agreement is divisible as it relates to personal property and real estate and for which there are separate considerations, which action seeks the amount of the value of the personal property which would have been received had the promisor performed his obligation as pleaded under the contract, is not barred by the general statute of frauds. Frantz v. Maher (Clark 1957) 106 Ohio App. 465, 155 N.E.2d 471, 7 O.O.2d 209. Frauds, Statute Of ⇨ 130(2)

6. Procedural issues

Statute requiring agreements to make a will to be in writing barred former daughter-in-law from seeking monetary damages for her former father-in-law's anticipatory breach of their alleged oral agreement that he would leave his business to her in his will. Gottfried-Smith v. Gottfried (Ohio App. 6 Dist., 05-30-1997) 119 Ohio App.3d 646, 695 N.E.2d 1229. Wills ⇨ 67

Allegations in former daughter-in-law's complaint failed to state any equitable cause of action that would entitle her to payment for value of services she rendered to her former father-in-law without pay, in alleged reliance on former father-in-law's oral promise that he would leave his business to her in his will; former daughter-in-law only referred to element of detrimental reliance in her complaint, which was insufficient to provide notice that she was asserting cause of action other than her claim for anticipatory repudiation. Gottfried-Smith v. Gottfried (Ohio App. 6 Dist., 05-30-1997) 119 Ohio App.3d 646, 695 N.E.2d 1229. Wills ⇨ 68

7. Unenforceable agreement

A written promise to pay a certain sum of money after the death of the maker, placed in the hands of a second person with injunctions to deliver it after his decease, is not good as a testamentary disposition. Hamor v. Moore's Adm'rs (Ohio 1858) 8 Ohio St. 239.

Hospice was not successor of hospital affiliate which provided in-home hospice care, for purposes of determining proper beneficiary under decedent's will and trust, which directed that, if hospital affiliate which provided in-home hospice care was no longer in existence, then residual estate passed to another specified charitable organization as contingent beneficiary; at cessation of affiliate, hospital did not transfer any of its assets or liabilities to hospital management company, but simply entered into an agreement so that its clients would have continuity of care, and when company ceased its hospice program, it did not transfer assets or liabilities to hospice. U.S. Bank, N.A. v. Hospice of Cincinnati (Ohio App. 1 Dist., Hamilton, 03-17-2006) No. C-050393, No. C-050394, No. C-050402, 2006-Ohio-1222, 2006 WL 664135, Unreported. Wills ⇨ 515

Alleged oral agreement relating to sons' expectations to share in inheritance of farms owned by parents amounted to an unenforceable contract to make a will; agreement to make a will or to make a devise or bequest by will was required to be in writing. Swank v. Estate of Swank (Ohio App. 5 Dist., Richland, 10-17-2005) No. 2004CA0110, No. 2004CA0111, No. 2004CA0112, 2005-Ohio-5524, 2005 WL 2660537, Unreported, appeal not allowed 108 Ohio St.3d 1489, 843 N.E.2d 794, 2006-Ohio-962. Wills ⇨ 58(1)

Will devising family farm to testator's "blood nephews" was consistent with limitation upon testator in contract to make will, providing that farm would be devised to testator's family, and, thus, contract to make will could not be specifically enforced to require devise to testator's nieces and grandnieces. Kretzer v. Brubaker (Ohio, 02-14-1996) 74 Ohio St.3d 519, 660 N.E.2d 446, 1996-Ohio-178. Specific Performance ⇨ 86; Wills ⇨ 66; Wills ⇨ 67

Alleged oral promise by decedent to convey business and real estate to employee when decedent died or "something happened to him" was unenforceable, either as oral contract to make will or oral contract for transfer of real estate which was barred by statute of frauds. Brannan v. Fowler (Ohio App. 4 Dist., 02-01-1995) 100 Ohio App.3d 577, 654 N.E.2d 434. Frauds, Statute Of ⇨ 74(1); Frauds, Statute Of ⇨ 75; Wills ⇨ 58(1)

An agreement to make a will or to make a devise or bequest by will is not enforceable under any circumstances unless it is in writing. Sherman v. Johnson (Ohio 1953) 159 Ohio St. 209, 112 N.E.2d 326, 50 O.O. 257.

An oral agreement to make a will is not enforceable; communications between attorney and clients are privileged and not admissible at request of third party to prove such an agreement, nor are concurrent wills sufficient to imply such an agreement. McGlone v. Gompert (N.D.Ohio 1953) 112 F.Supp. 840, 67 Ohio Law Abs. 76, 52 O.O. 77.

Where a plaintiff contends that he deeded property to the decedent upon decedent's oral promise to devise the property to the plaintiff in her will and decedent fails to do so, trial court properly refused to impose a constructive trust on such property where there is no evidence of fraud, duress, undue influence, mistake, breach of fiduciary duty or abuse of a confidential relationship on the part of the decedent. Veith v Maczuga, No. E–83–5 (6th Dist Ct App, Erie, 7–22–83).

8. Words of agreement

Where a will by which a decedent leaves his property to another person is executed the same day as a contract between the decedent and such other person, which contract contains no promise or agreement to make a will and which provides that "it is impossible to arrive at a definite figure… to be paid for the services to be rendered by" such other person and that such other person "will accept whatever" decedent "determines to be a just consideration for the services performed and to be performed," and the will makes no reference to the contract; neither the will nor the contract constitutes an enforceable contract entitling such other person to specific performance thereof, and such will is subject to revocation by a subsequently executed will. Stork v. Troeger (Defiance 1956) 103 Ohio App. 144, 144 N.E.2d 675, 3 O.O.2d 207, appeal dismissed 165 Ohio St. 405, 135 N.E.2d 675, 60 O.O. 33.

A revoked will which does not contain words which reasonably can be construed as words of promise or agreement or as an indication of any contract or agreement cannot be a memorandum or note of such agreement within RC 1335.05 or RC 2107.04, and a demurrer to a petition which alleges that it was such a contract admits only that the will was executed, and not that it was a contract. Wilson v. Dunkle (Ohio Com.Pl. 1955) 132 N.E.2d 483, 71 Ohio Law Abs. 483. Wills ⇨ 58(1)

Where a writing does not contain words which can be reasonably construed as words of promise or agreement or as an indication of any contract or agreement, such writing cannot be a memorandum or note of any agreement within the meaning of GC 8621 (RC 1335.05) or an agreement in writing within the meaning of this section. Sherman v. Johnson (Ohio 1953) 159 Ohio St. 209, 112 N.E.2d 326, 50 O.O. 257.

2107.05 Incorporation by reference

An existing document, book, record, or memorandum may be incorporated in a will by reference, if referred to as being in existence at the time the will is executed. Such document, book, record, or memorandum shall be deposited in the probate court when the will is probated or within thirty days thereafter, unless the court grants an extension of time for good cause shown. A copy may be substituted for the original document, book, record, or memorandum if such copy is certified to be correct by a person authorized to take acknowledgments on deeds.

(1953 H 1, eff. 10–1–53; GC 10504–4)

Historical and Statutory Notes

Pre–1953 H 1 Amendments: 114 v 346

Library References

Wills ⇨98.
Westlaw Topic No. 409.
C.J.S. Wills §§ 200, 209 to 213.

Research References

Encyclopedias

OH Jur. 3d Decedents' Estates § 293, Reference to Existing Instruments.

OH Jur. 3d Decedents' Estates § 296, Reference to Amendable Inter Vivos Trust; "Pour-Over" Provision.

OH Jur. 3d Decedents' Estates § 501, Testator's Knowledge of Law; Changes in Laws of Descent.

Forms

Ohio Forms Legal and Business § 25:6, Recordation.

Ohio Forms Legal and Business § 24:143, Drafting Will.

Ohio Forms Legal and Business § 24:311, General Clause.

Treatises and Practice Aids

Sowald & Morganstern, Baldwin's Ohio Practice Domestic Relations Law § 9:33, Effect of Signed Agreement—Incorporation, Integration, and Merger.

Carlin, Baldwin's Ohio Practice, Merrick-Rippner Probate Law § 27:3, Testamentary Formalities—Necessity for a Writing.

Carlin, Baldwin's Ohio Practice, Merrick-Rippner Probate Law § 31:1, Incorporation by Reference—Statutory Provisions.

Carlin, Baldwin's Ohio Practice, Merrick-Rippner Probate Law § 31:2, Incorporation by Reference—Pour-Over Will to a Trust.

Carlin, Baldwin's Ohio Practice, Merrick-Rippner Probate Law § 31:3, Incorporation by Reference—Practical Considerations.

Carlin, Baldwin's Ohio Practice, Merrick-Rippner Probate Law § 33:2, Trusts—Testamentary Addition to Existing Trust—Purpose of Pour-Over Statute.

Carlin, Baldwin's Ohio Practice, Merrick-Rippner Probate Law § 33:3, Trusts—Testamentary Addition to Existing Trust—Validity of Unfunded Trust.

Carlin, Baldwin's Ohio Practice, Merrick-Rippner Probate Law § 30:18, Drafting a Will—Beneficiary Clauses—Incorporation of Another Instrument.

Restatement (2d) of Property, Don. Trans. § 33.1, Meaning of a Will.

Restatement (3d) Property (Wills & Don. Trans.) § 3.6, Incorporation by Reference.

Law Review and Journal Commentaries

Problems with Pour-Over Wills, Robert J. Lynn. 47 Ohio St L J 47 (1986).

A Relaxation of the Requirement of a Self-Sufficient Integration, Note. 6 U Cin L Rev 295 (May 1932).

Notes of Decisions

Deposit into court   2
Inter vivos trust   1

---

1. Inter vivos trust

Where will contest action was dismissed, contestant could not thereafter maintain an action to set aside an inter vivos trust into which there was a "pour over" of the estate from the will. Hageman v. Cleveland Trust Co. (Ohio 1976) 45 Ohio St.2d 178, 343 N.E.2d 121, 74 O.O.2d 295.

Although attempted pour over to inter vivos trust was invalid by reason of an absence of a trust res, the trust instrument could be incorporated by reference in the will. Knowles v. Knowles (Ohio Prob. 1965) 4 Ohio Misc. 153, 212 N.E.2d 88, 33 O.O.2d 218.

An existing revocable and amendable living trust agreement, deed or settlement may be incorporated by reference in a will under this section. Bolles v. Toledo Trust Co. (Ohio 1944) 144 Ohio St. 195, 58 N.E.2d 381, 157 A.L.R. 1164, 29 O.O. 376. Wills ⚖ 98

Under Ohio law, decedent's putative daughter was not entitled under doctrine of deviation to be declared beneficiary of trust incorporated by reference in decedent's will, where compliance with terms of trust would not have been impossible or illegal, and would not have defeated or impaired purposes of trust because of circumstances not known to decedent. Rushford v. Firstar Bank, N.A. (C.A.6 (Ohio), 10-28-2002) No. 01-3487, 50 Fed.Appx. 202, 2002 WL 31424545, Unreported. Trusts ⚖ 58

2. Deposit into court

A provision of a will incorporating an extrinsic writing into the will, pursuant to RC 2107.05, has no effect unless such extrinsic writing is deposited with the probate court within thirty days after the will is probated, unless the court grants an extension of time for good cause shown. Hirsch v. Hirsch (Franklin 1972) 32 Ohio App.2d 200, 289 N.E.2d 386, 61 O.O.2d 212.

Contract to make a will was properly incorporated in testator's will even though contract was not deposited in court within thirty days of the date of probate of the will. Winkle v. U. S. (S.D.Ohio 1974) 381 F.Supp. 536.

Even though a trust agreement which is specifically referred to and incorporated into a will is not deposited with the probate court, where the trust was called to the attention of the court, exhibited to the appraisers of the estate and discussed with the court, there is substantial compliance with this section. Shawan v. City Bank Farmers Trust Co. (Ohio Prob. 1936) 1 Ohio Supp. 297, 21 Ohio Law Abs. 432, 6 O.O. 309.

2107.06 Persons under eighteen prohibited from witnessing will

No person under eighteen years of age shall witness a will executed pursuant to section 2107.03 of the Revised Code or an agreement to make a will or to make a devise or bequest by will pursuant to section 2107.04 of the Revised Code.

(2002 H 345, eff. 7–23–02)

Historical and Statutory Notes

Ed. Note: Former 2107.06 repealed by 1985 H 59, eff. 8–1–85; 131 v S 24; 1953 H 1; GC 10504–5.

Ed. Note: This statute was commonly referred to as the "Ohio Mortmain Statute."

Pre–1953 H 1 Amendments: 114 v 346

Library References

Wills ⚖ 116.
Westlaw Topic No. 409.
C.J.S. Wills §§ 253 to 255, 260 to 274.

Research References

Encyclopedias

OH Jur. 3d Decedents' Estates § 38, Law at Time of Intestate's Death as Controlling.

OH Jur. 3d Decedents' Estates § 233, Will's Validity Depends on Law at Death; Intent Determined With Reference to Law Applicable When Will is Executed.

OH Jur. 3d Decedents' Estates § 266, Public Authorities.

OH Jur. 3d Decedents' Estates § 268, Religious and Charitable Institutions; Former Mortmain Statute.

OH Jur. 3d Decedents' Estates § 310, Statutory Requirement of Attestation and Subscription.

OH Jur. 3d Decedents' Estates § 312, Attestation and Subscription Distinguished.

OH Jur. 3d Decedents' Estates § 313, Number of Witnesses.

OH Jur. 3d Decedents' Estates § 325, Application of the Usual Evidentiary Rules for Determining Competency.

OH Jur. 3d Decedents' Estates § 329, Testator's Spouse.

OH Jur. 3d Decedents' Estates § 410, Definition; Formal Requisites.

OH Jur. 3d Decedents' Estates § 429, Statutory Requirement of a Writing.

OH Jur. 3d Decedents' Estates § 442, Limitation of Actions.

OH Jur. 3d Decedents' Estates § 999, Requirements for Admission to Probate.

Forms

Ohio Forms Legal and Business § 24:115, Formal Requirements—Attestation by Witnesses.

Treatises and Practice Aids

Carlin, Baldwin's Ohio Practice, Merrick-Rippner Probate Law § 27:2, Testamentary Formalities—Compliance With Statute.

Carlin, Baldwin's Ohio Practice, Merrick-Rippner Probate Law § 27:9, Testamentary Formalities—Attesting Witnesses.

Carlin, Baldwin's Ohio Practice, Merrick-Rippner Probate Law § 28:2, Codicils—Requirements.

Carlin, Baldwin's Ohio Practice, Merrick-Rippner Probate Law § 32:1, Charitable Bequests—Mortmain Statute.

Carlin, Baldwin's Ohio Practice, Merrick-Rippner Probate Law § 34:5, Declaring the Validity of a Will—Procedure for Obtaining a Judgment—Judgment.

Carlin, Baldwin's Ohio Practice, Merrick-Rippner Probate Law § 36:1, Admission to Probate—Criteria.

Carlin, Baldwin's Ohio Practice, Merrick-Rippner Probate Law § 50:1, Agreement to Make a Will—RC 2107.04—Scope.

Carlin, Baldwin's Ohio Practice, Merrick-Rippner Probate Law § 50:3, Agreement to Make a Will—Essential Elements.

Carlin, Baldwin's Ohio Practice, Merrick-Rippner Probate Law § 50:7, Agreement to Make a Will—Part Performance And/Or Oral Contract.

Carlin, Baldwin's Ohio Practice, Merrick-Rippner Probate Law § 14:18, Payable on Death Accounts.

Carlin, Baldwin's Ohio Practice, Merrick-Rippner Probate Law § 30:42, Drafting a Will—Choosing Witnesses—in General.

Carlin, Baldwin's Ohio Practice, Merrick-Rippner Probate Law § 30:56, Malpractice Liability of Drafting Attorney; Professional Disciplinary Action.

Carlin, Baldwin's Ohio Practice, Merrick-Rippner Probate Law § 30:57, Simple Will—Form.

Carlin, Baldwin's Ohio Practice, Merrick-Rippner Probate Law § 43:26, Construing a Will—Words and Phrases—Issue.

Carlin, Baldwin's Ohio Practice, Merrick-Rippner Probate Law § 45:13, Rule Against Perpetuities—Effect.

Carlin, Baldwin's Ohio Practice, Merrick-Rippner Probate Law § 98:37, Adoption—Withdrawal of Consent.

Carlin, Baldwin's Ohio Practice, Merrick-Rippner Probate Law § 30:184, Attestation Clause of Witnesses—Form.

Carlin, Baldwin's Ohio Practice, Merrick-Rippner Probate Law § 30:189, Codicil—Form.

Carlin, Baldwin's Ohio Practice, Merrick-Rippner Probate Law § 30:190, Codicil-Alternate—Form.

Restatement (2d) of Property, Don. Trans. § 9.1, Restraints on Contests.

Restatement (2d) of Trusts § 362, Restrictions Upon the Creation of Charitable Trusts.

Restatement (3d) Property (Wills & Don. Trans.) § 9.7, Mortmain Abolished.

DEPOSIT

2107.07 Deposit of will

A will may be deposited by the maker, or by some person for the maker, in the office of the judge of the probate court in the county in which the testator lives. Such will shall be safely kept until delivered or disposed of as provided by section 2107.08 of the Revised Code. The judge, on being paid the fee of one dollar, shall receive, keep, and give a certificate of deposit for such will.

Every will which is to be deposited shall be enclosed in a sealed wrapper, which shall be indorsed with the name of the testator. The judge shall indorse thereon the date of delivery and the person by whom such will was delivered. The wrapper may be indorsed with the name of a person to whom it is to be delivered after the death of the testator. Such will shall not be opened or read until delivered to a person entitled to receive it, until the maker petitions the probate court for a declaratory judgment of the validity of the will pursuant to section 2107.081 of the Revised Code, or until otherwise disposed of as provided in section 2107.08 of the Revised Code.

(1978 H 505, eff. 1–1–79; 1953 H 1; GC 10504–6, 10504–7)

Historical and Statutory Notes

Pre–1953 H 1 Amendments: 114 v 346, 347

Library References

Wills ⬯127.
Westlaw Topic No. 409.
C.J.S. Wills §§ 441 to 442.

Research References

Encyclopedias

OH Jur. 3d Decedents' Estates § 445, Safekeeping by Court.
OH Jur. 3d Decedents' Estates § 446, Safekeeping by Court—Disposition During Testator's Lifetime.

Forms

Ohio Forms Legal and Business § 24:120, Safekeeping, Deposit, and Delivery of Will.

Treatises and Practice Aids

Carlin, Baldwin's Ohio Practice, Merrick-Rippner Probate Law § 30:54, Drafting a Will—Mechanical Recording of Execution of Will—Deposit of Will.

Carlin, Baldwin's Ohio Practice, Merrick-Rippner Probate Law § 98:40, Adoption—Consent Not Required—Putative Father.

Notes of Decisions

Deeds 1

---

1. Deeds

There being no statutory provisions governing the deposit of deeds in escrow with a probate judge, such deposit cannot be received by the probate judge in his official capacity; in absence of such statutory provision there is no implied reservation in the person depositing deeds in escrow with the probate judge to recall the same. Gordon v. Bartlett (Hardin 1938) 62 Ohio App. 295, 23 N.E.2d 964, 28 Ohio Law Abs. 161, 16 O.O. 13. Deposits And Escrows ⬯ 19

2107.08 Delivery of will

During the lifetime of a testator, the testator's will, deposited according to section 2107.07 of the Revised Code, shall be delivered only to him, to some person authorized by him by a written order, or to a probate court for a determination of its validity when the testator so requests. After the testator's death, the will shall be delivered to the person named in the indorsement on the wrapper of the will, if there is a person named who demands it. If the testator has petitioned the probate court for a judgment declaring the validity of the will pursuant to section 2107.081 of the Revised Code and the court has rendered the judgment, the probate judge with possession shall deliver the will to the proper probate court as determined under section 2107.11 of the Revised Code, upon the death of the testator, for probate.

If no person named in the indorsement demands the will and it is not one that has been declared valid pursuant to section 2107.084 of the Revised Code, it shall be publicly opened in the probate court within two months after notice of the testator's death and retained in the office of the probate judge until offered for probate. If the jurisdiction belongs to any other probate court, the will shall be delivered to the person entitled to its custody, to be presented for probate in the other court. If the probate judge who opens the will has jurisdiction of it, he immediately shall give notice of its existence to the executor named in the will or, if any, to the persons holding a power to nominate an executor as described in section 2107.65 of the Revised Code, or, if it is the case, to the executor named in the will and to the persons holding a power to nominate a coexecutor as described in that section. If no executor is named and no persons hold a power to nominate an executor as described in that section, the probate judge shall give notice to other persons immediately interested.

(1992 H 427, eff. 10–8–92; 1983 S 115; 1978 H 505; 1953 H 1; GC 10504–8, 10504–9)

Historical and Statutory Notes

Pre–1953 H 1 Amendments: 114 v 347

Cross References

Averments in indictment as to stolen, forged, destroyed, or secreted will or codicil, 2941.22
Securing writings by deception, 2913.43
Tampering with records, 2913.42

Library References

Wills ⚖128, 129.
Westlaw Topic No. 409.
C.J.S. Wills §§ 442 to 444.

Research References

Encyclopedias

OH Jur. 3d Decedents' Estates § 446, Safekeeping by Court—Disposition During Testator's Lifetime.
OH Jur. 3d Decedents' Estates § 447, Safekeeping by Court—Disposition After Testator's Death.

Forms

Ohio Forms Legal and Business § 24:120, Safekeeping, Deposit, and Delivery of Will.

Treatises and Practice Aids

Carlin, Baldwin's Ohio Practice, Merrick-Rippner Probate Law § 30:54, Drafting a Will—Mechanical Recording of Execution of Will—Deposit of Will.

DECLARATION OF VALIDITY OF WILL

2107.081 Petition by testator for declaration of validity of will; failure to file not evidence

(A) A person who executes a will allegedly in conformity with the laws of this state may petition the probate court of the county in which he is domiciled, if he is domiciled in this state, or the probate court of the county in which any of his real property is located, if he is not domiciled in this state, for a judgment declaring the validity of the will.

The petition may be filed in the form determined by the probate court of the county in which it is filed.

The petition shall name as parties defendant all persons named in the will as beneficiaries, and all of the persons who would be entitled to inherit from the testator under Chapter 2105. of the Revised Code had the testator died intestate on the date the petition was filed.

For the purposes of this section, "domicile" shall be determined at the time of filing the petition with the probate court.

(B) The failure of a testator to file a petition for a judgment declaring the validity of a will he has executed shall not be construed as evidence or an admission that the will was not properly executed pursuant to section 2107.03 of the Revised Code or any prior law of this state in effect at the time of execution or as evidence or an admission that the testator did not have the requisite testamentary capacity and freedom from undue influence under section 2107.02 of the Revised Code.

(1978 H 505, eff. 1–1–79)

Cross References

Validity of will, determination during testator's lifetime authorized, thereafter at request of interested party, 2721.03

Library References

Declaratory Judgment ⚖241.
Westlaw Topic No. 118A.
C.J.S. Declaratory Judgments § 104.

Research References

Encyclopedias

OH Jur. 3d Decedents' Estates § 411, Will Executed in Another State.
OH Jur. 3d Decedents' Estates § 449, Generally; Filing of Petition.
OH Jur. 3d Decedents' Estates § 653, Probate Court; Applicability of the Declaratory Judgment Act.

Forms

Ohio Forms Legal and Business § 24:120, Safekeeping, Deposit, and Delivery of Will.
Ohio Jurisprudence Pleading and Practice Forms § 2:6, Courts of Common Pleas—Probate Division.

Treatises and Practice Aids

Klein, Darling, & Terez, Baldwin's Ohio Practice Civil Practice § 4.4:2, Process: Service by Publication--Service by Publication Authorized by Law--In General.
Carlin, Baldwin's Ohio Practice, Merrick-Rippner Probate Law § 6:6, Declaratory Judgments—Probate Court Proceedings.
Carlin, Baldwin's Ohio Practice, Merrick-Rippner Probate Law § 27:1, Testamentary Formalities—Definition of Will; Testamentary Intent.
Carlin, Baldwin's Ohio Practice, Merrick-Rippner Probate Law § 28:1, Codicils—Definition.
Carlin, Baldwin's Ohio Practice, Merrick-Rippner Probate Law § 34:1, Declaring the Validity of a Will—Introduction.
Carlin, Baldwin's Ohio Practice, Merrick-Rippner Probate Law § 34:2, Declaring the Validity of a Will—Procedure for Obtaining a Judgment—Petitioner in Action.
Carlin, Baldwin's Ohio Practice, Merrick-Rippner Probate Law § 34:3, Declaring the Validity of a Will—Procedure for Obtaining a Judgment—Defendant in Action.
Carlin, Baldwin's Ohio Practice, Merrick-Rippner Probate Law § 34:4, Declaring the Validity of a Will—Procedure for Obtaining a Judgment—Hearing.
Carlin, Baldwin's Ohio Practice, Merrick-Rippner Probate Law § 34:8, Declaring the Validity of a Will—Effect on Will Contest.
Carlin, Baldwin's Ohio Practice, Merrick-Rippner Probate Law § 35:6, Contesting Jurisdiction to Probate—Interested Persons.
Carlin, Baldwin's Ohio Practice, Merrick-Rippner Probate Law § 38:2, Will Contests—Statutory Provisions.

Law Review and Journal Commentaries

The Ante Mortem Alternative to Probate Legislation in Ohio, Timothy R. Donovan. 9 Cap U L Rev 717 (Summer 1980).

Ante–Mortem Probate —Achieving Will Contest Invincibility, Gerry W. Beyer. 6 Prob L J Ohio 69 (May/June 1996).

Bullet–Proofing My Will or How to Guarantee the Validity of My Will, Gerald R. Walker. 12 Lake Legal Views 4 (February 1989).

Contemporary Ante–Mortem Statutory Formulations: Observations and Alternatives, Note. 32 Case W Res L Rev 823 (1982).

Notes of Decisions

Capacity of testator 2
Constitutional issues 1

---

1. Constitutional issues

The antemortem statutes are constitutional. Cooper v Woodard, No. CA–1724 (5th Dist Ct App, Tuscarawas, 7–27–83).

2. Capacity of testator

Competent and credible evidence failed to support finding that testator lacked testamentary capacity at time he executed will, where, other than physician's testimony, all evidence demonstrated that testator understood what property he owned and identity of his natural heirs when he executed will and physician's opinion that testator lacked testamentary capacity was based on nursing home records and physician's conclusions about possible effects of testator's illnesses and medications, rather than physician's personal observations of testator. In re Estate of Worstell v. Harold Todd, Inc., ex rel. Estate of Worstell (Ohio App. 2 Dist., Montgomery, 10-04-2002) No. 19133, 2002-Ohio-5385, 2002 WL 31243490, Unreported, appeal allowed 98 Ohio St.3d 1474, 784 N.E.2d 708, 2003-Ohio-904, motion granted 99 Ohio St.3d 1451, 790 N.E.2d 1216, 2003-Ohio-3396, appeal dismissed as improvidently allowed 100 Ohio St.3d 1258, 799 N.E.2d 636, 2003-Ohio-6387, reconsideration denied 101 Ohio St.3d 1470, 804 N.E.2d 43, 2004-Ohio-819. Wills ⚖ 55(5)

Where petitioner seeks an antemortem determination as to the validity of her will, the probate court may properly find such will to be valid even though the petitioner previously had been found mentally incompetent for purposes of guardianship where testimony concerning the petitioner's mental state at the time of the will's execution indicated that she knew she was about to execute her will, that she knew the members of her family and of her relationship to them, that she knew the extent of her property and that she was of sound mind. Fischer v Swartz, No. 82–CA–71 (2d Dist Ct App, Greene, 4–7–83).

2107.082 Service of process

Service of process in an action authorized by section 2107.081 of the Revised Code shall be made on every party defendant named in that action by the following methods:

(A) By certified mail, or any other valid personal service permitted by the Rules of Civil Procedure, if the party is an inhabitant of this state or is found within this state;

(B) By certified mail, with a copy of the summons and petition, to the party at his last known address or any other valid personal service permitted by the Rules of Civil Procedure, if the party is not an inhabitant of this state or is not found within this state;

(C) By publication, according to Civil Rule 4.4, in a newspaper of general circulation published in the county where the petition was filed, for three consecutive weeks, if the address of the party is unknown, if all methods of personal service permitted under division (B) of this section were attempted without success, or if the interest of the party under the will or in the estate of the testator should the will be declared invalid is unascertainable at that time.

(1978 H 505, eff. 1–1–79)

Cross References

Procedure in probate court, Civ R 73

Library References

Declaratory Judgment ⚖ 256.
Westlaw Topic No. 118A.

Research References

Encyclopedias

OH Jur. 3d Decedents' Estates § 450, Service of Process.
OH Jur. 3d Decedents' Estates § 456, Effect of Judgment—as Evidence in Other Proceedings.

Treatises and Practice Aids

Carlin, Baldwin's Ohio Practice, Merrick-Rippner Probate Law § 34:3, Declaring the Validity of a Will—Procedure for Obtaining a Judgment—Defendant in Action.
Carlin, Baldwin's Ohio Practice, Merrick-Rippner Probate Law § 34:6, Declaring the Validity of a Will—Post-Judgment Revocation or Modification.

2107.083 Validity of will, hearing

When a petition is filed pursuant to section 2107.081 of the Revised Code, the probate court shall conduct a hearing on the validity of the will. The hearing shall be adversary in nature and shall be conducted pursuant to section 2721.10 of the Revised Code, except as otherwise provided in sections 2107.081 to 2107.085 of the Revised Code.

(1978 H 505, eff. 1–1–79)

Library References

Declaratory Judgment ⚖ 364.
Westlaw Topic No. 118A.

Research References

Encyclopedias

OH Jur. 3d Decedents' Estates § 451, Hearing.

Treatises and Practice Aids

Carlin, Baldwin's Ohio Practice, Merrick-Rippner Probate Law § 34:2, Declaring the Validity of a Will—Procedure for Obtaining a Judgment—Petitioner in Action.
Carlin, Baldwin's Ohio Practice, Merrick-Rippner Probate Law § 34:4, Declaring the Validity of a Will—Procedure for Obtaining a Judgment—Hearing.
Carlin, Baldwin's Ohio Practice, Merrick-Rippner Probate Law § 34:5, Declaring the Validity of a Will—Procedure for Obtaining a Judgment—Judgment.

Law Review and Journal Commentaries

Ante–Mortem Probate —Achieving Will Contest Invincibility, Gerry W. Beyer. 6 Prob L J Ohio 69 (May/June 1996).

2107.084 Declaration of validity; effects; disposition; revocation or modification of will after declaration

(A) The probate court shall declare the will valid if, after conducting a proper hearing pursuant to section 2107.083 of the Revised Code, it finds that the will was properly executed pursuant to section 2107.03 of the Revised Code or under any prior law of this state that was in effect at the time of execution and that the testator had the requisite testamentary capacity and freedom from undue influence pursuant to section 2107.02 of the Revised Code.

Any such judgment declaring a will valid is binding in this state as to the validity of the will on all facts found, unless provided otherwise in this section, section 2107.33, or division (B) of section 2107.71 of the Revised Code, and, if the will remains valid, shall give the will full legal effect as the instrument of disposition of the testator's estate, unless the will has been modified or revoked according to law.

(B) Any declaration of validity issued as a judgment pursuant to this section shall be sealed in an envelope along with the will to which it pertains, and filed by the probate judge or his designated officer in the offices of that probate court. The filed will shall be available during the testator's lifetime only to the testator. If the testator removes a filed will from the possession of the probate judge, the declaration of validity rendered under division (A) of this section no longer has any effect.

(C) A testator may revoke or modify a will declared valid and filed with a probate court pursuant to this section by petitioning the probate court in possession of the will and asking that the will be revoked or modified. The petition shall include a document executed pursuant to sections 2107.02 and 2107.03 of the Revised Code, and shall name as parties defendant those persons who were parties defendant in any previous action declaring the will valid, those persons who are named in any modification as beneficiaries, and those persons who would be entitled because of the revocation or modification, to inherit from the testator under Chapter 2105. of the Revised Code had the testator died intestate on the date the petition was filed. Service of the petition and process shall be made on these parties by the methods authorized in section 2107.082 of the Revised Code.

Unless waived by all parties, the court shall conduct a hearing on the validity of the revocation or modification requested under this division in the same manner as it would on any initial petition for a judgment declaring a will to be valid under this section. If the court finds that the revocation or modification is valid, as defined in division (A) of this section, the revocation or modification shall take full effect and be binding, and revoke the will or modify it to the extent of the valid modification. The revocation or modification, the judgment declaring it valid, and the will itself shall be sealed in an envelope and filed with the probate court, and shall be available during the testator's lifetime only to the testator.

(D) A testator may also modify a will by any later will or codicil executed according to the laws of this state or any other state and may revoke a will by any method permitted under section 2107.33 of the Revised Code.

(E) A declaration of validity of a will, or of a revocation or modification of a will previously determined to be valid, given under division (C) of this section, is not subject to collateral attack, except by a person and in the manner specified in division (B) of section 2107.71 of the Revised Code, but is appealable subject to the terms of Chapter 2721. of the Revised Code.

(1978 H 505, eff. 1–1–79)

Cross References

Determination of validity of will during testator's lifetime allowed, 2721.03
Jurisdiction of probate court, 2101.24

Library References

Declaratory Judgment ⇐381, 390.
Wills ⇐167.
Westlaw Topic Nos. 118A, 409.
C.J.S. Wills §§ 386, 389, 1621.

Research References

Encyclopedias

OH Jur. 3d Decedents' Estates § 447, Safekeeping by Court—Disposition After Testator's Death.
OH Jur. 3d Decedents' Estates § 452, Judgment, Generally.
OH Jur. 3d Decedents' Estates § 453, Filing of Judgment and Will.
OH Jur. 3d Decedents' Estates § 454, Revocation or Modification of Will After Judgment.
OH Jur. 3d Decedents' Estates § 455, Effect of Judgment.
OH Jur. 3d Decedents' Estates § 868, Jurisdiction of Probate Court.
OH Jur. 3d Decedents' Estates § 996, Persons Entitled to Apply for Probate.
OH Jur. 3d Decedents' Estates § 999, Requirements for Admission to Probate.
OH Jur. 3d Decedents' Estates § 1012, Proof When Will Already Declared Valid.
OH Jur. 3d Declar. Judgments & Related Proceedings § 37, Jurisdiction, Generally—Probate Matters.

Forms

Ohio Forms Legal and Business § 24:120, Safekeeping, Deposit, and Delivery of Will.
Ohio Forms Legal and Business § 24:261, Prior Wills and Codicils.

Treatises and Practice Aids

Carlin, Baldwin's Ohio Practice, Merrick-Rippner Probate Law § 2:12, Probating the Will—Testimony of Witnesses Within the Discretion of Probate Court.
Carlin, Baldwin's Ohio Practice, Merrick-Rippner Probate Law § 34:1, Declaring the Validity of a Will—Introduction.
Carlin, Baldwin's Ohio Practice, Merrick-Rippner Probate Law § 34:5, Declaring the Validity of a Will—Procedure for Obtaining a Judgment—Judgment.
Carlin, Baldwin's Ohio Practice, Merrick-Rippner Probate Law § 34:6, Declaring the Validity of a Will—Post-Judgment Revocation or Modification.
Carlin, Baldwin's Ohio Practice, Merrick-Rippner Probate Law § 34:7, Declaring the Validity of a Will—Appeal and Collateral Attack.
Carlin, Baldwin's Ohio Practice, Merrick-Rippner Probate Law § 34:8, Declaring the Validity of a Will—Effect on Will Contest.
Carlin, Baldwin's Ohio Practice, Merrick-Rippner Probate Law § 36:1, Admission to Probate—Criteria.
Carlin, Baldwin's Ohio Practice, Merrick-Rippner Probate Law § 40:1, Revocation of Will—Introduction.
Carlin, Baldwin's Ohio Practice, Merrick-Rippner Probate Law § 49:1, Withholding a Will—Scope of RC 2107.10.
Carlin, Baldwin's Ohio Practice, Merrick-Rippner Probate Law § 49:4, Withholding a Will—Enforcing Production.
Carlin, Baldwin's Ohio Practice, Merrick-Rippner Probate Law § 2:121, Administration of Decedent's Estate—Checklist.

Law Review and Journal Commentaries

Ante–Mortem Probate —Achieving Will Contest Invincibility, Gerry W. Beyer. 6 Prob L J Ohio 69 (May/June 1996).

2107.085 Effects in relation to other matters

The finding of facts by a probate court in a proceeding brought under sections 2107.081 to 2107.085 of the Revised Code is not admissible as evidence in any proceeding other than one brought to determine the validity of a will.

The determination or judgment rendered in a proceeding under these sections is not binding upon the parties to such a proceeding in any action not brought to determine the validity of a will.

The failure of a testator to file a petition for a judgment declaring the validity of a will he has executed is not admissible as evidence in any proceeding to determine the validity of that will or any other will executed by the testator.

(1978 H 505, eff. 1–1–79)

Library References

Declaratory Judgment ⇐390.
Judgment ⇐644.
Westlaw Topic Nos. 118A, 228.
C.J.S. Judgments §§ 781, 784, 910 to 911, 913 to 917.

Research References

Encyclopedias

OH Jur. 3d Decedents' Estates § 456, Effect of Judgment—as Evidence in Other Proceedings.

Treatises and Practice Aids

Carlin, Baldwin's Ohio Practice, Merrick-Rippner Probate Law § 6:6, Declaratory Judgments—Probate Court Proceedings.
Carlin, Baldwin's Ohio Practice, Merrick-Rippner Probate Law § 34:1, Declaring the Validity of a Will—Introduction.
Carlin, Baldwin's Ohio Practice, Merrick-Rippner Probate Law § 34:4, Declaring the Validity of a Will—Procedure for Obtaining a Judgment—Hearing.

Law Review and Journal Commentaries

Ante–Mortem Probate —Achieving Will Contest Invincibility, Gerry W. Beyer. 6 Prob L J Ohio 69 (May/June 1996).

PRODUCTION

2107.09 Who may enforce production of a will; disposition of will previously declared valid

(A) If real or personal estate is devised or bequeathed by a last will, the executor, or any interested person, may cause such will to be brought before the probate court of the county in which the decedent was domiciled. By citation, attachment, or warrant or, if circumstances require it, by warrant or attachment in the first instance, such court may compel the person having the custody or control of such will to produce it before the court for the purpose of being proved.

If the person having the custody or control of the will intentionally conceals or withholds it or neglects or refuses to produce it for probate without reasonable cause, he may be committed to the county jail and kept in close custody until he produces the will. This person also shall be liable to any party aggrieved for the damages sustained by such neglect or refusal.

Any citation, attachment, or warrant issued pursuant to this section may be issued into any county in the state and shall be served and returned by the officer to whom it is delivered.

The officer to whom such process is delivered shall be liable for neglect in its service or return in like manner as sheriffs are liable for neglect in not serving or returning a capias issued upon an indictment.

(B) In the case of a will that has been declared valid pursuant to section 2107.084 of the Revised Code, the probate judge who made the declaration or who has possession of the will shall cause the will and the judgment declaring validity to be brought before the proper probate court as determined by section 2107.11 of the Revised Code at a time after the death of the testator. If the death of the testator is brought to the attention of the probate judge by an interested party, the judge shall cause the will to be brought before the proper probate court at that time.

(1978 H 505, eff. 1–1–79; 1953 H 1; GC 10504–10 to 10504–13)

Historical and Statutory Notes

Pre–1953 H 1 Amendments: 114 v 347, 348

Cross References

Securing writings by deception, 2913.43
Stealing or secreting will, indictment need not allege ownership or value, 2941.22
Tampering with records, 2913.42

Library References

Wills ⚖︎211, 249.
Westlaw Topic No. 409.
C.J.S. Wills §§ 453 to 456, 524 to 525.

Research References

Encyclopedias

OH Jur. 3d Decedents' Estates § 888, Where Testator was Domiciled in Ohio.
OH Jur. 3d Decedents' Estates § 971, Admission of Will to Probate; Notice.
OH Jur. 3d Decedents' Estates § 996, Persons Entitled to Apply for Probate.
OH Jur. 3d Decedents' Estates § 997, Compelling Production of a Will.

Treatises and Practice Aids

Klein, Darling, & Terez, Baldwin's Ohio Practice Civil Practice § 73:3, Probate Division--Venue.
Carlin, Baldwin's Ohio Practice, Merrick-Rippner Probate Law § 49:4, Withholding a Will—Enforcing Production.
Carlin, Baldwin's Ohio Practice, Merrick-Rippner Probate Law § 2:121, Administration of Decedent's Estate—Checklist.

Notes of Decisions

Jurisdiction and procedure 1
Presumption of revocation 2

---

1. Jurisdiction and procedure

Interested parties not served with notice of a former offer for probate may repropound the will notwithstanding its refusal. In re Stacey (Ohio Prob. 1897) 6 Ohio Dec. 142, 4 Ohio N.P. 143.

Proceedings to require production of will under this section, to admit will to probate under GC 10504–15 (RC 2107.11) and to establish lost, spoliated or destroyed will under GC 10504–35 (RC 2107.26) et seq. may be maintained only in probate court of county in which testator was domiciled at time of death. State ex rel. Overlander v. Brewer (Ohio 1947) 147 Ohio St. 386, 72 N.E.2d 84, 34 O.O. 338.

Jurisdiction over decedent's estate acquired by probate court of one county by appointment of administrator under GC 10509–1 (RC 2113.01) is not exclusive of jurisdiction over same estate later acquired by probate court of another county by virtue of proceedings under GC 10504–10 (RC 2107.09), 10504–15 (RC 2107.11), 10504–15 (RC 2107.26). State ex rel. Overlander v. Brewer (Ohio 1947) 147 Ohio St. 386, 72 N.E.2d 84, 34 O.O. 338.

2. Presumption of revocation

Where a testator executed a will in duplicate, keeping one copy and delivering the other to the executor-designate, and upon his death the copy retained by him cannot be found, a presumption arises that he revoked it, but this presumption can be overcome, and declarations of the testator may be shown for weakening or strengthening the presumption, and the court should admit newly discovered evidence at the hearing on a motion to probate the will. In re Wood's Estate (Cuyahoga 1951) 105 N.E.2d 589, 61 Ohio Law Abs. 548.

2107.10 Effect of withholding will; will previously declared valid in another county; knowledge of beneficiary

(A) No property or right, testate or intestate, shall pass to a beneficiary named in a will who knows of the existence of the will for three years and has the power to control it, and, without reasonable cause, intentionally conceals or withholds it or neglects or refuses within the three years to cause it to be offered for or admitted to probate. The estate devised to such devisee shall descend to the heirs of the testator, not including any heir who has concealed or withheld the will.

(B) No property or right, testate or intestate, passes to a beneficiary named in a will when the will was declared valid and filed with a probate judge pursuant to section 2107.084 of the Revised Code, the declaration and filing took place in a county different from the county in which the will of the testator would be probated under section 2107.11 of the Revised Code, and the named beneficiary knew of the declaration and filing and of the death of the testator and did not notify the probate judge with whom the will was filed. This division does not preclude a named beneficiary from acquiring property or rights from the estate of the testator for failing to notify a probate judge if it is his reasonable belief that the judge has previously been notified of the testator's death.

(1978 H 505, eff. 1–1–79; 1953 H 1; GC 10504–14)

Historical and Statutory Notes

Pre–1953 H 1 Amendments: 114 v 348

Cross References

Securing writings by deception, 2913.43
Stealing or secreting will, indictment need not allege ownership or value, 2941.22
Tampering with records, tampering with unrevoked will, 2913.42

Library References

Wills ⚖︎709.1.
Westlaw Topic No. 409.
C.J.S. Wills § 99.

Research References

Encyclopedias

OH Jur. 3d Decedents' Estates § 59, Effect of Withholding Will from Probate.
OH Jur. 3d Decedents' Estates § 676, Loss of Rights Under Will by Concealment or Neglect to Probate.
OH Jur. 3d Decedents' Estates § 677, Loss of Rights Under Will by Concealment or Neglect to Probate—Application to Foreign Wills.
OH Jur. 3d Decedents' Estates § 993, Time of Probate.
OH Jur. 3d Decedents' Estates § 994, Scope of Inquiry.
OH Jur. 3d Judgments § 193, Undivided Interests.

Treatises and Practice Aids

Carlin, Baldwin's Ohio Practice, Merrick-Rippner Probate Law § 49:1, Withholding a Will—Scope of RC 2107.10.

Carlin, Baldwin's Ohio Practice, Merrick-Rippner Probate Law § 49:2, Withholding a Will—Forfeiture—Nature of Intent Necessary to Trigger.

Carlin, Baldwin's Ohio Practice, Merrick-Rippner Probate Law § 49:3, Withholding a Will—Forfeiture—Defining the Penalty.

Bogert - the Law of Trusts and Trustees § 477, Title Obtained by Forgery—Probate Statutes.

Notes of Decisions

Effect of other laws 2
Forfeiture 1
Procedural issues 3

---

1. Forfeiture

Son, who knew of unprobated will devising everything to mother, is barred from asserting forfeiture of estate of mother because of lapse of three year period for probate under this section; adopted daughter of son, taking from her father by representation, is also barred by conduct of her father, from asserting claim. Lawrence v. Woodcox (Miami 1933) 16 Ohio Law Abs. 129.

A beneficiary under a will who fails to cause such will to be offered for probate within three years after knowing of its existence, is not deprived of his legacy or devise unless his withholding or neglect or concealment or refusal to cause it to be offered for probate is intentional and without reasonable cause, for the purpose of delaying its administration or defeating some rights or benefits given by the terms of the will. In re Kusar's Estate (Ohio Prob. 1965) 5 Ohio Misc. 23, 211 N.E.2d 535, 34 O.O.2d 32.

Widower by virtue of former GC 10542 (RC 2107.10) lost all rights given him in will; no action was required to divest him of such rights; statute of limitation as to forfeitures, GC 11225 (RC 2305.11), did not apply. Stillwell v. Tudor (Knox 1946) 80 Ohio App. 190, 75 N.E.2d 94, 35 O.O. 514.

Sole devisee barred under statute. Lawson v. Thomas (Lucas 1934) 48 Ohio App. 311, 193 N.E. 655, 16 Ohio Law Abs. 503, 1 O.O. 483.

The terms of the statute do not provide for the forfeiture of an interest that has vested, but prevents any estate from passing to the negligent devisee by the will. Barrow v. McCann (Lawrence 1927) 25 Ohio App. 520, 159 N.E. 104, 6 Ohio Law Abs. 127.

Where persons interested in the will of a decedent neglect to cause it to be offered for probate within statutory period, will becomes inoperative so far as vesting title to real estate in such persons is concerned, and realty devised to persons in default descends to the heirs of the testator. Loos v. Buffalo-Springfield Rubber Co. (Ohio App. 1922) 35 Ohio C.D. 809, 32 Ohio C.A. 443.

The limitation of RS 5943 for bringing an action under a statute for a forfeiture or penalty to one year applies to forfeitures under this section, and inasmuch as this statute is punitive in effect it must be strictly construed. Mitchell v. Long (Ohio Com.Pl. 1909) 20 Ohio Dec. 41, 9 Ohio N.P.N.S. 113.

2. Effect of other laws

Where a devisee neglects for three years to cause a copy of a probated foreign will to be recorded in the county where the devised property is situated, the devise will not lapse under the thirty-fourth section of the wills act of 1840, since that provision refers only to original probate. Carpenter v. Denoon (Ohio 1876) 29 Ohio St. 379.

Up to the time of probating a will the title held by the widow and heirs is one of inheritance, and the priority and validity of a levy during that interval upon the interest of one of the heirs cannot be questioned. Loos v. Buffalo-Springfield Rubber Co. (Ohio App. 1922) 35 Ohio C.D. 809, 32 Ohio C.A. 443. Descent And Distribution ⟶ 19; Execution ⟶ 112; Limitation Of Actions ⟶ 43; Wills ⟶ 77

Where a widow retains an attorney to assist her in being appointed administratrix of her late husband's estate, she is not entitled to information acquired by her counsel in a prior professional relationship concerning the will of her husband's brother, even though such knowledge might have enabled her to prevent the beneficiary from taking under such will under RS 5943 for failure to probate it until after the devisee's rights were forfeited. Long v. Bowersox (Ohio Com.Pl. 1909) 19 Ohio Dec. 494, 8 Ohio N.P.N.S. 249.

3. Procedural issues

The provision for forfeiture in RS 5943 does not declare a rule of property, and mere delay or lapse of time does not start the provision into operation; to do so requires that an action shall be brought and a decree entered declaring the forfeiture. Mitchell v. Long (Ohio Com.Pl. 1909) 20 Ohio Dec. 41, 9 Ohio N.P.N.S. 113.

The custodian of a will is not debarred by RS 5943 from taking as a devisee under a second will, by the fact that more than three years elapsed after the death of the testatrix before he offered it for probate, where a later will was probated within thirty days and was contested, and after a lapse of more than three years was set aside. Avery v. Howard (Ohio Com.Pl. 1908) 19 Ohio Dec. 71, 7 Ohio NP(NS) 97.

PROBATE

2107.11 Jurisdiction to probate

A will shall be admitted to probate:

(A) In the county in which the testator was domiciled if, at the time of his death, he was domiciled in this state;

(B) In any county of this state where any real or personal property of such testator is located if, at the time of his death, he was not domiciled in this state, and provided that such will has not previously been admitted to probate in this state or in the state of such testator's domicile;

(C) In the county of this state in which a probate court rendered a judgment declaring that the will was valid and where the will was filed with the probate court.

For the purpose of this section, intangible personal property is located in the place where the instrument evidencing a debt, obligation, stock, or chose in action is located or if there is no such instrument where the debtor resides.

(1978 H 505, eff. 1–1–79; 1953 H 1; GC 10504–15)

Historical and Statutory Notes

Pre–1953 H 1 Amendments: 120 v 649; 114 v 348

Cross References

Foreign wills, 2129.05, 2129.06
Jurisdiction in intestate estate, 2113.01

Library References

Wills ⟶249 to 251.
Westlaw Topic No. 409.
C.J.S. Wills §§ 524 to 525.

Research References

Encyclopedias

OH Jur. 3d Decedents' Estates § 884, Where Intestate was Not a Resident of Ohio.
OH Jur. 3d Decedents' Estates § 887, Domicil With Respect to Probate.
OH Jur. 3d Decedents' Estates § 888, Where Testator was Domiciled in Ohio.
OH Jur. 3d Decedents' Estates § 889, Where Testator was Not Domiciled in Ohio.
OH Jur. 3d Decedents' Estates § 890, Where Testator's Will Has Been Declared Valid.
OH Jur. 3d Decedents' Estates § 892, Venue.
OH Jur. 3d Decedents' Estates § 993, Time of Probate.

Forms

Ohio Forms Legal and Business § 24:120, Safekeeping, Deposit, and Delivery of Will.

Treatises and Practice Aids

Klein, Darling, & Terez, Baldwin's Ohio Practice Civil Practice § 73:3, Probate Division--Venue.

Carlin, Baldwin's Ohio Practice, Merrick-Rippner Probate Law § 2:11, Probating the Will—Initial Steps.

Carlin, Baldwin's Ohio Practice, Merrick-Rippner Probate Law § 2:14, Probating the Will—Appeal—Will Contest.

Carlin, Baldwin's Ohio Practice, Merrick-Rippner Probate Law § 3:13, Jurisdiction of Probate Court—Scope—Exclusive and Concurrent Jurisdiction.

Carlin, Baldwin's Ohio Practice, Merrick-Rippner Probate Law § 30:5, Drafting a Will—Introductory Clause—Statement of Testator's Residence.

Carlin, Baldwin's Ohio Practice, Merrick-Rippner Probate Law § 35:2, Domicile of Testator—Ohio.

Carlin, Baldwin's Ohio Practice, Merrick-Rippner Probate Law § 35:3, Domicile of Testator—Outside Ohio.

Carlin, Baldwin's Ohio Practice, Merrick-Rippner Probate Law § 36:5, Application to Probate Will—Form.

Carlin, Baldwin's Ohio Practice, Merrick-Rippner Probate Law § 49:1, Withholding a Will—Scope of RC 2107.10.

Carlin, Baldwin's Ohio Practice, Merrick-Rippner Probate Law § 49:4, Withholding a Will—Enforcing Production.

Carlin, Baldwin's Ohio Practice, Merrick-Rippner Probate Law § 68:1, Letters—in General—Jurisdiction.

Carlin, Baldwin's Ohio Practice, Merrick-Rippner Probate Law § 2:121, Administration of Decedent's Estate—Checklist.

Carlin, Baldwin's Ohio Practice, Merrick-Rippner Probate Law App B SPF 2.0, Application to Probate Will.

Carlin, Baldwin's Ohio Practice, Merrick-Rippner Probate Law App B SPF 2.0A, Application to Probate Will (Decedent Dying on or After 5-31-90).

Restatement (2d) of Conflicts § 314, Where Will May be Probated and Representative Appointed.

Law Review and Journal Commentaries

Change of Domicile from Ohio to Florida—Is the Juice Worth the Squeeze?, Jeffry L. Weiler. 3 Prob L J Ohio 45 (March/April 1993).

How a Will Is Admitted to Probate in Ohio. 50 Title Topics 6 (June 1983).

Probate Malpractice, Hon. Fred V. Skok. 14 Lake Legal Views 1 (February 1991).

Notes of Decisions

Domicile 2
Procedural issues 3
Real estate 1
State versus federal jurisdiction 4

---

1. Real estate

Statute addressing the jurisdiction of probate courts to probate a will did not give a probate court jurisdiction to administer an intestate nonresident decedent's non-Ohio property. State ex rel. Lee v. Trumbull County Probate Court (Ohio, 10-14-1998) 83 Ohio St.3d 369, 700 N.E.2d 4, 1998-Ohio-51, on remand 1999 WL 744032. Courts ⇔ 198; Courts ⇔ 200.7

Where an authenticated copy of a will, executed and proved according to the laws of the state of the decedent's domicile, has been admitted to record pursuant to RC 2129.05, and where it is not established that the widow who was domiciled in that state had claimed anything under that will or otherwise elected to take thereunder and where the testator owned real estate in Ohio at his death, such widow has the right, with respect to that Ohio real estate, to elect not to take under the testator's will but to take under the Ohio statute of descent and distribution, even though no such election is permitted by the law of the state of the testator's domicile at death. Pfau v. Moseley (Ohio 1966) 9 Ohio St.2d 13, 222 N.E.2d 639, 38 O.O.2d 8. Wills ⇔ 778

On the record will of decedent owning real property in Summit county and residing in West Germany could not properly be probated in Cuyahoga county. In re Paich's Estate (Cuyahoga 1962) 186 N.E.2d 755, 90 Ohio Law Abs. 470.

An Ohio probate court has jurisdiction to admit the will of a nonresident decedent to probate and to administer decedent's real and personal property located in Ohio. Gordon v. Holly Woods Acres, Inc. (C.A.6 (Ky.) 1964) 328 F.2d 253, 27 O.O.2d 188. Executors And Administrators ⇔ 12; Wills ⇔ 251

2. Domicile

Testator's brother failed to demonstrate that testator was not domiciled in Trumbull County, even though will indicated that testator was "presently residing" in a different county, and thus brother was not entitled to relief from judgment admitting will to probate in Trumbull County, where application to probate the will listed testator's domicile as Trumbull County, testator's funeral was held in, and her final place of interment was, Trumbull County, all of testator's next of kin, including her brother, received copies of the application to probate the will in Trumbull County and signed waivers agreeing that the facts set forth in the application were true, accurate, and correct, and the jurisdiction to probate the will was not contested. In re Estate of Mallory (Ohio App. 11 Dist., Trumbull, 03-17-2006) No. 2005-T-0028, 2006-Ohio-1265, 2006 WL 688008, Unreported. Wills ⇔ 249

Probate court had jurisdiction to probate decedent's estate, though decedent had not been domiciled in state, where decedent's intangible property was located in state and her will had not previously been admitted to probate elsewhere. Carlin v. Mambuca (Ohio App. 8 Dist., 05-23-1994) 96 Ohio App.3d 500, 645 N.E.2d 737, motion to certify allowed 70 Ohio St.3d 1475, 640 N.E.2d 848, cause dismissed 71 Ohio St.3d 1441, 643 N.E.2d 1152. Courts ⇔ 198

A purported will which upon presentation for probate contains eight separate black ink deletions, apparently made with a felt marking pen, the last blacking completely covering a testatrix's signature, is not a spoliated will, so that whether such purported will should be admitted to probate is governed by RC 2107.11 et seq., not by RC 2107.26 et seq., dealing with the probate of a spoliated will, as these sections existed at the time of decedent's death on August 29, 1975. In re Nash's Will (Ohio Com.Pl. 1976) 50 Ohio Misc. 4, 361 N.E.2d 558, 3 O.O.3d 347, 4 O.O.3d 33. Wills ⇔ 203; Wills ⇔ 231

The right of a widow in the estate of her deceased consort in an estate consisting of personalty is determined by the law of the decedent's domicile. In re McCombs' Estate (Ohio Prob. 1948) 80 N.E.2d 573, 52 Ohio Law Abs. 353. Descent And Distribution ⇔ 5

When on hearing probate court finds that testator at time of his death was resident in county in which application is made, judgment admitting will to probate, however erroneous, cannot be reviewed or set aside by superior court by prohibition. State ex rel. Barbee v. Allen (Ohio 1917) 96 Ohio St. 10, 117 N.E. 13, 15 Ohio Law Rep. 56, 15 Ohio Law Rep. 112. Courts ⇔ 202(4); Prohibition ⇔ 11; Wills ⇔ 356

A testator's declaration in his will as to his domicile, though not necessarily conclusive, will determine the question in the absence of more convincing proof to the contrary. Wilberding v. Miller (Ohio 1913) 88 Ohio St. 609, 90 Ohio St. 28, 106 N.E. 665, 11 Ohio Law Rep. 96, 11 Ohio Law Rep. 262, 11 Ohio Law Rep. 447. Domicile ⇔ 9; Domicile ⇔ 10

Jurisdiction over decedent's estate acquired by probate court of one county by appointment of administrator under GC 10509–1 (RC 2113.01) is not exclusive of jurisdiction over same estate later acquired by probate court of another county by virtue of proceedings under GC 10504–10 (RC 2107.09), 10504–15 (RC 2107.11) and 10504–35 (RC 2107.26). State ex rel. Overlander v. Brewer (Ohio 1947) 147 Ohio St. 386, 72 N.E.2d 84, 34 O.O. 338.

Proceedings to require production of will under GC 10504–10 (RC 2107.09), to admit will to probate under GC 10504–15 (RC 2107.11) and to establish lost, spoliated or destroyed will under GC 10504–35 (RC 2107.36) et seq. may be maintained only in probate court of county in which testator was domiciled at time of death. State ex rel. Overlander v. Brewer (Ohio 1947) 147 Ohio St. 386, 72 N.E.2d 84, 34 O.O. 338.

GC 10509–1 (RC 2113.01) is not in conflict with GC 10504–15 (RC 2107.11), as the former provides for appointment by probate court of administrator of estate of intestate who was resident of county of such court at time of death, while the latter section provides for admission to probate of decedent's will by probate court of county in which decedent was domiciled at time of death; term "resident" as used in GC 10509–1 (RC 2113.01) is not synonymous with term "domiciled" in either GC 10504–10 (RC 2107.09) or 10504–15 (RC 2107.11). State ex rel. Overlander v. Brewer (Ohio 1947) 147 Ohio St. 386, 72 N.E.2d 84, 34 O.O. 338.

Where a decedent who had cancer was moved to his sister's home for convalescent care following surgery and expressed a desire to stay in his sister's home until his death, he was domiciled in the county and state of his sister's home for purposes of RC 2107.11(A). In re Estate of Adams, No. 9–291 (11th Dist Ct App, Lake, 3–9–84).

3. Procedural issues

A probate court's original order admitting a will to probate is irrelevant to a court of appeals review of a will contest action since a will contest is not an appellate procedure but a trial de novo. Mattax v. Moore (Trumbull 1991) 72 Ohio App.3d 647, 595 N.E.2d 969, dismissed, jurisdictional motion overruled 61 Ohio St.3d 1419, 574 N.E.2d 1090.

In an original ancillary administration in Ohio, the Ohio probate law including the statute of descent and distribution is applied. Darrow v. Fifth Third Union Trust Co. (Ohio Com.Pl. 1954) 139 N.E.2d 112, 78 Ohio Law Abs. 303, 1 O.O.2d 104.

Where settlement in state-court personal injury action between minor victims and tortfeasor's automobile insurer had to be approved by probate court in order to be consummated, probate proceeding was not "civil action" subject to removal, but rather was ancillary to personal-injury action. Community Ins. Co. v. Rowe (S.D.Ohio, 08-12-1999) 85 F.Supp.2d 800. Removal Of Cases ⇐ 5

Under GC 10504–15 (RC 2107.11) and 10504–16 (RC 2107.12), "persons interested in its probate" include those whose interests are opposed to probate of the will; one who contends that there has been a former adjudication by a denial of probate may, under these sections, contest jurisdiction by asserting the defense of res judicata, and if aggrieved may prosecute error to the finding on such defense. State ex rel. Young v. Morrow (Ohio 1936) 131 Ohio St. 266, 2 N.E.2d 595, 5 O.O. 584.

The probate court's jurisdiction should be challenged when documents executed abroad are presented for probate and may not later be challenged on the basis that the decedent did not possess any property in Ohio. Fifth Third Bank v Montagu, No. C-820207 (1st Dist Ct App, Hamilton, 1–5–83).

An erroneous determination that a decedent was domiciled in the county where decedent's will was admitted to probate renders the judgment of the probate court voidable and such judgment may only be attacked by means of Civ R 60(B) or by direct appeal. In re Estate of Gavrilovich, No. 10718 (9th Dist Ct App, Summit, 10–27–82).

4. State versus federal jurisdiction

Wills and estates, probate exception to federal jurisdiction, tort claim asserted in bankruptcy proceeding, reversed and remanded, Marshall v. Marshall, 2006, 126 S.Ct. 1735.

Under probate exception, federal courts lack subject matter jurisdiction to probate a will or to administer a decedent's estate. Community Ins. Co. v. Rowe (S.D.Ohio, 08-12-1999) 85 F.Supp.2d 800. Federal Courts ⇐ 9

Probate exception to federal courts' subject matter jurisdiction did not apply in action to approve settlement of minors' personal-injury claims, so as to preclude removal, even though action was brought in state probate court, since action did not involve probate of will or proceedings concerning decedent's estate, and removal was sought on federal-question rather than diversity grounds. Community Ins. Co. v. Rowe (S.D.Ohio, 08-12-1999) 85 F.Supp.2d 800. Federal Courts ⇐ 9; Removal Of Cases ⇐ 19(1)

2107.12 Contest of jurisdiction

When a will is presented for probate or for a declaratory judgment of its validity pursuant to section 2107.081 of the Revised Code, persons interested in its outcome may contest the jurisdiction of the court to entertain the application. Preceding a hearing of a contest as to jurisdiction, all parties named in such will as legatees, devisees, trustees, or executors shall have notice thereof in such manner as may be ordered by the court.

When such contest is made, parties may call witnesses and shall be heard upon the question involved. The decision of the court as to its jurisdiction may be reviewed on error.

(1978 H 505, eff. 1-1-79; 1953 H 1; GC 10504–16; Source—GC 10504–15)

Historical and Statutory Notes

Pre–1953 H 1 Amendments: 114 v 348

Library References

Declaratory Judgment ⇐ 292, 393.
Wills ⇐ 229, 270, 400.
Westlaw Topic Nos. 118A, 409.
C.J.S. Wills §§ 503 to 506, 545 to 552, 778, 784.

Research References

Encyclopedias

OH Jur. 3d Decedents' Estates § 871, Jurisdiction of Probate Court—Contesting Jurisdiction.

Treatises and Practice Aids

Carlin, Baldwin's Ohio Practice, Merrick-Rippner Probate Law § 2:14, Probating the Will—Appeal—Will Contest.

Carlin, Baldwin's Ohio Practice, Merrick-Rippner Probate Law § 34:1, Declaring the Validity of a Will—Introduction.

Carlin, Baldwin's Ohio Practice, Merrick-Rippner Probate Law § 35:6, Contesting Jurisdiction to Probate—Interested Persons.

Carlin, Baldwin's Ohio Practice, Merrick-Rippner Probate Law § 35:7, Contesting Jurisdiction to Probate—Nature of Contest.

Carlin, Baldwin's Ohio Practice, Merrick-Rippner Probate Law § 35:9, Contesting Jurisdiction to Probate—Notice of Hearing.

Carlin, Baldwin's Ohio Practice, Merrick-Rippner Probate Law § 36:5, Application to Probate Will—Form.

Carlin, Baldwin's Ohio Practice, Merrick-Rippner Probate Law § 2:121, Administration of Decedent's Estate—Checklist.

Carlin, Baldwin's Ohio Practice, Merrick-Rippner Probate Law § 35:10, Appeal from Admission to Probate.

Carlin, Baldwin's Ohio Practice, Merrick-Rippner Probate Law § 35:11, Objection to Jurisdiction of Probate Court to Probate Will—Form.

Law Review and Journal Commentaries

How a Will Is Admitted to Probate in Ohio. 50 Title Topics 6 (June 1983).

Notes of Decisions

In general 1
Erroneous judgments 3
Procedural issues 4
Time and method of challenge 2

---

1. In general

By virtue of former GC 10520 (RC 2107.11) and 10521 (RC 2107.12), the judgment of a probate court as to the domicile of a testator is conclusive upon the courts of this state, although not binding upon the courts of other states. Hine v. Cowles (Ohio Cir. 1911) 33 Ohio C.D. 175, 18 Ohio C.C.(N.S.) 518, affirmed 86 Ohio St. 350, 99 N.E. 1124, 10 Ohio Law Rep. 118.

Testimony by the attorney-draftsman of the will as to the testator's instructions is admissible and supports the trial court's finding that the testatrix intended to create a demonstrative and not a specific legacy. Curl v Mardis, No. 9–81–8 (3d Dist Ct App, Marion, 3–8–82).

2. Time and method of challenge

A writ of prohibition may be issued to prevent the exercise of ultra vires jurisdiction by the probate court in administration of estates and probate of wills; when the proceeding merely involves a jurisdictional question during trial, the court has power to determine its own jurisdiction and a writ of prohibition will not lie to oust the court from jurisdiction. State ex rel. Young v. Morrow (Ohio 1936) 131 Ohio St. 266, 2 N.E.2d 595, 5 O.O. 584. Prohibition ⇐ 10(2)

The probate court's jurisdiction should be challenged when documents executed abroad are presented for probate and may not later be challenged on the basis that the decedent did not possess any property in Ohio. Fifth Third Bank v Montagu, No. C-820207 (1st Dist Ct App, Hamilton, 1–5–83).

3. Erroneous judgments

Once a court has jurisdiction of the subject matter and the parties to a case, it is immaterial how grossly irregular or manifestly erroneous its proceedings might have been; its final order cannot be regarded as a nullity and cannot therefore be collaterally impeached. Sheldon's Lessee v. Newton (Ohio 1854) 3 Ohio St. 494.

Where in a will contest action the jury returns a verdict establishing its validity, but mistakenly inserts the date of the will's execution as the date of its probate, and the record shows that only one will of the decedent was exhibited to the jury, it is not error for the court to treat the jury's date as mere surplusage and enter a judgment upon the verdict correcting the error and establishing the will's validity. Seal v. Goebel (Ohio Cir. 1908) 21 Ohio C.D. 286, 11 Ohio C.C.(N.S.) 433, affirmed 81 Ohio St. 523, 91 N.E. 1138, 7 Ohio Law Rep. 500.

An erroneous determination that a decedent was domiciled in the county where decedent's will was admitted to probate renders the judgment of the probate court voidable and such judgment may only be attacked by means of Civ R 60(B) or by direct appeal. In re Estate of Gavrilovich, No. 10718 (9th Dist Ct App, Summit, 10–27–82).

4. Procedural issues

Matters relating to substantive rights in personal property are still controlled by the law of the state of the decedent's domicile, and the legislature, by its amendments, merely subjected such assets to the statutory rules of procedure provided for the probate courts of Ohio. In re McCombs' Estate (Ohio Prob. 1948) 80 N.E.2d 573, 52 Ohio Law Abs. 353.

A testator's declaration in his will as to his domicile, though not necessarily conclusive, will determine the question in the absence of more convincing proof to the contrary. Wilberding v. Miller (Ohio 1913) 88 Ohio St. 609, 90 Ohio St. 28, 106 N.E. 665, 11 Ohio Law Rep. 96, 11 Ohio Law Rep. 262, 11 Ohio Law Rep. 447. Domicile ⇐ 9; Domicile ⇐ 10

Interested parties not served with notice of a former offer for probate may repropound the will notwithstanding its refusal. In re Stacey (Ohio Prob. 1897) 6 Ohio Dec. 142, 4 Ohio N.P. 143.

2107.15 Witness a devisee or legatee

If a devise or bequest is made to a person who is one of only two witnesses to a will, the devise or bequest is void. The witness shall then be competent to testify to the execution of the will, as if the devise or bequest had not been made. If the witness would have been entitled to a share of the testator's estate in case the will was not established, he takes so much of that share that does not exceed the bequest or devise to him. The devisees and legatees shall contribute for that purpose as for an absent or afterborn child under section 2107.34 of the Revised Code.

(1975 S 145, eff. 1–1–76; 1953 H 1; GC 10504–19)

Historical and Statutory Notes

Pre–1953 H 1 Amendments: 114 v 349

Legislative Service Commission

1975:

Under current law, if a witness to a will is needed to prove a will, the devise or bequest to him is void. Under this bill, the witnesses would not necessarily be examined in deciding whether a will is admitted to probate. This section would state that if the witness is one of only two witnesses to a will, the devise or bequest to him would be void.

Library References

Wills ⇐ 116, 712.
Westlaw Topic No. 409.
C.J.S. Wills §§ 88 to 92, 253 to 255, 260 to 274.

Research References

Encyclopedias

OH Jur. 3d Contribution, Indemnity, & Subrogation § 9, Contribution Governed by Statute.
OH Jur. 3d Decedents' Estates § 328, Devisees and Legatees.
OH Jur. 3d Decedents' Estates § 329, Testator's Spouse.
OH Jur. 3d Decedents' Estates § 330, Executors and Spouses of Executors.
OH Jur. 3d Decedents' Estates § 331, Trustee Named in Will.
OH Jur. 3d Decedents' Estates § 406, Number and Competency of Witnesses.
OH Jur. 3d Decedents' Estates § 1005, Competency of Witnesses.

Treatises and Practice Aids

Giannelli and Snyder, Baldwin's Ohio Practice, Evidence, R 601, General Rule of Competency.
Giannelli and Snyder, Baldwin's Ohio Practice, Evidence, § 601.16, Statutes; Dead Man Rule.
Carlin, Baldwin's Ohio Practice, Merrick-Rippner Probate Law § 27:9, Testamentary Formalities—Attesting Witnesses.
Carlin, Baldwin's Ohio Practice, Merrick-Rippner Probate Law § 36:3, Admission to Probate—Witness as Devisee or Legatee.
Carlin, Baldwin's Ohio Practice, Merrick-Rippner Probate Law § 30:42, Drafting a Will—Choosing Witnesses—in General.
Restatement (2d) of Property, Don. Trans. § 33.1, Meaning of a Will.
Restatement (3d) Property (Wills & Don. Trans.) § 3.1, Attested Wills.

Notes of Decisions

Executors 1
Interested parties 2
Verbal will 3

---

1. Executors

Where a written will is signed by a testator and attested and subscribed by two witnesses who are attorneys and partners, one of whom prepared such will, and who are nominated in such will as executor and alternate executor, respectively, such witnesses are competent and such will, if otherwise valid, is not thereby invalidated. Blankner v. Lathrop (Ohio 1959) 169 Ohio St. 229, 159 N.E.2d 229, 74 A.L.R.2d 279, 8 O.O.2d 221. Wills ⇐ 116

An executor may be a witness to a will, provided he is not a legatee or devisee. Blankner v. Lathrop (Franklin 1958) 154 N.E.2d 95, 79 Ohio Law Abs. 6, affirmed 169 Ohio St. 229, 159 N.E.2d 229, 74 A.L.R.2d 279, 8 O.O.2d 221.

A witness-executor or witness-trustee is not an incompetent subscribing witness to a will by reason of such fact. Fazekas v. Gobozy (Cuyahoga 1958) 150 N.E.2d 319, 78 Ohio Law Abs. 258.

2. Interested parties

Statute voiding a devise or bequest made to person who was one of only two witnesses to will did not apply to will which made residuary bequests to decedent's sisters, even though sisters signed will as interested witnesses, where the will was validly executed in Florida under Florida law. Hairelson v. Estate of Franks (Ohio App. 10 Dist., 12-10-1998) 130 Ohio App.3d 671, 720 N.E.2d 989. Wills ⇐ 240

A proponent of a will who is also its sole beneficiary is not automatically incompetent to testify as to the will's validity, since such a person is an interested party but not an interested witness to the will as contemplated by RC 2107.15, which makes a bequest to one of two attesting witnesses to a will void, where the person did not sign the will and was not a legal witness to it. In re Estate of Wachsmann (Cuyahoga 1988) 55 Ohio App.3d 265, 563 N.E.2d 734.

Interested witnesses to a written will are competent witnesses thereto if they otherwise meet the test of competency set forth in RC 2317.01. Rogers v. Helmes (Ohio 1982) 69 Ohio St.2d 323, 432 N.E.2d 186, 23 O.O.3d 301. Wills ⇐ 116

A devise or bequest made in a written will to an interested, supernumerary witness is not void. Rogers v. Helmes (Ohio 1982) 69 Ohio St.2d 323, 432 N.E.2d 186, 23 O.O.3d 301. Wills ⇐ 712

3. Verbal will

RS 5925, concerning the effect of a witness also being a devisee or legatee under the will, does not apply to verbal wills; at common law the will was void if a beneficiary named therein was a witness. Vrooman v. Powers (Ohio 1890) 47 Ohio St. 191, 23 W.L.B. 292, 24 N.E. 267.

2107.16 Will proved in certain cases; will previously declared valid

(A) When offered for probate, a will may be admitted to probate and allowed upon such proof as would be satisfactory, and in like manner as if an absent or incompetent witness were dead:

(1) If it appears to the probate court that a witness to such will has gone to parts unknown;

(2) If the witness was competent at the time of attesting its execution and afterward became incompetent;

(3) If testimony of a witness cannot be obtained within a reasonable time.

(B) When offered for probate, a will shall be admitted to probate and allowed when there has been a prior judgment by a probate court declaring that the will is valid pursuant to section 2107.084 of the Revised Code, if the will has not been removed from the possession of the probate judge and has not been modified or revoked under division (C) or (D) of section 2107.084 of the Revised Code.

(1978 H 505, eff. 1-1-79; 1953 H 1; GC 10504-20)

Historical and Statutory Notes

Pre-1953 H 1 Amendments: 114 v 349

Library References

Wills ⟜303(6).
Westlaw Topic No. 409.
C.J.S. Wills §§ 613 to 614, 625 to 626.

Research References

Encyclopedias

OH Jur. 3d Decedents' Estates § 1010, Proof When Witness Missing or Incompetent.

OH Jur. 3d Decedents' Estates § 1012, Proof When Will Already Declared Valid.

Treatises and Practice Aids

Giannelli and Snyder, Baldwin's Ohio Practice, Evidence, R 903, Subscribing Witness' Testimony Unnecessary.

Carlin, Baldwin's Ohio Practice, Merrick-Rippner Probate Law § 2:12, Probating the Will—Testimony of Witnesses Within the Discretion of Probate Court.

Carlin, Baldwin's Ohio Practice, Merrick-Rippner Probate Law § 36:1, Admission to Probate—Criteria.

Carlin, Baldwin's Ohio Practice, Merrick-Rippner Probate Law § 36:11, Examination of Witness to Signature—Form.

2107.17 Depositions may be taken by commission; legal effect

When a witness to a will, or other witness competent to testify at a probate or declaratory judgment proceeding, resides out of its jurisdiction, or resides within it but is infirm and unable to attend court, the probate court may issue a commission with the will annexed directed to any suitable person. In lieu of the original will, the probate court, in its discretion, may annex to the commission a copy of the will made by photostatic or any similar process. The person to whom the commission is directed shall take the deposition or authorize the taking of the deposition of the witness as provided by the Rules of Civil Procedure. The testimony, certified and returned, shall be admissible and have the same effect in the proceedings as if taken in open court.

(1978 H 505, eff. 1-1-79; 1975 S 145; 127 v 36; 1953 H 1; GC 10504-21)

Historical and Statutory Notes

Pre-1953 H 1 Amendments: 116 v 385; 114 v 349

OSBA Probate and Trust Law Section

1957:

This section provides for the sending of a will outside the jurisdiction of the court where it is necessary to obtain the sworn testimony, by deposition, of the attesting witnesses to a will who are not presently available in the court's jurisdiction.

The Committee believes that the frequency with which this section is employed warrants the inclusion of a provision which will enable the court to annex a "copy made by photostatic or similar process" of the original will with its commission for a deposition to be transmitted outside its jurisdiction. This will reduce the hazard of a possible loss of a will while it is out of the control and possession of the court having jurisdiction of probate, and save time in securing probate when the witnesses are in different localities for separate copies may be sent to each witness. Inasmuch as some counties may not have available reproducing equipment, the use of a "copy" is optional.

Cross References

Depositions, Civ R 27 to 32

Library References

Wills ⟜314.
Westlaw Topic No. 409.
C.J.S. Wills §§ 661 to 663.

Research References

Encyclopedias

OH Jur. 3d Boats, Ships, & Shipping § 8, Certificate of Title; Manufacturer's or Importer's Certificate—Application and Issuance.

OH Jur. 3d Decedents' Estates § 1011, Proof When Witness Resides Out of Jurisdiction or is Infirm.

OH Jur. 3d Decedents' Estates § 1688, Allowance to Children.

OH Jur. 3d Discovery & Depositions § 53, Depositions in Specified Proceedings.

Treatises and Practice Aids

Carlin, Baldwin's Ohio Practice, Merrick-Rippner Probate Law § 2:12, Probating the Will—Testimony of Witnesses Within the Discretion of Probate Court.

Carlin, Baldwin's Ohio Practice, Merrick-Rippner Probate Law § 36:12, Application for Court to Appoint Commissioner to Take Deposition of Witness to Will—Form.

Carlin, Baldwin's Ohio Practice, Merrick-Rippner Probate Law § 36:13, Entry to Issue Commission for Deposition of Witness to Will—Form.

Carlin, Baldwin's Ohio Practice, Merrick-Rippner Probate Law § 36:14, Commission to Take Deposition of Witness to Will—Form.

Carlin, Baldwin's Ohio Practice, Merrick-Rippner Probate Law § 36:15, Deposition of Witness to Will—Form.

Law Review and Journal Commentaries

How a Will Is Admitted to Probate in Ohio. 50 Title Topics 6 (June 1983).

2107.18 Admission to probate; will previously declared valid

The probate court shall admit a will to probate if it appears from the face of the will, or if the probate court requires, in its discretion, the testimony of the witnesses to a will and it appears from that testimony, that the execution of the will complies with the law in force at the time of the execution of the will in the jurisdiction in which it was executed, or with the law in force in this state at the time of the death of the testator, or with the law in force in the jurisdiction in which the testator was domiciled at the time of his death.

The probate court shall admit a will to probate when there has been a prior judgment by a probate court declaring that the will is valid, rendered pursuant to section 2107.084 of the Revised Code, if the will has not been removed from the possession of the probate judge and has not been modified or revoked under division (C) or (D) of section 2107.084 of the Revised Code.

(1990 H 346, eff. 5–31–90; 1978 H 505; 1975 S 145; 131 v S 25; 1953 H 1; GC 10504–22)

Uncodified Law

1990 H 346, § 3, eff. 5–31–90, reads:

(A) Sections 1 and 2 of this act shall apply only to the estates of decedents who die on or after the effective date of this act.

(B) It is the intent of the General Assembly in the outright repeal of sections 2107.13 and 2107.14 of the Revised Code and the amendments to sections 109.30, 2107.18, 2107.19, 2107.22, 2107.27, 2107.76, 2115.16, and 2703.14 of the Revised Code by this act, to respond to the dicta of the Supreme Court in *Palazzi v. Estate of Gardner* (1987), 32 Ohio St. 3d 169 and to enact statutory provisions relating to notice of probate proceedings that are not unconstitutional as potentially violative of the due process of law rights of nonresidents of this state.

Historical and Statutory Notes

Pre–1953 H 1 Amendments: 120 v 649; 114 v 349

Legislative Service Commission

1975:

This section currently provides the prerequisites before a will is to be admitted to probate including requirements of age, attestation, sound mind, and not under restraint. The witnesses have to testify before the will is admitted under current law. The bill would permit the admission of a will to probate if from the face of the will or if demanded, from the testimony of the witnesses, it appears that its execution complies with the law. In describing the law in force at the time of execution of the will, the bill would substitute the word "jurisdiction" for "state." The requirements of age, sound mind, etc. would be deleted.

Legislative Service Commission

1975 (Commentary from former RC 2107.14):

Under existing law, the execution of a notarized affidavit can be substituted for the appearance and testimony of the witnesses when proving a will. This current procedure that provides for the execution of this affidavit would be repealed by the bill. The bill would provide that the witnesses to a will would not have to be examined before the will is admitted to probate unless demanded by an interested party. If the witnesses were demanded, at least two of the witnesses to a will would have to come before the court and state those facts necessary to prove the will.

OSBA Probate and Trust Law Section

1957 (Commentary from former RC 2107.14):

In executing a will it is sometimes felt desirable to have more than two witnesses to the testator's signature. Section 2107.03 (10504–3), Revised Code of Ohio, provides a will shall be signed at the end by the party making it and be attested and subscribed in the presence of such party by two or more competent witnesses who saw the testator subscribe or heard him acknowledge his signature. When a will is presented for probate with more than two witnesses the question arises, must all of such subscribing witnesses to the will testify before such will is admitted to probate or is it necessary that only two of such witnesses be presented and examined?

Section 2107.14 (10504–18) as it now exists provides: The Probate Court shall cause *the witnesses to a will* and other witnesses whom a person interested in having such will admitted to probate may desire to have appear to come before the court.

This language has been interpreted to require the court to have *all witnesses*, however many there may be, to appear and testify as to the execution of the will. Such interpretation defeats the purpose of having more than two witnesses to a will.

The committee thinks it advisable that this section should be amended so as to require only the testimony of two witnesses to a will even though more than two witnesses signed the will.

Cross References

Probate court to keep record of wills, 2101.12
Proceedings to admit foreign will to record, 2129.07
Securing writings by deception, 2913.43
Stealing or secreting will, indictment need not allege ownership or value, 2941.22
Tampering with unrevoked will, 2913.42

Library References

Wills ⚖︎108, 344.
Westlaw Topic No. 409.
C.J.S. Wills §§ 217 to 221, 225, 734.
Baldwin's Ohio Legislative Service, 1990 Laws of Ohio, H 346—LSC Analysis, p 5–87

Research References

Encyclopedias

OH Jur. 3d Decedents' Estates § 281, Requisites of Execution of Foreign Wills.
OH Jur. 3d Decedents' Estates § 999, Requirements for Admission to Probate.
OH Jur. 3d Decedents' Estates § 1001, Prima Facie Case of Validity Required.
OH Jur. 3d Decedents' Estates § 1007, Witnesses Other Than the Subscribing Witnesses.
OH Jur. 3d Decedents' Estates § 1012, Proof When Will Already Declared Valid.
OH Jur. 3d Decedents' Estates § 1013, Cross-Examination of Witnesses.
OH Jur. 3d Decedents' Estates § 1015, Admission Mandatory Upon Proof of Valid Execution.
OH Jur. 3d Decedents' Estates § 1019, Sufficiency of Order of Probate.
OH Jur. 3d Decedents' Estates § 1050, Weight and Sufficiency of Evidence.

Forms

Ohio Jurisprudence Pleading and Practice Forms § 64:24, Necessity.

Treatises and Practice Aids

Baldwin's Ohio Handbook Series—Trial Handbook § 24:5, Authentication—Private Writing.
Giannelli and Snyder, Baldwin's Ohio Practice, Evidence, R 903, Subscribing Witness' Testimony Unnecessary.
Carlin, Baldwin's Ohio Practice, Merrick-Rippner Probate Law § 2:8, Preparation and Execution of Necessary Documents.
Carlin, Baldwin's Ohio Practice, Merrick-Rippner Probate Law § 2:11, Probating the Will—Initial Steps.
Carlin, Baldwin's Ohio Practice, Merrick-Rippner Probate Law § 2:12, Probating the Will—Testimony of Witnesses Within the Discretion of Probate Court.
Carlin, Baldwin's Ohio Practice, Merrick-Rippner Probate Law § 27:2, Testamentary Formalities—Compliance With Statute.
Carlin, Baldwin's Ohio Practice, Merrick-Rippner Probate Law § 27:9, Testamentary Formalities—Attesting Witnesses.
Carlin, Baldwin's Ohio Practice, Merrick-Rippner Probate Law § 28:2, Codicils—Requirements.
Carlin, Baldwin's Ohio Practice, Merrick-Rippner Probate Law § 34:5, Declaring the Validity of a Will—Procedure for Obtaining a Judgment—Judgment.
Carlin, Baldwin's Ohio Practice, Merrick-Rippner Probate Law § 35:7, Contesting Jurisdiction to Probate—Nature of Contest.
Carlin, Baldwin's Ohio Practice, Merrick-Rippner Probate Law § 36:1, Admission to Probate—Criteria.
Carlin, Baldwin's Ohio Practice, Merrick-Rippner Probate Law § 36:3, Admission to Probate—Witness as Devisee or Legatee.
Carlin, Baldwin's Ohio Practice, Merrick-Rippner Probate Law § 36:5, Application to Probate Will—Form.
Carlin, Baldwin's Ohio Practice, Merrick-Rippner Probate Law § 36:9, Subpoena for Witness to Will—Form.
Carlin, Baldwin's Ohio Practice, Merrick-Rippner Probate Law § 39:2, Lost, Spoliated, or Destroyed Will—Statutory Provisions for Admission to Probate.
Carlin, Baldwin's Ohio Practice, Merrick-Rippner Probate Law § 50:1, Agreement to Make a Will—RC 2107.04—Scope.
Carlin, Baldwin's Ohio Practice, Merrick-Rippner Probate Law § 50:3, Agreement to Make a Will—Essential Elements.
Carlin, Baldwin's Ohio Practice, Merrick-Rippner Probate Law § 50:7, Agreement to Make a Will—Part Performance And/Or Oral Contract.

Carlin, Baldwin's Ohio Practice, Merrick-Rippner Probate Law § 2:121, Administration of Decedent's Estate—Checklist.

Carlin, Baldwin's Ohio Practice, Merrick-Rippner Probate Law § 27:11, Testamentary Formalities—Foreign Will.

Carlin, Baldwin's Ohio Practice, Merrick-Rippner Probate Law § 30:42, Drafting a Will—Choosing Witnesses—in General.

Carlin, Baldwin's Ohio Practice, Merrick-Rippner Probate Law § 30:56, Malpractice Liability of Drafting Attorney; Professional Disciplinary Action.

Carlin, Baldwin's Ohio Practice, Merrick-Rippner Probate Law § 30:57, Simple Will—Form.

Carlin, Baldwin's Ohio Practice, Merrick-Rippner Probate Law § 36:10, Testimony of Witness—Form.

Carlin, Baldwin's Ohio Practice, Merrick-Rippner Probate Law § 36:11, Examination of Witness to Signature—Form.

Carlin, Baldwin's Ohio Practice, Merrick-Rippner Probate Law § 36:12, Application for Court to Appoint Commissioner to Take Deposition of Witness to Will—Form.

Carlin, Baldwin's Ohio Practice, Merrick-Rippner Probate Law § 36:13, Entry to Issue Commission for Deposition of Witness to Will—Form.

Carlin, Baldwin's Ohio Practice, Merrick-Rippner Probate Law § 36:16, Entry Admitting Will to Probate—Form.

Carlin, Baldwin's Ohio Practice, Merrick-Rippner Probate Law § 30:184, Attestation Clause of Witnesses—Form.

Carlin, Baldwin's Ohio Practice, Merrick-Rippner Probate Law § 30:189, Codicil—Form.

Carlin, Baldwin's Ohio Practice, Merrick-Rippner Probate Law § 30:190, Codicil-Alternate—Form.

Carlin, Baldwin's Ohio Practice, Merrick-Rippner Probate Law App B SPF 2.0, Application to Probate Will.

Carlin, Baldwin's Ohio Practice, Merrick-Rippner Probate Law App B SPF 2.0A, Application to Probate Will (Decedent Dying on or After 5-31-90).

Law Review and Journal Commentaries

Common Form Probate Is Here, Robert M. Brucken and Wiley Dinsmore. 1 Prob L J Ohio 3 (September/October 1990).

How a Will Is Admitted to Probate in Ohio. 50 Title Topics 6 (June 1983).

Notes of Decisions

Domicile 5
Jurisdiction 7
Limitation of action 6
Prima facie case 3
Review of order 2
Title to property 1
Witnesses and evidence 4

---

1. Title to property

All wills must be established by probate, and until a will has been duly probated no title can be set up under it, nor can it be received as evidence of claims made under it. Swazey's Lessee v. Blackman (Ohio 1837) 8 Ohio 5.

Until a will has been probated, a legatee under such will has no rights whatever, as a mere expectation of property in the future is not a vested right. Bielat v. Bielat (Ohio, 01-05-2000) 87 Ohio St.3d 350, 721 N.E.2d 28, 2000-Ohio-451. Wills ⇐ 628

Title of devisee is a new title and is not acquired until probate of the will. Douglass v. Miller (Ohio Com.Pl. 1896) 4 Ohio Dec. 414, 3 Ohio N.P. 220, reversed 20 Ohio C.D. 666, 11 Ohio C.C.(N.S.) 205.

Although a copy of a will admitted to probate in another state is not spread upon the record, where an order for admission to record is made and the regular uniform entry is used, the will is effectual to pass the title to lands in Ohio; by the law of Ohio since 1808, a will is not effectual to pass realty unless it be probated, if domestic, or recorded, if foreign. McClaskey v. Barr (C.C.S.D.Ohio 1893) 54 F. 781.

2. Review of order

An order of a probate court admitting a will to probate is not a final appealable order; the only available challenge to such an order is a will contest, which is in the nature of an original action or "trial de novo," in the court of common pleas. Carr v. Howard (Fayette 1969) 17 Ohio App.2d 233, 246 N.E.2d 563, 46 O.O.2d 360.

In a will contest the order of probate is prima-facie evidence of the attestation, execution and validity of the will; in order to prevail, the contestant must produce sufficient evidence to do more than merely meet the prima-facie case, or "presumption" arising from the order of probate. Carr v. Howard (Fayette 1969) 17 Ohio App.2d 233, 246 N.E.2d 563, 46 O.O.2d 360.

The probate court has no jurisdiction to consider an application to vacate the probate of a will and the appointment of an executor filed after the term in which the order of probate was made and more than six months after the will is probated and while an action to contest the will is pending in the common pleas court. State ex rel. Cleveland Trust Co. v. Probate Court of Cuyahoga County (Ohio 1961) 172 Ohio St. 1, 173 N.E.2d 100, 15 O.O.2d 43. Executors And Administrators ⇐ 32(2); Wills ⇐ 355; Wills ⇐ 368

The admission of a will to probate is not a final appealable order. State ex rel. Cleveland Trust Co. v. Probate Court of Cuyahoga County (Cuyahoga 1959) 113 Ohio App. 1, 162 N.E.2d 574, 82 Ohio Law Abs. 291, 17 O.O.2d 1.

An order of the probate court admitting a paper to probate as the last will is not reviewable on error, although a refusal so to do is reviewable. Hollrah v. Lasance (Ohio 1900) 63 Ohio St. 58, 44 W.L.B. 80, 57 N.E. 964. Wills ⇐ 356

An order admitting a will to probate is not reviewable on error. (See also Missionary Society of the M.E. Church v Ely, 56 OS 405, 47 NE 537 (1897); Mosier v Harmon, 29 OS 220 (1876).) Hollrah v. Lasance (Ohio 1900) 63 Ohio St. 58, 44 W.L.B. 80, 57 N.E. 964.

Application to probate court to admit an alleged will to probate is a special proceeding within the meaning of RS 6707, which provides that an order affecting a substantial right made in a special proceeding is a final order. Missionary Soc. of Methodist Episcopal Church v. Ely (Ohio 1897) 56 Ohio St. 405, 38 W.L.B. 13, 47 N.E. 537. Appeal And Error ⇐ 91(3); Courts ⇐ 202(5)

3. Prima facie case

The solemn adjudication of any court having jurisdiction of the subject matter, although erroneous, is not void, but is valid until reversed. Le Grange's Lessee v. Ward (Ohio 1842) 11 Ohio 257.

If the uncontradicted evidence adduced from the face of a will and/or from the testimony of the will's witnesses establishes as a matter of law that the testator was under restraint, the will's proponents fail to make a prima facie showing of the will's validity and the probate court may properly deny application to probate. In re Estate of Smith (Ohio App. 4 Dist., 06-02-1997) 120 Ohio App.3d 480, 698 N.E.2d 455. Wills ⇐ 288(1)

Probate court did not go beyond scope of application proceeding when it denied application to admit will to probate after determining that testator was under restraint; determination did not turn proceeding into will contest. In re Estate of Smith (Ohio App. 4 Dist., 06-02-1997) 120 Ohio App.3d 480, 698 N.E.2d 455. Wills ⇐ 222

Once a prima facie showing of will's validity is made out, the probate court must admit the will to probate, notwithstanding conflicts in the evidence; the probate court is not authorized to weigh the evidence or act as trier of fact. In re Estate of Smith (Ohio App. 4 Dist., 06-02-1997) 120 Ohio App.3d 480, 698 N.E.2d 455. Wills ⇐ 309

Will should be admitted to probate if it appears on its face to comply with statutory requirement for execution in effect at time of execution, unless interested person demands testimony of at least two witnesses to execution of will. In re Estate of Carmedy (Ohio App. 10 Dist., 08-18-1994) 95 Ohio App.3d 572, 642 N.E.2d 1170. Wills ⇐ 115

In admitting a will to probate, the court does not hold the content valid but only that the will was properly executed; thus, where a testator breached a contract by making a new will and revoking an older one, the disappointed individual must find his remedy in another action since the second will remains a valid instrument. Georgekopoulos v. Vasilopoulos (Summit 1984) 26 Ohio App.3d 43, 498 N.E.2d 165, 26 O.B.R. 216.

Under RC 2107.18 and RC 2107.181, a will must be admitted to probate when the proponents introduce substantial evidence tending to prove the validity of the will. In re Young (Summit 1978) 60 Ohio App.2d 390, 397 N.E.2d 1223, 14 O.O.3d 359.

The time frame of RC 2107.18 concerns the situation at the time the will was "made," and not the situation at the time it was presented for probate. In re Nash's Will (Ohio Com.Pl. 1976) 50 Ohio Misc. 4, 361 N.E.2d 558, 3 O.O.3d 347, 4 O.O.3d 33. Wills ⇐ 206

Once a will is "made" in the manner provided in RC 2107.03, it remains a will unless and until it is revoked by one of the means provided in RC 2107.33. In re Nash's Will (Ohio Com.Pl. 1976) 50 Ohio Misc. 4, 361 N.E.2d 558, 3 O.O.3d 347, 4 O.O.3d 33.

The record of the hearing in the probate court on the order of probate is not before the court of common pleas in a will contest; whether the same or different evidence is presented in the two proceedings is immaterial, because the same evidence may or may not be sufficient to overcome the presumption arising from the order of probate. Carr v. Howard (Fayette 1969) 17 Ohio App.2d 233, 246 N.E.2d 563, 46 O.O.2d 360. Wills ⇐ 289

In a will contest the order of probate is prima-facie evidence of the attestation, execution and validity of the will; in order to prevail, the contestant must produce sufficient evidence to do more than merely meet the prima-facie case, or "presumption" arising from the order of probate. Carr v. Howard (Fayette 1969) 17 Ohio App.2d 233, 246 N.E.2d 563, 46 O.O.2d 360.

Where all signatures to the instrument are genuine, the attesting clause is in due form, and there is oral testimony by one of the witnesses that she knew it was the will of the testatrix which she was signing, and that the testatrix was of full age, of sound mind and memory, and not under any restraint, a prima-facie case is established, and it is not necessary that both attesting witnesses orally testify that all the statutory requirements regarding the execution of the will had been complied with. In re McGraw's Will (Scioto 1967) 14 Ohio App.2d 87, 236 N.E.2d 684, 43 O.O.2d 207.

If the applicant for probate of a will makes a prima-facie case on the validity of the execution and attestation, and on the capacity and freedom from restraint of the testator, the will must be admitted to probate; and questions as to competency, revocation by implication, or whether the will violates a contract should be decided in a subsequent proceeding. In re Piasecki's Estate (Ohio Prob. 1964) 201 N.E.2d 840, 95 Ohio Law Abs. 257, 30 O.O.2d 169.

Where all signatures to the instrument are genuine, the attesting clause is in due form, and there is oral testimony by one of the witnesses that she knew it was the will of the testatrix which she was signing, and that the testatrix was of full age, of sound mind and memory, and not under any restraint, a prima-facie case is established to admit the will to probate, since it is not necessary that both attesting witnesses orally testify that all the statutory requirements regarding the execution of the will had been complied with. In re Schulz' Estate (Cuyahoga 1956) 102 Ohio App. 486, 136 N.E.2d 730, 3 O.O.2d 41. Wills ⇐ 300

A proceeding to probate a will is not an adversary one; when prima-facie case appears by substantial evidence it is mandatory upon the court to admit the will to probate. McWilliams v. Central Trust Co. (Hamilton 1935) 51 Ohio App. 246, 200 N.E. 532, 20 Ohio Law Abs. 544, 5 O.O. 104. Wills ⇐ 300

After probate the burden of proving incapacity is upon the contestant. Ousley v. Witheron (Ohio Cir. 1896) 7 Ohio C.D. 448.

When it appears that the will was duly attested and executed under RS 5929, the court shall admit it to probate. Wolf v. Menager (Ohio Com.Pl. 1903) 14 Ohio Dec. 128.

An instrument which makes no disposition of property should be admitted to probate as the last will and testament of the decedent, where an intention by the decedent to make a disposition of his property clearly appears. In re Williamson's Will (Ohio Com.Pl. 1898) 8 Ohio Dec. 47, 6 Ohio N.P. 79.

The burden of proof is upon those propounding the will to make out a prima facie case showing that the testator, at time of execution of the will, was of sound mind and memory. In re Ludlow's Estate (Ohio Prob. 1897) 6 Ohio Dec. 106, 4 Ohio N.P. 99.

4. Witnesses and evidence

The order of the court of probate, which recites that the will was presented for probate, that subscribing witnesses were sworn and examined in open court, and that their testimony was reduced to writing and filed by order of the court, and that thereupon the court ordered the will to be filed and admitted to record, is sufficient evidence that the will was proved according to law and ordered to be recorded. Holman v. Riddle (Ohio 1858) 8 Ohio St. 384.

Document presented to probate court by illegitimate child as prior will of decedent did not meet the requirements for a valid will, since it was not signed by the decedent or attested by any witnesses. In re Estate of Okos (Ohio App. 6 Dist., Lucas, 06-04-2004) No. L-03-1343, 2004-Ohio-2882, 2004 WL 1232041, Unreported. Wills ⇐ 111(1); Wills ⇐ 114

Challenger of will, which had been admitted in its entirety into probate, failed to overcome presumption that will was valid by presenting evidence that earlier separation of page three from pages one and two represented form of mutilation which equated with revocation. Mattax v. Moore (Trumbull 1991) 72 Ohio App.3d 647, 595 N.E.2d 969, dismissed, jurisdictional motion overruled 61 Ohio St.3d 1419, 574 N.E.2d 1090. Wills ⇐ 288(3)

A will is to be admitted to probate where there is evidence to support its validity even where the witnesses to the will do not remember the circumstances of their signing. In re Estate of Wachsmann (Cuyahoga 1988) 55 Ohio App.3d 265, 563 N.E.2d 734.

A proponent of a will who is also its sole beneficiary is not automatically incompetent to testify as to the will's validity, since such a person is an interested party but not an interested witness to the will as contemplated by RC 2107.15, which makes a bequest to one of two attesting witnesses to a will void, where the person did not sign the will and was not a legal witness to it. In re Estate of Wachsmann (Cuyahoga 1988) 55 Ohio App.3d 265, 563 N.E.2d 734.

RC 2107.18 does not require, as does RC 2107.27, that the will sought to be proved has been "unrevoked at the death of the testator." In re Nash's Will (Ohio Com.Pl. 1976) 50 Ohio Misc. 4, 361 N.E.2d 558, 3 O.O.3d 347, 4 O.O.3d 33.

Where the subscribing witnesses testify to the due and proper execution of a will, and that at the time of execution the instrument did not contain the black ink deletions apparent at the time of the hearing for probate, such will should be admitted to probate and record. In re Nash's Will (Ohio Com.Pl. 1976) 50 Ohio Misc. 4, 361 N.E.2d 558, 3 O.O.3d 347, 4 O.O.3d 33. Wills ⇐ 206

Where both witnesses to a will testified that the testatrix did not sign the will in their presence and that they did not see her signature on the will when they signed, there can be no probate of the will; no acknowledgment can be implied from the fact that the testatrix was a woman of some business experience. In re La Mar's Will (Ohio Prob. 1957) 146 N.E.2d 472, 77 Ohio Law Abs. 140.

In determining whether a will which is presented for probate and which is complete and regular in appearance and which apparently complies with all formalities should be admitted to probate, the probate court is not authorized to determine as a fact whether such will was attested and executed according to law, but is merely required to determine whether there is substantial evidence tending to prove that fact, i.e., evidence which will enable a finding of that fact by reasonable minds, and even though all who have apparently signed an instrument as attesting witnesses affirmatively testify that the instrument was not executed according to law, such execution and attestation may be established by other competent evidence. In re Lyons' Estate (Ohio 1957) 166 Ohio St. 207, 141 N.E.2d 151, 2 O.O.2d 26. Wills ⇐ 320

Under GC 10504–18 (RC 2107.14) and 10504–22 (RC 2107.18), the following principles govern hearing on an application to admit a will to probate: (a) no issue is presented for a contest of will between its proponents and opponents; (b) opponents of the will may cross-examine witnesses fully upon dueness of attestation and execution, mental capacity of testator and undue influence, but are not allowed to call witnesses against admission of will to probate; (c) a prima-facie case in favor of validity of will is all that is required, and when all evidence shows as a matter of law that such case is made out, court must admit will to probate, even though evidence is conflicting. In re Elvin's Will (Ohio 1946) 146 Ohio St. 448, 66 N.E.2d 629, 32 O.O. 534.

In a proceeding to probate a will court shall only determine whether there is substantial evidence tending to establish the essential facts necessary for the probate thereof as set forth in GC 10504–22 (RC 2107.18). McWilliams v. Central Trust Co. (Hamilton 1935) 51 Ohio App. 246, 200 N.E. 532, 20 Ohio Law Abs. 544, 5 O.O. 104. Wills ⇐ 302(1)

Where a proceeding to probate a will is pending in another state, in a court of record, and one fact necessary to establish the jurisdiction of the court is finding that the residence of deceased was, at death, within the court's territorial jurisdiction, and a person interested in such state as an heir of deceased and devisee enters appearance, admits the jurisdictional fact, consents to adjudication, and participates thereafter in the proceedings, and receives benefits thereunder, such person, and those claiming under him, are estopped by the judgment therein. Hopper v. Nicholas

Note 4

(Ohio 1922) 106 Ohio St. 292, 140 N.E. 186, 1 Ohio Law Abs. 100, 20 Ohio Law Rep. 492. Judgment ⇔ 822(1); Wills ⇔ 434

Witnesses other than subscribers may prove due signing. In re Leffel's Will (Ohio Prob. 1909) 8 Ohio NP(NS) 591, 54 W.L.B. 336.

Where a will was acknowledged by the testator as his will in the presence of three witnesses, the fact that one of them testifies that he does not remember the word "will" being used is not sufficient to defeat the will where at its probate the other witnesses present at its execution testify that the signature to the will was acknowledged by the testator to be his signature to his will. In re Leffel's Will (Ohio Prob. 1909) 8 Ohio NP(NS) 591, 54 W.L.B. 336.

In admitting a will to probate, the court cannot consider how the will is to operate, but is limited to a consideration of the testator's capacity and freedom from restraint, and whether the instrument has been duly attested and executed. Mitchell v. Long (Ohio Com.Pl. 1909) 20 Ohio Dec. 41, 9 Ohio N.P.N.S. 113.

Persons interested in resisting probate are not allowed to introduce evidence to contest its validity. In re Stacey (Ohio Prob. 1897) 6 Ohio Dec. 142, 4 Ohio N.P. 143.

In a will contest action where plaintiff demanded an examination of witnesses to the will and all witnesses are dead, the will may be admitted to probate where such will is valid on its face and plaintiff offers no further evidence concerning the invalidity of the will. Burian v Burian, No. 45646 (8th Dist Ct App, Cuyahoga, 8–4–83).

5. Domicile

The will of a person whose domicile is in this state at the time of his decease is properly admitted to original probate at the place of such domicile, without regard to where such will was made or where such person died. Converse v. Starr (Ohio 1872) 23 Ohio St. 491. Wills ⇔ 249

Under the laws of this state, the will of a testator domiciled within it at his decease may be admitted to probate in any county therein where the testator owned any real or personal estate, but letters testamentary can only issue from the probate court of the county in which he resided at the time of his death. Limes v. Irwin (Ohio 1866) 16 Ohio St. 488.

6. Limitation of action

Next of kin, not contesting forged will within year after arriving at majority because of ignorance of fraud, may maintain equitable suit within four years after discovering fraud. Seeds v. Seeds (Ohio 1927) 116 Ohio St. 144, 156 N.E. 193, 52 A.L.R. 761, 5 Ohio Law Abs. 174, 25 Ohio Law Rep. 259. Limitation Of Actions ⇔ 100(1); Wills ⇔ 260

7. Jurisdiction

Probate court had no jurisdiction to decide validity of will that had not been admitted to probate and to decide validity of testator's inter vivos transfers unrelated to administration of estate; only question properly before court was validity of will admitted for probate. Corron v. Corron (Ohio 1988) 40 Ohio St.3d 75, 531 N.E.2d 708. Wills ⇔ 255

2107.181 Will not entitled to probate; procedure

If it appears that the instrument purporting to be a will is not entitled to admission to probate, the court shall enter an interlocutory order denying probate of the instrument, and shall continue the matter for further hearing. The court shall order that not less than ten days' notice of the further hearing be given by the applicant, the executor named in the instrument, the persons holding a power to nominate an executor as described in section 2107.65 of the Revised Code, or a commissioner appointed by the court, to all persons named in the instrument as legatees, devisees, beneficiaries of a trust, trustees, executors, or persons holding a power to nominate an executor, coexecutor, successor executor, or successor coexecutor as described in section 2107.65 of the Revised Code. Upon further hearing, witnesses may be called, subpoenaed, examined, and cross-examined in open court or by deposition, and their testimony reduced to writing and filed in the same manner as in hearings for the admission of wills to probate. Thereupon, the court shall revoke its interlocutory order denying probate to the instrument, and admit it to probate, or enter a final order refusing to probate it. A final order refusing to probate the instrument may be reviewed on appeal.

(1983 S 115, eff. 10–14–83; 1975 S 145; 125 v 411)

Cross References

Notice to admit will involving charitable trust to probate, 109.30

Library References

Wills ⇔348.
Westlaw Topic No. 409.
C.J.S. Wills §§ 737, 814 to 815.

Research References

Encyclopedias

OH Jur. 3d Decedents' Estates § 1006, Contradiction of Attesting Witnesses.
OH Jur. 3d Decedents' Estates § 1007, Witnesses Other Than the Subscribing Witnesses.
OH Jur. 3d Decedents' Estates § 1013, Cross-Examination of Witnesses.
OH Jur. 3d Decedents' Estates § 1030, Generally; Hearing, Witnesses and Final Order.
OH Jur. 3d Decedents' Estates § 1031, Notice of Further Hearing.
OH Jur. 3d Decedents' Estates § 1032, Nature of Further Hearing.
OH Jur. 3d Decedents' Estates § 1033, Appeal.
OH Jur. 3d Decedents' Estates § 1056, Appeal from Denial of Probate.
OH Jur. 3d State of Ohio § 164, Registration and Reporting Requirements; Fees.

Treatises and Practice Aids

Carlin, Baldwin's Ohio Practice, Merrick-Rippner Probate Law § 2:14, Probating the Will—Appeal—Will Contest.
Carlin, Baldwin's Ohio Practice, Merrick-Rippner Probate Law § 37:1, Instrument Not Entitled to Probate—Procedure.
Carlin, Baldwin's Ohio Practice, Merrick-Rippner Probate Law § 37:2, Instrument Not Entitled to Probate—Appeal from Order Refusing to Probate.
Carlin, Baldwin's Ohio Practice, Merrick-Rippner Probate Law § 37:3, Interlocutory Entry Denying Probate of Will—Form.
Carlin, Baldwin's Ohio Practice, Merrick-Rippner Probate Law § 37:4, Notice of Hearing on Interlocutory Entry Denying Probate of Will—Form.
Carlin, Baldwin's Ohio Practice, Merrick-Rippner Probate Law § 37:5, Final Entry Denying Probate of Will—Form.

Law Review and Journal Commentaries

How a Will Is Admitted to Probate in Ohio. 50 Title Topics 6 (June 1983).

Notes of Decisions

Appeal 2
Evidence of validity 3
Findings of court 1

---

1. Findings of court

In determining whether a will which is presented for probate and which is complete and regular in appearance and which apparently complies with all formalities should be admitted to probate, the probate court is not authorized to determine as a fact whether such will has been attested and executed according to law, but is merely required to determine whether there is substantial evidence tending to prove that fact, i.e., evidence which will enable a finding of that fact by reasonable minds, and even though all who have apparently signed an instrument as attesting witnesses affirmatively testify that the instrument was not executed according to law, such execution and attestation may be established by other competent evidence. In re Lyons' Estate (Ohio 1957) 166 Ohio St. 207, 141 N.E.2d 151, 2 O.O.2d 26. Wills ⇔ 320

2. Appeal

An appeal lies to a common pleas court from an order of a probate court overruling an application to find and establish the contents of a lost will. Roth v. Siefert (Ohio 1908) 77 Ohio St. 417, 83 N.E. 611, 5 Ohio Law Rep. 565. Wills ☞ 358

An order of the probate court admitting a paper to probate as the last will is not reviewable on error, although a refusal so to do is reviewable. Hollrah v. Lasance (Ohio 1900) 63 Ohio St. 58, 44 W.L.B. 80, 57 N.E. 964. Wills ☞ 356

Application to probate court to admit an alleged will to probate is a special proceeding within the meaning of RS 6707, which provides that an order affecting a substantial right made in a special proceeding is a final order. Missionary Soc. of Methodist Episcopal Church v. Ely (Ohio 1897) 56 Ohio St. 405, 38 W.L.B. 13, 47 N.E. 537. Appeal And Error ☞ 91(3); Courts ☞ 202(5)

RS 5934, relating to proof of wills and admission to probate, relates exclusively to domestic wills, and an appeal does not lie to the court of common pleas from an order of the probate court refusing to admit a foreign will to record. Barr v. Closterman (Ohio Cir. 1887) 1 Ohio C.D. 546, affirmed.

3. Evidence of validity

Under RC 2107.18 and RC 2107.181, a will must be admitted to probate when the proponents introduce substantial evidence tending to prove the validity of the will. In re Young (Summit 1978) 60 Ohio App.2d 390, 397 N.E.2d 1223, 14 O.O.3d 359.

Every disposition of property must have a definite subject and a definite object; when the intent of the testator cannot be ascertained, either from the will, or by extraneous circumstances, the will is void and the estate must descend according to law. Cope v. Cope (Ohio 1888) 45 Ohio St. 464, 19 W.L.B. 98, 15 N.E. 206.

2107.19 Notice of admission of will to probate

(A)(1) Subject to divisions (A)(2) and (B) of this section, when a will has been admitted to probate, the fiduciary for the estate or another person specified in division (A)(4) of this section shall, within two weeks of the admission of the will to probate, give a notice as described in this division and in the manner provided by Civil Rule 73(E) to the surviving spouse of the testator, to all persons who would be entitled to inherit from the testator under Chapter 2105. of the Revised Code if the testator had died intestate, and to all legatees and devisees named in the will. The notice shall mention the probate of the will and, if a particular person being given the notice is a legatee or devisee named in the will, shall state that the person is named in the will as beneficiary. A copy of the will admitted to probate is not required to be given with the notice.

(2) A person entitled to be given the notice described in division (A)(1) of this section may waive that right by filing a written waiver of the right to receive the notice in the probate court. The person may file the waiver of the right to receive the notice at any time prior to or after the will has been admitted to probate.

(3) The fact that the notice described in division (A)(1) of this section has been given, subject to division (B) of this section, to all persons described in division (A)(1) of this section who have not waived their right to receive the notice, and, if applicable, the fact that certain persons described in that division have waived their right to receive the notice in accordance with division (A)(2) of this section, shall be evidenced by a certificate that shall be filed in the probate court in accordance with division (A)(4) of this section.

(4) The notice of the admission of the will to probate required by division (A)(1) of this section and the certificate of giving notice or waiver of notice required by division (A)(3) of this section shall be given or filed by the fiduciary for the estate or by the applicant for the admission of the will to probate, the applicant for a release from administration, any other interested person, or the attorney for the fiduciary or for any of the preceding persons. The certificate of giving notice shall be filed not later than two months after the appointment of the fiduciary or, if no fiduciary has been appointed, not later than two months after the admission of the will to probate, unless the court grants an extension of that time. Failure to file the certificate in a timely manner shall subject the fiduciary or applicant to the citation and penalty provisions of section 2109.31 of the Revised Code.

(B) The fiduciary or another person specified in division (A)(4) of this section is not required to give a notice pursuant to division (A)(1) of this section to persons who have been notified of the application for probate of the will or of a contest as to jurisdiction or to persons whose names or places of residence are unknown and cannot with reasonable diligence be ascertained, and a person authorized by division (A)(4) of this section to give notice shall file in the probate court a certificate to that effect.

(2003 H 51, eff. 4–8–04; 2001 H 85, eff. 10–31–01; 1994 H 208, eff. 6–23–94; 1990 H 346, eff. 5–31–90; 1953 H 1; GC 10504–23)

Uncodified Law

2004 H 161, § 3, eff. 4–8–04 reads, in part:

(C) Sections 2107.19, 2109.301, 2113.53, 2117.06, 2117.07, 2117.11, and 2117.12 of the Revised Code, as amended by this act, apply to estates of decedents who die on or after April 8, 2004.

1990 H 346, § 3, eff. 5–31–90, reads:

(A) Sections 1 and 2 of this act shall apply only to the estates of decedents who die on or after the effective date of this act.

(B) It is the intent of the General Assembly in the outright repeal of sections 2107.13 and 2107.14 of the Revised Code and the amendments to sections 109.30, 2107.18, 2107.19, 2107.22, 2107.27, 2107.76, 2115.16, and 2703.14 of the Revised Code by this act, to respond to the dicta of the Supreme Court in *Palazzi v. Estate of Gardner* (1987), 32 Ohio St. 3d 169 and to enact statutory provisions relating to notice of probate proceedings that are not unconstitutional as potentially violative of the due process of law rights of nonresidents of this state.

Historical and Statutory Notes

Pre–1953 H 1 Amendments: 114 v 349

Amendment Note: 2003 H 51 inserted "or, if no fiduciary has been appointed, not later than two months after the admission of the will to probate," following "the appointment of the fiduciary" and inserted "or applicant" following "subject the fiduciary" in division (A)(4).

Amendment Note: 2001 H 85 deleted "promptly" after "division (A)(4) of this section" and inserted ", within two weeks of the admission of the will to probate," in the first sentence of division (A)(1); added the last two sentences in division (A)(4); and made changes to reflect gender neutral language.

Amendment Note: 1994 H 208 substituted "fiduciary for the estate or another person specified in division (A)(4) of this section" for "executor" and "and in the manner provided by Civil Rule 73(E)" for "by certified mail" in and added the final sentence of division (A)(1); added the final sentence of division (A)(2); substituted "a certificate" for "an affidavit of the executor" in and added "in accordance with division (A)(4) of this section" at the end of division (A)(3); added division (A)(4); and substituted "The fiduciary or another person specified in division (A)(4) of this section" for "An executor", "a person authorized by division (A)(4) of this section to give notice" for "the executor", and "a certificate" for "an affidavit", in division (B).

Legislative Service Commission

1975 (Commentary from former RC 2107.13):

This section currently provides that notice be given to the surviving spouse before admission of the will to probate. It would be amended by the bill to provide that notice must be given to a surviving spouse only if known to the applicant.

OSBA Probate and Trust Law Section

1957 (Commentary from former RC 2107.13):

The Supreme Court has held that the requirement of notice of application for probate to be given to the surviving spouse and next of kin of the testator resident of the state is mandatory and jurisdictional. The statute in its present form has led to much uncertainty as to the validity of the probate of a will in the event the person offering the same notifies all next of kin known to him to be residents of the state when it subsequently develops that there are other residents of the state not known to him who have not been served. The proposed amendment removes this uncertainty by providing that the notice is to be given to the surviving spouse and to the persons known to the applicant to be residents of the state.

Cross References

Notice to admit will involving charitable trust to probate, 109.30
Service of notice, Civ R 73

Library References

Wills ⬅353.
Westlaw Topic No. 409.
C.J.S. Wills §§ 738, 818.
Baldwin's Ohio Legislative Service, 1990 Laws of Ohio, H 346—LSC Analysis, p 5–87

Research References

Encyclopedias

OH Jur. 3d Decedents' Estates § 948, Notice When Seeking Release from Administration.
OH Jur. 3d Decedents' Estates § 971, Admission of Will to Probate; Notice.
OH Jur. 3d Decedents' Estates § 998, Notice of Application for Probate.
OH Jur. 3d Decedents' Estates § 1016, Notice of Admission to Probate.
OH Jur. 3d Decedents' Estates § 1017, Notice of Admission to Probate—to Attorney General.
OH Jur. 3d Decedents' Estates § 1020, Admission to Probate of Will of Later Date.
OH Jur. 3d Decedents' Estates § 1022, Nature and Effect of Order.
OH Jur. 3d Decedents' Estates § 1028, Equitable Relief—Void Order Admitting Will to Probate.
OH Jur. 3d Decedents' Estates § 1116, Statutory Time Limitation, Generally.
OH Jur. 3d Decedents' Estates § 1118, When Action Commenced.
OH Jur. 3d Decedents' Estates § 1124, Applicability of Rules of Civil Procedure; Transfer of Venue—Process.
OH Jur. 3d Decedents' Estates § 1462, Hearing on Claim.

Treatises and Practice Aids

Carlin, Baldwin's Ohio Practice, Merrick-Rippner Probate Law § 2:13, Probating the Will—Notice of Admission of a Will to Probate.
Carlin, Baldwin's Ohio Practice, Merrick-Rippner Probate Law § 2:14, Probating the Will—Appeal—Will Contest.
Carlin, Baldwin's Ohio Practice, Merrick-Rippner Probate Law § 3:13, Jurisdiction of Probate Court—Scope—Exclusive and Concurrent Jurisdiction.
Carlin, Baldwin's Ohio Practice, Merrick-Rippner Probate Law § 36:2, Admission to Probate—Notice.
Carlin, Baldwin's Ohio Practice, Merrick-Rippner Probate Law § 36:6, Waiver of Notice of Hearing on Probate of Will—Form.
Carlin, Baldwin's Ohio Practice, Merrick-Rippner Probate Law § 36:7, Notice to Surviving Spouse and Next of Kin—Service by Sheriff—Form.
Carlin, Baldwin's Ohio Practice, Merrick-Rippner Probate Law § 36:8, Notice of Hearing to Probate Will—Form.
Carlin, Baldwin's Ohio Practice, Merrick-Rippner Probate Law § 38:2, Will Contests—Statutory Provisions.
Carlin, Baldwin's Ohio Practice, Merrick-Rippner Probate Law § 38:3, Will Contests—Later Will Admitted to Probate.
Carlin, Baldwin's Ohio Practice, Merrick-Rippner Probate Law § 38:6, Will Contests—Capacity to Contest a Will.
Carlin, Baldwin's Ohio Practice, Merrick-Rippner Probate Law § 38:7, Will Contests—Commencement of Action; Limitation of Actions.
Carlin, Baldwin's Ohio Practice, Merrick-Rippner Probate Law § 2:121, Administration of Decedent's Estate—Checklist.
Carlin, Baldwin's Ohio Practice, Merrick-Rippner Probate Law § 36:17, Notice of Probate of Will and Appointment of Executor—Form.
Carlin, Baldwin's Ohio Practice, Merrick-Rippner Probate Law § 36:18, Certificate of Executor of Notice of Admission to Probate—Form.
Carlin, Baldwin's Ohio Practice, Merrick-Rippner Probate Law § 36:19, Waiver of Notice of Admission of Will to Probate—Form.
Carlin, Baldwin's Ohio Practice, Merrick-Rippner Probate Law § 36:20, Certificate of Executor that Residence of Legatee or Devisee is Unknown—Form.
Carlin, Baldwin's Ohio Practice, Merrick-Rippner Probate Law § 36:21, Certificate of Executor that Notice Has Been Given—Form.
Carlin, Baldwin's Ohio Practice, Merrick-Rippner Probate Law § 54:10, Fiduciary Accounts—Citation to File Account.
Carlin, Baldwin's Ohio Practice, Merrick-Rippner Probate Law App B SPF 1.0, Surviving Spouse, Children, Next of Kin, Legatees and Devisees.
Carlin, Baldwin's Ohio Practice, Merrick-Rippner Probate Law App B SPF 2.0, Application to Probate Will.
Carlin, Baldwin's Ohio Practice, Merrick-Rippner Probate Law App B SPF 2.1, Waiver of Notice of Probate of Will.
Carlin, Baldwin's Ohio Practice, Merrick-Rippner Probate Law App B SPF 2.2, Notice of Probate of Will.
Carlin, Baldwin's Ohio Practice, Merrick-Rippner Probate Law App B SPF 2.4, Certificate of Service of Notice of Probate of Will.
Carlin, Baldwin's Ohio Practice, Merrick-Rippner Probate Law App B SPF 1.0A, Surviving Spouse, Next of Kin, Legatees and Devisees (Decedent Dying on or After 5-31-90).
Carlin, Baldwin's Ohio Practice, Merrick-Rippner Probate Law App B SPF 2.0A, Application to Probate Will (Decedent Dying on or After 5-31-90).
Carlin, Baldwin's Ohio Practice, Merrick-Rippner Probate Law App B SPF 2.1A, Waiver of Notice of Probate of Will (Decedent Dying on or After 5-31-90).
Carlin, Baldwin's Ohio Practice, Merrick-Rippner Probate Law App B SPF 2.2A, Notice of Probate of Will (Decedent Dying on or After 5-31-90).
Carlin, Baldwin's Ohio Practice, Merrick-Rippner Probate Law App B SPF 2.3A, Affidavit of Service of Notice of Probate of Will (Decedent Dying on or After 5-31-90).
Kuehnle and Levey, Ohio Real Estate Law and Practice § 18:1, Ohio State Bar Association Standards of Title Examination.

Law Review and Journal Commentaries

Changes to Ohio's Probate Notice Statutes, William F. Bates. 4 Prob L J Ohio 140 (May/June 1994).

Common Form Probate Is Here, Robert M. Brucken and Wiley Dinsmore. 1 Prob L J Ohio 3 (September/October 1990).

Cox v. Saadeh: A Warning to the Wary in Will Contests. Angela G. Carlin, 13 Prob L J Ohio 11 (September/October 2002).

House Bill 85, Probate Reform Bill 2001: A Noble Experiment. Marilyn J. Maag. 12 Prob L J Ohio 21 (November/December 2001).

How a Will Is Admitted to Probate in Ohio. 50 Title Topics 6 (June 1983).

Practical Application of House Bill 85 (Probate Reform 2001), Marilyn J. Maag. 13 Prob L J Ohio 19 (November/December 2002).

When In Doubt—Stop! Look! and Settle!, Ellis v Rippner. (Ed. note: Contains a sample chart to be used in deciding whether to contest a will.) Ohio B Ass'n Serv Letter, Probate Law Edition, July 1965.

Notes of Decisions

Ed. Note: This section contains annotations from former RC 2107.13.

Admission to probate 3
Constitutional issues 1
Parties entitled to notice 2
Procedural issues 4
Void order 5

---

1. Constitutional issues

RC 2107.13 does not violate the Due Process Clause of the US Constitution. (Ed. note: Ohio law construed by South Carolina Supreme Court.) Tripp v. Tripp (S.C. 1962) 240 S.C. 334, 126 S.E.2d 9, 93 Ohio Law Abs. 565, certiorari denied 83 S.Ct. 187, 371 U.S. 888, 9 L.Ed.2d 123.

2. Parties entitled to notice

The only persons held to three-month limitations period for filing will contests under former statute are those who must be given notice of a will's admission to probate, i.e., the surviving spouse of the testator, all persons who would be entitled to inherit from the testator if the testator had died intestate, and all legatees and devisees named in the will. Tomasik v. Tomasik (Ohio, 12-06-2006) 111 Ohio St.3d 481, 857 N.E.2d 127, 2006-Ohio-6109. Wills ⚖ 260

A nonresident heir who fails to bring an action challenging the constitutionality of the notice provision of RC 2107.13, as applied to nonresidents, within four months of receiving actual notice of his grandfather's death lacks standing to challenge RC 2107.13 as applied to him. Palazzi v. Estate of Gardner (Ohio 1987) 32 Ohio St.3d 169, 512 N.E.2d 971.

Notice to the surviving spouse of admission to probate of a will and appointment of an administrator with the will annexed is not necessary if the spouse is not a resident of the state. Armstrong v. Brufach (Ohio Com.Pl. 1950) 136 N.E.2d 463, 74 Ohio Law Abs. 370, 59 O.O. 352.

The words, "known to be residents of the state," as used in GC 10504–17 (RC 2107.13) mean that such knowledge must be had by either the proponent of the will or the court. In re Hammer's Estate (Seneca 1955) 99 Ohio App. 1, 130 N.E.2d 437, 58 O.O. 104.

The service of notice of the probate of the will of the father of a minor in military service should be made upon the minor at the family home. Case v. Case (Ohio Prob. 1955) 124 N.E.2d 856, 70 Ohio Law Abs. 2, 55 O.O. 317.

Nonresident next-of-kin who are legatees or devisees under a will are not thereby entitled to contest a will after expiration of the six month statutory period merely because they did not receive the notice to which they were entitled as legatees or devisees. Feeley v. First Nat. Bank & Trust Co. of Hamilton (Ohio Com.Pl. 1948) 124 N.E.2d 800, 69 Ohio Law Abs. 317, 55 O.O. 324.

Amendment of GC 10504–36 (RC 2107.27) by adding the words "known to be" before the words, "resident of the state" did not relieve the court from requiring notice to the next of kin of a testator who were then residents of the state of Ohio. Bowles' Estate v. Bowles' Heirs (Cuyahoga 1953) 96 Ohio App. 265, 114 N.E.2d 229, 66 Ohio Law Abs. 73, 54 O.O. 296.

Admission of will to probate ordinarily cannot determine rights of all interested parties, for only surviving spouse and next of kin known to be residents of state must be notified under this section. In re Frey's Estate (Ohio 1942) 139 Ohio St. 354, 40 N.E.2d 145, 22 O.O. 411.

The requirement of notice of application for probate to be given to the widow or husband and next of kin of the testator resident of the state is mandatory and jurisdictional, and an order of probate of a will without notice to and without waiver by such persons is void and subject to direct attack by those who neither received notice nor waived service of notice. Scholl v. Scholl (Ohio 1930) 123 Ohio St. 1, 173 N.E. 305, 8 Ohio Law Abs. 693.

3. Admission to probate

Where the son of decedent files an application to admit the decedent's will to probate, which application is accompanied by a waiver of notice signed by the applicant's sister but not by applicant; on the same day that the will is admitted to probate, applicant files an application to be appointed as executor, which includes his sworn statement that the will has been admitted to probate; and the applicant accepts the appointment and proceeds to administer the estate; the applicant and anyone else are estopped from denying that the will was duly admitted to probate, on the ground that the applicant neither received nor waived notice prior to the admission of the will to probate. In re Warrick's Estate (Montgomery 1962) 118 Ohio App. 542, 196 N.E.2d 132, 26 O.O.2d 62.

Where heirs join together as plaintiffs in a suit to set aside the probate of a will for the reason that one of such heirs was a resident of Ohio at the time of the probate of such will and had not been served with notice thereof, such heir, by bringing the will contest case, admits the probate of the will and is barred from making any attack upon the regularity of the order of probate or the authority and jurisdiction of the court that made it; and the heirs at law of such heir are bound by such election. In re Hammer's Estate (Seneca 1955) 99 Ohio App. 1, 130 N.E.2d 437, 58 O.O. 104.

4. Procedural issues

Former devisees and legatees, who had been named in decedent's prior will, but were not named in decedent's last will and testament, were not subject to three month statute of limitations applicable to will contests, where statute specifically applied only to surviving spouse, those who would inherit intestate, and those named in will, and former devisees and legatees were not such persons. Tomasik v. Tomasik (Ohio App. 9 Dist., Summit, 10-20-2004) No. 21980, 2004-Ohio-5558, 2004 WL 2348170, Unreported, appeal allowed 105 Ohio St.3d 1469, 824 N.E.2d 540, 2005-Ohio-1186. Wills ⚖ 260

Presumption that will contest complaint was untimely, arising from file-stamped date on pleading, was not rebutted by testimony that complaint naming wrong executor was timely filed nor receipt from clerk of court showing that filing fee was deposited in another case on last date for filing contest and, thus, contest complaint was untimely. Stevenson v. Wenner (Ohio App. 3 Dist., 03-30-1995) 102 Ohio App.3d 289, 656 N.E.2d 1386. Wills ⚖ 259

The Soldiers and Sailors Civil Relief Act does not apply to the proceedings for the probate of a will and issuance of letters of administration. Case v. Case (Ohio Prob. 1955) 124 N.E.2d 856, 70 Ohio Law Abs. 2, 55 O.O. 317.

5. Void order

The probate of a will without notice to the persons entitled thereto is void, and knowledge of the death and of the order of probate will not estop a plaintiff seeking to declare the probate void where the proponents were not prejudiced thereby. Vance v. Byerly (Ohio Com.Pl. 1957) 140 N.E.2d 912, 76 Ohio Law Abs. 72, 2 O.O.2d 216.

Fact that a person aggrieved by an order of probate court admitting a will to probate, made without service of notice upon next of kin resident in this state, could obtain relief in probate court by virtue of statutory provisions, does not preclude such person from recourse to a court of general equity jurisdiction, by original action, to have such order declared to be void. Young v. Guella (Summit 1941) 67 Ohio App. 11, 35 N.E.2d 997, 21 O.O. 66.

Order of probate court admitting a will to probate made without service of notice upon next of kin resident in this state, as required by this section, and without waiver thereof, is void. Young v. Guella (Summit 1941) 67 Ohio App. 11, 35 N.E.2d 997, 21 O.O. 66.

2107.20 Filing and recording of will; certified copy

When admitted to probate every will shall be filed in the office of the probate judge and recorded, together with any testimony or prior judgment of a probate court declaring the will valid, by him or the clerk of the probate court in a book to be kept for that purpose.

A copy of such recorded will, with a copy of the order of probate annexed thereto, certified by the judge under seal of his court, shall be as effectual in all cases as the original would be, if established by proof.

(1978 H 505, eff. 1–1–79; 1953 H 1; GC 10504–24, 10504–25)

Historical and Statutory Notes

Pre–1953 H 1 Amendments: 114 v 350

Cross References

Records kept by probate court, 2101.12

Library References

Wills ⚖353, 433.
Westlaw Topic No. 409.
C.J.S. Wills §§ 738, 807, 818.

Research References

Encyclopedias

OH Jur. 3d Decedents' Estates § 1018, Filing and Recording of Will.

Treatises and Practice Aids

Carlin, Baldwin's Ohio Practice, Merrick-Rippner Probate Law § 21:19, Rights of Surviving Spouse to Make Election—Effect of Election—Generally.

Carlin, Baldwin's Ohio Practice, Merrick-Rippner Probate Law § 36:22, Certificate of True Copy of Will—Form.

Notes of Decisions

Codicils 3
Copies 2
Recording 1

---

1. Recording

The duty of correctly recording a will is enjoined upon the probate judge by RS 5930, and misfeasance in that respect will not affect devisees or heirs. Wolf v. Menager (Ohio Com.Pl. 1903) 14 Ohio Dec. 128.

2. Copies

Where a foreign will executed and probated in a sister state, a copy of which has been admitted to record in this state, is attested, "signed, sealed, and published in presence," the will being signed at the end by the testator and three witnesses, in the absence of proof to the contrary, it will be presumed that the testator and the witnesses signed in presence of each other. Carpenter v. Denoon (Ohio 1876) 29 Ohio St. 379.

A copy of probate and record of a will, duly certified by the probate judge, is conclusive evidence of the validity of the will on the trial of a collateral issue between a stranger and a devisee under the will respecting the property devised, and is admissible in trial of such issue, notwithstanding the fact that proceedings are pending to contest the validity of the same at the time it is offered and admitted as evidence. Brown v. Burdick (Ohio 1874) 25 Ohio St. 260.

A copy of a record with, with a copy of the order of probate annexed, is as effectual as the original will if produced and proven, by virtue of RS 5931. Wolf v. Menager (Ohio Com.Pl. 1903) 14 Ohio Dec. 128.

3. Codicils

The provisions of this section apply also to the codicils appended to a will. Trull v. Patrick (Ohio Com.Pl. 1920) 31 Ohio Dec. 319, 22 Ohio N.P.N.S. 385.

2107.21 Recorded in each county where real estate is situated

If real estate devised by will is situated in any county other than that in which the will is proved, declared valid, or admitted to probate, an authenticated copy of the will and the order of probate or the judgment declaring validity shall be admitted to the record in the office of the probate judge of each county in which such real estate is situated upon the order of such judge. The authenticated copy shall have the same validity therein as if probate had been had in such county.

(1978 H 505, eff. 1–1–79; 1953 H 1; GC 10504–26)

Historical and Statutory Notes

Pre–1953 H 1 Amendments: 114 v 350

Cross References

Records kept by probate court, 2101.12

Library References

Wills ⚖=353.
Westlaw Topic No. 409.
C.J.S. Wills §§ 738, 818.

Research References

Encyclopedias

OH Jur. 3d Decedents' Estates § 1018, Filing and Recording of Will.

Treatises and Practice Aids

Carlin, Baldwin's Ohio Practice, Merrick-Rippner Probate Law § 36:23, Attestation of Certificate for Authenticated Copy—Form.

Carlin, Baldwin's Ohio Practice, Merrick-Rippner Probate Law § 36:24, Entry Admitting to Record Authenticated Copy of Will—Form.

Kuehnle and Levey, Ohio Real Estate Law and Practice § 10:51, Rights of Heirs When Owner Dies Resident Out of County, Preserving Marketability.

Law Review and Journal Commentaries

American Land Law Reform: Modernization of Recording Statutes (Part I), Robert N. Cook and Frederick M. Lombardi. 13 W Reserve U L Rev 639 (1962).

Notes of Decisions

Deeds of assignment 1
Foreign will 2

---

1. Deeds of assignment

The legislature, after establishing such a comprehensive system of land registration applicable by its terms to all conveyances, and affording each county notice of conveyances affecting lands within the county, meant to include deeds of assignment of lands lying in a county other than that of the assignor's residence in the requirement that such deeds be recorded in the county where the land is situated. Eggleston v. Harrison (Ohio 1900) 61 Ohio St. 397, 43 W.L.B. 62, 55 N.E. 993.

2. Foreign will

Where a devisee neglects for three years to cause a copy of a probated foreign will to be recorded in the county where the devised property is situated, the devise will not lapse under the thirty-fourth section of the wills act of 1840, since that provision refers only to original probate. Carpenter v. Denoon (Ohio 1876) 29 Ohio St. 379.

A foreign will must be recorded in Ohio before title in land vests in devisee. Wilson's Ex'rs v. Tappan (Ohio 1833) 6 Ohio 172.

2107.22 Probate of will of later date; will previously declared valid

(A)(1)(a) When a will has been admitted to probate by a probate court and another will of later date is presented to the same court for probate, notice of the will of later date shall be given to those persons required to be notified under section 2107.19 of the Revised Code, and to the fiduciaries and beneficiaries under the will of earlier date. The probate court may admit the will of later date to probate the same as if no earlier will had been so admitted if it appears from the face of the will of later date, or if an interested person makes a demand as described in division (A)(1)(b) of this section and it appears from the testimony of the witnesses to the will given in accordance with that division, that the execution of the will complies with the law in force at the time of the execution of the will in the jurisdiction in which it was executed, or with the law in force in this state at the time of the death of the testator, or with the law in force in the jurisdiction in which the testator was domiciled at the time of his death.

(b) Upon the demand of a person interested in having a will of later date admitted to probate, the probate court shall cause at least two of the witnesses to the will of later date, and any other witnesses that the interested person desires to have appear, to come before the probate court and provide testimony. If the interested person so requests, the probate court shall issue a subpoena to compel the presence of any such witness before the probate court to provide testimony.

Witnesses before the probate court pursuant to this division shall be examined, and may be cross-examined, in open court, and their testimony shall be reduced to writing and then filed in the records of the probate court pertaining to the testator's estate.

(2) When an authenticated copy of a will has been admitted to record by a probate court, and an authenticated copy of a will of later date that was executed and proved as required by law, is presented to the same court for record, it shall be admitted to record in the same manner as if no authenticated copy of the will of earlier date had been so admitted.

(3) If a probate court admits a will of later date to probate, or an authenticated copy of a will of later date to record, its order shall operate as a revocation of the order admitting the will of earlier date to probate, or shall operate as a revocation of the order admitting the authenticated copy of the will of earlier date to record. The probate court shall enter on the record of the earlier will a marginal note "later will admitted to probate ___" (giving the date admitted).

(B) When a will that has been declared valid pursuant to section 2107.084 of the Revised Code has been admitted to probate by a probate court, and an authenticated copy of another will of later date that was executed and proved as required by law is presented to the same court for record, the will of later date shall be admitted the same as if no other will had been admitted and the proceedings shall continue as provided in this section.

(1990 H 346, eff. 5–31–90; 1978 H 505; 130 v S 36; 1953 H 1; GC 10504–27, 10504–28)

Uncodified Law

1990 H 346, § 3, eff. 5–31–90, reads:

(A) Sections 1 and 2 of this act shall apply only to the estates of decedents who die on or after the effective date of this act.

(B) It is the intent of the General Assembly in the outright repeal of sections 2107.13 and 2107.14 of the Revised Code and the amendments to sections 109.30, 2107.18, 2107.19, 2107.22, 2107.27, 2107.76, 2115.16, and 2703.14 of the Revised Code by this act, to respond to the dicta of the Supreme Court in *Palazzi v. Estate of Gardner* (1987), 32 Ohio St. 3d 169 and to enact statutory provisions relating to notice of probate proceedings that are not unconstitutional as potentially violative of the due process of law rights of nonresidents of this state.

Historical and Statutory Notes

Pre–1953 H 1 Amendments: 114 v 350

Legislative Service Commission

1975 (Commentary from former RC 2107.14):

Under existing law, the execution of a notarized affidavit can be substituted for the appearance and testimony of the witnesses when proving a will. This current procedure that provides for the execution of this affidavit would be repealed by the bill. The bill would provide that the witnesses to a will would not have to be examined before the will is admitted to probate unless demanded by an interested party. If the witnesses were demanded, at least two of the witnesses to a will would have to come before the court and state those facts necessary to prove the will.

OSBA Probate and Trust Law Section

1963:

The first sentence of R.C. 2107.22... in its present form is unintelligible.... This section deals with the procedure for and effect of admission to probate of a will of later date. Upon consideration the Committee unanimously agrees that the language of the sentence should be corrected, and concluded that the entire section should be further clarified by dividing the first paragraph into two paragraphs, the first to define the procedure in admitting wills of later date, the second to cover procedure upon receipt of an authenticated copy of a will of later date, where the court has previously admitted an authenticated copy of a will to record.

1957 (Commentary from former RC 2107.14):

In executing a will it is sometimes felt desirable to have more than two witnesses to the testator's signature. Section 2107.03 (10504–3), Revised Code of Ohio, provides a will shall be signed at the end by the party making it and be attested and subscribed in the presence of such party by two or more competent witnesses who saw the testator subscribe or heard him acknowledge his signature. When a will is presented for probate with more than two witnesses the question arises, must all of such subscribing witnesses to the will testify before such will is admitted to probate or is it necessary that only two of such witnesses be presented and examined?

Section 2107.14 (10504–18) as it now exists provides: The Probate Court shall cause *the witnesses to a will* and other witnesses whom a person interested in having such will admitted to probate may desire to have appear to come before the court.

This language has been interpreted to require the court to have *all witnesses*, however many there may be, to appear and testify as to the execution of the will. Such interpretation defeats the purpose of having more than two witnesses to a will.

The committee thinks it advisable that this section should be amended so as to require only the testimony of two witnesses to a will even though more than two witnesses signed the will.

Baldwin's Ohio Legislative Service, 1990 Laws of Ohio, H 346—LSC Analysis, p 5–87

Library References

Wills ⚖221, 269, 355.
Westlaw Topic No. 409.
C.J.S. Wills §§ 553 to 556, 742 to 752, 817.

Research References

Encyclopedias

OH Jur. 3d Decedents' Estates § 999, Requirements for Admission to Probate.
OH Jur. 3d Decedents' Estates § 1006, Contradiction of Attesting Witnesses.
OH Jur. 3d Decedents' Estates § 1007, Witnesses Other Than the Subscribing Witnesses.
OH Jur. 3d Decedents' Estates § 1013, Cross-Examination of Witnesses.
OH Jur. 3d Decedents' Estates § 1016, Notice of Admission to Probate.
OH Jur. 3d Decedents' Estates § 1020, Admission to Probate of Will of Later Date.
OH Jur. 3d Decedents' Estates § 1045, Proof of Contents of Will.

Treatises and Practice Aids

Carlin, Baldwin's Ohio Practice, Merrick-Rippner Probate Law § 38:3, Will Contests—Later Will Admitted to Probate.

Notes of Decisions

Ed. Note: This section contains annotations from former RC 2107.14.

Appeal 3
Evidence and testimony 1
Procedural issues 2

---

1. Evidence and testimony

Where a will is probated and admitted to record on an application within the jurisdiction of the court, error will not lie to review the testimony upon which it was admitted. Mosier v. Harmon (Ohio 1876) 29 Ohio St. 220.

RC 2107.14, in addition to the witnesses to the purported will, authorizes the probate court to receive only the testimony of such other persons as may be presented by one interested in having the will admitted to probate, and the court may not receive any testimony offered by a person interested in having the paper denied admission to probate. In re Nash's Will (Ohio Com.Pl. 1976) 50 Ohio Misc. 4, 361 N.E.2d 558, 3 O.O.3d 347, 4 O.O.3d 33. Wills ⚖ 292

In a hearing on an application to admit a will to probate, it is error for the court to admit in evidence, over the objection of the proponent, letters written by the testator, intended to reflect upon his mental condition; this section does not contemplate the offering of evidence to controvert the testimony of the witnesses called by the proponent. In re Carson's Will (Champaign 1947) 83 Ohio App. 510, 75 N.E.2d 248, 50 Ohio Law Abs. 119, 38 O.O. 547.

An order admitting a will to probate is prima facie evidence only of its validity, and an argument in a will contest emphasizing probate to influence the jury constitutes misconduct of counsel. Wadsworth v. Purdy (Ohio Cir. 1908) 21 Ohio C.D. 110, 12 Ohio C.C.N.S. 8.

Witnesses other than subscribers may prove due signing. In re Leffel's Will (Ohio Prob. 1909) 8 Ohio NP(NS) 591, 54 W.L.B. 336.

2. Procedural issues

It is not required that those who are interested adversely should be summoned, as no issue is made for a contest between adverse parties. In re Hathaway's Will (Ohio 1854) 4 Ohio St. 383.

Friend of decedent who offered improperly executed document as will lacked standing to bring will contest challenging earlier will that had already been admitted to probate; friend was not interested party. In re Estate of Carmedy (Ohio App. 10 Dist., 08-18-1994) 95 Ohio App.3d 572, 642 N.E.2d 1170. Wills ☞ 229

Where a new executor is appointed under a later will, the period within which claims may be filed against the estate begins to run anew. Georgekopoulos v. Vasilopoulos (Summit 1984) 26 Ohio App.3d 43, 498 N.E.2d 165, 26 O.B.R. 216.

If the applicant for probate of a will makes a prima-facie case on the validity of the execution and attestation, and on the capacity and freedom from restraint of the testator, the will must be admitted to probate; and questions as to competency, revocation by implication, or whether the will violates a contract should be decided in a subsequent proceeding. In re Piasecki's Estate (Ohio Prob. 1964) 201 N.E.2d 840, 95 Ohio Law Abs. 257, 30 O.O.2d 169.

Even though all who have apparently signed an instrument as attesting witnesses affirmatively testify that the instrument was not executed according to law, such execution and attestation may be established by other competent evidence. In re Lyons's Estate (Ohio 1957) 166 Ohio St. 207, 141 N.E.2d 151, 2 O.O.2d 26. Wills ☞ 303(3)

Under GC 10504–18 (RC 2107.14) and 10504–22 (RC 2107.18), the following principles govern hearing on an application to admit a will to probate: (a) no issue is presented for a contest of will between its proponents and opponents; (b) opponents of will may cross-examine witnesses fully upon dueness of attestation and execution, mental capacity of testator and undue influence, but are not allowed to call witnesses against admission of will to probate; (c) a prima-facie case in favor of validity of will is all that is required, and when all evidence shows as a matter of law that such case is made out, court must admit will to probate, even though evidence is conflicting. In re Elvin's Will (Ohio 1946) 146 Ohio St. 448, 66 N.E.2d 629, 32 O.O. 534.

Earlier will cannot be probated where later will revoking it has been admitted to probate and probate stands unimpeached. Petitt v. Morton (Cuyahoga 1930) 38 Ohio App. 348, 176 N.E. 494, 10 Ohio Law Abs. 436, affirmed 124 Ohio St. 241, 177 N.E. 591, 10 Ohio Law Abs. 574. Wills ☞ 206

Under a statute requiring the probate court to set out the testimony and proof in admitting wills to probate, the failure to do so, while irregular, does not make the proceeding a nullity; where the court had jurisdiction, the proceeding cannot be collaterally attacked. Darling v. Hippel (Ohio Cir. 1897) 12 Ohio C.D. 754, affirmed 60 Ohio St. 591, 54 N.E. 1103.

3. Appeal

A later will supersedes the probate of a former will, and refusal of the probate court to admit the later will to probate is appealable. Stafford v. Todd (Ohio App. 2 Dist. 1921) 17 Ohio App. 114.

Order of probate court admitting instrument to probate as a last will is not reviewable on appeal. In re Frey's Estate (Ohio 1942) 139 Ohio St. 354, 40 N.E.2d 145, 22 O.O. 411. Appeal And Error ☞ 77(2)

2107.24 Probate court to treat document as will despite noncompliance with statute

(A) If a document that is executed that purports to be a will is not executed in compliance with the requirements of section 2107.03 of the Revised Code, that document shall be treated as if it had been executed as a will in compliance with the requirements of that section if a probate court, after holding a hearing, finds that the proponent of the document as a purported will has established, by clear and convincing evidence, all of the following:

(1) The decedent prepared the document or caused the document to be prepared.

(2) The decedent signed the document and intended the document to constitute the decedent's will.

(3) Two or more witnesses saw the decedent sign the document under division (A)(2) of this section.

(B) If the probate court holds a hearing pursuant to division (A) of this section and finds that the proponent of the document as a purported will has established by clear and convincing evidence the requirements under divisions (A)(1), (2), and (3) of this section, the executor may file an action in the probate court to recover court costs and attorney's fees from the attorney, if any, responsible for the execution of the document.

(2006 H 265, eff. 7–20–06)

Uncodified Law

2006 H 265, § 3, eff. 7–20–06, reads:

Section 2107.27 of the Revised Code, as amended by this act, and section 2107.24 of the Revised Code, as enacted by this act, apply to estates of decedents who die on or after the effective date of this act.

Historical and Statutory Notes

Ed. Note: Former RC 2107.24 repealed by 1976 S 466, eff. 5–26–76; 1953 H 1; GC 10504–33.

Pre–1953 H 1 Amendments: 114 v 351

Research References

Encyclopedias

OH Jur. 3d Decedents' Estates § 998, Notice of Application for Probate.
OH Jur. 3d Decedents' Estates § 1016, Notice of Admission to Probate.
OH Jur. 3d Decedents' Estates § 1040, When Court May Probate Lost, Spoliated, or Destroyed Will, Generally.
OH Jur. 3d Decedents' Estates § 1044, Notice.
OH Jur. 3d Decedents' Estates § 1050, Weight and Sufficiency of Evidence.
OH Jur. 3d Decedents' Estates § 1039.1, Document as a Purported Will.

Treatises and Practice Aids

Carlin, Baldwin's Ohio Practice, Merrick-Rippner Probate Law § 36:3, Admission to Probate—Witness as Devisee or Legatee.

LOST, SPOLIATED, OR DESTROYED WILLS

2107.26 Lost, spoliated, or destroyed wills may be admitted to probate

When an original will is lost, spoliated, or destroyed before or after the death of a testator, the probate court shall admit the lost, spoliated, or destroyed will to probate if both of the following apply:

(A) The proponent of the will establishes by clear and convincing evidence both of the following:

(1) The will was executed with the formalities required at the time of execution by the jurisdiction in which it was executed.

(2) The contents of the will.

(B) No person opposing the admission of the will to probate establishes by a preponderance of the evidence that the testator had revoked the will.

(1999 H 59, eff. 10–29–99; 1953 H 1, eff. 10–1–53; GC 10504–35)

Historical and Statutory Notes

Pre–1953 H 1 Amendments: 114 v 352

Amendment Note: 1999 H 59 rewrote the section, which prior thereto read:

"When an original will is lost, spoliated, or destroyed subsequent to the death of a testator, or before the death of such testator if the testator's lack of knowledge of such loss, spoliation, or destruction can be proved by clear and convincing testimony, or after he became incapable of making a will by reason of insanity, and such will cannot be produced in the probate court in as complete a manner as the originals of last wills and testaments which are actually produced therein for probate, the court may admit such lost, spoliated, or destroyed will to probate, if such court is satisfied the will was executed according to the law in force at the time of its execution and not revoked at the death of the testator."

Library References

Wills ⇌231, 345.
Westlaw Topic No. 409.
C.J.S. Wills §§ 510, 734, 740.

Research References

Encyclopedias

OH Jur. 3d Decedents' Estates § 361, Revocation Induced or Prevented by Fraud and Undue Influence.
OH Jur. 3d Decedents' Estates § 376, Presumption of Revocation When Will in Testator's Custody Cannot be Found.
OH Jur. 3d Decedents' Estates § 998, Notice of Application for Probate.
OH Jur. 3d Decedents' Estates § 1016, Notice of Admission to Probate.
OH Jur. 3d Decedents' Estates § 1040, When Court May Probate Lost, Spoliated, or Destroyed Will, Generally.
OH Jur. 3d Decedents' Estates § 1042, Jurisdiction.
OH Jur. 3d Decedents' Estates § 1044, Notice.
OH Jur. 3d Decedents' Estates § 1046, Burden of Proof.
OH Jur. 3d Decedents' Estates § 1050, Weight and Sufficiency of Evidence.
OH Jur. 3d Evidence & Witnesses § 966, Establishment of a Lost or Destroyed Instrument.

Treatises and Practice Aids

Klein, Darling, & Terez, Baldwin's Ohio Practice Civil Practice § 73:2, Probate Division--Applicability of Ohio Civil Rules.
Carlin, Baldwin's Ohio Practice, Merrick-Rippner Probate Law § 39:1, Lost, Spoliated, or Destroyed Will—Definition.
Carlin, Baldwin's Ohio Practice, Merrick-Rippner Probate Law § 39:2, Lost, Spoliated, or Destroyed Will—Statutory Provisions for Admission to Probate.
Carlin, Baldwin's Ohio Practice, Merrick-Rippner Probate Law § 39:3, Lost, Spoliated, or Destroyed Will—Evidence.
Carlin, Baldwin's Ohio Practice, Merrick-Rippner Probate Law § 39:4, Lost, Spoliated, or Destroyed Will—Effect of Probate.
Carlin, Baldwin's Ohio Practice, Merrick-Rippner Probate Law § 39:5, Application to Probate Lost, Spoliated, or Destroyed Will—Form.
Carlin, Baldwin's Ohio Practice, Merrick-Rippner Probate Law § 40:5, Revocation of Will—Physical Act—Presumption.
Carlin, Baldwin's Ohio Practice, Merrick-Rippner Probate Law § 2:121, Administration of Decedent's Estate—Checklist.

Law Review and Journal Commentaries

Lost, Spoliated and Destroyed Wills: Who Needs to be Notified? Jan M Frankel, 12 Prob L J Ohio 86 (May/June 2002).

Probate of a Lost Will—Is It Time to Modernize the Law?, Marvin R. Pliskin. 6 Prob L J Ohio 33 (January/February 1996).

Recent Legislation Makes It Easier to Admit Lost, Spoliated or Destroyed Wills, David Simmons. 10 Prob L J Ohio 2 (September/October 1999).

Notes of Decisions

Codicils 4
Copies 1
Presumptions and proof 3
Procedure and review 2

---

1. Copies

There can be but one original, effective, and dispositive instrument to be considered a last will and testament, and however so many copies of that original will, exact in every detail and executed by the testator and attested to by the witnesses there are, these copies remain just that: copies—copies useful to show what had existed in the case of a lost, spoliated, or destroyed will, but utterly ineffectual to be used as a substitute for the original will. In re Steel's Estate (Ohio Prob. 1966) 8 Ohio Misc. 133, 219 N.E.2d 236, 37 O.O.2d 70. Wills ⇌ 94

A copy or copies of a mutilated will cannot be used to supplant the original and only valid instrument. In re Steel's Estate (Ohio Prob. 1966) 8 Ohio Misc. 133, 219 N.E.2d 236, 37 O.O.2d 70. Wills ⇌ 171

2. Procedure and review

The spirit of the statute in respect to the establishment of spoliated wills is, to some extent, in odium spoliatoris, and to render the same practically effective, it must be so administered; not every variance between a spoliated will as made and the will as admitted to probate will avoid the latter. Banning v. Banning (Ohio 1861) 12 Ohio St. 437. Wills ⇌ 237

Exclusive jurisdiction in proceedings to establish spoliated, lost or destroyed wills is with the probate courts. Morningstar v. Selby (Ohio 1846) 15 Ohio 345, 45 Am.Dec. 579.

Statute allowing destroyed will to be admitted to probate did not apply to will which testator destroyed and threw away when executing new will, precluding friend of testator named as beneficiary under destroyed will from having interest needed to have standing to bring will contest on ground that new will was result of fraud or undue influence. Sheridan v. Harbison (Ohio App. 2 Dist., 02-15-1995) 101 Ohio App.3d 206, 655 N.E.2d 256, appeal not allowed 72 Ohio St.3d 1551, 650 N.E.2d 1370. Wills ⇌ 229; Wills ⇌ 234

Evidence that beneficiaries of most recent will abused testator until she destroyed previous will and executed new one in their favor did not negate fact that testator knew she was destroying old will and, thus, testator's friend who was alleged sole beneficiary under will destroyed by testator lacked standing to contest new will or show that testator destroyed previous will because of fraud or undue influence. Sheridan v. Harbison (Ohio App. 2 Dist., 02-15-1995) 101 Ohio App.3d 206, 655 N.E.2d 256, appeal not allowed 72 Ohio St.3d 1551, 650 N.E.2d 1370. Wills ⇌ 229

The proceeding to admit a lost, spoliated, or destroyed will is a special statutory proceeding in which the hearsay rule is inapplicable. In re Estate of Haynes (Ohio 1986) 25 Ohio St.3d 101, 495 N.E.2d 23, 25 O.B.R. 150. Wills ⇌ 293(4)

A purported will which upon presentation for probate contains eight separate black ink deletions, apparently made with a felt marking pen, the last blacking completely covering a testatrix's signature, is not a spoliated will, so that whether such purported will should be admitted to probate is governed by RC 2107.11 et seq., not by RC 2107.26 et seq., dealing with the probate of a spoliated will, as these sections existed at the time of decedent's death on August 29, 1975. In re Nash's Will (Ohio Com.Pl. 1976) 50 Ohio Misc. 4, 361 N.E.2d 558, 3 O.O.3d 347, 4 O.O.3d 33. Wills ⇌ 203; Wills ⇌ 231

In order to prevail in a will contest, the contestant must do more than merely meet the prima facie case; the record of a hearing in the probate court on the order of probate is not before the common pleas court in a will contest, but whether the same or different evidence is presented in the two proceedings is immaterial, since the same evidence may or may not be sufficient to overcome the presumption arising from the order of probate. Carr v. Howard (Fayette 1969) 17 Ohio App.2d 233, 246 N.E.2d 563, 46 O.O.2d 360.

When the contestants of a lost will which has been admitted to probate offer substantially the same evidence as that presented in opposition to its probate, the court must dismiss the petition. Carr v. Howard (Ohio Com.Pl. 1967) 15 Ohio Misc. 5, 237 N.E.2d 180, 42 O.O.2d 174, 44 O.O.2d 75, reversed 17 Ohio App.2d 233, 246 N.E.2d 563, 46 O.O.2d 360.

In a hearing on an application to probate a lost will declarations made by the decedent prior to his death may be introduced into evidence, provided the proper foundation is made therefor. In re Karras' Estate (Stark 1959) 109 Ohio App. 403, 166 N.E.2d 781, 11 O.O.2d 334. Wills ⇌ 297(3)

A decedent's brother, who makes application to probate an alleged lost will of such decedent, may not testify, in a hearing on an application to probate such will, concerning matters occurring prior to the death of such decedent. In re Karras' Estate (Stark 1959) 109 Ohio App. 403, 166 N.E.2d 781, 11 O.O.2d 334.

Proceedings to admit to probate lost, spoliated or destroyed wills, are statutory in nature, and in such cases the provisions of a lost, destroyed or spoliated will, whether it be a simple will or one containing trust provisions, will not operate to change the character of the statutory proceedings, and invoke the chancery powers of the Court of Appeals, and where appeal is prosecuted to the Court of Appeals on questions of law and fact, a motion to dismiss the appeal on questions of law and fact will be granted and the appeal retained as one on questions of law. (See also In re Estate of Bowles, 93 App 461, 113 NE(2d) 259 (1952).) Bowles' Estate v. Bowles'

Heirs (Cuyahoga 1953) 96 Ohio App. 265, 114 N.E.2d 229, 66 Ohio Law Abs. 73, 54 O.O. 296.

GC 11421–2 (RC 2315.22), providing for separate findings of fact and conclusions of law has no application to a proceeding in probate court to probate a lost will. In re Hughes' Estate (Butler 1948) 84 Ohio App. 275, 85 N.E.2d 583, 53 Ohio Law Abs. 410, 39 O.O. 404. Wills ⚖ 334

Order of probate court admitting instrument to probate as a last will is not reviewable on appeal. In re Frey's Estate (Ohio 1942) 139 Ohio St. 354, 40 N.E.2d 145, 22 O.O. 411. Appeal And Error ⚖ 77(2)

An appeal lies to a common pleas court from an order of a probate court overruling an application to find and establish the contents of a lost will. Roth v. Siefert (Ohio 1908) 77 Ohio St. 417, 83 N.E. 611, 5 Ohio Law Rep. 565. Wills ⚖ 358

An order of the probate court admitting a paper to probate as a last will and testament is not reviewable on petition in error, though an order refusing to admit such paper to probate is reviewable. Hollrah v. Lasance (Ohio 1900) 63 Ohio St. 58, 44 W.L.B. 80, 57 N.E. 964. Wills ⚖ 356

Proceedings to establish lost, spoliated or destroyed will under GC 10504–35 (RC 2107.26) et seq. may be maintained only in probate court of county in which testator was domiciled at time of death. State ex rel. Overlander v. Brewer (Ohio 1947) 147 Ohio St. 386, 72 N.E.2d 84, 34 O.O. 338.

Jurisdiction over decedent's estate acquired by probate court of one county by appointment of administrator under GC 10509–1 (RC 2113.01) is not exclusive of jurisdiction over same estate later acquired by probate court of another county by virtue of proceedings under GC 10504–10 (RC 2107.09), 10504–15 (RC 2107.11) and 10504–35 (RC 2107.26). State ex rel. Overlander v. Brewer (Ohio 1947) 147 Ohio St. 386, 72 N.E.2d 84, 34 O.O. 338.

3. Presumptions and proof

The omission of the record to state that the destruction of a will was subsequent to the testatrix's death does not render void the order admitting a transcript of such will to probate; such a will is entitled to the same prima facie effect as the statute gives to an order probating an original will. Converse v. Starr (Ohio 1872) 23 Ohio St. 491.

This section will not permit a will lost, spoliated, or destroyed to be established, unless it existed subsequent to the death of the testator. In re Sinclair's Will (Ohio 1855) 5 Ohio St. 290. Wills ⚖ 234

Presumption of revocation of a will is not overcome where the only testimony given at the hearing regarding the issue of revocation is that of a beneficiary under the terms of the will who would not benefit from the intestate succession of assets; the probate court could find that such testimony regarding the finding and location of a copy of the will lacks credibility. In re Estate of Brown (Ohio App. 2 Dist., Montgomery, 04-20-2001) No. 18611, 2001 WL 395346, Unreported.

Issues of fact are presented and a will contest is improperly dismissed where the attorney who prepared a lost will and the secretaries who would have witnessed it at the lawyer's office give testimony that is inconclusive about whether the will was properly executed, attested to, and witnessed, since they cannot specifically recall the testator signing the will. Springer v. Lee (Ohio App. 3 Dist., Hancock, 05-02-1996) No. 5-95-42, 1996 WL 223699, Unreported.

Statute permitting lost or destroyed will to be admitted to probate applies in instances where will is lost or destroyed subsequent to testator's death or if testator's lack of knowledge of predeath destruction of loss can be proved by clear and convincing evidence. Sheridan v. Harbison (Ohio App. 2 Dist., 02-15-1995) 101 Ohio App.3d 206, 655 N.E.2d 256, appeal not allowed 72 Ohio St.3d 1551, 650 N.E.2d 1370. Wills ⚖ 234

Statute permitting lost or destroyed will to be admitted to probate is intended to allow alleged beneficiary of lost or destroyed will opportunity to rebut presumption that will was disposed of by testator with intention of revoking it. Sheridan v. Harbison (Ohio App. 2 Dist., 02-15-1995) 101 Ohio App.3d 206, 655 N.E.2d 256, appeal not allowed 72 Ohio St.3d 1551, 650 N.E.2d 1370. Wills ⚖ 290

Beneficiary of lost or destroyed will may rebut presumption that will was disposed of by testator with intent to revoke by showing that will was not in testator's custody after being executed, that testator was otherwise not capable of exercising control over will, by proof of relationship between testator and persons involved, by showing that testator behaved as though she deemed will valid and unrevoked up to time of death, or by testimony that third party fraudulently destroyed will. Sheridan v. Harbison (Ohio App. 2 Dist., 02-15-1995) 101 Ohio App.3d 206, 655 N.E.2d 256, appeal not allowed 72 Ohio St.3d 1551, 650 N.E.2d 1370. Wills ⚖ 290

When will is in custody of testator and cannot be found following death of testator, presumption arises that testator destroyed will with intent to revoke it. Gockel v. Eble (Ohio App. 8 Dist., 10-17-1994) 98 Ohio App.3d 281, 648 N.E.2d 539, dismissed, appeal not allowed 71 Ohio St.3d 1491, 646 N.E.2d 466. Wills ⚖ 290

Presumption that testator destroyed new will that could not be found following testator's death may be rebutted by proof of declarations made by decedent, testimony that third party fraudulently destroyed will, or proof of testator's relationship to persons involved in will contest action. Gockel v. Eble (Ohio App. 8 Dist., 10-17-1994) 98 Ohio App.3d 281, 648 N.E.2d 539, dismissed, appeal not allowed 71 Ohio St.3d 1491, 646 N.E.2d 466. Wills ⚖ 290

Execution of will now alleged to be lost, spoliated, or destroyed must be demonstrated beyond reasonable doubt before such will may be admitted to probate. Gockel v. Eble (Ohio App. 8 Dist., 10-17-1994) 98 Ohio App.3d 281, 648 N.E.2d 539, dismissed, appeal not allowed 71 Ohio St.3d 1491, 646 N.E.2d 466. Wills ⚖ 302(8)

Destruction of will now alleged to be lost, spoliated, or destroyed must be established by clear and convincing evidence before such will may be admitted to probate. Gockel v. Eble (Ohio App. 8 Dist., 10-17-1994) 98 Ohio App.3d 281, 648 N.E.2d 539, dismissed, appeal not allowed 71 Ohio St.3d 1491, 646 N.E.2d 466. Wills ⚖ 302(8)

Evidence that testatrix properly executed allegedly destroyed will and evidence of contents of that will was required to establish fact question in will contest by heirs at law of testatrix, challenging validity of previous will which named her former live-in companion as sole legatee. Gockel v. Eble (Ohio App. 8 Dist., 10-17-1994) 98 Ohio App.3d 281, 648 N.E.2d 539, dismissed, appeal not allowed 71 Ohio St.3d 1491, 646 N.E.2d 466. Wills ⚖ 324(1)

Once a will is admitted to probate there is a presumption that it is valid, and a will contestant fails to overcome that presumption where he presents no evidence that an earlier separation of the last page of a will represented a form of mutilation which equated with revocation. Mattax v. Moore (Trumbull 1991) 72 Ohio App.3d 647, 595 N.E.2d 969, dismissed, jurisdictional motion overruled 61 Ohio St.3d 1419, 574 N.E.2d 1090.

The standard of proof necessary to admit a lost, spoliated, or destroyed will to probate is clear and convincing evidence that the loss, spoliation, or destruction of the original will occurred subsequent to the death of the testator or before the death of the testator, but without his knowledge. In re Estate of Haynes (Ohio 1986) 25 Ohio St.3d 101, 495 N.E.2d 23, 25 O.B.R. 150. Wills ⚖ 302(8)

When a lost will has been admitted to probate this establishes a presumption in a contest thereof that the probated document is the last will of the testator. Carr v. Howard (Ohio Com.Pl. 1967) 15 Ohio Misc. 5, 237 N.E.2d 180, 42 O.O.2d 174, 44 O.O.2d 75, reversed 17 Ohio App.2d 233, 246 N.E.2d 563, 46 O.O.2d 360.

"Spoliation," as used in RC 2107.26, is the doing of some act manifest on the face of the will, by someone other than the testator. In re Downie's Estate (Ohio Prob. 1966) 6 Ohio Misc. 36, 213 N.E.2d 833, 35 O.O.2d 31. Wills ⚖ 176

Where a portion of a will has been excised, but extrinsic evidence is available to establish the content of the excised portion, the will may be probated in its entirety. In re Downie's Estate (Ohio Prob. 1966) 6 Ohio Misc. 36, 213 N.E.2d 833, 35 O.O.2d 31.

On the evidence proponents failed to prove that will was lost rather than revoked. In re Simon's Estate (Ohio Prob. 1961) 177 N.E.2d 92, 86 Ohio Law Abs. 378, 86 Ohio Law Abs. 380, 20 O.O.2d 59.

Where the only issue presented in an application to probate a lost will is that the deceased did not have knowledge of such loss, the proponent must establish by clear and convincing evidence that testator did not know of its loss; and requiring the proponent to establish lack of knowledge "by the best evidence" constitutes reversible error. (See also In re Estate of Bowles, 93 App 461, 113 NE(2d) 259 (1952).) Bowles' Estate v. Bowles' Heirs (Cuyahoga 1953) 96 Ohio App. 265, 114 N.E.2d 229, 66 Ohio Law Abs. 73, 54 O.O. 296.

The plan of a will in remembering the persons who or charities that would be the natural objects of the testator's bounty, the care with which the will was drawn, the remarks of the testator thereafter that show a continuation of the state of mind of the testator at the time the will was drawn or small changes made in the general plan of the will by codicils all are relevant in support of the testator's lack of knowledge of the loss of the will. (See also In re Estate of Bowles, 93 App 461, 113 NE(2d) 259 (1952).) Bowles' Estate v. Bowles' Heirs (Cuyahoga 1953) 96 Ohio App. 265, 114 N.E.2d 229, 66 Ohio Law Abs. 73, 54 O.O. 296. Wills ⚖ 293(4)

Where a will is in the custody of the testator from the time of its execution until his death and is found among his effects after his death with the entire surname of testator's signature torn off and with "X" marks in ink through his initials which are on the margin of each page of the will, it will be presumed that the will was mutilated by the testator with the intention of revoking the same. In re Tyler's Estate (Ohio 1953) 159 Ohio St. 492, 112 N.E.2d 668, 50 O.O. 419. Wills ⇔ 290

To establish that the mutilation of a will occurred subsequent to the death of the testator, the evidence must satisfy the mind of the probate judge, and to establish a claim that the mutilation was made by some one other than the testator before his death and without his knowledge, the evidence must be clear and convincing. In re Tyler's Estate (Ohio 1953) 159 Ohio St. 492, 112 N.E.2d 668, 50 O.O. 419.

In probate proceedings involving issue as to whether will had been revoked by testator's destruction of copy retained by him, evidence that decedent had not left hospital from time he entered it until his death, that during such period, residuary legatee under prior will had had keys to decedent's house, that during visit to decedent at hospital such legatee had stated to decedent "I see you have changed your will" and other evidence with regard to statements made by decedent and such legatee at hospital was material on question of whether or not will had been revoked by testator, and such evidence should have been admitted. In re Wood's Estate (Cuyahoga 1951) 105 N.E.2d 589, 61 Ohio Law Abs. 548. Wills ⇔ 296

Where a will is lost or destroyed and testator becomes insane, the evidence to overcome the presumption that testator revoked it must be certain, satisfactory, and conclusive that it was unrevoked and in existence after he became insane. Cole v. McClure (Ohio 1913) 88 Ohio St. 1, 102 N.E. 264, 11 Ohio Law Rep. 39. Evidence ⇔ 596(1); Wills ⇔ 306

A will once known to have existed and to have been in the custody of the testator but not found after the testator's decease is presumed to have been destroyed by him with intent to revoke; testimony as to declarations of the testator is admissible to strengthen or repel the presumption of revocation, or to explain the act of destruction or cancellation. Behrens v. Behrens (Ohio 1890) 47 Ohio St. 323, 24 W.L.B. 286, 25 N.E. 209, 21 Am.St.Rep. 820.

A paper in seven pieces with one piece missing cannot be admitted to probate as a spoliated will under former GC 10543 (RC 2107.26) where it is shown that it became in such condition from being pocketworn, before testator's death. In re Miller (Ohio Prob. 1926) 26 Ohio NP(NS) 209, 4 Ohio Law Abs. 736. Wills ⇔ 234

Statutory requirements in case of lost will are to be liberally construed. (But see Banning v Banning, 12 OS 437 (1861).) In re Lasance's Estate (Ohio Prob. 1897) 7 Ohio Dec. 246, 5 Ohio N.P. 20.

The burden of proof is on the proponents. In re Lasance's Estate (Ohio Prob. 1897) 7 Ohio Dec. 246, 5 Ohio N.P. 20.

In the case of the probate of a spoliated will, the court must be judicially satisfied not only as to its proper execution and attestation, but also that the will was not revoked by the testator, and where the testator has removed his signature from the will, a presumption of revocation arises which must be overcome. In re Jones' Estate (Ohio Prob. 1895) 2 Ohio Dec. 409, 2 Ohio N.P. 190, 2 Ohio N.P. 194, 2 Ohio N.P. 209.

Where a testator, though enfeebled and on his death bed, obtains his will, tears off his signatures, and writes "destroyed by me" on it with the intent to revoke, such a will is not "spoliated" within the meaning of RS 5926 and may not be admitted to probate. In re Jones' Estate (Ohio Prob. 1895) 2 Ohio Dec. 409, 2 Ohio N.P. 190, 2 Ohio N.P. 194, 2 Ohio N.P. 209.

Where a will once known to have been in existence cannot be found, rebuttable presumption is that it was destroyed by the testator with the intention of revoking it. In re Ayres' Will (Ohio Prob. 1940) 5 Ohio Supp. 239, 33 Ohio Law Abs. 1, 19 O.O. 465, affirmed 43 N.E.2d 918, 36 Ohio Law Abs. 267. Wills ⇔ 290

4. Codicils

A codicil, however well preserved, is dependent upon a will for its force and effect and cannot be used to substitute for a will which is lost, or mutilated after the codicil was completed. In re Steel's Estate (Ohio Prob. 1966) 8 Ohio Misc. 133, 219 N.E.2d 236, 37 O.O.2d 70. Wills ⇔ 233

Where a codicil is executed by a testator, providing additional rights to beneficiaries under an existing will, which will is lost during the lifetime of testator, provisions of the codicil being such that they are completely dependent upon the will for their effectiveness, the codicil cannot be admitted to probate unless the will is also so admitted. (See also In re Estate of Bowles, 93 App 461, 113 NE(2d) 259 (1952).) Bowles' Estate v. Bowles' Heirs (Cuyahoga 1953) 96 Ohio App. 265, 114 N.E.2d 229, 66 Ohio Law Abs. 73, 54 O.O. 296.

2107.27 Notice of application; testimony; probate

(A) When application is made to the probate court to admit to probate a will that has been lost, spoliated, or destroyed as provided in section 2107.26 of the Revised Code or a document that is treated as a will as provided in section 2107.24 of the Revised Code, the party seeking to prove the will shall give a written notice by certified mail to the surviving spouse of the testator, to all persons who would be entitled to inherit from the testator under Chapter 2105. of the Revised Code if the testator had died intestate, to all legatees and devisees that are named in the will, and to all legatees and devisees that are named in the most recent will prior to the lost, spoliated, or destroyed will that is known to the applicant or in the most recent will prior to the document that is treated as a will if the most recent will is known to the applicant.

(B) In the cases described in division (A) of this section, the proponents and opponents of the will shall cause the witnesses to the will, and any other witnesses that have relevant and material knowledge about the will, to appear before the court to testify. If any witnesses reside out of its jurisdiction, or reside within its jurisdiction but are infirm or unable to attend, the probate court may order their testimony to be taken and reduced to writing by some competent person. The testimony shall be filed in the records of the probate court pertaining to the testator's estate.

(C) If upon such proof the court finds that the requirements of section 2107.24 or 2107.26 of the Revised Code, whichever is applicable, have been met, the probate court shall find and establish the contents of the will as near as can be ascertained. The contents of the will established under section 2107.26 of the Revised Code shall be as effectual for all purposes as if the original will had been admitted to probate and record. The contents of the will established under section 2107.24 of the Revised Code shall be as effectual for all purposes as if the document treated as a will had satisfied all of the requirements of section 2107.03 of the Revised Code and had been admitted to probate and record.

(2006 H 265, eff. 7–20–06; 2002 H 345, eff. 7–23–02; 1990 H 346, eff. 5–31–90; 1977 H 42; 1953 H 1; GC 10504–36, 10504–37, 10504–38, 10504–40)

Uncodified Law

2006 H 265, § 3: See Uncodified Law under RC 2107.24.

1990 H 346, § 3, eff. 5–31–90, reads:

(A) Sections 1 and 2 of this act shall apply only to the estates of decedents who die on or after the effective date of this act.

(B) It is the intent of the General Assembly in the outright repeal of sections 2107.13 and 2107.14 of the Revised Code and the amendments to sections 109.30, 2107.18, 2107.19, 2107.22, 2107.27, 2107.76, 2115.16, and 2703.14 of the Revised Code by this act, to respond to the dicta of the Supreme Court in *Palazzi v. Estate of Gardner* (1987), 32 Ohio St. 3d 169 and to enact statutory provisions relating to notice of probate proceedings that are not unconstitutional as potentially violative of the due process of law rights of nonresidents of this state.

Historical and Statutory Notes

Pre–1953 H 1 Amendments: 114 v 352, 353

Amendment Note: 2006 H 265 rewrote this section, which prior thereto read:

"(A) When application is made to the probate court to admit to probate a will that has been lost, spoliated, or destroyed, the party seeking to prove the will shall give a written notice by certified mail to the surviving spouse of the testator, to all persons who would be entitled to inherit from the testator under Chapter 2105. of the Revised Code if the testator had died intestate, to all legatees and devisees that are named in the will, and to all legatees and devisees that are named in the most recent will prior to the lost, spoliated, or destroyed will that is known to the applicant.

"(B) In the cases described in division (A) of this section, the proponents and opponents of the will shall cause the witnesses to the will, and any other witnesses that have relevant and material knowledge about the will, to appear before the court to testify. If any witnesses reside out of its jurisdiction, or reside within its jurisdiction but are infirm or unable to attend, the probate court may order their testimony to be taken and reduced to writing by some competent person. The testimony shall be filed in the records of the probate court pertaining to the testator's estate.

"(C) If upon such proof the court finds that the requirements of section 2107.26 of the Revised Code have been met, the probate court shall find and establish the contents of the will as near as can be ascertained. The contents of the will shall be as effectual for all purposes as if the original will had been admitted to probate and record."

Amendment Note: 2002 H 345 rewrote the section, which prior thereto read:

"(A) When application is made to the probate court to admit to probate a will that has been lost, spoliated, or destroyed, the party seeking to prove the will shall give a written notice by certified mail to the surviving spouse of the testator, to all persons who would be entitled to inherit from the testator under Chapter 2105. of the Revised Code if the testator had died intestate, to all legatees and devisees that are named in the will, and to all legatees and devisees that are named in the most recent will prior to the lost, spoliated, or destroyed will that is known to the applicant.

"(B) In the cases described in division (A) of this section, the proponents and opponents of the will shall cause the witnesses to the will, and any other witnesses that have relevant and material knowledge about the will, to appear before the court to testify. If any witnesses reside out of its jurisdiction, or reside within its jurisdiction but are infirm or unable to attend, the probate court may order their testimony to be taken and reduced to writing by some competent person. The testimony shall be filed in the records of the probate court pertaining to the testator's estate.

"(C) If upon such proof the court finds that the requirements of section 2107.26 of the Revised Code have been met, the probate court shall find and establish the contents of the will as near as can be ascertained. The contents of the will shall be as effectual for all purposes as if the original will had been admitted to probate and record."

Legislative Service Commission
1975 (Commentary from former RC 2107.13):

This section currently provides that notice be given to the surviving spouse before admission of the will to probate. It would be amended by the bill to provide that notice must be given to a surviving spouse only if known to the applicant.

OSBA Probate and Trust Law Section
1957 (Commentary from former RC 2107.13):

The Supreme Court has held that the requirement of notice of application for probate to be given to the surviving spouse and next of kin of the testator resident of the state is mandatory and jurisdictional. The statute in its present form has led to much uncertainty as to the validity of the probate of a will in the event the person offering the same notifies all next of kin known to him to be residents of the state when it subsequently develops that there are other residents of the state not known to him who have not been served. The proposed amendment removes this uncertainty by providing that the notice is to be given to the surviving spouse and to the persons known to the applicant to be residents of the state.

Cross References
Computation of time, 1.14
Determining next of kin, 2105.03
Legal advertising, 7.10 to 7.15

Library References
Wills ⟫269.
Westlaw Topic No. 409.
C.J.S. Wills §§ 553 to 556.
  Baldwin's Ohio Legislative Service, 1990 Laws of Ohio, H 346—LSC Analysis, p 5–87

Research References

Encyclopedias
OH Jur. 3d Decedents' Estates § 998, Notice of Application for Probate.
OH Jur. 3d Decedents' Estates § 999, Requirements for Admission to Probate.
OH Jur. 3d Decedents' Estates § 1007, Witnesses Other Than the Subscribing Witnesses.
OH Jur. 3d Decedents' Estates § 1016, Notice of Admission to Probate.
OH Jur. 3d Decedents' Estates § 1040, When Court May Probate Lost, Spoliated, or Destroyed Will, Generally.
OH Jur. 3d Decedents' Estates § 1044, Notice.
OH Jur. 3d Decedents' Estates § 1045, Proof of Contents of Will.
OH Jur. 3d Decedents' Estates § 1050, Weight and Sufficiency of Evidence.
OH Jur. 3d Decedents' Estates § 1057, Effect of Admission to Probate.
OH Jur. 3d Decedents' Estates § 1058, Admission to Record of Will Probated But Lost Before Recording.

Treatises and Practice Aids
Carlin, Baldwin's Ohio Practice, Merrick-Rippner Probate Law § 39:1, Lost, Spoliated, or Destroyed Will—Definition.
Carlin, Baldwin's Ohio Practice, Merrick-Rippner Probate Law § 39:2, Lost, Spoliated, or Destroyed Will—Statutory Provisions for Admission to Probate.
Carlin, Baldwin's Ohio Practice, Merrick-Rippner Probate Law § 39:3, Lost, Spoliated, or Destroyed Will—Evidence.
Carlin, Baldwin's Ohio Practice, Merrick-Rippner Probate Law § 39:5, Application to Probate Lost, Spoliated, or Destroyed Will—Form.
Carlin, Baldwin's Ohio Practice, Merrick-Rippner Probate Law § 39:6, Entry Setting for Hearing and Ordering Notice—Form.
Carlin, Baldwin's Ohio Practice, Merrick-Rippner Probate Law § 39:7, Entry Admitting Lost, Destroyed, or Spoliated Will to Probate—Form.
Carlin, Baldwin's Ohio Practice, Merrick-Rippner Probate Law § 40:5, Revocation of Will—Physical Act—Presumption.
Carlin, Baldwin's Ohio Practice, Merrick-Rippner Probate Law § 2:121, Administration of Decedent's Estate—Checklist.

Law Review and Journal Commentaries

Lost, Spoliated and Destroyed Wills: Who Needs to be Notified? Jan M Frankel, 12 Prob L J Ohio 86 (May/June 2002).

Notes of Decisions

Burden of proof; evidence   3
Notice   2
Procedure   1

---

1. Procedure

RC 2107.18 does not require, as does RC 2107.27, that the will sought to be proved has been "unrevoked at the death of the testator." In re Nash's Will (Ohio Com.Pl. 1976) 50 Ohio Misc. 4, 361 N.E.2d 558, 3 O.O.3d 347, 4 O.O.3d 33.

A purported will which upon presentation for probate contains eight separate black ink deletions, apparently made with a felt marking pen, the last blacking completely covering a testatrix's signature, is not a spoliated will, so that whether such purported will should be admitted to probate is governed by RC 2107.11 et seq., not by RC 2107.26 et seq., dealing with the probate of a spoliated will, as these sections existed at the time of decedent's death on August 29, 1975. In re Nash's Will (Ohio Com.Pl. 1976) 50 Ohio Misc. 4, 361 N.E.2d 558, 3 O.O.3d 347, 4 O.O.3d 33. Wills ⟫ 203; Wills ⟫ 231

Where the subscribing witnesses testify to the due and proper execution of a will, and that at the time of execution the instrument did not contain the black ink deletions apparent at the time of the hearing for probate, such will should be admitted to probate and record. In re Nash's Will (Ohio Com.Pl. 1976) 50 Ohio Misc. 4, 361 N.E.2d 558, 3 O.O.3d 347, 4 O.O.3d 33. Wills ⟫ 206

When the contestants of a lost will which has been admitted to probate offer substantially the same evidence as that presented in opposition to its probate, the court must dismiss the petition. Carr v. Howard (Ohio Com.Pl. 1967) 15 Ohio Misc. 5, 237 N.E.2d 180, 42 O.O.2d 174, 44 O.O.2d 75, reversed 17 Ohio App.2d 233, 246 N.E.2d 563, 46 O.O.2d 360.

In a hearing on an application to probate a lost will, declarations made by the decedent prior to his death may be introduced into evidence, provided the proper foundation is made therefor. In re Karras' Estate

(Stark 1959) 109 Ohio App. 403, 166 N.E.2d 781, 11 O.O.2d 334. Wills ⚖ 297(3)

A decedent's brother, who makes application to probate an alleged lost will of such decedent, may not testify, in a hearing on an application to probate such will, concerning matters occurring prior to the death of such decedent. In re Karras' Estate (Stark 1959) 109 Ohio App. 403, 166 N.E.2d 781, 11 O.O.2d 334.

Exclusion of an interested party in an action to probate an alleged lost will is error. (See also In re Estate of Bowles, 93 App 461, 113 NE(2d) 259 (1952).) Bowles' Estate v. Bowles' Heirs (Cuyahoga 1953) 96 Ohio App. 265, 114 N.E.2d 229, 66 Ohio Law Abs. 73, 54 O.O. 296.

Proceedings to admit to probate lost, spoliated or destroyed wills, are statutory in nature, and in such cases the provisions of a lost, destroyed or spoliated will, whether it be a simple will or one containing trust provisions, will not operate to change the character of the statutory proceedings, and invoke the chancery powers of the court of appeals, and where appeal is prosecuted to the court of appeals on questions of law and fact, a motion to dismiss the appeal on questions of law and fact will be granted and the appeal retained as one on questions of law. In re Bowles' Estate (Cuyahoga 1952) 93 Ohio App. 461, 113 N.E.2d 259, 65 Ohio Law Abs. 43, 51 O.O. 197.

Where the jury in a will contest action finds that the will propounded was not the testatrix's last will and testament, their answers of "don't know" to interrogatories which asked if the will was signed by the testatrix are not inconsistent with the general verdict. Bloor v. Platt (Ohio 1908) 78 Ohio St. 46, 84 N.E. 604, 5 Ohio Law Rep. 619, 14 Am.Ann.Cas. 332.

An appeal lies to a common pleas court from an order of a probate court overruling an application to find and establish the contents of a lost will. Roth v. Siefert (Ohio 1908) 77 Ohio St. 417, 83 N.E. 611, 5 Ohio Law Rep. 565. Wills ⚖ 358

An order of the probate court admitting a paper to probate as a last will and testament is not reviewable on petition in error, though an order refusing to admit such paper to probate is reviewable. Hollrah v. Lasance (Ohio 1900) 63 Ohio St. 58, 44 W.L.B. 80, 57 N.E. 964. Wills ⚖ 356

An order admitting a will to probate is not reviewable on error. (See also Missionary Society of the M.E. Church v Ely, 56 OS 405, 47 NE 537 (1897); Mosier v Harmon, 29 OS 220 (1876).) Hollrah v. Lasance (Ohio 1900) 63 Ohio St. 58, 44 W.L.B. 80, 57 N.E. 964.

A probate judge may allow counsel for a legatee not a party to the proceedings to cross-examine witnesses offered by proponents. In re Jones' Estate (Ohio Prob. 1895) 2 Ohio Dec. 409, 2 Ohio N.P. 190, 2 Ohio N.P. 194, 2 Ohio N.P. 209.

Where no statutory right existed on the part of opponents to a lost will to cross-examine the witnesses offered by proponents, such right was left to discretion of the court, and court permitted persons opposing the probate of the will to cross-examine witnesses of the other party because they might be able to bring out facts of value to the court in arriving at a proper disposition of the case. In re Ayres' Will (Ohio Prob. 1940) 5 Ohio Supp. 239, 33 Ohio Law Abs. 1, 19 O.O. 465, affirmed 43 N.E.2d 918, 36 Ohio Law Abs. 267.

2. Notice

Where there is no interested person residing in the county where application is made to admit to probate a lost, spoliated, or destroyed will, notice by publication must be given. Baugarth v. Miller (Ohio 1875) 26 Ohio St. 541.

Written notice of an application for probate of a lost will must be given to an administrator of the estate resident of the county and known to the applicant. In re Simon's Estate (Ohio Prob. 1961) 177 N.E.2d 92, 86 Ohio Law Abs. 378, 86 Ohio Law Abs. 380, 20 O.O.2d 59.

Amendment of GC 10504–36 (RC 2107.27) by adding the words "known to be" before the words, "resident of the state" did not relieve the court from requiring notice to the next of kin of a testator who were then residents of the state of Ohio. (See also In re Estate of Bowles, 93 App 461, 113 NE(2d) 259 (1952).) Bowles' Estate v. Bowles' Heirs (Cuyahoga 1953) 96 Ohio App. 265, 114 N.E.2d 229, 66 Ohio Law Abs. 73, 54 O.O. 296.

Where admission of a will to probate has been refused by the probate court persons having no notice of the proceedings and refusal until too late to perfect an appeal to the court of common pleas from the order of refusal are not concluded thereby and may repropound the will notwithstanding the former order of refusal has not been vacated. (See also In re Estate of Bowles, 93 App 461, 113 NE(2d) 259 (1952).) Bowles' Estate v. Bowles' Heirs (Cuyahoga 1953) 96 Ohio App. 265, 114 N.E.2d 229, 66 Ohio Law Abs. 73, 54 O.O. 296.

The act of May 3, 1852, relating to wills states that a party seeking to prove a will "which has been lost, spoliated, or destroyed... shall... give written notice to all persons whose interest it may be to resist the probate, and who reside in the county where the testator resided at the time of his death... five days before the day on which such proof is to be made, or to give notice, by publication in a newspaper printed in the county thirty days before the day set for the hearing of such proof" means that written notice must be given all interested individuals in the county; it is only when there are no interested individuals that publication will suffice. In re Jones' Estate (Ohio Prob. 1895) 2 Ohio Dec. 409, 2 Ohio N.P. 190, 2 Ohio N.P. 194, 2 Ohio N.P. 209.

3. Burden of proof; evidence

The record of the probate of a lost will is prima facie evidence, in a contest proceeding, not only of the due attestation on execution of will but also of its contents. Banning v. Banning (Ohio 1861) 12 Ohio St. 437.

Presumption of revocation of a will is not overcome where the only testimony given at the hearing regarding the issue of revocation is that of a beneficiary under the terms of the will who would not benefit from the intestate succession of assets; the probate court could find that such testimony regarding the finding and location of a copy of the will lacks credibility. In re Estate of Brown (Ohio App. 2 Dist., Montgomery, 04-20-2001) No. 18611, 2001 WL 395346, Unreported.

Neither individual whom stepson had accused of burning stepfather's will, nor daughter of stepfather's wife were jointly and severally liable, in stepson's action alleging that wife had engaged in fraud, fraudulent conveyance, and conversion; daughter merely assisted wife by driving her to financial institutions, and individual accused of burning stepfather's will testified that he had not been involved in burning the will. Kemp v. Kemp (Ohio App. 5 Dist., 06-17-2005) 161 Ohio App.3d 671, 831 N.E.2d 1038, 2005-Ohio-3120, stay granted 106 Ohio St.3d 1467, 831 N.E.2d 437, 2005-Ohio-3653, appeal not allowed 107 Ohio St.3d 1408, 836 N.E.2d 1228, 2005-Ohio-5859. Trover And Conversion ⚖ 25

Hearsay testimony that testatrix intended to execute new will, thereby revoking legacy to former live-in companion contained in offered will, and that testatrix believed she had executed new will revoking disputed legacy, together with evidence that companion took key to testatrix' safety deposit box shortly after her death, was inadmissible in contest challenging will naming companion as sole legatee in absence of evidence that testatrix did in fact execute new will with required formalities and of content of new will. Gockel v. Eble (Ohio App. 8 Dist., 10-17-1994) 98 Ohio App.3d 281, 648 N.E.2d 539, dismissed, appeal not allowed 71 Ohio St.3d 1491, 646 N.E.2d 466. Wills ⚖ 293(4)

In order to prevail in a will contest, the contestant must do more than merely meet the prima facie case; the record of a hearing in the probate court on the order of probate is not before the common pleas court in a will contest, but whether the same or different evidence is presented in the two proceedings is immaterial, since the same evidence may or may not be sufficient to overcome the presumption arising from the order of probate. Carr v. Howard (Fayette 1969) 17 Ohio App.2d 233, 246 N.E.2d 563, 46 O.O.2d 360.

When a lost will has been admitted to probate this establishes a presumption in a contest thereof that the probated document is the last will of the testator. Carr v. Howard (Ohio Com.Pl. 1967) 15 Ohio Misc. 5, 237 N.E.2d 180, 42 O.O.2d 174, 44 O.O.2d 75, reversed 17 Ohio App.2d 233, 246 N.E.2d 563, 46 O.O.2d 360.

An unwitnessed, but dated and signed, carbon copy of a will which was revoked by a later will subsequently lost, to which copy was attached a typewritten statement that "the original draft of my last will is in the hands of [my] attorney... I have destroyed the [later] will recently drawn" by another attorney, does not comply with the formal requirements for the re-execution of a will and codicil and is not effective to revive such first will. Shinn v. Phillips (Cuyahoga 1964) 8 Ohio App.2d 58, 220 N.E.2d 674.

Where the only issue presented in an application to probate a lost will is that the deceased did not have knowledge of such loss, the proponent must establish by clear and convincing evidence that testator did not know of its loss; and requiring the proponent to establish lack of knowledge "by the best evidence" constitutes reversible error. (See also In re Estate of Bowles, 93 App 461, 113 NE(2d) 259 (1952).) Bowles' Estate v. Bowles' Heirs (Cuyahoga 1953) 96 Ohio App. 265, 114 N.E.2d 229, 66 Ohio Law Abs. 73, 54 O.O. 296.

Although one who seeks to establish a lost will should be required to produce evidence that is clear, convincing and satisfactory, yet the burden put upon him should not be prohibitive and it is not necessary that the presumption of revocation be overcome by evidence that is free from doubt. (See also In re Estate of Bowles, 93 App 461, 113 NE(2d) 259 (1952).) Bowles' Estate v. Bowles' Heirs (Cuyahoga 1953) 96 Ohio App. 265, 114 N.E.2d 229, 66 Ohio Law Abs. 73, 54 O.O. 296. Wills ⇐ 302(8)

Execution of a codicil is almost irrefutable evidence that on the date of its execution the testator believed the original will to be in existence and if it had been lost the testator did not know it. (See also In re Estate of Bowles, 93 App 461, 113 NE(2d) 259 (1952).) Bowles' Estate v. Bowles' Heirs (Cuyahoga 1953) 96 Ohio App. 265, 114 N.E.2d 229, 66 Ohio Law Abs. 73, 54 O.O. 296.

The plan of a will in remembering the persons who or charities that would be the natural objects of the testator's bounty, the care with which the will was drawn, the remarks of the testator thereafter that show a continuation of the state of mind of the testator at the time the will was drawn or small changes made in the general plan of the will by codicils all are relevant in support of the testator's lack of knowledge of the loss of the will. (See also In re Estate of Bowles, 93 App 461, 113 NE(2d) 259 (1952).) Bowles' Estate v. Bowles' Heirs (Cuyahoga 1953) 96 Ohio App. 265, 114 N.E.2d 229, 66 Ohio Law Abs. 73, 54 O.O. 296. Wills ⇐ 293(4)

To establish that the mutilation of a will occurred subsequent to the death of the testator, the evidence must satisfy the mind of the probate judge, and to establish a claim that the mutilation was made by some one other than the testator before his death and without his knowledge, the evidence must be clear and convincing. In re Tyler's Estate (Ohio 1953) 159 Ohio St. 492, 112 N.E.2d 668, 50 O.O. 419.

A codicil to an alleged lost will reciting that sum given to named legatee in original will was withdrawn and given to another legatee, and removing two persons named in original will to make distribution of certain personal effects of deceased, and naming two others, was properly not admitted to probate, where probate court determined that proponents of the alleged lost will had failed in their proof and declined to admit the alleged lost will to probate. In re Ayres' Will (Franklin 1940) 43 N.E.2d 918, 36 Ohio Law Abs. 267. Wills ⇐ 302(8)

Where a will is lost or destroyed and testator becomes insane, the evidence to overcome the presumption that testator revoked it must be certain, satisfactory, and conclusive that it was unrevoked and in existence after he became insane. Cole v. McClure (Ohio 1913) 88 Ohio St. 1, 102 N.E. 264, 11 Ohio Law Rep. 39. Evidence ⇐ 596(1); Wills ⇐ 306

The order admitting a lost will to probate is prima facie evidence of its validity, and in order to set aside such probate plaintiff must prove by a preponderance of the evidence either lack of mental capacity, undue influence, or that the alleged writing was not the last will and testament of the testatrix. Bloor v. Platt (Ohio 1908) 78 Ohio St. 46, 84 N.E. 604, 5 Ohio Law Rep. 619, 14 Am.Ann.Cas. 332.

Where a will is made, and the testator retains the custody of it, and after his death it cannot be found, the presumption arises that he destroyed it with the intention of revoking it; but when a copy of it is admitted to probate, such presumption is necessarily rebutted, and the burden of proof in an action to contest such will is on the plaintiff to show that the testator in fact did revoke it before his death. Hutson v. Hartley (Ohio 1905) 72 Ohio St. 262, 74 N.E. 197, 3 Ohio Law Rep. 3.

When a copy of a lost will is probated, and the probate is introduced by the contestees, RS 5948 puts the burden of invalidating the will upon the contestant. Hutson v. Hartley (Ohio 1905) 72 Ohio St. 262, 74 N.E. 197, 3 Ohio Law Rep. 3.

Once the probate court has found and established the contents of a lost, spoliated, or destroyed will, the order of probate is prima facie evidence of its due attestation, execution, validity, and contents, and in a will contest action the burden of proof is upon the contestant to invalidate such a will. Behrens v. Behrens (Ohio 1890) 47 Ohio St. 323, 24 W.L.B. 286, 25 N.E. 209, 21 Am.St.Rep. 820. Wills ⇐ 288(3)

The burden is on the proponents to satisfy the court that a "lost" will was in existence and unrevoked at the time of the testator's death, and this fact can be established either by presumption or circumstantial evidence as well as by direct evidence. Gibson v. Gibson (Ohio Cir. 1904) 15 Ohio C.D. 698, 6 Ohio C.C.(N.S.) 269, affirmed 72 Ohio St. 677, 76 N.E. 1124, 3 Ohio Law Rep. 73.

Where the will was in the custody of another, failure to find it after death raises no presumption of revocation; if not in existence after death and the testator was incapable of revoking it or had not access to it, it must have been fraudulently destroyed and the legal result is the same as if it was in existence at the time of death, complying with former GC 10546 (RC 2107.27), authorizing probate if spoliated since death. In re Thompson's Will (Ohio Prob. 1914) 16 Ohio NP(NS) 121, 59 W.L.B. 344.

Before a lost will may be admitted to probate, it is necessary to prove that the will was lost at a time subsequent to the testator's death. In re Gibson's Will (Ohio Com.Pl. 1903) 14 Ohio Dec. 331, affirmed 15 Ohio C.D. 698, 6 Ohio C.C.(N.S.) 269, affirmed 72 Ohio St. 677, 76 N.E. 1124, 3 Ohio Law Rep. 73.

A copy of a will made shortly after the death of the testator by his attorney is admissible as proof of the contents of the last will. In re Lasance's Estate (Ohio Prob. 1897) 7 Ohio Dec. 246, 5 Ohio N.P. 20. Wills ⇐ 293(4); Wills ⇐ 298

The burden of proof is on the proponents of a will, and when subscribing witnesses are dead, secondary evidence, such as a copy of a will made by the testator's attorney, is admissible to prove its contents. In re Lasance's Estate (Ohio Prob. 1897) 7 Ohio Dec. 246, 5 Ohio N.P. 20.

Where a testator, though enfeebled and on his death bed, obtains his will, tears off his signatures, and writes "destroyed by me" on it with the intent to revoke, such a will is not "spoliated" within the meaning of RS 5926 and may not be admitted to probate. In re Jones' Estate (Ohio Prob. 1895) 2 Ohio Dec. 409, 2 Ohio N.P. 190, 2 Ohio N.P. 194, 2 Ohio N.P. 209.

2107.28 Will lost, spoliated, or destroyed after admission to probate

If a will is lost, spoliated, destroyed, mislaid, or stolen, after it has been admitted to probate but before it has been recorded, upon notice being given to the persons as provided by section 2107.27 of the Revised Code, the probate court may hear testimony. If the court is satisfied that the contents of the will have been substantially proved, the court may record the will as thus proven. The record shall have all the effects of a record of the original will.

(2002 H 345, eff. 7–23–02; 1953 H 1, eff. 10–1–53; GC 10504–39)

Historical and Statutory Notes

Amendment Note: 2002 H 345 rewrote the section, which prior thereto read:

"If a will is lost, spoliated, destroyed, mislaid, or stolen, after it has been admitted to probate but before it has been recorded, upon notice being given to the persons as provided by section 2107.27 of the Revised Code, the probate court may hear testimony. If the court is satisfied that the contents of the will have been substantially proved, the court may record the will as thus proven. The record shall have all the effects of a record of the original will."

Pre–1953 H 1 Amendments: 114 v 353

Cross References

Stealing or secreting will, indictment need not allege ownership or value, 2941.22

Tampering with unrevoked will, 2913.42

Library References

Wills ⇐353, 423.
Westlaw Topic No. 409.
C.J.S. Wills §§ 738, 800 to 806, 818.

Research References

Encyclopedias
OH Jur. 3d Decedents' Estates § 1058, Admission to Record of Will Probated But Lost Before Recording.

Treatises and Practice Aids
Carlin, Baldwin's Ohio Practice, Merrick-Rippner Probate Law § 39:1, Lost, Spoliated, or Destroyed Will—Definition.

Carlin, Baldwin's Ohio Practice, Merrick-Rippner Probate Law § 39:2, Lost, Spoliated, or Destroyed Will—Statutory Provisions for Admission to Probate.

Carlin, Baldwin's Ohio Practice, Merrick-Rippner Probate Law § 39:3, Lost, Spoliated, or Destroyed Will—Evidence.

Carlin, Baldwin's Ohio Practice, Merrick-Rippner Probate Law § 39:9, Application to Record Lost, Spoliated, or Destroyed Will After Its Admission to Probate—Form.

Carlin, Baldwin's Ohio Practice, Merrick-Rippner Probate Law § 40:5, Revocation of Will—Physical Act—Presumption.

Carlin, Baldwin's Ohio Practice, Merrick-Rippner Probate Law § 2:121, Administration of Decedent's Estate—Checklist.

Carlin, Baldwin's Ohio Practice, Merrick-Rippner Probate Law § 39:10, Entry Setting for Hearing and Ordering Notice—Form.

Carlin, Baldwin's Ohio Practice, Merrick-Rippner Probate Law § 39:11, Entry to Record Lost, Spoliated, or Destroyed Will After Its Admission to Probate—Form.

NEW RECORD OF PROBATE

2107.29 Record of will destroyed

When the record of a will is destroyed, a copy of such will or a copy of such will and its probate may be recorded by the probate court if it appears to the court's satisfaction that such record has been destroyed and if it appears, by reason of a certificate signed and sealed by the probate judge, or by the clerk of the court of common pleas, that such copy is a true copy of the original will or a true copy of the original will and its probate.

(1953 H 1, eff. 10–1–53; GC 10504–41)

Historical and Statutory Notes

Pre–1953 H 1 Amendments: 114 v 353

Cross References

Lost or destroyed wills, probate records; restoration, 2729.01 to 2729.08

Library References

Wills ⇐353.
Westlaw Topic No. 409.
C.J.S. Wills §§ 738, 818.

Research References

Encyclopedias

OH Jur. 3d Decedents' Estates § 1069, New Record of Probate.

2107.30 Original will may again be admitted to probate

When the record of a will has been destroyed, the original will may again be admitted to probate and record.

(1953 H 1, eff. 10–1–53; GC 10504–42)

Historical and Statutory Notes

Pre–1953 H 1 Amendments: 114 v 353

Library References

Wills ⇐353.
Westlaw Topic No. 409.
C.J.S. Wills §§ 738, 818.

Research References

Encyclopedias

OH Jur. 3d Decedents' Estates § 1070, New Probate of Will.

2107.31 Limitations as to contests

Sections 2107.29 and 2107.30 of the Revised Code do not affect the proceedings or extend the time for contesting the validity of any will or for asserting rights thereunder. The record provided for in such sections must show that the original record was destroyed, and the time, as near as may be, when the will was originally admitted to probate and record.

(1953 H 1, eff. 10–1–53; GC 10504–44)

Historical and Statutory Notes

Pre–1953 H 1 Amendments: 114 v 354

Library References

Wills ⇐260.
Westlaw Topic No. 409.
C.J.S. Wills §§ 532 to 534.

Research References

Encyclopedias

OH Jur. 3d Decedents' Estates § 1069, New Record of Probate.
OH Jur. 3d Decedents' Estates § 1122, Effect of Destruction of Record.

2107.32 Notice

Every probate judge who admits a will or copy of a will to record under sections 2107.29 to 2107.31, inclusive, of the Revised Code, immediately thereafter shall give notice for three consecutive weeks in two weekly newspapers of his county if two are published therein, or if not, in one newspaper of general circulation in the county, stating the name of the person the record of whose will has been destroyed and the day when such record was supplied. All persons interested in the record, at any time within five years from the making of such record, may come into the probate court and contest the question whether the record thus supplied is the same as the record destroyed.

(1953 H 1, eff. 10–1–53; GC 10504–45)

Historical and Statutory Notes

Pre–1953 H 1 Amendments: 114 v 354

Cross References

Newspaper of general circulation defined, 7.12

Library References

Wills ⇐353.
Westlaw Topic No. 409.
C.J.S. Wills §§ 738, 818.

Research References

Encyclopedias

OH Jur. 3d Decedents' Estates § 1071, Notice.
OH Jur. 3d Decedents' Estates § 1072, Contest of Authenticity of Record; Appeals.

Treatises and Practice Aids

Carlin, Baldwin's Ohio Practice, Merrick-Rippner Probate Law § 39:8, Notice of Admission to Record of Destroyed Record of Will—Form.

Carlin, Baldwin's Ohio Practice, Merrick-Rippner Probate Law § 39:12, Notice of Admission to Record of Lost, Spoliated, or Destroyed Will After Admission to Probate—Form.

REVOCATION

2107.33 Revocation of will; will previously declared valid

(A) A will shall be revoked in the following manners:

(1) By the testator by tearing, canceling, obliterating, or destroying it with the intention of revoking it;

(2) By some person, at the request of the testator and in the testator's presence, by tearing, canceling, obliterating, or destroying it with the intention of revoking it;

(3) By some person tearing, canceling, obliterating, or destroying it pursuant to the testator's express written direction;

(4) By some other written will or codicil, executed as prescribed by this chapter;

(5) By some other writing that is signed, attested, and subscribed in the manner provided by this chapter.

(B) A will that has been declared valid and is in the possession of a probate judge also may be revoked according to division (C) of section 2107.084 of the Revised Code.

(C) If a testator removes a will that has been declared valid and is in the possession of a probate judge pursuant to section 2107.084 of the Revised Code from the possession of the judge, the declaration of validity that was rendered no longer has any effect.

(D) If after executing a will, a testator is divorced, obtains a dissolution of marriage, has the testator's marriage annulled, or, upon actual separation from the testator's spouse, enters into a separation agreement pursuant to which the parties intend to fully and finally settle their prospective property rights in the property of the other, whether by expected inheritance or otherwise, any disposition or appointment of property made by the will to the former spouse or to a trust with powers created by or available to the former spouse, any provision in the will conferring a general or special power of appointment on the former spouse, and any nomination in the will of the former spouse as executor, trustee, or guardian shall be revoked unless the will expressly provides otherwise.

(E) Property prevented from passing to a former spouse or to a trust with powers created by or available to the former spouse because of revocation by this section shall pass as if the former spouse failed to survive the decedent, and other provisions conferring some power or office on the former spouse shall be interpreted as if the spouse failed to survive the decedent. If provisions are revoked solely by this section, they shall be deemed to be revived by the testator's remarriage with the former spouse or upon the termination of a separation agreement executed by them.

(F) A bond, agreement, or covenant made by a testator, for a valuable consideration, to convey property previously devised or bequeathed in a will does not revoke the devise or bequest. The property passes by the devise or bequest, subject to the remedies on the bond, agreement, or covenant, for a specific performance or otherwise, against the devisees or legatees, that might be had by law against the heirs of the testator, or the testator's next of kin, if the property had descended to them.

(G) A testator's revocation of a will shall be valid only if the testator, at the time of the revocation, has the same capacity as the law requires for the execution of a will.

(H) As used in this section:

(1) "Trust with powers created by or available to the former spouse" means a trust that is revocable by the former spouse, with respect to which the former spouse has a power of withdrawal, or with respect to which the former spouse may take a distribution that is not subject to an ascertainable standard but does not mean a trust in which those powers of the former spouse are revoked by section 5815.31 of the Revised Code or similar provisions in the law of another state.

(2) "Ascertainable standard" means a standard that is related to a trust beneficiary's health, maintenance, support, or education.

(2006 H 416, eff. 1–1–07; 1999 H 59, eff. 10–29–99; 1986 S 248, eff. 12–17–86; 1978 H 505; 1975 S 145; 1953 H 1; GC 10504–47, 10504–48)

Historical and Statutory Notes

Pre–1953 H 1 Amendments: 114 v 354, 355

Amendment Note: 2006 H 416 substituted "5815.31" for "1339.62" in division (H)(1).

Amendment Note: 1999 H 59 rewrote division (A) and designated the final sentence thereof as new division (B); redesignated former divisions (B) through (E) as new divisions (C) through (F); added division (G); redesignated former division (F) as division (H); and made changes the reflect gender neutral language and other nonsubstantive changes. Prior to amendment, division (A) read:

"(A) A will shall be revoked by the testator by tearing, canceling, obliterating, or destroying it with the intention of revoking it, or by some person in the testator's presence, or by the testator's express written direction, or by some other written will or codicil, executed as prescribed by sections 2107.01 to 2107.62 of the Revised Code, or by some other writing that is signed, attested, and subscribed in the manner provided by those sections. A will that has been declared valid and is in the possession of a probate judge may also be revoked according to division (C) of section 2107.084 of the Revised Code."

Legislative Service Commission

1975:

Current law provides that a divorce will revoke provisions of a will relating to the divorced spouse only where the parties enter into a full property settlement. *Younker v. Johnson*, 160 Ohio St. 409 (1954).

This amended section would provide that divorce, dissolution of marriage, annulment, or separation with a property settlement will revoke those provisions of a will that relate to the former spouse, unless the will expressly provides otherwise. If provisions of a will should be revoked by the operation of this section, they would be considered to be revived by the remarriage of the parties or upon the termination of the separation agreement executed by them.

OSBA Probate and Trust Law Section

1986:

These amendments are designed to cover the following situations:

H & W, while married, each execute a will and H, who owns the bulk of the property, executes a revocable inter-vivos trust. H's will pours his entire estate into the trust. W's will pours her estate over into H's trust. H and W are divorced and their property is settled between them. The wills and trusts are left unchanged.

The amendments to Section 2107.33 are drawn to provide that if W dies first, her bequest to H's trust will be deemed revoked.

The proposed legislation also covers the situation where powers of appointment or nominations of a divorced spouse are made by the documents.

Cross References

Effect of end of marriage on trust powers reserved by grantor, 1339.62

Library References

Wills ⚖167.
Westlaw Topic No. 409.
C.J.S. Wills §§ 386, 389, 1621.
Baldwin's Ohio Legislative Service Annotated, 2006 H 416 LSC Analysis, p 3/L-1709

Research References

Encyclopedias

OH Jur. 3d Conversion in Equity § 14, Effect at Law.
OH Jur. 3d Decedents' Estates § 357, Methods of Revocation; Strict Compliance With Statute.
OH Jur. 3d Decedents' Estates § 358, Methods of Revocation; Strict Compliance With Statute—Revocation by Oral Will.
OH Jur. 3d Decedents' Estates § 359, Intent to Revoke; Necessity of Overt Act.
OH Jur. 3d Decedents' Estates § 361, Revocation Induced or Prevented by Fraud and Undue Influence.
OH Jur. 3d Decedents' Estates § 362, Using Formally Executed Writings to Revoke Will, Generally.
OH Jur. 3d Decedents' Estates § 363, Express Revocation by a Later Will.
OH Jur. 3d Decedents' Estates § 368, Revocation by Codicil.
OH Jur. 3d Decedents' Estates § 370, Revocation by Other Nontestamentary Writings.
OH Jur. 3d Decedents' Estates § 371, Revocation by Other Nontestamentary Writings—Agreements, Generally.
OH Jur. 3d Decedents' Estates § 373, Destructive Act and Intention to Revoke, Generally.

OH Jur. 3d Decedents' Estates § 377, Partial Revocation by Destructive Act.

OH Jur. 3d Decedents' Estates § 378, Specific Acts; Tearing and Cutting.

OH Jur. 3d Decedents' Estates § 379, Specific Acts; Tearing and Cutting—Cancellation, Obliteration, or Other Destruction.

OH Jur. 3d Decedents' Estates § 387, Placing Encumbrance on Devised Property; Agreement to Convey.

OH Jur. 3d Decedents' Estates § 390, Divorce, Annulment, or Separation.

OH Jur. 3d Decedents' Estates § 397, Discovery of Fraud or Change in Testator's Legal Circumstances as Revival of Revoked Will.

OH Jur. 3d Decedents' Estates § 408, Revocation of Written Will by Oral Will.

OH Jur. 3d Decedents' Estates § 453, Filing of Judgment and Will.

OH Jur. 3d Decedents' Estates § 544, "Husband," "Wife," or "Widow".

OH Jur. 3d Decedents' Estates § 813, Disposal by Contract of Sale or Grant of Option.

OH Jur. 3d Real Property Sales & Exchanges § 228, Claimants Under Deceased Vendor.

OH Jur. 3d Trusts § 74, Effect of Incorporation Into Will.

Forms

Ohio Forms Legal and Business § 24:143, Drafting Will.

Ohio Forms Legal and Business § 24:161, Entire Estate to Spouse—Alternatively to Children—Guardianship of Minors.

Ohio Forms Legal and Business § 24:205, Residue to Trust for Spouse and Children.

Ohio Forms Legal and Business § 24:213, Separate Mutual Will—by Spouse Pursuant to Agreement With Other Spouse—Entire Estate to Survivor and to Children on Death of Survivor.

Ohio Forms Legal and Business § 24:261, Prior Wills and Codicils.

Ohio Forms Legal and Business § 24:264, Divorce or Annulment of Marriage Not to Revoke Will.

Ohio Forms Legal and Business § 24:428, Spouse If Marriage Terminated by Divorce, Annulment, or Dissolution.

Ohio Forms Legal and Business § 24:911, Codicil—General Form.

Ohio Forms Legal and Business § 24:991, Instrument Revoking Will—Inability to Find Previous Will—Declaration of Intention to Remain Intestate Until Testator Executes Another Will.

Ohio Forms and Transactions KP 30.13, Codicils or Amendments.

Treatises and Practice Aids

Sowald & Morganstern, Baldwin's Ohio Practice Domestic Relations Law § 8:7, Effect of Decree.

Carlin, Baldwin's Ohio Practice, Merrick-Rippner Probate Law § 28:4, Codicils—Revocation of Will.

Carlin, Baldwin's Ohio Practice, Merrick-Rippner Probate Law § 29:1, Oral Will—Disposition of Personal Property—Statutory Requirements.

Carlin, Baldwin's Ohio Practice, Merrick-Rippner Probate Law § 30:7, Drafting a Will—Introductory Clause—Revocation of Former Wills.

Carlin, Baldwin's Ohio Practice, Merrick-Rippner Probate Law § 34:5, Declaring the Validity of a Will—Procedure for Obtaining a Judgment—Judgment.

Carlin, Baldwin's Ohio Practice, Merrick-Rippner Probate Law § 34:6, Declaring the Validity of a Will—Post-Judgment Revocation or Modification.

Carlin, Baldwin's Ohio Practice, Merrick-Rippner Probate Law § 40:1, Revocation of Will—Introduction.

Carlin, Baldwin's Ohio Practice, Merrick-Rippner Probate Law § 40:2, Revocation of Will—Physical Act—Statutory Provision.

Carlin, Baldwin's Ohio Practice, Merrick-Rippner Probate Law § 40:3, Revocation of Will—Physical Act—Elements—Intent.

Carlin, Baldwin's Ohio Practice, Merrick-Rippner Probate Law § 40:4, Revocation of Will—Physical Act—Elements—Act.

Carlin, Baldwin's Ohio Practice, Merrick-Rippner Probate Law § 40:7, Revocation of Will—Subsequent Written Instrument—Statutory Provision.

Carlin, Baldwin's Ohio Practice, Merrick-Rippner Probate Law § 40:8, Revocation of Will—Subsequent Written Instrument—Types—Wills and Codicils.

Carlin, Baldwin's Ohio Practice, Merrick-Rippner Probate Law § 40:9, Revocation of Will—Subsequent Written Instrument—Types—Nontestamentary Writing.

Carlin, Baldwin's Ohio Practice, Merrick-Rippner Probate Law § 43:2, Construing a Will—Action for Instructions—Preferability of Declaratory Judgment Action.

Carlin, Baldwin's Ohio Practice, Merrick-Rippner Probate Law § 68:5, Letters of Administration—Specific Qualifications of Administrators—Preference of Suitable Persons—Surviving Spouse.

Carlin, Baldwin's Ohio Practice, Merrick-Rippner Probate Law § 21:85, Rights of Surviving Spouse—Termination of Rights Upon Divorce, Dissolution, or Annulment of Marriage.

Carlin, Baldwin's Ohio Practice, Merrick-Rippner Probate Law § 30:57, Simple Will—Form.

Carlin, Baldwin's Ohio Practice, Merrick-Rippner Probate Law § 30:59, Revocation Clause—Form.

Carlin, Baldwin's Ohio Practice, Merrick-Rippner Probate Law § 40:10, Revocation of Will—Subsequent Written Instrument—Defective Execution.

Carlin, Baldwin's Ohio Practice, Merrick-Rippner Probate Law § 40:12, Revocation of Interest.

Carlin, Baldwin's Ohio Practice, Merrick-Rippner Probate Law § 68:22, Letters Testamentary—Qualifications for Executors—Divorced Wife as Executor.

Carlin, Baldwin's Ohio Practice, Merrick-Rippner Probate Law § 68:27, Letters Testamentary—Refusal of Appointment of Executor by Probate Court.

Restatement (2d) of Property, Don. Trans. § 33.2, Multiple Wills.

Restatement (3d) Property (Wills & Don. Trans.) § 4.1, Revocation of Wills.

Law Review and Journal Commentaries

Legal Separation Proceedings, Dawn S. Garrett. 50 Dayton B Briefs 18 (February 2001).

Recent Legislation Makes It Easier to Admit Lost, Spoliated or Destroyed Wills, David Simmons. 10 Prob L J Ohio 2 (September/October 1999).

Notes of Decisions

By operation of law; will or codicil 3
Constitutional issues 1
Effect on other documents, contracts 4
Evidence and testimony 5
Legal effect; procedure 2

---

1. Constitutional issues

RC 2107.33, which became effective January 1, 1976, is applicable to a will which was executed prior to that date and does not violate the prohibition contained in O Const Art II, § 28, against the passage of retroactive laws. Buehler v. Buehler (Hamilton 1979) 67 Ohio App.2d 7, 425 N.E.2d 905, 21 O.O.3d 330.

2. Legal effect; procedure

Where a blind testator directs a person to destroy his will in a fire after feeling the seals on the document and identifying it as his will, but the person burns another paper in its place and keeps the will, such facts do not constitute a revocation under this section since no sign or symbol of such attempted revocation appears on the paper itself. Kent v. Mahaffey (Ohio 1859) 10 Ohio St. 204.

Sufficient evidence established that mother was competent on dates she revoked a revocable trust established on her behalf, executed a new will, and deeded certain property to three of her children, even though mother had two strokes and several physicians gave deposition testimony that mother's cognitive function and ability to express herself were impaired; psychiatrist who examined mother on and shortly before the relevant dates gave deposition testimony that mother was coherent and her memory was intact, and opined that mother was competent, and attorney who prepared the documents at issue testified that mother understood the documents and also opined that mother was competent. Hillis v. Humphrey (Ohio App. 5 Dist., Perry, 06-30-2005) No. 05CA6, 2005-Ohio-3459, 2005 WL 1579392, Unreported, appeal not allowed 107 Ohio St.3d 1410, 836 N.E.2d 1230, 2005-Ohio-5859, reconsideration denied 107 Ohio St.3d 1701, 840 N.E.2d 205, 2005-Ohio-6763. Wills ⇐ 55(5)

Where testatrix tore will, handed torn will to her son and directed him to burn will in conjunction with a signed statement to effect that she tore will with intention of revoking it, trial judge could hold that she did legally revoke her will. In re Eliker's Estate (Darke 1940) 32 Ohio Law Abs. 465.

This section does not require that a will be so torn as to separate it into parts, or in any particular manner in order to revoke it. In re Eliker's Estate (Darke 1940) 32 Ohio Law Abs. 465. Wills ⟐ 170; Wills ⟐ 171

Former husband's daughters, who were executors of his estate, had power of attorney to revoke alleged gift to former wife pursuant to document which conferred upon them "full power and authority to do and perform all and every act and thing necessary to be done, as fully to all intents and purposes as I might or could do if personally present, with full power of substitution and revocation" (Per opinion of McFarland, J., with two judges concurring in the result). Bobo v. Stansberry (Ohio App. 4 Dist., 07-29-2005) 162 Ohio App.3d 565, 834 N.E.2d 373, 2005-Ohio-3928. Principal And Agent ⟐ 51

To make effective revocation of previously made will, there must be strict compliance with provisions of statute setting forth exclusive methods by which will may be revoked. In re Estate of Mantalis (Ohio App. 2 Dist., 01-31-1996) 109 Ohio App.3d 61, 671 N.E.2d 1062. Wills ⟐ 167

Oral will is not means recognized by statute for revocation of prior will, written or oral. In re Estate of Mantalis (Ohio App. 2 Dist., 01-31-1996) 109 Ohio App.3d 61, 671 N.E.2d 1062. Wills ⟐ 179

Validly executed written will cannot be revoked by subsequent oral will, even if oral will has been reduced to writing in compliance with statute. In re Estate of Mantalis (Ohio App. 2 Dist., 01-31-1996) 109 Ohio App.3d 61, 671 N.E.2d 1062. Wills ⟐ 179

One-year limitations on claims against the deceased vendor's estate did not apply to action by vendee for specific performance of contract for sale and purchase of real estate brought against vendor's heirs, devisees, and estate; action was for specific performance of contract rather than claim against estate and estate was joined as party in that it would have right to resort to real estate or sale proceeds if there was insufficient personalty in estate to pay claims. Hackmann v. Dawley (Ohio App. 10 Dist., 07-18-1995) 105 Ohio App.3d 363, 663 N.E.2d 1342. Executors And Administrators ⟐ 437(3); Specific Performance ⟐ 105(2)

Once a will is admitted to probate there is a presumption that it is valid, and a will contestant fails to overcome that presumption where he presents no evidence that an earlier separation of the last page of a will represented a form of mutilation which equated with revocation. Mattax v. Moore (Trumbull 1991) 72 Ohio App.3d 647, 595 N.E.2d 969, dismissed, jurisdictional motion overruled 61 Ohio St.3d 1419, 574 N.E.2d 1090.

Where a bequest to a former spouse is revoked under RC 2107.33, an alternative bequest to be divided equally among decedent's natural born children and stepchildren by reason of marriage to the ineligible former spouse is valid. Bowling v. Deaton (Warren 1986) 31 Ohio App.3d 17, 507 N.E.2d 1152, 31 O.B.R. 31.

Once a will is "made" in the manner provided in RC 2107.03, it remains a will unless and until it is revoked by one of the means provided in RC 2107.33. In re Nash's Will (Ohio Com.Pl. 1976) 50 Ohio Misc. 4, 361 N.E.2d 558, 3 O.O.3d 347, 4 O.O.3d 33.

Where the subscribing witnesses testify to the due and proper execution of a will, and that at the time of execution the instrument did not contain the black ink deletions apparent at the time of the hearing for probate, such will should be admitted to probate and record. In re Nash's Will (Ohio Com.Pl. 1976) 50 Ohio Misc. 4, 361 N.E.2d 558, 3 O.O.3d 347, 4 O.O.3d 33. Wills ⟐ 206

The methods of revoking a will provided in RC 2107.33 being exclusive, an unsigned statement in the handwriting of a testatrix on the margin of her will that she intends to revoke a bequest contained therein, which writing does not touch that in the will itself, is not a cancellation of the will, but is a mere writing without the formalities required by statute for the making or revoking of a will. Kronauge v. Stoecklein (Montgomery 1972) 33 Ohio App.2d 229, 293 N.E.2d 320, 62 O.O.2d 321. Wills ⟐ 173

An unwitnessed, but dated and signed, carbon copy of a will which was revoked by a later will subsequently lost, to which copy was attached a typewritten statement that "the original draft of my last will is in the hands of [my] attorney… I have destroyed the [later] will recently drawn" by another attorney, does not comply with the formal requirements for the re-execution of a will and codicil and is not effective to revive such first will. Shinn v. Phillips (Cuyahoga 1964) 8 Ohio App.2d 58, 220 N.E.2d 674.

A will once revoked in Ohio cannot be revived by an instrument which does not comply with the formalities required for a will. Shinn v. Phillips (Cuyahoga 1964) 8 Ohio App.2d 58, 220 N.E.2d 674.

Where the evidence indicates that a testator deliberately and carefully tore his signature and those of the attesting witnesses off of the original copy of a will of which there were executed copies in existence, the will was revoked. In re Steel's Estate (Ohio Prob. 1966) 8 Ohio Misc. 133, 219 N.E.2d 236, 37 O.O.2d 70.

Where a portion of a will has been excised, but extrinsic evidence is available to establish the content of the excised portion, the will may be probated in its entirety. In re Downie's Estate (Ohio Prob. 1966) 6 Ohio Misc. 36, 213 N.E.2d 833, 35 O.O.2d 31.

If a portion only of a will is torn, canceled, obliterated, or destroyed with the intent to revoke that part only, but not with the intent to revoke the whole will, the act will be ineffective to revoke either the initialed portion or the will itself. In re Downie's Estate (Ohio Prob. 1966) 6 Ohio Misc. 36, 213 N.E.2d 833, 35 O.O.2d 31. Wills ⟐ 171

Where testatrix had drawn lines through one paragraph of will, and stated that she had cancelled that paragraph, but kept will in her possession, testatrix did not intend to revoke entire will, there was no partial revocation, and will was valid. Keferl v. Trimbach (Montgomery 1953) 125 N.E.2d 753, 69 Ohio Law Abs. 419. Wills ⟐ 170; Wills ⟐ 174

Where the act of obliterating a portion of a will is not so conclusive as to supply an intention to revoke the entire will, the act must be accompanied by a clear intention on the part of the testator to destroy it before there can be a revocation. Keferl v. Trimbach (Montgomery 1953) 125 N.E.2d 753, 69 Ohio Law Abs. 419.

Where a testator tears out one of a will's several pages and leaves the remainder intact, evincing an intent to preserve it, he has not revoked the will. Coghlin v. Coghlin (Ohio 1908) 79 Ohio St. 71, 85 N.E. 1058, 6 Ohio Law Rep. 517.

Drawing lines through a clause with intent to revoke it and not the whole will does not revoke the clause as intended; accordingly, the whole will should be admitted to probate, including that clause if it remains legible. Giffin v. Brooks (Ohio 1891) 48 Ohio St. 211, 31 N.E. 743.

A will once known to have existed and to have been in the custody of the testator but not found after the testator's decease is presumed to have been destroyed by him with intent to revoke; testimony as to declarations of the testator is admissible to strengthen or repel the presumption of revocation, or to explain the act of destruction or cancellation. Behrens v. Behrens (Ohio 1890) 47 Ohio St. 323, 24 W.L.B. 286, 25 N.E. 209, 21 Am.St.Rep. 820.

Where a will cannot be found after death of testator, it will be presumed to have been destroyed by him; such presumption may either be fortified or weakened by evidence of declarations made by the testator subsequent to the making of the will. Gurley v. Armentraut (Ohio Cir. 1905) 17 Ohio C.D. 199, 6 Ohio C.C.N.S. 156.

The burden is on the proponents to satisfy the court that a "lost" will was in existence and unrevoked at the time of the testator's death, and this fact can be established either by presumption or circumstantial evidence as well as by direct evidence. Gibson v. Gibson (Ohio Cir. 1904) 15 Ohio C.D. 698, 6 Ohio C.C.(N.S.) 269, affirmed 72 Ohio St. 677, 76 N.E. 1124, 3 Ohio Law Rep. 73.

Where signatures of witnesses to a will are partially obliterated through negligence of testator in preserving the instrument, the will can be admitted to probate if the witnesses can identify the portion of the signature remaining, and the will has not been legally revoked or cancelled. In re Miller (Ohio Prob. 1926) 26 Ohio NP(NS) 209, 4 Ohio Law Abs. 736.

Obliteration of portion of a will by its being negligently carried in the testator's pocket is not evidence of cancellation or obliteration. In re Miller (Ohio Prob. 1926) 26 Ohio NP(NS) 209, 4 Ohio Law Abs. 736.

A bequest cannot be revoked by simply crossing the words out. Porterfield v. Porterfield (Ohio Com.Pl. 1907) 17 Ohio Dec. 448, 4 Ohio N.P.N.S. 654.

In the case of the probate of a spoliated will, the court must be judicially satisfied not only as to its proper execution and attestation, but also that the will was not revoked by the testator, and where the testator has removed his signature from the will,, a presumption of revocation arises which must be overcome. In re Jones' Estate (Ohio Prob. 1895) 2 Ohio Dec. 409, 2 Ohio N.P. 190, 2 Ohio N.P. 194, 2 Ohio N.P. 209.

The capacity requisite to revoke a will is the capacity requisite to make a will, and there is a clear distinction between intelligence enough to destroy and capacity to revoke; the destruction of a will does not revoke it, unless done with the intention to revoke. In re Jones' Estate (Ohio Prob. 1895) 2 Ohio Dec. 409, 2 Ohio N.P. 190, 2 Ohio N.P. 194, 2 Ohio N.P. 209.

Where a testator, though enfeebled and on his death bed, obtains his will, tears off his signatures, and writes "destroyed by me" on it with the intent to revoke, such a will is not "spoliated" within the meaning of RS 5926 and may not be admitted to probate. In re Jones' Estate (Ohio Prob. 1895) 2 Ohio Dec. 409, 2 Ohio N.P. 190, 2 Ohio N.P. 194, 2 Ohio N.P. 209.

Testimony that decedent cut up her will constitutes competent, credible evidence to sustain the trial court's determination that decedent had revoked her will, pursuant to RC 2107.33. In re Estate of Evans, No. 82 CA 11 (4th Dist Ct App, Gallia, 8–19–83).

3. By operation of law; will or codicil

Where a testator makes a bequest to his "intended wife" in his will, divorces such wife, and dies without revoking his will, the procuring of a divorce does not necessarily imply a revocation of the will, for it is consistent with an intent to annul her right of dower only and the consequent right of election. Charlton v. Miller (Ohio 1875) 27 Ohio St. 298, 22 Am.Rep. 307.

As a will and codicil are to be taken and construed together as parts of the same instrument, and the intent of the testator gathered from the whole, a codicil to a will will not revoke the same any further than is clearly expressed or necessarily to be inferred from it. Collier v. Collier's Ex'rs (Ohio 1854) 3 Ohio St. 369.

A resident of Jamaica having made a written will there sufficient to pass his estate in Ohio cannot, in moving into Ohio, revoke such a former will in whole or in part by a nuncupative will. McCune's Devisees v. House (Ohio 1837) 8 Ohio 144, 31 Am.Dec. 438.

The trial court was not required to include wife's proposed provision, which released inheritance and other property rights by both parties, in legal separation agreement; the legal separation agreement made a full and final determination of the property rights between the parties, which implicitly waived each parties' rights as a surviving spouse. Hering v. Hering (Ohio App. 9 Dist., Lorain, 01-26-2005) No. 03CA008410, 2005-Ohio-262, 2005 WL 161171, Unreported. Husband And Wife ⊜ 278(3)

Destruction of a will after testatrix became incapable of making a will by reason of insanity will not revoke such will. In re Eliker's Estate (Darke 1940) 32 Ohio Law Abs. 465.

Decedent's prior written will and codicil were not revoked by alleged oral will declared by decedent on day before his death, even though oral will was subsequently reduced to writing, inasmuch as oral will was not statutorily recognized means of revoking prior will. In re Estate of Mantalis (Ohio App. 2 Dist., 01-31-1996) 109 Ohio App.3d 61, 671 N.E.2d 1062. Wills ⊜ 179

Where the testator executes a first will, then a second will, and later executes a codicil to the first will which includes a ratification and confirmation of the first will, the codicil operates as a republication of the first will and revives the first will, while revoking the second will. In re Estate of Stormont (Greene 1986) 34 Ohio App.3d 92, 517 N.E.2d 259.

Where it is shown that a testator obtained a divorce and executed a property settlement pursuant thereto, a court may validly conclude that by such acts he intended, within the provisions of RC 2107.33, to revoke his previously made last will and testament devising all of his property to his spouse. In re McQuay's Estate (Franklin 1975) 44 Ohio App.2d 74, 335 N.E.2d 746, 73 O.O.2d 63. Wills ⊜ 193

In determining whether a subsequent divorce and property settlement is sufficient to cause revocation by implication of the provisions in deceased husband's will for the wife, the substantially smaller distribution for her provided by later agreement is evidence of intent to revoke earlier plan. Davis v. Davis (Ohio Com.Pl. 1970) 24 Ohio Misc. 17, 258 N.E.2d 277, 51 O.O.2d 388, 53 O.O.2d 48.

Where the testator divorced the wife designated in his last will to be appointed executrix, but continued their business relationship, shortly resumed living together, and never completed their property settlement, no implied revocation resulted of her designation to be named executrix. In re Davis' Estate (Ohio Prob. 1969) 22 Ohio Misc. 14, 256 N.E.2d 281, 50 O.O.2d 37, 51 O.O.2d 28.

A codicil, however well preserved, is dependent upon a will for its force and effect and cannot be used to substitute for a will which is lost, or mutilated after the codicil was completed. In re Steel's Estate (Ohio Prob. 1966) 8 Ohio Misc. 133, 219 N.E.2d 236, 37 O.O.2d 70. Wills ⊜ 233

A divorce which includes a property settlement impliedly revokes provision made for a wife in a will executed prior to divorce. Skorapa v. Skorapa (Ohio Prob. 1961) 177 N.E.2d 310, 87 Ohio Law Abs. 232, 17 O.O.2d 97.

A subsequently executed instrument purporting to be a will which is not regular on its face cannot be presumed to have been validly executed so as to revoke a prior will. Dyce v. Koch (Columbiana 1958) 157 N.E.2d 130, 79 Ohio Law Abs. 596.

A divorce decree in effect restoring to the parties their separate property rights, but not coupled with a voluntary separation agreement contemplating a full settlement of their property rights, does not warrant a court finding an implied revocation of a will executed during marriage. Lang v. Leiter (Wood 1956) 103 Ohio App. 119, 144 N.E.2d 332, 3 O.O.2d 184. Wills ⊜ 193

Where husband during marriage executed will devising half of his property to his wife, and thereafter wife obtained divorce decree confirming fair and equitable property division, divorce impliedly revoked provision in will for benefit of wife. Younker v. Johnson (Ohio 1954) 160 Ohio St. 409, 116 N.E.2d 715, 52 O.O. 320. Wills ⊜ 193

Making of subsequent will which is inconsistent with earlier will, operates as a revocation of the earlier will without specific words of revocation, under this section, although such subsequent will is not in existence and could not be probated as a "lost, spoliated or destroyed" will under GC 10504–35 (RC 2107.26). Hennessy v. Volz (Hamilton 1938) 59 Ohio App. 1, 16 N.E.2d 1019, 27 Ohio Law Abs. 127, 12 O.O. 335.

A will is revoked by the execution of a second will duly executed, when the second will contains an express clause of revocation, or is utterly inconsistent with the provisions of the first will; if the second will be inconsistent in part with the first, it revokes the first will to that extent. Paully v. Crooks (Richland 1931) 41 Ohio App. 1, 179 N.E. 364, 11 Ohio Law Abs. 371, 35 Ohio Law Rep. 495. Wills ⊜ 179

In will contest, charge of the trial court that if the testator executed a second or subsequent will a former will would be revoked, is prejudicial error. Paully v. Crooks (Richland 1931) 41 Ohio App. 1, 179 N.E. 364, 11 Ohio Law Abs. 371, 35 Ohio Law Rep. 495.

"Codicil" does not revoke former will except to extent that its provisions are inconsistent with will, unless intent to revoke is expressed. Foye v. Foye (Ohio App. 1928) 35 Ohio App. 283, 172 N.E. 386, 27 Ohio Law Rep. 117. Wills ⊜ 184(3)

Mere divorce decree does not of itself revoke the will of a husband or wife made in favor of a surviving spouse. Pardee v. Grubiss (Cuyahoga 1929) 34 Ohio App. 474, 171 N.E. 375, 7 Ohio Law Abs. 459. Divorce ⊜ 321.5; Wills ⊜ 193

Where a divorce is coupled with settlement of property rights, there is an implied revocation of a prior will of one spouse in favor of the divorced spouse so far as said will makes bequest or devise to divorced spouse. Pardee v. Grubiss (Cuyahoga 1929) 34 Ohio App. 474, 171 N.E. 375, 7 Ohio Law Abs. 459.

A codicil operates not only as a new adoption of the will to which it refers, but also as a revocation of an intermediate will. In re Stocker's Will (Ohio Prob. 1926) 26 Ohio NP(NS) 112, 4 Ohio Law Abs. 205.

Two clauses written by the testatrix into her will and signed by her which direct a different distribution of two bequests are not codicils, as they were not witnessed as provided by law, nor do these clauses work a revocation of any provisions in the will. Porterfield v. Porterfield (Ohio Com.Pl. 1907) 17 Ohio Dec. 448, 4 Ohio N.P.N.S. 654. Wills ⊜ 184(2)

One may revoke or modify a will by a codicil, or revoke the codicil and allow the will to stand; but he cannot revoke a will and allow the codicil to stand, for the reason that a codicil is ancillary or supplemental to and depends upon the will. In re Ayres' Will (Ohio Prob. 1940) 5 Ohio Supp. 239, 33 Ohio Law Abs. 1, 19 O.O. 465, affirmed 43 N.E.2d 918, 36 Ohio Law Abs. 267. Wills ⊜ 175

4. Effect on other documents, contracts

The probate court has authority to determine whether a divorce decree constitutes an implied revocation of legacies to the wife in a will executed prior to the divorce. Davis v. Wallace (Belmont 1962) 192 N.E.2d 291, 91 Ohio Law Abs. 396, 27 O.O.2d 80.

A married woman who is named as a beneficiary in a policy of life insurance is entitled to the proceeds upon the death of her insured husband, notwithstanding a divorce obtained by her from the insured before his death. Cannon v. Hamilton (Ohio 1963) 174 Ohio St. 268, 189 N.E.2d 152, 22 O.O.2d 331. Insurance ⊜ 3481(1)

On the evidence, a release by two children of all claims against their stepmother did not affect the residuary clause of her will which left the residue of her estate to them. McFadyen v. Hanisch (Ohio 1959) 169 Ohio St. 471, 160 N.E.2d 272, 8 O.O.2d 477.

Where wife devised real estate to husband who had by virtue of power of attorney entered into contract of sale of property prior to her death,

2107.33
Note 4

property passes to husband subject to contract under this section. Sells v. Needles (Franklin 1946) 69 N.E.2d 770, 47 Ohio Law Abs. 425.

Where unrevoked and unamended, a revocable and amendable living trust has been incorporated in a will by reference, it does not invalidate a testamentary devise to the trustee of such trust to be administered according to the terms and conditions of the trust and is not repugnant to this section. Bolles v. Toledo Trust Co. (Ohio 1944) 144 Ohio St. 195, 58 N.E.2d 381, 157 A.L.R. 1164, 29 O.O. 376. Wills ⇐ 98; Wills ⇐ 168

The doctrine of implied revocation does not obtain as to after-acquired property devised by will, nor to devised specific property conveyed by a testator after the execution of the will and reconveyed to him before his death. Ridenour v. Callahan (Ohio Cir. 1906) 19 Ohio C.D. 65, 8 Ohio C.C.N.S. 585. Wills ⇐ 167; Wills ⇐ 194

Contract to sell land devised was an alteration but not a revocation of a devise of interest in said land. Rugg v. Larimore (Ohio Com.Pl. 1927) 27 Ohio N.P.N.S. 96.

Twin wills made by a husband and wife must each be the consideration for the other, reciprocity must pervade both wills, and the contract to make such wills must be clear; if a power is reserved to one party to alter or revoke without the consent of the other, the other will cannot be upheld. Albery v. Sessions (Ohio Com.Pl. 1895) 3 Ohio Dec. 330, 2 Ohio N.P. 237.

Where a husband and wife enter into a separation agreement due to a scheduled visit from the husband's mistress and where the husband and wife resume their marital relationship at the end of the visit, such separation agreement is deemed terminated and will provisions in favor of the surviving spouse are revived. In re Estate of Daneman, No. CA 85-07 (5th Dist Ct App, Knox, 12-4-85).

Where a divorce decree provides that each party to the divorce will maintain a will leaving their children at least their intestate share, failure of one party to comply with such provision does not relieve the other party of its obligation to make annual property settlement installment payments since the will provision is a tangential issue rather than a condition precedent to the property settlement. Thomas v Ferguson, Nos. 11019 and 11034 (9th Dist Ct App, Summit, 8-10-83).

5. Evidence and testimony

Trial court acted within its discretion in preventing will contestants from asking director of county humane society questions about society's treatment of animals, in proceedings involving will that left entire estate to humane society for care of pet cat, although contestants alleged that director's testimony would have confirmed that during certain period large number of animals were euthanized rather than adopted out, and that testimony was relevant to issue of whether testatrix intended to revoke will, where there was no evidence testatrix revoked will. Waldecker v. Pfefferle (Ohio App. 6 Dist., Erie, 11-08-2002) No. E-02-002, 2002-Ohio-6187, 2002 WL 31521467, Unreported, appeal not allowed 98 Ohio St.3d 1491, 785 N.E.2d 473, 2003-Ohio-1189. Wills ⇐ 296

Revocation of a will is supported by (1) direct evidence that the testator revoked the will after learning of her terminal illness immediately prior to her final hospitalization and death, (2) the testator's statement that the will was "no good" or "isn't right" is consistent with the sale of her home which is the subject of a specific bequest to the stepdaughter who has filed a claim to produce the will, and (3) the testator's specific instructions on the distribution of personal items to her husband's children at the time of revocation. Schroy v. Tignor (Ohio App. 5 Dist., Muskingum, 06-17-1998) No. CT97-0026, 1998 WL 346861, Unreported.

To obtain probate of a will allegedly lost before death of testatrix, proponent must prove that there was a will duly executed and unrevoked at death of testatrix and by clear and convincing testimony that testatrix did not know of its loss. In re Hughes' Estate (Butler 1948) 84 Ohio App. 275, 85 N.E.2d 583, 53 Ohio Law Abs. 410, 39 O.O. 404. Wills ⇐ 302(8)

In action to set aside will, copy of which had been probated because original could not be found after testator's death, jury could consider testimony that testator had said he had destroyed will, though there was no direct testimony of act of destruction by testator, and plaintiff was entitled to a charge to that effect. Chenoweth v. Cary (Madison 1939) 31 N.E.2d 716, 30 Ohio Law Abs. 98, 17 O.O. 76, appeal dismissed 136 Ohio St. 123, 23 N.E.2d 949, 17 O.O. 86. Evidence ⇐ 269(2); Trial ⇐ 207

2107.34 Afterborn or pretermitted heirs; effect on will

If, after making a last will and testament, a testator has a child born alive, or adopts a child, or designates an heir in the manner provided by section 2105.15 of the Revised Code, or if a child or designated heir who is absent and reported to be dead proves to be alive, and no provision has been made in such will or by settlement for such pretermitted child or heir, or for the issue thereof, the will shall not be revoked; but unless it appears by such will that it was the intention of the testator to disinherit such pretermitted child or heir, the devises and legacies granted by such will, except those to a surviving spouse, shall be abated proportionately, or in such other manner as is necessary to give effect to the intention of the testator as shown by the will, so that such pretermitted child or heir will receive a share equal to that which such person would have been entitled to receive out of the estate if such testator had died intestate with no surviving spouse, owning only that portion of the testator's estate not devised or bequeathed to or for the use and benefit of a surviving spouse. If such child or heir dies prior to the death of the testator, the issue of such deceased child or heir shall receive the share the parent would have received if living.

If such pretermitted child or heir supposed to be dead at the time of executing the will has lineal descendants, provision for whom is made by the testator, the other legatees and devisees need not contribute, but such pretermitted child or heir shall take the provision made for the pretermitted child's or heir's lineal descendants or such part of it as, in the opinion of the probate judge, may be equitable. In settling the claim of a pretermitted child or heir, any portion of the testator's estate received by a party interested, by way of advancement, is a portion of the estate and shall be charged to the party who has received it.

Though measured by Chapter 2105. of the Revised Code, the share taken by a pretermitted child or heir shall be considered as a testate succession. This section does not prejudice the right of any fiduciary to act under any power given by the will, nor shall the title of innocent purchasers for value of any of the property of the testator's estate be affected by any right given by this section to a pretermitted child or heir.

(2002 H 242, eff. 5-16-02; 129 v 7, eff. 10-5-61; 1953 H 1; GC 10504-49)

Historical and Statutory Notes

Pre-1953 H 1 Amendments: 114 v 355

Amendment Note: 2002 H 242 substituted "Chapter 2105." for "sections 2105.01 to 2105.21, inclusive" in the last paragraph; and made changes to reflect gender neutral language.

OSBA Probate and Trust Law Section

1961:

The committee now unanimously recommends that an amendment be sponsored to the After-Born or Pretermitted Heir Statute, Sec. 2107.34, R. C. Under this statute, as now constituted, if a testator has a living child, leaves it nothing in his will, there is no mention in the will of an after-born child, and the testator later has an after-born child without changing the will before his death, the living child is disinherited while the after-born child takes his intestate share.

A reading of the Ohio cases will show clearly that the purpose of the pretermitted heir statute is not to rewrite the testator's will nor to favor after-born children over living children, but is to protect the rights of children who were not born or not considered or who were overlooked at the time of the execution of the will. The statute in its present form, however, goes beyond this and actually benefits the after-born child where there is no mention of such child in the testator's will. Under the present statute, if the testator has a living child at the time his will is executed and no mention is made in the will of after-born children and the testator leaves all of his property to his wife, or someone else, the after-born child will take his intestate share and the living child will be disinherited. This is the inequity in the statute.

It is the opinion of the committee that the existing statute should be amended to correct this obvious injustice. This amendment should be made bearing in mind that it is not the purpose of this statute to violate the intention of the testator but merely to provide for the most equitable distribution of the property where children are born after the execution of the will and there is no evidence of the intention of the testator concerning the rights of the after-born child or children.

At Common Law, after-born children didn't inherit. Their rights have been allowed by statute in about all states.

The Pennsylvania statute does not permit the after-born child to have an interest in property passing to the surviving spouse. The Texas statute states that where a child was living when the will was executed, and the living child has been completely excluded from the testator's will and the surviving spouse is the principal beneficiary, the after-born has no right to any of testator's property. The Model Probate Code provides that if "substantially" all of testator's estate went to the surviving spouse, the after-born child has no right in the estate. There is no mention of designated heirs, grandchildren or more remote issue, abatement or advancements as there is in the Ohio Code.

It appears that under the Model Probate Code, the question of "substantially all" of the estate would always have to be litigated when more than token gifts were given to persons other than the surviving spouse. Also, the statute is not as inclusive as ours. The Texas statute has the disadvantage of revoking the will when there were no children living at the time the will was executed. The present Ohio statute corrected this situation in 1932 when it was adopted. The Pennsylvania statute simplifies the situation in that any property going to the surviving spouse is not subject to this statute. The committee is of the opinion that this is the most desirable result, and that if the Ohio statute were amended in this respect only, it would solve our problem and be a more inclusive statute than either the Pennsylvania or Texas statutes or the Model Probate Code.

Library References

Descent and Distribution ⟐47.
Wills ⟐191, 192, 804.
Westlaw Topic Nos. 124, 409.
C.J.S. Descent and Distribution §§ 50 to 54.
C.J.S. Wills §§ 417 to 419, 1719 to 1722.

Research References

Encyclopedias

OH Jur. 3d Contribution, Indemnity, & Subrogation § 9, Contribution Governed by Statute.
OH Jur. 3d Cotenancy & Partition § 82, Pretermitted Children.
OH Jur. 3d Decedents' Estates § 114, Designated Heirs—No Transmission of Right of Inheritance.
OH Jur. 3d Decedents' Estates § 169, Persons as to Whom Doctrine Applies.
OH Jur. 3d Decedents' Estates § 170, Generally; Time of Taking Effect.
OH Jur. 3d Decedents' Estates § 236, Restrictions as to Pretermitted Children.
OH Jur. 3d Decedents' Estates § 238, Restrictions as to Pretermitted Children—Effect of Provision by Will or Settlement.
OH Jur. 3d Decedents' Estates § 239, Restrictions as to Pretermitted Children—Pretermitted Heir's Share; When Interest in Real Property Passes.
OH Jur. 3d Decedents' Estates § 328, Devisees and Legatees.
OH Jur. 3d Decedents' Estates § 391, Birth or Adoption of Child.
OH Jur. 3d Decedents' Estates § 392, Designation of an Heir; Return of Child or Designated Heir Absent and Reported Dead.
OH Jur. 3d Decedents' Estates § 846, Abatement of Legacies to Pay Share of Pretermitted Child or Heir.

Forms

Ohio Forms Legal and Business § 24:91, Agreement—to Execute Joint or Mutual Wills—by Husband and Wife—Estate to Survivor.
Ohio Forms Legal and Business § 24:161, Entire Estate to Spouse—Alternatively to Children—Guardianship of Minors.
Ohio Forms Legal and Business § 24:205, Residue to Trust for Spouse and Children.
Ohio Forms Legal and Business § 24:421, General Clause.
Ohio Forms Legal and Business § 24:426, Child Born or Adopted After Execution of Will.
Ohio Forms Legal and Business § 24:761, Proportionate Abatement—Devises.
Ohio Forms and Transactions KP 30.07, Disinheritance of Children.

Treatises and Practice Aids

Carlin, Baldwin's Ohio Practice, Merrick-Rippner Probate Law § 17:2, Designation—Effect.
Carlin, Baldwin's Ohio Practice, Merrick-Rippner Probate Law § 20:5, Advancement—Rights of a Pretermitted Child.
Carlin, Baldwin's Ohio Practice, Merrick-Rippner Probate Law § 47:1, Afterborn or Pretermitted Heirs—Definitions.
Carlin, Baldwin's Ohio Practice, Merrick-Rippner Probate Law § 47:2, Afterborn or Pretermitted Heirs—Statutory Provisions.
Carlin, Baldwin's Ohio Practice, Merrick-Rippner Probate Law § 47:3, Afterborn or Pretermitted Heirs—Explanatory Chart 1.
Carlin, Baldwin's Ohio Practice, Merrick-Rippner Probate Law § 47:4, Afterborn or Pretermitted Heirs—Explanatory Chart 2.
Carlin, Baldwin's Ohio Practice, Merrick-Rippner Probate Law § 47:5, Afterborn or Pretermitted Heirs—Intent to Disinherit.
Carlin, Baldwin's Ohio Practice, Merrick-Rippner Probate Law § 30:21, Drafting a Will—Beneficiary Clauses—Disinheritance of Afterborn or Pretermitted Heirs.
Carlin, Baldwin's Ohio Practice, Merrick-Rippner Probate Law § 30:121, Disinheritance of Children—Form.
Restatement (2d) of Property, Don. Trans. § 34.2, Issue of Donor Omitted.
Restatement (3d) Property (Wills & Don. Trans.) § 9.6, Protection of Child or Descendant Against Unintentional Disinheritance.

Law Review and Journal Commentaries

Ghosts from the Grave-Inheriting Through the Predeceased Under Ohio Law. Kevin Purcell, 50 Clev St L Rev 189 (2002-03).

Notes of Decisions

Adopted children 1
Construction of will 5
Heir at law 3
Intention to disinherit 4
Procedural issues 6
Real estate 2
Revocation by birth 8
Settlement 7

---

1. Adopted children

An adopted grandchild is entitled to share in a trust as a beneficiary where the grandchild is adopted after the death of the settlor but before the eldest biological grandchild reaches the age of thirty, the time at which the trustee is directed to begin payments from the trust corpus and the time at which the class of beneficiaries closes. Bank One, Youngstown, N.A. v. Heltzel (Trumbull 1991) 76 Ohio App.3d 524, 602 N.E.2d 412, motion overruled 63 Ohio St.3d 1458, 590 N.E.2d 753.

Child adopted under former GC 8029 (RC 3107.07) and GC 8030 (RC 3107.09), has same rights as natural child to have will of parent, executed before adoption, set aside under this section. Surman v. Surman (Cuyahoga 1925) 21 Ohio App. 434, 153 N.E. 873, 3 Ohio Law Abs. 395, affirmed 114 Ohio St. 579, 151 N.E. 708, 4 Ohio Law Abs. 276, 24 Ohio Law Rep. 374.

A child adopted after the making of a will by the adopting parent is entitled to have the will revoked. Surman v. Surman (Ohio 1926) 114 Ohio St. 579, 151 N.E. 708, 4 Ohio Law Abs. 276, 24 Ohio Law Rep. 374.

2. Real estate

Where, in the administration of an estate, notwithstanding the fractional interest of a pretermitted child in the real estate of which the testator died seized, the testator's entire interest is transferred to the surviving spouse who is the sole beneficiary under the will, and subsequently the surviving spouse is adjudged an incompetent and, in guardianship proceedings, the fee simple title to such property is transferred to a purchaser for value by order of the probate court, neither res judicata nor estoppel by judgment is available to prevent such pretermitted child from claiming the fractional interest to which he is entitled. Twitchell v. Alexander & Liggett, Inc. (Franklin 1961) 115 Ohio App. 51, 184 N.E.2d 421, 20 O.O.2d 186.

When a person having a child or children executes his will and thereafter another child is born for whom no provision is made in the will or by codicil thereto, the testator, as to such after-born child, dies intestate, and if realty is part of his estate, after-born child may maintain action in partition to have set off to him in severalty his share of such realty.

Krueger v. Krueger (Ohio 1924) 111 Ohio St. 369, 145 N.E. 753, 2 Ohio Law Abs. 771, 22 Ohio Law Rep. 635.

A devise to a widow for life with remainder to the children generally, without naming them, is not a provision for an after-born child. Weiland v. Muntz (Ohio Cir. 1903) 15 Ohio C.D. 185, 2 Ohio C.C.N.S. 71.

3. Heir at law

Even though by explicit language in her will a testatrix, having one child, undertakes to disinherit an after-born child by devising her entire estate to her husband, such after-born child surviving the testatrix will inherit from the mother as her heir-at-law as if she died intestate. German Mut. Ins. Co. v. Lushey (Ohio 1902) 66 Ohio St. 233, 47 W.L.B. 500, 64 N.E. 120.

Where a testatrix having a child living devises all her estate to her husband, an afterborn child will inherit from the mother as an heir at law, notwithstanding that such testatrix undertook to disinherit such afterborn child. German Mut. Ins. Co. v. Lushey (Ohio 1902) 66 Ohio St. 233, 47 W.L.B. 500, 64 N.E. 120. Descent And Distribution ⟐ 47(3)

4. Intention to disinherit

In the probate of a will in which the surviving spouse is named as the sole beneficiary, evidence that at the time of the execution of the will the testator had three living children, and therefore in effect intended to disinherit such children, that thereafter the testator made no provision in his will for an after-born child but did make some provision for it by changes made in the beneficiaries of his life insurance policies, is insufficient to show an intention of the testator to disinherit such after-born child. Twitchell v. Alexander & Liggett, Inc. (Franklin 1961) 115 Ohio App. 51, 184 N.E.2d 421, 20 O.O.2d 186. Descent And Distribution ⟐ 47(2)

An intention to disinherit a pretermitted child can be implied from the facts and circumstances surrounding the testator at the time of execution of the will. Spieldenner v. Spieldenner (Ohio Prob. 1954) 122 N.E.2d 33, 69 Ohio Law Abs. 142, 54 O.O. 290.

Where testator leaves everything to his wife and further provides "This item shall continue in full force and effect regardless of whether or not any child or children may hereafter be born to my said wife and myself,…" such will under this section disinherits child adopted by testator and his wife after will was executed, even though item did not specifically refer to after-adopted children. York v. York (Montgomery 1944) 60 N.E.2d 70, 42 Ohio Law Abs. 242.

5. Construction of will

Where a testator in his will employs a term which standing alone may seem to designate a class of persons as his legatees, but when viewed in light of the circumstances and the construction of the whole will it is apparent that the term was used as a substitute for the legatees' names and to identify individuals, such words will not be held to embrace a class of persons, but will be confined to the individual persons designated. Starling's Ex'r v. Price (Ohio 1864) 16 Ohio St. 29.

Evidence supported trial court finding that child was a pretermitted heir of testator; testator executed a will prior to the birth of child, the will made no provisions for child, and the will did not indicate a desire to disinherit any after-born children. Dircksen v. Dircksen (Ohio App. 3 Dist., Shelby, 12-27-2004) No. 17-04-08, 2004-Ohio-7041, 2004 WL 2980658, Unreported. Descent And Distribution ⟐ 47(3)

A bequest to a class of persons "living at the time of my death" includes in such class a child en ventre sa mere who is a viable unborn child capable of sustaining life outside the mother's womb even though not born until three days after the time of the death of testatrix. Ebbs v. Smith (Ohio Com.Pl. 1979) 59 Ohio Misc. 133, 394 N.E.2d 1034, 11 O.O.3d 356, 13 O.O.3d 345.

The surviving children of a designated heir who predeceases his designator are not, upon the death of such designator, heirs at law or next of kin of such designator, and do not under the statute of descent and distribution have any right of inheritance in the estate of such designator, nor may they contest will, unless, under this section, the designation of the heir occurs after the execution of a last will and testament of the designator and no provision is made in such will or by settlement for such designated heir or his children; in such case, unless it appears by such will that it was the intention of the testator to disinherit such designated heir, the children of the latter receive a share equal to that which he, if living, would have been entitled to receive out of the estate if such designator-testator had died intestate. Kirsheman v. Paulin (Ohio 1951) 155 Ohio St. 137, 98 N.E.2d 26, 44 O.O. 134. Descent And Distribution ⟐ 28

Will providing that "the income of my said estate to be used for the purpose of maintaining, supporting and educating my said children until the youngest shall become twenty-five years, when a distribution shall be made between my said children, share and share alike," provides for children born after, as well as for those living at the time of, its execution, and there is no pretermission of such after-born children. Provident Sav. Bank & Trust Co. v. Nash (Hamilton 1945) 75 Ohio App. 493, 62 N.E.2d 736, 31 O.O. 290.

A devise to a widow for life with remainder to the children generally, without naming them, is not a provision for an after-born child. Weiland v. Muntz (Ohio Cir. 1903) 15 Ohio C.D. 185, 2 Ohio C.C.N.S. 71.

A child born after the making of the will but before the testator's death who is not provided for in the will takes an equal share of the testator's estate with the other children as if the testator had died intestate, notwithstanding specific bequests to the other children. Weiland v. Muntz (Ohio Cir. 1903) 15 Ohio C.D. 185, 2 Ohio C.C.N.S. 71.

Where a testator had no children at the time of executing his will and has made clear his intention that his will shall apply to unborn children, it is not for the court to inquire whether such provision was large or small, equal or unequal, vested or contingent, present or future. McMillan v. McMillan (Ohio Com.Pl. 1912) 23 Ohio Dec. 69, 12 Ohio NP(NS) 593. Wills ⟐ 497(7)

6. Procedural issues

A common pleas court has jurisdiction to determine and enforce the right to contribution given by the wills act to a child born after the execution of the will of its parent. McGarry v. Smith (Ohio 1871) 22 Ohio St. 190.

Testator's siblings waived their appellate argument that the pretermitted heir statute was unconstitutional, in action filed by testator's siblings challenging the parentage of testator's child, where siblings failed to raise the issue in the trial court, or object to the application of the statute. Dircksen v. Dircksen (Ohio App. 3 Dist., Shelby, 12-27-2004) No. 17-04-08, 2004-Ohio-7041, 2004 WL 2980658, Unreported. Children Out-of-wedlock ⟐ 88

Where in administration of an estate the existence of pretermitted heirs was overlooked, the estate could not, upon a reopening of the estate for redistribution of the assets, have a redetermination of the inheritance tax. In re Cones' Estate (Ohio Prob. 1961) 184 N.E.2d 776, 88 Ohio Law Abs. 577.

RS 5961 does not repeal RS 5914, permitting a testator to bequeath his property to any person to whom he may desire, but simply places a limitation upon the general power there conferred. German Mut. Ins. Co. v. Lushey (Ohio Cir. 1900) 11 Ohio C.D. 52, affirmed 66 Ohio St. 233, 47 W.L.B. 500, 64 N.E. 120.

A revoked will having been admitted to probate may be contested by one who would, if the will is set aside, take an estate in the property devised. Myers v. Barrow (Ohio Cir. 1888) 2 Ohio C.D. 52.

A will revoked by the operation of law before the death of the testator but probated after his death may be contested by one who would take an estate if will is set aside. Myers v. Barrow (Ohio Cir. 1888) 2 Ohio C.D. 52.

7. Settlement

A devise to wife for life "and after her death to the heirs of her body begotten," does not provide for a child subsequently born to him, under RS 5959, relating to the effect on a will where a child is born after the will is executed and there is no provision "made for such child by some settlement, or… in the will." Rhodes v. Weldy (Ohio 1889) 46 Ohio St. 234, 21 W.L.B. 110, 20 N.E. 461, 15 Am.St.Rep. 584. Wills ⟐ 191

Where decedent executed a will naming his wife and certain institutions as beneficiaries and subsequent to the making of such will adopted a child for whom he created an irrevocable trust, and later died without disturbing his will, such adopted child had no interest in the property of decedent at time of his death, since the creation of the trust constituted a "settlement" under this section, and child was precluded from taking under the will. City Nat. Bank & Trust Co. v. Kelly (Ohio Prob. 1939) 1 Ohio Supp. 311, 32 Ohio Law Abs. 559, 19 O.O. 231.

A "settlement" under this section is a provision made extraneous to a will for the benefit of an after-born or after-adopted child, with the intention on the part of the settlor that such provision shall preclude the child from taking any other portion of the testator's estate at the time of his death. City Nat. Bank & Trust Co. v. Kelly (Ohio Prob. 1939) 1 Ohio Supp. 311, 32 Ohio Law Abs. 559, 19 O.O. 231.

8. Revocation by birth

Where a child of a testator is born after the probate of his will, the birth of the child avoids the will. Evans v. Anderson (Ohio 1864) 15 Ohio St. 324. Wills ⇔ 417

Where a testatrix, having no child, made a will, but afterwards had a living child which she survived, it was held that the birth of the child revoked the will; the fact that the testatrix survived the child did not revive the will. Ash v. Ash (Ohio 1859) 9 Ohio St. 383. Wills ⇔ 191

2107.35 Encumbrances

An encumbrance upon real or personal estate for the purpose of securing the payment of money or the performance of a covenant shall not revoke a will previously executed and relating to such estate.

(127 v 36, eff. 9–4–57; 1953 H 1; GC 10504–50)

Historical and Statutory Notes

Pre–1953 H 1 Amendments: 114 v 356

OSBA Probate and Trust Law Section
1957:

The first part of the present section provides that a mortgage placed on property devised or bequeathed in a will *after* the will is executed does not revoke the will as to the property so mortgaged. However, the language of the latter part of this section, "but the devises or legacies thereon contained shall pass subject to such encumbrance" has raised the question whether such a mortgage encumbrance under the sections relating to presentment of claims, or under debt payment claims is to be paid as a debt of the estate and the property devised or bequeathed pass free and clear, or whether the encumbrance is to be paid by the devisee or legatee.

Cases of collateral interest to this section have arisen under the contribution-exoneration statute. The trend of theses cases indicate that mortgage indebtedness should be paid out of personalty and the mortgaged property pass free and clear unless the will discloses a contrary intention. This appears to be contrary to the rule expressed in the present section by the language now proposed to be omitted.

The inclusion of the customary "debt payment clause" in wills has been relied upon as an expressed intention to pay the mortgage indebtedness as a debt of the estate. No case in Ohio has been found on this point, but New York has held that such a clause is not such a manifestation of intent as to relieve the property devised or bequeathed of the burden of the encumbrance. Under a Missouri statute, which is practically identical to the Ohio statute, the effect of the debt payment clause has been similarly interpreted by the Missouri Supreme Court.

The Missouri statute provides that an encumbrance shall not revoke the will followed by language "but the devises and legacies therein contained shall pass and take effect, subject to such charge or encumbrance." The Missouri Court held this to be plain and unequivocal language to the effect that the encumbrance was not a debt of the estate in the absence of a clearly expressed intention to contrary in the will.

Under the present section it is apparently necessary to determine the date of the mortgage with relation to the date of execution of the will. Mortgages executed *before* the will are, by inference only and by the trend of cases on exoneration, to be paid as a debt of the estate out of personalty. Those mortgages executed *after* the will are to be paid by the devisee.

The Committee is of the unanimous opinion that encumbrances on property bequeathed or devised should be treated as debts of the estate to be paid by the executor and the property to pass free and clear of the encumbrance, unless the will clearly provides otherwise. It is believed this view is consonant with the desires and intentions of the majority of testators. There is no logical reason for distinguishing between encumbrances placed on the property before the will was executed and those subsequent to the execution of the will so long as the indebtedness does, in fact, exist at the date of death.

The problem is not confined to mortgages or encumbrances on real estate but arises as to all types of encumbrances on personalty. In view of the constant use of real and chattel mortgages in this day, it is certainly not the intention of most testators to leave their property to wives or members of the family encumbered by a debt.

In view of the New York and Missouri holdings with respect to the effect of the usual debt payment clause and the lack of authority in Ohio directly on this point, the Committee strongly recommends the deletion of that part of the present statute which gives rise to the question as a preventative measure to avoid that the Committee believes is an undesirable result, namely, that the present language would require a holding that the property must be burdened with the encumbrance.

Library References

Wills ⇔ 194.
Westlaw Topic No. 409.
C.J.S. Wills §§ 421 to 426.

Research References

Encyclopedias

OH Jur. 3d Decedents' Estates § 387, Placing Encumbrance on Devised Property; Agreement to Convey.

Treatises and Practice Aids

Carlin, Baldwin's Ohio Practice, Merrick-Rippner Probate Law § 41:1, Encumbrances—RC 2107.35.

Carlin, Baldwin's Ohio Practice, Merrick-Rippner Probate Law § 41:2, Encumbrances—Previous Form of RC 2107.35.

Notes of Decisions

Contract of sale 2
Indemnification 1

---

1. Indemnification

If the purchaser of an incumbered estate agrees to take it subject to the incumbrance, and an abatement is made in the price on that account, he is bound to indemnify his grantor against the incumbrance, whether he expressly promised to do so or not, since a promise to that effect is implied by the nature of the transaction. Thompson v. Thompson (Ohio 1854) 4 Ohio St. 333.

2. Contract of sale

Where wife devised real estate to husband who had by virtue of power of attorney entered into contract of sale of property prior to her death, property passes to husband subject to contract under this section. Sells v. Needles (Franklin 1946) 69 N.E.2d 770, 47 Ohio Law Abs. 425.

2107.36 Effect of alteration of property

An act of a testator which alters but does not wholly divest such testator's interest in property previously devised or bequeathed by him does not revoke the devise or bequest of such property, but such devise or bequest shall pass to the devisee or legatee the actual interest of the testator, which would otherwise descend to his heirs or pass to his next of kin; unless, in the instrument by which such alteration is made, the intention is declared that it shall operate as a revocation of such previous devise or bequest.

If the instrument by which such alteration is made is wholly inconsistent with the previous devise or bequest, such instrument will operate as a revocation thereof, unless such instrument depends on a condition or contingency, and such condition is not performed or such contingency does not happen.

(1953 H 1, eff. 10–1–53; GC 10504–51, 10504–52)

Historical and Statutory Notes

Pre–1953 H 1 Amendments: 114 v 356

Library References

Wills ⇔ 194.
Westlaw Topic No. 409.
C.J.S. Wills §§ 421 to 426.

Research References

Encyclopedias

OH Jur. 3d Decedents' Estates § 383, Alienation or Conveyance of Property.

OH Jur. 3d Decedents' Estates § 384, Alienation or Conveyance of Property—Beneficiary's Right to Trace the Proceeds of Sale.

OH Jur. 3d Decedents' Estates § 386, Effect of Alteration of Testator's Interest in Property.

OH Jur. 3d Decedents' Estates § 805, Ademption Compared With Revocation; Alteration of Testator's Interest, Generally.

OH Jur. 3d Decedents' Estates § 810, Change in Form of Subject Matter—Change from Absolute to Security Interest, or Vice Versa.

Forms

Ohio Forms Legal and Business § 24:781, Cash Bequests—in Lieu of Bequest or Devise Adeemed by Extinction.

Notes of Decisions

Personalty 2
Procedural issues 3
Real estate sale 1

---

1. Real estate sale

Where a devise is made of all of a testator's real and personal estate, and the real estate is sold before the testator's death, the sale changes the realty to personalty, and the devisee will take the proceeds of the real estate remaining and undisposed of at the testator's death as personalty; such a sale does not revoke the will. Kent v. Mahaffey (Ohio 1859) 10 Ohio St. 204.

Doctrine of ademption did not apply to devise of real estate by husband, notwithstanding that property was erroneously sold out of estate of wife who died three months earlier; property was part of husband's estate at time of his death, and thus all bequests made by husband were vested in legatees at his death; mere fact that property was erroneously sold as part of estate of wife by same executor for both estates before distribution did not work to defeat law of vesting. Estate of Parks v. Hodge (Cuyahoga 1993) 87 Ohio App.3d 831, 623 N.E.2d 227. Wills ⇐ 767

Ademption does not apply to the inter vivos transfer of realty listed in a will from decedent to his spouse when the spouse elects to take her statutory share against the will. King v. King (Montgomery 1992) 82 Ohio App.3d 747, 613 N.E.2d 251.

RC 2107.36 has no application where the testator sells real estate specifically devised. Mastics v. Kiraly (Ohio Prob. 1964) 196 N.E.2d 172, 93 Ohio Law Abs. 193, 26 O.O.2d 266.

Where testator devised land by will and thereafter conveyed said land reserving mineral rights, said mineral rights passed to the devisee upon his death. In re Knickel's Will (Ohio Prob. 1961) 185 N.E.2d 93, 89 Ohio Law Abs. 135.

Sale by a guardian, appointed upon grounds of physical incompetency, of real property theretofore devised by will of a ward with the ward's consent operates as an ademption of the devise. Roderick v. Fisher (Franklin 1954) 97 Ohio App. 95, 122 N.E.2d 475, 51 A.L.R.2d 762, 54 O.O. 264.

Where a testator, subsequent to the execution of a will specifically devising lands, voluntarily conveys the lands by an absolute conveyance, the will is revoked pro tanto. Gordon v. Bartlett (Hardin 1938) 62 Ohio App. 295, 23 N.E.2d 964, 28 Ohio Law Abs. 161, 16 O.O. 13. Wills ⇐ 194

The doctrine of implied revocation does not obtain as to after-acquired property devised by will, nor to devised specific property conveyed by a testator after the execution of the will and reconveyed to him before his death. Ridenour v. Callahan (Ohio Cir. 1906) 19 Ohio C.D. 65, 8 Ohio C.C.N.S. 585. Wills ⇐ 167; Wills ⇐ 194

A specific legacy of land to a niece and nephews is deemed where the testator before his death sells the land and invests the proceeds in a mortgage; such proceeds will pass to a sister to whom the testator bequeathed all his personal property. Sharp v. McPherson (Ohio Cir. 1895) 6 Ohio C.D. 634, 3 Ohio Dec. 468.

2. Personalty

A bequest of moneys and interest that may be recovered from a debtor of the decedent is a specific legacy, and the receipt of the money by the testator during his lifetime is an ademption of the bequest. Gilbreath v. Alban (Ohio 1840) 10 Ohio 64.

Where testator's will makes a specific bequest of a particular item of property, and the item does not exist as part of his estate at time of his death, the bequest is "adeemed," that is, it fails completely; such is true even if subject of the gift was lost, or was taken by eminent domain, such that it was not testator's intent that testamentary gift be adeemed; testator's intent to adeem or not to adeem is not controlling. Estate of Parks v. Hodge (Cuyahoga 1993) 87 Ohio App.3d 831, 623 N.E.2d 227. Wills ⇐ 764

Where gift of a specific legacy or devise is adeemed because it is not in existence as part of the testator's estate at his death, rights of the beneficiaries are extinguished; absent a contrary expression in the instrument, beneficiaries are denied the benefit of the thing given in the will or any property in lieu thereof. Estate of Parks v. Hodge (Cuyahoga 1993) 87 Ohio App.3d 831, 623 N.E.2d 227. Wills ⇐ 764

Where the beneficiary of a will files an exception to the inventory contending that certain items of personal property are missing, the trial court's finding that such items were given away by the testatrix before her death is proper if supported by some competent and credible evidence. In re Estate of Stein, No. CA 8100 (2d Dist Ct App, Montgomery, 6–23–83).

3. Procedural issues

A deed of conveyance made subsequent to a devise does not revoke the will unless it makes an entire disposition of the estate; the will attaches pro tanto to any part of the estate undisposed of and carries it to the devisees. Brush v. Brush (Ohio 1842) 11 Ohio 287.

Where a revoked codicil cannot be reproduced in full, and it cannot be determined what portions of the original will were revoked, and what parts remained unaffected by execution of the codicil, the original will must be refused admission to probate unless it can be shown that the original will was subsequently revived as provided by GC 10504–54 (RC 2107.38). In re Paulus' Will (Ohio Prob. 1943) 13 Ohio Supp. 7, 39 Ohio Law Abs. 456, 27 O.O. 283. Wills ⇐ 206

2107.37 Marriage does not revoke will

A will executed by an unmarried person is not revoked by a subsequent marriage.

(1975 S 145, eff. 1–1–76; 1953 H 1; GC 10504–53)

Historical and Statutory Notes

Pre–1953 H 1 Amendments: 114 v 356

Library References

Wills ⇐ 191.
Westlaw Topic No. 409.
C.J.S. Wills §§ 417 to 419.

Research References

Encyclopedias

OH Jur. 3d Decedents' Estates § 357, Methods of Revocation; Strict Compliance With Statute.

OH Jur. 3d Decedents' Estates § 389, Subsequent Marriage.

Forms

Ohio Forms Legal and Business § 24:335, Single Testator—Marriage Contemplated.

Ohio Forms Legal and Business § 24:924, Devise—to Spouse Married After Execution of Will.

Ohio Forms and Transactions KP 30.06, Rights of Surviving Spouse.

Treatises and Practice Aids

Carlin, Baldwin's Ohio Practice, Merrick-Rippner Probate Law § 26:3, Testamentary Capacity—Who May Make a Will—"A Person".

Notes of Decisions

Divorce after subsequent marriage 1

Effect of other statutes 2

1. Divorce after subsequent marriage

Where a testator makes a bequest to his "intended wife" in his will, divorces such wife, and dies without revoking his will, the procuring of a divorce does not necessarily imply a revocation of the will, for it is consistent with an intent to annul her right of dower only and the consequent right of election. Charlton v. Miller (Ohio 1875) 27 Ohio St. 298, 22 Am.Rep. 307.

2. Effect of other statutes

The common-law rule that marriage alone does not revoke the will of a husband made before marriage is not abrogated by a statute making the husband and the wife heirs of each other. Munday's Ex'rs v. Munday (Ohio Cir. 1897) 8 Ohio C.D. 44. Wills ⇌ 191

2107.38 Destruction of a subsequent will

If a testator executes a second will, the destruction, cancellation, or revocation of the second will shall not revive the first will unless the terms of such revocation show that it was such testator's intention to revive and give effect to his first will or unless, after such destruction, cancellation, or revocation, such testator republishes his first will.

(1953 H 1, eff. 10–1–53; GC 10504–54)

Historical and Statutory Notes

Pre–1953 H 1 Amendments: 114 v 356

Library References

Wills ⇌ 198.
Westlaw Topic No. 409.
C.J.S. Wills §§ 431 to 433, 435.

Research References

Encyclopedias

OH Jur. 3d Decedents' Estates § 399, Revocation of Subsequent Will as Revival of Earlier Will.
OH Jur. 3d Decedents' Estates § 1214, Stating Law Applicable to Issues.

Forms

Ohio Forms Legal and Business § 24:261, Prior Wills and Codicils.

Treatises and Practice Aids

Carlin, Baldwin's Ohio Practice, Merrick-Rippner Probate Law § 42:1, Destruction of Subsequent Will—Statutory Provision.
Restatement (2d) of Property, Don. Trans. § 33.2, Multiple Wills.
Restatement (3d) Property (Wills & Don. Trans.) § 4.2, Revival of Revoked Wills.

Notes of Decisions

Formal requirements for republication 1
Revocation 2
Time for contest 3

1. Formal requirements for republication

Where the testator executes a first will, then a second will, and later executes a codicil to the first will which includes a ratification and confirmation of the first will, the codicil operates as a republication of the first will and revives the first will, while revoking the second will. In re Estate of Stormont (Greene 1986) 34 Ohio App.3d 92, 517 N.E.2d 259.

An unwitnessed, but dated and signed, carbon copy of a will which was revoked by a later will subsequently lost, to which copy was attached a typewritten statement that "the original draft of my last will is in the hands of [my] attorney... I have destroyed the [later] will recently drawn" by another attorney, does not comply with the formal requirements for the re-execution of a will and codicil and is not effective to revive such first will. Shinn v. Phillips (Cuyahoga 1964) 8 Ohio App.2d 58, 220 N.E.2d 674.

A will once revoked in Ohio cannot be revived by an instrument which does not comply with the formalities required for a will. Shinn v. Phillips (Cuyahoga 1964) 8 Ohio App.2d 58, 220 N.E.2d 674.

To constitute a valid revivor of a revoked will under this section, the testator must acknowledge the instrument to be his last will before the witnesses who have already signed his will, or, if before other witnesses, they must sign the will at the request of the testator, or testator and two witnesses must sign some other instrument showing such intent, or such testator must republish his will with the same formalities as attended its original publication. Collins v. Collins (Ohio 1924) 110 Ohio St. 105, 143 N.E. 561, 38 A.L.R. 230, 2 Ohio Law Abs. 260, 22 Ohio Law Rep. 49.

Where a testator, by a codicil to a revoked anterior will in existence, confirms such will, the will, together with all previous codicils thereto, is thereby confirmed. In re Stocker's Will (Ohio Prob. 1926) 26 Ohio NP(NS) 112, 4 Ohio Law Abs. 205.

Cancellation or revocation of a second will does not revive a former will, unless the earlier will was republished with all the statutory formalities of its first publication, GC 10562 (RC 2107.38); this requires the first will to be produced to witnesses, and cannot be proved by parol. Crane v. Tunkey (Ohio Com.Pl. 1913) 58 W.L.B. 316, 11 Ohio Law Rep. 454.

2. Revocation

A will is revoked by the execution of, and is not revived by the subsequent destruction of, a second will duly executed, when the second will contains an express clause of revocation, or is utterly inconsistent with the provisions of the first will, and, further, that, if inconsistent in part with the provisions of the former will, it revokes the former will to that extent. Paully v. Crooks (Richland 1931) 41 Ohio App. 1, 179 N.E. 364, 11 Ohio Law Abs. 371, 35 Ohio Law Rep. 495.

A codicil operates not only as a new adoption of the will to which it refers, but also as a revocation of an intermediate will. In re Stocker's Will (Ohio Prob. 1926) 26 Ohio NP(NS) 112, 4 Ohio Law Abs. 205.

A second will does not revoke a first will under GC 10562 (RC 2107.38), unless it was in force at testator's death. In re Murray's Estate (Ohio Prob. 1917) 20 Ohio NP(NS) 305, 63 W.L.B. 81.

3. Time for contest

Will executed nine years before execution of probated will could not be admitted to probate, where latter will had been probated and unchallenged until long after period for contest had passed and only reason for probating earlier will was that under later will charitable bequests would be defeated. State ex rel. Haughey v. Lueders (Hamilton 1933) 46 Ohio App. 287, 187 N.E. 724, 15 Ohio Law Abs. 519, 39 Ohio Law Rep. 255. Wills ⇌ 206

CONSTRUCTION AND OPERATION

2107.46 Action by fiduciary

Any fiduciary may maintain an action in the probate court against creditors, legatees, distributees, or other parties, and ask the direction or judgment of the court in any matter respecting the trust, estate, or property to be administered, and the rights of the parties in interest.

If any fiduciary fails for thirty days to bring such an action after a written request from a party in interest, the party making the request may institute the suit.

(1975 S 145, eff. 1–1–76; 125 v 903; 1953 H 1; GC 10504–66, 10504–67)

Historical and Statutory Notes

Pre–1953 H 1 Amendments: 118 v 78, § 1; 114 v 358, 359

Cross References

Determination of rights or legal relations, 2721.05
Fiduciary defined, 2109.01
Reckoning time, 1.14

Library References

Wills ⟸697(3).
Westlaw Topic No. 409.
C.J.S. Wills §§ 1568 to 1570.

Research References

Encyclopedias

OH Jur. 3d Charities § 34, Action for Construction of Trust.
OH Jur. 3d Charities § 35, Who May Maintain Action to Enforce or Protect Trust.
OH Jur. 3d Decedents' Estates § 654, Probate Court; Applicability of the Declaratory Judgment Act—Action by a Fiduciary for Direction or Judgment of Court in Administration of Trust or Estate.
OH Jur. 3d Decedents' Estates § 657, Plaintiff; Fiduciaries.
OH Jur. 3d Decedents' Estates § 658, Plaintiff; Fiduciaries—"A Party in Interest".
OH Jur. 3d Decedents' Estates § 671, Appellate Review—Appeal by Fiduciary.
OH Jur. 3d Decedents' Estates § 965, Judicial Supervision of Representatives—Instructions and Advice on Request.
OH Jur. 3d Fiduciaries § 135, Generally, Jurisdiction.
OH Jur. 3d Fiduciaries § 136, Nature and Purpose of Action.
OH Jur. 3d Fiduciaries § 137, Cause of Action.
OH Jur. 3d Fiduciaries § 138, Parties.
OH Jur. 3d Fiduciaries § 142, Judgment or Order; Conclusiveness.
OH Jur. 3d Trusts § 371, Statutory Basis.
OH Jur. 3d Trusts § 538, in Equity—Particular Remedies.

Treatises and Practice Aids

Klein, Darling, & Terez, Baldwin's Ohio Practice Civil Practice § 73:3, Probate Division--Venue.
Carlin, Baldwin's Ohio Practice, Merrick-Rippner Probate Law § 4:53, Summons in Adversary Action—Form.
Carlin, Baldwin's Ohio Practice, Merrick-Rippner Probate Law § 43:1, Construing a Will—Action for Instructions—Scope.
Carlin, Baldwin's Ohio Practice, Merrick-Rippner Probate Law § 43:2, Construing a Will—Action for Instructions—Preferability of Declaratory Judgment Action.
Carlin, Baldwin's Ohio Practice, Merrick-Rippner Probate Law § 43:50, Complaint for Construction of Will by Fiduciary—Form.
Carlin, Baldwin's Ohio Practice, Merrick-Rippner Probate Law § 43:51, Complaint for Construction of Will by Party in Interest—Form.
Carlin, Baldwin's Ohio Practice, Merrick-Rippner Probate Law § 43:52, Entry Construing Will—Form.
Bogert - the Law of Trusts and Trustees § 559, Court Control—Advice as to Extent of Powers.
Bogert - the Law of Trusts and Trustees § 861, Remedies of the Beneficiary Against the Trustee.
Bogert - the Law of Trusts and Trustees § 870, Jurisdiction to Enforce Trust—Actions Available.
Restatement (3d) of Trusts § 71, Application to Court for Instructions.

Law Review and Journal Commentaries

Revisiting Firestone v. Galbreath and the Tort of Intentional Interference With an Expectancy, Angela G. Carlin. 6 Prob L J Ohio 17 (November/December 1995).

Notes of Decisions

Administration expenses 1
Charitable bequests 2
Executors' and trustees' actions 3
Future interests 4-8
    Fee simple determinable 4
    Fee simple subject to a condition subsequent 5
    Powers 6
    Remainders 7
    Reversions and executory devises 8
Procedure and appeal 9
Unauthorized actions 10
Will construction 11, 12
    Evidence 12
    Intent 11

1. Administration expenses

Order of probate court requiring inventory by administrator is not adjudication that there is no antenuptial contract defeating set-offs, nor is it interpretation of such contract. Keever v. Brown (Ohio App. 1930) 36 Ohio App. 1, 172 N.E. 626, 9 Ohio Law Abs. 296. Executors And Administrators ⟸ 5; Judgment ⟸ 640

A residuary devisee or legatee is presumed in law to be in the position of the last lienholder, after all prior lawful claims and charges have been satisfied out of the estate. Young Men's Christian Ass'n v. Davis (Ohio 1922) 106 Ohio St. 366, 140 N.E. 114, 1 Ohio Law Abs. 84, 20 Ohio Law Rep. 498, 20 Ohio Law Rep. 499, certiorari granted 43 S.Ct. 521, 262 U.S. 745, 67 L.Ed. 1211, rehearing granted 43 S.Ct. 699, 262 U.S. 739, 67 L.Ed. 1208, affirmed 44 S.Ct. 291, 264 U.S. 47, 68 L.Ed. 558. Wills ⟸ 827

Under will giving testator's widow all his property and requiring her to pay from any moneys of the estate debts and funeral expenses, widow, by electing to take under the will, did not render herself personally liable for the unpaid subscription price on stock of an insolvent corporation. John A. Roebling Sons Co. v. Shawnee Valley Coal & Iron Co. (Ohio 1908) 78 Ohio St. 408, 85 N.E. 1127, 6 Ohio Law Rep. 11. Wills ⟸ 803

The debts of a son to the estate of his father are superior to a mortgage or judgment liens against him on real estate coming to him by a general devise. Woodruff v. Woodruff (Ohio Cir. 1902) 13 Ohio C.D. 408, 3 Ohio C.C.N.S. 616.

The costs in an action under former GC 10857 (RC 2107.46), should first come out of the general estate; any deficiency should come pro rata out of securities or their proceeds which had been repledged rightfully, and any deficiency still remaining must come pro rata from those wrongfully repledged. Citizens Nat. Bank Co. v. Andrews (Ohio Com.Pl. 1923) 24 Ohio N.P.N.S. 361.

Where beneficiaries under will retained counsel to bring action for construction of will which action resulted in declaration that trust provision was invalid, thus entitling beneficiaries to funds which would otherwise go to trust, the fee paid to counsel for such action authorized by probate court was administration expense within United States Revenue Act. Schmalstig v. Conner (S.D.Ohio 1942) 46 F.Supp. 531, 24 O.O. 427.

2. Charitable bequests

An unincorporated society is entirely capable of taking a personal bequest, though it might be different as to realty. American Tract Soc. v. Atwater (Ohio 1876) 30 Ohio St. 77, 27 Am.Rep. 422.

A county can take real estate by devise, and where the devise is made to the county by name with no limitation on the property's use, it vests in the board of commissioners for the use of the county for any authorized county purposes. Carder v. Board of Com'rs of Fayette County (Ohio 1865) 16 Ohio St. 354.

It was testatrix' intent that bequest to "Diabetes Fund of Ohio" was to be used at local level; codicil in will emphasized testatrix' desire that gifts to nationally recognized charitable organizations be used solely at local divisions or units of those organizations to satisfy local needs and bequest to local units or chapters outside immediate county area were apparently limited to those charities based exclusively in location outside county area or those without county affiliate. American Diabetes Ass'n, Inc. v. Diabetes Soc. of Clinton County (Clinton 1986) 31 Ohio App.3d 136, 509 N.E.2d 84, 31 O.B.R. 224. Wills ⟸ 668

Residuary clause in will, providing that residue of estate was given and bequeathed to particular church "for the building fund" unequivocally constituted general, rather than specific charitable gift; thus, church remained residual beneficiary, despite contention that specific church building fund in existence at time of execution of will had ceased to exist, the building having been completed and indebtedness thereon satisfied prior to admission of subject will to probate. Hess v. Sommers (Mercer 1982) 4 Ohio App.3d 281, 448 N.E.2d 494, 4 O.B.R. 500. Charities ⟸ 37(6); Wills ⟸ 601(6)

A petition to terminate a charitable trust and to compel the trustees to account for maladministration is not an action for a declaratory judgment. Green v. Ryan (Hamilton 1953) 95 Ohio App. 345, 119 N.E.2d 668, 53 O.O. 311.

Charitable trust will not be terminated because of small changes in administration. Gearhart v. Richardson (Ohio 1924) 109 Ohio St. 418, 142 N.E. 890, 2 Ohio Law Abs. 181, 21 Ohio Law Rep. 578, 21 Ohio Law Rep. 579. Charities 29; Trusts 61(1)

A bequest for public charitable purposes attaching thereto a private charity which may conflict with the public charities sought to be created held void for uncertainty. Dirlam v. Morrow (Ohio 1921) 102 Ohio St. 279, 131 N.E. 365, 19 Ohio Law Rep. 50. Charities 10; Wills 104

Where property is devised to trustee for such charitable purposes as he may deem proper, trustee's judgment and discretion is essential to trust, and on death of trustee probate court has no authority to appoint successor under GC 10596 (repealed 1932. See § 10506–55). Rogers v. Rea (Ohio 1918) 98 Ohio St. 315, 120 N.E. 828, 16 Ohio Law Rep. 89. Charities 47; Trusts 169(1)

Under RS 4182 (repealed 1932. See GC 10503–12), providing that one, with the consent of the probate court, may designate the person named to stand in relation of heir, a person so named is not within he meaning of § 5915 (repealed 1932. See GC 10505–5), providing that, if any testator die leaving "issue of his body" or an adopted child, the will of such testator giving any part of his estate to any benefit, religious, educational, or charitable institution, shall be invalid, unless such will shall have been executed at least one year prior to testator's decease. Theobald v. Fugman (Ohio 1901) 64 Ohio St. 473, 45 W.L.B. 382, 60 N.E. 606. Charities 4; Wills 13(1)

Under the authority of RS 3975, a de facto board of education has the capacity to take a bequest made to it by will for school purposes. Rockwell v. Blaney (Ohio Com.Pl. 1910) 22 Ohio Dec. 107, 9 Ohio N.P.N.S. 495. Schools 64; Wills 10

3. Executors' and trustees' actions

By statute, authority is granted to an executor to maintain a civil action in the court of common pleas, asking the direction of the court in any manner affecting the trust, estate, or property to be administered, and the rights of the parties in interest. Merrick v. Merrick (Ohio 1881) 37 Ohio St. 126, 6 W.L.B. 423.

Where foreign real estate is converted into money which has been transmitted to Ohio, and a question arises as to the distribution of that property which is not controlled by the will, that question must be settled according to the laws of Ohio. Brewster v. Benedict (Ohio 1846) 14 Ohio 368.

Executrix failed to establish that independent living facility breached a duty owed to resident when escort failed to walk resident to her apartment after dinner, as required to support executrix's negligence claim, and resident fell and broke her wrist; executrix's negligence claim was based on facility's contractual duty to have escort walk resident to and from dinner until resident became familiar with the layout of facility, escort's failure to walk resident all the way to her apartment did not constitute a breach of a duty imposed by law. Corsaro v. ARC Westlake Village, Inc. (Ohio App. 8 Dist., Cuyahoga, 04-28-2005) No. 84858, 2005-Ohio-1982, 2005 WL 984502, Unreported. Asylums 7

Executrix failed to establish any damages resulted from independent living facility's escort leaving resident at elevator after resident indicated to escort that she could find her apartment on her own, in breach of contract case, even though resident fell after exiting elevator and fractured her wrist; resident's fall was not a natural consequence of escort failing to walk resident back to her apartment from dinner, fellow resident testified that he traveled with resident in the elevator and she did not appear unsteady and she did not ask him for directions, and facility was not notified the resident had a medical condition that caused a temporary loss of consciousness due to low blood pressure. Corsaro v. ARC Westlake Village, Inc. (Ohio App. 8 Dist., Cuyahoga, 04-28-2005) No. 84858, 2005-Ohio-1982, 2005 WL 984502, Unreported. Asylums 8

Executrix failed to establish that independent living facility breached its contract when escort, who was to walk resident to and from dinner until resident became familiar with the layout of facility, left resident by the elevator after resident indicated that she could find her apartment from there; resident chose to live at facility where she was free to come and go as she pleased, resident indicated when asked by her daughter if she wanted a dinner escort that "I don't think I need that," and resident chose to leave escort at the elevator and continue to her apartment alone. Corsaro v. ARC Westlake Village, Inc. (Ohio App. 8 Dist., Cuyahoga, 04-28-2005) No. 84858, 2005-Ohio-1982, 2005 WL 984502, Unreported. Asylums 5

In an executor's action against his father's estate to recover compensation for providing the father's personal and medical services and for maintaining his father's home and lawn, the mutuality of benefits test should be applied to determine whether a "family relationship" existed between the son and the decedent based on (1) the father-son relationship, (2) the nature of the services rendered, (3) the living arrangements, and (4) the respective financial conditions of the parties. In re Estate of Combs (Ohio App. 1 Dist., Hamilton, 03-13-1998) No. C-961056, 1998 WL 107664, Unreported.

Before a court of equity will undertake to construe a will, it must appear on the face of the instrument itself that an immediate necessity for such construction exists, such as the determination of a present or impending controversy, or that there is a provision of dubious or uncertain meaning under which the executor will be called to act soon. Beck v. Alliance First Nat. Bank (Stark 1929) 7 Ohio Law Abs. 723, 31 Ohio Law Rep. 213.

Trustees who brought action for declaratory relief seeking to have special testamentary powers of appointment given to adult sons of settlor, who were trust beneficiaries, and who were both unmarried and without issue, were provided sufficient notice that they had burden of persuasion, even though no person or entity with standing had opposed amendment of trust, where parties received notice of and did attend hearing on complaint for declaratory relief, and indicated in pretrial statement that they had burden. Fifth Third Bank v. Simpson (Ohio App. 1 Dist., 06-25-1999) 134 Ohio App.3d 71, 730 N.E.2d 406, appeal not allowed 87 Ohio St.3d 1432, 718 N.E.2d 448. Declaratory Judgment 342

Any error by trial court in failing to grant motion by executor of decedent's estate for determination that niece of decedent, who had held power of attorney for decedent, had burden of proof on issue of fairness of transaction challenged by executor, was harmless, where court ultimately considered evidence presented in accordance with executor's original request on nature of burden of proof. Gotthardt v. Candle (Ohio App. 7 Dist., 02-22-1999) 131 Ohio App.3d 831, 723 N.E.2d 1144, appeal not allowed 86 Ohio St.3d 1420, 711 N.E.2d 1014. Executors And Administrators 455

One who as a testamentary trustee and as an individual is interested in a provision of the will authorizing the removal of certain real estate from the trust and the substitution of a sum of money therefor may bring a declaratory judgment action in the probate court to secure a determination and declaration of his rights as trustee and as an individual. Sessions v. Skelton (Ohio 1955) 163 Ohio St. 409, 127 N.E.2d 378, 56 O.O. 370.

Causes of action by executor for money, checks, certificates of deposit, pass book, and other evidences of property removed from deceased's residence by defendant, held properly joined. Russ v. Wilson (Clermont 1927) 27 Ohio App. 34, 160 N.E. 735, 6 Ohio Law Abs. 342. Action 48(1); Executors And Administrators 86(2)

Where an executor dies or resigns without filing any account, his successor should compel an accounting and the payment to him of any balance due. Hocking Valley R. Co. v. White (Ohio 1913) 87 Ohio St. 413, 101 N.E. 354, 10 Ohio Law Rep. 611, Am.Ann.Cas. 1914A, 190. Executors And Administrators 464

An executor who has wrongfully paid out money upon distribution under mistake of law may not maintain an action to recover such money after it has already been paid out. Phillips v. McConica (Ohio 1898) 59 Ohio St. 1, 40 W.L.B. 293, 51 N.E. 445, 69 Am.St.Rep. 753.

A trustee should confine his acts to the carrying into effect of the provisions of the trust under which he is acting and, if in doubt, apply to the proper court for instruction. Jones v. Creamer (Ohio Cir. 1910) 22 Ohio C.D. 223, 13 Ohio C.C.(N.S.) 585, affirmed 87 Ohio St. 480, 102 N.E. 1126, 10 Ohio Law Rep. 480. Trusts 271.5

Powers of trustees may be defined in an action under RS 6202. City of Cincinnati v. McMicken (Ohio Cir. 1892) 3 Ohio C.D. 409, modified.

Where persons are not qualified as trustees under a will, they are not prejudiced by an order setting aside the will and voiding their acts as purported trustees. Noble v. Martin (Ohio Cir. 1890) 2 Ohio C.D. 598.

An action can be maintained by an executor, under RS 6202, only where a trust is involved, or where the executor has duties requiring the guidance of the court. Chase v. Isherwood (Ohio Com.Pl. 1894) 5 Ohio Dec. 1, 1 Ohio N.P. 31, 1 Ohio Leg. N. 133.

Applied in action by executor to determine validity of a gift inter vivos. McCoy v Gosser, 8 App 145, 30 CC(NS) 312 (1917).

A probate court has jurisdiction to consolidate a dispute between a trustee and a creditor with a trust action brought under RC 2107.46. In re Trust of Stum, No. 86 CA 28 (4th Dist Ct App, Pickaway, 12–2–87).

4. Future interests—Fee simple determinable

Where a testator directs that his executors sell land for the benefit of certain legatees, the title to the land descends to the heirs while the trust remains unexecuted, subject to be divested by the execution of the power; since both the legal and equitable title were united in the legatee/heirs, the rule which protects a bona fide purchaser without notice does not apply. Elstner v. Fife (Ohio 1877) 32 Ohio St. 358.

A condition in a will to be performed by the testator's son as executor may be imposed as a limitation upon a devise or bequest to the testator's other children, and when this condition precedent is performed, the estate vests. Scott v. Kramer (Ohio 1877) 31 Ohio St. 295.

Where a testator devises land to a tenant for life with the direction that at his death it be sold and the proceeds divided among his children, at his death the children may elect to take the land itself or to have it sold for their benefit; the estate of such children does not accrue until the life tenant's death, although his estate may be determined during his lifetime, and hence the estate devised is not in remainder. Holt v. Lamb (Ohio 1867) 17 Ohio St. 374.

Where a trust is declared in a will as to a tract of land but the legal title is left to descend to the heirs at law who would have a beneficial interest once the trust is either accomplished or fails, the legal title is held by the heirs as trustees and a creditor of one of the heirs who had obtained a judgment does not thereby acquire a lien on the land. Birchard v. Edwards (Ohio 1860) 11 Ohio St. 84. Wills ⚖ 869

Where a testator bequeaths an estate to his son to hold in trust for the use of his daughter during her life, giving such daughter the power to appoint absolutely to her heirs, the daughter takes an equitable fee simple as the first cestui que trust. Armstrong v. Zane's Heirs (Ohio 1843) 12 Ohio 287.

Where a testator leaves his widow all his estate and the proceeds therefrom, but directs his executors to lease the premises and after paying ground rents and taxes to pay the proceeds to the widow, the intention of the testator is that an interest in the proceeds of the estate should go to his wife, not a fee, and the title to the land is in the executors. Boyd's Lessee v. Talbert (Ohio 1843) 12 Ohio 212. Powers ⚖ 25; Wills ⚖ 692(1)

Where a testator devises land to his sons or the survivors and their heirs, to be divided when the youngest son reaches age twenty-one, the condition of survivorship relates to the death of the testator, cross remainders are not created, and the sons who survived the testator take a fee. Lawrence's Lessee v. McArter (Ohio 1840) 10 Ohio 37.

Where a testator bequeathed to his wife, so long as she remained his widow, his entire property, with power to sell and convey any realty in fee, she took only an estate for life, subject to termination on remarriage, though there was no limitation over, and, where she died without having remarried, the realty devised to her passed to testator's next of kin as an estate of remainder in fee simple. Fetter v. Rettig (Ohio 1918) 98 Ohio St. 428, 121 N.E. 696, 16 Ohio Law Rep. 89, 16 Ohio Law Rep. 401. Wills ⚖ 616(4)

Testator gave all the balance of his estate to his son and two daughters to be divided equally, and in case of the death of either of them the survivor or survivors were to inherit the property bequeathed to them; if more than one survivor it was to be divided share and share alike. Held, that the words "survivor or survivors" meant survivor or survivors at the time of testator's death, and the interest in the real estate devised was an estate in fee simple vesting immediately on the death of testator, so that on the death of the daughters' children after the death of the testator their interest passed to their representatives and not to their brother as survivor. Renner v. Williams (Ohio 1905) 71 Ohio St. 340, 73 N.E. 221, 2 Ohio Law Rep. 411. Wills ⚖ 539

5. —— Fee simple subject to a condition subsequent, future interests

A testator's pecuniary bequest to a married woman with a bequest over to his children if the legatee dies without issue vests the bequest in the first taker absolutely, and the divesting contingency cannot prevent the executor from paying the legacy. Lapham v. Martin (Ohio 1877) 33 Ohio St. 99.

A bequest of the residuary estate of a testator to his daughters "and their heirs" with a bequest over in case one daughter should die without issue rests the estate in the daughter first, upon the testator's death, with a divesting contingency over which does not defeat the daughter's right to possession. Ratliff v. Warner (Ohio 1877) 32 Ohio St. 334.

Where a testator devises real estate to his son "during his natural life and to his heirs" with a limitation over to certain nephews and nieces in case the son should die after attaining his majority and without legal issue, the word "heirs" will be construed as a word of limitation enlarging the life estate to a defeasible estate in fee simple when such construction conforms to the apparent scheme of disposition and is consistent with the will's other provisions. Carter v. Reddish (Ohio 1876) 32 Ohio St. 1.

Where a testator devised real estate to his granddaughter "and her issue and their heirs," but if she should die without issue before age twenty-one, a devise over to two daughters of the testator for their lives and then to their issue, upon the death of the granddaughter without issue after she attained age twenty-one, her husband is entitled to an estate by curtesy whether she died leaving issue or not, and the devise over to the daughters never took effect. Harkness v. Corning (Ohio 1873) 24 Ohio St. 416. Wills ⚖ 545(5)

Where a devise of real estate is made to a testatrix's husband in fee simple with the power to sell the premises on the condition that he care for the couple's imbecile daughter during their joint lives, and a devise is made to the testatrix's son with the same condition if the daughter survived her father, with the addition of words requiring a personal assumption of the care of his sister, where the son does assume such care, the condition is satisfied, and the estate in the son and those he sells to is absolute and fully discharged from the maintenance of the imbecile daughter. Huey v. Thomas (Ohio 1873) 23 Ohio St. 645.

A devise to the testator's wife of all his estate for life, to be divided upon her death among his children or the survivor of them, vests no interest in a child who dies before the widow, and such deceased child's child is not entitled to share in the estate as one of the "children" or "survivors" to whom it was to be distributed. Sinton v. Boyd (Ohio 1869) 19 Ohio St. 30, 2 Am.Rep. 369.

Where a testator devises real estate to his wife and daughter for life, and to the survivor of them the whole estate, and directs that if both should die without issue his wife's brother would take, upon the daughter's death without issue and the wife's death leaving issue by a second marriage, the wife's surviving issue is entitled to the estate under the will. Shaw v. Hoard (Ohio 1868) 18 Ohio St. 227. Wills ⚖ 498

Devise may have a condition annexed requiring an annuity to be paid to the widow of the testator. Carder v. Board of Com'rs of Fayette County (Ohio 1865) 16 Ohio St. 354.

While no particular form of words is necessary to raise a condition upon which an estate created by it may be defeated, to have such an effect, the testator's intention must be clear and unquestionable, since the courts will incline against conditions and limitations. Worman's Lessee v. Teagarden (Ohio 1853) 2 Ohio St. 380. Wills ⚖ 639

In a devise to heirs or the survivors that reach the age of twenty-one years with a remainder to the wife if all the heirs die before they come of age, the absolute estate is vested in the surviving one heir who reaches that age and dies shortly afterward. Ward's Lessee v. Barrows (Ohio 1853) 2 Ohio St. 241.

A will which gives to the testator's grandchildren certain real estate "provided they live to legal age" vests legal title to the land in the children, subject only to divestment upon their death before coming of age. Foster v. Wick's Lessee (Ohio 1848) 17 Ohio 250.

Where a testator makes a devise of real estate to a son, and in such devise provides that on the happening of an event, which may or may not occur, the lands devised to such son shall "go to and be vested in the heirs of the body" of such son, on the happening of the event which divests the son of his estate therein the children of the son take the lands of which the son has been divested, by devise from the testator in their own right, and not in a representative capacity. Rings v. Borton (Ohio 1923) 108 Ohio St. 280, 140 N.E. 515, 1 Ohio Law Abs. 485, 21 Ohio Law Rep. 150, 21 Ohio Law Rep. 152. Wills ⚖ 554

6. —— Powers, future interests

A devise of one-half of a testator's entire estate to his wife and one-half to his brothers and sisters, with a power given to the executor to sell and convey the real estate if necessary for the purpose of distributing the estate, confers only a naked power on the executor, the exercise of which must be limited to the purpose for which it was granted. Hoyt v. Day (Ohio 1877) 32 Ohio St. 101.

Where a power to distribute a testator's entire estate among his children is given to his wife to exercise as she deems best, and the wife does distribute some of the estate to the children, but dies seized of the remaining parcels, under the circumstances, the power never having been fully exercised, equity requires that the entire estate should be apportioned equally between all the children named, the partial distributions already made to stand as advancements on such equal portions. Stableton v. Ellison (Ohio 1871) 21 Ohio St. 527.

Where a testator devises to his wife all his property, real and personal, remaining after the payment of his debts, with full power to sell or convey during her life, and another clause bequeaths a legacy to be paid at the wife's death out of any moneys remaining, a deed by the wife is a sufficient execution of the power given to her by will and the exhaustion of the property prevents the payment of the legacy. Bishop v. Remple (Ohio 1860) 11 Ohio St. 277. Powers ⇐ 33(2); Wills ⇐ 692(5).

When an estate is settled or all claims against it are presumably satisfied by the lapse of time and no object of the testator remains to be attained, a power given to the executors by will to sell and convey land becomes legally inoperative and ceases to exist. Ward's Lessee v. Barrows (Ohio 1853) 2 Ohio St. 241. Powers ⇐ 13; Wills ⇐ 692(6).

In a bequest from a husband to his wife of lands to be used during her life which provides that the wife has the power to devise such land upon her death to whom she pleases, the wife does not take such an estate as would be liable for her debts and her devisee takes the estate unencumbered by her debt. Jones v. Shields (Ohio 1846) 14 Ohio 359.

Where an executor is given unlimited discretion in the sale and investment of lands of the testator, subject to the payment of a legacy to his granddaughter at age eighteen, and such executor sells all the lands and becomes insolvent before the legacy is to be paid, the trust does not create a charge on the testator's real estate in the hands of purchasers from the executor. Coonrod v. Coonrod (Ohio 1833) 6 Ohio 114.

Where a testator directs by will that his executor sell his real estate whenever, in her opinion, she could do so at good advantage, and the proceeds devised are to be distributed to the testator's children as they come of age, that power is connected with a trust entitling the executor to possession of the land. Dabney v. Manning (Ohio 1828) 3 Ohio 321, 17 Am.Dec. 597. Powers ⇐ 25; Wills ⇐ 692(7).

Where in a will the power to dispose of the testator's entire estate, real and personal, and the manner of doing it are limited only by the discretion of the executor, such executor has the power to convey land according to a trust agreement made between the testator and the defendant, though such trust is not mentioned as consideration for the conveyance. Steele v. Worthington (Ohio 1825) 2 Ohio 182.

Where testator directs his executor after the death of his wife to distribute among his legal heirs, it confers a contingent interest which does not vest until the period of distribution. Barr v. Denney (Ohio 1909) 79 Ohio St. 358, 87 N.E. 267, 6 Ohio Law Rep. 616. Remainders ⇐ 1; Wills ⇐ 634(7).

Where testator left his property in trust, the income to be paid to his daughters during life, free from all control of their husbands, with power of disposal by will, no marital trust was created to be ended as to each daughter on the death of her then living husband. Robbins v. Smith (Ohio 1905) 72 Ohio St. 1, 73 N.E. 1051, 2 Ohio Law Rep. 494. Trusts ⇐ 36; Wills ⇐ 671.

A will bequeathing to testator's wife all his estate in fee simple, with power to sell as she may see fit, and providing for the distribution of anything that remains on the widow's death in a certain manner, gives the widow power to convey the fee of the whole or any part of the real estate, and a deed good as against the widow is good against the second devisee. Bodmann German Protestant Widows' Home v. Lippardt (Ohio 1904) 70 Ohio St. 261, 71 N.E. 770, 2 Ohio Law Rep. 73. Powers ⇐ 36(1); Wills ⇐ 692(1).

Where land is devised in fee simple, with direction to the devisee to pay certain legacies as each legatee attains the age of 21 years, the devisee, on accepting the devise, becomes personally liable to pay the same as directed by the testator. Case v. Hall (Ohio 1894) 52 Ohio St. 24, 32 W.L.B. 366, 38 N.E. 618, 2 Ohio Leg. N. 91. Wills ⇐ 823.

Without an election by devisees of land to take the land instead of the proceeds to be derived from its sale, no incumbrance the devisees place upon it would affect, much less defeat, the right and power of the executor to convey away the title; the lien of a judgment against a devisee could operate no further than to bind the interest received. Smyth v Anderson, 31 OS 144 (1876).

The trial court erred in concluding the executor was granted a power coupled with an interest regarding a devise of land when he was granted such an interest in the rest and residue of the estate's property and his function to convey the land and have a survey conducted was purely ministerial. Bachman v Swearingen, No. 82–CA–24 (5th Dist Ct App, Delaware, 2–8–83).

7. —— Remainders, future interests

A devise to the testator's children when the youngest reaches age twenty-one, with the immediate estate devised to his wife, vests a remainder in the testator's children immediately on the testator's death, and is not defeated by the death of a devisee before the period named, in which case the devise would descend to the deceased's heirs by inheritance. Linton v. Laycock (Ohio 1877) 33 Ohio St. 128.

Under a devise to the testator's wife for life of a farm which was to be sold after her death and the proceeds divided between the testator's siblings or the children of any deceased sibling, the gift implied is of personalty, but as the fund could not be raised until the widow's death, and was to be divided among persons then living, the interest of the legatees therein remained contingent until that time. Richey v. Johnson (Ohio 1876) 30 Ohio St. 288.

Where a testator makes a bequest in trust for the benefit of his parents during their lives with a gift over upon their deaths to particular societies "for the advancement of the kingdom of Christ in the world," the bequest is not void for vagueness since the money is paid directly to the treasurers of such societies with no discretion left to anyone how the scheme should be carried out. American Tract Soc. v. Atwater (Ohio 1876) 30 Ohio St. 77, 27 Am.Rep. 422.

Conflicting provisions in a will should be reconciled to conform to the testator's manifest general intent, and only where such provisions are absolutely repugnant should either be rejected; thus, where words importing an absolute estate are contained in one clause and a remainder is given to another person, the first devisee takes a life estate and the limitation over is valid. Baxter v. Bowyer (Ohio 1869) 19 Ohio St. 490.

The rule which destroys a remainder in personalty when an absolute power of disposition is given to the first taker does not apply in any case where the repugnancy between the remainder and the prior interest is not total, and where there is no specific property that was to be consumed for the first taker's use, a gift of what may remain unappropriated is valid and legal. James v. Pruden (Ohio 1863) 14 Ohio St. 251. Remainders ⇐ 10; Wills ⇐ 616(8).

Where a testator sets up a trust with the interest to be paid to his son's widow for life and at her death the principal to be paid to her sons, and the sons predecease their mother without issue or debts, the trust fails by the occurrence of a contingency not provided for by the will, and the entire beneficial interest having vested in the mother as the boys' heir, she must be paid it directly without the delay and expense of successive administrations. Taylor v. Huber's Ex'rs (Ohio 1862) 13 Ohio St. 288.

A devise to life tenants and then to the children of the life tenants in fee simple with a limitation over if such tenant dies "without lawful heirs of their bodies" to the testator's brother's children is not void for uncertainty, since the intent of the testator was that, upon the death of the life tenant the children living were to take, and if any predeceased leaving a child or children such child or children should be substituted for its deceased parent; and if the life tenant died without issue, the fee would go immediately to the testator's brother's heirs. Stevenson v. Evans (Ohio 1859) 10 Ohio St. 307.

Where by will a father devises a life estate in land to his wife with an equal remainder in the premises going to his two sons upon the mother's death, but if one of the sons dies within the mother's lifetime the entire estate is to go to the other son, the contingent interest of one brother is releasable to the other during the mother's life, and passes by such release. Jeffers v. Lampson (Ohio 1859) 10 Ohio St. 101.

Where there is a devise in fee to A, but in case she dies "without issue" then to B in fee, the words "if she die without issue" or other words of similar import are to be interpreted according to their plain, popular and natural meaning, as referring to the time of the person's death, unless the contrary intention is plainly expressed in the will or is necessary to carry out its undoubted purposes. Parish's Heirs v. Ferris (Ohio 1856) 6 Ohio St. 563.

When testator gives trust and its remainder to one beneficiary, and that person dies prior to termination of the trust, resulting trust should be in favor of persons succeeding to beneficiary's interest, and not for testator. Summers v. Summers (Ohio App. 4 Dist., 06-09-1997) 121 Ohio App.3d 263, 699 N.E.2d 958, appeal not allowed 80 Ohio St.3d 1426, 685 N.E.2d 238. Wills ⇐ 682(1).

Portion of estate remaining unconsumed by life tenant held a vested remainder, subject to being divested. Tax Commission of Ohio v. Oswald (Ohio 1923) 109 Ohio St. 36, 141 N.E. 678, 1 Ohio Law Abs. 862, 21 Ohio Law Rep. 329. Remainders ⇐ 1; Wills ⇐ 634(4.1).

A devise of real estate to trustees, in trust to collect the rents, and pay a definite sum annually to the widow of the testator during her life, and to divide the residue equally among his children, "or their heirs," and at the death of his widow to convey an equal part of his lands to each of his children, "or their heirs," vests an equitable estate in each of his children at the death of the testator, in the absence of a clear intention to postpone the vesting to some later time. Bolton's Trustees v. Ohio Nat. Bank (Ohio 1893) 50 Ohio St. 290, 29 W.L.B. 329, 33 N.E. 1115. Remainders ⚫= 1; Wills ⚫= 634(8)

8. —— Reversions and executory devises, future interests

Where a testator devises real estate to his daughter for life with a remainder after her death to her children, as yet unborn, forever, without any further disposition of the inheritance, the reversion in fee descends to and vests in the heirs of the testator subject to divestment if the devisee for life should die leaving children. Gilpin v. Williams (Ohio 1874) 25 Ohio St. 283. Wills ⚫= 866

Where a testator devises a life estate in one-eighth of his real estate to his daughter with a remainder to her children in fee, and there is no provision in the will respecting a disposition of the remainder in case the daughter dies without issue and nothing showing a contrary intention of the testator, the daughter takes a life estate only and upon her death without issue the testator will have died intestate as to the contingent reversion of her share, and the same will revert to his general heirs. Gilpin v. Williams (Ohio 1867) 17 Ohio St. 396.

Where a testator directs that his executors should carry on his brewery for seven years for the benefit of the estate, and then deliver the brewery and its proceeds to the residuary legatees named in the will, the moneys and profits derived from the business are assets in the hands of the executors, and their sureties are liable upon their bond for the executor's failure to pay a just debt of the estate from such assets. Gandolfo v. Walker (Ohio 1864) 15 Ohio St. 251. Executors And Administrators ⚫= 41

Where a testator devises his estate to certain trustees and their successors to hold as joint tenants upon trusts, the limitation over to the successors is void as an attempt to create a perpetuity; the grantees take at law an estate for life, with a remainder for life during the life of the survivors, leaving the remainder in fee to descend to the heir, and during the life of the trustee or survivors the heir cannot maintain ejectment. Miles' Lessee v. Fisher (Ohio 1840) 10 Ohio 1, 36 Am.Dec. 61.

Where a testator gives a life estate in real estate to his widow as long as she remains his widow to raise his children, and if she ceases to be his widow the lands should not be disposed of until his youngest child comes of age, there can be no partition among the residuary devisees until the majority of such youngest child, even though the widow's estate is extinguished by her remarriage. Davison v. Wolf (Ohio 1839) 9 Ohio 73. Wills ⚫= 733(3)

Interests of children under will directing trustee to pay mortgages, sell real estate, and distribute proceeds among children held contingent, vesting at time of distribution. Webb v. Biles (Hamilton 1927) 27 Ohio App. 197, 161 N.E. 218, 5 Ohio Law Abs. 607, affirmed 118 Ohio St. 346, 161 N.E. 49, 6 Ohio Law Abs. 239, 26 Ohio Law Rep. 273. Wills ⚫= 630(4)

Where there is a devise or bequest to one, coupled with the provision that if he die without issue such property shall go to another, the words "die without issue" are to be interpreted as referring to the time of the death of the first taker, unless a contrary intention and purpose of the testator is clearly manifested. Briggs v. Hopkins (Ohio 1921) 103 Ohio St. 321, 132 N.E. 843, 19 Ohio Law Rep. 371. Wills ⚫= 545(2)

Where testator devises realty to a son for life and to his "heirs" in sense of "children," the realty, on death of son without children, does not go to his widow, but the remainder fails, and it reverts to son's brothers and sisters as heirs of testator. Cultice v. Mills (Ohio 1918) 97 Ohio St. 112, 119 N.E. 200, 15 Ohio Law Rep. 538, 15 Ohio Law Rep. 549. Reversions ⚫= 1; Wills ⚫= 866

Where there is a devise to a son, and if he dies without lineal descendants living at his death, then over, an estate by implication in the lineal descendants is not created, but the son takes a fee defeasible, on his death without lineal descendants, at the time of his decease, and in the event of lineal descendants living at such time, his fee becomes absolute, and the descendants have no interest under the will as against his grantee. Anderson v. United Realty Co. (Ohio 1908) 79 Ohio St. 23, 86 N.E. 644, 6 Ohio Law Rep. 516, affirmed 32 S.Ct. 50, 222 U.S. 164, 56 L.Ed. 144. Wills ⚫= 602(3)

A provision in a will giving a legatee the interest annually during his life of $1,000, which the executor is directed to invest, the money to be paid at the death of the legatee to his children or their issue, and, in case he die without children or issue, then to another, and which further provides that the legatee may secure the return of the money on his death, and on the offer of such security the sum shall be delivered to the legatee, is a provision for the payment of money only, and not for the delivery of the securities. Devenney v. Devenney (Ohio 1906) 74 Ohio St. 96, 77 N.E. 688, 3 Ohio Law Rep. 674, 4 Ohio Law Rep. 9. Trusts ⚫= 126; Wills ⚫= 684.8

A devise of lands to the two children of the testator, with the provision that, "should either die without heirs capable of inheriting, all such one's share and legacies under this will shall inure to the survivor," vests in each an estate in fee, determinable upon the contingency of death without children; and upon that contingency the estate of the deceased child passes to the other, by way of executory devise, although the deceased child leaves a husband surviving her. Durfee v. MacNeil (Ohio 1898) 58 Ohio St. 238, 39 W.L.B. 393, 50 N.E. 721. Wills ⚫= 602(3)

9. Procedure and appeal

A petition alleging a trust under a will and asking its construction without alleging that the executor has funds in his hands which will be involved, is not sufficient. Rothgeb v. Mauck (Ohio 1880) 35 Ohio St. 503.

An action cannot be maintained under this section for the mere purpose of obtaining the court's opinion as to the meaning or legal effect of a will, where the complainants make no case for any relief. Corry v. Fleming (Ohio 1876) 29 Ohio St. 147.

Where two religious societies are claiming as beneficiaries under a trust, the court may cause them to interplead without compelling either to establish its corporate rights at law. First Presbyterian Society of Tp. Gallipolis v. First Presbyterian Society of the Tp. Gallipolis (Ohio 1874) 25 Ohio St. 128.

Actions under this section may be appealed from the common pleas court to the district court of appeals. Swing v. Townsend (Ohio 1873) 24 Ohio St. 1.

A trustee may apply to a court of equity to define his powers and give judicial sanction to his acts, but the court will not order a sale of property where no adverse right is asserted. Wiswell v. First Congregational Church of Cincinnati (Ohio 1862) 14 Ohio St. 31. Trusts ⚫= 178

Genuine issues of material fact, precluding summary judgment for beneficiary's attorney in legal malpractice action by estate's administrator, existed as to whether attorney's representation of beneficiary began before statute of limitations expired on estate's wrongful death claim. DePugh v. Sladoje (Ohio App. 2 Dist., 06-14-1996) 111 Ohio App.3d 675, 676 N.E.2d 1231. Judgment ⚫= 181(16)

Genuine issues of material fact, precluding summary judgment for attorneys in legal malpractice action alleging that statute of limitations on administrator-beneficiary's wrongful death claim expired because attorneys made incorrect representations to client as a beneficiary about time in which that action needed to be filed, existed as to whether such alleged representations breached duty that attorneys owed to client in his personal capacity as a beneficiary. DePugh v. Sladoje (Ohio App. 2 Dist., 06-14-1996) 111 Ohio App.3d 675, 676 N.E.2d 1231. Judgment ⚫= 181(16)

Genuine issues of material fact, precluding summary judgment for beneficiary's attorney in legal malpractice action by estate's administrator, existed as to whether attorney breached duty owed to beneficiary by having estate's initial wrongful death claim dismissed, having administrator removed from that capacity, and failing to have beneficiary appointed administrator before statute of limitations on wrongful death claim expired. DePugh v. Sladoje (Ohio App. 2 Dist., 06-14-1996) 111 Ohio App.3d 675, 676 N.E.2d 1231. Judgment ⚫= 181(16)

Although legatees, devisees, heirs, executors, and other interested parties are necessary parties to will contest action, it does not follow that by bringing such action those who contest the will are making "claims against" any other opposing party; thus, counterclaim or cross claim is inappropriate manner in which to commence will contest action, since rule permitting counterclaim or cross claim is based upon existence of "claim against" opposing party or coparty. Hess v. Sommers (Mercer 1982) 4 Ohio App.3d 281, 448 N.E.2d 494, 4 O.B.R. 500. Wills ⚫= 280.1

The state of Ohio is not a necessary party in an action to construe a will where there has been no prior judicial determination of escheat to the state. Boulger v. Evans (Ohio 1978) 54 Ohio St.2d 371, 377 N.E.2d 753, 8 O.O.3d 388.

A judgment construing a will is res judicata, and the questions or facts necessarily determined therein cannot be disputed or relitigated in a subsequent action between the same parties or their successors in interest.

Tiedtke v. Tiedtke (Lucas 1951) 91 Ohio App. 442, 108 N.E.2d 578, 49 O.O. 36, appeal denied 156 Ohio St. 187, 101 N.E.2d 500, 46 O.O. 58, affirmed 157 Ohio St. 554, 106 N.E.2d 637, 47 O.O. 411. Wills ⇒ 705

A proceeding under an application to the probate court by a guardian for its direction as to the payment of a claim presented to such guardian is not an "action" within this section, when the claimant is not made a party to such proceeding. Sacks v. Johnston (Lucas 1943) 76 Ohio App. 143, 63 N.E.2d 246, 31 O.O. 438.

This section gives right of appeal from order or judgment of probate court in proceeding by executor to determine whether certain promissory notes were obligations belonging to estate and whether they should be set forth in inventory and appraisal. In re Doppes' Estate (Hamilton 1942) 70 Ohio App. 354, 42 N.E.2d 208, 35 Ohio Law Abs. 600, 25 O.O. 93.

Proceeding in probate court by executor for determination regarding who were entitled to share in decedent's estate under the plain language of his will was not a "proceeding to construe will" but was rather a "proceeding to determine heirship" and, therefore, judgment of probate court was not appealable to Court of Common Pleas on questions of fact and law but was appealable directly to Court of Appeals. Stewart v. Purget (Clark 1941) 37 N.E.2d 549, 34 Ohio Law Abs. 343. Appeal And Error ⇒ 240

An executor in its official capacity cannot be prejudiced in action for instructions respecting disposition of estate, by order simply directing the administration of the estate, and cannot appeal therefrom in its official capacity. First Nat. Bank of Cincinnati v. Rawson (Hamilton 1936) 54 Ohio App. 285, 7 N.E.2d 6, 23 Ohio Law Abs. 25, 8 O.O. 13.

Where action for instructions respecting disposition of estate is brought by an executor in official capacity and no interest or right in that capacity has been prejudiced by an erroneous judgment, such judgment will not be disturbed unless other persons interested in the will appeal, or unless the executor does so in its individual capacity. First Nat. Bank of Cincinnati v. Rawson (Hamilton 1936) 54 Ohio App. 285, 7 N.E.2d 6, 23 Ohio Law Abs. 25, 8 O.O. 13.

In an action brought by executors under this section, asking for the construction of a will, the petition raises all the issues in the case, no other pleadings are required, and a default judgment cannot be rendered against a party in interest for failure to answer. Hood v. Garrett (Highland 1936) 53 Ohio App. 464, 5 N.E.2d 937, 22 Ohio Law Abs. 694, 7 O.O. 316.

Proceeding by fiduciary for directions respecting estate not involving trust *held* not chancery case, and therefore not appealable to Court of Appeals (GC § 10857; Const Art IV, §6). Crowley v. Crowley (Ohio 1931) 124 Ohio St. 454, 179 N.E. 360, 11 Ohio Law Abs. 64, 35 Ohio Law Rep. 466. Appeal And Error ⇒ 4; Courts ⇒ 240

In action for construction of will, cause of action for a construction of the will by reason of its terms, and also by reason of agreement between the parties as to its construction, were both appealable. Grindle v. Warner (Clark 1929) 33 Ohio App. 532, 170 N.E. 31, error dismissed 121 Ohio St. 625, 172 N.E. 379.

Legatee under will is not entitled to file cross-petition for construction of will, where it was not shown that executor was requested in writing to file such action and failed for thirty days to do so. Snyder v. Heffner (Pickaway 1929) 33 Ohio App. 379, 169 N.E. 460. Declaratory Judgment ⇒ 300; Wills ⇒ 697(2)

After a widow has elected to take under a will leaving her all the testator's property in trust for their children, the legatees' action for a construction of the trust is not governed by RS 6202 and they are not impeded in pursuit of their rights. (See also Spreen v Sandman, 2 CC 441, 1 CD 577 (Hamilton 1887), appeal dismissed by 26 B 247 (OS 1891).) Cassidy v. Hynton (Ohio 1886) 44 Ohio St. 530, 16 W.L.B. 484, 9 N.E. 129.

Where the court of common pleas holds that there is no trust, the trustee may appeal to the circuit court in the interest of the cestui que trust. Hunt v. Edgerton (Ohio Cir. 1906) 19 Ohio C.D. 377, 9 Ohio C.C.(N.S.) 353, affirmed 75 Ohio St. 594, 80 N.E. 1126, 4 Ohio Law Rep. 521.

Where a will containing a charitable trust was made within a year of the testator's death and bequeathed money payable in two years, the executor need not wait two years before proceeding to have the will construed. Gordon v. Groesbeck (Ohio Cir. 1885) 1 Ohio C.D. 176. Wills ⇒ 259

Tortious interference with expectancy of inheritance redresses personal injury caused by intentional tort for which damages run directly from the tort-feasor to the injured plaintiff. Firestone v. Galbreath (C.A.6 (Ohio), 05-31-1994) 25 F.3d 323, on remand 895 F.Supp. 917. Torts ⇒ 289

Under Ohio law, fully vested testamentary right is not prerequisite for maintaining cause of action for tortious interference with expectancy of inheritance. Firestone v. Galbreath (C.A.6 (Ohio), 05-31-1994) 25 F.3d 323, on remand 895 F.Supp. 917. Torts ⇒ 289

Under Ohio law, res judicata, arising from state court determination that failure of family trust beneficiary to comply with demand provisions of probate code precluded family trust beneficiary from proceeding with tort claim, barred beneficiary from bringing same claim for tortious interference with expectancy in federal court; gist of both claims was that defendants wrongfully obtained property from settlor prior to her death which had become part of residual estate and bequeathed to family trust. Firestone v. Galbreath (S.D.Ohio, 08-09-1995) 895 F.Supp. 917. Judgment ⇒ 828.15(1)

10. Unauthorized actions

The heirs of an intestate cannot maintain an action in their own names to recover possession of assets belonging to the estate or to compel the executors of a party who had a life interest in such assets and has wrongly disposed of them by will to account for the assets, even after settlement by the administrator and where there are no outstanding debts. Davis v. Corwine (Ohio 1874) 25 Ohio St. 668. Descent And Distribution ⇒ 76

Trust beneficiary made demand of trustees to pursue claims against charitable foundation, and trustees failed to act within 30 days, and thus, beneficiary had standing to bring claims that foundation converted trust assets for its own benefit, even though statutory authority to sue was solely in fiduciary accountable to probate court to bring such claims and only Ohio Attorney General had standing to enforce or administer charitable foundation; statute only applied to testamentary trusts and trust was inter vivos trust, and claims did not purport to seek oversight of foundation's administration or enforce terms of charitable trust. Dater v. Charles H. Dater Foundation (Ohio App. 1 Dist., Hamilton, 12-30-2003) No. C-020675, No. C-020784, 2003-Ohio-7148, 2003 WL 23024026, Unreported, appeal not allowed 102 Ohio St.3d 1459, 809 N.E.2d 32, 2004-Ohio-2569. Charities ⇒ 49

Probate court acted within its discretion by refusing to amend testamentary trust to grant special testamentary powers of appointment to sons of settlor, who were trust beneficiaries, and who were both unmarried and without issue and were 66 and 75 years old respectively, even though such powers would have allowed sons to appoint half of trust estate to lineal descendants of their grandparents or to qualified charities, which would have minimized taxes on assets passing under trust; while settlor probably did not contemplate that none of his sons would have issue, trust language did not create duty to avoid taxation, or provide for special testamentary powers of appointment. Fifth Third Bank v. Simpson (Ohio App. 1 Dist., 06-25-1999) 134 Ohio App.3d 71, 730 N.E.2d 406, appeal not allowed 87 Ohio St.3d 1432, 718 N.E.2d 448. Trusts ⇒ 57

Where main question in proceeding was heirship under the plain language of a will, fact that wording of will required consideration was only incidental and hence, such proceeding did not come within this section. Stewart v. Purget (Clark 1941) 37 N.E.2d 549, 34 Ohio Law Abs. 343.

Statute authorizing fiduciary to sue for construction of will does not authorize heir, legatee, creditor, or even fiduciary to ask court to determine owner of realty devised. Wagner v. Schrembs (Stark 1932) 44 Ohio App. 44, 184 N.E. 292, 14 Ohio Law Abs. 187, 37 Ohio Law Rep. 595. Wills ⇒ 695(2)

A judgment in an action to construe a will brought by favor of former GC 10857 (RC 2107.46), was not conclusive against a beneficiary not a party thereto, and cannot be employed to justify an administration of the estate in a way contrary to the terms of the will. In re Kachelmacher's Estate (Hocking 1931) 40 Ohio App. 282, 178 N.E. 314, 11 Ohio Law Abs. 279.

A third party acquiring said estate from a widow by gift or fraud, or by collusion with her to the injury of the vested rights of those in remainder, and with knowledge of the will, holds the same, and the fruits thereof, as a trustee for the remainder-men, and is liable as such trustee to account to them in equity. Johnson v. Johnson (Ohio 1894) 51 Ohio St. 446, 32 W.L.B. 219, 38 N.E. 61.

In an action under RS 6202, the court cannot inquire whether trustees had done or omitted acts authorizing forfeiture. City of Cincinnati v. McMicken (Ohio Cir. 1892) 3 Ohio C.D. 409, modified.

11. Will construction—Intent

The meaning of a phrase in a will is to be ascertained by finding out what the testator intended by using it, and not what it may in legal effect mean. Forsythe v. Mintier (Ohio 1883) 39 Ohio St. 349, 10 W.L.B. 280.

In a will provision which directs that should the testator's wife claim dower, the balance of certain personal property bequeathed for her support "shall be shared equally among my heirs," the words "my heirs" will be construed as meaning "my heirs according to the statute of distribution, exclusive of my wife," though his wife, in case of intestacy, would have taken all the personal property under the statute. Jones v. Lloyd (Ohio 1878) 33 Ohio St. 572.

Where a testator vests the title to a specific portion of his real estate in his executors in trust with directions to sell the land and distribute the proceeds equally among the heirs, and it is claimed that a trust was created in all the land of the testator, though the will's language is entirely different as to that land, the trust is limited to the lands named specifically in the clause where it is found. Nimmons v. Westfall (Ohio 1877) 33 Ohio St. 213.

A testatrix's intention must be ascertained from the words of her will, and such words, if technical, must be taken in their technical sense, and if not technical, then in their ordinary sense, unless it appears from the context that they were used in some secondary sense; all parts of the will must be construed together and effect given to every word contained in it if possible. (See also Decker v Decker, 3 O 157 (1827); Linton v Laycock, 33 OS 128 (1877); but see Barr v Denney, 79 OS 358, 87 NE 267 (1909).) Townsend's Ex'rs v. Townsend (Ohio 1874) 25 Ohio St. 477.

Where a testator, by a condition in his will, excludes any one of his heirs who "goes to law to break his will" from any part or share in his estate, such a clause is valid and binding, and effect will be given to it in respect to devises of real estate as well as bequests of personalty. Bradford v. Bradford (Ohio 1869) 19 Ohio St. 546, 2 Am.Rep. 419.

A bequest of the right to take tolls upon a road, in trust to pay out of the tolls a specified sum monthly to the testator's mother for her life is not a demonstrative legacy but a trust fund payable from a specific legacy alone, and upon failure or insufficiency of the tolls, the monthly installments cannot be charged upon the estate. Morris v. Harris (Ohio 1869) 19 Ohio St. 15. Wills ⟲ 753

Where a testator bequeaths a legacy to one of his daughters in one clause, and in another clause directs that a second daughter who was devised land should pay a sum to the first daughter in installments, the sum is not to be applied to the first legacy, but is in addition thereto. Edwards v. Rainier's Ex'rs (Ohio 1867) 17 Ohio St. 597.

Whether a trust created by will be regarded as executed or executory, where the words of the will clearly point out what the trust is to be and distinctly specify its limitations, the same construction will be put on the will's language. Gilpin v. Williams (Ohio 1867) 17 Ohio St. 396.

Where a testator in his will employs a term which standing alone may seem to designate a class of persons as his legatees, but when viewed in light of the circumstances and the construction of the whole will it is apparent that the term was used as a substitute for the legatees' names and to identify individuals, such words will not be held to embrace a class of persons, but will be confined to the individual persons designated. Starling's Ex'r v. Price (Ohio 1864) 16 Ohio St. 29.

Words of exclusion in a testator's will cannot be used to disinherit one of his lawful heirs or to raise an estate by implication in favor of his other heirs where there is no attempt in the will to dispose of the property at issue or to create any interest thereon. Crane v. Doty's Ex'rs (Ohio 1853) 1 Ohio St. 279.

Where a testator has wholly failed to give his meaning and the residuary clause will admit of more than one construction, a court of equity will give it that construction which will be most favorable to the heir at law. Bane v. Wick (Ohio 1850) 19 Ohio 328.

A testator may use such words as he may please to convey his intention, and such intention, if clearly manifested, will be carried into effect if it is not unlawful and does not create an estate forbidden by law. (See also Carter v Reddish, 32 OS 1 (1876).) King v. Beck (Ohio 1846) 15 Ohio 559.

Where a testator bequeaths one half of all his personal property to his wife, and at her death, all of his stock to his daughter, the two bequests are repugnant and the latter, more specific bequest must prevail. Young v. McIntire's Ex'rs (Ohio 1828) 3 Ohio 498.

In prior appeal the Court of Appeals intended to remand probate case to determine whether "Extended Family Adult Care" as written in decedent's will was merely a misnomer for "Extended Family Adult Care Center," rather than to determine whether will's bequest to facility was to a place or to a business entity, for purposes of determining whether bequest of residuary of decedent's estate to facility was void, and thus remand was required to address former question, where trial court had mistakenly addressed later question in prior remand. Beaston v. Slingwine (Ohio App. 3 Dist., Seneca, 03-01-2004) No. 13-03-04, 2004-Ohio-924, 2004 WL 370408, Unreported. Wills ⟲ 706

Testator intended that share of testamentary trust of beneficiary who died childless before share was distributed to her would be distributed to co-beneficiaries equally; pursuant to terms of trust, lineal descendant's right to proceeds from trust was contingent upon descendant surviving full distribution of trust share, testator intended to keep trust corpus from being alienated outside bloodlines of his family or their descendants, and distribution would comport with intent of trust's spendthrift clause. Natl. City Bank v. Beyer (Ohio, 06-21-2000) 89 Ohio St.3d 152, 729 N.E.2d 711, 2000-Ohio-126. Wills ⟲ 682(1)

Beneficiaries, who had reached the age of 25 prior to their mother's death, had acquired a vested interest in the corpus of their father's testamentary trust, pursuant to its terms, because each had a present fixed right to future enjoyment of the trust assets. Natl. City Bank v. Beyer (Ohio, 06-21-2000) 89 Ohio St.3d 152, 729 N.E.2d 711, 2000-Ohio-126. Wills ⟲ 682(2)

Testator's mere placement of general bequest to his housekeeper in "Item One" of his will did not sufficiently show testator's intent to give that bequest any priority over other general bequests in "Item Two" for purposes of abatement, and thus burden of estate's debts fell on each general beneficiary pro rata. In re Estate of Oberstar (Ohio App. 11 Dist., 04-14-1998) 126 Ohio App.3d 30, 709 N.E.2d 872. Wills ⟲ 812

Where testator's will had created trust in favor of her son until son reached age of 25, at which time trust would be terminated and principal and interest distributed to son, son's death intestate at age 20 did not create resulting trust in favor of son's maternal grandparents, but rather, resulted in remainder interest passing to son's heirs at law; trust did not fail to exhaust res, since testator's intent was that son would ultimately receive trust property in fee simple, and trust did not fail for want of beneficiaries or any other cause. Summers v. Summers (Ohio App. 4 Dist., 06-09-1997) 121 Ohio App.3d 263, 699 N.E.2d 958, appeal not allowed 80 Ohio St.3d 1426, 685 N.E.2d 238. Trusts ⟲ 68

In construction of will, sole purpose of court is to ascertain and carry out intention of testator, which must be ascertained from words contained in will. Summers v. Summers (Ohio App. 4 Dist., 06-09-1997) 121 Ohio App.3d 263, 699 N.E.2d 958, appeal not allowed 80 Ohio St.3d 1426, 685 N.E.2d 238. Wills ⟲ 439; Wills ⟲ 440

Theory that testator would have drafted her will differently had she foreseen circumstances existing at her death does not justify altering manifest meaning of will. Summers v. Summers (Ohio App. 4 Dist., 06-09-1997) 121 Ohio App.3d 263, 699 N.E.2d 958, appeal not allowed 80 Ohio St.3d 1426, 685 N.E.2d 238. Wills ⟲ 483

A devise or bequest of a life interest must be clearly expressed to be effective. Margolis v. Pagano (Ohio Com.Pl. 1986) 39 Ohio Misc.2d 1, 528 N.E.2d 1331. Wills ⟲ 102

A clause is not uncertain and shows intent to transfer by will where the clause utilizes language such as "all the rest, residue, or remainder." Margolis v. Pagano (Ohio Com.Pl. 1986) 39 Ohio Misc.2d 1, 528 N.E.2d 1331. Wills ⟲ 587(1)

The subject matter of an ineffective legacy will pass in residue and not intestate, provided there is a valid residuary clause and the testator's intent was to cause the subject to pass through the will rather than pass intestate. Margolis v. Pagano (Ohio Com.Pl. 1986) 39 Ohio Misc.2d 1, 528 N.E.2d 1331. Wills ⟲ 858(1)

Where will provides that the executors are to hold a sum of money in trust to provide for the decoration of the graves of testatrix and other relatives, the executors have the right to arrange with a cemetery association to continue such plans, and will does not create a trust other than the executorship. Whiting v. Bertram (Hamilton 1935) 51 Ohio App. 40, 199 N.E. 367, 19 Ohio Law Abs. 363, 3 O.O. 292.

"Cy pres doctrine" means that, where literal execution of the trusts of a charitable gift is inexpedient or impracticable, equity will execute them as nearly as it can, according to original plan, but doctrine applies only where testator has manifested general intention to give to charity; where cy pres doctrine was inapplicable, bequests made for purposes of trust lapsed, and all property covered thereby passed by inheritance to next of kin. Allen v. City of Bellefontaine (Logan 1934) 47 Ohio App. 359, 191 N.E. 896, 17 Ohio Law Abs. 87, 40 Ohio Law Rep. 320. Charities ⟲ 37(1)

Testatrix' intention must be applied to facts existing at time will was written, or possibly at testatrix' death. Nelson v. Minton (Butler 1933) 46 Ohio App. 39, 187 N.E. 576, 14 Ohio Law Abs. 679, 38 Ohio Law Rep. 287. Wills ⟲ 481

In construction of clauses in a will, purpose of analysis is to reach intent of the maker. Cleveland Trust Co. v. Hickox (Ohio App. 1929) 32 Ohio App. 69, 167 N.E. 592, 29 Ohio Law Rep. 452.

Where testator stated in his will that it was made in case he met with an accident on a contemplated journey, but lived for one year and two months after such possible calamity had passed without change in his circumstances or those of the beneficiaries named in the will and without having changed or revoked the will which was in his personal custody, a strong presumption arises that the statement was not intended as a contingency or a condition precedent. McMerriman v. Schiel (Ohio 1923) 108 Ohio St. 334, 140 N.E. 600, 1 Ohio Law Abs. 883, 21 Ohio Law Rep. 151, 21 Ohio Law Rep. 152. Wills ⚖ 80

Where a will directed named persons to conduct moving picture business during the life of a lease, but did not authorize them to exercise option to renew lease, they were not entitled to a decree of specific performance to compel lessor to execute a renewal lease. Mills v. Connor (Ohio 1922) 104 Ohio St. 409, 135 N.E. 616, 20 Ohio Law Rep. 16, 20 Ohio Law Rep. 18. Landlord And Tenant ⚖ 86(1); Specific Performance ⚖ 17

Under GC 11494, disqualifying an attorney from testifying concerning a communication made to him by his client except by the client's express consent, an attorney, who acted as subscribing witness to client's will, could testify as to testamentary capacity or as to any other fact affecting validity of will, since client by procuring attorney as a subscribing witness consented that he might so testify. Knepper v. Knepper (Ohio 1921) 103 Ohio St. 529, 134 N.E. 476, 19 Ohio Law Rep. 462. Attorney And Client ⚖ 22; Witnesses ⚖ 219(3)

The changed value of money and property and the changed circumstances and needs of the beneficiary under a will do not justify a court in modifying its provisions to meet the changed circumstances and conditions, notwithstanding that, had testator foreseen them, he would have provided a different and larger income. Union Sav. Bank & Trust Co. v. Alter (Ohio 1921) 103 Ohio St. 188, 132 N.E. 834, 19 Ohio Law Rep. 178, 19 Ohio Law Rep. 179. Wills ⚖ 483

Where a will provided that on death of testator's widow all his estate then in existence should be equally divided between his and his wife's nearest of kin, "they sharing like and like," and where the next of kin of testator and of his widow were unequal in number, the intent was to give one-half to his own nearest of kin and one-half to her nearest of kin; the expression "they sharing like and like" referring to the proportionate share that each one of the two classes should take. Godfrey v. Epple (Ohio 1919) 100 Ohio St. 447, 126 N.E. 886, 11 A.L.R. 317, 17 Ohio Law Rep. 379, 17 Ohio Law Rep. 482. Wills ⚖ 531(3)

That the acts of a surviving consort may amount to an election, where the statutory method, GC 10566 et seq. (repealed 1932. See §10504–55 et seq.), is not followed, to take under the will, such acts must clearly demonstrate a purpose to accept the provisions of the will. Colored Industrial School of Cincinnati v. Bates (Ohio 1914) 90 Ohio St. 288, 107 N.E. 770, 12 Ohio Law Rep. 78, Am.Ann.Cas. 1916C,1198, Am.Ann.Cas. 1916C, 1198. Wills ⚖ 794

Though the presumption that a general description, coupled with an enumeration, covers only things ejusdem generis must yield to testator's intent, as gathered from the whole will, such presumption must prevail, when supported by such intention. Creamer v. Harris (Ohio 1914) 90 Ohio St. 160, 106 N.E. 967, 11 Ohio Law Rep. 519, Am.Ann.Cas. 1916C, 1137. Wills ⚖ 579

Where a will devises one-half of an estate to testator's lawful heirs and one-half to the lawful heirs of his wife, and provides for the disposition of stock bequeathed to his sister, and to the sister and brother of his wife, the persons included in the designation "lawful heirs" are to be ascertained as of the date of the death of testator or his wife, respectively. Wilberding v. Miller (Ohio 1913) 88 Ohio St. 609, 90 Ohio St. 28, 106 N.E. 665, 11 Ohio Law Rep. 96, 11 Ohio Law Rep. 262, 11 Ohio Law Rep. 447. Wills ⚖ 524(1)

An instrument, executed in compliance with the statute of wills, appointing an executor to settle up all property, both personal and real, and making the grand-daughters of testatrix equal "heirs" with her own children, is dispositive, and devised to the granddaughters each an equal share with the children of testatrix. Moon v. Stewart (Ohio 1913) 87 Ohio St. 349, 101 N.E. 344, 10 Ohio Law Rep. 601, Am.Ann.Cas. 1914A, 104. Wills ⚖ 525

In a will leaving a testator's wife the part of the estate secured to her by the laws of distribution, the word "distribution" held to extend to all the estate, real, personal and mixed. Foster v. Clifford (Ohio 1913) 87 Ohio St. 294, 101 N.E. 269, 10 Ohio Law Rep. 600, Am.Ann.Cas. 1915B, 65. Wills ⚖ 558(1)

Where there was not at the execution of a will any statute for the adoption of children, it is not required that testator should appear to have had the specific intention that the succession should be to the adopted child of a beneficiary for life, if it appears that the child by adoption comes within the terms by which the testator declared his general intentions. Smith v. Hunter (Ohio 1912) 86 Ohio St. 106, 99 N.E. 91, 10 Ohio Law Rep. 72. Adoption ⚖ 21; Wills ⚖ 506(5)

Where testatrix by will disposed of property belonging to her, and also of property belonging to the estate of her deceased husband, and certain of her children elected to insist on their proprietary rights in the lands of their deceased father, they did not by such election render other lands belonging to their mother, and disposed of by the will, intestate property, but they passed under the will to the devisee deprived of his interest in the lands of the father by such election, to the extent that may be necessary for his compensation. Bebout v. Quick (Ohio 1909) 81 Ohio St. 196, 90 N.E. 162, 7 Ohio Law Rep. 506. Wills ⚖ 802(1)

Technical rules of construction may be used as aids to interpretation of a will but cannot control if they are in conflict with the apparent intention of the testator. Barr v. Denney (Ohio 1909) 79 Ohio St. 358, 87 N.E. 267, 6 Ohio Law Rep. 616.

A trust created by will, the provisions of which are not repugnant to law or contrary to public policy, will not be decreed terminated where the objects of the trust have not been fully accomplished and their accomplishment has not been made impossible. Robbins v. Smith (Ohio 1905) 72 Ohio St. 1, 73 N.E. 1051, 2 Ohio Law Rep. 494. Trusts ⚖ 61(1)

Testator bequeathed his residuary estate to his lawful heirs, without other designation as to who were intended as his beneficiaries, and directed that the residuum should be equally divided "among my lawful heirs, share and share alike." Held, that all persons who at the time of testator's death were his lawful heirs were entitled to share in his residuary estate, regardless of their relationship to the testator, per capita. Mooney v. Purpus (Ohio 1904) 70 Ohio St. 57, 70 N.E. 894, 2 Ohio Law Rep. 3. Wills ⚖ 531(2)

Where a testator bequeathed all the net income of his estate to a trustee in trust for the education and support of a certain person for life, without other limitation, held, that the bequest so made is an absolute one, and is subject to the claim of creditors. Thornton v. Stanley (Ohio 1896) 55 Ohio St. 199, 36 W.L.B. 309, 45 N.E. 318. Wills ⚖ 614(3)

The word "heirs" where used by a testator having living children will be regarded as a synonym for children. Kuster v. Yeoman (Ohio Cir. 1911) 22 Ohio C.D. 476, 14 Ohio C.C.(N.S.) 264, affirmed 88 Ohio St. 592, 106 N.E. 1087, 11 Ohio Law Rep. 70. Wills ⚖ 506(4)

Where a testatrix in her will directs that her property shall go "as the law directs, with the following modifications," she has made a testamentary disposition of the property, and her heirs take nothing by descent (See also Woodruff v Woodruff, 3 CC(NS) 616, 13 CD 408 (Hamilton 1902).) Huber v. Carew (Ohio Cir. 1904) 16 Ohio C.D. 389, 7 Ohio C.C.(N.S.) 609, affirmed 74 Ohio St. 469, 78 N.E. 1127, 3 Ohio Law Rep. 674. Wills ⚖ 713

A presumption as to the intent of the testator will be considered in determining the extent of an estate devised, and the word "and" will not be regarded as equivalent to "and also" where the testator intended to make a distinction between two types of property devised. Silk v. Merry (Ohio Cir. 1901) 13 Ohio C.D. 218, 3 Ohio C.C.N.S. 91.

12. —— Evidence, will construction

In construing a will, in order to ascertain whether a disconnected piece of woodland was in fact part of one of "two farms" of the testator so as to pass under the devise, extrinsic evidence may be received to show the circumstances under which the will was made. Black v. Hill (Ohio 1877) 32 Ohio St. 313.

Where a will uses words that could be construed as the name of a place or a description equally, parol evidence is admissible to show in which of the two senses the testator intended them. Boggs v. Taylor (Ohio 1875) 26 Ohio St. 604.

The division of a township to which a devise has been made for school purposes does not affect the devise, and the student beneficiaries intended when the will was made, though in the township set off from the original one, partake of the fund created. Board of Education of Fairfield Tp. v. Ladd (Ohio 1875) 26 Ohio St. 210.

Where a clause in a testator's will gives his wife "and to her heirs and assigns forever" all his estate, real and personal, it passes a fee, and parol evidence offered by the grandchildren of the testator that the testator's intention was to give his wife a life estate and that she should devise the property to her children equally in her will will not be admitted to contradict, add to, or explain the will. Collins v. Hope (Ohio 1851) 20 Ohio 492.

In construing a will, to which are attached or added codicils, the whole is to be taken together as one instrument; the codicils constitute a part of the will. (See also Collier v Collier's Executors, 3 OS 369 (1854).) Negley v. Gard (Ohio 1851) 20 Ohio 310.

A bequest of moneys and interest that may be recovered from a debtor of the decedent is a specific legacy, and the receipt of the money by the testator during his lifetime is an ademption of the bequest. Gilbreath v. Alban (Ohio 1840) 10 Ohio 64.

Uncontroverted extrinsic evidence, in form of affidavit from attorney of testatrix, introduced by executor of testatrix's will, established that will contained latent ambiguity in that attorney erroneously named "Joyce" Smith as testatrix's beneficiary, instead of "George" Smith, and, thus inclusion of "Joyce" Smith in will was error on part of attorney, in declaratory judgment proceeding involving construction of will. Kaplan v. Fair (Ohio App. 6 Dist., Lucas, 06-30-2004) No. L-03-1300, 2004-Ohio-3457, 2004 WL 1468547, Unreported. Wills ☞ 488

Disinherited daughter had no right to testator's checks in possession of her sister who was sole beneficiary and executrix of testator's estate. Lakes v. Ryan (Ohio App. 12 Dist., Butler, 02-03-2003) No. CA2002-05-118, 2003-Ohio-504, 2003 WL 231272, Unreported. Wills ☞ 727

In a suit filed by an executor of a will seeking construction of the residual clause of the will wherein it is provided that the remainder of the estate is to go to hospices devoted primarily to the care of patients terminally ill with chronic obstructive pulmonary disease, affidavits filed by two hospices created genuine issues of material fact whether the hospices claiming under the will are devoted primarily to the care of patients terminally ill with chronic obstructive pulmonary disease and therefore, the trial court errs in granting the hospices motions for summary judgment. First Natl. Bank of Cincinnati v. Devlin (Warren 1989) 63 Ohio App.3d 708, 580 N.E.2d 25.

The court may consider extrinsic evidence to determine the testator's intention only when the language used in the will creates doubt as to the meaning of the will. Oliver v. Bank One, Dayton, N.A. (Ohio 1991) 60 Ohio St.3d 32, 573 N.E.2d 55. Wills ☞ 488

The distinction between specific and general legacies is that the former singles out the particular thing which testator intends donee to have, without regard to value, while general legacies may be satisfied on the general assets of estate (the residue), with the chief element being quantity or value. Boerstler v. Andrews (Hamilton 1986) 30 Ohio App.3d 63, 506 N.E.2d 279, 30 O.B.R. 118. Wills ☞ 753; Wills ☞ 756

The probate court has authority to determine whether a divorce decree constitutes an implied revocation of legacies to the wife in a will executed prior to the divorce. Davis v. Wallace (Belmont 1962) 192 N.E.2d 291, 91 Ohio Law Abs. 396, 27 O.O.2d 80.

In an action to construe a will the petition raises all issues of fact, but this general rule does not preclude the court from considering issues raised on the further pleadings of interested parties. Balduf v. Evans (Lucas 1953) 95 Ohio App. 292, 118 N.E.2d 848, 53 O.O. 208, reversed 165 Ohio St. 27, 133 N.E.2d 128, 59 O.O. 43. Pleading ☞ 350(7)

Where a latent ambiguity arises by reason of extraneous circumstances, known to the testator, extrinsic evidence of such circumstances may be admitted on the issue of testator's intention, and a reviewing court is not required to anticipate what evidence will be competent and material in relation to the trial of the issues raised on the pleadings. Balduf v. Evans (Lucas 1953) 95 Ohio App. 292, 118 N.E.2d 848, 53 O.O. 208, reversed 165 Ohio St. 27, 133 N.E.2d 128, 59 O.O. 43.

Language of will, if plain and obvious, cannot be qualified by court by conjecture or doubt that may arise from extraneous facts. Stahl v. Mohr (Holmes 1928) 35 Ohio App. 411, 172 N.E. 431. Wills ☞ 488

A petition, in a cause brought under RS 6202 (repealed 1932. See GC 10504–66, 10504–67), to obtain a construction of one item only of a will, which does not set forth the entire will, is bad on demurrer. Devenney v. Devenney (Ohio 1906) 74 Ohio St. 96, 77 N.E. 688, 3 Ohio Law Rep. 674, 4 Ohio Law Rep. 9. Declaratory Judgment ☞ 316; Wills ☞ 702

Courts of equity will not vacate a deed or set aside a will on the ground of influence or importunity, unless it has been unduly or improperly exercised; fair argument and persuasion, or appeals to the conscience or sense of duty of the testator, if fairly made, lay no foundation for setting aside a will. Gregg v. Moore (Ohio Cir. 1911) 23 Ohio C.D. 534, 14 Ohio C.C.N.S. 570.

Where a decedent bought money orders in the name of her sister intending to make a gift, but never had the opportunity to deliver them, the gift is incomplete since the buyer retains power to cancel money orders; the administrator of the estate is therefore entitled to the money in an action brought under GC 10857. McKelvey's Adm'r v. McKelvey (Ohio Cir. 1911) 23 Ohio C.D. 117, 14 Ohio C.C.(N.S.) 331.

A testator is not required to make an equitable will, and because he makes one with which the witnesses for the contestants do not agree does not mean he lacks testamentary capacity, even though the evidence shows some physical weaknesses, failure of memory, or a mistake of an unimportant character in connection with business affairs of the testator. Wilson v. Wilson (Ohio Cir. 1909) 22 Ohio C.D. 498, 14 Ohio C.C.N.S. 241.

In construing a will devising property "to Louisa Jane Barge, wife of my son, Robert T. Barge, and to his lawful heirs" to determine whether the devise is to the son's wife, the son, and his heirs or to the wife and the heirs only the court errs in ruling out testimony of the son's child as to the son's indebtedness, as this tends to show the father meant to exclude the son who would have lost the property to creditors had it been given to him. Kuster v. Yeoman (Ohio Cir. 1911) 22 Ohio C.D. 476, 14 Ohio C.C.(N.S.) 264, affirmed 88 Ohio St. 592, 106 N.E. 1087, 11 Ohio Law Rep. 70.

The subject of delusions of a testator is of no importance to court or jury; the only question is whether the delusions were carried to such an extent that they affected either the natural or selected objects of his bounty, distorting his judgment and preventing him from making a rational disposition of his property. Wadsworth v. Purdy (Ohio Cir. 1908) 21 Ohio C.D. 110, 12 Ohio C.C.N.S. 8.

The burden of proof is upon those propounding the will to make out a prima facie case showing that the testator, at time of execution of the will, was of sound mind and memory. In re Ludlow's Estate (Ohio Prob. 1897) 6 Ohio Dec. 106, 4 Ohio N.P. 99.

2107.47 Protection of purchaser against later will

(A) The title, estate, or interest of a bona fide purchaser, lessee, or encumbrancer, for value, in land situated in this state, that is derived from an heir of a decedent and acquired without knowledge of a will of the decedent that effectively disposes of it to another person, shall not be defeated by the production of a will of the decedent, unless, in the case of a resident decedent, the will is offered for probate within three months after the death of the decedent, or unless, in the case of a nonresident decedent, the will is offered for record in this state within three months after the death of the decedent.

(B) The title, estate, or interest of a bona fide purchaser, lessee, or encumbrancer, for value, in land situated in this state, that is derived from a beneficiary under a will of a decedent and acquired without knowledge of a later will of the decedent that effectively disposes of it to another person, shall not be defeated by the production of a later will of the decedent, unless, in the case of a resident decedent, the later will is offered for probate within three months after the death of the decedent, or unless, in the case of a nonresident decedent, the later will is offered for record in this state within three months after the death of the decedent.

(1996 H 391, eff. 10–1–96; 1981 H 262, eff. 2–2–82; 125 v 903; 1953 H 1; GC 10504–68)

Historical and Statutory Notes

Pre–1953 H 1 Amendments: 114 v 359

Amendment Note: 1996 H 391 substituted "death" for "date" and "decedent" for "appointment of the executor or administrator" throughout the section.

Cross References

Computation of time, 1.14
Marketable Title Act, 5301.47 to 5301.53

Library References

Vendor and Purchaser ☞220.

Wills ⚖︎845.
Westlaw Topic Nos. 400, 409.
C.J.S. Vendor and Purchaser §§ 482 to 483, 517.
C.J.S. Wills §§ 1943, 1955 to 1956, 1958 to 1964, 1966 to 1969, 1971.

Research References

Encyclopedias

OH Jur. 3d Decedents' Estates § 189, Interest Acquired by Transferee.
OH Jur. 3d Decedents' Estates § 1021, Admission to Probate of Will of Later Date—Protection of Bona Fide Purchaser.

Treatises and Practice Aids

Kuehnle and Levey, Ohio Real Estate Law and Practice § 16:13, Curative Acts—Decedent's Estates—Subsequently Produced Will, Rights of Purchaser from Fiduciary or Devisees or Heirs Under Prior Administered Estate.

Law Review and Journal Commentaries

Substitute House Bill 391—Omnibus Probate Bill, William B. McNeil. 7 Prob L J Ohio 2 (September/October 1996).

Notes of Decisions

Adverse possession 2
Recorded will 1

1. Recorded will

The true intent of the enactment of section of the wills act of 1852 (RC 2107.47) was to protect purchasers from the heirs of nonresidents against an unrecorded will, when no protection for such purchaser was intended as against the claims of devisees under a will already on record in this state in pursuance of law. Carpenter v. Denoon (Ohio 1876) 29 Ohio St. 379.

2. Adverse possession

A foreign will devising lands in Ohio but not probated in Ohio for forty years has no validity as against title by adverse possession. Hosler v. Haines (Ohio Cir. 1905) 18 Ohio C.D. 79, 7 Ohio C.C.(N.S.) 261, reversed 76 Ohio St. 588, 81 N.E. 1186, 4 Ohio Law Rep. 769.

2107.48 Foreign will cannot be contested here

There shall be no proceeding in this state to contest a will executed and proved according to the law of another state or of a foreign country, relative to property in this state; but if such will is set aside in the state or country in which it is executed and proved, it shall be invalid in this state as to persons claiming under it who have notice of its being set aside, and invalid as to all other persons from the time an authenticated copy of the final order or decree setting it aside is filed in the office of the probate judge of the county in which the will is recorded.

(1978 H 505, eff. 1-1-79; 1953 H 1; GC 10504-69)

Historical and Statutory Notes

Pre-1953 H 1 Amendments: 114 v 359

Cross References

Foreign wills, 2129.05
Proceedings to admit foreign will to record, 2129.07
Will contest, 2107.71 to 2107.77

Library References

Wills ⚖︎246.
Westlaw Topic No. 409.
C.J.S. Wills § 523.

Research References

Encyclopedias

OH Jur. 3d Decedents' Estates § 1081, Contest of Foreign Will.

Treatises and Practice Aids

Carlin, Baldwin's Ohio Practice, Merrick-Rippner Probate Law § 38:20, Will Contests—Foreign Will.

Notes of Decisions

Cases before Wills Act of 1852, standard 1
Invalid will 2

1. Cases before Wills Act of 1852, standard

A foreign will, not provable under laws of a sister state, will not be admitted to probate here. Barr v. Closterman (Ohio Cir. 1887) 1 Ohio C.D. 546, affirmed.

2. Invalid will

The provision of the wills act of 1852 which forbids the contest of a foreign will executed and proved according to the foreign law has reference to such foreign wills as, when made and proved in conformity with the foreign law are, by the laws of this state, valid to dispose of property therein situated, and does not apply to cases arising under former laws, of wills valid where made, but inoperative here because not executed according to our law. Jones v. Robinson (Ohio 1867) 17 Ohio St. 171.

2107.49 Rule in Shelley's case abolished

When lands, tenements, or hereditaments are given by deed or will to a person for his life, and after his death to his heirs in fee, the conveyance shall vest an estate for life only in such first taker and a remainder in fee simple in his heirs. If the remainder is given to the heirs of the body of the life tenant, the conveyance shall vest an estate for life only in such first taker and a remainder in fee simple in the heirs of his body. The rule in Shelley's case is abolished by this section and shall not be given effect.

(1953 H 1, eff. 10-1-53; GC 10504-70)

Historical and Statutory Notes

Pre-1953 H 1 Amendments: 119 v 348; 114 v 359

Library References

Wills ⚖︎608.
Westlaw Topic No. 409.
C.J.S. Wills §§ 1260 to 1261, 1263 to 1269.

Research References

Encyclopedias

OH Jur. 3d Deeds § 179, Rule in Shelley's Case.
OH Jur. 3d Estates, Pwrs., & Restrnts. on Alienat. § 46, Rule in Shelley's Case.

Treatises and Practice Aids

Carlin, Baldwin's Ohio Practice, Merrick-Rippner Probate Law § 44:2, Rule in Shelley's Case—Abolished.
Carlin, Baldwin's Ohio Practice, Merrick-Rippner Probate Law § 44:5, RC 2107.49—Purpose and Effect—Inter Vivos Trust.
Kuehnle and Levey, Ohio Real Estate Law and Practice § 2:10, Estates—Fee Simple Absolute—Rule in Shelley's Case—Abolished.
Restatement (2d) of Property, Don. Trans. § 30.1, Rule in Shelley's Case.
Restatement (3d) Property (Wills & Don. Trans.) § 16.2, Rule in Shelley's Case Repudiated.

Law Review and Journal Commentaries

The Rule In Shelley's Case Rears Its Ugly Head, Note. 17 U Dayton L Rev 253 (Fall 1991).

Notes of Decisions

Construction and language 3
Rule applicable 1

Rule inapplicable 2

1. Rule applicable

The rules of construction are intended to give a controlling effect to the clear intention of the testator and to forbid the application of the rule in Shelley's case when such application would defeat the manifest intention of the testator. Carter v. Reddish (Ohio 1876) 32 Ohio St. 1.

Where a testator bequeaths an estate to his son to hold in trust for the use of his daughter during her life, giving such daughter the power to appoint absolutely to her heirs, the daughter takes an equitable fee simple as the first cestui que trust. Armstrong v. Zane's Heirs (Ohio 1843) 12 Ohio 287.

The rule in Shelley's case, whereby the ancestor taking a freehold by deed or devise is limited either mediately or immediately to his heirs by the same conveyance, the word "heirs" is a word of limitation, not of purchase, and the fee rests in the ancestor, prevails in Ohio. (See also King v King, 12 O 390 (1843), reversed by 15 O 559 (1846); Armstrong v Zane, 12 O 287 (1843); but see Carter v Reddish, 32 OS 1 (1876).) McFeely's Lessee v. Moore's Heirs (Ohio 1832) 5 Ohio 464, 24 Am.Dec. 314.

Provisions of an inter vivos trust will be governed by the law existing at the time of its creation, absent a contrary intent stated within the instrument itself. Society Nat. Bank v. Jacobson (Ohio 1990) 54 Ohio St.3d 15, 560 N.E.2d 217, rehearing denied 55 Ohio St.3d 709, 563 N.E.2d 302. Trusts ⚖ 113

The rule of common law, known as the "rule in Shelley's case" was abolished as to deeds by a statute effective August 22, 1941, and the abolition thereof cannot be applied retroactively. Waters v. Monroe Coal Co., Inc. (Ohio Com.Pl. 1977) 54 Ohio Misc. 37, 376 N.E.2d 977, 8 O.O.3d 344.

The rule is that where an ancestor took a freehold for life and, by the same conveyance, was limited either mediately or immediately to his heirs, the word "heirs" was a word of limitation, not of purchase, and the fee vested in the ancestor; it is a rule of property rather than one of construction. Waters v. Monroe Coal Co., Inc. (Ohio Com.Pl. 1977) 54 Ohio Misc. 37, 376 N.E.2d 977, 8 O.O.3d 344. Deeds ⚖ 129(1).

Where property is deeded by a mother to her son for life, and then to the heirs of his body, and if he die without heirs of his body, the remainder to revert to the grantor, if living, and if not living, then the remainder to the grantor's heirs at law, it is incumbent upon the widow of the grantee-son, in an action to have quieted her title to such premises, to prove by a preponderance of the evidence that upon the death of the grantee-son without having had issue he had an absolute estate in fee simple in such premises which could pass to her as his heir or which could pass to her under the provisions of his will, i.e., that the grantor-mother had not successfully conveyed or devised away the reversion. Kohler v. Ichler (Hardin 1961) 116 Ohio App. 16, 186 N.E.2d 202, 21 O.O.2d 221. Quieting Title ⚖ 44(3)

Before the rule in Shelley's Case was, as to wills, abrogated in this state by the statute of 1840, a testator devised certain lands to his son for life, and at his death to go to his heirs, and, there being nothing else in the will to show that the testator used the word "heirs" to designate a more limited class, as children, held that, as the lands passed under the will precisely as they would have descended at law, the son took an estate in fee simple in the lands so devised. Brockschmidt v. Archer (Ohio 1901) 64 Ohio St. 502, 46 W.L.B. 4, 60 N.E. 623.

Before RS 5968 was enacted, a will devising land to the testator's son and after his death to his heirs, there being nothing else in the will to show that "heirs" designated a limited class, as children, the land passed to the son in fee simple. Brockschmidt v. Archer (Ohio 1901) 64 Ohio St. 502, 46 W.L.B. 4, 60 N.E. 623.

A devise to two devisees of certain lands of testator "to be equally divided between them, and to their heirs at their death" conveys the fees to the devisees named therein. Halley v. Hengstler (Ohio Cir. 1902) 13 Ohio C.D. 504, 3 Ohio C.C.(N.S.) 161, affirmed 70 Ohio St. 452, 72 N.E. 1158, 1 Ohio Law Rep. 1001.

A devise of land to a testator's daughter, providing that in the event of her death "leaving no legal heirs," the property so willed "is to descend to her brothers and sisters," passes to the daughter the entire estate in the lands devised. Darlington v. Compton (Ohio Cir. 1900) 11 Ohio C.D. 97. Wills ⚖ 601(1)

A devise of land by a testator to his sons where apt words are used to create a fee simple, the words being "to him and his heirs forever," but the habendum of a devise to the daughter is "to her, her lifetime, and to her heirs forever, or whosoever she pleases to will it to at her death," daughter takes a life estate only, but if such devise be prior to the act of 1840 abrogating the rule in Shelley's case, it vests a fee simple in the daughter. Kimball v. Kimball (Ohio Com.Pl. 1903) 13 Ohio Dec. 555.

The rule in Shelley's case in Ohio has been abolished as to wills in 1840, in pursuance of the state policy making the intention of the testator of paramount importance; the rule remains law in Ohio as to deeds, however. Davis v. Saunders (Ohio Com.Pl. 1900) 11 Ohio Dec. 259, 8 Ohio N.P. 161.

A conveyance to one in trust, requiring the trustee, if not needed to pay debts, to convey "to my daughter, Lucy, with life estate to her and remainder in fee to her heirs," is controlled by Shelley's case and a fee simple is taken by the trustee's deed to her; section applies to wills only and not to deeds of trust even though they may be testamentary. Neff v Abert, 9 App 286 (1918).

2. Rule inapplicable

Where a testator devised certain real property to his son F for life and then over to the heirs of F's body forever, with no residuary clause or other disposition of the property, and the son survived the testator and died testate without issue, it was held that the testator died intestate as to the reversion and that the son F became vested immediately with his undivided share of the reversion and title thereto was transmitted by his will. Chaffin v. Dixon (Ohio App. 2 Dist. 1920) 13 Ohio App. 1, 31 Ohio C.A. 97.

Where inter vivos trust executed prior to abolishment of rule in *Shelley's* case granted one quarter of trust income to beneficiary during his life, rule operated to create absolute gift in beneficiary; thus, upon beneficiary's death, trust income would be received by his adopted daughter, even though trust provided that if beneficiary left no "heirs of his body," his share of income would be distributed in another manner. Society Nat. Bank v. Jacobson (Ohio 1990) 54 Ohio St.3d 15, 560 N.E.2d 217, rehearing denied 55 Ohio St.3d 709, 563 N.E.2d 302. Trusts ⚖ 140(2)

Rule in Shelley's case could not apply where interest of life tenants was equitable rather than legal. Moysey v. Moysey (Ohio Com.Pl. 1974) 42 Ohio Misc. 27, 326 N.E.2d 870, 71 O.O.2d 191.

Doctrine of vested remainder held not to exclude designated heir of daughter under will devising daughter life estate with remainder to heirs. Laws v. Davis (Ohio App. 1929) 34 Ohio App. 157, 170 N.E. 601, 31 Ohio Law Rep. 419, error dismissed 121 Ohio St. 621, 172 N.E. 380. Wills ⚖ 524(6.1)

Under will devising realty for life to children and after their death to bodily heirs of named children or survivor of them, grandchildren and great-grandchild of testator had expectancy during continuance of intermediate estate; remainder devised being contingent and not vesting until contingency ceased. Pollock v. Brayton (Hamilton 1928) 29 Ohio App. 296, 163 N.E. 573, 6 Ohio Law Abs. 614.

Where those in expectancy under will creating contingent estate were different individuals at different periods of time during continuance of intermediate estate, the remainder is contingent and the fee vests when contingency ceases. Pollock v. Brayton (Hamilton 1924) 28 Ohio App. 172, 162 N.E. 608, 6 Ohio Law Abs. 616.

Where will devised real estate to testator's children and after their death to their bodily heirs in fee simple, remainder vested only after death of life tenants in their surviving children, and attempt by contingent remainder-man to dispose of interest in estate before death of life tenant was of no effect. Pollock v. Brayton (Hamilton 1924) 28 Ohio App. 172, 162 N.E. 608, 6 Ohio Law Abs. 616.

Provisions of a will devising an estate to a son with a limitation over if such son dies without lineal descendants pass to such son a defeasible fee. Anderson v. United Realty Co. (Ohio 1908) 79 Ohio St. 23, 86 N.E. 644, 6 Ohio Law Rep. 516, affirmed 32 S.Ct. 50, 222 U.S. 164, 56 L.Ed. 144.

The rule in Shelley's case will not apply as to a devise of Ohio lands by a foreign will, even if the rule is in force in the testator's state. Hosler v. Haines (Ohio Cir. 1905) 18 Ohio C.D. 79, 7 Ohio C.C.(N.S.) 261, reversed 76 Ohio St. 588, 81 N.E. 1186, 4 Ohio Law Rep. 769.

An estate in lands created by will or deed which, by the granting clause, would be an estate in fee simple may be limited by the habendum clause to an estate tail. Darling v. Hippel (Ohio Cir. 1897) 12 Ohio C.D. 754, affirmed 60 Ohio St. 591, 54 N.E. 1103.

A devise to a son, "and his heirs to the third generation," is an entailment within RS 4200, and the son takes a life estate and his heirs a fee simple. Naylor v. Loomis (Ohio Cir. 1894) 6 Ohio C.D. 41, 2 Ohio Dec. 114, dismissed. Estates In Property ⚖ 12; Wills ⚖ 607(2)

Where a testator devises land to his daughter and the heirs of her body, a fee tail in the daughter is created, and the daughter's children have no estate in the land during the life of their mother that they can alienate. Carter v. Grossnickle (Ohio Com.Pl. 1911) 22 Ohio Dec. 680, 11 Ohio N.P.N.S. 465.

A devise to sons with limitation over in case of death of sons without lineal descendants gives, by implication, life estate to sons and remainder to "lineal descendants." Anderson v. Messinger (C.C.A.6 (Ohio) 1906) 146 F. 929, 77 C.C.A. 179, 4 Ohio Law Rep. 361.

The clear intention of the general assembly in abolishing the rule in Shelley's case was to abolish its use under all circumstances; therefore, the rule has no applicability to a trust. Society Natl Bank v Jacobson, No. 55157 (8th Dist Ct App, Cuyahoga, 4–20–89), reversed by 15 OS(3d) 15 (1990).

When a lot is conveyed by deed to husband and wife, with these words "unto said grantees and the survivor of either, their heirs and assigns" and the habendum clause is "unto said grantees and the survivor of either, their heirs and assigns forever," this creates an estate in fee simple in the wife at the death of the husband by the right of survivorship clearly expressed and intended by the grantor; the rule in Shelley's case does not apply. In re Dennis' Estate (Ohio Com.Pl. 1928) 30 Ohio NP(NS) 118.

The Ohio act of December 17, 1812, that "all estates given in tail shall be and remain an absolute estate in fee-simple to the issue of the first donee in tail," does not apply to a devise of real estate to be held by trustees until the last-born child of any one of the sons or daughters of the testator should become of age, and then be divided between all his grandchildren taking per capita with the issue of any deceased taking per stirpes, with rents and profits divided meanwhile among the children and any grandchildren aged twenty-one or more years. McArthur v. Allen (C.C.S.D.Ohio 1878) 15 F.Cas. 1210, No. 8659.

3. Construction and language

A devise of lands to the testator's wife and son during the life of the wife or so long as she remained unmarried and on her death or remarriage to the testator's children or heirs forever gives the wife and sons estates for life determinable on the wife's death or remarriage with remainder in fee to the testator's heirs at law. Nimmons v. Westfall (Ohio 1877) 33 Ohio St. 213.

Where real estate is conveyed to C for life and after her death to her children by E and after their death to E and his heirs, the provision for the children is contingent upon their surviving their mother, and only such of the children as survive her take the estate. Smith v. Block (Ohio 1876) 29 Ohio St. 488. Deeds ⊯ 133(2); Life Estates ⊯ 3

A devise to John "through his natural life and then to his heirs," where in another part of the will "heirs" was used in sense of "children," creates a life estate in John and remainder to his children or issue, and not to heirs generally. Bunnell v. Evans (Ohio 1875) 26 Ohio St. 409. Reversions ⊯ 1; Wills ⊯ 614(6.1)

A devise of lands to a testator's daughter for life, with the remainder to her children, then unborn, forever, and without otherwise disposing of the inheritance, gives a reversion in fee to the heirs of the testator at his death, subject to divestment in case the daughter dies leaving surviving children. Gilpin v. Williams (Ohio 1874) 25 Ohio St. 283. Wills ⊯ 866

A devise of realty to one and his heirs, to be used by the devisee for life with remainder over to a third person, will not vest the fee in the devisee under the rule in Shelley's case, if such construction would defeat the manifest intention of the testator. King v. Beck (Ohio 1846) 15 Ohio 559. Estates In Property ⊯ 8; Wills ⊯ 608(2)

Rule in Shelley's case was abolished in Ohio long before will in this case was written; it is provided in substance in statute abrogating this rule that, when lands are given by will to person for his life, and after his death to his heirs in fee, or by words to that effect, such conveyance shall be construed to vest an estate for life only in life tenant and fee simple in remainder to his heirs; when this statutory provision is applied to testamentary disposition contained in will, heirs of son of testator take their interest in real estate not from son but from testator as devisees under his will. Hummel v. Davis (Franklin 1936) 22 Ohio Law Abs. 49.

Prior to its total abrogation in 1941, the rule in Shelley's case was a rule of property law in Ohio that was applicable to conveyances of both real and personal property by grant or deed. Society Nat. Bank v. Jacobson (Ohio 1990) 54 Ohio St.3d 15, 560 N.E.2d 217, rehearing denied 55 Ohio St.3d 709, 563 N.E.2d 302. Estates In Property ⊯ 8

Any attempt by a testator to restrain alienation on a grant of fee simple must be declared void. Margolis v. Pagano (Ohio Com.Pl. 1986) 39 Ohio Misc.2d 1, 528 N.E.2d 1331.

Children of deceased child of life tenant took, together with living children, under will devising land to testator's daughter for life, "and at her death to the 'issue' of her body then living." Watson v. Watson (Pickaway 1929) 34 Ohio App. 311, 171 N.E. 257. Wills ⊯ 498

Words of inheritance are not necessary to passing of estate in fee simple by will. Trumbull v. Stentz (Huron 1928) 30 Ohio App. 34, 164 N.E. 57, 6 Ohio Law Abs. 429. Wills ⊯ 598

The word "heirs" as used in a will is not a word of limitation where the testator's manifest intention was to dispose of a vested interest in the property devised, and the ambiguity in a later item of the will cannot be held to authorize a cutting down of the interest so conveyed. McDaniels v. Hayes (Ohio Cir. 1905) 22 Ohio C.D. 690, 6 Ohio C.C.(N.S.) 257, affirmed 15 Ohio Dec. 661, 6 Ohio N.P.(N.S.) 435, affirmed 74 Ohio St. 515, 78 N.E. 1131, 4 Ohio Law Rep. 158.

A clause in a will providing that property devised to the testator's widow for life with remainder to his heirs shall not be sold during the life of the widow is a clause against alienation, is repugnant to the devise made to the heirs, and is void. Toledo Loan Co. v. Larkin (Ohio Cir. 1903) 15 Ohio C.D. 209, 1 Ohio C.C.N.S. 473. Wills ⊯ 601(4)

The purpose of this section was to abrogate the rule in Shelley's case and not to resolve all doubtful cases into devises of estates for life with remainder over; the court is permitted to give controlling effect to the intention of the testator. Halley v. Hengstler (Ohio Cir. 1902) 13 Ohio C.D. 504, 3 Ohio C.C.(N.S.) 161, affirmed 70 Ohio St. 452, 72 N.E. 1158, 1 Ohio Law Rep. 1001.

Where the owner of land, in contemplation of marriage, conveys such land to a trustee for her sole use during her life, and in case of her death then to her husband, who is to receive the rents and profits during such survivorship, and then to the grantor's heirs, where the grantor dies before her husband, such property vests in her lawful heirs. Kirby v. Brownlee (Ohio Cir. 1894) 7 Ohio C.D. 460, affirmed 55 Ohio St. 676, 48 N.E. 1114. Deeds ⊯ 128; Husband And Wife ⊯ 31(4); Trusts ⊯ 129

Heirs may be construed in the sense of children. (See also Hoagland v Marsh, 4 CC 31, 2 CD 402 (Butler 1889).) Stewart v. Powers (Ohio Cir. 1894) 6 Ohio C.D. 101, 2 Ohio Dec. 219.

The word "heirs" in its ordinary sense is a word of limitation and not of purchase. McDaniel v. Hays (Ohio Com.Pl. 1905) 15 Ohio Dec. 661, 6 Ohio N.P.(N.S.) 435, affirmed 74 Ohio St. 515, 78 N.E. 1131, 4 Ohio Law Rep. 158. Wills ⊯ 466; Wills ⊯ 591

That specific real estate devised to a trustee in trust for the payment out of the rents and profits of a specified sum to testator's widow for life and remainder to the heirs shall not be sold during the life of the widow is repugnant to the devise to the heirs and is void. Mithoff v. Fritter (Ohio Com.Pl. 1904) 14 Ohio Dec. 321, 1 Ohio N.P.N.S. 433.

If real estate is devised to A generally, without any qualification or condition, but with a proviso that in case of his death without will, the property shall go to B, the limitation over is void, and A takes the entire estate in fee simple, unaffected by the proviso. Finlay Brewing Co. v. Dick (Ohio Com.Pl. 1903) 13 Ohio Dec. 581, 1 Ohio N.P.(N.S.) 592, affirmed 74 Ohio St. 468, 78 N.E. 1125, 3 Ohio Law Rep. 674.

To say that the rule in Shelley's case still applies in cases where the testator used the word "heirs" as a word of limitation is only to show in a different form that the testator's intentions govern a will; in other words, the fact is that the testator there simply chose to achieve the same result that the rule, before 1840, compelled. Kiersted v. Smith (Ohio Com.Pl. 1900) 10 Ohio Dec. 279, 8 Ohio N.P. 378.

Where the owner of a certain estate conveys a life estate and afterwards conveys the fee, the life estate will merge in the fee and give the grantee title in fee simple. Jenkins v Artz, 7 NP 371, 6 D 439 (CP, Delaware 1897).

Where the owner in fee conveys lands to his son during his natural life and then to pass exclusively to the heirs of his own body in fee simple forever, provided the son does not sell and convey said premises before his death, the title passes to the purchaser; in case of the reconveyance to the father in fee simple and then to the son's wife, the wife takes the estate in fee. Aikin v. Spellman (Ohio Cir. 1897) 6 Ohio Dec. 409, 4 Ohio N.P. 297. Estates In Property ⊯ 12

RS 5968, which removes the rule in Shelley's case from wills, does not defeat an intentional use of the word "heirs" as a word of limitation. Patterson v. Earhart (Ohio Com.Pl. 1895) 6 Ohio Dec. 16, 29 W.L.B. 313.

The clear intention of the general assembly in abolishing the rule in Shelley's case was to abolish its use under all circumstances; therefore, the rule has no applicability to a trust. Society Natl Bank v Jacobson, No. 55157 (8th Dist Ct App, Cuyahoga, 4–20–89), reversed by 54 OS(3d) 15 (1990).

2107.50 Property acquired subsequent to will

Any estate, right, or interest in any property of which a decedent was possessed at his decease shall pass under his will unless such will manifests a different intention.

(1953 H 1, eff. 10–1–53; GC 10504–71)

Historical and Statutory Notes

Pre–1953 H 1 Amendments: 114 v 359

Library References

Wills ⚖578.
Westlaw Topic No. 409.
C.J.S. Wills §§ 1085, 1099 to 1104.

Research References

Encyclopedias

OH Jur. 3d Decedents' Estates § 276, Power of Appointment.
OH Jur. 3d Decedents' Estates § 596, Passage of After-Acquired Property.

Forms

Ohio Forms Legal and Business § 24:581, Devises—Entire Estate.
Ohio Forms Legal and Business § 24:926, Devise—of After-Acquired Real Estate.

Treatises and Practice Aids

Carlin, Baldwin's Ohio Practice, Merrick-Rippner Probate Law § 30:57, Simple Will—Form.

Notes of Decisions

In general 1
Clearly and manifestly, construed 6
Intent of testator 2
Liberal construction 5
Predecease of testator 3
Residuary clause 4

---

1. In general

Doctrine of "ademption," applicable when property specifically bequeathed by testator is no longer in existence at his death or has been given away during his lifetime, had no application to specific bequest of real property that was never legally possessed by testator due to legal malpractice of attorney in failing to effectuate transfer of five-sixths interest in property to testator during his lifetime; because testator could not have conveyed property during his life, he could not adeem property. In re Estate of York (Ohio App. 12 Dist., 03-15-1999) 133 Ohio App.3d 234, 727 N.E.2d 607, appeal not allowed 86 Ohio St.3d 1442, 713 N.E.2d 1052. Wills ⚖ 766; Wills ⚖ 768

Under the former analogous section, after-acquired property passed under a will only if it manifestly appeared that the passing of such property was the intention of the testator, but under the present section, after-acquired property passes under the will unless the will manifests a different intention. Fitzgerald v. Bell (Ohio Prob. 1941) 6 Ohio Supp. 119, 33 Ohio Law Abs. 423, 20 O.O. 18, affirmed 39 N.E.2d 186, 34 Ohio Law Abs. 631.

2. Intent of testator

Lands acquired after the making of a will which disposes of all the testator's property owned by him at the time of his death for specified purposes, will pass under its provisions. James v. Pruden (Ohio 1863) 14 Ohio St. 251. Wills ⚖ 578(2.1)

Where a testator held by verbal contract of purchase a parcel of real estate at the time of making his will, and he subsequently took a deed to such land in his lifetime, a devise of the land by his will was operative. Smith's Lessee v. Jones (Ohio 1829) 4 Ohio 115.

Devise, by residuary clause, of remainder of property did not constitute exercise of general testamentary power of appointment over property, which was to pass to heirs in event of failure to exercise power, notwithstanding that testator was nonverbal deaf person and that his concept of property was broader than that of normal person or that he was hostile to heirs; specific devise of residence, one-half interest in which was subject to power, was not indisputable evidence of intent to exercise power with respect to rest of trust property. Dollar Sav. & Trust Co. v. Kirkham (Ohio Com.Pl. 1969) 21 Ohio Misc. 163, 255 N.E.2d 892, 50 O.O.2d 318, 50 O.O.2d 351. Powers ⚖ 36(1)

Where testatrix devised her one-half interest in a parcel of real estate and after the execution of her will acquired the other half interest, such after-acquired property does not pass under such devise. Graves v. Graves (Ohio Prob. 1956) 155 N.E.2d 540, 79 Ohio Law Abs. 262.

Lands acquired by a testator subsequent to the execution of his will do not pass thereby unless the testator's intention to include therein such after-acquired property clearly and manifestly appears on the face of the will itself. Wright v. Masters (Ohio 1909) 81 Ohio St. 304, 90 N.E. 797, 135 Am.St.Rep. 790, 7 Ohio Law Rep. 529, 7 Ohio Law Rep. 577, 18 Am.Ann.Cas. 165. Wills ⚖ 578(4)

The doctrine of implied revocation does not obtain as to after-acquired property devised by will, nor to devised specific property conveyed by a testator after the execution of the will and reconveyed to him before his death. Ridenour v. Callahan (Ohio Cir. 1906) 19 Ohio C.D. 65, 8 Ohio C.C.N.S. 585. Wills ⚖ 167; Wills ⚖ 194

A will devising all real estate passes realty acquired by descent after execution of will but before testator's death. McClaskey v. Barr (C.C.S.D.Ohio 1893) 54 F. 781.

Fact that a testatrix, at the time she executed her will, had no knowledge that she would receive a large inheritance under her cousin's will does not have any legal effect on the passing of such after-acquired property. Fitzgerald v. Bell (Ohio Prob. 1941) 6 Ohio Supp. 119, 33 Ohio Law Abs. 423, 20 O.O. 18, affirmed 39 N.E.2d 186, 34 Ohio Law Abs. 631.

Where a testator calls witnesses to his bedside and tells them that the paper he holds is his will previously executed and acknowledged, and the witnesses sign a certificate of reacknowledgment, it is not necessary that the witnesses see the testator sign the will but it is sufficient if he acknowledges his signature to the witnesses; the will is republished as of that date and disposes of real estate acquired after the will was first made and owned by the testator at his death. Reynolds' Lessee v. Shirley (Ohio 1836) 7 Ohio 39, PT. II.

3. Predecease of testator

The will of a surviving wife made twenty-five years before her death left all her real estate to her husband for life and after his death to her brother for life and after the death of both all the real estate "of which I die seized" to the children of the brother; this carries after-acquired real estate inherited from her husband, although the devise to him showed she expected him to survive her. Blacker v. Litten (Ohio App. 4 Dist. 1918) 10 Ohio App. 180, 29 Ohio C.A. 423.

Property willed by a husband to a wife with the power to dispose of as she sees fit does not pass by the wife's will made five years before the death of her husband. Lepley v. Smith (Ohio Cir. 1896) 7 Ohio C.D. 264.

4. Residuary clause

A testamentary power of appointment is an estate, right or interest in property within the meaning of RC 2107.50, and may be exercised by the general residuary clause of a donee's will, there being no different intention manifested. Dollar Sav. & Trust Co. v. First Nat. Bank of Boston (Ohio Com.Pl. 1972) 32 Ohio Misc. 81, 285 N.E.2d 768, 61 O.O.2d 134.

After-acquired real property passes under the residuary clauses of a will. Lee v. Scott (Ohio Cir. 1904) 16 Ohio C.D. 799, 5 Ohio C.C.N.S. 369.

When all the provisions of a will clearly indicate that the testator intended to dispose of all his estate, both real and personal, real estate acquired by him after the making of the will passes thereby, although the clause by which he devises the residuum of the lands contains a definite description of the residuum of the lands which he owned at the time of making his will. Farrar v. Fallestine (Ohio Cir. 1889) 2 Ohio C.D. 519. Wills ⚖ 578(3)

Where a residuary clause in a will is equivocal or of doubtful or uncertain meaning, its terms will be so construed as to prevent intestacy;

the doctrine of ejusdem generis is limited in its application to clauses not residuary, and the word "effects" in a residuary clause is not limited to property of the same general character as those specifically mentioned in the clause. Robinson v. Robinson (Ohio Com.Pl. 1913) 30 Ohio Dec. 666, 13 Ohio N.P.N.S. 613.

5. Liberal construction

Section should be liberally construed in favor of those seeking to take advantage of its provisions with respect to after-acquired personal property. Fitzgerald v. Bell (Ohio Prob. 1941) 6 Ohio Supp. 119, 33 Ohio Law Abs. 423, 20 O.O. 18, affirmed 39 N.E.2d 186, 34 Ohio Law Abs. 631.

6. Clearly and manifestly, construed

"Clearly and manifestly" as used in this section should receive but little consideration in construing wills. Carrel v. Carrel (Ohio Cir. 1903) 14 Ohio C.D. 416. Wills ⇔ 578(4).

2107.501 Rights of specific devisee or legatee on certain dispositions of subject property

(A) A specific devisee or legatee has the right of the remaining specifically devised or bequeathed property, and:

(1) Any balance on the purchase price, together with any security interest owing from a purchaser to the testator at death by reason of sale of the property;

(2) Any amount of condemnation award unpaid at death for the taking of the property;

(3) Any proceeds unpaid at death on fire or casualty insurance on the property;

(4) Property owned by the testator at death as a result of foreclosure, or obtained in lieu of foreclosure, of the security for a specifically devised or bequeathed obligation.

(B) If specifically devised or bequeathed property is sold by a guardian, by an agent acting within the authority of a power of attorney, or by an agent acting within the authority of a durable power of attorney, or if a condemnation award or insurance proceeds are paid to a guardian, to an agent acting within the authority of a power of attorney, or to an agent acting within the authority of a durable power of attorney as a result of condemnation, fire, or casualty to the property, the specific devisee or legatee has the right to a general pecuniary devise or bequest equal to the net proceeds of sale, the condemnation award, or the insurance proceeds, and such a devise or bequest shall be treated as property subject to section 2107.54 of the Revised Code. This section does not apply if subsequent to the sale, condemnation, fire, or casualty, it is adjudicated that the disability of the testator has ceased and the testator survives the adjudication by one year. The right of the specific devisee or legatee is reduced by any right the specific devisee or legatee has under division (A) of this section.

(2000 H 313, eff. 8–29–00; 1986 S 248, eff. 12–17–86; 1975 S 145)

Historical and Statutory Notes

Amendment Note: 2000 H 313 rewrote division (B), which prior thereto read:

"(B) If specifically devised or bequeathed property is sold by a guardian, or if a condemnation award or insurance proceeds are paid to a guardian as a result of condemnation, fire, or casualty to the property, the specific devisee or legatee has the right to a general pecuniary devise or bequest equal to the net proceeds of sale, the condemnation award, or the insurance proceeds, and such a devise or bequest shall be treated as property subject to section 2107.54 of the Revised Code. This section does not apply if subsequent to the sale, condemnation, or casualty, it is adjudicated that the disability of the testator has ceased and the testator survives the adjudication by one year. The right of the specific devisee or legatee is reduced by any right he has under division (A) of this section."

Legislative Service Commission

1975:

Nonademption. This new section would provide that if, during the period of guardianship of an incapable person specifically devised or bequeathed property is sold, condemned, or is converted into insurance proceeds because of fire or casualty, and the person dies before the disability is removed, the specific devisee or legatee is entitled to a specific pecuniary devise equal to the net proceeds of the sale, the condemnation award, or the insurance proceeds. This section would not apply if it is determined that the disability of the testator should cease after the sale, condemnation, or casualty and the testator survives the determination by one year.

However, in the case of a partial liquidation of a specific devise, the devisee would be entitled to any remaining property, and to any of the following:

(1) any balance on the purchase price and security interest;

(2) any unpaid amount of a condemnation award;

(3) any unpaid fire or casualty proceeds;

(4) property owned by the testator at death as a result or in lieu of foreclosure of the security for a specifically devised obligation.

OSBA Probate and Trust Law Section

1986:

This proposal makes absolutely no change in the text of the Ohio law. The proposed change is to reverse the order of the two paragraphs of the existing law....

By way of background, § 2107.501 of the Revised Code was added to our law in the 1975 Probate Reform Act and is borrowed directly from § 2–608 of the Uniform Probate Code.

After the Ohio legislation had copied the UPC section, the Joint Editorial Board of the UPC improved the section by reversing the order of the two paragraphs. The specific purpose of this change was to "correct an unintended interpretation of the section to the effect that all of the events described in subsections (a) and (b) had relevance only when the testator was under a conservatorship."

...

The order of paragraphs of the Ohio Revised Code was not changed after the order of paragraphs of the Uniform Probate Code was changed. Therefore, the erroneous implication continues to be present in our Ohio statute.

The Probate and Trust Law Section recommends that the order of paragraphs (A) and (B) of the Revised Code § 2107.501 be reversed, with no change in the text of the section.

Library References

Wills ⇔ 767.
Westlaw Topic No. 409.
C.J.S. Wills §§ 1751 to 1752, 1755 to 1759.

Research References

Encyclopedias

OH Jur. 3d Decedents' Estates § 384, Alienation or Conveyance of Property—Beneficiary's Right to Trace the Proceeds of Sale.

OH Jur. 3d Decedents' Estates § 385, Alienation or Conveyance of Property—Sale by Guardian; Condemnation Award or Insurance Proceeds.

OH Jur. 3d Decedents' Estates § 810, Change in Form of Subject Matter—Change from Absolute to Security Interest, or Vice Versa.

OH Jur. 3d Decedents' Estates § 811, Substitution of Property Purchased With Proceeds of Sale.

OH Jur. 3d Decedents' Estates § 812, Involuntary Conversion of Property.

OH Jur. 3d Decedents' Estates § 813, Disposal by Contract of Sale or Grant of Option.

OH Jur. 3d Decedents' Estates § 814, Sale By, or Payment Of, Condemnation Award or Insurance Proceeds To, Guardian.

Treatises and Practice Aids

Carlin, Baldwin's Ohio Practice, Merrick-Rippner Probate Law § 48:4, Property Chargeable With Payment of Debts—Ademption.

Carlin, Baldwin's Ohio Practice, Merrick-Rippner Probate Law § 96:7, Distribution of Proceeds—Sale of Specifically Devised or Bequeathed Property.

Carlin, Baldwin's Ohio Practice, Merrick-Rippner Probate Law § 43:48, Construing a Will—Apportionment of Estate—Rights of Specific Devisee or Legatee.

Carlin, Baldwin's Ohio Practice, Merrick-Rippner Probate Law § 97:19, Land Sale by Guardian—Proceeds.

Law Review and Journal Commentaries

A Costly Application of Strict Statutory Construction: The Ohio Supreme Court's Interpretation of Ohio's Nonademption Statute, Revised Code Section 2107.501(B), Christina Walsh. 28 U Tol L Rev 631 (Spring 1997).

Expansion of Exception to Ademption Rule to Include Specifically Devised or Bequeathed Property Sold By Attorney–In–Fact, Karen Moore. 10 Prob L J Ohio 68 (May/June 2000).

Hegel's Hobbled Heritage: The Ohio Supreme Court's Use of the Doctrine of Ademption to Prey on the Incompetent, David A. Onega. 26 Cap U L Rev 201 (1997).

The Traditional Wills Doctrine of Ademption and Its Exceptions Should be Extended to Revocable Trusts, Brian Layman. 13 Prob L J Ohio 119 (July/August 2003).

Notes of Decisions

Competency of testator, effect   1
Residuary clause containing specific devise or legacy   2
Sale by attorney-in-fact, effect   3

---

1. Competency of testator, effect

A specifically devised property of an incompetent testator that is sold under a durable power of attorney is not adeemed and the beneficiary is entitled to those proceeds not applied to the support or other expense of the principal. In re Estate of Hegel (Ohio, 08-28-1996) 76 Ohio St.3d 476, 668 N.E.2d 474, 1996-Ohio-77.

2. Residuary clause containing specific devise or legacy

Skilled nursing care facility, in which testamentary trust beneficiary resided prior to his death, was entitled to distribution under underlying will upon death of beneficiary and termination of trust together with long-term care group home where beneficiary resided prior to transfer to facility, where bequest anticipated that some institution other than home might provide residential care for beneficiary and, in that event, bequeathed one-half of bequest to home to that other institution, and there was no ambiguity in terms of bequest. Bank One Trust Co. v. Resident Home Ass'n for Mentally Retarded (Ohio App. 2 Dist., Montgomery, 07-18-2003) No. 19660, 2003-Ohio-3835, 2003 WL 21674987, Unreported. Wills ☞ 656

Where the residuary clause of a decedent's will states that the residue is to be divided equally amongst the children but then contains a sentence, "provided, however, that the share herein provided for my daughter, Judith, shall include whatever interest I own at the time of my death in my residence property," the intent of the testatrix was to divide her residue property, including her residence property, equally amongst her children, and it is error for the court to award the residence property solely to one child. Essig v. Tabbert (Ohio App. 9 Dist., Lorain, 10-26-1994) No. 94CA005845, 1994 WL 592380, Unreported, appeal not allowed 71 Ohio St.3d 1494, 646 N.E.2d 469.

3. Sale by attorney-in-fact, effect

Those acting under powers-of-attorney cannot be viewed the same as guardians, for purposes of determining whether statutory exception to ademption doctrine for sales by guardians applies to sales by attorneys-in-fact, since guardians are appointed by probate court and are subject to court's control, whereas attorneys-in-fact have much more freedom and can act without court approval as principal's alter ego. In re Estate of Hegel (Ohio, 08-28-1996) 76 Ohio St.3d 476, 668 N.E.2d 474, 1996-Ohio-77. Wills ☞ 767

Pursuant to statute which sets forth narrow exception to ademption doctrine, specific devisee or legatee's rights are protected and are not extinguished when guardian sells specifically devised or bequeathed property, but not when sale is made by attorney-in-fact. In re Estate of Hegel (Ohio, 08-28-1996) 76 Ohio St.3d 476, 668 N.E.2d 474, 1996-Ohio-77. Wills ☞ 767

Specific devise of testator's residence and its contents adeemed when property was sold by attorney-in-fact to third party prior to testator's death. In re Estate of Hegel (Ohio, 08-28-1996) 76 Ohio St.3d 476, 668 N.E.2d 474, 1996-Ohio-77. Wills ☞ 767

2107.51   When whole estate to pass

Every devise of lands, tenements, or hereditaments in a will shall convey all the estate of the devisor therein, unless it clearly appears by the will that the devisor intended to convey a less estate.

(1953 H 1, eff. 10–1–53; GC 10504–72)

Historical and Statutory Notes

Pre–1953 H 1 Amendments: 114 v 360

Library References

Wills ☞ 599.
Westlaw Topic No. 409.
C.J.S. Wills §§ 1197, 1210 to 1212.

Research References

Encyclopedias

OH Jur. 3d Estates, Pwrs., & Restrnts. on Alienat. § 13, Cutting Down Fee Simple.

OH Jur. 3d Estates, Pwrs., & Restrnts. on Alienat. § 20, Intent—Construction Against Forfeiture.

OH Jur. 3d Guardian & Ward § 92, Duties, Generally.

Treatises and Practice Aids

Carlin, Baldwin's Ohio Practice, Merrick-Rippner Probate Law § 3:13, Jurisdiction of Probate Court—Scope—Exclusive and Concurrent Jurisdiction.

Carlin, Baldwin's Ohio Practice, Merrick-Rippner Probate Law § 43:10, Construing a Will—Rules of Construction—Guides to Ascertain Testator's Intent.

Carlin, Baldwin's Ohio Practice, Merrick-Rippner Probate Law § 43:42, Construing a Will—Apportionment of Estate—Statutory Provision.

Carlin, Baldwin's Ohio Practice, Merrick-Rippner Probate Law § 43:43, Construing a Will—Apportionment of Estate—Construing a Fee Simple—When a Fee Simple Passes.

Kuehnle and Levey, Ohio Real Estate Law and Practice § 2:2, Estates—Fee Simple Absolute—Words of Inheritance Not Now Required.

Kuehnle and Levey, Ohio Real Estate Law and Practice § 3:17, Estates—Estates for Life—Income from Parcel.

Law Review and Journal Commentaries

Devise Of A Life Estate, Or Merely A Bequest Of Income For Life?, Robert A. Hausser. 56 Title Topics 6 (April 1989).

Life Estate or Fee?, Charles C. White. 1 U Cin L Rev 405 (November 1927).

Life Estate or Fee? A Sequel, Charles C. White. 6 U Cin L Rev 429 (November 1932).

Notes of Decisions

Inoperative or void provisions   3
Operation of language   2
Rules of construction   1
Vesting favored   4

---

1. Rules of construction

A devise by a testator of all of his property, of every description, after paying all his just debts, is a devise of the fee, without the aid of RS 5970. Piatt v. Sinton (Ohio 1881) 37 Ohio St. 353, 6 W.L.B. 799. Estates In Property ☞ 5; Wills ☞ 599

Where a testator devises a life estate to his daughter in land with a devise over if she should die without issue to her brothers and sisters, otherwise a remainder to the daughter's children subject to defeasance, if the daughter's children die without issue before age twenty-one, the fee simple estate in the daughter's children is contingent and not absolute during the life of their mother, and a deed of conveyance from the daughter and her children will not pass a fee simple to a grantee. Bates v. Zinsmeister (Ohio 1875) 26 Ohio St. 461.

Where a devise of real estate is made to a testatrix's husband in fee simple with the power to sell the premises on the condition that he care for the couple's imbecile daughter during their joint lives, and a devise is made to the testatrix's son with the same condition if the daughter survived her father, with the addition of words requiring a personal assumption of the care of his sister, where the son does assume such care, the condition is satisfied, and the estate in the son and those he sells to is absolute and fully discharged from the maintenance of the imbecile daughter. Huey v. Thomas (Ohio 1873) 23 Ohio St. 645.

A devise to a wife for life with the right of exclusive management of property in her and providing that after her death whatever part of the estate is left to be equally divided among all his children gives her only a life estate and life support, but not power to dispose of the property to some of the children to the exclusion of others. Huston v. Craighead (Ohio 1872) 23 Ohio St. 198.

Where a power to distribute a testator's entire estate among his children is given to his wife to exercise as she deems best, and the wife does distribute some of the estate to the children, but die seized of the remaining parcels, under the circumstances, the power never having been fully exercised, equity requires that the entire estate should be apportioned equally between all the children named, the partial distributions already made to stand as advancements on such equal portions. Stableton v. Ellison (Ohio 1871) 21 Ohio St. 527.

Where a testator devises to his wife all his property, real and personal, remaining after the payment of his debts, with full power to sell or convey during her life, and another clause bequeaths a legacy to be paid at the wife's death out of any moneys remaining, a deed by the wife is a sufficient execution of the power given to her by will and the exhaustion of the property prevents the payment of the legacy. Bishop v. Remple (Ohio 1860) 11 Ohio St. 277. Powers ⇨ 33(2); Wills ⇨ 692(5)

In a devise to heirs or the survivors that reach the age of twenty-one years with a remainder to the wife if all the heirs die before they come of age, the absolute estate is vested in the surviving one heir who reaches that age and dies shortly afterward. Ward's Lessee v. Barrows (Ohio 1853) 2 Ohio St. 241.

Where a testator has wholly failed to give his meaning and the residuary clause will admit of more than one construction, a court of equity will give it that construction which will be most favorable to the heir at law. Bane v. Wick (Ohio 1850) 19 Ohio 328.

A devise to a wife of one-half of all the testator's real estate is a devise in fee. Howe v. Fuller (Ohio 1850) 19 Ohio 51.

A residuary bequest of a testator who possesses a power of appointment over the assets of his father's estate and considerable property of his own, in the absence of any express intention to exercise the power, is insufficient for that purpose. Dollar Sav. & Trust Co. v. Kirkham (Ohio Com.Pl. 1969) 21 Ohio Misc. 163, 255 N.E.2d 892, 50 O.O.2d 318, 50 O.O.2d 351.

Courts favor the creation of a fee simple estate and cast the burden of proving that a lesser estate was created on the one asserting that a devise is of such lesser estate, but GC 10504–72 (RC 2107.51) provides a rule of construction to be employed only when it aids a court to ascertain the intention of testator. Perdue v. Morris (Belmont 1952) 93 Ohio App. 538, 114 N.E.2d 286, 51 O.O. 232. Wills ⇨ 601(1)

Under the provisions of section, in devises of real property an absolute fee simple title passes if nothing appears in the will showing a contrary intent; the use of words of inheritance in the devise is the expression of an intent that the devisee shall have a fee simple title. Jones v. Jones (Franklin 1933) 48 Ohio App. 138, 192 N.E. 811, 15 Ohio Law Abs. 39, 1 O.O. 111.

Stock distributed by a testator without naming the extent of his interest may be interpreted as to him as trustee for the benefit of others. Smith v. Rugg (Ohio Com.Pl. 1931) 28 Ohio NP(NS) 262, affirmed 40 Ohio App. 101, 177 N.E. 784, 9 Ohio Law Abs. 718, 34 Ohio Law Rep. 513.

A devise to a son, and if he dies without lineal descendants, then over, is not sufficient to per se immediately create or vest an estate in the son's lineal descendants. Anderson v. United Realty Co. (Ohio 1908) 79 Ohio St. 23, 86 N.E. 644, 6 Ohio Law Rep. 516, affirmed 32 S.Ct. 50, 222 U.S. 164, 56 L.Ed. 144.

A devise of lands is to be construed to be in fee; the limitation over in the event of the non-existence of lineal descendants does not of itself imply a devise to the lineal descendants. Anderson v. United Realty Co. (Ohio 1908) 79 Ohio St. 23, 86 N.E. 644, 6 Ohio Law Rep. 516, affirmed 32 S.Ct. 50, 222 U.S. 164, 56 L.Ed. 144.

Where land is devised under a will also directing the devisee to pay a legacy, the legacy is a charge upon the lands devised, and where the legacy is made a condition of the devise, acceptance of the devise creates a personal liability of the devisee to the legatee that can be enforced without resorting to the land; the lien on the land remains, however, as security. Case v. Hall (Ohio 1894) 52 Ohio St. 24, 32 W.L.B. 366, 38 N.E. 618, 2 Ohio Leg. N. 91.

A devise of all of a testator's property to his wife with power to sell and convey as she may deem best, and a provision that on her death property unconsumed shall go to others gives the wife a life estate, with power to sell for her support. Johnson v. Johnson (Ohio 1894) 51 Ohio St. 446, 32 W.L.B. 219, 38 N.E. 61.

Devise of a life estate with power to direct by will to whom the property shall then go does not pass a fee. Thurston v. Bissel (Ohio Cir. 1897) 7 Ohio C.D. 235.

Where the legal title to the undivided moiety of land is devised to a trust company in trust for certain purposes set forth in the will, the trustee for the purpose of protecting the title takes all of the estate of the devisor. Union Sav. Bank & Trust Co. v. Baltimore & O.S.W.R. Co. (Ohio Insolv. 1908) 7 Ohio NP(NS) 497, 53 W.L.B. 450.

RS 5970, stating that "Every devise… shall be construed to convey all the estate of the devisor… unless it shall clearly appear in the will that the devisor intended to convey a less estate," is by its terms a rule of construction only, not of property, to be employed when it aids in the ascertainment of the intention of the testator, and to be disregarded when its observance is plainly subversive thereof. Gillis v. Long (Ohio Com.Pl. 1908) 19 Ohio Dec. 253, 8 Ohio N.P.N.S. 1. Wills ⇨ 590

Where testatrix, on devise of land to museum for scientific purposes and preservation of relics thereon, reserved to herself no interest that could pass under residuary devise, she would at most have mere possibility of reverter therein. President and Fellows of Harvard College v. Jewett (C.C.A.6 (Ohio) 1925) 11 F.2d 119. Charities ⇨ 30; Partition ⇨ 116(1); Trusts ⇨ 153

2. Operation of language

A devise to John "through his natural life and then to his heirs," where in another part of the will "heirs" was used in sense of "children," creates a life estate in John and remainder to his children or issue, and not to heirs generally. Bunnell v. Evans (Ohio 1875) 26 Ohio St. 409. Reversions ⇨ 1; Wills ⇨ 614(6.1)

"I give and bequeath to M the remaining part of my real property," standing alone, is sufficient to pass a fee. Niles v. Gray (Ohio 1861) 12 Ohio St. 320.

No words of perpetuity are essential in a will to pass an estate of inheritance; therefore, if the language used, as descriptive of the estate, is general, and sufficient to comprehend the property, without any words of limitation, or provision in the will qualifying the interest devised, a fee in the land will pass. Thompson's Lessee v. Hoop (Ohio 1856) 6 Ohio St. 480. Wills ⇨ 598

The rigid rules of interpretation which are applied to deeds have never been considered applicable to wills, and thus the word "heirs" is not necessary to carry a fee, but any words which signify an intention to convey the whole interest of the testator are sufficient. Smith v. Berry (Ohio 1838) 8 Ohio 365.

A devise by a husband of all his real estate to his wife "to have and use for her own personal benefit and to distribute as she may direct," is an unconditional devise with power of disposition. Evans v. Molyneug (Muskingum 1927) 6 Ohio Law Abs. 165, 26 Ohio Law Rep. 102. Wills ⇨ 102

Where the testator does not use "fee simple absolute" language in a devise, but uses words that standing alone indicate an intent to convey a fee simple absolute, the court should determine whether the testator manifested an intent to create a fee simple absolute by looking to the limitations or powers connected to the devise. Dunkel v. Hilyard (Ohio App. 4 Dist., 10-15-2001) 146 Ohio App.3d 414, 766 N.E.2d 603, 2001-Ohio-2597, appeal not allowed 94 Ohio St.3d 1453, 762 N.E.2d 371. Wills ⇨ 597(1)

Testator devised property to wife in fee simple, not as life estate, although in another provision of will, he named brother's children as contingent devisees of "unexpended portion" of property, where will named wife as devisee "absolutely and in fee simple," and did not specify wife's powers over property. Dunkel v. Hilyard (Ohio App. 4 Dist., 10-15-2001) 146 Ohio App.3d 414, 766 N.E.2d 603, 2001-Ohio-2597, appeal not allowed 94 Ohio St.3d 1453, 762 N.E.2d 371. Wills ⇔ 601(1); Wills ⇔ 614(5)

To create a devise of less than fee simple followed by a remainder in a will, the first devise must contain some language indicating that a life estate or trust was intended; the mere existence of a remainder provision does not suffice to prove the testator's intent to devise less than the prima facie fee simple absolute. Dunkel v. Hilyard (Ohio App. 4 Dist., 10-15-2001) 146 Ohio App.3d 414, 766 N.E.2d 603, 2001-Ohio-2597, appeal not allowed 94 Ohio St.3d 1453, 762 N.E.2d 371. Wills ⇔ 622

Provision of will permitting the executor to make distributions of the estate to minors merely set forth the powers of the executor and did not limit or broaden the meaning of the technical words employed in the residuary clause. Polen v. Baker (Ohio, 08-22-2001) 92 Ohio St.3d 563, 752 N.E.2d 258, 2001-Ohio-1286. Wills ⇔ 587(5)

A devise or bequest of a life interest must be clearly expressed to be effective. Margolis v. Pagano (Ohio Com.Pl. 1986) 39 Ohio Misc.2d 1, 528 N.E.2d 1331. Wills ⇔ 102

A gift of property by testatrix to her husband followed by the provision "and after that to my children" creates a fee simple. Kohout v. Kohout (Ohio Prob. 1965) 4 Ohio Misc. 38, 203 N.E.2d 869, 31 O.O.2d 180.

A devise of real property "for the use and purpose hereinafter stated" to a county "to be held and occupied by the county as and for a county experiment farm" and conditioned upon the acceptance of such property for such use and purpose, otherwise the property to go to other persons, vests in the county a fee simple absolute, where the county so accepts the property. Taylor v. Dickerson (Madison 1961) 113 Ohio App. 344, 178 N.E.2d 46, 17 O.O.2d 367. Wills ⇔ 601(6)

Where a testator devises a life estate in real property to his wife and, at her death, to his son, but "should he die leaving no children" then to another, the words, "should he die leaving no children", refer to the death of the son without issue during the lifetime of his mother, and, where the son survives his mother title to such property becomes absolute in him. Trumbo v. Trumbo (Lawrence 1957) 106 Ohio App. 382, 155 N.E.2d 62, 7 O.O.2d 112.

A provision in a will devising certain property to one of the testator's children "and to her heirs when she shall arrive at the age of twenty-two years" vests in such daughter a fee simple estate at the date of distribution. Jones v. Jones (Franklin 1933) 48 Ohio App. 138, 192 N.E. 811, 15 Ohio Law Abs. 39, 1 O.O. 111. Wills ⇔ 601(1)

This section will not defeat intention of testator clearly expressed or implied in language of will. Heath v. City of Cleveland (Ohio 1926) 114 Ohio St. 535, 151 N.E. 649, 4 Ohio Law Abs. 257, 24 Ohio Law Rep. 366.

Where a testator bequeaths to his wife his estate in fee simple with the power to dispose of as she sees fit, with the remainder if any to be distributed to second devisees, RS 5970 places the burden on the second devisees to prove the devise is of a lesser estate. Bodmann German Protestant Widows' Home v. Lippardt (Ohio 1904) 70 Ohio St. 261, 71 N.E. 770, 2 Ohio Law Rep. 73.

Where a testator bequeaths to his wife his estate in fee simple with the power to dispose of it as she sees fit, with the remainder, if any, to be distributed to second devisees after her death, a deed evidencing conveyance of such property by the widow is good against the second devisees. Bodmann German Protestant Widows' Home v. Lippardt (Ohio 1904) 70 Ohio St. 261, 71 N.E. 770, 2 Ohio Law Rep. 73.

Where a testator devises 208 acres of land definitely described "and also" 83 acres of land on which "she now lives" to his daughter for life, the words "and also" indicate the intention to apply the limitation of the devise to a life estate to both tracts. Noble v. Ayers (Ohio 1900) 61 Ohio St. 491, 43 W.L.B. 112, 56 N.E. 199. Wills ⇔ 614(5)

A devise to two children on the condition that "should either die without heirs capable of inheriting such one's share under the will shall inure to survivor," vests a fee determinable upon the contingency of death without children. Durfee v. MacNeil (Ohio 1898) 58 Ohio St. 238, 39 W.L.B. 393, 50 N.E. 721.

A bequest of net income from a trust for life "for support and education" is an absolute bequest of the net income that can be reached by creditors, since it is not qualified by any exercise of judgment by the trustee as to what expenditures are necessary. Thornton v. Stanley (Ohio 1896) 55 Ohio St. 199, 36 W.L.B. 309, 45 N.E. 318.

Words of inheritance are not necessary to transmit realty under this section. Halley v. Hengstler (Ohio Cir. 1902) 13 Ohio C.D. 504, 3 Ohio C.C.(N.S.) 161, affirmed 70 Ohio St. 452, 72 N.E. 1158, 1 Ohio Law Rep. 1001. Wills ⇔ 598

Provision of a will by which all the testator's property is given to his wife "during her natural life, and to dispose of as she sees fit" confers the whole estate upon the wife, and the power of disposition enlarges the life estate into a fee. Lepley v. Smith (Ohio Cir. 1896) 7 Ohio C.D. 264. Wills ⇔ 616(1)

The language "the residue of my estate I give to my wife, to be expended for her support during her lifetime and to be disposed of by her in any way she may think proper," gives the wife an absolute title to the residue with a power of disposition. Clark v. Trustees of Hardwick Seminary (Ohio Cir. 1888) 2 Ohio C.D. 87, dismissed. Estates In Property ⇔ 5; Wills ⇔ 600(1)

Devise of lands to A for the term of his natural life, "with a gift over upon his dying under twenty-one" will not be construed by implication as a fee simple in "A." Hulse v. Hulse (Ohio Cir. 1885) 1 Ohio C.D. 202, affirmed. Estates In Property ⇔ 5; Wills ⇔ 617

Where property is to be "set off" and "partitioned" to daughters on attainment of majority but administered by a trustee who is to pay them income for life "with the fee simple to the heirs" only an impermissibly strained construction concludes the father meant the words "set off" and "partition" to convey a fee simple to the daughters. Kiersted v. Smith (Ohio Com.Pl. 1900) 10 Ohio Dec. 279, 8 Ohio N.P. 378.

3. Inoperative or void provisions

A provision in a devise that the two sons to whom estate are given shall not dispose of or encumber except to each other until ten years after one has reached the age of twenty-one is repugnant to the devise and contrary to public policy and absolute estates in fee simple vest at once. Anderson v. Cary (Ohio 1881) 36 Ohio St. 506, 38 Am.Rep. 602.

Where a testator by will devises to his children certain real estate in absolute language without words of limitation, and later in the same item attempts to limit or qualify the estate, there arises a repugnancy, the language forbidding alienation is void, such qualifying provision is in the nature of a precatory declaration, and the devisees take a fee simple estate. Heath v. Borst (Ohio App. 4 Dist. 1916) 13 Ohio App. 115, 32 Ohio C.A. 377.

The subject matter of an ineffective legacy will pass in residue and not intestate, provided there is a valid residuary clause and the testator's intent was to cause the subject to pass through the will rather than pass intestate. Margolis v. Pagano (Ohio Com.Pl. 1986) 39 Ohio Misc.2d 1, 528 N.E.2d 1331. Wills ⇔ 858(1)

A will by which testator provided "... I give, devise and bequeath all my property both real and personal to my wife,... At her demise, I request that each of our children... be given his or her proportionate share of the estate due consideration being given to those children and persons working and caring for the farm property," gives a fee simple title to testator's wife. Perdue v. Morris (Belmont 1952) 93 Ohio App. 538, 114 N.E.2d 286, 51 O.O. 232. Wills ⇔ 601(1)

Devise of real estate to a religious society "to be used as a parsonage," but with no provision for forfeiture or reversion, conveyed all of the estate the testator had therein to the devisee, and failure of the devisee to use the property as a parsonage will not cause the title to revert to the heirs of the testator. First Presbyterian Church of Salem v. Tarr (Columbiana 1939) 63 Ohio App. 286, 26 N.E.2d 597, 17 O.O. 57. Charities ⇔ 29

Mere statement in a will of the purpose for which property devised is to be used, will not be regarded as a condition subsequent, so as to debase the fee when the condition is broken, unless the intention of the testator is clearly shown to be otherwise. First Presbyterian Church of Salem v. Tarr (Columbiana 1939) 63 Ohio App. 286, 26 N.E.2d 597, 17 O.O. 57. Wills ⇔ 602(1)

Positive, express language creating a fee simple estate cannot be cut down by another disconnected provision of the will. Jones v. Jones (Franklin 1933) 48 Ohio App. 138, 192 N.E. 811, 15 Ohio Law Abs. 39, 1 O.O. 111. Wills ⇔ 601(1)

Where will bequeaths or devises property to person absolutely and in fee simple and then by subsequent provision attempts to ingraft remainder upon the fee, so-called remainder is void, and first taker will take property in fee simple. Trumbull v. Stentz (Huron 1928) 30 Ohio App. 34, 164 N.E. 57, 6 Ohio Law Abs. 429.

Where there is repugnancy in will between specific devise and provision against closing administration of estate for five years after death of testatrix, language forbidding alienation is void as in nature of precatory declaration, and devisees take fee simple estate. Baker v. Alexander (Richland 1926) 24 Ohio App. 117, 156 N.E. 223, 4 Ohio Law Abs. 583.

A devise of "the whole of said proceeds of said farm to the Preachers' Aid society, but said society are not to sell farm," is a devise to the society of the corpus of said farm absolutely and in fee; the words, "but said society are not to sell the farm," being inoperative and of no force or effect. Minor v. Shippley (Ohio App. 1923) 21 Ohio App. 236, 152 N.E. 768, 23 Ohio Law Rep. 551. Wills ⟾ 601(4)

Where an item in a will, standing alone, clearly conveys an absolute title without words of limitation, the devise cannot be reduced by subsequent vague and doubtful provisions. Martin v. Martin (Ohio App. 5 Dist. 1928) 27 Ohio Law Rep. 127.

Where the residuary clause of a will devises and bequeaths to the testator's wife all the residue of his estate both real and personal without using any express words of limitation to indicate the quantum of her interest, and a subsequent clause then states, "It is my desire and wish that after the death of my beloved wife, (naming her), and providing there remains sufficient property, to pay the following amounts hereafter specified; and if not sufficient that they be paid proportionately," following which certain parties are named and definite sums of money written after their names, the wife takes a fee simple estate in the realty and an absolute interest in the personalty, and the attempted limitations over are void. 1930 OAG 2537.

4. Vesting favored

Law favors vesting of all interest in testator's estate in devisee or legatee at earliest possible time on death of testator, unless contrary intention clearly appears; that testator directs property to be set apart or payment made at future time does not prevent vesting of estate on testator's death; that distribution of estate was postponed until death of widow did not indicate intention by testator to postpone vesting of interest of children until widow's death. Stahl v. Mohr (Holmes 1928) 35 Ohio App. 411, 172 N.E. 431.

Notwithstanding statute, an estate may be created by will that will not vest until the expiration of a definite period, or the happening of some event after the death of the testator, without the creation by will of an intervening estate upon which to rest it. Heath v. City of Cleveland (Ohio 1926) 114 Ohio St. 535, 151 N.E. 649, 4 Ohio Law Abs. 257, 24 Ohio Law Rep. 366. Wills ⟾ 630(8)

Where a will contains conflicting or inconsistent provisions, the law favors a construction establishing estates already vested, as opposed to estates merely contingent. Brown v. Brown (Ohio Com.Pl. 1919) 31 Ohio Dec. 407, 22 Ohio N.P.N.S. 410, 65 W.L.B. 463.

Where the item vesting a fee simple is clear and unambiguous, it cannot be modified by a subsequent attempt to lessen that fee already conferred, and if it is ever done, the item in the will modifying the item conveying the fee simple, or lessening it, must be clear and unambiguous, and must clearly show the intention of the testator to give only a life estate. Union Trust Co. v. Taylor (Ohio App. 8 Dist. 1930) 34 Ohio Law Rep. 327.

2107.52 Death of devisee or legatee

(A) As used in this section, "relative" means an individual who is related to a testator by consanguinity and an heir at law designated pursuant to section 2105.15 of the Revised Code.

(B) Unless a contrary intention is manifested in the will, if a devise of real property or a bequest of personal property is made to a relative of a testator and the relative was dead at the time the will was made or dies after that time, leaving issue surviving the testator, those issue shall take by representation the devised or bequeathed property as the devisee or legatee would have done if he had survived the testator. If the testator devised or bequeathed a residuary estate or the entire estate after debts, other general or specific devises and bequests, or an interest less than a fee or absolute ownership to that devisee or legatee and relatives of the testator and if that devisee or legatee leaves no issue, the estate devised or bequeathed shall vest in the other devisees or legatees surviving the testator in such proportions as the testamentary share of each devisee or legatee in the devised or bequeathed property bears to the total of the shares of all of the surviving devisees or legatees, unless a different disposition is made or required by the will.

(1992 H 427, eff. 10–8–92; 1953 H 1; GC 10504–73)

Uncodified Law

1992 H 427, § 3, eff. 10–8–92, reads: In amending sections 2107.01 and 2107.52 of the Revised Code, the General Assembly hereby declares its intent to supersede the effect of the holding of the Ohio Supreme Court on October 26, 1988, in *Dollar Savings & Trust Co. of Youngstown v. Turner* (1988), 39 Ohio St. 3d 182.

Historical and Statutory Notes

Pre–1953 H 1 Amendments: 114 v 360

Library References

Wills ⟾552.
Westlaw Topic No. 409.
C.J.S. Wills §§ 1809 to 1821.

Research References

ALR Library
86 ALR 5th 637, Right of Illegitimate Child to Maintain Action to Determine Paternity.

Encyclopedias
2 Am. Jur. Proof of Facts 2d 693, Mistake in Naming or Designating Beneficiary in Will.
OH Jur. 3d Decedents' Estates § 56, Lapsed Legacies or Devises.
OH Jur. 3d Decedents' Estates § 782, Intention as Preventing Lapse.
OH Jur. 3d Decedents' Estates § 788, Liberal Construction and Effect—Applicability to Class Gifts.
OH Jur. 3d Decedents' Estates § 790, Effect of Testator's Intention—Words of Survivorship.
OH Jur. 3d Decedents' Estates § 791, Beneficiary's Death Before Execution of Will.
OH Jur. 3d Decedents' Estates § 792, Who is a "Relative" Within Statute.
OH Jur. 3d Decedents' Estates § 793, Who is "Issue" of Relative Within Statute.
OH Jur. 3d Decedents' Estates § 794, Effect of Beneficiary's Indebtedness to Testator.
OH Jur. 3d Decedents' Estates § 802, Lapse in Share of Residuary Estate—Under Anti-Lapse Statute.
OH Jur. 3d Decedents' Estates § 1651, Persons Against Whom Right May be Asserted—Heirs of Predeceased Debtor-Beneficiary.
OH Jur. 3d Estates, Pwrs., & Restrnts. on Alienat. § 189, Lapse of Testamentary Appointment.
OH Jur. 3d Trusts § 215, Where Beneficiary of Testamentary Trust Predeceases Testator or Dies Before Reaching Specified Age.

Forms
Ohio Forms Legal and Business § 24:161, Entire Estate to Spouse—Alternatively to Children—Guardianship of Minors.
Ohio Forms Legal and Business § 24:201, Entire Estate to Specified Relatives or Issue—Provision for Future Spouse—Anatomical Dispositions—No Funeral Services.
Ohio Forms Legal and Business § 24:801, Bequest Not to Lapse on Death of Beneficiary Before Death of Testator.

Treatises and Practice Aids
Carlin, Baldwin's Ohio Practice, Merrick-Rippner Probate Law § 15:7, Descent and Distribution—Spouse as Heir at Law and Next of Kin.
Carlin, Baldwin's Ohio Practice, Merrick-Rippner Probate Law § 16:3, Statutory Presumption—Construed.
Carlin, Baldwin's Ohio Practice, Merrick-Rippner Probate Law § 46:1, Anti-Lapse Statute.
Carlin, Baldwin's Ohio Practice, Merrick-Rippner Probate Law § 46:2, Anti-Lapse Statute—"Relative" as Beneficiary.
Carlin, Baldwin's Ohio Practice, Merrick-Rippner Probate Law § 46:3, Anti-Lapse Statute—"Issue" as Beneficiary.
Carlin, Baldwin's Ohio Practice, Merrick-Rippner Probate Law § 46:4, Anti-Lapse Statute—Deceased Member of a Class as Beneficiary.
Carlin, Baldwin's Ohio Practice, Merrick-Rippner Probate Law § 46:5, Anti-Lapse Statute—Putative Child as Beneficiary.
Carlin, Baldwin's Ohio Practice, Merrick-Rippner Probate Law § 46:6, Anti-Lapse Statute—Application to "Living Trust Agreement".
Carlin, Baldwin's Ohio Practice, Merrick-Rippner Probate Law § 15:27, Descent and Distribution—Child Without Issue Predeceasing Parent.

Carlin, Baldwin's Ohio Practice, Merrick-Rippner Probate Law § 15:30, Descent and Distribution—Child Born Out of Wedlock.

Carlin, Baldwin's Ohio Practice, Merrick-Rippner Probate Law § 19:10, Uniform Parentage Act—Procedure in Action to Determine Father-Child Relationship.

Carlin, Baldwin's Ohio Practice, Merrick-Rippner Probate Law § 30:17, Drafting a Will—Beneficiary Clauses—Alternate Beneficiary.

Carlin, Baldwin's Ohio Practice, Merrick-Rippner Probate Law § 43:10, Construing a Will—Rules of Construction—Guides to Ascertain Testator's Intent.

Carlin, Baldwin's Ohio Practice, Merrick-Rippner Probate Law § 43:16, Construing a Will—Liberal Construction—Gifts to a Class: Construction Problems.

Carlin, Baldwin's Ohio Practice, Merrick-Rippner Probate Law § 43:30, Construing a Will—Words and Phrases—Per Stirpes.

Carlin, Baldwin's Ohio Practice, Merrick-Rippner Probate Law § 43:33, Construing a Will—Words and Phrases—Share and Share Alike—Per Capita.

Carlin, Baldwin's Ohio Practice, Merrick-Rippner Probate Law § 43:43, Construing a Will—Apportionment of Estate—Construing a Fee Simple—When a Fee Simple Passes.

Carlin, Baldwin's Ohio Practice, Merrick-Rippner Probate Law § 43:46, Construing a Will—Apportionment of Estate—Construing a Life Estate—When a Life Estate Does Not Pass.

Restatement (2d) of Property, Don. Trans. § 18.6, Operation of Antilapse Statutes With Reference to Appointments.

Restatement (2d) of Property, Don. Trans. § 27.1, Class Member Dies Before the Date the Dispositive Instrument is Executed.

Restatement (2d) of Property, Don. Trans. § 34.6, Donee Dies Before Donor.

Law Review and Journal Commentaries

Common Problems in Administration of Decedent's Estates, Daniel F. Carmack. 14 Clev–Marshall L Rev 179 (January 1965).

Existence of Survivorship Clause—Anti-lapse Statute Still Applies, Note. 28 Ohio St L J 135 (Winter 1967).

Ghosts from the Grave-Inheriting Through the Predeceased Under Ohio Law. Kevin Purcell, 50 Clev St L Rev 189 (2002-03).

Is The Anti–Lapse Statute, R.C. § 2107.52, Applicable Solely to Wills [Where The Devisee Of Real Or Personal Property Is A Relative And Predeceases The Testator]? Can It Apply Also to Distributions Under Inter Vivos Trusts Where the Beneficiary Is a Relative and Predeceases the Settlor?, Robert L. Hausser. 56 Title Topics 7 (December 1989).

Judicial Virus in the Probate Code: *Dollar Savings & Trust Co. v Turner*, William B. McNeil. 1 Prob L J Ohio 51 (January/February 1991).

Notes of Decisions

Intent of testator 5
Issue of deceased devisee taking estate 2
Lapse of devise 4
Residuary clause 3
Scope and construction 1

---

1. Scope and construction

Where a will devises property to my three children "and their legal representatives," such words are words of limitation and not of substitution, which construction is strengthened by use of "and" instead of "or" preceding "their legal representatives." Lansdowne v. Lansdowne (Darke 1935) 20 Ohio Law Abs. 520.

Fact question as to whether testator's greatgrandson, who predeceased testator and who was sole beneficiary of testator's estate, was father of putative daughter precluded summary judgment in action to determine heirship. Meckstroth v. Robinson (Ohio Com.Pl., 04-05-1996) 83 Ohio Misc.2d 57, 679 N.E.2d 744. Judgment 181(15.1).

In Ohio, the anti-lapse statute, RC 2107.52, applies only to "relatives" who are related by consanguinity, excluding those related by affinity. Oliver v. Bank One, Dayton, N.A. (Ohio 1991) 60 Ohio St.3d 32, 573 N.E.2d 55. Wills 552(3).

RC 2107.52 is applicable to trust agreements and will operate upon the death of the settlor to prevent the lapse of a gift contained therein so as to vest that portion of the trust res intended for a beneficiary who predeceases the settlor in the issue of the beneficiary. Dollar Sav. & Trust Co. of Youngstown v. Turner (Ohio 1988) 39 Ohio St.3d 182, 529 N.E.2d 1261. Trusts 124

The state of Ohio is not a necessary party in an action to construe a will where there has been no prior judicial determination of escheat to the state. Boulger v. Evans (Ohio 1978) 54 Ohio St.2d 371, 377 N.E.2d 753, 8 O.O.3d 388.

A bequest which contains a limitation to those of the group named who survive the testator is not subject to the anti-lapse statute. Shalkhauser v. Beach (Ohio Prob. 1968) 14 Ohio Misc. 1, 233 N.E.2d 527, 43 O.O.2d 20.

If a bequest once vests, the death of the legatee after that of the testator, but prior to payment or distribution of the bequest, does not cause a lapse, and in the absence of other provisions in the will, the bequest should be distributed to the executor or administrator of the deceased legatee. McSteen v. Barclays Bank Limited (Ohio Prob. 1967) 12 Ohio Misc. 29, 227 N.E.2d 280, 40 O.O.2d 489, 41 O.O.2d 23.

The lapse statute does not apply to a bequest to "all of my brothers who shall be living at the time of my decease." Day v. Brooks (Ohio Prob. 1967) 10 Ohio Misc. 273, 224 N.E.2d 557, 39 O.O.2d 441.

As used in RC 2107.52, the word "relative" is limited to persons related to the testator by consanguinity, and does not include those related by affinity. Kovar v. Kortan (Ohio Prob. 1965) 3 Ohio Misc. 63, 209 N.E.2d 762, 32 O.O.2d 302. Wills 552(3)

A devise of real property to the widow of the testator, for life, "and upon her death said property and the title thereto shall vest in the name and title of my sons... absolutely and in fee simple," which language anticipates absolute ownership of the property by the testator's sons, subject to the life estate of his widow, is a devise of vested remainders to the sons as of the death of the testator. Lane v. Lane (Miami 1961) 116 Ohio App. 100, 187 N.E.2d 71, 21 O.O.2d 375.

Where in a will six-sevenths of certain real property is given to testator's brother F, one seventh thereof is given to brother W, and the "rest, residue and remainder of my estate... which I own or have a right to dispose of" is given to F, or, in the event of F's predecease, the "residue" of the estate is given to W and sister S in equal shares, and where at the time of testator's death W is the sole survivor of the three named in the will, S having died without issue, the six-sevenths gift passes as a part of the residue, which in its entirety passes to W. Zangerle v. Thomas (Cuyahoga 1961) 115 Ohio App. 37, 176 N.E.2d 157, 87 Ohio Law Abs. 357, 17 O.O.2d 432.

As used in RC 2107.52, the phrase "relative of a testator" should be restricted to relationships which are consanguineous and excludes relationships which are merely affinitive. Schuck v. Schuck (Ohio Prob. 1958) 156 N.E.2d 351, 80 Ohio Law Abs. 394, 7 O.O.2d 198.

A devise by testatrix of certain property to her brother, his heirs and assigns, forever, does not lapse by virtue of the fact that such brother predeceased the testatrix. Graves v. Graves (Ohio Prob. 1956) 155 N.E.2d 540, 79 Ohio Law Abs. 262.

The phrase "If such devisee" appearing at beginning of second sentence of section, relative to succession on death of a devisee, refers back to phrase "child or other relative" appearing in first sentence of section. Heebsch v. Lonsway (Seneca 1947) 81 Ohio App. 361, 79 N.E.2d 663, 37 O.O. 207.

A bequest to legatee "if she has not remarried at time my trustee is ready to pay this legacy," vests immediately upon death of testator, subject to being divested, and in case where legatee not a blood relative of testator survives testator but dies before distribution, section designed to prevent lapsing of bequests in certain cases does not apply, but gift having vested on death of testator does not lapse because of death of beneficiary before time arrives for enjoyment in possession. Wilcox v. Central Nat. Bank (Ashtabula 1945) 69 N.E.2d 527, 46 Ohio Law Abs. 65.

While law of Ohio extends survivorship to descendants of "other relatives" of testator, that statute has no application to legacy under will of domiciliary of Indiana. Heater v. Mittendorf (Hamilton 1943) 72 Ohio App. 4, 50 N.E.2d 559, 38 Ohio Law Abs. 323, 26 O.O. 508.

Ohio court may not presume that the statutory law of Indiana is same as Ohio as to preventing lapse of bequest to relative of testator where relative predeceased testator, where only Indiana statute presented was one which prevented lapse of bequest to descendant of testator. Heater v. Mittendorf (Hamilton 1943) 72 Ohio App. 4, 50 N.E.2d 559, 38 Ohio Law Abs. 323, 26 O.O. 508.

A will which in fact disposes of the entire estate—after (a) debts, (b) other legacies and devises, general or specific, (c) a life estate, or (d) any other interest less than fee or absolute ownership—to relatives, some of whom have died leaving no issue surviving the testator, is subject to the provisions of this section. West v. Aigler (Ohio 1933) 127 Ohio St. 370, 188 N.E. 563, 39 Ohio Law Rep. 652.

The provisions of RS 5971 against failure of a devise apply to a devise to "children" as a class. (See also Mather v Copeland, 5 NP 151, 7 D 257 (CP, Jefferson 1898).) Woolley v. Paxson (Ohio 1889) 46 Ohio St. 307, 21 W.L.B. 303, 24 N.E. 599.

Husband is not a relative. Hess v. American Bible Soc. (Richland 1916) 28 Ohio C.D. 172, 26 Ohio C.C.(N.S.) 439.

Child or other relative in statute, means legitimate child, and not one who could not be an heir. Owens v. Humbert (Ohio App. 1916) 27 Ohio C.D. 307, 25 Ohio C.C.(N.S.) 522, 5 Ohio App. 312.

Section is confined to blood relatives, and the words heirs or assigns are words of limitation and not of substitution. Rea v. Griffin (Ohio Com.Pl. 1916) 29 Ohio Dec. 174, 21 Ohio N.P.(N.S.) 129, affirmed 98 Ohio St. 315, 120 N.E. 828, 16 Ohio Law Rep. 89.

The legatee included within the phrase "or other relative" must be related by blood, and not by marriage. Porterfield v. Porterfield (Ohio Com.Pl. 1907) 17 Ohio Dec. 448, 4 Ohio N.P.N.S. 654.

The doctrine of survivorship and lapsing of legacies and devises was, in olden times and even in early modern times, carried to such extremes that statutes like RS 5971 were enacted. Jackson v. Shinnick (Ohio Com.Pl. 1896) 6 Ohio Dec. 37, 3 Ohio N.P. 211.

The anti-lapse statute, RC 2107.52, is only applicable to wills and does not apply to testamentary trusts. Dollar Savings & Trust Co of Youngstown v Byrne, No. 85 CA 133 (7th Dist Ct App, Mahoning, 6–16–87).

Where a testator provided that if a beneficiary died within his lifetime, such deceased beneficiary's share should go to the surviving named beneficiaries, the anti-lapse provisions of RC 2107.52 were superseded by such provision of testator's will. In re Estate of Tertel v Tertel, No. L–83–286 (6th Dist Ct App, Lucas, 2–3–84).

A grandchild of a relative of a testator comes within the term "issue" as used in RC 2107.52. Third Nat. Bank & Trust Co. v Clendening, 175 NE(2d) 239, 17 OO(2d) 337 (Prob 1960).

2. Issue of deceased devisee taking estate

A devise to the testator's wife of all his estate for life, to be divided upon her death among his children or the survivor of them, vests no interest in a child who dies before the widow, and such deceased child's child is not entitled to share in the estate as one of the "children" or "survivors" to whom it was to be distributed. Sinton v. Boyd (Ohio 1869) 19 Ohio St. 30, 2 Am.Rep. 369.

A devise to life tenants and then to the children of the life tenants in fee simple with a limitation over if such tenant dies "without lawful heirs of their bodies" to the testator's brother's children is not void for uncertainty, since the intent of the testator was that, upon the death of the life tenant the children living were to take, and if any predeceased leaving a child or children such child or children should be substituted for its deceased parent; and if the life tenant died without issue, the fee would go immediately to the testator's brother's heirs. Stevenson v. Evans (Ohio 1859) 10 Ohio St. 307.

Right of issue of a deceased child to take its parent's share of an estate is based upon fact that testator devised an estate to such deceased child. Kelley v. Talifer (Shelby 1940) 31 Ohio Law Abs. 602.

Use of the phrase "or to the survivors thereof" in residuary clause evinced an intent to avoid operation of antilapse statute and to have the residuary estate vest only in those named beneficiaries who survived testatrix; testatrix intended for per capita distribution of the residuary estate to those named individuals who survived her, rather than per stirpes division to children of a named beneficiary who predeceased her. Polen v. Baker (Ohio, 08-22-2001) 92 Ohio St.3d 563, 752 N.E.2d 258, 2001-Ohio-1286. Wills ⊕ 587(5)

Son of testator, in whose favor will had created trust until son reached age 25, at which time trust would be terminated and principal and interest distributed to son, took immediate vested interest in trust estate at time of testator's death, which passed according to statute of descent and distribution after son's death intestate at age 20. Summers v. Summers (Ohio App. 4 Dist., 06-09-1997) 121 Ohio App.3d 263, 699 N.E.2d 958, appeal not allowed 80 Ohio St.3d 1426, 685 N.E.2d 238. Wills ⊕ 682(2)

When a testator bequeaths property to "nieces and nephews" of a named relative, whose living kin then included grandnieces and grandnephews only, it will be considered that the testator intended the logical result of a bequest to those persons who were able to receive it. Shalkhauser v. Beach (Ohio Prob. 1968) 14 Ohio Misc. 1, 233 N.E.2d 527, 43 O.O.2d 20.

Where property was devised to a relative "provided she be living at the time of my death," and such relative predeceased the testator leaving issue surviving, the anti-lapse statute will apply and such issue will take the bequest. Detzel v. Nieberding (Ohio Prob. 1966) 7 Ohio Misc. 262, 219 N.E.2d 327, 36 O.O.2d 358.

A testamentary provision for "lineal descendants of my blood" furnishes "other clear identification" as required by RC 3107.13(B) of the children of testator's predeceased son, without naming them, so as to enable them to succeed to a designated portion of testator's estate, although such children were previously adopted by nonrelatives. Saintignon v. Saintignon (Darke 1966) 5 Ohio App.2d 133, 214 N.E.2d 124, 34 O.O.2d 243.

The anti-lapse statute saves a gift to a relative who dies leaving issue before his gift becomes vested whether before or after the death of the testator. Schneider v. Dorr (Ohio Prob. 1965) 3 Ohio Misc. 103, 210 N.E.2d 311, 32 O.O.2d 391. Wills ⊕ 552(1)

Where a bequest was made to "my niece, Sarah Duckworth," and the only niece of such name had predeceased the testatrix, but there was a grandniece of such name and other grandnieces were called nieces, bequest was intended for such grandniece. Bartels v. Bartels (Ohio Prob. 1956) 139 N.E.2d 695, 75 Ohio Law Abs. 117, 1 O.O.2d 110.

A child of a person deceased at the date of the will is not entitled to take where the context shows that the naming of such deceased person in the will was mere inadvertence. Bartels v. Bartels (Ohio Prob. 1956) 139 N.E.2d 695, 75 Ohio Law Abs. 117, 1 O.O.2d 110. Wills ⊕ 552(4)

Where a testator devised the residue of his estate to his wife for life and upon her death provided that one fifth should go to each of four children and a fifth to the children of a deceased child, and that in event a child should die, that its interest should go to the heirs of its body, the remainder created was vested, not contingent. Cleveland Trust Co. v. Andrus (Lorain 1953) 95 Ohio App. 503, 121 N.E.2d 68, 54 O.O. 125.

When a remainder is given to persons named or otherwise definitely designated, and there is no clause of survivorship, the fact that a construction of the will which will render the remainder contingent may produce an intestacy as to the share of any of such persons who may die without leaving children surviving, during the continuance of the precedent estate, is a consideration which will influence the court to regard the remainder as a vested one. Cleveland Trust Co. v. Andrus (Lorain 1953) 95 Ohio App. 503, 121 N.E.2d 68, 54 O.O. 125. Wills ⊕ 634(12)

GC 10512-23 (RC 3107.13), as now in force, does not apply only to the rights of an adopted child under the anti-lapse statute, GC 10504–73 (RC 2107.52), it gives to an adopted child every right and privilege of inheritance which is given a natural child excepting only the inheritance of property "expressly limited to heirs of the body of the adopting parent or parents." In re Friedman's Estate (Cuyahoga 1949) 86 Ohio App. 97, 88 N.E.2d 230, 55 Ohio Law Abs. 22, 40 O.O. 510, reversed 154 Ohio St. 1, 93 N.E.2d 273, 42 O.O. 97.

Where testator bequeathed $1,000 to his wife's niece if she had not remarried when testator's trustee or executor was ready to pay the legacy, and she survived testator but died before payment was made to her by testator's executor, legacy vested at time of testator's death, and therefore administrator de bonis non of the estate of the niece of testator's wife was entitled to the legacy. Wilcox v. Central Nat. Bank (Ashtabula 1945) 69 N.E.2d 527, 46 Ohio Law Abs. 65. Wills ⊕ 630(8)

Where by her will testatrix left residue of her estate to two of her sisters, their heirs and assigns forever, and one of sisters predeceased testatrix leaving adopted daughter who survived testatrix, adopted daughter by virtue of GC 10504–73 (RC 2107.52) and 10512–19 (RC 3107.10), took estate given her adopting mother. Flynn v. Bredbeck (Ohio 1946) 147 Ohio St. 49, 68 N.E.2d 75, 33 O.O. 243. Wills ⊕ 552(3)

Under section providing that where devise of real or personal property is made to relative of testator and relative predeceases testator, leaving issue who survived testator, issue shall take estate devised and word "issue" embraces adopted child of original devisee. Flynn v. Bredbeck (Ohio 1946) 147 Ohio St. 49, 68 N.E.2d 75, 33 O.O. 243. Wills ⊕ 552(3)

The daughter of a testator's wife cannot, under statute, take property which such wife would have taken under her husband's will had she survived him. Kegler v. Kempter (Hamilton 1942) 74 Ohio App. 279, 58 N.E.2d 701, 29 O.O. 418.

Where a will bequeathing property to testatrix's brothers and sisters provides that if any of such brothers or sisters predecease testatrix, the share of the estate bequeathed to such brother or sister shall pass to his or her child or children, and a brother of testatrix dies leaving two children, one of whom predeceases testatrix, leaving issue, such issue will, under authority of section, share equally with the living child of the deceased brother. Thatcher v. Trouslot (Lucas 1935) 52 Ohio App. 74, 3 N.E.2d 57, 21 Ohio Law Abs. 301, 6 O.O. 134. Wills ⇔ 552(4)

Under RS 5971 (repealed 1932. See GC 10504–73), providing that on a devise to a child or other relative of the testator, if such child or relative was dead at the time of the making of the will, or shall die thereafter, leaving issue surviving the testator, in either case such issue shall take the share as the devisee would have done if he had lived, bequests to a child or other relative when such primary devisee dies before the testator, leaving issue which survives him, prevents the lapse of such bequests, unless to give it that effect would be subversive of the intent clearly expressed in the will. Larwill's Ex'rs v. Ewing (Ohio 1905) 73 Ohio St. 177, 76 N.E. 503, 3 Ohio Law Rep. 494. Wills ⇔ 552(1)

The effect of RS 5971 is to prevent the lapse of a devise to a relative of the testator who dies before the testator but leaves surviving issue, unless such effect is contrary to dispositive intention clearly expressed in the will. Larwill's Ex'rs v. Ewing (Ohio 1905) 73 Ohio St. 177, 76 N.E. 503, 3 Ohio Law Rep. 494.

Where a testator bequeaths his residuary estate to his three children per capita and directs that in the case of the death of any of them the survivor or survivors shall take the bequest of the deceased sibling or siblings, the words "survivor or survivors" refer specifically to the time of the testator's death. Renner v. Williams (Ohio 1905) 71 Ohio St. 340, 73 N.E. 221, 2 Ohio Law Rep. 411.

Under RS 5971 (repealed 1932. See GC 10504–73), providing that, where a devisee named in a will dies during the lifetime of the testator, leaving issue, such issue takes in the same manner the devisee would have done, if he had survived the testator, if the primary devisee is indebted to the estate of the testator, his issue is entitled to have and take only so much of the amount bequeathed to the parent as is left after the payment of the debt. Baker v. Carpenter (Ohio 1903) 69 Ohio St. 15, 48 W.L.B. 907, 68 N.E. 577, 1 Ohio Law Rep. 489, 1 Ohio Law Rep. 589. Wills ⇔ 731

Where a devisee named in a will dies during the lifetime of the testator, leaving issue, such issue takes the estate so devised in the same manner the devisee would have done, if he had survived the testator. Baker v. Carpenter (Ohio 1903) 69 Ohio St. 15, 48 W.L.B. 907, 68 N.E. 577, 1 Ohio Law Rep. 489, 1 Ohio Law Rep. 589.

Under RS 5971 (repealed 1932. See GC 10504–73), providing that where a devise is made to a child or other relative, if such child or other relative shall have been dead at the time of making the will or shall die thereafter leaving issue, such issue shall take the estate devised, there is no distinction between the issue of a devisee who died before the making of a will and of one who dies after it. Shumaker v. Pearson (Ohio 1902) 67 Ohio St. 330, 48 W.L.B. 147, 65 N.E. 1005. Wills ⇔ 552(4)

No distinction is permitted between the issue of a devisee who has died before the making of the will, and of one who dies after it. Shumaker v. Pearson (Ohio 1902) 67 Ohio St. 330, 48 W.L.B. 147, 65 N.E. 1005. Courts ⇔ 93(1); Wills ⇔ 849

When a legatee dies before the testator, the legacy lapses unless such legatee was a child or other relative of the testator, and left issue surviving the testator; an adopted child is not such issue. (See also Teobald v Fugman, 64 OS 473, 60 NE 606 (1901).) Phillips v. McConica (Ohio 1898) 59 Ohio St. 1, 40 W.L.B. 293, 51 N.E. 445, 69 Am.St.Rep. 753.

The heirs of a deceased devisee take by virtue of this section the residuary estate bequeathed to "legal heirs" of the deceased brother. Youngblood v. Youngblood (Ohio Cir. 1908) 20 Ohio C.D. 482, 11 Ohio C.C.(N.S.) 276, affirmed 78 Ohio St. 405, 85 N.E. 1135, 5 Ohio Law Rep. 625.

Where a widow dies before the probate of her husband's will, her heirs take the property given to her by that will as against the heirs of the husband. Hawkins v. Barrow (Ohio Cir. 1897) 8 Ohio C.D. 251.

Where payment of a legacy is postponed until the end of a life tenancy and made a specific lien on the remainder, the legacy vests in the legatee at the testator's death where it appears the postponement of payment is for the convenience of the remainderman on whose estate it is charged; consequently, where the legatee dies before the life tenant, the lien of the payment of the legacy does not lapse. Gillis v. Long (Ohio Com.Pl. 1908) 19 Ohio Dec. 253, 8 Ohio N.P.N.S. 1.

The word "issue" in RS 5971 includes grandchildren and is as broad as "heirs of the body" in the sense that where a testator devised property to a child who died before the testator and left issue who also died before the testator but left issue in turn, the great grandchild takes the devise. Moon v. Hepford (Ohio Com.Pl. 1895) 3 Ohio Dec. 508, 2 Ohio N.P. 365.

A husband is not the "issue" of his deceased wife for purposes of RS 5971, although he is next of kin by the statute of descent and distribution. Norwood v. Mills (Ohio Com.Pl. 1895) 3 Ohio Dec. 356, 1 Ohio N.P. 314.

Property of wife who left all of her property in her will to her husband, who preceded her in death by only two days after payment of a year's allowance and property not deemed assets to adopted granddaughter, would pass to issue of her husband including the adopted granddaughter as provided for in section. Harrison v. Hillegas (Ohio Prob. 1939) 1 Ohio Supp. 160, 28 Ohio Law Abs. 404, 13 O.O. 523. Descent And Distribution ⇔ 52(1)

3. Residuary clause

Skilled nursing care facility, in which testamentary trust beneficiary resided prior to his death, was entitled to distribution under underlying will upon death of beneficiary and termination of trust together with long-term care group home where beneficiary resided prior to transfer to facility, where bequest anticipated that some institution other than home might provide residential care for beneficiary and, in that event, bequeathed one-half of bequest to home to that other institution, and there was no ambiguity in terms of bequest. Bank One Trust Co. v. Resident Home Ass'n for Mentally Retarded (Ohio App. 2 Dist., Montgomery, 07-18-2003) No. 19660, 2003-Ohio-3835, 2003 WL 21674987, Unreported. Wills ⇔ 656

Where a will devises real estate to the brothers and sisters of the testatrix, individually, with no words of survivorship and no residuary clause, and one of such devisees predeceases the testatrix, leaving no issue, the devise as to the share of such devisee lapses. Bishop v. Jones (Licking 1929) 7 Ohio Law Abs. 484, 29 Ohio Law Rep. 48.

Testator's niece, who was to receive all funds in specific bank account under will, was only entitled to funds remaining in account at time of testator's death, and funds testator had removed from account and reinvested in certificate of deposit, which was not explicitly disposed of by will, became part of residue of estate. Church v. Morgan (Ohio App. 4 Dist., 11-01-1996) 115 Ohio App.3d 477, 685 N.E.2d 809. Wills ⇔ 767

Where testator bequeathed residue to "the heirs set forth in Item (naming pecuniary legatees) above, per stirpes," and where there was nothing in will or surrounding circumstances to overcome presumption that testator intended to make equal distribution among those who had equal claims upon his bounty, residue would be distributed pursuant to such presumption, and not in the same proportion as the specific bequests made in the item referred to, though pecuniary bequest therein to testator's sister-in-law was three times as much as amounts given to testator's own brothers and sister. Evans v. Cass (Ohio Prob. 1970) 23 Ohio Misc. 300, 256 N.E.2d 738, 51 O.O.2d 417, 52 O.O.2d 276. Wills ⇔ 860

Where testatrix created a trust for the benefit of her niece with a remainder in the niece's father, her brother, and the father predeceased testatrix, the remainder passes to the niece's estate on her death. Day v. Brooks (Ohio Prob. 1967) 10 Ohio Misc. 273, 224 N.E.2d 557, 39 O.O.2d 441.

A lapsed portion of the residue of an estate passes under the residuary provision to other persons entitled thereunder. Zangerle v. Thomas (Cuyahoga 1961) 115 Ohio App. 37, 176 N.E.2d 157, 87 Ohio Law Abs. 357, 17 O.O.2d 432.

Where testator devised his property in equal shares to his sister-in-law and his brother, and the sister-in-law survived him by only one day, the share which she would otherwise have taken passes to the brother as the sole residuary legatee. Schuck v. Schuck (Ohio Prob. 1958) 156 N.E.2d 351, 80 Ohio Law Abs. 394, 7 O.O.2d 198.

Where a will contains general residuary provisions for disposition of any and all of the testator's property not disposed of by other provisions of the will, if a bequest or devise of a part of the residue lapses or is otherwise ineffective, that part of the residue, except as provided by statute and in the absence of provisions of the will or surrounding circumstances justifying the conclusion that the testator expressed a different intention, will ordinarily pass under such residuary provisions of the will to any other parties entitled thereunder to portions of the residue, instead of passing as intestate property. Commerce Nat. Bank of Toledo v. Browning (Ohio 1952) 158 Ohio St. 54, 107 N.E.2d 120, 48 O.O. 28. Wills ⇔ 863

Petition by widow as sole devisee of residuary legatee under former GC 10857 (RC 2107.45) and GC 10858 (RC 2107.46), for construction of will of original testator, alleging that trustee, dividing rents and profits of estate among residuary legatees, refused to distribute any part of income to her after her husband's death, held to state cause of action under former GC 10581 (RC 2107.52), which provides for vesting of estate devised residuary legatee surviving testator, unless different disposition is required by will.

Webb v. Biles (Hamilton 1927) 27 Ohio App. 197, 161 N.E. 218, 5 Ohio Law Abs. 607, affirmed 118 Ohio St. 346, 161 N.E. 49, 6 Ohio Law Abs. 239, 26 Ohio Law Rep. 273.

A wife, having devised the residuary estate of her husband in accordance with his will and then dying before him, makes no disposition of the residue. Thomas v. Hobson (Ohio Cir. 1907) 20 Ohio C.D. 214, 10 Ohio C.C.N.S. 351.

The term "residuary estate" should receive its technical construction. Jewett v. Jewett (Ohio Cir. 1900) 12 Ohio C.D. 131, affirmed 67 Ohio St. 541, 67 N.E. 1098.

Section applies to cause distribution to surviving brothers and sisters of a bequest to a named sister providing that in case she predeceased the testator the bequest go to another named sister, and both sisters predeceased testator. Holman v. Warrick (Ohio Prob. 1942) 8 Ohio Supp. 132, 35 Ohio Law Abs. 520, 23 O.O. 397.

A general legacy made to a child or other relative who dies prior to the death of the testator, without issue, lapses unless the will shows a contrary intention. Stevens v. Hill (Ohio Prob. 1934) 2 Ohio Supp. 220, 33 Ohio Law Abs. 465, 1 O.O. 247.

A lapsed legacy passes under the residuary clause in a will unless such legacy is excluded from its provisions. Stevens v. Hill (Ohio Prob. 1934) 2 Ohio Supp. 220, 33 Ohio Law Abs. 465, 1 O.O. 247.

A residuary clause which reads "should there be a residue, I give and devise the same to..." does not exclude a lapsed bequest. Stevens v. Hill (Ohio Prob. 1934) 2 Ohio Supp. 220, 33 Ohio Law Abs. 465, 1 O.O. 247.

Where decedent's will contains a general residuary clause, a lapsed devise will pass under the residuary clause and not as intestate property. Clinton County Natl Bank & Trust Co v Smith, No. CA–460 (12th Dist Ct App, Clinton, 12–30–82).

4. Lapse of devise

Where a testator sets up a trust with the interest to be paid to his son's widow for life and at her death the principal to be paid to her sons, and the sons predecease their mother without issue or debts, the trust fails by the occurrence of a contingency not provided for by the will, and the entire beneficial interest having vested in the mother as the boys' heir, she must be paid it directly without the delay and expense of successive administrations. Taylor v. Huber's Ex'rs (Ohio 1862) 13 Ohio St. 288.

Testator is presumed to have known of existence and effect of antilapse statute. Martin v. Summers (Ohio App. 12 Dist., 02-21-1995) 101 Ohio App.3d 269, 655 N.E.2d 424. Evidence ⚖ 65

Antilapse statute did not apply and distribution was not made per stirpes, although daughter of testator was deceased where gift in will was not to daughter but to children of deceased daughter. Johnson v. Johnson (Ohio Com.Pl. 1984) 13 Ohio Misc.2d 15, 468 N.E.2d 945, 13 O.B.R. 302. Wills ⚖ 531(4); Wills ⚖ 552(1)

The anti-lapse statute does not apply to a member of a class who has predeceased testatrix where testatrix has expressly denied its application by limitation of the class of beneficiaries to those "who survive me." Cowgill v. Faulconer (Ohio Com.Pl. 1978) 57 Ohio Misc. 6, 385 N.E.2d 327, 8 O.O.3d 423, 11 O.O.3d 59. Wills ⚖ 552(5)

Testator's sister-in-law, being relative by affinity rather than consanguinity, was not covered by antilapse statute, and thus, where she predeceased testator without issue, pecuniary bequest to her, as well as any share which she might have had in residue, lapsed and passed to the other residuary legatees under the will, and not under statutes of descent and distribution. Evans v. Cass (Ohio Prob. 1970) 23 Ohio Misc. 300, 256 N.E.2d 738, 51 O.O.2d 417, 52 O.O.2d 276. Wills ⚖ 552(3); Wills ⚖ 863

A bequest to an uncle of testatrix who predeceased the testatrix leaving no issue lapses. Day v. Brooks (Ohio Prob. 1967) 10 Ohio Misc. 273, 224 N.E.2d 557, 39 O.O.2d 441.

The lapse statute does not apply to bequests to legatees who survive the testator and thereafter die. Central Trust Co. v. Bedinghaus (Ohio Prob. 1965) 8 Ohio Misc. 183, 219 N.E.2d 243, 36 O.O.2d 99, 37 O.O.2d 258.

Where the anti-lapse statute does not apply, if the named recipient of a general or specific devise or bequest is dead at the time of the execution of the will, or thereafter predeceases the testator, the gift lapses. Kellogg v. Campbell (Ohio Prob. 1965) 3 Ohio Misc. 27, 209 N.E.2d 645, 32 O.O.2d 252.

Where a devisee or legatee in a will dies prior to the testator, such devisee or legatee not being a child or other relative of the testator within RC 2107.52 and such will contains no residuary clause nor any provision showing any other intention of the testator, such legacy or devise lapses and such testator dies intestate as to such property named in such legacy or devise. Muckerheide v. Zink (Ohio Prob. 1963) 3 Ohio Misc. 33, 206 N.E.2d 436, 30 O.O.2d 512, affirmed 1 Ohio App.2d 76, 202 N.E.2d 725, 30 O.O.2d 103. Wills ⚖ 775; Wills ⚖ 865(1)

Where a husband named as a devisee in the will of his spouse dies prior to the time of the death of said spouse, or the time of his death comes within the "presumption of order of death" as stated in RC 2105.21, the devisee, not being a relative of the testatrix within the meaning of RC 2107.52 and the will not containing a residuary clause, nor any other provisions showing any other intention of the testatrix, the devise to the deceased spouse lapses and the testatrix dies intestate as to such property designated in such devise. Muckerheide v. Zink (Hamilton 1964) 1 Ohio App.2d 76, 202 N.E.2d 725, 30 O.O.2d 103.

Presumption is that testatrix knew that devises to persons known by her to be dead, and not her relatives, were void, since it is common knowledge that devises to such persons lapse. Nelson v. Minton (Butler 1933) 46 Ohio App. 39, 187 N.E. 576, 14 Ohio Law Abs. 679, 38 Ohio Law Rep. 287. Evidence ⚖ 65

Statute changing common-law rule relating to lapsing of devises and legacies should be liberally construed. Gale v. Keyes (Morrow 1933) 45 Ohio App. 61, 186 N.E. 755, 14 Ohio Law Abs. 549, 38 Ohio Law Rep. 227. Wills ⚖ 774

Will, whereby testator divided residuary estate among his children with devises over on alternate contingencies of death of any of children "leaving issue" or "leaving no issue," held referable to death of children at any time, notwithstanding statute preventing lapses. Ohio Nat. Bank of Columbus v. Harris (Ohio 1933) 126 Ohio St. 360, 185 N.E. 532, 37 Ohio Law Rep. 576. Wills ⚖ 545(2)

A devise, or legacy, lapses by the death of the devisee or legatee in the lifetime of the testator; this principle, however, has been modified in Ohio by the so-called statute against lapses, but only to the extent of exempting from its operation the issue of a "child or other relative," (of the testator) who was dead at the time the will was made, or dies thereafter leaving issue surviving the testator; in the instant case, it was held that a devise to "Henry H. Evers, and his heirs forever" is the devise of a fee simple estate in the property sought to be given, but Evers' death before the testator's death caused the legacy to lapse and the heirs of Evers got nothing by the instrument. Evers v. Williams (Ohio Com.Pl. 1931) 29 Ohio NP(NS) 197, affirmed 43 Ohio App. 555, 184 N.E. 19, 12 Ohio Law Abs. 726, 37 Ohio Law Rep. 291.

On lapse of devise or legacy in will containing no residuary clause, property descends as intestate property there. Foreman v. Medina County Nat. Bank (Ohio 1928) 119 Ohio St. 17, 162 N.E. 42, 6 Ohio Law Abs. 369, 26 Ohio Law Rep. 461. Wills ⚖ 849

Notwithstanding RS 5975 (repealed 1932. See GC 10504–77), relating to the lapse of legacies and devises, a devise of real estate by a wife to her husband will lapse if his death precedes hers, though he leaves issue of a former marriage surviving the testatrix. Schaefer v. Bernhardt (Ohio 1907) 76 Ohio St. 443, 81 N.E. 640, 5 Ohio Law Rep. 112, 10 Am.Ann.Cas. 919. Wills ⚖ 775

A devise of realty by a wife to her husband will lapse if his death precedes hers, although he leaves issue of a former marriage surviving the testatrix, as the phrase "other relative" in RS 5971 should be read to mean relative of blood and to exclude spouses. Schaefer v. Bernhardt (Ohio 1907) 76 Ohio St. 443, 81 N.E. 640, 5 Ohio Law Rep. 112, 10 Am.Ann.Cas. 919. Wills ⚖ 775

Where a legacy is given in payment of a debt by the express terms of a will, it does not lapse by the death of the legatee before the testator, but, where the intent of the testator was to confer a bounty, the legacy lapsed and evidence is inadmissible to show a different intent and that the legacy was given in payment of a debt. McNeal v. Pierce (Ohio 1905) 73 Ohio St. 7, 75 N.E. 938, 112 Am.St.Rep. 695, 3 Ohio Law Rep. 412. Wills ⚖ 775

A legacy to pay a debt does not lapse by the death of the legatee before the testator, but where by the express terms of the will it appears the intention of the testator was to confer a bounty, the legacy does lapse by the death of the legatee before the testator. McNeal v. Pierce (Ohio 1905) 73 Ohio St. 7, 75 N.E. 938, 112 Am.St.Rep. 695, 3 Ohio Law Rep. 412. Wills ⚖ 775

Where a devise was made to testator's two brothers and a sister individually and the brothers die before testator dies, the devise lapses as to them and the law directs as to the disposition of the property. Jewett v. Jewett (Ohio Cir. 1900) 12 Ohio C.D. 131, affirmed 67 Ohio St. 541, 67 N.E. 1098.

Note 4

Provision in a contract between a husband and wife that their wills were to be "unalterable and irrevocable as to the parties to the contract" only referred to the husband and wife as parties to the contract; even if the husband's original will was in force, the provision for his wife had lapsed by her earlier death and her heirs would not be entitled to anything under such will. Trustees of Reformed Church of Uniontown v. Wise's Ex'r (Ohio Cir. 1895) 6 Ohio C.D. 703, 3 Ohio Dec. 567.

Devise and legacy to a half-brother who died prior to deceased, and without leaving issue, does not pass under section and therefore lapses. Lane v. Berk (Ohio Prob. 1941) 7 Ohio Supp. 186, 35 Ohio Law Abs. 580, 23 O.O. 41.

Section has no application to the disposition of a general legacy to a child or other relative who dies prior to the death of the testator without issue. Stevens v. Hill (Ohio Prob. 1934) 2 Ohio Supp. 220, 33 Ohio Law Abs. 465, 1 O.O. 247.

5. Intent of testator

Most fundamental tenet for construction of a will mandates that court ascertain and carry out, within bounds of law, testator's intent. Church v. Morgan (Ohio App. 4 Dist., 11-01-1996) 115 Ohio App.3d 477, 685 N.E.2d 809. Wills ⇐ 439; Wills ⇐ 442

Since express language of will that bequeathed to testator's niece all funds located in specific bank accounts created no doubt as to its meaning, extrinsic evidence could not be considered to determine testator's intent. Church v. Morgan (Ohio App. 4 Dist., 11-01-1996) 115 Ohio App.3d 477, 685 N.E.2d 809. Wills ⇐ 490

Fiduciary of estate is obligated to ascertain and accomplish intention of testator from provisions contained in will. Meckstroth v. Robinson (Ohio Com.Pl., 04-05-1996) 83 Ohio Misc.2d 57, 679 N.E.2d 744. Wills ⇐ 440

Will provision directing testator's surviving wife and son to share in proceeds from sale of farm "equally, share and share alike" demonstrated testator's intent that his wife and son were to each receive half of sale proceeds and which permitted per capita, rather than per stirpes, distribution to testator's surviving wife and issue of son who predeceased testator. Martin v. Summers (Ohio App. 12 Dist., 02-21-1995) 101 Ohio App.3d 269, 655 N.E.2d 424. Wills ⇐ 533

Will provision dividing sale of farm proceeds "equally to my son and wife, share and share alike" did not manifest intent of testator to defeat antilapse statute and, thus, sale proceeds were distributed per stirpes between testator's surviving spouse and issue of testator's predeceased son; testator intended to make gifts to named individuals rather than to a class. Martin v. Summers (Ohio App. 12 Dist., 02-21-1995) 101 Ohio App.3d 269, 655 N.E.2d 424. Wills ⇐ 552(1)

The court may consider extrinsic evidence to determine the testator's intention only when the language in the will creates doubt as to the meaning of the will. Oliver v. Bank One, Dayton, N.A. (Ohio 1991) 60 Ohio St.3d 32, 573 N.E.2d 55. Wills ⇐ 488

The anti-lapse statute, RC 2107.52, may be avoided by sufficient expression of intent. Tootle v. Tootle (Ohio 1986) 22 Ohio St.3d 244, 490 N.E.2d 878, 22 O.B.R. 420. Wills ⇐ 552(1)

Where the terms of a will provide for a bequest or devise to a named person, per stirpes, without expressly designating the class of persons who are to take in the event that the named person does not survive the testatrix, and it is clear from the will taken as a whole, read in light of the circumstances surrounding the execution of the will, that a secondary gift was intended, then it will be assumed that a secondary gift is intended to go to the heirs at law of the named person as determined by the statute of descent and distribution. Richland Trust Co. v. Becvar (Ohio 1975) 44 Ohio St.2d 219, 339 N.E.2d 830, 73 O.O.2d 512.

Where a bequest was made to "my nephew William Holter," and testatrix had a nephew William Duckworth and a niece whose husband was named Wilbur Holter, bequest was intended for the nephew. Bartels v. Bartels (Ohio Prob. 1956) 139 N.E.2d 695, 75 Ohio Law Abs. 117, 1 O.O.2d 110.

On the evidence, testatrix's designation as legatees of "Albert Duckworth and Robert Duckworth, my two brothers" was intended to refer to her only living brothers Albert and Walter, and not to a deceased brother named John Robert or a nephew Robert. Bartels v. Bartels (Ohio Prob. 1956) 139 N.E.2d 695, 75 Ohio Law Abs. 117, 1 O.O.2d 110.

The words "as not organized and functioning" may be regarded as merely descriptive of a constituent beneficiary church in the absence of competent evidence tending to show that the testator intended a legacy to lapse as to a consolidated church corporation. In re Barker's Will (Ohio 1955) 162 Ohio St. 531, 124 N.E.2d 421, 55 O.O. 421.

Where will provided that residue should be divided equally among "my nieces and nephews that are living," testator intended that nephew, who had long been his agent, should have equal share in residue, notwithstanding such nephew predeceased testator; under a devise to a class, the devisees are not determined at the death of the testator but the issue of a deceased member of the class surviving the testator must take what the deceased would have taken had he survived. Gale v. Keyes (Morrow 1933) 45 Ohio App. 61, 186 N.E. 755, 14 Ohio Law Abs. 549, 38 Ohio Law Rep. 227. Wills ⇐ 524(2)

The expression "legal heirs" as used by a testator has a definite meaning, to wit, those upon whom the law would cast the estate if the testator had died intestate, the expression "to be divided in equal shares" merely points out how such persons are to take their interests. Youngblood v. Youngblood (Ohio Cir. 1908) 20 Ohio C.D. 482, 11 Ohio C.C.(N.S.) 276, affirmed 78 Ohio St. 405, 85 N.E. 1135, 5 Ohio Law Rep. 625.

Where a devise in a will fails for want of a beneficiary, the devisee having predeceased the testator, and there is a statute governing the descent of the property in such a case, the testator will be presumed to have had the statute in mind when he made the will, and to have intended that the property, in the event it could not descend to the devisee, should descend as provided by statute, in the absence of anything in the will showing a contrary intention. Ballman v. Ballman (Ohio Com.Pl. 1927) 25 Ohio Law Rep. 144.

2107.521 Only specific reference in will to testator's power of appointment effective

No provision of a will exercises a power of appointment held by the testator unless specific reference is made to the power.

(1980 S 317, eff. 3–23–81; 1975 S 145)

OSBA Probate and Trust Law Section

1980:

In 1975 Sec. 2107.521 was enacted to provide that a general residuary clause in a will does not exercise a power of appointment held by the testator unless specific reference is made to the power. Further analysis of the problem of exercise of powers of appointment by will has revealed a gap in this statute, in that it probably does not apply to a so-called "blanket exercise" clause, which thus may be construed to exercise a power without the specific reference required for a general residuary clause. Examples of blanket exercise clauses are, "I give the residue of my estate, including any property over which I have a power of appointment."

The Board believes that existing Sec. 2107.521 expresses a general policy that specific reference should be required for exercise of powers, and that this policy should also clearly apply in the case of a blanket exercise clause.

Library References

Wills ⇐ 589(6).
Westlaw Topic No. 409.

Research References

Encyclopedias

OH Jur. 3d Decedents' Estates § 276, Power of Appointment.
OH Jur. 3d Decedents' Estates § 472, Construction of Wills Exercising Powers.
OH Jur. 3d Estates, Pwrs., & Restrnts. on Alienat. § 179, Exercise by Will—by General Devise or Residuary Clause of Will.

Forms

Ohio Forms Legal and Business § 24:143, Drafting Will.
Ohio Forms Legal and Business § 24:361, Declaration of Intent to Exercise All Powers of Appointment.
Ohio Forms Legal and Business § 24:728, Devise of Residue—Including Property Over Which Testator Has Power of Appointment.

Treatises and Practice Aids

Carlin, Baldwin's Ohio Practice, Merrick-Rippner Probate Law § 30:20, Drafting a Will—Beneficiary Clauses—Property Under Power of Appointment.
Carlin, Baldwin's Ohio Practice, Merrick-Rippner Probate Law § 43:18, Construing a Will—Language—Actually Employed by Testator.
Carlin, Baldwin's Ohio Practice, Merrick-Rippner Probate Law § 43:19, Construing a Will—Language—Unambiguous.

Carlin, Baldwin's Ohio Practice, Merrick-Rippner Probate Law § 43:47, Construing a Will—Apportionment of Estate—Exercise of Power of Appointment.

Carlin, Baldwin's Ohio Practice, Merrick-Rippner Probate Law § 30:151, Reference to After-Acquired Property and Lapsed Legacies—Form.

Restatement (2d) of Property, Don. Trans. § 17.3, Disposition in Deed or Will of All the Donee's Property.

Restatement (2d) of Property, Don. Trans. § 17.4, Appointive Assets Identified in Dispositive Instrument of Donee.

Restatement (2d) of Property, Don. Trans. § 17.5, Other Circumstances Indicating that Donee Intended to Exercise a Power.

Notes of Decisions

Residuary clause   1
Specific reference   2

---

1. Residuary clause

A residuary clause which refers to specific property as included in the residue is a specific residuary clause as to that property, and not a "general residuary clause" as that phrase was used in former RC 2107.521, before its amendment by 1980 S 317, eff 3–23–81. Brouse v. Old Phoenix Nat. Bank of Medina (Summit 1985) 25 Ohio App.3d 9, 495 N.E.2d 42, 25 O.B.R. 38.

A residuary bequest of all property of which the testator has "the right to dispose of... by power of appointment or other wise," is ineffective to exercise the power, since there is no specific reference to the power as required by RC 2107.521. Murstein v. Central Nat. Bank of Cleveland (Cuyahoga 1985) 25 Ohio App.3d 6, 495 N.E.2d 37, 25 O.B.R. 35.

A general residuary clause in a will does not exercise a limited testamentary power of appointment when the clause does not specifically refer to the power. Clinton County Nat. Bank & Trust Co. v. First Nat. Bank of Cincinnati (Ohio 1980) 62 Ohio St.2d 90, 403 N.E.2d 968, 16 O.O.3d 99. Wills ⚖ 589(5)

A power of appointment is an estate, right, or interest in property within the meaning of RC 2107.50, and unless a contrary intention is manifested, is exercised by the general residuary clause of the donee's will. Dollar Sav. & Trust Co. v. First Nat. Bank of Boston (Ohio Com.Pl. 1972) 32 Ohio Misc. 81, 285 N.E.2d 768, 61 O.O.2d 134.

2. Specific reference

Testator's intent to exercise power of appointment must be manifested by his specific reference to the power and its subject matter. Arthur v. Odd Fellows' Beneficial Ass'n of Columbus (Ohio 1876) 29 Ohio St. 557.

California court's determination of intent of donee domiciled in California at time of power's exercise in exercising testamentary special power of appointment was binding in subsequent judicial proceedings in Ohio, and entitled to full faith and credit with respect thereto, even if California court failed to obtain personal jurisdiction over trust assets located in Ohio. Toledo Trust Co. v. Santa Barbara Foundation (Ohio 1987) 32 Ohio St.3d 141, 512 N.E.2d 664, certiorari denied 108 S.Ct. 1089, 485 U.S. 916, 99 L.Ed.2d 250. Judgment ⚖ 815

A disposition of "all... of the property... over which I may have any power of appointment" is sufficient to exercise the power. Cleveland Trust Co. v. Shuman (Ohio Com.Pl. 1974) 39 Ohio Misc. 136, 317 N.E.2d 256, 68 O.O.2d 332.

An intention to exercise a testamentary power of appointment may be shown either by referring to the power in the will, or by making a specific disposition of the subject matter of the power, or by showing that the will would not have any operation except as an exercise of the power. Kiplinger v. Armstrong (Summit 1930) 34 Ohio App. 348, 171 N.E. 245, 8 Ohio Law Abs. 286.

2107.53   Undevised real estate applied to debts

When part of the real estate of a testator descends to his heirs because it was not disposed of by his will, and his personal estate is insufficient to pay his debts, the undevised real estate shall be chargeable first with the debts, as far as it will go, in exoneration of the real estate that is devised, unless it appears from the will that a different arrangement of assets was made for the payment of such testator's debts, in which case such assets shall be applied for that purpose in conformity with the will.

(1953 H 1, eff. 10–1–53; GC 10504–74)

Historical and Statutory Notes

Pre–1953 H 1 Amendments: 114 v 360

Cross References

Sale of real property to pay debts, Ch 2127

Library References

Wills ⚖ 840.
Westlaw Topic No. 409.
C.J.S. Wills §§ 1943, 1949 to 1956, 1958 to 1969, 1971 to 1972.

Research References

Encyclopedias

OH Jur. 3d Decedents' Estates § 855, Enforcement of Contribution.

OH Jur. 3d Decedents' Estates § 1479, Undevised Real Estate Before Devised Real Estate.

OH Jur. 3d Decedents' Estates § 1480, Effect of Provisions of Will, Deed, or Other Instrument.

OH Jur. 3d Decedents' Estates § 1501, Determination of Particular Property or Quantity to be Sold.

Forms

Ohio Forms Legal and Business § 24:391, Payment of Debts—General Clause.

Ohio Forms Legal and Business § 24:394, Payment of Debts—Order of Sale of Realty.

Treatises and Practice Aids

Carlin, Baldwin's Ohio Practice, Merrick-Rippner Probate Law § 48:1, Property Chargeable With Payment of Debts—Statutory Provisions.

Carlin, Baldwin's Ohio Practice, Merrick-Rippner Probate Law § 92:1, Property Subject to Sale—General Rule.

Notes of Decisions

Debts as encumbrance on land   2
Noncupative will   3
Procedural issues   4
Widow's claim   1

---

1. Widow's claim

Where, in the probate of an estate, the only claims against the estate consist of the widow's claims for year's allowance, property exempt from administration and for reimbursement for funeral expenses paid by her, acceptance by the widow, the sole heir and devisee under the will, of transfer of all the assets of the estate effects a merger of such claims of the widow in the property transferred, constitutes a waiver by her of all her claims against the estate and, no debts of the estate remaining unpaid, a petition by the executor to sell land to pay debts consisting of the widow's claims for year's allowance, property exempt from administration and for reimbursement for funeral expenses paid will be denied. Kaczenski v. Kaczenski (Trumbull 1962) 118 Ohio App. 225, 193 N.E.2d 731, 25 O.O.2d 68. Executors And Administrators ⚖ 307

Where it appears that there is land enough to set off the dower of a widow who elects to take against the will without interfering with land specifically devised for life, it should be so done; otherwise, the disappointed devisees are equitably entitled to compensation out of the rejected provisions for the widow, and if they do not fully compensate such devisees, the resulting uncompensated loss should fall upon the residuary estate in preference to the specific devises, unless a contrary intention appears from the will. Dunlap v. McCloud (Ohio 1911) 84 Ohio St. 272, 95 N.E. 774, 9 Ohio Law Rep. 94. Wills ⚖ 802(5)

2. Debts as encumbrance on land

Where the personal assets of a decedent are exhausted, the remaining debts of the decedent are a lien on the land of which he died seized,

2107.53
Note 2

whether devised or cast by descent, which can only be removed by the payment of the debts. Ramsdall v. Craighill (Ohio 1839) 9 Ohio 197.

Where a purchaser of the legal title to lands from heirs has notice that such title is a trust for a decedent, he takes the land subject to the trust. Stiver v. Stiver's Heirs (Ohio 1837) 8 Ohio 217.

Mortgage on land inherited from wife by husband dying intestate leaving personalty sufficient to pay debts, should be paid from personalty. Medina County Nat. Bank v. Foreman (Medina 1927) 27 Ohio App. 400, 161 N.E. 366, 5 Ohio Law Abs. 787, affirmed 119 Ohio St. 17, 162 N.E. 42, 6 Ohio Law Abs. 369, 26 Ohio Law Rep. 461. Executors And Administrators ⇨ 272

3. Noncupative will

Where a testator, by a noncupative will attempts to give the whole of his estate, consisting of both real and personal property, to one not his heir, the debts and cost of administration should be paid from proceeds of the sale of real property. Skinner v. Blackburn (Ohio Cir. 1889) 2 Ohio C.D. 574.

4. Procedural issues

In determining the value of a life estate where real property was sold to pay debts the court could apply the proceeds of the personal estate to the indebtedness, deduct the remaining indebtedness from the proceeds of the sale of the real estate, and from the sum thus remaining compute the value of the life estate. Brooks v. Prince (Franklin 1952) 134 N.E.2d 78, 72 Ohio Law Abs. 161.

Where a decedent dies intestate as to a part of his real estate, the portions disposed of by will should be exonerated from contribution to the payment of the debts of the estate, in so far as the portion undisposed of together with the personalty will suffice to pay them. Gilson v. Gilson (Ohio Cir. 1907) 20 Ohio C.D. 322, 11 Ohio C.C.N.S. 49.

2107.54 Contribution; exception

(A) When real or personal property, devised or bequeathed, is taken from the devisee or legatee for the payment of a debt of the testator, the other devisees and legatees shall contribute their respective proportions of the loss to the person from whom such payment was taken so that the loss will fall equally on all the devisees and legatees according to the value of the property received by each of them.

If, by making a specific devise or bequest, the testator has exempted a devisee or legatee from liability to contribute to the payment of debts, of if the will makes a different provision for the payment of debts than the one prescribed in this section, the estate shall be applied in conformity with the will.

(B) A devisee or legatee shall not be prejudiced by the fact that the holder of a claim secured by lien on the property devised or bequeathed failed to present such claim to the executor or administrator for allowance within the time allowed by sections 2117.06 and 2117.07 of the Revised Code, and the devisee or legatee shall be restored by right of contribution, exoneration, or subrogation, to the position he would have occupied if such claim had been presented and allowed for such sum as is justly owing on it.

(C) A devisee of real estate that is subject to a mortgage lien that exists on the date of the testator's death, who does not have a right of exoneration that extends to that lien because of the operation of division (B) of section 2113.52 of the Revised Code, has a duty to contribute under this section to devisees and legatees who are burdened if the claim secured by the lien is presented and allowed pursuant to Chapter 2117. of the Revised Code.

(D) This section does not affect the liability of the whole estate of the testator for the payment of his debts. This section applies only to the marshaling of the assets as between those who hold or claim under the will.

(1983 S 115, eff. 10-14-83; 1953 H 1; GC 10504-75 to 10504-77)

Historical and Statutory Notes

Pre–1953 H 1 Amendments: 119 v 394, § 1; 114 v 360, 361

Library References

Wills ⇨736(2), 846.
Westlaw Topic No. 409.
C.J.S. Wills §§ 1623 to 1741, 1943, 1955, 1970.

Research References

Encyclopedias

OH Jur. 3d Contribution, Indemnity, & Subrogation § 4, Statutory Subrogation.

OH Jur. 3d Contribution, Indemnity, & Subrogation § 9, Contribution Governed by Statute.

OH Jur. 3d Contribution, Indemnity, & Subrogation § 16, Inequality of Benefits Received.

OH Jur. 3d Decedents' Estates § 823, Testator's Right to Designate Property Liable for Payment of Debts.

OH Jur. 3d Decedents' Estates § 844, Abatement in Absence of Expressed Intention.

OH Jur. 3d Decedents' Estates § 848, Contribution for Payment of Debts, Generally.

OH Jur. 3d Decedents' Estates § 849, as Between Devisees and Legatees.

OH Jur. 3d Decedents' Estates § 851, Devisee or Legatee of Encumbered Property.

OH Jur. 3d Decedents' Estates § 1370, Personal Liability of Representative for Attorneys' Fees—Whether Charged to General Estate or Apportioned.

OH Jur. 3d Decedents' Estates § 1480, Effect of Provisions of Will, Deed, or Other Instrument.

OH Jur. 3d Decedents' Estates § 1481, Contribution.

OH Jur. 3d Decedents' Estates § 1501, Determination of Particular Property or Quantity to be Sold.

Forms

Ohio Forms Legal and Business § 24:391, Payment of Debts—General Clause.

Ohio Forms and Transactions KP 30.09, Abatement of Legacies and Devises.

Treatises and Practice Aids

Carlin, Baldwin's Ohio Practice, Merrick-Rippner Probate Law § 48:1, Property Chargeable With Payment of Debts—Statutory Provisions.

Carlin, Baldwin's Ohio Practice, Merrick-Rippner Probate Law § 48:9, Beneficiaries Liable for Payment of Decedent's Debts—General Rules.

Carlin, Baldwin's Ohio Practice, Merrick-Rippner Probate Law § 96:7, Distribution of Proceeds—Sale of Specifically Devised or Bequeathed Property.

Carlin, Baldwin's Ohio Practice, Merrick-Rippner Probate Law § 43:48, Construing a Will—Apportionment of Estate—Rights of Specific Devisee or Legatee.

Carlin, Baldwin's Ohio Practice, Merrick-Rippner Probate Law § 48:10, Beneficiaries Liable for Payment of Decedent's Debts—Liability for Secured Claims.

Carlin, Baldwin's Ohio Practice, Merrick-Rippner Probate Law § 97:19, Land Sale by Guardian—Proceeds.

Restatement (3d) Property (Wills & Don. Trans.) § 1.1, Probate Estate.

Law Review and Journal Commentaries

Mortgage on Specifically—Devised Real Estate, Judge Richard B. Metcalf. 52 Title Topics 5 (July 1985).

S 115 and H 288: Steps Toward Logic and Fairness in the Ohio Probate Law, Note. 10 U Dayton L Rev 213 (Fall 1984).

Notes of Decisions

Construction and procedure   5
Encumbrance on estate   4
Federal estate tax   3
Type of devise or legacy   2

Widow's share   1

1. Widow's share

Uncompensated loss resulting from an election to take against the will falls upon all legatees equally rather than upon the residuary estate. Winters Nat. Bank & Trust Co. v. Riffe (Ohio Prob. 1963) 194 N.E.2d 921, 93 Ohio Law Abs. 171, 27 O.O.2d 261, reversed 2 Ohio St.2d 72, 206 N.E.2d 212, 31 O.O.2d 56.

Where it appears that there is land enough to set off the dower of a widow who elects to take against the will without interfering with land specifically devised for life, it should be so done; otherwise, the disappointed devisees are equitably entitled to compensation out of the rejected provisions for the widow, and if they do not fully compensate such devisees, the resulting uncompensated loss should fall upon the residuary estate in preference to the specific devises, unless a contrary intention appears from the will.   Dunlap v. McCloud (Ohio 1911) 84 Ohio St. 272, 95 N.E. 774, 9 Ohio Law Rep. 94.   Wills ⚖ 802(5)

When a testator devises one-sixth of his realty to his widow for life, at her death to their son, and devises the remaining five-sixths to others, and the widow elects to take her dower and distributive share, the value of which exceeds the value of her life estate in the one-sixth, the remainder in the one-sixth will not be accelerated, but the widow's life estate will be sequestered to compensate the disappointed devisees.   Holdren v. Holdren (Ohio 1908) 78 Ohio St. 276, 85 N.E. 537, 6 Ohio Law Rep. 109.   Remainders ⚖ 5; Wills ⚖ 853

When a widow is cited to elect, and it appears property specifically devised is required to pay debts, she is entitled to be judicially advised whether if she accepts she will be required to contribute to the person from whom the special legacy is taken.   Allen v. Tressenrider (Ohio 1905) 72 Ohio St. 77, 73 N.E. 1015, 2 Ohio Law Rep. 495, 2 Am.Ann.Cas. 974.

To determine whether a widow in electing to take under a will of her husband will be required to contribute to a legatee from whom a special devise is taken to pay debts, a consideration of the provisions of the will in connection with those of RS 5973 must be had.   Allen v. Tressenrider (Ohio 1905) 72 Ohio St. 77, 73 N.E. 1015, 2 Ohio Law Rep. 495, 2 Am.Ann.Cas. 974.

A widow who elects to take under the will of her husband in lieu of dower is not exempt from RS 5973, and will be required to contribute her proportion to a legatee from whom specially devised property is taken to pay debts.   Allen v. Tressenrider (Ohio 1905) 72 Ohio St. 77, 73 N.E. 1015, 2 Ohio Law Rep. 495, 2 Am.Ann.Cas. 974.   Wills ⚖ 802(5)

2. Type of devise or legacy

Where a will giving pecuniary legacies provides that they and the debts of the estate shall be paid out of the personal assets and proceeds of real estate directed to be sold for that purpose, the legacies are not demonstrative or in the nature of specific bequests but are to be regarded as mere general pecuniary legacies; if the fund thus provided is insufficient to pay the debts and legacies, the general pecuniary legatees cannot compel contribution from specific devises to equalize the loss arising from the deficiency.   Glass v. Dunn (Ohio 1867) 17 Ohio St. 413.   Wills ⚖ 812

Where a testator's will gives a life estate in real estate and a pecuniary legacy to his wife, gives a legacy to his minor daughter in trust and the entire residuary estate, real and personal, is left to his sons, the personal estate being insufficient to pay both the debts and the legacies, the daughter's legacy is chargeable upon the residuary real estate.   Moore v. Beckwith's Ex'r (Ohio 1862) 14 Ohio St. 129.

Trial court lawfully ordered a pro rata payment of estate's debts from will's specific bequests, where will only contained specific bequests, and residuary estate was not sufficient to pay debts.   In re Estate Of Morgan (Ohio App. 7 Dist., Mahoning, 11-24-2003) No. 02 CA 106, 2003-Ohio-6394, 2003 WL 22838734, Unreported.   Wills ⚖ 812

Bequest in will of any proceeds from sale of business and associated property was specific, rather than general, for purposes of determining whether bequest would be used to pay estate's debts; bequest did not provide for a specific value or amount of money to be paid to legatees.   In re Estate Of Morgan (Ohio App. 7 Dist., Mahoning, 11-24-2003) No. 02 CA 106, 2003-Ohio-6394, 2003 WL 22838734, Unreported.   Wills ⚖ 753

Statute providing that, when real or personal property is taken for payment of testator's debt, the other devisees and legatees must contribute their respective proportions of the loss, applies only to specific bequests, and not to general, pecuniary ones.   In re Estate of Oberstar (Ohio App. 11 Dist., 04-14-1998) 126 Ohio App.3d 30, 709 N.E.2d 872.   Wills ⚖ 807

Specific devises and bequests abate together.   Gionfriddo v. Palatrone (Ohio Prob. 1964) 196 N.E.2d 162, 93 Ohio Law Abs. 257, 26 O.O.2d 158.   Wills ⚖ 812

Under section a specific devisee or legatee is exempt from the liability to contribute to the payment of debts when there is a residuary estate out of which the debts may be paid.   In re Dickey's Estate (Montgomery 1949) 87 Ohio App. 255, 94 N.E.2d 223, 20 A.L.R.2d 1220, 57 Ohio Law Abs. 346, 42 O.O. 474.

The two main classes of legacies are general and specific, the distinguishing features being that the latter is a gift of specific property distinguishable from the balance of the estate, while the former is a gift not subject to identification but to come out of the general assets of the estate.   Shaw v. Shaw (Ohio App. 1928) 32 Ohio App. 168, 167 N.E. 611, 27 Ohio Law Rep. 414.

In order for a legacy to be demonstrative two elements must appear: (1) that the testator intended to make an unconditional gift in the nature of a general legacy; (2) that the bequest indicates the fund out of which it is payable.   Shaw v. Shaw (Ohio App. 1928) 32 Ohio App. 168, 167 N.E. 611, 27 Ohio Law Rep. 414.   Wills ⚖ 755

Use of the word "including," preceding certain properties specified in the residuary clause, precludes the possibility that the testator intended to segregate such properties as specific from the rest of the residuary clause, and by virtue of GC 10504–75 and 10504–76 (RC 2107.54), the property must be exhausted in the payment of costs and debts against the estate before resort is had to any specific devises and bequests.   Wilkinson v. Edwards (Ohio Prob. 1939) 3 Ohio Supp. 260, 29 Ohio Law Abs. 648, 15 O.O. 328.

Specific devisees and specific legatees must share equally in any loss resulting to one or more of them by reason of the insufficiency of funds for paying the testator's debts.   McArthur v McArthur, 93 Abs 367 (Prob, Cuyahoga 1961).

3. Federal estate tax

Whether the surviving spouse takes under the will or under the statute of descent and distribution, the federal estate tax is considered a debt against the entire estate and shall be deducted before a distribution.   Ginder v. Ginder (Ohio Prob. 1954) 134 N.E.2d 603, 72 Ohio Law Abs. 277, 82 Ohio Law Abs. 129, 59 O.O. 320.   Wills ⚖ 799

Where a widow elects to take under the statute of descent and distribution, the amount of the federal estate tax should be deducted before computing the widow's share thereof.   (See also Hall v Ball, 162 OS 299, 123 NE(2d) 259 (1954).)   Campbell v. Lloyd (Ohio 1954) 162 Ohio St. 203, 122 N.E.2d 695, 55 O.O. 102, certiorari denied 75 S.Ct. 600, 349 U.S. 911, 99 L.Ed. 1246, rehearing denied 75 S.Ct. 870, 349 U.S. 948, 99 L.Ed. 1274.

4. Encumbrance on estate

In a devise of an estate subject to payment by devisee of certain specific legacies, such legacies are a charge upon the real estate unless a contrary intention is expressed in the will.   Clyde v. Simpson (Ohio 1854) 4 Ohio St. 445.

Where a charge is imposed on property for the payment of legacies which are definitely ascertained and are to be paid immediately to the person entitled, the purchaser is bound to see that the money is actually applied to their discharge before the estate is relieved from the burden.   Clyde v. Simpson (Ohio 1854) 4 Ohio St. 445.

If the purchaser of an incumbered estate agrees to take it subject to the incumbrance, and an abatement is made in the price on that account, he is bound to indemnify his grantor against the incumbrance, whether he expressly promised to do so or not, since a promise to that effect is implied by the nature of the transaction.   Thompson v. Thompson (Ohio 1854) 4 Ohio St. 333.

On the death of an intestate, the law charges his debts as a general lien on his property.   (See also Straman v Rechtine, 58 OS 443, 51 NE 44 (1898).)   Sheldon's Lessee v. Newton (Ohio 1854) 3 Ohio St. 494.

Where the administrators of an estate obtain an order of court to sell the testator's land for the payment of debts, and such sales are regular and the title perfect, the purchasers hold such lands discharged of liens, but the proceeds are subject to the priorities of liens attached to such lands sold.   Bank of Muskingum v. Carpenter's Adm'rs (Ohio 1835) 7 Ohio 21, PT. I, 28 Am.Dec. 616.

A purchaser from the heir takes title charged with the ancestor's debts; he cannot buy without notice.   (See also Faran v Robinson, 17 OS 242 (1867).)   Piatt v St. Clair's Heirs, 6 Ohio 227 (1833).

Note 4

A condition in a the devise that the devisee pay at different periods to different persons certain sums creates a personal liability only during the lifetime of the devisee; after his death, they are a charge upon the land only. Decker's Ex'rs v. Decker's Ex'rs (Ohio 1827) 3 Ohio 157.

Under testatrix's will expenses of defending a will contest and of defending title to specifically bequeathed securities were properly a charge upon the residual of the estate. In re Jacoby's Estate (Ohio Prob. 1957) 155 N.E.2d 275, 79 Ohio Law Abs. 239.

A residuary devisee or legatee is presumed in law to be in the position of the last lienholder, after all prior lawful claims and charges have been satisfied out of the estate. Young Men's Christian Ass'n v. Davis (Ohio 1922) 106 Ohio St. 366, 140 N.E. 114, 1 Ohio Law Abs. 84, 20 Ohio Law Rep. 498, 20 Ohio Law Rep. 499, certiorari granted 43 S.Ct. 521, 262 U.S. 745, 67 L.Ed. 1211, rehearing granted 43 S.Ct. 699, 262 U.S. 739, 67 L.Ed. 1208, affirmed 44 S.Ct. 291, 264 U.S. 47, 68 L.Ed. 558. Wills ⚖ 827

5. Construction and procedure

The rule of pro rata contribution does not apply, in this state, to vendees of lands charged with the payment of legacies who become seized at different dates. Nellons v. Truax (Ohio 1856) 6 Ohio St. 97.

Remand of probate court's distribution of a cell tower lease that was devised equally to two devisees under the terms of decedent's will was required in order to condition one of the devisees' receipt of the lease on such devisee's payment of her share of the estate expenses, and for calculation of such expenses to reflect an amount proportionate to devisee's share of devises already taken to pay the estate's debts and expenses. In re Estate of Mahan (Ohio App. 11 Dist., Trumbull, 09-15-2006) No. 2005-T-0062, 2006-Ohio-4821, 2006 WL 2662723, Unreported. Wills ⚖ 848

Failure by daughters of testator to file transcript of trial court proceedings required affirmance of trial court's determination of the amounts of contribution to be paid by each devisee or legatee pursuant to statute governing contributions to pay testator's debts; absence of transcript made it impossible to determine whether daughters' claims were raised at trial court level, and prevented daughters from demonstrating any trial court error. In re Estate of Mahan (Ohio App. 11 Dist., Trumbull, 11-12-2004) No. 2003-T-0100, 2004-Ohio-6032, 2004 WL 2580595, Unreported. Executors And Administrators ⚖ 510(7)

Where a charge upon a particular fund is created by express terms or by necessary implication in favor of a creditor he may by petition in equity enforce payment without first obtaining judgment at law. Darst v Pittsburgh, Ft. Wayne & Chicago RR Co, 3 D Repr 199 (CP, Hardin 1859). Liens ⚖ 22; Railroads ⚖ 178

In the absence of proof of the law of a testator's domicile, the rule of abatement prescribed by Ohio law will be followed. Mastics v. Kiraly (Ohio Prob. 1964) 196 N.E.2d 172, 93 Ohio Law Abs. 193, 26 O.O.2d 266. Wills ⚖ 804

A change from the statutory rules for abatement must be provided in a will, and cannot be supplied by a separation agreement. Gionfriddo v. Palatrone (Ohio Prob. 1964) 196 N.E.2d 162, 93 Ohio Law Abs. 257, 26 O.O.2d 158.

The personal property of a decedent is primarily liable for his debts, even where there is one residuary clause applicable to personal property and another to real property. Ginder v. Ginder (Ohio Prob. 1954) 134 N.E.2d 603, 72 Ohio Law Abs. 277, 82 Ohio Law Abs. 129, 59 O.O. 320.

Compensation allowed counsel for executor in successful defense of a will contest suit, and other expenses incident to the defense of such action are necessary expenses of administering the estate, and where the will provided for payment of all debts, necessary expenses of administration, etc., such expenses of the will contest suit should be paid out of the general assets of the estate and the specific legatees and devisees should not bear any portion thereof. In re Dickey's Estate (Montgomery 1949) 87 Ohio App. 255, 94 N.E.2d 223, 20 A.L.R.2d 1220, 57 Ohio Law Abs. 346, 42 O.O. 474. Wills ⚖ 736(2)

2107.55 Portion of pretermitted heir, or of witness, subject to contribution

When a part of the estate of a testator descends to a child born or adopted, or to an heir designated, after the execution of the will, or to a child absent and reported to be dead at the time of execution of the will but later found to be alive, or to a witness to a will who is a devisee or legatee, such estate and the advancement made to such child, heir, or witness for all the purposes mentioned in section 2107.54 of the Revised Code shall be considered as if it had been devised to such child, heir, or witness and he shall be bound to contribute with the devisees and legatees, as provided by such section, and may claim contribution from them accordingly.

(1953 H 1, eff. 10–1–53; GC 10504–78)

Historical and Statutory Notes

Pre–1953 H 1 Amendments: 114 v 361

Cross References

Afterborn or pretermitted heirs, effect on will, 2107.34

Library References

Wills ⚖ 736(2), 846.
Westlaw Topic No. 409.
C.J.S. Wills §§ 1623 to 1741, 1943, 1955, 1970.

Research References

Encyclopedias

OH Jur. 3d Decedents' Estates § 11, Descent.
OH Jur. 3d Decedents' Estates § 853, Pretermitted Child or Heir; Subscribing Witness.

Forms

Ohio Forms Legal and Business § 24:391, Payment of Debts—General Clause.

Treatises and Practice Aids

Carlin, Baldwin's Ohio Practice, Merrick-Rippner Probate Law § 48:1, Property Chargeable With Payment of Debts—Statutory Provisions.

Notes of Decisions

Procedure 1

1. Procedure

A common pleas court has jurisdiction to determine and enforce the right to contribution given by the wills act to a child born after the execution of the will of its parent. McGarry v. Smith (Ohio 1871) 22 Ohio St. 190.

2107.56 Liability in case of insolvency

When any of the persons liable to contribute toward the discharge of a testator's debt according to sections 2107.54 and 2107.55 of the Revised Code, is insolvent, the others shall be severally liable to each other for the loss occasioned by such insolvency, each being liable in proportion to the value of the property received by him from the estate of the deceased. If any one of the persons liable dies without paying his proportion of such debt, his executors and administrators shall be liable therefor to the extent to which he would have been liable if living.

(1953 H 1, eff. 10–1–53; GC 10504–79)

Historical and Statutory Notes

Pre–1953 H 1 Amendments: 114 v 361

Library References

Wills ⚖ 736(2), 846.
Westlaw Topic No. 409.
C.J.S. Wills §§ 1623 to 1741, 1943, 1955, 1970.

Research References

Encyclopedias

OH Jur. 3d Contribution, Indemnity, & Subrogation § 18, Unavailable Co-Obligors.

OH Jur. 3d Decedents' Estates § 854, Effect of Insolvency of Person Liable to Contribute.

OH Jur. 3d Decedents' Estates § 1825, Causes Upon Which Actions May be Brought.

Forms

Ohio Forms Legal and Business § 24:391, Payment of Debts—General Clause.

Ohio Forms Legal and Business § 24:394, Payment of Debts—Order of Sale of Realty.

Treatises and Practice Aids

Carlin, Baldwin's Ohio Practice, Merrick-Rippner Probate Law § 48:1, Property Chargeable With Payment of Debts—Statutory Provisions.

Carlin, Baldwin's Ohio Practice, Merrick-Rippner Probate Law § 48:11, Liability for Payment of Claims Against Estate.

2107.57   Contribution enforced

All cases arising under sections 2107.01 to 2107.62, inclusive, of the Revised Code, in which devisees or legatees are required to contribute or in which contribution is to be made among devisees, legatees, and heirs, may be heard and determined in a single action.

(1953 H 1, eff. 10–1–53; GC 10504–80)

Historical and Statutory Notes

Pre–1953 H 1 Amendments: 114 v 361

Cross References

Permissive joinder of parties, Civ R 20

Library References

Wills ⇌736(2), 846.
Westlaw Topic No. 409.
C.J.S. Wills §§ 1623 to 1741, 1943, 1955, 1970.

Research References

Encyclopedias

OH Jur. 3d Decedents' Estates § 855, Enforcement of Contribution.

Notes of Decisions

Jurisdiction   1

1. Jurisdiction

A common pleas court has jurisdiction to determine and enforce the right to contribution given by the wills act to a child born after the execution of the will of its parent. McGarry v. Smith (Ohio 1871) 22 Ohio St. 190.

2107.58   Order of sale to pay debts

When a sale of lands aliened or unaliened by a devisee or heir is ordered for the payment of the debts of an estate, sections 2107.53 to 2107.57, inclusive, of the Revised Code do not prevent the probate court from making such order and decree for the sale of any portion of the aliened or unaliened land as is equitable between the several parties, and making an order of contribution and further order and decree to settle and adjust the various rights and liabilities of the parties.

(1953 H 1, eff. 10–1–53; GC 10504–81)

Historical and Statutory Notes

Pre–1953 H 1 Amendments: 114 v 361

Library References

Executors and Administrators ⇌322.

Wills ⇌736(2), 846.
Westlaw Topic Nos. 162, 409.
C.J.S. Executors and Administrators § 586.
C.J.S. Wills §§ 1623 to 1741, 1943, 1955, 1970.

Research References

Encyclopedias

OH Jur. 3d Contribution, Indemnity, & Subrogation § 26, Determination in Action by Obligee.

OH Jur. 3d Decedents' Estates § 855, Enforcement of Contribution.

OH Jur. 3d Decedents' Estates § 1501, Determination of Particular Property or Quantity to be Sold.

Forms

Ohio Forms Legal and Business § 24:394, Payment of Debts—Order of Sale of Realty.

Treatises and Practice Aids

Carlin, Baldwin's Ohio Practice, Merrick-Rippner Probate Law § 92:1, Property Subject to Sale—General Rule.

Notes of Decisions

Legacies   2
Rents   1

1. Rents

The real estate of an intestate descends at once to his legal heirs and the legal title is vested in them subject only to the right of the administrator to sell the land for the payment of the decedent's debts; thus, rents on the lands of an insolvent intestate accruing between the death of the intestate and the sale of the lands for the payment of debts by the administrator belong to the heir and not the administrator. Overturf v. Dugan (Ohio 1876) 29 Ohio St. 230.

2. Legacies

Where a testator's will gives a life estate in real estate and a pecuniary legacy to his wife, gives a legacy to his minor daughter in trust and the entire residuary estate, real and personal, is left to his sons, the personal estate being insufficient to pay both the debts and the legacies, the daughter's legacy is chargeable upon the residuary real estate. Moore v. Beckwith's Ex'r (Ohio 1862) 14 Ohio St. 129.

Where a charge is imposed on property for the payment of legacies which are definitely ascertained and are to be paid immediately to the person entitled, the purchaser is bound to see that the money is actually applied to their discharge before the estate is relieved from the burden. Clyde v. Simpson (Ohio 1854) 4 Ohio St. 445.

Even though decedent who willed his property to his wife for life and a life estate to his sister-in-law upon wife's death, died only two months prior to his wife, where his personal estate was an amount insufficient to pay his debts, a year's allowance to his widow and expenses of administration, Probate Court, in fixing value of sister-in-law's estate, properly first applied proceeds of personal estate to indebtedness of estate and then deducted remaining indebtedness from proceeds of sale of real estate and from sum thus remaining computed value of life estate; notwithstanding her contention that value of life estate should be determined upon full sale price of real estate. Brooks v. Prince (Franklin 1952) 134 N.E.2d 78, 72 Ohio Law Abs. 161. Wills ⇌ 732(7)

2107.59   Sale of land by executor's successor

When a last will and testament is admitted to probate, or a will made out of this state is admitted to record as provided by sections 2129.05 to 2129.07 of the Revised Code, and lands, tenements, or hereditaments are given or devised by such will to the executors named in the will, or nominated pursuant to a power as described in section 2107.65 of the Revised Code, to be sold or conveyed, or such estate thereby is ordered to be sold by such executors and one or more of the executors dies, refuses to act, or neglects to take upon himself the execution of the will, then all sales and conveyances of such estate by the executors who took upon themselves in this state the execution of the will, or the survivor of them, shall be as valid as if the remaining executors had joined in the sale and conveyance. But if none of such executors take upon themselves the execution of the will, or if all the executors who take out letters testamentary die, resign, or are removed before the sale and conveyance of such estate, or die, resign, or are removed after the sale and before the conveyance is made, the sale or conveyance, or both, shall be made by the administrator with the will annexed or, if any, by a successor executor or successor coexecutor nominated pursuant to a power as described in section 2107.65 of the Revised Code.

(1983 S 115, eff. 10–14–83; 1953 H 1; GC 10504–82)

Historical and Statutory Notes

Pre–1953 H 1 Amendments: 114 v 362

Library References

Executors and Administrators ⚖120(1).
Westlaw Topic No. 162.
C.J.S. Executors and Administrators §§ 941 to 946.

Research References

Encyclopedias

OH Jur. 3d Decedents' Estates § 1607, Exercise of Power by Coexecutors and Successors.

Forms

Ohio Forms Legal and Business § 24:394, Payment of Debts—Order of Sale of Realty.

Treatises and Practice Aids

Carlin, Baldwin's Ohio Practice, Merrick-Rippner Probate Law § 74:1, Decedent's Property—Authorization to Sell.

Carlin, Baldwin's Ohio Practice, Merrick-Rippner Probate Law § 91:20, Land Sale—Necessary Parties.

Law Review and Journal Commentaries

Does the Executor in Ohio Take An Estate or a Power? Does the Power Survive?, Charles C. White. 15 U Cin L Rev 1 (January 1941).

Notes of Decisions

Extent of authority 1
Interest of executor 3
Resignation of executor 2
Settlement of estate 4

---

1. Extent of authority

The power to sell lands, given by will to an executor, cannot be executed by an administrator with the will annexed. Wills v. Cowper (Ohio 1825) 2 Ohio 124, adhered to 3 Ohio 486. Executors And Administrators ⚖ 519(1)

The power to sell does not authorize exchange or barter of land, but sale for money only. (See also Fleischman v Shoemaker, 2 CC 152, 1 CD 415 (Hamilton 1881).) Taylor v. Galloway (Ohio 1823) 1 Ohio 232, 13 Am.Dec. 605. Powers ⚖ 20; Wills ⚖ 692(5)

Power given by will to executors to sell land may be executed by one executor, if one only accepts the office under the will. Taylor v. Galloway (Ohio 1823) 1 Ohio 232, 13 Am.Dec. 605.

Under this section, administrator with will annexed has same powers to sell as is given to executor named in will, and administrator with will annexed also has power to sell any and all property of estate and after payment of debts and legacies, if there be a balance, to pay balance to residuary legatees, as provided in will. Holly v. Phares (Butler 1936) 32 N.E.2d 64, 22 Ohio Law Abs. 162, 7 O.O. 236.

2. Resignation of executor

Where executors accept a trust in a testator's will giving them power to sell real estate for the benefit of certain legatees, and they resign without having executed the power, their authority to do so expires with their office, and the sale or conveyance may be made by an administrator with the will annexed. Elstner v. Fife (Ohio 1877) 32 Ohio St. 358.

3. Interest of executor

Full power conferred upon an executor to sell is a power coupled with an interest, vesting a fee simple in the executors so that the land does not descend to the testator's heirs; such a power is to be construed in order to carry out the intention of the testator. Williams' Lessee v. Veach (Ohio 1848) 17 Ohio 171, 49 Am.Dec. 453.

Although an executor cannot purchase at a sale by his coexecutors yet such a sale may be executed with the subsequent assent and ratification of the heirs. Mitchell v. Dunlap (Ohio 1840) 10 Ohio 117.

4. Settlement of estate

When an estate is settled or all claims against it are presumably satisfied by the lapse of time and no object of the testator remains to be attained, a power given to the executors by will to sell and convey land becomes legally inoperative and ceases to exist. Ward's Lessee v. Barrows (Ohio 1853) 2 Ohio St. 241. Powers ⚖ 13; Wills ⚖ 692(6)

NUNCUPATIVE WILLS

2107.60 Oral will

An oral will, made in the last sickness, shall be valid in respect to personal estate if reduced to writing and subscribed by two competent disinterested witnesses within ten days after the speaking of the testamentary words. Such witnesses must prove that the testator was of sound mind and memory, not under restraint, and that he called upon some person present at the time the testamentary words were spoken to bear testimony to such disposition as his will.

No oral will shall be admitted to record unless it is offered for probate within six months after the death of the testator.

(1953 H 1, eff. 10–1–53; GC 10504–83, 10504–84)

Historical and Statutory Notes

Pre–1953 H 1 Amendments: 114 v 362

Cross References

Computation of time, 1.14

Library References

Wills ⚖136 to 146, 260.
Westlaw Topic No. 409.
C.J.S. Wills §§ 328 to 336, 340, 532 to 534.

Research References

Encyclopedias

OH Jur. 3d Decedents' Estates § 358, Methods of Revocation; Strict Compliance With Statute—Revocation by Oral Will.

OH Jur. 3d Decedents' Estates § 402, Circumstances Under Which Allowed; Last Sickness.

OH Jur. 3d Decedents' Estates § 403, Limited to Personal Property.

OH Jur. 3d Decedents' Estates § 405, Necessity for and Form of Request to Bear Witness; Rogatio Testium.

OH Jur. 3d Decedents' Estates § 406, Number and Competency of Witnesses.

OH Jur. 3d Decedents' Estates § 407, Reduction to Writing.

OH Jur. 3d Decedents' Estates § 408, Revocation of Written Will by Oral Will.

OH Jur. 3d Decedents' Estates § 409, Time of Probate.

OH Jur. 3d Decedents' Estates § 1035, Oral Wills.

OH Jur. 3d Decedents' Estates § 1036, Oral Wills—Time of Probate.

Forms

Ohio Forms Legal and Business § 24:113, Formal Requirements—Necessity of Writing.

Ohio Forms Legal and Business § 24:114, Formal Requirements—Execution by Testator.

Ohio Forms Legal and Business § 24:155, Statement by Witnesses Reducing Oral Will to Writing.

Ohio Forms and Transactions KP 30.01, Validity and Form of Will.

Treatises and Practice Aids

Carlin, Baldwin's Ohio Practice, Merrick-Rippner Probate Law § 29:1, Oral Will—Disposition of Personal Property—Statutory Requirements.

Carlin, Baldwin's Ohio Practice, Merrick-Rippner Probate Law § 29:2, Oral Will—Purpose and Function of Witnesses.

Carlin, Baldwin's Ohio Practice, Merrick-Rippner Probate Law § 29:4, Entry Admitting Oral Will to Probate—Form.

Carlin, Baldwin's Ohio Practice, Merrick-Rippner Probate Law § 40:1, Revocation of Will—Introduction.

Carlin, Baldwin's Ohio Practice, Merrick-Rippner Probate Law § 40:7, Revocation of Will—Subsequent Written Instrument—Statutory Provision.

Carlin, Baldwin's Ohio Practice, Merrick-Rippner Probate Law § 40:8, Revocation of Will—Subsequent Written Instrument—Types—Wills and Codicils.

Restatement (2d) of Property, Don. Trans. § 33.1, Meaning of a Will.

Restatement (3d) Property (Wills & Don. Trans.) § 3.2, Holographic Wills.

Restatement (3d) Property (Wills & Don. Trans.) § 8.1, Requirement of Mental Capacity.

Notes of Decisions

Formalities required 1
Real estate 3
Revocation 4
Witnesses 2

---

1. Formalities required

Words not the same substantially as those actually spoken when admitted to probate are void, and this may be proved on contest. Bolles v. Harris (Ohio 1877) 34 Ohio St. 38.

Directions by an owner in respect to the disposition of his property which are to take effect after his death are of no validity, unless made through the medium of a last will and testament. Phipps v. Hope (Ohio 1866) 16 Ohio St. 586.

Nuncupative will is completed by testamentary statement and witnesses' signatures; attestation clause being surplusage. Kellner v. Hagood (Butler 1930) 39 Ohio App. 351, 177 N.E. 637, 10 Ohio Law Abs. 734. Wills ⇌ 143

Provisions of RS 5991 as to nuncupative wills must be strictly observed; it must be proved that a testator called upon some person present, at the time the testamentary words were spoken, to bear testimony to said disposition as his will, as provided by statute. Seever v. Seever (Ohio Cir. 1887) 1 Ohio C.D. 496. Wills ⇌ 145

The words "tell my folks to give M, my intended, one thousand dollars of my money," are not sufficient to serve as a basis for a nuncupative will, as they do not show that the decedent called upon witnesses as such to hear it as his will. Seever v. Seever (Ohio Cir. 1887) 1 Ohio C.D. 496.

2. Witnesses

Where a written will is signed by a testator and attested and subscribed by two witnesses who are attorneys and partners, one of whom prepared such will, and who are nominated in such will as executor and alternate executor, respectively, such witnesses are competent and such will, if otherwise valid, is not thereby invalidated. Blankner v. Lathrop (Ohio 1959) 169 Ohio St. 229, 159 N.E.2d 229, 74 A.L.R.2d 279, 8 O.O.2d 221. Wills ⇌ 116

Decedent's question to physician, "Will you be present?" held sufficient designation of witness to nuncupative will. Kellner v. Hagood (Butler 1930) 39 Ohio App. 351, 177 N.E. 637, 10 Ohio Law Abs. 734. Wills ⇌ 145

Under RS 5991 a verbal will must be subscribed, after being reduced to writing, by "two competent disinterested witnesses"; subscription by one disinterested and one interested witness is insufficient. Vrooman v. Powers (Ohio 1890) 47 Ohio St. 191, 23 W.L.B. 292, 24 N.E. 267.

Where the two witnesses to a nuncupative will were beneficiaries thereunder, their renunciation of their rights at the time of the probate thereof will not operate to make them "competent disinterested witnesses" within the meaning of RS 5991. Wass v. Guardian Trust Co. (Ohio Com.Pl. 1905) 15 Ohio Dec. 677.

3. Real estate

Under former acts (of 1808, 1810, 1816, 1824), relating to wills, a nuncupative will was valid to pass real estate in Ohio. Gillis' Lessee v. Weller (Ohio 1841) 10 Ohio 462. Wills ⇌ 138

Nuncupative wills are invalid as to real estate but valid as to personalty where the will attempts to dispose of both real and personal property. Parsons v. Wass (Ohio Cir. 1905) 31 Ohio C.D. 577, 16 Ohio C.C.N.S. 404.

Where, by a nuncupative will a whole estate is given to legatee, but as realty could not pass, and personalty was consumed by debts, the testator intended making the legatee a gift and the personalty was exonerated from payment of the debts. Skinner v. Blackburn (Ohio Cir. 1889) 2 Ohio C.D. 574.

A father's crediting before witnesses, in his account book, each of his children with their respective shares of his estate was not a nuncupative will as it relates to realty. Williams v Pope, W 406 (OS 1833).

4. Revocation

A resident of Jamaica having made a written will there sufficient to pass his estate in Ohio cannot, in moving into Ohio, revoke such a former will in whole or in part by a nuncupative will. McCune's Devisees v. House (Ohio 1837) 8 Ohio 144, 31 Am.Dec. 438.

Oral will is not means recognized by statute for revocation of prior will, written or oral. In re Estate of Mantalis (Ohio App. 2 Dist., 01-31-1996) 109 Ohio App.3d 61, 671 N.E.2d 1062. Wills ⇌ 179

Validly executed written will cannot be revoked by subsequent oral will, even if oral will has been reduced to writing in compliance with statute. In re Estate of Mantalis (Ohio App. 2 Dist., 01-31-1996) 109 Ohio App.3d 61, 671 N.E.2d 1062. Wills ⇌ 179

Decedent's prior written will and codicil were not revoked by alleged oral will declared by decedent on day before his death, even though oral will was subsequently reduced to writing, inasmuch as oral will was not statutorily recognized means of revoking prior will. In re Estate of Mantalis (Ohio App. 2 Dist., 01-31-1996) 109 Ohio App.3d 61, 671 N.E.2d 1062. Wills ⇌ 179

MISCELLANEOUS PROVISIONS

2107.61 Will ineffectual

Unless it has been admitted to probate or record, as provided in sections 2107.01 to 2107.62, inclusive, and 2129.05 to 2129.07, inclusive, of the Revised Code, no will is effectual to pass real or personal estate.

(1953 H 1, eff. 10–1–53; GC 10504–29)

Historical and Statutory Notes

Pre–1953 H 1 Amendments: 114 v 351

Cross References

Proceedings to admit foreign will to record, 2129.07

Library References

Wills ⇌205.
Westlaw Topic No. 409.
C.J.S. Wills §§ 451 to 452.

Research References

Encyclopedias

OH Jur. 3d Decedents' Estates § 218, Ambulatory Nature; Alterability and Revocability.

OH Jur. 3d Decedents' Estates § 674, When Title Vests in Devisee or Legatee.

OH Jur. 3d Decedents' Estates § 862, Necessity for Probate.

Notes of Decisions

Basis for claims 1
Procedural issues 2

1. Basis for claims

Where partition has been made of lands between coheirs, and afterward one of the heirs brings suit against the assignee of the other heirs to recover possession of a part of the lands allotted to them by the decree of partition, he will not be estopped by the decree in partition from setting up a title as devisee under the will of a common ancestor admitted to probate subsequent to the decree in partition. Woodbridge v. Banning (Ohio 1863) 14 Ohio St. 328.

All wills must be established by probate, and until a will has been duly probated no title can be set up under it, nor can it be received as evidence of claims made under it. Swazey's Lessee v. Blackman (Ohio 1837) 8 Ohio 5.

Under the statute, until will is probated, it has no legal standing as a basis for a suit in any court or as a basis for any claim to property or an interest therein on the part of the devisee of such instrument. Petitt v. Morton (Cuyahoga 1928) 28 Ohio App. 227, 162 N.E. 627, 6 Ohio Law Abs. 549, 26 Ohio Law Rep. 382.

Title of devisee is not acquired until the will is probated. Douglass v. Miller (Ohio Com.Pl. 1896) 4 Ohio Dec. 414, 3 Ohio N.P. 220, reversed 20 Ohio C.D. 666, 11 Ohio C.C.(N.S.) 205.

2. Procedural issues

General rule is that will is ambulatory and does not take effect until testator's death. In re Estate of Davis (Ohio App. 12 Dist., 02-05-1996) 109 Ohio App.3d 181, 671 N.E.2d 1302, appeal not allowed 76 Ohio St.3d 1424, 667 N.E.2d 26. Wills ⇐ 78

An action to set aside a deed upon the ground that the real estate involved was devised to plaintiff by will is subject to demurrer where the petition fails to disclose that the alleged will has ever been admitted to probate. Strawder v. Smith (Ohio Com.Pl. 1957) 143 N.E.2d 327, 75 Ohio Law Abs. 186.

Where will alleged to have been forged by testator's son was probated, under which son and his sisters took possession of property, and alleged forgery was not discovered until statute of limitations had run against right to contest will under the statute, nephew, being without interest either legal or equitable in the property and not being an heir at law, has no legal capacity to have trust declared in testator's son in favor of nephew. Petitt v. Morton (Cuyahoga 1928) 28 Ohio App. 227, 162 N.E. 627, 6 Ohio Law Abs. 549, 26 Ohio Law Rep. 382.

Although a copy of a will admitted to probate in another state is not spread upon the record, where an order for admission to record is made and the regular uniform entry is used, the will is effectual to pass the title to lands in Ohio; by the law of Ohio since 1808, a will is not effectual to pass realty unless it be probated, if domestic, or recorded, if foreign. McClaskey v. Barr (C.C.S.D.Ohio 1893) 54 F. 781.

2107.62 Expenses and fees

The expense of proving and recording wills and of any action for declaratory judgment of validity shall be paid by the party at whose instance this is done. The witnesses and officers shall have the same fees for attendance and services as in other cases. When the executor or administrator is appointed, the expense shall be reimbursed out of the estate.

(1978 H 505, eff. 1-1-79; 1953 H 1; GC 10504-85)

Historical and Statutory Notes

Pre-1953 H 1 Amendments: 114 v 362

Library References

Executors and Administrators ⇐511(3).
Wills ⇐404, 405.
Westlaw Topic Nos. 162, 409.
C.J.S. Executors and Administrators §§ 895 to 896, 898 to 899.

C.J.S. Wills § 787.

Research References

Encyclopedias

OH Jur. 3d Decedents' Estates § 855, Enforcement of Contribution.
OH Jur. 3d Decedents' Estates § 995, Expenses and Fees.
OH Jur. 3d Decedents' Estates § 1237, Costs, Generally.
OH Jur. 3d Decedents' Estates § 1372, Allowance of Counsel Fees Where Attorney is Retained by Third Person—Probate of Will; Declaration of Validity.
OH Jur. 3d Evidence & Witnesses § 656, Particular Cases.
OH Jur. 3d Evidence & Witnesses § 660, by Whom Witness Fees Payable.

Forms

Ohio Forms Legal and Business § 24:161, Entire Estate to Spouse—Alternatively to Children—Guardianship of Minors.
Ohio Forms Legal and Business § 24:261, Prior Wills and Codicils.

Treatises and Practice Aids

Carlin, Baldwin's Ohio Practice, Merrick-Rippner Probate Law § 40:8, Revocation of Will—Subsequent Written Instrument—Types—Wills and Codicils.

Notes of Decisions

Attorney's fees 1

1. Attorney's fees

Attorney's fees may be allowed to counsel successfully obtaining the probate of a will and defending it against contest for services rendered prior to the date of probate as well as thereafter. In re Woods' Estate (Ohio Prob. 1957) 159 N.E.2d 638, 80 Ohio Law Abs. 336.

Executor of will duly admitted to probate may include in his account items for attorney's fees incurred in establishing probate of such will, which was subsequently set aside as invalid. In re Hendrick's Estate (Franklin 1943) 71 Ohio App. 247, 49 N.E.2d 106, 39 Ohio Law Abs. 305, 26 O.O. 67, rehearing denied 52 N.E.2d 661. Executors And Administrators ⇐ 111(3)

Remand was required, in probate proceedings, to determine whether estate could pay attorney for executor $5,000 in attorney fees generated in separate concealment of assets action brought by executor through same attorney, although probate court denied application for attorney fees reasoning that relief had been previously granted in concealment of assets case, where executor, not attorney for executor, received judgment to recover attorney fees in concealment of assets action. In re Estate of Simons (Ohio App. 11 Dist., Trumbull, 08-30-2002) No. 2001-T-0130, 2002-Ohio-4518, 2002 WL 2022744, Unreported. Executors And Administrators ⇐ 455

TESTAMENTARY ADDITIONS TO TRUSTS

Comparative Laws

Uniform Testamentary Additions to Trusts Act
Table of Jurisdictions Wherein Act Has Been Adopted.

For text of Uniform Act, and variation notes and annotation materials for adopting jurisdictions, see Uniform Laws Annotated, Master Edition, Volume 8B.

Jurisdiction	Statutory Citation
Alaska	AS 13.12.511.
Arizona	A.R.S. § 14-2511.
Arkansas	A.C.A. § 28-27-101 to 28-27-106.
Colorado	West's C.R.S.A. § 15-11-511.
Connecticut	C.G.S.A. § 45a-260.
Delaware	12 Del.C. § 211, 211 note.
Hawaii	HRS § 560:2-511, 560:2-511 note.
Idaho	I.C. § 15-2-511.
Kentucky	KRS 394.076.
Minnesota	M.S.A. § 524.2-511.
Montana	MCA 72-2-531.
Nebraska	R.R.S. 1943, § 30-2336.

Jurisdiction	Statutory Citation
New Hampshire	RSA 563–A:1 to 563–A:4.
New Mexico	NMSA 1978, § 45–2–511.
North Dakota	NDCC 30.1–08–11.
Rhode Island	Gen. Laws 1956, § 18–14–1 to 18–14–6.
South Dakota	SDCL 29A–2–511.
Utah	U.C.A. 1953, 75–2–511.
Virginia	Code 1950, § 64.1 to 73.1.
West Virginia	Code, 41–3–8 to 41–3–11.

2107.63 Addition to trust estate

A testator may by will devise, bequeath, or appoint real or personal property or any interest in real or personal property to a trustee of a trust that is evidenced by a written instrument signed by the testator or any other settlor either before or on the same date of the execution of the will of the testator, that is identified in the will, and that has been signed, or is signed at any time after the execution of the testator's will, by the trustee or trustees identified in the will or their successors or by any other person lawfully serving, by court appointment or otherwise, as a trustee.

The property or interest so devised, bequeathed, or appointed to the trustee shall become a part of the trust estate, shall be subject to the jurisdiction of the court having jurisdiction of the trust, and shall be administered in accordance with the terms and provisions of the instrument creating the trust, including, unless the will specifically provides otherwise, any amendments or modifications of the trust made in writing before, concurrently with, or after the making of the will and prior to the death of the testator. The termination of the trust, or its entire revocation prior to the testator's death, shall invalidate the devise, bequest, or appointment to the trustee.

This section shall not affect any of the rights accorded to a surviving spouse under section 2106.01 of the Revised Code. This section applies, and shall be construed as applying, to the wills of decedents who die on or after the effective date of this amendment, regardless of the date of the execution of their wills.

(1992 H 427, eff. 10–8–92; 1990 H 346; 130 v H 1; 129 v 7)

Uncodified Law

1992 H 427, § 4, eff. 10–8–92, reads: In amending sections 1335.01 and 2107.63 of the Revised Code, the General Assembly hereby declares its intent to supersede the effect of the holding of the Probate Court of Cuyahoga County on August 3, 1965, in *Knowles, Exrx. v. Knowles*, 4 Ohio Misc. 153, that a testamentary pour-over to an inter vivos trust is valid only if the trust has a corpus to which the decedent's assets may be added.

1990 H 346, § 3, eff. 5–31–90, reads, in part: (A) Sections 1 and 2 of this act shall apply only to the estates of decedents who die on or after the effective date of this act.

Library References

Trusts ⇐36.
Wills ⇐9.
Westlaw Topic Nos. 390, 409.
C.J.S. Trusts § 61.
C.J.S. Wills §§ 69, 72, 95.

Research References

Encyclopedias

OH Jur. 3d Decedents' Estates § 295, Reference to Future Acts; Doctrine of Independent Significance.

OH Jur. 3d Decedents' Estates § 296, Reference to Amendable Inter Vivos Trust; "Pour-Over" Provision.

OH Jur. 3d Decedents' Estates § 372, Effect of Changes in Instrument Governing a Pour-Over Trust.

OH Jur. 3d Trusts § 73, Application of Statute of Wills.

Forms

Ohio Forms Legal and Business § 25:6, Recordation.

Ohio Forms Legal and Business § 25:53, Irrevocable Trusts—Husband and Wife as Grantors—Income to Children for Life—Remainder to Descendants.

Ohio Forms Legal and Business § 25:61, Trust for Minor Qualifying for Annual Gift Tax Exclusion—General Form.

Ohio Forms Legal and Business § 24:143, Drafting Will.

Ohio Forms Legal and Business § 24:205.10, Pour-Over Will—Residue to Trust.

Treatises and Practice Aids

Carlin, Baldwin's Ohio Practice, Merrick-Rippner Probate Law § 31:2, Incorporation by Reference—Pour-Over Will to a Trust.

Carlin, Baldwin's Ohio Practice, Merrick-Rippner Probate Law § 33:1, Trusts—Testamentary Addition to Existing Trust—Statutory Provisions for Pour-Over.

Carlin, Baldwin's Ohio Practice, Merrick-Rippner Probate Law § 33:2, Trusts—Testamentary Addition to Existing Trust—Purpose of Pour-Over Statute.

Carlin, Baldwin's Ohio Practice, Merrick-Rippner Probate Law § 33:3, Trusts—Testamentary Addition to Existing Trust—Validity of Unfunded Trust.

Bogert - the Law of Trusts and Trustees § 107, Recent Statutes Regarding Testamentary Additions to Trusts.

Bogert - the Law of Trusts and Trustees § 233, Revocable Trusts.

Restatement (2d) of Property, Don. Trans. § 33.1, Meaning of a Will.

Restatement (3d) Property (Wills & Don. Trans.) § 3.8, Pour-Over Devises.

Law Review and Journal Commentaries

The Ohio Mortmain Statute—as Amended, Richard W. Schwartz. 17 Case W Res L Rev 83 (October 1965).

Problems with Pour–Over Wills, Robert J. Lynn. 47 Ohio St L J 47 (1986).

Notes of Decisions

Corpus in existence 2
Surviving spouse 3
Will contest 1

---

1. Will contest

Where will contest action was dismissed, contestant could not thereafter maintain an action to set aside an inter vivos trust into which there was a "pour over" of the estate from the will. Hageman v. Cleveland Trust Co. (Ohio 1976) 45 Ohio St.2d 178, 343 N.E.2d 121, 74 O.O.2d 295.

The validity of a will and an inter vivos trust which is a beneficiary of that will must be considered separately because the trust possesses an independent legal significance, and the dismissal of a will contest action does not bar an action to determine the validity of the trust. Hageman v. Cleveland Trust Co. (Cuyahoga 1974) 41 Ohio App.2d 160, 324 N.E.2d 594, 70 O.O.2d 322, reversed 45 Ohio St.2d 178, 343 N.E.2d 121, 74 O.O.2d 295. Wills ⇐ 432

2. Corpus in existence

When a decedent has executed both a will and a trust and it is clear from the language of those instruments that the trust was intended to be an inter vivos trust, a bequest to that trust made in the will fails for want of a taker if a valid inter vivos trust was not in existence at the time of the decedent's death. Hageman v. Cleveland Trust Co. (Cuyahoga 1974) 41 Ohio App.2d 160, 324 N.E.2d 594, 70 O.O.2d 322, reversed 45 Ohio St.2d 178, 343 N.E.2d 121, 74 O.O.2d 295. Wills ⇐ 775

Although attempted pour-over to inter vivos trust was invalid by reason of an absence of a trust res, the trust instrument could be incorporated by reference in the will. Knowles v. Knowles (Ohio Prob. 1965) 4 Ohio Misc. 153, 212 N.E.2d 88, 33 O.O.2d 218.

RC 2107.63 requires that there be a corpus in existence at the time of the testator's death into which a pour-over can be made. Knowles v. Knowles (Ohio Prob. 1965) 4 Ohio Misc. 153, 212 N.E.2d 88, 33 O.O.2d 218.

3. Surviving spouse

Property in a revocable inter vivos trust created by the deceased spouse cannot be reached by a surviving spouse who rejects his deceased spouse's will, and the only rights he has are those specifically given to him by the trust agreement. Purcell v. Cleveland Trust Co. (Cuyahoga 1965) 6 Ohio App.2d 235, 217 N.E.2d 876, 35 O.O.2d 426. Wills ⟶ 801(6)

A surviving spouse who elects to take against the will is entitled to a share of property held in a revocable inter vivos trust created by the deceased spouse. Purcell v. Cleveland Trust Co. (Ohio Prob. 1964) 200 N.E.2d 602, 94 Ohio Law Abs. 455, 28 O.O.2d 262, reversed 6 Ohio App.2d 235, 217 N.E.2d 876, 35 O.O.2d 426. Wills ⟶ 801(6)

ASSORTED PROVISIONS

2107.64 Rights of testamentary trustee under life insurance or benefit plans

A policy of life insurance, or an employee or self-employed benefit plan including, but not limited to, an employee trust or annuity plan, a Keogh plan, an individual retirement account or annuity, or a retirement bond, may designate as beneficiary a trustee named by will. Upon qualification and issuance of letters of trusteeship, the proceeds of the insurance or benefit plan shall be payable to the trustee to be held and disposed of under the terms of the will as they exist as of the date of the death of the testator and in the same manner as other testamentary trusts are administered. However, if no qualified trustee makes claim to the proceeds from the insurance company or the trustee of or other person holding funds of the benefit plan within twelve months after the death of the insured or the person covered by the benefit plan, or if satisfactory evidence is furnished to the insurance company or the trustee of or other person holding funds of the benefit plan within that twelve-month period showing that there is or will be no trustee to receive the proceeds, payment shall be made by the insurance company or the trustee of or other person holding funds of the benefit plan to the executors, administrators, or assigns of the insured or person covered by the benefit plan, unless otherwise provided by agreement with the insurance company or the trustee of or other person holding funds of the benefit plan during the lifetime of the insured or the person covered by the benefit plan.

The proceeds of the insurance or of the benefit plan as received by the trustee shall not be subject to debts of the insured or the person covered by the benefit plan or to estate tax to any greater or lesser extent than if the proceeds were payable to the beneficiary or beneficiaries named in the trust and not to the estate of the insured or the person covered by the benefit plan.

The insurance proceeds, or the proceeds of the benefit plan, so held in trust may be commingled with any other assets that may properly come into the trust.

Nothing in this section shall affect the validity of any life insurance policy beneficiary designation made prior to August 10, 1965, or the validity of any benefit plan beneficiary designation made prior to the effective date of this amendment, naming trustees of a trust established by will.

(1980 S 317, eff. 3–23–81; 1971 H 1; 132 v S 326; 131 v S 25)

OSBA Probate and Trust Law Section

1980:

At present Section 2107.64 R. C. authorizes payment of insurance proceeds to a trustee named by the will. This Section was enacted to erase doubts as to whether life insurance could become part of a testamentary trust. The same question could arise as to pension benefits, since they are not mentioned in Section 2107.64. The proposed legislation is intended to remove that question.

Deductibility for Federal Estate Tax is covered by IRC 2039(c) and its interpretation by Rev. Rul. 73-404, in effect permitting deductibility of qualified plan benefits paid in installments to a testamentary trust provided the benefits aren't subject to claims of estate creditors. Thus, the proposed amendment would render eligible for deduction qualified plan benefits payable to a testamentary trustee.

Library References

Insurance ⟶3475(7).
Labor and Employment ⟶582.
Westlaw Topic Nos. 217, 231H.
C.J.S. Insurance § 1430.

Research References

Encyclopedias

OH Jur. 3d Insurance § 1195, Trustees.

Treatises and Practice Aids

Carlin, Baldwin's Ohio Practice, Merrick-Rippner Probate Law § 33:5, Trusts—Testamentary Trustee as Beneficiary of Life Insurance or Other Benefit Plan—Purpose and Scope of Statute Allowing Trustee-Beneficiary.

Carlin, Baldwin's Ohio Practice, Merrick-Rippner Probate Law § 33:6, Trusts—Testamentary Trustee as Beneficiary of Life Insurance or Other Benefit Plan—Statutory Provisions Regarding Trustee as Beneficiary.

Bogert - the Law of Trusts and Trustees § 239, Personal Life Insurance Trusts—Insurance Trusts and the Wills Acts.

2107.65 Power to nominate

A testator may confer in his will, upon one or more persons, the power to nominate, in writing, an executor, coexecutor, successor executor, or successor coexecutor, and also may provide in his will that persons so nominated may serve without bond. If a will confers such a power, the holders of it have the authority to nominate themselves as executor, coexecutor, successor executor, or successor coexecutor unless the will provides to the contrary.

(1983 S 115, eff. 10–14–83)

Cross References

Appointment and duties of a fiduciary, 2109.02
Executors and administrators, letters testamentary, letters of administration with the will annexed, 2113.05
Procedure if executor renounces, 2113.12

Library References

Executors and Administrators ⟶14.
Wills ⟶83.
Westlaw Topic Nos. 162, 409.
C.J.S. Executors and Administrators §§ 17 to 21.
C.J.S. Wills § 175.

Research References

Encyclopedias

OH Jur. 3d Decedents' Estates § 898, Generally; Definitions.
OH Jur. 3d Decedents' Estates § 919, Renunciation Of, or Failure to Accept, Appointment—Effect Where No Other Executor Named.
OH Jur. 3d Decedents' Estates § 1031, Notice of Further Hearing.
OH Jur. 3d Decedents' Estates § 1341, Funeral Expenses.
OH Jur. 3d Decedents' Estates § 1607, Exercise of Power by Coexecutors and Successors.
OH Jur. 3d Decedents' Estates § 1733, Who May be Appointed.

Forms

Ohio Forms Legal and Business § 24:120, Safekeeping, Deposit, and Delivery of Will.

Treatises and Practice Aids

Carlin, Baldwin's Ohio Practice, Merrick-Rippner Probate Law § 2:15, Appointment of Fiduciary—Appointment of Executor or Administrator.

Carlin, Baldwin's Ohio Practice, Merrick-Rippner Probate Law § 37:1, Instrument Not Entitled to Probate—Procedure.

Carlin, Baldwin's Ohio Practice, Merrick-Rippner Probate Law § 37:3, Interlocutory Entry Denying Probate of Will—Form.

Carlin, Baldwin's Ohio Practice, Merrick-Rippner Probate Law § 37:4, Notice of Hearing on Interlocutory Entry Denying Probate of Will—Form.

Carlin, Baldwin's Ohio Practice, Merrick-Rippner Probate Law § 37:5, Final Entry Denying Probate of Will—Form.

Carlin, Baldwin's Ohio Practice, Merrick-Rippner Probate Law § 52:4, Fiduciary's Bond—Exceptions to Requirement.

Carlin, Baldwin's Ohio Practice, Merrick-Rippner Probate Law § 2:121, Administration of Decedent's Estate—Checklist.

Carlin, Baldwin's Ohio Practice, Merrick-Rippner Probate Law § 30:34, Drafting a Will—Appointment of Executor, Alternate Executor; Ancillary Administrator.

Carlin, Baldwin's Ohio Practice, Merrick-Rippner Probate Law § 68:17, Letters Testamentary—Issuance.

Carlin, Baldwin's Ohio Practice, Merrick-Rippner Probate Law § 68:18, Letters Testamentary—Letters of Administration With the Will Annexed.

Carlin, Baldwin's Ohio Practice, Merrick-Rippner Probate Law § 68:28, Letters Testamentary—Refusal of Appointment of Executor by Nominee.

WILL CONTEST ACTION

2107.71 Venue of will contest; effects of previous declaration of validity; failure to seek

(A) A person interested in a will or codicil admitted to probate in the probate court, which will or codicil has not been declared valid by judgment of a probate court pursuant to section 2107.084 of the Revised Code, or which will or codicil has been declared valid by judgment of a probate court pursuant to section 2107.084 of the Revised Code, but which has been removed from the possession of the probate judge, may contest its validity by a civil action in the probate court in the county in which such will or codicil was admitted to probate.

(B) Except as otherwise provided in this division, no person may contest the validity of any will or codicil as to facts decided if it was submitted to a probate court by its maker during his lifetime and declared valid by judgment of the probate court and filed with the judge of the probate court pursuant to section 2107.084 of the Revised Code and if the will was not removed from the possession of the probate judge. A person may contest the validity of such a will, modification, or codicil as to such facts if the person is one who should have been named a party defendant in the action in which the will, modification, or codicil was declared valid, pursuant to section 2107.081 or 2107.084 of the Revised Code, and if the person was not named a defendant and properly served in such action. Upon the filing of an action contesting the validity of a will or codicil that is authorized by this division, the court shall proceed with the action in the same manner as if the will, modification, or codicil had not been previously declared valid under sections 2107.081 to 2107.085 of the Revised Code.

(C) No person may introduce, as evidence in an action authorized by this section contesting the validity of a will, the fact that the testator of the will did not file a petition for a judgment declaring its validity under section 2107.081 of the Revised Code.

(1978 H 505, eff. 1–1–79; 1975 S 145)

Historical and Statutory Notes

Ed. Note: 2107.71 contains provisions analogous to former 2741.01, repealed by 1975 S 145, eff. 1–1–76.

Cross References

Privileged communications and acts; will contests, 2317.02
Suits in which party adverse to personal representative cannot testify, exceptions, 2317.03

Library References

Wills ⇐229, 254 to 258.
Westlaw Topic No. 409.
C.J.S. Wills §§ 503 to 506, 527 to 529.

Research References

ALR Library

3 ALR 5th 590, What Constitutes Contest or Attempt to Defeat Will Within Provision Thereof Forfeiting Share of Contesting Beneficiary.

Encyclopedias

OH Jur. 3d Decedents' Estates § 361, Revocation Induced or Prevented by Fraud and Undue Influence.
OH Jur. 3d Decedents' Estates § 376, Presumption of Revocation When Will in Testator's Custody Cannot be Found.
OH Jur. 3d Decedents' Estates § 1022, Nature and Effect of Order.
OH Jur. 3d Decedents' Estates § 1079, Exclusiveness of Statutory Remedy.
OH Jur. 3d Decedents' Estates § 1080, Contest of Later Wills Admitted to Probate.
OH Jur. 3d Decedents' Estates § 1088, Nature and Extent of Interest.
OH Jur. 3d Decedents' Estates § 1100, The State of Ohio.
OH Jur. 3d Decedents' Estates § 1116, Statutory Time Limitation, Generally.
OH Jur. 3d Decedents' Estates § 1118, When Action Commenced.
OH Jur. 3d Decedents' Estates § 1123, Applicability of Rules of Civil Procedure; Transfer of Venue.
OH Jur. 3d Decedents' Estates § 1171, Evidence of Testator's Failure to File for Declaratory Judgment.

Forms

Ohio Forms Legal and Business § 24:951, Agreement Not to Contest Will—Between Testator and Heirs.

Treatises and Practice Aids

Klein, Darling, & Terez, Baldwin's Ohio Practice Civil Practice § 2:2, Civ. R. 1(C) Special Statutory Proceedings as Civil Actions.
Klein, Darling, & Terez, Baldwin's Ohio Practice Civil Practice § 82:5, Jurisdiction--Civil Rule Arguably Wholly Inapplicable Pursuant to Civ. R. 82.
Klein, Darling, & Terez, Baldwin's Ohio Practice Civil Practice § 24:12, Intervention of Right--Nonstatutory Intervention of Right--"The Applicant Claims an Interest Relating to the Property or Transaction Which is the Subject of the Action"--Interest...
Klein, Darling, & Terez, Baldwin's Ohio Practice Civil Practice § 4:180, Will Contest.
Giannelli and Snyder, Baldwin's Ohio Practice, Evidence, R 101, Scope of Rules: Applicability; Privileges; Exceptions.
Giannelli and Snyder, Baldwin's Ohio Practice, Evidence, § 101.17, Special Non-Adversary Statutory Proceedings.
Carlin, Baldwin's Ohio Practice, Merrick-Rippner Probate Law § 1:5, Constitutional and Legislative Provisions.
Carlin, Baldwin's Ohio Practice, Merrick-Rippner Probate Law § 3:3, Jurisdiction of Probate Court—Subject Matter—in General.
Carlin, Baldwin's Ohio Practice, Merrick-Rippner Probate Law § 3:8, Jurisdiction of Probate Court—Subject Matter—Specific Areas—Will Contests.
Carlin, Baldwin's Ohio Practice, Merrick-Rippner Probate Law § 5:8, Evidentiary Matters—Privileged Communications—Protected Relationships—Physician or Dentist and Patient—Waiver of the Privilege.
Carlin, Baldwin's Ohio Practice, Merrick-Rippner Probate Law § 17:2, Designation—Effect.
Carlin, Baldwin's Ohio Practice, Merrick-Rippner Probate Law § 2:14, Probating the Will—Appeal—Will Contest.
Carlin, Baldwin's Ohio Practice, Merrick-Rippner Probate Law § 28:1, Codicils—Definition.
Carlin, Baldwin's Ohio Practice, Merrick-Rippner Probate Law § 34:5, Declaring the Validity of a Will—Procedure for Obtaining a Judgment—Judgment.
Carlin, Baldwin's Ohio Practice, Merrick-Rippner Probate Law § 34:7, Declaring the Validity of a Will—Appeal and Collateral Attack.
Carlin, Baldwin's Ohio Practice, Merrick-Rippner Probate Law § 34:8, Declaring the Validity of a Will—Effect on Will Contest.

Carlin, Baldwin's Ohio Practice, Merrick-Rippner Probate Law § 36:1, Admission to Probate—Criteria.

Carlin, Baldwin's Ohio Practice, Merrick-Rippner Probate Law § 38:2, Will Contests—Statutory Provisions.

Carlin, Baldwin's Ohio Practice, Merrick-Rippner Probate Law § 38:3, Will Contests—Later Will Admitted to Probate.

Carlin, Baldwin's Ohio Practice, Merrick-Rippner Probate Law § 38:4, Will Contests—Interested Persons.

Carlin, Baldwin's Ohio Practice, Merrick-Rippner Probate Law § 38:6, Will Contests—Capacity to Contest a Will.

Carlin, Baldwin's Ohio Practice, Merrick-Rippner Probate Law § 38:7, Will Contests—Commencement of Action; Limitation of Actions.

Carlin, Baldwin's Ohio Practice, Merrick-Rippner Probate Law § 4:53, Summons in Adversary Action—Form.

Carlin, Baldwin's Ohio Practice, Merrick-Rippner Probate Law § 50:3, Agreement to Make a Will—Essential Elements.

Carlin, Baldwin's Ohio Practice, Merrick-Rippner Probate Law § 30:30, Drafting a Will—Clauses to Discourage a Will Contest Action—Designation of Heir.

Carlin, Baldwin's Ohio Practice, Merrick-Rippner Probate Law § 38:11, Will Contests—Pleadings.

Carlin, Baldwin's Ohio Practice, Merrick-Rippner Probate Law § 38:12, Will Contests—Pretrial Procedure.

Carlin, Baldwin's Ohio Practice, Merrick-Rippner Probate Law § 38:13, Will Contests—Trial—Procedure.

Carlin, Baldwin's Ohio Practice, Merrick-Rippner Probate Law § 38:22, Complaint for Contest of Will—Form.

Carlin, Baldwin's Ohio Practice, Merrick-Rippner Probate Law § 43:49, Construing a Will—Deviation or Modification of Trust Provisions; Resulting Trust.

Carlin, Baldwin's Ohio Practice, Merrick-Rippner Probate Law § 91:22, Land Sale—Necessary Parties Defendant—Heirs.

Carlin, Baldwin's Ohio Practice, Merrick-Rippner Probate Law App B SPF 13.10, Notice to Extend Administration.

Law Review and Journal Commentaries

Ante–Mortem Probate Revisited: Can an Idea Have a Life After Death?, Howard Fink. 37 Ohio St L J 264 (1976).

Crisis of Competence—Capacity to execute wills is tenuous for victims of Alzheimer's disease, Robert P. Friedland and James J. McMonagle. (Ed. note: Cleveland hospital neurogeriatrics head and hospital general counsel discuss legal capacity.) 82 A B A J 80 (May 1996).

Jurisprudential Drama: The Will Contest, Hon. Fred V. Skok. 13 Lake Legal Views 1 (February 1990).

Rest in Peace—or Thy Will Be Done, Ellis V. Rippner. 28 Ohio St L J 647 (1967).

The Standing of the Dead: Solving the Problem of Abandoned Graveyards. Comment, 32 Cap U L Rev 479 (Winter 2003).

Notes of Decisions

Ed. Note: This section contains annotations from former RC 2741.01, RC 2107.23, RC 2741.04, and RC 2741.02.

Attorney fees 1
Evidence 2, 3
    Admissibility 2
    Sufficiency 3
Jury trial 4
No contest clause 9
Presumptions 7
Procedure 6
Standing 5
Statute of limitation 8

1. Attorney fees

Plaintiffs' allegations that they were residual beneficiaries in prior wills prepared by decedent and that prior will was one of two reciprocal wills were sufficient to survive motion to dismiss based on defendant's claim that plaintiffs lacked standing to bring will contest. Vaia v. Young (Ohio App. 5 Dist., Licking, 12-02-2004) No. 2003CA00083, 2004-Ohio-6575, 2004 WL 2813093, Unreported. Pretrial Procedure ⇐ 652

A probate court in will contest is not bound by fees provided for in contingent fee contract; rather, the court must determine amount of fees which are reasonably necessary for services rendered to the estate and such determination does not preclude payment by beneficiaries of balance of contracted fee under terms of a contingent fee contract. In re Estate of Whitmore (Wayne 1983) 13 Ohio App.3d 170, 468 N.E.2d 769, 13 O.B.R. 205. Wills ⇐ 415

Where the trial court finds that an attorney acted more on behalf of a claimed beneficiary than for the estate in a will contest action, the trial court does not abuse its discretion in denying extraordinary fees to such attorney. Bank One Trust Co v Shaw, No. CA–1609 (5th Dist Ct App, Tuscarawas, 12–20–82).

2. Evidence—Admissibility

The opinion of a witness as to the testator's capacity to make a will is not admissible as involving a question of law and fact to be determined by the jury; the witness's opinion as to the testator's sanity must relate to the time of his examination, not to the time of the making of the will, to be admissible in a will contest action. Runyan v. Price (Ohio 1864) 15 Ohio St. 1, 86 Am.Dec. 459.

Although plaintiffs failed to state a claim for breach of promise to make a will when they failed to attach a written contract signed by decedent promising to make a will for plaintiffs' benefit, they stated a claim for constructive trust by alleging that decedent and live-in companion made reciprocal wills under which each left their estates to each other with plaintiffs and defendant named as residual beneficiaries. Vaia v. Young (Ohio App. 5 Dist., Licking, 12-02-2004) No. 2003CA00083, 2004-Ohio-6575, 2004 WL 2813093, Unreported. Trusts ⇐ 103(1); Wills ⇐ 68

Neither a finding of incompetence by the court nor a failure to find incompetence in a guardianship proceeding is to be used in a later will contest on the issue of the deceased ward's competence, which must be resolved de novo on the law and evidence in the will contest, even though some of the same evidence submitted in the guardianship proceeding may be used. In re Guardianship of Rudy (Ohio 1992) 65 Ohio St.3d 394, 604 N.E.2d 736, rehearing denied 65 Ohio St.3d 1482, 604 N.E.2d 759.

Medical information of a testator protected under the provisions of RC 2317.02 is not discoverable in a will contest action. Cline v. Finney (Franklin 1991) 71 Ohio App.3d 571, 594 N.E.2d 1100, motion overruled 62 Ohio St.3d 1409, 577 N.E.2d 361.

In a will contest action, the trial court erred in granting a motion in limine which prohibited testimony regarding undue influence and lack of testamentary capacity as to events which occurred three years before execution of the will. Rich v. Quinn (Warren 1983) 13 Ohio App.3d 102, 468 N.E.2d 365, 13 O.B.R. 119.

In an action to contest a will on the ground that it was not signed at the end thereof, as required by RS 5916 (repealed 1932. See GC 10504–3), its construction is not a subject for consideration, the only question being whether it has been executed in substantial compliance with the statute. Irwin v. Jacques (Ohio 1905) 71 Ohio St. 395, 73 N.E. 683, 2 Ohio Law Rep. 442. Wills ⇐ 311

Testimony as to the faithfulness and fidelity of a beneficiary to the testator is competent in a will contest, since it has bearing upon the reasonableness of the will as made. Moore v. Caldwell (Ohio Cir. 1904) 17 Ohio C.D. 449, 6 Ohio C.C.N.S. 484.

It is competent in a will contest in which the controlling question is whether the alleged will is a forgery or genuine to introduce the disputed will in evidence for comparison with other written documents in evidence which have been proven genuine, or to introduce forged papers where such papers will tend to show the evil purpose of the parties who may have forged the will in suit. Gurley v. Armentraut (Ohio Cir. 1905) 17 Ohio C.D. 199, 6 Ohio C.C.N.S. 156.

Declarations of a testatrix concerning her testamentary intentions made during her last sickness and shortly after the execution of her will are admissible to show the state of mind of the testatrix at the time with the will was executed, though they are not admissible to contradict the contents of the written will. Kuhl v. Reichert (Ohio Cir. 1903) 15 Ohio C.D. 693, 2 Ohio C.C.(N.S.) 42, affirmed 72 Ohio St. 661, 76 N.E. 1127, 3 Ohio Law Rep. 43.

Where the question in a will contest action is whether the will has been produced by undue influence, in connection with the question whether the testator had sufficient mental capacity to make a will, any testimony that might or would shed any light upon the question whether the will as made was probably his will or whether it was brought about by undue influence is competent. Kettemann v. Metzger (Ohio Cir. 1901) 13 Ohio C.D. 61, 3 Ohio C.C.N.S. 224.

Persons interested in resisting probate are not allowed to introduce evidence to contest its validity. In re Stacey (Ohio Prob. 1897) 6 Ohio Dec. 142, 4 Ohio N.P. 143.

3. —— Sufficiency, evidence

Court of Appeals would not consider claims by homeowner's fiance that probate court erred in granting summary judgment in favor of executor of homeowner's estate with respect to fiance's counterclaims for setting aside homeowner's will, slander, and intentional infliction of emotional distress, in action to recover possession of homeowner's real property, where fiance failed to cite to any legal authority in support of her claim. Tripp v. French (Ohio App. 9 Dist., Medina, 12-18-2002) No. 02CA0004-M, 2002-Ohio-6996, 2002 WL 31828886, Unreported. Executors And Administrators ⟹ 86(.5)

Will proponent was entitled to summary judgment on contestant's claim that will was product of testator's son's undue influence, where contestant failed to submit any evidence that testator was susceptible to influence, that son exerted or attempted to exert improper influence over testator, or that some result from the alleged improper influence occurred. Hamilton v. Hector (Ohio App. 3 Dist., 01-27-1997) 117 Ohio App.3d 816, 691 N.E.2d 745. Judgment ⟹ 185.3(1)

In a will contest action alleging undue influence, where the plaintiff asserted that the testator in ill health was held in isolation from his friends and relatives by the sole beneficiary of the testator's will, the trial court erred in granting summary judgment against the plaintiffs. Rich v. Quinn (Warren 1983) 13 Ohio App.3d 102, 468 N.E.2d 565, 13 O.B.R. 119.

Residuary clause in will, providing that residue of estate was given and bequeathed to particular church "for the building fund" unequivocally constituted general, rather than specific charitable gift; thus, church remained residual beneficiary, despite contention that specific church building fund in existence at time of execution of will had ceased to exist, the building having been completed and indebtedness thereon satisfied prior to admission of subject will to probate. Hess v. Sommers (Mercer 1982) 4 Ohio App.3d 281, 448 N.E.2d 494, 4 O.B.R. 500. Charities ⟹ 37(6); Wills ⟹ 601(6)

A judgment overturning a will in an action brought by brothers of the deceased wife of the testator upon representation that the testator died without issue will be vacated upon subsequent action by children of the testator. Donovan v. Decker (Franklin 1953) 98 Ohio App. 183, 122 N.E.2d 501, 68 Ohio Law Abs. 353, 57 O.O. 230.

It is error for a court in a will contest to charge that the law scrutinizes with greater care the acts of a son or daughter who is remembered in a will to a larger extent than are others bearing the same kinship, if such son or daughter is in a close relationship of trust or confidence or upon whom a testatrix would implicitly rely, than it would on others bearing no such relationship. Hall v. Hall (Ohio 1908) 78 Ohio St. 415, 85 N.E. 1125. Wills ⟹ 332

Where a woman after long deliberations executes a will in which she follows the written instructions of her deceased husband regarding the disposition of property received by her from him instead of giving all the property to her children as she had desired, she has executed her will freely and willingly and not under undue influence. Wilder v. Taylor (Ohio Cir. 1911) 23 Ohio C.D. 643, 14 Ohio C.C.(N.S.) 255, reversed 87 Ohio St. 520, 102 N.E. 1135, 10 Ohio Law Rep. 602.

Courts of equity will not vacate a deed or set aside a will on the ground of influence or importunity, unless it has been unduly or improperly exercised; fair argument and persuasion, or appeals to the conscience or sense of duty of the testator, if fairly made, lay no foundation for setting aside a will. Gregg v. Moore (Ohio Cir. 1911) 23 Ohio C.D. 534, 14 Ohio C.C.N.S. 570.

The testator's affliction with progressive locomotor ataxia for a number of years before his death is not sufficient to set aside his will where it appears that during all that time he directed the operation of large farms and did all that could have been done by a person of a sound and active mind, notwithstanding a slight forgetfulness on his part at times. Gregg v. Moore (Ohio Cir. 1911) 23 Ohio C.D. 534, 14 Ohio C.C.N.S. 570.

Where there is no evidence that a testator's will was made under the influence of liquor, the fact that the testator was intoxicated during the night after he returned home from making his will does not mean that he lacked mental capacity earlier while making it. Gregg v. Moore (Ohio Cir. 1911) 23 Ohio C.D. 534, 14 Ohio C.C.N.S. 570.

A verdict setting aside a will on the ground of undue influence is not justified by the mere fact of a beneficiary's presence at the place where the will was executed, nor by the fact that he gave advice to the testator concerning the will. Wilson v. Wilson (Ohio Cir. 1909) 22 Ohio C.D. 498, 14 Ohio C.C.N.S. 241.

In an action to contest a will the jury must be instructed that in order to set aside the will the evidence of the contestants should not only outweigh the defendant's evidence but also the presumption arising from the order admitting the will to probate; the declarations by a party to the record who is a legatee with others under the will are inadmissible to prove that the will was contrary to the testator's intentions or was procured by undue influence. Seal v. Goebel (Ohio Cir. 1908) 21 Ohio C.D. 286, 11 Ohio C.C.(N.S.) 433, affirmed 81 Ohio St. 523, 91 N.E. 1138, 7 Ohio Law Rep. 500.

Since a person may lack in capacity for the transaction of ordinary business and lack in contractual capacity and yet have testamentary capacity, a charge to the jury requiring "capacity enough to attend to ordinary business and to know and understand the business he was engaged in" lacks the essential requirements of testamentary capacity to make a will, and is thus misleading and prejudicial. Wadsworth v. Purdy (Ohio Cir. 1908) 21 Ohio C.D. 110, 12 Ohio C.C.N.S. 8.

The subject of delusions of a testator is of no importance to court or jury; the only question is whether the delusions were carried to such an extent that they affected either the natural or selected objects of his bounty, distorting his judgment and preventing him from making a rational disposition of his property. Wadsworth v. Purdy (Ohio Cir. 1908) 21 Ohio C.D. 110, 12 Ohio C.C.N.S. 8.

A delusion of a testator does not constitute mental incapacity to make a will unless it is an insane delusion, and in determining whether a testator was suffering from such a delusion at the time he made his will, the testimony offered on the subject should be considered by the jury. Moore v. Caldwell (Ohio Cir. 1904) 17 Ohio C.D. 449, 6 Ohio C.C.N.S. 484.

Jury instructions in a will contest action which shift the burden of proof onto the defendant to prove mental capacity and lack of undue influence are manifestly wrong and prejudicial to the defendant in view of the rule that an order of probate is prima facie evidence of the validity of the will, and the contesters have the burden of disproving such evidence. West v. Knoppenberger (Ohio Cir. 1903) 16 Ohio C.D. 168, 4 Ohio C.C.N.S. 305.

The question of the mental capacity of a testator when making his will is one of whether he had a disposing memory capable of recollecting his property, the manner of distributing it, and the objects of his bounty; the fact that the testator was eighty-four years of age and forgetful as to minor matters is not evidence of lack of testamentary capacity. Rewell v. Warden (Ohio Cir. 1903) 14 Ohio C.D. 344, 4 Ohio C.C.N.S. 545.

Where the weight of the testimony clearly indicates that the testator had sufficient mental capacity to make a will, and under the circumstances the will he made was a fair and natural one, a finding by a jury that such will was not the decedent's last will and testament should be set aside and a new trial had. Kettemann v. Metzger (Ohio Cir. 1901) 13 Ohio C.D. 61, 3 Ohio C.C.N.S. 224.

In a will contest action where the plaintiff asserts that decedent's will is void because of undue influence and where the plaintiff shows no evidence to support the fact of improper influence exerted or attempted, the trial court may properly grant a directed verdict in favor of the defendant. Pummill v Margerum, No. CA83–03–031 (12th Dist Ct App, Butler, 9–28–83).

In an action for concealment of assets of a decedent estate, the proper burden of proof on the claimant is a showing by a preponderance of the evidence; therefore, the trial court erred in adopting a burden of proof from the complainant requiring either clear and convincing evidence or proof beyond a reasonable doubt. In re Estate of Goodrich, No. 45867 (8th Dist Ct App, Cuyahoga, 8–9–83).

In a will contest action where there is little, if any, direct evidence of undue influence, sufficient competent and credible circumstantial evidence will support a finding of undue influence. Sestili v Rodgers, No. 3370 (9th Dist Ct App, Lorain, 11–24–82).

4. Jury trial

A party to a will contest action does not have the right to a jury trial; instead, a probate court has discretion to determine whether to sit as the trier of fact in a will contest action or to impanel a jury. State ex rel. Kear v. Court of Common Pleas of Lucas County, Probate Division (Ohio 1981) 67 Ohio St.2d 189, 423 N.E.2d 427, 21 O.O.3d 118. Jury ⟹ 19(7.5)

Whether a plaintiff has a right to maintain a will contest action is properly tried by the court as a preliminary issue and without the benefit of a jury. Comer v. Comer (Logan 1962) 119 Ohio App. 529, 200 N.E.2d 656, 28 O.O.2d 142, affirmed 175 Ohio St. 313, 194 N.E.2d 572, 25 O.O.2d 182. Wills ⇔ 312

The right to maintain an action to contest a will, where placed in issue, should be determined by the court without a jury before the trial on the issue of the validity of the will. Comer v. Comer (Ohio 1963) 175 Ohio St. 313, 194 N.E.2d 572, 25 O.O.2d 182.

Action to contest will, designated civil action by express terms of GC 12079, is subject to GC §11455 (repealed 1931. See § 11420–9), permitting rendition of verdict by jury on concurrence of three-fourths or more. Niemes v. Niemes (Ohio 1917) 97 Ohio St. 145, 119 N.E. 503, 15 Ohio Law Rep. 484, 15 Ohio Law Rep. 565. Trial ⇔ 321.5; Wills ⇔ 333

5. Standing

Decedent's son did not qualify as interested person that could initiate will contest action, and thus, trial court properly changed son from a party plaintiff to a party defendant in will contest; son only inherited if will was found valid. Roll v. Edwards (Ohio App. 4 Dist., Ross, 02-21-2006) No. 05CA2833, 2006-Ohio-830, 2006 WL 439423, Unreported. Wills ⇔ 266

Illegitimate child who failed to establish that he had a right to inherit from decedent through a prior will did not have a pecuniary interest in the decedent's estate and thus lacked standing to contest decedent's will. In re Estate of Okos (Ohio App. 6 Dist., Lucas, 06-04-2004) No. L-03-1343, 2004-Ohio-2882, 2004 WL 1232041, Unreported. Wills ⇔ 229

Statute allowing destroyed will to be admitted to probate did not apply to will which testator destroyed and threw away when executing new will, precluding friend of testator named as beneficiary under destroyed will from having interest needed to have standing to bring will contest on ground that new will was result of fraud or undue influence. Sheridan v. Harbison (Ohio App. 2 Dist., 02-15-1995) 101 Ohio App.3d 206, 655 N.E.2d 256, appeal not allowed 72 Ohio St.3d 1551, 650 N.E.2d 1370. Wills ⇔ 229; Wills ⇔ 234

Twin sisters placed for foster care by an agency in the home of a testatrix shortly after birth who live with the testatrix until her death 28 years later and who are never formally adopted by the testatrix who regards them as her "children" are not persons "interested in the will" within RC 2107.71. York v. Nunley (Cuyahoga 1992) 80 Ohio App.3d 697, 610 N.E.2d 576.

Contestants in a will contest action who reach agreement with fewer than all the legatees do not necessarily hold both under and against a will. Krischbaum v. Dillon (Ohio 1991) 58 Ohio St.3d 58, 567 N.E.2d 1291.

A testator's illegitimate child can contest the will if a parent-child relationship was established during the testator's life. Birman v. Sproat (Miami 1988) 47 Ohio App.3d 65, 546 N.E.2d 1354.

A will is ambulatory in nature, and until the death of the testator, after the law admits such instrument to probate, it gives no accrued rights to potential takers of benefit. Corron v. Corron (Ohio 1988) 40 Ohio St.3d 75, 531 N.E.2d 708. Wills ⇔ 78

Great-grandchildren of a decedent who are not legatees under the will are not "persons interested" in the will for purposes of bringing a will contest action under RC 2107.71; therefore, the fact that the great-grandchildren of decedent are under the legal disability of minority does not toll the four-month statute of limitations for filing a will contest, since the great-grandchildren have no standing to file such suit. Mayfield v. Herderick (Franklin 1986) 33 Ohio App.3d 44, 514 N.E.2d 441.

A person named executor under a will who qualifies and accepts appointment as such executor cannot maintain an action to contest the will under which he has accepted appointment as executor. Steinberg v. Central Trust Co. (Ohio 1969) 18 Ohio St.2d 33, 247 N.E.2d 303, 47 O.O.2d 154.

A surviving spouse may not contest a will when the same result may be achieved by electing to take against the will. Klicke v. Uhlenbrock (Ohio Com.Pl. 1964) 200 N.E.2d 497, 94 Ohio Law Abs. 402, 27 O.O.2d 290. Wills ⇔ 229

An individual named as executor in a prior will does not thereby acquire standing to contest a subsequent will admitted to probate. Hermann v. Crossen (Cuyahoga 1959) 160 N.E.2d 404, 81 Ohio Law Abs. 322.

An illegitimate son, designated as heir at law by his natural father pursuant to the provisions of GC 10503–12 (RC 2105.15), is not authorized under GC 12079 (RC 2741.01) to bring an action to contest the will of the brother of the natural father, which brother died subsequent to the decease of the natural father. Blackwell v. Bowman (Ohio 1948) 150 Ohio St. 34, 80 N.E.2d 493, 37 O.O. 323. Wills ⇔ 229

Right of one who without valid will would have property interest in estate, and who dies intestate before time limited for contesting will without having brought action or estopped himself, passes to his personal representative or heirs under statutes of descent and distribution. Chilcote v. Hoffman (Ohio 1918) 97 Ohio St. 98, 119 N.E. 364, 15 Ohio Law Rep. 538, 15 Ohio Law Rep. 549. Descent And Distribution ⇔ 8; Wills ⇔ 229

Right to maintain will contest, begun within statutory time, is not forfeited by contestant's written consent to probate of will and his acceptance of a legacy thereunder, where such consent was induced by executor's false and fraudulent representations. Kelley v. Hazzard (Ohio 1917) 96 Ohio St. 19, 117 N.E. 182, 15 Ohio Law Rep. 230

A judgment creditor or an heir, who has a lien by levy on property, which in the absence of a will would be the property of the heir by descent, is interested in the will, within RS 5858 (See GC § 12079), and therefore has legal capacity to sue to contest the validity of an alleged will disposing of such property other than to such heir. Bloor v. Platt (Ohio 1908) 78 Ohio St. 46, 84 N.E. 604, 5 Ohio Law Rep. 619, 14 Am.Ann.Cas. 332. Wills ⇔ 229

An individual having the interest of a remainderman under a will, and who would have no legal pecuniary interest in the estate were the testator to be found intestate, is not a "Person interested in a will" and accordingly cannot "contest the validity thereof in a civil action" under RS 5858. Leedy v. Cockley (Ohio Cir. 1911) 22 Ohio C.D. 299, 14 Ohio C.C.N.S. 72.

A daughter who enters into possession of land devised to her by the will of her father and proceeds to lease the land and collect rent after probate of the will is estopped thereby from contesting the will, nor can she raise this bar by surrendering to the executor or bringing into court the rents or money; had the father left a money legacy, restitution might have dispossessed her of the benefit bestowed by the will and made a contest possible. Leedy v. Cockley (Ohio Cir. 1911) 22 Ohio C.D. 299, 14 Ohio C.C.N.S. 72.

A will revoked by the operation of law before the death of the testator but probated after his death may be contested by one who would take an estate if will is set aside. Myers v. Barrow (Ohio Cir. 1888) 2 Ohio C.D. 52.

Under RS 5858, the right to contest a will admitted to probate is in those persons only who were interested in the will at the time of its probate; the right does not pass to the heirs of those individuals. Rockwell v. Blaney (Ohio Com.Pl. 1907) 18 Ohio Dec. 436, 5 Ohio N.P.N.S. 580. Wills ⇔ 229

6. Procedure

Will contestants, who challenged their deceased aunt's will that left her property to animal shelter, were barred on res judicata grounds from raising termination of trust claim, in which they argued that their aunt had intended to give her property to shelter in trust, after will contestants' had failed in their initial will challenge, in which contestants had alleged aunt had lacked testamentary capacity when she entered will; second claim involved same parties and transaction, and both claims were a challenge to aunt's thought process when she drafted her will. Waldecker v. Erie County Humane Society (Ohio App. 6 Dist., Erie, 02-27-2004) No. E-03-022, 2004-Ohio-892, 2004 WL 368098, Unreported, appeal not allowed 102 Ohio St.3d 1485, 810 N.E.2d 968, 2004-Ohio-3069. Wills ⇔ 427

Probate court's finding that testator's adopted daughter did not challenge prior will was irrelevant, for purposes of appeal from order declaring latter will to be valid. Lakes v. Ryan (Ohio App. 12 Dist., Butler, 02-03-2003) No. CA2002-05-118, 2003-Ohio-504, 2003 WL 231272, Unreported. Wills ⇔ 399

Person who would not stand to inherit from testator under intestate succession statutes must demonstrate prima facie validity of will under which he or she claims in order to establish required pecuniary interests to contest will. Sheridan v. Harbison (Ohio App. 2 Dist., 02-15-1995) 101 Ohio App.3d 206, 655 N.E.2d 256, appeal not allowed 72 Ohio St.3d 1551, 650 N.E.2d 1370. Wills ⇔ 229

A probate court's original order admitting a will to probate is irrelevant to a court of appeals review of a will contest action since a will contest is not an appellate procedure but a trial de novo. Mattax v. Moore (Trumbull 1991) 72 Ohio App.3d 647, 595 N.E.2d 969, dismissed, jurisdictional motion overruled 61 Ohio St.3d 1419, 574 N.E.2d 1090.

When, after the commencement of a will contest action, the probate court substitutes an administrator with will annexed for the executor originally appointed, and further substitutes the administrator with will annexed as a party to the will contest action, the probate court does not lose jurisdiction simply because no motion to substitute the administrator as a party has been served upon the other parties. Krischbaum v. Dillon (Ohio 1991) 58 Ohio St.3d 58, 567 N.E.2d 1291. Wills ⇔ 268

RC 2107.71 through 2107.77 are exclusive sections under which a will contest may be brought in the probate court. Corron v. Corron (Ohio 1988) 40 Ohio St.3d 75, 531 N.E.2d 708. Wills ⇔ 222

Will contestants, who failed to show that beneficiaries, which were required to be named as defendants in will contest but which were not so named, received notice of suit before end of four-month period for filing will contest, were not entitled to amend complaint to add those beneficiaries as defendants. Weaver v. Donnerberg (Shelby 1985) 26 Ohio App.3d 112, 498 N.E.2d 496, 26 O.B.R. 323. Limitation Of Actions ⇔ 124

Where an action to contest a will is mistakenly docketed in the general division of the court of common pleas rather than the probate division of that court, prejudicial error is committed if the court dismisses the complaint instead of transferring the action to the docket of the probate division, pursuant to a motion of the complainant. Siebenthal v. Summers (Franklin 1978) 56 Ohio App.2d 168, 381 N.E.2d 1344, 10 O.O.3d 186. Courts ⇔ 50; Wills ⇔ 400

In Ohio, the exclusive method of challenging a will alleged to be invalid on the ground of undue influence is by a will contest action brought pursuant to RC Ch 2741, and an action for declaratory judgment under RC Ch 2721 does not lie. Davidson v. Brate (Butler 1974) 44 Ohio App.2d 248, 337 N.E.2d 642, 73 O.O.2d 253. Declaratory Judgment ⇔ 241; Wills ⇔ 225

Where court in will contest proceeding directs verdict sua sponte on basis of compromise agreement made in private conference, which distributes devised property among claimants in attendance and all of parties in case are not parties to agreement, such verdict is void. Taylor v. Connell (Highland 1971) 26 Ohio App.2d 253, 271 N.E.2d 305, 55 O.O.2d 412.

Where a son and two daughters, sole heirs at law and next of kin of the testatrix, are nominated as coexecutors in her will and are appointed to said offices and are also beneficiaries under the will, as are their children, in a trust created by the will, and said coexecutors, as individuals, bring an action to contest the will, which if successful would cause the entire estate to pass to the plaintiffs under the statute of descent and distribution and deny any interest to other beneficiaries named in the will, and furthermore, as such coexecutors, there being no surviving spouse of the testatrix, use the authority conferred upon them by RC 2317.02 to their advantage during the trial, to grant or to refuse consent to the attorney of the testatrix or her physician, to testify relative to confidential communications of the testatrix when in the relationship of client and attorney, or patient and physician, and deny such privilege to other parties in interest, there is a conflict of interest created between plaintiffs, as individuals, and their obligations as coexecutors, and they may not maintain such will contest action without resigning as executors. Allison v. Allison (Ohio 1968) 15 Ohio St.2d 44, 238 N.E.2d 768, 44 O.O.2d 25.

Where, on the evidence in a will contest action on the preliminary issue of whether plaintiff comes within the classification of persons prescribed by the statutes as having the right to maintain the action (i.e., whether he is an heir at law of decedent) reasonable minds can differ as to the inferences to be drawn therefrom, a reviewing court cannot as a matter of law arrive at a different conclusion than the trial court on such evidence. Comer v. Comer (Logan 1962) 119 Ohio App. 529, 200 N.E.2d 656, 28 O.O.2d 142, affirmed 175 Ohio St. 313, 194 N.E.2d 572, 25 O.O.2d 182.

Where a petition is filed to set aside a will, service is obtained on all defendants, the case is never called for trial, is placed on the drop list and the plaintiff ordered to show cause why it should not be dropped, the attorney who filed the petition is deceased and his successor is not carried on the drop list and, therefore, fails to appear when the case is called, and the case is dismissed for want of prosecution, it is error to overrule a motion to reinstate the case, and there is a mandatory duty imposed upon the trial court to make up the issue by an order on the journal, where the issue is not made up by the pleadings, and submit the issue to the jury. Sharp v. Johnson (Franklin 1957) 103 Ohio App. 194, 144 N.E.2d 896, 3 O.O.2d 264. Wills ⇔ 307

This section and GC 12087 (RC 2741.09) afford the exclusive mode of setting aside a last will and testament. Madden v. Shallenberger (Ohio 1929) 121 Ohio St. 401, 169 N.E. 450, 8 Ohio Law Abs. 28, 30 Ohio Law Rep. 569. Wills ⇔ 222

In will contest where all necessary parties are joined and served either in person or by publication, a party defendant served by publication after period prescribed by statute for contest of will is not entitled to have judgment sustaining will opened and issue as to validity retried. McVeigh v. Fetterman (Ohio 1917) 95 Ohio St. 292, 116 N.E. 518, 15 Ohio Law Rep. 19, 15 Ohio Law Rep. 30. Wills ⇔ 355

Where the jury in a will contest action finds that the will propounded was not the testatrix's last will and testament, their answers of "don't know" to interrogatories which asked if the will was signed by the testatrix are not inconsistent with the general verdict. Bloor v. Platt (Ohio 1908) 78 Ohio St. 46, 84 N.E. 604, 5 Ohio Law Rep. 619, 14 Am.Ann.Cas. 332.

By bringing an action under RS 5858 (See GC 12079), to contest the validity of a will, plaintiffs admit the probate of the will so put in contest, and cannot question or deny either the regularity of the order of probate or the authority and jurisdiction of the court that made it. Stacey v. Cunningham (Ohio 1903) 69 Ohio St. 176, 48 W.L.B. 993, 68 N.E. 1001, 1 Ohio Law Rep. 583, 1 Ohio Law Rep. 717. Wills ⇔ 311

An order admitting a will to probate is not reviewable on error, but may only be challenged in a properly filed will contest action. Hollrah v. Lasance (Ohio 1900) 63 Ohio St. 58, 44 W.L.B. 80, 57 N.E. 964.

The issue in a will contest is "whether the writing produced is the last will or codicil of the testator, or not" and cannot be varied or restricted by averments in the pleadings. Dew v. Reid (Ohio 1895) 52 Ohio St. 519, 33 W.L.B. 275, 40 N.E. 718, 2 Ohio Leg. N. 516.

Where in a will contest action the jury returns a verdict establishing its validity, but mistakenly inserts the date of the will's execution as the date of its probate, and the record shows that only one will of the decedent was exhibited to the jury, it is not error for the court to treat the jury's date as mere surplusage and enter a judgment upon the verdict correcting the error and establishing the will's validity. Seal v. Goebel (Ohio Cir. 1908) 21 Ohio C.D. 286, 11 Ohio C.C.(N.S.) 433, affirmed 81 Ohio St. 523, 91 N.E. 1138, 7 Ohio Law Rep. 500.

A jury charge which states that in order to make a valid will "it is necessary that a person shall have sufficient mental capacity for the transactions of the ordinary affairs of life," when followed by the charge that "he need not have sufficient capacity to make a contract but must understand substantially what he or she is doing and the nature of the act in which he or she is engaged" is a correct statement of law and not error. Welsh Hills Baptist Church v. Wilson (Ohio Cir. 1905) 19 Ohio C.D. 391, 9 Ohio C.C.(N.S.) 611, affirmed 75 Ohio St. 636, 80 N.E. 1135, 4 Ohio Law Rep. 664.

In an action to construe a will, the probate court is without jurisdiction to determine the validity of the will. Bailey v McElroy, 120 App 85, 195 NE(2d) 559, 28 OO(2d) 286 (App 1963).

The will-contest provisions of RC Ch 2741 afford the exclusive remedy of contesting the validity of a will which has been duly admitted to probate. State ex rel. Cleveland Trust Co. v. Probate Court of Cuyahoga County (Cuyahoga 1959) 113 Ohio App. 1, 162 N.E.2d 574, 82 Ohio Law Abs. 291, 17 O.O.2d 1.

The trial court erred in granting a summary judgment when no opportunity was provided for the appellants to oppose the motion; the issue of whether the appellants, who were named in a first will, could contest the present will rests upon the determination of the validity of the later codicil and will. Barnhart v Barnhart, No. 921 (4th Dist Ct App, Ross, 1–27–83).

Where the child of the decedent consents to the probate of the decedent's will, the child may not later file an action in partition based on the law of pretermitted heirs but must bring a will contest action in order to challenge the validity of a will that has been admitted to probate. Reed v Reed, No. 82 CA 46 (7th Dist Ct App, Mahoning, 10–27–82).

The equitable remedy of a constructive trust is not available to a testator's heirs at law where allegedly the devisee under the will fraudulently failed to properly draw and execute a new will per the testator's request. Bensman v Schemmel, No. 17–81–17 (3d Dist Ct App, Shelby, 7–21–82).

7. Presumptions

Owner of adult care center had burden of establishing in will contest suit that deceased patient intended to bequest residuary of estate to center by leaving residuary of estate to the "Extended Family Adult Care," even though center's correct name was "Extended Family Adult Care Center." Beaston v. Slingwine (Ohio App. 3 Dist., Seneca, 03-01-2004) No. 13-03-04, 2004-Ohio-924, 2004 WL 370408, Unreported. Wills ⇔ 703

A testator is presumed to disinherit an illegitimate child whose existence he is aware of when he makes specific bequests to his other children but makes no mention of the illegitimate one. Birman v. Sproat (Miami 1988) 47 Ohio App.3d 65, 546 N.E.2d 1354.

Note 7

Actions to contest wills are inaugurated with a legal presumption in favor of the will and of the mental capacity of the testator and against undue influence. Beresford v. Stanley (Ohio Com.Pl. 1898) 9 Ohio Dec. 134, 6 Ohio N.P. 38.

8. Statute of limitation

Neither death nor the inability to sue due to a delay in the appointment of a legal representative is a "legal disability" under RC 2131.02 for purposes of tolling the four-month statute of limitations found in RC 2107.76 for bringing a will contest action under RC 2107.71. Mayfield v. Herderick (Franklin 1986) 33 Ohio App.3d 44, 514 N.E.2d 441.

The probate court has no jurisdiction to consider an application to vacate the probate of a will and the appointment of an executor filed after the term in which the order of probate was made and more than six months after the will is probated and while an action to contest the will is pending in the common pleas court. State ex rel. Cleveland Trust Co. v. Probate Court of Cuyahoga County (Ohio 1961) 172 Ohio St. 1, 173 N.E.2d 100, 15 O.O.2d 43. Executors And Administrators ⚖ 32(2); Wills ⚖ 355; Wills ⚖ 368

9. No contest clause

Testator's daughter who did not initiate will contest action, but was only named as a defendant, did not invoke no-contest clause in will by filing pleadings, and thus was not thereby barred from taking under the will. Modie v. Andrews (Ohio App. 9 Dist., Summit, 10-23-2002) No. C.A. 21029, 2002-Ohio-5765, 2002 WL 31386482, Unreported, appeal not allowed 98 Ohio St.3d 1480, 784 N.E.2d 712, 2003-Ohio-974. Wills ⚖ 665

There is no good-faith exception to "no contest" clauses in wills, by which testator denies or limits inheritance of named legatee or devisee is that person attempts to set aside, or break, or make invalid any provision of a will. Modie v. Andrews (Ohio App. 9 Dist., Summit, 10-23-2002) No. C.A. 21029, 2002-Ohio-5765, 2002 WL 31386482, Unreported, appeal not allowed 98 Ohio St.3d 1480, 784 N.E.2d 712, 2003-Ohio-974. Wills ⚖ 656

Will contest brought by testator's daughter action invoked the no-contest clause of the will, and thus, daughter was barred from taking under the will, even if she brought the action in good faith, where clause provided that if any heirs were dissatisfied and attempted to break the will under the law, they were debarred from any part of estate whatsoever. Modie v. Andrews (Ohio App. 9 Dist., Summit, 10-23-2002) No. C.A. 21029, 2002-Ohio-5765, 2002 WL 31386482, Unreported, appeal not allowed 98 Ohio St.3d 1480, 784 N.E.2d 712, 2003-Ohio-974. Wills ⚖ 665

2107.72 Rules of Civil Procedure govern; exception; right to jury trial upon demand

(A) The Rules of Civil Procedure govern all aspects of a will contest action, except as otherwise provided in sections 2107.71 to 2107.77 of the Revised Code.

(B)(1) Each party to a will contest action has the right to a jury trial of the action. To assert the right, a party shall demand a jury trial in the manner prescribed in the Rules of Civil Procedure. Subject to division (B)(2) of this section, if a party demands a jury trial in that manner, the action shall be tried to a jury.

(2) Notwithstanding any provision to the contrary in Civil Rule 38, a demand of a jury trial in a will contest action may be withdrawn, if either of the following applies:

(a) All parties to the action who are not in default of answer, consent to the withdrawal of the demand prior to the commencement of the trial;

(b) All parties to the action who are not in default of answer and who are present at the time of the commencement of the trial, consent to the withdrawal of the demand.

(1984 H 70, eff. 3–28–85; 1975 S 145)

Historical and Statutory Notes

Ed. Note: 2107.72 contains provisions analogous to former 2741.09, repealed by 1975 S 145, eff. 1–1–76.

Cross References

Procedure in probate court, Civ R 73

Library References

Jury ⚖ 19(7.5).
Wills ⚖ 312.
Westlaw Topic Nos. 230, 409.
C.J.S. Juries §§ 22, 45, 60, 63, 65, 73, 83, 99, 107, 126.
C.J.S. Wills § 639.

Research References

Encyclopedias

OH Jur. 3d Decedents' Estates § 1118, When Action Commenced.
OH Jur. 3d Decedents' Estates § 1123, Applicability of Rules of Civil Procedure; Transfer of Venue.
OH Jur. 3d Decedents' Estates § 1133, Issues.
OH Jur. 3d Decedents' Estates § 1167, Certified Copy of Testimony Given by Witness on Probate.
OH Jur. 3d Decedents' Estates § 1200, Dismissal of the Action.
OH Jur. 3d Decedents' Estates § 1201, Order of Evidence; Right to Open and Close.
OH Jur. 3d Decedents' Estates § 1205, Generally; Standard for Granting Motion.
OH Jur. 3d Decedents' Estates § 1211, Waiver of Jury.
OH Jur. 3d Decedents' Estates § 1219, Manner and Time of Giving.
OH Jur. 3d Decedents' Estates § 1223, Cautionary Instructions.
OH Jur. 3d Decedents' Estates § 1227, Rendition on Concurrence of Three-Fourths of Jury.
OH Jur. 3d Decedents' Estates § 1228, General Verdict and Interrogatories.
OH Jur. 3d Decedents' Estates § 1229, Correction of Minor Errors of Form in Verdict.
OH Jur. 3d Decedents' Estates § 1231, Generally; Judgment Upon and in Conformity to Verdict; Correction of Clerical Errors.
OH Jur. 3d Decedents' Estates § 1232, Judgment by Consent; by Default.
OH Jur. 3d Decedents' Estates § 1233, Judgment Notwithstanding the Verdict.
OH Jur. 3d Decedents' Estates § 1236, Vacation of Judgment.

Treatises and Practice Aids

Klein, Darling, & Terez, Baldwin's Ohio Practice Civil Practice § 82:5, Jurisdiction--Civil Rule Arguably Wholly Inapplicable Pursuant to Civ. R. 82.
Klein, Darling, & Terez, Baldwin's Ohio Practice Civil Practice § 38:15, Right to Jury Trial Under Ohio Statutes--Other Statutes.
Giannelli and Snyder, Baldwin's Ohio Practice, Evidence, R 101, Scope of Rules: Applicability; Privileges; Exceptions.
Carlin, Baldwin's Ohio Practice, Merrick-Rippner Probate Law § 3:49, Demand for Jury—Form.
Carlin, Baldwin's Ohio Practice, Merrick-Rippner Probate Law § 3:50, Entry to Draw Jury—Form.
Carlin, Baldwin's Ohio Practice, Merrick-Rippner Probate Law § 38:7, Will Contests—Commencement of Action; Limitation of Actions.
Carlin, Baldwin's Ohio Practice, Merrick-Rippner Probate Law § 38:8, Will Contests—Parties to Action—Necessary Parties.
Carlin, Baldwin's Ohio Practice, Merrick-Rippner Probate Law § 38:11, Will Contests—Pleadings.
Carlin, Baldwin's Ohio Practice, Merrick-Rippner Probate Law § 38:15, Will Contests—Trial—Juries.

Notes of Decisions

Ed. Note: This section contains annotations from former RC 2741.04, RC 2741.01, RC 2741.02, RC 2741.09, RC 2741.05, RC 2741.06, and RC 2107.23.

Amendment of pleadings; service 3
Burden of proof 4
Evidence and testimony 5
Jury trials 2
Procedural issues 1

Service 6

1. Procedural issues

A will contest action does not constitute such a claim as to be susceptible of pleading as a matter of right as a counterclaim or cross-claim. Hess v. Sommers (Mercer 1982) 4 Ohio App.3d 281, 448 N.E.2d 494, 4 O.B.R. 500. Wills ⇔ 280.1

Where an action to contest a will is mistakenly docketed in the general division of the court of common pleas rather than the probate division of that court, prejudicial error is committed if the court dismisses the complaint instead of transferring the action to the docket of the probate division, pursuant to a motion of the complainant. Siebenthal v. Summers (Franklin 1978) 56 Ohio App.2d 168, 381 N.E.2d 1344, 10 O.O.3d 186. Courts ⇔ 50; Wills ⇔ 400

The proper court may, under appropriate circumstances, approve a valid compromise agreement in which the beneficiary of a spendthrift testamentary trust releases her rights in the trust as part of an overall settlement of the will contest and in consideration of other payments made to her or for her benefit, when there is a genuine will contest pending; when the payment is made to one who is properly contesting the validity of the will; when the payment to the contestant (and the contestant's reciprocal surrender of her interest in the spendthrift trust) is reasonably necessary in order to protect the interest of the other beneficiaries in the will, which might be lost in the event that the will was wholly upset; and when the settlement appears by its terms to be fair and equitable. Central Nat. Bank of Cleveland v. Eells (Ohio Prob. 1965) 5 Ohio Misc. 187, 215 N.E.2d 77, 33 O.O.2d 418. Wills ⇔ 740(2)

A proceeding to contest a will is purely and exclusively statutory. Andes v. Shippe (Ohio 1956) 165 Ohio St. 275, 135 N.E.2d 396, 59 O.O. 363. Wills ⇔ 222

An interested person who initiates an action to contest a will within six months after probate may not thereafter dismiss the action over the protest of a defendant who wants the will set aside. Andes v. Shippe (Ohio 1956) 165 Ohio St. 275, 135 N.E.2d 396, 59 O.O. 363.

Provisions of statutes relative to action to contest validity of will are mandatory; the enjoyment of the right is dependent upon compliance with conditions and limitations therein contained. Case v. Smith (Ohio 1943) 142 Ohio St. 95, 50 N.E.2d 142, 26 O.O. 282. Wills ⇔ 260

On a trial of an action to contest a will, where it appears on its face that it was not signed as required by statute, it is not error to direct a verdict that the will is not a valid will. Sears v. Sears (Ohio 1907) 77 Ohio St. 104, 82 N.E. 1067, 5 Ohio Law Rep. 495, 11 Am.Ann.Cas. 1008. Wills ⇔ 327

Where a potential contestant of a will named as a nominal defendant in a will contest action wishes to continue the will contest proceedings and does not consent to the voluntary dismissal of such action by the plaintiff, such voluntary dismissal will be reversed. Maxey v Mason, No. 89 CA 02 (4th Dist Ct App, Hocking, 7-11-90).

Refusal to grant a fourth continuance in seven months to the plaintiff in a will contest for reasons of health is not an abuse of discretion, and the action may be dismissed for failure to prosecute. Rudolph v Lown, No. 84-CA-176 (7th Dist Ct App, Mahoning, 5-7-85).

2. Jury trials

Where a will has apparently been altered in a material provision and evidence is offered tending to show that such alteration was made since its execution, as well as to show that it was made before, it is the duty of the jury, in case the will is established, to determine the question in dispute and establish the will as it read when executed. Haynes v. Haynes (Ohio 1878) 33 Ohio St. 598, 31 Am.Rep. 579. Wills ⇔ 324(1)

The verdict of a jury is the only instrumentality given by which to set aside or invalidate the probate of a will, and it is error for a court to proceed by mere decree to set aside a will. Holt v. Lamb (Ohio 1867) 17 Ohio St. 374.

In a will contest proceeding, it is error to render final judgment on demurrer to an answer, since the statute requires that an issue be made up whether the writing produced is the last will and testament of the testator, which shall be tried to a jury. Walker v. Walker (Ohio 1862) 14 Ohio St. 157, 82 Am.Dec. 474.

A party to a will contest action does not have the right to a jury trial; instead, a probate court has discretion to determine whether to sit as the trier of fact in a will contest action or to impanel a jury. State ex rel. Kear v. Court of Common Pleas of Lucas County, Probate Division (Ohio 1981) 67 Ohio St.2d 189, 423 N.E.2d 427, 21 O.O.3d 118. Jury ⇔ 19(7.5)

The right to maintain an action to contest a will, where placed in issue, should be determined by the court without a jury before the trial on the issue of the validity of the will. Comer v. Comer (Ohio 1963) 175 Ohio St. 313, 194 N.E.2d 572, 25 O.O.2d 182.

Where in a will contest the entry setting forth the issue was dictated by the trial judge before the conclusion of the testimony, and then filed, and, at the time of impanelling the jury, such issue was given orally to the jury, there was no prejudicial error. Fazekas v. Gobozy (Cuyahoga 1958) 150 N.E.2d 319, 78 Ohio Law Abs. 258. Wills ⇔ 400

It is not error in a will contest action to refuse to give a special charge to the effect that the fact of the testatrix's belief in spiritualism does not afford grounds for setting aside the will, where the charge as requested does not embrace all the facts brought out at the trial concerning the belief and practice of spiritualism by the testatrix. Schoch v. Schoch (Ohio Cir. 1905) 17 Ohio C.D. 828, 6 Ohio C.C.N.S. 110.

A charge to the jury in a will contest action that "the important item of evidence bearing upon the condition of mind of the testator is the will itself" is erroneous, since the court invades the province of the jury by inviting a substituting of its opinion for that of the jury as to what item of evidence should be given more weight. Rapp v. Becker (Ohio Cir. 1904) 16 Ohio C.D. 321, 4 Ohio C.C.N.S. 139.

The materiality of facts assumed in a hypothetical question propounded to an expert are not for the jury; the questions should be framed so as to include only such facts as the evidence may warrant the jury in finding to exist, and not so as to allow the jury to speculate upon what is material and immaterial. West v. Knoppenberger (Ohio Cir. 1903) 16 Ohio C.D. 168, 4 Ohio C.C.N.S. 305.

Where the weight of the testimony clearly indicates that the testator had sufficient mental capacity to make a will, and under the circumstances the will he made was a fair and natural one, a finding by a jury that such will was not the decedent's last will and testament should be set aside and a new trial had. Kettemann v. Metzger (Ohio Cir. 1901) 13 Ohio C.D. 61, 3 Ohio C.C.N.S. 224.

3. Amendment of pleadings; service

Pursuant to RC 2107.72, the Rules of Civil Procedure govern all aspects of a will contest action, except as otherwise provided in RC 2107.71 to 2107.75; thus, the failure to name all necessary parties to a will contest action within the four-month period set forth in RC 2107.76 is not an absolute bar to a will contest action in Ohio since as long as one proper party files the action within four months after a will is admitted to probate, other necessary parties may be joined by amending the pleadings, which amendments will relate back to the date of the original filing pursuant to Civ R 15(C). Trubulas v. Doland (Hamilton 1987) 39 Ohio App.3d 62, 528 N.E.2d 1313, reversed in part 42 Ohio St.3d 8, 536 N.E.2d 642.

Amendments adding necessary parties may be made to a complaint in a will contest action and relate back to the date of the original filing pursuant to Civ R 15(C); due to a change in the law relating to will contest actions, the application of the rule no longer operates to expand the jurisdiction of probate courts in violation of Civ R 82. Smith v. Klem (Ohio 1983) 6 Ohio St.3d 16, 450 N.E.2d 1171, 6 O.B.R. 13.

In a will contest action, amendments may be made to a complaint to join necessary parties pursuant to Civ R 15, and such amendments relate back to the date of the original filing. Smith v. Klem (Ohio 1983) 6 Ohio St.3d 16, 450 N.E.2d 1171, 6 O.B.R. 13. Limitation Of Actions ⇔ 124; Parties ⇔ 95(1)

The will contest action is a special statutory proceeding and any civil rule which would permit the liberal amendment or joinder adding a necessary party relating the cause of action back to within the time limitation of RC 2741.09 would by its nature be clearly inapplicable as it would operate to extend the jurisdiction of the courts of this state in derogation of mandatory statutory language. (Superseded by statute as stated in Smith v Klem, 6 OS(3d) 16, 6 OBR 13, 450 NE(2d) 1171 (1983).) Holland v. Carlson (Cuyahoga 1974) 40 Ohio App.2d 325, 319 N.E.2d 362, 69 O.O.2d 299.

Where one service of summons in an action contesting a will is made within the time prescribed by RC 2741.09 upon a defendant occupying the positions of surviving spouse, devisee, and executrix and although such summons does not designate the specific relationship between the estate and the defendant, the various capacities of the defendant are clearly designated in the body of the complaint attached to the summons, an amendment of the original complaint after the expiration of the six-month statute of limitations prescribed by RC 2741.09, in order to formally add the same defendant in a different capacity, relates back to the date of the original pleading. Beverly v. Beverly (Erie 1973) 33 Ohio App.2d 199, 293 N.E.2d 562, 62 O.O.2d 303. Wills ⟿ 285

In a will contest, where a defendant who is not an heir and who is not a legatee under the will but is the duly appointed, qualified and acting executor of the testatrix's estate and is designated in the body of the petition as the executor of the estate, but in the caption of the petition and in the precipe which was issued there is no indication of his representative capacity, and the summons was served upon him in his individual capacity, there is sufficient compliance with RC 2741.09 to give the court jurisdiction of the action. Center v. St. Peter's Episcopal Church (Ohio 1967) 11 Ohio St.2d 64, 227 N.E.2d 599, 40 O.O.2d 68.

Where a will contest is brought within the statutory time provided therefor but the petition fails to disclose that the plaintiff is a party interested in the will involved, an amendment of the petition to allege facts showing that the plaintiff is an interested party will be in furtherance of justice, and such an amendment may be made after the statutory period for the bringing of such will contest. Morton v. Fast (Ohio 1953) 159 Ohio St. 380, 112 N.E.2d 385, 50 O.O. 335.

Under RC 2107.72, amendments may be made to a plaintiff's complaint to join necessary parties in a will contest action, which would, under Civ R 15(C), relate back to the date of the original filing. State, ex rel. Smith v. Court of Common Pleas, Probate Div. (Ohio 1982) 70 Ohio St.2d 213, 436 N.E.2d 1005, 24 O.O.3d 320.

4. Burden of proof

In a will contest, by virtue of the statute, the burden of proof is cast upon the contestant of the will and such burden never shifts from him, so that if the evidence produced furnishes only a basis for a choice among different possibilities he fails to sustain such burden. Kata v. Second Nat. Bank of Warren (Ohio 1971) 26 Ohio St.2d 210, 271 N.E.2d 292, 55 O.O.2d 458. Evidence ⟿ 94

In a proceeding to contest a will the court must overrule the defendant's motion for a directed verdict where the plaintiff has produced credible evidence of a substantial character sufficient to overcome the presumption of due attestation, execution, and validity of the will which arises from the order of probate. Truchess v. Brand (Lucas 1953) 98 Ohio App. 118, 128 N.E.2d 157, 57 O.O. 195.

When a person has been declared insane by a court of competent jurisdiction and is under guardianship, the presumption of sanity is not only removed but a presumption of insanity arises. Where a will of such a person, made after such adjudication, having been admitted to probate, becomes the subject of a will contest, the burden of proof by statute being cast upon the contestants of the will, the presumption of continuance of such insanity was a rebuttable one and would be removed when sufficient evidence had been introduced to overcome such presumption arising from the adjudication of insanity. Kennedy v. Walcutt (Ohio 1928) 118 Ohio St. 442, 161 N.E. 336, 6 Ohio Law Abs. 206, 26 Ohio Law Rep. 215.

Failure in a general charge in a will contest to restate, in connection with instructions as to testamentary capacity and undue influence, that the presumption arising from the probate of the will must be taken into consideration as part of the while evidence in arriving at a preponderance of the evidence in order that the contestant may prevail, held not prejudicial error, where a special finding for contestant on the issue of want of execution was supported by the evidence. West v. Lucas (Ohio 1922) 106 Ohio St. 255, 139 N.E. 859, 1 Ohio Law Abs. 72, 20 Ohio Law Rep. 470, 20 Ohio Law Rep. 471. Wills ⟿ 400

Jury instructions in a will contest action which shift the burden of proof onto the defendant to prove mental capacity and lack of undue influence are manifestly wrong and prejudicial to the defendant in view of the rule that an order of probate is prima facie evidence of the validity of the will, and the contesters have the burden of disproving such evidence. West v. Knoppenberger (Ohio Cir. 1903) 16 Ohio C.D. 168, 4 Ohio C.C.N.S. 305.

5. Evidence and testimony

The opinion of a witness as to the testator's capacity to make a will is not admissible as involving a question of law and fact to be determined by the jury; the witness's opinion as to the testator's sanity must relate to the time of his examination, not to the time of the making of the will, to be admissible in a will contest action. Runyan v. Price (Ohio 1864) 15 Ohio St. 1, 86 Am.Dec. 459.

Probate court exceeded limited statutory purposes in decedent's son's will contest action, where court did not explain reasons for granting summary judgment to decedent's wife on basis that net value of assets of estate was less than statutory allowance she was entitled to received as surviving spouse if will were declared invalid, and inventory had not been filed, and neither content nor value of estate had been determined; it was not probate court's function to determine content and value of estate's inventory. Dunaway v. Dunaway (Ohio App. 12 Dist., Brown, 02-18-2003) No. CA2002-07012, 2003-Ohio-706, 2003 WL 355719, Unreported. Wills ⟿ 351

Where there is no dispute as to any material fact, but only a dispute as to the law, a proper case is made for summary judgment. Shinn v. Phillips (Cuyahoga 1964) 8 Ohio App.2d 58, 220 N.E.2d 674.

Where the only issue in an action is whether testator used the legal requirements for expressing his intention to revive a revoked will, the case is a proper one for summary judgment. Shinn v. Phillips (Cuyahoga 1964) 8 Ohio App.2d 58, 220 N.E.2d 674.

The issue before the court on a petition, filed after term, for vacation of an earlier judgment and for new trial on the ground of the discovery of new and material evidence that a codicil found to be valid was "a fraudulent, fictitious and forged document," is not whether the codicil was a forgery but whether the alleged new evidence satisfies the requirements necessary to warrant the granting of a motion for a new trial based on the ground of newly discovered evidence. Rothstein v. Rothstein (Seneca 1958) 109 Ohio App. 234, 164 N.E.2d 768, 10 O.O.2d 466.

Where, in an action to contest a will, the claim is made that there was no will executed, a verdict should be directed for the proponents of the will, where the evidence shows the dictation of the will by the testator, the writing thereof in his presence and in the presence of the three subscribing witnesses and the due execution of the will by the testator as required by law. Brown v. Johnson (Montgomery 1957) 105 Ohio App. 159, 151 N.E.2d 692, 5 O.O.2d 431. Wills ⟿ 324(1)

In will contest, subscribing witness' affidavit, made and offered in probate court as proof of execution of will, held incompetent, where witness was in court. Fox v. Lynch (Perry 1932) 43 Ohio App. 305, 183 N.E. 177, 13 Ohio Law Abs. 142. Affidavits ⟿ 18; Wills ⟿ 294

In an action to contest a will the issue should be determined by the preponderance of all the evidence, regardless of which party adduced the evidence. Van Demark v. Tompkins (Ohio 1929) 121 Ohio St. 129, 167 N.E. 370, 7 Ohio Law Abs. 379, 29 Ohio Law Rep. 366.

In action to contest validity of will, lay witness, not subscribing witness, who has previously given testimony upon which opinion could reasonably be based, may state his opinion as to testator's soundness of mind. Niemes v. Niemes (Ohio 1917) 97 Ohio St. 145, 119 N.E. 503, 15 Ohio Law Rep. 484, 15 Ohio Law Rep. 565. Evidence ⟿ 472(8); Wills ⟿ 293(1)

It is error in a will contest to admit the testimony of witnesses who are not experts as to their opinions based upon a state of facts submitted to them in hypothetical questions rather than based upon facts and observations within their own knowledge. Gregg v. Moore (Ohio Cir. 1911) 23 Ohio C.D. 534, 14 Ohio C.C.N.S. 570.

Declarations of a witness which tend to show her state of mind and which afford circumstantial evidence of her ill-will toward the testatrix and her purpose and design in treating the testatrix with apparent but false affection in her last illness are competent. Schoch v. Schoch (Ohio Cir. 1905) 17 Ohio C.D. 828, 6 Ohio C.C.N.S. 110.

In an action to contest the will of an aged man, the testimony of lay witnesses is competent as to the mental capacity of the testator, where they are asked to state in detail circumstances upon which they have based an opinion as to whether the testator was subject to undue influence or had the capacity to make a will, and more reliance can often be based on such testimony than on that of experts whose testimony is based on hypothetical questions. Althans v Althans, 32 LR 400 (App, Cuyahoga 1930).

6. Service

Service upon one of the members of a class united in interest, if made within the limitation period, commences the action as to all the members of the class, and actual service of summons may be thereafter made at any time upon the remainder of the defendants of that class. Cook v. Sears (Wyandot 1967) 9 Ohio App.2d 197, 223 N.E.2d 613, 38 O.O.2d 209.

An action to contest a will admitted to probate on January 25 is brought within the statutory period where such action is instituted on July 25, on the same day there is filed a praecipe and summons issued for thirteen defendants, designated as heirs at law and devisees and who are served on July 26, and an affidavit and order for service by publication on two nonresident defendants, who with a cemetery are designated as the only other legatees and devisees, the first publication is made on July 26 and publication completed but no notice mailed to such two defendants and the cemetery is served on July 26. Cover v. Hildebran (Darke 1957) 103 Ohio App. 413, 145 N.E.2d 850, 3 O.O.2d 435.

Grandchildren who are made parties defendant to a will contest action and are served with summons within the time limited for the commencement of such action, are united in interest with grandchildren who are not made parties to such action or served with summons therein, and in such case such action may be considered as commenced, and there is not such a defect as would require a dismissal of such action for want of jurisdiction or of necessary parties. Carnicom v. Murphy (Sandusky 1956) 101 Ohio App. 416, 140 N.E.2d 3, 1 O.O.2d 337.

Even if the provisions of RC 2305.17 are applicable to cause commencement of an action to contest a will where no summons is issued to a necessary party until after the statutory period of six months has elapsed, it must be made to appear that such necessary party is "united in interest" with some party, other than an executor or administrator, to whom summons had been issued within such statutory period. Staley v. Scheck (Hamilton 1954) 99 Ohio App. 242, 133 N.E.2d 189, 58 O.O. 405.

Where plaintiff in a will contest action identifies a defendant as the "allegedly" executor of the estate, such language adequately identifies the executor and places the defendant on notice that he is a party to the suit as executor. Rismiller v Wagner, No. 1053 (2d Dist Ct App, Darke, 11–10–82).

2107.73 Necessary parties

Persons who are necessary parties to a will contest are as follows:

(A) Any person designated in a will to receive a testamentary disposition of real or personal property;

(B) Heirs who would take property pursuant to section 2105.06 of the Revised Code had the testator died intestate;

(C) The executor or the administrator with the will annexed;

(D) The attorney general as provided by section 109.25 of the Revised Code;

(E) Other interested parties.

(1976 S 466, eff. 5–26–76; 1975 S 145)

Historical and Statutory Notes

Ed. Note: 2107.73 contains provisions analogous to former 2741.02, repealed by 1975 S 145, eff. 1–1–76.

Cross References

Joinder of persons needed for just adjudication, Civ R 19

Library References

Wills ⚖︎265.1.
Westlaw Topic No. 409.
C.J.S. Wills § 540.

Research References

Encyclopedias

OH Jur. 3d Decedents' Estates § 1100, The State of Ohio.
OH Jur. 3d Decedents' Estates § 1103, Who Are Necessary Parties, Generally.
OH Jur. 3d Decedents' Estates § 1104, Devisees and Legatees.
OH Jur. 3d Decedents' Estates § 1105, Heirs of the Testator.
OH Jur. 3d Decedents' Estates § 1106, Executors or Administrators.
OH Jur. 3d Decedents' Estates § 1107, "Other Interested Parties".
OH Jur. 3d Decedents' Estates § 1119, Adding Necessary Parties by Amendment; Relation Back to Original Pleading.
OH Jur. 3d Decedents' Estates § 1123, Applicability of Rules of Civil Procedure; Transfer of Venue.

Treatises and Practice Aids

Klein, Darling, & Terez, Baldwin's Ohio Practice Civil Practice § 24:8, Intervention of Right--Statutory Intervention of Right--"A Statute of This State Confers an Unconditional Right to Intervene".
Giannelli and Snyder, Baldwin's Ohio Practice, Evidence, R 101, Scope of Rules: Applicability; Privileges; Exceptions.
Carlin, Baldwin's Ohio Practice, Merrick-Rippner Probate Law § 32:3, Charitable Trusts.
Carlin, Baldwin's Ohio Practice, Merrick-Rippner Probate Law § 38:7, Will Contests—Commencement of Action; Limitation of Actions.
Carlin, Baldwin's Ohio Practice, Merrick-Rippner Probate Law § 38:8, Will Contests—Parties to Action—Necessary Parties.
Carlin, Baldwin's Ohio Practice, Merrick-Rippner Probate Law § 4:31, Service—Summons—Specific Persons or Entities—Charitable Trust.
Carlin, Baldwin's Ohio Practice, Merrick-Rippner Probate Law § 38:10, Will Contests—Service of Process.

Law Review and Journal Commentaries

Cox v. Saadeh: A Warning to the Wary in Will Contests. Angela G. Carlin, 13 Prob L J Ohio 11 (September/October 2002).

Notes of Decisions

Ed. Note: This section contains annotations from former RC 2741.02, RC 2741.09, RC 2741.01, RC 2741.04, and RC 2741.07.

Beneficiaries and heirs 3
Executors 4
Interested person 5
Liberal construction 1
Procedure 2

---

1. Liberal construction

RC 2741.02 is a remedial statute, and the proceedings thereunder are to be liberally construed. Beverly v. Beverly (Erie 1973) 33 Ohio App.2d 199, 293 N.E.2d 562, 62 O.O.2d 303.

2. Procedure

A will contest proceeding binds only the parties to such proceeding and therefore although such parties, as between themselves, are estopped from setting up the will once it has been set aside in the proceeding, as to all other persons in interest it is to be regarded as a still subsisting will, and their rights are wholly unaffected by the proceeding. Holt v. Lamb (Ohio 1867) 17 Ohio St. 374.

Evidence that beneficiaries of most recent will abused testator until she destroyed previous will and executed new one in their favor did not negate fact that testator knew she was destroying old will and, thus, testator's friend who was alleged sole beneficiary under will destroyed by testator lacked standing to contest new will or show that testator destroyed previous will because of fraud or undue influence. Sheridan v. Harbison (Ohio App. 2 Dist., 02-15-1995) 101 Ohio App.3d 206, 655 N.E.2d 256, appeal not allowed 72 Ohio St.3d 1551, 650 N.E.2d 1370. Wills ⚖︎ 229

The amending of a complaint in a will contest to add a necessary party may relate back to the filing of the original complaint if the conditions listed in Civ R 15(C) are satisfied. Weaver v. Donnerberg (Shelby 1985) 26 Ohio App.3d 112, 498 N.E.2d 496, 26 O.B.R. 323.

In a will contest action, amendments may be made to a complaint to join necessary parties pursuant to Civ R 15, and such amendments relate back to the date of the original filing. Smith v. Klem (Ohio 1983) 6 Ohio St.3d 16, 450 N.E.2d 1171, 6 O.B.R. 13. Limitation Of Actions ⚖︎ 124; Parties ⚖︎ 95(1)

A party to a will contest action does not have the right to a jury trial; instead, a probate court has discretion to determine whether to sit as the trier of fact in a will contest action or to impanel a jury. State ex rel. Kear v. Court of Common Pleas of Lucas County, Probate Division (Ohio 1981) 67 Ohio St.2d 189, 423 N.E.2d 427, 21 O.O.3d 118. Jury ⚖︎ 19(7.5)

In a will contest action the complete and total failure to name a necessary party in any manner in the complaint for relief within the statutory limitation period is not a captious and purely technical ground for the trial court to deny jurisdiction. Holland v. Carlson (Cuyahoga 1974) 40 Ohio App.2d 325, 319 N.E.2d 362, 69 O.O.2d 291. Wills ⚖︎ 267

Where the captions of the complaint and the summons in an action contesting a will do not designate the specific legal relationship between the estate and a defendant occupying the positions of surviving spouse, devisee, and executrix, the requirements of RC 2741.02 are satisfied where service of summons within the time prescribed by RC 2741.09 is made upon such defendant with a copy of the complaint attached thereto and the body of the complaint concisely designates the capacities in which such person is named as defendant. Beverly v. Beverly (Erie 1973) 33 Ohio App.2d 199, 293 N.E.2d 562, 62 O.O.2d 303.

The names appearing in the caption of the case do not determine who are the parties to the suit. Gibbs v. Lemley (Lawrence 1972) 33 Ohio App.2d 220, 293 N.E.2d 324, 62 O.O.2d 315.

A will contest action, otherwise rightly brought within the meaning of RC 2741.09, will not fail under RC 2741.02 just because persons named testamentary trustees in the will, but not appointed to such capacity within six months following probate of the will, are not joined as parties in that capacity, where such persons have been timely made parties in the capacity of co-executors (having been so named in the will and appointed by the probate court), and all the beneficiaries of the testamentary trust have been timely made parties to the action. Hirsch v. Hirsch (Franklin 1972) 32 Ohio App.2d 200, 289 N.E.2d 386, 61 O.O.2d 212. Wills ☞ 265.1

Where court in will contest proceeding directs verdict sua sponte on basis of compromise agreement made in private conference, which distributes devised property among claimants in attendance and all of parties in case are not parties to agreement, such verdict is void. Taylor v. Connell (Highland 1971) 26 Ohio App.2d 253, 271 N.E.2d 305, 55 O.O.2d 412.

RC 2741.02, providing who must be made parties to a will contest, is a personal statute, and all of each class named therein must be made parties to such action by one of the methods of lawful service of summons. Collins v. Nurre (Hamilton 1969) 20 Ohio App.2d 53, 251 N.E.2d 621, 49 O.O.2d 70.

Where an organizational legatee has been named party defendant in a will contest action in the petition, precipe, summons and return of summons, with its name prefixed by the name and title of an agent upon whom service upon such organization may be had, and where it is apparent from an examination of the will and the petition that such agent has no relation to the estate except in behalf of his principal whose sole relationship to the estate is in the manner and capacity named as legatee in the will, the prefix of the name and office of the agent is mere surplusage, and the surplusage creates a mere misnomer, which may be waived by the organization by action constituting an entry of appearance or by failure to make timely objection thereto, so that on motion of another defendant, such misnomer may not be grounds for dismissal as constituting a failure of the plaintiff to make all necessary parties parties defendant. Cook v. Sears (Wyandot 1967) 9 Ohio App.2d 197, 223 N.E.2d 613, 38 O.O.2d 209.

The doctrine of virtual representation does not apply to a will contest action where it is apparent from the allegations in the petition that the persons interested in the action are not so numerous that it would be impracticable or inconvenient to make them all parties to the action, and such action is not brought as a class suit. McKinney v. McKinney (Allen 1960) 115 Ohio App. 379, 185 N.E.2d 319, 20 O.O.2d 453.

An action to contest the will of testator dying December 22, 1954, whose will was probated on January 6, 1955, could not be maintained where plaintiff failed to make personal service or secure service by publication upon the sole beneficiary under the will within six months from date of probate of will. Faust v. Cailor (Mahoning 1956) 146 N.E.2d 875, 76 Ohio Law Abs. 504. Limitation Of Actions ☞ 119(3)

Where an action to contest a will is actually begun so as to give the court jurisdiction of the subject matter, there is no specific limitation as to when the last interested individual party shall be brought in. Cover v. Hildebran (Darke 1957) 103 Ohio App. 413, 145 N.E.2d 850, 3 O.O.2d 435.

A party to a will contest action properly commenced within the statutory period of limitation and in conformity with statutory requirements may not withdraw from such action, and thereby defeat the right of the other parties to a jury trial to determine the validity of the will, and where a party to such action has been dismissed as a plaintiff, he may be made a party defendant; and where others in the same class have been properly served with summons, such party may be served after the six-month period of limitation. Frederick v. Brown (Scioto 1956) 102 Ohio App. 117, 141 N.E.2d 683, 2 O.O.2d 115.

Grandchildren who are made parties defendant to a will contest action and are served with summons within the time limited for the commencement of such action, are united in interest with grandchildren who are not made parties to such action or served with summons therein, and in such case such action may be considered as commenced, and there is not such a defect as would require a dismissal of such action for want of jurisdiction or of necessary parties. Carnicom v. Murphy (Sandusky 1956) 101 Ohio App. 416, 140 N.E.2d 3, 1 O.O.2d 337.

Where in will contest action brought by certain heirs at law the petition names as defendants the sole legatee and devisee, the executrix and three other heirs at law but fails to name numerous other heirs at law and no service of process is sought or secured on any of the defendant heirs within six months after the will has been admitted to probate, the addition as plaintiffs of the heirs at law not included in the petition and the defendant heirs at law not served with summons after the expiration of the statutory period of limitation does not confer jurisdiction on the court to hear such contest. Gravier v. Gluth (Ohio 1955) 163 Ohio St. 232, 126 N.E.2d 332, 56 O.O. 228. Wills ☞ 268

In will contest where all necessary parties are joined and served either in person or by publication, a party defendant served by publication after period prescribed by statute for contest of will is not entitled to have judgment sustaining will opened and issue as to validity retried. McVeigh v. Fetterman (Ohio 1917) 95 Ohio St. 292, 116 N.E. 518, 15 Ohio Law Rep. 19, 15 Ohio Law Rep. 30. Wills ☞ 355

3. Beneficiaries and heirs

The omission to make a legatee a party to a suit contesting the validity of a will is error for which the decree setting aside the will will be reversed, as in such a suit the legatees and devisees are indispensable parties. Reformed Presbyterian Church v. Nelson (Ohio 1880) 35 Ohio St. 638.

Beneficiaries of a testamentary trust whose father was the trustee and who settled a will contest with the testator's daughter twenty-eight years earlier affecting the terms of the trust, are not necessary parties to the will contest; since the trustee acted properly in securing the settlement, they have no basis to assert a claim against the trust. Fifth Third Bank v. Fifth Third Bank (Hamilton 1991) 77 Ohio App.3d 339, 602 N.E.2d 325, dismissed, jurisdictional motion overruled 63 Ohio St.3d 1409, 585 N.E.2d 834.

A legatee who would take under a will only if another legatee who survived had predeceased the testator or if such legatee were deprived of her interest by virtue of a no contest clause, is not a necessary party to an action contesting the will. Bazo v. Siegel (Ohio 1979) 58 Ohio St.2d 353, 390 N.E.2d 807, 12 O.O.3d 318.

A child, surrendered by its parents into the permanent custody of an institution established for the purpose of aiding, caring for and placing children in homes, under a written agreement pursuant to RC 5103.15, which agreement provides that the institution may appear in any legal proceeding for the adoption of such child and consent to the child's adoption, continues as an heir of its parents, either natural or adoptive, until such time as the child has been legally adopted pursuant to RC Ch 3107. Maurer v. Becker (Ohio 1971) 26 Ohio St.2d 254, 271 N.E.2d 255, 55 O.O.2d 486. Adoption ☞ 21

A person who is a beneficiary under a will has such an "interest" in a later will of the testator, which permits him to contest such subsequent will. Campbell v. Strasburger (Hamilton 1968) 17 Ohio App.2d 56, 244 N.E.2d 530, 46 O.O.2d 71. Wills ☞ 229

Co-executors of will, who are sole heirs and next of kin of testatrix and stand to inherit entire estate if will declared invalid, must, because of conflict between their duties as executors and interests as individuals, resign as executors before they can bring an action to contest the will. Allison v. Allison (Ohio 1968) 15 Ohio St.2d 44, 238 N.E.2d 768, 44 O.O.2d 25.

An "interested person" within the contemplation of RC 2109.33 is one who has some direct, pecuniary interest in the devolution of the testator's estate, and a surviving spouse who has entered into an antenuptial agreement whereby she relinquishes all claims which she might or could have in or to her deceased husband's estate is not such an interested person. In re Matusoff's Estate (Montgomery 1965) 10 Ohio App.2d 113, 226 N.E.2d 140, 39 O.O.2d 187.

Heirs or next of kin who would have been benefited by denial of probate are not entitled to share in consideration of contracts to which they are not parties. Hull v. Roseman (Ohio Com.Pl. 1964) 198 N.E.2d 792, 95 Ohio Law Abs. 218, 28 O.O.2d 31.

The illegitimate child of the widow of a testator is not his heir at law and, therefore, does not have sufficient interest to maintain a will contest, even though the testator married the child's mother after its birth and acknowledged the child as his own, unless he was in fact the father of the child. Comer v. Comer (Ohio 1963) 175 Ohio St. 313, 194 N.E.2d 572, 25 O.O.2d 182.

Where, in a will contest action, certain heirs of the testator are, without their consent or authority, joined as parties plaintiff and were not guilty of any fraud, bad faith or willful conduct which resulted in their being so joined, and such lack of authority or consent is known to the plaintiffs commencing such action, estoppel does not apply to preclude such nonconsenting heirs from moving to be dismissed as parties plaintiff. McKinney v. McKinney (Allen 1960) 115 Ohio App. 379, 185 N.E.2d 319, 20 O.O.2d 453.

The determination as to who is an heir of a decedent must be made from a consideration of the statutes of descent and distribution in effect at the time of the death of the decedent. Kluever v. Cleveland Trust Co. (Ohio 1962) 173 Ohio St. 177, 180 N.E.2d 579, 18 O.O.2d 461. Descent And Distribution ⚖ 6

The determination of the heirs of a decedent for the purpose of joinder of necessary parties in an action to contest a will must be made from a consideration of those who would take the decedent's estate in the event of an ultimate finding that such decedent died intestate. Kluever v. Cleveland Trust Co. (Ohio 1962) 173 Ohio St. 177, 180 N.E.2d 579, 18 O.O.2d 461. Wills ⚖ 265.1

A judgment overturning a will in an action brought by brothers of the deceased wife of the testator upon representation that the testator died without issue will be vacated upon subsequent action by children of the testator. Donovan v. Decker (Franklin 1953) 98 Ohio App. 183, 122 N.E.2d 501, 68 Ohio Law Abs. 353, 57 O.O. 230.

Action to contest validity of will is not commenced as to heirs at law of testator by service of summons upon such sole beneficiary within six months from date of probate where such sole beneficiary is neither heir at law nor next of kin of decedent. Case v. Smith (Ohio 1943) 142 Ohio St. 95, 50 N.E.2d 142, 26 O.O. 282.

Beneficiaries under prior unprobated purported will are not necessary parties to will contest. Machovina v. Machovina (Ohio 1936) 132 Ohio St. 171, 5 N.E.2d 496, 7 O.O. 253.

That executrix who was also sole beneficiary remained silent until after year for will contest expired held not waiver of her right to assert that she was not individually bound by judgment setting will aside in contest wherein she was not individually made party. Myers v. Hogue (Tuscarawas 1932) 45 Ohio App. 330, 187 N.E. 127, 15 Ohio Law Abs. 174, 39 Ohio Law Rep. 122. Wills ⚖ 432

An action to contest a will is not commenced as to the heirs of the testator and the devisees by the issuance of a summons for the executor, the executor not being "united in interest" with the heirs and devisees, within GC § 11230, providing that an action shall be deemed to have been commenced as to one defendant by issuance of summons for another defendant "united in interest" with him, in view of § 12080. McCord v. McCord (Ohio 1922) 104 Ohio St. 274, 135 N.E. 548, 19 Ohio Law Rep. 739. Wills ⚖ 260

An individual who is both a primary beneficiary and an executrix under a will is a necessary party under RC 2107.73(A) and when it is unclear if a complaint in a will contest names her individually, the complaint may be amended; however, where parties seek to amend their complaint twenty-nine months after they had notice of the defect, the trial court does not abuse its discretion in denying the motion to amend the complaint under Civ R 15(A). Fortney v Fortney, No. 45–CA–88 (5th Dist Ct App, Fairfield, 6–12–89).

4. Executors

When, after commencement of will contest action, probate court substitutes administrator with will annexed for executor originally appointed, and further substitutes administrator with will annexed as party in will contest action, probate court does not lose jurisdiction simply because no motion to substitute administrator as party has been served upon other parties. Krischbaum v. Dillon (Ohio 1991) 58 Ohio St.3d 58, 567 N.E.2d 1291. Wills ⚖ 268

Where, after probate of a will, the estate is relieved from administration and the nominated fiduciary is not appointed as such by the probate court until after six months following probate, such fiduciary is nonexistent for the purposes of, and is not a person interested in, a contest of the will. Hecker v. Schuler (Ohio 1967) 12 Ohio St.2d 58, 231 N.E.2d 877, 41 O.O.2d 277.

Although a fiduciary acting under a will has the right to defend the will, he has no duty so to do, and may cast that burden upon the legatees and devisees. Hecker v. Schuler (Ohio 1967) 12 Ohio St.2d 58, 231 N.E.2d 877, 41 O.O.2d 277. Executors And Administrators ⚖ 111(3)

In a will contest, where a defendant who is not an heir and who is not a legatee under the will but is the duly appointed, qualified and acting executor of the testatrix's estate and is designated in the body of the petition as the executor of the estate, but in the caption of the petition and in the precipe which was issued there is no indication of his representative capacity, and the summons was served upon him in his individual capacity, there is sufficient compliance with RC 2741.09 to give the court jurisdiction of the action. Center v. St. Peter's Episcopal Church (Ohio 1967) 11 Ohio St.2d 64, 227 N.E.2d 599, 40 O.O.2d 68.

Where in a timely brought action to contest a will, a defendant is designated in the body of the petition as the executor of the deceased testator's estate, but in the caption of the petition, in the precipe for summons and in the summons which is served on him he is named in an individual capacity, and it is apparent that his sole relation to the estate is that of executor, there is sufficient compliance with the provisions of RC 2741.02 to bring him into the action as executor, and a motion filed more than six months after the admission of the will to probate to dismiss the petition for failure to summon him as executor should be overruled. Porter v. Fenner (Ohio 1966) 5 Ohio St.2d 233, 215 N.E.2d 389, 34 O.O.2d 465.

In a will contest action, the necessity for service of summons on the executor is dispensed with where the executor files an answer, and thereby enters his appearance and becomes a party to the case. Claypole v. Norris (Hamilton 1960) 112 Ohio App. 549, 171 N.E.2d 352, 16 O.O.2d 457.

An agreement among all the heirs at law, devisees and legatees of a testator to divide the estate in a manner different from that provided in the will, should the will be set aside by a jury in a pending will contest action in which they are parties, is not contrary to public policy and is valid, and the executor is not a necessary party to such agreement where his interest in the proceedings is ex officio only, so that under the circumstances no right of such executor is prejudiced by his not being notified of and present at the trial of such will contest action. Skelly v. Graybill (Stark 1959) 109 Ohio App. 277, 165 N.E.2d 218, 11 O.O.2d 42. Wills ⚖ 740(2)

A person named as executor in a will, which appointment was revoked by a codicil duly probated as a part of such will, does not come within the category of "interested persons" and is not a necessary defendant in an action to contest such will and codicil. Bruckmann v. Shaffer (Hamilton 1958) 108 Ohio App. 531, 155 N.E.2d 491, 10 O.O.2d 20.

In a will contest, where the executor or administrator is made a party, is named in the caption of the petition as executor or administrator and in no other capacity, is described in the body of the petition as executor or administrator and in no other capacity, and in fact has no relation to such case in any other capacity, and where, attached to the petition, there is a precipe for the issuance of summons naming such executor or administrator but not with his title attached, and where service of summons is made upon such executor or administrator, with the caption of the petition upon the summons, in which caption the party is named as executor or administrator and in no other capacity, such executor or administrator is summoned as a party to the will contest in his fiduciary capacity. Abbott v. Dawson (Ohio 1958) 167 Ohio St. 238, 147 N.E.2d 609, 4 O.O.2d 288.

Where in an action to contest a will the administrator is named and served only in his individual capacity, such service is defective even though he could not have been a party in any other capacity. Mangan v. Hopkins (Ohio 1956) 166 Ohio St. 41, 138 N.E.2d 872, 1 O.O.2d 186.

Where devisee and legatee is sued and served in will contest action in that capacity but not in his capacity as executor, the court is without jurisdiction even though in the body of the petition plaintiff stated that defendant was appointed executor by the probate court. Bynner v. Jones (Ohio 1950) 154 Ohio St. 184, 93 N.E.2d 687, 42 O.O. 257.

Under this section, all the devisees, legatees, and heirs of the testator, and other interested persons, including the executor or administrator, must be made parties to an action to contest a will, and it is mandatory and jurisdictional that the executor be made a party to such action. Peters v. Moore (Ohio 1950) 154 Ohio St. 177, 93 N.E.2d 683, 42 O.O. 254. Wills ⚖ 267

It is not a compliance with the jurisdictional requirements of this section when a person occupying the positions of heir, legatee and sole executor is made a party in his individual capacity as heir and legatee but not in his distinctive, official, fiduciary capacity as executor, and another person is sued as executor. Peters v. Moore (Ohio 1950) 154 Ohio St. 177, 93 N.E.2d 683, 42 O.O. 254. Wills ⚖ 307

An individual who is both a primary beneficiary and an executrix under a will is a necessary party under RC 2107.73(A) and when it is unclear if a complaint in a will contest names her individually, the complaint may be amended; however, where parties seek to amend their complaint twenty-nine months after they had notice of the defect, the trial court does not abuse its discretion in denying the motion to amend the complaint under Civ R 15(A). Fortney v Fortney, No. 45–CA–88 (5th Dist Ct App, Fairfield, 6–12–89).

Where plaintiff in a will contest action identifies a defendant as the "allegedly" executor of the estate, such language adequately identifies the executor and places the defendant on notice that he is a party to the suit as executor. Rismiller v Wagner, No. 1053 (2d Dist Ct App, Darke, 11–10–82).

5. Interested person

Illegitimate child of testator had standing to bring will contest action based on determination of paternity in bastardy proceedings brought during testator's life. Birman v. Sproat (Miami 1988) 47 Ohio App.3d 65, 546 N.E.2d 1354. Wills ⇔ 229

Although legatees, devisees, heirs, executors and other interested parties are necessary parties to a will contest action, it does not follow that by bringing such an action those who contest the will are making claims against any other opposing party. Hess v. Sommers (Mercer 1982) 4 Ohio App.3d 281, 448 N.E.2d 494, 4 O.B.R. 500. Wills ⇔ 280.1

One who, at the commencement of a will contest action, has a direct, pecuniary interest in the estate which would be impaired or defeated if the instrument admitted to probate is a valid will, is a necessary party to such will contest action. Trustees of Diocese of Southern Ohio v. Gilchrist (Hamilton 1981) 3 Ohio App.3d 223, 444 N.E.2d 451, 3 O.B.R. 254. Wills ⇔ 265.1

RC 109.25 does not make the attorney general a necessary party to a will contest where the will in question merely contains an unconditional bequest to a trustee of a charitable trust, since a will with such a provision does not create a charitable trust. O'Neal v. Buckley (Morgan 1979) 67 Ohio App.2d 45, 425 N.E.2d 924, 21 O.O.3d 354.

An illegitimate child does not per se have a direct pecuniary interest in the estate of his natural father that would be defeated or impaired if the father's will, admitted to probate, is a valid will; thus, he has no standing to contest the will of his natural father. Moore v. Dague (Franklin 1975) 46 Ohio App.2d 75, 345 N.E.2d 449, 75 O.O.2d 68. Wills ⇔ 229

A provision of a will directing that a debt of the testator be paid does not make the creditor a legatee or a necessary party to a will contest action. Hirsch v. Hirsch (Franklin 1972) 32 Ohio App.2d 200, 289 N.E.2d 386, 61 O.O.2d 212.

A person interested in a will within the meaning of RC 2741.01 is one who, at the time of the commencement of an action to contest a will, has a direct, pecuniary interest in the estate of the putative testator, that would be impaired or defeated if the instrument admitted to probate is a valid will. Steinberg v. Central Trust Co. (Ohio 1969) 18 Ohio St.2d 33, 247 N.E.2d 303, 47 O.O.2d 154. Wills ⇔ 229

A nonexistent person cannot be an interested person in a will contest, and need not be joined as a party thereto. Hecker v. Schuler (Ohio 1967) 12 Ohio St.2d 58, 231 N.E.2d 877, 41 O.O.2d 277.

The character of a person's interest in a will necessary to require that he be made a party to an action to contest such will is the same as the character of the interest necessary to support such person's right to contest such will. Durbin v. Durbin (Hardin 1957) 106 Ohio App. 155, 153 N.E.2d 706, 6 O.O.2d 414.

Where stock in a bank is bequeathed to certain named legatees with the express direction that "none of said stock shall be sold by any of said legatees unless with the consent and approval of" the named president of such bank, such bank president is not an interested person in such will, and it is not necessary to make him a party in an action to contest such will. Durbin v. Durbin (Hardin 1957) 106 Ohio App. 155, 153 N.E.2d 706, 6 O.O.2d 414.

A person named as a beneficiary under a will and omitted as such under a subsequently executed will which revoked the former will, has an interest in it that, under GC 12079 (RC 2741.01), he is eligible to contest it. Caswell v. Lermann (Erie 1948) 85 Ohio App. 200, 88 N.E.2d 405, 40 O.O. 148.

A person who is a beneficiary under a will has such a pecuniary interest in the estate of the testator as entitles him to contest another alleged will of the same testator which would destroy, reduce or impair his share in such estate. Kennedy v. Walcutt (Ohio 1928) 118 Ohio St. 442, 161 N.E. 336, 6 Ohio Law Abs. 206, 26 Ohio Law Rep. 215.

"A person interested" who may contest a will, means one who has a direct pecuniary interest when the action is filed, which would be impaired if the will is valid. Chilcote v. Hoffman (Ohio 1918) 97 Ohio St. 98, 119 N.E. 364, 15 Ohio Law Rep. 538, 15 Ohio Law Rep. 549.

The grantee of a devisee of part of the land devised is an interested person, and if not made party to a contest of the will is not bound by an adverse result. Sears v. Stinehelfer (Ohio 1913) 89 Ohio St. 163, 105 N.E. 1047, 11 Ohio Law Rep. 347, 11 Ohio Law Rep. 447.

A judgment creditor of an heir, who has obtained a lien on property which in the absence of a will would belong to the debtor heir, is an interested party for purposes of a will contest action. Bloor v. Platt (Ohio 1908) 78 Ohio St. 46, 84 N.E. 604, 5 Ohio Law Rep. 619, 14 Am.Ann.Cas. 332.

2107.74 Effective order of probate

On the trial of any will contest under section 2107.71 of the Revised Code, the order of probate is prima-facie evidence of the attestation, execution, and validity of the will or codicil. The contesting party may call any witness to the will as upon cross examination.

(1975 S 145, eff. 1–1–76)

Historical and Statutory Notes

Ed. Note: 2107.74 contains provisions analogous to former 2741.05, repealed by 1975 S 145, eff. 1–1–76.

Cross References

Cross examination, scope; leading questions permitted, Evid R 611

Library References

Wills ⇔ 294, 427.

Westlaw Topic No. 409.

C.J.S. Wills §§ 595 to 597, 601, 604, 800 to 806.

Research References

Encyclopedias

OH Jur. 3d Decedents' Estates § 992, Generally; Nature of Proceedings.

OH Jur. 3d Decedents' Estates § 1123, Applicability of Rules of Civil Procedure; Transfer of Venue.

OH Jur. 3d Decedents' Estates § 1136, Order of Probate as Prima Facie Evidence of Validity of Will.

OH Jur. 3d Decedents' Estates § 1137, Order of Probate as Prima Facie Evidence of Validity of Will—Attestation and Execution.

OH Jur. 3d Decedents' Estates § 1140, Order of Probate as Prima Facie Evidence of Validity of Will—Lost, Spoliated, or Destroyed Will.

OH Jur. 3d Decedents' Estates § 1141, Order of Probate as Prima Facie Evidence of Validity of Will—Oral Will.

OH Jur. 3d Decedents' Estates § 1144, Undue Influence.

OH Jur. 3d Decedents' Estates § 1204, Witnesses.

Treatises and Practice Aids

Giannelli and Snyder, Baldwin's Ohio Practice, Evidence, R 611, Mode and Order of Interrogation and Presentation.

Giannelli and Snyder, Baldwin's Ohio Practice, Evidence, § 301.15, Selected Presumptions.

Carlin, Baldwin's Ohio Practice, Merrick-Rippner Probate Law § 26:7, Testamentary Capacity—Defining Capacity—Factors Bearing on Capacity—Insanity and Psychosis.

Carlin, Baldwin's Ohio Practice, Merrick-Rippner Probate Law § 38:13, Will Contests—Trial—Procedure.

Carlin, Baldwin's Ohio Practice, Merrick-Rippner Probate Law § 38:14, Will Contests—Trial—Attorney as Witness.

Law Review and Journal Commentaries

Destruction of a Testamentary Trust by Agreement as Incidental to the Compromise of a Will Contest, Note. 4 U Cin L Rev 524 (November 1930).

Notes of Decisions

Ed. Note: *This section contains annotations from former RC 2741.07, RC 2141.05, RC 2741.01, RC 2741.05, and RC 2107.23.*

Appeal 4
Burden of proof 2
Evidence 3
Prima facie evidence 1

Procedural issues 5

1. Prima facie evidence

A copy of probate and record of a will, duly certified by the probate judge, is conclusive evidence of the validity of the will on the trial of a collateral issue between a stranger and a devisee under the will respecting the property devised, and is admissible in trial of such issue, notwithstanding the fact that proceedings are pending to contest the validity of the same at the time it is offered and admitted as evidence. Brown v. Burdick (Ohio 1874) 25 Ohio St. 260.

The omission of the record to state that the destruction of a will was subsequent to the testatrix's death does not render void the order admitting a transcript of such will to probate; such a will is entitled to the same prima facie effect as the statute gives to an order probating an original will. Converse v. Starr (Ohio 1872) 23 Ohio St. 491.

The record of the probate of a lost will is prima facie evidence, in a contest proceeding, not only of the due attestation on execution of will but also of its contents. Banning v. Banning (Ohio 1861) 12 Ohio St. 437.

Although RC 2107.74 provides that the order admitting a will to probate is prima facie evidence of the attestation, execution, and validity of the will, that section does not create an irrebuttable presumption of validity. Krischbaum v. Dillon (Ohio 1991) 58 Ohio St.3d 58, 567 N.E.2d 1291.

Words appearing after the signature claimed to be meaningless and surplusage and not dispositive, do not as matter of law show that the will was not signed at the end, but the order of probate makes a prima facie case and the proponents are entitled to offer "other evidence" and the jury must determine whether the signature is at the end. Hane v. Kintner (Ohio 1924) 111 Ohio St. 297, 145 N.E. 326, 2 Ohio Law Abs. 676, 22 Ohio Law Rep. 522.

In a will contest action, it is error for the trial court to fail to explain in its charge to the jury that the order of probate is prima facie evidence of the validity of the will and raises the presumption that the writing is the last will and testament of the testatrix. Hall v. Hall (Ohio 1908) 78 Ohio St. 415, 85 N.E. 1125.

In a will contest action, the order of probate is prima facie evidence of the validity of the will, and the plaintiff may not attack the regularity of the order of probate, but must limit inquiry to the issue whether the writing admitted at probate was the testator's last will vel non. Stacey v. Cunningham (Ohio 1903) 69 Ohio St. 176, 48 W.L.B. 993, 68 N.E. 1001, 1 Ohio Law Rep. 583, 1 Ohio Law Rep. 717.

2. Burden of proof

Under this section, at the trial of a will contest, the order of probate shall be prima facie evidence of the due attestation, execution, and validity of the will, and after the order of probate is offered in evidence, the effect is to transfer the burden of proof from the propounders to the contestants of the will. Mears v. Mears (Ohio 1864) 15 Ohio St. 90. Wills ⟹ 288(3)

In a will contest, by virtue of the statute, the burden of proof is cast upon the contestant of the will and such burden never shifts from him, so that if the evidence produced furnishes only a basis for a choice among different possibilities he fails to sustain such burden. Kata v. Second Nat. Bank of Warren (Ohio 1971) 26 Ohio St.2d 210, 271 N.E.2d 292, 55 O.O.2d 458. Evidence ⟹ 94

In a will contest, the burden of proof is cast upon the contestant of the will before a jury would be justified in setting aside a will, the evidence adduced in the case against the will must outweigh both the evidence adduced in favor of the will and the presumption arising from the order of the probate court admitting the will to probate as the valid last will and testament of the testator. Kennedy v. Walcutt (Ohio 1928) 118 Ohio St. 442, 161 N.E. 336, 6 Ohio Law Abs. 206, 26 Ohio Law Rep. 215.

Instructions by the trial court in a will contest must clearly define the rule that the evidence introduced by contestant, in order that he may prevail, must be a preponderance, outweighing both the evidence produced by the contestee and the presumption of validity that arises from probate of the will. West v. Lucas (Ohio 1922) 106 Ohio St. 255, 139 N.E. 859, 1 Ohio Law Abs. 72, 20 Ohio Law Rep. 470, 20 Ohio Law Rep. 471. Wills ⟹ 329(3)

In a contest of a will admitted to probate as a lost will, where the allegation of the petition is that such paper was not the last will of the deceased, but that the testator revoked it by destroying it, and that the will was not lost or spoliated after his decease, and the proof of plaintiff tended to show only that the testator destroyed the will, and that it was in his custody shortly before his death, and could not be found shortly after it, it is not error to charge that the burden is on plaintiff to establish that the paper is not testator's last will, and to show by a preponderance of the evidence that testator did during his lifetime destroy the will with the intent of revoking it. Hutson v. Hartley (Ohio 1905) 72 Ohio St. 262, 74 N.E. 197, 3 Ohio Law Rep. 3. Wills ⟹ 331(2)

Where a will is made, and the testator retains the custody of it, and after his death it cannot be found, the presumption arises that he destroyed it with the intention of revoking it; but when a copy of it is admitted to probate, such presumption is necessarily rebutted, and the burden of proof in an action to contest such will is on the plaintiff to show that the testator in fact did revoke it before his death. Hutson v. Hartley (Ohio 1905) 72 Ohio St. 262, 74 N.E. 197, 3 Ohio Law Rep. 3.

The establishment by the probate court of a cost or listed will is prima facie evidence of the will thus abolished for all purposes, including all that relate to the rest of the same; thus, after the copy of the will as probated the probate record has been introduced by the contestees, burden of invalidating the will is upon the contestants. (See also Gurley v Armentraut, 6 CC(NS) 156, 17 CD 199 (Wayne 1904).) Hutson v. Hartley (Ohio 1905) 72 Ohio St. 262, 74 N.E. 197, 3 Ohio Law Rep. 3.

In an action to contest a will on the ground that it was not signed at the end thereof, as required by RS 5916 (repealed 1932. See GC 10504–3), its construction is not a subject for consideration, the only question being whether it has been executed in substantial compliance with the statute. Irwin v. Jacques (Ohio 1905) 71 Ohio St. 395, 73 N.E. 683, 2 Ohio Law Rep. 442. Wills ⟹ 311

Once the probate court has found and established the contents of a lost, spoliated, or destroyed will, the order of probate is prima facie evidence of its due attestation, execution, validity, and contents, and in a will contest action the burden of proof is upon the contestant to invalidate such a will. Behrens v. Behrens (Ohio 1890) 47 Ohio St. 323, 24 W.L.B. 286, 25 N.E. 209, 21 Am.St.Rep. 820. Wills ⟹ 288(3)

Jury instructions in a will contest action which shift the burden of proof onto the defendant to prove mental capacity and lack of undue influence are manifestly wrong and prejudicial to the defendant in view of the rule that an order of probate is prima facie evidence of the validity of the will, and the contesters have the burden of disproving such evidence. West v. Knoppenberger (Ohio Cir. 1903) 16 Ohio C.D. 168, 4 Ohio C.C.N.S. 305.

After probate the burden of proving incapacity is upon the contestant. Ousley v. Witheron (Ohio Cir. 1896) 7 Ohio C.D. 448.

The burden of proof is upon those propounding the will to make out a prima facie case showing that the testator, at time of execution of the will, was of sound mind and memory. In re Ludlow's Estate (Ohio Prob. 1897) 6 Ohio Dec. 106, 4 Ohio N.P. 99.

3. Evidence

Where a testatrix makes her will under the influence of her purported husband in an unlawful marriage, the will is not void for that reason alone, unless such influences were exerted in restraint of the will of the testatrix. Monroe v. Barclay (Ohio 1867) 17 Ohio St. 302, 93 Am.Dec. 620.

Particular objections to a will which has been admitted to probate can only be known as they may be developed in the testimony offered by those opposing the will, and to require those affirming the will either to finally rest their case on the order of probate or to introduce all the evidence they may have sustaining the will on every ground possible would not promote justice; thus, the contestees may introduce additional evidence sustaining the will after the contestants have introduced their testimony. Runyan v. Price (Ohio 1864) 15 Ohio St. 1, 86 Am.Dec. 459.

Declarations by a legatee who is a party to a will contest proceeding in reference to the mental capacity of the testator are not admissible in evidence to impeach the will where there are other legatees or devisees whose interests may be injuriously affected by the admission of such evidence. Thompson v. Thompson (Ohio 1862) 13 Ohio St. 356. Evidence ⟹ 226(4); Wills ⟹ 53(1)

Evidence supported trial court's finding that daughter did not exercise undue influence over mother's decision to change her will such that daughter would be main devisee, even though mother had long intended to equally divide her estate among her children; daughter took mother in to care, testimony indicated that mother was still competent during that time, and sibling was not denied access to mother while in daughter's care. Miscoi v. Rogers (Ohio App. 5 Dist., Stark, 10-27-2003) No. 2002CA00386, 2003-Ohio-5768, 2003 WL 22435255, Unreported. Wills ⟹ 166(2)

A claim of undue influence is unsupported by evidence to the contrary that the testator was an alert feisty older woman with a mind of her own who at the time of execution of her will understood the extent of her estate given her tendency to show off her beloved home and antiques to anyone who would listen or take time to view them and that she understood the identities of her natural heirs who inherit nothing under the will which leaves to the testator's stepdaughter an estate worth an estimated $600,000; the fact that the testator is diagnosed with dementia approximately ten months after she executes the will is no evidence of her state of mind at the time of the execution of the will. Wise v. Riddlebaugh (Ohio App. 3 Dist., Marion, 05-29-1997) No. 9-97-6, 1997 WL 280628, Unreported.

Psychiatrist's testimony was insufficient to satisfy conclusion that testatrix lacked testamentary capacity to execute will, even though psychiatrist diagnosed testatrix as having personality disorder with chronic alcoholism, where psychiatrist testified that testatrix was not mentally ill, was of above average intelligence with good memory other than short term memory infirmities created by alcohol, and did indeed manage her day to day affairs. Doyle v. Schott (Hamilton 1989) 65 Ohio App.3d 92, 582 N.E.2d 1057, motion overruled 49 Ohio St.3d 708, 551 N.E.2d 1304. Wills ⇔ 55(6)

In a will contest the order of probate is prima facie evidence of the attestation, execution and validity of the will; in order to prevail, the contestant must produce sufficient evidence to do more than merely to meet the prima facie case, or "presumption" arising from the order of probate. Carr v. Howard (Fayette 1969) 17 Ohio App.2d 233, 246 N.E.2d 563, 46 O.O.2d 360.

The mere existence of undue influence or an opportunity to exercise it, although coupled with an interest or motive to do so, is not sufficient to invalidate a will, but such influence must be actually exerted on the mind of the testator with respect to the execution of the will in question; and, in order to invalidate the will, it must be shown that the undue influence resulted in the making of testamentary dispositions which the testator would not otherwise have made. West v. Henry (Ohio 1962) 173 Ohio St. 498, 184 N.E.2d 200, 20 O.O.2d 119. Wills ⇔ 158

Where will of person is made after he has been adjudicated insane and will after being admitted to probate becomes subject of will contest, presumption of continuance of insanity is a rebuttable one and will be removed when sufficient evidence has been introduced to meet, extinguish, or overcome such presumption arising from the adjudication of insanity. Hermann v. Crossen (Cuyahoga 1959) 160 N.E.2d 404, 81 Ohio Law Abs. 322. Wills ⇔ 52(4)

Where testator subscribed will in presence of witnesses four days after they had subscribed will in testator's presence, resubscription by witnesses held unnecessary to validate will where they did not expressly disaffirm their signatures at time of testator's subscription in heir presence. Bloechle v. Davis (Ohio 1937) 132 Ohio St. 415, 8 N.E.2d 247, 8 O.O. 249. Wills ⇔ 123(4)

Order of probate is prima facie evidence of attestation as well as execution and validity of will. Instructions in will contest must clearly define rule that evidence introduced by contestant to warrant setting aside will must be preponderance, outweighing both evidence produced by contestee and presumption of validity arising from probate of will. Instruction to find against will if one or both of signatures of subscribing witnesses was not genuine held properly refused because instruction did not also incorporate presumption arising from probate of will. Steinle v. Kester (Darke 1932) 46 Ohio App. 245, 188 N.E. 395, 13 Ohio Law Abs. 497, 39 Ohio Law Rep. 415.

Instruction that, if deceased at time of executing alleged will labored under delusion, and paper was result thereof, paper was void, held erroneous, since only "insane" delusion affecting will invalidates it. Warn v. Whipple (Lucas 1932) 45 Ohio App. 285, 187 N.E. 88, 13 Ohio Law Abs. 461, 39 Ohio Law Rep. 49. Wills ⇔ 330(2)

In will contest, though petition did not allege specific grounds of contest, excluding evidence respecting relations between testator and favored son, unjustness of will, and incoherent talk by testator, held prejudicial error. Fox v. Lynch (Perry 1932) 43 Ohio App. 305, 183 N.E. 177, 13 Ohio Law Abs. 142. Wills ⇔ 400

Where bill of exceptions does not contain all evidence, alleged errors in exclusion of evidence cannot be considered on appeal. Aston v. Hauck (Hamilton 1926) 22 Ohio App. 430, 153 N.E. 277, 4 Ohio Law Abs. 319. Appeal And Error ⇔ 701(2); Exceptions, Bill Of ⇔ 12

Where testator stated in his will that it was made in case he met with an accident on a contemplated journey, but lived for one year and two months after such possible calamity had passed without change in his circumstances or those of the beneficiaries named in the will and without having changed or revoked the will which was in his personal custody, a strong presumption arises that the statement was not intended as a contingency or a condition precedent. McMerriman v. Schiel (Ohio 1923) 108 Ohio St. 334, 140 N.E. 600, 1 Ohio Law Abs. 883, 21 Ohio Law Rep. 151, 21 Ohio Law Rep. 152. Wills ⇔ 80

The fact that the evidence in a will contest case was sufficient to satisfy the judge that no undue influence was exerted, if he had tried the issue without a jury, is not alone sufficient to warrant withdrawing the issue from the jury. Board of Education of Pickaway Tp. Rural School Dist. v. Phillips (Ohio 1921) 103 Ohio St. 622, 134 N.E. 646, 19 Ohio Law Rep. 516. Wills ⇔ 324(3)

Courts cannot except from GC 11494, proceedings involving validity of will, it being presumed that Legislature in enacting sections 11494–11495, relating to competency of witness, had whole subject before it. Swetland v. Miles (Ohio 1920) 101 Ohio St. 501, 130 N.E. 22, 18 Ohio Law Rep. 309, 18 Ohio Law Rep. 432. Constitutional Law ⇔ 70.1(8); Witnesses ⇔ 36

In the contest of a will, a witness cannot give an opinion as to whether the testator had capacity to make a will; but, that the jury may determine such capacity, his physical and mental condition may be shown. Bahl v. Byal (Ohio 1914) 90 Ohio St. 129, 106 N.E. 766, 11 Ohio Law Rep. 519. Evidence ⇔ 478(1); Wills ⇔ 293(1)

A will was written on a blank form, folded in the middle, and containing three ruled pages marked with a printed heading. There were numerous testamentary clauses, and one naming the executor, occupying the first and a portion of the second page. Then a blank space was left between such clauses and the testimonium clause at the bottom of page 3. At the end of the testimonium clause testatrix signed her name, immediately following which was the attestation clause signed by two witnesses. There was no testamentary provision after her signature. Held, that the will was signed at the end thereof, as required by RS 5916 (repealed 1932. See GC 10504–3). Mader v. Apple (Ohio 1909) 80 Ohio St. 691, 89 N.E. 37, 131 Am.St.Rep. 719, 7 Ohio Law Rep. 117. Wills ⇔ 111(2)

The ground of contest of a will which had been admitted to probate was that testator had destroyed the will with intention of revoking it. The evidence showed that testator removed from the instrument and tore one of its several pages, leaving the will otherwise intact. Held not a revocation of the will within RS 5953 (repealed 1932. See GC 10504–47), providing that a will shall be revoked by tearing or destroying the same with the intention of revoking it. Coghlin v. Coghlin (Ohio 1908) 79 Ohio St. 71, 85 N.E. 1058, 6 Ohio Law Rep. 517. Wills ⇔ 174

Where a testator took care to separate one of several pages of his will and to preserve all of the instrument except that page, his conduct is inconsistent with intention to revoke the will, and in a will contest after such will has been admitted to probate, the allegation that the will was revoked is not sustained by such evidence. Coghlin v. Coghlin (Ohio 1908) 79 Ohio St. 71, 85 N.E. 1058, 6 Ohio Law Rep. 517.

Where, on application to the probate court, it was alleged that a will was in existence after death of testatrix and was lost, and a paper alleged to contain the substance of the lost will was admitted to probate, and in proceedings to set the probate aside the jury returned a verdict that the paper was not the last will of testatrix, and in answer to the question whether the paper claimed to be the last will was signed by testatrix answered "Don't know," and as to whether it was signed in her presence by subscribing witnesses answered "Don't know," such answers were not inconsistent with the general verdict. Bloor v. Platt (Ohio 1908) 78 Ohio St. 46, 84 N.E. 604, 5 Ohio Law Rep. 619, 14 Am.Ann.Cas. 332. Trial ⇔ 359(1); Wills ⇔ 333

The order admitting a lost will to probate is prima facie evidence of its validity, and in order to set aside such probate plaintiff must prove by a preponderance of the evidence either lack of mental capacity, undue influence, or that the alleged writing was not the last will and testament of the testatrix. Bloor v. Platt (Ohio 1908) 78 Ohio St. 46, 84 N.E. 604, 5 Ohio Law Rep. 619, 14 Am.Ann.Cas. 332.

A will is not signed at the end thereof, within RS 5916 (repealed 1932. See GC 10504–3), when it is written by the party making it on a printed blank form containing a testimonium clause, with blanks for the name of the place and the date of execution, which he fills, and immediately following a blank line for the signature, which he leaves blank, though he has written his name in the attestation clause, immediately following the testimonium clause, in a blank left for the name of testator, and may have intended such act as a signing. Sears v. Sears (Ohio 1907) 77 Ohio St. 104, 82 N.E. 1067, 5 Ohio Law Rep. 495, 11 Am.Ann.Cas. 1008. Wills ⇔ 111(2)

In an action to contest a will which has been admitted to probate, the issue to be tried, as prescribed by RS 1892, § 5861, is whether the writing produced is the last will or codicil of the testator, or not: and on the trial of this issue the question whether the will was properly admitted to probate is not involved and cannot be inquired into. Stacey v. Cunningham (Ohio 1903) 69 Ohio St. 176, 48 W.L.B. 993, 68 N.E. 1001, 1 Ohio Law Rep. 583, 1 Ohio Law Rep. 717. Wills ⚖ 311

Although the specific ground of contest to which the evidence relates is not alleged in the petition, upon trial any competent evidence tending to show that the writing produced is not the last will and testament of the testator is admissible and should receive proper consideration by the jury. Dew v. Reid (Ohio 1895) 52 Ohio St. 519, 33 W.L.B. 275, 40 N.E. 718, 2 Ohio Leg. N. 516.

A will may not be set aside due to the fact that the testator was afflicted with progressive locomotor ataxia and partially paralyzed, where during that time he directed the operation and management of a large farm business and did all that could have been done by a person of a sound and active mind, and the only testimony which went to the question of mental capacity was the testator's forgetfulness on certain occasions. Gregg v. Moore (Ohio Cir. 1911) 23 Ohio C.D. 534, 14 Ohio C.C.N.S. 570.

A testator is not required to make an equitable will, and because he makes one with which the witnesses for the contestants do not agree does not mean he lacks testamentary capacity, even though the evidence shows some physical weaknesses, failure of memory, or a mistake of an unimportant character in connection with business affairs of the testator. Wilson v. Wilson (Ohio Cir. 1909) 22 Ohio C.D. 498, 14 Ohio C.C.N.S. 241.

In an action to contest a will the jury must be instructed that in order to set aside the will the evidence of the contestants should not only outweigh the defendant's evidence but also the presumption arising from the order admitting the will to probate; the declarations by a party to the record who is a legatee with others under the will are inadmissible to prove that the will was contrary to the testator's intentions or was procured by undue influence. Seal v. Goebel (Ohio Cir. 1908) 21 Ohio C.D. 286, 11 Ohio C.C.(N.S.) 433, affirmed 81 Ohio St. 523, 91 N.E. 1138, 7 Ohio Law Rep. 500.

Where a witness to the execution of a will is not prevented by death or otherwise from being present to testify in a will contest, an affidavit of the witness made in connection with the admission of the will to probate is not competent evidence in the suit to break the will. Kettemann v. Metzger (Ohio Cir. 1901) 13 Ohio C.D. 61, 3 Ohio C.C.N.S. 224.

In a will contest action where plaintiff demanded an examination of witnesses to the will and all witnesses are dead, the will may be admitted to probate where such will is valid on its face and plaintiff offers no further evidence concerning the invalidity of the will. Burian v Burian, No. 45646 (8th Dist Ct App, Cuyahoga, 8–4–83).

4. Appeal

Where a will is probated and admitted to record on an application within the jurisdiction of the court, error will not lie to review the testimony upon which it was admitted. Mosier v. Harmon (Ohio 1876) 29 Ohio St. 220.

An order of a probate court admitting a will to probate is not a final appealable order; the only available challenge to such an order is a will contest, which is in the nature of an original action or "trial de novo," in the court of common pleas. Carr v. Howard (Fayette 1969) 17 Ohio App.2d 233, 246 N.E.2d 563, 46 O.O.2d 360.

Order of probate court admitting an instrument to probate as a last will is not reviewable on appeal. In re Frey's Estate (Ohio 1942) 139 Ohio St. 354, 40 N.E.2d 145, 22 O.O. 411. Appeal And Error ⚖ 77(2)

5. Procedural issues

The only mode of contesting the validity of a will that has been admitted to probate is expressly given by statute, is exclusive, and must be pursued in that manner or the contestants' rights shall be forever barred. Mosier v. Harmon (Ohio 1876) 29 Ohio St. 220.

A court sitting as a probate court in the trial of an issue made up to determine the validity of a will cannot be legally required to give construction of the provisions of the will or to pass upon the validity or invalidity of doubtful legacies or bequests therein contained; the jurisdiction of a probate court is limited to the probate of the will, and its construction is left to other tribunals. Mears v. Mears (Ohio 1864) 15 Ohio St. 90.

The order of probate of a will is not conclusive as against proper proceedings to establish and probate a later will. Stafford v. Todd (Ohio App. 2 Dist. 1921) 17 Ohio App. 114. Wills ⚖ 432

A party to a will contest action does not have the right to a jury trial; instead, a probate court has discretion to determine whether to sit as the trier of fact in a will contest action or to impanel a jury. State ex rel. Kear v. Court of Common Pleas of Lucas County, Probate Division (Ohio 1981) 67 Ohio St.2d 189, 423 N.E.2d 427, 21 O.O.3d 118. Jury ⚖ 19(7.5)

Request in will contest to charge jury that, if credible proof of forgery was adduced, jury could no longer entertain presumption that subscribing witness, testifying that will was duly executed, told truth, held properly refused. Scholl v. Sterkel (Richland 1933) 46 Ohio App. 389, 189 N.E. 15, 16 Ohio Law Abs. 491, 40 Ohio Law Rep. 9. Wills ⚖ 329(3)

Action to contest will, designated civil action by express terms of GC 12079, is subject to GC §11455 (repealed 1931. See § 11420–9), permitting rendition of verdict by jury on concurrence of three-fourths or more. Niemes v. Niemes (Ohio 1917) 97 Ohio St. 145, 119 N.E. 503, 15 Ohio Law Rep. 484, 15 Ohio Law Rep. 565. Trial ⚖ 321.5; Wills ⚖ 333

In the contest of a will, the admission of an answer to the question to a witness whether the testator had capacity to form an intent to dispose of his property is not error justifying the setting aside of a verdict sustaining the will. Dunlap v. Dunlap (Ohio 1913) 89 Ohio St. 28, 104 N.E. 1006, 11 Ohio Law Rep. 294, 11 Ohio Law Rep. 318. Wills ⚖ 400

An order admitting a will to probate is prima facie evidence only of its validity, and an argument in a will contest emphasizing probate to influence the jury constitutes misconduct of counsel. Wadsworth v. Purdy (Ohio Cir. 1908) 21 Ohio C.D. 110, 12 Ohio C.C.N.S. 8.

Under Ohio law, final judgment in prior state court action upholding validity of will in will contest action brought by decedent's putative daughter barred, under doctrine of res judicata, daughter's subsequent action in federal court seeking to invalidate trust incorporated by reference in decedent's will, where trustee was party to state action, issues concerning validity of trust were resolved in state action, and daughter had every reason to present all arguments challenging trust at state action. Rushford v. Firstar Bank, N.A. (C.A.6 (Ohio), 10-28-2002) No. 01-3487, 50 Fed. Appx. 202, 2002 WL 31424545, Unreported. Wills ⚖ 432

2107.75 Defense of questionable will taxed as cost of administration

When the jury or the court finds that the writing produced is not the last will and testament or codicil of the testator, the trial court shall allow as part of the costs of administration such amounts to the fiduciary and to the attorneys defending such purported last will or purported codicil as the trial court finds to be reasonable compensation for the services rendered in such contest. The court shall order such amounts to be paid out of the estate of the decedent.

(1975 S 145, eff. 1–1–76)

Historical and Statutory Notes

Ed. Note: 2107.75 contains provisions analogous to former 2741.04, repealed by 1975 S 145, eff. 1–1–76.

Library References

Wills ⚖405, 415.
Westlaw Topic No. 409.
C.J.S. Wills §§ 787, 792 to 795.

Research References

Encyclopedias

OH Jur. 3d Decedents' Estates § 1123, Applicability of Rules of Civil Procedure; Transfer of Venue.
OH Jur. 3d Decedents' Estates § 1238, Costs, Generally—Attorney's and Fiduciary's Fees.
OH Jur. 3d Decedents' Estates § 1366, When May Representative Employ Attorney: for Consultation—for the Prosecution and Defense of Suits.
OH Jur. 3d Decedents' Estates § 1367, When May Representative Employ Attorney: for Consultation—Will Contests.

Treatises and Practice Aids

Carlin, Baldwin's Ohio Practice, Merrick-Rippner Probate Law § 3:3, Jurisdiction of Probate Court—Subject Matter—in General.
Carlin, Baldwin's Ohio Practice, Merrick-Rippner Probate Law § 53:1, Fiduciary's Attorney—Appointment, Fees.

Carlin, Baldwin's Ohio Practice, Merrick-Rippner Probate Law § 80:1, Commissions—Statutory.

Carlin, Baldwin's Ohio Practice, Merrick-Rippner Probate Law § 80:3, Commissions—Determination of Compensation Other Than by Percentage.

Carlin, Baldwin's Ohio Practice, Merrick-Rippner Probate Law § 38:18, Will Contests—Attorney Fees.

Carlin, Baldwin's Ohio Practice, Merrick-Rippner Probate Law § 38:23, Verdict in Will Contest—Form.

Carlin, Baldwin's Ohio Practice, Merrick-Rippner Probate Law § 38:24, Judgment on Verdict—Form.

Carlin, Baldwin's Ohio Practice, Merrick-Rippner Probate Law § 80:10, Extraordinary Services—Compensation Allowed.

Carlin, Baldwin's Ohio Practice, Merrick-Rippner Probate Law § 80:13, Extraordinary Services—Procedure in Allowance of Fees to Fiduciary and Attorney.

Carlin, Baldwin's Ohio Practice, Merrick-Rippner Probate Law § 80:15, Attorney Fees—Allowed.

Notes of Decisions

Ed. Note: This section contains annotations from former RC 2741.04.

Constitutional issues 1
Contract for fees 5
Entitlement to compensation 4
Fee determination by court 2
Fiduciary services 3

---

1. Constitutional issues

Former GC 12082 (RC 2741.04), as amended effective July 4, 1945, and authorizing the allowance as a part of the costs of administration of a decedent's estate, attorney fees for an unsuccessful defense of a purported will, is not unconstitutional, does not deprive the contestees of property without due process of law, and is not unreasonable. Lindsey v. Markley (Tuscarawas 1950) 87 Ohio App. 529, 96 N.E.2d 311, 43 O.O. 317. Constitutional Law ⇐ 317(1); Wills ⇐ 413

2. Fee determination by court

Court of Appeals could not review whether beneficiaries were entitled to attorney fees related to will contest, where estate was still open, and there was no final order on the matter. Hoeck v. Varner (Ohio App. 7 Dist., Carroll, 12-16-2003) No. 02CA781, 2003-Ohio-7113, 2003 WL 23018731, Unreported. Wills ⇐ 394

Trial court acted reasonably in denying beneficiaries of estate attorney fees for costs incurred in prosecuting contempt proceedings against former executrix, even though executrix's actions were egregious, where consequences of executrix's actions were exacerbated by beneficiaries inaction. Hoeck v. Varner (Ohio App. 7 Dist., Carroll, 12-16-2003) No. 02CA781, 2003-Ohio-7113, 2003 WL 23018731, Unreported. Contempt ⇐ 68

In denying attorney's request for fees for unsuccessfully defending will contest, trial court was required to explain how and why it reached conclusion that attorney had not proven reasonableness of fees and expenses submitted. In re Estate of Szczotka (Ohio App. 11 Dist., 03-24-2006) 166 Ohio App.3d 302, 849 N.E.2d 302, 2006-Ohio-1449. Executors And Administrators ⇐ 111(3)

Statute providing for payment, as an administrative expense, of the fees incurred for the unsuccessful defense of a will contest is applicable only to the fiduciary and the fiduciary's attorney. In re Estate of Szczotka (Ohio App. 11 Dist., 03-24-2006) 166 Ohio App.3d 124, 849 N.E.2d 302, 2006-Ohio-1449. Executors And Administrators ⇐ 111(3)

Attorney who represented executor in unsuccessful will contest was entitled to reasonable attorney fees; executor, who was also beneficiary under will, was not acting solely for his own benefit, but also acted on behalf of co-beneficiary, and successful defense of will would have benefited entire estate as contemplated by will. In re Estate of Szczotka (Ohio App. 11 Dist., 03-24-2006) 166 Ohio App.3d 302, 849 N.E.2d 302, 2006-Ohio-1449. Executors And Administrators ⇐ 111(3)

A probate court has discretion under RC 2107.75 to determine the reasonable value, if any, of the services of an executor or an attorney defending a purported will in a will contest action, based on all the facts and circumstances of the particular case. Trubulas v. Doland (Hamilton 1987) 39 Ohio App.3d 62, 528 N.E.2d 1313, reversed in part 42 Ohio St.3d 8, 536 N.E.2d 642.

The fiduciary and attorneys defending a purported will in a will contest action are entitled to reasonable compensation for the services rendered in such contest, and no fees for services in appeals attacking a judgment finding such paper writing not to be the last will alleged are allowable; and, in the fixing of such fees, it is error to consider the grounds of the will contest. Logeman v. Wagner (Hamilton 1966) 7 Ohio App.2d 48, 218 N.E.2d 761, 36 O.O.2d 124.

3. Fiduciary services

Executor, who employed counsel to defend against testator's stepchildren's action to enforce antenuptial agreement, which required testator to leave her entire estate to stepchildren, was entitled to recover fees from the estate pursuant to statute allowing costs of defending a will to be taxed to the estate; although executor was also a beneficiary under testator's will, there was no evidence that she was merely trying to advance her personal interests rather than trying to determine whether decedent's last wishes could be carried out. In re Estate of Dawson (Ohio App. 2 Dist., 12-27-1996) 117 Ohio App.3d 51, 689 N.E.2d 1008. Executors And Administrators ⇐ 216(2)

Where a nominated trustee under a will undertakes and performs a duty ordinarily performed by the named executrix in the will, but which duty the named executrix fails and refuses to perform, such nominated trustee is entitled to reasonable compensation for the services rendered. In re Allison's Will (Clark 1965) 9 Ohio App.2d 333, 224 N.E.2d 386, 38 O.O.2d 388.

Where the executor of an estate under administration in the probate court, being under no obligation to participate in litigation involving principally the interests of the beneficiaries under the will, participates in such litigation at the request of such beneficiaries in order to protect their interests, he is entitled to compensation for extraordinary services, and consideration for such agreements consists of performance by the executor of services beyond the scope of his duties as executor. Doty v. Peters (Madison 1958) 106 Ohio App. 435, 155 N.E.2d 239, 7 O.O.2d 181. Wills ⇐ 749

4. Entitlement to compensation

RC 2107.75, which provides that the trial court shall allow as part of the costs of the administration to be paid out of the estate compensation to the fiduciary and to the attorneys defending a purported last will or purported codicil, is applicable only to the fiduciary and the fiduciary's attorney; neither the beneficiaries of a defeated will nor their attorneys are entitled to compensation under this statute. In re Estate of Zonas (Ohio 1989) 42 Ohio St.3d 8, 536 N.E.2d 642.

A probate court may allow, as a part of the expense in the administration of a decedent's estate, compensation to an executor and attorney for services rendered in the successful defense of such decedent's will. In re Teopas' Estate (Lucas 1960) 116 Ohio App. 506, 188 N.E.2d 616, 22 O.O.2d 322.

Where legal services provided by an attorney defending a will contest action primarily benefit the defendant-beneficiary and not the estate as a whole, an award of attorney fees to the defendant will be reversed. Vogel v Thiel, No. 16–89–6 (3d Dist Ct App, Wyandot, 6–26–90).

5. Contract for fees

Payment of attorney fees is proper in will contest actions, even if party defending the will is unsuccessful. In re Estate of Dawson (Ohio App. 2 Dist., 12-27-1996) 117 Ohio App.3d 51, 689 N.E.2d 1008. Wills ⇐ 412.1

RC 2741.04 does not prohibit a contract between an attorney and a beneficiary under a will, providing for the amount which is to be paid for services rendered in defending such will, and a probate court is not precluded from allowing, as a part of the expense in the administration of a decedent's estate, compensation to an executor and attorney for services rendered in the defense of such will. In re Teopas' Estate (Lucas 1960) 116 Ohio App. 506, 188 N.E.2d 616, 22 O.O.2d 322.

2107.76 Contest of will within three months; exceptions; rights not affected

(A) No person who has received or waived the right to receive the notice of the admission of a will to probate required by section 2107.19 of the Revised Code may commence an action permitted by section 2107.71 of the Revised Code to contest the validity of the will more than three months after the filing of the certificate described in division (A)(3) of section 2107.19 of the Revised Code. No other person may commence an action permitted by section 2107.71 of the Revised Code to contest the validity of the will more than three months after the initial filing of a certificate described in division (A)(3) of section 2107.19 of the Revised Code. A person under any legal disability nevertheless may commence an action permitted by section 2107.71 of the Revised Code to contest the validity of the will within three months after the disability is removed, but the rights saved shall not affect the rights of a purchaser, lessee, or encumbrancer for value in good faith and shall not impose any liability upon a fiduciary who has acted in good faith, or upon a person delivering or transferring property to any other person under authority of a will, whether or not the purchaser, lessee, encumbrancer, fiduciary, or other person had actual or constructive notice of the legal disability.

(B) Section 2305.19 of the Revised Code does not apply to an action permitted by section 2107.71 of the Revised Code to contest the validity of a will.

(2006 H 144, eff. 6–15–06; 2001 H 85, eff. 10–31–01; 1994 H 208, eff. 6–23–94; 1990 H 346, eff. 5–31–90; 1978 H 505; 1976 S 466)

Uncodified Law

1990 H 346, § 3, eff. 5–31–90, reads:

(A) Sections 1 and 2 of this act shall apply only to the estates of decedents who die on or after the effective date of this act.

(B) It is the intent of the General Assembly in the outright repeal of sections 2107.13 and 2107.14 of the Revised Code and the amendments to sections 109.30, 2107.18, 2107.19, 2107.22, 2107.27, 2107.76, 2115.16, and 2703.14 of the Revised Code by this act, to respond to the dicta of the Supreme Court in *Palazzi v. Estate of Gardner* (1987), 32 Ohio St. 3d 169 and to enact statutory provisions relating to notice of probate proceedings that are not unconstitutional as potentially violative of the due process of law rights of nonresidents of this state.

Historical and Statutory Notes

Ed. Note: 2107.76 contains provisions analogous to former 2107.23, repealed by 1976 S 466, eff. 5–26–76.

Amendment Note: 2006 H 144 designated division (A); added the second sentence in newly designated division (A); substituted "three" for "four" in the third sentence of newly designated division (A); and added new division (B).

Amendment Note: 2001 H 85 rewrote this section which prior thereto read:

"No person who has received or waived the right to receive the notice of the admission of a will to probate required by section 2107.19 of the Revised Code may commence an action permitted by section 2107.71 of the Revised Code to contest the validity of the will more than four months after the filing of the certificate described in division (A)(3) of section 2107.19 of the Revised Code certifying the giving of that notice to or the waiver of that notice by that person. No other person may commence an action permitted by section 2107.71 of the Revised Code to contest the validity of the will more than four months after the initial filing of a certificate described in division (A)(3) of section 2107.19 of the Revised Code. A person under any legal disability nevertheless may commence an action permitted by section 2107.71 of the Revised Code to contest the validity of the will within four months after the disability is removed, but the rights saved shall not affect the rights of a purchaser, lessee, or encumbrancer for value in good faith and shall not impose any liability upon a fiduciary who has acted in good faith, or upon a person delivering or transferring property to any other person under authority of a will, whether or not the purchaser, lessee, encumbrancer, fiduciary, or other person had actual or constructive notice of the legal disability."

Amendment Note: 1994 H 208 rewrote this section, which previously read:

"If, within four months after the filing by an executor of the affidavit described in division (A)(3) of section 2107.19 of the Revised Code, the filing of the affidavit described in division (B) of that section, or both types of affidavits, no person files an action permitted by section 2107.71 of the Revised Code to contest the validity of the will, the probate shall be forever binding, except as to persons under any legal disability, or to such persons for four months after such disability is removed. The rights saved shall not affect the rights of a purchaser, lessee, or encumbrancer for value in good faith, and shall not impose any liability upon a fiduciary who has acted in good faith, or upon a person delivering or transferring property to any other person under authority of a will, whether or not the purchaser, lessee, encumbrancer, fiduciary, or other person had actual or constructive notice of the legal disability."

Cross References

Marketable Title Act, 5301.47 to 5301.53
Reckoning time, 1.14

Library References

Wills ⚖=260.
Westlaw Topic No. 409.
C.J.S. Wills §§ 532 to 534.
  Baldwin's Ohio Legislative Service, 1990 Laws of Ohio, H 346—LSC Analysis, p 5–87

Research References

ALR Library
3 ALR 5th 590, What Constitutes Contest or Attempt to Defeat Will Within Provision Thereof Forfeiting Share of Contesting Beneficiary.

Encyclopedias
  OH Jur. 3d Actions § 175, Effect of "Savings Statute" on Recommencement of Action.
  OH Jur. 3d Decedents' Estates § 1022, Nature and Effect of Order.
  OH Jur. 3d Decedents' Estates § 1100, The State of Ohio.
  OH Jur. 3d Decedents' Estates § 1116, Statutory Time Limitation, Generally.
  OH Jur. 3d Decedents' Estates § 1117, Statutory Time Limitation, Generally—for Persons Under a Disability.
  OH Jur. 3d Decedents' Estates § 1118, When Action Commenced.
  OH Jur. 3d Limitations & Laches § 97, Infancy.

Treatises and Practice Aids
Carlin, Baldwin's Ohio Practice, Merrick-Rippner Probate Law § 2:14, Probating the Will—Appeal—Will Contest.
Carlin, Baldwin's Ohio Practice, Merrick-Rippner Probate Law § 38:2, Will Contests—Statutory Provisions.
Carlin, Baldwin's Ohio Practice, Merrick-Rippner Probate Law § 38:3, Will Contests—Later Will Admitted to Probate.
Carlin, Baldwin's Ohio Practice, Merrick-Rippner Probate Law § 38:4, Will Contests—Interested Persons.
Carlin, Baldwin's Ohio Practice, Merrick-Rippner Probate Law § 38:6, Will Contests—Capacity to Contest a Will.
Carlin, Baldwin's Ohio Practice, Merrick-Rippner Probate Law § 38:7, Will Contests—Commencement of Action; Limitation of Actions.
Carlin, Baldwin's Ohio Practice, Merrick-Rippner Probate Law § 38:8, Will Contests—Parties to Action—Necessary Parties.
Carlin, Baldwin's Ohio Practice, Merrick-Rippner Probate Law § 38:10, Will Contests—Service of Process.
Carlin, Baldwin's Ohio Practice, Merrick-Rippner Probate Law § 38:16, Will Contests—Termination Action—Dismissal Not on the Merits.
Carlin, Baldwin's Ohio Practice, Merrick-Rippner Probate Law § 38:17, Will Contests—Termination—Directed Verdict, Summary Judgment, and Judgment Notwithstanding the Verdict.
Carlin, Baldwin's Ohio Practice, Merrick-Rippner Probate Law App B SPF 2.0, Application to Probate Will.
Carlin, Baldwin's Ohio Practice, Merrick-Rippner Probate Law App B SPF 2.1, Waiver of Notice of Probate of Will.
Carlin, Baldwin's Ohio Practice, Merrick-Rippner Probate Law App B SPF 2.2, Notice of Probate of Will.
Kuehnle and Levey, Ohio Real Estate Law and Practice § 16:12, Curative Acts—Decedent's Estates—Validity of Sale, Lease, or Encumbrance by Fiduciary as Against Persons Under Disability Entitled to Contest Will.

Law Review and Journal Commentaries

Cox v. Saadeh: A Warning to the Wary in Will Contests. Angela G. Carlin, 13 Prob L J Ohio 11 (September/October 2002).

Rest in Peace—or Thy Will Be Done, Ellis V. Rippner. 28 Ohio St L J 647 (Fall 1967).

The Uniform Trust Code (2000) and Its Application to Ohio. David M. English, 12 Prob L J Ohio 1 (September/October 2001).

When the Savings Statute Does Not Save, Stanley B. Kent. 56 Clev B J 300 (October 1985).

Notes of Decisions

Ed. Note: This section contains annotations from former RC 2741.01, 2107.23, 2741.09, 2741.02, 2741.08, 2107.02, and 2741.04.

In general 1
Attorney misconduct in drafting will 5
Operation of statute of limitations and saving clause 2
Procedure and appeal 3
Spurious will, remedies 4

---

1. In general

The only mode of contesting the validity of a will that has been admitted to probate is expressly given by statute, is exclusive, and must be pursued in that manner or the contestants' rights shall be forever barred. Mosier v. Harmon (Ohio 1876) 29 Ohio St. 220.

Proposed written settlement agreement prepared by counsel for decedent's daughters, which sought to memorialize an oral settlement of daughters' will contest and which also addressed additional matters not covered by the oral settlement, did not constitute a counteroffer that executor of decedent's estate was free to reject; settlement was valid and binding once executor's oral offer was orally accepted. Brown v. Dillinger (Ohio App. 9 Dist., Medina, 03-22-2006) No. 05CA0040-M, 2006-Ohio-1307, 2006 WL 709117, Unreported. Wills ⇔ 212

Oral settlement offer by executor of estate to settle a will contest, which was orally accepted by decedent's daughters, did not have to be reduced to a written settlement agreement in order to constitute a valid settlement agreement. Brown v. Dillinger (Ohio App. 9 Dist., Medina, 03-22-2006) No. 05CA0040-M, 2006-Ohio-1307, 2006 WL 709117, Unreported. Wills ⇔ 212

Sufficient evidence established that decedent's two daughters orally accepted an offer by executor of decedent's estate to settle their will contest for a payment of $15,000 each, despite executor's contention that she withdrew her offer before the agreement was put into writing; daughters both testified that they accepted the offer once it was communicated to them, and there was no evidence executor conditioned the offer on the signing of a written settlement agreement, but rather executor attempted to further condition her original offer after it was accepted by daughters. Brown v. Dillinger (Ohio App. 9 Dist., Medina, 03-22-2006) No. 05CA0040-M, 2006-Ohio-1307, 2006 WL 709117, Unreported. Wills ⇔ 212

Allegedly misnamed party in will had burden of proving that party as named in will was a misnomer and that a legal entity was the intended beneficiary for bequest, otherwise gift would fail. Beaston v. Slingwine (Ohio App. 3 Dist., 12-15-2003) 155 Ohio App.3d 505, 801 N.E.2d 916, 2003-Ohio-6702, vacated and superseded on reconsideration 2004-Ohio-924, 2004 WL 370408. Wills ⇔ 703

Neither death nor the inability to sue due to a delay in the appointment of a legal representative is a "legal disability" under RC 2131.02 for purposes of tolling the four-month statute of limitations found in RC 2107.76 for bringing a will contest action under RC 2107.71. Mayfield v. Herderick (Franklin 1986) 33 Ohio App.3d 44, 514 N.E.2d 441.

The savings clause of RC 2305.19 is not applicable to an action to contest the validity of a will pursuant to RC 2107.76. Barnes v. Anderson (Ashtabula 1984) 17 Ohio App.3d 142, 478 N.E.2d 248, 17 O.B.R. 242.

The exercise of the right to contest a will is dependent upon compliance with the statutory requirements upon which such right is based, and any failure to comply with such statutes extinguishes such right. Donovan v. Decker (Franklin 1953) 98 Ohio App. 183, 122 N.E.2d 501, 68 Ohio Law Abs. 353, 57 O.O. 230.

Word "person" in this section, is defined in GC 10213 (RC 1.02, RC 1.10) and does not include the state of Ohio. State ex rel. Rich v. Page (Ohio Com.Pl. 1941) 6 Ohio Supp. 104, 33 Ohio Law Abs. 647, 20 O.O. 155.

2. Operation of statute of limitations and saving clause

Where a petition for a will contest is filed within the statutory period of limitation, although only part of the persons interested are made parties thereto, the right of action is saved as to all who are ultimately made parties, notwithstanding some of them are not brought into the case until after the period of limitations has expired. Bradford v. Andrews (Ohio 1870) 20 Ohio St. 208, 5 Am.Rep. 645. Limitation Of Actions ⇔ 124; Wills ⇔ 260

Where one heir is exempt from the statute of limitations by reason of her infancy, and upon reaching her majority has the decedent's will set aside within the limitation period, the statute avails for all the heirs since the interests under the will are nonseverable; the will is thus wholly annulled and the entire estate is distributed. Meese v. Keefe (Ohio 1841) 10 Ohio 362.

Former devisees and legatees, who had been named in decedent's prior will, but were not named in decedent's last will and testament, were not subject to three month statute of limitations applicable to will contests, where statute specifically applied only to surviving spouse, those who would inherit intestate, and those named in will, and former devisees and legatees were not such persons. Tomasik v. Tomasik (Ohio App. 9 Dist., Summit, 10-20-2004) No. 21980, 2004-Ohio-5558, 2004 WL 2348170, Unreported, appeal allowed 105 Ohio St.3d 1469, 824 N.E.2d 540, 2005-Ohio-1186. Wills ⇔ 260

Probate court was not authorized to grant executor's motion to dismiss action challenging validity of will, on grounds that claim involved was not timely filed, notwithstanding the fact that the motion mischaracterized the claim as jurisdictional rather than one asserting a prohibited statute of limitation defense, where executor did not plead failure to satisfy statute of limitation as an affirmative defense to claim in either of the two answers she filed. Chase v. Kiernan (Ohio App. 2 Dist., Greene, 05-28-2004) No. 2003CA70, 2004-Ohio-2745, 2004 WL 1178762, Unreported. Wills ⇔ 283

Saving statute, permitting refiling of actions that were initially timely filed but had failed on issues other than merits, applied to will contests and, thus, claimant, who had voluntarily dismissed will contest action without prejudice, could refile contest after statute of limitations had expired. Allen v. McBride (Ohio, 12-30-2004) 105 Ohio St.3d 21, 821 N.E.2d 1001, 2004-Ohio-7112. Limitation Of Actions ⇔ 130(5)

Three-month statute of limitations for bringing a will contest did not apply to testator's nieces and nephews who were not entitled to notice of admission of will to probate; even though prior and subsequent versions of statute set limitations period for persons not entitled to notice, the statute in effect at time of will contest contained no such provision and was unambiguous. Tomasik v. Tomasik (Ohio, 12-06-2006) 111 Ohio St.3d 481, 857 N.E.2d 127, 2006-Ohio-6109. Wills ⇔ 260

The only persons held to three-month limitations period for filing will contests under former statute are those who must be given notice of a will's admission to probate, i.e., the surviving spouse of the testator, all persons who would be entitled to inherit from the testator if the testator had died intestate, and all legatees and devisees named in the will. Tomasik v. Tomasik (Ohio, 12-06-2006) 111 Ohio St.3d 481, 857 N.E.2d 127, 2006-Ohio-6109. Wills ⇔ 260

Pursuant to RC 2107.72, the Rules of Civil Procedure govern all aspects of a will contest action, except as otherwise provided in RC 2107.71 to 2107.75; thus, the failure to name all necessary parties to a will contest action within the four-month period set forth in RC 2107.76 is not an absolute bar to a will contest action in Ohio since as long as one proper party files the action within four months after a will is admitted to probate, other necessary parties may be joined by amending the pleadings, which amendments will relate back to the date of the original filing pursuant to Civ R 15(C). Trubulas v. Doland (Hamilton 1987) 39 Ohio App.3d 62, 528 N.E.2d 1313, reversed in part 42 Ohio St.3d 8, 536 N.E.2d 642.

Great-grandchildren of a decedent who are not legatees under the will are not "persons interested" in the will for purposes of bringing a will contest action under RC 2107.71; therefore, the fact that the great-grandchildren of decedent are under the legal disability of minority does not toll the four-month statute of limitations for filing a will contest, since the great-grandchildren have no standing to file such suit. Mayfield v. Herderick (Franklin 1986) 33 Ohio App.3d 44, 514 N.E.2d 441.

A nonresident heir who fails to bring an action challenging the constitutionality of the notice provision of RC 2107.13, as applied to nonresidents, within four months of receiving actual notice of his grandfather's death lacks standing to challenge RC 2107.13 as applied to him. Palazzi v. Estate of Gardner (Ohio 1987) 32 Ohio St.3d 169, 512 N.E.2d 971.

The savings clause of RC 2305.19 does not apply to a cause of action created by statute (in this case, a will contest) which is unknown to the common law and which in terms contains its own statute of limitations. Alakiotis v. Lancione (Ohio Com.Pl. 1966) 12 Ohio Misc. 257, 232 N.E.2d 663, 41 O.O.2d 381.

In will contest, all necessary parties must be before court either as plaintiffs or defendants within statutory six months or contest is not properly filed and case should be dismissed. Kluever v. Cleveland Trust Co. (Cuyahoga 1961) 173 N.E.2d 183, 86 Ohio Law Abs. 79, affirmed 173 Ohio St. 177, 180 N.E.2d 579, 18 O.O.2d 461. Wills ⚖ 265.1

The interested persons in a will contest action must be named and made parties within six months after probate of the will. Fletcher v. First Nat. Bank of Zanesville (Ohio 1958) 167 Ohio St. 211, 147 N.E.2d 621, 4 O.O.2d 268. Wills ⚖ 265.1

Nonresident next-of-kin who are legatees or devisees under a will are not thereby entitled to contest a will after expiration of the six month statutory period merely because they did not receive the notice to which they were entitled as legatees or devisees. Feeley v. First Nat. Bank & Trust Co. of Hamilton (Ohio Com.Pl. 1948) 124 N.E.2d 800, 69 Ohio Law Abs. 317, 55 O.O. 324.

Where a petition to contest a will is filed and the executor, who is also a beneficiary, is named as a defendant in his individual capacity only, the court does not have jurisdiction to hear the cause, and such jurisdiction is not invoked by the filing of a cross-petition naming the executor in his fiduciary capacity as well as in his individual capacity where service of summons on such cross-petition was not made on the executor as such until after six months from the date of probate of the will. Woodruff v. Norvill (Hancock 1951) 91 Ohio App. 251, 107 N.E.2d 911, 48 O.O. 361. Wills ⚖ 260

Action to contest a will is not commenced within six months of probate, where an original petition and precipe, filed within the six months, are abandoned and a new precipe is attached to an amended petition filed after the six months have expired. It is not sufficient that a petition to contest and precipe for summons be filed within the time prescribed, but summons must also be issued within that time. Coughlin v. Passionist Monastery of the Holy Cross (Ohio App. 1938) 59 Ohio App. 433, 18 N.E.2d 496, 27 Ohio Law Abs. 353, 13 O.O. 199.

Where no devisees, legatees, or transferee of any legatee or devisee was summoned within one year after admitting will to probate, will contest would not lie. Sours v. Shuler (Hancock 1932) 42 Ohio App. 393, 181 N.E. 908, 12 Ohio Law Abs. 108, 36 Ohio Law Rep. 544. Wills ⚖ 260

Probate court cannot vacate order of probate after statutory period for contest, even if will is conclusively proven spurious. Petitt v. Morton (Cuyahoga 1930) 38 Ohio App. 348, 176 N.E. 494, 10 Ohio Law Abs. 436, affirmed 124 Ohio St. 241, 177 N.E. 591, 10 Ohio Law Abs. 574. Judgment ⚖ 386(7); Wills ⚖ 221

Under former GC 10531 (RC 2107.23) and 12087 (RC 2741.09), a court is without jurisdiction to entertain an action for the contest of a will commenced subsequent to the time prescribed therein. McCord v. McCord (Cuyahoga 1922) 104 Ohio St. 274, 135 N.E. 548, 19 Ohio Law Rep. 739.

Exceptions under GC 12087, extending the time for contesting a will to more than two years, are to be strictly construed, and cannot be enlarged by considerations of apparent hardship or inconvenience. McVeigh v. Fetterman (Ohio 1917) 95 Ohio St. 292, 116 N.E. 518, 15 Ohio Law Rep. 19, 15 Ohio Law Rep. 30. Wills ⚖ 260

RS 5933 and RS 5866 allow two years after probating of a will for a contest, saving, however, persons under disability, while the general savings provisions of RS 4989 prevent the two-year period from running against an individual disabled by absence from the state until he comes into Ohio; where the individual absent from the state is brought in by another standing in loco parentis, the time begins to elapse though the presence is short and notwithstanding the individual's minority, nor is the disability of absence revived by leaving the state. Powell v. Koehler (Ohio 1894) 52 Ohio St. 103, 33 W.L.B. 20, 39 N.E. 195, 49 Am.St.Rep. 705, 2 Ohio Leg. N. 192.

When a right of action to contest a will is saved under RS 5933 and RS 5866 because of disabilities such as infancy and absence from Ohio, the saving inures to the benefit of all other parties interested in the estate. Powell v. Koehler (Ohio 1894) 52 Ohio St. 103, 33 W.L.B. 20, 39 N.E. 195, 49 Am.St.Rep. 705, 2 Ohio Leg. N. 192. Limitation Of Actions ⚖ 70(1); Wills ⚖ 417

A granddaughter, upon attaining her majority and thirteen years after the probate of her grandmother's will, is not estopped from contesting the will by the fact that while she was a child of tender years the executors, one of whom was her guardian, distributed the available assets of the estate without filing an inventory or obtaining an order of distribution, or filing any report thereof. Swetland v. Miles (Knox 1920) 35 Ohio C.D. 458, 31 Ohio C.A. 529, affirmed 101 Ohio St. 501, 130 N.E. 22, 18 Ohio Law Rep. 309, 18 Ohio Law Rep. 432.

An action contesting a will dismissed for want of prosecution can be recommenced within one year of dismissal by virtue of RS 4991, even though the petition in this second action is not filed until after the two years allowed by the statute of limitations for original institution of a will contest have elapsed. Hunt v. Hunt (Ohio Com.Pl. 1904) 15 Ohio Dec. 571, 2 Ohio N.P.N.S. 577.

Where a will has been probated and the statutory period for contest has run, a disinherited heir has no standing to bring suit to revise or rescind a contract made by the decedent and a third party beneficiary, wherein decedent agreed to name the third party as beneficiary, as the validity of such contract will not affect the validity of the will. Weissberg v Kurtz, No. 44571 (8th Dist Ct App, Cuyahoga, 10–28–82).

Suit is not deemed commenced until date of issuance of summons which is properly served; unless such date is within time prescribed action will be defeated though waivers of service were obtained from some of defendants, which were not filed but held by counsel. (See also 12 Abs 268 (1932).) Wirt v Wirt, 13 Abs 11 (App, Mahoning 1932).

3. Procedure and appeal

Where a will is probated and admitted to record on an application within the jurisdiction of the court, error will not lie to review the testimony upon which it was admitted. Mosier v. Harmon (Ohio 1876) 29 Ohio St. 220.

Trial court did not commit prejudicial error when it sustained objection to hypothetical question posed to expert witness in will contest, regarding whether expert could form opinion as to whether or not it was probable testator suffered from extreme fatigue on date that she executed will; jurors were already aware that decedent was taking drugs that made her sleepy and tired before counsel asked hypothetical question about extreme fatigue. Roll v. Edwards (Ohio App. 4 Dist., Ross, 02-21-2006) No. 05CA2833, 2006-Ohio-830, 2006 WL 439423, Unreported. Wills ⚖ 400

Owner of adult care center had burden of establishing in will contest suit that deceased patient intended to bequest residuary of estate to center by leaving residuary of estate to the "Extended Family Adult Care," even though center's correct name was "Extended Family Adult Care Center." Beaston v. Slingwine (Ohio App. 3 Dist., Seneca, 03-01-2004) No. 13-03-04, 2004-Ohio-924, 2004 WL 370408, Unreported. Wills ⚖ 703

Evidence showing how testator's daughter from a prior marriage discovered that testator, and later testator's new wife, passed away did not establish the laches defense asserted by wife's estate, as to daughter's challenge to the validity of testator's will, in probate proceeding for testator's wife, who had been sole beneficiary of testator's will. Harmon-Butts v. Zoloty (Ohio App. 9 Dist., Medina, 04-30-2003) No. 02CA0075-M, 2003-Ohio-2155, 2003 WL 1984127, Unreported. Wills ⚖ 261

Trial court misunderstood question to be put to jury on remand in will contest case, and thus matter was subject to second remand so that proper question could be addressed, where Court of Appeals intended jury to determine whether inaccurately named business in will was merely a misnomer for correct name, but trial court asked jury to determine whether will intended gift to go to business named or to its owner. Beaston v. Slingwine (Ohio App. 3 Dist., 12-15-2003) 155 Ohio App.3d 505, 801 N.E.2d 916, 2003-Ohio-6702, vacated and superseded on reconsideration 2004-Ohio-924, 2004 WL 370408. Wills ⚖ 401

Presumption that will contest complaint was untimely, arising from file-stamped date on pleading, was not rebutted by testimony that complaint naming wrong executor was timely filed nor receipt from clerk of court showing that filing fee was deposited in another case on last date for filing contest and, thus, contest complaint was untimely. Stevenson v. Wenner (Ohio App. 3 Dist., 03-30-1995) 102 Ohio App.3d 289, 656 N.E.2d 1386. Wills ⚖ 259

The amending of a complaint in a will contest to add a necessary party may relate back to the filing of the original complaint if the conditions listed in Civ R 15(C) are satisfied. Weaver v. Donnerberg (Shelby 1985) 26 Ohio App.3d 112, 498 N.E.2d 496, 26 O.B.R. 323.

Amendments adding necessary parties may be made to a complaint in a will contest action and relate back to the date of the original filing pursuant to Civ R 15(C); due to a change in the law relating to will contest actions, the application of the rule no longer operates to expand the jurisdiction of probate courts in violation of Civ R 82. Smith v. Klem (Ohio 1983) 6 Ohio St.3d 16, 450 N.E.2d 1171, 6 O.B.R. 13.

The will contest action is a special statutory proceeding and any civil rule which would permit the liberal amendment or joinder adding a necessary party relating the cause of action back to within the time limitation of RC 2741.09 would by its nature be clearly inapplicable as it would operate to extend the jurisdiction of the courts of this state in derogation of mandatory statutory language. (Superseded by statute as stated in Smith v Klem, 6 OS(3d) 16, 6 OBR 13, 450 NE(2d) 1171 (1983).) Holland v. Carlson (Cuyahoga 1974) 40 Ohio App.2d 325, 319 N.E.2d 362, 69 O.O.2d 299.

An heir at law, who is not named as a party in a will contest action within a period of six months from the date of probate, cannot at a later date vitalize the contest action by filing in the action a waiver of service, entry of appearance, and consent to the prayer of the petition. Williams v. Wilfong (Summit 1961) 114 Ohio App. 183, 181 N.E.2d 314, 19 O.O.2d 63. Wills ⇐ 265.1

An action to contest a will admitted to probate on January 25 is brought within the statutory period where such action is instituted on July 25, on the same day there is filed a praecipe and summons issued for thirteen defendants, designated as heirs at law and devisees and who are served on July 26, and an affidavit and order for service by publication on two nonresident defendants, who with a cemetery are designated as the only other legatees and devisees, the first publication is made on July 26 and publication completed but no notice mailed to such two defendants and the cemetery is served on July 26. Cover v. Hildebran (Darke 1957) 103 Ohio App. 413, 145 N.E.2d 850, 3 O.O.2d 435.

A party to a will contest action properly commenced within the statutory period of limitation and in conformity with statutory requirements may not withdraw from such action, and thereby defeat the right of the other parties to a jury trial to determine the validity of the will, and where a party to such action has been dismissed as a plaintiff, he may be made a party defendant; and where others in the same class have been properly served with summons, such party may be served after the six-month period of limitation. Frederick v. Brown (Scioto 1956) 102 Ohio App. 117, 141 N.E.2d 683, 2 O.O.2d 115.

An interested person who initiates an action to contest a will within six months after probate may not thereafter dismiss the action over the protest of a defendant who wants the will set aside. Andes v. Shippe (Ohio 1956) 165 Ohio St. 275, 135 N.E.2d 396, 59 O.O. 363.

Where in will contest action brought by certain heirs at law the petition names as defendants the sole legatee and devisee, the executrix and three other heirs at law but fails to name numerous other heirs at law, and no service of process is sought or secured on any of the defendant heirs within six months after the will has been admitted to probate, the addition as plaintiffs of the heirs at law not included in the petition and the defendant heirs at law not served with summons after the expiration of the statutory period of limitation does not confer jurisdiction on the court to hear such contest. Gravier v. Gluth (Ohio 1955) 163 Ohio St. 232, 126 N.E.2d 332, 56 O.O. 228. Wills ⇐ 268

Where a will contest is brought within the statutory time provided therefor but the petition fails to disclose that the plaintiff is a party interested in the will involved, an amendment of the petition to allege facts showing that the plaintiff is an interested party will be in furtherance of justice; and such an amendment may be made after the statutory period for the bringing of such will contest. Morton v. Fast (Ohio 1953) 159 Ohio St. 380, 112 N.E.2d 385, 50 O.O. 335.

An order of the probate court admitting a paper to probate as a last will and testament is not reviewable on petition in error, though an order refusing to admit such paper to probate is reviewable. Hollrah v. Lasance (Ohio 1900) 63 Ohio St. 58, 44 W.L.B. 80, 57 N.E. 964. Wills ⇐ 356

An order admitting a will to probate is not reviewable on error, but may only be challenged in a properly filed will contest action. Hollrah v. Lasance (Ohio 1900) 63 Ohio St. 58, 44 W.L.B. 80, 57 N.E. 964.

After a will has been duly admitted to probate and the validity of the will has been sustained in a contest of will action, the probate court is without jurisdiction to thereafter entertain an action to redetermine the validity of the will. Bailey v McElroy, 120 App 85, 195 NE(2d) 559, 28 OO(2d) 286 (App 1963).

Where plaintiff alleges her failure to contest a will within the statutory limitation period was caused by a disability as evidenced by her physician's affidavit, the trial court properly dismisses such action where evidence is presented that the plaintiff consulted with her attorney, issued certain documents relative to the will contest action, and gave her daughter a general power of attorney during her alleged period of disability. Barber v Barber, No. 1241 (11th Dist Ct App, Portage, 12–23–82).

4. Spurious will, remedies

Probative value of testimony of attorney who prepared will, that he worked as a magistrate in probate/juvenile court, was substantially outweighed by unfair prejudice, in will contest; evidence of attorney's position as magistrate in same court where will contest was tried had little probative value, and unfair prejudice was substantial, since evidence could have enhanced attorney's credentials in the eyes of jurors, and jurors could have assigned more weight to his testimony based upon their knowledge of his current employment. Roll v. Edwards (Ohio App. 4 Dist., Ross, 02-21-2006) No. 05CA2833, 2006-Ohio-830, 2006 WL 439423, Unreported. Evidence ⇐ 146

Trial court's error, if any, in limiting cross-examination of executrix of estate, daughter of decedent, was harmless in will contest; although husband and son of decedent argued that they had right to cross-examine executrix for purpose of showing bias, executrix openly admitted that she had fights over the years with her father and her brother, and jury was well aware of her possible bias. Roll v. Edwards (Ohio App. 4 Dist., Ross, 02-21-2006) No. 05CA2833, 2006-Ohio-830, 2006 WL 439423, Unreported. Wills ⇐ 400

Husband and son of decedent waived issue on appeal in will contest that they had right to cross-examine executrix of estate for purpose of showing bias, where husband and son did not state on record purpose of bias at time when trial court could have considered it. Roll v. Edwards (Ohio App. 4 Dist., Ross, 02-21-2006) No. 05CA2833, 2006-Ohio-830, 2006 WL 439423, Unreported. Wills ⇐ 396

Trial court did not abuse its discretion in limiting cross-examination of executrix of estate in will contest; court, throughout trial, generally considered evidence irrelevant when it involved matters that occurred after will's execution, and evidence in question, financial decisions regarding administration of estate, involved matters that occurred after will's execution. Roll v. Edwards (Ohio App. 4 Dist., Ross, 02-21-2006) No. 05CA2833, 2006-Ohio-830, 2006 WL 439423, Unreported. Witnesses ⇐ 270(2)

Trial court was not required to give proposed jury instruction, which included added language that it was essential to validity of will that testator knew and understood its actual contents and that will could not be said to express testator's mind when testator was ignorant of contents of will, in will contest; court gave standard jury instruction regarding testamentary capacity, and instruction included all the elements of testamentary capacity, and thus, court's instruction was fair and correct statement of law. Roll v. Edwards (Ohio App. 4 Dist., Ross, 02-21-2006) No. 05CA2833, 2006-Ohio-830, 2006 WL 439423, Unreported. Wills ⇐ 330(1)

If, as alleged, defendants deliberately destroyed and suppressed will, and fabricated and forged another will, and had latter probated by aid of perjured testimony, devisee under first will had cause of action against defendants. Morton v. Petitt (Ohio 1931) 124 Ohio St. 241, 177 N.E. 591, 10 Ohio Law Abs. 574. Torts ⇐ 289; Wills ⇐ 211

Beneficiary of unprobated will, not contesting probated spurious will within statutory period, because of ignorance of fraud, may sue in tort the wrongdoers who suppress the true will and procure execution and probate of the spurious will. Petitt v. Morton (Cuyahoga 1930) 38 Ohio App. 348, 176 N.E. 494, 10 Ohio Law Abs. 436, affirmed 124 Ohio St. 241, 177 N.E. 591, 10 Ohio Law Abs. 574. Torts ⇐ 289; Wills ⇐ 211; Torts ⇐ 291

Where will has been forged by a person named in it as sole beneficiary and such person has obtained the probate of the will without notice to the next of kin and has obtained the transfer to him of the legal title to the property of the decedent, such person is trustee ex maleficio of such property for the benefit of the next of kin in a suit in equity brought by the next of kin within four years of his discovery of the fraud. Seeds v. Seeds (Ohio 1927) 116 Ohio St. 144, 156 N.E. 193, 52 A.L.R. 761, 5 Ohio Law Abs. 174, 25 Ohio Law Rep. 259.

5. Attorney misconduct in drafting will

The privity exception to the *Simon v. Zipperstein* rule, which provided than an attorney was immune from liability to third parties arising from his performance as an attorney in good faith unless such third party is in privity with the client or the attorney acts maliciously, applied to allow testator's two children to pursue a legal malpractice claim against attorney and law firm that assisted in the transfer of all of testator's stock in closely held corporation to her grandson; testator, as the majority shareholder in closely held corporation, owed a fiduciary duty to her two children, who were minority shareholders, and attorney and law firm owed a fiduciary duty to testator, their client, and thus testator's children were in privity with testator for the purpose of the stock transfer. LeRoy v. Allen Yurasek & Merklin (Ohio App. 3 Dist., Union, 08-29-2005) No. 14-04-49, 2005-Ohio-4452, 2005 WL 2064144, Unreported.

The maliciousness exception to the *Simon v. Zipperstein* rule, which provided than an attorney was immune from liability to third parties arising from his performance as an attorney in good faith unless such third party was in privity with the client or the attorney acted maliciously, applied to allow testator's two children to pursue a legal malpractice claim against attorney and law firm that executed testator's will; testator's children specifically alleged that there was a conflict of interest in attorney's representation of testator as well as testator's son and grandson, and children alleged that attorney and law firm committed acts in collusion with testator's son and grandson. LeRoy v. Allen Yurasek & Merklin (Ohio App. 3 Dist., Union, 08-29-2005) No. 14-04-49, 2005-Ohio-4452, 2005 WL 2064144, Unreported. Attorney And Client ☞ 26

The maliciousness exception to the *Simon v. Zipperstein* rule, which provided than an attorney was immune from liability to third parties arising from his performance as an attorney in good faith unless such third party was in privity with the client or the attorney acted maliciously, applied to allow testator's two children to pursue a legal malpractice claim against attorney and law firm that executed testator's will; testator's children specifically alleged that there was a conflict of interest in attorney's representation of testator as well as testator's son and grandson, and children alleged that attorney and law firm committed acts in collusion with testator's son and grandson. LeRoy v. Allen, Yurasek & Merklin (Ohio App. 3 Dist., 08-29-2005) 162 Ohio App.3d 155, 832 N.E.2d 1246, 2005-Ohio-4452, opinion vacated and superseded on reconsideration 2005-Ohio-4452, 2005 WL 2064144, appeal allowed 108 Ohio St.3d 1411, 841 N.E.2d 317, 2006-Ohio-179, appeal allowed 108 Ohio St.3d 1435, 842 N.E.2d 61, 2006-Ohio-421. Attorney And Client ☞ 26

Trial court was required to consider the alleged bad faith of attorney and law firm in drafting testator's will and transferring her stock shares to grandson as an element of fraud, collusion, or other malicious conduct, rather than considering it on its own, when determining whether attorney and law firm waived their immunity from legal malpractice suit brought by testator's children. LeRoy v. Allen, Yurasek & Merklin (Ohio App. 3 Dist., 08-29-2005) 162 Ohio App.3d 155, 832 N.E.2d 1246, 2005-Ohio-4452, opinion vacated and superseded on reconsideration 2005-Ohio-4452, 2005 WL 2064144, appeal allowed 108 Ohio St.3d 1411, 841 N.E.2d 317, 2006-Ohio-179, appeal allowed 108 Ohio St.3d 1435, 842 N.E.2d 61, 2006-Ohio-421. Attorney And Client ☞ 26

2107.77 Contest of later wills

Sections 2107.71 to 2107.76 of the Revised Code apply to later wills admitted to probate.

(1976 S 466, eff. 5–26–76)

Historical and Statutory Notes

Ed. Note: 2107.77 contains provisions analogous to former 2107.25 repealed by 1977 H 1, eff. 8–26–77.

Cross References

Privileged communications and acts; will contests, 2317.02

Library References

Wills ☞254 to 265.1.
Westlaw Topic No. 409.
C.J.S. Wills §§ 527 to 538, 540.

Research References

Encyclopedias

OH Jur. 3d Decedents' Estates § 1080, Contest of Later Wills Admitted to Probate.

Forms

Ohio Forms Legal and Business § 24:951, Agreement Not to Contest Will—Between Testator and Heirs.

Treatises and Practice Aids

Klein, Darling, & Terez, Baldwin's Ohio Practice Civil Practice § 82:5, Jurisdiction--Civil Rule Arguably Wholly Inapplicable Pursuant to Civ. R. 82.

Giannelli and Snyder, Baldwin's Ohio Practice, Evidence, R 101, Scope of Rules: Applicability; Privileges; Exceptions.

Giannelli and Snyder, Baldwin's Ohio Practice, Evidence, § 101.17, Special Non-Adversary Statutory Proceedings.

Carlin, Baldwin's Ohio Practice, Merrick-Rippner Probate Law § 3:3, Jurisdiction of Probate Court—Subject Matter—in General.

Carlin, Baldwin's Ohio Practice, Merrick-Rippner Probate Law § 5:8, Evidentiary Matters—Privileged Communications—Protected Relationships—Physician or Dentist and Patient—Waiver of the Privilege.

Carlin, Baldwin's Ohio Practice, Merrick-Rippner Probate Law § 38:2, Will Contests—Statutory Provisions.

Carlin, Baldwin's Ohio Practice, Merrick-Rippner Probate Law § 38:3, Will Contests—Later Will Admitted to Probate.

Carlin, Baldwin's Ohio Practice, Merrick-Rippner Probate Law § 38:11, Will Contests—Pleadings.

Carlin, Baldwin's Ohio Practice, Merrick-Rippner Probate Law § 38:12, Will Contests—Pretrial Procedure.

Carlin, Baldwin's Ohio Practice, Merrick-Rippner Probate Law § 38:13, Will Contests—Trial—Procedure.

CHAPTER 2108

HUMAN BODIES OR PARTS THEREOF

DEFINITIONS

Section	
2108.01	Definitions

ANATOMICAL GIFTS

Section	
2108.02	Gift of body or part; rights of next of kin to donate; when donee shall not accept; examination; rights of donee and of coroner conducting autopsy
2108.021	Protocol for facilitating procurement of anatomical gifts
2108.03	Permissible donees
2108.04	Instrument of gift
2108.05	Delivery or deposit of instrument
2108.06	Manner of amendment or revocation
2108.07	Acceptance and use of body; time of death
2108.071	Enucleation of eyes; definition
2108.08	Person who acts in good faith not liable
2108.09	Adoption of Uniform Anatomical Gift Act; uniform construction
2108.10	Forms of document of gift
2108.101	Validity of prior gift designations

MISCELLANEOUS PROVISIONS

Section	
2108.11	Transaction involving human fluids or body parts not a sale
2108.12	Sale of human body parts prohibited
2108.15	Second chance trust fund
2108.17	Second chance trust fund advisory committee
2108.18	Donor registry developed by motor vehicles bureau
2108.19	Toll–free telephone number maintained by motor vehicles bureau
2108.20	Immunities
2108.21	Seventeen–year–olds may donate blood; publicity

DETERMINATION OF DEATH

Section	
2108.30	Determination that death has occurred; immunity of physician

POST–MORTEM EXAMINATION

Section	
2108.50	Consent for post-mortem examination
2108.51	Exemption from liability
2108.52	Exceptions to requirement of consent for post-mortem examination

Section

2108.521 Petition for post-mortem examination upon suspicious death of mentally retarded or developmentally disabled person; hearing; order to perform post-mortem examination
2108.53 Pituitary gland may be removed; rights of next of kin
2108.60 Coroner may remove eye for medical use; right of next of kin to object; good faith action protected

DISPOSITION OF REMAINS AND PURCHASE OF GOODS AND SERVICES RELATED TO FUNERAL

2108.70 Assignment of right to direct disposition of remains after death and purchase goods and services related to funeral; designation of successor representative
2108.71 Vesting of assignment or reassignment of right of disposition
2108.72 Contents of declaration of assignment of right of disposition; form of written declaration
2108.73 Execution of written declaration
2108.74 Truthfulness of declaration
2108.75 Disqualification from serving as a representative or successor representative
2108.76 Former spouse as representative or successor representative
2108.77 Additional criteria for disqualification from serving as representative or successor representative
2108.78 Assignment of right of disposition relating to anatomical gifts
2108.79 Majority vote prevails when representative or successor representative is group or class of persons; probate court to decide when no majority decision
2108.80 Revocation of assignment
2108.81 Priority of assignment of right of disposition
2108.82 Probate court may assign right of disposition; criteria considered
2108.83 Disputes relating to right of disposition; immunity from liability
2108.84 Preservation of remains while dispute pending; cost
2108.85 Court costs; legal fees; criminal or civil liability for failure to bring legal action
2108.86 Right to good faith reliance on written declaration and instructions; criminal or civil liability
2108.87 Duty to independently investigate existence or locate representative or successor representative
2108.88 Resignation of right of disposition
2108.89 Liability for cost of goods and services relating to exercise of right of disposition
2108.90 Exclusive jurisdiction

PENALTY

2108.99 Penalty

Cross References

AIDS testing of anatomical gifts, informed consent, 3701.242

Law Review and Journal Commentaries

Advancing the Rights of Children and Adolescents to be Altruistic: Bone Marrow Donation by Minors, Jennifer K. Robbennolt, Victoria Weisz, Craig M. Lawson. 9 J L & Health 213 (1994–95).

Ancient Answers to Modern Questions: Death, Dying, and Organ Transplants—A Jewish Law Perspective, Stephen J. Merber. 11 J L & Health 13 (1996–1997).

Anencephalic Infants As Organ Donors: A Question Of Life Or Death, Note. 40 Case W Res L Rev 781 (1989–90).

Assessing Patient Compliance in the Selection of Organ Transplant Recipients, Note. 6 Health Matrix: J Law–Medicine 503 (Summer 1996).

Bioethics symposium: Thinking about biomedical advances: The role of ethics and law. Lance Tibbles et al., 31 Cap U L Rev 1 (2003).

The Concept of Death, Carl E. Wasmuth, Jr. 30 Ohio St L J 32 (Winter 1969).

Organ Transplantation: The Doctor's Dilemma and the Lawyer's Responsibility, Frank E. Woodside. 31 Ohio St L J 66 (Winter 1970).

Overcoming the Legal Obstacles to the Creation of a Futures Market in Bodily Organs, Gregory S. Crespi. 55 Ohio St L J 1 (1994).

A Paper Tiger: Lawsuits Against Doctors for Non–Disclosure of Economic Interests In Patients' Cells, Tissues and Organs, Note. 42 Case W Res L Rev 565 (1992).

Property interests in cadaverous organs: Changes to Ohio anatomical gift law and the erosion of family rights. Note, 17 J L & Health 37 (2002–03).

Right of disposition of remains/funeral, burial or cremation arrangements. Jeffry L. Weiler, 16 Prob L J Ohio 166 (July/August 2006).

Spleen for Sale: *Moore v. Regents of the University of California* and the Right to Sell Parts of Your Body, Comment. 51 Ohio St L J 499 (1990).

A Unified Approach To Organ Donor Recruitment, Organ Procurement, And Distribution, David A. Peters. 3 J L & Health 157 (1988–89).

DEFINITIONS

2108.01 Definitions

As used in sections 2108.01 to 2108.12 of the Revised Code:

(A) "Anatomical gift" means a donation of all or part of a human body to take effect upon or after death.

(B) "Decedent" means a deceased individual and includes a stillborn infant or fetus.

(C) If a will or other document by which an anatomical gift is made includes a valid specification of the intended donee, "donee" means the specified person or entity; otherwise, "donee" means, in the case of organs, an organ procurement organization that serves the region of the state where the body of the donor is located or, in the case of tissue or eyes, an organization entitled by law to recover the tissue or eyes from the donor's body.

(D) "Donor" means an individual who makes an anatomical gift.

(E) "Hospital" means any hospital operated in this state that is certified under Title XVIII of the "Social Security Act," 49 Stat. 620 (1935), 42 U.S.C. 301, as amended, or accredited by the joint commission on accreditation of healthcare organizations or the American osteopathic association. "Hospital" also means a facility licensed, accredited, registered, or approved as a hospital under the laws of any state, and includes a facility operated as a hospital by a state or a subdivision of the state, although not required to be licensed under state laws.

(F) "Identification card" means an identification card issued under sections 4507.50 and 4507.51 of the Revised Code.

(G) "Part" means any portion of a human body.

(H) "Tissue" means any body part other than an organ or eye.

(I) "Person" has the same meaning as in section 1.59 of the Revised Code and also includes a government or governmental subdivision or agency.

(J) "Physician" or "surgeon" means an individual who is licensed or authorized to practice medicine and surgery or osteopathic medicine and surgery under the laws of any state.

(K) "Recovery agency" means a nonprofit organization incorporated under Chapter 1702. of the Revised Code that is one of the following:

(1) An organ procurement organization designated by the secretary of health and human services pursuant to Title XVIII of the "Social Security Act," 49 Stat. 620 (1935), 42 U.S.C. 301, 1320b–8, as amended;

(2) An eye bank that is accredited by the eye bank association of America or that has applied for accreditation, is in substantial compliance with accreditation standards of the association, and

since applying for accreditation has been in operation for not longer than one year;

(3) A tissue bank that is certified by the American association of tissue banks or that has applied for certification, is in substantial compliance with certification standards of the association, and since applying for certification has been in operation for not longer than one year.

(2000 S 188, eff. 12-13-00; 1990 H 21, eff. 3-27-91; 1970 H 852; 1969 H 51)

Historical and Statutory Notes

Ed. Note: Former 2108.01 repealed by 1969 H 51, eff. 11-6-69; 132 v H 215; see now 2108.02 for provisions analogous to former 2108.01.

Amendment Note: 2000 S 188 added new division (C); redesignated former divisions (C) through (J) as new divisions (D) through (K); substituted "that is accredited" for "certified" and inserted "or that has applied for accreditation, is in substantial compliance with accreditation standards of the association, and since applying for accreditation has been in operation for not longer than one year" in new division (K)(2); inserted "and since applying for certification has been in operation for not longer than one year" in new division (K)(3); and made other nonsubstantive changes.

Cross References

Dilation and extraction procedure, hospital defined, 2919.16
Donation of perishable food, hospital defined, 2305.37
Durable power of attorney for health care, hospital defined, 1337.11
Instrument of gift other than will, 2133.16
Living wills, hospital defined, 2133.01

Research References

Encyclopedias

OH Jur. 3d Cemeteries & Dead Bodies § 74, Manner of Making Anatomical Gift—by Declarant Under Modified Uniform Rights of the Terminally Ill Act.

OH Jur. 3d Decedents' Estates § 277, Testator's Body; Uniform Anatomical Gift Act.

Forms

Ohio Forms Legal and Business § 24:141, Information Requested from Testator in Preparing Will.

Ohio Forms Legal and Business § 24:143, Drafting Will.

Ohio Forms Legal and Business § 24:201, Entire Estate to Specified Relatives or Issue—Provision for Future Spouse—Anatomical Dispositions—No Funeral Services.

Ohio Forms Legal and Business § 24:201.20, Entire Estate to Specified Relatives or Issue—Anatomical Gift Provisions.

Ohio Forms Legal and Business § 24:380.30, Anatomical Gift by Next of Kin or Other Authorized Person.

Treatises and Practice Aids

Carlin, Baldwin's Ohio Practice, Merrick-Rippner Probate Law § 3:61, Gift by Next of Kin or Other Authorized Person—Form.

Carlin, Baldwin's Ohio Practice, Merrick-Rippner Probate Law § 30:11, Drafting a Will—Funeral and Memorial Instructions—Anatomical Gifts.

Carlin, Baldwin's Ohio Practice, Merrick-Rippner Probate Law § 60:35.20, Declaration of Anatomical Gift.

Law Review and Journal Commentaries

Ancient Answers to Modern Questions: Death, Dying, and Organ Transplants—A Jewish Law Perspective, Stephen J. Merber. 11 J L & Health 13 (1996-1997).

ANATOMICAL GIFTS

Comparative Laws

Uniform Anatomical Gift Act

Table of Jurisdictions Wherein Act Has Been Adopted.

For text of Uniform Act, and variation notes and annotation materials for adopting jurisdictions, see Uniform Laws Annotated, Master Edition, Volume 8A.

Jurisdiction	Statutory Citation
Alabama	Code 1975, § 22-19-40 to 22-19-74.
Alaska	AS 13.50.010 to 13.50.090.
Colorado	West's C.R.S.A. § 12-34-101 to 12-34-110.
Delaware	16 Del.C. § 2710 to 2719.
District of Columbia	D.C. Official Code, 2001 Ed. § 7-1521.01 to 7-1521.11.
Florida	West's F.S.A. § 765.510 to 765.522.
Georgia	O.C.G.A. § 44-5-140 to 44-5-151.
Illinois	S.H.A. 755 ILCS 50/1 to 50/9.
Indiana	West's A.I.C. 29-2-16-1 to 29-2-16-16.
Kansas	K.S.A. 65-3209 to 65-3219.
Kentucky	KRS 311.165 to 311.235.
Louisiana	LSA-R.S. 17:2351 to 17:2359.
Maine	22 M.R.S.A. § 2901 to 2911.
Maryland	Code, Estates and Trusts, § 4-501 to 4-512.
Massachusetts	M.G.L.A. c. 113, § 7 to 14.
Michigan	M.C.L.A. § 333.10101 to 333.10109.
Mississippi	Code 1972, § 41-39-11, 41-39-31 to 41-39-53.
Missouri	V.A.M.S. § 194.210 to 194.290.
Nebraska	R.R.S.1943, § 71-4801 to 71-4820.
New Jersey	N.J.S.A. 26:6-57 to 26:6-65.
New York	McKinney's Public Health Law § 4300 to 4309.
North Carolina	G.S. § 130A-402 to 130A-412.2.
Oklahoma	63 Okl.St.Ann. § 2201 to 2218.
Pennsylvania	20 Pa.C.S.A. § 8601, 8611 to 8624.
South Carolina	Code 1976, § 44-43-310 to 44-43-420.
South Dakota	SDCL 34-26-20 to 34-26-41.
Tennessee	T.C.A. § 68-30-101 to 68-30-116.
Texas	V.T.C.A. Health & Safety Code, § 692.001 to 692.016.
Wyoming	Wyo.Stat.Ann., § 35-5-101 to 35-5-119.

2108.02 Gift of body or part; rights of next of kin to donate; when donee shall not accept; examination; rights of donee and of coroner conducting autopsy

(A) Any individual of sound mind may make an anatomical gift for any purpose specified in section 2108.03 of the Revised Code, the anatomical gift to take effect upon the individual's death, if either of the following conditions applies:

(1) The individual is eighteen years of age or more;

(2) The individual is less than eighteen years of age and a parent or guardian of the individual signs a document pursuant to division (B)(2) or a statement pursuant to division (C) of section 2108.04 of the Revised Code.

(B) Any of the following persons, in the order of priority stated, when persons in prior classes are not available at the time of death, and in the absence of actual notice of contrary indications by the decedent or actual notice of opposition by a member of the same or a prior class, may make an anatomical gift of all or any part of the body of a decedent for any purpose specified in section 2108.03 of the Revised Code:

(1) The spouse;

(2) An adult son or daughter;

(3) Either parent;

(4) An adult brother or sister;

(5) A grandparent;

(6) A guardian of the person of the decedent at the time of the decedent's death;

(7) Any other person authorized or under obligation to dispose of the body.

(C) The donee shall not accept the anatomical gift if the donee has actual notice of contrary indications by the decedent or if the anatomical gift is made pursuant to division (B) of this section and that an anatomical gift by a member of a class is opposed by a member of the same or a prior class. The persons authorized in division (B) of this section may make the anatomical gift after or immediately before death.

(D) An anatomical gift authorizes any examination necessary to ensure medical acceptability of the anatomical gift for the purpose intended.

(E) The rights of the donee created by the anatomical gift are paramount to the rights of others except that a coroner or, in the coroner's absence, a deputy coroner, who has, under section 313.13 of the Revised Code, taken charge of the decedent's dead body and decided that an autopsy is necessary, has a right to the dead body and any part that is paramount to the rights of the donee. The coroner, or in the coroner's absence, the deputy coroner, may waive this paramount right and permit the donee to take a donated part if the donated part is or will be unnecessary for successful completion of the autopsy or for evidence. If the coroner or deputy coroner does not waive this paramount right and later determines, while performing the autopsy, that the donated part is or will be unnecessary for successful completion of the autopsy or for evidence, the coroner or deputy coroner may thereupon waive the paramount right and permit the donee to take the donated part, either during the autopsy or after it is completed.

(F) The donee has a property right in an anatomical gift donated pursuant to sections 2108.02 and 2108.04 of the Revised Code and may enforce this right in an action for a declaratory judgment under Chapter 2721. of the Revised Code in the common pleas court of the county where the donor last resided or died or the county where the donee resides. The court shall give such an action precedence over other pending actions.

(G) Nothing in this section shall be construed as requiring a donee to accept an anatomical gift.

(2000 S 188, eff. 12-13-00; 1990 H 21, eff. 3-27-91; 1989 H 529; 1976 H 1182; 1969 H 51)

Historical and Statutory Notes

Ed. Note: 2108.02 contains provisions analogous to former 2108.01 repealed by 1969 H 51, eff. 11-6-69.

Ed. Note: Former 2108.02 repealed by 1969 H 51, eff. 11-6-69; 132 v H 215; see now 2108.03 for provisions analogous to former 2108.02.

Amendment Note: 2000 S 188 inserted "if the anatomical gift is made pursuant to division (B) of this section and" in division (C); added division (F); and made changes to reflect gender neutral language.

Cross References

Age of majority, 3109.01

Library References

Coroners ⚖14.
Dead Bodies ⚖1.
Health ⚖916.
Westlaw Topic Nos. 100, 116, 198H.
C.J.S. Coroners and Medical Examiners §§ 10 to 11, 14, 16.
C.J.S. Dead Bodies §§ 1 to 3.

Research References

Encyclopedias
OH Jur. 3d Cemeteries & Dead Bodies § 72, Who May Make Anatomical Gift; Who May Become Donee of Gift.
OH Jur. 3d Cemeteries & Dead Bodies § 73, Manner of Making Anatomical Gift.
OH Jur. 3d Cemeteries & Dead Bodies § 75, Rights of Donee; Acceptance or Rejection of Anatomical Gift by Donee.
OH Jur. 3d Decedents' Estates § 277, Testator's Body; Uniform Anatomical Gift Act.

Forms
Ohio Forms Legal and Business § 26:54, Introduction.
Ohio Forms Legal and Business § 26:56, Checklist—Drafting Donation of Anatomical Gift.
Ohio Forms Legal and Business § 26:61, Anatomical Gift—by Next of Kin or Other Authorized Person.
Ohio Forms Legal and Business § 26:62, Anatomical Gift—by Statement at Time of Application or Renewal of Driver's or Commercial Driver's License, Motorcycle Operator's License or Endorsement, or Identification Card.
Ohio Forms Legal and Business § 24:379, Gift of Body or Body Part.
Ohio Forms Legal and Business § 24:380.10, Uniform Donor Card.
Ohio Forms Legal and Business § 24:380.20, Anatomical Gift Made on Driver's License or Identification Card.
Ohio Forms Legal and Business § 24:380.30, Anatomical Gift by Next of Kin or Other Authorized Person.

Treatises and Practice Aids
Carlin, Baldwin's Ohio Practice, Merrick-Rippner Probate Law § 3:61, Gift by Next of Kin or Other Authorized Person—Form.
Carlin, Baldwin's Ohio Practice, Merrick-Rippner Probate Law § 30:11, Drafting a Will—Funeral and Memorial Instructions—Anatomical Gifts.
Carlin, Baldwin's Ohio Practice, Merrick-Rippner Probate Law § 64:10, Powers and Duties of Guardian—Ward's Person—Discretionary Acts—Donation of Body Parts/Autopsy.
Carlin, Baldwin's Ohio Practice, Merrick-Rippner Probate Law § 60:35.20, Declaration of Anatomical Gift.

Law Review and Journal Commentaries

Human Biological Material: A Proprietary Interest or Part of the Monistic Being?, Comment. 17 Ohio N U L Rev 805 (1991).

Organ Transplantation with an Incompetent Donor: Kentucky Resolves the Dilemma of Strunk v Strunk, Joe C. Savage. 58 Ky L J 129 (1969–70).

Notes of Decisions

Constitutional issues 1

---

1. Constitutional issues

The Ohio Uniform Anatomical Gift Act, as codified at RC 2108.02(B), expressly grants a widow the right to control the disposition of her deceased spouse's remains, and her interest in the husband's corneas rises to the level of a legitimate claim of entitlement protected by the Due Process Clause of US Const Am 14. Brotherton v. Cleveland (C.A.6 (Ohio) 1991) 923 F.2d 477, rehearing denied, on remand 908 F.Supp. 502.

A widow and children have no property interest in the remains of a decedent that allows them to sue a coroner for violation of due process rights after the coroner permits removal of the decedent's corneas for use as anatomical gifts without consent of the widow or children. Brotherton v. Cleveland (S.D.Ohio 1989) 733 F.Supp. 56, reversed 923 F.2d 477, rehearing denied, on remand 908 F.Supp. 502. Constitutional Law ⚖ 277(1)

2108.021 Protocol for facilitating procurement of anatomical gifts

Every hospital shall develop a protocol consistent with 42 C.F.R. section 482.45 for facilitating procurement of anatomical gifts.

(2000 S 188, eff. 12-13-00; 1999 H 283, eff. 9-29-99)

Historical and Statutory Notes

Ed. Note: Former 2108.021 repealed by 1999 H 283, eff. 9–29–99; 1990 H 21, eff. 3–27–91; 1986 H 770.

Amendment Note: 2000 S 188 rewrote the section, which prior thereto read:

"(A) Every hospital shall develop and implement a written protocol for facilitating procurement of anatomical gifts in consultation with all recovery agencies that work with the hospital in procuring and realizing anatomical gifts. The protocol shall include provisions under which the hospital shall do all of the following:

"(1) Enter into an agreement with an organ procurement organization that does all of the following:

"(a) Provides for the hospital to give timely notice as provided in division (B) of this section that an individual's death is imminent or the individual has died in the hospital;

"(b) Provides for the organ procurement organization to determine the medical suitability of the potential donor for organ donation;

"(c) On notification by the hospital of the death or imminent death of a potential eye or tissue donor, provides for the organ procurement organization or third party described in division (B) of this section to notify in a timely manner the eye and tissue banks the hospital has agreements with under division (C) of this section;

"(d) Unless an agreement the hospital has entered into with an eye bank or tissue bank under division (C) of this section provides for the eye or tissue bank to determine medical suitability of the potential donor for eye or tissue donation, provides for the organ procurement organization to determine medical suitability of each potential donor for eye and tissue donations.

"(2) Collaborate with the organ procurement organization to establish a procedure for requesting organ, eye, or tissue donations that ensures the family of each potential donor is notified of the option to donate organs, eyes, or tissues, or to decline to donate;

"(3) Encourage discretion and sensitivity with respect to the circumstances, opinions, and beliefs of the family of each potential donor;

"(4) Cooperate with the organ procurement organization and an eye bank and a tissue bank to do all of the following:

"(a) Educate staff on donation issues;

"(b) Review death certificates and other records to improve identification of potential donors;

"(c) Maintain the body of each potential donor while necessary testing and matching of potential donated organs, tissues, and eyes take place.

"(B) An organ procurement organization, in consultation and agreement with the eye banks and tissue banks the hospital has agreements with under division (C) of this section, may designate a third party to receive the notice required under division (A)(1)(a) of this section. If a third party is designated in accordance with this division, the agreement between the hospital and the organ procurement organization shall specify that the notice is to be given to the third party. If a third party is not designated in accordance with this division, the agreement between the hospital and the organ procurement organization shall require the hospital to give the notice to the organ procurement organization or a third party designated by the organ procurement organization.

"(C) Each hospital shall enter into an agreement with at least one eye bank and at least one tissue bank with which the hospital will cooperate to retrieve, process, preserve, store, and distribute all usable eyes and tissues that have been donated.

"An agreement between a hospital and an eye bank may provide for the eye bank to determine the medical suitability of each potential donor for eye donation. An agreement between a hospital and a tissue bank may provide for the tissue bank to determine the medical suitability of each potential donor for tissue donation.

"Nothing in an agreement entered into under this division shall interfere with the procurement of organs under an agreement entered into under division (A)(1) of this section."

Library References

Health ⇐256.
Westlaw Topic No. 198H.

Research References

Treatises and Practice Aids

Carlin, Baldwin's Ohio Practice, Merrick-Rippner Probate Law § 3:61, Gift by Next of Kin or Other Authorized Person—Form.

Carlin, Baldwin's Ohio Practice, Merrick-Rippner Probate Law § 30:11, Drafting a Will—Funeral and Memorial Instructions—Anatomical Gifts.

Law Review and Journal Commentaries

Ancient Answers to Modern Questions: Death, Dying, and Organ Transplants—A Jewish Law Perspective, Stephen J. Merber. 11 J L & Health 13 (1996–1997).

Assessing Patient Compliance in the Selection of Organ Transplant Recipients, Note. 6 Health Matrix: J Law–Medicine 503 (Summer 1996).

Notes of Decisions

Ed. Note: This section contains annotations from former RC 2108.021.

Certificate of request   1

---

1. Certificate of request

Although the legislature has changed RC 2108.021, effective March 27, 1991, to require hospitals to send with a body to the coroner a completed certificate of request for an anatomical gift, the amendment to RC 2108.021 does not apply retroactively to a negligence claim brought by a decedent's family against a hospital for the removal of the decedent's corneas by a coroner against the express wishes of the family as told to the hospital prior to its sending of the body to the coroner, since at the time, the hospital owed no duty to the family to pass on to the coroner any information it had received relative to anatomical gifts from the body of a subject within the coroner's jurisdiction. Brotherton v. Cleveland (Hamilton 1991) 76 Ohio App.3d 601, 602 N.E.2d 749, motion to dismiss denied 63 Ohio St.3d 1430, 588 N.E.2d 130, motion overruled 64 Ohio St.3d 1416, 593 N.E.2d 6, rehearing denied 64 Ohio St.3d 1444, 596 N.E.2d 474.

2108.03   Permissible donees

The following may become donees of anatomical gifts for the purposes stated:

(A) A hospital, surgeon, physician, or recovery agency, for transplantation, therapy, medical or dental education, research, or advancement of medical or dental science;

(B) An accredited medical or dental school, college, or university, for education, research, or advancement of medical or dental science.

(1990 H 21, eff. 3–27–91; 1969 H 51)

Historical and Statutory Notes

Ed. Note: 2108.03 contains provisions analogous to former 2108.02 repealed by 1969 H 51, eff. 11–6–69.

Ed. Note: Former 2108.03 repealed by 1969 H 51, eff. 11–6–69; 132 v H 215; see now 2108.08 for provisions analogous to former 2108.03.

Library References

Dead Bodies ⇐1.
Westlaw Topic No. 116.
C.J.S. Dead Bodies §§ 1 to 3.

Research References

Encyclopedias

OH Jur. 3d Cemeteries & Dead Bodies § 72, Who May Make Anatomical Gift; Who May Become Donee of Gift.

Forms

Ohio Forms Legal and Business § 26:56, Checklist—Drafting Donation of Anatomical Gift.

Ohio Forms Legal and Business § 26:61, Anatomical Gift—by Next of Kin or Other Authorized Person.

Ohio Forms Legal and Business § 24:380.30, Anatomical Gift by Next of Kin or Other Authorized Person.

Treatises and Practice Aids

Carlin, Baldwin's Ohio Practice, Merrick-Rippner Probate Law § 3:61, Gift by Next of Kin or Other Authorized Person—Form.

Carlin, Baldwin's Ohio Practice, Merrick-Rippner Probate Law § 30:11, Drafting a Will—Funeral and Memorial Instructions—Anatomical Gifts.

2108.04 Instrument of gift

(A) An individual eighteen years of age or older may make an anatomical gift by will under division (A) of section 2108.02 of the Revised Code. The anatomical gift becomes effective upon the death of the testator without waiting for probate. If the will is not probated or if it is declared invalid for testamentary purposes, the anatomical gift, to the extent that it has been acted upon in good faith, is nevertheless valid and effective.

(B)(1) An individual may also make an anatomical gift under division (A) of section 2108.02 of the Revised Code by a document other than a will. The anatomical gift becomes effective upon the death of the donor. The document, which may be a card designed to be carried on the person, shall be signed by the donor in the presence of two witnesses who shall sign the document in the donor's presence. If the donor cannot sign, the document may be signed for the donor at the donor's direction and in the presence of two witnesses, having no affiliation with the donee, who shall sign the document in the donor's presence. Delivery of the document of gift during the donor's lifetime is not necessary to make the anatomical gift valid.

(2) If a person less than eighteen years of age wishes to make an anatomical gift under division (B)(1) of this section, one of the witnesses who signs the document shall be a parent or guardian of that person.

(3) An individual who is a declarant may make an anatomical gift under division (A) of section 2108.02 of the Revised Code by specifying in the declaration the intent of the declarant to make an anatomical gift as provided in section 2133.16 of the Revised Code. A declaration that specifies the intent of a declarant to make an anatomical gift and satisfies the requirements of section 2133.02 of the Revised Code is considered as having satisfied the requirements of division (B)(1) of this section. The declaration is subject to sections 2108.01 to 2108.12 of the Revised Code to the extent that the declaration specifies the intent of the declarant to make an anatomical gift.

As used in division (B)(3) of this section, "declarant" and "declaration" have the same meanings as in section 2133.01 of the Revised Code.

(C) An anatomical gift under division (A) of section 2108.02 of the Revised Code may also be made by a designation, to be provided for on all Ohio driver's or commercial driver's licenses and motorcycle operator's licenses or endorsements, and on all identification cards. The anatomical gift becomes effective upon the death of the donor. The holder of the driver's or commercial driver's license or endorsement, or the holder of the identification card must sign a statement at the time of application or renewal of the license, endorsement, or identification card; except that when the holder of the license or card is less than eighteen years of age, the statement also shall be signed by a parent or guardian of the holder. Delivery of the license or identification card during the donor's lifetime is not necessary to make the anatomical gift valid. Revocation, suspension, or expiration of the license or endorsement will not invalidate the anatomical gift. The anatomical gift must be renewed upon renewal of each license, endorsement, or identification card.

(D) Except as provided in section 2108.07 of the Revised Code, the donee or other person authorized to accept the anatomical gift may employ or authorize any surgeon or physician to carry out the appropriate procedures.

(E) Any anatomical gift by a person specified in division (B) of section 2108.02 of the Revised Code shall be made in one of the following ways:

(1) By a document signed by the person;

(2) By telegram;

(3) By a telephone call in which two persons receive the message and one of them prepares written documentation of the message, or by a telephone call that is recorded mechanically or electronically.

(F) A valid declaration of an anatomical gift made under division (A), (B), or (C) of this section prevails over any contrary desires of the donor's family regarding the donor's corpse, but nothing in this section shall be construed as requiring a donee to accept an anatomical gift.

(2004 H 392, eff. 9–16–04; 2001 S 158, eff. 11–21–01; 2000 S 188, eff. 12–13–00; 1990 H 21, eff. 3–27–91; 1989 H 529, H 381; 1984 S 302; 1978 S 294; 1975 H 650; 1969 H 51)

Uncodified Law

1990 H 21, § 4: See Uncodified Law under 2108.10.

Historical and Statutory Notes

Amendment Note: 2004 H 392 amended the section by adding Subsec. (B)(3).

Amendment Note: 2001 S 158 rewrote division (C) which prior thereto read:

"(C) An anatomical gift under division (A) of section 2108.02 of the Revised Code may also be made by a designation, to be provided for on all Ohio driver's or commercial driver's licenses and motorcycle operator's licenses or endorsements, and on all identification cards. The anatomical gift becomes effective upon the death of the donor. The holder of the driver's or commercial driver's license or endorsement, or the holder of the identification card must sign a statement at the time of application or renewal of the license, endorsement, or identification card in the presence of two witnesses, who must sign the statement in the presence of the donor; except that when the holder of the license or card is less than eighteen years of age, one of the witnesses who signs shall be a parent or guardian of the holder. Delivery of the license or identification card during the donor's lifetime is not necessary to make the anatomical gift valid. Revocation, suspension, or expiration of the license or endorsement will not invalidate the anatomical gift. The anatomical gift must be renewed upon renewal of each license, endorsement, or identification card. If the statement is ambiguous as to whether a general or specific anatomical gift is intended by the donor, the statement shall be construed as evidencing the specific anatomical gift only."

Amendment Note: 2000 S 188 inserted ", or expiration" in division (C); added division (F); and made changes to reflect gender neutral language.

Cross References

Commercial driver's licenses, indication of intention to make anatomical gift, 4506.11

Commercial driver's licenses, intention to make anatomical gift on application, 4506.07

Driver's license law, application; social security numbers; willingness to make anatomical donation, 4507.51

Form and content of application for driver's license, provision for anatomical gift, 4507.06

Instrument of gift other than will, 2133.16

Library References

Dead Bodies ⇒1.
Wills ⇒5.
Westlaw Topic Nos. 116, 409.
C.J.S. Dead Bodies §§ 1 to 3.
C.J.S. Wills §§ 53, 57 to 61, 65 to 68.

Research References

Encyclopedias

OH Jur. 3d Automobiles & Other Vehicles § 104, Contents of License.
OH Jur. 3d Cemeteries & Dead Bodies § 72, Who May Make Anatomical Gift; Who May Become Donee of Gift.
OH Jur. 3d Cemeteries & Dead Bodies § 73, Manner of Making Anatomical Gift.
OH Jur. 3d Cemeteries & Dead Bodies § 74, Manner of Making Anatomical Gift—by Declarant Under Modified Uniform Rights of the Terminally Ill Act.
OH Jur. 3d Cemeteries & Dead Bodies § 75, Rights of Donee; Acceptance or Rejection of Anatomical Gift by Donee.
OH Jur. 3d Cvl. Servants & Pub. Officers & Employ. § 557, Disposition of Bodies.
OH Jur. 3d Decedents' Estates § 277, Testator's Body; Uniform Anatomical Gift Act.

Forms

Ohio Forms Legal and Business § 26:54, Introduction.
Ohio Forms Legal and Business § 26:55, Form Drafting Principles.
Ohio Forms Legal and Business § 26:56, Checklist—Drafting Donation of Anatomical Gift.
Ohio Forms Legal and Business § 26:57, Donor Card.
Ohio Forms Legal and Business § 26:62, Anatomical Gift—by Statement at Time of Application or Renewal of Driver's or Commercial Driver's License, Motorcycle Operator's License or Endorsement, or Identification Card.
Ohio Forms Legal and Business § 24:201, Entire Estate to Specified Relatives or Issue—Provision for Future Spouse—Anatomical Dispositions—No Funeral Services.
Ohio Forms Legal and Business § 24:379, Gift of Body or Body Part.
Ohio Forms Legal and Business § 24:201.20, Entire Estate to Specified Relatives or Issue—Anatomical Gift Provisions.
Ohio Forms Legal and Business § 24:380.10, Uniform Donor Card.
Ohio Forms Legal and Business § 24:380.20, Anatomical Gift Made on Driver's License or Identification Card.
Ohio Forms Legal and Business § 24:380.30, Anatomical Gift by Next of Kin or Other Authorized Person.

Treatises and Practice Aids

Carlin, Baldwin's Ohio Practice, Merrick-Rippner Probate Law § 30:11, Drafting a Will—Funeral and Memorial Instructions—Anatomical Gifts.
Carlin, Baldwin's Ohio Practice, Merrick-Rippner Probate Law § 30:65, Donation of Body for Scientific Research—Form.
Carlin, Baldwin's Ohio Practice, Merrick-Rippner Probate Law § 60:35.20, Declaration of Anatomical Gift.

Law Review and Journal Commentaries

Leaving a Legacy: the Issue of Organ/Tissue Donation, Carol J. Branch. Cin B Ass'n Rep 6 (December 1999).

2108.05 Delivery or deposit of instrument

The donor of an anatomical gift may deliver the will, card, or other document of gift or a copy of the document to a donee to expedite the appropriate procedures after death. Delivery is not necessary to the validity of the anatomical gift. The will, card, or other document, or an executed copy thereof, may be deposited in any hospital, recovery agency, or registry office that accepts it for safekeeping or for facilitation of procedures after death. On the request of any interested person made on or after the death of the donor, the person in possession of the document of gift shall allow the interested person to examine or copy the document.

(1990 H 21, eff. 3-27-91; 1969 H 51)

Library References

Dead Bodies ⚚1.
Wills ⚚127.
Westlaw Topic Nos. 116, 409.
C.J.S. Dead Bodies §§ 1 to 3.
C.J.S. Wills §§ 441 to 442.

Research References

Encyclopedias

OH Jur. 3d Cemeteries & Dead Bodies § 73, Manner of Making Anatomical Gift.
OH Jur. 3d Decedents' Estates § 277, Testator's Body; Uniform Anatomical Gift Act.

Forms

Ohio Forms Legal and Business § 24:201, Entire Estate to Specified Relatives or Issue—Provision for Future Spouse—Anatomical Dispositions—No Funeral Services.

2108.06 Manner of amendment or revocation

(A) If the will, card, or other document of gift or an executed copy thereof, has been delivered to a specified donee, the donor may amend or revoke the anatomical gift by any of the following means:

(1) The execution and delivery to the donee of a signed statement;

(2) An oral statement made in the presence of two persons and communicated to the donee;

(3) A statement during a terminal illness or injury addressed to the physician attending the donor and communicated to the donee;

(4) A signed card or document found on his person or in his effects.

(B) The donor may revoke any document of gift which has not been delivered to the donee, in any manner specified in division (A) of this section or by destruction, cancellation, or mutilation of the document and all executed copies of it.

(C) Any anatomical gift made by a will may also be amended or revoked in the manner provided for amendment or revocation of wills or as provided in division (A) of this section.

(1990 H 21, eff. 3-27-91; 1969 H 51)

Cross References

Instrument of gift other than will, 2133.16

Library References

Dead Bodies ⚚1.
Wills ⚚167.
Westlaw Topic Nos. 116, 409.
C.J.S. Dead Bodies §§ 1 to 3.
C.J.S. Wills §§ 386, 389, 1621.

Research References

Encyclopedias

OH Jur. 3d Cemeteries & Dead Bodies § 76, Amendment or Revocation of Anatomical Gift.
OH Jur. 3d Decedents' Estates § 277, Testator's Body; Uniform Anatomical Gift Act.

Forms

Ohio Forms Legal and Business § 26:56, Checklist—Drafting Donation of Anatomical Gift.
Ohio Forms Legal and Business § 26:63, Revocation of Prior Anatomical Gift.
Ohio Forms Legal and Business § 26:64, Amendment of Prior Anatomical Gift.
Ohio Forms Legal and Business § 24:201, Entire Estate to Specified Relatives or Issue—Provision for Future Spouse—Anatomical Dispositions—No Funeral Services.
Ohio Forms Legal and Business § 24:380.40, Revocation of Prior Anatomical Gift.

Law Review and Journal Commentaries

Leaving a Legacy: the Issue of Organ/Tissue Donation, Carol J. Branch. Cin B Ass'n Rep 6 (December 1999).

2108.07 Acceptance and use of body; time of death

A donee may accept or reject an anatomical gift. If a donee accepts an anatomical gift of an entire body, the surviving spouse or next of kin may, after consultation with the donee and subject to the terms of the anatomical gift, allow the embalming and use of the body in funeral services. If the anatomical gift is of a part of a body, the donee, upon the death of the donor and prior to embalming, shall cause the part to be removed without unnecessary disfigurement. After removal of the part, the custody of the remainder of the body vests in the surviving spouse, next of kin, or other persons under obligation to dispose of the body.

(B) The physician who attends the donor at death or, if none, the physician who certifies the death shall determine the time of death of the donor and record the time in writing. The physician determining the time of death or certifying the death shall not participate in the procedures for removing or transplanting a part.

(1990 H 21, eff. 3–27–91; 1969 H 51)

Library References

Dead Bodies ⚖=1.
Descent and Distribution ⚖=18.
Wills ⚖=167.
Westlaw Topic Nos. 116, 124, 409.
C.J.S. Dead Bodies §§ 1 to 3.
C.J.S. Wills §§ 386, 389, 1621.

Research References

Encyclopedias

OH Jur. 3d Cemeteries & Dead Bodies § 75, Rights of Donee; Acceptance or Rejection of Anatomical Gift by Donee.

OH Jur. 3d Decedents' Estates § 277, Testator's Body; Uniform Anatomical Gift Act.

Law Review and Journal Commentaries

Euthanasia and the Right to Die, Rowine Hayes Brown and Richard B. Truitt. 3 Ohio N U L Rev 615 (1976).

A Hypothetical: Quinlan Under Ohio Law, Comment. 10 Akron L Rev 145 (Summer 1976).

2108.071 Enucleation of eyes; definition

(A) With respect to the gift of an eye, an embalmer licensed pursuant to Chapter 4717. of the Revised Code who has completed a course in eye enucleation and has received a certificate of competency to that effect from a school of medicine recognized by the state medical board or from an eye bank that is a member of the eye bank association of America may enucleate eyes for the gift after proper certification of death by a physician and compliance with the intent of the gift as defined by sections 2108.01 to 2108.10 of the Revised Code.

(B) As used in this section, "eye enucleation" means the removal of the eyeball in such a way that it comes out clean and whole.

(1990 H 21, eff. 3–27–91; 1974 H 1242)

Library References

Dead Bodies ⚖=1.
Westlaw Topic No. 116.
C.J.S. Dead Bodies §§ 1 to 3.

Research References

Treatises and Practice Aids

Carlin, Baldwin's Ohio Practice, Merrick-Rippner Probate Law § 30:11, Drafting a Will—Funeral and Memorial Instructions—Anatomical Gifts.

2108.08 Person who acts in good faith not liable

A person who in good faith acts, or attempts to act, in accordance with sections 2108.01 to 2108.12, 2108.15, 2108.17, and 2108.18 of the Revised Code, or the anatomical gift laws of another state, is not liable for damages in any civil action or subject to prosecution in any criminal proceeding for his act.

(2001 S 158, eff. 11–21–01; 1990 H 21, eff. 3–27–91; 1970 H 852; 1969 H 51)

Historical and Statutory Notes

Ed. Note: 2108.08 contains provisions analogous to former 2108.03 repealed by 1969 H 51, eff. 11–6–69.

Amendment Note: 2001 S 158 inserted ", 2108.15, 2108.17, and 2108.18" after "2108.12".

Library References

Dead Bodies ⚖=1, 9.
Westlaw Topic No. 116.
C.J.S. Dead Bodies §§ 1 to 3, 12, 14 to 26.

Research References

Encyclopedias

OH Jur. 3d Decedents' Estates § 277, Testator's Body; Uniform Anatomical Gift Act.

Treatises and Practice Aids

Carlin, Baldwin's Ohio Practice, Merrick-Rippner Probate Law § 30:11, Drafting a Will—Funeral and Memorial Instructions—Anatomical Gifts.

2108.09 Adoption of Uniform Anatomical Gift Act; uniform construction

Sections 2108.01 to 2108.09, inclusive, of the Revised Code, are enacted to adopt the Uniform Anatomical Gift Act (1968), national conference of commissioners on uniform state laws, and shall be construed so as to effectuate its general purpose to make uniform the law of those states which enact it.

(1969 H 51, eff. 11–6–69)

Library References

Dead Bodies ⚖=1.
Westlaw Topic No. 116.
C.J.S. Dead Bodies §§ 1 to 3.

Research References

Encyclopedias

OH Jur. 3d Decedents' Estates § 277, Testator's Body; Uniform Anatomical Gift Act.

2108.10 Forms of document of gift

(A) The document of gift provided for in division (B)(1) of section 2108.04 of the Revised Code shall conform substantially to the following form:

"ANATOMICAL GIFT OF

....

(Print or type name of living donor)

In the hope that I may help others upon my death, I hereby give the following body parts: .... for any purpose authorized by law: transplantation, therapy, research, or education.

Signed by the donor and the following two witnesses in the presence of each other:

....
Signature of Donor

....
Date of Birth of Donor

....
Date Signed

....
Witness

....
Witness

This is a legal document under the Uniform Anatomical Gift Act or similar laws."

The statement of an anatomical gift provided for in division (B)(3) of section 2108.04 of the Revised Code and section 2133.16 of the Revised Code shall conform substantially to the form provided in division (B) of section 2133.07 of the Revised Code.

(B) The document of gift provided for in division (E) of section 2108.04 of the Revised Code shall conform substantially to the following form:

"ANATOMICAL GIFT BY A RELATIVE OR THE GUARDIAN OF THE
PERSON OF A DECEDENT

I hereby make this anatomical gift from the body of .... (name) who died on .... (date) in .... (city and state)

The marks in the appropriate squares and the words filled into the blanks below indicate my relationship to the decedent and my desires respecting the anatomical gift.

1. I survive the decedent as:
    1. [ ] spouse;
    2. [ ] adult son or daughter;
    3. [ ] parent;
    4. [ ] adult brother or sister;
    5. [ ] grandparent;
    6. [ ] guardian of the person;
    7. [ ] person authorized to dispose of the body
2. I hereby give the following body parts:

[ ] heart   [ ] liver   [ ] skin   [ ] middle ear
[ ] kidneys   [ ] lung   [ ] heart valves [ ] other ......
[ ] pancreas   [ ] eyes   [ ] bone/ligament

for: [ ] any purpose authorized by law
         [ ] transplantation
         [ ] therapy
         [ ] medical research and education

3. After the donated organs, tissues, or eyes are removed, the remains of the body shall be disposed of in the following manner: _____; at the expense of the following person:

....
Date ....   City and State ....
....
    Witness   Signature of Survivor
....
    Witness   Address of Survivor"

(C) The statement of gift provided for in division (C) of section 2108.04 of the Revised Code shall state the following:

"Upon my death, I make an anatomical gift of organs, tissues, and eyes for any purpose authorized by law."

The statement may be included on an application for a driver's license, commercial driver's license, motorcycle operator's license or endorsement, or state identification card. The donor shall sign the statement or the application containing the statement. If the donor is under eighteen years of age, a parent or guardian of the donor also must sign the statement or the application containing the statement.

(2004 H 392, eff. 9–16–04; 2001 S 158, eff. 11–21–01; 1990 H 21, eff. 3–27–91; 1981 H 54; 1978 S 294; 1970 H 852)

Uncodified Law

1990 H 21, § 4, eff. 3-27-91, reads: Notwithstanding the provisions of division (C) of section 2108.10 of the Revised Code specifying the form of the statement of gift provided for in division (C) of section 2108.04 of the Revised Code, any forms printed under former division (B) of section 2108.10 of the Revised Code may be used until the supply of those forms available on the effective date of this act is depleted.

Historical and Statutory Notes

Amendment Note: 2004 H 392 amended the section by adding the last paragraph of Subsec. (A).

Amendment Note: 2001 S 158 rewrote division (C), which prior thereto read:

"(C) The statement of gift provided for in division (C) of section 2108.04 of the Revised Code shall conform substantially to the following form:

"I hereby make an anatomical gift, to be effective upon my death, of:
(A) [ ] Any needed body parts
    or
(B) [ ] The following body part(s): (list)

_____
Date _____
Signature of donor _____
Witness _____
Witness _____"

Cross References

Instrument of gift other than will, 2133.16

Library References

Dead Bodies ⇐1.
Westlaw Topic No. 116.
C.J.S. Dead Bodies §§ 1 to 3.

Research References

Encyclopedias

OH Jur. 3d Cemeteries & Dead Bodies § 73, Manner of Making Anatomical Gift.
OH Jur. 3d Cemeteries & Dead Bodies § 74, Manner of Making Anatomical Gift—by Declarant Under Modified Uniform Rights of the Terminally Ill Act.

Forms

Ohio Forms Legal and Business § 26:55, Form Drafting Principles.
Ohio Forms Legal and Business § 26:57, Donor Card.
Ohio Forms Legal and Business § 26:61, Anatomical Gift—by Next of Kin or Other Authorized Person.
Ohio Forms Legal and Business § 24:380.10, Uniform Donor Card.
Ohio Forms Legal and Business § 24:380.20, Anatomical Gift Made on Driver's License or Identification Card.
Ohio Forms and Transactions F 30.05, Specific Bequests and Devises.

Treatises and Practice Aids

Carlin, Baldwin's Ohio Practice, Merrick-Rippner Probate Law § 3:60, Gift of All or Part of the Body—Form.
Carlin, Baldwin's Ohio Practice, Merrick-Rippner Probate Law § 3:61, Gift by Next of Kin or Other Authorized Person—Form.

Carlin, Baldwin's Ohio Practice, Merrick-Rippner Probate Law § 30:11, Drafting a Will—Funeral and Memorial Instructions—Anatomical Gifts.

Carlin, Baldwin's Ohio Practice, Merrick-Rippner Probate Law § 30:65, Donation of Body for Scientific Research—Form.

Carlin, Baldwin's Ohio Practice, Merrick-Rippner Probate Law § 60:35.20, Declaration of Anatomical Gift.

2108.101 Validity of prior gift designations

Any anatomical gift designation made prior to the effective date of this section by a person eighteen years old or older that includes that person's signature is valid regardless of whether it has been witnessed.

(2001 S 158, eff. 11–21–01)

Library References

Dead Bodies ⚖1.
Westlaw Topic No. 116.
C.J.S. Dead Bodies §§ 1 to 3.

Research References

Encyclopedias

OH Jur. 3d Cemeteries & Dead Bodies § 73, Manner of Making Anatomical Gift.

MISCELLANEOUS PROVISIONS

2108.11 Transaction involving human fluids or body parts not a sale

Subject to the prohibition in section 2108.12 of the Revised Code, the procuring, furnishing, donating, processing, distributing, or using human whole blood, plasma, blood products, blood derivatives, and products, corneas, bones, organs, or other human tissue except hair, for the purpose of injecting, transfusing, or transplanting the fluid or body part in another human body, is considered for all purposes as the rendition of a service by every person participating in the act and not a sale of any such fluid or body part. No warranties of any kind or description are applicable to the act.

(1990 H 21, eff. 3–27–91; 1969 H 439)

Library References

Dead Bodies ⚖1.
Westlaw Topic No. 116.
C.J.S. Dead Bodies §§ 1 to 3.

Research References

Encyclopedias

OH Jur. 3d Sales & Exchanges of Personal Property § 16, Sales Distinguished from Other Types of Transactions, Generally—Transactions Involving Human Blood and Tissue.

Law Review and Journal Commentaries

AIDS: Dealing With the Plague, Roger N. Braden. 19 N Ky L Rev 277 (1992).

Blood Bank Liability To Recipients Of HIV Contaminated Blood, Comment. 18 U Dayton L Rev 87 (Fall 1992).

2108.12 Sale of human body parts prohibited

(A) No person, for valuable consideration, shall knowingly acquire, receive, or otherwise transfer a human organ, tissue, or eye for transplantation.

(B) Valuable consideration does not include reasonable payments for the removal, processing, disposal, preservation, quality control, storage, transportation, or implantation of a part of a body.

(1990 H 21, eff. 3–27–91)

Cross References

Penalty: 2108.99
Instrument of gift other than will, 2133.16

Library References

Dead Bodies ⚖7.
Westlaw Topic No. 116.
C.J.S. Dead Bodies §§ 27 to 29.

Research References

Encyclopedias

OH Jur. 3d Cemeteries & Dead Bodies § 61, Sale of Human Body Parts.

OH Jur. 3d Cemeteries & Dead Bodies § 74, Manner of Making Anatomical Gift—by Declarant Under Modified Uniform Rights of the Terminally Ill Act.

Forms

Ohio Forms Legal and Business § 24:380.30, Anatomical Gift by Next of Kin or Other Authorized Person.

Treatises and Practice Aids

Carlin, Baldwin's Ohio Practice, Merrick-Rippner Probate Law § 30:11, Drafting a Will—Funeral and Memorial Instructions—Anatomical Gifts.

Carlin, Baldwin's Ohio Practice, Merrick-Rippner Probate Law § 60:35.20, Declaration of Anatomical Gift.

2108.15 Second chance trust fund

(A) There is hereby created in the state treasury the second chance trust fund. The fund shall consist of voluntary contributions deposited as provided in sections 4503.721, 4506.081, 4507.231, and 4507.501 of the Revised Code. All investment earnings of the fund shall be credited to the fund.

(B) The director of health shall use the money in the fund only for the following purposes:

(1) Development and implementation of a campaign that explains and promotes the second chance trust fund;

(2) Development and implementation of local and statewide public education programs about organ, tissue, and eye donation, including the informational material required to be provided under sections 4506.081, 4507.231, and 4507.501 of the Revised Code;

(3) Development and implementation of local and statewide donor awareness programs in schools;

(4) Development and implementation of local and statewide programs to recognize donor families;

(5) Development and distribution of materials promoting organ, tissue, and eye donation;

(6) Cooperation with the Ohio Supreme Court, Ohio State Bar Association, and law schools of this state to more effectively educate attorneys about the donation of anatomical gifts and to encourage them to assist their clients in donating anatomical gifts through anatomical gift declarations, durable powers of attorney for health care, declarations as defined in section 2133.01 of the Revised Code, wills, and any other appropriate means;

(7) Cooperation with the state medical board, state medical, osteopathic, and opthalmological associations, and colleges of medicine and osteopathic medicine in this state to more effectively educate physicians about the donation of anatomical gifts and to encourage them to assist their patients in making declarations of anatomical gifts;

(8) Development and initial implementation of the donor registry established pursuant to section 2108.18 of the Revised Code, except that the total amount expended shall not exceed one hundred fifty thousand dollars;

(9) Development of statewide hospital training programs to encourage and facilitate compliance with section 2108.021 of the Revised Code concerning circumstances under which an anatomical gift is required to be requested;

(10) Reimbursement of the bureau of motor vehicles for the administrative costs incurred in the performance of duties under sections 4506.081, 4507.231, and 4507.501 of the Revised Code;

(11) Reimbursement of the department of health for administrative costs incurred in the performance of duties under this section and section 2108.17 of the Revised Code;

(12) Reimbursement of members of the second chance fund advisory committee for actual and necessary expenses incurred in the performance of official duties.

(C) The director shall make the materials developed under division (B)(5) of this section available to other state agencies.

(D) The director shall consider recommendations made by the second chance trust fund advisory committee pursuant to section 2108.17 of the Revised Code. The director shall determine the appropriateness of and approve or disapprove projects recommended by the advisory committee for funding and approve or disapprove the disbursement of money from the second chance trust fund.

(2006 H 236, eff. 3–30–07; 2001 S 158, eff. 11–21–01; 2000 S 188, eff. 12–13–00; 1999 H 283, § 1, eff. 9–29–99; 1999 H 283, § 160, eff. 6–30–99; 1996 S 300, § 4, eff. 12–31–00; 1996 S 300, § 1, eff. 7–1–97)

Uncodified Law

1999 H 283, § 160, eff. 9–29–99, reads, in part:

It is the intent of this section to prevent the amendment of section 2108.15 of the Revised Code that was to have taken effect December 31, 2000. The combined effect of this action and a complementary amendment made to existing section 2108.15 of the Revised Code by Section 1 of this act is not substantive.

Historical and Statutory Notes

Ed. Note: The amendment of this section by 1996 S 300, § 4—to have taken effect 12–31–00—was repealed by 1999 H 283, § 160, eff. 6–30–99.

Amendment Note: 2006 H 236 inserted "4503.721" in division (A).

Amendment Note: 2001 S 158 deleted "secondary" before "schools" in division (B)(3).

Amendment Note: 2000 S 188 rewrote the section, which prior thereto read:

"There is hereby created in the state treasury the second chance trust fund. The fund shall consist of voluntary contributions deposited as provided in sections 4506.081, 4507.231, and 4507.501 of the Revised Code. All investment earnings of the fund shall be credited to the fund.

"The director of health shall use the money in the fund only for the following purposes:

"(A) Development and implementation of a campaign that explains and promotes the second chance trust fund;

"(B) Development and implementation of a statewide public education program about organ, tissue, and eye donation, including the informational material required to be provided under sections 4506.081, 4507.231, and 4507.501 of the Revised Code;

"(C) Development and implementation of statewide donor awareness programs in secondary schools;

"(D) Development and implementation of statewide programs to recognize donor families;

"(E) Development of statewide hospital training programs to encourage and facilitate compliance with the provisions of section 2108.021 of the Revised Code concerning circumstances under which an anatomical gift is required to be requested;

"(F) Reimbursement of the bureau of motor vehicles for the administrative costs incurred in the performance of duties under sections 4506.081, 4507.231, and 4507.501 of the Revised Code;

"(G) Payment of the compensation of a staff member of the department of health for the staff member's time spent monitoring hospital compliance with sections 2108.01 to 2108.09 of the Revised Code;

"(H) Until December 31, 2000, reimbursement of board members for actual and necessary expenses incurred in the performance of official duties.

"Until December 31, 2000, the director shall consider recommendations made by the second chance trust fund board pursuant to section 2108.16 of the Revised Code. Until December 31, 2000, the director shall determine the appropriateness of and approve or disapprove projects recommended by the board for funding. On and after December 31, 2000, the director shall determine the appropriateness of and approve or disapprove projects. The director shall approve or disapprove the disbursement of money from the second chance trust fund."

Amendment Note: 1999 H 283 deleted "division (A) of" before "section 2108.021" in division (E); inserted "Until December 31, 2000," at the beginning of division (H); and rewrote the final paragraph, which prior thereto read:

"The director shall consider recommendations made by the second chance trust fund board pursuant to section 2108.16 of the Revised Code. The director shall determine the appropriateness of and approve or disapprove projects recommended by the board for funding and approve or disapprove the disbursement of money from the second chance trust fund."

Cross References

"Donate Life" license plates, 4503.721

Library References

States ⇌127.
Westlaw Topic No. 360.
C.J.S. States § 228.

Research References

Encyclopedias

OH Jur. 3d Automobiles & Other Vehicles § 80, Application for License; Fees.

OH Jur. 3d Automobiles & Other Vehicles § 105, Identification Cards for Persons Not Licensed to Drive.

OH Jur. 3d Decedents' Estates § 277, Testator's Body; Uniform Anatomical Gift Act.

OH Jur. 3d Health & Sanitation § 41, Second Chance Fund.

2108.17 Second chance trust fund advisory committee

(A) There is hereby created within the department of health the second chance trust fund advisory committee, consisting of thirteen members. The members shall include the following:

(1) The chairs of the standing committees of the house of representatives and senate with primary responsibilities for health legislation;

(2) One representative of each of the following appointed by the director of health:

(a) An Ohio organ procurement organization that is a member of the Organ Procurement and Transplantation Network;

(b) An Ohio tissue bank that is an accredited member of the American association of tissue banks;

(c) An Ohio eye bank that is certified by the eye bank association of America;

(d) The Ohio solid organ transplantation consortium;

(e) A hospital to which both of the following apply:

(i) It is a member of the Ohio hospital association.

(ii) It has a transplant program or a facility that has been verified as a level I or level II trauma center by the American college of surgeons.

(f) The department of health.

(3) Except as provided in division (C) of this section, three members of the public appointed by the director who are not affiliated with recovery agencies;

(4) Two members appointed by the director who are either affiliated with recovery agencies or members of the public.

(B) Of the members first appointed under division (A)(2) of this section, the representatives of the organ procurement organization, tissue procurement organization, and eye bank shall serve terms of three years; the representatives of the department of health and Ohio solid organ transplantation consortium shall serve terms of two years; and the member representing the Ohio hospital association shall serve a term of one year. Thereafter, all members shall serve terms of three years.

(C) The members initially appointed under division (A)(3) of this section shall be representatives of the following:

(1) An organ procurement organization in Ohio designated by the United States secretary of health and human services that is not represented by the appointment under division (A)(2)(a) of this section;

(2) An Ohio tissue bank that is an accredited member of the American association of tissue banks, not affiliated with an organ procurement organization, and not represented by the appointment under division (A)(2)(b) of this section;

(3) An Ohio eye bank that is certified by the eye bank association of America, not affiliated with an organ procurement organization, and not represented by the appointment under division (A)(2)(c) of this section.

The three members shall serve until the proposed rules under section 2108.18 of the Revised Code are formulated. After the initial appointments, the director shall appoint three members of the public who are not affiliated with recovery agencies to serve terms of three years.

(D) Members appointed under division (A)(2), (3), or (4) of this section shall be geographically and demographically representative of the state. No more than a total of three members appointed under divisions (A)(2), (3), and (4) of this section shall be affiliated with the same recovery agency or group of recovery agencies. Recovery agencies that recover only one type of organ, tissue, or part, as well as recovery agencies that recover more than one type of organ, tissue, or part, shall be represented.

No individual appointed under division (A)(2), (3), or (4) of this section shall serve more than two consecutive terms, regardless of whether the terms were full or partial terms. Each member shall serve from the date of appointment until the member's successor is appointed. All vacancies on the committee shall be filled for the balance of the unexpired term in the same manner as the original appointment.

(E) The committee shall annually elect a chairperson from among its members and shall establish procedures for the governance of its operations. The committee shall meet at least semiannually. It shall submit an annual report of its activities and recommendations to the director of health.

(F) Committee members shall serve without compensation, but shall be reimbursed from the second chance trust fund for all actual and necessary expenses incurred in the performance of official duties.

(G) The committee shall do all of the following:

(1) Make recommendations to the director of health for projects for funding from the second chance trust fund;

(2) Consult with the registrar of motor vehicles in formulating proposed rules under division (C)(1) of section 2108.18 of the Revised Code;

(3) As requested, consult with the registrar or director on other matters related to organ donation;

(4) Approve brochures, written materials, and electronic media regarding anatomical gifts and anatomical gift procedures for use in driver training schools pursuant to section 4508.021 of the Revised Code.

(H) The committee is not subject to section 101.84 of the Revised Code.

(2004 H 392, eff. 9–16–04; 2002 H 407, eff. 10–11–02; 2000 S 188, eff. 12–13–00)

Historical and Statutory Notes

Amendment Note: 2004 H 392 amended the section by substituting "thirteen" for "eleven" in Subsec. (A); deleting "and is not affiliated with an organ procurement organization" from the end of Subsecs. (A)(2)(b) and (A)(2)(c); rewriting Subsec. (A)(2)(e), which previously read "(e) The Ohio hospital association;"; substituting "(C)" for "(D)" in Subsec. (A)(3); adding Subsec. (A)(4); deleting Subsec. (B); redesignating Subsecs. (C) and (D) as Subsecs. (B) and (C), respectively; rewriting Subsec. (E) and redesignating it as Subsec. (D); and redesignating Subsecs. (F) through (I) as Subsecs. (E) through (H), respectively. Prior to the deletion of Subsec. (B) and the amendment and redesignation of Subsec. (E), those subsections read as follows:

"(B) No two members appointed under divisions (A)(2)(a), (b), and (c) of this section shall be from the same organ procurement and distribution service area designated by the United States secretary of health and human services.

" * * *

"(E) No individual appointed under division (A)(2) or (3) of this section shall serve more than two consecutive terms, regardless of whether the terms were full or partial terms. Each member shall serve from the date of appointment until the member's successor is appointed. All vacancies on the committee shall be filled for the balance of the unexpired term in the same manner as the original appointment."

Amendment Note: 2002 H 407 added new division (H)(4).

Library References

States ⚞45.
Westlaw Topic No. 360.
C.J.S. States §§ 79 to 82, 136.

Research References

Encyclopedias
OH Jur. 3d Decedents' Estates § 277, Testator's Body; Uniform Anatomical Gift Act.

2108.18 Donor registry developed by motor vehicles bureau

(A)(1) The bureau of motor vehicles shall develop and maintain a donor registry that identifies each individual who has agreed to make an anatomical gift by a designation on a driver's or commercial driver's license or motorcycle operator's license or endorsement as provided in division (C) of section 2108.04 of the Revised Code. The registry shall be fully operational not later than July 1, 2002.

(2) Any person who provides to the bureau the form set forth in division (C)(2) of section 2133.07 of the Revised Code requesting to be included in the donor registry shall be included.

(B) The bureau shall maintain the registry in a manner that provides to organ procurement organizations, tissue banks, and eye banks immediate access to the information in the registry twenty-four hours a day and seven days a week.

(C)(1) The registrar of motor vehicles, in consultation with the director of health and the second chance trust fund advisory committee created under section 2108.17 of the Revised Code, shall formulate proposed rules that specify all of the following:

(a) The information to be included in the registry;

(b) A process, in addition to that provided for in section 2108.06 of the Revised Code, for an individual to revoke the individual's intent to make an anatomical gift and for updating information in the registry;

(c) How the registry will be made available to organ procurement organizations, tissue banks, and eye banks;

(d) Limitations on the use of and access to the registry;

(e) How information on organ, tissue, and eye donation will be developed and disseminated to the public by the bureau and the department of health;

(f) Anything else the registrar considers appropriate.

(2) In formulating the proposed rules under this division, the registrar may consult with any person or entity that expresses an interest in the matters to be dealt with in the rules.

(3) Following formulation of the proposed rules, but not later than January 1, 2002, the registrar shall adopt rules in accordance with Chapter 119. of the Revised Code.

(D) The costs of developing and initially implementing the registry shall be paid from the second chance trust fund created in section 2108.15 of the Revised Code.

(2004 H 392, eff. 9–16–04; 2000 S 188, eff. 12–13–00)

Historical and Statutory Notes

Amendment Note: 2004 H 392 amended this section be redesignating Subsec. (A) as Subsec. (A)(1); and adding Subsec. (A)(2).

Ohio Administrative Code References

Donor registry for anatomical gifts, OAC 4501:1–1–36

Library References

Automobiles ⇐10.
Dead Bodies ⇐1.
States ⇐127.
Westlaw Topic Nos. 116, 360, 48A.
C.J.S. Dead Bodies §§ 1 to 3.
C.J.S. Motor Vehicles §§ 38 to 40.
C.J.S. States § 228.

Research References

Encyclopedias

OH Jur. 3d Automobiles & Other Vehicles § 104, Contents of License.
OH Jur. 3d Cemeteries & Dead Bodies § 73, Manner of Making Anatomical Gift.
OH Jur. 3d Decedents' Estates § 277, Testator's Body; Uniform Anatomical Gift Act.

2108.19 Toll–free telephone number maintained by motor vehicles bureau

The bureau of motor vehicles shall maintain a toll-free telephone number available twenty-four hours a day that the public may use to obtain information on becoming an organ, tissue, or eye donor as provided in section 2108.04 of the Revised Code. The bureau of motor vehicles shall pay the costs of maintaining the toll-free telephone number.

(2000 S 188, eff. 12–13–00)

Library References

Automobiles ⇐10.
Dead Bodies ⇐1.
Westlaw Topic Nos. 116, 48A.
C.J.S. Dead Bodies §§ 1 to 3.
C.J.S. Motor Vehicles §§ 38 to 40.

2108.20 Immunities

The bureau of motor vehicles, registrar of motor vehicles, deputy registrars of motor vehicles, and agents and employees of the bureau of motor vehicles are not liable for damages in any civil action or subject to prosecution in a criminal proceeding for acting, attempting to act, or failing to act in accordance with section 2108.18, 2108.19, or 4501.024 of the Revised Code, unless the act, attempt, or omission was committed or omitted with malicious purpose, in bad faith, or in a wanton or reckless manner.

(2000 S 188, eff. 12–13–00)

Library References

Dead Bodies ⇐1, 7, 8.
Westlaw Topic No. 116.
C.J.S. Dead Bodies §§ 1 to 3, 27 to 29.

2108.21 Seventeen–year–olds may donate blood; publicity

Any person seventeen years of age or older may donate blood in a voluntary blood program, which is not operated for profit, without consent of his parent or guardian. Before obtaining blood donations from students at high schools, joint vocational schools, or technical schools, a blood program shall arrange for the dissemination of written donation information to students to be shared with their parents or guardians. This information shall include a statement that the students will be requested to donate blood.

(1983 H 162, eff. 9–22–83; 1970 S 455)

Cross References

Age of majority, 3109.01
AIDS carrier, sale or donation of blood by, 2927.13

Library References

Health ⇐911.
Infants ⇐28.
Westlaw Topic Nos. 198H, 211.
C.J.S. Infants §§ 135 to 139.

Law Review and Journal Commentaries

The Gift Of Life: New Laws, Old Dilemmas, And The Future Of Organ Procurement, Comment. 21 Akron L Rev 443 (Spring 1988).

DETERMINATION OF DEATH

Comparative Laws

Uniform Determination of Death Act

Table of Jurisdictions Wherein Act Has Been Adopted.

For text of Uniform Act, and variation notes and annotation materials for adopting jurisdictions, see Uniform Laws Annotated, Master Edition, Volume 12A.

Jurisdiction	Statutory Citation
Alabama	Code 1975, § 22–31–1 to 22–31–2.
Arkansas	A.C.A. § 20–17–101.
California	West's Ann.Cal.Health & Safety Code, § 7180.
Colorado	West's C.R.S.A. § 12–36–136.

Jurisdiction	Statutory Citation
Delaware	24 Del.C. § 1760.
Dist. of Columbia	D.C. Official Code, 2001 Ed. § 7–601.
Georgia	O.G.C.A. § 31-10-16.
Idaho	I.C. § 54-1819.
Indiana	West's A.I.C. 1-1-4-3.
Kansas	K.S.A. 77-204 to 77-206.
Maine	22 M.R.S.A. § 2811 to 2813.
Maryland	Code, Health-General, § 5-202.
Michigan	M.C.L.A. § 333.1031 to 333.1034.
Minnesota	M.S.A. § 145.135.
Mississippi	Code 1972, § 41-36-1, 41-36-3.
Missouri	V.A.M.S. § 194.005.
Montana	MCA § 50-22-101.
Nebraska	R.R.S.1943, § 71-7201 to 71-7203.
Nevada	N.R.S. 451.007.
New Hampshire	RSA 141-D:1 to 141-D:2.
New Mexico	NMSA 1978, § 12-2-4.
North Dakota	NDCC 23-06.3-01, 23-06.3-02.
Oklahoma	63 Okl.St.Ann. § 3121 to 3123.
Oregon	ORS 432.300.
Pennsylvania	35 P.S. § 10201 to 10203.
Rhode Island	Gen.Laws 1956, § 23-4-16.
South Carolina	Code 1976, § 44-43-450, 44-43-460.
South Dakota	SDCL 34-25-18.1.
Utah	U.C.A.1953, 26-34-1, 26-34-2.
Vermont	18 V.S.A. § 5218.
Virgin Islands	19 V.I.C. § 869.
West Virginia	Code, 16-10-1 to 16-10-4.
Wyoming	Wyo.Stat.Ann. § 35-19-101 to 35-19-103.

2108.30 Determination that death has occurred; immunity of physician

An individual is dead if he has sustained either irreversible cessation of circulatory and respiratory functions or irreversible cessation of all functions of the brain, including the brain stem, as determined in accordance with accepted medical standards. If the respiratory and circulatory functions of a person are being artificially sustained, under accepted medical standards a determination that death has occurred is made by a physician by observing and conducting a test to determine that the irreversible cessation of all functions of the brain has occurred.

A physician who makes a determination of death in accordance with this section and accepted medical standards is not liable for damages in any civil action or subject to prosecution in any criminal proceeding for his acts or the acts of others based on that determination.

Any person who acts in good faith in reliance on a determination of death made by a physician in accordance with this section and accepted medical standards is not liable for damages in any civil action or subject to prosecution in any criminal proceeding for his actions.

(1981 S 98, eff. 3-15-82)

Cross References

Death; establishing; presumptions, 2105.35

Library References

Coroners ⇐18.
Dead Bodies ⇐1, 7, 8.
Westlaw Topic Nos. 100, 116.

C.J.S. Coroners and Medical Examiners §§ 10 to 11, 14, 20.
C.J.S. Dead Bodies §§ 1 to 3, 27 to 29.

Research References

Encyclopedias

56 Am. Jur. Proof of Facts 3d 255, Proof of Survivorship of Common Disaster.

Treatises and Practice Aids

Katz, Giannelli, Blair and Lipton, Baldwin's Ohio Practice, Criminal Law, § 95:3, Proof of Life and Death.

Carlin, Baldwin's Ohio Practice, Merrick-Rippner Probate Law § 16:1, Statutory Provisions.

Carlin, Baldwin's Ohio Practice, Merrick-Rippner Probate Law § 30:11, Drafting a Will—Funeral and Memorial Instructions—Anatomical Gifts.

Law Review and Journal Commentaries

The Case of L.W.: An Argument for a Permanent Vegetative State Treatment Statute, Robyn S. Shapiro. 51 Ohio St L J 440 (1990).

The Gift Of Life: New Laws, Old Dilemmas, And The Future Of Organ Procurement, Comment. 21 Akron L Rev 443 (Spring 1988).

Reflecting on Values, Joan McIver Gibson. 51 Ohio St L J 452 (1990).

Relitigating Life and Death, Rebecca Dresser. 51 Ohio St L J 425 (1990).

Notes of Decisions

Brain death 1

---

1. Brain death

The offense of aggravated vehicular homicide does not occur until the death of the victim, and where the victim is revived by chemical means and placed on a life support system, the offense does not occur until the attending physician determines that brain death has occurred. State v. Long (Franklin 1983) 7 Ohio App.3d 248, 455 N.E.2d 534, 7 O.B.R. 327.

POST–MORTEM EXAMINATION

2108.50 Consent for post-mortem examination

(A) Subject to section 2108.521 of the Revised Code, an autopsy or post-mortem examination may be performed upon the body of a deceased person by a licensed physician or surgeon if consent has been given by the person who has the right of disposition under section 2108.70 or 2108.81 of the Revised Code.

(B) Consent to an autopsy or post-mortem examination given under this section may be revoked only by the person executing the consent and in the same manner as required for execution of consent under this section.

(2006 H 426, eff. 10–12–06; 2004 S 178, eff. 1–30–04; 2000 H 538, eff. 9–22–00; 1971 S 243, eff. 12–3–71; 1969 S 234)

Historical and Statutory Notes

Amendment Note: 2006 H 426 rewrote this section, which prior thereto read:

"(A) Subject to section 2108.521 of the Revised Code, an autopsy or post-mortem examination may be performed upon the body of a deceased person by a licensed physician or surgeon if consent has been given in the order named by one of the following persons of sound mind and eighteen years of age or older in a written instrument executed by the person or on the person's behalf at the person's express direction:

"(1) The deceased person during the deceased person's lifetime;

"(2) The decedent's spouse;

"(3) If there is no surviving spouse, if the address of the surviving spouse is unknown or outside the United States, if the surviving spouse is physically or mentally unable or incapable of giving consent, or if the deceased person was separated and living apart from such surviving spouse, then a person having the first named degree of relationship in the following list in which a relative of the deceased person survives and is physically and mentally able and capable of giving consent may execute consent:

"(a) Children;

"(b) Parents;

"(c) Brothers or sisters.

(4) If there are no surviving persons of any degree of relationship listed in division (A)(3) of this section, any other relative or person who assumes custody of the body for burial;

"(5) A person authorized by written instrument executed by the deceased person to make arrangements for burial;

"(6) A person who, at the time of death of the deceased person, was serving as guardian of the person for the deceased person.

"(B) Consent to an autopsy or post-mortem examination given under this section may be revoked only by the person executing the consent and in the same manner as required for execution of consent under this section.

"(C) As used in this section, 'written instrument' includes a telegram or cablegram."

Amendment Note: 2003 S 178 inserted "Subject to section 2108.521 of the Revised Code, an" at the beginning of the first paragraph; inserted "given under this section" in division (B); and made other nonsubstantive changes.

Amendment Note: 2000 H 538 designated the first paragraph as division (A) and redesignated former divisions (A) to (E) as subdivisions (1) to (5); added new subdivision (A)(6); redesignated former subdivisions (C)(1) to (3) as (A)(3)(a) to (c); designated new divisions (B) and (C); substituted "(A)(3)" for "(C)" in new subdivision (A)(4); inserted "to an autopsy or post-mortem examination" in newly designated division (B); made changes to reflect gender neutral language; and made other nonsubstantive changes.

Cross References

Abortion trafficking, 2919.14
Autopsy, official, 313.13
Duties of guardian of person, 2111.13

Ohio Administrative Code References

Abortions, disposition of fetus, autopsy, OAC 3701–47–05

Library References

Coroners ⚖14.
Dead Bodies ⚖1.
Westlaw Topic Nos. 100, 116.
C.J.S. Coroners and Medical Examiners §§ 10 to 11, 14, 16.
C.J.S. Dead Bodies §§ 1 to 3.

Research References

Encyclopedias

OH Jur. 3d Cemeteries & Dead Bodies § 68, Autopsies.
OH Jur. 3d Cemeteries & Dead Bodies § 69, Autopsies—Upon Suspicious Death of Mentally Retarded or Developmentally Disabled Person.
OH Jur. 3d Criminal Law § 806, Abortion Trafficking.
OH Jur. 3d Guardian & Ward § 79, Judicial Control.

Forms

Ohio Jurisprudence Pleading and Practice Forms § 40:5, Statutory and Common-Law Limitations.

Treatises and Practice Aids

Carlin, Baldwin's Ohio Practice, Merrick-Rippner Probate Law § 30:10, Drafting a Will—Funeral and Memorial Instructions—Autopsy or Post-Mortem Examination.

Carlin, Baldwin's Ohio Practice, Merrick-Rippner Probate Law § 62:44, Guardianship Proceedings—Consent to Autopsy or Post-Mortem Examination.

Carlin, Baldwin's Ohio Practice, Merrick-Rippner Probate Law § 64:10, Powers and Duties of Guardian—Ward's Person—Discretionary Acts—Donation of Body Parts/Autopsy.

Carlin, Baldwin's Ohio Practice, Merrick-Rippner Probate Law § 64:11, Powers and Duties of Guardian—Ward's Person—Discretionary Act—Consent to Autopsy or Post-Mortem Examination.

Notes of Decisions

Consent 2
Disinterment 1

---

1. Disinterment

Standard wording in insurance policies required by RC 3923.04(J), reserving right of insurance company to make autopsy, does not include right to order disinterment for autopsy purposes. Mutual of Omaha Ins. Co. v. Garrigan (Ohio Com.Pl. 1971) 31 Ohio Misc. 1, 285 N.E.2d 395, 60 O.O.2d 29.

Civ R 26 and Civ R 34 will not be construed to override long standing common law and statutory limitations on disinterment, under which court ordered disinterment only in rare instances and then only where insurance company presented evidence to indicate that examination may reveal something that will show fraud or mistake. Mutual of Omaha Ins. Co. v. Garrigan (Ohio Com.Pl. 1971) 31 Ohio Misc. 1, 285 N.E.2d 395, 60 O.O.2d 29.

2. Consent

A foundation acting at the behest of the coroner is entitled to the same exemption from the consent requirement of RC 2108.50 as the coroner is granted by RC 313.13. Hicks v. NLO, Inc. (S.D.Ohio 1986) 631 F.Supp. 1207.

2108.51 Exemption from liability

Any licensed physician or surgeon who, in good faith and acting in reliance upon an instrument of consent for an autopsy or post-mortem examination executed under section 2108.50 of the Revised Code and without actual knowledge of revocation of such consent, performs an autopsy or post-mortem examination is not liable in a civil or criminal action brought against him for such act.

(1969 S 234, eff. 11–27–69)

Library References

Coroners ⚖23, 25.
Dead Bodies ⚖7, 8.
Westlaw Topic Nos. 100, 116.
C.J.S. Coroners and Medical Examiners §§ 31, 33.
C.J.S. Dead Bodies §§ 27 to 29.

Research References

Encyclopedias

OH Jur. 3d Cemeteries & Dead Bodies § 68, Autopsies.

Treatises and Practice Aids

Carlin, Baldwin's Ohio Practice, Merrick-Rippner Probate Law § 30:10, Drafting a Will—Funeral and Memorial Instructions—Autopsy or Post-Mortem Examination.

2108.52 Exceptions to requirement of consent for post-mortem examination

The requirements of section 2108.50 of the Revised Code do not apply to a post-mortem or other examination performed under sections 313.01 to 313.22 of the Revised Code, or to medical, surgical, and anatomical study performed under sections 1713.34 to 1713.42 of the Revised Code.

(1975 H 1, eff. 6–13–75; 1969 S 234)

Library References

Coroners ⚖14.

Dead Bodies ⊙1.
Westlaw Topic Nos. 100, 116.
C.J.S. Coroners and Medical Examiners §§ 10 to 11, 14, 16.
C.J.S. Dead Bodies §§ 1 to 3.

Research References

Encyclopedias

OH Jur. 3d Cemeteries & Dead Bodies § 68, Autopsies.

2108.521 Petition for post-mortem examination upon suspicious death of mentally retarded or developmentally disabled person; hearing; order to perform post-mortem examination

(A) If a mentally retarded person or a developmentally disabled person dies, if the department of mental retardation and developmental disabilities or a county board of mental retardation and developmental disabilities has a good faith reason to believe that the deceased person's death occurred under suspicious circumstances, if the coroner was apprised of the circumstances of the death, and if the coroner after being so apprised of the circumstances declines to conduct an autopsy, the department or the board may file a petition in a court of common pleas seeking an order authorizing an autopsy or post-mortem examination under this section.

(B) Upon the filing of a petition under division (A) of this section, the court may conduct, but is not required to conduct, a hearing on the petition. The court may determine whether to grant the petition without a hearing. The department or board, and all other interested parties, may submit information and statements to the court that are relevant to the petition, and, if the court conducts a hearing, may present evidence and testimony at the hearing. The court shall order the requested autopsy or post-mortem examination if it finds that, under the circumstances, the department or board has demonstrated a need for the autopsy or post-mortem examination. The court shall order an autopsy or post-mortem examination in the circumstances specified in this division regardless of whether any consent has been given, or has been given and withdrawn, under section 2108.50 of the Revised Code, and regardless of whether any information was presented to the coroner pursuant to section 313.131 of the Revised Code or to the court under this section regarding an autopsy being contrary to the deceased person's religious beliefs.

(C) An autopsy or post-mortem examination ordered under this section may be performed upon the body of the deceased person by a licensed physician or surgeon. The court may identify in the order the person who is to perform the autopsy or post-mortem examination. If an autopsy or post-mortem examination is ordered under this section, the department or board that requested the autopsy or examination shall pay the physician or surgeon who performs the autopsy or examination for costs and expenses incurred in performing the autopsy or examination.

(2004 S 178, eff. 1–30–04)

Research References

Encyclopedias

OH Jur. 3d Cemeteries & Dead Bodies § 68, Autopsies.
OH Jur. 3d Cemeteries & Dead Bodies § 69, Autopsies—Upon Suspicious Death of Mentally Retarded or Developmentally Disabled Person.

Treatises and Practice Aids

Carlin, Baldwin's Ohio Practice, Merrick-Rippner Probate Law § 30:10, Drafting a Will—Funeral and Memorial Instructions—Autopsy or Post-Mortem Examination.

Carlin, Baldwin's Ohio Practice, Merrick-Rippner Probate Law § 62:44, Guardianship Proceedings—Consent to Autopsy or Post-Mortem Examination.

Carlin, Baldwin's Ohio Practice, Merrick-Rippner Probate Law § 64:11, Powers and Duties of Guardian—Ward's Person—Discretionary Act—Consent to Autopsy or Post-Mortem Examination.

2108.53 Pituitary gland may be removed; rights of next of kin

(A) A county coroner who performs an autopsy under section 313.13 of the Revised Code may, except as provided in divisions (B) and (C) of this section, remove the pituitary gland from the body and give it to the national pituitary agency to use for research and in manufacturing a hormone necessary for the physical growth of persons who are hypopituitary dwarfs, or to any other agency or organization to use for such research and manufacturing.

(B) If the pituitary gland is unnecessary for the successful completion of the autopsy or for evidence, the coroner shall not alter a gift made by the decedent or any other authorized person under Chapter 2108. of the Revised Code to an organization.

(C) If the pituitary gland is unnecessary for the successful completion of the autopsy or for evidence, the coroner shall not remove the pituitary gland under division (A) of this section if the next of kin of the decedent notifies the coroner that he objects to the actions of the coroner on the ground that the actions would violate the tenets of a well-recognized religion.

(1978 S 449, eff. 10–19–78)

Library References

Coroners ⊙8.
Dead Bodies ⊙1.
Westlaw Topic Nos. 100, 116.
C.J.S. Coroners and Medical Examiners §§ 8 to 9.
C.J.S. Dead Bodies §§ 1 to 3.

2108.60 Coroner may remove eye for medical use; right of next of kin to object; good faith action protected

(A) As used in this section:

(1) "Cornea" or "corneas" includes corneal tissue.

(2) "Eye bank" means a nonprofit corporation that is organized under the laws of this state, the purposes of which include obtaining, storing, and distributing corneas to be used for corneal transplants or other medical or medical research purposes, and that is exempt from federal taxation under subsection 501(c) of the Internal Revenue Code.

(3) "Eye bank official" means a person authorized by the trustees of an eye bank to make requests for corneas to be used for corneal transplants or other medical or medical research purposes.

(4) "Eye technician" means a person authorized by the medical director of an eye bank to remove the corneas of a decedent.

(5) "Internal Revenue Code" means the "Internal Revenue Code of 1954," 68A Stat. 3, 26 U.S.C. 1, as amended.

(B) A county coroner who performs an autopsy pursuant to section 313.13 of the Revised Code may remove one or both corneas of the decedent, or a coroner may authorize a deputy coroner, physician or surgeon licensed pursuant to section 4731.14 of the Revised Code, embalmer authorized under section 2108.071 of the Revised Code to enucleate eyes, or eye technician to remove one or both corneas of a decedent whose body is the subject of an autopsy performed pursuant to section 313.13 of the Revised Code, if all of the following apply:

(1) The corneas are not necessary for the successful completion of the autopsy or for evidence;

(2) An eye bank official has requested the removal of corneas and certified to the coroner in writing that the corneas will be used only for corneal transplants or other medical or medical research purposes;

(3) The removal of the corneas and gift to the eye bank do not alter a gift made by the decedent or any other person authorized under this chapter to an agency or organization other than the eye bank;

(4) The coroner, at the time he removes or authorizes the removal of the corneas, has no knowledge of an objection to the removal by any of the following:

(a) The decedent, as evidenced in a written document executed during his lifetime;

(b) The decedent's spouse;

(c) If there is no spouse, the decedent's adult children;

(d) If there is no spouse and no adult children, the decedent's parents;

(e) If there is no spouse, no adult children, and no parents, the decedent's brothers or sisters;

(f) If there is no spouse, no adult children, no parents, and no brothers or sisters, the guardian of the person of the decedent at the time of death;

(g) If there is no spouse, no adult children, no parents, no brothers or sisters, no guardian of the person of the decedent at the time of death, any other person authorized or under obligation to dispose of the body.

(C) Any person who acts in good faith under this section and without knowledge of an objection, as described in division (B)(4) of this section, to the removal of corneas is not liable in any civil or criminal action based on the removal.

(1983 H 239, eff. 3–28–84; 1979 H 415)

Library References

Coroners ⇔8.
Dead Bodies ⇔1.
Westlaw Topic Nos. 100, 116.
C.J.S. Coroners and Medical Examiners §§ 8 to 9.
C.J.S. Dead Bodies §§ 1 to 3.

Research References

Encyclopedias

OH Jur. 3d Decedents' Estates § 277, Testator's Body; Uniform Anatomical Gift Act.

Law Review and Journal Commentaries

Brotherton v. Cleveland: The Creation Of Property Rights By A Federal Court, Harry J. Finke, IV. 23 U Tol L Rev 555 (Spring 1992).

Brotherton v Cleveland: Transplant Organs, Property Rights, and the Constitution, Maxwell J. Mehlman. 2 Health L J Ohio 141 (May/June 1991).

Notes of Decisions

Constitutional issues 1
Liability and immunity 2

---

1. Constitutional issues

Coroner acted as county official, not state official, when he implemented cornea removal policy of "intentional ignorance" regarding wishes of deceased persons and their kin, and therefore was not entitled to Eleventh Amendment immunity from liability in his official capacity in 1983 action brought by widow whose objection to removal of deceased husband's corneas was not respected; county, rather than state, would satisfy any money judgment against coroner, who was elected county official, acted autonomously without state oversight, and was funded and defended by county, and Ohio law authorizing corneal harvesting did not compel coroner to craft policy at issue, so as to require that coroner be treated as state actor for purposes of case. Brotherton v. Cleveland (C.A.6 (Ohio), 04-14-1999) 173 F.3d 552, on remand 141 F.Supp.2d 894. Federal Courts ⇔ 269

Although it was nonprofit corporation and had been found to be state actor for purposes of case, eye bank association was not entitled to Eleventh Amendment immunity in 1983 action arising from removal of deceased husband's corneas over widow's objection; state did not exert control over association, apart from its regulation of all corporations operating within state, and Ohio laws did little more than give association's member eye banks permission to harvest corneas, making it unlikely that Ohio had financial involvement with association or would pay judgment against association. Brotherton v. Cleveland (C.A.6 (Ohio), 04-14-1999) 173 F.3d 552, on remand 141 F.Supp.2d 894. Federal Courts ⇔ 265

A county coroner's policy and custom to remove corneas after death without first reviewing medical records or paperwork to ascertain whether consent has been given for the removal, which results in the coroner taking corneas from the remains without considering the interest of any other party if the coroner has no knowledge of an objection, is considered an established state procedure so that the state must provide the process due before depriving the holder of that interest. Brotherton v. Cleveland (C.A.6 (Ohio) 1991) 923 F.2d 477, rehearing denied, on remand 908 F.Supp. 502. Constitutional Law ⇔ 274(2); Dead Bodies ⇔ 1

RC 2108.60(B) impinges on no fundamental right by permitting a county coroner performing an autopsy to remove corneas and consent to their use without the consent of survivors and would be upheld against a challenge based upon equal protection of the laws if rationally related to some legitimate state interest. Brotherton v. Cleveland (S.D.Ohio 1989) 733 F.Supp. 56, reversed 923 F.2d 477, rehearing denied, on remand 908 F.Supp. 502. Constitutional Law ⇔ 250.5

A widow and children have no property interest in the remains of a decedent that allows them to sue a coroner for violation of due process rights after the coroner permits removal of the decedent's corneas for use as anatomical gifts without consent of the widow or children. Brotherton v. Cleveland (S.D.Ohio 1989) 733 F.Supp. 56, reversed 923 F.2d 477, rehearing denied, on remand 908 F.Supp. 502. Constitutional Law ⇔ 277(1)

2. Liability and immunity

An attorney is not negligent for failing to prosecute a medical malpractice claim in a skillful and diligent manner where (1) plaintiffs claim that their decedent's corneas were removed without approval before an official pronouncement of death, (2) the attorney is hired to pursue claims for improper treatment and unauthorized removal, (3) plaintiffs would not have prevailed in the underlying action because documentary evidence demonstrates that the removal occurred at the coroner's office after death and lack of prior consent for the removal was not actionable pursuant to the law as it then existed under RC Ch 2108. Higgins v. McDonnell (Ohio App. 8 Dist., Cuyahoga, 05-15-1997) No. 71341, 1997 WL 253150, Unreported, appeal not allowed 80 Ohio St.3d 1415, 684 N.E.2d 706.

County coroner authorized removal of decedent's corneas without surviving family members' consent pursuant to Ohio statute, which allows coroner's office to take corneas from bodies of deceased without considering interest of any other parties so long as office has no knowledge of any objection to such removal, and coroner was therefore entitled to immunity in his official capacity, as policy of coroner's office not to review medical records or paperwork pertaining to corpse prior to removal of corneas was "induced" by Ohio law. Brotherton v. Cleveland (S.D.Ohio, 11-27-1995) 908 F.Supp. 502, affirmed in part, reversed in part and remanded 173 F.3d 552, on remand 141 F.Supp.2d 894. Federal Courts ⇔ 270

DISPOSITION OF REMAINS AND PURCHASE OF GOODS AND SERVICES RELATED TO FUNERAL

2108.70 Assignment of right to direct disposition of remains after death and purchase goods and services related to funeral; designation of successor representative

(A) As used in this section and sections 2108.71 to 2108.90 of the Revised Code:

(1) "Adult" means an individual who is eighteen years of age or older.

(2) "Declarant" means an adult who has executed a written declaration described in division (B) of this section.

(3) "Representative" means an adult or a group of adults, collectively, to whom a declarant has assigned the right of disposition.

(4) "Right of disposition" means one or more of the rights described in division (B) of this section that a declarant chooses to assign to a representative in a written declaration executed under that division or all of the rights described in division (B) of this section that are assigned to a person pursuant to section 2108.81 of the Revised Code.

(5) "Successor representative" means an adult or group of adults, collectively, to whom the right of disposition for a declarant has been reassigned because the declarant's representative is disqualified from exercising the right under section 2108.75 of the Revised Code. Each successor representative shall be considered in the order the representative is designated by the declarant.

(B) An adult who is of sound mind may execute at any time a written declaration assigning to a representative one or more of the following rights:

(1) The right to direct the disposition, after death, of the declarant's body or any part of the declarant's body that becomes separated from the body before death. This right includes the right to determine the location, manner, and conditions of the disposition of the declarant's bodily remains.

(2) The right to make arrangements and purchase goods and services for the declarant's funeral. This right includes the right to determine the location, manner, and condition of the declarant's funeral.

(3) The right to make arrangements and purchase goods and services for the declarant's burial, cremation, or other manner of final disposition. This right includes the right to determine the location, manner, and condition of the declarant's burial, cremation, or other manner of final disposition.

(C)(1) Subject to division (C)(2) of this section, a declarant may designate a successor representative.

(2) If a representative is a group of persons and not all of the persons in the group meet at least one criterion to be disqualified from serving as the representative, as described in section 2108.75 of the Revised Code, the persons in the group who are not disqualified shall remain the representative who has the right of disposition.

(D) The assignment or reassignment of a right of disposition to a representative and a successor representative supercedes an assignment of a right of disposition under section 2108.81 of the Revised Code.

(2006 H 426, eff. 10–12–06)

Cross References

Allowance for tombstone and cemetery lot, 2113.37
Antemortem cremation authorization, 4717.21
Authorizing agents, 4717.22
Duties of guardian of person, 2111.13
Fiduciaries, appointment and duties, 2109.02
Preneed cemetery merchandise and services contracts, 1721.211
Preneed funeral contracts, 1111.19
Reimbursement of funeral expenses to surviving spouse or person with right of disposition, 2106.20

Law Review and Journal Commentaries

Right of disposition of remains/funeral, burial or cremation arrangements. Jeffry L. Weiler, 16 Prob L J Ohio 166 (July/August 2006).

2108.71 Vesting of assignment or reassignment of right of disposition

The assignment or reassignment of a right of disposition by a declarant under section 2108.70 of the Revised Code vests in a representative or a successor representative at the time of the declarant's death.

(2006 H 426, eff. 10–12–06)

2108.72 Contents of declaration of assignment of right of disposition; form of written declaration

(A) The written declaration described in section 2108.70 of the Revised Code shall include all of the following:

(1) The declarant's legal name and present address;

(2) A statement that the declarant, an adult being of sound mind, willfully and voluntarily appoints a representative to have the declarant's right of disposition for the declarant's body upon the declarant's death;

(3) A statement that all decisions made by the declarant's representative with respect to the right of disposition are binding;

(4) The name, last known address, and last known telephone number of the representative or, if the representative is a group of persons, the name, last known address, and last known telephone number of each person in the group;

(5) If the declarant chooses to have a successor representative, a statement that if any person or group of persons named as the declarant's representative is disqualified from serving in such position as described in section 2108.75 of the Revised Code, the declarant appoints a successor representative;

(6) If applicable, the name, last known address, and last known telephone number of the successor representative or, if the successor representative is a group of persons, the name, last known address, and last known telephone number of each person in the group;

(7) A space where the declarant may indicate the declarant's preferences regarding how the right of disposition should be exercised, including any religious observances the declarant wishes the person with the right of disposition to consider;

(8) A space where the declarant may indicate one or more sources of funds that may be used to pay for goods and services associated with the exercise of the right of disposition;

(9) A statement that the declarant's written declaration becomes effective on the declarant's death;

(10) A statement that the declarant revokes any written declaration that the declarant executed, in accordance with section 2108.70 of the Revised Code, prior to the execution of the present written declaration.

(11) A space where the declarant can sign and date the written declaration;

(12) A space where a notary public or two witnesses can sign and date the written declaration as described in section 2108.73 of the Revised Code.

(B) A written declaration may take the following form:

APPOINTMENT OF REPRESENTATIVE FOR DISPOSITION OF BODILY REMAINS, FUNERAL ARRANGEMENTS, AND BURIAL OR CREMATION GOODS AND SERVICES:

I, ... (legal name and present address of declarant), an adult being of sound mind, willfully and voluntarily appoint my representative, named below, to have the right of disposition, as defined in section 2108.70 of the Revised Code, for my body upon my death. All decisions made by my representative with respect to the right of disposition shall be binding.

REPRESENTATIVE:

(If the representative is a group of persons, indicate the name, last known address, and telephone number of each person in the group.)

Name(s): ....

Address(es): ....

Telephone Number(s): ....

SUCCESSOR REPRESENTATIVE:

If my representative is disqualified from serving as my representative as described in section 2108.75 of the Revised Code, then I hereby appoint the following person or group of persons to serve as my successor representative.

(If the successor representative is a group of persons, indicate the name, last known address, and telephone number of each person in the group.)

Name(s): ....

Address(es): ....

Telephone Number(s): ....

PREFERENCES REGARDING HOW THE RIGHT OF DISPOSITION SHOULD BE EXERCISED, INCLUDING ANY RELIGIOUS OBSERVANCES THE DECLARANT WISHES A REPRESENTATIVE OR A SUCCESSOR REPRESENTATIVE TO CONSIDER:

....
....
....
....

ONE OR MORE SOURCES OF FUNDS THAT COULD BE USED TO PAY FOR GOODS AND SERVICES ASSOCIATED WITH AN EXERCISE OF THE RIGHT OF DISPOSITION:

....
....
....
....

DURATION:

The appointment of my representative and, if applicable, successor representative, becomes effective upon my death.

PRIOR APPOINTMENTS REVOKED:

I hereby revoke any written declaration that I executed in accordance with section 2108.70 of the Ohio Revised Code prior to the date of execution of this written declaration indicated below.

AUTHORIZATION TO ACT:

I hereby agree that any of the following that receives a copy of this written declaration may act under it:

- Cemetery organization;
- Crematory operator;
- Business operating a columbarium;
- Funeral director;
- Embalmer;
- Funeral home;
- Any other person asked to assist with my funeral, burial, cremation, or other manner of final disposition.

MODIFICATION AND REVOCATION—WHEN EFFECTIVE:

Any modification or revocation of this written declaration is not effective as to any party until that party receives actual notice of the modification or revocation.

LIABILITY:

No person who acts in accordance with a properly executed copy of this written declaration shall be liable for damages of any kind associated with the person's reliance on this declaration.

Signed this ...... day of ....

....
(Signature of declarant)

ACKNOWLEDGMENT OF ASSUMPTION OF OBLIGATIONS AND COSTS:

By signing below, the representative, or successor representative, if applicable, acknowledges that he or she, as representative or successor representative, assumes the right of disposition as defined in section 2108.70 of the Revised Code, and understands that he or she is liable for the reasonable costs of exercising the right, including any goods and services that are purchased.

ACCEPTANCE (OPTIONAL):

The undersigned hereby accepts this appointment as representative or successor representative, as applicable, for the right of disposition as defined in section 2108.70 of the Revised Code.

Signed this ...... day of ....

....
Signature of representative (if representative is a group of persons, each person in the group shall sign)

Signed this ...... day of ....

....
Signature of successor representative (if successor representative is a group of persons, each person in the group shall sign)

WITNESSES:

I attest that the declarant signed or acknowledged this assignment of the right of disposition under section 2108.70 of the Revised Code in my presence and that the declarant is at least eighteen years of age and appears to be of sound mind and not under or subject to duress, fraud, or undue influence. I further attest that I am not the declarant's representative or successor representative, I am at least eighteen years of age, and I am not related to the declarant by blood, marriage, or adoption.

First witness:
Name (printed):
.... Residing at: ....
Signature:
....
Date:
....

Second witness:
Name (printed):
.... Residing at: ....
Signature:
....
Date:
....

OR

NOTARY ACKNOWLEDGMENT:

State of Ohio

County of .... SS.

On ...., before me, the undersigned notary public, personally appeared ...., known to me or satisfactorily proven to be the person whose name is subscribed as the declarant, and who has acknowledged that he or she executed this written declaration under section 2108.70 of the Revised Code for the purposes expressed in that section. I attest that the declarant is at least eighteen years of age and appears to be of sound mind and not under or subject to duress, fraud, or undue influence.

Signature of notary public

....

My commission expires on: ....

(2006 H 426, eff. 10–12–06)

Cross References

Antemortem cremation authorization, 4717.21
Preneed cemetery merchandise and services contracts, 1721.211
Preneed funeral contracts, 1111.19

Law Review and Journal Commentaries

Right of disposition of remains/funeral, burial or cremation arrangements. Jeffry L. Weiler, 16 Prob L J Ohio 166 (July/August 2006).

2108.73 Execution of written declaration

A written declaration executed by a declarant under section 2108.70 of the Revised Code shall be signed and dated by the declarant in the presence of either of the following:

(A) A notary public who shall make the certification described in section 147.53 of the Revised Code.

(B) Two witnesses who are adults and who are not related by blood, marriage, or adoption to the declarant.

(2006 H 426, eff. 10–12–06)

2108.74 Truthfulness of declaration

A declarant who executes a written declaration in accordance with section 2108.73 of the Revised Code warrants the truthfulness of the entire content of the declaration.

(2006 H 426, eff. 10–12–06)

2108.75 Disqualification from serving as a representative or successor representative

(A) A person shall be disqualified from serving as a representative or successor representative, or from having the right of disposition for a deceased adult pursuant to section 2108.81 of the Revised Code, if any of the following occurs:

(1) The person dies.

(2) A probate court declares or determines that the person is incompetent.

(3) The person resigns or declines to exercise the right as described in section 2108.88 of the Revised Code.

(4) The person refuses to exercise the right within two days after notification of the declarant's death.

(5) The person cannot be located with reasonable effort.

(6) The person meets the criteria described in section 2108.76 or 2108.77 of the Revised Code.

(B) No owner, employee, or agent of a funeral home, cemetery, or crematory providing funeral, burial, or cremation services for a declarant shall serve as a representative or successor representative for the declarant unless the owner, employee, or agent is related to the declarant by blood, marriage, or adoption.

(C) Subject to divisions (C)(2) and (D)(2) of section 2108.70 of the Revised Code, if a person is disqualified from serving as the declarant's representative or successor representative, or from having the right of disposition for a deceased adult pursuant to section 2108.81 of the Revised Code, as described in division (A) of this section, the right is automatically reassigned to, and vests in, the next person who has the right pursuant to the declarant's written declaration or pursuant to the order of priority in section 2108.81 of the Revised Code.

(2006 H 426, eff. 10–12–06)

Cross References

Antemortem cremation authorization, 4717.21

2108.76 Former spouse as representative or successor representative

(A) Except as provided in division (B) of this section, if the person named as the declarant's representative or successor representative in a written declaration was the declarant's spouse at the time the declaration was executed, but is not the declarant's spouse at the time of the declarant's death, the former spouse shall no longer be qualified to serve as the declarant's representative or successor representative.

(B) Division (A) of this section shall not apply and a former spouse is qualified to serve as a declarant's representative or successor representative if the declarant signs and dates, after the termination of the marriage, a document stating the declarant's intent that the former spouse be the declarant's representative or successor representative. The document must be notarized or witnessed in accordance with the procedures described in section 2108.73 of the Revised Code.

(2006 H 426, eff. 10–12–06)

2108.77 Additional criteria for disqualification from serving as representative or successor representative

If the person named as the declarant's representative or successor representative in a written declaration, or the person who has a deceased adult's right of disposition pursuant to section 2108.81 of the Revised Code, meets any of the following criteria, the person shall be disqualified from serving as the representative or successor representative, or from having the right:

(A)(1) Subject to division (A)(2) of this section, the person has been charged with murder, aggravated murder, or voluntary manslaughter.

(2) If the charges against the person described in division (A)(1) of this section are dismissed or if the person is acquitted of such charges, the right is restored to the person.

(B)(1) Subject to division (B)(2) of this section, the person has been charged with an act of domestic violence under section 2919.25 of the Revised Code and it has been alleged in the charging instrument or accompanying papers that the act resulted in or contributed to the declarant's death.

(2) If the charges against the person described in division (B)(1) of this section are dismissed or if the person is acquitted of such charges, the right is restored to the person.

(C) The person and the declarant or deceased adult are spouses and an action to terminate the marriage pursuant to Chapter 3105. of the Revised Code was pending at the time of the declarant's or deceased adult's death.

(D) The person and the declarant or deceased adult are spouses and a probate court, on the motion of any other person or its own motion, determines that the declarant's or deceased adult's spouse and the declarant were estranged at the time of the declarant's or deceased adult's death. As used in this division, "estranged" means that a declarant's or a deceased adult's spouse and the declarant or deceased adult were physically and emotionally separated from each other, at the time of the declarant's or deceased adult's death, and had been separated for a period of time that clearly demonstrates an absence of due affection, trust, and regard between spouse and the declarant of deceased adult.

(2006 H 426, eff. 10–12–06)

2108.78 Assignment of right of disposition relating to anatomical gifts

If a declarant or deceased adult has made a valid declaration of an anatomical gift by will or any other document or means described in section 2108.04 of the Revised Code, any person to whom the declarant has assigned the right of disposition under section 2108.70 of the Revised Code, or who has the right as described in section 2108.81 of the Revised Code, is bound by the declaration of the anatomical gift and must follow the instructions associated with the gift before making any decisions or taking any other actions associated with the right.

(2006 H 426, eff. 10–12–06)

2108.79 Majority vote prevails when representative or successor representative is group or class of persons; probate court to decide when no majority decision

(A) Subject to divisions (B) and (C) of this section, if a declarant's representative or successor representative is a group of people in whom the right of disposition has vested as described in section 2108.71 of the Revised Code, or if a class of persons has the right as described in section 2108.81 of the Revised Code, and the persons in the group or class disagree regarding how the right is to be exercised, the decisions of the majority of the persons in the group or class shall prevail.

(B) If, after reasonable efforts, less than all of the persons in a group or class described in division (A) of this section have been located, the decisions of the majority of the persons in the group or class who have been located prevail.

(C) If a majority of persons cannot reach a decision under division (A) or (B) of this section, the probate court of the county in which the declarant or deceased person resided at the time of death shall make the decision in accordance with the criteria set forth in division (B) of section 2108.82 of the Revised Code.

(2006 H 426, eff. 10–12–06)

2108.80 Revocation of assignment

A declarant may revoke a written declaration executed under section 2108.70 of the Revised Code by indicating the declarant's desire to revoke the declaration in a document signed and dated by the declarant in the presence of either of the following:

(A) A notary public who shall make the certification described in section 147.53 of the Revised Code.

(B) Two witnesses who are adults and are not related by blood, marriage, or adoption to the declarant.

(2006 H 426, eff. 10–12–06)

2108.81 Priority of assignment of right of disposition

(A) If either of the following is true, division (B) of this section shall apply:

(1) An adult has not executed a written declaration pursuant to sections 2108.70 to 2108.73 of the Revised Code that remains in force at the time of the adult's death.

(2) Each person to whom the right of disposition has been assigned or reassigned pursuant to a written declaration is disqualified from exercising the right as described in section 2108.75 of the Revised Code.

(B) Subject to division (A) of this section and sections 2108.75 and 2108.79 of the Revised Code, the right of disposition is assigned to the following persons, if mentally competent adults who can be located with reasonable effort, in the order of priority stated:

(1) The deceased person's surviving spouse;

(2) The sole surviving child of the deceased person or, if there is more than one surviving child, all of the surviving children, collectively;

(3) The deceased person's surviving parent or parents;

(4) The deceased person's surviving sibling, whether of the whole or of the half blood or, if there is more than one sibling of the whole or of the half blood, all of the surviving siblings, collectively;

(5) The deceased person's surviving grandparent or grandparents;

(6) The lineal descendants of the deceased person's grandparents, as described in division (I) of section 2105.06 of the Revised Code;

(7) The person who was the deceased person's guardian at the time of the deceased person's death, if a guardian had been appointed;

(8) Any other person willing to assume the right of disposition, including the personal representative of the deceased person's estate or the licensed funeral director with custody of the deceased person's body, after attesting in writing that a good faith effort has been made to locate the persons in divisions (B)(1) to (7) of this section.

(2006 H 426, eff. 10–12–06)

Cross References

Allowance for tombstone and cemetery lot, 2113.37
Antemortem cremation authorization, 4717.21
Authorizing agents, 4717.22
Duties of guardian of person, 2111.13
Fiduciaries, appointment and duties, 2109.02
Preneed cemetery merchandise and services contracts, 1721.211
Preneed funeral contracts, 1111.19
Reimbursement of funeral expenses to surviving spouse or person with right of disposition, 2106.20

2108.82 Probate court may assign right of disposition; criteria considered

(A) Notwithstanding section 2108.81 of the Revised Code and in accordance with division (B) of this section, the probate court for the county in which the declarant or deceased person resided at the time of death may, on its own motion or the motion of another person, assign to any person the right of disposition for a declarant or deceased person.

(B) In making a determination for purposes of division (A) of this section and division (C) of section 2108.79 of the Revised Code, the court shall consider the following:

(1) Whether evidence presented to, or in the possession of the court, demonstrates that the person who is the subject of the motion and the declarant or deceased person had a close personal relationship;

(2) The reasonableness and practicality of any plans that the person who is the subject of the motion may have for the declarant's or deceased person's funeral, burial, cremation, or final disposition, including the degree to which such plans allow maximum participation by all persons who wish to pay their final respects to the deceased person;

(3) The willingness of the person who is the subject of the motion to assume the responsibility to pay for the declarant's or deceased person's funeral, burial, cremation, or final disposition and the desires of that person;

(4) The convenience and needs of other families and friends wishing to pay their final respects to the declarant or deceased person;

(5) The express written desires of the declarant or deceased person.

(C) Except to the extent considered under division (B)(3) of this section, the following persons do not have a greater claim to the right of disposition than such persons otherwise have pursuant to law:

(1) A person who is willing to assume the responsibility to pay for the declarant's or deceased person's funeral, burial, cremation, or final disposition;

(2) The personal representative of the declarant or deceased person.

(2006 H 426, eff. 10–12–06)

2108.83 Disputes relating to right of disposition; immunity from liability

In the event of a dispute regarding the right of disposition, a funeral home, funeral director, crematory operator, cemetery operator, cemetery organization, or other person asked to assist with a declarant's or deceased person's funeral, burial, cremation, or other manner of final disposition shall not be liable for damages of any kind for refusing to accept the remains, refusing to inter, cremate, or otherwise dispose of the remains, or refusing to complete funeral or other arrangements pertaining to final disposition until such funeral home, funeral director, crematory operator, cemetery operator, cemetery organization, or other person receives a court order or a written document that is executed by a person that the funeral home, funeral director, crematory operator, cemetery operator, cemetery organization, or other person reasonably believes has the right of disposition and that clearly expresses how the right of disposition is to be exercised.

(2006 H 426, eff. 10–12–06)

2108.84 Preservation of remains while dispute pending; cost

If a funeral home, funeral director, crematory operator, or other person asked to assist with a declarant's or deceased person's funeral, burial, cremation, or other manner of final disposition is in possession of a declarant's or deceased person's remains while a dispute described in section 2108.83 of the Revised Code is pending, the funeral home, funeral director, crematory operator, or other person may embalm or refrigerate and shelter the remains to preserve them and may add the cost of embalming, refrigeration, and sheltering to the final disposition costs to be charged.

(2006 H 426, eff. 10–12–06)

2108.85 Court costs; legal fees; criminal or civil liability for failure to bring legal action

(A) If a funeral home, funeral director, crematory operator, cemetery operator, cemetery organization, or other person asked to assist with a declarant's or deceased person's funeral, burial, cremation, or other manner of final disposition brings a legal action for purposes of section 2108.83 or 2108.84 of the Revised Code, the funeral home, funeral director, crematory operator, cemetery operator, cemetery organization, or other person may add to the costs the person charges for the goods and services the person provided the legal fees, if reasonable, and the court costs that the person incurred.

(B) The right created by division (A) of this section shall neither be construed to require, nor impose a duty on, a funeral home, funeral director, crematory operator, cemetery operator, cemetery organization, or other person asked to assist with a declarant's or deceased person's funeral, burial, cremation, or other manner of final disposition, to bring a legal action and such person shall not be held criminally or civilly liable for not bringing an action.

(2006 H 426, eff. 10–12–06)

2108.86 Right to good faith reliance on written declaration and instructions; criminal or civil liability

(A) A funeral home, funeral director, crematory operator, cemetery operator, cemetery organization, or other person asked to assist with a declarant's funeral, burial, cremation, or other manner of final disposition has the right to rely on the content of a written declaration and the instructions of the person or group of persons whom the funeral home, funeral director, crematory operator, cemetery operator, cemetery organization, or other person reasonably believes has the right of disposition.

(B) If the circumstances described in division (A) of section 2108.81 of the Revised Code apply, a funeral home, funeral director, crematory operator, cemetery operator, cemetery organization, or other person asked to assist with a deceased person's funeral, burial, cremation, or other manner of final disposition has the right to rely on the instructions of the person or group of persons the funeral home, funeral director, crematory operator, cemetery operator, cemetery organization, or other person reasonably believes has the right of disposition pursuant to section 2108.81 of the Revised Code.

(C) No funeral home, funeral director, crematory operator, cemetery operator, cemetery organization, or other person asked to assist with a deceased person's funeral, burial, cremation, or other manner of final disposition, who relies, pursuant to divisions (A) and (B) of this section, in good faith on the contents of a written declaration or the instructions of the person or group of persons the funeral home, funeral director, crematory operator, cemetery operator, cemetery organization, or other person reasonably believes has the right of disposition, shall be subject to criminal or civil liability or subject to disciplinary action for taking an action or not taking an action in reliance on such contents or instructions and for otherwise complying with sections 2108.70 to 2108.90 of the Revised Code.

(2006 H 426, eff. 10–12–06)

2108.87 Duty to independently investigate existence or locate representative or successor representative

(A) A funeral home, funeral director, crematory operator, cemetery operator, cemetery organization, or other person asked to assist with a deceased person's funeral, burial, cremation, or other manner of final disposition may independently investigate the existence of, or locate or contact, the following persons:

(1) A representative or successor representative named in a written declaration;

(2) A person listed in section 2108.81 of the Revised Code.

(B) In no circumstances shall a funeral home, funeral director, crematory operator, cemetery operator, cemetery organization, or other person asked to assist with a deceased person's funeral, burial, cremation, or other manner of final disposition have a duty to independently investigate the existence of, or locate or contact, the persons described in division (A) of this section.

(2006 H 426, eff. 10–12–06)

2108.88 Resignation of right of disposition

(A) A person to whom a declarant's or deceased person's right of disposition has been assigned or reassigned pursuant to section 2108.70 or 2108.81 of the Revised Code may decline to exercise the right or resign after beginning to exercise the right.

(B) A person described in division (A) of this section who resigns after beginning to exercise the right shall be subject to section 2108.89 of the Revised Code.

(2006 H 426, eff. 10–12–06)

2108.89 Liability for cost of goods and services relating to exercise of right of disposition

The following persons shall be liable for the reasonable costs of any goods or services purchased in connection with the exercise of the right of disposition for a declarant or deceased person:

(A) A representative or successor who assumes liability for the cost of such goods and services by signing a written declaration that states that such an assumption is made;

(B) A person to whom the right of disposition is assigned pursuant to section 2108.81 of the Revised Code and who has purchased goods or services associated with an exercise of the right.

(2006 H 426, eff. 10–12–06)

2108.90 Exclusive jurisdiction

Pursuant to division (A) of section 2101.24 of the Revised Code, the probate court for the county in which the declarant or deceased person resided at the time of death or the county in which a living person whose post-death arrangements are the subject of dispute resides shall have exclusive jurisdiction over any action that results from sections 2108.70 to 2108.89 of the Revised Code.

(2006 H 426, eff. 10–12–06)

Cross References

Application for summary release from administration by person obligated to pay decedent's funeral and burial expenses, 2113.031
Jurisdiction of probate court, 2101.24

PENALTY

2108.99 Penalty

Whoever violates section 2108.12 of the Revised Code is guilty of unlawful transfer of body parts, a felony of the fifth degree.

(1995 S 2, eff. 7–1–96; 1990 H 21, eff. 3–27–91)

Historical and Statutory Notes

Amendment Note: 1995 S 2 substituted "fifth" for "fourth".

Library References

Dead Bodies ⇌7.
Westlaw Topic No. 116.
C.J.S. Dead Bodies §§ 27 to 29.

Research References

Encyclopedias

OH Jur. 3d Cemeteries & Dead Bodies § 61, Sale of Human Body Parts.

Treatises and Practice Aids

Carlin, Baldwin's Ohio Practice, Merrick-Rippner Probate Law § 30:11, Drafting a Will—Funeral and Memorial Instructions—Anatomical Gifts.

CHAPTER 2109

FIDUCIARIES

PRELIMINARY PROVISIONS

Section	
2109.01	Definition
2109.02	Appointment and duties
2109.021	Certain documents may be filed by mail; exceptions
2109.022	Limitation on liability of fiduciary when certain powers granted to other persons
2109.03	Fiduciary's attorney

BOND; SURETIES

Section	
2109.04	Bond
2109.05	Bond; trust created by will
2109.06	New or additional bond
2109.07	Bond conditions of administrators; exemption of surviving spouse receiving entire net estate
2109.08	Bond conditions, special administrator
2109.09	Bond conditions, executors
2109.10	Bond when executor or administrator is sole residuary legatee or distributee
2109.11	Bond conditions, testamentary trustees
2109.12	Bond conditions, guardians
2109.13	Deposit of personal property in lieu of bond
2109.14	Deposit of works of art in museum authorized; reduction of bond
2109.15	Informality of bond
2109.16	One bond for two or more wards
2109.17	Sureties
2109.18	Release of a fiduciary's sureties
2109.19	Bond of indemnity to surety
2109.20	Guardian may give real estate mortgage to secure bond

QUALIFICATIONS AND MISCELLANEOUS PROVISIONS

Section	
2109.21	Residence qualifications of fiduciaries; nonresidents subject to conditions
2109.22	Marriage not a disqualification
2109.24	Resignation or removal of fiduciary
2109.25	Fiduciary in military service; removal and reinstatement

Section

2109.26	Vacancy before termination of the trust; accounting; successor fiduciary
2109.27	Surviving fiduciaries
2109.28	Merger of fiduciaries
2109.29	Rights as to shares in corporation

ACCOUNTS

2109.30	Accounts of executors and administrators
2109.301	Accounts of executors or administrators; requirements; final and distributive account; certificate of termination of estate
2109.302	Accounts of guardians or conservators
2109.303	Accounts of testamentary trustees or other fiduciaries
2109.31	Citation to file account
2109.32	Hearing on account; supplemental final account
2109.33	Notice of hearing; exceptions to account
2109.34	Representation in account proceeding
2109.35	Effect of order settling account; vacation of order
2109.36	Order of distribution
2109.361	Approval of third-party distribution

INVESTMENTS

2109.37	Investment powers
2109.371	Additional investment authority
2109.372	Temporary investments by fiduciaries; procedure
2109.38	Retention of other investments

POWERS, DUTIES, PROHIBITIONS, AND LIABILITIES

2109.39	Receiving distribution in kind
2109.40	Participation in corporate reorganization
2109.41	Deposit of funds
2109.42	Liability for failure to invest or deposit
2109.43	Personal use of trust property prohibited
2109.44	Fiduciaries not allowed to have dealings with estate; exception (first version)
2109.44	Fiduciaries not allowed to have dealings with estate; exception (second version)
2109.45	Statement before private sale confirmed

MORTGAGE BY FIDUCIARY

2109.46	Mortgage by fiduciary
2109.47	Report of investigators
2109.48	Amount of loan

INVESTIGATION OF TRUST

2109.49	Investigation of trust

CONCEALED OR EMBEZZLED ASSETS

2109.50	Proceeding when assets concealed or embezzled
2109.51	Imprisonment for disobeying citation
2109.52	Judgment on the complaint
2109.53	Judgment against fiduciary; removal
2109.54	Certificate of judgment; delivery to clerk of the court of common pleas
2109.55	Judgment in favor of state
2109.56	Conveyances

FUNDS OF UNKNOWN OR NONRESIDENT PERSONS

2109.57	Trustee of funds of unknown or nonresident

INVENTORY

2109.58	Inventory by fiduciary

COMPLAINT FOR DISTRIBUTION; ACTION ON BOND; TERMINATION OF TRUST

2109.59	Payment or distribution
2109.60	Probate court may send case to the court of common pleas
2109.61	Bond; parties to suit
2109.62	Termination of trust; distribution

ALLOCATION OF RECEIPTS AND EXPENDITURES

2109.68	Allocation by fiduciary
2109.69	Laws applicable to testamentary trusts

Comparative Laws

Del.—12 Del.C. § 3301 et seq.

Cross References

Custodian of minor's property; form of deed to successor, 1339.37
Executor or administrator not liable for consequences of exercise of powers granted to others, 1339.43
Fiduciary holding partnership interest in that capacity; limit on liability, 1339.65
Fiduciary law, Ch 1339
Grantee under deed as "trustee" or "agent"; effect of language, 5301.03
Ohio Transfers to Minors Act, 1339.31 to 1339.39
Procedure in probate court, Civ R 73

Law Review and Journal Commentaries

The Attorney's Role in Life Services Planning, Gregory S. French. Cin B Ass'n Rep 16 (April 1988).

Fiduciary Liability Under Superfund: Myth or Reality?, William Falsgraf. 1 Prob L J Ohio 97 (May/June 1991).

Fiduciary preludes: Likely issues for LLCs, Deborah A. DeMott. 66 U Colo L Rev 1043 (1995).

Ohio adopts new trust code—an overview of the new Ohio trust code and house bill 416. Alan Newman, 20 Ohio Law 9 (September/October 2006).

Special Provisions in a Will or Trust Occasioned by the Existence of a Business Interest, Howard M. Kohn. 13 W Reserve U L Rev 356 (1962).

The Structure of a General Theory of Nondisclosure, Christopher T. Wonnell. 41 Case W Res L Rev 329 (1991).

The Uniform Custodial Trust Act—A Useful New Forum of Title, Richard V. Wellman. 4 Prob L J Ohio 65 (January/February 1994).

PRELIMINARY PROVISIONS

2109.01 Definition

"Fiduciary" as used in Chapters 2101. to 2131. of the Revised Code, except as provided in section 2109.022 of the Revised Code, means any person, other than an assignee or trustee for an insolvent debtor or a guardian under sections 5905.01 to 5905.19 of the Revised Code, appointed by and accountable to the probate court and acting in a fiduciary capacity for any person, or charged with duties in relation to any property, interest, trust, or estate for the benefit of another; and includes an agency under contract with the department of mental retardation and developmental disabilities for the provision of protective service under sections 5123.55 to 5123.59 of the Revised Code, appointed by and accountable to the probate court as guardian or trustee with respect to mentally retarded or developmentally disabled persons.

(1990 H 569, eff. 7–1–91; 1989 S 46; 1985 S 129; 1980 H 900; 1971 H 290; 1953 H 1; GC 10506–1)

Historical and Statutory Notes

Pre–1953 H 1 Amendments: 114 v 364

Cross References

Discretionary distributions by fiduciaries, fiduciary defined, 1340.21

Research References

Encyclopedias

OH Jur. 3d Decedents' Estates § 657, Plaintiff; Fiduciaries.

OH Jur. 3d Fiduciaries § 4, Statutory Definitions; Generally—Under Probate Court Provisions.

OH Jur. 3d Fiduciaries § 45, Generally, Trustee for Absentee.

OH Jur. 3d Fiduciaries § 86, Additional Investment Authority; Prudent Person Standard.

OH Jur. 3d Fiduciaries § 129, Jurisdiction of Probate Division of the Court of Common Pleas.

OH Jur. 3d Fiduciaries § 171, Liability Under Statute; Corporation Dealing With Fiduciary as to Its Own Stock.

OH Jur. 3d Fiduciaries § 259, Jurisdiction of Probate Court.

OH Jur. 3d Trusts § 412, Where Trust Instrument Contains No Directions for Carrying Out Trust.

Forms

Ohio Forms Legal and Business § 25:58, Trust Agreement for Judgment Recovery for Minor.

Ohio Forms and Transactions KP 30.14, Trusts and Trustees.

Treatises and Practice Aids

Carlin, Baldwin's Ohio Practice, Merrick-Rippner Probate Law § 3:5, Jurisdiction of Probate Court—Subject Matter—Specific Areas—Fiduciaries.

Carlin, Baldwin's Ohio Practice, Merrick-Rippner Probate Law § 64:1, Powers and Duties of Guardian—Fiduciary Relationship.

Bogert - the Law of Trusts and Trustees § 651, Ohio.

Law Review and Journal Commentaries

The Fiduciary Duty of Care: A Perversion of Words. William A. Gregory, 38 Akron L Rev 181 (2005).

The Ohio uniform trust code takes shape. Alan Newman, 14 Prob L J Ohio 72 (March/April 2004).

The Uniform Trusts Act, Frank S. Rowley and Harry W. Vanneman. 5 Ohio St L J 145 (March 1939).

The Uniform Trusts Act, Frank S. Rowley and Harry W. Vanneman. 13 U Cin L Rev 157 (March 1939).

Notes of Decisions

Fiduciary relationship 1
Jurisdiction 3
Trusts and trustees 2

---

1. Fiduciary relationship

Statute requiring fiduciary to be provided hearing, with at least ten days prior notice, before fiduciary may be removed did not apply to trial court's removal of administrator of estate for failure to timely file account of estate, although statutory definition of "fiduciary" included administrators; statute governing failure to file account provided authority for administrator's immediate removal. In re Estate of Phelps (Ohio App. 7 Dist., Jefferson, 02-21-2006) No. 05 JE 19, 2006-Ohio-890, 2006 WL 459265, Unreported, reconsideration overruled 2006-Ohio-1471, 2006 WL 772017. Executors And Administrators ⇨ 35(16)

Service as both trustee and director of family corporation, whose stock was owned by trust, did not create conflict sufficient to establish breach of a fiduciary duty. Natl. City Bank v. Noble (Ohio App. 8 Dist., Cuyahoga, 12-08-2005) No. 85696, 2005-Ohio-6484, 2005 WL 3315034, Unreported. Trusts ⇨ 231(1)

First partner in partnership formed for purpose of purchasing building failed to establish that second partner breached fiduciary duty by failing to inform first partner that company, which purchased three floors of building by delivering promissory note and mortgage to partnership, intended to refinance promissory note; although second partner conceded it would have duty to disclose refinancing, first partner failed to demonstrate that second partner was aware of company's plan to refinance note as all of second partner's communications with company concerning financing related only to company's operating expenses. BI Properties, Inc. v. Vulcan Blanchester Realty Corp. (Ohio App. 1 Dist., Butler, 10-08-2004) No. C-040008, 2004-Ohio-5397, 2004 WL 2255029, Unreported, appeal not allowed 105 Ohio St.3d 1441, 822 N.E.2d 812, 2005-Ohio-531. Partnership ⇨ 121

Even if employer and corporation that resulted from merger of employer and another company owed fiduciary duty to executives related to stock options and performance awards, such alleged duty was not breached when decision was made that stock options and performance awards given to executives after employer announced that it would merge, but before merger closed, did not vest upon closing, where interpretation of stock plan by its administrator, providing that stock options and performance awards at issue did not vest upon closing, was reasonable and its interpretation was provided to employer and corporation. O'Planick v. Rubbermaid, Inc. (Ohio App. 9 Dist., Wayne, 09-22-2004) No. 03CA0060, 2004-Ohio-5168, 2004 WL 2244122, Unreported, appeal not allowed 105 Ohio St.3d 1439, 822 N.E.2d 811, 2005-Ohio-531. Corporations ⇨ 119; Corporations ⇨ 308(3)

Trust beneficiary made demand of trustees to pursue claims against charitable foundation, and trustees failed to act within 30 days, and thus, beneficiary had standing to bring claims that foundation converted trust assets for its own benefit, even though statutory authority to sue was solely in fiduciary accountable to probate court to bring such claims and only Ohio Attorney General had standing to enforce or administer charitable foundation; statute only applied to testamentary trusts and trust was inter vivos trust, and claims did not purport to seek oversight of foundation's administration or enforce terms of charitable trust. Dater v. Charles H. Dater Foundation (Ohio App. 1 Dist., Hamilton, 12-30-2003) No. C-020675, No. C-020784, 2003-Ohio-7148, 2003 WL 23024026, Unreported, appeal not allowed 102 Ohio St.3d 1459, 809 N.E.2d 32, 2004-Ohio-2569. Charities ⇨ 49

Genuine issues of material fact as to whether a fiduciary relationship was created when lender's agent told borrower to "drop their attorney" precluded summary judgment on borrower's negligence counterclaim in lender's action for nonpayment on note. National City Bank v. Slink & Taylor, LLC (Ohio App. 11 Dist., Portage, 12-12-2003) No. 2002-P-0045, 2003-Ohio-6693, 2003 WL 22931355, Unreported. Judgment ⇨ 181(26)

Statement by lender's agent, indicating that she would handle borrowers' transaction on her own, did not create a de facto fiduciary relationship between lender and borrowers so as to make lender liable to borrowers in negligence; shepherding a client through the borrowing process was a basic function of a loan officer and did not transform debtor/creditor relationship into a fiduciary relation. National City Bank v. Slink & Taylor, LLC (Ohio App. 11 Dist., Portage, 12-12-2003) No. 2002-P-0045, 2003-Ohio-6693, 2003 WL 22931355, Unreported. Banks And Banking ⇨ 111

"Express trust" is fiduciary relationship with respect to property, arising as result of manifestation of intention to create it and subjecting person in whom title is vested to equitable duties to deal with it for benefit of others. Gabel v. Richley (Ohio App. 2 Dist., 02-24-1995) 101 Ohio App.3d 356, 655 N.E.2d 773. Trusts ⇨ 1; Trusts ⇨ 270

In an action against a public service organization for breach of fiduciary duty and fraudulent misrepresentation relating a prior wrongful discharge suit which was ultimately settled and the conduct of an attorney who acted on behalf of the plaintiff, the complaint fails to allege facts sufficient to establish a fiduciary relationship where according to the record the organization did not refer, hire, or attempt to interfere with the attorney's conduct of the earlier litigation; the plaintiff alleged neither the existence of a fiduciary relationship nor any mutual understanding between himself and the organization that he reposed a special confidence in the organization and thus the existence of a de facto fiduciary relationship upon which a claim for breach of fiduciary duty may be based was not established. Applegate v. Fund for Constitutional Govt. (Franklin 1990) 70 Ohio App.3d 813, 592 N.E.2d 878.

Under Ohio law, "fiduciary relationship" is one in which special confidence and trust is reposed in integrity and fidelity of another and there is a resulting position of superiority or influence, acquired by virtues of this special trust; in this context, fiduciary's rule can be assumed through formal appointment, or it may arise de facto through more informal confidential relationship. Anchor v. O'Toole (C.A.6 (Ohio), 09-09-1996) 94 F.3d 1014, rehearing denied. Fraud ⇨ 7

Under Ohio law, "confidential relationship" is one where person comes to rely on and trust another in his important affairs and relations there involved are not necessarily legal, but may be moral, social, domestic, or merely personal; such a confidential relationship cannot be unilateral. Anchor v. O'Toole (C.A.6 (Ohio), 09-09-1996) 94 F.3d 1014, rehearing denied. Fraud ⇨ 7

Under Ohio law, "fiduciary duty" need not arise out of contract but may arise out of informal relationship where both parties understand that special trust or confidence has been reposed. NPF IV, Inc. v. Transitional Health Services (S.D.Ohio, 04-04-1996) 922 F.Supp. 77. Fraud ⇨ 7

Members of employer's board of directors may be "fiduciaries" with respect to employee welfare plan established by employer. Kuper v. Quantum Chemical Corp. (S.D.Ohio 1993) 838 F.Supp. 342. Labor And Employment ⇨ 463

Employer and its board of directors were not "fiduciaries," under ERISA, in connection with sale of division of employer and resulting trust-to-trust transfer of securities held in employee stock ownership plan for benefit of any employee of division, and thus, employer and its board of directors were not liable under ERISA in failing to prevent trust-to-trust transfer of assets and to allow distribution of assets to plan participants following sale of division and in failing to monitor financial condition of company and to protect plan assets, where employer and its board of directors were not named fiduciaries of plan, under terms of plan, employer and its directors did not have any discretionary authority over plan's management, administration or assets, and instead discretion was vested in committee members appointed by board, and employees failed to show that employer and board controlled decisions of committee or knew of wrongdoing by plan administrators. Kuper v. Quantum Chemical Corp. (S.D.Ohio 1993) 838 F.Supp. 342. Labor And Employment ⟲ 462; Labor And Employment ⟲ 463

Among the special relationships giving rise to a fiduciary duty are the duty owed by an innkeeper to a guest, a common carrier to a passenger, an individual who voluntarily takes custody of another under circumstances which prevent the other individual from protecting himself, and a possessor of land who leaves it open for public use. In re Donahue Securities, Inc. (Bkrtcy.S.D.Ohio, 10-07-2004) 318 B.R. 667, affirmed 337 B.R. 160. Carriers ⟲ 233; Fraud ⟲ 7

Ohio recognizes several special relationships that give rise to a fiduciary duty, including a psychotherapist to a third party harmed by his/her patient, an invitee of a business owner, a parent to prevent the abuse of their child, from an employer to an employee, and from a police officer to a prisoner in his/her custody. In re Donahue Securities, Inc. (Bkrtcy.S.D.Ohio, 10-07-2004) 318 B.R. 667, affirmed 337 B.R. 160. Fraud ⟲ 7; Health ⟲ 754; Parent And Child ⟲ 1

An individual's debt for fraud or defalcation while acting in a fiduciary capacity is excepted by 11 USC 523(a)(4) from debts the individual can discharge in bankruptcy proceedings; the definition of a "fiduciary" for purposes of this provision is a question of federal law but state law is considered relevant to the issue. In re Kern (Bkrtcy.S.D.Ohio 1989) 98 B.R. 321.

Superintendent of banks is not a fiduciary within this section. Fulton v Tischer, 17 Abs 449 (App, Montgomery 1934).

2. Trusts and trustees

Trust beneficiaries failed to allege sufficient facts to support claims that corporate and individual trustees' retention of stock in family corporation was done for their own pecuniary gain; under terms of trust agreement, trustees could retain investments without liability or depreciation, there was no allegation that trust contained an inordinate amount of corporate trustee's stock, and, while trust contained a large amount of stock in family company, value of trust increased since its inception. Natl. City Bank v. Noble (Ohio App. 8 Dist., Cuyahoga, 12-08-2005) No. 85696, 2005-Ohio-6484, 2005 WL 3315034, Unreported. Trusts ⟲ 261

Under specific language of trust document, stating that trustees were expressly empowered to retain as an investment, without liability for depreciation in value, any and all securities issued by family corporation, beneficiary's request for review of trust for diversification did not trigger a continuing duty on part of corporate trustee to monitor retention of stock in family corporation. Natl. City Bank v. Noble (Ohio App. 8 Dist., Cuyahoga, 12-08-2005) No. 85696, 2005-Ohio-6484, 2005 WL 3315034, Unreported. Trusts ⟲ 217.3(9)

Trial court's order allowing trustees to set off compensatory and punitive damages from beneficiary's share of trust property, which damages were assessed upon court's finding that beneficiary converted trust property, did not deprive beneficiary of the share of the trust to which he was entitled. Petefish v. Haselberger (Ohio App. 5 Dist., Ashland, 10-21-2005) No. 2005-COA-012, 2005-Ohio-5638, 2005 WL 2715634, Unreported. Trusts ⟲ 253

Trial court's award of compensatory damages to trustees, as reimbursement for unaccounted items missing from trust estate believed to have been among the items that beneficiary wrongfully converted from the trust estate, was warranted; there was competent and credible evidence in the record to support trial court's belief that beneficiary had all the property and to support trial court's valuation of the unaccounted property. Petefish v. Haselberger (Ohio App. 5 Dist., Ashland, 10-21-2005) No. 2005-COA-012, 2005-Ohio-5638, 2005 WL 2715634, Unreported. Trover And Conversion ⟲ 40(6)

No resulting trust existed on proceeds from fire policy on property which was corpus of pro tanto purchase-money resulting trust, since no funds from equitable beneficiaries was used to pay premiums and policy was not fraudulently or otherwise wrongfully obtained. Gabel v. Richley (Ohio App. 2 Dist., 02-24-1995) 101 Ohio App.3d 356, 655 N.E.2d 773. Trusts ⟲ 63.9

"Resulting trust" is based on intention of parties and is generally imposed in situations where express trust fails in whole or in part, where express trust is performed without exhausting trust estate, or where there is purchase-money trust. Gabel v. Richley (Ohio App. 2 Dist., 02-24-1995) 101 Ohio App.3d 356, 655 N.E.2d 773. Trusts ⟲ 65; Trusts ⟲ 67; Trusts ⟲ 72

"Purchase-money trust" arises where title to property is transferred to one person, but purchase price is paid by another; such situation raises inference that title-holder is not intended to possess beneficial interest in property. Gabel v. Richley (Ohio App. 2 Dist., 02-24-1995) 101 Ohio App.3d 356, 655 N.E.2d 773. Trusts ⟲ 72

"Pro tanto purchase-money trust" may arise where person other than title holder pays only portion of purchase price; equitable owner has interest in such proportion as amount paid toward total purchase price. Gabel v. Richley (Ohio App. 2 Dist., 02-24-1995) 101 Ohio App.3d 356, 655 N.E.2d 773. Trusts ⟲ 79

"Constructive trust" arises irrespective of intention of parties; "constructive trust" is an equitable remedy imposed to prevent fraud or unjust enrichment. Gabel v. Richley (Ohio App. 2 Dist., 02-24-1995) 101 Ohio App.3d 356, 655 N.E.2d 773. Trusts ⟲ 91

Spendthrift trusts are valid and enforceable in Ohio and the beneficiary has no interest liable to the execution of a judgment. Scott v. Bank One Trust Co., N.A. (Ohio 1991) 62 Ohio St.3d 39, 577 N.E.2d 1077.

RC 2109.44 is not applicable to the trustee of an inter vivos trust, because RC 2109.01 limits its purview to fiduciaries "appointed by and accountable to the probate court;" and hence such a trustee can properly purchase trust property for itself, provided court approval thereof is obtained after full disclosure. Central Nat. Bank of Cleveland v. Brewer (Ohio Com.Pl. 1966) 8 Ohio Misc. 409, 220 N.E.2d 846, 37 O.O.2d 323, 37 O.O.2d 393.

A residuary bequest to the United States for a permanent fund, the interest to be used for the relief of the various tribes of indigent American Indians, creates a valid charitable trust, and the federal government may serve as trustee and is not subject to the jurisdiction of the probate court. Edgeter v. Kemper (Ohio Prob. 1955) 136 N.E.2d 630, 73 Ohio Law Abs. 297. Charities ⟲ 11

Where trust funds were turned over to an Indiana charitable corporation by an Ohio probate court, a trustee appointed by the Ohio court seventeen years later could not demand a return of the property and an accounting. Hamrick v. Indianapolis Humane Soc., Inc. (S.D.Ind. 1959) 174 F.Supp. 403, 84 Ohio Law Abs. 70, 11 O.O.2d 150, affirmed 273 F.2d 7, 84 Ohio Law Abs. 78, 11 O.O.2d 400, certiorari denied 80 S.Ct. 671, 362 U.S. 919, 4 L.Ed.2d 739.

Under Ohio law, "express trust" is fiduciary relationship with respect to property, that arises as result of manifestation of intention to create it, and that subjects person in whom title is vested to equitable duties to deal with property for benefit of others. In re Pomainville (Bkrtcy.S.D.Ohio, 03-07-2000) 254 B.R. 699. Trusts ⟲ 1

In construing a trust agreement created in 1929, the terms "issue" and "grandchildren" clearly do not include illegitimate issue in the absence of an adverse showing since Ohio law as it existed in 1929 applies to the construction of the trust. First Natl Bank of Cincinnati v Simon, No. C-810587 (1st Dist Ct App, Hamilton, 3-31-82).

3. Jurisdiction

An action for money damages is not within jurisdiction of probate division of common pleas court, although filed as counterclaim to an action within jurisdiction of that division by trust adviser named in a will being administered under its authority. Kindt v. Cleveland Trust Co. (Ohio Com.Pl. 1971) 26 Ohio Misc. 1, 266 N.E.2d 84, 55 O.O.2d 53.

Contingent claims of defendants, who were former officers and directors of debtor, for indemnification and contribution against the debtor were sufficient to create "related to" bankruptcy jurisdiction, and thus constitute basis for removal of investors' state law claims against them for fraud, breach of contract, breach of fiduciary duty, negligence, misrepresentation, and securities fraud; defendants showed that their claims had a basis in contract, statute, corporate bylaws, and insurance policies, and had filed proofs of claim in the bankruptcy proceedings. In re National Century Financial Enterprises, Inc., Inv. Litigation (S.D.Ohio, 06-10-2004) 323 F.Supp.2d 861. Bankruptcy ⟲ 2053; Bankruptcy ⟲ 2088

The probate court has jurisdiction to render a declaratory judgment passing upon the capacity of a charitable beneficiary to take under an inter vivos trust as well as under a will, where, if the gift under the trust was ineffective, the property would become part of the estate. Natl City Bank v Baldwin, 90 Abs 228 (Prob, Cuyahoga 1962).

2109.02 Appointment and duties

Every fiduciary, before entering upon the execution of a trust, shall receive letters of appointment from a probate court having jurisdiction of the subject matter of the trust.

The duties of a fiduciary shall be those required by law, and such additional duties as the court orders. Letters of appointment shall not issue until a fiduciary has executed a written acceptance of the fiduciary's duties, acknowledging that the fiduciary is subject to removal for failure to perform the fiduciary's duties, and that the fiduciary is subject to possible penalties for conversion of property the fiduciary holds as a fiduciary. The written acceptance may be filed with the application for appointment.

No act or transaction by a fiduciary is valid prior to the issuance of letters of appointment to the fiduciary. This section does not prevent an executor named in a will, an executor nominated pursuant to a power as described in section 2107.65 of the Revised Code, or a person with the right of disposition under section 2108.70 or 2108.81 of the Revised Code from paying funeral expenses, or prevent necessary acts for the preservation of the trust estate prior to the issuance of such letters.

(2006 H 426, eff. 10–12–06; 1983 S 115, eff. 10–14–83; 1975 S 145; 1953 H 1; GC 10506–2, 10506–22)

Historical and Statutory Notes

Pre–1953 H 1 Amendments: 114 v 364, 368

Amendment Note: 2006 H 426 made changes throughout to reflect gender neutral language; inserted "or a person with the right of disposition under section 2108.70 or 2108.81 of the Revised Code" in the second sentence of the third paragraph; and made other nonsubstantive changes.

OSBA Probate and Trust Law Section

1983:
See the comment for 1983 following Sec. 2113.05.

Cross References

Advance payment of cost of appointing fiduciary may be demanded, 2101.21
Order in which debts to be paid, 2117.25

Library References

Executors and Administrators ⚖25, 27, 77.
Guardian and Ward ⚖13, 14, 16.
Mental Health ⚖120, 216.
Trusts ⚖160(1), 171, 225.
Westlaw Topic Nos. 162, 196, 257A, 390.
C.J.S. Executors and Administrators §§ 70, 79, 171.
C.J.S. Mental Health §§ 130, 132, 167 to 168, 177 to 178.
C.J.S. Trusts §§ 295 to 296, 318 to 320, 383, 388 to 390.

Research References

Encyclopedias
OH Jur. 3d Decedents' Estates § 954, Prerequisites to Issuance; Bond.
OH Jur. 3d Decedents' Estates § 959, Relation Back of Letters.
OH Jur. 3d Decedents' Estates § 967, Power Before Grant of Letters.
OH Jur. 3d Decedents' Estates § 1341, Funeral Expenses.
OH Jur. 3d Decedents' Estates § 1397, Right and Duty to Make Repairs; Liability in Tort.
OH Jur. 3d Fiduciaries § 10, Issuance of Letters of Appointment; Acceptance by Fiduciary.
OH Jur. 3d Fiduciaries § 11, Issuance of Letters of Appointment; Acceptance by Fiduciary—Actions Taken Prior to Appointment; Doctrine of "Relation Back."
OH Jur. 3d Guardian & Ward § 55, Generally; Vesting of Authority.
OH Jur. 3d Guardian & Ward § 56, Letter of Appointment.
OH Jur. 3d Guardian & Ward § 62, Effect of Order as Defining Scope of Guardian's Powers.
OH Jur. 3d Trusts § 168, Acceptance of Appointment.
OH Jur. 3d Trusts § 305, Source of Title in Property of Testamentary Trust.

Forms
Ohio Forms and Transactions KP 30.14, Trusts and Trustees.

Treatises and Practice Aids
Carlin, Baldwin's Ohio Practice, Merrick-Rippner Probate Law § 2:8, Preparation and Execution of Necessary Documents.
Carlin, Baldwin's Ohio Practice, Merrick-Rippner Probate Law § 2:15, Appointment of Fiduciary—Appointment of Executor or Administrator.
Carlin, Baldwin's Ohio Practice, Merrick-Rippner Probate Law § 68:2, Letters—in General—Issuance.
Carlin, Baldwin's Ohio Practice, Merrick-Rippner Probate Law § 69:5, Special Administrator—Entry for Appointment and for Bond—Form.
Carlin, Baldwin's Ohio Practice, Merrick-Rippner Probate Law § 2:121, Administration of Decedent's Estate—Checklist.
Carlin, Baldwin's Ohio Practice, Merrick-Rippner Probate Law § 33:22, Application for Appointment of Testamentary Trustee—Form.
Carlin, Baldwin's Ohio Practice, Merrick-Rippner Probate Law § 33:23, Application for Appointment of Testamentary Trustee—Form.
Carlin, Baldwin's Ohio Practice, Merrick-Rippner Probate Law § 33:24, Order Appointing Testamentary Trustee—Form.
Carlin, Baldwin's Ohio Practice, Merrick-Rippner Probate Law § 33:25, Letters of Testamentary Trusteeship—Form.
Carlin, Baldwin's Ohio Practice, Merrick-Rippner Probate Law § 62:21, Appointment of Guardian—Application—Appointment, Acceptance, and Bonding.
Carlin, Baldwin's Ohio Practice, Merrick-Rippner Probate Law § 62:83, Acceptance of Duties as Guardian of Minor—Form.
Carlin, Baldwin's Ohio Practice, Merrick-Rippner Probate Law § 62:86, Entry for Appointment of Guardian and Fixing Bond—Form.
Carlin, Baldwin's Ohio Practice, Merrick-Rippner Probate Law § 68:15, Letters of Administration—Written Acceptance of Duties.
Carlin, Baldwin's Ohio Practice, Merrick-Rippner Probate Law § 68:17, Letters Testamentary—Issuance.
Carlin, Baldwin's Ohio Practice, Merrick-Rippner Probate Law § 68:26, Letters Testamentary—Written Acceptance of Duties.
Carlin, Baldwin's Ohio Practice, Merrick-Rippner Probate Law § 68:47, Acceptance of Duties of Fiduciary—Form.
Carlin, Baldwin's Ohio Practice, Merrick-Rippner Probate Law § 109:69, Ohio Estate Tax—Release or Consent—Failure to Comply.
Carlin, Baldwin's Ohio Practice, Merrick-Rippner Probate Law App B SPF 4.0, Application for Authority to Administer Estate.
Bogert - the Law of Trusts and Trustees § 121, Selection of a Trustee.
Bogert - the Law of Trusts and Trustees § 151, Oath, Bond, and Letters of Trusteeship.
Restatement (3d) of Trusts § 32, Capacity of Individual to be Trustee.

Law Review and Journal Commentaries

Ohio adopts new trust code—an overview of the new Ohio trust code and house bill 416. Alan Newman, 20 Ohio Law 9 (September/October 2006).

The Fiduciary Duty of Care: A Perversion of Words. William A. Gregory, 38 Akron L Rev 181 (2005).

Using a Corporate Executor, Phillip B. Rosplock. 12 Lake Legal Views 5 (February 1989).

Notes of Decisions

Acts prior to appointment 1
Breach of fiduciary duties 3
Compensation 6
Jurisdiction 2
Powers and duties 4
Statute of limitations 5

---

1. Acts prior to appointment

A person nominated in a will as executrix of an estate may, prior to her formal appointment, collect assets and delegate funds; therefore, a person nominated as an executrix may properly close the decedent's accounts and pay money to his children according to her wishes where the executrix is the sole beneficiary and the estate has no debts. North Akron S. & L. Assn. v. Rondy (Summit 1990) 68 Ohio App.3d 518, 589 N.E.2d 82.

The doctrine of relation back to validate an executrix's actions prior to her formal appointment is applicable where the executrix, the sole legatee of an estate with no debts, directs that certain accounts of the decedent be closed and the proceeds distributed pursuant to her wishes. North Akron S. & L. Assn. v. Rondy (Summit 1990) 68 Ohio App.3d 518, 589 N.E.2d 82.

A financial institution is not liable to an estate for disbursing funds of a decedent to a party presenting tax waiver forms incorrectly naming the financial institution by omitting the word "North" from the institution's name where the party presenting the forms (1) has applied for executrix status pursuant to a will but at the time of disbursement had not yet been appointed executrix by the probate court, (2) presented to the institution's employee a valid power of attorney, and (3) possesses tax consent forms. North Akron S. & L. Assn. v. Rondy (Summit 1990) 68 Ohio App.3d 518, 589 N.E.2d 82.

A will contest action, otherwise rightly brought within the meaning of RC 2741.09, will not fail under RC 2741.02 just because persons named testamentary trustees in the will, but not appointed to such capacity within six months following probate of the will, are not joined as parties in that capacity, where such persons have been timely made parties in the capacity of co-executors (having been so named in the will and appointed by the probate court), and all the beneficiaries of the testamentary trust have been timely made parties to the action. Hirsch v. Hirsch (Franklin 1972) 32 Ohio App.2d 200, 289 N.E.2d 386, 61 O.O.2d 212. Wills ⊙— 265.1

The doctrine of "relation back" validates acts or transactions previous to the appointment of an administrator of an estate only in those instances where the doctrine results in a benefit to the estate. Wrinkle v. Trabert (Ohio 1963) 174 Ohio St. 233, 188 N.E.2d 587, 22 O.O.2d 248. Executors And Administrators ⊙— 29(1)

2. Jurisdiction

A residuary bequest to the United States for a permanent fund, the interest to be used for the relief of the various tribes of indigent American Indians, creates a valid charitable trust, and the federal government may serve as trustee and is not subject to the jurisdiction of the probate court. Edgeter v. Kemper (Ohio Prob. 1955) 136 N.E.2d 630, 73 Ohio Law Abs. 297. Charities ⊙— 11

Federal court does not have jurisdiction of an action against an executor or administrator involving an alleged breach of fiduciary duties. Starr v. Rupp (C.A.6 (Ohio) 1970) 25 Ohio Misc. 224, 421 F.2d 999, 12 A.L.R. Fed. 279, 53 O.O.2d 169, 54 O.O.2d 343.

An Ohio court has no jurisdiction over real property in the District of Columbia and a decision purporting to exercise such jurisdiction is not entitled to full faith and credit. Hughes v. Hughes (D.D.C. 1953) 112 F.Supp. 899, 67 Ohio Law Abs. 284, 52 O.O. 137.

3. Breach of fiduciary duties

Former husband's transfer of real property from trust of which he and former wife were co-grantors and co-trustees to himself individually without wife's knowledge or consent violated husband's fiduciary duties to trust, even though trust authorized trustees to dispose of trust assets and to act independently of each other; trust granted trustees such powers "to carry out the purposes and intents" of the trust, rather than to enable self-dealing. Sredniawa v. Sredniawa (Ohio App. 8 Dist., Cuyahoga, 03-30-2006) No. 86607, 2006-Ohio-1597, 2006 WL 832449, Unreported. Trusts ⊙— 239

Removing executrix was not abuse of probate court's discretion, where executrix admitted that she used decedent's checking account for her own, personal items such as groceries and spending money. In re Estate of Lindsay (Ohio App. 7 Dist., Mahoning, 11-02-2005) No. 04-MA-259, 2005-Ohio-5930, 2005 WL 2981647, Unreported. Executors And Administrators ⊙— 35(1)

First partner in partnership formed for purpose of purchasing building failed to establish that second partner breached fiduciary duty by rejecting first partner's efforts to purchase additional equity in partnership, where first partner did not tender sum agreed upon in partnership agreement to increase its share in partnership, but instead tendered lesser sum. BI Properties, Inc. v. Vulcan Blanchester Realty Corp. (Ohio App. 1 Dist., Butler, 10-08-2004) No. C-040008, 2004-Ohio-5397, 2004 WL 2255029, Unreported, appeal not allowed 105 Ohio St.3d 1441, 822 N.E.2d 812, 2005-Ohio-531. Partnership ⊙— 94

First partner in partnership formed for purpose of purchasing building failed to establish that second partner breached fiduciary duty by failing to inform first partner that company, which purchased three floors of building by delivering promissory note and mortgage to partnership, intended to refinance promissory note; although second partner conceded it would have duty to disclose refinancing, first partner failed to demonstrate that second partner was aware of company's plan to refinance note as all of second partner's communications with company concerning financing related only to company's operating expenses. BI Properties, Inc. v. Vulcan Blanchester Realty Corp. (Ohio App. 1 Dist., Butler, 10-08-2004) No. C-040008, 2004-Ohio-5397, 2004 WL 2255029, Unreported, appeal not allowed 105 Ohio St.3d 1441, 822 N.E.2d 812, 2005-Ohio-531. Partnership ⊙— 121

Executives, who received stock options and performance awards, failed to establish breach of contract claim against employer and corporation that resulted from merger of employer and another company based on failure of stock options and performance awards granted to executives after employer announced that it would merge, but before merger closed, to vest upon closing, where interpretation of stock plan by its administrator, providing that stock options and performance awards at issue did not vest upon closing, was reasonable and not result of gross mistake or bad faith and this interpretation was provided to employer and corporation. O'Planick v. Rubbermaid, Inc. (Ohio App. 9 Dist., Wayne, 09-22-2004) No. 03CA0060, 2004-Ohio-5168, 2004 WL 2244122, Unreported, appeal not allowed 105 Ohio St.3d 1439, 822 N.E.2d 811, 2005-Ohio-531. Corporations ⊙— 119; Corporations ⊙— 308(3)

Even if employer and corporation that resulted from merger of employer and another company owed fiduciary duty to executives related to stock options and performance awards, such alleged duty was not breached when decision was made that stock options and performance awards given to executives after employer announced that it would merge, but before merger closed, did not vest upon closing, where interpretation of stock plan by its administrator, providing that stock options and performance awards at issue did not vest upon closing, was reasonable and this interpretation was provided to employer and corporation. O'Planick v. Rubbermaid, Inc. (Ohio App. 9 Dist., Wayne, 09-22-2004) No. 03CA0060, 2004-Ohio-5168, 2004 WL 2244122, Unreported, appeal not allowed 105 Ohio St.3d 1439, 822 N.E.2d 811, 2005-Ohio-531. Corporations ⊙— 119; Corporations ⊙— 308(3)

Parishioner who alleged that church employee molested and sexually assaulted him stated cause of action for breach of fiduciary duty against diocese and church; diocese allowed employee to supervise and coach activities of youth organization, it was reasonable to claim that diocese had duty to protect participants in its youth program from its agents, a claim for breach of fiduciary duty against diocese depended upon existence of underlying tort claim and there was valid underlying tort claim against employee for sexual abuse, and despite numerous opportunities to discover abuse, church ignored the hundreds of acts of abuse which occurred in its rectory. Mills v. Deehr (Ohio App. 8 Dist., Cuyahoga, 05-06-2004) No. 82799, 2004-Ohio-2338, 2004 WL 1047720, Unreported, as amended nunc pro tunc. Religious Societies ⊙— 30

Trust beneficiaries were only entitled to their respective shares of trust corpus plus interest and were not entitled to any property purchased with trust funds; trustee was entitled to all of the profit or income derived from the trust corpus during her lifetime, and beneficiaries failed to provide evidence that either the trust or the trustee profited as a result of trustee's alleged failure to account for trust funds, commingling of trust property, and failure to notify beneficiaries of existence of trust. Jones v. Elsea (Ohio App. 4 Dist., Pickaway, 09-12-2003) No. 02-CA-27, 2003-Ohio-4900, 2003 WL 22133294, Unreported, appeal not allowed 101 Ohio St.3d 1422, 802 N.E.2d 153, 2004-Ohio-123. Trusts ⊙— 140(1); Trusts ⊙— 325

Trustee's use of trust funds for no-interest loan to purchase farm did not amount to breach of fiduciary duty, even though loan was a self-dealing transaction, where trustee was entitled to all of the profit or income derived from the trust corpus during her lifetime and her only duty was to ensure that trust corpus remained intact. Jones v. Elsea (Ohio App. 4 Dist., Pickaway, 09-12-2003) No. 02-CA-27, 2003-Ohio-4900, 2003 WL 22133294, Unreported, appeal not allowed 101 Ohio St.3d 1422, 802 N.E.2d 153, 2004-Ohio-123. Trusts ⊙— 231(2)

Trustees' selection of independent appraisers from two nationally known companies to value stock of family corporation precluded claim that trustees breached their duty to make reasonable efforts to sell trust assets at best price obtainable, even though beneficiary's expert reached different conclusion and higher value. Huntington Natl. Bank v. Wolfe (Ohio App. 10 Dist., 12-29-1994) 99 Ohio App.3d 585, 651 N.E.2d 458. Trusts ⊙— 195

Individual trustee did not violate duty of loyalty to beneficiary by determining to sell family corporation stock owned by trust and making distribution of beneficiary's share in cash, despite conflict of interest, given that trustee acted in good faith and corporate trustee, which had no conflicting interest, concurred in determination. Huntington Natl. Bank v. Wolfe (Ohio App. 10 Dist., 12-29-1994) 99 Ohio App.3d 585, 651 N.E.2d 458. Trusts ⚖ 231(1)

Even though one cotrustee may have conflict of interest, trust beneficiary must prove that conflict has resulted in prejudice to trust, or to beneficiary, in order to be entitled to relief based on alleged breach of duty of loyalty. Huntington Natl. Bank v. Wolfe (Ohio App. 10 Dist., 12-29-1994) 99 Ohio App.3d 585, 651 N.E.2d 458. Trusts ⚖ 262

Law indulges in presumption of misrepresentation if fiduciary relationship exists and fiduciary obtains benefit by virtue of relationship, but any such presumption may be rebutted by showing that plaintiff had competent and disinterested advice, that she entered into transaction voluntarily, deliberately, and advisedly, knowing its nature and effect, or that her consent was not obtained by reason of power of influence to which relation gave rise. Craggett v. Adell Ins. Agency (Ohio App. 8 Dist., 12-13-1993) 92 Ohio App.3d 443, 635 N.E.2d 1326. Fraud ⚖ 50

A school district treasurer who invests $100,000 at 10.5% interest in a bank ineligible under RC 135.03 to be a depository of public money, who receives a cashier's check for $110,500 that is dishonored after the investment matures, and who is convicted and imprisoned for bribery because he made the unauthorized investment in return for a $10,000 payment, owes a debt to the school district that cannot be discharged in his bankruptcy proceedings because under 11 USC 523(a)(4) the debt arises from defalcation of his fiduciary duties, whether it be the result of embezzlement, negligence, ignorance, or mere failure to account for the funds. In re Curth (Bkrtcy.S.D.Ohio 1989) 98 B.R. 324.

A fiduciary's inability, even if innocent or negligent, to account for a sum constitutes "defalcation" and renders the debt created by the breach of fiduciary duty nondischargeable under 11 USC 523(a)(4) in the fiduciary's bankruptcy proceedings. In re Kern (Bkrtcy.S.D.Ohio 1989) 98 B.R. 321.

4. Powers and duties

Personal representatives only can sue for damages and on them is the risk of ascertaining who is entitled thereto. Weidner v. Rankin (Ohio 1875) 26 Ohio St. 522.

A guardian derives his power to act from the appointment and bond; letters of guardianship need not in fact issue. Maxsom v. Sawyer (Ohio 1843) 12 Ohio 195.

Trustee did not violate any duties to settlor by allowing settlor to modify the trust instrument and to transfer additional assets into the trust and, thus, could not be held liable to settlor's son for negligence or breach of fiduciary duty arising out of the implementation of such changes, even if trustee had notice that settlor was suffering from Alzheimer's Disease at time she made the changes, where there was no evidence that settlor was legally incompetent when she made the changes, but rather vice president of trustee stated in affidavit that settlor was lucid and knew what she was doing at all times vice president dealt with her. Miller v. Keybank Natl. Assn. (Ohio App. 8 Dist., Cuyahoga, 04-06-2006) No. 86327, 2006-Ohio-1725, 2006 WL 871621, Unreported. Trusts ⚖ 58

Trust provision allowing the grantors to "add or withdraw" assets from the trust at any time did not allow former husband who, with former wife, was co-grantor and co-trustee of the trust, to transfer real property from the trust to himself individually; husband performed the transfer in his capacity as trustee, rather than as grantor, as evidenced by a trustee's deed filed in county recorder's office along with an affidavit of trustee invoking husband's powers as trustee in making the transfer. Sredniawa v. Sredniawa (Ohio App. 8 Dist., Cuyahoga, 03-30-2006) No. 86607, 2006-Ohio-1597, 2006 WL 832449, Unreported. Trusts ⚖ 231(1)

Fiduciary's role may be assumed by formal appointment, or it may arise de facto from more informal confidential relationship, but such a confidential relationship cannot be unilateral. Cairns v. Ohio Sav. Bank (Ohio App. 8 Dist., 03-04-1996) 109 Ohio App.3d 644, 672 N.E.2d 1058. Fraud ⚖ 7

Fiduciary duty may arise from informal relationship only if both parties understand that special trust or confidence has been reposed. Cairns v. Ohio Sav. Bank (Ohio App. 8 Dist., 03-04-1996) 109 Ohio App.3d 644, 672 N.E.2d 1058. Fraud ⚖ 7

Mortgagee did not owe fiduciary duty to mortgagors, even though mortgagee maintained escrow account on behalf of mortgagors, which was funded by monthly payments and used to pay property taxes and insurance premiums; there was nothing in mortgage agreement that expressly gave rise to fiduciary relationship between parties, and there was no allegation in complaint of de facto fiduciary relationship. Cairns v. Ohio Sav. Bank (Ohio App. 8 Dist., 03-04-1996) 109 Ohio App.3d 644, 672 N.E.2d 1058. Mortgages ⚖ 211

Trustees had authority to sell family corporation stock owned by trust and make distribution to beneficiary in cash, rather than in kind; any power of conversion did not apply in that trust was not terminated when trustees sold stock and trust agreement conferred "full power" upon trustees to sell any property. Huntington Natl. Bank v. Wolfe (Ohio App. 10 Dist., 12-29-1994) 99 Ohio App.3d 585, 651 N.E.2d 458. Trusts ⚖ 189; Trusts ⚖ 282

Mere existence of conflict of interest, known and anticipated by settlor, does not disqualify individual trustee from participating in decisions regarding trust; only requirement is that individual trustee having conflicting interest exercise judgment in good faith. Huntington Natl. Bank v. Wolfe (Ohio App. 10 Dist., 12-29-1994) 99 Ohio App.3d 585, 651 N.E.2d 458. Trusts ⚖ 231(1)

Absence of either self-dealing or breach of good faith by corporate trustee, in deciding to sell stock in family corporation and make distribution in cash, precluded finding that corporate trustee improperly delegated its duties to individual trustee. Huntington Natl. Bank v. Wolfe (Ohio App. 10 Dist., 12-29-1994) 99 Ohio App.3d 585, 651 N.E.2d 458. Trusts ⚖ 238.1

The administrator of a chattel mortgagor must administer the mortgaged chattels, and the mortgagee cannot have replevin. Lingler v. Wesco (Ohio 1908) 79 Ohio St. 225, 86 N.E. 1004, 128 Am.St.Rep. 714, 6 Ohio Law Rep. 572.

Administration is a prerequisite to the devolution of the personal estate of a decedent. McBride v. Vance (Ohio 1906) 73 Ohio St. 258, 76 N.E. 938, 112 Am.St.Rep. 723, 3 Ohio Law Rep. 569, 3 Ohio Law Rep. 574, 4 Am.Ann.Cas. 191. Executors And Administrators ⚖ 3(1)

Board of directors' fiduciary obligations under ERISA based on their power to appoint and remove plan fiduciaries are not unlimited; although under such circumstances board members exercise discretionary management or control with respect to management of plan, and are therefore fiduciaries, their fiduciary obligations are limited to selection and retention of plan fiduciaries. Kuper v. Quantum Chemical Corp. (S.D.Ohio 1993) 838 F.Supp. 342. Labor And Employment ⚖ 463

5. Statute of limitations

Trustee's trusteeship terminated, and four-year limitations period applicable to beneficiaries' action for breach of fiduciary duty began to run, when trustee transferred ownership of life insurance policies which served as sole means of funding trust to beneficiaries of trust. Cassner v. Bank One Trust Co., N.A. (Ohio App. 10 Dist., Franklin, 07-01-2004) No. 03AP-1114, 2004-Ohio-3484, 2004 WL 1470806, Unreported, cause dismissed 103 Ohio St.3d 1523, 817 N.E.2d 407, 2004-Ohio-5853. Limitation Of Actions ⚖ 103(1)

Beneficiaries' action against trustee for breach of fiduciary duty accrued, and four-year limitations period began to run, when trustee's trusteeship terminated, as opposed to when beneficiaries' interests were first impaired by breach, where action was not brought until after termination of trust. Cassner v. Bank One Trust Co., N.A. (Ohio App. 10 Dist., Franklin, 07-01-2004) No. 03AP-1114, 2004-Ohio-3484, 2004 WL 1470806, Unreported, cause dismissed 103 Ohio St.3d 1523, 817 N.E.2d 407, 2004-Ohio-5853. Limitation Of Actions ⚖ 103(1)

Allegations that trustee negligently managed life insurance policies which served as sole means of funding trust stated tort claim for breach of fiduciary duty, as opposed to claim for breach of contract, and thus four-year period of limitations applicable to tort claims, rather than 15-year period of limitations applicable to breach of contract claims, applied. Cassner v. Bank One Trust Co., N.A. (Ohio App. 10 Dist., Franklin, 07-01-2004) No. 03AP-1114, 2004-Ohio-3484, 2004 WL 1470806, Unreported, cause dismissed 103 Ohio St.3d 1523, 817 N.E.2d 407, 2004-Ohio-5853. Action ⚖ 27(1)

An action is not properly commenced so as to bar the defense of the statute of limitations, where such action is instituted within the statutory period of limitation against one acting as administrator whose letters of administration, although applied for within the period of limitation, were not issued until such period had elapsed. Wrinkle v. Trabert (Ohio 1963) 174 Ohio St. 233, 188 N.E.2d 587, 22 O.O.2d 248. Limitation Of Actions ⚖ 82

Where the letters of appointment of an administrator are not issued until after the statute of limitations has run as to a tort action against the estate, the administrator has no authority to validate an attempted defense of such action by him undertaken before the issuance of his letters of appointment. Wrinkle v. Trabert (Ohio 1963) 174 Ohio St. 233, 188 N.E.2d 587, 22 O.O.2d 248.

Where a probate court turned assets over to an Indiana charitable corporation in accordance with testamentary provisions and said charitable corporation never qualified as trustee of such charitable trust, the court could not seventeen years later appoint an individual as trustee of such trust. Hamrick v. Indianapolis Humane Soc., Inc. (C.A.7 (Ind.) 1959) 273 F.2d 7, 84 Ohio Law Abs. 78, 11 O.O.2d 400, certiorari denied 80 S.Ct. 671, 362 U.S. 919, 4 L.Ed.2d 739.

Where trust funds were turned over to an Indiana charitable corporation by an Ohio probate court, a trustee appointed by the Ohio court seventeen years later could not demand a return of the property and an accounting. Hamrick v. Indianapolis Humane Soc., Inc. (S.D.Ind. 1959) 174 F.Supp. 403, 84 Ohio Law Abs. 70, 11 O.O.2d 150, affirmed 273 F.2d 7, 84 Ohio Law Abs. 78, 11 O.O.2d 400, certiorari denied 80 S.Ct. 671, 362 U.S. 919, 4 L.Ed.2d 739.

6. Compensation

Order awarding co-executor of deceased's estate fiduciary fees was not against manifest weight of evidence, absent any showing that she did not faithfully perform duties as executor in appropriate manner. In re Bird (Ohio App. 8 Dist., Cuyahoga, 05-05-2005) No. 85130, 2005-Ohio-2186, 2005 WL 1048128, Unreported. Executors And Administrators ☞ 498

Fiduciary's compensation for services rendered to trust includes allowance for attorney fees. In re Estate of Bickham (Logan 1993) 85 Ohio App.3d 634, 620 N.E.2d 913. Trusts ☞ 313

2109.021 Certain documents may be filed by mail; exceptions

After letters of appointment are issued to a fiduciary, the court shall accept filings by mail in matters of estates, guardianships, or trusts, unless the court in writing notifies the fiduciary or attorney of record that a personal appearance is necessary, or a personal appearance is otherwise required by law. An improper or incomplete filing shall be rejected, and the court shall return it to the sender, and impose a cost of two dollars and fifty cents per improper or incomplete filing, chargeable against the estate.

(1976 S 466, eff. 5–26–76; 1975 S 145)

Legislative Service Commission

1975:

This new section would permit filings to be made by a fiduciary by mail for everything except accounts, unless the fiduciary is notified by the court that a personal appearance is required or unless a personal appearance is otherwise required by law. An improper filing under this section would be rejected by the court and returned, with costs of $2.50 per envelope to the estate.

Library References

Records ☞ 7.
Westlaw Topic No. 326.
C.J.S. Records §§ 4 to 8.

Research References

Encyclopedias

OH Jur. 3d Decedents' Estates § 972, Filing by Mail or Appearance in Person.

OH Jur. 3d Fiduciaries § 37, Right to Employ Attorney—Notice and Service of Process; Personal Appearance.

OH Jur. 3d Guardian & Ward § 60, Nomination of Attorney; Filings by Mail.

Treatises and Practice Aids

Carlin, Baldwin's Ohio Practice, Merrick-Rippner Probate Law § 2:3, Time for Administration of Decedent's Estate and Payment of Estate Taxes.

Carlin, Baldwin's Ohio Practice, Merrick-Rippner Probate Law § 54:3, Fiduciary Accounts—Filing—by Mail.

2109.022 Limitation on liability of fiduciary when certain powers granted to other persons

(A) As used in this section, "fiduciary" means a trustee under any testamentary or other trust, an executor or administrator, or any other person who is acting in a fiduciary capacity for any person, trust, or estate.

(B) When an instrument under which a fiduciary acts reserves to the grantor, or vests in an advisory or investment committee or in one or more other persons, including one or more fiduciaries, to the exclusion of the fiduciary or of one or more of several fiduciaries, any power, including, but not limited to, the authority to direct the acquisition, disposition, or retention of any investment or the power to authorize any act that an excluded fiduciary may propose, any excluded fiduciary is not liable, either individually or as a fiduciary, for either of the following:

(1) Any loss that results from compliance with an authorized direction of the grantor, committee, person, or persons;

(2) Any loss that results from a failure to take any action proposed by an excluded fiduciary that requires a prior authorization of the grantor, committee, person, or persons if that excluded fiduciary timely sought but failed to obtain that authorization.

(C) Any excluded fiduciary as described in division (B) of this section is relieved from any obligation to perform investment reviews and make recommendations with respect to any investments to the extent the grantor, an advisory or investment committee, or one or more other persons have authority to direct the acquisition, disposition, or retention of any investment.

(D) This section does not apply to the extent that the instrument under which an excluded fiduciary as described in division (B) of this section acts contains provisions that are inconsistent with this section.

(1988 S 228, eff. 3–22–89; 1985 S 129)

Uncodified Law

1988 S 228, § 3, eff. 3–22–89, reads: The amendments to sections 1339.43 and 2109.022 of the Revised Code contained in this act shall apply to all transactions that occur on or after the effective date of this act.

Cross References

Uniform Gifts to Minors Act, limitation on fiduciary's liability, 1339.43

Library References

Executors and Administrators ☞ 81, 116 to 119, 433.
Guardian and Ward ☞ 63 to 65, 70, 120.
Mental Health ☞ 179, 238, 476.
Trusts ☞ 232 to 235, 237, 240.
Westlaw Topic Nos. 162, 196, 257A, 390.
C.J.S. Executors and Administrators §§ 166, 267 to 276, 724.
C.J.S. Mental Health §§ 158 to 159, 179, 256 to 257.
C.J.S. Right to Die §§ 5, 8.
C.J.S. Trusts §§ 323, 326, 328 to 330, 338 to 339, 345 to 346, 376.

Baldwin's Ohio Legislative Service, 1988 Laws of Ohio, S 228—LSC Analysis, p 5–968

Research References

Encyclopedias

OH Jur. 3d Fiduciaries § 80, Necessity for Approval by Beneficiary or Third Person.

Treatises and Practice Aids

Bogert - the Law of Trusts and Trustees § 391, Powers of Trustees for Charity.

Law Review and Journal Commentaries

Fiduciary Liability Under Superfund: Myth or Reality?, William Falsgraf. 1 Prob L J Ohio 97 (May/June 1991).

2109.03 Fiduciary's attorney

At the time of the appointment of a fiduciary, such fiduciary shall file in the probate court the name of the attorney, if any, who will represent him in matters relating to the trust. After the name of an attorney has been filed, notices sent to such fiduciary in his official capacity shall also be sent by the court to such attorney who may sign waiver of service of any or all of such notices upon him. If the fiduciary is absent from the state, such attorney shall be the agent of the fiduciary upon whom summonses, citations, and notices may be served. Any summons, citation, or notice may be served upon the fiduciary by delivering duplicate copies thereof to the attorney designated by him. No probate judge shall permit any person to practice law in the probate court for compensation, unless he has been admitted to the practice of law within the state. This section does not prevent any person from representing his own interest in any estate, matter, action, or proceeding.

(1953 H 1, eff. 10–1–53; GC 10506–3)

Historical and Statutory Notes

Pre–1953 H 1 Amendments: 119 v 394, § 1; 114 v 364

Library References

Executors and Administrators ⚖441, 525.
Guardian and Ward ⚖129.
Mental Health ⚖499, 500.
Process ⚖80.
Trusts ⚖260.
Westlaw Topic Nos. 162, 196, 257A, 313, 390.
C.J.S. Executors and Administrators §§ 782 to 784, 933.
C.J.S. Mental Health §§ 264, 275 to 278.
C.J.S. Process §§ 50, 54, 73.
C.J.S. Trusts §§ 555 to 556, 575 to 576.

Research References

Encyclopedias

OH Jur. 3d Decedents' Estates § 954, Prerequisites to Issuance; Bond.
OH Jur. 3d Fiduciaries § 36, Right to Employ Attorney—Filing Attorney's Name.
OH Jur. 3d Fiduciaries § 37, Right to Employ Attorney—Notice and Service of Process; Personal Appearance.
OH Jur. 3d Guardian & Ward § 60, Nomination of Attorney; Filings by Mail.

Treatises and Practice Aids

Carlin, Baldwin's Ohio Practice, Merrick-Rippner Probate Law § 53:1, Fiduciary's Attorney—Appointment, Fees.
Carlin, Baldwin's Ohio Practice, Merrick-Rippner Probate Law § 53:2, Fiduciary's Attorney—Discretion in Appointment.
Carlin, Baldwin's Ohio Practice, Merrick-Rippner Probate Law § 53:3, Fiduciary's Attorney—Service of Notices from Probate Court.
Carlin, Baldwin's Ohio Practice, Merrick-Rippner Probate Law § 53:4, Fiduciary's Attorney—Service of Notices from Probate Court—Absence of Fiduciary from State.
Carlin, Baldwin's Ohio Practice, Merrick-Rippner Probate Law § 53:5, Fiduciary's Attorney—Agent.
Carlin, Baldwin's Ohio Practice, Merrick-Rippner Probate Law § 84:3, Creditor's Claims—Form of Claim.
Carlin, Baldwin's Ohio Practice, Merrick-Rippner Probate Law § 80:14, Attorney Fees—Determination.

Law Review and Journal Commentaries

Probate Malpractice, Hon. Fred V. Skok. 14 Lake Legal Views 1 (February 1991).

Notes of Decisions

Attorney 1, 2
   Designation in will 1
   Discretion of executor 2
Claim presentation 5
Negligent performance of duties 3
Service of summons 4

---

1. Attorney—Designation in will

A provision of a will which designates an attorney to represent the executor in the administration of the estate may not be considered as a condition precedent to the appointment of the executor, but is merely precatory and not binding on the fiduciary. In re Estate of Deardoff (Ohio 1984) 10 Ohio St.3d 108, 461 N.E.2d 1292, 10 O.B.R. 434. Executors And Administrators ⚖ 14

A testator, by the terms of his will, may not bind his designated fiduciary to the election of a specific attorney no matter how mandatory the language of the will. In re Estate of Deardoff, No. 136 (12th Dist Ct App, Warren, 6-29-83), affirmed by 10 OS(3d) 108, 10 OBR 434, 461 NE(2d) 1292 (1984).

2. —— Discretion of executor, attorney

Upon consideration of GC 10506–3 (RC 2109.03) and 10509–193 (RC 2113.36) it seems that relation contemplated therein is that of attorney and client or employer and employee and it is to be noted that fiduciary is required to file in probate court the name of the attorney who will represent him in administration of estate; this contemplates exercise of discretion on part of fiduciary in choice of his counsel; should legislature have had any other intention it certainly would have written statute in such a manner as to make it mandatory upon court to appoint counsel for fiduciary. (Ed. note: See also 10 U Cin L Rev 104; 2 Ohio St L J 77 (1937).) In re Shinnick's Estate (Ohio Prob. 1935) 1 Ohio Supp. 394, 19 Ohio Law Abs. 461, 3 O.O. 458.

3. Negligent performance of duties

A testamentary trustee who fails to call on beneficiaries and provide them with financial data as required by the trust is not entitled to attorney fees, even though the trustee's noncompliance did not harm the beneficiaries. In re Estate of Winograd (Cuyahoga 1989) 65 Ohio App.3d 76, 582 N.E.2d 1047, motion to certify overruled 50 Ohio St.3d 702, 553 N.E.2d 278.

A beneficiary whose interest in an estate is vested is in privity with the fiduciary of the estate, and where such privity exists the attorney for the fiduciary is not immune from liability to the vested beneficiary for damages arising from the attorney's negligent performance. (See also Scholler v Scholler, 10 OS(3d) 98, 10 OBR 426, 462 NE(2d) 158 (1984); Simon v Zipperstein, 32 OS(3d) 74, 512 NE(2d) 636 (1987).) Elam v. Hyatt Legal Services (Ohio 1989) 44 Ohio St.3d 175, 541 N.E.2d 616.

4. Service of summons

RC 2109.03 requires the one seeking the service of summons to affirmatively allege in the body of the petition that the fiduciary is absent from the state. Kaczenski v. Kaczenski (Trumbull 1959) 169 N.E.2d 36, 83 Ohio Law Abs. 469.

The provision in RC 2109.03 that if a fiduciary is absent from the state, his attorney shall be his agent upon whom summons may be served, and that any summons may be served upon the fiduciary by delivering copies thereof to such attorney, is all-inclusive and is not limited or restricted to summons in actions originating in the probate court. Meisner v. Flemion (Hancock 1958) 109 Ohio App. 117, 164 N.E.2d 183, 10 O.O.2d 302.

5. Claim presentation

Attorney named by executrix to represent her in administration of estate was proper party to receive presentment of claim against estate, so that presentment of claim to attorney one week before expiration of three-month period was timely, notwithstanding fact that attorney did not inform executrix of claim until approximately three weeks later. Peoples Nat. Bank v. Treon (Miami 1984) 16 Ohio App.3d 410, 476 N.E.2d 372, 16 O.B.R. 480. Executors And Administrators ⚖ 225(1); Executors And Administrators ⚖ 228(1)

The mailing of a claim to the regularly appointed attorney in the settlement of the estate, which claim was listed as being a claim against the executor, and the acknowledgment of the receipt of the claim by the attorney for the estate is a filing with the executor in compliance with RC 2117.06. In re Clark's Estate (Ohio Com.Pl. 1967) 11 Ohio Misc. 103, 229 N.E.2d 122, 40 O.O.2d 347.

2109.03 Note 5

The presentation of a claim against an estate to the agent of an insurance company appointed by the administrator as his agent does not constitute statutory presentation of such a claim to the administrator, and the claim is barred at the expiration of the statutory period. Beacon Mut. Indem. Co. v. Stalder (Summit 1954) 95 Ohio App. 441, 120 N.E.2d 743, 54 O.O. 69.

BOND; SURETIES

2109.04 Bond

(A)(1) Unless otherwise provided by law, every fiduciary, prior to the issuance of his letters as provided by section 2109.02 of the Revised Code, shall file in the probate court in which the letters are to be issued a bond with a penal sum in such amount as may be fixed by the court, but in no event less than double the probable value of the personal estate and of the annual real estate rentals which will come into such person's hands as a fiduciary. The bond of a fiduciary shall be in a form approved by the court and signed by two or more personal sureties or by one or more corporate sureties approved by the court. It shall be conditioned that the fiduciary faithfully and honestly will discharge the duties devolving upon him as fiduciary, and shall be conditioned further as may be provided by law.

(2) Except as otherwise provided in this division, if the instrument creating the trust dispenses with the giving of a bond, the court shall appoint a fiduciary without bond, unless the court is of the opinion that the interest of the trust demands it. If the court is of that opinion, it may require bond to be given in any amount it fixes. If a parent nominates a guardian for his child in a will and provides in the will that the guardian may serve without giving bond, the court may appoint the guardian without bond or require the guardian to give bond in accordance with division (A)(1) of this section.

(3) A guardian of the person only does not have to give bond unless, for good cause shown, the court considers a bond to be necessary. When a bond is required of a guardian of the person only, it shall be determined and filed in accordance with division (A)(1) of this section. This division does not apply to a guardian of the person only nominated in a parent's will if the will provides that the guardian may serve without giving bond.

(4) When the probable value of the personal estate and of the annual real estate rentals that will come into the guardian's hands as a fiduciary is less than ten thousand dollars, the court may waive or reduce a bond required by division (A)(1) of this section.

(B) When an executive director who is responsible for the administration of children services in the county is appointed as trustee of the estate of a ward pursuant to section 5153.18 of the Revised Code and has furnished bond under section 5153.13 of the Revised Code, or when an agency under contract with the department of mental retardation and developmental disabilities for the provision of protective service under sections 5123.55 to 5123.59 of the Revised Code is appointed as trustee of the estate of a ward under such sections and any employees of the agency having custody or control of funds or property of such a ward have furnished bond under section 5123.59 of the Revised Code, the court may dispense with the giving of a bond.

(C) When letters are granted without bond, at any later period on its own motion or upon the application of any party interested, the court may require bond to be given in such amount as may be fixed by the court. On failure to give such bond, the defaulting fiduciary shall be removed.

No instrument authorizing a fiduciary whom it names to serve without bond shall be construed to relieve a successor fiduciary from the necessity of giving bond, unless the instrument clearly evidences such intention.

The court by which a fiduciary is appointed may reduce the amount of the bond of such fiduciary at any time for good cause shown.

When two or more persons are appointed as joint fiduciaries, the court may take a separate bond from each or a joint bond from all.

(1991 H 82, eff. 9–10–91; 1989 S 46; 1984 H 263; 1980 H 900; 1971 H 290; 132 v H 1; 129 v 1623; 125 v 903; 1953 H 1; GC 10506–4, 10506–8, 10506–13, 10506–21)

Historical and Statutory Notes

Pre–1953 H 1 Amendments: 123 v 534; 116 v 385; 114 v 365, 366, 368

Cross References

Additional bond before sale of land by executor, administrator, or guardian, 2127.27
Appointment of guardian for hospitalized patients, 5122.41
Bond of foreign executor or administrator selling Ohio lands, 2129.26
Bond of foreign trustee of Ohio lands, 2129.28
Bonds signed in blank, 3.34
Limitation of action on official bond, 2305.12
Successor fiduciary completing land sale, additional bond, 2127.06
Surety company can be a bondsman, 3929.01, 3929.14, 3929.15
Veteran's guardian, bond, 5905.10

Library References

Executors and Administrators ⚖26.
Guardian and Ward ⚖15.
Mental Health ⚖166.
Trusts ⚖161.
Westlaw Topic Nos. 162, 196, 257A, 390.
C.J.S. Executors and Administrators §§ 71 to 77.
C.J.S. Mental Health § 141.
C.J.S. Trusts § 302.

Research References

Encyclopedias

OH Jur. 3d Decedents' Estates § 908, Joint Letters of Administration.
OH Jur. 3d Decedents' Estates § 954, Prerequisites to Issuance; Bond.
OH Jur. 3d Decedents' Estates § 1704, Duties and Powers of Special Administrator—Inventory and Account.
OH Jur. 3d Fiduciaries § 178, Bond Required After Letters Granted Without Bond.
OH Jur. 3d Fiduciaries § 180, Form and Amount of Bond.
OH Jur. 3d Fiduciaries § 181, Separate or Joint Bonds.
OH Jur. 3d Fiduciaries § 186, Dispensing With Bond.
OH Jur. 3d Fiduciaries § 310, Failure to Give Bond.
OH Jur. 3d Guardian & Ward § 57, Bond.
OH Jur. 3d Guardian & Ward § 59, Waiver of Bond.

Forms

Ohio Forms Legal and Business § 24:143, Drafting Will.
Ohio Forms Legal and Business § 24:161, Entire Estate to Spouse—Alternatively to Children—Guardianship of Minors.
Ohio Forms Legal and Business § 24:205, Residue to Trust for Spouse and Children.
Ohio Forms Legal and Business § 24:461, Appointment—General Clause.
Ohio Forms Legal and Business § 24:481, Appointment of Guardian—Person of Minor Children—Provision Expressing Desire Same Person be Appointed Guardian of Their Estates.
Ohio Forms Legal and Business § 24:913, Codicil—Appointing New Coexecutor.
Ohio Forms Legal and Business § 24:205.10, Pour-Over Will—Residue to Trust.
Ohio Forms and Transactions KP 30.10, Guardianship Clause.

Treatises and Practice Aids

Carlin, Baldwin's Ohio Practice, Merrick-Rippner Probate Law § 2:8, Preparation and Execution of Necessary Documents.
Carlin, Baldwin's Ohio Practice, Merrick-Rippner Probate Law § 2:16, Appointment of Fiduciary—Fiduciary's Bond.

Carlin, Baldwin's Ohio Practice, Merrick-Rippner Probate Law § 52:1, Fiduciary's Bond—Introduction.

Carlin, Baldwin's Ohio Practice, Merrick-Rippner Probate Law § 52:2, Fiduciary's Bond—in General.

Carlin, Baldwin's Ohio Practice, Merrick-Rippner Probate Law § 52:4, Fiduciary's Bond—Exceptions to Requirement.

Carlin, Baldwin's Ohio Practice, Merrick-Rippner Probate Law § 52:5, Fiduciary's Bond—Motion of Interested Party to Seek Bond.

Carlin, Baldwin's Ohio Practice, Merrick-Rippner Probate Law § 52:6, Fiduciary's Bond—Amount.

Carlin, Baldwin's Ohio Practice, Merrick-Rippner Probate Law § 52:7, Fiduciary's Bond—Amount—Reduction.

Carlin, Baldwin's Ohio Practice, Merrick-Rippner Probate Law § 52:8, Fiduciary's Bond—Joint Fiduciaries.

Carlin, Baldwin's Ohio Practice, Merrick-Rippner Probate Law § 12:30, Wrongful Death Trust Agreement—Form.

Carlin, Baldwin's Ohio Practice, Merrick-Rippner Probate Law § 2:121, Administration of Decedent's Estate—Checklist.

Carlin, Baldwin's Ohio Practice, Merrick-Rippner Probate Law § 30:35, Drafting a Will—Executor's Bond.

Carlin, Baldwin's Ohio Practice, Merrick-Rippner Probate Law § 30:57, Simple Will—Form.

Carlin, Baldwin's Ohio Practice, Merrick-Rippner Probate Law § 52:10, Fiduciary's Bond—Limitation of Action.

Carlin, Baldwin's Ohio Practice, Merrick-Rippner Probate Law § 52:11, Fiduciary's Bond—Special Bond of Sole Residuary Legatee or Distributee—Liability.

Carlin, Baldwin's Ohio Practice, Merrick-Rippner Probate Law § 52:12, Fiduciary's Bond—Special Bond of Sole Residuary Legatee or Distributee—Exception for Surviving Spouse.

Carlin, Baldwin's Ohio Practice, Merrick-Rippner Probate Law § 52:13, Fiduciary's Bond—Exceptions for Trustee of Estate of Ward.

Carlin, Baldwin's Ohio Practice, Merrick-Rippner Probate Law § 52:21, Fiduciary's Bond—Sureties—Introduction.

Carlin, Baldwin's Ohio Practice, Merrick-Rippner Probate Law § 52:31, Fiduciary's Bond—Mortgage Bond in Lieu of Surety.

Carlin, Baldwin's Ohio Practice, Merrick-Rippner Probate Law § 52:36, Motion to Require Executor to Give Bond—Form.

Carlin, Baldwin's Ohio Practice, Merrick-Rippner Probate Law § 52:37, Motion to Require Testamentary Trustee to Give Bond—Form.

Carlin, Baldwin's Ohio Practice, Merrick-Rippner Probate Law § 52:38, Bond of Fiduciary—Form.

Carlin, Baldwin's Ohio Practice, Merrick-Rippner Probate Law § 52:39, Bond of Executor—Form.

Carlin, Baldwin's Ohio Practice, Merrick-Rippner Probate Law § 52:46, Bond of Trustee—Funds of Unknown or Nonresident Person—Form.

Carlin, Baldwin's Ohio Practice, Merrick-Rippner Probate Law § 52:47, Application to Reduce Penalty on Bond—Form.

Carlin, Baldwin's Ohio Practice, Merrick-Rippner Probate Law § 52:48, Order Reducing Penalty on Bond—Form.

Carlin, Baldwin's Ohio Practice, Merrick-Rippner Probate Law § 52:58, Entry Approving Bond of Testamentary Trustee—Form.

Carlin, Baldwin's Ohio Practice, Merrick-Rippner Probate Law § 62:21, Appointment of Guardian—Application—Appointment, Acceptance, and Bonding.

Carlin, Baldwin's Ohio Practice, Merrick-Rippner Probate Law § 62:88, Exceptions to Bond of Guardian—Form.

Carlin, Baldwin's Ohio Practice, Merrick-Rippner Probate Law § 62:91, Entry Approving Bond and Ordering Letters of Guardianship for Minor—Form.

Carlin, Baldwin's Ohio Practice, Merrick-Rippner Probate Law § 64:20, Powers and Duties of Guardian—Ward's Estate—Mandatory Duties.

Carlin, Baldwin's Ohio Practice, Merrick-Rippner Probate Law § 68:20, Letters Testamentary—Qualifications for Executors—Age Requirement.

Carlin, Baldwin's Ohio Practice, Merrick-Rippner Probate Law § 68:44, Fiduciary's Bond—Form.

Carlin, Baldwin's Ohio Practice, Merrick-Rippner Probate Law § 97:16, Land Sale by Guardian—Additional Bond of Guardian.

Carlin, Baldwin's Ohio Practice, Merrick-Rippner Probate Law § 30:162, Bond Not Required of Executor Named in Will—Form.

Carlin, Baldwin's Ohio Practice, Merrick-Rippner Probate Law App B SPF 15.3, Guardian's Bond.

Bogert - the Law of Trusts and Trustees § 151, Oath, Bond, and Letters of Trusteeship.

Bogert - the Law of Trusts and Trustees § 563, Court Supervised Trusts.

Restatement (2d) of Conflicts § 267, Court Supervision of Administration.

Law Review and Journal Commentaries

Actions on Fiduciary Bonds in Probate Court, Jerome C. Tinianow. 59 Clev B J 120 (February 1988).

Notes of Decisions

Action on bond 3
Appointment of fiduciary 5
Bankruptcy of fiduciary, effect 6
Construction 4
Discretion of court in fixing bond 2
Liability on bond 1

---

1. Liability on bond

An administration bond is liable where the administrator fails to pay the proceeds of real estate sold to pay debts, to the heirs. Griswold v. Frink (Ohio 1871) 22 Ohio St. 79.

Where a debtor of a decedent is appointed administrator, the debt becomes assets and his bond is liable therefor. In re Raab's Estate (Ohio 1865) 16 Ohio St. 273.

Where co-trustees authorize one of their number to receive and control the trust fund, and are negligent in taking security and looking after the fund, and it is lost by the defalcation of the trustee having such control, all the trustees are responsible. State v. Guilford (Ohio 1846) 15 Ohio 593. Trusts ⇐ 240

Error in failing to require administrator with will annexed to secure bond did not invalidate administrator's sale of real property, which was newly discovered asset of decedent's estate, where there were no allegations of malfeasance against administrator, property was appraised by court-approved appraiser, and property was sold at appraised value. In re Estate of Hyer (Ohio App. 7 Dist., Monroe, 09-27-2004) No. 03 MO 9, 2004-Ohio-5359, 2004 WL 2334510, Unreported. Executors And Administrators ⇐ 143

Even if bank should have realized that there was something wrong with social security deposits being made to account of deceased person and should have prohibited administrator of estate from withdrawing such funds, administrator's bonding company was subject to liability for administrator's wrongful conversion of such funds while acting as bonded administrator. Bank One of Ohio N.A. v. Brown (Summit 1985) 22 Ohio App.3d 82, 488 N.E.2d 939, 22 O.B.R. 180. Executors And Administrators ⇐ 529

Where after twenty years the principal on the bond is cited to appear and judgment is taken against him without the surety's knowledge, the surety is not bound thereby. Gilbert v. Gilbert (Ohio Cir. 1896) 7 Ohio C.D. 58.

2. Discretion of court in fixing bond

The probate court has authority to reduce the amount of the bond of a trustee, accept a new bond, and discharge the trustees upon the former bond, where it finds such action to be to the best interest of the estate; such finding is justified by the saving of expense to the estate by a reduction in the amount of the bond; and the action of the court in accepting the new bond and releasing the sureties on the former bond is within the jurisdiction of the court, and not open to collateral attack. Wolfe v. Fidelity & Deposit Co. of Maryland (Ohio App. 2 Dist. 1919) 11 Ohio App. 58, 30 Ohio C.A. 593, affirmed 100 Ohio St. 332, 126 N.E. 414, 17 Ohio Law Rep. 345. Principal And Surety ⇐ 109; Trusts ⇐ 382

Trial court abused its discretion when it required son to provide a bond of $284,800 in order to serve as co-executor of estate but did not require a bond from the other co-executors; statute required the trial court to either take a separate bond from each of the co-executors or to require a joint bond from all of them. In re Estate of Laffin (Ohio App. 3 Dist., Auglaize, 06-05-2006) No. 2-05-41, 2006-Ohio-2779, 2006 WL 1519906, Unreported. Executors And Administrators ⇐ 26(1)

Unless a will creating a testamentary trust dispenses with the giving of bond, a trust company must give bond in an amount not less than double

Note 2

the probate value of the personal estate and of the annual real estate rentals which will come into its hands, before letters of appointment may be issued to it as testamentary trustee under such will; except at the time of issuance of such letters of appointment, full power is vested in the probate court to require bond from a trust company as a testamentary trustee, solely within the discretion of the court. Winters Nat. Bank & Trust Co. v. Ross (Ohio 1959) 169 Ohio St. 335, 159 N.E.2d 603, 8 O.O.2d 347. Trusts ⇔ 161

Testamentary trustees are "an interested party" within the last sentence of this section and, upon their application, the probate court may take a new bond for a smaller amount than the original bond and may discharge the original bond. Fidelity & Deposit Co. v. Wolfe (Ohio 1919) 100 Ohio St. 332, 126 N.E. 414, 17 Ohio Law Rep. 345.

Under GC 10506–4 (RC 2109.04) and former 10506–17 (RC 2109.21), a testator has the privilege of requesting that no bond be required of his executor, or of leaving the fixing of bond to the probate court. Tieman v. Smith (Ohio Com.Pl. 1933) 30 Ohio N.P.N.S. 544.

Where a testator requests that bond be given by his executor in a stated amount, it is the duty of the probate court to fix the amount of such bond in accordance with statute, and the probate court in such case has no discretion to follow the testator's request or suggestion as to amount of bond of executor, if same is less than double the estimated value of the personal estate. Tieman v. Smith (Ohio Com.Pl. 1933) 30 Ohio N.P.N.S. 544.

3. Action on bond

Where a bond has not been given, an order of the court for the sale of real estate, though it may be erroneous, is not void. Arrowsmith v. Harmoning (Ohio 1884) 42 Ohio St. 254, affirmed 6 S.Ct. 1023, 118 U.S. 194, 30 L.Ed. 243.

Executors and administrators who have not given bond in Ohio cannot appeal without giving an appeal bond. Dennison v. Talmage (Ohio 1876) 29 Ohio St. 433.

In an action brought on an administration bond against the surviving obligors and the administratrix of the estate, the plaintiff assumes as to such administratrix the character of a creditor of her intestate's estate; such action cannot be maintained until eighteen months after the date of her administration bond. Hammerle v. Kramer (Ohio 1861) 12 Ohio St. 252. Executors And Administrators ⇔ 537(5); Principal And Surety ⇔ 149

A demand and refusal to pay must be averred by a creditor to maintain an action on an administrator's bond. Woodson v. State for Use of Borland (Ohio 1848) 17 Ohio 161.

A suit on a bond and proceedings by citation are barred after ten years. Gilbert v. Marsh (Ohio Prob. 1897) 7 Ohio Dec. 230, 4 Ohio N.P. 338.

The administrator is the proper party defendant in an action on his bond, and is rightfully joined with the sureties thereon. Kehnast v. Daum (Ohio Com.Pl. 1897) 6 Ohio Dec. 401, 4 Ohio N.P. 366, affirmed 9 Ohio C.D. 867.

4. Construction

Bonds of executors and administrators are controlled by the laws in force at the time such bonds were given. McGovney v. State for Use of Lee's Adm'r (Ohio 1851) 20 Ohio 93.

The amendment in 1935 of GC 10506–4 (RC 2109.04) striking the words "unless otherwise provided by law," therefrom had the effect of repealing by implication the provisions of GC 710–161 (RC 1107.14) in respect only to the requirement of bond imposed upon every fiduciary prior to the issuance of letters of appointment as such by the probate court. Winters Nat. Bank & Trust Co. v. Ross (Ohio 1959) 169 Ohio St. 335, 159 N.E.2d 603, 8 O.O.2d 347.

The duty enjoined upon an administrator to give a bond, with conditions as therein provided, contemplates that such bond shall secure the faithful performance of the duties imposed upon the personal representative of a deceased person under former GC 10772 (RC 2125.02, RC 2125.03). U.S. Fidelity & Guaranty Co. v. Decker (Ohio 1930) 122 Ohio St. 285, 171 N.E. 333, 68 A.L.R. 1538, 8 Ohio Law Abs. 273, 31 Ohio Law Rep. 581.

Under the law of Ohio, the rules governing testamentary trusts and trustees are the same as those governing guardians and the administration of estates, and the provisions of RS 5981 and RS 5986 are simply directory as to what court shall appoint such a trustee. Boals v. Clingan (Ohio Com.Pl. 1905) 16 Ohio Dec. 267, 6 Ohio N.P.N.S. 609.

Breaking the will terminates the administration of an administrator with the will annexed. In re Schonacker's Estate (Ohio Prob. 1910) 55 W.L.B. 78.

5. Appointment of fiduciary

A guardian derives his power to act from the appointment and bond; letters of guardianship need not in fact issue. Maxsom v. Sawyer (Ohio 1843) 12 Ohio 195.

Failing to require administrator with will annexed to secure bond was error; although decedent's will eliminated bond requirement for named joint executrixes, this did not eliminate bond requirement for any other or subsequent estate fiduciaries. In re Estate of Hyer (Ohio App. 7 Dist., Monroe, 09-27-2004) No. 03 MO 9, 2004-Ohio-5359, 2004 WL 2334510, Unreported. Executors And Administrators ⇔ 26(2)

An order removing an administrator because his bond was not signed by an authorized agent is not in fact a "removal" of a fiduciary, but a refusal to appoint a fiduciary who has failed to qualify. (See also In re Estate of Anders, 83 Abs 351, 169 NE(2d) 302 (1959).) In re Anders' Estate (Franklin 1959) 110 Ohio App. 258, 162 N.E.2d 871, 81 Ohio Law Abs. 552, 13 O.O.2d 24.

When the persons named as executors of a will are also named as trustees of a trust created by that instrument, they should be appointed such trustees and give bond as such on the completion of their duties as executors. In re Kachelmacher's Estate (Hocking 1931) 40 Ohio App. 282, 178 N.E. 314, 11 Ohio Law Abs. 279.

An incorporated trust company which has deposited funds with treasurer of state as provided by law is required, notwithstanding provisions of GC 710–161 (RC 1107.14), to give a bond by reason of provisions of this section before being qualified to act as a fiduciary where its appointment is made and letters are issued by probate court. 1945 OAG 631.

6. Bankruptcy of fiduciary, effect

To establish the nondischargeability of a debt under the exception to discharge for a debtor's defalcation while acting in a fiduciary capacity, plaintiffs must show establishment of a trust, party in trust acting in fiduciary capacity, and breach of that relationship by at least "defalcation" of funds. In re Harris-Miles (Bkrtcy.N.D.Ohio, 09-12-1995) 187 B.R. 178. Bankruptcy ⇔ 3376(5)

2109.05 Bond; trust created by will

When deemed necessary by the probate court and not otherwise directed in the will, a bond, as provided by sections 2109.01 to 2109.58, inclusive, of the Revised Code, shall be required in all trusts created by will and not fully discharged, on the petition of an interested person and after notice to the trustee.

If such a trustee fails to give bond within the time ordered by the court, he shall be removed from his trust or be considered to have declined it. Another person may be appointed in his stead upon giving the required bond.

(1953 H 1, eff. 10–1–53; GC 10506–19, 10506–20)

Historical and Statutory Notes

Pre–1953 H 1 Amendments: 114 v 368

Library References

Trusts ⇔161.
Westlaw Topic No. 390.
C.J.S. Trusts § 302.

Research References

Encyclopedias

OH Jur. 3d Fiduciaries § 12, Appointment to Fill Vacancy in Office; Sole Fiduciary.

OH Jur. 3d Fiduciaries § 179, Bond Requirement for Testamentary Trust.

OH Jur. 3d Fiduciaries § 310, Failure to Give Bond.

Treatises and Practice Aids

Carlin, Baldwin's Ohio Practice, Merrick-Rippner Probate Law § 2:16, Appointment of Fiduciary—Fiduciary's Bond.

Carlin, Baldwin's Ohio Practice, Merrick-Rippner Probate Law § 52:41, Bond of Testamentary Trustee—Form.

Carlin, Baldwin's Ohio Practice, Merrick-Rippner Probate Law § 52:42, Bond of Trustee—Form.

Bogert - the Law of Trusts and Trustees § 150, Acceptance by the Trustee.

Bogert - the Law of Trusts and Trustees § 151, Oath, Bond, and Letters of Trusteeship.

Law Review and Journal Commentaries

Actions on Fiduciary Bonds in Probate Court, Jerome C. Tinianow. 59 Clev B J 120 (February 1988).

Notes of Decisions

Executor's actions 2
Management of trust 1

---

1. Management of trust

In equity, a trustee is not permitted to so manage the subject of his trust as to make profits or gain therefrom for himself, for the beneficiaries of the trust have a right to expect and require the exercise of his best judgment, care, and diligence on their behalf, and the gains resulting therefrom inure to their sole benefit; what such trustee may not do directly he is not permitted to do through the intervention of an agent or attorney. Cox v. John (Ohio 1877) 32 Ohio St. 532.

The general rule in equity is that a trustee can acquire no personal interest in the trust property; and where he is authorized to do so by statute the validity of his title depends, in equity, upon its bona fides. Rammelsberg v. Mitchell (Ohio 1875) 29 Ohio St. 22.

Where a trustee of a testamentary trust invests the trust fund according to the direction of the will of the testator and for the purpose of protecting the fund purchases property at a sheriff's sale taking title to the same in his own name as trustee, and the cestui que trust enters into possession of the land and uses and occupies it or accepts from the trustee the rents and revenues thereof in lieu of the interest earnings of the trust fund, such cestui que trust is estopped by his conduct from questioning the right or the authority of the trustee to make such purchase, and from demanding from him an accounting of an amount equal to the interest such fund would have earned during the time he so occupies the land or accepts the rents and revenues therefrom. Willis v. Holcomb (Ohio 1911) 83 Ohio St. 254, 94 N.E. 486, 8 Ohio Law Rep. 595. Trusts ⟾ 230; Wills ⟾ 681(1)

2. Executor's actions

Where a trustee under a will who is also executor wrongfully converts trust funds to his own use, for which he gave his note and mortgage to a third party for his beneficiaries, a promise by the beneficiaries to release the mortgage if he would resign is void. Withers v. Ewing (Ohio 1884) 40 Ohio St. 400, 10 W.L.B. 426.

As a general rule, the powers of an executor are coextensive with all the trusts devolved upon him by the will and all acts done by him in executing such trusts will be regarded as done in his capacity as executor, unless it plainly appears, from the whole will, that the testator intended to create a special trust to be managed by the person named as executor in the capacity of special trustee. Mathews v. Meek (Ohio 1872) 23 Ohio St. 272.

Where a party is appointed by will as both executor and trustee, separate bonds must be given for each position. P., C. & St. L.R. Co. v. Schmidt (Ohio Cir. 1894) 4 Ohio C.D. 535, 1 Ohio Dec. 639.

2109.06 New or additional bond

The probate court by which a fiduciary is appointed may, on its own motion or on the application of any interested party, and after notice to the fiduciary, require a new bond or sureties or an additional bond or sureties, whenever, in the opinion of such court, the interests of the trust demand it.

Immediately upon the filing of the inventory by a fiduciary, the court shall determine whether the amount of the bond of such fiduciary is sufficient and shall require new or additional bond if in the opinion of the court the interests of the trust demand it.

When a new bond is required as provided in this section, the sureties in the prior bond shall nevertheless be liable for all breaches of the conditions set forth in such bond which are committed before the new bond is approved by the court.

A fiduciary who fails within the time fixed by the court to furnish new or additional bond or sureties shall be removed and some other person appointed in his stead, as the circumstances of the case require.

(1953 H 1, eff. 10–1–53; GC 10506–9 to 10506–12)

Historical and Statutory Notes

Pre–1953 H 1 Amendments: 114 v 366

Library References

Executors and Administrators ⟾26.
Guardian and Ward ⟾15.
Mental Health ⟾166.
Trusts ⟾161.
Westlaw Topic Nos. 162, 196, 257A, 390.
C.J.S. Executors and Administrators §§ 71 to 77.
C.J.S. Mental Health § 141.
C.J.S. Trusts § 302.

Research References

Encyclopedias

OH Jur. 3d Fiduciaries § 12, Appointment to Fill Vacancy in Office; Sole Fiduciary.

OH Jur. 3d Fiduciaries § 180, Form and Amount of Bond.

OH Jur. 3d Fiduciaries § 182, New or Additional Bond.

OH Jur. 3d Fiduciaries § 206, Effect on Liability of New or Additional Bond or Sureties.

OH Jur. 3d Fiduciaries § 310, Failure to Give Bond.

Treatises and Practice Aids

Carlin, Baldwin's Ohio Practice, Merrick-Rippner Probate Law § 2:16, Appointment of Fiduciary—Fiduciary's Bond.

Carlin, Baldwin's Ohio Practice, Merrick-Rippner Probate Law § 52:1, Fiduciary's Bond—Introduction.

Carlin, Baldwin's Ohio Practice, Merrick-Rippner Probate Law § 52:5, Fiduciary's Bond—Motion of Interested Party to Seek Bond.

Carlin, Baldwin's Ohio Practice, Merrick-Rippner Probate Law § 81:1, Removal—Statutory Provisions.

Carlin, Baldwin's Ohio Practice, Merrick-Rippner Probate Law § 93:9, Additional Bond in Land Sale Proceedings—Form.

Carlin, Baldwin's Ohio Practice, Merrick-Rippner Probate Law § 33:18, Trusts—Ohio Principal and Income Act.

Carlin, Baldwin's Ohio Practice, Merrick-Rippner Probate Law § 52:14, Fiduciary's Bond—New or Additional.

Carlin, Baldwin's Ohio Practice, Merrick-Rippner Probate Law § 52:15, Fiduciary's Bond—Removal for Failure to Give.

Carlin, Baldwin's Ohio Practice, Merrick-Rippner Probate Law § 52:24, Fiduciary's Bond—Sureties—Statutory Requirements.

Carlin, Baldwin's Ohio Practice, Merrick-Rippner Probate Law § 52:28, Fiduciary's Bond—Sureties—Liability—New or Additional Bonds.

Carlin, Baldwin's Ohio Practice, Merrick-Rippner Probate Law § 62:88, Exceptions to Bond of Guardian—Form.

Carlin, Baldwin's Ohio Practice, Merrick-Rippner Probate Law § 62:89, Notice of Exceptions to Bond—Form.

Carlin, Baldwin's Ohio Practice, Merrick-Rippner Probate Law § 62:90, Order Sustaining Exceptions—Form.

Carlin, Baldwin's Ohio Practice, Merrick-Rippner Probate Law § 64:20, Powers and Duties of Guardian—Ward's Estate—Mandatory Duties.

Bogert - the Law of Trusts and Trustees § 151, Oath, Bond, and Letters of Trusteeship.

Notes of Decisions

Additional bond 2

New bond 1

---

1. New bond

The sureties on an administrator's original and new bonds in proceedings to sell real estate are liable for all the money passing into the hands of the administrator, whether it is the proceeds of real estate or personal property. Wade v. Graham (Ohio 1829) 4 Ohio 126.

Where an executor gives a new bond and is subsequently removed, but prior to giving the new bond he collects and converts to his own use all the assets of the estate, the sureties on the new bond are liable for the indebtedness of the executor to the estate. Foster v. Wise (Ohio 1888) 46 Ohio St. 20, 20 W.L.B. 55, 16 N.E. 687, 15 Am.St.Rep. 542.

Where no reason appears of record it will be presumed that a new bond is not an additional bond. Pummill v. Baumgartner (Ohio Com.Pl. 1895) 4 Ohio Dec. 69, 3 Ohio N.P. 40.

2. Additional bond

Sureties on an additional bond are liable for a breach of its conditions. King v. Bell (Ohio 1881) 36 Ohio St. 460.

In ordering the sale of real estate, an additional bond is not required unless the original bond is not sufficient. Wade v. Graham (Ohio 1829) 4 Ohio 126.

Where successive bonds have been given with different sureties and waste has occurred before the execution and approval of any of them, the liability of sureties in the subsequent bonds is secondary to that of the sureties on the bonds in force at the time the estate was wasted, and if the former have made good the loss, they may recover from the latter the full amount paid by them. Corrigan v. Foster (Ohio 1894) 51 Ohio St. 225, 31 W.L.B. 275, 37 N.E. 263.

2109.07 Bond conditions of administrators; exemption of surviving spouse receiving entire net estate

(A) The bond required of an administrator by section 2109.04 of the Revised Code shall not be required in either of the following cases:

(1) It shall not be required of a surviving spouse to administer the deceased spouse's estate if the surviving spouse is entitled to the entire net proceeds of the estate.

(2) It shall not be required of an administrator to administer an estate if there is no will, if the administrator is the next of kin, and if the administrator is entitled to the entire net proceeds of the estate.

(B) The bond otherwise required by section 2109.04 of the Revised Code of an administrator shall be conditioned as follows:

(1) To file with the probate court within the time required by section 2115.02 of the Revised Code an inventory of all tangible and intangible personal property of the deceased that is to be administered and that comes to the administrator's possession or knowledge and an inventory of the deceased's interest in real estate located in this state;

(2) To administer and distribute according to law all tangible and intangible personal property of the deceased, the proceeds of any action for wrongful death or of any settlement, with or without suit, of a wrongful death claim, and the proceeds of all real estate in which the deceased had an interest, that is located in this state, and that is sold, when the property or proceeds have come to the possession of the administrator or to the possession of a person for the administrator;

(3) To render a just and true account of the administrator's administration at the times required by section 2109.301 of the Revised Code;

(4) To deliver the letters of administration into court if a will of the deceased is proved and allowed.

(2001 H 85, eff. 10–31–01; 1999 H 59, eff. 10–29–99; 1996 H 391, eff. 10–1–96; 1992 H 427, eff. 10–8–92; 1975 S 145; 1953 H 1; GC 10506–14)

Uncodified Law

1999 H 59, § 5, eff. 10–29–99, reads:

Sections 2109.07, 2109.09, and 2109.10 of the Revised Code, as amended by this act, shall apply regarding all administrators and executors who are appointed on or after the effective date of this act.

Historical and Statutory Notes

Pre–1953 H 1 Amendments: 119 v 394, § 1; 114 v 366

Amendment Note: 2001 H 85 substituted "2109.301" for "2109.30" in division (B)(3).

Amendment Note: 1999 H 59 designated new division (A) and division (A)(1); added division (A)(2); designated new division (B); redesignated former divisions (A) through (D) as new divisions (B)(1) through (B)(4); and made other nonsubstantive changes.

Amendment Note: 1996 H 391 rewrote divisions (A) and (B); substituted "the administrator's" for "his"; and made nonsubstantive changes. Prior to amendment, divisions (A) and (B) read:

"(A) To make and return to the probate court within the time required by section 2115.02 of the Revised Code a true inventory of all moneys, chattels, rights, and credits of the deceased that are to be administered and that come to the administrator's possession or knowledge, and an inventory of the real estate of the deceased;

"(B) To administer and distribute according to law all the moneys, chattels, rights, and credits of the deceased, the proceeds of any action for wrongful death or of any settlement, with or without suit, of a wrongful death claim, and the proceeds of all his real estate sold that come to the possession of the administrator or to the possession of any person for him [.]"

Cross References

Bond of executor who is sole residuary legatee or distributee, 2109.10

Library References

Executors and Administrators ⚖═26(2).
Westlaw Topic No. 162.
C.J.S. Executors and Administrators §§ 71 to 77.

Research References

Encyclopedias

OH Jur. 3d Decedents' Estates § 925, Surviving Spouse.
OH Jur. 3d Decedents' Estates § 954, Prerequisites to Issuance; Bond.
OH Jur. 3d Decedents' Estates § 956, Effect of Proof of Will After Issuance of Letters of Administration.
OH Jur. 3d Fiduciaries § 186, Dispensing With Bond.
OH Jur. 3d Fiduciaries § 191, Administrator's Bond.

Treatises and Practice Aids

Carlin, Baldwin's Ohio Practice, Merrick-Rippner Probate Law § 2:16, Appointment of Fiduciary—Fiduciary's Bond.
Carlin, Baldwin's Ohio Practice, Merrick-Rippner Probate Law § 52:2, Fiduciary's Bond—in General.
Carlin, Baldwin's Ohio Practice, Merrick-Rippner Probate Law § 52:9, Fiduciary's Bond—Conditions.
Carlin, Baldwin's Ohio Practice, Merrick-Rippner Probate Law § 2:121, Administration of Decedent's Estate—Checklist.
Carlin, Baldwin's Ohio Practice, Merrick-Rippner Probate Law § 30:35, Drafting a Will—Executor's Bond.
Carlin, Baldwin's Ohio Practice, Merrick-Rippner Probate Law § 52:11, Fiduciary's Bond—Special Bond of Sole Residuary Legatee or Distributee—Liability.
Carlin, Baldwin's Ohio Practice, Merrick-Rippner Probate Law § 52:12, Fiduciary's Bond—Special Bond of Sole Residuary Legatee or Distributee—Exception for Surviving Spouse.

Carlin, Baldwin's Ohio Practice, Merrick-Rippner Probate Law § 52:38, Bond of Fiduciary—Form.

Carlin, Baldwin's Ohio Practice, Merrick-Rippner Probate Law § 52:40, Bond of Administrator—Form.

Carlin, Baldwin's Ohio Practice, Merrick-Rippner Probate Law § 52:44, Bond of Administrator When Sole Distributee—Form.

Carlin, Baldwin's Ohio Practice, Merrick-Rippner Probate Law § 30:162, Bond Not Required of Executor Named in Will—Form.

Carlin, Baldwin's Ohio Practice, Merrick-Rippner Probate Law App B SPF 4.0, Application for Authority to Administer Estate.

Notes of Decisions

Accounting   1
Forgery   3
Liability of administrator   4
Other fiduciaries   2

1. Accounting

An heir cannot sustain an action against security on an administrator's bond until the administrator's accounts are settled with the court or the plaintiff's right is established by judgment. Treasurer of Pickaway, for Use of N. Oulrey v. Hall's Ex'r (Ohio 1827) 3 Ohio 225. Executors And Administrators ⇐ 533; Principal And Surety ⇐ 140

The sureties upon an administrator's bond are liable for the debt of the administrator due the decedent regardless of the solvency or insolvency of said administrator. Perkins v. Scott (Ohio Cir. 1895) 6 Ohio C.D. 226, 2 Ohio Dec. 496, dismissed.

Proceeds of a life insurance policy which came into the hands of an administrator after his appointment become assets of the estate in his hands, and on his failure to account for the same his sureties on his bond become liable therefor to the extent of the penalty of the bond. Webb v. Roettinger (Ohio Cir. 1894) 4 Ohio C.D. 270, 1 Ohio Dec. 191, affirmed 55 Ohio St. 686, 48 N.E. 1119.

2. Other fiduciaries

Former GC 10634 (RC 2113.22) authorized an administrator de bonis non to maintain a suit against a former administrator or executor and his sureties upon an administration bond to recover for the default of such former administrator or executor arising out of the performance of the duties imposed by former GC 10772 (RC 2125.02, RC 2125.03). U.S. Fidelity & Guaranty Co. v. Decker (Ohio 1930) 122 Ohio St. 285, 171 N.E. 333, 68 A.L.R. 1538, 8 Ohio Law Abs. 273, 31 Ohio Law Rep. 581.

The duty enjoined upon an administrator to give a bond, with conditions as therein provided, contemplates that such bond shall secure the faithful performance of the duties imposed upon the personal representative of a deceased person under former GC 10772 (RC 2125.02, RC 2125.03). U.S. Fidelity & Guaranty Co. v. Decker (Ohio 1930) 122 Ohio St. 285, 171 N.E. 333, 68 A.L.R. 1538, 8 Ohio Law Abs. 273, 31 Ohio Law Rep. 581.

Duties of an administrator cum testamento annexo are similar to those of a guardian. Guthrie v. Cincinnati Gas & Elec. Co. (Ohio Super. 1904) 15 Ohio Dec. 23, 2 Ohio N.P.N.S. 117.

3. Forgery

A probate judge is not liable for accepting a bond of an administrator on which the names of the sureties have been forged. Ingersoll v Smith, OS Unrep 522, 36 B 302 (1896).

4. Liability of administrator

The sureties on an administrator's original and new bonds in proceedings to sell real estate are liable for all the money passing into the hands of the administrator, whether it is the proceeds of real estate or personal property. Wade v. Graham (Ohio 1829) 4 Ohio 126.

A devastavit by an administrator cannot be suggested and proved, in a suit on the administrator's bond, against the administrator and his securities. Stewart v. Treasurer of Champaign County (Ohio 1829) 4 Ohio 98.

Administrator must give bond securing faithful performance of duties to administer money arising from claim for wrongful death. U.S. Fidelity & Guaranty Co. v. Decker (Ohio 1930) 122 Ohio St. 285, 171 N.E. 333, 68 A.L.R. 1538, 8 Ohio Law Abs. 273, 31 Ohio Law Rep. 581. Executors And Administrators ⇐ 26(2)

2109.08 Bond conditions, special administrator

The bond required by section 2109.04 of the Revised Code of a special administrator shall be conditioned as follows:

(A) To file with the probate court within three months an inventory of the tangible and intangible personal property of the deceased that has or may come to the special administrator's possession or knowledge;

(B) To account for the tangible and intangible personal property of the deceased and for the debts of the deceased that the special administrator receives as special administrator, whenever required by the court, and deliver them to the person authorized to receive them.

(1996 H 391, eff. 10–1–96; 1992 H 427, eff. 10–8–92; 1953 H 1; GC 10506–15)

Historical and Statutory Notes

Pre–1953 H 1 Amendments: 114 v 367

Amendment Note: 1996 H 391 rewrote this section, which prior thereto read:

"The bond required by section 2109.04 of the Revised Code of a special administrator shall be conditioned as follows:

"(A) To make and return into the probate court within one month a true inventory of the moneys, chattels, rights, and credits of the deceased that have or may come to his possession or knowledge;

"(B) To account for the moneys, chattels, and debts of the deceased received by him as special administrator, whenever required by the court, and deliver them to the person authorized to receive them."

Cross References

Investment of trust funds, 1111.13

Library References

Executors and Administrators ⇐ 26(0.5).
Westlaw Topic No. 162.
C.J.S. Executors and Administrators §§ 71 to 77.

Research References

Encyclopedias

OH Jur. 3d Decedents' Estates § 1704, Duties and Powers of Special Administrator—Inventory and Account.
OH Jur. 3d Fiduciaries § 191, Administrator's Bond.

Treatises and Practice Aids

Carlin, Baldwin's Ohio Practice, Merrick-Rippner Probate Law § 69:6, Special Administrator—Bond—Form.

Carlin, Baldwin's Ohio Practice, Merrick-Rippner Probate Law § 52:45, Bond of Special Administrator—Form.

2109.09 Bond conditions, executors

(A) Unless the testator has specified otherwise in the will [1], the bond required of an executor by section 2109.04 of the Revised Code shall not be required of the executor to administer an estate in accordance with the will of the testator if the executor is the next of kin and if the executor is entitled to the entire net proceeds of the estate.

(B) The bond otherwise required of an executor by section 2109.04 of the Revised Code shall be conditioned as follows:

(1) To file with the probate court within the time required by section 2115.02 of the Revised Code an inventory of all the tangible and intangible personal property of the testator that is to be administered and that comes to the executor's possession or knowledge and an inventory of the testator's interest in real estate located in this state;

(2) To administer and distribute according to law and the will of the testator all the testator's tangible and intangible personal

property, the proceeds of any action for wrongful death or of any settlement, with or without suit, of a wrongful death claim, and the proceeds of all real estate in which the testator had an interest, that is located in this state, and that is sold, when the property or proceeds have come to the possession of the executor or to the possession of another person for the executor;

(3) To render a just and true account of the executor's administration at the times required by section 2109.301 of the Revised Code.

(2001 H 85, eff. 10–31–01; 1999 H 59, eff. 10–29–99; 1996 H 391, eff. 10–1–96; 1992 H 427, eff. 10–8–92; 1953 H 1; GC 10506–16)

[1] Prior and current versions differ; although no amendment to this language appeared in 2001 H 85, "in the will" appeared as "in the bill" in 1999 H 59.

Uncodified Law

1999 H 59, § 5, eff. 10–29–99, reads:

Sections 2109.07, 2109.09, and 2109.10 of the Revised Code, as amended by this act, shall apply regarding all administrators and executors who are appointed on or after the effective date of this act.

Historical and Statutory Notes

Pre–1953 H 1 Amendments: 119 v 394, § 1; 114 v 367

Amendment Note: 2001 H 85 substituted "2109.301" for "2109.30" in division (B)(3).

Amendment Note: 1999 H 59 rewrote and designated the former first paragraph as new division (A); and redesignated former divisions (A) through (C) as divisions (A)(1) through (A)(3). Prior to amendment, the former first paragraph read:

"The bond required by section 2109.04 of the Revised Code of an executor shall be conditioned as follows:"

Amendment Note: 1996 H 391 rewrote this section, which prior thereto read:

"The bond required by section 2109.04 of the Revised Code of an executor shall be conditioned as follows:

"(A) To make and return to the probate court within the time required by section 2115.02 of the Revised Code a true inventory of all the moneys, chattels, rights, and credits of the testator that are to be administered and that come to his possession or knowledge and an inventory of the real estate of the testator;

"(B) To administer and distribute according to law and the will of the testator all the testator's moneys, chattels, rights, and credits, the proceeds of any action for wrongful death or of any settlement, with or without suit, of a wrongful death claim, and the proceeds of all his real estate sold that come to the possession of the executor or to the possession of any other person for him;

"(C) To render a just and true account of his administration at the times required by section 2109.30 of the Revised Code."

Library References

Executors and Administrators ⚖ 26(1).
Westlaw Topic No. 162.
C.J.S. Executors and Administrators §§ 71 to 77.

Research References

Encyclopedias

OH Jur. 3d Decedents' Estates § 1256, Duty to Make and File Inventory.
OH Jur. 3d Fiduciaries § 186, Dispensing With Bond.
OH Jur. 3d Fiduciaries § 192, Executor's Bond.

Treatises and Practice Aids

Carlin, Baldwin's Ohio Practice, Merrick-Rippner Probate Law § 2:16, Appointment of Fiduciary—Fiduciary's Bond.
Carlin, Baldwin's Ohio Practice, Merrick-Rippner Probate Law § 52:2, Fiduciary's Bond—In General.
Carlin, Baldwin's Ohio Practice, Merrick-Rippner Probate Law § 2:121, Administration of Decedent's Estate—Checklist.
Carlin, Baldwin's Ohio Practice, Merrick-Rippner Probate Law § 30:35, Drafting a Will—Executor's Bond.
Carlin, Baldwin's Ohio Practice, Merrick-Rippner Probate Law § 52:11, Fiduciary's Bond—Special Bond of Sole Residuary Legatee or Distributee—Liability.
Carlin, Baldwin's Ohio Practice, Merrick-Rippner Probate Law § 30:162, Bond Not Required of Executor Named in Will—Form.

Law Review and Journal Commentaries

How a Will Is Admitted to Probate in Ohio. 50 Title Topics 6 (June 1983).

Notes of Decisions

Separate bonds 1

---

1. **Separate bonds**

Trial court abused its discretion when it required son to provide a bond of $284,800 in order to serve as co-executor of estate but did not require a bond from the other co-executors; statute required the trial court to either take a separate bond from each of the co-executors or to require a joint bond from all of them. In re Estate of Laffin (Ohio App. 3 Dist., Auglaize, 06-05-2006) No. 2-05-41, 2006-Ohio-2779, 2006 WL 1519906, Unreported. Executors And Administrators ⚖ 26(1)

Where a party is appointed by will as both executor and trustee, separate bonds must be given for each position. P., C. & St. L.R. Co. v. Schmidt (Ohio Cir. 1894) 4 Ohio C.D. 535, 1 Ohio Dec. 639.

2109.10 Bond when executor or administrator is sole residuary legatee or distributee

If an executor or administrator is sole residuary legatee or distributee and if division (A) of section 2109.07 or division (A) of section 2109.09 of the Revised Code does not apply, instead of giving the bond prescribed by section 2109.04 of the Revised Code, the executor or administrator may give a bond to the satisfaction of the probate court conditioned as follows:

(A) To pay the costs of administration and all the debts and legacies of the decedent to the extent of the assets of the estate;

(B) If there is a will, to pay over the testator's estate to the person entitled to the testator's estate if the will is set aside;

(C) If there is no will offered at the opening of the estate, to pay over the testator's estate to the person entitled to the testator's estate if a will is probated after the administrator's initial appointment.

The giving of such bond shall not discharge the lien on the decedent's real estate for the payment of the decedent's debts, except that part which has been lawfully sold by the executor or administrator.

(1999 H 59, eff. 10–29–99; 1953 H 1, eff. 10–1–53; GC 10506–18)

Uncodified Law

1999 H 59, § 5, eff. 10–29–99, reads:

Sections 2109.07, 2109.09, and 2109.10 of the Revised Code, as amended by this act, shall apply regarding all administrators and executors who are appointed on or after the effective date of this act.

Historical and Statutory Notes

Pre–1953 H 1 Amendments: 119 v 394, § 1; 114 v 368

Amendment Note: 1999 H 59 inserted "and if division (A) of section 2109.07 or division (A) of section 2109.09 of the Revised Code does not apply" in the first paragraph; substituted "If there is a will" for "If executor" in division (B); substituted "If there is no will offered at the opening of the estate" for "If administrator" and inserted "initial" in division (C); and made changes to reflect gender neutral language and other nonsubstantive changes.

Library References

Executors and Administrators ⚖26(1), 26(2).
Westlaw Topic No. 162.
C.J.S. Executors and Administrators §§ 71 to 77.

Research References

Encyclopedias

OH Jur. 3d Fiduciaries § 193, Bond of Administrator or Executor Who is Sole Distributee or Residuary Legatee.

Treatises and Practice Aids

Carlin, Baldwin's Ohio Practice, Merrick-Rippner Probate Law § 2:16, Appointment of Fiduciary—Fiduciary's Bond.

Carlin, Baldwin's Ohio Practice, Merrick-Rippner Probate Law § 2:121, Administration of Decedent's Estate—Checklist.

Carlin, Baldwin's Ohio Practice, Merrick-Rippner Probate Law § 30:35, Drafting a Will—Executor's Bond.

Carlin, Baldwin's Ohio Practice, Merrick-Rippner Probate Law § 52:11, Fiduciary's Bond—Special Bond of Sole Residuary Legatee or Distributee—Liability.

Carlin, Baldwin's Ohio Practice, Merrick-Rippner Probate Law § 52:38, Bond of Fiduciary—Form.

Carlin, Baldwin's Ohio Practice, Merrick-Rippner Probate Law § 52:43, Bond of Executor When Sole Residuary Legatee—Form.

Carlin, Baldwin's Ohio Practice, Merrick-Rippner Probate Law § 52:44, Bond of Administrator When Sole Distributee—Form.

Carlin, Baldwin's Ohio Practice, Merrick-Rippner Probate Law § 30:162, Bond Not Required of Executor Named in Will—Form.

Notes of Decisions

Action against executor 1
Indemnity 2

---

1. Action against executor

The petition in an action against an executor upon a bond given by him as residuary legatee need not show a presentment of the claim to the executor for allowance or rejection. Stevens v. Hartley (Ohio 1862) 13 Ohio St. 525.

Personal property of a decedent does not vest in the heirs until administration, and is then vested in the administrator by relation from the time of death, and no right of action on a note belonging to decedent is shown by a party in an action on the note by proof of possession and that he is sole heir. McBride v. Vance (Ohio 1906) 73 Ohio St. 258, 76 N.E. 938, 112 Am.St.Rep. 723, 3 Ohio Law Rep. 569, 3 Ohio Law Rep. 574, 4 Am.Ann.Cas. 191. Bills And Notes ⚖ 443(1); Descent And Distribution ⚖ 91(1); Executors And Administrators ⚖ 43

2. Indemnity

A surety on a bond under RS 5997 has a lien on the residuary share for indemnity. Tidd v. Bloch (Ohio Cir. 1904) 16 Ohio C.D. 113, 4 Ohio C.C.N.S. 216.

2109.11 Bond conditions, testamentary trustees

The bond required by section 2109.04 of the Revised Code of a testamentary trustee shall be conditioned as follows:

(A) To make and return to the probate court within the time required by section 2109.58 of the Revised Code a true inventory of all moneys, chattels, rights, credits and real estate belonging to the trust that come to the trustee's possession or knowledge;

(B) To administer and distribute according to law and the will of the testator all moneys, chattels, rights, credits, and real estate belonging to the trust that come to the possession of the trustee or to the possession of any other person for the trustee;

(C) To render a just and true account of the trustee's administration at the times required by section 2109.303 of the Revised Code.

(2001 H 85, eff. 10-31-01; 1992 H 427, eff. 10-8-92; 1953 H 1; GC 10506-18a)

Uncodified Law

2001 H 85, § 7, eff. 10-31-01, reads:

Sections 2109.11, 2109.18, 2109.24, and 2109.30 of the Revised Code, as amended by this act, and section 2109.303 of the Revised Code, as enacted by this act, apply to testamentary trustees or other fiduciaries of trusts that are in existence or are created on or after January 1, 2002 or to other fiduciaries under governing instruments that are in existence or are created on or after January 1, 2002.

As used in this section, "other fiduciary" has the same meaning as in section 2109.303 of the Revised Code, as enacted by this act.

Historical and Statutory Notes

Pre-1953 H 1 Amendments: 119 v 394, § 3

Amendment Note: 2001 H 85 substituted "2109.303" for "2109.30" in division (C); and made changes to reflect gender neutral language.

Library References

Trusts ⚖161.
Westlaw Topic No. 390.
C.J.S. Trusts § 302.

Research References

Encyclopedias

OH Jur. 3d Fiduciaries § 194, Testamentary Trustee's Bond.

Treatises and Practice Aids

Carlin, Baldwin's Ohio Practice, Merrick-Rippner Probate Law § 52:2, Fiduciary's Bond—in General.

Carlin, Baldwin's Ohio Practice, Merrick-Rippner Probate Law § 90:3, Persons Entitled to Bring Land Sale Actions—Testamentary Trustee.

Carlin, Baldwin's Ohio Practice, Merrick-Rippner Probate Law § 52:41, Bond of Testamentary Trustee—Form.

Carlin, Baldwin's Ohio Practice, Merrick-Rippner Probate Law § 52:42, Bond of Trustee—Form.

Carlin, Baldwin's Ohio Practice, Merrick-Rippner Probate Law § 68:44, Fiduciary's Bond—Form.

Bogert - the Law of Trusts and Trustees § 151, Oath, Bond, and Letters of Trusteeship.

Bogert - the Law of Trusts and Trustees § 597, Inventory and Appraisal.

2109.12 Bond conditions, guardians

Any bond required by or pursuant to section 2109.04 of the Revised Code of a guardian shall be conditioned as follows:

(A) If applicable, to make and return to the probate court within the time required by section 2111.14 of the Revised Code a true inventory of all moneys, chattels, rights, credits, and real estate belonging to the ward that come to the guardian's possession or knowledge;

(B) To administer and distribute according to law all moneys, chattels, rights, credits, and real estate belonging to the ward that come to the possession of the guardian or to the possession of any other person for the guardian;

(C) To render a just and true account of the guardian's administration at any times required by or pursuant to section 2109.302 of the Revised Code.

(2001 H 85, eff. 10-31-01; 1992 H 427, eff. 10-8-92; 1984 H 263; 1953 H 1; GC 10506-20a)

Uncodified Law

2001 H 85, § 6, eff. 10-31-01, reads:

Sections 2109.12, 2109.18, 2109.24, 2109.30, and 5905.11 of the Revised Code, as amended by this act, and section 2109.302 of the Revised Code, as enacted by this act, apply to guardians or conservators of wards' estates that are in existence or are created on or after January 1, 2002.

Historical and Statutory Notes

Pre–1953 H 1 Amendments: 119 v 394, § 4

Amendment Note: 2001 H 85 substituted "2109.302" for "2109.30" in division (C); and made changes to reflect gender neutral language.

Cross References

Veteran's guardian, bond, 5905.10

Library References

Guardian and Ward ⚖15.
Mental Health ⚖166.
Westlaw Topic Nos. 196, 257A.
C.J.S. Mental Health § 141.

Research References

Encyclopedias

OH Jur. 3d Fiduciaries § 195, Guardian's Bond.

Treatises and Practice Aids

Carlin, Baldwin's Ohio Practice, Merrick-Rippner Probate Law § 52:1, Fiduciary's Bond—Introduction.

Carlin, Baldwin's Ohio Practice, Merrick-Rippner Probate Law § 52:2, Fiduciary's Bond—in General.

Carlin, Baldwin's Ohio Practice, Merrick-Rippner Probate Law § 52:9, Fiduciary's Bond—Conditions.

Carlin, Baldwin's Ohio Practice, Merrick-Rippner Probate Law § 62:21, Appointment of Guardian—Application—Appointment, Acceptance, and Bonding.

Notes of Decisions

Accrual of right of action   1
Appointment   4
Mishandling of funds   3
Power over property and funds   7
Procedure and jurisdiction   2
Sureties   5
Termination   6

---

1. Accrual of right of action

A right of action on a guardian's bond to recover from sureties the amount remaining in the hands of the guardian accrues to the ward when the amount owing is determined by the probate court on final settlement of the account. Newton v. Hammond (Ohio 1882) 38 Ohio St. 430, 8 W.L.B. 241. Guardian And Ward ⚖ 182(3); Limitation Of Actions ⚖ 47(4).

A ward's right of action on a guardian's bond accrues when the guardian files his final account; the ward's delay in compelling the guardian to settle the account does not discharge sureties though the guardian becomes insolvent. Newton v. Hammond (Ohio 1882) 38 Ohio St. 430, 8 W.L.B. 241.

No cause of action on the bond of a guardian accrues in favor of the ward until the filing of the guardianship account and the settlement of the estate in the probate court. Wegner v Wiltsie, 3 CC(NS) 410, 13 CD 302 (Lucas 1902).

Where a guardian fraudulently transfers his property and his sureties are subsequently compelled to make good a deficit under the bond, their right of action as to the fraudulent transfer accrues at the time the transfer was made, not at the time of the payment made under the bond. Boies v Johnson, 1 CC(NS) 451, 15 CD 331 (Medina 1903), reversed by 72 OS 644, 76 NE 1126 (1905).

2. Procedure and jurisdiction

Jurisdiction of a probate court over the settlement of a guardian's account is exclusive; a suit in equity to compel an accounting cannot be maintained without showing that the powers and jurisdiction of the probate court are ineffectual to secure such accounting. Newton v. Hammond (Ohio 1882) 38 Ohio St. 430, 8 W.L.B. 241.

The four years within which suits are to be commenced against administrators applies to actions on guardians' bonds, and the disability of infancy will not save the plaintiff. Favorite v. Booher's Adm'r (Ohio 1867) 17 Ohio St. 548.

A suit against sureties on a guardian's bond may be maintained without a previous liquidation of the amount due from the principal. State for Use of Bartlet v. Humphreys (Ohio 1835) 7 Ohio 223, PT. I.

The death of a guardian without filing an account and without leaving books of account or memoranda from which his indebtedness to the estate can be ascertained does not give the common pleas court jurisdiction on the bond of the guardian to compel an accounting and payment to the ward of the amount found due him. Wegner v Wiltsie, 3 CC(NS) 410, 13 CD 302 (Lucas 1902).

An indebtedness paid by reason of suretyship on the bond of a guardian relates back to the date of the bond. Boies v Johnson, 1 CC(NS) 451, 15 CD 331 (Medina 1903), reversed by 72 OS 644, 76 NE 1126 (1905).

3. Mishandling of funds

Where a guardian receives money after giving a bond and embezzles such money and gives a new bond the surety on the first bond will not be exonerated as to such money though he was released. Eichelberger v. Gross (Ohio 1885) 42 Ohio St. 549, 13 W.L.B. 282.

Where, in a suit brought in the court of common pleas upon a guardian's bond to recover the amount of a judgment of a probate court rendered against the guardian upon settlement of his accounts, the defendant surety interposes an answer and cross-petition averring that the amount of the judgment is greatly in excess of the amount actually due from the guardian to his ward and was obtained by concealment and fraud by the guardian, the fact that the pleading fails to deny the amount so adjudged due in its entirety does not deprive the court of its power to grant relief if the facts so charged by the pleading are found upon trial to be true. Gantz v. Gease (Ohio 1910) 82 Ohio St. 34, 91 N.E. 872, 7 Ohio Law Rep. 638. Guardian And Ward ⚖ 182(5); Principal And Surety ⚖ 156

Where a guardian gives a bond on appointment and an additional bond on the sale of real estate and dies insolvent, defaulting to his ward, having commingled various funds with proceeds from the real estate, the sureties on both bonds are liable for the guardian's default. Swisher v. McWhinney (Ohio 1901) 64 Ohio St. 343, 45 W.L.B. 355, 60 N.E. 565.

Where a guardian of the person and estate of a minor receives, after giving bond, money belonging to his ward, and converting it to his own use, subsequently resigns and moves and is reappointed and qualified in another state, and files an account there in which he charges himself with the amount found due at the time of his resignation, the sureties on the first bond will not be exonerated with respect to the money so converted, but they will be liable upon the ground that the guardian failed to faithfully perform his duties. Penn v McBride, 1 CC 285, 1 CD 157 (Noble 1885).

4. Appointment

In a suit on a guardian's bond alleging appointment of the guardian by proper authority, the obligors are estopped to deny the fact thus recited or from questioning the appointment. Shroyer v. Richmond (Ohio 1866) 16 Ohio St. 455. Estoppel ⚖ 32(4); Mental Health ⚖ 187.1

The probate court is not authorized by law to appoint a guardian of the person of a minor who is without estate. In re Baier (Ohio Com.Pl. 1900) 11 Ohio Dec. 47, 8 Ohio N.P. 107.

A guardian's bond cannot be sued upon until the court has attempted to compel him to account. Schwab v Rappold, 9 D Repr 340, 12 B 197 (Hamilton 1883).

5. Sureties

In a settlement of a guardian's account when he was credited with payments not made, and the account was subsequently corrected during the ward's minority, sureties on the bond were not affected. Scobey v. Gano (Ohio 1880) 35 Ohio St. 550. Guardian And Ward ⚖ 177; Principal And Surety ⚖ 97

After final settlement the sureties on a guardian's bond cannot be heard in the absence of fraud to question the correctness of the guardian's final account. Braiden v. Mercer (Ohio 1886) 44 Ohio St. 339, 16 W.L.B. 29, 7 N.E. 155.

Settling a guardian's account without notice is not conclusive as to sureties. Gilbert v. Gilbert (Ohio Cir. 1896) 7 Ohio C.D. 58.

One surety on a guardian's bond is sufficient. Arrowsmith v. Gleason (U.S.Ohio 1889) 9 S.Ct. 237, 129 U.S. 86, 32 L.Ed. 630.

6. Termination

A guardian's refusal to pay over money to a minor or his attorney after termination of the guardianship will not enable the minor to maintain suit on the guardian's bond. Favorite v. Booher's Adm'r (Ohio 1867) 17 Ohio St. 548.

After a ward arrives at majority the guardianship ceases ipso facto, and his further dealings are those of a mere agent and are not covered by the bond. In re Streit's Estate (Ohio Com.Pl. 1901) 12 Ohio Dec. 158. Bonds ⚖ 61; Guardian And Ward ⚖ 20; Guardian And Ward ⚖ 175

7. Power over property and funds

A purchaser of notes of a guardian takes them charged with the trust if on their face they show that they are for trust funds. Strong v. Strauss (Ohio 1883) 40 Ohio St. 87, 9 W.L.B. 345.

A guardian for a minor, appointed by the court of common pleas, has no power to act or control the property of his ward, until he has given bond, with surety approved by the court. State, for Use of Carpenter v. Sloane (Ohio 1851) 20 Ohio 327. Guardian And Ward ⚖ 15

Duties of an administrator cum testamento annexo are similar to those of a guardian. Guthrie v. Cincinnati Gas & Elec. Co. (Ohio Super. 1904) 15 Ohio Dec. 23, 2 Ohio N.P.N.S. 117.

Where funds of a guardian come into the hands of an attorney he cannot retain his fees therefrom. Hurd v. Wheeling & L.E.R. Co. (Ohio Com.Pl. 1897) 6 Ohio Dec. 549, 4 Ohio N.P. 404.

2109.13 Deposit of personal property in lieu of bond

In any case in which a bond is required by the probate court from a fiduciary and the value of the estate or fund is such that the court deems it inexpedient to require security in the full amount prescribed by section 2109.04 of the Revised Code, the court may direct the deposit of any suitable personal property belonging to the estate or fund with a bank, savings bank, savings and loan association, credit union, or trust company incorporated under the laws of this state or of the United States, as may be designated by order of the court.

The deposit shall be made in the name of the fiduciary, and the personal property deposited shall not be withdrawn from the custody of the bank, savings bank, association, credit union, or trust company except upon the special order of the court. No fiduciary shall receive or collect the whole or any part of the principal represented by the personal property without the special order of the court. Such an order can be made in favor of the fiduciary only if the court within its discretion, having regard for the purpose for which the order is requested, the disposition to be made of the assets as may be released, the value of the assets as related to the total value of the estate, and the period of time the assets will remain in the possession of the fiduciary, finds that the original bond previously given and then in force will be sufficient to protect the estate; otherwise, the court, as a condition to the release of the personal property deposited, shall require the fiduciary to execute an additional bond in an amount that the court determines.

After the deposit has been made and after the filing with the court of a receipt for the personal property executed by the designated bank, savings bank, association, credit union, or company, which receipt shall acknowledge that the personal property is held by the bank, savings bank, association, credit union, or company subject to the order of the court, the court may fix or reduce the amount of the bond so that the amount of the penalty of the bond is determined with respect to the value of the remainder only of the estate or fund, without including the value of the personal property deposited. Neither the fiduciary nor the fiduciary's sureties shall be liable for any loss to the trust estate resulting from the deposit as is authorized and directed by the court pursuant to this section, if the fiduciary has acted in good faith.

This section may be invoked simultaneously with the initial application for appointment of the fiduciary if an interim receipt of the bank, savings bank, association, credit union, or company for which the application for appointment as depositary is being made, acknowledging that it already has received temporary deposit of the personal property described in the application for appointment as depositary, accompanies the simultaneous applications for appointment of fiduciary and for appointment of the depositary.

(2005 H 81, eff. 4–14–06; 1980 S 317, eff. 3–23–81; 130 v S 36; 127 v 36; 125 v 411; 1953 H 1; GC 10506–23 to 10506–25)

Historical and Statutory Notes

Pre–1953 H 1 Amendments: 116 v 385; 114 v 368, 369

Amendment Note: 2005 H 81 deleted "building and loan association" in the first paragraph; inserted "savings bank" and "credit union," throughout; substituted "the fiduciary's" for "his" in the third paragraph; and made other nonsubstantive changes.

OSBA Probate and Trust Law Section

1980:

The Board believes there is no reason to exclude savings and loan associations from serving as depositaries in situations where the fiduciary of an estate is depositing funds in order to avoid the expense of providing bond. Permitting the funds to be deposited in savings and loan associations offers the potential of increasing the income to the estate without sacrificing the safety of the funds.

1963:

Section 3929.15, R. C., specifies the premiums which may be paid for the bonds of fiduciaries, while Sec. 2109.13, R. C., permits a fiduciary upon court order to deposit assets with a bank or trust company and be relieved of bond with respect to such assets. In its present form, strictly and literally construed, a fiduciary cannot secure authority to make a deposit with resulting lowered bond, contemporaneously with his application for appointment, but must always give an initial bond covering the full value of the assets of the estate. Thereafter he may secure deposit authority and a reduction in the amount of bond, but this necessitates the payment of a full first year premium on the high bond.

Some probate courts, it was found, in an effort to reduce expense to the fiduciaries and their estates have been permitting deposit and ordering reduced bond contemporaneously with the appointment of the fiduciary. The Committee approves wholeheartedly of this objective, but feels strongly that this practice should not be followed without both statutory authority and complete protection to the estate with respect to the assets not to be bonded. The Committee has concluded that if the proposed Depositary first were to give a temporary receipt to the fiduciary for the property for which authority is sought to make permanent deposit, this would protect the estate, and the fiduciary could then contemporaneously make application for appointment, authority to make deposit and give bond covering only the assets not deposited. The Committee, believing that protection of the estate is of paramount importance, does not feel that any further modification of the bond requirement should be made, recognizing fully that the proposed Amendment in actual practice will apply only to assets which come into the possession of the prospective fiduciary prior to his appointment, and not apply to those which will prospectively come into his hands after appointment.

Cross References

Accounts of fiduciaries, 2109.30

Library References

Executors and Administrators ⚖26(0.5).
Guardian and Ward ⚖15.
Mental Health ⚖166.

Trusts ⟐161.
Westlaw Topic Nos. 162, 196, 257A, 390.
C.J.S. Executors and Administrators §§ 71 to 77.
C.J.S. Mental Health § 141.
C.J.S. Trusts § 302.

Research References

Encyclopedias

OH Jur. 3d Decedents' Estates § 1667, Contents and Designation of Accounts.
OH Jur. 3d Fiduciaries § 188, Fixing Amount of Bond for Remainder.
OH Jur. 3d Fiduciaries § 189, Effect of Deposit; Order for Withdrawal.
OH Jur. 3d Fiduciaries § 248, Waiver or Loss of Right to Compel Accounting—Waiver of Accounting by Certain Guardians.

Treatises and Practice Aids

Carlin, Baldwin's Ohio Practice, Merrick-Rippner Probate Law § 2:16, Appointment of Fiduciary—Fiduciary's Bond.
Carlin, Baldwin's Ohio Practice, Merrick-Rippner Probate Law § 52:1, Fiduciary's Bond—Introduction.
Carlin, Baldwin's Ohio Practice, Merrick-Rippner Probate Law § 52:4, Fiduciary's Bond—Exceptions to Requirement.
Carlin, Baldwin's Ohio Practice, Merrick-Rippner Probate Law § 54:6, Fiduciary Accounts—Exhibition of Assets.
Carlin, Baldwin's Ohio Practice, Merrick-Rippner Probate Law § 54:9, Fiduciary Accounts—Exceptions to Requirement to Account.
Carlin, Baldwin's Ohio Practice, Merrick-Rippner Probate Law § 12:30, Wrongful Death Trust Agreement—Form.
Carlin, Baldwin's Ohio Practice, Merrick-Rippner Probate Law § 2:121, Administration of Decedent's Estate—Checklist.
Carlin, Baldwin's Ohio Practice, Merrick-Rippner Probate Law § 52:49, Application for Deposit of Assets to Reduce Penalty on Bond—Form.
Carlin, Baldwin's Ohio Practice, Merrick-Rippner Probate Law § 52:50, Order for Deposit of Assets to Reduce Penalty on Bond—Form.
Carlin, Baldwin's Ohio Practice, Merrick-Rippner Probate Law § 52:51, Receipt of Depository—Form.
Carlin, Baldwin's Ohio Practice, Merrick-Rippner Probate Law § 52:52, Application for Special Order Directing Depository to Release Assets—Form.
Carlin, Baldwin's Ohio Practice, Merrick-Rippner Probate Law § 52:53, Special Order Directing Depository to Release Assets—Form.
Carlin, Baldwin's Ohio Practice, Merrick-Rippner Probate Law § 54:42, Certificate of Depository—Form.
Carlin, Baldwin's Ohio Practice, Merrick-Rippner Probate Law § 62:21, Appointment of Guardian—Application—Appointment, Acceptance, and Bonding.
Carlin, Baldwin's Ohio Practice, Merrick-Rippner Probate Law § 64:37, Account of Guardian—Form.
Carlin, Baldwin's Ohio Practice, Merrick-Rippner Probate Law App B SPF 22.2, Entry Approving Settlement of a Minor's Claim—Form.

Notes of Decisions

Application for appointment 1
Calculation of bond 4
Court's discretion 3
Sequestration order, copy to bank 2

1. Application for appointment

Provisions of section relative to furnishing of bonds by fiduciaries, are properly invoked by filing of two related applications, one for appointment of administrator de bonis non and other for designation of depository. In re Langenbach's Estate (Stark 1941) 70 Ohio App. 132, 45 N.E.2d 129, 24 O.O. 447. Executors And Administrators ⟐ 26(2)

2. Sequestration order, copy to bank

It was legislature's intent under RC 2109.13 for the designated bank to receive a copy of a sequestration order because without it a bank cannot take precautionary steps to protect itself from releasing funds to a fiduciary without a court order authorizing release. In re Guardianship of Jenkins, No. 92-P-0081, 1993 WL 419132 (11th Dist Ct App, Portage, 6-4-93).

3. Court's discretion

The court abuses its discretion in requiring a trustee to place $20,000 of trust funds in a custodial account in lieu of requiring posting of a bond. In re Trust of McGlinchey, No. 88AP-591 (10th Dist Ct App, Franklin, 3-28-89).

4. Calculation of bond

Where bonds belonging to incompetent's estate were deposited in bank subject only to probate court's order, and incompetent's guardian filed a surety bond with penal sum in not less than double the value of the remainder of the incompetent's estate, maximum amount probate court would allow surety for premium on bond was one-fourth of 1 per cent a year on the amount of the bond. In re Brown's Estate (Ohio Prob. 1948) 79 N.E.2d 340, 51 Ohio Law Abs. 129, 41 O.O. 354. Mental Health ⟐ 231.1

2109.14 Deposit of works of art in museum authorized; reduction of bond

If the estate held by a fiduciary consists in whole or in part of works of nature or of art which are suitable for preservation and exhibition in a museum or other similar institution, the probate court may authorize and direct that any or all of such works be deposited with a corporation conducting such a museum or other similar institution; provided that no such deposit shall be authorized or directed except with a corporation having a net worth of at least ten times the value of the works to be deposited. Such deposit shall be made in the name of the fiduciary and the property deposited shall not be withdrawn from the custody of such depository or otherwise deposited except upon the special order of the court. The probate judge may impose such conditions relative to insurance and the care and protection of the property deposited as the court thinks best for the interests of the estate and the beneficiaries thereof. After such deposit has been made, a receipt for said property executed by said corporation shall be filed with the court, which receipt shall acknowledge that said property is held by said corporation subject to the order of the court. When such receipt is filed, the court may fix or reduce the amount of the bond so that the amount of the penalty thereof is determined with respect to the value of the remainder only of the estate or fund, without including the value of the property deposited. Neither the fiduciary nor his sureties shall be liable for any loss to the trust estate resulting from a deposit authorized and directed by the court pursuant to this section, provided such fiduciary has acted in good faith.

(1953 H 1, eff. 10–1–53; GC 10506–25a)

Historical and Statutory Notes

Pre–1953 H 1 Amendments: 117 v 435, § 1

Library References

Executors and Administrators ⟐26(0.5).
Guardian and Ward ⟐15.
Mental Health ⟐166.
Trusts ⟐161.
Westlaw Topic Nos. 162, 196, 257A, 390.
C.J.S. Executors and Administrators §§ 71 to 77.
C.J.S. Mental Health § 141.
C.J.S. Trusts § 302.

Research References

Encyclopedias

OH Jur. 3d Fiduciaries § 188, Fixing Amount of Bond for Remainder.
OH Jur. 3d Fiduciaries § 189, Effect of Deposit; Order for Withdrawal.

Treatises and Practice Aids

Carlin, Baldwin's Ohio Practice, Merrick-Rippner Probate Law § 2:16, Appointment of Fiduciary—Fiduciary's Bond.

Carlin, Baldwin's Ohio Practice, Merrick-Rippner Probate Law § 2:121, Administration of Decedent's Estate—Checklist.

Carlin, Baldwin's Ohio Practice, Merrick-Rippner Probate Law § 62:21, Appointment of Guardian—Application—Appointment, Acceptance, and Bonding.

2109.15 Informality of bond

No bond executed by a fiduciary shall be void or held invalid because of any informality in such bond or because of informality or illegality in the appointment of such fiduciary. Such bond shall have the same effect as if the appointment had been legally made and the bond executed in proper form.

(1953 H 1, eff. 10–1–53; GC 10506–32)

Historical and Statutory Notes

Pre–1953 H 1 Amendments: 114 v 370

Cross References

Bonds signed in blank, 3.34

Library References

Executors and Administrators ⚖︎26(0.5).
Guardian and Ward ⚖︎15.
Mental Health ⚖︎166.
Trusts ⚖︎161.
Westlaw Topic Nos. 162, 196, 257A, 390.
C.J.S. Executors and Administrators §§ 71 to 77.
C.J.S. Mental Health § 141.
C.J.S. Trusts § 302.

Research References

Encyclopedias

OH Jur. 3d Fiduciaries § 184, Effect of Irregularities; Defects in Appointment.

Treatises and Practice Aids

Carlin, Baldwin's Ohio Practice, Merrick-Rippner Probate Law § 52:1, Fiduciary's Bond—Introduction.

Carlin, Baldwin's Ohio Practice, Merrick-Rippner Probate Law § 52:16, Fiduciary's Bond—Informality.

Carlin, Baldwin's Ohio Practice, Merrick-Rippner Probate Law § 52:17, Fiduciary's Bond—Defects in Appointment—Informality.

Carlin, Baldwin's Ohio Practice, Merrick-Rippner Probate Law § 52:18, Fiduciary's Bond—Defects in Appointment—Illegality.

Bogert - the Law of Trusts and Trustees § 151, Oath, Bond, and Letters of Trusteeship.

2109.16 One bond for two or more wards

When a person is appointed guardian of several minors who are children of the same parentage and inherit from the same estate, separate bonds shall not be required. In such cases, only one application for letters of guardianship is necessary, and the letters issued to such guardian shall be in one copy and not one copy for each minor. The probate court approving and recording the bond of the guardian, if any, and issuing such letters shall charge the fees allowed by section 2101.16 of the Revised Code for such services. Such fees shall be charged but once for all the wards and not once for each ward.

(1984 H 263, eff. 10–4–84; 1953 H 1; GC 10506–33)

Historical and Statutory Notes

Pre–1953 H 1 Amendments: 114 v 370

Library References

Guardian and Ward ⚖︎15.
Westlaw Topic No. 196.

Research References

Encyclopedias

OH Jur. 3d Fiduciaries § 181, Separate or Joint Bonds.
OH Jur. 3d Guardian & Ward § 38, Application for Appointment by Interested Person.
OH Jur. 3d Guardian & Ward § 56, Letter of Appointment.

Treatises and Practice Aids

Carlin, Baldwin's Ohio Practice, Merrick-Rippner Probate Law § 62:21, Appointment of Guardian—Application—Appointment, Acceptance, and Bonding.

Law Review and Journal Commentaries

Probation Publication Eliminated, Hon. Fred V. Skok. 17 Lake Legal Views 9 (July 1994).

2109.17 Sureties

If the bond of a fiduciary is executed by personal sureties, one or more of such sureties shall be a resident of the county in which such fiduciary applies for appointment. The sureties shall own real property worth double the sum to be secured, over and above all encumbrances, and shall have property in this state liable to execution equal to the sum to be secured. When two or more sureties are offered on the same bond they must have in the aggregate the qualifications prescribed in this section. Such sureties shall qualify under oath and may be required to exhibit to the probate court satisfactory evidence of the ownership of such real property.

No corporate surety shall be acceptable on a fiduciary's bond in such court unless such surety is acceptable to the United States government on surety bonds in like amount, as shown by the regulations issued by the secretary of the treasury of the United States, or in any other manner, to the satisfaction of the court. Such surety shall also be qualified to do business in this state.

A surety on the bond of a fiduciary shall not be held liable for any debt of such fiduciary to the estate represented by him existing at the time such fiduciary was appointed; but such surety shall be liable to the extent that such debt has been made uncollectible by wrongful act of such fiduciary after appointment.

(1953 H 1, eff. 10–1–53; GC 10506–6 to 10506–7a)

Historical and Statutory Notes

Pre–1953 H 1 Amendments: 119 v 394, § 2; 114 v 365

Library References

Executors and Administrators ⚖︎26(0.5).
Guardian and Ward ⚖︎15.
Mental Health ⚖︎166.
Trusts ⚖︎161.
Westlaw Topic Nos. 162, 196, 257A, 390.
C.J.S. Executors and Administrators §§ 71 to 77.
C.J.S. Mental Health § 141.
C.J.S. Trusts § 302.

Research References

Encyclopedias

OH Jur. 3d Fiduciaries § 198, Personal.
OH Jur. 3d Fiduciaries § 199, Corporate.
OH Jur. 3d Fiduciaries § 212, Acts Occurring Before Fiduciary's Appointment.
OH Jur. 3d Guardian & Ward § 155, Additional Bond for Guardian.

Treatises and Practice Aids

Carlin, Baldwin's Ohio Practice, Merrick-Rippner Probate Law § 52:22, Fiduciary's Bond—Sureties—Qualifications—Personal Sureties.

Carlin, Baldwin's Ohio Practice, Merrick-Rippner Probate Law § 52:23, Fiduciary's Bond—Sureties—Qualifications—Corporate Fiduciaries.

Carlin, Baldwin's Ohio Practice, Merrick-Rippner Probate Law § 52:27, Fiduciary's Bond—Sureties—Liability—Extent and Commencement.

Carlin, Baldwin's Ohio Practice, Merrick-Rippner Probate Law § 97:16, Land Sale by Guardian—Additional Bond of Guardian.

Notes of Decisions

Liability 2
Procedure and jurisdiction 1

1. Procedure and jurisdiction

Sureties on an executor's bond are estopped to deny the jurisdiction of the court which appointed the executor and approved their bond which caused the estate's assets to be turned over to the executor. Hoffman v. Fleming (Ohio 1902) 66 Ohio St. 143, 47 W.L.B. 430, 64 N.E. 63.

A surety on a joint administrator's bond may insist that the estates of both administrators be exhausted before he shall be compelled to pay for the defaults of one of them. Eckert v. Myers (Ohio 1888) 45 Ohio St. 525, 19 W.L.B. 325, 15 N.E. 862.

One surety on a guardian's bond is sufficient. Arrowsmith v. Gleason (U.S.Ohio 1889) 9 S.Ct. 237, 129 U.S. 86, 32 L.Ed. 630.

A bond given by a surety on the condition that another surety should be obtained is valid as to third parties and cannot be collaterally impeached by them. Arrowsmith v. Gleason (U.S.Ohio 1889) 9 S.Ct. 237, 129 U.S. 86, 32 L.Ed. 630.

A suit against sureties on a guardian's bond may be maintained without a previous liquidation of the amount due from the principal. State for Use of Bartlet v. Humphreys (Ohio 1835) 7 Ohio 223, PT. I.

2. Liability

Where a creditor obtains a judgment against an executor for the amount of the widow's debt, and the sureties had no knowledge thereof, the sureties are not answerable for the executor's refusal to pay over the proceeds of a sale according to the order of the court. Flickinger v. Saum (Ohio 1884) 40 Ohio St. 591.

Summary judgment is precluded where a genuine issue of material fact exists as to whether a successor guardian in an action may recover funds of a ward from the issuer of a guardian's bond which the original guardian wrongfully acquired and enjoyed when it is unclear when the original guardian committed the wrongful acts rendering the debt owed to the ward uncollectible. Ohio Cas. Group of Ins. Cos. v. Cochrane (Summit 1990) 67 Ohio App.3d 222, 586 N.E.2d 257. Judgment ⚖ 181(15.1)

The indebtedness of an executor to his testator is assets with which he is chargeable, at its maturity, as so much money in his hands; and the sureties on his bond are liable for his failure to administer and distribute the same according to law and the will, although he was insolvent at the time of his appointment, and continued to be so until the settlement of his final account. McGaughey v Jacoby, 54 OS 487, 44 NE 231 (1896). Executors And Administrators ⚖ 475; Executors And Administrators ⚖ 528(5).

A substituted surety is liable on a bond for the unpaid residue, whether or not the same is partly or entirely the proceeds of the sale of real estate. Tuttle v. Northrop (Ohio 1886) 44 Ohio St. 178, 15 W.L.B. 246, 5 N.E. 659.

2109.18 Release of a fiduciary's sureties

A surety of a fiduciary or the executor or administrator of a surety may make application at any time to the probate court to be released from the bond of such fiduciary. Such surety shall file a written request therefor with the probate judge of such court and give at least five days' notice in writing to such fiduciary. If, upon the hearing, the court is of the opinion that there is good reason therefor, it shall release such surety. The death of a surety shall always be good cause.

A fiduciary may make application at any time to the court for the release of the fiduciary's sureties. Such fiduciary shall file a written request therefor with the judge of such court and give at least five days' notice in writing to such sureties. If, upon the hearing, the court is of the opinion that there is good reason therefor, it shall order the fiduciary to file an account, as provided by section 2109.301, 2109.302, or 2109.303 of the Revised Code, and such sureties shall be released after the fiduciary files a new bond which is approved by the court.

If such fiduciary fails to give new bond as directed, the fiduciary shall be removed and the fiduciary's letters of appointment superseded. Such original sureties shall not be released until the fiduciary gives a bond, but shall be liable for such fiduciary's acts only from the time of executing the original bond to the filing and approval by the court of the new bond.

The costs of such proceeding shall be paid by the surety applying to be released, unless it appears to the court that the fiduciary is insolvent, incompetent, or is wasting the assets of the estate.

(2001 H 85, eff. 10–31–01; 1953 H 1, eff. 10–1–53; GC 10506–26 to 10506–29)

Uncodified Law

2001 H 85, § 6: See Uncodified Law under 2109.12.

2001 H 85, § 7: See Uncodified Law under 2109.11.

Historical and Statutory Notes

Pre–1953 H 1 Amendments: 114 v 369, 370

Amendment Note: 2001 H 85 substituted "2109.301, 2109.302, or 2109.303" for "2109.30" in the second paragraph; and made changes to reflect gender neutral language.

Cross References

Bond of county commissioners, oath of office, discharge, 305.04
Removal of executor or administrator, 2113.18

Library References

Executors and Administrators ⚖531.
Guardian and Ward ⚖177.
Mental Health ⚖190.
Trusts ⚖382.
Westlaw Topic Nos. 162, 196, 257A, 390.
C.J.S. Executors and Administrators § 910.
C.J.S. Trusts §§ 767 to 769.

Research References

Encyclopedias
OH Jur. 3d Fiduciaries § 202, Application to Court for Release.
OH Jur. 3d Fiduciaries § 206, Effect on Liability of New or Additional Bond or Sureties.
OH Jur. 3d Fiduciaries § 310, Failure to Give Bond.

Treatises and Practice Aids
Carlin, Baldwin's Ohio Practice, Merrick-Rippner Probate Law § 52:2, Fiduciary's Bond—in General.
Carlin, Baldwin's Ohio Practice, Merrick-Rippner Probate Law § 52:29, Fiduciary's Bond—Sureties—Liability—Merger of Fiduciaries.
Carlin, Baldwin's Ohio Practice, Merrick-Rippner Probate Law § 52:32, Fiduciary's Bond—Release—on Application of Surety.
Carlin, Baldwin's Ohio Practice, Merrick-Rippner Probate Law § 52:33, Fiduciary's Bond—Release—on Application of Fiduciary.
Carlin, Baldwin's Ohio Practice, Merrick-Rippner Probate Law § 52:54, Application for Release of Surety—Form.
Carlin, Baldwin's Ohio Practice, Merrick-Rippner Probate Law § 52:55, Entry for Notice of Hearing on Application to Release Surety—Form.
Carlin, Baldwin's Ohio Practice, Merrick-Rippner Probate Law § 52:56, Entry Releasing Surety—Form.
Carlin, Baldwin's Ohio Practice, Merrick-Rippner Probate Law § 52:57, Entry Approving New Bond—Form.

Notes of Decisions

Death of fiduciary 2
Liability 3

Mishandling or conversion of funds 1
New bond 4

1. Mishandling or conversion of funds

Where a guardian receives money after giving a bond and embezzles such money and gives a new bond the surety on the first bond will not be exonerated as to such money though he was released. Eichelberger v. Gross (Ohio 1885) 42 Ohio St. 549, 13 W.L.B. 282.

Sureties will not be discharged from liability by the fraud of the executor in procuring their execution of bonds where the beneficiaries of the estate, in whose interest the liability is sought to be enforced, are themselves innocent of the fraud. McGaughey v Jacoby, 54 OS 487, 44 NE 231 (1896). Executors And Administrators ⚖ 527(1); Executors And Administrators ⚖ 531; Executors And Administrators ⚖ 537(3); Principal And Surety ⚖ 41

Where an executor gives a new bond and is subsequently removed, but prior to giving the new bond he collects and converts to his own use all the assets of the estate, the sureties on the new bond are liable for the indebtedness of the executor to the estate. Foster v. Wise (Ohio 1888) 46 Ohio St. 20, 20 W.L.B. 55, 16 N.E. 687, 15 Am.St.Rep. 542.

Where a guardian's bond is broken by his failure to pay over to his ward the balance in his hands when the ward becomes of age, his sureties are not released by the mere fact that the ward shortly after becoming of age gave the guardian a receipt in full, without any payment in fact. Meier v. Herancourt (Ohio Super. 1882) 11 Am. Law Rec. 46, 8 W.L.B. 29.

Where a guardian of the person and estate of a minor receives, after giving bond, money belonging to his ward, and converting it to his own use, subsequently resigns and moves and is reappointed and qualified in another state, and files an account there in which he charges himself with the amount found due at the time of his resignation, the sureties on the first bond will not be exonerated with respect to the money so converted, but they will be liable upon the ground that the guardian failed to faithfully perform his duties. Penn v McBride, 1 CC 285, 1 CD 157 (Noble 1885).

2. Death of fiduciary

A succeeding fiduciary is not authorized to file an application in the probate court for the release of the sureties on the bond of a predecessor deceased fiduciary and such sureties may not be finally released prior to the approval of the final accounting of the representative of the deceased fiduciary. In re Gray's Estate (Ohio 1954) 162 Ohio St. 384, 123 N.E.2d 408, 55 O.O. 224. Executors And Administrators ⚖ 531

Where the amount due an estate of a decedent from the surety on the bond of a deceased fiduciary for certain delinquencies is not in dispute at the time a settlement is made with such surety, it is not necessary for the successor fiduciary to pay or tender back the amount received before pursuing any remedy available to him to recover from the surety for other and separate delinquencies. In re Gray's Estate (Ohio 1954) 162 Ohio St. 384, 123 N.E.2d 408, 55 O.O. 224. Compromise And Settlement ⚖ 18(3)

Where a guardian gives a bond on appointment and an additional bond on the sale of real estate and dies insolvent, defaulting to his ward, having commingled various funds with proceeds from the real estate, the sureties on both bonds are liable for the guardian's default. Swisher v. McWhinney (Ohio 1901) 64 Ohio St. 343, 45 W.L.B. 355, 60 N.E. 565.

3. Liability

A ward's right of action on a guardian's bond accrues when the guardian files his final account; the ward's delay in compelling the guardian to settle the account does not discharge sureties though the guardian becomes insolvent. Newton v. Hammond (Ohio 1882) 38 Ohio St. 430, 8 W.L.B. 241.

The sureties on an administrator's original and new bonds in proceedings to sell real estate are liable for all the money passing into the hands of the administrator, whether it is the proceeds of real estate or personal property. Wade v. Graham (Ohio 1829) 4 Ohio 126.

Where debtor was creditor's executor, his sureties, who were released after his removal as executor when he was appointed administrator de bonis non with new bond, cannot be held for amount of his unpaid debt to testator. U.S. Fidelity & Guaranty Co. of Baltimore, Md. v. Jones (Warren 1926) 22 Ohio App. 345, 153 N.E. 281, 4 Ohio Law Abs. 611. Executors And Administrators ⚖ 527(2)

Where a guardian sells land and gives a special bond and thereafter a surety on the bond is released and a new bond is given and the guardian defaults, the sureties on the first bond are liable. Tuttle v. Northrop (Ohio 1886) 44 Ohio St. 178, 15 W.L.B. 246, 5 N.E. 659.

Where after twenty years the principal on the bond is cited to appear and judgment is taken against him without the surety's knowledge, the surety is not bound thereby. Gilbert v. Gilbert (Ohio Cir. 1896) 7 Ohio C.D. 58.

The sureties upon an administrator's bond are liable for the debt of the administrator due the decedent regardless of the solvency or insolvency of said administrator. Perkins v. Scott (Ohio Cir. 1895) 6 Ohio C.D. 226, 2 Ohio Dec. 496, dismissed.

Where one of the sureties is insolvent, the proper remedy is in equity against all the other sureties on both bonds. Kehnast v. Daum (Ohio Com.Pl. 1897) 6 Ohio Dec. 401, 4 Ohio N.P. 366, affirmed 9 Ohio C.D. 867.

Sureties on the original bond and on the additional bond given in proceedings to sell real estate are all entitled to contribution. Kehnast v. Daum (Ohio Com.Pl. 1897) 6 Ohio Dec. 401, 4 Ohio N.P. 366, affirmed 9 Ohio C.D. 867.

Sureties on the original bond and on the additional bond given in proceedings to sell real estate are equally bound for all of the money that comes into the administrator's possession. Kehnast v. Daum (Ohio Com. Pl. 1897) 6 Ohio Dec. 401, 4 Ohio N.P. 366, affirmed 9 Ohio C.D. 867.

4. New bond

A surety shall not be released until a new bond is given. Howenstine v. Sweet (Ohio Cir. 1896) 7 Ohio C.D. 498.

The release by the probate court of one of two sureties on a joint and several guardian's bond, and the acceptance of another surety in his place, releases the cosurety, not having consented thereto. Dowell v Guion, 6 D Repr 634, 3 B 735 (CP, Hamilton 1877). Guardian And Ward ⚖ 177; Principal And Surety ⚖ 116

Where no reason appears of record it will be presumed that a new bond is not an additional bond. Pummill v. Baumgartner (Ohio Com.Pl. 1895) 4 Ohio Dec. 69, 3 Ohio N.P. 40.

Where it appears that administrator was given proper notice of hearing on application of his sureties to be released from their bond, and an order was made releasing such sureties and ordering a new bond, probate court could, without further notice, under provisions of this section, order removal of said administrator, as such action is not governed by provisions of former GC 10629 (RC 2109.24). Swartz v. Swartz (Wood 1931) 12 Ohio Law Abs. 158.

2109.19 Bond of indemnity to surety

If a fiduciary wastes or unfaithfully administers an estate, on the application of a surety on the fiduciary's bond the probate court granting letters of appointment to such fiduciary may order him to render an account and to execute to such surety a bond of indemnity with sureties approved by the court. Upon neglect or refusal to execute such bond within the time ordered, the court may remove such fiduciary, revoke his letters of appointment, and appoint another fiduciary in his place.

(125 v 903, eff. 10–1–53; 1953 H 1; GC 10506–30)

Historical and Statutory Notes

Pre–1953 H 1 Amendments: 114 v 370

Library References

Executors and Administrators ⚖26, 35(8), 460.
Guardian and Ward ⚖15, 25, 138.
Mental Health ⚖166, 175, 293.
Trusts ⚖161, 166(1), 291.
Westlaw Topic Nos. 162, 196, 257A, 390.
C.J.S. Executors and Administrators §§ 71 to 77, 104 to 110, 786.
C.J.S. Mental Health §§ 141, 148, 193.
C.J.S. Trusts §§ 302, 307, 594 to 597.

Research References

Encyclopedias

OH Jur. 3d Decedents' Estates § 979, Devastavit—Remedies.

OH Jur. 3d Fiduciaries § 12, Appointment to Fill Vacancy in Office; Sole Fiduciary.

OH Jur. 3d Fiduciaries § 231, Indemnification; Application for Bond Indemnifying Surety.

OH Jur. 3d Fiduciaries § 310, Failure to Give Bond.

Forms

Ohio Forms Legal and Business § 12:2, General Requirements.

Treatises and Practice Aids

Carlin, Baldwin's Ohio Practice, Merrick-Rippner Probate Law § 2:121, Administration of Decedent's Estate—Checklist.

Carlin, Baldwin's Ohio Practice, Merrick-Rippner Probate Law § 52:30, Fiduciary's Bond—Sureties—Liability—Bond of Indemnity to Surety.

Carlin, Baldwin's Ohio Practice, Merrick-Rippner Probate Law § 52:61, Application of Surety—Indemnity Bond—Form.

Carlin, Baldwin's Ohio Practice, Merrick-Rippner Probate Law § 52:62, Bond of Surety—Indemnity Bond—Form.

Notes of Decisions

Consideration 1
Losses covered 2

---

1. Consideration

It is sufficient consideration for an indemnity bond that it is given in a legal proceeding and continues the executor in charge of the trust. Buffington v. Bronson (Ohio 1899) 61 Ohio St. 231, 43 W.L.B. 230, 56 N.E. 762.

2. Losses covered

An indemnity bond is not limited to such loss as failure to pay over money, but includes losses on account of liability existing at the time of its execution and thereafter paid by the obligee. Buffington v. Bronson (Ohio 1899) 61 Ohio St. 231, 43 W.L.B. 230, 56 N.E. 762.

2109.20 Guardian may give real estate mortgage to secure bond

Instead of the sureties required on his bond by section 2109.04 of the Revised Code, a guardian of the person and estate or of the estate only of any ward may execute to the ward a mortgage upon unencumbered real estate. The guardian first shall furnish to the probate court a title guarantee or a mortgagee's title insurance policy for the benefit of the guardianship, with respect to the real estate, and it shall be shown to the court's satisfaction that, exclusive of improvements on the real estate, the real estate is of a value sufficient to secure the bond. The mortgage shall be recorded in the county in which the property is situated and filed with the court.

(1992 H 427, eff. 10–8–92; 1953 H 1; GC 10506–31)

Historical and Statutory Notes

Pre–1953 H 1 Amendments: 114 v 370

Library References

Guardian and Ward ⚖15, 45.
Mental Health ⚖166.
Westlaw Topic Nos. 196, 257A.
C.J.S. Mental Health § 141.

Research References

Encyclopedias

OH Jur. 3d Fiduciaries § 197, Mortgage to Secure Guardian's Bond in Lieu of Sureties.

Treatises and Practice Aids

Carlin, Baldwin's Ohio Practice, Merrick-Rippner Probate Law § 52:1, Fiduciary's Bond—Introduction.

Carlin, Baldwin's Ohio Practice, Merrick-Rippner Probate Law § 52:31, Fiduciary's Bond—Mortgage Bond in Lieu of Surety.

QUALIFICATIONS AND MISCELLANEOUS PROVISIONS

2109.21 Residence qualifications of fiduciaries; nonresidents subject to conditions

(A) An administrator, special administrator, administrator de bonis non, or administrator with the will annexed shall be a resident of this state and shall be removed on proof that the administrator is no longer a resident of this state.

(B)(1) To qualify for appointment as executor or trustee, an executor or a trustee named in a will or nominated in accordance with any power of nomination conferred in a will, may be a resident of this state or, as provided in this division, a nonresident of this state. To qualify for appointment, a nonresident executor or trustee named in, or nominated pursuant to, a will shall be an individual who is related to the maker of the will by consanguinity or affinity, or a person who resides in a state that has statutes or rules that authorize the appointment of a nonresident person who is not related to the maker of a will by consanguinity or affinity, as an executor or trustee when named in, or nominated pursuant to, a will. No such executor or trustee shall be refused appointment or removed solely because the executor or trustee is not a resident of this state.

The court may require that a nonresident executor or trustee named in, or nominated pursuant to, a will assure that all of the assets of the decedent that are in the county at the time of the death of the decedent will remain in the county until distribution or until the court determines that the assets may be removed from the county.

(2) In accordance with this division and section 2129.08 of the Revised Code, the court shall appoint as an ancillary administrator a person who is named in the will of a nonresident decedent, or who is nominated in accordance with any power of nomination conferred in the will of a nonresident decedent, as a general executor of the decedent's estate or as executor of the portion of the decedent's estate located in this state, whether or not the person so named or nominated is a resident of this state.

To qualify for appointment as an ancillary administrator, a person who is not a resident of this state and who is named or nominated as described in this division, shall be an individual who is related to the maker of the will by consanguinity or affinity, or a person who resides in a state that has statutes or rules that authorize the appointment of a nonresident of that state who is not related to the maker of a will by consanguinity or affinity, as an ancillary administrator when the nonresident is named in a will or nominated in accordance with any power of nomination conferred in a will. If a person who is not a resident of this state and who is named or nominated as described in this division so qualifies for appointment as an ancillary administrator and if the provisions of section 2129.08 of the Revised Code are satisfied, the court shall not refuse to appoint the person, and shall not remove the person, as ancillary administrator solely because the person is not a resident of this state.

The court may require that an ancillary administrator who is not a resident of this state and who is named or nominated as described in this division, assure that all of the assets of the decedent that are in the county at the time of the death of the decedent will remain in the county until distribution or until the court determines that the assets may be removed from the county.

(C) A guardian shall be a resident of the county, except that the court may appoint a nonresident of the county who is a resident of this state as guardian of the person, the estate, or both; that a nonresident of the county or of this state may be appointed a guardian, if named in a will by a parent of a minor or if selected by a minor over the age of fourteen years as provided by section 2111.12 of the Revised Code; that a nonresident of the county or of this state may be appointed a guardian if nominated in or pursuant to a durable power of attorney as described in division (D) of section 1337.09 of the Revised Code or a writing as described in division (A) of section 2111.121 of the Revised Code; and that a nonresident of the county or of this state may be appointed as a guardian if the nonresident was nominated as a guardian in or pursuant to a durable power of attorney as described in division (D) of section 1337.09 of the Revised Code or a writing described in division (A) of section 2111.121 of the Revised Code. A guardian, other than a guardian named in a will by a parent of a minor, selected by a minor over the age of fourteen years, or nominated in or pursuant to such a durable power of attorney or writing, may be removed on proof that the guardian is no longer a resident of the county in which the guardian resided at the time of the guardian's appointment, and shall be removed on proof that the guardian is no longer a resident of this state.

(D) Any fiduciary, whose residence qualifications are not defined in this section, shall be a resident of this state, and shall be removed on proof that the fiduciary is no longer a resident of this state.

(E) Any fiduciary, in order to assist in the carrying out of the fiduciary's fiduciary duties, may employ agents who are not residents of the county or of this state.

(1996 H 288, eff. 1–14–97; 1990 H 346, eff. 5–31–90; 1988 S 228; 1983 S 115; 1982 S 247; 1975 S 145; 1953 H 1; GC 10506–65)

Uncodified Law

1990 H 346, § 3, eff. 5–31–90, reads, in part: (A) Sections 1 and 2 of this act shall apply only to the estates of decedents who die on or after the effective date of this act.

Historical and Statutory Notes

Pre–1953 H 1 Amendments: 123 v 460; 114 v 378

Amendment Note: 1996 H 288 inserted "and that a nonresident of the county or of this state may be appointed as a guardian if the nonresident was nominated as a guardian in or pursuant to a durable power of attorney as described in division (D) of section 1337.09 of the Revised Code or a writing described in division (A) of section 2111.121 of the Revised Code" in division (C); and made changes to reflect gender neutral language and other nonsubstantive changes.

Legislative Service Commission

1975:

Current law requires an administrator to be a resident of this state. The probate court may also refuse to allow an executor or trustee named in a will to be a nonresident. Under the bill, an administrator, would still be required to be a resident of the state but the provision that permits the probate court to refuse to allow a nonresident executor or trustee would be repealed, and any other executor, except a surviving spouse or next of kin, would also have to be a resident of the state.

OSBA Probate and Trust Law Section

1983:

See the comment for 1983 following Sec. 2111.121 and Sec. 2113.05.

Cross References

Court appointment of guardian, 2111.02
Presentation of claims to ancillary administrator, 2129.12

Library References

Executors and Administrators ⚖︎15, 18, 21(1).
Guardian and Ward ⚖︎10.
Mental Health ⚖︎116.1.
Trusts ⚖︎159.
Westlaw Topic Nos. 162, 196, 257A, 390.
C.J.S. Executors and Administrators §§ 22 to 28, 44 to 49, 947.
C.J.S. Mental Health § 123.
C.J.S. Trusts §§ 284 to 287, 300 to 301.

Baldwin's Ohio Legislative Service, 1988 Laws of Ohio, S 228—LSC Analysis, p 5–968; 1990 Laws of Ohio, H 346—LSC Analysis, p 5–87

Research References

Encyclopedias

OH Jur. 3d Decedents' Estates § 913, Meaning of "Suitable" and "Competent", Generally—Nonresidency.
OH Jur. 3d Decedents' Estates § 937, Residence Required.
OH Jur. 3d Decedents' Estates § 1712, Authority of Administrators and Executors Appointed in Another State, Generally.
OH Jur. 3d Decedents' Estates § 1733, Who May be Appointed.
OH Jur. 3d Decedents' Estates § 1735, Appointment.
OH Jur. 3d Fiduciaries § 9, Qualification; Residency.
OH Jur. 3d Fiduciaries § 309, Change of Residence.
OH Jur. 3d Guardian & Ward § 21, Residence.
OH Jur. 3d Guardian & Ward § 206, Generally; Termination of Office.
OH Jur. 3d Trusts § 172, Nonresidents.

Forms

Ohio Forms Legal and Business § 24:481, Appointment of Guardian—Person of Minor Children—Provision Expressing Desire Same Person be Appointed Guardian of Their Estates.
Ohio Forms and Transactions KP 30.14, Trusts and Trustees.

Treatises and Practice Aids

Carlin, Baldwin's Ohio Practice, Merrick-Rippner Probate Law § 2:15, Appointment of Fiduciary—Appointment of Executor or Administrator.
Carlin, Baldwin's Ohio Practice, Merrick-Rippner Probate Law § 2:16, Appointment of Fiduciary—Fiduciary's Bond.
Carlin, Baldwin's Ohio Practice, Merrick-Rippner Probate Law § 51:1, Residency—Administrator.
Carlin, Baldwin's Ohio Practice, Merrick-Rippner Probate Law § 51:2, Residency—Executor or Testamentary Trustee.
Carlin, Baldwin's Ohio Practice, Merrick-Rippner Probate Law § 51:3, Residency—Executor or Trustee—Retention of Assets in County.
Carlin, Baldwin's Ohio Practice, Merrick-Rippner Probate Law § 51:4, Residency—Guardian.
Carlin, Baldwin's Ohio Practice, Merrick-Rippner Probate Law § 51:5, Residency—Guardian—Removal of Nonresident.
Carlin, Baldwin's Ohio Practice, Merrick-Rippner Probate Law § 51:6, Residency—Removal of Nonresident Fiduciary.
Carlin, Baldwin's Ohio Practice, Merrick-Rippner Probate Law § 51:7, Residency—Agents.
Carlin, Baldwin's Ohio Practice, Merrick-Rippner Probate Law § 57:2, Removal of Fiduciary—Introduction.
Carlin, Baldwin's Ohio Practice, Merrick-Rippner Probate Law § 57:5, Removal of Fiduciary—Grounds—Nonresidency of Fiduciary.
Carlin, Baldwin's Ohio Practice, Merrick-Rippner Probate Law § 60:9, Power of Attorney—Appointment of Guardian for Principal.
Carlin, Baldwin's Ohio Practice, Merrick-Rippner Probate Law § 66:1, Termination of Guardianship—Mandatory.
Carlin, Baldwin's Ohio Practice, Merrick-Rippner Probate Law § 68:4, Letters of Administration—Specific Qualifications of Administrators—Residency Requirement.
Carlin, Baldwin's Ohio Practice, Merrick-Rippner Probate Law § 75:4, Distribution—Voluntary—Liability—Executor or Administrator.
Carlin, Baldwin's Ohio Practice, Merrick-Rippner Probate Law § 81:1, Removal—Statutory Provisions.
Carlin, Baldwin's Ohio Practice, Merrick-Rippner Probate Law § 81:3, Removal—Application.
Carlin, Baldwin's Ohio Practice, Merrick-Rippner Probate Law § 2:121, Administration of Decedent's Estate—Checklist.

Carlin, Baldwin's Ohio Practice, Merrick-Rippner Probate Law § 30:31, Drafting a Will—Designation of Guardian, Trustee, and Attorney—Designation of Guardian of Minor Children.

Carlin, Baldwin's Ohio Practice, Merrick-Rippner Probate Law § 30:32, Drafting a Will—Designation of Guardian, Trustee, and Attorney—Designation of Testamentary Trustee.

Carlin, Baldwin's Ohio Practice, Merrick-Rippner Probate Law § 30:34, Drafting a Will—Appointment of Executor, Alternate Executor; Ancillary Administrator.

Carlin, Baldwin's Ohio Practice, Merrick-Rippner Probate Law § 60:10, Power of Attorney—"Standby Guardian" for Minor Child of Principal.

Carlin, Baldwin's Ohio Practice, Merrick-Rippner Probate Law § 62:16, Appointment of Guardian—Application—Who May Apply.

Carlin, Baldwin's Ohio Practice, Merrick-Rippner Probate Law § 62:23, Appointment of Guardian—Procedure—Guardian Nominated in Will, Power of Attorney, or Other Writing.

Carlin, Baldwin's Ohio Practice, Merrick-Rippner Probate Law § 62:24, Appointment of Guardian—Parent May Nominate Guardian for Minor by Will.

Carlin, Baldwin's Ohio Practice, Merrick-Rippner Probate Law § 62:29, Appointment of Guardian—Residency Requirements—Guardian.

Carlin, Baldwin's Ohio Practice, Merrick-Rippner Probate Law § 62:30, Appointment of Guardian—Miscellaneous—Minor Children of Ward.

Carlin, Baldwin's Ohio Practice, Merrick-Rippner Probate Law § 62:50, Appointment of Guardian of a Minor—Designation by Minor.

Carlin, Baldwin's Ohio Practice, Merrick-Rippner Probate Law § 62:52, Appointment of Guardian of a Minor—Testamentary Designation by Parent.

Carlin, Baldwin's Ohio Practice, Merrick-Rippner Probate Law § 64:13, Powers and Duties of Guardian—Ward's Person—Discretionary Acts—Employment of Agents.

Carlin, Baldwin's Ohio Practice, Merrick-Rippner Probate Law § 64:21, Powers and Duties of Guardian—Ward's Estate—Discretionary Acts.

Carlin, Baldwin's Ohio Practice, Merrick-Rippner Probate Law § 68:18, Letters Testamentary—Letters of Administration With the Will Annexed.

Carlin, Baldwin's Ohio Practice, Merrick-Rippner Probate Law § 68:21, Letters Testamentary—Qualifications for Executors—Trust Company.

Carlin, Baldwin's Ohio Practice, Merrick-Rippner Probate Law § 68:24, Letters Testamentary—Qualifications for Executors—Residency Requirement.

Carlin, Baldwin's Ohio Practice, Merrick-Rippner Probate Law § 30:171, Appointment of Guardian If Spouse Fails to Survive; Successor—Form.

Bogert - the Law of Trusts and Trustees § 132, Nonresidents and Foreign Corporations as Trustees.

Law Review and Journal Commentaries

Standby Guardianships—Substitute H.B. 288, Michael Stark. 7 Prob L J Ohio 65 (July/August 1997).

Notes of Decisions

Administrators 6
Corporations 3
Executors, guardians and trustees 5
Foreign decedents and creditors 4
Procedure and jurisdiction 1
Removal 2

1. Procedure and jurisdiction

Qualifications are not jurisdictional facts, nor is failure to file a statement of the nature of the estate. In re Ferguson's Estate (Ohio Com.Pl. 1904) 16 Ohio Dec. 486, 3 Ohio NP(NS) 549.

2. Removal

RC 2109.21 requires the removal of a guardian of a minor, who was not named in a will by the parent of such minor, upon proof that he is no longer a resident of the state. In re Guardianship of Lloyd (Cuyahoga 1964) 8 Ohio App.2d 223, 197 N.E.2d 377, 32 O.O.2d 128. Guardian And Ward ⇐ 25

A guardian who was a nonresident of the county at the time of her appointment may not subsequently be removed solely upon the ground of such nonresidence. In re Guardianship of Price (Ohio Prob. 1959) 162 N.E.2d 494, 83 Ohio Law Abs. 149.

When, without allowing a reasonable time for the next of kin to apply for letters of administration upon the estate of a deceased person, the probate court appoints a stranger as administrator, the appointment is illegal; and on application and appointment of the next of kin, the letters granted to the stranger should be revoked. In re Patterson's Estate (Ohio Com.Pl. 1927) 26 Ohio NP(NS) 580.

3. Corporations

A probate court is under no duty to appoint a nonresident corporation, licensed to do business in Ohio, as executor of the estate of a resident testator who designated such corporation to act in that capacity. In re Emery (Hamilton 1978) 59 Ohio App.2d 7, 391 N.E.2d 746, 13 O.O.3d 44, 9 A.L.R.4th 1214.

A foreign trust company may act as a testamentary trustee for a foreign testator. Union Sav. Bank & Trust Co. v. Baltimore & O.S.W.R. Co. (Ohio Insolv. 1908) 6 Ohio NP(NS) 454, 53 W.L.B. 180.

4. Foreign decedents and creditors

A foreign creditor can take out letters though a foreign administrator has been appointed. Bustard v. Dabney (Ohio 1829) 4 Ohio 68.

Italian consul had right by treaty to be appointed administrator of estate of Italian national who died resident in Ohio, but treaty could not and did not supersede domestic law nor divest probate court of its powers, and consul's right was thus subject to the discretion of the state probate court as to appointment of administrator. (See also In re Estate of Balbo, 16 NP(NS) 9, 29 D 603 (Prob, Stark 1914); In re Estate of Todarello, 15 NP(NS) 593, 62 B 201 (Prob, Mahoning 1913).) Pagano v. Cerri (Ohio 1916) 93 Ohio St. 345, 112 N.E. 1037, 13 Ohio Law Rep. 578.

The Italian consul has no paramount and exclusive right to be appointed administrator of a deceased Italian, but is relegated to the fourth class enumerated in former GC 10617 (RC 2113.06, RC 2113.07), and that only by virtue of treaty, for a consul is constructively a resident of his own country, and hence not qualified under our statute. (See also Pagano v Cerri, 93 OS 345, 112 NE 1037 (1916); In re Estate of Todarello, 15 NP(NS) 593, 62 B 201 (Prob, Mahoning 1913).) In re Balbo's Estate (Ohio Prob. 1914) 29 Ohio Dec. 603, 16 Ohio NP(NS) 9.

The right extends to the Italian consul to be appointed administrator of the estate of a citizen of Italy who died in this county, notwithstanding the provisions of RS 6005 as to whom letters of administration shall be granted. In re Arduino's Estate (Ohio Com.Pl. 1909) 20 Ohio Dec. 461, 9 Ohio NP(NS) 369.

5. Executors, guardians and trustees

The trial court's appointment of mother's second son, rather than the son mother had nominated as her prospective guardian, as guardian of mother was an abuse of discretion; nominated son had assisted mother in managing her affairs since her husband died, he paid her bills, he visited her often, and his name was on her checking and savings accounts, mother had executed a durable power of attorney that nominated son as her attorney in fact and prospective guardian, and there was no evidence that nominated son was incompetent to serve as mother's guardian. In re Guardianship of McHaney (Ohio App. 9 Dist., Summit, 11-10-2004) No. 22088, 2004-Ohio-5956, 2004 WL 2535414, Unreported, appeal not allowed 105 Ohio St.3d 1464, 824 N.E.2d 92, 2005-Ohio-1024. Guardian And Ward ⇐ 10

Fact that father of children who were under guardianship was not an Ohio resident did not preclude probate court from returning children to him, as a natural guardian, upon termination of formal guardianship. In re Guardianship of Grant (Ohio App. 3 Dist., Allen, 08-11-2003) No. 1-02-99, 2003-Ohio-4234, 2003 WL 21904749, Unreported. Guardian And Ward ⇐ 25; Guardian And Ward ⇐ 29

A probate court that erroneously appoints three nonresident coguardians for a woman declared incompetent may be precluded from determining subsequent guardianship matters due to lack of jurisdiction for failing to follow applicable statutes. In re Guardianship of Coller (Wood 1991) 74 Ohio App.3d 386, 599 N.E.2d 292, motion overruled 62 Ohio St.3d 1477, 581 N.E.2d 1099.

Rejection of a nonresident designated as an attorney-in-fact and nominated as guardian of the subject of a durable power of attorney, solely because the nominee is a nonresident, is reversible error. In re Medsker (Cuyahoga 1990) 66 Ohio App.3d 219, 583 N.E.2d 1091.

Appointment of a grandson as guardian of a physically incapacitated ward, nominated as guardian in a defective application, and rejection of the application of the ward's daughter, nominated as guardian in a properly executed durable power of attorney, on the ground that the daughter is a nonresident, is improper. In re Medsker (Cuyahoga 1990) 66 Ohio App.3d 219, 583 N.E.2d 1091.

Residency in and of itself was not a sufficient standard for adjudicating the fitness or competency of a potential trustee; only consideration pertaining to residency would be that trustee was resident of the state. In re Trust of Selsor (Madison 1983) 13 Ohio App.3d 164, 468 N.E.2d 745, 13 O.B.R. 198. Trusts ⇔ 159

That one of the executors named in a will is a nonresident does not justify refusal to appoint him, notwithstanding a rule of the court to the contrary. Seasongood v. Seasongood (Hamilton 1915) 27 Ohio C.D. 200, 23 Ohio C.C.(N.S.) 369.

Where the provisions of a trust provide that the surviving co-trustee shall appoint a successor trustee, the probate court erred in refusing to follow the surviving co-trustee's recommendation as to a successor on the grounds that the recommended trustee was not a resident of the county in which the court sat. In re Selsor, No. CA83–03–012 (12th Dist Ct App, Madison, 11–30–83).

6. Administrators

Appointment of an administratrix, who thereafter abandoned her residence in state of Ohio, is voidable at instance of proper party, but such appointment is not subject to attack by party who has no real interest in administration of assets of estate. In re Fannin's Estate (Darke 1970) 24 Ohio App.2d 1, 262 N.E.2d 883, 53 O.O.2d 26.

Due qualification of an administrator relates back to the date of his appointment as to acts for the benefit of the estate during the interim. Archdeacon v. Cincinnati Gas & Elec. Co. (Ohio 1907) 76 Ohio St. 97, 81 N.E. 152, 4 Ohio Law Rep. 739.

Nonresidents of this state are not eligible for appointment as administrators. In re Ulhorn's Estate (Ohio Cir. 1894) 4 Ohio C.D. 526, 1 Ohio Dec. 631.

Application by the next of kin of a deceased person for the appointment of a stranger as administrator and refusal by the court to appoint the stranger do not constitute a waiver of the rights of the next of kin to the appointment. In re Patterson's Estate (Ohio Com.Pl. 1927) 26 Ohio NP(NS) 580.

A county auditor may in the sound discretion of the probate court be appointed as the administrator of an estate. 1927 OAG 1350.

2109.22 Marriage not a disqualification

The marriage of any person does not disqualify him from acting as fiduciary, whether the marriage occurs before or after his appointment and qualification, and all of his acts in such capacity shall have the same validity as though he were unmarried.

(1975 S 145, eff. 1–1–76; 1953 H 1; GC 10506–66)

Historical and Statutory Notes

Pre–1953 H 1 Amendments: 114 v 378

Legislative Service Commission

1975:

This section currently provides that the marriage of a woman does not disqualify her from acting as a fiduciary. The bill would substitute "any person" for "woman."

Library References

Executors and Administrators ⇔18, 34.
Guardian and Ward ⇔10, 24.
Mental Health ⇔119, 166.
Trusts ⇔159, 163.
Westlaw Topic Nos. 162, 196, 257A, 390.
C.J.S. Executors and Administrators §§ 23 to 26, 44 to 49.
C.J.S. Mental Health §§ 123, 141.
C.J.S. Trusts §§ 284 to 287, 300 to 301.

Research References

Encyclopedias

OH Jur. 3d Decedents' Estates § 939, Meaning of "Competent" and "Suitable", Generally; Discretion of Court—Effect of Marriage.
OH Jur. 3d Fiduciaries § 9, Qualification; Residency.

Forms

Ohio Forms and Transactions KP 30.14, Trusts and Trustees.

Treatises and Practice Aids

Bogert - the Law of Trusts and Trustees § 127, Trustee Capable of Taking and Holding Title But Not of Administering the Trust.
Bogert - the Law of Trusts and Trustees § 975, Compensation of Trustees.

Notes of Decisions

After appointment 1
Foreign guardian 2

---

1. After appointment

An execution or an order of sale once begun is not abated by the marriage of the administratrix, in whose favor it issued. Craig, Adm'x v. Fox (Ohio 1847) 16 Ohio 563. Abatement And Revival ⇔ 68; Execution ⇔ 117; Executors And Administrators ⇔ 34

2. Foreign guardian

A foreign guardian, ineligible to an appointment as such in Ohio, will not be permitted to collect money due the ward in this state. Habighurst v Stevenson, 10 D Repr 162, 19 B 106 (Super, Cincinnati 1886). Guardian And Ward ⇔ 168

2109.24 Resignation or removal of fiduciary

The probate court at any time may accept the resignation of any fiduciary upon the fiduciary's proper accounting, if the fiduciary was appointed by, is under the control of, or is accountable to the court.

If a fiduciary fails to make and file an inventory as required by sections 2109.58, 2111.14, and 2115.02 of the Revised Code or to render a just and true account of the fiduciary's administration at the times required by section 2109.301, 2109.302, or 2109.303 of the Revised Code, and if the failure continues for thirty days after the fiduciary has been notified by the court of the expiration of the relevant time, the fiduciary forthwith may be removed by the court and shall receive no allowance for the fiduciary's services unless the court enters upon its journal its findings that the delay was necessary and reasonable.

The court may remove any fiduciary, after giving the fiduciary not less than ten days' notice, for habitual drunkenness, neglect of duty, incompetency, or fraudulent conduct, because the interest of the property, testamentary trust, or estate that the fiduciary is responsible for administering demands it, or for any other cause authorized by law.

The court may remove a testamentary trustee upon the written application of more than one-half of the persons having an interest in the estate controlled by the testamentary trustee, but the testamentary trustee is not to be considered as a person having an interest in the estate under the proceedings; except that no testamentary trustee appointed under a will shall be removed upon such written application unless for a good cause.

(2006 H 416, eff. 1–1–07; 2001 H 85, eff. 10–31–01; 1992 H 427, eff. 10–8–92; 1953 H 1; GC 10506–53)

Uncodified Law

2001 H 85, § 6: See Uncodified Law under 2109.12.

2001 H 85, § 7: See Uncodified Law under 2109.11.

Historical and Statutory Notes

Pre–1953 H 1 Amendments: 119 v 394, § 1; 114 v 375

Amendment Note: 2006 H 416 rewrote the third and fourth paragraph, which prior thereto read:

"The court may remove any such fiduciary, after giving the fiduciary not less than ten days' notice, for habitual drunkenness, neglect of duty, incompetency, or fraudulent conduct, because the interest of the trust demands it, or for any other cause authorized by law.

"The court may remove a trustee upon the written application of more than one-half of the persons having an interest in the estate controlled by the trustee, but the trustee is not to be considered as a person having an interest in the estate under the proceedings; except that no trustee appointed under a will shall be removed upon such written application unless for a good cause."

Amendment Note: 2001 H 85 substituted "2109.301, 2109.302, or 2109.303" for "2109.30" in the second paragraph; and made changes to reflect gender neutral language.

Library References

Executors and Administrators ⚖33, 35.
Guardian and Ward ⚖23, 25.
Mental Health ⚖167, 174.
Trusts ⚖162, 164.
Westlaw Topic Nos. 162, 196, 257A, 390.
C.J.S. Executors and Administrators §§ 89, 93, 104 to 120.
C.J.S. Mental Health §§ 146 to 148.
C.J.S. Trusts §§ 303 to 310.

Baldwin's Ohio Legislative Service Annotated, 2006 H 416 LSC Analysis, p 3/L-1709

Research References

Encyclopedias

OH Jur. 3d Charities § 26, Jurisdiction of Courts.
OH Jur. 3d Decedents' Estates § 938, Meaning of "Competent" and "Suitable", Generally; Discretion of Court.
OH Jur. 3d Decedents' Estates § 961, Resignation.
OH Jur. 3d Decedents' Estates § 1341, Funeral Expenses.
OH Jur. 3d Fiduciaries § 239, Accounting Upon Vacancy in Office—Resignation or Removal of Fiduciary.
OH Jur. 3d Fiduciaries § 258, Loss or Forfeiture of Right to Compensation—Statutory Grounds for Denial of Commission.
OH Jur. 3d Fiduciaries § 297, Resignation.
OH Jur. 3d Fiduciaries § 301, on Application of Persons Interested in Trust.
OH Jur. 3d Fiduciaries § 302, Failure to File Inventory or Account.
OH Jur. 3d Fiduciaries § 303, Overview of Other Causes.
OH Jur. 3d Fiduciaries § 304, Fraudulent Conduct.
OH Jur. 3d Fiduciaries § 305, Neglect of Duty; Mismanagement.
OH Jur. 3d Fiduciaries § 306, Interest of the Trust.
OH Jur. 3d Fiduciaries § 314, Generally; Jurisdiction.
OH Jur. 3d Fiduciaries § 316, Motion.
OH Jur. 3d Fiduciaries § 317, Notice.
OH Jur. 3d Trusts § 181, Resignation.
OH Jur. 3d Trusts § 184, Removal—Discretion of Court.

Treatises and Practice Aids

Carlin, Baldwin's Ohio Practice, Merrick-Rippner Probate Law § 2:15, Appointment of Fiduciary—Appointment of Executor or Administrator.
Carlin, Baldwin's Ohio Practice, Merrick-Rippner Probate Law § 57:1, Resignation of Fiduciary.
Carlin, Baldwin's Ohio Practice, Merrick-Rippner Probate Law § 57:2, Removal of Fiduciary—Introduction.
Carlin, Baldwin's Ohio Practice, Merrick-Rippner Probate Law § 57:3, Removal of Fiduciary—Trustee.
Carlin, Baldwin's Ohio Practice, Merrick-Rippner Probate Law § 57:4, Removal of Fiduciary—Grounds—Failure to File Inventory or Account.
Carlin, Baldwin's Ohio Practice, Merrick-Rippner Probate Law § 57:6, Removal of Fiduciary—Grounds—"Interest of Trust".
Carlin, Baldwin's Ohio Practice, Merrick-Rippner Probate Law § 57:7, Removal of Fiduciary—Other Grounds.
Carlin, Baldwin's Ohio Practice, Merrick-Rippner Probate Law § 57:9, Removal of Fiduciary—Procedure—Notice.
Carlin, Baldwin's Ohio Practice, Merrick-Rippner Probate Law § 66:2, Termination—Discretionary—Court; Removal.
Carlin, Baldwin's Ohio Practice, Merrick-Rippner Probate Law § 81:1, Removal—Statutory Provisions.
Carlin, Baldwin's Ohio Practice, Merrick-Rippner Probate Law § 81:5, Motion for Removal of Executor or Administrator—Forms.
Carlin, Baldwin's Ohio Practice, Merrick-Rippner Probate Law § 90:8, Authority for Land Sale Action—Insufficient Personal Property to Pay Debts.
Carlin, Baldwin's Ohio Practice, Merrick-Rippner Probate Law § 91:3, Land Sale—Motion to Commence Action and Proceed.
Carlin, Baldwin's Ohio Practice, Merrick-Rippner Probate Law § 57:13, Resignation of Fiduciary—Form.
Carlin, Baldwin's Ohio Practice, Merrick-Rippner Probate Law § 57:14, Entry on Resignation of Fiduciary With Account—Form.
Carlin, Baldwin's Ohio Practice, Merrick-Rippner Probate Law § 57:16, Motion for Removal of Fiduciary—Form.
Carlin, Baldwin's Ohio Practice, Merrick-Rippner Probate Law § 57:17, Order for Hearing and Notice on Removal of Fiduciary—Form.
Carlin, Baldwin's Ohio Practice, Merrick-Rippner Probate Law § 57:18, Notice to Executor or Administrator—Form.
Carlin, Baldwin's Ohio Practice, Merrick-Rippner Probate Law § 57:19, Order of Removal of Executor or Administrator—Form.
Carlin, Baldwin's Ohio Practice, Merrick-Rippner Probate Law § 66:10, Termination of Guardianship—Minor.
Carlin, Baldwin's Ohio Practice, Merrick-Rippner Probate Law § 68:19, Letters Testamentary—Qualifications of Executors—in General.
Carlin, Baldwin's Ohio Practice, Merrick-Rippner Probate Law § 79:41, Entry for Removal of Fiduciary—Form.
Bogert - the Law of Trusts and Trustees § 519, Removal of Trustees—Court's Power to Remove.
Bogert - the Law of Trusts and Trustees § 527, Grounds for Removal.
Bogert - the Law of Trusts and Trustees § 963, Duty to Render Formal Account in Court of Equity.
Bogert - the Law of Trusts and Trustees § 980, Power of Court to Reduce or Deny Compensation.
Restatement (3d) of Trusts § 37, Removal of Trustee.

Law Review and Journal Commentaries

The Uniform Trust Code (2000) and Its Application to Ohio. David M. English, 12 Prob L J Ohio 1 (September/October 2001).

Notes of Decisions

Fees 1
Jurisdiction 2
Removal of fiduciaries other than trustees 3-6
    For failure to file inventory 3
    For other cause 4
    Interest in estate 5
    Procedural issues 6
Removal of trustees 7
Resignation 8
Termination of authority 9

---

1. Fees

Statute dealing with removal or resignation of a fiduciary did not provide basis for denying all fiduciary fees to trustee, where probate court did not remove trustee as fiduciary. In re Testamentary Trust of Manning (Ohio App. 7 Dist., Mahoning, 09-09-2005) No. 05 MA 2, 2005-Ohio-4764, 2005 WL 2206732, Unreported. Trusts ⚖ 321

Under law of the case doctrine, probate court was required to follow mandate of Court of Appeals' decision which reversed probate court's total fee denial as an abuse of discretion and directed that, on remand, court determine an appropriate amount of reasonably discounted fiduciary fees that should be paid to trustee. In re Testamentary Trust of Manning (Ohio App. 7 Dist., Mahoning, 09-09-2005) No. 05 MA 2, 2005-Ohio-4764, 2005 WL 2206732, Unreported. Trusts ⚖ 329

A 30% discount of fiduciary fees, as trustee's officers proposed, represented a reasonable amount for trustee's error in taking fees in trust account without prior court approval and on a quarterly basis rather than an annual basis. In re Testamentary Trust of Manning (Ohio App. 7 Dist., Mahoning, 09-09-2005) No. 05 MA 2, 2005-Ohio-4764, 2005 WL 2206732, Unreported. Trusts ⚖ 321

Probate court had discretionary power with regard to authorizing payment of attorney fees in connection with action to remove guardian and whether the expenses were necessary or beneficial to the ward's interest was squarely within the exercise of the court's discretion. In re Guardianship of Escola (Stark 1987) 41 Ohio App.3d 42, 534 N.E.2d 866. Mental Health ⚖ 159

The application for payment of attorney fees in unsuccessfully resisting removal proceedings against a guardian will be denied where the guardian's removal was mandatorily required under RC 2109.21. In re Guardianship of Lloyd (Cuyahoga 1964) 8 Ohio App.2d 223, 197 N.E.2d 377, 32 O.O.2d 128.

Upon the settlement of the accounts of an administrator or executor who has resigned or been removed the court may order the amount due from him to be paid to his successor. Slagle v. Entrekin (Ohio 1887) 44 Ohio St. 637, 17 W.L.B. 211, 10 N.E. 675.

2. Jurisdiction

An order of the probate court appointing an executor, if made without jurisdiction, is void, and it may be disregarded in any other court; however, if the order is made in the exercise of proper jurisdiction over the subject matter and estate, although based on erroneous conclusions of law or fact, it cannot be collaterally attacked. Union Sav. Bank & Trust Co. v. Western Union Tel. Co. (Ohio 1908) 79 Ohio St. 89, 86 N.E. 478, 128 Am.St.Rep. 675, 6 Ohio Law Rep. 554. Courts ⚖ 202(4); Executors And Administrators ⚖ 29(3); Judgment ⚖ 475

The probate court having appointed a guardian does not lose jurisdiction of such guardianship by his removal from the state. Netting v. Strickland (Ohio Cir. 1899) 9 Ohio C.D. 841.

Appellate jurisdiction of a common pleas court to determine the right to remove executors is not inconsistent with the exclusive jurisdiction of the probate court. In re Sells' Estate (Ohio Com.Pl. 1909) 19 Ohio Dec. 567, 8 Ohio NP(NS) 175.

Appellate jurisdiction of a common pleas court to determine the right to remove executors is not inconsistent with the exclusive jurisdiction of the probate court. In re Sells' Estate (Ohio Com.Pl. 1909) 19 Ohio Dec. 567, 8 Ohio NP(NS) 175.

Reasons for removal are not jurisdictional and need not appear in the journal entry. In re Ferguson's Estate (Ohio Com.Pl. 1904) 16 Ohio Dec. 486, 3 Ohio NP(NS) 549.

Jurisdiction of the probate court in removing executors and administrators is exclusive. Munger v. Jeffries (Ohio Com.Pl. 1900) 10 Ohio Dec. 12, 7 Ohio N.P. 55.

3. Removal of fiduciaries other than trustees—For failure to file inventory

Statute requiring fiduciary to be provided hearing, with at least ten days prior notice, before fiduciary may be removed did not apply to trial court's removal of administrator of estate for failure to timely file account of estate, although statutory definition of "fiduciary" included administrators; statute governing failure to file account provided authority for administrator's immediate removal. In re Estate of Phelps (Ohio App. 7 Dist., Jefferson, 02-21-2006) No. 05 JE 19, 2006-Ohio-890, 2006 WL 459265, Unreported, reconsideration overruled 2006-Ohio-1471, 2006 WL 772017. Executors And Administrators ⚖ 35(16)

Removal of director of family services agency as ward's guardian was warranted, where director failed to render an account of the administration of the ward's estate, failed to file an inventory of the estate after appointment, and disregarded orders of the court. In re Guardianship of Monus (Ohio App. 7 Dist., Mahoning, 05-28-2004) No. 03 MA 128, No. 03 MA 131, No. 03 MA 129, No. 03 MA 132, No. 03 MA 130, No. 03 MA 153, 2004-Ohio-2808, 2004 WL 1194070, Unreported. Mental Health ⚖ 167

Removal of director of family services agency as ward's guardian was warranted, where director failed to file an inventory of the estate after appointment, failed to produce receipts for particular items purchased, made lump sum expenditures from estate, and failed to keep an itemized statement of receipts and disbursements that could be verified by vouchers or proof. In re Guardianship of Monus (Ohio App. 7 Dist., Mahoning, 05-28-2004) No. 03 MA 128, No. 03 MA 131, No. 03 MA 129, No. 03 MA 132, No. 03 MA 130, No. 03 MA 153, 2004-Ohio-2808, 2004 WL 1194070, Unreported. Guardian And Ward ⚖ 25

An administratrix may not be deprived of the compensation due to her for her services for mere delay in making and returning the inventory of the estate, when she has not been given an order requiring her, at an early day therein named, to return same, or has not been notified by the court of the expiration of the time to file such inventory. In re Burchett's Estate (Marion 1968) 16 Ohio App.2d 45, 241 N.E.2d 787, 45 O.O.2d 133. Executors And Administrators ⚖ 500

4. —— For other cause, removal of fiduciaries other than trustees

Removal of executor was not warranted, where executor's inventory of estate was not flawed. In re Estate of Shaw (Ohio App. 2 Dist., Greene, 09-09-2005) No. 2004 CA 111, 2005-Ohio-4743, 2005 WL 2179300, Unreported. Executors And Administrators ⚖ 35(1)

Probate court was required to adopt magistrate's findings of fact when deciding executor's objections to magistrate's decision, which granted beneficiary's motion to remove executor; executor failed to file transcript of hearing that was held before magistrate. In re Estate of Thompson (Ohio App. 9 Dist., Summit, 08-17-2005) No. 22403, 2005-Ohio-4261, 2005 WL 1963028, Unreported. Executors And Administrators ⚖ 35(19)

Probate court did not abuse its discretion, in considering beneficiary's motion to remove executor, by applying statute governing removal of executor based on unsettled claims between executor and estate, even though beneficiary sought removal pursuant to statute authorizing removal for habitual drunkenness, neglect of duty, incompetence, or fraudulent conduct; probate court was not limited to consideration of the statute cited by the parties, and beneficiary established that he instituted separate civil action against executor to recover estate funds allegedly withdrawn by executor and placed in a personal account. In re Estate of Levy (Ohio App. 2 Dist., Montgomery, 02-04-2005) No. CIV.A. 20509, 2005-Ohio-446, 2005 WL 281169, Unreported. Executors And Administrators ⚖ 35(1)

Removal of director of family services agency as ward's guardian was warranted, where director failed to seek court approval before expending funds, failed to file an accurate inventory, and disregarded orders of the court. In re Guardianship of Monus (Ohio App. 7 Dist., Mahoning, 05-28-2004) No. 03 MA 128, No. 03 MA 131, No. 03 MA 129, No. 03 MA 132, No. 03 MA 130, No. 03 MA 153, 2004-Ohio-2808, 2004 WL 1194070, Unreported. Guardian And Ward ⚖ 25

Guardian's failing to apply for Medicaid benefits on behalf of ward's estate for ten months after he knew that he should have applied for those benefits, along with his failure to pay ward's bills that were accumulating, was cause for guardian's removal. In re Ewanicky (Ohio App. 8 Dist., Cuyahoga, 06-26-2003) No. 81742, 2003-Ohio-3351, 2003 WL 21469181, Unreported, stay denied 99 Ohio St.3d 1534, 795 N.E.2d 55, 2003-Ohio-4677, appeal not allowed 100 Ohio St.3d 1506, 799 N.E.2d 186, 2003-Ohio-6161, reconsideration denied 101 Ohio St.3d 1425, 802 N.E.2d 155, 2004-Ohio-123. Guardian And Ward ⚖ 25

Court's discretion in matters of removal of administrators is very broad. Hopkins v. Barger (Lawrence 1935) 21 Ohio Law Abs. 386.

Removing executor for failing to reimburse beneficiary for decedent's funeral expenses was not an abuse of discretion; beneficiary's exceptions to executor's account and her motion for contempt and removal of executor put executor on notice of her demand for payment, such that executor was obligated to take some action on beneficiary's claim once it was filed, and beneficiary's viewing her mother's body, even given mother's wish to have a closed coffin, was not officious and meddlesome conduct that warranted not reimbursing her. In re Estate of Geanangel (Ohio App. 7 Dist., 02-25-2002) 147 Ohio App.3d 131, 768 N.E.2d 1235, 2002-Ohio-850. Executors And Administrators ⚖ 35(1)

Trial court did not apply "suitability" standard in removing executor; although trial court discussed statutory "suitable person" test, which applies when it appoints executor, trial court specifically removed executor by authority of statute governing removal of fiduciary, and not by authority of statute concerning her appointment. Pio v. Ramsier (Wayne 1993) 88 Ohio App.3d 133, 623 N.E.2d 174, motion overruled 67 Ohio St.3d 1482, 620 N.E.2d 854. Executors And Administrators ⚖ 35(.5)

Executor's refusal to waive physician-patient privilege may be basis for removal, provided that trial court accords executor hearing and opportuni-

Note 4

ty to present evidence on issues involved. Pio v. Ramsier (Wayne 1993) 88 Ohio App.3d 133, 623 N.E.2d 174, motion overruled 67 Ohio St.3d 1482, 620 N.E.2d 854. Executors And Administrators ⇒ 35(1)

It was not abuse of discretion to remove daughter as executor of her mother's estate, of which she was to receive substantial share, on ground that removal was in best interest of estate; there were allegations that mother may not have been competent and may have been subject to undue influence, and it was in best interest of estate to appoint impartial executor to consent to or deny consent to releasing mother's medical records. Pio v. Ramsier (Wayne 1993) 88 Ohio App.3d 133, 623 N.E.2d 174, motion overruled 67 Ohio St.3d 1482, 620 N.E.2d 854. Executors And Administrators ⇒ 35(2)

The executor of an estate may be removed for good cause sua sponte by the probate court; an order of removal need not be based on clear and convincing evidence, nor must the executor's actions amount to illegal acts, or even cause injury to the estate. In re Estate of Bost (Cuyahoga 1983) 10 Ohio App.3d 147, 460 N.E.2d 1156, 10 O.B.R. 199.

Where a guardian of a minor child has been validly appointed, the burden of proof is on one seeking the removal of such guardian, and the court must be clearly convinced that the interests of the ward cannot be preserved except by the removal; a mere showing that the movant might conceivably make a better guardian is inadequate. In re Guardianship of Conley (Ohio Prob. 1966) 10 Ohio Misc. 197, 224 N.E.2d 183, 39 O.O.2d 292.

It was an abuse of discretion for a court not to remove a guardian of an incompetent and his attorney in order to appoint the wife of the incompetent as guardian and the brother of the incompetent as attorney, when the latter both agreed to serve without compensation. In re Marshall's Guardianship (Shelby 1951) 120 N.E.2d 324, 67 Ohio Law Abs. 314.

Probate court has power, due opportunity for hearing having been given, to revoke letters of administration de bonis non where such appointment was obtained by fraud practiced upon court, or for refusal of such administrator to obey orders of court duly and lawfully made; and where such fraud and refusal to obey orders injuriously affect creditor of heir of estate, and such heir was active participant in such fraud, and he and administrator are benefited thereby, to detriment of creditor, creditor has such interest in administration of estate as entitles him to invoke exercise of said power by motion. In re Adams' Estate (Summit 1942) 71 Ohio App. 113, 48 N.E.2d 127, 25 O.O. 477.

One entitled to attack appointment of administrator under GC 10629 (repealed 1932. See §§10506–53, 10506–19) could challenge the appointment on the ground that it was not made in a county in which the decedent was an inhabitant or resident at the time of his death as required by section 10604 (repealed 1932. See §§10509–1, 10511–4). In re Gingery's Estate (Ohio 1921) 103 Ohio St. 559, 134 N.E. 449, 19 Ohio Law Rep. 463. Executors And Administrators ⇒ 32(1)

In a proceeding for the removal of an executor based on a motion filed under RS 6017 where the gist of the charge is fraud, it is error to grant an order of removal where no attempt has been made to show fraud. In re Breckinridge's Estate (Ohio Cir. 1905) 17 Ohio C.D. 688, 7 Ohio C.C.(N.S.) 86.

Grounds for removal are also grounds for refusal to appoint. In re Ulhorn's Estate (Ohio Cir. 1894) 4 Ohio C.D. 526, 1 Ohio Dec. 631.

An application for a removal must state the facts; it is not sufficient to charge neglect or mismanagement in general terms. Fox v. Keister (Ohio Com.Pl. 1899) 9 Ohio Dec. 316, 6 Ohio N.P. 327.

It is cause for removal of an executor if he moves out of the state. In re Pickands' Estate (Ohio Prob. 1898) 7 Ohio Dec. 476, 5 Ohio N.P. 493.

Where it is shown that a guardian, for some reason not explained, made alterations in her account and vouchers after they had been filed in due course in the probate court, ample ground exists for suspension of payments and removal of the guardian from office; and this was done in the present case, notwithstanding the guardian was the mother of the ward, and the money was used for the benefit of the ward, but in a different way from that shown by the account and vouchers filed; moreover, the display by the guardian of a disrespectful, obnoxious, refractory and recalcitrant demeanor toward the court and government officials, would of itself have fully warranted the action which has been taken, without reference to the falsification of the account and vouchers. In re Removal of Brock, 28 NP(NS) 62 (CP, Morgan 1930).

5. —— Interest in estate, removal of fiduciaries other than trustees

Son could be removed as executor of father's estate, even if he did not violate any statutory provisions governing executors; removal could be justified based on a finding that it was in the best interest of the estate. In re Estate of Wilkerson (Ohio App. 9 Dist., Summit, 01-19-2005) No. 22049, 2005-Ohio-159, 2005 WL 100788, Unreported, appeal not allowed 105 Ohio St.3d 1564, 828 N.E.2d 118, 2005-Ohio-2447, reconsideration denied 106 Ohio St.3d 1489, 832 N.E.2d 740, 2005-Ohio-3978. Executors And Administrators ⇒ 35(1)

Co-executors under decedent's second will breached fiduciary duties by repeatedly aligning themselves with potential beneficiary under second will, in challenges brought by first will's executor, and thus executors were subject to removal, where there was a controversy between beneficiaries under will and the heirs at law as to the meaning of residuary clause, and executor had a conflict with himself as a potential beneficiary. Beaston v. Slingwine (Ohio App. 3 Dist., Seneca, 12-15-2003) No. 13-03-29, 2003-Ohio-6709, 2003 WL 22939470, Unreported. Executors And Administrators ⇒ 35(2)

Joint guardians of estate of imbecile have no property right in trust as such, and probate court, for best interests of ward, has a wide discretion under this section in ordering their removal. Gorsuch v. Stabler (Butler 1933) 16 Ohio Law Abs. 250.

Conflict of interest is not a statutory ground for removing a guardian, and not every adverse interest warrants such removal. In re Guardianship of Price (Ohio Prob. 1959) 162 N.E.2d 494, 83 Ohio Law Abs. 149.

Insolvent qualifying as administrator of his surety's estate and paying his own notes as claims against the estate, is removable on the ground of unsettled claims or demands between him and estate. Yakey v. Strunk (Ohio Com.Pl. 1908) 18 Ohio Dec. 726, 7 Ohio N.P.(N.S.) 177, affirmed 81 Ohio St. 568, 91 N.E. 1143, 7 Ohio Law Rep. 610.

The individual rights of an executor who is interested in an estate are not prejudiced by his removal. Munger v. Jeffries (Ohio Com.Pl. 1900) 10 Ohio Dec. 12, 7 Ohio N.P. 55.

Where there are such hostile and adverse interests between a guardian and his incompetent ward that such parties cannot deal with each other on an impartial basis the trial court abused its discretion in refusing to remove the guardian. In re Guardianship of Ray, No. 14 (12th Dist Ct App, Warren, 7–28–82).

6. —— Procedural issues, removal of fiduciaries other than trustees

Where letters of administration are revoked, and an administrator de bonis non appointed, a scire facias cannot be sued out in the name of the removed administrator to revive a judgment obtained by him, as it must be sued out by the new administrator. Weaver v. Reese (Ohio 1834) 6 Ohio 418. Executors And Administrators ⇒ 453(4); Judgment ⇒ 870(1)

Removal of executrix and appointment of her successor were erroneous, where notice of removal was lacking and attorney was appointed, rather than consideration to decedent's children other than executrix or those indebted to estate. In re Mizer (Ohio App. 5 Dist., Tuscarawas, 02-24-2005) No. 2004 AP 04 0035, 2005-Ohio-862, 2005 WL 469268, Unreported. Executors And Administrators ⇒ 35(13)

Trial court denial of son's motion to remove his siblings as co-executors of their father's estate was not an abuse of discretion, even though son argued that executor's distribution of father's monetary assets as intervivos gifts was an unauthorized use of executor's power of attorney; executor's power of attorney expressly provided that she could distribute testator's property as gifts prior to his death, at the hearing on the motion to remove co-executors son failed to present any evidence regarding his motion to remove, instead he focused on executor's distribution of assets as gifts prior to their father's death, and there was no evidence that established that son and co-executors were subject to a viable controversy that required the removal of co-executors. In re Estate of Meloni (Ohio App. 11 Dist., Trumbull, 12-30-2004) No. 2003-T-0096, 2004-Ohio-7224, 2004 WL 3090190, Unreported, appeal not allowed 105 Ohio St.3d 1546, 827 N.E.2d 328, 2005-Ohio-2188. Executors And Administrators ⇒ 35(9)

Order denying son's motion to remove co-executors was a final appealable order; the denial of the motion to remove co-executors determined the action with respect to a "provisional remedy," the order prevented a judgment in the action in favor of son, and son would have no effective or meaningful remedy following the final resolution of the estate because the duties of co-executors would terminate. In re Estate of Meloni (Ohio App. 11 Dist., Trumbull, 12-30-2004) No. 2003-T-0096, 2004-Ohio-7224,

2004 WL 3090190, Unreported, appeal not allowed 105 Ohio St.3d 1546, 827 N.E.2d 328, 2005-Ohio-2188. Executors And Administrators ⇐ 35(19)

Removal of minor child's guardian cannot be grounded in statute governing removal of fiduciary by probate or juvenile court, though statute may be used to define the "good cause" needed to remove guardian. In re Guardianship of Sanders (Ohio App. 2 Dist., 03-07-1997) 118 Ohio App.3d 606, 693 N.E.2d 1101. Guardian And Ward ⇐ 25

Removal of executor rests within sound discretion of trial court and reviewing court will not reverse decision absent clear showing of abuse of discretion. Pio v. Ramsier (Wayne 1993) 88 Ohio App.3d 133, 623 N.E.2d 174, motion overruled 67 Ohio St.3d 1482, 620 N.E.2d 854. Executors And Administrators ⇐ 35(1); Executors And Administrators ⇐ 35(19)

The removal of a fiduciary under RC 2109.24 rests within the sound discretion of the trial court, and a reviewing court will not reverse that decision absent a clear showing of abuse of discretion. In re Estate of Russolillo (Franklin 1990) 69 Ohio App.3d 448, 590 N.E.2d 1324. Executors And Administrators ⇐ 35(1); Executors And Administrators ⇐ 35(19)

Where an application is filed for the removal of a fiduciary, the fiduciary is entitled to receive not less than ten days' notice and is entitled to a hearing on the charges made against him. In re Estate of Russolillo (Franklin 1990) 69 Ohio App.3d 448, 590 N.E.2d 1324.

It is the duty of the court to receive and hear all relevant and proper notice proffered on the issues made by the claims and denials of the respective parties in an action for removal of a fiduciary. In re Estate of Russolillo (Franklin 1990) 69 Ohio App.3d 448, 590 N.E.2d 1324.

Where no hearing is held upon an application for removal of a party as an executor of an estate, it is prejudicial error for the executor to be removed, even where the executor's refusal to waive the physician-patient privilege in the will contest could be a basis for removal; the executor must be given a hearing and an opportunity to present evidence. In re Estate of Russolillo (Franklin 1990) 69 Ohio App.3d 448, 590 N.E.2d 1324.

In action to remove guardian, notice is required to be given ten days before the hearing and is to be given to guardian only whereas, in termination action, notice is required to be reasonable and to be given to the guardian, the ward, and the person who initially applied for the appointment of a guardian. In re Guardianship of Escola (Stark 1987) 41 Ohio App.3d 42, 534 N.E.2d 866. Guardian And Ward ⇐ 25; Mental Health ⇐ 169; Mental Health ⇐ 176

The removal of a fiduciary pursuant to RC 2109.24 is within the sound discretion of the trial court, and absent a clear abuse of that discretion, a reviewing court will not reverse an order of a lower court removing a fiduciary. In re Jarvis Estate (Cuyahoga 1980) 67 Ohio App.2d 94, 425 N.E.2d 939, 21 O.O.3d 411.

Where, in an appeal from action of the probate court vacating an appointment of an administrator on the ground that the bond filed was not signed by an authorized agent, the appellant administrator fails to file a bill of exceptions, the appeal must be dismissed. In re Anders' Estate (Franklin 1959) 169 N.E.2d 302, 83 Ohio Law Abs. 351.

Upon an application for removal of a fiduciary upon a ground other than failure to make and file an inventory, the fiduciary is entitled to receive not less than ten days notice thereof, and is entitled to a hearing thereon; at such hearing the allegations in the application and the opening statements of counsel are not evidence, and it is prejudicial error to grant the application in the absence of evidence in support thereof and to refuse to permit the fiduciary to offer evidence in opposition. In re Paull's Estate (Cuyahoga 1950) 90 Ohio App. 403, 101 N.E.2d 209, 60 Ohio Law Abs. 333, 46 O.O. 52.

Any proper complaint which brings to attention of court matters complained of is sufficient to meet requirements of section and where there is no evidence to indicate that fiduciary was in any way inconvenienced, surprised or prejudiced by being required to proceed on complaint as filed, trial court does not abuse its discretion by overruling a motion to require movant to make motion for removal definite and certain by setting forth in detail facts on which he relied. (See also In re Trust of Marshall, 78 App 45, 65 NE(2d) 95 (1945).) In re Marshall's Will (Franklin 1946) 78 Ohio App. 1, 65 N.E.2d 523, 46 Ohio Law Abs. 344, 33 O.O. 375.

A proceeding for removal of a trustee under section may be instituted by filing a motion. (See also In re Trust of Marshall, 78 App 45, 65 NE(2d) 95 (1945).) In re Marshall's Will (Franklin 1946) 78 Ohio App. 1, 65 N.E.2d 523, 46 Ohio Law Abs. 344, 33 O.O. 375. Trusts ⇐ 167

The removal of a trustee is not subject to review. Stafford v. American Missionary Ass'n (Ohio Cir. 1901) 12 Ohio C.D. 442.

A proceeding to remove an administrator and a proceeding against him for concealing assets under RS 6407 may be joined, and such proceeding is appealable. Harris v. Westervelt (Ohio Cir. 1898) 8 Ohio C.D. 367.

Error does not lie to a removal, though it does to an order denying the right of a certain person to administer under RS 6005. In re Ferguson's Estate (Ohio Com.Pl. 1904) 16 Ohio Dec. 486, 3 Ohio NP(NS) 549.

7. Removal of trustees

Where one trustee dies and another moves to a place unknown, the probate court may fill such vacancies even where there is a surviving trustee. Sowers v. Cyrenius (Ohio 1883) 39 Ohio St. 29, 9 W.L.B. 175.

Ordering removal of bank as trustee and member of charitable trust's income distribution–appointing committee, disgorgement of previously approved fees, and vacatur of previously approved accounts of bank was abuse of probate court's discretion; bank and committee, who never claimed that taking additional fees was proper, emphasized that as soon as they realized impropriety of their actions, they remedied the situation, and there was no evidence supporting removal on grounds permitted by statute. In re the Trust Created Under Item IV of the Last Will and Testament of Watson (Ohio App. 7 Dist., Mahoning, 12-13-2004) No. 03 MA 154, 2004-Ohio-7063, 2004 WL 2980342, Unreported. Charities ⇐ 45(1)

Removal of director of family services agency as trustee of special needs trust for mentally handicapped beneficiary was warranted, where director repeatedly spent funds without court approval. In re Guardianship of Monus (Ohio App. 7 Dist., Mahoning, 05-28-2004) No. 03 MA 128, No. 03 MA 131, No. 03 MA 129, No. 03 MA 132, No. 03 MA 130, No. 03 MA 153, 2004-Ohio-2808, 2004 WL 1194070, Unreported. Trusts ⇐ 166(2)

Where beneficiaries have notice of an interest in trust and do not object to distribution of trust income to their mother until eight years after the opening of an active trust account, the evidence supports the conclusion that the beneficiaries ratified the trustee's actions and that they were estopped from asserting any claims even though the testamentary trustee breached its judiciary duty and abused its discretion by not inquiring into the financial circumstances of all the beneficiaries before distributing income to one beneficiary. In re Estate of Winograd (Cuyahoga 1989) 65 Ohio App.3d 76, 582 N.E.2d 1047, motion to certify overruled 50 Ohio St.3d 702, 553 N.E.2d 278.

A trustee's continuing duty to act reasonably and in the best interests of the beneficiaries is not altered by the testamentary trust's grant of broad administrative authority. In re Estate of Winograd (Cuyahoga 1989) 65 Ohio App.3d 76, 582 N.E.2d 1047, motion to certify overruled 50 Ohio St.3d 702, 553 N.E.2d 278. Trusts ⇐ 173

Where a testamentary trustee makes a good faith effort to carry out what it believed was the purpose of the trust, the trustee's distribution of income to one beneficiary and failure to consider needs of other beneficiaries does not warrant removal. In re Estate of Winograd (Cuyahoga 1989) 65 Ohio App.3d 76, 582 N.E.2d 1047, motion to certify overruled 50 Ohio St.3d 702, 553 N.E.2d 278.

Where beneficiaries of a testamentary trust are not prejudiced as a result of the trustee's distribution of trust income, they are not entitled to attorney fees. In re Estate of Winograd (Cuyahoga 1989) 65 Ohio App.3d 76, 582 N.E.2d 1047, motion to certify overruled 50 Ohio St.3d 702, 553 N.E.2d 278. Trusts ⇐ 377

Where a trustee who was being removed refused to transfer the trust assets to the successor trustee pursuant to court order, his refusal was punishable as contempt, regardless of whether the order was a "final" order of the court. Ollick v. Rice (Cuyahoga 1984) 16 Ohio App.3d 448, 476 N.E.2d 1062, 16 O.B.R. 519.

A trustee who is disloyal to the beneficiary of the trust may be removed from his office. In re Trustees Under Yost's Will (Belmont 1956) 102 Ohio App. 62, 141 N.E.2d 176, 2 O.O.2d 44.

Where a person is both executor and trustee, record of a hearing before a special master commissioner on exceptions to his account as executor and records of his administration of estate are admissible as evidence in proceedings to remove him as trustee. (See also In re Trust of Marshall, 78 App 45, 65 NE(2d) 95 (1945).) In re Marshall's Will (Franklin 1946) 78 Ohio App. 1, 65 N.E.2d 523, 46 Ohio Law Abs. 344, 33 O.O. 375.

Where all evidence on which trial court acted is not before reviewing court, it will be presumed that there was sufficient evidence to support judgment of trial court in removing trustee, and that trial court did not abuse its discretion. (See also In re Trust of Marshall, 78 App 45, 65 NE(2d) 95 (1945).) In re Marshall's Will (Franklin 1946) 78 Ohio App. 1, 65 N.E.2d 523, 46 Ohio Law Abs. 344, 33 O.O. 375.

Note 7

Under statute, notice of a removal proceeding is required to be given to fiduciary, but persons interested in trust are not considered necessary parties to determination of issue, and notice to them is not required. (See also In re Trust of Marshall, 78 App 45, 65 NE(2d) 95 (1945).) In re Marshall's Will (Franklin 1946) 78 Ohio App. 1, 65 N.E.2d 523, 46 Ohio Law Abs. 344, 33 O.O. 375.

Term "fiduciary" as used in statute includes "trustee," but a trustee appointed under a will may not be removed except for good cause. (See also In re Trust of Marshall, 78 App 45, 65 NE(2d) 95 (1945).) In re Marshall's Will (Franklin 1946) 78 Ohio App. 1, 65 N.E.2d 523, 46 Ohio Law Abs. 344, 33 O.O. 375.

Reviewing court will not reverse an order of probate court removing a trustee appointed under a will unless record discloses an abuse of discretion. (See also In re Trust of Marshall, 78 App 45, 65 NE(2d) 95 (1945).) In re Marshall's Will (Franklin 1946) 78 Ohio App. 1, 65 N.E.2d 523, 46 Ohio Law Abs. 344, 33 O.O. 375.

Broad discretion is given probate court in removal of a fiduciary under statute which, after enumerating certain specific causes, provides that a fiduciary may be removed "because interest of trust demands it." In re Marshall's Will (Franklin 1946) 78 Ohio App. 1, 65 N.E.2d 523, 46 Ohio Law Abs. 344, 33 O.O. 375.

The probate court has power to remove the trustee designated in a deed of trust of real estate and to appoint his successor. Pherson v Mitchell, 12 App 336, 31 CC(NS) 333 (1920).

The beneficiaries under a will are without authority to demand the removal of a successor trustee, appointed by the probate court in due course, where no ground is given for the removal, and there would be nothing to prevent a renewal of the application, following successive denials, until finally perhaps a trustee might be named who would be satisfactory to the applicants. In re Trust Under Hartman's Will, 28 NP(NS) 76 (Prob, Franklin 1930).

8. Resignation

Receiving and filing the resignation of an executor without formal acceptance and appointing a successor complies with former GC 10627 (RC 2107.37 and RC 2107.39), and the new appointment is valid. Johnston v. Schwenck (Ohio 1918) 99 Ohio St. 59, 124 N.E. 61, 8 A.L.R. 170, 16 Ohio Law Rep. 363, 17 Ohio Law Rep. 23.

By accepting the resignation of an administrator pending settlement of his accounts the probate court does not lose jurisdiction and may proceed to hear exception, and he and his sureties will be bound. Slagle v. Entrekin (Ohio 1887) 44 Ohio St. 637, 17 W.L.B. 211, 10 N.E. 675.

While earlier statute provides that the court may receive the administrator's resignation "if it thinks fit, and upon good cause shown," the absence of a specific finding that the court thought it fit or thought the cause sufficient cannot defeat what was actually done; such findings are not essential to the validity or effectiveness of the order. State ex rel. McCullough v. Moffitt (Ohio Cir. 1908) 23 Ohio C.D. 238, 13 Ohio C.C.(N.S.) 152, affirmed 82 Ohio St. 433, 92 N.E. 1124, 8 Ohio Law Rep. 90.

Making appointment of successor is not essential to taking effect of accepted resignation of administrator. State ex rel. McCullough v. Moffitt (Ohio Cir. 1908) 23 Ohio C.D. 238, 13 Ohio C.C.(N.S.) 152, affirmed 82 Ohio St. 433, 92 N.E. 1124, 8 Ohio Law Rep. 90.

Where an administrator submits to the probate court his resignation, he cannot be held liable for maladministration if he fails to answer a summons thereafter served on him in a proceeding involving the estate. State ex rel. McCullough v. Moffitt (Ohio Cir. 1908) 23 Ohio C.D. 238, 13 Ohio C.C.(N.S.) 152, affirmed 82 Ohio St. 433, 92 N.E. 1124, 8 Ohio Law Rep. 90.

If an executor resigns before or pending a will contest, the court should appoint an administrator to be made a party to the suit. McArthur v. Scott (U.S.Ohio 1885) 5 S.Ct. 652, 113 U.S. 340, 28 L.Ed. 1015.

9. Termination of authority

Removal terminates the authority of an administrator, and the right to recover on a judgment obtained by him is in his successor. Weaver v. Reese (Ohio 1834) 6 Ohio 418.

Where an administrator is appointed and a will is subsequently discovered naming an executor, it repeals the letters of administration, but acts done by the administrator before the discovery of the will are valid, as well as orders of the court made in reference to the estate. Bigelow's Ex'r v. Bigelow's Adm'rs (Ohio 1829) 4 Ohio 138, 19 Am.Dec. 591.

Conservatorship was terminated at the time of conservatee's death, and thus, removal of director of family services agency as conservator was warranted; the termination could not be reversed and the best interests of the conservatee were no longer an issue. In re Guardianship of Monus (Ohio App. 7 Dist., Mahoning, 05-28-2004) No. 03 MA 128, No. 03 MA 131, No. 03 MA 129, No. 03 MA 132, No. 03 MA 130, No. 03 MA 153, 2004-Ohio-2808, 2004 WL 1194070, Unreported. Guardian And Ward ⇐ 22; Guardian And Ward ⇐ 25

The authority of an executor or administrator continues until it is terminated by one of the modes provided by statute. Weyer v. Watt (Ohio 1891) 48 Ohio St. 545, 26 W.L.B. 284, 28 N.E. 670.

A probate court may remove or accept the resignation of an executor or administrator, but while choses in action or assets of the estate remain in his hands unadministered, his authority to administer same is not extinguished by an order, made upon what purports to be a settlement of his final account, directing that he be discharged. Weyer v. Watt (Ohio 1891) 48 Ohio St. 545, 26 W.L.B. 284, 28 N.E. 670.

The trust of a guardian expires at the date of his removal. Gorman v. Taylor (Ohio 1885) 43 Ohio St. 86, 13 W.L.B. 425, 1 N.E. 227.

Removal of a guardian from the state ipso facto terminates his authority to act. Merchants' & Clerks' Sav. Bank Co. v. Schirk (Ohio Cir. 1904) 17 Ohio C.D. 125, 5 Ohio C.C.N.S. 569.

Breaking of will terminates administration of an administrator with the will annexed. In re Schonacker's Estate (Ohio Prob. 1910) 55 W.L.B. 78.

2109.25 Fiduciary in military service; removal and reinstatement

Whenever it appears to the satisfaction of the probate court that a fiduciary is unable to perform his duties because he is engaged or is about to engage in military service as defined by this section, the court may remove such fiduciary and appoint a substitute or authorize the remaining fiduciaries to execute the trust. Such action may be taken on the court's own motion or on the application of any party in interest, including the fiduciary or cofiduciary, either without notice or upon notice to such persons and in such manner as the court shall direct.

If any of the duties of such office remain unexecuted when a fiduciary who has resigned or been removed on account of his military service ceases to be in such military service, he shall be reappointed as fiduciary upon his application to the court and upon such notice as the court may direct, provided he is at the time a suitable and competent person and has the qualifications as to residence required by section 2109.21 of the Revised Code. If such person is reappointed, the court shall remove the substitute fiduciary and revoke his letters of appointment, and make such further order or decree as justice requires.

"Military service," as used in this section, means any service, work, or occupation which in the opinion of the court is directly or indirectly in furtherance of any military effort of the United States. Such definition includes internment in an enemy country, residence in any foreign country, or residence in any possession or dependency of the United States, if by reason thereof the fiduciary is unable to return to this state.

(1953 H 1, eff. 10–1–53; GC 10506–54)

Historical and Statutory Notes

Pre–1953 H 1 Amendments: 120 v 649

Cross References

Trustee for absentee, 2119.01

Library References

Executors and Administrators ⇐35(1), 35(21).
Guardian and Ward ⇐25.
Mental Health ⇐175, 176.
Trusts ⇐166(1), 167.
Westlaw Topic Nos. 162, 196, 257A, 390.

C.J.S. Executors and Administrators §§ 104 to 110.
C.J.S. Mental Health § 148.
C.J.S. Trusts §§ 307, 309 to 310.

Research References

Encyclopedias

OH Jur. 3d Fiduciaries § 313, Military Service.

Forms

Ohio Forms and Transactions KP 30.14, Trusts and Trustees.

Treatises and Practice Aids

Carlin, Baldwin's Ohio Practice, Merrick-Rippner Probate Law § 57:7, Removal of Fiduciary—Other Grounds.

Bogert - the Law of Trusts and Trustees § 527, Grounds for Removal.

2109.26 Vacancy before termination of the trust; accounting; successor fiduciary

If a sole fiduciary dies, is dissolved, declines to accept, resigns, is removed, or becomes incapacitated prior to the termination of the trust, the probate court shall require a final account of all dealings of such trust to be filed forthwith by such fiduciary if a living person and able to act. If such fiduciary is a living person but unable to act, such final account shall be filed by his guardian, or if there is no guardian by some other suitable person in his behalf, appointed or approved by the court. If such fiduciary is a deceased person, such account shall be filed by his executor or administrator. If such fiduciary is a dissolved corporation, such account shall be filed by such persons as are charged by law with winding up the affairs of such corporation. Thereupon the court shall cause such proceedings to be had as are provided by sections 2109.30 to 2109.36, inclusive, of the Revised Code.

Whenever such a vacancy occurs and such contingency is not otherwise provided for by law or by the instrument creating the trust, or whenever such instrument names no fiduciary, the court shall, on its own motion or on the application of any person beneficially interested, issue letters of appointment as fiduciary to some competent person or persons who shall qualify according to law and execute the trust to its proper termination. Such vacancy and the appointment of a successor fiduciary shall not affect the liability of the former fiduciary or his sureties which was previously incurred.

(125 v 903, eff. 10–1–53; 1953 H 1; GC 10506–55)

Historical and Statutory Notes

Pre–1953 H 1 Amendments: 114 v 375

Library References

Executors and Administrators ⚖23, 459, 461.
Guardian and Ward ⚖27, 137, 139.
Mental Health ⚖178, 291, 293.
Trusts ⚖169, 289, 292.
Westlaw Topic Nos. 162, 196, 257A, 390.
C.J.S. Executors and Administrators §§ 52, 786.
C.J.S. Mental Health §§ 157, 183, 193.
C.J.S. Trusts §§ 288 to 294, 298 to 299, 587 to 589, 598 to 601.

Research References

Encyclopedias

OH Jur. 3d Decedents' Estates § 983, Appointment.

OH Jur. 3d Fiduciaries § 12, Appointment to Fill Vacancy in Office; Sole Fiduciary.

OH Jur. 3d Fiduciaries § 29, Successor Fiduciary.

OH Jur. 3d Fiduciaries § 201, on Termination of Office; Change or Discharge of Fiduciary.

OH Jur. 3d Fiduciaries § 238, Accounting Upon Vacancy in Office.

OH Jur. 3d Fiduciaries § 239, Accounting Upon Vacancy in Office—Resignation or Removal of Fiduciary.

OH Jur. 3d Trusts § 166, Want of a Trustee—Methods of Correcting Defect.

OH Jur. 3d Trusts § 182, Death.

Treatises and Practice Aids

Carlin, Baldwin's Ohio Practice, Merrick-Rippner Probate Law § 66:2, Termination—Discretionary—Court; Removal.

Carlin, Baldwin's Ohio Practice, Merrick-Rippner Probate Law § 70:5, Administrator De Bonis Non—Rights and Duties.

Carlin, Baldwin's Ohio Practice, Merrick-Rippner Probate Law § 30:57, Simple Will—Form.

Carlin, Baldwin's Ohio Practice, Merrick-Rippner Probate Law § 52:34, Fiduciary's Bond—Release—Death of Fiduciary.

Bogert - the Law of Trusts and Trustees § 514, Resignation Through Judicial Proceedings.

Bogert - the Law of Trusts and Trustees § 516, Conditional Acceptance of a Resignation.

Bogert - the Law of Trusts and Trustees § 532, Vacancies in the Trusteeship—Appointment of Successors.

Bogert - the Law of Trusts and Trustees § 963, Duty to Render Formal Account in Court of Equity.

Restatement (3d) of Trusts § 36, Resignation of Trustee.

Law Review and Journal Commentaries

Guardians—Powers and Duties: Revokable Living Trust—Durable Power of Attorney, Michael L. Stark. 2 Prob L J Ohio 105 (May/June 1992).

The Uniform Trusts Act, Frank S. Rowley and Harry W. Vanneman. 5 Ohio St L J 145 (March 1939).

The Uniform Trusts Act, Frank S. Rowley and Harry W. Vanneman. 13 U Cin L Rev 157 (March 1939).

Notes of Decisions

Appointment 4
Deceased fiduciary 1
Resigned fiduciary 2
Successor fiduciary 3

---

1. Deceased fiduciary

Where one trustee dies and another moves to a place unknown, the probate court may fill such vacancies even where there is a surviving trustee. Sowers v. Cyrenius (Ohio 1883) 39 Ohio St. 29, 9 W.L.B. 175.

Where the executor and trustee named in a will dies during the administration of the estate and trust, no application for the appointment of a trustee is filed by a person beneficially interested and the court, on its own motion, does not appoint a trustee but an administrator de bonis non with the will annexed is appointed but not as trustee, the duty devolves such administrator to act also as trustee and administer the trust until a trustee is appointed. In re Rothstein's Estate (Seneca 1958) 108 Ohio App. 487, 162 N.E.2d 547, 9 O.O.2d 469.

When an administrator dies it is the duty of his administrator to render a final account and then turn over the assets less fees due to the deceased administrator to the administrator de bonis non. Bates v. Creed (Hamilton 1913) 26 Ohio C.D. 338, 15 Ohio C.C.(N.S.) 433, 2 Ohio App. 59, affirmed 90 Ohio St. 288, 107 N.E. 770, 12 Ohio Law Rep. 78, Am.Ann. Cas. 1916C,1198, Am.Ann.Cas. 1916C, 1198.

Where an administrator dies pending exceptions to his account and his executrix files a final account for him to which similar exceptions are taken, she is incompetent to be a witness to any facts except those arising after her appointment. In re Runyan's Estate (Ohio Prob. 1897) 7 Ohio Dec. 236, 4 Ohio N.P. 335.

Statute gives to the probate court the right to appoint a successor to execute a trust under a will upon the death of the original trustee. In re Trust Under Hartman's Will, 28 NP(NS) 76 (Prob, Franklin 1930).

2. Resigned fiduciary

An executor by resigning does not thereby convey title to another named in the will to act in his stead in case of his resignation. Veazie v. McGugin (Ohio 1883) 40 Ohio St. 365.

The receiving of resignation of executor or administrator by probate court appointing him, and the filing of document by judge, followed by appointment of a successor, is a sufficient compliance with GC 10627 (repealed 1932. See §§10506–53, 10506–55) and new appointment is valid, in view of sections 10938, 11035 (repealed 1932. See §10506–53); §11147. Johnston v. Schwenck (Ohio 1918) 99 Ohio St. 59, 124 N.E. 61, 8 A.L.R. 170, 16 Ohio Law Rep. 363, 17 Ohio Law Rep. 23. Executors And Administrators ⚖ 33

The probate court, for good cause, may remove an executor or administrator, or accept his resignation; but while choses in action or other assets belonging to the estate remain in his hands unadministered, his authority to administer the same is not extinguished by an order, made upon what purports to be the settlement of his final account, directing that he be discharged from his trust. Weyer v. Watt (Ohio 1891) 48 Ohio St. 545, 26 W.L.B. 284, 28 N.E. 670.

By accepting the resignation of an administrator pending settlement of his accounts the probate court does not lose jurisdiction and may proceed to hear exception, and he and his sureties will be bound. Slagle v. Entrekin (Ohio 1887) 44 Ohio St. 637, 17 W.L.B. 211, 10 N.E. 675.

Making appointment of successor is not essential to the taking effect of accepted resignation of administrator. State ex rel. McCullough v. Moffitt (Ohio Cir. 1908) 23 Ohio C.D. 238, 13 Ohio C.C.(N.S.) 152, affirmed 82 Ohio St. 433, 92 N.E. 1124, 8 Ohio Law Rep. 90.

If an executor resigns before or pending a will contest, the court should appoint an administrator to be made a party to the suit. McArthur v. Scott (U.S.Ohio 1885) 5 S.Ct. 652, 113 U.S. 340, 28 L.Ed. 1015.

3. Successor fiduciary

Probate court abused its discretion in appointing successor trustee for family trust after trustee filed declaratory judgment action and resigned his position; trust instrument gave authority to appoint successor trustee to beneficiaries, and court did not give beneficiaries sufficient time to choose their own successor trustee inasmuch as beneficiaries lived throughout United States and court gave them only approximately one month to reach consensus and find trustee who was willing and qualified to serve. Galbreath v. del Valle (Ohio App. 10 Dist., 11-24-1993) 91 Ohio App.3d 829, 633 N.E.2d 1185, dismissed, jurisdictional motion overruled 69 Ohio St.3d 1414, 630 N.E.2d 376. Trusts ⚖ 169(1)

Probate court could require any successor trustee under family trust to qualify under state law. Galbreath v. del Valle (Ohio App. 10 Dist., 11-24-1993) 91 Ohio App.3d 829, 633 N.E.2d 1185, dismissed, jurisdictional motion overruled 69 Ohio St.3d 1414, 630 N.E.2d 376. Trusts ⚖ 169(1)

Where the amount due an estate of a decedent from the surety on the bond of a deceased fiduciary for certain delinquencies is not in dispute at the time a settlement is made with such surety, it is not necessary for the successor fiduciary to pay or tender back the amount received before pursuing any remedy available to him to recover from the surety for other and separate delinquencies. In re Gray's Estate (Ohio 1954) 162 Ohio St. 384, 123 N.E.2d 408, 55 O.O. 224. Compromise And Settlement ⚖ 18(3)

An administrator de bonis non with the will annexed succeeds to the management of a trust given to an executor. Francis v. Anthony (Stark 1933) 46 Ohio App. 121, 187 N.E. 782, 14 Ohio Law Abs. 20, 38 Ohio Law Rep. 69. Executors And Administrators ⚖ 120(2)

An administrator with the will annexed who has been appointed to succeed the deceased executor has the power to sell real estate without an order of the court where such power was conferred by the will upon the executor. Avery v. Howard (Ohio Com.Pl. 1908) 19 Ohio Dec. 71, 7 Ohio NP(NS) 97.

4. Appointment

Where testatrix granted power to appoint successor trustee to court and limited exercise of such power to nominees designated or selected by surviving trustee or trustees, thereby indicating that she intended surviving trustee to play important role in process of filling vacancy in other trustee position, it was duty of probate court to follow recommendation of surviving trustee as to who should be cotrustee unless person chosen as cotrustee was incompetent to administer trust and such appointment would be detrimental to trust. In re Trust of Selsor (Madison 1983) 13 Ohio App.3d 164, 468 N.E.2d 745, 13 O.B.R. 198. Trusts ⚖ 157

In a negligence action for the recovery of damages instituted under RC 2117.07 against an administrator seeking to recover only from the decedent's liability insurer, where the administrator of the estate of the decedent has been discharged and the estate closed, the probate court may reappoint the administrator for the purpose of accepting service of summons. In re George's Estate (Ohio 1970) 24 Ohio St.2d 18, 262 N.E.2d 872, 53 O.O.2d 10.

Where the final and distributive account of the administrators of an estate has been approved and settled and they have been discharged from their trust pursuant to RC 2109.32, and that order has not been vacated pursuant to RC 2109.35, where some asset remains upon which administration has not been exhausted and for some lawful purpose relating to that asset administration is required, an administrator may be appointed to complete such administration only in a manner similar to, and with the same formalities as, the original appointment of an administrator, and in such circumstances, where such asset consists of an automobile liability insurance policy of the decedent covering the claim of a person alleged to have received bodily injuries due to the alleged negligence of the decedent, such policy is an asset which will support the appointment of an administrator upon whom service may be made and with authority to defend suit. In re George's Estate (Hancock 1969) 20 Ohio App.2d 87, 252 N.E.2d 176, 49 O.O.2d 110. Executors And Administrators ⚖ 37(2); Executors And Administrators ⚖ 37(5)

Where widow and next of kin had signed waivers of right to the appointment of administrator of decedent's estate, probate court was authorized to make appointment of administrator for purpose of filing a final account, and this right existed regardless of whether decedent had any separate estate in his own right. In re Chambers' Estate (Montgomery 1939) 36 N.E.2d 175, 30 Ohio Law Abs. 420, 16 O.O. 519, appeal dismissed 136 Ohio St. 202, 24 N.E.2d 601, 16 O.O. 535, rehearing denied 43 N.E.2d 244.

Section is sufficient to prevent the failure of any valid trust merely for want of a trustee, and authorizes the court to appoint one. Rogers v. Rea (Ohio 1918) 98 Ohio St. 315, 120 N.E. 828, 16 Ohio Law Rep. 89.

History and effect of this section discussed. Clark v Neil, 24 NP(NS) 589 (CP, Franklin 1924).

2109.27 Surviving fiduciaries

When two or more fiduciaries have been appointed jointly to execute a trust and one or more of them dies, declines, resigns, or is removed, the title shall pass to the remaining fiduciaries who shall execute the trust, unless the creating instrument expresses a contrary intention or unless the probate court on the application of persons interested in the trust determines otherwise. The remaining fiduciaries shall within ninety days after the death, resignation, or removal of a cofiduciary, file in the court a complete account covering all matters to the time of such death, resignation, or removal.

(1953 H 1, eff. 10–1–53; GC 10506–56)

Historical and Statutory Notes

Pre–1953 H 1 Amendments: 114 v 376

Library References

Executors and Administrators ⚖127.
Guardian and Ward ⚖71.
Mental Health ⚖211, 293.
Trusts ⚖242.
Westlaw Topic Nos. 162, 196, 257A, 390.
C.J.S. Executors and Administrators § 961.
C.J.S. Mental Health §§ 165, 193.
C.J.S. Trusts § 345.

Research References

Encyclopedias

OH Jur. 3d Charities § 28, Appointment of Trustees—Successors to Trustees.
OH Jur. 3d Fiduciaries § 13, Appointment to Fill Vacancy in Office; Sole Fiduciary—Joint Fiduciaries.
OH Jur. 3d Fiduciaries § 28, Surviving Fiduciary.
OH Jur. 3d Fiduciaries § 238, Accounting Upon Vacancy in Office.
OH Jur. 3d Trusts § 303, Effect of Trustee's Death, Removal or Resignation.

Treatises and Practice Aids

Carlin, Baldwin's Ohio Practice, Merrick-Rippner Probate Law § 54:2, Fiduciary Accounts—Filing—Ordered or Requested.

Carlin, Baldwin's Ohio Practice, Merrick-Rippner Probate Law § 58:1, Passing of Title to Surviving Fiduciary.
Carlin, Baldwin's Ohio Practice, Merrick-Rippner Probate Law § 58:2, Purpose of RC 2109.27.
Carlin, Baldwin's Ohio Practice, Merrick-Rippner Probate Law § 58:5, Limitation on the Power of Probate Court.
Bogert - the Law of Trusts and Trustees § 530, Survivorship Among Co-Trustees.
Bogert - the Law of Trusts and Trustees § 553, Personal Powers and Powers Attached to the Office.
Restatement (3d) of Trusts § 34, Appointment of Trustees.

Notes of Decisions

Accounting 2
Intent of settlor 1
Successor trustees 3

1. Intent of settlor

Appointment by probate court of a successor cotrustee, under exceptions in section, on court's own motion without proper notice and hearing in absence of a contrary intention expressed in creating instrument, and in absence of an application by one or more of beneficiaries or other persons interested in trust in disregard of expressed or implied intent of settlor, is arbitrary and constitutes an abuse of discretion of court in appointment and removal of trustees. In re Labold's Will (Ohio 1947) 148 Ohio St. 332, 74 N.E.2d 251, 35 O.O. 318.

2. Accounting

Court may properly accept resignation of one of two administrators without his filing an account, as section requires an accounting by the remaining administrator and not the one resigning. Thrasher v. Kelly (Hamilton 1943) 73 Ohio App. 304, 55 N.E.2d 873, 40 Ohio Law Abs. 309, 28 O.O. 457.

3. Successor trustees

Where one executor of several declines to qualify the duty of executing the trust devolves under S. & C. 1629 upon the others. Collier v. Grimesey (Ohio 1880) 36 Ohio St. 17.

Where an estate is devised to certain trustees and their successors, the limitation over to the successors is void. Miles' Lessee v. Fisher (Ohio 1840) 10 Ohio 1, 36 Am.Dec. 61. Trusts ⟾ 155; Wills ⟾ 681(1)

Under section, where one of two cotrustees dies, probate court does not have power to appoint a successor cotrustee unless instrument creating trust provides for appointment or unless an application is made by one or more of beneficiaries or other persons interested in trust to have a successor cotrustee appointed. In re Labold's Will (Ohio 1947) 148 Ohio St. 332, 74 N.E.2d 251, 35 O.O. 318.

2109.28 Merger of fiduciaries

A trust company or state or national bank having trust powers, resulting from merger or consolidation shall, upon filing proof thereof in the probate court, and without a new appointment, succeed to the rights and duties of all predecessor companies, as fiduciary. A purchase of substantially all the assets and assumption of substantially all the liabilities is a merger for the purposes of sections 2109.01 to 2109.58, inclusive, of the Revised Code. In all cases of merger or consolidation the bond given by any predecessor fiduciary shall remain liable for all acts of the successor fiduciary except as to any surety released upon application as provided in section 2109.18 of the Revised Code.

(1953 H 1, eff. 10–1–53; GC 10506–57)

Historical and Statutory Notes

Pre–1953 H 1 Amendments: 114 v 376

Cross References

Trust companies, effect of reorganization, 1111.07

Library References

Executors and Administrators ⟾26, 37.
Guardian and Ward ⟾27.
Mental Health ⟾178.
Trusts ⟾169(1).
Westlaw Topic Nos. 162, 196, 257A, 390.
C.J.S. Executors and Administrators §§ 71 to 77, 935, 946.
C.J.S. Mental Health § 157.
C.J.S. Trusts §§ 288 to 293.

Research References

Encyclopedias

OH Jur. 3d Fiduciaries § 30, Successor Fiduciary—Acquisition of Trust Powers by Merger or Consolidation.
OH Jur. 3d Fiduciaries § 201, on Termination of Office; Change or Discharge of Fiduciary.
OH Jur. 3d Trusts § 176, Corporations, Partnerships, and Associations—Banks and Trust Companies.

Treatises and Practice Aids

Carlin, Baldwin's Ohio Practice, Merrick-Rippner Probate Law § 52:29, Fiduciary's Bond—Sureties—Liability—Merger of Fiduciaries.
Bogert - the Law of Trusts and Trustees § 531, Dissolution, Merger, Consolidation or Conversion of Corporate Trustees.

2109.29 Rights as to shares in corporation

A corporation need not, unless ordered by a court, take notice of any duty of a fiduciary, or any restriction or limitation of the right, capacity, authority, or interest of such fiduciary, or see to the performance of any duty or requirement imposed upon such fiduciary by Chapters 2101. to 2131., inclusive, of the Revised Code, as to any of such corporation's shares of record in the name of or owned by such fiduciary or in the name of or owned by a decedent, ward, or beneficiary for whom such fiduciary is acting.

(1953 H 1, eff. 10–1–53; GC 10506–58)

Historical and Statutory Notes

Pre–1953 H 1 Amendments: 114 v 376

Library References

Corporations ⟾135.
Westlaw Topic No. 101.
C.J.S. Corporations §§ 272, 282.

Research References

Encyclopedias

OH Jur. 3d Fiduciaries § 171, Liability Under Statute; Corporation Dealing With Fiduciary as to Its Own Stock.

Forms

Ohio Forms and Transactions F 5.12, Request to Transfer Stock to Fiduciary.

Treatises and Practice Aids

Carlin, Baldwin's Ohio Practice, Merrick-Rippner Probate Law § 54:54, Request to Transfer Shares to Fiduciary—Form.
Carlin, Baldwin's Ohio Practice, Merrick-Rippner Probate Law § 54:55, Complaint for Distribution of Stock—Form.
Carlin, Baldwin's Ohio Practice, Merrick-Rippner Probate Law § 54:56, Court Order for Distribution of Shares—Form.
Restatement (2d) of Trusts § 325, Registration of Transfer of Securities Held by Trustee.

ACCOUNTS

2109.30 Accounts of executors and administrators

(A) Every executor and administrator shall render an account of the executor's and administrator's administration at the time and in the manner prescribed in section 2109.301 of the Revised Code. Every guardian or conservator shall render an account of the ward's estate at the time and in the manner prescribed in section 2109.302 of the Revised Code. Every testamentary trustee and other fiduciary not subject to sections 2109.301 and 2109.302 of the Revised Code shall render an account of the testamentary trustee's or other fiduciary's administration at the time and in the manner prescribed in section 2109.303 of the Revised Code.

(B) An account showing complete administration before distribution of assets shall be designated "final account." An account filed subsequent to the final account and showing distribution of assets shall be designated "account of distribution." An account showing complete administration and distribution of assets shall be designated "final and distributive account."

(2001 H 85, eff. 10–31–01; 1996 H 538, eff. 1–1–97; 1994 H 208, eff. 6–23–94; 1992 H 427, eff. 10–8–92; 1984 H 263, S 171; 1980 S 317; 1975 S 145; 1972 S 500; 1970 S 185; 1969 H 176; 125 v 903; 1953 H 1; GC 10506–34)

Uncodified Law

2001 H 85, § 6: See Uncodified Law under 2109.12.

2001 H 85, § 7: See Uncodified Law under 2109.11.

Historical and Statutory Notes

Pre–1953 H 1 Amendments: 120 v 649

Amendment Note: 2001 H 85 rewrote this section which prior thereto read:

"(A) Except as provided in division (B) of this section, within nine months after appointment, every executor and administrator shall render an account of the executor's and administrator's administration. Except as provided in division (B) of this section, after the initial account is rendered, every executor and administrator shall render further accounts at least once each year. Except as provided in divisions (C) and (D) of this section, every fiduciary, other than an executor, administrator, or guardian of the person only, shall render an account of the administration of the fiduciary's estate or trust at least once in each two years. An account shall be rendered by a guardian of the person only at any time, or, subject to division (D) of this section, by any other fiduciary at any time other than those mentioned in this section, upon the order of the court either at its own instance, or upon the motion of any person interested in the estate or trust, for good cause shown. Except as provided in divisions (B) and (C) of this section, every fiduciary, other than a guardian of the person only, shall render a final account within thirty days after completing the administration of the estate or the termination of the fiduciary's trust or within any other period of time that the court may order.

"Every account shall include an itemized statement of all receipts of the fiduciary during the accounting period and of all disbursements and distributions made by the fiduciary during the accounting period. The itemized disbursements and distributions shall be verified by vouchers or proof, except in the case of an account rendered by a corporate fiduciary subject to section 1111.28 of the Revised Code. In addition, the account shall include an itemized statement of all funds, assets, and investments of the estate or trust known to or in the possession of the fiduciary at the end of the accounting period and shall show any changes in investments since the last previous account. The accounts of testamentary trustees shall, and the accounts of other fiduciaries may, show receipts and disbursements separately identified as to principal and income.

"Every account shall be upon the signature of the fiduciary. When an account is rendered by two or more joint fiduciaries, the court may allow the account upon the signature of one of them.

"Upon the filing of every account, the fiduciary, except corporate fiduciaries subject to section 1111.28 of the Revised Code, shall exhibit to the court, for its examination, the securities shown in the account as being in the hands of the fiduciary, or the certificate of the person in possession of the securities, if held as collateral or pursuant to section 2109.13 or 2131.21 of the Revised Code, and a passbook or certified bank statement showing as to each depository the fund deposited to the credit of the trust. The court may designate a deputy clerk, an agent of a corporate surety on the bond of the fiduciary, or another suitable person whom the court appoints as commissioner to make the examination and to report the person's findings to the court. When securities are located outside the county, the court may appoint a commissioner or request another probate court to make the examination and to report its findings to the court. The court may examine the fiduciary under oath concerning the account.

"When a fiduciary is authorized by law or by the instrument governing distribution to distribute the assets of the estate or trust, in whole or in part, the fiduciary may do so and include a report of the distribution in the fiduciary's succeeding account.

"An account showing complete administration before distribution of assets shall be designated "final account." An account filed subsequent to the final account and showing distribution of assets shall be designated "account of distribution." An account showing complete administration and distribution of assets shall be designated "final and distributive account."

"(B)(1) In estates of decedents in which the sole legatee, devisee, or heir also is the executor or administrator, no partial accountings are required, and no final account or final and distributive account shall be filed. The executor or administrator shall be discharged by filing with the court within thirty days after completing the administration of the estate a certificate of termination of an estate that states all of the following:

"(a) That all debts and claims presented to the estate have been paid in full or settled finally;

"(b) That an estate tax return, if required under Chapter 5731. of the Revised Code, has been filed, and any estate tax due under that chapter has been paid;

"(c) That all attorney's fees have been waived by or paid to counsel of record of the estate, and all fiduciary fees have been waived or paid;

"(d) The amount of attorney's fees and the amount of fiduciary fees that have been paid;

"(e) That all assets remaining after completion of the activities described in divisions (B)(1)(a) to (d) of this section have been distributed to the sole legatee, devisee, or heir.

"In estates of decedents in which none of the legatees, devisees, or heirs is under a legal disability, each partial accounting of an executor or administrator may be waived by the written consent of all the legatees, devisees, or heirs filed in lieu of a partial accounting otherwise required.

"(C)(1) The court may waive, by order, an account that division (A) of this section requires of a guardian of the estate or a guardian of the person and estate, other than an account made pursuant to court order, if any of the following circumstances applies:

"(a) The assets of the estate consist entirely of real property.

"(b) The assets of the estate consist entirely of personal property, that property is held by a bank, savings and loan association, or trust company in accordance with section 2109.13 of the Revised Code, and the court has authorized expenditures of not more than five thousand dollars annually for the support, maintenance, or, if applicable, education of the ward.

"(c) The assets of the estate consist entirely of real property and of personal property that is held by a bank, savings and loan association, or trust company in accordance with section 2109.13 of the Revised Code, and the court has authorized expenditures of not more than five thousand dollars annually for the support, maintenance, or, if applicable, education of the ward.

"(2) The order of a court entered pursuant to division (C)(1) of this section is prima-facie evidence that a guardian of the estate or a guardian of the person and estate has authority to make expenditures as described in division (C)(1)(b) or (c) of this section.

"(D)(1) As used in this division:

"(a) "Charitable trust" has the same meaning as in section 109.23 of the Revised Code.

"(b) "Qualified community foundation" means any foundation that is exempt from federal income taxation under sections 170(b)(1)(A)(vi) and 501(c)(3) of the "Internal Revenue Code of 1986," 100 Stat. 2085, as amended; that is further described in section 1.170A–9(10) and (11) of Title 26 of the Code of Federal Regulations, 26 C.F.R. 1.170A–9(10) and (11), as amended; and that publishes at least annually and circulates widely within its community an audited report of its fund balances, activities, and donors.

"(c) 'Testamentary charitable trust' means any charitable trust that is created by a will.

"(2) If the assets of a testamentary charitable trust are held and managed by a fiduciary who is an individual or by a corporate fiduciary and if the trust merges into a qualified community foundation, then, after the fiduciary files with the court a final and distributive account pertaining to the trust and activities up to the effective date of the merger, the fiduciary and any successors of the fiduciary shall not be required to render any accounting to the court pertaining to the merged trust and activities that follow the effective date of the merger."

Amendment Note: 1996 H 538 substituted "1111.28" for "1109.16" in the second and fourth paragraphs in division (A); and made changes to reflect gender neutral language.

Amendment Note: 1994 H 208 inserted "except as provided in division (B) of this section" throughout division (A); and rewrote division (B), which previously read:

"(B) In estates of decedents in which the sole legatee or heir also is the executor or administrator, no partial accountings are required.

"In estates of decedents in which none of the legatees or heirs is under a legal disability, each partial accounting of the executor or administrator may be waived by the written consent of all the legatees or heirs filed in lieu of a partial accounting otherwise required."

Cross References

Accounts, Sup R 64
Bond conditions of administrators, exemption of surviving spouse receiving entire net estate, 2109.07
Counsel fees, Sup R 71
Neither the judge nor a clerk may prepare an account, 2101.41
Trustee's compensation, Sup R 74
Veteran's guardian, annual account filed with the court, 5905.11

Library References

Executors and Administrators ⇐458, 459, 466.
Guardian and Ward ⇐137, 142, 143.
Mental Health ⇐291, 292.
Trusts ⇐289, 295, 296.
Westlaw Topic Nos. 162, 196, 257A, 390.
C.J.S. Executors and Administrators §§ 785 to 786.
C.J.S. Mental Health §§ 183 to 184.
C.J.S. Trusts §§ 587 to 589, 600 to 601.

Research References

Encyclopedias

OH Jur. 3d Decedents' Estates § 1491, Report of Sale.
OH Jur. 3d Decedents' Estates § 1633, Receipts, Acknowledgments, and Releases on Distribution.
OH Jur. 3d Decedents' Estates § 1666, When Accounts Are Filed; Waiver of Partial Account.
OH Jur. 3d Decedents' Estates § 1667, Contents and Designation of Accounts.
OH Jur. 3d Decedents' Estates § 1669, When Executor or Administrator is Sole Beneficiary; Certificate of Termination.
OH Jur. 3d Fiduciaries § 235, Duty to Account.
OH Jur. 3d Fiduciaries § 236, Periodic Accounting.
OH Jur. 3d Fiduciaries § 240, Final Accounting Upon Termination of Administration or Trust.
OH Jur. 3d Guardian & Ward § 170, by Guardian Appointed Under Veterans' Guardianship Law.

Treatises and Practice Aids

Carlin, Baldwin's Ohio Practice, Merrick-Rippner Probate Law § 2:92, Fiduciary's Account—Time for Filing.
Carlin, Baldwin's Ohio Practice, Merrick-Rippner Probate Law § 2:93, Fiduciary's Account—Contents.
Carlin, Baldwin's Ohio Practice, Merrick-Rippner Probate Law § 52:2, Fiduciary's Bond—in General.
Carlin, Baldwin's Ohio Practice, Merrick-Rippner Probate Law § 54:1, Fiduciary Accounts—Filing—Time.
Carlin, Baldwin's Ohio Practice, Merrick-Rippner Probate Law § 54:4, Fiduciary Accounts—Contents—Certificate of Service.
Carlin, Baldwin's Ohio Practice, Merrick-Rippner Probate Law § 54:5, Fiduciary Accounts—Verification.
Carlin, Baldwin's Ohio Practice, Merrick-Rippner Probate Law § 54:8, Fiduciary Accounts—Designation of Account.
Carlin, Baldwin's Ohio Practice, Merrick-Rippner Probate Law § 55:1, Fiduciary Misconduct—Deposit and Investment of Funds—Generally.
Carlin, Baldwin's Ohio Practice, Merrick-Rippner Probate Law § 57:4, Removal of Fiduciary—Grounds—Failure to File Inventory or Account.
Carlin, Baldwin's Ohio Practice, Merrick-Rippner Probate Law § 79:4, Inventory—Enforcement of Filing.
Carlin, Baldwin's Ohio Practice, Merrick-Rippner Probate Law § 2:105, Distribution of Assets—Order of Distribution.
Carlin, Baldwin's Ohio Practice, Merrick-Rippner Probate Law § 2:121, Administration of Decedent's Estate—Checklist.
Carlin, Baldwin's Ohio Practice, Merrick-Rippner Probate Law § 33:28, Account of Trustee—Form.
Carlin, Baldwin's Ohio Practice, Merrick-Rippner Probate Law § 54:10, Fiduciary Accounts—Citation to File Account.
Carlin, Baldwin's Ohio Practice, Merrick-Rippner Probate Law § 54:42, Certificate of Depository—Form.
Carlin, Baldwin's Ohio Practice, Merrick-Rippner Probate Law § 64:36, Motion to Require Guardian to File Account—Form.
Carlin, Baldwin's Ohio Practice, Merrick-Rippner Probate Law § 64:37, Account of Guardian—Form.
Carlin, Baldwin's Ohio Practice, Merrick-Rippner Probate Law § 64:38, Receipts and Disbursements—Form.
Carlin, Baldwin's Ohio Practice, Merrick-Rippner Probate Law § 65:32, Application for Appointment of Guardian Ad Litem, Approval and Finality of Accounts—Form.
Carlin, Baldwin's Ohio Practice, Merrick-Rippner Probate Law § 65:33, Order Appointing Guardian Ad Litem—Form.
Carlin, Baldwin's Ohio Practice, Merrick-Rippner Probate Law § 65:34, Answer of Guardian Ad Litem—Form.
Carlin, Baldwin's Ohio Practice, Merrick-Rippner Probate Law § 65:35, Entry Approving and Settling Account—Form.
Carlin, Baldwin's Ohio Practice, Merrick-Rippner Probate Law App B SPF 13.0, Fiduciary's Account.
Carlin, Baldwin's Ohio Practice, Merrick-Rippner Probate Law App B SPF 13.4, Waiver of Partial Account.
Carlin, Baldwin's Ohio Practice, Merrick-Rippner Probate Law App B SPF 13.6, Certificate of Termination.
Carlin, Baldwin's Ohio Practice, Merrick-Rippner Probate Law App B SPF 15.8, Guardian's Account.
Bogert - the Law of Trusts and Trustees § 963, Duty to Render Formal Account in Court of Equity.
Restatement (2d) of Property, Don. Trans. § 33.1, Meaning of a Will.

Law Review and Journal Commentaries

The Uniform Trust Code (2000) and Its Application to Ohio. David M. English, 12 Prob L J Ohio 1 (September/October 2001).

Notes of Decisions

Jurisdiction 3
Procedure 1
Sufficiency of account 2

---

1. Procedure

Probate courts of this state are vested with power, upon final settlement with the administrator of an intestate estate, to order distribution of the money remaining in his hands to the persons entitled thereto; such power is exhausted when the order of distribution is made, and the court cannot entertain a petition brought to enforce the collection of the amount distributed. McLaughlin v. McLaughlin (Ohio 1855) 4 Ohio St. 508, 64 Am.Dec. 603.

A hearing by a probate court for the purpose of settling the "final and distributive account" of a receiver is not one of the equitable actions encompassed by RC 2501.02. In re Wisser and Gabler (Ohio 1966) 5 Ohio St.2d 89, 214 N.E.2d 92, 34 O.O.2d 217. Appeal And Error ⇐ 15

Where a contingent claim against an estate accrues after complete distribution of the assets, the claimant's remedy for any deficiency is an action against the distributee, rather than seeking to vacate the order of final distribution and compelling the distributee to return the assets to the executor. In re Robbins' Estate (Ohio Prob. 1964) 200 N.E.2d 735, 94 Ohio Law Abs. 561, 28 O.O.2d 399.

Where an objection is raised and issue presented, the court must require the fiduciary to comply strictly with RC 2109.30. In re Brown's Estate (Fayette 1954) 98 Ohio App. 297, 129 N.E.2d 509, 57 O.O. 342.

Order of Probate Court approving final account of executor is final order and binding upon all those who approved account, and such order cannot be opened up by declaratory judgment proceeding. Fletcher v. Stanton (Ohio Prob. 1952) 124 N.E.2d 495, 69 Ohio Law Abs. 161, affirmed 124 N.E.2d 493, 69 Ohio Law Abs. 174. Declaratory Judgment ⇔ 114; Executors And Administrators ⇔ 513(4).

A petition to terminate a charitable trust and to compel the trustees to account for maladministration is not an action for a declaratory judgment. Green v. Ryan (Hamilton 1953) 95 Ohio App. 345, 119 N.E.2d 668, 53 O.O. 311.

Where an executor of an executor renders a final account under RS 6175 and exceptions are filed by an administrator de bonis non of the original unsettled estate, such executor is a party in fiduciary capacity within RS 6408 as to an appeal bond. In re Sidwell's Estate (Ohio 1903) 67 Ohio St. 464, 48 W.L.B. 277, 66 N.E. 521.

The settlement of the final account of an executor, showing the payment of money to a person not entitled thereto, is no bar to a subsequent action against him for the recovery of the money by one who is legally entitled to the same. Banning v. Gotshall (Ohio 1900) 62 Ohio St. 210, 43 W.L.B. 315, 56 N.E. 1030. Executors And Administrators ⇔ 513(9); Judgment ⇔ 688

The liability of the guardian to pay the wards the balance shown to be due in his final account, except as to the liability upon his bond, is both statutory and upon an account. Lamkin v. Robinson (Ohio Com.Pl. 1910) 21 Ohio Dec. 13, 10 Ohio N.P.(N.S.) 1, reversed 24 Ohio C.D. 91, 15 Ohio C.C.(N.S.) 126, affirmed 88 Ohio St. 603, 106 N.E. 1065, 11 Ohio Law Rep. 80.

A long delay on the part of a ward in filing exceptions to his guardian's account, there being no excuse for the delay, is laches, especially where the filing is delayed until after the death of the guardian, thus depriving his sureties of their main witness. In re Streit's Estate (Ohio Com.Pl. 1901) 12 Ohio Dec. 158.

Where a guardian receives money from an executor by order of court, the order being subsequently reversed for want of jurisdiction, in a proceeding to compel the guardian to charge himself with such money he is estopped from setting up the illegality of such order. In re Cloud's Estate (Ohio Prob. 1888) 20 W.L.B. 455. Estoppel ⇔ 9; Guardian And Ward ⇔ 61

No action accrues for a guardian against his ward upon account of advances made to the ward until the relation of guardian and ward is determined. Davis v. Ford's Adm'rs (Ohio 1836) 7 Ohio 104, PT. II.

Where at a guardian's sale the purchaser fails to pay and the property has to be resold, the guardian may recover from the purchaser the difference in price. Clawson v Beatty, OS Unrep 502, 36 B 214 (1896).

Where executrix has failed to timely file a schedule of debts and a preliminary notice as to taxes as statutorily required, it was not an abuse of discretion for probate court to order the removal of the executrix for misconduct even though executrix acted under advice from counsel and executrix was prepared at the time of hearing to file all delinquent papers. Baringer v Newell, No. 81–C–48 (7th Dist Ct App, Columbiana, 2–18–82).

No cause of action on the bond of a guardian accrues in favor of the ward until the filing of the guardianship account and the settlement of the estate in the probate court. Wegner v Wiltsie, 3 CC(NS) 410, 13 CD 302 (Lucas 1902).

The administrator of a deceased guardian should file the account of the deceased guardian and turn over the money in his hands to the newly appointed guardian immediately after his appointment. In re Estate of Bruckmann, 1 NP(NS) 7, 48 B 637 (Prob, Hamilton 1903).

2. Sufficiency of account

Upon the final settlement of an administrator's accounts, it is not the duty of the probate judge to provide for the payment of claims against the estate which no creditor is asserting. Cox v. John (Ohio 1877) 32 Ohio St. 532.

Where an account must be rendered by the guardian every two years, and it is approved by the probate court, it is final as between the guardian and the ward. Woodmansie v. Woodmansie (Ohio 1876) 32 Ohio St. 18.

Where a guardian induces the ward to sign a receipt as though the money had been paid and promises to become personally responsible for the money and interest, the ward can sue on such promise without opening up the guardian's account. Lindsay v. Lindsay (Ohio 1875) 28 Ohio St. 157. Guardian And Ward ⇔ 163

Burden was on executor, who was also attorney for the estate, to establish reasonableness of attorney fees charged to the estate, where the fees were subject to contest, even though trial court placed great emphasis on fact that the fees conformed to local court's rules. In re Estate of Secoy (Miami 1984) 19 Ohio App.3d 269, 484 N.E.2d 160, 19 O.B.R. 439. Executors And Administrators ⇔ 506(1)

Executor's approved and settled accounting could not be opened in declaratory judgment proceeding concerning whether certain charges should be made against income earned by trust assets while in hands of the executor. Third Nat. Bank & Trust Co. of Dayton v. Gardner (Ohio Com.Pl. 1970) 24 Ohio Misc. 223, 262 N.E.2d 430, 53 O.O.2d 261, 53 O.O.2d 290. Executors And Administrators ⇔ 513(2)

When in determining federal income tax liability on income derived from personal property, charitable deductions are taken by an executor in computing the taxable income of an estate, the income taxes paid on said income, unless otherwise provided in a decedent's will, are chargeable as a cost of administration, so that all residuary legatees, including the charitable residuary legatees, shall bear the burden of the tax. In re Gamble's Estate (Ohio Prob. 1966) 8 Ohio Misc. 314, 220 N.E.2d 621, 36 O.O.2d 388, 37 O.O.2d 337.

Executors are not required to show receipts and disbursements separately identified as to principal and income. In re Gamble's Estate (Ohio Prob. 1966) 8 Ohio Misc. 314, 220 N.E.2d 621, 36 O.O.2d 388, 37 O.O.2d 337.

Failure to account as required by RC 2109.30 justified indefinite suspension of attorney from practice of law. Columbus Bar Ass'n v. Margulis (Ohio 1963) 174 Ohio St. 263, 189 N.E.2d 88, 22 O.O.2d 328.

Where a final account shows only part of certain purchases from the estate, an exception thereto should be sustained. In re Brown's Estate (Ohio Prob. 1954) 129 N.E.2d 497, 67 Ohio Law Abs. 291, affirmed in part, reversed in part 98 Ohio App. 297, 129 N.E.2d 509, 57 O.O. 342.

Mere sworn statement without vouchers, filed by guardian in lieu of an itemized final account as provided for in section, is sufficient to authorize probate court to hear proof of the matters therein set forth, permit exceptions to be filed thereto and fully dispose of the matter in accordance with the provisions of GC 10501–53 (RC 2101.24) and 10506–39 (RC 2109.32). Marks v. Marks (Columbiana 1937) 58 Ohio App. 266, 16 N.E.2d 509, 12 O.O. 158. Mental Health ⇔ 299

When an administrator, by virtue of his office, takes the unexpired term of his decedent's lease for years, and sells the same, the proceeds of such sale are by law appropriated to the original lessor to the extent of the unpaid rents of the original lease, and such administrator will be required to account to his decedent's estate only for the excess beyond the sum required to pay the rents reserved in the original lease. Steward v. Barry (Ohio 1921) 102 Ohio St. 129, 131 N.E. 492, 18 Ohio Law Rep. 542, 18 Ohio Law Rep. 543. Executors And Administrators ⇔ 134

Amount of fees for attorney's services, rendered to executor or administrator, may be included as item in settlement-account, or application on due notice to all parties in interest may be made to probate court to allow claim and fix amount thereof. Trumpler v. Royer (Ohio 1917) 95 Ohio St. 194, 115 N.E. 1018, 14 Ohio Law Rep. 551. Executors And Administrators ⇔ 242

Under RS 1908, §§5996, 6188 (See GC §§10506–4, 10509–192, 10509–193, 10510–45), allowances to an administrator for extraordinary services in the settlement of the estate are part of the statement of his account, and all to be so considered by the court. McMahon v. Ambach & Co. (Ohio 1908) 79 Ohio St. 103, 86 N.E. 512, 6 Ohio Law Rep. 554. Executors And Administrators ⇔ 482

The allowance to an administrator for extraordinary services in the settlement of the estate is part of the statement of his account. McMahon v. Ambach & Co. (Ohio 1908) 79 Ohio St. 103, 86 N.E. 512, 6 Ohio Law Rep. 554. Executors And Administrators ⇔ 482

The legatees of a first estate may require an accounting from the administrator of a deceased executor who refused to allow a debt of the estate to the estate of the testator. Jones v. Willis (Ohio 1905) 72 Ohio St. 189, 74 N.E. 166, 2 Ohio Law Rep. 529.

After the executor delivered possession of the personal estate to the widow, he had administered the estate and executed the trust, and cannot thereafter be held responsible for any use or disposition made by her or be required to account therefor in a probate court. Posegate v. South (Ohio 1889) 46 Ohio St. 391, 21 W.L.B. 380, 21 N.E. 641.

A guardian is not required to keep separate accounts but only to render one account of all receipts and disbursements. Tuttle v. Northrop (Ohio 1886) 44 Ohio St. 178, 15 W.L.B. 246, 5 N.E. 659.

A fiduciary's inability, even if innocent or negligent, to account for a sum constitutes "defalcation" and renders the debt created by the breach of fiduciary duty nondischargeable under 11 USC 523(a)(4) in the fiduciary's bankruptcy proceedings. In re Kern (Bkrtcy.S.D.Ohio 1989) 98 B.R. 321.

Where the accounting required of a guardian by RC 2109.30 is impracticable or impossible, the probate court has plenary power under RC 2101.24 to substitute an alternative means of accounting such as a hearing upon statements offered in lien of a formal account; such a hearing, provided for by RC 2109.32, requires formal notice to all interested parties, so that an order closing a guardianship after a hearing held without notice to a ward must be reversed. In re Guardianship of Flesh, No. 84–CA–6 (2d Dist Ct App, Miami, 7–20–84).

Where a testamentary trust grants the trustee absolute discretion but provides for invasion of the trust principal to continue the beneficiary's standard of living only if such beneficiary's "income from all sources is insufficient," the trial court erred in approving the trustee's accounting which ignored the beneficiary's income. In re Short's Will, No. 82–CA–64 (2d Dist Ct App, Miami, 6–27–83).

Reinvestment of proceeds of sale of real estate under order of court does not relieve surety if fund is not finally accounted for and paid over to proper person. Huntington v Globe Indemnity Co, 6 Abs 99, 27 NP(NS) 12 (CP, Franklin 1927).

3. Jurisdiction

A creditor cannot, at his option, transfer the settlement of the estate of his deceased debtor from the probate court to a court in chancery. McDonald v. Aten (Ohio 1853) 1 Ohio St. 293. Courts ⇔ 472.4(4); Executors And Administrators ⇔ 473(2)

Jurisdiction of the person of an administrator until his accounts are settled is not ousted by the fact that after due notice the court requires him to make settlement, and by the same entry orders his removal and appoints a successor. In re Morrison's Estate (Ohio 1903) 68 Ohio St. 252, 48 W.L.B. 586, 67 N.E. 567, 1 Ohio Law Rep. 22, 1 Ohio Law Rep. 335. Courts ⇔ 30; Executors And Administrators ⇔ 469(2)

The appointment of an administrator by the probate court and his acceptance and qualification gives that court jurisdiction over the estate and the person of the administrator until his accounts are settled; such jurisdiction is not ousted by the fact that the court orders his removal and appoints a successor. In re Morrison's Estate (Ohio 1903) 68 Ohio St. 252, 48 W.L.B. 586, 67 N.E. 567, 1 Ohio Law Rep. 22, 1 Ohio Law Rep. 335. Executors And Administrators ⇔ 76

An Ohio probate court, although it has admitted to probate an Ohio will and has issued letters to the executor therein named, has no power to review the accounts of such executor respecting property situate in a foreign state for which he has duly accounted to the proper court of that state. In re Crawford (Ohio 1903) 68 Ohio St. 58, 48 W.L.B. 492, 67 N.E. 156, 96 Am.St.Rep. 648, 1 Ohio Law Rep. 91.

Where a trust is terminated by a mutual agreement and the former trustee obtains control over the property, he is an agent and can be compelled to account only in a court of general jurisdiction, and not an executor or administrator who can be compelled to account in a probate court. Culver v. Culver (Ohio 1898) 58 Ohio St. 172, 39 W.L.B. 371, 50 N.E. 505.

There is no federal diversity jurisdiction over probate matters; thus an action by heirs against an executrix seeking damages for alleged irregularities is properly dismissed from a district court. Bedo v. McGuire (C.A.6 (Ohio) 1985) 767 F.2d 305.

Federal court does not have jurisdiction of an action against an executor or administrator involving an alleged breach of fiduciary duties. Starr v. Rupp (C.A.6 (Ohio) 1970) 25 Ohio Misc. 224, 421 F.2d 999, 12 A.L.R. Fed. 279, 53 O.O.2d 169, 54 O.O.2d 343.

A clause in a deed of trust of real estate that the trustee "shall not be required to render any account of his trusteeship to any court but a settlement between the parties shall be final and conclusive," does not supersede the jurisdiction of the probate court over the accounting in case no settlement has been made between the parties. Pherson v Mitchell, 12 App 336, 31 CC(NS) 333 (1920).

The death of a guardian without filing an account and without leaving books of account or memoranda from which his indebtedness to the estate can be ascertained does not give the common pleas court jurisdiction on the bond of the guardian to compel an accounting and payment to the ward of the amount found due him. Wegner v Wiltsie, 3 CC(NS) 410, 13 CD 302 (Lucas 1902).

2109.301 Accounts of executors or administrators; requirements; final and distributive account; certificate of termination of estate

(A) An administrator or executor shall render an account at any time other than a time otherwise mentioned in this section upon an order of the probate court issued for good cause shown either at its own instance or upon the motion of any person interested in the estate. Except as otherwise provided in division (B)(2) of this section, an administrator or executor shall render a final account within thirty days after completing the administration of the estate or within any other period of time that the court may order.

Every account shall include an itemized statement of all receipts of the administrator or executor during the accounting period and of all disbursements and distributions made by the executor or administrator during the accounting period. In addition, the account shall include an itemized statement of all funds, assets, and investments of the estate known to or in the possession of the administrator or executor at the end of the accounting period and shall show any changes in investments since the last previous account.

Every account shall be upon the signature of the administrator or executor. When two or more administrators or executors render an account, the court may allow the account upon the signature of one of them. The court may examine the administrator or executor under oath concerning the account.

When an administrator or executor is authorized by law or by the instrument governing distribution to distribute the assets of the estate, in whole or in part, the administrator or executor may do so and include a report of the distribution in the administrator's or executor's succeeding account.

In estates of decedents in which none of the legatees, devisees, or heirs is under a legal disability, each partial accounting of an executor or administrator may be waived by the written consent of all the legatees, devisees, or heirs filed in lieu of a partial accounting otherwise required.

(B)(1) Every administrator and executor, within six months after appointment, shall render a final and distributive account of the administrator's or executor's administration of the estate unless one or more of the following circumstances apply:

(a) An Ohio estate tax return must be filed for the estate.

(b) A proceeding contesting the validity of the decedent's will pursuant to section 2107.71 of the Revised Code has been commenced.

(c) The surviving spouse has filed an election to take against the will.

(d) The administrator or executor is a party in a civil action.

(e) The estate is insolvent.

(f) For other reasons set forth by the administrator or executor, subject to court approval, it would be detrimental to the estate and its beneficiaries or heirs to file a final and distributive account.

(2) In estates of decedents in which the sole legatee, devisee, or heir is also the administrator or executor of the estate, no partial accountings are required. The administrator or executor of an estate of that type shall file a final account or final and distributive account or, in lieu of filing a final account, the

administrator or executor may file with the court within thirty days after completing the administration of the estate a certificate of termination of an estate that states all of the following:

(a) All debts and claims presented to the estate have been paid in full or settled finally.

(b) An estate tax return, if required under the provisions of the Internal Revenue Code or Chapter 5731. of the Revised Code, has been filed, and any estate tax has been paid.

(c) All attorney's fees have been waived by or paid to counsel of record of the estate, and all executor or administrator fees have been waived or paid.

(d) The amount of attorney's fees and the amount of administrator or executor fees that have been paid.

(e) All assets remaining after completion of the activities described in divisions (B)(2)(a) to (d) of this section have been distributed to the sole legatee, devisee, or heir.

(3) In an estate of the type described in division (B)(2) of this section, a sole legatee, devisee, or heir of a decedent may be liable to creditors for debts of and claims against the estate that are presented after the filing of the certificate of termination described in that division and within the time allowed by section 2117.06 of the Revised Code for presentation of the creditors' claims.

(4) Not later than thirteen months after appointment, every administrator and executor shall render an account of the administrator's or executor's administration, unless a certificate of termination is filed under division (B)(2) of this section. Except as provided in divisions (B)(1) and (2) of this section, after the initial account is rendered, every administrator and executor shall render further accounts at least once each year.

(2003 H 51, eff. 4–8–04; 2001 H 85, eff. 10–31–01)

Uncodified Law

2004 H 161, § 3, eff. 4–8–04 reads, in part:

(C) Sections 2107.19, 2109.301, 2113.53, 2117.06, 2117.07, 2117.11, and 2117.12 of the Revised Code, as amended by this act, apply to estates of decedents who die on or after April 8, 2004.

Historical and Statutory Notes

Amendment Note: 2003 H 51 substituted ". The administrator or executor of an estate of that type shall file" for ", and the administrator or executor shall not file" and substituted "or, in lieu of filing a final account, the administrator or executor may file" for ". In lieu of filing a final account, the administrator or executor of an estate of that type shall be discharged by filing" in division (B)(2); added new division (B)(3); and redesignated former division (B)(3) as division (B)(4).

Library References

Executors and Administrators ⇐459, 502.
Guardian and Ward ⇐137, 153.
Mental Health ⇐292, 299.
Trusts ⇐289, 322.
Westlaw Topic Nos. 162, 196, 257A, 390.
C.J.S. Executors and Administrators §§ 786, 847.
C.J.S. Mental Health §§ 183 to 184, 190.
C.J.S. Trusts §§ 587 to 589, 636.

Research References

Encyclopedias

OH Jur. 3d Decedents' Estates § 1491, Report of Sale.
OH Jur. 3d Decedents' Estates § 1633, Receipts, Acknowledgments, and Releases on Distribution.
OH Jur. 3d Decedents' Estates § 1666, When Accounts Are Filed; Waiver of Partial Account.
OH Jur. 3d Decedents' Estates § 1668, Hearing on Account; Notice; Exceptions to Account.
OH Jur. 3d Decedents' Estates § 1669, When Executor or Administrator is Sole Beneficiary; Certificate of Termination.
OH Jur. 3d Fiduciaries § 236, Periodic Accounting.
OH Jur. 3d Fiduciaries § 237, Periodic Accounting—Court Ordered Accounting.
OH Jur. 3d Fiduciaries § 240, Final Accounting Upon Termination of Administration or Trust.
OH Jur. 3d Fiduciaries § 244, Requirement Applicable to Executor or Administrator Who is Sole Beneficiary.
OH Jur. 3d Fiduciaries § 247, Waiver or Loss of Right to Compel Accounting.
OH Jur. 3d Fiduciaries § 250, Overview of Content.
OH Jur. 3d Fiduciaries § 253, Receipts and Disbursements.
OH Jur. 3d Fiduciaries § 255, Generally; Accrual Upon Accounting.
OH Jur. 3d Fiduciaries § 260, Examination of Fiduciary; Exhibiting Securities and Passbooks.

Treatises and Practice Aids

Carlin, Baldwin's Ohio Practice, Merrick-Rippner Probate Law § 2:3, Time for Administration of Decedent's Estate and Payment of Estate Taxes.
Carlin, Baldwin's Ohio Practice, Merrick-Rippner Probate Law § 2:92, Fiduciary's Account—Time for Filing.
Carlin, Baldwin's Ohio Practice, Merrick-Rippner Probate Law § 2:93, Fiduciary's Account—Contents.
Carlin, Baldwin's Ohio Practice, Merrick-Rippner Probate Law § 2:94, Fiduciary's Account—Hearing.
Carlin, Baldwin's Ohio Practice, Merrick-Rippner Probate Law § 2:95, Fiduciary's Account—Copy of Account to Interested Parties—Notice of Hearing; Exceptions to Account.
Carlin, Baldwin's Ohio Practice, Merrick-Rippner Probate Law § 2:96, Fiduciary's Account—Effect of Order Settling Account.
Carlin, Baldwin's Ohio Practice, Merrick-Rippner Probate Law § 2:98, Fiduciary's Account—Effect of Vacation; Supplemental Final Account.
Carlin, Baldwin's Ohio Practice, Merrick-Rippner Probate Law § 52:2, Fiduciary's Bond—in General.
Carlin, Baldwin's Ohio Practice, Merrick-Rippner Probate Law § 54:1, Fiduciary Accounts—Filing—Time.
Carlin, Baldwin's Ohio Practice, Merrick-Rippner Probate Law § 54:2, Fiduciary Accounts—Filing—Ordered or Requested.
Carlin, Baldwin's Ohio Practice, Merrick-Rippner Probate Law § 54:4, Fiduciary Accounts—Contents—Certificate of Service.
Carlin, Baldwin's Ohio Practice, Merrick-Rippner Probate Law § 54:5, Fiduciary Accounts—Verification.
Carlin, Baldwin's Ohio Practice, Merrick-Rippner Probate Law § 54:6, Fiduciary Accounts—Exhibition of Assets.
Carlin, Baldwin's Ohio Practice, Merrick-Rippner Probate Law § 54:7, Fiduciary Accounts—Report of Distribution.
Carlin, Baldwin's Ohio Practice, Merrick-Rippner Probate Law § 54:9, Fiduciary Accounts—Exceptions to Requirement to Account.
Carlin, Baldwin's Ohio Practice, Merrick-Rippner Probate Law § 57:4, Removal of Fiduciary—Grounds—Failure to File Inventory or Account.
Carlin, Baldwin's Ohio Practice, Merrick-Rippner Probate Law § 57:9, Removal of Fiduciary—Procedure—Notice.
Carlin, Baldwin's Ohio Practice, Merrick-Rippner Probate Law § 79:4, Inventory—Enforcement of Filing.
Carlin, Baldwin's Ohio Practice, Merrick-Rippner Probate Law § 2:105, Distribution of Assets—Order of Distribution.
Carlin, Baldwin's Ohio Practice, Merrick-Rippner Probate Law § 2:121, Administration of Decedent's Estate—Checklist.
Carlin, Baldwin's Ohio Practice, Merrick-Rippner Probate Law § 54:11, Fiduciary Accounts—Hearing on Account—Notice of Hearing—Copy of Account.
Carlin, Baldwin's Ohio Practice, Merrick-Rippner Probate Law § 54:13, Fiduciary Accounts—Approval of Final Account and Discharge of Fiduciary.
Carlin, Baldwin's Ohio Practice, Merrick-Rippner Probate Law § 54:44, Waiver of Partial Account—Form.
Carlin, Baldwin's Ohio Practice, Merrick-Rippner Probate Law § 54:45, Certificate of Termination—Form.
Carlin, Baldwin's Ohio Practice, Merrick-Rippner Probate Law § 54:46, Motion to Compel Fiduciary to File Account—Form.

Carlin, Baldwin's Ohio Practice, Merrick-Rippner Probate Law § 75:34, Complaint for Distribution—Form.

Carlin, Baldwin's Ohio Practice, Merrick-Rippner Probate Law App B SPF 13.0, Fiduciary's Account.

Carlin, Baldwin's Ohio Practice, Merrick-Rippner Probate Law App B SPF 13.8, Application and Entry to Extend Administration.

Carlin, Baldwin's Ohio Practice, Merrick-Rippner Probate Law App B SPF 13.10, Notice to Extend Administration.

Law Review and Journal Commentaries

Nonclaim Statute and Distributions: The Sooner the Better, Morton Bobowick. 13 Prob L J Ohio 21 (November/December 2002).

Practical Application of House Bill 85 (Probate Reform 2001), Marilyn J. Maag. 13 Prob L J Ohio 19 (November/December 2002).

Notes of Decisions

Final accounts   1

---

1. Final accounts

Guardians' failure to list value of contents of safe-deposit boxes did not prevent approval of guardians' first and final account of ward's estate, which was filed after ward's death; presumably, contents would be inventoried under required procedures by fiduciary of the estate. In re Rickels (Ohio App. 3 Dist., Paulding, 05-10-2004) No. 11-03-13, 2004-Ohio-2353, 2004 WL 1049120, Unreported. Guardian And Ward ⚖ 141

Disbursements for guardians' fees and ward's telephone bill would not be excepted from guardians' first and final account of ward's estate; disbursements had been previously approved and allowed by order of probate court. In re Rickels (Ohio App. 3 Dist., Paulding, 05-10-2004) No. 11-03-13, 2004-Ohio-2353, 2004 WL 1049120, Unreported. Guardian And Ward ⚖ 148; Guardian And Ward ⚖ 150

Financial accounts and real estate that were purportedly subject to pay-on-death and transfer-on-death conditions were required to be included in guardians' first and final account of ward's estate, which was filed after ward's death; financial accounts and real estate came into guardians' hands during existence of guardianship and thus were assets of the guardianship. In re Rickels (Ohio App. 3 Dist., Paulding, 05-10-2004) No. 11-03-13, 2004-Ohio-2353, 2004 WL 1049120, Unreported. Guardian And Ward ⚖ 141

2109.302   Accounts of guardians or conservators

(A) Every guardian or conservator shall render an account of the administration of the ward's estate at least once in each two years. The guardian or conservator shall render an account at any time other than a time otherwise mentioned in this section upon the order of the probate court issued for good cause shown either at its own instance or upon the motion of any person interested in the estate. Except as provided in division (B) of this section, every guardian or conservator shall render a final account within thirty days after completing the administration of the ward's estate or within any other period of time that the court may order.

Every account shall include an itemized statement of all receipts of the guardian or conservator during the accounting period and of all disbursements and distributions made by the guardian or conservator during the accounting period. The itemized disbursements and distributions shall be verified by vouchers or proof, except in the case of an account rendered by a corporate fiduciary subject to section 1111.28 of the Revised Code. In addition, the account shall include an itemized statement of all funds, assets, and investments of the estate known to or in the possession of the guardian or conservator at the end of the accounting period and shall show any changes in investments since the last previous account.

Every account shall be upon the signature of the guardian or conservator. When two or more guardians or conservators render an account, the court may allow the account upon the signature of one of the guardians or conservators.

Upon the filing of every account, the guardian or conservator, except a corporate fiduciary subject to section 1111.28 of the Revised Code, shall exhibit to the court for its examination both of the following: the securities shown in the account as being in the hands of the guardian or conservator, or the certificate of the person in possession of the securities, if held as collateral or pursuant to section 2109.13 or 2131.21 of the Revised Code; and a passbook or certified bank statement showing as to each depository the fund deposited to the credit of the ward's estate. The court may designate a deputy clerk, an agent of a corporate surety on the bond of the guardian or conservator, or another suitable person whom the court appoints as commissioner to make the examination and to report the person's findings to the court. When securities are located outside the county, the court may appoint a commissioner or request another probate court to make the examination and to report its findings to the court. The court may examine the guardian or conservator under oath concerning the account.

When a guardian or conservator is authorized by law to distribute the assets of the estate, in whole or in part, the guardian or conservator may do so and include a report of the distribution in the guardian's or conservator's succeeding account.

(B)(1) The court may waive, by order, an account that division (A) of this section requires of a guardian of the estate or of a guardian of the person and estate, other than an account made pursuant to court order, if any of the following circumstances apply:

(a) The assets of the estate consist entirely of real property.

(b) The assets of the estate consist entirely of personal property, that property is held by a bank, savings and loan association, or trust company in accordance with section 2109.13 of the Revised Code, and the court has authorized expenditures of not more than ten thousand dollars annually for the support, maintenance, or, if applicable, education of the ward.

(c) The assets of the estate consist entirely of real property and of personal property that is held by a bank, savings and loan association, or trust company in accordance with section 2109.13 of the Revised Code, and the court has authorized expenditures of not more than ten thousand dollars annually for the support, maintenance, or, if applicable, education of the ward.

(2) The order of a court entered pursuant to division (B)(1) of this section is prima-facie evidence that a guardian of the estate or a guardian of the person and estate has authority to make expenditures as described in divisions (B)(1)(b) and (c) of this section.

(3) Notwithstanding the requirements for accounts by other guardians under this section, a guardian of the person is not required to render an account except upon an order of the court that the court issues for good cause shown either at its own instance or upon the motion of any person interested in the estate.

(2001 H 85, eff. 10–31–01)

Uncodified Law

2001 H 85, § 6: See Uncodified Law under 2109.12.

Library References

Executors and Administrators ⚖458, 465.
Guardian and Ward ⚖137, 140, 141.
Mental Health ⚖292, 299.
Trusts ⚖289, 295.
Westlaw Topic Nos. 162, 196, 257A, 390.
C.J.S. Executors and Administrators §§ 785 to 786.
C.J.S. Mental Health §§ 183 to 184, 190.
C.J.S. Trusts §§ 587 to 589, 600 to 601.

Research References

Encyclopedias

OH Jur. 3d Decedents' Estates § 1666, When Accounts Are Filed; Waiver of Partial Account.

OH Jur. 3d Fiduciaries § 235, Duty to Account.

OH Jur. 3d Fiduciaries § 236, Periodic Accounting.

OH Jur. 3d Fiduciaries § 237, Periodic Accounting—Court Ordered Accounting.

OH Jur. 3d Fiduciaries § 240, Final Accounting Upon Termination of Administration or Trust.

OH Jur. 3d Fiduciaries § 248, Waiver or Loss of Right to Compel Accounting—Waiver of Accounting by Certain Guardians.

OH Jur. 3d Fiduciaries § 250, Overview of Content.

OH Jur. 3d Fiduciaries § 253, Receipts and Disbursements.

OH Jur. 3d Fiduciaries § 260, Examination of Fiduciary; Exhibiting Securities and Passbooks.

Treatises and Practice Aids

Carlin, Baldwin's Ohio Practice, Merrick-Rippner Probate Law § 2:92, Fiduciary's Account—Time for Filing.

Carlin, Baldwin's Ohio Practice, Merrick-Rippner Probate Law § 2:93, Fiduciary's Account—Contents.

Carlin, Baldwin's Ohio Practice, Merrick-Rippner Probate Law § 2:94, Fiduciary's Account—Hearing.

Carlin, Baldwin's Ohio Practice, Merrick-Rippner Probate Law § 2:96, Fiduciary's Account—Effect of Order Settling Account.

Carlin, Baldwin's Ohio Practice, Merrick-Rippner Probate Law § 54:1, Fiduciary Accounts—Filing—Time.

Carlin, Baldwin's Ohio Practice, Merrick-Rippner Probate Law § 54:2, Fiduciary Accounts—Filing—Ordered or Requested.

Carlin, Baldwin's Ohio Practice, Merrick-Rippner Probate Law § 54:4, Fiduciary Accounts—Contents—Certificate of Service.

Carlin, Baldwin's Ohio Practice, Merrick-Rippner Probate Law § 54:5, Fiduciary Accounts—Verification.

Carlin, Baldwin's Ohio Practice, Merrick-Rippner Probate Law § 54:6, Fiduciary Accounts—Exhibition of Assets.

Carlin, Baldwin's Ohio Practice, Merrick-Rippner Probate Law § 54:7, Fiduciary Accounts—Report of Distribution.

Carlin, Baldwin's Ohio Practice, Merrick-Rippner Probate Law § 54:9, Fiduciary Accounts—Exceptions to Requirement to Account.

Carlin, Baldwin's Ohio Practice, Merrick-Rippner Probate Law § 57:4, Removal of Fiduciary—Grounds—Failure to File Inventory or Account.

Carlin, Baldwin's Ohio Practice, Merrick-Rippner Probate Law § 57:9, Removal of Fiduciary—Procedure—Notice.

Carlin, Baldwin's Ohio Practice, Merrick-Rippner Probate Law § 64:4, Powers and Duties of Guardian—Accounting.

Carlin, Baldwin's Ohio Practice, Merrick-Rippner Probate Law § 79:4, Inventory—Enforcement of Filing.

Carlin, Baldwin's Ohio Practice, Merrick-Rippner Probate Law § 54:11, Fiduciary Accounts—Hearing on Account—Notice of Hearing—Copy of Account.

Carlin, Baldwin's Ohio Practice, Merrick-Rippner Probate Law § 54:46, Motion to Compel Fiduciary to File Account—Form.

Carlin, Baldwin's Ohio Practice, Merrick-Rippner Probate Law § 64:36, Motion to Require Guardian to File Account—Form.

Carlin, Baldwin's Ohio Practice, Merrick-Rippner Probate Law § 64:37, Account of Guardian—Form.

Carlin, Baldwin's Ohio Practice, Merrick-Rippner Probate Law § 64:38, Receipts and Disbursements—Form.

Carlin, Baldwin's Ohio Practice, Merrick-Rippner Probate Law § 65:32, Application for Appointment of Guardian Ad Litem, Approval and Finality of Accounts—Form.

Carlin, Baldwin's Ohio Practice, Merrick-Rippner Probate Law § 65:33, Order Appointing Guardian Ad Litem—Form.

Carlin, Baldwin's Ohio Practice, Merrick-Rippner Probate Law § 65:34, Answer of Guardian Ad Litem—Form.

Carlin, Baldwin's Ohio Practice, Merrick-Rippner Probate Law § 65:35, Entry Approving and Settling Account—Form.

Carlin, Baldwin's Ohio Practice, Merrick-Rippner Probate Law § 68:47, Acceptance of Duties of Fiduciary—Form.

Notes of Decisions

Failure to render account 2
Jurisdiction 1
Statement of receipts and disbursements 3

1. Jurisdiction

Trial court did not exceed its territorial jurisdiction in appointing conservator over funds located in financial institutions outside of county. In re Conservatorship of Ahmed (Ohio App. 7 Dist., Belmont, 06-16-2003) No. 01 BA 13, No. 01 BA 48, 2003-Ohio-3272, 2003 WL 21442314, Unreported, stay denied 99 Ohio St.3d 1540, 795 N.E.2d 680, 2003-Ohio-4671, appeal not allowed 100 Ohio St.3d 1433, 797 N.E.2d 512, 2003-Ohio-5396, reconsideration denied 100 Ohio St.3d 1511, 799 N.E.2d 188, 2003-Ohio-6161, motion denied 100 Ohio St.3d 1526, 100 Ohio St.3d 1527, 800 N.E.2d 44, 2003-Ohio-6510. Guardian And Ward ⇐ 8

2. Failure to render account

Removal of director of family services agency as ward's guardian was warranted, where director failed to render an account of the administration of the ward's estate, failed to file an inventory of the estate after appointment, and disregarded orders of the court. In re Guardianship of Monus (Ohio App. 7 Dist., Mahoning, 05-28-2004) No. 03 MA 128, No. 03 MA 131, No. 03 MA 129, No. 03 MA 132, No. 03 MA 130, No. 03 MA 153, 2004-Ohio-2808, 2004 WL 1194070, Unreported. Mental Health ⇐ 167

Removal of director of family services agency as ward's guardian was warranted, where director failed to seek court approval before expending funds, failed to file an accurate inventory, and disregarded orders of the court. In re Guardianship of Monus (Ohio App. 7 Dist., Mahoning, 05-28-2004) No. 03 MA 128, No. 03 MA 131, No. 03 MA 129, No. 03 MA 132, No. 03 MA 130, No. 03 MA 153, 2004-Ohio-2808, 2004 WL 1194070, Unreported. Guardian And Ward ⇐ 25

3. Statement of receipts and disbursements

Removal of director of family services agency as ward's guardian was warranted, where director failed to file an inventory of the estate after appointment, failed to produce receipts for particular items purchased, made lump sum expenditures from estate, and failed to keep an itemized statement of receipts and disbursements that could be verified by vouchers or proof. In re Guardianship of Monus (Ohio App. 7 Dist., Mahoning, 05-28-2004) No. 03 MA 128, No. 03 MA 131, No. 03 MA 129, No. 03 MA 132, No. 03 MA 130, No. 03 MA 153, 2004-Ohio-2808, 2004 WL 1194070, Unreported. Guardian And Ward ⇐ 25

2109.303 Accounts of testamentary trustees or other fiduciaries

(A) Except as provided in division (B) of this section, every testamentary trustee shall, and every other fiduciary not subject to section 2109.301 or 2109.302 of the Revised Code may, render an account of the trustee's or other fiduciary's administration of the estate or trust at least once in each two years. Any testamentary trustee or other fiduciary shall render an account, subject to division (B) of this section, at any time other than a time otherwise mentioned in this section upon an order of the court issued for good cause shown either at its own instance or upon the motion of any person interested in the estate or trust. Every testamentary trustee shall, and every other fiduciary may, render a final account within thirty days after completing the administration of the estate or trust or shall file a final account within any other period of time that the court may order.

Every account shall include an itemized statement of all receipts of the testamentary trustee or other fiduciary during the accounting period and of all disbursements and distributions made by the testamentary trustee or other fiduciary during the accounting period. The itemized disbursements and distributions shall be verified by vouchers or proof, except in the case of an account rendered by a corporate fiduciary subject to section 1111.28 of the Revised Code. In addition, the account shall include an itemized statement of all funds, assets, and investments of the estate or trust known to or in the possession of the testamentary trustee or other fiduciary at the end of the accounting period and shall show any changes in investments since the last previous account. The accounts of testamentary trustees shall, and the accounts of other fiduciaries may, show receipts and disbursements separately identified as to principal and income.

Every account shall be upon the signature of the testamentary trustee or other fiduciary. When two or more testamentary trustees or other fiduciaries render an account, the court may allow the account upon the signature of one of them.

Upon the filing of every account, the testamentary trustee or other fiduciary, except a corporate fiduciary subject to section 1111.28 of the Revised Code, shall exhibit to the court for its examination both of the following: the securities shown in the account as being in the hands of the testamentary trustee or other fiduciary, or the certificate of the person in possession of the securities, if held as collateral or pursuant to section 2109.13 or 2131.21 of the Revised Code; and a passbook or certified bank statement showing as to each depository the fund deposited to the credit of the estate or trust. The court may designate a deputy clerk, an agent of a corporate surety on the bond of the testamentary trustee or other fiduciary, or another suitable person whom the court appoints as commissioner to make the examination and to report the person's findings to the court. When securities are located outside the county, the court may appoint a commissioner or request another probate court to make the examination and to report its findings to the court. The court may examine the testamentary trustee or other fiduciary under oath concerning the account.

When a testamentary trustee or other fiduciary is authorized by law or by the instrument governing distribution to distribute the assets of the estate or trust, in whole or in part, the testamentary trustee or other fiduciary may do so and include a report of the distribution in the testamentary trustee's or fiduciary's succeeding account.

(B) If the assets of a testamentary charitable trust are held and managed by a testamentary trustee or other fiduciary who is an individual or by a corporate fiduciary and if the trust merges into a qualified community foundation, then, after the testamentary trustee or other fiduciary files with the court a final and distributive account pertaining to the trust and activities up to the effective date of the merger, the testamentary trustee or other fiduciary and any successors of the testamentary trustee or other fiduciary shall not be required to render any accounting to the court pertaining to the merged trust and activities that follow the effective date of the merger.

(C) As used in this section:

(1) "Charitable trust" has the same meaning as in section 109.23 of the Revised Code.

(2) "Qualified community foundation" means any foundation that is exempt from federal income taxation under sections 170(b)(1)(A)(vi) and 501(c)(3) of the "Internal Revenue Code of 1986," 100 Stat. 2085, 26 U.S.C. 170(b)(1)(A)(vi) and 501 (c)(3), as amended; that is further described in section 1.170A–9(10) and (11) of Title 26 of the Code of Federal Regulations, 26 C.F.R. 1.170A–9(10) and (11), as amended; and that publishes at least annually and circulates widely within its community an audited report of its fund balances, activities, and donors.

(3) "Testamentary charitable trust" means any charitable trust that is created by a will.

(4) "Other fiduciary" means a fiduciary other than an executor, administrator, guardian, conservator, or testamentary trustee.

(2001 H 85, eff. 10–31–01)

Uncodified Law

2001 H 85, § 7: See Uncodified Law under 2109.11.

Library References

Executors and Administrators ⚖︎458, 465.
Guardian and Ward ⚖︎137, 140, 141.
Mental Health ⚖︎292, 299.
Trusts ⚖︎289, 295.
Westlaw Topic Nos. 162, 196, 257A, 390.
C.J.S. Executors and Administrators §§ 785 to 786.
C.J.S. Mental Health §§ 183 to 184, 190.
C.J.S. Trusts §§ 587 to 589, 600 to 601.

Research References

Encyclopedias
OH Jur. 3d Fiduciaries § 235, Duty to Account.
OH Jur. 3d Fiduciaries § 236, Periodic Accounting.
OH Jur. 3d Fiduciaries § 237, Periodic Accounting—Court Ordered Accounting.
OH Jur. 3d Fiduciaries § 240, Final Accounting Upon Termination of Administration or Trust.
OH Jur. 3d Fiduciaries § 250, Overview of Content.
OH Jur. 3d Fiduciaries § 253, Receipts and Disbursements.
OH Jur. 3d Fiduciaries § 260, Examination of Fiduciary; Exhibiting Securities and Passbooks.

Treatises and Practice Aids
Carlin, Baldwin's Ohio Practice, Merrick-Rippner Probate Law § 2:92, Fiduciary's Account—Time for Filing.
Carlin, Baldwin's Ohio Practice, Merrick-Rippner Probate Law § 2:93, Fiduciary's Account—Contents.
Carlin, Baldwin's Ohio Practice, Merrick-Rippner Probate Law § 2:94, Fiduciary's Account—Hearing.
Carlin, Baldwin's Ohio Practice, Merrick-Rippner Probate Law § 2:96, Fiduciary's Account—Effect of Order Settling Account.
Carlin, Baldwin's Ohio Practice, Merrick-Rippner Probate Law § 54:1, Fiduciary Accounts—Filing—Time.
Carlin, Baldwin's Ohio Practice, Merrick-Rippner Probate Law § 54:4, Fiduciary Accounts—Contents—Certificate of Service.
Carlin, Baldwin's Ohio Practice, Merrick-Rippner Probate Law § 54:5, Fiduciary Accounts—Verification.
Carlin, Baldwin's Ohio Practice, Merrick-Rippner Probate Law § 54:6, Fiduciary Accounts—Exhibition of Assets.
Carlin, Baldwin's Ohio Practice, Merrick-Rippner Probate Law § 54:7, Fiduciary Accounts—Report of Distribution.
Carlin, Baldwin's Ohio Practice, Merrick-Rippner Probate Law § 54:9, Fiduciary Accounts—Exceptions to Requirement to Account.
Carlin, Baldwin's Ohio Practice, Merrick-Rippner Probate Law § 57:4, Removal of Fiduciary—Grounds—Failure to File Inventory or Account.
Carlin, Baldwin's Ohio Practice, Merrick-Rippner Probate Law § 57:9, Removal of Fiduciary—Procedure—Notice.
Carlin, Baldwin's Ohio Practice, Merrick-Rippner Probate Law § 64:4, Powers and Duties of Guardian—Accounting.
Carlin, Baldwin's Ohio Practice, Merrick-Rippner Probate Law § 79:4, Inventory—Enforcement of Filing.
Carlin, Baldwin's Ohio Practice, Merrick-Rippner Probate Law § 33:28, Account of Trustee—Form.
Carlin, Baldwin's Ohio Practice, Merrick-Rippner Probate Law § 54:11, Fiduciary Accounts—Hearing on Account—Notice of Hearing—Copy of Account.
Carlin, Baldwin's Ohio Practice, Merrick-Rippner Probate Law § 54:39, Fiduciary's Account—Trustee—Form.
Carlin, Baldwin's Ohio Practice, Merrick-Rippner Probate Law § 54:40, Statement of Receipts and Disbursements—Trustee—Form.
Carlin, Baldwin's Ohio Practice, Merrick-Rippner Probate Law § 54:41, Statement of Assets Remaining in Fiduciary's Hands—Trustee—Form.
Carlin, Baldwin's Ohio Practice, Merrick-Rippner Probate Law § 54:46, Motion to Compel Fiduciary to File Account—Form.
Carlin, Baldwin's Ohio Practice, Merrick-Rippner Probate Law § 68:47, Acceptance of Duties of Fiduciary—Form.

2109.31 Citation to file account

(A) If a fiduciary neglects or refuses to file an account, inventory, certificate of notice of probate of will, or report when due according to section 2107.19, 2109.30, 2111.49, or 2115.02 of the Revised Code or when ordered by the probate court, the court at its own instance may issue, and on the application of any interested party or of any of the next of kin of any ward shall issue, a citation as described in division (B) of this section to such fiduciary pursuant to Civil Rules 4.1 to 4.6 to compel the filing of the overdue account, inventory, certificate of notice of probate of will, or report.

(B) The citation that is required by division (A) of this section may contain any of the following:

(1) A statement that the particular account, inventory, certificate of notice of probate of will, or report is overdue;

(2) An order to the fiduciary to file the account, inventory, certificate of notice of probate of will, or report, or otherwise to appear before the court on a specified date;

(3) A statement that, upon the issuance of the citation, a continuance to file the account, inventory, certificate of notice of probate of will, or report may be obtained from the court only on or after the date specified pursuant to division (B)(2) of this section.

(C) If a citation is issued to a fiduciary in accordance with divisions (A) and (B) of this section and if the fiduciary fails to file the account, inventory, certificate of notice of probate of will, or report prior to the appearance date specified in the citation, the court may order, on that date, one or more of the following:

(1) The removal of the fiduciary;

(2) A denial of all or part of the fees to which the fiduciary otherwise would be entitled;

(3) A continuance of the time for filing the account, inventory, certificate of notice of probate of will, or report;

(4) An assessment against the fiduciary of a penalty of one hundred dollars and costs of twenty-five dollars for the hearing, or a suspension of all or part of the penalty and costs;

(5) That the fiduciary is in contempt of the court for the failure to comply with the citation and that a specified daily fine, imprisonment, or daily fine and imprisonment may be imposed against the fiduciary, beginning with the appearance date, until the account, inventory, certificate of notice of probate of will, or report is filed with the court;

(6) If the fiduciary does not appear in the court on the specified appearance date, that the fiduciary is in contempt of the court for the failure to comply with the citation, and that one of the following may occur:

(a) The fiduciary shall be taken into custody by the sheriff or a deputy sheriff and brought before the court.

(b) The fiduciary shall appear before the court on a specified date or otherwise be taken into custody by the sheriff or a deputy sheriff and brought before the court.

(D) The assessments, fines, and other sanctions that the court may impose upon a fiduciary pursuant to this section may be imposed only upon a fiduciary and shall not be imposed upon the surety of any fiduciary.

(2001 H 85, eff. 10–31–01; 1989 S 46, eff. 1–1–90; 1953 H 1; GC 10506–35)

Historical and Statutory Notes

Pre–1953 H 1 Amendments: 121 v 270; 120 v 649; 114 v 371

Amendment Note: 2001 H 85 inserted "2107.19" in division (A) and "certificate of notice of probate of will," throughout the section.

Cross References

Veteran's guardian, failure to file account, 5905.12

Library References

Executors and Administrators ⚖460, 472, 473.
Guardian and Ward ⚖138, 145.
Mental Health ⚖293, 295.
Trusts ⚖291, 301.
Westlaw Topic Nos. 162, 196, 257A, 390.
C.J.S. Executors and Administrators §§ 786, 801.
C.J.S. Mental Health §§ 189, 191 to 193.
C.J.S. Trusts §§ 594 to 597.

Research References

Encyclopedias

OH Jur. 3d Decedents' Estates § 948, Notice When Seeking Release from Administration.
OH Jur. 3d Decedents' Estates § 1016, Notice of Admission to Probate.
OH Jur. 3d Decedents' Estates § 1670, Remedy When Executor or Administrator Neglects or Fails to File Accounts.
OH Jur. 3d Fiduciaries § 246, Citation to File Account.
OH Jur. 3d Fiduciaries § 258, Loss or Forfeiture of Right to Compensation—Statutory Grounds for Denial of Commission.

Treatises and Practice Aids

Carlin, Baldwin's Ohio Practice, Merrick-Rippner Probate Law § 2:13, Probating the Will—Notice of Admission of a Will to Probate.
Carlin, Baldwin's Ohio Practice, Merrick-Rippner Probate Law § 2:14, Probating the Will—Appeal—Will Contest.
Carlin, Baldwin's Ohio Practice, Merrick-Rippner Probate Law § 2:92, Fiduciary's Account—Time for Filing.
Carlin, Baldwin's Ohio Practice, Merrick-Rippner Probate Law § 38:2, Will Contests—Statutory Provisions.
Carlin, Baldwin's Ohio Practice, Merrick-Rippner Probate Law § 38:7, Will Contests—Commencement of Action; Limitation of Actions.
Carlin, Baldwin's Ohio Practice, Merrick-Rippner Probate Law § 54:4, Fiduciary Accounts—Contents—Certificate of Service.
Carlin, Baldwin's Ohio Practice, Merrick-Rippner Probate Law § 55:1, Fiduciary Misconduct—Deposit and Investment of Funds—Generally.
Carlin, Baldwin's Ohio Practice, Merrick-Rippner Probate Law § 57:4, Removal of Fiduciary—Grounds—Failure to File Inventory or Account.
Carlin, Baldwin's Ohio Practice, Merrick-Rippner Probate Law § 64:4, Powers and Duties of Guardian—Accounting.
Carlin, Baldwin's Ohio Practice, Merrick-Rippner Probate Law § 64:5, Powers and Duties of Guardian—Removal for Failure to File an Account or Inventory.
Carlin, Baldwin's Ohio Practice, Merrick-Rippner Probate Law § 79:4, Inventory—Enforcement of Filing.
Carlin, Baldwin's Ohio Practice, Merrick-Rippner Probate Law § 54:10, Fiduciary Accounts—Citation to File Account.
Carlin, Baldwin's Ohio Practice, Merrick-Rippner Probate Law § 54:46, Motion to Compel Fiduciary to File Account—Form.
Carlin, Baldwin's Ohio Practice, Merrick-Rippner Probate Law § 54:47, Order to Issue Citation—Form.
Carlin, Baldwin's Ohio Practice, Merrick-Rippner Probate Law § 54:48, Citation to File Account—Form.
Carlin, Baldwin's Ohio Practice, Merrick-Rippner Probate Law § 64:36, Motion to Require Guardian to File Account—Form.
Bogert - the Law of Trusts and Trustees § 702, Breach of Duty to Invest.
Bogert - the Law of Trusts and Trustees § 706, Breach of Duty by Failing to Use Reasonable Skill and Prudence in Investing, Retaining or Selling.
Bogert - the Law of Trusts and Trustees § 861, Remedies of the Beneficiary Against the Trustee.
Bogert - the Law of Trusts and Trustees § 980, Power of Court to Reduce or Deny Compensation.

Law Review and Journal Commentaries

House Bill 85, Probate Reform Bill 2001: A Noble Experiment. Marilyn J. Maag, 12 Prob L J Ohio 21 (November/December 2001).

Notes of Decisions

Compensation 2
Failure to account 3
Time bar 1

1. Time bar

The power of proceeding by citation or attachment against a fiduciary for neglecting to file an account is a necessary incident to the proper exercise of the jurisdiction of a probate court; such proceeding is barred by such lapse of time after the default of the fiduciary as would be sufficient to bar an action on the administration bond. Philips v. State (Ohio 1855) 5 Ohio St. 122, 64 Am.Dec. 635. Contempt ⇔ 30

While probate court had jurisdiction to bar attorney for estate from practicing in probate court due to his failure to file proper account, that court was required to specify in its order that counsel was only barred until the delinquent pleading was submitted and approved. In re Estate of Orville (Ohio App. 7 Dist., Mahoning, 12-03-2004) No. 04 MA 97, No. 04 MA 100, 2004-Ohio-6510, 2004 WL 2808392, Unreported. Attorney And Client ⇔ 36(2)

No limitation of time exists which will bar the issuing of a citation requiring a guardian to file an account of his trust. McClelland v. State (Ohio 1920) 101 Ohio St. 42, 127 N.E. 409, 17 Ohio Law Rep. 488. Guardian And Ward ⇔ 145; Limitation Of Actions ⇔ 102(2)

A suit on a bond and proceedings by citation are barred after ten years. Gilbert v. Marsh (Ohio Prob. 1897) 7 Ohio Dec. 230, 4 Ohio N.P. 338.

2. Compensation

While denial of estate attorney's future fees was reasonable sanction for his continued failure to file a proper account, disgorgement of earned and approved fees was not. In re Estate of Orville (Ohio App. 7 Dist., Mahoning, 12-03-2004) No. 04 MA 97, No. 04 MA 100, 2004-Ohio-6510, 2004 WL 2808392, Unreported. Executors And Administrators ⇔ 511(1)

Appropriate sanction for violations of local court rules by fiduciary of trusts and guardianship accounts by taking fees without prior court approval and by taking quarterly rather than annual fees was reduction of fees, not denial of all fees, since there was no malfeasance, fees were not excessive, and fiduciary reimbursed all quarterly fees taken plus ten percent interest. In re Testamentary Trust of Manning (Ohio App. 7 Dist., Mahoning, 09-26-2002) No. 99 CA 92, 2002-Ohio-5239, 2002 WL 31169522, Unreported. Trusts ⇔ 321

An administratrix may not be deprived of the compensation due to her for her services for mere delay in making and returning the inventory of the estate when she has not been given an order requiring her, at an early day therein named, to return same, or has not been notified by the court of the expiration of the time to file such inventory. In re Burchett's Estate (Marion 1968) 16 Ohio App.2d 45, 241 N.E.2d 787, 45 O.O.2d 133. Executors And Administrators ⇔ 500

Compensation could not be denied a guardian because of failure to file an account when verbally ordered to, where no citation was served upon him, but compensation could be denied on ground he had failed to account for moneys received and had mismanaged estate. In re Guardianship of O'Brien (Darke 1955) 140 N.E.2d 806, 74 Ohio Law Abs. 366.

3. Failure to account

Statute requiring fiduciary to be provided hearing, with at least ten days prior notice, before fiduciary may be removed did not apply to trial court's removal of administrator of estate for failure to timely file account of estate, although statutory definition of "fiduciary" included administrators; statute governing failure to file account provided authority for administrator's immediate removal. In re Estate of Phelps (Ohio App. 7 Dist., Jefferson, 02-21-2006) No. 05 JE 19, 2006-Ohio-890, 2006 WL 459265, Unreported, reconsideration overruled 2006-Ohio-1471, 2006 WL 772017. Executors And Administrators ⇔ 35(16)

Probate court complied with statutory procedures when it held attorney for estate in contempt for failing to file proper account, since it gave written notice to attorney that it was considering holding him in contempt on the grounds of a delinquent account, citations on delinquent account stated why he could be held in contempt, order containing notice was entered in the journal, and hearing was conducted. In re Estate of Orville (Ohio App. 7 Dist., Mahoning, 12-03-2004) No. 04 MA 97, No. 04 MA 100, 2004-Ohio-6510, 2004 WL 2808392, Unreported. Contempt ⇔ 61(1)

Citation procedure contained in statute governing contempt in delinquent account cases applied to attorney for estate, as well as estate's fiduciary. In re Estate of Orville (Ohio App. 7 Dist., Mahoning, 12-03-2004) No. 04 MA 97, No. 04 MA 100, 2004-Ohio-6510, 2004 WL 2808392, Unreported. Contempt ⇔ 55

There was sufficient evidence that former attorney of record for ward's guardianship failed to file accounting of estate, to support removal of attorney as counsel of record and denial of compensation; record indicated court had ordered counsel and original guardian to file accounting, that no accounting was ever filed, and attorney failed to provide sufficient evidence that it was original guardian's neglect and failure to cooperate that caused lack of accounting. In re Guardianship of Ferranti (Ohio App. 7 Dist., Mahoning, 10-17-2003) No. 02 CA 69, 2003-Ohio-5538, 2003 WL 22382568, Unreported. Guardian And Ward ⇔ 157

Failure of administrator for probate estate to turn over probate estate property to the probate estate was a failure to perform his duties as estate administrator and a failure to account for estate funds. In re Reed (Bkrtcy.S.D.Ohio 1993) 155 B.R. 169. Executors And Administrators ⇔ 117; Executors And Administrators ⇔ 467

Material issues of fact concerning nature of workers' compensation carriers' claim against bankrupt debtor precluded summary judgment on issue of whether debt arising from defalcation by debtor, as administrator of probate estate for deceased worker, fell within Bankruptcy Code exception to discharge for defalcation. In re Reed (Bkrtcy.S.D.Ohio 1993) 155 B.R. 169. Federal Civil Procedure ⇔ 2486

2109.32 Hearing on account; supplemental final account

(A) Every fiduciary's account required by section 2109.301, 2109.302, or 2109.303 of the Revised Code shall be set for hearing before the probate court. The hearing on the account shall be set not earlier than thirty days after the filing of the account.

At the hearing upon an account required by section 2109.302 or 2109.303 of the Revised Code and, if ordered by the court, upon an account required by section 2109.301 of the Revised Code, the court shall inquire into, consider, and determine all matters relative to the account and the manner in which the fiduciary has executed the fiduciary's trust, including the investment of trust funds, and may order the account approved and settled or make any other order as the court considers proper. If, at the hearing upon an account, the court finds that the fiduciary has fully and lawfully administered the estate or trust and has distributed the assets of the estate or trust in accordance with the law or the instrument governing distribution, as shown in the account, the court shall order the account approved and settled and may order the fiduciary discharged. Upon approval of a final and distributive account required by division (B)(1) of section 2109.301 of the Revised Code, the court may order the surety bond for the fiduciary terminated. Unless otherwise ordered by the court, the fiduciary shall be discharged without further order twelve months following the approval of the final and distributive account.

(B)(1) An administrator or executor filing an account pursuant to section 2109.301 of the Revised Code shall provide at the time of filing the account a copy of the account to each heir of an intestate estate or to each beneficiary of a testate estate. An administrator or executor is not required to provide a copy of the account to any of the following:

(a) An heir or a beneficiary whose residence is unknown;

(b) A beneficiary of a specific bequest or devise who has received his or her distribution and for which a receipt has been filed or exhibited with the court.

(2) An administrator or executor filing an account pursuant to section 2109.301 of the Revised Code shall file with the probate

court a certificate of service of account prior to or simultaneously with the filing of the account.

(3) The probate court shall not approve the final account of any executor or administrator until the following events have occurred:

(a) Three months have passed since the death of the decedent.

(b) The surviving spouse has filed an election to take under or against the will, or the time for making the election has expired.

(4) If an administrator or executor learns of the existence of newly discovered assets after the filing of the final account or otherwise comes into possession of assets belonging to the estate after the filing of the final account, the executor or administrator shall file a supplemental final account with respect to the disposition of the assets and shall provide a copy of the supplemental final account to each heir of an intestate estate or to each beneficiary of a testate estate, as provided in division (B)(1) of this section and subject to the exceptions specified in divisions (B)(1)(a) and (b) of this section.

(C) The rights of any person with a pecuniary interest in the estate are not barred by approval of an account pursuant to divisions (A) and (B) of this section. These rights may be barred following a hearing on the account pursuant to section 2109.33 of the Revised Code.

(2003 H 51, eff. 4–8–04; 2001 H 85, eff. 10–31–01; 1994 H 208, eff. 6–23–94; 1975 S 145, eff. 1–1–76; 125 v 903; 1953 H 1; GC 10506–36, 10506–39)

Uncodified Law

2004 H 161, § 3, eff. 4–8–04 reads, in part:

(A) Sections 2106.01, 2106.02, and 2109.32 of the Revised Code, as amended by Am. Sub. H.B. 51 of the 125th General Assembly, apply to estates that are in existence or are initiated on or after April 8, 2004.

Historical and Statutory Notes

Pre–1953 H 1 Amendments: 121 v 270; 120 v 649; 114 v 371, 372

Amendment Note: 2003 H 51 added new division (B)(2) and redesignated former divisions (B)(2) and (B)(3) as divisions (B)(3) and (B)(4), respectively.

Amendment Note: 2001 H 85 rewrote this section which prior thereto read:

Every fiduciary's account required by section 2109.30 of the Revised Code shall be set for hearing before the probate court. The hearing on the account shall be set not earlier than thirty days after the filing of the account.

At the hearing upon an account, the court shall inquire into, consider, and determine all matters relative to the account and the manner in which the fiduciary has executed his trust, including the investment of trust funds, and may order the account approved and settled or make any other order as the court considers proper. If, at the hearing upon an account, the court finds that the fiduciary has fully and lawfully administered the estate or trust and has distributed the assets of the estate or trust in accordance with the law or the instrument governing distribution, as shown in the account, the court shall order the account approved and settled and may order the fiduciary discharged.

The probate court shall not approve the final account of any executor or administrator until the following events have occurred:

(A) Three months have passed since the death of the decedent;

(B) The surviving spouse has filed an election to take under or against the will, or the time for making the election has expired."

Amendment Note: 1994 H 208 rewrote this section, which previously read:

"Every fiduciary's account required by section 2109.30 of the Revised Code shall be set for hearing before the probate court. Within one month after an account is filed, the court shall cause notice of the filing of the account and the time and place of the hearing thereon to be published once in some newspaper of general circulation in the county. The hearing on the account shall be set not earlier than thirty days after the publication of the notice. The costs of the notice, if more than one account is specified in the same notice, shall be paid in equal proportions by the fiduciaries.

"At the hearing upon an account, the court shall inquire into, consider, and determine all matters relative to the account and the manner in which the fiduciary has executed his trust, including the investment of trust funds, and may order the account approved and settled or make any other order as the court deems proper. If, at the hearing upon an account, the court finds that the fiduciary has fully and lawfully administered the estate or trust and has distributed the assets thereof in accordance with the law or the instrument governing distribution, as shown in the account, the court shall order the account approved and settled and may order the fiduciary discharged.

"The probate court shall not approve the final account of any executor or administrator until the following events have occurred:

"(A) Four months have passed since the appointment of the executor or administrator;

"(B) The surviving spouse has filed an election to take under or against the will, or the time for making the election has expired."

Legislative Service Commission

1975:

This section currently provides that every fiduciary's account that is filed under section 2109.30 be set for hearing. If the court finds that the fiduciary has fully and lawfully administered the estate or trust and has distributed the assets of the estate or trust properly as shown in the account, present law requires the court to order the account approved and settled and the probate court may order the fiduciary discharged.

The bill would prohibit the probate court from approving the final account of any executor or administrator until four months after appointment and until the time for the surviving spouse to elect to take against the will has expired.

Cross References

Conditional grants or devises of real estate, 5301.27
Newspaper of general circulation defined, 7.12
Veteran's guardian, annual account filed with the court, 5905.11

Library References

Executors and Administrators ⟸471, 473, 507(0.5).
Guardian and Ward ⟸145, 158.
Mental Health ⟸295, 302.
Trusts ⟸302, 326.
Westlaw Topic Nos. 162, 196, 257A, 390.
C.J.S. Executors and Administrators §§ 799 to 801, 855.
C.J.S. Mental Health §§ 189, 191 to 193, 196.
C.J.S. Trusts §§ 605, 635, 639.

Research References

Encyclopedias

OH Jur. 3d Decedents' Estates § 1668, Hearing on Account; Notice; Exceptions to Account.
OH Jur. 3d Decedents' Estates § 1671, Effect of Order Settling the Accounts; Reopening the Estate.
OH Jur. 3d Fiduciaries § 241, Final Accounting Upon Termination of Administration or Trust—Supplemental Account.
OH Jur. 3d Fiduciaries § 251, Copies of Account to Heirs and Beneficiaries.
OH Jur. 3d Fiduciaries § 255, Generally; Accrual Upon Accounting.
OH Jur. 3d Fiduciaries § 259, Jurisdiction of Probate Court.
OH Jur. 3d Fiduciaries § 270, Scope of Hearing.
OH Jur. 3d Fiduciaries § 272, Conduct of Hearing.
OH Jur. 3d Fiduciaries § 280, Conclusiveness of Partial Account.
OH Jur. 3d Fiduciaries § 284, Discharge of Fiduciary.
OH Jur. 3d Guardian & Ward § 172, by Guardian Who Receives Benefits from Veterans' Administration—Notice and Hearing.
OH Jur. 3d Records & Recording § 52, Instruments Transferring Interests in or Encumbering Land—Conditional Grants and Devises.

Treatises and Practice Aids

Carlin, Baldwin's Ohio Practice, Merrick-Rippner Probate Law § 2:92, Fiduciary's Account—Time for Filing.
Carlin, Baldwin's Ohio Practice, Merrick-Rippner Probate Law § 2:93, Fiduciary's Account—Contents.

Carlin, Baldwin's Ohio Practice, Merrick-Rippner Probate Law § 2:94, Fiduciary's Account—Hearing.

Carlin, Baldwin's Ohio Practice, Merrick-Rippner Probate Law § 2:95, Fiduciary's Account—Copy of Account to Interested Parties—Notice of Hearing; Exceptions to Account.

Carlin, Baldwin's Ohio Practice, Merrick-Rippner Probate Law § 2:96, Fiduciary's Account—Effect of Order Settling Account.

Carlin, Baldwin's Ohio Practice, Merrick-Rippner Probate Law § 2:98, Fiduciary's Account—Effect of Vacation; Supplemental Final Account.

Carlin, Baldwin's Ohio Practice, Merrick-Rippner Probate Law § 54:1, Fiduciary Accounts—Filing—Time.

Carlin, Baldwin's Ohio Practice, Merrick-Rippner Probate Law § 54:4, Fiduciary Accounts—Contents—Certificate of Service.

Carlin, Baldwin's Ohio Practice, Merrick-Rippner Probate Law § 79:8, Inventory—Newly Discovered Assets.

Carlin, Baldwin's Ohio Practice, Merrick-Rippner Probate Law § 2:121, Administration of Decedent's Estate—Checklist.

Carlin, Baldwin's Ohio Practice, Merrick-Rippner Probate Law § 54:11, Fiduciary Accounts—Hearing on Account—Notice of Hearing—Copy of Account.

Carlin, Baldwin's Ohio Practice, Merrick-Rippner Probate Law § 54:12, Fiduciary Accounts—Jurisdiction to Settle.

Carlin, Baldwin's Ohio Practice, Merrick-Rippner Probate Law § 54:13, Fiduciary Accounts—Approval of Final Account and Discharge of Fiduciary.

Carlin, Baldwin's Ohio Practice, Merrick-Rippner Probate Law § 54:14, Fiduciary Accounts—Notice of Hearing—Service.

Carlin, Baldwin's Ohio Practice, Merrick-Rippner Probate Law § 54:20, Fiduciary Accounts—Representation in Account Proceedings.

Carlin, Baldwin's Ohio Practice, Merrick-Rippner Probate Law § 54:22, Fiduciary Accounts—Effect of Order Settling Account.

Carlin, Baldwin's Ohio Practice, Merrick-Rippner Probate Law § 54:29, Fiduciary Accounts—Vacation on Motion Where Notice was Solely by Newspaper Publication.

Carlin, Baldwin's Ohio Practice, Merrick-Rippner Probate Law § 54:32, Fiduciary Accounts—Notice of Hearing to Vacate.

Carlin, Baldwin's Ohio Practice, Merrick-Rippner Probate Law § 54:43, Entry Approving and Settling Account—Form.

Carlin, Baldwin's Ohio Practice, Merrick-Rippner Probate Law § 79:46, Report of Newly Discovered Assets and Application for Order Requalifying Executor or Administrator—Form.

Carlin, Baldwin's Ohio Practice, Merrick-Rippner Probate Law § 79:47, Order Reopening Estate and Requalifying Executor or Administrator—Form.

Carlin, Baldwin's Ohio Practice, Merrick-Rippner Probate Law App B SPF 13.0, Fiduciary's Account.

Carlin, Baldwin's Ohio Practice, Merrick-Rippner Probate Law App B SPF 13.3, Entry Approving and Settling Account.

Carlin, Baldwin's Ohio Practice, Merrick-Rippner Probate Law App B SPF 13.9, Certificate of Service of Account to Heirs and Beneficiaries.

Kuehnle and Levey, Ohio Real Estate Law and Practice § 9:21, Conditional Grant and Devise Liens.

Law Review and Journal Commentaries

Practical Application of House Bill 85 (Probate Reform 2001), Marilyn J. Maag. 13 Prob L J Ohio 19 (November/December 2002).

Notes of Decisions

Ed. Note: This section contains annotations from former RC 2109.23.

Action on bond   2
Attorney fees   8
Constitutional issues   1
Exceptions to account   7
Jurisdiction   5
Liability of fiduciary   4
Procedural issues   6
Time limitation   3

---

1. Constitutional issues

Although notice of hearing on trustee's first account, which was published in newspaper, complied with notice requirements of statute governing hearings on accounts, statute's notice by publication provision did not satisfy due process standard that notice be reasonably calculated to reach interested parties, and, therefore, order approving account was void ab initio due to failure of notice. In re Estate of Cullen (Ohio App. 12 Dist., 02-18-1997) 118 Ohio App.3d 256, 692 N.E.2d 650, dismissed, appeal not allowed 79 Ohio St.3d 1417, 680 N.E.2d 155. Trusts ⚖ 302.1

2. Action on bond

A ward's right of action on a guardian's bond accrues when the guardian files his final account; the ward's delay in compelling the guardian to settle the account does not discharge sureties though the guardian becomes insolvent. Newton v. Hammond (Ohio 1882) 38 Ohio St. 430, 8 W.L.B. 241.

Where the amount due an estate of a decedent from the surety on the bond of a deceased fiduciary for certain delinquencies is not in dispute at the time a settlement is made with such surety, it is not necessary for the successor fiduciary to pay or tender back the amount received before pursuing any remedy available to him to recover from the surety for other and separate delinquencies. In re Gray's Estate (Ohio 1954) 162 Ohio St. 384, 123 N.E.2d 408, 55 O.O. 224. Compromise And Settlement ⚖ 18(3)

Where no reason appears of record it will be presumed that a new bond is not an additional bond. Pummill v. Baumgartner (Ohio Com.Pl. 1895) 4 Ohio Dec. 69, 3 Ohio N.P. 40.

Citation may be issued to the sureties on a guardian's bond in a case where the guardian is in default as to filing his account and a citation issued to him has been returned "not found." State v McClelland, 30 CC(NS) 522, 35 CD 422 (Tuscarawas 1919), affirmed by 101 OS 42, 127 NE 409 (1920), McClelland v State.

3. Time limitation

Thirty-day time period in which to appeal the probate court's orders granting motions to quash subpoenas, limiting the scope of depositions, and awarding attorney and executor fees began to run from the date the final account of the estate, rather than the supplemental final account of the estate, was filed, in proceeding challenging the distribution of the estate of decedent; supplemental account was filed three months after the final account was filed and approved. In re Estate of Caplan (Ohio App. 8 Dist., Cuyahoga, 03-18-2004) No. 82634, 2004-Ohio-1258, 2004 WL 536460, Unreported. Executors And Administrators ⚖ 314(12)

No limitation of time exists which will bar the issue of a citation requiring a guardian to file an account of his trust. McClelland v. State (Ohio 1920) 101 Ohio St. 42, 127 N.E. 409, 17 Ohio Law Rep. 488. Guardian And Ward ⚖ 145; Limitation Of Actions ⚖ 102(2)

A suit on a bond and proceedings by citation are barred after ten years. Gilbert v. Marsh (Ohio Prob. 1897) 7 Ohio Dec. 230, 4 Ohio N.P. 338.

4. Liability of fiduciary

A probate court has jurisdiction to find a sum due from the guardian to be larger than the remaining assets. Loudon v. Patterson (Ohio 1884) 41 Ohio St. 206.

Where guardian induces the ward to sign a receipt as though money had been paid, agreeing to be responsible for the amount with interest, the ward may maintain a suit against the guardian on such agreement without opening up the guardian's account. Lindsay v. Lindsay (Ohio 1875) 28 Ohio St. 157. Guardian And Ward ⚖ 163

Trustees acting within their authority and using ordinary prudence, care, and diligence, are not accountable for losses of trust funds arising from their management. Miller v. Proctor (Ohio 1870) 20 Ohio St. 442.

Where a guardian converts his ward's money into real estate and fully accounts for it to his ward, the land is not held by him as a trustee to the ward. Davies v. Lowrey (Ohio 1846) 15 Ohio 655.

A guardian is appointed to keep the ward's funds safe, and if he fails to invest them productively when he can do so, and fails to show by oath or otherwise his inability to do so, he will be charged with the interest. Armstrong v. Miller (Ohio 1833) 6 Ohio 118.

Under O Const Art IV, § 8 and GC 10501–53 (RC 2101.24) and 10506–39 (RC 2109.32), probate court has plenary power at law and in equity to hear, determine and finally dispose of all matters relative to manner in which guardian has executed his trust and to require such guardian to account not only for estate of his ward which came into the guardian's hands but for estate of his ward which should have come into his hands through exercise of reasonable diligence and that care which reasonable man would have used in conduct of his own affairs as well. Guardianship of Zimmerman (Ohio 1943) 141 Ohio St. 207, 47 N.E.2d 782, 25 O.O. 326. Guardian And Ward 144

For purposes of exception to discharge for defalcation while acting in fiduciary capacity, "defalcation" involves failure to account for money or property held in fiduciary capacity; it does not require showing of intentional wrongdoing, and defalcation may result from negligence or ignorance. In re Harris-Miles (Bkrtcy.N.D.Ohio, 09-12-1995) 187 B.R. 178. Bankruptcy 3376(5)

To establish the nondischargeability of a debt under the exception to discharge for a debtor's defalcation while acting in a fiduciary capacity, plaintiffs must show establishment of a trust, party in trust acting in fiduciary capacity, and breach of that relationship by at least "defalcation" of funds. In re Harris-Miles (Bkrtcy.N.D.Ohio, 09-12-1995) 187 B.R. 178. Bankruptcy 3376(5)

5. Jurisdiction

Jurisdiction of a probate court over the settlement of a guardian's account is exclusive; a suit in equity to compel an accounting cannot be maintained without showing that the powers and jurisdiction of the probate court are ineffectual to secure such accounting. Newton v. Hammond (Ohio 1882) 38 Ohio St. 430, 8 W.L.B. 241.

Where the notice required by RS 6402 is omitted, a court is without jurisdiction to fix the amount of compensation of an executor. Ballard v. Mack (Ohio Cir. 1905) 17 Ohio C.D. 839, 3 Ohio Law Rep. 249.

The probate court having appointed a guardian does not lose jurisdiction of such guardianship by his removal from the state. Netting v. Strickland (Ohio Cir. 1899) 9 Ohio C.D. 841.

Where plaintiff brings a cause of action in malpractice for money damages against the attorney-executor of decedent's estate, such action is properly brought in the common pleas court since the probate court lacks jurisdiction. Elden v Sylvania Savings Bank Co, No. L–83–211 (6th Dist Ct App, Lucas, 10–21–83).

6. Procedural issues

Where guardians are required to file an account every two years and do so and they are approved by the court, the settlement is final unless an appeal is taken. Woodmansie v. Woodmansie (Ohio 1876) 32 Ohio St. 18.

Under S. & C. 673, a guardian may appear for an infant defendant in an action for dower. Rankin v. Kemp (Ohio 1871) 21 Ohio St. 651.

Since trust beneficiaries' motion to vacate order approving second account was timely, beneficiaries were without standing to challenge notice provisions of statute governing hearings on accounts, as they related to second account. In re Estate of Cullen (Ohio App. 12 Dist., 02-18-1997) 118 Ohio App.3d 256, 692 N.E.2d 650, dismissed, appeal not allowed 79 Ohio St.3d 1417, 680 N.E.2d 155. Trusts 328

Successor guardian met all requirements of statute for vacating order settling fiduciary's account; successor had no actual knowledge of hearings on accounts because she did not subscribe to newspaper in which notice was published and filed her motions to vacate within three years after orders settling accounts were made. In re Guardianship of McPheter (Ohio App. 6 Dist., 08-05-1994) 95 Ohio App.3d 440, 642 N.E.2d 690. Mental Health 304

In a negligence action for the recovery of damages instituted under RC 2117.07 against an administrator seeking to recover only from the decedent's liability insurer, where the administrator of the estate of the decedent has been discharged and the estate closed, the probate court may reappoint the administrator for the purpose of accepting service of summons. In re George's Estate (Ohio 1970) 24 Ohio St.2d 18, 262 N.E.2d 872, 53 O.O.2d 10.

Where the final and distributive account of the administrators of an estate has been approved and settled and they have been discharged from their trust pursuant to RC 2109.32, and that order has not been vacated pursuant to RC 2109.35, where some asset remains upon which administration has not been exhausted and for some lawful purpose relating to that asset administration is required, an administrator may be appointed to complete such administration only in a manner similar to, and with the same formalities as, the original appointment of an administrator, and in such circumstances, where such asset consists of an automobile liability insurance policy of the decedent covering the claim of a person alleged to have received bodily injuries due to the alleged negligence of the decedent, such policy is an asset which will support the appointment of an administrator upon whom service may be made and with authority to defend suit. In re George's Estate (Hancock 1969) 20 Ohio App.2d 87, 252 N.E.2d 176, 49 O.O.2d 110. Executors And Administrators 37(2); Executors And Administrators 37(5)

Where a nominated trustee under a will undertakes and performs a duty ordinarily performed by the named executrix in the will, but which duty the named executrix fails and refuses to perform, such nominated trustee is entitled to reasonable compensation for the services rendered. In re Allison's Will (Clark 1965) 9 Ohio App.2d 333, 224 N.E.2d 386, 38 O.O.2d 388.

Approval of an executor's account is a final order. In re Norris (Monroe 1959) 169 N.E.2d 639, 84 Ohio Law Abs. 92. Executors And Administrators 510(2)

A reviewing court will not reverse a judgment of the probate court allowing compensation to trustee for a missing person and for legal services rendered unless the compensation is so excessive as to show an abuse of discretion. In re Parrett (Franklin 1949) 86 Ohio App. 162, 90 N.E.2d 425, 41 O.O. 20. Absentees 5

Trial court was not required to approve administrator's unopposed final account of estate; although court was authorized to order the final account approved and settled if the court found that the fiduciary had fully and lawfully administered the estate and had distributed the assets of the estate in accordance with decedent's will, court had expressed concerns about the final account rendered by appellant, specifically, the amount of attorney fees and administrator fees, the apportionment of estate taxes, possible underpayment to the surviving spouse and payments made to administrator's family members for "clean up and auction preparation." In re Estate of Hadorn (Ohio App. 5 Dist., Tuscarawas, 05-31-2002) No. 2001 AP 08 0080, 2002-Ohio-2848, 2002 WL 1232939, Unreported. Executors And Administrators 504(1)

Where the accounting required of a guardian by RC 2109.30 is impracticable or impossible, the probate court has plenary power under RC 2101.24 to substitute an alternative means of accounting such as a hearing upon statements offered in lien of a formal account; such a hearing, provided for by RC 2109.32, requires formal notice to all interested parties, so that an order closing a guardianship after a hearing held without notice to a ward must be reversed. In re Guardianship of Flesh, No. 84–CA–6 (2d Dist Ct App, Miami, 7–20–84).

7. Exceptions to account

Trustee for testators' inter vivos trusts had standing to file exceptions to executor's final accounts of assets of testators' estates, even though none of the trust beneficiaries objected to the final accounts, since all trust beneficiaries could not yet be ascertained, and thus there was no unanimous consent by beneficiaries to final accounts. In re Estate of Herrick (Ohio App. 8 Dist., Cuyahoga, 06-12-2003) No. 82057, 2003-Ohio-3025, 2003 WL 21361664, Unreported, on subsequent appeal 2005-Ohio-5201, 2005 WL 2401242. Executors And Administrators 504(2)

There are no provisions in section, or any other statute, specifically making the allowance of a claim against an estate the subject of exceptions to an account. In re Blue's Estate (Union 1939) 67 Ohio App. 37, 32 N.E.2d 499, 29 Ohio Law Abs. 161, 14 O.O. 447.

The probate court has power, upon a hearing of exceptions to the account of an executor, to find that he has been guilty of fraudulent conduct and to charge him in his account therefor. Reed v. Brown (Ohio Cir. 1894) 6 Ohio C.D. 15, 2 Ohio Dec. 29, affirmed 56 Ohio St. 264, 37 W.L.B. 324, 46 N.E. 982.

8. Attorney fees

In an action objecting to an executor's accounts, a surcharge against the executor for the objecting party's attorney fees is in essence an award of attorney fees against the losing party and is forbidden by the American rule, absent conduct that is obdurate, vexatious, wanton, or undertaken for oppressive reasons or bad faith; a surcharge for accountant's fees is similarly unfounded. Whitaker v. Estate of Whitaker (Ohio App. 4 Dist., 06-26-1995) 105 Ohio App.3d 46, 663 N.E.2d 681.

2109.33 Notice of hearing; exceptions to account

A fiduciary may serve notice of the hearing upon his account to be conducted under section 2109.32 of the Revised Code, or may cause the notice to be served, upon any person who is interested in the estate or trust. The probate court, after notice to the fiduciary upon the motion of any interested person for good cause shown or at its own instance, may order that a notice of the hearing is to be served upon persons the court designates.

The notice shall set forth the time and place of the hearing and shall specify the account to be considered and acted upon by the court at the hearing and the period of time covered by the account. It shall contain a statement to the effect that the person notified is required to examine the account, to inquire into the contents of the account and into all matters that may come before the court at the hearing on the account, and to file any exceptions that the person may have to the account at least five days prior to the hearing on the account, and that upon his failure to file exceptions, the account may be approved without further notice. If the person to be notified was not a party to the proceeding in which any prior account was settled, the notice, for the purpose of barring any rights possessed by that person, may include and specify the prior accounts and the periods of time covered by them. In that event, the notice shall inform the person notified that the approval of the account filed most recently will terminate any rights possessed by him to vacate the order settling each prior account so specified, except as provided in section 2109.35 of the Revised Code, and shall further inform the person that, under penalty of losing those rights, he forthwith shall examine each prior account so specified, shall inquire into its contents, and, if he deems it necessary to protect his rights, shall take the action with respect to his rights that is permitted by law.

The notice of the hearing upon an account shall be served at least fifteen days prior to the hearing on the account. Any competent person may waive service of notice and consent to the approval of any account by the court. Waivers of service and consents to approval shall be recorded with the account.

Any person interested in an estate or trust may file exceptions to an account or to matters pertaining to the execution of the trust. All exceptions shall be specific and written. Exceptions shall be filed and a copy of them furnished to the fiduciary by the exceptor, not less than five days prior to the hearing on the account. The court for cause may allow further time to file exceptions. If exceptions are filed to an account, the court may allow further time for serving notice of the hearing upon any person who may be affected by an order disposing of the exceptions and who has not already been served with notice of the hearing in accordance with this section.

A probate court, by local rule, may require that notice of the hearing on a final account be given to all heirs in an intestate estate and to all residuary beneficiaries in a testate estate.

Any notice that is required or permitted by this section or by any local rule adopted under authority of this section shall be served, and any waiver of the right to receive any notice of those types may be waived, in accordance with the Rules of Civil Procedure.

(1994 H 208, eff. 6–23–94; 1992 H 427, eff. 10–8–92; 1953 H 1; GC 10506–37, 10506–38)

Historical and Statutory Notes

Pre–1953 H 1 Amendments: 121 v 270; 120 v 649; 114 v 371, 372

Amendment Note: 1994 H 208 deleted "In addition to the notice required by section 2109.32 of the Revised Code," from the beginning of, inserted "to be conducted under section 2109.32 of the Revised Code" in, and substituted "a notice of the hearing" for "additional notice" in, the first paragraph; and added the final two paragraphs.

Cross References

Conditional grants or devises of real estate, 5301.27

Library References

Executors and Administrators ⚖471, 504.
Guardian and Ward ⚖145, 155.
Mental Health ⚖295, 300.
Trusts ⚖303, 324.
Westlaw Topic Nos. 162, 196, 257A, 390.
C.J.S. Executors and Administrators §§ 799, 848 to 855, 861 to 863.
C.J.S. Mental Health §§ 189, 191 to 194.
C.J.S. Trusts §§ 635, 638.

Research References

ALR Library
3 ALR 5th 590, What Constitutes Contest or Attempt to Defeat Will Within Provision Thereof Forfeiting Share of Contesting Beneficiary.

Encyclopedias
OH Jur. 3d Decedents' Estates § 1360, Application for Extra Compensation and Review.
OH Jur. 3d Decedents' Estates § 1668, Hearing on Account; Notice; Exceptions to Account.
OH Jur. 3d Decedents' Estates § 1671, Effect of Order Settling the Accounts; Reopening the Estate.
OH Jur. 3d Decedents' Estates § 1672, Effect of Order Settling the Accounts; Reopening the Estate—Effect of Vacating Order Settling an Account on the Rights of Purchaser, Lessee, or Encumbrancer for Value in Good Faith.
OH Jur. 3d Fiduciaries § 261, Notice.
OH Jur. 3d Fiduciaries § 262, Notice—Content.
OH Jur. 3d Fiduciaries § 263, Notice—Waiver of Service and Consent to Court Approval of Account.
OH Jur. 3d Fiduciaries § 265, Generally; Notice and Form.
OH Jur. 3d Fiduciaries § 266, Who May File.
OH Jur. 3d Fiduciaries § 267, Subject Matter.
OH Jur. 3d Records & Recording § 52, Instruments Transferring Interests in or Encumbering Land—Conditional Grants and Devises.

Treatises and Practice Aids
Klein, Darling, & Terez, Baldwin's Ohio Practice Civil Practice § 6:4, Time--Computation--Day of Act, Event, or Default Not Included.
Klein, Darling, & Terez, Baldwin's Ohio Practice Civil Practice § 6:6, Time--Computation--Intermediate Saturdays, Sundays, and Legal Holidays Not Included If Time Period Less Than Seven Days.
Carlin, Baldwin's Ohio Practice, Merrick-Rippner Probate Law § 2:94, Fiduciary's Account—Hearing.
Carlin, Baldwin's Ohio Practice, Merrick-Rippner Probate Law § 2:95, Fiduciary's Account—Copy of Account to Interested Parties—Notice of Hearing; Exceptions to Account.
Carlin, Baldwin's Ohio Practice, Merrick-Rippner Probate Law § 2:96, Fiduciary's Account—Effect of Order Settling Account.
Carlin, Baldwin's Ohio Practice, Merrick-Rippner Probate Law § 64:5, Powers and Duties of Guardian—Removal for Failure to File an Account or Inventory.
Carlin, Baldwin's Ohio Practice, Merrick-Rippner Probate Law § 64:7, Powers and Duties of Guardian—Ward's Person—Mandatory Duties.
Carlin, Baldwin's Ohio Practice, Merrick-Rippner Probate Law § 66:2, Termination—Discretionary—Court; Removal.
Carlin, Baldwin's Ohio Practice, Merrick-Rippner Probate Law § 74:1, Decedent's Property—Authorization to Sell.
Carlin, Baldwin's Ohio Practice, Merrick-Rippner Probate Law § 2:121, Administration of Decedent's Estate—Checklist.
Carlin, Baldwin's Ohio Practice, Merrick-Rippner Probate Law § 33:28, Account of Trustee—Form.
Carlin, Baldwin's Ohio Practice, Merrick-Rippner Probate Law § 54:11, Fiduciary Accounts—Hearing on Account—Notice of Hearing—Copy of Account.
Carlin, Baldwin's Ohio Practice, Merrick-Rippner Probate Law § 54:14, Fiduciary Accounts—Notice of Hearing—Service.
Carlin, Baldwin's Ohio Practice, Merrick-Rippner Probate Law § 54:15, Fiduciary Accounts—Notice—Contents.

Carlin, Baldwin's Ohio Practice, Merrick-Rippner Probate Law § 54:16, Fiduciary Accounts—Prior Accounts.

Carlin, Baldwin's Ohio Practice, Merrick-Rippner Probate Law § 54:17, Fiduciary Accounts—Waiver of Service of Notice and Consent to Approval of Account.

Carlin, Baldwin's Ohio Practice, Merrick-Rippner Probate Law § 54:18, Fiduciary Accounts—Exceptions.

Carlin, Baldwin's Ohio Practice, Merrick-Rippner Probate Law § 54:27, Fiduciary Accounts—Who is Deemed a Party.

Carlin, Baldwin's Ohio Practice, Merrick-Rippner Probate Law § 54:29, Fiduciary Accounts—Vacation on Motion Where Notice was Solely by Newspaper Publication.

Carlin, Baldwin's Ohio Practice, Merrick-Rippner Probate Law § 54:32, Fiduciary Accounts—Notice of Hearing to Vacate.

Carlin, Baldwin's Ohio Practice, Merrick-Rippner Probate Law § 54:34, Fiduciary Accounts—Effect of Vacation of Order.

Carlin, Baldwin's Ohio Practice, Merrick-Rippner Probate Law § 54:49, Waiver of Notice and Consent to Approval of Account—Form.

Carlin, Baldwin's Ohio Practice, Merrick-Rippner Probate Law § 54:50, Exceptions to Account—Form.

Carlin, Baldwin's Ohio Practice, Merrick-Rippner Probate Law § 54:51, Order Setting Exceptions for Hearing and Ordering Notice—Form.

Carlin, Baldwin's Ohio Practice, Merrick-Rippner Probate Law § 64:37, Account of Guardian—Form.

Carlin, Baldwin's Ohio Practice, Merrick-Rippner Probate Law § 65:32, Application for Appointment of Guardian Ad Litem, Approval and Finality of Accounts—Form.

Carlin, Baldwin's Ohio Practice, Merrick-Rippner Probate Law § 65:33, Order Appointing Guardian Ad Litem—Form.

Carlin, Baldwin's Ohio Practice, Merrick-Rippner Probate Law § 65:34, Answer of Guardian Ad Litem—Form.

Carlin, Baldwin's Ohio Practice, Merrick-Rippner Probate Law § 65:35, Entry Approving and Settling Account—Form.

Carlin, Baldwin's Ohio Practice, Merrick-Rippner Probate Law § 75:33, Receipt, Waiver, and Consent on Final Distribution—Form.

Carlin, Baldwin's Ohio Practice, Merrick-Rippner Probate Law App B SPF 13.0, Fiduciary's Account.

Carlin, Baldwin's Ohio Practice, Merrick-Rippner Probate Law App B SPF 13.5, Notice of Hearing on Account.

Carlin, Baldwin's Ohio Practice, Merrick-Rippner Probate Law App B SPF 13.7, Waiver of Notice of Hearing on Account.

Bogert - the Law of Trusts and Trustees § 181, Beneficiaries With Various Types of Interests.

Bogert - the Law of Trusts and Trustees § 869, Remedies Against Third Persons for Other Wrongs.

Bogert - the Law of Trusts and Trustees § 970, Parties and Procedure on Accounting.

Kuehnle and Levey, Ohio Real Estate Law and Practice § 9:21, Conditional Grant and Devise Liens.

Law Review and Journal Commentaries

Practical Application of House Bill 85 (Probate Reform 2001), Marilyn J. Maag. 13 Prob L J Ohio 19 (November/December 2002).

Probation Publication Eliminated, Hon. Fred V. Skok. 17 Lake Legal Views 9 (July 1994).

Notes of Decisions

Due process 5
Duties of court 2
Procedural issues 3
Specificity requirement 4
Standing 1

---

1. Standing

Trustee for testators' inter vivos trusts had standing to file exceptions to executor's final accounts of assets of testators' estates, even though none of the trust beneficiaries objected to the final accounts, since all trust beneficiaries could not yet be ascertained, and thus there was no unanimous consent by beneficiaries to final accounts. In re Estate of Herrick (Ohio App. 8 Dist., Cuyahoga, 06-12-2003) No. 82057, 2003-Ohio-3025, 2003 WL 21361664, Unreported, on subsequent appeal 2005-Ohio-5201, 2005 WL 2401242. Executors And Administrators ⇌ 504(2)

Granddaughter of decedent, who was beneficiary of inter vivos trust named as residual beneficiary of decedent's will, had a direct, proprietary interest in estate, and thus was "person interested" in estate who had standing to file exceptions to an account by decedent's daughter, who was executor of estate under decedent's will, even though granddaughter's interest in estate was equitable rather than legal. In re Estate of Boll (Ohio App. 4 Dist., 03-05-1998) 126 Ohio App.3d 507, 710 N.E.2d 1139. Executors And Administrators ⇌ 504(2)

A person who does not have a direct pecuniary interest in a ward's estate, although he is the ward's stepson, is not an "interested person" within the meaning of RC 2109.33 and as such has no standing to except to an accounting where the ward's will specifically excludes the "exceptor" from participation in her testamentary estate. In re Guardianship of Dougherty (Montgomery 1989) 63 Ohio App.3d 289, 578 N.E.2d 832, dismissed, jurisdictional motion overruled 45 Ohio St.3d 713, 545 N.E.2d 901.

The beneficiary of an inter vivos trust which will ultimately be funded primarily from the estates of two decedents is a proper party to file exceptions to the accounts rendered and fees paid in such probate estates. Ollick v. Rice (Cuyahoga 1984) 16 Ohio App.3d 448, 476 N.E.2d 1062, 16 O.B.R. 529.

An "interested person" within the contemplation of RC 2109.33 is one who has some direct, pecuniary interest in the devolution of the testator's estate, and a surviving spouse who has entered into an antenuptial agreement whereby she relinquishes all claims which she might or could have in or to her deceased husband's estate is not such an interested person. In re Matusoff's Estate (Montgomery 1965) 10 Ohio App.2d 113, 226 N.E.2d 140, 39 O.O.2d 187.

Where a guardian of an estate is appointed solely on the ground of the ward's physical incapacity, the ward's mental capacity is not impaired, and such appointment is made with the consent of the ward, a daughter of such ward may file exceptions to such guardian's account. In re Guardianship of Tillman (Darke 1955) 100 Ohio App. 291, 136 N.E.2d 291, 60 O.O. 254.

Bonding company, surety on bond of joint guardians as to whose accounts exceptions have been sustained and findings made that large sums of money were due from guardians to wards, is interested party under section, and bonding company may maintain appeal from findings although no judgment has yet been entered against it; overruling of its exceptions being final order as to it in that proceeding. In re Zimmerman's Guardianship (Lucas 1945) 78 Ohio App. 297, 70 N.E.2d 153, 34 O.O. 17. Guardian And Ward ⇌ 145; Guardian And Ward ⇌ 161

After the death of a ward and the probate of her will disposing of the entire estate, persons not named in the will are without standing to take exception to the fiduciary's accounting. In re Guardianship of Fulks, No. 82-J-33 (7th Dist Ct App, Jefferson, 4–27–84).

2. Duties of court

Where exceptions have been heard and determined by the court, they cannot be again questioned by the same parties on the hearing of a subsequent account without leave of court. In re Stayner (Ohio 1878) 33 Ohio St. 481.

Exceptions may be filed to an administrator's account and the probate judge is required to determine the questions thereby raised. In re Raab's Estate (Ohio 1865) 16 Ohio St. 273.

Probate court's error in failing to notify legatee who filed objections to the executor's final account that the court would rule on the final account at a final pretrial conference, after previously excepting the objections from consideration, was prejudicial to legatee, even though legatee did not attend the pretrial conference as required by the court, given that had legatee known that the court would rule on the final account and his objections thereto, he may well have decided to appear at the hearing. In re Estate of Osborne (Ohio App. 4 Dist., 04-17-2006) 166 Ohio App.3d 732, 853 N.E.2d 323, 2006-Ohio-1952. Pretrial Procedure ⇌ 742.1

Probate court abused its discretion by enlarging hearing without notice to encompass the court's own exceptions to guardian's application for fees, and by refusing to grant a continuance to allow the parties to subpoena witnesses. In re Guardianship of Lauder (Ohio App. 10 Dist., 11-12-2002) 150 Ohio App.3d 277, 780 N.E.2d 1025, 2002-Ohio-6102, entered nunc pro tunc 2003-Ohio-406, 2003 WL 194760. Mental Health ⇌ 233

Where specific written exceptions to a final account of an executor have been timely filed, it is within the power of the probate court to sustain such exceptions to the account and modify an allowance of fees made at a prior term of court, where such an allowance was made without notice to the interested party and no objections were made by such party at the time of the determination of the amount of fees. In re Alexander's Estate (Franklin 1957) 103 Ohio App. 514, 146 N.E.2d 315, 4 O.O.2d 19. Executors And Administrators ⇐ 501

It is the duty of the probate court to examine accounts filed in that court, and sua sponte or on request of an interested party make such orders as are proper and necessary to secure a faithful and correct administration of the trust. Jones v. Creamer (Ohio Cir. 1910) 22 Ohio C.D. 223, 13 Ohio C.C.(N.S.) 585, affirmed 87 Ohio St. 480, 102 N.E. 1126, 10 Ohio Law Rep. 480. Executors And Administrators ⇐ 507(1); Executors And Administrators ⇐ 508(1)

A probate court errs where it allocates the entire burden of paying extraordinary compensation and attorney fees granted pursuant to RC 2113.36 to only one of four devisees, despite the fact that the extraordinary expenses and attorney fees were incurred by the estate in responding to exceptions filed by the one devisee to whom the probate court allocates the burden. In re Estate of Wiehe, No. C–830419 (1st Dist Ct App, Hamilton, 5–9–84).

A court lacks jurisdiction to modify a custody decree issued by a sister court to create a guardianship, and errs in refusing to terminate it upon motion of the original custodian, despite her earlier consent to the guardianship. Fraley v Perigo, No. CA83–09–033 (12th Dist Ct App, Madison, 4–30–84).

3. Procedural issues

Where a debtor of a decedent is appointed administrator, the debt becomes assets and on an exception that he has failed to charge himself therewith the court may hear evidence and determine the validity of the claim. In re Raab's Estate (Ohio 1865) 16 Ohio St. 273.

Surviving spouse's direct, pecuniary interest in decedent's estate made her an "interested person" who was required to adhere to statutory procedures for filing an exception to final accounting of estate; wife failed to set forth specific, written exceptions to final accounting and to comply with statute's five-day notice requirement, but was allowed to present evidence on her claim that she was entitled to be reimbursed for property taxes she paid on properties that belonged to herself and decedent jointly, as well as properties owned solely by decedent. In re Estate of Eyajan (Ohio App. 11 Dist., Ashtabula, 01-28-2005) No. 2002-A-0041, 2005-Ohio-351, 2005 WL 238146, Unreported, appeal not allowed 106 Ohio St.3d 1415, 830 N.E.2d 347, 2005-Ohio-3154. Executors And Administrators ⇐ 504(5)

Son failed to specifically challenge, during probate proceedings, rental value of deceased mother's property and failed to specifically file an exception to the account concerning rent, and thus son waived challenge to his liability to mother's estate for $9,000 in rent for son's occupancy of mother's home from time of her death to time son was removed from home. In re Estate of Endslow (Ohio App. 5 Dist., Delaware, 07-22-2003) No. 03-CAF-01001, 2003-Ohio-3916, 2003 WL 21694010, Unreported. Executors And Administrators ⇐ 510(4)

To properly challenge guardian's administration of ward's estate, nursing home was required to file exceptions to guardian's final account. Guardianship of Skrzyniecki (Ohio App. 6 Dist., 01-31-1997) 118 Ohio App.3d 67, 691 N.E.2d 1105. Mental Health ⇐ 300

Successor guardian met all requirements of statute for vacating order settling fiduciary's account; successor had no actual knowledge of hearings on accounts because she did not subscribe to newspaper in which notice was published and filed her motions to vacate within three years after orders settling accounts were made. In re Guardianship of McPheter (Ohio App. 6 Dist., 08-05-1994) 95 Ohio App.3d 440, 642 N.E.2d 690. Mental Health ⇐ 304

An order of the probate court which requires payment of attorney fees by an executor prior to the settlement of such fees in an account, where all interested parties are not bound by the order, is of doubtful validity, and an appeal by the executor from such an order will not be dismissed on preliminary motion but will be held for determination on the merits. (See also In re Estate of Verbeck, 173 OS 557, 184 NE(2d) 384 (1962).) In re Verbeck's Estate (Franklin 1961) 114 Ohio App. 155, 180 N.E.2d 615, 18 O.O.2d 465.

An executor has no right of appeal from an order of the probate court fixing the amount of attorney fees, on the ground that the amount of the fees fixed is excessive. (See also In re Estate of Verbeck, 173 OS 557, 184 NE(2d) 384 (1962).) In re Verbeck's Estate (Franklin 1961) 114 Ohio App. 155, 180 N.E.2d 615, 18 O.O.2d 465. Executors And Administrators ⇐ 256(3)

Where an heir seeks a citation against the administrator and another heir for withholding a portion of her distributive share of an estate in which a final account has been filed, and charges that her receipt for her share is a forgery, she must first have the order settling the final account vacated. In re Reitler's Estate (Ohio Prob. 1956) 137 N.E.2d 791, 73 Ohio Law Abs. 328.

Where testator devised property in trust to wife as trustee and as income beneficiary with right to use so much of principal as would bring yearly income up to $2,500 and with power of appointment as to principal and wife exercised power of appointment in her will by devising principal to named beneficiaries, but did not during her life file an account as required by statute, she did not in her discretion use principal of trust account for trust principal. In re Post's Will (Ashtabula 1949) 91 N.E.2d 698, 56 Ohio Law Abs. 240. Trusts ⇐ 304

Where statutory provisions as to notice of hearing on administrator's final account were strictly complied with and persons filing exceptions to account were not shown to have been without actual notice of filing of account and time set for hearing, filing of such exceptions within eight months after settlement of account was too late. In re Kopczynski's Estate (Cuyahoga 1942) 49 N.E.2d 960, 38 Ohio Law Abs. 306. Executors And Administrators ⇐ 504(3)

In computing the five-day period within which exceptions to a final account must be filed, Saturdays and Sundays are not to be included. In re Estate of Wanska, No. 12–221 (11th Dist Ct App, Lake, 7–29–88).

Where beneficiaries of a will file an action against the executor alleging conflict of interest and breach of fiduciary duty, concealment and embezzlement of assets, and an exception to inventory, the beneficiaries have not violated the provisions of a no contest clause. Estate of Riber v Peters, Nos. 81–CA–27 and 81–CA–28 (12th Dist Ct App, Fayette, 10–27–82).

4. Specificity requirement

Exceptions to fiduciary's account were sufficiently specific as to handling of estate by executrix, in that purchase of certain real estate was incorrectly listed, and note and mortgage were erroneously listed as a deduction as were certain equipment purchases, conveyance taxes, recording costs, real estate taxes and survey costs, all of which affected the share distributions. In re Mizer (Ohio App. 5 Dist., Tuscarawas, 02-24-2005) No. 2004 AP 04 0035, 2005-Ohio-862, 2005 WL 469268, Unreported. Executors And Administrators ⇐ 504(5)

Successor administrator's exceptions to former administrator's account of estate were sufficiently specific to satisfy statutory requirement, where successor administrator demanded that former administrator produce evidence that excepted disbursements were debts of the decedent properly payable by the estate, alleged that eight classifications of items, consisting mostly of various coins and silverplated flatware, should have been included in the estate, averred that the distributions to former administrator exceeded amount to which he was entitled to under the will, disputed former administrator's $23,567.67 claim against the estate and disbursement of any fiduciary fee or commission. Talbott v. Fisk (Ohio App. 10 Dist., Franklin, 12-17-2002) No. 02AP-427, No. 02AP-428, 2002-Ohio-6960, 2002 WL 31819671, Unreported. Executors And Administrators ⇐ 504(5)

5. Due process

Failure of decedent's daughter to file timely exceptions to inventory did not waive arguments as to later account; daughter was not given opportunity to timely file exceptions to inventory, since her first notice was not received until after scheduled hearing date, daughter was then never successfully served with continued inventory hearing notice, which would have extended her time for filing exceptions, and there was no indication that daughter was served with first partial account or given notice of hearing on account, and without being aware that account was filed, she could not be expected to file timely exceptions. In re Estate of Reinhart (Ohio App. 7 Dist., Mahoning, 09-13-2005) No. 05 MA 36, 2005-Ohio-4894, 2005 WL 2267397, Unreported. Executors And Administrators ⇐ 504(4)

Attorney's due process rights were violated by the Probate Court's actions in guardianship case, and thus reversal and remand of the case was required; Probate Court acted as an investigator and presented facts and acted as the adjudicator and determined whether the facts were sufficient, the court enlarged the hearing to review claims that attorney breached his fiduciary duty, had conflicts of interest, and committed fraud and self-dealing without notice to the parties, and the court failed to file exceptions on attorney. In re Guardianship of Lauder (Ohio App. 10 Dist., Franklin, 01-30-2003) No. 01AP-1180, No. 01AP-1181, No. 01AP-1182, 2003-Ohio-

406, 2003 WL 194760, Unreported. Constitutional Law ⬅ 255(5); Mental Health ⬅ 302

2109.34 Representation in account proceeding

If an interest in an estate or trust is or may be possessed by persons who will compose a certain class upon the happening of any future event, the unborn members of such class shall be deemed to be represented in any hearing upon a fiduciary's account required by section 2109.32 of the Revised Code, if any living member of the class is made a party to such proceeding or if a trustee for the proceeding is appointed by the probate court. The unborn members of such class need not be served by publication. An order made in such proceeding shall be binding upon all members of such class, except that such order may be vacated for fraud as provided in section 2109.35 of the Revised Code.

If the beneficiaries, both present and future, of a charitable trust are not represented by a trustee or an existing corporation or other organization they shall be represented in any such proceeding by the attorney general if he is made a party thereto. Any order made in the proceeding shall be binding upon such beneficiaries, except for fraud.

(125 v 903, eff. 10–1–53; 1953 H 1; GC 10506–38a)

Historical and Statutory Notes

Pre–1953 H 1 Amendments: 121 v 270

Cross References

Service of process on charitable trust, 109.25

Library References

Executors and Administrators ⬅471.
Trusts ⬅299.1, 302.1.
Westlaw Topic Nos. 162, 390.
C.J.S. Executors and Administrators § 799.
C.J.S. Trusts § 635.

Research References

Encyclopedias

OH Jur. 3d Decedents' Estates § 1671, Effect of Order Settling the Accounts; Reopening the Estate.
OH Jur. 3d Fiduciaries § 264, Parties; Persons Deemed Represented.
OH Jur. 3d State of Ohio § 163, Investigation of Trusts.

Treatises and Practice Aids

Carlin, Baldwin's Ohio Practice, Merrick-Rippner Probate Law § 54:20, Fiduciary Accounts—Representation in Account Proceedings.
Carlin, Baldwin's Ohio Practice, Merrick-Rippner Probate Law § 54:21, Fiduciary Accounts—Charitable Trust Representation.
Carlin, Baldwin's Ohio Practice, Merrick-Rippner Probate Law § 54:27, Fiduciary Accounts—Who is Deemed a Party.
Bogert - the Law of Trusts and Trustees § 871, Procedure—Parties—Costs and Fees.
Bogert - the Law of Trusts and Trustees § 970, Parties and Procedure on Accounting.

2109.35 Effect of order settling account; vacation of order

The order of the probate court upon the settlement of a fiduciary's account shall have the effect of a judgment and may be vacated only as follows:

(A) The order may be vacated for fraud, upon motion of any person affected by the order or upon the court's own order, if the motion is filed or order is made within one year after discovery of the existence of the fraud. Any person who is subject to any legal disability may file the motion at any time within one year after the removal of the legal disability or within one year after he discovers the existence of the fraud, whichever is later, or his guardian or a successor guardian may do so during the period of the legal disability. If the death of any person occurs during the period within which he could have filed the motion, his administrator or executor may file it within one year after the person's death.

(B) The order may be vacated for good cause shown, other than fraud, upon motion of any person affected by the order who was not a party to the proceeding in which the order was made and who had no knowledge of the proceeding in time to appear in it; provided that, if the account settled by the order is included and specified in the notice to that person of the proceeding in which a subsequent account is settled, the right of that person to vacate the order shall terminate upon the settlement of the subsequent account. A person affected by an order settling an account shall be deemed to have been a party to the proceeding in which the order was made if that person was served with notice of the hearing on the account in accordance with section 2109.33 of the Revised Code, waived that notice, consented to the approval of the account, filed exceptions to the account, or is bound by section 2109.34 of the Revised Code; but no person in being who is under legal disability at the time of that proceeding shall be deemed to have been a party to that proceeding unless he was represented in it as provided in section 2111.23 of the Revised Code. Neither the fiduciary nor his surety shall incur any liability as a result of the vacation of an order settling an account in accordance with this division, if the motion to vacate the order is filed more than three years following the settlement of the fiduciary's account showing complete distribution of assets; but the three-year period shall not affect the liability of any heir, devisee, or distributee either before or after the expiration of that period.

(C) The order may be vacated for good cause shown upon motion of the fiduciary, if the motion is filed prior to the settlement of the account showing that the fiduciary has fully discharged his trust.

A motion to vacate an order settling an account shall set forth the items of the account with respect to which complaint is made and the reasons for complaining of those items. The person filing a motion to vacate an order settling an account or another person the court may designate shall cause notice of the hearing on the motion to be served upon all interested parties who may be adversely affected by an order of the court granting the motion.

An order settling an account shall not be vacated unless the court determines that there is good cause for doing so, and the burden of proving good cause shall be upon the complaining party.

The vacation of an order settling an account, made after notice given in the manner provided in section 2109.33 of the Revised Code, shall not affect the rights of a purchaser for value in good faith, a lessee for value in good faith, or an encumbrancer for value in good faith; provided that, if the fiduciary has effected any such sale, lease, or encumbrance, any person prejudiced by it may proceed, after vacation of the order, against any distributee benefiting from the sale, lease, or encumbrance to the extent of the amount received by that distributee on distribution of the estate or trust, or if any heir, devisee, or distributee has effected any such sale, lease, or encumbrance, any person prejudiced by it may proceed, after the vacation of the order, against that heir, devisee, or distributee, to the extent of the value at the time of alienation of the property aliened by him, with legal interest.

(1994 H 208, eff. 6–23–94; 1992 H 427, eff. 10–8–92; 125 v 903; 1953 H 1; GC 10506–40)

Historical and Statutory Notes

Pre–1953 H 1 Amendments: 121 v 270; 120 v 649; 114 v 372

Amendment Note: 1994 H 208 deleted former division (C); redesignated former division (D) as division (C); and deleted a reference to section 2109.32 in the final paragraph. Prior to amendment, division (C) read:

"(C) The order may be vacated for good cause shown, other than fraud, upon motion of any person affected by the order who was a party to the proceeding in which the order was made solely by reason of his having been served by publication in a newspaper in accordance with section 2109.33 of the Revised Code, if the motion is filed within one year after that person acquires knowledge of the proceeding and, in any event, within three years after the order is made. The person shall establish to the satisfaction of the court that he had no knowledge of the proceeding in time to appear in it."

Cross References

Executor or administrator not liable, 2113.56

Library References

Executors and Administrators ⊂⊃516(7).
Guardian and Ward ⊂⊃165.
Mental Health ⊂⊃304.
Trusts ⊂⊃333.
Westlaw Topic Nos. 162, 196, 257A, 390.
C.J.S. Executors and Administrators §§ 872, 880.
C.J.S. Trusts §§ 642 to 644.

Research References

Encyclopedias

OH Jur. 3d Decedents' Estates § 1653, Liability of Representative, Generally.
OH Jur. 3d Decedents' Estates § 1668, Hearing on Account; Notice; Exceptions to Account.
OH Jur. 3d Decedents' Estates § 1671, Effect of Order Settling the Accounts; Reopening the Estate.
OH Jur. 3d Decedents' Estates § 1672, Effect of Order Settling the Accounts; Reopening the Estate—Effect of Vacating Order Settling an Account on the Rights of Purchaser, Lessee, or Encumbrancer for Value in Good Faith.
OH Jur. 3d Fiduciaries § 285, Generally, Jurisdiction.
OH Jur. 3d Fiduciaries § 286, Vacation on Grounds of Fraud.
OH Jur. 3d Fiduciaries § 287, Vacation on Grounds of Fraud—Good Cause Other Than Fraud.
OH Jur. 3d Fiduciaries § 288, Effect.
OH Jur. 3d Fiduciaries § 289, Persons Who May Commence Proceedings.
OH Jur. 3d Fiduciaries § 290, Time Limitations.
OH Jur. 3d Fiduciaries § 291, Content of Motion.
OH Jur. 3d Fiduciaries § 292, Notice and Hearing.
OH Jur. 3d Guardian & Ward § 224, Action Based on Final Accounting.

Treatises and Practice Aids

Carlin, Baldwin's Ohio Practice, Merrick-Rippner Probate Law § 3:9, Jurisdiction of Probate Court—Subject Matter—Specific Areas—Exhaustion of Jurisdiction—Estate Closed.
Carlin, Baldwin's Ohio Practice, Merrick-Rippner Probate Law § 2:83, Ohio Estate Tax—Determination of Tax Liability—Role of the Tax Commissioner.
Carlin, Baldwin's Ohio Practice, Merrick-Rippner Probate Law § 2:95, Fiduciary's Account—Copy of Account to Interested Parties—Notice of Hearing; Exceptions to Account.
Carlin, Baldwin's Ohio Practice, Merrick-Rippner Probate Law § 2:96, Fiduciary's Account—Effect of Order Settling Account.
Carlin, Baldwin's Ohio Practice, Merrick-Rippner Probate Law § 2:97, Fiduciary's Account—Motion to Vacate.
Carlin, Baldwin's Ohio Practice, Merrick-Rippner Probate Law § 2:98, Fiduciary's Account—Effect of Vacation; Supplemental Final Account.
Carlin, Baldwin's Ohio Practice, Merrick-Rippner Probate Law § 3:13, Jurisdiction of Probate Court—Scope—Exclusive and Concurrent Jurisdiction.
Carlin, Baldwin's Ohio Practice, Merrick-Rippner Probate Law § 64:5, Powers and Duties of Guardian—Removal for Failure to File an Account or Inventory.
Carlin, Baldwin's Ohio Practice, Merrick-Rippner Probate Law § 64:7, Powers and Duties of Guardian—Ward's Person—Mandatory Duties.
Carlin, Baldwin's Ohio Practice, Merrick-Rippner Probate Law § 66:2, Termination—Discretionary—Court; Removal.
Carlin, Baldwin's Ohio Practice, Merrick-Rippner Probate Law § 2:121, Administration of Decedent's Estate—Checklist.
Carlin, Baldwin's Ohio Practice, Merrick-Rippner Probate Law § 54:11, Fiduciary Accounts—Hearing on Account—Notice of Hearing—Copy of Account.
Carlin, Baldwin's Ohio Practice, Merrick-Rippner Probate Law § 54:12, Fiduciary Accounts—Jurisdiction to Settle.
Carlin, Baldwin's Ohio Practice, Merrick-Rippner Probate Law § 54:14, Fiduciary Accounts—Notice of Hearing—Service.
Carlin, Baldwin's Ohio Practice, Merrick-Rippner Probate Law § 54:16, Fiduciary Accounts—Prior Accounts.
Carlin, Baldwin's Ohio Practice, Merrick-Rippner Probate Law § 54:18, Fiduciary Accounts—Exceptions.
Carlin, Baldwin's Ohio Practice, Merrick-Rippner Probate Law § 54:20, Fiduciary Accounts—Representation in Account Proceedings.
Carlin, Baldwin's Ohio Practice, Merrick-Rippner Probate Law § 54:22, Fiduciary Accounts—Effect of Order Settling Account.
Carlin, Baldwin's Ohio Practice, Merrick-Rippner Probate Law § 54:23, Fiduciary Accounts—Vacation of Order of Settlement of Account for Fraud.
Carlin, Baldwin's Ohio Practice, Merrick-Rippner Probate Law § 54:24, Fiduciary Accounts—Person Under Legal Disability.
Carlin, Baldwin's Ohio Practice, Merrick-Rippner Probate Law § 54:25, Fiduciary Accounts—Death of Party.
Carlin, Baldwin's Ohio Practice, Merrick-Rippner Probate Law § 54:26, Fiduciary Accounts—Vacation for Good Cause on Motion of Person Not Party to Proceeding.
Carlin, Baldwin's Ohio Practice, Merrick-Rippner Probate Law § 54:27, Fiduciary Accounts—Who is Deemed a Party.
Carlin, Baldwin's Ohio Practice, Merrick-Rippner Probate Law § 54:28, Fiduciary Accounts—Liability of Fiduciary and Surety.
Carlin, Baldwin's Ohio Practice, Merrick-Rippner Probate Law § 54:29, Fiduciary Accounts—Vacation on Motion Where Notice was Solely by Newspaper Publication.
Carlin, Baldwin's Ohio Practice, Merrick-Rippner Probate Law § 54:30, Fiduciary Accounts—Vacation Upon Motion of Fiduciary.
Carlin, Baldwin's Ohio Practice, Merrick-Rippner Probate Law § 54:31, Fiduciary Accounts—Contents of Motion to Vacate.
Carlin, Baldwin's Ohio Practice, Merrick-Rippner Probate Law § 54:32, Fiduciary Accounts—Notice of Hearing to Vacate.
Carlin, Baldwin's Ohio Practice, Merrick-Rippner Probate Law § 54:33, Fiduciary Accounts—Burden of Proving Good Cause.
Carlin, Baldwin's Ohio Practice, Merrick-Rippner Probate Law § 54:34, Fiduciary Accounts—Effect of Vacation of Order.
Carlin, Baldwin's Ohio Practice, Merrick-Rippner Probate Law § 54:52, Motion to Vacate Order Approving Account—Form.
Carlin, Baldwin's Ohio Practice, Merrick-Rippner Probate Law § 75:19, Distribution—Remainderman's Interest—Without Security.
Carlin, Baldwin's Ohio Practice, Merrick-Rippner Probate Law § 109:49, Ohio Estate Tax—Correctness of Items on Return.
Bogert - the Law of Trusts and Trustees § 974, Effect of Account—When Opened up.

Notes of Decisions

Accounting 3
Final account 7
Foreign executor 11
Fraud 4
Insurance policy 8
Parties 10
Release or recovery from surety 2
Rights of surviving spouse 5
Settlement proceedings 6
Time requirements 9

Vacating court order 1

1. Vacating court order

Judgments and orders of a probate court including the approval of partial and final accounts of guardians import absolute verity between the parties and cannot be questioned collaterally. Eichelberger v. Gross (Ohio 1885) 42 Ohio St. 549, 13 W.L.B. 282.

Executor's failure to provide corroborating evidence of will beneficiary's debt to estate justified a grant of beneficiary's motion to vacate probate order, approving inventory that included a debt owed by beneficiary; beneficiary averred that she never borrowed money from decedent and never signed any loan agreement, executor provided no evidence of existence of loan, motion was filed within one-year limitations provision, and fairness required that executor provide corroborating documents to justify debt. Estate of Heffner v. Cornwall (Ohio App. 3 Dist., Mercer, 11-24-2003) No. 10-03-06, 2003-Ohio-6318, 2003 WL 22787613, Unreported. Executors And Administrators ⇐ 69

Good cause existed to vacate order approving trustee's second account, where probate court was not advised of pending suit brought by beneficiaries against trustee, and account demonstrated that funds which facially should have remained in the trust were transferred to the settlor's estate. In re Estate of Cullen (Ohio App. 12 Dist., 02-18-1997) 118 Ohio App.3d 256, 692 N.E.2d 650, dismissed, appeal not allowed 79 Ohio St.3d 1417, 680 N.E.2d 155. Trusts ⇐ 328

Statute providing that trial court may vacate estate settlement order if various conditions are met does not require court to vacate such order, even if all of statutory requirements have been satisfied. In re Estate of Keeler (Ohio App. 10 Dist., 06-13-1996) 111 Ohio App.3d 657, 676 N.E.2d 1220. Executors And Administrators ⇐ 509(.5)

Good cause exists to vacate estate settlement order if probate court approves final and distributive account without knowledge of existing claim, if there is mistake or error by probate court, or if there is mistake in proceeding of court of record in matters of law or fact. In re Estate of Keeler (Ohio App. 10 Dist., 06-13-1996) 111 Ohio App.3d 657, 676 N.E.2d 1220. Executors And Administrators ⇐ 509(4)

Trial court could not vacate estate settlement order pursuant to motion of Department of Taxation without first determining that Department had satisfied statutory requirement to file motion to vacate within one year after Department acquired actual knowledge of settlement proceeding. In re Estate of Keeler (Ohio App. 10 Dist., 06-13-1996) 111 Ohio App.3d 657, 676 N.E.2d 1220. Executors And Administrators ⇐ 509(5)

Successor guardian met all requirements of statute for vacating order settling fiduciary's account; successor had no actual knowledge of hearings on accounts because she did not subscribe to newspaper in which notice was published and filed her motions to vacate within three years after orders settling accounts were made. In re Guardianship of McPheter (Ohio App. 6 Dist., 08-05-1994) 95 Ohio App.3d 440, 642 N.E.2d 690. Mental Health ⇐ 304

There is "good cause," within the meaning of RC 2109.35, to vacate a settlement order giving approval of a final and distributive account where approval was given under a mistake of fact (without knowledge of a pending tort claim), as long as the other requirements of RC 2109.35(C) are met by the party seeking the vacation. Mathe v. Fowler (Lake 1983) 13 Ohio App.3d 273, 469 N.E.2d 89, 13 O.B.R. 337.

Account previously settled is not opened by declaratory judgment proceeding which calls into question certain decisions made by executor in allocating expenses between principal and income. Third Nat. Bank & Trust Co. of Dayton v. Gardner (Ohio Com.Pl. 1970) 24 Ohio Misc. 223, 262 N.E.2d 430, 53 O.O.2d 261, 53 O.O.2d 290.

Where a contingent claim against an estate accrues after complete distribution of the assets, the claimant's remedy for any deficiency is an action against the distributee, rather than seeking to vacate the order of final distribution and compelling the distributee to return the assets to the executor. In re Robbins' Estate (Ohio Prob. 1964) 200 N.E.2d 735, 94 Ohio Law Abs. 561, 28 O.O.2d 399.

Evidence established right of beneficiary under will to have orders approving accounts of executor vacated on ground that service of notice upon beneficiary was by publication and that she had no actual notice of proceedings. In re Bentley's Estate (Cuyahoga 1951) 116 N.E.2d 738, 66 Ohio Law Abs. 363, reversed 163 Ohio St. 568, 127 N.E.2d 749, 57 O.O. 5. Executors And Administrators ⇐ 509(8)

The account of an administrator, although no exceptions are filed, is not by RS 6187 conclusive. Lambright v. Lambright (Ohio 1906) 74 Ohio St. 198, 78 N.E. 265, 4 Ohio Law Rep. 38, 6 Am.Ann.Cas. 807.

The finding and judgment of a probate court as to the amount of indebtedness of a deceased executor to the estate of the testator is conclusive until reversed. Jones v. Willis (Ohio 1905) 72 Ohio St. 189, 74 N.E. 166, 2 Ohio Law Rep. 529.

The settlement of the final account of an executor or administrator showing the payment of money to a person not entitled thereto is no bar to a subsequent action against him for the recovery of the money by one who is legally entitled to the same. Banning v. Gotshall (Ohio 1900) 62 Ohio St. 210, 43 W.L.B. 315, 56 N.E. 1030. Executors And Administrators ⇐ 513(9); Judgment ⇐ 688

The rule that probate court findings cannot be attacked collaterally, except for fraud, applies to approval of accounts. Woodward v. Curtis (Ohio Cir. 1899) 10 Ohio C.D. 400.

An account containing items of credit to an administrator for commission, extra services, and attorney fees, after being duly allowed cannot be reopened on the filing of a second account. Campbell v. McCormick (Ohio Cir. 1886) 1 Ohio C.D. 281.

RS 6187, authorizing and regulating the opening of the accounts of executors and administrators, is remedial, and should receive a reasonable construction so as to suppress the mischief and advance the remedy. In re Exceptions of Accounts of Leidigh (Ohio Com.Pl. 1902) 15 Ohio Dec. 193.

Where the assets of an estate have been distributed in accordance with the terms of a will to life tenants, the estate has been closed, the final account has been settled and determined, and the life tenants die, in the absence of a motion, filed in accordance with RC 2109.35, to vacate the order of the probate court, such court lacks jurisdiction to entertain an application by the remaindermen to commit securities formerly in the estate to a trustee. State ex rel. Beedle v. Kiracofe (Ohio 1964) 176 Ohio St. 149, 198 N.E.2d 61, 27 O.O.2d 25.

2. Release or recovery from surety

In a settlement of a guardian's account when he was credited with payments not made, and the account was subsequently corrected during the ward's minority, sureties on the bond were not affected. Scobey v. Gano (Ohio 1880) 35 Ohio St. 550. Guardian And Ward ⇐ 177; Principal And Surety ⇐ 97

A succeeding fiduciary is not authorized to file an application in the probate court for the release of the sureties on the bond of a predecessor deceased fiduciary, and such sureties may not be finally released prior to the approval of the final accounting of the representative of the deceased fiduciary. In re Gray's Estate (Ohio 1954) 162 Ohio St. 384, 123 N.E.2d 408, 55 O.O. 224. Executors And Administrators ⇐ 531

Where the amount due an estate of a decedent from the surety on the bond of a deceased fiduciary for certain delinquencies is not in dispute at the time a settlement is made with such surety, it is not necessary for the successor fiduciary to pay or tender back the amount received before pursuing any remedy available to him to recover from the surety for other and separate delinquencies. In re Gray's Estate (Ohio 1954) 162 Ohio St. 384, 123 N.E.2d 408, 55 O.O. 224. Compromise And Settlement ⇐ 18(3)

After final settlement the sureties on a guardian's bond cannot be heard in the absence of fraud to question the correctness of the guardian's final account. Braiden v. Mercer (Ohio 1886) 44 Ohio St. 339, 16 W.L.B. 29, 7 N.E. 155.

3. Accounting

Upon every settlement of an account by an executor or administrator, all his former accounts may be so far opened as to correct any mistake or error therein, except as to matters in dispute between two parties which had been previously heard and determined by the court; this includes the power to correct all errors or mistakes of the court, as well as of the executor or administrator, found in former settlements, whether as to items embraced in or omitted from such former accounts. Watts v. Watts (Ohio 1882) 38 Ohio St. 480, 8 W.L.B. 287.

A right of action on a guardian's bond to recover from sureties the amount remaining in the hands of the guardian accrues to the ward when the amount owing is determined by the probate court on final settlement of the account. Newton v. Hammond (Ohio 1882) 38 Ohio St. 430, 8 W.L.B. 241. Guardian And Ward ⇐ 182(3); Limitation Of Actions ⇐ 47(4)

Award to estate of fees that guardian had received during periods covered by third, fourth and fifth accounts was not supported by competent, credible evidence; trial court found that guardian had devoted time and effort and rendered valuable services to ward. In re Guardianship of McPheter (Ohio App. 6 Dist., 08-05-1994) 95 Ohio App.3d 440, 642 N.E.2d 690. Mental Health ⚖ 301

Failure of the probate court, in overruling a motion to vacate the first and final account of an executor, to separately state its findings of fact and conclusions of law when requested does not constitute reversible error unless prejudicially erroneous. In re Sloane's Estate (Montgomery 1959) 109 Ohio App. 110, 163 N.E.2d 915, 10 O.O.2d 269.

Under section no motion for new trial is necessary to appeal from order of probate court overruling exceptions to guardian's final account. In re Bireley's Guardianship (Darke 1944) 59 N.E.2d 69, 41 Ohio Law Abs. 601.

It is proper for probate court upon a showing of error or mistake upon filing of final account by an executor, to open a first partial account to correct such error or mistake, even though no exceptions were taken at time of filing of such first partial account. In re Russell's Estate (Lake 1938) 60 Ohio App. 385, 21 N.E.2d 604, 28 Ohio Law Abs. 201, 13 O.O. 239. Executors And Administrators ⚖ 510(4)

Probate court could open up and reconsider accounts of executor previously adjudicated in partial account. U.S. Fidelity & Guaranty Co. of Baltimore, Md. v. Wood (Morrow 1929) 35 Ohio App. 224, 172 N.E. 383. Executors And Administrators ⚖ 514

One of the three executors of a last will and testament who has not joined the other two executors in filing an account is an interested party and may file exceptions to such account. Burke v. McKee (Hocking 1928) 30 Ohio App. 236, 164 N.E. 776. Executors And Administrators ⚖ 504(2)

A debt due from an heir, legatee, or creditor to an estate is an asset of the estate, and where the distributive portion of such heir, legatee, or the claim of such creditor is equal to, or greater than, his debt, the administrator or executor should charge himself with and account for the full amount of the same. Lambright v. Lambright (Ohio 1906) 74 Ohio St. 198, 78 N.E. 265, 4 Ohio Law Rep. 38, 6 Am.Ann.Cas. 807. Executors And Administrators ⚖ 49

A final account showing all debts paid and the estate closed is conclusive, and no jurisdiction remains in the probate or common pleas courts to entertain a petition to sell assets to pay debts on an order of court that the account shall stand open; the only remedy is to file a subsequent account showing debts and credits whereupon the first account may be opened under former GC 10835 (RC 2109.35), after which a sale to pay debts may be asked for. Hunter v. Yocum (Ohio Com.Pl. 1914) 27 Ohio Dec. 31, 18 Ohio N.P.N.S. 14.

Partial accounts filed and approved by court, without exceptions, cannot be reopened by a referee on exceptions to the final account, former GC 10835 (GC 10506–40, now RC 2109.35), for opening prior accounts to correct any error or mistake, does not authorize opening to disallow improper credits paid intentionally and not by error or mistake. In re Campbell (Ohio Com.Pl. 1912) 22 Ohio Dec. 578, 13 Ohio NP(NS) 386.

This section permitting court to open up all former accounts to correct a mistake, or error, was passed by legislature to meet just such a situation; where prior accounts were formerly approved by court, without exceptions being filed thereto, and inasmuch as court has never had a hearing upon the matter, exceptors in filing exceptions to second and final account can now open up all prior accounts for purpose of having court determine matters with reference to investment of trust funds. In re Conover's Trusteeship (Ohio Prob. 1933) 5 Ohio Supp. 330, 26 Ohio Law Abs. 184, 10 O.O. 481.

If the petition on an administrator's bond avers a settlement in probate court, and a balance is found, a demurrer will admit the balance and a final judgment may be rendered. Luce v Treasurer for Use of Mcdonald, W 654 (1834).

Probate court has jurisdiction to open up former accounts of a trustee when the trustee omits from his account proper items to be charged against himself, unless the question has been raised and determined at a former hearing, or the beneficiaries are barred by reason of acquiescence or laches. In re Trust of Hartman, 29 Abs 67 (App, Franklin 1939).

Former GC 11032 (GC 10506–40, now RC 2109.35) and GC 11206 (GC 10501–56, now RC 2101.42) only have application to accounts filed by trustees of nonresident idiot, imbecile or lunatic. In re Jaymes, 18 Abs 613 (App, Clark 1935).

The language of section must be construed to include not merely clerical errors and mistakes contained in former accounts, but matters of substance as well, such as the question of the lawfulness of an investment shown in such previous accounts. In re Guardianship of Lodge (Ohio Prob. 1934) 32 Ohio NP(NS) 40.

4. Fraud

The settlement of an account is conclusive as to parties with actual notice of all matters specified therein and cannot be impeached except for fraud or error. McAfee v. Phillips (Ohio 1874) 25 Ohio St. 374.

Trial court's denial of executor's motion to obtain a transcript at the estate's expense was not an abuse of discretion, in action alleging that executor and attorney committed fraud in the administration of estate; the cost of the transcript was over $9,000, and the trial court settled the record, which resulted in a factual statement that was admissible in the absence of a transcript. In re Estate of Fouras (Ohio App. 5 Dist., Licking, 10-14-2004) No. 2003CA00049, No. 2003CA00052, 2004-Ohio-5563, 2004 WL 2348511, Unreported, appeal not allowed 105 Ohio St.3d 1518, 826 N.E.2d 316, 2005-Ohio-1880. Executors And Administrators ⚖ 456(1)

Ward's guardian committed constructive fraud, as opposed to actual fraud, in breaching her fiduciary duties to handle ward's accounts, for purposes of determining whether a fraud was committed on the court so as to require that prior settlement-of-account orders be vacated, where guardian signed a fiduciary acceptance, guardian submitted false information regarding ward's assets to court, and court acted in reliance upon such misinformation. In re Guardianship of Guzay (Ohio App. 10 Dist., Franklin, 09-23-2003) No. 02AP-745, 2003-Ohio-5036, 2003 WL 22177106, Unreported. Mental Health ⚖ 311

Former employee was not liable to his former employer on claim of breach of fiduciary duty for employee's alleged betrayal in making false statements about employer's financial condition, where employer cited no facts to support showing that the relationship between the employee and employer was a fiduciary relationship, characterized by some special competence and trust. Laurel Valley Oil Co. v. 76 Lubricants Co. (Ohio App. 5 Dist., 09-26-2003) 154 Ohio App.3d 512, 797 N.E.2d 1033, 2003-Ohio-5163, appeal not allowed 101 Ohio St.3d 1467, 804 N.E.2d 41, 2004-Ohio-819. Labor And Employment ⚖ 111

In proceeding to set aside order of probate court approving and settling account due to alleged fraud in failure of administratrix to include a tort claim as a liability in the account, evidence was not sufficiently clear and convincing to find that administratrix intentionally omitted tort claim from account to defraud tort claimants, since there was a dispute as to sufficiency of complaint and the claim was not liquidated when account was filed. Mathe v. Fowler (Lake 1983) 13 Ohio App.3d 273, 469 N.E.2d 89, 13 O.B.R. 337. Executors And Administrators ⚖ 509(8)

A person bringing a motion to vacate, on the basis of fraud, an order of the probate court giving approval of a final and distributive account, must prove fraud by clear and convincing evidence. Mathe v. Fowler (Lake 1983) 13 Ohio App.3d 273, 469 N.E.2d 89, 13 O.B.R. 337.

Probate courts have no jurisdiction over claims for money damages resulting from fraud. Alexander v. Compton (Clinton 1978) 57 Ohio App.2d 89, 385 N.E.2d 638, 11 O.O.3d 81.

Where the probate court sustains motions to open four accounts filed by an executrix and to vacate the orders approving such accounts, the entry stating that "applicants have proved grounds for opening each of said four accounts and vacating each of the orders settling the same," the appellate court must assume in the absence of a bill of exceptions that the order was based upon proof of fraud. In re Hartford's Estate (Columbiana 1958) 158 N.E.2d 911, 80 Ohio Law Abs. 313.

Where executrix' accounts were opened and vacated long after approval of accounts and resignation and death of executrix, in absence of bill of exceptions showing that contrary, reviewing court would assume that words in trial court's journal entry that applicants had proved grounds for opening accounts and vacating order settling the same were based upon proof of fraud shown by the required degree. In re Hartford's Estate (Columbiana 1958) 158 N.E.2d 911, 80 Ohio Law Abs. 313. Executors And Administrators ⚖ 510(9)

Daughter, who claimed that her distributive share of her father's estate had been withheld from her, and that receipt for her share which administrator had filed with first and final account in February, 1945, was forgery, could not bring action in Probate Court under statute relating to case where fiduciary has concealed, embezzled or conveyed away property from estate, since no judgment could be rendered in favor of daughter herself, and no judgment could be rendered in favor of estate as long as order of settlement of final account stood. In re Reitler's Estate (Ohio Prob. 1956) 137 N.E.2d 791, 73 Ohio Law Abs. 328. Executors And Administrators ⚖ 85(9)

2109.35
Note 4

In proceedings on motion to vacate settlement of administrator's account because of his alleged fraud in distributing assets to one who had allegedly bigamously married decedent, evidence established that prior marriage relied upon by movant had been invalid because solemnized when other party thereto was in law and in fact the common-law wife of another. In re Nyhuis' Estate (Cuyahoga 1952) 113 N.E.2d 700, 65 Ohio Law Abs. 65. Marriage ⇨ 50(1)

A vacation of the settlement of the account of the administrator of an estate for "good cause" or "suspicion of fraud" without a finding by clear and convincing evidence that fraud has been established is erroneous. In re Nyhuis' Estate (Cuyahoga 1952) 113 N.E.2d 700, 65 Ohio Law Abs. 65.

In a proceeding arising under GC 10506–40 (RC 2109.35), prior to its amendment in 120 v 653, where fraud or collusion or a violation of rights which are saved by statute to persons under disability is shown to have been practiced in administration of an executor's trust, determination of probate court approving final account is thereby vacated. In re Stafford's Estate (Ohio 1946) 146 Ohio St. 253, 65 N.E.2d 701, 32 O.O. 262.

A representation by husband's administrator that the husband left no surviving spouse when in fact his wife lived for seven months after his death was a misstatement of fact sufficient to constitute a "fraud" on the probate court, within the meaning of the statute authorizing the probate court to reopen a decedent's estate, so as to permit the administrator of the estate of the wife to obtain a widow's exemption and allowance as part of the wife's estate. In re Shive's Estate (Columbiana 1940) 65 Ohio App. 167, 29 N.E.2d 565, 18 O.O. 358. Executors And Administrators ⇨ 509(4)

Representation by an administrator that decedent left no surviving spouse, when in fact the surviving spouse lived for seven months after her husband's death, is a misstatement of fact sufficient to constitute a fraud on the probate court, within meaning of statute. In re Shive's Estate (Columbiana 1940) 65 Ohio App. 167, 29 N.E.2d 565, 18 O.O. 358. Executors And Administrators ⇨ 509(4)

An order of the probate court reopening the final account of an executor on the application of a creditor for fraud and manifest error is maintainable either under the old law, former GC 10834, or under GC 10506–40 (RC 2109.35) and related sections of the probate code. In re Steltenpohl's Estate (Hamilton 1936) 53 Ohio App. 541, 5 N.E.2d 954, 22 Ohio Law Abs. 410, 7 O.O. 120.

It could not be presumed that fraud was perpetrated against surety in probate court in opening up trustee's final account. U.S. Fidelity & Guaranty Co. of Baltimore, Md. v. Wood (Morrow 1929) 35 Ohio App. 224, 172 N.E. 383. Trusts ⇨ 329

After the expiration of eight months allowed by RS 6187 for filing exceptions when the account is settled in the absence of a person interested and without actual notice to him, the judgment of a probate court settling the final account of an executor or administrator becomes absolute and conclusive and cannot be attacked except for fraud of the prevailing party. Crawford v. Zeigler (Ohio 1911) 84 Ohio St. 224, 95 N.E. 743, 9 Ohio Law Rep. 94. Executors And Administrators ⇨ 516(2); Courts ⇨ 202(4)

The rule that probate court findings cannot be attacked collaterally, except for fraud, applies to approval of accounts. Woodward v. Curtis (Ohio Cir. 1899) 10 Ohio C.D. 400.

Fraud by one standing in a fiduciary and confidential relation to the person affected will avoid the settlement of any account of a trustee, executor, or administrator induced thereby, and such final settlement may be attacked in a court of equity in an independent action upon a complaint that the final settlement was obtained by fraud, constructive or in fact, and the common pleas court has jurisdiction in such action. Rote v. Stratton (Ohio Com.Pl. 1895) 3 Ohio Dec. 156, 2 Ohio N.P. 27.

Where matters covered by the ninth account were not "in dispute" nor determined by the court as such at the time of its approval, the probate court was authorized to open the account and to vacate its order of settlement which had been secured by fraud. Massachusetts Bonding & Ins. Co. v. Winters Nat. Bank & Trust Co. of Dayton, Ohio (C.C.A.6 (Ohio) 1942) 130 F.2d 5, 24 O.O. 225, certiorari denied 63 S.Ct. 526, 317 U.S. 700, 87 L.Ed. 560.

The beneficiaries of a guardianship-trusteeship may not seek to vacate a court order, approving a final accounting of a trust and providing for the release of the trustee-mother by alleging fraud, more than one year after the discovery of the alleged fraud under Civ R 60(B)(5) because RC 2109.35 specifically limits such actions to a one year period. In re Guardianship–Trusteeship of Colletts, Nos. 684 and 690 (4th Dist Ct App, Highland, 11–3–88).

5. Rights of surviving spouse

Where one is required by statute to do an act as a prerequisite to the accrual of a cause of action, all persons, whether under disability or not, are bound thereby unless excepted from the operation of the statute by a saving clause. In re Sarver's Estate (Franklin 1954) 97 Ohio App. 199, 124 N.E.2d 749, 55 O.O. 453. Action ⇨ 10

Administrator of the estate of a surviving spouse who died subsequent to her husband and before receiving her statutory widow's exemption and allowance is entitled under section in case of fraud or collusion, to have the husband's estate reopened more than eight months after the filing of the final account in his estate, have an administrator de bonis non appointed therefor, and obtain the widow's exemption and allowance as a part of her estate. In re Shive's Estate (Columbiana 1940) 65 Ohio App. 167, 29 N.E.2d 565, 18 O.O. 358. Executors And Administrators ⇨ 37(2); Executors And Administrators ⇨ 509(4)

By virtue of statute an order of probate court settling first and final account of executrix of an estate of a husband from which account it appears that no allowance has been made to widow for her year's support and no property set off to her as exempt, and there is no balance in hands of executrix and that said estate has been fully administered, operates as a judgment at law or decree in equity adjudicating that widow had no right to any distributive share, allowance for year's support, or to exempt property in the estate. Eckhart v. Wiles (Henry 1938) 61 Ohio App. 32, 22 N.E.2d 289, 15 O.O. 61, appeal dismissed 134 Ohio St. 491, 17 N.E.2d 920, 13 O.O. 159. Executors And Administrators ⇨ 513(10)

Rights of a widow who elects to take under will of her deceased husband are governed by this section, subsection (b), where appraisers of personal property of her husband's estate fail to make an allowance to her for a year's support and to set off exempted property pursuant to provisions of GC 10509–54 (RC 2115.13), and omission of executrix to have same done by appraisers or court is not occasioned by fraud, and failure of widow or her representatives to file exceptions to final account of executrix of husband's estate in accordance therewith within prescribed time limit will bar any recovery thereafter. Eckhart v. Wiles (Henry 1938) 61 Ohio App. 32, 22 N.E.2d 289, 15 O.O. 61, appeal dismissed 134 Ohio St. 491, 17 N.E.2d 920, 13 O.O. 159.

Allowances to a widow made in a proceeding to sell real estate belonging to her deceased husband to pay debts, to which no error was prosecuted or appeal taken, cannot be collaterally attacked by exception to her account as administratrix of the said estate. In re Hess' Estate (Ohio Cir. 1911) 23 Ohio C.D. 449, 14 Ohio C.C.(N.S.) 463. Executors And Administrators ⇨ 194(6); Homestead ⇨ 150(2)

The settlement made by an administrator will not be opened up forty years after the estate was closed in order to let in the claim of the widow for her first year's support, where no such claim was asserted at the time the estate was being settled. Evans v. Evans (Ohio Cir. 1909) 21 Ohio C.D. 635, 13 Ohio C.C.(N.S.) 62, affirmed 83 Ohio St. 482, 94 N.E. 1106, 8 Ohio Law Rep. 525.

Where decedent and decedent's spouse held the family homestead as tenants by the entireties, the trial court erred in finding that the surviving spouse was only entitled to a contribution out of her husband's estate for one-half of the liability of the mortgage on such homestead where decedent's trust agreement provided that the mortgage be paid in full. Ohio Citizens Trust Co v Pribe, No. L–82–265 (6th Dist Ct App, Lucas, 12–23–82).

6. Settlement proceedings

Where the names of infants are signed to final settlements without lawful authority, they may disaffirm on coming of age and compel an accounting. Piatt v. Longworth's Devisees (Ohio 1875) 27 Ohio St. 159.

The settlement of an account is prima facie evidence only of its correctness and binds no rights except where made in conformity with the law. Bank of Muskingum v. Carpenter's Adm'rs (Ohio 1835) 7 Ohio 21, PT. I, 28 Am.Dec. 616.

Judgment for $16,800 against guardian for loss of rental income resulting from guardian's failure to rent ward's residence even though ward was in nursing home without any reasonable prospect of returning to her home was not against weight of evidence. In re Guardianship of McPheter (Ohio App. 6 Dist., 08-05-1994) 95 Ohio App.3d 440, 642 N.E.2d 690. Mental Health ⇨ 258.1; Mental Health ⇨ 274

Where a conditional sales contract is not filed of record, upon the death of the purchaser the property becomes a part of the assets of the decedent's estate and the status of the seller is that of a general creditor of the estate. In re Sloane's Estate (Montgomery 1959) 109 Ohio App. 110,

163 N.E.2d 915, 10 O.O.2d 269. Executors And Administrators ⊶ 56; Executors And Administrators ⊶ 264(1)

Where a claim is presented to an administrator and the administrator rejects the claim and in the same letter offers to settle it for a lesser amount, there is no unequivocal rejection of the claim and the claimant can thereafter obtain an order vacating the order settling the administrator's final account. In re Douglass' Estate (Ohio Prob. 1957) 144 N.E.2d 924, 77 Ohio Law Abs. 89.

In proceeding to settle guardianship account court may open up former accounts, even though they have been adjudicated before by probate court, in order to correct any errors or mistakes therein, particularly where party with adverse interests in settlement of those accounts was insane at the time and had no actual notice of the proceedings. Marks v. Marks (Columbiana 1937) 58 Ohio App. 266, 16 N.E.2d 509, 12 O.O. 158. Mental Health ⊶ 304

A settlement of a decedent's estate is not one entire proceeding, but each step constitutes a separate and distinct proceeding and is governed by the law in force at the time such proceeding is begun. In re Steltenpohl's Estate (Hamilton 1936) 53 Ohio App. 541, 5 N.E.2d 954, 22 Ohio Law Abs. 410, 7 O.O. 120.

A probate court may remove or accept the resignation of an executor or administrator, but while choses in action or assets of the estate remain in his hands unadministered, his authority to administer same is not extinguished by an order, made upon what purports to be a settlement of his final account, directing that he be discharged. Weyer v. Watt (Ohio 1891) 48 Ohio St. 545, 26 W.L.B. 284, 28 N.E. 670.

Settling a guardian's account without notice is not conclusive as to sureties. Gilbert v. Gilbert (Ohio Cir. 1896) 7 Ohio C.D. 58.

The probate court will not go back to a settlement made in the common pleas court which involves an adjustment of the same matters of dispute, but will look to the entry of the upper court for its limitation. In re Seeger's Estate (Ohio Prob. 1899) 1 Ohio Dec. 113, 7 Ohio N.P. 207.

Former GC 10834 and 10835 (GC 10506–40, now RC 2109.35) refer to settlements by executors and administrators and not to guardians. In re Jaymes, 18 Abs 613 (App, Clark 1935).

7. Final account

Previous accounts of a trustee, errors in which have not been subjected to any special hearing by the probate court, can be opened up under GC 11033 (GC 10506–40 (RC 2109.35)). In re Trusteeship of Couden (Ohio App. 1 Dist. 1917) 9 Ohio App. 207.

Order of probate court settling fiduciary's account has effect of judgment and cannot be attacked collaterally, except for fraud. Border v. Ohio Sav. & Trust Co. (Ohio Com.Pl. 1970) 26 Ohio Misc. 273, 267 N.E.2d 120, 55 O.O.2d 410, 55 O.O.2d 433.

Executor's approved and settled accounting could not be opened in declaratory judgment proceeding concerning whether certain charges should be made against income earned by trust assets while in hands of the executor. Third Nat. Bank & Trust Co. of Dayton v. Gardner (Ohio Com.Pl. 1970) 24 Ohio Misc. 223, 262 N.E.2d 430, 53 O.O.2d 261, 53 O.O.2d 290. Executors And Administrators ⊶ 513(2)

Approval of an executor's account is a final order. In re Norris (Monroe 1959) 169 N.E.2d 639, 84 Ohio Law Abs. 92. Executors And Administrators ⊶ 510(2)

Order of Probate Court approving final account of executor is final order and binding upon all those who approved account, and such order cannot be opened up by declaratory judgment proceeding. Fletcher v. Stanton (Ohio Prob. 1952) 124 N.E.2d 495, 69 Ohio Law Abs. 161, affirmed 124 N.E.2d 493, 69 Ohio Law Abs. 174. Declaratory Judgment ⊶ 114; Executors And Administrators ⊶ 513(4)

An order approving the final account of an executor is final and binding upon all those who approved the account. Fletcher v. Stanton (Ohio Prob. 1952) 124 N.E.2d 495, 69 Ohio Law Abs. 161, affirmed 124 N.E.2d 493, 69 Ohio Law Abs. 174. Declaratory Judgment ⊶ 114; Executors And Administrators ⊶ 513(4)

As used in GC 10506–40 (RC 2109.35) knowledge of the settling of a final account means actual knowledge. In re Bentley's Estate (Cuyahoga 1951) 116 N.E.2d 738, 66 Ohio Law Abs. 363, reversed 163 Ohio St. 568, 127 N.E.2d 749, 57 O.O. 5.

A proceeding by guardian to sell incompetent's realty was separate from guardianship proceedings, and, if invalid should have been challenged in the separate proceedings, and not by exceptions to guardian's first and final account. In re Bireley's Guardianship (Darke 1944) 59 N.E.2d 71, 41 Ohio Law Abs. 604. Mental Health ⊶ 264; Mental Health ⊶ 300

Words "and shall be final as to all persons having notice of the hearing" as used in statute do not include notice of publication, generally spoken of as constructive notice. In re Chambers' Estate (Montgomery 1939) 36 N.E.2d 175, 30 Ohio Law Abs. 420, 16 O.O. 519, appeal dismissed 136 Ohio St. 202, 24 N.E.2d 601, 16 O.O. 535, rehearing denied 43 N.E.2d 244.

Without alleging fraud, mistake, or misconduct, heirs of an imbecile cannot have the probate court open a guardian's account after settlement. Millen v. Young (Ohio Cir. 1892) 8 Ohio C.D. 391.

The final account of a guardian duly confirmed is unimpeachable for any cause in two years after the minors have become of age. Lamkin v. Robinson (Ohio Com.Pl. 1910) 21 Ohio Dec. 13, 10 Ohio N.P.(N.S.) 1, reversed 24 Ohio C.D. 91, 15 Ohio C.C.(N.S.) 126, affirmed 88 Ohio St. 603, 106 N.E. 1065, 11 Ohio Law Rep. 80.

Court may reopen, at its discretion, an account in which it finds error. In re Ziegler (Ohio Com.Pl. 1897) 6 Ohio Dec. 244, 4 Ohio N.P. 182.

When a final account has been filed and approved, it cannot be attacked in a collateral proceeding; probate courts being courts of record in the fullest sense, their records import absolute verity. Smith v. Hayward (Ohio Prob. 1898) 5 Ohio Dec. 462, 5 Ohio N.P. 501.

Where court on its own motion does not order formal hearing on final account of administrator as authorized by GC 10506–36 (RC 2109.32) to 10506–40 (RC 2109.35) within period after publication of notice of filing of said account as fixed by rule of court, or fiduciary or an interested party does not request such hearing within such time, the probate court has full power under O Const Art IV, § 8 to approve the final account of an administrator and order his discharge. In re Johnson's Estate (Ohio Prob. 1943) 12 Ohio Supp. 148, 39 Ohio Law Abs. 333, 27 O.O. 131.

Where a guardian's account has been approved by the probate court, such adjudication is conclusive; the ward or a subsequently appointed guardian cannot bring an action to recover money wrongfully paid. Lynch v Cogswell, 18 CC 641, 7 CD 12 (Cuyahoga 1899).

8. Insurance policy

In a negligence action for the recovery of damages, instituted under RC 2117.07 against an administrator seeking to recover only from decedent's liability insurer, where administrator of estate of decedent has been discharged and estate closed, probate court may reappoint administrator for purpose of accepting service of summons. In re George's Estate (Ohio 1970) 24 Ohio St.2d 18, 262 N.E.2d 872, 53 O.O.2d 10.

Where the final and distributive account of the administrators of an estate has been approved and settled and they have been discharged from their trust pursuant to RC 2109.32, and that order has not been vacated pursuant to RC 2109.35, where some asset remains upon which administration has not been exhausted and for some lawful purpose relating to that asset administration is required, an administrator may be appointed to complete such administration only in a manner similar to, and with the same formalities as, the original appointment of an administrator, and in such circumstances, where such asset consists of an automobile liability insurance policy of the decedent covering the claim of a person alleged to have received bodily injuries due to the alleged negligence of the decedent, such policy is an asset which will support the appointment of an administrator upon whom service may be made and with authority to defend suit. In re George's Estate (Hancock 1969) 20 Ohio App.2d 87, 252 N.E.2d 176, 49 O.O.2d 110. Executors And Administrators ⊶ 37(2); Executors And Administrators ⊶ 37(5)

9. Time requirements

A final account is not final so as to bar further inquiry; after an account has been settled the probate court may within the time limit of S. & C. 566 compel a further accounting. McAfee v. Phillips (Ohio 1874) 25 Ohio St. 374.

Administrator and beneficiary of wife's estate were not entitled to reimbursement from husband's estate of one half of husband's funeral expenses and real estate taxes, which had been paid by wife from a joint account, even though husband's will directed that his estate pay his funeral expenses and debts; claim for reimbursement was a claim against husband's estate, administrator and wife improperly filed claim in the proceedings to administer wife estate, and claim was filed more than two years after husband's death, after the one-year limitations period for claims against estate, and after estate had been closed. In re Estate of Lewis (Ohio App. 6 Dist., Lucas, 04-21-2006) No. L-05-1225, 2006-Ohio-1986, 2006 WL 1047478, Unreported. Executors And Administrators ⊶ 225(1)

Note 9

Judgment of probate court settling accounts of fiduciary may be vacated by probate court during time specified and for reasons set forth in RC 2109.35. Border v. Ohio Sav. & Trust Co. (Ohio Com.Pl. 1970) 26 Ohio Misc. 273, 267 N.E.2d 120, 55 O.O.2d 410, 55 O.O.2d 433.

Prior to amendment of GC 10506–40 (RC 2109.35) by 120 v 653, effective September 20, 1943, statutory law of this state prescribed no limitation of time within which approval of final account of an executor could be challenged and vacated on ground (a) that fraud or collusion had been practiced in connection with such final account, or (b) that such approval was against rights which are saved by statute to persons under disability. In re Stafford's Estate (Ohio 1946) 146 Ohio St. 253, 65 N.E.2d 701, 32 O.O. 262. Executors And Administrators ⊕ 509(5)

After the eight months allowed by RS 6187 (See GC 10506–40, 10509–184) for filing exceptions when the account of an administrator is settled in the absence of persons interested and without notice, the judgment of the probate court settling the final account of an administrator becomes absolute and cannot be attacked, except for fraud. Crawford v. Zeigler (Ohio 1911) 84 Ohio St. 224, 95 N.E. 743, 9 Ohio Law Rep. 94. Executors And Administrators ⊕ 516(2); Courts ⊕ 202(4)

The specific time requirements governing the vacation of an approved final accounting of a trust set forth in RC 2109.35 may not be extended by allegations of fraud contained in a motion for relief from judgment under Civ R 60(B)(5). In re Guardianship–Trusteeship of Colletts, Nos. 684 and 690 (4th Dist Ct App, Highland, 11–3–88).

10. Parties

The heirs of an intestate cannot maintain an action in their own names to recover possession of assets belonging to the estate or to compel the executors of a party who had a life interest in such assets and has wrongly disposed of them by will to account for the assets, even after settlement by the administrator and where there are no outstanding debts. Davis v. Corwine (Ohio 1874) 25 Ohio St. 668. Descent And Distribution ⊕ 76

Since trust beneficiaries' motion to vacate order approving second account was timely, beneficiaries were without standing to challenge notice provisions of statute governing hearings on accounts, as they related to second account. In re Estate of Cullen (Ohio App. 12 Dist., 02-18-1997) 118 Ohio App.3d 256, 692 N.E.2d 650, dismissed, appeal not allowed 79 Ohio St.3d 1417, 680 N.E.2d 155. Trusts ⊕ 328

Interest of beneficiary of all of probate estate, with the exception of three specific requests, was almost identical to that of beneficiary taking under testamentary trust, making beneficiary a proper party to file exceptions to the accounts rendered and fees paid in probate estate, although probate estate was bequeathed to an inter vivos trust created by another, of which she was beneficiary. Ollick v. Rice (Cuyahoga 1984) 16 Ohio App.3d 448, 476 N.E.2d 1062, 16 O.B.R. 529. Executors And Administrators ⊕ 504(2)

The beneficiary of an inter vivos trust which will ultimately be funded primarily from the estates of two decedents is a proper party to file exceptions to the accounts rendered and fees paid in such probate estates. Ollick v. Rice (Cuyahoga 1984) 16 Ohio App.3d 448, 476 N.E.2d 1062, 16 O.B.R. 529.

The sureties of a guardian may, on their own motion, become parties to the settlement of final account for the purpose of correcting errors in that or a former account. Porter v Brown, 9 D Repr 646, 16 B 69 (CP, Muskingum 1886). Guardian And Ward ⊕ 145

11. Foreign executor

The statutes of Michigan do not give an executor appointed in another state the right to administer the trust as to property in Michigan by force of the laws of such other state, and such executor must account for the disposition thereof to the proper court of such state, and the Ohio probate court, which has probated an Ohio will, and has issued letters testamentary, cannot review the accounts of the executor as to property situated in Michigan for which he has duly accounted to the probate court in that state. In re Crawford (Ohio 1903) 68 Ohio St. 58, 48 W.L.B. 492, 67 N.E. 156, 96 Am.St.Rep. 648, 1 Ohio Law Rep. 91. Executors And Administrators ⊕ 526

2109.36 Order of distribution

An application for an order of distribution of the assets of an estate or trust held by a fiduciary may be set for hearing before the probate court at such time as the court shall designate. The fiduciary may serve notice of the hearing upon such application, or cause such notice to be served, upon any person who may be affected by an order disposing thereof; or the court, upon motion of any interested person for good cause shown or at its own instance, may order such notice to be served upon any such person. Such notice shall set forth the time and place of the hearing and shall be accompanied by a statement of the proposed distribution. At the hearing upon the application the court shall inquire into, consider, and determine all matters relative thereto, and make such order as the court deems proper. If the court makes an order of distribution, the fiduciary shall comply therewith and shall account to the court for his distribution, verified by vouchers or proof. An order of distribution shall have the effect of a judgment. Such order may be reviewed upon appeal and may be vacated as provided in section 2109.35 of the Revised Code.

(1953 H 1, eff. 10–1–53; GC 10506–40a)

Historical and Statutory Notes

Pre–1953 H 1 Amendments: 121 v 270; 120 v 649

Library References

Executors and Administrators ⊕314(0.5) to 315.9.
Trusts ⊕271.5, 280, 282.
Westlaw Topic Nos. 162, 390.
C.J.S. Executors and Administrators §§ 559 to 579.
C.J.S. Trusts §§ 348, 531, 544 to 550.

Research References

Encyclopedias

OH Jur. 3d Decedents' Estates § 1630, Court Ordered Distribution.
OH Jur. 3d Fiduciaries § 285, Generally, Jurisdiction.
OH Jur. 3d Fiduciaries § 294, Application by Fiduciary; Notice.
OH Jur. 3d Fiduciaries § 295, Hearing and Order; Account of Distribution.

Treatises and Practice Aids

Carlin, Baldwin's Ohio Practice, Merrick-Rippner Probate Law § 64:4, Powers and Duties of Guardian—Accounting.
Carlin, Baldwin's Ohio Practice, Merrick-Rippner Probate Law § 75:7, Distribution—Upon Application—Introduction.
Carlin, Baldwin's Ohio Practice, Merrick-Rippner Probate Law § 2:105, Distribution of Assets—Order of Distribution.
Bogert - the Law of Trusts and Trustees § 972, Credits to Trustee on Accounting.

Law Review and Journal Commentaries

Gift Over Upon Death Before Distribution: Settlor's Intent Still the Lodestar in Ohio, Mary Clare Cullen. 11 Prob L J Ohio 8 (September/October 2000).

Notes of Decisions

Breach of fiduciary duties 3
Contract for distribution 2
Testamentary trust 1
Valuation 4

---

1. Testamentary trust

The probate court has jurisdiction to entertain an application by the beneficiary of a testamentary trust to direct and control the conduct of testamentary trustees in the payment, or the withholding of payment, of trust income which is payable to such beneficiary under the will of the decedent. In re Gallagher's Trust (Mahoning 1963) 118 Ohio App. 477, 195 N.E.2d 601, 25 O.O.2d 394. Trusts ⊕ 280

2. Contract for distribution

A probate court has no jurisdiction to consider the validity or effect of a contract between the distributees of a decedent's estate and one who contracted to collect their share of the estate for a percentage thereof, where the purported contract has no bearing on the assets of the estate, the duties of the administrator or the court's supervision of his administration. In re Porter's Estate (Ohio Prob. 1969) 17 Ohio Misc. 136, 243 N.E.2d 794, 46 O.O.2d 180.

3. **Breach of fiduciary duties**

Federal court does not have jurisdiction of an action against an executor or administrator involving an alleged breach of fiduciary duties. Starr v. Rupp (C.A.6 (Ohio) 1970) 25 Ohio Misc. 224, 421 F.2d 999, 12 A.L.R. Fed. 279, 53 O.O.2d 169, 54 O.O.2d 343.

4. **Valuation**

Trial court clarifying prior order in probate case properly determined that prior order required that farm, as part of residue of estate, be valued at time of termination of widow's life estate, not at testator's death, since will required distributions of residue to be of equal value, and value of distributions could not be determined until termination of testator's life estate regarding residue of estate. In re Estate of Smith (Ohio App. 3 Dist., Seneca, 04-16-2003) No. 13-02-37, 2003-Ohio-1910, 2003 WL 1877624, Unreported. Wills ⇐ 527

2109.361 Approval of third-party distribution

(A) As used in this section, "third-party distribution" means the distribution by a fiduciary of an estate or trust of the assets of that estate or trust when both of the following apply:

(1) The fiduciary makes the distribution to either of the following persons:

(a) The transferee of a beneficiary;

(b) Any person pursuant to an agreement, request, or instruction of a beneficiary or pursuant to a legal claim against a beneficiary.

(2) The distribution is the subject of an agreement between a beneficiary and any person that requires the fiduciary or beneficiary to pay a percentage of an inheritance or a dollar amount to any person other than the beneficiary.

(B) Prior to making a third-party distribution, the affected beneficiary or the affected beneficiary's guardian or other legal representative of the beneficiary may file an application for the approval of a third-party distribution with the probate court. An application filed pursuant to this division shall identify the person to whom the third-party distribution is to be made, disclose the basis for making the third-party distribution, and include a copy of any written agreement between the affected beneficiary and the person to whom the third-party distribution is to be made.

(C) The probate court shall hold a hearing on an application filed under division (B) of this section. The applicant shall serve notice of the hearing on all interested parties at least fifteen days prior to the hearing in accordance with Civil Rule 73. An interested party may waive notice of the hearing in accordance with Civil Rule 73.

(D) The probate court may approve the third-party distribution in whole or in part, as the court determines is just and equitable. To the extent that the application is approved, the court shall determine whether the third-party distribution is properly charged solely against the beneficiary's share of the estate or trust or whether some or all of the third-party distribution is properly charged against the residue of the affected estate or trust. The court may consider any relevant factors in evaluating the application, including, but not limited to, any of the following:

(1) The amount or percentage of the affected beneficiary's share that would be the subject of the proposed third-party distribution measured against the reasonable value of any goods or services the person to whom the third-party distribution would be made provided to the beneficiary or to the estate or trust;

(2) Whether the agreement, request, or instructions of the affected beneficiary were procured by duress, fraud, misrepresentation, undue influence, or other unfair means;

(3) Whether the amount of the proposed third-party distribution is fixed or contingent under the terms of the agreement between the affected beneficiary and the recipient of the proposed third-party distribution;

(4) Whether the beneficiary was represented by an attorney during the pendency of the probate action, or the beneficiary authorized the recipient of the proposed third-party distribution to retain an attorney who is licensed to practice law in Ohio for the beneficiary to formally represent the beneficiary in any proceeding regarding the decedent's estate, and the recipient of the proposed third-party distribution is responsible for paying the attorney's fees;

(5) The extent, if any, to which the recipient of the proposed third-party distribution incurred expenses in connection with the services provided to the affected beneficiary, estate, or trust;

(6) Whether the beneficiary was required to advance any payments for fees or expenses to the recipient of the proposed third-party distribution.

(E) Division (D)(4) of this section does not prohibit the beneficiary from retaining the beneficiary's own legal counsel.

(F) This section does not apply to third-party distributions to an attorney who represents a beneficiary and does not affect any other provision of law regarding the compensation of attorneys.

(2006 H 83, eff. 3–23–07)

INVESTMENTS

2109.37 Investment powers

(A) Except as otherwise provided by law, including division (D) of this section, or by the instrument creating the trust, a fiduciary having funds belonging to a trust which are to be invested may invest them in the following:

(1) Bonds or other obligations of the United States or of this state;

(2) Bonds or other interest-bearing obligations of any county, municipal corporation, school district, or other legally constituted political taxing subdivision within the state, provided that such county, municipal corporation, school district, or other subdivision has not defaulted in the payment of the interest on any of its bonds or interest-bearing obligations, for more than one hundred twenty days during the ten years immediately preceding the investment by the fiduciary in the bonds or other obligations, and provided that such county, municipal corporation, school district, or other subdivision, is not, at the time of the investment, in default in the payment of principal or interest on any of its bonds or other interest-bearing obligations;

(3) Bonds or other interest-bearing obligations of any other state of the United States which, within twenty years prior to the making of such investment, has not defaulted for more than ninety days in the payment of principal or interest on any of its bonds or other interest-bearing obligations;

(4) Any bonds issued by or for federal land banks and any debentures issued by or for federal intermediate credit banks under the "Federal Farm Loan Act of 1916," 39 Stat. 360, 12 U.S.C.A. 641, as amended; or any debentures issued by or for banks for cooperatives under the "Farm Credit Act of 1933," 48 Stat. 257, 12 U.S.C.A. 131, as amended;

(5) Notes which are: (a) secured by a first mortgage on real estate held in fee and located in the state, improved by a unit designed principally for residential use for not more than four families or by a combination of such dwelling unit and business property, the area designed or used for nonresidential purposes

not to exceed fifty per cent of the total floor area; (b) secured by a first mortgage on real estate held in fee and located in the state, improved with a building designed for residential use for more than four families or with a building used primarily for business purposes, if the unpaid principal of the notes secured by such mortgage does not exceed ten per cent of the value of the estate or trust or does not exceed five thousand dollars, whichever is greater; or (c) secured by a first mortgage on an improved farm held in fee and located in the state, provided that such mortgage requires that the buildings on the mortgaged property shall be well insured against loss by fire, and so kept, for the benefit of the mortgagee, until the debt is paid, and provided that the unpaid principal of the notes secured by the mortgage shall not exceed fifty per cent of the fair value of the mortgaged real estate at the time the investment is made, and the notes shall be payable not more than five years after the date on which the investment in them is made; except that the unpaid principal of the notes may equal sixty per cent of the fair value of the mortgaged real estate at the time the investment is made, and may be payable over a period of fifteen years following the date of the investment by the fiduciary if regular installment payments are required sufficient to amortize four per cent or more of the principal of the outstanding notes per annum and if the unpaid principal and interest become due and payable at the option of the holder upon any default in the payment of any installment of interest or principal upon the notes, or of taxes, assessments, or insurance premiums upon the mortgaged premises or upon the failure to cure any such default within any grace period provided therein not exceeding ninety days in duration;

(6) Life, endowment, or annuity contracts of legal reserve life insurance companies regulated by sections 3907.01 to 3907.21, 3909.01 to 3909.17, 3911. 01 to 3911.24, 3913.01 to 3913.10, 3915.01 to 3915.15, and 3917.01 to 3917.05 of the Revised Code, and licensed by the superintendent of insurance to transact business within the state, provided that the purchase of contracts authorized by this division shall be limited to executors or the successors to their powers when specifically authorized by will and to guardians and trustees, which contracts may be issued on the life of a ward, a beneficiary of a trust fund, or according to a will, or upon the life of a person in whom such ward or beneficiary has an insurable interest and the contracts shall be drawn by the insuring company so that the proceeds shall be the sole property of the person whose funds are so invested;

(7) Notes or bonds secured by mortgages and insured by the federal housing administrator or debentures issued by such administrator;

(8) Obligations issued by a federal home loan bank created under the "Federal Home Loan Bank Act of 1932," 47 Stat. 725, 12 U.S.C.A. 1421, as amended;

(9) Shares and certificates or other evidences of deposits issued by a federal savings and loan association organized and incorporated under the "Home Owners' Loan Act of 1933," 48 Stat. 128, 12 U.S.C.A. 1461, as amended, to the extent and only to the extent that those shares or certificates or other evidences of deposits are insured pursuant to the "Financial Institutions Reform, Recovery, and Enforcement Act of 1989," 103 Stat. 183, 12 U.S.C.A. 1811, as amended;

(10) Bonds issued by the home owners' loan corporation created under the "Home Owners' Act of 1933," 48 Stat. 128, 12 U.S.C.A. 1461, as amended;

(11) Obligations issued by the national mortgage association created under the "National Housing Act," 48 Stat. 1246 (1934), 12 U.S.C.A. 1701, as amended;

(12) Shares and certificates or other evidences of deposits issued by a domestic savings and loan association organized under the laws of the state, which association has obtained insurance of accounts pursuant to the "Financial Institutions Reform, Recovery, and Enforcement Act of 1989," 103 Stat. 183, 12 U.S.C.A. 1811, as amended, or as may be otherwise provided by law, only to the extent that such evidences of deposits are insured under that act, as amended;

(13) Shares and certificates or other evidences of deposits issued by a domestic savings and loan association organized under the laws of the state, provided that no fiduciary may invest such deposits except with the approval of the probate court, and then in an amount not to exceed the amount which the fiduciary is permitted to invest under division (A)(12) of this section;

(14) In savings accounts in, or certificates or other evidences of deposits issued by, a national bank located in the state or a state bank located in and organized under the laws of the state by depositing the funds in the bank, and such national or state bank when itself acting in a fiduciary capacity may deposit the funds in savings accounts in, or certificates or other evidences of deposits issued by, its own savings department or any bank subsidiary corporation owned or controlled by the bank holding company that owns or controls such national or state bank; provided that no deposit shall be made by any fiduciary, individual, or corporate, unless the deposits of the depository bank are insured by the federal deposit insurance corporation created under the "Federal Deposit Insurance Corporation Act of 1933," 48 Stat. 162, 12 U.S.C. 264, as amended, and provided that the deposit of the funds of any one trust in any such savings accounts in, or certificates or other evidences of deposits issued by, any one bank shall not exceed the sum insured under that act, as amended;

(15) Obligations consisting of notes, bonds, debentures, or equipment trust certificates issued under an indenture, which are the direct obligations, or in the case of equipment trust certificates are secured by direct obligations, of a railroad or industrial corporation, or a corporation engaged directly and primarily in the production, transportation, distribution, or sale of electricity or gas, or the operation of telephone or telegraph systems or waterworks, or in some combination of them; provided that the obligor corporation is one which is incorporated under the laws of the United States, any state, or the District of Columbia, and the obligations are rated at the time of purchase in the highest or next highest classification established by at least two standard rating services selected from a list of the standard rating services which shall be prescribed by the superintendent of financial institutions; provided that every such list shall be certified by the superintendent to the clerk of each probate court in the state, and shall continue in effect until a different list is prescribed and certified as provided in this division;

(16) Obligations issued, assumed, or guaranteed by the international finance corporation or by the international bank for reconstruction and development, the Asian development bank, the inter-American development bank, the African development bank, or other similar development bank in which the president, as authorized by congress and on behalf of the United States, has accepted membership, provided that the obligations are rated at the time of purchase in the highest or next highest classification established by at least one standard rating service selected from a list of standard rating services which shall be prescribed by the superintendent of financial institutions;

(17) Securities of any investment company, as defined in and registered under sections 3 and 8 of the "Investment Company Act of 1940," 54 Stat. 789, 15 U.S.C.A. 80a–3 and 80a–8, that are invested exclusively in forms of investment or in instruments that are fully collateralized by forms of investment in which the fiduciary is permitted to invest pursuant to divisions (A)(1) to (16) of this section, provided that, in addition to such forms of investment, the investment company may, for the purpose of reducing risk of loss or of stabilizing investment returns, engage in hedging transactions.

(B) No administrator or executor may invest funds belonging to an estate in any asset other than a direct obligation of the United States that has a maturity date not exceeding one year from the date of investment, or other than in a short-term investment fund that is invested exclusively in obligations of the

United States or of its agencies, or primarily in such obligations and otherwise only in variable demand notes, corporate money market instruments including, but not limited to, commercial paper, or fully collateralized repurchase agreements or other evidences of indebtedness that are payable on demand or generally have a maturity date not exceeding ninety-one days from the date of investment, except with the approval of the probate court or with the permission of the instruments creating the trust.

(C)(1) In addition to the investments allowed by this section, a guardian or trustee, with the approval of the court, may invest funds belonging to the trust in productive real estate located within the state, provided that neither the guardian nor the trustee nor any member of the family of either has any interest in such real estate or in the proceeds of the purchase price. The title to any real estate so purchased by a guardian must be taken in the name of the ward.

(2) Notwithstanding the provisions of division (C)(1) of this section, the court may permit the funds to be used to purchase or acquire a home for the ward or an interest in a home for the ward in which a member of the ward's family may have an interest.

(D) If the fiduciary is a trustee appointed by and accountable to the probate court, the fiduciary shall invest the trust's assets pursuant to the requirements and standards set forth in the Ohio Uniform Prudent Investor Act.

(2006 H 416, eff. 1–1–07; 1998 H 701, eff. 3–22–99; 1995 S 162, eff. 10–29–95; 1994 S 179, eff. 3–10–95; 1992 H 332, eff. 10–6–92; 1988 S 228; 1987 H 21; 1986 H 562; 1969 S 171, S 176; 131 v S 202, S 58; 129 v 582; 128 v 939; 127 v 27; 125 v 903; 1953 H 1; GC 10506–41)

Uncodified Law

1998 H 701, § 3, eff. 3–22–99, reads:

If, on the effective date of this act, a trust meets all of the following conditions, it is not subject to this act until January 1, 2000:

(A) The trust assets are invested and managed by a non-corporate trustee.

(B) The trust cannot be terminated by the grantor.

(C) The value of the trust, as of December 31, 1998, is less than $100,000.

Historical and Statutory Notes

Pre–1953 H 1 Amendments: 123 v 667; 119 v 394, § 1; 118 v 503, § 1; 117 v 458; 116 v 250; 115 v Pt 2, 284; 115 v 396; 114 v 372

Amendment Note: 2006 H 416 substituted "Ohio Uniform Prudent Investor Act" for "sections 1339.52 to 1339.61 of the Revised Code" in division (D).

Amendment Note: 1998 H 701 inserted ", including division (D) of this section," in the first paragraph in division (A); added division (D); and made other nonsubstantive changes.

Amendment Note: 1995 S 162 substituted "financial institutions" for "banks" in divisions (A)(15) and (16).

Amendment Note: 1994 S 179 inserted "the international finance corporation or by" in division (A)(16).

OSBA Probate and Trust Law Section

1965:

With respect to the amendment of R. C. 2109.37, it is recognized that bank and savings and loan company deposits usually have to be maintained for quarterly or semiannual periods before interest is paid. U. S. Obligations and particularly treasury bills can be purchased with almost any short term maturity desired. Executors or administrators liquidating assets and/or holding large sums to pay federal estate tax obligations are often reluctant to invest them in financial institutions in amounts in excess of the deposit guarantees and therefore turn to government short term obligations. It appears unnecessary to require an executor or administrator to secure court approval to invest in direct obligations of the United States having a maturity date not exceeding one year from the date of investment.

See also the comment for 1965 following Sec. 2109.371.

1957:

The proposed amendment to section 2109.37 of the probate chapter relating to investments of fiduciaries generally specifies that a trustee, in addition to a guardian, may invest in real estate. It also provides that a guardian may invest funds in a home for the ward. This fills a long felt need.

Cross References

Capital improvements projects, obligations as lawful investments, 164.09
Cemeteries, endowment care trusts, investments, 1721.21
Endowment care fund, cemetery association, 1721.21
Pet cemeteries, endowment care funds, 961.04
Preneed cemetery merchandise and services contracts, investments, 1721.211
Sale of entailed and other estates, investing proceeds, 5303.27
Trust companies, investment of trust funds, 1111.13
Veteran's guardian, investment of surplus funds of estate, 5905.14

Library References

Executors and Administrators ⟐102.
Guardian and Ward ⟐53.
Mental Health ⟐224.
Trusts ⟐216.
Westlaw Topic Nos. 162, 196, 257A, 390.
C.J.S. Executors and Administrators §§ 223 to 225.
C.J.S. Mental Health § 171.
C.J.S. Trusts §§ 482 to 511.
  Baldwin's Ohio Legislative Service Annotated, 2006 H 416 LSC Analysis, p 3/L–1709
  Baldwin's Ohio Legislative Service, 1988 Laws of Ohio, S 228—LSC Analysis, p 5–968

Research References

Encyclopedias

OH Jur. 3d Annuities § 6, Applicable Statutory Provisions.
OH Jur. 3d Fiduciaries § 72, Uniform Prudent Investor Act.
OH Jur. 3d Fiduciaries § 75, What Constitutes the Making of an Investment—Deposit as Investment; Time for Making Investment.
OH Jur. 3d Fiduciaries § 78, Necessity for Court Approval.
OH Jur. 3d Fiduciaries § 82, Instrument Authorizing Investments.
OH Jur. 3d Fiduciaries § 83, Investments Authorized by Statute; Effect of Change in Statute.
OH Jur. 3d Fiduciaries § 84, Legal List for Fiduciary Investment.
OH Jur. 3d Fiduciaries § 85, Legal List for Fiduciary Investment—Particular Investments Government Obligations.
OH Jur. 3d Fiduciaries § 86, Additional Investment Authority; Prudent Person Standard.
OH Jur. 3d Guardian & Ward § 124, Surplus Funds of Veterans' Administration Ward.
OH Jur. 3d Trusts § 430, Investments.

Forms

Ohio Forms Legal and Business § 2:1, Definition—General Background.
Ohio Forms Legal and Business § 25:58, Trust Agreement for Judgment Recovery for Minor.
Ohio Forms Legal and Business § 24:203, Entire Estate to Friend—Powers of Execution.
Ohio Forms and Transactions KP 30.22, Powers of Executor or Trustee.

Treatises and Practice Aids

Carlin, Baldwin's Ohio Practice, Merrick-Rippner Probate Law § 2:92, Fiduciary's Account—Time for Filing.
Carlin, Baldwin's Ohio Practice, Merrick-Rippner Probate Law § 48:9, Beneficiaries Liable for Payment of Decedent's Debts—General Rules.
Carlin, Baldwin's Ohio Practice, Merrick-Rippner Probate Law § 54:4, Fiduciary Accounts—Contents—Certificate of Service.
Carlin, Baldwin's Ohio Practice, Merrick-Rippner Probate Law § 55:1, Fiduciary Misconduct—Deposit and Investment of Funds—Generally.
Carlin, Baldwin's Ohio Practice, Merrick-Rippner Probate Law § 57:4, Removal of Fiduciary—Grounds—Failure to File Inventory or Account.

Carlin, Baldwin's Ohio Practice, Merrick-Rippner Probate Law § 33:17, Trusts—Ohio Uniform Prudent Investor Act.

Carlin, Baldwin's Ohio Practice, Merrick-Rippner Probate Law § 43:10, Construing a Will—Rules of Construction—Guides to Ascertain Testator's Intent.

Carlin, Baldwin's Ohio Practice, Merrick-Rippner Probate Law § 43:18, Construing a Will—Language—Actually Employed by Testator.

Carlin, Baldwin's Ohio Practice, Merrick-Rippner Probate Law § 54:35, Application for Approval of Investment in Real Property—Form.

Carlin, Baldwin's Ohio Practice, Merrick-Rippner Probate Law § 54:36, Order Approving Investment in Real Property—Form.

Carlin, Baldwin's Ohio Practice, Merrick-Rippner Probate Law § 54:37, Application to Invest or Expend Funds—Form.

Carlin, Baldwin's Ohio Practice, Merrick-Rippner Probate Law § 54:38, Order to Invest or Expend Funds—Form.

Carlin, Baldwin's Ohio Practice, Merrick-Rippner Probate Law § 64:20, Powers and Duties of Guardian—Ward's Estate—Mandatory Duties.

Carlin, Baldwin's Ohio Practice, Merrick-Rippner Probate Law § 64:21, Powers and Duties of Guardian—Ward's Estate—Discretionary Acts.

Carlin, Baldwin's Ohio Practice, Merrick-Rippner Probate Law § 64:41, Application to Purchase Home for Ward—Form.

Carlin, Baldwin's Ohio Practice, Merrick-Rippner Probate Law § 64:42, Entry Granting Application to Purchase Home for Ward—Form.

Carlin, Baldwin's Ohio Practice, Merrick-Rippner Probate Law § 64:43, Complaint to Purchase and Mortgage Real Estate—Form.

Carlin, Baldwin's Ohio Practice, Merrick-Rippner Probate Law § 64:45, Entry Approving Report of Plaintiff as to Terms, and Authorizing Investment and Directing Execution of Note and Mortgage—Form.

Bogert - the Law of Trusts and Trustees § 236, Personal Life Insurance Trusts—Methods of Creating a Personal Insurance Trust.

Bogert - the Law of Trusts and Trustees § 543, Trustee's Duty of Loyalty to the Beneficiaries.

Bogert - the Law of Trusts and Trustees § 598, Safe-Keeping—Safety Deposit Box and Bank Account.

Bogert - the Law of Trusts and Trustees § 651, Ohio.

Bogert - the Law of Trusts and Trustees § 672, Federal, State and Municipal Bonds.

Bogert - the Law of Trusts and Trustees § 674, Loans Secured by Mortgages.

Bogert - the Law of Trusts and Trustees § 676, Real Estate and Personal Property.

Bogert - the Law of Trusts and Trustees § 678, Loans Without Property Security.

Bogert - the Law of Trusts and Trustees § 680, Power of Settlor to Control Trust Investments.

Restatement (2d) of Trusts § 6, Trust and Executorship or Administratorship.

Restatement (2d) of Trusts § 227, Investments Which a Trustee Can Properly Make.

Law Review and Journal Commentaries

Drafting Trust Instruments, Robert P. Goldman. 5 U Cin L Rev 172 (March 1931).

Investment by Corporate Fiduciaries, Note. 6 Ohio St L J 63 (December 1939).

Investment Legals for Corporate Fiduciaries, Frank S. Rowley. 14 U Cin L Rev 156 (January 1940).

Investment of Trust Funds, Samuel Freifield. 5 U Cin L Rev 1 (January 1931).

Investments By Fiduciaries Under the New Ohio Probate Code, Samuel Freifield. 5 U Cin L Rev 429 (November 1931).

Land Trust Certificates with Relation to Ohio Law, Robert P. Goldman and Clyde M. Abbott. 2 U Cin L Rev 255 (May 1928).

Ohio's Prudent Man Rule—Present and Proposed, Harley A. Watkins. Ohio B Ass'n Serv Letter, Probate Law Edition, Oct, 1964.

The Proposed Ohio Prudent Investor Act and Its Impact on Current Ohio Trust Investment Law, Joanne E. Hindel. 7 Prob L J Ohio 66 (July/August 1997).

The Uniform Trusts Act, Frank S. Rowley and Harry W. Vanneman. 5 Ohio St L J 145 (March 1939).

The Uniform Trusts Act, Frank S. Rowley and Harry W. Vanneman. 13 U Cin L Rev 157 (March 1939).

Notes of Decisions

Fiduciary, duties or liabilities 5
Interest or loss on investment 4
Investment restrictions 2
Right or duty to reinvest 3
Rights of depositor or beneficiary 1

---

1. Rights of depositor or beneficiary

Provision for notice to ward of hearing on application to make investments or to approve investments already made is not contemplated by this section; in absence of language in statute securing to ward right to be notified of hearing upon application to make investment of his estate under this section, ward is not entitled to such notice and matter of authorization is one lodged with court to be exercised by it in its wisdom and discretion. Schick v. Kroeger (Franklin 1936) 22 Ohio Law Abs. 389.

Benefits paid to a veteran or his guardian under the World War Veterans Relief Act deposited in a checking account are exempt from creditors' claims, but if deposited in a savings account are classed as investments and not exempt. Guardianship of Pryor (Ohio Prob. 1952) 106 N.E.2d 672, 62 Ohio Law Abs. 548, 48 O.O. 175.

Where a will gives to a trustee certain shares of stock, the net income of which is to be paid to one person for life with remainder to another, all cash or property dividends declared thereon belong to the life tenant and all stock dividends belong to the remainderman. Lamb v. Lehmann (Ohio 1924) 110 Ohio St. 59, 143 N.E. 276, 42 A.L.R. 437, 2 Ohio Law Abs. 245, 22 Ohio Law Rep. 29.

Any doubt in respect to the legality of a challenged investment made by the guardian of the estate of an incompetent, must be resolved in favor of the ward, for whose benefit the legislation is enacted. In re Guardianship of Lodge (Ohio Prob. 1934) 32 Ohio NP(NS) 40.

When a guardian of an incompetent person or minor, with the approval of the probate court, purchases real estate, paying a portion of the purchase price thereof with funds received from the US veterans bureau by said guardian for said ward, the balance of said purchase price to be paid in installments or at a future time, and title to said real estate is taken in the name of such ward, the interest of said ward in said real estate, to the extent of the amount of the purchase price so paid, is exempt from taxation. 1932 OAG 4239.

2. Investment restrictions

If a particular form of investment of trust funds is directed by a will (as here to be put at interest with the same discretion as if acting for themselves), statute does not limit the kind of investments, but an order of the probate court is recommended. In re Trusteeship of Couden (Ohio App. 1 Dist. 1917) 9 Ohio App. 207.

Order of probate court reading: "it is hereby ordered that the said executor distribute the stocks and bonds among the distributees of the said estate as follows, viz.: "W. W. Witmeyer, Tr 10 shares preferred stock of Victor Rubber Company, par value $1000.00. Distributive value, $1000.00." constitutes approval of court of this investment as required under this section. Witmeyer v. Sheets (Clark 1937) 24 Ohio Law Abs. 59.

This section provides for a guardian's investment of his ward's funds with a building and loan association, if the same is approved by court, and where probate court approved previous deposits made and also authorized, ordered and directed guardian to place future funds in same institution, this authorization of court protected guardian in making of deposits irrespective of fact that court from time to time also approved his accounts from which it appeared that guardian was carrying investments with same institutions. Schick v. Kroeger (Franklin 1936) 22 Ohio Law Abs. 389.

Neither statute authorizing investment of principal in securities nor statute authorizing investment of principal in short term investment funds was successor to statute generally limiting investment of principal to government obligations, mortgage—backed securities, and investment company securities, so that will authorizing trustee to invest principal in "those investments permitted to fiduciaries under Section 2109.37 of the Ohio Revised Code or any successor statute" did not permit investments of the type permitted by the later statutes. Bank One Ohio Trust Co., N.A. v.

Hiram College (Ohio App. 7 Dist., 10-31-1996) 115 Ohio App.3d 159, 684 N.E.2d 1275. Wills ⇔ 681(1)

The word "securities" used in a codicil does not include savings accounts. Union Commerce Bank v. Kusse (Ohio Prob. 1969) 21 Ohio Misc. 217, 251 N.E.2d 884, 49 O.O.2d 413, 50 O.O.2d 423.

In an action brought in the probate court by a testamentary trustee pursuant to request of the beneficiaries thereof seeking authority to deviate from the administrative provisions of the will with respect to permissible investments and permission to invest in those investments authorized under RC 2109.37 and RC 2109.371, the court is without authority to permit a trustee to deviate from the terms of such trust unless it clearly appears that compliance would be illegal, impossible, or would defeat or substantially impair the accomplishment of the purpose of such trust. Toledo Trust Co. v. Toledo Hospital (Lucas 1962) 117 Ohio App. 425, 192 N.E.2d 674, 24 O.O.2d 237, affirmed 174 Ohio St. 124, 187 N.E.2d 36, 21 O.O.2d 386.

Where a testator, in leaving the residue of his estate in trust, provides for no specific amount of income to be paid to charitable beneficiaries and provides for no specific amount of the corpus of the trust to be distributed to the charitable beneficiaries but does provide "that all investments of capital… shall be in interest bearing securities issued by the United States of America or by any state of the United States of America or by any governmental subdivision of the state of Ohio," a court is not justified in the absence of an existing emergency in permitting the trustee to deviate from this restrictive investment provision because of general inflationary factors and changing economic conditions covering a twenty-year period. Toledo Trust Co. v. Toledo Hospital (Ohio 1962) 174 Ohio St. 124, 187 N.E.2d 36, 21 O.O.2d 386.

Language used in will, particularly that providing that trustee should be "fully authorized to invest…" a portion of the trust, gave authority to invest without regard to the statutory restrictions. Vacha v. Vacha (Ohio Prob. 1961) 179 N.E.2d 187, 87 Ohio Law Abs. 534, 19 O.O.2d 35.

Investments made by trustee which are approved by court are made "in manner provided by law," within authorization in will, by reason of former GC 11214 (GC 10506–41, now RC 2109.37), authorizing fiduciaries to make such investments "as court having control of administration of trust approves." In re Dimond (Clark 1942) 46 N.E.2d 788, 37 Ohio Law Abs. 248.

Fact that exceptions are not filed to a guardian's accounts does not relieve the probate court of the duty of examining the accounts and requiring a guardian to explain an investment which the court may consider improper, and it will be presumed that the probate court performed such duty. In re Baker's Guardianship (Columbiana 1940) 65 Ohio App. 550, 31 N.E.2d 869, 19 O.O. 252. Mental Health ⇔ 300; Mental Health ⇔ 306

Investment of guardianship funds in land trust certificates when former GC 11214 (GC 10506–41, now RC 2109.37) was in effect and authorized guardians to invest in securities approved by the probate court, may be approved by that court in an adversary proceeding after the repeal of that section and the enactment of this section, which omitted the authorization as to investing in securities approved by that court; and such an investment, without prior authority from the probate court, cannot be questioned after the probate court subsequently has given specific approval. In re Baker's Guardianship (Columbiana 1940) 65 Ohio App. 550, 31 N.E.2d 869, 19 O.O. 252.

The investment of trust funds by a testamentary trustee Dec. 1, 1928, is governed by the terms and provisions of former GC 11214 (GC 10506–41 (RC 2109.37)) in force and effect at that time. Home Savings & Loan Co. v. Strain (Ohio 1935) 130 Ohio St. 53, 196 N.E. 770, 99 A.L.R. 903, 3 O.O. 104.

Where will directed trustee to invest fund in safe securities of trustee's own choosing with approval of probate court, trustee's failure to secure court's express approval prior to making the investment merely placed burden on trustee, on exceptions to final account, to show legality of investment and absence of injudicious conduct. In re Tischer's Trusteeship (Montgomery 1933) 46 Ohio App. 405, 188 N.E. 876, 15 Ohio Law Abs. 54, 39 Ohio Law Rep. 451. Trusts ⇔ 325

Where will directed trustee to invest fund in safe securities of trustee's own choosing with approval of probate court, and trustee invested only in securities authorized by statute, and court subsequently approved trustee's reports, trustee's failure to obtain court's express approval prior to investment held not to render trustee liable for depreciation. In re Tischer's Trusteeship (Montgomery 1933) 46 Ohio App. 405, 188 N.E. 876, 15 Ohio Law Abs. 54, 39 Ohio Law Rep. 451. Trusts ⇔ 218(1)

Where by the terms of a will a trust fund is created and a trustee appointed with authority to invest the fund in securities of its own choosing by and with the approval of the probate court and the executors and trustees of the testator's estate, but the approval is not specifically required to be given in advance of investment, such investment, if of a kind permitted by statute, and otherwise made in accordance with the requirements of the will, is not affected by the fact that the approval of the probate court was not obtained until the filing of the trustee's account. In re Trusteeship of Tischer, 30 NP(NS) 419 (CP, Montgomery 1932), affirmed by 46 App 405, 188 NE 876 (1933).

Where a testator gives to his executor and trustee the power to sell from his personal estate and reinvest the proceeds, such provision has the effect of extending the scope of RS 6413 governing investments by trustees and relieves the trustee of the requirements of that section. Willis v. Braucher (Ohio 1909) 79 Ohio St. 290, 87 N.E. 185, 6 Ohio Law Rep. 605, 16 Am.Ann.Cas. 66.

Where no approval of investment in participating trust certificates, as required by former GC 11214 (GC 10506–41, now RC 2109.37), was asked of or given by probate court, not only is there no statutory authority for the establishing of trust for investment of fiduciary funds, but its use is contrary to law governing administration of fiduciary trusts which are under jurisdiction of probate court. In re Estate of Wright, 26 Abs 285, 7 OSupp 146 (Prob, Lucas 1935).

Investment by a guardian of funds of his ward in a building and loan association must be approved by probate court at the time when it is made under this section in order to be valid. In re Michael, 18 Abs 629 (App, Darke 1935).

Where trustee made an unauthorized investment with trust funds and afterwards reported the same in his final account which was confirmed and approved, such investment could not thereafter be held to be illegal, where the statute in force at the time permitted investment to be made "in such securities as the court having control of the administration of the trust approves." In re Trusteeship Under Will of Wilson, 32 NP(NS) 497 (Prob, Madison 1934).

A participating trust certificate is not within the definition of "first mortgage on real estate," as used in section and does not constitute an authorized investment. In re Guardianship of Lodge (Ohio Prob. 1934) 32 Ohio NP(NS) 40.

A state building and loan association is not authorized to invest in turnpike bonds. 1958 OAG 3215.

Under terms of statute, as amended in 1939, a fiduciary may invest such funds belonging to his trust, as are to be invested, in shares and certificates or other evidences of deposit issued by a state chartered building and loan association organized under the laws of Ohio, which has obtained insurance of accounts as provided in National Housing Act of 1934, Title 4, and amendments thereto; but where such state chartered building and loan association organized under the laws of Ohio has no insurance of accounts, fiduciary may invest such funds in shares or certificates of such association, provided he secures approval of probate court to make the investment, and amount which may be invested in such shares, certificates, or other evidences of deposits of any individual building and loan association shall not exceed $5000. 1939 OAG 1037.

Section as amended requires all fiduciaries, including trust companies administering estates with funds to be invested, to obtain the approval of the probate court for investing in the classes of investments authorized by said section. 1934 OAG 2780.

3. Right or duty to reinvest

The provisions of RC 2109.37 and RC 2109.42 are applicable to the proceeds of matured series G United States savings bonds which are no longer income-producing, and it is the duty of the guardian of an incompetent to cash or reinvest such bonds which are the property of the incompetent. In re Guardianship of Sachs (Ohio 1962) 173 Ohio St. 270, 181 N.E.2d 464, 19 O.O.2d 122.

In the absence of fraud or bad faith an executor is not liable for a failure to sell stocks belonging to the estate until such stocks had declined substantially in value. In re Bentley's Estate (Ohio 1955) 163 Ohio St. 568, 127 N.E.2d 749, 57 O.O. 5.

Where stock belonging to an estate is in danger of depreciation, a probate court can order the administrator with will annexed to sell and reinvest the stock, and after such order is made, equity will compel the corporation to transfer the stock. Guthrie v. Cincinnati Gas & Elec. Co. (Ohio Super. 1904) 15 Ohio Dec. 23, 2 Ohio N.P.N.S. 117.

4. Interest or loss on investment

Investment in the stock of a corporation on which dividends may possibly be continued is neither authorized by section, nor by the terms of a will requiring the funds to be put out at interest; six per cent will be charged against the trustee from the time dividends stopped. In re Trusteeship of Couden (Ohio App. 1 Dist. 1917) 9 Ohio App. 207.

Probate court has authority to require a negligent trustee to account to the trust for interest lost due to the trustee's negligence. In re Testamentary Trust of Hamm (Ohio App. 11 Dist., 12-01-1997) 124 Ohio App.3d 683, 707 N.E.2d 524. Trusts 189

A negligent trustee may be surcharged for unreasonable investments, including lost principle and lost interest; this award must be predicated upon a finding of negligence in a particular investment and supported by some evidence to show what a reasonable investment would have returned, during the time in which the funds were negligently managed. In re Testamentary Trust of Hamm (Ohio App. 11 Dist., 12-01-1997) 124 Ohio App.3d 683, 707 N.E.2d 524. Trusts 217.1; Trusts 262

Although defendant was resulting trustee for benefit of investors, defendant had separate insurable interest in corpus property to extent that he made contributions of capital and expenses, and trustee therefore was entitled to receive proceeds of fire insurance for which he alone paid premiums; trustee had no duty to insure property for beneficiaries, and equitable beneficiaries could have obtained insurance to protect their insurable interest. Gabel v. Richley (Ohio App. 2 Dist., 02-24-1995) 101 Ohio App.3d 356, 655 N.E.2d 773. Insurance 1790(1); Insurance 3443; Trusts 182

Where a testator provides that the amount of a legacy shall be invested in government bonds at all times and the maximum rate of interest paid on such bonds is two and one-half per cent per annum, it is not error to require the executor to pay interest at that rate instead of the statutory rate during the delay in paying the legacy beginning nine months after the notice of the executor's appointment. In re Shanafelt's Estate (Ohio 1955) 164 Ohio St. 258, 129 N.E.2d 816, 58 O.O. 7. Executors And Administrators 313

An executor is entitled to credits for losses on investments of funds of the estate only when he acted in good faith and exercised the care men of ordinary prudence would exercise in the management of their own affairs; burden of establishing the validity of such credits is upon the executor. In re Howison's Estate (Union 1934) 49 Ohio App. 421, 197 N.E. 333, 17 Ohio Law Abs. 361, 3 O.O. 301. Executors And Administrators 103

Allowing investments of the decedent to continue in a bank which the executor, because of an official connection therewith, knows to be in a precarious financial condition, is a failure to use proper care in investment, and the executor is not entitled to credits for consequent losses by failure of the bank. In re Howison's Estate (Union 1934) 49 Ohio App. 421, 197 N.E. 333, 17 Ohio Law Abs. 361, 3 O.O. 301. Executors And Administrators 105

Where losses on investments of the funds of an estate are due to the failure of a bank, for which losses the executor is not entitled to credits because of his negligent investments, and where a final account is necessitated by his resignation, the payment of the funds owing to the estate will not be deferred until complete liquidation of the bank and the ascertainment of the deficiency owing by the executor and his surety, they not being prejudiced thereby since they are entitled to be subrogated to the claim of the estate against the bank. In re Howison's Estate (Union 1934) 49 Ohio App. 421, 197 N.E. 333, 17 Ohio Law Abs. 361, 3 O.O. 301. Executors And Administrators 105

Money in the hands of an administrator which has yielded him no profit, and which he has not been ordered to pay out, or which is tied up by litigation in good faith, does not bear interest; this rule is applicable to debts which the administrator owes to the estate, and which is chargeable against him as money in his hands. James v. West (Ohio 1902) 67 Ohio St. 28, 47 W.L.B. 857, 65 N.E. 156. Executors And Administrators 104(1)

Where guardian-bank became insolvent after making unlawful investment of ward's funds by exchanging mortgages for participating trust certificates, successor-guardian, held entitled to equitable lien on certificates to secure repayment of amounts invested in trust certificates, with interest at six per cent. In re Guardianship of Lodge (Ohio Prob. 1934) 32 Ohio NP(NS) 40.

5. Fiduciary, duties or liabilities

A fiduciary who keeps trust funds in a checking account in his own name because he intends to use the funds to make necessary repairs on the beneficiary's house but is unable to do so due to working overtime, presents a fact question, judgment for the beneficiary is error. Kinzel v. Kinzel (Ohio App. 9 Dist., Lorain, 03-20-1996) No. 95CA006122, 1996 WL 121997, Unreported.

If an investment of trust funds is made illegally, trustee is liable for loss occasioned thereby, regardless of the question of due care. In re Testamentary Trust of Hamm (Ohio App. 11 Dist., 12-01-1997) 124 Ohio App.3d 683, 707 N.E.2d 524. Trusts 217.1

Trustees of resulting trusts stand in fiduciary relationship to trust beneficiaries but do not have same active management duties of trustees of express trusts; trustee of resulting trust is ordinarily under duty merely to convey property to beneficiary or in accordance with directions. Gabel v. Richley (Ohio App. 2 Dist., 02-24-1995) 101 Ohio App.3d 356, 655 N.E.2d 773. Trusts 182; Trusts 284

Under either constructive or resulting type of implied trust, trustee has duty to transfer title of property to equitable beneficiaries at their request. Gabel v. Richley (Ohio App. 2 Dist., 02-24-1995) 101 Ohio App.3d 356, 655 N.E.2d 773. Trusts 284

If, by the terms of a trust instrument, a trustee is specifically directed to retain certain investments, such trustee is subject to liability if such investments are not so retained, absent impossibility, illegality, or a judicially determined change of circumstances. Stevens v. National City Bank (Ohio 1989) 45 Ohio St.3d 276, 544 N.E.2d 612. Trusts 217.3(9)

If, by the terms of a trust instrument, a trustee is merely authorized, but not directed, to retain certain investments, the trustee may retain them, unless under the circumstances it would be an abuse of discretion to retain them, or the trustee may sell a portion of such securities to obtain a diversification of the trust assets. Stevens v. National City Bank (Ohio 1989) 45 Ohio St.3d 276, 544 N.E.2d 612. Trusts 217.3(9)

A provision in decedent's will which provides that a legatee's share is to be given to his sister, to be held in trust for him, and to be paid over in whole or in part to him as she may deem advisable, creates a valid discretionary trust. In re Ternansky's Estate (Summit 1957) 141 N.E.2d 189, 76 Ohio Law Abs. 203, 4 O.O.2d 329.

Where the trustee personally operates a business and is peculiarly valuable in its operation, it is consistent with sound business practice to insure the life of the trustee for the benefit of the trust, and the annual premiums on such insurance are properly chargeable to operating expense. Holmes v. Hrobon (Ohio 1953) 158 Ohio St. 508, 110 N.E.2d 574, 49 O.O. 450. Wills 684.5

The word, "fiduciary" as used in this section embraces the trustee of a testamentary trust. Holmes v. Hrobon (Franklin 1951) 93 Ohio App. 1, 103 N.E.2d 845, 61 Ohio Law Abs. 113, 61 Ohio Law Abs. 241, 50 O.O. 178, affirmed in part, reversed in part 158 Ohio St. 508, 110 N.E.2d 574, 49 O.O. 450.

Unless the terms of the will expressly authorize the trustee to purchase insurance on his own life, payable to the trust, and paid for out of trust assets or income, he has no authority to purchase such insurance. Holmes v. Hrobon (Franklin 1951) 93 Ohio App. 1, 103 N.E.2d 845, 61 Ohio Law Abs. 113, 61 Ohio Law Abs. 241, 50 O.O. 178, affirmed in part, reversed in part 158 Ohio St. 508, 110 N.E.2d 574, 49 O.O. 450.

Guardian who invests the funds of his ward by depositing them in a bank, such investment not being authorized by section, or by probate court, is liable for any loss that may be occasioned thereby, regardless of the question of due care on the part of the guardian. In re Flavin's Guardianship (Morrow 1938) 59 Ohio App 443, 18 N.E.2d 514, 27 Ohio Law Abs. 257, 12 O.O. 262. Guardian And Ward 55

A guardian of an incompetent cannot escape liability for an unauthorized investment of his ward's funds by showing that in an earlier account filed and approved by the probate court he listed such unauthorized securities as investments of the estate. Soliday v. Ash (Hocking 1931) 40 Ohio App. 498, 179 N.E. 150, 10 Ohio Law Abs. 364.

Money in the hands of an administrator which has yielded him no profit, and which he has not been ordered to pay out, or which is tied up by litigation in good faith, does not bear interest; this rule is applicable to debts which the administrator owes to the estate, and which is chargeable against him as money in his hands. James v. West (Ohio 1902) 67 Ohio St. 28, 47 W.L.B. 857, 65 N.E. 156. Executors And Administrators 104(1)

Words "except as may be otherwise provided by law" constitute no grant to corporate fiduciaries of investment powers not theretofore possessed by them. Neff v. Cleveland Trust Co. (Ohio Com.Pl. 1941) 7 Ohio Supp. 136, 35 Ohio Law Abs. 1, 21 O.O. 461.

A corporate trustee has power to be a limited partner in a limited partnership. Cleveland Trust Co v Ingalls, 91 Abs 70 (Prob, Cuyahoga 1963).

Transaction within trust department of guardian-bank by which ward's mortgages were sold to the trust department and became a part of the mortgages against which participating trust certificates were issued in exchange therefor, held invalid as contrary to the principle of equity that a fiduciary cannot deal with himself. In re Guardianship of Lodge (Ohio Prob. 1934) 32 Ohio NP(NS) 40.

Where a guardian holds purchase money, notes, and a mortgage received on the sale of real estate, sells them before maturity by representing that the proceeds are to be used to pay debts of the ward, but appropriates part of the proceeds, the buyers cannot recover as to such part on foreclosure. McFarland v Harper, 33 B 87 (Greene 1895).

2109.371 Additional investment authority

(A) In addition to those investments made eligible by section 2109.37 or 2109.372 of the Revised Code, investments may be made by a fiduciary other than a guardian under sections 5905.01 to 5905.19 of the Revised Code, and subject to the restriction placed on an administrator or executor by division (B) of section 2109.37 of the Revised Code, in any of the following kinds and classes of securities, provided that it may be lawfully sold in Ohio and investment is made only in such securities as would be acquired by prudent persons of discretion and intelligence in such matters who are seeking a reasonable income and the preservation of their capital:

(1) Securities of corporations organized and existing under the laws of the United States, the District of Columbia, or any state of the United States including, but not limited to, bonds, debentures, notes, equipment trust obligations, or other evidences of indebtedness, and shares of common and preferred stocks of such corporations;

(2) Subject to division (C) of this section, collective investment funds established in accordance with section 1111.14 of the Revised Code or securities of any investment company, including any affiliated investment company, whether or not the fiduciary has invested other funds held by it in an agency or other nonfiduciary capacity in the securities of the same investment company or affiliated investment company. Such investments may be made regardless of the eligibility of the underlying assets held by the fund portfolios of the investment company.

(3) Bonds or other interest-bearing obligations of any state or territory of the United States, or of any county, city, village, school district, or other legally constituted political taxing subdivision of any state or territory of the United States, not otherwise eligible under division (A)(2) or (3) of section 2109.37 of the Revised Code;

(4) Debt or equity securities of foreign corporations that trade on recognized United States domiciled exchanges.

(B) No investment shall be made pursuant to this section which, at the time such investment is made, causes the aggregate market value of the investments, not made eligible by section 2109.37 or 2109.372 of the Revised Code, to exceed sixty per cent of the aggregate market value at that time of all the property of the fund held by the fiduciary. No sale or other liquidation of any investment shall be required solely because of any change in the relative market value of those investments made eligible by this section and those made eligible by section 2109.37 or 2109.372 of the Revised Code; provided that, in the event of a sale of investments authorized by this section, the proceeds from the sale may be reinvested in the kinds and classes of securities authorized by this section without regard to the percentage limitation provided in this division. In determining the aggregate market value of the property of a fund and the percentage of a fund to be invested under this section, a fiduciary may rely upon published market quotations as to those investments for which such quotations are available and upon such valuations of other investments as, in the fiduciary's best judgment, seem fair and reasonable according to available information.

(C)(1)(a) A fiduciary making an investment of trust funds in securities of an affiliated investment company, or a bank subsidiary corporation or other corporation owned or controlled by the bank holding company that owns or controls the fiduciary, may charge a reasonable fee for investment advisory, brokerage, transfer agency, registrar, management, or other similar services provided to an affiliated investment company. The fee may be in addition to the compensation to which the fiduciary is otherwise entitled to receive from the trust, provided that the fee is charged as a percentage of either asset value or income earned or actual amount charged and is disclosed at least annually by prospectus, account statement, or any other written means to all persons entitled to receive statements of account activity. The fiduciary shall disclose the relationship between the fiduciary and the affiliated investment company, at least annually by account statement, whether or not the fee is charged.

(b) A fiduciary making an investment of trust funds in securities of an affiliated investment company pursuant to division (A)(2) of this section shall, when providing any periodic account statements to the trust fund, report the net asset value of the shares comprising the investment of the trust funds in the affiliated investment company.

(c) If a fiduciary making an investment of trust funds in securities of an affiliated investment company pursuant to division (A)(2) of this section invests such funds in any mutual fund, the fiduciary shall disclose, in at least ten-point boldface type, by prospectus, account statement, or any other written means to all persons entitled to receive statements of account activity, that the mutual fund is not insured or guaranteed by the federal deposit insurance corporation or by any other government-sponsored agency of the federal government or of this state.

(2) Unless the investment of trust funds in securities of an affiliated investment company can be made under the terms of the instrument creating the trust, an exception to the investment of trust funds in securities of an affiliated investment company may be filed with the probate court. Any exception filed pursuant to this division must be signed by all persons who would, at the time the exception is filed, be permitted to file an exception to an account pursuant to section 2109.33 of the Revised Code and must state that all such persons request that the current investment of trust funds in securities of an affiliated investment company be terminated within a reasonable time. If the probate court determines that the exception complies with the requirements of this division, the probate court shall establish a schedule for disposing of any current investments in securities of an affiliated investment company, and the fiduciary shall cause the trust to dispose of the investments in accordance with the schedule. The fiduciary shall not be liable for any loss incurred by the trust as a result of complying with division (C)(2) of this section.

(D) As used in this section, "affiliated investment company" and "reasonable fee" have the same meanings as in division (E) of section 1111.13 of the Revised Code.

(2002 H 509, eff. 3-14-03; 1998 H 701, eff. 3-22-99; 1996 H 538, eff. 1-1-97; 1996 S 129, eff. 5-30-96; 1988 H 708, eff. 4-19-88; 1987 H 287, H 21; 1970 H 655; 132 v H 1; 131 v S 202; 129 v 582; 125 v 812)

Uncodified Law

1998 H 701, § 3: See Uncodified Law under 2109.37.

1987 H 287, § 3: See Uncodified Law under 2109.38.

Historical and Statutory Notes

Amendment Note: 2002 H 509 added the last sentence to (A)(2); and added division (A)(4).

Amendment Note: 1998 H 701 added the third sentence in division (C)(1)(a); and removed a reference to the definition of investment company and substituted "1111.13" for "1109.10" in division (D).

Amendment Note: 1996 S 129 substituted "Subject to division (C) of this section, common trust funds established pursuant to section 1109.20 of the Revised Code or securities of any investment company, including any affiliated investment company, whether or not the fiduciary has invested other funds held by it in an agency or other nonfiduciary capacity in the securities of the same investment company or affiliated investment company;" for "Securities of any open-end or closed-end management type investment company or investment trust, or common trust funds that are established pursuant to section 1109.20 of the Revised Code;" in division (A)(2); added divisions (C) and (D); and made changes to reflect gender neutral language throughout.

Amendment Note: 1996 H 538 substituted "collective investment funds that are established in accordance with section 1111.14" for "common trust funds that are established pursuant to section 1109.20" in division (A)(2); and made changes to reflect gender neutral language.

Comparative Laws

Ark.—A.C.A. § 28-71-104.
Colo.—West's C.R.S.A. 15–1–304.
Ind.—West's A.I.C. 30–4–3–3.
Kan.—K.S.A. 17-5004 et seq.
Ky.—Baldwin's KRS 386.800 et seq.
Miss.—Code 1972, § 91–13–3.
N.H.—RSA 564:18.
N.J.—N.J.S.A. 3A:15-35.
Ore.—ORS 128.057.
Va.—Code 1950, § 26–45.1.
Wis.—W.S.A. 881.01.

OSBA Probate and Trust Law Section

1965:

After careful review and study the Committee recommends for resubmission to the General Assembly, without change, the amendments to Section 2109.371 passed at the 1963 session, and amendment to R. C. 2109.37 to permit an executor or administrator to purchase direct obligations of the United States having a maturity date not exceeding one year without probate court approval, and amendments to clarify and make consistent Sections 2109.38, 2109.41 and 2109.42 of the Revised Code.

... The continuing inflationary economy of the country, the decline in the purchasing power of fixed dollar investments, the proven ability of fiduciaries to achieve highly satisfactory investment results through investment in a diversified list of holdings, made either directly or through mutual funds, the widespread adoption of the policy of diversification as shown by analysis of the security holdings of universities, foundations and funds of corporations and individuals, under the guidance of competent investment counsel, coupled with the acceptance of the full Prudent Man Rule by most states with an accompanying satisfactory experience thereunder all strongly support the recommendations of the Committee. Important also as evidence of the conservatism of the proposals, are the points that they do not seek to authorize a full Prudent Man Rule, but adopt the policy of providing for a balanced fund under the 70% limitation and that they do not abolish the legal list, in order that any fiduciary at his option can continue to limit his investments to "legals." The unsophisticated or timid fiduciary can still pick from the legal list. He is not deprived of this safe haven and required necessarily to assume the risk of defending any or all of his investments as prudent.

Cross References

Capital improvements projects, obligations as lawful investments, 164.09
Cemeteries, endowment care trusts, investments, 1721.21
Investing proceeds from sale of entailed estates, 5303.27
Pet cemeteries, endowment care funds, 961.04
Preneed cemetery merchandise and services contracts, investments, 1721.211
Temporary investments by fiduciary, procedure, 1339.44
Trust companies, investment of trust funds, 1111.13

Library References

Executors and Administrators ⇔101.
Guardian and Ward ⇔53.
Mental Health ⇔224.
Trusts ⇔216.
Westlaw Topic Nos. 162, 196, 257A, 390.

C.J.S. Executors and Administrators §§ 223 to 225.
C.J.S. Mental Health § 171.
C.J.S. Trusts §§ 482 to 511.

Research References

Encyclopedias

OH Jur. 3d Fiduciaries § 75, What Constitutes the Making of an Investment—Deposit as Investment; Time for Making Investment.
OH Jur. 3d Fiduciaries § 78, Necessity for Court Approval.
OH Jur. 3d Fiduciaries § 82, Instrument Authorizing Investments.
OH Jur. 3d Fiduciaries § 84, Legal List for Fiduciary Investment.
OH Jur. 3d Fiduciaries § 86, Additional Investment Authority; Prudent Person Standard.

Forms

Ohio Forms Legal and Business § 24:203, Entire Estate to Friend—Powers of Execution.
Ohio Forms and Transactions KP 30.22, Powers of Executor or Trustee.

Treatises and Practice Aids

Carlin, Baldwin's Ohio Practice, Merrick-Rippner Probate Law § 2:92, Fiduciary's Account—Time for Filing.
Carlin, Baldwin's Ohio Practice, Merrick-Rippner Probate Law § 54:4, Fiduciary Accounts—Contents—Certificate of Service.
Carlin, Baldwin's Ohio Practice, Merrick-Rippner Probate Law § 55:1, Fiduciary Misconduct—Deposit and Investment of Funds—Generally.
Carlin, Baldwin's Ohio Practice, Merrick-Rippner Probate Law § 57:4, Removal of Fiduciary—Grounds—Failure to File Inventory or Account.
Carlin, Baldwin's Ohio Practice, Merrick-Rippner Probate Law § 33:17, Trusts—Ohio Uniform Prudent Investor Act.
Carlin, Baldwin's Ohio Practice, Merrick-Rippner Probate Law § 43:10, Construing a Will—Rules of Construction—Guides to Ascertain Testator's Intent.
Carlin, Baldwin's Ohio Practice, Merrick-Rippner Probate Law § 43:18, Construing a Will—Language—Actually Employed by Testator.
Carlin, Baldwin's Ohio Practice, Merrick-Rippner Probate Law § 54:35, Application for Approval of Investment in Real Property—Form.
Carlin, Baldwin's Ohio Practice, Merrick-Rippner Probate Law § 54:36, Order Approving Investment in Real Property—Form.
Carlin, Baldwin's Ohio Practice, Merrick-Rippner Probate Law § 54:37, Application to Invest or Expend Funds—Form.
Carlin, Baldwin's Ohio Practice, Merrick-Rippner Probate Law § 54:38, Order to Invest or Expend Funds—Form.
Bogert - the Law of Trusts and Trustees § 651, Ohio.
Bogert - the Law of Trusts and Trustees § 672, Federal, State and Municipal Bonds.
Bogert - the Law of Trusts and Trustees § 673, Corporate Stocks and Bonds.
Bogert - the Law of Trusts and Trustees § 676, Real Estate and Personal Property.
Bogert - the Law of Trusts and Trustees § 680, Power of Settlor to Control Trust Investments.
Restatement (2d) of Trusts § 227, Investments Which a Trustee Can Properly Make.

Law Review and Journal Commentaries

Liberalization of Ohio's Legal List for Fiduciary Investment: "Prudent Man" Standard Engrafted, Richard F. Sater. 26 Ohio St B Ass'n Rep 749 (November 2, 1953).

Ohio's Prudent Man Rule—Present and Proposed, Harley A. Watkins. Ohio B Ass'n Serv Letter, Probate Law Edition, Oct, 1964.

The Proposed Ohio Prudent Investor Act and Its Impact on Current Ohio Trust Investment Law, Joanne E. Hindel. 7 Prob L J Ohio 66 (July/August 1997).

Notes of Decisions

Statutory authority 2

Trust authority 1

1. Trust authority

The word "securities" used in a codicil does not include savings accounts. Union Commerce Bank v. Kusse (Ohio Prob. 1969) 21 Ohio Misc. 217, 251 N.E.2d 884, 49 O.O.2d 413, 50 O.O.2d 423.

In an action brought in the probate court by a testamentary trustee pursuant to request of the beneficiaries thereof seeking authority to deviate from the administrative provisions of the will with respect to permissible investments and permission to invest in those investments authorized under RC 2109.37 and RC 2109.371, the court is without authority to permit a trustee to deviate from the terms of such trust unless it clearly appears that compliance would be illegal, impossible, or would defeat or substantially impair the accomplishment of the purpose of such trust. Toledo Trust Co. v. Toledo Hospital (Lucas 1962) 117 Ohio App. 425, 192 N.E.2d 674, 24 O.O.2d 237, affirmed 174 Ohio St. 124, 187 N.E.2d 36, 21 O.O.2d 386.

Where a testator, in leaving the residue of his estate in trust, provides for no specific amount of income to be paid to charitable beneficiaries and provides for no specific amount of the corpus of the trust to be distributed to the charitable beneficiaries but does provide "that all investments of capital... shall be in interest bearing securities issued by the United States of America or by any state of the United States of America or by any governmental subdivision of the state of Ohio," a court is not justified in the absence of an existing emergency in permitting the trustee to deviate from this restrictive investment provision because of general inflationary factors and changing economic conditions covering a twenty-year period. Toledo Trust Co. v. Toledo Hospital (Ohio 1962) 174 Ohio St. 124, 187 N.E.2d 36, 21 O.O.2d 386.

Language used in will, particularly that providing that trustee should be "fully authorized to invest..." a portion of the trust, gave authority to invest without regard to the statutory restrictions. Vacha v. Vacha (Ohio Prob. 1961) 179 N.E.2d 187, 87 Ohio Law Abs. 534, 19 O.O.2d 35.

A corporate trustee has power to be a limited partner in a limited partnership. Cleveland Trust Co v Ingalls, 91 Abs 70 (Prob, Cuyahoga 1963).

2. Statutory authority

Neither statute authorizing investment of principal in securities nor statute authorizing investment of principal in short term investment funds was successor to statute generally limiting investment of principal to government obligations, mortgage—backed securities, and investment company securities, so that will authorizing trustee to invest principal in "those investments permitted to fiduciaries under Section 2109.37 of the Ohio Revised Code or any successor statute" did not permit investments of the type permitted by the later statutes. Bank One Ohio Trust Co., N.A. v. Hiram College (Ohio App. 7 Dist., 10-31-1996) 115 Ohio App.3d 159, 684 N.E.2d 1275. Wills ⇔ 681(1)

RC 135.14 does not alter the common-law standard of liability for loss of public funds by public officials where the investment is in violation of the maximum investment limitation embodied in the statute. State v. Herbert (Ohio 1976) 49 Ohio St.2d 88, 358 N.E.2d 1090, 3 O.O.3d 51.

2109.372 Temporary investments by fiduciaries; procedure

(A) As used in this section:

(1) "Short term trust-quality investment fund" means a short term investment fund that meets both of the following conditions:

(a) The fund may be either a collective investment fund established in accordance with section 1111.14 of the Revised Code or a registered investment company, including any affiliated investment company whether or not the fiduciary has invested other funds held by it in an agency or other nonfiduciary capacity in the securities of the same registered investment company or affiliated investment company.

(b) The fund is invested in any one or more of the following manners:

(i) In obligations of the United States or of its agencies;

(ii) In obligations of one or more of the states of the United States or their political subdivisions;

(iii) In variable demand notes, corporate money market instruments including, but not limited to, commercial paper rated at the time of purchase in either of the two highest classifications established by at least one nationally recognized standard rating service;

(iv) Deposits in banks, savings banks, or savings and loan associations, whose deposits are insured by the federal deposit insurance corporation, or in credit unions insured by the national credit union administration or by a credit union share guaranty corporation established under Chapter 1761. of the Revised Code, if the rate of interest paid on such deposits is at least equal to the rate of interest generally paid by such banks, savings banks, savings and loan associations, or credit unions on deposits of similar terms or amounts;

(v) In fully collateralized repurchase agreements or other evidences of indebtedness that are of trust quality and are payable on demand or have a maturity date consistent with the purpose of the fund and the duty of fiduciary prudence.

(2) "Registered investment company" means any investment company that is defined in and registered under sections 3 and 8 of the "Investment Company Act of 1940," 54 Stat. 789, 15 U.S.C.A. 80a–3 and 80a–8.

(3) "Affiliated investment company" has the same meaning as in division (E)(1) of section 1111.13 of the Revised Code.

(B) A fiduciary is not required to invest cash that belongs to the trust and may hold that cash for the period prior to distribution if either of the following applies:

(1) The fiduciary reasonably expects to do either of the following:

(a) Distribute the cash to beneficiaries of the trust on a quarterly or more frequent basis;

(b) Use the cash for the payment of debts, taxes, or expenses of administration within the ninety-day period following the receipt of the cash by the fiduciary.

(2) Determined on the basis of the facilities available to the fiduciary and the amount of the income that reasonably could be earned by the investment of the cash, the amount of the cash does not justify the administrative burden or expense associated with its investment.

(C) If a fiduciary wishes to hold funds that belong to the trust in liquid form and division (B) of this section does not apply, the fiduciary may so hold the funds as long as they are temporarily invested as described in division (D) of this section.

(D)(1) A fiduciary may make a temporary investment of cash that the fiduciary may hold uninvested in accordance with division (B) of this section, and shall make a temporary investment of funds held in liquid form pursuant to division (C) of this section, in any of the following investments, unless the governing instrument provides for other investments in which the temporary investment of cash or funds is permitted:

(a) A short term trust-quality investment fund;

(b) Direct obligations of the United States or of its agencies;

(c) A deposit with a bank, savings bank, savings and loan association, or credit union, including a deposit with the fiduciary itself or any bank subsidiary corporation owned or controlled by the bank holding company that owns or controls the fiduciary, whose deposits are insured by the federal deposit insurance corporation, if the rate of interest paid on that deposit is at least equal to the rate of interest generally paid by that bank, savings bank, savings and loan association, or credit union on deposits of similar terms or amounts.

(2) A fiduciary that makes a temporary investment of cash or funds pursuant to division (D)(1) of this section may charge a

reasonable fee for the services associated with that investment. The fee shall be in addition to the compensation to which the fiduciary is entitled for ordinary fiduciary services.

(3) Fiduciaries that make one or more temporary investments of cash or funds pursuant to division (D)(1) of this section shall provide to the beneficiaries of the trusts involved, that are currently receiving income or have a right to receive income, a written disclosure of their temporary investment practices and, if applicable, the method of computing reasonable fees for their temporary investment services pursuant to division (D)(2) of this section. Fiduciaries may comply with this requirement in any appropriate written document, including, but not limited to, any periodic statement or account.

(4) A fiduciary that makes a temporary investment of cash or funds in an affiliated investment company pursuant to division (D)(1)(a) of this section shall, when providing any periodic account statements of its temporary investment practices, report the net asset value of the shares comprising the investment in the affiliated investment company.

(5) If a fiduciary that makes a temporary investment of cash or funds in an affiliated investment company pursuant to division (D)(1)(a) of this section invests in any mutual fund, the fiduciary shall provide to the beneficiaries of the trust involved, that are currently receiving income or have a right to receive income, a written disclosure, in at least ten-point boldface type, that the mutual fund is not insured or guaranteed by the federal deposit insurance corporation or by any other government agency or government-sponsored agency of the federal government or of this state.

(2005 H 81, eff. 4–14–06; 1996 H 538, eff. 1–1–97; 1992 S 269, eff. 3–24–93; 1992 H 332; 1988 H 503; 1987 H 287)

Uncodified Law

1987 H 287, § 3: See Uncodified Law under 2109.38.

Historical and Statutory Notes

Amendment Note: 2005 H 81 rewrote division (A)(1)(b)(iv); inserted references to savings bank and credit union in division (D)(1)(c); and deleted "his" in the last sentence of division (D)(2). Prior to amendment, division (A)(1)(b)(iv) read:

"(iv) Deposits in banks or savings and loan associations whose deposits are insured by the federal deposit insurance corporation, if the rate of interest paid on such deposits is at least equal to the rate of interest generally paid by such banks or savings and loan associations on deposits of similar terms or amounts;"

Amendment Note: 1996 H 538 substituted "collective investment fund established in accordance with section 1111.14" for "common trust fund established pursuant to section 1109.20" in division (A)(1)(a); substituted "1111.13" for "1109.10" in division (A)(3); and made changes to reflect gender neutral language.

Cross References

Capital improvements projects, obligations as lawful investments, 164.09
Temporary investments by fiduciaries, money from sale of entailed estates, 5303.27
Temporary investments by fiduciary allowed, 1339.44
Trust companies, investment of trust funds, 1111.13
Uniform prudent investor act, prudent investments under, 1339.61

Library References

Executors and Administrators ⇐102.
Guardian and Ward ⇐53.
Mental Health ⇐224.
Trusts ⇐216.
Westlaw Topic Nos. 162, 196, 257A, 390.
C.J.S. Executors and Administrators §§ 223 to 225.
C.J.S. Mental Health § 171.
C.J.S. Trusts §§ 482 to 511.

Research References

Encyclopedias

OH Jur. 3d Fiduciaries § 73, Duty to Invest.
OH Jur. 3d Fiduciaries § 75, What Constitutes the Making of an Investment—Deposit as Investment; Time for Making Investment.
OH Jur. 3d Fiduciaries § 84, Legal List for Fiduciary Investment.
OH Jur. 3d Fiduciaries § 86, Additional Investment Authority; Prudent Person Standard.

Forms

Ohio Forms and Transactions KP 30.22, Powers of Executor or Trustee.

Treatises and Practice Aids

Carlin, Baldwin's Ohio Practice, Merrick-Rippner Probate Law § 33:17, Trusts—Ohio Uniform Prudent Investor Act.
Carlin, Baldwin's Ohio Practice, Merrick-Rippner Probate Law § 43:10, Construing a Will—Rules of Construction—Guides to Ascertain Testator's Intent.
Carlin, Baldwin's Ohio Practice, Merrick-Rippner Probate Law § 43:18, Construing a Will—Language—Actually Employed by Testator.
Carlin, Baldwin's Ohio Practice, Merrick-Rippner Probate Law § 64:20, Powers and Duties of Guardian—Ward's Estate—Mandatory Duties.
Bogert - the Law of Trusts and Trustees § 651, Ohio.
Bogert - the Law of Trusts and Trustees § 680, Power of Settlor to Control Trust Investments.

Notes of Decisions

Authorized investments   1

---

1. Authorized investments

Neither statute authorizing investment of principal in securities nor statute authorizing investment of principal in short term investment funds was successor to statute generally limiting investment of principal to government obligations, mortgage—backed securities, and investment company securities, so that will authorizing trustee to invest principal in "those investments permitted to fiduciaries under Section 2109.37 of the Ohio Revised Code or any successor statute" did not permit investments of the type permitted by the later statutes. Bank One Ohio Trust Co., N.A. v. Hiram College (Ohio App. 7 Dist., 10-31-1996) 115 Ohio App.3d 159, 684 N.E.2d 1275. Wills ⇐ 681(1)

2109.38   Retention of other investments

Sections 2109.37, 2109.371, and 2109.372 of the Revised Code do not prohibit a fiduciary from retaining any part of a trust estate as received by him even though such part is not of the class or percentage permitted to fiduciaries, or from retaining any investment made by him after such investment ceases to be of a class or exceeds the percentage permitted by law, provided the circumstances are not such as to require the fiduciary to dispose of such investment in the performance of his duties.

(1987 H 287, eff. 10–20–87; 131 v S 202; 1953 H 1; GC 10506–42)

Uncodified Law

1987 H 287, § 3, eff. 10–20–87, reads: Sections 1109.10, 2109.371, 2109.38, 2109.41, 2109.42, and 5303.27 of the Revised Code, as amended by this act, and sections 1339.44 and 2109.372 of the Revised Code, as enacted by this act, are intended as a declaration and clarification of statutory authority that existed prior to the effective date of this act.

Historical and Statutory Notes

Pre–1953 H 1 Amendments: 119 v 394, § 1; 114 v 373

OSBA Probate and Trust Law Section

1965:

See the comment for 1965 following Sec. 2109.371.

FIDUCIARIES

Cross References

Investment of trust funds, 1111.13

Library References

Executors and Administrators ⚖102.
Guardian and Ward ⚖53.
Mental Health ⚖225.
Trusts ⚖217.3(9).
Westlaw Topic Nos. 162, 196, 257A, 390.
C.J.S. Executors and Administrators §§ 223 to 225.
C.J.S. Mental Health § 171.
C.J.S. Trusts §§ 482, 491, 502 to 503.

Research References

Encyclopedias

OH Jur. 3d Fiduciaries § 66, Retention of Investments.

Forms

Ohio Forms and Transactions KP 30.22, Powers of Executor or Trustee.

Treatises and Practice Aids

Bogert - the Law of Trusts and Trustees § 686, Statutes Affecting the Duty to Sell Nonlegals.

Restatement (2d) of Trusts § 230, Duty to Dispose of Improper Investments.

Law Review and Journal Commentaries

Investments By Fiduciaries Under the New Ohio Probate Code, Samuel Freifield. 5 U Cin L Rev 429 (November 1931).

Notes of Decisions

Duties of fiduciary 3
Survivorship rights 2
Terms of trust 1

---

1. Terms of trust

If, by the terms of a trust instrument, a trustee is specifically directed to retain certain investments, such trustee is subject to liability if such investments are not so retained, absent impossibility, illegality, or a judicially determined change of circumstances. Stevens v. National City Bank (Ohio 1989) 45 Ohio St.3d 276, 544 N.E.2d 612. Trusts ⚖ 217.3(9)

If, by the terms of a trust instrument, a trustee is merely authorized, but not directed, to retain certain investments, the trustee may retain them, unless under the circumstances it would be an abuse of discretion to retain them, or the trustee may sell a portion of such securities to obtain a diversification of the trust assets. Stevens v. National City Bank (Ohio 1989) 45 Ohio St.3d 276, 544 N.E.2d 612. Trusts ⚖ 217.3(9)

2. Survivorship rights

Under circumstances where a surviving joint depositor would have been entitled to the balance of the account in the absence of any intervening incompetency of the decedent joint depositor, the facts of such incompetency and the appointment of a guardian of the incompetent's estate do not, in and of themselves, destroy the survivorship rights of the surviving depositor. Miller v. Yocum (Auglaize 1969) 18 Ohio App.2d 52, 246 N.E.2d 594, 47 O.O.2d 37, affirmed 21 Ohio St.2d 162, 256 N.E.2d 208, 50 O.O.2d 372.

3. Duties of fiduciary

The existence in a codicil of an express prohibition against selling securities in the estate at the time of the testator's death does not relieve the executor of the duty to apply for authority to sell any of such securities for which sale is indicated by the exercise of due care in the management of the assets of the estate. Union Commerce Bank v. Kusse (Ohio Prob. 1969) 21 Ohio Misc. 217, 251 N.E.2d 884, 49 O.O.2d 413, 50 O.O.2d 423.

POWERS, DUTIES, PROHIBITIONS, AND LIABILITIES

2109.39 Receiving distribution in kind

A fiduciary entitled to a distributive share of the assets of an estate or trust has the same right as other beneficiaries to accept or demand distribution in kind and may retain any security or investment so distributed to him as though it were a part of the original estate received by him.

(1953 H 1, eff. 10–1–53; GC 10506–43)

Historical and Statutory Notes

Pre–1953 H 1 Amendments: 114 v 373

Cross References

Distribution in kind by executor or administrator, 2113.55

Library References

Executors and Administrators ⚖303(1).
Trusts ⚖271, 282.
Westlaw Topic Nos. 162, 390.
C.J.S. Executors and Administrators § 543.
C.J.S. Trusts §§ 318 to 320, 531.

Research References

Encyclopedias

OH Jur. 3d Fiduciaries § 66, Retention of Investments.

Forms

Ohio Jurisprudence Pleading and Practice Forms § 2:31, Disqualification—Procedure and Remedies.

Treatises and Practice Aids

Bogert - the Law of Trusts and Trustees § 571, Continuation of a Decedent's Business by a Personal Representative or Trustee.

2109.40 Participation in corporate reorganization

Unless the instrument creating a trust forbids, a fiduciary may do all of the things which an individual holder might do with respect to securities held by him, including the exercise or sale of subscription rights, the acceptance of new stock in the same corporation in place of the stock held, or in the event of reorganization, sale, or merger in a different corporation, and with the approval of the probate court, the investment of additional funds where required of all shareholders participating in a reorganization.

(1953 H 1, eff. 10–1–53; GC 10506–44)

Historical and Statutory Notes

Pre–1953 H 1 Amendments: 114 v 373

Library References

Executors and Administrators ⚖102.
Guardian and Ward ⚖53.
Mental Health ⚖224.1, 225.
Trusts ⚖217.4.
Westlaw Topic Nos. 162, 196, 257A, 390.
C.J.S. Executors and Administrators §§ 223 to 225.
C.J.S. Mental Health § 171.
C.J.S. Trusts §§ 482, 498.

Research References

Encyclopedias

OH Jur. 3d Fiduciaries § 63, Fiduciary's Rights as Security Holder.

2109.40

Treatises and Practice Aids

Bogert - the Law of Trusts and Trustees § 551, Express and Implied Powers.

Bogert - the Law of Trusts and Trustees § 592, Duty to Collect Choses in Action.

Law Review and Journal Commentaries

The Uniform Trusts Act, Frank S. Rowley and Harry W. Vanneman. 5 Ohio St L J 145 (March 1939).

The Uniform Trusts Act, Frank S. Rowley and Harry W. Vanneman. 13 U Cin L Rev 157 (March 1939).

Notes of Decisions

Consent of probate court 1

---

1. Consent of probate court

By virtue of statute an administrator or an executor has the authority, when in his discretion it is advisable, to participate in the merger or reorganization of a corporation, to exchange shares of stock which are part of the assets of the estate for shares of stock in the new corporation, and it is not necessary, although probably advisable, to obtain the consent of the probate court to such transaction, unless it is necessary to invest additional funds from the estate in order to effect such merger. 1932 OAG 4108.

2109.41 Deposit of funds

Immediately after appointment and throughout the administration of a trust, but subject to section 2109.372 of the Revised Code, every fiduciary, pending payment of current obligations of the fiduciary's trust, distribution, or investment pursuant to law, shall deposit all funds received by the fiduciary in the fiduciary's name as such fiduciary in one or more depositaries. Each depositary shall be a bank, savings bank, savings and loan association, or credit union located in this state. A corporate fiduciary, authorized to receive deposits of fiduciaries, may be the depository of funds held by it as fiduciary. All deposits made pursuant to this section shall be in such class of account as will be most advantageous to the trust, and each depositary shall pay interest at the highest rate customarily paid to its patrons on deposits in accounts of the same class.

The placing of funds in such depositaries under the joint control of the fiduciary and a surety on the bond of the fiduciary shall not increase the liability of the fiduciary.

(2005 H 81, eff. 4–14–06; 1987 H 287, eff. 10–20–87; 131 v S 202; 129 v 345; 1953 H 1; GC 10506–45)

Uncodified Law

1987 H 287, § 3: See Uncodified Law under 2109.38.

Historical and Statutory Notes

Pre–1953 H 1 Amendments: 119 v 394, § 1; 118 v 503, § 1; 116 v 385; 114 v 374

Amendment Note: 2005 H 81 inserted ", savings bank," and ", or credit union" in the second sentence of the first paragraph; deleted "such" in the third sentence of the first paragraph and again in the second paragraph; made changes to reflect gender neutral language; and made other nonsubstantive changes.

OSBA Probate and Trust Law Section

1965:

See the comment for 1965 following Sec. 2109.371.

Library References

Deposits and Escrows ⇌13.
Executors and Administrators ⇌105.
Guardian and Ward ⇌55.
Mental Health ⇌229.
Trusts ⇌221.
Westlaw Topic Nos. 122A, 162, 196, 257A, 390.
C.J.S. Depositaries §§ 15 to 17.
C.J.S. Escrows § 8.
C.J.S. Executors and Administrators § 207.
C.J.S. Mental Health § 175.
C.J.S. Trusts §§ 379 to 380.

Research References

Encyclopedias

38 Am. Jur. Proof of Facts 3d 279, Self-Dealing by Trustee.
OH Jur. 3d Fiduciaries § 49, Form and Type of Account.
OH Jur. 3d Fiduciaries § 53, Effect of Agreement Limiting Control.
OH Jur. 3d Fiduciaries § 75, What Constitutes the Making of an Investment—Deposit as Investment; Time for Making Investment.
OH Jur. 3d Trusts § 424, Deposits in Banks.

Treatises and Practice Aids

Carlin, Baldwin's Ohio Practice, Merrick-Rippner Probate Law § 55:1, Fiduciary Misconduct—Deposit and Investment of Funds—Generally.

Carlin, Baldwin's Ohio Practice, Merrick-Rippner Probate Law § 64:20, Powers and Duties of Guardian—Ward's Estate—Mandatory Duties.

Bogert - the Law of Trusts and Trustees § 543, Trustee's Duty of Loyalty to the Beneficiaries.

Bogert - the Law of Trusts and Trustees § 598, Safe-Keeping—Safety Deposit Box and Bank Account.

Bogert - the Law of Trusts and Trustees § 678, Loans Without Property Security.

Law Review and Journal Commentaries

Investments By Fiduciaries Under the New Ohio Probate Code, Samuel Freifield. 5 U Cin L Rev 429 (November 1931).

Ohio's Prudent Man Rule—Present and Proposed, Harley A. Watkins. Ohio B Ass'n Serv Letter, Probate Law Edition, Oct, 1964.

"Trysting" with an Ethics Disaster, Albert L. Bell. 57 Ohio St B Ass'n Rep 72 (January 30, 1984).

The Uniform Trusts Act, Frank S. Rowley and Harry W. Vanneman. 5 Ohio St L J 145 (March 1939).

The Uniform Trusts Act, Frank S. Rowley and Harry W. Vanneman. 13 U Cin L Rev 157 (March 1939).

Notes of Decisions

Available investment 3
Bank outside of Ohio 5
Interest 4
Temporary deposit 2
Time pending investment 1

---

1. Time pending investment

What is a reasonable time for a guardian to leave his ward's funds on deposit pending investment, distribution or payment of current bills, must be determined from a consideration of the facts of each particular case. In re McIntire's Guardianship (Monroe 1940) 65 Ohio App. 143, 29 N.E.2d 568, 18 O.O. 349.

2. Temporary deposit

A guardian, exercising same measure of care and diligence as would be exercised by a man of ordinary prudence and skill in management of his own business, is not liable for loss of his ward's funds through failure of bank in which he temporarily deposited such funds, before enactment of section, earmarked to show their trust character, in good faith, for safe keeping, in a generally regarded financially sound and solvent incorporated bank situated in the state of residence of himself and his ward, with approval of probate court, pending distribution, investment or payment of current bills of the ward, for a reasonable time and without interest, but not as a permanent investment. In re McIntire's Guardianship (Monroe 1940) 65 Ohio App. 143, 29 N.E.2d 568, 18 O.O. 349.

Deposit by a guardian of his ward's money in a bank is permissible pending distribution or investment only, and not as a permanent investment. In re Flavin's Guardianship (Morrow 1938) 59 Ohio App. 443, 18 N.E.2d 514, 27 Ohio Law Abs. 257, 12 O.O. 262. Guardian And Ward ⇔ 55

Fiduciary is protected upon deposit of funds in accordance with section if possession of funds is to be longer than of a temporary nature and so long as no investment is available to him which in his judgment could be made under GC 10506–41 (RC 2109.37). In re Michael, 18 Abs 629 (App, Darke 1935).

An administrator holding funds awaiting distribution may deposit such money in a building association and such deposit does not constitute an investment. In re Smith's Estate (Ohio Prob. 1933) 32 Ohio NP(NS) 260.

An order of court to make a deposit in a building and loan association is not necessary, but even if it were, the confirmation of the administrator's account would constitute an approval of the administrator's act. In re Smith's Estate (Ohio Prob. 1933) 32 Ohio NP(NS) 260.

3. Available investment

Violation by attorney of RC 2109.41, RC 2109.43 and RC 2109.44 justified disbarment. Toledo Bar Ass'n v. Bartlett (Ohio 1974) 39 Ohio St.2d 100, 313 N.E.2d 834, 68 O.O.2d 59, stay denied 95 S.Ct. 301, 419 U.S. 989, 42 L.Ed.2d 264, certiorari denied 95 S.Ct. 663, 419 U.S. 1073, 42 L.Ed.2d 670, rehearing denied 95 S.Ct. 1153, 420 U.S. 939, 43 L.Ed.2d 418.

Obligation of fiduciary is to place funds in available investment under provisions of GC 10506–41 (RC 2109.37), and deposit of funds in accordance with this section will not be protected where there is an available investment. In re Michael, 18 Abs 629 (App, Darke 1935).

4. Interest

In response to successor trustee's motion to impose surcharge, burden was not upon former trustee of testamentary trust to validate his expenditures; rather, successor trustee bore initial burden to show some negligence in former trustee's management of trust funds with regard to investments made. In re Testamentary Trust of Hamm (Ohio App. 11 Dist., 12-01-1997) 124 Ohio App.3d 683, 707 N.E.2d 524. Trusts ⇔ 325

Surcharge of executor in excess of $16,000, for failing to invest estate funds, was properly calculated based on average cash balance in each of seven accounts of estate, using five percent interest rate. Whitaker v. Estate of Whitaker (Ohio App. 4 Dist., 06-26-1995) 105 Ohio App.3d 46, 663 N.E.2d 681. Executors And Administrators ⇔ 102

Probate court's award of interest, in action for concealment or embezzlement of estate assets, from date that first inventory and appraisal were filed in probate court by administrator of estate, was not abuse of discretion; if estate assets in heir's possession would have been properly turned over to administrator at that time, they would have been earning rate of return because of administrator's duty to invest. Wozniak v. Wozniak (Ohio App. 9 Dist., 09-22-1993) 90 Ohio App.3d 400, 629 N.E.2d 500, cause dismissed 68 Ohio St.3d 1440, 626 N.E.2d 124. Interest ⇔ 39(1)

5. Bank outside of Ohio

Statute governing deposit of funds received by a fiduciary did not give probate court the authority to sanction law firm for depositing settlement funds in a Pennsylvania bank rather than an Ohio bank. In re Estate of Black (Ohio App. 7 Dist., Mahoning, 11-02-2005) No. 04 MA 70, No. 04 MA 73, No. 04 MA 78, No. 04 MA 71, No. 04 MA 75, No. 04 MA 79, No. 04 MA 72, No. 04 MA 77, No. 04 MA 85, 2005- Attorney And Client ⇔ 24

2109.42 Liability for failure to invest or deposit

Subject to section 2109.372 of the Revised Code, a fiduciary who has funds belonging to a trust which are not required for payment of current obligations of his trust or distribution shall, unless otherwise ordered by the probate court, invest such funds within a reasonable time according to section 2109.37 or 2109.371 of the Revised Code. On failure to do so, such fiduciary shall account to the trust for such loss of interest as is found by the court to be due to his negligence.

(1987 H 287, eff. 10–20–87; 131 v S 202; 1953 H 1; GC 10506–46)

Uncodified Law

1987 H 287, § 3: See Uncodified Law under 2109.38.

Historical and Statutory Notes

Pre–1953 H 1 Amendments: 114 v 374

OSBA Probate and Trust Law Section

1965:
See the comment for 1965 following Sec. 2109.371.

Library References

Executors and Administrators ⇔104(2).
Guardian and Ward ⇔54, 55.
Mental Health ⇔228, 229.
Trusts ⇔219, 221.
Westlaw Topic Nos. 162, 196, 257A, 390.
C.J.S. Executors and Administrators §§ 227 to 228.
C.J.S. Mental Health § 175.
C.J.S. Trusts §§ 379 to 380, 512 to 524.

Research References

Encyclopedias

OH Jur. 3d Fiduciaries § 73, Duty to Invest.
OH Jur. 3d Fiduciaries § 75, What Constitutes the Making of an Investment—Deposit as Investment; Time for Making Investment.
OH Jur. 3d Fiduciaries § 87, Generally; Failure to Invest or Negligence.
OH Jur. 3d Fiduciaries § 88, Generally; Failure to Invest or Negligence—Procedure; Findings and Evidence of Negligence.
OH Jur. 3d Fiduciaries § 89, Generally; Failure to Invest or Negligence—Calculation of Surcharge.

Treatises and Practice Aids

Carlin, Baldwin's Ohio Practice, Merrick-Rippner Probate Law § 2:92, Fiduciary's Account—Time for Filing.
Carlin, Baldwin's Ohio Practice, Merrick-Rippner Probate Law § 54:4, Fiduciary Accounts—Contents—Certificate of Service.
Carlin, Baldwin's Ohio Practice, Merrick-Rippner Probate Law § 55:1, Fiduciary Misconduct—Deposit and Investment of Funds—Generally.
Carlin, Baldwin's Ohio Practice, Merrick-Rippner Probate Law § 57:4, Removal of Fiduciary—Grounds—Failure to File Inventory or Account.
Bogert - the Law of Trusts and Trustees § 702, Breach of Duty to Invest.
Bogert - the Law of Trusts and Trustees § 706, Breach of Duty by Failing to Use Reasonable Skill and Prudence in Investing, Retaining or Selling.
Bogert - the Law of Trusts and Trustees § 863, Liability for Interest.

Law Review and Journal Commentaries

Investments By Fiduciaries Under the New Ohio Probate Code, Samuel Freifield. 5 U Cin L Rev 429 (November 1931).

Notes of Decisions

Consequences of noninvestment, denial of fiduciary fees 3
Interest rate 2
Matured bonds 1

1. Matured bonds

The provisions of RC 2109.37 and RC 2109.42 are applicable to the proceeds of matured series G United States savings bonds which are no longer income producing, and it is the duty of the guardian of an incompetent to cash or reinvest such bonds which are the property of the incompetent. In re Guardianship of Sachs (Ohio 1962) 173 Ohio St. 270, 181 N.E.2d 464, 19 O.O.2d 122.

2. Interest rate

Beneficiary was entitled to interest on her share of estate that would have been earned if executor had not breached his fiduciary duty by failing to use due care and diligence in administration of estate; executor was obligated by statute to ensure that assets of estate were properly invested during time between decedent's death and the distribution of estate. Sudnick v. Klein (Ohio App. 11 Dist., Geauga, 12-31-2002) No. 2001-G-2356, No. 2001-G-2365, No. 2001-G-2357, No. 2001-G-2358, 2002-Ohio-7341, 2002 WL 31895117, Unreported, appeal not allowed 98 Ohio St.3d 1567, 787 N.E.2d 1231, 2003-Ohio-2242. Executors And Administrators ⇐ 104(1)

Probate court improperly calculated surcharge to be imposed against former trustee of testamentary trust by subtracting trust's expenditures from trust's beginning balance for period at issue, imposing ten percent interest compounded annually upon that difference and then subtracting trust's ending balance, where there was no evidence that former trustee's negligence caused any damage or loss to trust for the entire period he was its trustee, and there was no evidence that legal rate of ten percent was appropriate or that trust was entitled to receive such rate for entire period. In re Testamentary Trust of Hamm (Ohio App. 11 Dist., 12-01-1997) 124 Ohio App.3d 683, 707 N.E.2d 524. Trusts ⇐ 309; Trusts ⇐ 312

Surcharge of executor in excess of $16,000, for failing to invest estate funds, was properly calculated based on average cash balance in each of seven accounts of estate, using five percent interest rate. Whitaker v. Estate of Whitaker (Ohio App. 4 Dist., 06-26-1995) 105 Ohio App.3d 46, 663 N.E.2d 681. Executors And Administrators ⇐ 102

Where a testator provides that the amount of a legacy shall be invested in government bonds at all times and the maximum rate of interest paid on such bonds is two and one-half per cent per annum, it is not error to require the executor to pay interest at that rate instead of the statutory rate during the delay in paying the legacy beginning nine months after the notice of the executor's appointment. In re Shanafelt's Estate (Ohio 1955) 164 Ohio St. 258, 129 N.E.2d 816, 58 O.O. 7. Executors And Administrators ⇐ 313

Executors were bound to invest within a reasonable time estate funds not needed for current expenditures, but what was a reasonable time was for probate court to determine, and, before executors could be required to account for interest on funds of estate in their hands uninvested, court must find that interest was lost to the estate due to their neglect. Chapman v. Menke (Darke 1944) 68 N.E.2d 361, 45 Ohio Law Abs. 625. Executors And Administrators ⇐ 104(2)

3. Consequences of noninvestment, denial of fiduciary fees

Denying executor fiduciary fees was justified by executor's self-dealing, which resulted from making unauthorized loans to himself from estate funds and failing to invest estate funds. Whitaker v. Estate of Whitaker (Ohio App. 4 Dist., 06-26-1995) 105 Ohio App.3d 46, 663 N.E.2d 681. Executors And Administrators ⇐ 500

2109.43 Personal use of trust property prohibited

No fiduciary shall make any personal use of the funds or property belonging to a trust. For violation of this section, such fiduciary and his bond shall be liable in an action for any loss occasioned by such use and for such additional amount by way of forfeiture, not exceeding the amount of the loss occasioned by such use, as may be fixed by the probate court hearing such cause. Such amounts shall be payable for the benefit of the beneficiary, if living, and to his estate if he is deceased.

Any action under this section shall be brought not later than one year after the termination of the trust or the discovery of such loss.

(1953 H 1, eff. 10–1–53; GC 10506–47, 10506–48)

Historical and Statutory Notes

Pre–1953 H 1 Amendments: 114 v 374

Library References

Executors and Administrators ⇐ 115.
Guardian and Ward ⇐ 62.
Mental Health ⇐ 237.
Trusts ⇐ 231.
Westlaw Topic Nos. 162, 196, 257A, 390.
C.J.S. Executors and Administrators §§ 264 to 266, 343.
C.J.S. Mental Health § 179.
C.J.S. Trusts §§ 325, 327, 332 to 337.

Research References

Encyclopedias

38 Am. Jur. Proof of Facts 3d 279, Self-Dealing by Trustee.
OH Jur. 3d Fiduciaries § 104, Personal Use of Assets.
OH Jur. 3d Fiduciaries § 105, Personal Use of Assets—Action for Loss Resulting from Personal Use.
OH Jur. 3d Fiduciaries § 219, Statute of Limitations.
OH Jur. 3d Trusts § 417, Prohibition Against Trustee Benefiting from Trust.

Treatises and Practice Aids

Carlin, Baldwin's Ohio Practice, Merrick-Rippner Probate Law § 55:2, Fiduciary Misconduct—Prohibition Against Personal Use.
Carlin, Baldwin's Ohio Practice, Merrick-Rippner Probate Law § 55:3, Fiduciary Misconduct—Liability for Funds and Property of Trust.
Carlin, Baldwin's Ohio Practice, Merrick-Rippner Probate Law § 55:4, Fiduciary Misconduct—Time of Action Against Fiduciary.
Carlin, Baldwin's Ohio Practice, Merrick-Rippner Probate Law § 55:5, Fiduciary Misconduct—Exceptions Filed to Accounts.
Carlin, Baldwin's Ohio Practice, Merrick-Rippner Probate Law § 64:1, Powers and Duties of Guardian—Fiduciary Relationship.
Bogert - the Law of Trusts and Trustees § 541, General Duties—Duty to Exercise Ordinary Skill and Diligence.
Bogert - the Law of Trusts and Trustees § 543, Trustee's Duty of Loyalty to the Beneficiaries.
Bogert - the Law of Trusts and Trustees § 701, Scope of Chapter—General Underlying Principles.
Bogert - the Law of Trusts and Trustees § 861, Remedies of the Beneficiary Against the Trustee.
Bogert - the Law of Trusts and Trustees § 963, Duty to Render Formal Account in Court of Equity.

Law Review and Journal Commentaries

Probate Malpractice, Hon. Fred V. Skok. 14 Lake Legal Views 1 (February 1991).

The Trustee's Duties and Responsibilities, Karen M. Moore. 7 Prob L J Ohio 51 (May/June 1997).

Notes of Decisions

Compensation 2
Gifts 4
Procedural issues 3
Violations 1

---

1. Violations

Violation by attorney of RC 2109.41, RC 2109.43 and RC 2109.44 justified disbarment. Toledo Bar Ass'n v. Bartlett (Ohio 1974) 39 Ohio St.2d 100, 313 N.E.2d 834, 68 O.O.2d 59, stay denied 95 S.Ct. 301, 419 U.S. 989, 42 L.Ed.2d 264, certiorari denied 95 S.Ct. 663, 419 U.S. 1073, 42 L.Ed.2d 670, rehearing denied 95 S.Ct. 1153, 420 U.S. 939, 43 L.Ed.2d 418.

A guardian is not entitled to make personal use of his ward's car, nor to charge the expense thereof to the estate where the ward is no longer able to use such car. In re Guardianship of O'Brien (Darke 1955) 140 N.E.2d 806, 74 Ohio Law Abs. 366.

2. Compensation

Upon exceptions to a guardian's account the guardian should be required to account for compensation paid to himself for time spent selecting items for himself and others prior to a sale of personal property and for Christmas gifts made to himself and others, but not for payments to himself for care of the ward. (See also In re Guardianship of Tillman, 100 App 291, 136 NE(2d) 291 (1955).) In re Tillman (Ohio Prob. 1956) 137 N.E.2d 172, 73 Ohio Law Abs. 534.

3. Procedural issues

Section has no application to exceptions filed to the accounts of testamentary trustee by remaindermen and a hearing on such exceptions; the statutes relative to the filing of accounts and hearing of exceptions thereto apply. In re Deibel's Trust (Franklin 1949) 86 Ohio App. 346, 91 N.E.2d 812, 41 O.O. 380.

Where successor administrator, in action on surety bond given by defendant on first administrator, did not seek a penalty, limitations of GC 10506–47 and GC 10506–48 (RC 2109.43) were not applicable, and action was governed by limitations of GC 11226 (RC 2305.12). Massachusetts Bonding & Ins. Co. v. Winters Nat. Bank & Trust Co. of Dayton, Ohio (C.C.A.6 (Ohio) 1942) 130 F.2d 5, 24 O.O. 225, certiorari denied 63 S.Ct. 526, 317 U.S. 700, 87 L.Ed. 560.

4. Gifts

Power of guardian to make gifts on behalf of ward discussed. (See also In re Guardianship of Tillman, 100 App 291, 136 NE(2d) 291 (1955).) In re Tillman (Ohio Prob. 1956) 137 N.E.2d 172, 73 Ohio Law Abs. 534.

2109.44 Fiduciaries not allowed to have dealings with estate; exception (first version)

Note: See also following version of this section, and Publisher's Note.

Fiduciaries shall not buy from or sell to themselves and shall not have in their individual capacities any dealings with the estate, except as expressly authorized by the instrument creating the trust and then only with the approval of the probate court in each instance. No corporate fiduciary, other than a trust company, as defined in section 1101.01 of the Revised Code, shall be permitted to deal with the estate, any power in the instrument creating the trust to the contrary notwithstanding. This section does not prohibit a fiduciary from making an advancement when the advancement has been expressly authorized by the instrument creating the trust or when the probate court approves or from engaging in any act authorized by this chapter.

(1996 S 129, eff. 5–30–96; 1992 S 269, eff. 3–24–93; 1953 H 1; GC 10506–49)

Note: See also following version of this section, and Publisher's Note.

2109.44 Fiduciaries not allowed to have dealings with estate; exception (second version)

Note: See also preceding version of this section, and Publisher's Note.

Fiduciaries shall not buy from or sell to themselves nor shall they in their individual capacities have any dealings with the estate, except as expressly authorized by the instrument creating the trust and then only to the extent expressly permitted by section 1111.13 or 1111.14 of the Revised Code or with the approval of the probate court in each instance; but no corporate fiduciary that is not subject to examination or regulatory oversight by the superintendent of financial institutions, the comptroller of the currency, or the office of thrift supervision shall be permitted to deal with the estate, any power in the instrument creating the trust to the contrary notwithstanding. This section does not prohibit a fiduciary from making an advancement, when such advancement has been expressly authorized by the instrument creating the trust or when the probate court approves.

(1996 H 538, eff. 1–1–97; 1992 S 269, eff. 3–24–93; 1953 H 1; GC 10506–49)

Note: See also preceding version of this section, and Publisher's Note.

Historical and Statutory Notes

Publisher's Note: 2109.44 was amended by 1996 S 129, eff. 5–30–96, and 1996 H 538, eff. 1–1–97. Harmonization pursuant to section 1.52 of the Revised Code is in question. See *Baldwin's Ohio Legislative Service*, 1996, pages 2/L–84 and 7/L–2961, or the OH–LEGIS or OH–LEGIS–OLD database on Westlaw, for original versions of these Acts.

Pre–1953 H 1 Amendments: 116 v 385; 114 v 374

Amendment Note: 1996 S 129 rewrote the section, which formerly read:

"Fiduciaries shall not buy from or sell to themselves nor shall they in their individual capacities have any dealings with the estate, except as expressly authorized by the instrument creating the trust and then only to the extent expressly permitted by section 1109.10 or 1109.20 of the Revised Code or with the approval of the probate court in each instance; but no corporate fiduciary other than a trust company subject to Chapter 1109. of the Revised Code shall be permitted to deal with the estate, any power in the instrument creating the trust to the contrary notwithstanding. This section does not prohibit a fiduciary from making an advancement, when such advancement has been expressly authorized by the instrument creating the trust or when the probate court approves."

Amendment Note: 1996 H 538 substituted "1111.13 or 1111.14" for "1109.10 or 1109.20" and "that is not subject to examination or regulatory oversight by the superintendent of financial institutions, the comptroller of the currency, or the office of thrift supervision" for "other than a trust company subject to Chapter 1109. of the Revised Code".

Cross References

Investment of trust funds, 1111.13

Library References

Executors and Administrators ⚖115, 144, 163.
Guardian and Ward ⚖40, 62.
Mental Health ⚖237, 258.1.
Trusts ⚖198, 231.
Westlaw Topic Nos. 162, 196, 257A, 390.
C.J.S. Executors and Administrators §§ 264 to 266, 295, 312, 329, 336, 343.
C.J.S. Mental Health § 179.
C.J.S. Trusts §§ 325, 327, 332 to 337, 404, 450 to 453.

Research References

Encyclopedias

38 Am. Jur. Proof of Facts 3d 279, Self-Dealing by Trustee.
OH Jur. 3d Decedents' Estates § 1490, Manner and Form of Sale; Notice—Who May Purchase.
OH Jur. 3d Decedents' Estates § 1556, Who May Purchase; Executors and Administrators.
OH Jur. 3d Decedents' Estates § 1571, Remedies.
OH Jur. 3d Decedents' Estates § 1573, Liability of Executor or Administrator.
OH Jur. 3d Decedents' Estates § 1583, Rights of Subsequent Purchasers.
OH Jur. 3d Decedents' Estates § 1652, Advancements.
OH Jur. 3d Fiduciaries § 108, Statutory Prohibitions.
OH Jur. 3d Trusts § 389, Self Dealing.

Treatises and Practice Aids

Carlin, Baldwin's Ohio Practice, Merrick-Rippner Probate Law § 55:6, Fiduciary Misconduct—Self-Dealing.
Carlin, Baldwin's Ohio Practice, Merrick-Rippner Probate Law § 64:1, Powers and Duties of Guardian—Fiduciary Relationship.
Carlin, Baldwin's Ohio Practice, Merrick-Rippner Probate Law § 30:36, Drafting a Will—Authorization for Executor's Activity—Self-Dealing.
Carlin, Baldwin's Ohio Practice, Merrick-Rippner Probate Law § 30:37, Drafting a Will—Authorization for Executor's Activity—Advancements.
Bogert - the Law of Trusts and Trustees § 542, Exculpatory or Immunity Clauses—Required Standard of Care Reduced by Settlor.
Bogert - the Law of Trusts and Trustees § 543, Trustee's Duty of Loyalty to the Beneficiaries.
Bogert - the Law of Trusts and Trustees § 551, Express and Implied Powers.
Restatement (2d) of Trusts § 244, Expenses Properly Incurred.

Law Review and Journal Commentaries

The Trustee's Duties and Responsibilities, Karen M. Moore. 7 Prob L J Ohio 51 (May/June 1997).

The Uniform Trusts Act, Frank S. Rowley and Harry W. Vanneman. 5 Ohio St L J 145 (March 1939).

The Uniform Trusts Act, Frank S. Rowley and Harry W. Vanneman. 13 U Cin L Rev 157 (March 1939).

Notes of Decisions

Attorneys 1
Executors and administrators 2
Guardians 3
Trustees 4-9
    Government agency 4
    Losses and liens 6
    Multiple trusts 7
    Profits 5
    Purchase and allocation to trust 9
    Voting shares 8

1. Attorneys

Attorney's self-dealing and violation of fiduciary duty, consisting of 52 unauthorized transfers of funds totalling $75,800 into his business account from client's testamentary trust for which he was serving as trustee, violated disciplinary rules prohibiting dishonest conduct, accepting employment where one's judgment might be influenced by personal interests, and failing to properly maintain client funds, notwithstanding attorney's attempt to characterize the transfers as loans. Office of Disciplinary Counsel v. Kurtz (Ohio, 05-20-1998) 82 Ohio St.3d 55, 693 N.E.2d 1080, 1998-Ohio-278, reconsideration denied 82 Ohio St.3d 1470, 696 N.E.2d 226. Attorney And Client ⇔ 38; Attorney And Client ⇔ 44(2)

RC 2109.44, which prohibits self-dealings by an estate fiduciary, is equally applicable to the attorney employed by that fiduciary. Ollick v. Rice (Cuyahoga 1984) 16 Ohio App.3d 448, 476 N.E.2d 1062, 16 O.B.R. 529. Executors And Administrators ⇔ 115

Violation by attorney of RC 2109.41, RC 2109.43 and RC 2109.44 justified disbarment. Toledo Bar Ass'n v. Bartlett (Ohio 1974) 39 Ohio St.2d 100, 313 N.E.2d 834, 68 O.O.2d 59, stay denied 95 S.Ct. 301, 419 U.S. 989, 42 L.Ed.2d 264, certiorari denied 95 S.Ct. 663, 419 U.S. 1073, 42 L.Ed.2d 670, rehearing denied 95 S.Ct. 1153, 420 U.S. 939, 43 L.Ed.2d 418.

Where the executor of an estate also served as attorney to the estate, and four corporations comprising the estate assets paid retainers to the executor or his law firm during the period the estate was in probate, the prohibition against self-dealing of RC 2109.44 was not violated where testimony showed that the estate had benefitted by the executor's administration; further, the executor was not required to refund the retainers received from the corporations as a setoff against his attorney fees received pursuant to RC 2113.36. In re Estate of Lossman, No. 47312 (8th Dist Ct App, Cuyahoga, 4–5–84).

2. Executors and administrators

In absence of authorization in will for fiduciary to engage in any kind of self-dealing, executor was properly surcharged for $5,000 loan from estate which executor made to himself. Whitaker v. Estate of Whitaker (Ohio App. 4 Dist., 06-26-1995) 105 Ohio App.3d 46, 663 N.E.2d 681. Executors And Administrators ⇔ 115

Executor was properly surcharged in excess of $41,000 for expenses incurred in maintaining real property following transfers from estate to beneficiary; there was no statutory authority for maintaining properties that are no longer estate assets. Whitaker v. Estate of Whitaker (Ohio App. 4 Dist., 06-26-1995) 105 Ohio App.3d 46, 663 N.E.2d 681. Executors And Administrators ⇔ 132

An executor who is the beneficiary of an option to purchase real estate of the testator must, in order to purchase and obtain clear title to such property, not only exercise his option to purchase such property, but also make application to and obtain the approval of the probate court for such sale, and in such case, the probate court is not precluded from ordering a reappraisal of such real estate by the fact that an appraisal has been made and approved. Walters v. Wannemacher (Paulding 1964) 6 Ohio App.2d 226, 217 N.E.2d 695, 35 O.O.2d 385.

A sale of estate property by an administrator to his spouse is voidable at the election of the heirs, but in an equitable action by an heir to set aside such a sale, the defense of laches is applicable to such an heir who, with full knowledge of the circumstances of the sale and subsequent events, delays the filing of his action of a period of seventeen years. Christman v. Christman (Ohio 1960) 171 Ohio St. 152, 168 N.E.2d 153, 12 O.O.2d 172.

Where a court of probate issues an order for the private sale of realty by the administratrix of an estate and she then makes such a sale to her spouse, the sale is voidable at the election of the heirs. Magee v. Troutwine (Ohio 1957) 166 Ohio St. 466, 143 N.E.2d 581, 2 O.O.2d 471.

Where fiduciary made advancement to estate of her husband without obtaining prior approval of the probate court, contrary to statute, the approval of her final account by the probate court constitutes approval of the fiduciary's action. In re Outhwaite's Estate (Franklin 1950) 94 N.E.2d 59, 57 Ohio Law Abs. 238, 42 O.O. 445.

Where an executor attempts to purchase decedent's real estate through a corporation solely owned by such executor, and otherwise makes no bona fide effort to sell or rent such real estate, the probate court has sufficient grounds for his removal. In re Estate of Kuntz, No. 7355 (2d Dist Ct App, Montgomery, 5–19–83).

The public sale of a diamond ring to the spouse of the executor of an estate is voidable. In re Estate of Kellhofer, No. 943 (4th Dist Ct App, Ross, 2–18–83).

3. Guardians

Power of guardian to make gifts on behalf of ward discussed. (See also In re Guardianship of Tillman, 100 App 291, 136 NE(2d) 291 (1955).) In re Tillman (Ohio Prob. 1956) 137 N.E.2d 172, 73 Ohio Law Abs. 534.

Upon exceptions to a guardian's account the guardian should be required to account for compensation paid to himself for time spent selecting items for himself and others prior to a sale of personal property and for Christmas gifts made to himself and others, but not for payments to himself for care of the ward. (See also In re Guardianship of Tillman, 100 App 291, 136 NE(2d) 291 (1955).) In re Tillman (Ohio Prob. 1956) 137 N.E.2d 172, 73 Ohio Law Abs. 534.

4. Trustees—Government agency

Court would decline to award Veterans Administration (VA) patient's medical and physical care damages in form of trust, with full reversionary interest in government, where VA might, to greater or lesser extent, be responsible for patient's care; to allow government then to have reversionary interest in sums provided for patient's care would allow windfall to government. Smith v. U.S. Dept. of Veterans Affairs (N.D.Ohio 1994) 865 F.Supp. 433. United States ⇔ 144

5. —— Profits, trustees

Reasonable compensation may be charged by a bank for the organization and creation of a trust, the securities of which are later sold by it to another trust for which it is trustee; such bank cannot, through commissions, schemes of underwriting or guaranteeing the sale of securities so created in the parent trust, advance the price of such securities so as to claim profits for itself before they are sold or transferred to other trusts for which it is trustee. In re Binder's Estate (Ohio 1940) 137 Ohio St. 26, 27 N.E.2d 939, 129 A.L.R. 130, 17 O.O. 364. Trusts ⇔ 315(1)

Departmental banks are single corporate entities, managed by a single board of directors and owned by shareholders who participate in the combined profits and losses of the several departments, and therefore, transactions between separate departments of a bank, affecting a trust for which the bank is trustee, do not create any immunity against self-dealing as between the bank and the trust. In re Binder's Estate (Ohio 1940) 137 Ohio St. 26, 27 N.E.2d 939, 129 A.L.R. 130, 17 O.O. 364. Trusts ⇔ 231(1)

Trustee may not engage in self-dealing, and may, therefore, neither invest money left with him in trust in securities in which he is interested by way of commission, promotion or profit, nor sell to himself as trustee his individual property or property in which he has a personal or beneficial interest, and in such cases, it is immaterial that he acts in good faith in purchasing the property for the trust and that he pays a fair consideration therefor. In re Binder's Estate (Ohio 1940) 137 Ohio St. 26, 27 N.E.2d 939, 129 A.L.R. 130, 17 O.O. 364. Trusts ⇔ 231(2)

6. —— Losses and liens, trustees

Loan of money by trustee to his wife may be voidable but it is not necessarily void. In re Chambers' Estate (Montgomery 1939) 36 N.E.2d 175, 30 Ohio Law Abs. 420, 16 O.O. 519, appeal dismissed 136 Ohio St. 202, 24 N.E.2d 601, 16 O.O. 535, rehearing denied 43 N.E.2d 244.

There is no unjust enrichment to a beneficiary of a trust in allowing him to rescind a self-dealing transaction on the part of a bank as trustee in purchasing worthless securities for such trust, and to participate as a creditor in the distribution and liquidation of the assets of such bank on an equality with creditors of the other departments of the same bank. In re Binder's Estate (Ohio 1940) 137 Ohio St. 26, 27 N.E.2d 939, 129 A.L.R. 130, 17 O.O. 364. Banks And Banking ⇔ 317(3)

Where in a transaction relating to his trust a trustee has been guilty of self-dealing or breach of good faith and a loss has occurred, the trustee may be surcharged with any decline in the value of the property or securities purchased for the trust, notwithstanding any claim that he has acted in good faith and notwithstanding there may be no causal relation between his self-dealing and the loss or depreciation incurred. In re Binder's Estate (Ohio 1940) 137 Ohio St. 26, 27 N.E.2d 939, 129 A.L.R. 130, 17 O.O. 364. Trusts ⇔ 231(1)

Where in a transaction relating to his trust a trustee has been guilty of self-dealing or breach of good faith, such transaction is voidable and the right of the beneficiary of the trust to rescind does not depend on whether the estate has suffered a loss. In re Binder's Estate (Ohio 1940) 137 Ohio St. 26, 27 N.E.2d 939, 129 A.L.R. 130, 17 O.O. 364. Trusts ⇔ 231(1)

When, in the purchase of property or securities by a trustee for his trust, it becomes necessary to pay off prior liens or incumbrances on the property which is the security for such investments, the trustee may liquidate such liens even though they be owing to himself, provided the property is not taken and the liens paid for the purpose or with the result of liquidating a poor investment of his own. In re Binder's Estate (Ohio 1940) 137 Ohio St. 26, 27 N.E.2d 939, 129 A.L.R. 130, 17 O.O. 364. Trusts ⇔ 231(2)

7. —— Multiple trusts, trustees

There is no legal inhibition against a trustee setting up a special or independent trust in property other than his own and acting as trustee for the securities issued thereunder, even though done for the sole purpose of selling such securities as an investment to other trusts for which he may also be trustee, provided the transaction is free from self-dealing or profit-taking on his own account, is fair, and is made in good faith as between the several trusts. In re Binder's Estate (Ohio 1940) 137 Ohio St. 26, 27 N.E.2d 939, 129 A.L.R. 130, 17 O.O. 364. Trusts ⇔ 231(1)

Corporation or an individual authorized to act in a trust capacity is not inhibited by law from acting as trustee of multiple trusts, or from transferring securities from one of its trusts to another by purchase and sale, provided the trustee does not have a beneficial interest in the securities so transferred, and provided the terms of the sale and purchase are fair and made in good faith as between the several trusts. In re Binder's Estate (Ohio 1940) 137 Ohio St. 26, 27 N.E.2d 939, 129 A.L.R. 130, 17 O.O. 364. Trusts ⇔ 231(1)

8. —— Voting shares, trustees

As to any fiduciary relationship created on and after Jan 1, 1968, RC 1109.10 specifies whether and how a trust company may vote its own shares held by it in such fiduciary capacity. Cleveland Trust Co. v. Eaton (Ohio 1970) 21 Ohio St.2d 129, 256 N.E.2d 198, 50 O.O.2d 354. Banks And Banking ⇔ 313

RC 1701.47(C) providing that "no corporation shall directly or indirectly vote any shares issued by it," does not now apply to a banking corporation or a trust company. Cleveland Trust Co. v. Eaton (Ohio 1970) 21 Ohio St.2d 129, 256 N.E.2d 198, 50 O.O.2d 354. Banks And Banking ⇔ 313

9. —— Purchase and allocation to trust, trustees

Beneficiary of trust failed to demonstrate that trustee's sale of trust property to company created by trustee's husband, without listing the property and without negotiating the purchase price, injured beneficiary, precluding beneficiary's recovery on breach of fiduciary duty claim, where property was appraised at $163,000, valued by Internal Revenue Service at $178,024, and sold by trustee for $200,000. Biddulph v. Delorenzo (Ohio App. 8 Dist., Cuyahoga, 08-26-2004) No. 83808, 2004-Ohio-4502, 2004 WL 1902725, Unreported. Trusts ⇔ 231(2)

Trustee's sale of trust property to company created by her husband did not constitute self-dealing; trust instrument authorized a private sale, and statute requiring approval of sale by probate court did not apply to inter vivos trust. Biddulph v. Delorenzo (Ohio App. 8 Dist., Cuyahoga, 08-26-2004) No. 83808, 2004-Ohio-4502, 2004 WL 1902725, Unreported. Trusts ⇔ 231(2)

Trustee's 52 transfers of funds totalling $75,800 from testamentary trust into his own account were not "loans" even though he returned many of the funds to trust with interest above bank rates, where contemporaneous notations indicated otherwise, estate received no notes or other loan-evidencing documentation, trust instrument did not expressly authorize trustee to make loans to himself, and trustee never sought probate court approval. Office of Disciplinary Counsel v. Kurtz (Ohio, 05-20-1998) 82 Ohio St.3d 55, 693 N.E.2d 1080, 1998-Ohio-278, reconsideration denied 82 Ohio St.3d 1470, 696 N.E.2d 226. Trusts ⇔ 222; Trusts ⇔ 233

Will language authorizing trustee of testamentary trust to invest trust property "in such investment bonds and securities as may be selected by him, irrespective of any limitation prescribed by law or custom upon the investments of Trustees" did not "expressly" authorize trustee to make loans to himself, and thus such loans were prohibited under statute governing fiduciaries' dealings with estate. Office of Disciplinary Counsel v. Kurtz (Ohio, 05-20-1998) 82 Ohio St.3d 55, 693 N.E.2d 1080, 1998-Ohio-278, reconsideration denied 82 Ohio St.3d 1470, 696 N.E.2d 226. Wills ⇔ 681(1)

RC 2109.44 is not applicable to the trustee of an inter vivos trust, and hence such a trustee can properly purchase trust property for itself, provided court approval thereof is obtained. Central Nat. Bank of Cleveland v. Brewer (Ohio Com.Pl. 1966) 8 Ohio Misc. 409, 220 N.E.2d 846, 37 O.O.2d 323, 37 O.O.2d 393.

Self-dealing or breach of good faith on the part of a trustee, as distinguished from his failure to observe statutory directions as to the character of investments, cannot be excused on the ground that the instrument creating a trust and making him trustee gave him broad authority and unlimited discretion in the administration of the trust. In re Binder's Estate (Ohio 1940) 137 Ohio St. 26, 27 N.E.2d 939, 129 A.L.R. 130, 17 O.O. 364. Trusts ⇔ 231(1)

When investments are purchased by a trustee for the benefit of his trust, it is not only necessary that such purchases be made for the trust, but, in order to avoid a charge of self-dealing, that immediate transfer and allocation of the securities to the trust for which they were purchased be made, accompanied by clear evidence that they have been so purchased and allocated. In re Binder's Estate (Ohio 1940) 137 Ohio St. 26, 27 N.E.2d 939, 129 A.L.R. 130, 17 O.O. 364. Trusts ⇔ 231(2)

Trustee may advance money to purchase securities for his trust before all the money is available in the trust estate for that purpose, and may make a reasonable charge for the money so advanced; but the trustee may not purchase such securities in his own right, or acquire a beneficial interest therein before turning them over or allocating them to a trust for which he is trustee. In re Binder's Estate (Ohio 1940) 137 Ohio St. 26, 27 N.E.2d 939, 129 A.L.R. 130, 17 O.O. 364. Trusts ⇔ 231(2)

Trustee bank had authority to pledge assets of trust as collateral for loans by trustee bank to trust beneficiary to open a new restaurant, and trustee bank's actions did not constitute self-dealing or a breach of good faith, despite donor's claim that trustee bank was required to obtain written consent from donor or should have conducted an investigation into merits of loan transaction, as terms of trust gave trustee bank extremely broad authority over management of trust, including encumbrance of assets for benefit of beneficiaries, trustee bank obtained oral consent from donor, beneficiary had life-long experience in restaurant business and was successfully operating another restaurant, and donor had previously approved pledge for loan to another beneficiary. Saba v. Fifth Third Bank of NW Ohio, N.A. (Ohio App. 6 Dist., Lucas, 09-06-2002) No. L-01-1284, 2002-Ohio-4658, 2002 WL 31002781, Unreported. Trusts ⇔ 206(1); Trusts ⇔ 231(1)

2109.45 Statement before private sale confirmed

Before the probate court confirms a sale by an executor, administrator, guardian, assignee, or trustee made under an order allowing that officer to make a private sale, the court shall require that officer to file a statement indicating that the private sale was made after diligent endeavor to obtain the best price for the property and that the private sale was at the highest price he could get for the property.

(1992 H 427, eff. 10–8–92; 1953 H 1; GC 10506–51)

Historical and Statutory Notes

Pre–1953 H 1 Amendments: 114 v 375

Cross References

Application to sell personalty, Sup R 63
Sale of land by executor, administrator, or guardian, Ch 2127

Library References

Executors and Administrators ⚖︎375.
Guardian and Ward ⚖︎103.
Mental Health ⚖︎269.
Trusts ⚖︎200(2).
Westlaw Topic Nos. 162, 196, 257A, 390.
C.J.S. Executors and Administrators § 644.
C.J.S. Trusts §§ 404, 446 to 449, 460.

Research References

Encyclopedias

OH Jur. 3d Decedents' Estates § 1491, Report of Sale.
OH Jur. 3d Decedents' Estates § 1562, Return Where Private Sale Ordered.
OH Jur. 3d Fiduciaries § 46, Sale or Lease of Lands.
OH Jur. 3d Guardian & Ward § 164, Confirmation of Sale; Deed.
OH Jur. 3d Trusts § 388, Judicial Control—Statutory Provisions.

Treatises and Practice Aids

Carlin, Baldwin's Ohio Practice, Merrick-Rippner Probate Law § 74:9, Decedent's Property—Report of Sale.
Carlin, Baldwin's Ohio Practice, Merrick-Rippner Probate Law § 95:7, Private Sale—Procedure.
Carlin, Baldwin's Ohio Practice, Merrick-Rippner Probate Law § 96:2, Confirmation of Sale—Sufficiency.
Carlin, Baldwin's Ohio Practice, Merrick-Rippner Probate Law § 64:31, Statement of Guardian—Private Sale—Form.
Carlin, Baldwin's Ohio Practice, Merrick-Rippner Probate Law § 74:20, Statement of Fiduciary Before Private Sale Confirmed—Form.
Carlin, Baldwin's Ohio Practice, Merrick-Rippner Probate Law § 95:26, Report of Private Sale; Statement—Form.
Bogert - the Law of Trusts and Trustees § 745, Terms and Conditions of Sale—Duties of Trustee.

Notes of Decisions

Highest bidder 1

---

1. Highest bidder

RC 2109.45 governs the actions of the probate court in all sales of estate property made by executors and trustees pursuant to and under an order of the court "allowing" such officer to make a private sale, and where the record discloses that trustees sold for a price less than that offered by the highest responsible bidder the sale will be set aside and sale ordered to the highest bidder. Dombey v. Rindsfoos (Franklin 1958) 105 Ohio App. 335, 151 N.E.2d 563, 77 Ohio Law Abs. 522, 6 O.O.2d 123.

MORTGAGE BY FIDUCIARY

2109.46 Mortgage by fiduciary

When it appears to be for the best interests of the trust, a fiduciary other than an executor or administrator may, with the approval of the probate court, borrow money and mortgage real estate belonging to the trust, whether such real estate was acquired by purchase or by descent and distribution.

The fiduciary proposing so to borrow money must file in the probate court which appointed him a petition describing all of the real estate in the trust and stating the nature and amount of the encumbrances thereon, the date such encumbrances became or will become due, and the rate of interest thereon. The petition shall also contain a statement of the personal property in the trust, the income from such personal property, and the income from the real estate in such trust. Such petition if filed by a guardian shall state the names, ages, and residences of the ward and next of kin known to be resident in the state, including the spouse of such ward and persons holding liens on such real estate, all of whom must be made defendants and be notified of the pendency and prayer of the petition in such manner as the court directs. In addition such petition shall contain a statement of the nature of the imbecility or insanity, if any, of such ward, whether temporary or confirmed and its duration. Except as provided in this section, the defendants and notice thereto shall be the same as though the real estate proposed to be mortgaged were being sold by the fiduciary. The petition shall set forth the purpose of the loan, the amount required therefor, and such other facts as may be pertinent to the question whether such money should be borrowed and shall contain a prayer that the fiduciary be authorized to mortgage so much of the ward's lands as may be necessary to secure such loan.

Upon the filing of such petition, the proceedings as to pleadings and proof shall be the same as on petition to sell real estate belonging to the trust.

(1953 H 1, eff. 10–1–53; GC 10506–59, 10506–60, 10506–62)

Historical and Statutory Notes

Pre–1953 H 1 Amendments: 114 v 377

Cross References

Sale of land by executor, administrator, or guardian, Ch 2127

Library References

Executors and Administrators ⚖︎151.
Guardian and Ward ⚖︎45, 112.
Mental Health ⚖︎275.
Trusts ⚖︎206(1).
Westlaw Topic Nos. 162, 196, 257A, 390.
C.J.S. Executors and Administrators § 323.
C.J.S. Trusts §§ 462 to 464, 469.

Research References

Encyclopedias

OH Jur. 3d Fiduciaries § 47, Authority to Borrow Money and Mortgage Real Property; Procedures.
OH Jur. 3d Guardian & Ward § 122, Borrowing Money; Mortgaging Real Property; Report.
OH Jur. 3d Trusts § 499, on Contracts.

Treatises and Practice Aids

Carlin, Baldwin's Ohio Practice, Merrick-Rippner Probate Law § 73:5, Management of Real Estate—Termination of Authority.
Carlin, Baldwin's Ohio Practice, Merrick-Rippner Probate Law § 64:21, Powers and Duties of Guardian—Ward's Estate—Discretionary Acts.
Carlin, Baldwin's Ohio Practice, Merrick-Rippner Probate Law § 64:43, Complaint to Purchase and Mortgage Real Estate—Form.
Carlin, Baldwin's Ohio Practice, Merrick-Rippner Probate Law § 64:46, Complaint of Guardian to Mortgage Real Estate—Form.
Carlin, Baldwin's Ohio Practice, Merrick-Rippner Probate Law § 64:47, Entry Fixing Time of Hearing and Ordering Summons—Form.
Carlin, Baldwin's Ohio Practice, Merrick-Rippner Probate Law § 64:48, Notice to Defendants—Form.
Carlin, Baldwin's Ohio Practice, Merrick-Rippner Probate Law § 64:49, Answer of Spouse of Ward—Form.
Carlin, Baldwin's Ohio Practice, Merrick-Rippner Probate Law § 64:50, Entry of Findings of Court and Directing Plaintiff to Ascertain Terms—Form.
Bogert - the Law of Trusts and Trustees § 551, Express and Implied Powers.
Bogert - the Law of Trusts and Trustees § 763, Power Granted the Court by Statute.
Bogert - the Law of Trusts and Trustees § 764, Notice to the Beneficiaries.

2109.47 Report of investigators

Before the probate court makes an order authorizing a guardian to mortgage real estate for the purpose of borrowing money to make repairs or improvements, the court shall appoint three disinterested persons whose duty it shall be to investigate fully the necessity for and the advisability of making the repairs or improvements and their probable cost and to report their conclusions to the court.

(1992 H 427, eff. 10-8-92; 1953 H 1; GC 10506-61)

Historical and Statutory Notes

Pre–1953 H 1 Amendments: 114 v 377

Library References

Executors and Administrators ⊆151.
Guardian and Ward ⊆45, 84, 112.
Mental Health ⊆275.
Trusts ⊆206(0.5), 206(1).
Westlaw Topic Nos. 162, 196, 257A, 390.
C.J.S. Executors and Administrators § 323.
C.J.S. Trusts §§ 462 to 464, 469.

Research References

Encyclopedias

OH Jur. 3d Fiduciaries § 47, Authority to Borrow Money and Mortgage Real Property; Procedures.
OH Jur. 3d Guardian & Ward § 122, Borrowing Money; Mortgaging Real Property; Report.

Treatises and Practice Aids

Bogert - the Law of Trusts and Trustees § 763, Power Granted the Court by Statute.

2109.48 Amount of loan

If on the final hearing of a fiduciary's petition to borrow money and mortgage real estate belonging to the trust it appears to be for the best interests of the trust that the prayer of the petition be granted, the probate court shall fix the amount necessary to be borrowed, direct what lands shall be encumbered by mortgage to secure such amount, and issue an order to such fiduciary directing him to ascertain and report to the court the rate of interest and the length of time for which he can borrow such amount.

If such report and the terms proposed are satisfactory to the court, they may be accepted and confirmed and the fiduciary ordered, as fiduciary, to execute a note for such amount and a mortgage on the lands so designated, which shall be a valid lien thereon. The fiduciary in no way shall be personally liable for the payment of any part of the sum borrowed, but such mortgaged lands alone shall be bound therefor. Such court shall direct the distribution of the fund and the fiduciary shall report to the court, for its approval, the execution of such notes and mortgage and his distribution of the fund.

(1953 H 1, eff. 10-1-53; GC 10506-63, 10506-64)

Historical and Statutory Notes

Pre–1953 H 1 Amendments: 114 v 377, 378

Library References

Executors and Administrators ⊆151.
Guardian and Ward ⊆45, 112.
Mental Health ⊆275.
Trusts ⊆206(0.5).
Westlaw Topic Nos. 162, 196, 257A, 390.
C.J.S. Executors and Administrators § 323.
C.J.S. Trusts § 462.

Research References

Encyclopedias

OH Jur. 3d Fiduciaries § 47, Authority to Borrow Money and Mortgage Real Property; Procedures.
OH Jur. 3d Trusts § 499, on Contracts.

Treatises and Practice Aids

Carlin, Baldwin's Ohio Practice, Merrick-Rippner Probate Law § 64:44, Entry Directing Guardian to Ascertain Terms—Form.
Carlin, Baldwin's Ohio Practice, Merrick-Rippner Probate Law § 64:45, Entry Approving Report of Plaintiff as to Terms, and Authorizing Investment and Directing Execution of Note and Mortgage—Form.
Carlin, Baldwin's Ohio Practice, Merrick-Rippner Probate Law § 64:51, Report of Plaintiff as to Terms—Form.
Carlin, Baldwin's Ohio Practice, Merrick-Rippner Probate Law § 64:52, Entry Approving Report of Plaintiff as to Terms and Directing Execution of Note and Mortgage and Distribution of Fund—Form.
Carlin, Baldwin's Ohio Practice, Merrick-Rippner Probate Law § 64:53, Report of Plaintiff on Execution of Note and Mortgage and Distribution of Fund—Form.
Carlin, Baldwin's Ohio Practice, Merrick-Rippner Probate Law § 64:54, Entry Approving Execution of Note and Mortgage and Distribution of Fund—Form.
Carlin, Baldwin's Ohio Practice, Merrick-Rippner Probate Law § 64:55, Mortgage by Guardian—Form.
Carlin, Baldwin's Ohio Practice, Merrick-Rippner Probate Law § 64:56, Report of Guardian—Mortgage—Form.
Carlin, Baldwin's Ohio Practice, Merrick-Rippner Probate Law § 64:57, Entry Confirming Mortgage and Ordering Distribution—Form.
Bogert - the Law of Trusts and Trustees § 763, Power Granted the Court by Statute.
Bogert - the Law of Trusts and Trustees § 765, Terms of the Mortgage.

INVESTIGATION OF TRUST

2109.49 Investigation of trust

The probate judge, when the probate judge deems it necessary or upon the written application of any party interested in the trust estate, may appoint suitable persons to investigate the administration of the trust and report to the court. The expense thereof shall be taxed as costs against the party asking for such examination or the trust fund, as the court may decree. This section shall not apply to a corporate trustee which is subject to section 1111.28 of the Revised Code.

(1996 H 538, eff. 1-1-97; 129 v 1817, eff. 11-8-61; 129 v 582; 1953 H 1; GC 10506-50)

Historical and Statutory Notes

Pre–1953 H 1 Amendments: 114 v 374

Amendment Note: 1996 H 538 substituted "1111.28" for "1107.16"; and made changes to reflect gender neutral language.

Library References

Executors and Administrators ⊆116, 117, 468.
Guardian and Ward ⊆63, 64, 143.
Mental Health ⊆238, 295.
Trusts ⊆232, 233, 299.1.
Westlaw Topic Nos. 162, 196, 257A, 390.
C.J.S. Executors and Administrators §§ 267 to 270, 276, 795.
C.J.S. Mental Health §§ 179, 189, 191 to 193.
C.J.S. Trusts §§ 323, 326, 330, 376.

Research References

Encyclopedias

OH Jur. 3d Fiduciaries § 134, Appointment of Persons to Investigate Trust Administration.
OH Jur. 3d Trusts § 346, Probate Court.

Treatises and Practice Aids

Carlin, Baldwin's Ohio Practice, Merrick-Rippner Probate Law § 55:10, Application for Investigation of a Trust—Form.
Carlin, Baldwin's Ohio Practice, Merrick-Rippner Probate Law § 55:11, Order Setting Time for Hearing and Ordering Notice—Form.
Carlin, Baldwin's Ohio Practice, Merrick-Rippner Probate Law § 55:12, Notice of Hearing for Investigation of Trust—Form.

Carlin, Baldwin's Ohio Practice, Merrick-Rippner Probate Law § 55:13, Order to Investigate Trust—Form.

Notes of Decisions

Recovery of funds 1

1. Recovery of funds

Where a decedent, prior to her death, transfers assets from one bank account to another in violation of an injunction, such transfer will not support an action to recover the funds under RC 2109.49 against either the bank in which the funds reside or against decedent's joint tenant in the new account. Dodd v. Crowe (Summit 1976) 51 Ohio App.2d 40, 365 N.E.2d 1257, 5 O.O.3d 163.

CONCEALED OR EMBEZZLED ASSETS

2109.50 Proceeding when assets concealed or embezzled

Upon complaint made to the probate court of the county having jurisdiction of the administration of a trust estate or of the county wherein a person resides against whom the complaint is made, by a person interested in such trust estate or by the creditor of a person interested in such trust estate against any person suspected of having concealed, embezzled, or conveyed away or of being or having been in the possession of any moneys, chattels, or choses in action of such estate, said court shall by citation, attachment or warrant, or, if circumstances require it, by warrant or attachment in the first instance, compel the person or persons so suspected to forthwith appear before it to be examined, on oath, touching the matter of the complaint. Where necessary such citation, attachment or warrant may be issued into any county in the state and shall be served and returned by the officer to whom it is delivered. The officer to whom such process is delivered shall be liable for negligence in its service or return in like manner as sheriffs are liable for negligence in not serving or returning a capias issued upon an indictment. Before issuing an extra-county citation, attachment or warrant, the probate judge may require the complainant to post security with the probate court in such amount and in such form as the probate judge shall find acceptable in order to cover the costs of the proceeding under this section, including in such costs a reasonable allowance for the travelling expenses of the person or persons against whom an extra-county citation, attachment or warrant is to be issued. Such security may be in the form of a bond, the amount, terms, conditions and sureties of which shall be subject to the approval of the probate judge.

The probate court may initiate proceedings on its own motion.

The probate court shall forthwith proceed to hear and determine the matter.

The examinations, including questions and answers, shall be reduced to writing, signed by the party examined, and filed in the probate court.

If required by either party, the probate court shall swear such witnesses as may be offered by either party touching the matter of such complaint and cause the examination of every such witness, including questions and answers, to be reduced to writing, signed by the witness, and filed in the probate court.

All costs of such proceedings, including the reasonable travelling expenses of a person against whom an extra-county citation, attachment or warrant is issued, shall be assessed against and paid by the party making the complaint, except as provided by section 2109.52 of the Revised Code.

(128 v 76, eff. 11-9-59; 1953 H 1; GC 10506-67, 10506-68, 10506-70 to 10506-72)

Historical and Statutory Notes

Pre-1953 H 1 Amendments: 114 v 379

OSBA Probate and Trust Law Section

1959:

Sec. 2109.50 R. C. is the first section in a series of sections dealing with the recovery of concealed assets. In the case of *In Re Chance*, 88 Ohio App. 416 (1951), the Court of Appeals of Hamilton County held, in an opinion setting forth an extended statutory and constitutional analysis, that a Probate Court has no power to issue an extra-county citation in a summary proceeding under Sec. 2109.50, notwithstanding the broad powers granted it by the Legislature in Sec. 2101.22. There has been no further appeal or subsequent citation of the *Chance* case.

This decision obviously hampers the prompt and efficient administration of a decedent's estate. As the law now stands an executor, in order to recover assets being withheld or concealed in another county, must go into the probate or common pleas court of that county and institute a summary proceeding under Section 2109.50 R. C. The estate is thus put to additional expense and may, due to the notoriously crowded dockets in many counties in Ohio, be considerably delayed in its administration. The Committee believes that a probate court charged with administration of an estate should have jurisdiction throughout the state to compel the production of a decedent's assets without being required to go through the processes of a court of another county. Similar powers have been granted to probate courts to compel the production of a decedent's will by Section 2107.09. If the Probate Court is given statewide power in a summary proceeding for production of concealed assets there should be no need to give a common pleas court the concurrent jurisdiction provided by the present statute.

If Sec. 2109.50 R. C. is amended as indicated, then the Probate Court would have statewide power to compel attendance by arrest, if necessary. It is therefore recommended that the penalty of Sec. 2109.51 R. C. be restricted to compelling answer upon examination, as provided by the proposed amendment thereto. The proposed amendment to Sec. 2109.52 merely reflects changes required to keep it consistent with the proposed amendment to Sec. 2109.50.

Cross References

Offense of embezzlement, 2913.02

Library References

Executors and Administrators ⚖85.
Guardian and Ward ⚖33.
Mental Health ⚖219.
Trusts ⚖181(1).
Westlaw Topic Nos. 162, 196, 257A, 390.
C.J.S. Executors and Administrators §§ 174 to 181, 183 to 186.
C.J.S. Mental Health § 179.
C.J.S. Trusts §§ 361 to 364.

Research References

Encyclopedias

OH Jur. 3d Courts & Judges § 284, Jurisdiction Granted by Statute.
OH Jur. 3d Creditors' Rights & Remedies § 262, Applicability in County, Municipal and Small Claims Courts.
OH Jur. 3d Decedents' Estates § 868, Jurisdiction of Probate Court.
OH Jur. 3d Decedents' Estates § 980, Conversion.
OH Jur. 3d Decedents' Estates § 1274, Property Fraudulently Concealed or Embezzled.
OH Jur. 3d Decedents' Estates § 1316, Proceeds from Action for Wrongful Death.
OH Jur. 3d Decedents' Estates § 1803, Pleading, Generally.
OH Jur. 3d Decedents' Estates § 1820, Actions Affecting Personalty.
OH Jur. 3d Fiduciaries § 144, Purpose and Nature of Proceeding.
OH Jur. 3d Fiduciaries § 146, Purpose and Nature of Proceeding—Relation to Other Actions.
OH Jur. 3d Fiduciaries § 147, Purpose and Nature of Proceeding—Transfers in Avoidance of Proceeding.
OH Jur. 3d Fiduciaries § 148, Requisites for Relief, Generally.
OH Jur. 3d Fiduciaries § 149, Requisites for Relief, Generally—Wrongful Conduct; Possession.
OH Jur. 3d Fiduciaries § 150, Requisites for Relief, Generally—Title to Assets.
OH Jur. 3d Fiduciaries § 151, Generally; Application of Statute of Limitations.
OH Jur. 3d Fiduciaries § 152, Jurisdiction and Venue.

OH Jur. 3d Fiduciaries § 153, Parties; Who is an "Interested Person".
OH Jur. 3d Fiduciaries § 154, Pleadings; Complaint.
OH Jur. 3d Fiduciaries § 155, Pleadings; Complaint—Answer; Raising Defenses.
OH Jur. 3d Fiduciaries § 156, Pleadings; Complaint—Amendments; Conforming to Proof.
OH Jur. 3d Fiduciaries § 157, Citation, Attachment, or Warrant of Suspected Person or Persons Interested in Assets.
OH Jur. 3d Fiduciaries § 158, Citation, Attachment, or Warrant of Suspected Person or Persons Interested in Assets—Prejudgment Attachment; Limitations and Prerequisites.
OH Jur. 3d Fiduciaries § 160, Hearing; Submission to Jury or Referee.
OH Jur. 3d Fiduciaries § 161, Hearing; Submission to Jury or Referee—Burden and Degree of Proof; Evidence.
OH Jur. 3d Fiduciaries § 162, Hearing; Submission to Jury or Referee—Witnesses; Reduction of Examination to Writing.
OH Jur. 3d Fiduciaries § 163, Hearing; Submission to Jury or Referee—Determination of Questions of Title.
OH Jur. 3d Fiduciaries § 164, Judgment or Order; Award of Damages.
OH Jur. 3d Fiduciaries § 165, Judgment or Order; Award of Damages—Imposition of Penalty.
OH Jur. 3d Fiduciaries § 166, Judgment or Order; Award of Damages—Operation and Effect.
OH Jur. 3d Fiduciaries § 168, Costs.
OH Jur. 3d Fiduciaries § 218, Prerequisites to Action.
OH Jur. 3d Fiduciaries § 233, Subrogation.
OH Jur. 3d Gifts § 46, Admissibility of Evidence.
OH Jur. 3d Trusts § 538, in Equity—Particular Remedies.

Treatises and Practice Aids

Baldwin's Ohio Handbook Series—Trial Handbook § 2:8, Particular Duties and Powers of Judge.
Giannelli and Snyder, Baldwin's Ohio Practice, Evidence, § 614.3, Court-Called Witnesses.
Carlin, Baldwin's Ohio Practice, Merrick-Rippner Probate Law § 3:3, Jurisdiction of Probate Court—Subject Matter—in General.
Carlin, Baldwin's Ohio Practice, Merrick-Rippner Probate Law § 12:3, Wrongful Death—Jurisdiction of Probate Court.
Carlin, Baldwin's Ohio Practice, Merrick-Rippner Probate Law § 56:1, Concealed or Embezzled Assets—Scope of RC 2109.50 to RC 2109.56.
Carlin, Baldwin's Ohio Practice, Merrick-Rippner Probate Law § 56:2, Concealed or Embezzled Assets—Jurisdiction Over Complaint.
Carlin, Baldwin's Ohio Practice, Merrick-Rippner Probate Law § 56:3, Concealed or Embezzled Assets—Extra-County Powers.
Carlin, Baldwin's Ohio Practice, Merrick-Rippner Probate Law § 56:6, Concealed or Embezzled Assets—Quasi-Criminal Nature of Proceedings.
Carlin, Baldwin's Ohio Practice, Merrick-Rippner Probate Law § 56:8, Concealed or Embezzled Assets—Complaint for Recovery of Assets.
Carlin, Baldwin's Ohio Practice, Merrick-Rippner Probate Law § 56:9, Concealed or Embezzled Assets—Question of Title.
Carlin, Baldwin's Ohio Practice, Merrick-Rippner Probate Law § 64:3, Powers and Duties of Guardian—Inventory.
Carlin, Baldwin's Ohio Practice, Merrick-Rippner Probate Law § 64:4, Powers and Duties of Guardian—Accounting.
Carlin, Baldwin's Ohio Practice, Merrick-Rippner Probate Law § 65:1, Litigation Involving Guardians—Guardian May Sue or be Sued; Intervenor—Dispute Resolution Procedure.
Carlin, Baldwin's Ohio Practice, Merrick-Rippner Probate Law § 56:10, Concealed or Embezzled Assets—Dismissal of Complaint.
Carlin, Baldwin's Ohio Practice, Merrick-Rippner Probate Law § 56:11, Concealed or Embezzled Assets—Ex Parte Proceedings.
Carlin, Baldwin's Ohio Practice, Merrick-Rippner Probate Law § 56:12, Concealed or Embezzled Assets—Defense to Concealment Action.
Carlin, Baldwin's Ohio Practice, Merrick-Rippner Probate Law § 56:14, Concealed or Embezzled Assets—Evidence of Concealment.
Carlin, Baldwin's Ohio Practice, Merrick-Rippner Probate Law § 56:17, Concealed or Embezzled Assets—Declaratory Judgment; Summary Judgment.
Carlin, Baldwin's Ohio Practice, Merrick-Rippner Probate Law § 56:18, Concealed or Embezzled Assets—Dismissal of Appeal.
Carlin, Baldwin's Ohio Practice, Merrick-Rippner Probate Law § 56:19, Complaint for Concealing, Embezzling, Etc., of Assets—Form.
Carlin, Baldwin's Ohio Practice, Merrick-Rippner Probate Law § 56:20, Entry on Filing of Complaint—Form.
Carlin, Baldwin's Ohio Practice, Merrick-Rippner Probate Law § 56:21, Citation—Form.
Carlin, Baldwin's Ohio Practice, Merrick-Rippner Probate Law § 79:14, Inventory—Hearing.
Carlin, Baldwin's Ohio Practice, Merrick-Rippner Probate Law § 79:21, Inventory—Exceptions—Nature of Proceedings.
Carlin, Baldwin's Ohio Practice, Merrick-Rippner Probate Law § 79:24, Inventory—Exceptions—Burden of Proof and Evidence.

Law Review and Journal Commentaries

Revisiting Firestone v. Galbreath and the Tort of Intentional Interference With an Expectancy, Angela G. Carlin. 6 Prob L J Ohio 17 (November/December 1995).

Notes of Decisions

Attorney fees 6
Complaint and citation 3
Evidence and testimony 5
Examination and hearing 4
Procedural issues 2
Scope of action 1

---

1. Scope of action

Where a guardian receives money after giving a bond and embezzles such money and gives a new bond the surety on the first bond will not be exonerated as to such money though he was released. Eichelberger v. Gross (Ohio 1885) 42 Ohio St. 549, 13 W.L.B. 282.

Creditors, devisees, legatees, heirs or other interested persons are not authorized under RS 6053 to RS 6059 to prosecute summary proceedings against the executor or administrator of an estate. Meinzer v. Bevington (Ohio 1884) 42 Ohio St. 325.

Inter vivos transfers of stock and cash as gifts to recipients were invalid and title to those assets was in estate, and thus probate court had subject matter jurisdiction over estate's action for declaratory judgment that transfers were invalid and to recover those assets; transfers were invalidated as recipients failed to rebut presumption of undue influence arising from their confidential or fiduciary relationship with decedent. Rudloff v. Efstathiadis (Ohio App. 11 Dist., Trumbull, 12-12-2003) No. 2002-T-0119, 2003-Ohio-6686, 2003 WL 22931382, Unreported, appeal not allowed 102 Ohio St.3d 1412, 806 N.E.2d 563, 2004-Ohio-1763. Executors And Administrators ⟬⟭ 56; Gifts ⟬⟭ 38

Probate judge was entitled to judicial immunity in §§1983 lawsuit, even though he exceeded his authority through entry of prejudgment attachment order in prior case regarding embezzled funds from wrongful death actions; judge did not act in complete absence of all subject matter jurisdiction because he had jurisdiction to approve distribution of funds that were embezzled, and he had jurisdiction to initiate proceedings against any person suspected of concealing or embezzling estate assets. Goldberg v. Maloney (C.A.6 (Ohio), 02-03-2003) No. 01-4019, 57 Fed.Appx. 664, 2003 WL 247114, Unreported. Civil Rights ⟬⟭ 1376(8)

Joint and survivorship bank accounts were not probate assets, and thus probate court lacked subject matter jurisdiction to consider complaint for concealment of assets by joint owner against attorney-in-fact who removed funds from account; any cause of action concerning joint and survivorship accounts lay individually with joint owner against attorney-in-fact in Common Pleas Court. In re Estate of Jaric (Ohio App. 7 Dist., Mahoning, 09-18-2002) No. 00 CA 243, 2002-Ohio-5016, 2002 WL 31116088, Unreported, appeal not allowed 98 Ohio St.3d 1461, 783 N.E.2d 520, 2003-Ohio-644. Joint Tenancy ⟬⟭ 14

Under RC 2109.50, a probate court has subject matter jurisdiction to discover and secure possession of assets belonging to an estate but not to hear actions for recovery of damages for breach of fiduciary duty and fraud relating to power of attorney transactions occurring before decedent's death. Harpster v Castle, No. CA 1022, 1993 WL 274296 (5th Dist Ct App, Ashland, 6–28–93).

This section does not authorize bringing of any action by any of persons mentioned in this section for property transferred by decedent prior to her death whether such transfer was procured through coercion, duress, undue influence or other unlawful restraint. McMahan v. Jones (Hancock 1934) 17 Ohio Law Abs. 488.

Note 1

No additional penalty can be added where action is brought on theory of conversion of papers and securities of estate rather than an action under this section, which provides for imposition of a penalty. Fremont Savings Bank v. Bowlus (Sandusky 1933) 16 Ohio Law Abs. 551.

In determining the scope of a statutory concealment proceeding to discover the concealed or embezzled assets of an estate, the court must first look at the statute's language, reading words and phrases used in context and construing them according to the rules of grammar and common usage. Goldberg v. Maloney (Ohio, 11-08-2006) 111 Ohio St.3d 211, 855 N.E.2d 856, 2006-Ohio-5485. Executors And Administrators ⚖ 85(1.5)

Concealment action, rather than civil action for a money judgment or accounting, was not improper method of recovering funds withdrawn by ward's sister prior to guardianship proceeding; the ward's estate came into existence on the date sister received notice of ward's alleged incompetency, which was prior to sister's withdrawal of funds. Harrison v. Faseyitan (Ohio App. 7 Dist., 12-09-2004) 159 Ohio App.3d 325, 823 N.E.2d 925, 2004-Ohio-6808. Mental Health ⚖ 238

Statute limiting concealment proceedings to cases in which a person was suspected of concealing, embezzling, conveying away, or being or having been in possession of any money, chattel, or chose in action of an estate did not authorize probate court or its judge to issue prejudgment attachment order for proceeds from settlements of wrongful death claims, which were not estate assets. State ex rel. Goldberg v. Mahoning Cty. Probate Court (Ohio, 09-05-2001) 93 Ohio St.3d 160, 753 N.E.2d 192, 2001-Ohio-1297, reconsideration denied 93 Ohio St.3d 1464, 756 N.E.2d 1239. Attachment ⚖ 64

Purpose of statute governing proceedings to discover concealed or embezzled estate assets is not to furnish a substitute for a civil action to recover a judgment for money owing to an administrator, but rather to provide a speedy and effective method for discovering assets belonging to the estate and to secure possession of them for purposes of administration. Rinehart v. Bank One, Columbus, N.A. (Ohio App. 10 Dist., 03-31-1998) 125 Ohio App.3d 719, 709 N.E.2d 559, dismissed, appeal not allowed 82 Ohio St.3d 1480, 696 N.E.2d 1087. Mental Health ⚖ 238

Probate court had subject matter jurisdiction over action in which bonding company, as subrogee of ward's former guardian, alleged that bank had permitted guardian to withdraw funds from guardianship account for impermissible purposes. Rinehart v. Bank One, Columbus, N.A. (Ohio App. 10 Dist., 03-31-1998) 125 Ohio App.3d 719, 709 N.E.2d 559, dismissed, appeal not allowed 82 Ohio St.3d 1480, 696 N.E.2d 1087. Mental Health ⚖ 480

Financial institution which conveys funds to an authorized person, but under circumstances giving rise to liability to the estate, comes within ambit of statute specifically granting probate court jurisdiction over complaints by persons interested in a trust estate against fiduciaries or any other person suspected of having concealed or misappropriated an estate asset. Rinehart v. Bank One, Columbus, N.A. (Ohio App. 10 Dist., 03-31-1998) 125 Ohio App.3d 719, 709 N.E.2d 559, dismissed, appeal not allowed 82 Ohio St.3d 1480, 696 N.E.2d 1087. Mental Health ⚖ 480

Financial institution which conveys out money from estate in its possession to unauthorized individual without consent of customer or his estate comes within provisions of statute prohibiting wrongful or culpable withholding or concealing of estate assets. In re Estate of Popp (Ohio App. 8 Dist., 04-18-1994) 94 Ohio App.3d 640, 641 N.E.2d 739, dismissed 70 Ohio St.3d 1446, 639 N.E.2d 114, certiorari denied 115 S.Ct. 1256, 513 U.S. 1192, 131 L.Ed.2d 136. Executors And Administrators ⚖ 86(.5)

There is no absolute right to jury trial under statute prohibiting wrongful or culpable withholding or concealing of estate assets. In re Estate of Popp (Ohio App. 8 Dist., 04-18-1994) 94 Ohio App.3d 640, 641 N.E.2d 739, dismissed 70 Ohio St.3d 1446, 639 N.E.2d 114, certiorari denied 115 S.Ct. 1256, 513 U.S. 1192, 131 L.Ed.2d 136. Jury ⚖ 19(1)

Financial institution's conviction for wrongful conveyance under statute prohibiting wrongful or culpable withholding or concealing of estate assets could not be characterized as misdemeanor or felony and, therefore, institution could not prove violation of either constitutional or statutory right to speedy trial. In re Estate of Popp (Ohio App. 8 Dist., 04-18-1994) 94 Ohio App.3d 640, 641 N.E.2d 739, dismissed 70 Ohio St.3d 1446, 639 N.E.2d 114, certiorari denied 115 S.Ct. 1256, 513 U.S. 1192, 131 L.Ed.2d 136. Action ⚖ 18

Purpose of statute regarding concealment or embezzlement of assets from estate is to provide speedy and effective method of discovering assets belonging to estate and securing their recovery. Wozniak v. Wozniak (Ohio App. 9 Dist., 09-22-1993) 90 Ohio App.3d 400, 629 N.E.2d 500, cause dismissed 68 Ohio St.3d 1440, 626 N.E.2d 124. Executors And Administrators ⚖ 85(.5)

Action under statute regarding concealment or embezzlement of assets from estate involves unauthorized and wrongful concealment, embezzlement, or conveyance of estate property in denial of, and inconsistent with, rights of estate. Wozniak v. Wozniak (Ohio App. 9 Dist., 09-22-1993) 90 Ohio App.3d 400, 629 N.E.2d 500, cause dismissed 68 Ohio St.3d 1440, 626 N.E.2d 124. Executors And Administrators ⚖ 85(1)

Inquiry under statute regarding embezzlement or concealment of assets from estate focuses on ownership of asset and whether possession of asset is being impermissibly concealed or withheld from estate, and thus plaintiff states actionable cause of action if he alleges that asset is exclusive property of estate and that defendant has unauthorized possession of asset or in some way has impermissibly disposed of it. Wozniak v. Wozniak (Ohio App. 9 Dist., 09-22-1993) 90 Ohio App.3d 400, 629 N.E.2d 500, cause dismissed 68 Ohio St.3d 1440, 626 N.E.2d 124. Executors And Administrators ⚖ 85(5)

A probate court has jurisdiction to inquire into an incompetent's contractual affairs entered into prior to the appointment of a guardian where such person's mental capacity at the time of such dealings is questioned by the guardian. Grannen v. Ey (Hamilton 1974) 44 Ohio App.2d 55, 335 N.E.2d 735, 73 O.O.2d 52.

An agreement entered into by a person subsequently declared incompetent may be declared void when the benefiting party was aware of the person's deteriorating mental condition and took advantage of such to gain control of his property. Grannen v. Ey (Hamilton 1974) 44 Ohio App.2d 55, 335 N.E.2d 735, 73 O.O.2d 52.

A probate court has no jurisdiction to consider the validity or effect of a contract between the distributees of a decedent's estate and one who contracted to collect their share of the estate for a percentage thereof, where the purported contract has no bearing on the assets of the estate, the duties of the administrator or the court's supervision of his administration. In re Porter's Estate (Ohio Prob. 1969) 17 Ohio Misc. 136, 243 N.E.2d 794, 46 O.O.2d 180.

Probate court has no jurisdiction in a proceeding for the discovery of concealed or embezzled assets to determine the right to possession of stock certificates, where the right to the possession of such certificates depends upon the interpretation, application and validity of various contracts. Smith v. Simpson (Hardin 1959) 111 Ohio App. 36, 170 N.E.2d 433, 13 O.O.2d 388.

The purpose of RC 2109.50 is not to furnish a substitute for a civil action to recover judgment for money owing to a fiduciary, but rather to provide a speedy and effective method of discovering assets belonging to an estate to secure possession of them for the purpose of administration, and resort to the statute may not be had to collect a debt, obtain an accounting or adjudicate rights under a contract. In re Woods' Estate (Franklin 1959) 110 Ohio App. 277, 167 N.E.2d 122, 11 O.O.2d 302.

The surplus remaining from a land-forfeiture sale, after the payment of the taxes owing and the costs incident to such sale, is personal property, and the administrator of the estate of the former owner of such property has the right, as the real party in interest, to maintain an action to obtain such surplus. Floyd v. Clyne (Cuyahoga 1958) 108 Ohio App. 16, 154 N.E.2d 771, 80 Ohio Law Abs. 225, 9 O.O.2d 93.

Where grantees obtained a deed to certain property several months after the property had been forfeited to the state, the right to claim the balance in the hands of the county treasurer on the ground that the deed was a nullity is personal property and passes to the grantor's administrator. Floyd v. Clyne (Cuyahoga 1958) 108 Ohio App. 16, 154 N.E.2d 771, 80 Ohio Law Abs. 225, 9 O.O.2d 93.

Where there is a dispute between an executor and a party who had a joint bank account with the decedent and withdrew funds therefrom shortly before decedent's death, resort may not be had to RC 2109.50 to determine the rights therein. In re Stoltz' Estate (Ohio Prob. 1957) 143 N.E.2d 192, 75 Ohio Law Abs. 583.

The trustee of real property cannot attack mismanagement of a tenant through contempt proceedings. In re Schroder's Will (Darke 1950) 107 N.E.2d 143, 62 Ohio Law Abs. 239.

Resort may not be had to the summary procedure under this section to collect a debt due a decedent, to obtain an accounting and judgment for any balance found due, or to adjudicate rights under a contract. In re Leiby's Estate (Ohio 1952) 157 Ohio St. 374, 105 N.E.2d 583, 47 O.O. 265. Executors And Administrators ⚖ 85(1.5)

GC 10506–67 (RC 2109.50) and 10506–73 (RC 2109.52) provide a summary means, inquisitorial in nature, to recover specific property or the proceeds or value thereof belonging to a trust estate, title to which was in a decedent at his death or in a ward when his guardian was appointed, or to recover property belonging to a trust estate, concealed, taken or disposed of after the appointment of the fiduciary. In re Black's Estate (Ohio 1945) 145 Ohio St. 405, 62 N.E.2d 90, 31 O.O. 31. Guardian And Ward ⚖ 33; Trusts ⚖ 181(1)

Resort may not be had to GC 10506–67 (RC 2109.50) et seq. to collect a debt, obtain an accounting or adjudicate rights under a contract. In re Black's Estate (Ohio 1945) 145 Ohio St. 405, 62 N.E.2d 90, 31 O.O. 31.

Purpose of GC 10506–67 (RC 2109.50) et seq. is not to furnish a substitute for a civil action to recover judgment for money owing to an administrator or executor, but rather to provide a speedy and effective method for discovering assets belonging to the estate and to secure possession of them for the purpose of administration. Goodrich v. Anderson (Ohio 1940) 136 Ohio St. 509, 26 N.E.2d 1016, 17 O.O. 152. Executors And Administrators ⚖ 85(1)

An equitable action will not lie for the recovery of concealed assets. Ireland v. Loomis (Ohio Cir. 1898) 9 Ohio C.D. 393.

Question of who is a fiduciary, within meaning of fiduciary-fraud exception to discharge, is one of federal bankruptcy law; however, state law governs nature of legal interests involved. In re Dauterman (Bkrtcy. N.D.Ohio 1993) 156 B.R. 976. Bankruptcy ⚖ 3376(3)

Language of section does not authorize action by the fiduciary of another estate to invoke the provisions of the section to recover from a trust estate since the whole purpose of the section and those following it is to provide a speedy remedy through summary proceeding to place property in the hands of a fiduciary of a trust estate. Gregg v Kent, 27 Abs 628 (App, Madison 1938).

Common pleas court has no jurisdiction to hear and determine an action by executor of an estate against trustee of another trust estate to recover money and other property which allegedly belongs to deceased's estate where there is no evidence of wrongdoing on part of trustee. Gregg v Kent, 27 Abs 628 (App, Madison 1938).

2. Procedural issues

In action by estate executrix alleging that testator's agent by power of attorney concealed, embezzled, or conveyed assets of estate, probate court had subject matter jurisdiction to consider inter vivos transfers by power of attorney, transfers based upon contracts for services, and funds in a joint and survivorship account of testator and agent; the validity of the underlying transfers was challenged. Burwell v. Rains (Ohio App. 11 Dist., Trumbull, 04-22-2005) No. 2004-T-0042, 2005-Ohio-1893, 2005 WL 940580, Unreported. Executors And Administrators ⚖ 435

Ward's daughter, who was not the guardian, was not an interested party and lacked standing to sue her sister and brother-in-law for embezzlement or concealment of money from the guardianship; the legal guardian was the representative who could bring the action. In re Guardianship of Brady (Ohio App. 8 Dist., Cuyahoga, 11-10-2004) No. 83881, 2004-Ohio-5972, 2004 WL 2537048, Unreported, appeal not allowed 105 Ohio St.3d 1543, 827 N.E.2d 327, 2005-Ohio-2188. Mental Health ⚖ 481.1

Trial court failed to follow mandatory procedures for action for restoration of estate assets which were allegedly taken in a manner inconsistent with power of attorney by continuing hearing when defendant, who formally held power of attorney for ninety-seven-year-old and was accused of obtaining his funds under false pretenses and using them for her own purposes, did not appear, since, due to quasi-criminal nature of proceedings, defendant could have been imprisoned for failing to appear. Guardianship of Vasko v. Brown (Ohio App. 8 Dist., Cuyahoga, 12-18-2003) No. 82433, No. 82560, No. 82780, 2003-Ohio-6858, 2003 WL 22966198, Unreported. Principal And Agent ⚖ 79(6)

A concealment action to discover concealed or embezzled assets of an estate is quasi-criminal in nature. Goldberg v. Maloney (Ohio, 11-08-2006) 111 Ohio St.3d 211, 855 N.E.2d 856, 2006-Ohio-5485. Mental Health ⚖ 219

Attorney's bankruptcy action did not automatically stay probate court from proceeding in quasi-criminal proceeding against attorney for the discovery of concealed or embezzled assets of ward's estate. Goldberg v. Maloney (Ohio, 11-08-2006) 111 Ohio St.3d 211, 855 N.E.2d 856, 2006-Ohio-5485. Bankruptcy ⚖ 2395

A proceeding for the discovery of concealed or embezzled assets of an estate is a special proceeding of a summary, inquisitorial character whose purpose is to facilitate the administration of estates by summarily retrieving assets that rightfully belong there. Goldberg v. Maloney (Ohio, 11-08-2006) 111 Ohio St.3d 211, 855 N.E.2d 856, 2006-Ohio-5485. Executors And Administrators ⚖ 85(1)

Probate court did not patently and unambiguously lack jurisdiction to proceed in guardian's concealment action against attorney to determine whether preguardianship transactions, including settlement agreements that the guardian alleged ward never signed, wrongfully transferred assets that would revert to the estate if invalidated. Goldberg v. Maloney (Ohio, 11-08-2006) 111 Ohio St.3d 211, 855 N.E.2d 856, 2006-Ohio-5485. Mental Health ⚖ 219

Decedent's daughter was not required to file a concealment/embezzlement action or an action for declaratory judgment to determine title to family Bible, which she alleged decedent's son had improperly gifted to his daughter pursuant to a power of attorney during the decedent's lifetime; rather, Probate Court had jurisdiction to determine title to the bible, on objections by decedent's daughter to estate administrator's final account. In re Estate of Kelsey (Ohio App. 11 Dist., 03-10-2006) 165 Ohio App.3d 680, 847 N.E.2d 1277, 2006-Ohio-1171. Executors And Administrators ⚖ 85(1)

Even if wrongful death proceeds were "estate assets" for purposes of statute limiting concealment proceedings to cases in which a person was suspected of concealing, embezzling, conveying away, or being or having been in possession of any money, chattel, or chose in action of an estate, a concealment proceeding brought under statute would not authorize the prejudgment attachment of personal property ordered by probate court or its judge; statute was confined to authorizing prejudgment attachment of persons, not property, and required commencement of a civil action, rather than use of quasi-criminal proceeding. State ex rel. Goldberg v. Mahoning Cty. Probate Court (Ohio, 09-05-2001) 93 Ohio St.3d 160, 753 N.E.2d 192, 2001-Ohio-1297, reconsideration denied 93 Ohio St.3d 1464, 756 N.E.2d 1239. Attachment ⚖ 67; Attachment ⚖ 70

Statutes governing proceedings for the discovery of concealed or embezzled assets of an estate do not confer subject-matter jurisdiction on probate courts to issue prejudgment attachment orders relating to personal property. State ex rel. Goldberg v. Mahoning Cty. Probate Court (Ohio, 09-05-2001) 93 Ohio St.3d 160, 753 N.E.2d 192, 2001-Ohio-1297, reconsideration denied 93 Ohio St.3d 1464, 756 N.E.2d 1239. Executors And Administrators ⚖ 85(1)

A concealment action under statute governing proceedings for the discovery of concealed or embezzled assets of an estate is not a civil action; instead, it is a quasi-criminal proceeding that is not intended to be a substitute for a civil action to recover a judgment for money owing to an administrator. State ex rel. Goldberg v. Mahoning Cty. Probate Court (Ohio, 09-05-2001) 93 Ohio St.3d 160, 753 N.E.2d 192, 2001-Ohio-1297, reconsideration denied 93 Ohio St.3d 1464, 756 N.E.2d 1239. Executors And Administrators ⚖ 85(1)

Despite the quasi-criminal nature of a proceeding under statute governing actions to discover concealed or embezzled estate assets, the Rules of Civil Procedure, as practiced in the probate court, are applicable to such a proceeding. Rinehart v. Bank One, Columbus, N.A. (Ohio App. 10 Dist., 03-31-1998) 125 Ohio App.3d 719, 709 N.E.2d 559, dismissed, appeal not allowed 82 Ohio St.3d 1480, 696 N.E.2d 1087. Mental Health ⚖ 238

Decision to pursue a streamlined inquisitorial proceeding under statute governing actions to discover concealed or embezzled estate assets must be taken as an election of remedies in those cases where there is mutuality of parties and identity of factual issues, and a party pursuing this judicially economical remedy accepts the risk that res judicata will foreclose proceedings in another form, as would any litigant faced with a choice of procedural or geographical venues. Rinehart v. Bank One, Columbus, N.A. (Ohio App. 10 Dist., 03-31-1998) 125 Ohio App.3d 719, 709 N.E.2d 559, dismissed, appeal not allowed 82 Ohio St.3d 1480, 696 N.E.2d 1087. Mental Health ⚖ 238

Surety for former fiduciary of estate is not proper party to concealment action brought under statute against former fiduciary. Schraff v. Harrison (Ohio Com.Pl., 09-08-1998) 94 Ohio Misc.2d 104, 703 N.E.2d 877, affirmed 2000 WL 1732789, appeal not allowed 91 Ohio St.3d 1481, 744 N.E.2d 1194. Executors And Administrators ⚖ 438(1)

Proper method of determining liability of fiduciary, for purposes of triggering liability of surety on its bond, is to settle account of fiduciary; if fiduciary fails or refuses to file account, it is obligation of successor fiduciary appointed by court to file account for former fiduciary, and once liability of former fiduciary has been determined, it is appropriate to commence surcharge action against surety on former fiduciary's bond. Schraff v. Harrison (Ohio Com.Pl., 09-08-1998) 94 Ohio Misc.2d 104, 703 N.E.2d 877, affirmed 2000 WL 1732789, appeal not allowed 91 Ohio St.3d 1481, 744 N.E.2d 1194. Principal And Surety ⚖ 66(2); Principal And Surety ⚖ 140

Action against surety is commenced only after liability of fiduciary is established by court and determined by settlement of fiduciary's account. Schraff v. Harrison (Ohio Com.Pl., 09-08-1998) 94 Ohio Misc.2d 104, 703 N.E.2d 877, affirmed 2000 WL 1732789, appeal not allowed 91 Ohio St.3d 1481, 744 N.E.2d 1194. Principal And Surety ⚖ 140

2109.50
Note 2

Surety for former trustee of testamentary trust was not proper party to concealment action brought by successor trustee against former trustee. Schraff v. Harrison (Ohio Com.Pl., 09-08-1998) 94 Ohio Misc.2d 104, 703 N.E.2d 877, affirmed 2000 WL 1732789, appeal not allowed 91 Ohio St.3d 1481, 744 N.E.2d 1194. Trusts ⟺ 366(3)

Motion made by guardian of individual adjudicated incompetent against attorney, requesting that he show cause why he should not be held in contempt of court, was insufficient to give rise to jurisdiction in probate court, after incompetent's death, to hear statutory discovery proceeding attempting to recover allegedly excessive attorney fees charged by him with respect to incompetent's appeal from guardianship order; attorney purged himself of contempt citation at issue; and guardian never attempted to retrieve any funds from him. Burns v. Daily (Ohio App. 11 Dist., 10-28-1996) 114 Ohio App.3d 693, 683 N.E.2d 1164. Contempt ⟺ 55; Contempt ⟺ 81

Statute conferring jurisdiction on probate court to conduct summary proceedings to discover and retrieve specific property or proceeds or value thereof that belong to trust estate may not be used as substitute for action in general division of common pleas court to collect debt due a decedent, for accounting and judgment for any balance found due, or to adjudicate rights under contract. Burns v. Daily (Ohio App. 11 Dist., 10-28-1996) 114 Ohio App.3d 693, 683 N.E.2d 1164. Courts ⟺ 200.7

Court of Appeals reviews Probate Court's determination that it had subject–matter jurisdiction over statutory proceeding to recover assets de novo, without any deference to conclusion reached below, keeping in mind that complainant in such proceeding bears burden of demonstrating that subject matter of his complaint lies within contemplation of statute. Burns v. Daily (Ohio App. 11 Dist., 10-28-1996) 114 Ohio App.3d 693, 683 N.E.2d 1164. Courts ⟺ 202(5)

If title to personal property resides in decedent upon her death, title to that property passes over to executor or administrator of estate, and property can be properly considered "probate property" subject to statutory discovery proceeding. Burns v. Daily (Ohio App. 11 Dist., 10-28-1996) 114 Ohio App.3d 693, 683 N.E.2d 1164. Executors And Administrators ⟺ 43; Executors And Administrators ⟺ 85(3)

If title to personal property does not reside in decedent upon her death, but passed to third party by inter vivos transaction or gift, then such property may not be included as estate asset, and may not be retrieved by summary proceeding in probate court. Burns v. Daily (Ohio App. 11 Dist., 10-28-1996) 114 Ohio App.3d 693, 683 N.E.2d 1164. Executors And Administrators ⟺ 55

Money paid by trust settlor to her attorney for legal services was not asset of her estate recoverable in statutory summary proceeding; title thereto passed to attorney at time of payment, and therefore did not pass to her executor upon her death and did not become "probate property" subject to statutory discovery proceeding. Burns v. Daily (Ohio App. 11 Dist., 10-28-1996) 114 Ohio App.3d 693, 683 N.E.2d 1164. Executors And Administrators ⟺ 55

Freeze-asset order with respect to assets of individual subjected to incompetency proceeding was superseded by final order granting application to appoint guardian, and could no longer serve as continuing basis to assert probate court's jurisdiction over individual's attorney in proceeding to recapture assets. Burns v. Daily (Ohio App. 11 Dist., 10-28-1996) 114 Ohio App.3d 693, 683 N.E.2d 1164. Mental Health ⟺ 160.1

Probate court's reservation of jurisdiction over issue of whether fees charged by attorney for individual declared incompetent were excessive, pending state Supreme Court's resolution of such individual's direct appeal from guardianship order, was insufficient to preserve jurisdiction of probate court over attorney following reversal of guardianship order; reversal of guardianship gave rise to presumption of individual's competency at time she hired and paid attorney, and attorney was therefore not required to seek probate court's approval for his fees. Burns v. Daily (Ohio App. 11 Dist., 10-28-1996) 114 Ohio App.3d 693, 683 N.E.2d 1164. Mental Health ⟺ 159

Since guardian of ward's estate did not follow proper procedure for gaining possession of ward's assets allegedly taken by guardian of ward's person, lower court erred by approving inclusion in guardian's inventory of account receivable representing monies guardian of estate believed that guardian of person was paid or took from ward's account during period when he cared for ward prior to institution of guardianship. In re Guardianship of Maurer (Ohio App. 6 Dist., 12-22-1995) 108 Ohio App.3d 354, 670 N.E.2d 1030, cause dismissed 74 Ohio St.3d 1461, 656 N.E.2d 1297, dismissed, appeal not allowed 76 Ohio St.3d 1405, 666 N.E.2d 565. Guardian And Ward ⟺ 32

Denial of request by financial institution charged with wrongful conveyance under statute prohibiting wrongful or culpable withholding or concealing of estate assets to transfer action to court of common pleas and, instead, transfer of case to another probate court was proper, where probate court was not shown to be interested party as contemplated by statute. In re Estate of Popp (Ohio App. 8 Dist., 04-18-1994) 94 Ohio App.3d 640, 641 N.E.2d 739, dismissed 70 Ohio St.3d 1446, 639 N.E.2d 114, certiorari denied 115 S.Ct. 1256, 513 U.S. 1192, 131 L.Ed.2d 136. Courts ⟺ 484

Since administrator's complaint against financial institution for concealment or embezzlement of estate assets involved wrongful or culpable conduct on part of institution, jurisdiction was appropriate in probate court. In re Estate of Popp (Ohio App. 8 Dist., 04-18-1994) 94 Ohio App.3d 640, 641 N.E.2d 739, dismissed 70 Ohio St.3d 1446, 639 N.E.2d 114, certiorari denied 115 S.Ct. 1256, 513 U.S. 1192, 131 L.Ed.2d 136. Executors And Administrators ⟺ 85(4)

Actions under statute prohibiting wrongful or culpable withholding or concealing of estate assets are specifically to be brought in probate court. In re Estate of Popp (Ohio App. 8 Dist., 04-18-1994) 94 Ohio App.3d 640, 641 N.E.2d 739, dismissed 70 Ohio St.3d 1446, 639 N.E.2d 114, certiorari denied 115 S.Ct. 1256, 513 U.S. 1192, 131 L.Ed.2d 136. Executors And Administrators ⟺ 85(4)

Statute prohibiting wrongful or culpable withholding or concealing of estate assets is intended as summary proceeding to recover assets of estate that are alleged to be concealed, embezzled, or conveyed away; since it is special proceeding that does not require jail sentence but only recovery of assets or their face value and 10% fine where applicable, summary judgment may be granted by court. In re Estate of Popp (Ohio App. 8 Dist., 04-18-1994) 94 Ohio App.3d 640, 641 N.E.2d 739, dismissed 70 Ohio St.3d 1446, 639 N.E.2d 114, certiorari denied 115 S.Ct. 1256, 513 U.S. 1192, 131 L.Ed.2d 136. Judgment ⟺ 180

Statute regarding concealment or embezzlement of assets from estate was not intended as substitute for civil action to collect debt, obtain accounting, adjudicate rights under contract or recover judgment for money owing executor or administrator. Wozniak v. Wozniak (Ohio App. 9 Dist., 09-22-1993) 90 Ohio App.3d 400, 629 N.E.2d 500, cause dismissed 68 Ohio St.3d 1440, 626 N.E.2d 124. Executors And Administrators ⟺ 85(.5)

Proceeding under statute regarding concealment or embezzlement of assets from estate is quasi-criminal in nature, but it does not involve litigation of criminal act. Wozniak v. Wozniak (Ohio App. 9 Dist., 09-22-1993) 90 Ohio App.3d 400, 629 N.E.2d 500, cause dismissed 68 Ohio St.3d 1440, 626 N.E.2d 124. Executors And Administrators ⟺ 85(1)

Proceeding under statute regarding concealment or embezzlement of assets from estate is civil in character and law governing civil actions controls. Wozniak v. Wozniak (Ohio App. 9 Dist., 09-22-1993) 90 Ohio App.3d 400, 629 N.E.2d 500, cause dismissed 68 Ohio St.3d 1440, 626 N.E.2d 124. Executors And Administrators ⟺ 85(1)

To be "interested party" under statute regarding concealment or embezzlement of assets of estate, plaintiff must allege sufficient relationship to estate entitled to recover concealed assets. Wozniak v. Wozniak (Ohio App. 9 Dist., 09-22-1993) 90 Ohio App.3d 400, 629 N.E.2d 500, cause dismissed 68 Ohio St.3d 1440, 626 N.E.2d 124. Executors And Administrators ⟺ 85(2)

Ultimate beneficiary of estate's recovery of any concealed assets was "interested person" under statute regarding concealment or embezzlement of estate's assets. Wozniak v. Wozniak (Ohio App. 9 Dist., 09-22-1993) 90 Ohio App.3d 400, 629 N.E.2d 500, cause dismissed 68 Ohio St.3d 1440, 626 N.E.2d 124. Executors And Administrators ⟺ 85(2)

Nature of transaction by which defendant obtains possession of concealed assets is not dispositive of whether probate court has jurisdiction over action to recover assets allegedly concealed or embezzled from estate. Wozniak v. Wozniak (Ohio App. 9 Dist., 09-22-1993) 90 Ohio App.3d 400, 629 N.E.2d 500, cause dismissed 68 Ohio St.3d 1440, 626 N.E.2d 124. Executors And Administrators ⟺ 85(4)

Special proceeding which enables interested parties to recover concealed, embezzled, and conveyed assets of estate is quasi-criminal in nature, and specific procedural requirements of governing statute must be followed to effect recovery. Lauerman v. Destocki (Ross 1993) 87 Ohio App.3d 657, 622 N.E.2d 1122. Executors And Administrators ⟺ 86(.5)

Executor's action to recover stock certificates allegedly concealed from estate by employees of testator was properly conducted by probate court as summary proceeding, even though executor was allowed to present her entire case prior to any cross-examination of executor's witnesses by employees, where probate court allowed employees complete freedom to present any witnesses of their choosing and to cross-examine all of executor's witnesses, employees objected to evidence and court ruled on each objection, and employees made no jury request. Lauerman v.

Destocki (Ross 1993) 87 Ohio App.3d 657, 622 N.E.2d 1122. Executors And Administrators ☞ 86(.5)

A court of appeals lacks jurisdiction to consider a decedent's son's assignment of errors regarding a probate court's determination and order that a joint and survivorship account was an asset of the decedent's estate for which the son was to provide an accounting of the monies withdrawn by him, where the probate court's order appealed from does not constitute a final appealable order because it does not conform to the procedural requirements of RC 2109.52 directing the court to make a finding relative to the decedent's son's guilt or innocence on a charge that he concealed estate assets, and since no penalty was imposed against the son no substantial right of the decedent's son was affected. In re Estate of Meyer (Butler 1989) 63 Ohio App.3d 454, 579 N.E.2d 260.

An injunction, granted in a pending divorce proceeding, which restrains both parties from selling and encumbering assets, has no application in an action under RC 2109.50 to recover concealed assets of the estate of one of the parties so enjoined. Dodd v. Crowe (Summit 1976) 51 Ohio App.2d 40, 365 N.E.2d 1257, 5 O.O.3d 163. Divorce ☞ 206

Where a decedent, prior to her death, transfers assets from one bank account to another in violation of an injunction, such transfer will not support an action to recover the funds under RC 2109.49 against either the bank in which the funds reside or against decedent's joint tenant in the new account. Dodd v. Crowe (Summit 1976) 51 Ohio App.2d 40, 365 N.E.2d 1257, 5 O.O.3d 163.

If an executor, administrator, or other interested party discovers that an asset was not included in the inventory or supplemental inventory of a decedent and that the asset may belong to the estate, such party may bring an action in declaratory judgment under RC 2721.05, or use the special proceedings of RC 2109.50 to determine whether such asset belongs to the estate of the decedent. Eger v. Eger (Cuyahoga 1974) 39 Ohio App.2d 14, 314 N.E.2d 394, 68 O.O.2d 150. Declaratory Judgment ☞ 243; Executors And Administrators ☞ 85(1)

It is error for a court to order the substitution of the executor of a ward's estate as party in interest in place of the guardian of such ward in matters pertaining to a complaint filed by such guardian, prior to the ward's death, alleging the concealment of "monies, chattels or choses in action belonging to said ward's estate." Kelly v. Smith (Logan 1964) 7 Ohio App.2d 142, 219 N.E.2d 231, 36 O.O.2d 293.

Where an executor conveys property of the estate to himself as legatee less than one month after the approval of the inventory, a creditor of the executor may cause the estate to obtain judgment against such executor for such amount so improperly distributed. In re Walden's Estate (Ohio Prob. 1965) 6 Ohio Misc. 214, 214 N.E.2d 271, 34 O.O.2d 149.

The statutory proceeding for concealment of assets under the provisions of RC 2109.50 et seq. is quasi-criminal in nature. In re Woods' Estate (Franklin 1959) 110 Ohio App. 277, 167 N.E.2d 122, 11 O.O.2d 302.

Where an heir seeks a citation against the administrator and another heir for withholding a portion of her distributive share of an estate in which a final account has been filed, and charges that her receipt for her share is a forgery, she must first have the order settling the final account vacated. In re Reitler's Estate (Ohio Prob. 1956) 137 N.E.2d 791, 73 Ohio Law Abs. 328.

In a proceeding for the discovery of concealed or embezzled assets there is no absolute right to cross-examination of the defendant therein by the complaining party. In re Fife's Estate (Ohio 1956) 164 Ohio St. 449, 132 N.E.2d 185, 58 O.O. 293. Executors And Administrators ☞ 85(1)

The filing of exceptions to an executor's account, the exceptor alleging that the executor has failed to charge himself with all the assets of the estate, is not the proper procedure to obtain a determination as to the validity of a gift and transfer of possession during the lifetime of the decedent. In re Trent's Estate (Franklin 1954) 98 Ohio App. 238, 128 N.E.2d 839, 57 O.O. 266. Executors And Administrators ☞ 504(6)

It was an abuse of discretion not to grant a new trial upon exceptions to an inventory where newly discovered evidence showed that the decedent had died the day before a savings account withdrawal form was presented in her name. In re Warga's Estate (Cuyahoga 1953) 113 N.E.2d 39, 69 Ohio Law Abs. 1.

Proceeding for discovery of concealed or embezzled goods, etc., was appropriate to recover from an employee of decedent, funds which the employee had embezzled from decedent; action for accounting would not be. In re Leiby's Estate (Franklin 1951) 101 N.E.2d 214, 60 Ohio Law Abs. 245, appeal dismissed 156 Ohio St. 254, 101 N.E.2d 906, 46 O.O. 121; reversed 157 Ohio St. 374, 105 N.E.2d 583, 47 O.O. 265.

Action for discovery of concealed assets was properly referred to a master commissioner where no jury trial was requested. In re Leiby's Estate (Franklin 1951) 101 N.E.2d 214, 60 Ohio Law Abs. 245, appeal dismissed 156 Ohio St. 254, 101 N.E.2d 906, 46 O.O. 121, reversed 157 Ohio St. 374, 105 N.E.2d 583, 47 O.O. 265.

On appeal from judgment under this section for the discovery of concealed assets, there can be no stay of execution or supersedeas thereof unless bond is given in conformance with GC 12223–9 (RC 2505.09). In re Leiby's Estate (Franklin 1950) 101 N.E.2d 213, 60 Ohio Law Abs. 243. Appeal And Error ☞ 460(1)

A proceeding by the administrator of a decedent's estate for the recovery of concealed or embezzled assets is not a civil action and does not require appointment of a guardian ad litem for a minor defendant. Hiple v. Skolmutch (Stark 1950) 88 Ohio App. 529, 100 N.E.2d 642, 45 O.O. 281. Infants ☞ 78(1)

Appeal on law and fact does not lie from action brought under provisions of GC 10506–67 (RC 2109.50) et seq. for concealment of assets. Holbrook v. Frey (Franklin 1950) 97 N.E.2d 51, 58 Ohio Law Abs. 481.

In a proceeding under GC 10506–67 (RC 2109.50) et seq., a finding of guilty or not guilty is required with the imposition of a penalty upon a finding of guilty, and the statutes should not be extended by implication beyond their manifest purpose, to reach persons or matters not covered by the descriptive terms of the statutes. In re Black's Estate (Ohio 1945) 145 Ohio St. 405, 62 N.E.2d 90, 31 O.O. 31.

Under broad authority conferred on probate court in matters relating to administration of estates and in control of fiduciaries, including plenary power to dispose of any matter properly before it, a proceeding in such court based on section does not abate with death of a fiduciary charged with concealment of assets of an estate and may be revived in name of his executor. Sheets v. Hodes (Ohio 1944) 142 Ohio St. 559, 53 N.E.2d 804, 27 O.O. 498.

Proceedings brought under section are quasi-criminal in nature. In re Johnson's Estate (Cuyahoga 1943) 50 N.E.2d 273, 38 Ohio Law Abs. 372.

Right of action to set aside gifts of personal property by decedent only passed to personal representative who is real party in interest. Skehan v. Larkin (Lucas 1930) 41 Ohio App. 85, 179 N.E. 425, 8 Ohio Law Abs. 425, 11 Ohio Law Abs. 449. Executors And Administrators ☞ 49

Testatrix's brother, who was legatee, could not maintain action to set aside gifts of personal property by testatrix to executrix because not real party in interest. Skehan v. Larkin (Lucas 1930) 41 Ohio App. 85, 179 N.E. 425, 8 Ohio Law Abs. 425, 11 Ohio Law Abs. 449. Wills ☞ 748

Defendant sued in replevin for property obtained as administrator may interplead executors appointed under will probated after defendant's appointment. Lorain County Sav. & Trust Co. v. Haynes (Lorain 1927) 26 Ohio App. 552, 160 N.E. 516, 5 Ohio Law Abs. 723. Executors And Administrators ☞ 439

In summary proceeding under GC 10673 (RC 2109.50) for recovery of judgment and penalty against defendant claimed to have concealed, embezzled, or conveyed away money of decedent, the administratrix cannot recover possession of the specific money. Lindquist v. Hayes (Lucas 1926) 22 Ohio App. 141, 153 N.E. 297, 4 Ohio Law Abs. 451.

A proceeding under GC 10673 (RC 2109.50) to recover property belonging to a decedent's estate is a special proceeding and not barred by GC 11224 (RC 2305.09). State, on Complaint of Board of Education of Pickaway Tp. Rural School Dist., Pickaway County v. Steeley (Pickaway 1926) 21 Ohio App. 396, 153 N.E. 285, 4 Ohio Law Abs. 763. Executors And Administrators ☞ 85(1); Limitation Of Actions ☞ 16

A proceeding to remove an administrator and a proceeding against him for concealing assets under RS 6407 may be joined, and such proceeding is appealable. Harris v. Westervelt (Ohio Cir. 1898) 8 Ohio C.D. 367.

Probate court had jurisdiction to entertain action against attorney in fact for concealed or embezzled assets, as assets were withdrawn with a power of attorney and partly withdrawn from intervivos trust funds. Fox v. Stockmaster (Ohio App. 3 Dist., Seneca, 06-05-2002) No. 13-01-34, No. 13-01-35, 2002-Ohio-2824, 2002 WL 1299985, Unreported, appeal not allowed 96 Ohio St.3d 1525, 775 N.E.2d 864, 2002-Ohio-5099. Trusts ☞ 360

Where attorney who was given power of attorney had in his possession and failed to administer and account for assets of estate, trial court did not err in rendering judgment against attorney. Estate of Pearce v Dilley, No. 82 CA 11 (7th Dist Ct App, Mahoning, 9–28–83).

Former GC 10673 (RC 2109.50) et seq. provide for a trial in the probate court of the right of property, title to which is claimed to be in the estate of a decedent; and a judgment entered by that court in proceedings pursuant to said act may be pleaded in bar of another action to try title to or right of possession of the property involved in such proceeding. Tibbott v Cadisch, 32 CC(NS) 161, 35 CD 504 (Cuyahoga 1916).

3. Complaint and citation

In complaint under this section no pleadings are contemplated except original complaint, and no others are provided by statute. Hendrickson v. Hendrickson (Erie 1934) 17 Ohio Law Abs. 39.

Ten percent statutory penalty authorized in concealment actions did not warrant reduction of law firm's fees based on its alleged failure to deposit wrongful death settlement proceeds into approved estate accounts within the county, where there was no indication that any party had filed a concealment complaint. In re Estate of Traylor (Ohio App. 7 Dist., Mahoning, 12-01-2004) No. 03 MA 253, No. 03 MA 256, No. 03 MA 259, No. 03 MA 254, No. 03 MA 257, No. 03 MA 262, No. 03 MA 255, No. 03 MA 258, 2004-Ohio-6504, 2004 WL 2808402, Unreported, reconsideration overruled 2005-Ohio-1348, 2005 WL 678626, appeal not allowed 105 Ohio St.3d 1500, 825 N.E.2d 623, 2005-Ohio-1666. Attorney And Client ⇐ 153

If a defendant takes a person's money after that person died or after that person became a ward, meaning that an estate was in existence at the time the money was taken, then a concealment action is proper. Harrison v. Faseyitan (Ohio App. 7 Dist., 12-09-2004) 159 Ohio App.3d 325, 823 N.E.2d 925, 2004-Ohio-6808. Executors And Administrators ⇐ 49; Mental Health ⇐ 238

A concealment action is not a substitute for a civil action to obtain a money judgment or an accounting of a ward's estate; a concealment action is, however, the proper tool to recover assets or money taken from a ward's estate. Harrison v. Faseyitan (Ohio App. 7 Dist., 12-09-2004) 159 Ohio App.3d 325, 823 N.E.2d 925, 2004-Ohio-6808. Mental Health ⇐ 238

Complaint filed under statute prohibiting wrongful or culpable withholding or concealing of estate assets, although quasi-criminal in character, is controlled by laws governing civil proceedings in probate court. In re Estate of Popp (Ohio App. 8 Dist., 04-18-1994) 94 Ohio App.3d 640, 641 N.E.2d 739, dismissed 70 Ohio St.3d 1446, 639 N.E.2d 114, certiorari denied 115 S.Ct. 1256, 513 U.S. 1192, 131 L.Ed.2d 136. Executors And Administrators ⇐ 86(.5)

A petition and complaint comes within the provisions of RC 2109.50 where it alleges facts showing that the person filing it is a person interested in the estate of a decedent, and where it contains the further allegations that moneys deposited in a bank during the lifetime of the decedent in the joint names of the decedent and another with right of survivorship were so deposited for convenience only and in reality were the sole property of the decedent and belong in his estate, and that such other unauthorizedly withdrew the moneys from the account during the lifetime of the decedent and deposited the same in an account in such other's name where such moneys remain. Fecteau v. Cleveland Trust Co. (Ohio 1960) 171 Ohio St. 121, 167 N.E.2d 890, 12 O.O.2d 139. Executors And Administrators ⇐ 85(5)

In a proceeding to discover concealed assets in which the complaint is that the suspected person is in possession of certificates of corporate stock belonging to decedent's estate and it is shown that such certificates were issued to the decedent during his lifetime and stood in his name on the books of the corporation at the time of his death, a prima-facie case is made for the inclusion of such certificates as assets of the estate, but it may be rebutted and overcome by clear and convincing evidence that such certificates were assigned and delivered by way of gift to the suspected person by the decedent during his lifetime. In re Fife's Estate (Ohio 1956) 164 Ohio St. 449, 132 N.E.2d 185, 58 O.O. 293.

No relief for a probate court estate, upon a complaint to the probate court pursuant to GC 10506-67 (RC 2109.50) can be given except with respect to property of such estate. In re Sexton's Estate (Ohio 1955) 163 Ohio St. 124, 126 N.E.2d 129, 56 O.O. 178, certiorari denied 76 S.Ct. 75, 350 U.S. 838, 100 L.Ed. 747.

Probate court has power to issue citation to any person to appear before it when complaint is made that such person is concealing assets properly included in an estate in process of administration before it, but not to issue extracounty process in the service of such citation. In re Chance's Estate (Hamilton 1951) 88 Ohio App. 416, 100 N.E.2d 92, 60 Ohio Law Abs. 297, 45 O.O. 201. Executors And Administrators ⇐ 85(4.5)

When citation under this section has been issued by the probate court of Hamilton county, accompanied by extracounty process, such court commits no reversible error in quashing the service of such citation, issued to and served upon a resident appearing in said court solely for the purpose of moving to quash such service of citation in Franklin county. In re Chance's Estate (Hamilton 1951) 88 Ohio App. 416, 100 N.E.2d 92, 60 Ohio Law Abs. 297, 45 O.O. 201.

Where complaint filed under section alleges that defendant had "concealed, embezzled or conveyed away moneys" of decedent, and court finds defendant not guilty as charged but finds from evidence defendant guilty "of having been in possession of" moneys belonging to decedent, motion to dismiss complaint is properly overruled and it is not error for trial court to order complaint amended to conform to proof as provided in GC 11363 (RC 2309.58). In re Howard's Estate (Franklin 1947) 79 Ohio App. 203, 80 Ohio App. 80, 72 N.E.2d 502, 48 Ohio Law Abs. 189, 34 O.O. 537, 35 O.O. 447.

Complaint filed in probate court under provisions of section is quasi-criminal in character but laws governing civil proceedings in probate court are applicable to such proceeding. In re Howard's Estate (Franklin 1947) 79 Ohio App. 203, 80 Ohio App. 80, 72 N.E.2d 502, 48 Ohio Law Abs. 189, 34 O.O. 537, 35 O.O. 447.

Where complaint is filed in probate court under section, proof of allegation in complaint is necessary prerequisite to rendering money judgment under GC 10506-73 (RC 2109.52). In re Howard's Estate (Franklin 1947) 79 Ohio App. 203, 80 Ohio App. 80, 72 N.E.2d 502, 48 Ohio Law Abs. 189, 34 O.O. 537, 35 O.O. 447.

A complaint filed under section involves a charge of wrongful or criminal conduct on the part of the person accused. In re Black's Estate (Ohio 1945) 145 Ohio St. 405, 62 N.E.2d 90, 31 O.O. 31.

Where guardian of incompetent filed in the probate court on July 7, 1938, a complaint against certain individual to recover assets allegedly belonging to the guardianship estate, and named individual claimed to hold the assets by virtue of a trust created by the incompetent before appointment of the guardian, and guardian claimed that the ward was incompetent to create the trust, the probate court had jurisdiction under the Probate Code to try the issue as to the title of the assets. In re Sanderson's Guardianship (Summit 1940) 64 Ohio App. 177, 28 N.E.2d 565, 17 O.O. 562. Mental Health ⇐ 480

A complaint, filed in the probate court by an administrator of a decedent's estate under GC 10673 (RC 2109.50), asking that the defendant be required to answer under oath concerning the alleged concealment of certain property claimed to be a part of the estate, is a special proceeding and cannot, in reserving the case to the court of common pleas for hearing and determination, under authority of GC 10674 (RC 2109.50), be transmuted into a suit in equity to receive evidence or determine issues involving the mental incapacity of decedent as pertaining to his intention regarding inter vivos gifts. Halloran v. Merritt (Lucas 1934) 48 Ohio App. 135, 192 N.E. 542, 16 Ohio Law Abs. 548, 1 O.O. 85. Executors And Administrators ⇐ 85(1)

Petition by administrator of decedent's estate under GC 10673 (RC 2109.50), alleging that defendant has taken possession of and appropriated money and property of decedent to which administrator was entitled, states a good cause of action, allegation of criminality not being required, and GC 10678 (RC 2109.52) not being applicable. Losee v. Krieger (Lucas 1925) 22 Ohio App. 395, 153 N.E. 857, 3 Ohio Law Abs. 357.

Fraudulent or criminal intent is not a necessary element in making out administratrix's case under GC 10673 (RC 2109.50) against one concealing, embezzling, or conveying away money of decedent. Lindquist v. Hayes (Lucas 1926) 22 Ohio App. 141, 153 N.E. 297, 4 Ohio Law Abs. 451. Executors And Administrators ⇐ 85(5.1)

4. Examination and hearing

Trial court's hearing dealing with exceptions to accounts regarding deceased mother's estate was not limited to issue of whether son concealed mother's assets, and thus trial court had jurisdiction to consider whether son owed estate rent for occupying mother's house after her death. In re Estate of Endslow (Ohio App. 5 Dist., Delaware, 07-22-2003) No. 03-CAF-01001, 2003-Ohio-3916, 2003 WL 21694010, Unreported. Executors And Administrators ⇐ 507(1)

Evidence supported probate court's imputation, in action by decedent's daughter for accounting of probate estate assets, of $3,000 per month in living expenses, for months in which decedent had lived with decedent's son before decedent's death; decedent had refused to live in nursing home, decedent had told son the son could have his money if the son took care of him, and nursing home had cost $3,200 a month when decedent had to be placed there because of broken hip. Silcott v. Prebble (Ohio App. 12 Dist., Clermont, 02-03-2003) No. CA2002-04-028, 2003-Ohio-508, 2003 WL 231287, Unreported. Executors And Administrators ⇐ 221(5)

Evidence supported probate court's finding, in action by decedent's daughter for accounting of probate estate assets, that decedent's first son was not liable for imputed rent for using, in connection with family business, commercial building owned by decedent, and that second son was not liable for imputed rent for living in decedent's house; first son had operated business as partner with decedent, and first son had made deal with decedent that, in exchange for hiring second son and paying taxes on business, first son could use commercial building rent-free and second son could live in house if second son paid taxes on it. Silcott v. Prebble (Ohio App. 12 Dist., Clermont, 02-03-2003) No. CA2002-04-028, 2003-Ohio-508, 2003 WL 231287, Unreported. Executors And Administrators ⇌ 131

RC 2317.03 does not apply to proceedings under RC 2109.50. In re Brandt's Estate (Ohio Prob. 1964) 1 Ohio Misc. 37, 204 N.E.2d 270, 30 O.O.2d 615.

A proceeding under RC 2109.50 is inquisitorial, the witnesses testifying therein are the court's, and the rule of evidence against impeachment of a party's own witness does not apply. Jones v. Neu (Cuyahoga 1958) 106 Ohio App. 161, 150 N.E.2d 858, 78 Ohio Law Abs. 245, 6 O.O.2d 428.

A complainee in an action for concealing assets of an estate is entitled to testify in support of his defense regarding transactions with the decedent. In re Jones' Estate (Cuyahoga 1952) 122 N.E.2d 111, 68 Ohio Law Abs. 282.

In hearing on complaint filed by administrator, under section, letter written by decedent a short time before his death stating he had $5,000 in bank, which statement tended to refute claim of defendant, that such money had been given to her for certain purposes, was properly admitted in evidence. In re Howard's Estate (Franklin 1947) 79 Ohio App. 203, 80 Ohio App. 80, 72 N.E.2d 502, 48 Ohio Law Abs. 189, 34 O.O. 537, 35 O.O. 447.

In hearing on complaint under section, probate court is given jurisdiction to determine questions of title as provided by GC 10506–73 (RC 2109.52), and if defendant is found guilty under complaint, court has complete authority to render money judgment. In re Howard's Estate (Franklin 1947) 79 Ohio App. 203, 80 Ohio App. 80, 72 N.E.2d 502, 48 Ohio Law Abs. 189, 34 O.O. 537, 35 O.O. 447. Executors And Administrators ⇌ 85(6); Executors And Administrators ⇌ 85(8)

Where death of witness in action against fiduciary for concealment, etc., of assets, was conceded, and his examination on original trial was incorporated in bill of exceptions duly signed by trial judge, under GC 11496 (RC 2317.06) such examination was admissible in subsequent trial of proceeding, and fact that such examination was not signed by witness did not render it inadmissible. Sheets v. Hodes (Crawford 1943) 68 N.E.2d 342, 39 Ohio Law Abs. 492, affirmed 142 Ohio St. 559, 53 N.E.2d 804, 27 O.O. 498.

Section relating to examination of witnesses in proceedings against fiduciary for concealment or embezzlement of assets, being directory and not mandatory, examinations of witnesses as recorded by an official court stenographer and authenticated by his certificate and by certificate of trial judge and filed in the action, if otherwise admissible at subsequent trial of the proceedings, are not rendered inadmissible by fact that such examinations are not signed by the respective witnesses. Sheets v. Hodes (Crawford 1943) 68 N.E.2d 342, 39 Ohio Law Abs. 492, affirmed 142 Ohio St. 559, 53 N.E.2d 804, 27 O.O. 498.

In a special proceeding under GC 10506–67 (RC 2109.50) et seq., to discover assets of an estate, a defense that the articles in question were given to the defendant by the decedent, is good if proven, but evidence that the decedent was insolvent at the time of the alleged gift should be rejected. In re Raymond's Estate (Erie 1940) 66 Ohio App. 428, 34 N.E.2d 821, 20 O.O. 385.

A court may, in the exercise of its jurisdiction, compel an attorney appearing before it to pay over or account for moneys or to deliver papers which he has received in his official capacity and wrongfully withholds from his client; such attorney must be given an opportunity to answer and defend, and if the attorney in good faith claims title to the funds or papers in question, the client is not entitled to a summary order against him. In re Butler's Estate (Ohio 1940) 137 Ohio St. 115, 28 N.E.2d 196, 17 O.O. 440. Attorney And Client ⇌ 126(1)

In a proceeding brought pursuant to RC 2109.50, where there is no admission, but rather a denial, of possession of guardianship assets, the better practice is to proceed as in an adversary hearing, with the parties being given a full opportunity to present their respective assertions. In re Guardianship of Grandstaff, No. 1038 (4th Dist Ct App, Ross, 3–15–84).

5. Evidence and testimony

Son of decedent failed to prove by clear and convincing evidence that decedent made inter vivos gift of funds to him; decedent's direction to son that funds be used to pay for decedent's nursing home care and for any repairs that had to be done to decedent's house was inconsistent with complete relinquishment of dominion and control of funds. Rasnick v. Lenos (Ohio App. 12 Dist., Butler, 06-13-2005) No. CA2004-02-033, 2005-Ohio-2916, 2005 WL 1385218, Unreported, cause dismissed 106 Ohio St.3d 1523, 835 N.E.2d 41, 2005-Ohio-5122. Gifts ⇌ 49(5)

Power of attorney executed by decedent was insufficient to authorize decedent's son to transfer funds in decedent's accounts to son's own accounts, in form of gift; there was no provision in power of attorney that expressly and unambiguously authorized son to make gratuitous transfers of decedent's funds to himself or others, and language of power of attorney that authorized son to make withdrawals from decedent's accounts, when read in context, merely authorized son to take certain actions to conduct banking transactions or business for decedent in decedent's name. Rasnick v. Lenos (Ohio App. 12 Dist., Butler, 06-13-2005) No. CA2004-02-033, 2005-Ohio-2916, 2005 WL 1385218, Unreported, cause dismissed 106 Ohio St.3d 1523, 835 N.E.2d 41, 2005-Ohio-5122. Principal And Agent ⇌ 69(1)

Having stipulated to a proffer of his testimony, deceased mother's son could not claim on appeal that he was denied the opportunity to testify under oath during probate proceedings, and thus son waived any claim that court erred in not taking his testimony concerning whether he should be penalized for concealing deceased mother's assets, where son was given an opportunity to testify, and instead chose to have counsel represent to the court what he would say if called to testify. In re Estate of Endslow (Ohio App. 5 Dist., Delaware, 07-22-2003) No. 03-CAF-01001, 2003-Ohio-3916, 2003 WL 21694010, Unreported. Executors And Administrators ⇌ 510(4)

There was competent, credible evidence to support probate court judgment that executor acted outside his authority while conservator for ward in purchasing $100,000 certificate of deposit (CD) and later concealed it from the probate estate, where executor, as conservator of ward, consolidated three CDs in order to purchase one CD naming ward and executor's wife in joint and survivorship account, CD passed to wife upon ward's death and money was used for benefit of executor and his wife. Elliott v. Emig (Ohio App. 5 Dist., Coshocton, 01-17-2003) No. 02CA7, 2003-Ohio-226, 2003 WL 139759, Unreported. Executors And Administrators ⇌ 465

Probate court did not violate statutory directives for conducting concealment action against former estate administrator, even though witnesses did not sign their transcribed testimony and portions of the transcript were reported as "inaudible," where witnesses were examined under oath in presence of the probate court judge, a court reporter transcribed their testimony, no one objected to accuracy of the transcript, and portions identified as "inaudible" were brief and sporadic. Talbott v. Fisk (Ohio App. 10 Dist., Franklin, 12-17-2002) No. 02AP-427, No. 02AP-428, 2002-Ohio-6960, 2002 WL 31819671, Unreported. Executors And Administrators ⇌ 507(3)

Proceeds from the sale of the deceased parents' home as well as from life insurance policies do not belong to the parents' estates where there has been no breach of fiduciary duty or wrongful concealment of assets by defendant who holds a power of attorney in favor of his father and mother and transacts financial matters for them during the last months of their lives and subsequently cashes the checks and deposits the proceeds into his personal account. Shuerger v. Wehner (Ohio App. 8 Dist., Cuyahoga, 06-25-1998) No. 72477, 1998 WL 338072, Unreported.

Action by executrix to recover money which she claimed was value of bonds which were property of her decedent, and which she charged defendant had converted to his own use, was not an action under favor of this section, but merely one at common law for money as damages, and court properly confined testimony of defendant as a witness to matters that had occurred subsequent to death of testatrix. Hodge v. Weed (Meigs 1932) 12 Ohio Law Abs. 591. Witnesses ⇌ 139(1)

Certificates of deposit so drawn, with the knowledge of the wife, as to be payable to either husband or wife, and placed in a safe deposit box to which the wife had the key, were joint property during the lifetime of the husband and at his death became the exclusive property of the wife and were not subject to disposition by the husband in his will, and the wife in making use of them did not become subject to an action for embezzlement. In re Shangle's Estate (Perry 1930) 8 Ohio Law Abs. 621, 32 Ohio Law Rep. 185.

A plaintiff has stated an actionable cause for the discovery of concealed or embezzled assets of an estate if he alleges that the asset is the exclusive property of the estate and that the defendant has unauthorized possession of the asset or in some way has impermissibly disposed of it. Goldberg v. Maloney (Ohio, 11-08-2006) 111 Ohio St.3d 211, 855 N.E.2d 856, 2006-Ohio-5485. Executors And Administrators ⇌ 85(1)

There was insufficient evidence to support claim by ward's sister that ward instructed her to make withdrawals and distributions from ward's bank accounts, in concealment action brought by ward's guardian; presented no corroborating testimony or evidence, she failed to produce receipts or even state amounts for the alleged repairs, moving, and storage she paid for, she did not call the alleged recipients of the distributions to testify, and she did not seek to bring in as a third party anyone who received assets with notice of the pending guardianship. Harrison v. Faseyitan (Ohio

App. 7 Dist., 12-09-2004) 159 Ohio App.3d 325, 823 N.E.2d 925, 2004-Ohio-6808. Mental Health ⇐ 238

Concealment of ward's assets existed, arising from withdrawals made by ward's sister, even if the entire family met and agreed to the withdrawals and payments; it was no defense that the family agreed on how to spend the ward's or potential ward's money, but rather, the concealment action was to recover the assets that belonged to the ward in order to benefit the ward, not to benefit potential heirs of the ward. Harrison v. Faseyitan (Ohio App. 7 Dist., 12-09-2004) 159 Ohio App.3d 325, 823 N.E.2d 925, 2004-Ohio-6808. Mental Health ⇐ 238

Ward's sister could be found to have concealed assets, even though she did not try to hide withdrawals from ward's bank accounts; under statute, the assets or money need not have been "concealed" in the strict sense of the word, but rather the statute allowed examination of anyone suspected of having concealed, embezzled, or conveyed away or of being or having been in the possession of estate assets. Harrison v. Faseyitan (Ohio App. 7 Dist., 12-09-2004) 159 Ohio App.3d 325, 823 N.E.2d 925, 2004-Ohio-6808. Mental Health ⇐ 238

Unless there was evidence which could be interpreted as direction by either customer or her estate to bank to convey any money without reference to genuineness of endorsement, or prior course of dealing between customer and bank warranting such payment, bank was liable if payment was made on unauthorized endorsement; bank did not have to know that instrument was forged or that presenter had criminal intent. In re Estate of Popp (Ohio App. 8 Dist., 04-18-1994) 94 Ohio App.3d 640, 641 N.E.2d 739, dismissed 70 Ohio St.3d 1446, 639 N.E.2d 114, certiorari denied 115 S.Ct. 1256, 513 U.S. 1192, 131 L.Ed.2d 136. Banks And Banking ⇐ 148(2)

Financial institution charged with wrongful conveyance under statute prohibiting wrongful or culpable withholding or concealing of estate assets failed to show that it was prejudiced by common pleas court's refusal to allow questions put forth to administrator for purposes of establishing institution's defense of mens rea, where mens rea in conveying money belonging to estate was irrelevant to its conviction under statute. In re Estate of Popp (Ohio App. 8 Dist., 04-18-1994) 94 Ohio App.3d 640, 641 N.E.2d 739, dismissed 70 Ohio St.3d 1446, 639 N.E.2d 114, certiorari denied 115 S.Ct. 1256, 513 U.S. 1192, 131 L.Ed.2d 136. Executors And Administrators ⇐ 85(8)

In proceeding against financial institution for wrongful conveyance under statute prohibiting wrongful or culpable withholding or concealing of estate assets, it must first be established that there was conveyance made to wrong party, after which all that is required is to show by preponderance of evidence that money belonged to decedent; it is not necessary to establish that conveyance was made with fraudulent criminal intent. In re Estate of Popp (Ohio App. 8 Dist., 04-18-1994) 94 Ohio App.3d 640, 641 N.E.2d 739, dismissed 70 Ohio St.3d 1446, 639 N.E.2d 114, certiorari denied 115 S.Ct. 1256, 513 U.S. 1192, 131 L.Ed.2d 136. Executors And Administrators ⇐ 86(.5)

Heir stated claim against trustee of trust for concealment or embezzlement of trust assets, where he alleged that trustee transferred to himself assets belonging exclusively to estate and that he either concealed or disposed of those assets without authorization from grantor or representative of her estate. Wozniak v. Wozniak (Ohio App. 9 Dist., 09-22-1993) 90 Ohio App.3d 400, 629 N.E.2d 500, cause dismissed 68 Ohio St.3d 1440, 626 N.E.2d 124. Executors And Administrators ⇐ 85(5); Trusts ⇐ 261

In order to assert gift defense to charge of concealment in proceeding to discover concealed assets of estate, alleged donees must establish elements of inter vivos gift by clear and convincing evidence. Lauerman v. Destocki (Ross 1993) 87 Ohio App.3d 657, 622 N.E.2d 1122. Executors And Administrators ⇐ 86(.5)

A factual issue exists as to a lessor's intention to hold the property in a purchase money resulting trust when a lease defines the relationship as lessor-lessee and an addendum provides the lessee with an option to buy the property at the end of the lease term. Glick v. Dolin (Cuyahoga 1992) 80 Ohio App.3d 592, 609 N.E.2d 1338.

Where the executor's inventory incorrectly listed certain certificates of deposit as payable at death, and the probate court subsequently ruled that the certificates were part of the decedent's estate and ordered the persons who had received the proceeds to return them, the court did not abuse its discretion in failing to find the executor guilty of concealing estate assets and permitting him to continue as fiduciary. In re Estate of Clapsaddle (Washington 1992) 79 Ohio App.3d 747, 607 N.E.2d 1148, motion overruled 65 Ohio St.3d 1435, 600 N.E.2d 678.

Where a defendant has withheld assets of the decedent's estate under the mistaken but good faith belief that the decedent had legally given her such assets and the trial court finds that title to the assets lies in the estate,

the defendant is not guilty of concealing estate assets without a showing of more than mere possession. Ukrainiec v. Batz (Summit 1982) 24 Ohio App.3d 200, 493 N.E.2d 1368, 24 O.B.R. 323.

Circumstantial evidence relied upon to prove an essential element of a crime must be irreconcilable with any reasonable theory of an accused's innocence in order to support a finding of guilt. State v. Kulig (Ohio 1974) 37 Ohio St.2d 157, 309 N.E.2d 897, 66 O.O.2d 351.

Since the statutory proceeding for concealment of assets requires a finding of guilty, the burden is imposed upon the claimant or the court to at least produce evidence of such probative character that reasonable minds might reach different conclusions upon the guilt or innocence of the respondent. In re Woods' Estate (Franklin 1959) 110 Ohio App. 277, 167 N.E.2d 122, 11 O.O.2d 302. Executors And Administrators ⇐ 85(5.1)

In an action under GC 10506-67 (RC 2109.50) a written statement by the incompetent allegedly defrauded that a transfer was made under duress is admissible. In re Guardianship of Rost (Franklin 1952) 134 N.E.2d 863, 72 Ohio Law Abs. 261.

The giving of the key to a box taken from a closet, together with a key to a safe deposit box in a bank, with the direction that the donee is to "have everything in this box" and in the safe deposit box in the bank, is not sufficient to establish a gift causa mortis, where such box was still in the donor's room at the time of his death and the donee's residence was different from that of the donor, and in an action for a declaratory judgment brought by a person in possession of personal property claimed by the executor of decedent's estate and which the party in possession claims by virtue of a gift inter vivos, a probate court has jurisdiction to determine the title to such personal property. (See also Renee v Sanders, 160 OS 279, 116 NE(2d) 420 (1953).) Renee v. Sanders (Cuyahoga 1956) 102 Ohio App. 21, 131 N.E.2d 846, 73 Ohio Law Abs. 449, 2 O.O.2d 7.

Where one at all times openly and notoriously and under claim of right retains possession of an asset claimed by an estate, he is not guilty of "having concealed, embezzled or conveyed away" an asset of an estate under GC 10506-67 (RC 2109.50) and 10506-73 (RC 2109.52). In re Brooks' Estate (Cuyahoga 1949) 90 N.E.2d 605, 56 Ohio Law Abs. 15.

An executrix who obtained possession of assets rightfully and held them in her fiduciary capacity could not be held guilty of a "wrongful withholding" of assets from devisees within the statute authorizing summary proceedings against a fiduciary by the unexcused failure of listing them in her first inventory, where upon demand of devisees and upon advice of counsel executrix subsequently and within reasonable time disclosed such assets, all of which were still in her possession lawfully as executrix. In re Meyer's Estate (Ohio Prob. 1948) 82 N.E.2d 856, 53 Ohio Law Abs. 97. Executors And Administrators ⇐ 85(9)

Where complaint filed by administrator under section alleges that defendant "concealed, embezzled or conveyed away moneys" of decedent, and court after judgment in furtherance of justice orders complaint amended to conform to proof by inserting following allegation "or of being or having been in possession of" and evidence shows that defendant was in possession of large sums of money which she and decedent withdrew from his savings account which she claims decedent gave to her at different times for certain purposes and there is evidence offered to refute her claim, judgment of trial court that defendant was guilty of being in possession of moneys belonging to estate of decedent will not be reversed on weight of evidence. In re Howard's Estate (Franklin 1947) 79 Ohio App. 203, 80 Ohio App. 80, 72 N.E.2d 502, 48 Ohio Law Abs. 189, 34 O.O. 537, 35 O.O. 447.

Proceeding instituted by guardian under section to recover property alleged to belong to his ward's estate may not be successfully pursued where it appears from the evidence that title to such property had been transferred by the ward, pursuant to a valid agreement, prior to the guardianship. In re Black's Estate (Ohio 1945) 145 Ohio St. 405, 62 N.E.2d 90, 31 O.O. 31.

Where administrator is charged, in action brought under GC 10506-67 (RC 2109.50) et seq., with having concealed, embezzled, or conveyed away assets of estate, and evidence shows he conveyed away assets of small value, without attempt to conceal, and with consent of one whom he thought, upon advice of counsel, to be sole heir, a finding of "not guilty" by probate court, is justified. In re Johnson's Estate (Cuyahoga 1943) 50 N.E.2d 273, 38 Ohio Law Abs. 372.

In action by executrix to recover personal property held by another upon claim of valid gift by decedent, brought pursuant to section, it is error for court to exclude testimony of witnesses as to statements made by decedent to effect that property in question was placed in hands of one claiming title thereto for safekeeping only, and contradicting such person's testimony that valid gift was intended; and probate court, in such case, is authorized under GC 10506-73 (RC 2109.52), to hear and determine "questions of title." In re Evans' Estate (Franklin 1941) 71 Ohio App. 127, 41 N.E.2d 410, 35 Ohio Law Abs. 295, 25 O.O. 499.

In action by executrix to recover personal property held by another upon claim of valid gift by decedent, brought under section, utterances by decedent, made in connection with alleged delivery of property in question and purpose of such delivery, are of such importance for determination of issue presented, the intention of alleged donor, that they should be admitted as exception to hearsay rule. In re Evans' Estate (Franklin 1941) 71 Ohio App. 127, 41 N.E.2d 410, 35 Ohio Law Abs. 295, 25 O.O. 499.

Evidence by witnesses to the effect that deceased had delivered personal property to defendant for safekeeping may be admitted only to refute statements of defendant that the delivery to her was a gift. In re Evans' Estate (Franklin 1941) 71 Ohio App. 127, 41 N.E.2d 410, 35 Ohio Law Abs. 295, 25 O.O. 499.

In action under former GC 10673 (RC 2109.50) by administrator of decedent, alleging defendant had appropriated property of decedent, it was error to exclude evidence that property of decedent had been appropriated and withheld. Losee v. Krieger (Lucas 1925) 22 Ohio App. 395, 153 N.E. 857, 3 Ohio Law Abs. 357.

In action by administrator, alleging defendant had appropriated property belonging to the estate, evidence was admissible to show that decedent was incapacitated from transacting business at the time it was claimed she had disposed of some of her property. Losee v. Krieger (Lucas 1925) 22 Ohio App. 395, 153 N.E. 857, 3 Ohio Law Abs. 357.

A defendant in a summary proceeding under former GC 10673 (RC 2109.50) to recover money of decedent claimed to have been concealed, embezzled, or conveyed away, who admits withdrawal and retention of money from the bank, thereby admits conveying it away, and the administratrix, to establish a prima-facie case, need only establish by preponderance of evidence that the money belonged to decedent. Lindquist v. Hayes (Lucas 1926) 22 Ohio App. 141, 153 N.E. 297, 4 Ohio Law Abs. 451.

Where a stepfather receives an inheritance belonging to his stepchildren and innocently mingles it with his own means under the impression that his promise to support the children is a valid consideration therefor, a complaint by the children for having concealed or embezzled their inheritance, made after they attain their majority, will not lie. In re Ledig's Estate (Ohio Com.Pl. 1909) 21 Ohio Dec. 713, 9 Ohio NP(NS) 169.

The use by a guardian of his own money in his own business and its loss thereby, to constitute embezzlement, must be with a fraudulent purpose although the statute is silent as to intent. State v. Meyer (Ohio Com.Pl. 1890) 23 W.L.B. 251, reversed 2 Ohio C.D. 712.

To except debt from discharge as one for money obtained by debtor's fraud on defalcation in fiduciary capacity, creditor must demonstrate existence of express trust, that party in trust acted in fiduciary capacity, and breach of trust relationship by at least a defalcation of funds. In re Dauterman (Bkrtcy.N.D.Ohio 1993) 156 B.R. 976. Bankruptcy ⟐ 3376(1)

Debtor need not have acted intentionally or in bad faith in order to be guilty of "defalcation," such as may prevent discharge of resulting judgment debt. In re Dauterman (Bkrtcy.N.D.Ohio 1993) 156 B.R. 976. Bankruptcy ⟐ 3376(5)

Guardians' behavior, in using funds from ward's estate to purchase new appliances and furniture for their home and to repay creditor who had loaned them money to purchase home, rose at least to level of "defalcation," so as to preclude discharge of resulting judgment debt in bankruptcy as one for money obtained by guardians' fraud or defalcation in fiduciary capacity. In re Dauterman (Bkrtcy.N.D.Ohio 1993) 156 B.R. 976. Bankruptcy ⟐ 3376(5)

A valid inter vivos gift of funds from a testator to his son does not constitute unlawful concealment of assets of the estate from his other heirs. Leigh v Hurd, No. 4037 (11th Dist Ct App, Trumbull, 12–9–88).

6. Attorney fees

Attorney who represented executor of estate in concealment of assets action was not entitled to payment of $5,000 attorney fees from the estate, even though $5,000 attorney fees were awarded in the concealment of assets action, where executor, rather than the estate, was the real party in interest in the concealment action, and attorney was only entitled to seek attorney fees from the executor rather than from the estate. In re Estate of Simons (Ohio App. 11 Dist., Trumbull, 05-13-2005) No. 2004-T-0066, 2005-Ohio-2362, 2005 WL 1131775, Unreported. Executors And Administrators ⟐ 111(1)

Brother of husband could not recover travel and miscellaneous expenses incurred in defending action brought by husband's wife, alleging that brother conveyed away or concealed assets belong to husband's estate; brother was not issued an extra-county citation, as required to recover travel costs, and the miscellaneous expenses for facsimiles and photocopies were not statutory fees eligible for reimbursement. Arneault v. Arneault (Ohio App. 4 Dist., Washington, 05-21-2003) No. 02CA60, 2003-Ohio-4553, 2003 WL 22017263, Unreported. Executors And Administrators ⟐ 456(1)

Brother of husband could not recover attorney fees incurred in defending action brought by husband's wife, alleging that brother conveyed away or concealed assets belong to husband's estate; there was no statute specifically authorizing the probate court to award attorney fees, and probate court did not find that wife acted in bad faith by initiating her action. Arneault v. Arneault (Ohio App. 4 Dist., Washington, 05-21-2003) No. 02CA60, 2003-Ohio-4553, 2003 WL 22017263, Unreported. Executors And Administrators ⟐ 456(1)

2109.51 Imprisonment for disobeying citation

If a person compelled under section 2109.50 of the Revised Code to appear for examination refuses to answer interrogatories propounded, the probate court shall commit such person to the county jail and such person shall remain in close custody until he submits to the court's order.

(128 v 76, eff. 11–9–59; 1953 H 1; GC 10506–69)

Historical and Statutory Notes

Pre–1953 H 1 Amendments: 114 v 379

OSBA Probate and Trust Law Section

1959:
See the comment for 1959 following Sec. 2109.50.

Library References

Contempt ⟐ 20, 70.
Westlaw Topic No. 93.
C.J.S. Contempt §§ 14, 107 to 108, 110, 117, 119.

Research References

Encyclopedias
OH Jur. 3d Contempt § 46, Opportunity to Purge the Contempt.
OH Jur. 3d Fiduciaries § 159, Citation, Attachment, or Warrant of Suspected Person or Persons Interested in Assets—Punishment for Disobeying Citation.

Treatises and Practice Aids
Carlin, Baldwin's Ohio Practice, Merrick-Rippner Probate Law § 56:2, Concealed or Embezzled Assets—Jurisdiction Over Complaint.
Carlin, Baldwin's Ohio Practice, Merrick-Rippner Probate Law § 56:22, Entry for Attachment of Body—Form.
Carlin, Baldwin's Ohio Practice, Merrick-Rippner Probate Law § 56:23, Entry for Commitment—Form.
Carlin, Baldwin's Ohio Practice, Merrick-Rippner Probate Law § 56:24, Commitment to County Jail—Form.
Carlin, Baldwin's Ohio Practice, Merrick-Rippner Probate Law § 56:25, Sheriff's Return of Commitment—Form.

Notes of Decisions

Examination 1
Procedural issues 3
Self–incrimination 2

1. Examination

In a proceeding for the discovery of concealed or embezzled assets there is no absolute right to cross-examination of the defendant therein by the complaining party. In re Fife's Estate (Ohio 1956) 164 Ohio St. 449, 132 N.E.2d 185, 58 O.O. 293. Executors And Administrators ⟐ 85(1)

In a summary proceeding by an administratrix under former GC 10673 (RC 2109.50) to recover a judgment for money of decedent claimed to be concealed, embezzled, or conveyed away, questions as to form and disposition of the money withdrawn from bank were immaterial and irrelevant,

Note 1

and hence defendant could not be held for contempt under GC 10675 (RC 2109.51) for refusing to answer them. Lindquist v. Hayes (Lucas 1926) 22 Ohio App. 141, 153 N.E. 297, 4 Ohio Law Abs. 451.

2. Self–incrimination

A witness is not the sole judge as to whether the answer to a question will tend to incriminate him, but the question is one for the court. Lindquist v. Hayes (Lucas 1926) 22 Ohio App. 141, 153 N.E. 297, 4 Ohio Law Abs. 451. Witnesses ⚖ 308

If there is a reasonable ground for apprehending that the answer of a witness will tend to incriminate him, he cannot be required to answer. Lindquist v. Hayes (Lucas 1926) 22 Ohio App. 141, 153 N.E. 297, 4 Ohio Law Abs. 451. Witnesses ⚖ 297(1)

3. Procedural issues

In a complaint for concealment of personal property in an estate, the procedures of RC 2109.50 et seq. should be followed; thus, when 1) the mandatory language of RC 2109.51 is not adhered to because persons compelled to testify under that section did not and deposition testimony of one of those persons does not satisfy the statute and 2) the court did not make a finding of guilt or innocence as required by RC 2109.52, the case must be remanded for a hearing on the concealment of property. In re Estate of Holmes, No. 62749 (8th Dist Ct App, Cuyahoga, 6–10–93).

2109.52 Judgment on the complaint

When passing on a complaint made under section 2109.50 of the Revised Code, the probate court shall determine, by the verdict of a jury if either party requires it or without if not required, whether the person accused is guilty of having concealed, embezzled, conveyed away, or been in the possession of moneys, chattels, or choses in action of the trust estate. If such person is found guilty, the probate court shall assess the amount of damages to be recovered or the court may order the return of the specific thing concealed or embezzled or may order restoration in kind. The probate court may issue a citation into any county in this state, which citation shall be served and returned as provided in section 2109.50, requiring any person to appear before it who claims any interest in the assets alleged to have been concealed, embezzled, conveyed, or held in possession and at such hearing may hear and determine questions of title relating to such assets. In all cases, except when the person found guilty is the fiduciary, the probate court shall forthwith render judgment in favor of the fiduciary or if there is no fiduciary in this state, the probate court shall render judgment in favor of the state, against the person found guilty, for the amount of the moneys or the value of the chattels or choses in action concealed, embezzled, conveyed away, or held in possession, together with ten per cent penalty and all costs of such proceedings or complaint; except that such judgment shall be reduced to the extent of the value of any thing specifically restored or returned in kind as provided in this section.

If the person found guilty is the fiduciary, the probate court shall forthwith render judgment in favor of the state against him for such amount or value, together with penalty and costs as provided in this section.

(128 v 76, eff. 11–9–59; 1953 H 1; GC 10506–73)

Historical and Statutory Notes

Pre–1953 H 1 Amendments: 114 v 379

OSBA Probate and Trust Law Section

1959:
See the comment for 1959 following Sec. 2109.50.

Library References

Executors and Administrators ⚖85(8).
Guardian and Ward ⚖33.
Mental Health ⚖219.
Trusts ⚖181(1).
Westlaw Topic Nos. 162, 196, 257A, 390.
C.J.S. Executors and Administrators §§ 174, 176, 185 to 186.
C.J.S. Mental Health § 179.
C.J.S. Trusts §§ 361 to 364.

Research References

Encyclopedias

OH Jur. 3d Decedents' Estates § 1757, Action to Recover and Preserve Assets.
OH Jur. 3d Fiduciaries § 148, Requisites for Relief, Generally.
OH Jur. 3d Fiduciaries § 157, Citation, Attachment, or Warrant of Suspected Person or Persons Interested in Assets.
OH Jur. 3d Fiduciaries § 160, Hearing; Submission to Jury or Referee.
OH Jur. 3d Fiduciaries § 163, Hearing; Submission to Jury or Referee—Determination of Questions of Title.
OH Jur. 3d Fiduciaries § 164, Judgment or Order; Award of Damages.
OH Jur. 3d Fiduciaries § 165, Judgment or Order; Award of Damages—Imposition of Penalty.
OH Jur. 3d Fiduciaries § 168, Costs.

Treatises and Practice Aids

Carlin, Baldwin's Ohio Practice, Merrick-Rippner Probate Law § 56:3, Concealed or Embezzled Assets—Extra-County Powers.
Carlin, Baldwin's Ohio Practice, Merrick-Rippner Probate Law § 56:4, Concealed or Embezzled Assets—Judgment for Recovery.
Carlin, Baldwin's Ohio Practice, Merrick-Rippner Probate Law § 56:5, Concealed or Embezzled Assets—Guilty Finding.
Carlin, Baldwin's Ohio Practice, Merrick-Rippner Probate Law § 56:9, Concealed or Embezzled Assets—Question of Title.
Carlin, Baldwin's Ohio Practice, Merrick-Rippner Probate Law § 56:15, Concealed or Embezzled Assets—Right to Trial by Jury—Dispute Resolution Procedure.
Carlin, Baldwin's Ohio Practice, Merrick-Rippner Probate Law § 56:18, Concealed or Embezzled Assets—Dismissal of Appeal.
Carlin, Baldwin's Ohio Practice, Merrick-Rippner Probate Law § 56:26, Order on Complaint for Concealing Assets—Form.
Bogert - the Law of Trusts and Trustees § 862, Decree Against the Trustee for the Payment of Money—Damages.

Notes of Decisions

In general 1
Evidence 4
Jurisdiction to determine title 2
Procedural issues 3
Remedies 5

---

1. In general

Where grantees obtained a deed to certain property several months after the property had been forfeited to the state, the right to claim the balance in the hands of the county treasurer on the ground that the deed was a nullity is personal property and passes to the grantor's administrator. Floyd v. Clyne (Cuyahoga 1958) 108 Ohio App. 16, 154 N.E.2d 771, 80 Ohio Law Abs. 225, 9 O.O.2d 93.

GC 10506–67 (RC 2109.50) and this section provide a summary means, inquisitorial in nature, to recover specific property or the proceeds or value thereof belonging to a trust estate, title to which was in a decedent at his death or in a ward when his guardian was appointed, or to recover property belonging to a trust estate, concealed, taken or disposed of after the appointment of the fiduciary. In re Black's Estate (Ohio 1945) 145 Ohio St. 405, 62 N.E.2d 90, 31 O.O. 31. Guardian And Ward ⚖ 33; Trusts ⚖ 181(1)

GC 10506–67 (RC 2109.50) et seq. have been broadened by including within subject matter of examination property suspected of being or having been in possession of such persons so complained against. Jones v. Whaley (Ohio Com.Pl. 1937) 5 Ohio Supp. 174, 25 Ohio Law Abs. 513, 10 O.O. 87.

2. Jurisdiction to determine title

In an action in common pleas court for the recovery of concealed assets, any questions as to title of such assets may be heard and determined by virtue of section. Smith v. Ross (Darke 1939) 29 Ohio Law Abs. 553.

The giving of the key to a box taken from a closet, together with a key to a safe deposit box in a bank, with the direction that the donee is to "have everything in this box" and in the safe deposit box in the bank, is not sufficient to establish a gift causa mortis, where such box was still in the donor's room at the time of his death and the donee's residence was different from that of the donor, and in an action for a declaratory judgment brought by a person in possession of personal property claimed by the executor of decedent's estate and which the party in possession claims by virtue of a gift inter vivos, a probate court has jurisdiction to determine the title to such personal property. (See also Renee v Sanders, 160 OS 279, 116 NE(2d) 420 (1953).) Renee v. Sanders (Cuyahoga 1956) 102 Ohio App. 21, 131 N.E.2d 846, 73 Ohio Law Abs. 449, 2 O.O.2d 7.

Resort may not be had to the summary procedure under GC 10506–67 (RC 2109.50), to collect a debt due a decedent, to obtain an accounting and judgment for any balance due, or to adjudicate rights under a contract. In re Leiby's Estate (Ohio 1952) 157 Ohio St. 374, 105 N.E.2d 583, 47 O.O. 265. Executors And Administrators 85(1.5)

In hearing on complaint under GC 10506–67 (RC 2109.50), probate court is given jurisdiction to determine questions of title as provided by section, and if defendant is found guilty under complaint, court has complete authority to render money judgment. In re Howard's Estate (Franklin 1947) 79 Ohio App. 203, 80 Ohio App. 80, 72 N.E.2d 502, 48 Ohio Law Abs. 189, 34 O.O. 537, 35 O.O. 447. Executors And Administrators 85(6); Executors And Administrators 85(8)

In action by executrix to recover personal property held by another upon claim of valid gift by decedent, brought pursuant to GC 10506–67 (RC 2109.50), it is error for court to exclude testimony of witnesses as to statements made by decedent to effect that property in question was placed in hands of one claiming title thereto for safekeeping only, and contradicting such person's testimony that valid gift was intended; and probate court, in such case, is authorized under section, to hear and determine questions of title. In re Evans' Estate (Franklin 1941) 71 Ohio App. 127, 41 N.E.2d 410, 35 Ohio Law Abs. 295, 25 O.O. 499.

The change in section from the corresponding former section, among other things, is that the court is now given authority to hear and determine "the questions of title." In re Evans' Estate (Franklin 1941) 71 Ohio App. 127, 41 N.E.2d 410, 35 Ohio Law Abs. 295, 25 O.O. 499.

Where guardian of an incompetent filed, in a probate court, on July 7, 1938, a complaint against A, seeking to recover assets allegedly belonging to the guardianship estate, and A claimed to hold the assets by virtue of a trust created by the ward before the guardian was appointed, and the guardian claimed that his ward was incompetent to create the trust, the probate court, under the provisions of section, had jurisdiction to try the issue as to the title of said assets. In re Sanderson's Guardianship (Summit 1940) 64 Ohio App. 177, 28 N.E.2d 565, 17 O.O. 562. Mental Health 480

Probate court and common pleas court under said statutes are given a quick and summary jurisdiction for recovery of assets in favor of decedent's estate. Jones v. Whaley (Ohio Com.Pl. 1937) 5 Ohio Supp. 174, 25 Ohio Law Abs. 513, 10 O.O. 87.

3. Procedural issues

Having stipulated to a proffer of his testimony, deceased mother's son could not claim on appeal that he was denied the opportunity to testify under oath during probate proceedings, and thus son waived any claim that court erred in not taking his testimony concerning whether he should be penalized for concealing deceased mother's assets, where son was given an opportunity to testify, and instead chose to have counsel represent to the court what he would say if called to testify. In re Estate of Endslow (Ohio App. 5 Dist., Delaware, 07-22-2003) No. 03-CAF-01001, 2003-Ohio-3916, 2003 WL 21694010, Unreported. Executors And Administrators 510(4)

Probate court complied with statutory directive that it find former administrator "guilty" or "not guilty" in concealment action, even though it did not expressly state that administrator was "guilty," where probate court imposed statutory penalties against former administrator. Talbott v. Fisk (Ohio App. 10 Dist., Franklin, 12-17-2002) No. 02AP-427, No. 02AP-428, 2002-Ohio-6960, 2002 WL 31819671, Unreported. Executors And Administrators 508(1)

Bonding company which had brought action as prior guardian's subrogee, along with successor guardian, against bank from which prior guardian had allegedly been allowed to withdraw funds from guardianship account for impermissible purposes, did not have standing to, in effect, "amend" its complaint on appeal to request 10% statutory penalty for embezzlement of estate assets, where only successor guardian sought such relief in complaint, and successor did not appeal from judgment of trial court denying it

such relief. Rinehart v. Bank One, Columbus, N.A. (Ohio App. 10 Dist., 03-31-1998) 125 Ohio App.3d 719, 709 N.E.2d 559, dismissed, appeal not allowed 82 Ohio St.3d 1480, 696 N.E.2d 1087. Appeal And Error 888(1)

Executor's action to recover stock certificates allegedly concealed from estate by employees of testator was properly conducted by probate court as summary proceeding, even though executor was allowed to present her entire case prior to any cross-examination of executor's witnesses by employees, where probate court allowed employees complete freedom to present any witnesses of their choosing and to cross-examine all of executor's witnesses, employees objected to evidence and court ruled on each objection, and employees made no jury request. Lauerman v. Destocki (Ross 1993) 87 Ohio App.3d 657, 622 N.E.2d 1122. Executors And Administrators 86(.5)

A court of appeals lacks jurisdiction to consider a decedent's son's assignment of errors regarding a probate court's determination and order that a joint and survivorship account was an asset of the decedent's estate for which the son was to provide an accounting of the monies withdrawn by him, where the probate court's order appealed from does not constitute a final appealable order because it does not conform to the procedural requirements of RC 2109.52 directing the court to make a finding relative to the decedent's son's guilt or innocence on a charge that he concealed estate assets, and since no penalty was imposed against the son no substantial right of the decedent's son was affected. In re Estate of Meyer (Butler 1989) 63 Ohio App.3d 454, 579 N.E.2d 260.

It is error for a court to order the substitution of the executor of a ward's estate as party in interest in place of the guardian of such ward in matters pertaining to a complaint filed by such guardian, prior to the ward's death, alleging the concealment of "monies, chattels or choses in action belonging to said ward's estate." Kelly v. Smith (Logan 1964) 7 Ohio App.2d 142, 219 N.E.2d 231, 36 O.O.2d 293.

Where an heir seeks a citation against the administrator and another heir for withholding a portion of her distributive share of an estate in which a final account has been filed, and charges that her receipt for her share is a forgery, she must first have the order settling the final account vacated. In re Reitler's Estate (Ohio Prob. 1956) 137 N.E.2d 791, 73 Ohio Law Abs. 328.

In a proceeding for the discovery of concealed or embezzled assets there is no absolute right to cross-examination of the defendant therein by the complaining party. In re Fife's Estate (Ohio 1956) 164 Ohio St. 449, 132 N.E.2d 185, 58 O.O. 293. Executors And Administrators 85(1)

In a proceeding to discover concealed assets in which the complaint is that the suspected person is in possession of certificates of corporate stock belonging to decedent's estate and it is shown that such certificates were issued to the decedent during his lifetime and stood in his name on the books of the corporation at the time of his death, a prima-facie case is made for the inclusion of such certificates as assets of the estate, but it may be rebutted and overcome by clear and convincing evidence that such certificates were assigned and delivered by way of gift to the suspected person by the decedent during his lifetime. In re Fife's Estate (Ohio 1956) 164 Ohio St. 449, 132 N.E.2d 185, 58 O.O. 293.

Action for discovery of concealed assets was properly referred to a master commissioner where no jury trial was requested. In re Leiby's Estate (Franklin 1951) 101 N.E.2d 214, 60 Ohio Law Abs. 245, appeal dismissed 156 Ohio St. 254, 101 N.E.2d 906, 46 O.O. 121, reversed 157 Ohio St. 374, 105 N.E.2d 583, 47 O.O. 265.

On appeal from judgment for discovery of concealed assets, there can be no stay of execution or supersedeas unless bond is given in conformance with GC 12223–9 (RC 2505.09). (See also In re Estate of Leiby, 60 Abs 245, 101 NE(2d) 214 (1952); reversed by 157 OS 374, 105 NE(2d) 583 (1952).) In re Leiby's Estate (Franklin 1950) 101 N.E.2d 213, 60 Ohio Law Abs. 243.

Where complaint is filed in probate court under GC 10506–67 (RC 2109.50), proof of allegation in complaint is necessary prerequisite to rendering money judgment under section. In re Howard's Estate (Franklin 1947) 79 Ohio App. 203, 80 Ohio App. 80, 72 N.E.2d 502, 48 Ohio Law Abs. 189, 34 O.O. 537, 35 O.O. 447.

Where, in proceeding to discover concealed or embezzled assets of estate of decedent, the defendant is found not guilty of concealing or embezzling such assets, the court may not proceed to determine other issues, but has no alternative except to dismiss the complaint. Goodrich v. Anderson (Ohio 1940) 136 Ohio St. 509, 26 N.E.2d 1016, 17 O.O. 152. Executors And Administrators 85(1.5)

A judgment in an executor's proceeding against one who has carried away assets should be in favor of the executor, and not in favor of the

Note 3

state. Leonard v. State ex rel. Scott (Ohio App. 1914) 20 Ohio C.C.(N.S.) 340, 3 Ohio App. 313.

Under former GC 10678 (RC 2109.52), judgment in favor of a person charged with withholding certain assets belonging to an estate determines the right of property and may be pleaded in bar to a replevin previously brought but still pending. Tibbott v Cadish, 35 CD 504, 28 OCA 481 (Cuyahoga 1916).

In a complaint for concealment of personal property in an estate, the procedures of RC 2109.50 et seq. should be followed; thus, when 1) the mandatory language of RC 2109.51 is not adhered to because persons compelled to testify under that section did not and deposition testimony of one of those persons does not satisfy the statute and 2) the court did not make a finding of guilt or innocence as required by RC 2109.52, the case must be remanded for a hearing on the concealment of property. In re Estate of Holmes, No. 62749 (8th Dist Ct App, Cuyahoga, 6–10–93).

4. Evidence

Evidence supported probate court's imputation, in action by decedent's daughter for accounting of probate estate assets, of $3,000 per month in living expenses, for months in which decedent had lived with decedent's son before decedent's death; decedent had refused to live in nursing home, decedent had told son the son could have his money if the son took care of him, and nursing home had cost $3,200 a month when decedent had to be placed there because of broken hip. Silcott v. Prebble (Ohio App. 12 Dist., Clermont, 02-03-2003) No. CA2002-04-028, 2003-Ohio-508, 2003 WL 231287, Unreported. Executors And Administrators 221(5)

Evidence supported probate court's finding, in action by decedent's daughter for accounting of probate estate assets, that decedent's first son was not liable for imputed rent for using, in connection with family business, commercial building owned by decedent, and that second son was not liable for imputed rent for living in decedent's house; first son had operated business as partner with decedent, and first son had made deal with decedent that, in exchange for hiring second son and paying taxes on business, first son could use commercial building rent-free and second son could live in house if second son paid taxes on it. Silcott v. Prebble (Ohio App. 12 Dist., Clermont, 02-03-2003) No. CA2002-04-028, 2003-Ohio-508, 2003 WL 231287, Unreported. Executors And Administrators 131

Where the executor's inventory incorrectly listed certain certificates of deposit as payable at death, and the probate court subsequently ruled that the certificates were part of the decedent's estate and ordered the persons who had received the proceeds to return them, the court did not abuse its discretion in failing to find the executor guilty of concealing estate assets and permitting him to continue as fiduciary. In re Estate of Clapsaddle (Washington 1992) 79 Ohio App.3d 747, 607 N.E.2d 1148, motion overruled 65 Ohio St.3d 1435, 600 N.E.2d 678.

Circumstantial evidence relied upon to prove an essential element of a crime must be irreconcilable with any reasonable theory of an accused's innocence in order to support a finding of guilt. State v. Kulig (Ohio 1974) 37 Ohio St.2d 157, 309 N.E.2d 897, 66 O.O.2d 351.

Where an executor conveys property of the estate to himself as legatee less than one month after the approval of the inventory, a creditor of the executor may cause the estate to obtain judgment against such executor for such amount so improperly distributed. In re Walden's Estate (Ohio Prob. 1965) 6 Ohio Misc. 214, 214 N.E.2d 271, 34 O.O.2d 149.

It was an abuse of discretion not to grant a new trial upon exceptions to an inventory where newly discovered evidence showed that the decedent had died the day before a savings account withdrawal form was presented in her name. In re Warga's Estate (Cuyahoga 1953) 113 N.E.2d 39, 69 Ohio Law Abs. 1.

Where one at all times openly and notoriously and under claim of right retains possession of an asset claimed by an estate, he is not guilty of "having concealed, embezzled or conveyed away" an asset of an estate under GC 10506–67 (RC 2109.50) and this section. In re Brooks' Estate (Cuyahoga 1949) 90 N.E.2d 605, 56 Ohio Law Abs. 15.

Where the probate court finds that the administratrix of a decedent's estate is found to have held an auction of certain chattels of the estate without probate authority, the probate court may properly dismiss the complaint where no assets of any significance were sold, the items were sold by a licensed auctioneer and the administratrix properly accounted for the funds. Paumier v Adams, No. 1135 (11th Dist Ct App, Ashtabula, 6–3–83).

5. Remedies

In summary proceedings before the probate court under S. & C. 618 the court has no constitutional power to render judgment except for the amount admitted to have been embezzled. Howell v. Fry (Ohio 1869) 19 Ohio St. 556.

Under this section, authority of court and jury ends with a determination by jury of alleged guilt of accused, and if found guilty, with a determination of amount of damages on account thereof for which judgment must be given with a penalty of ten per cent. Wilson v. Wilson (Athens 1932) 12 Ohio Law Abs. 704. Executors And Administrators 85(6)

No relief for a probate court estate, upon a complaint to the probate court pursuant to GC 10506–67 (RC 2109.50), can be given except with respect to property of such estate. In re Sexton's Estate (Ohio 1955) 163 Ohio St. 124, 126 N.E.2d 129, 56 O.O. 178, certiorari denied 76 S.Ct. 75, 350 U.S. 838, 100 L.Ed. 747.

In a proceeding under GC 10506–67 (RC 2109.50) et seq., a finding of guilty or not guilty is required with the imposition of a penalty upon a finding of guilty, and the statutes should not be extended by implication beyond their manifest purpose, to reach persons or matters not covered by the descriptive terms of the statutes. In re Black's Estate (Ohio 1945) 145 Ohio St. 405, 62 N.E.2d 90, 31 O.O. 31.

Penalty of ten per cent imposed. Skehan v. Larkin (Lucas 1930) 41 Ohio App. 85, 179 N.E. 425, 8 Ohio Law Abs. 425, 11 Ohio Law Abs. 449.

To establish the nondischargeability of a debt under the exception to discharge for a debtor's defalcation while acting in a fiduciary capacity, plaintiffs must show establishment of a trust, party in trust acting in fiduciary capacity, and breach of that relationship by at least "defalcation" of funds. In re Harris-Miles (Bkrtcy.N.D.Ohio, 09-12-1995) 187 B.R. 178. Bankruptcy 3376(5)

Daughter had to repay only half of the amount that she wrongfully withdrew as attorney in fact from father's grants and trusts during his lifetime, as daughter acting as attorney in fact in essence misappropriated an equal amount of her own and her sister's trust money. Fox v. Stockmaster (Ohio App. 3 Dist., Seneca, 06-05-2002) No. 13-01-34, No. 13-01-35, 2002-Ohio-2824, 2002 WL 1299985, Unreported, appeal not allowed 96 Ohio St.3d 1525, 775 N.E.2d 864, 2002-Ohio-5099. Executors And Administrators 286

2109.53 Judgment against fiduciary; removal

If a judgment is rendered against a fiduciary under section 2109.52 of the Revised Code, he shall forthwith be removed by the probate court and that part of the trust not already administered shall be committed to some other person. A fiduciary so removed shall not receive compensation for acting as fiduciary and must be charged in his account with the amount of such judgment. Such fiduciary's property also shall be liable for the satisfaction of the judgment on execution issued thereon by his successor.

(1953 H 1, eff. 10–1–53; GC 10506–74)

Historical and Statutory Notes

Pre–1953 H 1 Amendments: 116 v 273; 114 v 380

Library References

Executors and Administrators 35(1).
Guardian and Ward 25.
Mental Health 175.
Trusts 166.
Westlaw Topic Nos. 162, 196, 257A, 390.
C.J.S. Executors and Administrators §§ 104 to 110.
C.J.S. Mental Health § 148.
C.J.S. Trusts §§ 307 to 308.

Research References

Encyclopedias

OH Jur. 3d Fiduciaries § 12, Appointment to Fill Vacancy in Office; Sole Fiduciary.
OH Jur. 3d Fiduciaries § 167, Judgment or Order; Award of Damages— Enforcement.

OH Jur. 3d Fiduciaries § 258, Loss or Forfeiture of Right to Compensation—Statutory Grounds for Denial of Commission.
OH Jur. 3d Fiduciaries § 311, Concealment or Embezzlement of Assets.
OH Jur. 3d Trusts § 186, Removal—Proceedings.

Treatises and Practice Aids

Carlin, Baldwin's Ohio Practice, Merrick-Rippner Probate Law § 56:4, Concealed or Embezzled Assets—Judgment for Recovery.

Carlin, Baldwin's Ohio Practice, Merrick-Rippner Probate Law § 81:1, Removal—Statutory Provisions.

Carlin, Baldwin's Ohio Practice, Merrick-Rippner Probate Law § 56:26, Order on Complaint for Concealing Assets—Form.

Bogert - the Law of Trusts and Trustees § 861, Remedies of the Beneficiary Against the Trustee.

Bogert - the Law of Trusts and Trustees § 980, Power of Court to Reduce or Deny Compensation.

Notes of Decisions

Duty of court   3
Evidence   1
Procedural issues   2

1. Evidence

Where the executor's inventory incorrectly listed certain certificates of deposit as payable at death, and the probate court subsequently ruled that the certificates were part of the decedent's estate and ordered the persons who had received the proceeds to return them, the court did not abuse its discretion in failing to find the executor guilty of concealing estate assets and permitting him to continue as fiduciary. In re Estate of Clapsaddle (Washington 1992) 79 Ohio App.3d 747, 607 N.E.2d 1148, motion overruled 65 Ohio St.3d 1435, 600 N.E.2d 678.

2. Procedural issues

Proceedings brought under statute regulating procedure when assets of an estate are concealed or embezzled are quasi-criminal in their character. In re Johnson's Estate (Cuyahoga 1943) 50 N.E.2d 273, 38 Ohio Law Abs. 372. Executors And Administrators ⚖ 85(9).

For purposes of exception to discharge for defalcation while acting in fiduciary capacity, defalcation may be found even though the debtor derived no personal gain therefrom; relevant issue under the defalcation exception to discharge is failure to deal properly with entrusted property and not with the identity of the improper recipient of the property. In re Reed (Bkrtcy.S.D.Ohio 1993) 155 B.R. 169. Bankruptcy ⚖ 3376(5)

Under exception to discharge for defalcation while acting in fiduciary capacity, neither ignorance of the law nor subjective mental state is relevant to finding of defalcation. In re Reed (Bkrtcy.S.D.Ohio 1993) 155 B.R. 169. Bankruptcy ⚖ 3376(5)

3. Duty of court

Debt owed to probate estate by Chapter 7 debtor who was probate estate administrator and who misapplied probate estate's workers' compensation proceeds fell within exception to discharge for defalcation while acting in fiduciary capacity. In re Reed (Bkrtcy.S.D.Ohio 1993) 155 B.R. 169. Bankruptcy ⚖ 3376(5)

The word "shall" used in RC 2109.53 creates a mandatory duty on a trial court that once a fiduciary is found guilty of embezzlement or concealment pursuant to RC 2109.52, the fiduciary must be removed forthwith. Schultz v Franklin, No. L–84–379 (6th Dist Ct App, Lucas, 2–15–85).

2109.54 Certificate of judgment; delivery to clerk of the court of common pleas

The fiduciary in whose favor a judgment has been rendered by the probate court under section 2109.52 of the Revised Code shall forthwith deliver to the clerk of the court of common pleas a certificate of such judgment in accordance with section 2329.04 of the Revised Code, which certificate the probate judge shall make out and deliver to such fiduciary on demand. The clerk shall forthwith issue an execution of the court of common pleas for the amount of the judgment and the costs that have accrued or that may accrue thereon. Thenceforth proceedings on execution shall be the same as if the judgment had been rendered in such court of common pleas.

(1953 H 1, eff. 10–1–53; GC 10506–75)

Historical and Statutory Notes

Pre–1953 H 1 Amendments: 116 v 273; 114 v 380

Library References

Executors and Administrators ⚖85(8).
Guardian and Ward ⚖33.
Mental Health ⚖219.
Trusts ⚖181(1).
Westlaw Topic Nos. 162, 196, 257A, 390.
C.J.S. Executors and Administrators §§ 174, 176, 185 to 186.
C.J.S. Mental Health § 179.
C.J.S. Trusts §§ 361 to 364.

Research References

Encyclopedias

OH Jur. 3d Enforcement & Execution of Judgments § 52, Probate Court.

OH Jur. 3d Fiduciaries § 167, Judgment or Order; Award of Damages—Enforcement.

Treatises and Practice Aids

Carlin, Baldwin's Ohio Practice, Merrick-Rippner Probate Law § 3:5, Jurisdiction of Probate Court—Subject Matter—Specific Areas—Fiduciaries.

Carlin, Baldwin's Ohio Practice, Merrick-Rippner Probate Law § 57:3, Removal of Fiduciary—Trustee.

2109.55 Judgment in favor of state

If a judgment is rendered in the name of the state under section 2109.52 of the Revised Code and there is no fiduciary within this state, the prosecuting attorney shall cause the certificate provided for in section 2109.54 of the Revised Code to be filed in the clerk's office and proceed thereon to execution as provided in such section. Such prosecuting attorney shall pay the money realized upon such execution to the county treasurer for the use of such trust, reserving such compensation to himself as the probate court allows.

(1953 H 1, eff. 10–1–53; GC 10506–76)

Historical and Statutory Notes

Pre–1953 H 1 Amendments: 116 v 273; 114 v 380

Library References

Executors and Administrators ⚖85(8).
Guardian and Ward ⚖33.
Mental Health ⚖219.
Trusts ⚖181(1).
Westlaw Topic Nos. 162, 196, 257A, 390.
C.J.S. Executors and Administrators §§ 174, 176, 185 to 186.
C.J.S. Mental Health § 179.
C.J.S. Trusts §§ 361 to 364.

Research References

Encyclopedias

OH Jur. 3d Cvl. Servants & Pub. Officers & Employ. § 466, Duties, Generally; Financial Matters.

OH Jur. 3d Fiduciaries § 147, Purpose and Nature of Proceeding—Transfers in Avoidance of Proceeding.

OH Jur. 3d Fiduciaries § 167, Judgment or Order; Award of Damages—Enforcement.

Treatises and Practice Aids

Carlin, Baldwin's Ohio Practice, Merrick-Rippner Probate Law § 56:4, Concealed or Embezzled Assets—Judgment for Recovery.

2109.56 Conveyances

All gifts, grants, or conveyances of land, tenements, hereditaments, rents, or chattels and all bonds, judgments, or executions made or obtained with intent to avoid the purpose of the proceedings set forth in sections 2109.50 to 2109.55, inclusive, of the Revised Code, or in contemplation of any examination or complaint provided for by such sections shall be void.

(1953 H 1, eff. 10–1–53; GC 10506–77)

Historical and Statutory Notes

Pre–1953 H 1 Amendments: 114 v 381

Library References

Fraudulent Conveyances ⚖=24(1).
Westlaw Topic No. 186.

Research References

Encyclopedias

OH Jur. 3d Fiduciaries § 144, Purpose and Nature of Proceeding.
OH Jur. 3d Fiduciaries § 146, Purpose and Nature of Proceeding—Relation to Other Actions.
OH Jur. 3d Fiduciaries § 147, Purpose and Nature of Proceeding—Transfers in Avoidance of Proceeding.
OH Jur. 3d Fiduciaries § 150, Requisites for Relief, Generally—Title to Assets.
OH Jur. 3d Fiduciaries § 151, Generally; Application of Statute of Limitations.
OH Jur. 3d Fiduciaries § 152, Jurisdiction and Venue.
OH Jur. 3d Fiduciaries § 154, Pleadings; Complaint.
OH Jur. 3d Fiduciaries § 156, Pleadings; Complaint—Amendments; Conforming to Proof.
OH Jur. 3d Fiduciaries § 158, Citation, Attachment, or Warrant of Suspected Person or Persons Interested in Assets—Prejudgment Attachment; Limitations and Prerequisites.
OH Jur. 3d Trusts § 538, in Equity—Particular Remedies.

Treatises and Practice Aids

Blackford, Baldwin's Ohio Practice Business Organizations § 16:12, Free Transferability of Shares.
Carlin, Baldwin's Ohio Practice, Merrick-Rippner Probate Law § 3:3, Jurisdiction of Probate Court—Subject Matter—in General.
Carlin, Baldwin's Ohio Practice, Merrick-Rippner Probate Law § 56:1, Concealed or Embezzled Assets—Scope of RC 2109.50 to RC 2109.56.
Carlin, Baldwin's Ohio Practice, Merrick-Rippner Probate Law § 56:2, Concealed or Embezzled Assets—Jurisdiction Over Complaint.
Carlin, Baldwin's Ohio Practice, Merrick-Rippner Probate Law § 56:4, Concealed or Embezzled Assets—Judgment for Recovery.
Carlin, Baldwin's Ohio Practice, Merrick-Rippner Probate Law § 56:6, Concealed or Embezzled Assets—Quasi-Criminal Nature of Proceedings.
Carlin, Baldwin's Ohio Practice, Merrick-Rippner Probate Law § 56:8, Concealed or Embezzled Assets—Complaint for Recovery of Assets.
Carlin, Baldwin's Ohio Practice, Merrick-Rippner Probate Law § 56:9, Concealed or Embezzled Assets—Question of Title.
Carlin, Baldwin's Ohio Practice, Merrick-Rippner Probate Law § 56:17, Concealed or Embezzled Assets—Declaratory Judgment; Summary Judgment.

Notes of Decisions

Constructive trust 2
Liability 1
Procedural issues 3

1. Liability

Sureties for executor, who was removed and subsequently appointed administrator de bonis non with will annexed with new bond, can be held for shortage existing at time of removal. U.S. Fidelity & Guaranty Co. of Baltimore, Md. v. Jones (Warren 1926) 22 Ohio App. 345, 153 N.E. 281, 4 Ohio Law Abs. 611. Executors And Administrators ⚖= 527(2)

Where debtor was creditor's executor, his sureties, who were released under former GC 10862 (RC 2109.18), upon his removal as executor and his appointment as administrator de bonis non, with will annexed, cannot be held liable for his debt to testator at time of his removal as executor, since liability for default in accounting for such sum could not be fixed until final settlement. U.S. Fidelity & Guaranty Co. of Baltimore, Md. v. Jones (Warren 1926) 22 Ohio App. 345, 153 N.E. 281, 4 Ohio Law Abs. 611. Executors And Administrators ⚖= 527(2)

Chapter 7 debtor vendors' intention to deceive purchasers of real property could be inferred for nondischargeability purposes from debtors' knowledge of judgment against them and failure to disclose the judgment through course of sale of real property. In re Lewis (Bkrtcy.N.D.Ohio 1993) 158 B.R. 89. Bankruptcy ⚖= 3403(7)

Debtor's conduct is not required to rise to level of fraud to support nondischargeability under Bankruptcy Code section making nondischargeable a debt for fraud or defalcation while acting in fiduciary capacity. In re Moran (Bkrtcy.S.D.Ohio 1993) 152 B.R. 493. Bankruptcy ⚖= 3376(1)

2. Constructive trust

Although plaintiff established unjust enrichment and presented substantial documentation to trace funds used for improvements on her former fiance's home, trial court did not err in failing to impose constructive trust against fiance's property for full $54,527 that plaintiff allegedly spent on fiance's behalf during their four year cohabitation, since court effectively engaged in constructive trust analysis and achieved equitable result, by tracing funds from plaintiff's $18,750 loan deposit to fiance's home improvements and granting restitution to plaintiff in that amount. Dixon v. Smith (Ohio App. 3 Dist., 04-23-1997) 119 Ohio App.3d 308, 695 N.E.2d 284. Trusts ⚖= 358(1)

No constructive trust is imposed on lessors who purchase a home with a downpayment furnished by the lessee and an independently obtained mortgage, which is paid by the lessee under a lease-option contract; a constructive trust is to only prevent fraud or unjust enrichment. Glick v. Dolin (Cuyahoga 1992) 80 Ohio App.3d 592, 609 N.E.2d 1338.

3. Procedural issues

In a complaint asserting that a realtor induced a seller to enter into a second contract of sale for the same real property and thus interfered with the existing contractual relationship between plaintiff and defendant, it is trial court error to award both specific performance and $20,000 in damages to the seller and fail to conduct an evidentiary hearing on the seller's request for damages. Crawford v Johnson, No. 94APE04-476, 1994 WL 694987 (10th Dist Ct App, Franklin, 12-8-94).

Complaint seeking determination that debt was nondischargeable for fraud or defalcation while acting in fiduciary capacity is not subject to specificity requirement for pleading fraud under civil rule. In re Moran (Bkrtcy.S.D.Ohio 1993) 152 B.R. 493. Bankruptcy ⚖= 3399

Failure of creditors in state court suit against Chapter 7 debtor to allege breach of fiduciary duty did not preclude creditors from seeking in bankruptcy court a determination that debt was nondischargeable for fraud or defalcation while acting in fiduciary capacity. In re Moran (Bkrtcy. S.D.Ohio 1993) 152 B.R. 493. Judgment ⚖= 828.21(2)

FUNDS OF UNKNOWN OR NONRESIDENT PERSONS

2109.57 Trustee of funds of unknown or nonresident

In any action or proceeding pending in a court of record, if it is made to appear to the court that any person entitled to all or a part of the proceeds of property sold in such action or proceeding is unknown or is a nonresident and not represented in such action or proceeding or that the person entitled cannot, at the time, definitely be ascertained, the probate court may appoint a trustee to whom the notes and mortgages for the unpaid part shall be made, delivered, and paid and to receive, hold, and manage such proceeds or part thereof. Such trustee shall collect the unpaid part of the proceeds of the property sold, by action or otherwise, and shall pay over such fund only on the order of the probate court appointing him.

Payment to such trustee shall be a bar to any claim thereafter made by any person and the persons or corporations paying such money in no case shall be required to see to the application of the money paid.

If a person entitled to any portion of the money held by such trustee fails for seven or more years after such trustee's appointment to make claim to the money and to present the proof necessary to entitle such person to such money, the prosecuting attorney of the county in which such trustee was appointed shall collect it, with the interest accrued thereon, from such trustee and pay it into such county's treasury, to be placed to the credit of the general fund.

When the probate court which appointed such trustee is satisfied that a person who appears and claims the moneys paid into the county treasury has a right to receive them, in whole or part, less the costs of collection by the prosecuting attorney, such court shall order the payment thereof to the person shown to be entitled to such moneys. Such person, on the judge's certificate, shall be given a warrant therefor by the county auditor.

(1953 H 1, eff. 10–1–53; GC 10506–78 to 10506–83)

Historical and Statutory Notes

Pre–1953 H 1 Amendments: 114 v 381, 382

Library References

Abandoned and Lost Property ⇐1 to 5.
Westlaw Topic No. 1.
C.J.S. Abandonment §§ 2 to 12.

Research References

Encyclopedias

OH Jur. 3d Abandoned, Lost, & Escheated Property § 27, Personal Property.
OH Jur. 3d Decedents' Estates § 1662, Unclaimed Money.
OH Jur. 3d Fiduciaries § 16, Trustee to Receive Proceeds from Sale for Unknown or Nonresident Person.
OH Jur. 3d Fiduciaries § 24, Trustee to Receive Proceeds from Sale for Unknown or Nonresident Person.
OH Jur. 3d Fiduciaries § 121, Trustee to Receive Proceeds from Sale for Unknown or Nonresident Person.

Treatises and Practice Aids

Carlin, Baldwin's Ohio Practice, Merrick-Rippner Probate Law § 33:29, Application for Appointment of Trustee—Unknown or Nonresident Person—Form.
Carlin, Baldwin's Ohio Practice, Merrick-Rippner Probate Law § 33:30, Entry Appointing Trustee and Fixing Bond—Form.
Carlin, Baldwin's Ohio Practice, Merrick-Rippner Probate Law § 33:31, Letters of Appointment of Trustee to Collect and Preserve Property—Unknown or Nonresident Person—Form.
Carlin, Baldwin's Ohio Practice, Merrick-Rippner Probate Law § 52:46, Bond of Trustee—Funds of Unknown or Nonresident Person—Form.
Carlin, Baldwin's Ohio Practice, Merrick-Rippner Probate Law § 52:59, Entry Approving Bond of Trustee, and Ordering Letters—Form.
Bogert - the Law of Trusts and Trustees § 246, Public Trusts: Statutory and Created by Court.

Notes of Decisions

Disposal of funds 1
Escheated money 2

---

1. Disposal of funds

Funds held by a county treasurer pursuant to RC 5723.11, RC 2109.57 and RC 2113.64 must be disposed of pursuant to instructions contained therein and are not available for diversion to other uses. OAG 72–122.

2. Escheated money

Money paid to county treasurer as property passing to the state of Ohio by escheat is not 'unclaimed money' within meaning of statutes vesting authority in the probate court to issue a certificate for the payment of unclaimed money. In re Schoenberner's Estate (Summit 1940) 44 N.E.2d 286, 36 Ohio Law Abs. 509. Deposits In Court ⇐ 11

INVENTORY

2109.58 Inventory by fiduciary

Each fiduciary as to whom definite provision is not made in sections 2111.14 and 2115.02 of the Revised Code shall make and file within three months after his appointment a full inventory of the real and personal property belonging to the trust, its value, and the value of the yearly rent of the real property.

Except as provided by section 2115.16 of the Revised Code, exceptions to the inventory of a fiduciary may be filed at any time within six months after the return of the inventory by any person interested in the trust or in any of the property included in the inventory, but the six-month period shall not apply in case of fraud or concealment of assets. At the hearing, the fiduciary and any witness may be examined under oath. The probate court shall enter its finding on the journal and tax the costs as may be equitable.

(1992 H 427, eff. 10–8–92; 1953 H 1; GC 10506–84, 10506–85)

Historical and Statutory Notes

Pre–1953 H 1 Amendments: 118 v 78, § 1; 114 v 382

Library References

Executors and Administrators ⇐62 to 73.
Guardian and Ward ⇐32.
Mental Health ⇐219.
Westlaw Topic Nos. 162, 196, 257A.
C.J.S. Executors and Administrators §§ 152 to 162.
C.J.S. Mental Health § 179.

Research References

Encyclopedias

OH Jur. 3d Fiduciaries § 44, Exceptions to Inventory.

Treatises and Practice Aids

Carlin, Baldwin's Ohio Practice, Merrick-Rippner Probate Law § 56:9, Concealed or Embezzled Assets—Question of Title.
Carlin, Baldwin's Ohio Practice, Merrick-Rippner Probate Law § 57:4, Removal of Fiduciary—Grounds—Failure to File Inventory or Account.
Carlin, Baldwin's Ohio Practice, Merrick-Rippner Probate Law § 64:3, Powers and Duties of Guardian—Inventory.
Carlin, Baldwin's Ohio Practice, Merrick-Rippner Probate Law § 33:26, Inventory for Trusteeship—Form.
Carlin, Baldwin's Ohio Practice, Merrick-Rippner Probate Law § 33:27, Inventory for Trusteeship—Form.
Carlin, Baldwin's Ohio Practice, Merrick-Rippner Probate Law § 56:14, Concealed or Embezzled Assets—Evidence of Concealment.
Carlin, Baldwin's Ohio Practice, Merrick-Rippner Probate Law § 68:47, Acceptance of Duties of Fiduciary—Form.
Carlin, Baldwin's Ohio Practice, Merrick-Rippner Probate Law § 79:14, Inventory—Hearing.
Carlin, Baldwin's Ohio Practice, Merrick-Rippner Probate Law § 79:21, Inventory—Exceptions—Nature of Proceedings.
Carlin, Baldwin's Ohio Practice, Merrick-Rippner Probate Law § 79:24, Inventory—Exceptions—Burden of Proof and Evidence.
Carlin, Baldwin's Ohio Practice, Merrick-Rippner Probate Law § 79:42, Exceptions to Inventory—Form.
Bogert - the Law of Trusts and Trustees § 597, Inventory and Appraisal.

Notes of Decisions

Jurisdiction 2
Parties 1
Witnesses 3

1. Parties

In a proceeding in the probate court, where an exception to the inventory and appraisement in an estate is filed on the ground that a claim against a certain person should be included in the inventory and appraisement, and an application by the executor of the estate is filed to amend the inventory and appraisement to include such claim against this person, the exceptor and the executor are parties in the proceeding, but the person against whom it is contended such claim should be made is not a party in such proceeding where he does not enter his appearance therein and oppose the proposed changes in the inventory. In re Haas' Estate (Ohio 1963) 174 Ohio St. 277, 189 N.E.2d 65, 22 O.O.2d 336.

Under guardianship of an incompetent person from physical disability alone where guardian is appointed with the consent of such incompetent, a brother is not an "interested person" who may file exceptions to an inventory or an account made or rendered by the guardian of such incompetent; but under guardianship of an imbecile the contrary is true, that is, a brother, or even a stranger, is an interested person who may file such exceptions. In re Faulder, 17 Abs 571 (CP, Auglaize 1934).

2. Jurisdiction

As an incident to a hearing upon exceptions to an inventory, the probate court has jurisdiction to determine the issue of a common-law marriage. In re Soeder's Estate (Cuyahoga 1966) 7 Ohio App.2d 271, 220 N.E.2d 547, 36 O.O.2d 404.

3. Witnesses

A beneficiary under a will who is not the executor can be properly excluded from a courtroom under a ruling ordering a separation of witnesses in a proceeding upon exceptions to an inventory brought pursuant to RC 2109.58. In re Soeder's Estate (Cuyahoga 1966) 7 Ohio App.2d 271, 220 N.E.2d 547, 36 O.O.2d 404.

COMPLAINT FOR DISTRIBUTION; ACTION ON BOND; TERMINATION OF TRUST

2109.59 Payment or distribution

If a fiduciary, upon demand, refuses or neglects to pay any creditor whose claim has been allowed by the fiduciary and not subsequently rejected or to pay any creditor or make distribution to any person interested in the estate whose claim or interest has been established by judgment, decree, or order of court, including an order of distribution, such creditor or other person may file a petition against the fiduciary in the probate court from which the fiduciary received his appointment to enforce such payment or distribution, briefly setting forth therein the amount and nature of his claim or interest. Such petition shall not be filed against an executor or administrator until the expiration of the period prescribed in section 2117.30 of the Revised Code.

When such petition is filed, the probate court shall issue a citation to the fiduciary setting forth the filing of the petition and the nature of the claim of the petitioner and commanding such fiduciary to appear before the court on the return day thereof to answer and show cause why a judgment should not be rendered or order entered against him. Such citation shall be returnable not less than twenty nor more than forty days from its date and shall be served and returned by an officer as in the case of summons. Such citation may issue to any county in the state.

On the return of the citation the cause shall be for hearing, unless for good cause shown it is continued. The probate court may hear and determine all questions necessary to ascertain and fix the amount due from the fiduciary to the petitioner and render such judgment or make such order as may be proper. If necessary, such court may hear, determine, and settle the rights and claims of all parties interested in the subject matter of the petition. For such purpose the probate court may cause all parties in interest to be made parties to such petition by amended, supplemental, or crosspetition. The court shall cause notice to be served on all such parties in the manner provided in this section for service of the citation upon the fiduciary.

In any such proceeding the sureties on the bond of the fiduciary, if made parties thereto, may make any defense that the fiduciary could make and the court may render such judgment or make such order with respect to the sureties as may be proper.

(1953 H 1, eff. 10–1–53; GC 10506–86 to 10506–89)

Historical and Statutory Notes

Pre–1953 H 1 Amendments: 119 v 394, § 5

Cross References

Service of process, Civ R 73

Library References

Executors and Administrators ⚖282, 283, 314.
Guardian and Ward ⚖67, 119.
Mental Health ⚖257, 476.
Trusts ⚖225, 250, 282, 345.
Westlaw Topic Nos. 162, 196, 257A, 390.
C.J.S. Executors and Administrators §§ 523 to 524, 559 to 569, 579.
C.J.S. Mental Health §§ 256 to 257.
C.J.S. Trusts §§ 383, 388 to 390, 531, 555, 557 to 561, 662 to 663.

Research References

Encyclopedias

OH Jur. 3d Decedents' Estates § 1774, Action on Allowed Claim.
OH Jur. 3d Fiduciaries § 122, Generally; Jurisdiction.
OH Jur. 3d Fiduciaries § 124, Parties; Pleading.
OH Jur. 3d Fiduciaries § 125, Citation to Answer Claim; Notice to Parties in Interest.
OH Jur. 3d Fiduciaries § 126, Hearing and Judgment.
OH Jur. 3d Guaranty & Suretyship § 173, Right to Sue Principal or Surety—Suit Against Surety Without Prior Action Against Principal.
OH Jur. 3d Guaranty & Suretyship § 268, Generally; Rendition.

Treatises and Practice Aids

Carlin, Baldwin's Ohio Practice, Merrick-Rippner Probate Law § 52:26, Fiduciary's Bond—Sureties—Liability—General.
Carlin, Baldwin's Ohio Practice, Merrick-Rippner Probate Law § 75:12, Distribution—Upon Application—Enforcement.
Carlin, Baldwin's Ohio Practice, Merrick-Rippner Probate Law § 75:34, Complaint for Distribution—Form.
Carlin, Baldwin's Ohio Practice, Merrick-Rippner Probate Law § 75:35, Entry for Citation—Form.
Carlin, Baldwin's Ohio Practice, Merrick-Rippner Probate Law § 75:36, Citation—Form.
Carlin, Baldwin's Ohio Practice, Merrick-Rippner Probate Law § 75:37, Entry on Complaint for Distribution—Form.
Carlin, Baldwin's Ohio Practice, Merrick-Rippner Probate Law § 88:11, Rejection of Claims—Jurisdiction.
Bogert - the Law of Trusts and Trustees § 1010, Powers and Duties of Trustee on Termination of Trust.

Law Review and Journal Commentaries

Gift Over Upon Death Before Distribution: Settlor's Intent Still the Lodestar in Ohio, Mary Clare Cullen. 11 Prob L J Ohio 8 (September/October 2000).

A Radical Theory of Jurisprudence: The "Decisionmaker" as the Source of Law—The Ohio Supreme Court's Adoption of the Spendthrift Trust Doctrine as a Model, Gerald P. Moran. 30 Akron L Rev 393 (Spring 1997).

Should Everyone Trust a Living Trust?, (Revisited), William A. Fields. 9 Prob L J Ohio 106 (July/August 1999).

Notes of Decisions

Judgment creditors 1
Procedural issues 3
Spendthrift trusts 4
Widow's allowance 2

---

1. Judgment creditors

When a joint action is commenced in probate court by a judgment creditor against a fiduciary and the surety on the bond of the fiduciary under RC 2109.59, the probate court may enter a judgment against the surety in behalf of a judgment creditor whose claim has been wrongfully rejected by the fiduciary where the court finds the fiduciary liable for the claim and the surety is made a party to the action. In re Grant (Cuyahoga 1978) 56 Ohio App.2d 207, 381 N.E.2d 1348, 10 O.O.3d 205. Executors And Administrators ⚖ 537(12)

The creditor of a decedent who obtains a judgment in a court of common pleas against the estate of the decedent pursuant to RC 2117.12 may commence a joint action against the fiduciary and the surety on the bond of the fiduciary under RC 2109.59 in the probate court of the county wherein the fiduciary received his appointment. In re Grant (Cuyahoga 1978) 56 Ohio App.2d 207, 381 N.E.2d 1348, 10 O.O.3d 205. Executors And Administrators ⚖ 537(4); Executors And Administrators ⚖ 537(7)

A judgment creditor, during administration of an estate in probate court and before an order of distribution is made, may maintain an action in nature of creditor's bill in court of common pleas to reach an interest of judgment debtor-legatee in funds or property in hands of executor of such estate. Union Properties v. Patterson (Ohio 1944) 143 Ohio St. 192, 54 N.E.2d 668, 28 O.O. 111. Debtor And Creditor ⚖ 11

2. Widow's allowance

The widow's allowance is a debt against her husband's estate and is a vested right which is not divested by the widow's death or any other contingency occurring after the amount thereof is fixed and allowed; it formerly constituted a preferred debt and is recoverable by her estate after her death, and interest is allowable thereon. Monger v. Jones (Jackson 1949) 91 Ohio App. 246, 108 N.E.2d 116, 48 O.O. 347. Constitutional Law ⚖ 92; Executors And Administrators ⚖ 195

3. Procedural issues

Sufficient evidence established that mother was competent on dates she revoked a revocable trust established on her behalf, executed a new will, and deeded certain property to three of her children, even though mother had two strokes and several physicians gave deposition testimony that mother's cognitive function and ability to express herself were impaired; psychiatrist who examined mother on and shortly before the relevant dates gave deposition testimony that mother was coherent and her memory was intact, and opined that mother was competent, and attorney who prepared the documents at issue testified that mother understood the documents and also opined that mother was competent. Hillis v. Humphrey (Ohio App. 5 Dist., Perry, 06-30-2005) No. 05CA6, 2005-Ohio-3459, 2005 WL 1579392, Unreported. Wills ⚖ 55(5)

A petition, filed in court of common pleas, by an alleged creditor of an estate against the administrators of the estate to enforce payment of his alleged claim, which petition does not allege that the claim was properly presented to the administrators and by them duly rejected, is subject to demurrer in that it does not state facts which show a cause of action, a presentation and a rejection of the claim being prerequisite to the right to bring the action. Wildermuth v. Liggett (Franklin 1944) 75 Ohio App. 410, 62 N.E.2d 522, 31 O.O. 240. Executors And Administrators ⚖ 283

If a fiduciary refuses to make payment to any creditor whose claim has been allowed by the fiduciary and not subsequently rejected, or to make payment to any creditor or other interested person whose claim has been established, such creditor, under GC 10506–86 (RC 2109.59), may file a petition to enforce payment, briefly setting forth the nature of his claim, only in the probate court from which the fiduciary received his appointment. Wildermuth v. Liggett (Franklin 1944) 75 Ohio App. 410, 62 N.E.2d 522, 31 O.O. 240. Executors And Administrators ⚖ 283; Courts ⚖ 472.4(1)

In an action for concealment of assets of a decedent estate, the proper burden of proof on the claimant is a showing by a preponderance of the evidence; therefore, the trial court erred in adopting a burden of proof from the complainant requiring either clear and convincing evidence or proof beyond a reasonable doubt. In re Estate of Goodrich, No. 45867 (8th Dist Ct App, Cuyahoga, 8–9–83).

4. Spendthrift trusts

Spendthrift trusts are valid and enforceable in Ohio and the beneficiary has no interest liable to the execution of a judgment. Scott v. Bank One Trust Co., N.A. (Ohio 1991) 62 Ohio St.3d 39, 577 N.E.2d 1077.

2109.60 Probate court may send case to the court of common pleas

When a proceeding set forth in section 2109.59 of the Revised Code is pending in the probate court, such court, on motion of any party thereto, may reserve and send such cause to the court of common pleas which shall hear, settle, and determine all issues as provided in such section. In case of such reservation, the probate court shall prepare a transcript of the proceedings in the cause, so far as it has progressed, which, with the petition and other papers therein, forthwith shall be filed with the clerk of the court of common pleas.

(1953 H 1, eff. 10–1–53; GC 10506–90)

Historical and Statutory Notes

Pre–1953 H 1 Amendments: 119 v 394, § 5

Cross References

Probate division of court of common pleas, O Const Art IV §4

Library References

Courts ⚖ 485.
Westlaw Topic No. 106.
C.J.S. Courts § 194.

Research References

Encyclopedias
OH Jur. 3d Fiduciaries § 127, Hearing and Judgment—Transfer to Another Division of Court of Common Pleas.

2109.61 Bond; parties to suit

An action may be prosecuted on the bond of a fiduciary against any one or more of the obligors thereof by any person who has been injured by reason of the breach of any condition of the bond. Such action shall be prosecuted for the benefit of all persons who are interested in the estate and who have been similarly injured. Any such person or any obligor on the bond who is not already a party to the action may intervene therein or be made a party thereto by supplemental, amended, or crosspetition.

If a surety on the bond of a fiduciary is not made a party to an action or proceeding against such fiduciary, the fact that a judgment was rendered or an order was entered against the fiduciary shall constitute only prima-facie evidence of the justice and validity of the claim in an action subsequently brought against the sureties on the bond of the fiduciary.

(1953 H 1, eff. 10–1–53; GC 10506–91, 10506–92)

Historical and Statutory Notes

Pre–1953 H 1 Amendments: 119 v 394, § 5

Library References

Executors and Administrators ⚖ 537.
Guardian and Ward ⚖ 182.
Mental Health ⚖ 192.
Trusts ⚖ 387.
Westlaw Topic Nos. 162, 196, 257A, 390.

C.J.S. Executors and Administrators §§ 900, 914.
C.J.S. Trusts §§ 770 to 777.

Research References

Encyclopedias

OH Jur. 3d Fiduciaries § 218, Prerequisites to Action.
OH Jur. 3d Fiduciaries § 220, Parties.
OH Jur. 3d Fiduciaries § 221, Parties—Successor Fiduciary as Plaintiff.
OH Jur. 3d Fiduciaries § 227, Evidence and Presumptions—Conclusiveness of Judgment Against Fiduciary.
OH Jur. 3d Guaranty & Suretyship § 173, Right to Sue Principal or Surety—Suit Against Surety Without Prior Action Against Principal.
OH Jur. 3d Guaranty & Suretyship § 185, Defendants in Suretyship Cases.

Treatises and Practice Aids

Carlin, Baldwin's Ohio Practice, Merrick-Rippner Probate Law § 52:57, Entry Approving New Bond—Form.

Law Review and Journal Commentaries

Actions on Fiduciary Bonds in Probate Court, Jerome C. Tinianow. 59 Clev B J 120 (February 1988).

Notes of Decisions

Constitutional issues 1
Debts 2
Joint action 3

1. Constitutional issues

Guardian's bondsman was not denied due process of law when the trial court adjudicated successor guardian's exceptions to settlement of ward's accounts prior to the court issuing an order setting aside and vacating the court's entries settling the guardian's first partial account and the guardian's second and final distributive account, even though court did not use specific language vacating prior settlement orders; it was implicit that prior orders were vacated, bondsman was aware that hearing before magistrate was on both relief from judgment and exception to accounts, and bondsman had a statutory right to a hearing on bond if it chose. In re Guardianship of Guzay (Ohio App. 10 Dist., Franklin, 09-23-2003) No. 02AP-745, 2003-Ohio-5036, 2003 WL 22177106, Unreported. Constitutional Law ⟹ 306(1); Mental Health ⟹ 304

A surety who is not given notice of an accounting proceeding against its fiduciary is denied the constitutional right to due process of law and cannot be compelled to pay any sum on its bond without further proceedings. In Matter of Guardianship of Edwards (Ohio App. 4 Dist., Ross, 09-25-1996) No. 95CA2134, 1996 WL 557807, Unreported, dismissed, appeal not allowed 78 Ohio St.3d 1409, 675 N.E.2d 1249.

2. Debts

Where a testator directs that his executors should carry on his brewery for seven years for the benefit of the estate, and then deliver the brewery and its proceeds to the residuary legatees named in the will, the moneys and profits derived from the business are assets in the hands of the executors, and their sureties are liable upon their bond for the executor's failure to pay a just debt of the estate from such assets. Gandolfo v. Walker (Ohio 1864) 15 Ohio St. 251. Executors And Administrators ⟹ 41

3. Joint action

When a joint action is commenced in probate court by a judgment creditor against a fiduciary and the surety on the bond of the fiduciary under RC 2109.59, the probate court may enter a judgment against the surety in behalf of a judgment creditor whose claim has been wrongfully rejected by the fiduciary where the court finds the fiduciary liable for the claim and the surety is made a party to the action. In re Grant (Cuyahoga 1978) 56 Ohio App.2d 207, 381 N.E.2d 1348, 10 O.O.3d 205. Executors And Administrators ⟹ 537(12)

The creditor of a decedent who obtains a judgment in a court of common pleas against the estate of the decedent pursuant to RC 2117.12 may commence a joint action against the fiduciary and the surety on the bond of the fiduciary under RC 2109.59 in the probate court of the county wherein the fiduciary received his appointment. In re Grant (Cuyahoga 1978) 56 Ohio App.2d 207, 381 N.E.2d 1348, 10 O.O.3d 205. Executors And Administrators ⟹ 537(4); Executors And Administrators ⟹ 537(7)

2109.62 Termination of trust; distribution

(A)(1) Upon the filing of a motion by a trustee with the court that has jurisdiction over the trust, upon the provision of reasonable notice to all beneficiaries who are known and in being and who have vested or contingent interests in the trust, and after holding a hearing, the court may terminate the trust, in whole or in part, if it determines that all of the following apply:

(a) It is no longer economically feasible to continue the trust.

(b) The termination of the trust is for the benefit of the beneficiaries.

(c) The termination of the trust is equitable and practical.

(d) The current value of the trust is less than one hundred thousand dollars.

(2) The existence of a spendthrift or similar provision in a trust instrument or will does not preclude the termination of a trust pursuant to this section.

(B) If property is to be distributed from an estate being probated to a trust and the termination of the trust pursuant to this section does not clearly defeat the intent of the testator, the probate court has jurisdiction to order the outright distribution of the property or to make the property custodial property under sections 5814.01 to 5814.09 of the Revised Code. A probate court may so order whether the application for the order is made by an inter vivos trustee named in the will of the decedent or by a testamentary trustee.

(C) Upon the termination of a trust pursuant to this section, the probate court shall order the distribution of the trust estate in accordance with any provision specified in the trust instrument for the premature termination of the trust. If there is no provision of that nature in the trust instrument, the probate court shall order the distribution of the trust estate among the beneficiaries of the trust in accordance with their respective beneficial interests and in a manner that the court determines to be equitable. For purposes of ordering the distribution of the trust estate among the beneficiaries of the trust under this division, the court shall consider all of the following:

(1) The existence of any agreement among the beneficiaries with respect to their beneficial interests;

(2) The actuarial values of the separate beneficial interests of the beneficiaries;

(3) Any expression of preference of the beneficiaries that is contained in the trust instrument.

(2006 H 416, eff. 1–1–07; 2003 S 64, eff. 10–21–03; 2002 H 345, eff. 7–23–02; 1986 H 139, eff. 7–24–86)

Uncodified Law

1986 H 139, § 3, eff. 7–24–86, reads, in part: Sections 1 and 2 of this act shall apply only to the estates of decedents whose death occurs on or after the effective date of this act.

Historical and Statutory Notes

Amendment Note: 2006 H 416 substituted "5814.01" for "1339.31" and "5814.09" for "1339.39" in the first sentence of division (B); and deleted division (D). Prior to amendment, division (D) read:

"(D) Unless otherwise represented or bound, a minor, an incapacitated or unborn person, or a person whose identity or location is unknown and is not reasonably ascertainable may be represented by or bound by another person who has a substantially identical interest in the trust as that minor, incapacitated or unborn person, or person whose identity or location is unknown and is not reasonably ascertainable, but only to the extent that there is no conflict of interest between the person who is represented or bound and the person who represents or binds that person. As used in this division, 'minor' means a person who is under eighteen years of age."

Amendment Note: 2003 S 64 added new divisions (C) and (D).

Amendment Note: 2002 H 345 substituted "one hundred" for "fifty" in division (A)(1)(d); and made other nonsubstantive changes.

Library References

Trusts ⚖=61.
Westlaw Topic No. 390.
C.J.S. Trusts §§ 117 to 127.
Baldwin's Ohio Legislative Service Annotated, 2006 H 416 LSC Analysis, p 3/L-1709

Research References

Encyclopedias

OH Jur. 3d Agency & Independent Contractors § 39, Termination or Revocation of Authority.
OH Jur. 3d Trusts § 162, Termination Sought by Trustee; Small Trusts.
OH Jur. 3d Trusts § 194, Validity and Effect.

Treatises and Practice Aids

Carlin, Baldwin's Ohio Practice, Merrick-Rippner Probate Law § 3:2, Jurisdiction of Probate Court—Statutory.
Carlin, Baldwin's Ohio Practice, Merrick-Rippner Probate Law § 3:4, Jurisdiction of Probate Court—Subject Matter—Specific Areas—Inter Vivos Trusts.
Carlin, Baldwin's Ohio Practice, Merrick-Rippner Probate Law § 3:6, Jurisdiction of Probate Court—Subject Matter—Specific Areas—Testamentary Trusts.
Carlin, Baldwin's Ohio Practice, Merrick-Rippner Probate Law § 33:8, Trusts—Spendthrift Provision.
Carlin, Baldwin's Ohio Practice, Merrick-Rippner Probate Law § 33:20.50, Termination of Small Trusts.
Bogert - the Law of Trusts and Trustees § 400, Termination of Charitable Trusts.
Kuehnle and Levey, Ohio Real Estate Law and Practice § 56:60, Conveyances—Motion for Judicial Termination of Trust Under $100,000.
Kuehnle and Levey, Ohio Real Estate Law and Practice § 56:62, Conveyances—Judgment Entry, Order Terminating Inter Vivos Trust.

Law Review and Journal Commentaries

Distribution Upon Termination of Small Trusts - Some Guidance, William B. McNeil. 13 Prob L J Ohio 28 (November/December 2002).

Ohio adopts new trust code—an overview of the new Ohio trust code and house bill 416. Alan Newman, 20 Ohio Law 9 (September/October 2006).

Termination of Small Trusts. William J. McGraw III, 12 Prob L J Ohio 80 (May/June 2002).

Notes of Decisions

Objects of trust 1

---

1. Objects of trust

Trust providing that upon the settlor's death the trust would be delivered to settlor's minor child unless child was under the age of 30, in which case it would continue for the health, maintenance, support, and education of child until she reached the age of 30, did not terminate on the death of settlor, where child was seven years old at time of settlor's death. Zhang Revocable Trust v. Ling (Ohio App. 11 Dist., Lake, 09-09-2005) No. 2004-L-114, 2005-Ohio-4775, 2005 WL 2211108, Unreported. Trusts ⚖ 61(2)

Trustee's failure to file motion to terminate testamentary trust did not preclude trial court from terminating trust after beneficiary disclaimed her interest in trust; statute governing termination of trust on motion by trustee was not the exclusive means of terminating trust, but rather trust could be terminated under doctrine of acceleration of remainders. In re Testamentary Trust of Flynn (Ohio App. 2 Dist., Montgomery, 08-05-2005) No. 20699, No. 20700, 2005-Ohio-4028, 2005 WL 1846520, Unreported. Trusts ⚖ 61(3)

Testamentary trust providing that, after death of testator's daughter, trust was to benefit testator's living lineal descendants, successively and per stirpes, indefinitely, subject to termination of trust 21 years after death of the last surviving of daughter and two grandchildren or if income generat-

ed was less than $5,000 per year, did not allow for distribution of a grandchild's equal share that was held and managed by trustee to grandchild's estate if grandchild died without surviving lineal descendants; trust contemplated that it would continue beyond lifetime of grandchildren by at least 21 years unless trust generated insufficient income, and that the principal and accumulated income would be divided among beneficiaries existing at time of termination. Bank One Trust Co., N.A. v. Reynolds (Ohio App. 2 Dist., Montgomery, 11-24-2004) No. 20386, No. 20402, 2004-Ohio-6670, 2004 WL 2849034, Unreported. Wills ⚖ 498

A trust created by will, the provisions of which are not repugnant to law or contrary to public policy, will not be decreed terminated where the objects of the trust have not been fully accomplished and their accomplishment has not been made impossible. Robbins v. Smith (Ohio 1905) 72 Ohio St. 1, 73 N.E. 1051, 2 Ohio Law Rep. 494. Trusts ⚖ 61(1)

ALLOCATION OF RECEIPTS AND EXPENDITURES

Comparative Laws

Uniform Principal and Income Act

Table of Jurisdictions Wherein Act Has Been Adopted.

For text of Uniform Act, and variation notes and annotation materials for adopting jurisdictions, see Uniform Laws Annotated, Master Edition, Volume 7B.

Jurisdiction	Statutory Citation
Alaska	AS 13.38.010 to 13.38.140.
Arizona	A.R.S. § 14–7401 to 14–7413.
Florida	West's F.S.A. § 738.01 to 738.15.
Georgia	O.C.G.A. § 53–12–210 to 53–12–219.
Hawaii	HRS § 557–1 to 557–16.
Idaho	I.C. § 68–1001 to 68–1016.
Illinois	760 ILCS 15/1 to 15/17.
Indiana	West's A.I.C. 30–4–5–1 to 30–4–5–11.
Kansas	K.S.A. 58–901 to 58–917.
Kentucky	KRS 386.191 to 386.349.
Maryland	Code, Estates and Trusts, § 14–201 to 14–214.
Michigan	M.C.L.A. § 555.51 to 555.68.
Minnesota	M.S.A. § 501B.59 to 501B.76.
Mississippi	Code 1972, § 91–17–1 to 91–17–31.
Montana	MCA 72–34–401 to 72–34–416.
Nebraska	R.R.S.1943, § 30–3101 to 30–3115.
Nevada	N.R.S. 164.140 to 164.370.
New Jersey	N.J.S.A. 3B:19A–1 to 3B:19A–35.
New Mexico	NMSA 1978, § 46–3–1 to 46–3–15.
New York	McKinney's EPTL 11–2.1.
North Carolina	G.S. § 37–16 to 37–40.
Oregon	ORS 129.005 to 129.125.
South Carolina	Code 1976, § 62–7–401 to 62–7–421.
South Dakota	SDCL 55–13–1 to 55–13–17.
Texas	V.T.C.A., Property Code § 113.101 to 113.111.
Utah	U.C.A.1953, 22–3–1 to 22–3–16.
Washington	West's RCWA 11.104.010 to 11.104.940.
Wisconsin	W.S.A. 701.20.
Wyoming	Wyo.Stat.Ann., § 2–3–601 to 2–3–614.

2109.68 Allocation by fiduciary

Allocation of receipts and expenditures between principal and income by an executor, administrator, or testamentary trustee shall be as prescribed in sections 5812.01 to 5812.52 of the Revised Code.

(2006 H 416, eff. 1–1–07; 2002 H 522, eff. 1–1–03; 1987 S 146, eff. 10–20–87)

Historical and Statutory Notes

Amendment Note: 2006 H 416 substituted "5812.01" for "1340.40" and "5812.52" for "1340.91".

Amendment Note: 2002 H 522 rewrote this section which prior thereto read:

"In all cases not covered by section 2109.66 or 2109.67 of the Revised Code, allocation of receipts and expenditures by an executor, administrator, or testamentary trustee shall be as prescribed in sections 1340.01 to 1340.13 of the Revised Code."

Library References

Trusts ⚖ 272, 274.
Wills ⚖ 684.3.
Westlaw Topic Nos. 390, 409.
C.J.S. Trusts §§ 391 to 400, 510 to 511, 551 to 554.
C.J.S. Wills §§ 1463, 1465 to 1479.

Baldwin's Ohio Legislative Service Annotated, 2006 H 416 LSC Analysis, p 3/L-1709

Research References

Forms

Ohio Forms Legal and Business § 25:51, Irrevocable Trusts—General Form.

Ohio Forms Legal and Business § 25:53, Irrevocable Trusts—Husband and Wife as Grantors—Income to Children for Life—Remainder to Descendants.

Ohio Forms Legal and Business § 25:358, General Provision.

Ohio Forms Legal and Business § 25:359, Allocation of Receipts and Expenses—in Trustee's Discretion.

Treatises and Practice Aids

Carlin, Baldwin's Ohio Practice, Merrick-Rippner Probate Law § 33:18, Trusts—Ohio Principal and Income Act.

Carlin, Baldwin's Ohio Practice, Merrick-Rippner Probate Law § 43:34, Construing a Will—Words and Phrases—Stocks and Stock Dividends.

2109.69 Laws applicable to testamentary trusts

(A) Subject to division (B) of this section, the provisions of Chapters 5801. to 5811. of the Revised Code apply to testamentary trusts except to the extent that any provision of those chapters conflicts with any provision of Chapter 2109. of the Revised Code, or with any other provision of the Revised Code, that applies specifically to testamentary trusts and except to the extent that any provision of Chapters 5801. to 5811. of the Revised Code is clearly inapplicable to testamentary trusts.

(B) Section 5808.13 of the Revised Code applies to testamentary trusts whether or not that section conflicts with any provision of Chapter 2109. of the Revised Code or any other provision of the Revised Code that applies specifically to testamentary trusts.

(2006 H 416, eff. 1–1–07)

Cross References

Applicability of title, 5801.02

Library References

Baldwin's Ohio Legislative Service Annotated, 2006 H 416 LSC Analysis, p 3/L-1709

CHAPTER 2111

GUARDIANS; CONSERVATORSHIPS

GENERAL PROVISIONS

Section	
2111.01	Definitions
2111.02	Appointment of guardian
2111.021	Conservatorship
2111.03	Application for appointment of guardian
2111.031	Appointment of physicians or others to examine alleged incompetent
2111.04	Notice
2111.041	Investigation of alleged incompetent
2111.042	Appointment of investigator; reports
2111.05	Estate not more than ten thousand dollars
2111.06	Guardian of the person or estate
2111.07	Powers of guardian of person and estate
2111.08	Parents are natural guardians; equal parental rights and responsibilities; guardianship jurisdiction
2111.09	Administrator or executor ineligible
2111.091	Restrictions on attorneys representing guardians
2111.10	Corporation as guardian
2111.11	Spouse may be appointed guardian
2111.12	Guardian of minor
2111.121	Nomination as guardian of person or estate; procedure

POWERS AND DUTIES OF GUARDIAN

Section	
2111.13	Duties of guardian of person
2111.131	How money may be handled for minor with no guardian of the estate
2111.14	Duties of guardian of estate
2111.141	Evidence to support inventory; verification of inventory
2111.15	Duties of guardian of person and estate
2111.151	Limitation on liability of guardians and conservators on contracts and debts
2111.16	Certain vouchers not allowed as credits
2111.17	Suits by guardians
2111.18	Claim for injury to ward or damage to property; settlement
2111.181	Settlement of claims of emancipated minors
2111.19	Completion of land contract by guardian
2111.20	Sale of personal estate
2111.21	Sale, compromise, adjustment, or mortgage of dower
2111.22	Release of ward's tax title by guardian
2111.23	Guardian ad litem
2111.24	Insolvency of ward

LEASE OF REAL PROPERTY

Section	
2111.25	Lease for not more than three years
2111.26	Lease for term of years
2111.27	Petition
2111.28	Parties
2111.29	Parties and proceedings
2111.30	Duties of appraisers
2111.31	Hearing and order
2111.32	Royalty

IMPROVEMENT OF REAL ESTATE

Section	
2111.33	Guardian may improve real estate; procedure
2111.34	Proceedings
2111.35	Amount to be used for improvement
2111.36	Guardian's report

Section

RESIDENT GUARDIAN OF NONRESIDENT WARD

2111.37 Guardian for nonresident
2111.38 Bond and duties
2111.39 Foreign guardian may collect money
2111.40 When nonresident ward becomes a resident

NONRESIDENT GUARDIAN OF NONRESIDENT WARD

2111.41 Removal in favor of foreign guardian when ward leaves the state
2111.42 Foreign guardians may receive property
2111.43 Foreign wards and guardians
2111.44 Sale of lands of foreign wards

TERMINATION OF GUARDIANSHIP

2111.45 Marriage of ward
2111.46 Guardianship of minors
2111.47 Wards other than minors
2111.471 Transfer of guardianship on removal of ward from county

MISCELLANEOUS PROVISIONS

2111.48 Certain acts validated
2111.49 Guardian's report; court intervention; hearing
2111.50 Probate court powers over guardianship
2111.51 Indigent guardianship fund

Cross References

Appointment of ancillary administrator, 2129.08
Community alternative homes, rights of residents adjudicated incompetent, 3724.07
Consent furnished by guardian, incompetent person, 5126.043
Court of claims, assistance to victims of crimes, payment of award to guardian of estate of minor, 2743.66
Custodian of minor's property; form of deed to successor, 1339.37
Durable power of attorney for health care, guardian defined, 1337.11
Fiduciary holding partnership interest in that capacity; limit on liability, 1339.65
Guardians are fiduciaries, 1339.01
Guardianship of mentally retarded minors, 5123.93
Guardianship or trusteeship appointments, conservator defined, 5123.55
Hospitalization of mentally ill, legal effect of indeterminate hospitalization, 5122.36
Issuer of securities may treat record holders as competent unless certified copy of decree received, 1339.02
Juvenile courts, guardian defined, 2151.011
Legal disability, defined, 2131.02
Legal rights service may serve as guardian, 5123.60
Living wills, guardian defined, 2133.01
Mentally retarded or developmentally disabled adults, consent to services by incompetents, 5126.31
Non-ademption of specific devise or bequest by ward when property sold during guardianship, 2107.501
Persons not to benefit from death, guardian bringing complaint to restore rights, 2105.19
Rights of residents of nursing or rest home, 3721.13

Law Review and Journal Commentaries

1990 Guardianship Law Safeguards Personal Rights Yet Protects Vulnerable Elderly, Comment. 24 Akron L Rev 161 (Summer 1990).

The Attorney's Role in Life Services Planning, Gregory S. French. Cin B Ass'n Rep 16 (April 1988).

Changes in Ohio's Guardianship Law, Wilma A. Sevcik. 63 Law & Fact 27 (November–December 1989).

Civil Incompetency in Ohio: Determination and Effect, Fred A. Dewey. 34 U Cin L Rev 419 (Fall 1965).

The Structure of a General Theory of Nondisclosure, Christopher T. Wonnell. 41 Case W Res L Rev 329 (1991).

The Uniform Custodial Trust Act—A Useful New Forum of Title, Richard V. Wellman. 4 Prob L J Ohio 65 (January/February 1994).

GENERAL PROVISIONS

2111.01 Definitions

As used in Chapters 2101. to 2131. of the Revised Code:

(A) "Guardian," other than a guardian under sections 5905.01 to 5905.19 of the Revised Code, means any person, association, or corporation appointed by the probate court to have the care and management of the person, the estate, or both of an incompetent or minor. When applicable, "guardian" includes, but is not limited to, a limited guardian, an interim guardian, a standby guardian, and an emergency guardian appointed pursuant to division (B) of section 2111.02 of the Revised Code. "Guardian" also includes an agency under contract with the department of mental retardation and developmental disabilities for the provision of protective service under sections 5123.55 to 5123.59 of the Revised Code when appointed by the probate court to have the care and management of the person of an incompetent.

(B) "Ward" means any person for whom a guardian is acting or for whom the probate court is acting pursuant to section 2111.50 of the Revised Code.

(C) "Resident guardian" means a guardian appointed by a probate court to have the care and management of property in this state that belongs to a nonresident ward.

(D) "Incompetent" means any person who is so mentally impaired as a result of a mental or physical illness or disability, or mental retardation, or as a result of chronic substance abuse, that the person is incapable of taking proper care of the person's self or property or fails to provide for the person's family or other persons for whom the person is charged by law to provide, or any person confined to a correctional institution within this state.

(E) "Next of kin" means any person who would be entitled to inherit from a ward under Chapter 2105. of the Revised Code if the ward dies intestate.

(F) "Conservator" means a conservator appointed by the probate court in an order of conservatorship issued pursuant to section 2111.021 of the Revised Code.

(G) "Parent" means a natural parent or adoptive parent of a minor child whose parental rights and responsibilities have not been terminated by a juvenile court or another court.

(1996 H 288, eff. 1–14–97; 1994 H 571, eff. 10–6–94; 1989 S 46, eff. 1–1–90; 1986 S 322; 1980 H 900; 1978 S 415; 1976 H 244; 1971 H 290; 1969 H 688; 129 v 1448; 1953 H 1; GC 10507–1)

Uncodified Law

1989 S 46, § 3, eff. 10–2–89, reads: The amendments to the definition of an incompetent in section 2111.01 of the Revised Code that are made by this act do not affect any guardianship of the person, the estate, or the person and estate of an incompetent that was established prior to the effective date of this act and that was based upon advanced age, chronic alcoholism, or physical disability or infirmity.

Historical and Statutory Notes

Pre–1953 H 1 Amendments: 114 v 382

Amendment Note: 1996 H 288 inserted "a standby guardian," in division (A); added division (G); and made changes to reflect gender neutral language.

Amendment Note: 1994 H 571 substituted "correctional" for "penal" in division (D).

Cross References

Body piercing and tattooing, guardian defined, 3730.01
Durable power of attorney for health care, incompetent defined, 1337.11
Incompetent ceases to be general partner, 1782.23
Infant hearing-impairment screening, guardian defined, 3701.503
Living wills, incompetent defined, 2133.01
Rights of executor or administrator of estate of limited partner, 1782.43

Seducer of incompetent aged eighteen or older, civil liability, 2305.29

Research References

Encyclopedias

OH Jur. 3d Contracts § 13, Capacity to Contract—as Affected by Age or Infirmities.

OH Jur. 3d Decedents' Estates § 1383, Administrator as Guardian.

OH Jur. 3d Guardian & Ward § 3, Nature of Guardian Ward Relationship.

OH Jur. 3d Guardian & Ward § 9, Definitions and Types of Guardians—Judicially Appointed Guardians.

OH Jur. 3d Guardian & Ward § 15, Generally; Estates Valued at $10,000 or Less.

OH Jur. 3d Guardian & Ward § 17, Persons Subject to Guardianship; Minors—Incompetents.

OH Jur. 3d Guardian & Ward § 19, Persons Subject to Guardianship; Minors—Nonresidents.

OH Jur. 3d Guardian & Ward § 39, Application for Appointment by Interested Person—on Motion of Court.

OH Jur. 3d Guardian & Ward § 42, Persons to be Served, Generally.

OH Jur. 3d Guardian & Ward § 52, Application for Guardian for Incompetent—Mental Condition Justifying Appointment on Incompetency Grounds.

OH Jur. 3d Incompetent Persons § 85, Generally; Definitions.

Forms

Ohio Forms Legal and Business § 12A:58, Lease—Provision for Arbitration of Certain Disputes.

Ohio Jurisprudence Pleading and Practice Forms § 22:8, Capacity of Minors and Incompetent Persons.

Treatises and Practice Aids

Sowald & Morganstern, Baldwin's Ohio Practice Domestic Relations Law § 7:8, Statutory Grounds—Mental Incompetency.

Carlin, Baldwin's Ohio Practice, Merrick-Rippner Probate Law § 3:18, Guardianship of Incompetent—Form.

Carlin, Baldwin's Ohio Practice, Merrick-Rippner Probate Law § 51:5, Residency—Guardian—Removal of Nonresident.

Carlin, Baldwin's Ohio Practice, Merrick-Rippner Probate Law § 51:6, Residency—Removal of Nonresident Fiduciary.

Carlin, Baldwin's Ohio Practice, Merrick-Rippner Probate Law § 57:5, Removal of Fiduciary—Grounds—Nonresidency of Fiduciary.

Carlin, Baldwin's Ohio Practice, Merrick-Rippner Probate Law § 61:3, Legal Disability—Person of Unsound Mind.

Carlin, Baldwin's Ohio Practice, Merrick-Rippner Probate Law § 62:1, Appointment of Guardian—Definitions—Incompetent.

Carlin, Baldwin's Ohio Practice, Merrick-Rippner Probate Law § 62:2, Appointment of Guardian—Definitions—Guardian.

Carlin, Baldwin's Ohio Practice, Merrick-Rippner Probate Law § 62:3, Appointment of Guardian—Definitions—Ward.

Carlin, Baldwin's Ohio Practice, Merrick-Rippner Probate Law § 62:4, Appointment of Guardian—Definitions—Resident Guardian.

Carlin, Baldwin's Ohio Practice, Merrick-Rippner Probate Law § 62:8, Appointment of Guardian—Definitions—Conservator.

Carlin, Baldwin's Ohio Practice, Merrick-Rippner Probate Law § 66:7, Termination of Guardianship—Incompetent—Standard of Proof.

Carlin, Baldwin's Ohio Practice, Merrick-Rippner Probate Law § 68:4, Letters of Administration—Specific Qualifications of Administrators—Residency Requirement.

Carlin, Baldwin's Ohio Practice, Merrick-Rippner Probate Law § 30:31, Drafting a Will—Designation of Guardian, Trustee, and Attorney—Designation of Guardian of Minor Children.

Carlin, Baldwin's Ohio Practice, Merrick-Rippner Probate Law § 60:10, Power of Attorney—"Standby Guardian" for Minor Child of Principal.

Carlin, Baldwin's Ohio Practice, Merrick-Rippner Probate Law § 62:16, Appointment of Guardian—Application—Who May Apply.

Carlin, Baldwin's Ohio Practice, Merrick-Rippner Probate Law § 62:23, Appointment of Guardian—Procedure—Guardian Nominated in Will, Power of Attorney, or Other Writing.

Carlin, Baldwin's Ohio Practice, Merrick-Rippner Probate Law § 62:30, Appointment of Guardian—Miscellaneous—Minor Children of Ward.

Carlin, Baldwin's Ohio Practice, Merrick-Rippner Probate Law § 62:34, Guardianship Proceedings—Determining When a Guardianship for Incompetent Required.

Carlin, Baldwin's Ohio Practice, Merrick-Rippner Probate Law § 62:43, Guardianship Proceedings—Who May Serve—Life Support Cases.

Carlin, Baldwin's Ohio Practice, Merrick-Rippner Probate Law § 62:45, Guardianship Proceedings—Role of Physician or Investigators.

Carlin, Baldwin's Ohio Practice, Merrick-Rippner Probate Law § 62:48, Guardianship Proceedings—Person Adjudged Not Incompetent.

Carlin, Baldwin's Ohio Practice, Merrick-Rippner Probate Law § 62:50, Appointment of Guardian of a Minor—Designation by Minor.

Carlin, Baldwin's Ohio Practice, Merrick-Rippner Probate Law § 62:80, Statement of Expert Evaluation—Form.

Carlin, Baldwin's Ohio Practice, Merrick-Rippner Probate Law § 65:14, Representing Ward's Best Interests—Ward or Guardian as Defendant—Necessary Party.

Carlin, Baldwin's Ohio Practice, Merrick-Rippner Probate Law § 65:22, Settlement of Suits—Generally—Approval of Court.

Carlin, Baldwin's Ohio Practice, Merrick-Rippner Probate Law § 65:24, Ratification of Contracts by Guardian.

Carlin, Baldwin's Ohio Practice, Merrick-Rippner Probate Law § 66:19, Motion to Terminate Guardianship of an Incompetent—Form.

Carlin, Baldwin's Ohio Practice, Merrick-Rippner Probate Law § 30:171, Appointment of Guardian If Spouse Fails to Survive; Successor—Form.

Carlin, Baldwin's Ohio Practice, Merrick-Rippner Probate Law App B SPF 17.0, Application for Appointment of Guardian (An Alleged Incompetent).

Carlin, Baldwin's Ohio Practice, Merrick-Rippner Probate Law App B SPF 17.1, Statement of Expert Evaluation.

Carlin, Baldwin's Ohio Practice, Merrick-Rippner Probate Law App B SPF 17.8, Investigator's Report.

White, Ohio Landlord Tenant Law § 2:22, Description of the Parties—Mental Capacity.

Kuehnle and Levey, Ohio Real Estate Law and Practice § 20:18, Conveyancing—Grantors—Capacity—Individuals—Minors and Persons Incarcerated.

Restatement (2d) of Contracts § 12, Capacity to Contract.

Law Review and Journal Commentaries

Hegel's Hobbled Heritage: The Ohio Supreme Court's Use of the Doctrine of Ademption to Prey on the Incompetent, David A. Onega. 8 Prob L J Ohio 25 (November/December 1997).

Standby Guardianships—Substitute H.B. 288, Michael Stark. 7 Prob L J Ohio 65 (July/August 1997).

Notes of Decisions

Appointment requirements and effects 6
Constitutional issues 1
Court's powers and duties 4
Guardian's powers and duties 5
Procedural issues 2
Standard for incompetency 3

---

1. Constitutional issues

Ward waived her appellate arguments that alleged the trial court lacked in personam jurisdiction over ward and that the trial court's failure to dismiss the action violated due process, where ward failed to appeal from order appointing guardian for ward. In re Helen Riva Guardianship (Ohio App. 5 Dist., Richland, 10-19-2006) No. 2006-CA-0067, 2006-Ohio-5547, 2006 WL 3020316, Unreported. Mental Health ⇔ 148.1

Earlier statute, making physical inability of a person to manage his property a ground for guardianship when he is mentally competent is in violation of O Const Art I, § 1. Schafer v. Haller (Ohio 1923) 108 Ohio St. 322, 140 N.E. 517, 30 A.L.R. 1378, 1 Ohio Law Abs. 485, 21 Ohio Law Rep. 150, 21 Ohio Law Rep. 152.

The term "advanced age" as used in RC 2111.01(D) is not unconstitutional or vague. In re Guardianship of Slaughter, No. 1135 (4th Dist Ct App, Athens, 1-21-83).

2. Procedural issues

Where a guardian is appointed on two grounds but the record does not show on which ground, it will be presumed that it was on both grounds. King v. Bell (Ohio 1881) 36 Ohio St. 460.

An imbecile, after a guardian has been appointed, may inquire into his imbecility in an action to enjoin guardian from control of his property. Messenger v. Bliss (Ohio 1880) 35 Ohio St. 587.

The appointment of a guardian for an imbecile is only prima facie evidence of imbecility. Messenger v. Bliss (Ohio 1880) 35 Ohio St. 587.

Probate court in guardianship proceeding conducted a full hearing regarding ward's objections to magistrate's decision declaring her to be incompetent; probate court held a hearing and addressed ward's objections one by one on the record. In re Guardianship of Castrataro (Ohio App. 8 Dist., Cuyahoga, 11-10-2005) No. 85697, 2005-Ohio-5984, 2005 WL 3007137, Unreported. Mental Health ⇐ 139

In a divorce action defended by the duly appointed guardian of an incompetent defendant who is confined under restraint in a psychiatric ward, the plaintiff wife cannot testify except as to facts which occurred after the appointment of the guardian. Matteo v. Matteo (Ashtabula 1952) 114 N.E.2d 439, 65 Ohio Law Abs. 339.

Since an insane wife is the owner of her own property and as this property can be placed in the hands of a guardian without notice to her, her husband, who has no interest in or control over her property, need not have notice of the appointment of a guardian for his wife. Heckman v. Adams (Ohio 1893) 50 Ohio St. 305, 29 W.L.B. 330, 34 N.E. 155.

An idiot must reside in a county twelve months before the court can appoint a guardian, as he is not otherwise legally settled there for purposes of RS 6203; this conclusion is based on the length of time relating to pauper relief in RS 1492. In re Canady (Ohio Prob. 1898) 7 Ohio Dec. 285, 4 Ohio N.P. 403.

3. Standard for incompetency

Sufficient medical reports substantiated magistrate's conclusion, in guardianship proceeding, that ward was incompetent; two physicians diagnosed ward with paranoid schizophrenia, and court investigator's report summarized the findings of the treatment team at hospital where ward was treated and concluded that ward was in need of a guardian. In re Guardianship of Castrataro (Ohio App. 8 Dist., Cuyahoga, 11-10-2005) No. 85697, 2005-Ohio-5984, 2005 WL 3007137, Unreported. Mental Health ⇐ 135

Evidence supported trial court's finding that mental health patient was incompetent and that appointment of guardian was warranted; although patient had some success living alone, doctor testified that patient suffered from schizophrenia and could not care for herself without help, patient had long history of not complying with treatment needs, and patient's resistance to taking medication repeatedly resulted in lengthy hospitalization. In re Guardianship of Ryan (Ohio App. 5 Dist., Ashland, 12-10-2004) No. 2004-COA-016, 2004-Ohio-6709, 2004 WL 2891933, Unreported. Mental Health ⇐ 105; Mental Health ⇐ 135

Evidence supported finding that proposed ward who suffered from mental illness, but who was able to make arrangements for his care in nursing home and to cause checks to be issued to pay for his care, was competent, precluding appointment of guardian; proposed ward was capable of handling his day-to-day affairs. In re Langenderfer (Ohio App. 6 Dist., Fulton, 08-06-2004) No. F-03-031, 2004-Ohio-4149, 2004 WL 1765463, Unreported. Mental Health ⇐ 135

Prisoner against whom various civil actions were commenced ultimately consented to guardianship over his estate, and thus was precluded from arguing that incarceration alone was insufficient to warrant finding of incompetence, which resulted in finding that guardianship was appropriate; prisoner correctly argued that nothing prevented incarcerated persons from entering into contracts and disposing of property, but this doctrine did not reach prisoners over whom guardianship had been established, and moreover, incarceration was clearly sufficient to warrant finding of incompetence under the statutory definition of "incompetent." In re Guardianship of Goins (Ohio App. 7 Dist., Mahoning, 02-25-2003) No. 02 CA 163, 2003-Ohio-931, 2003 WL 685878, Unreported, appeal not allowed 99 Ohio St.3d 1453, 790 N.E.2d 1218, 2003-Ohio-3396. Convicts ⇐ 3; Guardian And Ward ⇐ 9.5; Guardian And Ward ⇐ 13(8)

Evidence concerning the deplorable condition of a person's residence justifies a finding of incompetency and the appointment of a guardian based upon (1) refuse strewn throughout the home, (2) animal feces, insect infestations and rodents, (3) a fire hazard created by full and empty containers of kerosene, and (4) electricity that does not work. Davis v. Cuyahoga County Adult Protective Services (Ohio App. 8 Dist., Cuyahoga, 10-12-2000) No. 77116, 2000 WL 1513752, Unreported.

An elderly woman who is fatally injured by an underinsured driver who, prior to her unexpected death, is capable of caring for herself or of arranging for that care to be done by others is not a ward of the insured who brings a claim based on the underinsured motorist clause of her insurance policy seeking coverage for the deceased as a "relative" which includes a ward under the care of the insured; the elderly woman's choice to have the insured as her friend to live with her and care for her needs rather than hire a visiting nurse, bookkeeper, or other assistant does not transform the friend into the elderly woman's ward. Raines v. Florence (Ohio App. 9 Dist., Wayne, 10-06-1999) No. 98CA0044, 1999 WL 812923, Unreported, appeal not allowed 88 Ohio St.3d 1415, 723 N.E.2d 120.

Appointment of guardian of estate only is granted where there is clear and convincing evidence that respondent is unable to recall her monthly income and distributions from her checking account and neither understands nor remembers the documents she has signed. In re Guardianship of Stokes (Ohio App. 8 Dist., Cuyahoga, 01-30-1997) No. 70666, 1997 WL 37686, Unreported.

Evidence presented at woman's competency hearing clearly and convincingly showed that she was an incompetent person and thus that a guardianship was necessary; there was testimony that woman suffered from moderate dementia, that the condition had progressed and would not improve over time, that she was vulnerable to undue influence, that she was unable to make informed decisions regarding financial matters, and that she lacked a good understanding as to her medication, and there was evidence suggesting that persons had already taken financial advantage of woman. In re Guardianship of Thomas (Ohio App. 10 Dist., 03-12-2002) 148 Ohio App.3d 11, 771 N.E.2d 882, 2002-Ohio-1037. Mental Health ⇐ 135

Definition of "incompetent" under amendment to Code section allowing appointment of guardian did not allow person to be found incompetent based solely on physical disability; trial court had to find person mentally impaired before person could be found incompetent. In re Bolander (Lake 1993) 88 Ohio App.3d 498, 624 N.E.2d 322. Mental Health ⇐ 105

A patient confined in the psychiatric ward at a veterans hospital and unable to manage his affairs is insane within the meaning of GC 11495 (RC 2317.03). Matteo v. Matteo (Ashtabula 1952) 114 N.E.2d 439, 65 Ohio Law Abs. 339.

General rule that party is deemed to have waived disqualification of juror unless he is able to show upon hearing that with exercise of reasonable diligence he could not have objected to seating of such juror at his impaneling thereof, applies to juror who is incompetent person under section, and by reason of advanced age and mental and physical disability and infirmity is incapable of caring for his person and estate. Cottman v. Federman Co. (Summit 1942) 71 Ohio App. 89, 47 N.E.2d 1009, 25 O.O. 435. New Trial ⇐ 54

A person adjudged incompetent because of mental infirmity brought about by advanced age is "insane" within meaning of that term as defined by section. Jacobs v. Porter (Franklin 1941) 73 Ohio App. 286, 43 N.E.2d 879, 36 Ohio Law Abs. 282, 28 O.O. 449.

"Insane" in RS 5242 disqualifying parties as witnesses in certain cases, comprehends "imbeciles." Ross v. Todd (Ohio Cir. 1889) 2 Ohio C.D. 385.

One who has been wasting his property by bad contracts and squandering money, is an imbecile within the meaning of RS 6302 and the Bouvier's Law Dictionary definition of an imbecile as a person lacking "natural or acquired ideas… or… those faculties which acquaint us with the qualities and ordinary relation of things or… the morals and motives that regulate our relations and conduct towards our fellow men;" thus, a person who can govern himself and not need a guardian of the person may be an imbecile unable to manage his other affairs requiring a guardian of his estate. In re Emswiler (Ohio Prob. 1900) 11 Ohio Dec. 10, 8 Ohio N.P. 132.

That legislature, defining "imbecile" in section did not intend that it should mean "a condition of permanent and hopeless incapacity," is apparent from GC 10507–61 (RC 2111.47). Potts v. First–Central Trust Co. (Summit 1940) 47 N.E.2d 823, 37 Ohio Law Abs. 382.

4. Court's powers and duties

The trial court's denial of ward's motion to relocate to the State of Pennsylvania was not an abuse of discretion, even though ward preferred to relocate; two experts opined that ward needed constant assistance, and ward conceded that she needed assistance with daily life. In re Helen Riva Guardianship (Ohio App. 5 Dist., Richland, 10-19-2006) No. 2006-CA-

Note 4

0067, 2006-Ohio-5547, 2006 WL 3020316, Unreported. Mental Health ⚬⇨ 35

Probate court in guardianship proceeding could consider the testimony of ward's brother concerning ward's inappropriate behavior toward their parents; testimony was admissible and reliable, and decision to appoint guardian was not based solely on the testimony, but rather on evidence including expert reports, medical reports, and other testimony. In re Guardianship of Castrataro (Ohio App. 8 Dist., Cuyahoga, 11-10-2005) No. 85697, 2005-Ohio-5984, 2005 WL 3007137, Unreported. Mental Health ⚬⇨ 135

A probate court has authority to appoint a guardian for one incompetent by reason of physical disability even though prior to such appointment said incompetent was sued by his wife for divorce and restrained from disposing of his property. In re Guardianship of Stephens (Ohio Prob. 1964) 2 Ohio Misc. 47, 202 N.E.2d 458, 30 O.O.2d 325.

Appointment of guardian over person not possessing sufficient mentality properly to care for her property is within sound discretion of probate court. In re Wilson's Guardianship (Perry 1926) 23 Ohio App. 390, 155 N.E. 654, 4 Ohio Law Abs. 348. Mental Health ⚬⇨ 137.1.

Probate court, before appointing guardian for an alleged incompetent, should be fully satisfied that claimed infirmity prevents person from fully protecting herself and property from those who would be inclined to take advantage of such person by securing her property without consideration. In re Wilson's Guardianship (Perry 1926) 23 Ohio App. 390, 155 N.E. 654, 4 Ohio Law Abs. 348.

The common pleas court may appoint a guardian for an imbecile upon appeal from probate refusing to do so. In re Oliver's Guardianship (Ohio 1908) 77 Ohio St. 474, 83 N.E. 795, 5 Ohio Law Rep. 586.

The power of English chancery courts over the estates of infants, lunatics, idiots, and imbeciles has in Ohio been transferred to the probate courts. Kissell v. Gram (Ohio Prob. 1879) 7 Ohio Dec. 233, 4 Ohio N.P. 333.

The probate court has the duty to appoint a guardian for an imbecile when a proper application is filed even where he has been admitted to an infirmary and his property taken possession of by its officers. Kissell v. Gram (Ohio Prob. 1879) 7 Ohio Dec. 233, 4 Ohio N.P. 333.

5. Guardian's powers and duties

The guardian of an imbecile has no lawful right to pay an attorney's fee for fomented litigation; will be charged with interest on funds of the ward which came into his hands and were used as his own; cannot make disbursements to prospective heirs of the ward; is an incompetent witness as to the value of services rendered by himself on behalf of the ward before his appointment as guardian; and is liable to removal for mingling the ward's funds with his own and investing such funds in real estate taken in his own name, paying claims without investigation, and appropriating enormous fees for his own services. In re Oliver's Guardianship (Ohio Com.Pl. 1909) 20 Ohio Dec. 64, 9 Ohio NP(NS) 178.

Ohio statutes provide for appointment by probate court, when found necessary, of a guardian of person or estate of a minor, or of both, who will have care and management of the person or estate of such minor, or both, and that with certain exceptions, a minor over age of fourteen years may select a guardian, who, if a suitable person, shall be appointed; further, a father and a mother have equal rights to the custody of a minor, and a surviving parent may by last will appoint a guardian; there is a distinction between a parent acting as a natural guardian of his minor child with custody of the minor's person and the position of legal guardian appointed by the court for purpose of care and management of the estate of such minor. Chertoff v. C.I.R. (C.C.A.6 1947) 160 F.2d 691, 35 O.O. 399.

The executive secretary of the Lucas county child welfare board may be appointed legal guardian of a minor when said minor's funds, originally deposited under RC 2111.05, have increased to over $1,000, and by accepting the responsibilities of such a guardianship, he is performing the official duties and exercising the powers of his office as set forth in RC 5153.16 and is not entitled to receive guardianship compensation. OAG 68–036.

Under existing statutes, a guardian of an incompetent person, appointed under earlier statute as amended in 108 v p 1, p 387, has no control over the personal property of his ward, nor can the court grant such guardian an order to sell his ward's real estate. 1921 OAG p 246.

6. Appointment requirements and effects

A county cannot be charged with the maintenance of an idiot, lunatic, or insane pauper, until after a guardian is appointed by the court of common pleas. Brimfield Tp. v. Portage County Com'rs (Ohio 1840) 10 Ohio 283. Counties ⚬⇨ 133; Paupers ⚬⇨ 47

Appointment of guardian for woman who suffered from multiple sclerosis was supported by competent, credible evidence, including testimony of court-appointed psychiatrist that woman suffered from debilitating multiple sclerosis, dementia, and organic mood disorder, she had been rendered incapable of taking care of her person or her property, she was not capable of making decisions regarding medical treatment and died, and there was no chance woman would ever be capable of making decisions for herself. In re Poliksa (Ohio App. 1 Dist., Hamilton, 05-26-2006) No. C-050474, 2006-Ohio-2617, 2006 WL 1449533, Unreported. Mental Health ⚬⇨ 105

Guardianship of incompetent woman, a lottery winner, was more appropriate than less restrictive alternatives of placing her assets in preexisting inter vivos trust or having her remain in the care of her new husband at his residence; terms of preexisting trust were insufficient to provide the type of protection of her assets that the appointment of a guardian would provide, and there was evidence that husband had attempted to exert influence over woman because of her substantial wealth and concerns that if she remained at residence she would be vulnerable to husband and other individuals. In re Guardianship of Thomas (Ohio App. 10 Dist., 03-12-2002) 148 Ohio App.3d 11, 771 N.E.2d 882, 2002-Ohio-1037. Mental Health ⚬⇨ 105

Those acting under powers-of-attorney cannot be viewed the same as guardians, for purposes of determining whether statutory exception to ademption doctrine for sales by guardians applies to sales by attorneys-in-fact, since guardians are appointed by probate court and are subject to court's control, whereas attorneys-in-fact have much more freedom and can act without court approval as principal's alter ego. In re Estate of Hegel (Ohio, 08-28-1996) 76 Ohio St.3d 476, 668 N.E.2d 474, 1996-Ohio-77. Wills ⚬⇨ 767

Where the decedent's former spouse is given custody of their children he is not considered their "guardian" as that word is used in RC 2111.01 and as a result he is not subject to RC 2111.09, which forbids appointment of the same person as administrator and guardian. In re Estate of Robertson (Cuyahoga 1985) 26 Ohio App.3d 64, 498 N.E.2d 206, 26 O.B.R. 238.

Where ward gave consent to appointment of guardian of her estate on ground of incompetency due to physical disability without full knowledge of the legal implications of her act, it was not her free act as contemplated by GC 10507–2 (RC 2111.02), and if, upon motion of ward to terminate the guardianship, it appears that there is no necessity for the guardianship to continue, the motion should be granted. In re Luft's Guardianship (Franklin 1950) 91 Ohio App. 409, 97 N.E.2d 561, 59 Ohio Law Abs. 33, 45 O.O. 333.

Appointment of guardians by ex parte proceeding for the person and estate of a man eighty-one years of age, who had broken with his family by reason of his having adopted the religious belief of the "Russellites", including a belief in the "second coming" of Christ, is not justified. In re Smith's Guardianship (Ohio Prob. 1927) 26 Ohio N.P.(N.S.) 533.

The appointment of a guardian for an aged man on the ground of incapacity to care for his property imports a finding by the court of such infirmity, and a transfer of property by him after such an appointment has been made is void and may be set aside and the title quieted to the property thus sought to be conveyed. Fiorni v Goss, 23 NP(NS) 303 (CP, Montgomery 1921).

An individual who is appointed guardian of the person of a minor, pursuant to RC Ch 2111, has legal custody of the minor for purposes of RC 3313.64. OAG 94–033.

2111.02 Appointment of guardian

(A) When found necessary, the probate court on its own motion or on application by any interested party shall appoint, subject to divisions (C) and (D) of this section and to section 2109.21 and division (B) of section 2111.121 of the Revised Code, a guardian of the person, the estate, or both, of a minor or incompetent, provided the person for whom the guardian is to be appointed is a resident of the county or has a legal settlement in the county and, except in the case of a minor, has had the opportunity to have the assistance of counsel in the proceeding for the appointment of such guardian. An interested party includes, but is not limited to, a person nominated in a durable power of attorney as described in division (D) of section 1337.09 of the Revised Code or in a writing as described in division (A) of section 2111.121 of the Revised Code.

Except when the guardian of an incompetent is an agency under contract with the department of mental retardation and developmental disabilities for the provision of protective services under sections 5123.55 to 5123.59 of the Revised Code, the guardian of an incompetent, by virtue of such appointment, shall be the guardian of the minor children of the guardian's ward, unless the court appoints some other person as their guardian.

When the primary purpose of the appointment of a guardian is, or was, the collection, disbursement, or administration of moneys awarded by the veterans administration to the ward, or assets derived from such moneys, no court costs shall be charged in the proceeding for the appointment or in any subsequent proceedings made in pursuance of the appointment, unless the value of the estate, including the moneys then due under the veterans administration award, exceeds one thousand five hundred dollars.

(B)(1) If the probate court finds it to be in the best interest of an incompetent or minor, it may appoint pursuant to divisions (A) and (C) of this section, on its own motion or on application by an interested party, a limited guardian with specific limited powers. The sections of the Revised Code, rules, and procedures governing guardianships apply to a limited guardian, except that the order of appointment and letters of authority of a limited guardian shall state the reasons for, and specify the limited powers of, the guardian. The court may appoint a limited guardian for a definite or indefinite period. An incompetent or minor for whom a limited guardian has been appointed retains all of the incompetent's or minor's rights in all areas not affected by the court order appointing the limited guardian.

(2) If a guardian appointed pursuant to division (A) of this section is temporarily or permanently removed or resigns, and if the welfare of the ward requires immediate action, at any time after the removal or resignation, the probate court may appoint, ex parte and with or without notice to the ward or interested parties, an interim guardian for a maximum period of fifteen days. If the court appoints the interim guardian ex parte or without notice to the ward, the court, at its first opportunity, shall enter upon its journal with specificity the reason for acting ex parte or without notice, and, as soon as possible, shall serve upon the ward a copy of the order appointing the interim guardian. For good cause shown, after notice to the ward and interested parties and after hearing, the court may extend an interim guardianship for a specified period, but not to exceed an additional thirty days.

(3) If a minor or incompetent has not been placed under a guardianship pursuant to division (A) of this section and if an emergency exists, and if it is reasonably certain that immediate action is required to prevent significant injury to the person or estate of the minor or incompetent, at any time after it receives notice of the emergency, the court, ex parte, may issue any order that it considers necessary to prevent injury to the person or estate of the minor or incompetent, or may appoint an emergency guardian for a maximum period of seventy-two hours. A written copy of any order issued by a court under this division shall be served upon the incompetent or minor as soon as possible after its issuance. Failure to serve such an order after its issuance or prior to the taking of any action under its authority does not invalidate the order or the actions taken. The powers of an emergency guardian shall be specified in the letters of appointment, and shall be limited to those powers that are necessary to prevent injury to the person or estate of the minor or incompetent. If the court acts ex parte or without notice to the minor or incompetent, the court, at its first opportunity, shall enter upon its journal a record of the case and, with specificity, the reason for acting ex parte or without notice. For good cause shown, after notice to the minor or incompetent and interested parties, and after hearing, the court may extend an emergency guardianship for a specified period, but not to exceed an additional thirty days.

(C) Prior to the appointment of a guardian or limited guardian under division (A) or (B)(1) of this section, the court shall conduct a hearing on the matter of the appointment. The hearing shall be conducted in accordance with all of the following:

(1) The proposed guardian or limited guardian shall appear at the hearing and, if appointed, shall swear under oath that the proposed guardian or limited guardian has made and will continue to make diligent efforts to file a true inventory in accordance with section 2111.14 of the Revised Code and find and report all assets belonging to the estate of the ward and that the proposed guardian or limited guardian faithfully and completely will fulfill the other duties of guardian, including the filing of timely and accurate reports and accountings;

(2) If the hearing is conducted by a referee, the procedures set forth in Civil Rule 53 shall be followed;

(3) If the hearing concerns the appointment of a guardian or limited guardian for an alleged incompetent, the burden of proving incompetency shall be by clear and convincing evidence;

(4) Upon request of the applicant, the alleged incompetent for whom the appointment is sought or the alleged incompetent's counsel, or any interested party, a recording or record of the hearing shall be made;

(5) Evidence of a less restrictive alternative to guardianship may be introduced, and when introduced, shall be considered by the court;

(6) The court may deny a guardianship based upon a finding that a less restrictive alternative to guardianship exists;

(7) If the hearing concerns the appointment of a guardian or limited guardian for an alleged incompetent, the alleged incompetent has all of the following rights:

(a) The right to be represented by independent counsel of his choice;

(b) The right to have a friend or family member of his choice present;

(c) The right to have evidence of an independent expert evaluation introduced;

(d) If the alleged incompetent is indigent, upon his request:

(i) The right to have counsel and an independent expert evaluator appointed at court expense;

(ii) If the guardianship, limited guardianship, or standby guardianship decision is appealed, the right to have counsel appointed and necessary transcripts for appeal prepared at court expense.

(D) When a person has been nominated to be a guardian of the estate of a minor in or pursuant to a durable power of attorney as described in division (D) of section 1337.09 of the Revised Code or a writing as described in division (A) of section 2111.121 of the Revised Code, the person nominated has preference in appointment over a person selected by the minor. A person who has been nominated to be a guardian of the person of a minor in or pursuant to a durable power of attorney or writing of that nature does not have preference in appointment over a person selected by the minor, but the probate court may appoint the person named in the durable power of attorney or the writing, the person selected by the minor, or another person as guardian of the person of the minor.

(1996 H 288, eff. 1–14–97; 1989 S 46, eff. 1–1–90; 1988 S 228; 1983 S 115; 129 v 1448; 128 v 76; 1953 H 1; GC 10507–2)

Historical and Statutory Notes

Pre–1953 H 1 Amendments: 123 v 665; 114 v 383

Amendment Note: 1996 H 288 added the reference to division (D) in the first sentence in the first paragraph in division (A); added the references to limited guardian in division (C)(1); inserted ", or standby guardianship" in division (C)(7)(d)(ii); added division (D); and made changes to reflect gender neutral language and other nonsubstantive changes.

OSBA Probate and Trust Law Section

1983:

See the comment for 1983 following Sec. 2111.121.

Cross References

Appeal from probate court, 2101.42
Appointment of fiduciary, acceptance of duties, 2109.02
Attorney in fact may become guardian, 1337.09

Library References

Guardian and Ward ⚖13.
Mental Health ⚖120 to 143.
Westlaw Topic Nos. 196, 257A.
C.J.S. Mental Health §§ 130 to 139.
   Baldwin's Ohio Legislative Service, 1988 Laws of Ohio, S 228—LSC Analysis, p 5–968

Research References

Encyclopedias

8 Am. Jur. Trials 483, Incompetency and Commitment Proceedings.
26 Am. Jur. Trials 97, Representing the Mentally Ill: Civil Commitment Proceedings.
OH Jur. 3d Actions § 153, Unpreparedness; Continuance to Amend Pleadings.
OH Jur. 3d Agency & Independent Contractors § 42, Effect of Death or Incompetence of Principal—Durable Power of Attorney; Nomination of Guardian of Principal or Minor Children.
OH Jur. 3d Contracts § 13, Capacity to Contract—as Affected by Age or Infirmities.
OH Jur. 3d Guardian & Ward § 11, Definitions and Types of Guardians—Limited, Interim, and Emergency Guardians.
OH Jur. 3d Guardian & Ward § 16, Persons Subject to Guardianship; Minors.
OH Jur. 3d Guardian & Ward § 17, Persons Subject to Guardianship; Minors—Incompetents.
OH Jur. 3d Guardian & Ward § 32, Preference to Testamentary Guardian or Guardian Nominated by a Parent.
OH Jur. 3d Guardian & Ward § 35, Which Probate Court Has Jurisdiction.
OH Jur. 3d Guardian & Ward § 36, Resident Guardianship for Nonresident Ward.
OH Jur. 3d Guardian & Ward § 38, Application for Appointment by Interested Person.
OH Jur. 3d Guardian & Ward § 39, Application for Appointment by Interested Person—on Motion of Court.
OH Jur. 3d Guardian & Ward § 44, Persons to be Served, Generally—Application for Guardian for Incompetent.
OH Jur. 3d Guardian & Ward § 51, Application for Guardian for Incompetent—Rights of Allegedly Incompetent Person for Whom Appointment is Sought; Standard of Proof.
OH Jur. 3d Guardian & Ward § 62, Effect of Order as Defining Scope of Guardian's Powers.
OH Jur. 3d Guardian & Ward § 183, Administration of Moneys Awarded by Veterans' Administration.
OH Jur. 3d Mandamus, Procedendo, & Prohibition § 183, Effect of Patent and Unambiguous Lack of Jurisdiction.

Forms

Ohio Forms and Transactions KP 30.10, Guardianship Clause.

Treatises and Practice Aids

Giannelli and Snyder, Baldwin's Ohio Practice, Evidence, R 804, Hearsay Exceptions; Declarant Unavailable.
Carlin, Baldwin's Ohio Practice, Merrick-Rippner Probate Law § 51:5, Residency—Guardian—Removal of Nonresident.
Carlin, Baldwin's Ohio Practice, Merrick-Rippner Probate Law § 51:6, Residency—Removal of Nonresident Fiduciary.
Carlin, Baldwin's Ohio Practice, Merrick-Rippner Probate Law § 57:5, Removal of Fiduciary—Grounds—Nonresidency of Fiduciary.
Carlin, Baldwin's Ohio Practice, Merrick-Rippner Probate Law § 60:9, Power of Attorney—Appointment of Guardian for Principal.
Carlin, Baldwin's Ohio Practice, Merrick-Rippner Probate Law § 62:2, Appointment of Guardian—Definitions—Guardian.
Carlin, Baldwin's Ohio Practice, Merrick-Rippner Probate Law § 62:5, Appointment of Guardian—Definitions—Limited Guardian.
Carlin, Baldwin's Ohio Practice, Merrick-Rippner Probate Law § 62:6, Appointment of Guardian—Definitions—Interim Guardian.
Carlin, Baldwin's Ohio Practice, Merrick-Rippner Probate Law § 62:7, Appointment of Guardian—Definitions—Emergency Guardian.
Carlin, Baldwin's Ohio Practice, Merrick-Rippner Probate Law § 63:1, Notice of Guardianship Hearing.
Carlin, Baldwin's Ohio Practice, Merrick-Rippner Probate Law § 66:9, Termination of Guardianship—Incompetent—Least Restrictive Alternative.
Carlin, Baldwin's Ohio Practice, Merrick-Rippner Probate Law § 68:4, Letters of Administration—Specific Qualifications of Administrators—Residency Requirement.
Carlin, Baldwin's Ohio Practice, Merrick-Rippner Probate Law § 30:31, Drafting a Will—Designation of Guardian, Trustee, and Attorney—Designation of Guardian of Minor Children.
Carlin, Baldwin's Ohio Practice, Merrick-Rippner Probate Law § 60:10, Power of Attorney—"Standby Guardian" for Minor Child of Principal.
Carlin, Baldwin's Ohio Practice, Merrick-Rippner Probate Law § 62:10, Appointment of Guardian—Definitions—Legal Settlement.
Carlin, Baldwin's Ohio Practice, Merrick-Rippner Probate Law § 62:11, Appointment of Guardian—Definitions—Domicile.
Carlin, Baldwin's Ohio Practice, Merrick-Rippner Probate Law § 62:12, Appointment of Guardian—Definitions—Residence.
Carlin, Baldwin's Ohio Practice, Merrick-Rippner Probate Law § 62:13, Appointment of Guardian—Definitions—Least Restrictive Alternative.
Carlin, Baldwin's Ohio Practice, Merrick-Rippner Probate Law § 62:14, Appointment of Guardian—Application—Jurisdiction.
Carlin, Baldwin's Ohio Practice, Merrick-Rippner Probate Law § 62:15, Appointment of Guardian—Application—Venue.
Carlin, Baldwin's Ohio Practice, Merrick-Rippner Probate Law § 62:16, Appointment of Guardian—Application—Who May Apply.
Carlin, Baldwin's Ohio Practice, Merrick-Rippner Probate Law § 62:18, Appointment of Guardian—Application—Notice.
Carlin, Baldwin's Ohio Practice, Merrick-Rippner Probate Law § 62:19, Appointment of Guardian—Application—Investigations by Court.
Carlin, Baldwin's Ohio Practice, Merrick-Rippner Probate Law § 62:20, Appointment of Guardian—Application—Hearing.
Carlin, Baldwin's Ohio Practice, Merrick-Rippner Probate Law § 62:23, Appointment of Guardian—Procedure—Guardian Nominated in Will, Power of Attorney, or Other Writing.
Carlin, Baldwin's Ohio Practice, Merrick-Rippner Probate Law § 62:27, Appointment of Guardian—Residency Requirements—Resident Ward.
Carlin, Baldwin's Ohio Practice, Merrick-Rippner Probate Law § 62:30, Appointment of Guardian—Miscellaneous—Minor Children of Ward.
Carlin, Baldwin's Ohio Practice, Merrick-Rippner Probate Law § 62:31, Appointment of Guardian—Miscellaneous—Veteran's Guardianships.
Carlin, Baldwin's Ohio Practice, Merrick-Rippner Probate Law § 62:33, Guardianship Proceedings—Court's Jurisdiction.
Carlin, Baldwin's Ohio Practice, Merrick-Rippner Probate Law § 62:34, Guardianship Proceedings—Determining When a Guardianship for Incompetent Required.
Carlin, Baldwin's Ohio Practice, Merrick-Rippner Probate Law § 62:35, Guardianship Proceedings—Burden of Proof.
Carlin, Baldwin's Ohio Practice, Merrick-Rippner Probate Law § 62:37, Guardianship Proceedings—Least Restrictive Alternative.
Carlin, Baldwin's Ohio Practice, Merrick-Rippner Probate Law § 62:38, Guardianship Proceedings—Hearings.
Carlin, Baldwin's Ohio Practice, Merrick-Rippner Probate Law § 62:45, Guardianship Proceedings—Role of Physician or Investigators.
Carlin, Baldwin's Ohio Practice, Merrick-Rippner Probate Law § 62:48, Guardianship Proceedings—Person Adjudged Not Incompetent.

Carlin, Baldwin's Ohio Practice, Merrick-Rippner Probate Law § 62:50, Appointment of Guardian of a Minor—Designation by Minor.

Carlin, Baldwin's Ohio Practice, Merrick-Rippner Probate Law § 62:53, Appointment of Guardian of a Minor—Designation by Parent in a Power of Attorney or Writing.

Carlin, Baldwin's Ohio Practice, Merrick-Rippner Probate Law § 62:60, Limited Guardianship.

Carlin, Baldwin's Ohio Practice, Merrick-Rippner Probate Law § 62:61, Interim Guardianship.

Carlin, Baldwin's Ohio Practice, Merrick-Rippner Probate Law § 62:62, Emergency Guardianship.

Carlin, Baldwin's Ohio Practice, Merrick-Rippner Probate Law § 62:73, Entry Setting for Hearing and Ordering Notice—Form.

Carlin, Baldwin's Ohio Practice, Merrick-Rippner Probate Law § 62:76, Entry for Appointment of Guardian for Incompetent, and for Bond—Form.

Carlin, Baldwin's Ohio Practice, Merrick-Rippner Probate Law § 30:171, Appointment of Guardian If Spouse Fails to Survive; Successor—Form.

Carlin, Baldwin's Ohio Practice, Merrick-Rippner Probate Law App B SPF 15.4, Letters of Guardianship.

Carlin, Baldwin's Ohio Practice, Merrick-Rippner Probate Law App B SPF 15.9, Oath of Guardian.

Carlin, Baldwin's Ohio Practice, Merrick-Rippner Probate Law App B SPF 16.5, Judgment Entry—Appointment of Guardian of Minor.

Carlin, Baldwin's Ohio Practice, Merrick-Rippner Probate Law App B SPF 17.5, Judgment Entry—Appointment of Guardian for Incompetent Person.

Adrine & Ruden, Ohio Domestic Violence Law § 9:8, Relationships Covered—Parents and Children.

Law Review and Journal Commentaries

Guardianship and the Elderly: Oversight Not Overlooked, Norman Fell. 25 U Tol L Rev 189 (1994).

1990 Guardianship Law Safeguards Personal Rights Yet Protects Vulnerable Elderly, Comment. 24 Akron L Rev 161 (Summer 1990).

Limited Guardianships Should Be The Norm, Wiley Dinsmore. 2 Prob L J Ohio 1 (September/October 1991).

What are the Ethical Obligations for an Attorney Who Believes a Client is Mentally Impaired?, Lee A. Koosed. 68 Clev B J 13 (May 1997).

Notes of Decisions

Constitutional issues 1
Effect of appointment; termination 5
Evidence 8
Jurisdiction 7
Mental incompetence; minority 4
Physical disability 3
Procedure 2
Residence 6
Selection of guardian 9

---

1. Constitutional issues

The statute of January 5, 1871 which enables the court of common pleas to appoint a guardian of the property of habitual drunkards is not in conflict with the provision of O Const Art IV, § 8, defining the jurisdiction of probate courts. Hagany v. Cohnen (Ohio 1876) 29 Ohio St. 82. Constitutional Law ⟹ 56; Courts ⟹ 472.5; Chemical Dependents ⟹ 2; Guardian And Ward ⟹ 8.

Evidence supported finding that proposed ward who suffered from mental illness, but who was able to make arrangements for his care in nursing home and to cause checks to be issued to pay for his care, was competent, precluding appointment of guardian; proposed ward was capable of handling his day-to-day affairs. In re Langenderfer (Ohio App. 6 Dist., Fulton, 08-06-2004) No. F-03-031, 2004-Ohio-4149, 2004 WL 1765463, Unreported. Mental Health ⟹ 135

Proposed guardian waived for appellate review in guardianship proceeding her claim that trial court erred by giving full faith and credit to Indiana guardianship order that lacked proper authentication, where proposed guardian failed to raise any objections to foreign judgment at trial-court level. In re Guardianship of Replogle (Ohio App. 2 Dist., 10-14-2005) 2005-Ohio-5530, 2005 WL 2660550. Mental Health ⟹ 148.1

2. Procedure

Where the common pleas court in divorce proceedings decrees the custody of children to one of the parties, the probate court cannot interfere with such custody by letters of guardianship. Hoffman v. Hoffman (Ohio 1864) 15 Ohio St. 427.

Father was not prejudiced when guardian filed a separate application for guardianship for each of two sons; while guardianship statute provided that only one guardianship application was necessary to cover both children, statute did not say that it was illegal or improper to file an application for each child. In re Guardianship of Ahmed (Ohio App. 7 Dist., Belmont, 10-10-2003) No. 02 BE 56, 2003-Ohio-5463, 2003 WL 22344914, Unreported, reconsideration denied 2003-Ohio-6390, 2003 WL 22837720, appeal not allowed 101 Ohio St.3d 1487, 805 N.E.2d 539, 2004-Ohio-1293. Guardian And Ward ⟹ 13(3)

Alteration of the date and filing stamp on magistrate's decision did not prejudice sister, in proceeding to appoint guardian for second sister; the date and filing error did not effect sister's objections to the magistrate's decision, and sister failed to show an prejudicial consequences resulting from the error. In re Guardianship of Bush (Ohio App. 7 Dist., Mahoning, 09-30-2003) No. 02-CA-16, No. 02-CA-84, 2003-Ohio-5440, 2003 WL 22332941, Unreported. Guardian And Ward ⟹ 13(8)

The probate court's failure to appoint counsel for ward was not an abuse of discretion, in proceeding to appoint a guardian for ward; hearing was continued to allow ward an opportunity to obtain counsel, and ward failed to obtain counsel or request the appointment of counsel. In re Guardianship of Bush (Ohio App. 7 Dist., Mahoning, 09-30-2003) No. 02-CA-16, No. 02-CA-84, 2003-Ohio-5440, 2003 WL 22332941, Unreported. Guardian And Ward ⟹ 13(3)

While trial court had authority to appoint a guardian for dementia patient on its own, in order to comply with statutory notice requirements, it should have first given notice of proposed guardian, required proposed guardian to file his application with required statutory inventory, and then scheduled a hearing. In re Guardianship of Simmons (Ohio App. 6 Dist., Wood, 10-10-2003) No. WD-02-039, 2003-Ohio-5416, 2003 WL 22319415, Unreported. Mental Health ⟹ 126; Mental Health ⟹ 128; Mental Health ⟹ 137.1

Probate court abused its discretion in guardianship proceeding when it found that alleged incompetent's estate was worth $2 million, where probate court concluded that trust was not part of guardianship estate, but then added worth of trust to estate to determine estate's value. In re Guardianship of Poschner (Ohio App. 7 Dist., Mahoning, 09-26-2003) No. 03MA53, 2003-Ohio-5148, 2003 WL 22231711, Unreported, on subsequent appeal 2005-Ohio-2788, 2005 WL 1324748. Guardian And Ward ⟹ 32

Trial court's appointment of an attorney, rather than applicant, as guardian for applicant's father and step-mother, was not abuse of discretion, where appointment was with the consent of all the applicants, father's and step-mother's guardian ad litem recommended the attorney be appointed as guardian, and attorney was apparently competent to serve as guardian, as she had extensive experience dealing with the elderly, and was a neutral, detached, and objective person. In re Guardianship of Keller (Ohio App. 5 Dist., Licking, 06-16-2003) No. 02CA76, No. 02CA75, 2003-Ohio-3168, 2003 WL 21398964, Unreported. Mental Health ⟹ 116.1

Trial court did not abuse its discretion in guardianship proceeding involving incompetent adult by not admitting, in its entirety, psychologist's report on family of incompetent adult that was ordered by the domestic relations court; psychologist's opinions regarding the best interests of incompetent adult were presented to court from psychologist himself. In re Guardianship of Nease (Ohio App. 6 Dist., Lucas, 05-02-2003) No. L-02-1296, 2003-Ohio-2218, 2003 WL 2007729, Unreported. Mental Health ⟹ 135

Nothing prevented trial court from sua sponte imposing guardianship over estate of prisoner against whom various civil actions had been commenced; statute governing appointment of guardians specifically authorized probate court to appoint guardians on its own motion. In re Guardianship of Goins (Ohio App. 7 Dist., Mahoning, 02-25-2003) No. 02 CA 163, 2003-Ohio-931, 2003 WL 685878, Unreported, appeal not allowed 99 Ohio St.3d 1453, 790 N.E.2d 1218, 2003-Ohio-3396. Convicts ⟹ 3; Guardian And Ward ⟹ 13(3)

Aunt's nephew lacked standing to challenge on appeal trial court's appointment of attorney as guardian of aunt's estate and person, where nephew did not file an application for appointment and suffered no consequences adverse to his interests as a result of court's appointment of attorney. In re Guardianship of Lee (Ohio App. 2 Dist., Miami, 11-15-2002) No. 02CA3, 2002-Ohio-6194, 2002 WL 31528725, Unreported. Guardian And Ward ⇐ 13(8)

Mother, whose sons applied for appointment of guardian for her, was not entitled to writ of prohibition to prevent probate judge from using guardian ad litem (GAL) to conduct ex parte communications with mother outside presence of her counsel, from conducting ex parte communications with GAL, and from considering or using reports created by GAL through ex parte communications with mother, where mother had adequate remedy at law. State ex rel. Florence v. Zitter (Ohio, 08-10-2005) 106 Ohio St.3d 87, 831 N.E.2d 1003, 2005-Ohio-3804. Prohibition ⇐ 3(3)

Ward may challenge order appointing guardian by direct appeal on ground that letters of guardianship were in first instance improperly issued. Burns v. Daily (Ohio App. 11 Dist., 10-28-1996) 114 Ohio App.3d 693, 683 N.E.2d 1164. Mental Health ⇐ 151

Probate court could appoint guardian even though person appointed was not present at hearing on application for appointment of guardian, where no person had been proposed as guardian before application hearing; subsequently named guardian was not "proposed guardian" within meaning of statute requiring "proposed guardian" to appear at application hearing. In re Guardianship of Armstrong (Paulding 1993) 87 Ohio App.3d 452, 622 N.E.2d 441. Mental Health ⇐ 137.1

Appointment of a minor's maternal grandfather to the guardianship of the minor's estate is proper under RC 2111.02 when the court considers less restrictive alternatives and limits the guardianship to only those funds received under the mother's will, which stated a preference for the grandfather as guardian of the estate. In re Estate of Bednarczuk (Warren 1992) 80 Ohio App.3d 548, 609 N.E.2d 1310, motion overruled 65 Ohio St.3d 1444, 600 N.E.2d 686.

When the guardianship sought is over the estate, and not the person of the minor, the court need not determine that the father is unsuitable before it appoints the grandfather as guardian of the minor's estate, and RC 2111.08 does not grant the father a statutory entitlement to the minor's estate for which a showing of unsuitability is required. In re Estate of Bednarczuk (Warren 1992) 80 Ohio App.3d 548, 609 N.E.2d 1310, motion overruled 65 Ohio St.3d 1444, 600 N.E.2d 686.

Probate court improperly relied upon evidence subpoenaed sua sponte after hearing in order to affirm referee's report finding proposed ward incompetent where proposed ward received no notice that court intended to take additional evidence pertaining to competency. In re Guardianship of Schumacher (Summit 1987) 38 Ohio App.3d 37, 525 N.E.2d 833. Mental Health ⇐ 139

Pursuant to Civ R 17(B), a court other than a probate court has authority to appoint a guardian ad litem for an individual whom the court believes to be incompetent. Dailey v. Dailey (Montgomery 1983) 11 Ohio App.3d 121, 463 N.E.2d 427, 11 O.B.R. 176. Courts ⇐ 472.4(8)

A party seeking appointment as successor guardian of an incompetent does not have standing to file an affidavit of bias and prejudice against a probate judge. In re Guardianship of Hill (Ohio Prob. 1963) 196 N.E.2d 816, 93 Ohio Law Abs. 237, 29 O.O.2d 60.

A judgment of the probate court appointing a guardian for a minor is a nullity and may be directly attacked in any court in any proceeding, where the hearing provided in RC 2111.04 was set prior to the passing of the required three days. Horn v. Childers (Lawrence 1959) 116 Ohio App. 175, 187 N.E.2d 402, 22 O.O.2d 34.

An attorney who files an application for the appointment of a guardian of an incompetent on the recommendation of the superintendent of the county home where such incompetent resides makes such application as "an interested party." In re Guardianship of Titington (Ohio Prob. 1958) 162 N.E.2d 628, 82 Ohio Law Abs. 563.

No legal distinction exists in the administration of a "consent" guardianship and any other guardianship, and hence it is no defense to exceptions to a guardian's account that the expenditures involved were made at the direction of the ward. (See also In re Guardianship of Tillman, 100 App 291, 136 NE(2d) 291 (1955).) In re Tillman (Ohio Prob. 1956) 137 N.E.2d 172, 73 Ohio Law Abs. 534.

The appellate court will not substitute its judgment for that of the trial court on a law appeal from an order appointing a guardian of the person and estate of an incompetent. In re Guardianship of Harris (Franklin 1954) 136 N.E.2d 328, 73 Ohio Law Abs. 97.

An order appointing a stranger guardian of a minor is a final order affecting a substantial right of the father and is reviewable on error. Hare v. Sears (Ohio Com.Pl. 1906) 17 Ohio Dec. 590, 4 Ohio N.P.N.S. 566. Guardian And Ward ⇐ 13(8)

Trustees and guardians appointed by the probate court are regulated and controlled to a great extent by the same law by which administrators and executors are controlled. Boals v. Clingan (Ohio Com.Pl. 1905) 16 Ohio Dec. 267, 6 Ohio N.P.N.S. 609. Guardian And Ward ⇐ 3; Trusts ⇐ 171; Wills ⇐ 681(1)

Validity of lower court's order removing sister as limited guardian of her sibling and appointing disinterested third person was to be presumed in absence of transcript, statement of evidence, or agreed statement of record for review. In re Tinman (Ohio App. 6 Dist., Huron, 06-21-2002) No. H-01-061, 2002-Ohio-3149, 2002 WL 1396538, Unreported. Mental Health ⇐ 177

Although RC 2111.02(C)(1) states that the proposed guardian "shall" appear at the hearing on an application for the appointment of a guardian, such requirement does not apply where no particular guardian is proposed prior to the hearing and appointment. In re Guardianship of Armstrong, No. 11–92–10 (3d Dist Ct App, Paulding, 5–4–93).

In a proceeding for the appointment of a guardian for the person and estate of an individual allegedly physically and mentally incompetent, an indigent prospective ward has no right to court-appointed counsel. In re Guardianship of Yates, No. 84AP–902 (10th Dist Ct App, Franklin, 9–3–85).

An uncle ought to be interested in the welfare of his infant nephew and, accordingly, has standing in a proceeding for appointment of a guardian. In re Murray, 8 CC(NS) 498, 18 CD 652 (Lorain 1906).

As used in RC 2111.02 "court costs" includes fees of a sheriff for service in a guardianship proceeding, but does not include newspaper charges for publication of a notice of the appointment of the guardian. 1956 OAG 6592.

Court costs paid by mistake in a guardianship proceeding are not refundable by the probate court where such costs have become a part of the general fund of the county. 1956 OAG 6592.

3. Physical disability

Appointment of guardian for woman who suffered from multiple sclerosis was supported by competent, credible evidence, including testimony of court-appointed psychiatrist that woman suffered from debilitating multiple sclerosis, dementia, and organic mood disorder, she had been rendered incapable of taking care of her person or her property, she was not capable of making decisions regarding medical treatment and died, and there was no chance woman would ever be capable of making decisions for herself. In re Poliksa (Ohio App. 1 Dist., Hamilton, 05-26-2006) No. C-050474, 2006-Ohio-2617, 2006 WL 1449533, Unreported. Mental Health ⇐ 105

A ward who is an incompetent person because he is comatose due to pontine hemorrhage qualifies for the appointment of a guardian and the guardian has authority to authorize or approve the provision to the ward of medical treatment or services under normal circumstances. In re Guardianship of McInnis (Ohio Prob. 1991) 61 Ohio Misc.2d 790, 584 N.E.2d 1389.

Appointment of a grandson as guardian of a physically incapacitated ward, nominated as guardian in a defective application, and rejection of the application of the ward's daughter, nominated as guardian in a properly executed durable power of attorney, on the ground that the daughter is a nonresident, is improper. In re Medsker (Cuyahoga 1990) 66 Ohio App.3d 219, 583 N.E.2d 1091.

The spirit and purpose of the provision of RC 2111.02 that " [i]f a person is incompetent due to physical disability, the consent of the incompetent must first be obtained before the appointment of a guardian for him" requires that the "consent" should be in writing or made in open court by the proposed ward who is mentally competent. In re Guardianship of Gallagher (Madison 1981) 2 Ohio App.3d 218, 441 N.E.2d 593, 2 O.B.R. 238. Guardian And Ward ⇐ 9.5

A probate court has authority to appoint a guardian for one incompetent by reason of physical disability even though prior to such appointment said incompetent was sued by his wife for divorce and restrained from disposing of his property. In re Guardianship of Stephens (Ohio Prob. 1964) 2 Ohio Misc. 47, 202 N.E.2d 458, 30 O.O.2d 325.

Sale by a guardian, appointed upon grounds of physical incompetency, of real property theretofore devised by will of a ward with the ward's consent operates as an ademption of the devise. (Ed. note: But see 2107.501, 1975 S 145, eff. 1–1–76.) Roderick v. Fisher (Franklin 1954) 97 Ohio App. 95, 122 N.E.2d 475, 51 A.L.R.2d 762, 54 O.O. 264.

It is presumed that a ward for whom a guardian has been appointed upon grounds of physical incompetency is mentally competent and has testamentary power. Roderick v. Fisher (Franklin 1954) 97 Ohio App. 95, 122 N.E.2d 475, 51 A.L.R.2d 762, 54 O.O. 264.

Spirit and purpose of provision of section, "that if the incompetency" of an incompetent "be due to physical disability or infirmity the consent of the incompetent" to the appointment of a guardian "must first be obtained" require that the consent should be in writing or made in open court by the proposed ward who is mentally competent. In re Irvine's Guardianship (Knox 1943) 72 Ohio App. 405, 52 N.E.2d 536, 27 O.O. 332.

4. Mental incompetence; minority

Where a guardian is appointed for an infant who is of unsound mind, it not being stated on which ground the appointment was made, it will be presumed to have been made on both grounds. King v. Bell (Ohio 1881) 36 Ohio St. 460.

A minor must reside in the county where his guardian is appointed, or the court has no authority to appoint. Maxsom v. Sawyer (Ohio 1843) 12 Ohio 195.

Appointment of dementia patient's son as her guardian was not in her best interest in light of hostility and lack of communication between guardian and his siblings concerning patient's care and finances; better approach would have been to appoint a disinterested third party who could have relayed information and worked together with all interested parties. In re Guardianship of Simmons (Ohio App. 6 Dist., Wood, 10-10-2003) No. WD-02-039, 2003-Ohio-5416, 2003 WL 22319415, Unreported. Mental Health ⇌ 118

Prisoner against whom various civil actions were commenced ultimately consented to guardianship over his estate, and thus was precluded from arguing that incarceration alone was insufficient to warrant finding of incompetence, which resulted in finding that guardianship was appropriate; prisoner correctly argued that nothing prevented incarcerated persons from entering into contracts and disposing of property, but this doctrine did not reach prisoners over whom guardianship had been established, and moreover, incarceration was clearly sufficient to warrant finding of incompetence under the statutory definition of "incompetent." In re Guardianship of Goins (Ohio App. 7 Dist., Mahoning, 02-25-2003) No. 02 CA 163, 2003-Ohio-931, 2003 WL 685878, Unreported, appeal not allowed 99 Ohio St.3d 1453, 790 N.E.2d 1218, 2003-Ohio-3396. Convicts ⇌ 3; Guardian And Ward ⇌ 9.5; Guardian And Ward ⇌ 13(8)

Appointment of guardian of estate only is granted where there is clear and convincing evidence that respondent is unable to recall her monthly income and distributions from her checking account and neither understands nor remembers the documents she has signed. In re Guardianship of Stokes (Ohio App. 8 Dist., Cuyahoga, 01-30-1997) No. 70666, 1997 WL 37686, Unreported.

Guardian might be appointed in Ohio, even though the minor had his domicile in some other county or some other state. Langan v. Kessinger (Greene 1936) 23 Ohio Law Abs. 392. Guardian And Ward ⇌ 8

Woman was not entitled to continuance of proceeding to adjudicate her competence and appoint guardian over her person and estate, although she may have been effectively deprived of the opportunity to obtain an independent medical expert of her own choice; right to expert of her own choice was not mandated by statute, woman was examined by her own physician but did not present him as a witness, two prior continuances had been granted, purpose of requested examination was to determine future, not present, competence, and woman did not object to testimony of court-appointed medical expert. In re Guardianship of Thomas (Ohio App. 10 Dist., 03-12-2002) 148 Ohio App.3d 11, 771 N.E.2d 882, 2002-Ohio-1037. Pretrial Procedure ⇌ 717.1

Although advanced age has been removed from statutory definition of incompetency for purposes of appointment of guardian, it can remain consideration. Brown v. Haffey (Ohio App. 8 Dist., 09-06-1994) 96 Ohio App.3d 724, 645 N.E.2d 1295. Mental Health ⇌ 107

Definition of "incompetent" under amendment to Code section allowing appointment of guardian did not allow person to be found incompetent based solely on physical disability; trial court had to find person mentally impaired before person could be found incompetent. In re Bolander (Lake 1993) 88 Ohio App.3d 498, 624 N.E.2d 322. Mental Health ⇌ 105

Finding that person was "incompetent" as result of physical disability contained implicit finding that person was mentally impaired and thus person's consent was not needed to appointment of guardian. In re Bolander (Lake 1993) 88 Ohio App.3d 498, 624 N.E.2d 322. Mental Health ⇌ 104.1; Mental Health ⇌ 143

Guardianship of estate can be appointed over person who is physically disabled only if that disability has rendered person "incompetent," which is defined as mentally impaired. In re Bolander (Lake 1993) 88 Ohio App.3d 498, 624 N.E.2d 322. Mental Health ⇌ 105

RC 2111.02(B)(1) provides for limited guardianship only for minors or incompetent persons, and the appointment of a limited guardian is improper where the trial court did not make a specific finding that the elderly ward was incompetent but referred only to the ward's "incapacity" due to infirmity and need for regular assistance to obtain medical care, live in her own home, and manage her property. In re Guardianship of Rudy (Ohio 1992) 65 Ohio St.3d 394, 604 N.E.2d 736, rehearing denied 65 Ohio St.3d 1482, 604 N.E.2d 759.

Record supported finding that it was in incompetent's best interest to have guardian appointed with power to authorize forced administration of psychotropic drugs, in light of long history of paranoid delusions that, at least, bordered on schizophrenia when patient did not take her medication. In re Guardianship of Willis (Franklin 1991) 74 Ohio App.3d 554, 599 N.E.2d 745. Mental Health ⇌ 51.15; Mental Health ⇌ 155

A judicially declared incompetent ward may not enter into an installment contract and his estate has no obligation to honor the "contract" absent the guardian's ratification. Huntington Natl. Bank v. Toland (Franklin 1991) 71 Ohio App.3d 576, 594 N.E.2d 1103.

Good cause for ordering psychiatric evaluation of proposed ward in guardianship proceeding was not established, for purposes of civil rule providing for ordered examination of mental or physical condition of person that is in controversy; there were only statements of applicant for guardianship that proposed ward had Down's syndrome and that she had been in schools for mentally retarded and was unable to care for herself, there was no evidence of such facts, and good cause for examination could not be found solely on basis of statements in application and in camera arguments of counsel. In re Guardianship of Johnson (Franklin 1987) 35 Ohio App.3d 41, 519 N.E.2d 655. Pretrial Procedure ⇌ 455

Judgment of another state's court to effect that husband, who sought divorce from wife, who had been appointed his guardian, was incompetent was entitled to full faith and credit and thus, trial court could not make its own determination of husband's competency to bring divorce action. Pace v. Pace (Franklin 1986) 32 Ohio App.3d 47, 513 N.E.2d 1357. Judgment ⇌ 815

Probate court, in awarding guardianship of infant to maternal grandparents, had further authority to confer visitation rights on paternal grandparents. In re Zahoransky (Cuyahoga 1985) 22 Ohio App.3d 75, 488 N.E.2d 944, 22 O.B.R. 173. Child Custody ⇌ 284

Trial court's finding that proposed ward was mentally incompetent was not supported by sufficient weight of the evidence, where there was no personal interview of the proposed ward by the court and no medical report. In re Guardianship of Corless (Butler 1981) 2 Ohio App.3d 92, 440 N.E.2d 1203, 2 O.B.R. 104. Mental Health ⇌ 135

Probate court has discretion in appointing guardian over person not mentally able to care for her property. In re Wilson's Guardianship (Perry 1926) 23 Ohio App. 390, 155 N.E. 654, 4 Ohio Law Abs. 348. Mental Health ⇌ 137.1

This section authorizes the appointment of a guardian for the estate of a lunatic, without appointing a guardian of the person. Heckman v. Adams (Ohio 1893) 50 Ohio St. 305, 29 W.L.B. 330, 34 N.E. 155.

The father is natural guardian of his minor child and necessity for appointment of a guardian does not arise except for cause and where the father is shown to be an unsuitable person. Hare v. Sears (Ohio Com.Pl. 1906) 17 Ohio Dec. 590, 4 Ohio N.P.N.S. 566. Guardian And Ward ⇌ 9.5; Child Custody ⇌ 22

A seventy-seven year old woman who manages her household affairs, pays her taxes, insurance and water regularly, attends to market and visits her friends, but has hearing and memory impairment, will not have a guardian appointed for her on the ground that she is an imbecile. In re Shelleig (Ohio Prob. 1900) 11 Ohio Dec. 81, 8 Ohio N.P. 399.

Under RS 6529 and RS 6255, a guardian of the person of a minor can be appointed only where the minor has an estate; where a destitute child lacks support as a result of its parents' vagrancy, negligence, or misconduct the means to its improvement lie not in appointment of a guardian but in proceedings under RS 3140a, on the complaint of some reputable citizen of the county, whereby the child may be placed in an orphans' home while a home with fit and suitable persons is sought. In re Baier (Ohio Com.Pl. 1900) 11 Ohio Dec. 47, 8 Ohio N.P. 107.

If the record in the probate court of the appointment of a guardian of a minor affirmatively shows that such minor is without estate, such appointment is void, and upon habeas corpus the parent will be awarded the custody of the child against the guardian so appointed. In re Baier (Ohio Com.Pl. 1900) 11 Ohio Dec. 47, 8 Ohio N.P. 107.

It is not necessary, to justify the appointment of a guardian, that a person be an absolute imbecile without mind or capacity; a person may be an imbecile though able to govern himself so as not to need a guardian of his person but only his property. In re Emswiler (Ohio Prob. 1900) 11 Ohio Dec. 10, 8 Ohio N.P. 132.

The court must determine the custody of children with a paramount regard to the highest welfare and best interests of the child. In re Minors of Luck, 7 NP 49, 10 D 1 (Prob, Cuyahoga 1899).

A probate court may appoint a guardian for a minor but only if such minor's father and mother are dead or are both unsuitable persons to have the custody or tuition of such minor. Boescher v Boescher, 5 D 184, 7 NP 418 (CP 1895).

To justify the appointment of a guardian for a person as an imbecile, the infirmity of such person must render her incompetent to have charge of any affairs or do any business; mere weakness of mind or memory impairment will not warrant the appointment of a guardian. In re Tempest's Guardian (Ohio Prob. 1889) 21 W.L.B. 301.

The appointment of a guardian of an idiot, lunatic or imbecile is conclusive evidence of the incapacity of the ward to contract or do any binding act in regard to his property in conflict with the authority reposed by law in his guardian, so long as the guardianship continues. In re Dickson (Ohio Prob. 1886) 18 W.L.B. 37.

Ohio statutes provide for appointment by probate court, when found necessary, of a guardian of person or estate of a minor, or of both, who will have care and management of the person or estate of such minor, or both, and that with certain exceptions, a minor over age of fourteen years may select a guardian, who, if a suitable person, shall be appointed; further, a father and a mother have equal rights to the custody of a minor, and a surviving parent may by last will appoint a guardian; there is a distinction between a parent acting as a natural guardian of his minor child with custody of the minor's person and the position of legal guardian appointed by the court for purpose of care and management of the estate of such minor. Chertoff v. C.I.R. (C.C.A.6 1947) 160 F.2d 691, 35 O.O. 399.

The court with jurisdiction to appoint the guardian of an orphaned child is that in the last domicile of the parents. In re Murray, 8 CC(NS) 498, 18 CD 652 (Lorain 1906).

For purposes of RC 3313.64, the term "guardian" must be given a liberal construction, and can include a person who stands in loco parentis to an adult student. OAG 74–076.

The executive secretary of the Lucas county child welfare board may be appointed legal guardian of a minor when said minor's funds, originally deposited under RC 2111.05, have increased to over $1,000 and by accepting the responsibilities of such a guardianship, he is performing the official duties and exercising the powers of his office as set forth in RC 5153.16 and is not entitled to receive guardianship compensation. OAG 68–036.

5. Effect of appointment; termination

An order appointing a guardian cannot be collaterally impeached. Shroyer v. Richmond (Ohio 1866) 16 Ohio St. 455.

Letters of guardianship give no authority until a proper bond has been given. State, for Use of Carpenter v. Sloane (Ohio 1851) 20 Ohio 327.

The power of a guardian is derived from his appointment and giving bond, and letters of guardianship need not necessarily in fact issue. Maxsom v. Sawyer (Ohio 1843) 12 Ohio 195.

Probate court abused its discretion when it appointed corporate fiduciary as guardian of estate of alleged incompetent; probate court specifically acknowledged that alleged incompetent's brother-in-law, who sought appointment as guardian, was familiar with alleged incompetent's estate and that brother-in-law had been assisting his wife, who had been alleged incompetent's sister and conservator, in handling alleged incompetent's accounts, there were no allegations that brother-in-law had mismanaged accounts when helping as conservator, probate court had relied on erroneous excessive valuation of estate in appointing corporate fiduciary as guardian of estate, and corporate fiduciary had not requested to be guardian. In re Guardianship of Poschner (Ohio App. 7 Dist., Mahoning, 09-26-2003) No. 03MA53, 2003-Ohio-5148, 2003 WL 22231711, Unreported, on subsequent appeal 2005-Ohio-2788, 2005 WL 1324748. Guardian And Ward 10

Appellate court would not consider issue of appointment of guardian of incompetent individual's estate, where individual's daughter did not raise the issue in her notice of appeal from judgments finding individual incompetent and substituting guardian of estate as plaintiff in place of daughter. Brady ex rel. Brady v. Benzing (Ohio App. 8 Dist., Cuyahoga, 06-26-2003) No. 81894, 2003-Ohio-3354, 2003 WL 21469584, Unreported, appeal not allowed 100 Ohio St.3d 1487, 798 N.E.2d 1094, 2003-Ohio-5992. Mental Health 148.1

Prisoners may not be subjected to guardianship unless someone moves for appointment and appointment is found necessary. In re Guardianship of Goins (Ohio App. 7 Dist., Mahoning, 02-25-2003) No. 02 CA 163, 2003-Ohio-931, 2003 WL 685878, Unreported, appeal not allowed 99 Ohio St.3d 1453, 790 N.E.2d 1218, 2003-Ohio-3396. Convicts 3; Guardian And Ward 9.5

Trial court acted within its discretion when it scrutinized legal expenses which mother charged against assets of her child's estate, rejected mother's request to settle child's claim to insurance proceeds arising from father's automobile accident for $50,000, and appointed independent guardian to ensure that child received proper settlement, where court noted that $50,000 was significantly less than amount arrived at by applying child's jury award percentage to total settlement amount, and left amount of child's share to be determined by independent guardian subject to court's approval. In re Guardianship of Muehrcke (Ohio App. 8 Dist., Cuyahoga, 01-16-2003) No. 81353, 2003-Ohio-176, 2003 WL 132422, Unreported, appeal not allowed 99 Ohio St.3d 1412, 788 N.E.2d 648, 2003-Ohio-2454. Guardian And Ward 33

Trial court acted within its discretion, and in best interest of child, when court decided that monetary conflict of interest regarding settlement of father's insurance claims rendered mother unsuitable to become guardian of child's estate, where amount child would receive from settlement was inversely proportional to amount mother would receive. In re Guardianship of Muehrcke (Ohio App. 8 Dist., Cuyahoga, 01-16-2003) No. 81353, 2003-Ohio-176, 2003 WL 132422, Unreported, appeal not allowed 99 Ohio St.3d 1412, 788 N.E.2d 648, 2003-Ohio-2454. Guardian And Ward 10

Appointment of a person as guardian, subsequent to the appointment of another guardian by proper authority, who is discharging the duties of his trust, is void, and the subsequently appointed guardian is therefore not entitled to compensation, expenses, or attorney's fees. In re Fox' Estate (Ohio Prob. 1942) 36 Ohio Law Abs. 349. Guardian And Ward 150

A probate court's order appointing a guardian cannot be collaterally impeached, and actions taken by a guardian whose appointment is later successfully challenged are taken under color of law and may be upheld. In re Guardianship of Rudy (Ohio 1992) 65 Ohio St.3d 394, 604 N.E.2d 736, rehearing denied 65 Ohio St.3d 1482, 604 N.E.2d 759.

Denial of motion to terminate guardianship of ward's estate was properly denied where there was ample evidence that ward was not better able to care for her property at time of termination hearing than she was at time guardianship of her estate was established, her vision had worsened, she appeared confused, and she was unable to deal with important aspects of her personal, business, and legal affairs. In re Guardianship of Allen (Ohio 1990) 50 Ohio St.3d 142, 552 N.E.2d 934, rehearing denied 51 Ohio St.3d 705, 555 N.E.2d 322. Mental Health 170

An order appointing a guardian of an incompetent cannot be collaterally attacked. In re Guardianship of Titington (Ohio Prob. 1958) 162 N.E.2d 628, 82 Ohio Law Abs. 563.

In an attempt to terminate the guardianship, under physical disability, the incompetent must prove to the satisfaction of the court that she is now better able to care for her property than at the time of the appointment, or that conditions have changed and that a guardian of her estate is no longer necessary. In re Guardianship of Barr (Ohio Prob. 1958) 156 N.E.2d 357, 80 Ohio Law Abs. 488.

Where a guardian is appointed, the journal entry reciting that notice was given and the consent of the ward obtained, the probate court cannot four years later vacate such order nunc pro tunc upon the ground that such consent was not obtained. In re Gerstenek (Cuyahoga 1956) 139 N.E.2d 64, 76 Ohio Law Abs. 280.

Where a consent to appointment of a guardian was not voluntarily and freely given, the appointment is illegal and an application to dismiss the guardian should be granted. (See also In re Guardianship of Luft, 91 App 409, 97 NE(2d) 561 (1950).) In re Guardianship of Luft (Franklin 1951) 107 N.E.2d 259, 62 Ohio Law Abs. 157.

A guardianship should be terminated where it is disclosed that the ward's consent to the guardian's appointment was given under an apparent misapprehension of the ward's rights; in such a proceeding it is discretionary with the court to permit the guardian to contest his removal by entering an appearance, introducing evidence and cross-examining witnesses. In re Luft's Guardianship (Franklin 1950) 91 Ohio App. 409, 97 N.E.2d 561, 59 Ohio Law Abs. 33, 45 O.O. 333.

The appointment of a guardian of the person and estate of an habitual drunkard is only prima facie and not conclusive evidence of a lack of capacity to enter into and consummate a legal marriage. McCleary v. Barcalow (Ohio Cir. 1891) 3 Ohio C.D. 547.

The chief object to be attained by the appointment of a guardian for a minor is the welfare of the child. State ex rel. Fisher v. Madden (Ohio Com.Pl. 1901) 12 Ohio Dec. 83.

Where the guardian of an adjudged incompetent adult has been accused of accepting a low settlement of her ward's medical malpractice claim out of greed and subsequently such guardian resigns as guardian of her ward's estate, the court may properly refuse to appoint a new guardian where the ward's sole assets consist of pending claims which appear to be less than $10,000 and the former guardian can adequately represent the ward in the pending lawsuits as "next friend" pursuant to Civ R 17(B). In re Mihal, No. 45828 (8th Dist Ct App, Cuyahoga, 7–14–83).

6. Residence

Probate court of county in which prisoner resided prior to incarceration was entitled to institute guardianship proceedings against him, even though the prisoner was currently incarcerated elsewhere; incarceration did not change residence, and because there was always the possibility of obtaining reversal of his conviction or sentence, the prisoner was not necessarily prevented from forming intent to return to his residence. In re Guardianship of Goins (Ohio App. 7 Dist., Mahoning, 02-25-2003) No. 02 CA 163, 2003-Ohio-931, 2003 WL 685878, Unreported, appeal not allowed 99 Ohio St.3d 1453, 790 N.E.2d 1218, 2003-Ohio-3396. Convicts ⚖ 3; Guardian And Ward ⚖ 8

For purposes of guardianship statute, which allows probate court to appoint guardian for ward who resides in county in which court sits or had a legal settlement in county, "residence" requires the actual physical presence at some abode coupled with an intent to remain at that place for some period of time. In re Guardianship of Replogle (Ohio App. 2 Dist., 10-14-2005) 2005-Ohio-5530, 2005 WL 2660550. Mental Health ⚖ 110

Statute authorizing probate court to appoint a guardian prevents a court from providing a guardian for a ward who does not reside or have a legal settlement in the county in which the court sits. In re Guardianship of Replogle (Ohio App. 2 Dist., 10-14-2005) 2005-Ohio-5530, 2005 WL 2660550. Mental Health ⚖ 110

Proposed guardian failed to clearly establish that ward resided or had legal settlement in county in which probate court sat, as would support conclusion that court lacked jurisdiction to appoint a guardian, although there was evidence that ward had been in care facility located in county for approximately five months; evidence indicated the possibility that ward's Indiana guardian moved ward to Ohio solely for purpose of avoiding termination of her status as guardian in Indiana. In re Guardianship of Replogle (Ohio App. 2 Dist., 10-14-2005) 2005-Ohio-5530, 2005 WL 2660550. Mental Health ⚖ 110

Infant hospitalized within county on 24–hour, seven-day-per-week basis, while in persistent vegetative state, was a resident of that county, for purposes of statute giving probate court jurisdiction to appoint a guardian who resides in the county in which the infant resides. (Per Lundberg Stratton, J., with two Justices concurring and two Justices concurring separately.) In re Guardianship of Stein (Ohio, 12-30-2004) 105 Ohio St.3d 30, 821 N.E.2d 1008, 2004-Ohio-7114. Guardian And Ward ⚖ 8

For purposes of statute precluding court from providing guardian for ward who does not reside or have a legal settlement in the county, term "legal settlement" connotes one living in an area with some degree of permanency greater than a visit lasting a few days or weeks. State ex rel. Florence v. Zitter (Ohio, 08-10-2005) 106 Ohio St.3d 87, 831 N.E.2d 1003, 2005-Ohio-3804. Mental Health ⚖ 110

"Residence," for purposes of statute precluding court from providing guardian for a ward who does not reside or have a legal settlement in the county, requires the actual physical presence at some abode coupled with an intent to remain at that place for some period of time. State ex rel. Florence v. Zitter (Ohio, 08-10-2005) 106 Ohio St.3d 87, 831 N.E.2d 1003, 2005-Ohio-3804. Mental Health ⚖ 110

"Residence," for purposes of statute precluding court from providing guardian for a ward who does not reside or have a legal settlement in the county, requires actual physical presence at some abode coupled with an intent to remain at that place for some period of time. In re Guardianship of Fisher (Ohio App. 3 Dist., 10-20-1993) 91 Ohio App.3d 212, 632 N.E.2d 533. Mental Health ⚖ 110

For purposes of statute precluding court from providing guardian for ward who does not reside or have a legal settlement in the county, term "legal settlement" connotes one living in an area with some degree of permanency greater than a visit lasting a few days or weeks. In re Guardianship of Fisher (Ohio App. 3 Dist., 10-20-1993) 91 Ohio App.3d 212, 632 N.E.2d 533. Mental Health ⚖ 110

Ward was resident of or had legal settlement in county for purpose of statute governing appointment of guardian, though ward was placed in out-of-county facilities by order of probate court after being deemed incompetent; ward expressed desire and intent to return to home in county and was physically present at home in county on regular basis. In re Tripp (Ohio App. 6 Dist., 09-10-1993) 90 Ohio App.3d 209, 628 N.E.2d 139. Mental Health ⚖ 110

For a county to exercise jurisdictional power over the appointment of a guardian the proposed ward must actually dwell or have a legal settlement in that county; where a proposed ward is a resident of a particular county when guardianship proceedings are begun, that county's probate court has sole, exclusive jurisdiction to appoint a guardian. Le Sueur v. Robinson (Fulton 1988) 53 Ohio App.3d 9, 557 N.E.2d 796, motion overruled 39 Ohio St.3d 725, 534 N.E.2d 357.

Court will refuse to appoint older sister as guardian of her younger sister where the sole purpose of the action is to qualify the younger child as a resident of the older sister's community for the purpose of school attendance. In re DiSalvo (Ohio Prob. 1967) 11 Ohio Misc. 259, 227 N.E.2d 441, 40 O.O.2d 523.

A decree of guardianship of a minor resident of Ohio by a court in the state where the child has a technical domicile, which decree is made without personal service on either the child or the person with whom the child is living, is not entitled to such faith and credit as will nullify the prior appointment of a guardian of such minor by the probate court of the county of his residence. In re Fore (Ohio 1958) 168 Ohio St. 363, 155 N.E.2d 194, 7 O.O.2d 127, appeal dismissed, certiorari denied 79 S.Ct. 878, 359 U.S. 313, 3 L.Ed.2d 831. Judgment ⚖ 818(2)

Where there is no existing award of custody of an orphaned minor resident of Ohio by a foreign court, the probate court of the county of such residence has jurisdiction to appoint a guardian of the minor, irrespective of the fact that the domicile of such minor may be in another state. In re Fore (Ohio 1958) 168 Ohio St. 363, 155 N.E.2d 194, 7 O.O.2d 127, appeal dismissed, certiorari denied 79 S.Ct. 878, 359 U.S. 313, 3 L.Ed.2d 831. Guardian And Ward ⚖ 8

Where both parents of a child were killed in a common disaster in France and the maternal aunt brought such child to Ohio, and a paternal grandparent has obtained the right of "tutorship" from a Louisiana court in the parish of the grandmother's and hence the child's domicile, the Ohio courts have no authority to grant letters of guardianship to the maternal aunt. Petition of Fore (Cuyahoga 1958) 151 N.E.2d 777, 79 Ohio Law Abs. 15, reversed 168 Ohio St. 363, 155 N.E.2d 194, 7 O.O.2d 127, appeal dismissed, certiorari denied 79 S.Ct. 878, 359 U.S. 313, 3 L.Ed.2d 831.

A probate court cannot appoint a guardian for an idiot unless the idiot has resided within its county of jurisdiction for twelve consecutive months or has come into the county with some person having legal control over him with the intention of making such county his residence. In re Canady (Ohio Prob. 1898) 7 Ohio Dec. 285, 4 Ohio N.P. 403.

Where lack of facilities in Wood County in which mentally disabled woman's home was located required that she be placed in out-of-county facilities, and evidence shows woman stayed overnight at her residence on a one weekend per month basis, court found that woman was resident of or had legal settlement in Wood County for jurisdictional requirements of RC 2111.02(A), and probate court of Wood County had authority to appoint guardian of woman and her estate. In re Tripp, No. 93WD–58, 1993 WL 342598 (6th Dist Ct App, Wood, 9–10–93).

Where a party, released from a hospital, is unable to return to her home because it is being repaired and instead resides in another county for a few days before being admitted into a nursing home, such party's few days residence in the second county does not give the probate court jurisdiction to rule on an application for guardianship over the party since such party is neither a resident of the second county nor does she have a legal settlement there. In re Guardianship of Rawlins, No. 9–82–47 (3d Dist Ct App, Marion, 6–7–83).

A student who has reached the age of eighteen is entitled to attend school free in the district of his parents' or guardian's actual residence, or, if he works to support himself by his own labor, in the district in which he is employed. OAG 74–076.

7. Jurisdiction

Appointing a guardian is a proceeding in rem and the actual presence of the ward is not necessary for jurisdiction. Shroyer v. Richmond (Ohio 1866) 16 Ohio St. 455.

Note 7

Plenary and exclusive original jurisdiction is given to probate courts to appoint guardians and jurisdiction attaches whenever application is duly made. Shroyer v. Richmond (Ohio 1866) 16 Ohio St. 455.

The probate court lacked subject matter jurisdiction to enter order overruling its motion to vacate and ordering removal of guardian; guardian was appointed to file a complaint for personal injuries for ward due to the ward's minority, ward had turned 18 years of age before the probate court entered its order, and there was no finding in the record that ward was incompetent. In re Guardianship of Hollins (Ohio App. 8 Dist., Cuyahoga, 03-30-2006) No. 86412, No. 86574, 2006-Ohio-1543, 2006 WL 825389, Unreported. Guardian And Ward ⚖ 25

Juvenile court's dismissal of father's motion for visitation for lack of jurisdiction based on probate court's having taken prior jurisdiction of such questions in maternal grandparents' guardianship proceeding was not error and did not deny father due process to assert his parentage rights; probate court's plenary power over guardianship proceeding extended to visitation issues, as visitation rights fell within range of matters "touching the guardianship." In re Hoke (Ohio App. 10 Dist., Franklin, 09-04-2003) No. 02AP-1398, 2003-Ohio-4704, 2003 WL 22064121, Unreported. Constitutional Law ⚖ 274(5); Courts ⚖ 475(6); Guardian And Ward ⚖ 8

In Ohio action to appoint guardian, trial court acted within its discretion in finding that Indiana, which was where ward's guardianship had been pending for years, was more convenient forum than Ohio, and thus court's decision to decline to exercise jurisdiction over matter was warranted; Indiana guardian's decision to move ward to Ohio appeared to be attempt to circumvent proceedings in Indiana court relating to effort to remove Indiana guardian upon allegations of abuse. In re Guardianship of Replogle (Ohio App. 2 Dist., 10-14-2005) 2005-Ohio-5530, 2005 WL 2660550. Courts ⚖ 28

Mother, whose sons applied for appointment of guardian for her, was not entitled to writ of prohibition to prevent probate judge from exercising jurisdiction over guardianship case; although mother claimed that judge patently and unambiguously lacked jurisdiction over guardianship case since she was neither resident of nor had legal settlement in county at time that case commenced, statute precluding court from providing guardian for ward who did not reside or have legal settlement in county did not patently and unambiguously divest judge of jurisdiction over guardianship case, and mother had adequate remedy by way of appeal following final judgment to raise her claims. State ex rel. Florence v. Zitter (Ohio, 08-10-2005) 106 Ohio St.3d 87, 831 N.E.2d 1003, 2005-Ohio-3804. Prohibition ⚖ 10(2)

Where a probate court appoints a guardian for a minor child, the probate court retains continuing and exclusive jurisdiction over the ward and the guardian; thus, a juvenile court is without jurisdiction to grant custody of the ward to another person until the guardianship has been terminated. In re Miller (Cuyahoga 1986) 33 Ohio App.3d 224, 515 N.E.2d 635.

Where the application filed and notice served upon a ward in a guardianship proceeding sought the appointment of the applicant or some other interested person as guardian and then during the time the application was before the court it was withdrawn and the application of another applicant granted, the court had jurisdiction to appoint such latter applicant. In re Gerstenek (Cuyahoga 1956) 139 N.E.2d 64, 76 Ohio Law Abs. 280.

Once a probate court properly appoints a guardian for a minor, exclusive, continuing jurisdiction upon matters of custody remain in that court, even though the minor has his domicile in some other county or state. Weigel v. Grossnickle (Clermont 1954) 100 Ohio App. 106, 135 N.E.2d 894, 60 O.O. 66.

The probate court has exclusive original jurisdiction under RS 524 and RS 6254 to appoint and remove guardians, and the orders of that court in such proceedings are not subject to collateral attack. State ex rel. Fisher v. Madden (Ohio Com.Pl. 1901) 12 Ohio Dec. 83.

8. Evidence

Evidence supported trial court's finding that mental health patient was incompetent and that appointment of guardian was warranted; although patient had some success living alone, doctor testified that patient suffered from schizophrenia and could not care for herself without help, patient had long history of not complying with treatment needs, and patient's resistance to taking medication repeatedly resulted in lengthy hospitalization. In re Guardianship of Ryan (Ohio App. 5 Dist., Ashland, 12-10-2004) No. 2004-COA-016, 2004-Ohio-6709, 2004 WL 2891933, Unreported. Mental Health ⚖ 105; Mental Health ⚖ 135

Magistrate's decision in guardianship proceeding set forth sufficient facts on which probate court could make meaningful independent analysis in appointing guardian of estate of alleged incompetent; alleged incompetent's brother-in-law, who sought appointment as guardian, was 80 years old, he frequently visited alleged incompetent and was familiar with alleged incompetent's accounts as result of helping his wife, who was alleged incompetent's sister and conservator, with alleged incompetent's accounts, and magistrate determined that estate was valued at close to $2 million. In re Guardianship of Poschner (Ohio App. 7 Dist., Mahoning, 09-26-2003) No. 03MA53, 2003-Ohio-5148, 2003 WL 22231711, Unreported, on subsequent appeal 2005-Ohio-2788, 2005 WL 1324748. Guardian And Ward ⚖ 13(7)

Awarding guardianship of mentally ill hospital patient to a registered volunteer guardian rather than to patient's mother was not plain error, where court investigator's report indicated concerns pertaining to mother's ability to care for patient's health and mental needs, mother clandestinely provided prohibited food to patient despite his need for pureed food, she was disruptive and interfered with patient's care to the extent that a behavior contract was executed between herself and hospital, she minimized or withheld pertinent information regarding patient's alcohol, drug and violence issues, and guardianship statute did not provide a preference for natural parents. In re Guardianship of Koenig (Ohio App. 8 Dist., Cuyahoga, 04-03-2003) No. 81462, 2003-Ohio-1727, 2003 WL 1759603, Unreported. Mental Health ⚖ 156

Prisoner against whom various civil actions were commenced, which prompted trial court to impose guardianship over his estate, presented no evidence that less restrictive alternatives were available, and thus the trial court was not required to explore alternatives to guardianship; prisoner merely argued that his capacity to contract and dispose of property was undiminished by his incarceration. In re Guardianship of Goins (Ohio App. 7 Dist., Mahoning, 02-25-2003) No. 02 CA 163, 2003-Ohio-931, 2003 WL 685878, Unreported, appeal not allowed 99 Ohio St.3d 1453, 790 N.E.2d 1218, 2003-Ohio-3396. Convicts ⚖ 3; Guardian And Ward ⚖ 9.5

Evidence concerning the deplorable condition of a person's residence justifies a finding of incompetency and the appointment of a guardian based upon (1) refuse strewn throughout the home, (2) animal feces, insect infestations and rodents, (3) a fire hazard created by full and empty containers of kerosene, and (4) electricity that does not work. Davis v. Cuyahoga County Adult Protective Services (Ohio App. 8 Dist., Cuyahoga, 10-12-2000) No. 77116, 2000 WL 1513752, Unreported.

A judgment of incompetency and appointment of a guardian are supported by evidence in the case of a person who (1) is ninety years old, (2) suffers from leukemia, (3) is unable to administer his own medication properly, and (4) has short-term memory loss which manifests itself in ways that could result in serious harm to himself. Matter of Guardianship of Worth (Ohio App. 2 Dist., Darke, 06-20-1997) No. 1430, 1997 WL 335559, Unreported.

The court may appoint the grandfather, rather than the father, as guardian of a minor's estate when there is evidence that the grandfather would act in the child's best interest, the grandfather has a demonstrated ability in the management of the financial affairs of the estate in question, and evidence indicates the father is unacquainted with the child's assets. In re Estate of Bednarczuk (Warren 1992) 80 Ohio App.3d 548, 609 N.E.2d 1310, motion overruled 65 Ohio St.3d 1444, 600 N.E.2d 686.

The probate court's finding of "incapacity," based on an elderly and infirm ward's need for regular assistance to obtain medical care, live in her own home, and manage her property, cannot substitute for the finding of incompetence required for appointment of a limited guardian under RC 2111.02(B)(1), and while the court of appeals may review findings of fact for an abuse of discretion, it cannot make a finding of fact which should have been made by the trial court nor extract such finding from the trial court's opinion when no finding was made. In re Guardianship of Rudy (Ohio 1992) 65 Ohio St.3d 394, 604 N.E.2d 736, rehearing denied 65 Ohio St.3d 1482, 604 N.E.2d 759.

A probate court will not appoint guardians for the sole purpose to continue or withhold life-sustaining treatment; in the absence of advance directives the administration or the withdrawal of life-sustaining treatment should be based on medical expertise, consistent with the patient's wishes, as they are expressed by family members. In re Guardianship of McInnis (Ohio Prob. 1991) 61 Ohio Misc.2d 790, 584 N.E.2d 1389. Health ⚖ 915

The required degree of proof of mental incompetency is by clear and convincing evidence. In re Guardianship of Gallagher (Madison 1981) 2 Ohio App.3d 218, 441 N.E.2d 593, 2 O.B.R. 238. Mental Health ⚖ 135

Under section a guardian may be appointed for an alleged incompetent who objects to such appointment, only if in fact he is incompetent because of mental disability or infirmity. Jacobs v. Porter (Franklin 1941) 73 Ohio App. 286, 43 N.E.2d 879, 36 Ohio Law Abs. 282, 28 O.O. 449.

In any guardianship matter probate court has two things to determine: first, whether there are circumstances or conditions or both which would justify the appointment of a guardian, and second, whether a guardianship is necessary even though those circumstances or conditions exist. In re Joyce (Ohio Prob. 1940) 5 Ohio Supp. 16, 32 Ohio Law Abs. 553, 19 O.O. 506. Guardian And Ward ⇔ 13(1)

9. Selection of guardian

Statute governing appointment of a guardian creates no preference for the prospective ward's next of kin, nor does statute require their approval before a person who is not a next of kin files an application. In re Guardianship of Lee (Ohio App. 2 Dist., Miami, 11-15-2002) No. 02CA3, 2002-Ohio-6194, 2002 WL 31528725, Unreported. Guardian And Ward ⇔ 10

Statute governing appointment of persons to administer the estate of a decedent creates a preference for appointment of next of kin, however, it has no application to appointment of a guardian. In re Guardianship of Lee (Ohio App. 2 Dist., Miami, 11-15-2002) No. 02CA3, 2002-Ohio-6194, 2002 WL 31528725, Unreported. Executors And Administrators ⇔ 17(2); Guardian And Ward ⇔ 10

2111.021 Conservatorship

A competent adult who is physically infirm may petition the probate court of the county in which he resides, to place, for a definite or indefinite period of time, his person, any or all of his real or personal property, or both under a conservatorship with the court. A petitioner either may grant specific powers to the conservator or court or may limit any powers granted by law to the conservator or court, except that the petitioner may not limit the powers granted to the court by this section and may not limit the requirement for bond as determined by the court. The petition shall state whether the person of the competent adult will be placed under the conservatorship, shall state with particularity all real and personal property that will be placed under the conservatorship, shall state the powers granted and any limitation upon the powers of the conservator or court, and shall state the name of a proposed suitable conservator.

After a hearing, if the court finds that the petition was voluntarily filed and that the proposed conservator is suitable, the court shall issue an order of conservatorship. Upon issuance of the order, all sections of the Revised Code governing a guardianship of the person, the estate, or both, whichever is involved, except those sections the application of which specifically is limited by the petitioner, and all rules and procedures governing such a guardianship, shall apply to the conservatorship, including, but not limited to, applicable bond and accounting requirements.

A conservatorship shall terminate upon a judicial determination of incompetency, the death of the petitioner, the order of the probate court, or the execution of a written termination notice by the petitioner. A termination notice shall take effect upon execution by the petitioner, and shall be filed with the court and served upon the conservator. A termination notice executed by a petitioner relative to a conservatorship of the estate and the termination of a conservatorship of the estate based upon a termination notice are void unless the termination notice is filed with the court within fourteen days after its execution. Modification of the powers of a conservator or the court may be made by the petitioner upon motion to the court at any time during the conservatorship. Neither the establishment of a conservatorship nor the filing of a petition for conservatorship with the probate court shall be considered as evidence of mental impairment under section 2111.01 of the Revised Code.

Upon motion to the probate court and a showing of good cause, the court may make confidential, or remove from confidential status, any file, record, petition, motion, account, or paper, except for an index, docket, or journal, that pertains to a conservatorship and that is in the possession of the court.

(1989 S 46, eff. 1–1–90)

Library References

Guardian and Ward ⇔13.
Mental Health ⇔120 to 143.
Westlaw Topic Nos. 196, 257A.
C.J.S. Mental Health §§ 130 to 139.

Research References

Encyclopedias

OH Jur. 3d Guardian & Ward § 10, Definitions and Types of Guardians—Conservatorships.
OH Jur. 3d Guardian & Ward § 40, Application for a Conservator.

Treatises and Practice Aids

Carlin, Baldwin's Ohio Practice, Merrick-Rippner Probate Law § 62:1, Appointment of Guardian—Definitions—Incompetent.
Carlin, Baldwin's Ohio Practice, Merrick-Rippner Probate Law § 62:8, Appointment of Guardian—Definitions—Conservator.
Carlin, Baldwin's Ohio Practice, Merrick-Rippner Probate Law § 62:45, Guardianship Proceedings—Role of Physician or Investigators.
Carlin, Baldwin's Ohio Practice, Merrick-Rippner Probate Law § 62:63, Conservatorship.
Carlin, Baldwin's Ohio Practice, Merrick-Rippner Probate Law § 62:94, Application for Appointment of Conservator—Form.
Carlin, Baldwin's Ohio Practice, Merrick-Rippner Probate Law § 62:95, Judgment Entry for Appointment of Conservator—Form.
Carlin, Baldwin's Ohio Practice, Merrick-Rippner Probate Law § 66:14, Termination of Conservatorship.
Carlin, Baldwin's Ohio Practice, Merrick-Rippner Probate Law App B SPF 20.0, Application for Appointment of Conservator.
Carlin, Baldwin's Ohio Practice, Merrick-Rippner Probate Law App B SPF 20.1, Judgment Entry—Appointment of Conservator.

Notes of Decisions

Competent adult ward's powers 3
Conservatorship and guardianship distinguished 1
Jurisdiction 4
Procedural issues 2

---

1. Conservatorship and guardianship distinguished

Although the conservator of a physically infirm but competent adult ward stands in a fiduciary relationship with the ward, the obligations imposed are not the same as those imposed on guardians. Miebach v. Mathias (Ohio Com.Pl., 04-01-1998) 91 Ohio Misc.2d 72, 697 N.E.2d 297. Mental Health ⇔ 217

2. Procedural issues

Conservator's payment of expert witness fees out of conservatorship funds, pursuant to clause in application for appointment of conservator providing for payment of attorney fees and costs to private attorneys to represent conservatee in pending criminal cases, was proper. In re Conservatorship of Ahmed (Ohio App. 7 Dist., Belmont, 06-16-2003) No. 01 BA 13, No. 01 BA 48, 2003-Ohio-3272, 2003 WL 21442314, Unreported, stay denied 99 Ohio St.3d 1540, 795 N.E.2d 680, 2003-Ohio-4671, appeal not allowed 100 Ohio St.3d 1433, 797 N.E.2d 512, 2003-Ohio-5396, reconsideration denied 100 Ohio St.3d 1511, 799 N.E.2d 188, 2003-Ohio-6161, motion denied 100 Ohio St.3d 1526, 100 Ohio St.3d 1527, 800 N.E.2d 44, 2003-Ohio-6510. Guardian And Ward ⇔ 58

Probate court had authority to terminate conservatorship on motion of conservator and allow depletion of the conservatorship funds through payments to various individuals. In re Conservatorship of Ahmed (Ohio App. 7 Dist., Belmont, 06-16-2003) No. 01 BA 13, No. 01 BA 48, 2003-Ohio-3272, 2003 WL 21442314, Unreported, stay denied 99 Ohio St.3d 1540, 795 N.E.2d 680, 2003-Ohio-4671, appeal not allowed 100 Ohio St.3d 1433, 797 N.E.2d 512, 2003-Ohio-5396, reconsideration denied 100 Ohio St.3d 1511, 799 N.E.2d 188, 2003-Ohio-6161, motion denied 100 Ohio St.3d 1526, 100 Ohio St.3d 1527, 800 N.E.2d 44, 2003-Ohio-6510. Guardian And Ward ⇔ 25; Guardian And Ward ⇔ 58

Absent indication that notice of termination was filed within 14 days of execution, conservatee's notice of termination of voluntary conservatorship was void. In re Conservatorship of Ahmed (Ohio App. 7 Dist., Belmont,

2111.021
Note 2

06-16-2003) No. 01 BA 13, No. 01 BA 48, 2003-Ohio-3272, 2003 WL 21442314, Unreported, stay denied 99 Ohio St.3d 1540, 795 N.E.2d 680, 2003-Ohio-4671, appeal not allowed 100 Ohio St.3d 1433, 797 N.E.2d 512, 2003-Ohio-5396, reconsideration denied 100 Ohio St.3d 1511, 799 N.E.2d 188, 2003-Ohio-6161, motion denied 100 Ohio St.3d 1526, 100 Ohio St.3d 1527, 800 N.E.2d 44, 2003-Ohio-6510. Guardian And Ward ⊙— 25

Conservatee's failure to appeal from order refusing to terminate conservatorship and granting fees to conservator waived any arguments surrounding deficiencies in initial establishment of conservatorship, the failure to terminate conservatorship upon conservator's letter and written motion, the $700 payment to attorney, and the allowance of various fees to the conservator. In re Conservatorship of Ahmed (Ohio App. 7 Dist., Belmont, 06-16-2003) No. 01 BA 13, No. 01 BA 48, 2003-Ohio-3272, 2003 WL 21442314, Unreported, stay denied 99 Ohio St.3d 1540, 795 N.E.2d 680, 2003-Ohio-4671, appeal not allowed 100 Ohio St.3d 1433, 797 N.E.2d 512, 2003-Ohio-5396, reconsideration denied 100 Ohio St.3d 1511, 799 N.E.2d 188, 2003-Ohio-6161, motion denied 100 Ohio St.3d 1526, 100 Ohio St.3d 1527, 800 N.E.2d 44, 2003-Ohio-6510. Guardian And Ward ⊙— 161

Whether a physically infirm but competent adult ward of a conservatorship authorized the conservator's disbursements of the ward's assets for the conservator's own benefit presented a fact question that could not be decided by summary judgment, in an action by the ward's children against the conservator for breach of fiduciary duty. Miebach v. Mathias (Ohio Com.Pl., 04-01-1998) 91 Ohio Misc.2d 72, 697 N.E.2d 297. Judgment ⊙— 181(15.1)

3. Competent adult ward's powers

Physically infirm but competent adult ward of a conservatorship may request or authorize the conservator to make specific transactions falling with the scope of the conservatorship. Miebach v. Mathias (Ohio Com.Pl., 04-01-1998) 91 Ohio Misc.2d 72, 697 N.E.2d 297. Mental Health ⊙— 217

4. Jurisdiction

Trial court did not exceed its territorial jurisdiction in appointing conservator over funds located in financial institutions outside of county. In re Conservatorship of Ahmed (Ohio App. 7 Dist., Belmont, 06-16-2003) No. 01 BA 13, No. 01 BA 48, 2003-Ohio-3272, 2003 WL 21442314, Unreported, stay denied 99 Ohio St.3d 1540, 795 N.E.2d 680, 2003-Ohio-4671, appeal not allowed 100 Ohio St.3d 1433, 797 N.E.2d 512, 2003-Ohio-5396, reconsideration denied 100 Ohio St.3d 1511, 799 N.E.2d 188, 2003-Ohio-6161, motion denied 100 Ohio St.3d 1526, 100 Ohio St.3d 1527, 800 N.E.2d 44, 2003-Ohio-6510. Guardian And Ward ⊙— 8

2111.03 Application for appointment of guardian

A person applying for appointment as a guardian, including, but not limited to, as a limited guardian, pursuant to section 2111.02 of the Revised Code, shall file with the probate court an application that contains a statement of the whole estate of the ward, its probable value, and the probable annual rents of the ward's real property, and that also contains the following:

(A) A statement whether the applicant ever has been charged with or convicted of any crime involving theft, physical violence, or sexual, alcohol, or substance abuse, and, if the applicant has been so charged or convicted, the date and place of each charge and each conviction;

(B) A statement whether a limited guardianship is sought and, if sought, a specification of the limited powers that are requested and a statement whether the limited guardianship is to be for a definite or indefinite period;

(C) In the case of an application for the appointment of a guardian of a minor, all of the following:

(1) Name, age, and residence of the minor;

(2) Name and residence of each parent of the minor;

(3) Name, degree of kinship, age, and address of next of kin of the minor, if no parent is living or if a parent of the minor is absent, under disability, or for other reason cannot be notified;

(4) Name and residence address of the person having custody of the minor.

(D) In the case of an application for the appointment of a guardian of an alleged incompetent, all of the following:

(1) Name, age, and residence of the person for whom such appointment is sought;

(2) Facts upon which the application is based;

(3) Name, degree of kinship, age, and address of the next of kin of the alleged incompetent.

The court, on its own motion, shall proceed as provided in this chapter, upon suggestion by the bureau of workers' compensation that any person who has made application for or been awarded compensation or death benefits as an employee or the dependent of a killed employee is a minor or incompetent. In that case, no application need be filed and the bureau shall furnish the court with the name and residence of such person and the name, degree of kinship, age, and address of the father, mother, or next of kin of such person insofar as known by the bureau.

(1992 H 427, eff. 10–8–92; 1989 H 222, S 46; 129 v 1448; 1953 H 1; GC 10507–3)

Historical and Statutory Notes

Pre–1953 H 1 Amendments: 115 v 424; 114 v 424

Cross References

Appointment of fiduciary, acceptance of duties, 2109.02

Library References

Guardian and Ward ⊙—13(3).
Mental Health ⊙—126.
Westlaw Topic Nos. 196, 257A.
C.J.S. Mental Health § 133.
  Baldwin's Ohio Legislative Service, 1989 Laws of Ohio, H 222—LSC Analysis, p 5–832

Research References

Encyclopedias
  OH Jur. 3d Guardian & Ward § 38, Application for Appointment by Interested Person.
  OH Jur. 3d Guardian & Ward § 39, Application for Appointment by Interested Person—on Motion of Court.

Treatises and Practice Aids
Carlin, Baldwin's Ohio Practice, Merrick-Rippner Probate Law § 62:15, Appointment of Guardian—Application—Venue.
Carlin, Baldwin's Ohio Practice, Merrick-Rippner Probate Law § 62:17, Appointment of Guardian—Application—Contents.
Carlin, Baldwin's Ohio Practice, Merrick-Rippner Probate Law § 62:45, Guardianship Proceedings—Role of Physician or Investigators.
Carlin, Baldwin's Ohio Practice, Merrick-Rippner Probate Law § 62:81, Application for Appointment of Guardian of Minor—Form.
Carlin, Baldwin's Ohio Practice, Merrick-Rippner Probate Law § 62:82, Next of Kin in Guardianship—Form.
Carlin, Baldwin's Ohio Practice, Merrick-Rippner Probate Law § 62:84, Entry Setting Application for Hearing and Ordering Notice—Form.
Carlin, Baldwin's Ohio Practice, Merrick-Rippner Probate Law § 62:86, Entry for Appointment of Guardian and Fixing Bond—Form.
Carlin, Baldwin's Ohio Practice, Merrick-Rippner Probate Law § 62:91, Entry Approving Bond and Ordering Letters of Guardianship for Minor—Form.
Carlin, Baldwin's Ohio Practice, Merrick-Rippner Probate Law App B SPF 16.0, Application for Appointment of Guardian of Minor.
Carlin, Baldwin's Ohio Practice, Merrick-Rippner Probate Law App B SPF 17.0, Application for Appointment of Guardian (An Alleged Incompetent).

Law Review and Journal Commentaries

Guardianship and the Elderly: Oversight Not Overlooked, Norman Fell. 25 U Tol L Rev 189 (1994).

Guardianship of Adults with Mental Retardation: Towards a Presumption of Competence, Comment. 14 Akron L Rev 321 (Fall 1980).

Notes of Decisions

Application requirements 2
Procedural issues 1

---

1. Procedural issues

Under guardianship statutes, probate court has jurisdiction in appointment and control of guardians which extends to all matters touching guardianship, including custody of minor and visitation rights of third parties. In re Zahoransky (Cuyahoga 1985) 22 Ohio App.3d 75, 488 N.E.2d 944, 22 O.B.R. 173. Guardian And Ward ⟐ 8

A party seeking appointment as successor guardian of an incompetent does not have standing to file an affidavit of bias and prejudice against a probate judge. In re Guardianship of Hill (Ohio Prob. 1963) 196 N.E.2d 816, 93 Ohio Law Abs. 237, 29 O.O.2d 60.

A proceeding for the appointment of a guardian is not an ordinary civil proceeding in which there is a party plaintiff and a party defendant, but rather the proceeding is essentially one in the nature of a declaratory judgment; and no pleadings are provided for except that section provides that the application for appointment shall contain allegations of certain facts. In re Joyce (Ohio Prob. 1940) 5 Ohio Supp. 16, 32 Ohio Law Abs. 553, 19 O.O. 506.

2. Application requirements

Where two applications for the appointment of a guardian, neither of which was complete, but which were complete when considered together, were filed as one instrument, it was proper for the court to treat them as a valid application. Guardianship of Kollmeyer (Darke 1952) 113 N.E.2d 122, 64 Ohio Law Abs. 577, 64 Ohio Law Abs. 578.

2111.031 Appointment of physicians or others to examine alleged incompetent

In connection with an application for the appointment of a guardian for an alleged incompetent, the court may appoint physicians and other qualified persons to examine, investigate, or represent the alleged incompetent, to assist the court in deciding whether a guardianship is necessary. If the person is determined to be an incompetent and a guardian is appointed for him, the costs, fees, or expenses incurred to so assist the court shall be charged either against the estate of the person or against the applicant, unless the court determines, for good cause shown, that the costs, fees, or expenses are to be recovered from the county, in which case they shall be charged against the county. If the person is not determined to be an incompetent or a guardian is not appointed for him, the costs, fees, or expenses incurred to so assist the court shall be charged against the applicant, unless the court determines, for good cause shown, that the costs, fees, or expenses are to be recovered from the county, in which case they shall be charged against the county.

A court may require the applicant to make an advance deposit of an amount that the court determines is necessary to defray the anticipated costs of examinations of an alleged incompetent and to cover fees or expenses to be incurred to assist it in deciding whether a guardianship is necessary.

This section does not affect or apply to the duties of a probate court investigator under sections 2111.04 and 2111.041 of the Revised Code.

(1989 S 46, eff. 1–1–90; 1984 H 263)

Library References

Guardian and Ward ⟐13(1).
Mental Health ⟐120, 123, 158.
Westlaw Topic Nos. 196, 257A.
C.J.S. Mental Health §§ 130 to 132.

Research References

Encyclopedias
OH Jur. 3d Guardian & Ward § 53, Application for Guardian for Incompetent—Investigation of Circumstances of an Alleged Incompetent.
OH Jur. 3d Mandamus, Procedendo, & Prohibition § 183, Effect of Patent and Unambiguous Lack of Jurisdiction.

Treatises and Practice Aids
Carlin, Baldwin's Ohio Practice, Merrick-Rippner Probate Law § 62:17, Appointment of Guardian—Application—Contents.
Carlin, Baldwin's Ohio Practice, Merrick-Rippner Probate Law § 62:19, Appointment of Guardian—Application—Investigations by Court.
Carlin, Baldwin's Ohio Practice, Merrick-Rippner Probate Law § 62:38, Guardianship Proceedings—Hearings.
Carlin, Baldwin's Ohio Practice, Merrick-Rippner Probate Law § 62:45, Guardianship Proceedings—Role of Physician or Investigators.
Carlin, Baldwin's Ohio Practice, Merrick-Rippner Probate Law § 62:47, Guardianship Proceedings—Person Adjudged Incompetent.
Carlin, Baldwin's Ohio Practice, Merrick-Rippner Probate Law § 62:48, Guardianship Proceedings—Person Adjudged Not Incompetent.
Carlin, Baldwin's Ohio Practice, Merrick-Rippner Probate Law § 62:49, Guardianship Proceedings—Advance Deposit of Costs.

Notes of Decisions

Medical records 1

---

1. Medical records

A trial court may not base its determination of incompetency on medical records subpoenaed by the court sua sponte, and without any notice to the alleged incompetent ward, after a hearing before a referee. In re Guardianship of Schumacher (Summit 1987) 38 Ohio App.3d 37, 525 N.E.2d 833.

2111.04 Notice

(A) Except for an interim or emergency guardian appointed under division (B)(2) or (3) of section 2111.02 of the Revised Code, no guardian of the person, the estate, or both shall be appointed until at least seven days after the probate court has caused written notice, setting forth the time and place of the hearing, to be served as follows:

(1) In the appointment of the guardian of a minor, notice shall be served:

(a) Upon the minor, if over the age of fourteen, by personal service;

(b) Upon each parent of the minor whose name and address is known or with reasonable diligence can be ascertained, provided the parent is free from disability other than minority;

(c) Upon the next of kin of the minor who are known to reside in this state, if there is no living parent, the name and address of the parent cannot be ascertained, or the parent is under disability other than minority;

(d) Upon the person having the custody of the minor.

(2) In the appointment of the guardian of an incompetent, notice shall be served:

(a)(i) Upon the person for whom appointment is sought by personal service, by a probate court investigator, or in the manner provided in division (A)(2)(a)(ii) of this section. The notice shall be in boldface type and shall inform the alleged incompetent, in boldface type, of his rights to be present at the hearing, to contest any application for the appointment of a guardian for his person, estate, or both, and to be represented by an attorney and of all of the rights set forth in division (C)(7) of section 2111.02 of the Revised Code.

(ii) If the person for whom appointment is sought is a resident of, or has a legal settlement in, the county in which the court has jurisdiction, but is absent from that county, the probate court may designate, by order, a temporary probate court investigator, in lieu of a regular probate court investigator appointed or designated under section 2101.11 of the Revised Code, to make the personal service of the notice described in division (A)(2)(a)(i) of this section upon the person for whom appointment is sought.

(b) Upon the next of kin of the person for whom appointment is sought who are known to reside in this state.

(B) After service of notice in accordance with division (A) of this section and for good cause shown, the court may appoint a guardian prior to the time limitation specified in that division.

(C) Notice may not be waived by the person for whom the appointment is sought.

(D) From the service of notice until the hearing, no sale, gift, conveyance, or encumbrance of the property of an alleged incompetent shall be valid as to persons having notice of the proceeding.

(1989 S 46, eff. 1–1–90; 1975 S 145; 129 v 1448; 127 v 36; 1953 H 1; GC 10507–4)

Historical and Statutory Notes

Pre–1953 H 1 Amendments: 121 v 557; 114 v 384

Comparative Laws

Minn.—M.S.A. § 525.55.

Cross References

Issuer of securities may treat record holders as competent unless certified copy of decree received, 1339.02
Service of notice, Civ R 73

Library References

Guardian and Ward ⬉13(1).
Mental Health ⬉127.
Westlaw Topic Nos. 196, 257A.
C.J.S. Mental Health § 134.

Research References

Encyclopedias

OH Jur. 3d Decedents' Estates § 1274, Property Fraudulently Concealed or Embezzled.
OH Jur. 3d Guardian & Ward § 41, Generally; Sufficiency.
OH Jur. 3d Guardian & Ward § 43, Persons to be Served, Generally—Application for Guardian for Minor.
OH Jur. 3d Guardian & Ward § 44, Persons to be Served, Generally—Application for Guardian for Incompetent.
OH Jur. 3d Guardian & Ward § 45, Waiver of Service.
OH Jur. 3d Guardian & Ward § 46, Protection of Property Pending Hearing.
OH Jur. 3d Guardian & Ward § 51, Application for Guardian for Incompetent—Rights of Allegedly Incompetent Person for Whom Appointment is Sought; Standard of Proof.
OH Jur. 3d Guardian & Ward § 203, Notice and Hearing—Evidence.

Treatises and Practice Aids

Carlin, Baldwin's Ohio Practice, Merrick-Rippner Probate Law § 56:1, Concealed or Embezzled Assets—Scope of RC 2109.50 to RC 2109.56.
Carlin, Baldwin's Ohio Practice, Merrick-Rippner Probate Law § 56:2, Concealed or Embezzled Assets—Jurisdiction Over Complaint.
Carlin, Baldwin's Ohio Practice, Merrick-Rippner Probate Law § 63:1, Notice of Guardianship Hearing.
Carlin, Baldwin's Ohio Practice, Merrick-Rippner Probate Law § 63:2, Notice of Guardianship Hearing—Service—Guardianship of Minor.
Carlin, Baldwin's Ohio Practice, Merrick-Rippner Probate Law § 63:3, Notice of Guardianship Hearing—Service—Guardianship of Incompetent.
Carlin, Baldwin's Ohio Practice, Merrick-Rippner Probate Law § 63:5, Notice of Guardianship Proceedings—Effect.
Carlin, Baldwin's Ohio Practice, Merrick-Rippner Probate Law § 63:6, Notice of Guardianship Proceedings—Waiver.
Carlin, Baldwin's Ohio Practice, Merrick-Rippner Probate Law § 65:1, Litigation Involving Guardians—Guardian May Sue or be Sued; Intervenor—Dispute Resolution Procedure.
Carlin, Baldwin's Ohio Practice, Merrick-Rippner Probate Law § 14:18, Payable on Death Accounts.
Carlin, Baldwin's Ohio Practice, Merrick-Rippner Probate Law § 62:18, Appointment of Guardian—Application—Notice.
Carlin, Baldwin's Ohio Practice, Merrick-Rippner Probate Law § 62:19, Appointment of Guardian—Application—Investigations by Court.
Carlin, Baldwin's Ohio Practice, Merrick-Rippner Probate Law § 62:73, Entry Setting for Hearing and Ordering Notice—Form.
Carlin, Baldwin's Ohio Practice, Merrick-Rippner Probate Law § 62:74, Notice of Hearing to Ward—Form.
Carlin, Baldwin's Ohio Practice, Merrick-Rippner Probate Law § 62:75, Notice of Hearing on Guardianship—Form.
Carlin, Baldwin's Ohio Practice, Merrick-Rippner Probate Law § 62:82, Next of Kin in Guardianship—Form.
Carlin, Baldwin's Ohio Practice, Merrick-Rippner Probate Law § 62:84, Entry Setting Application for Hearing and Ordering Notice—Form.
Carlin, Baldwin's Ohio Practice, Merrick-Rippner Probate Law § 62:85, Notice of Filing of Application—Form.
Carlin, Baldwin's Ohio Practice, Merrick-Rippner Probate Law § 64:22, Powers and Duties of Guardian—Ward's Estate—Acts of the Ward—Payable on Death Accounts.
Carlin, Baldwin's Ohio Practice, Merrick-Rippner Probate Law App B SPF 15.0, Next of Kin of Proposed Ward.
Carlin, Baldwin's Ohio Practice, Merrick-Rippner Probate Law App B SPF 16.3, Notice of Hearing for Appointment of Guardian of Minor (To Minor Over Age Fourteen).
Carlin, Baldwin's Ohio Practice, Merrick-Rippner Probate Law App B SPF 16.4, Notice of Hearing on Application for Appointment of Guardian of Minor to Parent, Known Next of Kin and Person Having Custody.
Carlin, Baldwin's Ohio Practice, Merrick-Rippner Probate Law App B SPF 17.4, Notice of Hearing for Appointment of Guardian of Alleged Incompetent (To Spouse and Known Next of Kin).

Law Review and Journal Commentaries

Notice Requirements In Ohio Estate And Guardianship Proceedings—Why The Difference?, Comment. 20 Cap U L Rev 455 (Spring 1991).

Notes of Decisions

Constitutional issues 1
Incompetence 4
Minors 3
Personal service 6
Pre–appointment acts 2
Residence 5

---

1. Constitutional issues

RC 2111.04(B)(2), under which notice of guardianship proceedings is served only on the ward's next of kin known to reside in the county in which the application to appoint the guardian is made, does not offend the due process, equal protection, or privileges and immunities provisions of US Const Am 14. In re Guardianship of Bissmeyer (Hamilton 1988) 49 Ohio App.3d 42, 550 N.E.2d 210, cause dismissed 40 Ohio St.3d 705, 534 N.E.2d 842.

2. Pre–appointment acts

Sale and conveyance of deceased landowner's property through landowner's attorney in fact was valid and not subject to further challenge, even though guardian was subsequently appointed for landowner; property was transferred before attorney in fact had notice of guardianship, attorney in fact took no further action upon notice of guardian application, deed had already been delivered to escrow agent and signed, guardian was appointed a month after deed was recorded, buyer had no knowledge of guardian application, binding sale contract existed, and challenge to transaction was barred by res judicata, as matter could have been raised in exceptions to guardian's inventory and account. Biviano v. Edward C. Mahan Trust (Ohio App. 11 Dist., Trumbull, 12-12-2003) No. 2002-T-0089, 2003-Ohio-

6699, 2003 WL 22931350, Unreported. Guardian And Ward ⇌ 13(3); Guardian And Ward ⇌ 17; Guardian And Ward ⇌ 163; Principal And Agent ⇌ 63(1)

The change of a beneficiary on a payable on death account is not a sale, gift, conveyance, or encumbrance of the account within the meaning of RC 2111.04. Ogilvie v. Kehr (Fairfield 1988) 39 Ohio App.3d 170, 530 N.E.2d 957.

RC 2111.04 does not apply to payment of a debt after notice of the proceeding referred to therein. Beach v. Baker (Cuyahoga 1958) 151 N.E.2d 677, 79 Ohio Law Abs. 136.

Where evidence shows that decedent during her lifetime placed a sealed envelope containing personal property in a safety deposit box in a bank, face of envelope bearing a statement signed by decedent that all contents of envelope belong to a named person, authorized that person to enter box and on day prior to appointment of a guardian for decedent gave to named person a key to box with instructions to "get what was his out of her lock box," intention of decedent to give property in envelope to named person is apparent and giving of key and its acceptance constitute a delivery and acceptance of property in envelope, and under such a state of facts, provision of section, that from service of notice of a hearing for appointment of a guardian for an incompetent person until hearing, no gift of property of incompetent shall be valid as to persons having notice of proceeding, is inapplicable where evidence does not disclose that named person received notice of proceeding prior to delivery of key. In re Stevenson's Estate (Franklin 1946) 79 Ohio App. 315, 69 N.E.2d 426, 46 Ohio Law Abs. 547, 35 O.O. 78.

Notice of proceedings to appoint a guardian does not prohibit a drunkard from purchasing necessaries and paying for them before such guardian's appointment. Brockway v. Jewell (Ohio 1894) 52 Ohio St. 187, 3 W.L.B. 59, 39 N.E. 470, 2 Ohio Leg. N. 239.

Where guardian's appointment was limited to date of second hearing under terms of original appointment order, she was not entitled to additional notice, ten days prior to second hearing, that her status as guardian would be revoked. In re Tinman (Ohio App. 6 Dist., Huron, 06-21-2002) No. H-01-061, 2002-Ohio-3149, 2002 WL 1396538, Unreported. Mental Health ⇌ 176

3. Minors

A judgment of the probate court appointing a guardian for a minor is a nullity and may be directly attacked in any court in any proceeding, where the hearing provided in RC 2111.04 was set prior to the passing of the required three days. Horn v. Childers (Lawrence 1959) 116 Ohio App. 175, 187 N.E.2d 402, 22 O.O.2d 34.

Mother of a minor child for whom a guardian has been appointed over her objection may appeal from such order. In re Guardianship of Moyer (Lucas 1941) 68 Ohio App. 319, 40 N.E.2d 695, 22 O.O. 483.

It is not necessary to notify the minor of an application to appoint a guardian for her, but parents of such infant, unless they are themselves the applicants or participants in the proceeding, must undoubtedly be notified. State ex rel. Fisher v. Madden (Ohio Com.Pl. 1901) 12 Ohio Dec. 83.

4. Incompetence

Disputed portion of settlement given to attorney for representing incompetent minor in medical malpractice action were not probate assets because funds were passed to attorney prior to establishment of guardianship, and thus, because probate court exceeded its jurisdiction by proceeding with concealment action related to disputed portion of settlement funds, attorney was entitled to writ of prohibition to bar probate court from proceeding with concealment action hearing. Goldberg v. Maloney (Ohio App. 7 Dist., Mahoning, 12-23-2005) No. 05 MA 545, 2005-Ohio-7110, 2005 WL 3642688, Unreported. Prohibition ⇌ 10(2)

Statute that required notice to be served on the next of kin for the allegedly incompetent person for whom appointment of a guardian was sought was satisfied, where the allegedly incompetent person was present at the hearing, and his next of kin consented to the appointment of petitioner as guardian. In re Guardianship of Roth (Ohio App. 7 Dist., Mahoning, 09-21-2005) No. 04 MA 199, 2005-Ohio-5057, 2005 WL 2336126, Unreported. Mental Health ⇌ 130

Children's custodian could properly waive notice of trial court's judgment entry appointing guardian for estates of children; custodian was not person from whom guardianship was sought, and custodian was adult who was not suffering from mental illness. In re Guardianships of Ahmed (Ohio App. 7 Dist., Belmont, 11-24-2003) No. 02 BE 56, 2003-Ohio-6390, 2003 WL 22837720, Unreported, appeal not allowed 101 Ohio St.3d 1487, 805 N.E.2d 539, 2004-Ohio-1293. Guardian And Ward ⇌ 13(3)

Ward's sister, who made withdrawals from ward's bank accounts using her power of attorney, was required to prove by clear and convincing evidence that the withdrawals were gifts; statute per se invalidated any gifts made to or taken by a person with notice of an incompetency proceeding. Harrison v. Faseyitan (Ohio App. 7 Dist., 12-09-2004) 159 Ohio App.3d 325, 823 N.E.2d 925, 2004-Ohio-6808. Mental Health ⇌ 238

A trial court may not base its determination of incompetency on medical records subpoenaed by the court sua sponte, and without any notice to the alleged incompetent ward, after a hearing before a referee. In re Guardianship of Schumacher (Summit 1987) 38 Ohio App.3d 37, 525 N.E.2d 833.

Service of written notice upon the next of kin of an incompetent known to reside in the county in which application is made, setting forth the time and place of the hearing, is a condition precedent to the appointment of such guardian, and letters of appointment issued without such notice are improperly issued. In re Guardianship of Kelley (Crawford 1964) 1 Ohio App.2d 137, 204 N.E.2d 96, 30 O.O.2d 159.

Where a guardian of an estate is appointed on the ground of the ward's physical incapacity, the ward's mental capacity is not impaired, and such appointment is made with the consent of the ward, a daughter of such ward may file exceptions to such guardian's account. In re Guardianship of Tillman (Darke 1955) 100 Ohio App. 291, 136 N.E.2d 291, 60 O.O. 254.

A probate court judgment declaring a person incompetent is void for lack of due process when such person has not been personally served with notice, and the filing of a motion to vacate an adjudication of incompetency does not constitute an entry of appearance relating back to the time of notice of the original adjudication so as to give the court jurisdiction over the person of the alleged incompetent even though he was not personally served. In re Koenigshoff (Cuyahoga 1954) 99 Ohio App. 39, 119 N.E.2d 652, 69 Ohio Law Abs. 121, 58 O.O. 114.

Where plaintiff was declared incompetent and given notice of application for appointment of guardian, failure to give notice of subsequent application for appointment of defendant as such guardian was not such irregularity as to invalidate the appointment as plaintiff had notice of court's jurisdiction being invoked for appointment of a guardian and the identity of the appointee would not affect plaintiff's substantive rights. In re Bireley's Guardianship (Darke 1944) 59 N.E.2d 71, 41 Ohio Law Abs. 604.

Rule 27 of the uniform rules of practice in the probate courts of Ohio, adopted pursuant to GC 10501–13 (RC 2101.04), and providing that "in applications for the appointment of guardians for… incompetents,… the notice to the proposed ward must be served by the sheriff or some other disinterested person," is reasonable and salutary, supplements this section and does not contravene GC 10501–21 (RC 2101.26 et seq.). (Ed. note: See Civil Rule 73.) In re Irvine's Guardianship (Knox 1943) 72 Ohio App. 405, 52 N.E.2d 536, 27 O.O. 332.

Notice to insane person is not necessary to give probate court jurisdiction to appoint guardian, and failure to give notice is mere irregularity which cannot be raised collaterally, but must be complained of in a direct proceeding to set aside the appointment or by bringing error proceeding to reverse it. Oldham v. Winget (Shelby 1933) 47 Ohio App. 287, 191 N.E. 824, 17 Ohio Law Abs. 304, 40 Ohio Law Rep. 296.

Only notice which a person who is charged with being incompetent is entitled to under section is simply a notice that an application has been filed for appointment of a guardian, and this notice must be served upon him personally at least three days before date of the hearing. In re Joyce (Ohio Prob. 1940) 5 Ohio Supp. 16, 32 Ohio Law Abs. 553, 19 O.O. 506. Guardian And Ward ⇌ 13(3)

5. Residence

The phrase "known to reside in the county," as used in RC 2111.04 has reference to the knowledge had by those whose duty it is to give the notice in the first place, either the person applying for appointment as guardian or the court. In re Guardianship of Kelley (Crawford 1964) 1 Ohio App.2d 137, 204 N.E.2d 96, 30 O.O.2d 159. Mental Health ⇌ 129

In a proceeding for the appointment of a resident guardian for a nonresident confined person, compliance with RC 2111.04 with respect to notice to such confined person is requisite before the court acquires jurisdiction, and a judgment, without notice to such person as required by such section, finding such person confined in a hospital as a mentally ill person and appointing a resident guardian of the Ohio estate of such person, is void for lack of due process. In re Guardianship of Reynolds (Lucas 1956) 103 Ohio App. 102, 144 N.E.2d 501, 3 O.O.2d 175, appeal dismissed 168 Ohio St. 265, 153 N.E.2d 674, 6 O.O.2d 423.

6. Personal service

There was no evidence that father's children were citizens from another country, to support father's argument that trial court lacked subject matter jurisdiction over guardianship proceedings because guardian's waiver of notice was ineffective for non-citizens. In re Guardianships of Ahmed (Ohio App. 7 Dist., Belmont, 11-24-2003) No. 02 BE 56, 2003-Ohio-6390, 2003 WL 22837720, Unreported, appeal not allowed 101 Ohio St.3d 1487, 805 N.E.2d 539, 2004-Ohio-1293. Guardian And Ward ⚖ 8

There was no evidence that father was not given notice of trial court's judgment entry appointing guardian to father's sons, and thus that he was prevented from timely appealing judgment; record on appeal indicated a copy of judgment entry was mailed to father, and Court of Appeals lacked authority and power to conduct independent investigation to determine whether he received notice. In re Guardianships of Ahmed (Ohio App. 7 Dist., Belmont, 11-24-2003) No. 02 BE 56, 2003-Ohio-6390, 2003 WL 22837720, Unreported, appeal not allowed 101 Ohio St.3d 1487, 805 N.E.2d 539, 2004-Ohio-1293. Guardian And Ward ⚖ 13(8)

When an application for appointment of a guardian is made and personal service is not perfected on the person for whom appointment is sought pursuant to RC 2111.04(B)(1), the trial court is without jurisdiction to appoint a guardian for such person and the cause must be dismissed. In re Guardianship of Corless (Butler 1981) 2 Ohio App.3d 92, 440 N.E.2d 1203, 2 O.B.R. 104. Guardian And Ward ⚖ 13(3)

2111.041 Investigation of alleged incompetent

(A) At the time of the service of notice upon an alleged incompetent, as required by division (A)(2)(a) of section 2111.04 of the Revised Code, the court shall require a regular probate court investigator appointed or designated under section 2101.11 of the Revised Code or appoint a temporary probate court investigator to investigate the circumstances of the alleged incompetent, and, to the maximum extent feasible, to communicate to the alleged incompetent in a language or method of communication that he can understand, his rights as specified in that division, and subsequently to file with the court a report that contains all of the following:

(1) A statement indicating that the notice was served and describing the extent to which the alleged incompetent's rights to be present at the hearing, to contest any application for the appointment of a guardian for his person, estate, or both, and to be represented by an attorney were communicated to him in a language or method of communication understandable to the alleged incompetent;

(2) A brief description, as observed by the investigator, of the physical and mental condition of the alleged incompetent;

(3) A recommendation regarding the necessity for a guardianship or a less restrictive alternative;

(4) A recommendation regarding the necessity of appointing pursuant to section 2111.031 of the Revised Code, an attorney to represent the alleged incompetent.

(B) The report that is required by division (A) of this section shall be made a part of the record in the case and shall be considered by the court prior to establishing any guardianship for the alleged incompetent.

(1989 S 46, eff. 1–1–90)

Cross References

Cost of investigations, 2101.16

Library References

Mental Health ⚖ 123.
Westlaw Topic No. 257A.
C.J.S. Mental Health § 131.

Research References

Encyclopedias

OH Jur. 3d Guardian & Ward § 53, Application for Guardian for Incompetent—Investigation of Circumstances of an Alleged Incompetent.

Treatises and Practice Aids

Carlin, Baldwin's Ohio Practice, Merrick-Rippner Probate Law § 62:19, Appointment of Guardian—Application—Investigations by Court.

Carlin, Baldwin's Ohio Practice, Merrick-Rippner Probate Law § 62:38, Guardianship Proceedings—Hearings.

Carlin, Baldwin's Ohio Practice, Merrick-Rippner Probate Law App B SPF 17.8, Investigator's Report.

2111.042 Appointment of investigator; reports

(A) In connection with the appointment of a guardian for a minor or the functioning of the guardianship of a minor, the court may appoint a regular probate court investigator appointed or designated under section 2101.11 of the Revised Code or appoint a temporary probate court investigator to investigate the need for, or the circumstances of, the guardianship and to file with the court a report that contains all of the following:

(1) A brief description, as observed by the investigator, of the physical and mental condition of the minor;

(2) If a guardian already has been appointed, a brief description, as observed by the investigator, of the circumstances and functioning of the guardianship;

(3) If no guardian has been appointed, a brief recommendation regarding the necessity for a guardianship.

(B) The report that is required pursuant to division (A) of this section shall be made part of the record in the case and shall be considered by the court prior to establishing any guardianship for the minor, if no guardianship has been established, and prior to making any change in the guardianship or the functioning of the guardianship, if a guardian already has been appointed.

(1994 H 457, eff. 11–9–94)

Uncodified Law

1994 H 457, § 3: See Uncodified Law under 2101.16.

Cross References

Appointment of guardian or investigation, fees, 2101.16

Library References

Guardian and Ward ⚖ 13(1).
Westlaw Topic No. 196.

Research References

Encyclopedias

OH Jur. 3d Guardian & Ward § 54, Application for Guardian for Incompetent—Investigation of Circumstances of a Minor.

Treatises and Practice Aids

Carlin, Baldwin's Ohio Practice, Merrick-Rippner Probate Law § 62:19, Appointment of Guardian—Application—Investigations by Court.

Carlin, Baldwin's Ohio Practice, Merrick-Rippner Probate Law § 62:38, Guardianship Proceedings—Hearings.

Carlin, Baldwin's Ohio Practice, Merrick-Rippner Probate Law § 62:45, Guardianship Proceedings—Role of Physician or Investigators.

Carlin, Baldwin's Ohio Practice, Merrick-Rippner Probate Law § 62:49, Guardianship Proceedings—Advance Deposit of Costs.

Carlin, Baldwin's Ohio Practice, Merrick-Rippner Probate Law § 62:51, Appointment of Guardian of a Minor—Investigations.

2111.05 Estate not more than ten thousand dollars

When the whole estate of a ward, or of several wards jointly, under the same guardianship, does not exceed ten thousand dollars in value, the guardian may apply to the probate court for an order to terminate the guardianship. Upon proof that it would be for the best interest of the ward to terminate the guardianship, the court may order the guardianship terminated, and direct the guardian, if the ward is a minor, to deposit the assets of the guardianship in a depository authorized to receive fiduciary funds, payable to the ward when he attains majority, or the court may authorize the delivery of the assets to the natural guardian of the minor, to the person by whom the minor is maintained, to the executive director of children services in the county, or to the minor himself.

If the ward is an incompetent, and the court orders the guardianship terminated, the court may authorize the deposit of the assets of the guardianship in a depository authorized to receive fiduciary funds in the name of a suitable person to be designated by the court, or if the assets do not consist of money, the court may authorize delivery to a suitable person to be designated by the court. The person receiving the assets shall hold and dispose of them in the manner the court directs.

If the court refuses to grant the application to terminate the guardianship, or if no such application is presented to the court, the guardian only shall be required to render account upon the termination of his guardianship, upon order of the probate court made upon its own motion, or upon the order of the court made on the motion of a person interested in the wards or their property, for good cause shown, and set forth upon the journal of the court.

If the estate is ten thousand dollars or less and the ward is a minor, the court, without the appointment of a guardian by the court, or the giving of bond, may authorize the deposit in a depository authorized to receive fiduciary funds, payable to the guardian when appointed, or to the ward when he attains majority, or the court may authorize delivery to the natural guardian of the minor, to the person by whom the minor is maintained, to the executive director who is responsible for the administration of children services in the county, or to the minor himself.

If the whole estate of a person over eighteen years of age, who has been adjudged mentally ill or mentally retarded, does not exceed ten thousand dollars in value, the court, without the appointment of a guardian by the court or the giving of bond, may authorize the deposit of the estate in a depository authorized to receive fiduciary funds in the name of a suitable person to be designated by the court, or if the assets do not consist of money, the court may authorize delivery to a suitable person to be designated by the court. The person receiving the assets shall hold and dispose of them in the manner the court directs.

(1991 H 82, eff. 9–10–91; 1989 S 46; 1980 H 900; 1978 H 946; 1975 S 145; 1973 S 1; 1971 H 290; 130 v H 1; 129 v 1448; 127 v 378; 126 v 71; 1953 H 1; GC 10507–5)

Historical and Statutory Notes

Pre–1953 H 1 Amendments: 121 v 538; 119 v 394; 114 v 384

Cross References

County children services board, powers and duties relative to court proceedings, 5153.18
Court of claims, assistance to victims of crimes, payment of award to designated person or depository, 2743.66
Minor is sui juris for workers' compensation purposes, 4123.89

Ohio Administrative Code References

Workers' compensation, awards, OAC 4123–3–10

Library References

Guardian and Ward ⚖18.
Mental Health ⚖167.
Westlaw Topic Nos. 196, 257A.
C.J.S. Mental Health §§ 146 to 147.

Research References

Encyclopedias

OH Jur. 3d Guardian & Ward § 15, Generally; Estates Valued at $10,000 or Less.
OH Jur. 3d Guardian & Ward § 169, Generally; Estates Valued at $10,000 or Less.
OH Jur. 3d Guardian & Ward § 192, Estates Valued at $10,000 or Less.
OH Jur. 3d Workers' Compensation § 79, Minors.
OH Jur. 3d Workers' Compensation § 410, Payment Procedure, Generally—to Whom Payment is Made.

Forms

Ohio Forms and Transactions KP 30.10, Guardianship Clause.

Treatises and Practice Aids

Carlin, Baldwin's Ohio Practice, Merrick-Rippner Probate Law § 66:2, Termination—Discretionary—Court; Removal.
Carlin, Baldwin's Ohio Practice, Merrick-Rippner Probate Law § 66:6, Termination of Guardianship—Incompetent—Estate is Less Than $10,000.
Carlin, Baldwin's Ohio Practice, Merrick-Rippner Probate Law § 67:7, Alternatives to Guardianship—Adult Wards.
Carlin, Baldwin's Ohio Practice, Merrick-Rippner Probate Law § 67:8, Application for Release of Assets Without Appointment of Guardian—Incompetent—Form.
Carlin, Baldwin's Ohio Practice, Merrick-Rippner Probate Law § 67:9, Entry to Pay or Deliver Property of Incompetent Without Appointment of Guardian—Form.
Carlin, Baldwin's Ohio Practice, Merrick-Rippner Probate Law § 66:10, Termination of Guardianship—Minor.
Carlin, Baldwin's Ohio Practice, Merrick-Rippner Probate Law § 66:13, Termination of Guardianship—Effect of Order.
Carlin, Baldwin's Ohio Practice, Merrick-Rippner Probate Law § 67:10, Application for Release of Assets Without Appointment of Guardian—Minor—Form.
Carlin, Baldwin's Ohio Practice, Merrick-Rippner Probate Law § 67:11, Entry to Pay or Deliver Property of Minor Without Appointment of Guardian—Form.
Carlin, Baldwin's Ohio Practice, Merrick-Rippner Probate Law App B SPF 14.2, Entry Approving Settlement and Distribution of Wrongful Death and Survival Claims—Form.
Carlin, Baldwin's Ohio Practice, Merrick-Rippner Probate Law App B SPF 22.0, Application to Settle a Minor's Claim and Entry Setting Hearing—Form.
Carlin, Baldwin's Ohio Practice, Merrick-Rippner Probate Law App B SPF 22.3, Verification of Receipt and Deposit—Form.

Law Review and Journal Commentaries

Guardianship of Adults with Mental Retardation: Towards a Presumption of Competence, Comment. 14 Akron L Rev 321 (Fall 1980).

Notes of Decisions

Computation of estate 3
Court costs 4
Public official 1
Use of money 2

---

1. Public official

The executive secretary of the Lucas county child welfare board may be appointed legal guardian of a minor when said minor's funds, originally deposited under RC 2111.05, have increased to over $1,000 and by accepting the responsibilities of such a guardianship, he is performing the official duties and exercising the powers of his office as set forth in RC 5153.16 and is not entitled to receive guardianship compensation. OAG 68–036.

Note 1

The executive secretary of a county welfare board acting as the trustee of a minor's estate of less than one thousand dollars may administer those assets without being appointed guardian of such minor. 1959 OAG 826.

A child welfare board, when its executive secretary has been duly designated by the probate court as trustee of funds of one of its wards, is not empowered to make disposition of said funds except as authorized by or approved by the probate court who has jurisdiction in the matter. 1958 OAG 1990.

Funds of a ward of a child welfare board held in the custody of the county treasurer should be paid over to the legal guardian of such ward, or if not more than $1,000.00 in amount, should be paid over to the executive secretary of a child welfare board duly designated by the probate court as trustee, and the disposition of such funds by the guardian or trustee is subject to the authorization and approval of the probate court. 1958 OAG 1990.

2. Use of money

A guardian cannot legally terminate a guardianship by using up the ward's money to purchase stock in his business without applying to the probate court, particularly when no account is ever filed. In re Guardianship of Maunz (Van Wert 1991) 77 Ohio App.3d 760, 603 N.E.2d 1045.

The executive secretary of a county welfare board acting as trustee of an estate of a ward which is less than one thousand dollars may use those assets for medical and dental care of such child subject to the approval of the probate court. 1959 OAG 826.

3. Computation of estate

Under GC 10507–2 (RC 2111.02) only the amount of the veterans' administration award that is then on hand or has become due and payable should be included in the value of the estate; if a later account is filed showing that the value of the estate is $1500, only the costs of the later account should be collected; the court would not be required to collect all costs that have accumulated to the date of the later account. 1950 OAG 2401.

4. Court costs

GC 10507–2 (RC 2111.02) provides that no probate court costs shall be charged or taxed for the filing of accounts, applications for appointment of a guardian or any other subsequent proceedings made in pursuance of the appointment unless the value of the estate, including the moneys due under the veterans' administration award, exceeds $1500. 1950 OAG 1533.

2111.06 Guardian of the person or estate

If the powers of the person appointed as guardian of a minor or incompetent are not limited by the order of appointment, such person shall be guardian both of the person and estate of the ward. In every instance the court shall appoint the same person as guardian of the person and estate of any such ward, unless in the opinion of the court the interests of the ward will be promoted by the appointment of different persons as guardians of the person and of the estate.

A guardian of the person of a minor shall be appointed as to a minor having neither father nor mother, or whose parents are unsuitable persons to have the custody and tuition of such minor, or whose interests, in the opinion of the court, will be promoted thereby. A guardian of the person shall have the custody and provide for the maintenance of the ward, and if the ward is a minor, such guardian shall also provide for the education of such ward.

Before exercising its jurisdiction to appoint a guardian of a minor, the court shall comply with the jurisdictional standards of sections 3127.01 to 3127.53 of the Revised Code.

(2004 S 185, eff. 4–11–05; 1977 S 135, eff. 10–25–77; 129 v 1448; 1953 H 1; GC 10507–6)

Historical and Statutory Notes

Pre–1953 H 1 Amendments: 114 v 385

Amendment Note: 2004 S 185 substituted "3127.01 to 3127.53" for "3109.21 to 3109.37" in the last paragraph.

Library References

Guardian and Ward ⚖17, 29, 36.
Mental Health ⚖115.
Westlaw Topic Nos. 196, 257A.
C.J.S. Mental Health § 122.

Research References

ALR Library
69 ALR 5th 1, Grandparents' Visitation Rights Where Child's Parents Are Deceased, or Where Status of Parents is Unspecified.

Encyclopedias
OH Jur. 3d Guardian & Ward § 16, Persons Subject to Guardianship; Minors.
OH Jur. 3d Guardian & Ward § 27, Same Person as Guardian of Person and Estate.
OH Jur. 3d Guardian & Ward § 34, Generally; Jurisdiction of Probate Court.
OH Jur. 3d Guardian & Ward § 62, Effect of Order as Defining Scope of Guardian's Powers.
OH Jur. 3d Guardian & Ward § 82, Duties, Generally.

Treatises and Practice Aids
Sowald & Morganstern, Baldwin's Ohio Practice Domestic Relations Law § 17:2, UCCJA—Applicability.
Carlin, Baldwin's Ohio Practice, Merrick-Rippner Probate Law § 62:5, Appointment of Guardian—Definitions—Limited Guardian.
Carlin, Baldwin's Ohio Practice, Merrick-Rippner Probate Law § 62:9, Appointment of Guardian—Definitions—Guardianship of the Person And/Or Estate.
Carlin, Baldwin's Ohio Practice, Merrick-Rippner Probate Law § 62:33, Guardianship Proceedings—Court's Jurisdiction.
Carlin, Baldwin's Ohio Practice, Merrick-Rippner Probate Law § 62:43, Guardianship Proceedings—Who May Serve—Life Support Cases.
Carlin, Baldwin's Ohio Practice, Merrick-Rippner Probate Law § 62:55, Appointment of Guardian of a Minor—Custody Issues—Jurisdiction.
Carlin, Baldwin's Ohio Practice, Merrick-Rippner Probate Law § 62:58, Appointment of Guardian of a Minor—Custody Issues—Best Interests of Minor.
Carlin, Baldwin's Ohio Practice, Merrick-Rippner Probate Law § 62:60, Limited Guardianship.
Carlin, Baldwin's Ohio Practice, Merrick-Rippner Probate Law § 62:61, Interim Guardianship.
Carlin, Baldwin's Ohio Practice, Merrick-Rippner Probate Law § 62:66, Appellate Standard of Review—Discretion of Court.
Carlin, Baldwin's Ohio Practice, Merrick-Rippner Probate Law App B SPF 16.0, Application for Appointment of Guardian of Minor.

Law Review and Journal Commentaries

Guardianship of Adults with Mental Retardation: Towards a Presumption of Competence, Comment. 14 Akron L Rev 321 (Fall 1980).

Notes of Decisions

Adequate representation 3
Custody of minors 1
Discharge of patient 2
Limitations on guardian's power 5
Revocation of powers 4

---

1. Custody of minors

Probate court's disposition of mother's motion to terminate guardianship of her daughter under the domestic relation's best interest of the child standard, rather than the good cause standard, was improper, where mother consented to guardianship, and there was no final resolution of custody. In re Hammons (Ohio App. 8 Dist., Cuyahoga, 03-06-2003) No. 80570, 2003-Ohio-992, 2003 WL 760593, Unreported, appeal not allowed 99 Ohio St.3d 1467, 791 N.E.2d 983, 2003-Ohio-3669. Guardian And Ward ⚖ 25

Probate court's improper disposition of mother's motion to terminate guardianship of her daughter under the domestic relation's best interest of the child standard, rather than the good cause standard, was harmless; mother's failure to present evidence showing why the guardianship should be terminated was so complete that the probate court would have been justified in denying her motion to terminate the guardianship under the proper legal standard. In re Hammons (Ohio App. 8 Dist., Cuyahoga, 03-06-2003) No. 80570, 2003-Ohio-992, 2003 WL 760593, Unreported, appeal not allowed 99 Ohio St.3d 1467, 791 N.E.2d 983, 2003-Ohio-3669. Guardian And Ward ⇔ 13(8)

Probate court had jurisdiction to terminate guardianship of minor, but once guardianship was terminated, minor was no longer a ward of probate court, and juvenile court had exclusive jurisdiction to determine minor's custody. In re Guardianship of Harrison (Hamilton 1989) 60 Ohio App.3d 19, 572 N.E.2d 855, motion overruled 47 Ohio St.3d 708, 547 N.E.2d 992. Courts ⇔ 472.1; Guardian And Ward ⇔ 25

While juvenile court entered order granting temporary custody of minor child to county welfare department of social services upon adjudging minor child to be dependent child, when juvenile court terminated order and returned minor child to mother, jurisdiction of juvenile court ceased, so that when grandmother of minor child applied to probate court to become child's guardian, probate court acquired exclusive jurisdiction over ward and guardian, and juvenile court was without jurisdiction to grant custody over ward to another person until guardianship had been terminated. In re Miller (Cuyahoga 1986) 33 Ohio App.3d 224, 515 N.E.2d 635. Courts ⇔ 475(6)

Notice published in newspaper failed to state last known address of natural mother as required by rule, so that service of notice of motion brought by natural father seeking custody of minor child was defective; service by publication was method of last resort and therefore requirements of rule were mandatory and would be strictly enforced. In re Miller (Cuyahoga 1986) 33 Ohio App.3d 224, 515 N.E.2d 635. Child Custody ⇔ 409

Under guardianship statutes, probate court has jurisdiction in appointment and control of guardians which extends to all matters touching guardianship, including custody of minor and visitation rights of third parties. In re Zahoransky (Cuyahoga 1985) 22 Ohio App.3d 75, 488 N.E.2d 944, 22 O.B.R. 173. Guardian And Ward ⇔ 8

The Uniform Child Custody Jurisdiction Act, as adopted in Ohio, is applicable to and must be complied with in a guardianship termination proceeding. In re Wonderly's Guardianship (Ohio 1981) 67 Ohio St.2d 178, 423 N.E.2d 420, 21 O.O.3d 111. Guardian And Ward ⇔ 25

The court must determine the custody of children with a paramount regard to the highest welfare and best interests of the child. In re Minors of Luck, 7 NP 49, 10 D 1 (Prob, Cuyahoga 1899).

2. Discharge of patient

While superintendent of institution operated by department of mental hygiene and correction has no duty to provide for support of patient after final discharge, circumstances may be such as to require that, as part of his examination to determine patient's fitness for discharge, superintendent should inquire into and make sure that arrangement for his support exists if such support is necessary for his continued mental health. OAG 71–072.

3. Adequate representation

Incapacitated individual's daughter failed to establish, for purposes of intervening in action against her sister and brother-in-law for conversion of part of individual's estate, that guardian of the estate could not adequately represent her interest; guardian took over case after revoking daughter's power of attorney, and had fiduciary duty to protect estate assets. Brady ex rel. Brady v. Benzing (Ohio App. 8 Dist., Cuyahoga, 06-26-2003) No. 81894, 2003-Ohio-3354, 2003 WL 21469584, Unreported, appeal not allowed 100 Ohio St.3d 1487, 798 N.E.2d 1094, 2003-Ohio-5992. Parties ⇔ 41

4. Revocation of powers

Guardian of the estate of incompetent individual had authority under power-of-attorney statute to revoke power of attorney in favor of individual's daughter. Brady ex rel. Brady v. Benzing (Ohio App. 8 Dist., Cuyahoga, 06-26-2003) No. 81894, 2003-Ohio-3354, 2003 WL 21469584, Unreported, appeal not allowed 100 Ohio St.3d 1487, 798 N.E.2d 1094, 2003-Ohio-5992. Principal And Agent ⇔ 37

5. Limitations on guardian's power

Probate court's statutory authority to appoint a limited guardian for an infant did not give the probate court authority to vest the limited guardian with power to withdraw all life-sustaining support, in absence of termination of parental rights. (Per Lundberg Stratton, J., with two Justices concurring and two Justices concurring separately.) In re Guardianship of Stein (Ohio, 12-30-2004) 105 Ohio St.3d 30, 821 N.E.2d 1008, 2004-Ohio-7114. Health ⇔ 915

2111.07 Powers of guardian of person and estate

Each person appointed guardian of the person and estate of a minor shall have the custody and tuition of his ward and the management of such ward's estate during minority, unless such guardian is removed or discharged from such trust or the guardianship terminates from any of the causes specified in Chapters 2101. to 2131., inclusive, of the Revised Code.

(1953 H 1, eff. 10–1–53; GC 10507–7)

Historical and Statutory Notes

Pre–1953 H 1 Amendments: 114 v 385

Cross References

Gift of securities to minors, 1339.31 to 1339.39
Minor or incompetent person as party to action, Civ R 17

Library References

Guardian and Ward ⇔17.
Mental Health ⇔179.
Westlaw Topic Nos. 196, 257A.
C.J.S. Mental Health §§ 158 to 159.
C.J.S. Right to Die §§ 5, 8.

Research References

Encyclopedias
OH Jur. 3d Guardian & Ward § 78, Generally; Office of Guardian.

Law Review and Journal Commentaries

Guardianship and the Elderly: Oversight Not Overlooked, Norman Fell. 25 U Tol L Rev 189 (1994).

Notes of Decisions

Contracts   1
Incompetents   3
Minors   2
Trusts   4

---

1. Contracts

A ward cannot bind her guardianship estate to obligations based upon contract, unless ratified by the guardian. In re Guardianship of Allen (Ohio 1990) 50 Ohio St.3d 142, 552 N.E.2d 934, rehearing denied 51 Ohio St.3d 705, 555 N.E.2d 322. Mental Health ⇔ 374

2. Minors

The Uniform Child Custody Jurisdiction Act, as adopted in Ohio, is applicable to and must be complied with in a guardianship termination proceeding. In re Wonderly's Guardianship (Ohio 1981) 67 Ohio St.2d 178, 423 N.E.2d 420, 21 O.O.3d 111. Guardian And Ward ⇔ 25

Where the mother in divorce proceedings has been granted the custody of her child, she cannot by will transfer custody to anyone but its living father. Ex parte Coons (Ohio Cir. 1899) 11 Ohio C.D. 208.

3. Incompetents

The guardian of an imbecile has no lawful right to pay an attorney's fee for fomented litigation; will be charged with interest on funds of the ward which came into his hands and were used as his own; cannot make disbursements to prospective heirs of the ward; is an incompetent witness as to the value of services rendered by himself on behalf of the ward before his appointment as guardian; and is liable to removal for mingling the ward's funds with his own and investing such funds in real estate taken in his own name, paying claims without investigation, and appropriating enormous fees for his own services. In re Oliver's Guardianship (Ohio Com.Pl. 1909) 20 Ohio Dec. 64, 9 Ohio NP(NS) 178.

4. Trusts

A purchaser of notes of a guardian takes them charged with the trust if on their face they show that they are for trust funds. Strong v. Strauss (Ohio 1883) 40 Ohio St. 87, 9 W.L.B. 345.

Trusts for minors in which trustee could expend income for accident, illness, or other emergency did not qualify for $3,000 gift tax exclusion. Faber v. U. S. (S.D.Ohio 1969) 26 Ohio Misc. 277, 309 F.Supp. 818, 53 O.O.2d 246, 55 O.O.2d 433, affirmed 439 F.2d 1189.

2111.08 Parents are natural guardians; equal parental rights and responsibilities; guardianship jurisdiction

The wife and husband are the joint natural guardians of their minor children and are equally charged with their care, nurture, welfare, and education and the care and management of their estates. The wife and husband have equal powers, rights, and duties and neither parent has any right paramount to the right of the other concerning the parental rights and responsibilities for the care of the minor or the right to be the residential parent and legal custodian of the minor, the control of the services or the earnings of such minor, or any other matter affecting the minor; provided that if either parent, to the exclusion of the other, is maintaining and supporting the child, that parent shall have the paramount right to control the services and earnings of the child. Neither parent shall forcibly take a child from the guardianship of the parent who is the residential parent and legal custodian of the child.

If the wife and husband live apart, the court may award the guardianship of a minor to either parent, and the state in which the parent who is the residential parent and legal custodian or who otherwise has the lawful custody of the minor resides has jurisdiction to determine questions concerning the minor's guardianship.

(1990 S 3, eff. 4–11–91; 1953 H 1; GC 10507–8)

Historical and Statutory Notes

Pre–1953 H 1 Amendments: 114 v 385

Cross References

Parent removing child from custody of other parent, misdemeanor, 2905.04
Right of parent to custody of child, 3109.03

Library References

Child Custody ⚖101.
Guardian and Ward ⚖10.
Westlaw Topic Nos. 196, 76D.

Research References

Encyclopedias

OH Jur. 3d Family Law § 1057, Equal Rights of Parents to Their Children.
OH Jur. 3d Family Law § 1058, Relinquishment of Custody and Control to Other Parent.
OH Jur. 3d Family Law § 1075, Parent's Equality in Allocation.
OH Jur. 3d Family Law § 1076, Allocation Primarily to One Parent.
OH Jur. 3d Guardian & Ward § 28, Appointment of One Parent as Against the Other.
OH Jur. 3d Guardian & Ward § 34, Generally; Jurisdiction of Probate Court.

Forms

Ohio Forms Legal and Business § 28:1, Introduction.
Ohio Forms Legal and Business § 28:43, Introduction.
Ohio Forms Legal and Business § 28:69, Support of Children.
Ohio Forms Legal and Business § 28:81, Introduction.
Ohio Forms Legal and Business § 28:84, Introduction.
Ohio Forms and Transactions KP 30.10, Guardianship Clause.

Treatises and Practice Aids

Carlin, Baldwin's Ohio Practice, Merrick-Rippner Probate Law § 62:2, Appointment of Guardian—Definitions—Guardian.
Carlin, Baldwin's Ohio Practice, Merrick-Rippner Probate Law § 67:4, Alternatives to Guardianship—Statutory Authority for Payments to Minors Under $5,000 Annually.
Carlin, Baldwin's Ohio Practice, Merrick-Rippner Probate Law § 33:19, Trusts—Reports of Inter Vivos Trustees.
Carlin, Baldwin's Ohio Practice, Merrick-Rippner Probate Law § 62:54, Appointment of Guardian of a Minor—Custody Issues—Generally.
Carlin, Baldwin's Ohio Practice, Merrick-Rippner Probate Law § 62:57, Appointment of Guardian of a Minor—Custody Issues—Selection by the Minor.

Notes of Decisions

Abandonment 3
Adoption 7
Best interests of child 4
Control of minor's assets and earnings 1
Liability for minor's debts and support 2
Procedural issues 5
Suitability 6

---

1. Control of minor's assets and earnings

RC 2111.08, making husbands and wives "joint natural guardians" of their minor children and equally charged with "management of their estates" does not entitle an ex-husband parent to be guardian of an estate devised to the child by his former wife, the child's mother; no showing that the father is unsuitable is necessary as a prerequisite to the naming of another person as guardian. In re Estate of Bednarczuk (Warren 1992) 80 Ohio App.3d 548, 609 N.E.2d 1310, motion overruled 65 Ohio St.3d 1444, 600 N.E.2d 686.

The court may appoint the grandfather, rather than the father, as guardian of a minor's estate when there is evidence that the grandfather would act in the child's best interest, the grandfather has a demonstrated ability in the management of the financial affairs of the estate in question, and evidence indicates the father is unacquainted with the child's assets. In re Estate of Bednarczuk (Warren 1992) 80 Ohio App.3d 548, 609 N.E.2d 1310, motion overruled 65 Ohio St.3d 1444, 600 N.E.2d 686.

When the guardianship sought is over the estate, and not the person of the minor, the court need not determine that the father is unsuitable before it appoints the grandfather as guardian of the minor's estate, and RC 2111.08 does not grant the father a statutory entitlement to the minor's estate for which a showing of unsuitability is required. In re Estate of Bednarczuk (Warren 1992) 80 Ohio App.3d 548, 609 N.E.2d 1310, motion overruled 65 Ohio St.3d 1444, 600 N.E.2d 686.

A township trustee is not in violation of former RC 2919.10 in reference to the employment of his minor children by the municipality unless it clearly appears that he is interested in the profits of the contract of services performed by said children, and any presumption that he has any such interest is rebuttable. OAG 66–064.

2. Liability for minor's debts and support

A sentence of thirty days in jail was warranted for criminal contempt by a former husband for failing to pay child support for several years. In re Contemnor Caron (Ohio Com.Pl., 04-27-2000) 110 Ohio Misc.2d 58, 744 N.E.2d 787. Child Support ⚖ 444

Former husband was required to comply with child support orders until paternity claim was resolved. In re Contemnor Caron (Ohio Com.Pl., 04-27-2000) 110 Ohio Misc.2d 58, 744 N.E.2d 787. Child Support ⚖ 375

Where a husband and wife are divorced, the duty to support minor children is governed by RC 3109.05, so that a wife may be required to contribute to the support of her minor children who are in the custody of their father. Hacker v. Hacker (Fairfield 1981) 5 Ohio App.3d 46, 448 N.E.2d 831, 5 O.B.R. 50. Child Support ⇐ 60

A noncustodial father is not liable for an elective abortion performed on his minor daughter, which procedure was neither requested nor authorized by him, and where there was no showing that such parent had refused or neglected to provide for the minor child's support or medical care. Akron City Hospital v. Anderson (Ohio Mun. 1981) 68 Ohio Misc. 14, 428 N.E.2d 472, 22 O.O.3d 238. Child Support ⇐ 113

In an action by a hospital against the parents of a minor child for medical treatment provided to the minor child by the hospital, the mother of the child may not absolve herself of liability to the hospital, a third party, by reason of a provision in the divorce decree requiring the father of the child to pay for all medical expenses incurred by the child. Children's Hospital of Akron v. Johnson (Summit 1980) 68 Ohio App.2d 17, 426 N.E.2d 515, 22 O.O.3d 11.

Parents are liable for the payment of the personal property taxes of their minor children pursuant to RC 5711.05. OAG 72–102.

3. Abandonment

Evidence supported finding that mother's parents prevented communication between mother and biological father of child, for purposes of determining, in adoption proceeding, whether father willfully abandoned mother and child; record indicated that biological father was ordered to stay away from mother, that all attempts by father and his parents to contact mother's parents went unanswered, that father and his family were not given any information regarding child's birth, that every effort was made by mother's parents to keep father and his family away from both mother and child, and that, despite this, father made concerted effort to establish his potential parental rights. In re Adoption of Suvak (Ohio App. 3 Dist., Allen, 02-09-2004) No. 1-03-51, 2004-Ohio-536, 2004 WL 231494, Unreported. Adoption ⇐ 7.4(4)

Offers made by biological father's parents constituted offers for support, for purposes of determining, in adoption proceeding, whether father willfully abandoned mother and child; father's parents offered mother financial and emotional support throughout pregnancy, and father and parents attempted to contact both mother and her parents throughout the pregnancy but were met with repeated rejection. In re Adoption of Suvak (Ohio App. 3 Dist., Allen, 02-09-2004) No. 1-03-51, 2004-Ohio-536, 2004 WL 231494, Unreported. Adoption ⇐ 7.4(6)

Actions of biological father's parents were permissibly attributed to actions of father himself, for purposes of determining, in adoption proceeding, whether father willfully abandoned mother and child; father was a minor for whom parents were statutorily required to care, father was threatened with criminal charges and restraining order if he continued to contact mother, and father's parents offered home to mother, attempted to contact mother's parents, decided to help father and mother financially, and told father to give them money to establish savings account for child's needs. In re Adoption of Suvak (Ohio App. 3 Dist., Allen, 02-09-2004) No. 1-03-51, 2004-Ohio-536, 2004 WL 231494, Unreported. Adoption ⇐ 7.4(4)

Considerations of delay in genetic testing of child and of whether biological father was given notice regarding placement proceedings was proper in determining whether father willfully abandoned mother and child up to time of placement so as to dispense with his consent to adoption, as facts demonstrated extent of interference by mother's parents with father's involvement with child and showed that any abandonment by father of mother during pregnancy and up to time of placement was not voluntary choice by father. In re Adoption of Suvak (Ohio App. 3 Dist., Allen, 02-09-2004) No. 1-03-51, 2004-Ohio-536, 2004 WL 231494, Unreported. Adoption ⇐ 7.4(4)

Although parent who formerly abandoned his children is shown now to be proper person to have such custody, fact of children's grandparents having cared for them over several years must be considered, along with resulting affections, in determining present best interests of children. Baker v. Rose (Ohio Com.Pl. 1970) 28 Ohio Misc. 200, 270 N.E.2d 678, 57 O.O.2d 57, 57 O.O.2d 351.

Abandonment by parent of his minor child forfeits any preference under law to obtain custody of such child, but does not preclude his being considered as appropriate person to whom court might award custody. Baker v. Rose (Ohio Com.Pl. 1970) 28 Ohio Misc. 200, 270 N.E.2d 678, 57 O.O.2d 57, 57 O.O.2d 351.

4. Best interests of child

A court is not obligated to find parents unfit before awarding custody to the child's grandmother where the child (1) has adjusted to life at his grandmother's house, (2) is participating in school and community activities and (3) the grandmother is making an effort to preserve the child's relationships with the father and his extended family. Wright v. Wright (Ohio App. 8 Dist., Cuyahoga, 10-19-1995) No. 67884, 1995 WL 614500, Unreported.

A proposed settlement of child support and custody disputes was not in the best interests of the child; the former husband was five-and-one-half years delinquent in child support, and the former wife waived a major portion of the court-ordered entitlements for the benefit of the child. In re Contemnor Caron (Ohio Com.Pl., 04-27-2000) 110 Ohio Misc.2d 58, 744 N.E.2d 787. Child Custody ⇐ 35; Child Support ⇐ 44

The best interests of a child demand that the father pay to the mother, for the benefit of the child, all monies and expenses previously ordered by the court. In re Contemnor Caron (Ohio Com.Pl., 04-27-2000) 110 Ohio Misc.2d 58, 744 N.E.2d 787. Child Support ⇐ 430

Before the court may consider what disposition should be made of children for their best interest and welfare, there must first be an adjudication that said children are neglected or dependent, and where neglect and dependency existed at the time of the filing of the complaint, but said cause was not prosecuted further until more than four years afterwards and the conditions of the parents had changed sufficiently that evidence was lacking to establish neglect or dependency at the time of the hearing, said complaint must be dismissed. In re Burkhart (Ohio Juv. 1968) 15 Ohio Misc. 170, 239 N.E.2d 772, 44 O.O.2d 329.

Division of child welfare granted custody of minor children upon ground children's return to mother and maternal relatives would not serve the best interests of the children. In re Zerick, 129 NE(2d) 661, 74 Abs 525, 57 OO 331 (Juv. 1955).

Ohio statutes provide for appointment by probate court, when found necessary, of a guardian of person or estate of a minor, or of both, who will have care and management of the person or estate of such minor, or both, and that with certain exceptions, a minor over age of fourteen years may select a guardian, who, if a suitable person, shall be appointed; further, a father and a mother have equal rights to the custody of a minor, and a surviving parent may by last will appoint a guardian; there is a distinction between a parent acting as a natural guardian of his minor child with custody of the minor's person and the position of legal guardian appointed by the court for purpose of care and management of the estate of such minor. Chertoff v. C.I.R. (C.C.A.6 1947) 160 F.2d 691, 35 O.O. 399.

5. Procedural issues

Alabama was child's home state under Uniform Child Custody Jurisdiction Act (UCCJA), where both mother and father had equal parenting rights once father's domestic violence complaint against mother was dismissed, father had physical child custody for approximately five years, and child resided with father in Alabama for more than six consecutive months prior to time instant child custody action was brought. In re Sklenchar (Ohio App. 7 Dist., Mahoning, 08-18-2004) No. 04MA55, 2004-Ohio-4405, 2004 WL 1874572, Unreported. Child Custody ⇐ 736

Parents' failure to appeal from adjudication that children were dependent prevented them from raising alleged errors occurring at adjudication hearing on appeal of subsequent grant of permanent custody of children to county children services board; adjudication decision was final appealable order. In re Sessoms (Ohio App. 12 Dist., Butler, 10-06-2003) No. CA2002-11-280, 2003-Ohio-5281, 2003 WL 22283495, Unreported. Infants ⇐ 248.1

Mother, who sought guardianship over her adult incompetent son, failed to preserve for appellate review her claim that trial court's findings of fact that son's father had a degenerative eye disease that was likely to eventually result in blindness, was against the weight of the evidence, where mother failed to object to father's testimony at guardianship proceeding that he was going blind. In re Guardianship of Nease (Ohio App. 6 Dist., Lucas, 05-02-2003) No. L-02-1296, 2003-Ohio-2218, 2003 WL 2007729, Unreported. Mental Health ⇐ 148.1

There is a presumption that the best interests of a bastard child require it to be in its mother's custody, and the burden is upon the person disputing such mother's right to custody to prove that such child should not be in its mother's custody. In re Gary (Cuyahoga 1960) 112 Ohio App. 331, 167 N.E.2d 509, 83 Ohio Law Abs. 486, 14 O.O.2d 431.

A trial court that approved a separation agreement, thereafter adopted as a part of the judgment in a divorce, alimony and custody action, which agreement contained a provision regarding the custody of a minor child, is not bound by the terms of that agreement, in a subsequent hearing on a motion to modify the provisions of the judgment entry. Bastian v. Bastian

(Cuyahoga 1959) 160 N.E.2d 133, 73 A.L.R.2d 1440, 81 Ohio Law Abs. 408, 13 O.O.2d 267.

A child should be appointed a guardian ad litem and made a party to a legitimization proceeding, when it is clear that the mother, as natural guardian, has an adverse interest in the proceeding. Blackburn v Ludden, 1 OBR 340 (App, Trumbull 1982).

6. Suitability

Trial court acted within its discretion, and in best interest of child, when court decided that monetary conflict of interest regarding settlement of father's insurance claims rendered mother unsuitable to become guardian of child's estate, where amount child would receive from settlement was inversely proportional to amount mother would receive. In re Guardianship of Muehrcke (Ohio App. 8 Dist., Cuyahoga, 01-16-2003) No. 81353, 2003-Ohio-176, 2003 WL 132422, Unreported, appeal not allowed 99 Ohio St.3d 1412, 788 N.E.2d 648, 2003-Ohio-2454. Guardian And Ward ⟲ 10

Trial court acted within its discretion when it scrutinized legal expenses which mother charged against assets of her child's estate, rejected mother's request to settle child's claim to insurance proceeds arising from father's automobile accident for $50,000, and appointed independent guardian to ensure that child received proper settlement, where court noted that $50,000 was significantly less than amount arrived at by applying child's jury award percentage to total settlement amount, and left amount of child's share to be determined by independent guardian subject to court's approval. In re Guardianship of Muehrcke (Ohio App. 8 Dist., Cuyahoga, 01-16-2003) No. 81353, 2003-Ohio-176, 2003 WL 132422, Unreported, appeal not allowed 99 Ohio St.3d 1412, 788 N.E.2d 648, 2003-Ohio-2454. Guardian And Ward ⟲ 33

The father is natural guardian of his minor child and necessity for appointment of a guardian does not arise except for cause and where the father is shown to be an unsuitable person. Hare v. Sears (Ohio Com.Pl. 1906) 17 Ohio Dec. 590, 4 Ohio N.P.N.S. 566. Guardian And Ward ⟲ 9.5; Child Custody ⟲ 22

7. Adoption

A natural parent cannot be the sole adoptive parent of a natural child even with the consent of other natural parent as a matter of law. In re Adoption of Graham (Ohio Com.Pl. 1980) 63 Ohio Misc. 22, 409 N.E.2d 1067, 16 O.O.3d 347, 17 O.O.3d 341.

2111.09 Administrator or executor ineligible

Unless expressly appointed or designated to act both as guardian and executor by a last will in writing, no person who is or has been an administrator or executor of a last will shall, prior to the approval of his final account as such executor or administrator, be appointed a guardian of the person and estate or of the estate only of a ward who is interested in the estate administered upon or entitled to an interest under such will, except that a surviving spouse may be executor or administrator of the deceased spouse's estate and also guardian of the person and estate or of the estate only of a minor child of such surviving spouse, whether or not such minor child is interested in the estate of the deceased spouse. But an executor or an administrator may be appointed a guardian of the person only of a ward.

(127 v 36, eff. 9–4–57; 1953 H 1; GC 10507–9)

Historical and Statutory Notes

Pre–1953 H 1 Amendments: 114 v 386

Library References

Guardian and Ward ⟲10.
Mental Health ⟲116.
Westlaw Topic Nos. 196, 257A.
C.J.S. Mental Health § 123.

Research References

Encyclopedias
OH Jur. 3d Decedents' Estates § 1383, Administrator as Guardian.

OH Jur. 3d Guardian & Ward § 22, Administrator or Executor as Guardian.

Forms
Ohio Forms Legal and Business § 24:143, Drafting Will.

Ohio Forms Legal and Business § 24:481, Appointment of Guardian—Person of Minor Children—Provision Expressing Desire Same Person be Appointed Guardian of Their Estates.

Ohio Forms and Transactions F 30.11, Appointment of Guardian.

Treatises and Practice Aids
Carlin, Baldwin's Ohio Practice, Merrick-Rippner Probate Law § 30:31, Drafting a Will—Designation of Guardian, Trustee, and Attorney—Designation of Guardian of Minor Children.

Carlin, Baldwin's Ohio Practice, Merrick-Rippner Probate Law § 30:57, Simple Will—Form.

Carlin, Baldwin's Ohio Practice, Merrick-Rippner Probate Law § 62:41, Guardianship Proceedings—Who May Serve—Administrator/Executor.

Carlin, Baldwin's Ohio Practice, Merrick-Rippner Probate Law App B SPF 17.5, Judgment Entry—Appointment of Guardian for Incompetent Person.

Notes of Decisions

Eligible 2
Illegal appointment, effect 3
Ineligible 1

---

1. Ineligible

An administratrix of an estate in which a minor is interested is ineligible to be appointed guardian of the estate of such minor. Scobey v. Gano (Ohio 1880) 35 Ohio St. 550.

Under earlier statute (108 v Pt 2, 1162) in effect prior to January 1, 1932, no person who at the time was or had been an administratrix or executrix of a last will prior to approval of her final account as such executrix or administratrix might be appointed guardian of estate of minor who was interested in estate administered upon or entitled to interest under and by virtue of such will. Guardianship of Zimmerman (Ohio 1943) 141 Ohio St. 207, 47 N.E.2d 782, 25 O.O. 326. Guardian And Ward ⟲ 10

2. Eligible

Where the decedent's former spouse is given custody of their children he is not considered their "guardian" as that word is used in RC 2111.01 and as a result he is not subject to RC 2111.09, which forbids appointment of the same person as administrator and guardian. In re Estate of Robertson (Cuyahoga 1985) 26 Ohio App.3d 64, 498 N.E.2d 206, 26 O.B.R. 238.

3. Illegal appointment, effect

Where a guardian of a minor has been illegally appointed and the minor moves to another county, the probate court of the latter county can appoint another guardian though no order vacating the former appointment has been made. Scobey v. Gano (Ohio 1880) 35 Ohio St. 550.

The proceedings of the guardian of a minor to sell the minor's real estate, which are carried on in good faith and confirmed by probate court, are not a mere nullity notwithstanding the guardian held office illegally by reason of the fact that he was also executor of an estate in which the minor was interested. Easton v. Wittekind (Ohio Com.Pl. 1929) 27 Ohio N.P.N.S. 525.

2111.091 Restrictions on attorneys representing guardians

No attorney who represents any person other than himself who is appointed as a guardian under this chapter or under any other provision of the Revised Code shall do either of the following:

(A) Act as a person with co-responsibility for any guardianship asset for which the guardian he represents is responsible;

(B) Be a cosignatory on any financial account related to the guardianship, including any checking account, savings account, or other banking or trust account.

(1992 S 273, eff. 3–6–92)

Library References

Attorney and Client ⚖32(7), 78.
Westlaw Topic No. 45.
C.J.S. Attorney and Client §§ 6, 43 to 58, 86, 209 to 217.

Research References

Encyclopedias

OH Jur. 3d Guardian & Ward § 97, Particular Actions on Ward's Behalf; Exercise of Ward's Right of Election—Bringing or Defending Suits; Employment of Counsel.

Forms

Ohio Forms Legal and Business § 24:143, Drafting Will.
Ohio Forms Legal and Business § 24:481, Appointment of Guardian—Person of Minor Children—Provision Expressing Desire Same Person be Appointed Guardian of Their Estates.

Treatises and Practice Aids

Carlin, Baldwin's Ohio Practice, Merrick-Rippner Probate Law § 30:31, Drafting a Will—Designation of Guardian, Trustee, and Attorney—Designation of Guardian of Minor Children.

Carlin, Baldwin's Ohio Practice, Merrick-Rippner Probate Law § 64:25, Powers and Duties of Guardian—Ward's Estate—Acts of the Ward—Attorneys.

Notes of Decisions

Conflict of interest 2
Constitutional issues 1

---

1. Constitutional issues

Statute prohibiting attorney of guardian from acting as person with coresponsibility for any guardianship assets or from being cosignatory on any financial account related to guardianship was not unconstitutional interference with judiciary rulemaking, where record did not demonstrate adoption of local rule allowing such action in county probate court. In re Heggs (Hamilton 1994) 92 Ohio App.3d 102, 634 N.E.2d 269. Attorney And Client ⚖ 1; Constitutional Law ⚖ 55

2. Conflict of interest

Attorney, who was guardian of ward's estate, had a conflict of interest that required removal as guardian, where attorney had represented ward's son, who was guardian of ward's person, in several legal matters, including a divorce, he had advised son to transfer title of his property to his mother to avoid execution of judgment liens, and he had applied to the probate court for authority to release estate funds to son to pay off a lease on a truck that son was obligated to pay to his former spouse in a divorce. In re Guardianship of Walther (Ohio App. 2 Dist., Montgomery, 06-25-2004) No. 20095, 2004-Ohio-3396, 2004 WL 1454464, Unreported. Guardian And Ward ⚖ 25

Evidence regarding the representation by attorney, who was guardian of ward's estate, of ward's son, who was guardian of ward's person, was relevant to prove a conflict of interest in action by granddaughter of ward to remove attorney as guardian of estate. In re Guardianship of Walther (Ohio App. 2 Dist., Montgomery, 06-25-2004) No. 20095, 2004-Ohio-3396, 2004 WL 1454464, Unreported. Guardian And Ward ⚖ 25

2111.10 Corporation as guardian

As used in this section, "mentally retarded person" and "developmentally disabled person" have the same meanings as in section 5123.01 of the Revised Code.

Any appointment of a corporation as guardian shall apply to the estate only and not to the person, except that a nonprofit corporation organized under the laws of this state and entitled to tax exempt status under section 501(a) of the "Internal Revenue Code of 1986," 100 Stat. 2085, 26 U.S.C.A. 501, as amended, that has a contract with the department of mental retardation and developmental disabilities to provide protective services may be appointed as a guardian of the person of a mentally retarded or developmentally disabled person and may serve as guardian pursuant to sections 5123.55 to 5123.59 of the Revised Code.

(1990 H 569, eff. 7–1–91; 1980 H 900; 1978 S 415; 1953 H 1; GC 10507–10)

Historical and Statutory Notes

Pre–1953 H 1 Amendments: 114 v 386

Library References

Mental Health ⚖116.1.
Westlaw Topic No. 257A.
C.J.S. Mental Health § 123.

Research References

Encyclopedias

OH Jur. 3d Guardian & Ward § 23, Corporation as Guardian.

Forms

Ohio Forms Legal and Business § 24:481, Appointment of Guardian—Person of Minor Children—Provision Expressing Desire Same Person be Appointed Guardian of Their Estates.

Treatises and Practice Aids

Carlin, Baldwin's Ohio Practice, Merrick-Rippner Probate Law § 62:9, Appointment of Guardian—Definitions—Guardianship of the Person And/Or Estate.

2111.11 Spouse may be appointed guardian

When a guardian is appointed for a person having a spouse, the court may appoint such spouse as the guardian, if it is made to appear to the satisfaction of the court that such spouse is competent to discharge the duties of such appointment.

(1953 H 1, eff. 10–1–53; GC 10507–11)

Historical and Statutory Notes

Pre–1953 H 1 Amendments: 114 v 386

Library References

Guardian and Ward ⚖10.
Mental Health ⚖119.
Westlaw Topic Nos. 196, 257A.
C.J.S. Mental Health § 123.

Research References

Encyclopedias

OH Jur. 3d Guardian & Ward § 33, Guardian for Incompetent.

Treatises and Practice Aids

Carlin, Baldwin's Ohio Practice, Merrick-Rippner Probate Law § 62:42, Guardianship Proceedings—Who May Serve—Spouse.

Notes of Decisions

Authority of spouse 2
Notice to spouse 1

---

1. Notice to spouse

Before the amendment of RS 6302 in 1889, a guardian of the estate of an insane wife might be appointed without notice to her husband. Heckman v. Adams (Ohio 1893) 50 Ohio St. 305, 29 W.L.B. 330, 34 N.E. 155.

2. Authority of spouse

A spouse, individually and without the intervention of the court, and without the appointment of a guardian, has the authority to discontinue life-sustaining treatment. In re Guardianship of McInnis (Ohio Prob. 1991) 61 Ohio Misc.2d 790, 584 N.E.2d 1389. Health ⇐ 915

2111.12 Guardian of minor

(A) A minor over the age of fourteen years may select a guardian who shall be appointed if a suitable person. If such minor fails to select a suitable person, an appointment may be made without reference to the minor's wishes. The minor shall not select one person to be the guardian of the minor's estate only and another to be the guardian of the person only, unless the court which appoints is of the opinion that the interests of such minor will thereby be promoted.

(B) A surviving parent by last will in writing may appoint a guardian for any of the surviving parent's children, whether born at the time of making the will or afterward, to continue during the minority of the child or for a less time.

When the father or mother of a minor names a person as guardian of the estate of such minor in a will, the person named shall have preference in appointment over the person selected by such minor. A person named in such a will as guardian of the person of such minor shall have no preference in appointment over the person selected by such minor, but in such event the probate court may appoint the person named in the will, the person selected by the minor, or some other person.

Whenever a testamentary guardian is appointed, the testamentary guardian's duties, powers, and liabilities in all other respects shall be governed by the law regulating guardians not appointed by will.

(C) A parent pursuant to a durable power of attorney as described in division (D) of section 1337.09 or a writing as described in division (A) of section 2111.121 of the Revised Code may nominate a person to be a guardian for one or more of the parent's minor children, whether born at the time of the making of the petition or afterward.

(1996 H 288, eff. 1–14–97; 1953 H 1, eff. 10–1–53; GC 10507–12 to 10507–14)

Historical and Statutory Notes

Pre–1953 H 1 Amendments: 121 v 557; 114 v 386

Amendment Note: 1996 H 288 designated division (B); added division (C); and made changes to reflect gender neutral language.

Cross References

Residence qualifications of guardians, 2109.21

Library References

Guardian and Ward ⇐10, 13(1).
Westlaw Topic No. 196.

Research References

Encyclopedias

OH Jur. 3d Guardian & Ward § 7, Definitions and Types of Guardians—Guardianships by Nomination.

OH Jur. 3d Guardian & Ward § 8, Definitions and Types of Guardians—Testamentary Guardianships.

OH Jur. 3d Guardian & Ward § 21, Residence.

OH Jur. 3d Guardian & Ward § 27, Same Person as Guardian of Person and Estate.

OH Jur. 3d Guardian & Ward § 31, Minor's Right of Choice.

OH Jur. 3d Guardian & Ward § 32, Preference to Testamentary Guardian or Guardian Nominated by a Parent.

OH Jur. 3d Guardian & Ward § 104, Testamentary Guardian.

Forms

Ohio Forms Legal and Business § 24:143, Drafting Will.

Ohio Forms Legal and Business § 24:161, Entire Estate to Spouse—Alternatively to Children—Guardianship of Minors.

Ohio Forms Legal and Business § 24:282, Guardian.

Ohio Forms Legal and Business § 24:481, Appointment of Guardian—Person of Minor Children—Provision Expressing Desire Same Person be Appointed Guardian of Their Estates.

Ohio Forms Legal and Business § 24:486, Appointment of Coguardians—Persons of Minor Children—Provisions for Alternate or Successive Guardians.

Ohio Forms Legal and Business § 24:205.10, Pour-Over Will—Residue to Trust.

Treatises and Practice Aids

Carlin, Baldwin's Ohio Practice, Merrick-Rippner Probate Law § 51:4, Residency—Guardian.

Carlin, Baldwin's Ohio Practice, Merrick-Rippner Probate Law § 51:5, Residency—Guardian—Removal of Nonresident.

Carlin, Baldwin's Ohio Practice, Merrick-Rippner Probate Law § 51:6, Residency—Removal of Nonresident Fiduciary.

Carlin, Baldwin's Ohio Practice, Merrick-Rippner Probate Law § 57:5, Removal of Fiduciary—Grounds—Nonresidency of Fiduciary.

Carlin, Baldwin's Ohio Practice, Merrick-Rippner Probate Law § 68:4, Letters of Administration—Specific Qualifications of Administrators—Residency Requirement.

Carlin, Baldwin's Ohio Practice, Merrick-Rippner Probate Law § 30:31, Drafting a Will—Designation of Guardian, Trustee, and Attorney—Designation of Guardian of Minor Children.

Carlin, Baldwin's Ohio Practice, Merrick-Rippner Probate Law § 30:57, Simple Will—Form.

Carlin, Baldwin's Ohio Practice, Merrick-Rippner Probate Law § 60:10, Power of Attorney—"Standby Guardian" for Minor Child of Principal.

Carlin, Baldwin's Ohio Practice, Merrick-Rippner Probate Law § 62:16, Appointment of Guardian—Application—Who May Apply.

Carlin, Baldwin's Ohio Practice, Merrick-Rippner Probate Law § 62:23, Appointment of Guardian—Procedure—Guardian Nominated in Will, Power of Attorney, or Other Writing.

Carlin, Baldwin's Ohio Practice, Merrick-Rippner Probate Law § 62:24, Appointment of Guardian—Parent May Nominate Guardian for Minor by Will.

Carlin, Baldwin's Ohio Practice, Merrick-Rippner Probate Law § 62:30, Appointment of Guardian—Miscellaneous—Minor Children of Ward.

Carlin, Baldwin's Ohio Practice, Merrick-Rippner Probate Law § 62:39, Guardianship Proceedings—Who May Serve.

Carlin, Baldwin's Ohio Practice, Merrick-Rippner Probate Law § 62:50, Appointment of Guardian of a Minor—Designation by Minor.

Carlin, Baldwin's Ohio Practice, Merrick-Rippner Probate Law § 62:52, Appointment of Guardian of a Minor—Testamentary Designation by Parent.

Carlin, Baldwin's Ohio Practice, Merrick-Rippner Probate Law § 62:53, Appointment of Guardian of a Minor—Designation by Parent in a Power of Attorney or Writing.

Carlin, Baldwin's Ohio Practice, Merrick-Rippner Probate Law § 30:171, Appointment of Guardian If Spouse Fails to Survive; Successor—Form.

Carlin, Baldwin's Ohio Practice, Merrick-Rippner Probate Law App B SPF 16.2, Selection of Guardian by Minor Over Fourteen Years of Age.

Kuehnle and Levey, Ohio Real Estate Law and Practice § 52:20, Statutory Fiduciary Sales—Action for Sale by Guardian—Testamentary Power of Sale.

Law Review and Journal Commentaries

Standby Guardianships—Substitute H.B. 288, Michael Stark. 7 Prob L J Ohio 65 (July/August 1997).

Notes of Decisions

Choice of minor 2
Suitability 1
Testamentary guardian 3

Void appointment 4

1. Suitability

The court may appoint the grandfather, rather than the father, as guardian of a minor's estate when there is evidence that the grandfather would act in the child's best interest, the grandfather has a demonstrated ability in the management of the financial affairs of the estate in question, and evidence indicates the father is unacquainted with the child's assets. In re Estate of Bednarczuk (Warren 1992) 80 Ohio App.3d 548, 609 N.E.2d 1310, motion overruled 65 Ohio St.3d 1444, 600 N.E.2d 686.

When the guardianship sought is over the estate, and not the person of the minor, the court need not determine that the father is unsuitable before it appoints the grandfather as guardian of the minor's estate, and RC 2111.08 does not grant the father a statutory entitlement to the minor's estate for which a showing of unsuitability is required. In re Estate of Bednarczuk (Warren 1992) 80 Ohio App.3d 548, 609 N.E.2d 1310, motion overruled 65 Ohio St.3d 1444, 600 N.E.2d 686.

2. Choice of minor

A guardian appointed when a minor was too young to choose a guardian cannot, after the minor reaches the age where the original guardianship expires by law, maintain a suit to sell the ward's land. Perry's Lessee v. Brainard (Ohio 1842) 11 Ohio 442.

A minor may select one person as guardian of its estate and another for its person if the interests of such minor will be promoted by such choice. State ex rel. Fisher v. Madden (Ohio Com.Pl. 1901) 12 Ohio Dec. 83.

Ohio statutes provide for appointment by probate court, when found necessary, of a guardian of person or estate of a minor, or of both, who will have care and management of the person or estate of such minor, or both, and that with certain exceptions, a minor over age of fourteen years may select a guardian, who, if a suitable person, shall be appointed; further, a father and a mother have equal rights to the custody of a minor, and a surviving parent may by last will appoint a guardian; there is a distinction between a parent acting as a natural guardian of his minor child with custody of the minor's person and the position of legal guardian appointed by the court for purpose of care and management of the estate of such minor. Chertoff v. C.I.R. (C.C.A.6 1947) 160 F.2d 691, 35 O.O. 399.

3. Testamentary guardian

Where the mother in divorce proceedings has been granted the custody of her child, she cannot by will transfer custody to anyone but its living father. Ex parte Coons (Ohio Cir. 1899) 11 Ohio C.D. 208.

4. Void appointment

If the record in the probate court of the appointment of a guardian of a minor affirmatively shows that such minor is without estate, such appointment is void, and upon habeas corpus the parent will be awarded the custody of the child against the guardian so appointed. In re Baier (Ohio Com.Pl. 1900) 11 Ohio Dec. 47, 8 Ohio N.P. 107.

2111.121 Nomination as guardian of person or estate; procedure

(A) A person may nominate in a writing, as described in this division, another person to be the guardian of the nominator's person, estate, or both or the guardian of the person, the estate, or both, of one or more of the nominator's minor children, whether born at the time of the execution of the writing or afterward. The nomination is for consideration by a court if proceedings for the appointment of a guardian of the person, the estate, or both, for the person making the nomination or if proceedings for the appointment of a guardian as the guardian of the person, the estate, or both of one or more of the nominator's minor children are commenced at a later time. The person may authorize, in a writing of that nature, the person nominated as guardian to nominate a successor guardian for consideration by a court. The person also may direct, in a writing of that nature, that bond be waived for a person nominated as guardian in it or nominated as a successor guardian in accordance with an authorization in it.

To be effective as a nomination, the writing shall be signed by the person making the nomination in the presence of two witnesses; signed by the witnesses; contain, immediately prior to their signatures, an attestation of the witnesses that the person making the nomination signed the writing in their presence; and be acknowledged by the person making the nomination before a notary public.

(B) If a person has nominated, in a writing as described in division (A) of this section or in a durable power of attorney as described in division (D) of section 1337.09 of the Revised Code, another person to be the guardian of the nominator's person, estate, or both, and proceedings for the appointment of a guardian for the person are commenced at a later time, the court involved shall appoint the person nominated as guardian in the writing or durable power of attorney most recently executed if the person nominated is competent, suitable, and willing to accept the appointment. If the writing or durable power of attorney contains a waiver of bond, the court shall waive bond of the person nominated as guardian unless it is of the opinion that the interest of the trust demands it.

(C) Nomination of a person as a guardian or successor guardian of the person, the estate, or both of one or more of the nominator's minor children under division (A) of this section, and any subsequent appointment of the guardian or successor guardian as guardian under section 2111.02 of the Revised Code, does not vacate the jurisdiction of any other court that previously may have exercised jurisdiction over the person of the minor.

(D) The writing containing the nomination of a person to be the guardian of the person, the estate, or both of one or more of the nominator's minor children under division (A) of this section may be filed with the probate court for safekeeping, and the probate court shall designate the nomination as the nomination of a standby guardian.

(1996 H 288, eff. 1–14–97; 1988 S 228, eff. 3–22–89; 1983 S 115)

Historical and Statutory Notes

Amendment Note: 1996 H 288 inserted "or the guardian of the person, the estate, or both of one or more of the nominator's minor children, whether born at the time of the execution of the writing or afterward" and "or if proceedings for the appointment of a guardian as the guardian of the person, the estate, or both of one or more of the nominator's minor children" in the first paragraph in division (A); added division (C); and made changes to reflect gender neutral language and other nonsubstantive changes.

OSBA Probate and Trust Law Section

1983:

It had come to the attention to [sic] the Probate and Trust Law Board of Governors that certain financial institutions in the State of Ohio were failing to honor Durable Powers of Attorney which were not recently executed. It was thought this was an unfortunate problem which could be easily corrected by adding a provision to current law preventing invalidation due to age of a Durable Power of Attorney.

In studying the Durable Power of Attorney statute while addressing the above problem, it was thought the Durable Power of Attorney was a suitable tool to permit a principal to nominate his own guardian. Certainly an individual ought to be able to express a preference in the unfortunate event it becomes necessary to institute guardianship proceedings in his behalf. Some individuals may not want a Durable Power of Attorney but still wish to nominate their own guardian and therefore legislation is proposed to permit such a nomination by a separate writing. The question of residence requirements for a guardian was addressed and no good reason could be found for requiring different standards for a guardian so named.

The matter of the proper execution requirements for a Durable Power of Attorney was considered and it was decided that since a Durable Power of Attorney and separate writing in which a principal nominated his own guardian were of such sensitivity and importance, these instruments should be executed with the same formality as Powers of Attorney dealing with real estate.

The necessary conforming changes were made in existing Guardianship Section 2111.02 of the Revised Code.

Cross References

Residence qualifications of guardians, 2109.21

Library References

Guardian and Ward ⚖13(3).
Mental Health ⚖126.
Westlaw Topic Nos. 196, 257A.
C.J.S. Mental Health § 133.
  Baldwin's Ohio Legislative Service, 1988 Laws of Ohio, S 228—LSC Analysis, p 5–968

Research References

Encyclopedias

OH Jur. 3d Guardian & Ward § 7, Definitions and Types of Guardians—Guardianships by Nomination.
OH Jur. 3d Guardian & Ward § 21, Residence.
OH Jur. 3d Guardian & Ward § 25, Right to Nominate a Guardian.
OH Jur. 3d Guardian & Ward § 32, Preference to Testamentary Guardian or Guardian Nominated by a Parent.
OH Jur. 3d Guardian & Ward § 48, Where Ward Has Nominated a Guardian.
OH Jur. 3d Guardian & Ward § 59, Waiver of Bond.

Treatises and Practice Aids

Carlin, Baldwin's Ohio Practice, Merrick-Rippner Probate Law § 51:4, Residency—Guardian.
Carlin, Baldwin's Ohio Practice, Merrick-Rippner Probate Law § 51:5, Residency—Guardian—Removal of Nonresident.
Carlin, Baldwin's Ohio Practice, Merrick-Rippner Probate Law § 51:6, Residency—Removal of Nonresident Fiduciary.
Carlin, Baldwin's Ohio Practice, Merrick-Rippner Probate Law § 57:5, Removal of Fiduciary—Grounds—Nonresidency of Fiduciary.
Carlin, Baldwin's Ohio Practice, Merrick-Rippner Probate Law § 60:9, Power of Attorney—Appointment of Guardian for Principal.
Carlin, Baldwin's Ohio Practice, Merrick-Rippner Probate Law § 67:7, Alternatives to Guardianship—Adult Wards.
Carlin, Baldwin's Ohio Practice, Merrick-Rippner Probate Law § 68:4, Letters of Administration—Specific Qualifications of Administrators—Residency Requirement.
Carlin, Baldwin's Ohio Practice, Merrick-Rippner Probate Law § 30:31, Drafting a Will—Designation of Guardian, Trustee, and Attorney—Designation of Guardian of Minor Children.
Carlin, Baldwin's Ohio Practice, Merrick-Rippner Probate Law § 60:10, Power of Attorney—"Standby Guardian" for Minor Child of Principal.
Carlin, Baldwin's Ohio Practice, Merrick-Rippner Probate Law § 60:43, Guardian Designation—Form.
Carlin, Baldwin's Ohio Practice, Merrick-Rippner Probate Law § 62:14, Appointment of Guardian—Application—Jurisdiction.
Carlin, Baldwin's Ohio Practice, Merrick-Rippner Probate Law § 62:16, Appointment of Guardian—Application—Who May Apply.
Carlin, Baldwin's Ohio Practice, Merrick-Rippner Probate Law § 62:23, Appointment of Guardian—Procedure—Guardian Nominated in Will, Power of Attorney, or Other Writing.
Carlin, Baldwin's Ohio Practice, Merrick-Rippner Probate Law § 62:26, Appointment of Guardian—Nomination by Other Writing.
Carlin, Baldwin's Ohio Practice, Merrick-Rippner Probate Law § 62:30, Appointment of Guardian—Miscellaneous—Minor Children of Ward.
Carlin, Baldwin's Ohio Practice, Merrick-Rippner Probate Law § 62:39, Guardianship Proceedings—Who May Serve.
Carlin, Baldwin's Ohio Practice, Merrick-Rippner Probate Law § 62:50, Appointment of Guardian of a Minor—Designation by Minor.
Carlin, Baldwin's Ohio Practice, Merrick-Rippner Probate Law § 62:53, Appointment of Guardian of a Minor—Designation by Parent in a Power of Attorney or Writing.
Carlin, Baldwin's Ohio Practice, Merrick-Rippner Probate Law § 30:171, Appointment of Guardian If Spouse Fails to Survive; Successor—Form.

Law Review and Journal Commentaries

Guardianship versus Power of Attorney: A Clear Winner Emerges, Fred V. Skok. 12 Lake Legal Views 1 (February 1989).

Power of Attorney—How to Avoid Third Party Denial, Jane Hils Shea. Cin B Ass'n Rep 14 (February 1988).

Standby Guardianships—Substitute H.B. 288, Michael Stark. 7 Prob L J Ohio 65 (July/August 1997).

Notes of Decisions

Conflict of interest 2
Defective application 1

---

1. Defective application

The trial court's appointment of mother's second son, rather than the son mother had nominated as her prospective guardian, as guardian of mother was an abuse of discretion; nominated son had assisted mother in managing her affairs since her husband died, he paid her bills, he visited her often, and his name was on her checking and savings accounts, mother had executed a durable power of attorney that nominated son as her attorney in fact and prospective guardian, and there was no evidence that nominated son was incompetent to serve as mother's guardian. In re Guardianship of McHaney (Ohio App. 9 Dist., Summit, 11-10-2004) No. 22088, 2004-Ohio-5956, 2004 WL 2535414, Unreported, appeal not allowed 105 Ohio St.3d 1464, 824 N.E.2d 92, 2005-Ohio-1024. Guardian And Ward ⚖ 10

Appointment of a grandson as guardian of a physically incapacitated ward, nominated as guardian in a defective application, and rejection of the application of the ward's daughter, nominated as guardian in a properly executed durable power of attorney, on the ground that the daughter is a nonresident, is improper. In re Medsker (Cuyahoga 1990) 66 Ohio App.3d 219, 583 N.E.2d 1091.

2. Conflict of interest

Appointment of husband as guardian over wife's person was not in best interests of wife; wife did not nominate him as sole guardian but rather as co-guardian, and there was much evidence that husband took improper actions regarding wife's financial assets. In re Guardianship of Thomas (Ohio App. 10 Dist., 03-12-2002) 148 Ohio App.3d 11, 771 N.E.2d 882, 2002-Ohio-1037. Mental Health ⚖ 119

In investigating alleged conflict of interest between coguardians which could ultimately affect best interest of ward, court-appointed investigator was not required to communicate with ward pursuant to statute which applies to initial investigations of alleged incompetent and provides safeguards for due process rights of alleged incompetent; that statute was inapplicable, as ward had previously been adjudged incompetent. In re Guardianship of Coller (Wood 1991) 74 Ohio App.3d 386, 599 N.E.2d 292, motion overruled 62 Ohio St.3d 1477, 581 N.E.2d 1099. Mental Health ⚖ 120

POWERS AND DUTIES OF GUARDIAN

2111.13 Duties of guardian of person

(A) When a guardian is appointed to have the custody and maintenance of a ward, and to have charge of the education of the ward if the ward is a minor, the guardian's duties are as follows:

(1) To protect and control the person of the ward;

(2) To provide suitable maintenance for the ward when necessary, which shall be paid out of the estate of such ward upon the order of the guardian of the person;

(3) To provide such maintenance and education for such ward as the amount of the ward's estate justifies when the ward is a minor and has no father or mother, or has a father or mother who fails to maintain or educate the ward, which shall be paid out of such ward's estate upon the order of the guardian of the person;

(4) To obey all the orders and judgments of the probate court touching the guardianship.

(B) Except as provided in section 2111.131 of the Revised Code, no part of the ward's estate shall be used for the support, maintenance, or education of such ward unless ordered and approved by the court.

(C) A guardian of the person may authorize or approve the provision to the ward of medical, health, or other professional care, counsel, treatment, or services unless the ward or an interested party files objections with the probate court, or the court, by rule or order, provides otherwise.

(D) Unless a person with the right of disposition for a ward under section 2108.70 or 2108.81 of the Revised Code has made a decision regarding whether or not consent to an autopsy or post-mortem examination on the body of the deceased ward under section 2108.50 of the Revised Code shall be given, a guardian of the person of a ward who has died may consent to the autopsy or post-mortem examination.

(E) If a deceased ward did not have a guardian of the estate, the estate is not required to be administered by a probate court, and a person with the right of disposition for a ward, as described in section 2108.70 or 2108.81 of the Revised Code, has not made a decision regarding the disposition of the ward's body or remains, the guardian of the person of the ward may authorize the burial or cremation of the ward.

(F) A guardian who gives consent or authorization as described in divisions (D) and (E) of this section shall notify the probate court as soon as possible after giving the consent or authorization.

(2006 H 426, eff. 10–12–06; 2000 H 538, eff. 9–22–00; 1989 S 46, eff. 1–1–90; 1984 H 263; 1953 H 1; GC 10507–16)

Historical and Statutory Notes

Pre–1953 H 1 Amendments: 114 v 387

Amendment Note: 2006 H 426 rewrote division (E), which prior thereto read:

"(D) A guardian of the person of a ward who has died may consent to an autopsy or post-mortem examination upon the body of the deceased ward under section 2108.50 of the Revised Code and, if the deceased ward did not have a guardian of the estate and the estate is not required to be administered by a probate court, may authorize the burial or cremation of the deceased ward. A guardian who gives consent or authorization as described in this division shall notify the probate court as soon as possible after giving the consent or authorization."

Amendment Note: 2000 H 538 added division (D) and made changes to reflect gender neutral language.

Cross References

Excusing child from school attendance to perform necessary work for guardian, 3321.04
Guardian to send child to school, 3321.38
Truancy, notice to guardian, 3321.19

Library References

Guardian and Ward ⚖29.
Mental Health ⚖217.
Westlaw Topic Nos. 196, 257A.
C.J.S. Mental Health § 179.

Research References

ALR Library
69 ALR 5th 1, Grandparents' Visitation Rights Where Child's Parents Are Deceased, or Where Status of Parents is Unspecified.

Encyclopedias
OH Jur. 3d Guardian & Ward § 79, Judicial Control.
OH Jur. 3d Guardian & Ward § 82, Duties, Generally.
OH Jur. 3d Guardian & Ward § 84, Maintenance, Support, and Education of Ward; Medical and Other Health Matters.
OH Jur. 3d Guardian & Ward § 89, Court Authorization for Payment of Maintenance, Support, and Education; Indigent Guardianship Fund.
OH Jur. 3d Guardian & Ward § 97, Particular Actions on Ward's Behalf; Exercise of Ward's Right of Election—Bringing or Defending Suits; Employment of Counsel.
OH Jur. 3d Guardian & Ward § 175, Maintenance, Support, and Education of Ward and Dependents.

Forms
Ohio Forms Legal and Business § 24:481, Appointment of Guardian—Person of Minor Children—Provision Expressing Desire Same Person be Appointed Guardian of Their Estates.

Treatises and Practice Aids
Carlin, Baldwin's Ohio Practice, Merrick-Rippner Probate Law § 3:5, Jurisdiction of Probate Court—Subject Matter—Specific Areas—Fiduciaries.
Carlin, Baldwin's Ohio Practice, Merrick-Rippner Probate Law § 3:11, Jurisdiction of Probate Court—Subject Matter—Specific Areas—Removal of Life Support.
Carlin, Baldwin's Ohio Practice, Merrick-Rippner Probate Law § 64:2, Powers and Duties of Guardian—Probate Court is the Superior Guardian.
Carlin, Baldwin's Ohio Practice, Merrick-Rippner Probate Law § 64:7, Powers and Duties of Guardian—Ward's Person—Mandatory Duties.
Carlin, Baldwin's Ohio Practice, Merrick-Rippner Probate Law § 64:8, Powers and Duties of Guardian—Ward's Person—Discretionary Acts—Medical Care/Removal of Nutrition and Hydration.
Carlin, Baldwin's Ohio Practice, Merrick-Rippner Probate Law § 65:1, Litigation Involving Guardians—Guardian May Sue or be Sued; Intervenor—Dispute Resolution Procedure.
Carlin, Baldwin's Ohio Practice, Merrick-Rippner Probate Law § 60:27, Power of Attorney for Health Care—Decision in Absence of Valid Health Care Instrument; Probate Court Proceedings.
Carlin, Baldwin's Ohio Practice, Merrick-Rippner Probate Law § 62:43, Guardianship Proceedings—Who May Serve—Life Support Cases.
Carlin, Baldwin's Ohio Practice, Merrick-Rippner Probate Law § 62:44, Guardianship Proceedings—Consent to Autopsy or Post-Mortem Examination.
Carlin, Baldwin's Ohio Practice, Merrick-Rippner Probate Law § 64:11, Powers and Duties of Guardian—Ward's Person—Discretionary Act—Consent to Autopsy or Post-Mortem Examination.
Carlin, Baldwin's Ohio Practice, Merrick-Rippner Probate Law § 64:14, Powers and Duties of Guardian—Ward's Person—Prohibited Acts—Criminal Proceedings.
Carlin, Baldwin's Ohio Practice, Merrick-Rippner Probate Law § 64:32, Application for Authority to Expend Funds—Form.
Carlin, Baldwin's Ohio Practice, Merrick-Rippner Probate Law § 64:33, Entry Authorizing Expenditure of Funds—Form.

Law Review and Journal Commentaries

Guardianship and the Elderly: Oversight Not Overlooked, Norman Fell. 25 U Tol L Rev 189 (1994).

"Nowhere To Go and Chose To Stay": Using The Tort of False Imprisonment To Redress Involuntary Confinement of the Elderly In Nursing Homes and Hospitals, Comment. 137 U Pa L Rev 903 (January 1989).

The Right to Refuse Medical Treatment in Ohio after Cruzan: The Need for a Comprehensive Legislative Solution, Thomas J. Onusko and Patricia Casey Cuthbertson. 5 J L & Health 35 (1990–91).

Notes of Decisions

Construction 4
Control of ward 6
Jurisdiction 3
Order for payment 1
Standing to sue on ward's behalf 2
Suitable maintenance and expenses 7
Tax consequences 5

Testamentary dispositions 8

---

1. Order for payment

Guardian was not required to obtain approval of probate court to hire legal counsel to represent him on ward's motion to terminate guardianship in order to bind ward or her estate to pay for legal services rendered on behalf of guardian. Brown v. Haffey (Ohio App. 8 Dist., 09-06-1994) 96 Ohio App.3d 724, 645 N.E.2d 1295. Mental Health ⚖ 233

While RC 2111.13 provides that "no part of the ward's estate shall be used for the support, maintenance, or education of such ward unless ordered and approved by the court," the statute does not require that the order of the court for payment be made prior to the rendition of the services. In re Tillman (Ohio Prob. 1956) 137 N.E.2d 172, 73 Ohio Law Abs. 534.

Claim for nursing services rendered by guardian cannot be maintained by guardian against personal representative of deceased ward's estate where no order for payment of the claim was made in the guardianship proceedings. In re Burns' Estate (Darke 1948) 79 N.E.2d 234, 52 Ohio Law Abs. 134.

Ohio statutes make it the duty of husband to support his wife and minor children out of his property or by his labor and if he is unable to do so wife must assist him so far as she is able; no part of ward's estate shall be used for support, maintenance, or education of ward unless ordered or approved by court. There is a distinction between a parent acting as natural guardian of his minor child with custody of minor's person and the position of legal guardian appointed by court for purpose of care and management of the estate of such minor. Chertoff v. C.I.R. (C.C.A.6 1947) 160 F.2d 691, 35 O.O. 399.

While the new probate code provides that it is the duty of the guardian of a minor, when necessary, to provide for the maintenance and education of his ward, and that the cost thereof may be paid from the estate of the minor to the extent his estate justifies, it provides with equal positiveness that no part of the estate may be used for the purposes mentioned unless ordered and approved by the court having jurisdiction in the premises. 1932 OAG 4864.

2. Standing to sue on ward's behalf

Parent of minor beneficiaries of payment-on-death (POD) certificates did not have standing to bring suit on children's behalf against deceased depositor's estate and bank to challenge the liquidation of POD account by depositor's guardian 13 months before depositor's death; beneficiaries' legal interest did not vest until depositor's death. Ferguson v. Walsh (Ohio App. 10 Dist., Franklin, 08-26-2003) No. 02AP-1231, 2003-Ohio-4504, 2003 WL 22006833, Unreported. Banks And Banking ⚖ 129; Banks And Banking ⚖ 221; Executors And Administrators ⚖ 55

Upon proper determination by Department of Human Resources that ward no longer qualified for Medicaid benefits, it became incumbent upon guardian to petition probate court for disbursements of personal injury settlement funds to determine their availability for ward's care and well-being. Gorenflo v. Ohio Dept. of Human Serv. (Marion 1992) 81 Ohio App.3d 500, 611 N.E.2d 425. Mental Health ⚖ 217

A guardian of the person of a ward has no power under RC 2111.13 to bring an action on the ward's behalf, but a guardian of a ward's estate is empowered by RC 2111.14(E) to sue for the ward when suit is in the ward's best interest. Maylin v. Cleveland Psychiatric Institute (Franklin 1988) 52 Ohio App.3d 106, 557 N.E.2d 170.

3. Jurisdiction

The probate court has subject matter jurisdiction over all matters touching the guardianship pursuant to RC 2101.24 and 2111.13(A)(4), including all expenditures of a ward's funds and the proposed expenditure of a ward's funds to pay for the medical expenses of the ward's wife. In re Rauscher (Cuyahoga 1987) 40 Ohio App.3d 106, 531 N.E.2d 745. Guardian And Ward ⚖ 58

A probate court has jurisdiction to order a guardian to allow a third party to visit the ward, inasmuch as the order is one "touching the guardianship" within the meaning of RC 2111.13. In re Zahoransky (Cuyahoga 1985) 22 Ohio App.3d 75, 488 N.E.2d 944, 22 O.B.R. 173.

4. Construction

When ward dies in fact, his guardian dies in law. In re Estate of Curry (Montgomery 1986) 29 Ohio App.3d 361, 505 N.E.2d 641, 29 O.B.R. 491. Guardian And Ward ⚖ 22

Guardian sections of revised code neither include nor exclude right of guardian to exercise power to revoke inter vivos trust which is held by ward. Friedrich v. BancOhio Nat. Bank (Madison 1984) 14 Ohio App.3d 247, 470 N.E.2d 467, 53 A.L.R.4th 1285, 14 O.B.R. 276. Mental Health ⚖ 236

Ohio statutes provide for appointment by probate court, when found necessary, of a guardian of person or estate of a minor, or of both, who will have care and management of the person or estate of such minor, or both, and that with certain exceptions, a minor over age of fourteen years may select a guardian, who, if a suitable person, shall be appointed; further, a father and a mother have equal rights to the custody of a minor, and a surviving parent may by last will appoint a guardian; there is a distinction between a parent acting as a natural guardian of his minor child with custody of the minor's person and the position of legal guardian appointed by the court for purpose of care and management of the estate of such minor. Chertoff v. C.I.R. (C.C.A.6 1947) 160 F.2d 691, 35 O.O. 399.

Ohio law does not indicate that a guardian stands in an express relation of trust to his ward. In re Hiner (Bkrtcy.N.D.Ohio 1988) 94 B.R. 955.

5. Tax consequences

Trusts for minors in which trustee could expend income for accident, illness, or other emergency did not qualify for $3,000 gift tax exclusion. Faber v. U. S. (S.D.Ohio 1969) 26 Ohio Misc. 277, 309 F.Supp. 818, 53 O.O.2d 246, 55 O.O.2d 433, affirmed 439 F.2d 1189.

6. Control of ward

A guardian's authority to act for an incompetent is extinguished by virtue of the ward's death and a medical provider who files an action for services rendered to the incompetent before her death must file a motion for substitution of the parties pursuant to Civ R 25 after the death of the ward and upon the extinguishment of the guardianship. William Hicks, M.D., Inc. v. Duke (Ohio App. 10 Dist., Franklin, 11-04-1997) No. 97APG06-797, 1997 WL 703385, Unreported.

Failure of attorney for ward to object in trial court to guardian's representation by legal counsel on ward's motion to terminate guardianship and to raise issue of motivation of guardian's counsel in rendering legal services precluded attorney from doing so on appeal. Brown v. Haffey (Ohio App. 8 Dist., 09-06-1994) 96 Ohio App.3d 724, 645 N.E.2d 1295. Mental Health ⚖ 172

Under the best interest standard, a person who has been declared incompetent may be forced by the guardian to take psychotropic medication to control schizophrenic behavior. In re Guardianship of Willis (Franklin 1991) 74 Ohio App.3d 554, 599 N.E.2d 745.

7. Suitable maintenance and expenses

Granddaughter of ward, who was guardian of ward's person, was entitled to additional compensation from ward's estate for her services in providing 24-hour care to ward, where guardian was receiving $1.39 per hour under her original agreement to care for ward and she had additional expenses of food, housing, and utilities as a result of caring for ward. In re Guardianship of Walther (Ohio App. 2 Dist., Montgomery, 06-25-2004) No. 20095, 2004-Ohio-3396, 2004 WL 1454464, Unreported. Guardian And Ward ⚖ 152

Guardian of elderly woman has duty to provide care and maintenance according to her means and position in life. Disciplinary Counsel v. Clifton (Ohio, 10-01-1997) 79 Ohio St.3d 496, 684 N.E.2d 33. Guardian And Ward ⚖ 30(1)

Wasting elderly ward's considerable estate through negligence and design, while filling dual roles of guardian and attorney for guardianship, and failing to adequately provide for ward's care and comfort warranted permanent disbarment. Disciplinary Counsel v. Clifton (Ohio, 10-01-1997) 79 Ohio St.3d 496, 684 N.E.2d 33. Attorney And Client ⚖ 58

Trial court acted arbitrarily, and abused its discretion, in reversing Department of Human Resources' termination of Medicaid benefits on grounds that recipient had access to available resource greater than allowed for Medicaid recipients, where there was sufficient evidence to conclude that funds remaining from recipient's personal injury settlement were available to recipient for disbursement; settlement monies were not subject of express trust, and probate court had previously released monies upon petition of recipient's guardian. Gorenflo v. Ohio Dept. of Human Serv. (Marion 1992) 81 Ohio App.3d 500, 611 N.E.2d 425. Health ⇨ 512(3)

The "suitable maintenance" that a guardian of the person is supposed to provide for his ward under RC 2111.13(A)(2) includes medical expenses. Maylin v. Cleveland Psychiatric Institute (Franklin 1988) 52 Ohio App.3d 106, 557 N.E.2d 170. Mental Health ⇨ 179

A guardian who spends his own money for the support or benefit of his ward is entitled to full credit for such advancements; the guardian's cause of action to recover these expenses is separate and distinct from a cause of action of the ward and is thus not tolled by RC 2305.16. Maylin v. Cleveland Psychiatric Institute (Franklin 1988) 52 Ohio App.3d 106, 557 N.E.2d 170.

Absent a specific demonstration that the actions are beneficial to the estate or ward, a guardian may not be reimbursed from the estate for legal expenses incurred in proceedings relating solely to the determination of whether the guardian may serve in that capacity. In re Guardianship of Wonderly (Ohio 1984) 10 Ohio St.3d 40, 461 N.E.2d 879, 10 O.B.R. 304. Guardian And Ward ⇨ 68

The term "maintenance" as used in section relating to duties of a guardian to his ward, includes nursing and medical expenses. In re Burns' Estate (Darke 1948) 79 N.E.2d 234, 52 Ohio Law Abs. 134.

8. Testamentary dispositions

An incompetent for whom a guardian has been appointed may change the beneficiary designation of payable on death (P.O.D.) accounts as such designations are in the manner of testamentary dispositions and a guardian has no authority to make testamentary dispositions on behalf of a ward. Witt v. Ward (Preble 1989) 60 Ohio App.3d 21, 573 N.E.2d 201, motion overruled 43 Ohio St.3d 712, 541 N.E.2d 78.

2111.131 How money may be handled for minor with no guardian of the estate

(A) The probate court may enter an order that authorizes a person under a duty to pay or deliver money or personal property to a minor who does not have a guardian of the person and estate or a guardian of the estate, to perform that duty in amounts not exceeding five thousand dollars annually, by paying or delivering the money or property to any of the following:

(1) The guardian of the person only of the minor;

(2) The minor's natural guardians, if any, as determined pursuant to section 2111.08 of the Revised Code;

(3) The minor's own self;

(4) Any person who has the care and custody of the minor and with whom the minor resides, other than a guardian of the person only or a natural guardian;

(5) A financial institution incident to a deposit in a federally insured savings account in the sole name of the minor;

(6) A custodian designated by the court in its order, for the minor under sections 5814.01 to 5814.09 of the Revised Code.

(B) An order entered pursuant to division (A) of this section authorizes the person or entity specified in it, to receive the money or personal property on behalf of the minor from the person under the duty to pay or deliver it, in amounts not exceeding five thousand dollars annually. Money or personal property so received by guardians of the person only, natural guardians, and custodians as described in division (A)(4) of this section may be used by them only for the support, maintenance, or education of the minor involved. The order of the court is prima-facie evidence that a guardian of the person only, a natural guardian, or a custodian as described in division (A)(4) of this section has the authority to use the money or personal property received.

(C) A person who pays or delivers moneys or personal property in accordance with a court order entered pursuant to division (A) of this section is not responsible for the proper application of the moneys or property by the recipient.

(2006 H 416, eff. 1–1–07; 1984 H 263, eff. 10–4–84)

Historical and Statutory Notes

Amendment Note: 2006 H 416 substituted "5814.01" for "1339.31" and "5814.09" for "1339.39" in division (A)(6); and substituted "minor's own self" for "minor himself" in division (A)(3).

Library References

Guardian and Ward ⇨33.
Westlaw Topic No. 196.
  Baldwin's Ohio Legislative Service Annotated, 2006 H 416 LSC Analysis, p 3/L-1709

Research References

Encyclopedias
OH Jur. 3d Guardian & Ward § 82, Duties, Generally.

Treatises and Practice Aids
Carlin, Baldwin's Ohio Practice, Merrick-Rippner Probate Law § 67:4, Alternatives to Guardianship—Statutory Authority for Payments to Minors Under $5,000 Annually.

2111.14 Duties of guardian of estate

In addition to his other duties, every guardian appointed to take care of the estate of a ward shall have the following duties:

(A) To make and file within three months after his appointment a full inventory of the real and personal property of the ward, its value, and the value of the yearly rent of the real property, provided that, if the guardian fails to file the inventory for thirty days after he has been notified of the expiration of the time by the probate judge, the judge shall remove him and appoint a successor;

(B) To manage the estate for the best interest of the ward;

(C) To pay all just debts due from the ward out of the estate in his hands, collect all debts due to the ward, compound doubtful debts, and appear for and defend, or cause to be defended, all suits against the ward;

(D) To obey all orders and judgments of the courts touching the guardianship;

(E) To bring suit for the ward when a suit is in the best interests of the ward;

(F) To settle and adjust, when necessary or desirable, the assets that he may receive in kind from an executor or administrator to the greatest advantage of the ward. Before a settlement and adjustment is valid and binding, it shall be approved by the probate court and the approval shall be entered on its journal. The guardian also shall have the approval of the probate court to hold the assets as received from the executor or administrator or to hold what may be received in the settlement and adjustment of those assets.

No guardian appointed to take care of the estate of a ward may open a safety deposit box held in the name of the ward, until the contents of the box have been audited by an employee of the county auditor in the presence of the guardian and until a verified report of the audit has been filed by the auditor with the probate court, which then shall issue a release to the guardian permitting the guardian to have access to the safety deposit box of the ward.

(1992 H 427, eff. 10–8–92; 1969 S 42; 1953 H 1; GC 10507–15)

Historical and Statutory Notes

Pre–1953 H 1 Amendments: 114 v 387

Cross References

Appraisement may be dispensed with, new appraisement, appraisers, 2127.22
Appropriation of property, service of summons, 163.07
Bond conditions, guardians, 2109.12
Death or incompetence of bank customer, 1304.28
Fiduciary, resignation or removal, 2109.24
Guardian can act for ward in partition, 5307.19
Guardian liable for loss to ward occasioned by use of property for gambling, 3763.06
Guardian may contract for ward's support, 5121.10
Guardian to return personal property of ward for taxation, 5711.05
Inventory by fiduciary, 2109.58
Investment by fiduciary, 2109.37 to 2109.38
Temporary investments by fiduciary allowed, 1339.44

Library References

Guardian and Ward ⚖32 to 36.
Mental Health ⚖217, 219, 221.
Westlaw Topic Nos. 196, 257A.
C.J.S. Mental Health §§ 168, 179.

Research References

Encyclopedias

OH Jur. 3d Banks & Financial Institutions § 201, Title to Contents and Access to Box.
OH Jur. 3d Family Law § 871, Effect of Lack of Representation.
OH Jur. 3d Fiduciaries § 12, Appointment to Fill Vacancy in Office; Sole Fiduciary.
OH Jur. 3d Fiduciaries § 302, Failure to File Inventory or Account.
OH Jur. 3d Guardian & Ward § 92, Duties, Generally.
OH Jur. 3d Guardian & Ward § 93, Custody and Control of Property.
OH Jur. 3d Guardian & Ward § 97, Particular Actions on Ward's Behalf; Exercise of Ward's Right of Election—Bringing or Defending Suits; Employment of Counsel.
OH Jur. 3d Guardian & Ward § 118, Generally; Payment of Debts.
OH Jur. 3d Guardian & Ward § 119, Collection of Debts and Assets.
OH Jur. 3d Guardian & Ward § 120, Collection of Debts and Assets—Assets from Executor or Administrator.
OH Jur. 3d Guardian & Ward § 154, Appraisement of Property; Appointment and Removal of Appraisers.
OH Jur. 3d Guardian & Ward § 210, Types of Actions.
OH Jur. 3d Guardian & Ward § 216, Representation of Ward.

Forms

Ohio Forms Legal and Business § 24:481, Appointment of Guardian—Person of Minor Children—Provision Expressing Desire Same Person be Appointed Guardian of Their Estates.

Treatises and Practice Aids

Carlin, Baldwin's Ohio Practice, Merrick-Rippner Probate Law § 57:4, Removal of Fiduciary—Grounds—Failure to File Inventory or Account.
Carlin, Baldwin's Ohio Practice, Merrick-Rippner Probate Law § 64:2, Powers and Duties of Guardian—Probate Court is the Superior Guardian.
Carlin, Baldwin's Ohio Practice, Merrick-Rippner Probate Law § 64:3, Powers and Duties of Guardian—Inventory.
Carlin, Baldwin's Ohio Practice, Merrick-Rippner Probate Law § 64:5, Powers and Duties of Guardian—Removal for Failure to File an Account or Inventory.
Carlin, Baldwin's Ohio Practice, Merrick-Rippner Probate Law § 65:1, Litigation Involving Guardians—Guardian May Sue or be Sued; Intervenor—Dispute Resolution Procedure.
Carlin, Baldwin's Ohio Practice, Merrick-Rippner Probate Law § 93:1, Ordering Appraisal of Real Property.
Carlin, Baldwin's Ohio Practice, Merrick-Rippner Probate Law § 21:71, Rights of Surviving Spouse—Procedure for Purchase—Limitations on Purchase—Who May Make Election.
Carlin, Baldwin's Ohio Practice, Merrick-Rippner Probate Law § 64:20, Powers and Duties of Guardian—Ward's Estate—Mandatory Duties.
Carlin, Baldwin's Ohio Practice, Merrick-Rippner Probate Law § 64:27, Compensation—Attorneys.
Carlin, Baldwin's Ohio Practice, Merrick-Rippner Probate Law § 64:29, Application to Sell Personal Property—Form.
Carlin, Baldwin's Ohio Practice, Merrick-Rippner Probate Law § 64:30, Entry Authorizing Sale of Personal Property—Form.
Carlin, Baldwin's Ohio Practice, Merrick-Rippner Probate Law § 64:32, Application for Authority to Expend Funds—Form.
Carlin, Baldwin's Ohio Practice, Merrick-Rippner Probate Law § 64:33, Entry Authorizing Expenditure of Funds—Form.
Carlin, Baldwin's Ohio Practice, Merrick-Rippner Probate Law § 64:34, Inventory of Guardian—Form.
Carlin, Baldwin's Ohio Practice, Merrick-Rippner Probate Law § 64:35, Inventory of Guardian—Alternate—Form.
Carlin, Baldwin's Ohio Practice, Merrick-Rippner Probate Law § 64:36, Motion to Require Guardian to File Account—Form.
Carlin, Baldwin's Ohio Practice, Merrick-Rippner Probate Law § 64:39, Application for Order Authorizing Release of Contents of Safe Deposit Box of Ward—Form.
Carlin, Baldwin's Ohio Practice, Merrick-Rippner Probate Law § 64:40, Entry Authorizing Release of Contents of Safe Deposit Box of Ward—Form.
Carlin, Baldwin's Ohio Practice, Merrick-Rippner Probate Law § 65:10, Representing Ward's Best Interests—Ward or Guardian as Plaintiff—Duty to File Suit.
Carlin, Baldwin's Ohio Practice, Merrick-Rippner Probate Law § 65:13, Representing Ward's Best Interests—Ward or Guardian as Plaintiff—Other Actions.
Carlin, Baldwin's Ohio Practice, Merrick-Rippner Probate Law § 65:15, Representing Ward's Best Interests—Ward or Guardian as Defendant—Requirement that Guardian Defend.
Carlin, Baldwin's Ohio Practice, Merrick-Rippner Probate Law § 68:47, Acceptance of Duties of Fiduciary—Form.
Carlin, Baldwin's Ohio Practice, Merrick-Rippner Probate Law § 91:26, Land Sale—Necessary Parties Defendant—Person Under Disability.
Carlin, Baldwin's Ohio Practice, Merrick-Rippner Probate Law § 97:15, Land Sale by Guardian—Appraisal of Property to be Sold.
Carlin, Baldwin's Ohio Practice, Merrick-Rippner Probate Law App B SPF 15.2, Fiduciary's Acceptance—Guardian.
Carlin, Baldwin's Ohio Practice, Merrick-Rippner Probate Law App B SPF 15.5, Guardian's Inventory.

Law Review and Journal Commentaries

Guardianship of Adults with Mental Retardation: Towards a Presumption of Competence, Comment. 14 Akron L Rev 321 (Fall 1980).

Notes of Decisions

Ed. Note: This section contains annotations from former RC 2109.23.

Attorney fees 5
Construction 1
Limitations on guardian's power 7
Management of estate 3
Settlement of accounts 4
Suits involving wards 2
Survivorship 6

---

1. Construction

A stepmother who is appointed guardian of her stepson and supports him until he is sixteen years old by her own exertions is entitled to charge the child's estate for his support and education where such stepmother is without adequate means or income. Peters v. Scoble (Ohio Cir. 1906) 18 Ohio C.D. 541, 7 Ohio C.C.(N.S.) 417, affirmed 76 Ohio St. 564, 81 N.E. 1193, 4 Ohio Law Rep. 683.

The traditional meaning of a fiduciary as someone standing in a special relation of good faith, trust, and confidence is held by a federal bankruptcy court to be far too broad for purposes of federal bankruptcy laws such as 11 USC 523(a)(4), which prevents a "fiduciary" from discharging a debt resulting from fraud or defalcation. In re Hiner (Bkrtcy.N.D.Ohio 1988) 94 B.R. 955.

Ohio law does not indicate that a guardian stands in an express relation of trust to his ward. In re Hiner (Bkrtcy.N.D.Ohio 1988) 94 B.R. 955.

2. Suits involving wards

Where the promise of the defendants was to pay the guardian of the ward to whom they owed money, the guardian's right to sue upon such note is clear, and the fact that the ward comes of age during the pendency of the suit gives no ground to abate it. Gard v. Neff (Ohio 1884) 39 Ohio St. 607.

Unless a ward is made party to the original suit, a decree in equity against his guardian which touches the real estate of the ward does not affect the ward. Este v. Strong (Ohio 1826) 2 Ohio 401.

To properly challenge guardian's administration of ward's estate, nursing home was required to file exceptions to guardian's final account. Guardianship of Skrzyniecki (Ohio App. 6 Dist., 01-31-1997) 118 Ohio App.3d 67, 691 N.E.2d 1105. Mental Health 300

Probate court must act in best interests of minor child when making decisions which affect guardianship. In re Guardianship of Prince (Ohio App. 8 Dist., 06-19-1995) 104 Ohio App.3d 657, 662 N.E.2d 1125. Guardian And Ward 2

Guardian may file suit for ward if action is in ward's best interests. In re Guardianship of Prince (Ohio App. 8 Dist., 06-19-1995) 104 Ohio App.3d 657, 662 N.E.2d 1125. Guardian And Ward 116(1)

It would have been better choice for guardian to have ordered psychiatric examination of ward upon filing by ward of motion to terminate guardianship, than to contest motion. Brown v. Haffey (Ohio App. 8 Dist., 09-06-1994) 96 Ohio App.3d 724, 645 N.E.2d 1295. Mental Health 168.1

A guardian of the person of a ward has no power under RC 2111.13 to bring an action on the ward's behalf, but a guardian of a ward's estate is empowered by RC 2111.14(E) to sue for the ward when suit is in the ward's best interest. Maylin v. Cleveland Psychiatric Institute (Franklin 1988) 52 Ohio App.3d 106, 557 N.E.2d 170.

Incompetent ward cannot maintain action in his own name as long as adjudication of incompetency continues, but rather must be represented by his guardian. Pace v. Pace (Franklin 1986) 32 Ohio App.3d 47, 513 N.E.2d 1357. Mental Health 473

Under RC 3105.01(K) the granting of a divorce is within the discretion of the trial judge, and a divorce will not automatically be granted upon proof of two or more years of physical separation between the parties without cohabitation, unless there is evidence that the suing party wants the divorce, in a suit brought by the guardian of a ward previously adjudged incompetent, which suit is opposed by the ward's spouse on the ground that her husband can communicate and does not want the divorce. Boyd v. Edwards (Cuyahoga 1982) 4 Ohio App.3d 142, 446 N.E.2d 1151, 4 O.B.R. 234.

Where a guardian sues for divorce on behalf of her ward who has previously been adjudged incompetent, and the suit is opposed by the ward's spouse on the ground that the ward does not want a divorce, and there is testimony that the ward can communicate and express his feelings, the court may not grant a divorce under RC 3105.01(K) without first determining if the ward is competent to testify, and to express his intentions as to the divorce. Boyd v. Edwards (Cuyahoga 1982) 4 Ohio App.3d 142, 446 N.E.2d 1151, 4 O.B.R. 234. Divorce 146

The probate court cannot compel the dismissal and termination of an action in partition after the common pleas court has acquired full and complete jurisdiction of said partition action and has made and issued a valid order of sale. Child v. Snyder (Ohio Com.Pl. 1962) 181 N.E.2d 315, 88 Ohio Law Abs. 401, 20 O.O.2d 432. Courts 475(6)

A guardian does not have to have the approval of the probate court of an action in partition by him on behalf of his ward. Child v. Snyder (Ohio Com.Pl. 1962) 181 N.E.2d 315, 88 Ohio Law Abs. 401, 20 O.O.2d 432.

Where reasonable grounds for contest of a will exist, it is "for the best interests of the ward," within section, for guardian to contest any will under which ward receives substantially less than he would receive as an heir-at-law, had there been no will. In re Kowalke's Guardianship (Marion 1946) 80 Ohio App. 515, 76 N.E.2d 899, 36 O.O. 305.

A guardian, unrelated to and otherwise uninterested in the person or estate of his ward, who has been removed as guardian by court order, lacks capacity, either as an individual or as former guardian, to appeal from a subsequent court order appointing a successor guardian. In re Kowalke's Guardianship (Marion 1946) 80 Ohio App. 513, 76 N.E.2d 898, 36 O.O. 304. Guardian And Ward 27

The legally appointed guardian of an insane defendant may be joined with him as a party defendant in an action to recover damages for wrongful death brought in the county where the insane defendant has his legal residence. Stuard v. Porter (Ohio 1908) 79 Ohio St. 1, 85 N.E. 1062, 6 Ohio Law Rep. 516.

A judgment against a minor may be reversed upon petition in error filed by him within the statutory time after reading his majority, where he did not have his day in court in an action affecting his rights. Roberts v. Roberts (Ohio 1899) 61 Ohio St. 96, 42 W.L.B. 367, 55 N.E. 411. Infants 111

The appointment of a qualified guardian as a substitute for a disqualified guardian as a party to a suit is proper. Weiland v. Muntz (Ohio Cir. 1903) 15 Ohio C.D. 185, 2 Ohio C.C.N.S. 71.

Where a guardian surrenders possession of his ward's estate upon her coming of age before he can reimburse himself for advances to the ward, an equitable action may be maintained in his favor against the ward's general estate for indemnification. Fourth Natl Bank v Hopple, 8 NP 473, 11 D 483 (Super, Cincinnati 1900).

A suit for attorney fees by counsel employed to bring suit for wrongful death cannot be maintained against the guardian in his representative capacity. Hurd v. Wheeling & L.E.R. Co. (Ohio Com.Pl. 1897) 6 Ohio Dec. 549, 4 Ohio N.P. 404.

It is sufficient, in proceedings to sell a decedent's real estate by executors or administrators, if infant heirs enter an appearance by their general guardian. Ewing v. Hollister (Ohio 1836) 7 Ohio 138, PT. II.

The relation of guardian and ward must be determined before an action accrues for the guardian against his ward upon account of advances made to the ward. Davis v. Ford's Adm'rs (Ohio 1836) 7 Ohio 104, PT. II.

Minor wards who actually have an appearance entered for them in court by their guardian in a proceeding by an administrator to sell the decedent's real estate for the payment of debts are bound by the order of sale even though they are not named in the petition. Ewing v. Higby (Ohio 1835) 7 Ohio 198, PT. I.

The guardian of an incompetent ward may amend a divorce complaint to include as grounds living separate and apart for one year, RC 3105.01(K), where the divorce action was pending prior to the ward's incompetence and the ward had vacated the marital home prior to his incompetence; under such circumstances, a divorce may properly be granted on the ground of living separate and apart for one year. Heskett v Heskett, No. 91–CA–05, (2d Dist Ct App, Champaign, 11–25–91).

3. Management of estate

A guardian of minors has a duty of general management of his wards' real estate for purposes of taxation, and may represent his wards' estate under the statute relating to road and street improvements, either to ask for or oppose such improvements. Campbell v. Park (Ohio 1877) 32 Ohio St. 544.

Where guardians act within the scope of their authority given by will, and exercise such prudence, care, and diligence as reasonable men manifest in like matters of their own, they should not be held accountable for losses happening from their management of the ward's funds. Miller v. Proctor (Ohio 1870) 20 Ohio St. 442.

A guardian of a minor ward must keep his ward's funds safely and render them productive, and if he fails to invest them productively he is chargeable with interest, unless it can be shown he could not safely invest them productively by law. Armstrong v. Miller (Ohio 1833) 6 Ohio 118.

Where a guardian is legally empowered to make improvements upon his ward's property, and gives a lien upon the accruing rents for the payment of the costs of those improvements, it is not competent for the heirs, by the purchase of a paramount title, to defeat the previously legally acquired lien. Este v. Strong (Ohio 1826) 2 Ohio 401.

Removal of director of family services agency as ward's guardian was warranted, where director failed to render an account of the administration of the ward's estate, failed to file an inventory of the estate after appointment, and disregarded orders of the court. In re Guardianship of Monus (Ohio App. 7 Dist., Mahoning, 05-28-2004) No. 03 MA 128, No. 03 MA 131, No. 03 MA 129, No. 03 MA 132, No. 03 MA 130, No. 03 MA 153, 2004-Ohio-2808, 2004 WL 1194070, Unreported. Mental Health 167

Removal of director of family services agency as ward's guardian was warranted, where director failed to file an inventory of the estate after appointment, failed to produce receipts for particular items purchased, made lump sum expenditures from estate, and failed to keep an itemized statement of receipts and disbursements that could be verified by vouchers or proof. In re Guardianship of Monus (Ohio App. 7 Dist., Mahoning, 05-28-2004) No. 03 MA 128, No. 03 MA 131, No. 03 MA 129, No. 03 MA

132, No. 03 MA 130, No. 03 MA 153, 2004-Ohio-2808, 2004 WL 1194070, Unreported. Guardian And Ward ⊙— 25

Record did not reveal that counsel for proposed guardian of children's estates had conflict of interest or improperly represented proposed guardian; attorney, in filing application for guardian at request of relatives of children's deceased mother was not representing relatives, record did not indicate that she represented anyone with interest adverse to guardian or children, and that attorney was mother's attorney prior to her death and was attorney for mother's estate did not mean attorney had conflict of interest. In re Guardianships of Ahmed (Ohio App. 7 Dist., Belmont, 11-24-2003) No. 02 BE 56, 2003-Ohio-6390, 2003 WL 22837720, Unreported, appeal not allowed 101 Ohio St.3d 1487, 805 N.E.2d 539, 2004-Ohio-1293. Guardian And Ward ⊙— 13(1)

Evidence was sufficient to support determination that guardian was acting in good faith when she authorized unlicensed real estate agent to sell ward's house and paid agent commission; guardian testified she was not aware agent was ineligible for commission because license was in escrow and she was not working with broker, that house sold for more than appraisal value, that commission paid was less than would have been paid to real estate professionals, and that sale and commission fee benefitted estate. In re Guardianship of Rolfe (Ohio App. 12 Dist., Fayette, 11-03-2003) No. CA2003-04-004, 2003-Ohio-5879, 2003 WL 22470175, Unreported. Guardian And Ward ⊙— 157

Guardian of elderly woman has duty to provide care and maintenance according to her means and position in life. Disciplinary Counsel v. Clifton (Ohio, 10-01-1997) 79 Ohio St.3d 496, 684 N.E.2d 33. Guardian And Ward ⊙— 30(1)

Under R.C. §2111.20, guardian of estate may sell any part of personal estate of ward, without court approval, with such sales in interest of ward, and under R.C. §2111.14 burden of acting in best interest of ward is upon guardian; thus, guardian, who may completely alienate personal estate of ward without court order, has authority to pledge property as collateral for loan for benefit of ward. Cincinnati Ins. Co. v. Citizens Home Sav. (Lorain 1985) 22 Ohio App.3d 40, 488 N.E.2d 1255, 22 O.B.R. 117. Guardian And Ward ⊙— 43; Guardian And Ward ⊙— 45

A guardian of the person and estate of an adjudicated incompetent may not exercise her ward's right to revoke an inter vivos trust previously created by the ward without a court order following a showing of necessity for the ward's care, maintenance, and support. Friedrich v. BancOhio Nat. Bank (Madison 1984) 14 Ohio App.3d 247, 470 N.E.2d 467, 53 A.L.R.4th 1285, 14 O.B.R. 276.

The provisions of RC 2109.37 and RC 2109.42 are applicable to the proceeds of matured series G United States savings bonds which are no longer income-producing, and it is the duty of the guardian of an incompetent to cash or reinvest such bonds which are the property of the incompetent. In re Guardianship of Sachs (Ohio 1962) 173 Ohio St. 270, 181 N.E.2d 464, 19 O.O.2d 122.

Fact that the deceased had been hospitalized in a state hospital for a compensable injury for which she had received workmen's compensation benefits, did not require Bureau of Support to resort to Industrial Commission Fund for payment of expenses of hospitalization of decedent, and if duty lay upon anyone to collect money for this purpose it was the duty of the guardian and when the guardian did not do so, administratrix should have proceeded to collect claim as asset of estate. In re Moore's Estate (Ohio Prob. 1958) 154 N.E.2d 675, 79 Ohio Law Abs. 112. Executors And Administrators ⊙— 86(1); Mental Health ⊙— 82.1

A court authorized to determine in a proper proceeding and upon sufficient evidence, that one against whom a complaint has been filed is incompetent, and to appoint a guardian of the estate and person of such incompetent is without authority to authorize such guardian to modify or change the terms or conditions of the contracts of such ward where such changes or modifications are not necessary in the management or conservation of the ward's estate or the protection or care of his person. Zuber v. Zuber (Cuyahoga 1952) 93 Ohio App. 195, 112 N.E.2d 688, 50 O.O. 496.

Where a guardian who is the life tenant consents to the sale of the land for her minor children who are the remaindermen, such minors or their legal representatives are not estopped from recovering the possession of the land from the purchaser or those claiming under him upon the termination of the life estate. Ream v. Wolls (Ohio 1899) 61 Ohio St. 131, 42 W.L.B. 358, 55 N.E. 176.

Where the father is dead, the mother of a minor is liable for such minor child's maintenance, but where such child is the fee simple owner of real estate worth sixty-thousand dollars which is twice the income of his mother, his guardian should support and maintain the ward out of the ward's estate. Wing v. Hibbert (Ohio Cir. 1899) 11 Ohio C.D. 190.

As head of the family, the father is primarily responsible for the support of his children, but after his death the mother is bound to support them if she is able, and cannot claim reimbursement for necessaries from the estate left the children by their father; the guardian of the children's estate should not pay such a demand of the mother. Wing v. Hibbert (Ohio Com.Pl. 1897) 8 Ohio Dec. 65, 7 Ohio N.P. 124, affirmed in part, reversed in part 11 Ohio C.D. 190.

Where a guardian of minor children receives a fund whose principal is to be divided among the wards when they come of age, and the interest from such principal is to be paid to the minors' mother, the guardian holds the principal as guardian for his wards, and the interest thereon as trustee for the mother. In re Kaufman's Estate, 7 NP 552, 5 D 407 (Prob, Hamilton 1887).

It is the duty of the court, with or without complaint first being made, to enforce the performance of duties required by this section and all other requirements relating to the duties of guardians to preserve the estates of minors for whom such guardians may have been or shall be appointed. In re Strickland, 7 NP 233, 1 D 702 (Prob, Hamilton 1899). Guardian And Ward ⊙— 2

Ohio statutes provide for appointment by probate court, when found necessary, of a guardian of person or estate of a minor, or of both, who will have care and management of the person or estate of such minor, or both, and that with certain exceptions, a minor over age of fourteen years may select a guardian, who, if a suitable person, shall be appointed; further, a father and a mother have equal rights to the custody of a minor, and a surviving parent may by last will appoint a guardian; there is a distinction between a parent acting as a natural guardian of his minor child with custody of the minor's person and the position of legal guardian appointed by the court for purpose of care and management of the estate of such minor. Chertoff v. C.I.R. (C.C.A.6 1947) 160 F.2d 691, 35 O.O. 399.

Trusts for minors in which trustee could expend income for accident, illness, or other emergency did not qualify for $3,000 gift tax exclusion. Faber v. U. S. (S.D.Ohio 1969) 26 Ohio Misc. 277, 309 F.Supp. 818, 53 O.O.2d 246, 55 O.O.2d 433, affirmed 439 F.2d 1189.

A declaration that an individual is incompetent and the appointment of a guardian for him do not prevent him from seeking relief in bankruptcy through his next friend. In re Jones (Bkrtcy.S.D.Ohio 1989) 97 B.R. 901.

Even though RC 1339.42 implies that a guardian has fiduciary obligations, a federal bankruptcy court will not necessarily hold a guardian to be a fiduciary for purposes of 11 USC 523(a)(4), which prevents a fiduciary from discharging in bankruptcy a debt resulting from fraud or defalcation. In re Hiner (Bkrtcy.N.D.Ohio 1988) 94 B.R. 955.

Where a guardian introduces no evidence of his inability to invest the money of his ward, but merely states that if he had invested it in certain stocks considered the best in the city it would have been a total loss, all the banks having failed, such a statement does not excuse him from having interest on the money charged to him from the time it came into his hands. Armstrong v Miller, 6 O 118 (1833).

Where a purchaser of land at a guardian's sale fails to make the payments required by the terms of the sale, it is necessary to hold a resale by order of court at his risk for the difference in the price of his bid and the lower bid secured at the resale. Clawson v Beatty, 36 B 214 (OS Unrep 1896).

4. Settlement of accounts

The delay of a ward upon becoming of age to compel his guardian to settle his accounts in the probate court does not discharge the sureties on the guardian's bond, even though the guardian may have become insolvent in the meantime. Newton v. Hammond (Ohio 1882) 38 Ohio St. 430, 8 W.L.B. 241. Guardian And Ward ⊙— 177; Principal And Surety ⊙— 125

No action will lie against a guardian and his sureties on his bond as for breach thereof, for any balance due from the guardian to his late ward, in a court of law, until such balance shall have been fixed by final settlement in the probate court. Newton v. Hammond (Ohio 1882) 38 Ohio St. 430, 8 W.L.B. 241.

Where a guardian who is the father of his ward induces her to sign vouchers for money as though paid, promising to return the amount with interest, and closes his final account in the probate court, an action may be maintained upon the agreement by the ward, and the amount due from her guardian recovered without opening or reviewing the probate court's account. Lindsay v. Lindsay (Ohio 1875) 28 Ohio St. 157.

Parent of minor beneficiaries of payment-on-death (POD) certificates did not have standing to bring suit on children's behalf against deceased depositor's estate and bank to challenge the liquidation of POD account by depositor's guardian 13 months before depositor's death; beneficiaries' legal interest did not vest until depositor's death. Ferguson v. Walsh (Ohio App. 10 Dist., Franklin, 08-26-2003) No. 02AP-1231, 2003-Ohio-4504, 2003 WL 22006833, Unreported. Banks And Banking ⚖ 129; Banks And Banking ⚖ 221; Executors And Administrators ⚖ 55

Remand was required on petition for allowing expenses against minor ward's estate for findings of fact about which expenses were disallowed and additional information about basis for decision. In re Guardianship of Prince (Ohio App. 8 Dist., 06-19-1995) 104 Ohio App.3d 657, 662 N.E.2d 1125. Guardian And Ward ⚖ 135

A guardian who files periodic accounts without claiming the ordinary compensation may, in a subsequent account, claim compensation for past years. In re Guardianship of Webb (Ohio Prob. 1967) 11 Ohio Misc. 21, 225 N.E.2d 868, 40 O.O.2d 97.

Where an attorney procured the removal of a guardian and the appointment of a successor, and also succeeded in obtaining the release of the ward from a state hospital, his fees are not limited to the amount the estate was benefited, but should also include services which were beneficial to the ward. In re Miller's Guardianship (Darke 1952) 107 N.E.2d 626, 62 Ohio Law Abs. 505.

The proof of a contract to pay which is required between members of a family does not apply to a daughter's claim for services to an imbecile ward; the court will settle the allowance under earlier statute, and not being a personal claim against the ward, need not be presented to his administrator if he dies. Scattergood v. Ingram (Ohio 1912) 86 Ohio St. 76, 98 N.E. 923, 10 Ohio Law Rep. 23.

Where in a suit brought in common pleas court to recover upon a judgment rendered against a guardian upon the settlement of his accounts, the defendant surety in his answer and cross petition avers that the guardian did not owe the amount of the judgment to his ward, but that he had obtained such judgment by concealment and fraud, the mere fact that the pleading fails to deny the judgment amount in its entirety does not deprive the court of power to grant relief if the facts in the pleading are found to be true. Gantz v. Gease (Ohio 1910) 82 Ohio St. 34, 91 N.E. 872, 7 Ohio Law Rep. 638. Guardian And Ward ⚖ 182(5); Principal And Surety ⚖ 156

Sureties on a guardian's bond may not question the correctness of a final settlement of the account found by the probate court in the absence of fraud and collusion, or demand a rehearing of the accounts in an action upon the bond for the recovery of the amount found due the wards. Braiden v. Mercer (Ohio 1886) 44 Ohio St. 339, 16 W.L.B. 29, 7 N.E. 155.

An action may be prosecuted in equity on a guardian's bond for an account, but only where the ground of equitable jurisdiction is set forth in the petition; otherwise it will be assumed that they do not exist and the accounting will be left to the exclusive jurisdiction of the probate court. Gorman v. Taylor (Ohio 1885) 43 Ohio St. 86, 13 W.L.B. 425, 1 N.E. 227.

An action in equity may be maintained upon the bond of a guardian if for any reason the probate court loses jurisdiction of the guardian to compel an accounting, even though usually an accounting is first to take place to ascertain the amount due the ward. Gilbert v. Gilbert (Ohio Cir. 1896) 7 Ohio C.D. 58.

A guardian's sureties are not released where the ward, after coming of age, gave the guardian a receipt in full for amounts in the guardian's hands which he failed to pay over to the ward, which receipt was filed in court but not seen by the sureties and was without consideration or actual payment. Meier v. Herancourt (Ohio Super. 1882) 11 Am. Law Rec. 46, 8 W.L.B. 29.

Upon the settlement of the account of the guardian by the probate court after the wards come of age, the former legal relation of trustee and beneficiary existing between them ceases and the relation of debtor and creditor arises. Lamkin v. Robinson (Ohio Com.Pl. 1910) 21 Ohio Dec. 13, 10 Ohio N.P.(N.S.) 1, reversed 24 Ohio C.D. 91, 15 Ohio C.C.(N.S.) 126, affirmed 88 Ohio St. 603, 106 N.E. 1065, 11 Ohio Law Rep. 80. Guardian And Ward ⚖ 163

Where a ward does not file exceptions to his guardian's account until six years after reaching his majority and until after his guardian had died, without excuse, such a delay is laches, since the sureties are thus deprived of their main witness. In re Streit's Estate (Ohio Com.Pl. 1901) 12 Ohio Dec. 158.

Where a parent is able to support himself and his child and the child's estate is not abundant for her support, a parent will not be allowed to reimburse himself out of the estate of his ward for the expense of maintenance and support. In re Gould's Estate (Ohio Prob. 1893) 2 Ohio Dec. 398.

In the absence of an agreement that the guardian would take her wards and gratuitously furnish all their necessaries, the rules of law would justify a reasonable compensation and return for moneys expended in their behalf. In re Hough, 2 NP 382, 1 D 699 (Prob, Hamilton 1893).

Where moneys paid to a guardian by an executor under an order of court without jurisdiction actually belong to other persons, they must be accounted for as assets by him and his sureties, and they are estopped to set up the illegality or the title of others in a proceeding to compel an accounting. In re Cloud's Estate (Ohio Prob. 1888) 20 W.L.B. 455.

The administrator of a deceased guardian should file his account and turn over the money in his hands to the newly appointed guardian immediately after his appointment. In re Estate of Bruckman, 1 NP(NS) 7, 48 B 637 (Prob, Hamilton 1903).

The probate court's exclusive jurisdiction over the settlement of accounts extends to matters omitted from the account as well as those contained in it. State v Beatty, 33 B 109 (OS Unrep 1895).

5. Attorney fees

Petition of administrator of ward's estate was legally insufficient to state a viable claim for a writ of prohibition to prevent probate court judge from enforcing judgment awarding fees to attorney who had worked as a master commissioner for guardianship; administrator, who admitted that work performed by commissioner pertained to guardianship, would never be able to demonstrate that jurisdiction over fee issue was transferred to another court after ward's death, and administrator had an adequate legal remedy in appeal from probate judge's "fee" judgment. State ex rel. Estate of Hards v. Klammer (Ohio App. 11 Dist., Lake, 05-27-2005) No. 2004-L-189, 2005-Ohio-2655, 2005 WL 1272374, Unreported. Prohibition ⚖ 10(2)

Denying application for $5,000 in attorney fees and guardian fees filed by guardian, who brought collection proceedings that resulted in approximately $4,500 benefit to ward's estate, and failing to give guardian opportunity to make subsequent application for more reasonable fee was abuse of discretion, where guardian submitted itemized statement indicating that $16,795.99 in fees were incurred in collection action and it could not be said that guardian's efforts did not financially benefit estate. Mitchell v. Western Reserve Area Agency on Aging (Ohio App. 8 Dist., Cuyahoga, 08-19-2004) No. 83877, 2004-Ohio-4353, 2004 WL 1853156, Unreported. Guardian And Ward ⚖ 136

Probate court abused its discretion by requiring estate of minor to pay attorney fees incurred by attorney who had represented minor's paternal grandfather in connection with unsuccessful competing application to be appointed guardian of minor's estate, which was filed after minor's mother filed initial application, where grandfather at no time served as minor's guardian, and attorney failed to show that his representation of grandfather was beneficial to minor's estate in any way. In re Guardianship of Kufchak (Ohio App. 9 Dist., 02-25-1998) 126 Ohio App.3d 428, 710 N.E.2d 748. Guardian And Ward ⚖ 58; Guardian And Ward ⚖ 68

Probate court has discretion to determine appropriate amount of attorney fees to be authorized in connection with action brought on behalf of ward by guardian. In re Guardianship of Prince (Ohio App. 8 Dist., 06-19-1995) 104 Ohio App.3d 657, 662 N.E.2d 1125. Guardian And Ward ⚖ 58

Legal expenses incurred in connection with action filed on behalf of minor ward may be recovered from estate assets, but only to extent that expenses were incurred in furtherance of ward's interests. In re Guardianship of Prince (Ohio App. 8 Dist., 06-19-1995) 104 Ohio App.3d 657, 662 N.E.2d 1125. Guardian And Ward ⚖ 58

Legal services rendered on behalf of guardian on ward's motion to terminate guardianship were necessary, proper and performed for benefit of guardianship, entitling attorney to fees, where, by retaining attorney, guardian enabled ward and court to call him as witness, guardian and guardian's attorney had reservations regarding ward's competency which were not entirely unfounded, and attorney's cross-examination of witnesses provided court with information from alternative perspective in ruling on motion to terminate. Brown v. Haffey (Ohio App. 8 Dist., 09-06-1994) 96 Ohio App.3d 724, 645 N.E.2d 1295. Mental Health ⚖ 159

An award to a guardian's attorney of $9,702 in attorney fees for services rendered in defending a claim against the estate by the former guardian is proper even though the balance of the estate is only $17,000 since (1) the ward was directly benefeted by the legal expenses incurred because instead of the $25,000 payed for by the former guardian, only $1,050 was awarded; and (2) the fee charged by the attorney was reasonable under the Code of Professional Responsibility because the attorney actually worked 98.9 hours, but only billed the estate for 96 hours and $100 per hour rate charged was reasonable for services performed. In re Guardianship of Rider (Huron 1990) 68 Ohio App.3d 709, 589 N.E.2d 465.

In an action to terminate a guardianship, a probate court should determine whether an attorney acted in good faith, whether the services performed were in the nature of necessities, and whether the attorney's actions benefitted the guardianship, in order to determine if payment of attorney fees from the guardianship estate is merited. In re Guardianship of Allen (Ohio 1990) 50 Ohio St.3d 142, 552 N.E.2d 934, rehearing denied 51 Ohio St.3d 705, 555 N.E.2d 322. Mental Health ⚖ 159

Absent a specific demonstration that the actions are beneficial to the estate or ward, a guardian may not be reimbursed from the estate for legal expenses incurred in proceedings relating solely to the determination of whether the guardian may serve in that capacity. In re Guardianship of Wonderly (Ohio 1984) 10 Ohio St.3d 40, 461 N.E.2d 879, 10 O.B.R. 304. Guardian And Ward ⚖ 68

The guardian of an imbecile has no lawful right to pay an attorney's fee for fomented litigation; will be charged with interest on funds of the ward which came into his hands and were used as his own; cannot make disbursements to prospective heirs of the ward; is an incompetent witness as to the value of services rendered by himself on behalf of the ward before his appointment as guardian; and is liable to removal for mingling the ward's funds with his own and investing such funds in real estate taken in his own name, paying claims without investigation, and appropriating enormous fees for his own services. In re Oliver's Guardianship (Ohio Com.Pl. 1909) 20 Ohio Dec. 64, 9 Ohio NP(NS) 178.

6. Survivorship

Under circumstances where a surviving joint depositor would have been entitled to the balance of the account in the absence of any intervening incompetency of the decedent joint depositor, the facts of such incompetency and the appointment of a guardian of the incompetent's estate do not, in and of themselves, destroy the survivorship rights of the surviving depositor. Miller v. Yocum (Auglaize 1969) 18 Ohio App.2d 52, 246 N.E.2d 594, 47 O.O.2d 37, affirmed 21 Ohio St.2d 162, 256 N.E.2d 208, 50 O.O.2d 372.

Probate court, sitting as court of equity, had inherent power, independent of statute, to intervene and permit guardian of incompetent surviving spouse to exercise for her, the election to purchase mansion-house from estate at appraised value, in view of fact that failure to exercise such power would cause to be lost to incompetent surviving spouse such right, there being no statute which gives an incompetent surviving spouse an adequate remedy at law. Dorfmeier v. Dorfmeier (Ohio Prob. 1954) 123 N.E.2d 681, 69 Ohio Law Abs. 15. Mental Health ⚖ 214; Mental Health ⚖ 236

7. Limitations on guardian's power

Ward's guardian committed constructive fraud, as opposed to actual fraud, in breaching her fiduciary duties to handle ward's accounts, for purposes of determining whether a fraud was committed on the court so as to require that prior settlement-of-account orders be vacated, where guardian signed a fiduciary acceptance, guardian submitted false information regarding ward's assets to court, and court acted in reliance upon such misinformation. In re Guardianship of Guzay (Ohio App. 10 Dist., Franklin, 09-23-2003) No. 02AP-745, 2003-Ohio-5036, 2003 WL 22177106, Unreported. Mental Health ⚖ 311

Probate court was required to reconsider guardian's application to disburse funds from guardianship estate representing prepaid child support, in context of guardian acting as judgment creditor, after domestic relations court determined that father owed support arrearage; probate court was required to examine minors' needs and guardian's justification for request for lump-sum payment, and determine interim necessary support actually provided by guardian, as well as appropriateness of mother serving as guardian. In re Guardianship of Derakhshan (Ohio App. 11 Dist., 04-01-1996) 110 Ohio App.3d 190, 673 N.E.2d 954. Guardian And Ward ⚖ 69

Guardian has duty to manage estate in child's best interests. In re Guardianship of Prince (Ohio App. 8 Dist., 06-19-1995) 104 Ohio App.3d 657, 662 N.E.2d 1125. Guardian And Ward ⚖ 37

Guardian may retain attorney to initiate a lawsuit for ward. In re Guardianship of Prince (Ohio App. 8 Dist., 06-19-1995) 104 Ohio App.3d 657, 662 N.E.2d 1125. Guardian And Ward ⚖ 49

An incompetent for whom a guardian has been appointed may change the beneficiary designation of payable on death (P.O.D.) accounts as such designations are in the manner of testamentary dispositions and a guardian has no authority to make testamentary dispositions on behalf of a ward.

Witt v. Ward (Preble 1989) 60 Ohio App.3d 21, 573 N.E.2d 201, motion overruled 43 Ohio St.3d 712, 541 N.E.2d 78.

A probate court has authority to appoint a guardian for one incompetent by reason of physical disability even though prior to such appointment said incompetent was sued by his wife for divorce and restrained from disposing of his property. In re Guardianship of Stephens (Ohio Prob. 1964) 2 Ohio Misc. 47, 202 N.E.2d 458, 30 O.O.2d 325.

A guardian of an incompetent surviving spouse may obtain approval for the purchase of the mansion house of the decedent. Dorfmeier v. Dorfmeier (Ohio Prob. 1954) 123 N.E.2d 681, 69 Ohio Law Abs. 15.

Guardian having control over estate of insane ward only had no authority to dictate what her residence should be. Bishop v. Bishop (Lucas 1931) 40 Ohio App. 493, 179 N.E. 142, 10 Ohio Law Abs. 399.

Unless he is authorized to do so by statute, a guardian of a minor has no authority to waive the issuance and service of summons on his ward in an action affecting the ward's rights, nor to dispense with the appointment of a guardian ad litem. Roberts v. Roberts (Ohio 1899) 61 Ohio St. 96, 42 W.L.B. 367, 55 N.E. 411. Guardian And Ward ⚖ 129; Infants ⚖ 78(1); Infants ⚖ 89

Where it appears that a guardian is without authority to sell securities of his ward, good faith on the part of the purchaser is not material in an action against such purchaser for recovery of the amount of the proceeds which were misappropriated. Merchants' & Clerks' Sav. Bank Co. v. Schirk (Ohio Cir. 1904) 17 Ohio C.D. 125, 5 Ohio C.C.N.S. 569.

2111.141 Evidence to support inventory; verification of inventory

The court, by order or rule, may require that any inventory filed by a guardian pursuant to section 2111.14 of the Revised Code be supported by evidence that the inventory is a true and accurate inventory of the estate of the ward of the guardian, which evidence may include, but is not limited to, prior income tax returns, bank statements, and social security records of the ward or other documents that are relevant to determining the accuracy of the inventory. In order to verify the accuracy of an inventory, the court may order a guardian to produce any additional evidence that may tend to prove that the guardian is in possession of or has knowledge of assets that belong to the estate of his ward and that have not been included in the guardianship inventory, which evidence may include, but is not limited to, the guardian's income tax returns and bank statements and any other documents that are relevant to determining the accuracy of an inventory. The court may assign court employees or appoint an examiner to verify an inventory filed by a guardian. Upon appointment, the assigned court employees or appointed examiner shall conduct an investigation to verify the accuracy of the inventory filed by the guardian. Upon order of the court, the assigned court employees or appointed examiner may subpoena any documents necessary for his investigation. Upon completion of the investigation, the assigned court employees or appointed examiner shall file a report with the court. The court shall hold a hearing on the report with notice to all interested parties. At the hearing, the guardian shall have the right to examine and cross-examine any assigned court employees or appointed examiner who conducted the investigation and filed the report that is the subject of the hearing. The court shall charge any costs associated with the verification of an inventory filed by a guardian against the estate of the ward, except that, if the court determines that the guardian wrongfully withheld, or aided in the wrongful withholding, of assets from the inventory filed by the guardian, the court shall charge the costs against the guardian.

(1989 S 46, eff. 1–1–90)

Library References

Guardian and Ward ⚖32.
Mental Health ⚖219.
Westlaw Topic Nos. 196, 257A.
C.J.S. Mental Health § 179.

Research References

Encyclopedias

OH Jur. 3d Guardian & Ward § 92, Duties, Generally.

Treatises and Practice Aids

Carlin, Baldwin's Ohio Practice, Merrick-Rippner Probate Law § 56:9, Concealed or Embezzled Assets—Question of Title.

Carlin, Baldwin's Ohio Practice, Merrick-Rippner Probate Law § 64:3, Powers and Duties of Guardian—Inventory.

Carlin, Baldwin's Ohio Practice, Merrick-Rippner Probate Law § 56:14, Concealed or Embezzled Assets—Evidence of Concealment.

Carlin, Baldwin's Ohio Practice, Merrick-Rippner Probate Law § 64:20, Powers and Duties of Guardian—Ward's Estate—Mandatory Duties.

Carlin, Baldwin's Ohio Practice, Merrick-Rippner Probate Law § 79:14, Inventory—Hearing.

Carlin, Baldwin's Ohio Practice, Merrick-Rippner Probate Law § 79:21, Inventory—Exceptions—Nature of Proceedings.

Carlin, Baldwin's Ohio Practice, Merrick-Rippner Probate Law § 79:24, Inventory—Exceptions—Burden of Proof and Evidence.

Notes of Decisions

Hearing 1

1. Hearing

Trial court did not abuse its discretion by proceeding to final judgment on exceptions to guardian's inventory even though several discovery motions were pending. In re Guardianship of Maurer (Ohio App. 6 Dist., 12-22-1995) 108 Ohio App.3d 354, 670 N.E.2d 1030, cause dismissed 74 Ohio St.3d 1461, 656 N.E.2d 1297, dismissed, appeal not allowed 76 Ohio St.3d 1405, 666 N.E.2d 565. Guardian And Ward ⇐ 32

Guardian of person waived his argument that he was wrongfully denied evidentiary hearing on his exceptions to guardian's inventory by failing to object to hearing on merits. In re Guardianship of Maurer (Ohio App. 6 Dist., 12-22-1995) 108 Ohio App.3d 354, 670 N.E.2d 1030, cause dismissed 74 Ohio St.3d 1461, 656 N.E.2d 1297, dismissed, appeal not allowed 76 Ohio St.3d 1405, 666 N.E.2d 565. Guardian And Ward ⇐ 32

Hearing on exceptions to guardian's inventory does not have to be evidentiary hearing. In re Guardianship of Maurer (Ohio App. 6 Dist., 12-22-1995) 108 Ohio App.3d 354, 670 N.E.2d 1030, cause dismissed 74 Ohio St.3d 1461, 656 N.E.2d 1297, dismissed, appeal not allowed 76 Ohio St.3d 1405, 666 N.E.2d 565. Guardian And Ward ⇐ 32

Since prior judge's order scheduling evidentiary hearing on exceptions to guardian's inventory was interlocutory, second judge could modify it and hold hearing at different time. In re Guardianship of Maurer (Ohio App. 6 Dist., 12-22-1995) 108 Ohio App.3d 354, 670 N.E.2d 1030, cause dismissed 74 Ohio St.3d 1461, 656 N.E.2d 1297, dismissed, appeal not allowed 76 Ohio St.3d 1405, 666 N.E.2d 565. Guardian And Ward ⇐ 32; Judges ⇐ 24

2111.15 Duties of guardian of person and estate

When a person is appointed to have the custody of the person and to take charge of the estate of a ward, such person shall have all the duties required of a guardian of the estate and of a guardian of the person.

(1953 H 1, eff. 10–1–53; GC 10507–17)

Historical and Statutory Notes

Pre–1953 H 1 Amendments: 114 v 388

Cross References

Issuer of securities may treat record holders as competent unless certified copy of decree received, 1339.02

Library References

Guardian and Ward ⇐ 17.

Mental Health ⇐ 179.
Westlaw Topic Nos. 196, 257A.
C.J.S. Mental Health §§ 158 to 159.
C.J.S. Right to Die §§ 5, 8.

Research References

Encyclopedias

OH Jur. 3d Guardian & Ward § 78, Generally; Office of Guardian.

Treatises and Practice Aids

Carlin, Baldwin's Ohio Practice, Merrick-Rippner Probate Law § 64:20, Powers and Duties of Guardian—Ward's Estate—Mandatory Duties.

Notes of Decisions

Account of guardian 2
Powers of guardian 1

1. Powers of guardian

A guardian of the person and estate of an adjudicated incompetent may not exercise her ward's right to revoke an inter vivos trust previously created by the ward without a court order following a showing of necessity for the ward's care, maintenance, and support. Friedrich v. BancOhio Nat. Bank (Madison 1984) 14 Ohio App.3d 247, 470 N.E.2d 467, 53 A.L.R.4th 1285, 14 O.B.R. 276.

2. Account of guardian

Where a guardian's account showing a claim which is later claimed to be wrongfully paid has been approved by the probate court, such account is res judicata against the ward, and an action may not be maintained against the party receiving the payment for such claim to recover the money wrongfully paid to him. Lynch v Cogswell, 18 CC 641, 7 CD 12 (Cuyahoga 1899).

2111.151 Limitation on liability of guardians and conservators on contracts and debts

(A) If a guardian of the estate, a guardian of the person and estate, a guardian of the person, or a conservator enters into a contract in the representative capacity of the guardian or conservator, if the contract is within the authority of the guardian or conservator, and if the guardian or conservator discloses in the contract that it is being entered into in the representative capacity of the guardian or conservator, the guardian or conservator is not personally liable on the contract, unless the contract otherwise specifies. If the words "guardian," "as guardian," "conservator," "as conservator," or any other word or words indicating representative capacity as a guardian of the estate, a guardian of the person and estate, a guardian of the person, or a conservator are included in a contract following the name or signature of the guardian or conservator, the inclusion is sufficient disclosure for purposes of this division that the contract is being entered into in the guardian's representative capacity as guardian of the estate, guardian of the person and the estate, or guardian of the person or is being entered into in the conservator's representative capacity as conservator.

(B) A guardian of the estate, a guardian of the person and estate, a guardian of the person, or a conservator is not personally liable for any debt of the ward or, in the case of a conservator, the physically infirm, competent adult, unless one or more of the following applies:

(1) The guardian or conservator agrees to be personally responsible for the debt.

(2) The debt was incurred for the support of the ward or the physically infirm, competent adult, and the guardian or conservator is liable for that debt because of another legal relationship that gives rise to or results in a duty of support relative to the ward or the physically infirm, competent adult.

(3) The negligence of the guardian or conservator gave rise to or resulted in the debt.

(4) An act of the guardian or conservator that was beyond the guardian's or conservator's authority gave rise to or resulted in the debt.

(1996 H 391, eff. 10–1–96; 1993 S 113, eff. 10–29–93)

Uncodified Law

1996 H 391, § 3, eff. 10–1–96, reads: New section 1337.092 of the Revised Code, as enacted by this act, and the amendments to section 2111.151 of the Revised Code made in this act shall apply only to contracts entered into or debts incurred on or after the effective date of this act. The personal liability of or defenses to or immunity from personal liability of an attorney in fact in connection with contracts that were entered into prior to the effective date of this act and that pertain to the attorney in fact's principal and in connection with debts of an attorney in fact's principal, a guardian's ward, or a conservator's physically infirm, competent adult that were incurred prior to the effective date of this act shall be determined in accordance with the common law of this state and any applicable sections of the Revised Code in effect on the day immediately prior to the effective date of this act.

1993 S 113, § 2, eff. 10–29–93, reads: In enacting section 2111.151 of the Revised Code in this act, the General Assembly hereby declares its intent to supersede the effect of the February 16, 1990, holding of the Fifth District Court of Appeals in *Dearth Management, Inc. v Nentwich*, 1990 Ohio App. Lexis 646 [No. 89CA34 (5th Dist Ct App, Knox, 2–16–90)], relative to the personal liability of a guardian who signs a contract in his representative capacity as guardian of a ward.

Historical and Statutory Notes

Amendment Note: 1996 H 391 deleted "of the estate, guardian of the person and estate, guardian of the person," twice in division (A); deleted "other than from the assets of the ward or the assets of the physically infirm, competent adult," preceding "unless one or more of the following applies:" in division (B); inserted "personally" in division (B)(1); inserted "debt was incurred for the support of the ward or the physically infirm, competent adult, and the" in division (B)(2); made changes to reflect gender neutral language; and made other nonsubstantive changes.

Library References

Guardian and Ward ⟜45 to 52.
Mental Health ⟜179, 217, 222.
Westlaw Topic Nos. 196, 257A.
C.J.S. Mental Health §§ 158 to 159, 179.
C.J.S. Right to Die §§ 5, 8.

Research References

Encyclopedias

OH Jur. 3d Guardian & Ward § 102, Actions Against Guardian Involving Administration of Guardianship—on Guardian's Contract.

Treatises and Practice Aids

Carlin, Baldwin's Ohio Practice, Merrick-Rippner Probate Law § 62:68, Personal Liability of Guardian or Conservator.

Kuehnle and Levey, Ohio Real Estate Law and Practice § 25:15, Powers of Attorney—Personal Liability of Attorney-In-Fact.

Notes of Decisions

Guardian's liability for debt 1

---

1. Guardian's liability for debt

Absent evidence of amount Medicaid would have paid creditors on behalf of ward's estate, had guardian timely applied for Medicaid payments, guardian was required to satisfy the debt resulting from his failure to pay creditors for products and services rendered to estate. In re Ewanicky (Ohio App. 8 Dist., Cuyahoga, 06-26-2003) No. 81742, 2003-Ohio-3351, 2003 WL 21469181, Unreported, stay denied 99 Ohio St.3d 1534, 795 N.E.2d 55, 2003-Ohio-4677, appeal not allowed 100 Ohio St.3d 1506, 799 N.E.2d 186, 2003-Ohio-6161, reconsideration denied 101 Ohio St.3d 1425, 802 N.E.2d 155, 2004-Ohio-123. Guardian And Ward ⟜ 67

Guardian, whose negligent failure to pay ward's creditors caused estate to accrue debt, was personally liable to reimburse estate for such debt. In re Ewanicky (Ohio App. 8 Dist., Cuyahoga, 06-26-2003) No. 81742, 2003-Ohio-3351, 2003 WL 21469181, Unreported, stay denied 99 Ohio St.3d 1534, 795 N.E.2d 55, 2003-Ohio-4677, appeal not allowed 100 Ohio St.3d 1506, 799 N.E.2d 186, 2003-Ohio-6161, reconsideration denied 101 Ohio St.3d 1425, 802 N.E.2d 155, 2004-Ohio-123. Guardian And Ward ⟜ 67

2111.16 Certain vouchers not allowed as credits

Unless previously authorized by the court, no voucher shall be received from or allowed as a credit in the settlement of a guardian's account which is signed or purports to be signed by his ward.

(127 v 36, eff. 9–4–57; 1953 H 1; GC 10507–29)

Historical and Statutory Notes

Pre–1953 H 1 Amendments: 114 v 390

OSBA Probate and Trust Law Section

1957:

The application of the present provisions of this section in actual practice has raised some difficulties which the Committee believes could be avoided by amending the section as proposed.

The present section provides that no guardian can be allowed a credit in his account for a voucher signed by his ward. There are many cases, especially in the cases of minors, where as a practical matter, and in the best interests of the ward, it appears desirable to permit payment of certain amounts directly to the ward.

It is the opinion of the Committee that while the rule of the present section is generally a wise one, the proposed amendment should be adopted so that on a court order previously made it will be possible to accept vouchers from wards for any proper purpose subject to such limitations as may be determined by the court in those cases where the circumstances warrant. Under the proposed amendment, authority from the court will have to be obtained in each instance in advance before the guardian makes any payment directly to the ward and obtains a voucher directly from such ward.

Research References

Treatises and Practice Aids

Carlin, Baldwin's Ohio Practice, Merrick-Rippner Probate Law § 64:4, Powers and Duties of Guardian—Accounting.

Carlin, Baldwin's Ohio Practice, Merrick-Rippner Probate Law § 64:66, Application for Compensation—Guardian—Form.

Notes of Decisions

Reopening account 1

---

1. Reopening account

The probate court has no power to re-open an account rendered by the guardian of an imbecile after it has passed upon it in due form and having jurisdiction over the matter, upon the mere request of the heirs and without a showing of fraud or mistake. Millen v. Young (Ohio Cir. 1892) 8 Ohio C.D. 391.

2111.17 Suits by guardians

A guardian may sue in his own name, describing himself as guardian of the ward for whom he sues. When his guardianship ceases, actions or proceedings then pending shall not abate, if the right survives. His successor as guardian, the executor or administrator of the ward, or the ward himself, if the guardianship has terminated other than by the ward's death, shall be made party to the suit or other proceeding as the case requires, in the same manner an executor or administrator is made a party to a similar suit or proceeding where the plaintiff dies during its pendency.

(1953 H 1, eff. 10–1–53; GC 10507–18)

Historical and Statutory Notes

Pre–1953 H 1 Amendments: 114 v 388

Cross References

Civil action by guardian, Civ R 17
Suits in which party adverse to guardian cannot testify, exceptions, 2317.03

Library References

Guardian and Ward ⬅116(1).
Westlaw Topic No. 196.

Research References

Encyclopedias

OH Jur. 3d Actions § 116, Change In, or Termination Of, Office of Fiduciary.
OH Jur. 3d Guardian & Ward § 220, Pleadings.

Treatises and Practice Aids

Carlin, Baldwin's Ohio Practice, Merrick-Rippner Probate Law § 65:1, Litigation Involving Guardians—Guardian May Sue or be Sued; Intervenor—Dispute Resolution Procedure.
Carlin, Baldwin's Ohio Practice, Merrick-Rippner Probate Law § 65:6, Survival of Actions Beyond Term of Guardianship—Action to Proceed—Substitution of Parties.

Notes of Decisions

Advancements 2
Insane persons 1
Minority 3

---

1. Insane persons

An action against a lunatic for wrongful death is properly brought in the county in which the defendant has his legal residence and his guardian may be joined as a party defendant. Stuard v. Porter (Ohio 1908) 79 Ohio St. 1, 85 N.E. 1062, 6 Ohio Law Rep. 516. Mental Health ⬅ 480; Venue ⬅ 18

The insanity of a defendant in a divorce is not a bar to the adjudication of his property rights, and it is the duty of the court to appoint a trustee for the prosecution or defense of the suit on behalf of the insane party. Kerlik v. Kerlik (Ohio Cir. 1906) 20 Ohio C.D. 274, 10 Ohio C.C.(N.S.) 524.

2. Advancements

A guardian who spends his own money for the support or benefit of his ward is entitled to full credit for such advancements; the guardian's cause of action to recover these expenses is separate and distinct from a cause of action of the ward and is thus not tolled by RC 2305.16. Maylin v. Cleveland Psychiatric Institute (Franklin 1988) 52 Ohio App.3d 106, 557 N.E.2d 170.

No action accrues for a guardian against his ward upon account of advances made to the ward until the relation of guardian and ward is determined. Davis v. Ford's Adm'rs (Ohio 1836) 7 Ohio 104, PT. II.

3. Minority

An action by a guardian of a minor on an instrument payable to him in his capacity as guardian does not abate by the ward becoming of age. Gard v. Neff (Ohio 1884) 39 Ohio St. 607. Abatement And Revival ⬅ 45; Guardian And Ward ⬅ 128

2111.18 Claim for injury to ward or damage to property; settlement

When personal injury, damage to tangible or intangible property, or damage or loss on account of personal injury or damage to tangible or intangible property is caused to a ward by wrongful act, neglect, or default that would entitle the ward to maintain an action and recover damages for the injury, damage, or loss, and when any ward is entitled to maintain an action for damages or any other relief based on any claim or is subject to any claim to recover damages or any other relief based on any claim, the guardian of the estate of the ward may adjust and settle the claim with the advice, approval, and consent of the probate court. In the settlement, if the ward is a minor, the parent or parents may waive all claim for damages on account of loss of service of the minor, and that claim may be included in the settlement. However, when it is proposed that the claim involved be settled for ten thousand dollars or less, the court, upon application by any person whom the court may authorize to receive and receipt for the settlement, may authorize the settlement without the appointment of a guardian and authorize the delivery of the moneys to the natural guardian of the minor, to the person by whom the minor is maintained, or to the minor himself. The court may authorize the minor or person receiving the moneys to execute a complete release on account of the receipt. The payment shall be a complete and final discharge of any such claim.

(1990 H 346, eff. 5–31–90; 1980 S 317; 1976 H 1137; 127 v 380; 125 v 903; 1953 H 1; GC 10507–19)

Uncodified Law

1990 H 346, § 3, eff. 5–31–90, reads, in part: (A) Sections 1 and 2 of this act shall apply only to the estates of decedents who die on or after the effective date of this act.

Historical and Statutory Notes

Pre–1953 H 1 Amendments: 115 v 198; 114 v 388

Comparative Laws

Pa.—20 Pa.C.S.A. § 5521.

OSBA Probate and Trust Law Section

1990:

For change made by 1990 H 346, see comment following 2111.181.

Cross References

Settlement of claim for injury to minors, Sup R 68

Library References

Guardian and Ward ⬅116(1).
Westlaw Topic No. 196.
Baldwin's Ohio Legislative Service, 1990 Laws of Ohio, H 346—LSC Analysis, p 5–87

Research References

Encyclopedias

OH Jur. 3d Family Law § 263, Settlement of Emancipated Minor's Tort Claim.
OH Jur. 3d Family Law § 290, Loss or Waiver of Right of Action.
OH Jur. 3d Family Law § 878, Compromise or Settlement.
OH Jur. 3d Family Law § 879, Appeals and Rehearing.
OH Jur. 3d Guardian & Ward § 98, Particular Actions on Ward's Behalf; Exercise of Ward's Right of Election—Compromise and Release of Rights, Claims, Judgments.
OH Jur. 3d Guardian & Ward § 222, Enforcement of Judgment.

Forms

Ohio Forms Legal and Business § 15:6, Checklist—Drafting Compromise and Settlement Agreements.
Ohio Forms Legal and Business § 15:47, Form Drafting Principles.
Ohio Forms Legal and Business § 15:62, Release—by Guardian of Minors—Claims Based on Automobile Accident—With Covenant Not to Sue.
Ohio Forms Legal and Business § 28:83, Payment of Small Estate to Minor Without Guardian—Affidavit of Parent Requesting Payment on Behalf of Minor.
Ohio Forms and Transactions F 27.12, Release of Minor's Claim for $10,000 or Less With Court Approval, Including Parents' Claim for Loss of Services.
Ohio Forms and Transactions F 27.13, Release of Minor's Claim by Guardian With Court Approval (Multiple Releases).

Ohio Forms and Transactions KP 27.07, Release of Minor's Tort Claims Through Probate Court.

Treatises and Practice Aids

Carlin, Baldwin's Ohio Practice, Merrick-Rippner Probate Law § 12:1, Wrongful Death—Scope of RC Ch. 2125.

Carlin, Baldwin's Ohio Practice, Merrick-Rippner Probate Law § 64:15, Powers and Duties of Guardian—Special Matters Relating to Minor Wards—Settlement of Claims for Injury.

Carlin, Baldwin's Ohio Practice, Merrick-Rippner Probate Law § 64:21, Powers and Duties of Guardian—Ward's Estate—Discretionary Acts.

Carlin, Baldwin's Ohio Practice, Merrick-Rippner Probate Law § 65:22, Settlement of Suits—Generally—Approval of Court.

Carlin, Baldwin's Ohio Practice, Merrick-Rippner Probate Law § 65:23, Settlement of Suits—Attorney Fees in Cases Where Court Approval is Required.

Carlin, Baldwin's Ohio Practice, Merrick-Rippner Probate Law § 65:24, Ratification of Contracts by Guardian.

Carlin, Baldwin's Ohio Practice, Merrick-Rippner Probate Law § 65:25, Application by Guardian for Authority to Settle Claim for Injury or Damage to Ward—Form.

Carlin, Baldwin's Ohio Practice, Merrick-Rippner Probate Law § 65:26, Waiver of Notice and Consent of Parents to Claim of Minor—Form.

Carlin, Baldwin's Ohio Practice, Merrick-Rippner Probate Law § 65:27, Entry to Settle Claim for Injury or Damage—Form.

Carlin, Baldwin's Ohio Practice, Merrick-Rippner Probate Law § 65:28, Report of Settlement—Form.

Carlin, Baldwin's Ohio Practice, Merrick-Rippner Probate Law § 65:29, Entry Confirming Settlement of Claim—Form.

Carlin, Baldwin's Ohio Practice, Merrick-Rippner Probate Law § 67:12, Application for Authority to Settle Claim Not Over $10,000 Without Appointment of Guardian for Minor—Form.

Carlin, Baldwin's Ohio Practice, Merrick-Rippner Probate Law § 67:13, Entry Authorizing Settlement of Claim to Minor Without Appointment of Guardian—Form.

Carlin, Baldwin's Ohio Practice, Merrick-Rippner Probate Law § 67:14, Entry Approving Delivery of Funds—Form.

Carlin, Baldwin's Ohio Practice, Merrick-Rippner Probate Law § 80:14, Attorney Fees—Determination.

Carlin, Baldwin's Ohio Practice, Merrick-Rippner Probate Law App B SPF 22.0, Application to Settle a Minor's Claim and Entry Setting Hearing—Form.

Carlin, Baldwin's Ohio Practice, Merrick-Rippner Probate Law App B SPF 22.1, Waiver and Consent to Settle Minor's Claim—Form.

Notes of Decisions

Attorney fees   3
Counsel   5
Fraud   1
Minors   2
Procedural issues   6
Releases   4

---

1. Fraud

A release from liability obtained by fraud in the factum is void ab initio, while a release obtained by fraud in the inducement is only voidable; fraud in the factum can exist only where an act or misrepresentation of one party causes another to agree to the release without an understanding that he has done so and that the one released will no longer be liable on the claims concerned. Haller v. Borror Corp. (Ohio 1990) 50 Ohio St.3d 10, 552 N.E.2d 207, rehearing denied 51 Ohio St.3d 704, 555 N.E.2d 322.

A releasor may not attack the validity of a release for fraud in the inducement unless he first tenders back the consideration he received for making the release; where fraud in the factum is alleged, no tender is required. Haller v. Borror Corp. (Ohio 1990) 50 Ohio St.3d 10, 552 N.E.2d 207, rehearing denied 51 Ohio St.3d 704, 555 N.E.2d 322. Release ⇐ 24(2)

2. Minors

The settlement and release of a wrongful death claim brought by the administratrix of her husband's estate cannot be effective with respect to the children's claims where there is no indication that the settlement is reached and the release signed "with the advice, approval, and consent" of the probate court as contemplated by RC 2111.18. Brewer v. Akron General Medical Center (Ohio App. 9 Dist., Summit, 01-27-1999) No. 19068, 1999 WL 33382, Unreported.

Procedural irregularities warranted grant of relief from judgment, to minor, from probate court's judgment approving of father's $10,000 settlement of minor's claim against automobile manufacturer relating to minor's injuries from automobile accident; manufacturer did not disclose to probate court that father received additional compensation for damage to automobile and possibly for minor's medical expenses, manufacturer's failure to include restrictive endorsement on settlement check and father's failure to deposit check in bank account in minor's name allowed father to disburse settlement funds before child reached age of majority, no party to settlement disclosed letter from minor's family physician discussing minor's current medical condition, father did not provide meaningful representation to minor at settlement hearing, and settlement amount was the highest amount for which a settlement could be made without automatic appointment of guardian. (Per Carr, P.J., with one Judge concurring in judgment only.) In re Guardianship of Matyaszek (Ohio App. 9 Dist., 12-29-2004) 159 Ohio App.3d 424, 824 N.E.2d 132, 2004-Ohio-7167, appeal not allowed 105 Ohio St.3d 1562, 828 N.E.2d 117, 2005-Ohio-2447. Infants ⇐ 105

Guardian did not improperly raise a new issue or present a new theory on appeal, in guardian's appeal from probate court's denial of motion to vacate judgment approving of father's $10,000 settlement of claim against automobile manufacturer relating to infant ward's injuries in automobile accident, though in probate court guardian had contended manufacturer's counsel had perpetrated a fraud on the court by withholding letter written by ward's family physician regarding ward's current medical condition, but on appeal guardian contended manufacturer rather than its counsel had withheld the letter; guardian consistently alleged that failure to present letter to probate court prejudiced the proceedings with respect to approval of settlement, regardless of whether manufacturer or its counsel was responsible for such failure. (Per Carr, P.J., with one Judge concurring in judgment only.) In re Guardianship of Matyaszek (Ohio App. 9 Dist., 12-29-2004) 159 Ohio App.3d 424, 824 N.E.2d 132, 2004-Ohio-7167, appeal not allowed 105 Ohio St.3d 1562, 828 N.E.2d 117, 2005-Ohio-2447. Infants ⇐ 115

Automobile accident victim's minor children could pursue their claims for underinsured motorist (UIM) benefits for victim's wrongful death against his employer's automobile insurer and excess UIM carrier, even though their mother settled tort claim without protecting UIM carriers' subrogation rights; their mother lacked authority to release children's wrongful death claims, and the settlement agreement was thus not effective to release them. Davis v. Dembek (Ohio App. 10 Dist., 11-26-2002) 150 Ohio App.3d 423, 782 N.E.2d 80, 2002-Ohio-6443, appeal allowed, reversed 99 Ohio St.3d 49, 788 N.E.2d 1063, 2003-Ohio-2462. Insurance ⇐ 2793(1)

Statute setting forth procedure in probate court for settlement of minors' claims only grants probate court power to advise on, and approve and consent to, settlement that has already been entered into by guardian. In re Guardianship of Hicks (Ohio Com.Pl. 1993) 63 Ohio Misc.2d 280, 624 N.E.2d 1125. Compromise And Settlement ⇐ 53.1

A probate court's finding that a contingent fee agreement regarding a personal injury claim of a minor ward under which an attorney would have received one-third of a $90,000 settlement, was not an enforceable contract because (1) it was signed only by the parents, (2) it was signed when the parents were under great mental stress, and (3) it was not approved by the court prior to the agreement being entered into by the guardian as required by statute, and in the place of the agreement, awarding the attorney $9,142.50, the reasonable value of his services (60.95 hours X $150 per hour), plus costs and expenses advanced of $423.50, does not constitute an abuse of discretion. In re Guardianship of Patrick (Huron 1991) 66 Ohio App.3d 415, 584 N.E.2d 86.

Petition for authority to present claim of a minor for damages against an estate to the executor thereof after expiration of the time for presentment of claims was properly brought by minor through her father and next friend. In re Noie's Estate (Franklin 1960) 179 N.E.2d 536, 87 Ohio Law Abs. 276.

In the absence of a showing of prejudicial error in the proceedings or of fraud or collusion on the part of those involved, a settlement of an injured minor's claim for damages by his guardian in conformity with GC 10507–19 (RC 2111.18) is valid and binding on the minor and may not be set aside.

In re Guardianship of Kelley (Ohio 1961) 172 Ohio St. 177, 174 N.E.2d 244, 15 O.O.2d 327. Guardian And Ward ⇨ 33

A settlement by the guardian of an injured minor made in the best interests of the minor at the time, in good faith and more than two years after the injury to such minor, and where no fraud was involved, is valid and binding; and a judgment subsequently setting aside such settlement is against the weight of the evidence and will be reversed. In re Guardianship of Kelley (Clinton 1960) 113 Ohio App. 180, 168 N.E.2d 587, 15 O.O.2d 431, affirmed 172 Ohio St. 177, 174 N.E.2d 244, 15 O.O.2d 327.

When a minor reaches her majority and the probate court grants the request to terminate her guardianship the probate court loses jurisdiction over any matter pertaining to her including a personal injury claim from an automobile accident which occurs during minority. In re Layshock (Ohio App. 7 Dist., Mahoning, 12-28-2001) No. 00-C.A.-198, 2001-Ohio-3381, 2001 WL 1667872, Unreported.

3. Attorney fees

Probate court's denial of counsel's request for fees and expenses from guardianship allegedly incurred in underlying suit on behalf of ward against investment firm was not unreasonable; counsel had already received $15,000 from to file complaint more than three years after expiration of applicable statute of limitations, and there was no showing that legal expenses directly benefitted ward. In re Guardianship of Hards (Ohio App. 11 Dist., Lake, 03-14-2003) No. 2002-L-032, 2003-Ohio-1207, 2003 WL 1193779, Unreported. Mental Health ⇨ 251

Attorney's substantial rights were not affected by denial of discovery requests, in action to recover attorney fees and expenses from guardianship allegedly incurred in underlying suit brought on ward's behalf against investment firm, absent any showing guardian had sole possession of any evidence demonstrating benefits conferred on ward by attorney's services. In re Guardianship of Hards (Ohio App. 11 Dist., Lake, 03-14-2003) No. 2002-L-032, 2003-Ohio-1207, 2003 WL 1193779, Unreported. Pretrial Procedure ⇨ 36.1

Court of Appeals would not recognize "constructive" guardianship as basis for permitting attorney to settle personal injury claim on behalf of guardianship before formal guardianship was created. In re Guardianship of Freeman (Ohio App. 4 Dist., Adams, 11-20-2002) No. 02CA737, 2002-Ohio-6386, 2002 WL 31647801, Unreported, stay denied 98 Ohio St.3d 1459, 783 N.E.2d 518, 2003-Ohio-644, appeal not allowed 98 Ohio St.3d 1512, 786 N.E.2d 62, 2003-Ohio-1572. Guardian And Ward ⇨ 67

Attorney wrongfully withheld attorney fees from guardianship, and probate court, acting in best interest of ward and his guardianship estate, properly ordered their repayment, where attorney settled personal injury claim and paid himself fees before guardianship was created and trial court approved attorney fee award. In re Guardianship of Freeman (Ohio App. 4 Dist., Adams, 11-20-2002) No. 02CA737, 2002-Ohio-6386, 2002 WL 31647801, Unreported, stay denied 98 Ohio St.3d 1459, 783 N.E.2d 518, 2003-Ohio-644, appeal not allowed 98 Ohio St.3d 1512, 786 N.E.2d 62, 2003-Ohio-1572. Guardian And Ward ⇨ 58; Guardian And Ward ⇨ 67

Guardian of infant was required to obtain probate court authorization before entering into contingency-fee agreement in action on behalf of infant. In re Thompson (Ohio App. 1 Dist., 11-08-2002) 150 Ohio App.3d 98, 779 N.E.2d 816, 2002-Ohio-6065. Guardian And Ward ⇨ 136

A probate court, in order to maintain control over any personal injury settlement entered into on behalf of a ward under its protection, has subject matter jurisdiction over the entire amount of settlement funds, which includes attorney fees to be drawn therefrom. In re Guardianship of Jadwisiak (Ohio 1992) 64 Ohio St.3d 176, 593 N.E.2d 1379. Guardian And Ward ⇨ 123

A probate court's approval of a fee-splitting agreement between counsel without affording notice or opportunity to be heard to all parties in the agreement violates the right to due process. In re Guardianship of Jadwisiak (Ohio 1992) 64 Ohio St.3d 176, 593 N.E.2d 1379. Attorney And Client ⇨ 151; Constitutional Law ⇨ 306(1)

Reasonable value of legal services rendered by counsel who obtained settlement for minors struck by intoxicated motorist was $17,500 for representation of each minor; case did not present complex issues, thrust of counsel's representation had no novel or difficult connotation, there was no counsel resisting claims for insurance policy limits, no suit filed, no discovery, deposition or controverted facts, and there was never any risk of nonrecovery. In re Settlements of Betts (Ohio Com.Pl. 1991) 62 Ohio Misc.2d 30, 587 N.E.2d 997. Costs ⇨ 194.18

A probate court may, within the discretion granted it by RC 2111.18, refuse to approve a settlement of an action brought on behalf of a minor for less than $10,000 where a contingent arrangement awards the attorney one-third of such settlement as his fee. In re Guardianship of Davis, No. 87AP060049 (5th Dist Ct App, Tuscarawas, 12–22–87).

4. Releases

A pre-injury waiver of liability for injury to a minor which is executed by the parents for injury to their child who participates in an athletic event (1) is an implied covenant not to sue as the child's best friend, (2) is not against public policy, and (3) evinces the policy to promote recreational activities. Zivich v. Mentor Soccer Club, Inc. (Ohio App. 11 Dist., Lake, 04-18-1997) No. 95-L-184, 1997 WL 203646, Unreported, appeal allowed 79 Ohio St.3d 1489, 683 N.E.2d 791, appeal dismissed in part 80 Ohio St.3d 1474, 687 N.E.2d 471, affirmed on other grounds 82 Ohio St.3d 367, 696 N.E.2d 201, 1998-Ohio-389.

Guardian's motion to vacate judgment approving of father's $10,000 settlement of infant ward's claims against automobile manufacturer, relating to ward's injuries in automobile accident, was brought within reasonable time, as element for vacating judgment under catch-all provision of civil procedure rule for relief from judgment, though motion was brought 12 and one-half years after judgment and five years after father became aware of manufacturer's alleged fraud; ward's status as minor entitled him to greater flexibility as to time requirements, ward had incurred his injuries when he was two years old, father himself may have engaged in fraud with respect to presenting settlement to probate court, so that his knowledge would not be attributed to ward, and guardian brought motion within about a year of his appointment as guardian. (Per Carr, P.J., with one Judge concurring in judgment only.) In re Guardianship of Matyaszek (Ohio App. 9 Dist., 12-29-2004) 159 Ohio App.3d 424, 824 N.E.2d 132, 2004-Ohio-7167, appeal not allowed 105 Ohio St.3d 1562, 828 N.E.2d 117, 2005-Ohio-2447. Infants ⇨ 105

Wrongful death claims that had not accrued when automobile accident victim's surviving spouse and adult daughter settled tort claim prior to victim's death could be released and, therefore, were barred by settlement agreement with tort-feasor and her liability insurer. Davis v. Dembek (Ohio App. 10 Dist., 11-26-2002) 150 Ohio App.3d 423, 782 N.E.2d 80, 2002-Ohio-6443, appeal allowed, reversed 99 Ohio St.3d 49, 788 N.E.2d 1063, 2003-Ohio-2462. Insurance ⇨ 3390

Parent lacked the authority to release her children's future wrongful death claims exceeding $10,000 and arising out of their father's death after settlement of tort claim. Davis v. Dembek (Ohio App. 10 Dist., 11-26-2002) 150 Ohio App.3d 423, 782 N.E.2d 80, 2002-Ohio-6443, appeal allowed, reversed 99 Ohio St.3d 49, 788 N.E.2d 1063, 2003-Ohio-2462. Parent And Child ⇨ 8

The issue whether a release of a negligence claim executed in the probate court is void may be determined by a common pleas court in an action therein to recover for personal injury damages caused by such negligence. Carpenter v. Pontius (Stark 1963) 119 Ohio App. 383, 200 N.E.2d 682, 28 O.O.2d 12. Courts ⇨ 472.4(1)

5. Counsel

When a minor and the minor's parents are unrepresented by counsel during negotiation and settlement of the minor's injury claim, the attorney retained by the tortfeasor's insurer may prepare the application for guardianship appointment and the application for approval of settlement of the minor's claim and may appear before the court for final approval of the settlement, provided that (1) the attorney informs the minor and the minor's parents that the attorney is retained by the insurer and does not represent the minor; (2) the attorney informs the minor and the minor's parents that the attorney prepared the documents and that they may secure counsel to review the documents; and (3) the attorney makes these disclosures to the court. Throughout these interactions the attorney must not give legal advice to the unrepresented minor the minor's parents. Bd of Commrs on Grievances & Discipline Op 96–002 (2–2–96).

6. Procedural issues

Ward's daughter lacked standing to appeal trial court's decision granting guardian authority to settle lawsuit originally brought on ward's behalf by daughter; settlement was entirely within guardian's power, with court approval. In re Brady (Ohio App. 8 Dist., Cuyahoga, 01-27-2005) No. 84517, No. 84743, 2005-Ohio-287, 2005 WL 174773, Unreported, appeal not allowed 106 Ohio St.3d 1486, 832 N.E.2d 738, 2005-Ohio-3978. Guardian And Ward ⇨ 33

Trial court in guardianship proceedings was not required to issue findings of fact and conclusions of law to support its decision granting guardian authority to settle lawsuit originally brought on ward's behalf by ward's daughter; guardian's motion for authority to settle lawsuit did not ask court to decide any fact question, but rather whether settlement was in ward's best interest. In re Brady (Ohio App. 8 Dist., Cuyahoga, 01-27-2005) No. 84517, No. 84743, 2005-Ohio-287, 2005 WL 174773, Unreported, appeal not allowed 106 Ohio St.3d 1486, 832 N.E.2d 738, 2005-Ohio-3978. Guardian And Ward ⚖ 33

2111.181 Settlement of claims of emancipated minors

When personal injury, damage to tangible or intangible property, or damage or loss on account of personal injury or damage to tangible or intangible property is caused to a minor, who claims to be emancipated, by wrongful act, neglect, or default which would entitle the minor to maintain an action and recover damages for the injury, damage, or loss, and when any minor who claims to be emancipated is entitled to maintain an action for damages or any other relief based on any claim, or is subject to any claim to recover damages or any other relief based on any claim, the minor, who claims to be emancipated, may file an application in the probate court in the county where he then resides, praying for a finding by the court that the minor is in fact emancipated, and authorizing, approving, and consenting to the settlement of the claim by the minor without the appointment of a guardian. Upon hearing on the application, after five days' written notice of the time and place of the hearing has been given to each of the living parents of the minor, whose name and address is known, provided the parent is free from disability other than minority, or, if there is no living parent, after such notice to the next of kin of the minor known to reside in the county, the court may find the minor to be emancipated and may authorize, approve, and consent to the settlement of the claim by the minor without the appointment of a guardian and may authorize the minor to receive and receipt for the settlement and, upon the minor executing and delivering a full and complete release for the injuries, damages, losses, or claims, may authorize the delivery and payment of such moneys to the minor, to a trustee or guardian of the estate of the minor appointed by the court for the benefit of the minor, or to a depository authorized to receive fiduciary funds to hold the moneys payable to the ward when he attains majority, or for the benefit of the minor, as the court may direct.

Upon the finding of the probate court that the minor was, at the time of the injury, damage, loss, or claim, an emancipated minor, and provided the notice required by this section has been given to each living parent, whose name and address is known, then the release executed by the emancipated minor shall be a full and complete discharge and release of any claim which either or both of the parents might have by reason of the personal injury, damage to tangible or intangible property, damage or loss on account of personal injury, or damage to tangible or intangible property, or any other claim of the minor.

(1990 H 346, eff. 5-31-90; 129 v 205)

Uncodified Law

1990 H 346, § 3, eff. 5-31-90, reads, in part: (A) Sections 1 and 2 of this act shall apply only to the estates of decedents who die on or after the effective date of this act.

Library References

Guardian and Ward ⚖ 116(1).
Westlaw Topic No. 196.

   Baldwin's Ohio Legislative Service, 1990 Laws of Ohio, H 346—LSC Analysis, p 5-87

Research References

Encyclopedias

OH Jur. 3d Family Law § 263, Settlement of Emancipated Minor's Tort Claim.

OH Jur. 3d Family Law § 290, Loss or Waiver of Right of Action.

Forms

Ohio Forms Legal and Business § 15:6, Checklist—Drafting Compromise and Settlement Agreements.

Ohio Forms and Transactions F 27.14, Release of Emancipated Minor's Claim With Court Approval, and Receipt of Custodian for Settlement Proceeds.

Ohio Forms and Transactions KP 27.07, Release of Minor's Tort Claims Through Probate Court.

Treatises and Practice Aids

Carlin, Baldwin's Ohio Practice, Merrick-Rippner Probate Law § 64:15, Powers and Duties of Guardian—Special Matters Relating to Minor Wards—Settlement of Claims for Injury.

Carlin, Baldwin's Ohio Practice, Merrick-Rippner Probate Law § 64:21, Powers and Duties of Guardian—Ward's Estate—Discretionary Acts.

Carlin, Baldwin's Ohio Practice, Merrick-Rippner Probate Law § 67:15, Application for Determination of Emancipation and for Authority to Settle Claim for Personal Injuries to an Emancipated Minor Without Appointment of Guardian—Form.

Carlin, Baldwin's Ohio Practice, Merrick-Rippner Probate Law § 67:16, Entry for Notice of Application to Determine Emancipation, Etc—Form.

Carlin, Baldwin's Ohio Practice, Merrick-Rippner Probate Law § 67:17, Entry Finding that Minor is Emancipated and Approving Settlement of Claim for Personal Injuries and Damages Without Appointment of Guardian—Form.

OSBA Probate and Trust Law Section

1990:

The purpose of the amendments is to broaden the scope of minor claim settlements. The present two sections currently permit settlement only of a minor's personal injury and tangible or intangible property claims. Because minors can and do have other rights to sue in many other areas, such as claims against fiduciaries, contract and real property matters, to name a few, the amendment will provide broad authority to probate courts to authorize settlement of any minor claim regardless of its nature. The amendment also will allow settlement of any claim against a minor.

2111.19 Completion of land contract by guardian

A guardian, whether appointed by a court in this state or elsewhere, may complete the contracts of his ward for the purchase or sale of real estate or any authorized contract relating to real estate entered into by a guardian who has died or been removed. Said guardian shall proceed in the manner provided by sections 2113.48 to 2113.50, inclusive, of the Revised Code.

(129 v 257, eff. 10-5-61; 1953 H 1; GC 10507-21)

Historical and Statutory Notes

Pre-1953 H 1 Amendments: 114 v 388

Library References

Guardian and Ward ⚖ 38, 43.
Mental Health ⚖ 222.1.
Westlaw Topic Nos. 196, 257A.
C.J.S. Mental Health § 179.

Research References

Encyclopedias

OH Jur. 3d Guardian & Ward § 113, Real Property, Generally—Completion of Real Estate Contracts.

Treatises and Practice Aids

Carlin, Baldwin's Ohio Practice, Merrick-Rippner Probate Law § 90:2, Persons Entitled to Bring Land Sale Actions—Other Parties.

Carlin, Baldwin's Ohio Practice, Merrick-Rippner Probate Law § 64:21, Powers and Duties of Guardian—Ward's Estate—Discretionary Acts.

Kuehnle and Levey, Ohio Real Estate Law and Practice § 52:3, Statutory Fiduciary Sales—21 Statutory Proceedings.

2111.20 Sale of personal estate

The guardian of the person and estate, or of the estate only, may sell all or any part of the personal estate of the ward when such sale is for the interest of the ward.

(1953 H 1, eff. 10-1-53; GC 10507-22)

Historical and Statutory Notes

Pre-1953 H 1 Amendments: 114 v 388

Library References

Guardian and Ward ⚓40.
Mental Health ⚓259.
Westlaw Topic Nos. 196, 257A.

Research References

Encyclopedias

OH Jur. 3d Guardian & Ward § 93, Custody and Control of Property.

Treatises and Practice Aids

Carlin, Baldwin's Ohio Practice, Merrick-Rippner Probate Law § 64:21, Powers and Duties of Guardian—Ward's Estate—Discretionary Acts.

Carlin, Baldwin's Ohio Practice, Merrick-Rippner Probate Law § 64:29, Application to Sell Personal Property—Form.

Carlin, Baldwin's Ohio Practice, Merrick-Rippner Probate Law § 64:30, Entry Authorizing Sale of Personal Property—Form.

Carlin, Baldwin's Ohio Practice, Merrick-Rippner Probate Law § 64:31, Statement of Guardian—Private Sale—Form.

Notes of Decisions

Fraud 2
Interest of ward 1
Pledge of assets 3

---

1. Interest of ward

One who buys notes showing on their face that they are for a trust fund is charged with notice, and if the notes are sold against the interest of the ward the purchaser gets no title. Strong v. Strauss (Ohio 1883) 40 Ohio St. 87, 9 W.L.B. 345.

The guardian of a minor has the power to sell all or any part of the personal estate of his ward without an order of court; thus, the purchaser of notes from a guardian need not look to the application of the purchase money nor the necessity of sale. Strong v Hope, 7 D Repr 700, 4 B 1034 (Hamilton 1879), reversed sub nom Strong v Strauss, 40 OS 87 (1883).

2. Fraud

A federal circuit court has jurisdiction in equity to set aside a sale of an infant's property fraudulently made by his guardian. Arrowsmith v. Gleason (U.S.Ohio 1889) 9 S.Ct. 237, 129 U.S. 86, 32 L.Ed. 630.

3. Pledge of assets

A guardian may pledge assets of her wards' estate to secure loans without court approval. Cincinnati Ins. Co. v. Citizens Home Sav. (Lorain 1985) 22 Ohio App.3d 40, 488 N.E.2d 1255, 22 O.B.R. 117.

2111.21 Sale, compromise, adjustment, or mortgage of dower

The guardian of a ward who has or is claimed to have a right of dower, or a contingent right to it, in lands or tenements of which the spouse of such ward was or is seized as an estate of inheritance, where the dower has not been assigned, may sell, compromise, or adjust such dower or may release such contingent right of dower in the event the spouse of such ward desires to mortgage such property upon such terms as such guardian deems for the interests of such ward and upon such terms as the probate court of the county in which the guardian was appointed approves, or if such guardian was appointed in a foreign state, upon such terms as the probate court of the county wherein the land is situated approves. After such approval, the guardian may execute and deliver all the necessary deeds, mortgages, releases, and agreements for the sale, compromise, assignment, or mortgage of such dower or contingent right to dower. As a basis for computing the value of an inchoate dower right in any sale, compromise, or adjustment pursuant to this section, the value of the lands or tenements may be considered to be the sale price or, if there is no sale, the appraised value. Such sale, compromise, adjustment, or mortgage may be made upon application and entry in the pending proceedings.

(1953 H 1, eff. 10-1-53; GC 10507-23)

Historical and Statutory Notes

Pre-1953 H 1 Amendments: 122 v H 191; H 4 v 389

Cross References

Dower, Ch 5305

Library References

Guardian and Ward ⚓38, 42, 45.
Westlaw Topic No. 196.

Research References

Encyclopedias

OH Jur. 3d Family Law § 156, Insane and Other Incompetent Persons.

Treatises and Practice Aids

Carlin, Baldwin's Ohio Practice, Merrick-Rippner Probate Law § 90:2, Persons Entitled to Bring Land Sale Actions—Other Parties.

Carlin, Baldwin's Ohio Practice, Merrick-Rippner Probate Law § 64:21, Powers and Duties of Guardian—Ward's Estate—Discretionary Acts.

Carlin, Baldwin's Ohio Practice, Merrick-Rippner Probate Law § 64:49, Answer of Spouse of Ward—Form.

Carlin, Baldwin's Ohio Practice, Merrick-Rippner Probate Law § 64:52, Entry Approving Report of Plaintiff as to Terms and Directing Execution of Note and Mortgage and Distribution of Fund—Form.

Carlin, Baldwin's Ohio Practice, Merrick-Rippner Probate Law § 64:78, Application of Guardian for Sale of Dower Interest—Form.

Carlin, Baldwin's Ohio Practice, Merrick-Rippner Probate Law § 64:79, Entry Granting Application to Sell Dower Interest—Form.

Carlin, Baldwin's Ohio Practice, Merrick-Rippner Probate Law § 64:80, Application of Guardian to Release Contingent Dower for Purpose of Mortgage—Form.

Carlin, Baldwin's Ohio Practice, Merrick-Rippner Probate Law § 64:81, Order Granting Application to Release Contingent Dower for Purpose of Mortgage—Form.

Carlin, Baldwin's Ohio Practice, Merrick-Rippner Probate Law § 97:13, Land Sale by Guardian—Dower Interest of Ward.

Kuehnle and Levey, Ohio Real Estate Law and Practice § 52:3, Statutory Fiduciary Sales—21 Statutory Proceedings.

Law Review and Journal Commentaries

Power of Attorney—How to Avoid Third Party Denial, Jane Hils Shea. Cin B Ass'n Rep 14 (February 1988).

2111.22 Release of ward's tax title by guardian

When a ward has title to real estate by tax title only, the guardian, by deed of release and quitclaim, may convey such ward's interest or title to the person entitled to redeem such real estate, upon receiving from such person the amount paid for such tax title with the forfeiture and interest allowed by sections 319.52 and 323.121 of the Revised Code. If the guardian tenders such deed to the person entitled to redeem such real estate and he refuses to accept and pay for it, he shall not recover costs in any proceeding thereafter instituted to redeem such real estate.

(1982 H 379, eff. 9–21–82; 1953 H 1; GC 10507–24)

Historical and Statutory Notes

Pre–1953 H 1 Amendments: 114 v 389

Library References

Guardian and Ward ⚖38.
Westlaw Topic No. 196.

Research References

Encyclopedias

OH Jur. 3d Taxation § 768, Who May Redeem.

Treatises and Practice Aids

Carlin, Baldwin's Ohio Practice, Merrick-Rippner Probate Law § 64:21, Powers and Duties of Guardian—Ward's Estate—Discretionary Acts.

2111.23 Guardian ad litem

Whenever a ward, for whom a guardian of the estate or of the person and estate has been appointed, is interested in any suit or proceeding in the probate court, such guardian shall in all such suits or proceedings act as guardian ad litem for such ward, except as to suits or proceedings in which the guardian has an adverse interest. Whenever a minor or other person under legal disability, for whom no guardian of the estate or of the person and estate has been appointed, is interested in any suit or proceeding in such court, the court may appoint a guardian or a guardian ad litem. In a suit or proceeding in which the guardian has an adverse interest, the court shall appoint a guardian ad litem to represent such minor or other person under legal disability.

(125 v 411, eff. 10–16–53; 1953 H 1; GC 10507–26)

Historical and Statutory Notes

Pre–1953 H 1 Amendments: 114 v 389

Cross References

Appointment of guardian ad litem in appropriation of property, 163.11
Fiduciary, effect of order settling account, 2109.35
Minor or incompetent person as party to action, Civ R 17

Library References

Guardian and Ward ⚖28.
Infants ⚖77.
Mental Health ⚖179, 485.
Westlaw Topic Nos. 196, 211, 257A.
C.J.S. Infants §§ 222, 226 to 228.
C.J.S. Mental Health §§ 158 to 159, 264 to 274.
C.J.S. Right to Die §§ 5, 8.

Research References

Encyclopedias

OH Jur. 3d Decedents' Estates § 1671, Effect of Order Settling the Accounts; Reopening the Estate.
OH Jur. 3d Family Law § 864, Necessity of Appointment.
OH Jur. 3d Family Law § 865, Purpose of Appointment.
OH Jur. 3d Guardian & Ward § 217, Representation of Ward—in Probate Court.
OH Jur. 3d Mandamus, Procedendo, & Prohibition § 183, Effect of Patent and Unambiguous Lack of Jurisdiction
OH Jur. 3d Parties § 13, Actions by and Against Incompetents—Appointment of Guardian Ad Litem.

Treatises and Practice Aids

Carlin, Baldwin's Ohio Practice, Merrick-Rippner Probate Law § 98:4, Adoption—Parties—Who May Petition to Adopt.
Carlin, Baldwin's Ohio Practice, Merrick-Rippner Probate Law § 54:27, Fiduciary Accounts—Who is Deemed a Party.
Carlin, Baldwin's Ohio Practice, Merrick-Rippner Probate Law § 62:10, Appointment of Guardian—Definitions—Legal Settlement.
Carlin, Baldwin's Ohio Practice, Merrick-Rippner Probate Law § 62:11, Appointment of Guardian—Definitions—Domicile.
Carlin, Baldwin's Ohio Practice, Merrick-Rippner Probate Law § 62:12, Appointment of Guardian—Definitions—Residence.
Carlin, Baldwin's Ohio Practice, Merrick-Rippner Probate Law § 62:14, Appointment of Guardian—Application—Jurisdiction.
Carlin, Baldwin's Ohio Practice, Merrick-Rippner Probate Law § 62:33, Guardianship Proceedings—Court's Jurisdiction.
Carlin, Baldwin's Ohio Practice, Merrick-Rippner Probate Law § 65:18, Guardian Ad Litem—Appointment.
Carlin, Baldwin's Ohio Practice, Merrick-Rippner Probate Law § 65:30, Order Appointing Guardian Ad Litem on Court's Own Motion—Form.
Carlin, Baldwin's Ohio Practice, Merrick-Rippner Probate Law § 65:31, Answer of Guardian Ad Litem—Form.
Carlin, Baldwin's Ohio Practice, Merrick-Rippner Probate Law § 65:32, Application for Appointment of Guardian Ad Litem, Approval and Finality of Accounts—Form.
Carlin, Baldwin's Ohio Practice, Merrick-Rippner Probate Law § 65:33, Order Appointing Guardian Ad Litem—Form.
Carlin, Baldwin's Ohio Practice, Merrick-Rippner Probate Law § 65:34, Answer of Guardian Ad Litem—Form.
Carlin, Baldwin's Ohio Practice, Merrick-Rippner Probate Law § 65:35, Entry Approving and Settling Account—Form.
Carlin, Baldwin's Ohio Practice, Merrick-Rippner Probate Law § 91:26, Land Sale—Necessary Parties Defendant—Person Under Disability.
Carlin, Baldwin's Ohio Practice, Merrick-Rippner Probate Law § 98:44, Adoption—Hearing of Petition—Notice.
Kuehnle and Levey, Ohio Real Estate Law and Practice § 53:13, Land Sales—Parties Defendant—Guardian Ad Litem—Necessity for Appointment.

Notes of Decisions

Adverse interest 3
Appointment 4
Fees 2
Procedural issues 1

---

1. Procedural issues

An appearance and answer by the guardian ad litem of infant heirs in an administrator's sale of their lands is reasonable and proper. Biggs v. Bickel (Ohio 1861) 12 Ohio St. 49.

The failure to give notice to the heir in a proceeding to sell their land for debts of the testator does not deprive the court of jurisdiction it is enough that the heirs' guardian ad litem was before the court when the order was made. Sheldon's Lessee v. Newton (Ohio 1854) 3 Ohio St. 494.

A probate/juvenile judge in a custodial/guardianship proceeding for an infant lacks jurisdiction to appoint a guardian ad litem to prosecute a reparations award on behalf of the infant in the Court of Claims; therefore, the guardian ad litem's appointment is null and void. In re Traylor (Ohio Ct.Cl. 1989) 61 Ohio Misc.2d 772, 584 N.E.2d 1377. Infants ⚖ 77

Petition for authority to present claim of a minor for damages against an estate to the executor thereof after expiration of the time for presentment of claims was properly brought by minor through her father and next friend. In re Noie's Estate (Franklin 1960) 179 N.E.2d 536, 87 Ohio Law Abs. 276.

GC 11631, subds. 5 and 8 pertaining to vacation of judgments against infants, section 11603, dispensing with the necessity of reserving in a judgment the rights of a minor to show cause, and section 12270 (repealed 1936) limiting the time within which to sue to vacate judgments, are cumulative, and in addition to the right of an infant to impeach a judgment for fraud after arriving at majority, and such a cause based on proper grounds can be prosecuted by original suit begun in the court where the decree complained of was entered. Bennett v. Fleming (Ohio 1922) 105

Ohio St. 352, 137 N.E. 900, 1 Ohio Law Abs. 214, 20 Ohio Law Rep. 166, 20 Ohio Law Rep. 172. Action ⇨ 35; Infants ⇨ 111

Unless he is authorized to do so by statute, a guardian of a minor has no authority to waive the issuance and service of summons on his ward in an action affecting the ward's rights, nor to dispense with the appointment of a guardian ad litem. Roberts v. Roberts (Ohio 1899) 61 Ohio St. 96, 42 W.L.B. 367, 55 N.E. 411. Guardian And Ward ⇨ 129; Infants ⇨ 78(1); Infants ⇨ 89

Where idiot heirs are made parties to the record in an action by an administrator to sell real estate to pay debts by the filing of an answer and cross-petition by their guardian which admits the allegations and waives service of summons on such idiot heirs, they are bound by the sale made. Segal v Eagle Bldg Co, 11 CC(NS) 481, 21 CD 519 (Hamilton 1907).

2. Fees

Ruling on motion for guardian ad litem fees without conducting evidentiary hearing was not error in proceeding for modification of child support, where ex-husband filed objections to fees prior to court's ruling on fees such that court had ample information to determine reasonableness of fees and court had great deal of experience with case and parties. Fox v. Fox (Ohio App. 3 Dist., Hancock, 06-28-2004) No. 5-03-42, 2004-Ohio-3344, 2004 WL 1433553, Unreported. Infants ⇨ 83

No statutory authority exists authorizing the payment of guardian ad litem fees from county funds in a civil action involving negligent or intentional acts of an indigent minor in causing fire damage to a rental unit. Nationwide Mut. Ins. Co. v. Wymer (Franklin 1986) 33 Ohio App.3d 318, 515 N.E.2d 987.

In an action brought against a parent and his child for damages caused by a fire in a rental unit, where the court finds the child alone liable for such damages in that the child was responsible for starting the fire, the fees and expenses of a court-appointed guardian ad litem are properly charged to the indigent minor child and not to his parent, as part of the court costs. Nationwide Mut. Ins. Co. v. Wymer (Franklin 1986) 33 Ohio App.3d 318, 515 N.E.2d 987.

Transactions by which attorneys secured transfer of stock out of guardianship as compensation for services without any appointment of a guardian ad litem was a fraud upon the wards and will be set aside, despite prior approval of such transfer by the courts. Smith v. Merkle (Ohio Prob. 1956) 136 N.E.2d 749, 74 Ohio Law Abs. 33.

3. Adverse interest

Minor beneficiary of inter vivos trust did not have an "adverse interest" in proceedings to approve final account of trustors' estate such that guardian ad litem was required, although minor had an interest in the proceedings; rather, trustors' guardian, who was also the executor of the estate, had the "adverse interest" in the proceedings, which concerned guardian's payment of principal funds to individuals who were not direct principal recipients under the estate plans. In re Estate of Herrick (Ohio App. 8 Dist., Cuyahoga, 09-29-2005) No. 85695, 2005-Ohio-5201, 2005 WL 2401242, Unreported. Infants ⇨ 78(1)

Duly appointed guardian of an incompetent, who has no personal interest in the proceedings, may, in an action commenced by her to sell ward's interest in real estate, also act as party defendant by virtue of statute, which provides that guardian shall act as "guardian ad litem" for the ward. Hasty v. Weller (Ohio Prob. 1940) 6 Ohio Supp. 71, 33 Ohio Law Abs. 190, 19 O.O. 304.

Where the only interest which a guardian has in proceeding for the sale of ward's interest in real estate is the bringing of the action in her official capacity as guardian, such guardian is not "personally interested" within the meaning of section. Hasty v. Weller (Ohio Prob. 1940) 6 Ohio Supp. 71, 33 Ohio Law Abs. 190, 19 O.O. 304. Mental Health ⇨ 488

Where a trustee is also guardian of beneficiaries of the trust, but no adverse interest is shown, the denial of the appointment of a guardian ad litem will be upheld. In re Trust of Stum, No. 86 CA 28 (4th Dist Ct App, Pickaway, 12–2–87).

A child should be appointed a guardian ad litem and made a party to a legitimization proceeding, when it is clear that the mother, as natural guardian, has an adverse interest in the proceeding. Blackburn v Ludden, 1 OBR 340 (App, Trumbull 1982).

4. Appointment

Trial court did not abuse its discretion in refusing to appoint guardian ad litem for subject child, in proceedings to dispense with biological mother's consent to step-parent adoption, where trial court was statutorily required to assess child and step-parent to determine whether adoption was in child's best interests, and appointment of guardian ad litem was not statutorily mandated. In re Adoption of Haylett (Ohio App. 11 Dist., Portage, 02-18-2005) No. 2004-P-0063, 2005-Ohio-696, 2005 WL 407526, Unreported. Infants ⇨ 78(1)

Mother, whose sons applied for appointment of guardian for her, was not entitled to writ of prohibition to prevent probate judge from appointing guardian ad litem (GAL) for her in guardianship proceeding; given evidence that mother was confused and might not have intended to leave her home and probate court's interest in determining veracity of conflicting allegations of mother's children, that mother was incompetent and that son removed mother from her home despite her desire to remain there, judge did not patently and unambiguously lack jurisdiction to appoint GAL for mother. State ex rel. Florence v. Zitter (Ohio, 08-10-2005) 106 Ohio St.3d 87, 831 N.E.2d 1003, 2005-Ohio-3804. Prohibition ⇨ 10(2)

In adoption proceedings where a minor has no appointed guardian, neither RC 2111.23 nor Civ R 17(B) requires that a guardian ad litem be appointed. In re Adoption of Carnes (Portage 1983) 8 Ohio App.3d 435, 457 N.E.2d 903, 8 O.B.R. 560.

An appeal having been taken on behalf of a person adjudged incompetent for whom a guardian for such person's property in Ohio has been appointed, on motion of such guardian a trustee for the prosecution of such appeal will be appointed by the court of appeals. In re Guardianship of Reynolds (Lucas 1957) 106 Ohio App. 488, 155 N.E.2d 686, 7 O.O.2d 222.

Section expressly provides that the guardian shall act as guardian ad litem for the ward and, therefore, no additional appointment is necessary. Hasty v. Weller (Ohio Prob. 1940) 6 Ohio Supp. 71, 33 Ohio Law Abs. 190, 19 O.O. 304.

2111.24 Insolvency of ward

If the probate court finds that the estate of a ward is insolvent or will probably be insolvent, such estate shall be settled by the guardian in like manner as for the settlement of the insolvent estate of a deceased person under section 2117.15 of the Revised Code.

(1953 H 1, eff. 10–1–53; GC 10507–30)

Historical and Statutory Notes

Pre–1953 H 1 Amendments: 114 v 390

Library References

Guardian and Ward ⇨ 36, 67.
Mental Health ⇨ 211, 239.
Westlaw Topic Nos. 196, 257A.
C.J.S. Mental Health § 165.

Research References

Treatises and Practice Aids

Carlin, Baldwin's Ohio Practice, Merrick-Rippner Probate Law § 64:3, Powers and Duties of Guardian—Inventory.

Carlin, Baldwin's Ohio Practice, Merrick-Rippner Probate Law § 64:4, Powers and Duties of Guardian—Accounting.

Notes of Decisions

Judgment as lien 1
Medicaid eligibility issues 2

---

1. Judgment as lien

A judgment rendered against an imbecile, idiot, or lunatic during the existence of a guardianship is not a lien on the lands of such imbecile, idiot, or lunatic, since he has no estate in law or equity which could pass under sheriff's sale. Neff v. Cox (Ohio Prob. 1891) 5 Ohio Dec. 377, 5 Ohio N.P. 413.

2. Medicaid eligibility issues

Restrictions imposed by statute and local probate rule on ability of patient's guardian to deplete assets in patient's insolvent estate did not render such assets unavailable for purposes of Medicaid eligibility; statutes governing payment of debts of insolvent guardianship did not preclude guardian from expending funds for maintenance and support of patient, and rule barring court approval of any distribution of estate assets prior to filing of inventory was not a total bar to depletion of assets. Payne v. Ohio Dept. of Human Serv. (Ohio App. 10 Dist., 09-16-1997) 123 Ohio App.3d 341, 704 N.E.2d 270. Health ⚖ 471(1)

LEASE OF REAL PROPERTY

2111.25 Lease for not more than three years

A guardian, of the person and estate or of the estate only, without application to the probate court, may lease the possession or use of any real estate of his ward for a term not exceeding three years, provided such term does not extend beyond the minority, if the ward is a minor. If the lease extends beyond the death of the ward or beyond the removal of the disability of a ward other than a minor, such lease shall terminate on such death or removal of disability, unless confirmed by the ward or his legal representatives. In the event of such determination, the tenant shall have a lien on the premises for any sum expended by him in pursuance of the lease in making improvements for which compensation was not made in rent or otherwise.

(1953 H 1, eff. 10–1–53; GC 10507–31)

Historical and Statutory Notes

Pre–1953 H 1 Amendments: 114 v 391

Library References

Guardian and Ward ⚖ 44.
Mental Health ⚖ 259.
Westlaw Topic Nos. 196, 257A.

Research References

Encyclopedias

OH Jur. 3d Family Law § 157, Insane and Other Incompetent Persons—Dower Rights in the Property of Incompetents.

OH Jur. 3d Guardian & Ward § 133, Lease for Not More Than Three Years.

Forms

Ohio Forms Legal and Business § 8:33, Checklist—Drafting Commercial Property Lease.

Treatises and Practice Aids

Carlin, Baldwin's Ohio Practice, Merrick-Rippner Probate Law § 64:21, Powers and Duties of Guardian—Ward's Estate—Discretionary Acts.

Notes of Decisions

Removal 1

___

1. Removal

A covenant by a guardian to renew a lease for a second term is in excess of the power granted by RS 6295 and void. Globe Soap Co v Louisville & Nashville RR Co, 6 CC(NS) 496, 17 CD 759 (Hamilton 1905), affirmed by 76 OS 577, 81 NE 1189 (1907).

2111.26 Lease for term of years

A guardian may lease the possession and use of the real estate of his ward or any part of it for a term of years, renewable or otherwise, by perpetual lease, with or without the privilege of purchase, or may lease upon such terms and for such time as the probate court approves any lands belonging to the ward containing coal, gypsum, petroleum oil, natural gas, gravel, stone, or any other mineral substance for the purpose of drilling, mining, or excavating for and removing any of such substances, or such guardian may modify or change in any respect any lease previously made.

Such lease, or modification or change in a lease previously made, may be made when the guardian of the person and estate or of the estate only applies to the court by which he was appointed and such court finds that the lease or modification or change is necessary for the support of the ward or of his family, for the payment of the just debts of the ward, for the ward's education, if a minor, to secure the improvement of the real estate of the ward and increase the rent, to pay any liens or claims against said real estate, or if such court finds that such real estate is suffering unavoidable waste, or that in any other respect it will be for the best interests of the ward or those persons for whom the ward is required by law to provide.

(1953 H 1, eff. 10–1–53; GC 10507–32)

Historical and Statutory Notes

Pre–1953 H 1 Amendments: 114 v 391

Library References

Guardian and Ward ⚖ 44.
Mental Health ⚖ 259.
Westlaw Topic Nos. 196, 257A.

Research References

Forms

Ohio Forms Legal and Business § 8:33, Checklist—Drafting Commercial Property Lease.

Treatises and Practice Aids

Carlin, Baldwin's Ohio Practice, Merrick-Rippner Probate Law § 64:21, Powers and Duties of Guardian—Ward's Estate—Discretionary Acts.

Carlin, Baldwin's Ohio Practice, Merrick-Rippner Probate Law § 64:58, Complaint for Lease and Improvement of Real Property of Ward—Form.

Carlin, Baldwin's Ohio Practice, Merrick-Rippner Probate Law § 64:59, Answer of Spouse Consenting to Lease of Real Estate—Form.

Carlin, Baldwin's Ohio Practice, Merrick-Rippner Probate Law § 64:60, Entry Appointing Appraiser and Ordering Appraisal—Form.

Carlin, Baldwin's Ohio Practice, Merrick-Rippner Probate Law § 64:61, Order to Appraisers—Form.

Carlin, Baldwin's Ohio Practice, Merrick-Rippner Probate Law § 64:62, Report of Appraiser—Form.

Carlin, Baldwin's Ohio Practice, Merrick-Rippner Probate Law § 64:63, Entry Authorizing Lease and Improvement of Real Property of Ward—Form.

Carlin, Baldwin's Ohio Practice, Merrick-Rippner Probate Law § 64:64, Report of Guardian—Lease—Form.

Carlin, Baldwin's Ohio Practice, Merrick-Rippner Probate Law § 64:65, Entry Confirming Lease—Form

Notes of Decisions

Oil lease 2
Renewal 1

___

1. Renewal

In order to bring a lease with renewal provisions within RS 6296, the petition should contain averments showing the requisite conditions and the authority of the court. Globe Soap Co v Louisville & Nashville RR Co, 6 CC(NS) 496, 17 CD 759 (Hamilton 1905), affirmed by 76 OS 577, 81 NE 1189 (1907).

2. Oil lease

The superintendent of the Ohio soldiers and sailors orphans home has no authority to enter into a lease for oil and gas purposes on the real estate of his wards until he has obtained permission so to do from the probate court of Greene county. 1927 OAG 602.

2111.27 Petition

A guardian's application for authority to lease real estate of a ward shall be by petition setting forth:

(A) The legal capacity of the petitioner;

(B) The name of the ward, the character of his disability, and if it is idiocy, imbecility, or lunacy, whether such disability is curable or not, temporary, or confirmed, and its duration;

(C) The number, names, ages, and residence of the family of the ward, including the spouse and those residents of the county who have the next estate of inheritance from such ward, all of whom, as well as the ward, must be made defendants;

(D) The indebtedness of the ward, the expense of supporting and maintaining him, the expense of educating him if he is a minor, and any other expense of the ward;

(E) The value of all the property and effects of the ward including the real estate proposed to be leased;

(F) The income of the ward and the net annual value to the ward of the real estate proposed to be leased;

(G) A description of the real estate proposed to be leased and the probable amount for which such real estate can be leased;

(H) A detailed statement of the improvements proposed to be made to the real estate sought to be leased;

(I) The reasons for the proposed lease and the terms, covenants, conditions, and stipulations thereof, including the time for which it is proposed the real estate should be leased;

(J) Such other facts necessary to apprise the court fully of the necessity or benefit to the ward or the estate of the proposed lease, or such other facts as may be required by the court;

(K) A prayer for the proper authority.

(1953 H 1, eff. 10–1–53; GC 10507–33)

Historical and Statutory Notes

Pre–1953 H 1 Amendments: 114 v 391

Library References

Guardian and Ward ⚖86.
Mental Health ⚖265.
Westlaw Topic Nos. 196, 257A.

Research References

Encyclopedias
OH Jur. 3d Guardian & Ward § 135, Procedure, Generally.
OH Jur. 3d Guardian & Ward § 136, Parties; Consent by Ward's Spouse to Lease.

Treatises and Practice Aids
Carlin, Baldwin's Ohio Practice, Merrick-Rippner Probate Law § 64:21, Powers and Duties of Guardian—Ward's Estate—Discretionary Acts.

2111.28 Parties

In an application for authority to lease real estate of a ward under sections 2111.26 and 2111.27 of the Revised Code, the guardian may act for two or more wards and two or more guardians of different wards may unite, when all the wards are jointly or in common interested in the real estate. When the same person is guardian of two or more wards owning lands in common, such wards may be joined as defendants in the same petition.

The ward's spouse shall be made a defendant to such petition, and if the proposed lease is for the purpose of mining or removing mineral or other substances, and if such spouse files an answer consenting to the lease, free and discharged of all right and expectancy of dower therein, such answer shall be a full release of such spouse's expectancy of dower when the lease is confirmed. Unless in such answer an allowance in lieu of dower is waived, the court shall allow, out of the proceeds of the lease, such sum in money as is the just and reasonable value of such expectancy of dower.

(1953 H 1, eff. 10–1–53; GC 10507–34, 10507–35)

Historical and Statutory Notes

Pre–1953 H 1 Amendments: 114 v 392

Cross References

Dower, Ch 5305

Library References

Guardian and Ward ⚖83, 113.
Mental Health ⚖265, 274.
Westlaw Topic Nos. 196, 257A.

Research References

Encyclopedias
OH Jur. 3d Family Law § 111, Crops; Mines and Wells.
OH Jur. 3d Family Law § 157, Insane and Other Incompetent Persons—Dower Rights in the Property of Incompetents.
OH Jur. 3d Guardian & Ward § 136, Parties; Consent by Ward's Spouse to Lease.

2111.29 Parties and proceedings

When a guardian files an application for authority to lease the real estate of a ward, the same rules shall apply as to parties and, upon the filing of the petition described in section 2111.27 of the Revised Code, like proceedings shall be had as in an action to sell real estate belonging to the ward under sections 2127.01 to 2127.43, inclusive, of the Revised Code, including services of summons, notice, appraisal, pleading, rule days, and proof.

(1953 H 1, eff. 10–1–53; GC 10507–36)

Historical and Statutory Notes

Pre–1953 H 1 Amendments: 114 v 392

Library References

Guardian and Ward ⚖80.
Westlaw Topic No. 196.

Research References

Encyclopedias
OH Jur. 3d Guardian & Ward § 135, Procedure, Generally.
OH Jur. 3d Guardian & Ward § 136, Parties; Consent by Ward's Spouse to Lease.

2111.30 Duties of appraisers

When a guardian applies for authority to lease the real estate of a ward, the duties of the appraisers shall be the same as in proceedings to sell real estate belonging to the ward under sections 2127.22 and 2127.23 of the Revised Code, except that they shall appraise not only the value of the real estate but also the value of the annual rental upon the terms, covenants, conditions, and stipulations of the proposed lease. If said lease is for the mining or removal of mineral or other substances, the appraisers shall report in writing to the probate court their opinion as to the probability of the lands containing such substances, the probable quantity of such substances, and the terms upon which it would be advantageous to the ward to lease the lands for mining or removing such substances. In their report the appraisers shall state whether in their opinion, the proposed lease will be for the best interests of the ward, those whom he is required by law to support, or the estate. They may also suggest any change in the terms, covenants, and stipulations proposed in the petition. The report of the appraisers shall be returned on or before the day named in the order for the final hearing of the case. On the return of the appraisement, the guardian need not give an additional bond, but in case of sale under the terms of the lease, such guardian must give such bond before the confirmation of the sale.

(125 v 903, eff. 10–1–53; 1953 H 1; GC 10507–37)

Historical and Statutory Notes

Pre–1953 H 1 Amendments: 114 v 392

Library References

Guardian and Ward ⊜93.
Mental Health ⊜264.
Westlaw Topic Nos. 196, 257A.

Research References

Encyclopedias
OH Jur. 3d Guardian & Ward § 137, Appraisers and Appraisal.
OH Jur. 3d Guardian & Ward § 138, Hearing, Determination, and Order.

2111.31 Hearing and order

If the report of the appraisers under section 2111.30 of the Revised Code is favorable to the lease and on the final hearing the court is of the opinion that it will be to the advantage of the ward, those whom he is required by law to support, or the estate to lease the real estate, the probate court shall make an order authorizing the lease to be made by public or private letting, as it deems best, on such terms, covenants, conditions, and stipulations, either in accordance with those set forth in the petition or otherwise, as it directs, provided such terms, covenants, conditions, and stipulations are not less favorable to the ward than those reported by the appraisers. The lease shall not take effect until such lease and the security, if any, therein prescribed are approved and confirmed.

In the lease made in pursuance of such order it may be provided that the improvements shall be made by the tenant as part of the rent, or by the guardian, either out of the rent or other means of the ward as the court directs.

If the lease is for the mining or removal of mineral or other substances and the guardian is unable to lease the lands upon the terms ordered, he may report the fact to the court and such court may change the terms of leasing, but not below the customary royalty in the vicinity of such lands.

(125 v 903, eff. 10–1–53; 1953 H 1; GC 10507–38, 10507–39, 10507–41)

Historical and Statutory Notes

Pre–1953 H 1 Amendments: 114 v 393

Library References

Guardian and Ward ⊜88, 90.
Mental Health ⊜267.
Westlaw Topic Nos. 196, 257A.

Research References

Encyclopedias
OH Jur. 3d Guardian & Ward § 138, Hearing, Determination, and Order.

Treatises and Practice Aids
Carlin, Baldwin's Ohio Practice, Merrick-Rippner Probate Law § 66:13, Termination of Guardianship—Effect of Order.

2111.32 Royalty

If the lease made pursuant to court order, under section 2111.31 of the Revised Code is for the mining or removal of mineral or other substances on a royalty basis, within six months after the receipt of the first royalty under such lease the guardian shall report to the probate court the amount thereof, and the court shall then fix a bond which will cover such royalty. At any time the court deems the bond insufficient to secure the royalty, it may increase such bond or require a new one.

(1953 H 1, eff. 10–1–53; GC 10507–40)

Historical and Statutory Notes

Pre–1953 H 1 Amendments: 114 v 393

Library References

Guardian and Ward ⊜38.
Westlaw Topic No. 196.

Research References

Encyclopedias
OH Jur. 3d Guardian & Ward § 138, Hearing, Determination, and Order.

Treatises and Practice Aids
Carlin, Baldwin's Ohio Practice, Merrick-Rippner Probate Law § 64:21, Powers and Duties of Guardian—Ward's Estate—Discretionary Acts.

IMPROVEMENT OF REAL ESTATE

2111.33 Guardian may improve real estate; procedure

A guardian may use the moneys and personal estate of his ward to improve his ward's real estate. Such guardian shall file in the probate court in which he was appointed a petition containing the following:

(A) A description of the premises to be improved;

(B) The amount of rent the premises yield at the time the petition is filed;

(C) In what manner it is proposed to make such improvement;

(D) The proposed expenditures for such improvement;

(E) What rent the premises will probably yield when so improved;

(F) A statement of the value of the ward's personal estate;

(G) Other facts which are pertinent to the question whether the improvement should be made;

(H) A prayer that such guardian be authorized to use so much of his ward's money and personal estate as is necessary to make such improvement;

(I) The character of the disability of the ward, and if it is incompetency, whether such disability is curable or not, temporary, or confirmed, and its duration;

(J) The names, ages, and residence of the family of the ward, including the spouse and those known to be residents of the county who have the next estate of inheritance from the ward. All such persons, as well as the ward, must be made defendants and notified of the pendency and prayer of the petition in such manner as the court directs.

If the property is so situated that, to the best interest of the ward's estate, it can be advantageously improved in connection with the improvement of property adjacent to it, the petition shall show this and have a prayer in accordance therewith.

(129 v 1448, eff. 10-25-61; 125 v 903; 1953 H 1; GC 10507-42)

Historical and Statutory Notes

Pre-1953 H 1 Amendments: 114 v 394

Library References

Guardian and Ward ⚖58.
Mental Health ⚖234.
Westlaw Topic Nos. 196, 257A.
C.J.S. Mental Health § 176.

Research References

Encyclopedias

OH Jur. 3d Guardian & Ward § 127, Improvements to Property.
OH Jur. 3d Guardian & Ward § 128, Procedure; Petition.

Treatises and Practice Aids

Carlin, Baldwin's Ohio Practice, Merrick-Rippner Probate Law § 64:21, Powers and Duties of Guardian—Ward's Estate—Discretionary Acts.

Notes of Decisions

Liens 1

---

1. Liens

Where a guardian, with authority therefor, improves a ward's property and gives a lien on accruing rents, the ward cannot defeat the lien by purchasing a paramount title. Este v. Strong (Ohio 1826) 2 Ohio 401.

2111.34 Proceedings

Upon the filing of the petition described in section 2111.33 of the Revised Code, like proceedings shall be had as to pleadings and proof as on petition by a guardian to sell the real estate of a ward under sections 2127.01 to 2127.43, inclusive, of the Revised Code. The probate court shall appoint three disinterested freeholders of the county as commissioners to examine the premises to be improved, to examine the surroundings, and to report to the court their opinion whether the improvement proposed will be advantageous to the estate of the ward.

(1953 H 1, eff. 10-1-53; GC 10507-43)

Historical and Statutory Notes

Pre-1953 H 1 Amendments: 114 v 394

Library References

Guardian and Ward ⚖93.
Mental Health ⚖264.
Westlaw Topic Nos. 196, 257A.

Research References

Encyclopedias

OH Jur. 3d Guardian & Ward § 128, Procedure; Petition.
OH Jur. 3d Guardian & Ward § 129, Procedure; Petition—Examination of Premises.

2111.35 Amount to be used for improvement

On the final hearing of a guardian's proceeding to improve the real estate of his ward, if the prayer of the petition is granted, the probate court shall fix the amount of money and personal estate that may be used in making such improvement. Such court may authorize such guardian to unite with the owners of adjacent property, upon such equitable terms and conditions as the court approves, for the improvement of the premises of his ward and for the proper management and repair of the property when so improved.

(1953 H 1, eff. 10-1-53; GC 10507-44)

Historical and Statutory Notes

Pre-1953 H 1 Amendments: 114 v 394

Library References

Guardian and Ward ⚖90.
Mental Health ⚖267.
Westlaw Topic Nos. 196, 257A.

Research References

Encyclopedias

OH Jur. 3d Fiduciaries § 258, Loss or Forfeiture of Right to Compensation—Statutory Grounds for Denial of Commission.
OH Jur. 3d Guardian & Ward § 130, Procedure; Petition—Determination of Amount; Hearing.

2111.36 Guardian's report

A guardian shall distinctly report to the probate court the amount of money and personal property expended in making an improvement to the ward's real property under section 2111.35 of the Revised Code, within forty days after the improvement is completed. If the ward dies before the removal of the disability and there are heirs who inherit real property only from him, the money expended shall descend and pass the same as his other personal property and be a charge on the premises improved in favor of the heirs who inherit the personal property.

(1992 H 427, eff. 10-8-92; 1953 H 1; GC 10507-45)

Historical and Statutory Notes

Pre-1953 H 1 Amendments: 114 v 394

Library References

Guardian and Ward ⚖137.
Mental Health ⚖291.
Westlaw Topic Nos. 196, 257A.
C.J.S. Mental Health § 183.

Research References

Encyclopedias

OH Jur. 3d Guardian & Ward § 127, Improvements to Property.
OH Jur. 3d Guardian & Ward § 130, Procedure; Petition—Determination of Amount; Hearing.
OH Jur. 3d Guardian & Ward § 131, Procedure; Petition—Guardian's Report.

Treatises and Practice Aids

Carlin, Baldwin's Ohio Practice, Merrick-Rippner Probate Law § 64:21, Powers and Duties of Guardian—Ward's Estate—Discretionary Acts.

RESIDENT GUARDIAN OF NONRESIDENT WARD

2111.37 Guardian for nonresident

When a nonresident minor, incompetent, habitual drunkard, idiot, imbecile, lunatic, or person confined in a state, charitable, or correctional institution has real estate, chattels, rights, credits, or moneys in this state, the probate court of the county in which the property or a part of it is situated may appoint a resident guardian of the ward to manage, collect, lease, and take care of his property. The appointment may be made whether or not a ward has a guardian, trustee, or other conservator in the state of his residence, and, if he has a guardian, trustee, or other conservator in the state of his residence, the control and authority of the resident guardian appointed in Ohio shall be superior as to all property of the ward in Ohio.

The first appointment of a resident guardian of a nonresident ward shall extend to all the property and effects of the ward in this state and exclude the jurisdiction of the probate court of any other county.

(1994 H 571, eff. 10–6–94; 1953 H 1, eff. 10–1–53; GC 10507–46, 10507–47)

Historical and Statutory Notes

Pre–1953 H 1 Amendments: 114 v 395

Amendment Note: 1994 H 571 substituted "correctional" for "penal".

Library References

Guardian and Ward ⚖167.
Mental Health ⚖195.
Westlaw Topic Nos. 196, 257A.

Research References

Encyclopedias

OH Jur. 3d Guardian & Ward § 19, Persons Subject to Guardianship; Minors—Nonresidents.
OH Jur. 3d Guardian & Ward § 36, Resident Guardianship for Nonresident Ward.
OH Jur. 3d Guardian & Ward § 106, Resident Guardian for Nonresident Ward.

Treatises and Practice Aids

Carlin, Baldwin's Ohio Practice, Merrick-Rippner Probate Law § 62:28, Appointment of Guardian—Residency Requirements—Nonresident Ward.
Carlin, Baldwin's Ohio Practice, Merrick-Rippner Probate Law § 97:21, Land Sale by Guardian—Nonresident Ward.

Notes of Decisions

Competency 2
Resident trustee 1

---

1. Resident trustee

In hearing of application under statute for trusteeship of lunatic adjudged insane in foreign state and application by foreign guardian under statute to possess property of lunatic in state, probate court has discretion, in best interest of lunatic, to grant application for trusteeship and deny foreign guardian's application. George v. Cleveland Trust Co. (Cuyahoga 1926) 22 Ohio App. 1, 153 N.E. 914, 5 Ohio Law Abs. 292.

2. Competency

RC 2111.37 gives Ohio courts authority to determine the competency of nonresidents who own property in Ohio. In re Guardianship of Slaughter, No. 1135 (4th Dist Ct App, Athens, 1–21–83).

2111.38 Bond and duties

The resident guardian of a nonresident ward shall give bond and be bound and controlled by all the statutes of Ohio as though he were a guardian of a ward resident in this state, and shall have all of the authority of a guardian of a resident ward including the authority to lease or sell real estate belonging to the ward.

Unless removed by the probate court, a resident guardian of a nonresident minor shall hold his appointment until such minor dies or arrives at the age of majority, whether or not such minor is over fourteen years of age at the time of appointment. A resident guardian of any other nonresident ward shall hold his appointment until the death of the ward or until the court is satisfied that the necessity for the guardianship no longer exists.

All moneys due to such nonresident ward while such resident guardianship continues shall be paid over to his foreign guardian so far as necessary or proper for the ward's support and maintenance. If the ward dies, such moneys shall be paid to his ancillary administrator or other legal representative, provided that the court which appointed such resident guardian has satisfactory proof, as provided by section 2111.39 of the Revised Code, of the authority of such foreign guardian, administrator, or other legal representative to receive the moneys or estates of such nonresident ward, that the security given by such foreign guardian, administrator, or other legal representative is sufficient to protect such ward's interest or estate, and provided such court deems it best for him or his estate.

(1953 H 1, eff. 10–1–53; GC 10507–48 to 10507–50)

Historical and Statutory Notes

Pre–1953 H 1 Amendments: 114 v 395

Library References

Guardian and Ward ⚖167 to 169.
Mental Health ⚖195 to 196.
Westlaw Topic Nos. 196, 257A.

Research References

Encyclopedias

OH Jur. 3d Guardian & Ward § 106, Resident Guardian for Nonresident Ward.
OH Jur. 3d Guardian & Ward § 189, Removal of Resident Guardian for Nonresident Ward.
OH Jur. 3d Guardian & Ward § 196, Guardianship of Nonresident.

Treatises and Practice Aids

Carlin, Baldwin's Ohio Practice, Merrick-Rippner Probate Law § 62:21, Appointment of Guardian—Application—Appointment, Acceptance, and Bonding.
Carlin, Baldwin's Ohio Practice, Merrick-Rippner Probate Law § 64:20, Powers and Duties of Guardian—Ward's Estate—Mandatory Duties.
Carlin, Baldwin's Ohio Practice, Merrick-Rippner Probate Law § 64:21, Powers and Duties of Guardian—Ward's Estate—Discretionary Acts.
Carlin, Baldwin's Ohio Practice, Merrick-Rippner Probate Law § 97:21, Land Sale by Guardian—Nonresident Ward.

2111.39 Foreign guardian may collect money

When a foreign legal representative of a nonresident ward applies to have all or any of the moneys or property in the hands of the resident guardian of such ward paid or delivered to him, he must file his petition or motion in the probate court by which such resident guardian was appointed. Such resident guardian must be given thirty days' notice of the time of hearing thereon and such foreign representative must produce an exemplification under the seal of the office, if there be a seal, of the proper court of the state of his residence containing all the entries on record in relation to his appointment and qualification, authenticated as required by the act of congress in such cases. Upon the hearing thereof, the court shall make such order as it deems for the best interests of such nonresident ward or his estate.

(1953 H 1, eff. 10–1–53; GC 10507–51)

Historical and Statutory Notes

Pre–1953 H 1 Amendments: 114 v 396

Library References

Guardian and Ward ⟪168, 170.
Mental Health ⟪196.
Westlaw Topic Nos. 196, 257A.

Research References

Encyclopedias

OH Jur. 3d Guardian & Ward § 116, Application by Foreign Guardian to Obtain Property from Resident Guardian.

Treatises and Practice Aids

Carlin, Baldwin's Ohio Practice, Merrick-Rippner Probate Law § 64:21, Powers and Duties of Guardian—Ward's Estate—Discretionary Acts.

Carlin, Baldwin's Ohio Practice, Merrick-Rippner Probate Law § 64:70, Motion of Foreign Guardian for Transfer of Funds by Resident Guardian—Form.

Carlin, Baldwin's Ohio Practice, Merrick-Rippner Probate Law § 64:71, Entry Setting Motion for Hearing and Ordering Notice—Form.

Carlin, Baldwin's Ohio Practice, Merrick-Rippner Probate Law § 64:72, Notice of Filing Motion to Transfer Funds—Form.

Carlin, Baldwin's Ohio Practice, Merrick-Rippner Probate Law § 64:73, Entry to Transfer Funds to Foreign Guardian—Form.

2111.40 When nonresident ward becomes a resident

When a nonresident ward for whom a resident guardian was appointed has become a resident since the appointment and a guardian has been appointed for such ward, the probate court shall remove the resident guardian previously appointed and require an immediate settlement of his account.

(1953 H 1, eff. 10–1–53; GC 10507–52)

Historical and Statutory Notes

Pre–1953 H 1 Amendments: 114 v 396

Library References

Guardian and Ward ⟪167.
Mental Health ⟪195.
Westlaw Topic Nos. 196, 257A.

Research References

Encyclopedias

OH Jur. 3d Guardian & Ward § 189, Removal of Resident Guardian for Nonresident Ward.

Treatises and Practice Aids

Carlin, Baldwin's Ohio Practice, Merrick-Rippner Probate Law § 66:2, Termination—Discretionary—Court; Removal.

NONRESIDENT GUARDIAN OF NONRESIDENT WARD

2111.41 Removal in favor of foreign guardian when ward leaves the state

When a ward for whom a guardian has been appointed in this state removes to another state or territory, and a guardian of the ward is there appointed, the guardian in this state may be removed and required to settle his account.

Such a removal shall not be made unless the guardian appointed in another state or territory applies to the probate court in this state that made the former appointment, and files an exemplification from the record of the court making the foreign appointment containing all the entries and proceedings relating to his appointment, his giving bond, with a copy thereof, and of the letters of guardianship, all authenticated as required by the act of congress. Before such an application is heard or action taken by the court, at least thirty days' written notice shall be served on the guardian appointed in this state specifying the object of the application, and the time it is to be heard.

No such removal shall be made in favor of a foreign guardian, unless at the time of the hearing the state or territory in which he was appointed has a similar provision as to wards removing from that state or territory. The court shall grant the application unless it makes an affirmative finding that the removal of the guardian appointed in this state would not be in the interest of the ward.

If on such a hearing the court removes the guardian, it shall make all suitable orders for discharging the guardian and shall deliver to the foreign guardian all moneys and other property in the hands of the resident guardian after his settlement.

(1975 S 145, eff. 1–1–76; 125 v 903; 1953 H 1; GC 10507–53 to 10507–56)

Historical and Statutory Notes

Pre–1953 H 1 Amendments: 114 v 396, 397

Legislative Service Commission

1975:

Under present law, if a ward moves from this state to another, the guardian appointed in the other state may apply to this state for removal of the resident guardian and transfer of the ward's property. The court may deny this application, unless satisfied the removal of the resident guardian would be to the interest of the ward. This would be changed by the bill to require the court to grant the application of the nonresident guardian unless the court makes an affirmative finding that it would *not* be in the ward's interest.

Library References

Guardian and Ward ⟪25.
Mental Health ⟪175.
Westlaw Topic Nos. 196, 257A.
C.J.S. Mental Health § 148.

Research References

Encyclopedias

OH Jur. 3d Guardian & Ward § 186, Removal of Ohio Guardian After Ward Leaves Ohio.

OH Jur. 3d Guardian & Ward § 187, Removal of Ohio Guardian After Ward Leaves Ohio—Notice and Hearing.

OH Jur. 3d Guardian & Ward § 188, Removal of Ohio Guardian After Ward Leaves Ohio—Order of Removal; Appeal.

Treatises and Practice Aids

Carlin, Baldwin's Ohio Practice, Merrick-Rippner Probate Law § 66:3, Termination—Discretionary—Ward Relocation.

Carlin, Baldwin's Ohio Practice, Merrick-Rippner Probate Law § 62:55, Appointment of Guardian of a Minor—Custody Issues—Jurisdiction.

Carlin, Baldwin's Ohio Practice, Merrick-Rippner Probate Law § 64:74, Application by Foreign Guardian to Remove Guardian When Guardian Moves to Another State—Form.

Carlin, Baldwin's Ohio Practice, Merrick-Rippner Probate Law § 64:75, Entry Setting Application for Hearing and Ordering Notice—Form.

Carlin, Baldwin's Ohio Practice, Merrick-Rippner Probate Law § 64:76, Notice of Hearing—Form.

Notes of Decisions

Discretion of court 1

1. Discretion of court

Probate court has discretion in interest of ward, adjudged lunatic in foreign state, to grant application for trusteeship and deny application of foreign guardian to possess property in state. George v. Cleveland Trust Co. (Cuyahoga 1926) 22 Ohio App. 1, 153 N.E. 914, 5 Ohio Law Abs. 292. Mental Health ⇔ 196.

2111.42 Foreign guardians may receive property

If a guardian is appointed by a court of another state or territory or by a foreign country for a nonresident ward, and the ward is entitled to money or other property in the custody of an executor, administrator, or other person in this state, the executor, administrator, or other person may deliver the money or other property to the guardian of the nonresident ward.

(1984 H 263, eff. 10–4–84; 1975 S 145; 1953 H 1; GC 10507–57)

Historical and Statutory Notes

Pre–1953 H 1 Amendments: 119 v 394, § 1; 114 v 397

Library References

Guardian and Ward ⇔168.
Mental Health ⇔196.
Westlaw Topic Nos. 196, 257A.

Research References

Encyclopedias

OH Jur. 3d Guardian & Ward § 117, Application by Foreign Guardian to Obtain Property from Resident Guardian—from Other Persons.

Treatises and Practice Aids

Carlin, Baldwin's Ohio Practice, Merrick-Rippner Probate Law § 64:21, Powers and Duties of Guardian—Ward's Estate—Discretionary Acts.

Carlin, Baldwin's Ohio Practice, Merrick-Rippner Probate Law § 64:77, Entry for Removal of Resident Guardian and Transfer of Money and Property to Foreign Guardian—Form.

Carlin, Baldwin's Ohio Practice, Merrick-Rippner Probate Law § 97:22, Land Sale by Guardian—Nonresident Guardian.

Notes of Decisions

Death of guardian 2
Eligibility 3
Limitation on power 1

1. Limitation on power

Courts of Indiana held to be powerless to authorize conveyance of interest in real estate in Ohio by guardian of insane person, but such action should have been brought in courts of state of Ohio. Smith v. McKelvey (Lucas 1928) 28 Ohio App. 361, 162 N.E. 722, 6 Ohio Law Abs. 677. Courts ⇔ 18; Mental Health ⇔ 263.

Under statute, providing that properly qualified guardian of lunatic "may possess" ward's property within state, power of foreign guardian is limited to similar power possessed by guardians appointed by state courts. George v. Cleveland Trust Co. (Cuyahoga 1926) 22 Ohio App. 1, 153 N.E. 914, 5 Ohio Law Abs. 292.

2. Death of guardian

Where a guardian appointed in Pennsylvania receives assets of the ward and then moves to Ohio with the ward and dies without settlement, the ward can maintain an action in equity for an account against the guardian's administrator in the Ohio courts. Pedan v. Robb's Adm'r. (Ohio 1837) 8 Ohio 227.

3. Eligibility

Compliance by a foreign guardian with RS 6279 is necessary to entitle him to demand money belonging to his ward in the hands of an Ohio administrator. Banning v. Gotshall (Ohio 1900) 62 Ohio St. 210, 43 W.L.B. 315, 56 N.E. 1030.

A foreign guardian who is ineligible to an appointment as such in Ohio due to her remarriage will not be permitted to collect money due to her ward in this state. Nabighurst v Stevenson, 10 D Repr 162, 19 B 106 (Super, Cincinnati 1886).

2111.43 Foreign wards and guardians

Wards living outside this state and owning lands within it are entitled to the benefit of Chapters 2101. to 2131., inclusive, of the Revised Code. Guardians appointed by foreign courts for nonresident wards may bring and maintain actions and enforce the collection of judgments rendered in such cases in their favor in the manner and to the extent that they could if appointed in this state, upon giving security for the costs which may accrue therein as other nonresidents do under sections 2323.30 to 2323.36, inclusive, of the Revised Code.

(1953 H 1, eff. 10–1–53; GC 10507–58)

Historical and Statutory Notes

Pre–1953 H 1 Amendments: 114 v 397

Library References

Guardian and Ward ⇔166 to 172.
Mental Health ⇔194.
Westlaw Topic Nos. 196, 257A.

Research References

Encyclopedias

OH Jur. 3d Cotenancy & Partition § 79, Guardians.
OH Jur. 3d Guardian & Ward § 214, Parties—Nonresident Ward; Representation by Foreign Guardian.
OH Jur. 3d Guardian & Ward § 222, Enforcement of Judgment.

Treatises and Practice Aids

Carlin, Baldwin's Ohio Practice, Merrick-Rippner Probate Law § 64:20, Powers and Duties of Guardian—Ward's Estate—Mandatory Duties.

Carlin, Baldwin's Ohio Practice, Merrick-Rippner Probate Law § 64:21, Powers and Duties of Guardian—Ward's Estate—Discretionary Acts.

Carlin, Baldwin's Ohio Practice, Merrick-Rippner Probate Law § 97:22, Land Sale by Guardian—Nonresident Guardian.

Notes of Decisions

Actions 1
Authority to appoint 2

1. Actions

Under authority of former statute, a foreign guardian of a minor, resident of a foreign state, could answer for his ward in a partition action and, by doing so, enter the appearance of both. Kunzelmann v. Duval (Hamilton 1939) 61 Ohio App. 360, 22 N.E.2d 632, 29 Ohio Law Abs. 200, 14 O.O. 519. Guardian And Ward ⇔ 171

There is no authority for a foreign guardian to bring an action as such in a federal court sitting in another state. Smith v. Madden (C.C.N.D.Ohio 1896) 78 F. 833. Federal Courts ⇔ 71; Guardian And Ward ⇔ 170

A guardian appointed in Pennsylvania may maintain an action in Ohio to recover damages for personal injury to his minor ward who is a resident of Pennsylvania. Pennsylvania Co v Raub, 11 CC(NS) 157, 20 CD 542 (Mahoning 1907), affirmed by 79 OS 454, 87 NE 1139 (1908).

2. Authority to appoint

A minor must reside in the county where his guardian is appointed, or the court has no authority to appoint. Maxsom v. Sawyer (Ohio 1843) 12 Ohio 195.

2111.44 Sale of lands of foreign wards

Applications for the sale of real estate by guardians of wards who live out of this state shall be made in the county in which the land is situated. If such real estate is situated in two or more counties, such application shall be made in one of the counties in which a part of it is situated. Additional security, which may be approved by the probate court of the county in which the application is made, shall be required from such guardian when deemed necessary.

(1953 H 1, eff. 10–1–53; GC 10507–59)

Historical and Statutory Notes

Pre–1953 H 1 Amendments: 114 v 397

Cross References

Sale of lands of foreign wards, 2127.42

Library References

Guardian and Ward ⇌168.
Mental Health ⇌196.
Westlaw Topic Nos. 196, 257A.

Research References

Encyclopedias

OH Jur. 3d Guardian & Ward § 146, Generally; Jurisdiction and Venue.
OH Jur. 3d Guardian & Ward § 155, Additional Bond for Guardian.

Treatises and Practice Aids

Carlin, Baldwin's Ohio Practice, Merrick-Rippner Probate Law § 62:55, Appointment of Guardian of a Minor—Custody Issues—Jurisdiction.
Carlin, Baldwin's Ohio Practice, Merrick-Rippner Probate Law § 97:22, Land Sale by Guardian—Nonresident Guardian.

TERMINATION OF GUARDIANSHIP

2111.45 Marriage of ward

The marriage of a ward shall terminate the guardianship as to the person, but not as to the estate, of the ward.

(1989 S 46, eff. 1–1–90; 1975 S 145; 1953 H 1; GC 10507–20)

Historical and Statutory Notes

Pre–1953 H 1 Amendments: 114 v 388

Legislative Service Commission

1975:

This section currently provides that the marriage of a "female" ward will determine the guardianship as to person but not as to the estate of the female ward. This section would be amended by the bill to apply to all wards whether male or female.

Library References

Guardian and Ward ⇌21.
Mental Health ⇌167.
Westlaw Topic Nos. 196, 257A.
C.J.S. Mental Health §§ 146 to 147.

Research References

Encyclopedias

OH Jur. 3d Guardian & Ward § 193, Marriage of Ward.

Treatises and Practice Aids

Carlin, Baldwin's Ohio Practice, Merrick-Rippner Probate Law § 66:1, Termination of Guardianship—Mandatory.

Law Review and Journal Commentaries

Guardianship and the Elderly: Oversight Not Overlooked, Norman Fell. 25 U Tol L Rev 189 (1994).

2111.46 Guardianship of minors

When a guardian has been appointed for a minor before such minor is over fourteen years of age, such guardian's power shall continue until the ward arrives at the age of majority, unless removed for good cause or unless such ward selects another suitable guardian. After such selection is made and approved by the probate court and the person selected is appointed and qualified, the powers of the former guardian shall cease. Thereupon his final account as guardian shall be filed and settled in court.

Upon the termination of a guardianship of the person, estate, or both of a minor before such minor reaches eighteen years of age, if a successor guardian is not appointed and if the court finds that such minor is without proper care, the court shall certify a copy of its finding together with as much of the record and such further information as the court deems necessary, or as the juvenile court may request, to the juvenile court for further proceedings and thereupon such court shall have exclusive jurisdiction respecting such child.

(1953 H 1, eff. 10–1–53; GC 10507–60)

Historical and Statutory Notes

Pre–1953 H 1 Amendments: 121 v 557; 114 v 398

Cross References

Resignation or removal of fiduciary, 2109.24

Library References

Guardian and Ward ⇌20.
Westlaw Topic No. 196.

Research References

Encyclopedias

OH Jur. 3d Family Law § 1095, Child Residing With Third Party or in an Institution.
OH Jur. 3d Family Law § 1544, on Certification from Another Court.
OH Jur. 3d Guardian & Ward § 185, Selection by Minor of Another Suitable Guardian.
OH Jur. 3d Guardian & Ward § 195, Generally; Guardianship of Minor.
OH Jur. 3d Guardian & Ward § 207, Generally; Termination of Office—by Ward's Selection of Another Guardian on Becoming 14 Years of Age.

Treatises and Practice Aids

Carlin, Baldwin's Ohio Practice, Merrick-Rippner Probate Law § 66:1, Termination of Guardianship—Mandatory.
Carlin, Baldwin's Ohio Practice, Merrick-Rippner Probate Law § 66:2, Termination—Discretionary—Court; Removal.
Carlin, Baldwin's Ohio Practice, Merrick-Rippner Probate Law § 62:57, Appointment of Guardian of a Minor—Custody Issues—Selection by the Minor.
Carlin, Baldwin's Ohio Practice, Merrick-Rippner Probate Law § 66:10, Termination of Guardianship—Minor.
Carlin, Baldwin's Ohio Practice, Merrick-Rippner Probate Law § 66:15, Motion to Terminate Guardianship of Minor—Form.
Carlin, Baldwin's Ohio Practice, Merrick-Rippner Probate Law § 66:18, Entry Terminating Guardianship of Minor—Form.
Carlin, Baldwin's Ohio Practice, Merrick-Rippner Probate Law § 105:12, Juvenile Court—Certification from Probate Court.
Giannelli & Yeomans, Ohio Juvenile Law § 16:15, Certification or Transfer from Another Court.

Notes of Decisions

Attorney fees 5
Constitutional issues 1
Domicile 3
Majority 6
Standards for termination 2
Standing 4

---

1. Constitutional issues

Father, whose paternity was adjudicated after uncle was named legal guardian of minor child, clearly established he was the father of the child and supported decision to terminate guardianship; father immediately located child upon learning he was the father, and spent four hours with child, he consistently visited or called about his child, and several witnesses testified to his commitment to the child. In re Guardianship of Salisbury (Ohio App. 5 Dist., Holmes, 12-21-2004) No. 04CA013, 2004-Ohio-7118, 2004 WL 3001147, Unreported. Guardian And Ward ⇐ 25

Accepting certified copy of administrative order establishing father's paternity as substitute exhibit, after taking uncertified copy of order under advisement, was not abuse of discretion in proceeding on father's motion to terminate guardianship of minor child. In re Guardianship of Salisbury (Ohio App. 5 Dist., Holmes, 12-21-2004) No. 04CA013, 2004-Ohio-7118, 2004 WL 3001147, Unreported. Guardian And Ward ⇐ 25

Issue tried to court on father's motion was whether to terminate guardianship, not whether to remove guardian; father's paternity had not been adjudicated when guardianship was established and, as a result, he was unaware of any such proceedings and never relinquished or surrendered his custody rights. In re Guardianship of Salisbury (Ohio App. 5 Dist., Holmes, 12-21-2004) No. 04CA013, 2004-Ohio-7118, 2004 WL 3001147, Unreported. Guardian And Ward ⇐ 25

A decree of guardianship of a minor resident of Ohio by a court in the state where the child has a technical domicile, which decree is made without personal service on either the child or the person with whom the child is living, is not entitled, under US Const Art IV, § 1, to such faith and credit as will nullify the prior appointment of a guardian of such minor by the probate court of the county of his residence. In re Fore (Ohio 1958) 168 Ohio St. 363, 155 N.E.2d 194, 7 O.O.2d 127, appeal dismissed, certiorari denied 79 S.Ct. 878, 359 U.S. 313, 3 L.Ed.2d 831. Judgment ⇐ 818(2)

2. Standards for termination

Trial court did not commit reversible error by denying father's motion to terminate guardianship of estates of his two sons on the same day it was filed without giving guardian a chance to respond to motion, as neither father nor guardian was prejudiced in that court rendered judgment in guardian's favor and father had an opportunity to present his case. In re Guardianship of Ahmed (Ohio App. 7 Dist., Belmont, 10-10-2003) No. 02 BE 56, 2003-Ohio-5463, 2003 WL 22344914, Unreported, reconsideration denied 2003-Ohio-6390, 2003 WL 22837720, appeal not allowed 101 Ohio St.3d 1487, 805 N.E.2d 539, 2004-Ohio-1293. Guardian And Ward ⇐ 13(8)

Father, who was convicted of murdering his son's mother, could not raise in motion to terminate guardianship of their estates arguments that evidence was insufficient to support appointment of guardian, that a guardianship was unnecessary since son's estates had no assets, and that trial court improperly ignored his wish to have his brother appointed guardian, where father did not appeal appointment of guardian. In re Guardianship of Ahmed (Ohio App. 7 Dist., Belmont, 10-10-2003) No. 02 BE 56, 2003-Ohio-5463, 2003 WL 22344914, Unreported, reconsideration denied 2003-Ohio-6390, 2003 WL 22837720, appeal not allowed 101 Ohio St.3d 1487, 805 N.E.2d 539, 2004-Ohio-1293. Guardian And Ward ⇐ 25

Good cause existed for termination of the temporary guardianship of child; mother had a paramount right to custody of child, necessity for the guardianship no longer existed in that mother was now fit to assume custody, mother had finished cosmetology school, become gainfully employed and married since the time mother granted the guardianship, and mother was no longer mentally or emotionally unstable. In re Guardianship of Smith (Ohio App. 12 Dist., Preble, 08-11-2003) No. CA2002-12-012, 2003-Ohio-4247, 2003 WL 21905173, Unreported. Guardian And Ward ⇐ 25

Mother did not contract her rights away or abandon child, and thus, the guardianship was temporary, and because mother did not forfeit her paramount right to custody, the trial court did not err by failing to apply the "best interests" test in custody dispute between mother and guardians; mother testified that she never intended to give up permanent custody of child with either Indiana agreement or filing of Ohio guardianship, neither of these documents referred to the placement as permanent, Indiana agreement provided for termination with mutual consent of the parties, Ohio guardianship application signed by mother did not indicate it was permanent, and, at time mother granted the guardianship, she was unable to care for herself or child physically, emotionally or financially. In re Guardianship of Smith (Ohio App. 12 Dist., Preble, 08-11-2003) No. CA2002-12-012, 2003-Ohio-4247, 2003 WL 21905173, Unreported. Child Custody ⇐ 68; Child Custody ⇐ 76

Trial court's determination that good cause existed to grant mother's motion to terminate the grandparents' temporary guardianship of her child was not abuse of discretion, where condition leading to guardianship, that is, mother's inability to provide medical insurance to child, was no longer an issue, mother was currently a fit and suitable parent, in that she maintained regular employment, attended church regularly, had been diligent in her visitation with child throughout the five-year guardianship, had been married for nearly two years to a gainfully employed man, and resided in a four-bedroom home that was more than adequate. In re Guardianship of Godsey (Ohio App. 2 Dist., Clark, 05-23-2003) No. 2002-CA-69, 2003-Ohio-2692, 2003 WL 21213377, Unreported. Guardian And Ward ⇐ 25

In determining whether good cause existed to terminate guardianship of child, trial court properly placed substantial weight on issue of mother's current suitability to serve as child's parent, rather than determining whether some negative change had occurred in guardians' circumstances or in child's circumstances, where guardianship was temporary in nature and thus mother had not forfeited her paramount right to the custody of her child. In re Guardianship of Godsey (Ohio App. 2 Dist., Clark, 05-23-2003) No. 2002-CA-69, 2003-Ohio-2692, 2003 WL 21213377, Unreported. Guardian And Ward ⇐ 25

Temporary guardianship did not become permanent with the passage of five years, and thus, mother did not forfeit her paramount right to custody of the child, where mother remained involved with child throughout guardianship to the extent permitted by the guardians, in that she visited with child every week over the five year period, and while no court ordered support was paid by mother, no such order existed, guardians were in a better financial position than mother, and accepted military child allotment from the father, and mother presented child with gifts on birthdays and during summer visitation periods. In re Guardianship of Godsey (Ohio App. 2 Dist., Clark, 05-23-2003) No. 2002-CA-69, 2003-Ohio-2692, 2003 WL 21213377, Unreported. Guardian And Ward ⇐ 13(6); Guardian And Ward ⇐ 17

Guardianship in case was temporary, as would support finding that mother did not forfeit her paramount right to custody of the child, where guardians did not request guardianship for a definite duration, such as until the ward's eighteenth birthday, letters of guardianship described guardianship as being for an "indefinite time period," mother testified that guardianship was intended to be temporary, and child's need for medical insurance was expressed reason for guardians' application for guardianship. In re Guardianship of Godsey (Ohio App. 2 Dist., Clark, 05-23-2003) No. 2002-CA-69, 2003-Ohio-2692, 2003 WL 21213377, Unreported. Guardian And Ward ⇐ 13(6)

Probate court's improper disposition of mother's motion to terminate guardianship of her daughter under the domestic relation's best interest of the child standard, rather than the good cause standard, was harmless; mother's failure to present evidence showing why the guardianship should be terminated was so complete that the probate court would have been justified in denying her motion to terminate the guardianship under the proper legal standard. In re Hammons (Ohio App. 8 Dist., Cuyahoga, 03-06-2003) No. 80570, 2003-Ohio-992, 2003 WL 760593, Unreported, appeal not allowed 99 Ohio St.3d 1467, 791 N.E.2d 983, 2003-Ohio-3669. Guardian And Ward ⇐ 13(8)

Probate court's disposition of mother's motion to terminate guardianship of her daughter under the domestic relation's best interest of the child standard, rather than the good cause standard, was improper, where mother consented to guardianship, and there was no final resolution of custody. In re Hammons (Ohio App. 8 Dist., Cuyahoga, 03-06-2003) No. 80570, 2003-Ohio-992, 2003 WL 760593, Unreported, appeal not allowed 99 Ohio St.3d 1467, 791 N.E.2d 983, 2003-Ohio-3669. Guardian And Ward ⇐ 25

Since grandfather's guardianship of child was only meant to last until mother had resolved issues involving drug abuse, alcohol abuse and the criminal proceedings against her, the guardianship was temporary and could be terminated for "good cause," without applying the more stringent "best interest of the child" test. In re Termination of Guardianship of

Hendrickson (Ohio App. 7 Dist., 03-10-2003) 152 Ohio App.3d 116, 786 N.E.2d 937, 2003-Ohio-1220. Guardian And Ward ⇐ 25

Grandfather's guardianship of child was created so that child could be cared for until mother, who was arrested for drug trafficking, resolved problems arising from her drug abuse and trafficking, and good cause existed to terminate this temporary guardianship once the problems that engendered the guardianship were resolved; the criminal proceedings against mother had been completed, mother had a stable job, she had resolved her drug and alcohol problems, and she had presented a reasonable plan for integrating child back into her life. In re Termination of Guardianship of Hendrickson (Ohio App. 7 Dist., 03-10-2003) 152 Ohio App.3d 116, 786 N.E.2d 937, 2003-Ohio-1220. Guardian And Ward ⇐ 25

Removal of minor child's guardian cannot be grounded in statute governing removal of fiduciary by probate or juvenile court, though statute may be used to define the "good cause" needed to remove guardian. In re Guardianship of Sanders (Ohio App. 2 Dist., 03-07-1997) 118 Ohio App.3d 606, 693 N.E.2d 1101. Guardian And Ward ⇐ 25

Refusal of minor child's maternal grandmother, who was child's guardian, to permit visitation by child's mother did not require termination of guardianship. In re Guardianship of Sanders (Ohio App. 2 Dist., 03-07-1997) 118 Ohio App.3d 606, 693 N.E.2d 1101. Guardian And Ward ⇐ 25

Evidence, though conflicting, supported findings that parties intended maternal grandmother's guardianship of minor child to be permanent and that mother had relinquished her custody rights, in mother's proceeding to terminate guardianship; evidence included designation "non-limited" on guardianship application and judge's own recollection. In re Guardianship of Sanders (Ohio App. 2 Dist., 03-07-1997) 118 Ohio App.3d 606, 693 N.E.2d 1101. Guardian And Ward ⇐ 25

Evidence supported finding that minor child whose maternal grandmother had been appointed guardian had received primary care from grandmother for her entire life, in mother's proceeding to terminate guardianship, even though mother sometimes lived with them. In re Guardianship of Sanders (Ohio App. 2 Dist., 03-07-1997) 118 Ohio App.3d 606, 693 N.E.2d 1101. Guardian And Ward ⇐ 25

Evidence supported finding that minor child whose maternal grandmother had been appointed guardian was completely integrated into grandmother's household and was provided with loving care, in mother's proceeding to terminate guardianship; evidence showed church attendance, school enrollment, and vacations and included letter from school principal and testimony from neighbors. In re Guardianship of Sanders (Ohio App. 2 Dist., 03-07-1997) 118 Ohio App.3d 606, 693 N.E.2d 1101. Guardian And Ward ⇐ 25

Reliable, credible evidence supported finding of trial court that father relinquished right to custody of child; father specifically consented to having his child under care of grandparents, and also consented in written agreement to their being appointed his legal guardians, and later consented to a divorce decree which in essence incorporated his agreement to have child under care of grandparents. Masitto v. Masitto (Ohio 1986) 22 Ohio St.3d 63, 488 N.E.2d 857, 22 O.B.R. 81. Child Custody ⇐ 641

Where a guardian of a minor child has been validly appointed, the burden of proof is on one seeking the removal of such guardian, and the court must be clearly convinced that the interests of the ward cannot be preserved except by the removal; a mere showing that the movant might conceivably make a better guardian is inadequate. In re Guardianship of Conley (Ohio Prob. 1966) 10 Ohio Misc. 197, 224 N.E.2d 183, 39 O.O.2d 292.

Termination of a guardianship of seven months' duration, where the mother has not contracted away her rights, should be determined pursuant to a good cause test not a best interest standard. In re Spriggs, No. 89-CA–1803 (4th Dist Ct App, Scioto, 4–24–90).

3. Domicile

Where there is no existing award of custody of an orphaned minor resident of Ohio by a foreign court, the probate court of the county of such residence has jurisdiction to appoint a guardian of the minor, regardless of the fact that the domicile of such minor may be in another state. In re Fore (Ohio 1958) 168 Ohio St. 363, 155 N.E.2d 194, 7 O.O.2d 127, appeal dismissed, certiorari denied 79 S.Ct. 878, 359 U.S. 313, 3 L.Ed.2d 831. Guardian And Ward ⇐ 8

Where both parents of a child were killed in a common disaster in France and the maternal aunt brought such child to Ohio, and a paternal grandparent has obtained the right of "tutorship" from a Louisiana court in the parish of the grandmother's and hence the child's domicile, the Ohio courts have no authority to grant letters of guardianship to the maternal aunt. Petition of Fore (Cuyahoga 1958) 151 N.E.2d 777, 79 Ohio Law Abs. 15, reversed 168 Ohio St. 363, 155 N.E.2d 194, 7 O.O.2d 127, appeal dismissed, certiorari denied 79 S.Ct. 878, 359 U.S. 313, 3 L.Ed.2d 831.

4. Standing

The uncle of a minor has sufficient interest in such minor's welfare so as to have standing to challenge the jurisdiction of a court to make an appointment of a guardian, and upon overruling of his motion he may appeal to the common pleas court. In re Guardianship of Murray, 8 CC(NS) 498, 18 CD 652 (Lorain 1906).

5. Attorney fees

In an action to terminate a guardianship, the probate court should apply a three-part test to determine if payment of attorney fees from the guardianship estate is merited: (1) whether the attorney acted in good faith, (2) whether the services performed were in the nature of necessities, and (3) whether the attorney's actions benefited the guardianship. In re Guardianship of Allen (Ohio 1990) 50 Ohio St.3d 142, 552 N.E.2d 934, rehearing denied 51 Ohio St.3d 705, 555 N.E.2d 322. Mental Health ⇐ 159

6. Majority

The guardianship of a minor female expires by operation of law when she is twelve years of age; at that time she has a choice of her own guardian, to be approved by the probate court. Perry's Lessee v. Brainard (Ohio 1842) 11 Ohio 442.

After a ward arrives at majority, the guardianship ceases ipso facto, and further dealings by the guardian are those of a mere agent not covered by the bond. In re Streit's Estate (Ohio Com.Pl. 1901) 12 Ohio Dec. 158. Bonds ⇐ 61; Guardian And Ward ⇐ 20; Guardian And Ward ⇐ 175

2111.47 Wards other than minors

Upon reasonable notice to the guardian, to the ward, and to the person on whose application the appointment was made, and upon satisfactory proof that the necessity for the guardianship no longer exists or that the letters of appointment were improperly issued, the probate court shall order that the guardianship of an incompetent terminate and shall make an appropriate entry upon the journal. Thereupon the guardianship shall cease, the accounts of the guardian shall be settled by the court, and the ward shall be restored to the full control of his property as before the appointment. Such entry terminating the guardianship of an insane person shall have the same effect as a determination by the court that such person is restored to sanity.

(129 v 1448, eff. 10–25–61; 1953 H 1; GC 10507–61)

Historical and Statutory Notes

Pre–1953 H 1 Amendments: 114 v 398

Library References

Mental Health ⇐167.
Westlaw Topic No. 257A.
C.J.S. Mental Health §§ 146 to 147.

Research References

Encyclopedias

OH Jur. 3d Guardian & Ward § 65, Finality of Order.
OH Jur. 3d Guardian & Ward § 67, Appeal—Who May Appeal.
OH Jur. 3d Guardian & Ward § 202, Notice and Hearing.
OH Jur. 3d Guardian & Ward § 203, Notice and Hearing—Evidence.
OH Jur. 3d Guardian & Ward § 204, Order.

Treatises and Practice Aids

Carlin, Baldwin's Ohio Practice, Merrick-Rippner Probate Law § 66:1, Termination of Guardianship—Mandatory.
Carlin, Baldwin's Ohio Practice, Merrick-Rippner Probate Law § 66:4, Termination of Guardianship—Incompetent—Necessity No Longer Exists.
Carlin, Baldwin's Ohio Practice, Merrick-Rippner Probate Law § 66:7, Termination of Guardianship—Incompetent—Standard of Proof.

Carlin, Baldwin's Ohio Practice, Merrick-Rippner Probate Law § 66:11, Termination of Guardianship—Accounting.

Carlin, Baldwin's Ohio Practice, Merrick-Rippner Probate Law § 66:13, Termination of Guardianship—Effect of Order.

Carlin, Baldwin's Ohio Practice, Merrick-Rippner Probate Law § 66:16, Entry Setting for Hearing and Ordering Notice—Form.

Carlin, Baldwin's Ohio Practice, Merrick-Rippner Probate Law § 66:17, Notice of Hearing to Terminate Guardianship—Form.

Carlin, Baldwin's Ohio Practice, Merrick-Rippner Probate Law § 66:19, Motion to Terminate Guardianship of an Incompetent—Form.

Carlin, Baldwin's Ohio Practice, Merrick-Rippner Probate Law § 66:20, Entry Terminating Guardianship of Incompetent—Form.

Law Review and Journal Commentaries

Guardianship and the Elderly: Oversight Not Overlooked, Norman Fell. 25 U Tol L Rev 189 (1994).

Notes of Decisions

Appeal 3
Attorney fees 7
Collateral attack 6
Consent 5
Debts 9
Presumptions 2
Procedural issues 4
Removal 8
Standard for competency 1

---

1. Standard for competency

Trial court's determination that necessity for daughter's guardianship of her mother continued to exist was not against manifest weight of the evidence; physician noted that mother suffered from dementia due to Parkinson's disease, that mother exhibited impulsive behavior that prevented her from making "informed and reasoned decisions," and that mother's impulsive behavior placed her at risk for physical injury, physician noted that mother was on currently on at least seventeen different medications and that mother's behavior resulted in her failing to take her medications appropriately, and physician opined that mother's best interests and safety were served by continuing the guardianship. In re Guardianship of Morton (Ohio App. 2 Dist., Miami, 03-10-2006) No. 2005-CA-22, 2006-Ohio-1139, 2006 WL 574404, Unreported. Mental Health ⇔ 170

Once "satisfactory proof" that reasons for guardianship no longer exist is presented, probate court has mandatory duty to end guardianship; proof is satisfactory if some evidence of competency is presented. In re Bolander (Lake 1993) 88 Ohio App.3d 498, 624 N.E.2d 322. Mental Health ⇔ 170

Presentation of psychiatrist's report stating that person for whom guardian had been appointed was competent was sufficient to rebut presumption of continuing incompetence and warranted termination of guardianship; even if person wished to spend her money foolishly, as long as she was competent guardian was not required. In re Bolander (Lake 1993) 88 Ohio App.3d 498, 624 N.E.2d 322. Mental Health ⇔ 170

Judgment in action to terminate guardianship restores the ward to the full control over her person and property and is an adjudication that the ward has been restored to sanity. In re Guardianship of Escola (Stark 1987) 41 Ohio App.3d 42, 534 N.E.2d 866. Mental Health ⇔ 173

The sole issue before the court in a proceeding to terminate the guardianship of an incompetent is whether the ward has presented "satisfactory proof that the necessity for the guardianship no longer exists," and, where such "satisfactory proof" is presented, the court is under a mandatory duty to terminate the guardianship. In re Guardianship of Breece (Ohio 1962) 173 Ohio St. 542, 184 N.E.2d 386, 20 O.O.2d 155. Mental Health ⇔ 169; Mental Health ⇔ 170

In a proceeding, by a person adjudged mentally incompetent, to terminate guardianship and for restoration to competency, the test is whether such person has made substantial progress and whether he is at present competent to manage his own affairs. In re Guardianship of Nitschke (Franklin 1961) 113 Ohio App. 243, 177 N.E.2d 628, 17 O.O.2d 223. Mental Health ⇔ 168.1

In an attempt to terminate the guardianship, under physical disability, the incompetent must prove to the satisfaction of the court that she is now better able to care for her property than at the time of the appointment, or that conditions have changed and that a guardian of her estate is no longer necessary. In re Guardianship of Barr (Ohio Prob. 1958) 156 N.E.2d 357, 80 Ohio Law Abs. 488.

In application to terminate guardianship over applicant imposed for alleged mental incompetency, testimony by applicant which was clear and definite as to age, dates, children, and property, together with lack of testimony of any acts or omissions indicating applicant was not able to take care of his property, showed applicant was mentally qualified and able to possess and manage his estate, and should be restored to estate, under statute. Rhoads v. Rhoads (Fairfield 1927) 29 Ohio App. 449, 163 N.E. 724.

A nonexpert or lay witness should not be permitted to testify as to the mentality of ward until he shall have testified to facts within his knowledge, tending at least in some degree to indicate mental capacity or lack of same. Rhoads v. Rhoads (Fairfield 1927) 29 Ohio App. 449, 163 N.E. 724.

On application under section, to terminate guardianship over applicant alleged to be incompetent, question for final determination by court of appeals is whether, under facts as contained in record, and according to law pertaining to same, applicant is mentally competent to care for, preserve, and possess estate belonging to him and now in hands of his guardian. Rhoads v. Rhoads (Fairfield 1927) 29 Ohio App. 449, 163 N.E. 724.

The probate court may terminate a guardianship upon adjudication that a person is no longer incompetent pursuant to RC 2101.24(A)(4), 2101.24(A)(6) and 2111.47; such person then regains full control over his property and may validly revoke an inter vivos trust. Old Phoenix Natl Bank of Medina v Oenslager, No. 1586 (9th Dist Ct App, Medina, 10-14-87).

That legislature, defining "imbecile" in GC 10507-1 (RC 2111.01) did not intend that it should mean "a condition of permanent and hopeless incapacity," is apparent from this section. Potts v. First–Central Trust Co. (Summit 1940) 47 N.E.2d 823, 37 Ohio Law Abs. 382.

2. Presumptions

The appointment of a guardian for an imbecile is only prima facie evidence of imbecility; such fact may be inquired into through an action brought by the alleged imbecile to enjoin his guardian from interfering with the control and management of his property. Messenger v. Bliss (Ohio 1880) 35 Ohio St. 587. Mental Health ⇔ 161

In the absence of contrary proof, a condition of lack of mental capacity which has been judicially determined is presumed to continue; an intervening determination of another court on the subject may be given such weight as the court which made the original determination finds proper on a later consideration of the person's present condition. In re Moser (Ohio Com.Pl. 1967) 19 Ohio Misc. 81, 246 N.E.2d 626, 47 O.O.2d 420, 48 O.O.2d 253.

The presumption that a person adjudicated an incompetent continues to be incompetent is rebuttable and will not prevail where, in a proceeding to terminate the guardianship of an incompetent, there is substantial and overwhelming evidence that the necessity for the guardianship no longer exists. In re Guardianship of Breece (Ohio 1962) 173 Ohio St. 542, 184 N.E.2d 386, 20 O.O.2d 155. Mental Health ⇔ 18; Mental Health ⇔ 170

3. Appeal

A guardian of a mentally incompetent ward does not have a right of appeal under RC 2101.42 from an order of the probate court terminating the guardianship pursuant to RC 2111.47 upon satisfactory proof that the ward had regained his mental competency and the necessity for the guardianship has ceased to exist, where the record does not reflect any interest of the guardian adverse to the ward in such order of termination, or show that the guardian has been aggrieved in any manner by the order of termination. In re Guardianship of Love (Ohio 1969) 19 Ohio St.2d 111, 249 N.E.2d 794, 48 O.O.2d 107.

The right of an imbecile ward under section to move in the probate court to terminate the guardianship on the ground of restoration to reason or that the letters were improperly issued and to appeal to the common pleas from the order carries with it the right to prosecute error in his own name in the court of appeals from an adverse ruling in the common pleas. Robinson v. Wagner (Ohio 1917) 95 Ohio St. 300, 116 N.E. 514, 15 Ohio Law Rep. 19, 15 Ohio Law Rep. 32.

An appeal will lie from an order of the probate court overruling the motion of an imbecile to terminate his guardianship where letters were improperly issued and he has subsequently been fully restored to reason. Hiett v. Nebergall (Ohio 1888) 45 Ohio St. 702, 17 N.E. 558. Courts ⇔ 202(5); Mental Health ⇔ 45; Mental Health ⇔ 167

Where an order of the probate court is made upon application of the alleged imbecile himself terminating his guardianship, an appeal may be taken by the guardian in the interest of the trust. Kraner, Guardianship of (Ohio Com.Pl. 1909) 19 Ohio Dec. 444, 8 Ohio N.P.N.S. 217.

4. Procedural issues

The next friend of an incompetent adult may initiate proceedings for the termination of the guardianship of such ward on the ground that the letters of appointment were improperly issued. In re Guardianship of Kelley (Crawford 1964) 1 Ohio App.2d 137, 204 N.E.2d 96, 30 O.O.2d 159. Mental Health ⇒ 176

In a proceeding under RC 2111.47 to terminate guardianship of an incompetent, the probate court shall, after proper notice and upon satisfactory proof that the necessity for the guardianship no longer exists, order that the guardianship of the incompetent terminate and make an appropriate entry upon the journal. In re Guardianship of Nitschke (Franklin 1961) 113 Ohio App. 243, 177 N.E.2d 628, 17 O.O.2d 223. Mental Health ⇒ 169

Where petitioner has an adequate remedy at law a writ of habeas corpus should be denied; section provides an adequate remedy for the removal of a guardian and the exclusive method for the exercise of original jurisdiction in such a proceeding. In re Glendenning, 145 OS 82, 60 NE(2d) 676, 30 OO 301 (1945).

5. Consent

When one has voluntarily consented to the appointment of a guardian under the statutes providing for such appointment and the court has acted upon the matter and made the appointment, the ward cannot terminate the guardianship by merely withdrawing his consent. In re Guardianship of Williams (Franklin 1958) 151 N.E.2d 602, 78 Ohio Law Abs. 98, appeal dismissed 168 Ohio St. 248, 151 N.E.2d 706, 6 O.O.2d 27. Guardian And Ward ⇒ 25

Where a guardian of an estate is appointed solely on the ground of the ward's physical incapacity, the ward's mental capacity is not impaired, and such appointment is made with the consent of the ward, a daughter of such ward may file exceptions to such guardian's account. In re Guardianship of Tillman (Darke 1955) 100 Ohio App. 291, 136 N.E.2d 291, 60 O.O. 254.

A guardianship should be terminated where it is disclosed that the ward's consent to the guardian's appointment was given under an apparent misapprehension of the ward's rights; in such a proceeding it is discretionary with the court to permit the guardian to contest his removal by entering an appearance, introducing evidence and cross-examining witnesses. In re Luft's Guardianship (Franklin 1950) 91 Ohio App. 409, 97 N.E.2d 561, 59 Ohio Law Abs. 33, 45 O.O. 333.

6. Collateral attack

An order appointing a guardian of an incompetent cannot be collaterally attacked. In re Guardianship of Titington (Ohio Prob. 1958) 162 N.E.2d 628, 82 Ohio Law Abs. 563.

The guardianship of an insane wife cannot be attacked collaterally by her husband, since, where the record shows nothing to the contrary, it will be conclusively presumed that such order was made upon full proof of all the facts necessary to authorize it. Heckman v. Adams (Ohio 1893) 50 Ohio St. 305, 29 W.L.B. 330, 34 N.E. 155.

7. Attorney fees

In an action to terminate a guardianship, the probate court should apply a three-part test to determine if payment of attorney fees from the guardianship estate is merited: (1) whether the attorney acted in good faith, (2) whether the services performed were in the nature of necessities, and (3) whether the attorney's actions benefited the guardianship. In re Guardianship of Allen (Ohio 1990) 50 Ohio St.3d 142, 552 N.E.2d 934, rehearing denied 51 Ohio St.3d 705, 555 N.E.2d 322. Mental Health ⇒ 159

8. Removal

If the court believes that a guardian has rightly endeavored and reasonably well succeeded in managing the trust, it will not remove him merely because his ward has taken a violent dislike to him and will have no dealings with him. Frantz v. Frantz (Ohio Prob. 1892) 6 Ohio Dec. 560, 4 Ohio N.P. 278.

9. Debts

Upon the death of the ward, his unpaid debts or those of the guardian must be redressed through the personal representative of the ward's estate. Simpson v. Holmes (Ohio 1922) 106 Ohio St. 437, 140 N.E. 395, 1 Ohio Law Abs. 84, 20 Ohio Law Rep. 497, 20 Ohio Law Rep. 499. Guardian And Ward ⇒ 22; Guardian And Ward ⇒ 67; Mental Health ⇒ 218

2111.471 Transfer of guardianship on removal of ward from county

If the ward for whom a guardian has been appointed removes to another county within this state and acquires a new residence or legal settlement therein, the probate court having jurisdiction over the guardian and the ward, may, on its own motion, or on motion of the guardian or any interested party, with the consent of the probate court of the county to which such ward has removed, transfer the jurisdiction over said guardian and ward to such probate court, provided it appears that such transfer would be in the best interest of the ward.

Thereupon, the original probate court shall prepare certified copies of the appointment, letters of guardianship, bond, inventory, the last account, if any, a full and complete transcript of its docket and journal entries up to and including the order of transfer and copies of such other papers as may be requested by the receiving court, and shall cause the same to be filed in the probate court accepting jurisdiction, all costs to be paid by the guardian out of the assets of the estate of the ward.

Upon the filing of the certified copies of the original papers and the transcript, and the payment of costs, the probate court to which the proceedings have been transferred may assign a case number and by journal entry, accept jurisdiction. A copy of the entry accepting jurisdiction shall be returned to the court of original jurisdiction. Thereupon, the probate court to which the proceedings have been transferred shall acquire jurisdiction over the guardian and the ward as though such probate court had jurisdiction and appointed the guardian in the first instance, and the jurisdiction of the probate court from which the proceedings have been transferred shall cease.

(129 v 7, eff. 10–5–61)

OSBA Probate and Trust Law Section

1961:

The committee, working with the Probate Judges Committee on the subject, found a strong need for legislation to authorize the transfer of a guardianship from the county of original appointment to another county when convenience of all concerned so dictates. This would be when a ward removes to another county within the state. Families move and minors move with them. Adults under guardianship may go to live with relatives or be placed in an institution in another county.

Research References

Encyclopedias

OH Jur. 3d Guardian & Ward § 184, Generally; Transfer of Guardianship to Another County.

Treatises and Practice Aids

Carlin, Baldwin's Ohio Practice, Merrick-Rippner Probate Law § 62:14, Appointment of Guardian—Application—Jurisdiction.

Notes of Decisions

Jurisdiction   1

---

1. Jurisdiction

County in which proposed ward resided when guardianship proceedings were initiated had sole and exclusive jurisdiction to appoint guardian, even after ward moved to nursing home in another county, where proceedings were not transferred to that county. Le Sueur v. Robinson (Fulton 1988)

53 Ohio App.3d 9, 557 N.E.2d 796, motion overruled 39 Ohio St.3d 725, 534 N.E.2d 357. Mental Health ⇔ 112

MISCELLANEOUS PROVISIONS

2111.48 Certain acts validated

All sales, leases, encumbrances, or liens made or created on any real estate located in Ohio by guardians for persons who are incompetent by reason of advanced age or mental or physical disability since August 17, 1919, by order of any court of this state shall not be declared invalid for the reason that such guardians for incompetents were not vested with all the statutory powers given to guardians of idiots, imbeciles, and lunatics. Such acts of guardians for incompetents are legal and effective.

(1953 H 1, eff. 10–1–53; GC 10507–25)

Historical and Statutory Notes

Pre–1953 H 1 Amendments: 114 v 389

Research References

Encyclopedias
OH Jur. 3d Guardian & Ward § 39, Application for Appointment by Interested Person—on Motion of Court.
OH Jur. 3d Guardian & Ward § 111, Real Property, Generally.

Treatises and Practice Aids
Carlin, Baldwin's Ohio Practice, Merrick-Rippner Probate Law § 97:1, Land Sale by Guardian—Introduction.

2111.49 Guardian's report; court intervention; hearing

(A)(1) Subject to division (A)(3) of this section, the guardian of an incompetent person shall file a guardian's report with the court two years after the date of the issuance of the guardian's letters of appointment and biennially after that time, or at any other time upon the motion or a rule of the probate court. The report shall be in a form prescribed by the court and shall include all of the following.

(a) The present address of the place of residence of the ward;

(b) The present address of the guardian;

(c) If the place of residence of the ward is not the ward's personal home, the name of the facility at which the ward resides and the name of the person responsible for the ward's care;

(d) The approximate number of times during the period covered by the report that the guardian has had contact with the ward, the nature of those contacts, and the date that the ward was last seen by the guardian;

(e) Any major changes in the physical or mental condition of the ward observed by the guardian;

(f) The opinion of the guardian as to the necessity for the continuation of the guardianship;

(g) The opinion of the guardian as to the adequacy of the present care of the ward;

(h) The date that the ward was last examined or otherwise seen by a physician and the purpose of that visit;

(i) A statement by a licensed physician, licensed clinical psychologist, licensed independent social worker, licensed professional clinical counselor, or mental retardation team that has evaluated or examined the ward within three months prior to the date of the report as to the need for continuing the guardianship.

(2) The court shall review a report filed pursuant to division (A)(1) of this section to determine if a continued necessity for the guardianship exists. The court may direct a probate court investigator to verify aspects of the report.

(3) Division (A)(1) of this section applies to guardians appointed prior to, as well as on or after, the effective date of this section. A guardian appointed prior to that date shall file the first report in accordance with any applicable court rule or motion, or, in the absence of such a rule or motion, upon the next occurring date on which a report would have been due if division (A)(1) of this section had been in effect on the date of appointment as guardian, and shall file all subsequently due reports biennially after that time.

(B) If, upon review of any report required by division (A)(1) of this section, the court finds that it is necessary to intervene in a guardianship, the court shall take any action that it determines is necessary, including, but not limited to, terminating or modifying the guardianship.

(C) Except as provided in this division, for any guardianship, upon written request by the ward, the ward's attorney, or any other interested party made at any time after the expiration of one hundred twenty days from the date of the original appointment of the guardian, a hearing shall be held in accordance with section 2111.02 of the Revised Code to evaluate the continued necessity of the guardianship. Upon written request, the court shall conduct a minimum of one hearing under this division in the calendar year in which the guardian was appointed, and upon written request, shall conduct a minimum of one hearing in each of the following calendar years. Upon its own motion or upon written request, the court may, in its discretion, conduct a hearing within the first one hundred twenty days after appointment of the guardian or conduct more than one hearing in a calendar year. If the ward alleges competence, the burden of proving incompetence shall be upon the applicant for guardianship or the guardian, by clear and convincing evidence.

(1996 S 223, eff. 3–18–97; 1989 S 46, eff. 1–1–90)

Historical and Statutory Notes

Amendment Note: 1996 S 223 substituted "licensed independent social worker, licensed professional clinical counselor," for "or licensed clinical social worker" in division (A)(1)(i); and made changes to reflect gender neutral language and other nonsubstantive changes.

Cross References

Cost of investigations, 2101.16

Library References

Mental Health ⇔167, 179.
Westlaw Topic No. 257A.
C.J.S. Mental Health §§ 146 to 147, 158 to 159.
C.J.S. Right to Die §§ 5, 8.

Research References

Encyclopedias
OH Jur. 3d Guardian & Ward § 79, Judicial Control.

Treatises and Practice Aids
Carlin, Baldwin's Ohio Practice, Merrick-Rippner Probate Law § 64:6, Powers and Duties of Guardian—Biennial Report.
Carlin, Baldwin's Ohio Practice, Merrick-Rippner Probate Law § 66:1, Termination of Guardianship—Mandatory.
Carlin, Baldwin's Ohio Practice, Merrick-Rippner Probate Law § 66:4, Termination of Guardianship—Incompetent—Necessity No Longer Exists.
Carlin, Baldwin's Ohio Practice, Merrick-Rippner Probate Law § 66:5, Termination of Guardianship—Incompetent—Application of the Ward.
Carlin, Baldwin's Ohio Practice, Merrick-Rippner Probate Law § 66:7, Termination of Guardianship—Incompetent—Standard of Proof.
Carlin, Baldwin's Ohio Practice, Merrick-Rippner Probate Law § 79:4, Inventory—Enforcement of Filing.
Carlin, Baldwin's Ohio Practice, Merrick-Rippner Probate Law § 54:10, Fiduciary Accounts—Citation to File Account.

Carlin, Baldwin's Ohio Practice, Merrick-Rippner Probate Law § 62:35, Guardianship Proceedings—Burden of Proof.

Carlin, Baldwin's Ohio Practice, Merrick-Rippner Probate Law § 62:80, Statement of Expert Evaluation—Form.

Carlin, Baldwin's Ohio Practice, Merrick-Rippner Probate Law § 64:82, Guardian's Report—Biennial—Form.

Carlin, Baldwin's Ohio Practice, Merrick-Rippner Probate Law App B SPF 17.1, Statement of Expert Evaluation.

Carlin, Baldwin's Ohio Practice, Merrick-Rippner Probate Law App B SPF 17.7, Guardian's Report.

Notes of Decisions

Termination of guardianship 1

---

1. Termination of guardianship

It would have been better choice for guardian to have ordered psychiatric examination of ward upon filing by ward of motion to terminate guardianship, than to contest motion. Brown v. Haffey (Ohio App. 8 Dist., 09-06-1994) 96 Ohio App.3d 724, 645 N.E.2d 1295. Mental Health ⇐ 168.1

Legal services rendered on behalf of guardian on ward's motion to terminate guardianship were necessary, proper and performed for benefit of guardianship, entitling attorney to fees, where, by retaining attorney, guardian enabled ward and court to call him as witness, guardian and guardian's attorney had reservations regarding ward's competency which were not entirely unfounded, and attorney's cross-examination of witnesses provided court with information from alternative perspective in ruling on motion to terminate. Brown v. Haffey (Ohio App. 8 Dist., 09-06-1994) 96 Ohio App.3d 724, 645 N.E.2d 1295. Mental Health ⇐ 159

Guardians who possess good-faith belief that termination of guardianship is not in best interest of ward or estate have to testify should they wish to prove continuing incompetency by clear and convincing evidence. Brown v. Haffey (Ohio App. 8 Dist., 09-06-1994) 96 Ohio App.3d 724, 645 N.E.2d 1295. Mental Health ⇐ 170

2111.50 Probate court powers over guardianship

(A)(1) At all times, the probate court is the superior guardian of wards who are subject to its jurisdiction, and all guardians who are subject to the jurisdiction of the court shall obey all orders of the court that concern their wards or guardianships.

(2)(a) Subject to divisions (A)(2)(b) and (c) of this section, the control of a guardian over the person, the estate, or both of his ward is limited to the authority that is granted to the guardian by the Revised Code, relevant decisions of the courts of this state, and orders or rules of the probate court.

(b) Except for the powers specified in division (E) of this section and unless otherwise provided in or inconsistent with another section of the Revised Code, the probate court may confer upon a guardian any power that this section grants to the probate court in connection with wards.

(c) For good cause shown, the probate court may limit or deny, by order or rule, any power that is granted to a guardian by a section of the Revised Code or relevant decisions of the courts of this state.

(B) In connection with any person whom the probate court has found to be an incompetent or a minor subject to guardianship and for whom the court has appointed a guardian, the court has, subject to divisions (C) to (E) of this section, all the powers that relate to the person and estate of the person and that he could exercise if present and not a minor or under a disability, except the power to make or revoke a will. These powers include, but are not limited to, the power to do any of the following:

(1) Convey or release the present, contingent, or expectant interests in real or personal property of the person, including, but not limited to, dower and any right of survivorship incident to a survivorship tenancy, joint tenancy, or tenancy by the entireties;

(2) Exercise or release powers as a trustee, personal representative, custodian for a minor, guardian, or donee of a power of appointment;

(3) Enter into contracts, or create revocable trusts of property of the estate of the person, that may not extend beyond the minority, disability, or life of the person or ward;

(4) Exercise options to purchase securities or other property;

(5) Exercise rights to elect options under annuities and insurance policies, and to surrender an annuity or insurance policy for its cash value;

(6) Exercise the right to an elective share in the estate of the deceased spouse of the person pursuant to section 2107.45 of the Revised Code;

(7) Make gifts, in trust or otherwise, to relatives of the person and, consistent with any prior pattern of the person of giving to charities or of providing support for friends, to charities and friends of the person.

(C) Except for the powers specified in division (D) of this section, all powers of the probate court that are specified in this chapter and that relate either to any person whom it has found to be an incompetent or a minor subject to guardianship and for whom it has appointed a guardian and all powers of a guardian that relate to his ward or guardianship as described in division (A)(2) of this section, shall be exercised in the best interest, as determined in the court's or guardian's judgment, of the following:

(1) The person whom the probate court has found to be an incompetent or a minor subject to guardianship;

(2) The dependents of the person;

(3) The members of the household of the person.

(D) If the court is to exercise or direct the exercise, pursuant to division (B) of this section, of the power to make gifts in trust or otherwise, the following conditions shall apply:

(1) The exercise of the particular power shall not impair the financial ability of the estate of the person whom the probate court has found to be an incompetent or a minor subject to guardianship and for whom the court has appointed a guardian, to provide for his foreseeable needs for maintenance and care;

(2) If applicable, the court shall consider any of the following:

(a) The estate, income, and other tax advantages of the exercise of a particular power to the estate of a person whom the probate court has found to be an incompetent or a minor subject to guardianship and for whom the court has appointed a guardian;

(b) Any pattern of giving of, or any pattern of support provided by, the person prior to his incompetence;

(c) The disposition of property made by the will of the person;

(d) If there is no knowledge of a will of the person, his prospective heirs;

(e) Any relevant and trustworthy statements of the person, whether established by hearsay or other evidence.

(E)(1) The probate court shall cause notice as described in division (E)(2) of this section to be given and a hearing to be conducted prior to its exercise or direction of the exercise of any of the following powers pursuant to division (B) of this section:

(a) The exercise or release of powers as a donee of a power of appointment;

(b) Unless the amount of the gift is no more than one thousand dollars, the making of a gift, in trust or otherwise.

(2) The notice required by division (E)(1) of this section shall be given to the following persons:

(a) Unless a guardian of a ward has applied for the exercise of a power specified in division (E)(1) of this section, to the guardian;

(b) To the person whom the probate court has found to be an incompetent or a minor subject to guardianship;

(c) If known, to a guardian who applied for the exercise of a power specified in division (E)(1) of this section, to the prospective heirs of the person whom the probate court has found to be an incompetent or a minor subject to guardianship under section 2105.06 of the Revised Code, and any person who has a legal interest in property that may be divested or limited as the result of the exercise of a power specified in division (E)(1) of this section;

(d) To any other persons the court orders.

(F) When considering any question related to, and issuing orders for, medical or surgical care or treatment of incompetents or minors subject to guardianship, the probate court has full parens patriae powers unless otherwise provided by a section of the Revised Code.

(1989 S 46, eff. 1-1-90)

Cross References

Jurisdiction of probate courts, 2101.24

Library References

Courts ⚖198 to 201.
Guardian and Ward ⚖2, 8.
Mental Health ⚖109.
Westlaw Topic Nos. 106, 196, 257A.
C.J.S. Mental Health § 117.

Research References

Encyclopedias

OH Jur. 3d Guardian & Ward § 1, Generally; Jurisdiction Over Guardianship Matters.

OH Jur. 3d Guardian & Ward § 79, Judicial Control.

OH Jur. 3d Guardian & Ward § 84, Maintenance, Support, and Education of Ward; Medical and Other Health Matters.

Treatises and Practice Aids

Carlin, Baldwin's Ohio Practice, Merrick-Rippner Probate Law § 3:3, Jurisdiction of Probate Court—Subject Matter—in General.

Carlin, Baldwin's Ohio Practice, Merrick-Rippner Probate Law § 3:5, Jurisdiction of Probate Court—Subject Matter—Specific Areas—Fiduciaries.

Carlin, Baldwin's Ohio Practice, Merrick-Rippner Probate Law § 3:11, Jurisdiction of Probate Court—Subject Matter—Specific Areas—Removal of Life Support.

Carlin, Baldwin's Ohio Practice, Merrick-Rippner Probate Law § 62:3, Appointment of Guardian—Definitions—Ward.

Carlin, Baldwin's Ohio Practice, Merrick-Rippner Probate Law § 64:2, Powers and Duties of Guardian—Probate Court is the Superior Guardian.

Carlin, Baldwin's Ohio Practice, Merrick-Rippner Probate Law § 60:27, Power of Attorney for Health Care—Decision in Absence of Valid Health Care Instrument; Probate Court Proceedings.

Carlin, Baldwin's Ohio Practice, Merrick-Rippner Probate Law § 62:43, Guardianship Proceedings—Who May Serve—Life Support Cases.

Carlin, Baldwin's Ohio Practice, Merrick-Rippner Probate Law § 64:15, Powers and Duties of Guardian—Special Matters Relating to Minor Wards—Settlement of Claims for Injury.

Carlin, Baldwin's Ohio Practice, Merrick-Rippner Probate Law § 64:21, Powers and Duties of Guardian—Ward's Estate—Discretionary Acts.

Carlin, Baldwin's Ohio Practice, Merrick-Rippner Probate Law § 64:24, Powers and Duties of Guardian—Ward's Estate—Acts of the Ward—Trusts.

Carlin, Baldwin's Ohio Practice, Merrick-Rippner Probate Law § 65:22, Settlement of Suits—Generally—Approval of Court.

Carlin, Baldwin's Ohio Practice, Merrick-Rippner Probate Law § 65:23, Settlement of Suits—Attorney Fees in Cases Where Court Approval is Required.

Kuehnle and Levey, Ohio Real Estate Law and Practice § 6:26, Cotenancies—Survivorship Tenancies—Release by Minors and Incompetents.

Kuehnle and Levey, Ohio Real Estate Law and Practice § 21:11, Execution—Dower—Release of Inchoate Dower.

Law Review and Journal Commentaries

Guardians—Powers and Duties: Revokable Living Trust—Durable Power of Attorney, Michael L. Stark. 2 Prob L J Ohio 105 (May/June 1992).

The Lombardo Case, Michael Stark. (Ed. Note: Whether an irrevocable trust by an individual who is now incompetent may be revoked at the behest of the guardian is the subject of the article.) 9 Prob L J Ohio 104 (July/August 1999).

Notes of Decisions

Attorney fees 1
Best interest of ward 4
Property transfer 5
Removal of life support 2
Settlement of personal injury claim 3
Testamentary disposition of trust property 6

---

1. Attorney fees

Any debt arising out of the services of an attorney to a ward is in the nature of necessities, and it is for the probate court to determine what constitutes a necessary service. In re Guardianship of Allen (Ohio 1990) 50 Ohio St.3d 142, 552 N.E.2d 934, rehearing denied 51 Ohio St.3d 705, 555 N.E.2d 322. Mental Health ⚖ 233

In an action to terminate a guardianship, the probate court should apply a three-part test to determine if payment of attorney fees from the guardianship estate is merited: (1) whether the attorney acted in good faith, (2) whether the services performed were in the nature of necessities, and (3) whether the attorney's actions benefited the guardianship. In re Guardianship of Allen (Ohio 1990) 50 Ohio St.3d 142, 552 N.E.2d 934, rehearing denied 51 Ohio St.3d 705, 555 N.E.2d 322. Mental Health ⚖ 159

2. Removal of life support

Probate court's statutory authority to appoint a limited guardian for an infant did not give the probate court authority to vest the limited guardian with power to withdraw all life-sustaining support, in absence of termination of parental rights. (Per Lundberg Stratton, J., with two Justices concurring and two Justices concurring separately.) In re Guardianship of Stein (Ohio, 12-30-2004) 105 Ohio St.3d 30, 821 N.E.2d 1008, 2004-Ohio-7114. Health ⚖ 915

A court as guardian of a minor ward may approve the removal of nutrition and hydration when a minor ward is in a persistent vegetative state for three months with no reasonable hope of recovery and there is some evidence that the ward would not wish to be maintained on life supports; a court may render its decision based upon the best interest test and determine that a three-week death with proper comfort care does not outweigh years of inhumane and tortuous existence in a vegetative state with certain death of unknown duration at its end. In re Guardianship of Myers (Ohio Com.Pl. 1993) 62 Ohio Misc.2d 763, 610 N.E.2d 663.

A probate court has the jurisdiction and power to authorize the guardian of a minor or incompetent to refuse or terminate life-sustaining care of the ward who is in a chronic vegetative state; RC 1337.13 shows the express intent of the legislature to allow the guardian of a minor to be empowered to make health care decisions regarding the care of the ward. In re Guardianship of Crum (Ohio Prob. 1991) 61 Ohio Misc.2d 596, 580 N.E.2d 876.

The parents, as guardians, of a seventeen-year-old ward who has been in a chronic vegetative state for over five years may be granted authorization to terminate life-sustaining treatment, i.e., nutrition and hydration, being provided to the ward where it is shown that withdrawal of nutrition and hydration will not cause physical pain or discomfort to the ward. In re Guardianship of Crum (Ohio Prob. 1991) 61 Ohio Misc.2d 596, 580 N.E.2d 876.

3. Settlement of personal injury claim

Even if probate court had jurisdiction to interject itself into negotiations of minor's personal injury claim, doing so to require guardian to enter into settlement would be abuse of discretion; such action would involve probate court substituting its judgment for that of counsel, and would set dangerous precedent for all probate courts. In re Guardianship of Hicks (Ohio Com.Pl. 1993) 63 Ohio Misc.2d 280, 624 N.E.2d 1125. Compromise And Settlement ⟲ 54

Statute authorizing probate court to function as superior guardian did not authorize probate court to interject itself into negotiations of minor's personal injury claim and require guardian to enter into settlement. In re Guardianship of Hicks (Ohio Com.Pl. 1993) 63 Ohio Misc.2d 280, 624 N.E.2d 1125. Guardian And Ward ⟲ 28

4. Best interest of ward

Trial court, as part of its authority in matters involving guardianship of woman, could revoke power of attorney granted to woman's new husband; court found woman incompetent, and court assumed no greater right than woman would have been able to exercise if she had been competent. In re Guardianship of Thomas (Ohio App. 10 Dist., 03-12-2002) 148 Ohio App.3d 11, 771 N.E.2d 882, 2002-Ohio-1037. Mental Health ⟲ 139

Probate court has no authority to grant powers pertaining to a ward's estate beyond those powers that the ward, if present and competent, could exercise himself or herself. In re Guardianship of Lombardo (Ohio, 09-29-1999) 86 Ohio St.3d 600, 716 N.E.2d 189, 1999-Ohio-132. Guardian And Ward ⟲ 133

Although, by statute, major adverse intervention can be administered only when incompetent continues to engage in behavior destructive to herself or others, psychotropic drugs are not "major adverse intervention," and thus the best interest of the ward is the determinative issue when deciding if incompetent should be forced to take psychotropic medications. In re Guardianship of Willis (Franklin 1991) 74 Ohio App.3d 554, 599 N.E.2d 745. Mental Health ⟲ 51.15

5. Property transfer

Evidence was sufficient to support probate court's authorization of gift disbursements from trustors' guardianship estates by guardian, who was also executor of the estates, and approval of account of the estates, despite the large total amount of the gifts, guardian's failure to produce documents, and lack of information concerning testators' wishes regarding medical care and their prior pattern of giving; gifts did not impair the finances of the estates and did not interfere with provision for the testators, gifts resulted in some tax benefits, gifts furthered the testators' stated objectives of assisting grandchildren with their educations and treating the beneficiaries equally, no one other than the trustee objected to the gifts, trust did not bar inter vivos gifts, trust did not contemplate a specific amount of principal, and trust was ultimately funded with significant principal. In re Estate of Herrick (Ohio App. 8 Dist., Cuyahoga, 09-29-2005) No. 85695, 2005-Ohio-5201, 2005 WL 2401242, Unreported. Guardian And Ward ⟲ 57

An action involving the transfer for consideration of a one- third interest in property owned by a ward of the court to the ward's guardian requires notice to the department of human services that the probate court is planning to act on behalf of its ward, as medicaid eligibility may be affected by the transfer, but the department is not a necessary party to the transfer and has no equitable or financial interest in the transfer of property. In Matter of Guardianship of Stowell (Ohio App. 10 Dist., Franklin, 08-03-1995) No. 95APF01-128, 1995 WL 458963, Unreported.

6. Testamentary disposition of trust property

In original action in prohibition, alternative writ was warranted to prohibit the Court of Common Pleas from ruling on any motions in divorce proceeding until the record in domestic relations case, which pertained to husband's filing a complaint for divorce, and the record in probate case, in which a guardian was appointed for wife due to mental incompetence, could be reconciled. State ex rel. Downs v. Panioto (Ohio App. 1 Dist., Hamilton, 02-25-2005) No. C-040784, 2005-Ohio-778, 2005 WL 433438, Unreported. Courts ⟲ 207.5

Conflict did not exist between state statute, providing that probate court is superior guardian of wards subject to its jurisdiction, and has all powers ward would have if he or she were not under a disability, except the power to make or revoke a will, and federal laws governing special needs trusts which are a means of removing assets from consideration in assessing an individual's eligibility for supplemental security income (SSI) or Medicaid benefits which are distributed based on need, as special needs trusts do not require a testamentary disposition of trust property. In re Daniel J. Rosenbaum Trust (Ohio App. 8 Dist., Cuyahoga, 04-10-2003) No. 81213, 2003-Ohio-1830, 2003 WL 1849141, Unreported. Health ⟲ 471(6)

Proposed amendment to special needs trust document, specifically disposing of trust property following death of beneficiary, would have effectively made a will for ward and was therefore beyond the court's power as superior guardian of wards subject to its jurisdiction. In re Daniel J. Rosenbaum Trust (Ohio App. 8 Dist., Cuyahoga, 04-10-2003) No. 81213, 2003-Ohio-1830, 2003 WL 1849141, Unreported. Trusts ⟲ 58

2111.51 Indigent guardianship fund

Each county shall establish in the county treasury an indigent guardianship fund. All revenue that the general assembly appropriates to the indigent guardianship fund for a county, thirty dollars of the thirty-five-dollar fee collected pursuant to division (A)(34) of section 2101.16 of the Revised Code, and twenty dollars of the sixty-dollar fee collected pursuant to division (A)(59) of that section shall be deposited into the fund that is established in that county. Expenditures from the fund shall be made only upon order of the probate judge and only for payment of any cost, fee, charge, or expense associated with the establishment, opening, maintenance, or termination of a guardianship for an indigent ward.

If a probate court determines that there are reasonably sufficient funds in the indigent guardianship fund of the county in which the court is located to meet the needs of indigent guardianships in that county, the court, by order, may declare a surplus in the indigent guardianship fund and expend the surplus funds for other guardianship expenses or for other court purposes.

(1994 H 457, eff. 11–9–94; 1993 H 9, eff. 9–14–93; 1990 S 267; 1989 S 46)

Uncodified Law

1994 H 457, § 3: See Uncodified Law under 2101.16.

1993 H 9, § 3, eff. 9–14–93, reads: Sections 2101.16, 2111.51, and 2113.03 of the Revised Code, as amended by this act, shall apply to the estates of decedents who die on or after the effective date of this act.

Historical and Statutory Notes

Amendment Note: 1994 H 457 substituted "sixty" for "seventy" and deleted "(b)" after "(A)(59)" in the first paragraph.

Amendment Note: 1993 H 9 added "and twenty dollars of the seventy-dollar fee collected pursuant to division (A)(59)(b) of that section" in the first paragraph.

Library References

Counties ⟲161.
Westlaw Topic No. 104.
C.J.S. Counties § 195.

Research References

Encyclopedias

OH Jur. 3d Guardian & Ward § 89, Court Authorization for Payment of Maintenance, Support, and Education; Indigent Guardianship Fund.

Treatises and Practice Aids

Carlin, Baldwin's Ohio Practice, Merrick-Rippner Probate Law § 62:38, Guardianship Proceedings—Hearings.

Carlin, Baldwin's Ohio Practice, Merrick-Rippner Probate Law § 62:47, Guardianship Proceedings—Person Adjudged Incompetent.

Carlin, Baldwin's Ohio Practice, Merrick-Rippner Probate Law § 64:26, Compensation—Guardian.

CHAPTER 2113

EXECUTORS AND ADMINISTRATORS—APPOINTMENT; POWERS; DUTIES

APPOINTMENT; RELEASE FROM ADMINISTRATION

Section	
2113.01	What court shall grant letters
2113.02	Limitation for granting original administration
2113.03	Release from administration
2113.031	Application for summary release from administration by person obligated to pay decedent's funeral and burial expenses
2113.04	Release of decedent's wages without administration
2113.041	Estate recovery program; affidavit of program administrator; release of funds for cost of services provided to medicaid recipient
2113.05	Letters testamentary; letters of administration with the will annexed
2113.06	To whom letters of administration shall be granted
2113.07	Application for appointment as executor or administrator
2113.11	Notice when deceased was an alien
2113.12	Procedure if executor renounces
2113.13	Minority of an executor
2113.14	Executor of an executor not to administer

SPECIAL ADMINISTRATION

2113.15	Special administrator
2113.16	Powers of special administrator to cease
2113.17	Special administrator not liable to creditors

REMOVAL

2113.18	Removal of executor or administrator
2113.19	Administrator de bonis non
2113.20	Will proved after administration as of an intestate
2113.21	Powers of executors, administrators, and testamentary trustees during a will contest
2113.22	Proceedings against the former executor or administrator
2113.23	Sales of former executor or administrator valid

LIMITATIONS

2113.24	Limitations

COLLECTION OF ASSETS; NEW ADMINISTRATOR

2113.25	Assets to be collected
2113.26	Contents of application
2113.27	Extension of time limited
2113.28	Time allowed to collect assets not to defer account
2113.29	New administrator

GENERAL POWERS AND DUTIES

2113.30	Continuing decedent's business
2113.31	Responsibility of executor or administrator
2113.311	Management of real estate by executor or administrator
2113.32	Executors and administrators not to profit
2113.33	Not responsible for bad debts
2113.34	Chargeable with property consumed

COMMISSIONS AND ALLOWANCES

2113.35	Commissions
2113.36	Further allowance; review of all services; counsel fees
2113.37	Allowance for tombstone and cemetery lot

SALE OF PROPERTY

2113.39	Sale of property under authority of will
2113.40	Sale of personal property
2113.41	Public sale
2113.42	Report of sale
2113.43	Credit
2113.44	Sale of notes secured by mortgage
2113.45	Mortgaged premises to be considered personal assets; possession

Section	
2113.46	Who may discharge mortgage
2113.47	Foreclosure of mortgage
2113.48	Action to complete contract to sell land
2113.49	Court may order alteration or cancellation of contract for sale of real estate; venue
2113.50	Completion of decedent's contract to buy land
2113.51	Property may be delivered to legatee
2113.52	Devisee or heir takes subject to unpaid taxes; mortgage lien; right of exoneration

DISTRIBUTION AND PAYMENT

2113.53	Distribution of assets; liability of executor or administrator; provision for rejected claims; liabilities of beneficiary on unsatisfied claims
2113.531	Interest on general legacies
2113.54	Distribution upon application of legatee or distributee
2113.55	Distribution in kind
2113.56	Executor or administrator not liable
2113.57	Distribution after settlement
2113.58	Protection of remainderman's interest in personal property
2113.59	Lien on share of beneficiary

CERTIFICATE OF TRANSFER

2113.61	Application for certificate of transfer; duty of court
2113.62	Record by county recorder
2113.63	Fees

UNCLAIMED MONEY

2113.64	Investment of unclaimed money
2113.65	Disposition of investment
2113.66	Statute of limitations no defense
2113.67	Money paid to owner
2113.68	Responsibility for safekeeping of evidences of title

NEWLY DISCOVERED ASSETS

2113.69	Newly discovered assets

FOREIGN EXECUTORS AND ADMINISTRATORS

2113.70	Suit against foreign executors and administrators
2113.71	Jurisdiction
2113.72	Proceedings against foreign executor or administrator
2113.73	Security for distributees and indemnification for sureties
2113.74	Other remedies
2113.75	Foreign executor or administrator may prosecute suit in this state

TRUST FOR SAFEKEEPING FOR NONRESIDENT

2113.81	Money and property to be held in trust for safekeeping for nonresidents of United States
2113.82	Payments of money or property by county treasurer or trustee

TAX APPORTIONMENT

2113.85	Definitions
2113.86	Apportionment of federal and Ohio estate taxes among interested persons; exemptions; penalties
2113.861	Apportionment of generation-skipping transfer tax
2113.87	Objections to apportionment of taxes; determination by probate court; notice
2113.88	Withholding taxes from distribution; bond where property distributed prior to final tax apportionment
2113.89	Suit by fiduciary to recover tax; three months after determination; uncollectible amounts reapportioned
2113.90	When interested nonresidents may sue in this state; reciprocal rights

Cross References

Executor or administrator not liable for consequences of exercise of powers granted to others, 1339.43
Executors and administrators are fiduciaries, 1339.01
Fiduciaries, rights as to shares in corporation, 2109.29
Foreign wards and guardians, 2111.43
Liens; executors and administrators have same rights and liabilities as owner would have, 1311.21
Order in which debts to be paid, 2117.25
Payment of debts, 2117.15
Powers of guardian of person and estate, 2111.07
Powers of trustee for person who disappeared, 2119.03
Presentation and allowance of creditor's claims, procedure, 2117.06

Law Review and Journal Commentaries

Common Problems in Administration of Decedent's Estates, Daniel F. Carmack. 14 Clev–Marshall L Rev 179 (January 1965).

Fiduciary Liability Under Superfund: Myth or Reality?, William Falsgraf. 1 Prob L J Ohio 97 (May/June 1991).

Is Ohio Ready for Universal Succession?, Craig Frederickson. 1 Prob L J Ohio 81 (March/April 1991).

Using a Corporate Executor, Phillip B. Rosplock. 12 Lake Legal Views 5 (February 1989).

APPOINTMENT; RELEASE FROM ADMINISTRATION

2113.01 What court shall grant letters

Upon the death of a resident of this state intestate, letters of administration of his estate shall be granted by the probate court of the county in which he was a resident at the time he died.

If the will of any person is admitted to probate in this state, letters testamentary or of administration shall be granted by the probate court in which such will was admitted to probate.

(1953 H 1, eff. 10–1–53; GC 10509–1)

Historical and Statutory Notes

Pre–1953 H 1 Amendments: 120 v 649; 114 v 400

Cross References

Deceased partner, application by surviving partners for administration, 1779.02
Jurisdiction of probate court, 2101.24
Jurisdiction to probate will, 2107.11

Library References

Executors and Administrators ⚖9, 10.
Westlaw Topic No. 162.
C.J.S. Executors and Administrators §§ 12 to 14.

Research References

Encyclopedias

OH Jur. 3d Decedents' Estates § 883, Where Intestate was a Resident of Ohio.
OH Jur. 3d Decedents' Estates § 884, Where Intestate was Not a Resident of Ohio.
OH Jur. 3d Decedents' Estates § 885, Residence or Domicil of Decedent.
OH Jur. 3d Decedents' Estates § 1455, Requirement of Written Statement of Allowance of Claim—Effect of Allowance.

Forms

Ohio Forms Legal and Business § 24:205, Residue to Trust for Spouse and Children.
Ohio Forms and Transactions KP 30.11, Executor.

Treatises and Practice Aids

Carlin, Baldwin's Ohio Practice, Merrick-Rippner Probate Law § 2:11, Probating the Will—Initial Steps.
Carlin, Baldwin's Ohio Practice, Merrick-Rippner Probate Law § 3:13, Jurisdiction of Probate Court—Scope—Exclusive and Concurrent Jurisdiction.
Carlin, Baldwin's Ohio Practice, Merrick-Rippner Probate Law § 35:2, Domicile of Testator—Ohio.
Carlin, Baldwin's Ohio Practice, Merrick-Rippner Probate Law § 68:1, Letters,—in General—Jurisdiction.
Carlin, Baldwin's Ohio Practice, Merrick-Rippner Probate Law § 68:2, Letters—in General—Issuance.
Carlin, Baldwin's Ohio Practice, Merrick-Rippner Probate Law § 68:48, Entry Appointing Fiduciary; Letters of Authority—Form.

Law Review and Journal Commentaries

How a Will Is Admitted to Probate in Ohio. 50 Title Topics 6 (June 1983).

Notes of Decisions

Accounting 8
Assets of estate 7
Collateral attack 9
Constitutional issues 1
Equitable relief 6
Jurisdiction 3
Prisoners and inmates 5
Qualifications 2
Residence 4

---

1. Constitutional issues

The jurisdiction of the probate court to issue letters of administration on estates of persons who were domiciled in Ohio proceeds from O Const Art IV, § 8. Hill v. Blumenberg (Ohio App. 4 Dist. 1924) 19 Ohio App. 404.

While the probate court cannot, under statute, appoint an administrator on the estate of one not an "inhabitant" of the state, yet having general jurisdiction by O Const Art IV, § 6, it may make such appointment outside the statute by virtue of the treaty with Austria–Hungary and US Const Art VI, cl 2. Bucyrus Steel Castings Co. v. Farkas (Ohio Com.Pl. 1914) 27 Ohio Dec. 220, 15 Ohio N.P.N.S. 609.

2. Qualifications

Where an Italian subject dies intestate in Ohio, leaving a widow and two minor children residents and subjects of Italy, the italian consul is not entitled to the entire exclusive right of administration, but is eligible to such appointment under GC 10617, subd. 4 (repealed 1932. See §§ 10506–65, 10509–3, 10509–4) subject to the probate court's discretion. Pagano v. Cerri (Ohio 1916) 93 Ohio St. 345, 112 N.E. 1037, 13 Ohio Law Rep. 578. Executors And Administrators ⚖ 24

Qualification of an administrator relates back at least to the time of filing the petition as regards acts done in the interim for the benefit of the estate. Archdeacon v. Cincinnati Gas & Elec. Co. (Ohio 1907) 76 Ohio St. 97, 81 N.E. 152, 4 Ohio Law Rep. 739.

3. Jurisdiction

The probate court has constitutional jurisdiction to issue letters of administration upon the estates of all those having a legal domicile in Ohio, and statutory jurisdiction to issue such letters on the estates of inhabitants not domiciled in Ohio, and additional statutory jurisdiction over those having no residence of any kind in Ohio but possessed of property therein. Hill v. Blumenberg (Ohio App. 4 Dist. 1924) 19 Ohio App. 404.

Statute empowering the probate court to grant letters of administration upon the death of an intestate resident did not give a probate court jurisdiction to administer an intestate nonresident decedent's non-Ohio property, even if she was domiciled in Ohio. State ex rel. Lee v. Trumbull County Probate Court (Ohio, 10-14-1998) 83 Ohio St.3d 369, 700 N.E.2d 4, 1998-Ohio-51, on remand 1999 WL 744032. Courts ⚖ 198; Courts ⚖ 200.7

2113.01
Note 3

Jurisdiction of probate court, acquired under section to appoint administrator for estate of intestate who was resident of county of such court at time he died, is terminated and superseded by admission to probate of will of same decedent by probate court of another county in which decedent was domiciled at time of death; making and filing of affidavit by person to be appointed administrator that there is not to his knowledge a last will and testament of intestate is condition precedent to granting of letters of administration of estate. State ex rel. Overlander v. Brewer (Ohio 1947) 147 Ohio St. 386, 72 N.E.2d 84, 34 O.O. 338.

Jurisdiction attaches upon the filing of the petition for the appointment of an administrator in the probate court. In re Worthington's Estate (Ohio Prob. 1896) 4 Ohio Dec. 381.

The probate court first exercising jurisdiction will retain it to the exclusion of every other probate court in the state, as there can be but one grant of administration on the same estate in the same state. In re Worthington's Estate (Ohio Prob. 1896) 4 Ohio Dec. 381.

Jurisdiction over decedent's estate acquired by probate court of one county by appointment of administrator under section is not exclusive jurisdiction over same estate later acquired by probate court of another county by virtue of proceedings under GC 10504–10 (RC 2107.09), 10504–15 (RC 2107.11) and 10504–35 (RC 2107.06). State ex rel. Overlander v. Brewer (Ohio 1947) 147 Ohio St. 386, 72 N.E.2d 84, 34 O.O. 338.

Upon the death of an inhabitant of this state, the probate court of the county in which he was an inhabitant or resident at the time he died has sole jurisdiction to administer said inhabitant's estate. 1927 OAG 1000.

The question of the jurisdiction of the probate court to appoint executors or administrators for soldiers who die in the Ohio soldiers home is a question of fact to be determined by the court before which the application for administration is made. 1927 OAG 1000.

4. Residence

The estate of a nonresident leaving an estate in Ohio may be administered under Ohio law. Williams' Adm'rs v. Welton's Adm'r (Ohio 1876) 28 Ohio St. 451.

Where a married woman living in Ohio dies intestate and her husband obtains letters of administration in another state, a suit cannot be maintained in Ohio by her heirs for distribution while the matter is pending in the other state. Adams v. Adams (Ohio 1857) 7 Ohio St. 83.

In estate proceedings, trial court was required to conduct evidentiary hearing, permitting parties to present sworn testimony on disputed issue of jurisdiction and intestate decedent's residency at time of death; trial court's ruling based upon pleadings and affidavits filed with the court was insufficient. In re Estate of Quick (Ohio App. 5 Dist., Licking, 08-23-2004) No. 08232004, 2004-Ohio-4434, 2004 WL 1879696, Unreported. Executors And Administrators 10

"Domicile" is not synonymous with "residence." State ex rel. Lee v. Trumbull County Probate Court (Ohio, 10-14-1998) 83 Ohio St.3d 369, 700 N.E.2d 4, 1998-Ohio-51, on remand 1999 WL 744032. Domicile 2

Rights of widow of nonresident decedent in Ohio property owned by decedent, discussed. In re McCombs' Estate (Ohio Prob. 1948) 80 N.E.2d 573, 52 Ohio Law Abs. 353.

Section is not in conflict with GC 10504–15 (RC 2107.11), as the wording of former section provides for appointment by probate court of administrator of estate of intestate who was resident of county of such court at time of death, while the latter section provides for admission to probate of decedent's will by probate court of county in which decedent was domiciled at time of death; term "resident" as used in this section is not synonymous with term "domiciled" in either GC 10504–10 (RC 2107.09) or 10504–15 (RC 2107.11). State ex rel. Overlander v. Brewer (Ohio 1947) 147 Ohio St. 386, 72 N.E.2d 84, 34 O.O. 338.

5. Prisoners and inmates

A man sentenced to imprisonment for life in the penitentiary is not civilly dead, and letters of administration cannot be granted on his estate. Frazer v. Fulcher (Ohio 1848) 17 Ohio 260. Certiorari 28(2); Convicts 1; Executors And Administrators 4

Personal property, including money, of deceased inmate of institution under supervision of department of public welfare should be administered by proceedings had in probate court of county wherein such inmate resided at the time of his death, and if there be no living heirs to inherit, such property escheats to state and should not be placed in so-called industrial and entertainment fund or posthumous fund of institution. 1942 OAG 5728.

Personal property of a deceased inmate of a reformatory should be administered by the probate court of the county wherein such inmate resided at the time of his death, in accordance with the provisions of statute. 1921 OAG p 63.

6. Equitable relief

Where an adequate remedy at law exists, courts of equity may not be invoked to correct errors in final or partial settlements until legal remedies have been exhausted. Piatt v. Longworth's Devisees (Ohio 1875) 27 Ohio St. 159.

Where an estate has no debts to be paid or adjusted and has already been the subject of administration, courts of equity have ample jurisdiction to enforce trusts. Davis v. Corwine (Ohio 1874) 25 Ohio St. 668.

Where a trust in the hands of the executors fails due to deaths of successive beneficiaries, and the entire beneficial interest has vested in a party, equity allows payment directly to that party without the delay and expense of successive administrators. Taylor v. Huber's Ex'rs (Ohio 1862) 13 Ohio St. 288.

A creditor may not transfer the settlement of the estate of his deceased debtor from the probate court to a court in chancery although he may invoke its aid for the purpose of reaching and placing in the hands of the administrator certain assets which might not otherwise be reached. McDonald v. Aten (Ohio 1853) 1 Ohio St. 293. Courts 472.4(4); Executors And Administrators 473(2)

Under Ohio law a prerequisite to the devolution of a decedent's personal estate is administration of that estate or relief from administration; where this necessary condition does not exist, a surviving spouse cannot prove she ever had an interest in a ring of her late husband that he sold to a pawn shop, and as a consequence she cannot seek to avoid that sale as a "fraudulent transfer" in her own bankruptcy proceedings. In re Jackson (Bkrtcy.S.D.Ohio 1989) 105 B.R. 15.

7. Assets of estate

Administration is a prerequisite to the devolution of the personal estate of a decedent and the heir in possession of a promissory note belonging to the deceased may not bring an action on that note. McBride v. Vance (Ohio 1906) 73 Ohio St. 258, 76 N.E. 938, 112 Am.St.Rep. 723, 3 Ohio Law Rep. 569, 3 Ohio Law Rep. 574, 4 Am.Ann.Cas. 191. Executors And Administrators 3(1)

Where administration is granted upon the estate of a deceased ward, the assets vest immediately in the administrator, not in the former guardian, and the administrator is the proper person to list the estate for taxation. Sommers v. Boyd (Ohio 1891) 48 Ohio St. 648, 27 W.L.B. 27, 29 N.E. 497.

A wrongful death claim in property and is part of the special estate of the decedent, even if decedent had no other property, and an administrator may be appointed to recover the claim for the benefit of statutory beneficiaries. In re Arduino's Estate (Ohio Com.Pl. 1909) 20 Ohio Dec. 461, 9 Ohio NP(NS) 369.

8. Accounting

After removal, an administrator may be required to account to the probate court for transactions occurring prior to removal. In re Morrison's Estate (Ohio 1903) 68 Ohio St. 252, 48 W.L.B. 586, 67 N.E. 567, 1 Ohio Law Rep. 22, 1 Ohio Law Rep. 335.

9. Collateral attack

Sureties on a bond are estopped from showing in a collateral attack that their principal was not duly appointed as executor or that the will was not duly probated. Hoffman v. Fleming (Ohio 1902) 66 Ohio St. 143, 47 W.L.B. 430, 64 N.E. 63.

2113.02 Limitation for granting original administration

Administration shall not be originally granted as of right after the expiration of twenty years from the death of the testator or intestate. But, within his county, each probate judge may grant letters of original administration upon the estate of a deceased person after the expiration of twenty years upon the petition of interested persons or their agent and on good cause shown therefor. Before allowing the prayer of such petition, such judge may direct notice thereof to be given by publication, for a period not exceeding thirty days, in one or more of the newspapers published in the county where such petition is filed.

(1977 H 42, eff. 10–7–77; 1953 H 1; GC 10509–13)

Historical and Statutory Notes

Pre–1953 H 1 Amendments: 114 v 403

Library References

Executors and Administrators ⇐20(2).
Westlaw Topic No. 162.
C.J.S. Executors and Administrators §§ 35, 53, 56.

Research References

Encyclopedias

OH Jur. 3d Decedents' Estates § 946, Time for Application—Waiver by Delay or Lapse of Time.

Treatises and Practice Aids

Carlin, Baldwin's Ohio Practice, Merrick-Rippner Probate Law § 68:42, Application for Authority to Administer Estate—Form.

2113.03 Release from administration

(A) Subject to division (D) of this section, an estate may be released from administration under division (B) of this section if either of the following applies:

(1) The value of the assets of the estate is thirty-five thousand dollars or less.

(2) The value of the assets of the estate is one hundred thousand dollars or less and either of the following applies:

(a) The decedent devised and bequeathed in a valid will all of the assets of the decedent's estate to a person who is named in the will as the decedent's spouse, and the decedent is survived by that person.

(b) The decedent is survived by a spouse whose marriage to the decedent was solemnized in a manner consistent with Chapter 3101. of the Revised Code or with a similar law of another state or nation, the decedent died without a valid will, and the decedent's surviving spouse is entitled to receive all of the assets of the decedent's estate under section 2105.06 of the Revised Code or by the operation of that section and division (B)(1) or (2) of section 2106.13 of the Revised Code.

(B) Upon the application of any interested party, after notice of the filing of the application has been given to the surviving spouse and heirs at law in the manner and for the length of time the probate court directs, and after notice to all interested parties by publication in a newspaper of general circulation in the county, unless the notices are waived or found unnecessary, the court, when satisfied that division (A)(1) or (2) of this section is satisfied, may enter an order relieving the estate from administration and directing delivery of personal property and transfer of real estate to the persons entitled to the personal property or real estate.

For the purposes of this section, the value of an estate that reasonably can be considered to be in an amount specified in division (A)(1) or (2) of this section and that is not composed entirely of money, stocks, bonds, or other property the value of which is readily ascertainable, shall be determined by an appraiser selected by the applicant, subject to the approval of the court. The appraiser's valuation of the property shall be reported to the court in the application to relieve the estate from administration. The appraiser shall be paid in accordance with section 2115.06 of the Revised Code.

For the purposes of this section, the amount of property to be delivered or transferred to the surviving spouse, minor children, or both, of the decedent as the allowance for support shall be established in accordance with section 2106.13 of the Revised Code.

When a delivery, sale, or transfer of personal property has been ordered from an estate that has been relieved from administration, the court may appoint a commissioner to execute all necessary instruments of conveyance. The commissioner shall receipt for the property, distribute the proceeds of the conveyance upon court order, and report to the court after distribution.

When the decedent died testate, the will shall be presented for probate, and, if admitted to probate, the court may relieve the estate from administration and order distribution of the estate under the will.

An order of the court relieving an estate from administration shall have the same effect as administration proceedings in freeing land in the hands of an innocent purchaser for value from possible claims of unsecured creditors.

(C) Any delivery of personal property or transfer of real estate pursuant to an order relieving an estate from administration is made subject to the limitations pertaining to the claims of creditors set forth in divisions (B) and (C) of section 2117.06 of the Revised Code.

(D) The release of an estate from administration under this section does not affect any duty of any person to file an estate tax return and certificate under division (A) of section 5731.21 of the Revised Code and does not affect the duties of a probate court set forth in that division.

(E) This section does not affect the ability of qualified persons to file an application for a summary release from administration under section 2113.031 of the Revised Code or to file an application for the grant of letters testamentary or letters of administration.

(2000 H 313, eff. 8–29–00; 1998 H 366, eff. 3–18–99; 1994 H 457, eff. 11–9–94; 1993 H 9, eff. 9–14–93; 1992 H 89; 1990 H 346; 1987 H 21; 1976 S 466; 1975 S 145; 1973 S 25; 1971 S 54; 132 v H 68; 130 v H 414; 1953 H 1; GC 10509–5)

Uncodified Law

1998 H 366, § 3, eff. 3–18–99, reads:

Sections 2106.13 and 2113.03 of the Revised Code, as amended by this act, apply to the estates of decedents who die on or after the effective date of this act.

1994 H 457, § 3: See Uncodified Law under 2101.16.

1993 H 9, § 3, eff. 9–14–93, reads: Sections 2101.16, 2111.51, and 2113.03 of the Revised Code, as amended by this act, shall apply to the estates of decedents who die on or after the effective date of this act.

1992 H 89, § 3, eff. 4–16–93, reads: Sections 2101.16 and 2113.03 of the Revised Code, as amended by this act, shall apply to the estates of decedents who die on or after the effective date of this act.

1987 H 21, § 3, eff. 10–20–87, reads: Sections 2113.03 and 2129.02 of the Revised Code, as amended by this act, apply only to the estates of decedents who die on or after the effective date of this act.

Historical and Statutory Notes

Pre–1953 H 1 Amendments: 122 v 427; 116 v 385; 114 v 320

Amendment Note: 2000 H 313 added new division (E).

Amendment Note: 1998 H 366 increased the value of the assets of an estate that may be released from administration to one hundred thousand dollars from eighty-five thousand dollars in division (A)(2); and made changes to reflect gender neutral language and other nonsubstantive changes.

Amendment Note: 1994 H 457 substituted "thirty-five" for "twenty-five" in division (A)(1).

Amendment Note: 1993 H 9 substituted "eighty-five" for "fifty" in division (A)(2).

Cross References

Election of surviving spouse to receive mansion house, 2106.10
Fees; costs of investigations; advance deposit, 2101.16
Inheritance by parent of deceased abandoned child prohibited, 2105.10
Medicaid, disposition of personal needs allowance account upon death of resident, definitions, 5111.112
Medicaid, estate recovery program, 5111.11
Newspaper of general circulation defined, 7.12
Probate court jurisdiction, 2101.24
Survivorship deed, vesting of decedent's interest in survivor, 5302.17

Library References

Executors and Administrators ⇐3(1).
Westlaw Topic No. 162.
C.J.S. Executors and Administrators §§ 7, 9 to 10.

Research References

Encyclopedias

OH Jur. 3d Cvl. Servants & Pub. Officers & Employ. § 559, Disposition of Personal Effects.
OH Jur. 3d Decedents' Estates § 117, Under the Statute of Descent and Distribution—Rights in Mansion House.
OH Jur. 3d Decedents' Estates § 136, Abandoning a Minor Child.
OH Jur. 3d Decedents' Estates § 194, Family Settlements.
OH Jur. 3d Decedents' Estates § 860, Necessity of Administration.
OH Jur. 3d Decedents' Estates § 868, Jurisdiction of Probate Court.
OH Jur. 3d Decedents' Estates § 1676, Right to Receive Mansion House as Part of Intestate Share.
OH Jur. 3d Decedents' Estates § 1831, When Administration May be Dispensed With.
OH Jur. 3d Decedents' Estates § 1832, Application to Release, and Order Releasing, Estate from Administration.

Treatises and Practice Aids

Sowald & Morganstern, Baldwin's Ohio Practice Domestic Relations Law § 1:5, Terms.
Carlin, Baldwin's Ohio Practice, Merrick-Rippner Probate Law § 2:3, Time for Administration of Decedent's Estate and Payment of Estate Taxes.
Carlin, Baldwin's Ohio Practice, Merrick-Rippner Probate Law § 3:2, Jurisdiction of Probate Court—Statutory.
Carlin, Baldwin's Ohio Practice, Merrick-Rippner Probate Law § 2:15, Appointment of Fiduciary—Appointment of Executor or Administrator.
Carlin, Baldwin's Ohio Practice, Merrick-Rippner Probate Law § 2:22, Inventory and Appraisal—Family Allowance.
Carlin, Baldwin's Ohio Practice, Merrick-Rippner Probate Law § 2:27, Payment of Debts and Claims—Presentation of Claims.
Carlin, Baldwin's Ohio Practice, Merrick-Rippner Probate Law § 2:28, Payment of Debts and Claims—Notice to Creditors.
Carlin, Baldwin's Ohio Practice, Merrick-Rippner Probate Law § 2:38, Elective Rights of Surviving Spouse—Election to Take Under Law or Under the Will—Elective Share of Surviving Spouse Against the Will.
Carlin, Baldwin's Ohio Practice, Merrick-Rippner Probate Law § 2:45, Elective Rights of Surviving Spouse—Election of Surviving Spouse to Receive Property as Part of Intestate Share and Allowance for Support.
Carlin, Baldwin's Ohio Practice, Merrick-Rippner Probate Law § 21:5, Rights of Surviving Spouse to Make Election—Statutory Provisions—Effect.
Carlin, Baldwin's Ohio Practice, Merrick-Rippner Probate Law § 68:2, Letters—in General—Issuance.
Carlin, Baldwin's Ohio Practice, Merrick-Rippner Probate Law § 75:4, Distribution—Voluntary—Liability—Executor or Administrator.
Carlin, Baldwin's Ohio Practice, Merrick-Rippner Probate Law § 90:9, Authority for Land Sale Action—Overriding Rights of Surviving Spouse.
Carlin, Baldwin's Ohio Practice, Merrick-Rippner Probate Law § 2:108, Release from Administration.
Carlin, Baldwin's Ohio Practice, Merrick-Rippner Probate Law § 2:109, Release from Administration—Appraisal of Property.
Carlin, Baldwin's Ohio Practice, Merrick-Rippner Probate Law § 2:110, Release from Administration—Application; Notice.
Carlin, Baldwin's Ohio Practice, Merrick-Rippner Probate Law § 2:111, Release from Administration—Election of Surviving Spouse to Receive Mansion House.
Carlin, Baldwin's Ohio Practice, Merrick-Rippner Probate Law § 2:112, Summary Release from Administration Generally.
Carlin, Baldwin's Ohio Practice, Merrick-Rippner Probate Law § 2:114, Application for Summary Release from Administration.
Carlin, Baldwin's Ohio Practice, Merrick-Rippner Probate Law § 2:115, Probate Court Order.
Carlin, Baldwin's Ohio Practice, Merrick-Rippner Probate Law § 2:116, Effect of Probate Court Order.
Carlin, Baldwin's Ohio Practice, Merrick-Rippner Probate Law § 2:117, Election of Surviving Spouse to Receive Mansion House.
Carlin, Baldwin's Ohio Practice, Merrick-Rippner Probate Law § 2:122, Administration of Decedent's Estate—Release—Checklist.
Carlin, Baldwin's Ohio Practice, Merrick-Rippner Probate Law § 21:44, Rights of Surviving Spouse to Elect to Receive Mansion House—Statutory Right.
Carlin, Baldwin's Ohio Practice, Merrick-Rippner Probate Law § 21:47, Rights of Surviving Spouse to Elect to Receive Mansion House—Procedure—Election Where Estate Relieved from Administration.
Carlin, Baldwin's Ohio Practice, Merrick-Rippner Probate Law § 30:34, Drafting a Will—Appointment of Executor, Alternate Executor; Ancillary Administrator.
Carlin, Baldwin's Ohio Practice, Merrick-Rippner Probate Law § 33:16, Trusts—Medicaid-Qualifying.
Carlin, Baldwin's Ohio Practice, Merrick-Rippner Probate Law § 68:29, Application to Relieve Estate from Administration—Form.
Carlin, Baldwin's Ohio Practice, Merrick-Rippner Probate Law § 68:30, Assets and Liabilities of Estate to be Relieved from Administration—Form.
Carlin, Baldwin's Ohio Practice, Merrick-Rippner Probate Law § 68:31, Waiver of Notice of Application to Relieve Estate from Administration—Form.
Carlin, Baldwin's Ohio Practice, Merrick-Rippner Probate Law § 68:32, Notice of Application to Relieve Estate from Administration—Form.
Carlin, Baldwin's Ohio Practice, Merrick-Rippner Probate Law § 68:33, Publication of Notice—Single Estate—Form.
Carlin, Baldwin's Ohio Practice, Merrick-Rippner Probate Law § 68:34, Publication of Notice—Multiple Estates—Form.
Carlin, Baldwin's Ohio Practice, Merrick-Rippner Probate Law § 68:35, Entry Relieving Estate from Administration—Form.
Carlin, Baldwin's Ohio Practice, Merrick-Rippner Probate Law § 68:36, Commissioner's Findings—Form.
Carlin, Baldwin's Ohio Practice, Merrick-Rippner Probate Law § 68:37, Commissioner's Report of Distribution, and Judgment Entry—Form.
Carlin, Baldwin's Ohio Practice, Merrick-Rippner Probate Law § 68:38, Report of Distribution by Applicant or Commissioner—Form.
Carlin, Baldwin's Ohio Practice, Merrick-Rippner Probate Law § 68:39, Entry Confirming Report—Form.
Carlin, Baldwin's Ohio Practice, Merrick-Rippner Probate Law § 91:35, Entry Issuing Certificate of Transfer—Form.
Carlin, Baldwin's Ohio Practice, Merrick-Rippner Probate Law § 91:36, Certificate of Transfer—Form.
Carlin, Baldwin's Ohio Practice, Merrick-Rippner Probate Law § 84:39.50, Creditor's Claims—Medicaid Estate Recovery Program.
Carlin, Baldwin's Ohio Practice, Merrick-Rippner Probate Law App B SPF 5.0, Application to Relieve Estate from Administration.
Carlin, Baldwin's Ohio Practice, Merrick-Rippner Probate Law App B SPF 5.6, Entry Relieving Estate from Administration.
Carlin, Baldwin's Ohio Practice, Merrick-Rippner Probate Law App B SPF 12.1, Certificate of Transfer.
Carlin, Baldwin's Ohio Practice, Merrick-Rippner Probate Law App B SPF 5.10, Application for Summary Release from Administration.
Kuehnle and Levey, Ohio Real Estate Law and Practice § 18:1, Ohio State Bar Association Standards of Title Examination.
Kuehnle and Levey, Ohio Real Estate Law and Practice § 10:50, Person Inheriting from Estate Relieved from Administration.

Law Review and Journal Commentaries

Avoiding Probate of Decedents' Estates, Gilbert A. Sheard. 36 U Cin L Rev 70 (Winter 1967).

H.B. 66 and Medicaid recovery. William J. Browning, 16 Prob L J Ohio 42 (November/December 2005).

Releasing From Estate Administration A Decedent's Assets Not Exceeding $25,000: Can the Order Relieving Estate from Administration Actually Free the Land "in the hands of an innocent purchaser for value from possible claims of unsecured creditors"? (R.C. § 2113.03), Robert L. Hausser. 55 Title Topics 5 (December 1988).

Relief From Administration Provisions: Harbinger of Probate Simplification?, Robert G. Dykes. 5 Prob L J Ohio 37 (January/February 1995).

Notes of Decisions

Coroner's actions 3
Partial distribution 1
Real estate titles 2

---

1. Partial distribution

No authority exists for ordering a partial distribution of personal estate without formal administration where the estate exceeds $1000 in value. In re McKenzie's Estate (Ohio Prob. 1956) 139 N.E.2d 505, 74 Ohio Law Abs. 106, 1 O.O.2d 485.

2. Real estate titles

Where the real property of a deceased person passes by the laws of descent and there is no administration of the estate, the title to real property may be transferred through the probate court under GC 10509–5 (RC 2113.03) and GC 10509–102 (RC 2113.61), as amended. 1935 OAG 4793.

A probate court may relieve an estate from administration as provided in section; the necessary affidavit provided for in GC 2768 (RC 317.22) may be made by one or more of the next of kin and the county auditor and county recorder should accept such affidavit in transferring the title to the real estate from the deceased to the next of kin or heirs entitled to the real estate in estates in which administration has been dispensed with. 1933 OAG 910.

3. Coroner's actions

Where property, other than money, clothing and personal effects, is found in connection with or pertaining to the body of a deceased person, in a case where death resulted in circumstances requiring action by the county coroner, and where such property is taken in custody by the coroner, it becomes his duty to "deposit" such property with the probate court by making application to the court either for the appointment of an administrator or for relieving the estate of such deceased person from administration. 1958 OAG 2153.

2113.031 Application for summary release from administration by person obligated to pay decedent's funeral and burial expenses

(A) As used in this section:

(1) "Financial institution" has the same meaning as in section 5725.01 of the Revised Code. "Financial institution" also includes a credit union and a fiduciary that is not a trust company but that does trust business.

(2) "Funeral and burial expenses" means whichever of the following applies:

(a) The funeral and burial expenses of the decedent that are included in the bill of a funeral director;

(b) The funeral expenses of the decedent that are not included in the bill of a funeral director and that have been approved by the probate court;

(c) The funeral and burial expenses of the decedent that are described in divisions (A)(2)(a) and (b) of this section.

(3) "Surviving spouse" means either of the following:

(a) The surviving spouse of a decedent who died leaving the surviving spouse and no minor children;

(b) The surviving spouse of a decedent who died leaving the surviving spouse and minor children, all of whom are children of the decedent and the surviving spouse.

(B)(1) If the value of the assets of the decedent's estate does not exceed the lesser of five thousand dollars or the amount of the decedent's funeral and burial expenses, any person who is not a surviving spouse and who has paid or is obligated in writing to pay the decedent's funeral and burial expenses, including a person described in section 2108.89 of the Revised Code, may apply to the probate court for an order granting a summary release from administration in accordance with this section.

(2) If either of the following applies, the decedent's surviving spouse may apply to the probate court for an order granting a summary release from administration in accordance with this section:

(a) The decedent's funeral and burial expenses have been prepaid, and the value of the assets of the decedent's estate does not exceed the total of the following items:

(i) The allowance for support that is made under division (A) of section 2106.13 of the Revised Code to the surviving spouse and, if applicable, to the decedent's minor children and that is distributable in accordance with division (B)(1) or (2) of that section;

(ii) An amount, not exceeding five thousand dollars, for the decedent's funeral and burial expenses referred to in division (A)(2)(c) of this section.

(b) The decedent's funeral and burial expenses have not been prepaid, the decedent's surviving spouse has paid or is obligated in writing to pay the decedent's funeral and burial expenses, and the value of the assets of the decedent's estate does not exceed the total of the items referred to in divisions (B)(2)(a)(i) and (ii) of this section.

(C) A probate court shall order a summary release from administration in connection with a decedent's estate only if the court finds that all of the following are satisfied:

(1) A person described in division (B)(1) of this section is the applicant for a summary release from administration, and the value of the assets of the decedent's estate does not exceed the lesser of five thousand dollars or the amount of the decedent's funeral and burial expenses, or the applicant for a summary release from administration is the decedent's surviving spouse, and the circumstances described in division (B)(2)(a) or (b) of this section apply.

(2) The application for a summary release from administration does all of the following:

(a) Describes all assets of the decedent's estate that are known to the applicant;

(b) Is in the form that the supreme court prescribes pursuant to its powers of superintendence under Section 5 of Article IV, Ohio Constitution, and is consistent with the requirements of this division;

(c) Has been signed and acknowledged by the applicant in the presence of a notary public or a deputy clerk of the probate court;

(d) Sets forth the following information if the decedent's estate includes a described type of asset:

(i) If the decedent's estate includes a motor vehicle, the motor vehicle's year, make, model, body type, manufacturer's vehicle identification number, certificate of title number, and date of death value;

(ii) If the decedent's estate includes an account maintained by a financial institution, that institution's name and the account's complete identifying number and date of death balance;

(iii) If the decedent's estate includes one or more shares of stock or bonds, the total number of the shares and bonds and their total date of death value and, for each share or bond, its serial number, the name of its issuer, its date of death value, and, if any, the name and address of its transfer agent.

(3) The application for a summary release from administration is accompanied by all of the following that apply:

(a) A receipt, contract, written declaration as defined in section 2108. 70 of the Revised Code, or other document that confirms the applicant's payment or obligation to pay the decedent's funeral and burial expenses or, if applicable in the case of the decedent's surviving spouse, the prepayment of the decedent's funeral and burial expenses;

(b) An application for a certificate of transfer as described in section 2113.61 of the Revised Code, if an interest in real property is included in the assets of the decedent's estate;

(c) The fee required by division (A)(59) of section 2101.16 of the Revised Code.

(4) At the time of its determination on the application, there are no pending proceedings for the administration of the decedent's estate and no pending proceedings for relief of the decedent's estate from administration under section 2113.03 of the Revised Code.

(5) At the time of its determination on the application, there are no known assets of the decedent's estate other than the assets described in the application.

(D) If the probate court determines that the requirements of division (C) of this section are satisfied, the probate court shall issue an order that grants a summary release from administration in connection with the decedent's estate. The order has, and shall specify that it has, all of the following effects:

(1) It relieves the decedent's estate from administration.

(2) It directs the delivery to the applicant of the decedent's personal property together with the title to that property.

(3) It directs the transfer to the applicant of the title to any interests in real property included in the decedent's estate.

(4) It eliminates the need for a financial institution, corporation, or other entity or person referred to in any provision of divisions (A) to (F) of section 5731.39 of the Revised Code to obtain, as otherwise would be required by any of those divisions, the written consent of the tax commissioner prior to the delivery, transfer, or payment to the applicant of an asset of the decedent's estate.

(E) A certified copy of an order that grants a summary release from administration together with a certified copy of the application for that order constitutes sufficient authority for a financial institution, corporation, or other entity or person referred to in divisions (A) to (F) of section 5731.39 of the Revised Code or for a clerk of a court of common pleas to transfer title to an asset of the decedent's estate to the applicant for the summary release from administration.

(F) This section does not affect the ability of qualified persons to file an application to relieve an estate from administration under section 2113.03 of the Revised Code or to file an application for the grant of letters testamentary or letters of administration in connection with the decedent's estate.

(2006 H 426, eff. 10–12–06; 2002 H 675, eff. 12–13–02; 2000 H 313, eff. 8–29–00)

Historical and Statutory Notes

Amendment Note: 2006 H 426 substituted "five" for "two" in division (B)(1), division (B)(2)(a)(ii), and division (C)(1); inserted ", including a person described in section 2108.89 of the Revised Code,"; and inserted "written declaration as defined in section 2108.70 of the Revised Code," in division (C)(3)(a).

Amendment Note: 2002 H 675 deleted division (D)(4); and redesignated former division (D)(5) as new division (D)(4). Prior to deletion former division (D)(4) read:

"(4) It eliminates the duty of all persons to file an estate tax return and certificate under division (A) of section 5731.21 of the Revised Code in connection with the decedent's estate."

Cross References

Election of surviving spouse to receive mansion house, 2106.10
Estate tax returns; certificates, 5731.21
Fees; costs of investigations; advance deposit, 2101.16
Probate court jurisdiction, 2101.24
Records kept by probate court, 2101.12

Library References

Executors and Administrators ⇐3(1).
Westlaw Topic No. 162.
C.J.S. Executors and Administrators §§ 7, 9 to 10.

Research References

Encyclopedias

OH Jur. 3d Decedents' Estates § 1404, Certificate of Transfer of Real Estate by Inheritance or Devise.
OH Jur. 3d Decedents' Estates § 1831, When Administration May be Dispensed With.
OH Jur. 3d Decedents' Estates § 1832, Application to Release, and Order Releasing, Estate from Administration.

Treatises and Practice Aids

Carlin, Baldwin's Ohio Practice, Merrick-Rippner Probate Law § 2:3, Time for Administration of Decedent's Estate and Payment of Estate Taxes.
Carlin, Baldwin's Ohio Practice, Merrick-Rippner Probate Law § 3:2, Jurisdiction of Probate Court—Statutory.
Carlin, Baldwin's Ohio Practice, Merrick-Rippner Probate Law § 2:22, Inventory and Appraisal—Family Allowance.
Carlin, Baldwin's Ohio Practice, Merrick-Rippner Probate Law § 2:38, Elective Rights of Surviving Spouse—Election to Take Under Law or Under the Will—Elective Share of Surviving Spouse Against the Will.
Carlin, Baldwin's Ohio Practice, Merrick-Rippner Probate Law § 2:62, Ohio Estate Tax—Filing the Return.
Carlin, Baldwin's Ohio Practice, Merrick-Rippner Probate Law § 21:5, Rights of Surviving Spouse to Make Election—Statutory Provisions—Effect.
Carlin, Baldwin's Ohio Practice, Merrick-Rippner Probate Law § 73:5, Management of Real Estate—Termination of Authority.
Carlin, Baldwin's Ohio Practice, Merrick-Rippner Probate Law § 90:9, Authority for Land Sale Action—Overriding Rights of Surviving Spouse.
Carlin, Baldwin's Ohio Practice, Merrick-Rippner Probate Law § 2:106, Distribution of Assets—Transfer of Real Estate.
Carlin, Baldwin's Ohio Practice, Merrick-Rippner Probate Law § 2:108, Release from Administration.
Carlin, Baldwin's Ohio Practice, Merrick-Rippner Probate Law § 2:112, Summary Release from Administration Generally.
Carlin, Baldwin's Ohio Practice, Merrick-Rippner Probate Law § 2:113, Value of Decedent's Assets Which May be Transferred.
Carlin, Baldwin's Ohio Practice, Merrick-Rippner Probate Law § 2:114, Application for Summary Release from Administration.
Carlin, Baldwin's Ohio Practice, Merrick-Rippner Probate Law § 2:115, Probate Court Order.
Carlin, Baldwin's Ohio Practice, Merrick-Rippner Probate Law § 2:116, Effect of Probate Court Order.
Carlin, Baldwin's Ohio Practice, Merrick-Rippner Probate Law § 2:117, Election of Surviving Spouse to Receive Mansion House.

Carlin, Baldwin's Ohio Practice, Merrick-Rippner Probate Law § 2:118, Certificate of Transfer or Interest in Real Property.
Carlin, Baldwin's Ohio Practice, Merrick-Rippner Probate Law § 2:121, Administration of Decedent's Estate—Checklist.
Carlin, Baldwin's Ohio Practice, Merrick-Rippner Probate Law § 21:44, Rights of Surviving Spouse to Elect to Receive Mansion House—Statutory Right.
Carlin, Baldwin's Ohio Practice, Merrick-Rippner Probate Law § 21:47, Rights of Surviving Spouse to Elect to Receive Mansion House—Procedure—Election Where Estate Relieved from Administration.
Carlin, Baldwin's Ohio Practice, Merrick-Rippner Probate Law § 109:11, Ohio Estate Tax—Gross Estate—Joint and Survivorship Property—Rights of Survivor—Transfer on Death Deed—Summary Administration.
Carlin, Baldwin's Ohio Practice, Merrick-Rippner Probate Law § 109:37, Ohio Estate Tax—Return—Time for Filing; Exceptions by Tax Commissioner.
Carlin, Baldwin's Ohio Practice, Merrick-Rippner Probate Law § 109:41, Ohio Estate Tax—Return—Penalties for Failure to File or Pay.
Carlin, Baldwin's Ohio Practice, Merrick-Rippner Probate Law App B SPF 5.10, Application for Summary Release from Administration.
Carlin, Baldwin's Ohio Practice, Merrick-Rippner Probate Law App B SPF 5.11, Entry Granting Summary Release from Administration.

Law Review and Journal Commentaries

Did They Mean What They Said and Say What They Meant? Did Our Legislature Already Eliminate Ohio Estate Taxes? James R. Wade, 13 Prob L J Ohio 13 (September/October 2002).

Estate Tax Loophole Closed for Summary Release, James L. Lanham. 13 Prob L J Ohio 53 (January/February 2003).

Summary Release: A Solution For Transfer of Small Estate Assets, Walter C. Grosjean. 10 Prob L J Ohio 69 (May/June 2000).

2113.04 Release of decedent's wages without administration

Any employer, including the state or a political subdivision, at any time after the death of his or its employee, may pay all wages or personal earnings due to the deceased employee to: (A) the surviving spouse; (B) any one or more of the children eighteen years of age or older; or (C) the father or mother of the deceased employee, preference being given in the order named, without requiring letters testamentary or letters of administration to be issued upon the estate of the deceased employee, and without requiring an Ohio estate tax release where the wages or personal earnings do not exceed two thousand five hundred dollars. The payment of wages or personal earnings is a full discharge and release to the employer from any claim for the wages or personal earnings. If letters testamentary or letters of administration are thereafter issued upon the estate of the deceased employee, any person receiving payment of wages or personal earnings under this section is liable to the executor or administrator for the sum received by him.

(1978 H 901, eff. 2–28–79; 1975 S 145; 1953 H 1; GC 10509–5a)

Historical and Statutory Notes

Pre–1953 H 1 Amendments: 124 v 535; 119 v 394, § 6

Cross References

Compensation of judges, death benefit, 141.04
Payment for unused sick leave; death of employee, 124.384
Personal leave for state employees, 124.386
Salaries of elective state officers, death benefit, 141.01, 141.011
School district superintendent, treatment of vacation leave on superintendent's death, 3319.01
State employees' unused vacation leave, payment, 124.13
Vacation leave for employees exempt from collective bargaining law, 124.134
Vacation leave, holiday pay, county employees, 325.19
Vacation of nonteaching employees, compensation on separation, payment to dependents, 3319.084

Library References

Executors and Administrators ⟸3(1).
Labor and Employment ⟸222.
Westlaw Topic Nos. 162, 231H.
C.J.S. Executors and Administrators §§ 7, 9 to 10.

Research References

Encyclopedias

OH Jur. 3d Decedents' Estates § 1831, When Administration May be Dispensed With.
OH Jur. 3d Decedents' Estates § 1832, Application to Release, and Order Releasing, Estate from Administration.

Treatises and Practice Aids

Carlin, Baldwin's Ohio Practice, Merrick-Rippner Probate Law § 2:119, Matters Outside Formal Estate Administration.
Carlin, Baldwin's Ohio Practice, Merrick-Rippner Probate Law § 2:121, Administration of Decedent's Estate—Checklist.
Carlin, Baldwin's Ohio Practice, Merrick-Rippner Probate Law § 2:122, Administration of Decedent's Estate—Release—Checklist.
Carlin, Baldwin's Ohio Practice, Merrick-Rippner Probate Law § 109:62, Ohio Estate Tax—Release or Consent—Requirement.
Carlin, Baldwin's Ohio Practice, Merrick-Rippner Probate Law § 109:69, Ohio Estate Tax—Release or Consent—Failure to Comply.
Carlin, Baldwin's Ohio Practice, Merrick-Rippner Probate Law § 109:72, Ohio Estate Tax—Release or Consent—Not Required for Payment of Wages Less Than $2,500.
Employment Coordinator Compensation § 30:71, Ohio; Wages Upon Employee's Death.
Gotherman, Babbit and Lang, Baldwin's Ohio Practice, Local Government Law—Municipal, § 40:10, Ordinance Authorizing Payment of Vacation Pay to Next of Kin.
Hastings, Manoloff, Sheeran, & Stype, Ohio School Law § 7:9, Superintendent's Contract, Compensation-Contract, Termination.
Hastings, Manoloff, Sheeran, & Stype, Ohio School Law § 7:19, Administrators' Contracts-In General.

Law Review and Journal Commentaries

When an employee dies, Richard A. Slee. 38 Ohio Sch Boards Ass'n J 2 (May 1994).

Notes of Decisions

County employees 3
Public officials 1
School district employees 2
State employees 4

---

1. Public officials

A public officer, such as a county auditor, is not an employee as such word is used in RC 325.19, and, upon the death of such officer, no amount may be paid for earned but unused vacation leave under RC 2113.04 to his estate. 1962 OAG 3239.

2. School district employees

Neither RC 121.161 nor RC 2113.04 authorizes the payment of any amount of money to survivors or personal representatives of the estate of a deceased employee of a school district for unused vacation time accumulated by the employee before his death. 1961 OAG 2579.

3. County employees

The survivors or personal representatives of the estate of an employee of a county after his death have no right to receive pay for unused vacation time accumulated by the employee before his death. 1958 OAG 2374.

4. State employees

A state employee may accumulate vacation leave earned, but not used during his state service, and in case of the death of a state employee the monetary value of all such unused vacation leave, if not exceeding $300, should be paid in accordance with RC 2113.04 and if exceeding $300, to his estate. 1960 OAG 1575.

State employees paid vacation leave may not be accumulated as a matter of right, but any such unused leave may be considered in granting extensions of current leave in special cases, and there is no provision for compensation for unused leave except as set forth in RC 121.161 and RC 2113.04. 1956 OAG 6580.

2113.041 Estate recovery program; affidavit of program administrator; release of funds for cost of services provided to medicaid recipient

(A) The administrator of the estate recovery program established pursuant to section 5111.11 of the Revised Code may present an affidavit to a financial institution requesting that the financial institution release account proceeds to recover the cost of services correctly provided to a medicaid recipient who is subject to the estate recovery program. The affidavit shall include all of the following information:

(1) The name of the decedent;

(2) The name of any person who gave notice that the decedent was a medicaid recipient and that person's relationship to the decedent;

(3) The name of the financial institution;

(4) The account number;

(5) A description of the claim for estate recovery;

(6) The amount of funds to be recovered.

(B) A financial institution may release account proceeds to the administrator of the estate recovery program if all of the following apply:

(1) The decedent held an account at the financial institution that was in the decedent's name only.

(2) No estate has been, and it is reasonable to assume that no estate will be, opened for the decedent.

(3) The decedent has no outstanding debts known to the administrator of the estate recovery program.

(4) The financial institution has received no objections or has determined that no valid objections to release of proceeds have been received.

(C) If proceeds have been released pursuant to division (B) of this section and the department of job and family services receives notice of a valid claim to the proceeds that has a higher priority under section 2117.25 of the Revised Code than the claim of the estate recovery program, the department may refund the proceeds to the financial institution or pay them to the person or government entity with the claim.

(2005 H 66, eff. 6–30–05; 2003 H 95, eff. 9–26–03)

Historical and Statutory Notes

Amendment Note: 2005 H 66 inserted "who is subject to the estate recovery program" in the first paragraph of division (A).

Library References

Executors and Administrators ⟐205.
Westlaw Topic No. 162.
C.J.S. Executors and Administrators § 398.

Research References

Encyclopedias

OH Jur. 3d Public Welfare § 168, Recovery of Medicaid Payments from Recipient or Estate.

Treatises and Practice Aids

Carlin, Baldwin's Ohio Practice, Merrick-Rippner Probate Law § 75:4, Distribution—Voluntary—Liability—Executor or Administrator.

Carlin, Baldwin's Ohio Practice, Merrick-Rippner Probate Law § 2:121, Administration of Decedent's Estate—Checklist.

Carlin, Baldwin's Ohio Practice, Merrick-Rippner Probate Law § 33:16, Trusts—Medicaid-Qualifying.

Carlin, Baldwin's Ohio Practice, Merrick-Rippner Probate Law § 48:11, Liability for Payment of Claims Against Estate.

Carlin, Baldwin's Ohio Practice, Merrick-Rippner Probate Law § 84:39.50, Creditor's Claims—Medicaid Estate Recovery Program.

Law Review and Journal Commentaries

H.B. 66 and Medicaid recovery. William J. Browning, 16 Prob L J Ohio 42 (November/December 2005).

2113.05 Letters testamentary; letters of administration with the will annexed

When a will is approved and allowed, the probate court shall issue letters testamentary to the executor named in the will or to the executor nominated by holders of a power as described in section 2107.65 of the Revised Code, or to the executor named in the will and to a coexecutor nominated by holders of such a power, if he is suitable, competent, accepts the appointment, and gives bond if that is required.

If no executor is named in a will and no power as described in section 2107.65 of the Revised Code is conferred in the will, or if the executor named in a will or nominated pursuant to such a power dies, fails to accept the appointment, resigns, or is otherwise disqualified and the holders of such a power do not have authority to nominate another executor or no such power is conferred in the will, or if such a power is conferred in a will but the power cannot be exercised because of the death of a holder of the power, letters of administration with the will annexed shall be granted to a suitable person or persons, named as devisees or legatees in the will, who would have been entitled to administer the estate if the decedent had died intestate, unless the will indicates an intention that the person or persons shall not be granted letters of administration. Otherwise, the court shall grant letters of administration with the will annexed to some other suitable person.

(1983 S 115, eff. 10–14–83; 1982 S 247; 1975 S 145; 1970 S 134; 125 v 903; 1953 H 1; GC 10509–2)

Historical and Statutory Notes

Pre–1953 H 1 Amendments: 116 v 385; 114 v 401

OSBA Probate and Trust Law Section

1983:

The Board of Governors of the Probate and Trust Law Section recommends an amendment to §2113.05 of the Ohio Revised Code. Technical amendments to §2109.02 and §2109.21 are also required.

Although Amended Substitute Senate Bill Number 247 amended sections 2109.21 and 2113.05 effective March 15, 1983, the Board of Governors believes that further amendments are necessary.

At least in certain portions of the state, attorneys, under certain circumstances, have encountered difficulty in securing the appointment of an executor without providing bond. The particular situation generally arises when a testator has provided in his will that a particular person or persons may designate or nominate the executor. Some probate courts have taken the position that since the name of the executor is not spelled out in the will, the person designated or nominated should be required to post bond.

Although §2109.21 acknowledges the possibility of a power of nomination being conferred in a will, §2113.05 does not specifically provide for the appointment of that person without bond when the testamentary instrument so provides.

Consequently, the Board of Governors believes that an amendment of §2113.05 is in order to specifically provide that a testator may by will confer a power for the nomination of an executor to serve without bond.

Cross References

Residence qualifications of administrators and guardians, 2109.21

Library References

Executors and Administrators ⚖14, 21, 27.
Westlaw Topic No. 162.
C.J.S. Executors and Administrators §§ 17 to 21, 79, 947.

Research References

Encyclopedias

OH Jur. 3d Decedents' Estates § 898, Generally; Definitions.
OH Jur. 3d Decedents' Estates § 910, Requirement of Competency and Suitability.
OH Jur. 3d Decedents' Estates § 911, Meaning of "Suitable" and "Competent", Generally.
OH Jur. 3d Decedents' Estates § 913, Meaning of "Suitable" and "Competent", Generally—Nonresidency.
OH Jur. 3d Decedents' Estates § 919, Renunciation Of, or Failure to Accept, Appointment—Effect Where No Other Executor Named.
OH Jur. 3d Decedents' Estates § 983, Appointment.
OH Jur. 3d Fiduciaries § 9, Qualification; Residency.

Forms

Ohio Forms Legal and Business § 24:461, Appointment—General Clause.

Treatises and Practice Aids

Carlin, Baldwin's Ohio Practice, Merrick-Rippner Probate Law § 2:15, Appointment of Fiduciary—Appointment of Executor or Administrator.
Carlin, Baldwin's Ohio Practice, Merrick-Rippner Probate Law § 57:1, Resignation of Fiduciary.
Carlin, Baldwin's Ohio Practice, Merrick-Rippner Probate Law § 57:2, Removal of Fiduciary—Introduction.
Carlin, Baldwin's Ohio Practice, Merrick-Rippner Probate Law § 57:5, Removal of Fiduciary—Grounds—Nonresidency of Fiduciary.
Carlin, Baldwin's Ohio Practice, Merrick-Rippner Probate Law § 68:2, Letters—in General—Issuance.
Carlin, Baldwin's Ohio Practice, Merrick-Rippner Probate Law § 68:6, Letters of Administration—Specific Qualifications of Administrators—Preference of Suitable Persons—Next of Kin.
Carlin, Baldwin's Ohio Practice, Merrick-Rippner Probate Law § 70:1, Administrator De Bonis Non—Necessity.
Carlin, Baldwin's Ohio Practice, Merrick-Rippner Probate Law § 81:1, Removal—Statutory Provisions.
Carlin, Baldwin's Ohio Practice, Merrick-Rippner Probate Law § 2:121, Administration of Decedent's Estate—Checklist.
Carlin, Baldwin's Ohio Practice, Merrick-Rippner Probate Law § 30:34, Drafting a Will—Appointment of Executor, Alternate Executor; Ancillary Administrator.
Carlin, Baldwin's Ohio Practice, Merrick-Rippner Probate Law § 30:44, Drafting a Will—Choosing Witnesses—Executor as Witness.
Carlin, Baldwin's Ohio Practice, Merrick-Rippner Probate Law § 68:14, Letters of Administration—Discretion of Probate Court in Appointing Administrators; Appeal.
Carlin, Baldwin's Ohio Practice, Merrick-Rippner Probate Law § 68:17, Letters Testamentary—Issuance.
Carlin, Baldwin's Ohio Practice, Merrick-Rippner Probate Law § 68:18, Letters Testamentary—Letters of Administration With the Will Annexed.
Carlin, Baldwin's Ohio Practice, Merrick-Rippner Probate Law § 68:19, Letters Testamentary—Qualifications of Executors—in General.
Carlin, Baldwin's Ohio Practice, Merrick-Rippner Probate Law § 68:21, Letters Testamentary—Qualifications for Executors—Trust Company.
Carlin, Baldwin's Ohio Practice, Merrick-Rippner Probate Law § 68:24, Letters Testamentary—Qualifications for Executors—Residency Requirement.
Carlin, Baldwin's Ohio Practice, Merrick-Rippner Probate Law § 68:27, Letters Testamentary—Refusal of Appointment of Executor by Probate Court.
Carlin, Baldwin's Ohio Practice, Merrick-Rippner Probate Law § 68:28, Letters Testamentary—Refusal of Appointment of Executor by Nominee.
Carlin, Baldwin's Ohio Practice, Merrick-Rippner Probate Law § 68:42, Application for Authority to Administer Estate—Form.
Carlin, Baldwin's Ohio Practice, Merrick-Rippner Probate Law § 68:53, Declination by Executor Named in Will—Form.

Notes of Decisions

Conflict of interest 3
Discretion of court 5
Other suitable persons, construed 6
Procedural issues 2
Suitability standard 1
Surviving spouse 4

---

1. Suitability standard

Attorney, who was named as executor in deceased's will, was not a suitable person to administer the estate, where attorney did not file an application for authority to administer the estate until over 17 months after the death, he only filed the application after the court appointed executor brought a complaint against him for concealment of assets, and, as a result of attorney's failure to apply for administration, the estate incurred tax liabilities and penalties. In re Estate of Rice (Ohio App. 7 Dist., Belmont, 09-28-2005) No. 04-BE-36, 2005-Ohio-5311, 2005 WL 2447031, Unreported. Executors And Administrators ⚖ 15

Lack of expertise in a specialized area is not the equivalent of unsuitability to serve as executor of estate. In re Estate of Tyler (Ohio Com.Pl., 04-07-1999) 100 Ohio Misc.2d 17, 716 N.E.2d 1239. Executors And Administrators ⚖ 15

Daughter of testator, who was named as devisee in will and would have been person entitled to administer estate if testator had died intestate, would be appointed as administrator with will annexed after individual appointed as executor in will declined to accept appointment; while bank named in will as beneficiary trustee may have had areas of greater expertise, nothing indicated that daughter was unsuitable or incompetent to serve as administrator. In re Estate of Tyler (Ohio Com.Pl., 04-07-1999) 100 Ohio Misc.2d 17, 716 N.E.2d 1239. Executors And Administrators ⚖ 18

Person is "suitable" for position of executrix only if she is reasonably disinterested and in position to reasonably fulfill obligations of fiduciary. Gockel v. Eble (Ohio App. 8 Dist., 10-17-1994) 98 Ohio App.3d 281, 648 N.E.2d 539, dismissed, appeal not allowed 71 Ohio St.3d 1491, 646 N.E.2d 466. Executors And Administrators ⚖ 15

Niece of testatrix was not "suitable" to serve as executrix, even though niece was named as party defendant in will contest brought by niece's mother, given that niece maintained that testatrix had executed new will which revoked legacies contained in contested will and, thus, removing niece from position of executrix was not an abuse of discretion. Gockel v. Eble (Ohio App. 8 Dist., 10-17-1994) 98 Ohio App.3d 281, 648 N.E.2d 539, dismissed, appeal not allowed 71 Ohio St.3d 1491, 646 N.E.2d 466. Executors And Administrators ⚖ 15

In determining who is a suitable person to administer an estate, a court will look for someone reasonably disinterested and in a position to reasonably meet his fiduciary responsibilities. In re Estate of Roch (Wayne 1991) 81 Ohio App.3d 161, 610 N.E.2d 524.

In accordance with RC 2113.05, a "suitable" person qualified for appointment as executor is an applicant who is reasonably disinterested and in a position to reasonably fulfill the obligations of a fiduciary. In re Henne's Estate (Ohio 1981) 66 Ohio St.2d 232, 421 N.E.2d 506, 20 O.O.3d 228. Executors And Administrators ⚖ 15

While acknowledging deference to the testator's nomination of an executor, the court, in determining the limits of a reasonably disinterested applicant, may consider factors including, but not limited to: (1) the nature and extent of the hostility and distrust among the parties; (2) the degree of conflicting interests and obligations, both personal and financial; and (3) the underlying and aggregate complexities of the conflict. In re Henne's Estate (Ohio 1981) 66 Ohio St.2d 232, 421 N.E.2d 506, 20 O.O.3d 228. Executors And Administrators ⚖ 15; Executors And Administrators ⚖ 20(8)

Where a testator nominates one to be the executrix of his estate, such nominee is not disqualified merely because she was financially indebted to the decedent at the time of his death, and is entitled to such appointment unless she is clearly disqualified under RC 2113.05. In re Nagle's Estate (Scioto 1974) 40 Ohio App.2d 40, 317 N.E.2d 242, 69 O.O.2d 22. Executors And Administrators ⚖ 15

An executor named in a will who has some physical disability but whose mental alertness and capacity are demonstrated by extensive examination, in the absence of any medical testimony that his physical condition has some effect on his mental condition, is suitable within the meaning of RC 2113.05. In re Ruggles' Estate (Huron 1973) 39 Ohio App.2d 39, 315 N.E.2d 486, 71 A.L.R.3d 667, 68 O.O.2d 177.

The appointment by a probate court of an executor who is not in a position to reasonably fulfill the obligations of a fiduciary, and, therefore, not a "suitable" person to act in a fiduciary capacity, constitutes an abuse of discretion. In re Young's Estate (Franklin 1964) 4 Ohio App.2d 315, 212 N.E.2d 612, 33 O.O.2d 357, appeal dismissed 177 Ohio St. 76, 202 N.E.2d 308, 29 O.O.2d 196.

A "suitable" person, qualified for appointment as an executor under RC 2113.05, means a person who is reasonably disinterested in the estate and the legatees and beneficiaries under the will. In re Young's Estate (Franklin 1964) 4 Ohio App.2d 315, 212 N.E.2d 612, 33 O.O.2d 357, appeal dismissed 177 Ohio St. 76, 202 N.E.2d 308, 29 O.O.2d 196.

Unsuitableness of executrix, not amounting to incapacity, is not sufficient to deny issue of letters testamentary. In re Sells' Estate (Ohio Prob. 1907) 5 Ohio NP(NS) 629, 52 W.L.B. 610.

2. Procedural issues

Statutes governing removal of fiduciary or executor, not statute governing appointment of executor, applied when determining whether to remove executor. In re Estate of Rice (Ohio App. 9 Dist., 06-29-2005) 161 Ohio App.3d 847, 832 N.E.2d 139, 2005-Ohio-3301. Executors And Administrators 35(1).

An individual named as executor in a prior will does not thereby acquire standing to contest a subsequent will admitted to probate. Hermann v. Crossen (Cuyahoga 1959) 160 N.E.2d 404, 81 Ohio Law Abs. 322.

An order of the probate court appointing an executor, if made in the exercise of proper jurisdiction over the subject matter and the estate, cannot be collaterally attacked, although based upon erroneous conclusions of law and fact. Union Sav. Bank & Trust Co. v. Western Union Tel. Co. (Ohio 1908) 79 Ohio St. 89, 86 N.E. 478, 128 Am.St.Rep. 675, 6 Ohio Law Rep. 554. Courts 202(4); Executors And Administrators 29(3); Judgment 475

Where the individual named in the will as executor repudiates acting as such, notice to this individual of the probate proceedings does not constitute notice to the beneficiaries. Feuchter v. Keyl (Ohio 1891) 48 Ohio St. 357, 25 W.L.B. 399, 27 N.E. 860.

Breaking of will terminates the administration of administrator with the will annexed. In re Schonacker's Estate (Ohio Prob. 1910) 55 W.L.B. 78.

3. Conflict of interest

Executrix may neither commence will contest action nor concur as defendant with plaintiffs in will contest action while simultaneously performing duties of executrix. Gockel v. Eble (Ohio App. 8 Dist., 10-17-1994) 98 Ohio App.3d 281, 648 N.E.2d 539, dismissed, appeal not allowed 71 Ohio St.3d 1491, 646 N.E.2d 466. Executors And Administrators 15

A person named in a will as executrix, admittedly competent otherwise, is not entitled to the appointment as a matter of right if she is not, because of conflicting interests, a "suitable" person under the circumstances, the question of such suitability resting within the discretion of the probate court. In re Bowman's Estate (Cuyahoga 1957) 143 N.E.2d 150, 76 Ohio Law Abs. 597. Executors And Administrators 15

The appointment of an administratrix with the will annexed will not be overturned for conflict of interest where the administratrix is employed by and represented by the same law firm which represents the sole beneficiary under the will. In re Estate of Seligman, No. L-83-285 (6th Dist Ct App, Lucas, 2-17-84).

4. Surviving spouse

A probate court does not abuse its discretion where it determines that a decedent's surviving spouse is not a suitable person to administer the decedent's estate because the only purpose for such administration would be to bring a wrongful death action and the surviving spouse cannot be reasonably disinterested when the wrongful death action would be against her father and any award in the wrongful death action would bring the possibility of a reduction in the surviving spouse's potential inheritance from her father. In re Estate of Roch (Wayne 1991) 81 Ohio App.3d 161, 610 N.E.2d 524.

A court may properly refuse to appoint as executor the person nominated by the testator as executor where the surviving spouse-sole beneficiary who seeks appointment as administratrix with will attached is hostile to the nominated executor-lawyer due to her belief that the lawyer, the scrivener of the will, misled the testator as to his intention to collect fees for his duties as counsel and as fiduciary and that such a double fee arrangement would be detrimental to the estate. In re Estate of Pfahler (Crawford 1989) 64 Ohio App.3d 331, 581 N.E.2d 602.

5. Discretion of court

RC 2113.05 vests authority in the probate court to exercise discretion in determining if an applicant for letters testamentary is a suitable person; an order granting or refusing letters of appointment is reversible only upon a finding of an abuse of discretion. In re Henne's Estate (Ohio 1981) 66 Ohio St.2d 232, 421 N.E.2d 506, 20 O.O.3d 228. Executors And Administrators 20(10)

A probate court is under no duty to appoint a nonresident corporation, licensed to do business in Ohio, as executor of the estate of a resident testator who designated such corporation to act in that capacity. In re Emery (Hamilton 1978) 59 Ohio App.2d 7, 391 N.E.2d 746, 13 O.O.3d 44, 9 A.L.R.4th 1214.

A probate court has authority to exercise reasonable discretion in determining if an applicant for letters testamentary is a competent and suitable person, and an order granting or refusing letters of appointment is reviewable by a determination of whether there has been an abuse of discretion. In re Young's Estate (Franklin 1964) 4 Ohio App.2d 315, 212 N.E.2d 612, 33 O.O.2d 357, appeal dismissed 177 Ohio St. 76, 202 N.E.2d 308, 29 O.O.2d 196. Executors And Administrators 15; Executors And Administrators 20(10)

Although the refusal of the probate court to consider the application of the next of kin or of a creditor for letters of administration may be reviewed in the common pleas court, that court will not disturb a finding of the probate court of the unsuitability of the next of kin or the incompetence of the applying creditor unless it appears that the probate court abused its discretion. McCallip v. Sharp (Ohio Com.Pl. 1903) 13 Ohio Dec. 650, affirmed 81 Ohio St. 520, 91 N.E. 1133, 7 Ohio Law Rep. 499.

If executrix named in will should refuse to employ counsel named by testatrix, court should not refuse to permit her to qualify as such executrix. In re Shinnick's Estate (Ohio Prob. 1935) 1 Ohio Supp. 394, 19 Ohio Law Abs. 461, 3 O.O. 458.

The trial court abused its discretion in denying the appointment of the executor named in decedent's will on the grounds that hostility was present between the named executor and beneficiaries where the beneficiaries' objections to the named executor are based on dissatisfaction that a member of the family was not named executor. In re Estate of Schill, No. 83-02-014 (12th Dist Ct App, Butler, 7-20-83).

6. Other suitable persons, construed

Removal of executrix and appointment of her successor were erroneous, where notice of removal was lacking and attorney was appointed, rather than consideration to decedent's children other than executrix or those indebted to estate. In re Mizer (Ohio App. 5 Dist., Tuscarawas, 02-24-2005) No. 2004 AP 04 0035, 2005-Ohio-862, 2005 WL 469268, Unreported. Executors And Administrators 35(13)

Appointing attorney as special administratrix was not an abuse of discretion in that nominated executrix and remainder of testatrix' family were not suitable persons; family of testatrix joined in will contest challenging validity of will naming testatrix' former live-in companion as sole legatee. Gockel v. Eble (Ohio App. 8 Dist., 10-17-1994) 98 Ohio App.3d 281, 648 N.E.2d 539, dismissed, appeal not allowed 71 Ohio St.3d 1491, 646 N.E.2d 466. Executors And Administrators 22(1)

2113.06 To whom letters of administration shall be granted

Administration of the estate of an intestate shall be granted to persons mentioned in this section, in the following order:

(A) To the surviving spouse of the deceased, if resident of the state;

(B) To one of the next of kin of the deceased, resident of the state.

If the persons entitled to administer the estate fail to take or renounce administration voluntarily, they shall be cited by the probate court for that purpose.

If there are no persons entitled to administration, or if they are for any reason unsuitable for the discharge of the trust, or if without sufficient cause they neglect to apply within a reasonable time for the administration of the estate, their right to priority shall be lost, and the court shall commit the administration to some suitable person who is a resident of the state, or to the attorney general or the attorney general's designee, if the department of job and family services is seeking to recover medical assistance from the deceased pursuant to section 5111.11 or 5111.111 of the Revised Code. Such person may be a creditor of the estate.

This section applies to the appointment of an administrator de bonis non.

(1999 H 471, eff. 7–1–00; 1995 H 167, eff. 11–15–95; 1976 S 466, eff. 5–26–76; 1975 S 145; 1953 H 1; GC 10509–3)

Uncodified Law

1975 S 145, § 3, eff. 11–28–75, reads: Sections 1 and 2 of this act shall take effect on January 1, 1976, and apply only to estate resulting from deaths that occur on and after that date.

Historical and Statutory Notes

Pre–1953 H 1 Amendments: 116 v 385; 114 v 401

Amendment Note: 1999 H 471 substituted "job and family" for "human" in the second paragraph in division (B).

Amendment Note: 1995 H 167 inserted ", or to the attorney general or the attorney general's designee, if the department of human services is seeking to recover medical assistance from the deceased pursuant to section 5111.11 or 5111.111 of the Revised Code".

Cross References

Probate court jurisdiction, 2101.24

Library References

Executors and Administrators ⚖14, 17(1) to 17(3), 27.
Westlaw Topic No. 162.
C.J.S. Executors and Administrators §§ 17 to 21, 34 to 37, 79.

Research References

Encyclopedias

OH Jur. 3d Actions § 145, Parties to be Substituted.
OH Jur. 3d Decedents' Estates § 868, Jurisdiction of Probate Court.
OH Jur. 3d Decedents' Estates § 919, Renunciation Of, or Failure to Accept, Appointment—Effect Where No Other Executor Named.
OH Jur. 3d Decedents' Estates § 924, Preferential Rights to Appointment, Generally.
OH Jur. 3d Decedents' Estates § 925, Surviving Spouse.
OH Jur. 3d Decedents' Estates § 927, Surviving Spouse—Effect of Divorce.
OH Jur. 3d Decedents' Estates § 928, Next of Kin.
OH Jur. 3d Decedents' Estates § 929, Next of Kin—Who Are Next of Kin.
OH Jur. 3d Decedents' Estates § 930, Other Suitable Persons.
OH Jur. 3d Decedents' Estates § 931, Other Suitable Persons—Creditors.
OH Jur. 3d Decedents' Estates § 933, Other Suitable Persons—Representative of Foreign Government.
OH Jur. 3d Decedents' Estates § 937, Residence Required.
OH Jur. 3d Decedents' Estates § 938, Meaning of "Competent" and "Suitable", Generally; Discretion of Court.
OH Jur. 3d Decedents' Estates § 940, Meaning of "Competent" and "Suitable", Generally; Discretion of Court—Effect of Minority.
OH Jur. 3d Decedents' Estates § 945, Time for Application.
OH Jur. 3d Decedents' Estates § 946, Time for Application—Waiver by Delay or Lapse of Time.
OH Jur. 3d Decedents' Estates § 947, Citation.
OH Jur. 3d Decedents' Estates § 983, Appointment.
OH Jur. 3d Decedents' Estates § 1703, Duties and Powers of Special Administrator.
OH Jur. 3d Fiduciaries § 9, Qualification; Residency.
OH Jur. 3d Parties § 9, Who is a Real Party in Interest.
OH Jur. 3d Parties § 82, Death of a Party.

Treatises and Practice Aids

Klein, Darling, & Terez, Baldwin's Ohio Practice Civil Practice § 25:8, Death of a Party--Motion for Substitution--In General.
Sowald & Morganstern, Baldwin's Ohio Practice Domestic Relations Law § 1:5, Terms.
Carlin, Baldwin's Ohio Practice, Merrick-Rippner Probate Law § 2:8, Preparation and Execution of Necessary Documents.
Carlin, Baldwin's Ohio Practice, Merrick-Rippner Probate Law § 2:15, Appointment of Fiduciary—Appointment of Executor or Administrator.
Carlin, Baldwin's Ohio Practice, Merrick-Rippner Probate Law § 68:1, Letters—in General—Jurisdiction.
Carlin, Baldwin's Ohio Practice, Merrick-Rippner Probate Law § 68:2, Letters—in General—Issuance.
Carlin, Baldwin's Ohio Practice, Merrick-Rippner Probate Law § 68:3, Letters of Administration—General Qualifications of Administrators.
Carlin, Baldwin's Ohio Practice, Merrick-Rippner Probate Law § 68:5, Letters of Administration—Specific Qualifications of Administrators—Preference of Suitable Persons—Surviving Spouse.
Carlin, Baldwin's Ohio Practice, Merrick-Rippner Probate Law § 68:6, Letters of Administration—Specific Qualifications of Administrators—Preference of Suitable Persons—Next of Kin.
Carlin, Baldwin's Ohio Practice, Merrick-Rippner Probate Law § 70:1, Administrator De Bonis Non—Necessity.
Carlin, Baldwin's Ohio Practice, Merrick-Rippner Probate Law § 86:1, Death of Claimant—Substitution of Parties.
Carlin, Baldwin's Ohio Practice, Merrick-Rippner Probate Law § 2:121, Administration of Decedent's Estate—Checklist.
Carlin, Baldwin's Ohio Practice, Merrick-Rippner Probate Law § 52:40, Bond of Administrator—Form.
Carlin, Baldwin's Ohio Practice, Merrick-Rippner Probate Law § 68:11, Letters of Administration—Specific Qualifications of Administrators—Unsuitable Persons—Next of Kin.
Carlin, Baldwin's Ohio Practice, Merrick-Rippner Probate Law § 68:14, Letters of Administration—Discretion of Probate Court in Appointing Administrators; Appeal.
Carlin, Baldwin's Ohio Practice, Merrick-Rippner Probate Law § 68:16, Letters of Administration—Waiver of Right to Appointment.
Carlin, Baldwin's Ohio Practice, Merrick-Rippner Probate Law § 68:18, Letters Testamentary—Letters of Administration With the Will Annexed.
Carlin, Baldwin's Ohio Practice, Merrick-Rippner Probate Law § 68:42, Application for Authority to Administer Estate—Form.
Carlin, Baldwin's Ohio Practice, Merrick-Rippner Probate Law § 68:45, Waiver of Right to Administer—Form.
Carlin, Baldwin's Ohio Practice, Merrick-Rippner Probate Law § 84:10, Creditor's Claims—Claims Requiring Presentation—Examples from Case Law—Personal Injury Actions.
Carlin, Baldwin's Ohio Practice, Merrick-Rippner Probate Law App B SPF 4.0, Application for Authority to Administer Estate.
Carlin, Baldwin's Ohio Practice, Merrick-Rippner Probate Law App B SPF 4.4, Notice and Citation of Hearing on Appointment of Fiduciary.

Law Review and Journal Commentaries

Acknowledgement of Paternity—Changes in Statutes and Forms, Angela G. Carlin. 10 Prob L J Ohio 10 (September/October 1999).

Notes of Decisions

In general 1
Determination of suitability 3
Priority of persons entitled to administer estate 2
Procedural issues 6
Review of appointment or refusal 4

Statute of limitation; reasonable time 5

1. In general

An administration de son tort is not recognized in Ohio. Dixon v. Cassell (Ohio 1832) 5 Ohio 533.

A separation agreement whereby a husband releases all right to administer his wife's estate is enforceable after the wife's death and a court errs in setting aside the agreement and in denying a motion to remove the husband as administrator where the language of the separation agreement evidences intent that it be binding in the absence of a decree. In Matter of Driggers v. Osdyke (Ohio App. 11 Dist., Portage, 11-22-1996) No. 96-P-0004, 1996 WL 704339, Unreported.

Where one has a claim against an estate, it is incumbent upon him, if no administrator has been appointed, to procure the appointment of an administrator against whom he can proceed. Wrinkle v. Trabert (Ohio 1963) 174 Ohio St. 233, 188 N.E.2d 587, 22 O.O.2d 248. Limitation Of Actions ⇐ 83(2)

Where a will is duly proved it is mandatory upon the court to appoint the person therein named if he is legally competent and offers proper bond. In re Sultzbach (Ohio Prob. 1896) 5 Ohio Dec. 516, 5 Ohio N.P. 218.

2. Priority of persons entitled to administer estate

Probate court must appoint administrator of an estate from the preferred class described by section, if there is a competent person in such preferred class, and mere fact that all of the next of kin, entitled to administer an estate, have neither waived nor renounced in favor of an applicant and that such next of kin are unable to agree among themselves as to which of their number may administer said estate, does not constitute grounds in law for dismissal of application of a member of preferred class. In re Froebe's Estate (Logan 1938) 27 Ohio Law Abs. 594. Executors And Administrators ⇐ 17(1)

Appointing attorney as special administratrix was not an abuse of discretion in that nominated executrix and remainder of testatrix' family were not suitable persons; family of testatrix joined in will contest challenging validity of will naming testatrix' former live-in companion as sole legatee. Gockel v. Eble (Ohio App. 8 Dist., 10-17-1994) 98 Ohio App.3d 281, 648 N.E.2d 539, dismissed, appeal not allowed 71 Ohio St.3d 1491, 646 N.E.2d 466. Executors And Administrators ⇐ 22(1)

Where no action has been taken in the administration of an estate, the waiver of an heir of his right to appointment may be withdrawn. In re Garvin's Estate (Ohio Prob. 1961) 175 N.E.2d 551, 85 Ohio Law Abs. 560.

The provisions of RC 2113.06 setting forth the persons to whom, and the order in which, letters of administration shall be granted, are mandatory and require the probate court to appoint an administrator of an estate from the preferred class therein described. In re Vickers' Estate (Vinton 1959) 110 Ohio App. 499, 170 Ohio 2d 85, 13 O.O.2d 274. Executors And Administrators ⇐ 17(1)

An adult man and woman, each owning a substantial amount of property and each having grown children by prior marriages, may lawfully enter into a prenuptial agreement whereby each relinquishes every and all rights in the property of the other, and where such an agreement is duly executed, the parties subsequently marry and thereafter the husband dies, the widow is barred from any part of his estate, including the special benefits conferred on the widow by statute and the privilege of administering the estate, where the agreement by its clear wording shows that such a result was intended. Troha v. Sneller (Ohio 1959) 169 Ohio St. 397, 159 N.E.2d 899, 8 O.O.2d 435. Descent And Distribution ⇐ 62; Executors And Administrators ⇐ 19; Executors And Administrators ⇐ 185

A provision in a separation agreement that the parties thereto waive such rights as they may have to administer the estates of each other is a waiver of priority but not an absolute bar to such appointment. In re Williams' Estate (Ohio Prob. 1958) 153 N.E.2d 727, 79 Ohio Law Abs. 592.

Where a man and woman enter into a prenuptial agreement whereby each relinquishes all rights in the property of the other, the parties thereafter marry, and, subsequently, while they are on a trip to Europe, the husband dies, but the widow does not accompany his body on its return home but continues on the European trip for a period of three months without evincing any interest in the affairs of her deceased husband, she is barred from all rights in his estate, including statutory benefits and the priority in the right to administer the estate. Troha v. Sneller (Cuyahoga 1958) 108 Ohio App. 153, 151 N.E.2d 595, 79 Ohio Law Abs. 74, 9 O.O.2d 195, affirmed 169 Ohio St. 397, 159 N.E.2d 899, 8 O.O.2d 435.

The term, "next of kin," as used in GC 10509-3 (RC 2113.06) means only those persons who are entitled to inherit all or some portion of the estate of the deceased, and a person who is entitled to inherit nothing from the estate has no priority in appointment as administrator of the estate and has no capacity to attack the appointment of another person. In re Kelly's Estate (Franklin 1956) 102 Ohio App. 518, 144 N.E.2d 130, 3 O.O.2d 56. Executors And Administrators ⇐ 17(2)

"Next of kin" is used to signify the relations of a party who has died intestate, those relatives who would inherit in case of intestacy. Wimmer v. DeWeese (Miami 1951) 108 N.E.2d 165, 62 Ohio Law Abs. 577. Descent And Distribution ⇐ 21

Next of kin as provided in this section means those who would inherit in case of intestacy and the provisions of GC 10503-2 (RC 2105.03) have no application for determining the right of appointment as administrator. In re Applegate's Estate (Ohio Prob. 1951) 100 N.E.2d 322, 61 Ohio Law Abs. 277, 45 O.O. 24.

Where decedent's only blood relatives resident in county or state and entitled to receive anything under statutes of descent and distribution were minor grandchildren who were incompetent to administer estate, decedent's nephew, nieces and cousins, residents of state, were not "next of kin", and hence, were not entitled to priority of appointment as administrator de bonis non over a resident trust company. In re Cassell's Estate (Ohio Prob. 1948) 83 N.E.2d 72, 53 Ohio Law Abs. 65. Executors And Administrators ⇐ 17(2)

Provisions of section are mandatory and when a surviving spouse is a minor, one of next of kin of deceased and a resident of the county is entitled to appointment as administrator in absence of incompetency, unsuitability or neglect; right of priority of next of kin is not dependent upon extent of his interest in assets of estate. In re Golembiewski's Estate (Ohio 1946) 146 Ohio St. 551, 67 N.E.2d 328, 33 O.O. 41. Executors And Administrators ⇐ 17(3)

Under section, resident surviving spouse is entitled to priority in appointment as administrator of estate of an intestate unless such spouse is incompetent or is for any reason unsuitable for discharge of trust or has without sufficient cause neglected to apply within a reasonable time for administration of estate; in event of such incompetency, unsuitability or neglect, spouse's right to priority is lost. Where incompetency exists by reason of minority, a guardian of spouse is not eligible as such for appointment as administrator. In re Golembiewski's Estate (Ohio 1946) 146 Ohio St. 551, 67 N.E.2d 328, 33 O.O. 41. Executors And Administrators ⇐ 17(3)

Under section relating to granting of letters of administration, a grandson of decedent comes within meaning of "next of kin" even if there are surviving children of decedent; thus a grandson who is a resident of the county in which decedent died, is to be preferred for appointment as administrator, over a son of decedent, who is a resident of another county in the state. In re Fields' Estate (Greene 1944) 65 N.E.2d 70, 44 Ohio Law Abs. 284.

Where deceased leaves only a minor child as his only next of kin, probate court may, in its discretion, appoint deceased's mother-in-law as administrator of estate rather than deceased's brother; there is nothing in this section compelling court to appoint, in absence of next of kin, nearest relative in direct line. Shannon v. Hendrixson (Clermont 1935) 32 N.E.2d 431, 20 Ohio Law Abs. 316, 4 O.O. 517.

An Italian consul is not entitled by treaty or by former GC 10617 (RC 2113.06, RC 2113.07), to be appointed administrator of an intestate Italian where one of the next of kin is a resident of the state; nor is he entitled to notice of the death unless there are no known heirs here, and he is a resident of the county or has a representative in the county duly certified to the court. (See also Pagano v Cerri, 93 OS 345, 112 NE 1037 (1916); In re Estate of Balbo, 16 NP(NS) 9, 29 D 603 (1914).) In re Todarello's Estate (Ohio Prob. 1913) 15 Ohio NP(NS) 593, 62 W.L.B. 201.

RS 6005, defining who shall have the right to administer, vests legal right to administer in the order named, which the court cannot ignore and which cannot be waived except by persons having the right. Fox v. Kiester (Ohio Com.Pl. 1899) 8 Ohio Dec. 636, 6 Ohio N.P. 216.

Anyone entitled under section to administer an estate may decline and designate some other person, subject to approval of court, to act in his place, but the probate court is without power or authority to appoint the nominee over the protest of any one of the class entitled under section to administer. In re Welch's Estate (Ohio Prob. 1939) 1 Ohio Supp. 14, 29 Ohio Law Abs. 144, 15 O.O. 189.

The probate court properly vacated the appointment of the applicant as administratrix to the decedent's estate on the grounds that such applicant is not the surviving spouse of the decedent where evidence showed that the decedent had refused to go through with a formal marriage and had signed an oil and gas lease indicating he was single since such is sufficient evidence to refute the claim of common law marriage. Estate of Yerke v Yerke, No. 82 CA 27 (7th Dist Ct App, Mahoning, 4–15–83).

In the selection of administrators the provisions of RS 6005 are extended to the husband or widow, next of kin, or creditors, over strangers. In re Estate of Arkenberg, 1 NP(NS) 9, 13 D 656 (CP, Shelby 1903).

The probate court may not issue letters testamentary to a surviving partner causing the estate of the deceased partner to be administered without citing the widow or next of kin, if residents of the same county as the decedent's estate, to accept or reject the appointment, even though thirty days has elapsed since the death and they made no application for administration. Warnock v Page, 14 D 278 (CP, Franklin 1903), affirmed by 15 CD 695, 2 LR 528 (Franklin 1904).

3. Determination of suitability

A foreign creditor can take out letters though a foreign administrator has been appointed. Bustard v. Dabney (Ohio 1829) 4 Ohio 68.

A bill in equity to subject the real estate of a decedent who resided in Ohio, where the heirs reside in another state and no letters of administration have been taken in Ohio, cannot be sustained, but the creditor may take letters of administration and have a complete remedy in law. Bustard v. Dabney (Ohio 1829) 4 Ohio 68.

Lack of expertise in a specialized area is not the equivalent of unsuitability to serve as executor of estate. In re Estate of Tyler (Ohio Com.Pl., 04-07-1999) 100 Ohio Misc.2d 17, 716 N.E.2d 1239. Executors And Administrators ⚖ 15

Daughter of testator, who was named as devisee in will and would have been person entitled to administer estate if testator had died intestate, would be appointed as administrator with will annexed after individual appointed as executor in will declined to accept appointment; while bank named in will as beneficiary trustee may have had areas of greater expertise, nothing indicated that daughter was unsuitable or incompetent to serve as administrator. In re Estate of Tyler (Ohio Com.Pl., 04-07-1999) 100 Ohio Misc.2d 17, 716 N.E.2d 1239. Executors And Administrators ⚖ 18

Trial court finding that no present agreement to remarry existed between decedent and his divorced spouse, disqualifying spouse from serving as administrator of decedent's intestate estate as "surviving spouse," was supported by evidence that decedent and former spouse declared themselves single on federal and state income tax forms and bankruptcy petitions, former spouse shipped decedent's possessions to him when he lived in another state, decedent dated other women, and that parties intended to remarry in the future, despite cohabitation immediately before decedent's death. In re Estate of Shepherd (Ohio App. 3 Dist., 10-25-1994) 97 Ohio App.3d 280, 646 N.E.2d 561. Executors And Administrators ⚖ 17(3); Executors And Administrators ⚖ 20(7)

"Next of kin" for purposes of RC 2113.06 means individuals entitled to inherit all or part of the decedent's estate; thus, a divorced decedent's minor children are her next of kin, and their father may be appointed administrator of his former wife's estate under RC 2113.06 as a "suitable person" even though he is no longer eligible for appointment as a "surviving spouse." In re Estate of Robertson (Cuyahoga 1985) 26 Ohio App.3d 64, 498 N.E.2d 206, 26 O.B.R. 238.

The surviving spouse of a common-law marriage may be a suitable person under the provision of RC 2113.06 to be granted letters of administration. In re Hammonds' Estate (Ohio Com.Pl. 1973) 39 Ohio Misc. 96, 315 N.E.2d 843, 67 O.O.2d 27, 68 O.O.2d 267. Executors And Administrators ⚖ 17(3)

Where the priority as a matter of right is exhausted for lack of eligible persons, the probate court, in committing administration "to some suitable person resident of the county" is not compelled to appoint the nearest relative in the direct line of inheritance. In re Williams' Estate (Ohio Prob. 1958) 153 N.E.2d 727, 79 Ohio Law Abs. 592.

Where the widow applies for letters and a son of the deceased resists, the court may appoint the widow unless good cause is shown why it should not be done; an agreement to live separate in consideration of the payment of a certain sum and agreeing to make no claim against the property of her husband will not prevent the widow from being appointed. Garretson v. Garretson (Ohio Cir. 1890) 2 Ohio C.D. 581, affirmed.

The right extends to the Italian consul to be appointed administrator of the estate of a citizen of Italy who died in this county, notwithstanding the provisions of RS 6005 as to whom letters of administration shall be granted. In re Arduino's Estate (Ohio Com.Pl. 1909) 20 Ohio Dec. 461, 9 Ohio NP(NS) 369.

A treaty between the United States and a foreign government may provide the consul of that country the right to intervene in the administration of the estate of a citizen of that country. In re Arduino's Estate (Ohio Com.Pl. 1909) 20 Ohio Dec. 461, 9 Ohio NP(NS) 369.

The unsuitableness of an executrix, not amounting to incapacity, is not sufficient to deny the issue of letters testamentary. In re Sells' Estate (Ohio Com.Pl. 1909) 19 Ohio Dec. 567, 8 Ohio NP(NS) 175.

The court has discretion and may refuse to appoint if the applicant is unsuitable; such unsuitableness is not overcome by the fact that he offers to give ample bond. In re Diller (Ohio Prob. 1896) 6 Ohio Dec. 182, 5 Ohio N.P. 255.

The fact that an executor is antagonistic to legatees, and that his interests are antagonistic to theirs, is not sufficient reason for the court to refuse to appoint him. In re Sultzbach (Ohio Prob. 1896) 5 Ohio Dec. 516, 5 Ohio N.P. 218.

Even where the interests of the named executor are hostile to the other legatees, he must be appointed by the court if he is legally competent under the statute and offers proper bond. In re Sultzbach (Ohio Prob. 1896) 5 Ohio Dec. 516, 5 Ohio N.P. 218.

One need not be mentally or morally incompetent to justify the court in refusing to appoint him, if his appointment would be detrimental to the estate; one having a claim antagonistic to the devisees or legatees will not be appointed. In re Brennan (Ohio Prob. 1898) 5 Ohio Dec. 499, 5 Ohio N.P. 490.

An administrator ought to be one in whom all interested parties have complete confidence, and if the next of kin does not include such a person, the court may appoint a stranger. In re Brennan (Ohio Prob. 1898) 5 Ohio Dec. 499, 5 Ohio N.P. 490.

Surviving spouse of common law marriage is unsuitable person to be granted letters of administration. In re Woods' Estate (Ohio Prob. 1941) 6 Ohio Supp. 236, 34 Ohio Law Abs. 169, 21 O.O. 98.

One who has applied for letters of administration, and who clearly indicates that he does not intend to pursue an underinsured motorists' claim that would benefit the estate, is "unsuitable" to administer the subject estate, pursuant to RC 2113.06. In re Estate of Stanley, No. E–83–25 (6th Dist Ct App, Erie, 3–9–84).

Where an attorney represented a creditor of decedent's estate but the relationship between such attorney and creditor has terminated, the probate court may properly appoint the attorney as administrator de bonis non to the estate. Estate of Danolfo v Laird, No. 45197 (8th Dist Ct App, Cuyahoga, 5–12–83).

The secretary of state has no duty to accept for filing the articles of incorporation of a corporation other than a trust company, the purpose of which is to engage in the business of serving, for hire, as executor, administrator and guardian. 1956 OAG 6200.

4. Review of appointment or refusal

Review may be had in a common pleas court of an order of a probate court denying next of kin to administer the estate. Schumacher v. McCallip (Ohio 1904) 69 Ohio St. 500, 69 N.E. 986, 1 Ohio Law Rep. 789, 1 Ohio Law Rep. 945.

The court of common pleas has jurisdiction to review an order of the probate court denying the right to administer the estate of a deceased person which the statute confers upon the next of kin, if a suitable person. Schumacher v. McCallip (Ohio 1904) 69 Ohio St. 500, 69 N.E. 986, 1 Ohio Law Rep. 789, 1 Ohio Law Rep. 945. Courts ⚖ 202(5); Executors And Administrators ⚖ 20(10)

Other things being equal, the court will appoint as administrator the one desired by the beneficiaries; the appointment will not be set aside merely because the reviewing court might have made another selection. Sargent v. Corbley (Ohio Cir. 1905) 18 Ohio C.D. 125, 7 Ohio C.C.N.S. 226.

Where two parties are equally suitable, and have equal statutory right, a court may choose, without abusing its discretion, the one favored by the major portion of the trust's beneficiaries, and this choice does not furnish any grounds for review. Sargent v. Corbley (Ohio Cir. 1905) 18 Ohio C.D. 125, 7 Ohio C.C.N.S. 226.

Error does not lie to a removal, though it does to an order denying the right of a certain person to administer under RS 6005. In re Ferguson's Estate (Ohio Com.Pl. 1904) 16 Ohio Dec. 486, 3 Ohio NP(NS) 549.

Although the refusal of the probate court to consider the application of the next of kin or of a creditor for letters of administration may be reviewed in the common pleas court, that court will not disturb a finding of

Note 4

the probate court of the unsuitability of the next of kin or the incompetence of the applying creditor unless it appears that the probate court abused its discretion. McCallip v. Sharp (Ohio Com.Pl. 1903) 13 Ohio Dec. 650, affirmed 81 Ohio St. 520, 91 N.E. 1133, 7 Ohio Law Rep. 499.

If any presumption arises, it is that an administrator is beneficially interested in the estate, and whether an appeal is being prosecuted in the interest of the trust must be determined from the record. In re Estate of Arkenberg, 1 NP(NS) 9, 13 D 656 (CP, Shelby 1903).

5. Statute of limitation; reasonable time

Next of kin are entitled to a reasonable time in which to apply for letters of administration. Todhunter v. Stewart (Ohio 1883) 39 Ohio St. 181, 9 W.L.B. 358.

An application for letters of administration made within eighteen days after the death of the intestate by next of kin residing in another county is made within reasonable time. Todhunter v. Stewart (Ohio 1883) 39 Ohio St. 181, 9 W.L.B. 358. Executors And Administrators ⟲ 20(2).

When an action is brought by the filing of a complaint, within the statute of limitations, complainant has one year thereafter in which to cause the appointment of a suitable personal representative and obtain service of summons against him. Hayden v. Ours (Ohio Com.Pl. 1975) 44 Ohio Misc. 62, 337 N.E.2d 183, 73 O.O.2d 224. Limitation Of Actions ⟲ 83(2).

An action is not properly commenced so as to bar the defense of the statute of limitations, where such action is instituted within the statutory period of limitation against one acting as administrator whose letters of administration, although applied for within the period of limitation, were not issued until such period had elapsed. Wrinkle v. Trabert (Ohio 1963) 174 Ohio St. 233, 188 N.E.2d 587, 22 O.O.2d 248. Limitation Of Actions ⟲ 82.

When the statute of limitations on a personal injury claim began to run against a defendant during his lifetime, it is not interrupted or suspended by his death or by the absence of the appointment of an administrator. Parrish v. McKee (Ohio Com.Pl. 1956) 135 N.E.2d 486, 73 Ohio Law Abs. 65, 59 O.O. 316.

The statute of limitations does not begin to run against a debt based on a contract in writing which becomes due by reason of the decease of the debtor until the appointment of an administrator or executor on the estate of such debtor, and due notice thereof. Hoiles v. Riddle (Ohio 1906) 74 Ohio St. 173, 78 N.E. 219, 113 Am.St.Rep. 946, 4 Ohio Law Rep. 38. Limitation Of Actions ⟲ 83(2).

The next of kin of an intestate are entitled to a reasonable time within which to apply for letters of administration; and an application made within thirty days after death of the intestate, by the next of kin, residing in another county, is made within a reasonable time. In re Patterson's Estate (Ohio Com.Pl. 1927) 26 Ohio NP(NS) 580.

6. Procedural issues

Creditor who had been named special administrator of decedent's estate was "real party in interest," for purposes of his motion to be substituted as plaintiff in survival action after decedent's death, even though beneficiaries of estate did not wish to continue that action; under rule requiring that every action be prosecuted in name of real party in interest, administrator could sue in his name as representative without joining those for whose benefit action was brought. Yardley v. W. Ohio Conference of the United Methodist Church, Inc. (Ohio App. 10 Dist., 08-29-2000) 138 Ohio App.3d 872, 742 N.E.2d 723. Parties ⟲ 59(3)

Creditor who had been named special administrator of decedent's estate was entitled to be substituted as plaintiff in survival action after decedent's death, even though estate's beneficiaries did not wish to continue that action. Yardley v. W. Ohio Conference of the United Methodist Church, Inc. (Ohio App. 10 Dist., 08-29-2000) 138 Ohio App.3d 872, 742 N.E.2d 723. Parties ⟲ 59(3)

As an incident to a hearing upon an application for appointment of an administrator pursuant to RC 2113.06 the probate court has jurisdiction to determine the issue of common-law marriage. In re Hammonds' Estate (Ohio Com.Pl. 1973) 39 Ohio Misc. 96, 315 N.E.2d 843, 67 O.O.2d 27, 68 O.O.2d 267.

Where a defendant dies, the "proper party" under Civ R 25(A)(1) for purposes of substitution must be the person appointed by the probate court under RC 2113.06 based upon the representation that defendant died intestate. Highland View Hospital v. Dempsey (Ohio Mun. 1972) 33 Ohio Misc. 209, 294 N.E.2d 925, 62 O.O.2d 367.

In a negligence action for the recovery of damages, instituted under RC 2117.07 against an administrator seeking to recover only from decedent's liability insurer, where administrator of estate of decedent has been discharged and estate closed, probate court may reappoint administrator for purpose of accepting service of summons. In re George's Estate (Ohio 1970) 24 Ohio St.2d 18, 262 N.E.2d 872, 53 O.O.2d 10.

Where the final and distributive account of the administrators of an estate has been approved and settled and they have been discharged from their trust pursuant to RC 2109.32, and that order has not been vacated pursuant to RC 2109.35, where some asset remains upon which administration has not been exhausted and for some lawful purpose relating to that asset administration is required, an administrator may be appointed to complete such administration only in a manner similar to, and with the same formalities as, the original appointment of an administrator, and in such circumstances, where such asset consists of an automobile liability insurance policy of the decedent covering the claim of a person alleged to have received bodily injuries due to the alleged negligence of the decedent, such policy is an asset which will support the appointment of an administrator upon whom service may be made and with authority to defend suit. In re George's Estate (Hancock 1969) 20 Ohio App.2d 87, 252 N.E.2d 176, 49 O.O.2d 110. Executors And Administrators ⟲ 37(2); Executors And Administrators ⟲ 37(5)

Notice to the surviving spouse of admission to probate of a will and appointment of an administrator with the will annexed is not necessary if the spouse is not a resident of the state. Armstrong v. Brufach (Ohio Com.Pl. 1950) 136 N.E.2d 463, 74 Ohio Law Abs. 370, 59 O.O. 352.

Notice to the Italian consul of an application to appoint an administrator for a deceased Italian is not necessary where the applicant is a brother of decedent and a minor son eighteen years old is in court consenting thereto. In re Balbo's Estate (Ohio Prob. 1914) 29 Ohio Dec. 603, 16 Ohio NP(NS) 9.

2113.07 Application for appointment as executor or administrator

Before being appointed executor or administrator, every person shall make and file an application that shall contain the names of the surviving spouse and all the next of kin of the deceased known to the applicant, their post-office addresses if known, a statement in general terms as to what the estate consists of and its probable value, and a statement of any indebtedness the deceased had against the applicant.

The application may be accompanied by a waiver signed by the persons who have priority to administer the estate, and, in the absence of a waiver, those persons shall be cited by the probate court for the purpose of ascertaining whether they desire to take or renounce administration.

Letters of administration shall not be issued upon the estate of an intestate until the person to be appointed has made and filed a statement indicating that there is not to his knowledge a last will and testament of the intestate.

(1992 H 427, eff. 10–8–92; 1975 S 145; 1953 H 1; GC 10509–4)

Historical and Statutory Notes

Pre–1953 H 1 Amendments: 116 v Pt 2, 28; 116 v 307; 114 v 401

Cross References

Inheritance by parent of deceased abandoned child prohibited, 2105.10

Library References

Executors and Administrators ⟲20(5).
Westlaw Topic No. 162.
C.J.S. Executors and Administrators §§ 53, 59.

Research References

Encyclopedias

OH Jur. 3d Decedents' Estates § 136, Abandoning a Minor Child.
OH Jur. 3d Decedents' Estates § 944, Requirements as to Application.
OH Jur. 3d Decedents' Estates § 947, Citation.

Forms

Am. Jur. Pl & Pr Forms Executors & Administrators § 77, Ohio.

Treatises and Practice Aids

Carlin, Baldwin's Ohio Practice, Merrick-Rippner Probate Law § 81:4, Removal—Voidable Appointment.

Carlin, Baldwin's Ohio Practice, Merrick-Rippner Probate Law § 9:12, Presumption of Death—Judgment Entry—Form.

Carlin, Baldwin's Ohio Practice, Merrick-Rippner Probate Law § 2:121, Administration of Decedent's Estate—Checklist.

Carlin, Baldwin's Ohio Practice, Merrick-Rippner Probate Law § 68:41, List of Beneficiaries—Form.

Carlin, Baldwin's Ohio Practice, Merrick-Rippner Probate Law § 68:42, Application for Authority to Administer Estate—Form.

Carlin, Baldwin's Ohio Practice, Merrick-Rippner Probate Law § 68:46, Notice of Hearing on Appointment of Fiduciary—Form.

Carlin, Baldwin's Ohio Practice, Merrick-Rippner Probate Law App B SPF 1.0, Surviving Spouse, Children, Next of Kin, Legatees and Devisees.

Carlin, Baldwin's Ohio Practice, Merrick-Rippner Probate Law App B SPF 4.4, Notice and Citation of Hearing on Appointment of Fiduciary.

Law Review and Journal Commentaries

Practical Application of House Bill 85 (Probate Reform 2001), Marilyn J. Maag. 13 Prob L J Ohio 19 (November/December 2002).

Notes of Decisions

Ed. Note: This section contains annotations from former RC 2113.08.

Prenuptial agreements 1
Procedural issues 3
Requirements for application 2

---

1. Prenuptial agreements

Executor's principal duty was to accomplish testator's purpose by protecting, preserving, and distributing assets in accordance with provisions of will; accordingly, absent allegations as to invalidity of will, executor was required to determine whether antenuptial agreement between testator and her husband, which required testator to leave her entire estate to her stepchildren, was in fact valid, whether it had been revoked or modified, whether testator had breached agreement by executing new will after husband's death, and whether there were any defenses to stepchildren's action for breach of the agreement. In re Estate of Dawson (Ohio App. 2 Dist., 12-27-1996) 117 Ohio App.3d 51, 689 N.E.2d 1008. Executors And Administrators ⟐ 81

An adult man and woman, each owning a substantial amount of property and each having grown children by prior marriages, may lawfully enter into a prenuptial agreement whereby each relinquishes every and all rights in the property of the other, and where such an agreement is duly executed, the parties subsequently marry and thereafter the husband dies, the widow is barred from any part of his estate, including the special benefits conferred on the widow by statute and the privilege of administering the estate, where the agreement by its clear wording shows that such a result was intended. Troha v. Sneller (Ohio 1959) 169 Ohio St. 397, 159 N.E.2d 899, 8 O.O.2d 435. Descent And Distribution ⟐ 62; Executors And Administrators ⟐ 19; Executors And Administrators ⟐ 185

Where a man and woman enter into a prenuptial agreement whereby each relinquishes all rights in the property of the other, the parties thereafter marry, and, subsequently, while they are on a trip to Europe, the husband dies, but the widow does not accompany his body on its return home but continues on the European trip for a period of three months without evincing any interest in the affairs of her deceased husband, she is barred from all rights in his estate, including statutory benefits and the priority in the right to administer the estate. Troha v. Sneller (Cuyahoga 1958) 108 Ohio App. 153, 151 N.E.2d 595, 79 Ohio Law Abs. 74, 9 O.O.2d 195, affirmed 169 Ohio St. 397, 159 N.E.2d 899, 8 O.O.2d 435.

2. Requirements for application

A notice of appointment is good even when it consists merely of a demand officially signed by the administrator that all persons indebted to the estate come forward and make payment, and all persons having claims are notified to present them. Gilbert v. Little's Adm'r (Ohio 1853) 2 Ohio St. 156. Executors And Administrators ⟐ 27

The appointment of an executor or administrator of an estate, without the latter filing a statement of any indebtedness owed by kin to the estate is voidable and not void. McKelvey v. McKelvey (Holmes 1951) 90 Ohio App. 563, 107 N.E.2d 555, 48 O.O. 207. Executors And Administrators ⟐ 29(4)

Where an application for appointment as administrator is not accompanied by a waiver signed by resident next of kin and the applicant has not been cited to determine whether he desires to take or renounce such administration, a motion for removal of the administrator will be granted. In re Applegate's Estate (Ohio Prob. 1951) 100 N.E.2d 322, 61 Ohio Law Abs. 277, 45 O.O. 24.

Jurisdiction of probate court acquired under GC 10509–1 (RC 2113.01) to appoint administrator for estate of intestate who was resident of county of such court at time he died is terminated and superseded by admission to probate of will of same decedent by probate court of another county in which decedent was domiciled at time of death; making and filing of affidavit by person to be appointed administrator that there is not to his knowledge a last will and testament of intestate is condition precedent to granting of letters of administration of estate. State ex rel. Overlander v. Brewer (Ohio 1947) 147 Ohio St. 386, 72 N.E.2d 84, 34 O.O. 338.

3. Procedural issues

Trial court error, if any, in failing to conduct an evidentiary hearing on the issue of appointment of three co-executors for estate was invited error, where son, who sought to be appointed co-executor of estate with his two sisters, agreed to submit the issue on briefs, depositions, and exhibits in lieu of an evidentiary hearing, son alleged after the depositions had occurred that he had a digital recording that allegedly impeached the testimony of his sisters and brother, and son's failure to inform his attorney of the recording before the depositions prevented the attorney from cross-examining son's siblings about the recording during the depositions. In re Estate of Laffin (Ohio App. 3 Dist., Auglaize, 06-05-2006) No. 2-05-41, 2006-Ohio-2779, 2006 WL 1519906, Unreported. Executors And Administrators ⟐ 20(10)

Woman who filed application for authority to administer decedent's estate was not suitable person to serve as fiduciary of estate, even if she was surviving spouse of decedent, where applicant, without letters of appointment, negotiated some checks made payable to estate, gave tacit permission to other members of her family to take certain guns and other items of personal property belonging to decedent, without grant of letters of authority from probate court and prior to appointment of fiduciary, and suffered certain physical health problems including restricted mobility, and court determined that it would be in best interests of all concerned for neutral third-party with knowledge of probate law to be appointed as fiduciary. In re Estate of Dalton (Ohio Com.Pl., 01-27-1995) 68 Ohio Misc.2d 78, 647 N.E.2d 581. Executors And Administrators ⟐ 17(3)

Determinations of the probate court in the administration of an estate overruling exceptions to the inventory filed by the executor and refusing to remove such executor in removal proceedings brought against him do not estop the institution of concealment proceedings against him by an administrator, subsequently appointed with the will annexed, for concealment of assets of the estate during the time he served as executor, where the subject matter and the issues involved in such prior proceedings were not identical with those in the subsequent concealment proceedings. Gordon v. Dewan (Hamilton 1964) 4 Ohio App.2d 214, 202 N.E.2d 325, 33 O.O.2d 254.

The next of kin of an intestate are entitled to a reasonable time within which to apply for letters of administration; and an application made within thirty days after death of the intestate, by the next of kin, residing in another county, is made within a reasonable time. In re Patterson's Estate (Ohio Com.Pl. 1927) 26 Ohio NP(NS) 580.

2113.11 Notice when deceased was an alien

Upon the filing of an application for appointment as executor or administrator of the estate of a deceased alien with surviving heirs residing in a foreign country, or as soon thereafter during the administration of the estate as the probate court ascertains that the deceased was an alien, the court shall cause notice of the proceedings to be forwarded by registered mail to the nearest consular representative of the country of which the deceased was a citizen. The executor or administrator shall inform the court that the deceased was an alien as soon as such fact is ascertained by such executor or administrator, but failure to inform the court of such fact or to notify such consular representative as provided in this section shall not delay nor invalidate the administration proceedings or any part thereof.

(1953 H 1, eff. 10–1–53; GC 10509–8)

Historical and Statutory Notes

Pre–1953 H 1 Amendments: 114 v 402

Cross References

Service of notice, Civ R 73

Library References

Executors and Administrators ⚖20(4), 517.
Westlaw Topic No. 162.
C.J.S. Executors and Administrators §§ 53, 58, 915.

Research References

Encyclopedias

OH Jur. 3d Decedents' Estates § 933, Other Suitable Persons—Representative of Foreign Government.
OH Jur. 3d Decedents' Estates § 949, Notice to Consular Officer of Application for Appointment as Executor or Administrator of Estate of Deceased Alien.

Treatises and Practice Aids

Carlin, Baldwin's Ohio Practice, Merrick-Rippner Probate Law § 68:51, Notice to Consul for Foreign Heir—Form.

2113.12 Procedure if executor renounces

If a person named as executor in the will of a decedent, or nominated as an executor by holders of a power as described in section 2107.65 of the Revised Code, refuses to accept the trust, or, if after being cited for that purpose, neglects to appear and accept, or if he neglects for twenty days after the probate of the will to give any required bond, the probate court shall grant letters testamentary to the other executor, if there is one capable and willing to accept the trust, and if there is no such other executor named in the will or nominated by holders of a power as described in section 2107.65 of the Revised Code, the court shall commit administration of the estate, with the will annexed, to some suitable and competent person, pursuant to section 2113.05 of the Revised Code.

(1983 S 115, eff. 10–14–83; 1970 S 134; 1953 H 1; GC 10509–10)

Historical and Statutory Notes

Pre–1953 H 1 Amendments: 116 v 385; 114 v 403

Library References

Executors and Administrators ⚖19.
Westlaw Topic No. 162.
C.J.S. Executors and Administrators §§ 50 to 51.

Research References

Encyclopedias

OH Jur. 3d Decedents' Estates § 908, Joint Letters of Administration.
OH Jur. 3d Decedents' Estates § 918, Renunciation Of, or Failure to Accept, Appointment—Effect Where Second Executor Named.
OH Jur. 3d Decedents' Estates § 919, Renunciation Of, or Failure to Accept, Appointment—Effect Where No Other Executor Named.
OH Jur. 3d Decedents' Estates § 947, Citation.

Treatises and Practice Aids

Carlin, Baldwin's Ohio Practice, Merrick-Rippner Probate Law § 2:15, Appointment of Fiduciary—Appointment of Executor or Administrator.
Carlin, Baldwin's Ohio Practice, Merrick-Rippner Probate Law § 68:28, Letters Testamentary—Refusal of Appointment of Executor by Nominee.

Notes of Decisions

Notice 1
Sale of land 2

1. Notice

Revocation of appointment of an administrator with the will annexed on the ground that appointment and letters of administration were issued without notice to one of the heirs at law who was therefore given no opportunity to take or renounce administration and who did not waive his right to appointment or otherwise renounce administration of the estate is not supported by legal grounds where six months elapsed between probate of will and taking out of letters of administration and the named executor made no application for appointment and filed no bond. In re Evans' Estate (Darke 1938) 27 Ohio Law Abs. 550.

Where the individual named in the will as executor repudiates acting as such, notice to this individual of the probate proceedings does not constitute notice to the beneficiaries. Feuchter v. Keyl (Ohio 1891) 48 Ohio St. 357, 25 W.L.B. 399, 27 N.E. 860.

2. Sale of land

Where a will directs land to be sold by the executors and they resign without having executed that power, the sale may be made by an administrator with the will annexed. Elstner v. Fife (Ohio 1877) 32 Ohio St. 358. Executors And Administrators ⚖ 121(2); Powers ⚖ 30; Wills ⚖ 692(1)

2113.13 Minority of an executor

When a person appointed executor is under the age of eighteen years at the time of proving the will, administration may be granted with the will annexed during his minority, unless there is another executor who will accept the trust. If there is such an executor, the estate shall be administered by him until the minor arrives at full age when such former minor may be admitted as executor with him upon giving bond as provided in section 2109.04 of the Revised Code.

(1973 S 1, eff. 1–1–74; 1953 H 1; GC 10509–11)

Historical and Statutory Notes

Pre–1953 H 1 Amendments: 114 v 403

Library References

Executors and Administrators ⚖15.
Westlaw Topic No. 162.
C.J.S. Executors and Administrators §§ 22 to 28.

Research References

Encyclopedias

OH Jur. 3d Decedents' Estates § 914, Meaning of "Suitable" and "Competent", Generally—Minority.

Treatises and Practice Aids

Carlin, Baldwin's Ohio Practice, Merrick-Rippner Probate Law § 68:20, Letters Testamentary—Qualifications for Executors—Age Requirement.

2113.14 Executor of an executor not to administer

The executor of an executor has no authority, as such, to administer the estate of the first testator. On the death of the sole or surviving executor of a last will, administration of that part of the estate of the first testator not already administered may be granted, with the will annexed, to such person as the probate court appoints.

(1953 H 1, eff. 10–1–53; GC 10509–12)

Historical and Statutory Notes

Pre–1953 H 1 Amendments: 114 v 403

Library References

Executors and Administrators ⚖︎36, 128.
Westlaw Topic No. 162.
C.J.S. Executors and Administrators § 92.

Research References

Encyclopedias

OH Jur. 3d Decedents' Estates § 983, Appointment.

Treatises and Practice Aids

Carlin, Baldwin's Ohio Practice, Merrick-Rippner Probate Law § 70:5, Administrator De Bonis Non—Rights and Duties.

SPECIAL ADMINISTRATION

2113.15 Special administrator

When there is delay in granting letters testamentary or of administration, the probate court may appoint a special administrator to collect and preserve the effects of the deceased.

Such special administrator must collect the chattels and debts of the deceased and preserve them for the executor or administrator who thereafter is appointed. For that purpose such special administrator may begin and maintain suits as administrator and also sell such goods as the court orders sold. He shall be allowed such compensation for his services as the court thinks reasonable, if he forthwith delivers the property and effects of the estate to the executor or administrator who supersedes him.

(1953 H 1, eff. 10–1–53; GC 10509–14, 10509–15)

Historical and Statutory Notes

Pre–1953 H 1 Amendments: 114 v 403, 404

Library References

Executors and Administrators ⚖︎22.
Westlaw Topic No. 162.
C.J.S. Executors and Administrators §§ 951 to 956.

Research References

Encyclopedias

OH Jur. 3d Actions § 145, Parties to be Substituted.
OH Jur. 3d Decedents' Estates § 1362, Compensation to Special Administrator or Others Acting in Place of Representative.
OH Jur. 3d Decedents' Estates § 1702, Appointment of Special Administrator.
OH Jur. 3d Decedents' Estates § 1703, Duties and Powers of Special Administrator.
OH Jur. 3d Decedents' Estates § 1706, Compensation of Special Administrator.
OH Jur. 3d Decedents' Estates § 1707, Authority of Special Administrator to Sue; Survival of Actions to Successor.
OH Jur. 3d Parties § 9, Who is a Real Party in Interest.
OH Jur. 3d Parties § 82, Death of a Party.

Treatises and Practice Aids

Klein, Darling, & Terez, Baldwin's Ohio Practice Civil Practice § 17:5, Real Party in Interest by Statute.
Carlin, Baldwin's Ohio Practice, Merrick-Rippner Probate Law § 69:1, Special Administrator—Necessity.
Carlin, Baldwin's Ohio Practice, Merrick-Rippner Probate Law § 69:2, Special Administrator—Nature of Office and Duties.
Carlin, Baldwin's Ohio Practice, Merrick-Rippner Probate Law § 69:3, Special Administrator—Compensation.
Carlin, Baldwin's Ohio Practice, Merrick-Rippner Probate Law § 69:4, Special Administrator—Application for Appointment—Form.
Carlin, Baldwin's Ohio Practice, Merrick-Rippner Probate Law § 69:5, Special Administrator—Entry for Appointment and for Bond—Form.
Carlin, Baldwin's Ohio Practice, Merrick-Rippner Probate Law § 69:6, Special Administrator—Bond—Form.
Carlin, Baldwin's Ohio Practice, Merrick-Rippner Probate Law § 69:7, Special Administration—Letters—Form.
Carlin, Baldwin's Ohio Practice, Merrick-Rippner Probate Law § 52:45, Bond of Special Administrator—Form.

Notes of Decisions

Account 2
Interest of special administrator 3
Procedural issues 1

---

1. Procedural issues

Creditor who had been named special administrator of decedent's estate was "real party in interest," for purposes of his motion to be substituted as plaintiff in survival action after decedent's death, even though beneficiaries of estate did not wish to continue that action; under rule requiring that every action be prosecuted in name of real party in interest, administrator could sue in his name as representative without joining those for whose benefit action was brought. Yardley v. W. Ohio Conference of the United Methodist Church, Inc. (Ohio App. 10 Dist., 08-29-2000) 138 Ohio App.3d 872, 742 N.E.2d 723. Parties ⚖︎ 59(3)

Creditor who had been named special administrator of decedent's estate was entitled to be substituted as plaintiff in survival action after decedent's death, even though estate's beneficiaries did not wish to continue that action. Yardley v. W. Ohio Conference of the United Methodist Church, Inc. (Ohio App. 10 Dist., 08-29-2000) 138 Ohio App.3d 872, 742 N.E.2d 723. Parties ⚖︎ 59(3)

A trial court must grant a motion for revivor and substitution of the duly appointed and qualified executors of an estate, in an action instituted by a special administrator of the estate of their decedent, to recover a judgment for money claimed to be due the estate of such decedent. Heekin v. Palmer (Hamilton 1955) 101 Ohio App. 216, 138 N.E.2d 431, 1 O.O.2d 168.

Special administrator had no authority to contest foreign administration, and was entitled to no compensation or allowance for expenses incurred by reason thereof. Phares v. Lincoln Nat. Bank (Hamilton 1931) 42 Ohio App. 433, 182 N.E. 360, 12 Ohio Law Abs. 31, 36 Ohio Law Rep. 365, error dismissed 125 Ohio St. 634, 185 N.E. 883. Executors And Administrators ⚖︎ 122(1)

2. Account

On final account of special administrator, no written itemized statement of legal services to estate rendered by attorney was required to be filed by attorney or by administrator. Dicken v. Strasburger (Wood 1927) 31 Ohio App. 18, 166 N.E. 143, 6 Ohio Law Abs. 89. Executors And Administrators ⚖︎ 502

On final account of special administrator appointed to collect and preserve effects of deceased for executor, or administrator thereafter to be appointed, trial court properly disallowed claim for legal services of attorney, in so far as such charges were for services in litigation growing out of will contest, since special administrator was not concerned in that litigation, and was not even a party thereto. Dicken v. Strasburger (Wood 1927) 31 Ohio App. 18, 166 N.E. 143, 6 Ohio Law Abs. 89.

Statement of legal services rendered on behalf of estate to special administrator, though attached to administrator's account, is not properly before the court until offered in evidence. Dicken v. Strasburger (Wood 1927) 31 Ohio App. 18, 166 N.E. 143, 6 Ohio Law Abs. 89. Executors And Administrators ⚖︎ 507(2)

3. Interest of special administrator

Special administrator is mere stakeholder without interest in who shall be general administrator or whether administration shall be foreign or domestic. Phares v. Lincoln Nat. Bank (Hamilton 1931) 42 Ohio App. 433, 182 N.E. 360, 12 Ohio Law Abs. 31, 36 Ohio Law Rep. 365, error dismissed 125 Ohio St. 634, 185 N.E. 883. Executors And Administrators ⚖︎ 122(1)

2113.16 Powers of special administrator to cease

Upon granting of letters testamentary or of administration, the power of a special administrator appointed under section 2113.15 of the Revised Code shall cease and he forthwith must deliver to the executor or administrator all the chattels and moneys of the deceased in his hands. The executor or administrator may be admitted to prosecute any suit begun by the special administrator, as an administrator de bonis non is authorized to prosecute a suit commenced by a former executor or administrator.

If such special administrator neglects or refuses to deliver over the property and estate to the executor or administrator, the probate court may compel him to do so by citation and attachment. The executor or administrator also may proceed, by civil action, to recover the value of the assets from such special administrator and his sureties.

(1953 H 1, eff. 10–1–53; GC 10509–16, 10509–17)

Historical and Statutory Notes

Pre–1953 H 1 Amendments: 114 v 404

Library References

Executors and Administrators ⚖=22(1).
Westlaw Topic No. 162.
C.J.S. Executors and Administrators §§ 951 to 952, 954 to 956.

Research References

Encyclopedias

OH Jur. 3d Actions § 116, Change In, or Termination Of, Office of Fiduciary.
OH Jur. 3d Decedents' Estates § 1705, Termination of Authority of Special Administrator.
OH Jur. 3d Decedents' Estates § 1708, Actions Against Special Administrator.
OH Jur. 3d Decedents' Estates § 1802, Substitution of Successor Representative as Party.

Treatises and Practice Aids

Carlin, Baldwin's Ohio Practice, Merrick-Rippner Probate Law § 69:2, Special Administrator—Nature of Office and Duties.

Notes of Decisions

Compensation 2
Substitution 1

---

1. Substitution

A trial court must grant a motion for revivor and substitution of the duly appointed and qualified executors of an estate, in an action instituted by a special administrator of the estate of their decedent, to recover a judgment for money claimed to be due the estate of such decedent. Heekin v. Palmer (Hamilton 1955) 101 Ohio App. 216, 138 N.E.2d 431, 1 O.O.2d 168.

2. Compensation

Special administrator who refused to deliver estate forthwith to administrator with will annexed was entitled to no compensation or fees. Phares v. Lincoln Nat. Bank (Hamilton 1931) 42 Ohio App. 433, 182 N.E. 360, 12 Ohio Law Abs. 31, 36 Ohio Law Rep. 365, error dismissed 125 Ohio St. 634, 185 N.E. 883. Executors And Administrators ⚖= 500

2113.17 Special administrator not liable to creditors

A special administrator appointed under section 2113.15 of the Revised Code is not liable to an action by a creditor of the deceased. The time of limitation for suits against the estate shall begin to run from the time of granting letters testamentary or of administration in the usual form, as if such special administration had not been granted.

(1953 H 1, eff. 10–1–53; GC 10509–18)

Historical and Statutory Notes

Pre–1953 H 1 Amendments: 114 v 404

Library References

Executors and Administrators ⚖=428, 437(6).
Westlaw Topic No. 162.
C.J.S. Executors and Administrators §§ 709, 730, 747, 752.

Research References

Encyclopedias

OH Jur. 3d Decedents' Estates § 1708, Actions Against Special Administrator.

Treatises and Practice Aids

Carlin, Baldwin's Ohio Practice, Merrick-Rippner Probate Law § 69:1, Special Administrator—Necessity.
Carlin, Baldwin's Ohio Practice, Merrick-Rippner Probate Law § 69:2, Special Administrator—Nature of Office and Duties.

REMOVAL

2113.18 Removal of executor or administrator

(A) The probate court may remove any executor or administrator if there are unsettled claims existing between him and the estate, which the court thinks may be the subject of controversy or litigation between him and the estate or persons interested therein.

(B) The probate court may remove any executor or administrator upon motion of the surviving spouse, children, or other next of kin of the deceased person whose estate is administered by the executor or administrator if both of the following apply:

(1) The executor or administrator refuses to bring an action for wrongful death in the name of the deceased person;

(2) The court determines that a prima-facie case for a wrongful death action can be made from the information available to the executor or administrator.

(1982 S 176, eff. 6–1–82; 1953 H 1; GC 10509–19)

Historical and Statutory Notes

Pre–1953 H 1 Amendments: 114 v 404

Library References

Executors and Administrators ⚖=35(1), 35(2).
Westlaw Topic No. 162.
C.J.S. Executors and Administrators §§ 104 to 110.

Research References

Encyclopedias

OH Jur. 3d Decedents' Estates § 958, Appointment as Subject to Collateral Attack.
OH Jur. 3d Decedents' Estates § 962, Removal from Office or Revocation of Letters.
OH Jur. 3d Fiduciaries § 312, Removal of Fiduciary as Executor or Administrator of Estate.
OH Jur. 3d Fiduciaries § 315, Who May Apply.
OH Jur. 3d Fiduciaries § 317, Notice.

Forms

Ohio Jurisprudence Pleading and Practice Forms § 123:21, Removal of Fiduciary.

Treatises and Practice Aids

Carlin, Baldwin's Ohio Practice, Merrick-Rippner Probate Law § 2:15, Appointment of Fiduciary—Appointment of Executor or Administrator.

Carlin, Baldwin's Ohio Practice, Merrick-Rippner Probate Law § 57:2, Removal of Fiduciary—Introduction.

Carlin, Baldwin's Ohio Practice, Merrick-Rippner Probate Law § 81:1, Removal—Statutory Provisions.

Carlin, Baldwin's Ohio Practice, Merrick-Rippner Probate Law § 81:4, Removal—Voidable Appointment.

Carlin, Baldwin's Ohio Practice, Merrick-Rippner Probate Law § 81:5, Motion for Removal of Executor or Administrator—Forms.

Carlin, Baldwin's Ohio Practice, Merrick-Rippner Probate Law § 81:6, Entry Setting for Hearing and Giving Notice—Form.

Carlin, Baldwin's Ohio Practice, Merrick-Rippner Probate Law § 81:7, Entry of Removal of Executor or Administrator—Form.

Carlin, Baldwin's Ohio Practice, Merrick-Rippner Probate Law § 12:15, Wrongful Death—Failure of Fiduciary to File Action.

Carlin, Baldwin's Ohio Practice, Merrick-Rippner Probate Law § 68:19, Letters Testamentary—Qualifications of Executors—in General.

Carlin, Baldwin's Ohio Practice, Merrick-Rippner Probate Law § 91:20, Land Sale—Necessary Parties.

Law Review and Journal Commentaries

Revisiting Firestone v. Galbreath and the Tort of Intentional Interference With an Expectancy, Angela G. Carlin. 6 Prob L J Ohio 17 (November/December 1995).

Notes of Decisions

Accounting 1
Conflict of interest 3
Hearing 6
Procedural issues 5
Surviving spouse 4
Unsettled claims 2

---

1. Accounting

After removal, an administrator may be required to account to the probate court for transactions occurring prior to removal. In re Morrison's Estate (Ohio 1903) 68 Ohio St. 252, 48 W.L.B. 586, 67 N.E. 567, 1 Ohio Law Rep. 22, 1 Ohio Law Rep. 335.

The authority of an executor or administrator to represent the estate, unless terminated in one of the modes provided by statute, continues until the estate is fully settled, and his authority is not extinguished by an order made upon what purports to be the settlement of his final account, directing he be discharged from his trust. Weyer v. Watt (Ohio 1891) 48 Ohio St. 545, 26 W.L.B. 284, 28 N.E. 670.

2. Unsettled claims

Determinations of the probate court in the administration of an estate overruling exceptions to the inventory filed by the executor and refusing to remove such executor in removal proceedings brought against him do not estop the institution of concealment proceedings against him by an administrator, subsequently appointed with the will annexed, for concealment of assets of the estate during the time he served as executor, where the subject matter and the issues involved in such prior proceedings were not identical with those involved in the subsequent concealment proceedings. Gordon v. Dewan (Hamilton 1964) 4 Ohio App.2d 214, 202 N.E.2d 325, 33 O.O.2d 254.

Application to remove administrator should be sustained where he has unsettled claims and demands against the estate arising out of numerous transactions covering a period of years and aggregating an unliquidated amount of more than one fourth of total estate, which claims may be the subject of controversy between him and persons interested in the estate. In re Stauffer's Estate (Darke 1943) 57 N.E.2d 145, 40 Ohio Law Abs. 254.

The removal of an executor under RC 2113.18(A) because of unsettled claims between the executor and the estate is merely discretionary with the court; where the unsettled claim is between the estate and a corporation in which the executor owns stock, the court does not err in refusing to remove the executor. In re Estate of Wahl, No. 92-CA-1 (5th Dist Ct App, Licking, 7-15-92).

3. Conflict of interest

An executor may be removed under RC 2113.18(A) for conflict of interest arising subsequent to his appointment where he is also a life beneficiary in a business of the estate for which he must pay rent to another beneficiary with whom he is involved in litigation. Hoover v Gamblin, No. CA15707 (9th Dist Ct App, Summit, 1-27-93).

Probate courts are obligated under RC 2113.18 to remove any executor who financially benefits from the continuation of litigation or from the fraudulent behavior of another, or who is involved in a suit against himself; further, there is no time limit on this removal, so there can be no waiver of the right to object. Hoover v Gamblier, No. 15707 (9th Dist Ct App, Summit, 1-27-93).

4. Surviving spouse

The probate court properly vacated the appointment of the applicant as administratrix to the decedent's estate on the grounds that such applicant is not the surviving spouse of the decedent where evidence showed that the decedent had refused to go through with a formal marriage and had signed an oil and gas lease indicating he was single since such is sufficient evidence to refute the claim of common law marriage. Estate of Yerke v Yerke, No. 82 CA 27 (7th Dist Ct App, Mahoning, 4-15-83).

5. Procedural issues

Beneficiary of estate waived any objection to probate court's failure to rule on her motion to remove replacement executor of the estate; in the three years following beneficiary's motion, the parties engaged in numerous hearings and conferences without beneficiary asking probate court to rule on her motion, and beneficiary did not take advantage of any extraordinary remedies to compel a ruling. Masterson v. Weaver (Ohio App. 5 Dist., Morgan, 03-08-2006) No. CA-05-014, 2006-Ohio-1069, 2006 WL 561499, Unreported. Executors And Administrators ⇐ 35(19)

Attorney, who was named as executor in deceased's will, lacked standing to raise the issue of revoking the first administration of deceased's estate after her will was produced; attorney's minimal interest in case was extinguished when the trial court determined that he was unqualified to be the executor. In re Estate of Rice (Ohio App. 7 Dist., Belmont, 09-28-2005) No. 04-BE-36, 2005-Ohio-5311, 2005 WL 2447031, Unreported. Executors And Administrators ⇐ 32(2)

Trial court denial of son's motion to remove his siblings as co-executors of their father's estate was not an abuse of discretion, even though son argued that executor's distribution of father's monetary assets as intervivos gifts was an unauthorized use of executor's power of attorney; executor's power of attorney expressly provided that she could distribute testator's property as gifts prior to his death, at the hearing on the motion to remove co-executors son failed to present any evidence regarding his motion to remove, instead he focused on executor's distribution of assets as gifts prior to their father's death, and there was no evidence that established that son and co-executors were subject to a viable controversy that required the removal of co-executors. In re Estate of Meloni (Ohio App. 11 Dist., Trumbull, 12-30-2004) No. 2003-T-0096, 2004-Ohio-7224, 2004 WL 3090190, Unreported, appeal not allowed 105 Ohio St.3d 1546, 827 N.E.2d 328, 2005-Ohio-2188. Executors And Administrators ⇐ 35(9)

Heir's failure to arrange for court reporter to transcribe proceedings regarding his application to remove estate's executor left Court of Appeals without ability to counter presumption of validity of Probate Court's decision. In re Estate of Weiner (Ohio App. 2 Dist., Montgomery, 06-27-2003) No. 19533, No. 19564, 2003-Ohio-3408, 2003 WL 21488186, Unreported. Executors And Administrators ⇐ 35(19)

Statutes governing removal of fiduciary or executor, not statute governing appointment of executor, applied when determining whether to remove executor. In re Estate of Rice (Ohio App. 9 Dist., 06-29-2005) 161 Ohio App.3d 847, 832 N.E.2d 139, 2005-Ohio-3301. Executors And Administrators ⇐ 35(1)

Probate court had jurisdiction to act upon motion to remove as executor individual named both executor of estate and trustee of testamentary trust, even though less than one half of persons interested in estate applied for removal as executor, since statutory requirement of application by majority applies only to testamentary trustees proper. In re Estate of Bost (Cuyahoga 1983) 10 Ohio App.3d 147, 460 N.E.2d 1156, 10 O.B.R. 199. Executors And Administrators ⇐ 35(13.5)

Reasons for removal or qualifications of an administrator are not jurisdictional and need not be stated affirmatively in the journal entry. In re Ferguson's Estate (Ohio Com.Pl. 1904) 16 Ohio Dec. 486, 3 Ohio NP(NS) 549.

6. Hearing

Decedent's daughter received sufficient notice that the appointment of a new estate administrator would be addressed at hearing on motion to remove daughter as executrix of the estate, and thus daughter waived her right to challenge probate court's appointment of a new estate administrator by not attending hearing, where hearing notice and copy of motion were served upon daughter, and motion specifically requested trial court to appoint a new administrator. In re Estate of Pallay (Ohio App. 4 Dist., Washington, 06-28-2006) No. 05CA45, 2006-Ohio-3528, 2006 WL 1875899, Unreported. Executors And Administrators ⚖ 35(13)

2113.19 Administrator de bonis non

When a sole executor or administrator dies without having fully administered the estate, the probate court shall grant letters of administration, with the will annexed or otherwise as the case requires, to some suitable person pursuant to section 2113.05 or 2113.06 of the Revised Code. Such person shall administer the goods and estate of the deceased not administered, in case there is personal estate to be administered to the amount of twenty dollars or debts to that amount due from the estate.

(1970 S 134, eff. 6–12–70; 1953 H 1; GC 10509–20)

Historical and Statutory Notes

Pre–1953 H 1 Amendments: 114 v 404

Library References

Executors and Administrators ⚖ 37(1), 37(2), 37(5).
Westlaw Topic No. 162.
C.J.S. Executors and Administrators §§ 935, 946.

Research References

Encyclopedias

OH Jur. 3d Decedents' Estates § 983, Appointment.

Treatises and Practice Aids

Carlin, Baldwin's Ohio Practice, Merrick-Rippner Probate Law § 70:1, Administrator De Bonis Non—Necessity.

Carlin, Baldwin's Ohio Practice, Merrick-Rippner Probate Law § 70:3, Administrator De Bonis Non—Personal Property Requirement.

Carlin, Baldwin's Ohio Practice, Merrick-Rippner Probate Law § 81:1, Removal—Statutory Provisions.

Carlin, Baldwin's Ohio Practice, Merrick-Rippner Probate Law § 82:2, Applicability of Statute—Death of Executor.

Carlin, Baldwin's Ohio Practice, Merrick-Rippner Probate Law § 54:12, Fiduciary Accounts—Jurisdiction to Settle.

Carlin, Baldwin's Ohio Practice, Merrick-Rippner Probate Law § 54:22, Fiduciary Accounts—Effect of Order Settling Account.

Carlin, Baldwin's Ohio Practice, Merrick-Rippner Probate Law § 68:42, Application for Authority to Administer Estate—Form.

Carlin, Baldwin's Ohio Practice, Merrick-Rippner Probate Law § 91:20, Land Sale—Necessary Parties.

Notes of Decisions

Ed. Note: This section contains annotations from former RC 2113.10.

Accounting 6
Administrative bond 2
Debts 5
Jurisdiction 4
Personal estate 1
Recovery of assets 7
Widow's allowance 3

1. Personal estate

Court cannot appoint administrator de bonis non when there is no personal property to be administered, even though attorneys agree that appointment should be made, this could not confer jurisdiction on court. Hopkins v. Barger (Lawrence 1935) 21 Ohio Law Abs. 386.

To invoke jurisdiction of probate court to issue letters of administration under this section, it is necessary that court find that there is personal estate to be administered to amount of twenty dollars, or debts to that amount due from estate; application to administer an estate may be made by person interested in estate either as heir or creditor; but where application for administration is made by person other than heir, court in order to grant letters of administration must find that applicant is a creditor of estate besides finding existence of either one or both of jurisdictional grounds of above section. Cooney v. Orth (Hardin 1935) 20 Ohio Law Abs. 570.

Where corporate stock bequeathed to a legatee was ordered subjected to indebtedness of the legatee to the estate, and before the stock was judicially disposed of and accounted for by the executrix she died, an administrator de bonis non should be appointed. State ex rel., Voight v. Lueders (Ohio 1920) 101 Ohio St. 259, 128 N.E. 72, 18 Ohio Law Rep. 66. Executors And Administrators ⚖ 37(2)

2. Administrative bond

An administrator de bonis non, whose predecessor's powers have ceased by death, can neither maintain an action against the administrator of the estate of the deceased administrator, nor force a settlement by him in the probate court of the deceased administrator's account. The only available remedy is on the administrative bond of the deceased administrator. Douglas v. Day (Ohio 1875) 28 Ohio St. 175. Executors And Administrators ⚖ 460

An administrator de bonis non cannot maintain an action on a balance found due from the estate of the former administrator to the estate in question, but he must seek his remedy on the administrative bond of the deceased administrator. Curtis v. Lynch's Adm'rs (Ohio 1869) 19 Ohio St. 392. Executors And Administrators ⚖ 120(1)

3. Widow's allowance

Where a widow received the balance remaining in the hands of the administrator after settlement of her husband's estate without making any claim for an allowance for her first year's support, it is not competent for the probate court after the lapse of nearly forty years to grant an application for the appointment of an administrator de bonis non for the sole purpose of setting off to her said allowance. Evans v. Evans (Ohio Com.Pl. 1909) 20 Ohio Dec. 676, 9 Ohio N.P.(N.S.) 589, affirmed 21 Ohio C.D. 635, 13 Ohio C.C.(N.S.) 62, affirmed 83 Ohio St. 482, 94 N.E. 1106, 8 Ohio Law Rep. 525. Executors And Administrators ⚖ 37(1); Executors And Administrators ⚖ 190

An administrator de bonis non may not be appointed by the probate court forty years after an estate was settled by the widow of the deceased merely to allow the widow to receive a single year's allowance. Evans v. Evans (Ohio Com.Pl. 1909) 20 Ohio Dec. 676, 9 Ohio N.P.(N.S.) 589, affirmed 21 Ohio C.D. 635, 13 Ohio C.C.(N.S.) 62, affirmed 83 Ohio St. 482, 94 N.E. 1106, 8 Ohio Law Rep. 525.

4. Jurisdiction

In an application for the appointment of an administrator de bonis non, the court is without jurisdiction to determine whether the executor wrongfully paid out money where the will gave the executor discretion as to its payment. In re Hess' Estate (Ohio Prob. 1894) 4 Ohio Dec. 413, 3 Ohio N.P. 62.

5. Debts

Even where the entire estate is disposed of, an administrator de bonis non should be appointed if debts outstanding against the estate are before the court. Piatt v. St. Clair's Heirs (Ohio 1832) 5 Ohio 555.

Where an attorney represented a creditor of decedent's estate but the relationship between such attorney and creditor has terminated, the probate court may properly appoint the attorney as administrator de bonis non to the estate. Estate of Danolfo v Laird, No. 45197 (8th Dist Ct App, Cuyahoga, 5–12–83).

6. Accounting

The personal representative of a deceased executor who has died without filing any account should file an account for him, and pay over to the executor's successor any balance due the estate from the deceased executor. Hocking Valley R. Co. v. White (Ohio 1913) 87 Ohio St. 413,

101 N.E. 354, 10 Ohio Law Rep. 611, Am.Ann.Cas. 1914A, 190. Executors And Administrators ⚖ 464

7. Recovery of assets

An administrator de bonis non has the right and power to sue for and recover the assets of the estate wherever found. Jelke v. Goldsmith (Ohio 1895) 52 Ohio St. 499, 33 W.L.B. 193, 40 N.E. 167, 49 Am.St.Rep. 730, 2 Ohio Leg. N. 430.

2113.20 Will proved after administration as of an intestate

If a will of a deceased is proved and allowed after letters of administration have been granted as of an intestate estate, the first administration shall be revoked, unless before such revocation a petition contesting the probate of such will is filed in the court of common pleas. If such a petition is filed, the probate court may allow the administration to be continued in the hands of the original administrators until the final determination of such contest. If the will is sustained, the first administration must be revoked. In either case, upon the revocation of the first administration and the appointment of an executor or administrator with the will annexed, such executor or administrator shall be admitted to prosecute or defend any suit, proceeding, or matter begun by or against the original administrator, in like manner as an administrator de bonis non is authorized to prosecute or defend a suit commenced by a former executor or administrator.

(1953 H 1, eff. 10–1–53; GC 10509–21)

Historical and Statutory Notes

Pre–1953 H 1 Amendments: 114 v 405

Library References

Executors and Administrators ⚖ 21, 23, 32.
Westlaw Topic No. 162.
C.J.S. Executors and Administrators §§ 52, 95 to 103, 947.

Research References

Encyclopedias

OH Jur. 3d Actions § 116, Change In, or Termination Of, Office of Fiduciary.
OH Jur. 3d Decedents' Estates § 956, Effect of Proof of Will After Issuance of Letters of Administration.
OH Jur. 3d Decedents' Estates § 982, Definitions and Distinctions: Administrators De Bonis Non and Administrators With the Will Annexed.
OH Jur. 3d Decedents' Estates § 1802, Substitution of Successor Representative as Party.

Treatises and Practice Aids

Carlin, Baldwin's Ohio Practice, Merrick-Rippner Probate Law § 38:3, Will Contests—Later Will Admitted to Probate.
Carlin, Baldwin's Ohio Practice, Merrick-Rippner Probate Law § 81:1, Removal—Statutory Provisions.

Notes of Decisions

Deed 1

1. Deed

Administrator's deed not void where will subsequently probated. Gasienica v. Dec (Cuyahoga 1929) 31 Ohio App. 502, 166 N.E. 692, 7 Ohio Law Abs. 443.

2113.21 Powers of executors, administrators, and testamentary trustees during a will contest

When a will is contested, the executor, the administrator de bonis non, with the will annexed, or the testamentary trustee may, during the contest, do the following:

(A) Control all the real estate which is included in the will but not specifically devised and all the personal estate of the testator not administered before such contest;

(B) Collect the debts and convert all assets into money, except those which are specially bequeathed;

(C) Pay all taxes on such real and personal property and all debts;

(D) Repair buildings and make other improvements if necessary to preserve the real property from waste;

(E) Insure such buildings upon an order first obtained from the probate court having jurisdiction of such executor, administrator, or testamentary trustee;

(F) Advance or borrow money on the credit of such estate for such repairs, taxes, and insurance which shall be a charge thereon;

(G) Receive and receipt for a distributive share of an estate or trust to which such testator would have been entitled, if living.

The court may require such additional bonds as from time to time seems proper.

(1953 H 1, eff. 10–1–53; GC 10509–22)

Historical and Statutory Notes

Pre–1953 H 1 Amendments: 114 v 405

Library References

Executors and Administrators ⚖ 78.
Westlaw Topic No. 162.
C.J.S. Executors and Administrators § 172.

Research References

Encyclopedias

OH Jur. 3d Decedents' Estates § 968, Powers When Will Contested.
OH Jur. 3d Decedents' Estates § 1399, Right and Duty to Insure Property.
OH Jur. 3d Trusts § 383, Will Contest.

Treatises and Practice Aids

Carlin, Baldwin's Ohio Practice, Merrick-Rippner Probate Law § 71:1, Powers of Fiduciary During Will Contest—Statutory Provisions.

Notes of Decisions

Defense of will 1
Distribution 7
Necessary parties 2
Procedural issues 8
Repairs 6
Sales 3
Time for claims 5
Trusts 4

1. Defense of will

An executor is not required to assume the burden of the defense of a will contest brought by the heirs. Andrews Ex'rs v. His Adm'rs (Ohio 1857) 7 Ohio St. 143.

Although a fiduciary acting under a will has the right to defend the will, he has no duty so to do, and may cast that burden upon the legatees and devisees. Hecker v. Schuler (Ohio 1967) 12 Ohio St.2d 58, 231 N.E.2d 877, 41 O.O.2d 277. Executors And Administrators ⚖ 111(3)

Note 1

Where the will left a substantial legacy to the executrix, the estate is not required to bear the cost of defense of the will. Weir v. Weir (Ohio Cir. 1906) 18 Ohio C.D. 199, 7 Ohio C.C.N.S. 289.

2. Necessary parties

The attorney general is not a necessary party to a will contest case even though the proceeding may result in the nonexistence of a purported charitable trust created by the alleged will. Spang v. Cleveland Trust Co. (Ohio Com.Pl. 1956) 134 N.E.2d 586, 73 Ohio Law Abs. 164, 1 O.O.2d 288.

In an action to contest a will, where the executor has been discharged, an administrator de bonis non is a necessary party, but he is not a party united in interest with a testamentary trustee and where such administrator is not served with summons within the statutory time, the court obtains no jurisdiction of such administrator although the trustee was served within time. Campbell v. Johnson (Franklin 1948) 83 Ohio App. 225, 79 N.E.2d 147, 51 Ohio Law Abs. 258, 38 O.O. 301.

An action to contest a will is not commenced as to the heirs of the testator and the devisees by the issuance of a summons for the executor, the executor not being "united in interest" with the heirs and devisees, within Gen.Code, § 11230, providing that an action shall be deemed to have been commenced as to one defendant by issuance of summons for another defendant "united in interest" with him, in view of § 12080. McCord v. McCord (Ohio 1922) 104 Ohio St. 274, 135 N.E. 548, 19 Ohio Law Rep. 739. Wills ⇐ 260

3. Sales

Acting executor may, under devise to sell, sell alone. Taylor v. Galloway (Ohio 1823) 1 Ohio 232, 13 Am.Dec. 605.

Where an executor has borrowed money and used it to pay testator's debt, the creditor of the executor cannot intervene in a suit involving sale of the lands devised and have his claim against the executor paid from the proceeds of the sale. Smith v. Hayward (Ohio Prob. 1898) 5 Ohio Dec. 462, 5 Ohio N.P. 501.

4. Trusts

Powers of executor are coextensive with trusts created by will. Mathews v. Meek (Ohio 1872) 23 Ohio St. 272.

Where a testamentary trustee brought an action for forcible entry and detainer against a tenant who had paid the rent to the sole heir of the testator who was contesting a will, the Akron municipal court had jurisdiction to hear such action. Olds v. Morse (Summit 1954) 98 Ohio App. 382, 129 N.E.2d 644, 57 O.O. 419.

5. Time for claims

The filing of a petition to contest a decedent's will does not suspend or extend the time in which a creditor shall present his claim to the executor of said decedent's estate. In re Kehoe's Estate (Ohio Prob. 1963) 199 N.E.2d 29, 94 Ohio Law Abs. 469, 27 O.O.2d 35. Executors And Administrators ⇐ 225(2)

6. Repairs

While the executor is entitled to be reimbursed for repairs on real estate necessary to maintain the property in as good condition as when he received it, he is not entitled to make improvements or better the property at the estate's expense. In re Ullman (Ohio Cir. 1909) 21 Ohio C.D. 370, 12 Ohio C.C.(N.S.) 340.

7. Distribution

Evidence did not support claim by testator's daughter that executrix refused to relinquish daughter's personal property, as required to support action against executrix for conversion; executrix testified that daughter could retrieve personal items at her convenience. Lakes v. Ryan (Ohio App. 12 Dist., Butler, 02-03-2003) No. CA2002-05-118, 2003-Ohio-504, 2003 WL 231272, Unreported. Executors And Administrators ⇐ 450

The effect of a contest of a will upon the powers of executors during the contest is defined in section which is to clothe the administrator or executor with authority to carry on the mandatory obligations of the estate but to hold distribution in abeyance. Adams v. Gurklies (Champaign 1949) 88 Ohio App. 225, 91 N.E.2d 706, 56 Ohio Law Abs. 167, 44 O.O. 393.

8. Procedural issues

Judgment setting aside a will does not vacate the appointment of an administrator by the probate court. Sanker v. Mattison (Ohio Cir. 1900) 11 Ohio C.D. 125.

2113.22 Proceedings against the former executor or administrator

An administrator or executor appointed in the place of an executor or administrator who has resigned or been removed, whose letters have been revoked, or whose authority has been extinguished is entitled to the possession of all the personal effects and assets of the estate unadministered, and all other funds collected and unaccounted for by such executor or administrator, and may maintain a suit against the former executor or administrator and his sureties on the administration bond to recover such effects, assets and funds and for all damages arising from the maladministration or omissions of the former executor or administrator.

(128 v 76, eff. 11–9–59; 1953 H 1; GC 10509–23)

Historical and Statutory Notes

Pre–1953 H 1 Amendments: 114 v 405

OSBA Probate and Trust Law Section

1959:

The Committee now unanimously recommends that legislation be sponsored to enable an Executor or Administrator to manage real estate when necessary in order to conserve it and prevent injury or loss to the devisees or heirs. The powers proposed to be granted are limited in scope, and to be effective only upon probate court approval first had after hearing on proper application of which notice is to be given unless dispensed with for good cause by the court.

Devisees and heirs inherit the title to real estate upon death, subject only to divestment thereof if sold for the payment of debts. They are immediately entitled to possession and the rents. Yet sometimes the devisees and heirs are unknown, or if known cannot be located. Frequently they are unable to agree promptly upon management because of differences of opinion or scattered, diverse residence. Under such circumstances it is felt the executor or administrator should be authorized to step in and do a caretaking job in the real estate with limited but authorized powers under statutory authority until the devisees and heirs are in a position to act.

Presently no such powers or authority exist, and the fact that in the past in numerous cases executors and administrators have stepped in, managed real estate, collected rents and accounted for the proceeds without benefit of clergy, so to speak, emphasizes rather than dispenses with the need for legislation to define when real estate management by a fiduciary can be lawful, and the extent of the authority to be lawfully exercised, without risk of suit for well-meaning and often essential but unauthorized action.

Library References

Executors and Administrators ⇐120(0.5), 537(6).
Westlaw Topic No. 162.
C.J.S. Executors and Administrators §§ 900, 914, 941 to 942, 946.

Research References

Encyclopedias

OH Jur. 3d Decedents' Estates § 989, Rights and Powers—Right to Possession of Estate Assets.
OH Jur. 3d Decedents' Estates § 1759, Action to Recover and Preserve Assets—Action by Administrator De Bonis Non.
OH Jur. 3d Decedents' Estates § 1779, Action by Successor Representative Against Former Representative.
OH Jur. 3d Fiduciaries § 221, Parties—Successor Fiduciary as Plaintiff.

Treatises and Practice Aids

Carlin, Baldwin's Ohio Practice, Merrick-Rippner Probate Law § 70:5, Administrator De Bonis Non—Rights and Duties.
Carlin, Baldwin's Ohio Practice, Merrick-Rippner Probate Law § 82:1, Duties of New Executor or Administrator.

Carlin, Baldwin's Ohio Practice, Merrick-Rippner Probate Law § 82:2, Applicability of Statute—Death of Executor.

Law Review and Journal Commentaries

Actions on Fiduciary Bonds in Probate Court, Jerome C. Tinianow. 59 Clev B J 120 (February 1988).

Notes of Decisions

Assets of estate   2
Bond and sureties   1
Deceased administrator   3
Wrongful death suit   4

---

1. Bond and sureties

An administrator de bonis non cannot maintain an action on a balance found due from the estate of the former administrator to the estate in question, but he must seek his remedy on the administrative bond of the deceased administrator. Curtis v. Lynch's Adm'rs (Ohio 1869) 19 Ohio St. 392. Executors And Administrators ⇐ 120(1)

Where a removed administrator has settled with the court, and the balance in his hands is ascertained, suit may be sustained against his sureties without obtaining a separate judgment against him. Treasurer of Franklin County v. McElvain (Ohio 1831) 5 Ohio 200.

The sureties on an administration bond, given by an executor who has been removed, are liable thereon, to the administrator appointed in his place, for the indebtedness of such executor to the estate for assets received by him, and converted to his own use; and a recovery may be had therefor by the successor in a suit on the administration bond. Foster v. Wise (Ohio 1888) 46 Ohio St. 20, 20 W.L.B. 55, 16 N.E. 687, 15 Am.St.Rep. 542.

Omission by an administrator de bonis non of a bond with the proper number of sureties will not defeat his right to maintain an action against his predecessors. (See also Foster v Wise, 46 OS 20, 16 NE 687 (1888).) Slagle v. Entrekin (Ohio 1887) 44 Ohio St. 637, 17 W.L.B. 211, 10 N.E. 675. Executors And Administrators ⇐ 26(2); Executors And Administrators ⇐ 29(4)

A former administrator who has been removed or who has resigned is liable for the unadministered assets of the estate remaining in his hands and his sureties may be sued on his official bond. In re Miller's Account (Ohio Com.Pl. 1901) 11 Ohio Dec. 624, 8 Ohio N.P. 385.

2. Assets of estate

An administrator de bonis non can maintain a suit against a former administrator for assets not accounted for. O'Conner v. State, for use of Potter's Adm'r. (Ohio 1849) 18 Ohio 225.

Where a sole devisee appointed as executor sells as devisee lands of the estate at private sale, he must account for the full value thereof if necessary for the payment of the testator's debts, regardless of whether the sale was for less or full value. Hocking Valley R. Co. v. White (Ohio 1913) 87 Ohio St. 413, 101 N.E. 354, 10 Ohio Law Rep. 611, Am.Ann.Cas. 1914A, 190. Executors And Administrators ⇐ 40

Where the executor of a will died while indebted to his testator and the amount of the debt has been ascertained by court, this amount is considered an asset of the testator's estate and since the executor died without bond and before the account was due, it is his administrator's duty to provide for the satisfaction of the amount charged against the executor's estate by the probate court. Jones v. Willis (Ohio 1905) 72 Ohio St. 189, 74 N.E. 166, 2 Ohio Law Rep. 529.

An administrator de bonis non may maintain a suit against a former administrator who converted assets of estate for his own use or against the former administrator's sureties on his administrative bond. (See also Foster v Wise, 46 OS 20, 16 NE 687 (1888).) Slagle v. Entrekin (Ohio 1887) 44 Ohio St. 637, 17 W.L.B. 211, 10 N.E. 675.

3. Deceased administrator

An administrator de bonis non is authorized to maintain a suit against the prior executor or administrator, deceased or not, as the purpose of the statute is to transfer the entire estate to the administrator de bonis non. Tracy's Adm'x v. Card's Adm'r (Ohio 1853) 2 Ohio St. 431.

An administrator de bonis non may not bring an action under the statute or at common law against the representative of a deceased administrator who died in office or on his bond. Blizzard v. Filler (Ohio 1851) 20 Ohio 479.

The personal representative of an executor, who died in office before any account was had in reference to his trust, is not, under RS 6020 (See GC 10509–23) conferring on the successors of an executor who has resigned or who has been removed a right to sue the former executor of administrator on his bond, liable to the administrator de bonis non of the testator, in an action against him alone, as such personal representative, to recover the unadministered assets of the estate of such testator, when none came into the possession or control of such personal representative. Jones v. Willis (Ohio 1902) 66 Ohio St. 114, 47 W.L.B. 342, 63 N.E. 605. Executors And Administrators ⇐ 128

4. Wrongful death suit

This section authorizes an administrator de bonis non to maintain a suit against a former administrator or executor and his sureties upon an administration bond to recover for the default of such former administrator or executor arising out of the performance of the duties imposed by former GC 10772 (GC 10509–167, now RC 2125.02). U.S. Fidelity & Guaranty Co. v. Decker (Ohio 1930) 122 Ohio St. 285, 171 N.E. 333, 68 A.L.R. 1538, 8 Ohio Law Abs. 273, 31 Ohio Law Rep. 581.

2113.23 Sales of former executor or administrator valid

When letters of administration are revoked, when an executor or administrator, or administrator with the will annexed, is removed, resigns, or dies, when a will is declared invalid, or when an election to take under section 2105.06 of the Revised Code is made by or for a surviving spouse, all previous sales, leases, encumbrances, whether of real or personal property, made lawfully and in good faith by the executor or administrator, or administrator with the will annexed, and with good faith on the part of the purchasers, and all lawful acts done in the settlement of the estate or execution of the will shall be valid as to such executor, administrator, administrator with the will annexed, purchasers for value in good faith, lessees for value in good faith, encumbrancers for value in good faith, all other parties dealing with said fiduciary for value in good faith, and all parties lawfully claiming by, through or under any of them. But the sums paid out or distributed to legatees or other distributees, when necessary for the proper execution of a will or administration of an estate, may be recovered from the persons receiving them.

(125 v 411, eff. 10–16–53; 125 v 903; 1953 H 1; GC 10509–24)

Historical and Statutory Notes

Pre–1953 H 1 Amendments: 114 v 406

Cross References

Marketable Title Act, 5301.47 to 5301.53

Library References

Executors and Administrators ⇐ 137, 148, 167, 318.
Westlaw Topic No. 162.
C.J.S. Executors and Administrators §§ 295 to 298, 318, 321, 329, 336, 341, 343, 558.

Research References

Encyclopedias

OH Jur. 3d Decedents' Estates § 956, Effect of Proof of Will After Issuance of Letters of Administration.
OH Jur. 3d Decedents' Estates § 1654, Refunding by Legatees and Distributees.

Treatises and Practice Aids

Carlin, Baldwin's Ohio Practice, Merrick-Rippner Probate Law § 73:18, Deed of Fiduciary Under Power of Sale in Will—Form.
Kuehnle and Levey, Ohio Real Estate Law and Practice § 18:1, Ohio State Bar Association Standards of Title Examination.

Kuehnle and Levey, Ohio Real Estate Law and Practice § 16:11, Curative Acts—Decedent's Estates—Validity of Sale, Lease, or Encumbrance by Fiduciary When Fiduciary Removed, Resigns, or Dies, or When Will Declared Invalid or Surviving Spouse Elects to Take...

Kuehnle and Levey, Ohio Real Estate Law and Practice § 16:13, Curative Acts—Decedent's Estates—Subsequently Produced Will, Rights of Purchaser from Fiduciary or Devisees or Heirs Under Prior Administered Estate.

Notes of Decisions

Interest 3
Land sale 2
Settlement 1

1. Settlement

Where a will is discovered after full settlement by the administrator, the executor cannot compel an accounting or interfere with the settlement. Barkaloo's Adm'R v. Emerick Et Al (Ohio 1849) 18 Ohio 268.

2. Land sale

Under section a land sale proceeding brought by the administrator is binding on the administrator de bonis non with the will annexed. Kincaid v. Dawson (Franklin 1950) 87 Ohio App. 299, 93 N.E.2d 731, 57 Ohio Law Abs. 193, 43 O.O. 16. Executors And Administrators ☞ 325

3. Interest

Interest on refunded legacy on setting aside will begins when money in fact received. Bermont v. Gotshall (Ohio 1924) 110 Ohio St. 425, 144 N.E. 137, 22 Ohio Law Rep. 160. Executors And Administrators ☞ 317

An executor having received the amount of a legacy to him and being chargeable to return the same on the will being set aside, must pay interest thereon only from the date of filing exceptions. In re Thompson's Estate (Ohio Com.Pl. 1921) 23 Ohio NP(NS) 544.

LIMITATIONS

2113.24 Limitations

If any claim must be presented or any notice given to an executor or administrator, or if any action, suit, or proceeding must be instituted against him within any limited period of time prescribed by statute, and if during such period the administrator or executor dies, resigns, or is removed, or the office becomes vacant for any other reason, the time between such death, resignation, removal, or the occurrence of such vacancy and the appointment of a successor shall be excluded in computing the period of such time limitation.

(1953 H 1, eff. 10–1–53; GC 10509–122a)

Historical and Statutory Notes

Pre–1953 H 1 Amendments: 119 v 394, § 7

Library References

Executors and Administrators ☞225, 437.
Westlaw Topic No. 162.
C.J.S. Executors and Administrators §§ 426 to 435, 747 to 768.

Research References

Encyclopedias

OH Jur. 3d Decedents' Estates § 1446, Tolling of Statutes.
OH Jur. 3d Decedents' Estates § 1785, Effect of Termination of Office or Appointment of Successor.

Treatises and Practice Aids

Carlin, Baldwin's Ohio Practice, Merrick-Rippner Probate Law § 83:1, Fiduciary Claims—Time Limit.

Notes of Decisions

Completion of administration 1
Procedural issues 2

1. Completion of administration

In a negligence action for the recovery of damages instituted under RC 2117.07 against an administrator seeking to recover only from the decedent's liability insurer, where the administrator of the estate of the decedent has been discharged and the estate closed, the probate court may reappoint the administrator for the purpose of accepting service of summons. In re George's Estate (Ohio 1970) 24 Ohio St.2d 18, 262 N.E.2d 872, 53 O.O.2d 10.

Where the final and distributive account of the administrators of an estate has been approved and settled and they have been discharged from their trust pursuant to RC 2109.32, and that order has not been vacated pursuant to RC 2109.35, where some asset remains upon which administration has not been exhausted and for some lawful purpose relating to that asset administration is required, an administrator may be appointed to complete such administration only in a manner similar to, and with the same formalities as, the original appointment of an administrator, and in such circumstances, where such asset consists of an automobile liability insurance policy of the decedent covering the claim of a person alleged to have received bodily injuries due to the alleged negligence of the decedent, such policy is an asset which will support the appointment of an administrator upon whom service may be made and with authority to defend suit. In re George's Estate (Hancock 1969) 20 Ohio App.2d 87, 252 N.E.2d 176, 49 O.O.2d 110. Executors And Administrators ☞ 37(2); Executors And Administrators ☞ 37(5)

2. Procedural issues

Where a removed administrator has settled with the court, and the balance in his hands is ascertained, suit may be sustained against his sureties without obtaining a separate judgment against him. Treasurer of Franklin County v. McElvain (Ohio 1831) 5 Ohio 200.

The four-month period prescribed by RC 2117.02 for the presentment of claims by an executor or administrator to the probate court for allowance begins as of the date of the appointment of the executor or administrator and is not interrupted by the removal of the executor or administrator and the simultaneous appointment of his successor within such four-month period. Allen v. Hunter (Franklin 1964) 1 Ohio App.2d 278, 204 N.E.2d 545, 30 O.O.2d 296.

COLLECTION OF ASSETS; NEW ADMINISTRATOR

2113.25 Assets to be collected

So far as the executor or administrator is able, the executor or administrator of an estate shall collect the assets and complete the administration of that estate within thirteen months after the date of appointment.

Upon application of the executor or administrator and notice to the interested parties, if the probate court considers that notice necessary, the court may allow further time in which to collect assets, to convert assets into money, to pay creditors, to make distributions to legatees or distributees, to file partial, final, and distributive accounts, and to settle estates. The court, upon application of any interested party, may authorize the examination under oath in open court of the executor or administrator upon any matter relating to the administration of the estate.

(2001 H 85, eff. 10–31–01; 1953 H 1, eff. 10–1–53; GC 10509–85, 10509–86)

Historical and Statutory Notes

Pre–1953 H 1 Amendments: 119 v 394, § 1; 114 v 420

Amendment Note: 2001 H 85 substituted "the executor or administrator" for "he" and "thirteen" for "nine" in the first paragraph and "considers that" for "deems such" in the second paragraph; made other changes to reflect gender neutral language; and made other nonsubstantive changes.

Cross References

Death or incompetence of bank customer, 1304.28
Lottery prize, executor or administrator has one hundred eighty days to collect from day of award announcement, 3770.07
Partnership, partner's demise divests interest, 1775.24
Rest home or nursing home that managed resident's financial affairs shall give remainder to executor, administrator, or estate, 3721.15
Suits in which party adverse to personal representative cannot testify, exceptions, 2317.03
Survival of counterclaims against decedents, 2309.19
Temporary investments by fiduciary allowed, 1339.44

Library References

Executors and Administrators ⟬86, 459.
Westlaw Topic No. 162.
C.J.S. Executors and Administrators §§ 187 to 201, 786.

Research References

Encyclopedias

OH Jur. 3d Decedents' Estates § 1271, Generally; Duty to Collect Assets.
OH Jur. 3d Decedents' Estates § 1272, Time Allowed for Collection of Assets.
OH Jur. 3d Decedents' Estates § 1627, Duty to Make Distribution.
OH Jur. 3d Decedents' Estates § 1635, Time Allowed for Completing Administration.
OH Jur. 3d Decedents' Estates § 1636, Time for Paying of Legacies.

Forms

Ohio Forms Legal and Business § 24:861, Delayed Distribution of Legacies—Specification of Period.

Treatises and Practice Aids

Carlin, Baldwin's Ohio Practice, Merrick-Rippner Probate Law § 2:3, Time for Administration of Decedent's Estate and Payment of Estate Taxes.
Carlin, Baldwin's Ohio Practice, Merrick-Rippner Probate Law § 2:17, Inventory and Appraisal—Ascertaining Assets.
Carlin, Baldwin's Ohio Practice, Merrick-Rippner Probate Law § 2:121, Administration of Decedent's Estate—Checklist.
Carlin, Baldwin's Ohio Practice, Merrick-Rippner Probate Law § 74:22, Application for Extension of Time—Form.
Carlin, Baldwin's Ohio Practice, Merrick-Rippner Probate Law § 74:23, Entry Extending Time—Form.
Carlin, Baldwin's Ohio Practice, Merrick-Rippner Probate Law § 75:12, Distribution—Upon Application—Enforcement.
Carlin, Baldwin's Ohio Practice, Merrick-Rippner Probate Law § 80:19, Attorney Fees—Facts to be Considered.
Kuehnle and Levey, Ohio Real Estate Law and Practice § 52:22, Statutory Fiduciary Sales—Action to Set Aside Conveyance Made During Decedent's Lifetime.

Notes of Decisions

Ed. Note: This section contains annotations from former RC 2113.08.

Fraud on creditors 10
Gifts 5
Insurance policies 7
Interest 4
Invasion of privacy claim 12
Joint accounts 9
Land and rents 1
Notes 2
Procedural issues 3
Retirement benefits 11
Trusts 6
Wrongful death 8

1. Land and rents

After-acquired assets must be accounted for by the administrator, but rents of real estate accruing after death of intestate are not rents of the estate and the administrator has no duty in regard to them. Overturf v. Dugan (Ohio 1876) 29 Ohio St. 230.

An Ohio administrator may not bring an action to recover money which is the proceeds of lands of the intestate in Pennsylvania, sold by the guardian as the property of wards under the authority of the orphan's court of that state. Jones v. Shields (Ohio 1846) 14 Ohio 359. Guardian And Ward ⟬ 171

Petition filed by administrator, alleging that plaintiff's decedent, without consideration and under undue influence exercised by grantees, conveyed certain real property, that the conveyance was not decedent's voluntary act, and that the personal property of decedent is insufficient to pay the debts of the estate, consisting of medical and funeral expenses and costs of administration, and praying that the conveyance be set aside and realty sold to pay debts of the estate, states a cause of action and is warranted by section. Miller v. Bigelow (Wood 1941) 67 Ohio App. 371, 36 N.E.2d 860, 21 O.O. 324. Executors And Administrators ⟬ 129(3); Executors And Administrators ⟬ 336

An action by an administrator to recover from a railroad company compensation and damages for wrongfully taking and appropriating lands of the decedent during his lifetime cannot be maintained because such wrongful taking did not divest the decedent of his title to the land and the land, therefore, descended to his heirs. Lawrence R. Co. v. O'Harra (Ohio 1893) 50 Ohio St. 667, 36 N.E. 14. Descent And Distribution ⟬ 75; Eminent Domain ⟬ 284; Executors And Administrators ⟬ 49

2. Notes

If notes are delivered to an executor to indemnify the estate against liability where the testator was a surety, such notes and the money collected on them are not part of the estate, and the estate is not liable for the misconduct of the administrator in reference to such notes and money. Arbuckle's Ex'rs v. Tracy's Adm'rs (Ohio 1846) 15 Ohio 432. Executors And Administrators ⟬ 45

Under section, where administrator has in his hands as part of the assets of estate a note secured by a mortgage on realty, it is his duty to collect the note, and, if necessary, to foreclose the mortgage, and it is beyond his power to accept a conveyance of the realty in satisfaction of the indebtedness evidenced thereby. In re Tredway (Fulton 1927) 29 Ohio App. 265, 163 N.E. 223, 5 Ohio Law Abs. 805.

Where heirs of decedent treated as advancements certain notes given to decedent in his lifetime, the widow cannot claim her portion of the sum of those notes on distribution, as the statute only includes the personal property of the estate, collected by the administrator, and reduced to money, as assets for distribution. Young v Roberts, 7 CC 105, 3 CD 685 (Butler 1892), affirmed by 54 OS 622, 47 NE 1119 (1896).

3. Procedural issues

Order that distributed assets in probate case also included instructions for attorney to prepare judgment entry granting estate money judgment for property taxes mistakenly paid by estate, and thus, order was not a final judgment from which an appeal could be taken. In re Estate of Mahan (Ohio App. 11 Dist., Trumbull, 09-09-2005) No. 2005-T-0062, 2005-Ohio-4770, 2005 WL 2211085, Unreported. Executors And Administrators ⟬ 314(12)

An executor, who is also a beneficiary, cannot appeal from a judgment which does not prejudice him in his capacity as executor. Fried v. Fried (Cuyahoga 1989) 65 Ohio App.3d 61, 582 N.E.2d 1038. Appeal And Error ⟬ 151(3)

An executor cannot sue himself in the same action when he also acts as a beneficiary in an individual capacity. Fried v. Fried (Cuyahoga 1989) 65 Ohio App.3d 61, 582 N.E.2d 1038.

An action to recover public employees retirement system benefits is governed by a six-year limitations period; the statute does not begin to run as to the estate of a claimant until a personal representative becomes qualified. State ex rel. Hadinger v. City of Akron (Summit 1988) 48 Ohio App.3d 64, 548 N.E.2d 299, motion overruled 38 Ohio St.3d 723, 533 N.E.2d 1063.

In accordance with RC 2113.05, a "suitable" person qualified for appointment as executor is an applicant who is reasonably disinterested and in a position to reasonably fulfill the obligations of a fiduciary. In re Henne's Estate (Ohio 1981) 66 Ohio St.2d 232, 421 N.E.2d 506, 20 O.O.3d 228. Executors And Administrators ⇐ 15

Under GC 11235 (RC 2305.21), 11397 (RC 2311.21) and 11401 (RC 2311.25), a derivative stockholders suit, for benefit of the corporation, may be revived following the death of the plaintiff, in the name of plaintiff's administrator, and such remedy of revivor is a matter of right and not of discretion. Holmes v. Republic Steel Corp. of N. J. (Cuyahoga 1944) 64 N.E.2d 426, 44 Ohio Law Abs. 294. Abatement And Revival ⇐ 59.1

An administrator has the right and power to sue for and recover the assets of the estate wherever found. Jelke v. Goldsmith (Ohio 1895) 52 Ohio St. 499, 33 W.L.B. 193, 40 N.E. 167, 49 Am.St.Rep. 730, 2 Ohio Leg. N. 430. Executors And Administrators ⇐ 158; Executors And Administrators ⇐ 170

4. Interest

Where a testator provides that the amount of a legacy shall be invested in government bonds at all times and the maximum rate of interest paid on such bonds is two and one-half per cent per annum, it is not error to require the executor to pay interest at that rate instead of the statutory rate during the delay in paying the legacy beginning nine months after the notice of the executor's appointment. In re Shanafelt's Estate (Ohio 1955) 164 Ohio St. 258, 129 N.E.2d 816, 58 O.O. 7. Executors And Administrators ⇐ 313

A general legacy bears interest at the legal rate from the end of nine months from the date of the issuance of letters of appointment from the probate court to the executor, unless it be clearly apparent that the testator did not so intend, and a legatee is entitled to such interest from said date, unless the will provides otherwise, regardless of the pendency of a contest delaying the settlement of an estate and the participation in that contest by the legatees claiming interest; interest upon arrearages of annuities is recoverable from the time the installment of annuities became due and payable, which time shall be determined from the intent of the testator as shown by the terms of the will which created the annuity. In re Rothschild's Estate (Ohio Prob. 1948) 114 N.E.2d 143, 66 Ohio Law Abs. 237, 51 O.O. 110. Wills ⇐ 734(4); Wills ⇐ 734(8)

5. Gifts

Where a decedent bought money orders in the name of her sister intending to make a gift, but never had the opportunity to deliver them, the gift is incomplete since the buyer retains power to cancel money orders; the administrator of the estate is therefore entitled to the money in an action brought under GC 10857. McKelvey's Adm'r v. McKelvey (Ohio Cir. 1911) 23 Ohio C.D. 117, 14 Ohio C.C.(N.S.) 331.

6. Trusts

Where an entire estate is devised to the executor in trust and is thus received by the executor as trustee, no part of it becomes assets in his hands as executor except such part of the personalty as is necessary to settle the ordinary charges of administration. Union Sav. Bank & Trust Co. v. Baltimore & O.S.W.R. Co. (Ohio Insolv. 1908) 7 Ohio NP(NS) 497, 53 W.L.B. 450.

7. Insurance policies

Proceeds of a husband's insurance policy naming the wife individually as beneficiary are not part of his estate even though the husband's will mistakenly asserts they are, but where the wife as executrix treats the proceeds as part of the estate she gives, in effect, the money to the estate and the act binds not only herself but her heirs as well. Buehler v. Buehler (Ohio Com.Pl. 1904) 14 Ohio Dec. 693, 2 Ohio N.P.N.S. 430.

8. Wrongful death

An Ohio administrator cannot sue in Ohio under an Illinois wrongful death statute allowing the personal representative of the deceased to sue for the benefit of the widow or next of kin. Woodard v. Michigan Southern & Northern I.R. Co. (Ohio 1859) 10 Ohio St. 121.

9. Joint accounts

A petition and complaint comes within the provisions of RC 2109.50 where it alleges facts showing that the person filing it is a person interested in the estate of a decedent, and where it contains the further allegations that moneys deposited in a bank during the lifetime of the decedent in the joint names of the decedent and another with right of survivorship were so deposited for convenience only and in reality were the sole property of the decedent and belong in his estate, and that such other unauthorizedly withdrew the moneys from the account during the lifetime of the decedent and deposited the same in an account in such other's name where such moneys remain. Fecteau v. Cleveland Trust Co. (Ohio 1960) 171 Ohio St. 121, 167 N.E.2d 890, 12 O.O.2d 139. Executors And Administrators ⇐ 85(5)

10. Fraud on creditors

An administrator of an insolvent estate represents first the creditors and may bring a suit in equity to recover property transferred by the decedent to defraud the creditors. Mutual Life Ins. Co. of N.Y. v. Farmers' & Mechanics' Nat. Bank of Cadiz, Ohio (C.C.S.D.Ohio 1909) 173 F. 390.

11. Retirement benefits

An action to recover public employees retirement system benefits is governed by a six-year limitations period; the statute does not begin to run as to the estate of a claimant until a personal representative becomes qualified. State ex rel. Hadinger v. City of Akron (Summit 1988) 48 Ohio App.3d 64, 548 N.E.2d 299, motion overruled 38 Ohio St.3d 723, 533 N.E.2d 1063.

12. Invasion of privacy claim

Since an estate is not a living person it cannot suffer damages of shame or humiliation from invasion of privacy and a court properly dismisses the claim of an estate based upon release of medical and financial information regarding a potential resident of a home who is placed on a waiting list for admission and dies prior to entry; furthermore, a resident's right to confidential treatment of personal and medical records pursuant to RC 3721.13 cannot be enforced in this case since the deceased was never a resident of the home. Rothstein v Montefiore Home, 116 App(3d) 775, 689 NE(2d) 108 (Cuyahoga 1996).

2113.26 Contents of application

An application made by an executor or administrator under section 2113.25 of the Revised Code shall set forth the grounds of the application, the amount of money in the hands of the executor or administrator applicable on the debts of the deceased, and that he has used due diligence in performing the duties enumerated therein. Such application shall be supported by the affidavit of the executor or administrator.

(1953 H 1, eff. 10–1–53; GC 10509–87)

Historical and Statutory Notes

Pre–1953 H 1 Amendments: 119 v 394, § 1; 114 v 420

Library References

Executors and Administrators ⇐ 86(4).
Westlaw Topic No. 162.
C.J.S. Executors and Administrators §§ 187, 189, 196 to 198, 200 to 201.

Research References

Encyclopedias

OH Jur. 3d Decedents' Estates § 1635, Time Allowed for Completing Administration.

Treatises and Practice Aids

Carlin, Baldwin's Ohio Practice, Merrick-Rippner Probate Law § 74:22, Application for Extension of Time—Form.

Carlin, Baldwin's Ohio Practice, Merrick-Rippner Probate Law § 74:23, Entry Extending Time—Form.

2113.27 Extension of time limited

The probate court shall not at any one time grant an extension of more than six months from the date of application under sections 2113.25 and 2113.26 of the Revised Code, except that in cases where the estate is subject to estate or inheritance taxes which cannot be determined and paid within six months, the court may grant an extension for such longer period as it deems proper. The office of the executor or administrator shall not cease with the time allowed by law or the court for the performance of the duties enumerated in such sections.

(1953 H 1, eff. 10–1–53; GC 10509–88)

Historical and Statutory Notes

Pre–1953 H 1 Amendments: 119 v 394, § 1; 114 v 420

Library References

Executors and Administrators ⚖︎86(4).
Westlaw Topic No. 162.
C.J.S. Executors and Administrators §§ 187, 189, 196 to 198, 200 to 201.

Research References

Encyclopedias
OH Jur. 3d Decedents' Estates § 1635, Time Allowed for Completing Administration.

Notes of Decisions

Ed. Note: This section contains annotations from former RC 2113.10.

Assets not available 2
Continuation of office 3
Rejection of claim 1

---

1. Rejection of claim

Where a claim presented by a creditor to the administrator or executor is accepted, but is subsequently disallowed by the successor to the executor or administrator who allowed it, the four-year statute of limitation begins to run from the time of rejection of the claim. Bray v. Darby (Ohio 1910) 82 Ohio St. 47, 91 N.E. 861, 7 Ohio Law Rep. 638.

Notice of appointment must be given by a new administrator, otherwise an action brought more than six months after rejection of a claim lies. Croxton Mining Co. v. Hubbard (Ohio App. 1918) 30 Ohio C.D. 150, 8 Ohio App. 105, 28 Ohio C.A. 249.

2. Assets not available

Where the widow's homestead right terminated twenty years after the initial collection of assets, statute of limitations does not bar a suit to recover assets not available at the time the assets were first collected. Taylor v. Thorn (Ohio 1876) 29 Ohio St. 569.

3. Continuation of office

Unless the authority of the executor or administrator be terminated in some one of the ways pointed out in the statute, it is his duty to continue the administration of the estate until it shall be entirely settled, and shall administer according to law and the will of the testator all of his goods, chattels, rights, and credits, and one of the duties enjoined upon him is to collect the assets within one year from the date of his bond, or such further time as the probate court may allow, not exceeding five years; but the office of the executor does not cease "with the time allowed by law or the court for the collection of assets" and he is required to file and settle accounts of his administration in the proper court at the end of 18 months from the date of his bond, and from time to time thereafter, until the estate is fully administered. Weyer v. Watt (Ohio 1891) 48 Ohio St. 545, 26 W.L.B. 284, 28 N.E. 670.

2113.28 Time allowed to collect assets not to defer account

The time allowed by the probate court to collect the assets of an estate shall not operate as an allowance of further time to file the accounts required by section 2109.301 of the Revised Code.

(2001 H 85, eff. 10–31–01; 1953 H 1, eff. 10–1–53; GC 10509–171)

Historical and Statutory Notes

Pre–1953 H 1 Amendments: 114 v 439
Amendment Note: 2001 H 85 substituted "2109.301" for "2109.30".

Library References

Executors and Administrators ⚖︎459.
Westlaw Topic No. 162.
C.J.S. Executors and Administrators § 786.

2113.29 New administrator

When assets come to the hands of a new administrator, after any of the periods limited for the commencement of suits against him, he shall account for them and be liable to suits and proceedings on account thereof, as is provided with respect to an original administrator.

(1953 H 1, eff. 10–1–53; GC 10509–157)

Historical and Statutory Notes

Pre–1953 H 1 Amendments: 114 v 436

Cross References

Newly discovered assets, 2113.69

Library References

Executors and Administrators ⚖︎464.
Westlaw Topic No. 162.
C.J.S. Executors and Administrators § 786.

Research References

Encyclopedias
OH Jur. 3d Decedents' Estates § 991, Liabilities.

Notes of Decisions

Ed. Note: This section contains annotations from former RC 2113.10.

Notice 2
Rents 1

---

1. Rents

After-acquired assets must be accounted for by the administrator, but rents of real estate accruing after death of intestate are not rents of the estate and the administrator has no duty in regard to them. Overturf v. Dugan (Ohio 1876) 29 Ohio St. 230.

2. Notice

An order of the probate court directing that "notice of appointment of a new administrator" be given "in the same manner prescribed with respect to an original administrator," which order fixes the period of four months following such appointment wherein creditors shall present their claims to the new administrator is presumed valid in collateral proceedings unless it is made to appear that the action by the court is void for want of authority. Haag v. Meffley (Lucas 1951) 89 Ohio App. 471, 103 N.E.2d 37, 46 O.O. 274.

GENERAL POWERS AND DUTIES

2113.30 Continuing decedent's business

(A) Except as otherwise directed by the decedent in the decedent's last will and testament, an executor or administrator, without personal liability for losses incurred, may continue the decedent's business during four months next following the date of the appointment of that executor or administrator, unless the probate court directs otherwise, and for any further time that the court may authorize upon a hearing and after notice to the surviving spouse and distributees. In either case, no debts incurred or contracts entered into shall involve the estate beyond the assets used in that business immediately prior to the death of the decedent without first obtaining the approval of the court. During the time the business is continued, the executor or administrator shall file monthly reports in the court, setting forth the receipts and expenses of the business for the preceding month and any other pertinent information that the court may require. The executor or administrator may not bind the estate without court approval beyond the period during which the business is continued.

(B) As used in this section, "decedent's business" means a business that is owned by the decedent as a sole proprietor at the time of the decedent's death. "Decedent's business" does not include a business that is owned in whole or in part by the decedent as a shareholder of a corporation, a member of a limited liability company, or a partner of a partnership, or under any other form of ownership other than a sole proprietorship.

(2002 H 345, eff. 7–23–02; 1953 H 1, eff. 10–1–53; GC 10509–9)

Historical and Statutory Notes

Pre–1953 H 1 Amendments: 116 v 385

Amendment Note: 2002 H 345 designated division (A); substituted "four months" for "one month" in newly designated division (A); added new division (B); made changes to reflect gender neutral language; and made other nonsubstantive changes.

Cross References

Liens; executors and administrators have same rights and liabilities as owner would have, 1311.21

Library References

Executors and Administrators ⚖93(1).
Westlaw Topic No. 162.
C.J.S. Executors and Administrators §§ 205 to 206, 210 to 215.

Research References

Encyclopedias

OH Jur. 3d Decedents' Estates § 1411, Statutory Authority for Continuing Business.

OH Jur. 3d Decedents' Estates § 1414, Personal Liability for Continuing Business; Indemnification.

Forms

Ohio Forms Legal and Business § 24:466, Powers—to Carry on Interest in Partnership.

Ohio Forms Legal and Business § 24:467, Powers—to Carry on Business and to Sell and Encumber Property.

Ohio Forms Legal and Business § 24:661, Bequest of Business—Sole Proprietorship.

Treatises and Practice Aids

Carlin, Baldwin's Ohio Practice, Merrick-Rippner Probate Law § 2:6, Identification of Assets.

Carlin, Baldwin's Ohio Practice, Merrick-Rippner Probate Law § 2:47, Continuation of Decedent's Business—in General.

Carlin, Baldwin's Ohio Practice, Merrick-Rippner Probate Law § 2:48, Continuation of Decedent's Business—After Four Months.

Carlin, Baldwin's Ohio Practice, Merrick-Rippner Probate Law § 2:49, Continuation of Decedent's Business—Debts.

Carlin, Baldwin's Ohio Practice, Merrick-Rippner Probate Law § 72:1, Power to Continue Decedent's Business—Time Limit.

Carlin, Baldwin's Ohio Practice, Merrick-Rippner Probate Law § 72:2, Power to Continue Decedent's Business—Time Limit—Extension.

Carlin, Baldwin's Ohio Practice, Merrick-Rippner Probate Law § 72:3, Power to Continue Decedent's Business—Reports.

Carlin, Baldwin's Ohio Practice, Merrick-Rippner Probate Law § 30:38, Drafting a Will—Authorization for Executor's Activity—Continuation of Decedent's Business.

Carlin, Baldwin's Ohio Practice, Merrick-Rippner Probate Law § 30:57, Simple Will—Form.

Carlin, Baldwin's Ohio Practice, Merrick-Rippner Probate Law § 73:12, Application for Authority to Continue Business—Form.

Carlin, Baldwin's Ohio Practice, Merrick-Rippner Probate Law § 73:13, Entry Setting for Hearing and Ordering Notice—Form.

Carlin, Baldwin's Ohio Practice, Merrick-Rippner Probate Law § 73:14, Entry to Continue Decedent's Business—Form.

Carlin, Baldwin's Ohio Practice, Merrick-Rippner Probate Law § 91:18, Land Sale—Not to Pay for Continuing Business of Decedent.

Carlin, Baldwin's Ohio Practice, Merrick-Rippner Probate Law § 30:166, Continuation of Business—Form.

Bogert - the Law of Trusts and Trustees § 572, Statutes Affecting the Problem.

Bogert - the Law of Trusts and Trustees § 573, Court Orders for Continuance—Procedure and Contents of Order.

Bogert - the Law of Trusts and Trustees § 575, Authorized Continuance—Contract, Tort or Other Liability to Third Persons.

Law Review and Journal Commentaries

Continuing Decedent's Business After Death. William J. McGraw III, 12 Prob L J Ohio 82 (May/June 2002).

Notes of Decisions

"Business" construed 6
Expenses 2
General assets of estate 3
Lease renewal 4
Liquidation 1
Personal liability 5
Standard of care 7

---

1. Liquidation

RC 2113.30 does not apply where a business is being liquidated. In re Brown's Estate (Fayette 1954) 98 Ohio App. 297, 129 N.E.2d 509, 57 O.O. 342.

Where certain moneys are due from the exceptor to the purchaser at a private sale of the remaining portion of deceased's business being liquidated by the administrator, the failure of the exceptor to account for such moneys does not relieve the administrator of his duty to correctly report the full amount of the sale price. In re Brown's Estate (Fayette 1954) 98 Ohio App. 297, 129 N.E.2d 509, 57 O.O. 342. Executors And Administrators ⚖ 374

An administrator has no authority to give vacation pay to employees of the decedent's business to induce them to remain employed during the liquidation of the business, without court authority. In re Brown's Estate (Ohio Prob. 1954) 129 N.E.2d 497, 67 Ohio Law Abs. 291, affirmed in part, reversed in part 98 Ohio App. 297, 129 N.E.2d 509, 57 O.O. 342.

Payments made to an administrator for services rendered in liquidating a decedent's business more than one month following his appointment as administrator, without court authority, are unauthorized. In re Brown's Estate (Ohio Prob. 1954) 129 N.E.2d 497, 67 Ohio Law Abs. 291, affirmed in part, reversed in part 98 Ohio App. 297, 129 N.E.2d 509, 57 O.O. 342.

2. Expenses

Upon proper proof an executor is entitled to credit for expenses incurred in the operation of decedent's business for one month after his death, and the burden of proving such expenditures is upon the executor. In re Szakacs' Estate (Cuyahoga 1961) 175 N.E.2d 119, 86 Ohio Law Abs. 333.

3. General assets of estate

The general assets of the testator, not used in his former business, cannot be subjected to the liabilities incurred by the executor of the estate in carrying on such business after the testator's death where there is no clear and explicit authority conferred by the will, even though the executor acted in good faith. Lucht v. Behrens (Ohio 1876) 28 Ohio St. 231, 22 Am.Rep. 378.

Administrator of decedent's estate did not fail to preserve tractor, as an asset of estate, and, thus, estate should not have been penalized in the amount of $250 a month for ten months based upon alleged negligence of administrator. Booth v. Hendershot (Ohio App. 5 Dist., Guernsey, 12-10-2002) No. 02CA08, 2002-Ohio-6794, 2002 WL 31761445, Unreported. Executors And Administrators ⇐ 86(1)

Decedent's tractor was still an asset of the estate, and, thus, issue of valuation of tractor as of the date of alleged sale to decedent's son was moot. Booth v. Hendershot (Ohio App. 5 Dist., Guernsey, 12-10-2002) No. 02CA08, 2002-Ohio-6794, 2002 WL 31761445, Unreported. Executors And Administrators ⇐ 63

4. Lease renewal

Where a will directed named persons to conduct moving picture business during the life of a lease, but did not authorize them to exercise option to renew lease, they were not entitled to a decree of specific performance to compel lessor to execute a renewal lease. Mills v. Connor (Ohio 1922) 104 Ohio St. 409, 135 N.E. 616, 20 Ohio Law Rep. 16, 20 Ohio Law Rep. 18. Landlord And Tenant ⇐ 86(1); Specific Performance ⇐ 17

5. Personal liability

Companion of sole stockholder of corporation, who sought declaratory judgment that executor of stockholder's estate failed to properly invest and preserve the estate's assets and was liable for financial losses that occurred in estate while under his control, was not required to include a claim for specific monetary damages in order to obtain a monetary judgment; though it was clear that stockholder's companion did not expressly request monetary relief nor include a specific dollar amount in her complaint, a reasonable interpretation of complaint could lead to the conclusion she was requesting money damages for the amount of the loss suffered as a result of the failure of the executor to properly invest and preserve the assets of the estate. Sudnek v. Klein (Ohio App. 11 Dist., 09-29-1997) 125 Ohio App.3d 336, 708 N.E.2d 735, appeal allowed 81 Ohio St.3d 1445, 690 N.E.2d 16, appeal dismissed as improvidently allowed 84 Ohio St.3d 1243, 705 N.E.2d 359, 1999-Ohio-371. Declaratory Judgment ⇐ 321

6. "Business" construed

Statute authorizing continuance of the decedent's business by executor or administrator of estate for one month following date of appointment without personal liability for losses incurred, and for any further periods as court might authorize, applies to corporations that have a single shareholder. Sudnek v. Klein (Ohio App. 11 Dist., 09-29-1997) 125 Ohio App.3d 336, 708 N.E.2d 735, appeal allowed 81 Ohio St.3d 1445, 690 N.E.2d 16, appeal dismissed as improvidently allowed 84 Ohio St.3d 1243, 705 N.E.2d 359, 1999-Ohio-371. Executors And Administrators ⇐ 93(1)

7. Standard of care

Beneficiary's acquiescence to continued operation of decedent's business and failure to demand sale or liquidation of business did not lessen culpability of executor who failed to use due care and diligence in the administration of estate; substantial evidence indicated that during six years executor continued business beneficiary was not given necessary information to keep her sufficiently informed of corporation's financial standing, as executor did not make annual accountings to beneficiaries. Sudnick v. Klein (Ohio App. 11 Dist., Geauga, 12-31-2002) No. 2001-G-2356, No. 2001-G-2365, No. 2001-G-2357, No. 2001-G-2358, 2002-Ohio-7341, 2002 WL 31895117, Unreported, appeal not allowed 98 Ohio St.3d 1567, 787 N.E.2d 1231, 2003-Ohio-2242. Executors And Administrators ⇐ 93(1)

There was some competent, credible evidence to support probate court's finding that executor had failed to use due care and diligence in the administration of estate; executor failed to seek an order from the probate court authorizing the continuation of decedent's business, decedent's will did not specifically grant executor power to continue operating business after decedent's death, and value of business plummeted from $450,000, when executor was appointed, to $19,129, when executor decided to finally wind up estate in six years later. Sudnick v. Klein (Ohio App. 11 Dist., Geauga, 12-31-2002) No. 2001-G-2356, No. 2001-G-2365, No. 2001-G-2357, No. 2001-G-2358, 2002-Ohio-7341, 2002 WL 31895117, Unreported, appeal not allowed 98 Ohio St.3d 1567, 787 N.E.2d 1231, 2003-Ohio-2242. Executors And Administrators ⇐ 93(1)

2113.31 Responsibility of executor or administrator

Every executor or administrator is chargeable with all chattels, rights, and credits of the deceased which come into his hands and are to be administered, although not included in the inventory required by section 2115.02 of the Revised Code. Such executor or administrator is also chargeable with all the proceeds of personal property and real estate sold for the payment of debts or legacies, and all the interest, profit, and income that in any way comes to his hands from the personal estate of the deceased.

(1953 H 1, eff. 10–1–53; GC 10509–172)

Historical and Statutory Notes

Pre–1953 H 1 Amendments: 114 v 439

Cross References

Fiduciary holding partnership interest in that capacity; limit on liability, 1339.65
Liens; executors and administrators have same rights and liabilities as owner would have, 1311.21

Library References

Executors and Administrators ⇐ 86, 102, 104(1), 131, 147, 153, 166.
Westlaw Topic No. 162.
C.J.S. Executors and Administrators §§ 187 to 201, 223 to 225, 227 to 228, 284, 295, 316, 324, 329, 336, 343.

Research References

Encyclopedias

OH Jur. 3d Decedents' Estates § 974, for Assets Received.
OH Jur. 3d Decedents' Estates § 975, for Proceeds, Income, and Profits.
OH Jur. 3d Decedents' Estates § 976, in Regard to Realty.

Treatises and Practice Aids

Restatement (2d) of Property, Don. Trans. § 33.1, Meaning of a Will.

Notes of Decisions

Appeal   5
Debts due estate   1
Distribution   4
Interest   2
Joint and survivor accounts   6
Real estate   3
Third party funds   7

---

1. Debts due estate

The principle that the appointment of a debtor as administrator converts the debt into assets to be accounted for does not apply to one who is only conditionally liable to the estate. Shields v. Odell (Ohio 1875) 27 Ohio St. 398. Executors And Administrators ⇐ 50

Where the debtor of the deceased is appointed administrator, the debt becomes an asset in his hands, and the court may hear evidence as to whether he has properly charged himself in settling the final account. (See also Tracy v Card, 2 OS 431 (1853).) In re Raab's Estate (Ohio 1865) 16 Ohio St. 273.

When the obligor on a bond becomes administrator of the obligee, the bond is suspended, and the debt due becomes an asset in the hands of the debtor, as administrator. Bigelow's Ex'r v. Bigelow's Adm'rs (Ohio 1829) 4 Ohio 138, 19 Am.Dec. 591.

Absent evidence of precisely what repair bills represented, or any agreement between decedent and his son regarding who was responsible for bills, trial court could correctly assign any bills for repair of tractor, as estate's asset, to decedent's estate. Booth v. Hendershot (Ohio App. 5 Dist., Guernsey, 12-10-2002) No. 02CA08, 2002-Ohio-6794, 2002 WL 31761445, Unreported. Executors And Administrators ⇐ 205

To the extent decedent's son paid an obligation of the estate, when he tendered balance due to pay off promissory note encumbering tractor, he was entitled to reimbursement for the funds expended. Booth v. Hendershot (Ohio App. 5 Dist., Guernsey, 12-10-2002) No. 02CA08, 2002-Ohio-6794, 2002 WL 31761445, Unreported. Executors And Administrators ⇐ 202

2. Interest

An administrator is not chargeable with interest on money from an estate unless he uses it for himself or unreasonably delays settlement of the accounts. Cooch v. Irwin's Adm'r (Ohio 1857) 7 Ohio St. 22.

Assets in the hands of an administrator which have yielded no profit, have been tied up in litigation, and which the court has not ordered be distributed, do not bear interest and it is error to charge the administrator on such items, including debts which the administrator owes to the estate. James v. West (Ohio 1902) 67 Ohio St. 28, 47 W.L.B. 857, 65 N.E. 156.

Finding by probate court as to the debt due by the administrator is final, binding the sureties on the administrator's bond. Perkins v. Scott (Ohio Cir. 1895) 6 Ohio C.D. 226, 2 Ohio Dec. 496, dismissed.

3. Real estate

Absent any evidence that step-daughter exerted or attempted to exert improper influence over grantor, that there was any fiduciary relationship between step-daughter and grantor, or that transfer of grantor's marital residence to step-daughter was the result of fraud, assertion of administratrix of grantor's estate that transfer had to be the result of undue influence and fraud, because that is the only reasonable explanation for transfer, was insufficient to establish undue influence or fraud. In re Estate of Rickerson (Ohio App. 6 Dist., Lucas, 04-29-2005) No. L-04-1108, 2005-Ohio-2101, 2005 WL 1009919, Unreported. Executors And Administrators ☞ 56

Administratrix of estate was not required to expend her own personal funds to preserve estate property, and thus, administratrix did not breach her fiduciary duties, where there were no funds available to the estate to pay for repairs to condemned property. Smith v. Estate of Mattern (Ohio App. 5 Dist., Stark, 12-09-2002) No. 2002CA00215, 2002-Ohio-6883, 2002 WL 31812678, Unreported. Executors And Administrators ☞ 132

Administratrix of estate did not breach her fiduciary duty by not selling estate property, which was mortgaged, to pay off estate debts after foreclosure action was initiated; doctrine of lis pendens would have frustrated any attempted sale of the property once the foreclosure action was instituted and administratrix could not have conveyed clear title to property while foreclosure was pending. Smith v. Estate of Mattern (Ohio App. 5 Dist., Stark, 12-09-2002) No. 2002CA00215, 2002-Ohio-6883, 2002 WL 31812678, Unreported. Executors And Administrators ☞ 137

Administratrix of estate did not breach her fiduciary duty by waiting to sell estate property, which was mortgaged, to pay off estate debts, where mortgagee was considering accepting deed to property in lieu of foreclosure. Smith v. Estate of Mattern (Ohio App. 5 Dist., Stark, 12-09-2002) No. 2002CA00215, 2002-Ohio-6883, 2002 WL 31812678, Unreported. Executors And Administrators ☞ 137

Real estate of decedent descends directly to decedent's heirs or devisees, and administrator or executor, in absence of testamentary provision, has no right with respect to real estate unless he has ascertained that personal property is insufficient to pay debts. Hackmann v. Dawley (Ohio App. 10 Dist., 07-18-1995) 105 Ohio App.3d 363, 663 N.E.2d 1342. Descent And Distribution ☞ 75; Executors And Administrators ☞ 129(1); Wills ☞ 722

Where a sole devisee appointed as executor sells lands as devisee, the proceeds come into his hands as executor; and, where the personal estate is insufficient, he must apply such proceeds to the payment of testator's debts. Hocking Valley R. Co. v. White (Ohio 1913) 87 Ohio St. 413, 101 N.E. 354, 10 Ohio Law Rep. 611, Am.Ann.Cas. 1914A, 190. Executors And Administrators ☞ 40

An executor who in bad faith sells lands at a price manifestly less than their true value should be charged with the difference between the price received and the true value. Brown v. Reed (Ohio 1897) 56 Ohio St. 264, 37 W.L.B. 324, 46 N.E. 982. Executors And Administrators ☞ 138(9)

Rents received by an administrator from the real estate of the intestate may properly be charged to him on his account filed for settling the estate. Campbell v. McCormick (Ohio Cir. 1886) 1 Ohio C.D. 281. Executors And Administrators ☞ 477

Trial court did not commit plain error by admitting testimony by executor of estate to establish that the difference between sale price of estate property and assessed value was intended to be a partial satisfaction of rent arrearages, although this testimony violated parol evidence rule; admission did not seriously affect the basic fairness, integrity, or public reputation of the judicial process. Ejzak v. Remy (Ohio App. 5 Dist., Richland, 08-21-2002) No. 02CA8-2, 2002-Ohio-4385, 2002 WL 1969848, Unreported. Executors And Administrators ☞ 455

Executor of estate was not to be surcharged with $1,006 in uncollected rent from estate property, where that amount was part of $8,000 excess of sale price of property over assessed value, which was allowed as setoff against amount of rent arrearage to be surcharged. Ejzak v. Remy (Ohio App. 5 Dist., Richland, 08-21-2002) No. 02CA8-2, 2002-Ohio-4385, 2002 WL 1969848, Unreported. Executors And Administrators ☞ 131

Executrix of debtor's estate, who opened debt collection letters mailed to debtor, had standing to bring action against debt collector under Fair Debt Collection Practices Act (FDCPA). W v Finance Service of Norwalk, Inc, 22 F(3d) 647 (6th Cir O 1994).

4. Distribution

Debts due from the executor to the testator are regarded as assets chargeable as money in the hands of the executor and his sureties are liable for his failure to distribute this money. McGaughey v Jacoby, 54 OS 487, 44 NE 231 (1896).

5. Appeal

In probate court proceeding which affects only the rights of beneficiaries, executor/beneficiary must appeal in his individual capacity or he is presumed to be satisfied with judgment. In re Estate of Wirebaugh (Wood 1992) 84 Ohio App.3d 1, 616 N.E.2d 245. Appeal And Error ☞ 141

6. Joint and survivor accounts

Upon the death of one of the holders of joint and survivorship certificates of deposit in a bank, the survivor has the right to such certificates to the exclusion of the administrator of the decedent's estate, and such certificates may not be included in the inventory and appraisement of the estate notwithstanding the endorsement and delivery thereof to the administrator subsequent to the death of the decedent. Hoover v. Hoover (Wood 1950) 90 Ohio App. 148, 104 N.E.2d 41, 47 O.O. 37. Executors And Administrators ☞ 43; Executors And Administrators ☞ 66; Joint Tenancy ☞ 6

7. Third party funds

An administrator is responsible for any property he receives from a third party in his representative capacity; it follows that the administrator's surety is liable for funds converted by a bonded administrator. Bank One of Ohio N.A. v. Brown (Summit 1985) 22 Ohio App.3d 82, 488 N.E.2d 939, 22 O.B.R. 180. Executors And Administrators ☞ 86(3)

2113.311 Management of real estate by executor or administrator

(A) If, within a reasonable time after the appointment of the executor or administrator, no one in authority has taken over the management and rental of any real estate of which the decedent died seized, the executor or administrator, or an heir or devisee may, unless the will otherwise provides, make application to the probate court for an order authorizing the executor or administrator to assume such duties. Such application shall contain:

(1) A brief statement of the facts upon which the application is based and such other pertinent information as the court may require;

(2) A description or identification of the real estate and the interest owned by the decedent at the time of his death;

(3) The names and addresses, if known to the applicant, of the persons to whom such real estate passed by descent or devise.

Notice of the time of hearing on such application shall be given to the persons designated in sub-paragraph division (A)(3) of this section, unless for good cause the court dispenses with such notice, and also to the executor or administrator, unless the executor or administrator is the applicant.

If the court finds that the statements contained in the application are true and that it would be for the best interest of such heirs or devisees that the application be granted, it may authorize the executor or administrator to assume the management and rental of such real estate.

The court may require bond, new or additional, in an amount to be fixed by the court and conditioned that the executor or administrator will faithfully and honestly discharge the duties devolving upon him by the provisions of this section.

(B) In the exercise of such authority, the executor or administrator shall be authorized to do the following:

(1) Collect rents;

(2) From the rents collected:

(a) Pay all taxes and assessments due on such real estate, and all such usual operating expenses in connection with the management thereof;

(b) Make repairs when necessary to preserve such real estate from waste, provided that an order of the court shall first be obtained if the cost of such repairs exceeds one hundred dollars;

(c) Insure buildings against loss by fire or other casualty and against public liability;

(3) Advance money upon an order first obtained from the court, for such repairs, taxes, insurance, and all usual operating expenses, which shall be a charge on such real estate;

(4) Rent the property on a month to month basis, or, upon an order first obtained from the court, for a period not to exceed one year;

(5) Prosecute actions for forcible entry and detention of such real estate.

The executor or administrator shall, at intervals not to exceed twelve months, pay over to the heirs or devisees, if known, their share of the net rents, and shall account for all money received and paid out under authority of this section in his regular accounts of the administration of the estate, but in a separate schedule. If any share of the net rents remains unclaimed, it may be disposed of in the same manner as is provided for unclaimed money under section 2113.64 of the Revised Code.

The authority granted under this section shall terminate upon the transfer of the real estate to the heirs or devisees in accordance with section 2113.61 of the Revised Code, or upon a sale thereof, or upon application of the executor or administrator, or for a good cause shown, upon the application of an heir or devisee.

Upon application the court may allow compensation to the executor or administrator for extraordinary services, which shall be charged against the rents, and if said rents be insufficient, shall be a charge against such real estate.

Upon application the court may allow reasonable attorney fees paid by the executor or administrator when an attorney is employed in connection with the management and rental of such real estate, which shall be charged against the rents, and if said rents be insufficient, shall be a charge against such real estate.

(128 v 76, eff. 11–9–59)

Cross References

Liens; executors and administrators have same rights and liabilities as owner would have, 1311.21

Library References

Executors and Administrators ⚖130(1).
Westlaw Topic No. 162.
C.J.S. Executors and Administrators § 282.

Research References

Encyclopedias

OH Jur. 3d Decedents' Estates § 976, in Regard to Realty.
OH Jur. 3d Decedents' Estates § 1385, Statutory Authority Relating to the Management of Real Estate.
OH Jur. 3d Decedents' Estates § 1386, Statutory Authority Relating to the Management of Real Estate—Acts Specifically Authorized.
OH Jur. 3d Decedents' Estates § 1387, Statutory Authority Relating to the Management of Real Estate—Duty to Account for Rents Collected.
OH Jur. 3d Decedents' Estates § 1388, Statutory Authority Relating to the Management of Real Estate—Termination of Authority.
OH Jur. 3d Decedents' Estates § 1389, Title To, and Power Over, Real Estate Generally.
OH Jur. 3d Decedents' Estates § 1395, Powers and Liabilities as to Leases.
OH Jur. 3d Decedents' Estates § 1396, Powers and Liabilities as to Leases—Leases of Decedent.
OH Jur. 3d Decedents' Estates § 1397, Right and Duty to Make Repairs; Liability in Tort.
OH Jur. 3d Decedents' Estates § 1399, Right and Duty to Insure Property.
OH Jur. 3d Decedents' Estates § 1400, Duty to Pay Taxes.

Forms

Ohio Forms Legal and Business § 24:466, Powers—to Carry on Interest in Partnership.

Treatises and Practice Aids

Carlin, Baldwin's Ohio Practice, Merrick-Rippner Probate Law § 2:6, Identification of Assets.
Carlin, Baldwin's Ohio Practice, Merrick-Rippner Probate Law § 2:50, Management of Decedent's Real Estate.
Carlin, Baldwin's Ohio Practice, Merrick-Rippner Probate Law § 73:1, Management of Real Estate—Application.
Carlin, Baldwin's Ohio Practice, Merrick-Rippner Probate Law § 73:2, Management of Real Estate—Rental and Maintenance of Property.
Carlin, Baldwin's Ohio Practice, Merrick-Rippner Probate Law § 73:3, Management of Real Estate—Accounting for Rent Collected and Expenses.
Carlin, Baldwin's Ohio Practice, Merrick-Rippner Probate Law § 73:5, Management of Real Estate—Termination of Authority.
Carlin, Baldwin's Ohio Practice, Merrick-Rippner Probate Law § 82:1, Duties of New Executor or Administrator.
Carlin, Baldwin's Ohio Practice, Merrick-Rippner Probate Law § 73:15, Application to Take Over Management and Rental of Real Property—Form.
Carlin, Baldwin's Ohio Practice, Merrick-Rippner Probate Law § 73:16, Entry to Take Over Management and Rental of Real Property—Form.
Carlin, Baldwin's Ohio Practice, Merrick-Rippner Probate Law § 90:11, Collection of Rents and Management of Realty Before Land Sale.
Kuehnle and Levey, Ohio Real Estate Law and Practice § 52:12, Statutory Fiduciary Sales—Enjoining Creditors from Levying After Owner's Death.
Kuehnle and Levey, Ohio Real Estate Law and Practice § 52:23, Statutory Fiduciary Sales—Administrator's Action to Enjoin Creditors from Levying.
Kuehnle and Levey, Ohio Real Estate Law and Practice § 53:18, Land Sales—Interests Subject to Sale by Fiduciaries—Rents Accruing Between Death of Owner and Sale.

Law Review and Journal Commentaries

Fiduciary Liability Under Superfund: Myth or Reality?, William Falsgraf. 1 Prob L J Ohio 97 (May/June 1991).

Notes of Decisions

Duties of executor 3
Mortgage 2
Sale 1

---

1. Sale

Provision of will explicitly directing executor of estate to sell testator's real property as soon as practicable prevailed, pursuant to doctrine of equitable conversion, over will's residuary clause under which testator's three children were devised and bequeathed "all the rest, residue and remainder" of testator's real and personal property, and therefore executor could proceed with selling and converting testator's real property, though will's power of sale provision did not contain any order to distribute

Note 1

proceeds from sale of property. In re Estate of Line (Ohio App. 12 Dist., 08-18-1997) 122 Ohio App.3d 387, 701 N.E.2d 1028. Wills ⇨ 634(6); Wills ⇨ 692(5)

Beneficiary under will did not have option to take his share of testator's real property outright, though title passed to him under will, where executor of estate, who was also named beneficiary, found it to be in estate's best interest for property to be sold pursuant to testator's explicit direction, and executor had right of possession of real property in order to carry out testator's direction. In re Estate of Line (Ohio App. 12 Dist., 08-18-1997) 122 Ohio App.3d 387, 701 N.E.2d 1028. Wills ⇨ 727

An executor of a will is not required to comply with the procedural requirements of RC 2113.311 where the will specifically directs the executor to sell property. Bilikam, Huntington Nat. Bank of Columbus v. Bilikam (Franklin 1982) 2 Ohio App.3d 300, 441 N.E.2d 845, 2 O.B.R. 332. Executors And Administrators ⇨ 138(1)

2. Mortgage

Where a mortgagor dies and his executor obtains permission from the probate court to manage the real property of the mortgagor pursuant to RC 2113.311, the executor is required to use all rental incomes remaining after payment of the expenses authorized by RC 2113.311 to pay the mortgagee, even though the mortgage agreement does not contain a specific pledge of rental income. BancOhio Nat. Bank v. Andrew J. Haas Irrevocable Trust (Summit 1986) 33 Ohio App.3d 253, 515 N.E.2d 1024.

3. Duties of executor

Dispute between executor and heir of estate concerning executor's attempt to evict heir from real property belonging to estate did not constitute an unsettled claim between executor and estate, so as to support heir's motion to remove executor; heir was not the estate and was not acting on behalf of all heirs in challenging the executor's actions. In re Estate of Jacob (Ohio App. 8 Dist., Cuyahoga, 09-22-2005) No. 85640, 2005-Ohio-4998, 2005 WL 2304574, Unreported. Executors And Administrators ⇨ 35(2)

Trial court properly granted executor of estate authority to manage real property belonging to estate; estate's debts exceeded its available funds, and executor required the authority to pay operating expenses, perform repairs, rent the properties, and, if necessary, evict the occupants. In re Estate of Jacob (Ohio App. 8 Dist., Cuyahoga, 09-22-2005) No. 85640, 2005-Ohio-4998, 2005 WL 2304574, Unreported. Executors And Administrators ⇨ 129(1)

Nephew of testator, who was specifically directed by will to sell testator's home as executor of estate, was not required by statute to obtain probate court's approval before managing the real estate by paying expenses from estate funds, even though will also directed that proceeds of sale were to be given to nephew. In re Estate of Carpenter (Ohio App. 11 Dist., 09-11-1998) 129 Ohio App.3d 717, 719 N.E.2d 20. Executors And Administrators ⇨ 109(1)

Looking after real estate, collecting rents, and paying taxes for two years are not services required of an administrator or executor in the common course of duty. In re Wolfe's Estate (Ohio Prob. 1897) 7 Ohio Dec. 220, 4 Ohio N.P. 336. Executors And Administrators ⇨ 494

2113.32 Executors and administrators not to profit

No profits shall be made by executors or administrators by the increase of any part of an estate, nor shall they sustain any loss by the decrease or destruction of such estate without their fault.

(1953 H 1, eff. 10–1–53; GC 10509–173)

Historical and Statutory Notes

Pre–1953 H 1 Amendments: 114 v 440

Library References

Executors and Administrators ⇨115, 118.
Westlaw Topic No. 162.
C.J.S. Executors and Administrators §§ 264 to 266, 271 to 274, 343.

Research References

Encyclopedias

OH Jur. 3d Decedents' Estates § 974, for Assets Received.

Notes of Decisions

Claim settlement 1
Land 3
Loans 2

---

1. Claim settlement

An administrator may not through his attorney adjust or settle claims against the estate for less than face value and pocket the difference. Cox v. John (Ohio 1877) 32 Ohio St. 532.

Where the probate court acquired jurisdiction over the administrator of a deceased executor, and the question of the liability of the executor to the estate of his decedent, its findings and judgment as to the amount of a debt due by the executor to the estate are conclusive, until reversed or modified. Jones v. Willis (Ohio 1905) 72 Ohio St. 189, 74 N.E. 166, 2 Ohio Law Rep. 529. Executors And Administrators ⇨ 513(12); Judgment ⇨ 640

2. Loans

Where executors are empowered by the will to loan money, and they exercise such care as would men of ordinary prudence, they will not be held liable for a loss resulting from unforeseen defects in the security on the loan. Miller v. Proctor (Ohio 1870) 20 Ohio St. 442.

3. Land

Profits arising from either the natural increase in the value of the property or from the trustee's management are the absolute property of the beneficiary. Berkmeyer v. Kellerman (Ohio 1877) 32 Ohio St. 239, 30 Am.Rep. 577.

Because of the fiduciary nature of the position, an administrator may not buy land which he put up for public sale in the course of his administration, not even to cure a problem in the sale, and should a problem arise, the administrator must again offer the property for sale. (See also Sheldon v Newton, 3 OS 494 (1854); Caldwell v Caldwell, 45 OS 512, 15 NE 297 (1888).) Barrington v. Alexander (Ohio 1856) 6 Ohio St. 189.

2113.33 Not responsible for bad debts

An executor or administrator is not accountable for debts inventoried as due to the decedent, if it appears to the probate court that, without his fault, they remain uncollected.

(1953 H 1, eff. 10–1–53; GC 10509–174)

Historical and Statutory Notes

Pre–1953 H 1 Amendments: 114 v 440

Cross References

Liens; executors and administrators have same rights and liabilities as owner would have, 1311.21

Library References

Executors and Administrators ⇨89.
Westlaw Topic No. 162.
C.J.S. Executors and Administrators § 204.

Research References

Encyclopedias

OH Jur. 3d Decedents' Estates § 974, for Assets Received.

Notes of Decisions

Distribution 2
Interest 1

Untimely proof 3

1. Interest

Assets in the hands of an administrator which have yielded no profit, have been tied up in litigation, and which the court has not ordered be distributed, do not bear interest and it is error to charge the administrator on such items, including debts which the administrator owes to the estate. James v. West (Ohio 1902) 67 Ohio St. 28, 47 W.L.B. 857, 65 N.E. 156.

2. Distribution

Debts due from the executor to the testator are regarded as assets chargeable as money in the hands of the executor and his sureties are liable for his failure to distribute this money. McGaughey v Jacoby, 54 OS 487, 44 NE 231 (1896).

3. Untimely proof

Untimely proof of claim filed by executrix of creditor's estate was deemed allowed, where no objections to claim had been filed. In re Carlin Inv. Co. (Bkrtcy.N.D.Ohio 1993) 158 B.R. 690. Bankruptcy ⇐ 2923

Claimant, who filed untimely but allowed proof of claim in time to permit payment of claim, failed to establish that she did not receive notice or have actual knowledge of case in time to file proof of claim, for purposes of determining priority of distribution; notice was mailed to address of record of claimant's deceased husband but not returned, claimant retained same attorney through more than six years that litigation was pending in adversary proceeding which resulted in assets to distribute in Chapter 7 case, and both claimant and her attorney had notice or actual knowledge of case in time to file proof of claim by due date. In re Carlin Inv. Co. (Bkrtcy.N.D.Ohio 1993) 158 B.R. 690. Bankruptcy ⇐ 3443

2113.34 Chargeable with property consumed

If an executor or administrator neglects to sell personal property which he is required to sell, and retains, consumes, or disposes of it for his own benefit, he shall be charged therewith at double the value affixed thereto by the appraisers.

(125 v 903, eff. 10–1–53; 1953 H 1; GC 10509–175)

Historical and Statutory Notes

Pre–1953 H 1 Amendments: 114 v 440

Library References

Executors and Administrators ⇐115.
Westlaw Topic No. 162.
C.J.S. Executors and Administrators §§ 264 to 266, 343.

Research References

Encyclopedias
OH Jur. 3d Fiduciaries § 104, Personal Use of Assets.

COMMISSIONS AND ALLOWANCES

2113.35 Commissions

Executors and administrators shall be allowed commissions upon the amount of all the personal estate, including the income from the personal estate, that is received and accounted for by them and upon the proceeds of real estate that is sold, as follows:

(A) For the first one hundred thousand dollars, at the rate of four per cent;

(B) All above one hundred thousand dollars and not exceeding four hundred thousand dollars, at the rate of three per cent;

(C) All above four hundred thousand dollars, at the rate of two per cent.

Executors and administrators also shall be allowed a commission of one per cent on the value of real estate that is not sold.

Executors and administrators also shall be allowed a commission of one per cent on all property that is not subject to administration and that is includable for purposes of computing the Ohio estate tax, except joint and survivorship property.

The basis of valuation for the allowance of such commissions on real estate sold shall be the gross proceeds of sale, and for all other property the fair market value of the other property as of the date of death of the decedent. The commissions allowed to executors and administrators in this section shall be received in full compensation for all their ordinary services.

If the probate court finds, after hearing, that an executor or administrator, in any respect, has not faithfully discharged his duties as executor or administrator, the court may deny the executor or administrator any compensation whatsoever or may allow the executor or administrator the reduced compensation that the court thinks proper.

(1990 H 346, eff. 5–31–90; 1980 S 158; 1974 H 691; 1953 H 1; GC 10509–192)

Uncodified Law

1990 H 346, § 3, eff. 5–31–90, reads, in part: (A) Sections 1 and 2 of this act shall apply only to the estates of decedents who die on or after the effective date of this act.

Historical and Statutory Notes

Pre–1953 H 1 Amendments: 119 v 394, § 1; 116 v 385; 114 v 443

OSBA Probate and Trust Law Section

1990:

This Subcommittee was appointed to review the provisions of Section 2113.35 as it relates to commissions of executors.

The Committee's focus was on the next to last paragraph of the Statute, as the Board felt it was currently unclear whether the basis for valuing assets for purpose of fixing an executors commission is the date of death, the alternate valuation date if elected, or the special use valuation, if elected. There was concern that the fiduciary who in attempting to reduce the value of the gross estate and save taxes for the beneficiary, finds that he has thereby reduced his own fee and as result, the executor may be reluctant to use such tax reducing devises. It was the Committee's recommendation that this paragraph be amended to read in part as follows:

"The basis for valuation for the allowance of such commissions on REAL property shall be the gross proceeds of sale and for all other property the FAIR MARKET value of the other property AS OF THE DATE OF DEATH."

The Board believes that the Committee's proposal removes existing ambiguities and presents a good policy compromise, so that fiduciaries could focus on doing as good a job as possible without fear of losing commissions as a result.

The further recommendation of the Committee was to delete in the first paragraph, the words "under authority contained in a will", as obviously the administrators would not be operating under a will, and the words as presently included only create some confusion.

Library References

Executors and Administrators ⇐495.
Westlaw Topic No. 162.
C.J.S. Executors and Administrators §§ 821, 833 to 834.
Baldwin's Ohio Legislative Service, 1990 Laws of Ohio, H 346—LSC Analysis, p 5–87

Research References

Encyclopedias
OH Jur. 3d Decedents' Estates § 1348, Generally; Statutory Commissions.
OH Jur. 3d Decedents' Estates § 1350, Services and Property Covered by Commissions.
OH Jur. 3d Decedents' Estates § 1351, Percentage, Amount, and Apportionment of Commissions.

OH Jur. 3d Decedents' Estates § 1356, Allowance of Extra Compensation for Expenses and Extraordinary Services.

OH Jur. 3d Decedents' Estates § 1361, Waiver and Forfeiture of Compensation.

OH Jur. 3d Decedents' Estates § 1595, Commissions of Executor or Administrator.

OH Jur. 3d Decedents' Estates § 1596, Commissions of Executor or Administrator—Amount and Computation.

OH Jur. 3d Fiduciaries § 258, Loss or Forfeiture of Right to Compensation—Statutory Grounds for Denial of Commission.

Forms

Ohio Forms and Transactions KP 30.11, Executor.

Treatises and Practice Aids

Carlin, Baldwin's Ohio Practice, Merrick-Rippner Probate Law § 2:2, Explanation of Fees and Expenses.

Carlin, Baldwin's Ohio Practice, Merrick-Rippner Probate Law § 80:1, Commissions—Statutory.

Carlin, Baldwin's Ohio Practice, Merrick-Rippner Probate Law § 80:2, Commissions—Computation of Allowance.

Carlin, Baldwin's Ohio Practice, Merrick-Rippner Probate Law § 80:4, Commissions—Joint or Successor Executors or Administrators.

Carlin, Baldwin's Ohio Practice, Merrick-Rippner Probate Law § 80:5, Commissions—Denial or Reduction.

Carlin, Baldwin's Ohio Practice, Merrick-Rippner Probate Law § 80:7, Commissions—Attachment by Creditor of Fiduciary.

Carlin, Baldwin's Ohio Practice, Merrick-Rippner Probate Law § 80:8, Extraordinary Services—Allowance.

Carlin, Baldwin's Ohio Practice, Merrick-Rippner Probate Law § 80:16, Attorney Fees—Refused.

Carlin, Baldwin's Ohio Practice, Merrick-Rippner Probate Law § 96:12, Expenses of Sale—Compensation of Executor or Administrator.

Carlin, Baldwin's Ohio Practice, Merrick-Rippner Probate Law App B SPF 14.0, Application to Approve Settlement and Distribution of Wrongful Death and Survival Claims—Form.

Law Review and Journal Commentaries

Attorney as Both Executor and Attorney for Estate: Dual Roles = Dual Compensation, Robert G. Dykes & Brent A. Andrewsen. 13 Prob L J Ohio 58 (January/February 2003).

Ten Questions Arising in Settlement of Executor's Accounts, Harry Lewis Deibel. 31 Ohio L Rep 7 (January 30, 1930).

Notes of Decisions

Accounting 6
Attachment of commission 8
Attorney fees 5
Computation and apportionment 1
Interest 7
Inventory 4
Real estate sale 3
Unfaithful administration 2

---

1. Computation and apportionment

RS 6165 and RS 6188 are to be construed together in determining the percentage compensation for the sale of real estate and said compensation is to be computed on the aggregate amount arising from both real and personal estate, not on the proceeds of the real estate alone. Stone v. Strong (Ohio 1884) 42 Ohio St. 53.

The executor or administrator of a surviving partner who dies with partnership assets in his possession and is in the process of settling the partnership's accounts, is entitled to possession of such assets, and he is not precluded from receiving compensation out of the partnership funds for his services. Dayton v. Bartlett (Ohio 1882) 38 Ohio St. 357, 8 W.L.B. 212.

Commissions due to the administrator should be charged against the principal and income proportionally. Boggs v. Taylor (Ohio 1876) 29 Ohio St. 172. Life Estates ⟾ 15(1); Wills ⟾ 728

Computation is upon the entire personal estate and not merely on money handled, excluding stocks and bonds, the income of which is bequeathed to the executrix. Hegner v. Hegner (Ohio App. 1 Dist. 1917) 9 Ohio App. 147, 31 Ohio C.A. 418.

Because an award of extraordinary fiduciary fees must be adjusted so that the value of all the fiduciary's services to the estate correspond to the total compensation paid by the estate, a trial court's award of extraordinary fees without considering the regular commission is inappropriate; in addition, where the fee controversy involves a wrongful death settlement and the probate court is required to make an equitable distribution of the proceeds from the settlement, the court does not abuse discretion by awarding the executor a slightly larger share of the award after taking into consideration both the losses suffered by each beneficiary and the personal circumstances of each beneficiary. In re Estate of Thomas (Ohio App. 9 Dist., Summit, 04-12-2000) No. 19588, 2000 WL 372312, Unreported.

Probate court's reduction or denial of requested executor's commission will not be reversed on appeal absent abuse of discretion. Whitaker v. Estate of Whitaker (Ohio App. 4 Dist., 06-26-1995) 105 Ohio App.3d 46, 663 N.E.2d 681. Executors And Administrators ⟾ 501

Executor could not renounce provision in decedent's will which stated that she was to receive no fee for serving as executor and receive statutory commission based on amount of estate; statute did not authorize renouncement of nonexisting fee in order to receive a commission from the estate. In re Estate of Scheid (Ohio App. 6 Dist., 03-31-1995) 102 Ohio App.3d 345, 657 N.E.2d 311. Executors And Administrators ⟾ 490

Where administrator and executor had agreed that administrator could draw wages for period of sixty days in course of continuing or liquidating decedent's junk business, but no consent or approval was had as to further period, exception to payment of wages to administrator as employee of the business beyond sixty days would be sustained notwithstanding contention that continuance of operation was essential to liquidation, and notwithstanding alleged oral consent or authorization from the court. In re Brown's Estate (Ohio Prob. 1954) 129 N.E.2d 497, 67 Ohio Law Abs. 291, affirmed in part, reversed in part 98 Ohio App. 297, 129 N.E.2d 509, 57 O.O. 342. Executors And Administrators ⟾ 494

Where an executor resigns after collecting but not disbursing the assets, his commissions for ordinary services must be apportioned between him and his successor in proportion to the services of each. Thurston v. Ludwig (Ohio App. 1915) 25 Ohio C.C.(N.S.) 298, 4 Ohio App. 486.

The probate court has jurisdiction to apportion the statutory commission between two executors where the accounts of the estate have not yet been settled. Meyers v. Hopkins (Ohio Cir. 1905) 18 Ohio C.D. 208, 7 Ohio C.C.N.S. 240.

Where a will provides that increased legacies were in lieu of charges or commissions except for expenses actually incurred, the administrators are not entitled to statutory commissions. Rote v. Warner (Ohio Cir. 1899) 9 Ohio C.D. 536.

An administrator de bonis non may not charge the estate for amounts already paid to the previous administrator, but may charge the percentage that the previous administrator could have charged on money subsequently collected. In re Waring (Ohio Prob. 1887) 5 Ohio Dec. 415, 7 Ohio N.P. 553.

2. Unfaithful administration

Pursuant to RC 2113.35, a probate court has discretion to deny or reduce a commission to an executor if the court finds, after a hearing, that an executor has not faithfully discharged his duties in any respect; however, a probate court's denial of any commission to an executor based largely on the executor's refusal to turn over life insurance proceeds payable directly to the executor in his capacity as beneficiary rather than as executor or trustee, where there is no evidence of fraud or undue influence, constitutes an abuse of discretion and will be reversed and remanded. In re Estate of Justice, No. 93CA2, 1993 WL 335010 (4th Dist Ct App, Pickaway, 8–24–93).

Denying executor fiduciary fees was justified by executor's self-dealing, which resulted from making unauthorized loans to himself from estate funds and failing to invest estate funds. Whitaker v. Estate of Whitaker (Ohio App. 4 Dist., 06-26-1995) 105 Ohio App.3d 46, 663 N.E.2d 681. Executors And Administrators ⟾ 500

Executor's compensation may be reduced or denied when executor does not faithfully discharge duties. Whitaker v. Estate of Whitaker (Ohio App. 4 Dist., 06-26-1995) 105 Ohio App.3d 46, 663 N.E.2d 681. Executors And Administrators ⟾ 500

Where a nominated trustee under a will undertakes and performs a duty ordinarily performed by the named executrix in the will, but which duty the named executrix fails and refuses to perform, such nominated trustee is entitled to reasonable compensation for the services rendered. In re Allison's Will (Clark 1965) 9 Ohio App.2d 333, 224 N.E.2d 386, 38 O.O.2d 388.

The probate court may, in its discretion, deny allowance of an administrator's fee to an administrator who the court finds did not faithfully discharge his duties, and of counsel fees to such administrator who also acted as attorney for such estate. In re Gray's Estate (Franklin 1963) 118 Ohio App. 547, 196 N.E.2d 131, 26 O.O.2d 65.

The settlement of the account of an administrator is not a chancery case in the probate court, and hence the doctrine of equitable estoppel cannot be invoked to bar the administrator's fees and commissions; unfaithfulness in the discharge of his duties is the only basis for disallowance of compensation. In re Brown's Estate (Ohio Prob. 1954) 129 N.E.2d 497, 67 Ohio Law Abs. 291, affirmed in part, reversed in part 98 Ohio App. 297, 129 N.E.2d 509, 57 O.O. 342.

Unfaithfulness by an executor of a decedent's estate in discharge of his duties is sole basis on which a court can reduce or refuse to allow his compensation fixed by section, and where journal entry of trial court reducing compensation sets forth no specific finding of any unfaithfulness, court of appeals may not resort to opinion of trial court at variance with any inference necessary to sustain entry journalizing opinion, and must presume that entry is lawful and that trial court had facts before it sufficient to support entry. In re Marshall's Estate (Franklin 1946) 78 Ohio App. 457, 65 N.E.2d 527, 46 Ohio Law Abs. 350, 34 O.O. 183.

Where administrator improperly credited himself with certain items and the court found unfaithful administration, the administrator is not deprived of compensation for his services. Campbell v. McCormick (Ohio Cir. 1886) 1 Ohio C.D. 281.

Where a will confers a general power of sale of real estate on an executrix, she cannot be said to have unfaithfully discharged her duties, so as to warrant a reduction of commission under RC 2113.35, where she sold a piece of real estate over the objections of some of the beneficiaries under the will. In re Githens, No. CA83–06–039 (12th Dist Ct App, Warren, 2–13–84).

3. Real estate sale

An executor is not entitled to an order for the sale of premises to pay his percentage on legacies. Williams v. Williams's Ex'r (Ohio 1858) 8 Ohio St. 300.

Where the land offered for sale is bid in by a mortgage creditor whose mortgage is the first lien, and the bid is less than the secured debt, plus taxes and costs, there is no right to a percentage on the proceeds to the extent of the mortgage debt. Andrews v. Johns (Ohio 1898) 59 Ohio St. 65, 40 W.L.B. 332, 51 N.E. 880.

Costs and expenses of the sale do not include general or extraordinary costs of administration, but only such as are incident to a foreclosure. Sherman v. Millard (Ohio Cir. 1904) 17 Ohio C.D. 175, 6 Ohio C.C.N.S. 338.

An executor is not entitled to commissions on the sale of real estate when it was sold under agreement of the heirs. Union Sav. Bank & Trust Co. v. Smith (Ohio Cir. 1904) 16 Ohio C.D. 317, 4 Ohio C.C.(N.S.) 237, affirmed 74 Ohio St. 565, 78 N.E. 1137, 4 Ohio Law Rep. 61.

Where a probate court has accepted a final settlement of an estate, it cannot several months later make an allowance to the administrator for his commission without reopening the account and providing notice to the interested parties, particularly in the case of sale of the real estate of the deceased. Snider v. Graham (Ohio Cir. 1897) 8 Ohio C.D. 3.

4. Inventory

An administratrix may not be deprived of the compensation due to her for her services for mere delay in making and returning the inventory of the estate, when she has not been given an order requiring her, at an early day therein named, to return same, or has not been notified by the court of the expiration of the time to file such inventory. In re Burchett's Estate (Marion 1968) 16 Ohio App.2d 45, 241 N.E.2d 787, 45 O.O.2d 133. Executors And Administrators ⚖ 500

A probate court may not disallow the fees paid by an administratrix to an attorney employed by her in the administration of the estate as a penalty to him for failure to file an inventory within the time provided by law, but must exercise its discretion in determining what constitutes reasonable fees for attorney services taking into consideration the scope of the services performed and whether they were performed in a professional manner. In re Burchett's Estate (Marion 1968) 16 Ohio App.2d 45, 241 N.E.2d 787, 45 O.O.2d 133.

5. Attorney fees

Attorney, who represented executor and attorney for estate in action alleging that executor and attorney committed fraud in the administration of estate, was not a creditor of estate; executor's non-payment of fees owed to attorney did not convert attorney into a creditor of estate. In re Estate of Fouras (Ohio App. 5 Dist., Licking, 10-14-2004) No. 2003CA00049, No. 2003CA00052, 2004-Ohio-5563, 2004 WL 2348511, Unreported, appeal not allowed 105 Ohio St.3d 1518, 826 N.E.2d 316, 2005-Ohio-1880. Executors And Administrators ⚖ 216(2)

Award of $30,000 in attorney fees to attorney who represented executor and attorney for estate in action alleging fraud in the administration of estate, even though attorney had requested $51,589.82, was not against the manifest weight of the evidence. In re Estate of Fouras (Ohio App. 5 Dist., Licking, 10-14-2004) No. 2003CA00049, No. 2003CA00052, 2004-Ohio-5563, 2004 WL 2348511, Unreported, appeal not allowed 105 Ohio St.3d 1518, 826 N.E.2d 316, 2005-Ohio-1880. Executors And Administrators ⚖ 456(1)

Trial court order denying an award of executor's fees was not an abuse of discretion. In re Estate of Fouras (Ohio App. 5 Dist., Licking, 10-14-2004) No. 2003CA00049, No. 2003CA00052, 2004-Ohio-5563, 2004 WL 2348511, Unreported, appeal not allowed 105 Ohio St.3d 1518, 826 N.E.2d 316, 2005-Ohio-1880. Executors And Administrators ⚖ 488

Trial court award of $30,000 in attorney fees to attorney who represented executor and attorney for estate in action alleging that executor and attorney committed fraud in the administration of estate, rather than awarding attorney $51,589.82 that he requested, was not an abuse of discretion. In re Estate of Fouras (Ohio App. 5 Dist., Licking, 10-14-2004) No. 2003CA00049, No. 2003CA00052, 2004-Ohio-5563, 2004 WL 2348511, Unreported, appeal not allowed 105 Ohio St.3d 1518, 826 N.E.2d 316, 2005-Ohio-1880. Executors And Administrators ⚖ 456(1)

Remand was required to allow the trial court to identify the means or reason by which it determined to award attorney, who represented executor and the estate in action alleging that executor and attorney for estate committed fraud in the administration of estate, $30,000 in attorney fees; the trial court had previously been directed by the Court of Appeals to identify how the court arrived at the $30,000 figure. In re Estate of Fouras (Ohio App. 5 Dist., Licking, 10-14-2004) No. 2003CA00049, No. 2003CA00052, 2004-Ohio-5563, 2004 WL 2348511, Unreported, appeal not allowed 105 Ohio St.3d 1518, 826 N.E.2d 316, 2005-Ohio-1880. Executors And Administrators ⚖ 455

Awarding $7,500 in fees to attorney who assisted in administration of decedent's estate was not abuse of discretion; although attorney moved for approval of $20,372.19 in fees, attorney failed to offer any independent evidence regarding reasonableness of his billable hours and there was conflicting evidence regarding reasonableness of fees. In re Estate of Lazar (Ohio App. 11 Dist., Geauga, 04-16-2004) No. 2003-G-2509, 2004-Ohio-1964, 2004 WL 833455, Unreported, appeal not allowed 103 Ohio St.3d 1462, 815 N.E.2d 678, 2004-Ohio-5056. Executors And Administrators ⚖ 216(2)

Burden was on executor, who was also attorney for the estate, to establish reasonableness of attorney fees charged to the estate, where the fees were subject to contest, even though trial court placed great emphasis on fact that the fees conformed to local court's rules. In re Estate of Secoy (Miami 1984) 19 Ohio App.3d 269, 484 N.E.2d 160, 19 O.B.R. 439. Executors And Administrators ⚖ 506(1)

Probate judge is qualified to make determination, upon evidence, of reasonable fees to be paid from an estate to attorney for the estate without necessity of expert testimony; if expert testimony is presented, credibility of the testimony and weight to be given it along with other evidence presented is for probate court, as trier of facts, to determine. In re Estate of Secoy (Miami 1984) 19 Ohio App.3d 269, 484 N.E.2d 160, 19 O.B.R. 439. Executors And Administrators ⚖ 507(1)

A probate court may allow, as a part of the expense in the administration of a decedent's estate, compensation to an executor and attorney for services rendered in the successful defense of such decedent's will. In re Teopas' Estate (Lucas 1960) 116 Ohio App. 506, 188 N.E.2d 616, 22 O.O.2d 322.

RC 2741.04 does not prohibit a contract between an attorney and a beneficiary under a will, providing for the amount which is to be paid for services rendered in defending such will, and a probate court is not precluded from allowing, as a part of the expense in the administration of a decedent's estate, compensation to an executor and attorney for services rendered in the defense of such will. In re Teopas' Estate (Lucas 1960) 116 Ohio App. 506, 188 N.E.2d 616, 22 O.O.2d 322.

A formal written application is not a prerequisite to a grant of compensation to an administrator in excess of the statutory amount, nor for the payment of attorney fees. In re Brown's Estate (Fayette 1954) 98 Ohio App. 297, 129 N.E.2d 509, 57 O.O. 342.

Compensation for extraordinary services by a fiduciary and payment of attorney's fees in connection with the execution by the fiduciary of his duties discussed. In re Haggerty's Estate (Ohio Prob. 1955) 128 N.E.2d 680, 70 Ohio Law Abs. 463.

The determination of whether to apply the statutory attorney-fee standard in a case in which the attorney of the estate also acted as the executor of the estate was discretionary, and thus the probate court's mechanical application of the standard to award attorney half of his requested attorney fees warranted remand for reconsideration; the court was required to exercise reasonable judgment to determine whether the fee request was reasonable. In re Rothert (Ohio App. 1 Dist., Hamilton, 05-03-2002) No. C-010604, 2002-Ohio-2150, 2002 WL 834509, Unreported. Executors And Administrators ⇐ 455

6. Accounting

Burden of establishing validity of account is upon executor when objections are taken to executor's account. Whitaker v. Estate of Whitaker (Ohio App. 4 Dist., 06-26-1995) 105 Ohio App.3d 46, 663 N.E.2d 681. Executors And Administrators ⇐ 506(1)

Where acting probate judge found that administrator had not faithfully discharged his duties in that he had failed to include in first and final account an itemized statement of all receipts or an itemized statement of all expenditures, and in certain other respects, amounts of administrator's commissions, if any, and fees to which his attorney might be reasonably entitled, would be held in abeyance pending submission of an amended and supplemental final account. In re Brown's Estate (Ohio Prob. 1954) 129 N.E.2d 497, 67 Ohio Law Abs. 291, affirmed in part, reversed in part 98 Ohio App. 297, 129 N.E.2d 509, 57 O.O. 342. Executors And Administrators ⇐ 501

Probate court may in its discretion postpone judicial approval of commissions due executor until there is accounting for funds belonging to estate and on deposit in bank. In re Russell's Estate (Lake 1938) 60 Ohio App. 385, 21 N.E.2d 604, 28 Ohio Law Abs. 201, 13 O.O. 239. Executors And Administrators ⇐ 501

Trust company is not entitled to compensation for administration of an estate until the estate funds it has deposited in its own business, and which have since been impounded, are paid in full or to a sufficient extent to reach in part whatever compensation is then allowed. In re Baldwin's Estate (Ohio Prob. 1934) 2 Ohio Supp. 138, 33 Ohio Law Abs. 551, 1 O.O. 252.

7. Interest

Awarding executor of decedent's estate $5,000 in fiduciary fees was not abuse of discretion; although final distributive account filed by executor included $12,300 fiduciary fee, executor failed to timely administer estate and executor failed to timely file income tax return for estate, which resulted in unnecessary interest expense. In re Estate of Lazar (Ohio App. 11 Dist., Geauga, 04-16-2004) No. 2003-G-2509, 2004-Ohio-1964, 2004 WL 833455, Unreported, appeal not allowed 103 Ohio St.3d 1462, 815 N.E.2d 678, 2004-Ohio-5056. Executors And Administrators ⇐ 500

Interest is chargeable to a personal representative on sums wrongfully appropriated by him in payment of his commissions in advance of their judicial allowance from date of appropriation to date of allowance. In re Russell's Estate (Lake 1938) 60 Ohio App. 385, 21 N.E.2d 604, 28 Ohio Law Abs. 201, 13 O.O. 239. Executors And Administrators ⇐ 104(1)

8. Attachment of commission

Compensation and commissions of administrator or executor cannot be attached by his creditor until allowed by probate court. Overturf v. Gerlach (Ohio 1900) 62 Ohio St. 127, 43 W.L.B. 217, 56 N.E. 653, 78 Am.St.Rep. 704. Attachment ⇐ 61; Executors And Administrators ⇐ 488

The commissions of an administrator are not subject to attachment until allowed by the probate court. Overturf v. Gerlach (Ohio 1900) 62 Ohio St. 127, 43 W.L.B. 217, 56 N.E. 653, 78 Am.St.Rep. 704. Attachment ⇐ 61; Executors And Administrators ⇐ 488

2113.36 Further allowance; review of all services; counsel fees

Allowances, in addition to those provided by section 2113.35 of the Revised Code for an executor or administrator, which the probate court considers just and reasonable shall be made for actual and necessary expenses and for extraordinary services not required of an executor or administrator in the common course of his duty.

Upon the application of an executor or administrator for further allowances for extraordinary services rendered, the court shall review both ordinary and extraordinary services claimed to have been rendered. If the commissions payable pursuant to section 2113.35 of the Revised Code, exceed the reasonable value of such ordinary services rendered, the court must adjust any allowance made for extraordinary services so that total commissions and allowances to be made fairly reflect the reasonable value of both ordinary and extraordinary services.

When an attorney has been employed in the administration of the estate, reasonable attorney fees paid by the executor or administrator shall be allowed as a part of the expenses of administration. The court may at any time during administration fix the amount of such fees and, on application of the executor or administrator or the attorney, shall fix the amount thereof. When provision is made by the will of the deceased for compensation to an executor, the amount provided shall be a full satisfaction for his services, in lieu of such commissions or his share thereof, unless by an instrument filed in the court within four months after his appointment he renounces all claim to the compensation given by the will.

(1974 H 691, eff. 6–19–74; 1953 H 1; GC 10509–193)

Historical and Statutory Notes

Pre–1953 H 1 Amendments: 119 v 394, § 1; 114 v 443

Library References

Executors and Administrators ⇐111(5) to 111(9), 490, 497, 511.
Westlaw Topic No. 162.
C.J.S. Executors and Administrators §§ 237, 239, 251 to 255, 258 to 259, 261 to 263, 812, 826, 895 to 899.

Research References

Encyclopedias

OH Jur. 3d Appellate Review § 98, Orders of the Probate Division of the Court of Common Pleas.
OH Jur. 3d Decedents' Estates § 1354, Effect on Compensation of Provisions of Will.
OH Jur. 3d Decedents' Estates § 1356, Allowance of Extra Compensation for Expenses and Extraordinary Services.
OH Jur. 3d Decedents' Estates § 1360, Application for Extra Compensation and Review.
OH Jur. 3d Decedents' Estates § 1362, Compensation to Special Administrator or Others Acting in Place of Representative.
OH Jur. 3d Decedents' Estates § 1373, Amount of Attorneys' Fees.
OH Jur. 3d Decedents' Estates § 1375, Procedure for Allowance of Attorneys' Fees; Remedies.
OH Jur. 3d Decedents' Estates § 1595, Commissions of Executor or Administrator.

Forms

Ohio Forms and Transactions KP 30.11, Executor.

Treatises and Practice Aids

Carlin, Baldwin's Ohio Practice, Merrick-Rippner Probate Law § 2:2, Explanation of Fees and Expenses.
Carlin, Baldwin's Ohio Practice, Merrick-Rippner Probate Law § 3:13, Jurisdiction of Probate Court—Scope—Exclusive and Concurrent Jurisdiction.
Carlin, Baldwin's Ohio Practice, Merrick-Rippner Probate Law § 53:1, Fiduciary's Attorney—Appointment, Fees.

Carlin, Baldwin's Ohio Practice, Merrick-Rippner Probate Law § 80:1, Commissions—Statutory.

Carlin, Baldwin's Ohio Practice, Merrick-Rippner Probate Law § 80:3, Commissions—Determination of Compensation Other Than by Percentage.

Carlin, Baldwin's Ohio Practice, Merrick-Rippner Probate Law § 80:5, Commissions—Denial or Reduction.

Carlin, Baldwin's Ohio Practice, Merrick-Rippner Probate Law § 80:8, Extraordinary Services—Allowance.

Carlin, Baldwin's Ohio Practice, Merrick-Rippner Probate Law § 30:39, Drafting a Will—Authorization for Executor's Activity—Compensation of Executor.

Carlin, Baldwin's Ohio Practice, Merrick-Rippner Probate Law § 64:27, Compensation—Attorneys.

Carlin, Baldwin's Ohio Practice, Merrick-Rippner Probate Law § 80:10, Extraordinary Services—Compensation Allowed.

Carlin, Baldwin's Ohio Practice, Merrick-Rippner Probate Law § 80:12, Extraordinary Services—Compensation Provision in Will.

Carlin, Baldwin's Ohio Practice, Merrick-Rippner Probate Law § 80:13, Extraordinary Services—Procedure in Allowance of Fees to Fiduciary and Attorney.

Carlin, Baldwin's Ohio Practice, Merrick-Rippner Probate Law § 80:14, Attorney Fees—Determination.

Carlin, Baldwin's Ohio Practice, Merrick-Rippner Probate Law § 80:16, Attorney Fees—Refused.

Carlin, Baldwin's Ohio Practice, Merrick-Rippner Probate Law § 80:17, Attorney Fees—Allowed on Claims Rejected on Requisition.

Carlin, Baldwin's Ohio Practice, Merrick-Rippner Probate Law § 80:19, Attorney Fees—Facts to be Considered.

Carlin, Baldwin's Ohio Practice, Merrick-Rippner Probate Law § 80:24, Application for Extraordinary Compensation—Form.

Carlin, Baldwin's Ohio Practice, Merrick-Rippner Probate Law § 80:25, Entry for Extraordinary Compensation—Form.

Carlin, Baldwin's Ohio Practice, Merrick-Rippner Probate Law § 80:26, Application for Authority to Pay Attorney Fees—Form.

Carlin, Baldwin's Ohio Practice, Merrick-Rippner Probate Law § 80:27, Entry for Payment of Attorney Fees—Form.

Carlin, Baldwin's Ohio Practice, Merrick-Rippner Probate Law § 96:12, Expenses of Sale—Compensation of Executor or Administrator.

Carlin, Baldwin's Ohio Practice, Merrick-Rippner Probate Law § 30:169, Compensation: Specific Sum to Individual—Form.

Law Review and Journal Commentaries

Attorney as Both Executor and Attorney for Estate: Dual Roles = Dual Compensation, Robert G. Dykes & Brent A. Andrewsen. 13 Prob L J Ohio 58 (January/February 2003).

Barred Claims Statute, Appeals from Probate Court Discussed, Hon. Nelson J. Brewer. 8 Clev B J 83 (March 1937).

Ten Questions Arising in Settlement of Executor's Accounts, Harry Lewis Deibel. 31 Ohio L Rep 7 (January 30, 1930).

Notes of Decisions

Ed. Note: This section contains annotations from former RC 2109.23.

Attorney fees 1-5
   Beneficiaries and heirs 1
   Court's discretion 2
   Excessive 3
   Payment 4
   Reasonable value; factors 5
Beneficiaries and heirs, attorney fees 1
Court procedure; hearing 6
Court's discretion, attorney fees 2
Defense of will 7
Designation of attorney for estate 8
Excessive, attorney fees 3
Expenses of estate 9
Extraordinary fiduciary fees 10
Payment, attorney fees 4

Reasonable value; factors, attorney fees 5

1. Attorney fees—Beneficiaries and heirs

Estate beneficiary was not a prevailing party in action against estate, but rather was a party to a settlement agreement, and thus, beneficiary was not entitled to attorney fees outside of those agreed to in the settlement. In re Estate of Poling (Ohio App. 4 Dist., Hocking, 09-27-2005) No. 04CA18, 2005-Ohio-5147, 2005 WL 2386482, Unreported. Executors And Administrators ☞ 515

Under the terms of the settlement agreement entered into between co-executors and beneficiaries of estate, probate court was authorized to order estate's attorney to contact beneficiary's attorneys to determine if reimbursement to beneficiary for fees he paid to attorneys was warranted; under the terms of the agreement, the estate was required to pay up to $3000 of beneficiary's attorney fees. In re Estate of Poling (Ohio App. 4 Dist., Hocking, 09-27-2005) No. 04CA18, 2005-Ohio-5147, 2005 WL 2386482, Unreported. Executors And Administrators ☞ 515

Beneficiaries under testator's will were provided ample opportunity to present their case in opposition to request for attorney fees that was made by executor's attorney regarding beneficiaries' motion to remove executor; court advised beneficiaries of their right to cross examine attorney and expert witness, judge questioned attorney and expert witness on beneficiaries' behalf, and beneficiaries, who were acting pro se, were presumed as a matter of law to know proper procedure for presenting testimony and calling witnesses. In re Estate of Shaw (Ohio App. 2 Dist., Greene, 09-09-2005) No. 2004 CA 111, 2005-Ohio-4743, 2005 WL 2179300, Unreported. Executors And Administrators ☞ 35(18)

Trustee's attorney was entitled to attorney fees in beneficiary's action for accounting and breach of fiduciary duty, where beneficiary was not successful on his claims. Diemert v. Diemert (Ohio App. 8 Dist., Cuyahoga, 12-04-2003) No. 82597, 2003-Ohio-6496, 2003 WL 22862810, Unreported, appeal not allowed 102 Ohio St.3d 1446, 808 N.E.2d 397, 2004-Ohio-2263. Trusts ☞ 268; Trusts ☞ 330

Attorney was not entitled under common fund theory of recovery to award of attorney fees from estate for representing heir in motion to remove administrator of estate, in absence of evidence that attorney's actions resulted in a benefit to estate; attorney's actions did not result in beneficiaries receiving greater sums from estate than those they would have received had attorney's services not been rendered; nor could attorney recover payment for unsuccessful efforts rendered on beneficiary's behalf which, had the efforts been successful, would have created, augmented, or preserved the estate. In re Estate of Fugate (Meigs 1993) 86 Ohio App.3d 293, 620 N.E.2d 966. Attorney And Client ☞ 155

Executor/beneficiary, in his capacity as executor of estate, was not aggrieved by probate court judgment awarding attorney fees to other beneficiaries and against estate, and, thus, had no right to appeal question of whether amount of attorney fees awarded was excessive. In re Estate of Wirebaugh (Wood 1992) 84 Ohio App.3d 1, 616 N.E.2d 245. Executors And Administrators ☞ 256(3)

Probate court may authorize payment of reasonable attorney fees from estate to attorney employed by heir or beneficiary where attorney's services were rendered to benefit of whole estate. In re Estate of Brown (Butler 1992) 83 Ohio App.3d 540, 615 N.E.2d 319. Executors And Administrators ☞ 111(1)

Attorney fees incurred to defend against beneficiary's exceptions to inventory which resulted in title to approximately $276,000 remaining as estate assets benefitted estate and, thus, award of approximately $7,000 in attorney fees was required. In re Estate of Brown (Butler 1992) 83 Ohio App.3d 540, 615 N.E.2d 319. Executors And Administrators ☞ 111(1)

Where an attorney's services are necessarily and successfully rendered to the benefit of the whole estate, the probate court may allow the payment of reasonable attorney fees from the estate, even though the attorney is employed by an heir or beneficiary and not employed by the executor or administrator. In re Keller (Cuyahoga 1989) 65 Ohio App.3d 650, 584 N.E.2d 1312.

A probate court cannot allocate the burden of paying extraordinary attorney fees, incurred in connection with the administration of an estate, entirely to the beneficiary whose actions precipitated such extraordinary fees, since RC 2117.25 and other provisions implicitly require that such expenses are to be paid out of the estate as a whole, and the burden is to be equally shared by the beneficiaries. In re Estate of Coleman (Lucas 1988) 55 Ohio App.3d 261, 564 N.E.2d 116. Executors And Administrators ☞ 277

RC 2741.04 does not prohibit a contract between an attorney and a beneficiary under a will, providing for the amount which is to be paid for services rendered in defending such will, and a probate court is not precluded from allowing, as a part of the expense in the administration of a decedent's estate, compensation to an executor and attorney for services rendered in the defense of such will. In re Teopas' Estate (Lucas 1960) 116 Ohio App. 506, 188 N.E.2d 616, 22 O.O.2d 322.

Attorney fees paid for representation in a federal estate tax determination are not chargeable against the assets of the probate estate when the burden of the estate tax would have fallen solely on the beneficiary of nonprobate property. In re McKitrick's Estate (Ohio Prob. 1960) 172 N.E.2d 197, 85 Ohio Law Abs. 323, 15 O.O.2d 274.

Where services are rendered by an attorney for a widow in effecting a settlement of all her rights and claims in and to the estate of her deceased husband, the probate court has jurisdiction to hear and determine an application by the attorney for the allowance of compensation out of the estate; but, although it may have been fortuitous for the estate that a settlement of many problems may have been effected, such circumstances do not justify payment of attorney fees by the estate. In re Colosimo's Estate (Montgomery 1957) 104 Ohio App. 342, 149 N.E.2d 31, 5 O.O.2d 24.

An administrator who defends an action for specific performance of a contract, alleged to have been made by his decedent, to will the plaintiff all the residue of decedent's estate, in consideration of care and service for the rest of her life, after payment of all debts and costs, in a case in which the only heir at law is represented by counsel and actively contests the action, cannot, if unsuccessful in defending the action, charge the estate with attorney fees and expenses of litigation incurred in the contest. Foltz v. Boone (Ohio 1923) 107 Ohio St. 562, 140 N.E. 761, 1 Ohio Law Abs. 421, 1 Ohio Law Abs. 864, 21 Ohio Law Rep. 107, 21 Ohio Law Rep. 108. Executors And Administrators ⚖ 111(4)

2. —— Court's discretion, attorney fees

Probate court abused its discretion in reducing the amount of attorney fees requested by guardian of alleged incompetent's estate; facts and issues presented on appeal, including guardian's detailed billing statement, reflected that the services rendered and the requested fees appeared proportionate. In re Guardianship of Poschner (Ohio App. 7 Dist., Mahoning, 05-31-2005) No. 04 MA 160, 2005-Ohio-2788, 2005 WL 1324748, Unreported. Guardian And Ward ⚖ 162

Probate court did not abuse its discretion in guardianship proceedings and proceedings to administer ward's estate following ward's death by declining to award the full amount of attorney fees requested on behalf of attorney who represented guardian and estate; guardian and former administratrix of estate both were delinquent in filing their accounts. In re Guardianship of Papuska (Ohio App. 5 Dist., Stark, 02-22-2005) No. 2004-CA-00150, 2005-Ohio-741, 2005 WL 428031, Unreported. Guardian And Ward ⚖ 162

Probate court abused its discretion when if failed to pay attorney full amount of attorney fees it had previously approved, and instead proportionally divided money in estate between attorney and two remaining beneficiaries based on former executor's misappropriation of bulk of estate, where there was nothing in order indicating that probate court was reducing award as result of attorney's performance in case, court stated that reason it reduced award was to reach equitable result, and funds were available in estate to pay fee award at time of final distribution. In re Estate of Wyant (Ohio App. 11 Dist., Geauga, 12-06-2002) No. 2001-G-2388, 2002-Ohio-6706, 2002 WL 31744704, Unreported. Executors And Administrators ⚖ 511(1)

A probate court's reduction of the attorney's fee payable to counsel for the estate is an abuse of discretion where (1) the executrix expressly consents to and approves the requested fee, (2) the fee requested is the ordinary fee associated with services provided to the estate, and (3) the change is made without any notice to counsel. In Matter of Estate of Reardon (Ohio App. 7 Dist., Mahoning, 01-29-1997) No. 94 C.A. 206, 1997 WL 39896, Unreported.

Probate court is not bound by prior agreement of executor and estate attorney regarding attorney fees, and, where necessary, probate court may intervene to alter fee. In re Estate of York (Ohio App. 12 Dist., 03-15-1999) 133 Ohio App.3d 234, 727 N.E.2d 607, appeal not allowed 86 Ohio St.3d 1442, 713 N.E.2d 1052. Executors And Administrators ⚖ 216(2)

Executor was properly surcharged for estate funds paid to attorney without court approval and in absence of showing that fees were reasonable; probate court journal entry authorizing fee agreement providing for hourly fee and retainer was not authorization for executor to pay all legal fees. Whitaker v. Estate of Whitaker (Ohio App. 4 Dist., 06-26-1995) 105 Ohio App.3d 46, 663 N.E.2d 681. Executors And Administrators ⚖ 111(1)

Probate court has discretion when deciding reasonableness of attorney fees to award executor seeking reimbursement from estate. Whitaker v. Estate of Whitaker (Ohio App. 4 Dist., 06-26-1995) 105 Ohio App.3d 46, 663 N.E.2d 681. Executors And Administrators ⚖ 216(2)

Probate court has exclusive jurisdiction to determine whether fee charged by attorney employed in administration of estate is reasonable. In re Estate of Schaffer (Ohio App. 9 Dist., 03-08-1995) 101 Ohio App.3d 620, 656 N.E.2d 368. Courts ⚖ 472.4(2.1)

Attorney employed in administration of estate bears burden, in proceeding to recover fees, of introducing sufficient evidence of services performed and reasonable value of those services. In re Estate of Schaffer (Ohio App. 9 Dist., 03-08-1995) 101 Ohio App.3d 620, 656 N.E.2d 368. Executors And Administrators ⚖ 221(1.1)

Payment of reasonable attorney fees lies within sound discretion of probate court. In re Estate of Fugate (Meigs 1993) 86 Ohio App.3d 293, 620 N.E.2d 966. Executors And Administrators ⚖ 216(2)

Attorney who refused to comply with probate court order requiring him to return settlement funds previously distributed to him as attorney fees and expenses was properly held in contempt, notwithstanding attorney's claim that he had taken legal title to funds from fiduciary; probate court had in effect vacated its prior order distributing funds to attorney, and when attorney refused to comply with order, there was no court order of distribution of attorney fees. In re Kinross (Hamilton 1992) 84 Ohio App.3d 335, 616 N.E.2d 1128, dismissed, jurisdictional motion overruled 66 Ohio St.3d 1484, 612 N.E.2d 1241. Contempt ⚖ 20

Court of Appeals will not reverse probate court's finding of appropriate attorney fee award absent abuse of discretion. In re Estate of Wirebaugh (Wood 1992) 84 Ohio App.3d 1, 616 N.E.2d 245. Appeal And Error ⚖ 984(5)

The allocation of payment of attorney fees is within the sound discretion of the probate court and therefore the determination by a probate court of attorney fees surrounding the administration of an estate will not be reversed absent a showing that the award is against the manifest weight of the evidence or contrary to law. In re Estate of Ziechmann (Cuyahoga 1989) 63 Ohio App.3d 717, 580 N.E.2d 31. Executors And Administrators ⚖ 256(6)

An allocation of payments for attorney fees on behalf of a fiduciary charged with the administration of an estate is within the discretion of the court. In re Estate of Ziechmann (Cuyahoga 1987) 41 Ohio App.3d 214, 535 N.E.2d 374. Executors And Administrators ⚖ 111(1)

A compromise figure as to the legal fees for services performed by special tax counsel for an estate, agreed upon by and between counsel for the estate and the attorney for the special tax counsel, is in no way binding upon a probate court. Upon application to the court the sole question for determination is the reasonableness of the value of the services to the estate; this determination must be made by the probate court judge and his duty cannot be usurped by agreement of counsel. In re Cercone's Estate (Mahoning 1969) 18 Ohio App.2d 26, 246 N.E.2d 578, 47 O.O.2d 20. Executors And Administrators ⚖ 236

A probate court may not disallow the fees paid by an administratrix to an attorney employed by her in the administration of the estate as a penalty to him for failure to file an inventory within the time provided by law, but must exercise its discretion in determining what constitutes reasonable fees for the attorney's services taking into consideration the scope of the services performed and whether they were performed in a professional manner. In re Burchett's Estate (Marion 1968) 16 Ohio App.2d 45, 241 N.E.2d 787, 45 O.O.2d 133.

The probate court had jurisdiction upon application by executor to fix the amount of attorneys' fees for defense of the will against contest thereof begun by heirs at law in Common Pleas court and carried to Supreme Court, and hence writ of prohibition would not issue on petition of executor to prohibit probate court from making an entry nunc pro tunc modifying prior order fixing amount of such fees. State ex rel. Stephens v. Wiseman (Montgomery 1941) 42 N.E.2d 240, 35 Ohio Law Abs. 586. Prohibition ⚖ 10(2); Wills ⚖ 413

Allowance of fees for services of attorneys employed by an executor or administrator in the settlement of the estate in his hands is to be determined by probate court, and until so determined such fees do not constitute a valid claim against estate. Trumpler v. Royer (Ohio 1917) 95 Ohio St. 194, 115 N.E. 1018, 14 Ohio Law Rep. 551. Executors And Administrators ⚖ 513(1)

The determination of whether to apply the statutory attorney-fee standard in a case in which the attorney of the estate also acted as the executor of the estate was discretionary, and thus the probate court's mechanical application of the standard to award attorney half of his requested attorney fees warranted remand for reconsideration; the court was required to exercise reasonable judgment to determine whether the fee request was reasonable. In re Rothert (Ohio App. 1 Dist., Hamilton, 05-03-2002) No. C-010604, 2002-Ohio-2150, 2002 WL 834509, Unreported. Executors And Administrators 455

3. —— Excessive, attorney fees

Trial court's decision to reduce estate executor's allowable attorney fees from $8040 to $2500 was not arbitrary and unreasonable, where reduction was based in part on fact that much of executor's time was spent litigation not directed toward the general benefit of the estate, administration of the estate was legally unremarkable and relatively uncomplicated, and court expressed its position in its judgment entry that the award of attorneys fees was commensurate with the degree of work required for completing the administration of this estate, reviewed the evidence, considered the appropriate factors, and related its decision to the facts of the case. In re Estate of Bretschneider (Ohio App. 11 Dist., Geauga, 03-03-2006) No. 2005-G-2620, 2006-Ohio-1013, 2006 WL 533448, Unreported. Executors And Administrators 111(6)

Judgment allowing $15,000 in attorney fees in administration of estate reversed and remanded. In re Morgan's Estate (Cuyahoga 1961) 171 N.E.2d 921, 85 Ohio Law Abs. 481.

Upon an estate of $31,367.25 attorney fees of $1243.35 were reasonable; an added charge of $1000.00 was not. In re Brown's Estate (Ohio Prob. 1954) 129 N.E.2d 497, 67 Ohio Law Abs. 291, affirmed in part, reversed in part 98 Ohio App. 297, 129 N.E.2d 509, 57 O.O. 342.

An executor who is also an attorney can neither credit his account with payment to an outside counsel where nothing shows such employment was justified nor credit himself with a charge for making up his own accounts. In re Exceptions of Accounts of Leidigh (Ohio Com.Pl. 1902) 15 Ohio Dec. 193.

The trial court did not abuse its discretion when it held that the proper attorney fee was $650.00, and not $1,100.00, as the decedent's sister had the right to a bequest of all decedent's property pursuant to the will. Estate of Amber v Dilley, No. 82 CA 12 (7th Dist Ct App, Mahoning, 9–28–83).

4. —— Payment, attorney fees

Assuming estate co-executor was a prevailing party in action against estate, he was not entitled to attorney fees on his claim, where his attorney was not employed in the administration of the estate, but rather was retained to pursue co-executor's individual and beneficiary interests. In re Estate of Poling (Ohio App. 4 Dist., Hocking, 09-27-2005) No. 04CA18, 2005-Ohio-5147, 2005 WL 2386482, Unreported. Executors And Administrators 456(5)

Services of attorney in challenging probate court's valuation of testator's interest in company went to the personal benefit of executor of testator's estate, and thus, attorney fees were not compensable from the estate, where executor was the sole owner of company after death of testator and it was to his benefit to advocate for the lowest possible valuation of testator's interest for purposes of purchasing that interest. In re Estate of Murray (Ohio App. 11 Dist., Trumbull, 04-22-2005) No. 2004-T-0030, 2005-Ohio-1892, 2005 WL 940574, Unreported. Executors And Administrators 111(9)

Universal settlement of claims fixed the value of deceased's interest in company, and thus, executor of estate, who became sole member of company, was not entitled to return of the alleged overpayment company made in purchasing deceased's interest; overpayment did not constitute a fee owed to executor, but rather was a claim against the estate that was covered under universal settlement. In re Estate of Murray (Ohio App. 11 Dist., Trumbull, 04-22-2005) No. 2004-T-0030, 2005-Ohio-1892, 2005 WL 940574, Unreported. Executors And Administrators 496(1)

Although probate court was not bound in accepting estate attorney's itemization of services performed on behalf of estate for purposes of awarding attorney fees and court could reduce such fees, remand of fee reduction was warranted, where the court failed to indicate why it reduced requested attorney fees. In re Estate of Murray (Ohio App. 11 Dist., Trumbull, 04-22-2005) No. 2004-T-0030, 2005-Ohio-1892, 2005 WL 940574, Unreported. Executors And Administrators 455

Attorney for estate failed to explain why it was necessary to consult with outside attorneys regarding estate issues, and thus, probate court was entitled to deny attorney's request for fees associated with such consultation. In re Estate of Murray (Ohio App. 11 Dist., Trumbull, 04-22-2005) No. 2004-T-0030, 2005-Ohio-1892, 2005 WL 940574, Unreported. Executors And Administrators 111(1)

Although co-administrator's expert may have established that extraordinary attorney fees sought were reasonable from standpoint of attorney rendering services, he did not make the same point relative to the estate which would be charged, and thus, co-administrator could not recover attorney fees. In re Estate of Lewis (Ohio App. 6 Dist., Lucas, 12-31-2003) No. ES-00-1287, 2003-Ohio-7266, 2003 WL 23167308, Unreported. Executors And Administrators 216(2)

Estate attorney, who acted as both attorney and executor of a will, was entitled to attorney fees, even though he had received a fiduciary fee for his work as executor; the attorney fees were reasonable, the fees were for legal services, which differed from the work he had done as executor, and the attorney was not required to have his contract for legal services pre-approved by the probate court. In re Estate of Duffy (Ohio App. 11 Dist., 07-26-2002) 148 Ohio App.3d 574, 774 N.E.2d 344, 2002-Ohio-3844. Wills 414

Estate attorney, who acted as both attorney and executor of a will, was entitled to attorney fees, even though he had received a fiduciary fee for his work as executor; the attorney fees were reasonable, the fees were for legal services, which differed from the work he had done as executor, and the attorney was not required to have his contract for legal services pre-approved by the probate court. In re Estate of Duffy (Ohio App. 11 Dist., 07-26-2002) 148 Ohio App.3d 574, 774 N.E.2d 344, 2002-Ohio-3844. Wills 414

Probate court was authorized to award attorney fees to beneficiary who brought an action to remove executor, where action was successful and result was beneficial to estate. In re Estate of Geanangel (Ohio App. 7 Dist., 02-25-2002) 147 Ohio App.3d 131, 768 N.E.2d 1235, 2002-Ohio-850. Executors And Administrators 35(18)

Executor, who employed counsel to defend against testator's stepchildren's action to enforce antenuptial agreement, which required testator to leave her entire estate to stepchildren, was entitled to recover fees from the estate pursuant to statute allowing attorney fees to be paid as expenses of administration, since proper administration of estate required executor to retain counsel to represent estate in stepchildren's action. In re Estate of Dawson (Ohio App. 2 Dist., 12-27-1996) 117 Ohio App.3d 51, 689 N.E.2d 1008. Executors And Administrators 216(2)

Probate court had subject-matter jurisdiction over dispute between attorneys as to distribution of attorney fees from settlement fund resulting from wrongful death action brought on behalf of estate. In re Kinross (Hamilton 1992) 84 Ohio App.3d 335, 616 N.E.2d 1128, dismissed, jurisdictional motion overruled 66 Ohio St.3d 1484, 612 N.E.2d 1241. Executors And Administrators 314(2)

Determination of allocation of payment of attorney fees is matter within discretion of probate court. In re Estate of Wirebaugh (Wood 1992) 84 Ohio App.3d 1, 616 N.E.2d 245. Executors And Administrators 111(1)

Payment of attorney fees by estate may be justified where beneficiary is reasonably justified in bringing suit as long as fees benefit estate. In re Estate of Brown (Butler 1992) 83 Ohio App.3d 540, 615 N.E.2d 319. Executors And Administrators 111(1)

A formal written application is not a prerequisite to a grant of compensation to an administrator in excess of the statutory amount, nor for the payment of attorney fees. In re Brown's Estate (Fayette 1954) 98 Ohio App. 297, 129 N.E.2d 509, 57 O.O. 342.

Under section, no distinction is made between ordinary and extraordinary legal services rendered to the executor in the administration of an estate. In re Dickey's Estate (Montgomery 1949) 87 Ohio App. 255, 94 N.E.2d 223, 20 A.L.R.2d 1220, 57 Ohio Law Abs. 346, 42 O.O. 474.

Failure of an administrator to pay an attorney for services after the account is approved and ordered paid by the court is a breach of the administrative bond for which the surety is liable. Smith v. Rhodes (Ohio 1903) 68 Ohio St. 500, 48 W.L.B. 682, 68 N.E. 7, 1 Ohio Law Rep. 89, 1 Ohio Law Rep. 135, 1 Ohio Law Rep. 493.

5. —— Reasonable value; factors, attorney fees

Trial court considered applicable factors when awarding attorney's fees for estate administration, although it did not specifically recite each factor in its judgment entry, where court stated that it considered the factors to be considered as guides in determining the reasonableness of attorney fees. In re Estate of Bretschneider (Ohio App. 11 Dist., Geauga, 03-03-2006) No. 2005-G-2620, 2006-Ohio-1013, 2006 WL 533448, Unreported. Executors And Administrators 508(1)

Probate court based its decision upon improper factors and acted arbitrarily when it granted compensation to estate attorney in the amount of $3,600, despite the fact attorney produced a detailed list of time expenditures justifying request for $11,642.75 for 99.85 hours of service; trial court's electing not to conduct a hearing on fees made it difficult to discern how it reached its conclusion, and fact that most of fees generated by attorney were for out-of-court services was not adequate justification for so greatly reducing his attorney fees. In re Estate of Campbell (Ohio App. 7 Dist., Mahoning, 12-15-2003) No. 02 CA 186, No. 02 CA 187, 2003-Ohio-7040, 2003 WL 22999356, Unreported. Executors And Administrators ⚖ 111(6)

Beneficiary's testimony regarding attorney fees she incurred in pursuing action to remove executor, which was corroborated by detailed billing statements, was sufficient to demonstrate that fees were reasonable and were incurred in furtherance of the action. In re Estate of Geanangel (Ohio App. 7 Dist., 02-25-2002) 147 Ohio App.3d 131, 768 N.E.2d 1235, 2002-Ohio-850. Executors And Administrators ⚖ 35(18)

Probate court had power to review contingency fee agreement between estate and estate attorney, even though agreement had been approved earlier and may have been fair, customary, and reasonable at that time, where it appeared that case pursued by attorney on behalf of estate had not required much preparation and had been settled without trial. In re Estate of York (Ohio App. 12 Dist., 03-15-1999) 133 Ohio App.3d 234, 727 N.E.2d 607, appeal not allowed 86 Ohio St.3d 1442, 713 N.E.2d 1052. Executors And Administrators ⚖ 216(2)

Probate court was required to thoroughly review time, effort and skill of estate's attorney in pursuing litigation on behalf of estate and to provide sufficient justification, supported by the evidence, for decision to reduce fee from that provided for in contingency fee agreement when litigation settled before trial. In re Estate of York (Ohio App. 12 Dist., 03-15-1999) 133 Ohio App.3d 234, 727 N.E.2d 607, appeal not allowed 86 Ohio St.3d 1442, 713 N.E.2d 1052. Executors And Administrators ⚖ 216(2)

Burden is upon attorney seeking fees to introduce into the record sufficient evidence of services performed and reasonable value of such services. In re Estate of Haller (Ohio App. 10 Dist., 12-24-1996) 116 Ohio App.3d 866, 689 N.E.2d 612, dismissed, appeal not allowed 78 Ohio St.3d 1489, 678 N.E.2d 1227. Attorney And Client ⚖ 166(3)

Statute providing that fees paid by executor of estate to attorney employed in administration of estate are to be allowed as an administration expense gives exclusive original jurisdiction to probate court to determine reasonableness of attorney fees. In re Estate of Haller (Ohio App. 10 Dist., 12-24-1996) 116 Ohio App.3d 866, 689 N.E.2d 612, dismissed, appeal not allowed 78 Ohio St.3d 1489, 678 N.E.2d 1227. Executors And Administrators ⚖ 250

Probate court's determination that administrator's requested attorney fees were reasonable was adequately supported by itemized statement of fees and administrator's testimony that estate was "an absolute nightmare" to administer due to acrimony between beneficiaries; administrator was not required to introduce expert testimony as to reasonableness of fees. In re Estate of Haller (Ohio App. 10 Dist., 12-24-1996) 116 Ohio App.3d 866, 689 N.E.2d 612, dismissed, appeal not allowed 78 Ohio St.3d 1489, 678 N.E.2d 1227. Executors And Administrators ⚖ 252

Party seeking to obtain attorney fees from estate has burden of showing that fees are reasonable. Whitaker v. Estate of Whitaker (Ohio App. 4 Dist., 06-26-1995) 105 Ohio App.3d 46, 663 N.E.2d 681. Executors And Administrators ⚖ 221(1.1)

Unsworn certification of services performed by attorney employed in administration of estate and of reasonable value of those services is sufficient in uncontested matter seeking approval of attorney fees; unsworn certification is sufficient proof of reliability of time records and probate court may determine fees based on its own expertise. In re Estate of Schaffer (Ohio App. 9 Dist., 03-08-1995) 101 Ohio App.3d 620, 656 N.E.2d 368. Executors And Administrators ⚖ 221(4.1)

When evidentiary hearing is held on objections or exceptions to fee sought by attorney employed for administration of estate, attorney must ensure that evidence considered by court in its determination of fees, including time records, is introduced into record pursuant to rules of evidence. In re Estate of Schaffer (Ohio App. 9 Dist., 03-08-1995) 101 Ohio App.3d 620, 656 N.E.2d 368. Executors And Administrators ⚖ 252

Consideration of unauthenticated time records of attorney employed during estate administration, during evidentiary hearing on contested fee application, was harmless error given that no objection was made to reference by expert witness to attorney fee statements, attorney seeking fee answered questions of counsel and court, there was no objection to attorney fee statements on grounds that they were unsworn, and counsel's gratuitous waiver of oath requirement during attorney's testimony invited error. In re Estate of Schaffer (Ohio App. 9 Dist., 03-08-1995) 101 Ohio App.3d 620, 656 N.E.2d 368. Executors And Administrators ⚖ 256(6)

Fees awarded to attorney employed during estate administration totaling more than $12,000 was upheld, even though only $11,500 remained in estate to be distributed, in light of expert testimony that time spent was reasonable and necessary, estate became complex because of animosity between parties, rates charged were appropriate, and delegating work to paralegals was proper. In re Estate of Schaffer (Ohio App. 9 Dist., 03-08-1995) 101 Ohio App.3d 620, 656 N.E.2d 368. Executors And Administrators ⚖ 256(6)

In determining reasonableness of attorney fees charged against estate, probate court is not restricted to minimum or maximum figure, but, rather, is guided by factors in Code of Professional Responsibility. In re Estate of Wirebaugh (Wood 1992) 84 Ohio App.3d 1, 616 N.E.2d 245. Executors And Administrators ⚖ 111(6)

An award to a guardian's attorney of $9,702 in attorney fees for services rendered in defending a claim against the estate by the former guardian is proper even though the balance of the estate is only $17,000 since (1) the ward was directly benefited by the legal expenses incurred because instead of the $25,000 payed for by the former guardian, only $1,050 was awarded; and (2) the fee charged by the attorney was reasonable under the Code of Professional Responsibility because the attorney actually worked 98.9 hours, but only billed the estate for 96 hours and $100 per hour rate charged was reasonable for services performed. In re Guardianship of Rider (Huron 1990) 68 Ohio App.3d 709, 589 N.E.2d 465.

Where an attorney seeking fees for representing an estate has met the burden of presenting evidence of the reasonable value of the services performed, it is reversible error for the probate court, without explanation or evidentiary support, to disallow the $15,900 amount claimed in the attorney's fee application under an arrangement with the executor, who agreed that the attorney's rate would be $125 per hour, and instead to substitute the amount of $7,000 based on an hourly rate of $50, which under the agreement was to apply only as a minimum rate for work delegable to paralegal workers. Imler v. Cowan (Pickaway 1989) 65 Ohio App.3d 359, 583 N.E.2d 1355.

A probate court's award to an executrix of an estate of attorney fees representing approximately forty per cent of the estate assets does not constitute an abuse of discretion where the court had before it uncontested evidence substantiating the fees, including detailed itemized lists of costs and fees and evidence that the executrix and her attorneys were responsible for saving or adding over $100,000 to the estate through litigation and general administration and that the estate and the executrix were subject to a plethora of legal actions filed by the beneficiaries of a testamentary trust, which actions were all resolved in favor of the executrix and/or the estate; the record reflected that the court considered the factors enumerated in DR 2–106 and followed the law. In re Estate of Ziechmann (Cuyahoga 1989) 63 Ohio App.3d 717, 580 N.E.2d 31.

In determining an award of attorney fees, the time and labor of the attorney is only one of the many factors to be given consideration. In re Estate of Ziechmann (Cuyahoga 1987) 41 Ohio App.3d 214, 535 N.E.2d 374. Costs ⚖ 194.18

A probate judge is qualified to make a determination, upon evidence, of reasonable fees to be paid from an estate without the necessity of expert testimony; if expert testimony is presented, the credibility of such testimony and the weight to be given it is for the probate court, as the trier of fact, to determine. In re Estate of Secoy (Miami 1984) 19 Ohio App.3d 269, 484 N.E.2d 160, 19 O.B.R. 439. Executors And Administrators ⚖ 507(1)

The burden of proving the reasonableness of attorney fees under RC 2113.36 rests on the executor of the estate, and where the executor and the attorney are the same person, the value of the services provided by the attorney and their reasonableness must be demonstrated on the record by the executor. In re Estate of Secoy (Miami 1984) 19 Ohio App.3d 269, 484 N.E.2d 160, 19 O.B.R. 439.

Although a judge of a trial court is experienced in probate law, the determination of a reasonable attorney's fee in a matter before him must be based upon evidence adduced in open court and he may not substitute his own knowledge in its stead. In re Wood's Estate (Franklin 1977) 55 Ohio App.2d 67, 379 N.E.2d 256, 9 O.O.3d 225.

An attorney may not be compensated out of a guardianship estate for efforts to obtain personal compensation for the guardian. In re Guardianship of Webb (Ohio Prob. 1967) 11 Ohio Misc. 21, 225 N.E.2d 868, 40 O.O.2d 97.

Reasonable attorney fees allowed by the probate court as a part of the expenses of administering the estate must be based upon actual services performed by the attorneys and upon the reasonable value of those services as determined from the evidence which must substantiate the award of fees as being reasonable; a probate court judge is qualified to make a determination, upon evidence, of reasonable attorney fees to be paid from an estate without the necessity of expert testimony; if expert testimony is presented the credibility of such testimony and the weight to be given it along with the other evidence presented is for the probate court judge, as trier of the facts, to determine. In re Love's Estate (Franklin 1965) 1 Ohio App.2d 571, 206 N.E.2d 39, 30 O.O.2d 595.

In a proceeding to determine the amount of attorney fees in the administration of an estate the burden is upon the attorneys to introduce into the record sufficient evidence of the services performed and of the reasonable value of such services, to justify reasonable attorney fees in the amount awarded. In re Verbeck's Estate (Ohio 1962) 173 Ohio St. 557, 184 N.E.2d 384, 20 O.O.2d 163.

Compensation for extraordinary services by a fiduciary and payment of attorney's fees in connection with the execution by the fiduciary of his duties discussed. In re Haggerty's Estate (Ohio Prob. 1955) 128 N.E.2d 680, 70 Ohio Law Abs. 463.

The reasonable value of the services rendered by attorneys to an estate cannot be arrived at in a controverted case solely by the application of a predetermined formula of percentages of inventory values. In re Hickok's Estate (Ohio 1953) 159 Ohio St. 282, 111 N.E.2d 925, 50 O.O. 290.

A fiduciary who is an attorney may perform his own legal services, if he so desires, and shall be allowed a reasonable compensation for services so rendered. In re Cramer's Estate (Ohio Prob. 1946) 69 N.E.2d 204, 46 Ohio Law Abs. 521, 34 O.O. 316. Executors And Administrators ⬅ 497

Executors and administrators are personally liable for the services of attorneys employed by them, even though the services are for the benefit of the estate, and the executor or administrator may receive credit for reasonable expenditures in the settlement of his accounts. Thomas v. Moore (Ohio 1894) 52 Ohio St. 200, 33 W.L.B. 128, 39 N.E. 803, 2 Ohio Leg. N. 338. Executors And Administrators ⬅ 97; Executors And Administrators ⬅ 111(1); Executors And Administrators ⬅ 430; Executors And Administrators ⬅ 485

Equity entitles counsel not hired by the administrator who rendered services which benefitted the particular estate to reasonable fees. In re Oskamp's Estate (Ohio Prob. 1902) 1 Ohio NP(NS) 197, 49 W.L.B. 568.

Where the executor of an estate also served as attorney to the estate, and four corporations comprising the estate assets paid retainers to the executor or his law firm during the period the estate was in probate, the prohibition against self-dealing of RC 2109.44 was not violated where testimony showed that the estate had benefitted by the executor's administration; further, the executor was not required to refund the retainers received from the corporations as a setoff against his attorney fees received pursuant to RC 2113.36. In re Estate of Lossman, No. 47312 (8th Dist Ct App, Cuyahoga, 4–5–84).

Since travel was a requirement of employment, travel expenses of an attorney were not an important factor in fee determination. In re Estate of Kellhofer, No. 943 (4th Dist Ct App, Ross, 2–18–83).

6. Court procedure; hearing

Remand was required to permit trial court to hold a hearing on matter of attorney fees requested by attorneys that had represented decedent in litigation regarding his asbestos related injuries, so that evidence could be taken on matters including the time, effort, or skill of attorneys in representing estate. In re Estate of Campbell (Ohio App. 7 Dist., Mahoning, 12-15-2003) No. 02 CA 186, No. 02 CA 187, 2003-Ohio-7040, 2003 WL 22999356, Unreported. Executors And Administrators ⬅ 216(2)

Attorney that represented estate in probate proceedings was entitled to hearing on his request for attorney fees and trial court was required, on remand, to take evidence and judge the value of the work performed by attorney. In re Estate of Campbell (Ohio App. 7 Dist., Mahoning, 12-15-2003) No. 02 CA 186, No. 02 CA 187, 2003-Ohio-7040, 2003 WL 22999356, Unreported. Executors And Administrators ⬅ 253

Probate division of trial court was not required to conduct hearing before granting plaintiff's motion for attorneys' fees following defendant being held in contempt in action for writ of citation to produce testator's will, since defendant waived hearing by failing to request one, and attorney's affidavit and itemized statement provided ample evidence to support award. Pafford v. Woloszyn (Ohio App. 11 Dist., Lake, 12-27-2002) No. 2001-L-206, 2002-Ohio-7261, 2002 WL 31886678, Unreported. Wills ⬅ 416

Any error from probate court's sustaining objection to question about substance of individual discussions between estate administrator and his attorneys regarding the number of hours charged to administration of the estate, on basis of attorney-client privilege, at hearing on application for attorney fees, was harmless, given detailed invoice containing itemization of all tasks and time expended in administration of estate. In re Estate of Haller (Ohio App. 10 Dist., 12-24-1996) 116 Ohio App.3d 866, 689 N.E.2d 612, dismissed, appeal not allowed 78 Ohio St.3d 1489, 678 N.E.2d 1227. Executors And Administrators ⬅ 256(6)

Estate beneficiaries waived argument that probate court improperly sustained objection to request that administrator produce office file and any memos relating to discussions with counsel, on basis of attorney-client privilege, at hearing on application for attorney fees, when they failed to request in camera review of allegedly privileged materials. In re Estate of Haller (Ohio App. 10 Dist., 12-24-1996) 116 Ohio App.3d 866, 689 N.E.2d 612, dismissed, appeal not allowed 78 Ohio St.3d 1489, 678 N.E.2d 1227. Witnesses ⬅ 221

A probate court can, sua sponte, vacate an erroneous order fixing attorney's fees for services rendered to and expenses incurred for an estate and file a new journal entry for a lesser figure which he finds to be the reasonable value of the services rendered for the benefit of an estate. In re Cercone's Estate (Mahoning 1969) 18 Ohio App.2d 26, 246 N.E.2d 578, 47 O.O.2d 20. Executors And Administrators ⬅ 238

Reasonable counsel fees cannot be arrived at in a controverted case solely by the application of a rule of court fixing a predetermined formula of percentages of the proceeds of sale. Glimcher v. Doppelt (Richland 1966) 5 Ohio App.2d 269, 215 N.E.2d 423, 34 O.O.2d 435. Partition ⬅ 114(6)

A defendant from whose assets fees will be paid has a right to cross-examine the attorney to whom the fees are to be awarded as to the nature, extent and value of the services rendered; a denial of this right is prejudicial error. Glimcher v. Doppelt (Richland 1966) 5 Ohio App.2d 269, 215 N.E.2d 423, 34 O.O.2d 435.

Appeal from a determination of attorney fees can be only on questions of law, and, on appeal, the only questions before the appellate court are whether the judgment awarding fees is against the manifest weight of the evidence or contrary to law, and, if so, final judgment of modification cannot be rendered upon reversal, but the cause must be remanded to the probate court for further proceedings. In re Love's Estate (Franklin 1965) 1 Ohio App.2d 571, 206 N.E.2d 39, 30 O.O.2d 595. Executors And Administrators ⬅ 256(8)

An order of the probate court which requires payment of attorney fees by an executor prior to the settlement of such fees in an account, where all interested parties are not bound by the order, is of doubtful validity, and an appeal by the executor from such an order will not be dismissed on preliminary motion but will be held for determination on the merits. (See also In re Estate of Verbeck, 173 OS 557, 184 NE(2d) 384 (1962).) In re Verbeck's Estate (Franklin 1961) 114 Ohio App. 155, 180 N.E.2d 615, 18 O.O.2d 465.

In an appeal from an order of a probate court to the court of appeals, where the notice of appeal is signed by two persons in their representative capacities as co-executors, but such executors are without a right of appeal, and where one of such persons, who also has an interest in the estate in an individual capacity, participated in the probate court hearing without designation as to the capacity in which he appeared, the court of appeals may permit the notice of appeal to be amended to name such person as a party appellant in his individual capacity. (See also In re Estate of Verbeck, 173 OS 557, 184 NE(2d) 384 (1962).) In re Verbeck's Estate (Franklin 1961) 114 Ohio App. 155, 180 N.E.2d 615, 18 O.O.2d 465.

An executor has no right of appeal from an order of the probate court fixing the amount of attorney fees, on the ground that the amount of the fees fixed is excessive. (See also In re Estate of Verbeck, 173 OS 557, 184 NE(2d) 384 (1962).) In re Verbeck's Estate (Franklin 1961) 114 Ohio App. 155, 180 N.E.2d 615, 18 O.O.2d 465. Executors And Administrators ⬅ 256(3)

A determination by the probate court of the attorney fees to be paid to an attorney for the administrator of an estate is not appealable on questions of law and fact. In re Bancroft's Estate (Franklin 1959) 163 N.E.2d 68, 81 Ohio Law Abs. 548.

In absence of a showing of an abuse of discretion, a court is not authorized to interfere with the execution of a power granted by the will of a testator to his executrix to pay to herself from his estate such sum or sums as she deems proper compensation for legal services and unusual services rendered as executrix which in her judgment are necessary or advisable in the administration of his estate; and in such case, the executrix cannot be compelled to file an application for an allowance of attorney fees and for fees for services rendered as executrix and secure the approval of the probate court for such an allowance as provided by statute.

In re Ellis' Estate (Lake 1940) 66 Ohio App. 121, 32 N.E.2d 23, 19 O.O. 392.

Due to the wide latitude vested in a trial court in the allowance of attorney fees, a reviewing court will not reverse such allowance unless against the manifest weight of the evidence. Kern v. Heilker & Heilker (Hamilton 1937) 56 Ohio App. 371, 10 N.E.2d 1005, 24 Ohio Law Abs. 656, 9 O.O. 437. Appeal And Error ⚬▬ 1013

In awarding attorney fees for services rendered an estate, being an unliquidated amount, the court is not warranted in awarding interest or entering judgment for the amount against the estate, but the executor should pay the amount allowed and report the same in his account. Kern v. Heilker & Heilker (Hamilton 1937) 56 Ohio App. 371, 10 N.E.2d 1005, 24 Ohio Law Abs. 656, 9 O.O. 437.

Although the usual practice in the allowance of attorney fees, for services rendered an estate, is for the executor or administrator to credit an allowance for such in an account filed and ask approval of the probate court, yet it is not error to permit the application to be filed and the allowance made prior to the filing of any account by the executor or administrator. Kern v. Heilker & Heilker (Hamilton 1937) 56 Ohio App. 371, 10 N.E.2d 1005, 24 Ohio Law Abs. 656, 9 O.O. 437.

Where the will left a substantial legacy to the executrix, the estate is not required to bear the cost of defense of the will. Weir v. Weir (Ohio Cir. 1906) 18 Ohio C.D. 199, 7 Ohio C.C.N.S. 289.

Under this section it is incumbent upon administrator to present the claim for attorney fees to the probate court and request that he be given "further allowance" to reimburse him out of the assets of the estate for "reasonable attorney fees paid by" him but it is still within the province of the probate court to make the allowance in advance of payment and in anticipation of the filing of an account, so that the administrator may take a proper credit in his account after the court has determined the issue. In re Wellmeier's Estate (Ohio Prob. 1938) 2 Ohio Supp. 397, 26 Ohio Law Abs. 386, 11 O.O. 45.

A probate court errs where it allocates the entire burden of paying extraordinary compensation and attorney fees granted pursuant to RC 2113.36 to only one of four devisees, despite the fact that the extraordinary expenses and attorney fees were incurred by the estate in responding to exceptions filed by the one devisee to whom the probate court allocates the burden. In re Estate of Wiehe, No. C-830419 (1st Dist Ct App, Hamilton, 5-9-84).

Where original time sheets were lost for time erroneously posted to other accounts, testimony and reconstructed records by an attorney are sufficient to justify a fee. In re Estate of Lossman, No. 47312 (8th Dist Ct App, Cuyahoga, 4-5-84).

The trial court did not err in setting attorney's fees at an amount provided by local rules of court when the court reviewed files and considered evidence in the light of the value of the service to the estate. In re Estate of Kellhofer, No. 943 (4th Dist Ct App, Ross, 2-18-83).

7. Defense of will

Although estate fiduciary does not have duty to defend a will contest, he may nonetheless undertake to do so. In re Estate of Dawson (Ohio App. 2 Dist., 12-27-1996) 117 Ohio App.3d 51, 689 N.E.2d 1008. Executors And Administrators ⚬▬ 202

A probate court may allow, as a part of the expense in the administration of a decedent's estate, compensation to an executor and attorney for services rendered in the successful defense of such decedent's will. In re Teopas' Estate (Lucas 1960) 116 Ohio App. 506, 188 N.E.2d 616, 22 O.O.2d 322.

Attorney fees may be allowed to counsel successfully obtaining the probate of a will and defending it against contest for services rendered prior to the date of probate as well as thereafter. In re Woods' Estate (Ohio Prob. 1957) 159 N.E.2d 638, 80 Ohio Law Abs. 336.

Under testatrix's will expenses of defending a will contest and of defending title to specifically bequeathed securities were properly a charge upon the residual of the estate. In re Jacoby's Estate (Ohio Prob. 1957) 155 N.E.2d 275, 79 Ohio Law Abs. 239.

Even where an executor is a businessman, he is entitled to employ counsel to defend the will and receive a reasonable amount for counsel fees from the estate when the will is sustained. In re Ullman (Ohio Cir. 1909) 21 Ohio C.D. 370, 12 Ohio C.C.(N.S.) 340.

An executor who defends a will, resulting in upholding the will, is entitled to counsel fees. Union Sav. Bank & Trust Co. v. Smith (Ohio Cir. 1904) 16 Ohio C.D. 317, 4 Ohio C.C.(N.S.) 237, affirmed 74 Ohio St. 565, 78 N.E. 1137, 4 Ohio Law Rep. 61.

8. Designation of attorney for estate

A provision of a will which designates an attorney to represent the executor in the administration of the estate may not be considered as a condition precedent to the appointment of the executor, but is merely precatory and not binding on the fiduciary. In re Estate of Deardoff (Ohio 1984) 10 Ohio St.3d 108, 461 N.E.2d 1292, 10 O.B.R. 434. Executors And Administrators ⚬▬ 14

A testator, by the terms of his will, may not bind his designated fiduciary to the election of a specific attorney no matter how mandatory the language of the will. In re Estate of Deardoff, No. 136 (12th Dist Ct App, Warren, 6-29-83), affirmed by 10 OS(3d) 108, 10 OBR 434, 461 NE(2d) 1292 (1984).

9. Expenses of estate

To avoid abusing its discretion, probate court needed a more significant reason than amount of money which would be left in estate for reducing attorney fees requested by attorneys that had represented decedent in litigation regarding his asbestos related injuries. In re Estate of Campbell (Ohio App. 7 Dist., Mahoning, 12-15-2003) No. 02 CA 186, No. 02 CA 187, 2003-Ohio-7040, 2003 WL 22999356, Unreported. Executors And Administrators ⚬▬ 216(2)

Executor could not renounce provision in decedent's will which stated that she was to receive no fee for serving as executor and receive statutory commission based on amount of estate; statute did not authorize renouncement of nonexisting fee in order to receive a commission from the estate. In re Estate of Scheid (Ohio App. 6 Dist., 03-31-1995) 102 Ohio App.3d 345, 657 N.E.2d 311. Executors And Administrators ⚬▬ 490

Under a will directing that all of the just debts, funeral and "testamentary expenses" of the testatrix be paid out of her estate as soon after her death as may be found practicable, quoted words embrace those expenses that arose out of the protection and defense of the last will of the deceased and expenses incurred by the executor in defense of litigation involving shares of stock were chargeable upon the residual of the estate. In re Jacoby's Estate (Ohio Prob. 1958) 155 N.E.2d 282, 79 Ohio Law Abs. 247. Wills ⚬▬ 736(2)

Executor's claim against estate for expenses of funeral conducted by executor in his capacity as an undertaker was properly allowed in the amount of $350 though claim was not presented to probate court within time provided by statute. In re Winders' Estate (Noble 1945) 68 N.E.2d 677, 45 Ohio Law Abs. 353. Executors And Administrators ⚬▬ 233

For federal tax purposes, state law is controlling as to the deductibility of administrative expenses. Union Commerce Bank v. C.I.R. (C.A.6 (Ohio) 1964) 3 Ohio Misc. 189, 339 F.2d 163, 31 O.O.2d 252.

Truck rental and storage expenses required to maintain the testatrix's personal items are properly chargeable to the estate as actual and necessary, if reasonable. In re Estate of Kellhofer, No. 943 (4th Dist Ct App, Ross, 2-18-83).

10. Extraordinary fiduciary fees

Evidence was sufficient to support denial of estate executor's application for extraordinary fiduciary fees, although he made improvements to decedent's former residence; there was evidence that executor was living in the residence rent-free when improvements were made, and there was no evidence that estate actually benefited from the improvements. In re Estate of Bretschneider (Ohio App. 11 Dist., Geauga, 03-03-2006) No. 2005-G-2620, 2006-Ohio-1013, 2006 WL 533448, Unreported. Executors And Administrators ⚬▬ 506(3)

Because an award of extraordinary fiduciary fees must be adjusted so that the value of all the fiduciary's services to the estate correspond to the total compensation paid by the estate, a trial court's award of extraordinary fees without considering the regular commission is inappropriate; in addition, where the fee controversy involves a wrongful death settlement and the probate court is required to make an equitable distribution of the proceeds from the settlement, the court does not abuse discretion by awarding the executor a slightly larger share of the award after taking into consideration both the losses suffered by each beneficiary and the personal circumstances of each beneficiary. In re Estate of Thomas (Ohio App. 9 Dist., Summit, 04-12-2000) No. 19588, 2000 WL 372312, Unreported.

Executor was surcharged for unauthorized travel expenses, absent receipts or other documents demonstrating that expenses were necessary, just and reasonable. Whitaker v. Estate of Whitaker (Ohio App. 4 Dist., 06-

Surcharging executor for nearly $13,000 in interest which accrued due to deferral of estate taxes was not an abuse of discretion, even though tax laws authorized deferral, absent showing that accrued interest was actual and necessary estate expense. Whitaker v. Estate of Whitaker (Ohio App. 4 Dist., 06-26-1995) 105 Ohio App.3d 46, 663 N.E.2d 681. Executors And Administrators ⇐ 110

Disallowing executor's request for reimbursement of costs for repairing estate property was not abuse of discretion, absent showing that expenditure of estate funds was actual, necessary, just and reasonable. Whitaker v. Estate of Whitaker (Ohio App. 4 Dist., 06-26-1995) 105 Ohio App.3d 46, 663 N.E.2d 681. Executors And Administrators ⇐ 132

Executor could not be surcharged for accountant fees incurred in objecting to accounts absent statutory or other authority for surcharge. Whitaker v. Estate of Whitaker (Ohio App. 4 Dist., 06-26-1995) 105 Ohio App.3d 46, 663 N.E.2d 681. Executors And Administrators ⇐ 511(3)

Where an attorney acting as the executor of an estate testified that estate planning and estate tax preparation were areas of his expertise, and he paid his secretary $500 for the preparation of the estate's tax returns, the trial court did not abuse its discretion in finding that the subject payment was an extraneous fee remitted by the executor without application pursuant to RC 2113.36. Ollick v. Rice (Cuyahoga 1984) 16 Ohio App.3d 448, 476 N.E.2d 1062, 16 O.B.R. 529.

A fiduciary who wants to collect both an attorney fee and a broker's commission must demonstrate that he properly acted in a dual capacity, and that he actually performed extraordinary services as a broker which would justify any additional fees. Ollick v. Rice (Cuyahoga 1984) 16 Ohio App.3d 448, 476 N.E.2d 1062, 16 O.B.R. 529. Executors And Administrators ⇐ 495(2)

Where a nominated trustee under a will undertakes and performs a duty ordinarily performed by the named executrix in the will, but which duty the named executrix fails and refuses to perform, such nominated trustee is entitled to reasonable compensation for the services rendered. In re Allison's Will (Clark 1965) 9 Ohio App.2d 333, 224 N.E.2d 386, 38 O.O.2d 388.

The probate court may, in its discretion, deny allowance of an administrator's fee to an administrator who the court finds did not faithfully discharge his duties, and of counsel fees to such administrator who also acted as attorney for such estate. In re Gray's Estate (Franklin 1963) 118 Ohio App. 547, 196 N.E.2d 131, 26 O.O.2d 65.

Where title to real estate was transferred to the devisees and the executor thereafter sold the property pursuant to a power granted by will without having the certificate cancelled and refused to procure a quitclaim deed from the devisees, who were willing to give it, but such deed was finally given after the purchaser began litigation, the executor and his attorney were not entitled to additional compensation. In re Schoenleben's Estate (Darke 1955) 99 Ohio App. 212, 132 N.E.2d 245, 58 O.O. 366.

A bank's services, as cotrustee under will, in matters of advances to life beneficiary from principal of trust estate and kind of securities in which estate should be invested, as to which differences arose between bank and beneficiary and her husband, who was cotrustee, and defense of their action against bank for declaratory judgment regulating it as trustee in respect to such matters, were extraordinary services, for which bank was entitled to extra compensation. In re Haggerty's Estate (Ohio Prob. 1955) 128 N.E.2d 680, 70 Ohio Law Abs. 463. Trusts ⇐ 317

Compensation for extraordinary services by a fiduciary and payment of attorney fees in connection with the execution by the fiduciary of his duties discussed. In re Haggerty's Estate (Ohio Prob. 1955) 128 N.E.2d 680, 70 Ohio Law Abs. 463.

Where a fiduciary is an attorney, but never engaged in practice of law, did not have technical knowledge necessary to proper administration of estate and hired attorneys to represent estate, and where services which he performed were no more than those which any intelligent layman could have performed under same circumstances, he may be allowed compensation for extraordinary services rendered as a layman, but not as an attorney. In re Cramer's Estate (Ohio Prob. 1946) 69 N.E.2d 204, 46 Ohio Law Abs. 521, 34 O.O. 316.

Where executor, who was also funeral director, failed to file his claim for funeral expenses within time limit provided in GC 10509–106 (RC 2117.02) and failed to request authority to present claim after such time as provided by GC 10509–134 (RC 2117.07), probate court did not err in allowing subsequent claim to extent of $350 under authority in this section which allows executors further allowance for extraordinary services. In re Winders' Estate (Noble 1945) 68 N.E.2d 677, 45 Ohio Law Abs. 353.

Bank, as executor of deceased person who was heir at law and, until his death, administrator of estate of deceased brother, does not, after filing final account on behalf of administrator, have right, as representative of administrator, to intervene in appointment of administrator de bonis non for such deceased's estate, by moving that court's order designating depository for securities be vacated, and it is not entitled under section to allowance for legal services ordinarily "not required of executor... in common course of his duty." In re Langenbach's Estate (Stark 1941) 70 Ohio App. 132, 45 N.E.2d 129, 24 O.O. 447. Executors And Administrators ⇐ 497

The allowance to an administrator for extraordinary services in the settlement of the estate is part of the statement of his account and is to be considered by the court accordingly. McMahon v. Ambach & Co. (Ohio 1908) 79 Ohio St. 103, 86 N.E. 512, 6 Ohio Law Rep. 554. Executors And Administrators ⇐ 482

Neither attorneys fees incurred by the estate in a proceeding foreclosing the mortgage, nor costs of administration in the sale of real estate to pay debts, are extraordinary expenses under the statute. Sherman v. Millard (Ohio Cir. 1904) 17 Ohio C.D. 175, 6 Ohio C.C.N.S. 338.

An executor, by refusing to obey the court's order to file an account, is not entitled to extra allowance for extra services. Cairns v. Hedges (Ohio Cir. 1887) 1 Ohio C.D. 387. Executors And Administrators ⇐ 500

Claims presented by the administrator for extra services should be fully itemized for the benefit of the court and heir. In re Wolfe's Estate (Ohio Prob. 1897) 7 Ohio Dec. 220, 4 Ohio N.P. 336.

Extra compensation can only be allowed for extraordinary services, as GC 10837 is intended to cover ordinary service. In re Johnston's Estate (Ohio Prob. 1897) 7 Ohio Dec. 1, 4 Ohio N.P. 156.

Evidence that executor and spouse provided services in addition to standard home care services as a gift to decedent during the last years of his life was sufficient to support denial of quantum meruit damages for those services, where executor told decedent he was performing certain services because he loved him, not for the money, and spouse said it was in her nature to do "extra things" for decedent such as making meals. In re Estate of Bishop (Ohio App. 6 Dist., Lucas, 04-19-2002) No. L-01-1256, 2002-Ohio-1877, 2002 WL 597391, Unreported. Implied And Constructive Contracts ⇐ 99.1

The trial court did not abuse its discretion in disallowing the travel expenses of the executor. In re Estate of Kellhofer, No. 943 (4th Dist Ct App, Ross, 2–18–83).

The trial court did not abuse its discretion in failing to grant as an extraordinary expense the physical labor performed by the administrator and charged at hourly rates. In re Estate of Kellhofer, No. 943 (4th Dist Ct App, Ross, 2–18–83).

Compensation a little in excess of ten per cent of the total amount of money handled in the administration of trusts for the period covered by the final accounts is not excessive. Schieble v Phalen, 32 Abs 252 (App, Montgomery 1940).

2113.37 Allowance for tombstone and cemetery lot

The probate court, in settlement of an account, may allow as a credit to the following persons a just amount expended by the person for a tombstone or monument for the deceased and a just amount paid by the person to a cemetery association or corporation as a perpetual fund for caring for and preserving the lot on which the deceased is buried:

(A) An executor;

(B) An administrator;

(C) A person with the right of disposition under section 2108.70 or 2108.81 of the Revised Code.

It is not incumbent on such a person to procure a tombstone or monument or to pay any sum into such fund.

(2006 H 426, eff. 10–12–06; 1953 H 1, eff. 10–1–53; GC 10509–178)

Historical and Statutory Notes

Pre–1953 H 1 Amendments: 114 v 440

Amendment Note: 2006 H 426 rewrote this section, which prior thereto read:

"The probate court in settlement of an executor's or administrator's account may allow as a credit to the executor or administrator a just amount expended by him for a tombstone or monument for the deceased and a just amount paid by him to a cemetery association or corporation as a perpetual fund for caring for and preserving the lot on which the deceased is buried. It is not incumbent on an executor or administrator to procure a tombstone or monument or to pay any sum into such fund."

Cross References

Endowment care fund, cemetery association, 1721.12

Library References

Executors and Administrators ⚖109(2).
Westlaw Topic No. 162.
C.J.S. Executors and Administrators §§ 165, 237 to 239, 241 to 243, 245, 247, 249 to 250.

Research References

Encyclopedias

OH Jur. 3d Decedents' Estates § 1343, Expenses for Burial Lot, Monument, and Tombstone.

Treatises and Practice Aids

Carlin, Baldwin's Ohio Practice, Merrick-Rippner Probate Law § 30:12, Drafting a Will—Funeral and Memorial Instructions—Funeral and Burial Arrangements.

Carlin, Baldwin's Ohio Practice, Merrick-Rippner Probate Law § 30:60, Purchase of Burial Lot, Monument, Subject to Spouse's Approval—Form.

Carlin, Baldwin's Ohio Practice, Merrick-Rippner Probate Law § 30:61, Place of Burial; Permission for Others to Use Burial Plot—Form.

Carlin, Baldwin's Ohio Practice, Merrick-Rippner Probate Law § 30:66, Grave Marker—Form.

Carlin, Baldwin's Ohio Practice, Merrick-Rippner Probate Law § 30:67, Direction that Executor Purchase Perpetual Care Contract—Form.

Notes of Decisions

Authority to purchase 3
Court's discretion 2
Reasonableness of amount 1

---

1. Reasonableness of amount

Dependent upon the facts and circumstances in a particular case, the expenditure of a reasonable sum for a monument or marker for a deceased seventeen year old son in senior high school at the time of his death, caused by the wrongful act of a third person, may be considered as a necessary funeral expense. Caswell v Harry Miller Excavating Co, 20 Misc 46, 246 NE(2d) 921, 47 OO(2d) 307 (CP 1969).

The "justice" of the amount is a question between the executor or administrator and the successors to the estate; and the reasonableness or "justice" of the amount cannot be determined merely by comparing the amount with the gross amount of the testator's estate; the view seems to be generally sustained. 1921 OAG p 70.

2. Court's discretion

An order of the probate court allowing, as an administrative expense, payment in full of a testator's bequest to a cemetery association for the perpetual care of his cemetery lot is not a "just amount", and constitutes an abuse of discretion, where the assets of the estate are insufficient to pay all specific bequests in full, and such allowance would operate to reduce specific bequests rather than to reduce the general estate; and where, by a proportionate abatement and distribution affecting all specific bequests, payment of a part of the cemetery lot bequest would insure perpetual care for the decedent's lot. In re Nitschke's Estate (Franklin 1961) 114 Ohio App. 507, 183 N.E.2d 449, 20 O.O.2d 1. Executors And Administrators ⚖ 109(2)

Given the facts in record respecting the estate assets, debts, and expenses, and the fact that the testatrix made no provision in her will, the trial court was within its discretion in denying an expenditure for a grave marker. In re Estate of Kellhofer, No. 943 (4th Dist Ct App, Ross, 2–18–83).

3. Authority to purchase

The court is without jurisdiction in advance of the settlement of an estate to entertain an application by an administrator to fix a sum as a maximum or to order the administrator, in the event the widow or next of kin does not procure a monument, to erect a monument and charge the estate. In re Ferguson's Estate (Ohio 1909) 81 Ohio St. 58, 89 N.E. 1070, 7 Ohio Law Rep. 407.

A person other than the administrator may not purchase a monument for the deceased and charge it to his estate. Catlin v. Huestis (Ohio Cir. 1895) 5 Ohio C.D. 23.

The propriety of erecting a monument is in the exclusive discretion of the administrator, and only with reference to the deceased, although there is no room left for his widow's grave, but the court may determine the reasonableness of the cost. A reasonable expenditure may also be made for cornerstones of the cemetery lot and lettering thereon. In re Lones (Ohio Prob. 1911) 57 W.L.B. 122.

SALE OF PROPERTY

2113.39 Sale of property under authority of will

If a qualified executor, administrator, or testamentary trustee is authorized by will or devise to sell any class of personal property whatsoever or real estate, no order shall be required from the probate court to enable him to act in pursuance of the power vested in him. A power to sell authorizes a sale for any purpose deemed by such executor, administrator, or testamentary trustee to be for the best interest of the estate, unless the power is expressly limited by such will.

(1953 H 1, eff. 10–1–53; GC 10509–227)

Historical and Statutory Notes

Pre–1953 H 1 Amendments: 122 v H 281; 114 v 451

Cross References

Power of executor to compromise claims, 2117.05, 2117.09
Power of sale, written consent, 2127.011
Right of surviving spouse to one automobile of decedent, 2106.18

Library References

Executors and Administrators ⚖138(1), 138(2), 158.
Westlaw Topic No. 162.
C.J.S. Executors and Administrators §§ 295, 300, 329 to 332, 336, 343.

Research References

Encyclopedias

OH Jur. 3d Decedents' Estates § 1385, Statutory Authority Relating to the Management of Real Estate.
OH Jur. 3d Decedents' Estates § 1483, Property Subject to Sale.
OH Jur. 3d Decedents' Estates § 1610, Necessity of Court Order.
OH Jur. 3d Decedents' Estates § 1617, Purposes for Which Sale May be Made.
OH Jur. 3d Trusts § 388, Judicial Control—Statutory Provisions.

Forms

Ohio Forms Legal and Business § 24:465.20, Powers—to Sell House.

Treatises and Practice Aids

Carlin, Baldwin's Ohio Practice, Merrick-Rippner Probate Law § 2:51, Sale of Decedent's Personal Property.

Carlin, Baldwin's Ohio Practice, Merrick-Rippner Probate Law § 2:54, Sale of Land—Grounds for Land Sale.

Carlin, Baldwin's Ohio Practice, Merrick-Rippner Probate Law § 74:1, Decedent's Property—Authorization to Sell.

Carlin, Baldwin's Ohio Practice, Merrick-Rippner Probate Law § 90:3, Persons Entitled to Bring Land Sale Actions—Testamentary Trustee.

Carlin, Baldwin's Ohio Practice, Merrick-Rippner Probate Law § 90:4, Persons Entitled to Bring Land Sale Actions—Foreign Executor or Administrator.

Carlin, Baldwin's Ohio Practice, Merrick-Rippner Probate Law § 90:6, Authority for Land Sale Action—Testamentary Power.

Carlin, Baldwin's Ohio Practice, Merrick-Rippner Probate Law § 90:7, Authority for Land Sale Action—Consent or Demand of Beneficiaries.

Carlin, Baldwin's Ohio Practice, Merrick-Rippner Probate Law § 96:3, Confirmation of Sale—Effect.

Carlin, Baldwin's Ohio Practice, Merrick-Rippner Probate Law § 2:107, Distribution of Assets—Transfer of Titles to Motor Vehicles, Boat or Outboard Motor.

Carlin, Baldwin's Ohio Practice, Merrick-Rippner Probate Law § 2:121, Administration of Decedent's Estate—Checklist.

Carlin, Baldwin's Ohio Practice, Merrick-Rippner Probate Law § 21:81, Rights of Surviving Spouse—Right to Receive Motor Vehicles, Boat or Outboard Motor—Transfer Without Approval of Probate Court.

Carlin, Baldwin's Ohio Practice, Merrick-Rippner Probate Law § 30:57, Simple Will—Form.

Carlin, Baldwin's Ohio Practice, Merrick-Rippner Probate Law § 73:18, Deed of Fiduciary Under Power of Sale in Will—Form.

Carlin, Baldwin's Ohio Practice, Merrick-Rippner Probate Law § 75:17, Other Transfers of Automobiles, Watercraft and Outboard Motor.

Carlin, Baldwin's Ohio Practice, Merrick-Rippner Probate Law § 91:20, Land Sale—Necessary Parties.

Carlin, Baldwin's Ohio Practice, Merrick-Rippner Probate Law § 91:37, Fiduciary's Deed Under Testamentary Power—Form.

Carlin, Baldwin's Ohio Practice, Merrick-Rippner Probate Law § 30:164, Powers of Executor—Form.

Bogert - the Law of Trusts and Trustees § 743, Statutes Regarding Court or Trustee's Sales.

Kuehnle and Levey, Ohio Real Estate Law and Practice § 52:3, Statutory Fiduciary Sales—21 Statutory Proceedings.

Kuehnle and Levey, Ohio Real Estate Law and Practice § 52:15, Statutory Fiduciary Sales—Executor's Alternative Choice in Testamentary Power of Sale or by Complaint.

Kuehnle and Levey, Ohio Real Estate Law and Practice § 52:16, Statutory Fiduciary Sales—Scope of General Testamentary Power of Sale—Survival of Power in Administrator With Will Annexed.

Kuehnle and Levey, Ohio Real Estate Law and Practice § 52:21, Statutory Fiduciary Sales—Action by Trustee to Sell Trust Property.

Law Review and Journal Commentaries

Does the Executor in Ohio Take An Estate or a Power? Does the Power Survive?, Charles C. White. 15 U Cin L Rev 1 (January 1941).

Notes of Decisions

Administrator sale 3
Conditional power 4
Executor sale 2
Necessity 7
Price 6
Ratification 5
Trustee sale 1

1. Trustee sale

If, by the terms of a trust instrument, a trustee is specifically directed to retain certain investments, such trustee is subject to liability if such investments are not so retained, absent impossibility, illegality, or a judicially determined change of circumstances. Stevens v. National City Bank (Ohio 1989) 45 Ohio St.3d 276, 544 N.E.2d 612. Trusts ⚖ 217.3(9)

If, by the terms of a trust instrument, a trustee is merely authorized, but not directed, to retain certain investments, the trustee may retain them, unless under the circumstances it would be an abuse of discretion to retain them, or the trustee may sell a portion of such securities to obtain a diversification of the trust assets. Stevens v. National City Bank (Ohio 1989) 45 Ohio St.3d 276, 544 N.E.2d 612. Trusts ⚖ 217.3(9)

Section as amended to authorize testamentary trustees to sell property without order of court when so authorized by will or devise, cannot be given retroactive effect. Payer v. Black (Cuyahoga 1950) 96 N.E.2d 603, 58 Ohio Law Abs. 421.

2. Executor sale

Where the will states that the profits and benefits of the land are to be divided between legatees upon the occurrence of certain events, this is a mandate to sell the land upon the occurrence of those events and executors are empowered to make the sale. Collier v. Grimesey (Ohio 1880) 36 Ohio St. 17.

Power given to executors by the will to sell land becomes legally inoperative when the estate is settled. Ward's Lessee v. Barrows (Ohio 1853) 2 Ohio St. 241.

Where a will contains language conferring the power to dispose of real estate to the executors, it authorizes them to convey the real estate. Williams' Lessee v. Veach (Ohio 1848) 17 Ohio 171, 49 Am.Dec. 453.

Executor's power to sell real estate, given by the will, is a personal trust and cannot be executed by another administrator. Wills v. Cowper (Ohio 1825) 2 Ohio 124, adhered to 3 Ohio 486. Executors And Administrators ⚖ 519(1)

Power given to an executor to sell land does not authorize the executor to exchange or barter land, but to sell for money only. Taylor v. Galloway (Ohio 1823) 1 Ohio 232, 13 Am.Dec. 605. Executors And Administrators ⚖ 142; Powers ⚖ 20; Powers ⚖ 32; Wills ⚖ 692(5)

Power given by the will to the executors to sell land may be executed by one executor, if only one accepts the office under the will. Taylor v. Galloway (Ohio 1823) 1 Ohio 232, 13 Am.Dec. 605.

Executor was authorized to sell real estate in estate through auction without an order from the probate court and without being subject to statutory requirement that sale price equal at least 80% of appraised value of real estate, where property owner's last will and testament contained a power of sale clause. In re Phillipi (Ohio App. 5 Dist., Stark, 01-24-2005) No. 2004-CA-00144, 2005-Ohio-368, 2005 WL 267647, Unreported. Executors And Administrators ⚖ 142

Nephew of testator, who was specifically directed by will to sell testator's home as executor of estate, was not required by statute to obtain probate court's approval before managing the real estate by paying expenses from estate funds, even though will also directed that proceeds of sale were to be given to nephew. In re Estate of Carpenter (Ohio App. 11 Dist., 09-11-1998) 129 Ohio App.3d 717, 719 N.E.2d 20. Executors And Administrators ⚖ 109(1)

Determination that expenditures of approximately $7,665.55 in estate funds by executor of decedent's estate for payment of expenses relating to decedent's home prior to sale of home directed by will were not necessary expenditures of estate, so that nephew was required to reimburse estate for expenditures, was within trial court's discretion. In re Estate of Carpenter (Ohio App. 11 Dist., 09-11-1998) 129 Ohio App.3d 717, 719 N.E.2d 20. Executors And Administrators ⚖ 109(1)

Executor was not required to notify beneficiary prior to exercising power to sell estate property, where will gave executor power to sell property. In re Estate of Hughes (Ohio App. 9 Dist., 05-04-1994) 94 Ohio App.3d 551, 641 N.E.2d 248, appeal not allowed 70 Ohio St.3d 1441, 638 N.E.2d 1044. Executors And Administrators ⚖ 141

Executor's sale of estate property to executor's daughter did not constitute impermissible self-dealing, and thus was not voidable, though beneficiary offered higher price for property than did daughter; daughter offered to pay price equal to appraisal of property, there was no evidence that better price was available at time of sale to daughter because beneficiary did not make offer until seven days after contract with daughter was made, and there was no evidence that executor benefitted from sale. In re Estate of Hughes (Ohio App. 9 Dist., 05-04-1994) 94 Ohio App.3d 551, 641 N.E.2d 248, appeal not allowed 70 Ohio St.3d 1441, 638 N.E.2d 1044. Executors And Administrators ⚖ 143

The existence in a codicil of an express prohibition against selling securities in the estate at the time of the testator's death does not relieve the executor of the duty to apply for authority to sell any of such securities for which sale is indicated by the exercise of due care in the management of the assets of the estate. Union Commerce Bank v. Kusse (Ohio Prob. 1969) 21 Ohio Misc. 217, 251 N.E.2d 884, 49 O.O.2d 413, 50 O.O.2d 423.

Executors may not sell personal property which was specifically bequeathed to various legatees in order to pay debts of the estate before they have sold the real estate which passes under a residuary clause in the will. In re Boughton's Estate (Ohio Prob. 1959) 163 N.E.2d 423, 81 Ohio Law Abs. 589. Executors And Administrators ⚖ 158

Where a sole devisee appointed as executor sells as devisee lands of the estate at private sale, he must account for the full value thereof if necessary for the payment of the testator's debts, regardless of whether the sale was for less or full value. Hocking Valley R. Co. v. White (Ohio 1913) 87 Ohio St. 413, 101 N.E. 354, 10 Ohio Law Rep. 611, Am.Ann.Cas. 1914A, 190. Executors And Administrators ⇔ 40

Although authority was not expressly granted, the executor is empowered to sell the testator's house, if such authority can be inferred from the language of the will. Schaupp v. Jones (Ohio Cir. 1902) 13 Ohio C.D. 649, 3 Ohio C.C.N.S. 176.

Where the will gives the power to three executors to sell land and the contract is not executed by all three, the sale is not effective. Fleischman v. Shoemaker (Ohio Cir. 1887) 1 Ohio C.D. 415.

An attachment in an action against a devisee will not defeat the execution of a power of sale given by the testator to his executor, nor will such levy of attachment affect the title of the purchaser at the executor's sale. Smyth v Anderson, 31 OS 144 (1876).

3. Administrator sale

Where a will directs land to be sold by the executors and they resign without having executed that power, the sale may be made by an administrator with the will annexed. Elstner v. Fife (Ohio 1877) 32 Ohio St. 358. Executors And Administrators ⇔ 121(2); Powers ⇔ 30; Wills ⇔ 692(1)

Administrator with will annexed was not required to obtain written consent of devisees before selling real property, which was newly discovered asset of decedent's estate, where testamentary power of sale granted to executrixes was extended to administrator through probate court order providing that administrator had same powers to sell estate assets as those granted to executrixes. In re Estate of Hyer (Ohio App. 7 Dist., Monroe, 09-27-2004) No. 03 MO 9, 2004-Ohio-5359, 2004 WL 2334510, Unreported. Executors And Administrators ⇔ 121(2)

Administrator with will annexed had power to sell real property, which was newly discovered asset of decedent's estate; although will failed to specifically devise such real property, it generally devised residue and remainder of his real property to his children in fee simple, will authorized named executrixes to sell all or part of estate without court order, and probate court order provided that administrator had same powers to sell estate assets as those granted to executrixes. In re Estate of Hyer (Ohio App. 7 Dist., Monroe, 09-27-2004) No. 03 MO 9, 2004-Ohio-5359, 2004 WL 2334510, Unreported. Executors And Administrators ⇔ 121(2)

Where a will authorizes the sale of land by the administrators, the administrators must take out letters of administration before they have the authority to exercise this power, although they need no special order or license under the statute. In re Crawford's Estate (Ohio Cir. 1901) 11 Ohio C.D. 605, affirmed 68 Ohio St. 58, 48 W.L.B. 492, 67 N.E. 156, 96 Am.St.Rep. 648, 1 Ohio Law Rep. 91.

Administrator may sell an equitable title. Ewing v. Higby (Ohio 1835) 7 Ohio 198, PT. I.

Administrator may sell a part under an order of the court to sell the whole of a tract of land. Ewing v. Higby (Ohio 1835) 7 Ohio 198, PT. I.

4. Conditional power

Where power granted to the executor to sell land is conditional only if necessary to distribute the estate among the legatees, the devise is in fee of an undivided estate in land, not a bequest of the proceeds of the land, and the executor's power of sale is naked only and can only be exercised if necessary to make the distribution. Hoyt v. Day (Ohio 1877) 32 Ohio St. 101.

Where land is sold under authorization from a will to sell for debts, a purchaser for value is not required to ascertain whether there are debts. Smith v. McIntyre (C.C.A.6 (Ohio) 1899) 95 F. 585, 37 C.C.A. 177.

5. Ratification

Where executor's attorney makes a sale of land, and where the power to make such a sale is discretionary under the will and granted to the executor, the executor ratifies such sale by receipt of the purchase money. Although the discretionary power cannot be delegated, such transaction is equivalent to the exercise of power by the executor himself. Lake Shore & M.S. Ry. Co. v. Hutchins (Ohio 1881) 37 Ohio St. 282.

One executor may not purchase land at a sale by his coexecutor, although such sale may be executed with the subsequent assent and ratification of the heirs. Mitchell v. Dunlap (Ohio 1840) 10 Ohio 117.

Administrator with the will annexed (WWA) had authority under will to consent to modified closing date on sale of estate's real property without obtaining consent of probate court or beneficiaries; will provided that executor or executor's successor could sell estate's real property without court order or approval, and will did not require executor or administrator WWA to seek consent from any third party beneficiary. In re Estate of McCann (Ohio App. 6 Dist., Ottawa, 12-03-2004) No. OT-04-003, 2004-Ohio-6459, 2004 WL 2785291, Unreported. Executors And Administrators ⇔ 121(2)

6. Price

RC 2109.45 governs the actions of the probate court in all sales of estate property made by executors and trustees pursuant to and under an order of the court "allowing" such officer to make a private sale, and where the record discloses that trustees sold for a price less than that offered by the highest responsible bidder the sale will be set aside and sale ordered to the highest bidder. Dombey v. Rindsfoos (Franklin 1958) 105 Ohio App. 335, 151 N.E.2d 563, 77 Ohio Law Abs. 522, 6 O.O.2d 123.

An executor who, in the exercise of a testamentary power to sell lands for the payment of debts, in bad faith sells them for a price that is manifestly less than their true value, should, on exception to his account in the probate court, be charged with the difference between such inadequate price and the true value of the lands. Brown v. Reed (Ohio 1897) 56 Ohio St. 264, 37 W.L.B. 324, 46 N.E. 982. Executors And Administrators ⇔ 138(9)

Where the testator made a contract for the sale of land and in his will empowered the executor to sell the land, the executor cannot sell the land for less than one-third of the purchase price agreed upon by the executor. Pollock v. Pine (Ohio Cir. 1886) 1 Ohio C.D. 529.

7. Necessity

Where a will expressly authorized the widow to sell any of the property if necessary for maintenance, in an action in which the sale was attacked for want of authority to sell, the burden is on the attacking parties to show it was not necessary to sell, even where the attacking party is the widow herself seeking to repudiate the sale. Haren v. Block (Ohio Cir. 1906) 19 Ohio C.D. 460, 9 Ohio C.C.N.S. 328.

2113.40 Sale of personal property

At any time after the appointment of an executor or administrator, the probate court, when satisfied that it would be for the best interests of the estate, may authorize such executor or administrator to sell at public or private sale, at a fixed price or for the best price obtainable, and for cash or on such terms as the court may determine, any part or all of the personal property belonging to the estate, except:

(A) Such property as the surviving spouse desires to take at the appraised value;

(B) Property specifically bequeathed, when sale of such property is not necessary for the payment of debts, provided that such property may be sold with the consent of the person entitled thereto, including executors, administrators, guardians, and trustees;

(C) Property as to which distribution in kind has been demanded prior to the sale by the surviving spouse or other beneficiary entitled to such distribution in kind;

(D) Property which the court directs shall not be sold pursuant to a wish expressed by the decedent in his will; but at any later period, on application of a party interested, the court may, and for good cause shall, require such sale to be made.

In case of sale before expiration of the time within which the surviving spouse may elect to take at the appraised value, not less than ten days' notice of such sale shall be given to the surviving spouse, unless such surviving spouse consents to such sale or waives notice thereof. Such notice shall not be required as to perishable property.

The court may permit the itemized list of personal property being sold to be incorporated in documents and records relating to the sale, by reference to other documents and records which have been filed in the court. Provided that a court order shall not be required to permit the public sale of personal goods and chattels.

(1953 H 1, eff. 10–1–53; GC 10509–90)

Historical and Statutory Notes

Pre–1953 H 1 Amendments: 114 v 421

Cross References

Affidavit before private sale confirmed, 2109.45
Deceased partner, right of surviving partners to purchase property interest, 1779.04 to 1779.06, 1779.08
Precious metals dealers, duties of exempt persons in dealing with precious metals, 4728.12
Precious metals dealers, licenses, exemptions, 4728.11
Sale of escheated property, 109.41

Library References

Executors and Administrators ⚖157, 329(1).
Westlaw Topic No. 162.
C.J.S. Executors and Administrators §§ 329 to 343, 595.

Research References

Encyclopedias

OH Jur. 3d Abandoned, Lost, & Escheated Property § 26, Proceeding by Another State to Escheat Property of Ohio Citizen.
OH Jur. 3d Decedents' Estates § 1483, Property Subject to Sale.
OH Jur. 3d Decedents' Estates § 1486, Necessity of Court Order of Sale.
OH Jur. 3d Decedents' Estates § 1487, Necessity of Court Order of Sale—Effect of Failure to Obtain Order.

Treatises and Practice Aids

Carlin, Baldwin's Ohio Practice, Merrick-Rippner Probate Law § 2:51, Sale of Decedent's Personal Property.
Carlin, Baldwin's Ohio Practice, Merrick-Rippner Probate Law § 74:1, Decedent's Property—Authorization to Sell.
Carlin, Baldwin's Ohio Practice, Merrick-Rippner Probate Law § 2:121, Administration of Decedent's Estate—Checklist.
Carlin, Baldwin's Ohio Practice, Merrick-Rippner Probate Law § 74:10, Application to Sell Personal Property—Form.
Carlin, Baldwin's Ohio Practice, Merrick-Rippner Probate Law § 74:11, Schedule of Personal Property for Sale—Form.
Carlin, Baldwin's Ohio Practice, Merrick-Rippner Probate Law § 74:12, Notice of Sale of Personal Property—Form.
Carlin, Baldwin's Ohio Practice, Merrick-Rippner Probate Law § 74:13, Entry Authorizing Sale of Personal Property—Form.
Carlin, Baldwin's Ohio Practice, Merrick-Rippner Probate Law § 74:14, Order Authorizing Sale of Property Subject to Lien—Form.
Carlin, Baldwin's Ohio Practice, Merrick-Rippner Probate Law § 74:15, Notice to Lienholder—Form.
Carlin, Baldwin's Ohio Practice, Merrick-Rippner Probate Law § 74:16, Entry of Distribution—Form.
Carlin, Baldwin's Ohio Practice, Merrick-Rippner Probate Law § 74:21, Entry Approving and Confirming Sale—Private or Public Sale—Form.
Carlin, Baldwin's Ohio Practice, Merrick-Rippner Probate Law § 30:164, Powers of Executor—Form.
Carlin, Baldwin's Ohio Practice, Merrick-Rippner Probate Law App B SPF 9.0, Application to Sell Personal Property—Form.
Carlin, Baldwin's Ohio Practice, Merrick-Rippner Probate Law App B SPF 9.1, Entry Authorizing Sale of Personal Property—Form.
Carlin, Baldwin's Ohio Practice, Merrick-Rippner Probate Law App B SPF 9.2, Notice of Sale of Personal Property—Form.
Carlin, Baldwin's Ohio Practice, Merrick-Rippner Probate Law App B SPF 9.3, Entry Authorizing Sale of Personal Property—Form.

Notes of Decisions

Lease 2
Notes 1
Order of sale or distribution 4
Other laws, application 6
Securities 3
Voidable sale 5

---

1. Notes

An administrator has no power to sell or transfer notes secured by a mortgage which belonged to the deceased at the time of his death, and such notes taken up by a third party will be regarded and held as paid, as between the administrator and the third party. Miller v. Stark (Ohio 1900) 61 Ohio St. 413, 43 W.L.B. 116, 56 N.E. 11.

2. Lease

A lease of land for ninety-nine years, renewable forever, is a chattel that, upon the owner's decease, passes to his executor or administrator as any other chattel interest. Murdock v Ratcliff, 10 Ohio 119 (1840).

3. Securities

The existence in a codicil of an express prohibition against selling securities in the estate at the time of the testator's death does not relieve the executor of the duty to apply for authority to sell any of such securities for which sale is indicated by the exercise of due care in the management of the assets of the estate. Union Commerce Bank v. Kusse (Ohio Prob. 1969) 21 Ohio Misc. 217, 251 N.E.2d 884, 49 O.O.2d 413, 50 O.O.2d 423.

On the evidence, that the action of coexecutors and trustees in accepting an offer for the purchase of stock owned by the estate in preference to the highest price obtainable was contrary to the terms of the decedent's will and not for the best interest of the trust estate. Dombey v. Rindsfoos (Franklin 1958) 105 Ohio App. 335, 151 N.E.2d 563, 77 Ohio Law Abs. 522, 6 O.O.2d 123.

An order of the probate court authorizing an executor to sell corporate stock at the market value is not a compliance with GC 10704 (RC 2113.40), requiring the court to fix the lowest price; but this will not impair a bona fide sale at the market price. Burch v. Cincinnati Trust Co. (Ohio Cir. 1911) 23 Ohio C.D. 358, 14 Ohio C.C.N.S. 346.

While the order of the probate court not fixing a minimum price for the sale of shares of stock is defective, it does not impair the title to the stock where the sale conformed in all other respects to the statutes, the sale was for market price, and no collusion or fraud was found. Burch v. Cincinnati Trust Co. (Ohio Cir. 1911) 23 Ohio C.D. 358, 14 Ohio C.C.N.S. 346.

The probate court may order the sale of stocks which run the risk of depreciation and the reinvestment of the proceeds. Guthrie v. Cincinnati Gas & Elec. Co. (Ohio Super. 1904) 15 Ohio Dec. 23, 2 Ohio N.P.N.S. 117.

4. Order of sale or distribution

Executors may not sell personal property which was specifically bequeathed to various legatees in order to pay debts of the estate before they have sold the real estate which passes under a residuary clause in the will. In re Boughton's Estate (Ohio Prob. 1959) 163 N.E.2d 423, 81 Ohio Law Abs. 589. Executors And Administrators ⚖ 158

Under former section, probate court did not, through its order, effect a distribution of property because the only valid order of distribution which the probate court was authorized to enter was general and it had no power to designate distributees. Williamson v. C.I.R. (C.C.A.6 1938) 100 F.2d 735, 13 O.O. 493, certiorari denied 59 S.Ct. 827, 307 U.S. 623, 83 L.Ed. 1501.

5. Voidable sale

The public sale of a diamond ring to the spouse of the executor of an estate is voidable. In re Estate of Kellhofer, No. 943 (4th Dist Ct App, Ross, 2–18–83).

6. Other laws, application

The provisions of sections 8673–1 to 8673–7, inclusive, General Code, known as the Uniform Transfer Act, apply to trustees, executors, administrators, and other fiduciaries, where the validity of the transfer is not dependent upon the indorsement or assignment of such trustee, executor, administrator, or other fiduciary. Stoltz v. Carroll (Ohio 1919) 99 Ohio St. 289, 124 N.E. 226, 17 Ohio Law Rep. 7, 17 Ohio Law Rep. 22. Assignments ⚖ 31; Corporations ⚖ 125

2113.41 Public sale

Public sales of personal property mentioned in section 2113.40 of the Revised Code shall be at public auction and, unless otherwise directed by the probate court, after notice of such sale has been given:

(A) By advertisement appearing at least three times in a newspaper of general circulation in the county during a period of fifteen days next preceding such sale;

(B) By advertisement posted not less than fifteen days next preceding such sale in at least five public places in the township or municipal corporation where such sale is to take place;

(C) By both such forms of advertisement.

Such advertisement published or posted shall specify generally the property to be sold and the date, place, and terms of sale. The executor or administrator may employ an auctioneer or clerk, or both, to conduct such sale, and their reasonable fees and charges shall be deducted from the proceeds of the sale. The court for good cause may extend the time for sale.

(125 v 903, eff. 10–1–53; 1953 H 1; GC 10509–91)

Historical and Statutory Notes

Pre–1953 H 1 Amendments: 114 v 421

Library References

Executors and Administrators ⇔160, 363.
Westlaw Topic No. 162.
C.J.S. Executors and Administrators §§ 329, 334, 336, 343, 633.

Research References

Encyclopedias

OH Jur. 3d Decedents' Estates § 1488, Manner and Form of Sale; Notice.

Treatises and Practice Aids

Carlin, Baldwin's Ohio Practice, Merrick-Rippner Probate Law § 2:51, Sale of Decedent's Personal Property.

Carlin, Baldwin's Ohio Practice, Merrick-Rippner Probate Law § 74:5, Decedent's Property—Duty to Sell—Public Sale at Auction.

Carlin, Baldwin's Ohio Practice, Merrick-Rippner Probate Law § 2:121, Administration of Decedent's Estate—Checklist.

Carlin, Baldwin's Ohio Practice, Merrick-Rippner Probate Law § 74:13, Entry Authorizing Sale of Personal Property—Form.

Carlin, Baldwin's Ohio Practice, Merrick-Rippner Probate Law § 74:14, Order Authorizing Sale of Property Subject to Lien—Form.

Carlin, Baldwin's Ohio Practice, Merrick-Rippner Probate Law § 74:15, Notice to Lienholder—Form.

Carlin, Baldwin's Ohio Practice, Merrick-Rippner Probate Law § 74:16, Entry of Distribution—Form.

Carlin, Baldwin's Ohio Practice, Merrick-Rippner Probate Law § 74:18, Report of Sale of Personal Property—Public Sale—Form.

Carlin, Baldwin's Ohio Practice, Merrick-Rippner Probate Law § 74:21, Entry Approving and Confirming Sale—Private or Public Sale—Form.

Carlin, Baldwin's Ohio Practice, Merrick-Rippner Probate Law App B SPF 9.0, Application to Sell Personal Property—Form.

Carlin, Baldwin's Ohio Practice, Merrick-Rippner Probate Law App B SPF 9.1, Entry Authorizing Sale of Personal Property—Form.

Carlin, Baldwin's Ohio Practice, Merrick-Rippner Probate Law App B SPF 9.3, Entry Authorizing Sale of Personal Property—Form.

Notes of Decisions

Auctioneer 2
Liability of estate 4
Self–dealing 3
Voidable sale 1

---

1. Voidable sale

The public sale of a diamond ring to the spouse of the executor of an estate is voidable. In re Estate of Kellhofer, No. 943 (4th Dist Ct App, Ross, 2–18–83).

2. Auctioneer

In conducting a judicial sale of real estate at public sale an administrator may employ an auctioneer for a fee when such employment is authorized or approved by the court, and such auctioneer must be a licensed auctioneer. 1957 OAG 969.

3. Self–dealing

Because of the fiduciary nature of the position, an administrator may not buy land which he put up for public sale in the course of his administration, not even to cure a problem in the sale, and should a problem arise, the administrator must again offer the property for sale. (See also Sheldon v Newton, 3 OS 494 (1854); Caldwell v Caldwell, 45 OS 512, 15 NE 297 (1888).) Barrington v. Alexander (Ohio 1856) 6 Ohio St. 189.

4. Liability of estate

An administrator, in selling lands of his decedent which he conveys without covenants of warranty, cannot render the estate of the deceased liable in damages by false representations as to the condition of the title or the extent of existing incumbrances. Dunlap v. Robinson (Ohio 1861) 12 Ohio St. 530. Executors And Administrators ⇔ 388(4)

2113.42 Report of sale

Within thirty days after any public or private sale of the personal property of an estate, the executor or administrator shall make a report of the sale to the probate court. The report shall include proof of proper notice of the sale if it was at a public auction, and, if a clerk was employed for the sale, the report shall be accompanied by a sale bill signed by the clerk.

(1992 H 427, eff. 10–8–92; 1953 H 1; GC 10509–92)

Historical and Statutory Notes

Pre–1953 H 1 Amendments: 114 v 422

Cross References

Application to sell personalty, Sup R 63

Library References

Executors and Administrators ⇔374.
Westlaw Topic No. 162.
C.J.S. Executors and Administrators § 643.

Research References

Encyclopedias

OH Jur. 3d Decedents' Estates § 1491, Report of Sale.

Treatises and Practice Aids

Carlin, Baldwin's Ohio Practice, Merrick-Rippner Probate Law § 2:51, Sale of Decedent's Personal Property.

Carlin, Baldwin's Ohio Practice, Merrick-Rippner Probate Law § 74:9, Decedent's Property—Report of Sale.

Carlin, Baldwin's Ohio Practice, Merrick-Rippner Probate Law § 2:121, Administration of Decedent's Estate—Checklist.

Carlin, Baldwin's Ohio Practice, Merrick-Rippner Probate Law § 74:17, Report of Sale of Personal Property—Private Sale—Form.

Carlin, Baldwin's Ohio Practice, Merrick-Rippner Probate Law § 74:18, Report of Sale of Personal Property—Public Sale—Form.

Carlin, Baldwin's Ohio Practice, Merrick-Rippner Probate Law § 74:19, Sale Bill—Public Sale—Form.

2113.43 Credit

In all sales of the personal property of an estate the probate court may authorize the executor or administrator to sell on credit, the unpaid purchase price to be secured by notes or bonds with two or more sureties and approved by the executor or administrator. An executor or administrator shall not be responsible for loss due to the insolvency of the purchaser of any of such property if it appears that such executor or administrator acted with caution in extending credit pursuant to the authority of the court and has diligently tried to collect such notes and bonds.

(1953 H 1, eff. 10–1–53; GC 10509–93)

Historical and Statutory Notes

Pre–1953 H 1 Amendments: 114 v 422

Library References

Executors and Administrators ⚖︎146, 147, 368.
Westlaw Topic No. 162.
C.J.S. Executors and Administrators §§ 295, 315 to 316, 639.

Research References

Encyclopedias

OH Jur. 3d Decedents' Estates § 1489, Manner and Form of Sale; Notice—Terms of Sale.

Treatises and Practice Aids

Carlin, Baldwin's Ohio Practice, Merrick-Rippner Probate Law § 2:51, Sale of Decedent's Personal Property.

Carlin, Baldwin's Ohio Practice, Merrick-Rippner Probate Law § 74:1, Decedent's Property—Authorization to Sell.

Carlin, Baldwin's Ohio Practice, Merrick-Rippner Probate Law § 74:6, Decedent's Property—Duty to Sell—Sale on Credit.

Carlin, Baldwin's Ohio Practice, Merrick-Rippner Probate Law § 74:10, Application to Sell Personal Property—Form.

Carlin, Baldwin's Ohio Practice, Merrick-Rippner Probate Law App B SPF 9.0, Application to Sell Personal Property—Form.

Notes of Decisions

Loss 1
Sureties 2

---

1. Loss

Where a previous administrator permitted the widow to take a portion of the personal property for which she gave a note defective under the statute, and the administrator de bonis non thereafter voluntarily paid the balance due on her year's allowance, he is responsible for the loss arising from the uncollectable character of the note. White v. Moe (Ohio 1869) 19 Ohio St. 37.

2. Sureties

Administrator cannot arbitrarily reject sureties having the statutory qualifications, but a decision made with due caution, in good faith, will not be disturbed. Hamilton v. Bonham (Ohio Cir. 1900) 10 Ohio C.D. 834, reversed 66 Ohio St. 82, 47 W.L.B. 334, 63 N.E. 597.

2113.44 Sale of notes secured by mortgage

An executor or administrator, without court order, may sell and transfer, without recourse, any promissory notes secured by mortgage and the mortgage securing such notes at not less than the face value thereof with accrued interest.

(1953 H 1, eff. 10–1–53; GC 10509–94)

Historical and Statutory Notes

Pre–1953 H 1 Amendments: 114 v 422

Library References

Executors and Administrators ⚖︎166, 169, 170, 400, 402.
Westlaw Topic No. 162.
C.J.S. Executors and Administrators §§ 327, 329, 336, 343, 684 to 685.

Research References

Encyclopedias

OH Jur. 3d Decedents' Estates § 1484, Property Subject to Sale—Promissory Notes and Mortgage Securing the Notes.

OH Jur. 3d Decedents' Estates § 1486, Necessity of Court Order of Sale.

Treatises and Practice Aids

Carlin, Baldwin's Ohio Practice, Merrick-Rippner Probate Law § 74:7, Decedent's Property—Duty to Sell—Promissory Note.

2113.45 Mortgaged premises to be considered personal assets; possession

When a mortgagee of real estate, or an assignee of such mortgagee, dies without foreclosing the mortgage, the mortgaged premises and the debts secured thereby shall be considered personal assets in the hands of the executor or administrator of such mortgagee or assignee, and be administered and accounted for as such.

If the mortgagee or assignee did not obtain possession of the mortgage premises in his lifetime, his executor or administrator may take possession by open and peaceable entry or by action, as the deceased might have done if living.

(1953 H 1, eff. 10–1–53; GC 10509–68, 10509–69)

Historical and Statutory Notes

Pre–1953 H 1 Amendments: 114 v 416, 417

Comparative Laws

Ark.—A.C.A. § 28-49-102.
Ind.—West's A.I.C. 29–1–13–6.
Minn.—M.S.A. § 525.38.

Library References

Executors and Administrators ⚖︎151, 155.
Westlaw Topic No. 162.
C.J.S. Executors and Administrators §§ 323, 326.

Research References

Encyclopedias

OH Jur. 3d Decedents' Estates § 1300, Mortgages.

OH Jur. 3d Decedents' Estates § 1401, Powers and Duties in Relation to Mortgaged Property.

OH Jur. 3d Decedents' Estates § 1485, Property Subject to Sale—Mortgaged Premises Considered Personal Assets.

OH Jur. 3d Mortgages & Deeds of Trust § 141, Nature and Extent of Mortgagee's Rights.

Treatises and Practice Aids

Carlin, Baldwin's Ohio Practice, Merrick-Rippner Probate Law § 73:6, Mortgaged Property—Equitable Conversion and Obtaining Possession.

Carlin, Baldwin's Ohio Practice, Merrick-Rippner Probate Law § 73:9, Mortgaged Property—Action in Ejectment.

Notes of Decisions

Ejectment 2
Foreclosure 1
Jurisdiction 4

Personal assets 3

1. Foreclosure

Executor of a deceased mortgagee has capacity to bring action of foreclosure against heirs of deceased mortgagor and may obtain foreclosure without prayer for a right to personal judgment against heirs. Carter v. Holmes (Butler 1945) 77 Ohio App. 330, 67 N.E.2d 115, 45 Ohio Law Abs. 254, 33 O.O. 120.

2. Ejectment

Under this section interest of mortgagee could not upon his death pass to his heirs as real property and action of ejectment could not properly lie. Stafford v. Collins (Clark 1933) 16 Ohio Law Abs. 621. Descent And Distribution ⇒ 9; Executors And Administrators ⇒ 39; Executors And Administrators ⇒ 52

Mortgagee, by attempting to foreclose his note and mortgage in action in which court found fifteen-year statute of limitation had run on note and mortgage and therefore barred recovery, which finding of court was reduced to final judgment, was not estopped from thereafter maintaining action in ejectment on mortgage where twenty-one year statute of limitation had not run, and GC 10509–69 (RC 2113.45) specifically authorized administrator to bring such action. Taylor v. Quinn (Lucas 1941) 68 Ohio App. 164, 39 N.E.2d 627, 22 O.O. 292. Mortgages ⇒ 411

3. Personal assets

By virtue of this section, interest of mortgagee at time of his death in real estate upon which mortgage was given, must be considered personal assets of mortgagee and not real property. Stafford v. Collins (Clark 1933) 16 Ohio Law Abs. 621.

4. Jurisdiction

The probate court is not vested with jurisdiction to order an administrator specifically to perform an agreement alleged to have been made by his intestate. Jones v. Green (Ohio Cir. 1901) 11 Ohio C.D. 548.

2113.46 Who may discharge mortgage

In case of the redemption of a mortgage belonging to the estate of a decedent, the money paid thereon must be received by the executor or administrator and thereupon he shall release and discharge the mortgage. Until such redemption, the executor or administrator, if possession has been taken by him or by the decedent, shall be seized of the mortgaged premises in trust for the same persons who would be entitled to the money if the premises had been redeemed.

(1953 H 1, eff. 10–1–53; GC 10509–70)

Historical and Statutory Notes

Pre–1953 H 1 Amendments: 114 v 417

Library References

Executors and Administrators ⇒151, 155.
Westlaw Topic No. 162.
C.J.S. Executors and Administrators §§ 323, 326.

Research References

Encyclopedias

OH Jur. 3d Decedents' Estates § 1402, Powers and Duties in Relation to Mortgaged Property—Redemption.
OH Jur. 3d Decedents' Estates § 1507, Lands Subject to Liens.
OH Jur. 3d Mortgages & Deeds of Trust § 196, to Whom Payment Must be Made.
OH Jur. 3d Mortgages & Deeds of Trust § 217, Who May Release Mortgage.

Treatises and Practice Aids

Carlin, Baldwin's Ohio Practice, Merrick-Rippner Probate Law § 73:7, Mortgaged Property—Discharge of Mortgage.

2113.47 Foreclosure of mortgage

A mortgage belonging to an estate may be foreclosed by the executor or administrator.

(1953 H 1, eff. 10–1–53; GC 10509–71)

Historical and Statutory Notes

Pre–1953 H 1 Amendments: 114 v 417

Library References

Executors and Administrators ⇒133.
Westlaw Topic No. 162.
C.J.S. Executors and Administrators § 287.

Research References

Encyclopedias

OH Jur. 3d Decedents' Estates § 1403, Powers and Duties in Relation to Mortgaged Property—Foreclosure.
OH Jur. 3d Decedents' Estates § 1507, Lands Subject to Liens.
OH Jur. 3d Decedents' Estates § 1764, Actions Concerning Realty—Foreclosure of Mortgage.
OH Jur. 3d Mortgages & Deeds of Trust § 308, Mortgage.

Treatises and Practice Aids

Carlin, Baldwin's Ohio Practice, Merrick-Rippner Probate Law § 73:8, Mortgaged Property—Foreclosure.
Kuehnle and Levey, Ohio Real Estate Law and Practice § 52:2, Statutory Fiduciary Sales—Foreclosure by Executor or Administrator of Mortgagee.
Kuehnle and Levey, Ohio Real Estate Law and Practice § 36:21, Foreclosure—Parties—Plaintiff.

Law Review and Journal Commentaries

Will Mortgage Law Survive? A Commentary and Critique on Mortgage Law's Birth, Long Life, and Current Proposals for its Demise, Morris G. Shanker. 51 Case W Res L Rev 69 (Fall 2003). (Ed. note: Recent successes by lenders in imposing unfavorable terms upon borrowers are discussed.)

Notes of Decisions

Personal judgment 1

1. Personal judgment

Executor of a deceased mortgagee has capacity to bring action of foreclosure against heirs of deceased mortgagor and may obtain foreclosure without prayer for a right to personal judgment against such heirs. Carter v. Holmes (Butler 1945) 77 Ohio App. 330, 67 N.E.2d 115, 45 Ohio Law Abs. 254, 33 O.O. 120.

2113.48 Action to complete contract to sell land

When a person who has entered into a written contract for the sale and conveyance of an interest in real estate dies before its completion, his executor or administrator when not required to otherwise dispose of such contract, may, with the consent of the purchaser, obtain authority to complete such contract by filing an application therefor in the probate court of the county in which he was appointed. Notice of the time of hearing on such application shall be given to the surviving spouse and heirs, if the decedent died intestate, and to the surviving spouse, and devisees or legatees having an interest in such contract, if the decedent died testate. If the court is satisfied that it would be for the best interests of the estate, it may authorize the executor or administrator to complete said contract and to execute and deliver to the purchaser such instruments as are required to make the order of the court effective.

(1953 H 1, eff. 10–1–53; GC 10509–224)

Historical and Statutory Notes

Pre–1953 H 1 Amendments: 123 v 460; 114 v 450

Cross References

Completion of land contract by guardian, 2111.19

Library References

Executors and Administrators ⚖92.
Westlaw Topic No. 162.
C.J.S. Executors and Administrators §§ 205 to 206, 209 to 211.

Research References

Encyclopedias

OH Jur. 3d Conversion in Equity § 10, Conversion Resulting from Contract to Sell Realty.
OH Jur. 3d Decedents' Estates § 1406, Contracts Relating to Realty.
OH Jur. 3d Guardian & Ward § 113, Real Property, Generally—Completion of Real Estate Contracts.

Treatises and Practice Aids

Carlin, Baldwin's Ohio Practice, Merrick-Rippner Probate Law § 2:52, Sale of Land—Completion of Contracts Pertaining to Land.
Carlin, Baldwin's Ohio Practice, Merrick-Rippner Probate Law § 90:2, Persons Entitled to Bring Land Sale Actions—Other Parties.
Carlin, Baldwin's Ohio Practice, Merrick-Rippner Probate Law § 91:39, Application to Complete Contract for Sale and Conveyance of Real Estate—Form.
Carlin, Baldwin's Ohio Practice, Merrick-Rippner Probate Law § 91:40, Entry Granting Application to Complete Contract for Sale and Conveyance of Real Estate—Form.
Carlin, Baldwin's Ohio Practice, Merrick-Rippner Probate Law § 91:41, Fiduciary's Deed—Form.
Kuehnle and Levey, Ohio Real Estate Law and Practice § 52:3, Statutory Fiduciary Sales—21 Statutory Proceedings.

Notes of Decisions

Life estate 2
Procedural issues 1
Rescission 3

---

1. Procedural issues

A bill brought against the heirs on their ancestor's contract to convey land must make the personal representative a party defendant. Massie's Heirs v. Donaldson (Ohio 1838) 8 Ohio 377.

Procedure provided by section relative to completion of contracts of decedent under direction of court where other party consents, held to conform with due process. Kramer v. Gaskill (Cuyahoga 1943) 52 N.E.2d 674, 39 Ohio Law Abs. 310.

2. Life estate

Where devisee was given an estate for and during his natural life, with full power and authority to sell and convey any part, or all, and to use the proceeds in any manner as he might desire, the devisee had but a life estate, not a fee, and the remaindermen had a vested interest subject to divestment by principal being consumed; under these facts, upon death of life tenant, his administrator has power to complete an executory contract for the sale of part of the property enjoyed by deceased during his lifetime. Rippel v. Rippel (Ohio Prob. 1947) 78 N.E.2d 902, 52 Ohio Law Abs. 33, 38 O.O. 501.

3. Rescission

On a contract for the sale of land, where the buyer is in default and the contract gives the vendor the right to elect rescission or an action on the contract for unpaid money, this right may be exercised only by the administrator, and an action for rescission brought by the devisees of the deceased vendor is defective. Stang v. Newberger (Ohio Com.Pl. 1898) 8 Ohio Dec. 80, 6 Ohio N.P. 60.

2113.49 Court may order alteration or cancellation of contract for sale of real estate; venue

When a person who has entered into a written contract for the sale and conveyance of an interest in real estate dies before its completion, his executor or administrator, when not required to otherwise dispose of the contract, may file a petition for the alteration or cancellation of the contract, in the probate court of the county in which he was appointed, or in which the real estate or any part of it is situated. If the decedent died intestate, the surviving spouse and heirs, and if the decedent died testate, the surviving spouse, and devisees or legatees having an interest in the contract, when not plaintiffs, shall, together with the purchaser, be made parties defendant.

If, upon hearing, the court is satisfied that it is for the best interests of the estate, it may, with the consent of the purchaser, authorize the executor or administrator to agree to the alteration or cancellation of the contract, and to execute and deliver to the purchaser the instruments required to make the order of the court effective. Before making such an order, the court shall cause to be secured, to and for the benefit of the estate of the deceased, its just part of the consideration of the contract. The instruments executed and delivered pursuant to such an order shall recite the order, and be as binding on the heirs and other parties in interest, as if made by the deceased in his lifetime.

(1975 S 145, eff. 1–1–76; 1953 H 1; GC 10509–225)

Historical and Statutory Notes

Pre–1953 H 1 Amendments: 123 v 460; 114 v 450

Library References

Executors and Administrators ⚖135, 156.
Westlaw Topic No. 162.
C.J.S. Executors and Administrators §§ 291, 326.

Research References

Encyclopedias

OH Jur. 3d Conversion in Equity § 10, Conversion Resulting from Contract to Sell Realty.
OH Jur. 3d Decedents' Estates § 1408, Right to Alter, Cancel, or Compromise.

Treatises and Practice Aids

Klein, Darling, & Terez, Baldwin's Ohio Practice Civil Practice § 73:3, Probate Division--Venue.
Carlin, Baldwin's Ohio Practice, Merrick-Rippner Probate Law § 2:52, Sale of Land—Completion of Contracts Pertaining to Land.
Carlin, Baldwin's Ohio Practice, Merrick-Rippner Probate Law § 90:2, Persons Entitled to Bring Land Sale Actions—Other Parties.
Carlin, Baldwin's Ohio Practice, Merrick-Rippner Probate Law § 91:39, Application to Complete Contract for Sale and Conveyance of Real Estate—Form.

2113.50 Completion of decedent's contract to buy land

When a person who has entered into a written contract for the purchase of an interest in real estate dies before a conveyance thereof to him, his executor or administrator, or surviving spouse, or any heir, or any devisee or legatee having an interest in such contract, may file an application for authority to complete such contract in the probate court of the county in which the executor or administrator was appointed. Notice of the time of the hearing on such application shall be given to the surviving spouse and heirs, if the decedent died intestate, and to the surviving spouse, and devisees or legatees having an interest in such contract, if the decedent died testate, to the executor or administrator, if not the applicant, and to all other persons having an interest in such real estate. If the court is satisfied that it would be for the best interest of the estate it may, with the consent of the vendor, authorize the executor or administrator to complete the contract, pay to the vendor the amount due on the contract, and authorize a conveyance of the interest in the real estate to the persons entitled thereto. If, however, the court finds that the condition of the estate at the time of the hearing does not warrant the payment out of the estate of the amount due under the contract, it may authorize the persons entitled to the interest of the decedent in the contract to pay to the vendor the amount due on the contract. The real estate so conveyed shall thereafter be chargeable with the debts of the estate to the extent of the equitable interest of the estate therein, and may be sold in land sale proceedings, except that in the event of such sale, the persons to whom the real estate shall have been conveyed shall have a prior lien on the proceeds as against the estate to the extent of any portion of the purchase price paid by them.

The executor or administrator, or surviving spouse, or any heir, or any devisee or legatee having an interest in such a contract, may file a petition for the alteration or cancellation of the contract in the probate court of the county in which the executor or administrator was appointed. If the decedent died intestate, the surviving spouse and heirs, and if the decedent died testate, the surviving spouse, and devisees or legatees having an interest in such contract, and the executor or administrator, when not the plaintiff, together with the vendor, and all other persons having an interest in the real estate which is subject to the contract, shall be made parties defendant. If the court is satisfied that it would be for the best interests of the estate, the court, with the consent of the vendor, may authorize the executor or administrator to agree to the alteration or cancellation of the contract and to execute and deliver such deeds or other instruments to the vendor as are required to make the order of the court effective. Such deeds or other instruments as are executed and delivered pursuant to such order shall recite the order and be as binding on the parties to the suit as if made by the deceased in his lifetime.

(125 v 411, eff. 10–16–53; 1953 H 1; GC 10509–226)

Historical and Statutory Notes

Pre–1953 H 1 Amendments: 114 v 450

Cross References

Completion of land contract by guardian, 2111.19

Library References

Executors and Administrators ⟐135.
Westlaw Topic No. 162.
C.J.S. Executors and Administrators § 291.

Research References

Encyclopedias

OH Jur. 3d Conversion in Equity § 10, Conversion Resulting from Contract to Sell Realty.
OH Jur. 3d Decedents' Estates § 1406, Contracts Relating to Realty.
OH Jur. 3d Guardian & Ward § 113, Real Property, Generally—Completion of Real Estate Contracts.
OH Jur. 3d Real Property Sales & Exchanges § 230, Generally; Claimants Under Deceased Purchaser.

Treatises and Practice Aids

Carlin, Baldwin's Ohio Practice, Merrick-Rippner Probate Law § 2:52, Sale of Land—Completion of Contracts Pertaining to Land.
Carlin, Baldwin's Ohio Practice, Merrick-Rippner Probate Law § 91:39, Application to Complete Contract for Sale and Conveyance of Real Estate—Form.

Notes of Decisions

Purchase right 1

---

1. Purchase right

RC 2113.50 applies only where a decedent entered a completed, written purchase contract and all that remains is conveyance of the property under the terms of the contract; RC 2113.50 does not apply to preemptive rights to purchase property. Stratman v. Sheetz (Hamilton 1989) 60 Ohio App.3d 71, 573 N.E.2d 776. Executors And Administrators ⟐ 92

2113.51 Property may be delivered to legatee

The property of an estate which is specifically bequeathed may be delivered over to the legatee entitled thereto. Such legatee must secure its redelivery on demand to the executor or administrator. Otherwise, such property must remain in the hands of the executor or administrator to be distributed or sold, as required by law and the condition of the estate.

(1953 H 1, eff. 10–1–53; GC 10509–180)

Historical and Statutory Notes

Pre–1953 H 1 Amendments: 114 v 441

Library References

Executors and Administrators ⟐300.
Westlaw Topic No. 162.
C.J.S. Executors and Administrators § 543.

Research References

Encyclopedias

OH Jur. 3d Decedents' Estates § 1631, Distribution Without Court Order.
OH Jur. 3d Decedents' Estates § 1645, Delivery of Property Specifically Bequeathed to Legatee.
OH Jur. 3d Decedents' Estates § 1654, Refunding by Legatees and Distributees.

Treatises and Practice Aids

Carlin, Baldwin's Ohio Practice, Merrick-Rippner Probate Law § 2:100, Distribution of Assets—Property Specifically Bequeathed.

Notes of Decisions

Contract   1
Equitable interest   3
Succession rights   2

---

1. Contract

A probate court has no jurisdiction to consider the validity or effect of a contract between the distributees of a decedent's estate and one who contracted to collect their share of the estate for a percentage thereof, where the purported contract has no bearing on the assets of the estate, the duties of the administrator or the court's supervision of his administration. In re Porter's Estate (Ohio Prob. 1969) 17 Ohio Misc. 136, 243 N.E.2d 794, 46 O.O.2d 180.

2. Succession rights

A fiduciary of a decedent's estate has no right and, in fact, cannot be authorized by the probate court which appoints him to be a party to a compromise of the succession rights in a decedent's estate. In re Cantor's Estate (Ohio Prob. 1963) 200 N.E.2d 515, 94 Ohio Law Abs. 102, 31 O.O.2d 393, appeal dismissed 177 Ohio St. 59, 202 N.E.2d 307, 29 O.O.2d 155. Descent And Distribution ⟐ 82

3. Equitable interest

The equitable interest of a legatee has pecuniary value, is transferable, and can be brought under the dominion of the courts through a creditor's bill; consequently, a tax lien can attach to the equitable interest of a legatee who is a delinquent taxpayer. In re Granger (Bkrtcy.N.D.Ohio 1988) 90 B.R. 298.

2113.52 Devisee or heir takes subject to unpaid taxes; mortgage lien; right of exoneration

(A) A devisee taking real estate under a devise in a will, unless the will otherwise provides, or an heir taking real estate under the statutes of descent and distribution shall take the real estate subject to all taxes, penalties, interest, and assessments which are a lien against that real estate.

(B) If real estate devised in a will is subject to a mortgage lien that exists on the date of the testator's death, the person taking the real estate under the devise has no right of exoneration for the mortgage lien, regardless of a general direction in the will to pay the testator's debts, unless the will specifically provides a right of exoneration that extends to that lien.

(1983 S 115, eff. 10–14–83; 1982 H 379; 125 v 903; 1953 H 1; GC 10509–122b)

Historical and Statutory Notes

Pre–1953 H 1 Amendments: 119 v 394, § 7

Cross References

Devise of encumbered lands, probate court to record payment by devisee, 5301.27
Will or trust clause as to tax payment does not encompass "generation skipping transfer tax" unless so specified, 1339.45
Wills, contribution of others toward loss when one devisee's or legatee's property taken for debt, 2107.54

Library References

Descent and Distribution ⚖125.
Wills ⚖835.
Westlaw Topic Nos. 124, 409.
C.J.S. Descent and Distribution §§ 112, 114, 117 to 120.
C.J.S. Wills §§ 1943, 1945 to 1956, 1958 to 1969, 1971 to 1972.

Research References

Encyclopedias

OH Jur. 3d Conversion in Equity § 10, Conversion Resulting from Contract to Sell Realty.
OH Jur. 3d Decedents' Estates § 1335, Mortgages.
OH Jur. 3d Decedents' Estates § 1337, Taxes and Assessments.
OH Jur. 3d Decedents' Estates § 1402, Powers and Duties in Relation to Mortgaged Property—Redemption.
OH Jur. 3d Decedents' Estates § 1478, Personalty as Primary Fund—for Payment of Secured Debts.
OH Jur. 3d Decedents' Estates § 1515, Payment of Taxes.
OH Jur. 3d Decedents' Estates § 1516, Payment of Secured Debts.

Forms

Ohio Forms Legal and Business § 24:391, Payment of Debts—General Clause.

Treatises and Practice Aids

Carlin, Baldwin's Ohio Practice, Merrick-Rippner Probate Law § 2:34, Payment of Debts and Claims—Mortgage and Tax Liens.
Carlin, Baldwin's Ohio Practice, Merrick-Rippner Probate Law § 41:3, Encumbrances—Mortgage Lien—Exoneration.
Carlin, Baldwin's Ohio Practice, Merrick-Rippner Probate Law § 21:19, Rights of Surviving Spouse to Make Election—Effect of Election—Generally.
Carlin, Baldwin's Ohio Practice, Merrick-Rippner Probate Law § 48:10, Beneficiaries Liable for Payment of Decedent's Debts—Liability for Secured Claims.
Carlin, Baldwin's Ohio Practice, Merrick-Rippner Probate Law § 48:11, Liability for Payment of Claims Against Estate.
Carlin, Baldwin's Ohio Practice, Merrick-Rippner Probate Law § 91:15, Land Sale—Not to Pay for Mortgages.
Kuehnle and Levey, Ohio Real Estate Law and Practice § 6:8, Cotenancies—Tenancy in Common—Liability for Expenses—Taxes.

Law Review and Journal Commentaries

Devise or Descent of Real Property Subject to Taxes, Penalties, Interest and Assessments. 52 Title Topics 5 (February 1985).

Mortgage on Specifically—Devised Real Estate, Judge Richard B. Metcalf. 52 Title Topics 5 (July 1985).

S 115 and H 288: Steps Toward Logic and Fairness in the Ohio Probate Law, Note. 10 U Dayton L Rev 213 (Fall 1984).

Notes of Decisions

"Devisee" construed   1

---

1. "Devisee" construed

Devisee, in order to accept portion of real property that was divided between devisee and another devisee, was required to make contributions toward accrued real estate taxes and attorney fees arising from foreclosure proceedings on the property, in addition to contributions for mortgage indebtedness, in amounts that were proportionate to devisee's ownership interest in the property, even if such contributions substantially exceeded the value of devisee's inheritance; the amount of devisee's contributions could not be determined on an equitable basis. In re Estate of Mahan (Ohio App. 11 Dist., Trumbull, 09-15-2006) No. 2005-T-0062, 2006-Ohio-4821, 2006 WL 2662723, Unreported. Wills ⚖ 848

Provision of decedent's will directing that any real estate decedent owned at time of her death be sold, and that proceeds be given to her nephew, did not devise any interest in her homestead, but rather was a bequest of personalty, so that nephew, who was also named in will as executor of estate, never obtained an interest in property as beneficiary of will, and was not required to utilize his own funds during pendency of sale to cover mortgage for property or incidental expenses of its management. In re Estate of Carpenter (Ohio App. 11 Dist., 09-11-1998) 129 Ohio App.3d 717, 719 N.E.2d 20. Wills ⚖ 840

DISTRIBUTION AND PAYMENT

2113.53 Distribution of assets; liability of executor or administrator; provision for rejected claims; liabilities of beneficiary on unsatisfied claims

(A) At any time after the appointment of an executor or administrator, the executor or administrator may distribute to the beneficiaries entitled to assets of the estate under the will, if there is no action pending to set aside the will, or to the heirs entitled to assets of the estate by law, in cash or in kind, any part or all of the assets of the estate. Each beneficiary or heir is liable to return the assets or the proceeds from the assets to the estate if they are necessary to satisfy the share of a surviving spouse who elects to take against the will pursuant to section 2106.01 of the Revised Code or if the will is set aside.

(B) After distribution pursuant to division (A) of this section, a distributee shall be personally liable to a claimant who presents a valid claim within the time set forth in division (B) of section 2117.06 of the Revised Code, subject to the limitations described in this division.

If presentation of a claim is made pursuant to division (A)(2) of section 2117.06 of the Revised Code, only those distributees who have received timely presentation of the claim pursuant to division (B) of that section have any liability for the claim, subject to the limitations described in this division.

The personal liability of any distributee shall not exceed the lesser of the following:

(1) The amount the distributee has received reduced by the amount, if any, previously returned or otherwise used for the payment of the spouse's share or claims finally allowed;

(2) The distributee's proportionate share of the spouse's share or of claims finally allowed. Any distributee's proportionate

share of the spouse's share or of claims finally allowed shall be determined by the following fraction:

(a) The numerator shall be the total amount received by the distributee, reduced by all amounts, if any, previously returned or otherwise used for the payment of the spouse's share or claims finally allowed.

(b) The denominator shall be the total amount received by all distributees reduced by all amounts, if any, previously returned or otherwise used for the payment of the spouse's share or claims finally allowed.

(C) If there is a surviving spouse and if the executor or administrator distributes any part of the assets of the estate before the expiration of the times described in division (E) of section 2106.01 of the Revised Code for the making of an election by a surviving spouse, the executor or administrator shall be personally liable to any surviving spouse who subsequently elects to take against the will. If the executor or administrator distributes any part of the assets of the estate within three months after the death of the decedent, the executor or administrator shall be personally liable only to those claimants who present their claims within that three-month period. If the executor or administrator distributes any part of the assets of the estate more than three months but less than one year after the death of the decedent, the executor or administrator shall be personally liable only to those claimants who present their claims before the time of distribution and within the time set forth in division (B) of section 2117.06 of the Revised Code.

The executor or administrator shall be liable only to the extent that the sum of the remaining assets of the estate and the assets returned by the beneficiaries or heirs is insufficient to satisfy the share of the surviving spouse and to satisfy the claims against the estate. The executor or administrator shall not be liable in any case for an amount greater than the value of the estate that existed at the time that the distribution of assets was made and that was subject to the spouse's share or to the claims.

(D) The executor or administrator may provide for the payment of rejected claims or claims in suit by setting aside a sufficient amount of the assets of the estate for paying the claims. The assets shall be set aside for the payment of the claims in a manner approved by the probate court. Each claimant for whom assets are to be set aside shall be given notice, in the manner as the court shall order, of the hearing upon the application to set aside assets and shall have the right to be fully heard as to the nature and amount of the assets to be set aside for payment of the claim and as to all other conditions in connection with the claim. In any case in which the executor or administrator may set aside assets as provided in this section, the court, upon its own motion or upon application of the executor or administrator, as a condition precedent to any distribution, may require any beneficiary or heir to give a bond to the state with surety approved and in an amount fixed by the court, conditioned to secure the return of the assets to be distributed, or the proceeds from the assets or as much of the assets as may be necessary to satisfy the claims that may be recovered against the estate, and to indemnify the executor or administrator against loss and damage on account of such distribution. The bond may be in addition to the assets to be set aside or partially or wholly in lieu of the assets, as the court shall determine.

(2003 H 51, eff. 4–8–04; 2001 H 85, eff. 10–31–01; 1990 H 346, eff. 5–31–90; 1975 S 145; 1970 S 185; 1953 H 1; GC 10509–181)

Uncodified Law

2004 H 161, § 3, eff. 4–8–04 reads, in part:

(C) Sections 2107.19, 2109.301, 2113.53, 2117.06, 2117.07, 2117.11, and 2117.12 of the Revised Code, as amended by this act, apply to estates of decedents who die on or after April 8, 2004.

1990 H 346, § 3, eff. 5–31–90, reads, in part: (A) Sections 1 and 2 of this act shall apply only to the estates of decedents who die on or after the effective date of this act.

Historical and Statutory Notes

Pre–1953 H 1 Amendments: 119 v 394, § 1; 114 v 441

Amendment Note: 2003 H 51 inserted "to the estate" preceding "if they are necessary" and deleted ", if they are necessary to satisfy any claims against the estate as provided in this section," after "Revised Code" in division (A); and inserted "valid" preceding "claim within the time" and added the second paragraph of division (B).

Amendment Note: 2001 H 85 rewrote this section which prior thereto read:

"At any time after the appointment of an executor or administrator, the executor or administrator may distribute to the beneficiaries entitled to assets of the estate under the will, if there is no action pending to set aside the will, or to the heirs entitled to assets of the estate by law, in cash or in kind, any part or all of the assets of the estate. Each beneficiary or heir is liable to return the assets, or the proceeds from the assets, if they are necessary to satisfy the share of a surviving spouse who elects to take against the will pursuant to section 2106.01 of the Revised Code, or to satisfy any claims against the estate. If any executor or administrator distributes any part of the assets of the estate before the expiration of the times described in division (E) of section 2106.01 of the Revised Code for the making of an election by a surviving spouse, he is personally liable to any surviving spouse who subsequently elects to take against the will. If the executor or administrator distributes any part of the assets of the estate within three months after the death of the decedent, the executor or administrator is personally liable only to those claimants who present their claims within that three-month period. If the executor or administrator distributes any part of the assets of the estate more than three months but less than one year after the death of the decedent, the executor or administrator is personally liable only to those claimants who present their claims before the distribution. If the executor or administrator distributes any part of the assets of the estate more than one year after the death of the decedent, he is personally liable only to those claimants who present their claims within one year after the death of the decedent. The executor or administrator shall be liable only to the extent a claim is finally allowed.

"The executor or administrator shall be liable only to the extent that the sum of the remaining assets of the estate and the assets returned by the beneficiaries or heirs is insufficient to satisfy the share of the surviving spouse and to satisfy the claims against the estate. The executor or administrator shall not be liable in any case for an amount greater than the value of the estate that existed at the time that the distribution of assets was made and that was subject to the spouse's share or to the claims.

"Any executor or administrator may provide for the payment of rejected claims or claims in suit by setting aside a sufficient amount of the assets of the estate for paying the claims. The assets shall be set aside for the payment of the claims in a manner approved by the probate court. Each claimant for whom assets are to be set aside shall be given notice, in the manner as the court shall order, of the hearing upon the application to set aside assets and shall have the right to be fully heard as to the nature and amount of the assets to be set aside for payment of his claim and as to all other conditions in connection with the claim. In any case in which the executor or administrator may set aside assets as provided in this section, the court, upon its own motion or upon application of the executor or administrator, as a condition precedent to any distribution, may require any beneficiary or heir to give a bond to the state with surety approved and in an amount fixed by the court, conditioned to secure the return of the assets to be distributed, or the proceeds from the assets or as much of the assets as may be necessary to satisfy the claims that may be recovered against the estate, and to indemnify the executor or administrator against loss and damage on account of such distribution. The bond may be in addition to the assets to be set aside or partially or wholly in lieu of the assets, as the court shall determine."

Legislative Service Commission

1975:

Under current law, an executor or administrator cannot distribute the assets of the estate to beneficiaries until six months after the appointment of the executor or administrator, one month after the approval of the inventory, after the spouse's election, and after provision has been made for paying debts. The executor or administrator may set aside enough assets to pay rejected claims and claims in suit. Each legatee and distributee is liable to return the assets that he receives if necessary to pay such claims. If assets are to be set aside for a claimant, the claimant must be given notice of such. The court may require legatees and distributees to give a bond to cover the rejected claims and claims in suit.

The bill would allow an executor or administrator to distribute the the assets of the estate to beneficiaries and heirs at any time after appointment. The beneficiaries and heirs (these words would replace legatee and distributee) would be liable to return assets if necessary to satisfy the share of a surviving spouse who elects to take against the will or to satisfy any claims against the estate. If the distribution is made before the expiration of the time for the spouse's election or before the expiration of the time for filing claims, the executor or administrator would be personally liable to a spouse who elects to take against the will or to any claimant who subsequently establishes his claim against the estate. His liability would be limited to the extent that the remaining assets of the estate are insufficient to pay the claims and the elective share and would never be an amount greater than the value of the estate assets when he made the distribution. The executor or administrator would be permitted to set aside, in a manner approved by the court, sufficient assets to satisfy the spouse's share and the claims against the estate. The beneficiaries and heirs could still be required to supply a bond to secure the return of assets to cover the spouse's share and the claims against the estate.

Cross References

Disclaimer of succession to interest in property; procedure; distributor unaware of disclaimer not liable, 1339.60
End of trust; disposition of property meant to go to trust from an estate, 1339.66
Liability when claim presented before and after filing of final account, 2117.06
Manner of distribution meant to qualify for federal estate tax marital deduction, 1339.41
Will or trust clause as to tax payment does not encompass "generation skipping transfer tax" unless so specified, 1339.45

Library References

Executors and Administrators ⟺288, 295.
Westlaw Topic No. 162.
C.J.S. Executors and Administrators §§ 533, 538.
    Baldwin's Ohio Legislative Service, 1990 Laws of Ohio, H 346—LSC Analysis, p 5–87

Research References

Encyclopedias

OH Jur. 3d Decedents' Estates § 1628, Prerequisites to Distribution.
OH Jur. 3d Decedents' Estates § 1629, Prerequisites to Distribution—Making Provisions for Debts.
OH Jur. 3d Decedents' Estates § 1631, Distribution Without Court Order.
OH Jur. 3d Decedents' Estates § 1639, Distribution in Kind.
OH Jur. 3d Decedents' Estates § 1653, Liability of Representative, Generally.
OH Jur. 3d Decedents' Estates § 1654, Refunding by Legatees and Distributees.
OH Jur. 3d Decedents' Estates § 1656, Limitation of Representative's Liability.
OH Jur. 3d Decedents' Estates § 1659, Application to Provide for Claims Not Paid.
OH Jur. 3d Decedents' Estates § 1660, Application of Legatee or Distributee for Distribution.
OH Jur. 3d Decedents' Estates § 1693, Report of Insolvency and Application for Instructions.
OH Jur. 3d Decedents' Estates § 1786, Action on Rejected Claim.

Forms

Ohio Forms Legal and Business § 12:2, General Requirements.

Treatises and Practice Aids

Carlin, Baldwin's Ohio Practice, Merrick-Rippner Probate Law § 2:3, Time for Administration of Decedent's Estate and Payment of Estate Taxes.
Carlin, Baldwin's Ohio Practice, Merrick-Rippner Probate Law § 48:9, Beneficiaries Liable for Payment of Decedent's Debts—General Rules.
Carlin, Baldwin's Ohio Practice, Merrick-Rippner Probate Law § 56:8, Concealed or Embezzled Assets—Complaint for Recovery of Assets.
Carlin, Baldwin's Ohio Practice, Merrick-Rippner Probate Law § 71:1, Powers of Fiduciary During Will Contest—Statutory Provisions.
Carlin, Baldwin's Ohio Practice, Merrick-Rippner Probate Law § 75:1, Distribution—Voluntary—Time.
Carlin, Baldwin's Ohio Practice, Merrick-Rippner Probate Law § 75:2, Distribution—Voluntary—Required Notice to Distributee.
Carlin, Baldwin's Ohio Practice, Merrick-Rippner Probate Law § 75:3, Distribution—Voluntary—Liability—Beneficiaries or Heirs.
Carlin, Baldwin's Ohio Practice, Merrick-Rippner Probate Law § 75:4, Distribution—Voluntary—Liability—Executor or Administrator.
Carlin, Baldwin's Ohio Practice, Merrick-Rippner Probate Law § 75:5, Distribution—Voluntary—Rejected Claims and Claims in Suit.
Carlin, Baldwin's Ohio Practice, Merrick-Rippner Probate Law § 75:8, Distribution—Upon Application—Five-Month Time Limit.
Carlin, Baldwin's Ohio Practice, Merrick-Rippner Probate Law § 84:1, Creditor's Claims—Introduction.
Carlin, Baldwin's Ohio Practice, Merrick-Rippner Probate Law § 2:101, Distribution of Assets—Legacies and Distributions.
Carlin, Baldwin's Ohio Practice, Merrick-Rippner Probate Law § 2:121, Administration of Decedent's Estate—Checklist.
Carlin, Baldwin's Ohio Practice, Merrick-Rippner Probate Law § 48:11, Liability for Payment of Claims Against Estate.
Carlin, Baldwin's Ohio Practice, Merrick-Rippner Probate Law § 54:23, Fiduciary Accounts—Vacation of Order of Settlement of Account for Fraud.
Carlin, Baldwin's Ohio Practice, Merrick-Rippner Probate Law § 75:11, Distribution—Upon Application—Bond of Legatee or Distributee.
Carlin, Baldwin's Ohio Practice, Merrick-Rippner Probate Law § 75:23, Report of Distribution in Kind—Form.
Carlin, Baldwin's Ohio Practice, Merrick-Rippner Probate Law § 75:25, Indemnifying Bond of Legatee or Distributee—Form.
Carlin, Baldwin's Ohio Practice, Merrick-Rippner Probate Law § 75:26, Application for Distribution and for Setting Aside Assets to Pay Claims—Form.
Carlin, Baldwin's Ohio Practice, Merrick-Rippner Probate Law § 75:27, Entry for Distribution and for Setting Aside Assets to Pay Claim—Form.
Carlin, Baldwin's Ohio Practice, Merrick-Rippner Probate Law § 75:28, Application for Transfer of Registered Government Bonds—Form.
Carlin, Baldwin's Ohio Practice, Merrick-Rippner Probate Law § 75:29, Entry and Authenticated Copy of Order to Transfer Bonds—Form.
Carlin, Baldwin's Ohio Practice, Merrick-Rippner Probate Law § 84:28, Creditor's Claims—Claims Not Requiring Presentation—Contingent Claims—Setting Aside Assets to Cover.
Carlin, Baldwin's Ohio Practice, Merrick-Rippner Probate Law § 84:39, Creditor's Claims—Notice to Distributees Before Expiration of Claim Period.

Law Review and Journal Commentaries

Avoiding Probate of Decedents' Estates, Gilbert A. Sheard. 36 U Cin L Rev 70 (Winter 1967).

Distribution and Accounts, C. Terry Johnson. 43 Ohio St B Ass'n Rep 291 (March 9, 1970).

Nonclaim Statute and Distributions: The Sooner the Better, Morton Bobowick. 13 Prob L J Ohio 21 (November/December 2002).

Practical Application of House Bill 85 (Probate Reform 2001), Marilyn J. Maag. 13 Prob L J Ohio 19 (November/December 2002).

A Scrivener's "Delight"—The Marital Deduction Formula Clause, John H. Minan. 37 Ohio St L J 81 (1976).

Notes of Decisions

Court's responsibility 2
Debts 5
Improper distribution 1
Remedy 4
Taxation 3

---

1. Improper distribution

Where an executor conveys property of the estate to himself as legatee less than one month after the approval of the inventory, a creditor of the executor may cause the estate to obtain judgment against such executor for such amount so improperly distributed. In re Walden's Estate (Ohio Prob. 1965) 6 Ohio Misc. 214, 214 N.E.2d 271, 34 O.O.2d 149.

Note 1

An executor who has wrongfully paid out money upon distribution under mistake of law may not maintain an action to recover such money after it has already been paid out. Phillips v. McConica (Ohio 1898) 59 Ohio St. 1, 40 W.L.B. 293, 51 N.E. 445, 69 Am.St.Rep. 753.

2. Court's responsibility

Sufficient evidence supported trial court's conclusions that decedent never relinquished control of money in box under his bed, and that there was $35,000 in the box when he died, so as to support entry of $35,000 judgment in favor of estate against beneficiary of estate who took the box after decedent's death; decedent never gave up possession of the box or the money, and beneficiary testified several times that there was $35,000 in the box. Masterson v. Weaver (Ohio App. 5 Dist., Morgan, 03-08-2006) No. CA-05-014, 2006-Ohio-1069, 2006 WL 561499, Unreported. Executors And Administrators ⬩ 59

Trial court clarifying prior order in probate case properly determined that prior order required that farm, as part of residue of estate, be valued at time of termination of widow's life estate, not at testator's death, since will required distributions of residue to be of equal value, and value of distributions could not be determined until termination of testator's life estate regarding residue of estate. In re Estate of Smith (Ohio App. 3 Dist., Seneca, 04-16-2003) No. 13-02-37, 2003-Ohio-1910, 2003 WL 1877624, Unreported. Wills ⬩ 527

Probate court exceeded limited statutory purposes in decedent's son's will contest action, where court did not explain reasons for granting summary judgment to decedent's wife on basis that net value of assets of estate was less than statutory allowance she was entitled to received as surviving spouse if will were declared invalid, and inventory had not been filed, and neither content nor value of estate had been determined; it was not probate court's function to determine content and value of estate's inventory. Dunaway v. Dunaway (Ohio App. 12 Dist., Brown, 02-18-2003) No. CA2002-07012, 2003-Ohio-706, 2003 WL 355719, Unreported. Wills ⬩ 351

Executor as trustee, after paying debts of estate, may distribute personalty without prior order of distribution or approval of final account. Central Nat. Bank, Savings & Trust Co. v. Gilchrist (Cuyahoga 1926) 23 Ohio App. 87, 154 N.E. 811, 4 Ohio Law Abs. 331. Executors And Administrators ⬩ 309

In administering the distribution statute, a probate court assumes no responsibility and makes no finding that those whose assent the executor has procured, or proposes to procure, are in fact entitled to the estate. Brown v. Routzahn (N.D.Ohio 1931) 58 F.2d 329, reversed 63 F.2d 914, certiorari denied 54 S.Ct. 60, 290 U.S. 641, 78 L.Ed. 557. Executors And Administrators ⬩ 315.1

3. Taxation

Where distributee under a will was required to return securities and income therefrom after the distribution was declared invalid, he was entitled to recover payment of federal tax on income, which he had paid at the time of distribution. Ford v. Nauts (N.D.Ohio 1928) 25 F.2d 1015.

Provision in will which provided that wife's interest should go to another if the wife entered upon her duties as executrix and failed to complete the administration created a terminable interest not qualified for the marital deduction. Kidd v. U. S. (S.D.Ohio 1971) 334 F.Supp. 631, 61 O.O.2d 120, affirmed 451 F.2d 1026.

4. Remedy

Determining that checking account was an asset of estate was not abuse of probate court's discretion, given fact that former executrix who claimed survivorship right in account could not testify as to decedent's intent and given the fact that will seemed to direct executrix to use the account money to pay funeral expenses and debts without any rights to reimbursement. In re Estate of Lindsay (Ohio App. 7 Dist., Mahoning, 11-02-2005) No. 04-MA-259, 2005-Ohio-5930, 2005 WL 2981647, Unreported. Executors And Administrators ⬩ 55

Where a contingent claim against an estate accrues after complete distribution of the assets, the claimant's remedy for any deficiency is an action against the distributee, rather than seeking to vacate the order of final distribution and compelling the distributee to return the assets to the executor. In re Robbins' Estate (Ohio Prob. 1964) 200 N.E.2d 735, 94 Ohio Law Abs. 561, 28 O.O.2d 399.

Where decedent and her son held joint and survivorship accounts, such son testified he never deposited any of his own money in such accounts, and decedent spent the last year of her life attempting to regain possession of the funds which her son had withdrawn from such accounts, the trial court properly ruled that such accounts belonged to the estate. Crawford v Potter, No. WD–82–46 (6th Dist Ct App, Wood, 12–17–82).

5. Debts

Where administration of an estate is granted to one who is a debtor of the intestate on a bond, the amount due upon it becomes merged, and is chargeable against such administrator as assets in his hands. Bigelow's Ex'r v. Bigelow's Adm'rs (Ohio 1829) 4 Ohio 138, 19 Am.Dec. 591.

Legatee's interest in estate remains equitable, and thus, only attachable through creditor's bill until such time as executor has definite amount ready for distribution to legatee; once this occurs, legatee's interest becomes legal and may be attached by garnishment order. In re Estate of Dorothy Mason (Ohio App. 3 Dist., Hancock, 10-25-2004) No. 5-04-01, 2004-Ohio-5644, 2004 WL 2377865, Unreported, appeal allowed 106 Ohio St.3d 1410, 830 N.E.2d 344, 2005-Ohio-3154, affirmed 109 Ohio St.3d 532, 849 N.E.2d 998, 2006-Ohio-3256. Wills ⬩ 867

2113.531 Interest on general legacies

General legacies shall bear no interest unless specifically provided in the will.

(127 v 381, eff. 9–4–57)

Library References

Wills ⬩734.
Westlaw Topic No. 409.
C.J.S. Wills §§ 2002 to 2025.

Research References

Encyclopedias

OH Jur. 3d Decedents' Estates § 857, Payment of Interest.
OH Jur. 3d Decedents' Estates § 1632, Allowance of Interest.

Treatises and Practice Aids

Carlin, Baldwin's Ohio Practice, Merrick-Rippner Probate Law § 75:6, Distribution—Voluntary—Interest on General Legacies.

2113.54 Distribution upon application of legatee or distributee

When five months have expired after the appointment of an executor or administrator and the surviving spouse has made an election under section 2106.01 of the Revised Code, a legatee or distributee may apply to the probate court for an order requiring the executor or administrator to distribute the assets of the estate, either in whole or in part, in cash or in kind. Upon notice to the executor or administrator, the court shall inquire into the condition of the estate, and if all claims have been paid, or adequate provision has been or can be made for their payment, the court shall make such order with reference to distribution of the estate as the condition of the estate and the protection of all parties interested in the estate may demand. The order of the court shall provide that assets be set aside for the payment of claims rejected within two months or in suit, and each claimant for whom assets are to be set aside shall be entitled to be fully heard as to the nature and amount of the assets to be set aside for payment of his claim, and as to all other conditions in connection with the claim. Each legatee or distributee receiving distribution from the estate shall be liable to return the assets distributed to him, or the proceeds from the assets, if they are necessary to pay such claims. The court, upon its own motion or upon application of the executor or administrator, as a condition precedent to any distribution, may require any legatee or distributee to give bond to the state with surety approved and in an amount fixed by the court, conditioned as provided in section 2113.53 of the Revised Code or as may be directed by the court. Such bond may be in addition to the assets to be set aside or partially or wholly in lieu of those assets, as the court shall determine.

(1990 H 346, eff. 5–31–90; 1975 S 145; 1970 S 185; 125 v 903; 1953 H 1; GC 10509–182)

Uncodified Law

1990 H 346, § 3, eff. 5–31–90, reads, in part: (A) Sections 1 and 2 of this act shall apply only to the estates of decedents who die on or after the effective date of this act.

Historical and Statutory Notes

Pre–1953 H 1 Amendments: 119 v 394, § 1; 114 v 441

Library References

Executors and Administrators ⇐288 to 318.
Westlaw Topic No. 162.
C.J.S. Executors and Administrators §§ 533 to 579.

Research References

Encyclopedias

OH Jur. 3d Decedents' Estates § 1628, Prerequisites to Distribution.
OH Jur. 3d Decedents' Estates § 1629, Prerequisites to Distribution—Making Provisions for Debts.
OH Jur. 3d Decedents' Estates § 1637, Time When Legatee or Distributee May Apply for Distribution.
OH Jur. 3d Decedents' Estates § 1639, Distribution in Kind.
OH Jur. 3d Decedents' Estates § 1653, Liability of Representative, Generally.
OH Jur. 3d Decedents' Estates § 1659, Application to Provide for Claims Not Paid.
OH Jur. 3d Decedents' Estates § 1660, Application of Legatee or Distributee for Distribution.

Forms

Ohio Forms Legal and Business § 24:861, Delayed Distribution of Legacies—Specification of Period.

Treatises and Practice Aids

Carlin, Baldwin's Ohio Practice, Merrick-Rippner Probate Law § 75:7, Distribution—Upon Application—Introduction.
Carlin, Baldwin's Ohio Practice, Merrick-Rippner Probate Law § 75:8, Distribution—Upon Application—Five-Month Time Limit.
Carlin, Baldwin's Ohio Practice, Merrick-Rippner Probate Law § 75:9, Distribution—Upon Application—Notice and Inquiry of Court.
Carlin, Baldwin's Ohio Practice, Merrick-Rippner Probate Law § 2:101, Distribution of Assets—Legacies and Distributions.
Carlin, Baldwin's Ohio Practice, Merrick-Rippner Probate Law § 2:121, Administration of Decedent's Estate—Checklist.
Carlin, Baldwin's Ohio Practice, Merrick-Rippner Probate Law § 75:10, Distribution—Upon Application—Payment to Creditors.
Carlin, Baldwin's Ohio Practice, Merrick-Rippner Probate Law § 75:11, Distribution—Upon Application—Bond of Legatee or Distributee.
Carlin, Baldwin's Ohio Practice, Merrick-Rippner Probate Law § 75:30, Application for Distribution by Legatee or Distributee—Form.
Carlin, Baldwin's Ohio Practice, Merrick-Rippner Probate Law § 75:31, Indemnifying Bond of Legatee or Distributee—Form.
Carlin, Baldwin's Ohio Practice, Merrick-Rippner Probate Law § 75:32, Entry of Distribution to Legatee or Distributee—Form.

Notes of Decisions

Attachment or garnishment   1

---

1. Attachment or garnishment

Money or property held by an executor or administrator in his representative capacity before an order of distribution cannot be reached by attachment or garnishment in an action against the heir or legatee, under the Ohio rule of Orlopp v Schueller, 72 OS 41, 73 NE 1012 (1905). In re Granger (Bkrtcy.N.D.Ohio 1988) 90 B.R. 298. Attachment ⇐ 60; Garnishment ⇐ 35

2113.55   Distribution in kind

Before making distribution in kind of property which is not specifically bequeathed, an executor or administrator shall obtain the approval of the probate court or the consent of all of the legatees or distributees whose interests may be affected by such distribution. A distribution in kind may be made to any beneficiary, including an executor, administrator, trustee, guardian, and the surviving spouse.

(1953 H 1, eff. 10–1–53; GC 10509–183)

Historical and Statutory Notes

Pre–1953 H 1 Amendments: 119 v 394, § 1; 114 v 441

Cross References

Right of surviving spouse to one automobile of decedent, 2106.18

Library References

Executors and Administrators ⇐303(1).
Westlaw Topic No. 162.
C.J.S. Executors and Administrators § 543.

Research References

Encyclopedias

OH Jur. 3d Decedents' Estates § 743, Election Between Property and Proceeds.
OH Jur. 3d Decedents' Estates § 1639, Distribution in Kind.
OH Jur. 3d Decedents' Estates § 1653, Liability of Representative, Generally.

Forms

Ohio Forms and Transactions KP 30.12, Distribution in Kind.
Ohio Forms and Transactions KP 30.22, Powers of Executor or Trustee.

Treatises and Practice Aids

Carlin, Baldwin's Ohio Practice, Merrick-Rippner Probate Law § 2:103, Distribution of Assets—in Kind.
Carlin, Baldwin's Ohio Practice, Merrick-Rippner Probate Law § 2:107, Distribution of Assets—Transfer of Titles to Motor Vehicles, Boat or Outboard Motor.
Carlin, Baldwin's Ohio Practice, Merrick-Rippner Probate Law § 2:121, Administration of Decedent's Estate—Checklist.
Carlin, Baldwin's Ohio Practice, Merrick-Rippner Probate Law § 21:81, Rights of Surviving Spouse—Right to Receive Motor Vehicles, Boat or Outboard Motor—Transfer Without Approval of Probate Court.
Carlin, Baldwin's Ohio Practice, Merrick-Rippner Probate Law § 75:13, Distribution—in Kind—Methods.
Carlin, Baldwin's Ohio Practice, Merrick-Rippner Probate Law § 75:17, Other Transfers of Automobiles, Watercraft and Outboard Motor.
Carlin, Baldwin's Ohio Practice, Merrick-Rippner Probate Law § 75:20, Application to Distribute in Kind—Form.
Carlin, Baldwin's Ohio Practice, Merrick-Rippner Probate Law § 75:21, Schedule of Property to be Distributed in Kind—Form.
Carlin, Baldwin's Ohio Practice, Merrick-Rippner Probate Law § 75:22, Notice of Hearing on Application to Distribute in Kind—Form.
Carlin, Baldwin's Ohio Practice, Merrick-Rippner Probate Law § 75:24, Entry Approving Distribution in Kind—Form.
Carlin, Baldwin's Ohio Practice, Merrick-Rippner Probate Law § 75:33, Receipt, Waiver, and Consent on Final Distribution—Form.
Carlin, Baldwin's Ohio Practice, Merrick-Rippner Probate Law § 30:137, Division by Agreement, Two Named Children—Form.
Carlin, Baldwin's Ohio Practice, Merrick-Rippner Probate Law App B SPF 10.0, Application to Distribute in Kind—Form.
Carlin, Baldwin's Ohio Practice, Merrick-Rippner Probate Law App B SPF 10.1, Entry Approving Distribution in Kind—Form.
Carlin, Baldwin's Ohio Practice, Merrick-Rippner Probate Law App B SPF 10.2, Notice of Hearing on Application to Distribute in Kind—Form.
Carlin, Baldwin's Ohio Practice, Merrick-Rippner Probate Law App B SPF 10.3, Entry Approving Distribution in Kind.

Notes of Decisions

Partial distribution 2
Premature distribution 3
Surviving spouse 1

1. Surviving spouse

Where a deceased husband, by his will, made a specific bequest of a certain number of shares of stock in a corporation for the creation of a trust for the benefit of one of his employees, and where the remaining portion of his estate is sufficient, after the payment of all debts and other obligations, to provide his relict, who elected not to take under the will, with the share of his net estate to which she is entitled under RC 2105.06, the relict's share of the net estate is an undivided fractional interest in the real estate plus such additional amount of personal property not specifically bequeathed under the will, either in kind or in money, as shall make her total share of the net estate that amount to which she is entitled under the provisions of the statute. Winters Nat. Bank & Trust Co. v. Riffe (Ohio 1965) 2 Ohio St.2d 72, 206 N.E.2d 212, 31 O.O.2d 56.

2. Partial distribution

Where executor, after final settlement, distributes the balance on hand to only part of the distributees, he remains liable to those distributees who have not yet received their shares. Negley v. Gard (Ohio 1851) 20 Ohio 310.

Trial court acted within its discretion during probate proceedings in providing for an in-kind distribution of ten acres of real estate to decedent's son at value of $20,040, despite claims of self-dealing and that property was actually valued at $55,000, where administrator filed application for instructions, specifically requesting whether to distribute property, the court allowed distribution following a hearing, $55,000 valuation was conducted two years after property was transferred, and there was no evidence of self-dealing. In re Estate of Endslow (Ohio App. 5 Dist., Delaware, 07-22-2003) No. 03-CAF-01001, 2003-Ohio-3916, 2003 WL 21694010, Unreported. Executors And Administrators ⚖ 314(11)

3. Premature distribution

Where distribution in kind is made of a promissory note, an asset of an estate, before the time has elapsed within which creditors' claims may be filed with executrix, and no indemnifying bond is given by distributee, the distribution in kind is premature and ineffective to transfer the note and mortgage. Sager v. Breisach (Lucas 1938) 61 Ohio App. 413, 22 N.E.2d 644, 15 O.O. 266. Executors And Administrators ⚖ 295

2113.56 Executor or administrator not liable

An executor or administrator is not liable for any distribution made in compliance with sections 2113.53, 2113.54, and 2113.55 of the Revised Code, except that an order of distribution made pursuant to any of such sections may be vacated as provided in section 2109.35 of the Revised Code relating to accounts.

(1953 H 1, eff. 10–1–53; GC 10509–183a)

Historical and Statutory Notes

Pre–1953 H 1 Amendments: 121 v 270; 119 v 394

Library References

Executors and Administrators ⚖ 315.4.
Westlaw Topic No. 162.
C.J.S. Executors and Administrators § 570.

Research References

Encyclopedias

OH Jur. 3d Decedents' Estates § 1631, Distribution Without Court Order.
OH Jur. 3d Decedents' Estates § 1653, Liability of Representative, Generally.
OH Jur. 3d Fiduciaries § 285, Generally, Jurisdiction.

Treatises and Practice Aids

Carlin, Baldwin's Ohio Practice, Merrick-Rippner Probate Law § 97:19, Land Sale by Guardian—Proceeds.

2113.57 Distribution after settlement

If upon hearing and settlement of an executor's or administrator's account, a balance due the estate remains in the hands of the executor or administrator, the court may order distribution to be made by him.

(1953 H 1, eff. 10–1–53; GC 10509–184)

Historical and Statutory Notes

Pre–1953 H 1 Amendments: 114 v 441

Library References

Executors and Administrators ⚖ 296, 315.1.
Westlaw Topic No. 162.
C.J.S. Executors and Administrators §§ 538, 570.

Notes of Decisions

Amounts 1
Enforcement 2

1. Amounts

Settlement agreement regarding distribution of estate's assets that outlined the sale of property to one estate beneficiary did not reference the insurance proceeds the estate obtained from a fire on the property that occurred prior to the sale, and thus, beneficiary was not entitled to those insurance proceeds. In re Estate of Poling (Ohio App. 4 Dist., Hocking, 09-27-2005) No. 04CA18, 2005-Ohio-5147, 2005 WL 2386482, Unreported. Executors And Administrators ⚖ 515

A general finding of a balance in the hands of the executor and an order to distribute the amount under RS 6211 is not a sufficient foundation for the action, as the specific amount due the plaintiff must first have been fixed by the court. Henry v. Doyle (Ohio 1910) 82 Ohio St. 113, 91 N.E. 990, 137 Am.St.Rep. 769, 8 Ohio Law Rep. 31. Executors And Administrators ⚖ 537(2)

The probate court lacks jurisdiction, in making an order of distribution under RS 524, to determine the persons to whom distribution is to be made and the amount going to each; it may only enter a general order of distribution. First Nat. Bank of Cadiz v. Beebe (Ohio 1900) 62 Ohio St. 41, 43 W.L.B. 191, 56 N.E. 485. Courts ⚖ 198; Executors And Administrators ⚖ 314(2)

2. Enforcement

Where the administrator has a balance of the estate payable to distributees, the probate court lacks jurisdiction, upon final settlement, to inquire on its own into the administrator's accounts, and it must wait until the distributees seek an order of distribution to be enforced. Cox v. John (Ohio 1877) 32 Ohio St. 532.

Negotiations for settlement of beneficiary's claims to certain estate property did not constitute blackmail, and thus, the settlement agreement was not void, where the estate and counsel for other beneficiaries advised beneficiary that if he refused to settle his claims by purchasing the disputed real estate, the case would go before the probate court and the property would likely be sold at public auction. In re Estate of Poling (Ohio App. 4 Dist., Hocking, 09-27-2005) No. 04CA18, 2005-Ohio-5147, 2005 WL 2386482, Unreported. Executors And Administrators ⚖ 515

Evidence was sufficient to support trial court's finding that provision in settlement agreement that distributed deceased wife's assets, which provision released attorneys and agents, was part of the document that son signed; father testified that handwritten provision was drafted prior to son's signature, and son's attorney testified that provision was included prior to signature. Comer, Sr. v. Early Auction Co. (Ohio App. 12 Dist., Clermont, 04-26-2004) No. CA2003-07-061, 2004-Ohio-2073, 2004 WL 877856, Unreported, appeal not allowed 103 Ohio St.3d 1428, 814 N.E.2d 491, 2004-Ohio-4524. Executors And Administrators ⚖ 515

2113.58 Protection of remainderman's interest in personal property

When by a last will and testament the use or income of personal property is given to a person for a term of years or for life and some other person has an interest in such property as remainderman, the probate court, unless such last will and testament otherwise provides, may deliver such personal property to the person having the limited estate, with or without bond, as the court may determine; or the court may order that such property be held by the executor or some other trustee, with or without bond, for the benefit of the person having the limited estate. If bond is required of the person having the limited estate, or of the trustee, it may be increased or decreased, and if bond is not required in the first instance it may be required by the court at any time prior to the termination of the limited estate.

(1953 H 1, eff. 10-1-53; GC 10509-185)

Historical and Statutory Notes

Pre-1953 H 1 Amendments: 114 v 442

Library References

Executors and Administrators ⟐298.
Westlaw Topic No. 162.
C.J.S. Executors and Administrators § 541.

Research References

Encyclopedias
OH Jur. 3d Decedents' Estates § 1661, Protection of Remainder Interest in Personalty.
OH Jur. 3d Estates, Pwrs., & Restrnts. on Alienat. § 123, Rights, Generally.

Treatises and Practice Aids
Carlin, Baldwin's Ohio Practice, Merrick-Rippner Probate Law § 2:104, Distribution of Assets—Remainder Interests in Personal Property.
Carlin, Baldwin's Ohio Practice, Merrick-Rippner Probate Law § 2:121, Administration of Decedent's Estate—Checklist.
Carlin, Baldwin's Ohio Practice, Merrick-Rippner Probate Law § 75:18, Distribution—Remainderman's Interest.

Notes of Decisions

Life tenant's expenses 4
Personal property 1
Trustee 3
Will construction 2

---

1. Personal property

The conversion of real property to personalty does not destroy the rights of a life tenant or those of vested remaindermen. Kurtz v. Brown (Ottawa 1976) 53 Ohio App.2d 190, 372 N.E.2d 1338, 7 O.O.3d 255.

Under RC 2113.58 the probate court may, at its discretion and after distribution to the person having a life estate in personal property, require from such person a bond at any time prior to the termination of such life estate. In re Kyle's Estate (Miami 1958) 106 Ohio App. 502, 155 N.E.2d 498, 7 O.O.2d 229. Executors And Administrators ⟐ 298

Where a will expresses an intention that possession of the residue of the testator's personal estate should be delivered to those to whom he has given only life interest therein and does not provide for the taking of security therefor, such expressed intention may be given effect; and the executor under such will may lawfully distribute such residue to those having such life interests therein without requiring any security from them; and such personal property or its proceeds will not thereafter be or, on the death of the life tenant, will it again become property of such estate. In re Sexton's Estate (Ohio 1955) 163 Ohio St. 124, 126 N.E.2d 129, 56 O.O. 178, certiorari denied 76 S.Ct. 75, 350 U.S. 838, 100 L.Ed. 747.

2. Will construction

In construing GC 10509-185 (RC 2113.58) the clause following the semicolon and the word "or," and reading "or the court may in its discretion order that such property be held by the executor or some other trustee, with or without bond, for the benefit of the person having the limited estate," should be considered as a separate and independent grant of power to the probate court unconditioned and unlimited by the clause reading "unless such last will and testament otherwise provides," which appears in the preceding portion of that section. In re Miller's Estate (Ohio 1954) 160 Ohio St. 529, 117 N.E.2d 598, 46 A.L.R.2d 493, 52 O.O. 437.

3. Trustee

Will which provides for trust fund but fails to designate trustee falls within this section giving probate court authority to determine by whom property may be held and whether or not bond shall be given, unless such last will and testament otherwise provides. Moses v. Zook (Wayne 1934) 18 Ohio Law Abs. 373.

Where a will provides that a life tenant shall have the power to sell and convey the testator's real property as is necessary for her care and maintenance, the life tenant is a quasi-trustee for the remaindermen as to the amount not necessary for her care and maintenance. Kurtz v. Brown (Ottawa 1976) 53 Ohio App.2d 190, 372 N.E.2d 1338, 7 O.O.3d 255.

Where personal property is bequeathed to a life tenant, with a remainder to her children, and such life tenant is shown to be financially irresponsible, a probate court may direct that the property be held by a trustee, even though the will expressly directs otherwise. In re Miller's Estate (Franklin 1953) 95 Ohio App. 457, 121 N.E.2d 26, 54 O.O. 98, affirmed 160 Ohio St. 529, 117 N.E.2d 598, 46 A.L.R.2d 493, 52 O.O. 437.

The value of a charitable remainder is presently ascertainable where the testator intended to make a bequest of the corpus of the trust to a university and Ohio law requires trustees to administer trusts in a manner consistent with testamentary intent, thus precluding the trustees from eroding the principal of the trust without preserving the corpus intact for the benefit of the charity; therefore, the value of the charitable remainder is presently ascertainable and the charitable deduction for the present value of the testamentary trust remainder interest can be taken. Toulmin's Estate v. U. S. (S.D.Ohio 1971) 32 Ohio Misc. 176, 326 F.Supp. 1028, 60 O.O.2d 69, 61 O.O.2d 314, affirmed 462 F.2d 978, 65 O.O.2d 172. Internal Revenue ⟐ 4172(3)

Where the assets of an estate have been distributed in accordance with the terms of a will to life tenants, the estate has been closed, the final account has been settled and determined, and the life tenants die, in the absence of a motion, filed in accordance with RC 2109.35, to vacate the order of the probate court, such court lacks jurisdiction to entertain an application by the remaindermen to commit securities formerly in the estate to a trustee. State ex rel. Beedle v. Kiracofe (Ohio 1964) 176 Ohio St. 149, 198 N.E.2d 61, 27 O.O.2d 25.

4. Life tenant's expenses

Where a life tenant fails to exercise her power to consume, the executrix of her estate may exercise the power to consume and invade the testator's estate, but only to the extent necessary to pay unpaid debts for the care and maintenance of the life tenant, the expenses of her last illness, and her funeral expenses. Kurtz v. Brown (Ottawa 1976) 53 Ohio App.2d 190, 372 N.E.2d 1338, 7 O.O.3d 255.

2113.59 Lien on share of beneficiary

When a beneficiary of an estate is indebted to such estate, the amount of the indebtedness if due, or the present worth of the indebtedness if not due, may be set off by the executor or administrator against any testate or intestate share of the estate to which such beneficiary is entitled.

(1953 H 1, eff. 10-1-53; GC 10509-186)

Historical and Statutory Notes

Pre-1953 H 1 Amendments: 114 v 442

Library References

Descent and Distribution ⟐80.

Executors and Administrators ⚖=294.
Wills ⚖=731.
Westlaw Topic Nos. 124, 162, 409.
C.J.S. Descent and Distribution § 70.
C.J.S. Executors and Administrators § 543.
C.J.S. Wills §§ 1705 to 1707.

Research References

Encyclopedias

OH Jur. 3d Decedents' Estates § 1280, Debts of Heirs, Legatees, or Distributees.

Treatises and Practice Aids

Carlin, Baldwin's Ohio Practice, Merrick-Rippner Probate Law § 76:1, Equitable Setoff.

Notes of Decisions

Descent and distribution   4
Divestment of estate   5
Priority of liens   3
Set off   6
Surviving spouse   2
Time–barred debt   1

1. Time–barred debt

The indebtedness of a beneficiary of an estate to an estate, referred to in this section, embraces only legally enforceable indebtedness and does not include debts of the beneficiary to the estate which were barred by the statute of limitations at the time of the death of the creditor whose estate is being settled. Summers v. Connolly (Ohio 1953) 159 Ohio St. 396, 112 N.E.2d 391, 39 A.L.R.2d 661, 50 O.O. 352.

A debt due an intestate may not be retained out of, or set off against, the debtor's distributive share of the estate, where the debt was barred by the statute of limitation during the decedent's lifetime. Harrod v. Carder's Adm'r (Ohio Cir. 1888) 2 Ohio C.D. 274. Descent And Distribution ⚖= 80; Equity ⚖= 87(3); Limitation Of Actions ⚖= 16

2. Surviving spouse

Indebtedness due decedent from surviving spouse is a setoff under section against any sum awarded to surviving spouse as exempt from any administration under GC 10509–54 (RC 2115.13), and probate court has exclusive original jurisdiction to control executor as to his duty in that respect. Saluppo v. Santangelo (Hamilton 1942) 71 Ohio App. 185, 48 N.E.2d 903, 39 Ohio Law Abs. 169, 26 O.O. 10.

Where a life estate is devised to testator's wife "so long as she remains my widow," and the remainder is left equally to testator's two children, the children take vested remainders in fee, subject to the interest of the widow, which remainders may be alienated or mortgaged. Eastman v. Sohl (Franklin 1940) 66 Ohio App. 383, 34 N.E.2d 291, 33 Ohio Law Abs. 160, 20 O.O. 305. Life Estates ⚖= 3; Wills ⚖= 634(1)

3. Priority of liens

Where there is a distribution of stock in kind to one of the two remaindermen, prior to the termination of the widow's life estate, consented to by the probate court and all interested parties, and, subsequently, at the end of the life estate there is not sufficient personalty remaining to give a like amount to the other remainderman under the will, such other remainderman, in an action to partition the real estate, is entitled to a lien on the proceeds of the sale in partition up to the amount advanced to the first remainderman, before the fund so obtained shall be divided equally between them; but, where the transfer of the real estate to the persons named in the will has been ordered by the court to be made on the tax duplicate and where the certificate of transfer has been issued and recorded, the lien of such other remainderman is inferior to the liens of creditors against the interest of such first remainderman. Eastman v. Sohl (Franklin 1940) 66 Ohio App. 383, 34 N.E.2d 291, 33 Ohio Law Abs. 160, 20 O.O. 305.

Where a will gives all of the property to the widow for life and then to the children, the devise to the son is general, not specific, and a debt which the son owes the estate is superior to a mortgage or judgment lien against him on real estate coming to him by general devise. Woodruff v. Woodruff (Ohio Cir. 1902) 13 Ohio C.D. 408, 3 Ohio C.C.N.S. 616.

4. Descent and distribution

Nieces and nephews of an intestate decedent are subject to having a debt of their father, who predeceased the decedent, set off against their distributive share, when decedent has a brother and sister still living. Gruhler v. Hossapaus (Ohio Prob. 1963) 195 N.E.2d 387, 93 Ohio Law Abs. 71, 28 O.O.2d 477.

5. Divestment of estate

Where a testator devises real estate to a son, and provides that on the happening of an uncertain event the lands are to go to and be vested in the heirs of the body of such son, on the happening of the event the lands pass to the heirs of the body of the son free from the burden of the debts of the son to the estate of the testator. Rings v. Borton (Ohio 1923) 108 Ohio St. 280, 140 N.E. 515, 1 Ohio Law Abs. 485, 21 Ohio Law Rep. 150, 21 Ohio Law Rep. 152. Wills ⚖= 731

6. Set off

In conversion action brought by administrator of estate of brokerage account holder against joint account holder, joint account holder waived issue of whether he was entitled to setoff to judgment amount under statute permitting estate administrator to set off a beneficiary's debt against any share of the estate to which the beneficiary is entitled, where joint account holder failed to plead the same as affirmative defense. Toma v. Toma (Ohio App. 8 Dist., Cuyahoga, 08-14-2003) No. 82118, 2003-Ohio-4344, 2003 WL 21957022, Unreported, appeal not allowed 100 Ohio St.3d 1532, 800 N.E.2d 48, 2003-Ohio-6458. Executors And Administrators ⚖= 443(2)

CERTIFICATE OF TRANSFER

2113.61 Application for certificate of transfer; duty of court

(A)(1) When real property passes by the laws of intestate succession or under a will, the administrator or executor shall file in probate court, at any time after the filing of an inventory that includes the real property but prior to the filing of the administrator's or executor's final account, an application requesting the court to issue a certificate of transfer as to the real property. Real property sold by an executor or administrator or land registered under Chapters 5309. and 5310. of the Revised Code is excepted from the application requirement. Cases in which an order has been made under section 2113.03 of the Revised Code relieving an estate from administration and in which the order directing transfer of real property to the person entitled to it may be substituted for the certificate of transfer also are excepted from the application requirement.

(2) In accordance with division (C)(3)(b) of section 2113.031 of the Revised Code, an application for a certificate of transfer of an interest in real property included in the assets of the decedent's estate shall accompany an application for a summary release from administration under that section. This section applies to the application for and the issuance of the requested certificate of transfer except to the extent that the probate court determines that the nature of any of the provisions of this section is inconsistent with the nature of a grant of a summary release from administration.

(B) Subject to division (A)(2) of this section, the application for a certificate of transfer shall contain all of the following:

(1) The name, place of residence at death, and date of death of the decedent;

(2) A statement whether the decedent died testate or intestate;

(3) The fact and date of the filing and probate of the will, if applicable, and the fact and date of the appointment of the administrator or executor;

(4) A description of each parcel of real property situated in this state that is owned by the decedent at the time of death;

(5) Insofar as they can be ascertained, the names, ages, places of residence, and relationship to the decedent of the persons to whom each parcel of real property described in division (B)(4) of this section passed by descent or devise;

(6) A statement that all the known debts of the decedent's estate have been paid or secured to be paid, or that sufficient other assets are in hand to complete the payment of those debts;

(7) Other pertinent information that the court requires.

(C) Subject to division (A)(2) of this section, within five days following the filing of an application for a certificate of transfer that complies with division (B) of this section, the court shall issue a certificate of transfer for record in each county in this state in which real property so passing is situated, that shall recite all of the following:

(1) The name and date of death of the decedent;

(2) Whether the decedent died testate or intestate and, if testate, the volume and page of the record of the will;

(3) The volume and page of the probate court record of the administration of the estate;

(4) The names and places of residence of the devisees, the interests passing to them, the names and places of residence of the persons inheriting intestate, and the interests inherited by them, in each parcel of real property described in division (B)(4) of this section;

(5) A description of each parcel of real property described in division (B)(4) of this section;

(6) Other information that in the opinion of the court should be included.

(D) If an executor or administrator has failed to file an application for a certificate of transfer before being discharged, the application may be filed by an heir or devisee, or a successor in interest, in the probate court in which the testator's will was probated or, in the case of intestate estates, in the probate court in which administration was had. If no administration was had on an estate and if no administration is contemplated, except in the case of the grant of or contemplated application for the grant of an order of a summary release from administration under section 2113.031 of the Revised Code, an application for a certificate of transfer may be filed by an heir or devisee, or a successor in interest, in the probate court of the county in which the decedent was a resident at the time of death.

A foreign executor or administrator, when no ancillary administration proceedings have been had or are being had in this state, may file in accordance with this section an application for a certificate of transfer in the probate court of any county of this state in which real property of the decedent is located.

When a person who has entered into a written contract for the sale and conveyance of an interest in real property dies before its completion, the interest of the decedent in the contract and the record title to the real property described in the contract may be transferred to the persons, legatees, devisees, or heirs at law entitled to the interest of the decedent in the real property, in the same manner as provided in this section and sections 2113.62 and 2113.63 of the Revised Code for the transfer of real property. The application for the certificate of transfer and the certificate itself also shall recite that the real property described in the application or certificate is subject to a written contract for its sale and conveyance.

(2002 H 345, eff. 7-23-02; 2000 H 313, eff. 8-29-00; 1992 H 427, eff. 10-8-92; 130 v S 154; 1953 H 1; GC 10509-102)

Historical and Statutory Notes

Pre–1953 H 1 Amendments: 123 v 460; 116 v 385; 114 v 424

Amendment Note: 2002 H 345 inserted "at any time after the filing of an inventory that includes the real property but" in division (A)(1); and inserted "within five days following the filing of an application for a certificate of transfer that complies with division (B) of this section" in the first sentence of division (C).

Amendment Note: 2000 H 313 designated division (A)(1) and inserted "under section 2113.03 of the Revised Code"; added new divisions (A)(2) and (A)(3); inserted "Subject to division (A)(2) of this section, the" in divisions (B) and (C); inserted "except in the case of the grant of or contemplated application for the grant of an order of a summary release from administration under section 2113.031 of the Revised Code," in division (D); made changes to reflect gender neutral language; and made other nonsubstantive changes.

Cross References

Ancillary administrator, application for certificate of transfer, 2129.19
Bond of surviving partners electing to purchase, assignment of interest and certificate of title, 1779.05
County auditor compensation for services, 319.54
Death of survivorship tenant, evidence, 5309.081
Descent and distribution of title to real property, certificate of transfer, 2105.061
Election of surviving spouse to receive mansion house, 2106.10
Land registration, death of applicant pending; completion of proceeding, 5309.22
Registered landowner, personal representative may apply for new registration, 5309.45
Survivorship deed, transfer under may be recorded, 5302.17

Library References

Executors and Administrators ⇌300, 303(1), 305, 314(0.5), 315.1.
Westlaw Topic No. 162.
C.J.S. Executors and Administrators §§ 539, 543, 559, 564, 570.

Research References

Encyclopedias

OH Jur. 3d Abstracts & Land Titles § 41, Transfer of Interest of Deceased Survivorship Tenant.
OH Jur. 3d Decedents' Estates § 117, Under the Statute of Descent and Distribution—Rights in Mansion House.
OH Jur. 3d Decedents' Estates § 138, Nature of Heir's Title; Parcenary.
OH Jur. 3d Decedents' Estates § 146, Record of Transfer.
OH Jur. 3d Decedents' Estates § 1404, Certificate of Transfer of Real Estate by Inheritance or Devise.
OH Jur. 3d Decedents' Estates § 1676, Right to Receive Mansion House as Part of Intestate Share.
OH Jur. 3d Decedents' Estates § 1719, Application for Certificate of Transfer of Realty.

Forms

Ohio Forms Legal and Business § 2:14, Recordation.
Ohio Forms Legal and Business § 2:53, Survivorship Tenancy.

Treatises and Practice Aids

Carlin, Baldwin's Ohio Practice, Merrick-Rippner Probate Law § 2:22, Inventory and Appraisal—Family Allowance.
Carlin, Baldwin's Ohio Practice, Merrick-Rippner Probate Law § 2:38, Elective Rights of Surviving Spouse—Election to Take Under Law or Under the Will—Elective Share of Surviving Spouse Against the Will.
Carlin, Baldwin's Ohio Practice, Merrick-Rippner Probate Law § 2:45, Elective Rights of Surviving Spouse—Election of Surviving Spouse to Receive Property as Part of Intestate Share and Allowance for Support.
Carlin, Baldwin's Ohio Practice, Merrick-Rippner Probate Law § 2:50, Management of Decedent's Real Estate.
Carlin, Baldwin's Ohio Practice, Merrick-Rippner Probate Law § 21:5, Rights of Surviving Spouse to Make Election—Statutory Provisions—Effect.
Carlin, Baldwin's Ohio Practice, Merrick-Rippner Probate Law § 73:5, Management of Real Estate—Termination of Authority.

Carlin, Baldwin's Ohio Practice, Merrick-Rippner Probate Law § 90:9, Authority for Land Sale Action—Overriding Rights of Surviving Spouse.

Carlin, Baldwin's Ohio Practice, Merrick-Rippner Probate Law § 2:106, Distribution of Assets—Transfer of Real Estate.

Carlin, Baldwin's Ohio Practice, Merrick-Rippner Probate Law § 2:114, Application for Summary Release from Administration.

Carlin, Baldwin's Ohio Practice, Merrick-Rippner Probate Law § 2:117, Election of Surviving Spouse to Receive Mansion House.

Carlin, Baldwin's Ohio Practice, Merrick-Rippner Probate Law § 2:118, Certificate of Transfer or Interest in Real Property.

Carlin, Baldwin's Ohio Practice, Merrick-Rippner Probate Law § 2:121, Administration of Decedent's Estate—Checklist.

Carlin, Baldwin's Ohio Practice, Merrick-Rippner Probate Law § 21:44, Rights of Surviving Spouse to Elect to Receive Mansion House—Statutory Right.

Carlin, Baldwin's Ohio Practice, Merrick-Rippner Probate Law § 21:46, Rights of Surviving Spouse to Elect to Receive Mansion House—Procedure—Application for Certificate of Transfer.

Carlin, Baldwin's Ohio Practice, Merrick-Rippner Probate Law § 21:47, Rights of Surviving Spouse to Elect to Receive Mansion House—Procedure—Election Where Estate Relieved from Administration.

Carlin, Baldwin's Ohio Practice, Merrick-Rippner Probate Law § 21:50, Rights of Surviving Spouse to Payment of Specific Monetary Share—Monetary Share as Charge on Real Estate.

Carlin, Baldwin's Ohio Practice, Merrick-Rippner Probate Law § 59:31, Application to Transfer Realty of Deceased Partner—Form.

Carlin, Baldwin's Ohio Practice, Merrick-Rippner Probate Law § 91:34, Application for Certificate of Transfer—Form.

Carlin, Baldwin's Ohio Practice, Merrick-Rippner Probate Law § 91:35, Entry Issuing Certificate of Transfer—Form.

Carlin, Baldwin's Ohio Practice, Merrick-Rippner Probate Law § 91:36, Certificate of Transfer—Form.

Carlin, Baldwin's Ohio Practice, Merrick-Rippner Probate Law App B SPF 12.0, Application for Certificate of Transfer.

Carlin, Baldwin's Ohio Practice, Merrick-Rippner Probate Law App B SPF 12.1, Certificate of Transfer.

Kuehnle and Levey, Ohio Real Estate Law and Practice § 6:17, Cotenancies—Statutory Tenancy by the Entireties (1972-1985)—Creation.

Kuehnle and Levey, Ohio Real Estate Law and Practice § 6:22, Cotenancies—Statutory Joint Tenancy—Transfer to Survivor.

Kuehnle and Levey, Ohio Real Estate Law and Practice § 10:50, Person Inheriting from Estate Relieved from Administration.

Kuehnle and Levey, Ohio Real Estate Law and Practice § 10:51, Rights of Heirs When Owner Dies Resident Out of County, Preserving Marketability.

Kuehnle and Levey, Ohio Real Estate Law and Practice § 21:27, Execution—Ohio State Conveyance Fee—RC 319.54(F)(3).

Kuehnle and Levey, Ohio Real Estate Law and Practice § 53:18, Land Sales—Interests Subject to Sale by Fiduciaries—Rents Accruing Between Death of Owner and Sale.

Law Review and Journal Commentaries

American Land Law Reform: Modernization of Recording Statutes (Part I), Robert N. Cook and Frederick M. Lombardi. 13 W Reserve U L Rev 639 (1962).

Specific Timing of Issuance of Certificate of Transfer of Real Estate. Daniel J. Hoffheimer, 12 Prob L J Ohio 78 (May/June 2002).

Timing of Issuance of Certificate of Transfer of Real Estate: "Reunification" of Statute and Common Law, Daniel J. Hoffheimer. 10 Prob L J Ohio 85 (July/August 2000).

When RC 2113.61 Authorizes Transfer of "Real Estate" by Certificate of Transfer, Does This Include Decedent's Ownership of Equitable Interests? Mortgages? Installment Land Contracts?, Robert L. Hausser. 54 Title Topics 8 (July 1987).

Notes of Decisions

Fees 1
Ownership 3
Partial distribution 2
Relief from administration 4
Torrens land 5

---

1. Fees

A certificate of transfer issued by the probate court is not subject to the real property transfer fee imposed by RC 319.54. OAG 68–068.

No duty rests upon county recorder to accept for filing or recording certificates of transfer from the probate court, provided under section, until the necessary fees provided by GC 2778 (RC 317.32) have been paid by executor or administrator of estate or by grantor or grantees in such conveyance. 1938 OAG 1897.

2. Partial distribution

No authority exists for ordering a partial distribution of personal estate without formal administration where the estate exceeds $1000 in value. In re McKenzie's Estate (Ohio Prob. 1956) 139 N.E.2d 505, 74 Ohio Law Abs. 106, 1 O.O.2d 485.

3. Ownership

Probate court is without authority to require certificate of transfer, issued under authority of section, to be returned to his court by county recorder or any other person for purpose of being filed with other papers in case; such certificate of transfer should be and is property of grantee or grantees therein, whether transfer is made under intestate laws of this state or by devise under will. 1938 OAG 1897.

4. Relief from administration

A probate judge has permissive power to grant an application for the certificate to transfer real estate in an estate consisting of real estate only, exceeding $500 in value, and where no administration of the estate is had or intended, providing the application is made by an heir or devisee or a successor in interest, in accordance with the provisions of section. 1936 OAG 5193.

5. Torrens land

Where real property is registered on the Torrens land title register and is held as an estate by the entireties, surviving spouse need not comply with the requirements of statutes setting forth the procedure to be followed in transferring the registration of Torrenized property upon death of the registered owner since that statute only applies to property which is part of decedent's estate; where real property is held by husband and wife as an estate by the entireties, at death of one of the spouses the entire property automatically vests in the surviving spouse by operation of law and the property does not become part of the decedent's estate. Application of County Recorder to Certify Question to Common Pleas Court per R.C. 5309.43 (Cuyahoga 1984) 13 Ohio App.3d 292, 468 N.E.2d 1147, 13 O.B.R. 358.

2113.62 Record by county recorder

Upon receipt of the certificate provided for in section 2113.61 of the Revised Code, the county recorder shall record it in the books provided for the recording of deeds and index such records in the name of the decedent as grantor and the person to whom the real estate passes as grantee in the index provided for the record of deeds.

(1953 H 1, eff. 10–1–53; GC 10509–103)

Historical and Statutory Notes

Pre–1953 H 1 Amendments: 114 v 424

Library References

Records ⚖5.
Westlaw Topic No. 326.
C.J.S. Records §§ 19 to 20.

Research References

Encyclopedias

OH Jur. 3d Decedents' Estates § 1404, Certificate of Transfer of Real Estate by Inheritance or Devise.

Treatises and Practice Aids

Carlin, Baldwin's Ohio Practice, Merrick-Rippner Probate Law § 2:106, Distribution of Assets—Transfer of Real Estate.

Carlin, Baldwin's Ohio Practice, Merrick-Rippner Probate Law § 2:121, Administration of Decedent's Estate—Checklist.

2113.63 Fees

For recording and indexing the certificate provided for in section 2113.61 of the Revised Code, the county recorder shall be paid in fees provided by section 317.32 of the Revised Code for the recording and indexing of deeds, and the probate court shall be allowed the fees provided by section 2101.16 of the Revised Code for similar certificates. The probate judge shall tax and collect, as other costs of administering the estate, the fees of the recorder and the court.

(1985 H 419, eff. 3–13–86; 1969 H 1; 1953 H 1; GC 10509–104)

Historical and Statutory Notes

Pre–1953 H 1 Amendments: 114 v 424

Cross References

Transfer and indorsement by auditor before recording deed, 317.22

Library References

Records ⊗9(13.5).
Westlaw Topic No. 326.

Research References

Encyclopedias

OH Jur. 3d Decedents' Estates § 1404, Certificate of Transfer of Real Estate by Inheritance or Devise.

Treatises and Practice Aids

Carlin, Baldwin's Ohio Practice, Merrick-Rippner Probate Law § 2:121, Administration of Decedent's Estate—Checklist.

UNCLAIMED MONEY

2113.64 Investment of unclaimed money

If a sum of money to be distributed to heirs, next of kin, or legatees, or owing from an estate to a creditor of the estate, remains unclaimed prior to the filing of a final account, the court may order it turned into the county treasury as provided in section 2113.65 of the Revised Code, or may order the executor or administrator to invest it as the court directs for a period not to exceed two years, to accumulate for the benefit of the persons entitled to the sum of money. Such investment shall be made in the name of the probate judge of the court for the time being and shall be subject to the order of the judge and the judge's successors in office.

(2001 H 85, eff. 10-31-01; 1953 H 1, eff. 10-1-53; GC 10509-194)

Historical and Statutory Notes

Pre–1953 H 1 Amendments: 123 v 460; 114 v 443

Amendment Note: 2001 H 85 rewrote this section which prior thereto read:

"If a sum of money directed by a decree or order of the probate court to be distributed to heirs, next of kin, or legatees, or owing from an estate to a creditor thereof, remains for six months unclaimed, the court may order it turned into the county treasury as provided in section 2113.65 of the Revised Code, or may order the executor or administrator to invest it as the court directs for a period not to exceed one year, to accumulate for the benefit of the persons entitled thereto. Such investment shall be made in the name of the probate judge of the court for the time being and shall be subject to the order of the judge and his successors in office."

Library References

Escheat ⊗3.
Executors and Administrators ⊗303(3), 312, 313.
Westlaw Topic Nos. 152, 162.
C.J.S. Escheat § 4.
C.J.S. Executors and Administrators §§ 543, 555 to 556.

Research References

Encyclopedias

OH Jur. 3d Decedents' Estates § 1662, Unclaimed Money.

Treatises and Practice Aids

Carlin, Baldwin's Ohio Practice, Merrick-Rippner Probate Law § 77:1, Unclaimed Money—Disposition.

Carlin, Baldwin's Ohio Practice, Merrick-Rippner Probate Law § 77:3, Unclaimed Money—Escheat Distinguished.

Carlin, Baldwin's Ohio Practice, Merrick-Rippner Probate Law § 77:4, Unclaimed Money—Application for Authority to Invest—Form.

Carlin, Baldwin's Ohio Practice, Merrick-Rippner Probate Law § 77:5, Unclaimed Money—Entry Directing Investment—Form.

Carlin, Baldwin's Ohio Practice, Merrick-Rippner Probate Law § 77:6, Unclaimed Money—Memorandum of Investment—Form.

Carlin, Baldwin's Ohio Practice, Merrick-Rippner Probate Law § 77:7, Unclaimed Money—Entry Approving Investment—Form.

Notes of Decisions

Duty of administrator 1
Use of funds 2

---

1. Duty of administrator

Executor having private interest in unclaimed bequest liable for conversion for failure to use diligence to locate and notify legatee. Morris v. Mull (Ohio 1924) 110 Ohio St. 623, 144 N.E. 436, 39 A.L.R. 323, 2 Ohio Law Abs. 406, 22 Ohio Law Rep. 175. Executors And Administrators ⊗ 312; Wills ⊗ 663

In old statute, language stating that administrator "may" apply to court for order permitting him to invest funds for heirs not yet found means "must," and imposes a duty on the administrator. In re Thornton's Estate (Ohio Com.Pl. 1894) 5 Ohio Dec. 151, 7 Ohio N.P. 335, 1 Ohio Leg. N. 29.

2. Use of funds

Funds held by a county treasurer pursuant to RC 5723.11, RC 2109.57 and RC 2113.64 must be disposed of pursuant to instructions contained therein and are not available for diversion to other uses. OAG 72–122.

2113.65 Disposition of investment

The person investing unclaimed money under section 2113.64 of the Revised Code shall file in the probate court a memorandum thereof, with the original certificates or evidences of title representing such investment, which shall be allowed as a sufficient voucher for such payment under the order or decree. If the amount is unclaimed at the end of the period of such investment, it shall be turned into the county treasury and credited to the general fund, without liability for interest thereon. The receipt of the county treasurer taken for it and filed is a sufficient voucher.

(1953 H 1, eff. 10–1–53; GC 10509–195)

Historical and Statutory Notes

Pre–1953 H 1 Amendments: 123 v 460; 114 v 444

Library References

Escheat ⇐1.
Executors and Administrators ⇐303(3).
Westlaw Topic Nos. 152, 162.
C.J.S. Escheat § 2.
C.J.S. Executors and Administrators § 543.

Research References

Encyclopedias

OH Jur. 3d Decedents' Estates § 1662, Unclaimed Money.

Treatises and Practice Aids

Carlin, Baldwin's Ohio Practice, Merrick-Rippner Probate Law § 77:1, Unclaimed Money—Disposition.

Carlin, Baldwin's Ohio Practice, Merrick-Rippner Probate Law § 77:6, Unclaimed Money—Memorandum of Investment—Form.

Carlin, Baldwin's Ohio Practice, Merrick-Rippner Probate Law § 77:7, Unclaimed Money—Entry Approving Investment—Form.

2113.66 Statute of limitations no defense

The statute of limitations shall not be set up as a defense or bar to an action against an executor or administrator who fails or neglects to comply with the requirements of sections 2113.64 and 2113.65 of the Revised Code.

(1953 H 1, eff. 10–1–53; GC 10509–196)

Historical and Statutory Notes

Pre–1953 H 1 Amendments: 114 v 444

Library References

Executors and Administrators ⇐437(3).
Westlaw Topic No. 162.
C.J.S. Executors and Administrators §§ 747, 749 to 753, 766 to 768.

Research References

Encyclopedias

OH Jur. 3d Decedents' Estates § 1662, Unclaimed Money.

Treatises and Practice Aids

Carlin, Baldwin's Ohio Practice, Merrick-Rippner Probate Law § 77:2, Unclaimed Money—Statute of Limitation.

2113.67 Money paid to owner

When a person entitled to the money invested or turned into the county treasury under section 2113.64 of the Revised Code satisfies the probate court of his right to receive it, the court shall order it to be paid over and transferred to him. In case it has been turned into the treasury, the county auditor shall give to him a warrant therefor upon the certificate of the probate judge.

(1953 H 1, eff. 10–1–53; GC 10509–197)

Historical and Statutory Notes

Pre–1953 H 1 Amendments: 114 v 444

Library References

Escheat ⇐8(2).
Executors and Administrators ⇐303(3).
Westlaw Topic Nos. 152, 162.
C.J.S. Escheat §§ 22 to 23.
C.J.S. Executors and Administrators § 543.

Research References

Encyclopedias

OH Jur. 3d Abandoned, Lost, & Escheated Property § 27, Personal Property.

OH Jur. 3d Decedents' Estates § 1663, Unclaimed Money—Payment to Owner.

Treatises and Practice Aids

Carlin, Baldwin's Ohio Practice, Merrick-Rippner Probate Law § 77:1, Unclaimed Money—Disposition.

Carlin, Baldwin's Ohio Practice, Merrick-Rippner Probate Law § 77:8, Unclaimed Money—Application for Order to Receive—Form.

Carlin, Baldwin's Ohio Practice, Merrick-Rippner Probate Law § 77:9, Unclaimed Money—Entry Transferring—Form.

2113.68 Responsibility for safekeeping of evidences of title

The probate judge with whom the certificates or evidences of title required by section 2113.65 of the Revised Code are deposited and each succeeding judge to whom they come, and his sureties, shall be responsible for their safekeeping and application, as provided in sections 2113.64 to 2113.67, inclusive, of the Revised Code.

(1953 H 1, eff. 10–1–53; GC 10509–198)

Historical and Statutory Notes

Pre–1953 H 1 Amendments: 114 v 444

Library References

Records ⇐13.
Westlaw Topic No. 326.
C.J.S. Records § 32.

Research References

Encyclopedias

OH Jur. 3d Decedents' Estates § 1662, Unclaimed Money.

Treatises and Practice Aids

Carlin, Baldwin's Ohio Practice, Merrick-Rippner Probate Law § 77:1, Unclaimed Money—Disposition.

Carlin, Baldwin's Ohio Practice, Merrick-Rippner Probate Law § 77:3, Unclaimed Money—Escheat Distinguished.

NEWLY DISCOVERED ASSETS

2113.69 Newly discovered assets

When newly discovered assets come into the hands of an executor or administrator after the filing of the original inventory required by section 2115.02 of the Revised Code, he shall administer, account for, and distribute such assets in like manner as if received prior to the filing of such inventory. Within thirty days, he shall file in the probate court an itemized report of such assets, with an estimate of the value thereof, but shall not be required to make an inventory or appraisement of the same unless ordered to do so by the court, either upon its own motion or upon the application of any interested party.

(1953 H 1, eff. 10–1–53; GC 10509–147)

Historical and Statutory Notes

Pre–1953 H 1 Amendments: 119 v 394, § 1; 114 v 434

Cross References

New administrator receiving assets, 2113.29

Library References

Executors and Administrators ⇐66, 71.
Westlaw Topic No. 162.
C.J.S. Executors and Administrators §§ 155 to 156.

Research References

Encyclopedias

OH Jur. 3d Decedents' Estates § 1258, Newly Discovered Assets.

Treatises and Practice Aids

Carlin, Baldwin's Ohio Practice, Merrick-Rippner Probate Law § 79:8, Inventory—Newly Discovered Assets.

Carlin, Baldwin's Ohio Practice, Merrick-Rippner Probate Law § 2:121, Administration of Decedent's Estate—Checklist.

Carlin, Baldwin's Ohio Practice, Merrick-Rippner Probate Law § 79:45, Report of Newly Discovered Assets—Form.

Carlin, Baldwin's Ohio Practice, Merrick-Rippner Probate Law § 79:46, Report of Newly Discovered Assets and Application for Order Requalifying Executor or Administrator—Form.

Carlin, Baldwin's Ohio Practice, Merrick-Rippner Probate Law § 79:47, Order Reopening Estate and Requalifying Executor or Administrator—Form.

Carlin, Baldwin's Ohio Practice, Merrick-Rippner Probate Law § 79:48, Application to Reopen and Close Estate Immediately—Form.

Carlin, Baldwin's Ohio Practice, Merrick-Rippner Probate Law § 79:49, Entry on Application to Reopen and Close Estate Immediately—Form.

Notes of Decisions

Procedural issues 1
Surplus assets 2

---

1. Procedural issues

Error in failing to require administrator with will annexed to secure bond did not invalidate administrator's sale of real property, which was newly discovered asset of decedent's estate, where there were no allegations of malfeasance against administrator, property was appraised by court-approved appraiser, and property was sold at appraised value. In re Estate of Hyer (Ohio App. 7 Dist., Monroe, 09-27-2004) No. 03 MO 9, 2004-Ohio-5359, 2004 WL 2334510, Unreported. Executors And Administrators ⇐ 143

Administrator with will annexed could sell real property, which was newly discovered asset of decedent's estate, without filing report of newly discovered assets as amended inventory and appraisal and without hearing being conducted on inventory, where probate court's order authorized administrator to distribute assets without being required to make inventory or appraisal of assets and administrator had previously filed inventory and appraisal. In re Estate of Hyer (Ohio App. 7 Dist., Monroe, 09-27-2004) No. 03 MO 9, 2004-Ohio-5359, 2004 WL 2334510, Unreported. Executors And Administrators ⇐ 70

Casualty insurance claim, arising from damage to decedent's former real estate, was a chose in action that passed on death to decedent's executor, and thus proceeds from real estate that had been devised in equal shares to two brothers, who were co-executors of estate, passed equally to brothers, even though one brother had sold his interest in real estate to other brother; insurance claim antedated decedent's death, and one brother's contact with decedent's former insurer and meeting with its adjuster was no more than a fulfillment of his duty as a co-executor, giving him no greater legal or equitable claim to the insurance proceeds than his brother. In re Estate of Ray (Ohio App. 6 Dist., Wood, 04-18-2003) No. WD-02-049, 2003-Ohio-2001, 2003 WL 1904412, Unreported, appeal not allowed 99 Ohio St.3d 1515, 792 N.E.2d 201, 2003-Ohio-3957. Executors And Administrators ⇐ 49; Wills ⇐ 740(4)

No law requires or authorizes the filing with the probate court of an application by an administrator to determine the nature of a claim allegedly due an estate and to determine whether such amount should be included as an asset of such estate upon the filing of an amended inventory and appraisement; nor is there any law authorizing any order based upon such an application, unless such application can be construed as a petition for a declaratory judgment, which it cannot be where the application is not adversary in character, where there is no party plaintiff or party defendant, and where the facts set forth do not allege any justiciable controversy. In re Uhl's Estate (Marion 1954) 98 Ohio App. 145, 128 N.E.2d 142, 57 O.O. 212.

Where administratrix died after having completely administered estate, trust company's application for appointment as administrator de bonis non to administer newly discovered assets in the form of personal property of "undetermined" value, which assets consisted merely of a claim against estate of former administratrix for an alleged wrongful act was defective on its face for failure to allege a value of over $20 and because such claim is not an "asset" within contemplation of statute relating to administration of newly discovered assets. In re Cassell's Estate (Ohio Prob. 1948) 83 N.E.2d 72, 53 Ohio Law Abs. 65. Executors And Administrators ⇐ 37(2)

Where, at the time of appointment of the administrator, an estate is totally without assets, and no inventory is filed until twenty-two months thereafter, at which time certain bonds are received by the administrator as a result of a legal action in another county, an action by a creditor of the estate, commenced within two months of the filing of such inventory, may be maintained under favor of this section. Carrier v. Morrissey (Ohio Com.Pl. 1933) 32 Ohio N.P.N.S. 362.

2. Surplus assets

The surplus remaining from a land-forfeiture sale, after the payment of the taxes owing and the costs incident to such sale, is personal property, and the administrator of the estate of the former owner of such property has the right, as the real party in interest, to maintain an action to obtain such surplus. Floyd v. Clyne (Cuyahoga 1958) 108 Ohio App. 16, 154 N.E.2d 771, 80 Ohio Law Abs. 225, 9 O.O.2d 93.

FOREIGN EXECUTORS AND ADMINISTRATORS

2113.70 Suit against foreign executors and administrators

An executor or administrator appointed in any other state or country, or his legal representatives, may be prosecuted in any appropriate court in this state in his capacity of executor or administrator.

(125 v 903, eff. 10–1–53; 1953 H 1; GC 10509–160)

Historical and Statutory Notes

Pre–1953 H 1 Amendments: 114 v 437

Cross References

Ancillary administration, Ch 2129

Library References

Executors and Administrators ⇐525.
Westlaw Topic No. 162.
C.J.S. Executors and Administrators § 933.

Research References

Encyclopedias

OH Jur. 3d Decedents' Estates § 1721, Actions Against Foreign Executor or Administrator.

OH Jur. 3d Decedents' Estates § 1729, When Ancillary Administration is Necessary or Available, Generally—Necessity.

Treatises and Practice Aids

Restatement (2d) of Conflicts § 358, Suit Against Foreign Executor or Administrator.

Notes of Decisions

Administrator's power 3
Court's power 2
Jurisdiction over foreign administrator 1

---

1. Jurisdiction over foreign administrator

Where a foreign administrator brings suit in Ohio which is subsequently dismissed, the foreign administrator cannot thereafter assert that the court lacked jurisdiction. Hamilton v Taylor, 13 D Repr 975 (Super, Cincinnati 1873).

Where the court has subject matter jurisdiction, a foreign executor may be served within the county and ensuing judgment will be valid in Ohio.

Craig v. Toledo, A.A. & N.M.R. Co. (Ohio Com.Pl. 1895) 3 Ohio Dec. 146, 2 Ohio N.P. 64.

A foreign administrator may not be sued in Ohio, except as to the decedent's property within the state. Feldman v. Gross (N.D.Ohio 1952) 106 F.Supp. 308, 64 Ohio Law Abs. 545, 49 O.O. 415.

Foreign administrator may not be sued in Ohio for damages arising out of automobile collision, when no property of estate was to be found in Ohio. Feldman v. Gross (N.D.Ohio 1952) 106 F.Supp. 308, 64 Ohio Law Abs. 545, 49 O.O. 415.

2. Court's power

An Ohio probate court, admitting into probate an Ohio will and issuing letters testamentary to the executor therein named, does not have the power to review accounts of the executor respecting property situated in Michigan and for which the executor duly accounted to the proper Michigan court. In re Crawford (Ohio 1903) 68 Ohio St. 58, 48 W.L.B. 492, 67 N.E. 156, 96 Am.St.Rep. 648, 1 Ohio Law Rep. 91.

A foreign administrator may voluntarily appear in our courts, but he cannot be compelled to appear. Lampton v Nichols, 13 D Repr 765 (Super, Cincinnati 1870).

3. Administrator's power

Foreign administrators have full power to make a complete settlement of the estate of a deceased nonresident. In re McCreight (Ohio Prob. 1895) 9 Ohio Dec. 454, 6 Ohio N.P. 481.

2113.71 Jurisdiction

The several probate courts, courts of common pleas, and superior courts have the same authority over foreign executors and administrators as if they were appointed in this state.

(125 v 903, eff. 10–1–53; 1953 H 1; GC 10509–161)

Historical and Statutory Notes

Pre–1953 H 1 Amendments: 114 v 437

Library References

Executors and Administrators ⟐525.
Westlaw Topic No. 162.
C.J.S. Executors and Administrators § 933.

Research References

Encyclopedias

OH Jur. 3d Decedents' Estates § 1721, Actions Against Foreign Executor or Administrator.

Notes of Decisions

Procedural issues   1
Property in state   2

---

1. Procedural issues

In a suit brought against a life insurance company in the state where the company is located by the widow, where the company obtains a order requiring the administrator, an Ohio resident, to appear and interplead with the widow as to their respective claims under the policy, service in Ohio does not give the foreign court personal jurisdiction over the administrator, and a judgment barring him from any other action against the widow is void. Cross v. Armstrong (Ohio 1887) 44 Ohio St. 613, 10 N.E. 160.

2. Property in state

Ohio court had jurisdiction to determine if property located in county belonged in deceased's estate, even though Kentucky law controlled the administration of the estate, where the property was located in Ohio and no other court had ruled that it had to be included in the estate. Comer, Sr. v. Early Auction Co. (Ohio App. 12 Dist., Clermont, 04-26-2004) No. CA2003-07-061, 2004-Ohio-2073, 2004 WL 877856, Unreported, appeal not allowed 103 Ohio St.3d 1428, 814 N.E.2d 491, 2004-Ohio-4524. Executors And Administrators ⟐ 2

This statute is merely declaratory of common law rule permitting suits against foreign administrators to extent of decedent's property within state, and when no property of estate was in Ohio, foreign administrator could not be sued in Ohio for damages arising out of automobile collision. Feldman v. Gross (N.D.Ohio 1952) 106 F.Supp. 308, 64 Ohio Law Abs. 545, 49 O.O. 415.

2113.72 Proceedings against foreign executor or administrator

Any court of common pleas may compel a foreign administrator or executor residing in this state, or having assets or property herein, to account at the suit of an heir, distributee, or legatee, who is resident in this state, and make distribution of the amount found in his hands to the respective heirs, distributees, or legatees according to the law of the state granting such letters. When suits are pending or there are unsettled demands against such estate, the court also may require a refunding bond to be given to such executor or administrator by the heirs, distributees, or legatees entitled thereto in case the amount paid is needed to pay debts of the estate.

(1953 H 1, eff. 10–1–53; GC 10509–162)

Historical and Statutory Notes

Pre–1953 H 1 Amendments: 114 v 437

Library References

Executors and Administrators ⟐526.
Westlaw Topic No. 162.
C.J.S. Executors and Administrators §§ 934 to 935.

Research References

Encyclopedias

OH Jur. 3d Decedents' Estates § 1711, Accounting.
OH Jur. 3d Decedents' Estates § 1721, Actions Against Foreign Executor or Administrator.
OH Jur. 3d Decedents' Estates § 1724, Compelling Distribution.

Forms

Ohio Forms Legal and Business § 24:464, Appointment—Ancillary Executor—Corporation.

2113.73 Security for distributees and indemnification for sureties

When a foreign administrator or executor has wasted, misapplied, or converted assets of an estate, or has insufficient property to discharge his liability on account of the trust, or his sureties are irresponsible, distributees, heirs, or legatees, in any court of common pleas or probate court may compel him to secure the amounts respectively due to them and any of his sureties may require indemnity on account of their liability as bail.

(1953 H 1, eff. 10–1–53; GC 10509–163)

Historical and Statutory Notes

Pre–1953 H 1 Amendments: 114 v 437

Library References

Executors and Administrators ⟐519(1), 521, 523.
Westlaw Topic No. 162.
C.J.S. Executors and Administrators §§ 924, 927, 929 to 930.

Research References

Encyclopedias

OH Jur. 3d Decedents' Estates § 1721, Actions Against Foreign Executor or Administrator.

OH Jur. 3d Decedents' Estates § 1723, Compelling Foreign Representative to Give Security.

Notes of Decisions

Pending in other state   1

---

1. **Pending in other state**

Where a married woman living in Ohio dies intestate and her husband obtains letters of administration in another state, a suit cannot be maintained in Ohio by her heirs for distribution while the matter is pending in the other state. Adams v. Adams (Ohio 1857) 7 Ohio St. 83.

2113.74   Other remedies

The several provisional remedies and proceedings authorized by sections 2113.70 to 2113.73, inclusive, of the Revised Code, against a foreign executor or administrator also apply to the person and property of a foreign administrator or executor. The probate court or the court of common pleas may make any order or decree touching his property and effects, or the assets of such estate, necessary for the security of those interested therein.

(1953 H 1, eff. 10–1–53; GC 10509–164)

Historical and Statutory Notes

Pre–1953 H 1 Amendments: 114 v 438

Library References

Executors and Administrators ⇐525.
Westlaw Topic No. 162.
C.J.S. Executors and Administrators § 933.

Research References

Encyclopedias

OH Jur. 3d Decedents' Estates § 1721, Actions Against Foreign Executor or Administrator.

2113.75   Foreign executor or administrator may prosecute suit in this state

An executor or administrator appointed in any other state or country may commence and prosecute an action or proceeding in any court in this state, in his capacity as executor or administrator, in like manner and under like restrictions as a nonresident is permitted to sue.

(1953 H 1, eff. 10–1–53; GC 10509–165)

Historical and Statutory Notes

Pre–1953 H 1 Amendments: 114 v 438

Library References

Executors and Administrators ⇐524(0.5), 524(1).
Westlaw Topic No. 162.
C.J.S. Executors and Administrators § 931.

Research References

Encyclopedias

OH Jur. 3d Death § 120, Foreign Representative.
OH Jur. 3d Death § 183, Generally; Proper Party Plaintiff.
OH Jur. 3d Decedents' Estates § 1712, Authority of Administrators and Executors Appointed in Another State, Generally.
OH Jur. 3d Decedents' Estates § 1717, Actions by Foreign Executor or Administrator.
OH Jur. 3d Decedents' Estates § 1729, When Ancillary Administration is Necessary or Available, Generally—Necessity.

Treatises and Practice Aids

Carlin, Baldwin's Ohio Practice, Merrick-Rippner Probate Law § 12:2, Wrongful Death—Who May Bring Action.

Notes of Decisions

Appeal   4
Debts   2
Real property   3
Wrongful death   1

---

1. **Wrongful death**

Where decedent was killed in Indiana, administrator was appointed in Indiana, and where Indiana has a wrongful death right of action and reciprocity with Ohio, the administrator may maintain an action in Ohio subject to the same restrictions as a nonresident permitted to sue under RS 6133. Cincinnati, H. & D.R. Co. v. Thiebaud (C.C.A.6 (Ohio) 1900) 114 F. 918, 52 C.C.A. 538.

Where widow of decedent killed in Ohio accident executed release in Georgia, her place of residence, said release barred recovery by decedent or minor children in Ohio wrongful death action. McCluskey v. Rob San Services, Inc. (S.D.Ohio 1977) 443 F.Supp. 65, 10 O.O.3d 248.

Foreign personal representatives can maintain actions for wrongful death in Ohio courts. Glenn v. Trans World Airlines, Inc. (E.D.N.Y. 1962) 210 F.Supp. 31, 22 O.O.2d 431. Death ⇐ 31(4)

A personal representative appointed in another state may institute and maintain a wrongful death action in Ohio pursuant to RC 2113.75 and 2125.02, where a personal representative appointed in Ohio has not already done so. Ahlrichs v. Tri-Tex Corp. (Hamilton 1987) 41 Ohio App.3d 207, 534 N.E.2d 1231.

2. **Debts**

Payment of a debt owed the decedent at the time of his death by an Ohio debtor to a foreign administrator before the appointment of an Ohio administrator satisfies the debt. Crawford v. Foreign Christian Missionary Soc. (Ohio Com.Pl. 1910) 22 Ohio Dec. 804, 10 Ohio N.P.N.S. 676.

Where a promise to pay out an in-state deposit to a foreign administrator is made without notice of appointment to the Ohio administrator and paid out after notice, the Ohio administrator cannot recover, as a foreign administrator is authorized to collect debts in Ohio. Weizell v Cincinnati Savings Institution, 1 D Repr 55, 1 WLJ 393 (OS 1844).

3. **Real property**

A foreign trust company appointed to act as executor of a foreign testator's will may sue in Ohio courts where the will includes real property in Ohio. Union Sav. Bank & Trust Co. v. Baltimore & O.S.W.R. Co. (Ohio Insolv. 1908) 6 Ohio NP(NS) 454, 53 W.L.B. 180.

4. **Appeal**

A foreign executor who has never given bond in Ohio cannot appeal without giving an appeal bond. Work v. Massie (Ohio 1834) 6 Ohio 503.

TRUST FOR SAFEKEEPING FOR NONRESIDENT

2113.81   Money and property to be held in trust for safekeeping for nonresidents of United States

Where it appears that a legatee or a distributee, or a beneficiary of a trust not residing within the United States or its territories will not have the benefit or use or control of the money or other property due him from an estate, because of circumstances prevailing at the place of residence of such legatee, distributee, or a beneficiary of a trust, the probate court may direct that such money be paid into the county treasury to be held in trust or the probate court may direct that such money or other property be delivered to a trustee which trustee shall have the same powers and duties provided in section 2119.03 of the Revised Code for such legatee, distributee, beneficiary of a trust or such persons who may thereafter be entitled thereto. Such money or other property held in trust by such county treasurer or trustee shall be paid out by order of the probate judge in accordance with section 2113.82 of the Revised Code.

The county treasury shall not be liable for interest on such money held in trust.

(126 v 946, eff. 10–6–55)

Cross References

Heirs of aliens may inherit, aliens may hold lands, 2105.16

Library References

Executors and Administrators ⇐303(3).
Westlaw Topic No. 162.
C.J.S. Executors and Administrators § 543.

Research References

Encyclopedias

OH Jur. 3d Aliens & Citizens § 16, Rights in Estates of Deceased Persons—Effect of Statute Creating Trust for Nonresident for Safekeeping.

OH Jur. 3d Decedents' Estates § 1664, Beneficiary Residing in Certain Foreign Countries.

Forms

Ohio Forms and Transactions F 30.07, Conditional Bequests and Devises.

Treatises and Practice Aids

Carlin, Baldwin's Ohio Practice, Merrick-Rippner Probate Law § 78:1, Statutory Provisions.

Law Review and Journal Commentaries

Legatees Behind the Iron Curtain, Carl H. Fulda. 16 Ohio St L J 496 (Autumn 1956).

Notes of Decisions

Constitutional issues   1
Contingent beneficiaries   2
Right to receive property   3

1. Constitutional issues

A state statute such as RC 2113.81, which directs that funds in a decedent's estate which would otherwise be distributable be held in trust because it appears that the distributee resides outside the United States and its territories at a location where the prevailing circumstances will prevent his having the benefit, use, or control of the money due him, is invalid under US Const Art I, § 10, which grants exclusive power over the foreign affairs of this country to the federal government. First Nat. Bank of Cincinnati v. Fishman (Ohio Prob. 1968) 16 Ohio Misc. 185, 239 N.E.2d 270, 43 O.O.2d 384, 45 O.O.2d 147.

RC 2113.81 is unconstitutional if applied on any basis other than consideration of the statutory law of the foreign country involved. Mora v. Battin (N.D.Ohio 1969) 20 Ohio Misc. 208, 303 F.Supp. 660, 49 O.O.2d 133, 49 O.O.2d 303.

2. Contingent beneficiaries

It is not error for a court, in construing a will—where the testator gives the residue of his estate to certain named domestic legatees as contingent beneficiaries in the event the legacies bequeathed to certain persons resident of Czechoslovakia, or their lineal descendants, cannot, at the time of testator's death or within one year thereafter, "for any reason, be delivered to any or all of" them—to find that such legacies should be paid to the contingent domestic heirs rather than to the primary foreign heirs, where the evidence shows that an effective delivery of the legacies could not be made to the benefit of such foreign heirs at the time of testator's death, or within one year thereafter, because of economic and political conditions then in existence in Czechoslovakia. Queen v. Gastan (Hamilton 1965) 5 Ohio App.2d 278, 215 N.E.2d 408, 34 O.O.2d 439. Wills ⇐ 660

3. Right to receive property

Property distributable under the laws of intestate succession to heirs residing in the USSR should be held in trust until such time as the persons entitled thereto satisfy the court of their right to receive it. First Nat. Bank of Cincinnati v. Fishman (Ohio Prob. 1966) 7 Ohio Misc. 130, 217 N.E.2d 60, 35 O.O.2d 64.

2113.82 Payments of money or property by county treasurer or trustee

When a person entitled to money or other property invested or turned into the county treasurer or to a trustee under section 2113.81 of the Revised Code satisfies the probate court of his right to receive it, the court shall order the county treasurer or the trustee to pay it over to such person.

(126 v 946, eff. 10–6–55)

Library References

Executors and Administrators ⇐303(3).
Westlaw Topic No. 162.
C.J.S. Executors and Administrators § 543.

Research References

Encyclopedias

OH Jur. 3d Decedents' Estates § 1664, Beneficiary Residing in Certain Foreign Countries.

Treatises and Practice Aids

Carlin, Baldwin's Ohio Practice, Merrick-Rippner Probate Law § 78:1, Statutory Provisions.

Notes of Decisions

Constitutional issues   1
Delivery   2

1. Constitutional issues

A state statute such as RC 2113.81 which directs that funds in a decedent's estate which would otherwise be distributable be held in trust because it appears that the distributee resides outside the United States and its territories at a location where the prevailing circumstances will prevent his having the benefit, use, or control of the money due him is invalid under US Const Art I, § 10, which grants exclusive power over the foreign affairs of this country to the federal government. First Nat. Bank of Cincinnati v. Fishman (Ohio Prob. 1968) 16 Ohio Misc. 185, 239 N.E.2d 270, 43 O.O.2d 384, 45 O.O.2d 147.

2. Delivery

It is not error for a court, in construing a will—where the testator gives the residue of his estate to certain named domestic legatees as contingent beneficiaries in the event the legacies bequeathed to certain persons resident of Czechoslovakia, or their lineal descendants, cannot, at the time of testator's death or within one year thereafter, "for any reason, be delivered to any or all of" them—to find that such legacies should be paid to the contingent domestic heirs rather than to the primary foreign heirs, where the evidence shows that an effective delivery of the legacies could not be made to the benefit of such foreign heirs at the time of testator's death, or within one year thereafter, because of economic and political conditions then in existence in Czechoslovakia. Queen v. Gastan (Hamilton 1965) 5 Ohio App.2d 278, 215 N.E.2d 408, 34 O.O.2d 439. Wills ⇐ 660

TAX APPORTIONMENT

2113.85 Definitions

As used in sections 2113.85 to 2113.90 of the Revised Code:

(A) "Estate" means the gross estate of a decedent who is domiciled in this state, as determined for federal estate tax purposes under Subtitle B of the Internal Revenue Code of 1954,

26 U.S.C. 2001, as amended, for Ohio estate tax purposes under Chapter 5731. of the Revised Code, and for estate tax purposes of any other jurisdiction that imposes a tax on the transfer of property by a decedent who is domiciled in this state.

(B) "Person interested in the estate" means any person who is entitled to receive, or who has received, any property or property interest included in the decedent's estate. A "person interested in the estate" includes, but is not limited to, a personal representative, guardian, and trustee. A "person interested in the estate" does not include a creditor of the decedent or of his estate.

(C) "Tax" means the federal estate tax determined under Subtitle B of the Internal Revenue Code of 1954, 26 U.S.C. 2001, as amended, an Ohio estate tax determined under Chapter 5731. of the Revised Code, and the estate tax determined by any other jurisdiction that imposes a tax on the transfer of property by a decedent who is domiciled in this state.

(D) "Fiduciary" means an executor, administrator, or other person who, by virtue of his representation of the decedent's estate, is required to pay the tax.

(1986 H 139, eff. 7–24–86; 1980 S 317)

Uncodified Law

1986 H 139, § 3, eff. 7–24–86, reads, in part: Sections 1 and 2 of this act shall apply only to the estates of decedents whose death occurs on or after the effective date of this act.

Research References

ALR Library

56 ALR 5th 133, Construction and Application of "Pay-All-Taxes" Provision in Will, as Including Liability of Nontestamentary Property for Inheritance and Estate Taxes.

Encyclopedias

OH Jur. 3d Taxation § 977, Introduction.
OH Jur. 3d Taxation § 978, General Rule of Apportionment.
OH Jur. 3d Taxation § 990, Objections to Apportionment.

Forms

Ohio Forms Legal and Business § 24:51, Apportionment of Federal and Ohio Estate Taxes.

Treatises and Practice Aids

Carlin, Baldwin's Ohio Practice, Merrick-Rippner Probate Law § 2:81, Ohio Estate Tax—Determining the Gross Estate—Apportioning the Tax.

Carlin, Baldwin's Ohio Practice, Merrick-Rippner Probate Law § 30:9, Drafting a Will—Payment of Debts, Administration Expenses, and Taxes.

Carlin, Baldwin's Ohio Practice, Merrick-Rippner Probate Law § 110:1, Apportionment Law—Overview.

Carlin, Baldwin's Ohio Practice, Merrick-Rippner Probate Law § 110:2, Apportionment of Federal and Ohio Estate Taxes Among Interested Persons.

Carlin, Baldwin's Ohio Practice, Merrick-Rippner Probate Law § 110:4, Tax Not Reapportioned to Federal Tax Deduction Property.

Carlin, Baldwin's Ohio Practice, Merrick-Rippner Probate Law § 110:5, Marital or Charitable Deductions, Exceptions.

Carlin, Baldwin's Ohio Practice, Merrick-Rippner Probate Law § 109:58, Ohio Estate Tax—Liability—General Rules.

Carlin, Baldwin's Ohio Practice, Merrick-Rippner Probate Law § 111:19, Federal Estate Tax—Liability of Fiduciary for Payment.

Carlin, Baldwin's Ohio Practice, Merrick-Rippner Probate Law § 30:176, Death Taxes on Property Passing Under Will to be Paid Out of Residue—Form.

Notes of Decisions

Inter vivos gift 1

---

1. Inter vivos gift

Where an inter vivos gift of municipal bonds is made in contemplation of death, the bonds are not part of the estate for federal estate tax purposes; however, the bonds are part of the estate for Ohio estate tax purposes. In re Estate of Finke (Ohio 1987) 31 Ohio St.3d 1, 508 N.E.2d 158, 31 O.B.R. 1.

2113.86 Apportionment of federal and Ohio estate taxes among interested persons; exemptions; penalties

(A) Unless a will or another governing instrument otherwise provides, and except as otherwise provided in this section, a tax shall be apportioned equitably in accordance with the provisions of this section among all persons interested in an estate in proportion to the value of the interest of each person as determined for estate tax purposes.

(B) Except as otherwise provided in this division, any tax that is apportioned against a gift made in a clause of a will other than a residuary clause or in a provision of an inter vivos trust other than a residuary provision, shall be reapportioned to the residue of the estate or trust. It shall be charged in the same manner as a general administration expense. However, when a portion of the residue of the estate or trust is allowable as a deduction for estate tax purposes, the tax shall be reapportioned to the extent possible to the portion of the residue that is not so allowable.

(C)(1) A tax shall not be apportioned against an interest that is allowable as an estate tax marital or charitable deduction, except to the extent that the interest is a part of the residue of an estate or trust against which tax is reapportioned pursuant to division (B) of this section.

(2) Estate tax of this state or another jurisdiction shall not be reapportioned against an interest that is allowable as a deduction for federal estate tax purposes, to the extent that there is other property in the estate or trust that is not allowable as a deduction for federal estate tax purposes and against which estate tax of this state or another jurisdiction can be apportioned.

(D) A tax shall not be apportioned against property that passes to a surviving spouse as an elective share under section 2106.01 of the Revised Code or as an intestate share under section 2105.06 of the Revised Code, to the extent that there is other property in the estate that is not allowable as a deduction for estate tax purposes against which the tax can be apportioned.

(E)(1) Any federal estate tax credit for state or foreign death taxes on property that is includible in an estate for federal estate tax purposes, shall inure to the benefit of the persons chargeable with the payment of the state or foreign death taxes in proportion to the amount of the taxes paid by each person, but any federal estate tax credit for state or foreign death taxes inuring to the benefit of a person cannot exceed the federal estate tax apportioned to that person.

(2) Any federal estate tax credit for gift taxes paid by a donee of a gift shall inure to the benefit of that donee for purposes of this section.

(3) Credits against tax not covered by division (E)(1) or (2) of this section shall be apportioned equitably among persons in the manner in which the tax is apportioned among them.

(F) Any additional estate tax that is due because a qualified heir has disposed of qualified farm property in a manner not authorized by law or ceased to use any part of the qualified farm property for a qualified use, shall be apportioned against the interest of the qualified heir.

(G) If both a present interest and a future interest in property are involved, a tax shall be apportioned entirely to the principal. This shall be the case even if the future interest qualifies for an estate tax charitable deduction, even if the holder of the present interest also has rights in the principal, and even if the principal is otherwise exempt from apportionment.

(H) Penalties shall be apportioned in the same manner as a tax, and interest on tax shall be apportioned to the income of the estate or trust, unless a court directs a different apportionment of penalties or interest based on a finding that special circumstances make an apportionment as provided in this division inequitable.

(I) If any part of an estate consists of property, the value of which is included in the gross estate of the decedent by reason of section 2044 of the "Internal Revenue Code of 1986," 100 Stat. 2085, 26 U.S.C.A. 2044, as amended, or of section 5731.131 of the Revised Code, the estate is entitled to recover from the persons holding or receiving the property any amount by which the estate tax payable exceeds the estate tax that would have been payable if the value of the property had not been included in the gross estate of the decedent. This division does not apply if a decedent provides otherwise in his will or another governing instrument and the will or instrument refers to either section mentioned in this division or to qualified terminable interest marital deduction property.

(1990 H 346, eff. 5–31–90; 1986 H 139)

Uncodified Law

1990 H 346, § 3, eff. 5–31–90, reads, in part: (A) Sections 1 and 2 of this act shall apply only to the estates of decedents who die on or after the effective date of this act.

1986 H 139, § 3 and 6, eff. 7–24–86, read, in part:

Section 3. Except as provided in Sections... 6 of this act..., Sections 1 and 2 of this act shall apply only to the estates of decedents whose death occurs on or after the effective date of this act.

Section 6. The amendments made to division (C) of section 2107.39 and to former sections 2113.86 and 2113.87 of the Revised Code as they existed prior to the effective date of this act, the enactment of new section 2113.86 except for its division (I), and the enactment of section 2113.861 of the Revised Code, by Section 1 of this act, are clarifying amendments or enactments and generally are declaratory of the law of this state prior to the effective date of this act. The provisions of new section 2113.86 and section 2113.861 of the Revised Code as enacted by Section 1 of this act, the provisions of division (C) of section 2107.39 of the Revised Code as amended by Section 1 of this act, and the provisions of former sections 2113.86 and 2113.87 of the Revised Code as amended by Section 1 of this act, shall apply to the estates of decedents who died on or after March 23, 1981.

Historical and Statutory Notes

Ed. Note: Former 2113.86 amended and recodified as 2113.87 by 1986 H 139, eff. 7–24–86; 1980 S 317.

Cross References

Wills, election by surviving spouse, net estate determined before taxes paid, 2106.01

Library References

Internal Revenue ⇌4818 to 4821.
Taxation ⇌888, 903.
Westlaw Topic Nos. 220, 371.
C.J.S. Internal Revenue §§ 497, 723 to 724, 729.
C.J.S. Social Security and Public Welfare § 203.
C.J.S. Taxation §§ 1889 to 1897, 1976.

Research References

Encyclopedias

OH Jur. 3d Taxation § 978, General Rule of Apportionment.
OH Jur. 3d Taxation § 979, Effect of Will or Trust Agreement.
OH Jur. 3d Taxation § 981, Reapportionment to Residuary Estate.
OH Jur. 3d Taxation § 982, Exemption of Property Subject to Deductions.
OH Jur. 3d Taxation § 983, Exemption of Spouse's Share.
OH Jur. 3d Taxation § 984, Apportionment of Credits.
OH Jur. 3d Taxation § 985, Apportionment of Recapture Tax.
OH Jur. 3d Taxation § 986, Apportionment Among Present and Future Interests.
OH Jur. 3d Taxation § 987, Apportionment of Penalties and Interest.
OH Jur. 3d Taxation § 988, Recovery from Persons Holding Qualified Terminable Interest Property.
OH Jur. 3d Taxation § 989, Apportionment of Generation-Skipping Transfer Tax.

Forms

Ohio Forms Legal and Business § 24:51, Apportionment of Federal and Ohio Estate Taxes.
Ohio Forms Legal and Business § 24:168, Bequests and Devises to Children, Children Born Out of Wedlock, and Parents—Residuary Estate to Spouse—Bequests of Void Legacies.
Ohio Forms Legal and Business § 24:401, Death Taxes on Both Probate and Nonprobate Estate to be Paid from Residue.
Ohio Forms Legal and Business § 25:116, Marital Deduction Trust—Husband or Wife as Single Trustor—Lifetime Income and Power of Appointment in Beneficiary Spouse—Residuary Trust.

Treatises and Practice Aids

Carlin, Baldwin's Ohio Practice, Merrick-Rippner Probate Law § 2:38, Elective Rights of Surviving Spouse—Election to Take Under Law or Under the Will—Elective Share of Surviving Spouse Against the Will.
Carlin, Baldwin's Ohio Practice, Merrick-Rippner Probate Law § 21:5, Rights of Surviving Spouse to Make Election—Statutory Provisions—Effect.
Carlin, Baldwin's Ohio Practice, Merrick-Rippner Probate Law § 48:8, Property Liable for Payment of Debts—Personal Property—Effect of Spousal Election.
Carlin, Baldwin's Ohio Practice, Merrick-Rippner Probate Law § 109:4, Ohio Estate Tax—Gross Estate—Transfers in Contemplation of Death.
Carlin, Baldwin's Ohio Practice, Merrick-Rippner Probate Law § 110:1, Apportionment Law—Overview.
Carlin, Baldwin's Ohio Practice, Merrick-Rippner Probate Law § 110:2, Apportionment of Federal and Ohio Estate Taxes Among Interested Persons.
Carlin, Baldwin's Ohio Practice, Merrick-Rippner Probate Law § 110:3, Reapportionment of Tax on Interest Not Part of Residuary Estate.
Carlin, Baldwin's Ohio Practice, Merrick-Rippner Probate Law § 110:4, Tax Not Reapportioned to Federal Tax Deduction Property.
Carlin, Baldwin's Ohio Practice, Merrick-Rippner Probate Law § 110:5, Marital or Charitable Deductions, Exceptions.
Carlin, Baldwin's Ohio Practice, Merrick-Rippner Probate Law § 110:6, Elective Share or Intestate Share of Surviving Spouse.
Carlin, Baldwin's Ohio Practice, Merrick-Rippner Probate Law § 110:7, Federal Estate Tax Credit for State or Foreign Death Taxes.
Carlin, Baldwin's Ohio Practice, Merrick-Rippner Probate Law § 110:8, Federal Gift Tax Credit.
Carlin, Baldwin's Ohio Practice, Merrick-Rippner Probate Law § 110:9, Other Credits.
Carlin, Baldwin's Ohio Practice, Merrick-Rippner Probate Law § 21:24, Rights of Surviving Spouse to Make Election—Effect of Taxes on Election.
Carlin, Baldwin's Ohio Practice, Merrick-Rippner Probate Law § 30:29, Drafting a Will—Clauses to Discourage a Will Contest Action—in Terrorem Clause.
Carlin, Baldwin's Ohio Practice, Merrick-Rippner Probate Law § 89:17, Payment of Debts—Allowance for Support of Surviving Spouse and Minor Children—Preference Under Federal Law.
Carlin, Baldwin's Ohio Practice, Merrick-Rippner Probate Law § 109:58, Ohio Estate Tax—Liability—General Rules.
Carlin, Baldwin's Ohio Practice, Merrick-Rippner Probate Law § 110:10, Qualified Farm Property.
Carlin, Baldwin's Ohio Practice, Merrick-Rippner Probate Law § 110:11, Present and Future Interests.
Carlin, Baldwin's Ohio Practice, Merrick-Rippner Probate Law § 110:12, Apportionment of Penalties and Interest.
Carlin, Baldwin's Ohio Practice, Merrick-Rippner Probate Law § 110:13, Qualified Terminable Interest Property (Qtip), Effect on Apportionment.
Carlin, Baldwin's Ohio Practice, Merrick-Rippner Probate Law § 110:14, Generation-Skipping Transfer Tax, Effect on Apportionment.
Carlin, Baldwin's Ohio Practice, Merrick-Rippner Probate Law § 110:16, Objection to Apportionment and Determination of Apportionment by Probate Court.
Carlin, Baldwin's Ohio Practice, Merrick-Rippner Probate Law § 111:19, Federal Estate Tax—Liability of Fiduciary for Payment.

Bogert - the Law of Trusts and Trustees § 286.5, Apportionment of Death Taxes.

Law Review and Journal Commentaries

Recently Enacted Ohio Estate Tax Changes, Wayne A. Jenkins. 10 Prob L J Ohio 81 (July/August 2000).

U.S. Tax Court Misinterprets Ohio Tax Apportionment Act, Marvin R. Pliskin. 5 Prob L J Ohio 45 (March/April 1995).

Notes of Decisions

Ed. Note: This section contains annotations from former RC 2113.88.

Apportionment 3
Exemption 1
Intent of testator 2
Surviving spouse 4

1. Exemption

Where a credit is directly attributable to gifts made by a donor prior to death, and the credit is greater than the amount of Ohio estate tax attributable to the gifts under RC 2113.86, the credit shall inure to the benefit of the inter vivos donees under RC 2113.88 so as to exempt them from apportionment of the tax. In re Estate of Finke (Ohio 1987) 31 Ohio St.3d 1, 508 N.E.2d 158, 31 O.B.R. 1. Taxation ⇔ 3344

Donees of an inter vivos gift of municipal bonds are exempt from apportionment for estate taxes when the amount apportioned to the donees is less than the amount of the unified gift tax credit attributable to the bonds. In re Estate of Finke (Ohio 1987) 31 Ohio St.3d 1, 508 N.E.2d 158, 31 O.B.R. 1.

2. Intent of testator

An intent on the part of the testator that estate taxes are to be paid in a manner contrary to the apportionment method set forth in RC 2113.86 must be clearly expressed in the will; a provision in a will directing the executor to pay "all just debts" does not clearly evince such an intent. In re Estate of Drosos (Cuyahoga 1989) 62 Ohio App.3d 295, 575 N.E.2d 495. Taxation ⇔ 3346

3. Apportionment

RC 2113.88, read together with RC 2113.86(B), provides the following priority for apportionment of estate tax against classes of beneficiaries: (1) nonexempt residuary beneficiaries, (2) exempt residuary beneficiaries, (3) nonexempt specific or general beneficiaries, and (4) exempt specific or general beneficiaries. Matter of Estate of Widener (Franklin 1986) 31 O.B.R. 304.

Probate court's judgment entry apportioning estate taxes equally in proportion to the value of the interest of each beneficiary in the trust and assets received outside the trust not paid by the residuary assets of the estate was not a final appealable order, where the entry did not state whether taxes were owed in excess of the residuary assets, what amount of taxes might be left for apportionment, what proportion of tax liability was imposed on beneficiaries, and what figures were to be used to determine apportioned amounts. In re Estate of Kmowlton (Ohio App. 5 Dist., Delaware, 06-10-2003) No. 02CAF-12-061, 2003-Ohio-2991, 2003 WL 21350248, Unreported. Wills ⇔ 394

Under statute governing apportionment of estate taxes among interested persons, taxes are first apportioned against the residuary estate; however, if the tax apportioned to the residuary estate exceeds the value of the residue, then the tax is apportioned among specific and other nonresiduary bequests. Burkholder v. Haller (Ohio App. 10 Dist., 06-02-1998) 127 Ohio App.3d 618, 713 N.E.2d 523. Internal Revenue ⇔ 4821; Taxation ⇔ 3344

Will which contained provision requiring executor to charge against share of any devisee, legatee, or beneficiary all estate or inheritance taxes or other governmental charges imposed by reason of testator's death did not clearly, specifically, and unambiguously express intent that taxes be apportioned in manner other than that described by statute. Burkholder v. Haller (Ohio App. 10 Dist., 06-02-1998) 127 Ohio App.3d 618, 713 N.E.2d 523. Internal Revenue ⇔ 4824; Taxation ⇔ 3346

Since will contained specific devises, trial court was required to first apportion estate taxes equitably among all persons interested in estate in proportion to value of interest each person held as determined for estate tax purposes and then reapportion any tax that was apportioned against specific devise or inter vivos trust to residue of estate and charge them in same manner as general administration expense. In re Estate of Sherer (App. 7 Dist., 01-22-1997) 116 Ohio App.3d 345, 688 N.E.2d 46. Taxation ⇔ 3344

Where gifts are made by a donor prior to death, and such gifts are included in the donor's estate for Ohio estate tax purposes, the inter vivos donees are generally subject to apportionment of the tax under RC 2113.86 unless they are exempted by action of RC 2113.88. In re Estate of Finke (Ohio 1987) 31 Ohio St.3d 1, 508 N.E.2d 158, 31 O.B.R. 1. Taxation ⇔ 3370

Ohio estate taxes are first charged to residuary estate; only if tax apportioned to residuary portion exceeds value of residue is there apportionment among specific and other nonresiduary bequests. Boerstler v. Andrews (Hamilton 1986) 30 Ohio App.3d 63, 506 N.E.2d 279, 30 O.B.R. 118. Taxation ⇔ 3344

4. Surviving spouse

The interest of a surviving spouse electing to take against the will under RC 2107.39 is determined after deducting federal estate taxes from the estate, notwithstanding RC 2113.88, which exempts from apportionment of federal taxes only the share of a spouse whose interest is created by the will, as indicated by use of the words "legatee, devisee, or donee." In re Estate of McVicker (Ohio Com.Pl. 1985) 23 Ohio Misc.2d 43, 492 N.E.2d 491, 23 O.B.R. 437.

2113.861 Apportionment of generation-skipping transfer tax

Except as provided in section 5815.27 of the Revised Code, the generation-skipping transfer tax imposed by Chapter 13 of subtitle B of the Internal Revenue Code of 1986, 100 Stat. 2718, 26 U.S.C. 2601–2624, as amended, and the generation-skipping tax levied by division (B) of section 5731.181 of the Revised Code shall be apportioned in the manner described in section 2113.86 of the Revised Code.

(2006 H 416, eff. 1–1–07; 1990 H 286, eff. 11–8–90; 1986 H 139)

Uncodified Law

1990 H 286, § 3, eff. 11–8–90, reads: Sections 1 and 2 of this act apply only to the estates of decedents who die on or after the effective date of this act.

1986 H 139, § 3 and 6, eff. 7–24–86, read, in part:

Section 3. Except as provided in Sections... 6 of this act..., Sections 1 and 2 of this act shall apply only to the estates of decedents whose death occurs on or after the effective date of this act.

Section 6. The amendments made to division (C) of section 2107.39 and to former sections 2113.86 and 2113.87 of the Revised Code as they existed prior to the effective date of this act, the enactment of new section 2113.86 except for its division (I), and the enactment of section 2113.861 of the Revised Code, by Section 1 of this act, are clarifying amendments or enactments and generally are declaratory of the law of this state prior to the effective date of this act. The provisions of new section 2113.86 and section 2113.861 of the Revised Code as enacted by Section 1 of this act, the provisions of division (C) of section 2107.39 of the Revised Code as amended by Section 1 of this act, and the provisions of former sections 2113.86 and 2113.87 of the Revised Code as amended by Section 1 of this act, shall apply to the estates of decedents who died on or after March 23, 1981.

Historical and Statutory Notes

Ed. Note: 2113.861 contains provisions analogous to former 2113.91 repealed by 1986 H 139, eff. 7–24–86.

Amendment Note: 2006 H 416 substituted "5815.27" for "1339.45".

Cross References

Wills, election by surviving spouse, net estate determined before taxes paid, 2106.01

Library References

Internal Revenue ⇔4818 to 4820.

Taxation ⚖︎903.
Westlaw Topic Nos. 220, 371.
C.J.S. Internal Revenue §§ 497, 723 to 724.
C.J.S. Social Security and Public Welfare § 203.
C.J.S. Taxation § 1976.

Baldwin's Ohio Legislative Service Annotated, 2006 H 416 LSC Analysis, p 3/L-1709

Research References

Encyclopedias

OH Jur. 3d Taxation § 977, Introduction.
OH Jur. 3d Taxation § 989, Apportionment of Generation-Skipping Transfer Tax.

Treatises and Practice Aids

Carlin, Baldwin's Ohio Practice, Merrick-Rippner Probate Law § 2:38, Elective Rights of Surviving Spouse—Election to Take Under Law or Under the Will—Elective Share of Surviving Spouse Against the Will.

Carlin, Baldwin's Ohio Practice, Merrick-Rippner Probate Law § 21:5, Rights of Surviving Spouse to Make Election—Statutory Provisions—Effect.

Carlin, Baldwin's Ohio Practice, Merrick-Rippner Probate Law § 48:8, Property Liable for Payment of Debts—Personal Property—Effect of Spousal Election.

Carlin, Baldwin's Ohio Practice, Merrick-Rippner Probate Law § 21:24, Rights of Surviving Spouse to Make Election—Effect of Taxes on Election.

Carlin, Baldwin's Ohio Practice, Merrick-Rippner Probate Law § 89:17, Payment of Debts—Allowance for Support of Surviving Spouse and Minor Children—Preference Under Federal Law.

Carlin, Baldwin's Ohio Practice, Merrick-Rippner Probate Law § 110:14, Generation-Skipping Transfer Tax, Effect on Apportionment.

Carlin, Baldwin's Ohio Practice, Merrick-Rippner Probate Law § 111:19, Federal Estate Tax—Liability of Fiduciary for Payment.

Law Review and Journal Commentaries

Estate Planning and the Generation-Skipping Transfer Tax, Harold G. Wren. 32 Case W Res L Rev 105 (Fall 1981).

2113.87 Objections to apportionment of taxes; determination by probate court; notice

(A) The fiduciary, or any person interested in the estate who objects to the manner of apportionment of a tax, may apply to the court that has jurisdiction of the estate and request the court to determine the apportionment of the tax. If there are no probate proceedings, the probate court of the county in which the decedent was domiciled at death, upon application by the fiduciary or any other person interested in the estate who objects to the manner of apportionment of a tax, shall determine the apportionment of the tax.

(B) The fiduciary may notify any person interested in the estate of the manner of the apportionment of tax determined by the fiduciary. Upon receipt of such a notice, a person interested in the estate, within thirty days after the date of receipt of the notice, may indicate his objection to the manner of apportionment by application to a probate court as described in division (A) of this section. If the person interested in the estate fails to make the application within the thirty-day period, he is bound by the manner of apportionment determined by the fiduciary.

(C) If a probate court finds that an assessment of penalties and interest assessed with respect to a tax is due to delay caused by the negligence of the fiduciary, the court may charge the fiduciary with the amount of the assessed penalties and interest. In any suit or judicial proceeding to recover from any person interested in the estate the amount of the tax apportioned to that person, the determination of the probate court is conclusive.

(1986 H 139, eff. 7–24–86)

Uncodified Law

1986 H 139, § 3 and 6, eff. 7–24–86, read, in part:

Section 3. Except as provided in Sections... 6 of this act..., Sections 1 and 2 of this act shall apply only to the estates of decedents whose death occurs on or after the effective date of this act.

Section 6. The amendments made to division (C) of section 2107.39 and to former sections 2113.86 and 2113.87 of the Revised Code as they existed prior to the effective date of this act, the enactment of new section 2113.86 except for its division (I), and the enactment of section 2113.861 of the Revised Code, by Section 1 of this act, are clarifying amendments or enactments and generally are declaratory of the law of this state prior to the effective date of this act. The provisions of new section 2113.86 and section 2113.861 of the Revised Code as enacted by Section 1 of this act, the provisions of division (C) of section 2107.39 of the Revised Code as amended by Section 1 of this act, and the provisions of former sections 2113.86 and 2113.87 of the Revised Code as amended by Section 1 of this act, shall apply to the estates of decedents who died on or after March 23, 1981.

Historical and Statutory Notes

Ed. Note: 2113.87 is former 2113.86 amended and recodified by 1986 H 139, eff. 7–24–86; 1980 S 317.

Ed. Note: Former 2113.87 recodified as 2113.88 by 1986 H 139, eff. 7–24–86; 1980 S 317.

Library References

Internal Revenue ⚖︎4818 to 4820.
Taxation ⚖︎903.
Westlaw Topic Nos. 220, 371.
C.J.S. Internal Revenue §§ 497, 723 to 724.
C.J.S. Social Security and Public Welfare § 203.
C.J.S. Taxation § 1976.

Research References

Encyclopedias

OH Jur. 3d Taxation § 990, Objections to Apportionment.
OH Jur. 3d Taxation § 991, Objections to Apportionment—Notice by Fiduciary; Time for Filing Objections.
OH Jur. 3d Taxation § 993, Suits by Fiduciaries.
OH Jur. 3d Taxation § 995, Liability of Fiduciary for Negligence.

Treatises and Practice Aids

Carlin, Baldwin's Ohio Practice, Merrick-Rippner Probate Law § 30:29, Drafting a Will—Clauses to Discourage a Will Contest Action—in Terrorem Clause.

Carlin, Baldwin's Ohio Practice, Merrick-Rippner Probate Law § 110:15, Notice of Apportionment.

Carlin, Baldwin's Ohio Practice, Merrick-Rippner Probate Law § 110:16, Objection to Apportionment and Determination of Apportionment by Probate Court.

Carlin, Baldwin's Ohio Practice, Merrick-Rippner Probate Law § 110:17, Penalties and Interest Charged Against Fiduciary.

Notes of Decisions

Ed. Note: This section contains annotations from former RC 2113.86.

Intent of testator 3
Priority for apportionment 1
Time limit for objections 2

---

1. Priority for apportionment

RC 2113.88, read together with RC 2113.86(B), provides the following priority for apportionment of estate tax against classes of beneficiaries: (1) nonexempt residuary beneficiaries, (2) exempt residuary beneficiaries, (3) nonexempt specific or general beneficiaries, and (4) exempt specific or general beneficiaries. Matter of Estate of Widener (Franklin 1986) 31 O.B.R. 304.

Statute governing apportionment of tax against estate does not require fiduciary to notify persons interested in estate of manner in which taxes are to be apportioned; rather, notification is at the discretion of the fiduciary.

Burkholder v. Haller (Ohio App. 10 Dist., 06-02-1998) 127 Ohio App.3d 618, 713 N.E.2d 523. Internal Revenue ⇐ 4821; Taxation ⇐ 3344

Beneficiary of estate was bound by apportionment of estate tax made by fiduciary, where beneficiary never filed objection regarding manner of apportionment with probate court, and did not request that probate court apportion taxes, even though beneficiary informally complained about apportionment, and may even have filed objection with fiduciary. Burkholder v. Haller (Ohio App. 10 Dist., 06-02-1998) 127 Ohio App.3d 618, 713 N.E.2d 523. Internal Revenue ⇐ 4821; Taxation ⇐ 3367

Estate taxes are first charged to the residuary estate under RC 2113.86 prior to amendment by 1986 H 139, eff. 7–24–86. If and only if the tax apportioned to the residuary portion exceeds the value of the residue, there is an apportionment among the specific and other nonresiduary bequests. Boerstler v. Andrews (Hamilton 1986) 30 Ohio App.3d 63, 506 N.E.2d 279, 30 O.B.R. 118. Taxation ⇐ 3344

2. Time limit for objections

Hearing was not required in connection with fiduciary's apportionment of taxes on estate where beneficiary of estate failed to make objection to apportionment as required by statute. Burkholder v. Haller (Ohio App. 10 Dist., 06-02-1998) 127 Ohio App.3d 618, 713 N.E.2d 523. Internal Revenue ⇐ 4821; Taxation ⇐ 3367

The statutory time limit for objections to tax apportionment does not apply where the testator has directed that all taxes be paid from the principal of the estate, and not apportioned as provided by RC 2113.86. Evans v Robe, No. 1165 (4th Dist Ct App, Athens, 8–31–84).

3. Intent of testator

Where testator died before the effective date of RC 2113.86, the trial court erred in ordering that estate taxes be paid both from general legacies and specific legacies absent the testator's instructions that estate taxes should be paid from specific legacies. Baldauf v St. John the Baptist Church, No. 1–82–53 (3d Dist Ct App, Allen, 3–28–83).

2113.88 Withholding taxes from distribution; bond where property distributed prior to final tax apportionment

(A) The fiduciary may withhold from any property distributable to any person interested in the estate the amount of tax attributable to the person's interest. If the property in possession of the fiduciary and distributable to any person interested in the estate is insufficient to satisfy the proportionate amount of the tax determined to be due from that person, the fiduciary may recover the deficiency from that person. If the property is not in the possession of the fiduciary, the fiduciary may recover from any person interested in the estate the amount of the tax apportioned to that person in accordance with this section.

(B) If the property held by the fiduciary is distributed prior to final apportionment of the tax, the distributee shall provide a bond or other security for the apportionment liability in the form and amount prescribed by the fiduciary, with the approval of the probate court that has jurisdiction of the administration of the estate.

(1986 H 139, eff. 7–24–86)

Uncodified Law

1986 H 139, § 3 and 6, eff. 7–24–86, read, in part:

Section 3. Except as provided in Sections... 6 of this act..., Sections 1 and 2 of this act shall apply only to the estates of decedents whose death occurs on or after the effective date of this act.

Section 6. The amendments made to division (C) of section 2107.39 and to former sections 2113.86 and 2113.87 of the Revised Code as they existed prior to the effective date of this act, the enactment of new section 2113.86 except for its division (I), and the enactment of section 2113.861 of the Revised Code, by Section 1 of this act, are clarifying amendments or enactments and generally are declaratory of the law of this state prior to the effective date of this act. The provisions of new section 2113.86 and section 2113.861 of the Revised Code as enacted by Section 1 of this act, the provisions of division (C) of section 2107.39 of the Revised Code as amended by Section 1 of this act, and the provisions of former sections 2113.86 and 2113.87 of the Revised Code as amended by Section 1 of this act, shall apply to the estates of decedents who died on or after March 23, 1981.

Historical and Statutory Notes

Ed. Note: 2113.88 is former 2113.87 recodified by 1986 H 139, eff. 7–24–86; 1980 S 317.

Ed. Note: Former 2113.88 repealed by 1986 H 139, eff. 7–24–86; 1980 S 317.

Library References

Executors and Administrators ⇐ 316.
Westlaw Topic No. 162.
C.J.S. Executors and Administrators § 557.

Research References

Encyclopedias

OH Jur. 3d Taxation § 992, Collection of Tax by Fiduciary.

Forms

Ohio Forms Legal and Business § 24:52, Recovery by Fiduciary of Taxes.

Treatises and Practice Aids

Carlin, Baldwin's Ohio Practice, Merrick-Rippner Probate Law § 110:4, Tax Not Reapportioned to Federal Tax Deduction Property.

Carlin, Baldwin's Ohio Practice, Merrick-Rippner Probate Law § 110:5, Marital or Charitable Deductions, Exceptions.

Carlin, Baldwin's Ohio Practice, Merrick-Rippner Probate Law § 110:6, Elective Share or Intestate Share of Surviving Spouse.

Carlin, Baldwin's Ohio Practice, Merrick-Rippner Probate Law § 110:18, Withholding Taxes from Distribution and Recovery of Deficiency.

Carlin, Baldwin's Ohio Practice, Merrick-Rippner Probate Law § 110:19, Bond of Distributee.

Notes of Decisions

Ed. Note: This section contains annotations from former RC 2113.88.

Charitable bequests 2
Inter vivos gifts 4
Surviving spouse 3
Tax return 1

1. Tax return

RC 2113.88 applies to all estates, not merely to those large enough to require the filing of a federal estate tax return. Williams v Williams, No. 536 (4th Dist Ct App, Highland, 5–23–84).

2. Charitable bequests

Under will provision that residue, except federal and state estate taxes, should be divided into 100 equal parts and that 36 of those higher parts were to be devised to 18 named charitable institutions and remainder to 18 named individuals, the implication was that charitable bequests not be reduced by any portion of federal estate tax. Wittenberg University v. Waterworth (Hamilton 1984) 13 Ohio App.3d 452, 469 N.E.2d 970, 13 O.B.R. 542. Internal Revenue ⇐ 4824

3. Surviving spouse

When a surviving spouse elects to take against the will of a decedent spouse, federal estate tax is to be apportioned to the estate prior to determining the interest of the surviving spouse. In re Estate of McVicker (Ohio Com.Pl. 1985) 23 Ohio Misc.2d 43, 492 N.E.2d 491, 23 O.B.R. 437. Internal Revenue ⇐ 4821

4. Inter vivos gifts

Where gifts are made by donor prior to death, and such gifts are included in donor's estate for Ohio estate tax purposes, inter vivos donees are generally subject to apportionment of tax unless they are excepted by action of statute inuring credit directly attributable to particular gift to

2113.88 Note 4

benefit of donee. In re Estate of Finke (Ohio 1987) 31 Ohio St.3d 1, 508 N.E.2d 158, 31 O.B.R. 1. Taxation ⇐ 3370

2113.89 Suit by fiduciary to recover tax; three months after determination; uncollectible amounts reapportioned

The fiduciary is not required to institute any suit or proceeding to recover from any person interested in the estate the amount of the tax apportioned to the person until three months after the final determination of the tax. A fiduciary who institutes a suit or proceedings within the three-month period shall not be subject to any liability or surcharge because any portion of the tax apportioned to any person interested in the estate was collectible at a time following the death of the decedent but after that time became uncollectible. If, after making a reasonable attempt to collect the tax, the fiduciary cannot collect from any person interested in the estate the amount of the tax apportioned to that person, the amount not recoverable shall be equitably apportioned among the other persons interested in the estate who are subject to apportionment.

(1980 S 317, eff. 3–23–81)

Library References

Internal Revenue ⇐4818 to 4820.
Taxation ⇐903.
Westlaw Topic Nos. 220, 371.
C.J.S. Internal Revenue §§ 497, 723 to 724.
C.J.S. Social Security and Public Welfare § 203.
C.J.S. Taxation § 1976.

Research References

Encyclopedias

OH Jur. 3d Taxation § 992, Collection of Tax by Fiduciary.
OH Jur. 3d Taxation § 993, Suits by Fiduciaries.

Forms

Ohio Forms Legal and Business § 24:52, Recovery by Fiduciary of Taxes.

Treatises and Practice Aids

Carlin, Baldwin's Ohio Practice, Merrick-Rippner Probate Law § 110:20, Suit by Fiduciary to Recover Tax—Three-Month Period After Determination.

2113.90 When interested nonresidents may sue in this state; reciprocal rights

(A) A fiduciary who is acting in another state or a person required to pay the tax who is domiciled in another state may institute an action in the courts of this state and may recover a proportionate amount of the federal estate tax determined under Subtitle B of the "Internal Revenue Code of 1954," 68 Stat. 373, 26 U.S.C.A. 2001, as amended, of an estate tax payable to another state, or of a death duty by a decedent's estate to another state, from a person interested in the estate who is either domiciled in this state or who owns property in this state subject to attachment or execution. For the purposes of the action brought pursuant to this section, the determination of apportionment by the court that has jurisdiction of the administration of the decedent's estate in the other state shall be prima-facie correct.

(B) This section applies only if either of the following apply:

(1) The other state affords a remedy substantially similar to that afforded in division (A) of this section;

(2) With respect to the federal estate tax, if apportionment is authorized by the congress of the United States.

(1980 S 317, eff. 3–23–81)

Library References

Internal Revenue ⇐4818 to 4821, 4835.
Taxation ⇐888 to 891.5.
Westlaw Topic Nos. 220, 371.
C.J.S. Internal Revenue §§ 497, 723 to 724, 729, 734.
C.J.S. Social Security and Public Welfare § 203.
C.J.S. Taxation §§ 1889 to 1899, 1988.

Research References

Encyclopedias

OH Jur. 3d Taxation § 994, Actions by Nonresident Fiduciaries or Persons Obligated to Pay Tax.

Forms

Ohio Forms Legal and Business § 24:52, Recovery by Fiduciary of Taxes.

Treatises and Practice Aids

Carlin, Baldwin's Ohio Practice, Merrick-Rippner Probate Law § 2:81, Ohio Estate Tax—Determining the Gross Estate—Apportioning the Tax.

Carlin, Baldwin's Ohio Practice, Merrick-Rippner Probate Law § 30:9, Drafting a Will—Payment of Debts, Administration Expenses, and Taxes.

Carlin, Baldwin's Ohio Practice, Merrick-Rippner Probate Law § 110:1, Apportionment Law—Overview.

Carlin, Baldwin's Ohio Practice, Merrick-Rippner Probate Law § 110:22, Suit of Interested Nonresidents.

Carlin, Baldwin's Ohio Practice, Merrick-Rippner Probate Law § 110:23, Reciprocal Rights Where Nonresidents Involved.

Carlin, Baldwin's Ohio Practice, Merrick-Rippner Probate Law § 111:19, Federal Estate Tax—Liability of Fiduciary for Payment.

CHAPTER 2115

EXECUTORS AND ADMINISTRATORS—INVENTORY

GENERAL PROVISIONS

Section	
2115.01	"Inventory" defined
2115.02	Inventory; appraisal
2115.03	Proceedings on refusal to file inventory
2115.04	Notice of inventory
2115.05	Who shall make inventory
2115.06	Appraisers; compensation; fees charged against estate
2115.07	Duties of appraisers
2115.09	Inventory contents
2115.10	Emblements are assets

Section

DISCHARGE OF DEBT

2115.11	Discharge of a debt in a will
2115.12	Naming of person executor does not discharge debt

FILING AND APPROVAL

2115.15	Signing, certifying, and return of inventory
2115.16	Hearing on inventory
2115.17	Real estate appraisal conclusive

Cross References

Order in which debts to be paid, 2117.25
Payment of debts after three months, 2117.15

EXECUTORS AND ADMINISTRATORS—INVENTORY

Powers of guardian of person and estate, 2111.07
Presentation and allowance of creditor's claims, procedure, 2117.06

GENERAL PROVISIONS

2115.01 "Inventory" defined

As used in Chapters 2113. to 2125., inclusive, of the Revised Code, "inventory" includes appraisement.

(1953 H 1, eff. 10–1–53; GC 10509–40)

Historical and Statutory Notes

Pre–1953 H 1 Amendments: 114 v 411

Research References

Encyclopedias

OH Jur. 3d Decedents' Estates § 1257, Form and Contents of Inventory.
OH Jur. 3d Decedents' Estates § 1259, Appraisal; Dispensing With Appraisal.

Treatises and Practice Aids

Carlin, Baldwin's Ohio Practice, Merrick-Rippner Probate Law § 79:1, Inventory—Purpose.

Notes of Decisions

Revision of appraisal 1

1. Revision of appraisal

Under the plenary power conferred upon the probate court incident to the administration of estates it has authority, upon exceptions to an inventory, to revise the appraised value of any security listed in such inventory, but such authority should be exercised after hearing and determined upon the evidence adduced. In re Berman's Estate (Lucas 1963) 118 Ohio App. 354, 194 N.E.2d 794, 25 O.O.2d 226.

Where one who is both administrator and heir procures a low appraisement of the property in order to minimize taxes he can not ask a reappraisal when the widow has elected to take at the appraisal, he being responsible for the thing of which he complains; the inventory includes an appraisement, hence the right to except to the inventory, and to appeal from the ruling includes the right to except to the appraisal and to appeal. Sprankle v. Odell (Ohio Cir. 1907) 33 Ohio C.D. 685, 22 Ohio C.C.(N.S.) 480, affirmed 78 Ohio St. 404, 85 N.E. 1132, 5 Ohio Law Rep. 625.

2115.02 Inventory; appraisal

Within three months after the date of the executor's or administrator's appointment, unless the probate court grants an extension of time for good cause shown, the executor or administrator shall file with the court an inventory of the decedent's interest in real estate located in this state and of the tangible and intangible personal property of the decedent that is to be administered and that has come to the executor's or administrator's possession or knowledge. The inventory shall set forth values as of the date of death of the decedent. If a prior executor or administrator has done so, a successor executor or administrator need not file an inventory, unless, in the opinion of the court, it is necessary.

Any asset, the value of which is readily ascertainable, is not required to be appraised but shall be included in the inventory.

(1996 H 391, eff. 10–1–96; 1992 H 427, eff. 10–8–92; 1988 S 228; 1975 S 145; 1970 S 185; 1953 H 1; GC 10509–41)

Uncodified Law

1988 S 228, § 4, eff. 3–22–89, reads: The amendments to sections 2107.39, 2115.02, and 2117.06 of the Revised Code contained in this act shall apply only with respect to the estates of decedents whose deaths occur on or after the effective date of this act.

Historical and Statutory Notes

Pre–1953 H 1 Amendments: 116 v 385; 114 v 411

Amendment Note: 1996 H 391 rewrote this section, which prior thereto read:

"Within one month after the date of his appointment, unless the probate court grants an extension of time for good cause shown, every executor or administrator shall make and return into court a true inventory of the real estate of the decedent located in this state, and the chattels, moneys, rights, and credits of the decedent that are to be administered and that have come to his possession or knowledge. The inventory is to be based on values as of the date of death of the decedent. If his predecessors have done so, a fiduciary need not return and file an inventory, unless, in the opinion of the court, it is necessary.

"Any asset, the value of which is readily ascertainable without the exercise of judgment on the part of an appraiser, shall not be appraised. The value of these assets shall be shown in the inventory, and the administrator or executor shall provide evidence of value as the court requires."

Legislative Service Commission

1975:

This section now requires the filing of an inventory with appraisal within one month after appointment of an executor or administrator. No appraisal is necessary if there is no spouse or children and the value of the property is less than $500, or its value is readily ascertainable and the court approves. This exception from the general requirement for an appraisal would be repealed.

The bill would provide that an appraisal would not be needed if certain assets have readily ascertainable values. The value of the assets would have to be verified by the administrator or executor. He would be required to prove their value if the court demands it.

Cross References

Bond conditions, administrators, exemption of surviving spouse receiving entire net estate, 2109.07
Bond conditions, executors, 2109.09
Death or incompetence of bank customer, 1304.28
Deceased partner, appraisal of partnership property required, 1779.01, 1779.03
Distribution of assets, provision for rejected claims, liabilities of beneficiary on unsatisfied claims, 2113.53
Fiduciaries, citation to file inventory, 2109.31
Inventory by fiduciary, 2109.58
Newly discovered assets, 2113.69
No allowance to tax inquisitors, 2117.19
Resignation or removal of fiduciary, 2109.24
Responsibility of executor or administrator for chattels, rights, and credits outside the inventory, 2113.31
Sale of personal property, 2113.40
Surviving spouse may purchase property, 2106.16

Library References

Executors and Administrators ⚖62, 68.
Westlaw Topic No. 162.
C.J.S. Executors and Administrators §§ 152, 154, 158.
Baldwin's Ohio Legislative Service, 1988 Laws of Ohio, S 228—LSC Analysis, p 5–968

Research References

Encyclopedias

OH Jur. 3d Agriculture & Crops § 4, Emblements; Ownership of Crops on Land Belonging to Another.
OH Jur. 3d Decedents' Estates § 990, Duties.
OH Jur. 3d Decedents' Estates § 1256, Duty to Make and File Inventory.
OH Jur. 3d Decedents' Estates § 1257, Form and Contents of Inventory.
OH Jur. 3d Decedents' Estates § 1259, Appraisal; Dispensing With Appraisal.
OH Jur. 3d Decedents' Estates § 1263, Time for Hearing on Inventory Filed; Notice.
OH Jur. 3d Decedents' Estates § 1269, Effect of Approval of Inventory.
OH Jur. 3d Decedents' Estates § 1681, Proceedings for Purchase.
OH Jur. 3d Fiduciaries § 302, Failure to File Inventory or Account.

Treatises and Practice Aids

Carlin, Baldwin's Ohio Practice, Merrick-Rippner Probate Law § 2:17, Inventory and Appraisal—Ascertaining Assets.

Carlin, Baldwin's Ohio Practice, Merrick-Rippner Probate Law § 2:18, Inventory and Appraisal—Appraisal of Assets.

Carlin, Baldwin's Ohio Practice, Merrick-Rippner Probate Law § 2:19, Inventory and Appraisal—Listing and Valuation of Probate Assets.

Carlin, Baldwin's Ohio Practice, Merrick-Rippner Probate Law § 2:23, Inventory and Appraisal—Filing of Inventory.

Carlin, Baldwin's Ohio Practice, Merrick-Rippner Probate Law § 57:4, Removal of Fiduciary—Grounds—Failure to File Inventory or Account.

Carlin, Baldwin's Ohio Practice, Merrick-Rippner Probate Law § 79:2, Inventory—Time for Making.

Carlin, Baldwin's Ohio Practice, Merrick-Rippner Probate Law § 79:3, Inventory—Mandatory Requirement of Filing.

Carlin, Baldwin's Ohio Practice, Merrick-Rippner Probate Law § 79:4, Inventory—Enforcement of Filing.

Carlin, Baldwin's Ohio Practice, Merrick-Rippner Probate Law § 79:7, Inventory—Exclusion of Nonprobate Assets.

Carlin, Baldwin's Ohio Practice, Merrick-Rippner Probate Law § 90:9, Authority for Land Sale Action—Overriding Rights of Surviving Spouse.

Carlin, Baldwin's Ohio Practice, Merrick-Rippner Probate Law § 93:1, Ordering Appraisal of Real Property.

Carlin, Baldwin's Ohio Practice, Merrick-Rippner Probate Law § 2:121, Administration of Decedent's Estate—Checklist.

Carlin, Baldwin's Ohio Practice, Merrick-Rippner Probate Law § 2:122, Administration of Decedent's Estate—Release—Checklist.

Carlin, Baldwin's Ohio Practice, Merrick-Rippner Probate Law § 21:64, Rights of Surviving Spouse—Procedure for Purchase—Limitation on Time to Elect.

Carlin, Baldwin's Ohio Practice, Merrick-Rippner Probate Law § 54:10, Fiduciary Accounts—Citation to File Account.

Carlin, Baldwin's Ohio Practice, Merrick-Rippner Probate Law § 79:10, Inventory—Appraisal and Value.

Carlin, Baldwin's Ohio Practice, Merrick-Rippner Probate Law § 79:12, Inventory—When Appraisal Unnecessary.

Carlin, Baldwin's Ohio Practice, Merrick-Rippner Probate Law § 79:26, Inventory—Appeal of Judgment.

Carlin, Baldwin's Ohio Practice, Merrick-Rippner Probate Law § 79:27, Order Authorizing Inventory Without Appraisal—Form.

Carlin, Baldwin's Ohio Practice, Merrick-Rippner Probate Law § 79:28, Inventory Without Appraisal—Form.

Carlin, Baldwin's Ohio Practice, Merrick-Rippner Probate Law § 79:29, Appointment of Appraiser—Form.

Carlin, Baldwin's Ohio Practice, Merrick-Rippner Probate Law § 79:34, Inventory and Appraisal.

Carlin, Baldwin's Ohio Practice, Merrick-Rippner Probate Law App B SPF 6.0, Inventory and Appraisal—Form.

Restatement (2d) of Property, Don. Trans. § 33.1, Meaning of a Will.

Law Review and Journal Commentaries

Avoiding Probate of Decedents' Estates, Gilbert A. Sheard. 36 U Cin L Rev 70 (Winter 1967).

Practical Application of House Bill 85 (Probate Reform 2001), Marilyn J. Maag. 13 Prob L J Ohio 19 (November/December 2002).

Substitute House Bill 391—Omnibus Probate Bill, William B. McNeil. 7 Prob L J Ohio 2 (September/October 1996).

Notes of Decisions

Assets 7
Automobile 5
Gifts 6
Joint and survivorship accounts 4
Procedural issues 3
Rents 2
Surviving spouse 1

1. Surviving spouse

Parcels of land are properly conveyed as joint property with a right of survivorship and are not the sole property of the decedent nor included in his estate, since it passes to his surviving spouse by operation of law. In re Estate of Ault (Fayette 1992) 80 Ohio App.3d 399, 609 N.E.2d 568.

When devisees, other than the surviving spouse, have added substantial value to the mansion house after the appraisement, the surviving spouse is not entitled to purchase the property at the appraisement price. Wobser v. Tanner (Ohio 1979) 60 Ohio St.2d 28, 396 N.E.2d 753, 14 O.O.3d 195.

Where, in the administration of an estate, a motion to vacate and set aside an order previously entered approving and confirming an inventory filed therein is timely filed by the surviving spouse although not within one month after such order approving such inventory, and is subsequently found to be well taken and an order is thereupon entered that such previously approved inventory be modified by the deletion therefrom of certain personal property and by increasing the amount of the widow's year's allowance, such order of modification does not constitute a vacation of the previous order of approval so as to reinstate in such surviving spouse the right of election to purchase the mansion house for the one-month period from the date of such order of modification. In re Hrabnicky's Estate (Ohio 1958) 167 Ohio St. 507, 149 N.E.2d 909, 5 O.O.2d 181. Executors And Administrators 67; Executors And Administrators 191

2. Rents

Rents are not apportionable between the administrator of a tenant for life and the remainderman where the estate of the latter becomes an estate in possession immediately on the death of the life tenant and puts an end to the lease made by him. Noble v. Tyler (Ohio 1900) 61 Ohio St. 432, 43 W.L.B. 127, 56 N.E. 191.

As between the executor of the owner of a fee and a devisee, the devisee is entitled to all rents becoming due after the death of the testatrix. Dye v. Dimick (Ohio Com.Pl. 1897) 6 Ohio Dec. 231, 4 Ohio N.P. 185.

Where a tenant for life rented to another to raise a crop of corn and died in July and the crop was gathered and the renter paid the rent to the executor of the life tenant, the tenant in reversion cannot prevail in a suit to recover a share of the rent. Van Hayes v West, 3 CC 64, 2 CD 37 (Hamilton 1888).

3. Procedural issues

Res judicata did not prevent decedent's daughter from challenging the exclusion of the family Bible from the inventory of decedent's estate, although she did not raise the issue at the time the probate court approved the inventory of the estate; title to the family Bible was disputed, issue of whether the family Bible was properly an asset of the estate had never been raised, litigated, or determined, and, as trial court had determined that son's gifting of the family Bible to his own child was invalid, the Bible had the status of a concealed asset of the estate such that there was no time limit on the filing of exceptions to the exclusion of that asset from the estate. In re Estate of Kelsey (Ohio App. 11 Dist., 03-10-2006) 165 Ohio App.3d 680, 847 N.E.2d 1277, 2006-Ohio-1171. Executors And Administrators 72

An administratrix may not be deprived of the compensation due to her for her services for mere delay in making and returning the inventory of the estate, when she has not been given an order requiring her, at an early day therein named, to return same, or has not been notified by the court of the expiration of the time to file such inventory. In re Burchett's Estate (Marion 1968) 16 Ohio App.2d 45, 241 N.E.2d 787, 45 O.O.2d 133. Executors And Administrators 500

Where an executor conveys property of the estate to himself as legatee less than one month after the approval of the inventory, a creditor of the executor may cause the estate to obtain judgment against such executor for such amount so improperly distributed. In re Walden's Estate (Ohio Prob. 1965) 6 Ohio Misc. 214, 214 N.E.2d 271, 34 O.O.2d 149.

No law requires or authorizes the filing with the probate court of an application by an administrator to determine the nature of a claim allegedly due an estate and to determine whether such amount should be included as an asset of such estate upon the filing of an amended inventory and appraisement; nor is there any law authorizing any order based upon such an application, unless such application can be construed as a petition for a declaratory judgment, which it cannot be where the application is not adversary in character, where there is no party plaintiff or party defendant, and where the facts set forth do not allege any justiciable controversy. In re Uhl's Estate (Marion 1954) 98 Ohio App. 145, 128 N.E.2d 142, 57 O.O. 212.

4. Joint and survivorship accounts

At the death of one of the owners of a joint and survivorship bank account, it is not property of the deceased such as should be included in the inventory filed in his estate under RC 2115.02. In re Cecere's Estate (Ohio Prob. 1968) 17 Ohio Misc. 101, 242 N.E.2d 701, 46 O.O.2d 134.

Where the debts of an estate, including the year's allowance and exempt property allowance, exceed the assets in the estate as of the date of death, only so much may be deducted as does not exceed such assets, and joint bank accounts may not be included in the estate for computing such deductions. In re Williams' Estate (Ohio Prob. 1956) 138 N.E.2d 189, 73 Ohio Law Abs. 441.

Where a joint survivorship bank account was by a decedent created with the understanding that the funds would be used only to pay decedent's bills, and that if any money were left in the account at the time of decedent's death, the joint owner would be entitled to the money, such account is an asset of the decedent's estate and must be included in the inventory. In re Estate of Celinski, Nos. 47198 and 47206 (8th Dist Ct App, Cuyahoga, 3–22–84).

5. Automobile

Where the value of a car included in decedent's estate is determined arbitrarily to be $2,500 by the fiduciary and the basis for such determination was that two hundred ($200) dollars was paid for the car and the fiduciary and the decedent had worked on the car putting over $2,000 in it, the trial court erred in accepting such value. In re Estate of Drake, No. 9–82–29 (3d Dist Ct App, Marion, 9–26–83).

6. Gifts

In submitting estate inventory to probate court, executor was required to collect and account for all assets of testator's estate, including those items of personal property that were distributed to various family members prior to executor's appointment, even if prior distribution was fair to all parties. In re Estate of Ewing (Ohio App. 3 Dist., Hancock, 09-08-2003) No. 5-03-03, 2003-Ohio-4734, 2003 WL 22071471, Unreported. Executors And Administrators ☞ 66; Executors And Administrators ☞ 86(2)

Res judicata did not prevent decedent's daughter from challenging the exclusion of the family Bible from the inventory of decedent's estate, although she did not raise the issue at the time the probate court approved the inventory of the estate; title to the family Bible was disputed, issue of whether the family Bible was properly an asset of the estate had never been raised, litigated, or determined, and, as trial court had determined that son's gifting of the family Bible to his own child was invalid, the Bible had the status of a concealed asset of the estate such that there was no time limit on the filing of exceptions to the exclusion of that asset from the estate. In re Estate of Kelsey (Ohio App. 11 Dist., 03-10-2006) 165 Ohio App.3d 680, 847 N.E.2d 1277, 2006-Ohio-1171. Executors And Administrators ☞ 72

Language in settlement agreement which provided that decedent's son and daughter "fully and finally" released each other "from any and all claims" regarding the decedent's estate did not bar daughter's claim to family Bible which son had gifted to his own daughter, although title to the Bible was disputed; provision conflicted with another provision of the agreement providing that both parties may make claims to particular items of personal property and that the administrator should sell property that is claimed by both parties, no approved inventory of the estate and no itemized appraisal of decedent's personal property had been filed with the probate court at the time the parties entered into the agreement, and the agreement did not purport to define the personal property that belonged to the estate. In re Estate of Kelsey (Ohio App. 11 Dist., 03-10-2006) 165 Ohio App.3d 680, 847 N.E.2d 1277, 2006-Ohio-1171.

Presumption of undue influence in transactions involving fiduciaries, rather than family gift presumption, applied to transfer of family Bible by decedent's son, who had power of attorney, to his own daughter while decedent was still alive, although daughter was not in a fiduciary relationship to the decedent; power of attorney did not grant son authority to make gifts on decedent's behalf. In re Estate of Kelsey (Ohio App. 11 Dist., 03-10-2006) 165 Ohio App.3d 680, 847 N.E.2d 1277, 2006-Ohio-1171. Principal And Agent ☞ 79(5)

Where a decedent left a noninterest bearing note and mortgage with his lawyer for delivery upon his order or death to the makers thereof, but reserved to himself the right to receive the principal thereon at a fixed monthly rate until his death, there was no gift thereof and hence such note was properly included as an asset of decedent's estate. In re Gardner's Estate (Ohio Prob. 1959) 162 N.E.2d 579, 82 Ohio Law Abs. 185.

Where the beneficiary of a will files an exception to the inventory contending that certain items of personal property are missing, the trial court's finding that such items were given away by the testatrix before her death is proper if supported by some competent and credible evidence. In re Estate of Stein, No. CA 8100 (2d Dist Ct App, Montgomery, 6–23–83).

7. Assets

Materials prepared for a building are personal and not real assets. Gray v. Hawkins's Adm'rx (Ohio 1858) 8 Ohio St. 449, 72 Am.Dec. 600.

In deciding beneficiaries' motion to remove executor, evidence supported trial court's finding that inventory of estate was not flawed; evidence indicated that testator had given bank saw and drill press to grandson before death, microwave had been thrown away before testator died, executor took nothing out of house after testator died, and inventory was amended to include additional cash. In re Estate of Shaw (Ohio App. 2 Dist., Greene, 09-09-2005) No. 2004 CA 111, 2005-Ohio-4743, 2005 WL 2179300, Unreported. Executors And Administrators ☞ 35(15)

Probate court's conclusion that family Bible was not an asset of the decedent's estate for the purpose of inventorying the estate did not divest the court of jurisdiction to determine title to the Bible, as conclusion was based on the fact that the Bible was not in the decedent's possession and that there had been an attempted transfer of title, and dispute existed regarding title. In re Estate of Kelsey (Ohio App. 11 Dist., 03-10-2006) 165 Ohio App.3d 680, 847 N.E.2d 1277, 2006-Ohio-1171. Executors And Administrators ☞ 72

Where judgment ordered that certain property be included in inventory of estate, judgment would affect executor personally and in his representative capacity, if his allegation that property could not be located were true, and executor was proper party to appeal within statute permitting appeal from judgments of probate court by person whom it affects. In re Byerly's Estate (Madison 1956) 141 N.E.2d 771, 74 Ohio Law Abs. 586. Executors And Administrators ☞ 65

2115.03 Proceedings on refusal to file inventory

If an executor or administrator neglects or refuses to return an inventory as provided by section 2115.02 of the Revised Code, the probate court shall issue an order requiring him, at an early day specified in the order, to return an inventory. After personal service of the order by a person authorized to make the service, if the executor or administrator, by the day appointed, does not return the inventory or fails to obtain further time from the court to return it, or if the order cannot be served personally by reason of his absconding or concealing himself, the court may remove the executor or administrator and new letters shall be granted. The letters shall supersede all former letters testamentary or of administration, deprive the former executor or administrator of all power, authority, or control over the estate of the deceased, and entitle the person appointed to take, demand, and receive the effects of the deceased wherever they are found.

In every case of the revocation of letters under this section, the bond given by the former executor or administrator shall be prosecuted and a recovery had on the bond to the full extent of any injury sustained by the estate of the deceased by the former executor's or administrator's acts or omissions, and to the full value of all the property of the deceased received and not administered by him.

(1992 H 427, eff. 10–8–92; 1953 H 1; GC 10509–62 to 10509–65)

Historical and Statutory Notes

Pre–1953 H 1 Amendments: 114 v 415, 416

Cross References

Bond, parties to suit, 2109.61

Library References

Executors and Administrators ⚖︎65, 73.
Westlaw Topic No. 162.
C.J.S. Executors and Administrators §§ 158, 162.

Research References

Encyclopedias

OH Jur. 3d Decedents' Estates § 962, Removal from Office or Revocation of Letters.
OH Jur. 3d Decedents' Estates § 983, Appointment.
OH Jur. 3d Decedents' Estates § 989, Rights and Powers—Right to Possession of Estate Assets.
OH Jur. 3d Decedents' Estates § 990, Duties.
OH Jur. 3d Decedents' Estates § 1262, Proceedings to Compel Filing.
OH Jur. 3d Decedents' Estates § 1759, Action to Recover and Preserve Assets—Action by Administrator De Bonis Non.
OH Jur. 3d Fiduciaries § 302, Failure to File Inventory or Account.

Treatises and Practice Aids

Carlin, Baldwin's Ohio Practice, Merrick-Rippner Probate Law § 81:1, Removal—Statutory Provisions.
Carlin, Baldwin's Ohio Practice, Merrick-Rippner Probate Law § 81:5, Motion for Removal of Executor or Administrator—Forms.
Carlin, Baldwin's Ohio Practice, Merrick-Rippner Probate Law § 79:38, Application for Citation to File Inventory—Form.
Carlin, Baldwin's Ohio Practice, Merrick-Rippner Probate Law § 79:39, Entry to Issue Citation—Form.
Carlin, Baldwin's Ohio Practice, Merrick-Rippner Probate Law § 79:40, Citation—Form.
Carlin, Baldwin's Ohio Practice, Merrick-Rippner Probate Law § 79:41, Entry for Removal of Fiduciary—Form.

Notes of Decisions

Compensation 1
Time limits 2

---

1. Compensation

An administratrix may not be deprived of the compensation due to her for her services for mere delay in making and returning the inventory of the estate, when she has not been given an order requiring her, at an early day therein named, to return same, or has not been notified by the court of the expiration of the time to file such inventory. In re Burchett's Estate (Marion 1968) 16 Ohio App.2d 45, 241 N.E.2d 787, 45 O.O.2d 133. Executors And Administrators ⚖︎ 500

2. Time limits

A motion for citation and attachment proceedings against an administrator will lie under RS 6178 and RS 6040 until more than ten years have elapsed from the date of hearing of the last account filed by such administrator. Gilbert v. Marsh (Ohio Prob. 1897) 7 Ohio Dec. 230, 4 Ohio N.P. 338. Executors And Administrators ⚖︎ 470

2115.04 Notice of inventory

Not less than five days previous thereto, a written notice stating the time and place of making the inventory required by section 2115.02 of the Revised Code, must be served by the executor or administrator on the surviving spouse, but such notice may be waived in writing by such surviving spouse.

(1953 H 1, eff. 10–1–53; GC 10509–45)

Historical and Statutory Notes

Pre–1953 H 1 Amendments: 114 v 412

Library References

Executors and Administrators ⚖︎62.
Westlaw Topic No. 162.
C.J.S. Executors and Administrators §§ 152, 158.

Research References

Encyclopedias

OH Jur. 3d Decedents' Estates § 1255, Notice of Making Inventory.

Treatises and Practice Aids

Carlin, Baldwin's Ohio Practice, Merrick-Rippner Probate Law § 2:20, Inventory and Appraisal—Notice of Inventory.
Carlin, Baldwin's Ohio Practice, Merrick-Rippner Probate Law § 2:121, Administration of Decedent's Estate—Checklist.
Carlin, Baldwin's Ohio Practice, Merrick-Rippner Probate Law § 79:13, Inventory—Notice.
Carlin, Baldwin's Ohio Practice, Merrick-Rippner Probate Law App B SPF 6.0, Inventory and Appraisal—Form.

2115.05 Who shall make inventory

After giving the notice required in section 2115.04 of the Revised Code, the executor or administrator, with the aid of the appraiser, if an appraisement is to be made, shall make the inventory required by section 2115.02 of the Revised Code.

(1970 S 185, eff. 1–1–71; 1953 H 1; GC 10509–44)

Historical and Statutory Notes

Pre–1953 H 1 Amendments: 114 v 412

Library References

Executors and Administrators ⚖︎62 to 73.
Westlaw Topic No. 162.
C.J.S. Executors and Administrators §§ 152 to 162.

Research References

Encyclopedias

OH Jur. 3d Decedents' Estates § 1256, Duty to Make and File Inventory.

2115.06 Appraisers; compensation; fees charged against estate

The real estate and personal property comprised in the inventory required by section 2115.02 of the Revised Code, unless an appraisement thereof has been dispensed with by an order of the probate court, shall be appraised by one suitable disinterested person appointed by the executor or administrator, subject to the approval of the court and sworn to a faithful discharge of his trust. The executor or administrator, subject to the approval of the court, may appoint separate appraisers of property located in any other county and appoint separate appraisers for each asset.

If appraisers fail to attend to the performance of their duty, the executor or administrator, subject to the approval of the probate judge may appoint others to supply the place of such delinquents.

Each appraiser shall be paid such amount for his services as determined by the executor or administrator, subject to the approval of the probate judge, taking into consideration his training, qualifications, experience, time reasonably required, and the value of the property appraised. The amount of such fees may be charged against the estate as part of the cost of the proceeding.

(1976 S 466, eff. 5–26–76; 1975 S 145; 1970 S 185; 125 v 52; 1953 H 1; GC 10509–42, 10509–43, 10509–58)

Historical and Statutory Notes

Pre–1953 H 1 Amendments: 114 v 412, 415

Cross References

Property with value readily ascertainable without appraisal, 2115.02

Release from administration, form of application, 2113.03

Library References

Executors and Administrators ⚖︎67, 109(3).
Westlaw Topic No. 162.
C.J.S. Executors and Administrators §§ 157, 237 to 239, 241, 243, 245 to 247, 249 to 250.

Research References

Encyclopedias

OH Jur. 3d Decedents' Estates § 1259, Appraisal; Dispensing With Appraisal.

Treatises and Practice Aids

Carlin, Baldwin's Ohio Practice, Merrick-Rippner Probate Law § 2:18, Inventory and Appraisal—Appraisal of Assets.

Carlin, Baldwin's Ohio Practice, Merrick-Rippner Probate Law § 93:2, Appraisers—Appointment, Compensation, Removal.

Carlin, Baldwin's Ohio Practice, Merrick-Rippner Probate Law § 2:109, Release from Administration—Appraisal of Property.

Carlin, Baldwin's Ohio Practice, Merrick-Rippner Probate Law § 2:121, Administration of Decedent's Estate—Checklist.

Carlin, Baldwin's Ohio Practice, Merrick-Rippner Probate Law § 68:29, Application to Relieve Estate from Administration—Form.

Carlin, Baldwin's Ohio Practice, Merrick-Rippner Probate Law § 68:42, Application for Authority to Administer Estate—Form.

Carlin, Baldwin's Ohio Practice, Merrick-Rippner Probate Law § 79:11, Inventory—Appraisal and Value—Appraisers.

Carlin, Baldwin's Ohio Practice, Merrick-Rippner Probate Law § 79:30, Appointment of Appraiser to Fill Vacancy—Form.

Carlin, Baldwin's Ohio Practice, Merrick-Rippner Probate Law § 79:31, Appointment of Special Appraiser—Form.

Carlin, Baldwin's Ohio Practice, Merrick-Rippner Probate Law § 79:32, Appointment of Appraiser for Out-Of-County Property—Form.

Carlin, Baldwin's Ohio Practice, Merrick-Rippner Probate Law § 97:15, Land Sale by Guardian—Appraisal of Property to be Sold.

Notes of Decisions

Approval of court 1
Notice 2

---

1. Approval of court

A writ of mandamus will not be issued at the request of an appraiser to compel a probate court to approve the appraiser as selected by a fiduciary, even where no objections are raised as to the qualifications of the appraiser. State ex rel. Matasy v. Morley (Ohio 1986) 25 Ohio St.3d 22, 494 N.E.2d 1146, 25 O.B.R. 18.

Probate court, at hearing on exceptions to inventory of decedent's estate, was not empowered to impress constructive trust upon savings bonds, which had been issued in names of decedent and one of her relatives as co-owners, on ground that decedent fraudulently used her husband's funds to purchase the bonds. In re Estate of Etzensperger (Ohio 1984) 9 Ohio St.3d 19, 457 N.E.2d 1161, 9 O.B.R. 112. Executors And Administrators ⚖︎ 85(8)

2. Notice

An executor or administrator should be given notice of proceedings to appoint new appraisers, and of the act of such appraisers in making an allowance to the widow for a year's support, such allowance not having been made by the original appraisers. Heck v. Heck (Ohio 1878) 34 Ohio St. 369, 3 W.L.B. 363.

2115.07 Duties of appraisers

Before proceeding to the execution of their duties, the appraisers of a decedent's estate shall agree that they will truly, honestly, and impartially appraise the estate and property exhibited to them and perform the other duties required in the premises according to the best of their knowledge and ability.

In the presence of the surviving spouse, next of kin, legatees, devisees, or creditors of the testator or intestate, or such of them as attend, the appraisers of a decedent's estate shall proceed to estimate and appraise the property and estate. Each item shall be set down separately, with its value in dollars and cents in distinct figures opposite that item.

(1992 H 427, eff. 10–8–92; 1953 H 1; GC 10509–46, 10509–47)

Historical and Statutory Notes

Pre–1953 H 1 Amendments: 114 v 412

Library References

Executors and Administrators ⚖︎67.
Westlaw Topic No. 162.
C.J.S. Executors and Administrators § 157.

Research References

Encyclopedias

OH Jur. 3d Decedents' Estates § 1257, Form and Contents of Inventory.
OH Jur. 3d Decedents' Estates § 1259, Appraisal; Dispensing With Appraisal.

Treatises and Practice Aids

Carlin, Baldwin's Ohio Practice, Merrick-Rippner Probate Law § 2:20, Inventory and Appraisal—Notice of Inventory.

Carlin, Baldwin's Ohio Practice, Merrick-Rippner Probate Law § 79:5, Inventory—Contents—"Each Item" Listed Separately.

Carlin, Baldwin's Ohio Practice, Merrick-Rippner Probate Law § 2:121, Administration of Decedent's Estate—Checklist.

Carlin, Baldwin's Ohio Practice, Merrick-Rippner Probate Law § 79:33, Oath of Appraiser—Form.

Carlin, Baldwin's Ohio Practice, Merrick-Rippner Probate Law App B SPF 5.1, Assets and Liabilities of Estate to be Relieved from Administration—Form.

Notes of Decisions

Revision of appraisal 1
Separate items 2

---

1. Revision of appraisal

Under the plenary power conferred upon the probate court incident to the administration of estates it has authority, upon exceptions to an inventory, to revise the appraised value of any security listed in such inventory, but such authority should be exercised after hearing and determined upon the evidence adduced. In re Berman's Estate (Lucas 1963) 118 Ohio App. 354, 194 N.E.2d 794, 25 O.O.2d 226.

2. Separate items

Requirement of section, providing that in inventory of estate property "each article or item must be set down separately" with its value, is mandatory and neither appraisers nor probate court has discretion to group articles in one general classification. In re McConney's Estate (Huron 1942) 72 Ohio App. 286, 51 N.E.2d 239, 27 O.O. 121.

2115.09 Inventory contents

The inventory required by section 2115.02 of the Revised Code shall contain a particular statement of all securities for the payment of money that belong to the deceased and are known to the executor or administrator. Such inventory shall specify the name of the debtor in each security, the date, the sum originally payable, the indorsements thereon with their dates, the serial numbers or other identifying data as to each security, and the sum that, in the judgment of the appraisers, can be collected on each claim.

Such inventory shall contain a statement of all debts and accounts belonging to the deceased that are known to such executor or administrator and specify the name of the debtor, the date, the balance or thing due, and the value or sum that can be collected thereon, in the judgment of the appraisers.

Such inventory shall contain an account of all moneys that belong to the deceased and have come to the hands of the executor or administrator. If none has come to the executor's or administrator's hands, the fact shall be stated in the inventory.

The inventory shall contain a statement whether or not, insofar as it can be ascertained, the filing of an Ohio estate tax return will be required.

(2001 H 85, eff. 10–31–01; 1953 H 1, eff. 10–1–53; GC 10509–51 to 10509–53)

Historical and Statutory Notes

Pre–1953 H 1 Amendments: 114 v 413

Amendment Note: 2001 H 85 rewrote this section which prior thereto read:

"The inventory required by section 2115.02 of the Revised Code shall contain a particular statement of all securities for the payment of money which belong to the deceased and are known to such executor or administrator. Such inventory shall specify the name of the debtor in each security, the date, the sum originally payable, the indorsements thereon with their dates, the serial numbers or other identifying data as to each security, and the sum which, in the judgment of the appraisers, can be collected on each claim.

"Such inventory must contain a statement of all debts and accounts belonging to the deceased which are known to such executor or administrator and specify the name of the debtor, the date, the balance or thing due, and the value or sum which can be collected thereon, in the judgment of the appraisers.

"Such inventory must contain an account of all moneys which belong to the deceased and have come to the hands of the executor or administrator. If none has come to his hands, the fact must be stated in the inventory."

Library References

Executors and Administrators ⊘66, 68.
Westlaw Topic No. 162.
C.J.S. Executors and Administrators §§ 154 to 155.

Research References

Encyclopedias

OH Jur. 3d Decedents' Estates § 1257, Form and Contents of Inventory.

Treatises and Practice Aids

Carlin, Baldwin's Ohio Practice, Merrick-Rippner Probate Law § 2:23, Inventory and Appraisal—Filing of Inventory.

Carlin, Baldwin's Ohio Practice, Merrick-Rippner Probate Law § 79:5, Inventory—Contents—"Each Item" Listed Separately.

Carlin, Baldwin's Ohio Practice, Merrick-Rippner Probate Law § 2:121, Administration of Decedent's Estate—Checklist.

Carlin, Baldwin's Ohio Practice, Merrick-Rippner Probate Law App B SPF 6.0, Inventory and Appraisal—Form.

Notes of Decisions

Business and partnership assets   5
Conveyance of land   6
Notes   1
Procedural issues   4
Statute of limitations   3
Trust funds   7
Wrongful death   2

1. Notes

Notes delivered to an executor to indemnify the estate against the liability of the testator as surety are not assets of the estate, nor is money collected on them; thus, the estate is not liable for the misconduct of the executor regarding such notes and money. Arbuckle's Ex'rs v. Tracy's Adm'rs (Ohio 1846) 15 Ohio 432. Executors And Administrators ⊘ 45

Where the owner of a life estate leases in August for a year and the crops had all been cultivated and harvested before the lessor's death except corn, and the rent was secured by a note, the note is an asset of the estate of the deceased life tenant. Noble v. Tyler (Ohio 1900) 61 Ohio St. 432, 43 W.L.B. 127, 56 N.E. 191. Crops ⊘ 2; Life Estates ⊘ 15(1)

2. Wrongful death

Money realized on a judgment for causing wrongful death is not to be treated as a part of the assets of the estate, but must be distributed according to the statute of descent and distribution. Steel v. Kurtz (Ohio 1876) 28 Ohio St. 191.

3. Statute of limitations

Money arising from the sale of land sold to pay debts and money received from a guardian of heirs to save their land from sale are not new assets and will not extend the four-year period of limitation of actions. Favorite v. Booher's Adm'r (Ohio 1867) 17 Ohio St. 548.

Under the plenary power conferred upon the probate court incident to the administration of estates it has authority, upon exceptions to an inventory, to revise the appraised value of any security listed in such inventory, but such authority should be exercised after hearing and determined upon the evidence adduced. In re Berman's Estate (Lucas 1963) 118 Ohio App. 354, 194 N.E.2d 794, 25 O.O.2d 226.

The right of a widow to a year's allowance in the estate of her deceased husband vests immediately upon death, becomes a preferred and secured debt of his estate, and, when it has not been paid to the widow during her lifetime, such allowance survives as an asset of her estate and is includable in the inventory of her estate as a debt due from the estate of her deceased husband, but if an exception to the inventory, based on the running of the statute of limitations against such debt, is filed by several of such children, upon a hearing on exceptions to the inventory the probate court may summarily determine only whether such year's allowance is includable in the inventory as a debt but has no power to determine whether the debt is uncollectible by reason of the statute of limitations. In re Wreede's Estate (Van Wert 1958) 106 Ohio App. 324, 154 N.E.2d 756, 7 O.O.2d 75.

4. Procedural issues

No law requires or authorizes the filing with the probate court of an application by an administrator to determine the nature of a claim allegedly due an estate and to determine whether such amount should be included as an asset of such estate upon the filing of an amended inventory and appraisement; nor is there any law authorizing any order based upon such an application, unless such application can be construed as a petition for a declaratory judgment, which it cannot be where the application is not adversary in character, where there is no party plaintiff or party defendant, and where the facts set forth do not allege any justiciable controversy. In re Uhl's Estate (Marion 1954) 98 Ohio App. 145, 128 N.E.2d 142, 57 O.O. 212.

In an action for concealment of assets of a decedent estate, the proper burden of proof on the claimant is a showing by a preponderance of the evidence; therefore, the trial court erred in adopting a burden of proof from the complainant requiring either clear and convincing evidence or proof beyond a reasonable doubt. In re Estate of Goodrich, No. 45867 (8th Dist Ct App, Cuyahoga, 8–9–83).

5. Business and partnership assets

An executor or administrator of a surviving partner who dies with partnership assets in his possession and while he is engaged in settling the partnership business is entitled to the possession of such assets and is charged with the duty of completing such settlement. Dayton v. Bartlett (Ohio 1882) 38 Ohio St. 357, 8 W.L.B. 212.

Where by the direction of the testator his business has been continued after his death, the profits made are assets in the hands of the administrator. Gandolfo v. Walker (Ohio 1864) 15 Ohio St. 251.

Farm equipment is not properly listed as an asset of the estate of the deceased where (1) the mother of the deceased is listed on sales receipts as the purchaser of the equipment, (2) the equipment is located on the mother's farm at the time of deceased's death, (3) the brother and former wife of the deceased believe that the mother owns the equipment, and (4) the deceased did not list any of the equipment as assets in his separation agreement with his former wife. In re Estate of Nuss, No. CA93-11-214, 1994 WL 506223 (12th Dist Ct App, Butler, 9-19-94).

6. Conveyance of land

The rents of lands accruing between the death of the intestate and a sale of the land to pay debts belong to the heir and not to the administrator. Overturf v. Dugan (Ohio 1876) 29 Ohio St. 230. Descent And Distribution ⚖ 79; Executors And Administrators ⚖ 131; Executors And Administrators ⚖ 413

Where the intestate conveyed land to secure a debt and the administrator sells the land and pays the debt, the balance of the purchase money is assets of the estate. Stiver v. Stiver's Heirs (Ohio 1837) 8 Ohio 217.

The county auditor's certificate of a sale of land for taxes upon the death of the holder passes to the heir at law. Rice's Lessee v. White (Ohio 1837) 8 Ohio 216.

7. Trust funds

Trust funds in the hands of the deceased passing to the administrator are no part of his estate and will not authorize the beneficiary to proceed on the administrator's bond. Quinby v. Walker (Ohio 1863) 14 Ohio St. 193.

2115.10 Emblements are assets

The emblements raised by labor, whether severed or not from the land of the deceased at the time of his death, are assets in the hands of the executor or administrator and shall be included in the inventory required by section 2115.02 of the Revised Code.

The executor or administrator, or the person to whom he sells such emblements, at all reasonable times may enter upon the lands to cultivate, sever, and gather them.

(1953 H 1, eff. 10–1–53; GC 10509–49, 10509–50)

Historical and Statutory Notes

Pre–1953 H 1 Amendments: 114 v 413

Library References

Executors and Administrators ⚖66.
Westlaw Topic No. 162.
C.J.S. Executors and Administrators § 155.

Research References

Encyclopedias

OH Jur. 3d Agriculture & Crops § 4, Emblements; Ownership of Crops on Land Belonging to Another.
OH Jur. 3d Decedents' Estates § 1257, Form and Contents of Inventory.
OH Jur. 3d Decedents' Estates § 1308, Crops or Emblements.
OH Jur. 3d Estates, Pwrs., & Restrnts. on Alienat. § 62, Crops; Livestock.

Treatises and Practice Aids

Carlin, Baldwin's Ohio Practice, Merrick-Rippner Probate Law § 2:121, Administration of Decedent's Estate—Checklist.

Notes of Decisions

Growing crops 2
Rent 3
Will 1

---

1. Will

Former GC 10642 and GC 10643 (GC 10509–49 and GC 10509–50, now RC 2115.10), relating to emblements, constitute no limitation on power of testator to dispose of them, and where estate of widow of testator, whatever its nature, was created by will and not by law, her rights are limited to such rights as were conferred by the will which created the estate. Snyder v. Heffner (Pickaway 1929) 33 Ohio App. 379, 169 N.E. 460.

2. Growing crops

The administrator of the estate of a tenant for life, or his lessee, is entitled under RS 6026 and RS 6027 to the "annual crops raised by labor," as assets of the estate of the deceased, whether severed or not at his death. Noble v. Tyler (Ohio 1900) 61 Ohio St. 432, 43 W.L.B. 127, 56 N.E. 191. Crops ⚖ 2; Life Estates ⚖ 14

Growing grapes should be included in the inventory. Mason v Lemmon, OS Unrep 677, 38 B 197 (1897).

3. Rent

The mere fact that land is to be farmed will not convert the rent to be paid for it into emblements and it should not be inventoried. Dye v. Dimick (Ohio Com.Pl. 1897) 6 Ohio Dec. 231, 4 Ohio N.P. 185.

DISCHARGE OF DEBT

2115.11 Discharge of a debt in a will

The discharge or bequest, in a will, of a debt or demand of a testator against an executor named therein, or against any other person, is not valid as against the decedent's creditors, but is only a specific bequest of such debt or demand. The amount thereof must be included in the inventory of the credits and effects of the deceased and, if necessary, such amount must be applied in the payment of his debts. If not necessary for that purpose, such amount shall be paid in the same manner and proportion as other specific legacies.

(1953 H 1, eff. 10–1–53; GC 10509–66)

Historical and Statutory Notes

Pre–1953 H 1 Amendments: 114 v 416

Library References

Executors and Administrators ⚖66, 294.
Wills ⚖574, 731.
Westlaw Topic Nos. 162, 409.
C.J.S. Executors and Administrators §§ 155, 543.
C.J.S. Wills §§ 1085, 1135 to 1136, 1170, 1705 to 1707.

Research References

Encyclopedias

OH Jur. 3d Decedents' Estates § 1257, Form and Contents of Inventory.
OH Jur. 3d Decedents' Estates § 1285, Discharge of Debt in Will.

Forms

Ohio Forms and Transactions F 30.14, Alternate or Additional Will Clauses.

Treatises and Practice Aids

Carlin, Baldwin's Ohio Practice, Merrick-Rippner Probate Law § 79:9, Inventory—Discharge of Debt in Will—Professional Association.
Carlin, Baldwin's Ohio Practice, Merrick-Rippner Probate Law § 2:121, Administration of Decedent's Estate—Checklist.

Notes of Decisions

General devise 2
Predeceased devisee 1

---

1. Predeceased devisee

Where a devisee died before the testator, a debt due from the devisee to the estate must be deducted from the amount the deceased devisee's issue is entitled to take. Baker v. Carpenter (Ohio 1903) 69 Ohio St. 15, 48 W.L.B. 907, 68 N.E. 577, 1 Ohio Law Rep. 489, 1 Ohio Law Rep. 589.

2. General devise

A debt due an estate by a son is superior to a mortgage or judgment liens against him on real estate coming to him from his father by way of

2115.12 Naming of person executor does not discharge debt

The naming of a person as executor in a will shall not operate as a discharge or bequest of a just claim which the testator had against such executor. Such claim shall be included among the assets of the deceased in the inventory required by section 2115.02 of the Revised Code. The executor shall be liable for it as for so much money in his hands at the time such debt or demand becomes due, and must apply and distribute it as part of the personal estate of the deceased.

(1953 H 1, eff. 10–1–53; GC 10509–67)

Historical and Statutory Notes

Pre–1953 H 1 Amendments: 119 v 394, § 1; 116 v Pt 2, 255; 114 v 416

Library References

Executors and Administrators ⟶29(1), 66.
Westlaw Topic No. 162.
C.J.S. Executors and Administrators §§ 82, 85, 87, 155, 171.

Research References

Encyclopedias

OH Jur. 3d Decedents' Estates § 1257, Form and Contents of Inventory.
OH Jur. 3d Decedents' Estates § 1281, Debts of Executor or Administrator.
OH Jur. 3d Decedents' Estates § 1283, Debts of Executor or Administrator—Effect of Insolvency.
OH Jur. 3d Decedents' Estates § 1284, Debts of Executor or Administrator—Effect on Liens.

Notes of Decisions

Action against executor 6
Death of executor 1
Debt as asset 8
Debt of testator to executor or administrator 9
Individual debt 4
Insolvency of executor 2
Inventory 10
Mortgages and real estate 5
Procedural issues 3
Sureties 7

---

1. Death of executor

Where a debtor executor dies before rendering an account, the amount of his debt being ascertained, it is to be treated as money in the hands of his administrator due the the estate of the testator. Jones v. Willis (Ohio 1905) 72 Ohio St. 189, 74 N.E. 166, 2 Ohio Law Rep. 529.

2. Insolvency of executor

The sureties on an administrator's bond are liable if he fails to account for a debt due from him to the estate as assets in his hands though he is insolvent. McGaughey v Jacoby, 54 OS 487, 44 NE 231 (1896).

Where an administrator was insolvent when appointed and remained so thereafter during his administratorship, he should not be held accountable for a debt due from him to the estate. McCoy v. Allen (Ohio Cir. 1895) 6 Ohio C.D. 659, 3 Ohio Dec. 511, reversed 57 Ohio St. 641, 50 N.E. 1126.

Sureties on an administrator's bond are liable for the debt of the administrator due the estate regardless of the insolvency of the administrator. Perkins v. Scott (Ohio Cir. 1895) 6 Ohio C.D. 226, 2 Ohio Dec. 496, dismissed.

Although one of two joint executors is insolvent throughout his executorship, a claim due from him to his testator ought to be included in the inventory, but such executors will not be held liable for the same as money in their hands or to distribute the same. Brown v. Harshman (Ohio Cir. 1894) 6 Ohio C.D. 10, 2 Ohio Dec. 10.

An insolvent principal maker of a note, who is named as executor in the will of his surety and accepts and qualifies as such, and who pays his own notes as they subsequently fall due as claims against the estate, is properly chargeable as for so much money in his hands. Yakey v. Strunk (Ohio Com.Pl. 1908) 18 Ohio Dec. 726, 7 Ohio N.P.(N.S.) 177, affirmed 81 Ohio St. 568, 91 N.E. 1143, 7 Ohio Law Rep. 610. Executors And Administrators ⟶ 50

Where an agent appropriates trust funds for his own use and dies insolvent, his stock of goods into which the trust fund can be traced passes to his administrator charged with the trust, and the court may order its payment as a preferred claim. Deering Harvester Co v Keifer, 20 CC 311, 11 CD 270 (Hancock 1900).

3. Procedural issues

Under the plenary power conferred upon the probate court incident to the administration of estates it has authority, upon exceptions to an inventory, to revise the appraised value of any security listed in such inventory, but such authority should be exercised after hearing and determined upon the evidence adduced. In re Berman's Estate (Lucas 1963) 118 Ohio App. 354, 194 N.E.2d 794, 25 O.O.2d 226.

The filing of exceptions to an executor's account, the exceptor alleging that the executor has failed to charge himself with all the assets of the estate, is not the proper procedure to obtain a determination as to the validity of a gift and transfer of possession during the lifetime of the decedent. In re Trent's Estate (Franklin 1954) 98 Ohio App. 238, 128 N.E.2d 839, 57 O.O. 266. Executors And Administrators ⟶ 504(6)

Judgment approving executor's final account estopped heirs from asserting executor's indebtedness by reason of having received advancements. First & Citizens' Nat. Bank of Elizabeth City, N.C. v. Seip (Ross 1931) 43 Ohio App. 440, 183 N.E. 448, 14 Ohio Law Abs. 98. Executors And Administrators ⟶ 513(10); Judgment ⟶ 688

4. Individual debt

Debts owing by an administrator to the estate are to be treated as assets in his hands, but such debt must be one owed individually by the administrator. Bigelow's Ex'r v. Bigelow's Adm'rs (Ohio 1829) 4 Ohio 138, 19 Am.Dec. 591.

Rule that debts owing by executor to estate are to be regarded and treated as assets in his hands is confined to cases in which executor owes debt individually and unconditionally, and not to joint and several obligation of four co-makers, whereupon executor appeared only as surety. Alderfer v. Hammond (Medina 1935) 18 Ohio Law Abs. 540. Executors And Administrators ⟶ 50

5. Mortgages and real estate

A mortgagee by making his debtor his executor does not thereby extinguish the mortgage; an administrator de bonis non may institute proceedings in chancery to foreclose the mortgage. Miller v. Donaldson (Ohio 1848) 17 Ohio 264.

Where one who had agreed to convey land to another died and the vendee was appointed administrator, the vendee's debt is not thereby extinguished. Bigelow's Ex'r v. Bigelow's Adm'rs (Ohio 1829) 4 Ohio 138, 19 Am.Dec. 591.

Debt created by a joint mortgage is a primary obligation of all signers of mortgage deed, and in case of death of one of joint mortgagors, his estate becomes primarily liable, and it is not error for executor to list mortgage debt in schedule of debts of the estate, and joint obligation of executor with estate on such mortgage is not a sufficient basis for removal of executor on ground of an adverse interest. In re Fiebig's Estate (Hamilton 1938) 61 Ohio App. 40, 22 N.E.2d 288, 28 Ohio Law Abs. 373, 14 O.O. 216.

6. Action against executor

Where the debtor of a deceased person is appointed administrator, the debt becomes assets in his hands, and on exception to his final account that he has omitted to charge himself with such debt, the court may hear evidence and determine the claim. In re Raab's Estate (Ohio 1865) 16 Ohio St. 273.

An appointment as executor or administrator does not extinguish the debt of the executor or administrator to the estate of his testator or intestate, and judgment may be had against him in a proceeding by an administrator de bonis non. Tracy's Adm'x v. Card's Adm'r (Ohio 1853) 2 Ohio St. 431.

Judgment approving executor's final account estopped heirs from asserting executor's indebtedness by reason of having received advancements. First & Citizens' Nat. Bank of Elizabeth City, N.C. v. Seip (Ross 1931) 43 Ohio App. 440, 183 N.E. 448, 14 Ohio Law Abs. 98. Executors And Administrators ⇐ 513(10); Judgment ⇐ 688

7. Sureties

Appointing as administrator de bonis non a surety on the bond of the previous executor does not make a debt due the estate from such executor assets in the hands of such administrator by reason of his suretyship, as such principle does not apply to one who is only conditionally liable. Shields v. Odell (Ohio 1875) 27 Ohio St. 398. Executors And Administrators ⇐ 50

Where debtor was creditor's executor, his sureties, who were released after his removal as executor when he was appointed administrator de bonis non with new bond, cannot be held for amount of his unpaid debt to testator. U.S. Fidelity & Guaranty Co. of Baltimore, Md. v. Jones (Warren 1926) 22 Ohio App. 345, 153 N.E. 281, 4 Ohio Law Abs. 611. Executors And Administrators ⇐ 527(2)

When debtor is appointed administrator or executor to creditor, debt becomes asset in his hands, and his sureties are liable for his failure to administer and distribute it. U.S. Fidelity & Guaranty Co. of Baltimore, Md. v. Jones (Warren 1926) 22 Ohio App. 345, 153 N.E. 281, 4 Ohio Law Abs. 611. Executors And Administrators ⇐ 528(5)

The sureties on the bond of an insolvent administrator are liable for money in his hands arising from debts owing by him to the estate to the same extent that the sureties of an insolvent executor are liable for such money. James v. West (Ohio 1902) 67 Ohio St. 28, 47 W.L.B. 857, 65 N.E. 156. Executors And Administrators ⇐ 528(5)

8. Debt as asset

A debt due from an administrator to the estate is assets, although created after the decedent's death. Martin v. Train (Ohio Cir. 1891) 3 Ohio C.D. 344.

Executor paying his indebtedness out of his surety's estate held chargeable with excess over beneficial interest. Yakey v. Strunk (Ohio Com.Pl. 1908) 18 Ohio Dec. 726, 7 Ohio N.P.(N.S.) 177, affirmed 81 Ohio St. 568, 91 N.E. 1143, 7 Ohio Law Rep. 610.

Debt existing in the lifetime of the testator against one who becomes executor of his last will, is transmuted into money in the hands of such executor by the force of section; and no act of the executor can turn it again into the character of a mere demand or obligation. In re Koons' Estate (Ohio Prob. 1938) 6 Ohio Supp. 320, 26 Ohio Law Abs. 512, 11 O.O. 389. Executors And Administrators ⇐ 88

9. Debt of testator to executor or administrator

Where a creditor is appointed administrator of his debtor the debt is not to be regarded as paid or extinguished. Hall v. Pratt (Ohio 1831) 5 Ohio 72.

10. Inventory

A contract between an heir and other heirs by which the heir agreed to pay debts in consideration of receiving all personalty of decedent, if made, did not operate to dispense with the absolute duty imposed on administrator by code to make and return a true inventory of all the property of decedent which has come to administrator's possession or knowledge. In re Specht's Estate (Butler 1941) 36 N.E.2d 865, 34 Ohio Law Abs. 201. Executors And Administrators ⇐ 63

FILING AND APPROVAL

2115.15 Signing, certifying, and return of inventory

Upon the completion of the inventory required by section 2115.02 of the Revised Code, it shall be signed by the appraisers at its end, and the appraisers shall certify that the inventory is a true and correct appraisement of the property exhibited to them. It is not necessary for the appraisers to sign each schedule of the inventory. A copy of the inventory shall be retained by the executor or administrator who shall return the original to the probate court.

(1992 H 427, eff. 10–8–92; 1953 H 1; GC 10509–56)

Historical and Statutory Notes

Pre–1953 H 1 Amendments: 114 v 414

Library References

Executors and Administrators ⇐ 68.
Westlaw Topic No. 162.
C.J.S. Executors and Administrators § 154.

Research References

Encyclopedias
OH Jur. 3d Decedents' Estates § 1257, Form and Contents of Inventory.

Treatises and Practice Aids
Carlin, Baldwin's Ohio Practice, Merrick-Rippner Probate Law § 79:17, Inventory—Signing and Certifying Return.
Carlin, Baldwin's Ohio Practice, Merrick-Rippner Probate Law § 79:35, Schedule of Assets—Form.
Carlin, Baldwin's Ohio Practice, Merrick-Rippner Probate Law App B SPF 6.1, Schedule of Assets—Form.

Notes of Decisions

Military pension money 2
Partition sale proceeds 1

---

1. Partition sale proceeds

Moneys received by an administrator under a sale in partition are within the conditions of his bond. Cambell v English, W 119 (1832).

2. Military pension money

The act of congress of June 19, 1804, constitutes the administrator a trustee to receive and pay over pension money. Chapman v. Loveland (Ohio 1860) 11 Ohio St. 214. Executors And Administrators ⇐ 91; Pensions ⇐ 2

2115.16 Hearing on inventory

Upon the filing of the inventory required by section 2115.02 of the Revised Code, the probate court forthwith shall set a day, not later than one month after the day the inventory was filed, for a hearing on the inventory.

The executor or administrator may serve notice of the hearing, or may cause the notice to be served, upon any person who is interested in the estate. The probate court, after notice to the executor or administrator, either upon the motion of any interested party for good cause shown or at its own instance, may order that notice of the hearing is to be served upon persons the court designates.

For good cause, the hearing may be continued for the time that the court considers reasonable. Exceptions to the inventory or to the allowance for support provided by section 2106.13 of the Revised Code may be filed at any time prior to five days before the date set for the hearing or the date to which the hearing has been continued by any person interested in the estate or in any of the property included in the inventory, but the time limit for the filing of exceptions shall not apply in case of fraud or concealment of assets. When exceptions are filed, notice of them and the time of the hearing on them forthwith shall be given to the executor or administrator and his attorney by certified mail or by personal service, unless the notice is waived. At the hearing, the executor or administrator and any witness may be examined under oath. The court shall enter its finding on the journal and tax the costs as may be equitable.

(1994 H 208, eff. 6–23–94; 1990 H 346, eff. 5–31–90; 126 v 392; 125 v 903; 1953 H 1; GC 10509–59)

Uncodified Law

1990 H 346, § 3, eff. 5–31–90, reads:

(A) Sections 1 and 2 of this act shall apply only to the estates of decedents who die on or after the effective date of this act.

(B) It is the intent of the General Assembly in the outright repeal of sections 2107.13 and 2107.14 of the Revised Code and the amendments to sections 109.30, 2107.18, 2107.19, 2107.22, 2107.27, 2107.76, 2115.16, and 2703.14 of the Revised Code by this act, to respond to the dicta of the Supreme Court in *Palazzi v. Estate of Gardner* (1987), 32 Ohio St. 3d 169 and to enact statutory provisions relating to notice of probate proceedings that are not unconstitutional as potentially violative of the due process of law rights of nonresidents of this state.

Historical and Statutory Notes

Pre–1953 H 1 Amendments: 116 v 385

Amendment Note: 1994 H 208 rewrote this section, which previously read;

"Upon the filing of the inventory required by section 2115.02 of the Revised Code, the probate court shall forthwith set a day, not later than one month after the day the inventory was filed, for a hearing on the inventory and shall give at least ten days' notice by certified mail or otherwise of the hearing to the executor or administrator and to each of the following whose place of residence is known:

"(A) Surviving spouse;

"(B) Next of kin;

"(C) Beneficiaries under the will;

"(D) The attorneys, if known, representing any of the persons described in divisions (A) to (C) of this section.

"Such notice may be waived in writing by any of the persons described in divisions (A) to (D) of this section. For good cause, the hearing may be continued for such time as the court considers reasonable. Exceptions to the inventory or to the allowance for support provided by section 2106.13 of the Revised Code may be filed at any time prior to five days before the date set for the hearing or the date to which the hearing has been continued, by any person interested in the estate or in any of the property included in the inventory, but the time limit for the filing of exceptions shall not apply in case of fraud or concealment of assets. When exceptions are filed, notice of them and the time of the hearing on them shall forthwith be given to the executor or administrator and his attorney by certified mail or by personal service, unless the notice is waived. At the hearing, the executor or administrator and any witness may be examined under oath. The court shall enter its finding on the journal and tax the costs as may be equitable."

Legislative Service Commission

1975 (Commentary from former RC 2107.13):

This section currently provides that notice be given to the surviving spouse before admission of the will to probate. It would be amended by the bill to provide that notice must be given to a surviving spouse only if known to the applicant.

OSBA Probate and Trust Law Section

1957 (Commentary from former RC 2107.13):

The Supreme Court has held that the requirement of notice of application for probate to be given to the surviving spouse and next of kin of the testator resident of the state is mandatory and jurisdictional. The statute in its present form has led to much uncertainty as to the validity of the probate of a will in the event the person offering the same notifies all next of kin known to him to be residents of the state when it subsequently develops that there are other residents of the state not known to him who have not been served. The proposed amendment removes this uncertainty by providing that the notice is to be given to the surviving spouse and to the persons known to the applicant to be residents of the state.

Library References

Executors and Administrators ⚖62.
Westlaw Topic No. 162.
C.J.S. Executors and Administrators §§ 152, 158.
Baldwin's Ohio Legislative Service, 1990 Laws of Ohio, H 346—LSC Analysis, p 5–87

Research References

Encyclopedias

OH Jur. 3d Decedents' Estates § 1263, Time for Hearing on Inventory Filed; Notice.
OH Jur. 3d Decedents' Estates § 1264, Time for Filing Exceptions to Inventory; Notice.
OH Jur. 3d Decedents' Estates § 1265, Hearing on Inventory and Exceptions Thereto.
OH Jur. 3d Decedents' Estates § 1266, Who Are Parties to Hearing on Exceptions.
OH Jur. 3d Decedents' Estates § 1269, Effect of Approval of Inventory.
OH Jur. 3d Fiduciaries § 44, Exceptions to Inventory.

Treatises and Practice Aids

Carlin, Baldwin's Ohio Practice, Merrick-Rippner Probate Law § 3:3, Jurisdiction of Probate Court—Subject Matter—in General.
Carlin, Baldwin's Ohio Practice, Merrick-Rippner Probate Law § 2:23, Inventory and Appraisal—Filing of Inventory.
Carlin, Baldwin's Ohio Practice, Merrick-Rippner Probate Law § 56:9, Concealed or Embezzled Assets—Question of Title.
Carlin, Baldwin's Ohio Practice, Merrick-Rippner Probate Law § 64:3, Powers and Duties of Guardian—Inventory.
Carlin, Baldwin's Ohio Practice, Merrick-Rippner Probate Law § 83:7, Fiduciary Claims—Jurisdiction to Allow.
Carlin, Baldwin's Ohio Practice, Merrick-Rippner Probate Law § 2:121, Administration of Decedent's Estate—Checklist.
Carlin, Baldwin's Ohio Practice, Merrick-Rippner Probate Law § 56:11, Concealed or Embezzled Assets—Ex Parte Proceedings.
Carlin, Baldwin's Ohio Practice, Merrick-Rippner Probate Law § 56:14, Concealed or Embezzled Assets—Evidence of Concealment.
Carlin, Baldwin's Ohio Practice, Merrick-Rippner Probate Law § 79:14, Inventory—Hearing.
Carlin, Baldwin's Ohio Practice, Merrick-Rippner Probate Law § 79:15, Inventory—Hearing—Witnesses.
Carlin, Baldwin's Ohio Practice, Merrick-Rippner Probate Law § 79:16, Inventory—Hearing—Journal Entry.
Carlin, Baldwin's Ohio Practice, Merrick-Rippner Probate Law § 79:18, Inventory—Exceptions—Time Limit for Filing.
Carlin, Baldwin's Ohio Practice, Merrick-Rippner Probate Law § 79:19, Inventory—Exceptions—Who May File.
Carlin, Baldwin's Ohio Practice, Merrick-Rippner Probate Law § 79:20, Inventory—Exceptions—Hearing.
Carlin, Baldwin's Ohio Practice, Merrick-Rippner Probate Law § 79:21, Inventory—Exceptions—Nature of Proceedings.
Carlin, Baldwin's Ohio Practice, Merrick-Rippner Probate Law § 79:22, Inventory—Exceptions—Questions Raised.
Carlin, Baldwin's Ohio Practice, Merrick-Rippner Probate Law § 79:23, Inventory—Exceptions—Discretionary Jurisdiction.
Carlin, Baldwin's Ohio Practice, Merrick-Rippner Probate Law § 79:24, Inventory—Exceptions—Burden of Proof and Evidence.
Carlin, Baldwin's Ohio Practice, Merrick-Rippner Probate Law § 79:25, Inventory—Exceptions—Res Judicata as Defense.
Carlin, Baldwin's Ohio Practice, Merrick-Rippner Probate Law § 79:36, Waiver of Notice of Hearing on Inventory—Form.
Carlin, Baldwin's Ohio Practice, Merrick-Rippner Probate Law § 79:37, Notice of Hearing on Inventory—Form.
Carlin, Baldwin's Ohio Practice, Merrick-Rippner Probate Law § 79:42, Exceptions to Inventory—Form.
Carlin, Baldwin's Ohio Practice, Merrick-Rippner Probate Law § 79:43, Notice—Form.
Carlin, Baldwin's Ohio Practice, Merrick-Rippner Probate Law § 79:44, Entry on Exceptions and Hearing on Inventory—Form.
Carlin, Baldwin's Ohio Practice, Merrick-Rippner Probate Law App B SPF 6.3, Notice of Hearing on Inventory.

Law Review and Journal Commentaries

Ten Questions Arising in Settlement of Executor's Accounts, Harry Lewis Deibel. 31 Ohio L Rep 7 (January 30, 1930).

Notes of Decisions

Court's authority and jurisdiction 5
Notice 4
Parties 2
Procedural issues 1
Surviving spouse 3
Time limitations 7
Witnesses 6

---

1. Procedural issues

Hearing was required in order to address merits of objections of decedent's daughter as to magistrate's decision approving partial account filed by decedent's son, the executor of estate; although court made pronouncements concerning merits of some of daughter's objections, court's opinion relied on incorrect findings that daughter, who was never successfully served, waived arguments by failing to file timely objections to inventory, and daughter was never given opportunity to present her arguments on the merits. In re Estate of Reinhart (Ohio App. 7 Dist., Mahoning, 09-13-2005) No. 05 MA 36, 2005-Ohio-4894, 2005 WL 2267397, Unreported. Executors And Administrators ⇐ 504(7)

Complainant was entitled to remedial advantages of additional features of section and her right to file exceptions, as owner of property inventoried, after this section became effective, was not curtailed simply because estate was in process of administration while former GC 10639 (RC 2115.16) was in effect. In re Milliken's Estate (Summit 1937) 24 Ohio Law Abs. 650.

Res judicata did not prevent decedent's daughter from challenging the exclusion of the family Bible from the inventory of decedent's estate, although she did not raise the issue at the time the probate court approved the inventory of the estate; title to the family Bible was disputed, issue of whether the family Bible was properly an asset of the estate had never been raised, litigated, or determined, and, as trial court had determined that son's gifting of the family Bible to his own child was invalid, the Bible had the status of a concealed asset of the estate such that there was no time limit on the filing of exceptions to the exclusion of that asset from the estate. In re Estate of Kelsey (Ohio App. 11 Dist., 03-10-2006) 165 Ohio App.3d 680, 847 N.E.2d 1277, 2006-Ohio-1171. Executors And Administrators ⇐ 72

A hearing of exceptions to an inventory, pursuant to probate statute, is a summary proceeding conducted by the probate court to determine whether those charged with the responsibility of filing an inventory have included in the decedent's estate more or less than the decedent owned at the time of his or her death. In re Estate of Platt (Ohio App. 11 Dist., 06-28-2002) 148 Ohio App.3d 132, 772 N.E.2d 198, 2002-Ohio-3382. Executors And Administrators ⇐ 69

Trial court did not abuse its discretion by proceeding to final judgment on exceptions to guardian's inventory even though several discovery motions were pending. In re Guardianship of Maurer (Ohio App. 6 Dist., 12-22-1995) 108 Ohio App.3d 354, 670 N.E.2d 1030, cause dismissed 74 Ohio St.3d 1461, 656 N.E.2d 1297, dismissed, appeal not allowed 76 Ohio St.3d 1405, 666 N.E.2d 565. Guardian And Ward ⇐ 32

Guardian of person waived his argument that he was wrongfully denied evidentiary hearing on his exceptions to guardian's inventory by failing to object to hearing on merits. In re Guardianship of Maurer (Ohio App. 6 Dist., 12-22-1995) 108 Ohio App.3d 354, 670 N.E.2d 1030, cause dismissed 74 Ohio St.3d 1461, 656 N.E.2d 1297, dismissed, appeal not allowed 76 Ohio St.3d 1405, 666 N.E.2d 565. Guardian And Ward ⇐ 32

Hearing on exceptions to guardian's inventory does not have to be evidentiary hearing. In re Guardianship of Maurer (Ohio App. 6 Dist., 12-22-1995) 108 Ohio App.3d 354, 670 N.E.2d 1030, cause dismissed 74 Ohio St.3d 1461, 656 N.E.2d 1297, dismissed, appeal not allowed 76 Ohio St.3d 1405, 666 N.E.2d 565. Guardian And Ward ⇐ 32

Since prior judge's order scheduling evidentiary hearing on exceptions to guardian's inventory was interlocutory, second judge could modify it and hold hearing at different time. In re Guardianship of Maurer (Ohio App. 6 Dist., 12-22-1995) 108 Ohio App.3d 354, 670 N.E.2d 1030, cause dismissed 74 Ohio St.3d 1461, 656 N.E.2d 1297, dismissed, appeal not allowed 76 Ohio St.3d 1405, 666 N.E.2d 565. Guardian And Ward ⇐ 32; Judges ⇐ 24

Probate court's decision on whether to take evidence on exceptions to guardian's inventory is subject to review for abuse of discretion. In re Guardianship of Maurer (Ohio App. 6 Dist., 12-22-1995) 108 Ohio App.3d 354, 670 N.E.2d 1030, cause dismissed 74 Ohio St.3d 1461, 656 N.E.2d 1297, dismissed, appeal not allowed 76 Ohio St.3d 1405, 666 N.E.2d 565. Guardian And Ward ⇐ 32

Where guardian of ward's person did not present any evidence supporting his challenges to inventory prepared by guardian of ward's estate, trial court did not abuse its discretion by approving inventory without requiring guardian of ward's estate to prove his calculations. In re Guardianship of Maurer (Ohio App. 6 Dist., 12-22-1995) 108 Ohio App.3d 354, 670 N.E.2d 1030, cause dismissed 74 Ohio St.3d 1461, 656 N.E.2d 1297, dismissed, appeal not allowed 76 Ohio St.3d 1405, 666 N.E.2d 565. Guardian And Ward ⇐ 32

A probate court does not abuse its discretion when it approves, without an evidentiary hearing, an estate inventory that includes a condominium to which relatives of the deceased claim prior title by virtue of a purchase-money resulting trust; because an inventory hearing under RC 2115.16 is a summary proceeding, the inclusion of the condominium in the estate inventory raises no res judicata bar to a subsequent declaratory action. In re Estate of Ross (Geauga 1989) 65 Ohio App.3d 395, 583 N.E.2d 1379, dismissed 50 Ohio St.3d 717, 553 N.E.2d 1363.

The entry of a probate court overruling exceptions to the inventory of an estate is a final, appealable order within the meaning of RC 2505.02. Sheets v. Antes (Franklin 1984) 14 Ohio App.3d 278, 470 N.E.2d 931, 14 O.B.R. 307.

Notwithstanding RC 2101.24, the probate court does not have the authority under RC 2115.16 to impress a constructive trust on savings bonds at a hearing on exceptions, since such a hearing is a summary proceeding conducted by the probate court solely to determine whether all of the proper assets and liabilities have been included in a decedent's estate; the issue of the fraudulent appropriation of the purchase money for the bonds should be brought pursuant to RC 2117.02. In re Estate of Etzensperger (Ohio 1984) 9 Ohio St.3d 19, 457 N.E.2d 1161, 9 O.B.R. 112.

In evaluating the value of limited partnership interest in a decedent's estate the restrictions on disposition imposed by RC 1783.05 must be taken into consideration. In re Lerch's Estate (Ohio Prob. 1964) 200 N.E.2d 513, 95 Ohio Law Abs. 242, 27 O.O.2d 221.

Where a person claims title to and right of immediate possession of specific personal property, and that such property is being wrongfully detained from him, he may institute an action in common pleas court for its recovery against the administrator of an estate who is wrongfully detaining possession of the property from the owner, where there is no question of a divided interest or ownership between the owner and the estate. Service Transport Co. v. Matyas (Ohio 1953) 159 Ohio St. 300, 112 N.E.2d 20, 42 A.L.R.2d 413, 50 O.O. 298.

An alleged owner cannot ordinarily bring a replevin action in common pleas court against an executor or administrator of an estate in the course of administration in probate court. Service Transport Co. v. Matyas (Cuyahoga 1952) 108 N.E.2d 741, 63 Ohio Law Abs. 236, 63 Ohio Law Abs. 244, reversed 159 Ohio St. 300, 112 N.E.2d 20, 42 A.L.R.2d 413, 50 O.O. 298.

Inclusion of real estate in the inventory of a grantor's estate, to which no exception was filed and no actual hearing conducted by the probate court, is not res judicata, and does not estop a grantee from asserting title to the real estate. Scott v. Mofford (Hamilton 1940) 64 Ohio App. 457, 28 N.E.2d 947, 31 Ohio Law Abs. 535, 18 O.O. 197.

2. Parties

Where complainant excepted specifically to inventory filed on January 9, 1937, by administrator de bonis non and filed exceptions as "the sole heir and legatee" of said deceased and claimed ownership of property listed in inventory, classified herself as one falling within provisions of amended GC 10509–59 (RC 2115.16) in force in 1936 and in 1937 to date, both as a person "interested in the estate," and as one interested "in... property included in the inventory." In re Milliken's Estate (Summit 1937) 24 Ohio Law Abs. 650. Executors And Administrators ⇐ 69

The only parties to a hearing on exceptions to an inventory filed in the probate court pursuant to 2115.16 are the exceptor and the executor, unless other persons voluntarily appear and are allowed by the court to be made parties to the proceeding. Cole v. Ottawa Home & Sav. Ass'n (Ohio 1969) 18 Ohio St.2d 1, 246 N.E.2d 542, 47 O.O.2d 1. Executors And Administrators ⇐ 69

The determination by the probate court, in the summary proceeding provided for by RC 2115.16, that assets should be included in an estate makes the question of title res judicata as between all parties to the proceeding, but the judgment of the probate court may be attacked in a subsequent action by other interested persons who were not parties to the proceeding in probate court. Cole v. Ottawa Home & Sav. Ass'n (Ohio 1969) 18 Ohio St.2d 1, 246 N.E.2d 542, 47 O.O.2d 1. Judgment ⇨ 475; Judgment ⇨ 640

In a proceeding in the probate court, where an exception to the inventory and appraisement in an estate is filed on the ground that a claim against a certain person should be included in the inventory and appraisement, and an application by the executor of the estate is filed to amend the inventory and appraisement to include such claim against this person, the exceptor and the executor are parties in the proceeding, but the person against whom it is contended such claim should be made is not a party in such proceeding where he does not enter his appearance therein and oppose the proposed changes in the inventory. In re Haas' Estate (Ohio 1963) 174 Ohio St. 277, 189 N.E.2d 65, 22 O.O.2d 336.

An administrator of a decedent's estate may file exceptions to an inventory filed in another estate upon the ground that an asset (a joint bank account) shown in such estate is actually the property of his decedent. In re Ray's Estate (Ohio Prob. 1958) 156 N.E.2d 210, 79 Ohio Law Abs. 368.

Where upon sustaining exceptions to an inventory the court orders the executor to include certain property in the inventory which the executor claims he cannot locate, the executor is an interested party and may appeal therefrom. In re Byerly's Estate (Madison 1956) 141 N.E.2d 771, 74 Ohio Law Abs. 586.

Next of kin, contesting will by which they will receive nothing from estate are "persons interested," within terms of section, and have right to file exceptions to inventory. In re McConney's Estate (Huron 1942) 72 Ohio App. 286, 51 N.E.2d 239, 27 O.O. 121.

A creditor of an heir at law or distributee of a decedent cannot file exceptions to an account. In re Sturges' Estate (Ohio Com.Pl. 1908) 18 Ohio Dec. 344, 6 Ohio NP(NS) 331.

3. Surviving spouse

The surplus of the proceeds of a sale of real estate by an administrator, remaining in his hands on final settlement, are to be disposed of as real estate, and the widow of the intestate is not entitled to any part thereof as a distributee of the personal estate. Griswold v. Frink (Ohio 1871) 22 Ohio St. 79.

A year's allowance may be challenged either under RC 2115.16 or RC 2117.22. In re Stump's Estate (Ohio Prob. 1962) 185 N.E.2d 334, 89 Ohio Law Abs. 570.

The right of a widow to a year's allowance in the estate of her deceased husband vests immediately upon death, becomes a preferred and secured debt of his estate, and, when it has not been paid to the widow during her lifetime, such allowance survives as an asset of her estate and is includable in the inventory of her estate as a debt due from the estate of her deceased husband, but if an exception to the inventory, based on the running of the statute of limitations against such debt, is filed by several of such children, upon a hearing on exceptions to the inventory the probate court may summarily determine only whether such year's allowance is includable in the inventory as a debt but has no power to determine whether the debt is uncollectible by reason of the statute of limitations. In re Wreede's Estate (Van Wert 1958) 106 Ohio App. 324, 154 N.E.2d 756, 7 O.O.2d 75.

The question of whether a decedent left a widow entitled to an allowance for support is properly raised by exception to the allowance in the inventory. In re Scott's Estate (Ohio Com.Pl. 1909) 19 Ohio Dec. 577, 8 Ohio NP(NS) 279.

In a hearing on exceptions to inventory where decedent's nieces and nephews asserted that savings bonds co-owned by the decedent and the nieces and nephews should not be included in the inventory, the probate court was without jurisdiction to impose a constructive trust on one-half of the savings bonds for the benefit of decedent's surviving spouse. Etzensperger v Hurst, No. OT-82-18 (6th Dist Ct App, Ottawa, 12-3-82), affirmed by 9 OS(3d) 19, 9 OBR 112, 457 NE(2d) 1161 (1984).

4. Notice

Notice of filing of inventory and hearing thereon should be by registered mail or by such reasonable notice as probate judge should conclude to be sufficient in the exercise of a sound discretion. In re Keller's Estate (Cuyahoga 1940) 32 Ohio Law Abs. 624.

Notice of the filing of an estate inventory need not be by registered mail; notice of the filing of an estate inventory in a newspaper of general circulation is sufficient. In re Estate of Sliwa (Medina 1989) 58 Ohio App.3d 82, 568 N.E.2d 741, dismissed 47 Ohio St.3d 702, 547 N.E.2d 986.

5. Court's authority and jurisdiction

In deciding beneficiaries' motion to remove executor, evidence supported trial court's finding that inventory of estate was not flawed; evidence indicated that testator had given bank saw and drill press to grandson before death, microwave had been thrown away before testator died, executor took nothing out of house after testator died, and inventory was amended to include additional cash. In re Estate of Shaw (Ohio App. 2 Dist., Greene, 09-09-2005) No. 2004 CA 111, 2005-Ohio-4743, 2005 WL 2179300, Unreported. Executors And Administrators ⇨ 35(15)

Administrator with will annexed could sell real property, which was newly discovered asset of decedent's estate, without filing report of newly discovered assets as amended inventory and appraisal and without hearing being conducted on inventory, where probate court's order authorized administrator to distribute assets without being required to make inventory or appraisal of assets and administrator had previously filed inventory and appraisal. In re Estate of Hyer (Ohio App. 7 Dist., Monroe, 09-27-2004) No. 03 MO 9, 2004-Ohio-5359, 2004 WL 2334510, Unreported. Executors And Administrators ⇨ 70

Under the plenary power conferred upon the probate court incident to the administration of estates it has authority, upon exceptions to an inventory, to revise the appraised value of any security listed in such inventory, but such authority should be exercised after hearing and determined upon the evidence adduced. In re Berman's Estate (Lucas 1963) 118 Ohio App. 354, 194 N.E.2d 794, 25 O.O.2d 226.

Where an inventory lists a margin account of a decedent with a broker which account allegedly contains shares of stock claimed to be owned by an exceptor to the inventory, and where such shares of stock were voluntarily placed in said account by the broker, it is not an abuse of discretion for the probate court upon the hearing of exceptions to the inventory to refuse to conduct an accounting between the exceptor and the executor of decedent's estate and to permit exceptor to pursue such other remedies as may be available. In re Gottwald's Estate (Ohio 1956) 164 Ohio St. 405, 131 N.E.2d 586, 58 O.O. 235. Executors And Administrators ⇨ 69

Upon a hearing of exceptions to an inventory, a probate court, or common pleas court to whom the matter has been referred, has jurisdiction to employ the summary proceedings of impressing a trust and ordering an accounting. In re Barnes' Estate (Ohio Com.Pl. 1950) 108 N.E.2d 88, 64 Ohio Law Abs. 6, affirmed 108 N.E.2d 101, 64 Ohio Law Abs. 28.

Where bonds are stricken from an inventory of estate assets because the name of a survivor as well as the name of the decedent appears on the face of each bond, the probate court is without authority to determine ownership of the bonds or to order their delivery to the survivors by the executor. Etzensperger v Hurst, No. OT–84–21 (6th Dist Ct App, Ottawa, 12–14–84).

6. Witnesses

A beneficiary under a will who is not the executor can be properly excluded from a courtroom under a ruling ordering a separation of witnesses in a proceeding upon exceptions to an inventory brought pursuant to RC 2109.58. In re Soeder's Estate (Cuyahoga 1966) 7 Ohio App.2d 271, 220 N.E.2d 547, 36 O.O.2d 404.

A person who is not included in any of the classes of persons to whom notice of the filing of an inventory, the hearing thereon, the filing of exceptions, or the hearing thereon, is required to be given and who was never served with such notice but merely appeared as a witness at the hearing on exceptions to the inventory, claiming ownership of certain items of personal property claimed by the exceptor to belong to the estate, cannot appeal from a judgment of the probate court ordering such property included in the inventory. In re Apger's Estate (Van Wert 1960) 111 Ohio App. 164, 171 N.E.2d 347, 14 O.O.2d 54.

7. Time limitations

Failure of decedent's daughter to file timely exceptions to inventory did not waive arguments as to later account; daughter was not given opportunity to timely file exceptions to inventory, since her first notice was not received until after scheduled hearing date, daughter was then never successfully served with continued inventory hearing notice, which would have extended her time for filing exceptions, and there was no indication that daughter was served with first partial account or given notice of hearing on account, and without being aware that account was filed, she could not be expected to file timely exceptions. In re Estate of Reinhart

(Ohio App. 7 Dist., Mahoning, 09-13-2005) No. 05 MA 36, 2005-Ohio-4894, 2005 WL 2267397, Unreported. Executors And Administrators ⚖ 504(4)

Reasons advanced by probate court for taking of additional inventory of estate have no bearing upon right to except to such subsequent inventory if done within limitations of this section and under former GC 10639 (RC 2115.16) period of six months within which exceptions may be filed by persons falling within class specified in said statute began to run from date of filing of particular inventory to which exception was taken. In re Milliken's Estate (Summit 1937) 24 Ohio Law Abs. 650.

Res judicata did not prevent decedent's daughter from challenging the exclusion of the family Bible from the inventory of decedent's estate, although she did not raise the issue at the time the probate court approved the inventory of the estate; title to the family Bible was disputed, issue of whether the family Bible was properly an asset of the estate had never been raised, litigated, or determined, and, as trial court had determined that son's gifting of the family Bible to his own child was invalid, the Bible had the status of a concealed asset of the estate such that there was no time limit on the filing of exceptions to the exclusion of that asset from the estate. In re Estate of Kelsey (Ohio App. 11 Dist., 03-10-2006) 165 Ohio App.3d 680, 847 N.E.2d 1277, 2006-Ohio-1171. Executors And Administrators ⚖ 72

The fact that a hearing on an inventory and appraisement was not had within one month after the filing thereof does not invalidate the proceeding because such time limit is directory and not mandatory. In re Ray's Estate (Ohio Prob. 1958) 156 N.E.2d 210, 79 Ohio Law Abs. 368.

Where the rules of probate court prescribe the time within which a petition shall be filed to secure a review of a widow's allowance, the court does not have authority to diminish such allowance upon a petition filed after such time has expired. In re Johnson's Estate (Cuyahoga 1958) 150 N.E.2d 501, 80 Ohio Law Abs. 180.

2115.17 Real estate appraisal conclusive

When the inventory required by section 2115.02 of the Revised Code has been approved by the probate court, the appraisement of the real estate as set forth therein shall be conclusive for all purposes except estate tax, unless a reappraisal is ordered by the court.

(132 v S 326, eff. 7–1–68; 1953 H 1; GC 10509–61)

Historical and Statutory Notes

Pre–1953 H 1 Amendments: 114 v 415

Library References

Executors and Administrators ⚖67, 72.
Westlaw Topic No. 162.
C.J.S. Executors and Administrators §§ 157, 160.

Research References

Encyclopedias
OH Jur. 3d Decedents' Estates § 1260, Appraisal; Dispensing With Appraisal—Reappraisal.
OH Jur. 3d Decedents' Estates § 1269, Effect of Approval of Inventory.

Treatises and Practice Aids
Carlin, Baldwin's Ohio Practice, Merrick-Rippner Probate Law § 2:23, Inventory and Appraisal—Filing of Inventory.
Carlin, Baldwin's Ohio Practice, Merrick-Rippner Probate Law § 2:44, Elective Rights of Surviving Spouse—Election of Surviving Spouse to Purchase Property—Application or Complaint to Purchase, Notice and Hearing.
Carlin, Baldwin's Ohio Practice, Merrick-Rippner Probate Law § 2:121, Administration of Decedent's Estate—Checklist.
Carlin, Baldwin's Ohio Practice, Merrick-Rippner Probate Law § 21:68, Rights of Surviving Spouse—Procedure for Purchase—Objections to Appraised Value.

Notes of Decisions

Modification of appraisement 1
Reappraisal 2

---

1. Modification of appraisement

Inclusion of disputed personal property in estate inventory was not a binding determination that the estate owned such property, with respect to subsequent litigation on ownership issue, absent filed exceptions and a hearing thereon. Poling v. Poling (Ohio App. 4 Dist., Hocking, 10-17-2003) No. 03CA3, 2003-Ohio-5601, 2003 WL 22390093, Unreported, on subsequent appeal 2005-Ohio-5147, 2005 WL 2386482. Executors And Administrators ⚖ 72

When devisees, other than the surviving spouse, have added substantial value to the mansion house after the appraisement, the surviving spouse is not entitled to purchase the property at the appraisement price. Wobser v. Tanner (Ohio 1979) 60 Ohio St.2d 28, 396 N.E.2d 753, 14 O.O.3d 195.

Where, in the administration of an estate, a motion to vacate and set aside an order previously entered approving and confirming an inventory filed therein is timely filed by the surviving spouse, although not within one month after such order approving such inventory, and is subsequently found to be well taken and an order is thereupon entered that such previously approved inventory be modified by the deletion therefrom of certain personal property and by increasing the amount of the widow's year's allowance, such order of modification does not constitute a vacation of the previous order of approval so as to reinstate in such surviving spouse the right of election to purchase the mansion house for the one-month period from the date of such order of modification. In re Hrabnicky's Estate (Ohio 1958) 167 Ohio St. 507, 149 N.E.2d 909, 5 O.O.2d 181. Executors And Administrators ⚖ 67; Executors And Administrators ⚖ 191

2. Reappraisal

RC 2113.38 contemplates an adversary-type proceeding in which the defendants—the heirs, devisees, legatees, lienholders et al.—are given the opportunity to show the presence of fraud, collusion or the manifest inadequacy of the price fixed in the inventory, and if the evidence obtained shows fraud, collusion or the manifest inadequacy of the price, the court shall order a reappraisal as provided in RC 2115.17; if these items are not shown, the price fixed in the inventory is final. Bratanov v. Riemenschneider (Summit 1980) 1 Ohio App.3d 42, 439 N.E.2d 434, 1 O.B.R. 251.

An executor who is the beneficiary of an option to purchase real estate of the testator must, in order to purchase and obtain clear title to such property, not only exercise his option to purchase such property, but also make application to and obtain the approval of the probate court for such sale, and in such case, the probate court is not precluded from ordering a reappraisal of such real estate by the fact that an appraisal has been made and approved. Walters v. Wannemacher (Paulding 1964) 6 Ohio App.2d 226, 217 N.E.2d 695, 35 O.O.2d 385.

When the inventory has been approved by the probate court, the appraisement of the real estate as set forth therein becomes conclusive for all purposes except inheritance tax, unless a reappraisal is ordered by the court. In re Fouts' Estate (Clark 1957) 103 Ohio App. 313, 145 N.E.2d 440, 3 O.O.2d 353.

CHAPTER 2117

PRESENTMENT OF CLAIMS AGAINST ESTATE

DEBTS DUE EXECUTOR OR ADMINISTRATOR
Section
2117.01 Debts due an executor or administrator

Section
2117.02 Presentation of claim to probate court
2117.03 Disinterested person to represent estate

Section
2117.04 Appeals

CLAIMS OF CREDITORS
2117.05 Compromise and settlement of claims
2117.06 Presentation and allowance of creditor's claims; procedure
2117.061 Decedent aged fifty-five years or older; notice to administrator of estate recovery program
2117.07 Acceleration of bar against claims against estate
2117.08 Authentication of claims
2117.09 Disputed claims
2117.10 Failure of lienholder to present claim

REJECTION OF CLAIMS
2117.11 Rejection of claim
2117.12 Action on rejected claim barred
2117.13 Claims rejected on requisition of heir, devisee, or creditor
2117.14 Parties to action on claim rejected on requisition
2117.15 Payment of debts

HEARING ON CLAIMS
2117.17 Hearing on allowed claims; optional

TAXES
2117.18 Taxes or forfeitures
2117.19 No allowance to tax inquisitors

PAYMENT OF DEBTS
2117.25 Order in which debts to be paid
2117.251 Liability for funeral expenses when irrevocable pre-need funeral contract purchased
2117.27 Vendor's lien not preferred
2117.28 Debts not due
2117.29 Beneficiary taking subject to mortgage

SUITS AGAINST EXECUTOR OR ADMINISTRATOR
2117.30 Time for filing suits against estate
2117.31 Estate of deceased joint debtor
2117.33 Claims previously barred
2117.34 Execution; limitations
2117.35 Executions against executor or administrator

REAL ESTATE NOT LIABLE FOR DEBTS
2117.36 Real estate not liable for debts

CONTINGENT CLAIMS
2117.37 Presentation of contingent claims
2117.38 Assets from which payment to be made
2117.39 Contingent claims not to be presented
2117.40 Estate of deceased in the hands of heirs
2117.41 Payment of contingent claims after settlement of estate
2117.42 Creditors may proceed against all in one action

Cross References

Claims against estate for support of patient, waiver, contract for payment, 5121.10
Executor or administrator of surety may require creditor to sue principal or forfeit right to payment, 1341.05
Falsification, 2921.13
Paternity proceedings, limitation of action to determine father and child relationship, 3111.05
Wills, contribution of others toward loss of one legatee's or devisee's property taken for debt, 2107.54

Law Review and Journal Commentaries

Bankruptcy Basics—Death and Bankruptcy. 48 Dayton B Briefs 22 (October 1998).

Estate Planning and Conflict of Laws, John W. Ester and Eugene F. Scoles. 24 Ohio St L J 270 (Winter 1963).

Insolvent estates: Priority of debts and payment of claims. John D. Clark, 14 Prob L J Ohio 52 (January/February 2004).

The Use of Will Substitutes to Disinherit the Surviving Spouse, William A. Polster. 13 W Reserve U L Rev 674 (1962).

DEBTS DUE EXECUTOR OR ADMINISTRATOR

2117.01 Debts due an executor or administrator

No part of the assets of a deceased shall be retained by an executor or administrator in satisfaction of his own claim, until it has been proved to and allowed by the probate court. Such debt is not entitled to preference over others of the same class.

(1953 H 1, eff. 10–1–53; GC 10509–105)

Historical and Statutory Notes

Pre–1953 H 1 Amendments: 114 v 425

Cross References

Claims against estate for support of a patient, waiver, contract for payment, 5121.10
Claims against estate of deceased patient or relative, contracts for fixed annual payment on behalf of living patient, 5121.52

Library References

Executors and Administrators ⇐219, 265.
Westlaw Topic No. 162.
C.J.S. Executors and Administrators §§ 419, 513.

Research References

Encyclopedias

OH Jur. 3d Decedents' Estates § 1327, Claims of Executors or Administrators.
OH Jur. 3d Incompetent Persons § 165, Liability of Patient or Patient's Estate.

Treatises and Practice Aids

Carlin, Baldwin's Ohio Practice, Merrick-Rippner Probate Law § 83:1, Fiduciary Claims—Time Limit.
Carlin, Baldwin's Ohio Practice, Merrick-Rippner Probate Law § 89:7, Payment of Debts—Funeral Expenses—General Rule.
Carlin, Baldwin's Ohio Practice, Merrick-Rippner Probate Law § 2:121, Administration of Decedent's Estate—Checklist.
Carlin, Baldwin's Ohio Practice, Merrick-Rippner Probate Law § 84:22, Creditor's Claims—Claims Not Requiring Presentation—Promissory Notes; Mortgage Liens.
Carlin, Baldwin's Ohio Practice, Merrick-Rippner Probate Law § 99:11, Application to Change Name of Minor—Form.
Carlin, Baldwin's Ohio Practice, Merrick-Rippner Probate Law § 99:14, Consent of Parent to Minor's Change of Name—Form.

Law Review and Journal Commentaries

Insolvent estates: Priority of debts and payment of claims. John D. Clark, 14 Prob L J Ohio 52 (January/February 2004).

Notes of Decisions

Loans 2
Mandatory requirements 1
Parties 3
Preference 4

---

1. Mandatory requirements

Executor of decedent's estate, who had recorded mortgage lien on decedent's residence which was filed before decedent's death, was not required to present his claim to probate court for allowance, since his lien was secured claim. In re Estate of Cogan (App. 8 Dist., 10-06-1997) 123 Ohio App.3d 186, 703 N.E.2d 858, dismissed, jurisdictional motion overruled 81 Ohio St.3d 1442, 690 N.E.2d 14. Executors And Administrators ⇐222(1)

Sections are mandatory as to how a personal representative's claim against the estate he is administering shall be allowed, and an administrator must follow them in regard to allowing a claim by his co-administrator.

Fulton v. Roderick (Stark 1936) 55 Ohio App. 327, 9 N.E.2d 876, 24 Ohio Law Abs. 453, 9 O.O. 69.

The provisions of sections, governing the manner of presentation and allowance of claims of an executor or administrator against the estate which he represents, are mandatory, and cannot be circumvented by the payment of such claims, the listing of them in accounts, and the approval by the probate court of such accounts; nor by the listing of such claims in a petition to determine inheritance taxes. Trustees of Masonic Temple Ass'n of Sidney v. Emmons (Shelby 1934) 49 Ohio App. 87, 195 N.E. 259, 18 Ohio Law Abs. 526, 1 O.O. 286. Executors And Administrators ⇔ 228(1)

A claim alleged to be due a law firm, in which an executor is a partner, is subject to the mandatory requirements of section. Trustees of Masonic Temple Ass'n of Sidney v. Emmons (Shelby 1934) 49 Ohio App. 87, 195 N.E. 259, 18 Ohio Law Abs. 526, 1 O.O. 286.

2. Loans

Based upon usage of trade and the particular course of dealings between the parties, a decedent's delivery of an unendorsed stock certificate along with stock powers to a bank is additional collateral for a pre-existing loan and creates a perfected security agreement when the bank retains possession of the stock, entitling it to the proceeds of the sale of the stock, rather than the estate. Higley v Toledo Trust Co, No. L–82–282 (6th Dist Ct App, Lucas, 3–18–83).

The probate court was within its sound discretion in determining no loan contract existed where a wife-executrix wrote various checks to her husband and there was no written loan agreement, no evidence of interest payments, or a repayment schedule. In re Estate of Sheban, No. 82 CA 33 (7th Dist Ct App, Mahoning, 1–26–83).

3. Parties

In a proceeding for the allowance of a claim of an executor against the estate his co-executor is not a necessary party. Downing v Downing, 3 CC(NS) 623, 13 CD 389 (Trumbull 1902).

4. Preference

An administratrix cannot retain the assets of the estate until the claim has been allowed by the probate court, and her debt cannot be entitled to any preference over others of the same class. Liggett v. Liggett's Estate (Ohio Prob. 1905) 3 Ohio N.P.N.S. 518, 51 W.L.B. 59. Executors And Administrators ⇔ 219; Executors And Administrators ⇔ 228(3)

2117.02 Presentation of claim to probate court

An executor or administrator within three months after the date of his appointment shall present any claim he has against the estate to the probate court for allowance. The claim shall not be paid unless allowed by the court. When an executor or administrator presents a claim amounting to five hundred dollars or more, the court shall fix a day not less than four nor more than six weeks from its presentation, when the testimony touching it shall be heard. The court forthwith shall issue an order directed to the executor or administrator requiring him to give notice in writing to all the heirs, legatees, or devisees of the decedent interested in the estate, and to the creditors named in the order. The notice shall contain a statement of the amount claimed, designate the time fixed for hearing the testimony, and be served upon the persons named in the order at least twenty days before the time for hearing. If any persons mentioned in the order are not residents of the county, service of notice may be made upon them by publication for three consecutive weeks in a newspaper published or circulating in the county, or as the court may direct. All persons named in the order shall be parties to the proceeding, and any other person having an interest in the estate may be made a party.

(1975 S 145, eff. 1–1–76; 1973 H 566; 129 v 7; 1953 H 1; GC 10509–106)

Historical and Statutory Notes

Pre–1953 H 1 Amendments: 114 v 425

Cross References

Service of notice, Civ R 73

Library References

Executors and Administrators ⇔225(4), 219, 222 to 228(5).
Westlaw Topic No. 162.
C.J.S. Executors and Administrators §§ 419, 422 to 450, 454.

Research References

Encyclopedias
OH Jur. 3d Alternative Dispute Resolution § 225, Waiver or Loss of Right to Arbitrate.
OH Jur. 3d Alternative Dispute Resolution § 249, Stay of Trial.
OH Jur. 3d Appellate Review § 66, Rulings on Continuances and Stay Applications.
OH Jur. 3d Decedents' Estates § 1327, Claims of Executors or Administrators.
OH Jur. 3d Decedents' Estates § 1375, Procedure for Allowance of Attorneys' Fees; Remedies.
OH Jur. 3d Decedents' Estates § 1427, Claims Required to be Presented.
OH Jur. 3d Decedents' Estates § 1461, Presentation of Claim to Probate Court.
OH Jur. 3d Decedents' Estates § 1462, Hearing on Claim.
OH Jur. 3d Employment Relations § 536, Enforcement of Arbitration Agreements.

Treatises and Practice Aids
Carlin, Baldwin's Ohio Practice, Merrick-Rippner Probate Law § 3:3, Jurisdiction of Probate Court—Subject Matter—in General.
Carlin, Baldwin's Ohio Practice, Merrick-Rippner Probate Law § 2:27, Payment of Debts and Claims—Presentation of Claims.
Carlin, Baldwin's Ohio Practice, Merrick-Rippner Probate Law § 83:1, Fiduciary Claims—Time Limit.
Carlin, Baldwin's Ohio Practice, Merrick-Rippner Probate Law § 83:2, Fiduciary Claims—Hearings and Notice.
Carlin, Baldwin's Ohio Practice, Merrick-Rippner Probate Law § 83:7, Fiduciary Claims—Jurisdiction to Allow.
Carlin, Baldwin's Ohio Practice, Merrick-Rippner Probate Law § 83:8, Fiduciary Claims—Estate Tax Deductions.
Carlin, Baldwin's Ohio Practice, Merrick-Rippner Probate Law § 83:9, Presentation of Claim by Administrator or Executor—Form.
Carlin, Baldwin's Ohio Practice, Merrick-Rippner Probate Law § 89:7, Payment of Debts—Funeral Expenses—General Rule.
Carlin, Baldwin's Ohio Practice, Merrick-Rippner Probate Law § 2:121, Administration of Decedent's Estate—Checklist.
Carlin, Baldwin's Ohio Practice, Merrick-Rippner Probate Law § 57:10, Removal of Fiduciary—Procedure—Discretion of Probate Court.
Carlin, Baldwin's Ohio Practice, Merrick-Rippner Probate Law § 79:20, Inventory—Exceptions—Hearing.
Carlin, Baldwin's Ohio Practice, Merrick-Rippner Probate Law § 83:10, Entry Setting Claim for Hearing and Ordering Notice—Form.
Carlin, Baldwin's Ohio Practice, Merrick-Rippner Probate Law § 83:11, Notice of Hearing on Claim—Form.
Carlin, Baldwin's Ohio Practice, Merrick-Rippner Probate Law § 83:12, Notice of Publication—Form.
Carlin, Baldwin's Ohio Practice, Merrick-Rippner Probate Law § 83:15, Entry Allowing Claim—Form.
Carlin, Baldwin's Ohio Practice, Merrick-Rippner Probate Law § 84:22, Creditor's Claims—Claims Not Requiring Presentation—Promissory Notes; Mortgage Liens.

Law Review and Journal Commentaries

Notice Requirements In Ohio Estate And Guardianship Proceedings—Why The Difference?, Comment. 20 Cap U L Rev 455 (Spring 1991).

Notes of Decisions

Allowance 2
Jurisdiction 5
Notice 6
Parties 3
Procedural issues 1

Time limitations 4

1. Procedural issues

Executor of murder victim's estate and other individual could not recover punitive damages in action against victim's mother-in-law for intentional infliction of emotional distress and other claims that was based on mother-in-law's alleged failure to disclose information regarding murder and location of victim's remains during 20 years prior to arrest of victim's husband for her murder, where there was no award of compensatory damages against mother-in-law. Hartman v. Smith (Ohio App. 9 Dist., Wayne, 06-29-2005) No. 04CA0079, 2005-Ohio-3299, 2005 WL 1523862, Unreported. Dead Bodies ⇔ 9

Notwithstanding RC 2101.24, the probate court does not have the authority under RC 2115.16 to impress a constructive trust on savings bonds at a hearing on exceptions, since such a hearing is a summary proceeding conducted by the probate court solely to determine whether all of the proper assets and liabilities have been included in a decedent's estate; the issue of the fraudulent appropriation of the purchase money for the bonds should be brought pursuant to RC 2117.02. In re Estate of Etzensperger (Ohio 1984) 9 Ohio St.3d 19, 457 N.E.2d 1161, 9 O.B.R. 112.

The provisions of RC 2117.01 through RC 2117.04 are mandatory and provide the exclusive method for presentation and allowance of claims by an executor against the estate which he represents. Wilhoit v. Powell's Estate (Butler 1980) 70 Ohio App.2d 61, 434 N.E.2d 742, 24 O.O.3d 75. Executors And Administrators ⇔ 219

An executor's or administrator's claim need not be personally signed by the executor or administrator to be valid. In re McClintock (Ohio Com.Pl. 1978) 58 Ohio Misc. 5, 388 N.E.2d 762, 12 O.O.3d 60. Executors And Administrators ⇔ 227(7)

In a proceeding under this section to have a claim on a promissory note paid, payments by an insured decedent on a policy assigned to him by the payee of the note cannot be set off. Claypool v. Claypool (Ohio Cir. 1903) 15 Ohio C.D. 327, 4 Ohio C.C.(N.S.) 577, affirmed 75 Ohio St. 578, 80 N.E. 1125, 4 Ohio Law Rep. 479.

A proceeding commenced by an administrator for the allowance of a claim which he owns himself is an action in his behalf, and so far as that proceeding is concerned he is not the executor of the estate; the probate judge sits in his place as the statute provides and the proceeding is treated in all respects as an action in favor of the claimant. In re Ward's Estate (Ohio Cir. 1900) 12 Ohio C.D. 44.

2. Allowance

Executor of decedent's estate, who had recorded mortgage lien on decedent's residence which was filed before decedent's death, was not required to present his claim to probate court for allowance, since his lien was secured claim. In re Estate of Cogan (App. 8 Dist., 10-06-1997) 123 Ohio App.3d 186, 703 N.E.2d 858, dismissed, jurisdictional motion overruled 81 Ohio St.3d 1442, 690 N.E.2d 14. Executors And Administrators ⇔ 222(1)

Where a fine is imposed upon the conviction of a defendant and that defendant dies prior to the collection of the fine and before there has been a levy against the property of the defendant, the fine cannot be collected from the estate of the defendant. State v. Blake (Cuyahoga 1977) 53 Ohio App.2d 101, 371 N.E.2d 843, 7 O.O.3d 71. Executors And Administrators ⇔ 202

Where the claim of an executor against the estate which he represents is not presented to the probate court and allowed, such claim cannot be allowed as a deductible debt against the estate in the determination of the inheritance tax. In re Beckman's Estate (Mercer 1951) 91 Ohio App. 42, 107 N.E.2d 538, 48 O.O. 236. Taxation ⇔ 3355

An administratrix cannot retain the assets of the estate until the claim has been allowed by the probate court, and her debt cannot be entitled to any preference over others of the same class. Liggett v. Liggett's Estate (Ohio Prob. 1905) 3 Ohio N.P.N.S. 518, 51 W.L.B. 529. Executors And Administrators ⇔ 219; Executors And Administrators ⇔ 228(3)

A promissory note which is payable at a decedent's death is valid and enforceable, and it therefore is deductible for estate tax purposes. Wilder v. C.I.R. (N.D.Ohio 1983) 581 F.Supp. 86. Internal Revenue ⇔ 4177.10(3)

3. Parties

Fact that residuary beneficiary, who inherited real property upon his father's death, benefited from the denial of his brother's claim for a share of balance of money mother loaned to father to purchase the land, did not result in unjust enrichment of residuary beneficiary; father and mother entered into agreement regarding the loan for the money, expressly stating that promissory note for the loan was not to be entered as an asset or debit in father's or mother's estate, and thus doctrine of unjust enrichment, which operates in absence of an express contract, did not apply, and brother failed to plead operative facts allowing a claim for unjust enrichment. Davidson v. Davidson (Ohio App. 3 Dist., Auglaize, 12-05-2005) No. 17-05-12, 2005-Ohio-6414, 2005 WL 3274853, Unreported. Executors And Administrators ⇔ 202.10

Testator's son stated a claim against testator's estate for payments on promissory note accrued prior to testator's death, although terms of the note specifically excluded entering the note as an asset or debit in testator's estate, where testator had stopped making payments on note several years prior to his death, and note, which specifically excluded promissory note from estate, was silent on the enforcement of the accrued payments, thereby implying that payments accrued prior to testator's death should be enforced against his estate. Davidson v. Davidson (Ohio App. 3 Dist., Auglaize, 12-05-2005) No. 17-05-12, 2005-Ohio-6414, 2005 WL 3274853, Unreported. Executors And Administrators ⇔ 202.10

Bank, as testamentary trustee of testator's estate pursuant to will, was necessary party to proceedings in which executor of testator's estate filed claim against estate for work done to improve property. In re Townsend (Ohio App. 12 Dist., Fayette, 06-14-2004) No. CA2003-08-009, 2004-Ohio-3016, 2004 WL 1300318, Unreported. Executors And Administrators ⇔ 251

In a proceeding under RC 2117.02 in which executor seeks allowance of his personal claim against his wife's estate in amount equal to one-half the gross estate, tax commissioner is a proper party, as "person having an interest in the estate," as result of potential reduction in estate tax liability upon allowance of claim. In re Taylor's Estate (Ohio Prob. 1970) 23 Ohio Misc. 142, 254 N.E.2d 925, 51 O.O.2d 89, 52 O.O.2d 169.

A "suitable" person, qualified for appointment as an executor under RC 2113.05, means a person who is reasonably disinterested in the estate and the legatees and beneficiaries under the will. In re Young's Estate (Franklin 1964) 4 Ohio App.2d 315, 212 N.E.2d 612, 33 O.O.2d 357, appeal dismissed 177 Ohio St. 76, 202 N.E.2d 308, 29 O.O.2d 196.

Where interest of administrator and his wife in claim for services against his decedent's estate was joint or united, and value of services by one of them for decedent during her lifetime could not be separated from value of similar services by the other, wife was not only a proper but also a necessary party to proceedings in probate court by administrator for allowance of his claim against his decedent's estate. In re Smith's Estate (Ohio Prob. 1952) 120 N.E.2d 632, 67 Ohio Law Abs. 409. Executors And Administrators ⇔ 251

In a proceeding for the allowance of a claim of an executor against the estate his co-executor is not a necessary party. Downing v Downing, 3 CC(NS) 623, 13 CD 389 (Trumbull 1902).

4. Time limitations

Provision of promissory note, stating that note was not to be entered as an asset or debit against estate of promisor or promisee, extinguished any further obligation under the note at time of promisor's death, and thus note could not be enforced against promisor's estate. Davidson v. Davidson (Ohio App. 3 Dist., Auglaize, 12-05-2005) No. 17-05-12, 2005-Ohio-6414, 2005 WL 3274853, Unreported. Executors And Administrators ⇔ 202.10

Statute of limitation requiring executor or administrator of estate to present claim against the estate to probate court within three months after date of his appointment applied, barring decedent's son from bringing claim against estate, asserted more than one year after his appointment as co-executor, for specific performance of alleged oral contract to transfer farm. Poling v. Poling (Ohio App. 4 Dist., Hocking, 10-17-2003) No. 03CA3, 2003-Ohio-5601, 2003 WL 22390093, Unreported, on subsequent appeal 2005-Ohio-5147, 2005 WL 2386482. Executors And Administrators ⇔ 225(4)

Executor's failure to comply with three-month statute of limitations for presentment of claims against estates by executors cannot be excused. In re Estate of Waterman (Ohio App. 2 Dist., Champaign, 06-27-2003) No. 2002-CA-28, 2003-Ohio-3406, 2003 WL 21487863, Unreported. Executors And Administrators ⇔ 225(4)

This section is a statute of limitations, and executor or administrator who does not present his claim to probate court within three months after his appointment is barred thereafter. In re Grube's Estate (Clark 1935) 21 Ohio Law Abs. 1. Executors And Administrators ⇐ 225(4)

A failure to hear testimony regarding an executor's or administrator's claim within the time limits of RC 2117.02 does not result in a lack of jurisdiction by the court over the claim. In re McClintock (Ohio Com.Pl. 1978) 58 Ohio Misc. 5, 388 N.E.2d 762, 12 O.O.3d 60.

The time provisions of RC 2117.02 as to when testimony regarding an executor's or administrator's claim must be heard, are directory not mandatory. In re McClintock (Ohio Com.Pl. 1978) 58 Ohio Misc. 5, 388 N.E.2d 762, 12 O.O.3d 60.

The period prescribed by RC 2117.02 for the presentment of claims by an executor or administrator to the probate court for allowance begins as of the date of the appointment of the executor or administrator and is not interrupted by the removal of the executor or administrator and the simultaneous appointment of his successor within such four-month period. Allen v. Hunter (Franklin 1964) 1 Ohio App.2d 278, 204 N.E.2d 545, 30 O.O.2d 296.

The provisions of RC 2117.02 that an executor or administrator shall present any claim which he has against the estate to the probate court for allowance within the time prescribed is mandatory and constitutes a statute of limitation. Allen v. Hunter (Franklin 1964) 1 Ohio App.2d 278, 204 N.E.2d 545, 30 O.O.2d 296.

A claim due to a law firm in which an executor is a partner is subject to the limitations in RC 2117.02, which is a statute of limitations, and the executor or administrator who does not present his claim to probate court within the time allowed after his appointment is barred thereafter. In re Crawford's Estate (Ohio Prob. 1962) 184 N.E.2d 779, 89 Ohio Law Abs. 530, 21 O.O.2d 215.

An administrator must file his claim against an estate within three months after his appointment, and his resignation after expiration of the three month period does not permit the filing of the claim against the successor administrator. In re Grindle's Estate (Ohio Prob. 1961) 182 N.E.2d 887, 88 Ohio Law Abs. 289, 23 O.O.2d 442.

Executor's claim against estate for expenses of funeral conducted by executor in his capacity as an undertaker was properly allowed in the amount of $350 though claim was not presented to probate court within time provided by statute. In re Winders' Estate (Noble 1945) 68 N.E.2d 677, 45 Ohio Law Abs. 353. Executors And Administrators ⇐ 233

Where executor, who was also funeral director, failed to file his claim for funeral expenses within time limit provided in section and failed to request authority to present claim after such time as provided by GC 10509–134 (RC 2117.07), probate court did not err in allowing subsequent claim to extent of $350 under authority in GC 10509–193 (RC 2113.36) which allows executors further allowance for extraordinary services. In re Winders' Estate (Noble 1945) 68 N.E.2d 677, 45 Ohio Law Abs. 353.

Claims against estate which were not filed within three months of appointment of executor or administrator as required by statute were not barred where decedent died before effective date of statute. Mott v. Fulton (Ohio 1936) 131 Ohio St. 500, 3 N.E.2d 404, 6 O.O. 163. Executors And Administrators ⇐ 223

A claim by the executor of his mother's estate that he is entitled to compensation for services in running her farm is barred under RS 6100 within six years from his appointment and qualification as executor. In re Ward's Estate (Ohio Cir. 1900) 12 Ohio C.D. 44.

An executor or administrator must present his unsecured claim against the estate to the probate court for allowance within three months after the date of his appointment or be forever barred from maintaining an action thereon. Cribbs v. Sturman (Ohio Prob. 1933) 32 Ohio N.P.N.S. 29.

5. Jurisdiction

A probate court has jurisdiction to pass upon a claim against an estate filed individually by one of the co-administrators of such estate, but such court has no jurisdiction in such proceeding to examine into a claim of such estate against such co-administrator and her husband for moneys allegedly owing the estate on promissory notes. In re Stutz's Estate (Darke 1964) 1 Ohio App.2d 188, 204 N.E.2d 248, 30 O.O.2d 212. Courts ⇐ 201; Executors And Administrators ⇐ 250

Where a co-administrator and his wife hold a joint claim against an estate for services rendered, the probate court has jurisdiction to pass on the claim. In re Smith's Estate (Ohio Prob. 1952) 120 N.E.2d 632, 67 Ohio Law Abs. 409.

Where a claim for an allowance to the parents of a deceased child out of the child's estate is brought and an exception to the rule disallowing such a claim is presented, the power conferred by RS 6100 carries with it the necessary equitable jurisdiction. Spink v. Spink (Ohio Cir. 1905) 18 Ohio C.D. 94, 7 Ohio C.C.(N.S.) 89, affirmed 78 Ohio St. 390, 85 N.E. 1131, 5 Ohio Law Rep. 607.

6. Notice

A person who is appointed administratrix of an estate on the assumption that she is the sole heir at law of the decedent and who is also the only creditor of the estate is not required to present her claim to the probate court and serve notice thereof on herself as such sole heir. Haag v. Meffley (Lucas 1951) 89 Ohio App. 471, 103 N.E.2d 37, 46 O.O. 274.

Where husband created a trust for the benefit of his wife and brother, and wife during her lifetime entered into an agreement with the brother whereby wife was to have full benefit of trust during her lifetime and brother was to be entitled to the principal of the trust on death of wife, and wife in her will acknowledged that principal of trust belonged to husband's brother on her death, and wife died, fact that claim of brother to principal of trust was listed in the inventory in estate proceedings was sufficient notice to the state, which claimed that inheritance tax was due on principal of trust. In re Matthews' Estate (Hamilton 1951) 101 N.E.2d 303, 60 Ohio Law Abs. 385. Taxation ⇐ 3349

2117.03 Disinterested person to represent estate

At any time after the presentation by an executor or administrator of a claim which he owns against the estate he represents to the probate court for allowance, the court on its own motion, or on motion by any interested party, may appoint an attorney to represent the estate, who shall receive such compensation from the estate as may be fixed by the court. The court shall thereupon require the executor or administrator to make available to such attorney, for use in connection with the proceeding, all documents belonging to the estate relating to the subject matter of such claim.

(1953 H 1, eff. 10–1–53; GC 10509–107)

Historical and Statutory Notes

Pre–1953 H 1 Amendments: 114 v 425

Library References

Executors and Administrators ⇐111(8), 219, 251.

Westlaw Topic No. 162.

C.J.S. Executors and Administrators §§ 237, 239, 251 to 254, 258 to 259, 261, 263, 419, 480, 483 to 485.

Research References

Encyclopedias

OH Jur. 3d Alternative Dispute Resolution § 250, Court Order Compelling Arbitration.

OH Jur. 3d Alternative Dispute Resolution § 251, Court Order Compelling Arbitration—Effect of Dispute as to Existence or Performance of Arbitration Agreement.

OH Jur. 3d Decedents' Estates § 1362, Compensation to Special Administrator or Others Acting in Place of Representative.

OH Jur. 3d Decedents' Estates § 1463, Hearing on Claim—Representation of Estate by Disinterested Person.

Treatises and Practice Aids

Carlin, Baldwin's Ohio Practice, Merrick-Rippner Probate Law § 83:3, Fiduciary Claims—Inquiry.

Carlin, Baldwin's Ohio Practice, Merrick-Rippner Probate Law § 83:13, Motion for Appointment of Attorney to Represent Estate—Form.

Carlin, Baldwin's Ohio Practice, Merrick-Rippner Probate Law § 83:14, Entry Appointing Attorney to Represent Estate—Form.

Notes of Decisions

Time limitations 1

---

1. Time limitations

A claim due to a law firm in which an executor is a partner is subject to the limitations in RC 2117.02, which is a statute of limitations, and the executor or administrator who does not present his claim to probate court within the time allowed after his appointment is barred thereafter. In re Crawford's Estate (Ohio Prob. 1962) 184 N.E.2d 779, 89 Ohio Law Abs. 530, 21 O.O.2d 215.

2117.04 Appeals

Upon the hearing as to the allowance of an executor's or administrator's claim against the estate he represents, an appeal may be taken from a final order or judgment of the probate court upon a matter of law by any person affected by the order or judgment.

(1986 H 412, eff. 3–17–87; 1953 H 1; GC 10509–108)

Historical and Statutory Notes

Pre–1953 H 1 Amendments: 114 v 425

Library References

Executors and Administrators ⚖=256(2), 256(3).
Westlaw Topic No. 162.
C.J.S. Executors and Administrators §§ 491 to 493.

Research References

Encyclopedias

OH Jur. 3d Decedents' Estates § 1327, Claims of Executors or Administrators.

OH Jur. 3d Decedents' Estates § 1464, Exceptions and Appeals.

Treatises and Practice Aids

Carlin, Baldwin's Ohio Practice, Merrick-Rippner Probate Law § 83:1, Fiduciary Claims—Time Limit.

Carlin, Baldwin's Ohio Practice, Merrick-Rippner Probate Law § 2:121, Administration of Decedent's Estate—Checklist.

Painter & Dennis, Ohio Appellate Practice § 1:23, Right to Appeal-Appeal from Lower to Higher Court.

CLAIMS OF CREDITORS

2117.05 Compromise and settlement of claims

On the application of an executor or administrator for authority to compromise and settle a claim in favor of or against a decedent's estate, the probate court, upon hearing on such application and after reasonable notice has been given to all persons who would be adversely affected thereby as determined by the court, may authorize or direct the executor or administrator to compromise and settle such claim on such terms as the court deems to be for the best interest of the estate. The court may dispense with the notice of such hearing if it deems notice to be unnecessary. An executor authorized by the will to make such compromise and settlement may but shall not be required to apply to the court for such authority.

(1953 H 1, eff. 10–1–53; GC 10509–72)

Historical and Statutory Notes

Pre–1953 H 1 Amendments: 119 v 394, § 1; 114 v 417

Cross References

Deceased partner, rights and priority of creditors, 1775.40

Library References

Executors and Administrators ⚖=87.
Westlaw Topic No. 162.
C.J.S. Executors and Administrators § 202.

Research References

Encyclopedias

OH Jur. 3d Decedents' Estates § 1421, Compromise of Claims Due or Against the Estate.

Treatises and Practice Aids

Carlin, Baldwin's Ohio Practice, Merrick-Rippner Probate Law § 2:30, Payment of Debts and Claims—Options of Fiduciary.

Carlin, Baldwin's Ohio Practice, Merrick-Rippner Probate Law § 2:121, Administration of Decedent's Estate—Checklist.

Carlin, Baldwin's Ohio Practice, Merrick-Rippner Probate Law § 84:40, Application for Authority to Compromise Claim—Form.

Carlin, Baldwin's Ohio Practice, Merrick-Rippner Probate Law § 84:41, Entry to Compromise Claim—Form.

Carlin, Baldwin's Ohio Practice, Merrick-Rippner Probate Law App B SPF 14.0, Application to Approve Settlement and Distribution of Wrongful Death and Survival Claims—Form.

Restatement (2d) of Property, Don. Trans. § 33.1, Meaning of a Will.

Law Review and Journal Commentaries

Bankruptcy Basics—Death and Bankruptcy. 48 Dayton B Briefs 22 (October 1998).

Notes of Decisions

Deficiencies 1
Estate's best interest 2
Executor's debt 4
Parties 3

---

1. Deficiencies

Where the amount due an estate of a decedent from the surety on the bond of a deceased fiduciary for certain delinquencies is not in dispute at the time a settlement is made with such surety, it is not necessary for the successor fiduciary to pay or tender back the amount received before pursuing any remedy available to him to recover from the surety for other and separate delinquencies. In re Gray's Estate (Ohio 1954) 162 Ohio St. 384, 123 N.E.2d 408, 55 O.O. 224. Compromise And Settlement ⚖= 18(3)

2. Estate's best interest

An administrator or executor of an estate need not obtain prior court approval of a settlement or compromise of a claim against the estate, as long as the settlement or compromise is bona fide, reasonable and beneficial to the estate. Surber v. Woodruff (Ohio Com.Pl. 1983) 10 Ohio Misc.2d 1, 460 N.E.2d 1164, 10 O.B.R. 87. Executors And Administrators ⚖= 269

3. Parties

A fiduciary of a decedent's estate has no right and, in fact, cannot be authorized by the probate court which appoints him to be a party to a compromise of the succession rights in a decedent's estate. In re Cantor's Estate (Ohio Prob. 1963) 200 N.E.2d 515, 94 Ohio Law Abs. 102, 31 O.O.2d 393, appeal dismissed 177 Ohio St. 59, 202 N.E.2d 307, 29 O.O.2d 155. Descent And Distribution ⚖= 82

4. Executor's debt

This section does not contemplate a debt owed to estate by executor thereof, since it is neither reasonable nor just that a debtor should compromise a claim with himself. In re Koons' Estate (Ohio Prob. 1938) 6 Ohio Supp. 320, 26 Ohio Law Abs. 512, 11 O.O. 389.

2117.06 Presentation and allowance of creditor's claims; procedure

(A) All creditors having claims against an estate, including claims arising out of contract, out of tort, on cognovit notes, or on judgments, whether due or not due, secured or unsecured, liquidated or unliquidated, shall present their claims in one of the following manners:

(1) After the appointment of an executor or administrator and prior to the filing of a final account or a certificate of termination, in one of the following manners:

(a) To the executor or administrator in a writing;

(b) To the executor or administrator in a writing, and to the probate court by filing a copy of the writing with it;

(c) In a writing that is sent by ordinary mail addressed to the decedent and that is actually received by the executor or administrator within the appropriate time specified in division (B) of this section. For purposes of this division, if an executor or administrator is not a natural person, the writing shall be considered as being actually received by the executor or administrator only if the person charged with the primary responsibility of administering the estate of the decedent actually receives the writing within the appropriate time specified in division (B) of this section.

(2) If the final account or certificate of termination has been filed, in a writing to those distributees of the decedent's estate who may share liability for the payment of the claim.

(B) Except as provided in section 2117.061 of the Revised Code, all claims shall be presented within six months after the death of the decedent, whether or not the estate is released from administration or an executor or administrator is appointed during that six-month period. Every claim presented shall set forth the claimant's address.

(C) Except as provided in section 2117.061 of the Revised Code, a claim that is not presented within six months after the death of the decedent shall be forever barred as to all parties, including, but not limited to, devisees, legatees, and distributees. No payment shall be made on the claim and no action shall be maintained on the claim, except as otherwise provided in sections 2117.37 to 2117.42 of the Revised Code with reference to contingent claims.

(D) In the absence of any prior demand for allowance, the executor or administrator shall allow or reject all claims, except tax assessment claims, within thirty days after their presentation, provided that failure of the executor or administrator to allow or reject within that time shall not prevent the executor or administrator from doing so after that time and shall not prejudice the rights of any claimant. Upon the allowance of a claim, the executor or the administrator, on demand of the creditor, shall furnish the creditor with a written statement or memorandum of the fact and date of the allowance.

(E) If the executor or administrator has actual knowledge of a pending action commenced against the decedent prior to the decedent's death in a court of record in this state, the executor or administrator shall file a notice of the appointment of the executor or administrator in the pending action within ten days after acquiring that knowledge. If the administrator or executor is not a natural person, actual knowledge of a pending suit against the decedent shall be limited to the actual knowledge of the person charged with the primary responsibility of administering the estate of the decedent. Failure to file the notice within the ten-day period does not extend the claim period established by this section.

(F) This section applies to any person who is required to give written notice to the executor or administrator of a motion or application to revive an action pending against the decedent at the date of the death of the decedent.

(G) Nothing in this section or in section 2117.07 of the Revised Code shall be construed to reduce the periods of limitation or periods prior to repose in section 2125.02 or Chapter 2305. of the Revised Code, provided that no portion of any recovery on a claim brought pursuant to that section or any section in that chapter shall come from the assets of an estate unless the claim has been presented against the estate in accordance with Chapter 2117. of the Revised Code.

(H) Any person whose claim has been presented and has not been rejected after presentment is a creditor as that term is used in Chapters 2113. to 2125. of the Revised Code. Claims that are contingent need not be presented except as provided in sections 2117.37 to 2117.42 of the Revised Code, but, whether presented pursuant to those sections or this section, contingent claims may be presented in any of the manners described in division (A) of this section.

(I) If a creditor presents a claim against an estate in accordance with division (A)(1)(b) of this section, the probate court shall not close the administration of the estate until that claim is allowed or rejected.

(J) The probate court shall not require an executor or administrator to make and return into the court a schedule of claims against the estate.

(K) If the executor or administrator makes a distribution of the assets of the estate pursuant to section 2113.53 of the Revised Code and prior to the expiration of the time for the presentation of claims as set forth in this section, the executor or administrator shall provide notice on the account delivered to each distributee that the distributee may be liable to the estate if a claim is presented prior to the filing of the final account and may be liable to the claimant if the claim is presented after the filing of the final account up to the value of the distribution and may be required to return all or any part of the value of the distribution if a valid claim is subsequently made against the estate within the time permitted under this section.

(2004 S 80, eff. 4–7–05; 2003 H 51, eff. 4–8–04; 2003 H 95, eff. 9–26–03; 2002 S 281, eff. 4–11–03; 2001 S 108, § 2.01, eff. 7–6–01; 2001 S 108, § 2.02, eff. 7–6–01; 2001 H 85, eff. 10–31–01; 1996 H 350, eff. 1–27–97 [1]; 1990 H 346, eff. 5–31–90; 1988 S 228; 1984 H 37; 1983 H 291, S 115; 1982 H 379; 1975 S 145; 1969 H 363; 131 v H 580; 127 v 701; 1953 H 1; GC 10509–112)

[1] See Notes of Decisions, *State ex rel. Ohio Academy of Trial Lawyers v. Sheward* (Ohio 1999), 86 Ohio St.3d 451, 715 N.E.2d 1062.

Uncodified Law

2004 H 161, § 3, eff. 4–8–04 reads, in part:

(C) Sections 2107.19, 2109.301, 2113.53, 2117.06, 2117.07, 2117.11, and 2117.12 of the Revised Code, as amended by this act, apply to estates of decedents who die on or after April 8, 2004.

2002 S 281, § 6 through 8, eff. 4–11–03, read:

Section 6. (A) Sections 1751.67, 2117.06, 2305.11, 2305.15, 2305.234, 2317.02, 2317.54, 2323.56, 2711.21, 2711.22, 2711.23, 2711.24, 2743.02, 2743.43, 2919.16, 3923.63, 3923.64, 3929.71, and 5111.018 of the Revised Code, as amended by this act, and sections 2303.23, 2305.113, 2323.41, 2323.42, 2323.43, and 2323.55 of the Revised Code, as enacted by this act, apply to civil actions upon a medical claim, dental claim, optometric claim, or chiropractic claim in which the act or omission that constitutes the alleged basis of the claim occurs on or after the effective date of this act.

(B) As used in this section, "medical claim," "dental claim," "optometric claim," and "chiropractic claim" have the same meanings as in section 2305.113 of the Revised Code.

Section 7. If any item of law that constitutes the whole or part of a section of law contained in this act, or if any application of any item of law that constitutes the whole or part of a section of law contained in this act, is held invalid, the invalidity does not affect other items of law or applications of items of law that can be given effect without the invalid item of law or application. To this end, the items of law of which the sections contained in this act are composed, and their applications, are independent and severable.

Section 8. If any item of law that constitutes the whole or part of a section of law contained in this act, or if any application of any item of law contained in this act, is held to be preempted by federal law, the preemption of the item of law or its application does not affect other items of law or applications that can be given affect. The items of law of which the sections of this act are composed, and their applications, are independent and severable.

2001 S 108, § 1, eff. 7–6–01, reads:

It is the intent of this act (1) to repeal the Tort Reform Act, Am. Sub. H.B. 350 of the 121st General Assembly, 146 Ohio Laws 3867, in conformity with the Supreme Court of Ohio's decision in *State, ex rel. Ohio Academy of Trial Lawyers, v. Sheward* (1999), 86 Ohio St.3d 451; (2) to clarify the status of the law; and (3) to revive the law as it existed prior to the Tort Reform Act.

2001 S 108, § 3, eff. 7–6–01, reads, in part:

(A) In Section 2.01 of this act:

(3) Sections 109.36, 2117.06, 2125.01, 2125.02, 2125.04, 2305.10, 2305.16, 2305.27, 2305.38, 2307.31, 2307.32, 2307.75, 2307.80, 2315.01, 2315.19, 2501.02, 2744.06, 3722.08, 4112.14, 4113.52, 4171.10, and 4399.18 of the Revised Code are revived and amended, supersede the versions of the same sections that are repealed by Section 2.02 of this act, and include amendments that gender neutralize the language of the sections (as contemplated by section 1.31 of the Revised Code) and that correct apparent error.

1990 H 346, § 3, eff. 5–31–90, reads, in part: (A) Sections 1 and 2 of this act shall apply only to the estates of decedents who die on or after the effective date of this act.

1990 H 346, § 4, eff. 5–31–90, reads: The General Assembly hereby requests the supreme court to exercise its general superintendence authority over courts in this state, pursuant to section 5(A)(1) of Article IV, Ohio Constitution, to adopt standard probate forms that provide notice, to all distributees of an estate when assets are distributed prior to the one-year bar on claims established under section 2117.06 of the Revised Code, of their potential liabilities with respect to claims filed within the statutory time limitation.

1988 S 228, § 4, eff. 3–22–89, reads: The amendments to sections 2107.39, 2115.02, and 2117.06 of the Revised Code contained in this act shall apply only with respect to the estates of decedents whose deaths occur on or after the effective date of this act.

1983 H 291, § 127, eff. 7–1–83, reads: The amendment of sections 2117.06, 5731.01, 5731.011, 5731.02, 5731.05, 5731.09, 5731.14, 5731.15, 5731.16, 5731.18, 5731.21, 5731.22, 5731.26, 5731.42, and 5731.48, the enactment of sections 5731.131, 5731.181, 5731.231, and 5731.99, and the repeal of section 5731.20 of the Revised Code, all by this act, shall apply to the estate of any decedent whose death occurs on or after July 1, 1983.

Historical and Statutory Notes

Ed. Note: The amendment of this section by 1996 H 350, eff. 1–27–97, was repealed by 2001 S 108, § 2.02, eff. 7–6–01. See *Baldwin's Ohio Legislative Service Annotated*, 1996, page 10/L–3378, and 2001, page 6/L–1441, or the OH–LEGIS or OH–LEGIS–OLD database on Westlaw, for original versions of these Acts.

Pre–1953 H 1 Amendments: 119 v 394, § 1; 114 v 426

Amendment Note: 2004 S 80 rewrote subdivision (G), which prior thereto read:

"(G) Nothing in this section or in section 2117.07 of the Revised Code shall be construed to reduce the time mentioned in section 2125.02, 2305.09, 2305.10, 2305.11, 2305.113, or 2305.12 of the Revised Code, provided that no portion of any recovery on a claim brought pursuant to any of those sections shall come from the assets of an estate unless the claim has been presented against the estate in accordance with Chapter 2117. of the Revised Code."

Amendment Note: 2003 H 51 added new divisions (A)(1) and (A)(2); and redesignated former divisions (A)(1) to (3) as new subdivisions (A)(1)(a) to (c), respectfully; substituted "six months" for "one year" in divisions (B) and (C); substituted "(A)(1)(b)" for "(A)(2)" in division (I); inserted "pursuant to section 2113.53 of the Revised Code and" and "if a claim is presented prior to the filing of the final account and may be liable to the claimant if the claim is presented after the filing of the final account" in division (K); substituted "presentation" for "filing" in division (K); and made other nonsubstantive changes.

Amendment Note: 2003 H 95 substituted "Except as provided in section 2117.061 of the Revised Code, all" for "All" in division (B); and substituted "Except as provided in section 2117.061 of the Revised Code, a" for "A" in division (C).

Amendment Note: 2002 S 281 inserted "2305.113" in division (G); and made changes to reflect gender neutral language.

Amendment Note: 2001 H 85 inserted "of the executor or administrator" after "appointment" in division (E); rewrote divisions (H) and (K); made changes to reflect gender neutral language; and made other nonsubstantive changes. Prior to amendment divisions (H) and (K) read:

"(H) Any person whose claim has been presented, and not thereafter rejected, is a creditor as that term is used in Chapters 2113. to 2125. of the Revised Code. Claims that are contingent need not be presented except as provided in sections 2117.37 to 2117.42 of the Revised Code, but whether presented pursuant to those sections or this section, contingent claims may be presented in any of the manners described in division (A) of this section.

"(K) If the executor or administrator makes a distribution of the assets of the estate prior to the expiration of the time for the filing of claims as set forth in this section, he shall provide notice to each distributee as provided in section 2113.533 of the Revised Code."

Amendment Note: 1996 H 350 rewrote division (G); and made changes to reflect gender neutral language and other nonsubstantive changes. Prior to amendment, division (G) read:

"(G) Nothing in this section or in section 2117.07 of the Revised Code shall be construed to reduce the time mentioned in section 2125.02, 2305.09, 2305.10, 2305.11, or 2305.12 of the Revised Code, provided that no portion of any recovery on a claim brought pursuant to any of those sections shall come from the assets of an estate, unless the claim has been presented against the estate in accordance with Chapter 2117. of the Revised Code."

OSBA Probate and Trust Law Section

1983:

Situations exist where a Creditor does not wish to institute litigation to enforce his claim but does not want his claim to be overlooked or forgotten. The Board of Governors believes that the instant legislation would help in this situation since it directs the Probate Court not to close an estate administration prior to such claims being either allowed or rejected.

Cross References

Claims filed with the court, Sup R 62
Estates, release from administration, 2113.03
Final order, 2505.02
Institution caring for incompetent, claim for cost authorized, 5121.10
Liability for claim, limitations, 2113.53
Liability for debts and claims against estate after filing of certification of termination, 2109.301
Presentation of claims to ancillary administrator, 2129.12
Proceedings by nonresident executor or administrator to bar creditor's claims, 2129.02
Substitution of parties, Civ R 25
Wills, contribution of others toward loss of one legatee's or devisee's property taken for debt, exception, 2107.54

Ohio Administrative Code References

Judicial enforcement actions, OAC 5101:12–50–50

Library References

Executors and Administrators ⚖227, 228.
Westlaw Topic No. 162.
C.J.S. Executors and Administrators §§ 438 to 439, 441 to 450, 454.
 Baldwin's Ohio Legislative Service, 1988 Laws of Ohio, S 228—LSC Analysis, p 5–968; 1990 Laws of Ohio, H 346—LSC Analysis, p 5–87

Research References

Encyclopedias

OH Jur. 3d Criminal Law § 1441, Conveying Prohibited Items Onto Grounds of Criminal Justice Facility—Defenses.
OH Jur. 3d Decedents' Estates § 1341, Funeral Expenses.
OH Jur. 3d Decedents' Estates § 1424, Statutory Requirement for Presentation of Creditors Claims, Generally.
OH Jur. 3d Decedents' Estates § 1426, Purposes of Statutory Requirement—Application.

OH Jur. 3d Decedents' Estates § 1427, Claims Required to be Presented.
OH Jur. 3d Decedents' Estates § 1428, Contingent Claims.
OH Jur. 3d Decedents' Estates § 1430, Excuse for Failure to Present Claim—Waiver of Presentation.
OH Jur. 3d Decedents' Estates § 1432, Claims Expressly Excepted by Statute.
OH Jur. 3d Decedents' Estates § 1434, Claims Secured by Mortgages or Liens.
OH Jur. 3d Decedents' Estates § 1437, Requirement that Presentation be in Writing and Contain Claimant's Address.
OH Jur. 3d Decedents' Estates § 1438, Requirement that Claim be Presented to Representative.
OH Jur. 3d Decedents' Estates § 1441, Statute Requiring Presentation of Claims Within One Year.
OH Jur. 3d Decedents' Estates § 1445, Relation of Statutes to Other Limitation Statutes.
OH Jur. 3d Decedents' Estates § 1448, Effect of Failure to Present Claims Within Limitation Periods.
OH Jur. 3d Decedents' Estates § 1450, Time for Investigating Claim.
OH Jur. 3d Decedents' Estates § 1453, Requirement of Written Statement of Allowance of Claim.
OH Jur. 3d Decedents' Estates § 1454, Requirement of Written Statement of Allowance of Claim—What Constitutes Allowance.
OH Jur. 3d Decedents' Estates § 1455, Requirement of Written Statement of Allowance of Claim—Effect of Allowance.
OH Jur. 3d Decedents' Estates § 1628, Prerequisites to Distribution.
OH Jur. 3d Decedents' Estates § 1629, Prerequisites to Distribution—Making Provisions for Debts.
OH Jur. 3d Decedents' Estates § 1633, Receipts, Acknowledgments, and Releases on Distribution.
OH Jur. 3d Decedents' Estates § 1696, Liability for Excess Payments.
OH Jur. 3d Decedents' Estates § 1714, Presentation, Payment, or Bar of Claims of Creditors.
OH Jur. 3d Decedents' Estates § 1789, Action on Contingent Claims.
OH Jur. 3d Decedents' Estates § 1791, Action on Claim Neither Allowed Nor Rejected.
OH Jur. 3d Decedents' Estates § 1832, Application to Release, and Order Releasing, Estate from Administration.
OH Jur. 3d Limitations & Laches § 88, Effect of Death—Effect of Nonclaim Statute in Wrongful Death Action Where Tortfeasor Dies.

Forms

Ohio Forms Legal and Business § 16:101, Assignment of Creditor's Claims Against Estate.
Ohio Jurisprudence Pleading and Practice Forms § 12:11, Checklist—Statutes of Limitations.

Treatises and Practice Aids

Carlin, Baldwin's Ohio Practice, Merrick-Rippner Probate Law § 2:3, Time for Administration of Decedent's Estate and Payment of Estate Taxes.
Carlin, Baldwin's Ohio Practice, Merrick-Rippner Probate Law § 2:27, Payment of Debts and Claims—Presentation of Claims.
Carlin, Baldwin's Ohio Practice, Merrick-Rippner Probate Law § 2:28, Payment of Debts and Claims—Notice to Creditors.
Carlin, Baldwin's Ohio Practice, Merrick-Rippner Probate Law § 2:30, Payment of Debts and Claims—Options of Fiduciary.
Carlin, Baldwin's Ohio Practice, Merrick-Rippner Probate Law § 2:33, Payment of Debts and Claims—Schedule of Debts.
Carlin, Baldwin's Ohio Practice, Merrick-Rippner Probate Law § 2:34, Payment of Debts and Claims—Mortgage and Tax Liens.
Carlin, Baldwin's Ohio Practice, Merrick-Rippner Probate Law § 2:92, Fiduciary's Account—Time for Filing.
Carlin, Baldwin's Ohio Practice, Merrick-Rippner Probate Law § 30:9, Drafting a Will—Payment of Debts, Administration Expenses, and Taxes.
Carlin, Baldwin's Ohio Practice, Merrick-Rippner Probate Law § 48:9, Beneficiaries Liable for Payment of Decedent's Debts—General Rules.
Carlin, Baldwin's Ohio Practice, Merrick-Rippner Probate Law § 50:4, Agreement to Make a Will—Effect.
Carlin, Baldwin's Ohio Practice, Merrick-Rippner Probate Law § 53:5, Fiduciary's Attorney—Agent.
Carlin, Baldwin's Ohio Practice, Merrick-Rippner Probate Law § 54:1, Fiduciary Accounts—Filing—Time.
Carlin, Baldwin's Ohio Practice, Merrick-Rippner Probate Law § 54:9, Fiduciary Accounts—Exceptions to Requirement to Account.
Carlin, Baldwin's Ohio Practice, Merrick-Rippner Probate Law § 75:2, Distribution—Voluntary—Required Notice to Distributee.
Carlin, Baldwin's Ohio Practice, Merrick-Rippner Probate Law § 75:3, Distribution—Voluntary—Liability—Beneficiaries or Heirs.
Carlin, Baldwin's Ohio Practice, Merrick-Rippner Probate Law § 75:4, Distribution—Voluntary—Liability—Executor or Administrator.
Carlin, Baldwin's Ohio Practice, Merrick-Rippner Probate Law § 75:5, Distribution—Voluntary—Rejected Claims and Claims in Suit.
Carlin, Baldwin's Ohio Practice, Merrick-Rippner Probate Law § 81:3, Removal—Application.
Carlin, Baldwin's Ohio Practice, Merrick-Rippner Probate Law § 84:1, Creditor's Claims—Introduction.
Carlin, Baldwin's Ohio Practice, Merrick-Rippner Probate Law § 84:2, Creditor's Claims—Purpose of Statutes.
Carlin, Baldwin's Ohio Practice, Merrick-Rippner Probate Law § 84:3, Creditor's Claims—Form of Claim.
Carlin, Baldwin's Ohio Practice, Merrick-Rippner Probate Law § 84:4, Creditors Claims—Creditor Defined.
Carlin, Baldwin's Ohio Practice, Merrick-Rippner Probate Law § 84:5, Creditor's Claims—Claims Requiring Presentation—Statutory Provision.
Carlin, Baldwin's Ohio Practice, Merrick-Rippner Probate Law § 84:6, Creditor's Claims—Claims Requiring Presentation—Examples from Case Law.
Carlin, Baldwin's Ohio Practice, Merrick-Rippner Probate Law § 84:8, Creditor's Claims—Claims Requiring Presentation—Examples from Case Law—Rents.
Carlin, Baldwin's Ohio Practice, Merrick-Rippner Probate Law § 85:1, Acceleration of Claims—Introduction and Purpose of Statute.
Carlin, Baldwin's Ohio Practice, Merrick-Rippner Probate Law § 85:2, Acceleration of Claims—Effect on Other Statutes of Limitations.
Carlin, Baldwin's Ohio Practice, Merrick-Rippner Probate Law § 86:3, Death of Claimant—Motion for Substitution Within Ninety Days.
Carlin, Baldwin's Ohio Practice, Merrick-Rippner Probate Law § 87:1, Hearings on Claims—Rule Requiring Resolution of All Claims.
Carlin, Baldwin's Ohio Practice, Merrick-Rippner Probate Law § 88:1, Rejection of Claims—Purpose of Statute.
Carlin, Baldwin's Ohio Practice, Merrick-Rippner Probate Law § 88:2, Rejection of Claims—Manner of Rejection; Constructive Rejection.
Carlin, Baldwin's Ohio Practice, Merrick-Rippner Probate Law § 88:3, Rejection of Claims—Procedure.
Carlin, Baldwin's Ohio Practice, Merrick-Rippner Probate Law § 88:4, Rejection of Claims—Forced Rejection.
Carlin, Baldwin's Ohio Practice, Merrick-Rippner Probate Law § 88:8, Rejection of Claims—Action on Rejected Claim—Suit Within Two Months of Rejection.
Carlin, Baldwin's Ohio Practice, Merrick-Rippner Probate Law § 88:9, Rejection of Claims—Action on Rejected Claim—Commencement.
Carlin, Baldwin's Ohio Practice, Merrick-Rippner Probate Law § 89:7, Payment of Debts—Funeral Expenses—General Rule.
Carlin, Baldwin's Ohio Practice, Merrick-Rippner Probate Law § 2:101, Distribution of Assets—Legacies and Distributions.
Carlin, Baldwin's Ohio Practice, Merrick-Rippner Probate Law § 2:106, Distribution of Assets—Transfer of Real Estate.
Carlin, Baldwin's Ohio Practice, Merrick-Rippner Probate Law § 2:118, Certificate of Transfer or Interest in Real Property.
Carlin, Baldwin's Ohio Practice, Merrick-Rippner Probate Law § 2:121, Administration of Decedent's Estate—Checklist.
Carlin, Baldwin's Ohio Practice, Merrick-Rippner Probate Law § 48:10, Beneficiaries Liable for Payment of Decedent's Debts—Liability for Secured Claims.
Carlin, Baldwin's Ohio Practice, Merrick-Rippner Probate Law § 48:11, Liability for Payment of Claims Against Estate.
Carlin, Baldwin's Ohio Practice, Merrick-Rippner Probate Law § 64:27, Compensation—Attorneys.
Carlin, Baldwin's Ohio Practice, Merrick-Rippner Probate Law § 80:10, Extraordinary Services—Compensation Allowed.
Carlin, Baldwin's Ohio Practice, Merrick-Rippner Probate Law § 84:10, Creditor's Claims—Claims Requiring Presentation—Examples from Case Law—Personal Injury Actions.
Carlin, Baldwin's Ohio Practice, Merrick-Rippner Probate Law § 84:12, Creditor's Claims—Claims Requiring Presentation—Examples from Case Law—Counterclaims.

Carlin, Baldwin's Ohio Practice, Merrick-Rippner Probate Law § 84:13, Creditor's Claims—Claims Requiring Presentation—Examples from Case Law—Buy-Sell Agreements; Contract.

Carlin, Baldwin's Ohio Practice, Merrick-Rippner Probate Law § 84:14, Creditor's Claims—Claims Requiring Presentation—Guardian or Attorney Fees.

Carlin, Baldwin's Ohio Practice, Merrick-Rippner Probate Law § 84:16, Creditor's Claims—Claims Not Requiring Presentation—Federal Taxes—State Claim.

Carlin, Baldwin's Ohio Practice, Merrick-Rippner Probate Law § 84:17, Creditor's Claims—Claims Not Requiring Presentation—Trust Property.

Carlin, Baldwin's Ohio Practice, Merrick-Rippner Probate Law § 84:23, Creditor's Claims—Claims Not Requiring Presentation—Ownership of Assets in an Estate.

Carlin, Baldwin's Ohio Practice, Merrick-Rippner Probate Law § 84:24, Creditor's Claims—Claims Not Requiring Presentation—Contingent Claims—Definition.

Carlin, Baldwin's Ohio Practice, Merrick-Rippner Probate Law § 84:25, Creditor's Claims—Claims Not Requiring Presentation—Contingent Claims—Mandatory Presentation.

Carlin, Baldwin's Ohio Practice, Merrick-Rippner Probate Law § 84:29, Creditor's Claims—Statute of Limitations.

Carlin, Baldwin's Ohio Practice, Merrick-Rippner Probate Law § 84:30, Creditor's Claims—Acceleration of Bar Against Claims Against Estate.

Carlin, Baldwin's Ohio Practice, Merrick-Rippner Probate Law § 84:31, Creditor's Claims—No Savings Clause.

Carlin, Baldwin's Ohio Practice, Merrick-Rippner Probate Law § 84:32, Creditor's Claims—Setoff of Barred Claim.

Carlin, Baldwin's Ohio Practice, Merrick-Rippner Probate Law § 84:33, Creditor's Claims—Laches as Defense.

Carlin, Baldwin's Ohio Practice, Merrick-Rippner Probate Law § 84:34, Creditor's Claims—Allowance or Rejection.

Carlin, Baldwin's Ohio Practice, Merrick-Rippner Probate Law § 84:35, Creditor's Claims—Suit on Rejected Claims; Constructive Rejection; Jurisdiction of Probate Court.

Carlin, Baldwin's Ohio Practice, Merrick-Rippner Probate Law § 84:36, Creditor's Claims—Waiver of Claim Against Estate.

Carlin, Baldwin's Ohio Practice, Merrick-Rippner Probate Law § 84:37, Creditor's Claims—Application to Revive Action.

Carlin, Baldwin's Ohio Practice, Merrick-Rippner Probate Law § 84:38, Creditor's Claims—Effect on Other Statutes of Limitations.

Carlin, Baldwin's Ohio Practice, Merrick-Rippner Probate Law § 84:39, Creditor's Claims—Notice to Distributees Before Expiration of Claim Period.

Carlin, Baldwin's Ohio Practice, Merrick-Rippner Probate Law § 84:42, Presentation of Claim Against Estate—Form.

Carlin, Baldwin's Ohio Practice, Merrick-Rippner Probate Law § 84:43, Complaint for Money Only—Form.

Carlin, Baldwin's Ohio Practice, Merrick-Rippner Probate Law § 88:14, Rejection of Claim Against Estate—Form.

Carlin, Baldwin's Ohio Practice, Merrick-Rippner Probate Law § 91:24, Land Sale—Necessary Parties Defendant—Lienholders.

Carlin, Baldwin's Ohio Practice, Merrick-Rippner Probate Law App B SPF 13.0, Fiduciary's Account.

Ohio Personal Injury Practice App. C, Appendix C. Ohio Academy of Trial Lawyers v. Sheward.

Kuehnle and Levey, Ohio Real Estate Law and Practice § 18:1, Ohio State Bar Association Standards of Title Examination.

Kuehnle and Levey, Ohio Real Estate Law and Practice § 10:17, Judgment Lien—Filing Certificate After Death of Debtor.

Kuehnle and Levey, Ohio Real Estate Law and Practice § 10:52, Debts of Decedent After First Year of Death.

Kuehnle and Levey, Ohio Real Estate Law and Practice § 41:17, Sales—Remedies—Specific Performance Against Heirs—Statute of Limitations.

Kuehnle and Levey, Ohio Real Estate Law and Practice § 52:13, Statutory Fiduciary Sales—Four-Year Limitations on Creditor's Suit.

Restatement (2d) of Property, Don. Trans. § 34.3, Creditors of Donor.

Restatement (3d) Property (Wills & Don. Trans.) § 1.1, Probate Estate.

Law Review and Journal Commentaries

Barred Claims Statute, Appeals from Probate Court Discussed, Hon. Nelson J. Brewer. 8 Clev B J 83 (March 1937).

Bankruptcy Basics—Death and Bankruptcy. 48 Dayton B Briefs 22 (October 1998).

Expanding the Rights of Creditors to Nonprobate Property: A Sensible Proposal to Close Ohio's Antiquated Loopholes, Daniel J. Hoffheimer. 13 Prob L J Ohio 23 (November/December 2002).

The New Right of Subrogation in Creditor's Claims. Walter C. Grosjean, 12 Prob L J Ohio 79 (May/June 2002).

Nonclaim Statute and Distributions: The Sooner the Better, Morton Bobowick. 13 Prob L J Ohio 21 (November/December 2002).

Notice By Publication To Creditors Insufficient, Russell J. Meraglio, Jr. 12 Lake Legal Views 8 (February 1989).

Payment of Debts of Decedent's Estate, Judge Richard B. Metcalf. 52 Title Topics 3 (July 1985).

Practical Application of House Bill 85 (Probate Reform 2001), Marilyn J. Maag. 13 Prob L J Ohio 19 (November/December 2002).

S 115 and H 288: Steps Toward Logic and Fairness in the Ohio Probate Law, Note. 10 U Dayton L Rev 213 (Fall 1984).

Notes of Decisions

Ed. Note: This section contains annotations from former RC 2113.08.

Barred claims   12
Claims includable   2
Constitutional issues   1
Defenses   9
Exceptions   5
Foreign creditors   14
Mailing claim   8
Mandatory requirements   10
Notice   13
Presentation   4
Procedural issues   3
Rejection   7
Revivor and late filing   6
Statute of limitations   11

---

1. Constitutional issues

1996 H 350, which amended more than 100 statutes and a variety of rules relating to tort and other civil actions, and which was an attempt to reenact provisions of law previously held unconstitutional by the Supreme Court of Ohio, is an act of usurpation of judicial power in violation of the doctrine of separation of powers; for that reason, and because of violation of the one-subject rule of the Ohio Constitution, 1996 H 350 is unconstitutional. State ex rel. Ohio Academy of Trial Lawyers v. Sheward (Ohio, 08-16-1999) 86 Ohio St.3d 451, 715 N.E.2d 1062, 1999-Ohio-123, reconsideration denied 87 Ohio St.3d 1409, 716 N.E.2d 1170.

A state probate code provision that creditors have two months to present claims to the executor after notice is published of the commencement of probate proceedings deprives creditors whose identities are known "or reasonably ascertainable" of property without due process of law; such creditors must be notified by mail or another means ensuring actual notice. (Ed. note: Oklahoma statute construed in light of federal constitution.) Tulsa Professional Collection Services, Inc. v. Pope (U.S.Okl. 1988) 108 S.Ct. 1340, 485 U.S. 478, 99 L.Ed.2d 565.

2. Claims includable

Claim against deceased successor attorney's estate was made in accord with statute in action by original attorney against successor attorneys to recover for services rendered to client, where trial was pending at the time of death, deceased successor attorney's counsel filed notice of suggestion of death, original attorney filed a motion to substitute party, motion was served upon counsel of record for decedent and upon executrix of decedent's estate, trial court granted the motion, and a copy of the order and entry granting the motion was sent to both counsel for decedent and executrix. Harraman v. Howlett (Ohio App. 5 Dist., Morrow, 10-08-2004)

No. 03CA0023, 2004-Ohio-5566, 2004 WL 2348514, Unreported. Executors And Administrators ⇨ 228(3)

Mortgage lien against land owned by decedent did not fall within rule requiring creditors to present any claims against the estate to the executor or administrator. Beneficial Mortg. Co. of Ohio v. Currie (Ohio App. 5 Dist., Stark, 09-27-2004) No. 2003CA00238, 2004-Ohio-5190, 2004 WL 2260678, Unreported. Executors And Administrators ⇨ 224

Creditor's claim statute did not bar claim of decedent's former wife to property which probate court had transferred to decedent's heirs following his death, as former wife, rather than decedent, held title to the property and thus her claim was to recover an asset wrongfully held in an estate. In re Estate of Dinsio (Ohio App. 7 Dist., 11-09-2004) 159 Ohio App.3d 98, 823 N.E.2d 43, 2004-Ohio-6036. Executors And Administrators ⇨ 225(1)

Person other than surviving spouse who pays deceased's funeral expenses, not as officious volunteer or meddler but out of necessity of occasion, is entitled to reimbursement from estate of deceased, provided bill is reasonable. Osborne v. Osborne (Ohio App. 2 Dist., 09-27-1996) 114 Ohio App.3d 412, 683 N.E.2d 365. Executors And Administrators ⇨ 214

Conduct of decedent's parents in paying for burial expenses after decedent's wife told them she had no money to pay those costs did not establish that payments were loan or gift to decedent's estate, so as to excuse estate from its duty of reimbursement. Osborne v. Osborne (Ohio App. 2 Dist., 09-27-1996) 114 Ohio App.3d 412, 683 N.E.2d 365. Executors And Administrators ⇨ 217; Gifts ⇨ 4

Requirement that creditors present claims against estate within limited time following appointment of executor or administrator applies only to those claims which may be allowed as debts payable out of assets of an estate. Lewis v. Steinreich (Ohio, 08-23-1995) 73 Ohio St.3d 299, 652 N.E.2d 981, 1995-Ohio-133, reconsideration denied 74 Ohio St.3d 1409, 655 N.E.2d 188. Executors And Administrators ⇨ 224

Contingent claim against estate is one in which liability depends upon some uncertain future event which may or may not occur. In re Estate of Bickham (Logan 1993) 85 Ohio App.3d 634, 620 N.E.2d 913. Executors And Administrators ⇨ 202.2

In deciding whether claim for guardian and attorney fees arising from guardianship are contingent, determinative factors are certainty of claims and extent to which their existence depends on uncertain future events. In re Estate of Bickham (Logan 1993) 85 Ohio App.3d 634, 620 N.E.2d 913. Executors And Administrators ⇨ 202.2

Guardian who had faithfully and honestly discharged duties of his or her trust is entitled to be compensated for his or her services from ward's estate. In re Estate of Bickham (Logan 1993) 85 Ohio App.3d 634, 620 N.E.2d 913. Executors And Administrators ⇨ 219.9; Guardian And Ward ⇨ 150

Where an equitable claim of ownership exists by virtue of an alleged contract with the decedent and only arises upon or subsequent to the death of the decedent, it is a claim against the estate and must be presented within the time limit prescribed by RC 2117.06(B). Spaceway Distribution & Storage Co., Inc. v. Williamson (Franklin 1987) 41 Ohio App.3d 187, 535 N.E.2d 321. Executors And Administrators ⇨ 225(1)

A letter of credit executed to secure a fixed underlying debt constitutes a contingent claim exempt from the three-month presentment requirement of RC 2117.06, where there is uncertainty as to when and under what circumstances the letter of credit may be drawn upon. Carter v. Bank One of Columbus, N.A. (Franklin 1986) 31 Ohio App.3d 82, 508 N.E.2d 1023, 31 O.B.R. 124.

Where a fine is imposed upon the conviction of a defendant and that defendant dies prior to the collection of the fine and before there has been a levy against the property of the defendant, the fine cannot be collected from the estate of the defendant. State v. Blake (Cuyahoga 1977) 53 Ohio App.2d 101, 371 N.E.2d 843, 7 O.O.3d 71. Executors And Administrators ⇨ 202

The filing of a petition in an action against an administratrix which contains the address of the plaintiff and sets forth a cause of action on a claim of negligence against the estate of defendant's decedent, which claim, under the facts alleged therein, will not be affected by the insolvency of the estate and which claim is based on facts occurring prior to the decedent's death, and the service of summons and a copy of the petition upon the administratrix within four months of her appointment, is a compliance with the mandatory requirements of RC 2117.06. Fortelka v. Meifert (Cuyahoga 1963) 120 Ohio App. 294, 193 N.E.2d 170, 93 Ohio Law Abs. 1, 27 O.O.2d 175, appeal certified to 120 Ohio App. 294, 193 N.E.2d 305, 93 Ohio Law Abs. 8, 27 O.O.2d 78, affirmed 176 Ohio St. 476, 200 N.E.2d 318, 27 O.O.2d 439.

In an action against an executor to recover under an implied contract for personal services alleged to have been rendered at the special instance and request of the decedent, where the record shows that plaintiffs bore no relationship to the decedent, that plaintiffs performed the services alleged, that such services were rendered at the request of the decedent and there is evidence from which the jury had a right to draw an inference that plaintiffs expected to be compensated, a question of fact as to whether plaintiffs rendered the services gratuitously or expected to be compensated is presented for the determination of the jury. Evans v. McInturff (Champaign 1960) 111 Ohio App. 445, 173 N.E.2d 162, 15 O.O.2d 62.

RC 2117.06 applies to claims arising out of both contract and tort. Hammond v. Richards (Ohio Com.Pl. 1959) 164 N.E.2d 919, 83 Ohio Law Abs. 482, 13 O.O.2d 30.

Where a decedent, eighty-two years old at the time of his death, is ill during his residence with his daughter-in-law, thereby necessitating personal care and attention by her, is rendered valuable personal services by her, is a personal and financial burden on her, and contributes nothing in the way of finances or services to the household, there is an absence of reciprocal and mutual benefits between the parties and a family relationship does not exist; and a claim by such daughter-in-law for such services is properly established. In re Bowman's Estate (Darke 1956) 102 Ohio App. 121, 141 N.E.2d 499, 2 O.O.2d 118.

Where the administrator of an estate allows a claim against the estate for services rendered the decedent, the burden to establish the validity of such claim is on the administrator. In re Bowman's Estate (Darke 1956) 102 Ohio App. 121, 141 N.E.2d 499, 2 O.O.2d 118. Executors And Administrators ⇨ 506(1)

Where a co-administrator and his wife hold a joint claim against an estate for services rendered, the probate court has jurisdiction to pass on the claim. In re Smith's Estate (Ohio Prob. 1952) 120 N.E.2d 632, 67 Ohio Law Abs. 409.

A person claiming ownership of certain chattels may bring a replevin action in common pleas court to recover possession of such property from the administrator of an estate who is wrongfully detaining it, for the reason that such owner is not interested in the inventory and has no claim against the estate. Service Transport Co. v. Matyas (Ohio 1953) 159 Ohio St. 300, 112 N.E.2d 20, 42 A.L.R.2d 413, 50 O.O. 298.

An alleged owner cannot ordinarily bring a replevin action in common pleas court against an executor or administrator of an estate in the course of administration in probate court. Service Transport Co. v. Matyas (Cuyahoga 1952) 108 N.E.2d 741, 63 Ohio Law Abs. 236, 63 Ohio Law Abs. 244, reversed 159 Ohio St. 300, 112 N.E.2d 20, 42 A.L.R.2d 413, 50 O.O. 298.

Where plaintiff prays for rescission and cancellation of contract to sell real property to defendant's decedent and that he may retain all moneys according to the terms of said contract as and for stipulated damages, the plaintiff is claiming damages and was required to file claim with decedent's administratrix. Buydden v. Mitchell (Montgomery 1951) 102 N.E.2d 21, 60 Ohio Law Abs. 493.

Where a court of chancery finds that the res of a trust is in the hands of the personal representatives of a deceased trustee, such res is not a debt and may be recovered from such personal representatives without compliance by the cestui que trust with the provisions of the section. Staley v. Kreinbihl (Ohio 1949) 152 Ohio St. 315, 89 N.E.2d 593, 40 O.O. 361.

A person having an unliquidated claim for damages arising out of tort is a creditor within the meaning of section, requiring presentation of claims by creditors to the executor or administrator within a specified time. Pierce v. Johnson (Ohio 1939) 136 Ohio St. 95, 23 N.E.2d 993, 125 A.L.R. 867, 16 O.O. 34. Executors And Administrators ⇨ 225(3)

Where a divorced wife of a deceased person brings an action against the administrator of the deceased to recover the aggregate amount of alimony due her under a decree of the court granting the divorce, the amount of such delinquencies is a proper subject for investigation by the administrator, and the claim for such amount must be presented to the administrator for allowance or rejection as required by section; the rule which excepts from the requirements of section such claims as conclusively prove themselves, leaving no discretion to the administrator to reject them, is wholly inapplicable to a case of an unadjudicated claim, based on the failure to comply with a court order, for an aggregate amount undetermined and indeterminate at the time that the order was made. Swearingin v. Rendigs (Hamilton 1935) 53 Ohio App. 221, 4 N.E.2d 695, 20 Ohio Law Abs. 317, 5 O.O. 457.

Presentment to the executor of a physician's claim for services rendered during the last sickness of the decedent is necessary although the executor had knowledge of the claim before the death of the testatrix and had negotiated concerning the same; the fact that the will directed payment of debts and expenses of the last sickness does not excuse presentment of the claim. Devers v. Schreiber (Hamilton 1935) 50 Ohio App. 442, 198 N.E. 601, 19 Ohio Law Abs. 549, 4 O.O. 183.

Where testator provided in will for payment of services rendered to him by legatee without designating amount therefor, and executor and legatee could not agree on amount of payment, compensation for such services held for jury. Fair v. Fair (Holmes 1933) 46 Ohio App. 51, 187 N.E. 727, 15 Ohio Law Abs. 149, 38 Ohio Law Rep. 291. Executors And Administrators ⇨ 451(2)

A formal indorsement of allowance by the administrator is not indispensable, and where a claim is presented to an administrator and not disputed or rejected by him, that is a sufficient allowance of the claim by him to authorize a suit to be brought thereon for the money. Smock v. Bouse (Ohio Cir. 1896) 5 Ohio C.D. 293.

Money or property held by an executor or administrator in his representative capacity before an order of distribution cannot be reached by attachment or garnishment in an action against the heir or legatee, under the Ohio rule of Orlopp v Schueller, 72 OS 41, 73 NE 1012 (1905). In re Granger (Bkrtcy.N.D.Ohio 1988) 90 B.R. 298. Attachment ⇨ 60; Garnishment ⇨ 35

Upon examination of this section there seems to be no restriction placed upon type or kind of claim that may be presented to executor or administrator, and use of word "shall" seems to make presentment of all claims, other than that of later maturing negotiable instruments, mandatory. In re Christopher's Estate (Ohio Prob. 1937) 4 Ohio Supp. 327, 24 Ohio Law Abs. 245, 8 O.O. 546, affirmed 35 N.E.2d 454, 26 Ohio Law Abs. 422, 11 O.O. 251.

Claims, whether due or not due, accrued or accruing within nine months following appointment of an executor or administrator and any further time that may be allowed by the court for collection of assets of the estate comes within the provisions of GC 10509–112 (RC 2117.06), 10509–133 (RC 2117.12) and 10509–134 (RC 2117.07). State ex rel. Squire v. Cleveland Trust Co. (Cuyahoga 1937) 58 Ohio App. 16, 15 N.E.2d 640, 26 Ohio Law Abs. 340, 11 O.O. 420.

When an agreement to purchase stocks is entered into by two individuals six months prior to the death of the purchaser, and that agreement provides for periodic payments as part of the purchase price of the stock, the seller may recover the balance due for the stock purchase from the estate of the purchaser after his death. Ross v Brown–Holcomb, No. 63277 (8th Dist Ct App, Cuyahoga, 2–4–93).

A claim against an estate for recovery of wages of the claimant withheld by the decedent to enable the claimant to build a house in the future arises out of a contract; thus, such claim is governed by the provisions of RC 2117.06, including applicable time limitations. Willis v McDermott; appeal dismissed by 47 OS(3d) 608, 546 NE(2d) 932 (1989), No. 53820 (8th Dist Ct App, Cuyahoga, 6–30–88).

Services rendered to a decedent during life are presumed to be performed in expectation of payment where there is no "family relationship" between the performer and the beneficiary of the services, defined not by affinity or consanguinity but by mutuality of benefit, and it is error to deny a claim for the reasonable value of such services. Estate of Fleming v Fleming, No. CA 83–08–009 (12th Dist Ct App, Clinton, 6–25–84).

While expenses of a last sickness are made before the death of the decedent and the funeral expenses are made after, both are preferred claims against the estate, and as such should be presented to the executor or administrator for his acceptance or rejection. In re Estate of Miller, 12 D 563 (CP, Hamilton 1902).

3. Procedural issues

Creditors are required to present their claims to administrator or executor within four months after date of his appointment; if not so presented creditor or person deriving title from him may petition probate court under GC 10509–134 (RC 2117.07) for leave to file his claim for allowance and that court may permit such claim to be filed. (See also Holmberg v Third Natl Bank & Trust Co, 27 Abs 58, 102 NE(2d) 23 (App, Montgomery 1938).) Holmberg v. Third Nat. Bank & Trust Co. (Montgomery 1936) 23 Ohio Law Abs. 631.

One-year limitations on claims against the deceased vendor's estate did not apply to action by vendee for specific performance of contract for sale and purchase of real estate brought against vendor's heirs, devisees, and estate; action was for specific performance of contract rather than claim against estate and estate was joined as party in that it would have right to resort to real estate or sale proceeds if there was insufficient personalty in estate to pay claims. Hackmann v. Dawley (Ohio App. 10 Dist., 07-18-1995) 105 Ohio App.3d 363, 663 N.E.2d 1342. Executors And Administrators ⇨ 437(3); Specific Performance ⇨ 105(2)

Procedural statute requiring presentment of creditors' claim within three months after appointment of executor or administrator does not apply to action in which claimant alleged ownership of property that was being wrongfully withheld by an estate; ownership claim is not a creditor's claim under statute. Lewis v. Steinreich (Ohio, 08-23-1995) 73 Ohio St.3d 299, 652 N.E.2d 981, 1995-Ohio-133, reconsideration denied 74 Ohio St.3d 1409, 655 N.E.2d 188. Executors And Administrators ⇨ 224

Tort plaintiff's claim against deceased defendant's estate was timely, though plaintiff did not file formal independent action on her claim against estate within two months of administrator's rejection of claim, where she timely substituted administrator for decedent in her tort action. Carlin v. Mambuca (Ohio App. 8 Dist., 05-23-1994) 96 Ohio App.3d 500, 645 N.E.2d 737, motion to certify allowed 70 Ohio St.3d 1475, 640 N.E.2d 848, cause dismissed 71 Ohio St.3d 1441, 643 N.E.2d 1152. Executors And Administrators ⇨ 437(2)

Although RC 2117.06 extinguishes the right to make any claim against an estate after the expiration of three months, the failure to timely assert a claim against an estate does not preclude asserting such claim in a cross-demand against the estate pursuant to RC 2309.19; however, the defendant is limited to pleading his claim as an extinguishment or abatement only and as a defense to the demand made by the administrator and the defendant may not recover from the administrator any surplus his claim may have over the amount of the demand made by the estate. Eaver v. McGinnis (Summit 1987) 41 Ohio App.3d 153, 534 N.E.2d 959.

A claim against a decedent's estate need not be in any particular form so long as it is in substantial compliance with RC 2117.06 and recognized by the fiduciary as a claim against the estate. Gladman v. Carns (Miami 1964) 9 Ohio App.2d 135, 223 N.E.2d 378, 38 O.O.2d 149.

A petition in an action against an executor of the estate of a decedent which alleges an oral presentation of a claim against the estate to, and an oral rejection of the claim by, the executor does not state facts which show a cause of action and is subject to demurrer. Morgan v. City Nat. Bank & Trust Co. (Franklin 1964) 4 Ohio App.2d 417, 212 N.E.2d 822, 33 O.O.2d 504.

Where a contingent claim against an estate accrues after complete distribution of the assets, the claimant's remedy for any deficiency is an action against the distributee, rather than seeking to vacate the order of final distribution and compelling the distributee to return the assets to the executor. In re Robbins' Estate (Ohio Prob. 1964) 200 N.E.2d 735, 94 Ohio Law Abs. 561, 28 O.O.2d 399.

Where, in an action against an administrator for damages for personal injuries, the petition did not allege that the claim sued on was presented to the administrator, and at the close of plaintiff's case the defendant moved for a directed verdict, plaintiff's oral motion to dismiss the action without prejudice was granted, and the jury dismissed, it is not prejudicially erroneous for the court to overrule plaintiff's motion for leave to withdraw the oral motion and to have the case set for trial, in the absence of a showing of abuse of discretion. Robinson v. Engle (Greene 1953) 96 Ohio App. 238, 120 N.E.2d 611, 54 O.O. 278.

In an action by an administrator to recover on a contractual obligation, a judgment on a cross-demand cannot be had unless cross-claimant has complied with GC 10509–112 (RC 2117.06) and 10509–113 (RC 2117.11), and presented such claim to administrator for allowance as therein required. Benson v. Rosine (Lucas 1945) 76 Ohio App. 439, 64 N.E.2d 845, 32 O.O. 195.

In action for wrongful death between administrators of the estates of two decedents killed in a common accident, the pleadings show on their face and by admission the date of appointment of plaintiff administrator to be more than four months after the date of appointment of defendant administrator, thus rendering it impossible for plaintiff administrator to have presented the tort claim to defendant administrator within the time prescribed by section, and fact that such plaintiff's amended reply denies the allegation contained in the second defense of the amended answer of failure to present the claim, which denial is consistent with possible proof of presentment of the claim by a proper beneficiary of the wrongful death statute, presents no issue of fact and a motion for judgment on the pleadings is properly sustained. Stange v. Campbell (Hamilton 1945) 75 Ohio App. 316, 62 N.E.2d 185, 43 Ohio Law Abs. 365, 31 O.O. 77.

Provisions of section requiring the filing of a claim against an administrator as a condition precedent to the bringing of an action against him on the claim, apply to a suit brought by a minor on such a claim, and the disability of infancy will not save him from the operation of the statute; and a petition by or for the benefit of a minor on such a claim which does not allege that the claim has been so presented, does not state facts sufficient to constitute a cause of action. Breen v. Conn (Summit 1940) 64 Ohio App. 325, 28 N.E.2d 684, 30 Ohio Law Abs. 483, 18 O.O. 133. Executors And Administrators ⇔ 431(2)

Where a creditor of a decedent contends that a claim against an estate should not be barred where the administrator had knowledge of the creditor's claim within the statutory period and there was no Ohio case squarely in point, the granting of summary judgment was improper. Hart v. Johnston (C.A.6 (Ohio) 1968) 24 Ohio Misc. 178, 389 F.2d 239, 44 O.O.2d 221, 53 O.O.2d 205.

The plaintiff in an action for money having died and the cause having been revived in the name of his administratrix, a cross-petition filed thereafter asserting a claim against the estate is subject to a demurrer unless it alleges that the claim was presented to the administratrix within four months of her appointment, as required by RC 2117.06. National–Ben Franklin Fire Ins. Co. v. Woolcott (Lucas 1949) 86 Ohio App. 462, 93 N.E.2d 31, 42 O.O. 67.

4. Presentation

Acknowledgement by executrix of debtor's estate of balance remaining on contract did not amount to written presentment of claim against estate, as statutory condition precedent for bringing suit on contract against estate. Widrich v. Diamond (Ohio App. 8 Dist., Cuyahoga, 10-24-2002) No. 80492, 2002-Ohio-5836, 2002 WL 31401561, Unreported, appeal not allowed 98 Ohio St.3d 1490, 785 N.E.2d 473, 2003-Ohio-1189. Executors And Administrators ⇔ 228(3)

Section which provides that claims must be presented to the executor or administrator within four months after the date of his appointment, does not have the effect of extending the time for bringing action after claim is rejected, but such action must be commenced within two months, as provided in GC 10509–133 (RC 2117.12). Chronerberry v. Bartel (Miami 1940) 32 Ohio Law Abs. 284. Executors And Administrators ⇔ 225(1); Executors And Administrators ⇔ 437(7)

The purpose of one-year presentation requirement for claims against estate is both to facilitate the prompt administration of estates and to bar claimants who, through indifference, carelessness, or a dilatory attitude, fail to make an effort to file their claims on time. Secrest v. Citizens Natl. Bank of Norwalk (Ohio App. 6 Dist., 09-05-2003) 154 Ohio App.3d 245, 796 N.E.2d 999, 2003-Ohio-4731, corrected 2003-Ohio-4974, 2003 WL 22149670. Executors And Administrators ⇔ 225(1)

Executor of estate lacked authority to waive mandatory one-year presentation requirement for claims against estate. Secrest v. Citizens Natl. Bank of Norwalk (Ohio App. 6 Dist., 09-05-2003) 154 Ohio App.3d 245, 796 N.E.2d 999, 2003-Ohio-4731, corrected 2003-Ohio-4974, 2003 WL 22149670. Executors And Administrators ⇔ 225(1)

Claim against decedent's estate presented to executor's attorney satisfies statutory requirements that claims be presented to executor or administrator of decedent's estate. Caldwell v. Brown (Ohio App. 2 Dist., 03-01-1996) 109 Ohio App.3d 609, 672 N.E.2d 1037. Executors And Administrators ⇔ 228(3)

Filing certificate of judgment with clerk of court, coupled with statute requiring all lienholders to be made parties to action to sell real estate owned by estate, did not constitute "presentment" of claim to executor for purposes of one-year limitation on presentment of claims. In re Estate of Knepper (Ohio App. 3 Dist., 11-03-1995) 107 Ohio App.3d 78, 667 N.E.2d 1039. Executors And Administrators ⇔ 228(3)

If property held by decedent at time of death is actually owned by another from whom possession is wrongfully withheld, such property does not properly belong to estate and party claiming ownership is not creditor of the estate for purposes of procedural statute requiring presentment of creditors' claims within limited time. Lewis v. Steinreich (Ohio, 08-23-1995) 73 Ohio St.3d 299, 652 N.E.2d 981, 1995-Ohio-133, reconsideration denied 74 Ohio St.3d 1409, 655 N.E.2d 188. Executors And Administrators ⇔ 224

Purpose of presentment of claim, upon death of contract obligor, to administrator or executor of obligor's estate is to promote early completion of administration and prompt settlement of estates. Priestman v. Elder (Ohio App. 6 Dist., 09-16-1994) 97 Ohio App.3d 86, 646 N.E.2d 234. Executors And Administrators ⇔ 222(1)

One who seeks to enforce contract binding party's heirs and assigns to pay money after party's death is not relieved of making presentment of claim, upon death of contract obligor, to administrator or executor of obligor's estate. Priestman v. Elder (Ohio App. 6 Dist., 09-16-1994) 97 Ohio App.3d 86, 646 N.E.2d 234. Executors And Administrators ⇔ 224

Only written presentment provided to the administrator during the statutory time period can constitute presentment of claim against the estate within meaning of statute; presentment of claim in writing to the administrator of the estate is condition precedent to creditor bringing suit on that claim. Varisco v. Varisco (Ohio App. 9 Dist., 11-10-1993) 91 Ohio App.3d 542, 632 N.E.2d 1341. Executors And Administrators ⇔ 222(2); Executors And Administrators ⇔ 228(3)

Creditor did not satisfy statutory presentment requirements by discussing debt with administrator, even though administrator was in possession of decedent's notation of the debt owed to the creditor. Varisco v. Varisco (Ohio App. 9 Dist., 11-10-1993) 91 Ohio App.3d 542, 632 N.E.2d 1341. Executors And Administrators ⇔ 228(3)

Judgment creditors' timely presentment of claims against judgment debtor's estate would not have created liens upon debtor's real estate. Brandon v. Keaton (Ohio App. 2 Dist., 09-29-1993) 90 Ohio App.3d 542, 630 N.E.2d 17, dismissed, jurisdictional motion overruled 68 Ohio St.3d 1449, 626 N.E.2d 690. Judgment ⇔ 754

If claim is properly presented, silence by executor should not bar claimant from joining class of creditors of estate or prevent creditor from suing on claim. Children's Med. Ctr. v. Ward (Montgomery 1993) 87 Ohio App.3d 504, 622 N.E.2d 692, motion overruled 67 Ohio St.3d 1481, 620 N.E.2d 854. Executors And Administrators ⇔ 234; Executors And Administrators ⇔ 431(1)

Time requirement for presenting claim to estate is mandatory. Children's Med. Ctr. v. Ward (Montgomery 1993) 87 Ohio App.3d 504, 622 N.E.2d 692, motion overruled 67 Ohio St.3d 1481, 620 N.E.2d 854. Executors And Administrators ⇔ 225(1)

Statute permitting presentment of claim to executor or administrator in writing is satisfied by computer generated billing statement that clearly indicates creditor's name, address, and precise amount due, identifies decedent as debtor, and is timely received by administrator. Children's Med. Ctr. v. Ward (Montgomery 1993) 87 Ohio App.3d 504, 622 N.E.2d 692, motion overruled 67 Ohio St.3d 1481, 620 N.E.2d 854. Executors And Administrators ⇔ 227(1)

No strict form requirements are imposed on presentment of claims to executor. Children's Med. Ctr. v. Ward (Montgomery 1993) 87 Ohio App.3d 504, 622 N.E.2d 692, motion overruled 67 Ohio St.3d 1481, 620 N.E.2d 854. Executors And Administrators ⇔ 227(1); Executors And Administrators ⇔ 228(1)

Generally, it is responsibility of claimant to ascertain who and where executor is, and executors or legal representatives of estate have no duty to advise potential claimants on procedure for properly presenting claims. Children's Med. Ctr. v. Ward (Montgomery 1993) 87 Ohio App.3d 504, 622 N.E.2d 692, motion overruled 67 Ohio St.3d 1481, 620 N.E.2d 854. Executors And Administrators ⇔ 228(1)

Guardianship of an incompetent terminates upon the death of the incompetent; thus, a claim for necessaries supplied to an incompetent decedent during his lifetime pursuant to an agreement with the guardian must be brought in the probate court as a claim against the estate. In re Estate of Curry (Montgomery 1986) 29 Ohio App.3d 361, 505 N.E.2d 641, 29 O.B.R. 491. Executors And Administrators ⇔ 249

A claim against an estate is presented to the estate within the three-month period required by RC 2117.06 where the claim is presented to the attorney for the estate within the three-month period, although the attorney does not notify the executrix of the claim until after the three-month period has run. Peoples Nat. Bank v. Treon (Miami 1984) 16 Ohio App.3d 410, 476 N.E.2d 372, 16 O.B.R. 480.

The requirement of RC 2117.06 that all claims of creditors must be presented in writing to the administrator is met when a summons and complaint are served in a timely manner on the administrator. Mathe v. Fowler (Lake 1983) 13 Ohio App.3d 273, 469 N.E.2d 89, 13 O.B.R. 337. Executors And Administrators ⇔ 228(3)

If a defendant debtor is deceased, a claim for wrongful death must be presented to his legal representative in the manner and within the time limitations set forth in RC 2117.06 and RC 2117.07, even though the complaint filed specifically states that damages are sought from assets other than those of the debtor's estate. King v. Hargis (Clermont 1973) 37 Ohio App.2d 92, 307 N.E.2d 40, 66 O.O.2d 142. Executors And Administrators ⇔ 224

The presentation to the executor or administrator of a claim for wrongful death by one of the statutory beneficiaries of that action is sufficient compliance with RC 2117.06 and RC 2117.07. Burwell v. Maynard (Ohio 1970) 21 Ohio St.2d 108, 255 N.E.2d 628, 50 O.O.2d 268.

The filing of a petition against an administrator of a decedent's estate, setting forth a cause of action against the estate within four months of the administrator's appointment and accompanied by service of summons and a copy of the petition upon the administrator, constitutes a valid presentation of plaintiff's claim to the administrator and meets the requirements of RC 2117.06. Fortelka v. Meifert (Ohio 1964) 176 Ohio St. 476, 200 N.E.2d 318, 27 O.O.2d 439. Executors And Administrators ⇔ 227(1)

Presentment of a claim to an insurance company is not presentment to the administrator within the meaning of RC 2117.06. Wilcox v. Ceschiat (Ohio Com.Pl. 1960) 179 N.E.2d 544, 87 Ohio Law Abs. 225.

Presentment of a claim for injuries suffered in a motor vehicle accident to decedent's insurer does not constitute a presentment of the claim to the administrator in writing. Simmons v. Bartley (Ohio Com.Pl. 1960) 177 N.E.2d 77, 86 Ohio Law Abs. 321, 19 O.O.2d 335.

The claim of a cotenant for the reasonable rental value of her interest in property occupied by a deceased cotenant must be presented to the administrator or executor of the deceased cotenant's estate within the time prescribed by law. Evans v. May (Ohio Prob. 1961) 176 N.E.2d 189, 86 Ohio Law Abs. 65, 18 O.O.2d 459.

On the facts a creditor was entitled to present a claim more than four months after the appointment of an executor. In re Dulle's Estate (Ohio Prob. 1955) 130 N.E.2d 253, 71 Ohio Law Abs. 114.

Counsel for the administrator of a deceased's estate has no duty to advise a claimant of the name of the administrator, nor to advise such claimant of his error in wrongfully presenting his claim to the decedent's widow under the mistaken belief that she was the administratrix of the decedent's estate instead of to the court-appointed administrator. In re Miller's Estate (Columbiana 1954) 98 Ohio App. 445, 129 N.E.2d 838, 57 O.O. 481. Attorney And Client ⇔ 26

The presentation of a claim against an estate to the agent of an insurance company appointed by the administrator as his agent does not constitute statutory presentation of such a claim to the administrator, and the claim is barred at the expiration of the statutory period. Beacon Mut. Indem. Co. v. Stalder (Summit 1954) 95 Ohio App. 441, 120 N.E.2d 743, 54 O.O. 69.

Under statute providing that all claimants shall present their claims to executor or administrator in writing, including claims arising out of contract, out of tort, on cognovit notes or on judgments, whether due or not due, secured or unsecured, liquidated or unliquidated, vendor who sought rescission and cancellation of land contract and right to retain all monies according to terms of contract as and for stipulated damages for nonfulfillment of terms by now deceased purchaser was required to file claim with administratrix of purchaser's estate as prerequisite to right to rescind contract without restoration of consideration. Buydden v. Mitchell (Montgomery 1951) 102 N.E.2d 21, 60 Ohio Law Abs. 493. Executors And Administrators ⇔ 224

Where there is no evidence to indicate the amount of earnings received by a deceased trustee on trust funds, a court of chancery may not allow as part of the trust res any amount which the chancellor deems the trustee should have earned; the earnings which the trustee should have gained on the trust res may be recovered from such trustee's executors only as damages and only if the claim is properly presented to the executors and allowed by them. Staley v. Kreinbihl (Ohio 1949) 152 Ohio St. 315, 89 N.E.2d 593, 40 O.O. 361. Executors And Administrators ⇔ 224

Where corporation's note was signed by stockholders individually, the liability of each being limited to a specific amount in proportion to his stock holdings, payments to corporation by executors of deceased stockholder to apply on carrying charges and interest due payee of note did not constitute a "waiver" of obligation placed on payee to present its claim to executor or administrator within four months of appointment as required by statutes. Prudential Ins. Co. of America v. Joyce Bldg. Realty Co. (Franklin 1943) 65 N.E.2d 516, 44 Ohio Law Abs. 481, affirmed 143 Ohio St. 564, 56 N.E.2d 168, 28 O.O. 480. Executors And Administrators ⇔ 228(5)

Filing of a cross-petition for a money judgment in an action by an administrator is not presentation of asserted claim to administrator as required by GC 10509–112 (RC 2117.06) and 10509–113 (RC 2117.11), even if it is filed within four months of appointment of administrator. Benson v. Rosine (Lucas 1945) 76 Ohio App. 439, 64 N.E.2d 845, 32 O.O. 195. Executors And Administrators ⇔ 434(5)

It is not mandatory under this section that all claims be presented for allowance. Roberts v. Hickerson (Morgan 1936) 36 N.E.2d 282, 26 Ohio Law Abs. 616, 11 O.O. 471.

In action brought in a municipal court against an administratrix on a claim rejected by her, it is error for court to hold claim barred as a matter of law, where probate court, under GC 10509–134 (RC 2117.07), has decreed that the claimant be allowed to present its claim to the administratrix, although the evidence shows that it was not presented within time prescribed by this section. Busse & Borgmann Co. v. Upchurch (Hamilton 1938) 60 Ohio App. 349, 21 N.E.2d 349, 27 Ohio Law Abs. 575, 12 O.O. 493.

In order that lapse of time may bar an action upon claim against the administrator, notice of the appointment of the administrator must be given in accordance with the statute, and the burden of proving all conditions necessary to start the running of the statute is on the administrator; notwithstanding this, since section places the duty of publishing notice of such appointment upon the probate judge, under GC 11331 (RC 2309.29), publication is not required to be alleged in the answer, as there is a presumption of law that an official has performed the duties of his office, and presumptions of law need not be pleaded; the fact is established by the presumption in the absence of countervailing evidence. Swearingin v. Rendigs (Hamilton 1935) 53 Ohio App. 221, 4 N.E.2d 695, 20 Ohio Law Abs. 317, 5 O.O. 457.

This section and GC 10509–134 (RC 2117.07) (114 v 320), do not require the owner of a promissory note to present his claim thereunder to an executor or administrator when the executor or administrator at the time of his appointment is already in possession of the note for collection. Gerhold v. Papathanasion (Ohio 1936) 130 Ohio St. 342, 199 N.E. 353, 103 A.L.R. 334, 4 O.O. 425.

Unless the administrator requires proof by vouchers and affidavit, such strict formal presentation is not necessary. Morgan v. Bartlette (Ohio Cir. 1888) 2 Ohio C.D. 244. Executors And Administrators ⇔ 234

It is essential to prove a presentation to the administrator of a claim on an account alleged to be due from an intestate, and its rejection or the equivalent by him, or to show some other reason why the administrator is liable to be sued. Yager v. Greiss (Ohio Cir. 1886) 1 Ohio C.D. 296.

Where the estate and minor heirs derive a benefit from a third person's use of his own money in paying taxes and saving the land from sacrifice, at the executrix's request, the estate is liable for such indebtedness, and because of the nature of such a claim it is not necessary to its validity that it be formally presented to the executrix within the prescribed time. Stillman v. Holmes (Ohio Com.Pl. 1909) 20 Ohio Dec. 84, 9 Ohio N.P.N.S. 193.

It is not a necessary prerequisite to the enforcement of stockholders' liability against the estate of a decedent that the claim be presented to the executor; such a claim is by nature unliquidated and impossible to present since its extent cannot be ascertained except by court proceedings. (See also Hull v Standard Coal and Iron Co, 7 NP 157, 7 D 527 (CP, Licking 1897).) John A. Roebling Sons Co. v. Shawnee Val. Coal & Iron Co. (Ohio Com.Pl. 1906) 17 Ohio Dec. 8, 4 Ohio N.P.(N.S.) 113, affirmed 78 Ohio St. 408, 85 N.E. 1127, 6 Ohio Law Rep. 11.

Under Ohio law, presentation of claims to executor of estate within prescribed time is mandatory, and may not be waived by executor. Firestone v. Galbreath (S.D.Ohio, 08-09-1995) 895 F.Supp. 917. Executors And Administrators ⇔ 225(1); Executors And Administrators ⇔ 228(5)

The presentment requirements of RC 2117.06(A)(1) are satisfied where a creditor hospital timely sends computer-generated billing statements to the administratrix of the decedent's estate and the billings clearly indicate the creditor's name, address, and precise amount of the obligation due and identify the decedent as the debtor. Children's Medical Ctr v Ward, No. 13596, 1993 WL 125447 (2d Dist Ct App, Montgomery, 4–23–93).

5. Exceptions

Removing executor for failing to reimburse beneficiary for decedent's funeral expenses was not an abuse of discretion; beneficiary's exceptions to executor's account and her motion for contempt and removal of executor put executor on notice of her demand for payment, such that executor was obligated to take some action on beneficiary's claim once it was filed, and beneficiary's viewing her mother's body, even given mother's wish to have a closed coffin, was not officious and meddlesome conduct that warranted not reimbursing her. In re Estate of Geanangel (Ohio App. 7 Dist., 02-25-2002) 147 Ohio App.3d 131, 768 N.E.2d 1235, 2002-Ohio-850. Executors And Administrators ⇔ 35(1)

Filing requirements in RC 2117.06 and 2117.12 do not apply to a preemptive right to purchase property. Stratman v. Sheetz (Hamilton 1989) 60 Ohio App.3d 71, 573 N.E.2d 776.

An action seeking recovery of certain estate assets from a decedent's administratrix, in which it is alleged that the administratrix fraudulently concealed material facts from claimant, is governed by the four-year limitation provisions of RC 2305.09(C). Thompson v. Stein (Hamilton 1981) 2 Ohio App.3d 319, 441 N.E.2d 1123, 2 O.B.R. 362.

Where it is alleged in an action for bodily injuries that such injuries were proximately caused by negligence of a decedent and that he had a policy of insurance insuring him against liability for such negligence, and it does not appear that any other claims covered by such insurance have been asserted, such action may be brought against executor or administrator of such decedent and decedent's liability insurer, at any time within statute of limitations on such action without presenting a claim against estate within time specified in RC 2117.06 or RC 2117.07, and timely service of summons upon insurer-defendant is sufficient to commence action. Heuser v. Crum (Ohio 1972) 31 Ohio St.2d 90, 285 N.E.2d 340, 60 O.O.2d 56. Executors And Administrators ⇐ 224; Limitation Of Actions ⇐ 119(4)

Where it does not appear that any claim covered by an automobile liability insurance policy of decedent has been filed against estate of decedent within period specified in RC 2117.06, or as provided in and within time specified in RC 2117.07, such policy is not an asset of the decedent's estate within meaning of RC 2117.07. Heuser v. Crum (Ohio 1972) 31 Ohio St.2d 90, 285 N.E.2d 340, 60 O.O.2d 56. Executors And Administrators ⇐ 225(2)

In a negligence action for the recovery of damages, instituted under RC 2117.07 against an administrator seeking to recover only from decedent's liability insurer, where administrator of estate of decedent has been discharged and estate closed, probate court may reappoint administrator for purpose of accepting service of summons. In re George's Estate (Ohio 1970) 24 Ohio St.2d 18, 262 N.E.2d 872, 53 O.O.2d 10.

Where it is alleged in an action for bodily injuries and property damage that such injuries and damage were proximately caused by the negligence of a decedent and that he had a policy of insurance insuring him against liability for such negligence, and it does not appear that any other claims covered by such insurance have been asserted, such action may be brought against the executor or administrator of such decedent at any time within two years after the cause thereof arose without presenting a claim against the estate within the four-month time specified in RC 2117.06, or as provided in and within the nine-month time specified in RC 2117.07. Meinberg v. Glaser (Ohio 1968) 14 Ohio St.2d 193, 237 N.E.2d 605, 43 O.O.2d 296.

The federal government is not required to comply with the statutes relating to presentment of claims in order to collect social security taxes due from a decedent. Baker v. Charles (Ohio Prob. 1963) 202 N.E.2d 646, 95 Ohio Law Abs. 97, 31 O.O.2d 310.

Institution of a suit against an administrator within four months of his appointment upon a claim based on decedent's negligence which by terms of his insurance would not be barred by his bankruptcy constitutes substantial performance of the requirements for presentment of a claim. Simmons v. Bartley (Ohio Com.Pl. 1960) 177 N.E.2d 77, 86 Ohio Law Abs. 321, 19 O.O.2d 335.

Persons claiming as donee beneficiaries under an antenuptial contract are not creditors within the meaning of the statutes relating to presentment of claims. Cantor v. Cantor (Ohio Prob. 1959) 174 N.E.2d 304, 86 Ohio Law Abs. 452, 15 O.O.2d 148.

An administrator is not excused from liability for claims of the state of Ohio for support of decedent in a mental hospital by the failure of the state to file such claim against the estate within the time specified by law. In re Moore's Estate (Ohio Prob. 1958) 154 N.E.2d 675, 79 Ohio Law Abs. 112.

RC 5121.10 places the responsibility of ascertaining whether the state's claim for support of an inmate of a mental hospital has been paid, on the executor or administrator of such inmate's estate and dispenses with compliance with RC 2117.06, such claim being a preferred claim. In re Sowards' Estate (Trumbull 1957) 105 Ohio App. 239, 152 N.E.2d 146, 6 O.O.2d 59.

The bureau of support of the department of mental hygiene and correction cannot be barred by a statute of limitation from asserting a claim against an estate for money due for the support of a deceased inmate of a department benevolent institution. In re Sowards' Estate (Trumbull 1957) 105 Ohio App. 239, 152 N.E.2d 146, 6 O.O.2d 59.

When a spouse dies possessed of a mansion house which is encumbered with a mortgage given to secure a note of the deceased spouse, and the surviving spouse elects to purchase said mansion house at the appraised value as fixed by the appraisers, such surviving spouse is not required to pay the balance due on said mortgage in addition to the value fixed by the appraisers, and the executor shall pay it even though the mortgagee did not present its claim within four months. McAdams v. Bolsinger (Ohio Prob. 1950) 129 N.E.2d 878, 71 Ohio Law Abs. 531, 57 O.O. 338.

It is an abuse of discretion for a probate court to refuse to permit a claimant to file an alleged claim with an administrator more then four months after the latter's appointment where there is a clear showing of legal disability on the claimant's part. In re Gogan's Estate (Cuyahoga 1951) 108 N.E.2d 170, 63 Ohio Law Abs. 69.

The holder of a contingent claim is not required to present such claim under provisions of GC 10509–112 (RC 2117.06) or 10509–134 (RC 2117.07). Keifer v. Kissell (Clark 1947) 83 Ohio App. 133, 75 N.E.2d 692, 50 Ohio Law Abs. 375, 38 O.O. 224.

Where action against a deceased defendant has been revived properly it is not necessary for the plaintiff in such revived action to present his claim in writing to the executor or administrator as provided in section. Goehring v. Dillard (Ohio 1945) 145 Ohio St. 41, 60 N.E.2d 704, 158 A.L.R. 299, 30 O.O. 274. Executors And Administrators ⇐ 222(2)

An unliquidated claim for damages arising out of tort does not fall within the exception contained in section pertaining to contingent claims; suit thereon must be instituted within two months from the date of receipt of actual notice of disallowance of such claim by the executor or administrator, or be forever barred under the provisions of GC 10509–133 (RC 2117.12). Pierce v. Johnson (Ohio 1939) 136 Ohio St. 95, 23 N.E.2d 993, 125 A.L.R. 867, 16 O.O. 34.

Legatee held not required to present to executor claim for services rendered deceased testator during his lifetime, where will provided for payment of such services. Fair v. Fair (Holmes 1933) 46 Ohio App. 51, 187 N.E. 727, 15 Ohio Law Abs. 149, 38 Ohio Law Rep. 291. Executors And Administrators ⇐ 224

Wills and estates, probate exception to federal jurisdiction, tort claim asserted in bankruptcy proceeding, reversed and remanded, Marshall v. Marshall, 2006, 126 S.Ct. 1735.

Absence of a fiduciary against whom the federal government may bring an action to collect the unpaid tax liability tolls the six-year period of limitation for the bringing of an action provided by Internal Revenue Code of 1954, 26 USC 6502, inasmuch as under applicable Ohio probate law both a claim and an action against an estate may only proceed against a fiduciary of an estate, so that the absence of appointment of a fiduciary tolls the time in which claims may be presented against the estate. U. S. v. Besase (N.D.Ohio 1970) 29 Ohio Misc. 166, 319 F.Supp. 1064, 57 O.O.2d 51.

In an action in a federal district court in Pennsylvania against the Ohio administrator of an Ohio decedent involved in a motor vehicle accident in Pennsylvania, the Ohio statutes with respect to a time limit for presentation of claims against a decedent's estate do not constitute a defense. Colman v. Pitzer (W.D.Pa. 1958) 160 F.Supp. 862, 82 Ohio Law Abs. 452, 6 O.O.2d 476.

Where petitioner's claim had not accrued until long after decedent's death and long after time prescribed by statute for presentation of claims to administrator for allowance, probate court must conclude that such claim was not the kind of claim covered by section, which at least by implication embraces only actual claims and not claims which have not yet accrued or which do not exist; and, therefore, this section and GC 10509–134 (RC 2117.07) not being applicable to such claim, petitioner may present his claim and if refused, may sue thereon. In re Runcie's Estate (Ohio Prob. 1937) 3 Ohio Supp. 42, 33 Ohio Law Abs. 69, 20 O.O. 327.

Funeral expenses paid by sons of a decedent do not constitute a debt due at the time of death; thus the presentment requirement in RC 2117.06 is not applicable and the administrator may sell realty out of the assets of the estate to pay such expenses even without presentment of a claim. Michael v Byerly, No. CA89–04–005 (12th Dist Ct App, Madison, 12–11–89).

6. Revivor and late filing

If, within three months after a defendant's death, a claim is properly revived against the administratrix of the defendant's estate in her representative capacity and judgment is entered against the estate, resubmissions of such claim and judgment are not required under RC 2117.06, RC 2117.07 or RC 2117.12, and RC 2117.17 is irrelevant to such a case. Blanchard v. Morgan (Portage 1983) 10 Ohio App.3d 117, 460 N.E.2d 715, 10 O.B.R. 141. Abatement And Revival ⇐ 77

Where the defendant in a pending action for the recovery of damages dies and no attempt is made by the plaintiff to revive the action against the decedent's personal representative for more than nine months after the appointment of such personal representative, the cause of action is extinguished irrespective of whether recovery is sought against estate or nonestate assets. Smith v. Ralph (Franklin 1969) 18 Ohio App.2d 235, 248 N.E.2d 208, 47 O.O.2d 362.

Attorney for estate who received claim which should have been addressed to executor but did not so advise claimant until after lapse of four month period was not guilty wrongful act so as to justify late filing. In re Clark's Estate (Ohio Com.Pl. 1967) 11 Ohio Misc. 103, 229 N.E.2d 122, 40 O.O.2d 347.

Where, following an automobile accident upon an Ohio highway, a nonresident defendant dies after an action has been commenced against him pursuant to RC 2703.20, if there has been no administration in Ohio, the time limitation of RC 2311.31 and RC 2117.06 has not commenced to run, and under RC 2311.25 and RC 2703.20 the pending action may be revived any time before judgment against the nonresident decedent's executor or administrator appointed in another state. Kibbey v. Mercer (Scioto 1967) 11 Ohio App.2d 51, 228 N.E.2d 337, 40 O.O.2d 223. Abatement And Revival ⬄ 74(1)

The authority to file a claim against a decedent's estate after the four-month period must be in conformance with RC 2117.07, and cannot be predicated on general equitable principles outside the purview of the statute. In re Andres' Estate (Greene 1961) 114 Ohio App. 167, 180 N.E.2d 855, 19 O.O.2d 21. Executors And Administrators ⬄ 225(1)

Where a claim has not been presented within the four months prescribed by statute, the proper procedure is to file a petition or application for permission to reinstate the claim, and upon failure to do so, the claim is barred. Wilcox v. Ceschiat (Ohio Com.Pl. 1960) 179 N.E.2d 544, 87 Ohio Law Abs. 225.

A probate court is guilty of an abuse of discretion in refusing a claimant the right to file a claim with an executor after the expiration of the four-month time limit when such refusal to allow the claim to be filed prevents the revivor of an action pending against the executor's decedent in the court of common pleas, where the uncontradicted evidence establishes that the claimant was under a legal disability. In re Fuller's Estate (Medina 1960) 112 Ohio App. 25, 174 N.E.2d 613, 15 O.O.2d 378.

Where the time limit for filing revivor applications for pending actions is fixed as "the time provided for the presentation of claims by creditors in section 2117.06 of the Revised Code," such section must be read in pari materia with RC 2117.07. In re Fuller's Estate (Medina 1960) 112 Ohio App. 25, 174 N.E.2d 613, 15 O.O.2d 378. Statutes ⬄ 223.2(12)

After a written notice of the application or proceedings for a revivor is given to the executor or administrator of a deceased defendant in an action for money which survives, it is not required that a subsequent written notice of such application or proceedings be given to a succeeding executor or administrator. Miller v. Andre (Ohio 1957) 167 Ohio St. 83, 146 N.E.2d 598, 4 O.O.2d 52.

Where the defendant in an action for money, which survives, dies, and his executor is substituted as defendant, and where, thereafter, plaintiff files a motion for a conditional order of revivor and a summons with a copy of the petition is served upon the substituted defendant, such service constitutes sufficient written notice of the application or proceedings for revivor as required by RC 2311.31. Miller v. Andre (Ohio 1957) 167 Ohio St. 83, 146 N.E.2d 598, 4 O.O.2d 52.

Where claimant had knowledge of decedent's death but was not aware of the county of decedent's legal residence and examined the court records only in the county of decedent's post office address, the probate court erroneously denied claimant the right to file a claim after four months after the appointment of an executor. In re Lathrop's Estate (Auglaize 1956) 103 Ohio App. 392, 141 N.E.2d 212, 75 Ohio Law Abs. 458, 1 O.O.2d 482.

In a proceeding to file late claims against the estate of a decedent by claimants who charge that such physician had concealed his negligence in a surgical operation, the alleged wrongful acts of the physician do not qualify claimant's belated claim where it is not claimed that there was any wrongful act on the part of the administratrix or her attorney which would qualify claimants for relief under this section, as the acts of decedent are not imputed to the administratrix or her attorney. In re Natherson's Estate (Cuyahoga 1956) 102 Ohio App. 475, 134 N.E.2d 852, 57 A.L.R.2d 1297, 74 Ohio Law Abs. 387, 3 O.O.2d 35. Executors And Administrators ⬄ 225(2)

Where pedestrian, who brought action against motorist to recover for injuries sustained when struck by automobile, failed to make application to revive action against executor of motorist within maximum time allowed by statute providing for presentation of claims by creditors against estate of deceased, after death of motorist, court properly sustained motion to dismiss action, though pedestrian was a minor. Overman v. Yake (Clark 1952) 109 N.E.2d 697, 68 Ohio Law Abs. 248. Abatement And Revival ⬄ 74(1)

One who has a claim against a decedent's estate and fails to present the same in writing to the executor or administrator within four months of his appointment may, after the expiration of such time petition the probate court for leave to do so. Where the probate court, upon hearing the evidence, discloses that claimant actually knew of the decedent's death and his place of residence shortly after the death occurred and that in the exercise of reasonable diligence the claimant could have learned of the appointment of an administrator and thereafter had a fair opportunity to present his claim within the four months, it was not error to deny the authority to present such claim. In re Marrs' Estate (Ohio 1952) 158 Ohio St. 95, 107 N.E.2d 148, 48 O.O. 46.

Provisions of GC 10509–134 (RC 2117.07), relating to reinstatement of claim against an estate may be invoked only when such claim has not been presented or its presentation has not been waived within four months after the appointment of the estate's legal representative, in accordance with requirements of this section. In re Erbaugh's Estate (Montgomery 1943) 73 Ohio App. 533, 57 N.E.2d 294, 38 Ohio Law Abs. 574, 29 O.O. 177. Executors And Administrators ⬄ 233

Publication of notice of appointment is for the protection of the administrator, not to satisfy notice requirements to creditors, and the two-year limitation within which actions may be brought begins from the date of giving of bond by the administrator. Ardrey v. Shell (Ohio 1907) 77 Ohio St. 218, 82 N.E. 1075, 5 Ohio Law Rep. 505.

Where a cause of action is revived as against the administrator of the estate of the defendant without objection and may proceed to judgment against the deceased provided the petition states facts sufficient to constitute a cause of action against the decedent, no presentation or rejection of the claim is necessary. Glass v. Buzzard (Ohio Cir. 1910) 23 Ohio C.D. 144, 14 Ohio C.C.(N.S.) 427, affirmed 85 Ohio St. 461, 98 N.E. 1120, 9 Ohio Law Rep. 416.

Where plaintiff had failed to present a claim against decedent's estate within the period required by Ohio law, a federal court cannot obtain jurisdiction of the cause of action on the ground that it was presented to an agent of the administrator or that the administrator is estopped to contest the claim; the proper procedure would be to obtain reinstatement of a barred claim in the probate court. Hart v. Johnston (S.D.Ohio 1966) 9 Ohio Misc. 88, 253 F.Supp. 621, 36 O.O.2d 366, 38 O.O.2d 115, reversed 24 Ohio Misc. 178, 389 F.2d 239, 44 O.O.2d 221, 53 O.O.2d 205.

Purpose of enacting section and subsequent sections was to expedite handling and settlement of estates and sections are clear both in language and in purpose, and where in failing to exercise their rights petitioners were undoubtedly guilty of "culpable neglect," permission to reinstate their claim would be an abuse of judicial discretion. In re Christopher's Estate (Ohio Prob. 1937) 4 Ohio Supp. 327, 24 Ohio Law Abs. 245, 8 O.O. 546, affirmed 35 N.E.2d 454, 26 Ohio Law Abs. 422, 11 O.O. 251.

7. Rejection

Appropriate time to litigate applicability of equitable relief concerning creditor's rejected claim against decedent's estate was after filing of complaint on rejected claim. Smith v. Estate of Grilli (Ohio App. 5 Dist., Fairfield, 10-13-2005) No. 05CA33, 2005-Ohio-5711, 2005 WL 2806664, Unreported. Executors And Administrators ⬄ 437(7)

Letters to creditor from attorney for executor of decedent's estate did not make clear and unequivocal rejection of creditor's claim against decedent's estate, as required to commence running of two-month statute of limitations for actions on rejected claims; attorney's first letter at most indicated deficiencies in form arising from creditor's incorrect identification of decedent and made unqualified denial of claim against estate of person bearing incorrect name used by creditor, but did not treat claim as one against decedent's estate or reject it on its merits, and attorney's second letter simply referred to earlier letter rejecting creditor's first, incorrect, claim. Caldwell v. Brown (Ohio App. 2 Dist., 03-01-1996) 109 Ohio App.3d 609, 672 N.E.2d 1037. Executors And Administrators ⬄ 437(7)

There is no reason to consider implicit rejection by executor to be anything but final rejection, in that executor has no affirmative duty to notify potential claimant that submitted bill was improperly presented. Children's Med. Ctr. v. Ward (Montgomery 1993) 87 Ohio App.3d 504, 622 N.E.2d 692, motion overruled 67 Ohio St.3d 1481, 620 N.E.2d 854. Executors And Administrators ⬄ 234

Lack of response by administrator cannot be considered rejection of claim; lack of response does not prevent executor from later either rejecting or allowing claim. Children's Med. Ctr. v. Ward (Montgomery 1993) 87 Ohio App.3d 504, 622 N.E.2d 692, motion overruled 67 Ohio St.3d 1481, 620 N.E.2d 854. Executors And Administrators ⬄ 234

Executor's challenge to form of presentment must be considered at least implicit rejection. Children's Med. Ctr. v. Ward (Montgomery 1993) 87 Ohio App.3d 504, 622 N.E.2d 692, motion overruled 67 Ohio St.3d 1481, 620 N.E.2d 854. Executors And Administrators ⬄ 234

Executor who has actual knowledge of legitimate debt of estate, personally receives proper statement of debt, and does not accept claim within 30–day time period effects constructive rejection of claim. Children's Med. Ctr. v. Ward (Montgomery 1993) 87 Ohio App.3d 504, 622 N.E.2d 692, motion overruled 67 Ohio St.3d 1481, 620 N.E.2d 854. Executors And Administrators ⊂⊃ 234

Where a tort claim was presented to an Ohio administratrix and rejected, a judgment obtained in the court of another state in an action filed seven months after the rejection cannot be collected out of the assets of the Ohio estate. In re Rettig's Estate (Ohio Prob. 1964) 8 Ohio Misc. 38, 216 N.E.2d 924, 35 O.O.2d 141.

Where a claim is presented to an administrator and the administrator rejects the claim and in the same letter offers to settle it for a lesser amount, there is no unequivocal rejection of the claim and the claimant can thereafter obtain an order vacating the order settling the administrator's final account. In re Douglass' Estate (Ohio Prob. 1957) 144 N.E.2d 924, 77 Ohio Law Abs. 89.

Where the affidavit in proof of the claim is informal but no objection is taken, and the claim is rejected on its merits, the informality of the affidavit is waived. Morgan v. Bartlette (Ohio Cir. 1888) 2 Ohio C.D. 244. Executors And Administrators ⊂⊃ 227(4)

Where a claim against an estate requests acceptance "within the time provided by law," but does not specify what law is referred to, and where the estate sends the claimant written rejection of the claim beyond the thirty-day period in RC 2117.06(D), this rejection is nevertheless effective under RC 2117.06(D) and precludes the automatic rejection after five days provided for by RC 2117.11 even if the written rejection specifically cites RC 2117.11; the rejection is deemed effective when the writing is delivered and the two-month period for filing an action against the estate prescribed by RC 2117.12 commences then. Bush v Estate of O'Dell, No. CA–3705 (5th Dist Ct App, Licking, 2–26–92).

8. Mailing claim

Where sufficient evidence is presented to the trial court that a creditor's claim was mailed to the executor of an estate well within the statutorily required time period and was correctly addressed and posted, and sufficient evidence is presented that the delivery date for such claim is one hundred per cent within three days of mailing, it is within the trial court's discretion to weigh the evidence provided to determine whether presentment pursuant to RC 2117.06 was effectuated. Cannell v. Bulicek (Cuyahoga 1983) 8 Ohio App.3d 331, 457 N.E.2d 891, 8 O.B.R. 441. Executors And Administrators ⊂⊃ 225(1)

The mailing of a claim to the regularly appointed attorney in the settlement of the estate, which claim was listed as being a claim against the executor, and the acknowledgment of the receipt of the claim by the attorney for the estate is a filing with the executor in compliance with RC 2117.06. In re Clark's Estate (Ohio Com.Pl. 1967) 11 Ohio Misc. 103, 229 N.E.2d 122, 40 O.O.2d 347.

Claim mailed to executor within four month period but not delivered until after expiration thereof because of executor's absence from jurisdiction could be filed after expiration of period. In re McCracken's Estate (Ohio Prob. 1967) 9 Ohio Misc. 195, 224 N.E.2d 181, 38 O.O.2d 283.

Late filing of a claim against an estate will not be permitted although the late filing was the result of the claimant's mailing the claim originally to an erroneous address supplied by the clerical staff of the probate court. Krash v. Jarvis (Jefferson 1962) 187 N.E.2d 409, 90 Ohio Law Abs. 99, 25 O.O.2d 133.

9. Defenses

While assertion that payments decedent's parents made for burial expenses were loan or gift to decedent's wife may have been defense available to wife in any claim made or action for reimbursement brought against her personally, such defense would have no application to claim or action brought against her as personal representative of estate, absent evidence that those defenses were available to estate, as well. Osborne v. Osborne (Ohio App. 2 Dist., 09-27-1996) 114 Ohio App.3d 412, 683 N.E.2d 365. Executors And Administrators ⊂⊃ 214; Executors And Administrators ⊂⊃ 217

Where the maker of a note claimed by the administrator of an estate to be an asset of the estate asserts the defense of payment, it is not necessary, as a condition precedent to his right to assert such defense, that he comply with the requirement of RC 2117.06. Fox v. McCreary (Adams 1957) 103 Ohio App. 73, 144 N.E.2d 546, 3 O.O.2d 155.

Although a claim of a defendant against a plaintiff may be barred by the statute of limitation at the time the plaintiff institutes his action, such defendant may set up such claim as a setoff or defense to the extent it will equalize the claim of the plaintiff. Shriner v. Price (Hamilton 1944) 74 Ohio App. 373, 59 N.E.2d 152, 42 Ohio Law Abs. 308, 29 O.O. 542.

Where it is claimed that an administrator failed to set up the bar provided in GC 10509–133 (RC 2117.12) as a defense to an action on a rejected claim commenced under GC 10509–133 (RC 2117.12), as amended, the burden is upon exceptors to show that such action was not duly commenced within two months after receipt by claimant of actual notice of rejection by administrator of a claim duly presented under this section. In re Lamberton's Estate (Ohio 1944) 142 Ohio St. 417, 52 N.E.2d 855, 27 O.O. 356.

10. Mandatory requirements

Where plaintiff files a claim against a husband and wife and the husband dies and plaintiff files an amended complaint against the wife in her capacity as executrix, the executrix's motion for summary judgment on the grounds that the complaint against the estate was not presented in the manner or within the time limit provided by RC 2117.06 is properly overruled since while the requirements of RC 2117.06 are mandatory, any method that satisfies the manifest object and purpose of the statute is permissible and the wife, already a party to the action, knew of the existence, amount and nature of plaintiff's claim within one year after her husband's death. Sealy v. Davidson (Ohio App. 2 Dist., Montgomery, 10-12-1994) No. 14346, 1994 WL 558977, Unreported.

To distinguish claims subject to rejection by silence from those claims that are simply pending an allowance decision by an estate's personal representative the creditor's demand must refer to RC 2117.11 and its five day response period. In re Estate of Baughman (Ohio, 04-01-1998) 81 Ohio St.3d 302, 691 N.E.2d 257, 1998-Ohio-473. Executors And Administrators ⊂⊃ 234

The executor or administrator of an estate may not waive the requirement in RC 2117.06 that all claims against the estate be presented within three months after the date of the appointment of such executor or administrator. In re Estate of Fisher (Warren 1983) 12 Ohio App.3d 150, 467 N.E.2d 898, 12 O.B.R. 474.

The provisions of RC 2117.01 through RC 2117.04 are mandatory and provide the exclusive method for presentation and allowance of claims by an executor against the estate which he represents. Wilhoit v. Powell's Estate (Butler 1980) 70 Ohio App.2d 61, 434 N.E.2d 742, 24 O.O.3d 75. Executors And Administrators ⊂⊃ 219

The requirements of RC 2117.06 that all persons having claims against an estate shall present their claims to the executor or administrator in writing, within four months after the appointment of the executor or administrator and set forth the claimant's address, are mandatory. Fortelka v. Meifert (Cuyahoga 1963) 120 Ohio App. 294, 193 N.E.2d 170, 93 Ohio Law Abs. 1, 27 O.O.2d 175, appeal certified to 120 Ohio App. 294, 193 N.E.2d 305, 93 Ohio Law Abs. 8, 27 O.O.2d 78, affirmed 176 Ohio St. 476, 200 N.E.2d 318, 27 O.O.2d 439.

Claims filed against estates of decedents more than four months after the appointment of an administrator or executor must be filed in conformity with the statutes and not predicated on general principles of equity outside the purview of the statutes, as the statutes provide the exclusive remedy to file belated claims. In re Natherson's Estate (Cuyahoga 1956) 102 Ohio App. 475, 134 N.E.2d 852, 57 A.L.R.2d 1297, 74 Ohio Law Abs. 387, 3 O.O.2d 35. Executors And Administrators ⊂⊃ 233

Where one is required by statute to do an act as a prerequisite to the accrual of a cause of action, all persons, whether under disability or not, are bound thereby unless excepted from the operation of the statute by a saving clause. In re Sarver's Estate (Franklin 1954) 97 Ohio App. 199, 124 N.E.2d 749, 55 O.O. 453. Action ⊂⊃ 10

Requirements of section, that "creditors shall present their claims, whether due or not due, to the executor or administrator within four months after the date of his appointment" are mandatory and may not be waived by him. Prudential Ins. Co. of America v. Joyce Bldg. Realty Co. (Ohio 1944) 143 Ohio St. 564, 56 N.E.2d 168, 28 O.O. 480. Executors And Administrators ⊂⊃ 228(5)

Purpose of this section is that of presenting claims for allowance or rejection, and law suit in another court, although involving same party, is not in compliance with statutes. In re Christopher's Estate (Ohio Prob. 1937) 4 Ohio Supp. 327, 24 Ohio Law Abs. 245, 8 O.O. 546, affirmed 35 N.E.2d 454, 26 Ohio Law Abs. 422, 11 O.O. 251. Executors And Administrators ⊂⊃ 228(3)

11. Statute of limitations

Attorney met applicable level of reasonable representation in client's probate matter concerning the administration of client's mother's estate, precluding client from succeeding on her legal malpractice claim against attorney, despite client's assertions that attorney negligently failed to pursue potential claims against the estate or pursue client's potential options, including a claim for reimbursement against the estate and an option to purchase mother's house; some of the potential claims were time-barred by statute, and attorney made strategic decisions in the course of representation that did not prejudice the client. Holik v. Richard (Ohio App. 11 Dist., Ashtabula, 05-26-2006) No. 2005-A-0006, 2006-Ohio-2644, 2006 WL 1459677, Unreported. Attorney And Client ⇐ 112

Administrator and beneficiary of wife's estate were not entitled to reimbursement from husband's estate of one half of husband's funeral expenses and real estate taxes, which had been paid by wife from a joint account, even though husband's will directed that his estate pay his funeral expenses and debts; claim for reimbursement was a claim against husband's estate, administrator and wife improperly filed claim in the proceedings to administer wife estate, and claim was filed more than two years after husband's death, after the one-year limitations period for claims against estate, and after estate had been closed. In re Estate of Lewis (Ohio App. 6 Dist., Lucas, 04-21-2006) No. L-05-1225, 2006-Ohio-1986, 2006 WL 1047478, Unreported. Executors And Administrators ⇐ 225(1)

Ten-year limitations period applicable to action on bond of estate administrator, rather than one-year limitations period applicable to creditor's claims against decedent's estate, applied to claim by administrator de bonis non, with will annexed, of decedent's estate against original administrator of estate related to breach of duties, and thus, such ten-year limitations period applied to surcharge action brought by administrator de bonis non, with will annexed, of decedent's estate against insurer as surety for original administrator; liability of surety is ordinarily measure by liability of principal. In re Estate of Bishop (Ohio App. 2 Dist., Montgomery, 04-30-2004) No. 20102, 2004-Ohio-2197, 2004 WL 917693, Unreported, on subsequent appeal 165 Ohio App.3d 761, 848 N.E.2d 567, 2006-Ohio-1252. Executors And Administrators ⇐ 437(2)

Executor's statement two days before deadline for son to file claim against mother's estate that it would accept a late claim from son did not estop estate from relying on limitations period as a defense, because son's failure to file claim for over two years past deadline did not warrant equitable relief. Secrest v. Citizens Natl. Bank of Norwalk (Ohio App. 6 Dist., 09-05-2003) 154 Ohio App.3d 245, 796 N.E.2d 999, 2003-Ohio-4731, corrected 2003-Ohio-4974, 2003 WL 22149670. Executors And Administrators ⇐ 225(7)

Action to recover Medicaid payments brought by Ohio Department of Human Services (ODHS) against executors of decedent's estate were not barred by limitations or non-claim provisions of probate statute governing presentation of claims against estate; statute did not run against the state. Ohio Dept. of Human Serv. v. Eastman (Ohio App. 9 Dist., 08-01-2001) 145 Ohio App.3d 369, 763 N.E.2d 193. Executors And Administrators ⇐ 225(1); Limitation Of Actions ⇐ 11(1)

Purpose of statute, requiring creditor to make claims to executor in writing within one year after death of decedent, is to facilitate prompt administration of estates and to bar creditors who fail to make effort to file claims on time. In re Estate of Knepper (Ohio App. 3 Dist., 11-03-1995) 107 Ohio App.3d 78, 667 N.E.2d 1039. Executors And Administrators ⇐ 225(1); Executors And Administrators ⇐ 227(1)

Claim against estate by judgment creditor was barred as untimely when asserted more than one year after debtor's death, even though creditor was not notified of sale of real estate owned by estate. In re Estate of Knepper (Ohio App. 3 Dist., 11-03-1995) 107 Ohio App.3d 78, 667 N.E.2d 1039. Executors And Administrators ⇐ 225(1)

Filing of certificate of judgment with clerk of court did not give rise to presumption that executor had notice of claim against debtor's estate for purposes of one-year limitation for presenting claim against estate. In re Estate of Knepper (Ohio App. 3 Dist., 11-03-1995) 107 Ohio App.3d 78, 667 N.E.2d 1039. Executors And Administrators ⇐ 228(5)

Claims for guardian and attorney fees, not brought within one year after decedent's death, were barred; claims for guardian and attorney fees stemming from guardianship were not contingent, which would make them exempt from one-year time limit, where services of guardian and attorney had already occurred and claims did not depend upon occurrence of uncertain future event. In re Estate of Bickham (Logan 1993) 85 Ohio App.3d 634, 620 N.E.2d 913. Executors And Administrators ⇐ 225(1)

The three-month period within which all claims against an estate must be presented commences to run on the day of the appointment of the executor. Waterman v. Kitrick (Franklin 1990) 60 Ohio App.3d 7, 572 N.E.2d 250, motion to certify allowed 52 Ohio St.3d 707, 557 N.E.2d 1216, appeal dismissed 57 Ohio St.3d 618, 566 N.E.2d 1244, motion to vacate denied 59 Ohio St.3d 707, 571 N.E.2d 133. Executors And Administrators ⇐ 437(4)

The tolling provisions of RC 2305.16 are not applicable to the filing of claims against an estate, RC Ch 2117 which deals specifically with the filing of claims against an estate in probate court is controlling. In re Estate of Kennedy (Franklin 1988) 46 Ohio App.3d 128, 546 N.E.2d 220.

Where a new executor is appointed under a later will, the period within which claims may be filed against the estate begins to run anew. Georgekopoulos v. Vasilopoulos (Summit 1984) 26 Ohio App.3d 43, 498 N.E.2d 165, 26 O.B.R. 216.

An action for wrongful death caused proximately by the negligence of a decedent cannot be brought against the executor or administrator of that decedent unless a claim therefor is presented within the four-month time specified in RC 2117.06 or the nine-month time specified in RC 2117.07. Collins v. Yanity (Ohio 1968) 14 Ohio St.2d 202, 237 N.E.2d 611, 43 O.O.2d 301.

Where it does not appear that any claim covered by an automobile liability insurance policy of a decedent has been filed against the estate of the decedent within the four-month period specified in RC 2117.06 or the nine-month period specified in RC 2117.07, such policy is not an asset of the estate of the decedent within the meaning of those words as used in RC 2117.07. Meinberg v. Glaser (Ohio 1968) 14 Ohio St.2d 193, 237 N.E.2d 605, 43 O.O.2d 296.

The filing of a petition to contest a decedent's will does not suspend or extend the time in which a creditor shall present his claim to the executor of said decedent's estate. In re Kehoe's Estate (Ohio Prob. 1963) 199 N.E.2d 29, 94 Ohio Law Abs. 469, 27 O.O.2d 35. Executors And Administrators ⇐ 225(2)

The right of a part owner who pays the tax on the whole tract of which he is part owner to have a lien on the part of the other part owner for the tax paid on such part is subject to the statutes of limitation requiring presentation of claims to executors and administrators. Kuhnle v. Rusmisel (Miami 1960) 113 Ohio App. 389, 178 N.E.2d 810, 17 O.O.2d 465. Executors And Administrators ⇐ 224

The thirty day period specified in RC 2117.06 is directory rather than mandatory. In re Douglass' Estate (Ohio Prob. 1957) 144 N.E.2d 924, 77 Ohio Law Abs. 89.

Where creditor actually learned of death of decedent and of appointment of executrix more than four months after such appointment and creditor had no prior knowledge of such facts, the statute required that Probate Court authorize creditor to present his claim to executrix even though the four-month period for presentation of claims had expired. In re Dulle's Estate (Ohio Prob. 1955) 130 N.E.2d 253, 71 Ohio Law Abs. 114. Executors And Administrators ⇐ 233

GC 10509–112 (RC 2117.06) is a "nonclaim statute," or a statute of limitation. In re Sarver's Estate (Franklin 1954) 97 Ohio App. 199, 124 N.E.2d 749, 55 O.O. 453.

GC 10509–134 (RC 2117.07) creates the right to an adjudication of right to present a claim to an executor or administrator, when such claim has not been presented within the four-month period provided for by this section, and the proviso of the former section is a limitation on that right, which limitation is tolled by the institution of a proceeding under the section within nine months after appointment of executor and administrator. In re Erbaugh's Estate (Montgomery 1943) 73 Ohio App. 533, 57 N.E.2d 294, 38 Ohio Law Abs. 574, 29 O.O. 177. Executors And Administrators ⇐ 233

Where conveyance of realty in compensation for series rendered was adjudged void after grantor's death, grantee's claim for such services was at time of grantor's death "contingent", and action thereon, which was commenced within two months after rejection of claim which was presented to administratrix within two months after entry of decree voiding conveyance, was not barred by limitations. Yenzer v. Burton (Lucas 1944) 55 N.E.2d 665. Executors And Administrators ⇐ 437(7)

This section and GC 10509–134 (RC 2117.07) are statutes of limitation (or nonclaim statutes) which bar creditor's claims unless presented to executor or administrator within four months after the date of appointment. Beach v. Mizner (Ohio 1936) 131 Ohio St. 481, 3 N.E.2d 417, 6 O.O. 155.

The statute of limitations begins to run upon a claim that becomes due at the death of a debtor upon the appointment of an administrator. Hoiles v. Riddle (Ohio 1906) 74 Ohio St. 173, 78 N.E. 219, 113 Am.St.Rep. 946, 4 Ohio Law Rep. 38.

In general, presentation of notice to an insurance company is insufficient to comply with Ohio statute's requirement that notice of a claim against an estate be provided to the executor or administrator of the estate within one year after the death of the decedent. Lukowski v. CSX Transp., Inc. (C.A.6 (Ohio), 07-19-2005) 416 F.3d 478. Executors And Administrators ⟶ 228(3)

In Ohio law action for emotional distress injuries by crew members of train that collided with truck against estate of truck driver, crew members' notification of truck's insurer of claim against estate within one year of driver's death did not excuse failure to comply with Ohio statute requiring that notice of claim against estate be provided to executor or administrator of estate within one year after decedent's death, since crew members did not allege and prove that they sought recovery only from liability insurance policy, and not from assets of estate. Lukowski v. CSX Transp., Inc. (C.A.6 (Ohio), 07-19-2005) 416 F.3d 478. Executors And Administrators ⟶ 225(1)

This section and GC 10509–134 (RC 2117.07) (114 v 320), must be construed together and are statutes of limitation which bar creditors' claims unless presented to an executor or administrator within four months after date of appointment. Prudential Ins. Co. of America v. Joyce Bldg. Realty Co. (Ohio 1944) 143 Ohio St. 564, 56 N.E.2d 168, 28 O.O. 480.

This section and GC 10509–134 (RC 2117.07) must be construed together and are statutes of limitations (or nonclaim statutes) which bar creditors' claims unless presented to executor or administrator within four months after the date of appointment. State ex rel. Fulton v. Coburn (Ohio 1938) 133 Ohio St. 192, 12 N.E.2d 471, 10 O.O. 249.

The subrogee of a tort claim does not have a contingent claim within the meaning of RC 2117.37, and therefore must bring its claim within the time set forth in RC 2117.06. Marcum v Burnham, No. 8411 (2d Dist Ct App, Montgomery, 4–16–84).

Since there is no living person for the statute to run against until an executor or administrator is appointed for a decedent's estate, the statute of limitations does not run against a claim for funeral expenses until such appointment; as to expenses of the last sickness, the statute runs from the date of account. In re Estate of Miller, 12 D 563 (CP, Hamilton 1902).

12. Barred claims

Silence by executor in response to submitted bill does not save improperly presented claim from being time barred. Children's Med. Ctr. v. Ward (Montgomery 1993) 87 Ohio App.3d 504, 622 N.E.2d 692, motion overruled 67 Ohio St.3d 1481, 620 N.E.2d 854. Executors And Administrators ⟶ 228(5)

Where claimant presented her claim to the executrix on June 4, 1982 and such executrix was appointed on March 3, 1982, the executrix properly rejected such claim as being untimely filed. In re Estate of Fisher (Warren 1983) 12 Ohio App.3d 150, 467 N.E.2d 898, 12 O.B.R. 474.

Where a person having a claim against a decedent's estate knew of the decedent's death, resided in the same county where decedent resided, did not make inquiry about the appointment of an executor or administrator of the estate, failed to present his claim within the four-month period prescribed by statute and does not show any facts or circumstances within the purview of statute that would justify such failure, he may not properly be authorized by the probate court to present his claim after such four-month period. In re Andres' Estate (Greene 1961) 114 Ohio App. 167, 180 N.E.2d 855, 19 O.O.2d 21. Executors And Administrators ⟶ 225(1)

Failure to file a claim against a decedent's estate for loss of earning capacity resulting from an accident allegedly caused by decedent's negligence within four months of the administrator's appointment bars such claim. Lewis v. Knight (Mahoning 1955) 144 N.E.2d 551, 75 Ohio Law Abs. 589.

Where a claimant seeking to file a belated claim actually knew of decedent's death and in the exercise of reasonable diligence could have learned of the appointment of an administrator and thereafter had a fair opportunity to present his claim within four months, the probate court is chargeable with no error or abuse of discretion in denying such claimant authority to present such claim. In re Miller's Estate (Columbiana 1954) 98 Ohio App. 445, 129 N.E.2d 838, 57 O.O. 481. Executors And Administrators ⟶ 225(7)

A claim for damages for injuries resulting from a motor vehicle accident which was not presented to the defendant's executor within nine months of such appointment cannot be revived even if the plaintiff is a minor. Overman v. Yake (Clark 1952) 109 N.E.2d 697, 68 Ohio Law Abs. 248.

Claimant who foregoes the filing of his claim, whether the same be absolute or contingent, liquidated or unliquidated, may lose his right to participate in the disbursement of the estate funds. Roberts v. Hickerson (Morgan 1936) 36 N.E.2d 282, 26 Ohio Law Abs. 616, 11 O.O. 471.

RC 2117.06 is applicable to an assignee of a stock subscription who sues an executor for the unpaid balance due from the decedent, and in the absence of averments that the claim was duly presented within the four-month period and that the same was rejected, the petition does not state a cause of action, and the claim is barred; in such case the claim can only be reinstated under authority of and in the manner prescribed by GC 10509–134 (RC 2117.07), which vests jurisdiction over such claims in the probate court. Beach v. Mizner (Cuyahoga 1935) 52 Ohio App. 348, 3 N.E.2d 642, 20 Ohio Law Abs. 380, 4 O.O. 253, affirmed 131 Ohio St. 481, 3 N.E.2d 417, 6 O.O. 155.

13. Notice

The failure of an executrix to file a notice of her appointment in a suit pending against the decedent, as required by RC 2117.06, does not justify a finding that the plaintiff failed to file his claim against the defendant's estate within four months after the appointment of the executrix, such as would permit a delayed filing of the claim under RC 2117.07, where the defendant's attorneys of record notified the plaintiff's attorneys of record by letter of such death and appointment in ample time to permit filing of the claim within the four-month limitation. In re Herron's Estate (Ohio Prob. 1968) 21 Ohio Misc. 212, 252 N.E.2d 332, 49 O.O.2d 27, 50 O.O.2d 422.

Where probate court permitted a claimant with no actual notice of decedent's death or appointment of an executrix to present a claim after expiration of the four month period, it did not abuse its discretion. Bronson v. Haywood (Mahoning 1959) 172 N.E.2d 332, 84 Ohio Law Abs. 471.

If a personal representative knows or could ascertain in a reasonable way the identity of a creditor, a state "nonclaim" statute cannot bar the creditor's claim unless the creditor was given actual notice of the decedent's death and the need to file a claim; notice by publication alone is insufficient. In re Highway Equipment Co. (Bkrtcy.S.D.Ohio 1988) 91 B.R. 454.

14. Foreign creditors

Estate of Ohio resident had no valid interest in brokerage account assets which resident acquired as surviving joint tenant; disputed brokerage accounts were created by Florida resident with no intent to give Ohio resident present interest in account assets, as required for valid joint and survivorship interest to be created under Florida law. Lewis v. Steinreich (Ohio, 08-23-1995) 73 Ohio St.3d 299, 652 N.E.2d 981, 1995-Ohio-133, reconsideration denied 74 Ohio St.3d 1409, 655 N.E.2d 188. Executors And Administrators ⟶ 55; Joint Tenancy ⟶ 3

Claim to brokerage account assets by guardian ad litem for estate of Florida resident who created account against estate of Ohio resident who received assets as surviving joint tenant, claiming ownership of account assets on ground that joint tenancy with right of survivorship was not intended when account was created, was not subject to statutory requirement that creditors' claims against estate within limited time; claim was to ownership of account assets rather than claim for debt by creditor. Lewis v. Steinreich (Ohio, 08-23-1995) 73 Ohio St.3d 299, 652 N.E.2d 981, 1995-Ohio-133, reconsideration denied 74 Ohio St.3d 1409, 655 N.E.2d 188. Executors And Administrators ⟶ 224

Under statute conferring jurisdiction upon probate court in ancillary administration to order residuum to be paid over to domiciliary administrator or executor, or to such persons entitled thereto, probate court, upon ordering payment from residuum of ancillary estate to legatees and distributees who are residents of state, and to nonresident legatees of specific property within the state, should order balance of residuum remaining after such payments to be paid to the domiciliary executor or administrator, since rights of nonresident creditors and distributees and legatees other than legatees of specific property within state in residuum were subject to adjudication only in domiciliary administration proceeding. In re Kelley's Estate (Hancock 1940) 68 Ohio App. 51, 34 N.E.2d 34, 33 Ohio Law Abs. 258, 22 O.O. 158. Executors And Administrators ⟶ 519(1)

A claim is properly revived against an estate where the administratrix in defending that action has sufficient notice of the claim and the possible liability to the estate and such claim is timely and not barred by RC 2117.12 so that an independent action on the claim need not be filed even though the administratrix fails to honor it. Carlin v Mambuca, No. 65217, 1994 WL 189559 (8th Dist Ct App, Cuyahoga, 5–12–94).

2117.061 Decedent aged fifty-five years or older; notice to administrator of estate recovery program

(A) As used in this section:

(1) "Medicaid estate recovery program" means the program instituted under section 5111.11 of the Revised Code.

(2) "Permanently institutionalized individual" has the same meaning as in section 5111.11 of the Revised Code.

(3) "Person responsible for the estate" means the executor, administrator, commissioner, or person who filed pursuant to section 2113.03 of the Revised Code for release from administration of an estate.

(B) If a decedent, at the time of death, was fifty-five years of age or older or a permanently institutionalized individual, the person responsible for the decedent's estate shall determine whether the decedent was, at any time during the decedent's life, a medicaid recipient under Chapter 5111. of the Revised Code. If the decedent was a medicaid recipient, the person responsible for the estate shall submit a properly completed medicaid estate recovery reporting form prescribed under division (D) of this section to the administrator of the medicaid estate recovery program not later than thirty days after the occurrence of any of the following:

(1) The granting of letters testamentary;

(2) The administration of the estate;

(3) The filing of an application for release from administration or summary release from administration.

(C) The person responsible for the estate shall mark the appropriate box on the appropriate probate form to indicate compliance with the requirements of division (B) of this section.

The probate court shall send a copy of the completed probate form to the administrator of the medicaid estate recovery program.

(D) The administrator of the estate recovery program shall prescribe a medicaid estate recovery reporting form for the purpose of division (B) of this section. The form shall require, at a minimum, that the person responsible for the estate list all of the decedent's real and personal property and other assets that are part of the decedent's estate as defined in section 5111.11 of the Revised Code. The administrator shall include on the form a statement printed in bold letters informing the person responsible for the estate that knowingly making a false statement on the form is falsification under section 2921.13 of the Revised Code, a misdemeanor of the first degree.

(E) The estate recovery program administrator shall present a claim for estate recovery to the person responsible for the estate or the person's legal representative not later than ninety days after the date on which the medicaid estate recovery reporting form is received under division (B) of this section or one year after the decedent's death, whichever is later.

(2005 H 66, eff. 6–30–05; 2003 H 95, eff. 9–26–03)

Historical and Statutory Notes

Amendment Note: 2005 H 66 rewrote this section, which prior thereto read:

"(A) As used in this section, 'person responsible for the estate' means the executor, administrator, commissioner, or person who filed pursuant to section 2113.03 of the Revised Code for release from administration of an estate.

"(B) If the decedent was fifty-five years of age or older at the time of death, the person responsible for an estate shall determine whether the decedent was a recipient of medical assistance under Chapter 5111. of the Revised Code. If the decedent was a recipient, the person responsible for the estate shall give written notice to that effect to the administrator of the estate recovery program instituted under section 5111.11 of the Revised Code not later than thirty days after the occurrence of any of the following:

"(1) The granting of letters testamentary;

"(2) The administration of the estate;

"(3) The filing of an application for release from administration or summary release from administration.

"(C) The person responsible for an estate shall mark the appropriate box on the appropriate probate form to indicate compliance with the requirements of division (B) of this section.

"(D) The estate recovery program administrator shall present a claim for estate recovery to the person responsible for the estate or the person's legal representative not later than ninety days after the date on which notice is received under division (B) of this section or one year after the decedent's death, whichever is later."

Library References

Executors and Administrators ⚖226.
Westlaw Topic No. 162.
C.J.S. Executors and Administrators § 440.

Research References

Encyclopedias

OH Jur. 3d Public Welfare § 168, Recovery of Medicaid Payments from Recipient or Estate.

Treatises and Practice Aids

Carlin, Baldwin's Ohio Practice, Merrick-Rippner Probate Law § 2:15, Appointment of Fiduciary—Appointment of Executor or Administrator.

Carlin, Baldwin's Ohio Practice, Merrick-Rippner Probate Law § 2:27, Payment of Debts and Claims—Presentation of Claims.

Carlin, Baldwin's Ohio Practice, Merrick-Rippner Probate Law § 2:28, Payment of Debts and Claims—Notice to Creditors.

Carlin, Baldwin's Ohio Practice, Merrick-Rippner Probate Law § 68:1, Letters—in General—Jurisdiction.

Carlin, Baldwin's Ohio Practice, Merrick-Rippner Probate Law § 68:2, Letters—in General—Issuance.

Carlin, Baldwin's Ohio Practice, Merrick-Rippner Probate Law § 75:4, Distribution—Voluntary—Liability—Executor or Administrator.

Carlin, Baldwin's Ohio Practice, Merrick-Rippner Probate Law § 84:1, Creditor's Claims—Introduction.

Carlin, Baldwin's Ohio Practice, Merrick-Rippner Probate Law § 84:3, Creditor's Claims—Form of Claim.

Carlin, Baldwin's Ohio Practice, Merrick-Rippner Probate Law § 84:5, Creditor's Claims—Claims Requiring Presentation—Statutory Provision.

Carlin, Baldwin's Ohio Practice, Merrick-Rippner Probate Law § 89:4, Payment of Debts—Order of Payment.

Carlin, Baldwin's Ohio Practice, Merrick-Rippner Probate Law § 2:108, Release from Administration.

Carlin, Baldwin's Ohio Practice, Merrick-Rippner Probate Law § 2:110, Release from Administration—Application; Notice.

Carlin, Baldwin's Ohio Practice, Merrick-Rippner Probate Law § 2:112, Summary Release from Administration Generally.

Carlin, Baldwin's Ohio Practice, Merrick-Rippner Probate Law § 2:114, Application for Summary Release from Administration.

Carlin, Baldwin's Ohio Practice, Merrick-Rippner Probate Law § 2:121, Administration of Decedent's Estate—Checklist.

Carlin, Baldwin's Ohio Practice, Merrick-Rippner Probate Law § 2:122, Administration of Decedent's Estate—Release—Checklist.

Carlin, Baldwin's Ohio Practice, Merrick-Rippner Probate Law § 30:34, Drafting a Will—Appointment of Executor, Alternate Executor; Ancillary Administrator.

Carlin, Baldwin's Ohio Practice, Merrick-Rippner Probate Law § 33:16, Trusts—Medicaid-Qualifying.

Carlin, Baldwin's Ohio Practice, Merrick-Rippner Probate Law § 84:29, Creditor's Claims—Statute of Limitations.

Carlin, Baldwin's Ohio Practice, Merrick-Rippner Probate Law § 84:39.50, Creditor's Claims—Medicaid Estate Recovery Program.

Carlin, Baldwin's Ohio Practice, Merrick-Rippner Probate Law App B SPF 7.0, Notice of Administrator of Estate Recovery Program—Form.

Law Review and Journal Commentaries

Ambiguity in the New Medicaid Estate Recovery Statute of Limitations: Who's Kicking Whom?, James J. Lanham. 14 Prob L J Ohio 27 (November/December 2003).

H.B. 66 and Medicaid recovery. William J. Browning, 16 Prob L J Ohio 42 (November/December 2005).

2117.07 Acceleration of bar against claims against estate

An executor or administrator may accelerate the bar against claims against the estate established by section 2117.06 of the Revised Code by giving written notice to a potential claimant that identifies the decedent by name, states the date of the death of the decedent, identifies the executor or administrator by name and mailing address, and informs the potential claimant that any claims the claimant may have against the estate are required to be presented to the executor or administrator in a writing within the earlier of thirty days after receipt of the notice by the potential claimant or six months after the date of the death of the decedent. A claim of that potential claimant that is not presented in the manner provided by section 2117.06 of the Revised Code within the earlier of thirty days after receipt of the notice by the potential claimant or six months after the date of the death of the decedent is barred by section 2117.06 of the Revised Code in the same manner as if it was not presented within six months after the date of the death of the decedent.

(2003 H 51, eff. 4–8–04; 1990 H 346, eff. 5–31–90)

Uncodified Law

2004 H 161, § 3. See Uncodified Law under 2117.06

1990 H 346, § 3, eff. 5–31–90, reads, in part: (A) Sections 1 and 2 of this act shall apply only to the estates of decedents who die on or after the effective date of this act.

Historical and Statutory Notes

Ed. Note: Former 2117.07 repealed by 1990 H 346, eff. 5–31–90; 1975 S 145; 1970 S 185; 1969 S 103; 130 v H 13; 125 v 903; 1953 H 1; GC 10509–134.

Pre–1953 H 1 Amendments: 119 v 394, § 1; 114 v 431

Amendment Note: 2003 H 51 substituted "the claimant" for "he" and substituted "six months" for "one year".

Library References

Executors and Administrators ⇐225(1), 225(2), 232, 233.
Westlaw Topic No. 162.
C.J.S. Executors and Administrators §§ 435, 452.

Research References

Encyclopedias

OH Jur. 3d Decedents' Estates § 1432, Claims Expressly Excepted by Statute.
OH Jur. 3d Decedents' Estates § 1442, Acceleration of the Time for Presenting Claims.
OH Jur. 3d Decedents' Estates § 1445, Relation of Statutes to Other Limitation Statutes.
OH Jur. 3d Decedents' Estates § 1448, Effect of Failure to Present Claims Within Limitation Periods.
OH Jur. 3d Decedents' Estates § 1696, Liability for Excess Payments.
OH Jur. 3d Decedents' Estates § 1789, Action on Contingent Claims.
OH Jur. 3d Decedents' Estates § 1791, Action on Claim Neither Allowed Nor Rejected.
OH Jur. 3d Notice & Notices § 2, Actual and Constructive Notice.

Forms

Ohio Jurisprudence Pleading and Practice Forms § 12:11, Checklist—Statutes of Limitations.

Treatises and Practice Aids

Carlin, Baldwin's Ohio Practice, Merrick-Rippner Probate Law § 2:27, Payment of Debts and Claims—Presentation of Claims.
Carlin, Baldwin's Ohio Practice, Merrick-Rippner Probate Law § 2:28, Payment of Debts and Claims—Notice to Creditors.
Carlin, Baldwin's Ohio Practice, Merrick-Rippner Probate Law § 2:34, Payment of Debts and Claims—Mortgage and Tax Liens.
Carlin, Baldwin's Ohio Practice, Merrick-Rippner Probate Law § 70:4, Administrator De Bonis Non—Personal Injury Actions.
Carlin, Baldwin's Ohio Practice, Merrick-Rippner Probate Law § 75:4, Distribution—Voluntary—Liability—Executor or Administrator.
Carlin, Baldwin's Ohio Practice, Merrick-Rippner Probate Law § 84:1, Creditor's Claims—Introduction.
Carlin, Baldwin's Ohio Practice, Merrick-Rippner Probate Law § 84:2, Creditor's Claims—Purpose of Statutes.
Carlin, Baldwin's Ohio Practice, Merrick-Rippner Probate Law § 84:3, Creditor's Claims—Form of Claim.
Carlin, Baldwin's Ohio Practice, Merrick-Rippner Probate Law § 84:8, Creditor's Claims—Claims Requiring Presentation—Examples from Case Law—Rents.
Carlin, Baldwin's Ohio Practice, Merrick-Rippner Probate Law § 85:1, Acceleration of Claims—Introduction and Purpose of Statute.
Carlin, Baldwin's Ohio Practice, Merrick-Rippner Probate Law § 85:2, Acceleration of Claims—Effect on Other Statutes of Limitations.
Carlin, Baldwin's Ohio Practice, Merrick-Rippner Probate Law § 86:3, Death of Claimant—Motion for Substitution Within Ninety Days.
Carlin, Baldwin's Ohio Practice, Merrick-Rippner Probate Law § 2:121, Administration of Decedent's Estate—Checklist.
Carlin, Baldwin's Ohio Practice, Merrick-Rippner Probate Law § 54:13, Fiduciary Accounts—Approval of Final Account and Discharge of Fiduciary.
Carlin, Baldwin's Ohio Practice, Merrick-Rippner Probate Law § 54:22, Fiduciary Accounts—Effect of Order Settling Account.
Carlin, Baldwin's Ohio Practice, Merrick-Rippner Probate Law § 68:14, Letters of Administration—Discretion of Probate Court in Appointing Administrators; Appeal.
Carlin, Baldwin's Ohio Practice, Merrick-Rippner Probate Law § 84:10, Creditor's Claims—Claims Requiring Presentation—Examples from Case Law—Personal Injury Actions.
Carlin, Baldwin's Ohio Practice, Merrick-Rippner Probate Law § 84:16, Creditor's Claims—Claims Not Requiring Presentation—Federal Taxes—State Claim.
Carlin, Baldwin's Ohio Practice, Merrick-Rippner Probate Law § 84:24, Creditor's Claims—Claims Not Requiring Presentation—Contingent Claims—Definition.
Carlin, Baldwin's Ohio Practice, Merrick-Rippner Probate Law § 84:25, Creditor's Claims—Claims Not Requiring Presentation—Contingent Claims—Mandatory Presentation.
Carlin, Baldwin's Ohio Practice, Merrick-Rippner Probate Law § 84:29, Creditor's Claims—Statute of Limitations.
Carlin, Baldwin's Ohio Practice, Merrick-Rippner Probate Law § 84:30, Creditor's Claims—Acceleration of Bar Against Claims Against Estate.
Carlin, Baldwin's Ohio Practice, Merrick-Rippner Probate Law § 84:31, Creditor's Claims—No Savings Clause.
Carlin, Baldwin's Ohio Practice, Merrick-Rippner Probate Law § 84:35, Creditor's Claims—Suit on Rejected Claims; Constructive Rejection; Jurisdiction of Probate Court.
Carlin, Baldwin's Ohio Practice, Merrick-Rippner Probate Law § 84:37, Creditor's Claims—Application to Revive Action.
Carlin, Baldwin's Ohio Practice, Merrick-Rippner Probate Law § 84:38, Creditor's Claims—Effect on Other Statutes of Limitations.
Carlin, Baldwin's Ohio Practice, Merrick-Rippner Probate Law § 88:10, Rejection of Claims—Governmental Claim.
Kuehnle and Levey, Ohio Real Estate Law and Practice § 20:18, Conveyancing—Grantors—Capacity—Individuals—Minors and Persons Incarcerated.
Kuehnle and Levey, Ohio Real Estate Law and Practice § 36:23, Foreclosure—Parties—Defendants—Parties Liable on Debt—Personal Representative of Deceased Mortgagor.

Law Review and Journal Commentaries

Deciphering Polikoff and the Demise of Amato, Irene C. Keyse–Walker. 65 Clev B J 10 (November 1993).

Notes of Decisions

Ed. Note: This section contains annotations from former RC 2117.07.

Absence of executor or wrongful act or statement   5
Actual notice of death of decedent or appointment of executor   4
Claim barred   7
Exceptions   3
Final order; appeal   8
Legal disability of claimant   6
Scope; hearing and petition   1
Statute of limitations; procedure   2

---

1. Scope; hearing and petition

Relief granted by this section is exclusively and completely statutory and section is not intended to classify the remedy as equitable. In re Baumann's Estate (Montgomery 1938) 26 Ohio Law Abs. 595.

This section does not confer upon probate court authority to permit executor or administrator, who has not presented his claim within period of three months after his appointment, to then present same to probate court. In re Grube's Estate (Clark 1935) 21 Ohio Law Abs. 1. Executors And Administrators ⇐ 225(4)

This section applies to a claim that "has not been presented within the time prescribed by law," and there is nothing in the section indicating that it has any application to a claim which has been presented and allowed and which the probate court has ordered rejected under GC 10509–135 (RC 2117.13). Homan v. Lightner (Wayne 1935) 20 Ohio Law Abs. 76.

If, within three months after a defendant's death, a claim is properly revived against the administratrix of the defendant's estate in her representative capacity and judgment is entered against the estate, resubmissions of such claim and judgment are not required under RC 2117.06, RC 2117.07 or RC 2117.12, and RC 2117.17 is irrelevant to such a case. Blanchard v. Morgan (Portage 1983) 10 Ohio App.3d 117, 460 N.E.2d 715, 10 O.B.R. 141. Abatement And Revival ⇐ 77

The presentation to the executor or administrator of a claim for wrongful death by one of the statutory beneficiaries of that action is sufficient compliance with RC 2117.06 and RC 2117.07. Burwell v. Maynard (Ohio 1970) 21 Ohio St.2d 108, 255 N.E.2d 628, 50 O.O.2d 268.

A petition in an action against an executor of the estate of a decedent which alleges an oral presentation of a claim against the estate to, and an oral rejection of the claim by, the executor does not state facts which show a cause of action and is subject to demurrer. Morgan v. City Nat. Bank & Trust Co. (Franklin 1964) 4 Ohio App.2d 417, 212 N.E.2d 822, 33 O.O.2d 504.

The federal government is not required to comply with the statutes relating to presentment of claims in order to collect social security taxes due from a decedent. Baker v. Charles (Ohio Prob. 1963) 202 N.E.2d 646, 95 Ohio Law Abs. 97, 31 O.O.2d 310.

The filing of a petition to contest a decedent's will does not suspend or extend the time in which a creditor shall present his claim to the executor of said decedent's estate. In re Kehoe's Estate (Ohio Prob. 1963) 199 N.E.2d 29, 94 Ohio Law Abs. 469, 27 O.O.2d 35. Executors And Administrators ⇐ 225(2)

The filing of a petition in an action against an administratrix which contains the address of the plaintiff and sets forth a cause of action on a claim of negligence against the estate of defendant's decedent, which claim, under the facts alleged therein, will not be affected by the insolvency of the estate and which claim is based on facts occurring prior to the decedent's death, and the service of summons and a copy of the petition upon the administratrix within four months of her appointment, is a compliance with the mandatory requirements of RC 2117.06. Fortelka v. Meifert (Cuyahoga 1963) 120 Ohio App. 294, 193 N.E.2d 170, 93 Ohio Law Abs. 1, 27 O.O.2d 175, appeal certified to 120 Ohio App. 294, 193 N.E.2d 305, 93 Ohio Law Abs. 8, 27 O.O.2d 78, affirmed 176 Ohio St. 476, 200 N.E.2d 318, 27 O.O.2d 439.

The authority to file a claim against a decedent's estate after the four-month period must be in conformance with RC 2117.07, and cannot be predicated on general equitable principles outside the purview of the statute. In re Andres' Estate (Greene 1961) 114 Ohio App. 167, 180 N.E.2d 855, 19 O.O.2d 21. Executors And Administrators ⇐ 225(1)

The right of a part owner who pays the tax on the whole tract of which he is part owner to have a lien on the part of the other part owner for the tax paid on such part is subject to the statutes of limitation requiring presentation of claims to executors and administrators. Kuhnle v. Rusmisel (Miami 1960) 113 Ohio App. 389, 178 N.E.2d 810, 17 O.O.2d 465. Executors And Administrators ⇐ 224

Where the time limit for filing revivor applications for pending actions is fixed as "the time provided for the presentation of claims by creditors in section 2117.06 of the Revised Code," such section must be read in pari materia with RC 2117.07. In re Fuller's Estate (Medina 1960) 112 Ohio App. 25, 174 N.E.2d 613, 15 O.O.2d 378. Statutes ⇐ 223.2(12)

Persons claiming as donee beneficiaries under an antenuptial contract are not creditors within the meaning of the statutes relating to presentment of claims. Cantor v. Cantor (Ohio Prob. 1959) 174 N.E.2d 304, 86 Ohio Law Abs. 452, 15 O.O.2d 148.

Where the defendant in an action for money, which survives, dies, and his executor is substituted as defendant, and where, thereafter, plaintiff files a motion for a conditional order of revivor and a summons with a copy of the petition is served upon the substituted defendant, such service constitutes sufficient written notice of the application or proceedings for revivor as required by RC 2311.31. Miller v. Andre (Ohio 1957) 167 Ohio St. 83, 146 N.E.2d 598, 4 O.O.2d 52.

After a written notice of the application or proceedings for a revivor is given to the executor or administrator of a deceased defendant in an action for money which survives, it is not required that a subsequent written notice of such application or proceedings be given to a succeeding executor or administrator. Miller v. Andre (Ohio 1957) 167 Ohio St. 83, 146 N.E.2d 598, 4 O.O.2d 52.

The hearing of an application to the probate court under RC 2117.07 is a special proceeding and an order granting such authority is one affecting a substantial right, and, where a record is made in such special proceeding, the order is properly appealable on questions of law to the court of appeals. In re Wyckoff's Estate (Ohio 1957) 166 Ohio St. 354, 142 N.E.2d 660, 66 A.L.R.2d 653, 2 O.O.2d 257.

Claims filed against estates of decedents more than four months after the appointment of an administrator or executor must be filed in conformity with the statutes and not predicated on general principles of equity outside the purview of the statutes, as the statutes provide the exclusive remedy to file belated claims. In re Natherson's Estate (Cuyahoga 1956) 102 Ohio App. 475, 134 N.E.2d 852, 57 A.L.R.2d 1297, 74 Ohio Law Abs. 387, 3 O.O.2d 35. Executors And Administrators ⇐ 233

On the facts a creditor was entitled to present a claim more than four months after the appointment of an executor. In re Dulle's Estate (Ohio Prob. 1955) 130 N.E.2d 253, 71 Ohio Law Abs. 114.

The holder of a contingent claim is not required to present such claim under provisions of GC 10509–112 (RC 2117.06) or 10509–134 (RC 2117.07). Keifer v. Kissell (Clark 1947) 83 Ohio App. 133, 75 N.E.2d 692, 50 Ohio Law Abs. 375, 38 O.O. 224.

Provisions of section, relating to reinstatement of claim against an estate may be invoked only when such claim has not been presented or its presentation has not been waived within four months after the appointment of the estate's legal representative, in accordance with requirements of GC 10509–112 (RC 2117.06). In re Erbaugh's Estate (Montgomery 1943) 73 Ohio App. 533, 57 N.E.2d 294, 38 Ohio Law Abs. 574, 29 O.O. 177. Executors And Administrators ⇐ 233

Equity requires reinstatement of claim where no injury could result to creditors who have filed their claims in time or to others by allowance of such claim. Home Owners' Loan Corp. v. Doolittle (Cuyahoga 1937) 57 Ohio App. 329, 13 N.E.2d 920, 25 Ohio Law Abs. 195, 10 O.O. 225. Executors And Administrators ⇐ 233

In an action in a federal district court in Pennsylvania against the Ohio administrator of an Ohio decedent involved in a motor vehicle accident in Pennsylvania, the Ohio statutes with respect to a time limit for presentation of claims against a decedent's estate do not constitute a defense. Colman v. Pitzer (W.D.Pa. 1958) 160 F.Supp. 862, 82 Ohio Law Abs. 452, 6 O.O.2d 476.

Express language of this section requires court, before permitting petitioner to file his claim for allowance, to find, first, that in justice and equity the court should permit the claim to be filed, and second, that petitioner is not chargeable with culpable neglect in failing to present his claim within time so prescribed. In re Weimer's Estate (Ohio Prob. 1937) 4 Ohio Supp. 315, 23 Ohio Law Abs. 636, 8 O.O. 314.

Where superintendent of banks made no demand upon decedent during his lifetime, nor upon executor of estate of said decedent during time allowed by law for presentation of claims against estates, and first demand that was made was on application of state superintendent in filing application in court to reinstate claim under provisions of this section, interest must be allowed from date state superintendent of banks filed his application for reinstatement in court. Squire v Oerter, 4 Ohio Supp. 304 (Prob 1937).

While language of this section is somewhat vague, two things should be determined by court under this section: first, whether or not a claimant has been guilty of culpable neglect in filing a claim; second, whether or not a valid claim exists and court determines both questions in favor of claimant, order should be entered directing executor or administrator to pay same if such order is asked. In re McGuire's Estate (Ohio Prob. 1937) 4 Ohio Supp. 302, 24 Ohio Law Abs. 101, 8 O.O. 409.

In hearing brought under this section, court must determine two things: first, whether or not claimant has been guilty of culpable neglect in filing his claim; and second, whether or not a valid claim exists. Squire v Oerter, 24 Abs 249, 4 OSupp 304 (Prob, Tuscarawas 1937), modified by 25 Abs 225, 4 OSupp 307 (Prob, Tuscarawas 1937).

2. Statute of limitations; procedure

Tort plaintiff's claim against deceased defendant's estate was timely, though plaintiff did not file formal independent action on her claim against estate within two months of administrator's rejection of claim, where she timely substituted administrator for decedent in her tort action. Carlin v. Mambuca (Ohio App. 8 Dist., 05-23-1994) 96 Ohio App.3d 500, 645 N.E.2d 737, motion to certify allowed 70 Ohio St.3d 1475, 640 N.E.2d 848, cause dismissed 71 Ohio St.3d 1441, 643 N.E.2d 1152. Executors And Administrators ⚬— 437(2)

The tolling provisions of RC 2305.16 are not applicable to the filing of claims against an estate, RC Ch 2117 which deals specifically with the filing of claims against an estate in probate court is controlling. In re Estate of Kennedy (Franklin 1988) 46 Ohio App.3d 128, 546 N.E.2d 220.

A timely complaint in negligence which designates as a defendant one who died after the cause of action accrued but before the complaint was filed may be amended to substitute the executrix of the deceased defendant's estate for the original defendant after the limitations period has expired where the executrix, still bonded and acting at the time of the complaint and service of process, accepted service of summons within the one-year period for perfecting service after the filing of the complaint and voluntarily had the trial court substitute her as a party-defendant in the action. Gentile v. Carr (Jefferson 1981) 4 Ohio App.3d 55, 446 N.E.2d 477, 4 O.B.R. 104. Limitation Of Actions ⚬— 121(2)

When an action is brought by the filing of a complaint, within the statute of limitations, complainant has one year thereafter in which to cause the appointment of a suitable personal representative and obtain service of summons against him. Hayden v. Ours (Ohio Com.Pl. 1975) 44 Ohio Misc. 62, 337 N.E.2d 183, 73 O.O.2d 224. Limitation Of Actions ⚬— 83(2)

If a defendant debtor is deceased, a claim for wrongful death must be presented to his legal representative in the manner and within the time limitations set forth in RC 2117.06 and RC 2117.07, even though the complaint filed specifically states that damages are sought from assets other than those of the debtor's estate. King v. Hargis (Clermont 1973) 37 Ohio App.2d 92, 307 N.E.2d 40, 66 O.O.2d 142. Executors And Administrators ⚬— 224

A person claiming a right of action which may be filed pursuant to the last paragraph of RC 2117.07 should be granted the right to reopen the estate of the decedent for that purpose. In re McDonald's Estate (Ohio Prob. 1966) 15 Ohio Misc. 74, 239 N.E.2d 277, 44 O.O.2d 262.

The 1963 amendment to RC 2117.07 does not apply to a wrongful death action against an executor or administrator which is commenced within two years after the cause of such action arose, even where no portion of any recovery is sought from assets of the estate. Collins v. Yanity (Ohio 1968) 14 Ohio St.2d 202, 237 N.E.2d 611, 43 O.O.2d 301.

Where a claim has not been presented within the four months prescribed by statute, the proper procedure is to file a petition or application for permission to reinstate the claim, and upon failure to do so, the claim is barred. Wilcox v. Ceschiat (Ohio Com.Pl. 1960) 179 N.E.2d 544, 87 Ohio Law Abs. 225.

Where a petition is filed and summons issued in a negligence action, wherein the executor of an estate is defendant, on the last day before the expiration of the time for commencing such action, which petition contains allegations that a petition had been filed in the probate court for authority to present plaintiff's claim to such executor, and, on the same day, the petition to present such claim is filed in the probate court pursuant to RC 2117.07, the order of the probate court, entered after the expiration of the statutory time for bringing such negligence action, and the presentation of such claim relate back to the time of the filing of the petition in the negligence action, and such action is deemed commenced as required by law. Smith v. Boyers (Ottawa 1959) 110 Ohio App. 291, 169 N.E.2d 479, 13 O.O.2d 70.

Where a petition for authority to present a claim after the expiration of four months is filed under favor of RC 2117.07 the nine-month period provided therein dates from the filing of such petition. In re Howe's Estate (Stark 1958) 107 Ohio App. 361, 159 N.E.2d 622, 8 O.O.2d 321. Executors And Administrators ⚬— 233

GC 10509–134 (RC 2117.07) requires that a claim must be presented within nine months or be forever barred. In re Sarver's Estate (Franklin 1954) 97 Ohio App. 199, 124 N.E.2d 749, 55 O.O. 453.

Section must be construed liberally in favor of the claimant. In re Price's Estate (Darke 1949) 87 Ohio App. 23, 93 N.E.2d 769, 42 O.O. 272.

Where corporation's note was signed by stockholders individually, the liability of each being limited to a specific amount in proportion to his stock holdings, payments to corporation by executors of deceased stockholder to apply on carrying charges and interest due payee of note did not constitute a "waiver" of obligation placed on payee to present its claim to executor or administrator within four months of appointment as required by statutes. Prudential Ins. Co. of America v. Joyce Bldg. Realty Co. (Franklin 1943) 65 N.E.2d 516, 44 Ohio Law Abs. 481, affirmed 143 Ohio St. 564, 56 N.E.2d 168, 28 O.O. 480. Executors And Administrators ⚬— 228(5)

Where claimants filed petition in probate court on last day of nine-month period after appointment of administratrix of estate, seeking a court order allowing their claim to be presented to such administratrix under authority of provisions of section, the court's adjudication of their right to present such claim was legally determined as of the date of such filing even though such court's order was not actually made until after the expiration of more than fifteen months from the date of such administratrix's appointment. In re Erbaugh's Estate (Montgomery 1943) 73 Ohio App. 533, 57 N.E.2d 294, 38 Ohio Law Abs. 574, 29 O.O. 177. Executors And Administrators ⚬— 233

Section is a statute of limitation. In re Erbaugh's Estate (Montgomery 1943) 73 Ohio App. 533, 57 N.E.2d 294, 38 Ohio Law Abs. 574, 29 O.O. 177.

Where a creditor of a decedent contends that a claim against an estate should not be barred where the administrator had knowledge of the creditor's claim within the statutory period and there was no Ohio case squarely in point, the granting of summary judgment was improper. Hart v. Johnston (C.A.6 (Ohio) 1968) 24 Ohio Misc. 178, 389 F.2d 239, 44 O.O.2d 221, 53 O.O.2d 205.

Where plaintiff had failed to present a claim against decedent's estate within the period required by Ohio law, a federal court cannot obtain jurisdiction of the cause of action on the ground that it was presented to an agent of the administrator or that the administrator is estopped to contest the claim; the proper procedure would be to obtain reinstatement of a barred claim in the probate court. Hart v. Johnston (S.D.Ohio 1966) 9 Ohio Misc. 88, 253 F.Supp. 621, 36 O.O.2d 366, 38 O.O.2d 115, reversed 24 Ohio Misc. 178, 389 F.2d 239, 44 O.O.2d 221, 53 O.O.2d 205.

GC 10509–112 (RC 2117.06) and 10509–134 (RC 2117.07) (114 v 320) must be construed together and are statutes of limitation (or nonclaim statutes) which bar creditors' claims unless presented to an executor or administrator within four months after date of appointment. Prudential Ins. Co. of America v. Joyce Bldg. Realty Co. (Ohio 1944) 143 Ohio St. 564, 56 N.E.2d 168, 28 O.O. 480.

3. Exceptions

Where it is alleged in an action for bodily injuries that such injuries were proximately caused by negligence of a decedent and that he had a policy of insurance insuring him against liability for such negligence, and it does not appear that any other claims covered by such insurance have been asserted, such action may be brought against executor or administrator of such decedent and decedent's liability insurer, at any time within statute of limitations on such action without presenting a claim against estate within time specified in RC 2117.06 or RC 2117.07, and timely service of summons upon insurer-defendant is sufficient to commence action. Heuser v. Crum (Ohio 1972) 31 Ohio St.2d 90, 285 N.E.2d 340, 60 O.O.2d 56. Executors And Administrators ⚬— 224; Limitation Of Actions ⚬— 119(4)

Where it does not appear that any claim covered by an automobile liability insurance policy of decedent has been filed against estate of

2117.07
Note 3

decedent within period specified in RC 2117.06, or as provided in and within time specified in RC 2117.07, such policy is not an asset of the decedent's estate within meaning of RC 2117.07. Heuser v. Crum (Ohio 1972) 31 Ohio St.2d 90, 285 N.E.2d 340, 60 O.O.2d 56. Executors And Administrators ⇌ 225(2)

In a negligence action for the recovery of damages, instituted under RC 2117.07 against an administrator seeking to recover only from decedent's liability insurer, where administrator of estate of decedent has been discharged and estate closed, probate court may reappoint administrator for purpose of accepting service of summons. In re George's Estate (Ohio 1970) 24 Ohio St.2d 18, 262 N.E.2d 872, 53 O.O.2d 10.

Where the final and distributive account of the administrators of an estate has been approved and settled and they have been discharged from their trust pursuant to RC 2109.32, and that order has not been vacated pursuant to RC 2109.35, where some asset remains upon which administration has not been exhausted and for some lawful purpose relating to that asset administration is required, an administrator may be appointed to complete such administration only in a manner similar to, and with the same formalities as, the original appointment of an administrator, and in such circumstances, where such asset consists of an automobile liability insurance policy of the decedent covering the claim of a person alleged to have received bodily injuries due to the alleged negligence of the decedent, such policy is an asset which will support the appointment of an administrator upon whom service may be made and with authority to defend suit. In re George's Estate (Hancock 1969) 20 Ohio App.2d 87, 252 N.E.2d 176, 49 O.O.2d 110. Executors And Administrators ⇌ 37(2); Executors And Administrators ⇌ 37(5)

The 1963 amendment of RC 2117.07 permits an action for bodily injury or injuring personal property to be pursued against an executor without compliance with the requirements of that section for presentation of claims, provided that any recovery thereby adjudged is not permitted to be satisfied from the assets of the estate. In re McDonald's Estate (Ohio Prob. 1966) 15 Ohio Misc. 74, 239 N.E.2d 277, 44 O.O.2d 262.

An action which is filed against an executor pursuant to the last paragraph of RC 2117.07 may result in a judgment which can be satisfied from the rights accruing under a policy of liability insurance issued to the decedent. In re McDonald's Estate (Ohio Prob. 1966) 15 Ohio Misc. 74, 239 N.E.2d 277, 44 O.O.2d 262. Executors And Administrators ⇌ 233

The 1963 amendment to RC 2117.07 applies only to actions for bodily injury and injuring personal property. Collins v. Yanity (Ohio 1968) 14 Ohio St.2d 202, 237 N.E.2d 611, 43 O.O.2d 301.

The failure to file suit within two months of the rejection by the administrator of the estate of a claim against the estate for bodily injury does not bar an action for that bodily injury against that administrator where no part of the recovery sought is to come from "assets of the estate" as that term is defined in RC 2117.07. Collins v. Yanity (Ohio 1968) 14 Ohio St.2d 202, 237 N.E.2d 611, 43 O.O.2d 301. Executors And Administrators ⇌ 437(3)

The words, "assets of the estate," as used in the 1963 amendment of RC 2117.07, include only assets (1) which "may lawfully" be "paid out or distributed" by the executor or administrator, or (2) from which "payment or distribution" may be made to "creditors, legatees, and distributees" or to a surviving spouse, or (3) which may be executor or administrator. Meinberg v. Glaser (Ohio 1968) 14 Ohio St.2d 193, 237 N.E.2d 605, 43 O.O.2d 296.

Where it is alleged in an action for bodily injuries and property damage that such injuries and damage were proximately caused by the negligence of a decedent and that he had a policy of insurance insuring him against liability for such negligence and it does not appear that any other claims covered by such insurance have been asserted, such action may be brought against the executor or administrator of such decedent at any time within two years after the cause thereof arose without presenting a claim against the estate within the four-month time specified in RC 2117.06, or as provided in and within the nine-month time specified in RC 2117.07. Meinberg v. Glaser (Ohio 1968) 14 Ohio St.2d 193, 237 N.E.2d 605, 43 O.O.2d 296.

Where it does not appear that any claim covered by an automobile liability insurance policy of a decedent has been filed against the estate of the decedent within the four-month period specified in RC 2117.06 or the nine-month period specified in RC 2117.07, such policy is not an asset of the estate of the decedent within the meaning of those words as used in RC 2117.07. Meinberg v. Glaser (Ohio 1968) 14 Ohio St.2d 193, 237 N.E.2d 605, 43 O.O.2d 296.

The amendment of RC 2117.07 to state that it does not reduce the time for filing an action prescribed by RC 2305.10, provided that there shall be no recovery from the assets of an estate unless a claim was filed pursuant to RC Ch 2117, does not authorize the prosecution of an action against an estate where no claim has been so filed, although it is alleged that liability insurance is available to satisfy any judgment. Meinberg v. Glaser (Ohio Com.Pl. 1967) 14 Ohio Misc. 126, 237 N.E.2d 339, reversed 14 Ohio St.2d 193, 237 N.E.2d 605, 43 O.O.2d 296. Executors And Administrators ⇌ 225(1)

Where, following an automobile accident upon an Ohio highway, a nonresident defendant dies after an action has been commenced against him pursuant to RC 2703.20, if there has been no administration in Ohio, the time limitation of RC 2311.31 and RC 2117.06 has not commenced to run, and under RC 2311.25 and RC 2703.20 the pending action may be revived any time before judgment against the nonresident decedent's executor or administrator appointed in another state. Kibbey v. Mercer (Scioto 1967) 11 Ohio App.2d 51, 228 N.E.2d 337, 40 O.O.2d 223. Abatement And Revival ⇌ 74(1)

Where executor, who was also funeral director, failed to file his claim for funeral expenses within time limit provided in GC 10509–106 (RC 2117.02) and failed to request authority to present claim after such time as provided by this section, probate court did not err in allowing subsequent claim to extent of $350 under authority in GC 10509–193 (RC 2113.36) which allows executors further allowance for extraordinary services. In re Winders' Estate (Noble 1945) 68 N.E.2d 677, 45 Ohio Law Abs. 353.

4. Actual notice of death of decedent or appointment of executor

The failure of an executrix to file a notice of her appointment in a suit pending against the decedent, as required by RC 2117.06, does not justify a finding that the plaintiff failed to file his claim against the defendant's estate within four months after the appointment of the executrix, such as would permit a delayed filing of the claim under RC 2117.07, where the defendant's attorneys of record notified the plaintiff's attorneys of record by letter of such death and appointment in ample time to permit filing of the claim within the four-month limitation. In re Herron's Estate (Ohio Prob. 1968) 21 Ohio Misc. 212, 252 N.E.2d 332, 49 O.O.2d 27, 50 O.O.2d 422.

Where a person having a claim against a decedent's estate knew of the decedent's death, resided in the same county where decedent resided, did not make inquiry about the appointment of an executor or administrator of the estate, failed to present his claim within the four-month period prescribed by statute and does not show any facts or circumstances within the purview of statute that would justify such failure, he may not properly be authorized by the probate court to present his claim after such four-month period. In re Andres' Estate (Greene 1961) 114 Ohio App. 167, 180 N.E.2d 855, 19 O.O.2d 21. Executors And Administrators ⇌ 225(1)

Where probate court permitted a claimant with no actual notice of decedent's death or appointment of an executrix to present a claim after expiration of the four month period, it did not abuse its discretion. Bronson v. Haywood (Mahoning 1959) 172 N.E.2d 332, 84 Ohio Law Abs. 471.

In order to be permitted to present a claim against a decedent's estate after the expiration of four months, the claimant must have notice of neither the decedent's death nor the administrator's appointment. Redifer Bus Co. v. Lumme (Ohio 1961) 171 Ohio St. 471, 172 N.E.2d 304, 14 O.O.2d 374.

Where a claimant seeking recovery for the death of his decedent from the estate of another testifies on direct examination positively that he did not have actual notice of the death of such other person in the accident in which his decedent was killed but his testimony on cross-examination shows that he did have such notice, it is error to hold that such claimant did not have notice of the death of such other person, and the knowledge of a person as an individual is attributable to such person in his representative capacity as administrator of an estate. In re Wyckoff's Estate (Licking 1958) 105 Ohio App. 212, 152 N.E.2d 141, 6 O.O.2d 42. Evidence ⇌ 591

Mere knowledge by a claimant only of the death of a decedent shortly after it occurred is not, of itself, sufficient to bar the presenting of a belated claim. In re Lathrop's Estate (Auglaize 1956) 103 Ohio App. 392, 141 N.E.2d 212, 75 Ohio Law Abs. 458, 1 O.O.2d 482.

Knowledge of a decedent's post office address is not synonymous with knowledge of his place of legal residence. In re Lathrop's Estate (Auglaize 1956) 103 Ohio App. 392, 141 N.E.2d 212, 75 Ohio Law Abs. 458, 1 O.O.2d 482.

Where claimant had knowledge of decedent's death but was not aware of the county of decedent's legal residence and examined the court records only in the county of decedent's post office address, the probate court erroneously denied claimant the right to file a claim after four months from date of appointment of an executor. In re Lathrop's Estate (Auglaize 1956) 103 Ohio App. 392, 141 N.E.2d 212, 75 Ohio Law Abs. 458, 1 O.O.2d 482.

Actual knowledge of a decedent's death, acquired on the date following such death by a claimant presenting a claim against such decedent's estate after the expiration of the statutory period for the presentation of such claims, negatives such claimant's contention that he had no actual knowledge of the appointment of the administrator of such decedent's estate. In re Christman's Estate (Crawford 1955) 100 Ohio App. 133, 136 N.E.2d 80, 60 O.O. 129.

Late claims against the estate of a deceased physician may not be allowed where claimants had actual notice of the decedent's death at or about the time thereof by reading newspaper articles published at the time of that event. In re Natherson's Estate (Cuyahoga 1956) 102 Ohio App. 475, 134 N.E.2d 852, 57 A.L.R.2d 1297, 74 Ohio Law Abs. 387, 3 O.O.2d 35.

Where a claimant seeking to file a belated claim actually knew of decedent's death and in the exercise of reasonable diligence could have learned of the appointment of an administrator and thereafter had a fair opportunity to present his claim within four months, the probate court is chargeable with no error or abuse of discretion in denying such claimant authority to present such claim. In re Miller's Estate (Columbiana 1954) 98 Ohio App. 445, 129 N.E.2d 838, 57 O.O. 481. Executors And Administrators ⋘ 225(7)

Where claim agent of motor bus company had knowledge of truck driver's death and place of his residence, and in exercise of reasonable diligence company could have learned of appointment of administrator and could have timely filed claim against driver's estate for damages to motor bus which had collided with truck, company had "actual notice" of appointment of administrator, and probate court's refusal to permit company to file after expiration of time limited for filing claims was proper. In re Marrs' Estate (Shelby 1951) 111 N.E.2d 604, 64 Ohio Law Abs. 161, affirmed 158 Ohio St. 95, 107 N.E.2d 148, 48 O.O. 46. Executors And Administrators ⋘ 232

One who has a claim against a decedent's estate and fails to present the same in writing to the executor or administrator within four months of his appointment may, after the expiration of such time petition the probate court for leave to do so. Where the probate court, upon hearing the evidence, discloses that claimant actually knew of the decedent's death and his place of residence shortly after the death occurred and that in the exercise of reasonable diligence the claimant could have learned of the appointment of an administrator and thereafter had a fair opportunity to present his claim within the four months, it was not error to deny the authority to present such claim. In re Marrs' Estate (Ohio 1952) 158 Ohio St. 95, 107 N.E.2d 148, 48 O.O. 46.

In the absence of evidence that a creditor of a decedent has read a notice of the death or the appointment of an administrator of a decedent, proof of publication of such notice is insufficient to establish "actual notice" thereof. In re Fahle's Estate (Lucas 1950) 90 Ohio App. 195, 105 N.E.2d 429, 47 O.O. 231. Executors And Administrators ⋘ 225(2)

Under provisions of section, the probate court may authorize the reinstatement of a claim against an estate when it finds, from the evidence with the burden of proof on the claimant, either that the claimant did not have actual notice of decedent's death or that claimant did not have notice of appointment of estate's legal representative. In re Erbaugh's Estate (Montgomery 1943) 73 Ohio App. 533, 57 N.E.2d 294, 38 Ohio Law Abs. 574, 29 O.O. 177. Executors And Administrators ⋘ 232

While a probate court should not have admitted claimants' testimony relating to transactions with an insurance company concerning their claim, given at a hearing in such court on their petition for reinstatement of claims under authority of section, where the sole issue was whether such claimants had actual notice of the appointment of the administratrix of the estate of the deceased person within sufficient time to present the claims within the time prescribed by law, the admission of such evidence, which did not reflect on such issue, was not error prejudicial to such administratrix. In re Erbaugh's Estate (Montgomery 1943) 73 Ohio App. 533, 57 N.E.2d 294, 38 Ohio Law Abs. 574, 29 O.O. 177.

Mortgagee which had no actual notice or knowledge of death of mortgagor, and did not file its claim with administrator within four months, as required by GC 10509-112 (RC 2117.06), was not guilty of culpable neglect, and claim should be reinstated under section. Home Owners' Loan Corp. v. Doolittle (Cuyahoga 1937) 57 Ohio App. 329, 13 N.E.2d 920, 25 Ohio Law Abs. 195, 10 O.O. 225. Executors And Administrators ⋘ 232

Where a creditor of a decedent contends that a claim against an estate should not be barred where the administrator had knowledge of the creditor's claim within the statutory period and there was no Ohio case squarely in point, the granting of summary judgment was improper. Hart v. Johnston (C.A.6 (Ohio) 1968) 24 Ohio Misc. 178, 389 F.2d 239, 44 O.O.2d 221, 53 O.O.2d 205.

Allegation of lack of knowledge of death of decedent, is not sufficient ground to reinstate a barred claim and to hold creditor not guilty of culpable neglect. In re Dudley's Estate (Ohio Prob. 1937) 2 Ohio Supp. 95, 23 Ohio Law Abs. 522, 8 O.O. 404.

5. **Absence of executor or wrongful act or statement**

Claim mailed to executor within four month period but not delivered until after expiration thereof because of executor's absence from jurisdiction could be filed after expiration of period. In re McCracken's Estate (Ohio Prob. 1967) 9 Ohio Misc. 195, 224 N.E.2d 181, 38 O.O.2d 283.

Late filing of a claim against an estate will not be permitted although the late filing was the result of the claimant's mailing the claim originally to an erroneous address supplied by the clerical staff of the probate court. Krash v. Jarvis (Jefferson 1962) 187 N.E.2d 409, 90 Ohio Law Abs. 99, 25 O.O.2d 133.

Where the driver of a motor vehicle in an accident with claimant died on August 17 in a county other than the county in which the accident occurred at a time at which negotiations were in progress with the adjuster of his insurer but such adjuster did not advise claimant's attorney of the driver's death until December and then stated it occurred in November, or that an administrator had been appointed and claimant's attorney was advised of such appointment by the probate court two days after the running of the four-month limitation period, it was an abuse of discretion for the trial court not to allow the claimant to present his claim after such period. In re Howe's Estate (Stark 1958) 107 Ohio App. 361, 159 N.E.2d 622, 8 O.O.2d 321.

RC 2117.07(B) does not extend to a wrongful act or statement on the part of the decedent. In re Natherson's Estate (Cuyahoga 1956) 102 Ohio App. 475, 134 N.E.2d 852, 57 A.L.R.2d 1297, 74 Ohio Law Abs. 387, 3 O.O.2d 35.

In a proceeding to file late claims against the estate of a decedent by claimants who charge that such physician had concealed his negligence in a surgical operation, the alleged wrongful acts of the physician do not qualify claimant's belated claim where it is not claimed that there was any wrongful act on the part of the administratrix or her attorney which would qualify claimants for relief under this section, as the acts of decedent are not imputed to the administratrix or her attorney. In re Natherson's Estate (Cuyahoga 1956) 102 Ohio App. 475, 134 N.E.2d 852, 57 A.L.R.2d 1297, 74 Ohio Law Abs. 387, 3 O.O.2d 35. Executors And Administrators ⋘ 225(2)

Counsel for the administrator of a deceased's estate has no duty to advise a claimant of the name of the administrator, nor to advise the claimant of his error in wrongfully presenting his claim to the decedent's widow under the mistaken belief that she was the administratrix of the decedent's estate instead of to the court-appointed administrator. In re Miller's Estate (Columbiana 1954) 98 Ohio App. 445, 129 N.E.2d 838, 57 O.O. 481. Attorney And Client ⋘ 26

A person confined in a county jail is a person in captivity as defined in GC 10512-2 (RC 2131.02). In re Gogan's Estate (Cuyahoga 1951) 108 N.E.2d 170, 63 Ohio Law Abs. 69.

Under section, probate court is justified in reinstating claim against estate barred by expiration of four month period, where evidence shows that claimant's failure to file his claim on time was due to pending negotiations by claimant to purchase the assets of the estate, and due to statements by the executor when the claim was mentioned that it could not be allowed if presented at that time as he had ascertained that part of it had been paid by another. Valencic's Estate v. Valencic (Cuyahoga 1943) 60 N.E.2d 722, 42 Ohio Law Abs. 478.

One who holds, as payee, the notes of a decedent, and through mistake of fact and law accepts in payment thereof a note executed under mistaken authority by decedent's executrix and secured by a mortgage on realty in which the executrix, by the terms of decedent's will, holds only a life estate, and as a result thereof does not present his claim within the statutory time, is not chargeable with culpable neglect in failing to present his claim within the time so prescribed, and is entitled to have his claim reinstated under the provisions of section. Schindler v. Schindler (Richland 1935) 50 Ohio App. 517, 198 N.E. 879, 19 Ohio Law Abs. 63, 2 O.O. 95. Executors And Administrators ⋘ 233

Where both claimant and fiduciary have acted under mutual mistake of fact, and claim was presented to counsel for administrator thinking that counsel was administrator, and counsel for administrator, not knowing that claimant was mistaken and receipted for presentation of claim at place intended for signature of administrator, not knowing that in signing receipt, claimant believed it was presented and receipted by administrator, so that each side was ignorant of mistake made by other, claimant is not guilty of "culpable neglect," as this term is used in this section for failure to present claim within time limit prescribed by law, if mistake was not discovered until after expiration of time limit. In re Keenan's Estate (Ohio Prob. 1937) 2 Ohio Supp. 390, 25 Ohio Law Abs. 447, 10 O.O. 42.

A probate court properly allows the late presentation of a claim pursuant to RC 2117.07 where: (1) the claimant had several conversations with the estate's attorney regarding the claim during the three-month period; (2) the estate's attorney also acted as the claimant's attorney; and (3) the estate's attorney never informed the claimant of the need to file a claim or of the possible conflict of interest. Kinnunen v Schulz, No. 1144 (11th Dist Ct App, Ashtabula, 5–18–84).

6. Legal disability of claimant

Attorney for estate who received claim which should have been addressed to executor but did not so advise claimant until after lapse of four month period was not guilty of wrongful act so as to justify late filing. In re Clark's Estate (Ohio Com.Pl. 1967) 11 Ohio Misc. 103, 229 N.E.2d 122, 40 O.O.2d 347.

RC 5123.57 does not apply as a defense to a party to an action on a contract until such party establishes by credible evidence an adjudication of mental incapacity and a lawful commitment to a state institution by a probate court. Elder v. Baker (Cuyahoga 1962) 115 Ohio App. 372, 180 N.E.2d 858, 20 O.O.2d 448.

A person committed to a mental hospital for mental incompetency is of unsound mind within the definition of legal disability contained in RC 2117.07 and RC 2131.02, and under RC 5123.57 such mental incompetency continues until it is finally dissolved by an order of court; and a person legally a person of unsound mind (even though not necessarily so in fact) during a part of the four-month period who, during such period, is, by proper application on order of court legally restored to mental competency, may be allowed to present a late claim, such legal disability of a person as an individual being attributable to such person as a "claimant" under RC 2117.07. In re Wyckoff's Estate (Licking 1958) 105 Ohio App. 212, 152 N.E.2d 141, 6 O.O.2d 42.

Physical aches and pains, headaches, dizziness and inability to walk around or drive an automobile are not legal excuses for failure to comply with the statutory provisions for the presentation of claims against an estate, and where such claimant for the four-month period following the appointment of the administrator was able to and did go about and look into his business and affairs, he was not under legal disability. In re Christman's Estate (Crawford 1955) 100 Ohio App. 133, 136 N.E.2d 80, 60 O.O. 129.

A claim for damages for injuries resulting from a motor vehicle accident which was not presented to the defendant's executor within nine months of such appointment cannot be revived even if the plaintiff is a minor. Overman v. Yake (Clark 1952) 109 N.E.2d 697, 68 Ohio Law Abs. 248.

It is an abuse of discretion for a probate court to refuse to permit a claimant to file an alleged claim with an administrator more than four months after the latter's appointment where there is a clear showing of legal disability on the claimant's part. In re Gogan's Estate (Cuyahoga 1951) 108 N.E.2d 170, 63 Ohio Law Abs. 69.

If the claimant is subject to any legal disability during the four-month period, or any part thereof, he is entitled to the benefits of section. In re Price's Estate (Darke 1949) 87 Ohio App. 23, 93 N.E.2d 769, 42 O.O. 272.

Where a claimant against a decedent's estate was injured in an automobile accident, out of which his claim arose, and as a result of such injuries he suffered from shock, and for a period of six to eight weeks after the accident he was kept under sedatives and suffered from mental confusion, so that he was unable to look into his affairs, properly consult with counsel, prepare and present his case and assert and protect his rights in a court of justice, which condition covered approximately one-half of the four-month period, referred to in section, the trial court did not commit error in granting claimant authority to present his claim after the expiration of the four-month period. In re Price's Estate (Darke 1949) 87 Ohio App. 23, 93 N.E.2d 769, 42 O.O. 272.

The term, "legal disability", as used in section, is defined in GC 10512–2 (RC 2131.02) and applies to "persons of unsound mind"; the words, "of unsound mind" under the provisions of GC 10213 (RC 1.02, RC 1.10) include every species of mental deficiency or derangement. In re Price's Estate (Darke 1949) 87 Ohio App. 23, 93 N.E.2d 769, 42 O.O. 272.

7. Claim barred

Where the defendant in a pending action for the recovery of damages dies and no attempt is made by the plaintiff to revive the action against the decedent's personal representative for more than nine months after the appointment of such personal representative, the cause of action is extinguished irrespective of whether recovery is sought against estate or nonestate assets. Smith v. Ralph (Franklin 1969) 18 Ohio App.2d 235, 248 N.E.2d 208, 47 O.O.2d 362.

An action for wrongful death caused proximately by the negligence of a decedent cannot be brought against the executor or administrator of that decedent unless a claim therefor is presented within the four-month time specified in RC 2117.06 or the nine-month time specified in RC 2117.07. Collins v. Yanity (Ohio 1968) 14 Ohio St.2d 202, 237 N.E.2d 611, 43 O.O.2d 301.

A claim for wrongful death which was "forever barred as to all parties" for failure of presentment within nine months of the appointment of the administratrix, pursuant to RC 2117.07, prior to the amendment of that section effective August 9, 1963, is not revived by such amendment. Baker v. Farish (Ohio Com.Pl. 1964) 1 Ohio Misc. 1, 202 N.E.2d 331, 30 O.O.2d 606.

Where a claimant knew of decedent's death but failed to file a claim for personal injuries against decedent's estate and instead dealt with decedent's insurer until four months had elapsed after the appointment of an administrator of decedent's estate, the probate court properly declined to grant leave to file the claim. In re Kiko's Estate (Carroll 1959) 169 N.E.2d 138, 83 Ohio Law Abs. 555.

Where a claimant was negotiating with decedent's insurance company without knowledge of his death, such claimant could not file a claim with decedent's administrator after expiration of nine months from the date of the appointment of such administrator, since his claim for injuries sustained in an automobile accident was not a contingent one. In re Tomko's Estate (Ohio Prob. 1955) 146 N.E.2d 757, 77 Ohio Law Abs. 313, 3 O.O.2d 371, affirmed 146 N.E.2d 761, 3 O.O.2d 374.

GC 10509–134 (RC 2117.07) requires that a claim must be presented within nine months or be forever barred. In re Sarver's Estate (Franklin 1954) 97 Ohio App. 199, 124 N.E.2d 749, 55 O.O. 453.

Section creates the right to an adjudication of right to present a claim to an executor or administrator when such claim has not been presented within the four-month period provided for by GC 10509–112 (RC 2117.06), and the proviso of the former section is a limitation on that right, which limitation is tolled by the institution of a proceeding under the section within nine months after appointment of executor and administrator. In re Erbaugh's Estate (Montgomery 1943) 73 Ohio App. 533, 57 N.E.2d 294, 38 Ohio Law Abs. 574, 29 O.O. 177. Executors And Administrators ⇒ 233

Section is a statute of limitation. In re Erbaugh's Estate (Montgomery 1943) 73 Ohio App. 533, 57 N.E.2d 294, 38 Ohio Law Abs. 574, 29 O.O. 177.

Only effect of reinstatement of barred claim is to require the executor upon presentation to allow or reject it as provided by GC 10509–113 (RC 2117.11). In re Shartle's Estate (Montgomery 1940) 36 N.E.2d 534, 34 Ohio Law Abs. 203.

In action brought in a municipal court against an administratrix on a claim rejected by her, it is error for court to hold claim barred as a matter of law, where probate court, under section, has decreed that the claimant be allowed to present its claim to the administratrix, although the evidence shows that it was not presented within time prescribed by GC 10509–112 (RC 2117.06). Busse & Borgmann Co. v. Upchurch (Hamilton 1938) 60 Ohio App. 349, 21 N.E.2d 349, 27 Ohio Law Abs. 575, 12 O.O. 493.

GC 10509–112 (RC 2117.06) and 10509–134 (RC 2117.07) are statutes of limitation (or nonclaim statutes) which bar creditors' claims unless presented to an executor or administrator within four months after the date of appointment. Beach v. Mizner (Ohio 1936) 131 Ohio St. 481, 3 N.E.2d 417, 6 O.O. 155.

A barred claim may be reinstated and presented to an executor or administrator upon leave first obtained from the probate court in the manner provided in section. Beach v. Mizner (Ohio 1936) 131 Ohio St. 481, 3 N.E.2d 417, 6 O.O. 155. Executors And Administrators ⇒ 233

Where claim becomes due more than nine months after appointment of executor, is presented to and rejected by executor, and where no action is filed for recovery of such claim within two months from time of its rejection or within two months from date of its accrual, such claim is barred by law unless probate court, by virtue of section, permits petitioner to file his claim for allowance. State ex rel. Fulton v. Coburn (Ohio 1938) 133 Ohio St. 192, 12 N.E.2d 471, 10 O.O. 249.

The presentation of a claim against an estate to the agent of an insurance company appointed by the administrator as his agent does not constitute statutory presentation of such a claim to the administrator, and the claim is barred at the expiration of the statutory period. Beacon Mut. Indem. Co. v. Stalder (Summit 1954) 95 Ohio App. 441, 120 N.E.2d 743, 54 O.O. 69.

8. Final order; appeal

The order of a probate court authorizing the presentation of so-called late claims to the executor of an estate pursuant to RC 2117.07 is a final order affecting a substantial right in a special proceeding, and such order is subject to review on appeal. Smith v. Boyers (Ottawa 1959) 110 Ohio App. 291, 169 N.E.2d 479, 13 O.O.2d 70. Appeal And Error ⇐ 91(3)

The hearing of an application to the probate court under RC 2117.07 is a special proceeding and an order granting such authority is one affecting a substantial right, and, where a record is made in such special proceeding, the order is properly appealable on questions of law to the Court of Appeals. In re Wyckoff's Estate (Ohio 1957) 166 Ohio St. 354, 142 N.E.2d 660, 66 A.L.R.2d 653, 2 O.O.2d 257.

Where, in an action against an administrator for damages for personal injuries, the petition did not allege that the claim sued on was presented to the administrator, and at the close of plaintiff's case the defendant moved for a directed verdict, plaintiff's oral motion to dismiss the action without prejudice was granted, and the jury dismissed, it is not prejudicially erroneous for the court to overrule plaintiff's motion for leave to withdraw the oral motion and to have the case set for trial, in the absence of a showing of abuse of discretion. Robinson v. Engle (Greene 1953) 96 Ohio App. 238, 120 N.E.2d 611, 54 O.O. 278.

An order granting leave to present a claim under this section is a final order from which an appeal can be taken. In re Fahle's Estate (Lucas 1950) 90 Ohio App. 195, 105 N.E.2d 429, 47 O.O. 231. Appeal And Error ⇐ 77(2)

Action of probate court reinstating claim cannot be collaterally attacked when there was evidence that claim had not been previously rejected. Busse & Borgmann Co. v. Upchurch (Hamilton 1938) 60 Ohio App. 349, 21 N.E.2d 349, 27 Ohio Law Abs. 575, 12 O.O. 493.

Legislature clearly intended by section, to open door for payment of just debts of decedent when justice and equity require it; broad discretion of probate court should be exercised with view to carrying out spirit of statute; discretion should be exercised toward sustaining right granted to creditor rather than to defeat that right. Home Owners' Loan Corp. v. Doolittle (Cuyahoga 1937) 57 Ohio App. 329, 13 N.E.2d 920, 25 Ohio Law Abs. 195, 10 O.O. 225.

This section undoubtedly gives probate courts large discretion in allowing reinstatement of barred claims, but limits and removes right to exercise such discretion in instances where creditor is guilty of culpable neglect. In re Christopher's Estate (Ohio Prob. 1937) 4 Ohio Supp. 327, 24 Ohio Law Abs. 245, 8 O.O. 546, affirmed 35 N.E.2d 454, 26 Ohio Law Abs. 422, 11 O.O. 251.

Subject to limitations therein prescribed, section confers broad discretion upon probate court to permit or deny a petitioner the right to file his claim for allowance where such claim has not been presented to an administrator or executor within time prescribed by law. State ex rel. Fulton v. Coburn (Ohio 1938) 133 Ohio St. 192, 12 N.E.2d 471, 10 O.O. 249.

Where discretion has not been abused, decision rendered by probate court under section will not be disturbed by reviewing court. State ex rel. Fulton v. Coburn (Ohio 1938) 133 Ohio St. 192, 12 N.E.2d 471, 10 O.O. 249.

Where claim, filed with executor but not within time required by law, is rejected by executor, and thereafter an action is filed in common pleas court on same claim but not within time required by law, refusal of probate court at later time to permit such claim to be filed for allowance is not abuse of its discretion vested by section. State ex rel. Fulton v. Coburn (Ohio 1938) 133 Ohio St. 192, 12 N.E.2d 471, 10 O.O. 249.

2117.08 Authentication of claims

When a claim is presented against the estate of a deceased person, the executor or administrator may require satisfactory written proof in support of it and also the affidavit of the claimant that such claim is justly due, that no payments have been made thereon, and that there are no counterclaims against it to his knowledge. Such affidavit shall set forth any security held for the payment of said claim and, if the claim is not due, the date of maturity. If said claim arises out of tort, or if preference in payment is claimed, the facts in connection with the alleged tort or showing the right to such preference shall be briefly set forth.

(1953 H 1, eff. 10–1–53; GC 10509–114)

Historical and Statutory Notes

Pre–1953 H 1 Amendments: 119 v 394, § 1; 114 v 427

Cross References

Executor or administrator of surety may require creditor to sue principal or forfeit right to payment, 1341.05

Library References

Executors and Administrators ⇐ 227(2), 227(3).
Westlaw Topic No. 162.
C.J.S. Executors and Administrators §§ 443 to 446.

Research References

Encyclopedias
OH Jur. 3d Decedents' Estates § 1451, Request for Authentication of Claim.

Forms
Ohio Forms Legal and Business § 16:101, Assignment of Creditor's Claims Against Estate.

Treatises and Practice Aids
Carlin, Baldwin's Ohio Practice, Merrick-Rippner Probate Law § 2:30, Payment of Debts and Claims—Options of Fiduciary.

Carlin, Baldwin's Ohio Practice, Merrick-Rippner Probate Law § 2:121, Administration of Decedent's Estate—Checklist.

Carlin, Baldwin's Ohio Practice, Merrick-Rippner Probate Law § 87:10, Affidavit of Claimant—Form.

Notes of Decisions

Allowance 3
Formal requirements 1
Presentation 2
Rejection 5
Waiver 4

---

1. Formal requirements

Simply receiving and examining a claim and comparing it with the decedent's books is neither an allowance nor a rejection; the statute requires that there be proof of a request to indorse an allowance of the claim and a refusal to do so before a suit may be maintained against the estate. Keenan v. Saxton's Adm'rs (Ohio 1844) 13 Ohio 41.

An administrator's admission is prima facie evidence of the indebtedness of the estate he represents, though it is not conclusive; creditors are not required to go beyond his acts unless fraud or mistake is shown. Matoon v. Clapp's Heirs (Ohio 1837) 8 Ohio 248.

Trial court ruling on alleged caregiver's claim for compensation from estate did not commit plain error by failing to consider whether decedent and alleged caregiver, decedent's neighbor, had family relationship; the court reviewed the testimony concerning the nature of the relationship, mentioned acknowledgement that the two were "boyfriend-girlfriend" in the beginning, and noted evolution into a care-giving relationship as decedent required more care. Spradley v. Milliner (Ohio App. 12 Dist., Clinton, 12-16-2002) No. CA2002-04-019, 2002-Ohio-6882, 2002 WL 31798766, Unreported, appeal not allowed 98 Ohio St.3d 1565, 787 N.E.2d 1230, 2003-Ohio-2242. Executors And Administrators ⇐ 256(4)

Estate fiduciary cannot blindly pay debt allegedly owed by decedent without first determining whether it is valid; moreover, if litigation ensues, unless validity of debt cannot reasonably be disputed, fiduciary is obliged to defend the estate. In re Estate of Dawson (Ohio App. 2 Dist., 12-27-1996) 117 Ohio App.3d 51, 689 N.E.2d 1008. Executors And Administrators ⇐ 202

2117.08
Note 1

A claim against a decedent's estate need not be in any particular form so long as it is in substantial compliance with RC 2117.06 and recognized by the fiduciary as a claim against the estate. Gladman v. Carns (Miami 1964) 9 Ohio App.2d 135, 223 N.E.2d 378, 38 O.O.2d 149.

It is not necessary that a claimant formally present his claim against an estate with a demand that the administrator indorse his allowance thereon; a presentation of a note executed by the decedent to the administrator with a request for partial payment where the holder also says that there is no hurry is a sufficient exhibition of the claim. Miller v. Ewing (Ohio 1903) 68 Ohio St. 176, 48 W.L.B. 529, 67 N.E. 292, 1 Ohio Law Rep. 273.

2. Presentation

Where the same person is administrator of the creditor as well as the debtor estate, no formal presentation or allowance of claim is necessary. Thomas v. Chamberlain (Ohio 1883) 39 Ohio St. 112, 9 W.L.B. 258. Executors And Administrators ⟾ 222(1).

When evidence is in conflict as to whether a claim against an estate has been orally presented to the representative and orally allowed by him, a fact question is raised and must be decided by the jury or the court if it is trying the fact issues. Weber v. Kohn (Lucas 1938) 60 Ohio App. 64, 19 N.E.2d 534, 13 O.O. 424. Appeal And Error ⟾ 1008.2

Claim against an estate may be orally presented to the executor or administrator, and may be orally allowed by him. Weber v. Kohn (Lucas 1938) 60 Ohio App. 64, 19 N.E.2d 534, 13 O.O. 424. Executors And Administrators ⟾ 228(3); Executors And Administrators ⟾ 234

Where the holder of a note executed by decedent presents the note to his administrator and requires a partial payment thereon, such presentation sufficiently "exhibits" the claim, as required by Rev.St. 1892, §6097 (See GC 10509–133, 10509–113) and it is not necessary that the claimant shall demand that the administrator indorse his allowance thereon. Miller v. Ewing (Ohio 1903) 68 Ohio St. 176, 48 W.L.B. 529, 67 N.E. 292, 1 Ohio Law Rep. 273. Executors And Administrators ⟾ 228(3)

3. Allowance

An agreement between the holder of decrees for sale of mortgaged premises and the executor of the judgment debtor that the executor should sell the lands under a power given in the debtor's will and pay the decrees from the proceeds is in effect an allowance of the decrees as valid claims against the debtor's estate. Western Reserve Bank v. McIntire (Ohio 1884) 40 Ohio St. 528.

A claim against an estate which has been duly presented to and allowed by an administrator need not be further allowed by a succeeding administrator de bonis non. Thomas v. Chamberlain (Ohio 1883) 39 Ohio St. 112, 9 W.L.B. 258. Executors And Administrators ⟾ 241

The allowance of a claim is not conclusive of its validity against the estate, but it may be afterward contested by the administrator who allows it. Thomas v. Chamberlain (Ohio 1883) 39 Ohio St. 112, 9 W.L.B. 258. Executors And Administrators ⟾ 241

Payment of part of a claim without disputing the balance is sufficient allowance. Thomas v. Chamberlain (Ohio 1883) 39 Ohio St. 112, 9 W.L.B. 258. Executors And Administrators ⟾ 234; Payment ⟾ 32

An award of $16,664 for caring for neighbor in caregiver's home was reasonable compensation that caregiver sought from neighbor's estate for services over a four-year period; it amounted to approximately $80 per week. Spradley v. Milliner (Ohio App. 12 Dist., Clinton, 12-16-2002) No. CA2002-04-019, 2002-Ohio-6882, 2002 WL 31798766, Unreported, appeal not allowed 98 Ohio St.3d 1565, 787 N.E.2d 1230, 2003-Ohio-2242. Executors And Administrators ⟾ 206(4)

Evidence supported conclusions that caregiver provided services to neighbor in response to an implied agreement to pay and was entitled to compensation from his estate on quantum meruit theory; the neighbor moved in with caregiver. Spradley v. Milliner (Ohio App. 12 Dist., Clinton, 12-16-2002) No. CA2002-04-019, 2002-Ohio-6882, 2002 WL 31798766, Unreported, appeal not allowed 98 Ohio St.3d 1565, 787 N.E.2d 1230, 2003-Ohio-2242. Executors And Administrators ⟾ 252

Where an administrator pays the interest on a principal note for five years after it became due, such payments are part of the claim and are an allowance. Kemper v. Apollo Bldg. & Loan Co. (Ohio Com.Pl. 1907) 18 Ohio Dec. 484, 5 Ohio NP(NS) 403, affirmed 20 Ohio C.D. 700, 11 Ohio C.C.(N.S.) 372, affirmed 80 Ohio St. 732, 89 N.E. 1121.

4. Waiver

The objection that the claim was not presented for allowance before suit is waived where the administrator goes to trial without objection. Pepper v. Sidwell (Ohio 1881) 36 Ohio St. 454. Executors And Administrators ⟾ 443(7); Pleading ⟾ 406(5)

Where a creditor asks the administrator to allow an account and is refused, and the claim is present in the owner's pocket and is not formally presented to the administrator, the refusal to allow the account is a waiver of such formal presentation. Cheeseman v. Kyle (Ohio 1864) 15 Ohio St. 15.

5. Rejection

Presenting a claim for allowance and being told by the executor to consider it rejected constitutes a legal rejection, though no rejection is indorsed on the claim at the time; the six months' limitation begins to run from such rejection. Harter, Trump, Wikidal & Co. v. Taggart's Ex'rs (Ohio 1862) 14 Ohio St. 122.

Estate of property owner in whose backyard pool a four-year-old child drowned during a party could not be held liable to child's estate or mother for negligence absent evidence of reckless or intentional conduct by owner; child and mother were engaged in the recreational activity of swimming, mother knew that child could not swim and was not wearing any flotation devices, mother and father were in and around the pool area and were responsible for supervising child, and there was no evidence property owner knew of any problem with the pool or should have known of child's inability to swim. Estate of Vince v. Estate of Smallwood (Ohio App. 11 Dist., Trumbull, 03-31-2006) No. 2005-T-0017, 2006-Ohio-1697, 2006 WL 847440, Unreported. Negligence ⟾ 1129

The failure to authenticate a claim as provided in RC 2117.08 will not deny the claimant access to the courts to pursue the claim when the claim is rejected by the executor; RC 2117.12 allows a creditor two months following a rejection to bring his action on his claim or it will be barred. Johnson v. Middleton (Marion 1989) 66 Ohio App.3d 783, 586 N.E.2d 1093.

Representative of an estate, having allowed a claim against it, may later reject it. Weber v. Kohn (Lucas 1938) 60 Ohio App. 64, 19 N.E.2d 534, 13 O.O. 424.

2117.09 Disputed claims

If an executor or administrator doubts the justice of any claim presented against the estate he represents, he may enter into an agreement in writing with the claimant to refer the matter in controversy to three disinterested persons, who must be approved by the probate judge.

Upon filing the agreement of reference in the probate court of the county in which the letters testamentary or of administration were issued, the judge shall docket the cause and make an order referring the matter in controversy to the referees selected.

The referees thereupon must proceed to hear and determine the matter and make their report to the court. The referees shall have the same powers and be entitled to the same compensation and the same proceedings shall be followed as if the reference were made under the provisions for arbitrations under a rule of the court of common pleas. The court may set aside the report of the referees, appoint others in their places, or confirm such report and adjudge costs as in actions against executors and administrators. The judgment of the court thereupon shall be valid and effectual.

(1953 H 1, eff. 10–1–53; GC 10509–115 to 10509–117)

Historical and Statutory Notes

Pre–1953 H 1 Amendments: 114 v 427

Cross References

Arbitration, Ch 2711

Library References

Executors and Administrators ⚖246.
Westlaw Topic No. 162.
C.J.S. Executors and Administrators §§ 477 to 478.

Research References

Encyclopedias

OH Jur. 3d Alternative Dispute Resolution § 234, Fiduciaries.
OH Jur. 3d Alternative Dispute Resolution § 241, Particular Matters Arbitrable Pursuant to Special Statutes.
OH Jur. 3d Decedents' Estates § 1422, Submission of Disputed Claims to Referees.

Forms

Ohio Forms Legal and Business § 12A:3, Statutory Arbitration.
Ohio Jurisprudence Pleading and Practice Forms § 98:5, Special Controversies.

Treatises and Practice Aids

Carlin, Baldwin's Ohio Practice, Merrick-Rippner Probate Law § 2:30, Payment of Debts and Claims—Options of Fiduciary.
Carlin, Baldwin's Ohio Practice, Merrick-Rippner Probate Law § 2:121, Administration of Decedent's Estate—Checklist.
Carlin, Baldwin's Ohio Practice, Merrick-Rippner Probate Law § 87:11, Agreement to Refer Disputed Claim—Form.
Carlin, Baldwin's Ohio Practice, Merrick-Rippner Probate Law § 87:12, Entry Appointing Magistrates, Notification and Meeting—Form.
Carlin, Baldwin's Ohio Practice, Merrick-Rippner Probate Law § 87:13, Notice to Magistrates—Form.
Carlin, Baldwin's Ohio Practice, Merrick-Rippner Probate Law § 87:14, Magistrate's Decision—Form.
Carlin, Baldwin's Ohio Practice, Merrick-Rippner Probate Law § 87:15, Entry on Magistrate's Decision—Form.

Notes of Decisions

Arbitration 5
Burden of proof 2
Common pleas court's power 1
Judgment 4
Legatees and devisees 6
Settlement 3

1. Common pleas court's power

The probate court cannot receive the report of the referees on a disputed claim and act on it, as the common pleas court has this power. Anderson v. Baker (Ohio 1864) 15 Ohio St. 173.

Since the arbitration provisions referred to in section were repealed, a probate judge, in fixing referees' fees and taxing them as costs, may follow GC 11486 (RC 2315.36), relating to like matters in the common pleas courts, by reason of GC 10501–22 (RC 2101.32), which makes the common pleas rules applicable to probate courts where there are no probate rules on the same subject. In re Murnan's Estate (Franklin 1941) 38 N.E.2d 92, 34 Ohio Law Abs. 491.

2. Burden of proof

Evidence supported conclusion that loan contract, rather than gift, between decedent and wife regarding purchase of automobile was not proved in action filed by executor of estate, seeking recovery on balance of alleged contract; trial court was best able to determine credibility of evidence, and wife testified that, although she made some payments to "keep peace in the family," decedent had told her that if he died, payments could cease. Davis v. Davis (Ohio App. 5 Dist., Stark, 02-23-2004) No. 2003CA00243, 2004-Ohio-820, 2004 WL 333131, Unreported. Husband And Wife ⚖ 49.2(10)

Trial court's application of burden of proof in civil action brought by executor of decedent's estate, seeking recovery of balance of alleged contract between decedent and decedent's wife, reasoning that trial court was not convinced by preponderance of evidence that loan, rather than gift, was made to wife, was not error; executor was plaintiff in civil action, asserting on behalf of his father's estate that wife was debtor to decedent. Davis v. Davis (Ohio App. 5 Dist., Stark, 02-23-2004) No. 2003CA00243, 2004-Ohio-820, 2004 WL 333131, Unreported. Executors And Administrators ⚖ 450; Husband And Wife ⚖ 49.2(9); Husband And Wife ⚖ 49.2(10)

Where the administrator of an estate allows a claim against the estate for services rendered the decedent, the burden to establish the validity of such claim is on the administrator. In re Bowman's Estate (Darke 1956) 102 Ohio App. 121, 141 N.E.2d 499, 2 O.O.2d 118. Executors And Administrators ⚖ 506(1)

Where the only evidence offered by the next of kin in opposition of the widow's appointment as administrator of her husband's estate is a post-nuptial agreement made ten years previously between the husband and wife in which the wife agreed not to lay any claim to the property of her husband, and there is no proof the agreement was ever carried out or that it was fair and reasonable, the court is not bound to give any weight to it. Garretson v. Garretson (Ohio Cir. 1890) 2 Ohio C.D. 581, affirmed.

3. Settlement

In a claim against an estate involving ownership of an automobile where a party retains an attorney to represent him in his claim against the estate and a coin flip is part of the process for resolving that claim, where the attorney is at the coin flip on behalf of his client who is not present, the attorney has at least the apparent authority, if not implied authority, to negotiate ministerial details such as his client's time for performance in the transfer of ownership. Matter of Estate of Roush (Ohio App. 2 Dist., Clark, 06-15-1994) No. 3110, 1994 WL 264246, Unreported.

Proper claim which is provable may be settled if disputed by the probate court under GC 10509–115 to 10509–117 (RC 2117.09). Roberts v. Hickerson (Morgan 1936) 36 N.E.2d 282, 26 Ohio Law Abs. 616, 11 O.O. 471.

4. Judgment

In a proceeding by an administrator to sell real estate to pay judgments entered on awards, the heir may attack the judgments for fraud by way of cross-petition. Conway v. Duncan (Ohio 1875) 28 Ohio St. 102.

Where a cause of action is revived as against the administrator of the estate of the defendant without objection and may proceed to judgment against the deceased provided the petition states facts sufficient to constitute a cause of action against the decedent, no presentation or rejection of the claim is necessary. Glass v. Buzzard (Ohio Cir. 1910) 23 Ohio C.D. 144, 14 Ohio C.C.(N.S.) 427, affirmed 85 Ohio St. 461, 98 N.E. 1120, 9 Ohio Law Rep. 416.

Under this section it is not necessary that an action be brought on the award, but the court may enter judgment as soon as it is made. Bradstreet v. Pross (Ohio Dist. 1884) 11 W.L.B. 117.

A judgment against an administrator of a deceased partner may be had on a partnership judgment for a firm debt. Williams v Bradley, 5 CC 114, 3 CD 58 (Butler 1890).

5. Arbitration

An administrator has a common law right to submit a disputed claim against the estate he represents to arbitration, and this power is not affected by the provisions of the statute authorizing submission of disputed claims to referees. Childs v. Updyke (Ohio 1859) 9 Ohio St. 333.

Where, at time of enactment of statute entitling referees appointed to determine justice of claim against estate to same compensation as if reference were made under provisions for arbitrations under rule of common pleas court, statute pertaining to arbitrations had been repealed and substituted statutes did not provide for arbitrations under rule of court nor for compensation, probate court could allow referees' fees and charge them as "costs" payable by claimant, since inoperative provision would be disregarded and statutory provisions governing civil proceedings in court of common pleas would become operative. In re Murnan's Estate (Franklin 1941) 38 N.E.2d 92, 34 Ohio Law Abs. 491. Executors And Administrators ⚖ 235; Executors And Administrators ⚖ 240

Rejection by the administrator does not estop him from submitting the claim to arbitration. Bradstreet v. Pross (Ohio Dist. 1884) 11 W.L.B. 117.

6. Legatees and devisees

An annuity is a legacy, not a claim, and a devisee is not an heir under a will; in the first case the legatee need not file his claim with the executor for allowance or disallowance, and in the second case the devisee is not authorized to file a written requisition with the administrator as an heir to

2117.10 Failure of lienholder to present claim

The failure of the holder of a valid lien upon any of the assets of an estate to present his claim upon the indebtedness secured by such lien, as provided in Chapter 2117. of the Revised Code, shall not affect such lien if the same is evidenced by a document admitted to public record, or is evidenced by actual possession of the real or personal property which is subject to such lien.

(130 v H 1, eff. 1–23–63; 1953 H 1; GC 10509–123)

Historical and Statutory Notes

Pre–1953 H 1 Amendments: 119 v 394, § 1; 114 v 429

Library References

Executors and Administrators ⚖231.
Westlaw Topic No. 162.
C.J.S. Executors and Administrators § 452.

Research References

Encyclopedias

OH Jur. 3d Decedents' Estates § 1434, Claims Secured by Mortgages or Liens.

Treatises and Practice Aids

Carlin, Baldwin's Ohio Practice, Merrick-Rippner Probate Law § 2:27, Payment of Debts and Claims—Presentation of Claims.

Carlin, Baldwin's Ohio Practice, Merrick-Rippner Probate Law § 2:34, Payment of Debts and Claims—Mortgage and Tax Liens.

Carlin, Baldwin's Ohio Practice, Merrick-Rippner Probate Law § 2:121, Administration of Decedent's Estate—Checklist.

Notes of Decisions

Evidence 4
Mortgages 1
Part owner 3
Priorities 2
Taxes 5

---

1. Mortgages

Where a mortgagor dies in possession of property subject to a void chattel mortgage, it is the duty of his administrator to defend such possession against the claim of the mortgagee. Kilbourne v. Fay (Ohio 1876) 29 Ohio St. 264, 23 Am.Rep. 741.

Where a chattel mortgagor dies in possession of the goods, even after the condition is broken, and the administrator takes possession in his trust capacity, the mortgagee cannot maintain replevin, since the interest of the mortgagee in the property is transferred to the fund arising from the administrator's sale. Lingler v. Wesco (Ohio 1908) 79 Ohio St. 225, 86 N.E. 1004, 128 Am.St.Rep. 714, 6 Ohio Law Rep. 572. Executors And Administrators ⚖155

Where mortgaged property is taken possession of by the administrator and sold by him, the mortgagee, even if he had a valid lien thereon, is not authorized to maintain in the court of common pleas an action against the administrator and the purchaser of the property to foreclose the mortgage. Whiteley v. Weber (Ohio Cir. 1887) 1 Ohio C.D. 517.

Where a mortgagor in possession of goods dies and such goods are administered along with the rest of the estate, the mortgagee cannot maintain an action of replevin against the administrator for the possession of the mortgaged property notwithstanding the mortgagor's death broke the condition of the mortgage; in such a case the mortgagee's interest in the property is transferred to the fund arising from the sale by the administrator. Linghler v. Kraft (Ohio Com.Pl. 1905) 16 Ohio Dec. 474, 3 Ohio N.P.N.S. 653.

disallow a claim against the estate. Hunt v. Hayes (Ohio Cir. 1898) 10 Ohio C.D. 388, affirmed 63 Ohio St. 599, 60 N.E. 1131.

2. Priorities

Upon the decease of a debtor, his estate is subject to the payment of his general creditors alike, and one creditor cannot by superior diligence acquire priority. McDonald v. Aten (Ohio 1853) 1 Ohio St. 293. Executors And Administrators ⚖263

Separate individual creditors of a deceased member of a firm cannot claim a preference in the decedent's individual estate against the creditors of the firm. Seth Grosvenor & Co. v. Austin's Adm'rs (Ohio 1833) 6 Ohio 103, 25 Am.Dec. 743.

3. Part owner

The right of a part owner who pays the tax on the whole tract of which he is part owner to have a lien on the part of the other part owner for the tax paid on such part is subject to the statutes of limitation requiring presentation of claims to executors and administrators. Kuhnle v. Rusmisel (Miami 1960) 113 Ohio App. 389, 178 N.E.2d 810, 17 O.O.2d 465. Executors And Administrators ⚖224

4. Evidence

The exceptions provided in RC 2117.10 are conditioned upon the requirement that the excepted lien be "evidenced" by a public record or by actual possession. Kuhnle v. Rusmisel (Miami 1960) 113 Ohio App. 389, 178 N.E.2d 810, 17 O.O.2d 465.

5. Taxes

Daughter was subject to inheritance tax on property standing in the name of her deceased mother even though she had furnished most of the consideration therefor. In re Philhower's Estate (Ohio Prob. 1964) 7 Ohio Misc. 179, 215 N.E.2d 627, 34 O.O.2d 415.

REJECTION OF CLAIMS

2117.11 Rejection of claim

An executor or administrator, or a distributee who receives the presentation of a claim as provided in division (A)(2) of section 2117.06 of the Revised Code, shall reject a creditor's claim against the estate by giving the claimant written notice of the disallowance of the claim. The notice shall be given to the claimant pursuant to Civil Rule 73. Notice by mail shall be effective on delivery of the mail at the address given. A claim may be rejected in whole or in part. A claim that has been allowed may be rejected at any time after allowance of the claim.

A claim is rejected if the executor or administrator, or a distributee who receives the presentation of a claim as provided in division (A)(2) of section 2117.06 of the Revised Code, on demand in writing by the claimant for an allowance of the claim within five days, which demand may be made at presentation or at any time after presentation, fails to give to the claimant, within that five-day period, a written statement of the allowance of the claim. The rejection shall become effective at the expiration of that period.

(2003 H 51, eff. 4–8–04; 1953 H 1, eff. 10–1–53; GC 10509–113)

Uncodified Law

2004 H 161, § 3. See Uncodified Law under 2117.06

Historical and Statutory Notes

Pre–1953 H 1 Amendments: 119 v 394, § 1; 114 v 426

Amendment Note: 2003 H 51 inserted ", or a distributee who receives the presentation of a claim as provided in division (A)(2) of section 2117.06 of the Revised Code,"; substituted "pursuant to Civil Rule 73" for "personally or by registered mail with return receipt requested, addressed to the claimant at the address given on the claim"; substituted "after allowance of the claim" for "thereafter" following "rejected at any time"; inserted ", or a distributee who receives the presentation of a claim as provided in division (A)(2) of section 2117.06 of the Revised Code"; substituted "after presentation" for "thereafter" following "at presentation or at any time"; substituted "that five-day" for "such" following "to the claimant, within"; and made other nonsubstantive changes.

Cross References

Execution against assets of estate, limitations, 2117.34
Presentation of contingent claims, 2117.37

Library References

Executors and Administrators ⚖234.
Westlaw Topic No. 162.
C.J.S. Executors and Administrators §§ 455 to 456.

Research References

Encyclopedias

OH Jur. 3d Decedents' Estates § 1321, Effect of Order Disapproving or Confirming Claim.
OH Jur. 3d Decedents' Estates § 1341, Funeral Expenses.
OH Jur. 3d Decedents' Estates § 1457, Written Notice of Disallowance as Rejection.
OH Jur. 3d Decedents' Estates § 1458, Nonaction by Representative as Rejection.
OH Jur. 3d Decedents' Estates § 1791, Action on Claim Neither Allowed Nor Rejected.

Treatises and Practice Aids

Carlin, Baldwin's Ohio Practice, Merrick-Rippner Probate Law § 2:30, Payment of Debts and Claims—Options of Fiduciary.
Carlin, Baldwin's Ohio Practice, Merrick-Rippner Probate Law § 75:5, Distribution—Voluntary—Rejected Claims and Claims in Suit.
Carlin, Baldwin's Ohio Practice, Merrick-Rippner Probate Law § 88:1, Rejection of Claims—Purpose of Statute.
Carlin, Baldwin's Ohio Practice, Merrick-Rippner Probate Law § 88:2, Rejection of Claims—Manner of Rejection; Constructive Rejection.
Carlin, Baldwin's Ohio Practice, Merrick-Rippner Probate Law § 88:3, Rejection of Claims—Procedure.
Carlin, Baldwin's Ohio Practice, Merrick-Rippner Probate Law § 88:4, Rejection of Claims—Forced Rejection.
Carlin, Baldwin's Ohio Practice, Merrick-Rippner Probate Law § 2:121, Administration of Decedent's Estate—Checklist.
Carlin, Baldwin's Ohio Practice, Merrick-Rippner Probate Law § 84:34, Creditor's Claims—Allowance or Rejection.
Carlin, Baldwin's Ohio Practice, Merrick-Rippner Probate Law § 84:35, Creditor's Claims—Suit on Rejected Claims; Constructive Rejection; Jurisdiction of Probate Court.
Carlin, Baldwin's Ohio Practice, Merrick-Rippner Probate Law § 88:14, Rejection of Claim Against Estate—Form.

Notes of Decisions

In general 1
Action against the estate 5
Demand for allowance 2
Statute of limitations 4
Unequivocal rejection 3
Waiver 6

1. In general

A judicially declared incompetent ward may not enter into an installment contract and his estate has no obligation to honor the "contract" absent the guardian's ratification. Huntington Natl. Bank v. Toland (Franklin 1991) 71 Ohio App.3d 576, 594 N.E.2d 1103.

Where an administrator pays the interest on a principal note for five years after it became due, such payments are part of the claim and are an allowance. Kemper v. Apollo Bldg. & Loan Co. (Ohio Com.Pl. 1907) 18 Ohio Dec. 484, 5 Ohio NP(NS) 403, affirmed 20 Ohio C.D. 700, 11 Ohio C.C.(N.S.) 372, affirmed 80 Ohio St. 732, 89 N.E. 1121.

The probate court is not precluded by the fact that an executor has allowed a claim from inquiring into the validity of the claim as a proper deduction for inheritance tax purposes. In re Cooke, 93 Abs 311 (Prob, Franklin 1963).

2. Demand for allowance

In an action against a decedent's estate it is not necessary to aver or prove that a specific demand was made for the indorsement of the executor or administrator's allowance of the claim at the time the claim was rejected. Stambaugh v. Smith (Ohio 1873) 23 Ohio St. 584.

Removing executor for failing to reimburse beneficiary for decedent's funeral expenses was not an abuse of discretion; beneficiary's exceptions to executor's account and her motion for contempt and removal of executor put executor on notice of her demand for payment, such that executor was obligated to take some action on beneficiary's claim once it was filed, and beneficiary's viewing her mother's body, even given mother's wish to have a closed coffin, was not officious and meddlesome conduct that warranted not reimbursing her. In re Estate of Geanangel (Ohio App. 7 Dist., 02-25-2002) 147 Ohio App.3d 131, 768 N.E.2d 1235, 2002-Ohio-850. Executors And Administrators ⚖ 35(1)

A claimant does not have any duty to make a demand for allowance of a claim on the executor or administrator. In re Douglass' Estate (Ohio Prob. 1957) 144 N.E.2d 924, 77 Ohio Law Abs. 89.

Filing of a cross-petition for money judgment in an action by an administrator is not presentation of asserted claim to administrator as required by GC 10509–112 (RC 2117.06) and 10509–113 (RC 2117.11), even if it is filed within four months of appointment of administrator. Benson v. Rosine (Lucas 1945) 76 Ohio App. 439, 64 N.E.2d 845, 32 O.O. 195. Executors And Administrators ⚖ 434(5)

In an action by an administrator to recover on a contractual obligation, a judgment on a cross-demand cannot be had unless cross-claimant has complied with GC 10509–112 (RC 2117.06) and 10509–113 (RC 2117.11), and presented such claim to administrator for allowance as therein required. Benson v. Rosine (Lucas 1945) 76 Ohio App. 439, 64 N.E.2d 845, 32 O.O. 195.

It is essential to prove a presentation to the administrator of a claim on an account alleged to be due from an intestate, and its rejection or the equivalent by him, or to show some other reason why the administrator is liable to be sued. Yager v. Greiss (Ohio Cir. 1886) 1 Ohio C.D. 296.

A probate court has no jurisdiction to instruct an administrator whether to allow or reject a claim on a deceased's note. Jackson v. Jackson (Ohio Dist. 1880) 5 W.L.B. 647. Executors And Administrators ⚖ 234

A creditor's demand for payment of a "Guaranty of Payment of Promissory Note and Mortgage" does not constitute a demand for allowance of a claim against the estate and does not trigger application of the rejection by silence provision of RC 2117.11 where the executor fails to respond to the creditor's demand for payment. In re Estate of Baughman, No. CA96–02–018, 1996 WL 622561 (12th Dist Ct App, Warren, 10–28–96), affirmed 81 Ohio St.3d 302 (1998).

3. Unequivocal rejection

Successor administrator's exception to the former administrator's claim against estate gave former administrator plain and unequivocal notice of his disallowance of the claim and was a proper response by the successor administrator to the claim. Talbott v. Fisk (Ohio App. 10 Dist., Franklin, 12-17-2002) No. 02AP-427, No. 02AP-428, 2002-Ohio-6960, 2002 WL 31819671, Unreported. Executors And Administrators ⚖ 234

A rejection of a creditor's claim against an estate by a personal representative pursuant to the provisions of RC 2117.11 must be plain and unequivocal. Hawkes Hosp. of Mt. Carmel v. Colley (Ohio 1982) 2 Ohio St.3d 40, 442 N.E.2d 761, 36 A.L.R.4th 680, 2 O.B.R. 584. Executors And Administrators ⚖ 234

Where a claim is presented to an administrator and the administrator rejects the claim and in the same letter offers to settle it for a lesser amount, there is no unequivocal rejection of the claim and the claimant can thereafter obtain an order vacating the order settling the administrator's final account. In re Douglass' Estate (Ohio Prob. 1957) 144 N.E.2d 924, 77 Ohio Law Abs. 89.

4. Statute of limitations

Presenting a claim for allowance and being told by the executor to consider it rejected constitutes a legal rejection, though no rejection is indorsed on the claim at the time; the six months' limitation begins to run from such rejection. Harter, Trump, Wikidal & Co. v. Taggart's Ex'rs (Ohio 1862) 14 Ohio St. 122.

Claimants desiring to make amendment on rejected claims may protect themselves from the time limitation by presenting same immediately to the personal representative with demand for endorsement of allowance as provided under section, and upon refusal of the personal representative to make such endorsement of allowance, it becomes at once a disputed or rejected claim. Chronerberry v. Bartel (Miami 1940) 32 Ohio Law Abs. 284. Executors And Administrators ⇐ 437(7)

The tolling provisions of RC 2305.16 are not applicable to the filing of claims against an estate, RC Ch 2117 which deals specifically with the filing of claims against an estate in probate court is controlling. In re Estate of Kennedy (Franklin 1988) 46 Ohio App.3d 128, 546 N.E.2d 220.

Where a claim against an estate requests acceptance "within the time provided by law," but does not specify what law is referred to, and where the estate sends the claimant written rejection of the claim beyond the thirty-day period in RC 2117.06(D), this rejection is nevertheless effective under RC 2117.06(D) and precludes the automatic rejection after five days provided for by RC 2117.11 even if the written rejection specifically cites RC 2117.11; the rejection is deemed effective when the writing is delivered and the two-month period for filing an action against the estate prescribed by RC 2117.12 commences then. Bush v Estate of O'Dell, No. CA–3705 (5th Dist Ct App, Licking, 2–26–92).

Where the administrator of decedent's estate fails to give the state a written statement of allowance of a claim within five days, where such claim seeks recovery for support of decedent's daughter in a state institution, such failure constitutes a rejection by operation of law and commences the running of the statute of limitations for claims against the estate. Dept of Mental Health, Office of Support v Reynolds, No. C–820545 (1st Dist Ct App, Hamilton, 5–11–83).

5. Action against the estate

Simply receiving and examining a claim and comparing it with the decedent's books is neither an allowance nor a rejection; the statute requires that there be proof of a request to indorse an allowance of the claim and a refusal to do so before a suit may be maintained against the estate. Keenan v. Saxton's Adm'rs (Ohio 1844) 13 Ohio 41.

Notice of disallowance of creditor's claim against an estate by a fiduciary must be plain and unequivocal. In re Estate of Baughman (Ohio, 04-01-1998) 81 Ohio St.3d 302, 691 N.E.2d 257, 1998-Ohio-473. Executors And Administrators ⇐ 234

To distinguish claims subject to rejection by silence from those claims that are simply pending an allowance decision by an estate's personal representative the creditor's demand must refer to RC 2117.11 and its five day response period. In re Estate of Baughman (Ohio, 04-01-1998) 81 Ohio St.3d 302, 691 N.E.2d 257, 1998-Ohio-473. Executors And Administrators ⇐ 234

A petition in an action against an executor of the estate of a decedent which alleges an oral presentation of a claim against the estate to, and an oral rejection of the claim by, the executor does not state facts which show a cause of action and is subject to demurrer. Morgan v. City Nat. Bank & Trust Co. (Franklin 1964) 4 Ohio App.2d 417, 212 N.E.2d 822, 33 O.O.2d 504.

Probate court is without authority to determine and pass upon merits of claim rejected by an administrator in compliance with section; claimant's exclusive recourse, after such rejection, is the commencement of an independent action within the time prescribed in GC 10509–133 (RC 2117.12). In re Buchanan's Estate (Hamilton 1948) 82 Ohio App. 240, 81 N.E.2d 409, 37 O.O. 557.

Where by mistake the amount of the claim is stated too low and the claim is rejected, it amounts to a rejection of the whole claim and suit may be brought at once. Morgan v. Bartlette (Ohio Cir. 1888) 2 Ohio C.D. 244.

A formal endorsement of rejection on a claim against an estate by the administrator is not a prerequisite to the right to bring suit; a party may bring suit when, having presented the claim for allowance, and after ample time and opportunity for examining its merits, the same has been unequivocally rejected by the executor or administrator. Treasurer of Erie County v. Walker (Ohio Com.Pl. 1889) 22 W.L.B. 106. Executors And Administrators ⇐ 429

6. Waiver

Where the state of Ohio accepts modified payments of less than the prescribed statutory weekly amounts of support during the lifetime of a patient in a state mental institution, it does not thereby waive any right to further payments for such support; and any unpaid balance for the support of such patient is a valid claim against his estate. State v. Security Central Nat. Bank of Portsmouth (Scioto 1955) 100 Ohio App. 425, 137 N.E.2d 158, 60 O.O. 346. Executors And Administrators ⇐ 219.8; Mental Health ⇐ 73

2117.12 Action on rejected claim barred

When a claim against an estate has been rejected in whole or in part but not referred to referees, or when a claim has been allowed in whole or in part and thereafter rejected, the claimant must commence an action on the claim, or that part of the claim that was rejected, within two months after the rejection if the debt or that part of the debt that was rejected is then due, or within two months after that debt or part of the debt that was rejected becomes due, or be forever barred from maintaining an action on the claim or part of the claim that was rejected. If the executor or administrator dies, resigns, or is removed within that two-month period and before action is commenced on the claim or part of the claim that was rejected, the action may be commenced within two months after the appointment of a successor.

For the purposes of this section, the action of a claimant is commenced when the complaint and praecipe for service of summons on the executor or administrator, or on the distributee who received the presentation of the claim as provided in division (A)(2) of section 2117.06 of the Revised Code, have been filed.

(2003 H 51, eff. 4–8–04; 1953 H 1, eff. 10–1–53; GC 10509–133)

Uncodified Law

2004 H 161, § 3. See Uncodified Law under 2117.06

Historical and Statutory Notes

Pre–1953 H 1 Amendments: 119 v 394, § 1; 116 v 385; 114 v 431

Amendment Note: 2003 H 51 substituted "of the claim that was" for "thereof" and substituted "of the debt that was" for "thereof"; substituted "that debt or part of the debt that was rejected" for "the same" preceding "becomes due, or be forever"; substituted "on the claim or part of the claim that was rejected" for "thereon" following "maintaining an action" and following "action is commenced"; substituted "complaint" for "petition"; inserted ", or on the distributee who received the presentation of the claim as provided in division (A)(2) of section 2117.06 of the Revised Code,"; and made other nonsubstantive changes.

Library References

Executors and Administrators ⇐248.1, 437(2) to 437(4).
Westlaw Topic No. 162.
C.J.S. Executors and Administrators §§ 480, 747, 749 to 768.

Research References

Encyclopedias
OH Jur. 3d Decedents' Estates § 1428, Contingent Claims.
OH Jur. 3d Decedents' Estates § 1464, Exceptions and Appeals.
OH Jur. 3d Decedents' Estates § 1785, Effect of Termination of Office or Appointment of Successor.
OH Jur. 3d Decedents' Estates § 1786, Action on Rejected Claim.
OH Jur. 3d Decedents' Estates § 1787, Action on Rejected Claim—Exceptions to General Rule If Debt Not Due or If Successor Fiduciary Appointed.
OH Jur. 3d Decedents' Estates § 1788, Action on Rejected Claim—Purpose and Application to Sovereign Bodies.
OH Jur. 3d Decedents' Estates § 1789, Action on Contingent Claims.
OH Jur. 3d Decedents' Estates § 1790, Action on Allowed Claim.
OH Jur. 3d Decedents' Estates § 1800, Parties Defendant—in Action on Claim Rejected on Requisition.
OH Jur. 3d Decedents' Estates § 1819, Suits on Claim Rejected on Requisition.
OH Jur. 3d Fiduciaries § 124, Parties; Pleading.
OH Jur. 3d Limitations & Laches § 157, Governmental Bodies; State and United States.
OH Jur. 3d Time § 37, Extension After Service by Mail.

Forms
Ohio Jurisprudence Pleading and Practice Forms § 12:11, Checklist—Statutes of Limitations.

PRESENTMENT OF CLAIMS AGAINST ESTATE

2117.12
Note 1

Treatises and Practice Aids

Klein, Darling, & Terez, Baldwin's Ohio Practice Civil Practice § 4:2, Issuance of Summons--Obligations of the Plaintiff.

Klein, Darling, & Terez, Baldwin's Ohio Practice Civil Practice § 6:44, Time--Additional Three Days After Service by Mail--Civ. R. 6(E) Inapplicable to Special Statutory Proceeding Pursuant to Civ. R. 1.

Klein, Darling, & Terez, Baldwin's Ohio Practice Civil Practice § 73:2, Probate Division--Applicability of Ohio Civil Rules.

Carlin, Baldwin's Ohio Practice, Merrick-Rippner Probate Law § 2:31, Payment of Debts and Claims—Filing Suit on a Rejected Claim.

Carlin, Baldwin's Ohio Practice, Merrick-Rippner Probate Law § 84:3, Creditor's Claims—Form of Claim.

Carlin, Baldwin's Ohio Practice, Merrick-Rippner Probate Law § 85:2, Acceleration of Claims—Effect on Other Statutes of Limitations.

Carlin, Baldwin's Ohio Practice, Merrick-Rippner Probate Law § 86:3, Death of Claimant—Motion for Substitution Within Ninety Days.

Carlin, Baldwin's Ohio Practice, Merrick-Rippner Probate Law § 88:2, Rejection of Claims—Manner of Rejection; Constructive Rejection.

Carlin, Baldwin's Ohio Practice, Merrick-Rippner Probate Law § 88:8, Rejection of Claims—Action on Rejected Claim—Suit Within Two Months of Rejection.

Carlin, Baldwin's Ohio Practice, Merrick-Rippner Probate Law § 88:9, Rejection of Claims—Action on Rejected Claim—Commencement.

Carlin, Baldwin's Ohio Practice, Merrick-Rippner Probate Law § 2:121, Administration of Decedent's Estate—Checklist.

Carlin, Baldwin's Ohio Practice, Merrick-Rippner Probate Law § 52:26, Fiduciary's Bond—Sureties—Liability—General.

Carlin, Baldwin's Ohio Practice, Merrick-Rippner Probate Law § 84:16, Creditor's Claims—Claims Not Requiring Presentation—Federal Taxes—State Claim.

Carlin, Baldwin's Ohio Practice, Merrick-Rippner Probate Law § 84:24, Creditor's Claims—Claims Not Requiring Presentation—Contingent Claims—Definition.

Carlin, Baldwin's Ohio Practice, Merrick-Rippner Probate Law § 84:31, Creditor's Claims—No Savings Clause.

Carlin, Baldwin's Ohio Practice, Merrick-Rippner Probate Law § 84:35, Creditor's Claims—Suit on Rejected Claims; Constructive Rejection; Jurisdiction of Probate Court.

Carlin, Baldwin's Ohio Practice, Merrick-Rippner Probate Law § 84:43, Complaint for Money Only—Form.

Carlin, Baldwin's Ohio Practice, Merrick-Rippner Probate Law § 88:10, Rejection of Claims—Governmental Claim.

Carlin, Baldwin's Ohio Practice, Merrick-Rippner Probate Law § 88:11, Rejection of Claims—Jurisdiction.

Carlin, Baldwin's Ohio Practice, Merrick-Rippner Probate Law § 88:14, Rejection of Claim Against Estate—Form.

Carlin, Baldwin's Ohio Practice, Merrick-Rippner Probate Law § 92:11, Sale of Land Subject to Encumbrances—Equities and Priorities Among Lienholders.

Notes of Decisions

Action barred 7
Evidence and burden of proof 3
Joint action 4
Jurisdiction 5
Procedural issues 1
Rejection 2
Running, statute of limitations 8
Statute of limitations 8, 9
    Running 8
    Tolling 9
Tolling, statute of limitations 9
Waiver 6

---

1. Procedural issues

Count of complaint filed by testator's son, providing that statute governing rejection of claims against the estate required son to file complaint within two months of receiving rejection of his claim, and otherwise alleging only facts, satisfied requirements of the statute, and thus would be sustained on appeal. Davidson v. Davidson (Ohio App. 3 Dist., Auglaize, 12-05-2005) No. 17-05-12, 2005-Ohio-6414, 2005 WL 3274853, Unreported. Executors And Administrators ⇐ 251

Purchaser's claims against vendor's estate for reimbursement of rental payments, which by oral agreement were to be credited toward purchase price of property, were governed by 60-day statute of limitations for claims rejected by estate, rather than six-year statute of limitations for claims on an oral contract. Evans Property, Inc. v. Altiere (Ohio App. 11 Dist., Geauga, 05-07-2004) No. 2003-G-2494, 2004-Ohio-2305, 2004 WL 1043418, Unreported, appeal not allowed 103 Ohio St.3d 1429, 814 N.E.2d 491, 2004-Ohio-4524. Executors And Administrators ⇐ 225(1)

Tort plaintiff's claim against deceased defendant's estate was timely, though plaintiff did not file formal independent action on her claim against estate within two months of administrator's rejection of claim, where she timely substituted administrator for decedent in her tort action. Carlin v. Mambuca (Ohio App. 8 Dist., 05-23-1994) 96 Ohio App.3d 500, 645 N.E.2d 737, motion to certify allowed 70 Ohio St.3d 1475, 640 N.E.2d 848, cause dismissed 71 Ohio St.3d 1441, 643 N.E.2d 1152. Executors And Administrators ⇐ 437(2)

Failure of executor of deceased land installment contract vendor's estate to comply with statutory requirements for authentication of claims prior to bringing action against deceased purchaser's estate to recover amount claimed due under contract did not require dismissal of action, where claim had been rejected in its entirety by executor of deceased purchaser's estate. Johnson v. Middleton (Marion 1989) 66 Ohio App.3d 783, 586 N.E.2d 1093. Executors And Administrators ⇐ 431(1)

Filing requirements in RC 2117.06 and 2117.12 do not apply to a preemptive right to purchase property. Stratman v. Sheetz (Hamilton 1989) 60 Ohio App.3d 71, 573 N.E.2d 776.

RC 2117.12, which requires that an action against an estate on a rejected claim be filed within two months of the rejection, provides a special statutory proceeding within the meaning of Civ R 1(C); hence Civ R 6(E) does not apply to allow additional time after service by mail. Stull v. Jentes (Wayne 1985) 24 Ohio App.3d 127, 493 N.E.2d 567, 24 O.B.R. 198.

If, within three months after a defendant's death, a claim is properly revived against the administratrix of the defendant's estate in her representative capacity and judgment is entered against the estate, resubmissions of such claim and judgment are not required under RC 2117.06, RC 2117.07 or RC 2117.12, and RC 2117.17 is irrelevant to such a case. Blanchard v. Morgan (Portage 1983) 10 Ohio App.3d 117, 460 N.E.2d 715, 10 O.B.R. 141. Abatement And Revival ⇐ 77

The provisions of Civ R 3(A) and Civ R 4 are fully applicable to proceedings brought under RC 2117.12, so that the requirement that a praecipe be filed, to either commence an action or generate the process of issuing a summons, is eliminated. Yancey v. Pyles (Hamilton 1975) 44 Ohio App.2d 410, 339 N.E.2d 835, 73 O.O.2d 530.

Probate court is without authority to determine and pass upon merits of claim rejected by an administrator in compliance with GC 10509–113 (RC 2117.11); claimant's exclusive recourse, after such rejection, is the commencement of an independent action within the time prescribed in this section. In re Buchanan's Estate (Hamilton 1948) 82 Ohio App. 240, 81 N.E.2d 409, 37 O.O. 557.

Section which provided that suit on a rejected claim must be brought within two months after rejection, did not prescribe an exclusive, but only an alternative remedy. In re Hedges' Estate (Marion 1943) 75 Ohio App. 518, 62 N.E.2d 643, 31 O.O. 301. Executors And Administrators ⇐ 504(7)

The statute authorizing probate court to allow a claimant not chargeable with culpable neglect in failing to present claim against an estate within required time to thereafter file claim was not intended to render ineffective provision requiring presentation of claim to executor or administrator within four months, but was only intended to authorize probate court to soften rigid requirements of statute to prevent rank injustice to creditors. State ex rel. Fulton v. Coburn (Ohio 1938) 133 Ohio St. 192, 12 N.E.2d 471, 10 O.O. 249. Executors And Administrators ⇐ 233

Whether presentation of the claim is, or is not required, if such claim is in fact presented and rejected, GC 10509–133 (RC 2117.12) and 10509–144 (Repealed) apply, inasmuch as neither section is limited in application to claims that are required to be presented for allowance. Swearingin v. Rendigs (Hamilton 1935) 53 Ohio App. 221, 4 N.E.2d 695, 20 Ohio Law Abs. 317, 5 O.O. 457.

Where claim was presented to and rejected by administrator and no action was brought thereon, such a claim was not a "pending proceeding" within meaning of GC 26 (RC 1.20) before this section became effective. Philadelphia Nat. Bank v. Raff (C.C.A.6 (Ohio) 1935) 76 F.2d 843, certiorari denied 56 S.Ct. 118, 296 U.S. 601, 80 L.Ed. 426.

Note 1

Failure of administrator to plead administrative statute of limitations in action against the trust makes him personally liable for any judgment had against estate and paid out of funds of estate. In re Lamberton's Estate (Ohio Prob. 1942) 10 Ohio Supp. 91, 37 Ohio Law Abs. 186, 25 O.O. 14, reversed 142 Ohio St. 417, 52 N.E.2d 855, 27 O.O. 356.

Probate claim statutes are considered as nonclaim statutes and must be pleaded by the fiduciary. In re Lamberton's Estate (Ohio Prob. 1942) 10 Ohio Supp. 91, 37 Ohio Law Abs. 186, 25 O.O. 14, reversed 142 Ohio St. 417, 52 N.E.2d 855, 27 O.O. 356. Executors And Administrators ☞ 213

A pleading designated a "supplemental" complaint is actually an amendment where it concerns events that took place before the filing of the original complaint; where the pleading adds a claim arising from the same transaction as the original complaint it relates back to the filing date of the original complaint. Gardner v Cooke, No. CA–84–12–087 (12th Dist Ct App, Warren, 7–31–85).

A suit brought in the common pleas court on a rejected claim is a civil action, not a special proceeding, and may be appealed to the circuit court. Kennedy v Thompson, 3 CC 446, 2 CD 254 (Butler 1888).

2. Rejection

Appropriate time to litigate applicability of equitable relief concerning creditor's rejected claim against decedent's estate was after filing of complaint on rejected claim. Smith v. Estate of Grilli (Ohio App. 5 Dist., Fairfield, 10-13-2005) No. 05CA33, 2005-Ohio-5711, 2005 WL 2806664, Unreported. Executors And Administrators ☞ 437(7)

Creditor's claim brought against testator's estate by testator's companion was unequivocally rejected by estate, despite estate's action for declaratory judgment with respect to claim; in answer to estate's complaint, companion admitted that she had received certified letter from estate that rejected companion's claim in full. Kraus v. Hanna (Ohio App. 11 Dist., Portage, 07-23-2004) No. 2002-P-0093, 2004-Ohio-3928, 2004 WL 1662248, Unreported, appeal not allowed 104 Ohio St.3d 1426, 819 N.E.2d 709, 2004-Ohio-6585. Executors And Administrators ☞ 234

Claimants desiring to make amendment on rejected claims may protect themselves from the time limitation by presenting same immediately to the personal representative with demand for endorsement of allowance as provided under GC 10509–113 (RC 2117.11), and upon refusal of the personal representative to make such endorsement of allowance, it becomes at once a disputed or rejected claim. Chronerberry v. Bartel (Miami 1940) 32 Ohio Law Abs. 284. Executors And Administrators ☞ 437(7)

Letters to creditor from attorney for executor of decedent's estate did not make clear and unequivocal rejection of creditor's claim against decedent's estate, as required to commence running of two-month statute of limitations for actions on rejected claims; attorney's first letter at most indicated deficiencies in form arising from creditor's incorrect identification of decedent and made unqualified denial of claim against estate of person bearing incorrect name used by creditor, but did not treat claim as one against decedent's estate or reject it on its merits, and attorney's second letter simply referred to earlier letter rejecting creditor's first, incorrect, claim. Caldwell v. Brown (Ohio App. 2 Dist., 03-01-1996) 109 Ohio App.3d 609, 672 N.E.2d 1037. Executors And Administrators ☞ 437(7)

Inasmuch as purpose of statute imposing two-month limitation period for actions on rejected claims against estate is to provide short time period within which litigation must be commenced once claimant has been put on notice of rejection, it is essential that claimant be put on notice, and rejection of claim must be plain and unequivocal. Caldwell v. Brown (Ohio App. 2 Dist., 03-01-1996) 109 Ohio App.3d 609, 672 N.E.2d 1037. Executors And Administrators ☞ 437(7)

Letter sent by attorney for executor of estate to creditor did not constitute sufficient rejection of creditor's claim against estate where there was inconsistency in content of letter as to whether rejection of the claim was being made, and thus letter did not commence running of two-month statute of limitations. Hawkes Hosp. of Mt. Carmel v. Colley (Ohio 1982) 2 Ohio St.3d 40, 442 N.E.2d 761, 36 A.L.R.4th 680, 2 O.B.R. 584. Executors And Administrators ☞ 234

Action to compel surety of administrator to pay claim allegedly allowed by administrator is not barred in statutory time for bringing action against administrator on rejected claim. Bowman v. Delaney (Lucas 1933) 46 Ohio App. 109, 187 N.E. 788, 14 Ohio Law Abs. 337, 39 Ohio Law Rep. 264. Executors And Administrators ☞ 537(5)

Where by mistake the amount of the claim is stated too low and the claim is rejected, it amounts to a rejection of the whole claim and suit may be brought at once. Morgan v. Bartlette (Ohio Cir. 1888) 2 Ohio C.D. 244.

A claimant whose claim has been reduced or rejected by an executor or administrator can bring an action under the provisions of this section, or file exceptions to the schedule of debts. In re Czatt's Estate (Ohio Prob. 1933) 30 Ohio NP(NS) 355.

3. Evidence and burden of proof

In an action against a decedent's estate it is not necessary to aver or prove that a specific demand was made for the indorsement of the executor or administrator's allowance of the claim at the time the claim was rejected. Stambaugh v. Smith (Ohio 1873) 23 Ohio St. 584.

Where an administrator makes admissions respecting a claim against the estate when not in the act of accepting or rejecting the claim, such admissions are not admissible as evidence in a suit which is brought after the person making the admissions has been divested of his functions, and this is true notwithstanding that the said administrator is one of the heirs of the estate. Hueston's Adm'rs v. Hueston (Ohio 1853) 2 Ohio St. 488. Evidence ☞ 251(2); Executors And Administrators ☞ 252

Where it is claimed that an administrator failed to set up the bar provided in section as a defense to an action on a rejected claim commenced under section, the burden is upon exceptors to show that such action was not duly commenced within two months after receipt by claimant of actual notice of rejection by administrator of a claim duly presented under GC 10509–112 (RC 2117.06) (114 v 320). In re Lamberton's Estate (Ohio 1944) 142 Ohio St. 417, 52 N.E.2d 855, 27 O.O. 356.

4. Joint action

The creditor of a decedent who obtains a judgment in a court of common pleas against the estate of the decedent pursuant to RC 2117.12 may commence a joint action against the fiduciary and the surety on the bond of the fiduciary under RC 2109.59 in the probate court of the county wherein the fiduciary received his appointment. In re Grant (Cuyahoga 1978) 56 Ohio App.2d 207, 381 N.E.2d 1348, 10 O.O.3d 205. Executors And Administrators ☞ 537(4); Executors And Administrators ☞ 537(7)

Where a co-administrator and his wife hold a joint claim against an estate for services rendered, the probate court has jurisdiction to pass on the claim. In re Smith's Estate (Ohio Prob. 1952) 120 N.E.2d 632, 67 Ohio Law Abs. 409.

5. Jurisdiction

Probate court lacked subject matter jurisdiction or jurisdiction under plenary power to consider declaratory judgment with respect to creditor's claim against estate by testator's companion that was rejected by estate, and claims that she was entitled to appropriate equity share of estate and that de facto partnership existed between testator and herself; remedy for claims was for action in common pleas court. (Per William O'Neill, J., with two judges concurring in judgment only). Kraus v. Hanna (Ohio App. 11 Dist., Portage, 07-23-2004) No. 2002-P-0093, 2004-Ohio-3928, 2004 WL 1662248, Unreported, appeal not allowed 104 Ohio St.3d 1426, 819 N.E.2d 709, 2004-Ohio-6585. Declaratory Judgment ☞ 273

Probate court's judgment that creditor's claims against estate were untimely brought did not create a res judicata bar to creditor's action against estate in the general division of the Court of Common Pleas; probate court lacked subject matter jurisdiction to consider merits of creditor's claims, and thus doctrine of res judicata did not apply. Bank One v. Johnson (Ohio App. 2 Dist., Greene, 12-19-2003) No. 03CA0039, 2003-Ohio-6906, 2003 WL 22973304, Unreported. Executors And Administrators ☞ 255

In a dispute involving a paramour's claims to (1) joint ownership of the residence she and the deceased purchased for themselves and their child, and (2) support until the child's eighteenth birthday, where the wife, who is sole heir, rejects the claims in her capacity as executrix, the claims are properly before the court of common pleas as matters within its jurisdiction. Palmentera v. Marino (Ohio App. 9 Dist., Summit, 03-27-1996) No. 17430, 1996 WL 137424, Unreported.

A probate court cannot assert jurisdiction over an action on a rejected claim through the device of a declaratory judgment or an action for specific performance. Mainline Const. Co. v. Warren (Ohio Prob. 1967) 11 Ohio Misc. 233, 227 N.E.2d 432, 40 O.O.2d 509.

Where a claim of a funeral director for funeral expenses in excess of $350 founded on a contract made with decedent in his lifetime is rejected by executor the funeral director may, under provisions of section, maintain an action against the executor on such claim in some court other than probate court. Schroyer v. Hopwood (Franklin 1940) 65 Ohio App. 443, 30 N.E.2d 440, 32 Ohio Law Abs. 511, 19 O.O. 45.

Exceptions filed to a schedule of debts in a probate court do not, in and of themselves, preclude the exemptor from pursuing his claim by action in the court of common pleas, if such suit is brought in compliance with the provisions of section. Pfeiffer v Sheffield, 64 App 1, 27 NE(2d) 494, 17 OO 305 (App 1940). Courts ⟵ 475(2)

The probate court has no jurisdiction to order an administrator, against his objection, specifically to perform an agreement alleged to have been made by his intestate. Jones v. Green (Ohio Cir. 1901) 11 Ohio C.D. 548.

The requirement that a claim against the estate of a deceased person be presented to the administrator of the estate and be rejected by him before suit can be brought on it against the administrator, is not jurisdictional and may be waived by the administrator in answering the suit and going to trial on the merits of the case. Barman v. Feid (Ohio Com.Pl. 1929) 27 Ohio N.P.N.S. 409.

Where no part of the debt was due, claimant had no right of action which could be prosecuted in any court upon merits of claim. In re Method's Estate (Ohio Prob. 1936) 2 Ohio Supp. 225, 26 Ohio Law Abs. 209, 10 O.O. 489.

6. Waiver

Where the state of Ohio accepts modified payments of less than the prescribed statutory weekly amounts of support during the lifetime of a patient in a state mental institution, it does not thereby waive any right to further payments for such support; and any unpaid balance for the support of such patient is a valid claim against his estate. State v. Security Central Nat. Bank of Portsmouth (Scioto 1955) 100 Ohio App. 425, 137 N.E.2d 158, 60 O.O. 346. Executors And Administrators ⟵ 219.8; Mental Health ⟵ 73

Administrator is without authority to waive any statute providing for limitations of action set forth in probate act affecting administration of estates. In re Lamberton's Estate (Ohio Prob. 1942) 10 Ohio Supp. 91, 37 Ohio Law Abs. 186, 25 O.O. 14, reversed 142 Ohio St. 417, 52 N.E.2d 855, 27 O.O. 356. Executors And Administrators ⟵ 213

7. Action barred

This section providing that claimant against estate, whose claim has been rejected by executor or administrator, must file his suit on said claim within two months, clearly applies to creditors other than executor or administrator. In re Grube's Estate (Clark 1935) 21 Ohio Law Abs. 1. Executors And Administrators ⟵ 437(4)

Where a tort claim was presented to an Ohio administratrix and rejected, a judgment obtained in the court of another state in an action filed seven months after the rejection cannot be collected out of the assets of the Ohio estate. In re Rettig's Estate (Ohio Prob. 1964) 8 Ohio Misc. 38, 216 N.E.2d 924, 35 O.O.2d 141.

A petition in an action against an executor of the estate of a decedent which alleges an oral presentation of a claim against the estate to, and an oral rejection of the claim by, the executor does not state facts which show a cause of action and is subject to demurrer. Morgan v. City Nat. Bank & Trust Co. (Franklin 1964) 4 Ohio App.2d 417, 212 N.E.2d 822, 33 O.O.2d 504.

The division of aid for the aged is not subject to the provisions of RC 2117.12 barring an action on a rejected claim against an estate where not commenced within the time allowed. Division of Aid for Aged, Dept. of Public Welfare v. Mull (Franklin 1957) 105 Ohio App. 305, 152 N.E.2d 295, 6 O.O.2d 100. Limitation Of Actions ⟵ 11(1)

The division of aid for the aged, although an agency of the state of Ohio must commence an action upon its claim against the estate of a deceased person within two months after receipt of actual notice of rejection or reduction of such claim by the executor or administrator thereof. State v. Drake (Ohio Com.Pl. 1952) 106 N.E.2d 91, 64 Ohio Law Abs. 177, 47 O.O. 401.

State of Ohio and its agencies are bound by limitation of section providing that actions on claims against estate of decedent must be commenced within two months from receipt of actual notice of rejection of claim. Division of Aid for the Aged in Dept. of Welfare v. Wargo (Cuyahoga 1947) 73 N.E.2d 701, 48 Ohio Law Abs. 47. Executors And Administrators ⟵ 437(2)

The State Department of Public Welfare, by delaying bringing its claim against administrator for rejecting its claim against estate of decedent for old age assistance furnished to decedent until after approval of final account of distribution, after having received notice that administrator was to close the estate, was estopped from asserting its claim against the administrator. Division of Aid for Aged in Dept. of Public Welfare v. Marshall (Franklin 1944) 59 N.E.2d 942, 42 Ohio Law Abs. 131. Executors And Administrators ⟵ 437(7)

Where an authenticated copy of letters of appointment of the executor of the estate of a deceased nonresident is filed in a probate court in this state in accordance with GC 10511–2 (RC 2129.02), the filing in such court of a claim against such estate within six months from the filing of the copy of the letters, is within time and is not governed by this section, which provides that suit on a claim must be brought within two months after such claim is disallowed. Foulks v. Talbott (Crawford 1943) 74 Ohio App. 281, 58 N.E.2d 790, 29 O.O. 434. Executors And Administrators ⟵ 521

Where action against administrator on a claim for services rendered was not filed until more than four months after rejection of the claim by administrator, the action was barred by statute, then in force, limiting the time to two months within which actions could be brought. Heitz v. Iredale (Hamilton 1942) 44 N.E.2d 720, 36 Ohio Law Abs. 558. Executors And Administrators ⟵ 437(7)

An unliquidated claim for damages arising out of tort does not fall within the exception contained in GC 10509–112 (RC 2117.06), pertaining to contingent claims; suit thereon must be instituted within two months from the date of receipt of actual notice of disallowance of such claim by the executor or administrator, or be forever barred under the provisions of this section. Pierce v. Johnson (Ohio 1939) 136 Ohio St. 95, 23 N.E.2d 993, 125 A.L.R. 867, 16 O.O. 34.

When a claim against an estate has been allowed and later rejected, the statute of limitations begins to run from the time of such rejection. Weber v. Kohn (Lucas 1938) 60 Ohio App. 64, 19 N.E.2d 534, 13 O.O. 424. Limitation Of Actions ⟵ 105(1)

Where superintendent of banks' action against an executor appointed April 9, 1932, on claim accruing in May, 1933, was barred by limitations because it had not been commenced within two months after accrual of claim, the statutory bar could not be avoided by filing another claim for same liability and then filing a supplemental petition within two months after the rejection of that claim. State ex rel. Fulton v. Coburn (Ohio 1938) 133 Ohio St. 192, 12 N.E.2d 471, 10 O.O. 249. Executors And Administrators ⟵ 437(7)

Where a claim for the super-added liability is presented by the superintendent of banks to the personal representative of a decedent for allowance and such personal representative rejects such claim and the superintendent of banks does not within two months thereafter commence his suit for recovery against such personal representative, he is forever barred from maintaining an action thereon, as provided by section. State ex rel. Fulton v. Bremer (Ohio 1935) 130 Ohio St. 227, 198 N.E. 874, 4 O.O. 242.

Statute of limitations becoming effective ninety days after it was filed with secretary of state provided reasonable time for prosecution of causes of action then existing so as not to be unconstitutional because of retroactive effect. Matthews v. Raff (Stark 1933) 45 Ohio App. 242, 186 N.E. 887, 15 Ohio Law Abs. 94, 39 Ohio Law Rep. 58, error dismissed 126 Ohio St. 511, 186 N.E. 402, 38 Ohio Law Rep. 478. Constitutional Law ⟵ 191

Action for services rendered to decedent commenced approximately six months after administrator rejected claim held barred by two-month statute of limitations. Matthews v. Raff (Stark 1933) 45 Ohio App. 242, 186 N.E. 887, 15 Ohio Law Abs. 94, 39 Ohio Law Rep. 58, error dismissed 126 Ohio St. 511, 186 N.E. 402, 38 Ohio Law Rep. 478. Executors And Administrators ⟵ 437(3)

If within a reasonable time after exhibition of a note executed by the decedent the administrator informs the claimant that his claim is rejected, the six months' statute will then begin to run, and after the expiration of six months the administrator cannot by estoppel or in any other manner waive the statute and bind the estate. Miller v. Ewing (Ohio 1903) 68 Ohio St. 176, 48 W.L.B. 529, 67 N.E. 292, 1 Ohio Law Rep. 273. Executors And Administrators ⟵ 437(7)

The cause of action upon a legacy accrues when, by the terms of the will or by rule of law it becomes due and payable and the executor has sufficient assets to pay it; it is not necessary that the legatee have actual notice of the legacy or will to start the statute running, and its bar, once complete, will not be defeated by an order of the probate court directing final settlement and distribution of the estate or by the payment of other legacies by the executor. Webster v. American Bible Soc. (Ohio 1893) 50 Ohio St. 1, 29 W.L.B. 141, 33 N.E. 297. Wills ⟵ 748

Where a claim against a decedent's estate is disallowed more than six months prior to the commencement of an action, it is error for the court to render judgment against the estate, and the failure of the executor to plead

8. Statute of limitations—Running

Presenting a claim for allowance and being told by the executor to consider it rejected constitutes a legal rejection, though no rejection is indorsed on the claim at the time; the six months' limitation begins to run from such rejection. Harter, Trump, Wikidal & Co. v. Taggart's Ex'rs (Ohio 1862) 14 Ohio St. 122.

Saving statute, which permitted actions dismissed other than on the merits to be refiled within one year, applied to actions involving claims against an estate, and thus two-month limitations period for filing such actions following rejection of the underlying claims by an estate's executor or administrator did not bar claimants who voluntarily dismissed an action against decedent's estate from refiling their action less than a year later; original action was commenced within the two-month period, nothing in statute governing presentation of claims against an estate indicated that saving statute should not apply, and saving statute was a remedial statute to be construed broadly. Vitantonio v. Baxter (Ohio App. 11 Dist., Lake, 03-31-2006) No. 2005-L-004, 2006-Ohio-1685, 2006 WL 847229, Unreported. Limitation Of Actions ⇐ 130(5)

Rejection of a claim by an executor or administrator must be plain and unequivocal in order to start running the statute of limitations. Chronerberry v. Bartel (Miami 1940) 32 Ohio Law Abs. 284. Executors And Administrators ⇐ 437(7)

Claimant has four months within which to present his claim, but when presented and rejected, either by direct action of the administrator or executor or by operation of law under GC 10509-113 (RC 2117.11), the two months' period of limitation starts to run. Chronerberry v. Bartel (Miami 1940) 32 Ohio Law Abs. 284.

The failure to file suit within two months of the rejection by the administrator of the estate of a claim against the estate for bodily injury does not bar an action for that bodily injury against that administrator where no part of the recovery sought is to come from "assets of the estate" as that term is defined in RC 2117.07. Collins v. Yanity (Ohio 1968) 14 Ohio St.2d 202, 237 N.E.2d 611, 43 O.O.2d 301. Executors And Administrators ⇐ 437(3)

When an administrator rejects a claim he starts in motion a new statute of limitations. Parrish v. McKee (Ohio Com.Pl. 1956) 135 N.E.2d 486, 73 Ohio Law Abs. 65, 59 O.O. 316.

Plaintiff's presentation of claim against administrator and its rejection held not "commencement of action" so as to constitute "pending proceeding" before effective date of two-month statute of limitations. Matthews v. Raff (Stark 1933) 45 Ohio App. 242, 186 N.E. 887, 15 Ohio Law Abs. 94, 39 Ohio Law Rep. 58, error dismissed 126 Ohio St. 511, 186 N.E. 402, 38 Ohio Law Rep. 478. Limitation Of Actions ⇐ 132

That administratrix had made final account, distributed assets, and had been discharged, did not bar action on claim commenced within 6 months from day claim was rejected and within 18 months from day administratrix qualified. Beck v. Schmidt (Seneca 1930) 38 Ohio App. 476, 176 N.E. 595, 9 Ohio Law Abs. 168. Executors And Administrators ⇐ 513(11)

Where a claim presented by a creditor to an administrator is accepted and allowed, but is subsequently disallowed and rejected by the administrator's successor the four-year limitation prescribed by RS 6113 (Gen.Code, §10509-144, repealed 1935), providing that no administrator after giving notice of his appointment shall be held to answer to the suit if a creditor of decedent, unless commenced within four years from the time of the administrator's giving bond, with certain exceptions, begins to run only from the time of the rejection of the claim. Bray v. Darby (Ohio 1910) 82 Ohio St. 47, 91 N.E. 861, 7 Ohio Law Rep. 638. Executors And Administrators ⇐ 437(4)

This section relates to the limitation upon commencing suit on a rejected claim after the effective date of the law, and not to the commencement of suit upon claims rejected after its effective date; the statute deals with the time for pursuing the remedy, and not with the time that the right to pursue it arises. Philadelphia Nat. Bank v. Raff (N.D.Ohio 1933) 4 F.Supp. 230, affirmed 76 F.2d 843, certiorari denied 56 S.Ct. 118, 296 U.S. 601, 80 L.Ed. 426.

Where the administrator of decedent's estate fails to give the state a written statement of allowance of a claim within five days, where such claim seeks recovery for support of decedent's daughter in a state institution, such failure constitutes a rejection by operation of law and commences the running of the statute of limitations for claims against the estate. Dept of Mental Health, Office of Support v Reynolds, No. C–820545 (1st Dist Ct App, Hamilton, 5–11–83).

9. ——— Tolling, statute of limitations

The statute limiting the right of action to six months after the claim is rejected does not apply to a case where the claim is allowed upon presentation and afterwards is disputed; such suit must be commenced within six months of the rejection. (See also Bray v Darby, 82 OS 47, 91 NE 861 (1910); Royer v Hall, 82 OS 453, 92 NE 1122 (1910).) Thomas v. Chamberlain (Ohio 1883) 39 Ohio St. 112, 9 W.L.B. 258.

As between the estate of a deceased debtor and its creditors, the statute of limitations ceases to run against the claims of the latter upon their presentment to and allowance by the executor or administrator. Taylor v. Thorn (Ohio 1876) 29 Ohio St. 569. Executors And Administrators ⇐ 437(4); Limitation Of Actions ⇐ 132

Amendments may be made on rejected claims against estates at any time before the expiration of the two months' period of limitation, but the amendment will not extend the time for bringing action. Chronerberry v. Bartel (Miami 1940) 32 Ohio Law Abs. 284. Executors And Administrators ⇐ 227(5); Executors And Administrators ⇐ 437(7)

Statement by executor in letter to claimant with reference to claim, that "if this is reformed, itemized and placed in the proper manner, with all credits, etc., attached, I would be glad to take up the matter of payment of the claim but in the form in which the claim now is, I am compelled to refuse it," was not such unequivocal rejection as to start running of time within which action must have been commenced on claim. Martin v. Spellman (Franklin 1939) 30 Ohio Law Abs. 225. Executors And Administrators ⇐ 234; Limitation Of Actions ⇐ 132

Automobile insurer, as subrogee of insured, individually and as executor of estate of her insured husband, was statutorily barred from filing complaint against estate of third-party tortfeasor who allegedly caused automobile accident at issue, where insured was statutorily barred from filing complaint against tort-feasor's estate due to her failure to respond to estate's notice of rejection of claim within two-month limitations period; insurer did not have separate and distinct claim against estate. Ohio Mut. Ins. Assn., United Ohio Ins. Co. v. Warlaumont (Ohio App. 12 Dist., 12-01-1997) 124 Ohio App.3d 473, 706 N.E.2d 793. Insurance ⇐ 3523(3)

The federal government is not required to comply with the statutes relating to presentment of claims in order to collect social security taxes due from a decedent. Baker v. Charles (Ohio Prob. 1963) 202 N.E.2d 646, 95 Ohio Law Abs. 97, 31 O.O.2d 310.

RC 2217.12 is a statute of limitations and does not bind the federal government. Baker v. Charles (Ohio Prob. 1963) 202 N.E.2d 646, 95 Ohio Law Abs. 97, 31 O.O.2d 310.

Upon hearing on exceptions to administrator's account, it is error for probate court to assume the date of rejection of a claim and actual notice thereof to claimant from mere lapse of time between date of administrator's appointment and commencement of an action against him on rejected claim; under section, the bar of that statute did not begin to run until two months after receipt by claimant of actual notice of rejection of the claim. In re Lamberton's Estate (Ohio 1944) 142 Ohio St. 417, 52 N.E.2d 855, 27 O.O. 356.

Once a claim has been barred by RS 6113, a subsequent allowance or disallowance of the claim by an administrator de bonis non will not revive it to run again from the time of such disallowance. Crouse v. Frybarger (Ohio Cir. 1901) 12 Ohio C.D. 254.

This section must be construed with GC 11233 which prolongs the time for a suit to be commenced where there was a proper attempt to sue in time and within a reasonable time a judgment for the plaintiff is reversed or he fails otherwise than upon the merits. Burgoyne v. Moore (Ohio Cir. 1890) 5 Ohio C.D. 522, affirmed 51 Ohio St. 626.

Absence of a fiduciary against whom the federal government may bring an action to collect the unpaid tax liability tolls the six-year period of limitation for the bringing of an action provided by Internal Revenue Code of 1954, 26 USC 6502, inasmuch as under applicable Ohio probate law both a claim and an action against an estate may only proceed against a fiduciary of an estate, so that the absence of appointment of a fiduciary tolls the time in which claims may be presented against the estate. U. S. v. Besase (N.D.Ohio 1970) 29 Ohio Misc. 166, 319 F.Supp. 1064, 57 O.O.2d 51.

Where a claim against an estate requests acceptance "within the time provided by law," but does not specify what law is referred to, and where the estate sends the claimant written rejection of the claim beyond the thirty-day period in RC 2117.06(D), this rejection is nevertheless effective under RC 2117.06(D) and precludes the automatic rejection after five days provided for by RC 2117.11 even if the written rejection specifically cites RC 2117.11; the rejection is deemed effective when the writing is delivered and the two-month period for filing an action against the estate prescribed by RC 2117.12 commences then. Bush v Estate of O'Dell, No. CA-3705 (5th Dist Ct App, Licking, 2-26-92).

2117.13 Claims rejected on requisition of heir, devisee, or creditor

If a devisee, legatee, heir, creditor, or other interested party files in the probate court a written requisition on the executor or administrator to reject a claim presented for allowance against the estate he represents, whether the claim has been allowed or not, but which has not been paid in full and enters into a sufficient bond running to such executor or administrator, the amount, terms, and surety of which are to be approved by the probate judge, the claim shall be rejected by the executor or administrator. The notice of rejection shall inform the claimant of the filing of the requisition and of the name of the party filing the same. The condition of the bond shall be to pay all costs and expenses of contesting such claim, including such reasonable fee as the court allows to the attorney for the executor or administrator, in case the claim finally is allowed in whole, and if such claim is allowed only in part, to pay such part of the expenses as the court may determine, including such reasonable fee as the court may allow to the attorney for the executor or administrator.

(1953 H 1, eff. 10-1-53; GC 10509-135)

Historical and Statutory Notes

Pre-1953 H 1 Amendments: 119 v 394, § 1; 114 v 431

Library References

Executors and Administrators ⚖234.
Westlaw Topic No. 162.
C.J.S. Executors and Administrators §§ 455 to 456.

Research References

Encyclopedias
OH Jur. 3d Decedents' Estates § 1459, Rejection on Requisition by Interested Party.
OH Jur. 3d Decedents' Estates § 1776, Action on Claim Rejected on Requisition.
OH Jur. 3d Decedents' Estates § 1819, Suits on Claim Rejected on Requisition.

Treatises and Practice Aids
Carlin, Baldwin's Ohio Practice, Merrick-Rippner Probate Law § 2:30, Payment of Debts and Claims—Options of Fiduciary.
Carlin, Baldwin's Ohio Practice, Merrick-Rippner Probate Law § 87:8, Hearings on Claims—Court's Order of Allowance or Rejection.
Carlin, Baldwin's Ohio Practice, Merrick-Rippner Probate Law § 88:6, Rejection of Claims—Requisition—Statutory Procedure.
Carlin, Baldwin's Ohio Practice, Merrick-Rippner Probate Law § 88:7, Rejection of Claims—Requisition—Attorney Fees.
Carlin, Baldwin's Ohio Practice, Merrick-Rippner Probate Law § 80:17, Attorney Fees—Allowed on Claims Rejected on Requisition.
Carlin, Baldwin's Ohio Practice, Merrick-Rippner Probate Law § 88:15, Requisition to Disallow and Reject Claim—Form.
Carlin, Baldwin's Ohio Practice, Merrick-Rippner Probate Law § 88:16, Entry on Requisition, Approving Bond and Ordering Notice—Form.
Carlin, Baldwin's Ohio Practice, Merrick-Rippner Probate Law § 88:17, Bond on Requisition to Disallow or Reject Claim—Form.
Carlin, Baldwin's Ohio Practice, Merrick-Rippner Probate Law § 88:18, Notice to Fiduciary—Form.

Notes of Decisions

Costs   4
Evidence   3
Heirs   1
Parties   2

---

1. Heirs

Suit on claim against estate need not be brought within six months after rejection against heirs, who may be joined any time before trial. Baughn v. Duncan (Greene 1929) 31 Ohio App. 518, 167 N.E. 490. Executors And Administrators ⚖ 437(7)

Where the heirs request the rejection of a claim against the estate and execute a bond, administrator is required to reject said claim, and suit, if brought thereon, must be brought against the administrator within six months after such rejection, but the heirs demanding such rejection may be brought in at any time before trial. Baughn v. Duncan (Greene 1929) 31 Ohio App. 518, 167 N.E. 490.

The word "heirs" may mean devisees and legatees, and as such have the right to request the executor to reject a claim presented for allowance. Todd v. Todd (Ohio Cir. 1905) 17 Ohio C.D. 224, 6 Ohio C.C.N.S. 105.

An annuity is a legacy, not a claim, and a devisee is not an heir under a will; in the first case the legatee need not file his claim with the executor for allowance or disallowance, and in the second case the devisee is not authorized to file a written requisition with the administrator as an heir to disallow a claim against the estate. Hunt v. Hayes (Ohio Cir. 1898) 10 Ohio C.D. 388, affirmed 63 Ohio St. 599, 60 N.E. 1131.

A surviving husband entitled to curtesy is not an heir, creditor or a person who has purchased from an heir the real estate sought to be sold; therefore, his rights are not affected by the claims of decedent's creditors, and he has no right to contest such claims. Pirmann v. Gerhold (Ohio Prob. 1887) 5 Ohio Dec. 414, 7 Ohio N.P. 664.

2. Parties

In actions by creditors of a decedent to enforce their claims, where the personal representative of the decedent refuses or neglects to defend, an heir of the decedent may be permitted to come in and defend although he is ordinarily neither a proper nor a necessary party defendant. Gerardot v. Parrish (Paulding 1975) 44 Ohio App.2d 293, 338 N.E.2d 531, 73 O.O.2d 360.

Where an heir who has not requisitioned the disallowance of a claim against a decedent's estate under the provisions of RC 2117.13 et seq., but said claim is disallowed by the probate court pursuant to hearing of the schedule of claims, the heir is permitted by the common pleas court to intervene as a party defendant in a suit filed therein against the administrator of the decedent's estate by the claimant, and in which suit the administrator fails to join issue or defend against the claim, and the intervening heir, in effect, is substituted for the administrator to defend in such representative capacity the decedent's estate against the claim, and the relation of the parties and the competency of their testimony under the provisions of the dead man's statute are to be determined as if the administrator were the sole party defendant actively resisting the plaintiff's claim, and the presence of the heir as an intervening defendant in the suit shall not be deemed to add to or detract from the protection offered to the estate by the provisions of the statute. Gerardot v. Parrish (Paulding 1975) 44 Ohio App.2d 293, 338 N.E.2d 531, 73 O.O.2d 360.

The provisions of RS 6098 which authorize the heirs in such action to make any defense to the action which the administrator or executor could make necessarily carries with it the right to test the regularity of the proceedings in the trial court in the same manner as the administrator or executor can do, including an appeal to the circuit court, notwithstanding that the heirs were not parties to the judgment. Spaulding v. Allen (Ohio Cir. 1899) 10 Ohio C.D. 259.

The party giving the bond must be made a party to the suit upon the rejected claim or he will not be liable for costs. Fullerton v. Davis (Ohio Cir. 1886) 1 Ohio C.D. 320.

3. Evidence

Verbal notice given to the administrator of an estate by the widow of the deceased not to allow a claim is not sufficient proof of fraud on the part of the administrator for afterwards allowing the claim. Thomas v. Chamberlain (Ohio 1883) 39 Ohio St. 112, 9 W.L.B. 258. Executors And Administrators ⚖ 234

Excluding testimony of sole heir, who had filed bond to pay costs of contesting claim against estate, regarding what occurred before testator's death relating to claim, held error. Anderson v. Houpt (Richland 1932) 43

2117.13
Note 3

Ohio App. 538, 184 N.E. 29, 13 Ohio Law Abs. 16, 37 Ohio Law Rep. 234. Witnesses ⚖ 133

In a suit by an administrator on a bond given under this section, it is not necessary for him to prove that the requirements of the section have been strictly complied with. Fullerton v. Davis (Ohio Cir. 1886) 1 Ohio C.D. 320.

4. Costs

Sole legatee of deceased who entered into bond to pay expenses of contesting claim against deceased's estate could plead and make defense to action. Anderson v. Houpt (Richland 1932) 43 Ohio App. 538, 184 N.E. 29, 13 Ohio Law Abs. 16, 37 Ohio Law Rep. 234. Executors And Administrators ⚖ 244

Where claimant against estate has claim sustained after heir's requisition for rejection, costs are taxed against requisitor. Koelble v. Runyan (Brown 1927) 25 Ohio App. 426, 158 N.E. 279, 6 Ohio Law Abs. 41. Executors And Administrators ⚖ 240

2117.14 Parties to action on claim rejected on requisition

The devisee, legatee, heir, creditor, or other interested party filing the requisition referred to in section 2117.13 of the Revised Code, shall be made a party defendant with the executor or administrator to any action on a claim rejected on requisition and have a right to plead and make any defense thereto. Any judgment in favor of the claimant shall be against the executor or administrator only.

(1953 H 1, eff. 10–1–53; GC 10509–136)

Historical and Statutory Notes

Pre–1953 H 1 Amendments: 119 v 394, § 1; 114 v 431

Library References

Executors and Administrators ⚖248.1, 438(5), 438(7).
Westlaw Topic No. 162.
C.J.S. Executors and Administrators §§ 480, 769 to 772, 776, 779 to 780.

Research References

Encyclopedias

OH Jur. 3d Decedents' Estates § 1776, Action on Claim Rejected on Requisition.
OH Jur. 3d Decedents' Estates § 1800, Parties Defendant—in Action on Claim Rejected on Requisition.
OH Jur. 3d Decedents' Estates § 1819, Suits on Claim Rejected on Requisition.

Treatises and Practice Aids

Carlin, Baldwin's Ohio Practice, Merrick-Rippner Probate Law § 2:30, Payment of Debts and Claims—Options of Fiduciary.
Carlin, Baldwin's Ohio Practice, Merrick-Rippner Probate Law § 64:3, Powers and Duties of Guardian—Inventory.
Carlin, Baldwin's Ohio Practice, Merrick-Rippner Probate Law § 64:4, Powers and Duties of Guardian—Accounting.
Carlin, Baldwin's Ohio Practice, Merrick-Rippner Probate Law § 87:8, Hearings on Claims—Court's Order of Allowance or Rejection.

Notes of Decisions

Creditors 2
Legatees 1
Procedure and jurisdiction 4
Testimony 3

1. Legatees

Sole legatee of deceased who entered into bond to pay expenses of contesting claim against deceased's estate could plead and make defense to action. Anderson v. Houpt (Richland 1932) 43 Ohio App. 538, 184 N.E. 29, 13 Ohio Law Abs. 16, 37 Ohio Law Rep. 234. Executors And Administrators ⚖ 244

Suit on claim against estate need not be brought within six months after rejection against heirs, who may be joined any time before trial. Baughn v. Duncan (Greene 1929) 31 Ohio App. 518, 167 N.E. 490. Executors And Administrators ⚖ 437(7)

2. Creditors

In actions by creditors of a decedent to enforce their claims, where the personal representative of the decedent refuses or neglects to defend, an heir of the decedent may be permitted to come in and defend although he is ordinarily neither a proper nor a necessary party defendant. Gerardot v. Parrish (Paulding 1975) 44 Ohio App.2d 293, 338 N.E.2d 531, 73 O.O.2d 360.

3. Testimony

In action against executor and heirs on note alleged to have been executed by deceased, the heirs, as well as the executor, are entitled to call plaintiff as a witness for cross-examination, notwithstanding GC 11495 (RC 2317.03) forbidding parties to testify in certain cases. Atley v. Atley (Clinton 1926) 20 Ohio App. 497, 152 N.E. 761, 3 Ohio Law Abs. 687.

4. Procedure and jurisdiction

Where, pending an action against an estate, one of heirs dies who would have been one of contestants, it is not error to refuse continuance because of death of said heir and refusal of court to substitute parties for such heir. Homan v. Lightner (Wayne 1935) 20 Ohio Law Abs. 78.

Suit may be brought on a previously allowed and subsequently rejected claim within six months of notice of such rejection, notwithstanding that the statute of limitations would have run between the time of allowance and rejection of the claim. (See also Eicher v Darby, 17 D 780, 5 LR 102 (CP, Hamilton 1907); affirmed sub nom Glenn v Eicher, 81 OS 553, 91 NE 1129 (1910).) Speidel v. Phillips (Ohio 1908) 78 Ohio St. 194, 85 N.E. 53, 6 Ohio Law Rep. 90.

A claim against an executor for board and lodging of the decedent praying for allowance of the claim and for judgment is recognized in GC 10725 (RC 2117.14) as a civil action for money and is therefore within the jurisdiction of the municipal court. Keck v. Bahlke (Ohio App. 1916) 27 Ohio C.D. 390, 26 Ohio C.C.(N.S.) 398, 6 Ohio App. 246.

2117.15 Payment of debts

An executor or administrator may proceed to pay the debts due from the estate in accordance with Chapters 2113. to 2125. of the Revised Code. If it appears at any time that the estate is insolvent, the executor or administrator may report that fact to the court, and apply for any order that he considers necessary because of the insolvency. In case of insolvency, a creditor who has been paid according to law shall not be required to make any refund.

(1990 H 346, eff. 5–31–90; 1975 S 145; 1953 H 1; GC 10509–127)

Uncodified Law

1990 H 346, § 3, eff. 5–31–90, reads, in part: (A) Sections 1 and 2 of this act shall apply only to the estates of decedents who die on or after the effective date of this act.

Historical and Statutory Notes

Pre–1953 H 1 Amendments: 119 v 394, § 1; 114 v 429

Comparative Laws

Ind.—West's A.I.C. 29–1–14–19.
Tex.—V.A.T.S. Probate Code § 319.

Cross References

Insolvency of ward, 2111.24
Will or trust clause as to tax payment does not encompass "generation skipping transfer tax" unless so specified, 1339.45

Library References

Executors and Administrators ⚖︎277, 408, 416 to 417.
Westlaw Topic No. 162.
C.J.S. Executors and Administrators §§ 517, 693, 703 to 704.
    Baldwin's Ohio Legislative Service, 1990 Laws of Ohio, H 346—LSC Analysis, p 5–87

Research References

Encyclopedias

OH Jur. 3d Decedents' Estates § 1466, Debts to be Paid, Generally.
OH Jur. 3d Decedents' Estates § 1693, Report of Insolvency and Application for Instructions.
OH Jur. 3d Decedents' Estates § 1696, Liability for Excess Payments.
OH Jur. 3d Decedents' Estates § 1697, Recovery Back of Overpayment to Creditor.

Treatises and Practice Aids

Carlin, Baldwin's Ohio Practice, Merrick-Rippner Probate Law § 89:1, Payment of Debts.
Carlin, Baldwin's Ohio Practice, Merrick-Rippner Probate Law § 89:2, Payment of Debts—Insolvent Estates.
Carlin, Baldwin's Ohio Practice, Merrick-Rippner Probate Law § 87:16, Representation of Insolvency—Form.
Carlin, Baldwin's Ohio Practice, Merrick-Rippner Probate Law § 87:17, Entry on Filing Representation of Insolvency, and Ordering Notice—Form.
Carlin, Baldwin's Ohio Practice, Merrick-Rippner Probate Law § 87:18, Notice to Creditors of Insolvency—Form.

Notes of Decisions

Court's authority 1
Payment methods and priority 3
Procedure 2

1. Court's authority

In a hearing on application filed under section, the court is without authority to question the validity of a land sale proceeding or the correctness or validity of the inventory and appraisement, to disallow a claim of a creditor of the estate when the claim has been allowed by the administrator, and to adjudicate the question of the ownership of joint and survivorship bank accounts held in the name of the decedent and his wife; the attempt to adjudicate such matters was a nullity. In re Murphy's Estate (Franklin 1950) 88 Ohio App. 167, 95 N.E.2d 590, 58 Ohio Law Abs. 123, 44 O.O. 193.

In an application filed by an administrator under section, the court is limited to making an inquiry whether the report of insolvency is correct and instructing the administrator in what manner and to whom the assets should be distributed, but is without authority to do more. In re Murphy's Estate (Franklin 1950) 88 Ohio App. 167, 95 N.E.2d 590, 58 Ohio Law Abs. 123, 44 O.O. 193. Executors And Administrators ⚖︎ 410

2. Procedure

The provision in section, for reporting the insolvency of the estate to the court and making an application for any order that the executor or administrator deems necessary, is permissive and contemplates an ex parte hearing. In re Murphy's Estate (Franklin 1950) 88 Ohio App. 167, 95 N.E.2d 590, 58 Ohio Law Abs. 123, 44 O.O. 193. Executors And Administrators ⚖︎ 410

3. Payment methods and priority

Restrictions imposed by statute and local probate rule on ability of patient's guardian to deplete assets in patient's insolvent estate did not render such assets unavailable for purposes of Medicaid eligibility; statutes governing payment of debts of insolvency guardianship did not preclude guardian from expending funds for maintenance and support of patient, and rule barring court approval of any distribution of estate assets prior to filing of inventory was not a total bar to depletion of assets. Payne v. Ohio Dept. of Human Serv. (Ohio App. 10 Dist., 09-16-1997) 123 Ohio App.3d 341, 704 N.E.2d 270. Health ⚖︎ 471(1)

Where an estate is insolvent because of a claim of the department of public welfare, the funeral director can receive a maximum of $300.00 ahead of the state and is a general creditor as to any amount in excess of $300.00. In re Young's Estate (Ohio Prob. 1956) 140 N.E.2d 792, 74 Ohio Law Abs. 129.

GC 10509–130 (Repealed) (114 v 320), which provided that creditors of an estate would not be liable to refund any payment to them, must be applied in relation to other sections of the code pertaining to the payment of debts of an estate; payment of a creditor's claim by the executor when he did not know that the estate was then insolvent was payment under a mistake of fact, and the sum thus paid may be recovered back. Howe v. Citizens Central Bank of Nelsonville (Athens 1942) 74 Ohio App. 131, 57 N.E.2d 821, 29 O.O. 291.

Where an administrator, having notice of a creditor's claim pays all the others in full, thereby exhausting the funds in his hands so that such creditor would have no part, such administrator is individually liable to such creditor for the full amount of his claim, notwithstanding that the omitted creditor may only have received a proportional part of his claim if he had been considered in the general distribution. In re Wakefield's Estate (Ohio Prob. 1885) 5 Ohio Dec. 395, 7 Ohio N.P. 562. Executors And Administrators ⚖︎ 281

HEARING ON CLAIMS

2117.17 Hearing on allowed claims; optional

The probate court on its own motion may, and on motion of the executor or administrator shall, assign all claims against the estate that have been presented and any other known valid debts of the estate for hearing on a day certain. Forthwith upon such assignment, and in no case less than ten days before the date fixed for hearing or such longer period as the court may order, the executor or administrator shall cause written notice of the hearing to be served upon the following persons who have not waived the notice in writing or otherwise voluntarily entered their appearance:

(A) If it appears that the estate is fully solvent, such notice shall be given to the surviving spouse and all other persons having an interest in the estate as devisees, legatees, heirs, and distributees.

(B) If it appears probable that there will not be sufficient assets to pay all of the valid debts of the estate in full, then such notice also shall be given to all creditors and claimants whose claims have been rejected and whose rights have not been finally determined by judgment, reference, or lapse of time.

The notice required by this section shall state that a hearing concerning the debts has been scheduled, shall set forth the time and place of the hearing, and shall state that the action of the executor or administrator in allowing and classifying claims will be confirmed at such hearing unless cause to the contrary is shown. The notice shall be served personally or by certified mail in the manner specified for service of notice of the rejection of a claim under section 2117.11 of the Revised Code. Proof of service of the notice to the satisfaction of the court, by affidavit or otherwise, and all waivers of service shall be filed in court at the time of the hearing. At any time before hearing, any interested person may file exceptions in writing to the allowance or classification of any specific claim. The court may cause or permit other interested persons to be served with notice and witnesses to be subpoenaed as may be required to present the issues fully.

The court, upon hearing, shall determine whether the executor or administrator acted properly in allowing and classifying each claim and shall make an order confirming or disapproving such action.

An order of the court disapproving the allowance of a claim shall have the same effect as a rejection of the claim on the date on which the claimant is served with notice of the court's order. Notice of the court's order shall be served personally or by certified mail in the manner specified for service of notice of the rejection of a claim under section 2117.11 of the Revised Code.

An order of the court confirming the allowance or classification of a claim shall constitute a final order and shall have the same effect as a judgment at law or decree in equity, and shall be final as to all persons having notice of the hearing and as to claimants subsequently presenting their claims, though without notice of such hearing. In the absence of fraud, the allowance and classification of a claim and the subsequent payment of it in good faith shall not be subject to question upon exceptions to the executor's or administrator's accounts. The confirmation of a claim by the court shall not preclude the executor or administrator from thereafter rejecting the claim on discovery of error in his previous action or on requisition as provided in sections 2117.13 and 2117.14 of the Revised Code.

(1990 H 346, eff. 5-31-90; 1983 S 115; 1970 S 185; 1953 H 1; GC 10509-119)

Uncodified Law

1990 H 346, § 3, eff. 5-31-90, reads, in part: (A) Sections 1 and 2 of this act shall apply only to the estates of decedents who die on or after the effective date of this act.

Historical and Statutory Notes

Pre-1953 H 1 Amendments: 119 v 394, § 1; 116 v 385; 114 v 428

Cross References

Claims filed with the court, Sup R 62

Library References

Executors and Administrators ⚖236, 415.
Westlaw Topic No. 162.
C.J.S. Executors and Administrators §§ 455, 458 to 459, 701.
  Baldwin's Ohio Legislative Service, 1990 Laws of Ohio, H 346—LSC Analysis, p 5-87

Research References

Encyclopedias

OH Jur. 3d Actions § 110, Jurisdictional Considerations.
OH Jur. 3d Decedents' Estates § 1319, Hearing on Allowed Claims.
OH Jur. 3d Decedents' Estates § 1320, Notice of Hearing.
OH Jur. 3d Decedents' Estates § 1321, Effect of Order Disapproving or Confirming Claim.
OH Jur. 3d Decedents' Estates § 1459, Rejection on Requisition by Interested Party.
OH Jur. 3d Decedents' Estates § 1474, Equal Distribution Among Creditors of Same Class.

Treatises and Practice Aids

Carlin, Baldwin's Ohio Practice, Merrick-Rippner Probate Law § 2:29, Payment of Debts and Claims—Hearing.
Carlin, Baldwin's Ohio Practice, Merrick-Rippner Probate Law § 2:30, Payment of Debts and Claims—Options of Fiduciary.
Carlin, Baldwin's Ohio Practice, Merrick-Rippner Probate Law § 2:33, Payment of Debts and Claims—Schedule of Debts.
Carlin, Baldwin's Ohio Practice, Merrick-Rippner Probate Law § 84:3, Creditor's Claims—Form of Claim.
Carlin, Baldwin's Ohio Practice, Merrick-Rippner Probate Law § 86:3, Death of Claimant—Motion for Substitution Within Ninety Days.
Carlin, Baldwin's Ohio Practice, Merrick-Rippner Probate Law § 87:1, Hearings on Claims—Rule Requiring Resolution of All Claims.
Carlin, Baldwin's Ohio Practice, Merrick-Rippner Probate Law § 87:2, Hearings on Claims—Schedule of Claims.
Carlin, Baldwin's Ohio Practice, Merrick-Rippner Probate Law § 87:3, Hearings on Claims—Motion to Assign for Hearing.
Carlin, Baldwin's Ohio Practice, Merrick-Rippner Probate Law § 87:4, Hearings on Claims—Notice.
Carlin, Baldwin's Ohio Practice, Merrick-Rippner Probate Law § 87:5, Hearings on Claims—Contents and Service—Notice.
Carlin, Baldwin's Ohio Practice, Merrick-Rippner Probate Law § 87:6, Hearings on Claims—Exceptions to Allowance.
Carlin, Baldwin's Ohio Practice, Merrick-Rippner Probate Law § 87:7, Hearings on Claims—Witnesses.
Carlin, Baldwin's Ohio Practice, Merrick-Rippner Probate Law § 87:8, Hearings on Claims—Court's Order of Allowance or Rejection.
Carlin, Baldwin's Ohio Practice, Merrick-Rippner Probate Law § 109:52, Ohio Estate Tax—Appeal to Probate Court—Jurisdiction Over Tax Matters.

Law Review and Journal Commentaries

Barred Claims Statute, Appeals from Probate Court Discussed, Hon. Nelson J. Brewer. 8 Clev B J 83 (March 1937).

Notes of Decisions

Ed. Note: This section contains annotations from former RC 2117.16.

Constitutional issues 1
Court authority and jurisdiction 4
Final order 3
Procedure 2

---

1. Constitutional issues

Provisions of section, as to a hearing, without the intervention of a jury, on a schedule of debts and exceptions, if any thereto, do not violate any constitutional right to trial by jury. In re Blue's Estate (Union 1939) 67 Ohio App. 37, 32 N.E.2d 499, 29 Ohio Law Abs. 161, 14 O.O. 447.

2. Procedure

Where creditor presented its claim to executor as provided by GC 10509-112 (RC 2117.06) and claim was rejected and action was instituted in court of common pleas in accord with provisions of GC 10509-133 (RC 2117.12), and thereafter, exceptions involving same claim were filed against schedule of claims, debts and liabilities under authority of this section, this latter action of creditor was abated by reason of pendency of cause in common pleas court. In re Perkins' Estate (Cuyahoga 1936) 22 Ohio Law Abs. 513.

Attendance at a hearing for creditors who have been notified pursuant to RC 2117.17(B) is not a prerequisite to a creditor's right to a prorated recovery on his claim. In re Estate of Bochik (Cuyahoga 1985) 24 Ohio App.3d 98, 493 N.E.2d 297, 24 O.B.R. 168.

If, within three months after a defendant's death, a claim is properly revived against the administratrix of the defendant's estate in her representative capacity and judgment is entered against the estate, resubmissions of such claim and judgment are not required under RC 2117.06, RC 2117.07 or RC 2117.12, and RC 2117.17 is irrelevant to such a case. Blanchard v. Morgan (Portage 1983) 10 Ohio App.3d 117, 460 N.E.2d 715, 10 O.B.R. 141. Abatement And Revival ⚖ 77

An executor is under no legal duty to disclose to the probate court that a person holding claims against the estate is under legal disability during the period from such executor's appointment until his discharge. In re Sarver's Estate (Franklin 1954) 97 Ohio App. 199, 124 N.E.2d 749, 55 O.O. 453. Executors And Administrators ⚖ 242

Where heirs elected to invoke action of probate court upon validity of allowance of questioned claims contained in schedule of debts, heirs could not, while such proceeding was in process of determination and judgment, elect to requisition the administratrix under statute regarding contest of claim by heir. In re Throckmorton's Estate (Shelby 1941) 36 N.E.2d 792, 34 Ohio Law Abs. 219. Executors And Administrators ⚖ 244

Hearing on a schedule of debts under section is an in rem proceeding. In re Blue's Estate (Union 1939) 67 Ohio App. 37, 32 N.E.2d 499, 29 Ohio Law Abs. 161, 14 O.O. 447.

An administrator is the only proper party in the character of a defendant to a proceeding on exceptions to the account of an administrator to surcharge such administrator. In re Butler's Estate (Ohio 1940) 137 Ohio St. 115, 28 N.E.2d 196, 17 O.O. 440. Executors And Administrators ⚖ 504(7)

When validity of a credit taken by an administrator in his account is challenged by exceptions, duly filed, the burden of establishing the validity of such credit is upon him. In re Butler's Estate (Ohio 1940) 137 Ohio St. 96, 28 N.E.2d 186, 17 O.O. 432. Executors And Administrators ⚖ 506(1)

Where no exceptions have been filed in probate court to a schedule of debts against a decedent's estate as permitted by GC 10509-118 (RC

2117.16) and although the schedule of debts as filed has been approved by probate court and the claims listed therein paid by the administrator, the validity of such claims may still be challenged by exceptions of a legatee to the account of the administrator which shows that the latter has allowed and paid such claims. In re Butler's Estate (Ohio 1940) 137 Ohio St. 96, 28 N.E.2d 186, 17 O.O. 432.

Where a claim has been rejected by an administratrix, the above section does not prevent the operation of GC 10509–136 (RC 2117.14), which requires that suit be brought on such claim against the administratrix within two months after her rejection of the same. Locotosh v. Brothers (Lake 1935) 52 Ohio App. 158, 3 N.E.2d 556, 21 Ohio Law Abs. 521, 6 O.O. 274.

A claimant whose claim has been reduced or rejected by an executor or administrator can bring an action under the provisions of GC 10509–133 (RC 2117.12), or file exceptions to the schedule of debts. In re Czatt's Estate (Ohio Prob. 1933) 30 Ohio NP(NS) 355.

3. Final order

Under section, a probate court's approval of a claim against an estate, on a hearing of a schedule of debts and exceptions filed thereto, is final as to all persons interested in the estate, subject to a right of review and to be vacated or set aside under GC 10501–17 (RC 2101.23), or to be opened up for fraud, collusion or mistake. In re Blue's Estate (Union 1939) 67 Ohio App. 37, 32 N.E.2d 499, 29 Ohio Law Abs. 161, 14 O.O. 447.

Order of probate court entered on hearing of schedule of debts and exceptions thereto, affirming allowance of claims in controversy became final, in absence of an appeal from said order by a party thereto, as to all persons interested in said estate, subject only to statutory right of exceptor and persons voluntarily appearing as parties in said proceeding to have the same set aside for fraud, collusion or mistake, and rights of such persons and other persons interested in estate to have the same vacated or modified under the provisions of GC 10501–17 (RC 2101.33). In re Blue's Estate (Union 1939) 67 Ohio App. 37, 32 N.E.2d 499, 29 Ohio Law Abs. 161, 14 O.O. 447. Executors And Administrators ⇐ 255

Under provisions of section, the finding and order of the probate court overruling exceptions to an item contained in the schedule of debts involving a claim upon which the probate court is authorized by these provisions to act, are final as to parties filing exceptions or otherwise voluntarily entering their appearance, subject only to the right of review or to be opened up for fraud, collusion or mistake. In re Beabout's Estate (Ohio 1940) 136 Ohio St. 412, 26 N.E.2d 211, 16 O.O. 575.

Validity of a claim against an estate cannot be challenged by exceptions of a legatee to the final account of an administrator when such claim had theretofore been allowed and paid following a hearing by the probate court and a valid order overruling the exceptions of such legatee to the claim when duly presented in the schedule of debts, no appeal having been taken from the order overruling the exceptions or any action instituted to set the same aside on the ground of fraud, collusion or mistake. In re Beabout's Estate (Ohio 1940) 136 Ohio St. 412, 26 N.E.2d 211, 16 O.O. 575. Executors And Administrators ⇐ 241

An order of the probate court allowing claims against an estate which substantially and adversely affect the property rights of three beneficiaries of the estate is a binding determination that the claims are valid for federal estate tax purposes. Goodwin's Estate v. C.I.R. (C.A.6 (Ohio) 1953) 201 F.2d 576, 67 Ohio Law Abs. 233, 51 O.O. 73.

4. Court authority and jurisdiction

This section grants to probate court powers in examination of executor or administrator and creditor and its jurisdiction is exhausted when it has ordered that schedule of claims, debts and liabilities be approved and confirmed in accordance with facts of presentment, allowance or rejection of claims as same are produced at hearing on exceptions. In re Perkins' Estate (Cuyahoga 1936) 22 Ohio Law Abs. 513.

The tax commissioner has no authority to overrule a decision by the probate court; thus, where a claim has been made against an estate and held by the probate court to be valid, the tax commissioner may not contest the validity of that claim; he may, however, determine the tax implications of the allowed claim. In re Beasley's Estate (Athens 1980) 70 Ohio App.2d 131, 435 N.E.2d 91, 24 O.O.3d 167. Taxation ⇐ 3455

A probate court cannot assert jurisdiction over an action on a rejected claim through the device of a declaratory judgment or an action for specific performance. Mainline Const. Co. v. Warren (Ohio Prob. 1967) 11 Ohio Misc. 233, 227 N.E.2d 432, 40 O.O.2d 509.

Where services are rendered by an attorney for a widow in effecting a settlement of all her rights and claims in and to the estate of her deceased husband, the probate court has jurisdiction to hear and determine an application by the attorney for the allowance of compensation out of the estate; but, although it may have been fortuitous for the estate that a settlement of many problems may have been effected, such circumstances do not justify payment of attorney fees by the estate. In re Colosimo's Estate (Montgomery 1957) 104 Ohio App. 342, 149 N.E.2d 31, 5 O.O.2d 24.

The probate court has the statutory authority to disapprove, and thus, in effect, order rejected, a claim which the executor had classified as an allowed debt or claim, but it cannot act arbitrarily and this power can be exercised only upon a showing that the executor allowed the claim without due examination as to the validity of such claim, and where there is no evidence offered to refute the conclusion as to validity reached by the executor, the probate court is required to find that the executor acted properly in allowing and classifying the claim. In re Koplin's Estate (Summit 1956) 100 Ohio App. 553, 137 N.E.2d 424, 60 O.O. 421.

Probate court had express authority under section, without the intervention of a jury, to affirm, modify or reverse the action of an executor or administrator as to any items contained in the schedule of debts, except claims on which suit had been brought or which had been referred to referees or disallowed by requisition. In re Hedges' Estate (Marion 1943) 75 Ohio App. 518, 62 N.E.2d 643, 31 O.O. 301. Jury ⇐ 19(7)

Section does not give probate court jurisdiction to review the judgment of an administrator or an executor as to the allowance or rejection of claims. Locotosh v. Brothers (Lake 1935) 52 Ohio App. 158, 3 N.E.2d 556, 21 Ohio Law Abs. 521, 6 O.O. 274. Executors And Administrators ⇐ 250

Where executrix has failed to timely file a schedule of debts and a preliminary notice as to taxes as statutorily required, it was not an abuse of discretion for probate court to order the removal of the executrix for misconduct even though executrix acted under advice from counsel and executrix was prepared at the time of hearing to file all delinquent papers. Baringer v Newell, No. 81–C–48 (7th Dist Ct App, Columbiana, 2–18–82).

The probate court is not precluded by the fact that an executor has allowed a claim from inquiring into the validity of the claim as a proper deduction for inheritance tax purposes. In re Cooke, 93 Abs 311 (Prob, Franklin 1963).

TAXES

2117.18 Taxes or forfeitures

Taxes, penalties, and interest placed on a duplicate or added by the county auditor or the tax commissioner because of a failure to make a return or because of a false or incomplete return for taxation shall be a debt of a decedent and have the same priority and be paid as other taxes. Such taxes, penalties, and interest shall be collectible out of the property of the estate either before or after distribution, by any means provided for collecting other taxes. No distribution or payment of inferior debts or claims shall defeat such collection; but no such tax, penalty, or interest can be added before notice to the executor or administrator, and before an opportunity is given him to be heard. All taxes omitted by the deceased must be charged on the tax lists and duplicate in his name.

In all such additions to the personal tax lists and duplicate, each succeeding tax year shall be considered as beginning at the time of the completion of the annual settlement of the duplicate for the previous year with the county treasurer.

(1982 H 379, eff. 9–21–82; 125 v 903; 1953 H 1; GC 10509–81, 10509–82)

Historical and Statutory Notes

Pre–1953 H 1 Amendments: 114 v 419, 774

Library References

Executors and Administrators ⇐ 212, 261.
Westlaw Topic No. 162.
C.J.S. Executors and Administrators §§ 409, 504, 506 to 510.

Research References

Encyclopedias

OH Jur. 3d Decedents' Estates § 1337, Taxes and Assessments.

Treatises and Practice Aids

Carlin, Baldwin's Ohio Practice, Merrick-Rippner Probate Law § 91:11, Land Sale—to Pay Taxes—State.

Law Review and Journal Commentaries

The Apportionment Doctrine—A Proposed Ohio Estate Tax Apportionment Statute, Note. 41 U Cin L Rev 897 (1972).

Personal Judgment May Not Be Rendered in Ohio for Delinquent General Taxes and Special Assessments on Real Estate, Ansel B. Curtiss. 6 U Cin L Rev 251 (May 1932).

Real Estate Taxes in Ohio Are Charges Ad Rem Only, Ansel B. Curtiss. 10 U Cin L Rev 1 (January 1936).

Notes of Decisions

Omitted property 1
Types of taxes 2

---

1. Omitted property

The term "any omissions of property" was intended to include all omissions past, present and future, and the law authorizes contracts which have a prospective operation. State ex rel Wilson v Lewis, 4 NP(NS) 454, 17 D 370 (Super, Cincinnati 1906), reversed on other grounds by 74 OS 403, 78 NE 523 (1906).

A tax inquisitor may discover the existence of omitted property from inventories filed in the probate court, and is not excluded from furnishing evidence of omitted property to be listed in the name of the decedent. State ex rel. Seymour v. Gilfillan (Ohio Com.Pl. 1905) 15 Ohio Dec. 756, 3 Ohio N.P.(N.S.) 153, affirmed 19 Ohio C.D. 709, 3 Ohio Law Rep. 476, vacated 76 Ohio St. 341, 81 N.E. 437, 118 Am.St.Rep. 884, 4 Ohio Law Rep. 169, 5 Ohio Law Rep. 67.

2. Types of taxes

A municipal income tax ordinance which declares that such taxes may be collected as other debts and that those not paid when due become "a debt due the city from the taxpayer," has the effect of creating a debt once the tax liability is determined. City of Cincinnati v. Degoyer (Ohio Mun. 1968) 16 Ohio Misc. 229, 241 N.E.2d 769, 45 O.O.2d 92, 45 O.O.2d 181, reversed 26 Ohio App.2d 178, 270 N.E.2d 663, 55 O.O.2d 317, affirmed 25 Ohio St.2d 101, 267 N.E.2d 282, 48 A.L.R.3d 1318, 54 O.O.2d 232.

This section applies only to taxes other than real estate taxes. In re Kastelic's Estate (Ohio Com.Pl. 1935) 2 Ohio Supp. 297, 19 Ohio Law Abs. 109, 3 O.O. 164.

2117.19 No allowance to tax inquisitors

For the years during which property is required to be listed in the name of an executor or administrator, no percentage or part of any increased tax on such property of an estate, covered by an inventory required by section 2115.02 of the Revised Code, shall be allowed or paid to a person under a contract for securing for taxation, or putting on the tax list or duplicate, property omitted, or not listed or returned for taxation.

(1953 H 1, eff. 10–1–53; GC 10509–84)

Historical and Statutory Notes

Pre–1953 H 1 Amendments: 114 v 419

Library References

Executors and Administrators ⬄212.
Westlaw Topic No. 162.
C.J.S. Executors and Administrators § 409.

Notes of Decisions

Inventory 1

---

1. Inventory

A tax inquisitor is not entitled to commission on omitted property which has been placed upon the duplicate from information derived from the inventories of the probate court. State ex rel. McGoldrick v. Lewis (Ohio Super. 1901) 12 Ohio Dec. 46.

PAYMENT OF DEBTS

2117.25 Order in which debts to be paid

(A) Every executor or administrator shall proceed with diligence to pay the debts of the decedent and shall apply the assets in the following order:

(1) Costs and expenses of administration;

(2) An amount, not exceeding four thousand dollars, for funeral expenses that are included in the bill of a funeral director, funeral expenses other than those in the bill of a funeral director that are approved by the probate court, and an amount, not exceeding three thousand dollars, for burial and cemetery expenses, including that portion of the funeral director's bill allocated to cemetery expenses that have been paid to the cemetery by the funeral director.

For purposes of this division, burial and cemetery expenses shall be limited to the following:

(a) The purchase of a right of interment;

(b) Monuments or other markers;

(c) The outer burial container;

(d) The cost of opening and closing the place of interment;

(e) The urn.

(3) The allowance for support made to the surviving spouse, minor children, or both under section 2106.13 of the Revised Code;

(4) Debts entitled to a preference under the laws of the United States;

(5) Expenses of the last sickness of the decedent;

(6) If the total bill of a funeral director for funeral expenses exceeds four thousand dollars, then, in addition to the amount described in division (A)(2) of this section, an amount, not exceeding two thousand dollars, for funeral expenses that are included in the bill and that exceed four thousand dollars;

(7) Personal property taxes, claims made under the estate recovery program instituted pursuant to section 5111.11 of the Revised Code, and obligations for which the decedent was personally liable to the state or any of its subdivisions;

(8) Debts for manual labor performed for the decedent within twelve months preceding the decedent's death, not exceeding three hundred dollars to any one person;

(9) Other debts for which claims have been presented and finally allowed.

(B) The part of the bill of a funeral director that exceeds the total of six thousand dollars as described in divisions (A)(2) and (6) of this section, and the part of a claim included in division (A)(8) of this section that exceeds three hundred dollars shall be included as a debt under division (A)(9) of this section, depending upon the time when the claim for the additional amount is presented.

(C) Any natural person or fiduciary who pays a claim of any creditor described in division (A) of this section shall be subrogated to the rights of that creditor proportionate to the amount of the payment and shall be entitled to reimbursement for that amount in accordance with the priority of payments set forth in that division.

(D)(1) Chapters 2113. to 2125. of the Revised Code, relating to the manner in which and the time within which claims shall be presented, shall apply to claims set forth in divisions (A)(2), (6), and (8) of this section. Claims for an expense of administration or for the allowance for support need not be presented. The executor or administrator shall pay debts included in divisions (A)(4) and (7) of this section, of which the executor or administrator has knowledge, regardless of presentation.

(2) The giving of written notice to an executor or administrator of a motion or application to revive an action pending against the decedent at the date of death shall be equivalent to the presentation of a claim to the executor or administrator for the purpose of determining the order of payment of any judgment rendered or decree entered in such an action.

(E) No payments shall be made to creditors of one class until all those of the preceding class are fully paid or provided for. If the assets are insufficient to pay all the claims of one class, the creditors of that class shall be paid ratably.

(F) If it appears at any time that the assets have been exhausted in paying prior or preferred charges, allowances, or claims, those payments shall be a bar to an action on any claim not entitled to that priority or preference.

(2006 H 426, eff. 10–12–06; 2003 H 95, eff. 9–26–03; 2002 H 345, eff. 7–23–02; 1999 H 18, eff. 10–20–99; 1990 H 346, eff. 5–31–90; 1988 S 252; 1977 H 1; 1975 S 145; 1974 H 162; 1973 S 318; 128 v 320; 1953 H 1; GC 10509–121, 10509–122)

Uncodified Law

1990 H 346, § 3, eff. 5–31–90, reads, in part: (A) Sections 1 and 2 of this act shall apply only to the estates of decedents who die on or after the effective date of this act.

Historical and Statutory Notes

Pre–1953 H 1 Amendments: 121 v 115; 119 v 394, § 1; 116 v 385; 114 v 428, 429

Amendment Note: 2006 H 426 substituted "four" for "two" before "thousand dollars, for funeral expenses" and "three" for "two" before "thousand dollars, for burial and cemetery expenses" in division (A)(2); substituted "right" for "place" in division (A)(2)(a); substituted "four" for "two" before "thousand dollars, then, in addition to", "two" for "one" before "thousand dollars, for funeral expenses", and "four" for "two" before "thousand dollars;" in division (A)(2)(6); and substituted "six" for "three" before thousand dollars as described in" in division (B).

Amendment Note: 2003 H 95 inserted ", claims made under the estate recovery program instituted pursuant to section 5111.11 of the Revised Code," in division (A)(7).

Amendment Note: 2002 H 345 rewrote this section, which prior thereto read:

"Every executor or administrator shall proceed with diligence to pay the debts of the decedent, and shall apply the assets in the following order:

"(A) Costs and expenses of administration;

"(B) An amount, not exceeding two thousand dollars, for funeral expenses that are included in the bill of a funeral director, funeral expenses other than those in the bill of a funeral director that are approved by the probate court, and an amount, not exceeding two thousand dollars, for burial and cemetery expenses, including that portion of the funeral director's bill allocated to cemetery expenses that have been paid to the cemetery by the funeral director.

"For purposes of this division, burial and cemetery expenses shall be limited to the following:

"(1) The purchase of a place of interment;

"(2) Monuments or other markers;

"(3) The outer burial container;

"(4) The cost of opening and closing the place of interment;

"(5) The urn.

"(C) The allowance for support made to the surviving spouse, minor children, or both under section 2106.13 of the Revised Code;

"(D) Debts entitled to a preference under the laws of the United States;

"(E) Expenses of the last sickness of the decedent;

"(F) If the total bill of a funeral director for funeral expenses exceeds two thousand dollars, then, in addition to the amount described in division (B) of this section, an amount, not exceeding one thousand dollars, for funeral expenses that are included in the bill and that exceed two thousand dollars;

"(G) Personal property taxes and obligations for which the decedent was personally liable to the state or any of its subdivisions;

"(H) Debts for manual labor performed for the decedent within twelve months preceding the decedent's death, not exceeding three hundred dollars to any one person;

"(I) Other debts for which claims have been presented and finally allowed.

"The part of the bill of a funeral director that exceeds the total of three thousand dollars as described in divisions (B) and (F) of this section, and the part of a claim included in division (H) of this section that exceeds three hundred dollars shall be included as a debt under division (I) of this section, depending upon the time when the claim for the additional amount is presented.

"Chapters 2113. to 2125. of the Revised Code, relating to the manner in which and the time within which claims shall be presented, shall apply to claims set forth in divisions (B), (F), and (H) of this section. Claims for an expense of administration or for the allowance for support need not be presented. The executor or administrator shall pay debts included in divisions (D) and (G) of this section, of which the executor or administrator has knowledge, regardless of presentation.

"The giving of written notice to an executor or administrator of a motion or application to revive an action pending against the decedent at the date of death shall be equivalent to the presentation of a claim to the executor or administrator for the purpose of determining the order of payment of any judgment rendered or decree entered in such an action.

"No payments shall be made to creditors of one class until all those of the preceding class are fully paid or provided for. If the assets are insufficient to pay all the claims of one class, the creditors of that class shall be paid ratably.

"If it appears at any time that the assets have been exhausted in paying prior or preferred charges, allowances, or claims, such payments shall be a bar to an action on any claim not entitled to such priority or preference."

Amendment Note: 1999 H 18 rewrote division (B); deleted "Except as provided in section 2117.251 of the Revised Code," from the beginning of divisions (F) and (I); deleted "and burial" before "expenses" twice in division (F); and made changes to reflect gender neutral language and other nonsubstantive changes.

Legislative Service Commission

1975:

This section would be amended to provide that the new allowance for a spouse and children has the same priority as the current widow's allowance. The maximum amount for debts for manual labor having priority would be increased from $150 to $300. The bill would also change the time limit from four to three months for determining the priority of claims not specifically referred to in the section. Terminology would be changed to reflect new section 2117.20.

Cross References

Allowance for support, 2106.13
Contribution of others toward loss of one devisee's or legatee's property taken for debt, exception, 2107.54
Court costs, 2101.16
Death or incompetence of bank customer, 1304.28
Deceased partner, rights and priority of creditors, 1775.40
Estate recovery program; affidavit of program administrator; release of funds for cost of services provided to medicaid recipient, 2113.041.
Extraordinary services, counsel fees, 2113.36
Representatives commission, 2113.35, 2127.37
Undevised real estate applied to debts, 2107.53

Ohio Administrative Code References

Receipt and use of individual's funds, OAC 5123–9–05

Library References

Executors and Administrators ⟸259.
Westlaw Topic No. 162.
C.J.S. Executors and Administrators §§ 504, 506 to 512.
Baldwin's Ohio Legislative Service, 1990 Laws of Ohio, H 346—LSC Analysis, p 5–87

Research References

Encyclopedias

OH Jur. 3d Decedents' Estates § 470, Ejusdem Generis Rule—Specific vs General.
OH Jur. 3d Decedents' Estates § 1319, Hearing on Allowed Claims.
OH Jur. 3d Decedents' Estates § 1323, Expenses of Administration.
OH Jur. 3d Decedents' Estates § 1326, Claims for Support Furnished by Public or Governmental Agency.
OH Jur. 3d Decedents' Estates § 1339, Expenses of Last Illness.
OH Jur. 3d Decedents' Estates § 1341, Funeral Expenses.
OH Jur. 3d Decedents' Estates § 1342, Funeral Expenses—Amount of Expenses.
OH Jur. 3d Decedents' Estates § 1344, Liability for Funeral Expenses of Spouse.
OH Jur. 3d Decedents' Estates § 1346, Liability for Funeral Expenses of Spouse—Liability of Wife's Estate for Her Expenses.
OH Jur. 3d Decedents' Estates § 1378, Requirements as to Care and Diligence.
OH Jur. 3d Decedents' Estates § 1427, Claims Required to be Presented.
OH Jur. 3d Decedents' Estates § 1432, Claims Expressly Excepted by Statute.
OH Jur. 3d Decedents' Estates § 1435, Claims Known to Representative or Directed to be Paid.
OH Jur. 3d Decedents' Estates § 1439, Filing or Revival of Action Against Representative as Presentation.
OH Jur. 3d Decedents' Estates § 1441, Statute Requiring Presentation of Claims Within One Year.
OH Jur. 3d Decedents' Estates § 1465, Generally; Duty of Representative to Pay Decedent's Debts.
OH Jur. 3d Decedents' Estates § 1466, Debts to be Paid, Generally.
OH Jur. 3d Decedents' Estates § 1471, Statutory Order of Payment.
OH Jur. 3d Decedents' Estates § 1472, Statutory Order of Payment—Funeral Expenses.
OH Jur. 3d Decedents' Estates § 1473, Statutory Order of Payment—Debts Entitled to Preference Under the Laws of the United States.
OH Jur. 3d Decedents' Estates § 1474, Equal Distribution Among Creditors of Same Class.
OH Jur. 3d Decedents' Estates § 1684, Nature, Purpose, and Effect of Allowance.
OH Jur. 3d Decedents' Estates § 1689, Property Out of Which Allowance May be Made.
OH Jur. 3d Decedents' Estates § 1694, Order of Payment of Claims.
OH Jur. 3d Decedents' Estates § 1695, Order of Payment of Claims—Debts Due the United States.
OH Jur. 3d Decedents' Estates § 1698, Payment of Secured Claims.
OH Jur. 3d Decedents' Estates § 1700, Exhaustion of Assets Bars Subordinate Claims.
OH Jur. 3d Public Welfare § 168, Recovery of Medicaid Payments from Recipient or Estate.

Forms

Ohio Forms and Transactions F 30.01, General Form of Will.
Ohio Forms and Transactions KP 30.09, Abatement of Legacies and Devises.

Treatises and Practice Aids

Carlin, Baldwin's Ohio Practice, Merrick-Rippner Probate Law § 2:26, Payment of Debts and Claims—Statutory Preference.
Carlin, Baldwin's Ohio Practice, Merrick-Rippner Probate Law § 2:27, Payment of Debts and Claims—Presentation of Claims.
Carlin, Baldwin's Ohio Practice, Merrick-Rippner Probate Law § 30:9, Drafting a Will—Payment of Debts, Administration Expenses, and Taxes.
Carlin, Baldwin's Ohio Practice, Merrick-Rippner Probate Law § 48:7, Property Liable for Payment of Debts—Personal Property—Primary Liability Altered by Will.
Carlin, Baldwin's Ohio Practice, Merrick-Rippner Probate Law § 75:4, Distribution—Voluntary—Liability—Executor or Administrator.
Carlin, Baldwin's Ohio Practice, Merrick-Rippner Probate Law § 84:1, Creditor's Claims—Introduction.
Carlin, Baldwin's Ohio Practice, Merrick-Rippner Probate Law § 89:4, Payment of Debts—Order of Payment.
Carlin, Baldwin's Ohio Practice, Merrick-Rippner Probate Law § 89:5, Payment of Debts—Preference in Payment.
Carlin, Baldwin's Ohio Practice, Merrick-Rippner Probate Law § 89:6, Payment of Debts—Cost of Administration.
Carlin, Baldwin's Ohio Practice, Merrick-Rippner Probate Law § 89:7, Payment of Debts—Funeral Expenses—General Rule.
Carlin, Baldwin's Ohio Practice, Merrick-Rippner Probate Law § 91:7, Land Sale—to Pay Medical and Funeral Expenses.
Carlin, Baldwin's Ohio Practice, Merrick-Rippner Probate Law § 2:112, Summary Release from Administration Generally.
Carlin, Baldwin's Ohio Practice, Merrick-Rippner Probate Law § 2:121, Administration of Decedent's Estate—Checklist.
Carlin, Baldwin's Ohio Practice, Merrick-Rippner Probate Law § 21:19, Rights of Surviving Spouse to Make Election—Effect of Election—Generally.
Carlin, Baldwin's Ohio Practice, Merrick-Rippner Probate Law § 21:58, Rights of Surviving Spouse—Mansion House—Right to Remain in House for One Year.
Carlin, Baldwin's Ohio Practice, Merrick-Rippner Probate Law § 33:16, Trusts—Medicaid-Qualifying.
Carlin, Baldwin's Ohio Practice, Merrick-Rippner Probate Law § 48:11, Liability for Payment of Claims Against Estate.
Carlin, Baldwin's Ohio Practice, Merrick-Rippner Probate Law § 80:19, Attorney Fees—Facts to be Considered.
Carlin, Baldwin's Ohio Practice, Merrick-Rippner Probate Law § 84:32, Creditor's Claims—Setoff of Barred Claim.
Carlin, Baldwin's Ohio Practice, Merrick-Rippner Probate Law § 89:17, Payment of Debts—Allowance for Support of Surviving Spouse and Minor Children—Preference Under Federal Law.
Carlin, Baldwin's Ohio Practice, Merrick-Rippner Probate Law § 89:18, Payment of Debts—Expenses of Decedent's Last Sickness.
Carlin, Baldwin's Ohio Practice, Merrick-Rippner Probate Law § 89:19, Payment of Debts—Presentation of Claims Affecting Preference.
Carlin, Baldwin's Ohio Practice, Merrick-Rippner Probate Law § 91:11, Land Sale—to Pay Taxes—State.
Carlin, Baldwin's Ohio Practice, Merrick-Rippner Probate Law § 84:39.50, Creditor's Claims—Medicaid Estate Recovery Program.
Carlin, Baldwin's Ohio Practice, Merrick-Rippner Probate Law App B SPF 12.0, Application for Certificate of Transfer.

Law Review and Journal Commentaries

Liability of Husband and Wife's Estate for Funeral Expenses of Wife, Note. 4 U Cin L Rev 486 (November 1930).

The New Right of Subrogation in Creditor's Claims. Walter C. Grosjean, 12 Prob L J Ohio 79 (May/June 2002).

Payment of Debts of Decedent's Estate, Judge Richard B. Metcalf. 52 Title Topics 3 (July 1985).

Personal Judgment May Not Be Rendered in Ohio for Delinquent General Taxes and Special Assessments on Real Estate, Ansel B. Curtiss. 6 U Cin L Rev 251 (May 1932).

Real Estate Taxes in Ohio Are Charges Ad Rem Only, Ansel B. Curtiss. 10 U Cin L Rev 1 (January 1936).

Summary Release: A Solution For Transfer of Small Estate Assets, Walter C. Grosjean. 10 Prob L J Ohio 69 (May/June 2000).

Wills, Probate Practice: Claim for Funeral Expenses, Comment. 7 Ohio St L J 472 (June 1941).

Notes of Decisions

Attorney fees 6
Exceptions 5
Funeral expenses 7
Last illness 8
Procedure; priorities 3
Relation to other statutes 9
Setoff; secured creditors 4
Spousal obligation 2

1. Taxation

Where there are two administrators residing in different counties, the money credit and investments of the estate must be listed for taxation where the administrator having actual possession resides. Brown v. Noble (Ohio 1884) 42 Ohio St. 405, 15 W.L.B. 95.

Taxes accumulating upon a decedent's real estate which the personal representative has no funds to pay are debts for which the land may be ordered sold. Welsh v. Perkins (Ohio 1837) 8 Ohio 52.

The heir is bound to pay the taxes accruing after the death of the intestate. Piatt v St. Clair's Heirs, 6 Ohio 227 (1833).

When in determining federal income tax liability on income derived from personal property, charitable deductions are taken by an executor in computing the taxable income of an estate, the income taxes paid on said income, unless otherwise provided in a decedent's will, are chargeable as a cost of administration, so that all residuary legatees, including the charitable residuary legatees, shall bear the burden of the tax. In re Gamble's Estate (Ohio Prob. 1966) 8 Ohio Misc. 314, 220 N.E.2d 621, 36 O.O.2d 388, 37 O.O.2d 337.

The federal government is not required to comply with the statutes relating to presentment of claims in order to collect social security taxes due from a decedent. Baker v. Charles (Ohio Prob. 1963) 202 N.E.2d 646, 95 Ohio Law Abs. 97, 31 O.O.2d 310.

Whether the surviving spouse takes under the will or under the statute of descent and distribution, the federal estate tax is considered a debt against the entire estate and shall be deducted before a distribution. Ginder v. Ginder (Ohio Prob. 1954) 134 N.E.2d 603, 72 Ohio Law Abs. 277, 82 Ohio Law Abs. 129, 59 O.O. 320. Wills ⇔ 799

For federal tax purposes, state law is controlling as to the deductibility of administrative expenses. Union Commerce Bank v. C.I.R. (C.A.6 (Ohio) 1964) 3 Ohio Misc. 189, 339 F.2d 163, 31 O.O.2d 252.

Under federal statutes, in an insolvent estate of a decedent being administered in Ohio, the claim of United States for income taxes has priority over all claims against estate, except costs and expenses of administration, bill of funeral director, not exceeding $350.00, such other funeral expenses as are approved by court and allowance made to widow and children for their support for twelve months. In re Fackler's Estate (Ohio Prob. 1943) 12 Ohio Supp. 145, 39 Ohio Law Abs. 328, 27 O.O. 232.

Even if Ohio estate taxes were considered a cost of administration when paid by the estate, when that obligation was paid by testator's daughter her claim for reimbursement was a claim against the estate to be considered with other creditor's claims, which were accorded the lowest level of priority. In re Estate of Palasz (Ohio App. 8 Dist., Cuyahoga, 06-13-2002) No. 80211, 2002-Ohio-2960, 2002 WL 1299861, Unreported. Executors And Administrators ⇔ 263

Even if Ohio estate taxes were considered a cost of administration when paid by the estate, when that obligation was paid by testator's daughter her claim for reimbursement was a claim against the estate to be considered with other creditor's claims, which were accorded the lowest level of priority. In re Estate of Palasz (Ohio App. 8 Dist., Cuyahoga, 06-13-2002) No. 80211, 2002-Ohio-2960, 2002 WL 1299861, Unreported. Executors And Administrators ⇔ 263

2. Spousal obligation

The year's allowance to a widow and minor children is a debt of the estate, and payment of such allowance by the executrix is a proper credit on her account. Watts v. Watts (Ohio 1882) 38 Ohio St. 480, 8 W.L.B. 287. Executors And Administrators ⇔ 192

A year's allowance for the support of the widow and her child is a debt for which real estate may be ordered sold by the court. Allen v. Allen's Adm'r (Ohio 1868) 18 Ohio St. 234.

Under the doctrine of ejusdem generis, deceased's will, which authorized the payment out of deceased's TIAA-CREF account for expenses of his last illness, funeral expenses, costs of administration, and claims allowed in the administration of the estate, also authorized the account to be used for the allowance for spousal support, a federal and state income tax, and the costs of preparing those taxes; all of the expenses paid for with the account came from statute that set forth the order of priority in which an executor paid debts and there was no distinction between the items individually listed in the will and the other debts paid with the account. In re Estate of Hernton (Ohio App. 9 Dist., 11-02-2005) 164 Ohio App.3d 306, 842 N.E.2d 104, 2005-Ohio-5805. Wills ⇔ 455

The right of a widow to a year's allowance in the estate of her deceased husband vests immediately upon death, becomes a preferred and secured debt of his estate, and, when it has not been paid to the widow during her lifetime, such allowance survives as an asset of her estate and is includable in the inventory of her estate as a debt due from the estate of her deceased husband, but if an exception to the inventory, based on the running of the statute of limitations against such debt, is filed by several of such children, upon a hearing on exceptions to the inventory the probate court may summarily determine only whether such year's allowance is includable in the inventory as a debt but has no power to determine whether the debt is uncollectible by reason of the statute of limitations. In re Wreede's Estate (Van Wert 1958) 106 Ohio App. 324, 154 N.E.2d 756, 7 O.O.2d 75.

Where a testator bequeaths specific legacies with remainder to individual and charitable legatees, all the residuary legatees, including the charities, bear the burden of the tax. Hall v. Ball (Ohio 1954) 162 Ohio St. 299, 123 N.E.2d 259, 55 O.O. 175.

Where a widow elects to take under the statute of descent and distribution, the amount of the federal estate tax should be deducted before computing the widow's share thereof. (See also Hall v Ball, 162 OS 299, 123 NE(2d) 259 (1954).) Campbell v. Lloyd (Ohio 1954) 162 Ohio St. 203, 122 N.E.2d 695, 55 O.O. 102, certiorari denied 75 S.Ct. 600, 349 U.S. 911, 99 L.Ed. 1246, rehearing denied 75 S.Ct. 870, 349 U.S. 948, 99 L.Ed. 1274.

When a surviving spouse elects to take an intestate share rather than under the will of the deceased spouse, she takes such share free of the burden of any federal estate taxes not directly assessed by reason of her inheritance, and when her statutory share is less than the maximum marital deduction, she takes free of taxes. Miller v. Hammond (Ohio 1952) 156 Ohio St. 475, 104 N.E.2d 9, 46 O.O. 405.

GC 10509–54 (RC 2115.13), which makes provision for a certain amount or percentage of decedent's estate to be set aside in favor of surviving spouse, gives such surviving spouse a claim superior to all unsecured claims, including funeral expenses, costs in probate court and fees of executor and his attorneys, notwithstanding this section, prescribing order in which debts shall be paid. In re Bremer's Estate (Hamilton 1941) 67 Ohio App. 144, 36 N.E.2d 48, 34 Ohio Law Abs. 146, 21 O.O. 150.

After paying the funeral expenses, those of the last sickness, and the expenses of administration, the administrator is justified in paying the allowance to the widow and children as made by the appraisers, and is not liable to the creditors for the amount of a subsequent reduction by the court in such allowance, until he has recovered such amount from the widow. Steward v. Barry (Ohio 1921) 102 Ohio St. 129, 131 N.E. 492, 18 Ohio Law Rep. 542, 18 Ohio Law Rep. 543.

The priority of statutory allowances to a widow and minor son is fixed as of the date of the allowances, and cannot be defeated by a claim for double liability subsequently acquired by a bank against the estate as owner of shares of its stock. Swackhammer v. Fulton (Ohio Com.Pl. 1934) 32 Ohio N.P.N.S. 100.

A widow cannot prevent appraisers from setting off to her provisional alimony, or the administrator from paying it as a preferred debt out of the funds in his hands. Neeley v Neeley, 1 NP(NS) 97, 48 WLB 929 (Prob 1903).

Where the property consumed by the widow is greater than the allowance to her, which was made after her death, the allowance will be held to have been paid. In re McDermott's Estate (Ohio Com.Pl. 1902) 13 Ohio Dec. 390.

The widow and children of a deceased bankrupt are entitled to payment of a year's allowance even though the assets are in the hands of the trustee in bankruptcy. Siegel v. Wells (C.C.A.6 (Ohio) 1932) 55 F.2d 877, 12 Ohio Law Abs. 202, certiorari denied 52 S.Ct. 501, 286 U.S. 549, 76 L.Ed. 1285.

3. Procedure; priorities

An administrator cannot profit by settling accounts against the estate for less than full value, though he acts through an attorney while the attorney acts for him personally or in his official capacity, or for him and others. Cox v. John (Ohio 1877) 32 Ohio St. 532.

Where a lease has not expired at the time of the intestate's death and he had contracted to pay at the expiration of the term for buildings erected by the lessee, his executrix may pay for the buildings and such sum may be collected from the estate. Jackson v. O'Brannin (Ohio 1862) 14 Ohio St. 177.

2117.25
Note 3

Building materials prepared for a homestead prior to the death of the intestate are personal property and contracts for them may be rescinded or affirmed by the administrator as is best for the estate subject to court approval. Gray v. Hawkins's Adm'rx (Ohio 1858) 8 Ohio St. 449, 72 Am.Dec. 600.

Where a creditor's claim has been allowed against an estate and the executor or administrator has funds in hand applicable to its payment, the creditor is by law entitled to its payment within the eighteen months from the date of the administration bond, and an order for further time to collect assets of the estate is no bar to the action. Greer v. Ohio, for Use of Greer (Ohio 1853) 2 Ohio St. 574. Executors And Administrators ⇌ 537(5)

Each heir is subject to the payment of the ancestor's debts to the amount of assets received, and not for a greater sum; therefore, a joint action cannot be maintained against several heirs or devisees where there is no joint contract either express or implied, nor any joint reception of the assets. Spicer v. Giselman (Ohio 1846) 15 Ohio 338.

This section is a provision for payment of debts of deceased and the determination of priority in which they shall be paid; in no sense does it secure payment of any debt but if there is money to pay some but not all of debts, then they are paid in order of priority set forth in statute. Howett v. Howett (Miami 1937) 25 Ohio Law Abs. 150.

Under the doctrine of ejusdem generis, deceased's will, which authorized the payment out of deceased's TIAA-CREF account for expenses of his last illness, funeral expenses, costs of administration, and claims allowed in the administration of the estate, also authorized the account to be used for the allowance for spousal support, a federal and state income tax, and the costs of preparing those taxes; all of the expenses paid for with the account came from statute that set forth the order of priority in which an executor paid debts and there was no distinction between the items individually listed in the will and the other debts paid with the account. In re Estate of Hernton (Ohio App. 9 Dist., 11-02-2005) 164 Ohio App.3d 306, 842 N.E.2d 104, 2005-Ohio-5805. Wills ⇌ 455

Attendance at a hearing for creditors who have been notified pursuant to RC 2117.17(B) is not a prerequisite to a creditor's right to a prorated recovery on his claim. In re Estate of Bochik (Cuyahoga 1985) 24 Ohio App.3d 98, 493 N.E.2d 297, 24 O.B.R. 168.

Where an item in a will recites that which a statute makes mandatory, such cannot be used to prove the testator had a specific intent in its insertion. Spoerl v. Schriever (Butler 1975) 44 Ohio App.2d 161, 336 N.E.2d 851, 73 O.O.2d 159. Wills ⇌ 487(3)

In the absence of a provision to the contrary, where there is intestate personalty resulting from the lapse of a bequest in a will, such shall first be applied to the payment of debts and the costs of administration. Spoerl v. Schriever (Butler 1975) 44 Ohio App.2d 161, 336 N.E.2d 851, 73 O.O.2d 159. Wills ⇌ 827

The personal property of a decedent is primarily liable for his debts where there is one residuary clause applicable to personal property and another to real property. Ginder v. Ginder (Ohio Prob. 1954) 134 N.E.2d 603, 72 Ohio Law Abs. 277, 82 Ohio Law Abs. 129, 59 O.O. 320.

When all preferred claims against estate of deceased person have been paid in accordance with provisions of section, and such estate thereafter becomes insolvent, a pro rata distribution of remaining funds therein must be made among general creditors in accordance with GC 10509–122 (RC 2117.25). Moore v. Midland Buckeye Federal Savings & Loan Ass'n (Mahoning 1943) 72 Ohio App. 323, 51 N.E.2d 758, 27 O.O. 224.

The charges imposed by law on an intestate must first be paid out of the estate as a whole, before payment of the charges imposed on the estate by the will of the testator. Young Men's Christian Ass'n v. Davis (Ohio 1922) 106 Ohio St. 366, 140 N.E. 114, 1 Ohio Law Abs. 84, 20 Ohio Law Rep. 498, 20 Ohio Law Rep. 499, certiorari granted 43 S.Ct. 521, 262 U.S. 745, 67 L.Ed. 1211, rehearing granted 43 S.Ct. 699, 262 U.S. 739, 67 L.Ed. 1208, affirmed 44 S.Ct. 291, 264 U.S. 47, 68 L.Ed. 558. Executors And Administrators ⇌ 212

Where a testator requires by his will that the executor of his estate reject any and all claims by the testator's children and provides that if one of such children should recover upon a claim against the estate, that amount should be deducted from his share under the will; the amount recovered by an assignee of one of the children must be deducted from the assignor's share. Scheets v. Hunter (Ohio 1897) 56 Ohio St. 761, 37 W.L.B. 283, 49 N.E. 1116.

Attorney fees cannot be paid out of funds realized from the sale of lands to pay debts, as they are not included in the costs and expenses "of the sale." Sherman v. Millard (Ohio Cir. 1904) 17 Ohio C.D. 175, 6 Ohio C.C.N.S. 338.

In insolvent estate of decedent administered in Ohio, debts of deceased due to United States shall be paid to extent of assets available therefor after making deductions for costs and expenses of administration, preferred claims for funeral expenses, and amount fixed as year's allowance for support of widow and children of deceased; and after paying claim of United States for debts of deceased to extent of assets available therefor, the assets remaining shall be paid on claims in the priority listed in section, disregarding further consideration of item 4 thereof. In re Fackler's Estate (Ohio Prob. 1943) 12 Ohio Supp. 145, 39 Ohio Law Abs. 328, 27 O.O. 232.

Where a vendee dies leaving an unexecuted contract for purchase of real estate and his administrator for the benefit of the estate cancels it, equity will not thereafter decree specific performance. Howard v. Babcock (Ohio 1836) 7 Ohio 73, PT. II.

"Preferred" claim of division of aid for the aged versus a recipient's estate, under GC 1359–7 (RC 5105.13), has priority only over general claims, but not over the other preferred claims provided for in section. (See also Rogers v Peoples Bldg & Savings Co, 27 Abs 265 (Prob, Greene 1938).) Bush v. Cleaver (Fayette 1939) 29 Ohio Law Abs. 284.

A claim of the division of aid for the aged against a recipient's estate is a preferred claim, which gives it priority over the claims set forth in GC 10509–121. Rogers v Peoples Bldg & Savings Co, 27 Abs 265 (Prob, Greene 1938).

While expenses of a last sickness are made before the death of the decedent and the funeral expenses are made after, both are preferred claims against the estate, and as such should be presented to the executor or administrator for his acceptance or rejection. In re Estate of Miller, 12 D 563 (CP, Hamilton 1902).

4. Setoff; secured creditors

An unfiled chattel mortgage is void as against the creditors of the estate of a deceased mortgagor who died in possession of such mortgaged property, notwithstanding that such mortgage was a valid lien against the mortgagor, and such property becomes assets in the hands of the executor of the deceased mortgagor. Kilbourne v. Fay (Ohio 1876) 29 Ohio St. 264, 23 Am.Rep. 741.

Where an administrator of a vendee for the benefit of the estate rescinds an executory land contract, equity will not disturb the rescission on the application of the heirs after a lapse of many years. Ludlow's Heirs v. Cooper's Devisees (Ohio 1854) 4 Ohio St. 1.

An unsecured creditor does not become a secured creditor against the estate of a deceased contractor by virtue of a mechanic's lien against a property owner. In re Estate of Gilbert (Ohio Com.Pl. 1991) 61 Ohio Misc.2d 452, 579 N.E.2d 811. Mechanics' Liens ⇌ 187

A certificate of judgment cannot operate as a lien on lands of a decedent if the certificate is filed after the death. Ohio Citizens Bank v. Meyer (Henry 1985) 23 Ohio App.3d 74, 491 N.E.2d 319, 23 O.B.R. 138.

Creditors' rights against a debtor become fixed upon the death of the debtor and cannot be improved by a judgment obtained after the death. Ohio Citizens Bank v. Meyer (Henry 1985) 23 Ohio App.3d 74, 491 N.E.2d 319, 23 O.B.R. 138.

In action by administrator against bank to recover money deposited in bank, bank may set off against claim of administrator a contractual obligation of administrator's decedent acquired by bank after commencement of action by administrator, where estate is solvent and allowance of setoff will not disturb statutory order of distribution among creditors. Haefner v. First Nat. Bank of Elmwood Place (Hamilton 1941) 67 Ohio App. 213, 36 N.E.2d 308, 34 Ohio Law Abs. 523, 21 O.O. 197. Executors And Administrators ⇌ 434(1.1)

Where a chattel mortgagor dies in possession of the goods, even after the condition is broken, and the administrator takes possession in his trust capacity, the mortgagee cannot maintain replevin, since the interest of the mortgagee in the property is transferred to the fund arising from the administrator's sale. Lingler v. Wesco (Ohio 1908) 79 Ohio St. 225, 86 N.E. 1004, 128 Am.St.Rep. 714, 6 Ohio Law Rep. 572. Executors And Administrators ⇌ 155

Where mortgaged property is taken possession of by the administrator and sold by him, the mortgagee, even if he had a valid lien thereon, is not authorized to maintain in the court of common pleas an action against the administrator and the purchaser of the property to foreclose the mortgage. Whiteley v. Weber (Ohio Cir. 1887) 1 Ohio C.D. 517.

A widow's allowance does not take precedence upon sale of real estate over judgment liens. Jones v. Allen (Ohio Com.Pl. 1898) 8 Ohio Dec. 338, 6 Ohio N.P. 518.

The costs and expenses for gathering crops growing at the time of the decedent's death which crops were afterwards sold by the administrators to benefit the heirs are proper items, and the administrators are entitled to a credit. In re Turpin's Estate (Ohio Prob. 1887) 5 Ohio Dec. 410, 7 Ohio N.P. 569.

A lien created by the Bankruptcy Act giving the trustee the right of a lien creditor is merely in and of the trustee's duty to collect, hold, and administer the bankrupt estate, and does not create such a lien as would preclude the allowance to the bankrupt's widow. Siegel v. Wells (C.C.A.6 (Ohio) 1932) 55 F.2d 877, 12 Ohio Law Abs. 202, certiorari denied 52 S.Ct. 501, 286 U.S. 549, 76 L.Ed. 1285. Bankruptcy ⇐ 2514

By section 47a (2) of the Federal Bankruptcy Act, the trustee has the favored position of a lien or judgment creditor; former GC 10714 (GC 10509–121, now RC 2117.25) and GC 10715 (GC 10509–122, now RC 2117.25) provided for the order of priority for the payment of debts, of which the allowance to the widow and children was one, payable after funeral, medical, and administration expenses; former GC 10716 (GC 10509–123, now RC 2117.10) expressly provided that creditors' or other persons' liens should not be affected by the distribution provided under former GC 10714 (GC 10509–121, now RC 2117.25) and GC 10715 (GC 10509–122, now RC 2117.25). In re Seigel (D.C.Ohio 1931) 53 F.2d 269, reversed 55 F.2d 877, 12 Ohio Law Abs. 202, certiorari denied 52 S.Ct. 501, 286 U.S. 549, 76 L.Ed. 1285.

Where a bank issues bank checks to a savings account customer who pays for the bank checks with worthless checks from another bank and such customer dies with the savings account as his only asset, the bank issuing the bank checks may not set off its loss against the savings account. Hughes v Alliance Federal Savings and Loan Assn, No. CA–5954 (5th Dist Ct App, Stark, 12–21–82).

5. Exceptions

The general assets of a testator in the hands of an administrator de bonis non are not liable for debts incurred by the executor of the estate in carrying out the business of the testator where he had no authority to do so, even if done in good faith. Lucht v. Behrens (Ohio 1876) 28 Ohio St. 231, 22 Am.Rep. 378.

Removing executor for failing to reimburse beneficiary for decedent's funeral expenses was not an abuse of discretion; beneficiary's exceptions to executor's account and her motion for contempt and removal of executor put executor on notice of her demand for payment, such that executor was obligated to take some action on beneficiary's claim once it was filed, and beneficiary's viewing her mother's body, even given mother's wish to have a closed coffin, was not officious and meddlesome conduct that warranted not reimbursing her. In re Estate of Geanangel (Ohio App. 7 Dist., 02-25-2002) 147 Ohio App.3d 131, 768 N.E.2d 1235, 2002-Ohio-850. Executors And Administrators ⇐ 35(1)

By the terms of RC 5105.24 and the lien-certificate provided for therein in which the wife of a recipient of aid for the aged joins and "grant [s], to the... Division of Aid for the Aged all those rights, liens and uses set forth in" RC Ch 5105 "in the real estate" of such recipient, the lien of the division of aid for the aged takes priority over the claim of the surviving spouse for the property exempt from administration and her year's allowance. Division of Aid for Aged, Dept. of Public Welfare v. Huff (Columbiana 1960) 110 Ohio App. 483, 168 N.E.2d 316, 11 O.O.2d 397, concurring opinion 110 Ohio App. 483, 168 N.E.2d 582, 11 O.O.2d 397.

RC 5105.13 is a special statute covering only the administration of estates in which a claim of the division of aid for the aged is involved; constitutes an exception to RC 2117.25, and governs the amount allowable as a preferred claim for funeral expenses against an estate in which the division of aid for the aged has a claim (a sum not exceeding $300). In re Pfeiffer's Estate (Marion 1959) 109 Ohio App. 331, 165 N.E.2d 795, 11 O.O.2d 132.

GC 1359–7 (RC 5105.13) is a special section covering a particular subject matter and must be read as an exception to this section. 1940 OAG 1853.

Pursuant to GC 1359–7 (RC 5105.13), claim of division of aid for the aged for old age assistance given deceased recipient thereof is preferred claim against estate of such deceased recipient; such preferred claim is prior to all claims specifically set forth in section. 1938 OAG 2111.

6. Attorney fees

A probate court cannot allocate the burden of paying extraordinary attorney fees, incurred in connection with the administration of an estate, entirely to the beneficiary whose actions precipitated such extraordinary fees, since RC 2117.25 and other provisions implicitly require that such expenses are to be paid out of the estate as a whole, and the burden is to be equally shared by the beneficiaries. In re Estate of Coleman (Lucas 1988) 55 Ohio App.3d 261, 564 N.E.2d 116. Executors And Administrators ⇐ 277

Where an administrator is required to file an account of the expenses of his administration, and such account includes an amount due his attorney for services and expenses, and said account is allowed, and the administrator ordered to pay to such attorney the sum so found due, a failure to comply with such order is a breach of the administration bond. Smith v. Rhodes (Ohio 1903) 68 Ohio St. 500, 48 W.L.B. 682, 68 N.E. 7, 1 Ohio Law Rep. 89, 1 Ohio Law Rep. 135, 1 Ohio Law Rep. 493. Executors And Administrators ⇐ 532

Where the expenses of an administrator for attorney fees have been approved and ordered paid by the court, a failure to pay them is a breach of duty and the surety is liable on the administrator's bond. Smith v. Rhodes (Ohio 1903) 68 Ohio St. 500, 48 W.L.B. 682, 68 N.E. 7, 1 Ohio Law Rep. 89, 1 Ohio Law Rep. 135, 1 Ohio Law Rep. 493.

Executors and administrators are personally liable for the fees of attorneys employed by them, and their contracts therefor do not bind the estate. Thomas v. Moore (Ohio 1894) 52 Ohio St. 200, 33 W.L.B. 128, 39 N.E. 803, 2 Ohio Leg. N. 338.

7. Funeral expenses

Former executrix was not entitled to reimbursement for decedent's funeral expenses and other bills paid with estate funds and not with executrix's own personal funds. In re Estate of Lindsay (Ohio App. 7 Dist., Mahoning, 11-02-2005) No. 04-MA-259, 2005-Ohio-5930, 2005 WL 2981647, Unreported. Executors And Administrators ⇐ 488

Third party who paid decedent's funeral expenses was not limited to $4,000 provided by claim statute for funeral expenses, rather, the excess was to be paid out of surviving spouse's share of insolvent estate; it was surviving spouse's duty to pay funeral expenses. In re Estate of Bowens Jackson (Ohio App. 2 Dist., Montgomery, 04-09-2004) No. 20008, 2004-Ohio-1815, 2004 WL 758398, Unreported, appeal not allowed 103 Ohio St.3d 1442, 814 N.E.2d 869, 2004-Ohio-4626. Executors And Administrators ⇐ 214; Executors And Administrators ⇐ 417

Probate court has no power to allow amount in excess of maximum of $350 for funeral expenses under section, paragraph 1 and 7, so as to make the additional amount payable under paragraph 1. (See also Rogers v Peoples Bldg & Savings Co, 27 Abs 265 (Prob, Greene 1938).) Bush v. Cleaver (Fayette 1939) 29 Ohio Law Abs. 284.

In distributing proceeds from decedent's estate, mortgage indebtedness shall be paid from proceeds of sale of real estate before payment of funeral expenses. In re Estate of Cogan (App. 8 Dist., 10-06-1997) 123 Ohio App.3d 186, 703 N.E.2d 858, dismissed, jurisdictional motion overruled 81 Ohio St.3d 1442, 690 N.E.2d 14. Executors And Administrators ⇐ 261

Fraud is shown where three children of a decedent assign the proceeds of their mother's life insurance policy to a mortuary to secure payment of its services, but one of the children presents only the life insurance policy naming the children as beneficiaries to the insurer, and although the mortuary may make a claim against the estate to recover the value of its services, the assignment is valid and the children are liable for their one-third share of the funerary expenses; the child who presented the policy for payment absent the assignment shall bear all interest costs as his action was taken without the consent of the other beneficiaries but because there is no intent to permanently deprive the mortuary of payment, punitive damages are unwarranted. Busse & Borgmann Co. v. Muse (Ohio Mun. 1991) 62 Ohio Misc.2d 60, 590 N.E.2d 913.

A personal representative of a deceased, liable for funeral expenses of the deceased under the statute, may recover such expenses for the benefit of the estate from a tort feasor who negligently caused the death. Adams v. Malik (Lorain 1957) 106 Ohio App. 461, 155 N.E.2d 237, 7 O.O.2d 196.

Where an estate is insolvent because of a claim of the department of public welfare, the funeral director can receive a maximum of $300.00 ahead of the state and is a general creditor as to any amount in excess of $300.00. In re Young's Estate (Ohio Prob. 1956) 140 N.E.2d 792, 74 Ohio Law Abs. 129.

An administrator may bring an action for recovery of funeral expenses against one whose wrongful act is alleged to have caused the decedent's death. Hunter v. McKinney (Ohio Com.Pl. 1951) 101 N.E.2d 810, 69 Ohio Law Abs. 237, 46 O.O. 17.

Section does not require the approval of probate court to the allowance of a claim of a funeral director in excess of $350 founded on a contract made with the decedent in his lifetime, since such a contract fixing a price

2117.25 Note 7

in excess of $350 for services rendered by the funeral director is valid. Schroyer v. Hopwood (Franklin 1940) 65 Ohio App. 443, 30 N.E.2d 440, 32 Ohio Law Abs. 511, 19 O.O. 45.

The common law liability of a husband for the funeral expenses of his wife still exists and may be enforced, notwithstanding her duly probated will directs that her funeral expenses shall be paid out of her own estate. Lee v. Hempy (Seneca 1929) 35 Ohio App. 402, 172 N.E. 421, 8 Ohio Law Abs. 155, 31 Ohio Law Rep. 246.

A probate judge has a duty to scan closely the amounts claimed to have been paid for funeral expenses, and in the absence of statutory or testamentary provisions the allowance for such expenditures must be reasonable considering the amount of the estate and the station in life of the deceased; if extravagant and unreasonable, the expenses should be disallowed even as against legatees and next of kin. Kroll v. Close (Ohio 1910) 82 Ohio St. 190, 92 N.E. 29, 8 Ohio Law Rep. 70.

Where a deceased, in her last illness, had called a physician, and her executor had purchased a coffin and other articles for her funeral, such executor may properly allow such expenses and pay them from the assets of the estate, notwithstanding that the testatrix left a husband surviving owning property. McClellan v. Filson (Ohio 1886) 44 Ohio St. 184, 15 W.L.B. 273, 5 N.E. 861, 58 Am.Rep. 814.

Where a decedent who was a simple and frugal man leaves an estate of eight hundred dollars, an expenditure of one hundred fifty dollars for a casket is extravagant and unreasonable and should be disallowed notwithstanding the consent of the sole heir. In re Kaercher's Estate (Ohio Prob. 1908) 6 Ohio NP(NS) 459, 52 W.L.B. 107.

Where a wife was living separate and apart from her husband and died during the pendency of a divorce action and after an allowance for alimony pendente lite had been made to her, the husband is liable for the funeral expenses. Eveland & Motsinger v. Sherman (Ohio Com.Pl. 1910) 21 Ohio Dec. 726, 9 Ohio N.P.N.S. 559.

Where a husband and wife are both possessed of ample estates, and the husband pays the funeral expenses of his wife out of his own money, he is not entitled to reimbursement from his wife's estate, since both statute and common law recognize the duty of the husband to pay the expenses of his wife's funeral as part of her support. Phillips v. Tolerton (Ohio Com.Pl. 1908) 20 Ohio Dec. 249, 9 Ohio N.P.(N.S.) 565, affirmed 82 Ohio St. 403, 92 N.E. 1121, 7 Ohio Law Rep. 645.

Parents who agree to pay their son's funeral and burial expenses at the request of his wife who is legally responsible to pay such expenses but does not have the money to do so are entitled to reimbursement from the deceased's estate if monies are available. Osborne v Osborne, 114 App(3d) 412, 683 NE(2d) 365 (Greene 1996).

Where an executor or administrator voluntarily or under process pays the funeral expenses of a deceased wife out of her estate, the estate is not entitled to reimbursement from her husband. In re Guthrie's Estate (Ohio Prob. 1931) 28 Ohio NP(NS) 447.

8. Last illness

Nursing home and pharmacy expenses incurred to treat the decedent's chronic illnesses and before decedent was released to his home were not entitled to priority treatment as last illness expenses, given that stroke, from which decedent never recovered and which prevented decedent from resuming independent life, occurred some two months later; however, expenses actually incurred during "last illness" were entitled to priority. In re Estate of Wilson (Ohio Com.Pl., 10-25-1995) 75 Ohio Misc.2d 11, 662 N.E.2d 104. Executors And Administrators ⇐ 261

Where decedent left the residue of her property to the person who cared for her during her last illness, such last illness occurred during the one day period following a coronary occlusion and preceding her death, and no one was entitled to the bequest. Holmes v. Krause (Ohio Prob. 1954) 123 N.E.2d 755, 69 Ohio Law Abs. 337, 56 O.O. 272.

The surviving husband, rather than the deceased wife's estate, is liable for the expenses of her last illness. In re Shields' Estate (Ohio Prob. 1953) 116 N.E.2d 828, 67 Ohio Law Abs. 457.

The fact that by statute a deceased wife's estate is liable for the expenses of her last sickness does not modify husband's obligation with regard to medical services furnished the wife. Heym v. Juhasz (Cuyahoga 1943) 68 N.E.2d 119, 45 Ohio Law Abs. 571. Husband And Wife ⇐ 19(16)

Fact that by reason of section, estate of a deceased wife is liable for expenses of her last sickness, does not in any way modify husband's obligation with regard to medical services furnished his wife, if he would otherwise be liable for them. Heym v. Juhasz (Cuyahoga 1943) 68 N.E.2d 119, 45 Ohio Law Abs. 571. Husband And Wife ⇐ 19(16)

Where a physician, for a period of several months, treated a patient for a particular disease, and upon discontinuance of the treatment the patient resumed her usual occupation for nearly a year, at the end of which period treatments for the same disease were again resumed by the same physician, the fees for the treatments given prior to the interim when she ceased to be a patient and resumed work, are not "expenses of the last sickness," within the meaning of section, so as to be a preferred claim against the assets of the estate of the patient, although the disease of which the patient died was that for which the physician first examined and treated her. Murphy v. Langa (Lucas 1939) 62 Ohio App. 192, 23 N.E.2d 516, 15 O.O. 500. Executors And Administrators ⇐ 261

A husband is liable for medical services rendered to his wife unless she bound her estate for them by special contract, and this is not shown by an averment that they were rendered at her special instance and request; nor is he relieved by a provision in her will that all her just debts be paid; nor by former GC 10714 (GC 10509–121, now RC 2117.25) and GC 10715 (GC 10509–122, now RC 2117.25), requiring executors to apply assets, first, to pay funeral and last sickness expenses. Withrow v. Boone (Ohio Com.Pl. 1914) 25 Ohio Dec. 402, 16 Ohio N.P.N.S. 506.

9. Relation to other statutes

Legislature, in enacting this section, had in contemplation a larger group of obligations than was anticipated in GC 10510–2 (RC 2127.02); the two sections were enacted at same time and must be construed in light of each other, and with an intention to make both of them operative. McDonald v. McDonald (Ohio Prob. 1936) 1 Ohio Supp. 327, 20 Ohio Law Abs. 421, 5 O.O. 132. Statutes ⇐ 223.2(12)

2117.251 Liability for funeral expenses when irrevocable preneed funeral contract purchased

A claim under the bill of a funeral director pursuant to section 2117.25 of the Revised Code arises subsequent to the death of the decedent and is not in satisfaction of a personal obligation of the individual during the individual's lifetime. If a decedent during the decedent's lifetime has purchased an irrevocable preneed funeral contract pursuant to section 1111.19 of the Revised Code, then those provisions of section 2117.25 of the Revised Code that relate to the bill of a funeral director, including divisions (A) and (B) of that section, do not apply to the estate of the decedent and the estate is not liable for the funeral expenses of the decedent.

(2006 H 426, eff. 10–12–06)

Historical and Statutory Notes

Ed. Note: Former RC 2117.251 repealed by 1999 H 18, eff. 10–20–99; 1996 H 538, eff. 1–1–97; 1990 H 346, eff. 5–31–90.

Research References

Encyclopedias

OH Jur. 3d Decedents' Estates § 1341, Funeral Expenses.
OH Jur. 3d Decedents' Estates § 1471, Statutory Order of Payment.
OH Jur. 3d Decedents' Estates § 1472, Statutory Order of Payment—Funeral Expenses.

Treatises and Practice Aids

Carlin, Baldwin's Ohio Practice, Merrick-Rippner Probate Law § 89:4, Payment of Debts—Order of Payment.
Carlin, Baldwin's Ohio Practice, Merrick-Rippner Probate Law § 89:7, Payment of Debts—Funeral Expenses—General Rule.

2117.27 Vendor's lien not preferred

A vendor's lien not disclosed of record shall not, after the death of the vendee, have priority as against general creditors of the deceased.

(1953 H 1, eff. 10–1–53; GC 10509–126)

Historical and Statutory Notes

Pre–1953 H 1 Amendments: 114 v 429

Library References

Executors and Administrators ⚖ 261, 264(1).
Westlaw Topic No. 162.
C.J.S. Executors and Administrators §§ 397, 504, 506 to 510.

Research References

Encyclopedias

OH Jur. 3d Decedents' Estates § 1471, Statutory Order of Payment.
OH Jur. 3d Real Property Sales & Exchanges § 161, Persons Subject to Lien, Generally—Statutory Requirements.

Treatises and Practice Aids

Kuehnle and Levey, Ohio Real Estate Law and Practice § 33:7, Mortgages—Vendor's Lien.

2117.28 Debts not due

Debts not due may, and on demand of the creditor shall, if assets are available therefor, be paid by the executor or administrator according to the class to which they belong. If the debt does not bear interest before maturity, it shall be discounted at the legal rate of interest; otherwise the stipulated rate of interest shall be paid to time of payment. If a creditor whose claim is not due refuses to accept payment as provided in this section, the executor or administrator shall set aside assets to satisfy such claim. The sufficiency of such assets and the manner and place of holding and preserving the same shall be first approved by the probate judge after notice to the creditor, and if such assets thereafter become insufficient to pay such claim in full because of depreciation or loss without fault of the executor or administrator, neither the executor nor administrator nor the remaining assets of the estate shall be liable to such creditor by reason thereof.

After setting aside such assets, the executor or administrator may proceed to make payment and distribution of the remaining assets of the estate and to settle the same without recourse by such creditor to the assets so distributed.

(1953 H 1, eff. 10–1–53; GC 10509–124)

Historical and Statutory Notes

Pre–1953 H 1 Amendments: 119 v 394, § 1; 116 v 385; 114 v 429

Cross References

Distribution of assets, provision for rejected claims, liabilities of beneficiary on unsatisfied claims, 2113.53

Library References

Executors and Administrators ⚖ 202.2, 261.
Westlaw Topic No. 162.
C.J.S. Executors and Administrators §§ 405, 504, 506 to 510.

Research References

Encyclopedias

OH Jur. 3d Decedents' Estates § 1466, Debts to be Paid, Generally.
OH Jur. 3d Decedents' Estates § 1467, Debts to be Paid, Generally—Debts Not Due.
OH Jur. 3d Decedents' Estates § 1629, Prerequisites to Distribution—Making Provisions for Debts.
OH Jur. 3d Decedents' Estates § 1659, Application to Provide for Claims Not Paid.

Treatises and Practice Aids

Carlin, Baldwin's Ohio Practice, Merrick-Rippner Probate Law § 89:20, Application to Set Aside Assets for Payment of Debts Not Due—Form.
Carlin, Baldwin's Ohio Practice, Merrick-Rippner Probate Law § 89:21, Entry to Set Aside Assets to Pay Debts Not Due—Form.
Carlin, Baldwin's Ohio Practice, Merrick-Rippner Probate Law § 92:12, Sale of Land Subject to Encumbrances—Release and Satisfaction of Liens Against Real Property.

Notes of Decisions

Claims not covered 2
Court's authority 1

---

1. Court's authority

Section, conferring power to pay debts not due, carries authority to allow a sale of real estate for the purpose, especially if the creditor is willing to accept the money. Hunter v. Yocum (Ohio Com.Pl. 1914) 27 Ohio Dec. 31, 18 Ohio N.P.N.S. 14.

The probate court has exclusive jurisdiction over the subject matter of an estate and such court, incident to the exercise of such power, may order the cancellation of a mortgage securing a note not yet due, and the common pleas court has no jurisdiction to order the payment of such note. Denmead v. Sharp (Ohio Com.Pl. 1903) 14 Ohio Dec. 300.

2. Claims not covered

Claim against estate of a lessee of a ninety-nine year lease, renewable forever, for installments of rent which become due after death of such lessee, is not a "debt not due" within meaning of that phrase as used in section, which provides for the payment of "debts not due," where the lessee during his lifetime had assigned the lease with the consent of the lessors, and in such case there is no privity of estate between the lessors and lessee after the assignment of the lease, and the lessee's estate will not be impounded in order to secure the lessors in the future installments of rent. Meek v. City Nat. Bank & Trust Co. (Franklin 1940) 65 Ohio App. 349, 30 N.E.2d 347, 32 Ohio Law Abs. 201, 18 O.O. 523. Executors And Administrators ⚖ 202.2.

Section only applies to claims which have been allowed, and which are not disputed by anyone, but which are not due. In re Method's Estate (Ohio Prob. 1936) 2 Ohio Supp. 225, 26 Ohio Law Abs. 209, 10 O.O. 489.

2117.29 Beneficiary taking subject to mortgage

When the only debts of an estate remaining unpaid are secured by liens on property of the estate, the devisees, legatees, or heirs entitled to receive such property may be permitted to take the same subject to such liens, if all the lienholders consent and waive recourse to all the other assets of the estate in the event such property so taken is insufficient to pay the debts secured by such liens.

(129 v 582, eff. 1–10–61; 1953 H 1; GC 10509–132)

Historical and Statutory Notes

Pre–1953 H 1 Amendments: 119 v 394, § 1; 114 v 430

Library References

Descent and Distribution ⚖ 129.
Wills ⚖ 840.
Westlaw Topic Nos. 124, 409.
C.J.S. Descent and Distribution §§ 114, 119.
C.J.S. Wills §§ 1943, 1949 to 1956, 1958 to 1969, 1971 to 1972.

Research References

Encyclopedias

OH Jur. 3d Decedents' Estates § 1335, Mortgages.
OH Jur. 3d Decedents' Estates § 1629, Prerequisites to Distribution—Making Provisions for Debts.

Treatises and Practice Aids

Carlin, Baldwin's Ohio Practice, Merrick-Rippner Probate Law § 89:22, Application for Release of Estate by Mortgagee—Form.
Carlin, Baldwin's Ohio Practice, Merrick-Rippner Probate Law § 89:23, Entry of Release of Estate by Mortgagee—Form.

Notes of Decisions

Consent 1
Unrecorded mortgage 2

1. Consent

A son who inherits mortgaged real property from his parents is not personally liable on the parents' mortgage where the bank does not consent to a transfer of the mortgage, and where there is no consent the son is not entitled under RC 2117.29 to take the property subject to the mortgage; the fact the bank accepted the son's payments until he ceased to make them does not estop the bank from denying the son's liability on the mortgage where the bank was unaware of the transfer and did not know the son was making his parents' payments. In re Wilkinson (Bkrtcy. N.D.Ohio 1989) 99 B.R. 366.

2. Unrecorded mortgage

Mortgage on property owned by mortgagor who died three months after executing promissory note and mortgage was valid, and thus mortgagor's heirs took the property subject to the mortgage lien, even though mortgage was not recorded until seven and a half months after mortgagor's death; mortgage and note were enforceable against mortgagor during her lifetime even if not recorded, and purpose of recording was simply to put other lien holders on notice and prioritize liens. GMAC Mtge. Corp. v. McElroy (Ohio App. 5 Dist., Stark, 06-06-2005) No. 2004-CA-00380, 2005-Ohio-2837, 2005 WL 1364580, Unreported. Mortgages ⇐ 173

SUITS AGAINST EXECUTOR OR ADMINISTRATOR

2117.30 Time for filing suits against estate

No suit shall be brought against an executor or administrator by a creditor of the decedent or by any other party interested in the estate until after five months from the time of the appointment of the executor or administrator, or the expiration of the further time allowed by the probate court for the collection of the assets of the estate, except in the following cases:

(A) On claims rejected in whole or in part;

(B) For the enforcement of a lien against or involving title to specific property;

(C) For the recovery of a claim that would not be affected by the insolvency of the estate;

(D) On account of fraud, conversion, or concealment of assets;

(E) Any other action as to which a different rule is prescribed by statute.

When an executor or administrator dies, resigns, or is removed without having fully administered the estate of the deceased, the time between his death, resignation, or removal and the appointment of a successor shall be excluded in computing the five months or longer period provided in this section. In any event, his successor shall not be held to answer the suit until after the expiration of four months from the date of the successor's appointment, or a further time allowed him by the court for the collection of the assets of the estate.

(1975 S 145, eff. 1-1-76; 1970 S 185; 1953 H 1; GC 10509-138)

Historical and Statutory Notes

Pre-1953 H 1 Amendments: 119 v 394, § 1; 116 v 385; 114 v 432

Cross References

Action on rejected claim barred, 2117.12
Fiduciary refusing payment or distribution, limitation period on claim, 2109.59
Personal use of trust property by fiduciary prohibited, action for loss to be brought within one year, 2109.43

Library References

Executors and Administrators ⇐ 437(2) to 437(4).
Westlaw Topic No. 162.
C.J.S. Executors and Administrators §§ 747, 749 to 768.

Research References

Encyclopedias

OH Jur. 3d Decedents' Estates § 1769, Period During Which Actions Are Prohibited.
OH Jur. 3d Decedents' Estates § 1770, Period During Which Actions Are Prohibited—Appointment of Successor Representative.
OH Jur. 3d Fiduciaries § 219, Statute of Limitations.
OH Jur. 3d Mortgages & Deeds of Trust § 291, Time When Right Accrues.

Treatises and Practice Aids

Carlin, Baldwin's Ohio Practice, Merrick-Rippner Probate Law § 84:3, Creditor's Claims—Form of Claim.
Carlin, Baldwin's Ohio Practice, Merrick-Rippner Probate Law § 75:12, Distribution—Upon Application—Enforcement.
Carlin, Baldwin's Ohio Practice, Merrick-Rippner Probate Law § 75:34, Complaint for Distribution—Form.
Carlin, Baldwin's Ohio Practice, Merrick-Rippner Probate Law § 84:29, Creditor's Claims—Statute of Limitations.

Law Review and Journal Commentaries

Avoiding probate of decedents' estates, Gilbert A. Sheard. 36 U Cin L Rev 70 (Winter 1967).

Mortgage Foreclosure in Ohio When Fee Owner is Deceased, Leonard C. Hirsch. 36 Ohio L Rep 330 (May 9, 1932).

Notes of Decisions

Interest rate 2
Mandatory requirements 1
Rejection 3
Replevin 4
Statute of limitations 5

1. Mandatory requirements

When an action is brought by the filing of a complaint, within the statute of limitations, complainant has one year thereafter in which to cause the appointment of a suitable personal representative and obtain service of summons against him. Hayden v. Ours (Ohio Com.Pl. 1975) 44 Ohio Misc. 62, 337 N.E.2d 183, 73 O.O.2d 224. Limitation Of Actions ⇐ 83(2)

The filing of a petition against an administrator of a decedent's estate, setting forth a cause of action against the estate within four months of the administrator's appointment and accompanied by service of summons and a copy of the petition upon the administrator, constitutes a valid presentation of plaintiff's claim to the administrator and meets the requirements of RC 2117.06. Fortelka v. Meifert (Ohio 1964) 176 Ohio St. 476, 200 N.E.2d 318, 27 O.O.2d 439. Executors And Administrators ⇐ 227(1)

The filing of a petition in an action against an administratrix which contains the address of the plaintiff and sets forth a cause of action on a claim of negligence against the estate of defendant's decedent, which claim, under the facts alleged therein, will not be affected by the insolvency of the estate and which claim is based on facts occurring prior to the decedent's death, and the service of summons and a copy of the petition upon the administratrix within four months of her appointment, is a compliance with the mandatory requirements of RC 2117.06. Fortelka v. Meifert (Cuyahoga 1963) 120 Ohio App. 294, 193 N.E.2d 170, 93 Ohio Law Abs. 1, 27 O.O.2d 175, appeal certified to 120 Ohio App. 294, 193 N.E.2d 305, 93 Ohio Law Abs. 8, 27 O.O.2d 78, affirmed 176 Ohio St. 476, 200 N.E.2d 318, 27 O.O.2d 439.

Institution of a suit against an administrator within four months of his appointment upon a claim based on decedent's negligence which by terms of his insurance would not be barred by his bankruptcy constitutes substantial performance of the requirements for presentment of a claim. Simmons v. Bartley (Ohio Com.Pl. 1960) 177 N.E.2d 77, 86 Ohio Law Abs. 321, 19 O.O.2d 335.

Presentment of a claim for injuries suffered in a motor vehicle accident to decedent's insurer does not constitute a presentment of the claim to the administrator in writing. Simmons v. Bartley (Ohio Com.Pl. 1960) 177 N.E.2d 77, 86 Ohio Law Abs. 321, 19 O.O.2d 335.

Where a plaintiff in a personal injury action filed suit against the administrator of the defendant's estate two days before the running of the statute of limitations without presenting a claim to him, such petition is demurrable. Parrish v. McKee (Ohio Com.Pl. 1956) 135 N.E.2d 486, 73 Ohio Law Abs. 65, 59 O.O. 316.

Section is not violated by failure of plaintiffs to aver when administrator was appointed. Roberts v. Hickerson (Morgan 1936) 36 N.E.2d 282, 26 Ohio Law Abs. 616, 11 O.O. 471.

In a proceeding to enforce liability of a deceased surety on a cost bond, the estate of such surety having passed to his heir and distributee, although it had not been fully settled, a judgment against the administrator is proper, and not a judgment against the heir. McClaskey v. Barr (C.C.S.D.Ohio 1897) 79 F. 408. Descent And Distribution ⇔ 139; Executors And Administrators ⇔ 423

2. Interest rate

A general legacy bears interest at the legal rate from the end of nine months from the date of the issuance of letters of appointment from the probate court to the executor, unless it be clearly apparent that the testator did not so intend, and a legatee is entitled to such interest from said date, unless the will provides otherwise, regardless of the pendency of a contest delaying the settlement of an estate and the participation in that contest by the legatees claiming interest; interest upon arrearages of annuities is recoverable from the time the installment of annuities became due and payable, which time shall be determined from the intent of the testator as shown by the terms of the will which created the annuity. In re Rothschild's Estate (Ohio Prob. 1948) 114 N.E.2d 143, 66 Ohio Law Abs. 237, 51 O.O. 110. Wills ⇔ 734(4); Wills ⇔ 734(8)

A general legacy bears interest at the legal rate from the expiration of one year from the date of notice of the appointment of the executor, unless it is clearly apparent that the testator did not so intend. Kunneke v. Mapel (Ohio 1899) 60 Ohio St. 1, 41 W.L.B. 223, 53 N.E. 259.

3. Rejection

When an administrator rejects a claim he starts in motion a new statute of limitations. Parrish v. McKee (Ohio Com.Pl. 1956) 135 N.E.2d 486, 73 Ohio Law Abs. 65, 59 O.O. 316.

Where suit is brought on a claim within eighteen months it must appear that the claim has been rejected. Morgan v. Bartlette (Ohio Cir. 1888) 2 Ohio C.D. 244.

4. Replevin

A person claiming ownership of certain chattels may bring a replevin action in common pleas court to recover possession of such property from the administrator of an estate who is wrongfully detaining it, for the reason that such owner is not interested in the inventory and has no claim against the estate. Service Transport Co. v. Matyas (Ohio 1953) 159 Ohio St. 300, 112 N.E.2d 20, 42 A.L.R.2d 413, 50 O.O. 298.

An alleged owner cannot ordinarily bring a replevin action in common pleas court against an executor or administrator of an estate in the course of administration in probate court. Service Transport Co. v. Matyas (Cuyahoga 1952) 108 N.E.2d 741, 63 Ohio Law Abs. 236, 63 Ohio Law Abs. 244, reversed 159 Ohio St. 300, 112 N.E.2d 20, 42 A.L.R.2d 413, 50 O.O. 298.

5. Statute of limitations

When an individual chargeable with negligence dies in the episode resulting from his own lack of care, or within the day immediately thereafter, an action may be brought by the filing of a complaint against him within the period of the statute of limitations where no administration of his estate is had. Hayden v. Ours (Ohio Com.Pl. 1975) 44 Ohio Misc. 62, 337 N.E.2d 183, 73 O.O.2d 224. Limitation Of Actions ⇔ 83(2)

Where a claim has not been presented within the four months prescribed by statute, the proper procedure is to file a petition or application for permission to reinstate the claim, and upon failure to do so, the claim is barred. Wilcox v. Ceschiat (Ohio Com.Pl. 1960) 179 N.E.2d 544, 87 Ohio Law Abs. 225.

Absence of a fiduciary against whom the federal government may bring an action to collect the unpaid tax liability tolls the six-year period of limitation for the bringing of an action provided by Internal Revenue Code of 1954, 26 USC 6502, inasmuch as under applicable Ohio probate law both a claim and an action against an estate may only proceed against a fiduciary of an estate, so that the absence of appointment of a fiduciary tolls the time in which claims may be presented against the estate. U. S. v. Besase (N.D.Ohio 1970) 29 Ohio Misc. 166, 319 F.Supp. 1064, 57 O.O.2d 51.

2117.31 Estate of deceased joint debtor

When two or more persons are indebted in a joint contract, or upon a judgment founded on such contract, and either of them dies, his estate shall be liable therefor as if the contract had been joint and several, or as if the judgment had been against himself alone. This section shall not affect the rights of a surety, when certified as such, in a judgment rendered jointly against him and his principal.

(1953 H 1, eff. 10–1–53; GC 10509–139)

Historical and Statutory Notes

Pre–1953 H 1 Amendments: 114 v 432

Library References

Executors and Administrators ⇔203.
Westlaw Topic No. 162.
C.J.S. Executors and Administrators § 396.

Research References

Encyclopedias

OH Jur. 3d Actions § 120, Construction and Application of Survival Statute, Generally.
OH Jur. 3d Decedents' Estates § 1331, Claims Against Estate of Joint Debtor.
OH Jur. 3d Decedents' Estates § 1777, Action on Joint Contract.
OH Jur. 3d Parties § 33, Persons Jointly Liable on Contract—Effect of Death of Joint Contractor.

Notes of Decisions

Common law rule abrogated 1
Contribution from estate 3
Notes and negotiable instruments 5
Partnerships 2
Procedure 4

1. Common law rule abrogated

This section abrogates the common law principle that the death of one of the joint makers of an obligation extinguished all remedy at law against his estate; the estate is now made liable in the same manner as if the contract had been joint and several. Burgoyne v. Ohio Life Ins. & Trust Co. (Ohio 1855) 5 Ohio St. 586.

This section was intended to abrogate common law rule which made joint liability on contract cease as to joint liability, at death of one jointly liable, and to make estate of such deceased person responsible as though liability had been joint and several, but there is no language indicative of purpose to affect power of attorney to enter one's appearance and confess judgment. Griffeth v. Bender (Crawford 1935) 19 Ohio Law Abs. 135.

This section was no doubt enacted to alleviate the harsh rule of the common law that death of a joint maker of an obligation extinguished all remedy at law against his estate. Simon v. Rudner (Stark 1932) 43 Ohio App. 38, 182 N.E. 650, 12 Ohio Law Abs. 705.

Common law liability of surviving joint obligors is in no way affected by section, such statute merely creating a liability against estate of a deceased obligor which did not theretofore exist. Yoder v Medbury–Ward Co, 10 Abs 493 (App, Lucas 1931).

2. Partnerships

Where partners are indebted, and one of them dies, the only remedy at common law was against the surviving partner, but this section changed this rule so that the administrator of a deceased partner could be sued on the claim as well. Weil v. Guerin (Ohio 1884) 42 Ohio St. 299.

Where a testator's will provides that after his death his partner should carry on the business for two years for the joint benefit of the estate and the said co-partner, only the business then conducted by the firm and the capital engaged therein so far as the testator's interest is concerned are liable for the debts contracted by such co-partner, not the testator's individual estate. Covington City Bank v Wight's Executors, 4 NP 173, 6 D 350 (CP, Montgomery 1897). Partnership ⇐ 180; Partnership ⇐ 187; Partnership ⇐ 255(3)

Unless there is some provision in partnership articles to provide otherwise, death of one partner dissolves firm and upon death of one of two or more joint defendants, right of action becomes joint and several and one may maintain an action either severally or jointly. Fechheimer v Kiefer, 5 Abs 265 (App, Hamilton 1927).

Where a member of an insolvent partnership dies, the rule giving priority in his assets to individual creditors is not changed. Williams v Bradley, 7 CC 227, 4 CD 570 (Butler 1892).

A judgment against an administrator of a deceased partner may be had on a partnership judgment for a firm debt. Williams v Bradley, 5 CC 114, 3 CD 58 (Butler 1890).

3. Contribution from estate

Where a surviving joint obligor on a note has made no payment on the obligation, such obligor is not entitled to contribution from the estate of the deceased obligor for half of the obligation. In re McClintock (Ohio Com.Pl. 1978) 58 Ohio Misc. 5, 388 N.E.2d 762, 12 O.O.3d 60. Executors And Administrators ⇐ 217

A surviving joint obligor's right to contribution from the estate of the deceased joint obligor stems from the debt, and not from the ownership of the property which secures the joint obligation. In re McClintock (Ohio Com.Pl. 1978) 58 Ohio Misc. 5, 388 N.E.2d 762, 12 O.O.3d 60. Executors And Administrators ⇐ 217

A surviving spouse, who owned real property with her husband as a joint tenant with the right of survivorship, is entitled to receive contribution from her husband's estate where she has since sold the property and discharged all liability on a joint and several mortgage note which had been signed by both herself and the decedent. Pietro v. Leonetti (Ohio 1972) 30 Ohio St.2d 178, 283 N.E.2d 172, 59 O.O.2d 186. Executors And Administrators ⇐ 217

A signature in the lower right hand corner of a negotiable instrument indicates an intent to sign as the maker of the note or the drawer of a draft; therefore, where a decedent has ostensibly signed as a maker and it is not proved that the decedent was an accommodation party, the decedent's spouse is entitled to contributions from the estate for his pro-rata share of a joint indebtedness. Blumenthal v Abrams, No. 7797 (2d Dist Ct App, Montgomery, 2-16-83).

4. Procedure

Death of one joint contractor renders contract in effect joint and several and permits action against either survivor or administrator of deceased. Cornfeldt v. Rihacek (Lucas 1930) 39 Ohio App. 292, 177 N.E. 522, 8 Ohio Law Abs. 676. Contracts ⇐ 182(2); Parties ⇐ 19

Where two administrators give a joint bond and waste of the estate is committed by one of them after the decease of the other, it is the right of their sureties that the property of both shall be exhausted before the sureties can be compelled to pay. Eckert v. Myers (Ohio 1888) 45 Ohio St. 525, 19 W.L.B. 325, 15 N.E. 862.

Where there are several plaintiffs or defendants, and one of them dies, if a right of action remains against the remaining parties the action may proceed against all jointly or against the partners and legal representatives separately. Gaines v. S. Thorman & Co. (Ohio Com.Pl. 1909) 20 Ohio Dec. 95, 8 Ohio NP(NS) 521.

5. Notes and negotiable instruments

Where joint promissory notes are executed by a decedent and a person who becomes the administrator for the decedent's estate and such notes are paid by the estate, the administrator's account must be surcharged for his share of the indebtedness. In re Fouts' Estate (Clark 1957) 103 Ohio App. 313, 145 N.E.2d 440, 3 O.O.2d 353. Executors And Administrators ⇐ 475

If joint promissory notes made by the decedent and the one who became his administrator are paid by the latter out of the estate, his account must be surcharged with his share, since former GC 10733 (GC 10509–139, now RC 2117.31), and GC 10734 (GC 11258, now RC 2307.22) do not exempt him from liability. In re Lones (Ohio Prob. 1911) 57 W.L.B. 122.

If a negotiable instrument is ambiguous as to the signer's status, he must be regarded as an accommodation party; two primary factors are indicative of accommodation status: (1) no benefits from the proceeds of the instrument are received by the accommodation party; and (2) the signature is needed by the maker to acquire the loan. Blumenthal v Abrams, No. 7797 (2d Dist Ct App, Montgomery, 2-16-83).

2117.33 Claims previously barred

No law relating to limitation of actions against a new administrator shall revive a claim which is barred, during the continuance in office of the original executor or administrator, or of a former administrator de bonis non.

(1953 H 1, eff. 10–1–53; GC 10509–156)

Historical and Statutory Notes

Pre–1953 H 1 Amendments: 114 v 435

Library References

Executors and Administrators ⇐ 225(1).
Westlaw Topic No. 162.
C.J.S. Executors and Administrators § 435.

Research References

Encyclopedias

OH Jur. 3d Decedents' Estates § 1785, Effect of Termination of Office or Appointment of Successor.

Notes of Decisions

Resignation of administrator 1

---

1. Resignation of administrator

An administrator must file his claim against an estate within three months after his appointment, and his resignation after expiration of the three month period does not permit the filing of the claim against the successor administrator. In re Grindle's Estate (Ohio Prob. 1961) 182 N.E.2d 887, 88 Ohio Law Abs. 289, 23 O.O.2d 442.

2117.34 Execution; limitations

No execution against the assets of an estate shall issue upon a judgment against an executor or administrator unless upon the order of the probate court which appointed him. If an account has been rendered by such executor or administrator and settled by the court, such execution shall issue only for the sum that appeared, on settlement of such account, to be a just proportion of the assets applicable to the judgment. The order of the court allowing such execution shall fix the amount for which the same shall issue.

(1953 H 1, eff. 10–1–53; GC 10509–140)

Historical and Statutory Notes

Pre–1953 H 1 Amendments: 119 v 394, § 1; 114 v 432

Cross References

Execution, 2101.35

Library References

Executors and Administrators ⇐ 454.
Westlaw Topic No. 162.

Research References

Encyclopedias

OH Jur. 3d Decedents' Estates § 881, Interposition of Equity in Matters of Administration—Creditors' Suits.

OH Jur. 3d Decedents' Estates § 1812, Enforcement of Judgment; Execution.

Treatises and Practice Aids

Carlin, Baldwin's Ohio Practice, Merrick-Rippner Probate Law § 89:24, Application for Execution on Claim Against Estate—Form.

Carlin, Baldwin's Ohio Practice, Merrick-Rippner Probate Law § 89:25, Entry Setting for Hearing and Ordering Notice—Form.

Carlin, Baldwin's Ohio Practice, Merrick-Rippner Probate Law § 89:26, Entry Issuing Execution—Form.

Carlin, Baldwin's Ohio Practice, Merrick-Rippner Probate Law § 89:27, Execution—Form.

Carlin, Baldwin's Ohio Practice, Merrick-Rippner Probate Law § 89:28, Sheriff's Return of Execution—Form.

Notes of Decisions

Dismissal 2
Order of court 1

---

1. Order of court

Probate court did not abuse its discretion in refusing to stay its determination of whether claim against estate was barred as untimely pending prosecution of claim in foreign state in which cause of action arose. Carlin v. Mambuca (Ohio App. 8 Dist., 05-23-1994) 96 Ohio App.3d 500, 645 N.E.2d 737, motion to certify allowed 70 Ohio St.3d 1475, 640 N.E.2d 848, cause dismissed 71 Ohio St.3d 1441, 643 N.E.2d 1152. Executors And Administrators ⇐ 437(7)

Judgment creditor cannot enforce execution against estate where execution did not issue on order of probate court, and year after judgment had not expired. Kohn v. Kohn (Lucas 1941) 67 Ohio App. 404, 36 N.E.2d 1009, 21 O.O. 348.

Judgment creditor cannot enforce execution against estate where execution did not issue an order of probate court, and year after judgment had not expired. Buerhaus v. Adams (Muskingum 1930) 35 Ohio App. 347, 172 N.E. 440. Executors And Administrators ⇐ 454

2. Dismissal

A judgment dismissing proceedings in aid of execution brought before the expiration of eighteen months is not a bar against an adjudication of the same issues between the same parties, as the former judgment merely decided that the plaintiffs were not at that time permitted to proceed against the administratrix, and was in no way an adjudication of the rights of the parties in the matter. Lauer v. Smith (Ohio Cir. 1899) 14 Ohio C.D. 47, 1 Ohio C.C.(N.S.) 121, affirmed 65 Ohio St. 563, 63 N.E. 1133.

2117.35 Executions against executor or administrator

All executions against executors and administrators for debts due from the deceased shall run against the goods and estate of the deceased in their hands.

(1953 H 1, eff. 10–1–53; GC 10509–141)

Historical and Statutory Notes

Pre–1953 H 1 Amendments: 114 v 432

Library References

Executors and Administrators ⇐454.
Westlaw Topic No. 162.

Research References

Encyclopedias

OH Jur. 3d Decedents' Estates § 1334, Liens.

OH Jur. 3d Decedents' Estates § 1813, Property Subject to Execution.

Notes of Decisions

Defenses 3
Equitable estate 1
Liability of administrator or executor 2

---

1. Equitable estate

An action against the estate of a deceased executor may be maintained by legatees upon equitable as well as under the method provided by statute. Jones v. Willis (Ohio 1905) 72 Ohio St. 189, 74 N.E. 166, 2 Ohio Law Rep. 529.

The remedial provisions of RS 5464 are available for every judgment creditor entitled to an execution against property of the judgement debtor, authorizing a proceeding in aid of execution by action to subject any equitable estate or money of the debtor in the hands of an administratrix to the payment of the judgment. Lauer v. Smith (Ohio Cir. 1899) 14 Ohio C.D. 47, 1 Ohio C.C.(N.S.) 121, affirmed 65 Ohio St. 563, 63 N.E. 1133. Execution ⇐ 386; Executors And Administrators ⇐ 454

2. Liability of administrator or executor

Where an executor is given unlimited discretion in the sale and investment of lands of the testator, subject to the payment of a legacy to his granddaughter at age eighteen, and such executor sells all the lands and becomes insolvent before the legacy is to be paid, the trust does not create a charge on the testator's real estate in the hands of purchasers from the executor. Coonrod v. Coonrod (Ohio 1833) 6 Ohio 114.

The omission in a judgment "that it shall be levied on goods and chattels of the decedent" does not render the administrator personally liable. Kemper v. Apollo Bldg. & Loan Co. (Ohio Com.Pl. 1907) 18 Ohio Dec. 484, 5 Ohio NP(NS) 403, affirmed 20 Ohio C.D. 700, 11 Ohio C.C.(N.S.) 372, affirmed 80 Ohio St. 732, 89 N.E. 1121.

3. Defenses

The defense of a want of consideration for a contract made by the decedent is a good one, even though the instrument sued upon is a specialty under seal. Louderman v Judy, 1 CD 526 (Cir. 1887).

REAL ESTATE NOT LIABLE FOR DEBTS

2117.36 Real estate not liable for debts

No real estate of a deceased person which has been aliened or encumbered by the decedent's heirs prior to the issuing of letters testamentary or of administration shall be liable while in the hands of a bona fide purchaser for value or to the prejudice of a bona fide lessee or encumbrancer for value for debts of the deceased person unless letters testamentary or of administration are granted within four years from the date of death of such deceased person. No real estate of a deceased person which has been aliened or encumbered by the decedent's heirs or devisees after the issue of letters testamentary or of administration shall be liable while in the hands of a bona fide purchaser for value or to the prejudice of a bona fide lessee or encumbrancer for value for debts of a deceased person unless suit is brought to subject such real estate to the payment of such debts prior to the settlement of the executor's or administrator's final account or what purports to be his final account; provided that if such final account is not filed and settled within four years after the granting of letters testamentary or of administration, but excluding for the purposes hereof the time that any action is pending against the executors or administrators for the establishment or collection of any claim against the deceased, such real estate so aliened shall not be liable for the debts of the deceased unless suit is brought to subject such real estate thereto within such four-year period. The heir or devisee aliening such real estate shall be liable for the value thereof, with legal interest from the time of alienation, to the creditors of the deceased in the manner and within the limitations provided by law. This section does not enlarge or extend the right of the creditors of any deceased person against his real estate, or repeal any limitations contained in other sections of the Revised Code, or apply to mortgages or liens of record at the time of the death of such deceased person.

(1953 H 1, eff. 10–1–53; GC 10509–159)

Historical and Statutory Notes

Pre–1953 H 1 Amendments: 114 v 436

Library References

Executors and Administrators ⇔272.
Westlaw Topic No. 162.
C.J.S. Executors and Administrators § 529.

Research References

Encyclopedias

OH Jur. 3d Decedents' Estates § 190, Alienation as Affecting Liability for Ancestor's Debts.
OH Jur. 3d Decedents' Estates § 1298, Land Aliened or Encumbered by Heirs or Devisees.
OH Jur. 3d Decedents' Estates § 1509, Lands Aliened by Heirs or Devisees—Rights of Purchasers.
OH Jur. 3d Decedents' Estates § 1529, Time Within Which Action Must be Brought.

Treatises and Practice Aids

Carlin, Baldwin's Ohio Practice, Merrick-Rippner Probate Law § 91:5, Land Sale—Statute of Limitations.
Kuehnle and Levey, Ohio Real Estate Law and Practice § 18:1, Ohio State Bar Association Standards of Title Examination.
Kuehnle and Levey, Ohio Real Estate Law and Practice § 10:52, Debts of Decedent After First Year of Death.
Kuehnle and Levey, Ohio Real Estate Law and Practice § 10:53, Unpaid Debts in Estate Administration After Lapse of Four Years.
Kuehnle and Levey, Ohio Real Estate Law and Practice § 52:13, Statutory Fiduciary Sales—Four-Year Limitations on Creditor's Suit.

Notes of Decisions

Contribution 1
Creditors 2
Statute of limitations 3

---

1. Contribution

Debts of a decedent are a lien upon his real estate and the rule caveat emptor applies as to purchasers; if their lands are sold out from under them, they must look to any guaranties or warranties as they may have set up, or to rights they may have to contribution from their co-partitioners. Faran v. Robinson (Ohio 1867) 17 Ohio St. 242, 93 Am.Dec. 617.

Where the personal property has been exhausted in paying debts and the estate settled and afterwards a judgment is obtained against the administrator, real estate may be sold to pay the same, though it may have already been partitioned among the heirs and sold and conveyed by them. Faran v. Robinson (Ohio 1867) 17 Ohio St. 242, 93 Am.Dec. 617.

2. Creditors

A creditor acquires no specific lien upon his debtor's death, as his position with respect to other creditors remains unchanged. Gill v. Pinney's Adm'r (Ohio 1861) 12 Ohio St. 38.

3. Statute of limitations

Under section, time that any action is pending against an executrix on a claim against her decedent extends to that extent the four-year period, provided for in that section, within which an action may be commenced to subject real estate of a decedent to the payment of his debts. Kohn v. Kohn (Lucas 1941) 67 Ohio App. 404, 36 N.E.2d 1009, 21 O.O. 348.

CONTINGENT CLAIMS

2117.37 Presentation of contingent claims

If a claim is contingent at the time of a decedent's death and a cause of action subsequently accrues on the claim, it shall be presented to the executor or administrator, in the same manner as other claims, before the expiration of one year after the date of death of the decedent, or before the expiration of two months after the cause of action accrues, whichever is later, except as provided in section 2117.39 of the Revised Code. The executor or administrator shall allow or reject the claim in the same manner as other claims are allowed or rejected. If the claim is allowed, the executor or administrator shall proceed to pay it. If the claim is rejected, the claimant shall commence an action on the claim within two months after the rejection or be forever barred from maintaining an action on the claim.

(1990 H 346, eff. 5–31–90; 1975 S 145; 1953 H 1; GC 10509–216)

Uncodified Law

1990 H 346, § 3, eff. 5–31–90, reads, in part: (A) Sections 1 and 2 of this act shall apply only to the estates of decedents who die on or after the effective date of this act.

Historical and Statutory Notes

Pre–1953 H 1 Amendments: 119 v 394, § 1; 114 v 448

Cross References

Petition for authority to make late presentation of claim, 2117.07
Presentation and allowance of creditor's claims; procedure, 2117.06

Library References

Executors and Administrators ⇔225(3).
Westlaw Topic No. 162.
C.J.S. Executors and Administrators §§ 426, 435.
Baldwin's Ohio Legislative Service, 1990 Laws of Ohio, H 346—LSC Analysis, p 5–87

Research References

Encyclopedias

OH Jur. 3d Decedents' Estates § 1428, Contingent Claims.
OH Jur. 3d Decedents' Estates § 1443, Special Provisions as to Presentation of Contingent Claims.
OH Jur. 3d Decedents' Estates § 1448, Effect of Failure to Present Claims Within Limitation Periods.
OH Jur. 3d Decedents' Estates § 1455, Requirement of Written Statement of Allowance of Claim—Effect of Allowance.
OH Jur. 3d Decedents' Estates § 1468, Debts to be Paid, Generally—Contingent Claims.
OH Jur. 3d Decedents' Estates § 1789, Action on Contingent Claims.
OH Jur. 3d Decedents' Estates § 1825, Causes Upon Which Actions May be Brought.
OH Jur. 3d Decedents' Estates § 1826, Time for Bringing Action.
OH Jur. 3d Decedents' Estates § 1827, Extent of Liability.

Forms

Ohio Jurisprudence Pleading and Practice Forms § 12:11, Checklist—Statutes of Limitations.

Treatises and Practice Aids

Carlin, Baldwin's Ohio Practice, Merrick-Rippner Probate Law § 2:27, Payment of Debts and Claims—Presentation of Claims.
Carlin, Baldwin's Ohio Practice, Merrick-Rippner Probate Law § 84:1, Creditor's Claims—Introduction.
Carlin, Baldwin's Ohio Practice, Merrick-Rippner Probate Law § 85:1, Acceleration of Claims—Introduction and Purpose of Statute.
Carlin, Baldwin's Ohio Practice, Merrick-Rippner Probate Law § 54:23, Fiduciary Accounts—Vacation of Order of Settlement of Account for Fraud.
Carlin, Baldwin's Ohio Practice, Merrick-Rippner Probate Law § 64:27, Compensation—Attorneys.

Carlin, Baldwin's Ohio Practice, Merrick-Rippner Probate Law § 84:14, Creditor's Claims—Claims Requiring Presentation—Guardian or Attorney Fees.

Carlin, Baldwin's Ohio Practice, Merrick-Rippner Probate Law § 84:24, Creditor's Claims—Claims Not Requiring Presentation—Contingent Claims—Definition.

Carlin, Baldwin's Ohio Practice, Merrick-Rippner Probate Law § 84:25, Creditor's Claims—Claims Not Requiring Presentation—Contingent Claims—Mandatory Presentation.

Carlin, Baldwin's Ohio Practice, Merrick-Rippner Probate Law § 84:27, Creditor's Claims—Claims Not Requiring Presentation—Contingent Claims—Allowance or Rejection of Contingent Claim.

Carlin, Baldwin's Ohio Practice, Merrick-Rippner Probate Law § 84:29, Creditor's Claims—Statute of Limitations.

Notes of Decisions

Accrual of action 2
Barred claim 3
Minors 1
Subrogees 5
Sureties 4

---

1. Minors

The doctrine of parental immunity does not bar an action in negligence brought against the estate of a deceased parent and her liability insurance company by the unemancipated minor children. Dorsey v. State Farm Mut. Auto. Ins. Co. (Ohio 1984) 9 Ohio St.3d 27, 457 N.E.2d 1169, 9 O.B.R. 119. Parent And Child ⇐ 11

A claim for damages for injuries resulting from a motor vehicle accident which was not presented to the defendant's executor within nine months of such appointment cannot be revived even if the plaintiff is a minor. Overman v. Yake (Clark 1952) 109 N.E.2d 697, 68 Ohio Law Abs. 248.

2. Accrual of action

A "contingent claim," within meaning of limitations period for presenting a claim to executor or administrator, and thereafter filing an action if the claim is rejected, as to a claim that was contingent at the time of death, means a claim in which the liability thereon is dependent upon some uncertain future event that may or may not occur. Shearer v. Echelberger (Ohio App. 5 Dist., 08-09-2001) 145 Ohio App.3d 106, 761 N.E.2d 1136. Executors And Administrators ⇐ 225(3)

Purchasers' fraud claim against estate was not a "contingent claim," within meaning of limitations period for presenting a claim to executor or administrator, and thereafter filing an action if the claim is rejected, as to a claim that was contingent at the time of death, where the allegedly fraudulent conduct regarding the description of the property's acreage and boundaries arose after decedent's death, though purchasers improperly filed a proof of contingent claim in probate court. Shearer v. Echelberger (Ohio App. 5 Dist., 08-09-2001) 145 Ohio App.3d 106, 761 N.E.2d 1136. Executors And Administrators ⇐ 225(3)

Filing requirements of statute governing creditors' claims against estate do not apply to preemptive right to purchase real property because statute governing contingent interests provides that time periods for contingent claims do not begin to run until cause of action subsequently accrues thereon, i.e., when property owner decides to sell and breaches preemptive provision. Stratman v. Sheetz (Hamilton 1989) 60 Ohio App.3d 71, 573 N.E.2d 776. Limitation Of Actions ⇐ 46(6)

Where a contingent claim against an estate accrues after complete distribution of the assets, the claimant's remedy for any deficiency is an action against the distributee, rather than seeking to vacate the order of final distribution and compelling the distributee to return the assets to the executor. In re Robbins' Estate (Ohio Prob. 1964) 200 N.E.2d 735, 94 Ohio Law Abs. 561, 28 O.O.2d 399.

Where a cause of action accrues seventeen months after the decedent's death and a claim is not presented within two months of such accrual, the claim is barred by the limitations provision of RC 2117.37; the fact that letters referring to the contingent claim were sent to the executors within three months of the decedent's death is irrelevant, as the cause of action had not yet accrued. Morris v Continental Insurance Co, No. 1676 (11th Dist Ct App, Portage, 3-27-87).

When an action accrues before the expiration of the time in which the executor could be sued, an action against the heirs cannot be maintained. Bevitt v Diehl, 12 D 383 (CP, Clarke 1902).

3. Barred claim

Where there is no levy during the lifetime of the judgment debtor, and the judgment is not a lien at the time of his decease but in personam, it cannot be revived and enforced against the heirs of the judgment debtor. Miller v. Taylor (Ohio 1876) 29 Ohio St. 257.

Claims for guardian and attorney fees, not brought within one year after decedent's death, were barred; claims for guardian and attorney fees stemming from guardianship were not contingent, which would make them exempt from one-year time limit, where services of guardian and attorney had already occurred and claims did not depend upon occurrence of uncertain future event. In re Estate of Bickham (Logan 1993) 85 Ohio App.3d 634, 620 N.E.2d 913. Executors And Administrators ⇐ 225(1)

Failure to file a claim against a decedent's estate for loss of earning capacity resulting from an accident allegedly caused by decedent's negligence within four months of the administrator's appointment bars such claim. Lewis v. Knight (Mahoning 1955) 144 N.E.2d 551, 75 Ohio Law Abs. 589.

An express trust is a continuing and subsisting trust until it is openly disavowed or repudiated by the trustees and such disavowal is brought to the knowledge of the cestui que trustent, and an action for its desecration is not barred by the statute of limitations. Central Trust Co v Burke, 1 NP 169, 2 D 96 (CP, Franklin 1895). Limitation Of Actions ⇐ 102(4); Trusts ⇐ 365(1)

4. Sureties

Where decedent signed a promissory note as surety, which was secured by mortgage on the real estate of decedent, and where upon sale of such real estate the executor of the estate of the surety was required to pay the balance due on the note, the estate of the surety is required to present such claim to the administratrix of the estate of the deceased principal as a contingent claim under the provisions of section. Keifer v. Kissell (Clark 1947) 83 Ohio App. 133, 75 N.E.2d 692, 50 Ohio Law Abs. 375, 38 O.O. 224.

5. Subrogees

The subrogee of a tort claim does not have a contingent claim within the meaning of RC 2117.37, and therefore must bring its claim within the time set forth in RC 2117.06. Marcum v Burnham, No. 8411 (2d Dist Ct App, Montgomery, 4–16–84).

2117.38 Assets from which payment to be made

If an executor or administrator has made a partial distribution of the assets of the estate at the time a claim is presented under section 2117.37 of the Revised Code, and if the claim is allowed or after rejection is found to be due from the estate, but the assets remaining in the possession of the executor or administrator are insufficient to pay the claim in full, the assets remaining shall first be exhausted before proceeding to recover against the distributees of the assets of the estate. If a contingent claim is allowed or if after rejection it is found to be due from the estate, the creditor may bring an action thereon to recover from the distributees of the decedent's estate as provided in sections 2117.41 and 2117.42, inclusive, of the Revised Code, within two months after the final payment on account thereof by the executor or administrator, if such recovery is necessary for the payment of the claim in full.

(1953 H 1, eff. 10–1–53; GC 10509–216a)

Historical and Statutory Notes

Pre–1953 H 1 Amendments: 119 v 394, § 9

Library References

Executors and Administrators ⇐ 284, 318.
Westlaw Topic No. 162.
C.J.S. Executors and Administrators § 558.

Research References

Encyclopedias

OH Jur. 3d Decedents' Estates § 1468, Debts to be Paid, Generally—Contingent Claims.

OH Jur. 3d Decedents' Estates § 1825, Causes Upon Which Actions May be Brought.

OH Jur. 3d Decedents' Estates § 1826, Time for Bringing Action.

Notes of Decisions

Administrator, action against 2
Distributee, action against 1

---

1. Distributee, action against

Where a contingent claim against an estate accrues after complete distribution of the assets, the claimant's remedy for any deficiency is an action against the distributee, rather than seeking to vacate the order of final distribution and compelling the distributee to return the assets to the executor. In re Robbins' Estate (Ohio Prob. 1964) 200 N.E.2d 735, 94 Ohio Law Abs. 561, 28 O.O.2d 399.

2. Administrator, action against

In a proceeding to enforce liability of a deceased surety on a cost bond, the estate of such surety having passed to his heir and distributee, although it had not been fully settled, a judgment against the administrator is proper, and not a judgment against the heir. McClaskey v. Barr (C.C.S.D.Ohio 1897) 79 F. 408. Descent And Distribution ⚖ 139; Executors And Administrators ⚖ 423

2117.39 Contingent claims not to be presented

If at the time a cause of action accrues on a contingent claim against a decedent's estate, or if within two months thereafter an account of final distribution has been filed, no claim need be presented to the executor or administrator and the claimant may proceed by civil action against the distributees of the decedent's estate as provided in sections 2117.41 and 2117.42 of the Revised Code.

(1953 H 1, eff. 10–1–53; GC 10509–216b)

Historical and Statutory Notes

Pre–1953 H 1 Amendments: 119 v 394, § 9

Library References

Executors and Administrators ⚖ 224.
Westlaw Topic No. 162.
C.J.S. Executors and Administrators §§ 422, 426.

Research References

Encyclopedias

OH Jur. 3d Decedents' Estates § 1428, Contingent Claims.

OH Jur. 3d Decedents' Estates § 1443, Special Provisions as to Presentation of Contingent Claims.

OH Jur. 3d Decedents' Estates § 1789, Action on Contingent Claims.

OH Jur. 3d Decedents' Estates § 1825, Causes Upon Which Actions May be Brought.

Treatises and Practice Aids

Carlin, Baldwin's Ohio Practice, Merrick-Rippner Probate Law § 84:24, Creditor's Claims—Claims Not Requiring Presentation—Contingent Claims—Definition.

Carlin, Baldwin's Ohio Practice, Merrick-Rippner Probate Law § 84:25, Creditor's Claims—Claims Not Requiring Presentation—Contingent Claims—Mandatory Presentation.

Carlin, Baldwin's Ohio Practice, Merrick-Rippner Probate Law § 84:26, Creditor's Claims—Claims Not Requiring Presentation—Contingent Claims—Exception to Presentation of Contingent Claim.

Carlin, Baldwin's Ohio Practice, Merrick-Rippner Probate Law § 84:27, Creditor's Claims—Claims Not Requiring Presentation—Contingent Claims—Allowance or Rejection of Contingent Claim.

Notes of Decisions

Distributee, action against 1

---

1. Distributee, action against

Where a contingent claim against an estate accrues after complete distribution of the assets, the claimant's remedy for any deficiency is an action against the distributee, rather than seeking to vacate the order of final distribution and compelling the distributee to return the assets to the executor. In re Robbins' Estate (Ohio Prob. 1964) 200 N.E.2d 735, 94 Ohio Law Abs. 561, 28 O.O.2d 399.

2117.40 Estate of deceased in the hands of heirs

If a cause of action on a contingent claim accrues after the settlement of an estate or at such time that a claim thereon does not have to be presented to the executor or administrator, or if a contingent claim is presented to the executor or administrator as provided by section 2117.37 of the Revised Code, but the assets of the estate are insufficient for payment of the claim in full, then the heirs, next of kin, surviving spouse as next of kin, devisees, and legatees shall be liable for the payment of such claim or the unpaid balance thereof in an action in the court of common pleas as provided in sections 2117.41 and 2117.42 of the Revised Code.

(1953 H 1, eff. 10–1–53; GC 10509–216c)

Historical and Statutory Notes

Pre–1953 H 1 Amendments: 119 v 394, § 9

Library References

Descent and Distribution ⚖119(1), 138.
Wills ⚖827, 847(1).
Westlaw Topic Nos. 124, 409.
C.J.S. Descent and Distribution §§ 112, 114, 123.
C.J.S. Wills §§ 1943 to 1944.

Research References

Encyclopedias

OH Jur. 3d Decedents' Estates § 182, Personal Liability of Heirs; Contingent Claims.

OH Jur. 3d Decedents' Estates § 1825, Causes Upon Which Actions May be Brought.

OH Jur. 3d Decedents' Estates § 1828, Practice and Procedure.

Treatises and Practice Aids

Carlin, Baldwin's Ohio Practice, Merrick-Rippner Probate Law § 15:7, Descent and Distribution—Spouse as Heir at Law and Next of Kin.

Notes of Decisions

Advances 3
Heir's liability 2
Real estate 1

---

1. Real estate

Debts of a decedent are a lien upon his real estate and the rule caveat emptor applies as to purchasers; if their lands are sold out from under them, they must look to any guaranties or warranties as they may have set up, or to rights they may have to contribution from their co-partitioners. Faran v. Robinson (Ohio 1867) 17 Ohio St. 242, 93 Am.Dec. 617.

Where the personal property has been exhausted in paying debts and the estate settled and afterwards a judgment is obtained against the administrator, real estate may be sold to pay the same, though it may have already been partitioned among the heirs and sold and conveyed by them. Faran v. Robinson (Ohio 1867) 17 Ohio St. 242, 93 Am.Dec. 617.

2. Heir's liability

Each heir is subject to the payment of the ancestor's debts to the amount of assets received, and not for a greater sum; therefore, a joint action cannot be maintained against several heirs or devisees where there is no joint contract either express or implied, nor any joint reception of the assets. Spicer v. Giselman (Ohio 1846) 15 Ohio 338.

The heir takes the property subject to the right of sale to pay debts of the decedent. Piatt v St. Clair's Heirs, 6 Ohio 227 (1833).

The heir is bound to pay the taxes accruing after the death of the intestate. Piatt v St. Clair's Heirs, 6 Ohio 227 (1833).

Where a contingent claim against an estate accrues after complete distribution of the assets, the claimant's remedy for any deficiency is an action against the distributee, rather than seeking to vacate the order of final distribution and compelling the distributee to return the assets to the executor. In re Robbins' Estate (Ohio Prob. 1964) 200 N.E.2d 735, 94 Ohio Law Abs. 561, 28 O.O.2d 399.

3. Advances

A person who advances money to pay the intestate's debts acquires no lien upon the lands of the intestate in the hands of the heir. Lieby v. Ludlow's Heirs (Ohio 1831) 4 Ohio 469.

2117.41 Payment of contingent claims after settlement of estate

A claimant whose cause of action accrues as provided in section 2117.37 of the Revised Code may bring suit to recover thereon against the heirs, next of kin, surviving spouse as next of kin, devisees, and legatees under the decedent's will, each of whom shall be liable to the claimant in an amount not exceeding the value of the real and personal estate that he received under the will or on distribution of the estate. If, by the will of the deceased, any part of the estate or any one or more of the devisees and legatees is made exclusively liable for the debt, in exoneration of the residue of the estate or of the other devisees or legatees, the terms of the will shall be complied with in that respect and the persons and estate so exempt by the will shall be liable for only so much of the debt as cannot be recovered from those first chargeable therewith.

No such suit shall be maintained unless commenced within six months next after the time when the cause of action first accrues, except in case the suit is for the balance due after a payment by the executor or administrator, in which case suit shall be brought within two months after the final payment by the executor or administrator. If the person entitled to bring such suit is under legal disability, he may bring such action within one year after his disability is removed.

If any of such heirs, next of kin, surviving spouse as next of kin, devisees, or legatees dies without having paid his just proportion of such debt, his executors or administrators shall be liable therefor to the extent he would have been if living.

(1953 H 1, eff. 10–1–53; GC 10509–217 to 10509–219)

Historical and Statutory Notes

Pre–1953 H 1 Amendments: 119 v 394, § 1; 114 v 448, 449

Comparative Laws

Ark.—A.C.A. § 28-50-111.
Ind.—West's A.I.C. 29-1-14-8.
Minn.—M.S.A. § 524.3-810.

Library References

Descent and Distribution ⚖139.
Wills ⚖847(2).
Westlaw Topic Nos. 124, 409.
C.J.S. Descent and Distribution § 124.
C.J.S. Wills § 1943.

Research References

Encyclopedias

OH Jur. 3d Decedents' Estates § 1338, Miscellaneous.
OH Jur. 3d Decedents' Estates § 1789, Action on Contingent Claims.
OH Jur. 3d Decedents' Estates § 1825, Causes Upon Which Actions May be Brought.
OH Jur. 3d Decedents' Estates § 1826, Time for Bringing Action.
OH Jur. 3d Decedents' Estates § 1827, Extent of Liability.
OH Jur. 3d Decedents' Estates § 1829, Practice and Procedure—Parties.
OH Jur. 3d Decedents' Estates § 1830, Practice and Procedure—Determination and Apportionment of Liability.

Treatises and Practice Aids

Carlin, Baldwin's Ohio Practice, Merrick-Rippner Probate Law § 15:7, Descent and Distribution—Spouse as Heir at Law and Next of Kin.
Carlin, Baldwin's Ohio Practice, Merrick-Rippner Probate Law § 84:24, Creditor's Claims—Claims Not Requiring Presentation—Contingent Claims—Definition.
Carlin, Baldwin's Ohio Practice, Merrick-Rippner Probate Law § 84:26, Creditor's Claims—Claims Not Requiring Presentation—Contingent Claims—Exception to Presentation of Contingent Claim.
Carlin, Baldwin's Ohio Practice, Merrick-Rippner Probate Law § 84:27, Creditor's Claims—Claims Not Requiring Presentation—Contingent Claims—Allowance or Rejection of Contingent Claim.

Law Review and Journal Commentaries

Expanding the Rights of Creditors to Nonprobate Property: A Sensible Proposal to Close Ohio's Antiquated Loopholes, Daniel J. Hoffheimer. 13 Prob L J Ohio 23 (November/December 2002).

Notes of Decisions

Heirs, action against 2
Statute of limitations 1

---

1. Statute of limitations

The mere delay of a ward to compel his guardian to settle his accounts in the probate court does not discharge the sureties even though the guardian has become insolvent in the meantime. Newton v. Hammond (Ohio 1882) 38 Ohio St. 430, 8 W.L.B. 241. Guardian And Ward ⚖ 177; Principal And Surety ⚖ 125

Broker's claim for real estate commission was contingent claim against estate that was statutorily barred by not being brought within six months of accrual when purchaser exercised its option to purchase. Priestman v. Elder (Ohio App. 6 Dist., 09-16-1994) 97 Ohio App.3d 86, 646 N.E.2d 234. Executors And Administrators ⚖ 225(3); Executors And Administrators ⚖ 231

Broker's commission claim against estate accrued, at the latest, when conveyance to purchaser was recorded, rather than when broker discovered that sale occurred, where recording of conveyance of property provided broker with constructive notice of sale, and broker knew that he had commission claim if property was purchased by lessee or its successor at end of primary lease, requiring him to exercise reasonable care in monitoring progress of his potential claim. Priestman v. Elder (Ohio App. 6 Dist., 09-16-1994) 97 Ohio App.3d 86, 646 N.E.2d 234. Executors And Administrators ⚖ 225(3)

The one year's time within which under former section, to pursue the distributees of an estate which had been fully settled without paying a claim is not a mere limitation but qualifies the right; and it makes no difference that the ancestor's debt was as surety on a bond where the limitation as to him, if alive, would have been ten years, for the special statute excludes the general. Roth v Hummel, 1 App 361, 17 CC(NS) 252, 25 CD 355 (1913).

Whenever the right of action in a trustee who is vested with the legal estate and is competent to sue is barred by limitation, the right of the cestui que trust is also barred and this rule applies whether the cestui que trust is sui juris, or under disability during the period of limitation, except where application of the rule is abrogated by statute. Rogers v. Schuller (Mahoning 1938) 27 Ohio Law Abs. 449. Limitation Of Actions ⚖ 174(2); Trusts ⚖ 256

Heirs who set aside a will over one year after administration of estate of one of legatees cannot recover back money received by heirs of that

2117.41 Note 1

legatee, as requirement that action be brought within one year goes to basis of plaintiff's right. Swetland v Miles, 2 Abs 187 (App, Knox 1923).

A claim for damages for injuries resulting from a motor vehicle accident which was not presented to the defendant's executor within nine months of such appointment cannot be revived even if the plaintiff is a minor. Overman v. Yake (Clark 1952) 109 N.E.2d 697, 68 Ohio Law Abs. 248.

2. Heirs, action against

In an action by the creditor of a decedent against the heirs after the estate has been fully settled the same defenses may be made as in an action against the personal representative. Camp v. Bostwick (Ohio 1870) 20 Ohio St. 337, 5 Am.Rep. 669.

Where a debt has been reduced to judgment in an action against the administrator of an estate, an action by the judgment creditor against the heirs in equity cannot be maintained. Haynes v. Colvin (Ohio 1850) 19 Ohio 392.

A mere return of "no goods found" on an execution is not sufficient to authorize a sale of land; the heirs have the right to contest the truth of the sheriff's return by showing that other assets remain in the hands of the administrators. Jones v. Shields (Ohio 1846) 14 Ohio 359.

Language in settlement agreement which provided that decedent's son and daughter "fully and finally" released each other "from any and all claims" regarding the decedent's estate did not bar daughter's claim to family Bible which son had gifted to his own daughter, although title to the Bible was disputed; provision conflicted with another provision of the agreement providing that both parties may make claims to particular items of personal property and that the administrator should sell property that is claimed by both parties, no approved inventory of the estate and no itemized appraisal of decedent's personal property had been filed with the probate court at the time the parties entered into the agreement, and the agreement did not purport to define the personal property that belonged to the estate. In re Estate of Kelsey (Ohio App. 11 Dist., 03-10-2006) 165 Ohio App.3d 680, 847 N.E.2d 1277, 2006-Ohio-1171.

Where a contingent claim against an estate accrues after complete distribution of the assets, the claimant's remedy for any deficiency is an action against the distributee, rather than seeking to vacate the order of final distribution and compelling the distributee to return the assets to the executor. In re Robbins' Estate (Ohio Prob. 1964) 200 N.E.2d 735, 94 Ohio Law Abs. 561, 28 O.O.2d 399.

A suit for specific performance of a contract to execute a will in favor of the plaintiff is not an "action against the heirs, devisees or next of kin" within former GC 10878 (GC 10509–218, now RC 2117.41). Ohlendiek v. Schuler (C.C.A.6 (Ohio) 1924) 299 F. 182, certiorari denied 45 S.Ct. 93, 266 U.S. 608, 69 L.Ed. 465. Executors And Administrators ⇐ 437(2)

A widow who is the sole legatee and is settling the estate without administration is not liable as an heir in an action by creditors, for an heir cannot be sued for assets received until the estate has been settled by the executor or administrator. Arbaugh v Millett, 5 CC 295, 3 CD 146 (Darke 1891).

When an action accrues before the expiration of the time in which the executor could be sued, an action against the heirs cannot be maintained. Bevitt v Diehl, 12 D 383 (CP, Clarke 1902).

2117.42 Creditors may proceed against all in one action

If, in the cases specified in section 2117.41 of the Revised Code, more than one person is liable for the debt, the creditor shall proceed by one action to recover such debt against all so liable, or as many of them as are within the reach of process. Thereupon, by the verdict of a jury if either party requires it, the court must determine what sum is due to the plaintiff. They also, according to the equities of the case, shall decide how much each of the defendants is liable to pay toward the satisfaction of the debt and the court shall render judgment accordingly.

No suit shall be dismissed or debarred for not making all the persons defendants who might have been included as such. In any stage of the cause the court may award process to bring in other parties and allow amendments necessary to charge them, as defendants, upon such terms as it deems reasonable.

If any of the persons who were originally liable for the debt is insolvent or unable to pay his proportion, or is beyond the reach of process, the others nevertheless shall be liable to the creditor for the whole amount of his debt; except that no one shall be compelled to pay more than the amount received by him from the decedent's estate.

If, in consequence of insolvency, absence or other cause, any of the persons liable for such debt fails to pay his just proportion to the creditor, he shall be liable to indemnify all who, by reason of such failure on his part, have paid more than their just proportion of the debt, such indemnity to be recovered by all of them jointly or in separate actions, by any one or more for his or their parts respectively, at their election.

(1953 H 1, eff. 10–1–53; GC 10509–220 to 10509–223)

Historical and Statutory Notes

Pre–1953 H 1 Amendments: 114 v 449

Comparative Laws

Mass.—M.G.L.A. c. 197, § 28.
Wis.—W.S.A. 777.18 et seq.

Library References

Descent and Distribution ⇐144.
Wills ⇐847(3).
Westlaw Topic Nos. 124, 409.
C.J.S. Descent and Distribution § 127.
C.J.S. Wills § 1943.

Research References

Encyclopedias

OH Jur. 3d Contribution, Indemnity, & Subrogation § 18, Unavailable Co-Obligors.
OH Jur. 3d Decedents' Estates § 1428, Contingent Claims.
OH Jur. 3d Decedents' Estates § 1448, Effect of Failure to Present Claims Within Limitation Periods.
OH Jur. 3d Decedents' Estates § 1789, Action on Contingent Claims.
OH Jur. 3d Decedents' Estates § 1825, Causes Upon Which Actions May be Brought.
OH Jur. 3d Decedents' Estates § 1829, Practice and Procedure—Parties.
OH Jur. 3d Decedents' Estates § 1830, Practice and Procedure—Determination and Apportionment of Liability.

Treatises and Practice Aids

Carlin, Baldwin's Ohio Practice, Merrick-Rippner Probate Law § 2:27, Payment of Debts and Claims—Presentation of Claims.
Carlin, Baldwin's Ohio Practice, Merrick-Rippner Probate Law § 84:1, Creditor's Claims—Introduction.
Carlin, Baldwin's Ohio Practice, Merrick-Rippner Probate Law § 85:1, Acceleration of Claims—Introduction and Purpose of Statute.
Carlin, Baldwin's Ohio Practice, Merrick-Rippner Probate Law § 84:24, Creditor's Claims—Claims Not Requiring Presentation—Contingent Claims—Definition.
Carlin, Baldwin's Ohio Practice, Merrick-Rippner Probate Law § 84:26, Creditor's Claims—Claims Not Requiring Presentation—Contingent Claims—Exception to Presentation of Contingent Claim.
Carlin, Baldwin's Ohio Practice, Merrick-Rippner Probate Law § 84:29, Creditor's Claims—Statute of Limitations.

Notes of Decisions

Joint action 1
Value of estate 2

---

1. Joint action

Each heir is subject to the payment of the ancestor's debts to the amount of assets received, and not for a greater sum; therefore, a joint action cannot be maintained against several heirs or devisees where there is no joint contract either express or implied, nor any joint reception of the assets. Spicer v. Giselman (Ohio 1846) 15 Ohio 338.

2. Value of estate

In suit against distributees of bondsman's estate, based on bondsman's obligation under surety bond, distributees are liable only to extent of value of that part of estate actually received by them, and plaintiff must produce proof of such value. City of New Philadelphia v. Hurst (Tuscarawas 1937) 57 Ohio App. 479, 14 N.E.2d 1021, 26 Ohio Law Abs. 302, 11 O.O. 240. Descent And Distribution ⚖ 119(1)

CHAPTER 2119

TRUSTEE FOR ABSENTEE

Section
2119.01 Trustee for absentee
2119.02 Notice
2119.03 Powers of trustee
2119.04 Mortgage, lease, or sale of real estate; sale of personal property
2119.05 Termination of trust; final account

Cross References

Order in which debts to be paid, 2117.25
Payment of debts after three months, 2117.15
Presentation and allowance of creditor's claims, procedure, 2117.06

2119.01 Trustee for absentee

When a person owning property in this state has disappeared and has not been heard from, after diligent inquiry and for at least three months, under circumstances that afford reasonable ground to believe that he is dead, cannot return, or refuses to return to his home, and his estate requires attention, supervision, and care, or is needed for the maintenance of his dependents, the probate court may, on application of the spouse or of one of the next of kin, appoint a trustee to take possession and charge of the property of such person, other than the property with respect to which such person has made provision by written instrument designating an agent or attorney in fact. Such application shall be filed in the county in which such person last resided or if his last known residence was without this state, such application may be filed in any county in which any such property is situated.

(1953 H 1, eff. 10–1–53; GC 10509–39)

Historical and Statutory Notes

Pre–1953 H 1 Amendments: 120 v 649

Comparative Laws

Fla.—West's F.S.A. § 733.209.
Ind.—West's A.I.C. 29–2–5–1.
N.Y.—McKinney's SCPA 901 et seq.

Library References

Absentees ⚖5.
Westlaw Topic No. 5.
C.J.S. Absentees §§ 7 to 14.

Research References

Encyclopedias
OH Jur. 3d Cotenancy & Partition § 68, Missing or Absentee Owners.
OH Jur. 3d Fiduciaries § 14, Trustee for Absentee.
OH Jur. 3d Fiduciaries § 15, Trustee for Absentee—Application for Appointment; Notice.
OH Jur. 3d Fiduciaries § 23, Generally; Trustee for Absentee.

Treatises and Practice Aids
Carlin, Baldwin's Ohio Practice, Merrick-Rippner Probate Law § 33:29, Application for Appointment of Trustee—Unknown or Nonresident Person—Form.
Carlin, Baldwin's Ohio Practice, Merrick-Rippner Probate Law § 33:32, Application for Appointment of Trustee for Absent Person—Form.
Carlin, Baldwin's Ohio Practice, Merrick-Rippner Probate Law § 33:33, Entry Setting for Hearing and Ordering Notice—Form.
Carlin, Baldwin's Ohio Practice, Merrick-Rippner Probate Law § 33:34, Entry Appointing Trustee for Absent Person—Form.
Carlin, Baldwin's Ohio Practice, Merrick-Rippner Probate Law § 33:35, Letters of Authority of Trustee of Absent Person—Form.
Carlin, Baldwin's Ohio Practice, Merrick-Rippner Probate Law § 52:60, Entry Approving Bond of Trustee of Absentee—Form.
Bogert - the Law of Trusts and Trustees § 246, Public Trusts: Statutory and Created by Court.
Kuehnle and Levey, Ohio Real Estate Law and Practice § 52:3, Statutory Fiduciary Sales—21 Statutory Proceedings.
Kuehnle and Levey, Ohio Real Estate Law and Practice § 52:21, Statutory Fiduciary Sales—Action by Trustee to Sell Trust Property.

Notes of Decisions

Partition 3
Retirement benefits 1
Time limit 2

1. Retirement benefits

Mandamus will not lie to compel public retirement benefits to trustee where retirant has disappeared and has not thereafter been heard from. State ex rel. Hammond v. Public Emp. Retirement System (Ohio 1972) 29 Ohio St.2d 192, 280 N.E.2d 904, 58 O.O.2d 403.

2. Time limit

Where a trustee for a missing person was appointed pursuant to section, the authority of such trustee to act as such is not terminated with the expiration of the period of seven years' absence of such missing person, but such trustee may continue to act as such until the missing person returns or an administrator or executor of his estate is appointed. In re Parrett (Franklin 1949) 86 Ohio App. 162, 90 N.E.2d 425, 41 O.O. 20. Absentees ⚖ 5

3. Partition

On authority granted by the probate court and on a proper showing being made, a trustee for a missing person, appointed under section, may maintain an action for equitable partition of lands in which the missing person owned a fractional interest. In re Parrett (Franklin 1949) 86 Ohio App. 162, 90 N.E.2d 425, 41 O.O. 20. Absentees ⚖ 7

2119.02 Notice

The probate court, before appointing a trustee for an absentee, shall cause notice of the filing of the application under section 2119.01 of the Revised Code and of the time and place of hearing thereon to be published once a week for four consecutive weeks in some newspaper of general circulation in the county and shall cause copies of such notice to be mailed to the spouse and next of kin of the absentee residing within the state, excepting the applicant, and to the absentee residing at his last known address. The court may order notice to be given to such other persons in such manner as it deems best.

(1953 H 1, eff. 10–1–53; GC 10509–39a)

Historical and Statutory Notes

Pre–1953 H 1 Amendments: 120 v 649

Cross References

Service of notice, Civ R 73

Library References

Absentees ⇐5.
Westlaw Topic No. 5.
C.J.S. Absentees §§ 7 to 14.

Research References

Encyclopedias

OH Jur. 3d Fiduciaries § 15, Trustee for Absentee—Application for Appointment; Notice.

2119.03 Powers of trustee

The trustee appointed under section 2119.01 of the Revised Code may proceed without order of the probate court:

(A) To take possession of the property of the absentee wherever situated within the state;

(B) To collect all debts due to the absentee;

(C) To retain and invest the estate in accordance with Chapters 2113. to 2125. of the Revised Code.

The trustee may pay such part or all of the income or principal of the estate as the court, from time to time, may direct for the maintenance and support of the absentee's dependents and, under the order of the court, may bring and defend suits on behalf of the absentee, compromise claims in favor of and against the absentee, and pay such debts of the absentee as the court finds necessary for the protection of his dependents, including insurance premiums, orders for an award of spousal support, and other obligations. The court may make such other orders as it deems proper for the care and custody of the property and its proceeds.

(1990 H 514, eff. 1–1–91; 1953 H 1; GC 10509–39b)

Historical and Statutory Notes

Pre–1953 H 1 Amendments: 120 v 649

Cross References

Money and property to be held in trust for safekeeping for nonresidents of United States, 2113.81

Library References

Absentees ⇐5.
Westlaw Topic No. 5.
C.J.S. Absentees §§ 7 to 14.

Research References

Encyclopedias

OH Jur. 3d Decedents' Estates § 1664, Beneficiary Residing in Certain Foreign Countries.
OH Jur. 3d Fiduciaries § 23, Generally; Trustee for Absentee.
OH Jur. 3d Fiduciaries § 120, Trustee for Absentee.

Treatises and Practice Aids

Carlin, Baldwin's Ohio Practice, Merrick-Rippner Probate Law § 78:1, Statutory Provisions.
Carlin, Baldwin's Ohio Practice, Merrick-Rippner Probate Law § 90:2, Persons Entitled to Bring Land Sale Actions—Other Parties.
Carlin, Baldwin's Ohio Practice, Merrick-Rippner Probate Law § 97:1, Land Sale by Guardian—Introduction.

Notes of Decisions

Constitutional issues 1

---

1. Constitutional issues

A state statute such as RC 2113.81 which directs that funds in a decedent's estate which would otherwise be distributable be held in trust because it appears that the distributee resides outside the United States and its territories at a location where the prevailing circumstances will prevent his having the benefit, use, or control of the money due him is invalid under US Const Art I, § 10, which grants exclusive power over the foreign affairs of this country to the federal government. First Nat. Bank of Cincinnati v. Fishman (Ohio Prob. 1968) 16 Ohio Misc. 185, 239 N.E.2d 270, 43 O.O.2d 384, 45 O.O.2d 147.

2119.04 Mortgage, lease, or sale of real estate; sale of personal property

In order to provide money for the payments authorized by section 2119.03 of the Revised Code, proceedings may be had for the mortgaging, leasing, or sale of the real estate of an absentee in the same manner as provided by sections 2127.01 to 2127.43, inclusive, of the Revised Code, for sales of real estate by executors and administrators. The probate court, upon notice to the spouse and such other persons and in such manner as the court directs, may order all or any part of the personal estate to be sold.

(1953 H 1, eff. 10–1–53; GC 10509–39c)

Historical and Statutory Notes

Pre–1953 H 1 Amendments: 120 v 649

Library References

Absentees ⇐6.
Westlaw Topic No. 5.
C.J.S. Absentees § 5.

Research References

Encyclopedias

OH Jur. 3d Fiduciaries § 45, Generally, Trustee for Absentee.

Treatises and Practice Aids

Carlin, Baldwin's Ohio Practice, Merrick-Rippner Probate Law § 90:2, Persons Entitled to Bring Land Sale Actions—Other Parties.
Carlin, Baldwin's Ohio Practice, Merrick-Rippner Probate Law § 97:1, Land Sale by Guardian—Introduction.
Kuehnle and Levey, Ohio Real Estate Law and Practice § 52:3, Statutory Fiduciary Sales—21 Statutory Proceedings.
Kuehnle and Levey, Ohio Real Estate Law and Practice § 52:21, Statutory Fiduciary Sales—Action by Trustee to Sell Trust Property.

2119.05 Termination of trust; final account

If at any time the absentee returns and makes application to the probate court for the termination of the trust established under section 2119.01 of the Revised Code, the court shall, on notice to the trustee and other interested parties, order the trustee to file his final account and on settlement thereof shall terminate the trust and order all remaining property returned. If an executor, administrator, or guardian is appointed for the estate of such absentee, the court shall thereupon order the trustee to file his final account and on settlement thereof shall terminate the trust and order all of the property remaining in the hands of the trustee to be delivered to the fiduciary entitled thereto.

(1953 H 1, eff. 10–1–53; GC 10509–39d)

Historical and Statutory Notes

Pre–1953 H 1 Amendments: 120 v 649

Library References

Absentees ⇐5.
Westlaw Topic No. 5.
C.J.S. Absentees §§ 7 to 14.

Research References

Encyclopedias

OH Jur. 3d Decedents' Estates § 1314, Trust Funds.

OH Jur. 3d Fiduciaries § 242, Final Accounting Upon Termination of Administration or Trust—Trust for Absentee.
OH Jur. 3d Fiduciaries § 298, on Absentee's Return or Presumed Death.

Treatises and Practice Aids

Bogert - the Law of Trusts and Trustees § 246, Public Trusts: Statutory and Created by Court.

CHAPTER 2121

PRESUMED DECEDENTS' LAW

Section	
2121.01	When presumption of death arises
2121.02	Complaint to establish presumption; parties; notice
2121.03	Evidence admissible
2121.04	Decree of presumption of death; effects
2121.05	Administration of estate of presumed decedent; orders; conditions; bonds
2121.06	Title to real estate; limits on transfer; bond
2121.07	Distribution of personal property; bond
2121.08	Vacation of decree; effects; set off
2121.09	Substitution of person erroneously presumed dead as party to actions

Cross References

Appointment of ancillary administrator, 2129.08
Order in which debts to be paid, 2117.25
Payment of debts after three months, 2117.15
Powers of trustee for person who has disappeared, 2119.03
Presentation and allowance of creditor's claims; procedure, 2117.06

2121.01 When presumption of death arises

(A) Except as provided in division (B) of this section, a presumption of the death of a person arises:

(1) When the person has disappeared and been continuously absent from his place of last domicile for a five-year period without being heard from during the period;

(2) When the person has disappeared and been continuously absent from his place of last domicile without being heard from and was at the beginning of his absence exposed to a specific peril of death, even though the absence has continued for less than a five-year period.

(B) When a person who is on active duty in the armed services of the United States has been officially determined to be absent in a status of "missing" or "missing in action," a presumption of death arises when the head of the federal department concerned has made a finding of death pursuant to the "Federal Missing Persons Act," 80 Stat. 625 (1966), 37 U.S.C.A. 551, as amended and hereafter amended.

(1974 S 349, eff. 9–30–74)

Historical and Statutory Notes

Ed. Note: Former 2121.01 repealed by 1974 S 349, eff. 9–30–74; 1953 H 1; GC 10509–25.

Pre–1953 H 1 Amendments: 122 v H 50; 114 v 406

Cross References

Presumption of order of death where death of two or more persons occurs, 2105.21

Library References

Death ⇐2.
Westlaw Topic No. 117.
C.J.S. Death §§ 8 to 14.

Research References

Encyclopedias

OH Jur. 3d Death § 15, Presumption of Death.
OH Jur. 3d Decedents' Estates § 81, Heirs and Next of Kin as Successors Under the Statute of Descent and Distribution—Absentees and Presumed Decedents; Unknown Heirs.
OH Jur. 3d Decedents' Estates § 145, Realty of a Presumed Decedent.
OH Jur. 3d Decedents' Estates § 865, Death—Presumed Death.
OH Jur. 3d Decedents' Estates § 1039, Wills of Presumed Decedents.
OH Jur. 3d Decedents' Estates § 1736, Appointment in Case of Nonresident Presumed Decedent.
OH Jur. 3d Insurance § 1427, Presumption of Death in Case of Disappearance of Insured.

Treatises and Practice Aids

Baldwin's Ohio Handbook Series—Trial Handbook § 21:7, Death After Seven Years' Absence.
Sowald & Morganstern, Baldwin's Ohio Practice Domestic Relations Law § 2:65, Termination of Marriage.
Giannelli and Snyder, Baldwin's Ohio Practice, Evidence, R 301, Presumptions in General in Civil Actions and Proceedings.
Giannelli and Snyder, Baldwin's Ohio Practice, Evidence, § 301.15, Selected Presumptions.
Carlin, Baldwin's Ohio Practice, Merrick-Rippner Probate Law § 9:1, Presumption of Death—Statutory.
Carlin, Baldwin's Ohio Practice, Merrick-Rippner Probate Law § 9:6, Presumption of Death—Procedure for Establishing—Burden.
Carlin, Baldwin's Ohio Practice, Merrick-Rippner Probate Law § 9:9, Presumption of Death—Complaint—Form.

Notes of Decisions

Ed. Note: This section contains annotations from former RC 2121.01.

Common law rule 4
Effect of other laws 5
Peril of death 2
Rebuttal of presumption 3
Survivorship 1

---

1. Survivorship

The provisions of the Presumed Decedents Act may not be applied to determine the date of death of a person who has been absent from the place of his last domicile for more than seven years, so as to make such date subsequent to the death of another person from whom such absentee would have inherited an estate had he survived such other person, and thus make such date available as an item of evidence in the determination of the right to share in the estate of such other person. Baker v. Myers (Ohio 1953) 160 Ohio St. 376, 116 N.E.2d 711, 52 O.O. 239. Death ⇐ 6

Note 2

2. Peril of death

Evidence that three-year-old child dressed only in lightweight nylon warmup outfit disappeared in 28–degree weather while playing in backyard adjacent to his home was insufficient to establish exposure to specific peril of death at beginning of his absence and thus to support presumption of death under exception to five-year waiting period. Stepp v. Stepp (Ohio App. 10 Dist., 06-24-1999) 133 Ohio App.3d 749, 729 N.E.2d 836. Death ⇐ 2(1)

Evidence of hazardous conditions in an Alaskan wilderness area and of finding a missing person's backpack in a river supports a finding that the missing person is dead and that the river itself constitutes a specific peril of death within the meaning of RC 2121.01(A)(2). Skele v. Mutual Ben. Life Ins. Co. (Miami 1984) 20 Ohio App.3d 213, 485 N.E.2d 770, 20 O.B.R. 259.

3. Rebuttal of presumption

Under normal circumstances, an individual must be missing for a period of five years in order to raise a presumption of death. Stepp v. Stepp (Ohio App. 10 Dist., 06-24-1999) 133 Ohio App.3d 749, 729 N.E.2d 836. Death ⇐ 2(1)

Person, who for seven years has not been heard of by those who, had he been alive, would naturally have heard of him, is presumed to be dead unless circumstances of case are such as to account for his not having been heard of, without assuming his death. Doty v. Ohio Nat. Life Ins. Co. (Franklin 1937) 58 Ohio App. 1, 15 N.E.2d 544, 25 Ohio Law Abs. 673, 10 O.O. 177. Death ⇐ 2(1)

4. Common law rule

The common-law presumption arising after seven years absence has not been abrogated by the presumed decedents act which provides the procedure for administering an estate of one who is presumed to be dead on account of seven or more years absence from the place of his last domicile. White v. Industrial Commission (Franklin 1956) 102 Ohio App. 236, 142 N.E.2d 549, 2 O.O.2d 264. Death ⇐ 2(1)

The common law rule as to the presumption of death arising seven years after the time of disappearance has not been abrogated by the Presumed Decedents Act in Ohio. Freiberg v. Schloss (Ohio Prob. 1953) 112 N.E.2d 352, 65 Ohio Law Abs. 331, 50 O.O. 156. Death ⇐ 2(1)

At common law, where a person leaves his home or usual place of residence and goes to parts unknown and is not heard of or known to be living for a period of seven years, the legal presumption arises that he is dead; the rule, so far as the administration of decedents' estates is concerned, has been modified by the Presumed Decedents Act, and under such act the presumption of death in the case of unexplained absence for seven or more years arises as of the date of the decree of the probate court authorized by GC 10509–28 (RC 2121.04). In re McWilson's Estate (Ohio 1951) 155 Ohio St. 261, 98 N.E.2d 289, 44 O.O. 262.

Language of GC 10509–25 (RC 2121.01) et seq. does not indicate that the general assembly intended to abrogate the common law rule that a person is presumed dead seven years after date he left his home and was not heard of again. Blythe v. Vail (Ohio Com.Pl. 1938) 7 Ohio Supp. 1, 26 Ohio Law Abs. 516, 11 O.O. 393.

Common law rule that unexplained absence from usual place of residence for seven years raises presumption of death, held not abrogated by this section. Morrissey v Smith, 17 Abs 240, 39 LR 329 (App, Brown 1933).

5. Effect of other laws

In absence of evidence that retired railroad employee, who disappeared from county home in which he had been placed, died before expiration of seven-year period of absence during which he was unheard from, his daughters were entitled to recover unpaid monthly payments of annuity and as of expiration of seven years after his disappearance, the lump-sum death payment provided by Railroad Retirement Act. Tobin v. United States Railroad Retirement Board (C.A.6 1961) 286 F.2d 480, 16 O.O.2d 138. Social Security And Public Welfare ⇐ 166.1

2121.02 Complaint to establish presumption; parties; notice

(A) When such a presumption of death arises under section 2121.01 of the Revised Code with respect to a person who at the time of disappearance was domiciled in this state, the attorney general of this state or any person entitled under the last will of such presumed decedent or under Chapter 2105. of the Revised Code to any share in the presumed decedent's property within this state, or any person or entity who, under the terms of any contract, beneficiary designation, trust, or otherwise, may be entitled to any property, right, or interest by reason of the death of the presumed decedent, may file a complaint setting forth the facts which raise the presumption of death in the probate court of the county of the presumed decedent's last residence.

(B) When a presumption of death arises pursuant to section 2121.01 of the Revised Code with respect to a person who at the time of the person's disappearance was domiciled at a place other than within the state, and the presumed decedent owns real property within this state, the complaint may be filed in the county where any part of the real property of the presumed decedent is located by any of the persons or entities referred to in division (A) of this section, or by any domiciliary executor or administrator of the decedent. A foreign fiduciary shall include with the complaint an exemplified copy of the domiciliary proceedings pursuant to which the foreign fiduciary was appointed.

(C) In the case of a presumed decedent who was domiciled in this state, the complainant shall name as parties defendant the presumed decedent and each of the following that do not join in the complaint:

(1) The presumed decedent's surviving spouse, if any;

(2) All persons known to the complainant who are entitled under the presumed decedent's last will and all persons who are entitled under Chapter 2105. of the Revised Code to any share of the presumed decedent's property;

(3) All persons or entities known to the complainant who have or would have by reason of the presumed decedent's death any right or interest under any contract, beneficiary designation, trust, or otherwise;

(4) All contract obligors known to the complainant whose rights or obligations would be affected by a determination that the presumed decedent is in fact dead.

(D) In the case of a presumed decedent who was not domiciled in this state but who owned real estate in this state, the complainant shall name as parties defendant each of the following that do not join in the complaint:

(1) The presumed decedent's surviving spouse, if any;

(2) All persons known to the complainant who are entitled under the presumed decedent's last will and all persons who are entitled under Chapter 2105. of the Revised Code to any share of the presumed decedent's real property within this state.

(E) All parties defendant, other than the presumed decedent, shall be served with summons in the same manner as provided by the Rules of Civil Procedure.

(F) The complainant shall cause to be advertised once a week for four consecutive weeks in a newspaper published in the county, the fact that the complaint has been filed together with a notice that on a day certain, which shall be at least four weeks after the last appearance of the advertisement, or after the final publication where any defendant is being served by publication, whichever is later, the probate court will hear evidence relevant to the allegations of the complaint.

(G) No guardian ad litem, trustee for the suit, or other representative shall be required to be appointed to represent the presumed decedent in the proceeding.

(2002 H 242, eff. 5–16–02; 1974 S 349, eff. 9–30–74)

Historical and Statutory Notes

Ed. Note: Former 2121.02 repealed by 1974 S 349, eff. 9–30–74; 1953 H 1; GC 10509–26.

Pre–1953 H 1 Amendments: 122 v H 50; 114 v 406

Amendment Note: 2002 H 242 substituted "Chapter 2105." for "sections 2105.06 to 2105.21" throughout the section; and made changes to reflect gender neutral language.

Cross References

Appointment of ancillary administrator, 2129.08
Service of process, Civ R 73

Library References

Death ⟾2.
Westlaw Topic No. 117.
C.J.S. Death §§ 8 to 14.

Research References

Encyclopedias

OH Jur. 3d Death § 16, Proceedings; Complaint.
OH Jur. 3d Death § 17, Proceedings; Complaint—Parties.
OH Jur. 3d Death § 18, Proceedings; Complaint—Service of Summons.
OH Jur. 3d Death § 19, Hearing and Decree.
OH Jur. 3d Decedents' Estates § 883, Where Intestate was a Resident of Ohio.
OH Jur. 3d Decedents' Estates § 884, Where Intestate was Not a Resident of Ohio.
OH Jur. 3d Decedents' Estates § 1039, Wills of Presumed Decedents.

Treatises and Practice Aids

Carlin, Baldwin's Ohio Practice, Merrick-Rippner Probate Law § 9:1, Presumption of Death—Statutory.
Carlin, Baldwin's Ohio Practice, Merrick-Rippner Probate Law § 9:2, Presumption of Death—Procedure for Establishing—Jurisdiction.
Carlin, Baldwin's Ohio Practice, Merrick-Rippner Probate Law § 9:3, Presumption of Death—Procedure for Establishing—Necessary Parties Defendant.
Carlin, Baldwin's Ohio Practice, Merrick-Rippner Probate Law § 9:4, Presumption of Death—Procedure for Establishing—Notice.
Carlin, Baldwin's Ohio Practice, Merrick-Rippner Probate Law § 9:5, Presumption of Death—Procedure for Establishing—Filing Complaint.
Carlin, Baldwin's Ohio Practice, Merrick-Rippner Probate Law § 9:7, Presumption of Death—Effect of Decree.
Carlin, Baldwin's Ohio Practice, Merrick-Rippner Probate Law § 9:9, Presumption of Death—Complaint—Form.
Carlin, Baldwin's Ohio Practice, Merrick-Rippner Probate Law § 9:10, Presumption of Death—Entry Setting for Hearing, Ordering Notice, and Service of Summons—Form.
Carlin, Baldwin's Ohio Practice, Merrick-Rippner Probate Law § 9:11, Presumption of Death—Legal Notice—Form.

Notes of Decisions

Ed. Note: This section contains annotations from former RC 2121.04.

Retirement benefits 1

---

1. Retirement benefits

Mandamus will not lie to compel public retirement benefits to trustee where retirant has disappeared and has not thereafter been heard from. State ex rel. Hammond v. Public Emp. Retirement System (Ohio 1972) 29 Ohio St.2d 192, 280 N.E.2d 904, 58 O.O.2d 403.

2121.03 Evidence admissible

At the hearing the probate court shall hear such legally admissible evidence as is offered for the purpose of ascertaining whether the presumption of death is established. No person shall be disqualified to testify by reason of relationship as husband or wife to the presumed decedent, or by reason of an interest in the presumed decedent's property, or because of a right or interest under the terms of a contract, beneficiary designation, trust, or otherwise, arising by reason of the death of the presumed decedent.

(1974 S 349, eff. 9–30–74)

Historical and Statutory Notes

Ed. Note: Former 2121.03 repealed by 1974 S 349, eff. 9–30–74; 1953 H 1; GC 10509–27.

Pre–1953 H 1 Amendments: 114 v 407

Library References

Death ⟾3.
Westlaw Topic No. 117.
C.J.S. Death §§ 4 to 5, 8.

Research References

Encyclopedias

OH Jur. 3d Death § 19, Hearing and Decree.

Notes of Decisions

Ed. Note: This section contains annotations from former RC 2121.01.

Burden of proof 1
Date of death 3
Insurance policy 2

---

1. Burden of proof

Given clear and unequivocal language of amendments to trusts as to grantor's daughter, language of the original trust was essentially irrelevant in determining whether grantor intended to disinherit daughter and her lineal descendants. Henson v. Casey (Ohio App. 4 Dist., Pickaway, 11-01-2004) No. 04CA9, 2004-Ohio-5848, 2004 WL 2474264, Unreported, appeal not allowed 105 Ohio St.3d 1454, 823 N.E.2d 458, 2005-Ohio-763. Trusts ⟾ 112

Where one is appointed administrator of estate of an individual presumed to be dead by reason of seven or more years unexplained absence under Presumed Decedents Act and brings action to collect proceeds of a policy of insurance issued on the life of presumed decedent, payable upon his death, burden rests upon plaintiff to establish material averments of his cause of action by a preponderance of all evidence, which burden never shifts; where plaintiff produces evidence that absentee has been away from his usual place of residence, unheard from, for a period of more than seven years and relies solely upon presumption of death to establish his case, and defendant introduces evidence which in its cumulative effect at least counterbalances such presumption, the plaintiff must fail; in such action described, where upon all the evidence adduced reasonable minds could not fairly conclude that the presumption should stand, it disappears, and if in addition to such presumption there is no evidence tending to show that the absentee is in fact dead, the duty devolves upon the trial court to direct a verdict or render judgment for the defendant and his motion therefor. Brunny v. Prudential Ins. Co. of America (Ohio 1949) 151 Ohio St. 86, 84 N.E.2d 504, 38 O.O. 533.

If the administrator of the presumed decedent or any other interested party can rebut the presumption of death by evidence, he has a right to do so, but the presumption cannot be destroyed by any finding or any failure to find by the probate court in appointing the administrator of the presumed decedent. Morrissey v Smith, 17 Abs 240, 39 LR 329 (App, Brown 1933).

2. Insurance policy

"Due proof" of death required by insurance policy, which would entitle beneficiary to demand payment, need only be such as could be furnished under circumstances; absence of insured for period of seven years is presumptive evidence of death and if "due proof" of this is submitted to company and not questioned, it is sufficient to be basis of demand for payment under policy. Doty v. Ohio Nat. Life Ins. Co. (Franklin 1937) 58 Ohio App. 1, 15 N.E.2d 544, 25 Ohio Law Abs. 673, 10 O.O. 177.

Note 3

3. Date of death

A probate court, in an action brought by an executor for a declaratory judgment, where a devisee has been missing from the place of his last domicile, may declare and decree when proven by a preponderance of the evidence that said devisee is in fact dead, may fix the actual date of his death, when proven by a preponderance of the evidence, at any time between the date of the devisee's disappearance from his last domicile and the date of the court's decree, and may determine what rights, if any, he has under a testator's will. Freiberg v. Schloss (Ohio Prob. 1953) 112 N.E.2d 352, 65 Ohio Law Abs. 331, 50 O.O. 156. Declaratory Judgment ⚖ 243

2121.04 Decree of presumption of death; effects

(A) If satisfied that a presumption of death has been established, as provided in section 2121.01 of the Revised Code, the probate court shall so decree.

(B) The death of such presumed decedent shall for all purposes under the law of this state be regarded as having occurred as of the date of such decree.

(C) If the presumed decedent is married on the date of the decree, the presumed decedent's marriage is dissolved by the decree. No subsequent vacation of the decree, as provided in section 2121.08 of the Revised Code, shall affect the dissolution of the marriage.

(1974 S 349, eff. 9–30–74)

Historical and Statutory Notes

Ed. Note: Former 2121.04 repealed by 1974 S 349, eff. 9–30–74; 1953 H 1; GC 10509–28.

Pre–1953 H 1 Amendments: 114 v 407

Library References

Death ⚖ 2(1).
Westlaw Topic No. 117.
C.J.S. Death §§ 8 to 12.

Research References

Encyclopedias

OH Jur. 3d Death § 19, Hearing and Decree.
OH Jur. 3d Death § 20, Effect of Decree.
OH Jur. 3d Death § 21, Vacating Decree and Effect Thereof.

Treatises and Practice Aids

Carlin, Baldwin's Ohio Practice, Merrick-Rippner Probate Law § 9:1, Presumption of Death—Statutory.

Carlin, Baldwin's Ohio Practice, Merrick-Rippner Probate Law § 9:7, Presumption of Death—Effect of Decree.

Carlin, Baldwin's Ohio Practice, Merrick-Rippner Probate Law § 9:9, Presumption of Death—Complaint—Form.

Carlin, Baldwin's Ohio Practice, Merrick-Rippner Probate Law § 9:12, Presumption of Death—Judgment Entry—Form.

Notes of Decisions

Ed. Note: This section contains annotations from former RC 2121.01 and RC 2121.04.

Constitutional issues   1
Date of death   2

1. Constitutional issues

That part of GC 10509–28 (RC 2121.04) which provides that the "presumption of death shall be regarded as having arisen as of the date of such decree," is unconstitutional and ineffective to control the probate court as to the date the presumptive death arises. Blythe v. Vail (Ohio Com.Pl. 1938) 7 Ohio Supp. 1, 26 Ohio Law Abs. 516, 11 O.O. 393.

2. Date of death

Common sense of language of amendments to trusts was that, for the purposes of determining appropriate action to be taken at the time of grantor's death, daughter was presumed to be dead and assets to pass to other beneficiaries; plain language of amendments not only "presumed" the prior death of daughter, but spelled out the consequences of specific presumption that "shall" take place. Henson v. Casey (Ohio App. 4 Dist., Pickaway, 11-01-2004) No. 04CA9, 2004-Ohio-5848, 2004 WL 2474264, Unreported, appeal not allowed 105 Ohio St.3d 1454, 823 N.E.2d 458, 2005-Ohio-763. Trusts ⚖ 124

The provisions of the Presumed Decedents Act may not be applied to determine the date of death of a person who has been absent from the place of his last domicile for more than seven years, so as to make such date subsequent to the death of another person from whom such absentee would have inherited an estate had he survived such other person, and thus make such date available as an item of evidence in the determination of the right to share in the estate of such other person. Baker v. Myers (Ohio 1953) 160 Ohio St. 376, 116 N.E.2d 711, 52 O.O. 239. Death ⚖ 6

When it can be proven that a missing person died on a certain date, either within seven or more years absence from the place of his last domicile, his date of death shall be regarded as having arisen on such proven date, rather than on the date of the decree when he is merely presumed to be dead. Freiberg v. Schloss (Ohio Prob. 1953) 112 N.E.2d 352, 65 Ohio Law Abs. 331, 50 O.O. 156. Death ⚖ 2(2)

The date fixed by the probate court as the date when the presumption of death arises, cannot conclude strangers to the judgment which fixes the date, and cannot prevent such other parties from asserting in an independent action that the presumption of death is complete at the end of the seven year period specified by the common law rule. Morrissey v Smith, 17 Abs 240, 39 LR 329 (App, Brown 1933).

Where property rights depended upon an accurate determination of the date when the presumption of death arose, it was the mandatory duty of the probate court to fix such date. 1930 OAG 2125.

2121.05 Administration of estate of presumed decedent; orders; conditions; bonds

(A) Except as provided otherwise in Chapter 2121. of the Revised Code, all of the proceedings for the probate of the decedent's last will, if any, and all the proceedings, domiciliary or ancillary, for the administration of the decedent's estate that are set forth in the Revised Code for use upon the death of a decedent, shall upon the signing of the decree be instituted and carried on in the same manner as if the presumed decedent were in fact dead. All acts pursuant to these proceedings shall be as valid as if the presumed decedent were in fact dead.

(B) Following the decree the court may make such supplementary orders as in its discretion are necessary to consummate any right or interest arising by reason of the death of the presumed decedent under any contract, trust, or other nonprobate property interest of any person or entity who was a party to the proceedings. The court may condition the granting of any such order by requiring any person or entity who would benefit thereby to furnish bond for a three-year period after the decree in the form and amount, with or without sureties, as the court shall order. If any supplementary order is directed to the holder of assets of the presumed decedent which were created by the decree of presumed death, the court, at the request of the party defendant to whom the order is directed, shall condition the granting of any such order by requiring any person or entity who would benefit thereby to furnish a suretyship bond for a three-year period after the decree in the amount of the assets so created by the decree with interest for the period of the bond at the rate specified in the order.

(C) The term "assets of the presumed decedent which were created by the decree of presumed death" as used in division (B) of this section and division (D) of section 2121.08 of the Revised Code, means those potential assets of the presumed decedent in which the presumed decedent had a contractual or other right, contingent upon the presumed decedent's death, to have such assets paid to his designee and the decree of presumed death would fulfill the contingency. Only that portion of the proceeds of life insurance policies on the life of the presumed decedent that exceeds any net cash surrender value of such policies on the date of the decree is within the definition of the term "assets of the presumed decedent which were created by the decree of presumed death."

(D) The bond shall provide that, if within the three-year period after the decree is entered by the court it is established that the presumed decedent is alive, such person or entity shall on the subsequent order of the court refund or return any sums, with interest as provided in the court order, or property received by virtue of such order, to the presumed decedent or to the person or entity who, by reason of the erroneous finding of death of the presumed decedent, made such payment or delivered such property. The bond shall be further conditioned on returning the fair value of the property if the same shall have been sold or otherwise disposed of in the interim.

(E) If the person or entity who would benefit by an order, as provided in division (B) of this section, fails to provide a bond for the amount of the assets of the presumed decedent which were created by the decree, with interest as specified in the order, the holder shall hold those assets for the three-year period they would have been bonded. In that event, the holder shall pay interest at the same rate specified in the order as a condition of the bond and the interest shall accumulate and be held throughout that period.

(F) Nothing in this section shall preclude such person or entity from selling, encumbering, or otherwise disposing of any property so received and any purchaser, transferee or mortgagee acquires good title to such property free and clear of any claim of the presumed decedent.

(1974 S 349, eff. 9–30–74)

Historical and Statutory Notes

Ed. Note: Former 2121.05 repealed by 1974 S 349, eff. 9–30–74; 1953 H 1; GC 10509–29.

Pre–1953 H 1 Amendments: 114 v 407

Cross References

Appointment of ancillary administrator, 2129.08

Library References

Executors and Administrators ⚖4, 299.
Wills ⚖210.
Westlaw Topic Nos. 162, 409.
C.J.S. Executors and Administrators §§ 13, 541.
C.J.S. Wills § 467.

Research References

Encyclopedias
OH Jur. 3d Death § 20, Effect of Decree.
OH Jur. 3d Decedents' Estates § 40, Death of Intestate.
OH Jur. 3d Decedents' Estates § 1654, Refunding by Legatees and Distributees.

Treatises and Practice Aids
Carlin, Baldwin's Ohio Practice, Merrick-Rippner Probate Law § 9:1, Presumption of Death—Statutory.
Carlin, Baldwin's Ohio Practice, Merrick-Rippner Probate Law § 9:7, Presumption of Death—Effect of Decree.
Carlin, Baldwin's Ohio Practice, Merrick-Rippner Probate Law § 36:11, Examination of Witness to Signature—Form.
Carlin, Baldwin's Ohio Practice, Merrick-Rippner Probate Law § 36:13, Entry to Issue Commission for Deposition of Witness to Will—Form.

Notes of Decisions

Ed. Note: *This section contains annotations from former RC 2121.01.*

Common law 2
Inmates 4
Known estate 3
Procedural issues 1

---

1. Procedural issues

There was nothing inconsistent or redundant in conclusion that grantor intended to disinherit daughter and her lineal descendants while allowing daughter to remain as a beneficiary under lifetime benefits of trusts. Henson v. Casey (Ohio App. 4 Dist., Pickaway, 11-01-2004) No. 04CA9, 2004-Ohio-5848, 2004 WL 2474264, Unreported, appeal not allowed 105 Ohio St.3d 1454, 823 N.E.2d 458, 2005-Ohio-763. Trusts ⚖ 124

Language of original trust dispelled conclusion that language used in amendments to trusts was intended to counter the five year statutory period of the Presumed Decedents Law; original trust was clear and unequivocal in using a technique to deal with an absent beneficiary different than that imposed in amendments. Henson v. Casey (Ohio App. 4 Dist., Pickaway, 11-01-2004) No. 04CA9, 2004-Ohio-5848, 2004 WL 2474264, Unreported, appeal not allowed 105 Ohio St.3d 1454, 823 N.E.2d 458, 2005-Ohio-763. Trusts ⚖ 124

Where one is appointed administrator of estate of an individual presumed to be dead by reason of seven or more years unexplained absence under Presumed Decedents Act and brings action to collect proceeds of a policy of insurance issued on the life of presumed decedent, payable upon his death, burden rests upon plaintiff to establish material averments of his cause of action by a preponderance of all evidence, which burden never shifts; where plaintiff produces evidence that absentee has been away from his usual place of residence, unheard from, for a period of more than seven years and relies solely upon presumption of death to establish his case, and defendant introduces evidence which in its cumulative effect at least counterbalances such presumption, the plaintiff must fail; in such action described, where upon all the evidence adduced reasonable minds could not fairly conclude that the presumption should stand, it disappears, and if in addition to such presumption there is no evidence tending to show that the absentee is in fact dead, the duty devolves upon the trial court to direct a verdict or render judgment for the defendant and his motion therefor. Brunny v. Prudential Ins. Co. of America (Ohio 1949) 151 Ohio St. 86, 84 N.E.2d 504, 38 O.O. 533.

This section is a procedural statute and confined by its terms to the administration of the known estate of the presumed decedent. Morrissey v Smith, 17 Abs 240, 39 LR 329 (App, Brown 1933).

2. Common law

The common law rule as to the presumption of death arising seven years after the time of disappearance has not been abrogated by the Presumed Decedents Act in Ohio. Freiberg v. Schloss (Ohio Prob. 1953) 112 N.E.2d 352, 65 Ohio Law Abs. 331, 50 O.O. 156. Death ⚖ 2(1)

At common law, where a person leaves his home or usual place of residence and goes to parts unknown and is not heard of or known to be living for a period of seven years, the legal presumption arises that he is dead; the rule, so far as the administration of decedents' estates is concerned, has been modified by the Presumed Decedents Act, and under such act the presumption of death in the case of unexplained absence for seven or more years arises as of the date of the decree of the probate court authorized by GC 10509–28 (RC 2121.04). In re McWilson's Estate (Ohio 1951) 155 Ohio St. 261, 98 N.E.2d 289, 44 O.O. 262.

3. Known estate

The presumed decedents act is not intended to apply when a presumed decedent leaves no estate to be administered, but is confined by its terms to the administration of the known estate of a presumed decedent. Freiberg v. Schloss (Ohio Prob. 1953) 112 N.E.2d 352, 65 Ohio Law Abs. 331, 50 O.O. 156.

4. Inmates

Proceedings may be instituted under GC 10509–25 (RC 2121.01) et seq. to have legally presumed dead an inmate of a state institution who has escaped and has not been heard from for seven or more years, and money on deposit in the name of the superintendent of such state institution, as trustee for such inmate, may be closed out and distributed according to law after a legal presumption of death has been made out. 1934 OAG 3053.

2121.06 Title to real estate; limits on transfer; bond

Upon the signing of the decree establishing the death of the presumed decedent, the real estate of the presumed decedent passes and devolves[1] as in the case of actual death and the persons entitled by will, or under Chapter 2105. of the Revised Code, may enter and take possession. Persons taking the real estate may sell or mortgage it and the purchaser or mortgagee takes a good title, free and discharged of any interest or claim of the presumed decedent. The persons taking such real estate shall not sell, convey, or mortgage any part thereof within the three-year period specified in section 2121.08 of the Revised Code without first giving bond in an amount to be fixed by the probate court and with sureties to be approved by the court. In the discretion of the court the bond may be taken without sureties. Such bond shall be conditioned to account for and pay over to the presumed decedent, in case within the three-year period after the decree is entered by the court it is established that the presumed decedent is still alive, the value of the real estate sold or conveyed, or in the case of the making of a mortgage, to pay the amount of the mortgage and interest thereon, or in case of a foreclosure of such mortgage, to account for and pay over the value of the real estate mortgaged.

(2002 H 242, eff. 5–16–02; 1977 S 112, eff. 11–1–77; 1974 S 349)

[1] So in original; 2002 H 242.

Historical and Statutory Notes

Ed. Note: Former 2121.06 repealed by 1974 S 349, eff. 9–30–74; 1953 H 1; GC 10509–30.

Pre–1953 H 1 Amendments: 114 v 408

Amendment Note: 2002 H 242 substituted "Chapter 2105." for "sections 2105.01 to 2105.21" in the first sentence of the section.

Library References

Descent and Distribution ⚖75.
Executors and Administrators ⚖299.
Wills ⚖722.
Westlaw Topic Nos. 124, 162, 409.
C.J.S. Descent and Distribution § 73.
C.J.S. Executors and Administrators § 541.
C.J.S. Wills §§ 1614 to 1615.

Research References

Encyclopedias
OH Jur. 3d Death § 20, Effect of Decree.
OH Jur. 3d Decedents' Estates § 40, Death of Intestate.
OH Jur. 3d Decedents' Estates § 145, Realty of a Presumed Decedent.
OH Jur. 3d Decedents' Estates § 188, Sale or Mortgage of Realty After Presumption of Death Established.

Treatises and Practice Aids
Carlin, Baldwin's Ohio Practice, Merrick-Rippner Probate Law § 9:7, Presumption of Death—Effect of Decree.

2121.07 Distribution of personal property; bond

(A) Before any distribution of personal property is made from the estate of a presumed decedent, the persons entitled to receive such property may in the discretion of the court and as a condition of distribution be required to give bond in the form and amount, with or without sureties, as the court orders, with the condition that if within a three-year period after the decree is entered by the court it is established that the presumed decedent is alive, the distributee will upon subsequent order of the court refund or return the property to the presumed decedent, or the fair market value of property if the same shall have been sold or otherwise disposed of in the interim.

(B) Nothing in this section shall preclude a distributee from selling, encumbering, or otherwise disposing of any property so distributed and any purchaser, transferee, or mortgagee acquires good title to such property free and clear of any claim of the presumed decedent.

(1974 S 349, eff. 9–30–74)

Historical and Statutory Notes

Ed. Note: 2121.07 contains provisions analogous to former 2121.08 repealed by 1974 S 349, eff. 9–30–74.

Ed. Note: Former 2121.07 repealed by 1974 S 349, eff. 9–30–74; 1953 H 1; GC 10509–31.

Pre–1953 H 1 Amendments: 114 v 408

Library References

Executors and Administrators ⚖299.
Westlaw Topic No. 162.
C.J.S. Executors and Administrators § 541.

Research References

Encyclopedias
OH Jur. 3d Death § 20, Effect of Decree.

2121.08 Vacation of decree; effects; set off

(A) The probate court may at any time within a three-year period from the date of the decree establishing the death of a presumed decedent, upon proof satisfactory to the court that the presumed decedent is in fact alive, vacate the decree establishing the presumption of his death. After the decree has been vacated all the powers of the executor or administrator of the presumed decedent cease, but all proceedings had and steps taken with respect to the administration of the estate of the presumed decedent prior to the vacating of such decree remain valid. The executor or administrator of the estate of such presumed decedent who is found to be alive shall settle his account of his administration down to the time of the vacating of the decree and shall transfer all assets remaining in his hands to the person as whose executor or administrator he has acted, or to such person's authorized agent or attorney.

(B) The title of any person to any money, property, right, or interest as surviving spouse, next of kin, heir, legatee, devisee, co-owner with right of survivorship, beneficiary or other contractual payee, successor to a trust interest, or otherwise of the presumed decedent shall be subject to this section, and upon vacating of such decree as provided in this section any property, money, right, or interest, or the fair value thereof if the same shall have been sold or otherwise disposed of, may be recovered from the person who had received any such property.

(C) Except as provided in division (D) of this section, in any action against a beneficiary for the recovery of property or the value thereof, or upon the bond given as condition for delivery of money, other personal property, or sale or encumbrance of real property, the beneficiary may set off as against such claim, an allowance for services rendered in maintaining or preserving the property, and for any moneys or other considerations made or given by the beneficiary for the preservation, care, or maintenance of the property during the period of absence of the person erroneously presumed to be dead, and the reasonable value of any part of the property used for support by those whom the person erroneously presumed to be dead had a legal obligation to support during his absence.

(D) There shall be no set off as against those assets defined in division (C) of section 2121.05 of the Revised Code to be assets of the presumed decedent which were created by the decree of presumed death. Those assets created by the erroneous decree of presumed death shall be returned with interest to the person entitled thereto.

(E) Any net cash surrender value on any policies of life insurance on the life of a person erroneously presumed to be dead are subject to the set off provision in division (C) of this section. The person erroneously presumed to be dead, or persons claiming under him, may recover whatever remains of cash values from the person to whom paid. Such claimants have no recourse against the insurance company which made such payments, and it is discharged from liability on the policies affected.

(1977 S 112, eff. 11–1–77; 1974 S 349)

Historical and Statutory Notes

Ed. Note: 2121.08 contains provisions analogous to former 2121.09 repealed by 1974 S 349, eff. 9–30–74.

Ed. Note: Former 2121.08 repealed by 1974 S 349, eff. 9–30–74; 1953 H 1; GC 10509–32; see now 2121.07 for provisions analogous to former 2121.08.

Pre–1953 H 1 Amendments: 114 v 409

Library References

Death ⚖2(1).
Westlaw Topic No. 117.
C.J.S. Death §§ 8 to 12.

Research References

Encyclopedias
OH Jur. 3d Death § 21, Vacating Decree and Effect Thereof.
OH Jur. 3d Decedents' Estates § 962, Removal from Office or Revocation of Letters.

Treatises and Practice Aids
Carlin, Baldwin's Ohio Practice, Merrick-Rippner Probate Law § 9:7, Presumption of Death—Effect of Decree.
Carlin, Baldwin's Ohio Practice, Merrick-Rippner Probate Law § 9:8, Presumption of Death—Vacating Decree.

2121.09 Substitution of person erroneously presumed dead as party to actions

After vacation of the decree of the presumption of death has been established, as provided by section 2121.08 of the Revised Code, the person erroneously presumed to be dead may, on motion filed of record stating the facts, be substituted as plaintiff or petitioner in all actions or proceedings brought by the executor or administrator, whether prosecuted to judgment or decree or otherwise. Such person may, in all actions or proceedings previously brought against the executor or administrator, be substituted as defendant or respondent, on motion filed by him or on his behalf, but shall not be compelled to go to trial in less than three months from the time of filing of such motion. Judgments or decrees recovered against the executor or administrator, before the vacation of the decree, may be opened on application made by the person erroneously presumed to be dead within three months after the vacating of the decree, provided it is supported by an affidavit alleging the existence of facts which would be a valid defense. If the application is not made within the three months or is made but the supporting alleged facts are adjudged an insufficient defense, the judgment or decree is conclusive to all intents, saving the defendant's right to review as in other cases on appeal.

(1974 S 349, eff. 9–30–74)

Historical and Statutory Notes

Ed. Note: 2121.09 contains provisions analogous to former 2121.10 repealed by 1974 S 349, eff. 9–30–74.

Ed. Note: Former 2121.09 repealed by 1974 S 349, eff. 9–30–74; 1953 H 1; GC 10509–33; see now 2121.08 for provisions analogous to former 2121.09.

Pre–1953 H 1 Amendments: 114 v 409

Library References

Executors and Administrators ⚖438(1).
Parties ⚖59(1).
Westlaw Topic Nos. 162, 287.
C.J.S. Executors and Administrators §§ 769 to 770, 776, 779 to 780.
C.J.S. Parties §§ 76 to 78.

Research References

Encyclopedias
OH Jur. 3d Death § 21, Vacating Decree and Effect Thereof.
OH Jur. 3d Decedents' Estates § 145, Realty of a Presumed Decedent.
OH Jur. 3d Decedents' Estates § 865, Death—Presumed Death.
OH Jur. 3d Decedents' Estates § 1039, Wills of Presumed Decedents.
OH Jur. 3d Decedents' Estates § 1736, Appointment in Case of Nonresident Presumed Decedent.

Treatises and Practice Aids
Baldwin's Ohio Handbook Series—Trial Handbook § 21:7, Death After Seven Years' Absence.
Carlin, Baldwin's Ohio Practice, Merrick-Rippner Probate Law § 9:7, Presumption of Death—Effect of Decree.

CHAPTER 2123

DETERMINATION OF HEIRSHIP

Section
2123.01 When proceedings to determine heirship may be had
2123.02 Petition; defendants
2123.03 Service of summons
2123.04 Service by publication
2123.05 Finding and order
2123.06 Other persons may ask for determination
2123.07 Effect of determination

Cross References

Inheritance by parent of deceased abandoned child prohibited, 2105.10
Order in which debts to be paid, 2117.25
Paternity proceedings, limitation of action to determine father and child relationship, 3111.05
Payment of debts after three months, 2117.15
Powers of trustee, 2119.03
Presentation and allowance of creditor's claims, procedure, 2117.06

2123.01 When proceedings to determine heirship may be had

Whenever property passes by the laws of intestate succession, or under a will to a beneficiary not named in such will, proceedings may be had in the probate court to determine the persons entitled to such property.

(1953 H 1, eff. 10–1–53; GC 10509–95)

Historical and Statutory Notes

Pre–1953 H 1 Amendments: 114 v 422

Cross References

Ancillary administration, determination of heirship, 2129.18

Determination of rights or legal relations, 2721.05
Law of descent, Ch 2105
Wills, Ch 2107

Library References

Descent and Distribution ☞71.
Westlaw Topic No. 124.
C.J.S. Descent and Distribution §§ 77, 82 to 88.

Research References

Encyclopedias

OH Jur. 3d Decedents' Estates § 196, Heirship, Generally.
OH Jur. 3d Decedents' Estates § 197, Purpose of Special Proceedings for Determination of Heirship.
OH Jur. 3d Decedents' Estates § 198, When Special Proceedings Lie.
OH Jur. 3d Decedents' Estates § 199, Jurisdiction and Venue.
OH Jur. 3d Decedents' Estates § 962, Removal from Office or Revocation of Letters.

Treatises and Practice Aids

Klein, Darling, & Terez, Baldwin's Ohio Practice Civil Practice § 4.4:2, Process: Service by Publication--Service by Publication Authorized by Law--In General.
Carlin, Baldwin's Ohio Practice, Merrick-Rippner Probate Law § 6:6, Declaratory Judgments—Probate Court Proceedings.
Carlin, Baldwin's Ohio Practice, Merrick-Rippner Probate Law § 43:2, Construing a Will—Action for Instructions—Preferability of Declaratory Judgment Action.

Notes of Decisions

Adoption 4
Escheat 5
Marriage 1
Paternity 6
Procedural issues 3
Will 2

---

1. Marriage

As an incident to a hearing upon exceptions to an inventory, the probate court has jurisdiction to determine the issue of a common-law marriage. In re Soeder's Estate (Cuyahoga 1966) 7 Ohio App.2d 271, 220 N.E.2d 547, 36 O.O.2d 404.

In a proceeding for determination of heirship, the petitioner is not entitled to a jury trial; in such proceeding, where petitioner claims to be the commonlaw wife of the decedent and the adverse parties defend as heirs and administrator of the estate of decedent, the petitioner is incompetent to testify, over objection, as to facts tending to establish the alleged common law marriage. Brawley v. Thomas (Athens 1947) 82 Ohio App. 400, 81 N.E.2d 719, 38 O.O. 61. Witnesses ☞ 136

Where plaintiff submitted documentary evidence of her marriage to decedent in foreign country, attorney testified to marriage laws in such country, and it was incumbent on plaintiff to prove such marriage in action brought under this section to determine heirs, supreme court will not disturb affirmance by appellate court of finding by probate court in favor of defendant as court does not weigh the evidence, the appellate court having found insufficient evidence to establish authenticity of documentary evidence. Olijan v. Lublin (Gudlin) (Ohio 1944) 143 Ohio St. 417, 55 N.E.2d 658, 28 O.O. 354.

Where plaintiff instituted an action to be declared the sole surviving spouse of decedent based upon a common law marriage, a promise by the decedent to marry the plaintiff once everything was straightened out does not constitute an agreement to marry in praesenti. Pasquinelli v Pasquinelli, No. 1386 (4th Dist Ct App, Scioto, 8–10–83).

2. Will

Where testator devised realty to his wife for life with the power to sell the realty and enjoy the proceeds thereof if necessary for proper maintenance and provided that, if the realty was not sold by the wife, it should go to testator's two sisters, share and share alike, forever, the estate vested in the sisters on the death of the testator as an "estate in remainder", subject to be divested on a sale of the realty under power granted to the wife.

Schaefer v. Gebhart (Butler 1942) 42 N.E.2d 931, 36 Ohio Law Abs. 73. Wills ☞ 634(4.1)

Where there was an ambiguity in the body of the will, the probate court properly admitted extrinsic evidence in order to determine the actual intent of the testator. First Natl Bank of Cincinnati v Comisar, Nos. C–820897, C–820947, and C–820948 (1st Dist Ct App, Hamilton, 1–18–84).

Probate court may properly dismiss a petition to determine heirship where an unchallenged will stands in the probate court and there is no intestate property for which heirs need to be determined. Bank One Trust Co v Shaw, No. CA–1609 (5th Dist Ct App, Tuscarawas, 12–20–82).

3. Procedural issues

Motion to dismiss was not the proper procedural mechanism for an intestate decedent's daughter to seek removal of decedent's purported son as administrator of decedent's estate and to challenge his status as heir on the ground that a legal parent-child relationship had never been established; daughter should have filed a petition to determine heirship. In re Estate of Kinder (Ohio App. 3 Dist., 06-12-1998) 128 Ohio App.3d 316, 714 N.E.2d 964. Executors And Administrators ☞ 35(10)

In an action in the probate court for a determination of heirship where the state of the record makes it impossible to intelligently determine the heirs entitled to the estate, time should be given for additional testimony and evidence pertinent to the issue of relationship, and "letters rogatory" should be issued accordingly; and an application therefore should be allowed, even where the trial court has already rendered an opinion adverse to the applicant, but on which no judgment has been entered. Maurer v. Mihalyne (Stark 1957) 105 Ohio App. 83, 151 N.E.2d 383, 5 O.O.2d 367. Pretrial Procedure ☞ 122; Descent And Distribution ☞ 71(7)

Action for determination of heirship is statutory proceeding in which any relief granted is in accordance with legal and not equitable principles. Minnix v. Hague (Franklin 1952) 125 N.E.2d 739, 69 Ohio Law Abs. 418. Descent And Distribution ☞ 71(1)

In an action to determine who are heirs to property passing by intestate succession, an alleged heir is not disqualified from testifying. O'Shaughnessy v Stofft, 117 NE(2d) 734, 67 Abs 389, 55 OO 352 (Prob 1953).

The provisions of the Presumed Decedents Act may not be applied to determine the date of death of a person who has been absent from the place of his last domicile for more than seven years, so as to make such date subsequent to the death of another person from whom such absentee would have inherited an estate had he survived such other person, and thus make such date available as an item of evidence in the determination of the right to share in the estate of such other person. Baker v. Myers (Ohio 1953) 160 Ohio St. 376, 116 N.E.2d 711, 52 O.O. 239. Death ☞ 6

Probate court has jurisdiction to adjudicate rights of parties in specific items of property upon filing in such court of a pleading captioned "Petition to determine heirship," under authority conferred by GC 10509–95 (RC 2123.01) et seq. and under 10501–53 (RC 2101.24), conferring plenary power upon probate court to dispose of any matter properly before it, which power is exclusive "unless otherwise provided by law," such court has exclusive jurisdiction to make such an adjudication irrespective of such captioned pleading, when prayer therein asks for determination not only of names of heirs but also of interest each inherits. Speidel v. Schaller (Clermont 1943) 73 Ohio App. 141, 55 N.E.2d 346, 40 Ohio Law Abs. 190, 28 O.O. 252.

Proceeding in probate court by executor for determination regarding who were entitled to share in decedent's estate under the plain language of his will was not a "proceeding to construe will" but was rather a "proceeding to determine heirship" and, therefore, judgment of probate court was not appealable to Court of Common Pleas on questions of fact and law but was appealable directly to Court of Appeals. Stewart v. Purget (Clark 1941) 37 N.E.2d 549, 34 Ohio Law Abs. 343. Appeal And Error ☞ 240

The finding of the trial court that: "The Court is unable to determine the heirs of the decedent" is not a final order; therefore such order cannot be used as a basis for relief under Civ R 59 or Civ R 60. Estate of Curran v Corbett, No. CA–6035 (5th Dist Ct App, Stark, 5–23–83).

4. Adoption

A declaration or finding in a proceeding begun by an adopting father under the provisions of GC 10512–21 (Repealed), that an adoption is null and void on grounds therein set forth, operates prospectively only and does not cut off rights acquired by the adopted child prior to such declaration; in such case, in an action under section to determine who is entitled to next estate of inheritance of adopting mother, who died prior to such declaration without issue or surviving spouse, the adopted child is entitled to the next estate of inheritance of the deceased adopting mother. Steiner v. Rainer (Mahoning 1941) 69 Ohio App. 6, 42 N.E.2d 684, 23 O.O. 306.

In a suit to determine heirs for the purpose of distributing a decedent's estate under the laws of intestate succession, the doctrine of equitable adoption does not apply if there is no evidence of a purported contract or agreement to adopt, and the trial court's order of escheat to the state was proper. Boulger v Unknown Heirs of Robertson, No. 951 (4th Dist Ct App, Ross, 7–1–83).

5. Escheat

There is no authority for escheating property to the state, where there is no finding of an absence of heirs. Maurer v. Mihalyne (Stark 1957) 105 Ohio App. 83, 151 N.E.2d 383, 5 O.O.2d 367.

6. Paternity

Application to determine heirship which is in essence action to establish paternity is governed by statute which states that action to determine parentage must be brought within five years after child reaches his or her majority. Garrison v. Smith (Lucas 1988) 55 Ohio App.3d 14, 561 N.E.2d 1041. Children Out-of-wedlock ⟺ 38

2123.02 Petition; defendants

In a situation described in section 2123.01 of the Revised Code, the executor or administrator may file in the probate court of the county where the estate is being administered a petition signed by such executor or administrator or his attorney, which petition shall be verified. The surviving spouse and the legatees and devisees, or the heirs and distributees of the decedent, including those whose names are unknown, shall be made parties defendant. The petition shall contain a concise statement of the pertinent facts and shall conclude with a prayer for the determination of the heirs and distributees of such decedent or of the devisees or legatees not named in the will and their respective interests in the estate.

(1953 H 1, eff. 10–1–53; GC 10509–96)

Historical and Statutory Notes

Pre–1953 H 1 Amendments: 116 v 385; 114 v 422

Cross References

Inheritance by parent of deceased abandoned child prohibited, 2105.10
Pleadings need not be verified, exceptions, Civ R 11

Library References

Descent and Distribution ⟺71(3).
Westlaw Topic No. 124.
C.J.S. Descent and Distribution §§ 77, 82, 84.

Research References

Encyclopedias

OH Jur. 3d Decedents' Estates § 136, Abandoning a Minor Child.
OH Jur. 3d Decedents' Estates § 199, Jurisdiction and Venue.
OH Jur. 3d Decedents' Estates § 200, Petitioners.
OH Jur. 3d Decedents' Estates § 201, Defendants.
OH Jur. 3d Decedents' Estates § 203, Petition.
OH Jur. 3d Decedents' Estates § 962, Removal from Office or Revocation of Letters.
OH Jur. 3d Decedents' Estates § 1268, Nature and Scope of Hearing on Exceptions.

Treatises and Practice Aids

Klein, Darling, & Terez, Baldwin's Ohio Practice Civil Practice § 4.4:2, Process: Service by Publication--Service by Publication Authorized by Law--In General.
Carlin, Baldwin's Ohio Practice, Merrick-Rippner Probate Law § 3:62, Fiduciary Complaint for Determination of Heirs—Form.

Carlin, Baldwin's Ohio Practice, Merrick-Rippner Probate Law § 15:52, Descent and Distribution—Denial of Inheritance to Parent Who Abandons Minor—Filing of Petition in Probate Court.
Kuehnle and Levey, Ohio Real Estate Law and Practice § 53:12, Land Sales—Parties Defendant—Determination of Heirship Prior to Action to Sell.

Notes of Decisions

Marriage 1
Procedural issues 3
Termination of parental rights, effect 4
Testimony 2

---

1. Marriage

As an incident to a hearing upon exceptions to an inventory, the probate court has jurisdiction to determine the issue of a common-law marriage. In re Soeder's Estate (Cuyahoga 1966) 7 Ohio App.2d 271, 220 N.E.2d 547, 36 O.O.2d 404.

In a proceeding to determine heirs an alleged common law wife of the decedent is not competent to testify as to the marriage over the objections of decedent's children. Lynch v. Romas (Franklin 1956) 139 N.E.2d 352, 74 Ohio Law Abs. 1.

2. Testimony

In an action to determine who are heirs to property passing by intestate succession, an alleged heir is not disqualified from testifying. O'Shaughnessy v Stofft, 117 NE(2d) 734, 67 Abs 389, 55 OO 352 (Prob 1953).

3. Procedural issues

Motion to dismiss was not the proper procedural mechanism for an intestate decedent's daughter to seek removal of decedent's purported son as administrator of decedent's estate and to challenge his status as heir on the ground that a legal parent-child relationship had never been established; daughter should have filed a petition to determine heirship. In re Estate of Kinder (Ohio App. 3 Dist., 06-12-1998) 128 Ohio App.3d 316, 714 N.E.2d 964. Executors And Administrators ⟺ 35(10)

Where an estate is in the process of administration, the administrator is the only person entitled to bring an action to determine the heirs of the decedent. Stofft v. O'Shaughnessy (Ohio Prob. 1952) 107 N.E.2d 643, 62 Ohio Law Abs. 595, 48 O.O. 143.

4. Termination of parental rights, effect

Termination of parental rights does not divest children of rights to inheritance from their mother until such time as the children have been legally adopted where (1) the mother loses custody of her children after an auto accident which leaves her mentally and physically disabled, (2) the mother dies while the appeal of custody is pending, (3) a lawsuit arising out of the accident is settled leaving a substantial sum of money with the estate, and (4) the administratrix files a complaint in probate court to determine heirship pursuant to RC 2123.02. Pledgure v. Goutras (Ohio App. 5 Dist., Stark, 04-03-2000) No. 2000CA00035, 2000 WL 492578, Unreported.

2123.03 Service of summons

Upon the filing of the petition mentioned in section 2123.02 of the Revised Code the same proceedings, pleadings, and rule days as in civil actions in the court of common pleas shall apply. All parties defendant who are known to be residents of the state and whose place of residence is known shall be served with summons, as provided for the service of summons in civil actions in such court.

(1953 H 1, eff. 10–1–53; GC 10509–97)

Historical and Statutory Notes

Pre–1953 H 1 Amendments: 116 v 385; 114 v 423

Cross References

Service of summons, Civ R 73

Library References

Descent and Distribution ⚖71(1).
Process ⚖48.
Westlaw Topic Nos. 124, 313.
C.J.S. Descent and Distribution §§ 77, 82.
C.J.S. Process §§ 26, 33, 49.

Research References

Encyclopedias

OH Jur. 3d Decedents' Estates § 202, Service of Summons.
OH Jur. 3d Decedents' Estates § 204, Trial or Hearing.

Treatises and Practice Aids

Klein, Darling, & Terez, Baldwin's Ohio Practice Civil Practice § 73:5, Probate Division--Service and Filing of Pleadings and Papers Subsequent to the Original Complaint.

Carlin, Baldwin's Ohio Practice, Merrick-Rippner Probate Law § 3:68, Entry on Filing and Setting for Hearing and Issuing Summons—Form.

2123.04 Service by publication

In a proceeding to determine heirship, nonresident defendants and defendants whose names or places of residence are unknown shall be served by publication as in civil actions in the court of common pleas.

(1953 H 1, eff. 10–1–53; GC 10509–98)

Historical and Statutory Notes

Pre–1953 H 1 Amendments: 116 v 385; 114 v 423

Cross References

Publication of notice, necessary party unknown, 2703.24
Service of summons, Civ R 73

Library References

Descent and Distribution ⚖71(1).
Process ⚖84.
Westlaw Topic Nos. 124, 313.
C.J.S. Descent and Distribution §§ 77, 82.
C.J.S. Process § 58.

Research References

Encyclopedias

OH Jur. 3d Decedents' Estates § 202, Service of Summons.

Treatises and Practice Aids

Klein, Darling, & Terez, Baldwin's Ohio Practice Civil Practice § 73:5, Probate Division--Service and Filing of Pleadings and Papers Subsequent to the Original Complaint.

Carlin, Baldwin's Ohio Practice, Merrick-Rippner Probate Law § 4:22, Service—Summons—Publication—When Permitted.

Carlin, Baldwin's Ohio Practice, Merrick-Rippner Probate Law § 4:23, Service—Summons—Publication—Application to Probate Jurisdiction.

2123.05 Finding and order

At the time assigned for the hearing of a proceeding set forth under section 2123.01 of the Revised Code, or at any time to which said hearing may be adjourned, the probate court may hear proof taken by commission, or by witnesses produced in open court, of the facts set forth in the petition, and shall, if satisfied from the evidence, find and adjudge who are or were the heirs or next of kin of the decedent, and entitled by the laws of this state to inherit the estate of the deceased, or the devisees or legatees named or unnamed in the will, which finding and adjudication shall be entered on the journal of the court, which entry, or a certified copy thereof, shall be prima facie evidence of the facts therein found.

(1953 H 1, eff. 10–1–53; GC 10509–99)

Historical and Statutory Notes

Pre–1953 H 1 Amendments: 114 v 423

Cross References

Inheritance by parent of deceased abandoned child prohibited, 2105.10

Library References

Descent and Distribution ⚖71(7).
Westlaw Topic No. 124.
C.J.S. Descent and Distribution §§ 77, 82, 87 to 88.

Research References

Encyclopedias

OH Jur. 3d Decedents' Estates § 136, Abandoning a Minor Child.
OH Jur. 3d Decedents' Estates § 198, When Special Proceedings Lie.
OH Jur. 3d Decedents' Estates § 204, Trial or Hearing.
OH Jur. 3d Decedents' Estates § 205, Findings and Order.
OH Jur. 3d Decedents' Estates § 207, Effect of Determination.
OH Jur. 3d Decedents' Estates § 962, Removal from Office or Revocation of Letters.

Treatises and Practice Aids

Carlin, Baldwin's Ohio Practice, Merrick-Rippner Probate Law § 19:3, Legitimation—Constitutional Issues.

Carlin, Baldwin's Ohio Practice, Merrick-Rippner Probate Law § 3:69, Entry Determining Heirship—Form.

Carlin, Baldwin's Ohio Practice, Merrick-Rippner Probate Law § 57:10, Removal of Fiduciary—Procedure—Discretion of Probate Court.

Law Review and Journal Commentaries

Legal Applicability of Blood Group Tests, Comment. 1 Ohio St L J 47 (January 1935).

The Use of the Blood Tests for Disputed Paternity in the Courts of Ohio, Harriet S. Hyman and Lawrence H. Snyder. 2 Ohio St L J 203 (May 1936).

Notes of Decisions

Appeals 5
Common law marriage 4
Constitutional issues 1
Evidence and testimony 3
Jurisdiction 2
Procedural issues 6

---

1. Constitutional issues

Purported son of an intestate decedent was denied due process of law when he was determined not to be an heir and removed as administrator of decedent's estate without a hearing and by the inappropriate procedural mechanism of a motion to dismiss. In re Estate of Kinder (Ohio App. 3 Dist., 06-12-1998) 128 Ohio App.3d 316, 714 N.E.2d 964. Constitutional Law ⚖306(1); Executors And Administrators ⚖35(16)

Purported son of an intestate decedent deserved a hearing on the issue of heirship, which was raised when decedent's daughter sought removal of him as administrator of decedent's estate on the ground that a legal parent-child relationship had never been established, where the issue turned on whether the relationship had been timely established under a sister state's paternity law and this question could not properly be answered without full examination of the evidence and the law, particularly since the purported son asked for more time to prepare. In re Estate of Kinder (Ohio App. 3 Dist., 06-12-1998) 128 Ohio App.3d 316, 714 N.E.2d 964. Executors And Administrators ⚖35(16)

2. Jurisdiction

Michigan law governed whether a now-deceased father had timely legitimated his purported son and thereby established him as a legal heir under the Ohio laws of intestate succession, where the purported son was born in Michigan, the father resided there at the time of the birth and continued to reside there for at least 30 years, and a Michigan court had ruled that prima facie proof of paternity existed under Michigan law. In re Estate of Kinder (Ohio App. 3 Dist., 06-12-1998) 128 Ohio App.3d 316, 714 N.E.2d 964. Children Out-of-wedlock ⇔ 81

Probate court has jurisdiction to adjudicate rights of parties in specific items of property upon filing in such court of a pleading captioned "Petition to determine heirship," under authority conferred by GC 10509–95 (RC 2123.01) et seq., and 10501–53 (RC 2101.24), conferring plenary power upon probate court to dispose of any matter properly before it, which power is exclusive "unless otherwise provided by law," such court has exclusive jurisdiction to make such an adjudication irrespective of such captioned pleading, when prayer therein asks for determination not only of names of the heirs but also of the interest each inherits. Speidel v. Schaller (Clermont 1943) 73 Ohio App. 141, 55 N.E.2d 346, 40 Ohio Law Abs. 190, 28 O.O. 252.

3. Evidence and testimony

In an action in the probate court for a determination of heirship where the state of the record makes it impossible to intelligently determine the heirs entitled to the estate, time should be given for additional testimony and evidence pertinent to the issue of relationship, and "letters rogatory" should be issued accordingly; and an application therefore should be allowed, even where the trial court has already rendered an opinion adverse to the applicant but on which no judgment has been entered. Maurer v. Mihalyne (Stark 1957) 105 Ohio App. 83, 151 N.E.2d 383, 5 O.O.2d 367. Pretrial Procedure ⇔ 122; Descent And Distribution ⇔ 71(7)

GC 11564 (RC 2321.05) does not require a bill of exceptions to be filed if the error complained of is manifest independently of a bill of exceptions; thus, where court, in action to determine heirship and construe a will, following section, sets in detail his findings on the evidence, and enters same upon journal, no bill of exceptions need be filed. Stewart v. Purget (Clark 1942) 45 N.E.2d 792, 37 Ohio Law Abs. 105.

4. Common law marriage

As an incident to a hearing upon exceptions to an inventory, the probate court has jurisdiction to determine the issue of a common-law marriage. In re Soeder's Estate (Cuyahoga 1966) 7 Ohio App.2d 271, 220 N.E.2d 547, 36 O.O.2d 404.

In a proceeding to determine heirs an alleged common law wife of the decedent is not competent to testify as to the marriage over the objections of decedent's children. Lynch v. Romas (Franklin 1956) 139 N.E.2d 352, 74 Ohio Law Abs. 1.

In a proceeding for determination of heirship the petitioner is not entitled to a jury trial; in such proceeding, where the petitioner claims to be the common-law wife of the decedent and the adverse parties defend as heirs and administrator of the estate of decedent, the petitioner is incompetent to testify, over objection, as to facts tending to establish the alleged common law marriage. Brawley v. Thomas (Athens 1947) 82 Ohio App. 400, 81 N.E.2d 719, 38 O.O. 61. Witnesses ⇔ 136

In a hearing to determine heirship, the probate court properly found that the decedent and plaintiff were married at common law where the agreement to marry was originally made in a state which does not recognize common law marriages, since the subsequent actions of the decedent and plaintiff reaffirmed that agreement in this state. In re Yeagley Estate, No. 444 (7th Dist Ct App, Carroll, 9–8–82).

5. Appeals

Proceeding in probate court by executor for determination regarding who were entitled to share in decedent's estate under the plain language of his will was not a "proceeding to construe will" but was rather a "proceeding to determine heirship" and, therefore, judgment of probate court was not appealable to Court of Common Pleas on questions of fact and law but was appealable directly to Court of Appeals. Stewart v. Purget (Clark 1941) 37 N.E.2d 549, 34 Ohio Law Abs. 343. Appeal And Error ⇔ 240

6. Procedural issues

Motion to dismiss was not the proper procedural mechanism for an intestate decedent's daughter to seek removal of decedent's purported son as administrator of decedent's estate and to challenge his status as heir on the ground that a legal parent-child relationship had never been established; daughter should have filed a petition to determine heirship. In re Estate of Kinder (Ohio App. 3 Dist., 06-12-1998) 128 Ohio App.3d 316, 714 N.E.2d 964. Executors And Administrators ⇔ 35(10)

2123.06 Other persons may ask for determination

Whenever it is necessary for any person other than an executor or administrator to determine who are or were the heirs at law of a deceased person, on the petition of any interested party and proceedings like those set forth in sections 2123.01 to 2123.05, inclusive, of the Revised Code, the probate court may make a determination thereof.

(1953 H 1, eff. 10–1–53; GC 10509–100)

Historical and Statutory Notes

Pre–1953 H 1 Amendments: 114 v 423

Library References

Descent and Distribution ⇔71(3).
Westlaw Topic No. 124.
C.J.S. Descent and Distribution §§ 77, 82, 84.

Research References

Encyclopedias

OH Jur. 3d Decedents' Estates § 199, Jurisdiction and Venue.
OH Jur. 3d Decedents' Estates § 200, Petitioners.
OH Jur. 3d Decedents' Estates § 962, Removal from Office or Revocation of Letters.

Treatises and Practice Aids

Carlin, Baldwin's Ohio Practice, Merrick-Rippner Probate Law § 3:67, Interested Party Complaint for Determination of Heirs—Form.
Kuehnle and Levey, Ohio Real Estate Law and Practice § 53:12, Land Sales—Parties Defendant—Determination of Heirship Prior to Action to Sell.

Notes of Decisions

Administration of estate 2
Common law marriage 1
Procedural issues 3

---

1. Common law marriage

As an incident to a hearing upon exceptions to an inventory, the probate court has jurisdiction to determine the issue of a common-law marriage. In re Soeder's Estate (Cuyahoga 1966) 7 Ohio App.2d 271, 220 N.E.2d 547, 36 O.O.2d 404.

2. Administration of estate

Where an estate is in the process of administration, the administrator is the only person entitled to bring an action to determine the heirs of the decedent. Stofft v. O'Shaughnessy (Ohio Prob. 1952) 107 N.E.2d 643, 62 Ohio Law Abs. 595, 48 O.O. 143.

3. Procedural issues

Motion to dismiss was not the proper procedural mechanism for an intestate decedent's daughter to seek removal of decedent's purported son as administrator of decedent's estate and to challenge his status as heir on the ground that a legal parent-child relationship had never been established; daughter should have filed a petition to determine heirship. In re Estate of Kinder (Ohio App. 3 Dist., 06-12-1998) 128 Ohio App.3d 316, 714 N.E.2d 964. Executors And Administrators ⇔ 35(10)

2123.07 Effect of determination

Any fiduciary may make a final distribution of an estate or take any other appropriate action respecting a trust, upon the determination set forth in section 2123.05 of the Revised Code, and shall thereupon, together with the surety, be discharged from liability arising from such determined interest, and the title to any property thereupon purchased from such fiduciary shall be free from such determined interest.

(1953 H 1, eff. 10–1–53; GC 10509–101)

Historical and Statutory Notes

Pre–1953 H 1 Amendments: 114 v 423

Library References

Descent and Distribution ⚖71(7).
Westlaw Topic No. 124.
C.J.S. Descent and Distribution §§ 77, 82, 87 to 88.

Research References

Encyclopedias

OH Jur. 3d Decedents' Estates § 197, Purpose of Special Proceedings for Determination of Heirship.
OH Jur. 3d Decedents' Estates § 207, Effect of Determination.

Treatises and Practice Aids

Kuehnle and Levey, Ohio Real Estate Law and Practice § 52:9, Statutory Fiduciary Sales—Grounds for Judicial Sale—Consent of Beneficiaries.

Notes of Decisions

Common law marriage 1

---

1. Common law marriage

As an incident to a hearing upon exceptions to an inventory, the probate court has jurisdiction to determine the issue of a common-law marriage. In re Soeder's Estate (Cuyahoga 1966) 7 Ohio App.2d 271, 220 N.E.2d 547, 36 O.O.2d 404.

CHAPTER 2125

ACTION FOR WRONGFUL DEATH

Section
2125.01 Civil action for wrongful death
2125.02 Proceedings; damages allowable; limitation of actions; statute of repose for product liability claims; abandonment of deceased child; definitions
2125.03 Distribution of award
2125.04 New action

Uncodified Law

1987 H 1, § 3, eff. 1–5–88, reads, in part: (D) It is the intent of the General Assembly in enacting section 2315.21 of the Revised Code in this act to recognize that punitive or exemplary damages are not recoverable in wrongful death actions under Chapter 2125. of the Revised Code, as found by the Supreme Court in *Rubeck v. Huffman*, 54 Ohio St. 2d 20 (1978).

Comparative Laws

Ill.—ILCS 740 180/1 et seq.
Ind.—West's A.I.C. 34–1–1–2.
Ky.—Baldwin's KRS 411.130 et seq.
Mich.—M.C.L.A. § 600.2922.

Cross References

Actions against political subdivisions, 2744.05
Civil action for injury caused by criminal act barred by certain criminal convictions arising out of same act, tort action defined, 2307.60
Foreign wards and guardians, 2111.43
Law not to limit damages for wrongful death, O Const Art I §19a
Limitation on damages recoverable against state university or college, exception for wrongful death action, 3345.40
Motor vehicle insurance, policies allowed to treat all claims for bodily injury to one person as single claim, 3937.44
Order in which debts to be paid, 2117.25
Payment of debts after three months, 2117.15
Powers of guardian of person and estate, 2111.07
Powers of trustee for person who has disappeared, 2119.03
Presentation and allowance of creditor's claims; procedure, 2117.06
Product liability actions, claimant defined, 2307.71
Uninsured and underinsured motorist coverage, 3937.18

Law Review and Journal Commentaries

The Criminal Corporation: Is Ohio Prepared for Corporate Criminal Prosecutions for Workplace Fatalities?, Comment. 45 Clev St L Rev 135 (1997).

Damages Recoverable in Survivorship Actions as Compared to Wrongful Death Actions, William K. McCarter and Sean A. McCarter. 21 Lake Legal Views 10 (April 1998).

Punitive Damages in Wrongful Death, Gary N. Holthus. 20 Clev St L Rev 301 (May 1971).

Tort Law: Protection Of Prenatal Life Through Wrongful Death Statutes—Critique Of *Giardina v. Bennett*, 111 N.J. 412, 545 A.2d 139 (1988), Note. 15 U Dayton L Rev 157 (Fall 1989).

Wrongful Death Suits for Fetuses Gain, David E. Rovella. 18 Nat'l L J A6 (July 15, 1996).

2125.01 Civil action for wrongful death

When the death of a person is caused by wrongful act, neglect, or default which would have entitled the party injured to maintain an action and recover damages if death had not ensued, the person who would have been liable if death had not ensued, or the administrator or executor of the estate of such person, as such administrator or executor, shall be liable to an action for damages, notwithstanding the death of the person injured and although the death was caused under circumstances which make it aggravated murder, murder, or manslaughter. When the action is against such administrator or executor, the damages recovered shall be a valid claim against the estate of such deceased person. No action for the wrongful death of a person may be maintained against the owner or lessee of the real property upon which the death occurred if the cause of the death was the violent unprovoked act of a party other than the owner, lessee, or a person under the control of the owner or lessee, unless the acts or omissions of the owner, lessee, or person under the control of the owner or lessee constitute gross negligence.

When death is caused by a wrongful act, neglect, or default in another state or foreign country, for which a right to maintain an action and recover damages is given by a statute of such other state or foreign country, such right of action may be enforced in this state. Every such action shall be commenced within the time prescribed for the commencement of such actions by the statute of such other state or foreign country.

The same remedy shall apply to any such cause of action now existing and to any such action commenced before January 1, 1932, or attempted to be commenced in proper time and now appearing on the files of any court within this state, and no prior law of this state shall prevent the maintenance of such cause of action.

(2001 S 108, § 2.01, eff. 7–6–01; 2001 S 108, § 2.02, eff. 7–6–01; 1996 H 350, eff. 1–27–97 [1]*; 1981 H 332, eff. 2–5–82; 1953 H 1; GC 10509–166)*

[1] See Notes of Decisions, *State ex rel. Ohio Academy of Trial Lawyers v. Sheward* (Ohio 1999), 86 Ohio St.3d 451, 715 N.E.2d 1062.

Uncodified Law

2001 S 108, § 1, eff. 7–6–01, reads:

It is the intent of this act (1) to repeal the Tort Reform Act, Am. Sub. H.B. 350 of the 121st General Assembly, 146 Ohio Laws 3867, in conformity with the Supreme Court of Ohio's decision in *State, ex rel. Ohio Academy of Trial Lawyers, v. Sheward* (1999), 86 Ohio St.3d 451; (2) to clarify the status of the law; and (3) to revive the law as it existed prior to the Tort Reform Act.

2001 S 108, § 3, eff. 7–6–01, reads, in part:

(A) In Section 2.01 of this act:

(3) Sections 109.36, 2117.06, 2125.01, 2125.02, 2125.04, 2305.10, 2305.16, 2305.27, 2305.38, 2307.31, 2307.32, 2307.75, 2307.80, 2315.01, 2315.19, 2501.02, 2744.06, 3722.08, 4112.14, 4113.52, 4171.10, and 4399.18 of the Revised Code are revived and amended, supersede the versions of the same sections that are repealed by Section 2.02 of this act, and include amendments that gender neutralize the language of the sections (as contemplated by section 1.31 of the Revised Code) and that correct apparent error.

Historical and Statutory Notes

Ed. Note: The amendment of this section by 1996 H 350, eff. 1–27–97, was repealed by 2001 S 108, § 2.02, eff. 7–6–01. See *Baldwin's Ohio Legislative Service Annotated*, 1996, page 10/L–3379, and 2001, page 6/L–1441, or the OH–LEGIS or OH–LEGIS–OLD database on Westlaw, for original versions of these Acts.

Pre–1953 H 1 Amendments: 114 v 438

Amendment Note: 1996 H 350 rewrote this section, which prior thereto read:

"When the death of a person is caused by wrongful act, neglect, or default which would have entitled the party injured to maintain an action and recover damages if death had not ensued, the person who would have been liable if death had not ensued, or the administrator or executor of the estate of such person, as such administrator or executor, shall be liable to an action for damages, notwithstanding the death of the person injured and although the death was caused under circumstances which make it aggravated murder, murder, or manslaughter. When the action is against such administrator or executor, the damages recovered shall be a valid claim against the estate of such deceased person. No action for the wrongful death of a person may be maintained against the owner or lessee of the real property upon which the death occurred if the cause of the death was the violent unprovoked act of a party other than the owner, lessee, or a person under the control of the owner or lessee, unless the acts or omissions of the owner, lessee, or person under the control of the owner or lessee constitute gross negligence.

"When death is caused by a wrongful act, neglect, or default in another state or foreign country, for which a right to maintain an action and recover damages is given by a statute of such other state or foreign country, such right of action may be enforced in this state. Every such action shall be commenced within the time prescribed for the commencement of such actions by the statute of such other state or foreign country.

"The same remedy shall apply to any such cause of action now existing and to any such action commenced before January 1, 1932, or attempted to be commenced in proper time and now appearing on the files of any court within this state, and no prior law of this state shall prevent the maintenance of such cause of action."

Cross References

Amendment of pleadings to conform to the evidence, Civ R 15
Amount of recovery in tort action to be determined, 2315.80
Asbestos claims, applicability, 2307.95
Counterclaim and crossclaim, Civ R 13
Damages for wrongful death not to be limited by law, O Const Art I, § 19a
Joinder of claims and remedies, Civ R 18
Liability of employer, insurance provision, 4113.09
Requirements for prima-facie showing of physical impairment for certain tort actions involving asbestos exposure, 2307.92
Requirements for prima-facie showing of physical impairment for certain tort actions involving mixed dust exposure, 2307.86
Requirements for prima-facie showing of physical impairment for certain tort actions involving silica exposure, 2307.85

Library References

Death ⚖15, 43.
Westlaw Topic No. 117.
C.J.S. Death §§ 34, 36, 68, 113 to 114.

Research References

Encyclopedias

OH Jur. 3d Actions § 126, Physical Injuries to Person—Where Death Results from Injury; Relationship to Action for Wrongful Death.
OH Jur. 3d Actions § 128, Physical Injuries to Person—Survival of Death Action Against Tortfeasor's Estate.
OH Jur. 3d Aliens & Citizens § 20, Actions by Aliens—Actions for Wrongful Death.
OH Jur. 3d Appellate Review § 47, Orders in Special Proceedings—Examples of Special Proceedings.
OH Jur. 3d Boats, Ships, & Shipping § 42, Injuries to or Death of Ship's Personnel.
OH Jur. 3d Conflict of Laws § 56, Statute of Limitations.
OH Jur. 3d Death § 34, Generally; Common-Law Rule.
OH Jur. 3d Death § 35, Ohio Wrongful Death Statute.
OH Jur. 3d Death § 36, Ohio Wrongful Death Statute—Constitutionality.
OH Jur. 3d Death § 37, Ohio Wrongful Death Statute—Applicability, Generally.
OH Jur. 3d Death § 39, Effect of Other Statutes Authorizing Recovery for Death Upon Right of Action Under General Wrongful Death Statute—Workers' Compensation Law.
OH Jur. 3d Death § 50, Generally; Necessity of Violation of Legal Duty.
OH Jur. 3d Death § 51, Willful or Intentional Act.
OH Jur. 3d Death § 52, Negligence.
OH Jur. 3d Death § 57, Existence of Cause of Action in Decedent.
OH Jur. 3d Death § 58, Existence of Cause of Action in Decedent—Requisites as to Time When Cause Exists.
OH Jur. 3d Death § 72, Executor or Administrator of Wrongdoer.
OH Jur. 3d Death § 74, Defenses Based Upon Criminal Act of Wrongdoer or Decedent.
OH Jur. 3d Death § 79, Generally; by Decedent After Injury.
OH Jur. 3d Death § 85, Constitutional Prohibition Against Limitation on Amount.
OH Jur. 3d Death § 115, Generally; Jurisdiction.
OH Jur. 3d Death § 117, Limitation of Actions; Statute of Repose.
OH Jur. 3d Death § 125, Defendants.
OH Jur. 3d Death § 175, Action Based on Foreign Statute.
OH Jur. 3d Death § 177, Grounds of Action.
OH Jur. 3d Death § 182, Maximum Amount.
OH Jur. 3d Death § 183, Generally; Proper Party Plaintiff.
OH Jur. 3d Decedents' Estates § 1316, Proceeds from Action for Wrongful Death.
OH Jur. 3d Decedents' Estates § 1332, Damages for Wrongful Death.
OH Jur. 3d Decedents' Estates § 1445, Relation of Statutes to Other Limitation Statutes.
OH Jur. 3d Employment Relations § 333, Setoff of Amount Contributed or Paid by Employer for Insurance, Relief, Benefit, or Indemnity.
OH Jur. 3d Government Tort Liability § 87, Wrongful Death.
OH Jur. 3d Limitations & Laches § 15, Applicability of Foreign Wrongful Death Statutes.
OH Jur. 3d Premises Liability § 41, Liability for Acts of Third Persons.

Forms

Ohio Jurisprudence Pleading and Practice Forms § 22:4, Those Not Real Parties in Interest.
Ohio Jurisprudence Pleading and Practice Forms § 123:9, Conflict of Laws.
Ohio Jurisprudence Pleading and Practice Forms § 114:20, Rollover—Sport Utility Vehicle.
Ohio Jurisprudence Pleading and Practice Forms § 123:12, Negligent Medical Care—Cancer.
Ohio Jurisprudence Pleading and Practice Forms § 123:13, Nuisance in Maintenance and Elimination of Crosswalk.

Treatises and Practice Aids

Baldwin's Ohio Handbook Series—Trial Handbook § 34:53, Wrongful Death Actions.

Klein, Darling, & Terez, Baldwin's Ohio Practice Civil Practice § 4:184, Wrongful Death and Survival Action Joined.

Carlin, Baldwin's Ohio Practice, Merrick-Rippner Probate Law § 12:1, Wrongful Death—Scope of RC Ch. 2125.

Carlin, Baldwin's Ohio Practice, Merrick-Rippner Probate Law § 12:3, Wrongful Death—Jurisdiction of Probate Court.

Carlin, Baldwin's Ohio Practice, Merrick-Rippner Probate Law § 12:14, Wrongful Death—Statute of Limitations—Savings Statute.

Carlin, Baldwin's Ohio Practice, Merrick-Rippner Probate Law § 12:21, Wrongful Death—Denial of Damages to Parent Who Abandoned Child—Hearing; Burden of Proof; Order; Effect.

Carlin, Baldwin's Ohio Practice, Merrick-Rippner Probate Law § 12:22, Wrongful Death—Release by Decedent.

Carlin, Baldwin's Ohio Practice, Merrick-Rippner Probate Law § 12:23, Application to Approve Wrongful Death Settlement or Distribution—Form.

Ohio Personal Injury Practice § 4:6, Wrongful Death and Survival Claims—Wrongful Death—Requirements for Bringing a Wrongful Death Action.

Ohio Personal Injury Practice § 3:10, Parties Plaintiff—Wrongful Death Complaint.

Ohio Personal Injury Practice § 3:13, Pleading Damages—Wrongful Death Damages.

Ohio Personal Injury Practice App. C, Appendix C. Ohio Academy of Trial Lawyers v. Sheward.

Law Review and Journal Commentaries

Comparison of the "Old" and "New" Wrongful Death Statutes, Evelyn J. Stratton. 39 Columbus B Briefs 7 (April 15, 1983).

Feticide: Time to End Ohio's Blind Imitation of the Past, Comment. 18 Ohio N U L Rev 659 (1991).

Interspousal Immunity in Ohio After *Prem v. Cox*, Note. 17 Akron L Rev 647 (Spring 1984).

McMullen v. Ohio State University Hospitals: This Isn't Vegas, But Don't Tell the Courts—Playing with Percentages and the Loss-of-Chance Doctrine, Note. 34 Akron L Rev 767 (2001).

Ohio's New Wrongful Death Statute: An Expanded Scope of Recoverable Damages, Comment. 53 U Cin L Rev 1083 (1984).

Parents Who Abandon or Fail to Support their Children and Apportionment of Wrongful Death Damages, Note. 27 J Fam L 871 (1988–89).

Person v. Potential: judicial struggles to decide claims arising from the death of an embryo or fetus and Michigan's struggle to settle the question. Dena M. Marks, 37 Akron L R 41 (2004, No. 1).

Pleading: Joinder of Actions in Wrongful Death Cases, Comment. 4 Ohio St L J 127 (December 1937).

Recovery for the Wrongful Death of a Viable Fetus: Werling v. Sandy, Note. 19 Akron L Rev 127 (Summer 1985).

Recovery of Punitive Damages in Ohio Wrongful Death Actions: A Preferred Approach, James J. Ross. 6 U Dayton L Rev 175 (Summer 1981).

Stomping at *Savoie*, Jay R. Carson. 32 U Tol L Rev 509 (Summer 2001).

Torts—Actions and Defenses—Wrongful Death—Privileges and Immunities—The Doctrine of Interspousal Immunity Does Not Bar a Wrongful Death Action Brought By the Estate of a Deceased Spouse Against the Surviving Spouse, Note. 52 U Cin L Rev 936 (1983).

Valid Release Executed Prior to Death Not a Bar to Wrongful Death Action in Ohio, Note. 6 U Cin L Rev 212 (March 1932).

Wrongful Death Damages: Recovery of Investment in and Society and Companionship of a Child, Note. 27 Ohio St L J 355 (Spring 1966).

Wrongful Death Suits for Fetuses Gain, David E. Rovella. 18 Nat'l L J A6 (July 15, 1996).

The Wrongful Death of Willie McCord—Or—Beware of "Free" Public Parks—The Ghosts of Immunity and the Ohio Guest Statute Still Roam!, Lawrence P. Wilkins. 47 U Cin L Rev 591 (1979).

Notes of Decisions

Act, neglect, or default in foreign state 6
Action for benefit of heirs 2
Automobile insurance 15
Choice of law 18
Civil rights action 21
Constitutional issues 1
Contributory negligence and assumption of risk 19
Covenants not to sue 22
Damages 8
Effect of action 11
Evidence 20
Foreign right of action 5
Joinder 7
Limitation and bar of action 12
Negligence 9
Other statute pertinent or applicable 13
Pleading 4
Procedural issues 3
Proximate cause 10
Standards for action 16
Vicarious liability 14
Wrongful life 17

---

1. Constitutional issues

Lack of tolling provisions in two-year limitations period for wrongful death actions does not violate equal protection rights of minors on basis that minors lack standing to bring an action before the court, as any wrongful death action, whether on behalf of minors or adult beneficiaries, must be brought by personal representative of decedent. Schaffer v. Gateway Harvestore, Inc. (Ohio App. 3 Dist., 08-19-1998) 129 Ohio App.3d 448, 717 N.E.2d 1179, dismissed, appeal not allowed 84 Ohio St.3d 1436, 702 N.E.2d 1214. Constitutional Law ⇐ 249(3); Death ⇐ 9

1996 H 350, which amended more than 100 statutes and a variety of rules relating to tort and other civil actions, and which was an attempt to reenact provisions of law previously held unconstitutional by the Supreme Court of Ohio, is an act of usurpation of judicial power in violation of the doctrine of separation of powers; for that reason, and because of violation of the one-subject rule of the Ohio Constitution, 1996 H 350 is unconstitutional. State ex rel. Ohio Academy of Trial Lawyers v. Sheward (Ohio, 08-16-1999) 86 Ohio St.3d 451, 715 N.E.2d 1062, 1999-Ohio-123, reconsideration denied 87 Ohio St.3d 1409, 716 N.E.2d 1170.

2. Action for benefit of heirs

In a wrongful death claim against a city seeking damages for the death of a twenty-four-year-old blind pedestrian who is struck while walking in a marked crosswalk, the city is not immune from liability because the city's four month delay in implementing its decision to install an audible signal device at the intersection is unreasonable where funding is easily obtained from the department's ongoing budget and the device which is in stock would take less than one day to install. Hemenway v. City of Columbus (Ohio App. 10 Dist., Franklin, 01-19-1999) No. 98AP-513, 1999 WL 25543, Unreported, appeal not allowed 85 Ohio St.3d 1489, 709 N.E.2d 1216.

Wrongful death proceeds do not become part of a decedent's estate; an action for wrongful death is a purely statutory action providing for damages for the beneficiaries as defined by the wrongful death statute. In re Estate of Robertson (Ohio App. 7 Dist., 12-02-2004) 159 Ohio App.3d 297, 823 N.E.2d 904, 2004-Ohio-6509, appeal not allowed 105 Ohio St.3d 1500, 825 N.E.2d 624, 2005-Ohio-1666. Death ⇐ 11; Death ⇐ 31(1); Executors And Administrators ⇐ 51

The statutory right to bring a wrongful death action is the only civil remedy available to compensate surviving beneficiaries. Griffiths v. Doctors Hosp. (Ohio App. 5 Dist., 11-12-2002) 150 Ohio App.3d 234, 780 N.E.2d 603, 2002-Ohio-6173, appeal not allowed 98 Ohio St.3d 1491, 785 N.E.2d 473, 2003-Ohio-1189. Death ⇐ 7

An action for wrongful death is a statutory action providing for damages proportioned to the pecuniary injury resulting to the persons for whose benefit the action is brought. Griffiths v. Doctors Hosp. (Ohio App. 5 Dist., 11-12-2002) 150 Ohio App.3d 234, 780 N.E.2d 603, 2002-Ohio-6173, appeal not allowed 98 Ohio St.3d 1491, 785 N.E.2d 473, 2003-Ohio-1189. Death ⇐ 11; Death ⇐ 85

For purposes of determining whether a fetus is viable, and thus whether a wrongful death action can be brought on fetus's behalf, the term "viable" refers to the point in prenatal development at which time a fetus is capable of independent existence if removed from the mother's womb. Griffiths v. Doctors Hosp. (Ohio App. 5 Dist., 11-12-2002) 150 Ohio App.3d 234, 780 N.E.2d 603, 2002-Ohio-6173, appeal not allowed 98 Ohio St.3d 1491, 785 N.E.2d 473, 2003-Ohio-1189. Death ⇨ 15

Considering that prematurely born twins lived for one and one-half hours outside womb, genuine issue of material fact existed as to whether twins were viable at time of their birth at 21 weeks' gestation, precluding summary judgment for doctors and clinic on father's wrongful death action. Griffiths v. Doctors Hosp. (Ohio App. 5 Dist., 11-12-2002) 150 Ohio App.3d 234, 780 N.E.2d 603, 2002-Ohio-6173, appeal not allowed 98 Ohio St.3d 1491, 785 N.E.2d 473, 2003-Ohio-1189. Judgment ⇨ 185.3(21)

Household exclusion of liability coverage for injury to an insured under a homeowners' policy applied to death of named insured's grandmother, even though her heirs were not insureds and their wrongful death claim benefitted them, not the grandmother's estate. Brown v. Madison (Ohio App. 8 Dist., 10-30-2000) 139 Ohio App.3d 867, 745 N.E.2d 1141. Insurance ⇨ 2356

In an action for wrongful death, the surviving statutory beneficiaries have the right to recover damages suffered by reason of the wrongful death of the decedent. Clark v. Scarpelli (Ohio, 04-11-2001) 91 Ohio St.3d 271, 744 N.E.2d 719, 2001-Ohio-39, reconsideration denied 91 Ohio St.3d 1530, 747 N.E.2d 254. Death ⇨ 7

Each statutory wrongful death beneficiary's claim is considered separate and distinct from the claim of the estate, and from each other. Clark v. Scarpelli (Ohio, 04-11-2001) 91 Ohio St.3d 271, 744 N.E.2d 719, 2001-Ohio-39, reconsideration denied 91 Ohio St.3d 1530, 747 N.E.2d 254. Death ⇨ 7

To maintain successful wrongful death action, plaintiff must show the existence of a duty owed to decedent, breach of that duty, and that the breach was proximate cause of death. Pena v. Northeast Ohio Emergency Affiliates, Inc. (Ohio App. 9 Dist., 12-20-1995) 108 Ohio App.3d 96, 670 N.E.2d 268, dismissed, appeal not allowed 75 Ohio St.3d 1494, 664 N.E.2d 1291. Death ⇨ 13; Death ⇨ 17

In a wrongful death action against a truck driver and driver's employer involving a collision between the truck driver and a motorist, dismissal is proper on the basis that the plaintiff could not maintain a wrongful death suit on behalf of an alleged minor child of the motorist where the plaintiff and the motorist were not married, the motorist did not in probate court formally acknowledge the child as his with consent of the mother, and the motorist did not designate the child as his heir-at-law, adopt the child, or make provision for the child in his will, and, although a parentage action was brought by the plaintiff and her son, the action was brought after the death of the motorist; thus, as a matter of law, the child cannot inherit from the decedent's estate, including any recovery from the wrongful death action. Hunter–Martin v. Winchester Transp., Inc. (Shelby 1991) 71 Ohio App.3d 273, 593 N.E.2d 383, motion overruled 62 Ohio St.3d 1408, 577 N.E.2d 361.

A cause of action does not exist for the wrongful death of a viable fetus caused by negligent care resulting in stillbirth. Werling v Sandy, No. 1-83-4 (3d Dist Ct App, Allen, 4-30-84), reversed by 17 OS(3d) 45, 17 OBR 37, 476 NE(2d) 1053 (1985).

A cause of action exists for the wrongful death of a viable unborn child which is subsequently stillborn. Stidam v. Ashmore (Madison 1959) 109 Ohio App. 431, 167 N.E.2d 106, 11 O.O.2d 383. Death ⇨ 13

Where, during the pendency of an action for wrongful death brought under GC 10509–166 (RC 2125.01), the only heir and next of kin of the decedent, who has sustained pecuniary injury by reason of such death, dies, no one remains in whose behalf the action may be further prosecuted, and the sustaining of a motion by the defendant for a directed verdict or for a dismissal of the action is proper. Danis v. New York Central R. Co. (Ohio 1954) 160 Ohio St. 474, 117 N.E.2d 39, 43 A.L.R.2d 1286, 52 O.O. 356.

Under the wrongful-death statute, the administrator of the estate of a child who, while viable, suffered a prenatal injury through the alleged negligent act of another and who died approximately three months after its birth as a result of such injury has a cause of action against such other for damages for the benefit of the parents of such infant. Jasinsky v. Potts (Ohio 1950) 153 Ohio St. 529, 92 N.E.2d 809, 42 O.O. 9. Death ⇨ 15

The rights of the next of kin in an action for wrongful death begin where those of the decedent end, are rights over which decedent can have no control and are not affected by what may have happened to decedent's right of action. DeHart v. Ohio Fuel Gas Co. (Huron 1948) 84 Ohio App. 62, 85 N.E.2d 586, 39 O.O. 101.

A judgment denying recovery for personal injuries is not a bar to an action, under this and following sections, for the benefit of the next of kin of the injured person who died as a result of such injuries. DeHart v. Ohio Fuel Gas Co. (Huron 1948) 84 Ohio App. 62, 85 N.E.2d 586, 39 O.O. 101.

Charge to jury that whatever rights decedent had because of an accident, are preserved by statute to his next of kin, though inaccurate, is not prejudicially erroneous when followed by a correct charge as to nature of case and measure of damages. Chowning v. Ajax Motor Service (Hamilton 1938) 60 Ohio App. 470, 21 N.E.2d 1021, 28 Ohio Law Abs. 293, 14 O.O. 507.

Separate releases of husband and wife of cause of action for personal injuries sustained by wife, executed before wife's death from injuries, are not a bar to action for wrongful death brought by administratrix for benefit of children. Phillips v. Community Traction Co. (Lucas 1933) 46 Ohio App. 483, 189 N.E. 444, 16 Ohio Law Abs. 159, 40 Ohio Law Rep. 92. Death ⇨ 25

Action for wrongful death by administrator on behalf of wife's sisters and brother, against husband who killed wife, held not to lie. Demos v. Freemas (Franklin 1931) 43 Ohio App. 426, 183 N.E. 395, 13 Ohio Law Abs. 318. Death ⇨ 31(5); Executors And Administrators ⇨ 426

Sections 10770 and 10772 General Code, give an independent right of action for the benefit of the persons named in section 10772 where death has resulted from the injuries, to recover for such pecuniary injury resulting from such death, where such right arises from an act, neglect or default, such as would have entitled such person to maintain an action and recover damages in respect thereof, if death had not ensued. May Coal Co. v. Robinette (Ohio 1929) 120 Ohio St. 110, 165 N.E. 576, 64 A.L.R. 441, 7 Ohio Law Abs. 173, 28 Ohio Law Rep. 542.

Proof that deceased's next of kin were dependent when last seen might afford rebuttable inference of present dependency. Fini v. Perry (Ohio 1928) 119 Ohio St. 367, 164 N.E. 358. Death ⇨ 58(1); Evidence ⇨ 67(1)

When action was brought by administrator for the brothers and sisters of the deceased, who were in Italy, proof of the fact that they were so living at such time would give rise to the rebuttable presumption that they continued to live; proof of the fact that they were at such time dependent, together with proof of their physical infirmities, their history, and their financial inability to attend at the trial, might well afford a reasonable rebuttable inference of present dependency. Fini v. Perry (Ohio 1928) 119 Ohio St. 367, 164 N.E. 358.

Cause of action for personal injury survives death of injured party, and all rights, privileges, incidents, and options which injured party may have had in lifetime inure to benefit of his personal representatives or next of kin, respectively, unless statutes clearly provide otherwise. Wellston Iron Furnace Co. v. Rinehart (Ohio 1923) 108 Ohio St. 117, 140 N.E. 623, 1 Ohio Law Abs. 453, 1 Ohio Law Abs. 867, 21 Ohio Law Rep. 137. Abatement And Revival ⇨ 54; Death ⇨ 10; Executors And Administrators ⇨ 52

The right given by Rev. St. §§ 6134, 6135, to prosecute an action for damages for wrongfully causing the death of another, is not such species of "property" as will pass to the heirs or next of kin of those to whom the right is given. Doyle v. Baltimore & O.R. Co. (Ohio 1909) 81 Ohio St. 184, 90 N.E. 165, 135 Am.St.Rep. 775, 7 Ohio Law Rep. 506. Death ⇨ 29; Descent And Distribution ⇨ 8

The parent of a deceased may not give in evidence his opinion of the value of the services of the deceased child to him and his family, as that determination is for the jury. Cincinnati Traction Co. v. Stephens (Ohio 1906) 75 Ohio St. 171, 79 N.E. 235, 4 Ohio Law Rep. 504, 4 Ohio Law Rep. 508. Evidence ⇨ 487

Evidence tending to show the financial circumstances of the beneficiaries and what aid they would need and receive from the deceased, as well as the age, health and thrift of the deceased is admissible to determine the amount of damages. Cincinnati St. Ry. Co. v. Altemeier (Ohio 1899) 60 Ohio St. 10, 41 W.L.B. 245, 53 N.E. 300.

The statutes providing for wrongful death actions are not construed to be a revivor or survival of the cause of action for the injury nor to be a double liability for the same wrong; such an action merely succeeds the cause of action abated by the death of the injured person and takes its place in favor of his next of kin. Solor Refining Co. v. Elliott (Ohio Cir. 1898) 8 Ohio C.D. 225. Death ⇨ 7

A claim for wrongful death is a chose in action and as such is property and a part of the special estate of the decedent to be recovered in the name of the administrator for the benefit of the persons named in the statute and distributed as the statute provides. In re Arduino's Estate

(Ohio Com.Pl. 1909) 20 Ohio Dec. 461, 9 Ohio NP(NS) 369. Death ⇒ 31(3.1); Executors And Administrators ⇒ 51

This section was creative of a new cause of action, wholly unknown to the common law, and the right of action was not given to the person suffering the injury, since no man could sue for his own death, but to his widow or personal representatives; it was not survivorship of the cause of action which the legislature meant to provide for by this section, but the creation of an original cause of action in favor of a surviving widow or personal representative. Chambers v. Baltimore & O.R. Co. (U.S.Ohio 1907) 28 S.Ct. 34, 207 U.S. 142, 52 L.Ed. 143, 6 Ohio Law Rep. 498.

The Ohio Wrongful Death Act provides that recovery shall be for the exclusive benefit of the wife or husband and children, and if there be none, then to the parents and next of kin, and thus an action under that statute is properly brought by the parents and next of kin of the decedent, even though by the statute of descents his property would go to his brothers and sisters only. Toledo, St. L. & W.R. Co. v. Connolly (C.C.A.6 (Ohio) 1907) 149 F. 398, 79 C.C.A. 218.

Under Ohio law, survivorship claim exists separate and apart from a wrongful death claim. Wingrove v. Forshey (S.D.Ohio, 11-13-2002) 230 F.Supp.2d 808. Death ⇒ 10

Under Ohio law, wrongful death is independent, not derivative, cause of action; statute creates new cause of action that is asserted on behalf of decedent's survivors, distinct and apart from the right of action which the injured person may have had. Wingrove v. Forshey (S.D.Ohio, 11-13-2002) 230 F.Supp.2d 808. Death ⇒ 11; Death ⇒ 15

Under Ohio law, right to bring a wrongful death action does not depend on the existence of a separate cause of action that was or could have been asserted by the decedent immediately prior to his death. Wingrove v. Forshey (S.D.Ohio, 11-13-2002) 230 F.Supp.2d 808. Death ⇒ 15

An underage intoxicated patron has no cause of action against a liquor permit holder where the underage patron dies in a car he is driving in a one-car accident after consuming alcoholic beverages on the licensee's premises; the administrator of the decedent's estate cannot maintain a wrongful death action against a permit holder pursuant to RC 2125.01 through RC 2125.03 for the benefit of the next of kin of the decedent. Steed v Chances Entertainment, Inc, No. CT95–0030, 1996 WL 488850 (5th Dist Ct App, Muskingum, 7–25–96).

3. Procedural issues

The right to commence an action for wrongfully causing death abates by the death of the wrongdoers. Russell v. Sunbury (Ohio 1881) 37 Ohio St. 372, 6 W.L.B. 785, 41 Am.Rep. 523. Abatement And Revival ⇒ 63; Death ⇒ 30

Where the deceased commenced the affray in which he lost his life, and the defense requests an instruction that if the wrong or fault of the deceased contributed to the injury no recovery could be had, the instruction was properly refused. Darling v. Williams (Ohio 1878) 35 Ohio St. 58.

Local rule that allowed probate court to reduce attorney fees award to law firm that represented estate in wrongful death action due to firm's failure to fully and accurately disclose particulars of settlements did not apply retroactively to law firm, which applied for fees prior to the enactment of rule, and thus, probate court was not authorized to reduce attorney fees in accordance with rule. In re Estate of Covington (Ohio App. 7 Dist., Mahoning, 06-24-2004) No. 03MA98, 2004-Ohio-3649, 2004 WL 1534126, Unreported. Executors And Administrators ⇒ 216(2)

Statute allowing liability insurers, including automobile liability insurers, to treat all claims for bodily injury to one person, including death, as single claim did not violate state constitutional provision prohibiting limits on recovery for wrongful death. Fleming v. Wallace (Ohio App. 7 Dist., Belmont, 10-29-2002) No. 01-BA-64, 2002-Ohio-6003, 2002 WL 31443550, Unreported, appeal not allowed 98 Ohio St.3d 1463, 783 N.E.2d 521, 2003-Ohio-644. Insurance ⇒ 2281(2); Insurance ⇒ 2756(3)

In a wrongful death claim on behalf of decedent's estate, where the issue is whether the treating physician had conformed to the standard of care in deciding to perform a particular diagnostic procedure for gastric symptoms, the defendant is prejudiced by the trial court's erroneous instruction to "consider whether the physician ought to have foreseen that the natural and probable result of this act would cause harm." Needham v. Gaylor (Ohio App. 2 Dist., Montgomery, 09-20-1996) No. 14834, 1996 WL 531596, Unreported, appeal not allowed 77 Ohio St.3d 1526, 674 N.E.2d 377.

In a claim for medical malpractice and wrongful death, relevant expert testimony is required in order to evaluate whether the physicians' conduct constitutes medical malpractice where the testimony establishes (1) the patient required kidney dialysis prior to two emergency visits and while he was hospitalized, (2) the acceptable standard of care for an emergency department physician who lacks admitting privileges and expertise or training in nephrology, and (3) had the physicians ordered or performed dialysis as a treatment plan their conduct would have deviated from the appropriate standard of care; consequently, the court does not err in its denial of a motion in limine by the administratrix of the estate to exclude the testimony of the medical expert. Jones v. Emergency Dept. Physicians, Inc. (Ohio App. 8 Dist., Cuyahoga, 09-05-1996) No. 68576, 1996 WL 502158, Unreported.

Re-reading, to jury during deliberations, of expert testimony was not an abuse of discretion, in wrongful death action alleging medical malpractice; jury had asked for re-reading of all expert testimony, trial court inquired into jury's concerns and consulted with counsel, and counsel for defendant radiologist acquiesced to limiting the testimony re-read to jury, with an appropriate limiting instruction. Viox v. Weinberg (Ohio App. 1 Dist., 09-29-2006) 2006-Ohio-5075, 2006 WL 2788502. Trial ⇒ 308

Defendant radiologist could not predicate error, in wrongful death action asserting medical malpractice, on closing argument of counsel for patient's estate, which began to refer to deposition testimony of non-party doctor, given in separate proceeding, on stages of lung cancer; radiologist's counsel objected and trial court agreed that estate's counsel could not comment on matters not in evidence, thereby effectively sustaining the objection, and radiologist's counsel did not ask for curative instruction. Viox v. Weinberg (Ohio App. 1 Dist., 09-29-2006) 2006-Ohio-5075, 2006 WL 2788502. Appeal And Error ⇒ 216(3)

Closing arguments of counsel for patient's estate, referring to wealth disparity between defendant radiologist, patient, and patient's surviving daughter, and attacking the character of radiologist's trial counsel, did not constitute plain error, in wrongful death action asserting medical malpractice; such arguments did not seriously affect basic fairness, integrity, or public reputation of judicial process. Viox v. Weinberg (Ohio App. 1 Dist., 09-29-2006) 2006-Ohio-5075, 2006 WL 2788502. Appeal And Error ⇒ 207

Trial court had duty to intervene sua sponte to admonish defense counsel and to correct prejudicial effects of defense counsel's comments in action that was brought by patient's widower for medical malpractice and wrongful death; counsel consciously engaged throughout trial in pattern of misconduct that was designed to inflame jury's passion and prejudice, counsel told jurors that widower's witnesses, attorney, and expert witnesses had manipulated and lied to jurors to win big verdict, and counsel's comments that jurors were to consider only whether doctor had done his best were extremely pervasive and prejudicial. Thamann v. Bartish (Ohio App. 1 Dist., 06-30-2006) 2006-Ohio-3346, 2006 WL 1791403. Trial ⇒ 133.4

Order compelling administrator of patient's estate to produce nurse paralegal for estate's attorney for deposition on sole issue of how reports of estate's expert witnesses were generated, which deposition hospital sought after learning that paralegal had written reports of estate's experts, did not impermissibly allow hospital unfettered access to nurse paralegal to discover thoughts and strategies for trial, such as would violate rule prohibiting discovery of attorney work-product, for purposes of administrator's wrongful death action against hospital and others. Stanton v. Univ. Hosps. Health Sys., Inc. (Ohio App. 8 Dist., 05-11-2006) 166 Ohio App.3d 758, 853 N.E.2d 343, 2006-Ohio-2297. Pretrial Procedure ⇒ 184

Administrator of airplane accident victim's estate waived argument about interpretation of liability policy limits, where he did not argue that issue in his declaratory judgment action on enforceability of the limits. Michael v. Reliance Natl. Ins. Co. (Ohio App. 10 Dist., 06-08-2000) 140 Ohio App.3d 346, 747 N.E.2d 835, appeal allowed 90 Ohio St.3d 1451, 737 N.E.2d 55, appeal dismissed as improvidently allowed 91 Ohio St.3d 1262, 746 N.E.2d 604, 2001-Ohio-78, reconsideration denied 92 Ohio St.3d 1433, 749 N.E.2d 759. Declaratory Judgment ⇒ 393

Defendant in wrongful death and survivorship action was not entitled, based on his pro se status, to special consideration with respect to his failure to provide timely responses to request for admissions, especially in view of fact that defendant not only failed to respond to that request for nearly 18 months, but also ignored several notices of depositions during that time and generally refused to participate in discovery process. Holman v. Keegan (Ohio App. 6 Dist., 09-22-2000) 139 Ohio App.3d 911, 746 N.E.2d 209, appeal not allowed 91 Ohio St.3d 1432, 741 N.E.2d 895. Attorney And Client ⇒ 62

Jury trial was required, in wrongful death and survival action against motorist in which decedent's automobile insurance company intervened, where decedent's estate demanded jury trial in original complaint and there was no stipulation among the parties to waive the demand, no determination of an involuntary waiver, and no consent by other parties to estate's withdrawal of the demand. Holman v. Keegan (Ohio App. 6 Dist., 09-22-2000) 139 Ohio App.3d 911, 746 N.E.2d 209, appeal not allowed 91 Ohio St.3d 1432, 741 N.E.2d 895. Jury ⚖ 25(11)

Wrongful death action was ordinary civil action, and not special proceeding within meaning of statute designating final orders, and thus order denying city's motion for summary judgment based on immunity in action arising out of automobile accident was not appealable, as wrongful death action was recognized at common law, statute did not create action but only substituted right of representative to sue in place of deceased, and statute was enacted in 1851. Stevens v. Ackman (Ohio, 03-28-2001) 91 Ohio St.3d 182, 743 N.E.2d 901, 2001-Ohio-249. Appeal And Error ⚖ 78(1)

Grant of summary judgment in favor of village and police officer in action brought by motorcycle passenger who was injured in high-speed chase with officer did not preclude later wrongful death action by motorcyclist's estate against village and officer; even though village and officer brought estate into prior action as a third-party defendant for indemnification/contribution, it was in estate's best interest that village and officer were found to be immune from liability, thereby rendering indemnification/contribution claim moot. Wagner v. Heavlin (Ohio App. 7 Dist., 02-14-2000) 136 Ohio App.3d 719, 737 N.E.2d 989. Judgment ⚖ 634

Plaintiffs in wrongful death action against motorist who ran over motorcyclist after motorcyclist fell off motorcycle had burden of showing motorcyclist was alive when car struck him. Reidling v. Valle (Ohio App. 6 Dist., 02-19-1999) 132 Ohio App.3d 310, 724 N.E.2d 1222, appeal not allowed 86 Ohio St.3d 1420, 711 N.E.2d 1014. Death ⚖ 58(1)

To prevail against hospital on a claim of medical malpractice or professional negligence, plaintiff must first prove that defendant's resident doctors or nurses committed medical malpractice. Trisdale v. Ohio Dept. of Mental Health (Ohio Ct.Cl., 06-04-1999) 103 Ohio Misc.2d 5, 724 N.E.2d 868. Health ⚖ 782

Genuine issue of material fact as to what 26-year-old patient, who was mildly retarded, and his mother, had told hospital personnel after patient went to hospital complaining that he was sick, precluded summary judgment in wrongful death action based on alleged medical malpractice which was brought after patient was not treated by a physician at hospital, and instead went home with his mother, where he suffered a fatal heart attack. Walker v. E. End Community Health Ctr., Inc. (Ohio App. 1 Dist., 05-01-1998) 131 Ohio App.3d 322, 722 N.E.2d 550. Judgment ⚖ 181(33)

Defendants in a wrongful death action brought by the discharged administrator of the decedent's estate lacked standing to appeal a probate court's vacatur of the discharge order, which relief the discharged administrator had sought to clear up a question about his right to pursue the wrongful death action. In re Estate of Johnson (Ohio App. 8 Dist., 06-08-1998) 128 Ohio App.3d 148, 713 N.E.2d 1149. Courts ⚖ 202(5)

Plaintiff asserting a wrongful-death claim against a clinic based on the failure of an orthopedic surgeon employed by the clinic to refer the decedent to a mental health professional was not entitled to depose the director of the clinic's orthopedic residency program about the clinic's compliance with accreditation and licensing requirements, where the director lacked personal knowledge of the underlying claim. Freeman v. Cleveland Clinic Found. (Ohio App. 8 Dist., 04-27-1998) 127 Ohio App.3d 378, 713 N.E.2d 33, appeal not allowed 83 Ohio St.3d 1419, 698 N.E.2d 1007. Pretrial Procedure ⚖ 100

Trial court did not abuse its discretion by denying a wrongful death plaintiff's motion to amend his complaint to add the theory of diminished chance of recovery or survival in the wake of the theory's revival by the state's high court, where the motion was untimely and the plaintiff did not show how the theory applied to the decedent's death, which was by suicide. Freeman v. Cleveland Clinic Found. (Ohio App. 8 Dist., 04-27-1998) 127 Ohio App.3d 378, 713 N.E.2d 33, appeal not allowed 83 Ohio St.3d 1419, 698 N.E.2d 1007. Pleading ⚖ 236(7)

Where contingent fee agreement between administrator of estate and attorney hired to pursue wrongful death action was held to be invalid, attorney had no interest in fate of wrongful death action, and did not have standing to seek enforcement of settlement agreement in that action. In re Estate of Hamrick (Ohio App. 9 Dist., 03-18-1998) 126 Ohio App.3d 624, 710 N.E.2d 1213, dismissed, appeal not allowed 82 Ohio St.3d 1450, 695 N.E.2d 1148. Compromise And Settlement ⚖ 21

Whether physician-patient relationship existed between patient and on-call cardiologist who was consulted by emergency room physician, was question for jury in medical malpractice wrongful death action brought by executrix of patient's estate. McKinney v. Schlatter (Ohio App. 12 Dist., 02-18-1997) 118 Ohio App.3d 328, 692 N.E.2d 1045, dismissed 78 Ohio St.3d 1471, 678 N.E.2d 580, appeal not allowed 79 Ohio St.3d 1421, 680 N.E.2d 158. Health ⚖ 825

Trial court committed reversible error by refusing to allow counsel for plaintiff in wrongful death action to make reference during closing argument to testimony of family members relating to loss of future support resulting from death of 11-year-old decedent. Howard v. Seidler (Ohio App. 7 Dist., 12-04-1996) 116 Ohio App.3d 800, 689 N.E.2d 572, appeal not allowed 78 Ohio St.3d 1494, 678 N.E.2d 1230. Appeal And Error ⚖ 1060.1(5)

Wrongful death is not derivative action, but rather is independent cause of action. Dougherty v. Fecsik (Ohio App. 8 Dist., 12-16-1996) 116 Ohio App.3d 456, 688 N.E.2d 555. Death ⚖ 7

Fact that there was no administrator for decedent's estate when statute of limitations on wrongful death claim expired did not preclude beneficiary's legal malpractice claim against attorneys for subsequently appointed administrator, as attorneys may have committed malpractice by failing to effect administrator's appointment prior to expiration of statute of limitations. DePugh v. Sladoje (Ohio App. 2 Dist., 06-14-1996) 111 Ohio App.3d 675, 676 N.E.2d 1231. Attorney And Client ⚖ 112

In order to prevail in survival and wrongful death action, plaintiff must show that defendant owed decedent duty, that defendant breached that duty, and that defendant's breach of duty was proximate cause of decedent's injuries and death. Garcia v. Puskas Family Flowers, Inc. (Ohio App. 9 Dist., 01-24-1996) 108 Ohio App.3d 683, 671 N.E.2d 607, cause dismissed 75 Ohio St.3d 1472, 663 N.E.2d 1300, appeal not allowed 75 Ohio St.3d 1477, 663 N.E.2d 1304. Death ⚖ 13

Intentional injury exclusion in employer's liability endorsement to commercial general liability (CGL) policy did not preclude duty to defend against survivorship claims arising from death of employee who was allegedly directed to work in unsafe environment without proper safety equipment or training; it was possible that fact finder would conclude that injury was accidental, not expected or intended, and thus within coverage. Beacon Ins. Co. of Am. v. Kleoudis (Ohio App. 8 Dist., 03-27-1995) 100 Ohio App.3d 79, 652 N.E.2d 1. Insurance ⚖ 2278(3)

Admission of testimony of grief expert in wrongful death action was not abuse of discretion. Sharp v. Norfolk & W. Ry. Co. (Ohio, 06-14-1995) 72 Ohio St.3d 307, 649 N.E.2d 1219, 1995-Ohio-224, clarified 73 Ohio St.3d 1429, 652 N.E.2d 801. Evidence ⚖ 532

When person is injured by tortious conduct of another and person later dies from injury, two claims arise: first is claim for malpractice or personal injury, enforced by either injured person herself or by her representative in survival action, and second is wrongful death claim, enforced by decedent's personal representative on behalf of decedent's beneficiaries. Thompson v. Wing (Ohio, 08-31-1994) 70 Ohio St.3d 176, 637 N.E.2d 917, 1994-Ohio-358. Death ⚖ 7

RC 2125.01 et seq. may not be applied retrospectively. French v Dwiggins, appeal following reconsideration 9 OS(3d) 32, 458 NE(2d) 827, 9 OBR 123, 5 OBR 431 (App, Licking 1982).

Provisions of Wrongful Death Act adopted on February 5, 1982 are to be given retroactive effect. Robinson v. Parker-Hannifin Corp. (Ohio Com.Pl. 1982) 4 Ohio Misc.2d 6, 447 N.E.2d 781, 4 O.B.R. 257. Death ⚖ 9

Statutes providing that actions shall not abate by the death of a party and may be revived against personal representatives are substantive rather than remedial and will not be applied retroactively. Spriggs v. Dredge (Clark 1955) 140 N.E.2d 45, 74 Ohio Law Abs. 264.

It is not error for the court in instructing the jury to call attention to statutes which make it unlawful to sell a poisonous drug without labeling it "poison." Davis v. Guarnieri (Ohio 1887) 45 Ohio St. 470, 19 W.L.B. 204, 15 N.E. 350, 4 Am.St.Rep. 548.

The acceptance by a widow of benefits from the railroad employees' relief association provided for in her husband's contract does not bar her as administratrix from bringing an action for wrongful death. Baltimore & O.R. Co. v. McCamey (Ohio Cir. 1896) 5 Ohio C.D. 631.

Where an action for personal injuries is commenced by a person who suffered the injuries because of another's negligence, and during the pendency of the action the plaintiff dies from such injuries, the action cannot be revived in the name of the deceased's administrator; the only action that can be maintained after his death is one for wrongful death under RS 6134 and RS 6135. Gallagher v. River Furnace & Dock Co. (Ohio Com.Pl. 1905) 15 Ohio Dec. 789, 2 Ohio N.P.N.S. 661.

An attorney may retain a portion of the judgment in payment of his fees for acting as attorney in a wrongful death case. Merrill v McMahon; appeal dismissed by 42 B 252 (1899), 5 NP 77, 7 D 136 (Super, Cincinnati 1898).

The standards for deciding whether the lex loci delicti applies in a personal injury suit and whether it applies in a wrongful death suit are virtually identical. Bowman v. Koch Transfer Co. (C.A.6 (Ohio) 1988) 862 F.2d 1257.

Where a plaintiff sues in forma pauperis as administratrix of her deceased husband's estate to recover damages for his wrongful death under RS 6135, her affidavit of poverty should show that neither the estate nor the beneficiaries of the action are able to prepay or secure the costs. Reed v. Pennsylvania Co. (C.C.A.6 1901) 111 F. 714, 49 C.C.A. 572. Costs ⟻ 132(6)

State court ruling in original action was void, such that it had no effect on issues raised in civil rights and wrongful death and survival action in federal court, where at time state court made ruling it lacked subject matter jurisdiction as result of plaintiffs' voluntary dismissal of state action. Wingrove v. Forshey (S.D.Ohio, 11-13-2002) 230 F.Supp.2d 808. Judgment ⟻ 828.11(1)

Violation of state law in the use of a motor vehicle does not in itself make the violator's acts "willful" or "malicious" for purposes of 11 USC 523(a)(6), which would prevent the discharge in bankruptcy of a debt arising from the violator's misconduct. In re Roberson (Bkrtcy.S.D.Ohio 1988) 92 B.R. 263.

Decedent's personal representative and children were not barred by doctrine of collateral estoppel from bringing wrongful-death action against driver and insurers, although decedent and personal representative had signed a settlement agreement discharging driver from liability; decedent did not actually and directly litigate prior action against driver. Kissinger v. Pavlus (Ohio App. 10 Dist., Franklin, 05-21-2002) No. 01AP-1203, 2002-Ohio-3083, 2002 WL 1013085, Unreported. Compromise And Settlement ⟻ 17(1)

The provisions of RC 2125.01 and RC 2125.02 of the Wrongful Death Act, as amended by 1982 H 332, eff. 2–5–82, are to be applied retroactively. Robinson v. Parker–Hannifin Corp. (Ohio Com.Pl. 1982) 4 Ohio Misc.2d 6, 447 N.E.2d 781, 4 O.B.R. 257.

RC 2125.01, RC 2125.02, and RC 2125.03 are expressly retroactive. McKinney v Kidwell, 2 OBR 353 (CP, Hamilton 1982).

In an action for wrongful death, jurors are not disqualified by reason of their familiarity with the crossing where the death occurred. Lake Shore & Michigan Southern Railway Co v Reynolds, 21 CC 402, 11 CD 701 (Lake 1900).

4. Pleading

Estate of deceased patient adequately pleaded wrongful death cause of action in complaint that also alleged medical malpractice against medical personnel; although complaint did not specifically use the phrase "wrongful death" to describe the cause of action and did not state that defendants' negligence was the "proximate cause" of death, complaint alleged that defendants either misdiagnosed or mistreated patient's lung infection and that patient developed pneumonia and died, estate stated in leave to file an amended complaint that purpose of amendment was to make it clear that original complaint was describing wrongful death claim, and amended complaint clarified that claim was being pursued on behalf of patient's next of kin. Samonas v. St. Elizabeth Health Center (Ohio App. 7 Dist., Mahoning, 02-06-2006) No. 05 MA 83, 2006-Ohio-671, 2006 WL 338366, Unreported. Death ⟻ 46

Attempt to avoid payment for valid wrongful death claims by narrowly defining who is "insured" is impermissible attempt to eliminate underinsured motorist (UIM) coverage where claim or claims of such persons arise from causes of action recognized by tort law. Holt v. Grange Mut. Cas. Co. (Ohio, 09-24-1997) 79 Ohio St.3d 401, 683 N.E.2d 1080, 1997-Ohio-375. Insurance ⟻ 2774; Insurance ⟻ 2780

In a wrongful death action involving police officers' response to an emergency call which resulted in one of the officers killing the victim, who was attempting suicide, material issues of fact exist which preclude the granting of summary judgment in favor of the police officers when it is unclear whether the officers had (1) adequately questioned the victim's wife, (2) escalated the situation, (3) properly obtained necessary help, and (4) restrained the victim by means of reasonable force. Lytle v. Columbus (Franklin 1990) 70 Ohio App.3d 99, 590 N.E.2d 421. Judgment ⟻ 181(27)

In a medical malpractice and wrongful death action, the refusal of a trial court to instruct a jury on the "assumed duty" doctrine does not constitute prejudicial error where even assuming that obstetricians have a duty to refer to a cardiologist a pregnant patient who has a history of corrected coarctation of the aorta and other cardiovascular disorders and who suffers from hypertension during pregnancy, and that the obstetricians breach that duty, the administrator of the patient's estate still fails to show that the treatment received by the patient was in some way inferior to the treatment she would have received from a cardiologist in good standing and under like circumstances. Schmitz v. Blanchard Valley OB–GYN, Inc. (Hancock 1989) 63 Ohio App.3d 756, 580 N.E.2d 55, motion overruled 49 Ohio St.3d 705, 551 N.E.2d 617.

RC 2125.01 and 2125.02 are procedural and remedial in nature and should be given a liberal construction; thus, a complaint which states that the defendant aided and abetted in the commission of a wrongful act which caused the death of plaintiff's decedents states a claim for relief. Burton v. DePew (Butler 1988) 47 Ohio App.3d 107, 547 N.E.2d 995.

"Action" and "cause of action" distinguished (Alabama law construed). Spriggs v. Dredge (Clark 1955) 140 N.E.2d 45, 74 Ohio Law Abs. 264.

It is not error to permit the substitution as plaintiff in a wrongful death action of the original administratrix of the estate of a nonresident for an ancillary administrator after the expiration of the period of limitations. Kyes v. Pennsylvania R. Co. (Ohio 1952) 158 Ohio St. 362, 109 N.E.2d 503, 49 O.O. 239.

Where a suit commenced in a state court has been removed on the motion of the defendant to a United States court having concurrent jurisdiction of the cause of action, and has by such court, on the application of plaintiff, been dismissed without prejudice to plaintiff's right to bring a new action, there is no merger of the cause of action, and a new suit may be brought thereon within proper time in any court of competent jurisdiction as though no previous suit had been brought. Baltimore & O.R. Co. v. Larwill (Ohio 1910) 83 Ohio St. 108, 93 N.E. 619, 8 Ohio Law Rep. 448.

The transaction resulting in death may consist of a number of cooperating acts, and the plaintiff need not plead each as a separate cause of action. Schweinfurth v. Cleveland, C.C. & St. L. Ry. Co. (Ohio 1899) 60 Ohio St. 215, 42 W.L.B. 2, 54 N.E. 89.

Where case is removed to federal court and there disposed of otherwise than upon the merits, plaintiff cannot recommence in state court. Baltimore & O.R. Co. v. Fulton (Ohio 1899) 59 Ohio St. 575, 41 W.L.B. 229, 53 N.E. 265. Removal Of Cases ⟻ 97

It is not necessary to allege in a petition all the facts which contributed to the primary act complained of or which tend to establish the negligence of such act. Davis v. Guarnieri (Ohio 1887) 45 Ohio St. 470, 19 W.L.B. 204, 15 N.E. 350, 4 Am.St.Rep. 548. Negligence ⟻ 1512

Where there are no allegations in reference to the laws of another state it will be presumed that they are the same as in Ohio; thus, an action in Ohio for wrongfully causing death in Michigan need not set forth Michigan decisions or statutes. Lake Shore & M.S.R. Co. v. Andrews (Ohio Cir. 1897) 8 Ohio C.D. 73, reversed 58 Ohio St. 426, 40 W.L.B. 45, 51 N.E. 26.

An order striking allegations relating to unseaworthiness under general maritime law and the Ohio Wrongful Death Act is apparently a final order. Gillespie v. U. S. Steel Corp. (C.A.6 (Ohio) 1963) 321 F.2d 518, 25 O.O.2d 22, certiorari granted 84 S.Ct. 487, 375 U.S. 962, 11 L.Ed.2d 413, affirmed 85 S.Ct. 308, 379 U.S. 148, 13 L.Ed.2d 199.

A judgment in a wrongful death action cannot be discharged in the defendant's bankruptcy proceeding where the defendant's conduct was willful and malicious; an injury inflicted in an auto accident by a legally intoxicated driver is willful and malicious. Matter of Gibbs (Bkrtcy. S.D.Ohio 1984) 53 B.R. 503.

In an action for wrongful death it is sufficient if the facts constituting the negligence causing the injury resulting in the death of the person are such that if the person lived he could have maintained an action therefor; the averment that the deceased would have had a cause of action and recover damages for injuries had he lived is a conclusion, not facts. Lima Electric Light & Power Co v Deubler; appeal dismissed by 27 B 268 (OS 1892), 7 CC 185, 3 CD 720 (Allen 1892).

5. Foreign right of action

The act of March 25, 1851 allowing an action by the representatives of a party whose death was caused by the wrongful act of another, does not extend to cases where the wrongful act which caused the death was committed outside the state of Ohio. (See also Brooks v Railway Co, 53 OS 655, 44 NE 1131 (1895). Hover v. Pennsylvania Co. (Ohio 1874) 25 Ohio St. 667. Death ⟻ 35

An administrator appointed in this state cannot maintain an action for wrongful death in the courts of this state under an Illinois statute similar to the Ohio statute, as it cannot be supposed that Illinois intended to impose a trust or duty upon officers not appointed or acting under its laws.

Woodard v. Michigan Southern & Northern I.R. Co. (Ohio 1859) 10 Ohio St. 121.

Louisiana, rather than Ohio, law governed claim by Ohio insured to recover underinsured motorist (UIM) benefits from Ohio insurer for death of child as result of accident in Louisiana with resident of that state; child had no permanent residence, and Louisiana had dominating interest in determining whether its resident's conduct was tortious and whether insured's interest was entitled to legal protection. Amon v. Grange Mut. Cas. Co. (Ohio App. 11 Dist., 07-08-1996) 112 Ohio App.3d 407, 678 N.E.2d 1002, appeal not allowed 77 Ohio St.3d 1493, 673 N.E.2d 149. Insurance ⇐ 1091(11).

Under Louisiana law, Louisiana driver had no legal liability to parent of driver of other vehicle for death of driver of other vehicle as result of automobile accident, and, thus, parent was not entitled to underinsured motorist (UIM) benefits under automobile policy. Amon v. Grange Mut. Cas. Co. (Ohio App. 11 Dist., 07-08-1996) 112 Ohio App.3d 407, 678 N.E.2d 1002, appeal not allowed 77 Ohio St.3d 1493, 673 N.E.2d 149. Insurance ⇐ 2782.

Ohio court could not exercise personal jurisdiction over resident of Federal Republic of Germany for his involvement in fatal automobile accident with citizen of Ohio, where accident occurred in Federal Republic of Germany, and foreign resident had no known contacts with Ohio other than his attempt to extricate himself from being sued there. State ex rel. Connor v. McGough (Ohio 1989) 46 Ohio St.3d 188, 546 N.E.2d 407. Courts ⇐ 12(2.25).

An action for wrongful death is an asset of the decedent's estate and is, therefore, sufficient to justify the appointment of an administrator or an ancillary administrator in this state, even though there existed no other necessity for such an appointment, and the deceased was not domiciled in this state, and left no property in this state, and in such a case, the court for the county where the injury was received and the deceased died may properly entertain such jurisdiction. De Garza v. Chetister (Lucas 1978) 62 Ohio App.2d 149, 405 N.E.2d 331, 16 O.O.3d 335.

Where Ohio administrator of Ohio resident's estate sues Ohio executor of another Ohio resident's estate for damages for wrongful death arising from an airplane crash occurring in another state, the case is governed by the substantive law of Ohio. Moats v. Metropolitan Bank of Lima (Ohio 1974) 40 Ohio St.2d 47, 319 N.E.2d 603, 69 O.O.2d 323. Aviation ⇐ 173

RC 2125.01, which provides right of action for death caused by wrongful act in another state "for which a right to maintain an action and recover damages is given by a statute of such other state," does not require application of that state's limitation of amount of damages recoverable. Fox v. Morrison Motor Freight, Inc. (Ohio 1971) 25 Ohio St.2d 193, 267 N.E.2d 405, 54 O.O.2d 301, certiorari denied 91 S.Ct. 2254, 403 U.S. 931, 29 L.Ed.2d 710.

In action brought in Ohio under RC 2125.01, by Ohio administrator of estate of Ohio resident who was killed in motor vehicle collision in another state, where there was no citizen or resident of that state involved in collision, and there is no issue of liability, Ohio has all substantial governmental interests and law of Ohio is determinative of damages recoverable. Fox v. Morrison Motor Freight, Inc. (Ohio 1971) 25 Ohio St.2d 193, 267 N.E.2d 405, 54 O.O.2d 301, certiorari denied 91 S.Ct. 2254, 403 U.S. 931, 29 L.Ed.2d 710.

Where a nonresident of the state of Ohio is killed in an automobile accident which occurs in Ohio, his personal representative may bring an action in this state against a nonresident motor vehicle operator who is alleged to have caused the death, and the case is governed by both the substantive and procedural laws of Ohio. (See also Moats v Metropolitan Bank of Lima, 40 OS(2d) 47, 319 NE(2d) 603 (1974).) Ellis v. Garwood (Ohio 1958) 168 Ohio St. 241, 152 N.E.2d 100, 6 O.O.2d 22. Death ⇐ 31(4)

Although workmen's compensation had been paid under New York law which barred recovery for death caused by acts of a fellow employee, an action could be maintained in Ohio for wrongful death in Ohio of New York employee, against a fellow employee who was also resident of New York, notwithstanding the full faith and credit clause. Ellis v. Garwood (Cuyahoga 1957) 143 N.E.2d 715, 80 Ohio Law Abs. 443, affirmed 168 Ohio St. 241, 152 N.E.2d 100, 6 O.O.2d 22. Workers' Compensation ⇐ 2168

Wrongful death statute of another state may be pleaded in Ohio court under section, where action is brought in Ohio for accident and death which occurred in such other state. Shaffer v. New York Cent. R. Co. (Williams 1940) 66 Ohio App. 417, 34 N.E.2d 792, 20 O.O. 346.

Nonresident aliens are entitled to benefits under the Wrongful Death Act, and an action may be maintained for their benefit for negligence causing death in Ohio. Pittsburgh, C., C. & St. L. R. Co. v. Naylor (Ohio 1905) 73 Ohio St. 115, 76 N.E. 505, 112 Am.St.Rep. 701, 3 Ohio Law Rep. 466.

An action accruing in another state cannot be brought here unless the person wrongfully killed was a citizen of Ohio. Baltimore & O.R. Co. v. Chambers (Ohio 1905) 73 Ohio St. 16, 76 N.E. 91, 3 Ohio Law Rep. 412, affirmed 28 S.Ct. 34, 207 U.S. 142, 52 L.Ed. 143, 6 Ohio Law Rep. 498.

Where a statute of a sister state gives the personal representative of one who has been killed by the wrongful act of another a cause of action to recover in all cases in which the deceased could have maintained an action for injury had he lived, and a subsequent act regulating the liability of corporations for injuries to its employees provides that statutes of another state shall not be pleaded in defense, both laws must be read in pari materia in determining whether such laws allow the enforcement in its courts of the Ohio statute of like character; and where such statutes of a foreign state are not the equivalent of the Ohio statute, courts of Ohio have no jurisdiction to hear a suit brought to recover for the wrongful death of a railroad employee in Indiana. Wabash R. Co. v. Fox (Ohio 1901) 64 Ohio St. 133, 45 W.L.B. 193, 59 N.E. 888, 83 Am.St.Rep. 739. Death ⇐ 9; Statutes ⇐ 223.2(1.1)

A right given by the statute of a state to revive a pending action for personal injuries in the name of the personal representative of a deceased plaintiff is not lost upon removal of the case to federal court. Baltimore & O. R. Co. v. Joy (U.S.Ohio 1899) 19 S.Ct. 387, 173 U.S. 226, 43 L.Ed. 677. Abatement And Revival ⇐ 74(1)

Under Rev.St.Ohio, §6133 (See GC 10509–165), which authorizes an executor or administrator duly appointed in another state to maintain an action in the courts of Ohio in his official capacity, "in like manner and under like restrictions as a nonresident may be permitted to sue," and section 6134a, which provides that a right of action for wrongful death accruing under the laws of another state may be enforced in Ohio "in all cases where such other state... allows the enforcement in its courts of the statute of this state of like character," an administrator appointed in Indiana, where his decedent was killed, and who is given by the Indiana statute a right of action for the death in his official capacity, may maintain an action thereon in Ohio. Cincinnati, H. & D.R. Co. v. Thiebaud (C.C.A.6 (Ohio) 1900) 114 F. 918, 52 C.C.A. 538. Death ⇐ 31(4); Executors And Administrators ⇐ 524(1)

The citizenship of the administrator, not the beneficiaries is to be considered in determining whether a federal court has jurisdiction of a wrongful death action, since such administrator sues as trustee, not merely as a formal party without interest. Cincinnati, H. & D.R. Co. v. Thiebaud (C.C.A.6 (Ohio) 1900) 114 F. 918, 52 C.C.A. 538.

A foreign administrator may maintain an action for wrongful death in Ohio under RS 6133 on behalf of nonresident beneficiaries in a like manner as nonresidents may sue. Popp v. Cincinnati, H. & D.R. Co. (C.C.S.D.Ohio 1899) 96 F. 465.

The administrator of a decedent who was killed by the wrongful act of another is not a nominal party, but the real party in interest so far as the prosecution of the suit is concerned; consequently a foreign administrator may bring the action in federal court although the beneficiaries reside in the state where the death occurred. Popp v. Cincinnati, H. & D.R. Co. (C.C.S.D.Ohio 1899) 96 F. 465. Federal Courts ⇐ 289; Death ⇐ 31(3.1); Executors And Administrators ⇐ 153; Parties ⇐ 4

Under RC 2125.01, where an Ohio corporation is sued by the personal representative of a Michigan resident in a wrongful death action based on an accident in Georgia, the statute of limitations that applies to the suit will be determined by the law of Georgia. Jones v. Mid America Expositions, Inc. (S.D.Ohio 1989) 708 F.Supp. 173.

The words "caused by a wrongful act, neglect, or default in another state" in RC 2125.01 do not mean that another state's statute of limitations applies only when the tortious conduct giving rise to the injury occurred in the foreign state; instead, Ohio and common law principles indicate RC 2125.01 refers to the place where injury occurred. Vaughn v. J.C. Penney, Inc. (S.D.Ohio 1986) 645 F.Supp. 12.

Where widow of decedent killed in Ohio accident executed release in Georgia, her place of residence, said release barred recovery by decedent or minor children in Ohio wrongful death action. McCluskey v. Rob San Services, Inc. (S.D.Ohio 1977) 443 F.Supp. 65, 10 O.O.3d 248.

In suit under foreign wrongful death statute, Ohio court will determine rights and liabilities, including joinder of parties, under the law of the other state; federal court sitting in Ohio must do likewise. Carlson v. Glenn L. Martin Co. (N.D.Ohio 1952) 103 F.Supp. 153, 64 Ohio Law Abs. 312, 48 O.O. 409.

Damages recovered for the wrongful death of a husband, a resident of Ohio, occurring in the state of New York, are payable to his widow where he left no issue, notwithstanding the general rule that such damages are to be distributed in accordance with the statutes of the state in which the wrongful act was done. Miller v Miller, 9 CC(NS) 315, 19 CD 353 (Cuyahoga 1907).

6. Act, neglect, or default in foreign state

A wrongful death action by the administrator of a divorced Ohio resident who was struck by a truck in Illinois while riding a bicycle from Akron to Denver, Colorado will be decided under Illinois law by a federal court, where all the defendants reside in Illinois and the woman does not have custody of her children, who in any event live outside Ohio; in this case, Ohio's interest in assuring the full compensation of victims in wrongful death actions is outweighed by Illinois' interest in the liabilities of its citizens sued for torts occurring within the state. Bowman v. Koch Transfer Co. (C.A.6 (Ohio) 1988) 862 F.2d 1257.

7. Joinder

Evidence was insufficient in medical negligence and wrongful death action to find that the correctional facility breached any duty of care in respect to interpreting inmate's chest x-ray in a timely manner, obtaining adequate medical records, and classifying inmate's health condition upon admission to the corrections reception center (CRC); three-day period for interpreting inmate's x-ray was reasonable, since it was a routine screening x-ray, facility properly categorized inmate as a class 2 inmate upon his admission due to his mobility problems and asthma, and his stage four cancer had not been diagnosed, and the inmate transfer sheet provided enough information about inmate's health in order for the facility to render medical care to him. Spencer, Admr. v. Ohio Dept. of Rehab. & Corr. (Ohio Ct.Cl., 04-09-2002) No. 99-03961, 2002-Ohio-1714, 2002 WL 31974396, Unreported. States ⇐ 112.2(4)

Insurance carriers for deceased passenger's parents' employers were not indispensable or necessary in parents' action against passenger's employer's carrier for underinsured motorist (UIM) coverage, as passenger's employer's carrier was the primary UIM carrier. Roberts v. Wausau Business Ins. Co. (Ohio App. 10 Dist., 09-10-2002) 149 Ohio App.3d 612, 778 N.E.2d 594, 2002-Ohio-4734, appeal allowed 98 Ohio St.3d 1460, 783 N.E.2d 519, 2003-Ohio-644, reversed 100 Ohio St.3d 302, 798 N.E.2d 1077, 2003-Ohio-5888, motion stricken 100 Ohio St.3d 1497, 799 N.E.2d 179, 2003-Ohio-6267, motion granted 100 Ohio St.3d 1498, 799 N.E.2d 180, 2003-Ohio-6267. Insurance ⇐ 3567

Two distinct rights of action in wrongful death cases are recognized in Ohio, each maintainable by the personal representative of the deceased person—one for the exclusive, pecuniary benefit of the next of kin, and the other for the benefit of the estate. Moss v. Hirzel Canning Co. (Wood 1955) 100 Ohio App. 509, 137 N.E.2d 440, 60 O.O. 397. Death ⇐ 32; Death ⇐ 31(3.1).

Funeral and burial expenses incurred by a surviving spouse for the funeral and burial of his wife, who has sustained a fatal injury by the wrongful act of a third person, are recoverable in a direct action by the husband, on the ground that it is the husband's duty to provide for the funeral and burial of his wife; a plaintiff's petition therefor states a good cause of action; the expenses incurred thereby are not regarded as a pecuniary loss to the wife's estate or recoverable under the wrongful death statute; and a demurrer to plaintiff's petition is not well taken. Moss v. Hirzel Canning Co. (Wood 1955) 100 Ohio App. 509, 137 N.E.2d 440, 60 O.O. 397.

An administrator's cause of action for pain and suffering of his decedent may not be joined with a cause of action for the wrongful death of the same decedent. Fielder v. Ohio Edison Co. (Ohio 1952) 158 Ohio St. 375, 109 N.E.2d 855, 35 A.L.R.2d 1365, 49 O.O. 265.

An action under section by an administrator to recover damages for the wrongful death of his decedent, and an action theretofore instituted by the decedent in his lifetime against the same defendant to recover damages for the injuries ultimately resulting in his death, which action was settled and dismissed, are not actions "upon the same matter between the same parties." Gorman v. Columbus & Southern Ohio Elec. Co. (Ohio 1945) 144 Ohio St. 593, 60 N.E.2d 700, 30 O.O. 194.

An action for wrongful death may be brought against an insane person in the county where he has his legal residence, and his legal guardian may be joined with him as a party defendant. Stuard v. Porter (Ohio 1908) 79 Ohio St. 1, 85 N.E. 1062, 6 Ohio Law Rep. 516. Mental Health ⇐ 480; Venue ⇐ 18

8. Damages

A medical doctor and a professional liability insurer may agree that the insurer's liability for all damages sustained from the death of one person is subject to the monetary limit declared for "each claim," irrespective of the number of wrongful-death claimants. Katz v. Ohio Ins. Guar. Assn. (Ohio, 08-18-2004) 103 Ohio St.3d 4, 812 N.E.2d 1266, 2004-Ohio-4109. Insurance ⇐ 2281(2)

Swimming pool owner did not breach duty to deceased child to make pool reasonably safe so as to be liable in wrongful death action brought by child's parents, and thus parents could not establish any damages resulting from any alleged willful destruction of records so as to establish owner's liability for spoliation of evidence, even though parents claimed spoiled evidence would have established that there were sometimes 50 bathers at pool or that pool was otherwise unsafe, where at no time during inspection of pool were there 50 bathers, and witness testified that no more than six persons were present at pool on day of child's death. Bae v. Dragoo & Assoc., Inc. (Ohio App. 10 Dist., 02-03-2004) 156 Ohio App.3d 103, 804 N.E.2d 1007, 2004-Ohio-544, reconsideration denied 2004-Ohio-1297, 2004 WL 541021, appeal not allowed 102 Ohio St.3d 1473, 809 N.E.2d 1159, 2004-Ohio-2830. Torts ⇐ 306

When uninsurance/underinsurance provider pays proceeds for wrongful death of policyholder, those proceeds are characterized as "damages" recovered by personal representative, regardless of how or why they are paid; even though damages ultimately go to beneficiaries, proceeds are payable due to fact that "insured" party—the decedent—suffered wrongful death. Holt v. Grange Mut. Cas. Co. (Ohio, 09-24-1997) 79 Ohio St.3d 401, 683 N.E.2d 1080, 1997-Ohio-375. Death ⇐ 78

Each person who was covered by uninsured and underinsured motorist policy and who was entitled to recover for wrongful death of coinsured had separate claim for proceeds of policy; accordingly, each person could recover per person policy limit of $250,000 subject to per occurrence limit of $500,000. Garlikov v. Continental Cas. Co. (Ohio 1993) 68 Ohio St.3d 91, 623 N.E.2d 1183, rehearing denied 68 Ohio St.3d 1448, 626 N.E.2d 689. Insurance ⇐ 2796

Each person who is presumed to have been damaged as a result of wrongful death may, to the extent of his or her damages, collect from tortfeasor's liability policy up to its per person limits, subject to any per accident limits; liability policy provisions which purport to consolidate wrongful death damages suffered by individuals into one "each person" policy limit are unenforceable; overruling State Farm Auto. Ins. v Rose, 61 OS(3d) 528, 575 NE(2d) 459; Burris v Grange Mut. Cos., 46 OS(3d) 84, 545 N.E.3d 83. Savoie v. Grange Mut. Ins. Co. (Ohio 1993) 67 Ohio St.3d 500, 620 N.E.2d 809, rehearing denied 68 Ohio St.3d 1216, 625 N.E.2d 619. Insurance ⇐ 2281(2); Insurance ⇐ 2756(3)

Each person who is covered by uninsured/underinsured policy and is presumed to be damaged by wrongful death has a separate claim subject to separate per person policy limits. Savoie v. Grange Mut. Ins. Co. (Ohio 1993) 67 Ohio St.3d 500, 620 N.E.2d 809, rehearing denied 68 Ohio St.3d 1216, 625 N.E.2d 619. Insurance ⇐ 2796

Damages caused by an intentional trespasser need not be foreseeable to be compensable, and therefore, in wrongful death action brought against intentional trespassers, trial court erred in instructing jury that only foreseeable damages could result in liability. Baker v. Shymkiv (Ohio 1983) 6 Ohio St.3d 151, 451 N.E.2d 811, 6 O.B.R. 206. Trespass ⇐ 47

In an action under section, based upon a tortious act which proximately accelerated the death of a decedent, the trial court should fully charge the jury as to the consideration it should give to the length of the period by which decedent's life was shortened and what damages flowed only therefrom. Larrissey v. Norwalk Truck Lines (Ohio 1951) 155 Ohio St. 207, 98 N.E.2d 419, 44 O.O. 238. Death ⇐ 104(3)

In an action based upon malpractice by a physician resulting in the death of the patient, a husband may recover for the loss of his wife's services only between the time she sustained the injury and her resulting death. Shaweker v. Spinell (Ohio 1932) 125 Ohio St. 423, 181 N.E. 896, 36 Ohio Law Rep. 421.

An instruction to the jury in a case wherein damages are sought for the death of a child ten years of age, that "[t]he jury may take into account any pecuniary injury from loss of society, comfort and protection which may apply alike to all beneficiaries," is erroneous and prejudicial. Kennedy v. Byers (Ohio 1923) 107 Ohio St. 90, 140 N.E. 630, 20 Ohio Law Rep. 610. Death ⇐ 104(5); Parent And Child ⇐ 7(14); Appeal And Error ⇐ 1064.1(7); Death ⇐ 108

In a wrongful death action, damages which may be recovered are limited to the pecuniary loss sustained by the beneficiaries and do not include such elements as bereavement, or mental pain and suffering of the beneficiaries, or the loss of the society or comfort of the deceased. Kennedy v. Byers (Ohio 1923) 107 Ohio St. 90, 140 N.E. 630, 20 Ohio Law Rep. 610. Death ⚖ 89

In actions for wrongful death the amount of pecuniary injuries sustained is an issuable fact, and, when denied, must be determined from the evidence peculiar to each case; and, if the damages are found to be excessive by a reviewing court, such finding involves the weight of the evidence. Schendel v. Bradford (Ohio 1922) 106 Ohio St. 387, 140 N.E. 155, 1 Ohio Law Abs. 105, 20 Ohio Law Rep. 495, 20 Ohio Law Rep. 499. Appeal And Error ⚖ 1004(9); Death ⚖ 108; Evidence ⚖ 597

In an action by the administrator of the deceased wife for the benefit of her surviving husband and children, for wrongfully causing her death, evidence that the husband had again married, and that his second wife performed like services and duties and contributed in like manner as the first wife to the support of the family and the accumulation of property, is not admissible in mitigation of damages. Davis v. Guarnieri (Ohio 1887) 45 Ohio St. 470, 19 W.L.B. 204, 15 N.E. 350, 4 Am.St.Rep. 548. Death ⚖ 64; Death ⚖ 91

Issues of whether 11-year-old child who was injured when he was struck by automobile would have provided support to his family members, particularly his mother, after his emancipation, and dollar amount of that support, were for jury in wrongful death action; testimony was presented regarding child's age, mental and physical characteristics, and future plans, and also regarding child's family background and education and earning capacity of other members of his family. Howard v. Seidler (Ohio App. 7 Dist., 12-04-1996) 116 Ohio App.3d 800, 689 N.E.2d 572, appeal not allowed 78 Ohio St.3d 1494, 678 N.E.2d 1230. Death ⚖ 103(4)

As matter of course, jury in wrongful death action must weigh evidence in determining probability of lost future earnings of decedent, whether decedent is adult with wage earning history or child too young to have been wage earner at time of death. Howard v. Seidler (Ohio App. 7 Dist., 12-04-1996) 116 Ohio App.3d 800, 689 N.E.2d 572, appeal not allowed 78 Ohio St.3d 1494, 678 N.E.2d 1230. Death ⚖ 103(4)

In order to recover on wrongful death claim involving medical malpractice, it is not necessary to allege that such malpractice reduced victim's probability of survival by more than 50%; it is sufficient to allege that physician's negligence was cause of death. Safranic v. Belany (Trumbull 1993) 89 Ohio App.3d 65, 623 N.E.2d 611, motion overruled 67 Ohio St.3d 1506, 622 N.E.2d 654. Health ⚖ 813

In an action for wrongful death based on medical malpractice, there is no need to introduce evidence concerning the length of time the victim may have lived but for the malpractice; however, the defendant may introduce evidence showing that the victim would have survived only a short time in mitigation of damages. Taylor v. C. Lawrence Decker, M.D., Inc. (Hamilton 1986) 33 Ohio App.3d 118, 514 N.E.2d 754. Health ⚖ 826

In an action for wrongful death, based upon alleged medical malpractice, neither RC 2125.01 nor Ohio case law recognizes any recovery for the loss of any chance of survival. Williams v. Grant (Erie 1979) 65 Ohio App.2d 225, 417 N.E.2d 586, 19 O.O.3d 168. Death ⚖ 13

A personal representative of a deceased, liable for funeral expenses of the deceased under the statute, may recover such expenses for the benefit of the estate from a tort feasor who negligently caused the death. Adams v. Malik (Lorain 1957) 106 Ohio App. 461, 155 N.E.2d 237, 7 O.O.2d 196.

An action by an executor or administrator for wrongful death arises from liability created by statute, recognized by the Constitution; the jury may use its own experience in determining damages. Minglewood Coal & Ice Co. v. Carson (Wayne 1928) 31 Ohio App. 237, 166 N.E. 237.

RC 2125.02(B) is not retrospective. Lawrence v Erie Insurance Group, 5 OBR 536 (App, Franklin 1983).

Dependent upon the facts and circumstances in a particular case, the expenditure of a reasonable sum for a monument or marker for a deceased seventeen year old son in senior high school at the time of his death, caused by the wrongful act of a third person, may be considered as a necessary funeral expense. Caswell v Harry Miller Excavating Co, 20 Misc 46, 246 NE(2d) 921, 47 OO(2d) 307, (CP 1969)

Funeral expenses incurred by a father for the funeral and burial of a seventeen year old minor son who sustained a fatal injury by reason of the wrongful act of a third person are not part of the damages recoverable for pecuniary loss for the death of said son under the wrongful death statutes, so that a father may recover such necessary funeral expenses from a wrongdoer who causes the death of such minor child. Caswell v Harry Miller Excavating Co, 20 Misc 46, 246 NE(2d) 921, 47 OO(2d) 307, (CP 1969).

Funeral expenses incurred by a husband for the funeral and burial of his wife who has sustained a fatal injury by the wrongful act of a third person, are not to be considered as a pecuniary injury under the wrongful death statutes. Barcus v. Union Hospital Ass'n (Ohio Com.Pl. 1965) 14 Ohio Misc. 168, 236 N.E.2d 232, 43 O.O.2d 407. Death ⚖ 84

Medical expenses accruing during the lifetime of a deceased wife because of an injury resulting in death sustained by the wrongful action of a third person do not constitute an element of damages in a wrongful death action. Barcus v. Union Hospital Ass'n (Ohio Com.Pl. 1965) 14 Ohio Misc. 168, 236 N.E.2d 232, 43 O.O.2d 407.

In an action for the wrongful death of her husband, a plaintiff who has remarried is entitled to an order directing that she be referred to only by her former name and that opposing counsel be directed not to indicate the remarriage. Helmick v Netzley, 12 Misc 97, 229 NE(2d) 476, 40 OO(2d) 104 (CP 1967).

The common law rule that no recovery could be had by a husband for injury to his wife, resulting in her death, has been modified by statute to the extent of permitting recovery for loss of companionship and services, from the date of injury to that of death, but not for the period following her death to some time in the future. Spinell v. Shaweker (Tuscarawas 1931) 11 Ohio Law Abs. 289, 36 Ohio Law Rep. 20, reversed 125 Ohio St. 423, 181 N.E. 896, 36 Ohio Law Rep. 421.

Punitive damages are not available in wrongful death actions, but may be available in survivor actions. Robinson v. Parker–Hannifin Corp. (Ohio Com.Pl. 1982) 444 N.E.2d 1084. Death ⚖ 93

Funeral expenses are recoverable as damages in a wrongful death action. McManus v. Buskirk (Ohio Com.Pl. 1962) 183 N.E.2d 473, 89 Ohio Law Abs. 97, 21 O.O.2d 243, reversed 176 Ohio St. 75, 197 N.E.2d 560, 26 O.O.2d 373.

An administrator may bring an action for recovery of funeral expenses against one whose wrongful act is alleged to have caused the decedent's death. Hunter v. McKinney (Ohio Com.Pl. 1951) 101 N.E.2d 810, 69 Ohio Law Abs. 237, 46 O.O. 17.

The apportionment of damages in a wrongful death suit is of no concern to the negligent party against whom damages are recovered, and where instructions are given to the jury to consider the value of a child's services to its father, mother and next of kin and the father is the only one with a pecuniary interest in such services, the jury should allow the full value for such services, and not suppose that the value is multiplied by the number of beneficiaries. Toledo Railways & Light Co. v. Wettstein (Ohio Cir. 1908) 23 Ohio C.D. 15, 14 Ohio C.C.(N.S.) 441, affirmed 79 Ohio St. 439, 87 N.E. 1142, 6 Ohio Law Rep. 518.

RS 5306 which provides that "a new trial shall not be granted on account of the smallness of damages in an action for an injury to the person or reputation, nor in any other action where the damages equal the actual pecuniary injury to the plaintiff" cannot be read as a proviso to RS 6134, and therefore is not a rule of property binding on the federal courts in an action for wrongful death. Hughey v. Sullivan (C.C.S.D.Ohio 1897) 80 F. 72. Federal Civil Procedure ⚖ 2312; New Trial ⚖ 75(5)

9. Negligence

Where a person is at the station house of a railroad by mere tacit permission and to get in out of a violent storm, and not to conduct any business with the railroad, the railroad is not liable for the death of such person resulting from its failure to exercise ordinary skill and care in erecting or maintaining the station house. Pittsburgh, Ft. W. & C.R. Co. v. Bingham (Ohio 1876) 29 Ohio St. 364.

An action for wrongful death may not be defeated by proof that some of the next of kin of the intestates for whose benefit the action was brought were guilty of contributory negligence where the intestates were not guilty of contributory negligence themselves. Cleveland, C. & C.R. Co. v. Crawford (Ohio 1874) 24 Ohio St. 631, 15 Am.Rep. 633.

Where death results from combined causes, namely the cooperation of negligent conduct on the part of both the defendant and the deceased, the plaintiff has no right to recover. Pittsburg, Ft. W. & C.R. Co. v. Krichbaum's Adm'r (Ohio 1873) 24 Ohio St. 119.

It is error to charge that if the deceased has contributed to the injury, the defendant must show that he was without fault himself. Pendleton St. R. Co. v. Stallmann (Ohio 1871) 22 Ohio St. 1.

Medical staff employed by Department of Rehabilitation and Correction (DRC) did not commit medical malpractice in failing to more quickly diagnose and treat sixty-nine year old inmate's prostate cancer; staff complied with all applicable standards of care concerning prostate-specific antigen (PSA) screening, doctor ordered PSA screening when inmate first

Note 9

complained of pelvic pain, inmate's oncological expert agreed that medical staff responded properly and provided adequate medical treatment both before and after prostate cancer was diagnosed, conclusion that an earlier screening would have detected cancer was speculative, and earlier diagnosis would not have changed prognosis, given the aggressive nature of the cancer and its failure to respond to treatment. Bingman v. Ohio Dept. of Rehab. & Corr. (Ohio Ct.Cl., 11-02-2005) No. 2004-06828, 2005-Ohio-6314, 2005 WL 3163945, Unreported. Evidence ⟸ 571(3)

Jury issue existed in wrongful death action as to whether physician's failure to diagnose patient's heart condition breached standard of care for family practice physicians. Kassmakis v. Dasani (Ohio App. 6 Dist., Lucas, 12-03-2004) No. L-04-1041, 2004-Ohio-6463, 2004 WL 2785295, Unreported. Health ⟸ 825

Genuine issue of material fact existed as to whether electrical company breached its duty to maintain its power lines and equipment and whether tree trimming company was negligent in the performance of its contractual obligations, precluding summary judgment for companies in wrongful death action brought by administrator of estate of resident who was electrocuted while trimming a dead tree that extended over his yard. Brady Fray v. Toledo Edison Co. (Ohio App. 6 Dist., Lucas, 06-30-2003) No. L-02-1260, 2003-Ohio-3422, 2003 WL 21489416, Unreported, appeal not allowed 100 Ohio St.3d 1472, 798 N.E.2d 407, 2003-Ohio-5772, reconsideration granted 100 Ohio St.3d 1551, 800 N.E.2d 755, 2003-Ohio-6789, motion denied 102 Ohio St.3d 1408, 806 N.E.2d 560, 2004-Ohio-1763, appeal dismissed as improvidently allowed 102 Ohio St.3d 1244, 811 N.E.2d 545, 2004-Ohio-3591. Judgment ⟸ 181(33)

Blame for a fatal accident cannot be reasonably imposed upon parents whose fourteen-year-old daughter allows a friend to ride her father's all-terrain vehicle contrary to her parents' repeated instruction to refrain from using the ATV while they are not at home. Paxton v. Ruff, Inc. (Ohio App. 12 Dist., Butler, 01-12-1998) No. CA97-04-089, 1998 WL 8695, Unreported, appeal not allowed 81 Ohio St.3d 1526, 692 N.E.2d 1027.

In order to prove wrongful death claim grounded in negligence, plaintiff must show that defendant owed duty of care towards plaintiff, that defendant breached that standard of care, and that breach was proximate cause of plaintiff's injury. Hitch v. Ohio Dept. of Mental Health (Ohio Ct.Cl., 11-13-1995) 75 Ohio Misc.2d 15, 662 N.E.2d 106, affirmed 114 Ohio App.3d 229, 683 N.E.2d 38. Negligence ⟸ 202

In wrongful death action predicated on medical malpractice, duty that physician owes patient is same in all cases: to treat patient in manner that physician of ordinary skill, care and diligence would under similar circumstances. Oiler v. Willke (Ohio App. 4 Dist., 06-30-1994) 95 Ohio App.3d 404, 642 N.E.2d 667. Health ⟸ 619

Loss of chance of recovery does not fulfill standard of proof required in wrongful death case involving medical malpractice; there must be evidence from which jury could conclude that survival would have been more likely than not, but for negligence. Safranic v. Belany (Trumbull 1993) 89 Ohio App.3d 65, 623 N.E.2d 611, motion overruled 67 Ohio St.3d 1506, 622 N.E.2d 654. Health ⟸ 633

To maintain wrongful death action on theory of negligence or malpractice, plaintiff must demonstrate: existence of duty owing to plaintiff's decedent; breach of that duty; and proximate causation between breach of duty and death. Hubbard v. Laurelwood Hosp. (Lake 1993) 85 Ohio App.3d 607, 620 N.E.2d 895, dismissed, jurisdictional motion overruled 67 Ohio St.3d 1450, 619 N.E.2d 419. Negligence ⟸ 321

An electrical utility company that erects equipment and connects lines at an insufficient height over the roof of a corporation is under a duty to exercise the "highest degree of care" in its installation; the electrical utility's later relinquishment of ownership and maintenance of the lines does not extinguish the duty if the original construction has remained unaltered. Fortman v. Dayton Power & Light Co. (Montgomery 1992) 80 Ohio App.3d 525, 609 N.E.2d 1296.

A company hired to investigate a potential insurance agent prior to his being hired by an insurance company that fails to discover the potential agent's conviction for aggravated burglary which resulted in the agent being hired and then meeting, marrying, and murdering a woman he met as a result of his employment by the insurance company, is not liable in a wrongful death action brought by the decedent's estate on a claim of negligent investigation and reporting, since the investigation company owed no duty to the decedent's estate upon which a claim for negligence could be maintained, the agent's criminal act was not reasonably foreseeable and cannot be linked to the alleged negligence of the investigation company, and the alleged negligence cannot be said to have proximately caused the death of the agent's wife. Caliman v. Mize (Hamilton 1989) 63 Ohio App.3d 231, 578 N.E.2d 531.

A cause of action does not exist for the wrongful death of a viable fetus caused by negligent care resulting in stillbirth. Werling v Sandy, No. 1-83-4 (3d Dist Ct App, Allen, 4-30-84), reversed by 17 OS(3d) 45, 17 OBR 37, 476 NE(2d) 1053 (1985).

In an action for wrongful death pursuant to RC 2125.01, the contributory negligence of a beneficiary is a partial defense only as to such beneficiary's share of the right to recovery of damages, but does not constitute a defense as against other, non-negligent, beneficiaries; this issue of whether the contributory negligence of a beneficiary is the proximate cause of the wrongful death must be submitted to the jury pursuant to the comparative negligence provisions of RC 2315.19(A)(1). Shinaver v. Szymanski (Ohio 1984) 14 Ohio St.3d 51, 471 N.E.2d 477, 14 O.B.R. 446.

In a suit by an owner-passenger against the driver of an automobile, the negligence of the driver may not be imputed to the owner-passenger. Parrish v. Walsh (Ohio 1982) 69 Ohio St.2d 11, 429 N.E.2d 1176, 23 O.O.3d 7, 21 A.L.R.4th 454.

It is not necessary in a wrongful death action arising out of the shooting of a game protector for plaintiff to prove that the shooting was intentional. Patrick v. Baldridge (Fayette 1958) 107 Ohio App. 331, 159 N.E.2d 461, 80 Ohio Law Abs. 522, 8 O.O.2d 259.

Police officer who, acting under orders from police headquarters, discovered men attempting to burglarize a bakery, was not guilty of using excessive force in apprehending such persons where they chose to flee from scene upon being discovered and refused to halt after repeated orders to surrender, given by officer who did not direct his firing at them until their escape seemed probable; police officer is not liable under section for death of one of such criminals who was shot while thus fleeing. Clark v. Carney (Hamilton 1942) 71 Ohio App. 14, 42 N.E.2d 938, 36 Ohio Law Abs. 68, 25 O.O. 347.

If there was a scintilla of evidence tending to prove negligence against the defendant railroad company, and the plaintiff's evidence did not raise the presumption of contributory negligence as a matter of law, the case should have been submitted to the jury on the issue of common-law negligence; this view is supported in principle by the case of Gartner v Corwine, 57 OS 246, 48 NE 945 (1897). La Dow v. Baltimore & O.R. Co. (Hamilton 1931) 40 Ohio App. 458, 178 N.E. 697, 11 Ohio Law Abs. 491, certiorari denied 52 S.Ct. 496, 286 U.S. 544, 76 L.Ed. 1281.

In action against railroad for alleged wrongful death through a grade crossing collision, admission of opinion evidence as to whether speed of train was fair, reasonable, and proper, though error, was harmless, in absence of facts and circumstances which would make speed an element of negligence, collision occurring at a crossing in open country. Tyler v. Hocking Val. Ry. Co. (Franklin 1926) 28 Ohio App. 88, 162 N.E. 623, 5 Ohio Law Abs. 546.

In action for death of passenger in automobile in collision with train at grade crossing, refusal to admit in evidence rule requiring fireman to keep a careful watch on track when not otherwise engaged was not error, in that rule, if properly made and enforced, imposed no duty on fireman other than enjoined by law. Tyler v. Hocking Val. Ry. Co. (Franklin 1926) 28 Ohio App. 88, 162 N.E. 623, 5 Ohio Law Abs. 546.

Landlord held liable for injury to tenant's child playing on walk, caused by falling wall which landlord failed to keep in reasonably safe condition. Foti v. Lewis (Ohio App. 1925) 27 Ohio App. 535, 161 N.E. 365, 3 Ohio Law Abs. 69. Landlord And Tenant ⟸ 164(1); Negligence ⟸ 1115

In an action for wrongful death of child of tenant, where a landlord expressly or impliedly reserves to himself, for the common use of his tenants, the control of a portion of the premises, he owes a duty to his tenants and their invitees to exercise ordinary care and prudence, to the end that such portion of the premises be maintained in a reasonably safe condition. Foti v. Lewis (Ohio App. 1925) 27 Ohio App. 535, 161 N.E. 365, 3 Ohio Law Abs. 69.

An action to recover damages from one who performed an illegal operation to produce an abortion may be maintained by the administrator of the woman whose death resulted from such act, even though she consented thereto. Milliken v. Heddesheimer (Ohio 1924) 110 Ohio St. 381, 144 N.E. 264, 33 A.L.R. 53, 2 Ohio Law Abs. 375, 22 Ohio Law Rep. 160.

Under GC 5838 (RC 955.28), former 10770 (RC 2125.01) and 10772 (RC 2125.02), an action may be brought against the owner of a dog for the death of a person caused by a bite of a dog, without alleging or proving the known vicious character of the dog or the negligence of the owner. Lisk v. Hora (Ohio 1924) 109 Ohio St. 519, 143 N.E. 545, 2 Ohio Law Abs. 198, 21 Ohio Law Rep. 604.

In a petition claiming damages for negligence, an allegation that a sand bank is operated on a portion of defendant's premises, and that the children of the neighborhood were accustomed to use said premises for the purposes of a playground, and that defendant "permitted, allowed, and acquiesced" in such use, will not be construed as an invitation, either express or implied. Hannan v. Ehrlich (Ohio 1921) 102 Ohio St. 176, 131 N.E. 504, 19 Ohio Law Rep. 5. Negligence ⟐ 1067; Pleading ⟐ 34(5)

The personal representative of a passenger who is killed while riding on a freight train with the permission of a conductor though in violation of railroad rules against passengers on freight trains cannot recover in an action for wrongful death against the railroad company, since there was no duty of care owed by the railroad to the deceased. Baltimore & O. S. W. R. Co. v. Cox (Ohio 1902) 66 Ohio St. 276, 47 W.L.B. 529, 64 N.E. 119, 90 Am.St.Rep. 583.

Where a party goes to a drugstore and inquires for a harmless drug without stating what it is to be used for, and the druggist by mistake puts up a poisonous drug which the party gives to his wife who dies instantly from its effects, an action may be maintained against the druggist for wrongful death. Davis v. Guarnieri (Ohio 1887) 45 Ohio St. 470, 19 W.L.B. 204, 15 N.E. 350, 4 Am.St.Rep. 548.

All that is necessary at a street crossing of an electric railway is that a warning be given as a car approaches the crossing under circumstances where an ordinary prudent person would give a warning; it is error in an action for the wrongful death of a pedestrian who was hit by a car for a judge to charge the jury that the company had a duty to ring a gong as a car was about to cross a street. Cincinnati Traction Co. v. Charles (Ohio Cir. 1912) 23 Ohio C.D. 437, 14 Ohio C.C.(N.S.) 506, affirmed 87 Ohio St. 475, 102 N.E. 1120, 10 Ohio Law Rep. 469.

Where a street car runs down a little girl who had fallen on the track 150 to 200 feet ahead of the car, there is a fair inference that the motorman was negligent in that he was inattentive or was running the car at a reckless rate of speed, and such facts would warrant a verdict against the company. Toledo Railways & Light Co. v. Wettstein (Ohio Cir. 1908) 23 Ohio C.D. 15, 14 Ohio C.C.(N.S.) 441, affirmed 79 Ohio St. 439, 87 N.E. 1142, 6 Ohio Law Rep. 518. Urban Railroads ⟐ 25

Where an inexperienced young employee is directed to perform a dangerous task and is not given any instructions or warning by the foreman or anyone in the shop, and is killed during the performance of such task, it is a jury question whether the danger was so apparent that instructions were not necessary and whether the deceased was guilty of contributory negligence. Jackson Knife & Shear Co. v. Hathaway (Ohio Cir. 1903) 17 Ohio C.D. 745, 7 Ohio C.C.(N.S.) 242, affirmed 72 Ohio St. 623, 76 N.E. 1126, 2 Ohio Law Rep. 535.

Employees of a street railway company have a right to rely on assurances from their superiors that a bridge said to be dangerous is safe to cross, and by continuing to work on the bridge the employee is not guilty of contributory negligence. Toledo Consol. St. Ry. Co. v. Mammet (Ohio Cir. 1895) 6 Ohio C.D. 244, 2 Ohio Dec. 532.

Where it is admitted by the defendant in a wrongful death action that the death was due to the injuries received, it is not error to admit testimony as to the nature of the injuries where such testimony may support the allegations in the petition of the defendant's negligence. Cincinnati Traction Co. v. Moeller (Ohio Super. 1906) 17 Ohio Dec. 22.

A trial court properly entered judgment in a wrongful death action by estate of university student shot by university security guard in which remittitur was required and accepted. Jones v. Wittenberg University (C.A.6 (Ohio) 1976) 534 F.2d 1203, 3 O.O.3d 311.

Error of judgment in time of emergency where there is no opportunity for mature consideration is not negligence. Hutchinson v. Dickie (C.C.A.6 (Ohio) 1947) 162 F.2d 103, certiorari denied 68 S.Ct. 208, 332 U.S. 830, 92 L.Ed. 404.

One who boards a construction train without permission, conceals himself, and is killed in a collision, caused by the negligence of the railroad's employees, cannot recover. Singleton v. Felton (C.C.A.6 (Ohio) 1900) 101 F. 526, 42 C.C.A. 57.

Administrator's action was sustained where the negligence was not wilful. Rankine v Pennsylvania & Ohio Coal Co, 15 CC(NS) 17, 23 CD 349 (Jefferson 1911), affirmed by 88 OS 555, 106 NE 1071 (1913).

Where a licensee is struck on the track of an interurban railway and he and others use every possible means to signal the motorman of the problem but the motorman fails to stop though he sees the people on the track and runs the licensee down, such is evidence sufficient to find the railroad company negligent. Cincinnati, Georgetown & Portsmouth RR Co v Dameron, 14 CC(NS) 49, 23 CD 123 (Hamilton 1911), affirmed by 86 OS 321, 99 NE 1122 (1912).

The verdict in a wrongful death suit must be based on the negligence alleged in the petition and not on that stated in the charge of the court. Lake Shore & Michigan Southern Railway Co v Reynolds, 21 CC 402, 11 CD 701 (Lake 1900).

An action for wrongful death may be maintained against a municipal corporation where the deceased fell from a bridge maintained by the municipality without any railings or guards to prevent persons from falling into the stream. Boyd v Cambridge, 4 CC 519, 2 CD 683 (Guernsey 1890), affirmed by 26 B 228 (1891).

10. Proximate cause

Where a conductor, under his legal right and duty, expels a drunken and unruly passenger from a train after the other passengers are endangered, and does so in a prudent manner so as not to put him in peril, but the drunk is run over by another train later, the expulsion itself is not such proximate cause of death as will make the company liable. Railway Co. v. Valleley (Ohio 1877) 32 Ohio St. 345, 30 Am.Rep. 601.

Damages resulting from the death of an intoxicated person cannot be recovered in an action under the act of April 18, 1870 for injury to means of support in consequence of intoxication. Davis v. Justice (Ohio 1877) 31 Ohio St. 359, 27 Am.Rep. 514. Death ⟐ 14(1); Intoxicating Liquors ⟐ 312

Trial court's failure to define proximate cause in its jury instructions was not plain error in action of decedent's grandson under his underinsured motorist coverage for the wrongful death of decedent in car accident, where court correctly defined proximate cause for jury once it had been advised of its omission in the court's instructions. Hiner v. Nationwide Mut. Ins. Co. (Ohio App. 5 Dist., Stark, 12-13-2005) No. 2005CA00034, 2005-Ohio-6660, 2005 WL 3446322, Unreported. Appeal And Error ⟐ 216(2)

Representative of deceased patient's estate failed to establish that doctor's negligence in failing to perform electrocardiogram (EKG) on patient was proximate cause of patient's death eight months later following cardiac bypass surgery; doctor diagnosed patient as having pneumonia, patient's symptoms at that time were consistent with pneumonia and condition responded to antibiotic treatment, evidence did not establish that patient had heart failure at time doctor saw him, evidence was inconclusive on question of whether scarring on patient's heart would have been present if EKG had been taken when doctor saw patient, and death was known risk of bypass surgery, even if patient had received bypass surgery earlier. Xirafakis v. Custodio (Ohio App. 8 Dist., Cuyahoga, 06-02-2005) No. 84818, 2005-Ohio-2707, 2005 WL 1303196, Unreported. Death ⟐ 17

The *Smith* rule, that statutes prohibiting liquor permit holders from knowingly furnishing alcohol to underage individuals do not offer any relief to a patron against a liquor permit holder for injury or death to the patron that occurs as a proximate result of the patron's voluntary intoxication, applied to claims for wrongful death and pain and suffering brought derivatively by deceased underage patron's estate, for exclusive benefit of patron's next of kin. Kirchner v. Shooters on the Water, Inc. (Ohio App. 8 Dist., 07-13-2006) 2006-Ohio-3583, 2006 WL 1918335. Intoxicating Liquors ⟐ 295

Loss-of-chance doctrine was inapplicable in wrongful death action where negligence of hospital personnel did not merely combine with preexisting condition to create the ultimate harm, but instead directly caused the ultimate harm by setting in motion another, independent force that directly caused patient's death when nurses, without an order from physician, removed endotracheal tube and thereafter the re-intubation of patient was delayed, causing 29 percent oxygen saturation level in patient's blood that was inconsistent with life. McMullen v. Ohio State Univ. Hosp. (Ohio, 04-12-2000) 88 Ohio St.3d 332, 725 N.E.2d 1117, 2000-Ohio-342. Health ⟐ 656

Testimony of plaintiff's expert witness that there was a proximal relationship between nurse's failure while visiting outpatient to determine whether patient was taking anti-seizure medication and patient's death three days later was sufficient to allow trial court to find that death of patient was probably caused by nurse's omission, even though same expert later testified that the "most proximate cause" of death was patient's decision not to take medication. Hitch v. Ohio Dept. of Mental Health (Ohio App. 10 Dist., 09-24-1996) 114 Ohio App.3d 229, 683 N.E.2d 38. Evidence ⟐ 571(9)

Department of Mental Health's (DMH) breach of duty to monitor psychiatric patient's medication caused patient to suffer seizure, and resulted in his death, and thus failure to monitor medicine was proximate cause of patient's death. Hitch v. Ohio Dept. of Mental Health (Ohio Ct.Cl., 11-13-1995) 75 Ohio Misc.2d 15, 662 N.E.2d 106, affirmed 114 Ohio App.3d 229, 683 N.E.2d 38. Mental Health ⟐ 51.5

Statute bars wrongful death action against owner or operator of premises for death caused by violent act of third person while on premises unless cause proximately resulted from gross negligence of owner or operator, or cause was provoked by owner or operator's act or omission. Monnin v. Fifth Third Bank of Miami Valley, N.A. (Ohio App. 2 Dist., 03-29-1995) 103 Ohio App.3d 213, 658 N.E.2d 1140, appeal not allowed 73 Ohio St.3d 1428, 652 N.E.2d 801. Death ☞ 14(1); Death ☞ 14(2)

In order to maintain wrongful death action, plaintiff must generally show existence of duty owed to decedent, and that breach of that duty was proximate cause of death. Oiler v. Willke (Ohio App. 4 Dist., 06-30-1994) 95 Ohio App.3d 404, 642 N.E.2d 667. Death ☞ 13; Death ☞ 17

Foreseeability determinations are but manner of addressing limits of actor's legal responsibility, regardless of whether analysis is conducted under element of duty or proximate cause. Oiler v. Willke (Ohio App. 4 Dist., 06-30-1994) 95 Ohio App.3d 404, 642 N.E.2d 667. Negligence ☞ 213; Negligence ☞ 387

In wrongful death case in which medical malpractice is predicate, complaining party must establish that doctor, nurses, and/or staff did not satisfy standard of care required, and that such deviation proximately caused death. Safranic v. Belany (Trumbull 1993) 89 Ohio App.3d 65, 623 N.E.2d 611, motion overruled 67 Ohio St.3d 1506, 622 N.E.2d 654. Health ☞ 623; Health ☞ 632

Firing a shotgun in the direction of a deer where the shootist should know that "drivers" on the deer drive in which the hunter is participating will be located constitutes reckless conduct; thus, summary judgment in favor of the hunter is improper. Hoover v. Shipley (Perry 1991) 70 Ohio App.3d 256, 590 N.E.2d 905, motion overruled 63 Ohio St.3d 1418, 586 N.E.2d 125.

Physician named as defendant in medical malpractice action was properly allowed to testify that patient's death was caused by factors other than his negligence; although physician's stipulation admitted his negligence proximately caused injury and death, he did not stipulate that all damages alleged by patient's family were proximately caused by his negligence, and thus was entitled to present evidence tending to prove that patient would have lived only a short time had her death not been accelerated by his wrongful act. Miller v. Marrocco (Hamilton 1989) 63 Ohio App.3d 293, 578 N.E.2d 834, motion overruled 45 Ohio St.3d 719, 545 N.E.2d 908. Stipulations ☞ 18(4)

A company hired to investigate a potential insurance agent prior to his being hired by an insurance company that fails to discover the potential agent's conviction for aggravated burglary which resulted in the agent being hired and then meeting, marrying, and murdering a woman he met as a result of his employment by the insurance company, is not liable in a wrongful death action brought by the decedent's estate on a claim of negligent investigation and reporting, since the investigation company owed no duty to the decedent's estate upon which a claim for negligence could be maintained, the agent's criminal act was not reasonably foreseeable and cannot be linked to the alleged negligence of the investigation company, and the alleged negligence cannot be said to have proximately caused the death of the agent's wife. Caliman v. Mize (Hamilton 1989) 63 Ohio App.3d 231, 578 N.E.2d 531.

Under section, a wrongful death action may properly be based upon a tortious act which proximately accelerated the death; in such an action, the plaintiff has the burden of proving that the tortious act was the proximate cause of the acceleration of death, and in mitigation of damages the defendant may offer evidence as to the weakness, diseased condition, impaired earning power or lack of activity of the decedent or other facts tending to prove that he would have lived only a very short time had his death not been accelerated by the tortious act. Larrissey v. Norwalk Truck Lines (Ohio 1951) 155 Ohio St. 207, 98 N.E.2d 419, 44 O.O. 238. Death ☞ 65; Death ☞ 66; Death ☞ 67

Plaintiff required to establish defendant's negligence as sole and proximate cause. Avra v. Karshner (Butler 1929) 32 Ohio App. 492, 168 N.E. 237. Negligence ☞ 1741

In action to recover damages for wrongful death, instruction to find for defendants if death was result of "unavoidable accident" held erroneous, where allegations of both petition and answer charged negligence, and "unavoidable accident" is necessarily accident occurring without apparent cause or fault attributable to any one. Avra v. Karshner (Butler 1929) 32 Ohio App. 492, 168 N.E. 237.

For plaintiff to recover in action for wrongful death, negligence of defendant must be proximate cause of injury, and instruction requiring defendant's negligence to be sole and proximate cause of injury placed greater burden on plaintiff than law required and was erroneous. Avra v. Karshner (Butler 1929) 32 Ohio App. 492, 168 N.E. 237.

Where an intoxicated person buys strychnine from a druggist who fails to label the poison as such, and then the intoxicated person drinks the strychnine and dies, his act is the intervening and proximate cause of his own death, rendering the sale and failure to label the poison remote acts not resulting in the death of such person. Ronker v. St. John (Ohio Cir. 1900) 11 Ohio C.D. 434.

In a wrongful death suit, admissions by the deceased as to the manner in which the accident happened and as to her condition tending to show that the accident was not the cause of her death are admissible in such a case. Bond Hill v. Atkinson (Ohio Cir. 1898) 9 Ohio C.D. 185.

Evidence that an equally convenient road had been constructed under the railroad for the purpose of avoiding a dangerous crossing, and that by reason thereof such crossing was little used by the public to the knowledge of the railway company, is competent as bearing on the question of the wrongfulness of such company in running its trains at high speed over the crossing. Lake Shore & Michigan Southern Railway Co v Reynolds, 21 CC 402, 11 CD 701 (Lake 1900).

11. Effect of action

Wrongful death proceeds are recovered for exclusive distribution to those beneficiaries designated under wrongful death statute and form no part of decedent's estate. Brookbank v. Gray (Ohio, 01-17-1996) 74 Ohio St.3d 279, 658 N.E.2d 724, 1996-Ohio-135. Death ☞ 101

Wrongful death action does not arise until death of injured person and, thus, injured person cannot defeat beneficiaries' right to have wrongful death action brought on their behalf, as action has not yet arisen during injured person's lifetime; injured persons may release their own claims, but cannot release claims that are not yet in existence and that accrue in favor of persons other than themselves. Thompson v. Wing (Ohio, 08-31-1994) 70 Ohio St.3d 176, 637 N.E.2d 917, 1994-Ohio-358. Death ☞ 25

Recovery in medical malpractice action by decedent during his or her lifetime does not bar subsequent wrongful death action brought on behalf of decedent's beneficiaries pursuant to wrongful death statute, providing for such action if decedent would have been entitled to maintain action and recover damages "if death had not ensued"; wrongful death action is independent cause of action and, thus, right to bring action cannot depend on existence of separate cause of action held by injured person immediately before his or her death. Thompson v. Wing (Ohio, 08-31-1994) 70 Ohio St.3d 176, 637 N.E.2d 917, 1994-Ohio-358. Death ☞ 27

Wrongful death is new cause of action distinct and apart from the right of action which the injured person may have had. Prem v. Cox (Ohio 1983) 2 Ohio St.3d 149, 443 N.E.2d 511, 2 O.B.R. 694. Death ☞ 11

An action for personal injuries begun by the decedent and prosecuted by his personal representative after his death, is not a bar to recovery by such representative for wrongful death. Mahoning Valley Ry. Co. v. Van Alstine (Ohio 1908) 77 Ohio St. 395, 83 N.E. 601, 5 Ohio Law Rep. 565.

Where a case is duly removed from a state to a federal court, the state court's jurisdiction over the matter ceases and it can take no further steps thereon; and if the case is thereafter disposed of other than on the merits, it cannot be recommenced in the state court, although such action might have been taken had the case not been removed. Baltimore & O.R. Co. v. Fulton (Ohio 1899) 59 Ohio St. 575, 41 W.L.B. 229, 53 N.E. 265.

A decree in equity, other than for a conveyance, release or acquittance of title to realty, acts only in personam, and does not execute itself so as to transfer personalty. Jelke v. Goldsmith (Ohio 1895) 52 Ohio St. 499, 33 W.L.B. 193, 40 N.E. 167, 49 Am.St.Rep. 730, 2 Ohio Leg. N. 430. Equity ☞ 63; Equity ☞ 431; Judgment ☞ 528

12. Limitation and bar of action

Security guard, who fatally shot assailant who was attempting to rob security guard, was justified in using deadly force in shooting assailant in self-defense, and thus security guard was not liable in wrongful death action for assailant's death; assailant waived what appeared to be real gun at security guard, and security guard reasonably believed that he was in danger of death or serious bodily harm, and that he could prevent such harm to himself only by immediate use of deadly force. Ashford v. Betleyoun (Ohio App. 9 Dist., Summit, 05-24-2006) No. 22930, 2006-Ohio-2554, 2006 WL 1409793, Unreported. Assault And Battery ☞ 13

Husband was not precluded from bringing wrongful death action by fact that he married wife after she was diagnosed with cancer. DeVine v. Blanchard Valley Med. Assoc., Inc. (Ohio Com.Pl., 07-01-1999) 103 Ohio Misc.2d 40, 725 N.E.2d 366. Death ☞ 31(6)

Statute of limitations for action against company that installed manure-handling system on farm, brought on behalf of minors whose fathers were found dead at bottom of pit of manure, was two-year limitations period for wrongful death actions and began running with deaths of fathers; ten–year statute of repose for action to recover for injuries arising out of defective and unsafe condition of an improvement to real property, and related provision tolling statute of repose for minors, did not even come into play unless two-year limitations period for wrongful death was satisfied. Schaffer v. Gateway Harvestore, Inc. (Ohio App. 3 Dist., 08-19-1998) 129 Ohio App.3d 448, 717 N.E.2d 1179, dismissed, appeal not allowed 84 Ohio St.3d 1436, 702 N.E.2d 1214. Death 👉 38; Death 👉 39

Time limits prescribed in wrongful death statute cannot be diminished or embellished based on the underlying wrongful act that caused the death of the decedent in a particular case. Schaffer v. Gateway Harvestore, Inc. (Ohio App. 3 Dist., 08-19-1998) 129 Ohio App.3d 448, 717 N.E.2d 1179, dismissed, appeal not allowed 84 Ohio St.3d 1436, 702 N.E.2d 1214. Death 👉 39

Genuine issues of material fact, precluding summary judgment for beneficiary's attorney in legal malpractice action by estate's administrator, existed as to whether attorney's representation of beneficiary began before statute of limitations expired on estate's wrongful death claim. DePugh v. Sladoje (Ohio App. 2 Dist., 06-14-1996) 111 Ohio App.3d 675, 676 N.E.2d 1231. Judgment 👉 181(16)

Reappointed administrator of decedent's estate failed to show that when statute of limitations expired on wrongful death claim, he had attorney-client relationship with attorneys who had initially represented him in his capacity as administrator, thus precluding his recovery in that capacity in legal malpractice action against those attorneys; although attorneys represented estate when administrator initially served in that capacity, they withdrew as attorneys of record in probate proceedings after administrator asked to be removed from that capacity, at which point attorney-client relationship ended. DePugh v. Sladoje (Ohio App. 2 Dist., 06-14-1996) 111 Ohio App.3d 675, 676 N.E.2d 1231. Attorney And Client 👉 112

Estate's settlement of wrongful death claim against county, entered after statute of limitations on that claim had run, was no defense to estate's administrator's legal malpractice action, which was based on defendant attorneys' alleged mistaken advice that, upon dismissal of wrongful death claim before statute of limitations expired, savings statute gave estate one year from date of dismissal to refile case; failure to file before statute of limitations expired amounted to "malpractice per se." DePugh v. Sladoje (Ohio App. 2 Dist., 06-14-1996) 111 Ohio App.3d 675, 676 N.E.2d 1231. Attorney And Client 👉 112

Estate's administrator's ability to appeal trial court's approval of settlement of estate's wrongful death claim against county did not preclude administrator's legal malpractice claim against attorneys whose allegedly negligent advice permitted statute of limitations on wrongful death claim to expire; because statute of limitations had run, estate had no recourse against county if its settlement offer were rejected. DePugh v. Sladoje (Ohio App. 2 Dist., 06-14-1996) 111 Ohio App.3d 675, 676 N.E.2d 1231. Attorney And Client 👉 112

Genuine issues of material fact, precluding summary judgment for attorneys in legal malpractice action alleging that statute of limitations on administrator-beneficiary's wrongful death claim expired because attorneys made incorrect representations to client as a beneficiary about time in which that action needed to be filed, existed as to whether such alleged representations breached duty that attorneys owed to client in his personal capacity as a beneficiary. DePugh v. Sladoje (Ohio App. 2 Dist., 06-14-1996) 111 Ohio App.3d 675, 676 N.E.2d 1231. Judgment 👉 181(16)

Genuine issues of material fact, precluding summary judgment for beneficiary's attorney in legal malpractice action by estate's administrator, existed as to whether attorney breached duty owed to beneficiary by having estate's initial wrongful death claim dismissed, having administrator removed from that capacity, and failing to have beneficiary appointed administrator before statute of limitations on wrongful death claim expired. DePugh v. Sladoje (Ohio App. 2 Dist., 06-14-1996) 111 Ohio App.3d 675, 676 N.E.2d 1231. Judgment 👉 181(16)

Client was not required to present expert testimony to defeat defendant attorneys' summary judgment motion in legal malpractice action alleging that statute of limitations on client's wrongful death claim expired because attorneys made incorrect representations to client about time in which that action needed to be refiled, as that alleged breach of duty was sufficiently obvious. DePugh v. Sladoje (Ohio App. 2 Dist., 06-14-1996) 111 Ohio App.3d 675, 676 N.E.2d 1231. Judgment 👉 185.3(4)

Beneficiaries in wrongful death action are in privity with decedent and, thus, they are collaterally estopped from relitigating issues decided in decedent's own action. Thompson v. Wing (Ohio, 08-31-1994) 70 Ohio St.3d 176, 637 N.E.2d 917, 1994-Ohio-358. Judgment 👉 686

Claims for wrongful death and for medical malpractice are distinct even though originating in the same wrongful act; the time limit for wrongful death is governed by RC 2125.02(D), and the cause of action survives even though the decedent's claim in malpractice was time-barred when he died. Brosse v. Cumming (Cuyahoga 1984) 20 Ohio App.3d 260, 485 N.E.2d 803, 20 O.B.R. 322.

Doctrine of interspousal immunity does not bar an action for wrongful death brought by the estate of a deceased spouse against the surviving spouse. Prem v. Cox (Ohio 1983) 2 Ohio St.3d 149, 443 N.E.2d 511, 2 O.B.R. 694. Death 👉 15

Prohibition will lie to prevent a judge from proceeding with a wrongful death action on the basis of an occupational injury more than three years prior to the date of death. State ex rel. Allied Chemical Corp., Plastics Division v. Earhart (Ohio 1974) 37 Ohio St.2d 153, 310 N.E.2d 230, 66 O.O.2d 313.

Under principles of res judicata and estoppel by judgment, a judgment in a wrongful death action that defendant was not negligent bars daughter of decedent, who was a real party in interest in the action and who was injured by the same accident which caused the death of her father, from subsequently bringing an action against the same defendant to recover for her injuries. Brinkman v. Baltimore & O. R. Co. (Montgomery 1960) 111 Ohio App. 317, 172 N.E.2d 154, 14 O.O.2d 286. Judgment 👉 668(2)

General release executed by parents after death of child, who had no spouse or children, was a bar to wrongful death action brought by administrator of estate of infant. Featherolf v. Casserly (Franklin 1956) 144 N.E.2d 114, 75 Ohio Law Abs. 332. Death 👉 25

A general release, issued by both parents after the accrual of a cause of action which might have been maintained against a tort feasor for their benefit, constitutes a bar to an action by the administrator of the estate of the child of such parents who died prior to the execution of such release as a consequence of alleged pre-natal injuries. Featherolf v. Casserly (Franklin 1956) 144 N.E.2d 114, 75 Ohio Law Abs. 332.

Separate releases of husband and wife of cause of action for personal injuries sustained by wife, executed before wife's death from injuries, *held* not bar to action for wrongful death brought by administratrix for benefit of children. Phillips v. Community Traction Co. (Lucas 1933) 46 Ohio App. 483, 189 N.E. 444, 16 Ohio Law Abs. 159, 40 Ohio Law Rep. 92. Death 👉 25

Where the appointment of an administrator for a decedent who was killed by the negligence of another is not completed within two years of the wrongful death, an action brought before the cause abated but before the appointment of the administrator was completed cannot be maintained, and once the action abated by statutory limitation it could not be revived. Archdeacon v Cincinnati Gas & Electric Co, 3 NP(NS) 45, 15 D 585 (Super, Cincinnati 1905), affirmed by 3 NP(NS) 606, 16 D 775 (Super, Cincinnati 1906); reversed by 76 OS 97, 81 NE 152 (1907).

Contributory negligence on the part of some of the beneficiaries will not bar the rest of the beneficiaries from having an action brought for their benefit. Wolf v. Lake Erie & W.R. Co. (Ohio 1896) 55 Ohio St. 517, 37 W.L.B. 23, 45 N.E. 708. Death 👉 24

Where a deceased during his lifetime barred himself from recovery for injuries, and had no cause of action at the time of his death, no action will arise in favor of his next of kin at his death, and his administrator would be precluded from manifesting a wrongful death action. Solor Refining Co. v. Elliott (Ohio Cir. 1898) 8 Ohio C.D. 225.

RC 2125.01, by which a wrongful death action in Ohio based on a "wrongful act, neglect, or default in another state" must be brought within the other state's limitation period, is construed to make a foreign state's statute of limitations applicable if injury was incurred there, even if the wrongful act itself occurred in Ohio. Vaughn v. J.C. Penney Co., Inc. (C.A.6 (Ohio) 1987) 822 F.2d 605.

A suit for wrongful death is not barred by a former suit by the same administrator to recover the value of a horse and wagon injured in the same accident. Peake v. Baltimore & O.R. Co. (C.C.S.D.Ohio 1886) 26 F. 495.

Decedent's husband could not bring wrongful-death action against driver in his own capacity, where he and decedent had released driver from liability in settlement of prior negligence action. Kissinger v. Pavlus (Ohio App. 10 Dist., Franklin, 05-21-2002) No. 01AP-1203, 2002-Ohio-3083, 2002 WL 1013085, Unreported. Death 👉 25

Settlement made by wrongdoer with next of kin and release executed and delivered by next of kin to wrongdoer during lifetime of decedent is a bar to an action for wrongful death. Pilkington v Saas, 25 Abs 663 (App, Franklin 1937).

Where plaintiff's decedents were drowned on July 11, 1952 and action was filed and personal service obtained on defendant November 1, 1954, actions were barred by the two year statute of limitations, notwithstanding allegation that a suit for death was filed and dismissed without prejudice on September 27, 1954, where the petition failed to state that the action was filed within the two year period. Bronikowski v Bigham, affirmed 145 NE(2d) 331, 143 NE(2d) 490, 75 Abs 65 (CP 1955).

13. Other statute pertinent or applicable

The act of congress of July 7, 1838, 5 Stat 306, which provides "for the better security of the lives of passengers on board vessels propelled in whole or in part by steam" applies to actions brought for wrongfully causing death in Ohio. Bradley v. Northern Transp. Co. (Ohio 1864) 15 Ohio St. 553.

Sheriff was acting within course and scope of employment in responding to crime in progress when he shot plaintiffs' decedent who was attempting to break into sheriff's home after decedent ignored sheriff's warnings, and thus, sheriff was immune from liability for wrongful death, even though sheriff was off-duty at time, absent any showing that sheriff was acting maliciously, wantonly, or recklessly. Kendzierski v. Carney (Ohio App. 9 Dist., Summit, 12-21-2005) No. 22739, 2005-Ohio-6735, 2005 WL 3482397, Unreported. Sheriffs And Constables ⬭ 99

Judgment of dismissal in federal civil rights action brought by motorcyclist's estate against village and police officer did not preclude estate from filing state wrongful death action against village and officer; although facts giving rise to both actions were identical, federal claim required evidence that officer's conduct during high-speed chase shocked the conscience, while state law claims depended on whether officer's actions amounted to willful or wanton misconduct. Wagner v. Heavlin (Ohio App. 7 Dist., 02-14-2000) 136 Ohio App.3d 719, 737 N.E.2d 989. Judgment ⬭ 829(3)

Statutory prohibitions against criminal child endangerment and wrongful death did not expressly impose liability upon county or its employee and did not limit county's or employee's sovereign immunity from liability for death to child that occurred during fishing trip sponsored by county child services agency for children in its custody. Colling v. Franklin Cty. Children Serv. (Franklin 1993) 89 Ohio App.3d 245, 624 N.E.2d 230, dismissed, jurisdictional motion overruled 67 Ohio St.3d 1511, 622 N.E.2d 658, rehearing denied 68 Ohio St.3d 1431, 624 N.E.2d 1067. Counties ⬭ 146

Each person entitled to recover damages pursuant to RC 2125.02 for wrongful death, and who is an insured under an underinsured motorist provision in an insurance policy, has a separate claim and such separate claims may not be made subject to the single person limit of liability in the underinsured motorist provision. Wood v. Shepard (Ohio 1988) 38 Ohio St.3d 86, 526 N.E.2d 1089. Insurance ⬭ 2796

The contributory negligence of a driver of a vehicle which results in the death of his passenger is not imputed to his passenger and therefore does not affect the passenger's right of action for injuries and medical expenses proximately caused by the negligence of another driver; this right of action is maintainable under the general survival statute, RC 2305.21, and is independent of the wrongful death action pursuant to RC 2125.01. Shinaver v. Szymanski (Ohio 1984) 14 Ohio St.3d 51, 471 N.E.2d 477, 14 O.B.R. 446. Automobiles ⬭ 227.5

Where an alleged negligent act was such as would have, if death had not ensued, entitled a person to maintain an action therefor, a cause of action for wrongful death exists in such decedent's personal representative, and such cause of action for wrongful death cannot be defeated merely by reason of the bar of limitation which would have been applicable to decedent's action. Klema v. St. Elizabeth's Hospital of Youngstown (Ohio 1960) 170 Ohio St. 519, 166 N.E.2d 765, 11 O.O.2d 326.

The options given to an employee or his legal representative by GC 1465–76 (repealed 1931), are confined to employees injured in the course of employment, and comprehend only those cases where the injury has arisen from the willful act of the employer or from his failure to observe a lawful requirement; and in such cases the employee or his representative may exercise his option either to institute proceedings under the act for damages or to make application for an award, but the selection of one of such remedies is a waiver of the right to pursue the other. Conrad v. Youghiogheny & Ohio Coal Co. (Ohio 1923) 107 Ohio St. 387, 140 N.E. 482, 36 A.L.R. 1288, 1 Ohio Law Abs. 357, 21 Ohio Law Rep. 32, 21 Ohio Law Rep. 33. Election Of Remedies ⬭ 7(1); Workers' Compensation ⬭ 2105

The cause of action upon such a legacy accrues when, by the terms of the will or rules of law, it becomes due and payable, and the executor has sufficient assets applicable thereto; where the right of action accrued before the Code, but the action has been commenced since, it is governed by the statute in force when the right accrued. Webster v. American Bible Soc. (Ohio 1893) 50 Ohio St. 1, 29 W.L.B. 141, 33 N.E. 297. Executors And Administrators ⬭ 429

GC 9017, which qualifies the liability of railroad companies for injuries to their employees, is properly applied in an action for damages on account of the death of a locomotive engineer due to a defective engine and track. Pittsburgh, C., C. & St. L. Ry. v. Francis (Ohio Cir. 1910) 22 Ohio C.D. 189, 13 Ohio C.C.(N.S.) 167, affirmed 83 Ohio St. 520, 94 N.E. 1113, 8 Ohio Law Rep. 610.

Where an express agent on a railroad train is acting in the capacity of a baggage master under the employ and control of the railroad company in addition to carrying out his duties for the express company, and he is injured through the negligence of railroad employees, he is only entitled to the rights of an employee of the railroad for such injury. Baltimore & O.R. Co. v. McCamey (Ohio Cir. 1896) 5 Ohio C.D. 631.

Where an employee's death results from defective machinery or appliances which had not been inspected with proper care and diligence, the provisions of 95 O L 114 relating to the liability of employers for injury or wrongful death of employees gives an employee who was in the exercise of due care and diligence at the time of the accident a right of action. Clark's Adm'x v. Stillwell–Bierce & Smith–Vaile Co. (Ohio Com.Pl. 1905) 18 Ohio Dec. 741, 6 Ohio N.P.(N.S.) 448, affirmed 76 Ohio St. 576, 81 N.E. 1183, 4 Ohio Law Rep. 707.

Wrongful death and survival actions, accidents to nonseamen in territorial waters, preemption by federal maritime law. Yamaha Motor Corp., U.S.A. v. Calhoun (U.S.Pa., 01-09-1996) 116 S.Ct. 619, 516 U.S. 199, 133 L.Ed.2d 578. Admiralty ⬭ 1.20(6); States ⬭ 18.57

In a federal court wrongful death suit based on diversity of state citizenship brought against a railroad by the widow of a driver whose truck was struck, claims that the train was speeding are preempted by the Federal Railroad Safety Act of 1970, 45 USC 421 to 447, but claims based on absence of adequate warning devices at the railroad crossing are not preempted. CSX Transp., Inc. v. Easterwood (U.S.Ga. 1993) 113 S.Ct. 1732, 507 U.S. 658, 123 L.Ed.2d 387.

A state wrongful death suit filed in state court alleging miners' deaths were proximately caused by fraudulent and negligent acts of their union in connection with safety inspections conducted by the union pursuant to the collective bargaining agreement is a claim not independent of the agreement, since union representatives took part in the inspections, and, as a result, is preempted by the Labor Management Relations Act, 1947, 29 USC 185(a). United Steelworkers of America, AFL–CIO–CLC v. Rawson (U.S.Idaho 1990) 110 S.Ct. 1904, 495 U.S. 362, 109 L.Ed.2d 362.

The Jones Act supersedes all state statutes which might otherwise be applied to maritime deaths. Gillespie v. U. S. Steel Corp. (U.S.Ohio 1964) 85 S.Ct. 308, 379 U.S. 148, 13 L.Ed.2d 199.

Survivorship claim may be asserted only on behalf of the decedent by executor or administrator for benefit of his estate. Wingrove v. Forshey (S.D.Ohio, 11-13-2002) 230 F.Supp.2d 808. Death ⬭ 31(3.1)

Where the widow of an employee injured in the course of employment is notified in her capacity as widow that her late husband is listed on the employer's schedule in bankruptcy proceedings as holding an unsecured, unliquidated claim for workers' compensation benefits, and is notified of the bar date for filing claims, leave to file a late proof of a wrongful death claim against the employer on an intentional tort theory will not be granted notwithstanding the lack of separate notice to the widow in her capacity as executrix of the decedent's estate. In re Terex Corp. (Bkrtcy.N.D.Ohio 1985) 45 B.R. 290.

RC 2125.01 and 4 USC 51, create as substantive law the legal liability for the wrongful death of another. Matz v. Erie–Lackawanna R. Co. (Summit 1965) 2 Ohio App.2d 136, 207 N.E.2d 250, 31 O.O.2d 241.

14. Vicarious liability

Where a railway employee is killed by a train while riding to a destination where he was to unload gravel, and although he and the train's engineer are engaged in a common service the position of each gave no right of control over the other, the railroad company is not liable for the negligence of the engineer as long as it was not negligent in hiring the engineer. Kumler v. Junction R. Co. (Ohio 1877) 33 Ohio St. 150.

Where a receiver operating a railroad by order of court has exclusive control of the road and agents and employees in the business, in the same manner as the railroad itself, an action may be maintained against such receiver for the negligent discharge of his duties by himself or his agents causing injury or death in the same manner as the railroad company.

Murphy v. Holbrook (Ohio 1870) 20 Ohio St. 137, 5 Am.Rep. 633. Railroads ⇐ 265

Neither an intoxicated adult patron nor the administrator of the patron's estate may maintain a cause of action against a liquor permit holder for injury, death, or property damage caused by the negligent actions of the intoxicated adult patron regardless of whether the injury, death, or property damage occurred on or off the permit holder's premises. Miller v. Sports Page (Ohio App. 11 Dist., Lake, 09-30-1998) No. 97-G-2104, 1998 WL 682382, Unreported, dismissed, appeal not allowed 84 Ohio St.3d 1483, 705 N.E.2d 364.

Death of bank customer resulting from shot fired by perpetrator during robbery was not caused by gross negligence on part of bank and its agents and employees, as would allow recovery by administrator of customer's estate in wrongful death action against bank. Monnin v. Fifth Third Bank of Miami Valley, N.A. (Ohio App. 2 Dist., 03-29-1995) 103 Ohio App.3d 213, 658 N.E.2d 1140, appeal not allowed 73 Ohio St.3d 1428, 652 N.E.2d 801. Death ⇐ 14(2)

Fact issue as to whether bank had failed to take reasonable safeguards to protect customer who was fatally shot by perpetrator during robbery, precluding summary judgment in wrongful death action based on premises liability, was presented by evidence that bank had been robbed twice, by expert testimony that bank employee's statement to perpetrator that she knew his mother was type of statement which increased prospect of violence, and by testimony of employee that she had never been instructed to avoid alerting robber that she could identify him, even though robber acted intentionally in firing shots. Monnin v. Fifth Third Bank of Miami Valley, N.A. (Ohio App. 2 Dist., 03-29-1995) 103 Ohio App.3d 213, 658 N.E.2d 1140, appeal not allowed 73 Ohio St.3d 1428, 652 N.E.2d 801. Judgment ⇐ 185.3(21)

Fact issue as to whether fatal shooting of bank customer by perpetrator during robbery was provoked by bank employees, precluding summary judgment in wrongful death action against bank, was presented by evidence that at time of shooting perpetrator was acting out of excited state created by statement of bank employee that she knew perpetrator's mother, which indicated to perpetrator that he could be identified; employee's remark, while innocent of any malicious purpose, may have provoked perpetrator to shoot, and was chargeable to bank. Monnin v. Fifth Third Bank of Miami Valley, N.A. (Ohio App. 2 Dist., 03-29-1995) 103 Ohio App.3d 213, 658 N.E.2d 1140, appeal not allowed 73 Ohio St.3d 1428, 652 N.E.2d 801. Judgment ⇐ 185.3(21)

Any negligence on part of employee of bank who acted within scope of her employment in responding to perpetrator of robbery was chargeable to bank in action brought by administrator of estate of customer who was fatally wounded by perpetrator during robbery, and bank was also chargeable with any negligence on its part in instructing or directing employee if that negligence proximately caused customer's death. Monnin v. Fifth Third Bank of Miami Valley, N.A. (Ohio App. 2 Dist., 03-29-1995) 103 Ohio App.3d 213, 658 N.E.2d 1140, appeal not allowed 73 Ohio St.3d 1428, 652 N.E.2d 801. Labor And Employment ⇐ 3053

A psychiatrist will not be liable for a wrongful death caused by the violent acts of a voluntarily hospitalized mental patient after the patient's discharge if (1) the patient did not manifest violent propensities while being hospitalized and there was no reason to suspect the patient would become violent after discharge; or (2) a thorough evaluation of the patient's propensity for violence was conducted, taking into account all relevant factors, and a good faith decision was made by the psychiatrist that the patient had no violent propensity; or (3) the patient was diagnosed as having violent propensities and, after a thorough evaluation of the severity of the propensities and a balancing of the patient's interests and the interests of potential victims, a treatment plan was formulated in good faith which included discharge of the patient. Littleton v. Good Samaritan Hosp. & Health Center (Ohio 1988) 39 Ohio St.3d 86, 529 N.E.2d 449. Health ⇐ 757

Where a wrongful act which has caused injury was done by the servants or agents of a municipality in the performance of a purely ministerial act which was the proximate cause of the injury without fault on the part of the injured person, respondeat superior applies and the municipality is liable. Fowler v. City of Cleveland (Ohio 1919) 100 Ohio St. 158, 126 N.E. 72, 9 A.L.R. 131, 17 Ohio Law Rep. 153, 17 Ohio Law Rep. 192. Automobiles ⇐ 187(2); Municipal Corporations ⇐ 705(12)

A death caused by defective apparatus of a city's fire department does not make the city liable for the death. Frederick v. City of Columbus (Ohio 1898) 58 Ohio St. 538, 40 W.L.B. 83, 51 N.E. 35.

The administrators of one whose death is the result of the negligence of the county commissioners in failing to keep a county bridge in repair may maintain an action for wrongful death against such county commissioners in their official capacity. Rahe v. Commissioners of Cuyahoga County (Ohio Cir. 1904) 16 Ohio C.D. 489, 5 Ohio C.C.(N.S.) 97.

An action cannot be maintained against a village for damages sustained on account of defects in a sidewalk where a person voluntarily attempts to pass over the sidewalk knowing it to be defective or unsafe and which he might easily have avoided, since such actions cannot be regarded as exercising ordinary prudence, notwithstanding the village's negligence in allowing such defects to exist. Bond Hill v. Atkinson (Ohio Cir. 1898) 9 Ohio C.D. 185.

Under Ohio law, vicarious liability could not be imposed on parent corporation of manufacturer of storage tank which was incorporated into integrated manure handling system in wrongful death action brought after farmer drowned in manure pit which was part of system where plaintiffs did not plead basis for vicarious liability and did not meet burden of overcoming the presumption that parent and its subsidiary were separate entities and entitled to be treated as such. Schaffer by Schaffer v. A.O. Smith Harvestore Products, Inc. (C.A.6 (Ohio), 02-06-1996) 74 F.3d 722, rehearing denied. Corporations ⇐ 268(1); Corporations ⇐ 269(1)

15. Automobile insurance

The aunt and grandmother of an insured killed in an automobile collision resulting from the negligence of an uninsured motorist are not entitled to recover their own per person policy limit under the decedent's uninsured motorist coverage. Villagomez v. State Farm Mut. Auto. Ins. Co. (Ohio App. 3 Dist., Putnam, 06-05-1996) No. 12-96-2, 1996 WL 368237, Unreported, dismissed, appeal not allowed 77 Ohio St.3d 1472, 673 N.E.2d 137.

Survivorship actions, unlike wrongful death claims, require a demonstration of conscious pain and suffering by a decedent prior to death; furthermore, compensatory damages are properly denied siblings who assert a claim under an individual policy based upon the brother's death where conditions of the policy are not met because (1) none of the siblings personally suffers any bodily injury, (2) the decedent did not reside in the same household with any of the siblings who are filing claims, and therefore (3) none of the siblings is a "relative" of the decedent for purposes of "bodily injury" coverage. Nationwide Mut. Ins. Co. v. Wright (Ohio App. 9 Dist., Lorain, 06-05-1996) No. 95CA006190, 1996 WL 304205, Unreported, cause dismissed 76 Ohio St.3d 1471, 669 N.E.2d 854, appeal not allowed 76 Ohio St.3d 1478, 669 N.E.2d 860.

Deceased passenger was an "insured" under her employer's commercial automobile policy which contained underinsured motorist (UIM) coverage, even though passenger was not acting in scope and course of her employment at time of accident, as provisions specifically making school employees insureds when they were acting in scope and course of employment applied by express terms only to liability coverage and not to UIM coverage. Roberts v. Wausau Business Ins. Co. (Ohio App. 10 Dist., 09-10-2002) 149 Ohio App.3d 612, 778 N.E.2d 594, 2002-Ohio-4734, appeal allowed 98 Ohio St.3d 1460, 783 N.E.2d 519, 2003-Ohio-644, reversed 100 Ohio St.3d 302, 798 N.E.2d 1077, 2003-Ohio-5888, motion stricken 100 Ohio St.3d 1497, 799 N.E.2d 179, 2003-Ohio-6267, motion granted 100 Ohio St.3d 1498, 799 N.E.2d 180, 2003-Ohio-6267. Insurance ⇐ 2660

Because passenger's employer's business automobile insurance policy insured the passenger herself and therefore her estate, that policy was the primary underinsured motorist (UIM) coverage as compared to automobile policies issued to the individual beneficiaries of passenger's estate. Roberts v. Wausau Business Ins. Co. (Ohio App. 10 Dist., 09-10-2002) 149 Ohio App.3d 612, 778 N.E.2d 594, 2002-Ohio-4734, appeal allowed 98 Ohio St.3d 1460, 783 N.E.2d 519, 2003-Ohio-644, reversed 100 Ohio St.3d 302, 798 N.E.2d 1077, 2003-Ohio-5888, motion stricken 100 Ohio St.3d 1497, 799 N.E.2d 179, 2003-Ohio-6267, motion granted 100 Ohio St.3d 1498, 799 N.E.2d 180, 2003-Ohio-6267. Insurance ⇐ 2800

Underinsured motorist (UIM) coverage in automobile policy of passenger killed in accident was not triggered, as that policy contained provisions limiting all claims arising from a single wrongful death to the per person limits contained in the policy, policy contained valid anti-stacking provisions, and passenger's estate received amount under tortfeasors' liability policies that was greater than the UIM limits in driver's and passenger's policies. Roberts v. Wausau Business Ins. Co. (Ohio App. 10 Dist., 09-10-2002) 149 Ohio App.3d 612, 778 N.E.2d 594, 2002-Ohio-4734, appeal allowed 98 Ohio St.3d 1460, 783 N.E.2d 519, 2003-Ohio-644, reversed 100 Ohio St.3d 302, 798 N.E.2d 1077, 2003-Ohio-5888, motion stricken 100 Ohio St.3d 1497, 799 N.E.2d 179, 2003-Ohio-6267, motion granted 100 Ohio St.3d 1498, 799 N.E.2d 180, 2003-Ohio-6267. Insurance ⇐ 2787

Automobile insurer had standing only to contest damages in wrongful death and survivorship action by insured's estate in which insurer intervened to protect its interest with regard to potential uninsured or underinsured motorist coverage, where policy language relating to uninsured motorist coverage stated that any judgment for damages arising out of a suit brought without insurer's consent was not binding on insurer, but did not reserve any rights with respect to liability. Holman v. Keegan (Ohio App. 6 Dist., 09-22-2000) 139 Ohio App.3d 911, 746 N.E.2d 209, appeal not allowed 91 Ohio St.3d 1432, 741 N.E.2d 895. Parties ⟜ 48

Automobile liability insurers must include language within their policies of insurance that clearly and unambiguously consolidates all individual wrongful death claims arising out of any one person's bodily injury into a single claim to limit all wrongful death damages to a single per-person policy limit. Clark v. Scarpelli (Ohio, 04-11-2001) 91 Ohio St.3d 271, 744 N.E.2d 719, 2001-Ohio-39, reconsideration denied 91 Ohio St.3d 1530, 747 N.E.2d 254. Insurance ⟜ 2756(3)

Automobile liability insurance policy clearly and unambiguously limited all losses that resulted from insured's death to a single per-person policy limit; inclusion of phrases "loss of consortium" and "injury to the relationship" did not render provision ambiguous and encompassed all derivative claims, including claims for wrongful death. Clark v. Scarpelli (Ohio, 04-11-2001) 91 Ohio St.3d 271, 744 N.E.2d 719, 2001-Ohio-39, reconsideration denied 91 Ohio St.3d 1530, 747 N.E.2d 254. Insurance ⟜ 2756(3)

Insured's recovery under her uninsured motorist coverage for death of her mother, who was struck and killed while insured's sister was driving uninsured vehicle, was limited to automobile policy's $100,000 "per person" limit, rather than its $300,000 "per accident" limit; insured was the only named insured on her policy, and was the only one entitled to collect from insurer under that policy for the wrongful death of her mother. Plesz v. Plesz (Ohio Com.Pl., 04-06-2000) 106 Ohio Misc.2d 1, 732 N.E.2d 1071. Insurance ⟜ 2796

Uninsurance/underinsurance motorist (UM/UIM) coverage provider's use of restrictive policy language defining "insured" is ineffectual to exclude from coverage claim of uncompensated wrongful death statutory beneficiary seeking to recover UM/UIM benefits, since correct focus for wrongful death recovery under decedent's policy of UM/UIM coverage is whether decedent was "insured"; abrogating *Thompson v Utomo*(Oct. 27, 1995), 1995 WL 628242; *Estate of Simone v. Nationwide Ins. Co.*(Nov. 3, 1994), Cuyahoga App. No. 67081, 1994 WL 613876; *Berleman v. State Farm Mut. Auto. Ins. Co.*(1992), 76 Ohio App.3d 81, 600 N.E.2d 1145. Holt v. Grange Mut. Cas. Co. (Ohio, 09-24-1997) 79 Ohio St.3d 401, 683 N.E.2d 1080, 1997-Ohio-375. Insurance ⟜ 2780; Insurance ⟜ 3460

Attempt of underinsured motorist (UIM) carrier to deny coverage for claims of insured's children, since they were not insureds, but sought benefits as statutory beneficiaries for insured's wrongful death, was invalid; obligation to provide coverage arose due to fact that insured suffered wrongful death, and carrier's attempted reliance on definition of "insured" was functionally equivalent of attempt to deny coverage to insured decedent. Holt v. Grange Mut. Cas. Co. (Ohio, 09-24-1997) 79 Ohio St.3d 401, 683 N.E.2d 1080, 1997-Ohio-375. Insurance ⟜ 2780; Insurance ⟜ 3460

Wrongful death claimants seeking recovery as statutory beneficiaries of insured need not be in privity with automobile insurer, i.e., they need not be insureds, in order to recover underinsured motorist (UIM) benefits; it is sufficient if insured decedent is in privity with insurer. Holt v. Grange Mut. Cas. Co. (Ohio, 09-24-1997) 79 Ohio St.3d 401, 683 N.E.2d 1080, 1997-Ohio-375. Insurance ⟜ 3460

Insured's children, as wrongful death claimants and statutory beneficiaries, were entitled to recover under uninsured/underinsured motorist (UM/UIM) provisions of insured's policy, even though children were not insureds under the policy. Holt v. Grange Mut. Cas. Co. (Ohio, 09-24-1997) 79 Ohio St.3d 401, 683 N.E.2d 1080, 1997-Ohio-375. Insurance ⟜ 3460

Insured and his children were not entitled to underinsured motorist (UM) benefits for wrongful death of insured's parent who was not member of insured's household when struck by automobile while crossing street as pedestrian. Visocky v. Farmers Ins. of Columbus (Ohio App. 8 Dist., 09-01-1994) 98 Ohio App.3d 118, 648 N.E.2d 6, motion to certify allowed 71 Ohio St.3d 1422, 642 N.E.2d 387, appeal allowed 71 Ohio St.3d 1422, 642 N.E.2d 387, cause dismissed 71 Ohio St.3d 1487, 646 N.E.2d 463, cause dismissed 71 Ohio St.3d 1488, 646 N.E.2d 463. Insurance ⟜ 2661

The mother of a decedent may recover from her insurer under an uninsured motorist provision notwithstanding the fact that the mother has shared in the proceeds of a wrongful death action brought by the decedent's father where the mother's policy does not contain an antistacking provision. Fay v. Motorists Ins. Co. (Geauga 1992) 80 Ohio App.3d 63, 608 N.E.2d 836, motion overruled 65 Ohio St.3d 1436, 600 N.E.2d 679.

An insurer issuing a homeowner's policy excluding intentional acts has no duty to defend an insured estate in a wrongful death action where the insured, suffering from Alzheimer's disease, shoots and kills another person and then commits suicide where there is evidence that the shooting was not the result of the Alzheimer's disease and the insured's acts were not unintentional; thus, a court does not err in determining that the insured was not insane at the time of the killing. Midwestern Indemn. Co. v. Manthey (Lucas 1990) 68 Ohio App.3d 539, 589 N.E.2d 95.

The parents and sister of an adult automobile accident victim may not bring wrongful death claims against their own insurers under policies which did not include the decedent as a named insured nor the vehicle in which she was travelling as an insured vehicle. Smith v. Erie Ins. Group (Stark 1990) 61 Ohio App.3d 794, 573 N.E.2d 1174, dismissed 54 Ohio St.3d 703, 561 N.E.2d 543.

Each person entitled to recover damages pursuant to RC 2125.02 for wrongful death, and who is an insured under an underinsured motorist provision in an insurance policy, has a separate claim and such separate claims may not be made subject to the single person limit of liability in the underinsured motorist provision. Wood v. Shepard (Ohio 1988) 38 Ohio St.3d 86, 526 N.E.2d 1089. Insurance ⟜ 2796

An insured father is entitled to recover those damages, which he was legally obligated to pay, under his uninsured motorist coverage for the wrongful death of a minor child, even if the child was not an insured according to the terms of the policy. Sexton v. State Farm Mut. Auto. Ins. Co. (Ohio 1982) 69 Ohio St.2d 431, 433 N.E.2d 555, 23 O.O.3d 385.

The father of an unemancipated minor child is legally entitled to recover on his uninsured motorist coverage for the wrongful death of that minor child even if such child at the time of the injury and death was not a member of the father's household. Motorists Mut. Ins. Co. v. Speck (Summit 1977) 59 Ohio App.2d 224, 393 N.E.2d 500, 13 O.O.3d 239.

16. Standards for action

Where (1) a decedent had neither complaints nor symptoms following a medical procedure, (2) nothing in his medical chart would ordinarily have resulted in a longer stay in the hospital, and (3) it is not more likely or probable that he would have survived if hospitalized, then his early discharge is not actionable in a wrongful death suit. Czerwinski v. St. Luke's Medical Center (Ohio App. 8 Dist., Cuyahoga, 07-25-1996) No. 70032, 1996 WL 417138, Unreported.

Notwithstanding a wrongful death case may sound in contract as well as in tort, the wrongful death statute supplies a complete remedy, and it is consistent with reason that it should be regarded as the exclusive remedy. Spinell v. Shaweker (Tuscarawas 1931) 11 Ohio Law Abs. 289, 36 Ohio Law Rep. 20, reversed 125 Ohio St. 423, 181 N.E. 896, 36 Ohio Law Rep. 421.

Action in which plaintiff alleged that defendants' failure to provide proper medical care caused death of plaintiff's decedent was properly treated as a medical malpractice wrongful death action, even though plaintiff had alleged nine claims for relief in his complaint. Walker v. E. End Community Health Ctr., Inc. (Ohio App. 1 Dist., 05-01-1998) 131 Ohio App.3d 322, 722 N.E.2d 550. Health ⟜ 800

Homeowners' policy issued to mother, under which sons were also insureds, excluded liability coverage for wrongful death claim against mother arising out of accidental shooting death of son under exclusion for claims based on bodily injury to insured, notwithstanding that wrongful death plaintiff, father, was not insured under policy and did not suffer bodily injury, as any injury to father arose solely from bodily injury that his insured son sustained. Cincinnati Indemn. Co. v. Martin (Ohio, 06-16-1999) 85 Ohio St.3d 604, 710 N.E.2d 677, 1999-Ohio-322. Insurance ⟜ 2356

An insurer has no duty to defend or indemnify its insured in a wrongful death lawsuit brought by a noninsured based on the death of an insured where the policy excludes liability coverage for claims based on bodily injury to an insured. Cincinnati Indemn. Co. v. Martin (Ohio, 06-16-1999) 85 Ohio St.3d 604, 710 N.E.2d 677, 1999-Ohio-322. Insurance ⟜ 2278(1)

Actions for wrongful death and survivorship are statutory, and operate as exceptions to common-law rule that death terminates all claims for relief that otherwise might be brought; wrongful death and survivorship are not claims for relief, as such, but are statutory actions by which certain claims for relief may be brought. Monnin v. Fifth Third Bank of Miami Valley, N.A. (Ohio App. 2 Dist., 03-29-1995) 103 Ohio App.3d 213, 658 N.E.2d 1140, appeal not allowed 73 Ohio St.3d 1428, 652 N.E.2d 801. Death ⟜ 7

Action for wrongful death is created by statute, and affords civil remedy which compensates others for death of person caused by wrongful act, neglect, or default of third person. Monnin v. Fifth Third Bank of Miami Valley, N.A. (Ohio App. 2 Dist., 03-29-1995) 103 Ohio App.3d 213, 658 N.E.2d 1140, appeal not allowed 73 Ohio St.3d 1428, 652 N.E.2d 801. Death ⟜ 7

Having prevailed in wrongful death action against decedent's employer, decedent's wife and two minor children each had separate "covered claim" on which state insurance guaranty association was obligated to pay due to insolvency of employer's excess liability insurer, where excess liability policy did not limit coverage for such claims. Dickerson v. Thompson (Cuyahoga 1993) 89 Ohio App.3d 399, 624 N.E.2d 784. Insurance ⇌ 1499

In Ohio, there is no recovery in wrongful death for loss of any chance of survival on account of medical malpractice; rather, there must be sufficient evidence to show that with proper diagnosis, treatment, and surgery, patient probably would have survived. Lambert v. Shearer (Franklin 1992) 84 Ohio App.3d 266, 616 N.E.2d 965. Death ⇌ 81

Viable fetus which was negligently injured en ventre sa mere and subsequently stillborn could be basis for wrongful death action pursuant to statute. Werling v. Sandy (Ohio 1985) 17 Ohio St.3d 45, 476 N.E.2d 1053, 17 O.B.R. 37. Death ⇌ 15

A viable fetus which is negligently injured in its mother's womb and subsequently stillborn can be the basis for a wrongful death action pursuant to RC 2125.01. Werling v. Sandy (Ohio 1985) 17 Ohio St.3d 45, 476 N.E.2d 1053, 17 O.B.R. 37. Death ⇌ 15

The doctrine of interspousal immunity does not bar an action for wrongful death brought by the estate of a deceased against the surviving spouse. Prem v. Cox (Ohio 1983) 2 Ohio St.3d 149, 443 N.E.2d 511, 2 O.B.R. 694. Death ⇌ 15

Section authorizing bringing of an action for wrongful death creates a new cause or right of action distinct and apart from right of action which injured person might have had and upon existence of which new right is conditioned; statute is an innovation to principles of common law and affords only civil remedy to compensate others for death resulting from injuries. Karr v. Sixt (Ohio 1946) 146 Ohio St. 527, 67 N.E.2d 331, 33 O.O. 14. Death ⇌ 11; Death ⇌ 15

Action for wrongful death by administrator on behalf of wife's sisters and brother, against husband who killed wife, held not to lie. Demos v. Freemas (Franklin 1931) 43 Ohio App. 426, 183 N.E. 395, 13 Ohio Law Abs. 318. Death ⇌ 31(5); Executors And Administrators ⇌ 426

Section substantially follows Lord Campbell's Act, not only in its general features, but also in the requirement that it is essential to the maintenance of an action for death that the wrongful act, negligence, carelessness, unskillfulness, or default out of which the action arises must be of such character as would, if death had not ensued, have entitled the person to maintain an action and recover damages in respect thereof. May Coal Co. v. Robinette (Ohio 1929) 120 Ohio St. 110, 165 N.E. 576, 64 A.L.R. 441, 7 Ohio Law Abs. 173, 28 Ohio Law Rep. 542.

An action to recover damages from one who performed an illegal operation to produce an abortion may be maintained by the administrator of the woman whose death resulted from such wrongful act, even though she consented thereto. Milliken v. Heddesheimer (Ohio 1924) 110 Ohio St. 381, 144 N.E. 264, 33 A.L.R. 53, 2 Ohio Law Abs. 375, 22 Ohio Law Rep. 160.

Where the widow of a railroad employee makes a settlement with the railroad company without knowledge of her attorneys hired to bring the wrongful death suit, an action cannot be maintained against the widow in her representative capacity for attorney fees. Hurd v. Wheeling & L.E.R. Co. (Ohio Com.Pl. 1897) 6 Ohio Dec. 549, 4 Ohio N.P. 404.

Wrongful death, carriers, accident, unexpected or unusual event, refusal to move asthmatic passenger to seat away from smoking section. Olympic Airways v. Husain (U.S., 02-24-2004) 124 S.Ct. 1221, 540 U.S. 644, 157 L.Ed.2d 1146, rehearing denied 124 S.Ct. 2065, 541 U.S. 1007, 158 L.Ed.2d 527.

Changes in Ohio statutes regarding wrongful death and comparative negligence do not apply to accident occurring prior thereto. Tackett v. Consolidated Rail Corp. (S.D.Ohio 1982) 536 F.Supp. 409.

Decedent's wife and each minor child has a covered claim as defined in RC 3955.01 where each has a separate compensable claim under RC 2125.01 and the employer's excess liability insurance policy does not limit coverage in this regard. Dickerson v Thompson, No. 62640, 1993 WL 328753 (8th Dist Ct App, Cuyahoga, 8–26–93).

If a wife is killed instantly in an accident, there can be no action maintained for the loss of her services. Bauman v Pittsburgh, Cincinnati, Chicago & St. Louis Railway Co, 9 NP(NS) 320, 20 D 509 (CP, Licking 1909).

17. Wrongful life

Prolonging of patient's life by resuscitating him after he suffered ventricular fibrillation was not wrongful living; life is not a compensable harm. Anderson v. St. Francis–St. George Hosp. (Hamilton 1992) 83 Ohio App.3d 221, 614 N.E.2d 841, motion to certify overruled 66 Ohio St.3d 1459, 610 N.E.2d 423. Health ⇌ 917

18. Choice of law

An action for wrongful death may be brought in any county in the state where the defendant or any one of the defendants resides or may be served. Drea v. Carrington (Ohio 1877) 32 Ohio St. 595. Death ⇌ 36; Venue ⇌ 8.2

In wrongful death action brought against manufacturers and suppliers of vinyl chloride, Court of Appeals would decline to use Ohio's discovery rule to toll Michigan's three-year limitations period applicable to claim brought by widow of worker, who died after developing brain tumor allegedly caused from occupational exposure to vinyl chloride; Ohio's wrongful death statute does not create right to sue for alleged wrongful death occurring in another state, but allows for enforcement of that right and, if that right no longer exists because of bar by statute of limitations in state where cause of action accrued, it seems untenable to extend time period by use of Ohio's discovery rule. Mayor v. Ford Motor Co. (Ohio App. 8 Dist., Cuyahoga, 06-24-2004) No. 83297, 2004-Ohio-3289, 2004 WL 1402692, Unreported, appeal not allowed 103 Ohio St.3d 1526, 817 N.E.2d 409, 2004-Ohio-5852. Death ⇌ 39

Under borrowing provision of wrongful death statute, Michigan's statute of limitations applied in wrongful death action brought against manufacturers and suppliers of vinyl chloride by widow of worker, who died after developing brain tumor allegedly caused from occupational exposure to vinyl chloride; although widow alleged wrongful acts occurred in Ohio as that was where vinyl chloride was manufactured and allegedly conspiratorial meetings occurred, worker was allegedly exposed to vinyl chloride, became sick, and died in Michigan. Mayor v. Ford Motor Co. (Ohio App. 8 Dist., Cuyahoga, 06-24-2004) No. 83297, 2004-Ohio-3289, 2004 WL 1402692, Unreported, appeal not allowed 103 Ohio St.3d 1526, 817 N.E.2d 409, 2004-Ohio-5852. Death ⇌ 8

Plaintiff's decedent may maintain an action for wrongful death in Ohio when the decedent and the defendant were fellow employees resident in New York but temporarily in Ohio, where the accident and death occurred, although plaintiff obtained benefits under the New York workmen's compensation law, which bars a recovery for death caused by a fellow employee if such benefits have been paid. (See also Moats v Metropolitan Bank of Lima, 40 OS(2d) 47, 319 NE(2d) 603 (1974).) Ellis v. Garwood (Cuyahoga 1957) 143 N.E.2d 715, 80 Ohio Law Abs. 443, affirmed 168 Ohio St. 241, 152 N.E.2d 100, 6 O.O.2d 22.

Action for injuries by dog maintainable either under statute or at common law. Lisk v. Hora (Ohio 1924) 109 Ohio St. 519, 143 N.E. 545, 2 Ohio Law Abs. 198, 21 Ohio Law Rep. 604. Animals ⇌ 68; Common Law ⇌ 14

In action brought under Ohio wrongful death law, in which death occurs in another state as result of negligent act precipitated in Ohio, Ohio court would apply statute of limitations of state in which death occurs; thus, action brought against kerosene heater seller and kerosene manufacturer on behalf of Ohio residents who died in camper in Tennessee allegedly as result of inhaling noxious fumes emitted by heater, which was purchased in Ohio and which was fueled by kerosene purchased in Ohio, was barred by Tennessee one-year limitations period. Vaughn v. J.C. Penney Co., Inc. (C.A.6 (Ohio) 1987) 822 F.2d 605. Death ⇌ 8; Death ⇌ 38

Under Ohio law, survivorship claim exists separate and apart from a wrongful death claim. Wingrove v. Forshey (S.D.Ohio, 11-13-2002) 230 F.Supp.2d 808. Death ⇌ 10

Under Ohio law, statute of limitations applicable to wrongful death claim of personal representative of deceased Michigan resident against Ohio corporation arising out of accident in Georgia would be determined under Georgia law. Jones v. Mid America Expositions, Inc. (S.D.Ohio 1989) 708 F.Supp. 173. Death ⇌ 8

Conflict of laws provision in Ohio statute which provides exclusive remedy in Ohio for death caused by injury, directs trial court to apply statute of limitations in state in which injury occurred. Vaughn v. J.C. Penney, Inc. (S.D.Ohio 1986) 645 F.Supp. 12. Limitation Of Actions ⇌ 2(3)

In a wrongful death action brought in Ohio by daughter, against out-of-state corporation, allegedly because mother had taken drug while pregnant which caused cancer in daughter, the Ohio wrongful death law applied.

Bruck v. Eli Lilly and Co. (S.D.Ohio 1981) 523 F.Supp. 480, appeal dismissed 698 F.2d 1217.

Ohio's wrongful death statute, RC 2125.01, dictates who may bring the action; when a person dies from a tortfeasor's negligence, the probate court appoints an administrator as fiduciary to pursue the decedent's claims, and any wrongful death proceeds recovered by the administrator are distributed to the beneficiaries of the decedent according to Ohio law. Sansone v. State Farm Mut. Auto. Ins. Co. (S.D.Ohio 1993) 815 F.Supp. 1096.

19. Contributory negligence and assumption of risk

Genuine issue of material fact existed as to whether resident and resident's helper were acting in a negligent manner by cutting tree limbs that extended over resident's yard, precluding summary judgment for electrical company and tree trimming company in wrongful death action brought against companies by administrator of estate of resident who was electrocuted while trimming tree limbs. Brady Fray v. Toledo Edison Co. (Ohio App. 6 Dist., Lucas, 06-30-2003) No. L-02-1260, 2003-Ohio-3422, 2003 WL 21489416, Unreported, appeal not allowed 100 Ohio St.3d 1472, 798 N.E.2d 407, 2003-Ohio-5772, reconsideration granted 100 Ohio St.3d 1551, 800 N.E.2d 755, 2003-Ohio-6789, motion denied 102 Ohio St.3d 1408, 806 N.E.2d 560, 2004-Ohio-1763, appeal dismissed as improvidently allowed 102 Ohio St.3d 1244, 811 N.E.2d 545, 2004-Ohio-3591. Judgment ⇔ 181(33)

Contributory negligence of driver which resulted in death of passenger was not imputed to passenger and did not affect passenger's right of action for injuries and medical expenses proximately caused by negligence of another driver, which right of action was maintainable under general survival statute and was independent of wrongful death action. Shinaver v. Szymanski (Ohio 1984) 14 Ohio St.3d 51, 471 N.E.2d 477, 14 O.B.R. 446. Automobiles ⇔ 227.5

Under statutes requiring employer to furnish employees safe place of employment and regarding prevention of injuries, doctrine of assumption of risk no longer obtains. Hauer v. French Bros. Bauer Co. (Hamilton 1931) 43 Ohio App. 333, 183 N.E. 186, 11 Ohio Law Abs. 217, 36 Ohio Law Rep. 51. Labor And Employment ⇔ 2957

Where, in an action for damages for wrongful death, there was a verdict for defendant, and plaintiff prosecutes error, and it appears that on trial before court and jury there was evidence tending to show actionable negligence on the part of the defendant and the evidence does not show the decedent to be guilty of contributory negligence as a matter of law, the defendant in error is not entitled to an affirmance on the ground that the trial court should have directed a verdict in his favor. Fach v. Canton Yellow Cab Co. (Stark 1929) 36 Ohio App. 247, 173 N.E. 245, 9 Ohio Law Abs. 189. Appeal And Error ⇔ 1062.1; Trial ⇔ 134

Deceased on public road, electrocuted when coming near high-voltage wires, held not contributorily negligent as matter of law. Ohio Power Co. v. Fittro (Hardin 1930) 36 Ohio App. 186, 173 N.E. 33, 8 Ohio Law Abs. 617, 32 Ohio Law Rep. 227. Electricity ⇔ 19(12)

20. Evidence

Credible evidence in wrongful death case supported jury finding that defendant was not responsible for the hit-and-run death of bicyclist; defendant testified that he did not strike bicyclist with his van, deputy sheriff, who saw van four days after accident testified that he did not see damage or signs of recent repair to van, expert testified to a reasonable degree of scientific probability that defendant's van was not involved in the hit and run, defendant required a decal on his windshield to drive into his workplace, all experts agreed that the hit and run would have caused defendant's windshield to shatter, and defendant never requested a new decal from his work near the time of the accident. Starinchak v. Sapp (Ohio App. 10 Dist., Franklin, 06-02-2005) No. 04AP-484, 2005-Ohio-2715, 2005 WL 1303212, Unreported, appeal not allowed 106 Ohio St.3d 1558, 836 N.E.2d 582, 2005-Ohio-5531. Evidence ⇔ 571(6)

Evidence established that correctional facility breached a duty it owed to inmate when it failed to render follow-up care for treatment of possible pneumonia, that pneumonia was a proximate cause of inmate's death, and that inmate suffered physical harm when he was in facility's custody and control due to facility's failure to render follow-up care; medical expert for inmate's surviving sister testified that early intervention was important in any infection, especially pneumonia, medical notes from state medical center revealed inmate was treated for dehydration and possible aspiration pneumonia three days before he died, and inmate's chest x-ray showed signs suspicious for pneumonia and a follow-up recommendation. Spencer, Admr. v. Ohio Dept. of Rehab. & Corr. (Ohio Ct.Cl., 04-09-2002) No. 99-03961, 2002-Ohio-1714, 2002 WL 31974396, Unreported. States ⇔ 112.2(4)

Question of whether actions of physician were independent of actions of nurse and thus constituted intervening cause of patient's death was for jury, in action for medical malpractice and wrongful death involving actions of nurse; evidence showed that nurse did not follow written policy and procedures requiring her to ask physician to set patient's infusion rates, but set rate according to what she believed physician would routinely choose, and physician did not specify infusion rate or review infusion rate when he checked on patient. Czarney v. Porter (Ohio App. 8 Dist., 05-18-2006) 166 Ohio App.3d 830, 853 N.E.2d 692, 2006-Ohio-2471. Health ⇔ 826

Parents of deceased child failed to properly set forth a claim for spoliation of evidence in their wrongful death complaint, where nowhere in the complaint was there an actual count for spoliation of evidence, there was no indication in the facts set forth that such a claim would be raised, complaint merely stated proper records were not kept, and complaint was never amended to include claim after parents' counsel was apparently dissatisfied with discovery responses. Bae v. Dragoo & Assoc., Inc. (Ohio App. 10 Dist., 02-03-2004) 156 Ohio App.3d 103, 804 N.E.2d 1007, 2004-Ohio-544, reconsideration denied 2004-Ohio-1297, 2004 WL 541021, appeal not allowed 102 Ohio St.3d 1473, 809 N.E.2d 1159, 2004-Ohio-2830. Torts ⇔ 313

Evidence that emergency vehicle had its emergency lights and siren running did not establish that city firefighter did not act wantonly or recklessly in crossing center line of street at speed allegedly as high as 61 miles per hour on street on which speed limit was 35 miles per hour, for purposes of determining whether city and firefighter were immune from wrongful death action brought by deceased motorist's husband and her estate, alleging firefighter's negligence in striking motorist's vehicle with emergency vehicle. Hunter v. Columbus (Ohio App. 10 Dist., 12-05-2000) 139 Ohio App.3d 962, 746 N.E.2d 246, appeal not allowed 91 Ohio St.3d 1493, 745 N.E.2d 439. Automobiles ⇔ 187(2)

City's fire department's rule that an emergency vehicle should not proceed over 20 miles per hour when proceeding left of the center line of a road was not determinative of whether city firefighter acted wantonly or recklessly in crossing center line of street, during winter, at speed allegedly as high as 61 miles per hour, for purposes of determining whether city and firefighter were immune from wrongful death action brought by deceased motorist's husband and her estate, alleging firefighter's negligence in striking motorist's vehicle with emergency vehicle, but city's rule could be taken into consideration in determining what a reasonable speed was to protect the safety of all concerned. Hunter v. Columbus (Ohio App. 10 Dist., 12-05-2000) 139 Ohio App.3d 962, 746 N.E.2d 246, appeal not allowed 91 Ohio St.3d 1493, 745 N.E.2d 439. Automobiles ⇔ 187(2)

Adequate foundation was laid, in wrongful death action against motorist whose vehicle ran over motorcyclist who was lying in roadway after falling off motorcycle, for results of motorcyclist's blood-alcohol tests, where state trooper testified that coroner drew blood from motorcyclist and gave sample to trooper, that trooper then mailed sample to state laboratory, that he prepared chain-of-evidence document, and that both that document and the results of laboratory analysis were part of his report. Reidling v. Valle (Ohio App. 6 Dist., 02-19-1999) 132 Ohio App.3d 310, 724 N.E.2d 1222, appeal not allowed 86 Ohio St.3d 1420, 711 N.E.2d 1014. Evidence ⇔ 150

Trial court in wrongful death action committed reversible error by excluding testimony of economics expert regarding future lost earnings of 11–year–old child, who was fatally injured when he was struck by automobile; testimony would have been helpful to jury's determination as to what, if anything, child would have contributed to support of his mother. Howard v. Seidler (Ohio App. 7 Dist., 12-04-1996) 116 Ohio App.3d 800, 689 N.E.2d 572, appeal not allowed 78 Ohio St.3d 1494, 678 N.E.2d 1230. Appeal And Error ⇔ 1056.1(3)

There was ample evidence upon which jury could base finding that death of 11–year–old child, who was fatally struck by automobile while child was running on roadway, was caused by actions of teenagers who had threatened child and chased him into roadway, thus breaching their duty to leave child alone. Howard v. Seidler (Ohio App. 7 Dist., 12-04-1996) 116 Ohio App.3d 800, 689 N.E.2d 572, appeal not allowed 78 Ohio St.3d 1494, 678 N.E.2d 1230. Automobiles ⇔ 245(57)

Evidence of loss of support from reasonably expected earning capacity of decedent is admissible in wrongful death action where decedent was a minor at time of death and had never been gainfully employed. Howard v. Seidler (Ohio App. 7 Dist., 12-04-1996) 116 Ohio App.3d 800, 689 N.E.2d 572, appeal not allowed 78 Ohio St.3d 1494, 678 N.E.2d 1230. Death ⇔ 64

Neither failure to secure boat with holes in hull to shore nor failure to warn children of boat's dangerousness was willful or wanton misconduct, precluding liability of property owner for death of nine-year-old child who, while nondiscovered trespasser, drowned after falling out of sinking boat. Garcia v. Puskas Family Flowers, Inc. (Ohio App. 9 Dist., 01-24-1996) 108 Ohio App.3d 683, 671 N.E.2d 607, cause dismissed 75 Ohio St.3d 1472, 663 N.E.2d 1300, appeal not allowed 75 Ohio St.3d 1477, 663 N.E.2d 1304. Negligence ⚖ 1130

Determination of whether violent act of third person while on premises was provoked by owner or operator of premises, as will allow owner or operator to be held liable in wrongful death action, looks to act which is alleged to be provocation and to result it creates, not to purpose or motivation of person who offers alleged provocation; provocation may be intentional or inadvertent, and act or acts which provoke cause may be negligent as well as intentional. Monnin v. Fifth Third Bank of Miami Valley, N.A. (Ohio App. 2 Dist., 03-29-1995) 103 Ohio App.3d 213, 658 N.E.2d 1140, appeal not allowed 73 Ohio St.3d 1428, 652 N.E.2d 801. Death ⚖ 14(1)

In the trial of an action brought by an administrator to recover damages, under sections 6134 and 6135, Rev. St., it is competent for the defendant to introduce as evidence what the deceased said while in his right mind after the injury, tending to show that the injury was caused by his own fault, negligence, or carelessness. Helman v. Pittsburgh, C., C. & St. L. Ry. Co. (Ohio 1898) 58 Ohio St. 400, 40 W.L.B. 51, 50 N.E. 986. Death ⚖ 61; Evidence ⚖ 236(1)

21. Civil rights action

Members of decedent's immediate family may not bring 1983 action to recover for deprivation of parent-child relationship in wrongful death context. Kelly v. Wehrum (S.D.Ohio, 03-10-1997) 956 F.Supp. 1369. Civil Rights ⚖ 1332(1)

22. Covenants not to sue

Document executed by estate administrator and radiologist was a covenant-not-to-sue as opposed to a general release, although there was language stating that there was full and final consideration of all claims, as such finality was between administrator and radiologist, and document expressly stated that payment to administrator was not full and complete compensation, it did not release any action against others but only promised to cease suing radiologist, and it reserved administrator's right to sue other persons or corporations. Leon v. Parma Community Gen. Hosp. (Ohio App. 8 Dist., 10-23-2000) 140 Ohio App.3d 95, 746 N.E.2d 689. Release ⚖ 31; Release ⚖ 37

Estate administrator's covenant not to sue radiologist and radiology group did not operate to preclude the administrator from suing hospital and, in turn, did not preclude hospital's third-party complaint for indemnification against radiologist and radiology group. Leon v. Parma Community Gen. Hosp. (Ohio App. 8 Dist., 10-23-2000) 140 Ohio App.3d 95, 746 N.E.2d 689. Release ⚖ 37

2125.02 Proceedings; damages allowable; limitation of actions; statute of repose for product liability claims; abandonment of deceased child; definitions

(A)(1) Except as provided in this division, a civil action for wrongful death shall be brought in the name of the personal representative of the decedent for the exclusive benefit of the surviving spouse, the children, and the parents of the decedent, all of whom are rebuttably presumed to have suffered damages by reason of the wrongful death, and for the exclusive benefit of the other next of kin of the decedent. A parent who abandoned a minor child who is the decedent shall not receive a benefit in a civil action for wrongful death brought under this division.

(2) The jury, or the court if the civil action for wrongful death is not tried to a jury, may award damages authorized by division (B) of this section, as it determines are proportioned to the injury and loss resulting to the beneficiaries described in division (A)(1) of this section by reason of the wrongful death and may award the reasonable funeral and burial expenses incurred as a result of the wrongful death. In its verdict, the jury or court shall set forth separately the amount, if any, awarded for the reasonable funeral and burial expenses incurred as a result of the wrongful death.

(3)(a) The date of the decedent's death fixes, subject to division (A)(3)(b)(iii) of this section, the status of all beneficiaries of the civil action for wrongful death for purposes of determining the damages suffered by them and the amount of damages to be awarded. A person who is conceived prior to the decedent's death and who is born alive after the decedent's death is a beneficiary of the action.

(b)(i) In determining the amount of damages to be awarded, the jury or court may consider all factors existing at the time of the decedent's death that are relevant to a determination of the damages suffered by reason of the wrongful death.

(ii) Consistent with the Rules of Evidence, a party to a civil action for wrongful death may present evidence of the cost of an annuity in connection with an issue of recoverable future damages. If that evidence is presented, then, in addition to the factors described in division (A)(3)(b)(i) of this section and, if applicable, division (A)(3)(b)(iii) of this section, the jury or court may consider that evidence in determining the future damages suffered by reason of the wrongful death. If that evidence is presented, the present value in dollars of an annuity is its cost.

(iii) Consistent with the Rules of Evidence, a party to a civil action for wrongful death may present evidence that the surviving spouse of the decedent is remarried. If that evidence is presented, then, in addition to the factors described in divisions (A)(3)(b)(i) and (ii) of this section, the jury or court may consider that evidence in determining the damages suffered by the surviving spouse by reason of the wrongful death.

(B) Compensatory damages may be awarded in a civil action for wrongful death and may include damages for the following:

(1) Loss of support from the reasonably expected earning capacity of the decedent;

(2) Loss of services of the decedent;

(3) Loss of the society of the decedent, including loss of companionship, consortium, care, assistance, attention, protection, advice, guidance, counsel, instruction, training, and education, suffered by the surviving spouse, dependent children, parents, or next of kin of the decedent;

(4) Loss of prospective inheritance to the decedent's heirs at law at the time of the decedent's death;

(5) The mental anguish incurred by the surviving spouse, dependent children, parents, or next of kin of the decedent.

(C) A personal representative appointed in this state, with the consent of the court making the appointment and at any time before or after the commencement of a civil action for wrongful death, may settle with the defendant the amount to be paid.

(D) (1) Except as provided in division (D)(2) of this section, a civil action for wrongful death shall be commenced within two years after the decedent's death.

(2)(a) Except as otherwise provided in divisions (D)(2)(b), (c), (d), (e), (f), and (g) of this section or in section 2125.04 of the Revised Code, no cause of action for wrongful death involving a product liability claim shall accrue against the manufacturer or supplier of a product later than ten years from the date that the product was delivered to its first purchaser or first lessee who was not engaged in a business in which the product was used as a component in the production, construction, creation, assembly, or rebuilding of another product.

(b) Division (D)(2)(a) of this section does not apply if the manufacturer or supplier of a product engaged in fraud in regard to information about the product and the fraud contributed to the harm that is alleged in a product liability claim involving that product.

(c) Division (D)(2)(a) of this section does not bar a civil action for wrongful death involving a product liability claim against a manufacturer or supplier of a product who made an express, written warranty as to the safety of the product that was for a period longer than ten years and that, at the time of the decedent's death, has not expired in accordance with the terms of that warranty.

(d) If the decedent's death occurs during the ten-year period described in division (D)(2)(a) of this section but less than two years prior to the expiration of that period, a civil action for wrongful death involving a product liability claim may be commenced within two years after the decedent's death.

(e) If the decedent's death occurs during the ten-year period described in division (D)(2)(a) of this section and the claimant cannot commence an action during that period due to a disability described in section 2305.16 of the Revised Code, a civil action for wrongful death involving a product liability claim may be commenced within two years after the disability is removed.

(f)(i) Division (D)(2)(a) of this section does not bar a civil action for wrongful death based on a product liability claim against a manufacturer or supplier of a product if the product involved is a substance or device described in division (B)(1), (2), (3), or (4) of section 2305.10 of the Revised Code and the decedent's death resulted from exposure to the product during the ten-year period described in division (D)(2)(a) of this section.

(ii) If division (D)(2)(f)(i) of this section applies regarding a civil action for wrongful death, the cause of action that is the basis of the action accrues upon the date on which the claimant is informed by competent medical authority that the decedent's death was related to the exposure to the product or upon the date on which by the exercise of reasonable diligence the claimant should have known that the decedent's death was related to the exposure to the product, whichever date occurs first. A civil action for wrongful death based on a cause of action described in division (D)(2)(f)(i) of this section shall be commenced within two years after the cause of action accrues and shall not be commenced more than two years after the cause of action accrues.

(g) Division (D)(2)(a) of this section does not bar a civil action for wrongful death based on a product liability claim against a manufacturer or supplier of a product if the product involved is a substance or device described in division (B)(5) of section 2315.10 of the Revised Code. If division (D)(2)(g) of this section applies regarding a civil action for wrongful death, the cause of action that is the basis of the action accrues upon the date on which the claimant is informed by competent medical authority that the decedent's death was related to the exposure to the product or upon the date on which by the exercise of reasonable diligence the claimant should have known that the decedent's death was related to the exposure to the product, whichever date occurs first. A civil action for wrongful death based on a cause of action described in division (D)(2)(g) of this section shall be commenced within two years after the cause of action accrues and shall not be commenced more than two years after the cause of action accrues.

(E)(1) If the personal representative of a deceased minor has actual knowledge or reasonable cause to believe that the minor was abandoned by a parent seeking to benefit from a civil action for wrongful death or if any person listed in division (A)(1) of this section who is permitted to benefit from a civil action for wrongful death commenced in relation to a deceased minor has actual knowledge or reasonable cause to believe that the minor was abandoned by a parent seeking to benefit from the action, the personal representative or the person may file a motion in the court in which the action is commenced requesting the court to issue an order finding that the parent abandoned the minor and is not entitled to recover damages in the action based on the death of the minor.

(2) The movant who files a motion described in division (E)(1) of this section shall name the parent who abandoned the deceased minor and, whether or not that parent is a resident of this state, the parent shall be served with a summons and a copy of the motion in accordance with the Rules of Civil Procedure.

Upon the filing of the motion, the court shall conduct a hearing. In the hearing on the motion, the movant has the burden of proving, by a preponderance of the evidence, that the parent abandoned the minor. If, at the hearing, the court finds that the movant has sustained that burden of proof, the court shall issue an order that includes its findings that the parent abandoned the minor and that, because of the prohibition set forth in division (A)(1) of this section, the parent is not entitled to recover damages in the action based on the death of the minor.

(3) A motion requesting a court to issue an order finding that a specified parent abandoned a minor child and is not entitled to recover damages in a civil action for wrongful death based on the death of the minor may be filed at any time during the pendency of the action.

(F) This section does not create a new cause of action or substantive legal right against any person involving a product liability claim.

(G) As used in this section:

(1) "Annuity" means an annuity that would be purchased from either of the following types of insurance companies:

(a) An insurance company that the A. M. Best Company, in its most recently published rating guide of life insurance companies, has rated A or better and has rated XII or higher as to financial size or strength;

(b)(i) An insurance company that the superintendent of insurance, under rules adopted pursuant to Chapter 119. of the Revised Code for purposes of implementing this division, determines is licensed to do business in this state and, considering the factors described in division (G)(1)(b)(ii) of this section, is a stable insurance company that issues annuities that are safe and desirable.

(ii) In making determinations as described in division (G)(1)(b)(i) of this section, the superintendent shall be guided by the principle that the jury or court in a civil action for wrongful death should be presented only with evidence as to the cost of annuities that are safe and desirable for the beneficiaries of the action who are awarded compensatory damages under this section. In making the determinations, the superintendent shall consider the financial condition, general standing, operating results, profitability, leverage, liquidity, amount and soundness of reinsurance, adequacy of reserves, and the management of a particular insurance company involved and also may consider ratings, grades, and classifications of any nationally recognized rating services of insurance companies and any other factors relevant to the making of the determinations.

(2) "Future damages" means damages that result from the wrongful death and that will accrue after the verdict or determination of liability by the jury or court is rendered in the civil action for wrongful death.

(3) "Abandoned" means that a parent of a minor failed without justifiable cause to communicate with the minor, care for the minor, and provide for the maintenance or support of the minor as required by law or judicial decree for a period of at least one year immediately prior to the date of the death of the minor.

(4) "Minor" means a person who is less than eighteen years of age.

(5) "Harm" means death.

(6) "Manufacturer," "product," " product liability claim," and "supplier" have the same meanings as in section 2307.71 of the Revised Code.

(H) Divisions (D), (G)(5), and (G)(6) of this section shall be considered to be purely remedial in operation and shall be applied in a remedial manner in any civil action commenced on or after the effective date of this amendment, in which those divisions are relevant, regardless of when the cause of action accrued and notwithstanding any other section of the Revised

Code or prior rule of law of this state, but shall not be construed to apply to any civil action pending prior to the effective date of this amendment.

(2004 S 80, eff. 4–7–05; 2001 S 108, § 2.01, eff. 7–6–01; 2001 S 108, § 2.02, eff. 7–6–01; 1996 H 350, eff. 1–27–97 [1]; 1992 H 166, eff. 8–3–92; 1987 H 1; 1981 H 332; 1969 S 104; 125 v 903; 1953 H 1; GC 10509–167)

[1] See Notes of Decisions, *State ex rel. Ohio Academy of Trial Lawyers v. Sheward* (Ohio 1999), 86 Ohio St.3d 451, 715 N.E.2d 1062.

Uncodified Law

2004 S 80, § 3, eff. 4–7–05, reads, in part:

(C) In enacting division (D)(2) of section 2125.02 and division (C) of section 2305.10 of the Revised Code in this act, it is the intent of the General Assembly to do all of the following:

(1) To declare that the ten-year statute of repose prescribed by division (D)(2) of section 2125.02 and division (C) of section 2305.10 of the Revised Code, as enacted by this act, are specific provisions intended to promote a greater interest than the interest underlying the general four-year statute of limitations prescribed by section 2305.09 of the Revised Code, the general two-year statutes of limitations prescribed by sections 2125.02 and 2305.10 of the Revised Code, and other general statutes of limitations prescribed by the Revised Code;

(2) To declare that, subject to the two-year exceptions prescribed in division (D)(2)(d) of section 2125.02 and in division (C)(4) of section 2305.10 of the Revised Code, the ten-year statutes of repose shall serve as a limitation upon the commencement of a civil action in accordance with an otherwise applicable statute of limitations prescribed by the Revised Code;

(3) To recognize that subsequent to the delivery of a product, the manufacturer or supplier lacks control over the product, over the uses made of the product, and over the conditions under which the product is used;

(4) To recognize that under the circumstances described in division (C)(3) of this section, it is more appropriate for the party or parties who have had control over the product during the intervening time period to be responsible for any harm caused by the product;

(5) To recognize that, more than ten years after a product has been delivered, it is very difficult for a manufacturer or supplier to locate reliable evidence and witnesses regarding the design, production, or marketing of the product, thus severely disadvantaging manufacturers or suppliers in their efforts to defend actions based on a product liability claim;

(6) To recognize the inappropriateness of applying current legal and technological standards to products manufactured many years prior to the commencement of an action based on a product liability claim;

(7) To recognize that a statute of repose for product liability claims would enhance the competitiveness of Ohio manufacturers by reducing their exposure to disruptive and protracted liability with respect to products long out of their control, by increasing finality in commercial transactions, and by allowing manufacturers to conduct their affairs with increased certainty;

(8) To declare that division (D)(2) of section 2125.02 and division (C) of section 2305.10 of the Revised Code, as enacted by this act, strike a rational balance between the rights of prospective claimants and the rights of product manufacturers and suppliers and to declare that the ten-year statutes of repose prescribed in those sections are rational periods of repose intended to preclude the problems of stale litigation but not to affect civil actions against those in actual control and possession of a product at the time that the product causes an injury to real or personal property, bodily injury, or wrongful death;

2001 S 108, § 1 and 3: See Uncodified Law under 2125.01.

1992 H 166, § 3, eff. 8–3–92, reads, in part: The amendments to sections 2125.02 and 2125.03 of the Revised Code, as amended by this act, shall apply to all parents of minors who die on or after the effective date of this act, whether or not the abandonment, as described in section 2125.02 of the Revised Code, as amended by this act, commenced prior to, on, or after the effective date of this act.

1987 H 1, § 3, eff. 1–5–88, provides, in part, that the amendments to 2125.02 made in 1987 H 1, § 1, "shall apply only to tort or other civil actions that are commenced on and after the effective date of this act and that are based upon claims for relief that arise on or after that date, and only to tortious conduct that occurs on or after that date."

Historical and Statutory Notes

Ed. Note: The amendment of this section by 1996 H 350, eff. 1–27–97, was repealed by 2001 S 108, § 2.02, eff. 7–6–01. See *Baldwin's Ohio Legislative Service Annotated*, 1996, page 10/L–3380, and 2001, page 6/L–1441, or the OH–LEGIS or OH–LEGIS–OLD database on Westlaw, for original versions of these Acts.

Pre–1953 H 1 Amendments: 114 v 438

Amendment Note: 2004 S 80 rewrote this section, which prior thereto read:

"(A)(1) Except as provided in this division, an action for wrongful death shall be brought in the name of the personal representative of the decedent for the exclusive benefit of the surviving spouse, the children, and the parents of the decedent, all of whom are rebuttably presumed to have suffered damages by reason of the wrongful death, and for the exclusive benefit of the other next of kin of the decedent. A parent who abandoned a minor child who is the decedent shall not receive any benefit in a wrongful death action brought under this division.

"(2) The jury, or the court if the action is not tried to a jury, may award damages authorized by division (B) of this section, as it determines are proportioned to the injury and loss resulting to the beneficiaries described in division (A)(1) of this section by reason of the wrongful death and may award the reasonable funeral and burial expenses incurred as a result of the wrongful death. In its verdict, the jury or court shall set forth separately the amount, if any, awarded for the reasonable funeral and burial expenses incurred as a result of the wrongful death.

"(3)(a) The date of the decedent's death fixes, subject to division (A)(3)(b)(iii) of this section, the status of all beneficiaries of the action for purposes of determining the damages suffered by them and the amount of damages to be awarded. A person who is conceived prior to the decedent's death and who is born alive after the decedent's death is a beneficiary of the action.

"(b)(i) In determining the amount of damages to be awarded, the jury or court may consider all factors existing at the time of the decedent's death that are relevant to a determination of the damages suffered by reason of the wrongful death.

"(ii) Consistent with the Rules of Evidence, any party to an action for wrongful death may present evidence of the cost of an annuity in connection with any issue of recoverable future damages. If such evidence is presented, then, in addition to the factors described in division (A)(3)(b)(i) of this section and, if applicable, division (A)(3)(b)(iii) of this section, the jury or court may consider that evidence in determining the future damages suffered by reason of the wrongful death. If such evidence is presented, the present value in dollars of any annuity is its cost.

"(iii) Consistent with the Rules of Evidence, any party to an action for wrongful death may present evidence that the surviving spouse of the decedent is remarried. If such evidence is presented, then, in addition to the factors described in divisions (A)(3)(b)(i) and (ii) of this section, the jury or court may consider that evidence in determining the damages suffered by the surviving spouse by reason of the wrongful death.

"(B) Compensatory damages may be awarded in an action for wrongful death and may include damages for the following:

"(1) Loss of support from the reasonably expected earning capacity of the decedent;

"(2) Loss of services of the decedent;

"(3) Loss of the society of the decedent, including loss of companionship, consortium, care, assistance, attention, protection, advice, guidance, counsel, instruction, training, and education, suffered by the surviving spouse, minor children, parents, or next of kin ;

"(4) Loss of prospective inheritance to the decedent's heirs at law at the time of the decedent's death;

"(5) The mental anguish incurred by the surviving spouse, minor children, parents, or next of kin.

"(C) A personal representative appointed in this state, with the consent of the court making the appointment and at any time before or after the commencement of an action for wrongful death, may settle with the defendant the amount to be paid.

"(D) An action for wrongful death shall be commenced within two years after the decedent's death.

"(E)(1) If the personal representative of a deceased minor has actual knowledge or reasonable cause to believe that the minor was abandoned by a parent seeking to benefit from the wrongful death action or if any person listed in division (A)(1) of this section who is permitted to benefit in a wrongful death action filed in relation to a deceased minor has actual knowledge or reasonable cause to believe that the minor was abandoned by a parent seeking to benefit from the wrongful death action, the personal representative or the person may file a motion in the court in which the wrongful death action is filed requesting the court to issue an order finding that the parent abandoned the child and is not entitled to recover damages in the wrongful death action based on the death of the deceased minor child.

"(2) The movant who files a motion described in division (E)(1) of this section shall name the parent who abandoned the child and, whether or not that parent is a resident of this state, the parent shall be served with a summons and a copy of the motion in accordance with the Rules of Civil Procedure. Upon the filing of the motion, the court shall conduct a hearing. In the hearing on the motion, the movant has the burden of proving, by a preponderance of the evidence, that the parent abandoned the deceased minor child. If, at the hearing, the court finds that the movant has sustained that burden of proof, the court shall issue an order that includes its finding that the parent abandoned the deceased minor child and, because of the prohibition set forth in division (A) of this section, the parent is not entitled to recover damages in the wrongful death action based on the death of the deceased minor child.

"(3) A motion requesting a court to issue an order finding that the specified parent abandoned the child and is not entitled to recover damages in the wrongful death action based on the death of the deceased minor child may be filed at any time during the pendency of the wrongful death action.

"As used in this section:

"(1) 'Annuity' means an annuity that would be purchased from either of the following types of insurance companies:

"(a) An insurance company that the A. M. Best Company, in its most recently published rating guide of life insurance companies, has rated A or better and has rated XII or higher as to financial size or strength;

"(b)(i) An insurance company that the superintendent of insurance, under rules adopted pursuant to Chapter 119. of the Revised Code for purposes of implementing this division, determines is licensed to do business in this state and, considering the factors described in division (F)(1)(b)(ii) of this section, is a stable insurance company that issues annuities that are safe and desirable.

"(ii) In making determinations as described in division (F)(1)(b)(i) of this section, the superintendent shall be guided by the principle that the jury or court in an action for wrongful death should be presented only with evidence as to the cost of annuities that are safe and desirable for the beneficiaries of such an action who are awarded compensatory damages under this section. In making such determinations, the superintendent shall consider the financial condition, general standing, operating results, profitability, leverage, liquidity, amount and soundness of reinsurance, adequacy of reserves, and the management of any insurance company in question and also may consider ratings, grades, and classifications of any nationally recognized rating services of insurance companies and any other factors relevant to the making of such determinations.

"(2) 'Future damages' means damages that result from the wrongful death and that will accrue after the verdict or determination of liability by the jury or court is rendered in the action for wrongful death.

"(3) 'Abandoned' means that a parent of a minor failed without justifiable cause to communicate with the minor, care for the minor, and provide for the maintenance or support of the minor as required by law or judicial decree for a period of at least one year immediately prior to the date of the death of the minor.

"(4) 'Minor' means a person who is less than eighteen years of age."

Amendment Note: 1996 H 350 rewrote this section, which prior thereto read:

"(A)(1) Except as provided in this division, an action for wrongful death shall be brought in the name of the personal representative of the decedent for the exclusive benefit of the surviving spouse, the children, and the parents of the decedent, all of whom are rebuttably presumed to have suffered damages by reason of the wrongful death, and for the exclusive benefit of the other next of kin of the decedent. A parent who abandoned a minor child who is the decedent shall not receive any benefit in a wrongful death action brought under this division.

"(2) The jury, or the court if the action is not tried to a jury, may award damages authorized by division (B) of this section, as it determines are proportioned to the injury and loss resulting to the beneficiaries described in division (A)(1) of this section by reason of the wrongful death and may award the reasonable funeral and burial expenses incurred as a result of the wrongful death. In its verdict, the jury or court shall set forth separately the amount, if any, awarded for the reasonable funeral and burial expenses incurred as a result of the wrongful death.

"(3)(a) The date of the decedent's death fixes, subject to division (A)(3)(b)(iii) of this section, the status of all beneficiaries of the action for purposes of determining the damages suffered by them and the amount of damages to be awarded. A person who is conceived prior to the decedent's death and who is born alive after his death is a beneficiary of the action.

"(b)(i) In determining the amount of damages to be awarded, the jury or court may consider all factors existing at the time of the decedent's death that are relevant to a determination of the damages suffered by reason of the wrongful death.

"(ii) Consistent with the Rules of Evidence, any party to an action for wrongful death may present evidence of the cost of an annuity in connection with any issue of recoverable future damages. If such evidence is presented, then, in addition to the factors described in division (A)(3)(b)(i) of this section and, if applicable, division (A)(3)(b)(iii) of this section, the jury or court may consider that evidence in determining the future damages suffered by reason of the wrongful death. If such evidence is presented, the present value in dollars of any annuity is its cost.

"(iii) Consistent with the Rules of Evidence, any party to an action for wrongful death may present evidence that the surviving spouse of the decedent is remarried. If such evidence is presented, then, in addition to the factors described in divisions (A)(3)(b)(i) and (ii) of this section, the jury or court may consider that evidence in determining the damages suffered by the surviving spouse by reason of the wrongful death.

"(B) Compensatory damages may be awarded in an action for wrongful death and may include damages for the following:

"(1) Loss of support from the reasonably expected earning capacity of the decedent;

"(2) Loss of services of the decedent;

"(3) Loss of the society of the decedent, including loss of companionship, consortium, care, assistance, attention, protection, advice, guidance, counsel, instruction, training, and education, suffered by the surviving spouse, minor children, parents, or next of kin;

"(4) Loss of prospective inheritance to the decedent's heirs at law at the time of his death;

"(5) The mental anguish incurred by the surviving spouse, minor children, parents, or next of kin.

"(C) A personal representative appointed in this state, with the consent of the court making the appointment and at any time before or after the commencement of an action for wrongful death, may settle with the defendant the amount to be paid.

"(D) An action for wrongful death shall be commenced within two years after the decedent's death.

"(E)(1) If the personal representative of a deceased minor has actual knowledge or reasonable cause to believe that the minor was abandoned by a parent seeking to benefit from the wrongful death action or if any person listed in division (A)(1) of this section who is permitted to benefit in a wrongful death action filed in relation to a deceased minor has actual knowledge or reasonable cause to believe that the minor was abandoned by a parent seeking to benefit from the wrongful death action, the personal representative or the person may file a motion in the court in which the wrongful death action is filed requesting the court to issue an order finding that the parent abandoned the child and is not entitled to recover damages in the wrongful death action based on the death of the deceased minor child.

"(2) The movant who files a motion described in division (E)(1) of this section shall name the parent who abandoned the child and, whether or not that parent is a resident of this state, the parent shall be served with a summons and a copy of the motion in accordance with the Rules of Civil Procedure. Upon the filing of the motion, the court shall conduct a hearing. In the hearing on the motion, the movant has the burden of proving, by a preponderance of the evidence, that the parent abandoned the deceased minor child. If, at the hearing, the court finds that the movant has sustained that burden of proof, the court shall issue an order that includes its finding that the parent abandoned the deceased minor child and, because of the prohibition set forth in division (A) of this section, the parent is not entitled to recover damages in the wrongful death action based on the death of the deceased minor child.

"(3) A motion requesting a court to issue an order finding that the specified parent abandoned the child and is not entitled to recover damages in the wrongful death action based on the death of the deceased minor child may be filed at any time during the pendency of the wrongful death action.

"(F) As used in this section:

"(1) "Annuity" means an annuity that would be purchased from either of the following types of insurance companies:

"(a) An insurance company that the A. M. Best Company, in its most recently published rating guide of life insurance companies, has rated A or better and has rated XII or higher as to financial size or strength;

"(b)(i) An insurance company that the superintendent of insurance, under rules adopted pursuant to Chapter 119. of the Revised Code for purposes of implementing this division, determines is licensed to do business in this state and, considering the factors described in division (F)(1)(b)(ii) of this section, is a stable insurance company that issues annuities that are safe and desirable.

"(ii) In making determinations as described in division (F)(1)(b)(i) of this section, the superintendent shall be guided by the principle that the jury or court in an action for wrongful death should be presented only with evidence as to the cost of annuities that are safe and desirable for the beneficiaries of such an action who are awarded compensatory damages under this section. In making such determinations, the superintendent shall consider the financial condition, general standing, operating results, profitability, leverage, liquidity, amount and soundness of reinsurance, adequacy of reserves, and the management of any insurance company in question and also may consider ratings, grades, and classifications of any nationally recognized rating services of insurance companies and any other factors relevant to the making of such determinations.

"(2) "Future damages" means damages that result from the wrongful death and that will accrue after the verdict or determination of liability by the jury or court is rendered in the action for wrongful death.

"(3) "Abandoned" means that a parent of a minor failed without justifiable cause to communicate with the minor, care for him, and provide for his maintenance or support as required by law or judicial decree for a period of at least one year immediately prior to the date of the death of the minor.

"(4) "Minor" means a person who is less than eighteen years of age."

Cross References

Cost of annuity, evidence, 2317.62
Dalkon shield intrauterine device claims, limitation of actions, 2305.101
Final order, 2505.02
Limitation of action for damages based on defective and unsafe condition of improvement to real property, 2305.131
Presentation and allowance of creditor's claims, 2117.06
Suits in which party adverse to personal representative cannot testify, exceptions, 2317.03

Library References

Death ⇌31, 37 to 39, 78 to 89.
Westlaw Topic No. 117.
C.J.S. Death §§ 34, 46 to 47, 49 to 58, 98 to 104, 107 to 112, 171 to 172, 180 to 187, 189 to 205.

Research References

ALR Library

84 ALR 5th 687, Who, Other Than Parent, May Recover for Loss of Consortium on Death of Minor Child.
42 ALR 5th 465, Wrongful Death Damages for Loss of Expectancy of Inheritance from Decedent.
43 ALR 5th 87, Medical Malpractice in Connection With Diagnosis, Care, or Treatment of Diabetes.
33 ALR 5th 303, Intoxication of Automobile Driver as Basis for Awarding Punitive Damages.

Encyclopedias

11 Am. Jur. Trials 1, Representation of Survivors in Death Actions.
12 Am. Jur. Trials 317, Wrongful Death Actions.
32 Am. Jur. Trials 375, Pharmacist Liability.
OH Jur. 3d Damages § 41, Impairment of Earning Capacity, Generally.
OH Jur. 3d Death § 35, Ohio Wrongful Death Statute.
OH Jur. 3d Death § 36, Ohio Wrongful Death Statute—Constitutionality.
OH Jur. 3d Death § 66, Children.
OH Jur. 3d Death § 68, Parents; Adoptive Parents.
OH Jur. 3d Death § 69, Parents; Adoptive Parents—Effect of Abandonment of Child.
OH Jur. 3d Death § 70, Other Next of Kin.
OH Jur. 3d Death § 78, Beneficiaries.
OH Jur. 3d Death § 81, Settlement or Release; by Personal Representative.
OH Jur. 3d Death § 84, Punitive Damages.
OH Jur. 3d Death § 87, Mental Anguish.
OH Jur. 3d Death § 88, Loss of Financial Support and Inheritance.
OH Jur. 3d Death § 89, Loss of Service and Society of the Decedent.
OH Jur. 3d Death § 90, Funeral and Burial Expenses.
OH Jur. 3d Death § 92, Remarriage of Surviving Spouse.
OH Jur. 3d Death § 95, Financial Status and Prospects.
OH Jur. 3d Death § 117, Limitation of Actions; Statute of Repose.
OH Jur. 3d Death § 119, Capacity in Which Representative Sues.
OH Jur. 3d Death § 141, Presumption of Damages.
OH Jur. 3d Death § 151, Evidence Regarding Party Plaintiff and Beneficiaries.
OH Jur. 3d Death § 154, Standard of Proof; Capacity to Sue.
OH Jur. 3d Death § 164, Damages as Question for Jury.
OH Jur. 3d Death § 166, Damages as Question for Jury—Limitation on Jury's Authority.
OH Jur. 3d Death § 172, Verdict.
OH Jur. 3d Death § 183, Generally; Proper Party Plaintiff.
OH Jur. 3d Decedents' Estates § 86, Illegitimate Blood Relationship.
OH Jur. 3d Decedents' Estates § 87, Illegitimate Blood Relationship—Ohio Parentage Act.
OH Jur. 3d Decedents' Estates § 1316, Proceeds from Action for Wrongful Death.
OH Jur. 3d Decedents' Estates § 1445, Relation of Statutes to Other Limitation Statutes.
OH Jur. 3d Decedents' Estates § 1791, Action on Claim Neither Allowed Nor Rejected.
OH Jur. 3d Limitations & Laches § 4, Special Statutes, Generally—Limitation on Wrongful Death Action.
OH Jur. 3d Limitations & Laches § 27, Action for Wrongful Death.
OH Jur. 3d Limitations & Laches § 53, Wrongful Death Actions.
OH Jur. 3d Limitations & Laches § 97, Infancy.
OH Jur. 3d Limitations & Laches § 128, Special Statutory Actions—Action for Wrongful Death.
OH Jur. 3d Malpractice § 21, Liability to Third Persons.
OH Jur. 3d Parties § 15, Exceptions to Real-Party-In-Interest Requirement—Persons Authorized by Statute to Bring Actions.
OH Jur. 3d Products Liability § 58, Limitations.

Forms

Ohio Jurisprudence Pleading and Practice Forms § 22:2, Real Parties in Interest Enumerated in Civil Rule 17(a).
Ohio Jurisprudence Pleading and Practice Forms § 22:4, Those Not Real Parties in Interest.
Ohio Jurisprudence Pleading and Practice Forms § 12:11, Checklist—Statutes of Limitations.
Ohio Jurisprudence Pleading and Practice Forms § 123:2, Nature of Action.
Ohio Jurisprudence Pleading and Practice Forms § 123:4, Defenses.
Ohio Jurisprudence Pleading and Practice Forms § 123:5, Recoverable Damages.
Ohio Jurisprudence Pleading and Practice Forms § 123:7, Distribution Among Beneficiaries.
Ohio Jurisprudence Pleading and Practice Forms § 114:20, Rollover—Sport Utility Vehicle.
Ohio Jurisprudence Pleading and Practice Forms § 120:13, Wrongful Death—Medical Malpractice.
Ohio Jurisprudence Pleading and Practice Forms § 123:12, Negligent Medical Care—Cancer.
Ohio Jurisprudence Pleading and Practice Forms § 123:13, Nuisance in Maintenance and Elimination of Crosswalk.
Ohio Jurisprudence Pleading and Practice Forms § 123:20, for Order of Abandonment.
Ohio Jurisprudence Pleading and Practice Forms § 123:23, to Support Motion for Abandonment.

Treatises and Practice Aids

Baldwin's Ohio Handbook Series—Trial Handbook § 34:53, Wrongful Death Actions.
Klein, Darling, & Terez, Baldwin's Ohio Practice Civil Practice § 6:5, Time--Computation--Last Day Included Unless it is a Saturday, Sunday, or Legal Holiday.

Klein, Darling, & Terez, Baldwin's Ohio Practice Civil Practice § 6:8, Time--Computation--Relation of Civ. R. 6(A) and RC 1.14.

Klein, Darling, & Terez, Baldwin's Ohio Practice Civil Practice § 17:5, Real Party in Interest by Statute.

Klein, Darling, & Terez, Baldwin's Ohio Practice Civil Practice § 3:14, Commencement--Secondary Consequences Which May Accompany Failure of Commencement Under Civ. R. 3(A)--Failure to Satisfy a Statute of Limitations.

Klein, Darling, & Terez, Baldwin's Ohio Practice Civil Practice § 3:78, Review of Venue Determinations--Appeal.

Carlin, Baldwin's Ohio Practice, Merrick-Rippner Probate Law § 3:5, Jurisdiction of Probate Court—Subject Matter—Specific Areas—Fiduciaries.

Carlin, Baldwin's Ohio Practice, Merrick-Rippner Probate Law § 5:8, Evidentiary Matters—Privileged Communications—Protected Relationships—Physician or Dentist and Patient—Waiver of the Privilege.

Carlin, Baldwin's Ohio Practice, Merrick-Rippner Probate Law § 8:2, Appeal—Final Appealable Orders.

Carlin, Baldwin's Ohio Practice, Merrick-Rippner Probate Law § 12:1, Wrongful Death—Scope of RC Ch. 2125.

Carlin, Baldwin's Ohio Practice, Merrick-Rippner Probate Law § 12:2, Wrongful Death—Who May Bring Action.

Carlin, Baldwin's Ohio Practice, Merrick-Rippner Probate Law § 12:3, Wrongful Death—Jurisdiction of Probate Court.

Carlin, Baldwin's Ohio Practice, Merrick-Rippner Probate Law § 12:4, Wrongful Death—Trial.

Carlin, Baldwin's Ohio Practice, Merrick-Rippner Probate Law § 12:6, Wrongful Death—Burial Expenses Part of Award.

Carlin, Baldwin's Ohio Practice, Merrick-Rippner Probate Law § 12:7, Wrongful Death—Status of Beneficiaries Fixed at Death of Decedent.

Carlin, Baldwin's Ohio Practice, Merrick-Rippner Probate Law § 12:8, Wrongful Death—Afterborn Beneficiary; Next of Kin.

Carlin, Baldwin's Ohio Practice, Merrick-Rippner Probate Law § 53:7, Fiduciary's Attorney—Responsibilities.

Carlin, Baldwin's Ohio Practice, Merrick-Rippner Probate Law § 75:4, Distribution—Voluntary—Liability—Executor or Administrator.

Carlin, Baldwin's Ohio Practice, Merrick-Rippner Probate Law § 84:1, Creditor's Claims—Introduction.

Carlin, Baldwin's Ohio Practice, Merrick-Rippner Probate Law § 84:3, Creditor's Claims—Form of Claim.

Carlin, Baldwin's Ohio Practice, Merrick-Rippner Probate Law § 85:2, Acceleration of Claims—Effect on Other Statutes of Limitations.

Carlin, Baldwin's Ohio Practice, Merrick-Rippner Probate Law § 12:11, Wrongful Death—Damages—Compensatory.

Carlin, Baldwin's Ohio Practice, Merrick-Rippner Probate Law § 12:12, Wrongful Death—Damages—Apportionment.

Carlin, Baldwin's Ohio Practice, Merrick-Rippner Probate Law § 12:13, Wrongful Death—Damages—Stacking of Uninsured/Underinsured Motorist Coverage.

Carlin, Baldwin's Ohio Practice, Merrick-Rippner Probate Law § 12:14, Wrongful Death—Statute of Limitations—Savings Statute.

Carlin, Baldwin's Ohio Practice, Merrick-Rippner Probate Law § 12:16, Wrongful Death—Interspousal and Parental Immunities Not Applicable.

Carlin, Baldwin's Ohio Practice, Merrick-Rippner Probate Law § 12:19, Wrongful Death—Denial of Damages to Parent Who Abandoned Child—in General.

Carlin, Baldwin's Ohio Practice, Merrick-Rippner Probate Law § 12:20, Wrongful Death—Denial of Damages to Parent Who Abandoned Child—Motion to Deny Damages.

Carlin, Baldwin's Ohio Practice, Merrick-Rippner Probate Law § 12:21, Wrongful Death—Denial of Damages to Parent Who Abandoned Child—Hearing; Burden of Proof; Order; Effect.

Carlin, Baldwin's Ohio Practice, Merrick-Rippner Probate Law § 12:22, Wrongful Death—Release by Decedent.

Carlin, Baldwin's Ohio Practice, Merrick-Rippner Probate Law § 12:24, Entry Approving Settlement or Distributing Wrongful Death Proceeds—Form.

Carlin, Baldwin's Ohio Practice, Merrick-Rippner Probate Law § 12:25, Report of Distribution of Wrongful Death Proceeds—Form.

Carlin, Baldwin's Ohio Practice, Merrick-Rippner Probate Law § 15:20, Descent and Distribution—Children or Lineal Descendants—in General.

Carlin, Baldwin's Ohio Practice, Merrick-Rippner Probate Law § 30:56, Malpractice Liability of Drafting Attorney; Professional Disciplinary Action.

Carlin, Baldwin's Ohio Practice, Merrick-Rippner Probate Law § 64:15, Powers and Duties of Guardian—Special Matters Relating to Minor Wards—Settlement of Claims for Injury.

Carlin, Baldwin's Ohio Practice, Merrick-Rippner Probate Law § 84:10, Creditor's Claims—Claims Requiring Presentation—Examples from Case Law—Personal Injury Actions.

Carlin, Baldwin's Ohio Practice, Merrick-Rippner Probate Law § 84:24, Creditor's Claims—Claims Not Requiring Presentation—Contingent Claims—Definition.

Carlin, Baldwin's Ohio Practice, Merrick-Rippner Probate Law § 84:25, Creditor's Claims—Claims Not Requiring Presentation—Contingent Claims—Mandatory Presentation.

Carlin, Baldwin's Ohio Practice, Merrick-Rippner Probate Law § 84:29, Creditor's Claims—Statute of Limitations.

Carlin, Baldwin's Ohio Practice, Merrick-Rippner Probate Law § 84:30, Creditor's Claims—Acceleration of Bar Against Claims Against Estate.

Carlin, Baldwin's Ohio Practice, Merrick-Rippner Probate Law § 84:38, Creditor's Claims—Effect on Other Statutes of Limitations.

Carlin, Baldwin's Ohio Practice, Merrick-Rippner Probate Law § 12:22.50, Wrongful Death—Post-Judgment Review; Appeal.

Carlin, Baldwin's Ohio Practice, Merrick-Rippner Probate Law App B SPF 14.0, Application to Approve Settlement and Distribution of Wrongful Death and Survival Claims—Form.

Ohio Personal Injury Practice § 4:7, Wrongful Death and Survival Claims—Wrongful Death—Who Takes Under the Wrongful Death Statute.

Ohio Personal Injury Practice § 4:8, Wrongful Death and Survival Claims—Wrongful Death—Damages Available Under the Wrongful Death Statute.

Ohio Personal Injury Practice § 4:9, Wrongful Death and Survival Claims—Wrongful Death—Statute of Limitations.

Ohio Personal Injury Practice § 1:43, Sample Diary Card Form.

Ohio Personal Injury Practice § 11:3, Preparing for Summation—Considerations—Order of Argument.

Ohio Personal Injury Practice § 3:10, Parties Plaintiff—Wrongful Death Complaint.

Ohio Personal Injury Practice § 3:13, Pleading Damages—Wrongful Death Damages.

Ohio Personal Injury Practice § 4:10, Wrongful Death and Survival Claims—Wrongful Death—Wrongful Death and Medical Malpractice.

Ohio Personal Injury Practice § 6:23, Motions for Summary Judgment Filed by Defendants in Medical Malpractice Actions—Summary Judgment Alleging Failure to Comply With Statute of Limitations in Medical Malpractice.

Ohio Personal Injury Practice App. C, Appendix C. Ohio Academy of Trial Lawyers v. Sheward.

Ohio Personal Injury Practice § 11:15, Preparing for Summation—Organizing the Summation—Wrongful Death Damages.

Ohio Personal Injury Practice § 15:47, Damages May be Paid Through Structured Settlements.

Law Review and Journal Commentaries

Application Of The Discovery Rule To The Ohio Wrongful Death Statute, Note. 3 J L & Health 237 (1988–89).

Cincinnati Insurance Company v. Phillips: The Ohio Supreme Court Attempts To Reconcile Limitation Of Liability Language With Ohio's Wrongful Death Statute, Comment. 20 Cap U L Rev 781 (Summer 1991).

Comparison of the "Old" and "New" Wrongful Death Statutes, Evelyn J. Stratton. 39 Columbus B Briefs 7 (April 15, 1983).

Damages in Wrongful Death Actions, Stanley B. Kent. 17 Clev–Marshall L Rev 233 (May 1968).

Damages Recoverable in Survivorship Actions as Compared to Wrongful Death Actions, William K. McCarter and Sean A. McCarter. 21 Lake Legal Views 10 (April 1998).

Expanding Loss of Consortium Claims, Stanley B. Kent. 65 Clev B J 3 (January 1994).

H.B. 350—Dramatic Changes. 44 Tol B Ass'n News 11 (December 1996).

Hedonic damages in wrongful death and survival actions: Impact of Alzheimer's disease. 2 Elder L J 249 (1994).

How to Prove Reduction to Present Worth, Russell E. Leasure. 21 Ohio St L J 204 (Spring 1960).

Issues Complicating Rights of Spouses, Parents, and Children to Sue for Wrongful Death, Comment. 19 Akron L Rev 419 (Winter 1986).

Loss of Consortium: Should Marriage Be Retained as a Prerequisite?, Comment. 52 U Cin L Rev 842 (1983).

McMullen v. Ohio State University Hospitals: Legal Recovery for Terminally Ill and Injured Patients Without the Lost Chance Doctrine, Jason Perkins. 32 U Tol L Rev 451 (Spring 2001).

Ohio Tort Reform Acts to Produce Major Change, Timothy Scanlon. 28 Akron B Ass'n Examiner 6 (January 1988).

Ohio Tort Reform in 1998: The War Continues, Stephen J. Werber. 45 Clev St L Rev 539 (1997).

Person v. Potential: judicial struggles to decide claims arising from the death of an embryo or fetus and Michigan's struggle to settle the question. Dena M. Marks, 37 Akron L R 41 (2004, No. 1).

Recovery of Punitive Damages in Ohio Wrongful Death Actions: A Preferred Approach, James J. Ross. 6 U Dayton L Rev 175 (Summer 1981).

The Structured Judgment as an Alternative to Caps on Personal Injury Damages, Henry M. Brown. 16 N Ky L Rev 481 (1989).

Tort Reform—Why Not? 44 Tol B Ass'n News 9 (December 1996).

The Value Of Life, Lewis A. Kornhauser. 38 Clev St L Rev 209 (1990).

Why Tort Deform Injures Ohio Citizens—(Deform v. to Deface; disfigure), Jay Harris. 44 Tol B Ass'n News 8 (December 1996).

Wrongful Death Damages and the Remarried Spouse, Stanley B. Kent. 68 Clev B J 14 (March 1997).

Wrongful Death Damages: Recovery of Investment in and Society and Companionship of a Child, Note. 27 Ohio St L J 355 (Spring 1966).

The Wrongful Death Statute Omission, Stanley B. Kent. 63 Clev B J 344 (September 1992).

Wrongful Death Suits for Fetuses Gain, David E. Rovella. 18 Nat'l L J A6 (July 15, 1996).

Notes of Decisions

Action in name of personal representative 1
Bankruptcy effect 2
Classes of kin included, scope; action for benefit of heirs, scope; action for benefit of heirs 10
Commenced within two years, statutes of limitation 12
Constitutional issues, damages 3
Constitutional issues, statutes of limitation 13
Damages 3-6
    Constitutional issues 3
    Determination of pecuniary injury 4
    Nonrecoverable amounts 5
    Valuation; apportionment 6
Determination of pecuniary injury, damages 4
Evidence 7
Joinder 8
Nonrecoverable amounts, damages 5
Other statutes of limitation, effect, statutes of limitation 14
Pleading, statutes of limitation 15
Scope; action for benefit of heirs 9, 10
    In general 9
    Classes of kin included, scope; action for benefit of heirs 10
Settlement 11
Statutes of limitation 12-15
    Commenced within two years 12
    Constitutional issues 13

Statutes of limitation—Cont'd
    Other statutes of limitation, effect 14
    Pleading 15
Valuation; apportionment, damages 6

---

1. Action in name of personal representative

Where the widow or one of the next of kin is appointed administrator after the action has been commenced, it is not sufficient to render such person the "personal representative" of the deceased so that they may maintain the action. Weidner v. Rankin (Ohio 1875) 26 Ohio St. 522.

A wrongful death action must be brought in th e name of the personal representative of the deceased, even though the statutory beneficiaries are the real parties in interest and the personal representative acts merely as a nominal party. Yardley v. W. Ohio Conference of the United Methodist Church, Inc. (Ohio App. 10 Dist., 08-29-2000) 138 Ohio App.3d 872, 742 N.E.2d 723. Death ⚖ 41

Though the representative is not acting on behalf of the estate in a wrongful death action, neither is he the agent of the statutory beneficiaries of the wrongful death action. Hooks v. Owen (Ohio App. 7 Dist., 09-23-1998) 130 Ohio App.3d 38, 719 N.E.2d 581, dismissed, appeal not allowed 85 Ohio St.3d 1405, 706 N.E.2d 787. Death ⚖ 31(3.1)

Statute requiring probate court approval when a decedent's personal representative settles a wrongful death claim applied to a release evidencing such a representative's settlement of a claim for uninsured motorist (UM) benefits against the decedent's automobile insurer; without such approval, the release was of no force and effect. Stacy v. Nationwide Mut. Ins. Co. (Ohio App. 6 Dist., 02-27-1998) 125 Ohio App.3d 658, 709 N.E.2d 519, appeal allowed 82 Ohio St.3d 1433, 694 N.E.2d 982, appeal dismissed as improvidently allowed 85 Ohio St.3d 1203, 707 N.E.2d 507, 1999-Ohio-451, reconsideration stricken 85 Ohio St.3d 1453, 708 N.E.2d 1008, reconsideration denied 85 Ohio St.3d 1481, 709 N.E.2d 851. Insurance ⚖ 3383

Personal representative of decedent is sole person authorized to pursue beneficiaries' claims against the tortfeasor in wrongful death suit. Gibson v. State Farm Mut. Auto. Ins. Co. (Ohio App. 2 Dist., 08-22-1997) 123 Ohio App.3d 216, 704 N.E.2d 1. Death ⚖ 31(3.1)

Uninsured motorist (UM) or underinsured motorist (UIM) benefits recovered by insured's personal representative for insured's wrongful death are "wrongful death proceeds" to be distributed to surviving spouse, children, and parents as statutory beneficiaries. Holt v. Grange Mut. Cas. Co. (Ohio, 09-24-1997) 79 Ohio St.3d 401, 683 N.E.2d 1080, 1997-Ohio-375. Death ⚖ 101

Payment of underinsured motorist (UIM) benefits to insured's estate for his wrongful death were received by insured's personal representative in that capacity, not as executor of his estate. Holt v. Grange Mut. Cas. Co. (Ohio, 09-24-1997) 79 Ohio St.3d 401, 683 N.E.2d 1080, 1997-Ohio-375. Executors And Administrators ⚖ 51

Action to recover underinsured motorist (UIM) benefits under sister's automobile policy for death of decedent had to be brought in name of administrator of decedent's estate. Miller v. Allstate Ins. Co. (Ohio App. 11 Dist., 06-10-1996) 111 Ohio App.3d 575, 676 N.E.2d 943. Death ⚖ 31(1); Insurance ⚖ 2790

Decedent's sister could recover damages due to her death although sister was not entitled to rebuttable presumption that she was in fact legally damaged by wrongful death and was required to prove her damages. Miller v. Allstate Ins. Co. (Ohio App. 11 Dist., 06-10-1996) 111 Ohio App.3d 575, 676 N.E.2d 943. Death ⚖ 32; Death ⚖ 58(2)

Insured was entitled to uninsured motorist (UM)/underinsured motorist (UIM) benefits for presumed damages as result of wrongful death of her child, even though child was not insured under her policy; overruling *Hill v State Farm Ins. Co.*, Lucas App. No. L–87–382; *Rotsinger v. State Farm Ins. Co.*, 78 Ohio App.3d 696, 605 N.E.2d 1281. Cincinnati Ins. Co. v. Jarvis (Ohio App. 6 Dist., 10-21-1994) 98 Ohio App.3d 155, 648 N.E.2d 30. Insurance ⚖ 2772

Insured's claim for underinsured motorist (UIM) benefits for wrongful death of her child did not need to be made through executor of child's estate. Cincinnati Ins. Co. v. Jarvis (Ohio App. 6 Dist., 10-21-1994) 98 Ohio App.3d 155, 648 N.E.2d 30. Insurance ⚖ 3567

A limitation placed on wrongful death actions is that they must be brought in the name of the decedent's personal representative. Tennant v. State Farm Mut. Ins. Co. (Summit 1991) 81 Ohio App.3d 20, 610 N.E.2d 437, motion overruled 62 Ohio St.3d 1434, 578 N.E.2d 826. Death ⚖ 31(3.1)

Note 1

A surviving husband cannot compromise or settle an action as an individual in the wrongful death of his wife because Ohio law mandates that wrongful death actions must be brought in the name of the deceased's personal representative. Tennant v. State Farm Mut. Ins. Co. (Summit 1991) 81 Ohio App.3d 20, 610 N.E.2d 437, motion overruled 62 Ohio St.3d 1434, 578 N.E.2d 826.

When a husband signs a release in his capacity as personal representative of his deceased wife's estate upon settlement of a wrongful death action, he is acting on behalf of all beneficiaries, of which he is one; he is thus barred from further prosecution in his individual capacity. Tennant v. State Farm Mut. Ins. Co. (Summit 1991) 81 Ohio App.3d 20, 610 N.E.2d 437, motion overruled 62 Ohio St.3d 1434, 578 N.E.2d 826.

An administrator and personal representative of a decedent's estate must file a wrongful death and survivorship action in her representative capacity rather than in her individual capacity. Colling v. Franklin Cty. Children Serv. (Franklin 1991) 76 Ohio App.3d 736, 603 N.E.2d 338, dismissed, jurisdictional motion overruled 63 Ohio St.3d 1467, 590 N.E.2d 1267.

In a wrongful death action brought by the mother of the decedent as the personal representative of his estate, documents governing the mother's psychologist-patient relationship are potentially relevant since the mother sought damages for mental anguish on behalf of the wrongful death action beneficiaries, including herself in her capacity as a beneficiary. Colling v. Franklin Cty. Children Serv. (Franklin 1991) 76 Ohio App.3d 736, 603 N.E.2d 338, dismissed, jurisdictional motion overruled 63 Ohio St.3d 1467, 590 N.E.2d 1267.

A personal representative of an estate who recovers moneys pursuant to a wrongful death statute for exclusive distribution to statutory beneficiaries is not precluded from recovering accidental death benefits allegedly due under the terms of an automobile insurance policy since the moneys recovered under the wrongful death statute were not an asset of the decedent's estate to be administered by the personal representative as executor and thus were not subject to the right of subrogation of the automobile insurer. Fogt v. United Ohio Ins. Co. (Shelby 1991) 76 Ohio App.3d 24, 600 N.E.2d 1109.

Appointment of counsel in a wrongful death action is to be made by the personal representative of the estate, who serves as a trustee for the wrongful death beneficiaries and not as their agent; the beneficiaries have no right to name independent counsel to represent their interests in the litigation. In re Estate of Ross (Geauga 1989) 65 Ohio App.3d 395, 583 N.E.2d 1379, dismissed 50 Ohio St.3d 717, 553 N.E.2d 1363.

Probate court exercising jurisdiction granted by statute to approve wrongful death settlement by personal representative of decedent has limited plenary jurisdiction to construe policy of liability insurance for purpose of determining amount of insurance coverage available to settle the wrongful death claim. Burris v. Grange Mut. Companies (Ohio 1989) 46 Ohio St.3d 84, 545 N.E.2d 83, rehearing denied 46 Ohio St.3d 717, 546 N.E.2d 1335, rehearing denied 53 Ohio St.3d 718, 560 N.E.2d 779. Courts ⇒ 198

Administrator appointed for decedent's estate in Alabama was not entitled to be substituted for administrator earlier appointed for same estate in Ohio in wrongful death action instituted by Ohio administrator, although interest of surviving spouse who had been presumed dead was purportedly represented by Alabama administrator, while putative surviving spouse had acquiesced in Ohio appointment; there was no transfer of interest between the two administrators which would warrant substitution, as wrongful death actions were brought for benefit of decedent's next of kin and personal representatives were merely nominal parties. Ahlrichs v. Tri-Tex Corp. (Hamilton 1987) 41 Ohio App.3d 207, 534 N.E.2d 1231. Death ⇒ 44

Ohio law was applicable in determining amount of damages recoverable in an action commenced in Ohio by Ohio representatives of an Ohio decedent killed in a foreign state to recover under a policy of insurance issued in Ohio which limited recovery from underinsured motorist to those damages which insureds were "legally entitled to recover." Paul v. West American Ins. Co. (Hamilton 1984) 19 Ohio App.3d 82, 482 N.E.2d 1309, 19 O.B.R. 166. Insurance ⇒ 1091(11)

A viable fetus which is negligently injured in its mother's womb and subsequently stillborn can be the basis for a wrongful death action pursuant to RC 2125.01. Werling v. Sandy (Ohio 1985) 17 Ohio St.3d 45, 476 N.E.2d 1053, 17 O.B.R. 37. Death ⇒ 15

An action for wrongful death is an asset of the decedent's estate and is, therefore, sufficient to justify the appointment of an administrator or an ancillary administrator in this state, even though there existed no other necessity for such an appointment, and the deceased was not domiciled in this state, and left no property in this state, and in such a case, the court for the county where the injury was received and the deceased died may properly entertain such jurisdiction. De Garza v. Chetister (Lucas 1978) 62 Ohio App.2d 149, 405 N.E.2d 331, 16 O.O.3d 335.

RC 2125.02 requires that an action for wrongful death be brought in the name of the personal representative of the deceased person, and Civ R 17(A) specifically allows this as an exception to the general rule that an action must be prosecuted in the name of the real party in interest. De Garza v. Chetister (Lucas 1978) 62 Ohio App.2d 149, 405 N.E.2d 331, 16 O.O.3d 335.

A viable unborn fetus is not a "person" within the meaning of RC 4511.181. State v. Dickinson (Ohio 1971) 28 Ohio St.2d 65, 275 N.E.2d 599, 57 O.O.2d 255.

A cause of action exists for the wrongful death of a viable unborn child which is subsequently stillborn. (Ed. note: But see 28 OS(2d) 65, 275 NE(2d) 599 (1971), State v Dickinson, holding that a viable unborn fetus is not a "person" within the meaning of homicide statutes, and suggesting in dictum that child must survive independent of mother for some period of time to give rise to cause of action for wrongful death of child.) Stidam v. Ashmore (Madison 1959) 109 Ohio App. 431, 167 N.E.2d 106, 11 O.O.2d 383.

In an action for wrongful death properly brought in a court of competent jurisdiction by the personal representative of the decedent under authority of section, such personal representative is but a nominal party and the designated beneficiaries for whose exclusive benefit the action is maintainable are the real parties in interest. Gibson v. Solomon (Ohio 1939) 136 Ohio St. 101, 23 N.E.2d 996, 125 A.L.R. 903, 16 O.O. 36.

Negligence of administrator suing for death of boy could not bar right to recover. Fach v. Canton Yellow Cab Co. (Stark 1929) 36 Ohio App. 247, 173 N.E. 245, 9 Ohio Law Abs. 189. Death ⇒ 24; Executors And Administrators ⇒ 432

A judgment adverse to the administrator of a decedent in his action to recover damages for the benefit of the estate of his decedent, arising out of a personal injury, is not a bar to the subsequent prosecution by the administrator of an action for the benefit of the wife, husband, and children, or parents and next of kin of the decedent. May Coal Co. v. Robinette (Ohio 1929) 120 Ohio St. 110, 165 N.E. 576, 64 A.L.R. 441, 7 Ohio Law Abs. 173, 28 Ohio Law Rep. 542.

The administrator is a mere nominal party in a suit for wrongful death, having no interest in the case for himself or the estate he represents, and the action is for the exclusive benefit of the next of kin of the decedent. Wolf v. Lake Erie & W.R. Co. (Ohio 1896) 55 Ohio St. 517, 37 W.L.B. 23, 45 N.E. 708.

In wrongful death actions in the name of an administrator under RS 6134 and RS 6135, the administrator is a mere nominal party having no interest in the case for himself or the estate he represents, and such actions are for the exclusive benefit of the beneficiaries named in such sections. Wolf v. Lake Erie & W.R. Co. (Ohio 1896) 55 Ohio St. 517, 37 W.L.B. 23, 45 N.E. 708.

The personal representative of a decedent may maintain an action for death caused by wrongful act once letters of administration have been issued, even though such letters disclose the fact that the deceased left no estate real or personal, and fail to indicate that the appointment was made for the bringing of suit. Solor Refining Co. v. Elliott (Ohio Cir. 1898) 8 Ohio C.D. 225.

An action for wrongful death may be brought by the deceased's executor as well as an administrator as personal representative of the deceased. Wittman's Executrix v C, H & D Railway Co, 8 NP 279, 10 D 563 (CP, Montgomery 1900).

Gen.Code Ohio, § 12993, prohibits employment of a boy under 15 years of age in any mill, factory, etc., and section 13007–9 makes a violation of such provision a penal offense on the part of both the employer and a parent or guardian who permits such employment. Section 10772 of such Code (repealed 1932. See §§ 10509–167, 10509–168), gives a right of action for death caused by negligence, which would have entitled the deceased to recover if he had survived the injury, for the benefit of next of kin. Held, under the law of the state as established by its courts, that an action against the employer for the death of a boy under 15, killed while employed in a mill or factory in violation of the statute cannot be maintained for the benefit of a parent who consented to such employment. Star Fire Clay Co. v. Budno (C.C.A.6 (Ohio) 1920) 269 F. 508. Death ⇒ 24; Labor And Employment ⇒ 2985; Labor And Employment ⇒ 2788

Where a plaintiff sues in forma pauperis as administratrix of her deceased husband's estate to recover damages for his wrongful death under RS 6135, her affidavit of poverty should show that neither the estate nor the beneficiaries of the action are able to prepay or secure the costs.

Reed v. Pennsylvania Co. (C.C.A.6 1901) 111 F. 714, 49 C.C.A. 572. Costs ⇐ 132(6)

The administrator of a decedent who was killed by the wrongful act of another is not a nominal party, but the real party in interest so far as the prosecution of the suit is concerned; consequently a foreign administrator may bring the action in federal court although the beneficiaries reside in the state where the death occurred. Popp v. Cincinnati, H. & D.R. Co. (C.C.S.D.Ohio 1899) 96 F. 465. Federal Courts ⇐ 289; Death ⇐ 31(3.1); Executors And Administrators ⇐ 153; Parties ⇐ 4

While under Ohio law the administrator when appointed of the estate of a fourteen-year-old boy, drowned while working on defendant's vessel, would be only person who could bring suit for wrongful death, notification to vessel's owner by parents of deceased boy constituted notice by a "claimant" under the federal act, and filing of petition for exoneration by vessel's owner more than six months after receiving notice from such parents violated the federal act and was dismissed. Petition of Donnelly (N.D.Ohio 1954) 138 F.Supp. 823, 60 O.O. 142.

A personal representative appointed in another state may institute and maintain a wrongful death action in Ohio pursuant to RC 2113.75 and 2125.02, where a personal representative appointed in Ohio has not already done so. Ahlrichs v. Tri–Tex Corp. (Hamilton 1987) 41 Ohio App.3d 207, 534 N.E.2d 1231.

RC 2125.02(A)(1) mandates that an action for wrongful death be brought in the name of the personal representative of the decedent for the exclusive benefit of the surviving spouse, the children, and other next of kin of the decedent; thus, a personal representative is merely a nominal party and the real parties in interest are the surviving spouse, children, and other next of kin and a change in the class of beneficiaries whom an administrator represents does not alter the nominal role of the administrator under RC 2125.02. Ahlrichs v. Tri–Tex Corp. (Hamilton 1987) 41 Ohio App.3d 207, 534 N.E.2d 1231.

RC 2125.02 provides a specific remedy for the wrongful death of another by prescribing that the cause of action must be brought in the name of the personal representative of the decedent, and that such personal representative, with the consent of the court making the appointment of such personal representative, may settle with the defendant the amount to be paid as damages. Matz v. Erie–Lackawanna R. Co. (Summit 1965) 2 Ohio App.2d 136, 207 N.E.2d 250, 31 O.O.2d 241.

The statutory procedure under RC 2125.02 providing for the settlement of a claim for wrongful death is exclusive in the personal representative of the deceased person, subject to the approval of the probate court making the appointment of such personal representative. Matz v. Erie–Lackawanna R. Co. (Summit 1965) 2 Ohio App.2d 136, 207 N.E.2d 250, 31 O.O.2d 241.

The beneficiaries of an estate have no right to name independent counsel to represent their interests in a wrongful death action; the appointment of counsel is to be made by the personal representative of the estate. Ross v Roulette Pontiac, No. 13–014 (11th Dist Ct App, Lake, 11–24–89).

2. **Bankruptcy effect**

Debtor's bare denial that his operation of motor vehicle which blood-alcohol content of .232% was cause of accident which resulted in death of passenger in vehicle was not sufficient to preclude entry of summary judgment for passenger's relatives in adversary proceeding to except debtor's obligation on their wrongful death claim from discharge in Chapter 7, as debt for death or personal injury caused by debtor's unlawful operation of vehicle while intoxicated. In re Mellott (Bkrtcy.N.D.Ohio, 06-23-1995) 187 B.R. 578. Bankruptcy ⇐ 2164.1

Debtor's obligation on wrongful death claim arising out of his operation of motor vehicle with blood-alcohol content more than twice the legal limit would be excepted from discharge in Chapter 7, as debt for death or personal injury caused by debtor's unlawful operation of motor vehicle while he was intoxicated; debtor's violation of Ohio statute prohibiting any motorist from operating vehicle with blood-alcohol content of .10% or more established his intoxication for bankruptcy dischargeability purposes. In re Mellott (Bkrtcy.N.D.Ohio, 06-23-1995) 187 B.R. 578. Bankruptcy ⇐ 3374(12)

Statutory exception to discharge, for debts for personal injury or death caused by debtor's driving while intoxicated, is designed to deter drunk driving, to ensure that those who cause injury by driving while intoxicated do not escape civil liability through bankruptcy laws, and to protect victims of drunk driving. In re Mellott (Bkrtcy.N.D.Ohio, 06-23-1995) 187 B.R. 578. Bankruptcy ⇐ 3374(12)

To except debt from discharge as obligation for personal injury or death caused by debtor's driving while intoxicated, creditor must demonstrate, by preponderance of evidence, that debtor was legally intoxicated under state law at time of accident. In re Mellott (Bkrtcy.N.D.Ohio, 06-23-1995) 187 B.R. 578. Bankruptcy ⇐ 3405(14)

3. **Damages—Constitutional issues**

Automobile insurer's denial, consistent with the uninsured/underinsured motorist (UM/UIM) statute, of UM/UIM coverage for the wrongful death of a nonresident relative of the insured did not violate the spirit of the wrongful death statute, the state constitution's Equal Protection Clause, or the state constitutional prohibition against limiting tort damages, nor did it abrogate the state constitutional right to a remedy for injury. Clark v. Forney (Ohio App. 6 Dist., 09-30-1998) 129 Ohio App.3d 844, 719 N.E.2d 106, appeal allowed 84 Ohio St.3d 1493, 705 N.E.2d 689, cause dismissed 86 Ohio St.3d 1482, 716 N.E.2d 215. Constitutional Law ⇐ 245(3); Constitutional Law ⇐ 321; Insurance ⇐ 2650

Fifteen-year statute of repose for actions involving a product liability claim violated provision of State Constitution guaranteeing a right to a remedy. State ex rel. Ohio Academy of Trial Lawyers v. Sheward (Ohio, 08-16-1999) 86 Ohio St.3d 451, 715 N.E.2d 1062, 1999-Ohio-123, reconsideration denied 87 Ohio St.3d 1409, 716 N.E.2d 1170. Constitutional Law ⇐ 321; Limitation Of Actions ⇐ 4(2)

1996 H 350, which amended more than 100 statutes and a variety of rules relating to tort and other civil actions, and which was an attempt to reenact provisions of law previously held unconstitutional by the Supreme Court of Ohio, is an act of usurpation of judicial power in violation of the doctrine of separation of powers; for that reason, and because of violation of the one-subject rule of the Ohio Constitution, 1996 H 350 is unconstitutional. State ex rel. Ohio Academy of Trial Lawyers v. Sheward (Ohio, 08-16-1999) 86 Ohio St.3d 451, 715 N.E.2d 1062, 1999-Ohio-123, reconsideration denied 87 Ohio St.3d 1409, 716 N.E.2d 1170.

Statute permitting party to wrongful death action to present evidence that surviving spouse of decedent has remarried does not violate prohibition in Ohio Constitution against limiting by law the amount of damages recoverable in a wrongful death action; statute does not specifically limit amount of recoverable damages, but permits trier of fact to consider remarriage of surviving spouse as one of many factors that may be relevant to assessing surviving spouse's losses. Pena v. Northeast Ohio Emergency Affiliates, Inc. (Ohio App. 9 Dist., 12-20-1995) 108 Ohio App.3d 96, 670 N.E.2d 268, dismissed, appeal not allowed 75 Ohio St.3d 1494, 664 N.E.2d 1291. Death ⇐ 9

Interpretation of wrongful death statute to exclude unacknowledged illegitimate children from recovery would violate equal protection, as statute already provided protection against uninjured or undeserving potential distributees, in that damages were keyed to losses suffered by surviving beneficiaries and amount of damages was determined on basis of pecuniary and dependency-related factors, and two-year time limitation was not merely on remedy but on right of action itself. Brookbank v. Gray (Ohio, 01-17-1996) 74 Ohio St.3d 279, 658 N.E.2d 724, 1996-Ohio-135. Constitutional Law ⇐ 245(3); Death ⇐ 9

"Pecuniary injury," as used in RC 2125.02, does not include loss of society, comfort, and companionship of the decedent, and such limitation does not deny equal protection of the laws to the parents and siblings of a fatally injured minor child. Keaton v. Ribbeck (Ohio 1979) 58 Ohio St.2d 443, 391 N.E.2d 307, 12 O.O.3d 375. Death ⇐ 88

Ohio Wrongful Death Statute did not violate equal protection by requiring that formal acknowledgment of paternity be made for children born out of wedlock to have standing to bring suit; requirement of formal acknowledgement of paternity is rationally related to legitimate state interest in avoiding spurious wrongful death claim, and children born out of wedlock were not discriminated against per se. Martin v. Daily Express, Inc. (N.D.Ohio, 02-28-1995) 878 F.Supp. 91. Constitutional Law ⇐ 245(3); Death ⇐ 9

Application of two-year date of death statute of limitations to wrongful death action did not deny plaintiff due course of law or due process of law under Ohio or Federal Constitution on basis that limitation period should have run from date of discovery of causal relation between death of plaintiff's decedent and decedent's industrial exposure to dangerous film, dust and particles; two-year limit of statute was part of "due course of law" by which person was entitled to remedy. Bazdar v. Koppers Co., Inc. (N.D.Ohio 1981) 524 F.Supp. 1194, appeal dismissed 705 F.2d 451, appeal dismissed 705 F.2d 454. Constitutional Law ⇐ 308; Limitation Of Actions ⇐ 4(2)

4. —— Determination of pecuniary injury, damages

Under the wrongful death act, persons who had no legal claim for support from the deceased may, as next of kin, have an action maintained for their benefit to recover the compensation allowed by the statute; and in determining the pecuniary injury resulting from the death, the reasonable expectation of what the next of kin might have received from the deceased, had he lived, is a proper subject for the jury. Grotenkemper v. Harris (Ohio 1874) 25 Ohio St. 510.

It is not necessary in order to recover for wrongful death that the widow and next of kin should have a legal claim on the deceased for their support, although the reasonable expectation of what the next of kin might have received from the deceased had he lived is a proper subject for the jury to consider. Grotenkemper v. Harris (Ohio 1874) 25 Ohio St. 510.

In actions brought for wrongful death, it is within the discretion of the jury to make such award as they consider proper and reasonable for the pecuniary injury, and a verdict so rendered will not be set aside by a reviewing court unless the amount awarded is so excessive as to have been given under the influence of passion or prejudice or as a result of the jury's misunderstanding of their duties and obligations under the law. Cincinnati Traction Co. v. Cahill (Ohio App. 1 Dist. 1922) 16 Ohio App. 496.

Evidence that decedent was killed by a drunk driver was not relevant in action by decedent's grandson against his insurer under his underinsured motorist coverage for wrongful death; damages, not liability, for the accident was at issue. Hiner v. Nationwide Mut. Ins. Co. (Ohio App. 5 Dist., Stark, 12-13-2005) No. 2005CA00034, 2005-Ohio-6660, 2005 WL 3446322, Unreported. Death 61

Weight of evidence supported jury finding that decedent's grandson did not suffer damages under wrongful death statute for loss of society and mental anguish upon decedent's death in car accident; grandson, an adult married male, testified that decedent had been like a second mother to him since he was 13 and that her death caused him mental anguish, but admitted decedent had terminal cancer and had returned to the state to put her affairs in order, and there was no evidence that grandson had received counseling after decedent's death. Hiner v. Nationwide Mut. Ins. Co. (Ohio App. 5 Dist., Stark, 12-13-2005) No. 2005CA00034, 2005-Ohio-6660, 2005 WL 3446322, Unreported. Death 77

RC 3937.18 as amended requires that insurers provide coverage for losses resulting from bodily harm or death that the insured personally sustains and denies coverage to insureds who are siblings claiming "injury" they suffer in the wrongful death of their mother who is fatally injured while riding as a passenger in her husband's car. Spence v. National Mut. Ins. Co. (Ohio App. 7 Dist., Monroe, 06-30-1999) No. 812, No. 803, No. 804, 1999 WL 476015, Unreported, motion to certify allowed 87 Ohio St.3d 1407, 716 N.E.2d 1169, appeal allowed 87 Ohio St.3d 1408, 716 N.E.2d 1169, reversed and remanded 88 Ohio St.3d 403, 727 N.E.2d 592, 2000-Ohio-361, reversed and remanded 88 Ohio St.3d 403, 727 N.E.2d 593, reversed and remanded 88 Ohio St.3d 446, 727 N.E.2d 900, 2000-Ohio-378.

A father's visit with his son less than six months before the child's death precludes a finding of abandonment for purposes of wrongful death proceeds and if the parties are unable to equitably divide the proceeds according to RC 2125.03(A)(1) the court should consider the father's (1) failure to take any steps during the child's life to formally acknowledge parentage, (2) minimal contact with the child, (3) failure to pay child support, and (4) insignificant involvement and support compared to the mother's participation in the child's tragically short life. Wrongful Death of Turner (Ohio App. 2 Dist., Champaign, 11-25-1998) No. 98 CA 2, 1998 WL 811598, Unreported.

Damages may be awarded in wrongful death action to the next of kin, other than spouse, children of parents of decedent, only for proven, actual losses suffered by them as a result of the decedent's death. Hooks v. Owen (Ohio App. 7 Dist., 09-23-1998) 130 Ohio App.3d 38, 719 N.E.2d 581, dismissed, appeal not allowed 85 Ohio St.3d 1405, 706 N.E.2d 787. Death 31(5); Death 85

Claim for $100 in property damage, for destruction of clothing and eyeglasses, which was asserted in wrongful death action brought against railroad by administrator of estate of vehicle passenger killed in collision with train, was sufficient to support award of punitive damages in amount of $6 million. Gollihue v. Consolidated Rail Corp. (Ohio App. 3 Dist., 07-07-1997) 120 Ohio App.3d 378, 697 N.E.2d 1109, dismissed, appeal not allowed 80 Ohio St.3d 1444, 686 N.E.2d 273, reconsideration denied 80 Ohio St.3d 1481, 687 N.E.2d 476, reconsideration denied 80 Ohio St.3d 1482, 687 N.E.2d 476. Labor And Employment 2825

Funeral and burial expenses are element of damages that may be recovered under wrongful death statute. Morrison v. Fleck (Ohio App. 9 Dist., 06-11-1997) 120 Ohio App.3d 307, 697 N.E.2d 1064. Death 84

Issues of whether 11-year-old child who was injured when he was struck by automobile would have provided support to his family members, particularly his mother, after his emancipation, and dollar amount of that support, were for jury in wrongful death action; testimony was presented regarding child's age, mental and physical characteristics, and future plans, and also regarding child's family background and education and earning capacity of other members of his family. Howard v. Seidler (Ohio App. 7 Dist., 12-04-1996) 116 Ohio App.3d 800, 689 N.E.2d 572, appeal not allowed 78 Ohio St.3d 1494, 678 N.E.2d 1230. Death 103(4)

Evidence of loss of support from reasonably expected earning capacity of decedent is admissible in wrongful death action where decedent was a minor at time of death and had never been gainfully employed. Howard v. Seidler (Ohio App. 7 Dist., 12-04-1996) 116 Ohio App.3d 800, 689 N.E.2d 572, appeal not allowed 78 Ohio St.3d 1494, 678 N.E.2d 1230. Death 64

When uninsurance/underinsurance provider pays proceeds for wrongful death of policyholder, those proceeds are characterized as "damages" recovered by personal representative, regardless of how or why they are paid; even though damages ultimately go to beneficiaries, proceeds are payable due to fact that "insured" party—the decedent—suffered wrongful death. Holt v. Grange Mut. Cas. Co. (Ohio, 09-24-1997) 79 Ohio St.3d 401, 683 N.E.2d 1080, 1997-Ohio-375. Death 78

Even if trial court in wrongful death action arising out of railroad crossing accident erred in submitting punitive damages issue to jury, such error was cured by jury's defense verdict on punitive damages. Sheets v. Norfolk S. Corp. (Ohio App. 3 Dist., 02-12-1996) 109 Ohio App.3d 278, 671 N.E.2d 1364. Appeal And Error 1062.1

Evidence supported jury's award of $2.5 million in general damages to estate of ten-year-old passenger who was killed in railroad crossing accident, notwithstanding passenger's age and alleged fact that passenger's beneficiaries suffered no loss of earnings or pecuniary loss. Sheets v. Norfolk S. Corp. (Ohio App. 3 Dist., 02-12-1996) 109 Ohio App.3d 278, 671 N.E.2d 1364. Death 99(3)

Trial court's determination of which questions regarding the circumstances of surviving spouse's remarriage are relevant to jury's assessment of damages in wrongful death action will not be disturbed on appeal absent an abuse of discretion. Pena v. Northeast Ohio Emergency Affiliates, Inc. (Ohio App. 9 Dist., 12-20-1995) 108 Ohio App.3d 96, 670 N.E.2d 268, dismissed, appeal not allowed 75 Ohio St.3d 1494, 664 N.E.2d 1291. Appeal And Error 974(1)

Trial court did not abuse discretion, in wrongful death action by surviving spouse who had remarried, in finding that questions relating to how long plaintiff had known second wife, what services she performed for the family, and whether she was employed outside the home were relevant to jury's assessment of how plaintiff's remarriage affected his compensable losses under wrongful death statute. Pena v. Northeast Ohio Emergency Affiliates, Inc. (Ohio App. 9 Dist., 12-20-1995) 108 Ohio App.3d 96, 670 N.E.2d 268, dismissed, appeal not allowed 75 Ohio St.3d 1494, 664 N.E.2d 1291. Death 60

Provision of statutory scheme dealing with rights of nursing home patients expressly established basis for private cause of action for personal injuries and wrongful death of patient whose rights were allegedly violated. Sprosty v. Pearlview, Inc. (Ohio App. 8 Dist., 10-02-1995) 106 Ohio App.3d 679, 666 N.E.2d 1180, dismissed, appeal not allowed 75 Ohio St.3d 1405, 661 N.E.2d 754. Health 603

Wrongful death statute provides for persons permitted as plaintiffs to claim loss of consortium as compensable loss under statute; statute affords exclusive civil remedy to compensate others for death resulting from injuries. Miller v. Boden (Ohio App. 3 Dist., 05-10-1995) 103 Ohio App.3d 73, 658 N.E.2d 809, appeal not allowed 74 Ohio St.3d 1409, 655 N.E.2d 187. Death 7; Death 88

Evidence that biological father had effectively abandoned his son rebutted presumption arising in wrongful death action that father suffered loss by reason of son's death. In re Estate of Marinelli (Ohio App. 11 Dist., 12-19-1994) 99 Ohio App.3d 372, 650 N.E.2d 935. Death 58(2)

Provision of wrongful death statute prohibiting parent who has abandoned minor child from benefitting in wrongful death action applies only in instances where decedent is a minor. In re Estate of Marinelli (Ohio App. 11 Dist., 12-19-1994) 99 Ohio App.3d 372, 650 N.E.2d 935. Death 101

Doctrine of law of the case did not preclude award of punitive damages in wrongful death action brought by snowmobile operator's estate against railroad, where Supreme Court, in its order remanding case for new trial, did not limit issues or claims be retried. Sharp v. Norfolk & W. Ry. Co. (Ohio, 06-14-1995) 72 Ohio St.3d 307, 649 N.E.2d 1219, 1995-Ohio-224, clarified 73 Ohio St.3d 1429, 652 N.E.2d 801. Appeal And Error ⇨ 1195(1)

Award of $1 million to parents of snowmobile operator who died in collision with flatbed train car that was stopped at unlit crossing was not excessive. Sharp v. Norfolk & W. Ry. Co. (Ohio, 06-14-1995) 72 Ohio St.3d 307, 649 N.E.2d 1219, 1995-Ohio-224, clarified 73 Ohio St.3d 1429, 652 N.E.2d 801. Death ⇨ 99(5)

Trial court abused its discretion in determining that jury verdict awarding $2.5 million to husband of decedent and $240,000 to estate of decedent in wrongful death action based on medical malpractice was excessive and granting remittitur which reduced award to husband to $1,650,000 and award to decedent's estate to $120,000 where trial court noted that award was largest in history of county, placed significance on fact that decedent had been married only short time before death, noted that counsel had made dismally low appraisal of case, made conjecture that decedent's age, empathy for widow and decedent's parents, exceptional lawyering, and demeanor of physician had affect upon jury, and used arbitrary factors in reducing awards; ruling demonstrated nothing more than subjective disagreement with size of verdict, and invaded province of jury. Betz v. Timken Mercy Med. Ctr. (Ohio App. 5 Dist., 07-25-1994) 96 Ohio App.3d 211, 644 N.E.2d 1058, appeal not allowed 71 Ohio St.3d 1436, 643 N.E.2d 142, reconsideration denied 71 Ohio St.3d 1467, 644 N.E.2d 1389. Death ⇨ 99(1); Death ⇨ 99(4)

Statute governing wrongful death damages accords jury wide discretion, and statute no longer confines damages to pecuniary injuries sustained by beneficiaries of action. Ryne v. Garvey (Montgomery 1993) 87 Ohio App.3d 145, 621 N.E.2d 1320. Death ⇨ 78; Death ⇨ 81

Evidence supported future damages award for patient who had died following heart stress test administered by physician; expert had testified as to probability and degree of patient's life expectancy. Ryne v. Garvey (Montgomery 1993) 87 Ohio App.3d 145, 621 N.E.2d 1320. Health ⇨ 823(11)

Monies recovered by personal representative of estate pursuant to wrongful death statute for exclusive distribution to statutory beneficiaries were not asset of decedent's estate to be administered by personal representative as executor, and thus, monies recovered were not subject to right of subrogation of automobile insurer so as to render estate's claim for accidental death benefits pursuant to automobile policy moot. Fogt v. United Ohio Ins. Co. (Shelby 1991) 76 Ohio App.3d 24, 600 N.E.2d 1109. Insurance ⇨ 3519(1)

A new trial as to damages is properly granted after a verdict awarding $1,000,000 in a wrongful death action for a mother's mental anguish from the shooting death of her son by a police officer because the verdict is so excessive as to be the product of passion or prejudice where it is shown that the mother and the child did not enjoy a close relationship, and the mother had been the subject of the deceased child's battering. Fields v. Dailey (Franklin 1990) 68 Ohio App.3d 33, 587 N.E.2d 400, motion to certify overruled 56 Ohio St.3d 703, 564 N.E.2d 707, rehearing denied 57 Ohio St.3d 706, 566 N.E.2d 171.

Damages flowing from a life shortened by a physician's negligence are compensable, therefore, where a physician admits that he misread an X-ray containing a malignant lesion and there is evidence that this negligence accelerated the decedent's death, a judgment denying damages is against the manifest weight of the evidence. Miller v. Marrocco (Hamilton 1989) 63 Ohio App.3d 293, 578 N.E.2d 834, motion overruled 45 Ohio St.3d 719, 545 N.E.2d 908.

In an action for wrongful death based on medical malpractice, there is no need to introduce evidence concerning the length of time the victim may have lived but for the malpractice; however, the defendant may introduce evidence showing that the victim would have survived only a short time in mitigation of damages. Taylor v. C. Lawrence Decker, M.D., Inc. (Hamilton 1986) 33 Ohio App.3d 118, 514 N.E.2d 754. Health ⇨ 826

Wrongful death statute, as amended, differs from original statute in that it no longer limits recovery to pecuniary loss sustained by decedent's beneficiaries and reasonable funeral expenses, but allows beneficiaries to recover for their mental suffering or loss of companionship, society or consortium resulting from decedent's death. French v. Dwiggins (Ohio 1984) 9 Ohio St.3d 32, 458 N.E.2d 827, 9 O.B.R. 123. Death ⇨ 88; Death ⇨ 89

In wrongful death action, jury verdict of no pecuniary damages for family of 22-year-old dental hygienist who helped parents with their rental properties, cut her brothers' hair, cleaned her family's teeth, and whose death resulted in loss of rental and related expenses to sister and loss from consequent inability to repay educational loans parents had made to her was against manifest weight of evidence. Terveer v. Baschnagel (Franklin 1982) 3 Ohio App.3d 312, 445 N.E.2d 264, 3 O.B.R. 365. Death ⇨ 77

The contingency of marriage may be considered by the trier of fact in determining the amount recoverable by surviving parents for the wrongful death of their child. Terveer v. Baschnagel (Franklin 1982) 3 Ohio App.3d 312, 445 N.E.2d 264, 3 O.B.R. 365. Death ⇨ 81

RC 2125.02, as amended by 1981 H 332, eff. 2–5–82, substantially alters the dimension and character of wrongful death actions and cannot be given a retroactive effect. Rivers v. Kairis (Ohio Com.Pl. 1982) 2 Ohio Misc.2d 6, 442 N.E.2d 494.

The law presumes a pecuniary loss to a parent or parents entitled to the services and earnings of their minor child by the wrongful death of such child even before it has reached an age when it is actually able to render services or assistance of a pecuniary nature. Nelson v. Horton (Clermont 1971) 31 Ohio App.2d 159, 287 N.E.2d 108, 60 O.O.2d 246. Death ⇨ 58(1)

In order to support judgment of recovery in wrongful death action under RC 2125.02, it must be shown that beneficiaries of such judgment received financial aid from decedent during his lifetime and would likely have continued to receive such aid and/or would have, in reasonable probability, inherited from an accumulating estate program cut short by death of decedent; circumstances, age, health and means of support of such beneficiaries; and age, health, disposition and thrift of decedent are factors to be considered in determining whether there has been "pecuniary injury" to such beneficiaries. Murray v. Long (Ashland 1968) 21 Ohio App.2d 194, 256 N.E.2d 225, 50 O.O.2d 332. Death ⇨ 58(2)

Damages recoverable in wrongful death action brought for benefit of those named in RC 2125.02 must be "proportioned to the pecuniary injury" resulting from death. Murray v. Long (Ashland 1968) 21 Ohio App.2d 194, 256 N.E.2d 225, 50 O.O.2d 332. Death ⇨ 101

Where, in wrongful death action brought under RC 2125.02 on behalf of the decedent's parents, there is no evidence that at time of his death son contributed to support of either parent or that either parent could reasonably have anticipated contributions in the future or would need support money, or that the son was in the process of accumulating an estate which either parent might inherit, claim that either parent suffered "pecuniary injury" is not supported, and they cannot recover for the death of such son. Murray v. Long (Ashland 1968) 21 Ohio App.2d 194, 256 N.E.2d 225, 50 O.O.2d 332.

Generally, damages recoverable for wrongful death are to be determined by considering the victim's life expectancy, character, health, habits, talents, prospects, prior earnings, probable future earnings, and needs of and contributions to dependents and current returns on investments. Sutfin v. Burton (Cuyahoga 1951) 91 Ohio App. 177, 104 N.E.2d 53, 61 Ohio Law Abs. 281, 48 O.O. 298. Death ⇨ 86(1)

Where an action is brought under section for pecuniary injury resulting from the wrongful death of an infant, there is no exact rule regarding the amount of damages which a jury may award; factors for consideration by the jury are the age, sex and physical and mental condition of the child and the position in life, occupation and physical and economic conditions of the parents. It cannot be said as a matter of law that there is no pecuniary damage to the parents of an infant whose death is caused by the wrongful act of another nor can it be said that the expense of maintaining and educating the child would necessarily exceed any pecuniary advantage which the parents could have derived from his services had he lived. Immel v. Richards (Ohio 1950) 154 Ohio St. 52, 93 N.E.2d 474, 42 O.O. 128.

Term "pecuniary injury" as used in this section comprehends essentially injury measured by prospective advantages of a pecuniary nature which have been cut off by premature death of person from whom they would have preceded; term does not embrace such elements as bereavement or mental pain and suffering of beneficiaries or loss of society or comfort of deceased. Karr v. Sixt (Ohio 1946) 146 Ohio St. 527, 67 N.E.2d 331, 33 O.O. 14. Death ⇨ 86(1); Death ⇨ 88; Death ⇨ 89

Under section providing that in an action for wrongful death any award of damages is to be governed by "pecuniary injury" resulting from death, a presumption of pecuniary injury ordinarily exists in favor of those persons legally entitled to services, earnings or support from decedent; no such presumption obtains as to collateral kindred having no legal claims on decedent, and infliction of "pecuniary injury" on them by reason of death ought to appear from evidence before they may be considered in award of damages. Karr v. Sixt (Ohio 1946) 146 Ohio St. 527, 67 N.E.2d 331, 33 O.O. 14. Death ⇨ 58(2)

Proof that deceased's next of kin were dependent when last seen might afford rebuttable inference of present dependency. Fini v. Perry (Ohio

1928) 119 Ohio St. 367, 164 N.E. 358. Death ⇨ 58(1); Evidence ⇨ 67(1)

Instruction on damages for minor's death held not erroneous for failure to exclude earnings he might have made. John Shillito Co. v. Shanley (Hamilton 1926) 21 Ohio App. 12, 153 N.E. 102, 4 Ohio Law Abs. 750. Death ⇨ 104(5); Parent And Child ⇨ 7(14)

Where a fifty-two year old fireman is killed by the negligence of another, leaving a wife and grown-up children, in the absence of evidence, the law will presume that he supported his wife for purposes of assessing pecuniary loss. Toledo Ry. & Light Co. v. Ward (Ohio Cir. 1903) 15 Ohio C.D. 399, 2 Ohio C.C.(N.S.) 256, affirmed 71 Ohio St. 492, 74 N.E. 1142, 2 Ohio Law Rep. 295.

Wrongful death, Warsaw Convention actions for death in a plane crash on the high seas, loss of society damages. Zicherman v. Korean Air Lines Co., Ltd. (U.S.N.Y., 01-16-1996) 116 S.Ct. 629, 516 U.S. 217, 133 L.Ed.2d 596, on remand 92 F.3d 126.

A federal jury's $45,000 verdict for wrongful death that is supported by the evidence and within the "universe of possible awards" is not grossly inadequate. Molton v. City of Cleveland (C.A.6 (Ohio) 1988) 839 F.2d 240, certiorari denied 109 S.Ct. 1345, 489 U.S. 1068, 103 L.Ed.2d 814.

A wrongful death award must be reduced, under Ohio law, by the percentage of responsibility attributed to the plaintiff's decedent, but no reduction of an award based upon an intentional tort will be made. Molton v. City of Cleveland (C.A.6 (Ohio) 1988) 839 F.2d 240, certiorari denied 109 S.Ct. 1345, 489 U.S. 1068, 103 L.Ed.2d 814. Death ⇨ 23

In a survivorship action and a cause of action for wrongful death, brought by the mother of a decedent who alleges negligence with resultant pain and suffering, it is error to grant a defendant university hospital's motion and dismiss the entire action, where the trial court has failed to make findings and conclusions on the survivorship cause of action in regard to pain and suffering because of a hospital's failure to administer a scheduled dose of morphine to the decedent, and the plaintiff contends that her decedent should recover for pain and suffering as a result of the defendant university hospital's failure to administer pain medication as ordered. Moore v University of Cincinnati, No. 93API08-1156, 1994 WL 49769 (10th Dist Ct App, Franklin, 2-15-94).

In determining the amount of damages which may be awarded to a parent for the wrongful death of a child, the jury should consider the age and sex of the child, the parent's mode of living, and other helpful facts existing at the time of the child's death. Burns–Bowe Baking Co v Pakos, 9 Abs 262, 32 LR 593 (App, Cuyahoga 1930).

5. —— Nonrecoverable amounts, damages

Damages cannot be awarded on account of the bereavement, mental suffering, or as a solace for such wrongful death. Steel v. Kurtz (Ohio 1876) 28 Ohio St. 191.

An insurance policy exclusion that limits uninsured-underinsured motorist coverage to bodily injury or death sustained by an insured does not violate RC 3937.18(A); and where plaintiff's brother is killed by a vehicle driven by an uninsured motorist, plaintiff is not entitled to coverage for his derivative wrongful death damages since the deceased does not qualify as an "insured person" under the policy. Kocel v. Farmers Ins. of Columbus (Ohio App. 8 Dist., Cuyahoga, 03-07-1996) No. 69058, 1996 WL 100943, Unreported, appeal allowed 76 Ohio St.3d 1495, 670 N.E.2d 242, appeal dismissed as improvidently allowed 79 Ohio St.3d 1235, 684 N.E.2d 83, 1997-Ohio-135, reconsideration denied 80 Ohio St.3d 1450, 686 N.E.2d 276.

There can be no punitive damages in a wrongful death cause of action. McGill v. Newark Surgery Ctr. (Ohio Com.Pl., 04-03-2001) 113 Ohio Misc.2d 21, 756 N.E.2d 762. Death ⇨ 93

Widow of patient who alleged that patient had lost chance of survival due to medical malpractice could not recover for negligent infliction of serious emotional distress in action against hospital and physicians where widow was barred from recovery in underlying wrongful death action due to fact that negligence had caused at most loss of 20 to 30 percent chance of survival. Schlachet v. Cleveland Clinic Found. (Ohio App. 8 Dist., 05-30-1995) 104 Ohio App.3d 160, 661 N.E.2d 259, appeal not allowed 74 Ohio St.3d 1422, 655 N.E.2d 741. Damages ⇨ 57.18

The estate of a deceased minor child may not claim as damages the child's medical expenses in a medical malpractice action as the child's parents, not the child, are responsible for payment of a child's medical expenses and are therefore the proper party in interest. Blakeman v. Condorodis (Hamilton 1991) 75 Ohio App.3d 393, 599 N.E.2d 776, motion overruled 62 Ohio St.3d 1478, 581 N.E.2d 1099.

An injured party's right to punitive damages may survive his death and be pursued by the representative of his estate under RC 2305.21, although punitive damages are not available in a wrongful death action. Schaefer v. D & J Produce, Inc. (Erie 1978) 62 Ohio App.2d 53, 403 N.E.2d 1015, 16 O.O.3d 108.

While punitive damages are not recoverable in a wrongful death action, such damages can be awarded in an action that survives the decedent pursuant to RC 2305.21, where it can be proved that the decedent suffered personal injury or property loss before he died as a result of another's intentional, reckless, wanton, willful, gross, or malicious acts. Rubeck v. Huffman (Ohio 1978) 54 Ohio St.2d 20, 374 N.E.2d 411, 8 O.O.3d 11.

Funeral expenses incurred by a husband for the funeral and burial of his wife who has sustained a fatal injury by the wrongful act of a third person, are not to be considered as a pecuniary injury under wrongful death statutes. Barcus v. Union Hospital Ass'n (Ohio Com.Pl. 1965) 14 Ohio Misc. 168, 236 N.E.2d 232, 43 O.O.2d 407. Death ⇨ 84

Medical expenses accruing during the lifetime of a deceased wife because of an injury resulting in death sustained by the wrongful action of a third person do not constitute an element of damages in a wrongful death action. Barcus v. Union Hospital Ass'n (Ohio Com.Pl. 1965) 14 Ohio Misc. 168, 236 N.E.2d 232, 43 O.O.2d 407.

Funeral and burial expenses incurred by a surviving spouse for the funeral and burial of his wife, who has sustained a fatal injury by the wrongful act of a third person, are recoverable in a direct action by the husband, on the ground that it is the husband's duty to provide for the funeral and burial of his wife; a plaintiff's petition therefor states a good cause of action; the expenses incurred thereby are not regarded as a pecuniary loss to the wife's estate or recoverable under the wrongful death statute; and a demurrer to plaintiff's petition is not well taken. Moss v. Hirzel Canning Co. (Wood 1955) 100 Ohio App. 509, 137 N.E.2d 440, 60 O.O. 397.

Expenses for hospital, doctor and funeral bills are not expenses for pecuniary injuries to the beneficiaries and by virtue of section are not allowable as part of damages in an action for wrongful death. Sprung v. E.I. Dupont De Nemours & Co. (Franklin 1939) 34 N.E.2d 41, 30 Ohio Law Abs. 278, 16 O.O. 352, 16 O.O. 364, appeal dismissed 136 Ohio St. 94, 23 N.E.2d 947, 16 O.O. 368.

In an action for wrongful death brought under this and preceding section, the funeral expenses of the decedent, not being a pecuniary injury to any of the specified beneficiaries, are not recoverable. (Superseded by statute in 1969 S 104, eff. 11–21–69.) Gaus v. Pennsylvania R. Co. (Allen 1937) 56 Ohio App. 299, 10 N.E.2d 635, 25 Ohio Law Abs. 24, 9 O.O. 389. Death ⇨ 84

Funeral expenses constitute a part of the pecuniary loss of a husband whose wife was killed in an accident at a railroad crossing, as they cannot be recovered by her administrator in an action under RS 6134. Cincinnati, H. & D. Ry. v. Taylor (Ohio Cir. 1905) 17 Ohio C.D. 757, 3 Ohio Law Rep. 30.

The limits of liability for death of one person contained in policies of uninsured motorist insurance in a clear, conspicuous, and unambiguous manner is valid and enforceable under the provisions of RC 3937.18 and 2125.02. Berleman v. State Farm Mut. Auto. Ins. Co. (Hamilton 1992) 76 Ohio App.3d 81, 600 N.E.2d 1145.

Funeral expenses are not recoverable in an action brought by a widower, as administrator, for damages on account of the wrongful death of his late wife. Harry v Seibel, 29 NP(NS) 82 (CP, Montgomery 1932).

6. —— Valuation; apportionment, damages

Trial court's finding that decedent's sister suffered loss of her only brother and that they had shared close relationship was sufficient to support distribution of wrongful death settlement proceeds equally among sister and decedent's wife and son. In Re Estate of Steigerwald (Ohio App. 5 Dist., Tuscarawas, 07-13-2004) No. 2003-AP-10-0079, 2004-Ohio-3834, 2004 WL 1615851, Unreported. Death ⇨ 101

Insurance companies may limit all claims arising out of one bodily injury to a single per-person limit, including wrongful death claims. Clark v. Scarpelli (Ohio App. 2 Dist., Montgomery, 12-17-1999) No. 17883, 1999 WL 1206662, Unreported, motion to certify allowed 88 Ohio St.3d 1500, 727 N.E.2d 923, affirmed 91 Ohio St.3d 271, 744 N.E.2d 719, 2001-Ohio-39, reconsideration denied 91 Ohio St.3d 1530, 747 N.E.2d 254.

In a wrongful death matter, failure to instruct the jury on comparative negligence is error where evidence suggests that the decedent, despite her husband's requesting her to do so, declined to have a biopsy performed, and that her physician had explained the potential risk if the lump was malignant; these circumstances, coupled with the deceased's ten month delay in returning to the doctor's office, were sufficient to create a factual issue from which reasonable minds might reach the conclusion that the decedent was negligent as well. Ponti v. Erieside Clinic, Inc. (Ohio App. 11 Dist., Lake, 03-17-1995) No. 93-L-205, 1995 WL 237063, Unreported.

Provision of professional liability policy which made the limit for each claim the limit of liability for all damages because of all claims or suits first made during the policy period because of injury to or death of any one person was a limit of liability provision, rather than a consolidation clause; the provision did not consolidate into one claim all claims recognized as lawful under the wrongful-death statute. Katz v. Ohio Ins. Guar. Assn. (Ohio, 08-18-2004) 103 Ohio St.3d 4, 812 N.E.2d 1266, 2004-Ohio-4109. Insurance ⇐ 2281(2)

Automobile liability insurers must include language within their policies of insurance that clearly and unambiguously consolidates all individual wrongful death claims arising out of any one person's bodily injury into a single claim to limit all wrongful death damages to a single per-person policy limit. Clark v. Scarpelli (Ohio, 04-11-2001) 91 Ohio St.3d 271, 744 N.E.2d 719, 2001-Ohio-39, reconsideration denied 91 Ohio St.3d 1530, 747 N.E.2d 254. Insurance ⇐ 2756(3)

Automobile liability insurance policy clearly and unambiguously limited all losses that resulted from insured's death to a single per-person policy limit; inclusion of phrases "loss of consortium" and "injury to the relationship" did not render provision ambiguous and encompassed all derivative claims, including claims for wrongful death. Clark v. Scarpelli (Ohio, 04-11-2001) 91 Ohio St.3d 271, 744 N.E.2d 719, 2001-Ohio-39, reconsideration denied 91 Ohio St.3d 1530, 747 N.E.2d 254. Insurance ⇐ 2756(3)

Damage award of $75,000 to plaintiff whose brother's death from seizure was found to have been proximately caused by negligence of state agency in failing to check whether he was properly taking his medication was not so inadequate as to shock the conscience, and thus would not be disturbed; plaintiff's compensable damages, aside from funeral expenses, were limited to loss of society and mental anguish, and those noneconomic damages were not subject to straightforward mathematical calculation. Hitch v. Ohio Dept. of Mental Health (Ohio App. 10 Dist., 09-24-1996) 114 Ohio App.3d 229, 683 N.E.2d 38. Death ⇐ 98

Each insured presumed to have been damaged as result of wrongful death claim may, to extent of damages, collect up to per person limits of tort-feasor's liability policy; regardless of number of insureds, total amount collected by insureds may not exceed tort-feasor's per accident liability coverage. Anderson v. Hartford Underwriters Ins. Co. (Ohio App. 8 Dist., 08-08-1994) 96 Ohio App.3d 341, 645 N.E.2d 75. Insurance ⇐ 2756(3)

Under uninsured motorist (UM) policy providing $100,000 per person and $300,000 per occurrence coverage, each of two insured daughters of insured who was killed in accident with uninsured motorist was entitled to recover up to $100,000 per person limits on their wrongful death claims, and survivorship claim for pain and suffering experienced by insured from time of her injury until time of death was also subject to coverage up to $100,000. Anderson v. Hartford Underwriters Ins. Co. (Ohio App. 8 Dist., 08-08-1994) 96 Ohio App.3d 341, 645 N.E.2d 75. Insurance ⇐ 2796

While some of damages recoverable for bodily injury and wrongful death claims, such as medical expenses, lost wages, and funeral expenses, are objective in nature and are directly related to identifiable monetary loss, others such as pain and suffering, loss of society, and mental anguish, are subjective in nature in that they are less easily quantifiable, less tangible, or unliquidated. Betz v. Timken Mercy Med. Ctr. (Ohio App. 5 Dist., 07-25-1994) 96 Ohio App.3d 211, 644 N.E.2d 1058, appeal not allowed 71 Ohio St.3d 1436, 643 N.E.2d 142, reconsideration denied 71 Ohio St.3d 1467, 644 N.E.2d 1389. Damages ⇐ 30

Each person who is presumed to have been damaged as result of another's wrongful death may, to the extent of his or her damages, recover under tort-feasor's liability policy up to its per person limits, subject to any per accident limits; liability policy provisions which purport to make all damages suffered from any one wrongful death subject to one "each person" policy limit are unenforceable. Newman v. United Ohio Ins. Co. (Ohio 1994) 68 Ohio St.3d 170, 624 N.E.2d 728, reconsideration denied 69 Ohio St.3d 1204, 631 N.E.2d 157. Insurance ⇐ 2756(3)

Trial court is not required by statute to provide for or approve funeral and burial expenses in wrongful death settlement, in light of plain language of statute which renders discretionary whether to allocate settlement funds for such expenses. In re Estate of Craig (Butler 1993) 89 Ohio App.3d 80, 623 N.E.2d 620. Death ⇐ 101

Probate court did not abuse its discretion in refusing to allocate funds from wrongful death settlement to pay for funeral and burial expenses of victim of automobile accident, in light of probate court's express reliance on valid court order requiring driver to pay funeral and burial expenses as part of driver's sentence for vehicular homicide. In re Estate of Craig (Butler 1993) 89 Ohio App.3d 80, 623 N.E.2d 620. Death ⇐ 101

Settlement funds recovered by administrator of estate in wrongful death action for exclusive distribution to statutory beneficiaries were not assets of automobile accident victim's estate and, thus, probate court had no obligation to allocate portion of proceeds to intestate estate for either general claims against estate or potential survivor claims, even if administrator had executed valid release of accident victim's potential survivor claim against driver. In re Estate of Craig (Butler 1993) 89 Ohio App.3d 80, 623 N.E.2d 620. Death ⇐ 101

The limitation of underinsured motorist coverage when the underinsured motorist provision tracks the limits of liability and the policy unambiguously sets forth the limitation is permissible where the policy uses the language "due to" bodily injury to limit coverage. Yearling v. State Farm Ins. Co. (Franklin 1992) 76 Ohio App.3d 559, 602 N.E.2d 434, motion overruled 65 Ohio St.3d 1420, 598 N.E.2d 1171.

An insurer may be liable in a wrongful death action payable under the terms of an uninsured motorist endorsement up to the per person limits of the policy to each party entitled to share in the proceeds of a wrongful death action; the extent of the insurer's liability is governed by the per person limits of coverage, not the per occurrence limits. Nilsen v. Nationwide Mut. Ins. Co. (Miami 1990) 64 Ohio App.3d 563, 582 N.E.2d 38, motion overruled 53 Ohio St.3d 706, 558 N.E.2d 61.

Statute requiring court to subtract certain collateral benefits from compensatory damage award received by plaintiff in wrongful death verdict limits amount of damages recoverable by plaintiff in wrongful death action in violation of Ohio Constitution. Samuels v. Coil Bar Corp. (Ohio Com.Pl. 1991) 61 Ohio Misc.2d 407, 579 N.E.2d 558. Damages ⇐ 59

Automobile liability policy may apply single limit to separate claims arising out of single bodily injury provided policy limitation tracks corresponding limitation on liability coverage and is unambiguously stated. State Farm Auto. Ins. Co. v. Rose (Ohio 1991) 61 Ohio St.3d 528, 575 N.E.2d 459. Insurance ⇐ 2756(3)

An automobile liability insurance policy may apply a single limit to separate claims arising out of a single bodily injury, provided the policy limitation tracks the corresponding limitation on liability coverage and is unambiguously stated. State Farm Auto. Ins. Co. v. Rose (Ohio 1991) 61 Ohio St.3d 528, 575 N.E.2d 459. Insurance ⇐ 2756(3)

Each person entitled to recover damages pursuant to RC 2125.02 for wrongful death has a separate claim and such separate claims may not be made subject to the single-person limit of liability in a tortfeasor's liability insurance policy. Cincinnati Ins. Co. v. Phillips (Ohio 1990) 52 Ohio St.3d 162, 556 N.E.2d 1150.

An automobile liability insurance provision that limits coverage for all damages arising out of bodily injury, including death, sustained by one person to a single limit of liability is a valid restriction. Burris v. Grange Mut. Companies (Ohio 1989) 46 Ohio St.3d 84, 545 N.E.2d 83, rehearing denied 46 Ohio St.3d 717, 546 N.E.2d 1335, rehearing denied 53 Ohio St.3d 718, 560 N.E.2d 779. Insurance ⇐ 2756(3)

A probate court exercising jurisdiction granted by RC 2125.02(C) to approve a wrongful death settlement by the personal representative of the decedent has limited plenary jurisdiction under RC 2101.24 to construe a policy of liability insurance for the purpose of determining the amount of insurance coverage available to settle the wrongful death claim. Burris v. Grange Mut. Companies (Ohio 1989) 46 Ohio St.3d 84, 545 N.E.2d 83, rehearing denied 46 Ohio St.3d 717, 546 N.E.2d 1335, rehearing denied 53 Ohio St.3d 718, 560 N.E.2d 779. Courts ⇐ 198

The law of Ohio is well-settled that an injured party is entitled to only one satisfaction for his injuries "and that receipt of full compensation from one of several persons whose concurrent acts of negligence are the basis of a suit for damages for personal injuries releases all." Seifert v. Burroughs (Ohio 1988) 38 Ohio St.3d 108, 526 N.E.2d 813. Release ⇐ 29(1)

Verdicts of 2.5 million dollars for wrongful death and one million dollars for survivorship in wrongful death action against hospital were not result of jury passion or prejudice, where jury had opportunity to return punitive damage award and did not. Duren v. Suburban Community Hosp. (Ohio Com.Pl. 1985) 24 Ohio Misc.2d 25, 495 N.E.2d 51, 24 O.B.R. 450. New Trial ⇐ 77(2)

Survivorship award of $1,000,000 against hospital for pain and suffering of decedent who had been left unattended for several hours in hospital was excessive to extent it exceeded $500,000. Duren v. Suburban Community Hosp. (Ohio Com.Pl. 1985) 24 Ohio Misc.2d 25, 495 N.E.2d 51, 24 O.B.R. 450. Death ⇐ 99(2)

In its legal sense to support award of punitive damages, "malice" does not necessarily signal ill will to particular individual, but denotes that condition of the mind which is manifested by the intentional doing of wrongful act without just cause or excuse; hence, the law implies malice where one causes injury to another in an unlawful manner. Robinson v. Parker–Hannifin Corp. (Ohio Com.Pl. 1982) 4 Ohio Misc.2d 6, 447 N.E.2d 781, 4 O.B.R. 257. Damages ☞ 91.5(1)

The jury in a wrongful death action is to consider the gross income of a decedent rather than the net income after taxes, and thus it is improper for the trial court to instruct the jury that its award is not subject to federal income taxes or that in calculating any loss based on future earnings of decedent, the jury should deduct federal income taxes from those earnings. Terveer v. Baschnagel (Franklin 1982) 3 Ohio App.3d 312, 445 N.E.2d 264, 3 O.B.R. 365.

RC 2125.01, which provides right of action for death caused by wrongful act in another state "for which a right to maintain an action and recover damages is given by a statute of such other state," does not require application of that state's limitation of amount of damages recoverable. Fox v. Morrison Motor Freight, Inc. (Ohio 1971) 25 Ohio St.2d 193, 267 N.E.2d 405, 54 O.O.2d 301, certiorari denied 91 S.Ct. 2254, 403 U.S. 931, 29 L.Ed.2d 710.

In action brought in Ohio under RC 2125.01, by Ohio administrator of estate of Ohio resident who was killed in motor vehicle collision in another state, where there was no citizen or resident of that state involved in collision, and there is no issue of liability, Ohio has all substantial governmental interests and law of Ohio is determinative of damages recoverable. Fox v. Morrison Motor Freight, Inc. (Ohio 1971) 25 Ohio St.2d 193, 267 N.E.2d 405, 54 O.O.2d 301, certiorari denied 91 S.Ct. 2254, 403 U.S. 931, 29 L.Ed.2d 710.

As to the issue of excessiveness of a jury verdict, a reviewing court must subscribe to the sensible rule that it is not to substitute its judgment for that of the jury when there is sufficient evidence before the jury to resolve the issue. Diener v. White Consol. Industries, Inc. (Mahoning 1968) 15 Ohio App.2d 172, 239 N.E.2d 421, 44 O.O.2d 301. Appeal And Error ☞ 1004(9)

Damages of $10,000 for death of eleven year old boy struck by truck held not manifestly against the weight of the evidence. Crider v. Columbus Plastic Products, Inc. (Franklin 1956) 190 N.E.2d 63, 90 Ohio Law Abs. 605. Death ☞ 99(3)

On the evidence, $10,000 verdict in wrongful death action for death of eighteen year old watchmaker was not excessive. Flory v. New York Cent. R. Co. (Ohio 1959) 170 Ohio St. 185, 163 N.E.2d 902, 10 O.O.2d 126.

An administrator may bring an action for recovery of funeral expenses against one whose wrongful act is alleged to have caused the decedent's death. Hunter v. McKinney (Ohio Com.Pl. 1951) 101 N.E.2d 810, 69 Ohio Law Abs. 237, 46 O.O. 17.

Where an action for wrongful death of a minor child is brought for benefit of his parents and his brothers and sisters as beneficiaries, court should instruct jury as to considerations to be applied to each in fixing amount of any damage award. Karr v. Sixt (Ohio 1946) 146 Ohio St. 527, 67 N.E.2d 331, 33 O.O. 14. Death ☞ 104(5)

$14,000 damages for death of plumber, forty-two years, earning $1,500 yearly, and sole support of wife and two children, held not excessive. Ohio Power Co. v. Fittro (Hardin 1930) 36 Ohio App. 186, 173 N.E. 33, 8 Ohio Law Abs. 617, 32 Ohio Law Rep. 227. Death ☞ 99(4)

A verdict of $1.00 for death of young, able-bodied man held so inadequate as to demand a new trial; such verdict indicating a compromise by the jury instead of a decision of the issue submitted to them. Greer v. Board of Com'rs of Knox County (Ohio App. 1927) 33 Ohio App. 539, 169 N.E. 709, 27 Ohio Law Rep. 53.

$1 for death of young, able-bodied man held so inadequate as to require new trial. Greer v. Board of Com'rs of Knox County (Ohio App. 1927) 33 Ohio App. 539, 169 N.E. 709, 27 Ohio Law Rep. 53. Death ☞ 98; New Trial ☞ 75(5)

The law giving the right to recover damages for unlawful death, not providing any rule to determine the amount of damages recoverable, except that "the jury may give such damages as it may think proportioned to the pecuniary injury resulting from such death," the jury may use their own experience in the conduct of human affairs in arriving at the amount of their verdict, based upon the facts established. Minglewood Coal & Ice Co. v. Carson (Wayne 1928) 31 Ohio App. 237, 166 N.E. 237.

In actions for wrongful death, there are no definite standards for determining the amount which the beneficiaries might reasonably expect to receive, and the amount is purely matter of opinion, and in no sense a matter of computation. Chester Park Co. v. Schulte (Ohio 1929) 120 Ohio St. 273, 166 N.E. 186, 7 Ohio Law Abs. 221, 29 Ohio Law Rep. 6.

In action for death of minor for benefit of heirs and next of kin, failure of instruction on damages to exclude any earnings minor might have made before arriving at twenty-one years of age was not erroneous, notwithstanding that action was not for exclusive benefit of parents. John Shillito Co. v. Shanley (Hamilton 1926) 21 Ohio App. 12, 153 N.E. 102, 4 Ohio Law Abs. 750.

In an action for wrongful death, it is error to permit the plaintiff, the parent of deceased to give his opinion as to the value of his child's services to him and his family; that being a question for the jury on the evidence. Cincinnati Traction Co. v. Stephens (Ohio 1906) 75 Ohio St. 171, 79 N.E. 235, 4 Ohio Law Rep. 504, 4 Ohio Law Rep. 508. Evidence ☞ 487

In arriving at the total amount of damages in wrongful death cases, the jury should consider the pecuniary injury to each separate beneficiary and add the sums together. Wolf v. Lake Erie & W.R. Co. (Ohio 1896) 55 Ohio St. 517, 37 W.L.B. 23, 45 N.E. 708.

The apportionment of damages in a wrongful death suit is of no concern to the negligent party against whom damages are recovered, and where instructions are given to the jury to consider the value of a child's services to its father, mother and next of kin and the father is the only one with a pecuniary interest in such services, the jury should allow the full value for such services, and not suppose that the value is multiplied by the number of beneficiaries. Toledo Railways & Light Co. v. Wettstein (Ohio Cir. 1908) 23 Ohio C.D. 15, 14 Ohio C.C.(N.S.) 441, affirmed 79 Ohio St. 439, 87 N.E. 1142, 6 Ohio Law Rep. 518.

The measure of damages in a wrongful death suit under RS 6135 is the reasonable expectancy of what the family or next of kin might have received from the decedent and not the amount it is reasonably certain they would have received. New York, C. & St. L. Ry. Co. v. Roe (Ohio Cir. 1903) 15 Ohio C.D. 628, 4 Ohio C.C.(N.S.) 284, affirmed 73 Ohio St. 382, 78 N.E. 1133, 3 Ohio Law Rep. 484.

In an action for wrongful death brought about by a fall on a defective sidewalk, where the deceased was a frail sixty-eight year old woman suffering from organic heart disease and from the consequences of a previous fall, a verdict of $2500.00 is excessive. Bond Hill v. Atkinson (Ohio Cir. 1898) 9 Ohio C.D. 185.

In passing upon a verdict under the wrongful death statute, the court has no right to apply to it any rule from any mortality tables; the jury should give such sum as they deem reasonable in proportion to the pecuniary injury of the next of kin, and it is not the intention of the statute that they use such mathematical tables. Toledo Consol. St. Ry. Co. v. Mammet (Ohio Cir. 1895) 6 Ohio C.D. 244, 2 Ohio Dec. 532.

In an action for wrongful death, a request for special charges that the jury apportion the damages among the beneficiaries is properly refused; the probate court has plenary powers to determine all questions of distribution. Cincinnati Traction Co. v. Room (Ohio Super. 1905) 16 Ohio Dec. 101, 3 Ohio Law Rep. 36.

A county's negligent placement of signs warning of a bridge closing will not prevent the jury in a wrongful death action from considering the contributory negligence of a drunken motorcyclist who crashed through a barricade at eighty-three miles per hour. Cravens v. County of Wood, Ohio (C.A.6 (Ohio) 1988) 856 F.2d 753.

A wrongful death award must be reduced, under Ohio law, by the percentage of responsibility attributed to the plaintiff's decedent, but no reduction of an award based upon an intentional tort will be made. Molton v. City of Cleveland (C.A.6 (Ohio) 1988) 839 F.2d 240, certiorari denied 109 S.Ct. 1345, 489 U.S. 1068, 103 L.Ed.2d 814.

Trial court properly entered judgment in wrongful death action by estate of university student shot by university security guard in which remittitur was required and accepted. Jones v. Wittenberg University (C.A.6 (Ohio) 1976) 534 F.2d 1203, 3 O.O.3d 311.

Under Ohio law, $100,000 award for wrongful death of 67–year–old housewife who had life expectancy of 14.6 years, whose husband had life expectancy of 9.2 years, and whose attendance upon her children involved both family members moving into her home and her moving into theirs, often for extended periods of time, was not excessive. Blasky v. Wheatley Trucking, Inc. (C.A.6 (Ohio) 1973) 482 F.2d 497. Death ☞ 99(4)

Under Ohio wrongful death statute, damage award of $3,500,000 was excessive; despite evidence of loss of society and mental anguish, amount awarded for such items, $2,750,000, was unreasonable considering lack of evidence that despair and anguish of family prevented them from gathering themselves together and continuing on with their lives, or evidence that psychological help was needed or sought or that any member of the family had difficulty with dealing with the ordinary demands of life. Urseth v. City of Dayton (S.D.Ohio 1987) 680 F.Supp. 1150. Death ☞ 99(1)

Ohio law will be applied in determining the measure of damages for wrongful death in an action against the United States. Wasilko v. U. S. (N.D.Ohio 1967) 300 F.Supp. 573, 50 O.O.2d 290, affirmed 412 F.2d 859. United States ⟶ 78(14)

A separate award for funeral and burial expenses pursuant to an action for wrongful death under RC 2125.02 is not subject to the comparative negligence reduction formula set forth in RC 2315.19. Amick v Mitchell, No. CA–1892 (5th Dist Ct App, Tuscarawas, 7–5–85).

RC 2125.02(B) is not retrospective. Lawrence v Erie Insurance Group, 5 OBR 536 (App, Franklin 1983).

Where the next of kin was an invalid father, and the decedent was a son who earned $325 a month, and was accustomed to give to his father $100 to $125 each month together with other help, and the father's expectancy of life was 13.82 years, a verdict of $12,000 was not excessive and requires no intervention by a reviewing court. Burns–Bowe Baking Co v Pakos, 9 Abs 262, 32 LR 593 (App, Cuyahoga 1930).

7. Evidence

Even if the issue was properly preserved for appellate review, evidence that mentioned two other fatalities resulting from the same vehicular accident that killed decedent was relevant and was not unfairly prejudicial, warranting admission of the evidence in wrongful death action brought by decedent's estate; one of the other passengers was plaintiff's husband and his death was relevant to a determination of damages, evidence of the other fatalities was not used to arouse the jurors' emotions, and jury received limiting instructions on the evidence. Conway v. Dravenstott (Ohio App. 3 Dist., Crawford, 09-18-2006) No. 3-06-05, 2006-Ohio-4840, 2006 WL 2664241, Unreported. Death ⟶ 60

Any probative value of evidence that decedent was killed by a drunk driver was outweighed by danger of unfair prejudice to insurer in action brought by decedent's grandson under his underinsured motorist coverage for the wrongful death of decedent in car accident; jury might have been more inclined to award damages to grandson out of moral outrage or be confused by the issues if such evidence had been admitted. Hiner v. Nationwide Mut. Ins. Co. (Ohio App. 5 Dist., Stark, 12-13-2005) No. 2005CA00034, 2005-Ohio-6660, 2005 WL 3446322, Unreported. Evidence ⟶ 146

Second decedent did not negligently cause the death of first decedent while committing suicide by carbon monoxide poisoning, and thus second decedent's estate was not liable based on wrongful death theory to first decedent's estate for first decedent's death, where coroner could not determine that cause of second decedent's death was suicide, and it could not be determined from other evidence that second decedent had intended to commit suicide by leaving motor vehicle running. Fuerst v. Ford (Ohio App. 3 Dist., Allen, 03-29-2004) No. 1-03-81, 2004-Ohio-1510, 2004 WL 603521, Unreported. Death ⟶ 17

Evidence in wrongful death action supported conclusions that patient at psychiatric facility had a close relationship with his family, provided services to his family, which included general maintenance, plumbing, roofing, carpentry, and child-care, and would have continued to provide services and financial support in the future. Bhola v. Northcoast Behavioral Health Care Ctr. (Ohio Ct.Cl., 02-04-2004) 127 Ohio Misc.2d 10, 804 N.E.2d 1050, 2004-Ohio-648. Death ⟶ 86(2); Death ⟶ 87

Security company that owner of manufacturing plant hired to guard its property was "independent contractor," for purposes of determining owner's potential liability for security guard's alleged negligence in fatally shooting individual who entered parking lot, where owner specified only the result to be accomplished, i.e., deterrence of vandals and thieves, but left details of how to accomplish result to company except for requiring periodic patrolling, and company hired, paid, and assigned guards and was responsible for their training and certification. Pusey v. Bator (Ohio, 02-27-2002) 94 Ohio St.3d 275, 762 N.E.2d 968, 2002-Ohio-795, appeal after new trial 2005-Ohio-4691, 2005 WL 2174007. Labor And Employment ⟶ 30

Health care providers, whose alleged negligent failure to diagnose and treat patient's cancer formed basis of wrongful death action by spouse who married patient after patient was diagnosed with cancer, would be permitted to present evidence concerning the couple's relationship and knowledge of patient's condition, along with other relevant facts, to dispute any claim for damages raised by spouse. DeVine v. Blanchard Valley Med. Assoc., Inc. (Ohio Com.Pl., 07-01-1999) 103 Ohio Misc.2d 40, 725 N.E.2d 366. Death ⟶ 69

Statute allowing party to wrongful death action to present evidence that surviving spouse of decedent has remarried does not limit defendant to presenting only evidence of the remarriage; purpose of statute is to permit jury to consider not only the fact of remarriage, but also the circumstances of the remarriage which trial court determines are relevant to assessing surviving spouse's losses. Pena v. Northeast Ohio Emergency Affiliates, Inc. (Ohio App. 9 Dist., 12-20-1995) 108 Ohio App.3d 96, 670 N.E.2d 268, dismissed, appeal not allowed 75 Ohio St.3d 1494, 664 N.E.2d 1291. Death ⟶ 60

Awards of $1 plus $5,970.42 in funeral expenses for wrongful death of expectant mother at hospital, and $1 plus $90 in funeral expenses for wrongful death of unborn child, were not sustained by weight of the evidence and were inadequate, thus warranting new trial; while jury could consider husband's remarriage within three months of wife's death in determining his damages, it should not have considered remarriage in determining the amount of damages suffered by decedent's children, parents, and next of kin as result of her death, or the damages the unborn child's beneficiaries suffered because of his death. Pena v. Northeast Ohio Emergency Affiliates, Inc. (Ohio App. 9 Dist., 12-20-1995) 108 Ohio App.3d 96, 670 N.E.2d 268, dismissed, appeal not allowed 75 Ohio St.3d 1494, 664 N.E.2d 1291. Death ⟶ 98

Evidence that as result of medical malpractice patient had lost 20 to 30 percent chance of survival was insufficient to allow recovery in wrongful death action based on medical malpractice. Schlachet v. Cleveland Clinic Found. (Ohio App. 8 Dist., 05-30-1995) 104 Ohio App.3d 160, 661 N.E.2d 259, appeal not allowed 74 Ohio St.3d 1422, 655 N.E.2d 741. Health ⟶ 822(3)

In action for wrongful death where medical malpractice is alleged as proximate cause of death and plaintiff's evidence indicates that failure to diagnose injury prevented patient from opportunity to be operated on which eliminated any chance of patient's survival, issue of proximate cause can be submitted to jury only if there is sufficient evidence showing that with proper diagnosis, treatment, and surgery, patient probably would have survived. Schlachet v. Cleveland Clinic Found. (Ohio App. 8 Dist., 05-30-1995) 104 Ohio App.3d 160, 661 N.E.2d 259, appeal not allowed 74 Ohio St.3d 1422, 655 N.E.2d 741. Health ⟶ 826

The diary of an unwed mother-to-be who dies following surgery before the birth of the child is properly admitted in a malpractice action to show that the woman was anxiously awaiting the birth of her child. Shoemaker v. Crawford (Franklin 1991) 78 Ohio App.3d 53, 603 N.E.2d 1114, motion allowed 63 Ohio St.3d 1473, 591 N.E.2d 243, cause dismissed 64 Ohio St.3d 1434, 595 N.E.2d 943.

Documents governing personal representative's psychologist-patient relationship were potentially relevant in wrongful death action, where representative sought damages for mental anguish on behalf of beneficiaries of wrongful death action, including herself in her capacity as beneficiary, and, thus, the psychologist's records could arguably be calculated to lead to discovery of admissible evidence with which defendant could rebut representative's presumption of damages for mental anguish. Colling v. Franklin Cty. Children Serv. (Franklin 1991) 76 Ohio App.3d 736, 603 N.E.2d 338, dismissed, jurisdictional motion overruled 63 Ohio St.3d 1467, 590 N.E.2d 1267. Pretrial Procedure ⟶ 407

Wrongful death plaintiff, suing electric utility for failure to timely repair downed wire, was not entitled to instruction on punitive damages absent sufficient evidence from which reasonable minds could differ as to whether utility consciously disregarded injured party's rights or safety. Wilburn v. Cleveland Elec. Illum. Co. (Cuyahoga 1991) 74 Ohio App.3d 401, 599 N.E.2d 301. Death ⟶ 104(4)

In a suit against an emergency room nurse, physician, the physician's employer, and the hospital to recover for the wrongful death of a two-year-old following a visit to the emergency room, a trial court properly denies the employer's and the physician's motion for a directed verdict on the issue of proximate cause where the plaintiff presents substantial competent evidence upon which reasonable minds could differ, including expert testimony that the physician was negligent and that his failure was the proximate cause of the child's death, notwithstanding the defendants' assertion that the expert testimony was contradicted on cross-examination; the court finds no preclusive contradiction where the expert was asked hypothetical questions different from the facts in the case. Ramage v. Central Ohio Emergency Serv., Inc. (Ohio 1992) 64 Ohio St.3d 97, 592 N.E.2d 828.

Expert testimony is required to establish the prevailing standard of care, breach of that standard, and whether the negligence was the proximate cause of the injury where the plaintiff alleges that the emergency room health professionals failed to properly diagnose, treat, and care for a two-year-old girl who was brought to a hospital emergency room shaking and vomiting with a high temperature and other signs of distress, and was then discharged 75 minutes later after administration of Tylenol and fluids and a decrease in her temperature, and died at home less than two hours after discharge; expert testimony is required where the issues involve the professional skill and judgment of the emergency room professionals, which matters are not within the common knowledge and experience of laypersons, and where the claim is not merely one of ordinary negligence. Ramage v. Central Ohio Emergency Serv., Inc. (Ohio 1992) 64 Ohio St.3d 97, 592 N.E.2d 828.

In a suit against an emergency room nurse, physician, the physician's employer, and the hospital to recover for the wrongful death of a two-year-old girl following a visit to the emergency room, a trial court does not err in permitting the plaintiff's counsel to inquire of his expert witness whether the X-rays of the girl taken at the hospital, which the expert had not read prior to trial, were consistent with his opinion that the girl should not have been discharged from the emergency room or in permitting the expert's response which made passing reference to the cause of death as small bowel obstruction, a theory of liability not revealed through discovery; the testimony does not present any new theory of liability, and the court did not permit the plaintiff to present any evidence that the defendant physician had breached any standard of care with respect to this theory of liability. Ramage v. Central Ohio Emergency Serv., Inc. (Ohio 1992) 64 Ohio St.3d 97, 592 N.E.2d 828.

In a suit against an emergency room nurse, physician, the physician's employer, and the hospital to recover for the wrongful death of a two-year-old following a visit to the emergency room, a plaintiff may, during the direct examination of its expert witness, inquire whether that expert agrees with the opinions expressed in a publication by the defendant's witnesses although the defendant chooses not to call the expert to testify at trial where (1) the passage from the book is not used as substantive evidence, (2) the passage from the book is used in anticipation of live testimony, and (3) the defendant's expert, the author of the book, was asked about the particular passage in his deposition filed by the plaintiff prior to trial. Ramage v. Central Ohio Emergency Serv., Inc. (Ohio 1992) 64 Ohio St.3d 97, 592 N.E.2d 828.

In a suit against an emergency room nurse, physician, the physician's employer, and the hospital to recover for the wrongful death of a two-year-old following a visit to the emergency room, a trial court properly denies the hospital's request to question its own witness as if on cross-examination on the alternative grounds that the witness was hostile or closely identified with the plaintiff because she is his sister where (1) the witness is also an employee of the hospital, (2) the witness was generally cooperative in answering questions posed by the hospital's counsel, (3) the trial court indicated that it would reconsider its ruling if the hospital established that the witness was hostile and the hospital neither requested reconsideration nor demonstrated hostility, (4) the hospital had ample opportunity to impeach the witness, and (5) the hospital was able to elicit the admission from the witness that her trial testimony regarding the care given at the hospital to the child differed from the testimony given at her deposition. Ramage v. Central Ohio Emergency Serv., Inc. (Ohio 1992) 64 Ohio St.3d 97, 592 N.E.2d 828.

In wrongful death action arising out of physician's alleged negligent failure to diagnose patient's lung cancer when it was curable, evidence of patient's husband's remarriage was properly admitted for the limited purpose of showing mitigation of losses such as companionship. Miller v. Marrocco (Hamilton 1989) 63 Ohio App.3d 293, 578 N.E.2d 834, motion overruled 45 Ohio St.3d 719, 545 N.E.2d 908. Death ⇨ 77

Although a physician in a malpractice action has stipulated his liability in proximately causing the decedent's death, he may properly present evidence in mitigation of damages that the decedent would have lived only a short time had her death not been accelerated by the physician's negligence. Miller v. Marrocco (Hamilton 1989) 63 Ohio App.3d 293, 578 N.E.2d 834, motion overruled 45 Ohio St.3d 719, 545 N.E.2d 908.

Evidence of a surviving spouse's remarriage may properly be admitted for the limited purpose of showing a mitigation of damages such as companionship in a wrongful death action. Miller v. Marrocco (Hamilton 1989) 63 Ohio App.3d 293, 578 N.E.2d 834, motion overruled 45 Ohio St.3d 719, 545 N.E.2d 908.

Evidence that plaintiff's decedent, an inmate at correctional institution, spat up blood in presence of nurses charged with her care and that incident was ignored, that plaintiff's decedent was refused assistance to obtain aspirin or to get to toilet when she appeared unable to assist herself, that correctional employees were told plaintiff's decedent was "faking" her illness, and that apparently critical condition of plaintiff's decedent was not monitored during day's proceeding or transportation to hospital where she died warranted jury instruction on punitive damages in suit by administrator of decedent's estate against city, correctional institution's superintendent, doctor, and nurses, and various other city officials; jury could infer from that evidence that defendants acted with actual malice. White v. Moody (Franklin 1988) 51 Ohio App.3d 16, 554 N.E.2d 115, motion allowed 39 Ohio St.3d 721, 534 N.E.2d 355, cause dismissed 40 Ohio St.3d 703, 534 N.E.2d 853. Damages ⇨ 215(1)

Wrongful death complaint stated cause of action when it alleged that defendant aided and abetted wrongful act that caused death. Burton v. DePew (Butler 1988) 47 Ohio App.3d 107, 547 N.E.2d 995. Death ⇨ 46

Where a board of township trustees erects a stop sign at a railroad crossing absent any statutory duty to do so, its later removal of the sign for failure to obtain prior approval from the department of transportation is irrelevant in a wrongful death action based on a train-motor vehicle collision. Mozena v. Consolidated Rail Corp. (Lorain 1988) 46 Ohio App.3d 9, 544 N.E.2d 937, motion overruled 41 Ohio St.3d 706, 534 N.E.2d 1211.

Where an action for wrongful death against a board of township trustees is based on the board's failure to provide pavement markings at a railroad crossing, and there is no evidence concerning the actual prevailing speed at the crossing or the feasibility of pavement markings at the crossing, it is error for a trial court to grant summary judgment in favor of the board of township trustees. Mozena v. Consolidated Rail Corp. (Lorain 1988) 46 Ohio App.3d 9, 544 N.E.2d 937, motion overruled 41 Ohio St.3d 706, 534 N.E.2d 1211.

In an action for wrongful death based on medical malpractice, there is no need to introduce evidence concerning the length of time the victim may have lived but for the malpractice; however, the defendant may introduce evidence showing that the victim would have survived only a short time in mitigation of damages. Taylor v. C. Lawrence Decker, M.D., Inc. (Hamilton 1986) 33 Ohio App.3d 118, 514 N.E.2d 754. Health ⇨ 826

A viable fetus which is negligently injured in its mother's womb and subsequently stillborn can be the basis for a wrongful death action pursuant to RC 2125.01. Werling v. Sandy (Ohio 1985) 17 Ohio St.3d 45, 476 N.E.2d 1053, 17 O.B.R. 37. Death ⇨ 15

In a wrongful death action, where it is claimed that the death was accelerated by the wrongful act of the defendant, recovery can be had only where it is shown by the evidence that death was accelerated by an appreciable period of time as a direct result of the wrongful act. Lopresti v. Community Traction Co. (Ohio 1954) 160 Ohio St. 480, 117 N.E.2d 2, 52 O.O. 359.

In an action for wrongful death resulting from injuries received while previous section was in force, a charge to the jury including the added beneficiaries provided for by amended section, whose respective pecuniary losses were matters for the consideration by the jury, is prejudicial error. City of Cincinnati v. Bachmann (Hamilton 1935) 51 Ohio App. 108, 199 N.E. 853, 19 Ohio Law Abs. 389, 3 O.O. 271.

In suit for wrongful death, excluding deceased's declaration made shortly after accident relating to manner he was injured held error. Hauer v. French Bros. Bauer Co. (Hamilton 1931) 43 Ohio App. 333, 183 N.E. 186, 11 Ohio Law Abs. 217, 36 Ohio Law Rep. 51. Death ⇨ 61; Evidence ⇨ 126(1)

Evidence in action for wrongful death of plumber held sufficient to show pecuniary loss or dependency of next of kin. Paul A. Sorg Paper Co. v. Hayes (Butler 1932) 43 Ohio App. 140, 182 N.E. 886, 12 Ohio Law Abs. 61. Death ⇨ 77

Charge to deny recovery for wrongful death if decedent's knowledge of defective floor equalled that of defendant, held properly refused as assuming decedent's knowledge of danger. Paul A. Sorg Paper Co. v. Hayes (Butler 1932) 43 Ohio App. 140, 182 N.E. 886, 12 Ohio Law Abs. 61. Death ⇨ 104(2); Negligence ⇨ 1745; Trial ⇨ 191(7)

Where, in an action for damages for wrongful death, there was a verdict for defendant, and plaintiff prosecutes error, and it appears that on trial before court and jury there was evidence tending to show actionable negligence on the part of the defendant, and the evidence does not show the decedent to be guilty of contributory negligence as a matter of law, the defendant in error is not entitled to an affirmance on the ground that the trial court should have directed a verdict in his favor. Fach v. Canton Yellow Cab Co. (Stark 1929) 36 Ohio App. 247, 173 N.E. 245, 9 Ohio Law Abs. 189. Appeal And Error ⇨ 1062.1; Trial ⇨ 134

In an action for wrongful death, any evidence which tends to show amount of pecuniary injuries sustained by beneficiaries of decedent or which tends to show that such beneficiaries received financial aid from deceased during his lifetime and that they would likely have continued to receive such aid had he lived, is competent; and, to show that such beneficiaries needed and would likely have received such aid, the circumstances, age, health, and means of support of beneficiary, if parent or next of kin of decedent, as well as age, health, disposition, and thrift of decedent, may be shown. Greer v. Board of Com'rs of Knox County (Ohio App. 1927) 33 Ohio App. 539, 169 N.E. 709, 27 Ohio Law Rep. 53.

In action for death of minor, charge by court on contributory negligence is not prejudicial to defendant. John Shillito Co. v. Shanley (Hamilton 1926) 21 Ohio App. 12, 153 N.E. 102, 4 Ohio Law Abs. 750. Appeal And Error ☞ 1033(5); Death ☞ 108

The doctrine of imputed evidence does not prevail and the negligence of a husband is not to be imputed to the wife in an action for wrongfully causing her death. Davis v. Guarnieri (Ohio 1887) 45 Ohio St. 470, 19 W.L.B. 204, 15 N.E. 350, 4 Am.St.Rep. 548.

It is not error for the court in instructing the jury to call attention to statutes which make it unlawful to sell a poisonous drug without labeling it "poison." Davis v. Guarnieri (Ohio 1887) 45 Ohio St. 470, 19 W.L.B. 204, 15 N.E. 350, 4 Am.St.Rep. 548.

Where the death of a wife is wrongly caused and an action has been brought to recover damages, evidence cannot be shown in mitigation of damages that the husband has remarried. Davis v. Guarnieri (Ohio 1887) 45 Ohio St. 470, 19 W.L.B. 204, 15 N.E. 350, 4 Am.St.Rep. 548.

In an action for wrongful death, the petition need not allege that the next of kin of the decedent have sustained pecuniary loss by his death; where the proper allegations are made under the statute it is presumed that nominal pecuniary damages at least were sustained by the next of kin, and the amount of the prayer is also a sufficient allegation of damages. Jackson Knife & Shear Co. v. Hathaway (Ohio Cir. 1903) 17 Ohio C.D. 745, 7 Ohio C.C.(N.S.) 242, affirmed 72 Ohio St. 623, 76 N.E. 1126, 2 Ohio Law Rep. 535.

Evidence of the subsequent repair of a defective sidewalk is admissible on cross-examination by the plaintiff after the contractor in charge of maintaining such sidewalk testifies that he inspected the sidewalk at the point in question and found no defects. Bond Hill v. Atkinson (Ohio Cir. 1898) 9 Ohio C.D. 185.

In a wrongful death suit, admissions by the deceased as to the manner in which the accident happened and as to her condition tending to show that the accident was not the cause of her death are admissible in such a case. Bond Hill v. Atkinson (Ohio Cir. 1898) 9 Ohio C.D. 185.

Negligence of a railway company in constructing one of its bridges is a question for the jury. Lake Shore & M.S.R. Co. v. Andrews (Ohio Cir. 1897) 8 Ohio C.D. 73, reversed 58 Ohio St. 426, 40 W.L.B. 45, 51 N.E. 26.

Evidence in a wrongful death action must show who the beneficiaries are, their circumstances, and the pecuniary loss sustained by each; no presumptions will be indulged. Cincinnati Traction Co. v. Moeller (Ohio Super. 1906) 17 Ohio Dec. 22.

Dying declarations of the deceased are not admissible in an action for wrongful death although the defendant admits killing the deceased; such declarations are admissible only in homicide prosecutions on grounds of policy. Cosgrove v. Schafer (Ohio Super. 1885) 15 W.L.B. 8.

Passenger ticket to seagoing vessel, the cover of which boldly and specifically alerted passenger that it contained a contractual limitation on the time to sue, provided reasonable notice of the liability limitation, as required to enforce the limitation against passenger's survivorship and wrongful death claims arising from death of passenger's mother aboard the vessel; although passenger and his mother received their tickets a few minutes prior to boarding, they retained the portion containing the notice and the limitation clause and could have perused it during and after the voyage. U.S. v. Miller (N.D.Ohio, 08-25-2006) 448 F.Supp.2d 860. Shipping ☞ 166(2)

Decedent's supplying minors with money, allowing them to visit on weekends, and allowing them to call him dad was not formal acknowledgment of child in probate court and could not be basis for children born out of wedlock to establish standing under Ohio Wrongful Death Statute. Martin v. Daily Express, Inc. (N.D.Ohio, 02-28-1995) 878 F.Supp. 91. Death ☞ 31(8)

In an action for the wrongful death of her husband, a plaintiff who has remarried is entitled to an order directing that she be referred to only by her former name and that opposing counsel be directed not to indicate the remarriage. Helmick v Netzley, 12 Misc 97, 229 NE(2d) 476, 40 OO(2d) 104 (CP 1967).

Evidence of the poverty of the widow and next of kin of the decedent is incompetent in a wrongful death action. Lake Shore & Michigan Southern Railway Co v Reynolds, 21 CC 402, 11 CD 701 (Lake 1900).

8. Joinder

Persons acting in loco parentis for child whose death has resulted from another's negligence are permitted to join in wrongful death suit only after establishing, by clear and convincing evidence, that: natural parents of child have disclaimed or abandoned parental rights to child; claimant has performed obligations of parenthood for a substantial period of time; child and claimant have held themselves out to be parent and child for substantial period of time; and relationship between child and claimant has been publicly recognized. Miller v. Boden (Ohio App. 3 Dist., 05-10-1995) 103 Ohio App.3d 73, 658 N.E.2d 809, appeal not allowed 74 Ohio St.3d 1409, 655 N.E.2d 187. Death ☞ 31(7); Death ☞ 44

Dismissal of decedent's personal injury claim for failure to timely substitute estate as party plaintiff did not affect necessarily joined claims for loss of consortium or wrongful death. Perry v. Eagle–Picher Industries, Inc. (Ohio 1990) 52 Ohio St.3d 168, 556 N.E.2d 484. Pretrial Procedure ☞ 693.1

Two distinct rights of action in wrongful death cases are recognized in Ohio, each maintainable by the personal representative of the deceased person—one for the exclusive, pecuniary benefit of the next of kin, and the other for the benefit of the estate. Moss v. Hirzel Canning Co. (Wood 1955) 100 Ohio App. 509, 137 N.E.2d 440, 60 O.O. 397. Death ☞ 32; Death ☞ 31(3.1)

An administrator's cause of action for pain and suffering of his decedent may not be joined with a cause of action for the wrongful death of the same decedent. Fielder v. Ohio Edison Co. (Ohio 1952) 158 Ohio St. 375, 109 N.E.2d 855, 35 A.L.R.2d 1365, 49 O.O. 265.

Where administrator brings action under section to recover for wrongful death of his decedent in an automobile collision, he acts as a trustee for sole benefit of decedent's next of kin; a counterclaim interposed in that action by defendant to recover for personal injuries sustained by defendant in same collision, presents a claim against estate of decedent; in such situation administrator acts in different capacities as to each cause of action, there is no mutuality of parties as required by rule governing counterclaims, and an order requiring counterclaim of defendant to be docketed as an independent action is proper. Epinger v. Wade (Summit 1943) 73 Ohio App. 231, 55 N.E.2d 679, 28 O.O. 358, affirmed 142 Ohio St. 460, 52 N.E.2d 852, 27 O.O. 397. Executors And Administrators ☞ 434(1.1)

In a diversity action, Ohio law controls the standard to be applied in determining the damages under its wrongful death statute. Blasky v. Wheatley Trucking, Inc. (C.A.6 (Ohio) 1973) 482 F.2d 497. Federal Courts ☞ 431

The Ohio wrongful death statute allows recovery only for pecuniary loss. Blasky v. Wheatley Trucking, Inc. (C.A.6 (Ohio) 1973) 482 F.2d 497.

9. Scope; action for benefit of heirs—In general

Jury award to decedent's estate of $1,824,522.60 was not influenced by passion or prejudice, in trial to determine damages for the wrongful death of car passenger who died after vehicular accident caused by defendant, despite admission of evidence as to two other fatalities that arose from the same vehicular accident; the evidence as to the other fatalities was not unfairly prejudicial, and the size of the award was not so disproportionate as to evidence prejudice. Conway v. Dravenstott (Ohio App. 3 Dist., Crawford, 09-18-2006) No. 3-06-05, 2006-Ohio-4840, 2006 WL 2664241, Unreported. Death ☞ 99(1)

Intentional tort claims brought against employer and employer's corporate parent in connection with employee's death in industrial accident amounted to wrongful death claims and were thus governed by wrongful death statute. Haga v. Albex Aluminum, Inc. (Ohio App. 5 Dist., Stark, 03-07-2005) No. 2003CA00312, 2005-Ohio-1059, 2005 WL 567449, Unreported. Death ☞ 7

Probate division of court of common pleas, through its exclusive jurisdiction to approve settlements in actions for wrongful death and to order distribution of settlement proceeds, rather than general division of court of common pleas, through its jurisdiction over declaratory judgment actions, had subject matter jurisdiction over action by decedent's daughter, brought after she had reached age of majority, alleging that settlement agreement in wrongful death action against physician and liability insurer, purportedly executed on her behalf by her mother, was void for fraud in the factum. Comer v. Bench (Ohio App. 2 Dist., Montgomery, 05-30-2003) No. CIV.A. 19229, 2003-Ohio-2821, 2003 WL 21267232, Unreported. Courts ☞ 472.4(2.1); Courts ☞ 472.5

A fund arising out of a wrongful death claim is not a part of the assets of the estate of the decedent; it is not property which belonged to the decedent in his lifetime, and the claim did not come into existence until his death. State ex rel. Goldberg v. Mahoning Cty. Probate Court (Ohio, 09-05-2001) 93 Ohio St.3d 160, 753 N.E.2d 192, 2001-Ohio-1297, reconsideration denied 93 Ohio St.3d 1464, 756 N.E.2d 1239. Executors And Administrators ☞ 51

Note 9

Statutory beneficiaries could not show that probate court's distribution of proceeds from wrongful death settlement for payment of attorney fees adversely affected their rights, considering that the probate court reviewed the application for attorney fees to determine reasonableness, and beneficiaries had no authority over the matter in determining reasonableness. In re Estate of Kenington (Ohio App. 12 Dist., Clermont, 05-19-2003) No. CA2002-01-005, 2003-Ohio-2549, 2003 WL 21135469, Unreported. Executors And Administrators ☞ 216(2)

In an action for wrongful death, the surviving statutory beneficiaries have the right to recover damages suffered by reason of the wrongful death of the decedent. Clark v. Scarpelli (Ohio, 04-11-2001) 91 Ohio St.3d 271, 744 N.E.2d 719, 2001-Ohio-39, reconsideration denied 91 Ohio St.3d 1530, 747 N.E.2d 254. Death ☞ 7

Each statutory wrongful death beneficiary's claim is considered separate and distinct from the claim of the estate, and from each other. Clark v. Scarpelli (Ohio, 04-11-2001) 91 Ohio St.3d 271, 744 N.E.2d 719, 2001-Ohio-39, reconsideration denied 91 Ohio St.3d 1530, 747 N.E.2d 254. Death ☞ 7

Wrongful death claimant who is a statutory beneficiary of an insured decedent, but not named insured under decedent's uninsured or underinsured motorist (UM/UIM) policy, may recover benefits under policy either individually or through administratrix of decedent's estate. Yepko v. State Farm Mut. Ins. Co. (Ohio, 09-24-1997) 79 Ohio St.3d 414, 683 N.E.2d 1090, 1997-Ohio-373. Insurance ☞ 3460

Attempt to avoid payment for valid wrongful death claims by narrowly defining who is "insured" is impermissible attempt to eliminate underinsured motorist (UIM) coverage where claim or claims of such persons arise from causes of action recognized by tort law. Holt v. Grange Mut. Cas. Co. (Ohio, 09-24-1997) 79 Ohio St.3d 401, 683 N.E.2d 1080, 1997-Ohio-375. Insurance ☞ 2774; Insurance ☞ 2780

Uninsurance/underinsurance motorist (UM/UIM) coverage provider's use of restrictive policy language defining "insured" is ineffectual to exclude from coverage claim of uncompensated wrongful death statutory beneficiary seeking to recover UM/UIM benefits, since correct focus for wrongful death recovery under decedent's policy of UM/UIM coverage is whether decedent was "insured"; abrogating *Thompson v Utomo* (Oct. 27, 1995), 1995 WL 628242; *Estate of Simone v. Nationwide Ins. Co.* (Nov. 3, 1994), Cuyahoga App. No. 67081, 1994 WL 613876; *Berleman v. State Farm Mut. Auto. Ins. Co.* (1992), 76 Ohio App.3d 81, 600 N.E.2d 1145. Holt v. Grange Mut. Cas. Co. (Ohio, 09-24-1997) 79 Ohio St.3d 401, 683 N.E.2d 1080, 1997-Ohio-375. Insurance ☞ 2780; Insurance ☞ 3460

Attempt of underinsured motorist (UIM) carrier to deny coverage for claims of insured's children, since they were not insureds, but sought benefits as statutory beneficiaries for insured's wrongful death, was invalid; obligation to provide coverage arose due to fact that insured suffered wrongful death, and carrier's attempted reliance on definition of "insured" was functionally equivalent of attempt to deny coverage to insured decedent. Holt v. Grange Mut. Cas. Co. (Ohio, 09-24-1997) 79 Ohio St.3d 401, 683 N.E.2d 1080, 1997-Ohio-375. Insurance ☞ 2780; Insurance ☞ 3460

Wrongful death claimants seeking recovery as statutory beneficiaries of insured need not be in privity with automobile insurer, i.e., they need not be insureds, in order to recover underinsured motorist (UIM) benefits; it is sufficient if insured decedent is in privity with insurer. Holt v. Grange Mut. Cas. Co. (Ohio, 09-24-1997) 79 Ohio St.3d 401, 683 N.E.2d 1080, 1997-Ohio-375. Insurance ☞ 3460

Wrongful death statute does not incorporate "heirship" into its provisions; in fact, beneficiaries may include relatives who would not be eligible to inherit under statute of descent and distribution. Brookbank v. Gray (Ohio, 01-17-1996) 74 Ohio St.3d 279, 658 N.E.2d 724, 1996-Ohio-135. Death ☞ 32

Wrongful death claim of automobile accident victim, whose spouse died in the accident, was separate from victim's claim for personal injuries and was not subject to single-person limit of liability in tort-feasor's automobile policy; therefore, at least three justiciable claims arose out of the accident: spouse's personal injury/survivorship claim, victim's personal injury claim, and wrongful death claim. Cincinnati Ins. Co. v. Phillips (Ohio 1990) 52 Ohio St.3d 162, 556 N.E.2d 1150. Insurance ☞ 2756(3)

Where, under the Ohio wrongful death statutes, one who is neither a natural nor an adoptive parent seeks to recover from a tortfeasor, such a claim will lie only where the following four tests are met by clear and convincing evidence: (1) the natural parents of the child have disclaimed or abandoned parental rights to the child; (2) the one claiming to be parent has performed the obligations of parenthood for a substantial period of time; (3) the child and the one claiming to be parent have held themselves out to be parent and child for a substantial period of time; and (4) the relationship between the child and the one claiming to be parent

has been publicly recognized. Lawson v. Atwood (Ohio 1989) 42 Ohio St.3d 69, 536 N.E.2d 1167, certiorari denied 110 S.Ct. 176, 493 U.S. 862, 107 L.Ed.2d 132. Death ☞ 31(7)

Each person entitled to recover damages pursuant to RC 2125.02 for wrongful death, and who is an insured under an underinsured motorist provision in an insurance policy, has a separate claim and such separate claims may not be made subject to the single person limit of liability in the underinsured motorist provision. Wood v. Shepard (Ohio 1988) 38 Ohio St.3d 86, 526 N.E.2d 1089. Insurance ☞ 2796

RC 2125.02 as amended by 1981 H 332, eff. 2-5-82, is remedial in nature as written and promulgated by the general assembly, and applies to all wrongful death actions tried in any forum on or after that date. French v. Dwiggins (Ohio 1984) 9 Ohio St.3d 32, 458 N.E.2d 827, 9 O.B.R. 123. Death ☞ 9

There is no common law cause of action for wrongful death. Keaton v. Ribbeck (Ohio 1979) 58 Ohio St.2d 443, 391 N.E.2d 307, 12 O.O.3d 375. Death ☞ 11

An action for personal injuries begun by the decedent and prosecuted by his personal representative after his death, is not a bar to recovery by such representative for wrongful death. Mahoning Valley Ry. Co. v. Van Alstine (Ohio 1908) 77 Ohio St. 395, 83 N.E. 601, 5 Ohio Law Rep. 565.

Where next of kin of person whose death is alleged to have been caused by negligence of railroad are aliens, nonresident in state, administrator of such decedent may sue under Rev.St. 1892, §§6134, 6135 (See GC 10509-166 to 10509-168), for benefit of such next of kin in same manner as may be done in behalf of citizens of state or aliens resident therein. Pittsburgh, C., C. & St. L.R. Co. v. Naylor (Ohio 1905) 73 Ohio St. 115, 76 N.E. 505, 112 Am.St.Rep. 701, 3 Ohio Law Rep. 466. Aliens ☞ 16; Death ☞ 31(2); Executors And Administrators ☞ 426

Nonresident aliens are entitled to benefits under the wrongful death act, and an action may be maintained for their benefit for negligence causing death in Ohio. Pittsburgh, C., C. & St. L.R. Co. v. Naylor (Ohio 1905) 73 Ohio St. 115, 76 N.E. 505, 112 Am.St.Rep. 701, 3 Ohio Law Rep. 466.

Contributory negligence on the part of some of the beneficiaries will not bar the rest of the beneficiaries from having an action brought for their benefit. Wolf v. Lake Erie & W.R. Co. (Ohio 1896) 55 Ohio St. 517, 37 W.L.B. 23, 45 N.E. 708. Death ☞ 24

Administrator of estate was in privity with the statutory beneficiaries, and thus, the attorney-client relationship existing between the administrator and estate's attorneys extended to the mother and siblings of woman killed in head-on collision, for purposes of maintaining legal malpractice action against attorneys for failure to represent beneficiaries' interests in wrongful death action. Brinkman v. Doughty (Ohio App. 2 Dist., 11-17-2000) 140 Ohio App.3d 494, 748 N.E.2d 116, appeal not allowed 91 Ohio St.3d 1480, 744 N.E.2d 1194. Attorney And Client ☞ 129(1)

Beneficiaries in a wrongful death action are each entitled to a separate per-person limit of coverage under an uninsured policy. Gibson v. State Farm Mut. Auto. Ins. Co. (Ohio App. 2 Dist., 08-22-1997) 123 Ohio App.3d 216, 704 N.E.2d 1. Insurance ☞ 2796

Because estate's administrator was in privity with estate's beneficiary, administrator had standing to maintain legal malpractice action against beneficiary's attorneys, who allegedly gave incorrect advice to beneficiary (who later served as interim administrator) as to when wrongful death action was required to be refiled. DePugh v. Sladoje (Ohio App. 2 Dist., 06-14-1996) 111 Ohio App.3d 675, 676 N.E.2d 1231. Attorney And Client ☞ 129(1)

Irrevocable trust for benefit of minor children created with proceeds from wrongful death of their natural mother did not terminate on subsequent adoption of children; interests of children in trust vested when shares of all beneficiaries were adjusted in wrongful death proceeding and children were proper beneficiaries. Sawyer v. Lebanon Citizens Natl. Bank (Ohio App. 12 Dist., 07-31-1995) 105 Ohio App.3d 464, 664 N.E.2d 571, dismissed, appeal not allowed 74 Ohio St.3d 1476, 657 N.E.2d 783. Adoption ☞ 20; Trusts ☞ 61(1)

Bodily injury exclusion in employer's catastrophe policy did not apply to wrongful death claims where it did not specifically omit wrongful death claims from coverage; claim for wrongful death, although derivative of claim for bodily injury, was a separate claim for personal injury under Ohio law. Beacon Ins. Co. of Am. v. Kleoudis (Ohio App. 8 Dist., 03-27-1995) 100 Ohio App.3d 79, 652 N.E.2d 1. Insurance ☞ 2397

Insureds were entitled to underinsured motorist (UIM) benefits for wrongful death of parent, even though parent was not insured under their policies and did not reside in their household, and even though neither insureds nor their automobiles were involved in the fatal accident; policies required insurer to pay damages for bodily injury that insured was legally entitled to collect from owner or driver of uninsured motor vehicle, they did not require that bodily injury be sustained by insured or that insured or covered automobile actually be involved in accident, and they merely required that insured be legally entitled to collect damages from uninsured/underinsured motorist. Dudash v. State Farm Mut. Auto. Ins. Co. (Ohio App. 8 Dist., 08-08-1994) 96 Ohio App.3d 348, 645 N.E.2d 79. Insurance ⚖ 2780

Wrongful death cause of action was not recognized at common law, but rather is strictly creation of statute which is subject to rights and limitations imposed by statute. Buchert v. Newman (Ohio App. 1 Dist., 09-22-1993) 90 Ohio App.3d 382, 629 N.E.2d 489, dismissed, jurisdictional motion overruled 68 Ohio St.3d 1449, 626 N.E.2d 690. Death ⚖ 7; Death ⚖ 11

Wrongful death statute is remedial in nature and, thus, must be liberally construed to promote its object. Buchert v. Newman (Ohio App. 1 Dist., 09-22-1993) 90 Ohio App.3d 382, 629 N.E.2d 489, dismissed, jurisdictional motion overruled 68 Ohio St.3d 1449, 626 N.E.2d 690. Death ⚖ 9

Even assuming that church's interior egress ramp was in violation of basic building code regulation requiring that egress ramps be surfaced with approved nonslip materials wherever use of ramp is such as to involve dangerous slipping, this violation did not rise to status of negligence per se, so as to render church liable for death of woman who fell from ramp while attending bingo game at church; regulation was not such a specific, detailed requirement as to invoke negligence per se upon its violation, since it required intervention of human thought process, judgment, and decision making to determine what sorts of nonslip materials were appropriate for particular ramp and to determine whether ramp use involved dangerous slipping conditions. Zimmerman v. St. Peter's Catholic Church (Montgomery 1993) 87 Ohio App.3d 752, 622 N.E.2d 1184. Religious Societies ⚖ 30

Introduction of evidence that patient's minor daughter was adopted by her stepfather after patient's death was prejudicial error in patient's estate's medical malpractice action, as status of daughter was fixed at time of patient's death, before his daughter's adoption, and child's statutory rights derived from and through patient were not restricted by child's subsequent adoption. Ulmer v. Ackerman (Allen 1993) 87 Ohio App.3d 137, 621 N.E.2d 1315, dismissed, jurisdictional motion overruled 67 Ohio St.3d 1434, 617 N.E.2d 685. Appeal And Error ⚖ 1050.1(6); Death ⚖ 60

In Ohio, one's right to sue for wrongful death is a right created by statute and any limitations on that right are also imposed by statute. Tennant v. State Farm Mut. Ins. Co. (Summit 1991) 81 Ohio App.3d 20, 610 N.E.2d 437, motion overruled 62 Ohio St.3d 1434, 578 N.E.2d 826.

The intention of a wrongful death action in Ohio is not to compensate the decedent or the estate for personal injury, pain, and suffering; any damages recovered do not become assets of the decedent's estate but rather are to be distributed to the beneficiaries. Tennant v. State Farm Mut. Ins. Co. (Summit 1991) 81 Ohio App.3d 20, 610 N.E.2d 437, motion overruled 62 Ohio St.3d 1434, 578 N.E.2d 826. Death ⚖ 101

The mother of an adult daughter killed in an automobile accident is entitled to make a claim under the wrongful death statute, but cannot claim compensation under the underinsured motorist provision of her own insurance policy where the deceased daughter is not named in the policy and does not meet the policy definition of "insured," and none of the automobiles involved in the accident are covered under the policy. Rotsinger v. State Farm Ins. Co. (Erie 1992) 78 Ohio App.3d 696, 605 N.E.2d 1281, cause dismissed 64 Ohio St.3d 1420, 593 N.E.2d 305.

In a wrongful death action, the recovery from underinsured motorist coverage is not limited to out-of-pocket expenses but includes instead all damages which are recoverable in the action. Nationwide Mut. Ins. Co. v. Chivington (Franklin 1991) 72 Ohio App.3d 700, 595 N.E.2d 1002, cause dismissed 61 Ohio St.3d 1433, 575 N.E.2d 465. Insurance ⚖ 2803

The recovery by an insured of uninsured motorist coverage for the death of his mother who was struck and killed by an uninsured motorist is permissible even though the mother was not an insured under the policy; thus, the provision in the automobile policy which provides that with respect to uninsured motorist coverage, damages must result from bodily injury sustained by the insured caused by an accident is void since it is inconsistent with RC 3937.18(A)(1). Barr v. Insurance Co. of North America (Franklin 1991) 72 Ohio App.3d 595, 595 N.E.2d 531. Insurance ⚖ 2780

Determination adverse to widow in workers' compensation proceeding did not present res judicata or collateral estoppel bar to widow's pursuit of wrongful death and survivorship claims against husband's employer, as requirement of identity of parties or their privies was lacking; in compensation proceeding, widow appeared effectively in her individual capacity, but she asserted instant claims as administratrix of husband's estate,

representing number of potential beneficiaries who were not party to compensation proceeding. Altvater v. Claycraft Co. (Franklin 1991) 71 Ohio App.3d 264, 593 N.E.2d 377, motion overruled 62 Ohio St.3d 1408, 577 N.E.2d 361. Workers' Compensation ⚖ 1792

In a wrongful death and survivorship claim, res judicata or collateral estoppel is not a bar where the decedent died from silicosis and his widow, as dependent, filed suit for death benefits under the Workers' Compensation Act, the industrial commission denied the claim based upon its determination that the death was caused by a condition unrelated to the decedent's occupation and the widow then filed a complaint as administratrix, alleging that the intentional conduct of the employer proximately caused the wrongful death of her husband, suing not solely in her own right as "dependent," but as the administratrix on behalf of a number of potential beneficiaries who were not a party to the prior workers' compensation claim; although the widow appears in both actions, the required element of "identity of parties" is lacking between the proceedings since the widow sued in different capacities in each and brought suit in each proceeding on behalf of different beneficiaries. Altvater v. Claycraft Co. (Franklin 1991) 71 Ohio App.3d 264, 593 N.E.2d 377, motion overruled 62 Ohio St.3d 1408, 577 N.E.2d 361.

RC 2125.01 and 2125.02 are procedural and remedial in nature and should be given a liberal construction; thus, a complaint which states that the defendant aided and abetted in the commission of a wrongful act which caused the death of plaintiff's decedents states a claim for relief. Burton v. DePew (Butler 1988) 47 Ohio App.3d 107, 547 N.E.2d 995.

Although each surviving member of a decedent's immediate family may be entitled to receive damages as the result of an underinsured motorist's negligence, there is only one cause of action for the recovery of those damages under Ohio's wrongful death statute, RC 2125.02. Dick v. Allstate Ins. Co. (Hamilton 1986) 34 Ohio App.3d 28, 516 N.E.2d 1266, 31 O.B.R. 143. Insurance ⚖ 2772

In action for wrongful death based on medical malpractice, issue of proximate cause can be submitted to jury if there is sufficient evidence that, with proper diagnosis and treatment, patient would have survived his illness; there is no requirement of evidence as to specific length of time patient may have survived, although defendant may show that patient would have survived only a short time in mitigation of damages. Taylor v. C. Lawrence Decker, M.D., Inc. (Hamilton 1986) 33 Ohio App.3d 118, 514 N.E.2d 754. Health ⚖ 826

In a wrongful death action, it is within the discretion of the trial court to exclude from the courtroom the children of the decedent who are of tender years. Long v. Maxwell Co. (Fayette 1962) 118 Ohio App. 134, 193 N.E.2d 423, 24 O.O.2d 446.

Under principles of res judicata and estoppel by judgment, a judgment in a wrongful death action that defendant was not negligent bars daughter of decedent, who was a real party in interest in the action and who was injured by the same accident which caused the death of her father, from subsequently bringing an action against the same defendant to recover for her injuries. Brinkman v. Baltimore & O. R. Co. (Montgomery 1960) 111 Ohio App. 317, 172 N.E.2d 154, 14 O.O.2d 286. Judgment ⚖ 668(2)

A judgment denying recovery for personal injuries is not a bar to an action, under this and preceding section, for the benefit of the next of kin of the injured person who died as a result of such injuries. DeHart v. Ohio Fuel Gas Co. (Huron 1948) 84 Ohio App. 62, 85 N.E.2d 586, 39 O.O. 101.

Provisions of GC 10216 (RC 1.14) are applicable to this section. Young v. New York Cent. R. Co. (Lorain 1939) 64 Ohio App. 362, 28 N.E.2d 687, 18 O.O. 149.

Under RC 2125.02 the statutory beneficiaries are the real parties in interest in a lawful death claim; a decedent's estate has no claim to wrongful death benefits and is not entitled to recover uninsured motorists benefits under the decedent's motor vehicle policy. Mack v Allstate Insurance Co, No. CA96–12–261, 1997 WL 374733 (12th Dist Ct App, Butler, 7–7–97).

Settlement and release against a physician who renders negligent treatment serves to extinguish the hospital's vicarious liability for its agent, the treating physician. Radcliffe v. Mercy Hosp. Anderson (Ohio App. 1 Dist., Hamilton, 05-14-1997) No. C-960424, No. C-960425, 1997 WL 249436, Unreported.

The amendments to RC 2125.02 made by 1981 H 332, eff. 2–5–82, may not be applied retrospectively. Falasca v Haas, No. 46137 (8th Dist Ct App, Cuyahoga, 12–1–83).

The provisions of RC 2125.01 and RC 2125.02 of the Wrongful Death Act, as amended by 1982 H 332, eff. 2–5–82, are to be applied retroactively. Robinson v. Parker–Hannifin Corp. (Ohio Com.Pl. 1982) 4 Ohio Misc.2d 6, 447 N.E.2d 781, 4 O.B.R. 257.

Wrongful death statute which deals with procedures in a wrongful death action was remedial and procedural in nature, and thus amendment to such statute could be applied retrospectively. Wright v. Conney (Ohio Com.Pl. 1982) 3 Ohio Misc.2d 9, 444 N.E.2d 1088, 3 O.B.R. 298. Death ⊜ 9

RC 2125.02, as amended by 1981 H 332, eff. 2–5–82, and dealing with the procedures in a wrongful death action, is remedial and procedural in nature and may be applied retrospectively. Wright v. Conney (Ohio Com.Pl. 1982) 3 Ohio Misc.2d 9, 444 N.E.2d 1088, 3 O.B.R. 298.

RC 2125.01, RC 2125.02, and RC 2125.03 are expressly retroactive. McKinney v Kidwell, 2 OBR 353 (CP, Hamilton 1982).

A verdict and judgment against a person who is a beneficiary of one who was killed, in an action for personal injuries, is res judicata against him as a beneficiary in a wrongful death suit growing out of the same accident where such beneficiary's contributory negligence and want of fault of the defendant is proven in the first case. Haines v. Cincinnati Interurban Co. (Ohio Com.Pl. 1909) 7 Ohio Law Rep. 48.

If a plaintiff in a wrongful death action has no right of action in the state where the accident occurred, the action cannot be maintained in Ohio. Ott v. Lake Shore & M.S. Ry. Co. (Ohio Cir. 1899) 10 Ohio C.D. 85.

The statutes providing for wrongful death actions are not construed to be a revivor or survival of the cause of action for the injury nor to be a double liability for the same wrong; such an action merely succeeds the cause of action abated by the death of the injured person and takes its place in favor of his next of kin. Solor Refining Co. v. Elliott (Ohio Cir. 1898) 8 Ohio C.D. 225. Death ⊜ 7

A justice of the peace has no jurisdiction to try an action for wrongfully causing death. Sponseller v Cleveland Terminal & Valley Railway Co, 6 NP 422, 8 D 307 (CP, Summit 1897). Death ⊜ 34.1; Justices Of The Peace ⊜ 38(1)

A claim for wrongful death is a chose in action and as such is property and a part of the special estate of the decedent to be recovered in the name of the administrator for the benefit of the persons named in the statute and distributed as the statute provides. In re Arduino's Estate (Ohio Com.Pl. 1909) 20 Ohio Dec. 461, 9 Ohio NP(NS) 369. Death ⊜ 31(3.1); Executors And Administrators ⊜ 51

Under Gen.Code Ohio, §10772 (repealed 1932. See §§10509–167, 10509–168) an administrator suing for wrongful death is not a mere nominal party, but the real party, whose citizenship, and not that of the beneficiaries, controls the question of federal jurisdiction. Laubscher v. Fay (N.D.Ohio 1912) 197 F. 879, 10 Ohio Law Rep. 456. Federal Courts ⊜ 291; Death ⊜ 31(3.1); Executors And Administrators ⊜ 153; Parties ⊜ 4

A foreign administrator may maintain an action for wrongful death in Ohio under RS 6133 on behalf of nonresident beneficiaries in a like manner as nonresidents may sue. Popp v. Cincinnati, H. & D.R. Co. (C.C.S.D.Ohio 1899) 96 F. 465.

Probate court order declaring heirship did not establish standing of minor children born out of wedlock to bring suit under Ohio Wrongful Death Statute for death of alleged father; decedent did not acknowledge paternity, mother did not consent to alleged acknowledgment, and no action to establish paternity was taken during decedent's life. Martin v. Daily Express, Inc. (N.D.Ohio, 02-28-1995) 878 F.Supp. 91. Death ⊜ 31(8)

Naming children born out of wedlock as devisees, without suggesting that children were testator's, was not formal acknowledgment of paternity needed for children to have standing to bring suit for death of testator under Ohio Wrongful Death Statute. Martin v. Daily Express, Inc. (N.D.Ohio, 02-28-1995) 878 F.Supp. 91. Death ⊜ 31(8)

Ohio law provides that child born out of wedlock may establish standing as a person's child, for purposes of state's wrongful death statute, by using any of recognized legal methods through which child can establish right of inheritance. Martin v. Daily Express, Inc. (N.D.Ohio, 02-28-1995) 878 F.Supp. 91. Death ⊜ 31(8)

Ohio's wrongful death statute, RC 2125.01, dictates who may bring the action; when a person dies from a tortfeasor's negligence, the probate court appoints an administrator as fiduciary to pursue the decedent's claims, and any wrongful death proceeds recovered by the administrator are distributed to the beneficiaries of the decedent according to Ohio law. Sansone v. State Farm Mut. Auto. Ins. Co. (S.D.Ohio 1993) 815 F.Supp. 1096.

Changes in Ohio statutes regarding wrongful death and comparative negligence do not apply to accident occurring prior thereto. Tackett v. Consolidated Rail Corp. (S.D.Ohio 1982) 536 F.Supp. 409.

Where decedent's death occurred in Wisconsin where he was temporarily installing machinery, and all of his heirs were residents of Ohio where decedent was employed, Ohio law will apply to distribution to the beneficiaries. Satchwill v. Vollrath Co. (E.D.Wis. 1968) 293 F.Supp. 533, 47 O.O.2d 75.

10. —— Classes of kin included, scope; action for benefit of heirs

The surviving husband is, within the meaning of the Wrongful Death Act, the next of kin, if the deceased left no children. Steel v. Kurtz (Ohio 1876) 28 Ohio St. 191.

The risk of ascertaining the persons entitled to the benefit of the recovery, and the duty of making the distribution, are not imposed on the defendant, but on the personal representatives of the deceased; if the widow and next of kin could recover in their own names a joint judgment against the defendant, the judgment might be satisfied by payment to either of the plaintiffs, and thus defeat the distribution required by the statute. Weidner v. Rankin (Ohio 1875) 26 Ohio St. 522.

The amount recovered in a wrongful death action is for the exclusive benefit of the widow and next of kin, and is to be distributed among them in the proportions provided by law in relation to the distribution of personal estates of persons dying intestate. Weidner v. Rankin (Ohio 1875) 26 Ohio St. 522.

The fact of the legitimacy or illegitimacy of the deceased's child has no effect on the right to sue. Muhl's Adm'r v. Michigan Southern R. Co. (Ohio 1859) 10 Ohio St. 272.

An action may be maintained for the next of kin of a deceased who left no widow or children, even though the petition does not state special circumstances rendering the death a pecuniary injury to them. Johnston v. Cleveland & T.R. Co. (Ohio 1857) 7 Ohio St. 336, 70 Am.Dec. 75. Death ⊜ 52; Pleading ⊜ 71

Adoption of grandchild by stepmother terminated relationship between grandchild and grandparents and relationship between great grandchildren and grandparents, and thus grandchild and great grandchildren could not maintain wrongful death beneficiary claims following death of grandparents in automobile accident. Turvey v. Ocheltree (Ohio App. 5 Dist., Tuscarawas, 07-29-2005) No. 2005 AP 01 0002, 2005-Ohio-4114, 2005 WL 1897848, Unreported. Death ⊜ 31(8)

Decedent's aunt was not "other next of kin" for purposes of wrongful death statute who was entitled to a share of settlement proceeds from grandmother's claim against her insurer for uninsured motorist (UM) benefits, even though decedent, who had no children or spouse and his parents had abandoned him, had no relative in the first degree of kinship; grandmother was second degree of kinship while aunt was of the third degree of kinship, and grandmother was the only person in the "next" degree of relationship to decedent. In re Estate of Payne (Ohio App. 10 Dist., Franklin, 05-17-2005) No. 04AP-1176, 2005-Ohio-2391, 2005 WL 1155891, Unreported. Descent And Distribution ⊜ 36

Following the insureds' fatal automobile accident, decedents' estates are not entitled to recover underinsured motorists coverage from decedents' insurer merely because they have cause of action under the wrongful death statute. Wickline v. Western Reserve Group Mut. Cas. Co. (Ohio App. 10 Dist., Franklin, 05-09-1996) No. 95APE11-1498, 1996 WL 239636, Unreported, appeal not allowed 77 Ohio St.3d 1480, 673 N.E.2d 142.

In a wrongful death case involving a motor vehicle accident where the brother of the deceased is a passenger and brings a claim for emotional distress, the claim is a separate bodily injury and is subject to a separate per person limit of coverage in combination with his bodily injury claim. Thompson v. Utomo (Ohio App. 6 Dist., Lucas, 10-27-1995) No. L-95-034, 1995 WL 628242, Unreported, appeal dismissed 74 Ohio St.3d 1502, 659 N.E.2d 794, motion to certify allowed 74 Ohio St.3d 1524, 660 N.E.2d 743, appeal allowed 74 Ohio St.3d 1524, 660 N.E.2d 744, cause dismissed 75 Ohio St.3d 1444, 663 N.E.2d 326, stay granted 75 Ohio St.3d 1456, 663 N.E.2d 646.

Pursuant to a driver's insurance policy, a passenger fatally injured in a collision with an automobile driven by an uninsured motorist is an insured under the policy, so that coverage extends to the parents of the decedent as well as the decedent's two brothers and sister; although the siblings are not presumed to have sustained damages, each may recover for the death of their brother where evidence is presented supporting their claim of loss due to their brother's wrongful death. Viccarone v. Colonial Penn Ins. Co.

(Ohio App. 8 Dist., Cuyahoga, 02-23-1995) No. 66822, 1995 WL 79789, Unreported, appeal dismissed 72 Ohio St.3d 1533, 650 N.E.2d 110.

Interest of mother and siblings of woman killed in head-on collision in woman's wrongful death action was vested, not contingent, even if they had to prove their damages, and thus, mother and siblings were in privity with estate's administrator so as to extend attorney-client relationship between the administrator and estate's attorneys for purposes of maintaining legal malpractice action against attorneys for failure to represent their interests in the wrongful death action; wrongful death statute required administrator to bring the action for the exclusive benefit of the surviving spouse, children, parents, and other next of kin, and fixed status of all beneficiaries of the action as of date of death. Brinkman v. Doughty (Ohio App. 2 Dist., 11-17-2000) 140 Ohio App.3d 494, 748 N.E.2d 116, appeal not allowed 91 Ohio St.3d 1480, 744 N.E.2d 1194. Attorney And Client ⬅ 129(1).

Neither natural father of decedent's child nor maternal grandmother had right to give up child's right to recover under wrongful death action. Yardley v. W. Ohio Conference of the United Methodist Church, Inc. (Ohio App. 10 Dist., 08-29-2000) 138 Ohio App.3d 872, 742 N.E.2d 723. Death ⬅ 25.

Three adult brothers of named insured, who was killed in automobile accident while riding as passenger in vehicle driven by tortfeasor, were "insureds" within meaning of underinsured motorist provisions of automobile insurance policy, which defined "insured" to include any person who was entitled to recover damages from tortfeasor because of bodily injury that occurred to any family member of named insured; parents were named insureds under policy, decedent was family member of her parents, and brothers were potential beneficiaries under wrongful death statute. King v. W. Res. Group (Ohio App. 7 Dist., 12-01-1997) 125 Ohio App.3d 1, 707 N.E.2d 947, appeal not allowed 81 Ohio St.3d 1502, 691 N.E.2d 1062. Insurance ⬅ 2661.

Insured's children, as wrongful death claimants and statutory beneficiaries, were entitled to recover under uninsured/underinsured motorist (UM/UIM) provisions of insured's policy, even though children were not insureds under the policy. Holt v. Grange Mut. Cas. Co. (Ohio, 09-24-1997) 79 Ohio St.3d 401, 683 N.E.2d 1080, 1997-Ohio-375. Insurance ⬅ 3460.

State had rational basis for treating surviving spouses who remarry differently from those who live with another person, by enacting statute that allows party to wrongful death action to present evidence that surviving spouse of decedent has remarried, and thus statute survives equal protection scrutiny; state has legitimate interest in ensuring surviving spouse receives fair and just award, and legislature could reasonably have concluded that surviving spouse's remarriage has more permanent effect on compensable losses than the act of cohabiting with another. Pena v. Northeast Ohio Emergency Affiliates, Inc. (Ohio App. 9 Dist., 12-20-1995) 108 Ohio App.3d 96, 670 N.E.2d 268, dismissed, appeal not allowed 75 Ohio St.3d 1494, 664 N.E.2d 1291. Constitutional Law ⬅ 245(3); Death ⬅ 9.

Statute permitting party to wrongful death action to present evidence that surviving spouse of decedent has remarried does not infringe on fundamental right to marry protected by due process clause; while statute may have some incidental effect on decision to marry, it does not directly prohibit or discourage marriage. Pena v. Northeast Ohio Emergency Affiliates, Inc. (Ohio App. 9 Dist., 12-20-1995) 108 Ohio App.3d 96, 670 N.E.2d 268, dismissed, appeal not allowed 75 Ohio St.3d 1494, 664 N.E.2d 1291. Constitutional Law ⬅ 274(5); Constitutional Law ⬅ 301(3); Death ⬅ 9; Marriage ⬅ 2.

Action for wrongful death must be brought for exclusive benefit of surviving spouse, children, and parents of decedent, who are rebuttably presumed to have suffered damages by reason of death. Sawyer v. Lebanon Citizens Natl. Bank (Ohio App. 12 Dist., 07-31-1995) 105 Ohio App.3d 464, 664 N.E.2d 571, dismissed, appeal not allowed 74 Ohio St.3d 1476, 657 N.E.2d 783. Death ⬅ 32; Death ⬅ 58(2).

When negligence or medical malpractice results in death of victim, two distinct causes of action arise; first is wrongful death action brought on behalf of surviving spouse and next-of-kin, and second is malpractice or personal injury action, which is enforced by either injured person or representative of injured person in survival action. Evans v. S. Ohio Med. Ctr. (Ohio App. 4 Dist., 05-04-1995) 103 Ohio App.3d 250, 659 N.E.2d 326. Death ⬅ 7; Health ⬅ 810.

Maintenance of loving relationship between minor wrongful death victim and biological mother precluded finding that mother had "disclaimed or abandoned parental rights," and precluded victim's stepmother from recovering loss of consortium damages under wrongful death statute, regardless of whether stepmother had assumed parental role. Miller v. Boden (Ohio App. 3 Dist., 05-10-1995) 103 Ohio App.3d 73, 658 N.E.2d 809, appeal not allowed 74 Ohio St.3d 1409, 655 N.E.2d 187. Death ⬅ 31(7); Death ⬅ 88.

Term "children" as used in wrongful death statute, includes all natural or adopted children, whether legitimate, acknowledged or illegitimate. Brookbank v. Gray (Ohio, 01-17-1996) 74 Ohio St.3d 279, 658 N.E.2d 724, 1996-Ohio-135. Death ⬅ 32.

Child born out of wedlock is not foreclosed from recovering damages for wrongful death of child's putative father, simply because paternity has not been established during putative father's lifetime; paternity may be established after death of decedent in order to permit illegitimate child recovery under Wrongful Death Act for death of child's father. Brookbank v. Gray (Ohio, 01-17-1996) 74 Ohio St.3d 279, 658 N.E.2d 724, 1996-Ohio-135. Death ⬅ 32.

"Personal injury" coverage in employer's catastrophe policy potentially covered wrongful death claims for mental anguish of surviving spouse and children of employee killed in work-related fall where it provided coverage for personal injury arising out of mental anguish, mental injury, fright, shock and humiliation. Beacon Ins. Co. of Am. v. Kleoudis (Ohio App. 8 Dist., 03-27-1995) 100 Ohio App.3d 79, 652 N.E.2d 1. Insurance ⬅ 2276.

Considering classes of persons who may qualify as beneficiaries of wrongful death proceeds was not error. In re Estate of Marinelli (Ohio App. 11 Dist., 12-19-1994) 99 Ohio App.3d 372, 650 N.E.2d 935. Death ⬅ 101.

Excluding decedent's biological father from distribution of wrongful death settlement proceeds was not an abuse of discretion in light of evidence that father had effectively abandoned son. In re Estate of Marinelli (Ohio App. 11 Dist., 12-19-1994) 99 Ohio App.3d 372, 650 N.E.2d 935. Death ⬅ 101.

Convent was not "other next of kin" of convent member killed in automobile accident under liberal construction of term in wrongful death statute, which thus precluded wrongful death claim on behalf of convent even assuming that convent sustained economic loss from member's death. Buchert v. Newman (Ohio App. 1 Dist., 09-22-1993) 90 Ohio App.3d 382, 629 N.E.2d 489, dismissed, jurisdictional motion overruled 68 Ohio St.3d 1449, 626 N.E.2d 690. Death ⬅ 31(5).

Generally, "viability," as required to bring wrongful death action based on death of fetus, may vary with each pregnancy, and thus, determination of whether particular fetus is viable is matter of judgment for medical profession. Egan v. Smith (Huron 1993) 87 Ohio App.3d 763, 622 N.E.2d 1191. Death ⬅ 15; Death ⬅ 75.

Wrongful death action may not lie for death of nonviable fetus, even if fetus is "quick" or capable of movement in womb. Egan v. Smith (Huron 1993) 87 Ohio App.3d 763, 622 N.E.2d 1191. Death ⬅ 15.

Recovery of damages in a wrongful death action is for the exclusive benefit of the decedent's surviving spouse, children, and other next of kin. Tennant v. State Farm Mut. Ins. Co. (Summit 1991) 81 Ohio App.3d 20, 610 N.E.2d 437, motion overruled 62 Ohio St.3d 1434, 578 N.E.2d 826. Death ⬅ 32.

Next of kin, as contained in RC 2125.02(B)(5), are not limited to recovery for mental anguish if there is a surviving spouse, parents, or minor children; adult siblings of a decedent may be included in the term "next of kin" and may recover for mental anguish caused by the death of a sibling although a surviving spouse, parents, or minor children of the decedent are living. Shoemaker v. Crawford (Franklin 1991) 78 Ohio App.3d 53, 603 N.E.2d 1114, motion allowed 63 Ohio St.3d 1473, 591 N.E.2d 243, cause dismissed 64 Ohio St.3d 1434, 595 N.E.2d 943.

Insured brothers, whose father was killed in automobile accident caused by negligence of uninsured motorist, were entitled to uninsured motorist coverage under their automobile policies for damages caused by wrongful death of their father, notwithstanding that father did not live in same household with either insured and despite any limiting language in either policy to the contrary. Senig v. Nationwide Mut. Ins. Co. (Franklin 1992) 76 Ohio App.3d 565, 602 N.E.2d 438. Insurance ⬅ 2661.

Insured children of a parent killed in a collision with an uninsured motorist may recover from the insured motorist provisions of their policies although the deceased parent did not reside with them notwithstanding policy language denying such coverage. Senig v. Nationwide Mut. Ins. Co. (Franklin 1992) 76 Ohio App.3d 565, 602 N.E.2d 438.

Grandchildren may be other next of kin entitled to recovery for the death of a grandparent by an uninsured motorist although the decedent has surviving children. Senig v. Nationwide Mut. Ins. Co. (Franklin 1992) 76 Ohio App.3d 565, 602 N.E.2d 438.

Insured could recover under his underinsured motorist coverage for death of his mother who was struck and killed by an uninsured motorist, even though the mother was not an insured under the policy; insured could recover damages which he was legally entitled to recover from the uninsured motorist pursuant to the wrongful death statute. Barr v. Insurance Co. of North America (Franklin 1991) 72 Ohio App.3d 595, 595 N.E.2d 531. Insurance ⇨ 2780

Illegitimate child could not maintain wrongful death action on behalf of his deceased father, where paternity action to establish parent-child relationship was brought after purported father was killed in automobile accident. Hunter–Martin v. Winchester Transp., Inc. (Shelby 1991) 71 Ohio App.3d 273, 593 N.E.2d 383, motion overruled 62 Ohio St.3d 1408, 577 N.E.2d 361. Death ⇨ 31(8)

Under the wrongful death statute, next of kin, although not presumed to have sustained damages, may recover damages for mental anguish and loss of society upon proper proof thereof even though there is a surviving parent, spouse, or minor children. Wise v. Timmons (Ohio 1992) 64 Ohio St.3d 113, 592 N.E.2d 840. Death ⇨ 88; Death ⇨ 89

In a wrongful death suit seeking damages for loss of society and mental anguish on behalf of the father, sisters, and brother of a disabled twenty-one-year-old killed in a car accident against the estate of the driver, the trial court errs in granting the plaintiff's motion for a directed verdict on the issue of negligence where, although the parties stipulated that the accident caused the death of the decedent, there were no eyewitnesses to the events leading up to the crash and there is no evidence on the issues of whether (1) the vehicle was free from defect, (2) the driver was suffering from a medical condition causing the loss of control, and (3) the driver was reacting to an emergency; there is a presumption that a driver exercises due care and, while evidence may support an inference of negligence, that inference is for the jury. Wise v. Timmons (Ohio 1992) 64 Ohio St.3d 113, 592 N.E.2d 840.

In a wrongful death suit against the estate of the driver of a car, initiated by the decedent's father on behalf of himself and the decedent's sisters and brother and later, after the death of the father, on behalf of decedent's siblings seeking damages for loss of society and mental anguish, a trial court does not err in instructing the jury to consider the mental anguish and loss of society, if any, of the siblings on the occasion of their brother's death; the siblings are not precluded from recovering although the father survived his son's death since according to Ramage v Central Ohio Emergency Services, Inc, 64 OS(3d) 97 (1992), RC 2125.02 permits the recovery of next-of-kin who, although not presumed to have sustained damages, may recover mental anguish and loss of society damages upon proper proof even where there is a surviving parent, spouse, or minor children. Wise v. Timmons (Ohio 1992) 64 Ohio St.3d 113, 592 N.E.2d 840.

Pursuant to the Ohio wrongful death statute, "other next of kin," although not presumed to have sustained damages, may recover damages for mental anguish and loss of society upon proper proof thereof, even though there is a surviving parent, spouse, or minor children. Ramage v. Central Ohio Emergency Serv., Inc. (Ohio 1992) 64 Ohio St.3d 97, 592 N.E.2d 828. Death ⇨ 88; Death ⇨ 89

Next-of-kin, other than those categories set forth in RC 2125.02, may recover for mental anguish suffered from the loss of a loved one without regard to whether there remains a living parent, spouse, or minor child, but other next-of-kin are not presumed to have sustained damages and instead may recover upon proper proof of mental anguish and loss of services; grandparents are not foreclosed from recovering by the disjunctive use of the word "or" in both subsections of the statute since "or" may be read as "and" if appropriate, and since the law is intended to be remedial in nature and must be construed liberally to achieve its remedial ends. Ramage v. Central Ohio Emergency Serv., Inc. (Ohio 1992) 64 Ohio St.3d 97, 592 N.E.2d 828.

The live-in grandparents of a two-year-old decedent may testify about, and recover for, the mental anguish and loss of society resulting from the death of their granddaughter where the plaintiff, decedent's father, alleges that the emergency room health professionals failed to properly diagnose, treat, and care for the two-year-old girl who was brought to hospital emergency shaking and vomiting with a high temperature and other signs of distress, and then was discharged seventy-five minutes later after administration of Tylenol and fluids and a decrease in her temperature several degrees and who died at home less than two hours after discharge. Ramage v. Central Ohio Emergency Serv., Inc. (Ohio 1992) 64 Ohio St.3d 97, 592 N.E.2d 828.

A trial court does not err in dismissing the claim for damages of two minor children of a man who is severely injured in a motor vehicle accident against the driver of the other vehicle and his employer because a child does not have a cause of action for loss of parental consortium against a third-party tortfeasor who negligently or intentionally injures the child's parent; unlike the case of the parent who dies, the father of these minor children is still living and can assert a claim for his own injuries and be compensated for loss of earnings and the inability to care for his children. High v. Howard (Ohio 1992) 64 Ohio St.3d 82, 592 N.E.2d 818.

Adult children of decedent were "next of kin" within meaning of wrongful death statute permitting next of kin to recover damages irrespective of status as surviving spouse, minor children, or parents. Ellenwood v. Flower Memorial Hosp. (Ohio Com.Pl. 1991) 62 Ohio Misc.2d 43, 587 N.E.2d 1006. Death ⇨ 31(8)

Denial of beneficiaries' request to have separate trial counsel appointed to represent their interests in wrongful death action brought by personal representative of decedent's estate was not abuse of discretion, absent showing that personal representative had breached fiduciary duty owed to beneficiaries. In re Estate of Ross (Geauga 1989) 65 Ohio App.3d 395, 583 N.E.2d 1379, dismissed 50 Ohio St.3d 717, 553 N.E.2d 1363. Trial ⇨ 107

Care giver was parent for purposes of bringing wrongful death action, although care giver was not natural or adoptive parent of fatally injured child, where only known or knowable natural parent of child had disclaimed status as parent, care giver had performed obligations and enjoyed rights of parenthood for continuous period of 16 years, child had been held out as child of care giver, and parent-child relationship was recognized not only in public schools but also in court of law which awarded custody of child to care giver in dispute between care giver and his former wife. Lawson v. Atwood (Ohio 1989) 42 Ohio St.3d 69, 536 N.E.2d 1167, certiorari denied 110 S.Ct. 176, 493 U.S. 862, 107 L.Ed.2d 132. Death ⇨ 31(7)

Surviving spouse and children of decedent have the right to recover damages suffered by reason of wrongful death, even though action must be brought in name of personal representative of decedent. Wood v. Shepard (Ohio 1988) 38 Ohio St.3d 86, 526 N.E.2d 1089. Death ⇨ 32

Although each surviving member of insured's immediate family may be entitled to receive damages as a result of negligence of underinsured motorist, there is only one cause of action for recovery of those damages under wrongful death statute. Dick v. Allstate Ins. Co. (Hamilton 1986) 34 Ohio App.3d 28, 516 N.E.2d 1266, 31 O.B.R. 143. Insurance ⇨ 2772

Passenger, who was directly involved in accident killing her boyfriend, was entitled to recover damages for mental anguish caused by his death and predicated upon involvement in accident, rather than mere fact of his death, even though mental anguish over death of relative was compensable in wrongful death action. Binns v. Fredendall (Ohio 1987) 32 Ohio St.3d 244, 513 N.E.2d 278. Damages ⇨ 57.29

The father of an unemancipated minor child is legally entitled to recover on his uninsured motorist coverage for the wrongful death of that minor child even if such child at the time of the injury and death was not a member of the father's household. Motorists Mut. Ins. Co. v. Speck (Summit 1977) 59 Ohio App.2d 224, 393 N.E.2d 500, 13 O.O.3d 239.

The survivors of decedent in a wrongful death action are the real parties in interest and it is necessary that the personal representative, as plaintiff, name in the petition who are "the surviving spouse," or "the children," or the "other next of kin of the decedent," for if no known person comes under the classes of survivors named in the statute, there would not be any pecuniary loss to anyone, and an action for wrongful death would not lie; but an action under the so-called survivor statute, RC 2305.21, is for the benefit of the estate generally, by reason of the injuries and their concomitants for which the decedent would have had a right of action during his lifetime, and the survivors named in the wrongful death statute need not be named in this action. Fisher v. Butler (Ohio Com.Pl. 1966) 11 Ohio Misc. 116, 224 N.E.2d 923, 40 O.O.2d 139, 40 O.O.2d 355.

Wrongful death damages may be apportioned only among those beneficiaries listed in RC 2125.02. In re Cline's Estate (Ohio Prob. 1964) 1 Ohio Misc. 28, 202 N.E.2d 736, 30 O.O.2d 221.

On the evidence the court erred in awarding the entire proceeds of the settlement of a wrongful death claim to the widow to the exclusion of the children. In re Miller's Estate (Sandusky 1955) 102 Ohio App. 493, 127 N.E.2d 409, 72 Ohio Law Abs. 546, 59 O.O. 425.

A child born out of wedlock after the death of the reputed father may not have a recovery in a wrongful death action. Bonewit v. Weber (Summit 1952) 95 Ohio App. 428, 120 N.E.2d 738, 54 O.O. 20.

Where, during the pendency of an action for wrongful death brought under GC 10509–166 (RC 2125.01), the only heir and next of kin of the decedent, who has sustained pecuniary injury by reason of such death, dies, no one remains in whose behalf the action may be further prosecuted, and the sustaining of a motion by the defendant for a directed verdict or for a dismissal of the action is proper. Danis v. New York Central R. Co. (Ohio 1954) 160 Ohio St. 474, 117 N.E.2d 39, 43 A.L.R.2d 1286, 52 O.O. 356.

An illegitimate child recognized and acknowledged by the alleged father as his, is a dependent under the wrongful death statute although he is born after the father's death. Bonewit v. Weber (Ohio Com.Pl. 1952) 105 N.E.2d 683, 66 Ohio Law Abs. 519, affirmed 95 Ohio App. 428, 120 N.E.2d 738, 54 O.O. 20, appeal denied 158 Ohio St. 507, 110 N.E.2d 424, 49 O.O. 449.

Evidence was insufficient to establish that putative father of illegitimate child, born almost 8 1/2 months after putative father's death, had so acknowledged that child was his as to permit child to be considered as a dependent in death action predicated upon putative father's death. Bonewit v. Weber (Ohio Com.Pl. 1952) 105 N.E.2d 683, 66 Ohio Law Abs. 519, affirmed 95 Ohio App. 428, 120 N.E.2d 738, 54 O.O. 20, appeal denied 158 Ohio St. 507, 110 N.E.2d 424, 49 O.O. 449. Death ⇐ 75

Within meaning of section reciting that an action for wrongful death is "for exclusive benefit of surviving spouse, children and other next of kin," the phrase "and other next of kin" is used in a broad sense and includes brothers and sisters of a decedent as well as his parents, when both classes of kindred are in existence. Karr v. Sixt (Ohio 1946) 146 Ohio St. 527, 67 N.E.2d 331, 33 O.O. 14. Death ⇐ 32

Section creates a new right in the additional beneficiaries named therein, thereby affecting the amount of recovery, and cannot be given a retroactive effect. City of Cincinnati v. Bachmann (Hamilton 1935) 51 Ohio App. 108, 199 N.E. 853, 19 Ohio Law Abs. 389, 3 O.O. 271.

Action for wrongful death by administrator on behalf of wife's sisters and brother, against husband who killed wife, held not to lie. Demos v. Freemas (Franklin 1931) 43 Ohio App. 426, 183 N.E. 395, 13 Ohio Law Abs. 318. Death ⇐ 31(5); Executors And Administrators ⇐ 426

This section vests a right of action in the personal representative of the deceased for the benefit of the class existing when the right is enforced by suit, so that a right of action for the death of a person leaving no issue does not abate upon the death of his wife, but may be brought for the benefit of the parents and next of kin of the deceased. Garrard v. Mahoning Valley Ry. Co. (Ohio 1919) 100 Ohio St. 212, 126 N.E. 53, 17 Ohio Law Rep. 153, 17 Ohio Law Rep. 164.

A husband and wife sustained personal injuries causing the death of both, but the latter survived her husband a few hours; after the death of the wife, the husband's personal representative instituted suit, under the section named, for the benefit of the husband's father, mother, brothers, and sisters, there being no children of the deceased: held, the action was properly brought. Garrard v. Mahoning Valley Ry. Co. (Ohio 1919) 100 Ohio St. 212, 126 N.E. 53, 17 Ohio Law Rep. 153, 17 Ohio Law Rep. 164. Abatement And Revival ⇐ 72(2)

An action brought by a widow for the wrongful death of her husband fails upon her death for want of a beneficiary, where the widow was the sole heir and next of kin, and the husband left no children or parents or their next of kin but only some collateral heirs. Doyle v. Baltimore & O.R. Co. (Ohio 1909) 81 Ohio St. 184, 90 N.E. 165, 135 Am.St.Rep. 775, 7 Ohio Law Rep. 506.

The "parents" spoken of in RS 6135 for whose benefit an action for damages for wrongfully causing death may be brought, are the "parents" of the person whose death is thus caused. Doyle v. Baltimore & O.R. Co. (Ohio 1909) 81 Ohio St. 184, 90 N.E. 165, 135 Am.St.Rep. 775, 7 Ohio Law Rep. 506. Death ⇐ 32

Verdict of $45,000 in wrongful death action was not grossly inadequate and would not be set aside, and decedent's brother would not be excluded as beneficiary based on determination that he was not "next of kin" within meaning of Ohio statute. Molton v. City of Cleveland (C.A.6 (Ohio) 1988) 839 F.2d 240, certiorari denied 109 S.Ct. 1345, 489 U.S. 1068, 103 L.Ed.2d 814. Death ⇐ 98

Under RC 2125.02 the "next of kin" can recover for loss of the decedent's society only where no spouse, minor child, or parent survives the decedent. Molton v. City of Cleveland (C.A.6 (Ohio) 1988) 839 F.2d 240, certiorari denied 109 S.Ct. 1345, 489 U.S. 1068, 103 L.Ed.2d 814.

Where the decedent killed by a wrongful act left a father and mother and brothers and sisters, the action was properly brought for their joint benefit, and not for the benefit of his next of kin excluding his parents, though on the decedent's death his personal estate would have passed to his brothers and sisters, and not to his parents; the distribution under the wrongful death act is not to be made strictly in accordance with the laws of descent, since the court is required to consider the age and condition of the beneficiaries as well. Toledo, St. L. & W.R. Co. v. Connolly (C.C.A.6 (Ohio) 1907) 149 F. 398, 79 C.C.A. 218.

RC 2125.02(A)(1) mandates that an action for wrongful death be brought in the name of the personal representative of the decedent for the exclusive benefit of the surviving spouse, the children, and other next of kin of the decedent; thus, a personal representative is merely a nominal party and the real parties in interest are the surviving spouse, children, and other next of kin and a change in the class of beneficiaries whom an administrator represents does not alter the nominal role of the administrator under RC 2125.02. Ahlrichs v. Tri-Tex Corp. (Hamilton 1987) 41 Ohio App.3d 207, 534 N.E.2d 1231.

An action for wrongful death may be maintained and pecuniary and noneconomic damages may be recovered, pursuant to RC 2125.02, by the sister of the decedent, but damages are not presumed and the sister bears the burden of proof for such damages. In re Estate of Forbes, No. 54226 (8th Dist Ct App, Cuyahoga, 8–25–88).

A single person limitation in an insurance policy does not defeat the right of classes of kin protected under RC 2125.02 to recover on a wrongful death action. Price v Drumm, No. CA–3361 (5th Dist Ct App, Licking, 8–16–88).

A putative father who fails to establish a legal child-parent relationship prior to the child's death does not qualify as a "parent" for purposes of RC 2125.02 and thus is precluded from participation in the proceeds from a wrongful death action pursuant to RC 2125.02. Ginter v Woodell, No. 2392 (2d Dist Ct App, Clark, 5–17–88).

The adult children of a decedent are "next of kin" under RC 2125.02 which permits next of kin to recover damages irrespective of status of surviving spouse, minor children, or parents since a liberal interpretation of Ohio's wrongful death statute that would permit adult children to recover in every case is required by rules of construction, case law from Ohio appellate courts, and the requirements of equal protection of the law. Ellenwood v. Flower Memorial Hosp. (Ohio Com.Pl. 1991) 62 Ohio Misc.2d 43, 587 N.E.2d 1006.

The right to sue for the benefit of parents if there is no spouse or children, does not include adopting parents for they are neither heirs nor distributees of the adopted child's estate. Boswell v Lake Shore Electric Railway Co, 22 CC(NS) 251, 25 CD 522 (Huron 1913), affirmed by 88 OS 563, 105 NE 767 (1913).

Recovery for wrongful death is for the exclusive benefit of the husband or wife and children, hence the father is not entitled to share as a distributee. Miller v Miller, 9 CC(NS) 315, 19 CD 353 (Cuyahoga 1907).

An action for wrongful death may be maintained by the deceased's wife and for her benefit where the deceased left no children, as the surviving widow is the "next of kin" of the deceased within the meaning of the statute. Lima Electric Light & Power Co v Deubler; appeal dismissed by 27 B 268 (OS 1892), 7 CC 185, 3 CD 720 (Allen 1892).

11. Settlement

Wrongful death settlement proceeds did not belong to decedents' estates, but rather to the persons designated by the wrongful death statutes, and thus settlement funds could not be deposited into estate accounts without direction from the probate court concerning the status and proposed distribution of those funds. In re Estate of Traylor (Ohio App. 7 Dist., Mahoning, 12-01-2004) No. 03 MA 253, No. 03 MA 256, No. 03 MA 259, No. 03 MA 254, No. 03 MA 257, No. 03 MA 262, No. 03 MA 255, No. 03 MA 258, 2004-Ohio-6504, 2004 WL 2808402, Unreported, reconsideration overruled 2005-Ohio-1348, 2005 WL 678626, appeal not allowed 105 Ohio St.3d 1500, 825 N.E.2d 623, 2005-Ohio-1666. Death ⇐ 101; Executors And Administrators ⇐ 51

Beneficiaries of decedent's estate had no power to direct administratrix in prosecution of wrongful death claim, and thus, settlement of estate's wrongful death action with decedent's uninsured motorist carrier, together with probate court's approval of such settlement as adequate compensation, complied with statutory requirements for wrongful death settlements, even though administratrix accepted $245,000 in settlement despite policy limits of $300,000. In re Estate of Kenington (Ohio App. 12 Dist., Clermont, 05-19-2003) No. CA2002-01-005, 2003-Ohio-2549, 2003 WL 21135469, Unreported. Executors And Administrators ⇐ 87

The settlement and release of a wrongful death claim brought by the administratrix of her husband's estate cannot be effective with respect to the children's claims where there is no indication that the settlement is reached and the release signed "with the advice, approval, and consent" of the probate court as contemplated by RC 2111.18. Brewer v. Akron General Medical Center (Ohio App. 9 Dist., Summit, 01-27-1999) No. 19068, 1999 WL 33382, Unreported.

A person seeking to assert an underinsured motorist claim based on wrongful death must first qualify as an insured under the policy providing that coverage; an ex-husband is excluded from his ex-wife's policy pursuant to the accidental death of their son because he is not a "relative" since he is not related to his ex-wife by marriage and was not residing with her at the time of their son's accident. McDonald v. Nationwide Mut. Ins. Co. (Ohio App. 8 Dist., Cuyahoga, 08-08-1996) No. 69419, 1996 WL 447980, Unreported, appeal allowed 77 Ohio St.3d 1523, 674 N.E.2d 375, reversed 79 Ohio St.3d 413, 683 N.E.2d 1089, 1997-Ohio-374.

A wrongful death claim is a claim derived from bodily injury under a motor vehicle insurance policy which limits the amount payable "for all legal damages, including all derivative claims, claimed by anyone for bodily injury to one person as the result of one occurrence"; therefore, both a survivorship claim on behalf of an estate for pain and suffering a decedent suffered prior to death and a wrongful death claim on behalf of an estate for the benefit of the decedent's husband and children are subject to a $100,000 per person limitation; stated differently, the estate is limited to recover $100,000 in total, against the policy, for both claims. Estate of Springer v Nationwide Insurance Co, No. 92-A-1688, 1993 WL 317446 (11th Dist Ct App, Ashtabula, 8-6-93).

Law firm's failure to deposit proceeds of wrongful death action in bank account belonging to decedent's estate, as required by local rule, did not justify imposition of ten percent sanction against law firm's attorney fees award; settlement had not been approved by probate court, and proceeds of settlement had not been allocated among decedent's beneficiaries. In re Estate of Robertson (Ohio App. 7 Dist., 12-02-2004) 159 Ohio App.3d 297, 823 N.E.2d 904, 2004-Ohio-6509, appeal not allowed 105 Ohio St.3d 1500, 825 N.E.2d 624, 2005-Ohio-1666. Death ⇨ 109

Automobile accident victim's spouse who settled tort claim as victim's court-appointed guardian before his death was not acting as his personal representative for purposes of the wrongful death statute and, therefore, lacked authority to act for his next of kin when she executed the settlement agreement; thus, the wrongful death claims of the next of kin who were not parties to the settlement agreement were not released thereby. Davis v. Dembek (Ohio App. 10 Dist., 11-26-2002) 150 Ohio App.3d 423, 782 N.E.2d 80, 2002-Ohio-6443, appeal allowed, reversed 99 Ohio St.3d 49, 788 N.E.2d 1063, 2003-Ohio-2462. Compromise And Settlement ⇨ 4.5; Compromise And Settlement ⇨ 17(2)

Physician waived appellate review of claim that his personal responsibility under settlement agreement in wrongful death action was contingent upon his insurer paying full settlement amount, where trial court did not address issue, and appeal filed by executor of patient's estate and hospital's cross-appeal included physician as a party to settlement agreement, but physician did not file a cross-appeal. Kostelnik v. Helper (Ohio, 07-03-2002) 96 Ohio St.3d 1, 770 N.E.2d 58, 2002-Ohio-2985, reconsideration denied 96 Ohio St.3d 1489, 774 N.E.2d 764, 2002-Ohio-4478. Appeal And Error ⇨ 878(2)

The letter from counsel for hospital confirming settlement agreement in wrongful death action, releases, and actions of executor of patient's estate, in seeking relief from settlement against physician only in the amount of $1,100,000, established, as a matter of law, that executor settled with hospital for $100,000 and that $1,100,000 was physician's separate obligation; $1,200,000 settlement was merely sum of two separate settlements and not a joint and several liability. Kostelnik v. Helper (Ohio, 07-03-2002) 96 Ohio St.3d 1, 770 N.E.2d 58, 2002-Ohio-2985, reconsideration denied 96 Ohio St.3d 1489, 774 N.E.2d 764, 2002-Ohio-4478. Compromise And Settlement ⇨ 5(1); Compromise And Settlement ⇨ 11

Claim of attorneys in legal malpractice action that privity was lacking with regard to all beneficiaries of decedent's estate because the estate beneficiaries disclaimed any interest in the proceeds of the wrongful death settlement were not stipulated in the trial court, nor addressed by argument below, and thus, could not be considered on appeal. Brinkman v. Doughty (Ohio App. 2 Dist., 11-17-2000) 140 Ohio App.3d 494, 748 N.E.2d 116, appeal not allowed 91 Ohio St.3d 1480, 744 N.E.2d 1194. Appeal And Error ⇨ 173(13)

Undesignated settlement arising out of patient's death, which was negotiated by estate attorneys and paid by Pennsylvania hospital to patient's Ohio estate, was to be characterized as survivorship proceeds for benefit of estate, rather than wrongful death proceeds payable to next of kin under Ohio law, as it was inconceivable that hospital would have settled wrongful death matter for which it had no statutory liability under Pennsylvania law. Hooks v. Owen (Ohio App. 7 Dist., 09-23-1998) 130 Ohio App.3d 38, 719 N.E.2d 581, dismissed, appeal not allowed 85 Ohio St.3d 1405, 706 N.E.2d 787. Death ⇨ 101

Settlement funds recovered by the personal representative in a wrongful death action, where designated by the remitter for exclusive distribution to the statutory beneficiaries, are not an asset of the estate. Hooks v. Owen (Ohio App. 7 Dist., 09-23-1998) 130 Ohio App.3d 38, 719 N.E.2d 581, dismissed, appeal not allowed 85 Ohio St.3d 1405, 706 N.E.2d 787. Death ⇨ 101

Personal representative of decedent's estate does not require consent of the beneficiaries prior to the settlement. Gibson v. State Farm Mut. Auto. Ins. Co. (Ohio App. 2 Dist., 08-22-1997) 123 Ohio App.3d 216, 704 N.E.2d 1. Compromise And Settlement ⇨ 4.5

Personal representative's settlement of wrongful death claim and release of tortfeasor without consent of beneficiary's insurer did not result in breach by beneficiary of consent to settle provisions of her auto policy so as to preclude claim for underinsurance benefits for death of decedent under beneficiary's own policy. Gibson v. State Farm Mut. Auto. Ins. Co. (Ohio App. 2 Dist., 08-22-1997) 123 Ohio App.3d 216, 704 N.E.2d 1. Insurance ⇨ 2793(2)

Automobile insurance policy provision which eliminates underinsured motorist coverage for persons insured thereunder who are injured under Ohio's wrongful death statute, but are not the personal representative, when personal representative settles claim, violates underinsurance statute and is therefore invalid. Gibson v. State Farm Mut. Auto. Ins. Co. (Ohio App. 2 Dist., 08-22-1997) 123 Ohio App.3d 216, 704 N.E.2d 1. Insurance ⇨ 3367

Because it is statutory beneficiaries who are real parties in interest in wrongful death action, and because the amount received as result of action, whether by settlement or otherwise, is to be distributed to them, justice requires that they, in turn, be bound by execution of any general release which is a condition thereof. Morrison v. Fleck (Ohio App. 9 Dist., 06-11-1997) 120 Ohio App.3d 307, 697 N.E.2d 1064. Death ⇨ 25

Settlement which was entered into by administrator of decedent's estate in wrongful death action, which released defendant from any and all past, present and future claims, barred subsequent common-law claim for recovery of funeral and burial expenses, even though settlement did not specifically refer to such expenses. Morrison v. Fleck (Ohio App. 9 Dist., 06-11-1997) 120 Ohio App.3d 307, 697 N.E.2d 1064. Compromise And Settlement ⇨ 16(2)

Insured whose brother had died in an automobile accident did not breach the notice requirement of the subrogation clause in her underinsured motorist (UIM) policy by failing to tell the insurer about a wrongful death settlement between her brother's personal representative and the tort-feasor's liability insurer until two years after the probate court approved it, where the notice requirement applied only to settlements involving the "insured," and she did not participate in the settlement or receive any of its proceeds, did not know about it or even that the representative was acting for her until after approval, and took no affirmative steps to destroy her insurer's subrogation rights. Weiker v. Motorists Mut. Ins. Co. (Ohio, 06-17-1998) 82 Ohio St.3d 182, 694 N.E.2d 966, 1998-Ohio-265, 1998-Ohio-373. Insurance ⇨ 2793(1)

Administrator's settlement of wrongful death claims and release of tortfeasor and tort-feasor's liability insurer following decedent's death in automobile accident did not mean that decedent's siblings were no longer "legally entitled to recover" tort damages, and thus they could still seek underinsured motorist (UIM) benefits, where UIM insurer consented to settlement. Bentley v. Grange Mut. Cas. Ins. Co. (App. 10 Dist., 04-10-1997) 119 Ohio App.3d 93, 694 N.E.2d 526. Insurance ⇨ 2793(2)

Estate's administrator's ability to appeal trial court's approval of settlement of estate's wrongful death claim against county did not preclude administrator's legal malpractice claim against attorneys whose allegedly negligent advice permitted statute of limitations on wrongful death claim to expire; because statute of limitations had run, estate had no recourse against county if its settlement offer were rejected. DePugh v. Sladoje (Ohio App. 2 Dist., 06-14-1996) 111 Ohio App.3d 675, 676 N.E.2d 1231. Attorney And Client ⇨ 112

Personal representative appointed by probate court must obtain court's consent regarding settlement agreement in wrongful death action. Fosnight v. Esquivel (Ohio App. 3 Dist., 09-18-1995) 106 Ohio App.3d 372, 666 N.E.2d 273. Compromise And Settlement ⇨ 4.5

Wrongful death settlement was not enforceable, where personal representative of estate of decedent killed as a result of automobile collision, who was appointed by probate court, entered into it without court's consent. Fosnight v. Esquivel (Ohio App. 3 Dist., 09-18-1995) 106 Ohio App.3d 372, 666 N.E.2d 273. Compromise And Settlement ⇨ 4.5

Administrator of decedents' estate has exclusive right to settle with tortfeasor amount to be paid under wrongful death statute. Love v. Nationwide Mut. Ins. Co. (Ohio App. 10 Dist., 06-22-1995) 104 Ohio App.3d 804, 663 N.E.2d 407, appeal not allowed 74 Ohio St.3d 1459, 656 N.E.2d 952. Compromise And Settlement ⇨ 4.5

Absent fraud or other similar ground, proper settlement of administrator of decedent's estate with tort-feasor, if approved by probate court and executed by court-appointed administrator, is binding upon beneficiaries and bars any further prosecution of wrongful death claim. Love v. Nationwide Mut. Ins. Co. (Ohio App. 10 Dist., 06-22-1995) 104 Ohio App.3d 804, 663 N.E.2d 407, appeal not allowed 74 Ohio St.3d 1459, 656

N.E.2d 952. Compromise And Settlement ☞ 7.1; Compromise And Settlement ☞ 17(1)

Beneficiaries in wrongful death action were barred from seeking underinsurance compensation provided in their personal policies of auto insurance after administrator of decedents' estate settled wrongful death claims and released tort-feasor from further liability. Love v. Nationwide Mut. Ins. Co. (Ohio App. 10 Dist., 06-22-1995) 104 Ohio App.3d 804, 663 N.E.2d 407, appeal not allowed 74 Ohio St.3d 1459, 656 N.E.2d 952. Insurance ☞ 2793(1)

General release of tort-feasor executed by administrator of decedents' estate binds beneficiaries of wrongful death action. Love v. Nationwide Mut. Ins. Co. (Ohio App. 10 Dist., 06-22-1995) 104 Ohio App.3d 804, 663 N.E.2d 407, appeal not allowed 74 Ohio St.3d 1459, 656 N.E.2d 952. Release ☞ 31

Three-month period between insured's letter to underinsured motorist (UIM) carrier and settlement of estate's wrongful death claim with liability insurer was reasonable, and letter, which named executor's insurer and stated that that insurer gave attorney for insured and executor permission to settle with liability insurer, provided reasonable notice that settlement negotiations were going on; thus carrier had duty, and sufficient time, to act to protect its subrogation rights. Cincinnati Ins. Co. v. Jarvis (Ohio App. 6 Dist., 10-21-1994) 98 Ohio App.3d 155, 648 N.E.2d 30. Insurance ☞ 3517

A surviving husband cannot compromise or settle an action as an individual in the wrongful death of his wife because Ohio law mandates that wrongful death actions must be brought in the name of the deceased's personal representative. Tennant v. State Farm Mut. Ins. Co. (Summit 1991) 81 Ohio App.3d 20, 610 N.E.2d 437, motion overruled 62 Ohio St.3d 1434, 578 N.E.2d 826.

The personal representative of the decedent, if appointed in Ohio, may, at any time prior to or after commencement of the lawsuit with the consent of the appointing court, make a financial settlement with the defendant, and this right to make a settlement is exclusive to the personal representative, who acts on behalf of all interested parties. Tennant v. State Farm Mut. Ins. Co. (Summit 1991) 81 Ohio App.3d 20, 610 N.E.2d 437, motion overruled 62 Ohio St.3d 1434, 578 N.E.2d 826.

Where a personal representative settles an action with the consent of the court which appointed him, the settlement is binding on all beneficiaries and is a bar to further prosecution of a wrongful death claim. Tennant v. State Farm Mut. Ins. Co. (Summit 1991) 81 Ohio App.3d 20, 610 N.E.2d 437, motion overruled 62 Ohio St.3d 1434, 578 N.E.2d 826.

When a husband signs a release in his capacity as personal representative of his deceased wife's estate upon settlement of a wrongful death action, he is acting on behalf of all beneficiaries, of which he is one; he is thus barred from further prosecution in his individual capacity. Tennant v. State Farm Mut. Ins. Co. (Summit 1991) 81 Ohio App.3d 20, 610 N.E.2d 437, motion overruled 62 Ohio St.3d 1434, 578 N.E.2d 826.

An insurer on a single-limit underinsured motorist policy may not set off against the single limit of liability the total amount paid by the underinsured tortfeasor's insurer when the claims of each of the claimants taken individually do not reach that limit as reduced by the amount paid to each claimant by the tortfeasor; under such circumstances, the amount paid to each claimant by the tortfeasor's insurer shall be deducted from the claimant's total claim to determine the amount of the unsatisfied claim and each claimant shall take a proportional share of the remainder of the limit as reduced by his proportional share of the setoff. Derr v. Westfield Cos. (Ohio 1992) 63 Ohio St.3d 537, 589 N.E.2d 1278.

Upon death of insured, settlement proceeds under uninsured motorist provisions were to be considered damages distributable under the Wrongful Death Act R.C. §2125.02 rather than as proceeds of insurance contract payable to deceased insured's estate. In re Estate of Reeck (Ohio 1986) 21 Ohio St.3d 126, 488 N.E.2d 195, 21 O.B.R. 429. Executors And Administrators ☞ 51

In the case of the death of an insured, the settlement proceeds under an uninsured motorist provision are to be distributed among those persons who are entitled by statute to bring a wrongful death action. In re Estate of Reeck (Ohio 1986) 21 Ohio St.3d 126, 488 N.E.2d 195, 21 O.B.R. 429.

Where applications are made in probate court by a widow and her adult sons for an order of distribution of funds received by her, as executrix, from a railroad company engaged in interstate commerce, in settlement for death of her husband who had been killed in the course of his employment with such company, the Federal Employers Liability Act, 45 U.S.C. Ch 2 § 51 et seq., rather than GC 10509–167 (RC 2125.02) and 10509–168 (RC 2125.03), apply as to such distribution. In re Backus' Estate (Licking 1943) 73 Ohio App. 262, 55 N.E.2d 811, 28 O.O. 432. Death ☞ 101

The obtaining of a consent from the probate court by an administrator under GC 10772 (repealed 1932. See §§10509–167, 10509–168), to make settlement for injuries resulting in the death of his decedent while in the course of his employment, and the execution of a release of damage by the dependent, do not constitute a waiver by the latter of her claim for compensation, nor do they preclude such dependent from thereafter making application therefor. State ex rel. Trumbull Steel Co. v. Industrial Commission (Ohio 1922) 106 Ohio St. 82, 138 N.E. 530, 1 Ohio Law Abs. 10, 1 Ohio Law Abs. 278, 20 Ohio Law Rep. 427. Death ☞ 25; Workers' Compensation ☞ 1103

A settlement by the administrator, under this section, with the approval of the probate court does not preclude a subsequent application to the industrial commission under the workmen's compensation law. State ex rel. Trumbull Steel Co. v. Industrial Commission (Ohio 1922) 106 Ohio St. 82, 138 N.E. 530, 1 Ohio Law Abs. 10, 1 Ohio Law Abs. 278, 20 Ohio Law Rep. 427.

Where it does not appear that the probate court consented to and approved of a settlement made by the widow and administratrix of a decedent killed by a wrongful act, such settlement is void as against the minor children of the deceased. Baltimore & O. Ry. Co. v. Hottman (Ohio Cir. 1903) 15 Ohio C.D. 140, 1 Ohio C.C.(N.S.) 17, affirmed 70 Ohio St. 475, 72 N.E. 1154, 2 Ohio Law Rep. 25.

A contract by a widow fixing an attorney's fees in an action for wrongful death is valid, and where a widow settles directly with the railroad attorney she is still liable for the amount she contracted to pay her attorney for prosecuting the case. Connell v. Brumback (Ohio Cir. 1899) 10 Ohio C.D. 149.

Where a person has made a contract for settlement in his lifetime with the person whose unlawful act is the cause of his death, the terms of which were complied with, the pleading and establishment of such a settlement is a bar to an action by his administrator under RS 6134. Solor Refining Co. v. Elliott (Ohio Cir. 1898) 8 Ohio C.D. 225.

Consent of the probate court to a settlement by the administrator is not part of the contract but merely authorizes it and cannot be withdrawn after the compromise is consummated; hence, such settlement and release can be pleaded in bar to a second action unless it can be set aside on some proper ground. Bragg v. Ohio Elec. Ry. Co. (Ohio Com.Pl. 1920) 31 Ohio Dec. 125, 23 Ohio N.P.(N.S.) 140.

The probate court may not withdraw a consent given by it to a settlement of damages for death by wrongful act made by the administrator of the decedent. Bragg v. Ohio Elec. Ry. Co. (Ohio Com.Pl. 1920) 31 Ohio Dec. 125, 23 Ohio N.P.(N.S.) 140.

A sole beneficiary is authorized to make a contract that will release the railroad. Cullison v Baltimore & Ohio RR Co, 4 NP 360, 7 D 269 (CP, Licking 1897).

A widow receiving a settlement as beneficiary from the relief department of a railroad company cannot recover thereafter when suing as administratrix under this section. Cullison v Baltimore & Ohio RR Co, 4 NP 360, 7 D 269 (CP, Licking 1897).

Where widow of decedent killed in Ohio accident executed release in Georgia, her place of residence, said release barred recovery by decedent or minor children in Ohio wrongful death action. McCluskey v. Rob San Services, Inc. (S.D.Ohio 1977) 443 F.Supp. 65, 10 O.O.3d 248.

Where an employee executes a release in full for all claims for damages for injuries sustained by him in his employment, his estate is barred from further recovery in the event of his subsequent death from such injuries, but any claim for loss sustained by the widow or next of kin remains intact. Maguire v Cincinnati Traction Co, 14 CC(NS) 431, 23 CD 24 (Hamilton 1911), affirmed by 87 OS 512, 102 NE 1121 (1913).

12. Statutes of limitation—Commenced within two years

The wrongful death act gave an action to the personal representative of the deceased provided such action is commenced within two years after the death of such deceased person; the proviso therein is a condition qualifying the right of action, and not a mere limitation on the remedy. (See also Sabol v Pekoc, 148 OS 545, 76 NE(2d) 84 (1947).) Pittsburg, C. & St. L. Ry. Co. v. Hine (Ohio 1874) 25 Ohio St. 629. Death ☞ 37; Limitation Of Actions ☞ 6(1)

Two-year limitations period applicable to wrongful death action, which applied to claim by decedent's children for uninsured motorist (UM) benefits under automobile insurance policy issued to decedent's mother, was not tolled by fact that children were minors. Russ v. Nationwide Mut. Ins. Co. (Ohio App. 10 Dist., Franklin, 03-30-2004) No. 03AP-783, 2004-Ohio-1616, 2004 WL 626156, Unreported. Death ☞ 39

2125.02
Note 12

Assuming statutory "legally entitled to recover" qualification applied to underinsured motorist (UIM) coverage, fact that insured's employees, as survivors of deceased infant, did not seek UIM coverage until after expiration of two year statute of limitations for wrongful death claims did not serve as a basis to deny UM/UIM coverage; UIM statute was ambiguous as to when insured had to be "legally entitled to recover" and provision was a remedial statute that was to be liberally construed to give effect to remedy provided. Welsh v. Indiana Ins. Co. (Ohio App. 5 Dist., Stark, 09-22-2003) No. 2002CA00370, 2003-Ohio-5026, 2003 WL 22176824, Unreported, appeal not allowed 102 Ohio St.3d 1482, 810 N.E.2d 966, 2004-Ohio-3069. Insurance ⇔ 2782

Trial court erred in holding that survivors were not "legally entitled to recover" from tortfeasor, since they failed to file suit against tortfeasor before expiration of two year statute of limitations for wrongful death, and that survivors were, therefore, precluded from receiving uninsured/underinsured motorist (UIM) benefits under commercial automobile insurance policy issued to decedent's employer; phrase "legally entitled to recover," as used in statute, was ambiguous since statute did not specify at what point in time determination of whether an insured was legally entitled to recover damages from owner or operator of an uninsured vehicle was to be made. Ponser v. St. Paul Fire & Marine Ins. Co. (Ohio App. 5 Dist., Licking, 08-18-2003) No. 2002CA00072, 2003-Ohio-4377, 2003 WL 21962548, Unreported, appeal allowed, reversed in part 101 Ohio St.3d 214, 803 N.E.2d 814, 2004-Ohio-714, affirmed 104 Ohio St.3d 621, 821 N.E.2d 173, 2004-Ohio-7105. Insurance ⇔ 2782

Saving statute did not apply to provide a one-year extension for estate to re-file wrongful death action against village and police officer, which action estate had voluntarily dismissed prior to the expiration of two-year statute of limitations for such actions. Wagner v. Heavlin (Ohio App. 7 Dist., 02-14-2000) 136 Ohio App.3d 719, 737 N.E.2d 989. Limitation Of Actions ⇔ 130(5)

Saving statute provided a one-year extension for estate to re-file state law wrongful death claim against village and police officer, where estate's federal action, which included a state law wrongful death claim, was dismissed without prejudice after the expiration of the two-year statute of limitation. Wagner v. Heavlin (Ohio App. 7 Dist., 02-14-2000) 136 Ohio App.3d 719, 737 N.E.2d 989. Limitation Of Actions ⇔ 130(5)

Statute of limitations for action against company that installed manure-handling system on farm, brought on behalf of minors whose fathers were found dead at bottom of pit of manure, was two-year limitations period for wrongful death actions and began running with deaths of fathers; ten-year statute of repose for action to recover for injuries arising out of defective and unsafe condition of an improvement to real property, and related provision tolling statute of repose for minors, did not even come into play unless two-year limitations period for wrongful death was satisfied. Schafer v. Gateway Harvestore, Inc. (Ohio App. 3 Dist., 08-19-1998) 129 Ohio App.3d 448, 717 N.E.2d 1179, dismissed, appeal not allowed 84 Ohio St.3d 1436, 702 N.E.2d 1214. Death ⇔ 38; Death ⇔ 39

Discovery rule applies to toll two-year statute of limitations for wrongful death claims; overruling *Shover v Cordis Corp.*, 61 Ohio St.3d 213, 574 N.E.2d. Collins v. Sotka (Ohio, 04-29-1998) 81 Ohio St.3d 506, 692 N.E.2d 581. Death ⇔ 39

Wrongful death action that stems from murder accrues when victim's survivors discover, or through exercise of reasonable diligence, should have discovered, that defendant has been convicted and sentenced for murder; death, in and of itself, does not trigger limitations period. Collins v. Sotka (Ohio, 04-29-1998) 81 Ohio St.3d 506, 692 N.E.2d 581. Death ⇔ 39

Wrongful death action stemming from murder accrued when court entered order sentencing defendant for murder of plaintiffs' decedent. Collins v. Sotka (Ohio, 04-29-1998) 81 Ohio St.3d 506, 692 N.E.2d 581. Death ⇔ 39

Wrongful death action does not accrue until death of injured person. Dougherty v. Fecsik (Ohio App. 8 Dist., 12-16-1996) 116 Ohio App.3d 456, 688 N.E.2d 555. Death ⇔ 39

Plaintiff in wrongful death action who voluntarily dismisses action prior to expiration of statute of limitations has two years from date of death of injured person in which to refile case; savings statute permitting refiling of action within one year of dismissal only applies if dismissal occurred after expiration of statute of limitations. Dougherty v. Fecsik (Ohio App. 8 Dist., 12-16-1996) 116 Ohio App.3d 456, 688 N.E.2d 555. Limitation Of Actions ⇔ 130(5)

Wrongful death claims accrue upon death of decedent, and are subject to two-year statute of limitations. Evans v. S. Ohio Med. Ctr. (Ohio App. 4 Dist., 05-04-1995) 103 Ohio App.3d 250, 659 N.E.2d 326. Death ⇔ 38; Death ⇔ 39

In case of death alleged to have been caused by medical malpractice, even where plaintiff fails to file negligence action or malpractice action within applicable statute of limitations, wrongful death claim is not time barred as long as it is filed within two years after decedent's death. Evans v. S. Ohio Med. Ctr. (Ohio App. 4 Dist., 05-04-1995) 103 Ohio App.3d 250, 659 N.E.2d 326. Death ⇔ 38

Claim for wrongful death began to run at time of child's death. Fetterolf v. Hoffmann-LaRoche, Inc. (Ohio App. 11 Dist., 03-27-1995) 102 Ohio App.3d 106, 656 N.E.2d 1020, reconsideration granted, opinion vacated, on reconsideration 104 Ohio App.3d 272, 661 N.E.2d 811, dismissed, appeal not allowed 73 Ohio St.3d 1411, 651 N.E.2d 1309. Death ⇔ 39

That tort action for wrongful death of pilot trainee was brought at least in part on behalf of his minor daughter did not toll running of applicable two-year period of limitations for wrongful death. Sponagle v. USAir Group, Inc. (Montgomery 1992) 81 Ohio App.3d 789, 612 N.E.2d 395. Limitation Of Actions ⇔ 55(4)

If wrongful death claim is filed within required time, that claim is not barred due to decedent's failure to timely pursue related tort action while he was alive. Anderson v. Brush-Wellman, Inc. (Ottawa 1991) 77 Ohio App.3d 657, 603 N.E.2d 284. Death ⇔ 15

A mother's wrongful death action brought against physicians for the death of her child, who was born with complications and who died at age three, began to run on the date of the child's death rather than on the date, over two years after the child's death, that the mother discovered through another doctor that her child's complications and ultimate death could have been caused by an improper forceps delivery. Burris v. Romaker (Allen 1991) 71 Ohio App.3d 772, 595 N.E.2d 425, dismissed, jurisdictional motion overruled 62 Ohio St.3d 1414, 577 N.E.2d 660.

A wrongful death action brought by a decedent's estate alleging negligent investigation and reporting by an investigator hired by the insurance company to investigate a potential insurance agent, who after being hired murdered his wife, the decedent, whom he met while selling insurance, is time-barred since the action accrued when the alleged acts of negligence occurred rather than at the time of the decedent's death. Caliman v. Mize (Hamilton 1989) 63 Ohio App.3d 231, 578 N.E.2d 531.

Failure to file claim for wrongful death within prescribed statutory time frame results in failure to plead all necessary elements of action. Shover v. Cordis Corp. (Ohio 1991) 61 Ohio St.3d 213, 574 N.E.2d 457, rehearing denied 62 Ohio St.3d 1410, 577 N.E.2d 362. Death ⇔ 51

Discovery rule for bodily injury actions will not be extended to apply to wrongful death claims in view of clear legislative intent that action be commenced within two years after decedent's death. Shover v. Cordis Corp. (Ohio 1991) 61 Ohio St.3d 213, 574 N.E.2d 457, rehearing denied 62 Ohio St.3d 1410, 577 N.E.2d 362. Death ⇔ 39

RC 1.14 and Civ R 6(A) apply to the computation of the limitations period of RC 2125.02(D) for wrongful death actions; therefore, where the two-year limitations period of RC 2125.02(D) expires on a Saturday, Sunday, or legal holiday, those days are excluded from the computation of the limitations period, and a complaint filed on the next day which is not a Saturday, Sunday, or a legal holiday is timely. Ritz v. Brown (Putnam 1989) 61 Ohio App.3d 65, 572 N.E.2d 159. Time ⇔ 10(4)

Action commenced against decedent's employer on July 2, 1982, for wrongful death of decedent, which occurred on March 25, 1980, as result of third and fourth-degree burns sustained at work, was barred by two-year limitations period of R.C. §2125.02. Ball v. Victor K. Browning & Co., Inc. (Ashtabula 1984) 21 Ohio App.3d 175, 487 N.E.2d 326, 21 O.B.R. 186. Death ⇔ 37

Neither the minority of a person entitled to bring an action in wrongful death nor RC 2305.16, which tolls statutes of limitation during minority, has any bearing on RC 2125.02 because the two-year time within which a wrongful death action may be brought under RC 2125.02 is not a time limitation on the remedy but an element of the right of action itself. Taylor v. Black & Decker Mfg. Co. (Warren 1984) 21 Ohio App.3d 186, 486 N.E.2d 1173, 21 O.B.R. 199.

Even if patient's right to bring medical malpractice action was barred by one-year statute of limitations before patient died, administratrix of deceased patient's estate was not precluded from bringing action for wrongful death arising out of same alleged medical malpractice where wrongful death action was brought within two years after decedent's death. Brosse v. Cumming (Cuyahoga 1984) 20 Ohio App.3d 260, 485 N.E.2d 803, 20 O.B.R. 322. Death ⇔ 38

Where the petition in a wrongful death action is filed, and summons thereon is issued within the two-year limitation prescribed by RC 2125.02 but service of summons is not obtained, the voluntary appearance by the defendant within sixty days thereafter is equivalent to service of summons and the action is deemed "commenced" within the time prescribed for commencement of the action. Bakin v. Marti (Trumbull 1963) 118 Ohio App. 244, 194 N.E.2d 145, 25 O.O.2d 87.

Common pleas court was vested with power to substitute correct party plaintiff, administratrix of decedent's estate, for ancillary administrator, who was dismissed for want of interest, in wrongful death action after statute of limitations had run against filing of new action for alleged wrongful death, and substitution related back to date of filing of action. Renner v. Pennsylvania R. Co. (Columbiana 1951) 103 N.E.2d 832, 61 Ohio Law Abs. 298. Death ⇐ 39

Language used in section providing for the term within which an action for wrongful death must be commenced after the death of the deceased person, must be construed so that the first day of the period named is excluded and the last named day included. Young v. New York Cent. R. Co. (Lorain 1939) 64 Ohio App. 362, 28 N.E.2d 687, 18 O.O. 149.

Amended petition of a widow who institutes an action, as administratrix, for damages for wrongful death of her husband under mistaken belief that she had been duly appointed and had qualified as such, and thereafter discovers her error and amends her petition so as to show that she was appointed administratrix after expiration of statute of limitation applicable to such action, will relate back to date of filing of petition, and action will be deemed commenced within time limited by statute. Douglas v. Daniels Bros. Coal Co. (Ohio 1939) 135 Ohio St. 641, 22 N.E.2d 195, 123 A.L.R. 761, 15 O.O. 12. Death ⇐ 39; Limitation Of Actions ⇐ 125

Cause of action for wrongful death held extinguished as against defendant by lapse of two-year period before procuring service. Knight v. Schlachter (Wood 1927) 28 Ohio App. 70, 162 N.E. 455, 6 Ohio Law Abs. 196. Death ⇐ 38; Limitation Of Actions ⇐ 119(3)

Cause of action to recover for wrongful death was extinguished by failure to procure service upon defendant within two years; court had power of its own motion to dismiss action as to such defendant on motion to quash service of summons. Knight v. Schlachter (Wood 1927) 28 Ohio App. 70, 162 N.E. 455, 6 Ohio Law Abs. 196. Death ⇐ 38

Where the appointment of an administrator for a decedent who was killed by the negligence of another is not completed within two years of the wrongful death, an action brought before the cause abated but before the appointment of the administrator was completed cannot be maintained, and once the action abated by statutory limitation it could not be revived. Archdeacon v Cincinnati Gas & Electric Co, 3 NP(NS) 45, 15 D 585 (Super, Cincinnati 1905), affirmed by 3 NP(NS) 606, 16 D 775 (Super, Cincinnati 1906); reversed by 76 OS 97, 81 NE 152 (1907).

The two-year limitation upon the bringing of an action for wrongful death, imposed by the Ohio statute, is without application during a period of war, where the beneficiaries under the statute are alien enemies. Borovitz v. American Hard Rubber Co. (N.D.Ohio 1923) 287 F. 368, 1 Ohio Law Abs. 342, 21 Ohio Law Rep. 175.

If suit for wrongful death is not commenced within the two years prescribed, the right to sue expires. Borovitz v. American Hard Rubber Co. (N.D.Ohio 1923) 287 F. 368, 1 Ohio Law Abs. 342, 21 Ohio Law Rep. 175.

Section requiring an action for wrongful death to be brought within two years after death occurred is subject to the implied exception that in an action on behalf of alien enemies, the period of the war will be excluded from the computation of the two years. Borovitz v. American Hard Rubber Co. (N.D.Ohio 1923) 287 F. 368, 1 Ohio Law Abs. 342, 21 Ohio Law Rep. 175. Death ⇐ 38; Limitation Of Actions ⇐ 113; War And National Emergency ⇐ 10(2)

The fact that the nominal plaintiff in an action is the administrator does not prevent suspension of the running of the two-year period by reason of war, where the beneficiaries are alien enemies. Borovitz v. American Hard Rubber Co. (N.D.Ohio 1923) 287 F. 368, 1 Ohio Law Abs. 342, 21 Ohio Law Rep. 175.

Amended complaint to add new party defendant in wrongful death action involving asbestos-related tort related back to date on which motion for leave to file amended complaint was filed, and that motion for leave having been filed within Ohio limitations period applicable to wrongful death actions, amended complaint as against the new defendant was timely. Chaddock v. Johns–Manville Sales Corp. (S.D.Ohio 1984) 577 F.Supp. 937. Limitation Of Actions ⇐ 124

Survival and wrongful death actions brought against a manufacturer of equipment used by steel plant where plaintiffs were employed, for exposure to fumes, dust and asbestos particles, were barred by two-year statute of limitations. (See also Bazdar v Koppers Co, 524 FSupp 1194 (ND Ohio 1981).) Johnson v. Koppers Co., Inc. (N.D.Ohio 1981) 524 F.Supp. 1182, appeal dismissed 705 F.2d 451, appeal dismissed 705 F.2d 454.

Plaintiff could not use savings statute more than once to save wrongful death action, and thus complaint, which was refiled twice, was barred by statute of limitations; plaintiff voluntarily dismissed original complaint after expiration of statute of limitations, plaintiff refiled complaint within one year as required by statute, plaintiff failed to obtain service on defendant, that action was involuntarily dismissed without prejudice, and plaintiff subsequently refiled complaint a second time. Brubaker v. Ross (Ohio App. 10 Dist., Franklin, 08-22-2002) No. 01AP-1431, 2002-Ohio-4396, 2002 WL 1938422, Unreported. Limitation Of Actions ⇐ 130(5); Limitation Of Actions ⇐ 130(9)

Neither fraud nor the discovery rule can toll RC 2125.02(D), Ohio's statute setting forth the time within which to commence wrongful death actions. Shover v. Cordis Corp. (Ohio 1991) 61 Ohio St.3d 213, 574 N.E.2d 457, rehearing denied 62 Ohio St.3d 1410, 577 N.E.2d 362.

Where an insured commences an action under the uninsured motorist coverage of an insurance policy for the wrongful death of her sister, a two-year statute of limitations applies; however, the insurer's failure to raise the statute of limitations as a defense to the action constitutes a waiver of the defense. Hutchison v State Automobile Mutual Insurance Co, No. 1304 (4th Dist Ct App, Ross, 8–11–87).

Where service of summons in wrongful death action was attempted but was quashed on September 27, 1954 petitioner was not entitled to benefit of rule authorizing an extender of one year in addition to the two years within which action may be brought under wrongful death statute, since the action was neither commenced nor attempted to be commenced within due time. Bronikowski v Bigham, 145 NE(2d) 331 (App 1956).

Where plaintiff's decedents were drowned on July 11, 1952 and action was filed and personal service obtained on defendant November 1, 1954, actions were barred by the two year statute of limitations, notwithstanding allegation that a suit for death was filed and dismissed without prejudice on September 27, 1954, where the petition failed to state that the action was filed within the two year period. Bronikowski v Bigham, affirmed 145 NE(2d) 331, 143 NE(2d) 490, 75 Abs 65 (CP 1955).

13. —— Constitutional issues, statutes of limitation

Lack of tolling provisions in two-year limitations period for wrongful death actions does not violate equal protection rights of minors on basis that minors lack standing to bring an action before the court, as any wrongful death action, whether on behalf of minors or adult beneficiaries, must be brought by personal representative of decedent. Schaffer v. Gateway Harvestore, Inc. (Ohio App. 3 Dist., 08-19-1998) 129 Ohio App.3d 448, 717 N.E.2d 1179, dismissed, appeal not allowed 84 Ohio St.3d 1436, 702 N.E.2d 1214. Constitutional Law ⇐ 249(3); Death ⇐ 9

14. —— Other statutes of limitation, effect, statutes of limitation

Two-year limitations period applicable to wrongful death action, rather than 15-year limitations period applicable to insured's action against insurer for benefits, applied to claim by decedent's wife and children for uninsured motorist (UM) benefits under automobile insurance policy issued to decedent's mother, where policy conditioned payment of benefits on plaintiffs having legal right to recover against tortfeasor. Russ v. Nationwide Mut. Ins. Co. (Ohio App. 10 Dist., Franklin, 03-30-2004) No. 03AP-783, 2004-Ohio-1616, 2004 WL 626156, Unreported. Death ⇐ 38; Insurance ⇐ 3560

Decedent's estate was not entitled to uninsured/underinsured motorist (UIM) coverage under decedent's father's employer's business automobile policy, because it was not "legally entitled to recover" damages against tortfeasor as two year limitation period for wrongful death action had expired; estate was required to prove all elements of wrongful death claim, including compliance with two year statute of limitations, as a precondition to UM/UIM coverage. Fish v. Ohio Cas. Ins. Co. (Ohio App. 5 Dist., Stark, 08-18-2003) No. 2003CA00030, 2003-Ohio-4380, 2003 WL 21962560, Unreported, cause dismissed 100 Ohio St.3d 1504, 799 N.E.2d 184, 2003-Ohio-6161, appeal not allowed 100 Ohio St.3d 1509, 799 N.E.2d 187, 2003-Ohio-6161. Insurance ⇐ 2782

Decedent's brother was not entitled to uninsured/underinsured motorist (UIM) coverage under commercial auto liability policy issued to his employer, because he was not "legally entitled to recover" damages against tortfeasor as two year limitation period for wrongful death action had expired; brother was required to prove all elements of wrongful death claim, including compliance with two year statute of limitations, as a precondition to UM/UIM coverage. Fish v. Ohio Cas. Ins. Co. (Ohio

App. 5 Dist., Stark, 08-11-2003) No. 2003CA00041, 2003-Ohio-4276, 2003 WL 21919885, Unreported, cause dismissed 100 Ohio St.3d 1504, 799 N.E.2d 184, 2003-Ohio-6161, appeal not allowed 100 Ohio St.3d 1509, 799 N.E.2d 187, 2003-Ohio-6161. Insurance ⚖ 2782

Time limits prescribed in wrongful death statute cannot be diminished or embellished based on the underlying wrongful act that caused the death of the decedent in a particular case. Schaffer v. Gateway Harvestore, Inc. (Ohio App. 3 Dist., 08-19-1998) 129 Ohio App.3d 448, 717 N.E.2d 1179, dismissed, appeal not allowed 84 Ohio St.3d 1436, 702 N.E.2d 1214. Death ⚖ 39

Reappointed administrator of decedent's estate failed to show that when statute of limitations expired on wrongful death claim, he had attorney-client relationship with attorneys who had initially represented him in his capacity as administrator, thus precluding his recovery in that capacity in legal malpractice action against those attorneys; although attorneys represented estate when administrator initially served in that capacity, they withdrew as attorneys of record in probate proceedings after administrator asked to be removed from that capacity, at which point attorney-client relationship ended. DePugh v. Sladoje (Ohio App. 2 Dist., 06-14-1996) 111 Ohio App.3d 675, 676 N.E.2d 1231. Attorney And Client ⚖ 112

Fact that there was no administrator for decedent's estate when statute of limitations on wrongful death claim expired did not preclude beneficiary's legal malpractice claim against attorneys for subsequently appointed administrator, as attorneys may have committed malpractice by failing to effect administrator's appointment prior to expiration of statute of limitations. DePugh v. Sladoje (Ohio App. 2 Dist., 06-14-1996) 111 Ohio App.3d 675, 676 N.E.2d 1231. Attorney And Client ⚖ 112

Estate's settlement of wrongful death claim against county, entered after statute of limitations on that claim had run, was no defense to estate's administrator's legal malpractice action, which was based on defendant attorneys' alleged mistaken advice that, upon dismissal of wrongful death claim before statute of limitations expired, savings statute gave estate one year from date of dismissal to refile case; failure to file before statute of limitations expired amounted to "malpractice per se." DePugh v. Sladoje (Ohio App. 2 Dist., 06-14-1996) 111 Ohio App.3d 675, 676 N.E.2d 1231. Attorney And Client ⚖ 112

Tort claims which were timely filed against defendant in another state, within applicable Ohio limitations period, but which were dismissed on forum non conveniens grounds, subject to condition imposed by law of other state that any statute of limitations defense be waived if action was commenced in another forum within six months, could be raised in present action, despite running of statute of limitations, against defendant who had moved for forum non conveniens relief, but not against defendant who had not so moved. Sponagle v. USAir Group, Inc. (Montgomery 1992) 81 Ohio App.3d 789, 612 N.E.2d 395. Limitation Of Actions ⚖ 55(4)

The administratrix of the estate of an employee who, having contracted berylliosis, failed to timely file an action against his employer for intentional tort, is not barred from bringing a wrongful death action based on the same claim. Anderson v. Brush–Wellman, Inc. (Ottawa 1991) 77 Ohio App.3d 657, 603 N.E.2d 284.

Conditions that may ordinarily toll pure statutes of limitations have no effect on special statutory limitations qualifying given right; however, extension of time under provisions excluding Saturday, Sunday, or legal holiday from computation of limitations period when limitations period expires on Saturday, Sunday, or legal holiday is not "tolling." Ritz v. Brown (Putnam 1989) 61 Ohio App.3d 65, 572 N.E.2d 159. Time ⚖ 10(4)

Claims for wrongful death and for medical malpractice are distinct even though originating in the same wrongful act; the time limit for wrongful death is governed by RC 2125.02(D), and the cause of action survives even though the decedent's claim in malpractice was time-barred when he died. Brosse v. Cumming (Cuyahoga 1984) 20 Ohio App.3d 260, 485 N.E.2d 803, 20 O.B.R. 322.

The statute of limitations in a malpractice action does not bar an action for wrongful death. Koler v. St. Joseph Hospital (Ohio 1982) 69 Ohio St.2d 477, 432 N.E.2d 821, 23 O.O.3d 413.

The provision of RC 2305.17 that "an attempt to commence an action is equivalent to its commencement, when the party diligently endeavors to procure a service, if such attempt is followed by service within sixty days" applies not only to the general limitation of action statutes enumerated in such section but also to any special statutory limitation. Bakin v. Marti (Trumbull 1963) 118 Ohio App. 244, 194 N.E.2d 145, 25 O.O.2d 87.

Where an alleged negligent act was such as would have, if death had not ensued, entitled a person to maintain an action therefor, a cause of action for wrongful death exists in such decedent's personal representative, and such cause of action for wrongful death cannot be defeated merely by reason of the bar of limitation which would have been applicable to decedent's action. Klema v. St. Elizabeth's Hospital of Youngstown (Ohio 1960) 170 Ohio St. 519, 166 N.E.2d 765, 11 O.O.2d 326.

An action by an administrator for wrongful death, where the death occurred nine days after the alleged wrongful act, claimed to be malpractice of a physician, may be brought at any time within two years after the death, as provided in section; such cause of action is not controlled by GC 11225 (RC 2305.11), which relates to the time within which an action for malpractice must be brought. Naticchioni v. Felter (Hamilton 1936) 54 Ohio App. 180, 6 N.E.2d 764, 22 Ohio Law Abs. 485, 7 O.O. 55.

Judgment, in action for death of employee while application for compensation was pending before Industrial Commission, held not subject to collateral attack, notwithstanding action was not commenced within statutory period. Straka v. Cleveland Ry. Co. (Cuyahoga 1929) 34 Ohio App. 252, 170 N.E. 611. Judgment ⚖ 501; Workers' Compensation ⚖ 2150

The limitation of actions in a wrongful death suit runs from the death of the person injured by the wrongful act; the right to maintain the action is not affected by the lapse of time between the injury and death unless the deceased would have already been barred by the statute of limitations at the time of his death. Solor Refining Co. v. Elliott (Ohio Cir. 1898) 8 Ohio C.D. 225.

The Ohio "savings statute" has no application to a cause of action against which the statute of limitations has run where the cause has failed other than on the merits in another jurisdiction. Andrew v. Bendix Corp. (C.A.6 (Ohio) 1971) 452 F.2d 961, 61 O.O.2d 81, certiorari denied 92 S.Ct. 1773, 406 U.S. 920, 32 L.Ed.2d 119.

GC 10773–1 (repealed 1932. See § 10509–169), requiring an action for wrongful death to be brought within two years after death occurred, is subject to an implied exception excluding from computation of the period, in an action on behalf of alien enemies, the period of the war. Borovitz v. American Hard Rubber Co. (N.D.Ohio 1923) 287 F. 368, 1 Ohio Law Abs. 342, 21 Ohio Law Rep. 175. Death ⚖ 38; Limitation Of Actions ⚖ 113; War And National Emergency ⚖ 10(2)

When action was brought in Pennsylvania against manufacturer of aircraft in which Ohio resident was killed in North Carolina, Pennsylvania statute of limitations applied and barred wrongful death action but not survival action. Schenk v. Piper Aircraft Corp. (W.D.Pa. 1974) 377 F.Supp. 477, affirmed 521 F.2d 1399, affirmed 577 F.2d 742.

Where an action for wrongful death is filed within the time limits set by RC 2125.02(D), the trial court errs in using a bodily injury statute of limitation in RC 2305.10 to bar the action for wrongful death in a case where (1) a party dies from silicosis he contracted nine years before his death and had filed no action for bodily injury against the employer, and (2) the administratrix of the husband's estate, within two years of her husband's death, files a wrongful death action against her husband's former employer seeking compensation for herself and her children. Heck v Thiem Corp, No. 93–C–55, 1994 WL 705001 (7th Dist Ct App, Columbiana, 12–13–94).

In order to establish that a claimant for wrongful death, under the uninsured motorist coverage of a motor vehicle insurance policy, is "legally entitled to recovery from the owner or operator of an uninsured auto," RC 3937.18(A)(1), compliance with the two-year statute of limitations for wrongful death which is included in and considered to be an element of a claim for wrongful death under RC 2125.02 is mandatory, notwithstanding the fifteen-year statute of limitations for actions based on contract. Hutchison v Midwestern Indemnity Co, No. 1352 (4th Dist Ct App, Ross, 8–11–87).

The two year statute of limitations contained in RC 2125.02 rather than the one year statute of limitations contained in RC 2305.11 applies in a wrongful death action which arises originally from what is typically characterized as medical malpractice. Frost v Jonson, No. CA80–11–0124 (12th Dist Ct App, Butler, 1–29–82).

Where service of summons upon a defendant is quashed upon the ground that it was not left at his usual place of residence, plaintiff does not qualify for the extender of the statute of limitations granted by GC 10509–169 (RC 2125.04). Bronikowski v Bigham, affirmed 145 NE(2d) 331, 143 NE(2d) 490, 75 Abs 65 (CP 1955).

15. —— Pleading, statutes of limitation

Because estate's administrator was in privity with estate's beneficiary, administrator had standing to maintain legal malpractice action against beneficiary's attorneys, who allegedly gave incorrect advice to beneficiary (who later served as interim administrator) as to when wrongful death action was required to be refiled. DePugh v. Sladoje (Ohio App. 2 Dist.,

06-14-1996) 111 Ohio App.3d 675, 676 N.E.2d 1231. Attorney And Client ⇒ 129(1)

Commencement date for wrongful death action was date of death, rather than date mother discovered through discussion with another physician that child's death might have been attributable to improper medical care at time of birth. Burris v. Romaker (Allen 1991) 71 Ohio App.3d 772, 595 N.E.2d 425, dismissed, jurisdictional motion overruled 62 Ohio St.3d 1414, 577 N.E.2d 660. Death ⇒ 39

RC 2125.02 as amended by 1981 H 332, eff. 2–5–82, applies to all wrongful death actions tried on or after that date in any forum. Ball v. Victor K. Browning & Co., Inc. (Ashtabula 1984) 21 Ohio App.3d 175, 487 N.E.2d 326, 21 O.B.R. 186.

The presentation to the executor or administrator of a claim for wrongful death by one of the statutory beneficiaries of that action is sufficient compliance with RC 2117.06 and RC 2117.07. Burwell v. Maynard (Ohio 1970) 21 Ohio St.2d 108, 255 N.E.2d 628, 50 O.O.2d 268.

It is not error to permit the substitution as plaintiff in a wrongful death action of the original administratrix of the estate of a nonresident for an ancillary administrator after the expiration of the period of limitations. Kyes v. Pennsylvania R. Co. (Ohio 1952) 158 Ohio St. 362, 109 N.E.2d 503, 49 O.O. 239.

The court has the power to substitute a proper party plaintiff in a wrongful death action after the statute of limitations has run. Renner v. Pennsylvania R. Co. (Columbiana 1951) 103 N.E.2d 832, 61 Ohio Law Abs. 298.

In a wrongful-death action by the administrator of the decedent, the petition alleging that plaintiff's "decedent died leaving... his mother, a dependent, and that by reason of his wrongful death resulting from the negligence of defendant's decedent, the estate of plaintiff's decedent has been damaged in the sum of $10,000," sets forth such mother's dependency and pecuniary loss occasioned by the death of her son and states a cause of action. Ebeling v. Harman (Darke 1948) 83 Ohio App. 519, 80 N.E.2d 704, 52 Ohio Law Abs. 78, 38 O.O. 567, adhered to 83 Ohio App. 519, 82 N.E.2d 425, 52 Ohio Law Abs. 78, 38 O.O. 567.

Where administratrix commenced action for damages for wrongful death of decedent, and probate court removed her as administratrix because she was minor at time of filing application for appointment, motion of administrator de bonis non to be substituted as plaintiff should have been granted. Skalski v. Krieger (Lucas 1925) 26 Ohio App. 186, 159 N.E. 851, 3 Ohio Law Abs. 522.

In suit where answer admits that plaintiff is duly qualified administrator, and case is reached for trial more than two years after death, and defendant asks leave to amend his answer by denial of appointment and qualifications of plaintiff to interpose two-year bar of the statute, amendment will be denied. Where amended answer reaffirms all allegations of original answer except that plaintiff was duly qualified administrator, and then avers only that he was at a subsequent date, more than two years after death, appointed and qualified, legal effect is to leave in force admission of original answer of due appointment at commencement of suit. Archdeacon v. Cincinnati Gas & Elec. Co. (Ohio 1907) 76 Ohio St. 97, 81 N.E. 152, 4 Ohio Law Rep. 739. Death ⇒ 55; Executors And Administrators ⇒ 448

Where in a suit by an administrator for wrongful death, the answer admits plaintiff is the duly qualified administrator and the case being reached more than two years after the death, the defendant will not be permitted to amend his answer to deny the due appointment of the administrator for the sole purpose of interposing the two year bar of the statute. Archdeacon v. Cincinnati Gas & Elec. Co. (Ohio 1907) 76 Ohio St. 97, 81 N.E. 152, 4 Ohio Law Rep. 739.

It is not necessary to allege in a petition all the facts which contributed to the primary act complained of or which tend to establish the negligence of such act. Davis v. Guarnieri (Ohio 1887) 45 Ohio St. 470, 19 W.L.B. 204, 15 N.E. 350, 4 Am.St.Rep. 548. Negligence ⇒ 1512

Where rule of a railroad company has been continuously violated for fourteen years it is to be regarded as abrogated. Lake Shore & M.S.R. Co. v. Andrews (Ohio Cir. 1897) 8 Ohio C.D. 73, reversed 58 Ohio St. 426, 40 W.L.B. 45, 51 N.E. 26.

Where there are no allegations in reference to the laws of another state it will be presumed that they are the same as in Ohio; thus, an action in Ohio for wrongfully causing death in Michigan need not set forth Michigan decisions or statutes. Lake Shore & M.S.R. Co. v. Andrews (Ohio Cir. 1897) 8 Ohio C.D. 73, reversed 58 Ohio St. 426, 40 W.L.B. 45, 51 N.E. 26.

A petition by an administrator in an action for wrongful death must set out who the beneficiaries of such action are who are entitled to receive the funds if the plaintiff should recover. Hartzell v Shannon, 6 D Repr 1093 (DC, Hamilton 1881).

The amendment of a complaint to add a new party defendant in a wrongful death action based on an asbestos-related tort relates back to the date when the motion for leave to file an amended complaint was filed; if that motion was filed in a timely manner, the amended complaint against the new defendant is timely. Chaddock v. Johns–Manville Sales Corp. (S.D.Ohio 1984) 577 F.Supp. 937. Limitation Of Actions ⇒ 124

Where a plaintiff files a wrongful death action within two years in one county but no service is had upon the defendant, and after two years the case was dismissed for failure of service of summons and subsequently the plaintiff files an identical suit in another county, the plaintiff cannot be considered as having failed "otherwise than upon the merits" so as to authorize him to commence an action within one year thereafter under RC 2125.04. Bronikowski v Bigham, affirmed 145 NE(2d) 331, 143 NE(2d) 490, 75 Abs 65 (CP 1955).

2125.03 Distribution of award

(A)(1) The amount received by a personal representative in an action for wrongful death under sections 2125.01 and 2125.02 of the Revised Code, whether by settlement or otherwise, shall be distributed to the beneficiaries or any one or more of them. The court that appointed the personal representative, except when all of the beneficiaries are on an equal degree of consanguinity to the deceased person, shall adjust the share of each beneficiary in a manner that is equitable, having due regard for the injury and loss to each beneficiary resulting from the death and for the age and condition of the beneficiaries. If all of the beneficiaries are on an equal degree of consanguinity to the deceased person, the beneficiaries may adjust the share of each beneficiary among themselves. If the beneficiaries do not adjust their shares among themselves, the court shall adjust the share of each beneficiary in the same manner as the court adjusts the shares of beneficiaries who are not on an equal degree of consanguinity to the deceased person.

(2) The court may create a trust for any beneficiary who is under twenty-five years of age by ordering that the portion of the amount received by the personal representative for that beneficiary be deposited in trust for the benefit of that beneficiary, until the beneficiary reaches twenty-five years of age, and order the distribution of the amount in accordance with the provisions of the trust. Prior to appointment as a trustee of a trust created pursuant to this section, the person to be appointed shall be approved by each adult beneficiary and by the guardian of each minor beneficiary of the trust.

(3) The personal representative shall not distribute any amount received in an action for wrongful death under sections 2125.01 and 2125.02 of the Revised Code to any person in relation to whom the court has entered an order pursuant to division (E)(2) of section 2125.02 of the Revised Code.

(B) The court shall distribute the amount of funeral and burial expenses awarded, or received by settlement, by reason of the death to the personal representative of the decedent, to be expended by the personal representative for the payment, or as reimbursement for the payment, of the expenses.

(1996 H 391, eff. 10–1–96; 1992 H 166, eff. 8–3–92; 1981 H 332; 1980 H 387; 1969 S 104; 1953 H 1; GC 10509–168)

Uncodified Law

1992 H 166, § 3: See Uncodified Law under 2125.02.

Historical and Statutory Notes

Pre–1953 H 1 Amendments: 114 v 439

Amendment Note: 1996 H 391 substituted "any beneficiary who is under twenty-five years of age" for "children of the decedent", "that beneficiary" for "such children", and "that beneficiary" for "one or more of the beneficiaries" in division (A)(2); and made other nonsubstantive changes.

Library References

Death ⇐101.
Westlaw Topic No. 117.
C.J.S. Death §§ 58 to 66.

Research References

Encyclopedias

OH Jur. 3d Death § 113, by Whom Made.
OH Jur. 3d Declar. Judgments & Related Proceedings § 37, Jurisdiction, Generally—Probate Matters.

Treatises and Practice Aids

Carlin, Baldwin's Ohio Practice, Merrick-Rippner Probate Law § 12:1, Wrongful Death—Scope of RC Ch. 2125.

Carlin, Baldwin's Ohio Practice, Merrick-Rippner Probate Law § 12:6, Wrongful Death—Burial Expenses Part of Award.

Carlin, Baldwin's Ohio Practice, Merrick-Rippner Probate Law § 12:7, Wrongful Death—Status of Beneficiaries Fixed at Death of Decedent.

Carlin, Baldwin's Ohio Practice, Merrick-Rippner Probate Law § 12:10, Wrongful Death—Damages—Loss of Chance Doctrine.

Carlin, Baldwin's Ohio Practice, Merrick-Rippner Probate Law § 12:11, Wrongful Death—Damages—Compensatory.

Carlin, Baldwin's Ohio Practice, Merrick-Rippner Probate Law § 12:12, Wrongful Death—Damages—Apportionment.

Carlin, Baldwin's Ohio Practice, Merrick-Rippner Probate Law § 12:24, Entry Approving Settlement or Distributing Wrongful Death Proceeds—Form.

Carlin, Baldwin's Ohio Practice, Merrick-Rippner Probate Law § 12:25, Report of Distribution of Wrongful Death Proceeds—Form.

Carlin, Baldwin's Ohio Practice, Merrick-Rippner Probate Law § 12:26, Application for Apportionment by the Court After Judgment—Form.

Carlin, Baldwin's Ohio Practice, Merrick-Rippner Probate Law § 12:27, Entry of Apportionment by the Court—Form.

Carlin, Baldwin's Ohio Practice, Merrick-Rippner Probate Law § 12:28, Application for Appointment of Wrongful Death Trustee—Form.

Carlin, Baldwin's Ohio Practice, Merrick-Rippner Probate Law § 12:29, Consent to Trustee—Form.

Carlin, Baldwin's Ohio Practice, Merrick-Rippner Probate Law § 12:30, Wrongful Death Trust Agreement—Form.

Carlin, Baldwin's Ohio Practice, Merrick-Rippner Probate Law § 12:31, Judgment Entry—Form.

Carlin, Baldwin's Ohio Practice, Merrick-Rippner Probate Law App B SPF 14.0, Application to Approve Settlement and Distribution of Wrongful Death and Survival Claims—Form.

Carlin, Baldwin's Ohio Practice, Merrick-Rippner Probate Law App B SPF 14.1, Waiver and Consent Wrongful Death and Survival Claims—Form.

Carlin, Baldwin's Ohio Practice, Merrick-Rippner Probate Law App B SPF 14.2, Entry Approving Settlement and Distribution of Wrongful Death and Survival Claims—Form.

Ohio Personal Injury Practice § 15:47, Damages May be Paid Through Structured Settlements.

Law Review and Journal Commentaries

Damages in Wrongful Death Actions, Stanley B. Kent. 17 Clev-Marshall L Rev 233 (May 1968).

Probate prevents privacy. John W. Eilers, 15 Prob L J. Ohio 141 (July/August 2004).

Substitute House Bill 391—Omnibus Probate Bill, William B. McNeil. 7 Prob L J Ohio 2 (September/October 1996).

Who is Winning the Collateral Source Rule War?, The Battleground in the Sixth Circuit States, Nora J. Pasman-Green & Ronald S. Richards Jr. 31 U Tol L Rev 425 (Spring 2000).

Notes of Decisions

Apportionment 5
Attorney fees 1
Funeral expenses 3
Pecuniary injury or loss 2
Procedural issues 4
Workers' compensation award, effect 6

---

1. Attorney fees

Local probate rule that permitted probate court to deduct from attorney fees request the interest lost while wrongful death settlement proceeds were held in an attorney's trust account was improperly applied retroactively to reduce attorney fee award and costs awarded to law firm that prosecuted wrongful death action; rule was not in effect at time first application for fees was made, and rule affected a substantive right of law firm as to distribution of fees. In re Estate of Windsor (Ohio App. 7 Dist., Mahoning, 11-15-2004) No. 03 MA 184, 2004-Ohio-6213, 2004 WL 2650286, Unreported, appeal not allowed 105 Ohio St.3d 1471, 824 N.E.2d 541, 2005-Ohio-1186. Executors And Administrators ⇐ 485

An attorney who acts as cocounsel in a wrongful death action is entitled to recover his share of legal fees from the other attorney holding the proceeds of the action in trust for the clients who were vested beneficiaries, since the unpaid attorney was in privity with the clients, who were liable for his fees. Weisberger v. Home Ins. Cos. (Cuyahoga 1991) 76 Ohio App.3d 391, 601 N.E.2d 660, dismissed, jurisdictional motion overruled 63 Ohio St.3d 1455, 590 N.E.2d 750.

An attorney who acts as cocounsel in a wrongful death action is not barred from bringing an action to recover his share of legal fees from another attorney holding the proceeds of the action in trust for the clients by virtue of an exclusionary provision in the attorney's legal malpractice policy since the exclusion means that damages did not include legal fees incurred by cocounsel in obtaining judgment against the attorney. Weisberger v. Home Ins. Cos. (Cuyahoga 1991) 76 Ohio App.3d 391, 601 N.E.2d 660, dismissed, jurisdictional motion overruled 63 Ohio St.3d 1455, 590 N.E.2d 750.

Under an exclusionary provision of an attorney's legal malpractice policy, an arrangement by which the attorney received and distributed proceeds from a wrongful death action is not a "business enterprise" since no profit or business purpose was involved in the arrangement, which was a trust; thus, the exclusion does not bar an action by the attorney's cocounsel to recover judgment for unpaid legal fees and costs from the attorney's malpractice insurer. Weisberger v. Home Ins. Cos. (Cuyahoga 1991) 76 Ohio App.3d 391, 601 N.E.2d 660, dismissed, jurisdictional motion overruled 63 Ohio St.3d 1455, 590 N.E.2d 750. Insurance ⇐ 2391(2)

In a cocounsel's attorney's action against another attorney to recover his share of unpaid legal fees, summary judgment is improperly granted on the attorney's insurer's liability to cocounsel for an unpaid judgment against the insured attorney since a question of fact existed whether the attorney's failure to pay cocounsel's attorney fees and costs was negligent. Weisberger v. Home Ins. Cos. (Cuyahoga 1991) 76 Ohio App.3d 391, 601 N.E.2d 660, dismissed, jurisdictional motion overruled 63 Ohio St.3d 1455, 590 N.E.2d 750.

Where an attorney representing an administrator in the enforcement of a claim for wrongful death files a report in the probate court with regard to distribution of the proceeds of a settlement of that claim and showing a payment to such attorney of $525 for counsel fees and where the rules of that probate court require that the court shall be advised as to the arrangement for and shall review such fees and where at the time of the filing of such report such attorney has already been paid $975 for such counsel fees, the filing of such report may constitute a contempt of the probate court, regardless of whether the foregoing rules of court are or are not valid. In re La Penta's Estate (Ohio 1958) 167 Ohio St. 536, 150 N.E.2d 404, 5 O.O.2d 211.

2. Pecuniary injury or loss

Attempt of underinsured motorist (UIM) carrier to deny coverage for claims of insured's children, since they were not insureds, but sought benefits as statutory beneficiaries for insured's wrongful death, was invalid; obligation to provide coverage arose due to fact that insured suffered wrongful death, and carrier's attempted reliance on definition of "insured" was functionally equivalent of attempt to deny coverage to insured decedent. Holt v. Grange Mut. Cas. Co. (Ohio, 09-24-1997) 79 Ohio St.3d 401, 683 N.E.2d 1080, 1997-Ohio-375. Insurance ⇐ 2780; Insurance ⇐ 3460

In apportioning wrongful death damages, prospective advantages of a pecuniary nature which have been cut off by the premature death of the person from whom they would have proceeded should be considered, and with regard to a deceased child, one of the important considerations is the disposition of the deceased to support the beneficiary-claimant. In re

Cline's Estate (Ohio Prob. 1964) 1 Ohio Misc. 28, 202 N.E.2d 736, 30 O.O.2d 221. Death ☞ 101

In apportioning wrongful death benefits among beneficiaries, the principal standards to be considered by the court are the pecuniary injury, if any, suffered by the applicants and their age and condition. In re Cline's Estate (Ohio Prob. 1964) 1 Ohio Misc. 28, 202 N.E.2d 736, 30 O.O.2d 221.

The presumption that there is a pecuniary injury to persons legally entitled to care and support from a decedent, in an action for wrongful death, is negatived as to a widow where such widow was accorded no care and support, and none was expected or required by her from her husband, and her income is adequate for her needs; and where the adult children of such decedent are without money and living on a hand-to-mouth basis and the decedent had permitted them to live on certain of his properties rent free, and where it is probable that they will have to pay rent for the future use of such properties, such children have suffered a direct pecuniary loss through the death of the decedent and qualify for participation in the proceeds from such wrongful death claim. In re Miller's Estate (Sandusky 1955) 102 Ohio App. 493, 127 N.E.2d 409, 72 Ohio Law Abs. 546, 59 O.O. 425.

Instruction on damages for minor's death held not erroneous for failure to exclude earnings he might have made. John Shillito Co. v. Shanley (Hamilton 1926) 21 Ohio App. 12, 153 N.E. 102, 4 Ohio Law Abs. 750. Death ☞ 104(5); Parent And Child ☞ 7(14)

3. Funeral expenses

Trial court was required to approve the distribution of funds for funeral and burial expenses that were earmarked in a wrongful death settlement agreement, and thus, statutory beneficiaries could not show that probate court's distribution of $4,326.88 from proceeds from wrongful death settlement for payment funeral expenses adversely affected their rights. In re Estate of Kenington (Ohio App. 12 Dist., Clermont, 05-19-2003) No. CA2002-01-005, 2003-Ohio-2549, 2003 WL 21135469, Unreported. Executors And Administrators ☞ 214

Trial court is not required by statute to provide for or approve funeral and burial expenses in wrongful death settlement, in light of plain language of statute which renders discretionary whether to allocate settlement funds for such expenses. In re Estate of Craig (Butler 1993) 89 Ohio App.3d 80, 623 N.E.2d 620. Death ☞ 101

Probate court did not abuse its discretion in refusing to allocate funds from wrongful death settlement to pay for funeral and burial expenses of victim of automobile accident, in light of probate court's express reliance on valid court order requiring driver to pay funeral and burial expenses as part of driver's sentence for vehicular homicide. In re Estate of Craig (Butler 1993) 89 Ohio App.3d 80, 623 N.E.2d 620. Death ☞ 101

Funeral expenses incurred by a father for the funeral and burial of a seventeen year old minor son who sustained a fatal injury by reason of the wrongful act of a third person are not part of the damages recoverable for pecuniary loss for the death of said son under the wrongful death statutes, so that a father may recover such necessary funeral expenses from a wrongdoer who causes the death of such minor child. (Ed. note: Superseded by statutory amendment in 1969 S 104, eff. 11–21–69.) Caswell v. Harry Miller Excavating Co. (Ohio Com.Pl. 1969) 20 Ohio Misc. 46, 246 N.E.2d 921, 47 O.O.2d 307, 49 O.O.2d 75.

By the terms of section, the probate court, in making a distribution of the proceeds of such action among the beneficiaries, may consider funeral expenses incurred by any of the beneficiaries by reason of the death. Gaus v. Pennsylvania R. Co. (Allen 1937) 56 Ohio App. 299, 10 N.E.2d 635, 25 Ohio Law Abs. 24, 9 O.O. 389.

Where one of the beneficiaries for whose benefit the action was brought, by his own negligence contributed toward the injury which caused the death, damages cannot be awarded on account of the pecuniary loss to such beneficiary, and such beneficiary is not entitled to share in the proceeds of the action by reason of his having incurred funeral expenses. Gaus v. Pennsylvania R. Co. (Allen 1937) 56 Ohio App. 299, 10 N.E.2d 635, 25 Ohio Law Abs. 24, 9 O.O. 389.

RC 2125.03 does not require a probate court to order a personal representative to reimburse anyone for decedent's burial expenses, but rather the court is required to distribute the amount of funeral and burial expenses to the personal representative; any claim against the estate for reimbursement for funeral and burial expenses would then be required to be submitted to the personal representative according to law. In re Estate of Turnbaugh, No. 1356 (11th Dist Ct App, Portage, 3–30–84).

4. Procedural issues

Probate division of court of common pleas, through its exclusive jurisdiction to approve settlements in actions for wrongful death and to order distribution of settlement proceeds, rather than general division of court of common pleas, through its jurisdiction over declaratory judgment actions, had subject matter jurisdiction over action by decedent's daughter, brought after she had reached age of majority, alleging that settlement agreement in wrongful death action against physician and liability insurer, purportedly executed on her behalf by her mother, was void for fraud in the factum. Comer v. Bench (Ohio App. 2 Dist., Montgomery, 05-30-2003) No. CIV.A. 19229, 2003-Ohio-2821, 2003 WL 21267232, Unreported. Courts ☞ 472.4(2.1); Courts ☞ 472.5

The settlement and release of a wrongful death claim brought by the administratrix of her husband's estate cannot be effective with respect to the children's claims where there is no indication that the settlement is reached and the release signed "with the advice, approval, and consent" of the probate court as contemplated by RC 2111.18. Brewer v. Akron General Medical Center (Ohio App. 9 Dist., Summit, 01-27-1999) No. 19068, 1999 WL 33382, Unreported.

At best, the proceeds of a wrongful death claim are "assets" of the decedent's estate for procedural and accounting purposes only, the award being the actual property of the statutory beneficiaries, which cannot be used to satisfy the decedent's debts. State ex rel. Goldberg v. Mahoning Cty. Probate Court (Ohio, 09-05-2001) 93 Ohio St.3d 160, 753 N.E.2d 192, 2001-Ohio-1297, reconsideration denied 93 Ohio St.3d 1464, 756 N.E.2d 1239. Death ☞ 101; Executors And Administrators ☞ 51

Probate Court's statutory jurisdiction to distribute among the beneficiaries the amount received by a personal representative in an action for wrongful death does not empower the probate court to determine collateral-source deductions in actions brought against a state university, and that function remains exclusively with the Court of Claims. McMullen v. Ohio State Univ. Hosp. (Ohio, 04-12-2000) 88 Ohio St.3d 332, 725 N.E.2d 1117, 2000-Ohio-342. States ☞ 184.32

Wrongful death claimant who is a statutory beneficiary of an insured decedent, but not named insured under decedent's uninsured or underinsured motorist (UM/UIM) policy, may recover benefits under policy either individually or through administratrix of decedent's estate. Yepko v. State Farm Mut. Ins. Co. (Ohio, 09-24-1997) 79 Ohio St.3d 414, 683 N.E.2d 1090, 1997-Ohio-373. Insurance ☞ 3460

Attempt to avoid payment for valid wrongful death claims by narrowly defining who is "insured" is impermissible attempt to eliminate underinsured motorist (UIM) coverage where claim or claims of such persons arise from causes of action recognized by tort law. Holt v. Grange Mut. Cas. Co. (Ohio, 09-24-1997) 79 Ohio St.3d 401, 683 N.E.2d 1080, 1997-Ohio-375. Insurance ☞ 2774; Insurance ☞ 2780

Wrongful death claimants seeking recovery as statutory beneficiaries of insured need not be in privity with automobile insurer, i.e., they need not be insureds, in order to recover underinsured motorist (UIM) benefits; it is sufficient if insured decedent is in privity with insurer. Holt v. Grange Mut. Cas. Co. (Ohio, 09-24-1997) 79 Ohio St.3d 401, 683 N.E.2d 1080, 1997-Ohio-375. Insurance ☞ 3460

Payment of underinsured motorist (UIM) benefits to insured's estate for his wrongful death were received by insured's personal representative in that capacity, not as executor of his estate. Holt v. Grange Mut. Cas. Co. (Ohio, 09-24-1997) 79 Ohio St.3d 401, 683 N.E.2d 1080, 1997-Ohio-375. Executors And Administrators ☞ 51

When some or all beneficiaries of wrongful death action are children, trial court may order amount received for children to be placed in trust for their benefit until children reach age 25. Sawyer v. Lebanon Citizens Natl. Bank (Ohio App. 12 Dist., 07-31-1995) 105 Ohio App.3d 464, 664 N.E.2d 571, dismissed, appeal not allowed 74 Ohio St.3d 1476, 657 N.E.2d 783. Death ☞ 101

Contingency language in irrevocable trust agreement created for benefit of minor children with proceeds of wrongful death suit for death of their natural mother, purporting to transfer children's trust fund to mother's next of kin in event of children's untimely death, was invalid as against public policy; only children could dispose of trust funds vested in them. Sawyer v. Lebanon Citizens Natl. Bank (Ohio App. 12 Dist., 07-31-1995) 105 Ohio App.3d 464, 664 N.E.2d 571, dismissed, appeal not allowed 74 Ohio St.3d 1476, 657 N.E.2d 783. Trusts ☞ 52; Trusts ☞ 147(1)

Probate court has discretion to determine equitable distribution of wrongful death award or settlement proceeds. In re Estate of Marinelli (Ohio App. 11 Dist., 12-19-1994) 99 Ohio App.3d 372, 650 N.E.2d 935. Death ☞ 101

Note 4

A personal representative of an estate who recovers moneys pursuant to a wrongful death statute for exclusive distribution to statutory beneficiaries is not precluded from recovering accidental death benefits allegedly due under the terms of an automobile insurance policy since the moneys recovered under the wrongful death statute were not an asset of the decedent's estate to be administered by the personal representative as executor and thus were not subject to the right of subrogation of the automobile insurer. Fogt v. United Ohio Ins. Co. (Shelby 1991) 76 Ohio App.3d 24, 600 N.E.2d 1109.

Where no record is made in the probate court, the common pleas court has complete jurisdiction on appeal to entertain the cause and conduct a full hearing de novo to determine the issues involved, and in such hearing de novo to determine the apportionment of a part of the settlement of a wrongful death claim the refusal of such court to receive in evidence the entire record of the administration of the estate in probate court does not constitute error. In re Miller's Estate (Sandusky 1955) 102 Ohio App. 493, 127 N.E.2d 409, 72 Ohio Law Abs. 546, 59 O.O. 425.

Distribution of funds received in settlement of the death of an employee in interstate commerce are to be made per the federal employer's liability act and section has no bearing. In re Backus' Estate (Licking 1943) 73 Ohio App. 262, 55 N.E.2d 811, 28 O.O. 432.

Provisions of section apply to the duty of the probate court in making a distribution of the amount received by the personal representative, and they have no bearing on the trial of the action in the common pleas court. Gaus v. Pennsylvania R. Co. (Allen 1937) 56 Ohio App. 299, 10 N.E.2d 635, 25 Ohio Law Abs. 24, 9 O.O. 389.

Contributory negligence on the part of some of the beneficiaries will not bar the rest of the beneficiaries from having an action brought for their benefit. Wolf v. Lake Erie & W.R. Co. (Ohio 1896) 55 Ohio St. 517, 37 W.L.B. 23, 45 N.E. 708. Death ☞ 24

In a wrongful death action brought by the administrator of the estate of a divorced woman who did not have custody of her children, a federal trial court does not err by refusing to instruct the jury that when the children reached the age of twelve an Ohio court could let them choose under RC 3109.04 which parent to live with; the administrator's argument that it is "reasonable and probable that... each... would have selected the mother" is unfounded, and the proposed change would require the jury to speculate. Bowman v. Koch Transfer Co. (C.A.6 (Ohio) 1988) 862 F.2d 1257.

Uninsured motorist (UM) carrier should have paid the settlement of surviving insureds' wrongful death claims to the insured's personal representative, rather the surviving insureds. Yepko v. State Farm Mut. Auto. Ins. Co. (N.D.Ohio, 10-29-1998) 25 F.Supp.2d 831. Death ☞ 101; Insurance ☞ 3460

Changes in Ohio statutes regarding wrongful death and comparative negligence do not apply to accident occurring prior thereto. Tackett v. Consolidated Rail Corp. (S.D.Ohio 1982) 536 F.Supp. 409.

Where decedent's death occurred in Wisconsin where he was temporarily installing machinery, and all of his heirs were residents of Ohio where decedent was employed, Ohio law will apply to distribution to the beneficiaries. Satchwill v. Vollrath Co. (E.D.Wis. 1968) 293 F.Supp. 533, 47 O.O.2d 75.

RC 2125.01, RC 2125.02, and RC 2125.03 are expressly retroactive. McKinney v Kidwell, 2 OBR 353 (CP, Hamilton 1982).

5. Apportionment

The personal representatives are trustees of the fund received for damages in causing death and must distribute the same according to the statutes of descent. Steel v. Kurtz (Ohio 1876) 28 Ohio St. 191.

The amount recovered in a wrongful death action is for the exclusive benefit of the widow and next of kin, and is to be distributed among them in the proportions provided by law in relation to the distribution of personal estates of persons dying intestate. Weidner v. Rankin (Ohio 1875) 26 Ohio St. 522.

Where a testator's will gives a life estate in real estate and a pecuniary legacy to his wife, gives a legacy to his minor daughter in trust and the entire residuary estate, real and personal, is left to his sons, the personal estate being insufficient to pay both the debts and the legacies, the daughter's legacy is chargeable upon the residuary real estate. Moore v. Beckwith's Ex'r (Ohio 1862) 14 Ohio St. 129.

In a wrongful death action brought by the husband of the deceased, next of kin are entitled to distribution of a wrongful death settlement where the deceased had a "good and close" relationship with her father, an unusually close relationship with her sister and the death was traumatic for her brother; each of these individuals suffers damage by reason of the death and each is entitled to a portion of the wrongful death settlement. In re Estate of Cochran (Ohio App. 12 Dist., Clermont, 03-19-2001) No. CA2000-05-030, 2001 WL 273644, Unreported.

Because an award of extraordinary fiduciary fees must be adjusted so that the value of all the fiduciary's services to the estate correspond to the total compensation paid by the estate, a trial court's award of extraordinary fees without considering the regular commission is inappropriate; in addition, where the fee controversy involves a wrongful death settlement and the probate court is required to make an equitable distribution of the proceeds from the settlement, the court does not abuse discretion by awarding the executor a slightly larger share of the award after taking into consideration both the losses suffered by each beneficiary and the personal circumstances of each beneficiary. In re Estate of Thomas (Ohio App. 9 Dist., Summit, 04-12-2000) No. 19588, 2000 WL 372312, Unreported.

A father's visit with his son less than six months before the child's death precludes a finding of abandonment for purposes of wrongful death proceeds and if the parties are unable to equitably divide the proceeds according to RC 2125.03(A)(1) the court should consider the father's (1) failure to take any steps during the child's life to formally acknowledge parentage, (2) minimal contact with the child, (3) failure to pay child support, and (4) insignificant involvement and support compared to the mother's participation in the child's tragically short life. Wrongful Death of Turner (Ohio App. 2 Dist., Champaign, 11-25-1998) No. 98 CA 2, 1998 WL 811598, Unreported.

Court of Claims could not make collateral source deductions from award against state university hospital in wrongful death action until probate court had determined the proportionate shares to which deceased patient's beneficiaries were entitled. McMullen v. Ohio State Univ. Hosp. (Ohio, 04-12-2000) 88 Ohio St.3d 332, 725 N.E.2d 1117, 2000-Ohio-342. States ☞ 184.32

Uninsured motorist (UM) or underinsured motorist (UIM) benefits recovered by insured's personal representative for insured's wrongful death are "wrongful death proceeds" to be distributed to surviving spouse, children, and parents as statutory beneficiaries. Holt v. Grange Mut. Cas. Co. (Ohio, 09-24-1997) 79 Ohio St.3d 401, 683 N.E.2d 1080, 1997-Ohio-375. Death ☞ 101

RC 2125.03 was intended to vest discretion in the court in apportioning distribution in accordance with established principles of equity, without regard to the statute of descent and distribution, and without regard for any precise mathematical formula. In re Cline's Estate (Ohio Prob. 1964) 1 Ohio Misc. 28, 202 N.E.2d 736, 30 O.O.2d 221.

Wrongful death damages may be apportioned only among those beneficiaries listed in RC 2125.02. In re Cline's Estate (Ohio Prob. 1964) 1 Ohio Misc. 28, 202 N.E.2d 736, 30 O.O.2d 221.

On the evidence the court erred in awarding the entire proceeds of the settlement of a wrongful death claim to the widow to the exclusion of the children. In re Miller's Estate (Sandusky 1955) 102 Ohio App. 493, 127 N.E.2d 409, 72 Ohio Law Abs. 546, 59 O.O. 425.

A father as administrator of estate of deceased son, having received a sum of money in settlement of an action for wrongful death of that son, may, under authority of section, apportion said sum between himself and decedent's children, and when he invests the sum apportioned to the children in land, title being placed in name of one child, a court of equity will not, at the instance of the trustee in bankruptcy of the father's estate, order a reconveyance of the land to the father, who was adjudged a bankrupt within four months thereafter. Harry v. Russell (Wood 1941) 68 Ohio App. 377, 41 N.E.2d 424, 23 O.O. 67.

Probate court, not uninsured motorist (UM) carrier, had the sole authority to determine the share of the wrongful death proceeds to which the surviving insureds were entitled. Yepko v. State Farm Mut. Auto. Ins. Co. (N.D.Ohio, 10-29-1998) 25 F.Supp.2d 831. Death ☞ 101

In a wrongful death action, where the parents of the decedent were divorced subsequent to the decedent's death, and where all of the proceeds of the settlement were dispersed to the mother without the father being notified of the disbursement hearing, the father was divested of a property right without due process of law. In re Estate of Waselich, No. 83 C.A. 91 (7th Dist Ct App, Mahoning, 3–21–84).

6. Workers' compensation award, effect

In wrongful death cases where there are multiple beneficiaries, only person who has received workers' compensation award is subject to subrogation laws of payor's state. Thomas v. Cook Drilling Corp. (Ohio, 10-01-1997) 79 Ohio St.3d 547, 684 N.E.2d 75, 1997-Ohio-365. Workers' Compensation ☞ 2189

Insurer had no interest in survival and wrongful death action, and thus court did not abuse its discretion by denying insurer's eleventh-hour motion to intervene to assert subrogation claim for workers' compensation benefits paid to deceased worker's estate pursuant to Pennsylvania law; late filing of motion, only four weeks before rescheduled trial date, allowed court to determine that settlement monies obtained in action belonged to worker's next of kin, with nothing going to worker's estate, and insurer's right to subrogation under Pennsylvania law only applied to monies paid to the estate, the recipients of workers' compensation benefits. Thomas v. Cook Drilling Corp. (Ohio, 10-01-1997) 79 Ohio St.3d 547, 684 N.E.2d 75, 1997-Ohio-365. Workers' Compensation ⚖ 2225

2125.04 New action

In every civil action for wrongful death commenced or attempted to be commenced within the time specified by division (D)(1) or (D)(2)(c), (d), (e), (f), or (g) of section 2125.02 of the Revised Code, if a judgment for the plaintiff is reversed or the plaintiff fails otherwise than upon the merits and if the time limited by any of those divisions for the commencement of the action has expired at the date of the reversal or failure, the plaintiff or, if the plaintiff dies and the cause of action survives, the personal representative of the plaintiff may commence a new civil action for wrongful death within one year after that date.

(2004 S 80, eff. 4–7–05; 2001 S 108, § 2.01, eff. 7–6–01; 2001 S 108, § 2.02, eff. 7–6–01; 1996 H 350, eff. 1–27–97 [1]; 1953 H 1, eff. 10–1–53; GC 10509–169)

[1] See Notes of Decisions, *State ex rel. Ohio Academy of Trial Lawyers v. Sheward* (Ohio 1999), 86 Ohio St.3d 451, 715 N.E.2d 1062.

Uncodified Law

2001 S 108, § 1 and 3: See Uncodified Law under 2125.01.

Historical and Statutory Notes

Ed. Note: The amendment of this section by 1996 H 350, eff. 1–27–97, was repealed by 2001 S 108, § 2.02, eff. 7–6–01. See *Baldwin's Ohio Legislative Service Annotated*, 1996, page 10/L–3383, and 2001, page 6/L–1441, or the OH–LEGIS or OH–LEGIS–OLD database on Westlaw, for original versions of these Acts.

Pre–1953 H 1 Amendments: 114 v 439

Amendment Note: 2004 S 80 rewrote this section, which prior thereto read:

"In every action for wrongful death commenced or attempted to be commenced within the time specified by section 2125.02 of the Revised Code, if a judgment for the plaintiff is reversed or if the plaintiff fails otherwise than upon the merits, and the time limited by such section for the commencement of such action has expired at the date of such reversal or failure, the plaintiff or, if the plaintiff dies and the cause of action survives, the personal representative of the plaintiff may commence a new action within one year after such date."

Amendment Note: 1996 H 350 rewrote this section, which prior thereto read:

"In every action for wrongful death commenced or attempted to be commenced within the time specified by section 2125.02 of the Revised Code, if a judgment for the plaintiff is reversed or if the plaintiff fails otherwise than upon the merits, and the time limited by such section for the commencement of such action has expired at the date of such reversal or failure, the plaintiff or, if he dies and the cause of action survives, his representative may commence a new action within one year after such date."

Cross References

Saving clause in case of reversal, 2305.19

Library References

Death ⚖ 39.
Westlaw Topic No. 117.
C.J.S. Death §§ 100 to 101, 103 to 104.

Research References

Encyclopedias

OH Jur. 3d Actions § 126, Physical Injuries to Person—Where Death Results from Injury; Relationship to Action for Wrongful Death.

OH Jur. 3d Death § 35, Ohio Wrongful Death Statute.

OH Jur. 3d Death § 39, Effect of Other Statutes Authorizing Recovery for Death Upon Right of Action Under General Wrongful Death Statute—Workers' Compensation Law.

OH Jur. 3d Death § 85, Constitutional Prohibition Against Limitation on Amount.

OH Jur. 3d Death § 115, Generally; Jurisdiction.

OH Jur. 3d Death § 121, Effect of Death of Representative or Cessation of Powers.

OH Jur. 3d Decedents' Estates § 1316, Proceeds from Action for Wrongful Death.

OH Jur. 3d Decedents' Estates § 1455, Requirement of Written Statement of Allowance of Claim—Effect of Allowance.

OH Jur. 3d Employment Relations § 333, Setoff of Amount Contributed or Paid by Employer for Insurance, Relief, Benefit, or Indemnity.

OH Jur. 3d Limitations & Laches § 128, Special Statutory Actions—Action for Wrongful Death.

Treatises and Practice Aids

Klein, Darling, & Terez, Baldwin's Ohio Practice Civil Practice § 3:15, [Deleted] Commencement--Secondary Consequences Which May Accompany Failure of Commencement Under Civ. R. 3(A)--Failure to Qualify for Protection of Savings Statute.

Carlin, Baldwin's Ohio Practice, Merrick-Rippner Probate Law § 12:1, Wrongful Death—Scope of RC Ch. 2125.

Carlin, Baldwin's Ohio Practice, Merrick-Rippner Probate Law § 12:14, Wrongful Death—Statute of Limitations—Savings Statute.

Ohio Personal Injury Practice § 3:10, Parties Plaintiff—Wrongful Death Complaint.

Ohio Personal Injury Practice App. C, Appendix C. Ohio Academy of Trial Lawyers v. Sheward.

Law Review and Journal Commentaries

R.C. 2305.19: When There's No Salvation In The Savings Statute, J. Patrick Browne. 89–7 PRO/GRAM 1 (July 1989).

Notes of Decisions

Bar to action 3
Constitutional issues 1
Service of summons 2

---

1. Constitutional issues

1996 H 350, which amended more than 100 statutes and a variety of rules relating to tort and other civil actions, and which was an attempt to reenact provisions of law previously held unconstitutional by the Supreme Court of Ohio, is an act of usurpation of judicial power in violation of the doctrine of separation of powers; for that reason, and because of violation of the one-subject rule of the Ohio Constitution, 1996 H 350 is unconstitutional. State ex rel. Ohio Academy of Trial Lawyers v. Sheward (Ohio, 08-16-1999) 86 Ohio St.3d 451, 715 N.E.2d 1062, 1999-Ohio-123, reconsideration denied 87 Ohio St.3d 1409, 716 N.E.2d 1170.

2. Service of summons

Filing complaint without serving it was not attempted commencement of action required for protection under wrongful-death saving statute. Motorists Mut. Ins. Co. v. Huron Rd. Hosp. (Ohio, 08-30-1995) 73 Ohio St.3d 391, 653 N.E.2d 235, 1995-Ohio-119. Death ⚖ 39

Wrongful-death savings statute requires commencement or attempted commencement of action before expiration of statute of limitations, and failure otherwise than upon merits. Motorists Mut. Ins. Co. v. Huron Rd. Hosp. (Ohio, 08-30-1995) 73 Ohio St.3d 391, 653 N.E.2d 235, 1995-Ohio-119. Death ⚖ 39

Mere filing of complaint is not attempted commencement of action for purposes of wrongful-death savings statute. Motorists Mut. Ins. Co. v. Huron Rd. Hosp. (Ohio, 08-30-1995) 73 Ohio St.3d 391, 653 N.E.2d 235, 1995-Ohio-119. Death ⚖ 39

Note 2

Where service of summons upon a defendant is quashed upon the ground that it was not left at his usual place of residence, plaintiff does not qualify for the extender of the statute of limitations granted by GC 10509–169 (RC 2125.04). Bronikowski v Bigham, affirmed 145 NE(2d) 331, 143 NE(2d) 490, 75 Abs 65 (CP 1955).

Where a plaintiff files a wrongful death action within two years in one county but no service is had upon the defendant, and after two years the case was dismissed for failure of service of summons and subsequently the plaintiff files an identical suit in another county, the plaintiff cannot be considered as having failed "otherwise than upon the merits" so as to authorize him to commence an action within one year thereafter under RC 2125.04. Bronikowski v Bigham, affirmed 145 NE(2d) 331, 143 NE(2d) 490, 75 Abs 65 (CP 1955).

3. Bar to action

Failure to force the establishment of an estate means that plaintiff has not attempted to commence an action against the estate for the purposes of savings statutes. Sorrell v. Estate of Datko (Ohio App. 7 Dist., 11-29-2001) 147 Ohio App.3d 319, 770 N.E.2d 608, 2001-Ohio-3460, appeal not allowed 95 Ohio St.3d 1408, 765 N.E.2d 876, 2002-Ohio-5728. Limitation Of Actions ⇨ 130(8)

Administrator of passenger's estate failed to commence or attempt to commence an action against driver's estate within statute of limitations, and thus, administrator could not avail himself of savings statute, as administrator filed action against estate that was not in existence at the time of filing and administrator failed to force the opening of an estate, such that there was no valid demand of service, and instead, his filing upon an entity that did not exist was invalid. Sorrell v. Estate of Datko (Ohio App. 7 Dist., 11-29-2001) 147 Ohio App.3d 319, 770 N.E.2d 608, 2001-Ohio-3460, appeal not allowed 95 Ohio St.3d 1408, 765 N.E.2d 876, 2002-Ohio-5728. Limitation Of Actions ⇨ 130(8)

Plaintiff in wrongful death action who voluntarily dismisses action prior to expiration of statute of limitations has two years from date of death of injured person in which to refile case; savings statute permitting refiling of action within one year of dismissal only applies if dismissal occurred after expiration of statute of limitations. Dougherty v. Fecsik (Ohio App. 8 Dist., 12-16-1996) 116 Ohio App.3d 456, 688 N.E.2d 555. Limitation Of Actions ⇨ 130(5)

Where an action for wrongful death has been brought within two years after death, and after two years have elapsed and action has been disposed of otherwise than upon merits, section does not permit commencing of a new action based on same death against a different person within one year after date of disposition of former action. Sabol v. Pekoc (Ohio 1947) 148 Ohio St. 545, 76 N.E.2d 84, 36 O.O. 182.

CHAPTER 2127

SALE OF LANDS

WHEN EXECUTOR OR ADMINISTRATOR MAY SELL

Section
2127.01 Sale of lands by executors, administrators and guardians
2127.011 Power of sale, written consent
2127.02 Action for sale to pay debts
2127.03 Action for sale to pay legacy
2127.04 Action for sale in other circumstances

WHEN GUARDIAN MAY SELL

2127.05 Guardian may sell

PROVISIONS APPLICABLE TO EXECUTORS, ADMINISTRATORS, AND GUARDIANS

2127.06 Successor fiduciary shall complete sale proceedings
2127.07 Real estate subject to sale
2127.08 Fractional interests; sale of entire interest
2127.09 Venue
2127.10 Complaint in action to sell real estate
2127.11 Summary proceeding if value of land less than three thousand dollars
2127.12 Necessary parties in sale by executor or administrator
2127.13 Necessary parties in sale by guardian
2127.14 Service of summons
2127.15 Pleadings and procedure
2127.16 Sale to be free of dower
2127.17 Costs when there are objections to granting order for sale
2127.18 Equities and priorities
2127.19 Release of liens
2127.20 Sale subject to mortgage
2127.21 Petition of guardian to have land laid out in town lots

APPRAISEMENT; BOND; SALE

2127.22 Appraisement may be dispensed with; new appraisement; appraisers
2127.23 Duties of appraisers
2127.24 Vacancy in appraisers
2127.25 Compensation of appraisers
2127.27 Additional bond before sale
2127.28 Expense of sale
2127.29 Order of sale
2127.30 Order of sale when an equitable estate is included
2127.31 Persons interested may give bond to prevent sale
2127.32 Public or private sale

Section
2127.33 Price at which real estate may be sold
2127.34 Terms of sale
2127.35 Confirmation of sale; deed
2127.36 Security for deferred payments
2127.37 Compensation of executor, administrator, or guardian
2127.38 Distribution of proceeds of sale
2127.39 When proceeds of sale marshaled in conformity with will

FRAUDULENT CONVEYANCES

2127.40 Sale by executor or administrator of real estate fraudulently transferred by decedent

PARTITION

2127.41 Proceeds arising from partition of real estate may be reached by the executor or administrator

NONRESIDENTS

2127.42 Sale of the lands of foreign wards
2127.43 Sale of real estate by trustees of nonresidents

Publisher's Note: Until 1968, when the Modern Courts Amendment to the Ohio Constitution was adopted, Ohio court procedure was governed entirely by statute and case law. The Modern Courts Amendment required the Supreme Court of Ohio, subject to the approval of the General Assembly, to "prescribe rules governing practice and procedure in all courts of the state." Rules of practice and procedure are the Civil, Criminal, Appellate, and Juvenile Rules, Rules of the Court of Claims, and the Ohio Rules of Evidence. Pursuant to Ohio Constitution Article IV, Section 5(B), such rules "shall not abridge, enlarge, or modify any substantive right," and " [a]ll laws in conflict with such rules shall be of no further force or effect." Provisions of Chapter 2127 should be read with this in mind.

Comparative Laws

Ark.—A.C.A. § 28-51-102.
Fla.—West's F.S.A. § 733.613.
Ind.—West's A.I.C. 29-1-15-2.
Tex.—V.A.T.S. Probate Code § 332.

Cross References

County homes, county shall seek possession of property of persons entering, 5155.23
Disposition of escheated lands, alternate method of sale, 2105.09
Dower, defined, 2103.02
Fiduciaries, rights as to shares in corporation, 2109.29

SALE OF LANDS 2127.011

Fiduciary, defined, 2109.01
Forcible entry and detainer action, applicability to sales by executors, administrators, and guardians, 1923.02
Foreign wards and guardians, 2111.43
Guardians, parties and proceedings, 2111.29, 2111.34
Land sales, Sup R 65
Legal disability, defined, 2131.02
Powers of guardian of person and estate, 2111.07
Procedure in probate court, Civ R 73
Will, defined, 2107.01

Law Review and Journal Commentaries

Real Property in Probate Court Administrations—Overview of the Ohio Law and Procedures of Devolution of Title of Decedents, and Sales, Lawrence A. Belskis. 52 Title Topics 3 (October 1985).

WHEN EXECUTOR OR ADMINISTRATOR MAY SELL

2127.01 Sale of lands by executors, administrators and guardians

All proceedings for the sale of lands by executors, administrators, and guardians shall be in accordance with section 2127.01 to 2127.43, inclusive, of the Revised Code, except where the executor has testamentary power of sale, and in that case the executor may proceed under such sections or under the will.

(1953 H 1, eff. 10–1–53; GC 10510–1)

Historical and Statutory Notes

Pre–1953 H 1 Amendments: 119 v 394, § 1; 114 v 451

Cross References

Deceased partner, right of surviving partner's to purchase property interest, 1779.04 to 1779.06, 1779.08
Foreign executor or administrator may be authorized to sell real estate, 2129.25
Mortgage, lease, or sale of real estate; sale of personal property, 2119.04
Sale of real estate, ancillary administration, 2129.13

Library References

Executors and Administrators ⚖136.1.
Westlaw Topic No. 162.
C.J.S. Executors and Administrators § 295.

Research References

Encyclopedias
OH Jur. 3d Abandoned, Lost, & Escheated Property § 28, Real Property.
OH Jur. 3d Decedents' Estates § 180, Real Property of Ancestor.
OH Jur. 3d Decedents' Estates § 1718, Proceedings for Sale of Real Estate.
OH Jur. 3d Fiduciaries § 46, Sale or Lease of Lands.
OH Jur. 3d Guardian & Ward § 145, Property Subject to Sale—Property of Nonresident or Foreign Ward.
OH Jur. 3d Guardian & Ward § 146, Generally; Jurisdiction and Venue.

Forms
Ohio Forms Legal and Business § 24:394, Payment of Debts—Order of Sale of Realty.
Ohio Forms Legal and Business § 24:465.20, Powers—to Sell House.

Treatises and Practice Aids
Carlin, Baldwin's Ohio Practice, Merrick-Rippner Probate Law § 97:1, Land Sale by Guardian—Introduction.
Carlin, Baldwin's Ohio Practice, Merrick-Rippner Probate Law § 73:18, Deed of Fiduciary Under Power of Sale in Will—Form.
Kuehnle and Levey, Ohio Real Estate Law and Practice § 52:3, Statutory Fiduciary Sales—21 Statutory Proceedings.
Kuehnle and Levey, Ohio Real Estate Law and Practice § 52:7, Statutory Fiduciary Sales—Grounds for Judicial Sale—Payment of Debts.
Kuehnle and Levey, Ohio Real Estate Law and Practice § 52:15, Statutory Fiduciary Sales—Executor's Alternative Choice in Testamentary Power of Sale or by Complaint.

Notes of Decisions

Fiduciary duty 4
Partition 3
Purchaser's rights 1
Settled estate 2

---

1. Purchaser's rights

Where neither party has the legal title to land, the rule which protects a bona fide purchaser does not apply, and the party with the oldest equity must prevail; and where a party unites in himself both the legal and equitable title, the other party cannot be protected against such rights on the ground that he is a purchaser without notice. Elstner v. Fife (Ohio 1877) 32 Ohio St. 358.

2. Settled estate

When an estate is settled or all claims against it are presumptively satisfied by lapse of time and no object of the testator remains to be attained, a power given by the will to sell and convey land becomes legally inoperative and ceases to exist. Ward's Lessee v. Barrows (Ohio 1853) 2 Ohio St. 241. Powers ⚖ 13; Wills ⚖ 692(6)

3. Partition

A guardian does not have to have the approval of the probate court of an action in partition by him on behalf of his ward. Child v. Snyder (Ohio Com.Pl. 1962) 181 N.E.2d 315, 88 Ohio Law Abs. 401, 20 O.O.2d 432.

The probate court cannot compel the dismissal and termination of an action in partition after the common pleas court has acquired full and complete jurisdiction of said partition action and has made and issued a valid order of sale. Child v. Snyder (Ohio Com.Pl. 1962) 181 N.E.2d 315, 88 Ohio Law Abs. 401, 20 O.O.2d 432. Courts ⚖ 475(6)

4. Fiduciary duty

Executor was authorized to sell real estate in estate through auction without an order from the probate court and without being subject to statutory requirement that sale price equal at least 80% of appraised value of real estate, where property owner's last will and testament contained a power of sale clause. In re Phillipi (Ohio App. 5 Dist., Stark, 01-24-2005) No. 2004-CA-00144, 2005-Ohio-368, 2005 WL 267647, Unreported. Executors And Administrators ⚖ 142

Administrator with will annexed was not required to obtain written consent of devisees before selling real property, which was newly discovered asset of decedent's estate, where testamentary power of sale granted to executrixes was extended to administrator through probate court order providing that administrator had same powers to sell estate assets as those granted to executrixes. In re Estate of Hyer (Ohio App. 7 Dist., Monroe, 09-27-2004) No. 03 MO 9, 2004-Ohio-5359, 2004 WL 2334510, Unreported. Executors And Administrators ⚖ 121(2)

Administratrix of estate did not breach her fiduciary duty by not selling estate property, which was mortgaged, to pay off estate debts after foreclosure action was initiated; doctrine of lis pendens would have frustrated any attempted sale of the property once the foreclosure action was instituted and administratrix could not have conveyed clear title to property while foreclosure was pending. Smith v. Estate of Mattern (Ohio App. 5 Dist., Stark, 12-09-2002) No. 2002CA00215, 2002-Ohio-6883, 2002 WL 31812678, Unreported. Executors And Administrators ⚖ 137

Administratrix of estate did not breach her fiduciary duty by waiting to sell estate property, which was mortgaged, to pay off estate debts, where mortgagee was considering accepting deed to property in lieu of foreclosure. Smith v. Estate of Mattern (Ohio App. 5 Dist., Stark, 12-09-2002) No. 2002CA00215, 2002-Ohio-6883, 2002 WL 31812678, Unreported. Executors And Administrators ⚖ 137

2127.011 Power of sale, written consent

(A) In addition to the other methods provided by law or in the will and unless expressly prohibited by the will, an executor or administrator may sell at public or private sale, grant options to sell, exchange, re-exchange, or otherwise dispose of any parcel of real estate belonging to the estate at any time at prices and upon terms as are consistent with this section and may execute and deliver deeds and other instruments of conveyance if all of the following conditions are met:

(1) The surviving spouse, all of the legatees and devisees in the case of testacy, and all of the heirs in the case of intestacy, give written consent to a power of sale for a particular parcel of real estate or to a power of sale for all the real estate belonging to the estate. Each consent to a power of sale provided for in this section shall be filed in the probate court.

(2) Any sale under a power of sale authorized pursuant to this section shall be made at a price of at least eighty per cent of the appraised value, as set forth in an approved inventory.

(3) No power of sale provided for in this section is effective if the surviving spouse, any legatee, devisee, or heir is a minor. No person may give the consent of the minor that is required by this section.

(B) A surviving spouse who is the executor or administrator may sell real estate to himself pursuant to this section.

(1976 S 466, eff. 5–26–76; 1975 S 145)

Legislative Service Commission

1975:

Under current law, if a fiduciary is not given a testamentary power to sell real estate, he must initiate a land sale proceeding if he wishes to sell estate real property. This procedure involves the filing of a petition, and a court hearing under most circumstances.

This new section would authorize an executor or administrator, unless restricted by the will or otherwise provided by law, to sell at public or private sale, grant options to sell, exchange, re-exchange, or otherwise dispose of real estate, if all the legatees, devisees or heirs give their written consent, the sale is made at not less than 80% of the appraised value, and the executor or administrator files a report of sale with the probate court and obtains a confirmation of sale from the court. A minor who is an heir or legatee could not give his consent to this general power. The written consents to the power of sale would have to be filed in probate court. A surviving spouse who is also the executor or administrator could sell real estate to himself under this section. The surviving spouse and all legatees, devisees, and heirs may in writing revoke the powers granted by this section prior to the filing of the report of sale and confirmation by the court. Any surviving spouse, legatee, devisee, or heir would be permitted to apply to the probate court for revocation of the consent; if the consent is obtained by fraud, duress, or undue influences, the probate court would order the consent revoked.

Cross References

Forcible entry and detainer action, applicability to sales by executors, administrators, and guardians, 1923.02
Sale of property under authority of will, 2113.39

Library References

Executors and Administrators ⇌137.
Westlaw Topic No. 162.
C.J.S. Executors and Administrators §§ 295 to 296, 298, 321.

Research References

Encyclopedias

OH Jur. 3d Decedents' Estates § 1496, Power of Representative to Sell—Special Power to Dispose If Particular Statutory Conditions Are Met.
OH Jur. 3d Decedents' Estates § 1519, Purposes Demanded, or Consented To, by Beneficiaries.

Treatises and Practice Aids

Carlin, Baldwin's Ohio Practice, Merrick-Rippner Probate Law § 2:53, Sale of Land—Power of Sale.
Carlin, Baldwin's Ohio Practice, Merrick-Rippner Probate Law § 2:54, Sale of Land—Grounds for Land Sale.
Carlin, Baldwin's Ohio Practice, Merrick-Rippner Probate Law § 74:1, Decedent's Property—Authorization to Sell.
Carlin, Baldwin's Ohio Practice, Merrick-Rippner Probate Law § 90:1, Persons Entitled to Bring Land Sale Actions—Executors and Administrators.
Carlin, Baldwin's Ohio Practice, Merrick-Rippner Probate Law § 90:7, Authority for Land Sale Action—Consent or Demand of Beneficiaries.
Carlin, Baldwin's Ohio Practice, Merrick-Rippner Probate Law § 2:121, Administration of Decedent's Estate—Checklist.
Carlin, Baldwin's Ohio Practice, Merrick-Rippner Probate Law § 60:36, Power of Attorney—Short Form—Form.
Carlin, Baldwin's Ohio Practice, Merrick-Rippner Probate Law § 91:30, Land Sale—Service of Summons.
Carlin, Baldwin's Ohio Practice, Merrick-Rippner Probate Law § 91:33, Consent to Power to Sell Real Estate—Form.
Carlin, Baldwin's Ohio Practice, Merrick-Rippner Probate Law § 91:44, Complaint for Authority to Sell Real Property to Pay Legacies—Form.
Carlin, Baldwin's Ohio Practice, Merrick-Rippner Probate Law § 91:50, Complaint for Authority to Sell Real Estate, and for Order of Private Sale—Form.
Kuehnle and Levey, Ohio Real Estate Law and Practice § 52:4, Statutory Fiduciary Sales—With Consent of Surviving Spouse, Legatees, Devisees, or Heirs—Sale at Not Less Than 80%.

Notes of Decisions

Attorney fees 3
Consent 1
Fiduciary duty 2

---

1. Consent

Administrator with will annexed was not required to obtain written consent of devisees before selling real property, which was newly discovered asset of decedent's estate, where testamentary power of sale granted to executrixes was extended to administrator through probate court order providing that administrator had same powers to sell estate assets as those granted to executrixes. In re Estate of Hyer (Ohio App. 7 Dist., Monroe, 09-27-2004) No. 03 MO 9, 2004-Ohio-5359, 2004 WL 2334510, Unreported. Executors And Administrators ⇌ 121(2)

Probate court was first court to assert jurisdiction over deceased mortgagor's property, and thus, probate court's exclusive jurisdiction precluded mortgagee from bringing mortgage foreclosure action in general division of common pleas court; successor administrator of mortgagor's estate had filed with the probate court a written consent to power of sale signed by mortgagor's sole heir, and successor administrator had taken several actions pursuant to the consent, e.g., she had signed a listing agreement to sell the property to a bona fide purchaser, had served an eviction notice on property's occupant, and had ordered title work. U.S. Bank, N.A. v. Webb (Ohio Com.Pl., 07-14-2006) 2006-Ohio-5462, 2006 WL 3041272. Courts ⇌ 474

Statute requiring executor of decedent's estate to obtain legatees' written consent before selling real estate does not apply to estates of decedents who die testate. In re Estate of Cogan (App. 8 Dist., 10-06-1997) 123 Ohio App.3d 186, 703 N.E.2d 858, dismissed, jurisdictional motion overruled 81 Ohio St.3d 1442, 690 N.E.2d 14. Executors And Administrators ⇌ 138(1)

The administrator of an estate, who executed a contract with plaintiff for the sale of the decedent's real property, did not breach that contract by selling the realty to other purchasers at private sale where the contract with plaintiff contained the clause "subject to the approval of the probate court," such approval was never obtained, and where the heirs never gave consent to the sale of the property to plaintiff, as required by RC 2127.04 and RC 2127.011. Bilang v. Benson (Lucas 1978) 62 Ohio App.2d 134, 405 N.E.2d 311, 16 O.O.3d 297. Executors And Administrators ⇌ 142

Decedent's estate held real property in trust for decedent's youngest child, and youngest child's interest in property was not immaterial, even if the remaining five adult children transferred their interest in property when they issued quit-claim deeds releasing their rights and title in the property, and thus estate administrator did not have authority to complete a sale of the property, where terms of trust divided land between all six children when youngest reached age of 21, and youngest child had never relinquished any interest he had in the real estate. In re Smeller (Ohio

App. 9 Dist., 06-21-2006) 167 Ohio App.3d 444, 2006-Ohio-3112. Executors And Administrators ⇐ 137

2. Fiduciary duty

Administratrix of estate did not breach her fiduciary duty by waiting to sell estate property, which was mortgaged, to pay off estate debts, where mortgagee was considering accepting deed to property in lieu of foreclosure. Smith v. Estate of Mattern (Ohio App. 5 Dist., Stark, 12-09-2002) No. 2002CA00215, 2002-Ohio-6883, 2002 WL 31812678, Unreported. Executors And Administrators ⇐ 137

Administratrix of estate did not breach her fiduciary duty by not selling estate property, which was mortgaged, to pay off estate debts after foreclosure action was initiated; doctrine of lis pendens would have frustrated any attempted sale of the property once the foreclosure action was instituted and administratrix could not have conveyed clear title to property while foreclosure was pending. Smith v. Estate of Mattern (Ohio App. 5 Dist., Stark, 12-09-2002) No. 2002CA00215, 2002-Ohio-6883, 2002 WL 31812678, Unreported. Executors And Administrators ⇐ 137

3. Attorney fees

Successor administrator of estate of deceased mortgagor was not entitled to attorney fees, under civil procedure rule governing venue for probate proceedings, with respect to obtaining dismissal of mortgage foreclosure action which mortgagee filed in general division of common pleas court after probate court had asserted jurisdiction over the mortgaged property. U.S. Bank, N.A. v. Webb (Ohio Com.Pl., 07-14-2006) 2006-Ohio-5462, 2006 WL 3041207. Executors And Administrators ⇐ 456(1)

2127.02 Action for sale to pay debts

As soon as an executor or administrator ascertains that the personal property in his hands is insufficient to pay all the debts of the decedent, together with the allowance for support to the surviving spouse, minor children, or surviving spouse and minor children of the decedent as provided in section 2106.13 of the Revised Code, and the costs of administering the estate, he shall commence a civil action in the probate court for authority to sell the decedent's real property.

(1990 H 346, eff. 5–31–90; 1975 S 145; 1953 H 1; GC 10510–2)

Uncodified Law

1990 H 346, § 3, eff. 5–31–90, reads, in part: (A) Sections 1 and 2 of this act shall apply only to the estates of decedents who die on or after the effective date of this act.

Historical and Statutory Notes

Pre–1953 H 1 Amendments: 114 v 451

Legislative Service Commission

1975:

This existing section requires executors and administrators, upon determining that personal property of the estate will be insufficient to pay debts and provide the widow's allowance, to institute a civil action in probate or common pleas court to sell the realty. The bill would strike "widow" and substitute "surviving spouse" and also strike "court of common pleas," making the probate court the sole forum for such actions. These changes conform to earlier themes of the bill.

Library References

Executors and Administrators ⇐325.
Westlaw Topic No. 162.
C.J.S. Executors and Administrators § 586.

Baldwin's Ohio Legislative Service, 1990 Laws of Ohio, H 346—LSC Analysis, p 5–87

Research References

Encyclopedias

OH Jur. 3d Decedents' Estates § 144, Executor's or Administrator's Power to Sell Realty.
OH Jur. 3d Decedents' Estates § 180, Real Property of Ancestor.
OH Jur. 3d Decedents' Estates § 1510, Statutory Grounds, Generally.
OH Jur. 3d Decedents' Estates § 1511, Insufficiency of Personalty to Pay Debts as Condition Precedent.
OH Jur. 3d Decedents' Estates § 1513, Allowances to Surviving Spouse and Children.
OH Jur. 3d Decedents' Estates § 1514, Costs of Administration.
OH Jur. 3d Decedents' Estates § 1522, Institution by Action by Representative for Authority to Sell.
OH Jur. 3d Decedents' Estates § 1524, Jurisdiction and Powers of the Probate Court.
OH Jur. 3d Decedents' Estates § 1527, Jurisdiction and Powers of the Probate Court—Exclusive Jurisdiction of One Court.
OH Jur. 3d Mortgages & Deeds of Trust § 300, Courts Having Jurisdiction—After Death of Mortgagor.

Forms

Ohio Forms Legal and Business § 24:394, Payment of Debts—Order of Sale of Realty.
Ohio Forms and Transactions F 30.05, Specific Bequests and Devises.
Ohio Forms and Transactions KP 30.09, Abatement of Legacies and Devises.
Ohio Jurisprudence Pleading and Practice Forms § 106:5, Statutory Liens.

Treatises and Practice Aids

Klein, Darling, & Terez, Baldwin's Ohio Practice Civil Practice § 73:3, Probate Division--Venue.
Carlin, Baldwin's Ohio Practice, Merrick-Rippner Probate Law § 2:54, Sale of Land—Grounds for Land Sale.
Carlin, Baldwin's Ohio Practice, Merrick-Rippner Probate Law § 90:1, Persons Entitled to Bring Land Sale Actions—Executors and Administrators.
Carlin, Baldwin's Ohio Practice, Merrick-Rippner Probate Law § 90:8, Authority for Land Sale Action—Insufficient Personal Property to Pay Debts.
Carlin, Baldwin's Ohio Practice, Merrick-Rippner Probate Law § 91:3, Land Sale—Motion to Commence Action and Proceed.
Carlin, Baldwin's Ohio Practice, Merrick-Rippner Probate Law § 91:9, Land Sale—to Pay Family Allowance.
Carlin, Baldwin's Ohio Practice, Merrick-Rippner Probate Law § 92:6, Property Not Subject to Sale.
Carlin, Baldwin's Ohio Practice, Merrick-Rippner Probate Law § 92:9, Sale of Land Subject to Encumbrances—Real Property Conveyed by Heirs.
Carlin, Baldwin's Ohio Practice, Merrick-Rippner Probate Law § 94:2, Bond of Interested Person to Prevent Sale.
Carlin, Baldwin's Ohio Practice, Merrick-Rippner Probate Law § 2:121, Administration of Decedent's Estate—Checklist.
Carlin, Baldwin's Ohio Practice, Merrick-Rippner Probate Law § 90:13, Land Sale Action—Jurisdiction of Probate Court.
Carlin, Baldwin's Ohio Practice, Merrick-Rippner Probate Law § 91:43, Complaint for Authority to Sell Decedent's Real Estate to Pay Debts—Form.
Carlin, Baldwin's Ohio Practice, Merrick-Rippner Probate Law § 96:10, Expenses of Sale—Jurisdiction to Determine Costs and Expenses.
Kuehnle and Levey, Ohio Real Estate Law and Practice § 51:5, Partition—Persons Entitled to Partition—Devisees, Next of Kin, Fiduciaries.
Kuehnle and Levey, Ohio Real Estate Law and Practice § 52:7, Statutory Fiduciary Sales—Grounds for Judicial Sale—Payment of Debts.
Kuehnle and Levey, Ohio Real Estate Law and Practice § 52:12, Statutory Fiduciary Sales—Enjoining Creditors from Levying After Owner's Death.
Kuehnle and Levey, Ohio Real Estate Law and Practice § 52:23, Statutory Fiduciary Sales—Administrator's Action to Enjoin Creditors from Levying.
Kuehnle and Levey, Ohio Real Estate Law and Practice § 52:24, Statutory Fiduciary Sales—Partition of Decedent's Real Estate.
Restatement (2d) of Conflicts § 335, When Land May be Sold to Pay Claims Proved Locally.

Law Review and Journal Commentaries

Mortgage Foreclosure in Ohio When Fee Owner is Deceased, Leonard C. Hirsch. 36 Ohio L Rep 330 (May 9, 1932).

Sale of Real Estate, Construction of Wills, and Inheritance Taxes Are Discussed, Hon. Nelson J. Brewer. 11 Clev B J 121 (May 1940).

Notes of Decisions

Administrative powers and duties   1
Allowance to spouse and children   6
Appeal   7
Civil action   10
Court's powers   12
Dower   5
Jurisdiction   8
Nature of debt justifying sale of land   2
Partition and contribution   9
Procedural issues   3
Rights of purchaser   4
Statute of limitation   11

---

1. Administrative powers and duties

Where an administrator of a decedent's estate is made a defendant in an action for partition brought by one of the heirs and answers that it is necessary to sell such property for the payment of debts of the decedent, such administrator is entitled to an order of sale, and the statutes of limitations have no application in favor of the heirs as they hold title subject to the right of the administrator to sell the land for that purpose. Lafferty v. Shinn (Ohio 1882) 38 Ohio St. 46.

Rents accruing upon real estate of an insolvent intestate between his death and the sale of the lands for the payment of debts by the administrator belong to the heir and not to the administrator. Overturf v. Dugan (Ohio 1876) 29 Ohio St. 230. Descent And Distribution ⇐ 79; Executors And Administrators ⇐ 131; Executors And Administrators ⇐ 413

An administrator, in selling lands of his decedent, which he conveys without covenants of warranty, can not render the estate of the deceased liable in damages, by false representations as to the condition of the title, or the extent of existing incumbrances; as administrator he could only sell the interest or estate of the deceased in the premises, and covenants of warranty, unauthorized by the will, or the order of the court under which the sale was made could only bind himself personally. Dunlap v. Robinson (Ohio 1861) 12 Ohio St. 530. Executors And Administrators ⇐ 388(4)

Where the testator directed certain legacies to be paid by his executors, and devised certain lands to A. charged with the payment of the legacies and costs of administration, so far as funds might be needed by the executors for the payment of the same and A. paid and took receipts from the legatees and tendered the amount of costs of administration to the executors, exclusive of any per cent on the legacies, the executors were not entitled to an order for the sale of the premises, to pay a per cent on the legacies; in such case the executors are not entitled to a per cent, but whether in seeing to the discharge of the legacies by the legatees the executors performed extraordinary services not in the common course of duty will be a matter for the consideration of the jury. Williams v. Williams's Ex'r (Ohio 1858) 8 Ohio St. 300.

A power given to executors by will to sell and convey land becomes legally inoperative and ceases to exist, when the estate is settled, or all claims against it are presumptively satisfied by lapse of time, and no object of the testator remains to be attained. Ward's Lessee v. Barrows (Ohio 1853) 2 Ohio St. 241. Powers ⇐ 13; Wills ⇐ 692(6)

If an administrator pays out all the personal assets of the estate to one creditor, where the estate would be solvent upon sale of the realty, his failure to apply for such a sale is a waste of the assets of the estate. Abbott v. Cole (Ohio 1831) 5 Ohio 86.

Where administrators of an estate make a sale of the decedent's real estate to pay his debts without an order of sale by the court on the record, such sale is void. Goforth's Lessee v. Longworth (Ohio 1829) 4 Ohio 129, 19 Am.Dec. 588.

All the control that administrators have over real estate is by virtue of statutes. Ludlow's Heirs v. Johnston (Ohio 1828) 3 Ohio 553, 17 Am.Dec. 609.

Under RC 2127.38 proceeds of land sale proceeding of guardian must be held and finally distributed in same manner as would have been done had there been no sale, but such proceeds are subject to bear proportionate part of expenses of supporting the ward. Guerra v. Guerra (Ohio Com.Pl. 1970) 25 Ohio Misc. 1, 265 N.E.2d 818, 54 O.O.2d 14. Mental Health ⇐ 273

When an executor or an administrator ascertains that the personal property is insufficient to pay the debts of the deceased, together with the allowance to the widow, it is his duty to bring an action to sell the real estate to pay debts. Kincaid v. Dawson (Franklin 1950) 87 Ohio App. 299, 93 N.E.2d 731, 57 Ohio Law Abs. 193, 43 O.O. 16. Executors And Administrators ⇐ 325

Executor directed by probate court to sell lands to pay debts may sue for wrongful destruction of market value of such premises, where it appears that rights of creditor will be prejudiced thereby, in view of constitutional provisions that person for injury done him in land or goods shall have remedy by due course of law. Clark v. McClain Fire Brick Co. (Ohio 1919) 100 Ohio St. 110, 125 N.E. 877, 17 Ohio Law Rep. 154, 17 Ohio Law Rep. 164. Constitutional Law ⇐ 321; Executors And Administrators ⇐ 129(1)

Under the statutes of Ohio, the personal representative of the deceased is the only person authorized to maintain an action to subject the realty of the deceased to the payment of his debts. Rheinfrank v. Hurr (Ohio 1918) 98 Ohio St. 439, 121 N.E. 645, 15 Ohio Law Rep. 599. Executors And Administrators ⇐ 328

The right of an administrator to subject lands of his intestate to the payment of debts is superior to the rights of the heirs to have partition of the lands. Stout v. Stout (Ohio 1910) 82 Ohio St. 358, 92 N.E. 465, 137 Am.St.Rep. 785, 8 Ohio Law Rep. 118. Executors And Administrators ⇐ 323; Executors And Administrators ⇐ 338

An executor who, in the exercise of a testamentary power to sell lands for the payment of debts, in bad faith sells them for a price that is manifestly less than their true value, should, on exception to his account in the probate court, be charged with the difference between such inadequate price and the true value of the lands. Brown v. Reed (Ohio 1897) 56 Ohio St. 264, 37 W.L.B. 324, 46 N.E. 982. Executors And Administrators ⇐ 138(9)

Where an executor, after obtaining an order to sell his decedent's lands, resigns and then buys the property at his own sale, the sale will not be set aside where it does not appear that he did anything to stifle competition and paid a fair price for such property. Woodward v. Curtis (Ohio Cir. 1899) 10 Ohio C.D. 400.

Where administrators were ordered by the court to sell real estate and before the sale was made the law allowing such an order was repealed, the power of the administrators to sell terminated with the law's repeal; thus, a sale made by such administrators after the repeal was void. Bank of Hamilton v. Dudley's Lessee (U.S.Ohio 1829) 27 U.S. 492, 2 Pet. 492, 7 L.Ed. 496.

Where a will gives the executor power to dispose of all of the real estate of the decedent, the levy of an attachment in an action against a devisee will not defeat such power of sale, nor will it affect the title of the purchaser at the executor's sale. Smyth v Anderson, 31 OS 144 (1876).

Administrators de bonis non with the will annexed have the same power to sell at private sale granted by the will to the executors. In re Hanna's Estate (Ohio Prob. 1932) 29 Ohio N.P.(N.S.) 338.

2. Nature of debt justifying sale of land

Where, after the administrator of an estate has made a settlement he believes to be final and all the personal estate of the decedent has been exhausted, a judgment is recovered against the administrator on a liability contracted by the intestate, the administrator is entitled to an order for the sale of enough of the decedent's land to pay the judgment even though such land has been partitioned among the heirs and sold by them. Faran v. Robinson (Ohio 1867) 17 Ohio St. 242, 93 Am.Dec. 617.

Where an administrator in good faith and on the advice of family members received the rents of the real estate which descended from the testator to his infant heir and paid the testator's debts with such rents in order to save the land from sale, and such arrangement is beneficial to the infant heir, upon such infant's death his administrator cannot recover the rents from the administrator of the ancestor, even though the arrangement changes the distribution of the infant's estate. White v. Turpin (Ohio 1865) 16 Ohio St. 270.

Where devisees pay the legacies charged on the land, the executor cannot sell the land to pay his commission on such disbursement. Williams v. Williams's Ex'r (Ohio 1858) 8 Ohio St. 300.

Where summons has been served on only two of those named as defendants in an action to sell the land of their ancestor, and a judgment is rendered against all the defendants, only the title of the heirs served will pass to a purchaser at the sheriff's sale. Douglass' Lessee v. Massie (Ohio 1847) 16 Ohio 271, 47 Am.Dec. 375.

By marriage the husband becomes immediately entitled to all the wife's personal property, and where a husband and wife unite to sell property, the proceeds are personalty and by operation of law belong to the husband; and land purchased with such proceeds belongs to the husband and upon his death is subjected to the payment of his debts. Ramsdall v. Craighill (Ohio 1839) 9 Ohio 197.

A decedent's lands may be ordered to sale for the payment of taxes accumulating on such real estate which the personal representative has no funds to pay. Welsh v. Perkins (Ohio 1837) 8 Ohio 52.

In payment of costs of administration of decedent's estate, an item of specifically bequeathed personal property must be charged before proceeds from a land sale proceeding conducted by decedent's guardian can be reached. Guerra v. Guerra (Ohio Com.Pl. 1970) 25 Ohio Misc. 1, 265 N.E.2d 818, 54 O.O.2d 14. Executors And Administrators ⇨ 272

Special legislation authorizing apportionment of certain allowed exemptions in assessing Ohio tax on succession of Ohio property from a nonresident decedent did not authorize the deduction of all or proportionate part of the estate's debts, costs of administration or federal estate tax from appraised value of Ohio realty passing under residuary clause of nonresident's will where will authorized the executor to sell, lease, mortgage or otherwise dispose of the Ohio realty and where the estate contains sufficient personalty to pay the debts, taxes and costs. In re Packard's Estate (Ohio 1963) 174 Ohio St. 349, 189 N.E.2d 434, 22 O.O.2d 409. Taxation ⇨ 3355; Taxation ⇨ 3356

Administrative practice in determining state succession tax of allowing deduction of debts and expenses of out-of-state administration from personal property in state when decedent domiciled in state dies owning realty outside state was not only persuasive, in militating against requiring a deduction of portion of part of federal estate tax from value of state realty passing under residuary clause of nonresident's will where personal property outside state was sufficient to pay expenses of administration of nonresident's estate, but was of sufficient long standing to bear up unless judicial construction made it imperative to set it aside. In re Packard's Estate (Ohio 1963) 174 Ohio St. 349, 189 N.E.2d 434, 22 O.O.2d 409. Statutes ⇨ 219(10)

Administrator may maintain action to sell realty as assets of estate only when personal property of decedent is insufficient to pay debts of estate, such debts including not only decedent's actual debts, but also debts arising out of medical and funeral expenses and costs of administration. Miller v. Bigelow (Wood 1941) 67 Ohio App. 371, 36 N.E.2d 860, 21 O.O. 324. Executors And Administrators ⇨ 325

When, in the administration of his estate, it becomes necessary to sell the real estate of a decedent to pay debts, the statutes authorizing such sale provide that the mortgage indebtedness thereon shall be paid from the proceeds of sale before payment therefrom of funeral expenses. Nolan v. Kroll (Erie 1930) 37 Ohio App. 350, 174 N.E. 750, 8 Ohio Law Abs. 676, 33 Ohio Law Rep. 222. Executors And Administrators ⇨ 402

Debt, though secured by mortgage on realty, must be paid primarily from the personalty if personal debt of intestate. Foreman v. Medina County Nat. Bank (Ohio 1928) 119 Ohio St. 17, 162 N.E. 42, 6 Ohio Law Abs. 369, 26 Ohio Law Rep. 461. Executors And Administrators ⇨ 272

Fees of administratrix and attorney were properly disallowed priority over mortgage, where purchase price was insufficient to discharge mortgage. Watson v. Watson (Hamilton 1927) 24 Ohio App. 45, 156 N.E. 241. Executors And Administrators ⇨ 402

The lands of an intestate descend to his heirs, subject, however, to the payment of his debts and the year's allowance to the widow and minor children, in case the personalty is insufficient, and charges of administration incident to a sale of the land, but cannot be sold to pay costs of administration alone. Carr v. Hull (Ohio 1901) 65 Ohio St. 394, 62 N.E. 439, 87 Am.St.Rep. 623. Executors And Administrators ⇨ 321

The lands of an intestate descend to his heirs subject to the payment of debts and the year's allowance to the widow and minor children in case the personal estate is insufficient, and charges incident to the land sale; but the lands cannot be sold for the payment of administration costs alone. Carr v. Hull (Ohio 1901) 65 Ohio St. 394, 62 N.E. 439, 87 Am.St.Rep. 623. Executors And Administrators ⇨ 321

A judgment which is a subsisting lien on the lands of the debtor at the time of his death is entitled to share in the proceeds of the land when sold by the decedent's personal representative according to its priority at the time of the debtor's death; it is not necessary to issue execution on the judgment to preserve the lien. Ambrose v. Byrne (Ohio 1899) 61 Ohio St. 146, 42 W.L.B. 360, 55 N.E. 408. Executors And Administrators ⇨ 402

When the personal estate in the hands of an administrator is sufficient to pay the costs of administering the estate, and all the debts of the decedent, except such as are amply secured by mortgage executed by him in his lifetime on lands of which he died seised, an action cannot be maintained by the administrator to subject to sale, for the payment of mortgage indebtedness, other lands which the intestate had conveyed away with intent to hinder, delay, and defraud his creditors. McCall v. Pixley (Ohio 1891) 48 Ohio St. 379, 25 W.L.B. 417, 27 N.E. 887. Executors And Administrators ⇨ 329(1); Fraudulent Conveyances ⇨ 226

Where the personal estate will pay all the debts except those amply secured by mortgage, an action by the administrator to sell land to pay mortgage indebtedness cannot be maintained. McCall v. Pixley (Ohio 1891) 48 Ohio St. 379, 25 W.L.B. 417, 27 N.E. 887.

In construing GC 5336 (RC 5731.17) together with this section legislature did empower administrator to file action to pay inheritance taxes, which action is similar in character to one brought for purpose of paying debts of decedent. Kingrey v. Oldfather (Ohio Prob. 1938) 3 Ohio Supp. 245, 26 Ohio Law Abs. 148, 10 O.O. 524. Executors And Administrators ⇨ 324

Legislature did not regard inheritance taxes as debts of decedent within meaning of this section. Kingrey v. Oldfather (Ohio Prob. 1938) 3 Ohio Supp. 245, 26 Ohio Law Abs. 148, 10 O.O. 524.

Expense incurred in burial of testator's wife under terms and provisions of his will was not a "debt of deceased" within provision of this section. Kingrey v. Oldfather (Ohio Prob. 1938) 3 Ohio Supp. 245, 26 Ohio Law Abs. 148, 10 O.O. 524.

This section limits the purposes for which real estate may be sold. It may be sold, first, for payment of debts of decedent, and second, for allowance to widow and children, third, for cost of administering estate. McDonald v. McDonald (Ohio Prob. 1936) 1 Ohio Supp. 327, 20 Ohio Law Abs. 421, 5 O.O. 132.

An administrator may sell an undivided one-half interest in realty out of the assets of the estate to pay the funeral expenses of the decedent. Michael v Byerly, No. CA89–04–005 (12th Dist Ct App, Madison, 12–11–89).

Where the executrix of an estate filed an action for permission to sell a remainder interest held by the decedent to pay debts and the trial court properly determined that the owner of the deed was incompetent at the time the interest was transferred to the decedent, the transaction was void. Beery v Beery, Nos. 82AP–474 and 82AP–534 (10th Dist Ct App, Franklin, 1–20–83).

3. Procedural issues

In a proceeding to sell land to pay judgment creditors pending in the court of common pleas it is competent for the heir, who still retains an interest in the subject-matter, by cross-petition to attack such judgments on the ground of fraud. Sidener v. Hawes (Ohio 1882) 37 Ohio St. 532.

The sale of land by the sole heir of a decedent without an order of court at a private sale and the application of such proceeds in satisfaction of preferred claims is no bar to an action by an administrator to sell the land to pay debts. Sidener v. Hawes (Ohio 1882) 37 Ohio St. 532.

In a proceeding by an administrator to sell real estate to pay judgments entered upon awards of arbitrators it is competent for the heir, upon a cross-petition in the same proceeding, to attack said judgments for fraud, and it is error to hold that such judgments are conclusive as to the fact and amount of indebtedness, thus precluding any examination into the question of alleged fraud and collusion. Conway v. Duncan (Ohio 1875) 28 Ohio St. 102.

In a proceeding by an administrator to sell real estate to pay judgments entered upon awards of arbitrators, a cross-petition may be filed by the heirs and the judgment attacked for fraud in the same way that it might be in an original proceeding for that purpose. Conway v. Duncan (Ohio 1875) 28 Ohio St. 102.

An order of a court of record to sell an estate cannot be proven by parol. Ludlow's Heirs v. Johnston (Ohio 1828) 3 Ohio 553, 17 Am.Dec. 609.

Where the executor of an estate may sell, lease, mortgage or otherwise dispose of any properties, real or personal, included in the residuary clause of the will of a nonresident decedent, and at the time of the decedent's death the property situated in Ohio is realty, the succession to which is subject to the Ohio succession tax, the debts, including federal estate taxes and costs of administration, should not be deducted in whole or on a proportionate basis from the appraised value of such realty in assessing the succession tax if there is sufficient personalty in such estate to pay such debts, taxes and costs. In re Packard's Estate (Ohio 1963) 174 Ohio St. 349, 189 N.E.2d 434, 22 O.O.2d 409.

2127.02
Note 3

The personal property of a decedent is primarily liable for his debts where there is one residuary clause applicable to personal property and another to real property. Ginder v. Ginder (Ohio Prob. 1954) 134 N.E.2d 603, 72 Ohio Law Abs. 277, 82 Ohio Law Abs. 129, 59 O.O. 320.

Collateral attack may not be made upon an order of the probate court ordering a sale of the real estate of a decedent. Doughty v. Beard (Ohio Com.Pl. 1952) 132 N.E.2d 288, 72 Ohio Law Abs. 188.

Judgment entered in action brought in Probate Court to obtain sale of property to satisfy debts of estate, in which action Probate Court had acquired exclusive jurisdiction to determine all questions arising, could not be collaterally attacked in Court of Common Pleas by heirs at law on ground that they were not made parties to Probate Court proceedings but rather if any attack was to be made in proceedings such attack must be made in the Probate Court. Doughty v. Beard (Ohio Com.Pl. 1952) 132 N.E.2d 288, 72 Ohio Law Abs. 188. Judgment ⇒ 475

Where executor's petition in Probate Court for sale of decedent's real property to pay debts and determine equities contained allegation that decedent had died seized of premises, and another allegation that decedent had prior to death executed deed to grandson, who was executor, and that such deed should be set aside to enable executor to pay decedent's debts, allegations were not so inconsistent as to require executor to elect whether he would proceed on theory that decedent died seized of premises or on theory that decedent had conveyed premises. Piatt v. Piatt (Darke 1952) 114 N.E.2d 441, 65 Ohio Law Abs. 284. Pleading ⇒ 369(1)

When in an action to subject a decedent's property to sale in order to pay debts it is determined that title is not in the decedent, the action should be dismissed. Piatt v. Piatt (Darke 1952) 114 N.E.2d 441, 65 Ohio Law Abs. 284.

Objection to petition to sell decedent's real estate to pay debts of his estate, on ground that there is no allegation that the personal assets in decedent's estate at the time of his death were insufficient to pay his debts cannot be raised for the first time in an appellate court where evidence at trial shows that it was necessary to sell decedent's real estate to pay his debts. Kohn v. Kohn (Lucas 1941) 67 Ohio App. 404, 36 N.E.2d 1009, 21 O.O. 348. Executors And Administrators ⇒ 358(.5)

Where a judgment is a subsisting lien on the lands of the debtor at the time of his death, it is not necessary thereafter to issue execution upon it in order to preserve the lien; it is entitled to share in the proceeds of the land, when sold by the personal representative, according to its priority at the time of the debtor's death, although execution be not issued thereon within five years from its rendition or the date of the last execution. Ambrose v. Byrne (Ohio 1899) 61 Ohio St. 146, 42 W.L.B. 360, 55 N.E. 408.

An averment that there is no personal property sufficient to pay the decedent's debts is imperative under RS 6136 to RS 6141, and this requirement is not dispensed with by an allegation that the land in question had been fraudulently conveyed by the decedent. Baen v. Weller (Ohio Com.Pl. 1901) 12 Ohio Dec. 128.

A county auditor may require that all deeds and other instruments of conveyance be submitted to the county engineer for a determination as to whether the descriptions contained in said instruments are legally sufficient prior to submission to the county auditor for transfer of the real property upon the tax list pursuant to RC 319.20. OAG 86–028, overruled in part by OAG 94–066.

When a holder of a deed for real estate, which has been legally purchased from an administrator or executor of an estate through the probate court under procedure set forth in GC 10510–2 (RC 2127.02) et seq., makes application to the county auditor of the county in which the real estate is situated for transfer of such real estate by said deed properly describing such real estate, and presented therewith the deed and order of the probate court for the execution of such deed, it is the mandatory duty of the said county auditor to endorse on such deed "transferred", pursuant to GC 2573 (RC 319.20) and GC 2768 (Repealed), and he may not refuse to make such transfer for the reason that the county surveyor has not checked and approved the description of the property contained in such deed. 1936 OAG 6120; overruled by OAG 86–028.

4. Rights of purchaser

Where a sale of land for the payment of debts is in conformity with the requirements of the statute, the purchaser takes the land discharged of all creditors' liens, and the priorities given by such liens are transferred by statute to the fund arising from the sale of lands; the purchaser is not responsible for the administrator's application of such fund. Defrees v. Greenham (Ohio 1860) 11 Ohio St. 486. Executors And Administrators ⇒ 385

Where summons has been served on only two of those named as defendants in an action to sell the land of their ancestor, and a judgment is rendered against all the defendants, only the title of the heirs served will pass to a purchaser at the sheriff's sale. Douglass' Lessee v. Massie (Ohio 1847) 16 Ohio 271, 47 Am.Dec. 375.

A sale of land by the administrator of a decedent for the payment of debts extinguishes his widow's right of dower and transfers an unencumbered title to the purchaser where the wife had joined in a mortgage on the land containing a renunciation of her dower. St. Clair v. Morris (Ohio 1839) 9 Ohio 15, 34 Am.Dec. 415. Dower And Curtesy ⇒ 46; Executors And Administrators ⇒ 387

A purchaser of lands of a decedent who has had the dower interest of the divorced wife of the decedent set off from his land cannot maintain an action to recover back a portion of the purchase price to compensate him for the loss sustained by reason of the assignment of dower since the rule caveat emptor is applicable. Arnold v. Donaldson (Ohio 1888) 46 Ohio St. 73, 20 W.L.B. 431, 18 N.E. 540.

The levy of an attachment in an action against a devisee will not defeat or prevent the execution of a power of sale, given by the testator to his executor nor will such levy affect the title of the purchaser at the executor's sale. Smyth v Anderson, 31 OS 144 (1876).

Where a will gives the executor power to dispose of all of the real estate of the decedent, the levy of an attachment in an action against a devisee will not defeat such power of sale, nor will it affect the title of the purchaser at the executor's sale. Smyth v Anderson, 31 OS 144 (1876).

5. Dower

A sale of land by the administrator of a decedent for the payment of debts extinguishes his widow's right of dower and transfers an unencumbered title to the purchaser where the wife had joined in a mortgage on the land containing a renunciation of her dower. St. Clair v. Morris (Ohio 1839) 9 Ohio 15, 34 Am.Dec. 415. Dower And Curtesy ⇒ 46; Executors And Administrators ⇒ 387

Where, in the probate of an estate, the only claims against the estate consist of the widow's claims for year's allowance, property exempt from administration and for reimbursement for funeral expenses paid by her, acceptance by the widow, the sole heir and devisee under the will, of transfer of all the assets of the estate effects a merger of such claims of the widow in the property transferred, constitutes a waiver by her of all her claims against the estate and, no debts of the estate remaining unpaid, a petition by the executor to sell land to pay debts consisting of the widow's claims for year's allowance, property exempt from administration and for reimbursement for funeral expenses paid will be denied. Kaczenski v. Kaczenski (Trumbull 1962) 118 Ohio App. 225, 193 N.E.2d 731, 25 O.O.2d 68. Executors And Administrators ⇒ 307

A purchaser of lands of a decedent who has had the dower interest of the divorced wife of the decedent set off from his land cannot maintain an action to recover back a portion of the purchase price to compensate him for the loss sustained by reason of the assignment of dower since the rule caveat emptor is applicable. Arnold v. Donaldson (Ohio 1888) 46 Ohio St. 73, 20 W.L.B. 431, 18 N.E. 540.

6. Allowance to spouse and children

Where a homestead has been set aside for the widow and unmarried children of the decedent, an order of court to the executor to sell the land subject to the homestead is void while the premises is occupied as such homestead. Wehrle v. Wehrle (Ohio 1883) 39 Ohio St. 365, 10 W.L.B. 322.

Where a widow elects to take under the statute of descent and distribution, the amount of the federal estate tax should be deducted before computing the widow's share thereof. (See also Hall v Ball, 162 OS 299, 123 NE(2d) 259 (1954).) Campbell v. Lloyd (Ohio 1954) 162 Ohio St. 203, 122 N.E.2d 695, 55 O.O. 102, certiorari denied 75 S.Ct. 600, 349 U.S. 911, 99 L.Ed. 1246, rehearing denied 75 S.Ct. 870, 349 U.S. 948, 99 L.Ed. 1274.

7. Appeal

An action by executors against devisees, distributees, and heirs asking the direction and judgment of the court touching the construction of the testator's will and the duties of the executors thereunder, and praying, among other things, for an order to sell lands in pursuance of the supposed intention of the testator for the payment of legacies, is appealable from the Common Pleas to the District Court. Swing v. Townsend (Ohio 1873) 24 Ohio St. 1.

An action to construe a will and asking for sale of lands to pay debts is appealable. Swing v. Townsend (Ohio 1873) 24 Ohio St. 1.

An appeal may be taken to the court of common pleas from a decree of a court of insolvency or probate court confirming a sale of real estate made by an assignee for the benefit of creditors. Browne v. Wallace (Ohio 1899) 60 Ohio St. 177, 41 W.L.B. 359, 53 N.E. 957. Debtor And Creditor ⚖ 5; Courts ⚖ 185; Courts ⚖ 202(5).

8. Jurisdiction

The court of common pleas when acting as a probate court is a court of limited jurisdiction, and the same rule must be observed as though it possessed no other powers. Ludlow's Heirs v. Johnston (Ohio 1828) 3 Ohio 553, 17 Am.Dec. 609.

Where, in an action for the partition of the real property of a deceased person brought in the court of common pleas within one year from the decedent's death, it is disclosed that the personal property is insufficient to pay debts of the estate and that the administrator has instituted an action in the probate court to sell the real property to pay debts of the estate, the court of common pleas is without jurisdiction to grant partition of such lands. Burrier v. Kiefer (Crawford 1951) 90 Ohio App. 571, 107 N.E.2d 565, 48 O.O. 210. Courts ⚖ 475(2)

In proceedings to sell the real estate of a decedent to pay debts, the jurisdiction of the probate court is limited by GC 10783 (repealed 1932. See §10510–21) and it cannot on distribution of the proceeds in such a proceeding render personal judgment against the legatee who has been made a party. State ex rel. Voight v. Lueders (Ohio 1920) 101 Ohio St. 211, 128 N.E. 70. Executors And Administrators ⚖ 315.1

The probate court has jurisdiction to try any question of fact arising in such action and may give the parties a jury trial if the nature of the issues entitles them thereto. Doan v. Biteley (Ohio 1892) 49 Ohio St. 588, 32 N.E. 600.

An action begun by administrator to sell land in the probate court and appealed to the common pleas court gives that court jurisdiction as if it was originally started there. Tidd v. Bloch (Ohio Cir. 1904) 16 Ohio C.D. 113, 4 Ohio C.C.N.S. 216.

The probate court of county appointing a testamentary trustee has jurisdiction to order the sale of realty located in another county. Boals v. Clingan (Ohio Com.Pl. 1905) 16 Ohio Dec. 267, 6 Ohio N.P.N.S. 609.

9. Partition and contribution

Where an administrator has made a settlement believed by him to be final of the estate of his intestate and the personalty of the estate has been exhausted in the payment of debts and of statutory allowances to the widow, and afterward an action is brought against the administrator on a liability contracted by the intestate resulting, though contested in good faith and with due diligence, in a judgment against the administrator, such judgment remaining unreversed and unsatisfied, is conclusive evidence of indebtedness against the estate and can not be collaterally impeached for mere error; in such case, the administrator is entitled to an order for the sale of so much of the real estate of which the intestate died seized as may be necessary to satisfy the judgment, although such real estate may have been partitioned among the heirs of the intestate and by them sold and conveyed, wholly or in part to purchasers thereof. Faran v. Robinson (Ohio 1867) 17 Ohio St. 242, 93 Am.Dec. 617.

Filing of a partition action in common pleas court does not bar an executor or administrator from subjecting the land to the payment of the estate's debts. Fox v. Holcomb (Darke 1955) 132 N.E.2d 130, 71 Ohio Law Abs. 334.

Where the personal property of a deceased person is insufficient to pay debts of the estate, and partition proceedings are instituted in the court of common pleas for the partition of decedent's real property, the executor or administrator of the estate of such decedent may elect either to bring an action in the probate court to sell the real property to pay debts, or to secure and file a certificate in the court in which the partition proceedings are pending. Burrier v. Kiefer (Crawford 1951) 90 Ohio App. 571, 107 N.E.2d 565, 48 O.O. 210.

A suit in partition does not prevent a sale by the administrator to pay debts. Myers v. Myers (Ohio Cir. 1907) 19 Ohio C.D. 396, 9 Ohio C.C.N.S. 449.

Specific devisees and specific legatees must share equally in any loss resulting to one or more of them by reason of the insufficiency of funds for paying the testator's debts. McArther v McArther, 93 Abs 367 (Prob, Cuyahoga 1961).

10. Civil action

The proceeding of an executor or administrator to sell the real estate of the deceased, to pay the debts and costs of administering his estate, whether prosecuted in the court of common pleas or the probate court, is a civil action, in which any person may be made a defendant who has or claims an interest in the land, or who is a necessary party to a complete determination of any question involved in the action. Doan v. Biteley (Ohio 1892) 49 Ohio St. 588, 32 N.E. 600.

A proceeding in probate or common pleas court to sell land to pay debts is a civil action and any person claiming an interest in the land may be made a party. Doan v. Biteley (Ohio 1892) 49 Ohio St. 588, 32 N.E. 600.

An action by an administrator to sell lands is a civil action. Tidd v. Bloch (Ohio Cir. 1904) 16 Ohio C.D. 113, 4 Ohio C.C.N.S. 216.

This section, as well as former sections, which it superseded, provides that a proceeding to sell real estate is a "civil action." The determination of heirship under GC 10509–95 (RC 2123.01) et seq. is a civil action. It is, therefore, evident that at least these two proceedings are not affected by GC 26 (RC 1.20) if started after January 1, 1932, because they are made independent civil actions by statute. In re Murphy's Estate (Ohio Prob. 1932) 29 Ohio NP(NS) 183.

11. Statute of limitation

As between the estate of a deceased debtor and the creditors thereof, including the widow claiming her allowance, the statute of limitations does not run against their claims after they have been presented to and allowed by the executor or administrator. Fox v. Holcomb (Darke 1955) 132 N.E.2d 130, 71 Ohio Law Abs. 334.

Where allowances were made to a widow for her support, statute of limitations did not run against such allowed claim and therefore fact that administrator made payments upon the debts owing the widow within six years prior to his application to sell realty to pay such debt was immaterial. Fox v. Holcomb (Darke 1955) 132 N.E.2d 130, 71 Ohio Law Abs. 334. Limitation Of Actions ⚖ 132

After the running of the six-year statute of limitations on a proceeding to subject lands of a decedent to the payment of his debts, it is the right of an owner of an estate in remainder, though not in possession, to bring an action to quiet title in said estate against the claims of the administrator. Ling v. Strome (Ohio Cir. 1909) 21 Ohio C.D. 569, 12 Ohio C.C.N.S. 161.

The bar of the statute of limitations on the administrator's right to sell the decedent's lands to pay debts falls six years from the time the administrator ascertains that the personal estate in his hands is insufficient to pay all the debts, and such knowledge will be attributed to him not later than the filing of his account. Kemper v. Apollo Bldg. & Loan Co. (Ohio Com.Pl. 1907) 18 Ohio Dec. 484, 5 Ohio NP(NS) 403, affirmed 20 Ohio C.D. 700, 11 Ohio C.C.(N.S.) 372, affirmed 80 Ohio St. 732, 89 N.E. 1121.

12. Court's powers

In proceedings by an executor or administrator for the sale of real estate to pay debts where the same is encumbered by mortgages or other liens, the court is to settle the priorities among lien-holders and order a sale free from such liens. Stone v. Strong (Ohio 1884) 42 Ohio St. 53.

By the law of 1795 the orphan's court's power over an intestate's real estate is in express terms limited to the lands within the county where the court is. Ludlow's Heirs' Lessee v. McBride (Ohio 1827) 3 Ohio 240.

A mistake in a deed to a purchaser made by an administrator in proceedings to sell the lands of an intestate for the payment of debts may be corrected by a court of general jurisdiction in equity, and such court may correct the mistake in the proceedings of the probate court as well as in the deed. Gill v. Pelkey (Ohio 1896) 54 Ohio St. 348, 35 W.L.B. 276, 43 N.E. 991.

Before a probate court can make the necessary order for an entry of a release and satisfaction of mortgage the court must first follow the procedures of RC 2127.18 and determine the equities among the parties and the priorities of liens on the subject real estate prior to its sale. In re Estate of Marquis, No. L–97–1453, 1998 WL 769786 (6th Dist Ct App, Lucas, 11–6–98).

2127.03 Action for sale to pay legacy

When by operation of law or the provisions of a will, a legacy is effectual to charge real property, and the personal property is insufficient to pay the legacy, together with all the debts, the allowance to the surviving spouse, minor children, or surviving spouse and minor children as provided in section 2106.13 of the Revised Code, and the costs of administering the estate, the executor, administrator, or administrator with the will annexed shall commence a civil action in the probate court for authority to sell the real property so charged.

If the executor, administrator, or administrator with the will annexed fails to commence the action mentioned in this section or section 2127.02 of the Revised Code, the probate court in which letters testamentary have been granted, upon its own motion or upon motion by a creditor or legatee, shall order the executor, administrator, or administrator with the will annexed to commence such an action, and proceed in the manner prescribed in this chapter.

(1990 H 346, eff. 5–31–90; 1975 S 145; 1953 H 1; GC 10510–3, 10510–4)

Uncodified Law

1990 H 346, § 3, eff. 5–31–90, reads, in part: (A) Sections 1 and 2 of this act shall apply only to the estates of decedents who die on or after the effective date of this act.

Historical and Statutory Notes

Pre–1953 H 1 Amendments: 114 v 451

Cross References

Proceeds of sale to be marshaled in conformity with will, 2127.39

Library References

Executors and Administrators ⇌ 325, 326, 332.
Westlaw Topic No. 162.
C.J.S. Executors and Administrators §§ 586 to 591, 601.
  Baldwin's Ohio Legislative Service, 1990 Laws of Ohio, H 346—LSC Analysis, p 5–87

Research References

Encyclopedias
OH Jur. 3d Decedents' Estates § 1510, Statutory Grounds, Generally.
OH Jur. 3d Decedents' Estates § 1518, Payment of Legacies.

Treatises and Practice Aids
Carlin, Baldwin's Ohio Practice, Merrick-Rippner Probate Law § 2:54, Sale of Land—Grounds for Land Sale.
Carlin, Baldwin's Ohio Practice, Merrick-Rippner Probate Law § 90:1, Persons Entitled to Bring Land Sale Actions—Executors and Administrators.
Carlin, Baldwin's Ohio Practice, Merrick-Rippner Probate Law § 90:8, Authority for Land Sale Action—Insufficient Personal Property to Pay Debts.
Carlin, Baldwin's Ohio Practice, Merrick-Rippner Probate Law § 91:3, Land Sale—Motion to Commence Action and Proceed.
Carlin, Baldwin's Ohio Practice, Merrick-Rippner Probate Law § 91:6, Land Sale—to Pay Legacies.
Carlin, Baldwin's Ohio Practice, Merrick-Rippner Probate Law § 91:8, Land Sale—to Pay Debts.
Carlin, Baldwin's Ohio Practice, Merrick-Rippner Probate Law § 91:9, Land Sale—to Pay Family Allowance.
Carlin, Baldwin's Ohio Practice, Merrick-Rippner Probate Law § 94:2, Bond of Interested Person to Prevent Sale.
Carlin, Baldwin's Ohio Practice, Merrick-Rippner Probate Law § 91:44, Complaint for Authority to Sell Real Property to Pay Legacies—Form.
Kuehnle and Levey, Ohio Real Estate Law and Practice § 52:8, Statutory Fiduciary Sales—Grounds for Judicial Sale—Payment of Legacies.
Kuehnle and Levey, Ohio Real Estate Law and Practice § 52:11, Statutory Fiduciary Sales—Compelling Sale to Pay Debts or Legacies.

Notes of Decisions

Intent of testator 1
Residuary estate 2
Void devises 3

---

1. Intent of testator

Where a testatrix made money bequests largely in excess of her personal estate, and this fact was known to her at the time of the making of the will, it will be presumed that she intended to charge the real estate with the payment of such legacies. Townsend's Ex'rs v. Townsend (Ohio 1874) 25 Ohio St. 477.

A testator's express words in his will are not required to change pecuniary legacies upon the real estate; an intention to do so may be derived by implication, and where a devisee is required to pay them as consideration for the property, the law attaches an equitable lien for the security of the legatees, unless it appears that the testator intended to exonerate the property from the charge. Clyde v. Simpson (Ohio 1854) 4 Ohio St. 445.

Testamentary legacies are not payable out of real property specifically devised, unless the testator expresses such intention by the terms of his will. Snyder v. La Due (Lucas 1955) 100 Ohio App. 526, 137 N.E.2d 432, 60 O.O. 407. Wills ⇌ 821(1)

The testator's intention to charge legacies on real estate specifically devised must clearly appear or be clearly deducible from the language of the will, but the charge need not be made in express terms or by any particular language. Knepper v. Knepper (Ohio 1921) 103 Ohio St. 529, 134 N.E. 476, 19 Ohio Law Rep. 462. Wills ⇌ 821(1)

Legacies not specifically charged upon real estate will nevertheless be held to be charged upon such real estate, and be a lien thereon, where it appears that the testator, at the time the will was made and at his decease, had no moneys or personal estate of any kind out of which such legacies could be paid, unless a contrary intention is manifest from the whole will. Theobald v. Fugman (Ohio 1901) 64 Ohio St. 473, 45 W.L.B. 382, 60 N.E. 606. Wills ⇌ 820(3)

2. Residuary estate

Where a testator's will gives a life estate in real estate and a pecuniary legacy to his wife, gives a legacy to his minor daughter in trust and the entire residuary estate, real and personal, is left to his sons, the personal estate being insufficient to pay both the debts and the legacies, the daughter's legacy is chargeable upon the residuary real estate. Moore v. Beckwith's Ex'r (Ohio 1862) 14 Ohio St. 129.

Rule that general legacy, unprovided for, is charge on whole residuary estate, applicable only where satisfaction out of residuary estate is necessary. Koontz v. Hubley (Ohio 1924) 111 Ohio St. 414, 145 N.E. 590, 2 Ohio Law Abs. 117, 2 Ohio Law Abs. 772, 22 Ohio Law Rep. 636. Wills ⇌ 822

A devise of money legacies and devises of real estate and a devise of the residue, real and personal, authorizes the implication that the testator intended in case of failure of personal assets to make the legacy a charge upon the realty. Hunt v. Hayes (Ohio Cir. 1898) 10 Ohio C.D. 388, affirmed 63 Ohio St. 599, 60 N.E. 1131.

3. Void devises

Where devise to church was void, interest in realty became part of testatrix' general estate, subject to payment of legacies under will. Ward v. Worthington (Butler 1928) 28 Ohio App. 325, 162 N.E. 714, 6 Ohio Law Abs. 646. Wills ⇌ 849

2127.04 Action for sale in other circumstances

(A) With the consent of all persons entitled to share in an estate upon distribution, the executor, administrator, or administrator with the will annexed may, and upon the request of these persons shall, commence an action in the probate court for authority to sell any part or all of the decedent's real estate, even though the real estate is not required to be sold to pay debts or legacies. A guardian may make a request under this division, or give consent, on behalf of the guardian's ward.

(B) An executor, administrator, or administrator with the will annexed may commence an action in the probate court, on the executor or administrator's own motion, to sell any part or all of the decedent's real estate, even though the real estate is not required to be sold to pay debts or legacies. The court shall not issue an order of sale in the action unless one of the categories specified in divisions (B)(1)(a), (b), and (c), (B)(2)(a), (b), and (c), and (B)(3) of this section applies:

(1)(a) At least fifty per cent of all the persons interested in the real estate proposed to be sold have consented to the sale.

(b) Prior to the issuance of the order, no written objection is filed with the court by any person or persons who hold aggregate interests in the interest of the decedent in the real estate proposed to be sold, that total in excess of twenty-five per cent.

(c) The court determines that the sale is in the best interest of the decedent's estate.

(2)(a) No person's interest in the interest of the decedent in the real estate proposed to be sold exceeds ten per cent.

(b) Prior to the issuance of the order, no written objection is filed with the court by any person or persons who hold aggregate interests in the interest of the decedent in the real estate proposed to be sold, that total in excess of twenty-five per cent.

(c) The court determines that the sale is in the best interest of the decedent's estate.

(3) The real estate proposed to be sold escheats to the state under division (K) of section 2105.06 of the Revised Code.

(C) Notwithstanding any provision of the Revised Code, an executor, administrator, or administrator with the will annexed shall commence an action in the probate court to sell any part or all of the decedent's real estate if any person who is entitled to inherit all or part of the real estate cannot be found after a due and diligent search. The court shall not issue an order of sale in the action unless the sale is in the best interest of the person who cannot be found and in the best interest of the decedent's estate.

If a sale is ordered under this division, the costs of its administration shall be taken from the proceeds of the sale.

(D) A surviving spouse who is an executor or administrator of the decedent spouse's estate is not disqualified, by reason of being executor or administrator, as a person to whom a parcel of real estate may be sold pursuant to this section.

(2000 S 152, eff. 3–22–01; 1981 H 271, eff. 2–2–82; 1975 S 145; 1953 H 1; GC 10510–5)

Historical and Statutory Notes

Pre–1953 H 1 Amendments: 114 v 452

Amendment Note: 2000 S 152 inserted "the real estate is" and "under this division" in division (A); substituted "the real estate" for "it", deleted "following" before "categories", and inserted "specified in divisions (B)(1)(a), (b), and (c), (B)(2)(a), (b). and (c), and (B)(3) of this section" in division (B); designated divisions (B)(1)(a) to (B)(2)(c); substituted "(K)" for "(J)" in division (B)(3); and made other nonsubstantive changes.

Library References

Executors and Administrators ⚖ 319, 328, 332, 401.
Westlaw Topic No. 162.
C.J.S. Executors and Administrators §§ 584 to 585, 593, 601, 684.

Research References

Encyclopedias

OH Jur. 3d Decedents' Estates § 1510, Statutory Grounds, Generally.
OH Jur. 3d Decedents' Estates § 1519, Purposes Demanded, or Consented To, by Beneficiaries.
OH Jur. 3d Decedents' Estates § 1522, Institution by Action by Representative for Authority to Sell.
OH Jur. 3d Decedents' Estates § 1524, Jurisdiction and Powers of the Probate Court.
OH Jur. 3d Decedents' Estates § 1556, Who May Purchase; Executors and Administrators.
OH Jur. 3d Decedents' Estates § 1563, Refusal to Confirm; Resale.

Treatises and Practice Aids

Carlin, Baldwin's Ohio Practice, Merrick-Rippner Probate Law § 2:53, Sale of Land—Power of Sale.
Carlin, Baldwin's Ohio Practice, Merrick-Rippner Probate Law § 2:54, Sale of Land—Grounds for Land Sale.
Carlin, Baldwin's Ohio Practice, Merrick-Rippner Probate Law § 4:34, Service—Summons—Waiver.
Carlin, Baldwin's Ohio Practice, Merrick-Rippner Probate Law § 90:1, Persons Entitled to Bring Land Sale Actions—Executors and Administrators.
Carlin, Baldwin's Ohio Practice, Merrick-Rippner Probate Law § 90:4, Persons Entitled to Bring Land Sale Actions—Foreign Executor or Administrator.
Carlin, Baldwin's Ohio Practice, Merrick-Rippner Probate Law § 90:7, Authority for Land Sale Action—Consent or Demand of Beneficiaries.
Carlin, Baldwin's Ohio Practice, Merrick-Rippner Probate Law § 97:2, Land Sale by Guardian—Statutory Authority.
Carlin, Baldwin's Ohio Practice, Merrick-Rippner Probate Law § 2:121, Administration of Decedent's Estate—Checklist.
Carlin, Baldwin's Ohio Practice, Merrick-Rippner Probate Law § 91:17, Land Sale—Not to Pay for Disputed Title.
Carlin, Baldwin's Ohio Practice, Merrick-Rippner Probate Law § 91:45, Complaint for Authority to Sell Real Estate With Consent of Distributees—Form.
Carlin, Baldwin's Ohio Practice, Merrick-Rippner Probate Law § 91:46, Complaint for Authority to Sell Real Estate With Consent of Less Than All Interested Persons—Form.
Carlin, Baldwin's Ohio Practice, Merrick-Rippner Probate Law § 91:48, Entry Authorizing Sale of Real Estate and Appraisal—Form.
Carlin, Baldwin's Ohio Practice, Merrick-Rippner Probate Law § 91:52, Complaint for Sale of Decedent's Real Estate—Alternate Circumstances—Form.
Carlin, Baldwin's Ohio Practice, Merrick-Rippner Probate Law § 91:53, Consent of Beneficiary to Sale—Form.
Carlin, Baldwin's Ohio Practice, Merrick-Rippner Probate Law § 91:54, Consent of Guardian for Ward to Sale—Form.
Carlin, Baldwin's Ohio Practice, Merrick-Rippner Probate Law § 95:21, Entry Authorizing Sale of Real Estate at Private Sale—Form.
Carlin, Baldwin's Ohio Practice, Merrick-Rippner Probate Law § 97:12, Land Sale by Guardian—Consent.
Kuehnle and Levey, Ohio Real Estate Law and Practice § 52:3, Statutory Fiduciary Sales—21 Statutory Proceedings.
Kuehnle and Levey, Ohio Real Estate Law and Practice § 52:5, Statutory Fiduciary Sales—Sales With Consent of 50% of All Interested Parties; Where No Person's Interest Exceeds 10%; or When Property Escheats.
Kuehnle and Levey, Ohio Real Estate Law and Practice § 52:6, Statutory Fiduciary Sales—Sale by Fiduciary If Any Person Entitled to Inherit Cannot be Found.
Kuehnle and Levey, Ohio Real Estate Law and Practice § 52:9, Statutory Fiduciary Sales—Grounds for Judicial Sale—Consent of Beneficiaries.
Kuehnle and Levey, Ohio Real Estate Law and Practice § 52:12, Statutory Fiduciary Sales—Enjoining Creditors from Levying After Owner's Death.
Kuehnle and Levey, Ohio Real Estate Law and Practice § 52:23, Statutory Fiduciary Sales—Administrator's Action to Enjoin Creditors from Levying.

Notes of Decisions

Amendment of statute, effect 1
Contract for sale 2

---

1. **Amendment of statute, effect**

The application of RC 2127.04(B)(1), as amended by 1981 H 271, eff. 2–2–82, to the estate of a decedent who died before February 2, 1982, is violative of RC 1.58, because it denies a nonconsenting beneficiary a right he held under the statute prior to its amendment. Duffy v. Heffernan (Franklin 1983) 9 Ohio App.3d 273, 459 N.E.2d 898, 9 O.B.R. 487.

2127.04
Note 1

Real estate of a decedent who died before the effective date of 1981 H 271, eff. 2–2–82, amending RC 2127.04(B)(1), may not be sold pursuant to RC 2127.04(B)(1). Duffy v. Heffernan (Franklin 1983) 9 Ohio App.3d 273, 459 N.E.2d 898, 9 O.B.R. 487.

2. Contract for sale

The administrator of an estate, who executed a contract with plaintiff for the sale of the decedent's real property, did not breach that contract by selling the realty to other purchasers at private sale, where the contract with plaintiff contained the clause "subject to the approval of the probate court," such approval was never obtained, and where the heirs never gave consent to the sale of the property to plaintiff, as required by RC 2127.04 and RC 2127.011. Bilang v. Benson (Lucas 1978) 62 Ohio App.2d 134, 405 N.E.2d 311, 16 O.O.3d 297. Executors And Administrators ⇔ 142

WHEN GUARDIAN MAY SELL

2127.05 Guardian may sell

Whenever necessary for the education, support, or the payment of the just debts of the ward, or for the discharge of liens on the real estate of the ward, or wherever the real estate of the ward is suffering unavoidable waste, or a better investment of its value can be made, or whenever it appears that a sale of the real estate will be for the benefit of the ward or his children, the guardian of the person and estate or of the estate only of a minor, person unable to manage his property because of mental illness or deficiency, habitual drunkard, confined person, or other person under disability may commence a civil action in the probate court for authority to sell all or any part of the real estate of the ward. If it appears to the advantage of the ward to lay out all or any part of the land in town lots, application for such authority may also be made in the action.

When the same person is guardian for two or more wards whose real estate is owned by them jointly or in common, the actions may be joined, and in one complaint the guardian may ask for the sale of the interest of all or any number of his wards in the real estate. If different persons are guardians of wards interested jointly or in common in the same real estate, they may join as parties plaintiff in the same action. On the hearing, in either case, the court may authorize the sale of the interest of one or more of the wards.

(1975 S 145, eff. 1–1–76; 125 v 903; 1953 H 1; GC 10510–6, 10510–7)

Historical and Statutory Notes

Pre–1953 H 1 Amendments: 114 v 452

Cross References

Forcible entry and detainer action, applicability to sales by executors, administrators, and guardians, 1923.02
Guardian for nonresident, 2111.37
Partition, guardian's powers and duties, 5307.19
Sale of lands of foreign wards, 2111.44, 2127.42
Sale of real estate by trustees of nonresident, 2127.43

Library References

Guardian and Ward ⇔75.
Mental Health ⇔258.1 to 260.
Westlaw Topic Nos. 196, 257A.

Research References

Encyclopedias

OH Jur. 3d Family Law § 157, Insane and Other Incompetent Persons—Dower Rights in the Property of Incompetents.
OH Jur. 3d Guardian & Ward § 142, Generally; Purpose of Sale.
OH Jur. 3d Guardian & Ward § 143, Property Subject to Sale.
OH Jur. 3d Guardian & Ward § 144, Property Subject to Sale—Fractional or Undivided Interests.
OH Jur. 3d Guardian & Ward § 146, Generally; Jurisdiction and Venue.
OH Jur. 3d Guardian & Ward § 147, Parties; Plaintiff.
OH Jur. 3d Guardian & Ward § 150, Pleadings; Complaint.

Treatises and Practice Aids

Klein, Darling, & Terez, Baldwin's Ohio Practice Civil Practice § 73:3, Probate Division--Venue.
Carlin, Baldwin's Ohio Practice, Merrick-Rippner Probate Law § 90:1, Persons Entitled to Bring Land Sale Actions—Executors and Administrators.
Carlin, Baldwin's Ohio Practice, Merrick-Rippner Probate Law § 97:2, Land Sale by Guardian—Statutory Authority.
Carlin, Baldwin's Ohio Practice, Merrick-Rippner Probate Law § 97:4, Land Sale by Guardian—Joining Interests of Several Wards.
Carlin, Baldwin's Ohio Practice, Merrick-Rippner Probate Law § 64:21, Powers and Duties of Guardian—Ward's Estate—Discretionary Acts.
Carlin, Baldwin's Ohio Practice, Merrick-Rippner Probate Law § 90:13, Land Sale Action—Jurisdiction of Probate Court.
Carlin, Baldwin's Ohio Practice, Merrick-Rippner Probate Law § 91:47, Complaint of Guardian for Authority to Sell Real Estate—Form.
Carlin, Baldwin's Ohio Practice, Merrick-Rippner Probate Law § 91:48, Entry Authorizing Sale of Real Estate and Appraisal—Form.
Carlin, Baldwin's Ohio Practice, Merrick-Rippner Probate Law § 95:21, Entry Authorizing Sale of Real Estate at Private Sale—Form.
Kuehnle and Levey, Ohio Real Estate Law and Practice § 52:18, Statutory Fiduciary Sales—Action to Sell by Guardian.

Notes of Decisions

Court's power 5
Death of ward 1
Encumbrances 3
Female wards 4
Fraudulent sale 7
Grounds 8
Guardian's powers 9
Partition 6
Trust 2

---

1. Death of ward

Where a ward dies pending an appeal from an action ordering property of the ward sold and a new appraisement made, the guardianship terminates and the appeal is moot. Becker v. Becker (Summit 1952) 125 N.E.2d 563, 69 Ohio Law Abs. 414.

Where property inherited by a minor has undergone several transmutations from realty to personalty and back through sales by his guardian, and at the time of the minor's death the property is in the form of realty, it does not retain its character as ancestral property and must be treated as an acquisition of such minor for purposes of descent and distribution. McCammon v. Cooper (Ohio 1904) 69 Ohio St. 366, 69 N.E. 658, 1 Ohio Law Rep. 753, 1 Ohio Law Rep. 869.

2. Trust

Where a guardian sells his wards' real estate and takes purchase money notes for deferred payments, which notes plainly reveal that they are part of a trust fund, the purchaser of such notes is put on inquiry and buys at his peril under circumstances furnishing reasonable grounds to believe the sale was against the wards' interest; such purchaser can acquire no title to the property if the guardian appropriates the proceeds of the sale. Strong v. Strauss (Ohio 1883) 40 Ohio St. 87, 9 W.L.B. 345.

Where the guardian of a minor and such minor's mother, the widow of a deceased soldier, join to assign the military land warrant issued to them to a person knowing the facts, and do so without the authorization from the probate court, the purchaser holds such warrant in trust for the minor. (See also Stoddard v Smith, 11 OS 581 (1860).) Mack v. Brammer (Ohio 1876) 28 Ohio St. 508.

3. Encumbrances

A guardian has no power to convey the lands of a minor to county commissioners for a public use, nor to incumber the estate with a permanent easement without authority from the probate court. State v.

Commissioners of Hamilton County (Ohio 1883) 39 Ohio St. 58, 9 W.L.B. 173.

4. Female wards

This section does not authorize the courts of common pleas to order a sale of the lands of an infant femme covert upon the application of her husband, though it does allow the courts to appoint guardians to sell the lands of minors in general. Dengenhart v. Cracraft (Ohio 1881) 36 Ohio St. 549, 6 W.L.B. 156.

Under an earlier statute it was held where a guardian is appointed before a female ward arrives at the age of twelve years, he cannot after she becomes twelve sell the ward's land. Perry's Lessee v. Brainard (Ohio 1842) 11 Ohio 442.

5. Court's power

Under former laws, the only power to authorize a guardian to sell his ward's real estate, prior to the creation of the probate court, was vested in the common pleas court of the county in which the guardian was appointed. Foresman v. Haag (Ohio 1880) 36 Ohio St. 102, supplemented 37 Ohio St. 143.

A guardian for a minor must be appointed in the county in which he resides, and the court of common pleas that appointed a guardian may empower him to sell the minor's land situated in another county. Maxsom v. Sawyer (Ohio 1843) 12 Ohio 195.

Where a guardian sought to enforce a lien or charge by a sale of the interest of his ward in certain realty which had been devised to defendant, who sought to set up the equitable principle of exoneration, admitting that the ward's support was a charge on his land, but alleging that a special fund had been provided for such support, and sought to compel the guardian's resort to that fund before selling defendant's interest in the premises, the case was one of chancery jurisdiction, and therefore appealable to the Court of Appeals, under Const. art. IV, § 6, giving the Court of Appeals appellate jurisdiction in the trial of chancery cases. Best v. McClure (Ohio 1923) 108 Ohio St. 481, 141 N.E. 217, 1 Ohio Law Abs. 828, 21 Ohio Law Rep. 296.

6. Partition

When minors all claim land in one right, their guardian may institute partition without process, as such proceedings are not of an adversary character. Goudy's Lessee v. Shank (Ohio 1838) 8 Ohio 415.

7. Fraudulent sale

A federal circuit court has jurisdiction in equity to set aside a sale of a minor's lands fraudulently made by his guardian. Arrowsmith v. Gleason (U.S.Ohio 1889) 9 S.Ct. 237, 129 U.S. 86, 32 L.Ed. 630.

8. Grounds

Any one of the grounds asserted in RC 2127.05 will justify the sale of a ward's real estate. BancOhio/Ohio Natl Bank v Adkins, No. 83–CA–3 (4th Dist Ct App, Pickaway, 3–15–84).

9. Guardian's powers

Land script or certificates for money paid by S., were issued under the act of congress of May 23, 1828 (U.S. Stat. vol. 4, 286), to A., B. and C., minors, and in trust for the other heirs of S.; the certificates were not assignable on their face, and were payable in lands; the following note was appended to the certificates: "The indorsement to be executed by" (L.) "guardian of said heirs." The certificates indorsed by A., B., C. and L., guardian of said heirs, were used by L. and his partners in the purchase of lands, and the title taken by H., one of the partners, for their common benefit, the partners agreeing, respectively, to pay L. their portions of the amount of the certificates in money. In a proceeding by the unnamed heirs of S. against H., and others in interest, charging said lands, L. had no authority, as guardian of A., B. and C., to dispose of, or transfer the interest of the other heirs in the certificates. Stoddard v. Smith (Ohio 1860) 11 Ohio St. 581. Public Lands ⇔ 135(4)

PROVISIONS APPLICABLE TO EXECUTORS, ADMINISTRATORS, AND GUARDIANS

2127.06 Successor fiduciary shall complete sale proceedings

If the fiduciary who brings an action under section 2127.01 to 2127.43, inclusive, of the Revised Code, dies, resigns, or is removed, or his powers cease at any time before the real estate sold is conveyed, a successor fiduciary may be substituted as a party to the action and may convey land, whether sold before or after his appointment. He may also be required to give an additional bond.

(1953 H 1, eff. 10–1–53; GC 10510–8)

Historical and Statutory Notes

Pre–1953 H 1 Amendments: 114 v 452

Cross References

Bond of fiduciary, 2109.04 to 2109.20
Deed of fiduciary, 5302.09

Library References

Executors and Administrators ⇔120(1), 335, 351.
Guardian and Ward ⇔72, 83, 92.
Mental Health ⇔178, 264, 265.
Westlaw Topic Nos. 162, 196, 257A.
C.J.S. Executors and Administrators §§ 604, 630, 941 to 946.
C.J.S. Mental Health § 157.

Research References

Encyclopedias

OH Jur. 3d Actions § 116, Change In, or Termination Of, Office of Fiduciary.
OH Jur. 3d Decedents' Estates § 1533, Parties, Generally—Substitution of Successor Representative.
OH Jur. 3d Guardian & Ward § 147, Parties; Plaintiff.

Treatises and Practice Aids

Kuehnle and Levey, Ohio Real Estate Law and Practice § 53:16, Land Sales—Parties Defendant—Substituted Party Plaintiff.
Carlin, Baldwin's Ohio Practice, Merrick-Rippner Probate Law § 91:59, Application to be Substituted Party Plaintiff—Form.
Carlin, Baldwin's Ohio Practice, Merrick-Rippner Probate Law § 91:60, Entry Granting Application to be Substituted Party Plaintiff—Form.
Carlin, Baldwin's Ohio Practice, Merrick-Rippner Probate Law § 96:5, Deed of Fiduciary.
Carlin, Baldwin's Ohio Practice, Merrick-Rippner Probate Law § 97:7, Land Sale by Guardian—Death of Guardian.
Carlin, Baldwin's Ohio Practice, Merrick-Rippner Probate Law § 91:20, Land Sale—Necessary Parties.

Notes of Decisions

Resignation   1

---

1. Resignation

Where executors resign their office after accepting the trust, their authority to execute the power of sale conferred on them by the will as executors expires with their office, and a deed made by them afterward of land sold by them while in office conveys no title to the land. Elstner v. Fife (Ohio 1877) 32 Ohio St. 358.

2127.07 Real estate subject to sale

Any interest in real estate, whether legal or equitable, which the deceased had a right to sell or dispose of at the time of his decease, or of which the ward was seized at the time the action was brought, including coal, iron ore, limestone, fireclay, or other mineral upon or under such real estate, or the right to mine them, may be sold by an executor, administrator, or guardian under sections 2127.01 to 2127.43, inclusive, of the Revised Code. This section does not give an executor or administrator with the will annexed authority to sell real estate for the payment of legacies, other than as charged by the testator or by operation of law. This section does not give a guardian authority to sell an equitable estate in real estate placed by deed of trust, beyond the power of the ward to sell, convey, or assign.

(1953 H 1, eff. 10–1–53; GC 10510–9)

Historical and Statutory Notes

Pre–1953 H 1 Amendments: 114 v 452

Library References

Executors and Administrators ⚖329(1).
Guardian and Ward ⚖79.
Mental Health ⚖262.
Westlaw Topic Nos. 162, 196, 257A.
C.J.S. Executors and Administrators § 595.

Research References

Encyclopedias

OH Jur. 3d Decedents' Estates § 1503, Equitable Interest in Realty.
OH Jur. 3d Guardian & Ward § 143, Property Subject to Sale.

Treatises and Practice Aids

Carlin, Baldwin's Ohio Practice, Merrick-Rippner Probate Law § 92:1, Property Subject to Sale—General Rule.
Carlin, Baldwin's Ohio Practice, Merrick-Rippner Probate Law § 92:2, Property Subject to Sale—Equitable Interests in Real Property.
Carlin, Baldwin's Ohio Practice, Merrick-Rippner Probate Law § 92:6, Property Not Subject to Sale.
Carlin, Baldwin's Ohio Practice, Merrick-Rippner Probate Law § 97:5, Land Sale by Guardian—Selling Fractional Interests.
Kuehnle and Levey, Ohio Real Estate Law and Practice § 53:19, Land Sales—Interests Subject to Sale by Fiduciaries—Legal and Equitable.
Kuehnle and Levey, Ohio Real Estate Law and Practice § 53:20, Land Sales—Interests Subject to Sale by Fiduciaries—Mineral Rights.

Law Review and Journal Commentaries

Equitable Charges on Devised Realty, Note. 4 U Cin L Rev 467 (November 1930).

Notes of Decisions

Contracts and options 2
Equitable interests 1
Legacies 3

1. Equitable interests

A conveyance in trust on condition for a reconveyance creates an equitable estate that may be sold to pay debts. Biggs v. Bickel (Ohio 1861) 12 Ohio St. 49.

Equity in lands passes to the heirs and may be sold by the personal representative of the deceased for the payment of the estate's debts. Avery's Lessee v. Dufrees (Ohio 1839) 9 Ohio 145.

Any fractional interest of a decedent will support a land sale proceeding; and an equitable interest is subject to sale in such proceeding. Weaver v. Crommes (Miami 1959) 109 Ohio App. 470, 167 N.E.2d 661, 12 O.O.2d 15.

2. Contracts and options

Personal representative may perform or rescind personal contracts of the intestate subject to the approval of the court. Gray v. Hawkins's Adm'rx (Ohio 1858) 8 Ohio St. 449, 72 Am.Dec. 600.

Where an administrator for the benefit of the estate cancels an unexecuted contract, equity will not set it up again upon the request of the heirs. Howard v Babcock, 7 O 359 (1836).

Where the plaintiff had purchased real estate with the decedent and the probate court approved the sale of such real estate to a third party unless the plaintiff exercised her option to buy within a set amount of time, the probate court may properly authorize the sale to the third party after the plaintiff failed to timely exercise her option. Estate of Etts v Etts, No. L–83–045 (6th Dist Ct App, Lucas, 5–13–83).

3. Legacies

Testamentary legacies are not payable out of real property specifically devised, unless the testator expresses such intention by the terms of his will. Snyder v. La Due (Lucas 1955) 100 Ohio App. 526, 137 N.E.2d 432, 60 O.O. 407. Wills ⚖821(1)

2127.08 Fractional interests; sale of entire interest

When the interest of a decedent or ward in real estate is fractional and undivided, the action for authority to sell such real estate shall include only such undivided fractional interest, except that the executor, administrator, or guardian, or the owner of any other fractional interest, or any lienholder may, by pleading filed in the cause setting forth all interests in the property and liens thereon, require that the action include the entire interest in the property, and the owner of said interests and liens shall receive his respective share of the proceeds of sale after payment has been made of the expenses of sale including reasonable attorney fees for services in the case, which fees must be paid to the plaintiff's attorney unless the court awards some part thereof to other counsel for services in the case for the common benefit of all the parties, having regard to the interest of the parties, the benefit each may derive from the sale, and the equities of the case. The fees of the executor, administrator, or guardian shall be a charge only against such portion of the proceeds of sale as represents the interests of the decedent or ward.

(1953 H 1, eff. 10–1–53; GC 10510–10)

Historical and Statutory Notes

Pre–1953 H 1 Amendments: 123 v 460; 114 v 453

Library References

Executors and Administrators ⚖329(1).
Guardian and Ward ⚖79.
Mental Health ⚖262.
Westlaw Topic Nos. 162, 196, 257A.
C.J.S. Executors and Administrators § 595.

Research References

Encyclopedias

OH Jur. 3d Cotenancy & Partition § 49, Effect of Rights of Decedent's Creditors.
OH Jur. 3d Decedents' Estates § 1502, Fractional Interests in Realty.
OH Jur. 3d Decedents' Estates § 1592, Where Sale was of Entire Property in Which Decedent Owned Fractional Interest.
OH Jur. 3d Guardian & Ward § 144, Property Subject to Sale—Fractional or Undivided Interests.
OH Jur. 3d Guardian & Ward § 168, Proceeds from Sale of Property in Which Ward Had Fractional Interest or Interest Subject to Dower.

Treatises and Practice Aids

Carlin, Baldwin's Ohio Practice, Merrick-Rippner Probate Law § 2:54, Sale of Land—Grounds for Land Sale.
Carlin, Baldwin's Ohio Practice, Merrick-Rippner Probate Law § 90:1, Persons Entitled to Bring Land Sale Actions—Executors and Administrators.
Carlin, Baldwin's Ohio Practice, Merrick-Rippner Probate Law § 90:6, Authority for Land Sale Action—Testamentary Power.

Carlin, Baldwin's Ohio Practice, Merrick-Rippner Probate Law § 90:7, Authority for Land Sale Action—Consent or Demand of Beneficiaries.
Carlin, Baldwin's Ohio Practice, Merrick-Rippner Probate Law § 92:3, Property Subject to Sale—Fractional Interests in Real Property.
Carlin, Baldwin's Ohio Practice, Merrick-Rippner Probate Law § 92:4, Attorney and Other Fiduciary Fees.
Carlin, Baldwin's Ohio Practice, Merrick-Rippner Probate Law § 93:1, Ordering Appraisal of Real Property.
Carlin, Baldwin's Ohio Practice, Merrick-Rippner Probate Law § 96:9, Distribution of Proceeds—Method.
Carlin, Baldwin's Ohio Practice, Merrick-Rippner Probate Law § 97:5, Land Sale by Guardian—Selling Fractional Interests.
Carlin, Baldwin's Ohio Practice, Merrick-Rippner Probate Law § 91:25, Land Sale—Necessary Parties Defendant—Person With Dower Interest.
Carlin, Baldwin's Ohio Practice, Merrick-Rippner Probate Law § 91:49, Complaint for Authority to Sell Entire Interest in Real Estate—Form.
Carlin, Baldwin's Ohio Practice, Merrick-Rippner Probate Law § 91:51, Entry Granting Complaint and Ordering Appraisal of Entire Interest—Form.
Carlin, Baldwin's Ohio Practice, Merrick-Rippner Probate Law § 96:12, Expenses of Sale—Compensation of Executor or Administrator.
Carlin, Baldwin's Ohio Practice, Merrick-Rippner Probate Law § 96:17, Entry Confirming Sale, Ordering Deed and Distribution Where Entire Interest in Real Estate Sold—Form.
Carlin, Baldwin's Ohio Practice, Merrick-Rippner Probate Law § 97:20, Land Sale by Guardian—Fees and Expenses.
Kuehnle and Levey, Ohio Real Estate Law and Practice § 53:3, Land Sales—Parties Defendant—Spouses of Defendants as Necessary Parties.
Kuehnle and Levey, Ohio Real Estate Law and Practice § 53:21, Land Sales—Interests Subject to Sale by Fiduciaries—Fractional Interests.

Notes of Decisions

Constitutional issues 1
Equitable interest 3
Fees of executor or attorney 5
Funeral expenses 4
Procedural issues 2

---

1. Constitutional issues

This section is constitutional and not in violation of O Const Art II, § 28 or O Const Art I, § 19, or US Const Am 14. Hatch v. Tipton (Ohio 1936) 131 Ohio St. 364, 2 N.E.2d 875, 6 O.O. 68.

GC 10501–53 and 10510–10 (RC 2101.24 and 2127.08), are not unconstitutional as violative of O Const Art IV, § 8. Hatch v. Buckeye State Bldg. & Loan Co. (Ohio Prob. 1934) 32 Ohio N.P.N.S. 297, 16 Ohio Law Abs. 661.

Section does not deprive a cotenant of any existing rights, does not impair the right of partition, but provides an additional remedy to an executor or personal representative, where the decedent was a cotenant, and his interest is required to be sold for the payment of his debts, hence, the statute is not in violation of any provision of the Ohio or US Constitutions. Hatch v. Buckeye State Bldg. & Loan Co. (Ohio Prob. 1934) 32 Ohio N.P.N.S. 297, 16 Ohio Law Abs. 661.

2. Procedural issues

Where an action in partition has been instituted following the death of a co-owner and subsequent thereto the executor or administrator of such deceased co-owner institutes land sale proceedings under section, the latter supersedes and prevails over the former. Hatch v. Tipton (Ohio 1936) 131 Ohio St. 364, 2 N.E.2d 875, 6 O.O. 68. Partition ⇐ 27

3. Equitable interest

Any fractional interest of a decedent will support a land sale proceeding; and an equitable interest is subject to sale in such proceeding. Weaver v. Crommes (Miami 1959) 109 Ohio App. 470, 167 N.E.2d 661, 12 O.O.2d 15.

4. Funeral expenses

An administrator may sell an undivided one-half interest in realty out of the assets of the estate to pay the funeral expenses of the decedent. Michael v Byerly, No. CA89–04–005 (12th Dist Ct App, Madison, 12–11–89).

5. Fees of executor or attorney

The legislature provided that the fees of the executor or administrator and of his attorney shall be a charge only against the interest of the decedent in cases where there is a sale of a fractional interest of the decedent in connection with the sale of the other interests in real estate. Fulton v. Griffith (Ohio Com.Pl. 1932) 29 Ohio NP(NS) 435, 11 Ohio Law Abs. 673.

2127.09 Venue

An action by an executor, administrator, or guardian to obtain authority to sell real estate shall be brought in the county in which he was appointed or in which the real estate subject to sale or any part thereof is situated. If the action is brought in a county other than that in which the real estate or a part thereof is situated, a certified transcript of the record of all proceedings had therein shall be filed with and recorded by the probate court of each county in which such real estate or any part thereof is situated.

(1953 H 1, eff. 10–1–53; GC 10510–11)

Historical and Statutory Notes

Pre–1953 H 1 Amendments: 114 v 453

Cross References

Commencement of action, venue, Civ R 3

Library References

Executors and Administrators ⇐333.
Guardian and Ward ⇐81.
Mental Health ⇐263.
Westlaw Topic Nos. 162, 196, 257A.
C.J.S. Executors and Administrators § 603.

Research References

Encyclopedias

OH Jur. 3d Decedents' Estates § 1524, Jurisdiction and Powers of the Probate Court.
OH Jur. 3d Decedents' Estates § 1528, Venue.
OH Jur. 3d Guardian & Ward § 146, Generally; Jurisdiction and Venue.

Treatises and Practice Aids

Klein, Darling, & Terez, Baldwin's Ohio Practice Civil Practice § 3:70, Lis Pendens and Related Matters--In General.
Klein, Darling, & Terez, Baldwin's Ohio Practice Civil Practice § 73:2, Probate Division--Applicability of Ohio Civil Rules.
Klein, Darling, & Terez, Baldwin's Ohio Practice Civil Practice § 73:3, Probate Division--Venue.
Carlin, Baldwin's Ohio Practice, Merrick-Rippner Probate Law § 2:55, Sale of Land—Procedure for Commencement of Action.
Carlin, Baldwin's Ohio Practice, Merrick-Rippner Probate Law § 90:15, Land Sale Actions—Venue.
Carlin, Baldwin's Ohio Practice, Merrick-Rippner Probate Law § 97:11, Land Sale by Guardian—Venue.
Carlin, Baldwin's Ohio Practice, Merrick-Rippner Probate Law § 97:21, Land Sale by Guardian—Nonresident Ward.
Kuehnle and Levey, Ohio Real Estate Law and Practice § 53:30, Land Sales—Applicability of Ohio Civil Rules to Probate Court Proceedings—Notice.

2127.10 Complaint in action to sell real estate

An action to obtain authority to sell real estate shall be commenced by the executor, administrator, or guardian by filing a complaint with the probate court.

The complaint shall contain a description of the real estate proposed to be sold and its value, as near as can be ascertained, a statement of the nature of the interest of the decedent or ward in the real estate, a recital of all mortgages and liens upon and adverse interests in the real estate, the facts showing the reason or necessity for the sale, and any additional facts necessary to constitute the cause of action under the section of the Revised Code on which the action is predicated.

(1975 S 145, eff. 1-1-76; 1953 H 1; GC 10510-12, 10510-13)

Historical and Statutory Notes

Pre–1953 H 1 Amendments: 114 v 453

Library References

Executors and Administrators ⚖=336.
Guardian and Ward ⚖=86.
Mental Health ⚖=265.
Westlaw Topic Nos. 162, 196, 257A.
C.J.S. Executors and Administrators § 605.

Research References

Encyclopedias

OH Jur. 3d Decedents' Estates § 1501, Determination of Particular Property or Quantity to be Sold.
OH Jur. 3d Decedents' Estates § 1535, Practice and Procedure, Generally—Complaint.
OH Jur. 3d Guardian & Ward § 150, Pleadings; Complaint.

Treatises and Practice Aids

Klein, Darling, & Terez, Baldwin's Ohio Practice Civil Practice § 73:2, Probate Division--Applicability of Ohio Civil Rules.
Klein, Darling, & Terez, Baldwin's Ohio Practice Civil Practice § 73:3, Probate Division--Venue.
Carlin, Baldwin's Ohio Practice, Merrick-Rippner Probate Law § 2:55, Sale of Land—Procedure for Commencement of Action.
Carlin, Baldwin's Ohio Practice, Merrick-Rippner Probate Law § 91:1, Land Sale—Lis Pendens.
Carlin, Baldwin's Ohio Practice, Merrick-Rippner Probate Law § 91:2, Land Sale—Complaint.
Carlin, Baldwin's Ohio Practice, Merrick-Rippner Probate Law § 97:9, Land Sale by Guardian—Complaint.
Carlin, Baldwin's Ohio Practice, Merrick-Rippner Probate Law § 91:43, Complaint for Authority to Sell Decedent's Real Estate to Pay Debts—Form.
Carlin, Baldwin's Ohio Practice, Merrick-Rippner Probate Law § 91:50, Complaint for Authority to Sell Real Estate, and for Order of Private Sale—Form.
Carlin, Baldwin's Ohio Practice, Merrick-Rippner Probate Law § 95:21, Entry Authorizing Sale of Real Estate at Private Sale—Form.
Kuehnle and Levey, Ohio Real Estate Law and Practice § 53:35, Land Sales—Service—Lis Pendens.
Kuehnle and Levey, Ohio Real Estate Law and Practice § 53:36, Land Sales—Pleadings.

Notes of Decisions

Court powers 2
Grounds for action 3
Procedural issues 1

---

1. Procedural issues

The petition must describe all the land of the ward. Mauarr v. Parrish (Ohio 1875) 26 Ohio St. 636.

The failure of the court to require a new bond may be erroneous but does not render the proceedings void. Mauarr v. Parrish (Ohio 1875) 26 Ohio St. 636. Guardian And Ward ⚖= 92; Judicial Sales ⚖= 4

Where there is enough in the petition to give the court jurisdiction, a wrong numbering of the lots is not fatal. Mauarr v. Parrish (Ohio 1875) 26 Ohio St. 636.

Judicial proceedings in sales of real estate are to be sustained if possible. Stall v Macalester, 9 O 19 (1839).

The erroneous admission of a real estate appraiser's report in a hearing pursuant to RC 2127.10 constitutes harmless error where the court was otherwise aware of the approximate value of the land. BancOhio/Ohio Natl Bank v Adkins, No. 83–CA–3 (4th Dist Ct App, Pickaway, 3–15–84).

The failure to aver value in a complaint pursuant to RC 2127.10 is a procedural defect which may be remedied pursuant to the Rules of Civil Procedure in order to mete out substantial justice between the parties. BancOhio/Ohio Natl Bank v Adkins, No. 83–CA–3 (4th Dist Ct App, Pickaway, 3–15–84).

2. Court powers

Under former laws, the only power to authorize a guardian to sell his ward's real estate, prior to the creation of the probate court, was vested in the common pleas court of the county in which the guardian was appointed. Foresman v. Haag (Ohio 1880) 36 Ohio St. 102, supplemented 37 Ohio St. 143.

A guardian for a minor must be appointed in the county in which he resides, and the court of common pleas that appointed a guardian may empower him to sell the minor's land situated in another county. Maxsom v. Sawyer (Ohio 1843) 12 Ohio 195.

3. Grounds for action

When the personal estate in the hands of the administrator is sufficient to pay the costs of administering the estate and all the debts except those secured by a mortgage executed by the testator in his lifetime on lands of which he died seized, an action cannot be maintained to subject other lands which the testator had conveyed away to defraud his creditors to the payment of the mortgage debt. McCall v. Pixley (Ohio 1891) 48 Ohio St. 379, 25 W.L.B. 417, 27 N.E. 887. Executors And Administrators ⚖= 329(1); Fraudulent Conveyances ⚖= 226

An averment that there is not sufficient personalty to pay debts is imperative, and this requirement is not dispensed with by an allegation that the land had been fraudulently conveyed. Baen v. Weller (Ohio Com.Pl. 1901) 12 Ohio Dec. 128.

Under Ohio fraudulent transfer law, upon simultaneous conveyance of devised property to taxpayer and his brother, which was done without consideration and which left estate insolvent, taxpayer became derivatively liable after brother declared bankruptcy for estate tax deficiency subsequently assessed due to reappraisal of property devised to brother, notwithstanding that taxpayer and brother had agreed between themselves at time of conveyance that brother would be liable for any increased taxes on property devised him if estate was reappraised. Ewart v. C.I.R. (C.A.6 1987) 814 F.2d 321. Internal Revenue ⚖= 4820

Purchaser at guardian's sale refusing to complete is liable. Clawson v Beatty, OS Unrep 502, 36 B 214 (1896).

Real estate cannot be sold by an administrator with the guardian joined solely to maintain the ward and improve the property. Newcomb's Lessee v Smith, W 208 (Hamilton 1833).

2127.11 Summary proceeding if value of land less than three thousand dollars

When the actual market value of a decedent's or ward's real estate to be sold is less than three thousand dollars, and the court so finds, it may by summary order authorize the sale and conveyance of the land at private sale, on such terms as it deems proper, and in such a proceeding, all requirements of sections 2127.01 to 2127.43 of the Revised Code, as to service of summons, appraisal, and additional bond, shall be waived.

(1975 S 145, eff. 1-1-76; 128 v 154; 1953 H 1; GC 10510-14)

Historical and Statutory Notes

Pre–1953 H 1 Amendments: 114 v 454

Library References

Executors and Administrators ⚖332.
Guardian and Ward ⚖80.
Mental Health ⚖264.
Westlaw Topic Nos. 162, 196, 257A.
C.J.S. Executors and Administrators § 601.

Research References

Encyclopedias

OH Jur. 3d Decedents' Estates § 1537, Practice and Procedure, Generally—Service of Summons.
OH Jur. 3d Decedents' Estates § 1543, Order of Sale, Generally.
OH Jur. 3d Decedents' Estates § 1551, Summary Order for Sale of Real Property Valued at Less Than Statutory Amount.
OH Jur. 3d Guardian & Ward § 159, Summary Proceeding to Sell Property Worth Less Than $3,000.

Treatises and Practice Aids

Carlin, Baldwin's Ohio Practice, Merrick-Rippner Probate Law § 2:60, Sale of Land—Summary Proceedings.
Carlin, Baldwin's Ohio Practice, Merrick-Rippner Probate Law § 91:4, Land Sale—Summary Proceedings.
Carlin, Baldwin's Ohio Practice, Merrick-Rippner Probate Law § 97:8, Land Sale by Guardian—Summary Proceeding.
Carlin, Baldwin's Ohio Practice, Merrick-Rippner Probate Law § 91:61, Complaint for Summary Proceedings to Sell Land Valued at Less Than Three Thousand Dollars—Form.
Carlin, Baldwin's Ohio Practice, Merrick-Rippner Probate Law § 91:62, Entry Granting Complaint for Summary Proceedings and Ordering Private Sale—Form.
Kuehnle and Levey, Ohio Real Estate Law and Practice § 18:1, Ohio State Bar Association Standards of Title Examination.
Kuehnle and Levey, Ohio Real Estate Law and Practice § 52:3, Statutory Fiduciary Sales—21 Statutory Proceedings.

2127.12 Necessary parties in sale by executor or administrator

In an action by an executor or administrator to obtain authority to sell real estate, the following persons shall be made parties defendant:

(A) The surviving spouse;

(B) The heirs, devisees, or persons entitled to the next estate of inheritance from the decedent in the real estate and having an interest in it, but their spouses need not be made parties defendant;

(C) All mortgagees and other lienholders whose claims affect the real estate or any part of it;

(D) If the interest subject to sale is equitable, all persons holding legal title to the interest or any part of it, and those who are entitled to the purchase money for it, other than creditors;

(E) If a fraudulent transfer is sought to be set aside, all persons holding or claiming under the transfer;

(F) All other persons having an interest in the real estate.

(1990 H 506, eff. 9–28–90; 1953 H 1; GC 10510–15)

Historical and Statutory Notes

Pre–1953 H 1 Amendments: 120 v 284; 114 v 454

Library References

Executors and Administrators ⚖335.
Westlaw Topic No. 162.
C.J.S. Executors and Administrators § 604.

Research References

Encyclopedias

OH Jur. 3d Decedents' Estates § 1530, Parties, Generally.
OH Jur. 3d Decedents' Estates § 1531, Parties, Generally—Mortgagees and Other Lienholders.
OH Jur. 3d Decedents' Estates § 1532, Parties, Generally—Other Persons.
OH Jur. 3d Decedents' Estates § 1566, Effect on Liens—Mortgage Liens.

Treatises and Practice Aids

Carlin, Baldwin's Ohio Practice, Merrick-Rippner Probate Law § 2:55, Sale of Land—Procedure for Commencement of Action.
Carlin, Baldwin's Ohio Practice, Merrick-Rippner Probate Law § 84:6, Creditor's Claims—Claims Requiring Presentation—Examples from Case Law.
Carlin, Baldwin's Ohio Practice, Merrick-Rippner Probate Law § 91:21, Land Sale—Necessary Parties Defendant—List.
Carlin, Baldwin's Ohio Practice, Merrick-Rippner Probate Law § 91:22, Land Sale—Necessary Parties Defendant—Heirs.
Carlin, Baldwin's Ohio Practice, Merrick-Rippner Probate Law § 91:23, Land Sale—Necessary Parties Defendant—Legatees.
Carlin, Baldwin's Ohio Practice, Merrick-Rippner Probate Law § 91:24, Land Sale—Necessary Parties Defendant—Lienholders.
Carlin, Baldwin's Ohio Practice, Merrick-Rippner Probate Law § 91:25, Land Sale—Necessary Parties Defendant—Person With Dower Interest.
Carlin, Baldwin's Ohio Practice, Merrick-Rippner Probate Law § 91:29, Land Sale—Necessary Parties Defendant—Exclusions.
Carlin, Baldwin's Ohio Practice, Merrick-Rippner Probate Law § 91:43, Complaint for Authority to Sell Decedent's Real Estate to Pay Debts—Form.
Carlin, Baldwin's Ohio Practice, Merrick-Rippner Probate Law § 91:44, Complaint for Authority to Sell Real Property to Pay Legacies—Form.
Carlin, Baldwin's Ohio Practice, Merrick-Rippner Probate Law § 91:45, Complaint for Authority to Sell Real Estate With Consent of Distributees—Form.
Carlin, Baldwin's Ohio Practice, Merrick-Rippner Probate Law § 91:49, Complaint for Authority to Sell Entire Interest in Real Estate—Form.
Carlin, Baldwin's Ohio Practice, Merrick-Rippner Probate Law § 91:52, Complaint for Sale of Decedent's Real Estate—Alternate Circumstances—Form.
Kuehnle and Levey, Ohio Real Estate Law and Practice § 53:1, Land Sales—Parties Defendant—Necessary Parties Defendant—Action by Administrator or Executor.
Kuehnle and Levey, Ohio Real Estate Law and Practice § 53:2, Land Sales—Parties Defendant—Heirs of Decedent as Necessary Parties.
Kuehnle and Levey, Ohio Real Estate Law and Practice § 53:3, Land Sales—Parties Defendant—Spouses of Defendants as Necessary Parties.
Kuehnle and Levey, Ohio Real Estate Law and Practice § 53:4, Land Sales—Parties Defendant—Mortgagees and Other Lienholders.
Kuehnle and Levey, Ohio Real Estate Law and Practice § 53:6, Land Sales—Parties Defendant—Mortgagees—Other Lien Claimants of Interest Inherited by Devisees—Heirs.
Kuehnle and Levey, Ohio Real Estate Law and Practice § 53:7, Land Sales—Parties Defendant—Legatees and Persons Entitled to Distribution.
Kuehnle and Levey, Ohio Real Estate Law and Practice § 53:8, Land Sales—Parties Defendant—General Creditors of Decedent.
Kuehnle and Levey, Ohio Real Estate Law and Practice § 53:35, Land Sales—Service—Lis Pendens.

Notes of Decisions

Creditors 7
Guardian of minor 6
Heirs and devisees 2
Mortagees and lienholders 3
Procedural issues 1
Purchaser 5
Self–dealing by administrator 4

Tenants 8

1. Procedural issues

Where, in an action against an insane defendant for wrongful death, his guardian is made a party and enters his appearance, and summons is issued to another county for the insane defendant, and was personally served upon him, and subsequently the plaintiff dismissed the action as to the guardian only, it is error to quash the service on the insane defendant, and dismiss the action for want of jurisdiction over his person. Stuard v. Porter (Ohio 1908) 79 Ohio St. 1, 85 N.E. 1062, 6 Ohio Law Rep. 516. Mental Health ☞ 498.1

A proceeding in probate or common pleas court to sell land to pay debts is a civil action and any person claiming an interest in the land may be made a party. Doan v. Biteley (Ohio 1892) 49 Ohio St. 588, 32 N.E. 600.

The fiduciary relation of the administrator to the land is not terminated by sale but continues until full payment of the purchase price and delivery of proper deeds. Barrington v. Alexander (Ohio 1856) 6 Ohio St. 189.

In proceedings to sell a decedent's real estate for the payment of debts brought by an executor or administrator, persons in interest who enter an appearance are properly parties on the record, though not named in the petition. Ewing v. Hollister (Ohio 1836) 7 Ohio 138, PT. II.

Filing certificate of judgment with clerk of court, coupled with statute requiring all lienholders to be made parties to action to sell real estate owned by estate, did not constitute "presentment" of claim to executor for purposes of one-year limitation on presentment of claims. In re Estate of Knepper (Ohio App. 3 Dist., 11-03-1995) 107 Ohio App.3d 78, 667 N.E.2d 1039. Executors And Administrators ☞ 228(3)

Claim against estate by judgment creditor was barred as untimely when asserted more than one year after debtor's death, even though creditor was not notified of sale of real estate owned by estate. In re Estate of Knepper (Ohio App. 3 Dist., 11-03-1995) 107 Ohio App.3d 78, 667 N.E.2d 1039. Executors And Administrators ☞ 225(1)

A person who, upon the death of his father, is immediately vested with an interest in real property of which his father died seized, and who was not given notice of or made a party to a proceeding to sell land to pay debts of the estate, is entitled to assert his interest in such real estate in an action in partition. Shackelford v. Alford (Franklin 1963) 119 Ohio App. 63, 196 N.E.2d 609, 26 O.O.2d 152.

A public sale by executors need not be held at the court house. Smiley v. Cook (Ohio Prob. 1907) 8 Ohio N.P.(N.S.) 191, 52 W.L.B. 156, 4 Ohio Law Rep. 737, affirmed 79 Ohio St. 452, 87 N.E. 1131, 6 Ohio Law Rep. 565.

In an action by an administrator to sell real estate of an infant's ancestor, the guardian of such minor may waive process and enter an appearance for his ward. Sprague v Litherberry, 2 OFD 574 (6th Cir Ohio 1848).

2. Heirs and devisees

"Devisee" denotes one to whom real property passes by will. Ruff v. Baker (Ohio 1946) 146 Ohio St. 456, 66 N.E.2d 540, 32 O.O. 537. Wills ☞ 466

Word "devisees" as used in section is qualified by words "having next estate of inheritance from him." Ruff v. Baker (Ohio 1946) 146 Ohio St. 456, 66 N.E.2d 540, 32 O.O. 537.

Where a testator devised real property to G for life with remainder to his unborn issue or in default of such issue to issue of W, and where an action was brought by decedent's executor to sell devised real property to pay debts, G was a necessary party under section, but neither of remaindermen was a necessary or proper party and there was no necessity for contingent remaindermen to be represented in action. Ruff v. Baker (Ohio 1946) 146 Ohio St. 456, 66 N.E.2d 540, 32 O.O. 537. Executors And Administrators ☞ 335

This section does not require that the spouse of an heir be made a party to executor's or administrator's proceeding to sell real estate to pay debts. Carmack v. Carmack (Ohio Prob. 1936) 3 Ohio Supp. 111, 22 Ohio Law Abs. 702, 7 O.O. 313.

A judgment creditor of a devisee of land is not a lienholder as used in this section, and is not a necessary party. Kummer v Lapp, 1 NP(NS) 209, 13 D 491 (CP, Franklin 1903).

3. Mortagees and lienholders

The lien of a mortgagee who is not made a party remains unaffected by an order for sale and the proceedings thereunder. Holloway v. Stuart (Ohio 1869) 19 Ohio St. 472.

Under section, all who may have a lien upon all or any part of the real estate sought to be sold by an administrator to pay debts, are necessary parties to the action whether the liens existed upon the real estate at the time of the death of the decedent or are acquired upon the share of an heir at law therein, after the death of the ancestor from whom the estate came, and before the petition is filed by the administrator. Keenan v. Wilson (Summit 1925) 19 Ohio App. 499, 3 Ohio Law Abs. 445.

Though it appears that it is necessary to make the county treasurer a party to an action to sell real estate to pay debts, it is not a fatal defect because personal representative is charged with knowledge of this lien and by the terms of GC 5692 (RC 5719.25), when the real estate is sold, it is the obligation of the court to order the taxes and penalties, and the interest thereon, against such lands, to be discharged out of the proceeds of such sale. (See also Grafton v Mong, 134 OS 416, 17 NE(2d) 649 (1938).) In re Saviers' Estate (Franklin 1936) 23 Ohio Law Abs. 166.

The part of section which provides that "all mortgagees and other lienholders whose claims affect such real estate or any part thereof" shall be made defendants in action by administrator to sell real estate to pay debts of estate, is directory, and failure to make judgment lienholder party defendant does not, in and of itself, deprive court of jurisdiction to order sale. Schmidt v. Weather–Seal, Inc. (Summit 1943) 71 Ohio App. 387, 50 N.E.2d 362, 26 O.O. 322. Executors And Administrators ☞ 335

Legatees, if necessary parties to a proceeding to sell real estate to pay debts of a deceased person, are before the court for all purposes when summoned on a cross-petition of a mortgagee setting up his interest in the real estate to be sold. J. H. Day Co. v. Morris (Hamilton 1935) 49 Ohio App. 181, 195 N.E. 870, 19 Ohio Law Abs. 9, 2 O.O. 203. Executors And Administrators ☞ 386

4. Self–dealing by administrator

An administrator cannot act as agent for others in purchasing at his own sale with a view of making a profit therefrom. Piatt v. Longworth's Devisees (Ohio 1875) 27 Ohio St. 159.

An administrator cannot purchase at his own sale. Barrington v. Alexander (Ohio 1856) 6 Ohio St. 189.

To guard against the uncertainty and hazard of attempting to prove unfairness in a purchase by the administrator, the cestui que trusts may come into court without showing actual fraud and have the property resold. Barrington v. Alexander (Ohio 1856) 6 Ohio St. 189.

Where an administrator has enjoyed the land under a sale made by himself an accounting of the improvements made and rents received will be ordered and the balance retained for the use of the estate. Barrington v. Alexander (Ohio 1856) 6 Ohio St. 189.

Acquisition by the administrator raises an appearance of unfairness, and the sale may be set aside on the application of the cestui que trust. Barrington v. Alexander (Ohio 1856) 6 Ohio St. 189.

5. Purchaser

Purchasers of real estate at a sale made under order of court are proper parties to an appeal from an order of court denying motion to set aside sale, after the sale was approved and confirmed by the court thereby vesting their interest in the real estate. Ozias v. Renner (Preble 1945) 78 Ohio App. 166, 64 N.E.2d 325, 44 Ohio Law Abs. 415, 33 O.O. 504.

Where the devisee of real estate transfers it after probate, the grantee is an interested person within GC 12,080, and a necessary party to a subsequent action to contest the will. Sears v. Stinehelfer (Ohio 1913) 89 Ohio St. 163, 105 N.E. 1047, 11 Ohio Law Rep. 347, 11 Ohio Law Rep. 447. Wills ☞ 267

Mortgagors who have parted with their title to the land mortgaged and are not in possession of it, are not necessary parties to a proceeding brought by the executor of the purchaser to obtain an order to sell the land for the payment of debts. Denison University v. Manning (Ohio 1901) 65 Ohio St. 138, 46 W.L.B. 228, 61 N.E. 706. Executors And Administrators ☞ 335

An executor under an order issued by the probate court sold lands to pay the debts of the decedent without making the former wife of the decedent who had obtained a divorce from him on account of his aggressions a party to the suit, and the purchaser being advised by counsel that the title to the lands was clear and unincumbered and that wife had no dower estate therein, bought the lands at their full value in money and entered into possession of the premises; however, the court of common pleas afterwards adjudged that the divorced wife was dowable of the lands, set off dower therein to her and held that the purchaser cannot maintain an action to recover back sufficient of the purchase money to compensate him for the loss he has sustained by reason of the assignment of dower, and that the rule caveat emptor is applicable. Arnold v. Donaldson (Ohio 1888) 46 Ohio St. 73, 20 W.L.B. 431, 18 N.E. 540.

6. Guardian of minor

An actual service of process upon a minor heir is not necessary to give the court jurisdiction, or even to the regularity of the proceeding; it is enough that a guardian having the care and custody of the minor's person and estate or specially appointed for the purpose of representing them in the sale of their lands is before the court when the order is made. Sheldon's Lessee v. Newton (Ohio 1854) 3 Ohio St. 494.

Where an intestate left four children at his death including some minors, and in the petition by his administrator to sell his land for the payment of debts only three of the children are named, the order of sale is not void where the guardian ad litem of such minors appears and acknowledges such appearance as such guardian. Snevely v. Lowe (Ohio 1849) 18 Ohio 368.

Even though there is no proof that infant heirs were served with process; where a guardian ad litem was appointed for them and appeared and answered for them, an order for the sale of real estate is not void. Robb v. Irwin's Lessee (Ohio 1846) 15 Ohio 689.

7. Creditors

Action for determination of validity and amount of certain claims against estate of a testator, and asking for order to sell under terms of a will is not such an action as is referred to in this section, but is more in nature of action to quiet title, and a judgment creditor of a devisee is not a necessary party to such an action. employment is authorized or approved by the court, and such auctioneer must be a licensed auctioneer. Gauthier v. Ozark Land Co. (Summit 1932) 11 Ohio Law Abs. 311.

Where the division of aid for the aged agreed that if the grandson of a recipient of old age assistance would move into her house and care for her, it would waive the priority of a lien acquired by a mortgage to it, the claim of the grandson's wife for care, nursing and medical expenses is that of an unsecured creditor and she is not a proper party to a land sale proceeding although the waiver agreement is valid. Piatt v. Piatt (Darke 1952) 114 N.E.2d 441, 65 Ohio Law Abs. 284.

A judgment creditor or an heir, who has a lien by levy on property, which in the absence of a will would be the property of the heir by descent, is interested in the will, within RS 5858 (See Gen.Code § 12079), and therefore has legal capacity to sue to contest the validity of an alleged will disposing of such property other than to such heir. Bloor v. Platt (Ohio 1908) 78 Ohio St. 46, 84 N.E. 604, 5 Ohio Law Rep. 619, 14 Am.Ann.Cas. 332. Wills ⚖︎ 229

A creditor of an heir's testator is neither a necessary nor proper party defendant in an action brought by the heir's administrator to pay his debts. Smith v. Hayward (Ohio Prob. 1898) 5 Ohio Dec. 462, 5 Ohio N.P. 501.

8. Tenants

Spouses of cotenants are not essential parties to a partition action by one cotenant against another. Dunkle v. Dunkle (Ohio Com.Pl. 1956) 137 N.E.2d 170, 73 Ohio Law Abs. 477, 2 O.O.2d 399.

2127.13 Necessary parties in sale by guardian

In an action by a guardian to obtain authority to sell the real estate of his ward the following persons shall be made parties defendant:

(A) The ward;

(B) The spouse of the ward;

(C) All persons entitled to the next estate of inheritance from the ward in such real estate who are known to reside in Ohio, but their spouses need not be made parties defendant;

(D) All lienholders whose claims affect such real estate or any part thereof;

(E) If the interest subject to such sale is equitable, all persons holding legal title thereto or any part thereof;

(F) All other persons having an interest in such real estate, other than creditors.

(1953 H 1, eff. 10–1–53; GC 10510–16)

Historical and Statutory Notes

Pre–1953 H 1 Amendments: 120 v 244; 119 v 394, § 1; 114 v 454

Library References

Guardian and Ward ⚖︎83.
Mental Health ⚖︎265.
Westlaw Topic Nos. 196, 257A.

Research References

Encyclopedias

OH Jur. 3d Guardian & Ward § 148, Parties; Plaintiff—Defendant.

Treatises and Practice Aids

Carlin, Baldwin's Ohio Practice, Merrick-Rippner Probate Law § 91:47, Complaint of Guardian for Authority to Sell Real Estate—Form.

Carlin, Baldwin's Ohio Practice, Merrick-Rippner Probate Law § 97:10, Land Sale by Guardian—Necessary Parties Defendant.

Kuehnle and Levey, Ohio Real Estate Law and Practice § 53:9, Land Sales—Parties Defendant—Necessary Parties—Action by Guardian.

Kuehnle and Levey, Ohio Real Estate Law and Practice § 53:32, Land Sales—Service Upon Incompetent Persons.

Notes of Decisions

All other persons, construed   1

---

1. All other persons, construed

An action involving the transfer for consideration of a one-third interest in property owned by a ward of the court to the ward's guardian requires notice to the department of human services that the probate court is planning to act on behalf of its ward, as medicaid eligibility may be affected by the transfer, but the department is not a necessary party to the transfer and has no equitable or financial interest in the transfer of property. In Matter of Guardianship of Stowell (Ohio App. 10 Dist., Franklin, 08-03-1995) No. 95APF01-128, 1995 WL 458963, Unreported.

2127.14 Service of summons

Service of summons, actual or constructive, in an action to sell the real estate of a decedent or a ward shall be had as in other civil actions, but if any competent person in interest enters appearance or consents in writing to the sale, service on such person shall not be necessary. If all parties consent in writing to the sale, an order therefor may issue forthwith.

(1953 H 1, eff. 10–1–53; GC 10510–17)

Historical and Statutory Notes

Pre–1953 H 1 Amendments: 114 v 454

Cross References

Minor or incompetent person as party to action, Civ R 17
Process: who may be served, Civ R 4.2
Service of summons, Civ R 73
Substitution of parties, incompetent person, Civ R 25

Library References

Process ⚖︎48.
Westlaw Topic No. 313.
C.J.S. Process §§ 26, 33, 49.

Research References

Encyclopedias

OH Jur. 3d Decedents' Estates § 1537, Practice and Procedure, Generally—Service of Summons.

OH Jur. 3d Decedents' Estates § 1543, Order of Sale, Generally.

OH Jur. 3d Guardian & Ward § 149, Service of Process.

OH Jur. 3d Guardian & Ward § 152, Hearing and Determination of Necessity of Sale.

Treatises and Practice Aids

Klein, Darling, & Terez, Baldwin's Ohio Practice Civil Practice § 73:5, Probate Division--Service and Filing of Pleadings and Papers Subsequent to the Original Complaint.

Carlin, Baldwin's Ohio Practice, Merrick-Rippner Probate Law § 2:55, Sale of Land—Procedure for Commencement of Action.

Carlin, Baldwin's Ohio Practice, Merrick-Rippner Probate Law § 4:22, Service—Summons—Publication—When Permitted.

Carlin, Baldwin's Ohio Practice, Merrick-Rippner Probate Law § 4:23, Service—Summons—Publication—Application to Probate Jurisdiction.

Carlin, Baldwin's Ohio Practice, Merrick-Rippner Probate Law § 91:30, Land Sale—Service of Summons.

Carlin, Baldwin's Ohio Practice, Merrick-Rippner Probate Law § 91:63, Entry of Appearance and Consent to Sale—Form.

Carlin, Baldwin's Ohio Practice, Merrick-Rippner Probate Law § 91:67, Affidavit for Service by Publication—Residence Unknown—Form.

Carlin, Baldwin's Ohio Practice, Merrick-Rippner Probate Law § 91:68, Affidavit for Service by Publication—Including Unknown Heirs—Form.

Carlin, Baldwin's Ohio Practice, Merrick-Rippner Probate Law § 91:69, Entry for Service by Publication—Form.

Carlin, Baldwin's Ohio Practice, Merrick-Rippner Probate Law § 91:70, Notice by Publication on Known and Unknown Defendants—Form.

Carlin, Baldwin's Ohio Practice, Merrick-Rippner Probate Law § 91:71, Affidavit of Notice and Proof of Publication.

Kuehnle and Levey, Ohio Real Estate Law and Practice § 53:31, Land Sales—Service—Waiver.

Notes of Decisions

Corporations 4
Guardian of minors and incompetents 1
Jurisdiction 2
Procedural issues 5
Service by publication 3

---

1. Guardian of minors and incompetents

Even though there is no proof that infant heirs were served with process; where a guardian ad litem was appointed for them and appeared and answered for them, an order for the sale of real estate is not void. Robb v. Irwin's Lessee (Ohio 1846) 15 Ohio 689.

The guardian of a minor has no authority to waive the service of summons upon his ward in an action affecting the ward's rights, nor to dispense with the appointment of a guardian ad litem, unless authorized by statute; a judgment against a minor who did not have his day in court may be reversed upon petition by him within the statutory time after he reaches his age of majority. Roberts v. Roberts (Ohio 1899) 61 Ohio St. 96, 42 W.L.B. 367, 55 N.E. 411. Infants ⟶ 115

In proceedings to sell a decedents real estate it is sufficient if infant heirs appear by their general guardian. (See also Ewing v Higby, 7 O (pt 1) 198 (1835).) Ewing v. Hollister (Ohio 1836) 7 Ohio 138, PT. II.

In an action by an administrator to sell real estate to pay debts, heirs who are idiots are made parties to the record by the filing of an answer and cross-petition by their guardian, wherein the allegations of the petition are admitted, service of summons waived, and the court is asked to grant the prayer of the petition. Segal v Eagle Bldg Co, 11 CC(NS) 481, 21 CD 519 (Hamilton 1907).

In the event the service on a minor is made under former GC 10781 (RC 2127.14 and RC 2127.15) in connection with the sale of real estate by an executor or an administrator and service is made by the plaintiff or some person other than the sheriff, summons must be served by personally delivering copies to the minor, and guardian, father, mother or custodian, as the case requires. 1930 OAG 2560.

2. Jurisdiction

Evidence will not be received to contradict a finding of the court in a proceeding to sell the lands of a decedent to pay debts that "due notice had been given the defendant"; where the jurisdiction of the court is shown or must be presumed, the judgment or order of the court cannot be collaterally impeached. Richards v. Skiff (Ohio 1858) 8 Ohio St. 586.

Where the record of the court affirmatively shows that minor heirs have not been served with process, the presumption of jurisdiction over them is rebutted and a decree of such court purporting to determine such minors' rights is void. Moore's Lessee v. Starks (Ohio 1853) 1 Ohio St. 369.

3. Service by publication

The language of the statute providing that nonresident defendants may be served by publication in a newspaper refers to lunatic defendants as well as to sane persons. Sturges v. Longworth (Ohio 1853) 1 Ohio St. 544, motion overruled 4 Ohio St. 690, bill dismissed 6 Ohio St. 143. Mental Health ⟶ 498.1; Process ⟶ 87

4. Corporations

In order to make the service of a summons against a corporation by serving a subordinate officer at the usual place of business good, it must affirmatively appear on the return of service that neither the chief officer of the corporation nor any specified subordinate officers could be found in the county. Fee v. Big Sand Iron Co. (Ohio 1862) 13 Ohio St. 563.

5. Procedural issues

This section authorizes jury trial. Doan v. Biteley (Ohio 1892) 49 Ohio St. 588, 32 N.E. 600.

The lien of a magistrate's judgment may be set up in a proceeding in the probate court to sell the property of a decedent to pay debts, where the party against whom the lien was obtained has an interest in the property as an heir; such a proceeding is not one requiring the issuance of summons for the party against whom the lien was obtained, and an order claim can not be collaterally attacked. In re Seitz' Estate (Ohio Cir. 1908) 21 Ohio C.D. 32, 11 Ohio C.C.(N.S.) 204.

Persons interested, but not named in the petition by entering appearance, are parties of record. Ewing v. Hollister (Ohio 1836) 7 Ohio 138, PT. II.

2127.15 Pleadings and procedure

All pleadings and proceedings in an action to obtain authority to sell the real estate of a decedent or a ward in the probate court shall be the same as in other civil actions, except as otherwise provided in sections 2127.01 to 2127.43 of the Revised Code.

(1975 S 145, eff. 1–1–76; 1953 H 1; GC 10510–18)

Historical and Statutory Notes

Pre–1953 H 1 Amendments: 114 v 455

Cross References

Procedure in probate court, Civ R 73

Library References

Executors and Administrators ⟶336.
Guardian and Ward ⟶86.
Mental Health ⟶264, 265.
Westlaw Topic Nos. 162, 196, 257A.
C.J.S. Executors and Administrators § 605.

Research References

Encyclopedias

OH Jur. 3d Decedents' Estates § 1534, Practice and Procedure, Generally.

OH Jur. 3d Fiduciaries § 46, Sale or Lease of Lands.

OH Jur. 3d Guardian & Ward § 146, Generally; Jurisdiction and Venue.

Treatises and Practice Aids

Klein, Darling, & Terez, Baldwin's Ohio Practice Civil Practice § 73:2, Probate Division--Applicability of Ohio Civil Rules.

Carlin, Baldwin's Ohio Practice, Merrick-Rippner Probate Law § 91:1, Land Sale—Lis Pendens.

Carlin, Baldwin's Ohio Practice, Merrick-Rippner Probate Law § 91:31, Land Sale—Trial by Jury.

Carlin, Baldwin's Ohio Practice, Merrick-Rippner Probate Law § 92:21, Answer and Cross-Claim of Mortgagee—Form.

Notes of Decisions

General denial 1
Parties 2

1. General denial

Where a guardian ad litem for minor heirs answers a petition by an administrator to sell lands alleging his ignorance of matters in the petition and praying for the protection of his wards' rights, such an answer has the effect of a general denial and requires proof of all the material averments in the administrator's petition. Wood v. Butler (Ohio 1872) 23 Ohio St. 520.

2. Parties

The proceeding of an executor or administrator to sell the real estate of the deceased, to pay the debts and costs of administering his estate, whether prosecuted in the court of common pleas or the probate court, is a civil action, in which any person may be made a defendant who has or claims an interest in the land, or who is a necessary party to a complete determination of any question involved in the action. Doan v. Biteley (Ohio 1892) 49 Ohio St. 588, 32 N.E. 600.

2127.16 Sale to be free of dower

In a sale of real estate by an executor, administrator, or guardian, such real estate shall be sold free of all right and expectancy of dower therein, but out of the proceeds of the sale, in lieu of dower, the court shall allow to the person having any dower interest in the property such sum in money as is the just and reasonable value of such dower, unless the answer of such person waives such allowance.

(1953 H 1, eff. 10–1–53; GC 10510–19)

Historical and Statutory Notes

Pre–1953 H 1 Amendments: 114 v 455

Library References

Dower and Curtesy ⚙︎34.

Executors and Administrators ⚙︎387.

Westlaw Topic Nos. 136, 162.

C.J.S. Dower and Curtesy § 46.

C.J.S. Executors and Administrators § 670.

Research References

Encyclopedias

OH Jur. 3d Decedents' Estates § 1550, Disposition of Liens and Other Prior Rights; Generally—Spouse's Dower Rights.

OH Jur. 3d Decedents' Estates § 1590, Generally; Statutory Order.

OH Jur. 3d Family Law § 177, Proceeding to Sell Realty for Payment of Decedent's Debts.

OH Jur. 3d Guardian & Ward § 151, Pleadings; Complaint—Answer.

OH Jur. 3d Guardian & Ward § 156, Order Authorizing Sale.

OH Jur. 3d Guardian & Ward § 168, Proceeds from Sale of Property in Which Ward Had Fractional Interest or Interest Subject to Dower.

Treatises and Practice Aids

Carlin, Baldwin's Ohio Practice, Merrick-Rippner Probate Law § 91:48, Entry Authorizing Sale of Real Estate and Appraisal—Form.

Carlin, Baldwin's Ohio Practice, Merrick-Rippner Probate Law § 91:49, Complaint for Authority to Sell Entire Interest in Real Estate—Form.

Carlin, Baldwin's Ohio Practice, Merrick-Rippner Probate Law § 91:51, Entry Granting Complaint and Ordering Appraisal of Entire Interest—Form.

Carlin, Baldwin's Ohio Practice, Merrick-Rippner Probate Law § 92:14, Dower—Nature of Interest.

Carlin, Baldwin's Ohio Practice, Merrick-Rippner Probate Law § 92:19, Dower—Sale of Land Subject to Interest.

Carlin, Baldwin's Ohio Practice, Merrick-Rippner Probate Law § 92:23, Answer of Spouse—Form.

Carlin, Baldwin's Ohio Practice, Merrick-Rippner Probate Law § 96:16, Entry Confirming Sale, Ordering Deed and Distribution—Form.

Carlin, Baldwin's Ohio Practice, Merrick-Rippner Probate Law § 96:17, Entry Confirming Sale, Ordering Deed and Distribution Where Entire Interest in Real Estate Sold—Form.

Carlin, Baldwin's Ohio Practice, Merrick-Rippner Probate Law § 97:13, Land Sale by Guardian—Dower Interest of Ward.

Kuehnle and Levey, Ohio Real Estate Law and Practice § 53:23, Land Sales—Interests Subject to Sale by Fiduciaries—Dower.

Notes of Decisions

Election to take under will 2
Exception to account 3
Interest in estate 4
Mortgages 1

1. Mortgages

Where a testator dies leaving lands encumbered by a mortgage joined by his wife who survived him, and she elects to take against the will, upon the sale of the land and the payment of all debts including the mortgage, the widow is entitled to dower in the equity of redemption, and thus in the entire proceeds of the land as against the devisees. Kling v. Ballentine (Ohio 1883) 40 Ohio St. 391.

Where a mortgage is made for purchase money before marriage, and the property sold by the deceased mortgagor's executor, to pay the mortgage debt, the mortgagor's widow is not entitled to dower in the entire proceeds, but only in the surplus remaining after satisfying the mortgage. Nichols v. French (Ohio 1910) 83 Ohio St. 162, 93 N.E. 897, 8 Ohio Law Rep. 521, 8 Ohio Law Rep. 524.

Where the wife has joined a mortgage of the husband's lands to secure his debt, upon a judicial sale of the premises she may have the value of her contingent right of dower in the entire proceeds ascertained, and the husband's entire interest therein shall be exhausted to pay the debt before resorting to the interest of the wife therein. Mandel v. McClave (Ohio 1889) 46 Ohio St. 407, 22 W.L.B. 267, 22 N.E. 290, 15 Am.St.Rep. 627.

Ed. Note: *The following Note of Decision is reprinted to correct an error as printed in the main volume.*

2. Election to take under will

Where a will gives the widow a life estate in one-third of the property and directs a sale to pay debts, a sale by the administrator under order of the court to sell subject to dower passes title to the whole estate notwithstanding the widow's election to take under the will. Hamilton v. Stewart (Ohio Com.Pl. 1907) 18 Ohio Dec. 130, 5 Ohio N.P.(N.S.) 553, affirmed 80 Ohio St. 740, 89 N.E. 1120, 7 Ohio Law Rep. 85.

3. Exception to account

Where an order for the sale of a decedent's real estate for the payment of debts has been made and the widow's allowance and dower set off to her, and no error was prosecuted or appeal taken from it, such order cannot be collaterally attacked by exception to the widow's account as administratrix of the estate. In re Hess' Estate (Ohio Cir. 1911) 23 Ohio C.D. 449, 14 Ohio C.C.(N.S.) 463. Executors And Administrators ⚙︎ 194(6); Homestead ⚙︎ 150(2)

2127.16 Note 4

4. Interest in estate

It has always been held in this state that a mere technical seizin, without a beneficial interest in the estate, is not sufficient to entitle the widow to dower; thus, when the husband during coverture has purchased lands with the money of another and has taken the title in his own name under such circumstances as to raise a resulting trust in favor of the party whose money was so invested, the widow of the husband so seized was not entitled to dower. Welch v. Buckins (Ohio 1859) 9 Ohio St. 331.

2127.17 Costs when there are objections to granting order for sale

In an action to obtain authority to sell real estate, if a party in his answer objects to an order for the sale of real estate by an executor, administrator, or guardian, and on hearing it appears to the court that either the complaint or the objection is unreasonable, it may award costs to the party prevailing on that issue.

(1975 S 145, eff. 1–1–76; 1953 H 1; GC 10510–20)

Historical and Statutory Notes

Pre–1953 H 1 Amendments: 114 v 455

Library References

Executors and Administrators ⚖401.
Guardian and Ward ⚖114, 136.
Mental Health ⚖273.
Westlaw Topic Nos. 162, 196, 257A.
C.J.S. Executors and Administrators § 684.

Research References

Encyclopedias

OH Jur. 3d Decedents' Estates § 1547, Order of Sale, Generally—Costs Where Order is Objected to.
OH Jur. 3d Guardian & Ward § 151, Pleadings; Complaint—Answer.
OH Jur. 3d Guardian & Ward § 153, Hearing and Determination of Necessity of Sale—Costs.

2127.18 Equities and priorities

Upon the hearing of an action to obtain authority to sell real estate by an executor, administrator, or guardian, if satisfied that all necessary parties defendant are properly before the court, and that the demand for relief ought to be granted, the court may determine the equities among the parties and the priorities of lien of the several lien holders on the real estate, and order a distribution of the money arising from the sale in accordance with its determination. The court may in the same cause order contributions among all parties in interest.

(1975 S 145, eff. 1–1–76; 1953 H 1; GC 10510–21)

Historical and Statutory Notes

Pre–1953 H 1 Amendments: 114 v 455

Library References

Executors and Administrators ⚖400.
Guardian and Ward ⚖114.
Mental Health ⚖273.
Westlaw Topic Nos. 162, 196, 257A.
C.J.S. Executors and Administrators § 684.

Research References

Encyclopedias

OH Jur. 3d Decedents' Estates § 1525, Jurisdiction and Powers of the Probate Court—Equity Jurisdiction; Determination of Priorities.
OH Jur. 3d Decedents' Estates § 1548, Disposition of Liens and Other Prior Rights; Generally.
OH Jur. 3d Guardian & Ward § 157, Order Authorizing Sale—Disposition of Liens and Other Prior Rights.

Treatises and Practice Aids

Carlin, Baldwin's Ohio Practice, Merrick-Rippner Probate Law § 2:56, Sale of Land—Hearing and Order Granting Authority to Sell.
Carlin, Baldwin's Ohio Practice, Merrick-Rippner Probate Law § 92:11, Sale of Land Subject to Encumbrances—Equities and Priorities Among Lienholders.
Kuehnle and Levey, Ohio Real Estate Law and Practice § 53:2, Land Sales—Parties Defendant—Heirs of Decedent as Necessary Parties.

Notes of Decisions

Court powers 1
Judgment liens and court decrees 6
Jurisdiction 2
Parties 5
Procedural issues 3
Purchasers' rights 4
Subrogation 7

---

1. Court powers

In proceedings to sell lands to pay debts the probate court should settle priorities among lienholders and order sale free of liens. Stone v. Strong (Ohio 1884) 42 Ohio St. 53.

The probate court has chancery powers to determine questions arising in proceedings to sell lands to pay debts. Borntraeger v. Borntraeger (Ohio Dist. 1878) 3 W.L.B. 891.

Where the probate court has same power as a chancery court to determine equities and priorities of liens, a judgment is conclusive as to parties, whether they participated actively or not. Farmers' Nat. Bank of Greenville, Ohio v. Green (C.C.S.D.Ohio 1880) 4 F. 609.

2. Jurisdiction

Where evidence shows that deed executed by decedent and wife was intended merely as security for payment of a loan, subject to reconveyance on payment of loan, probate court had jurisdiction over proceedings by administratrix to determine rights and equities of parties in property of decedent, and to have same sold to pay debts. Helmbold v. Helmbold (Lucas 1926) 25 Ohio App. 32, 158 N.E. 499, 4 Ohio Law Abs. 532.

Probate court has concurrent jurisdiction with common pleas court in proceedings to sell real estate to pay debts of estate. Helmbold v. Helmbold (Lucas 1926) 25 Ohio App. 32, 158 N.E. 499, 4 Ohio Law Abs. 532. Courts ⚖472.4(2.1); Executors And Administrators ⚖333

The jurisdiction of the probate court in proceedings to sell real estate of a decedent to pay debts is limited by this section, and it is not authorized, on distribution of the proceeds in such proceeding, to render a personal judgment against a legatee of the estate, who has been made a party to the proceeding. State ex rel. Voight v. Lueders (Ohio 1920) 101 Ohio St. 211, 128 N.E. 70. Executors And Administrators ⚖315.1

Jurisdiction of the common pleas court of an action in the nature of a creditor's bill is not ousted by proceedings in probate court to sell lands for the benefit of creditors. Vandenbark v. Mattingly (Ohio 1900) 62 Ohio St. 25, 43 W.L.B. 238, 56 N.E. 473.

The probate court has jurisdiction to try all questions of fact before the court or before a jury. Doan v. Biteley (Ohio 1892) 49 Ohio St. 588, 32 N.E. 600.

3. Procedural issues

In proceeding by administratrix to sell property to pay debts of decedent, administratrix has burden of proving claim that deed to property executed by deceased was intended as a mortgage and not as an absolute conveyance. Helmbold v. Helmbold (Lucas 1926) 25 Ohio App. 32, 158 N.E. 499, 4 Ohio Law Abs. 532. Executors And Administrators ⚖339; Mortgages ⚖36

A judgment which is a subsisting lien on the lands of the debtor at the time of his death is entitled to share in the proceeds of the land when sold by the decedent's personal representative according to its priority at the time of the debtor's death; it is not necessary to issue execution on the judgment to preserve the lien. Ambrose v. Byrne (Ohio 1899) 61 Ohio St. 146, 42 W.L.B. 360, 55 N.E. 408. Executors And Administrators ⇐ 402.

The lien of a magistrate's judgment may be set up in a proceeding in the probate court to sell the property of a decedent to pay debts, where the party against whom the lien was obtained has an interest in the property as an heir; such a proceeding is not one requiring the issuance of summons for the party against whom the lien was obtained, and an order claim can not be collaterally attacked. In re Seitz' Estate (Ohio Cir. 1908) 21 Ohio C.D. 32, 11 Ohio C.C.(N.S.) 204.

4. Purchasers' rights

Where a sale of land for the payment of debts is in conformity with the requirements of the statute, the purchaser takes the land discharged of all creditors' liens, and the priorities given by such liens are transferred by statute to the fund arising from the sale of lands; the purchaser is not responsible for the administrator's application of such fund. Defrees v. Greenham (Ohio 1860) 11 Ohio St. 486. Executors And Administrators ⇐ 385.

Purchasers hold the land discharged of the prior liens but the proceeds are subject to such liens. Bank of Muskingum v. Carpenter's Adm'rs (Ohio 1835) 7 Ohio 21, PT. I, 28 Am.Dec. 616.

5. Parties

All persons claiming an interest should be brought before the court and all questions affecting title settled. Doan v. Biteley (Ohio 1892) 49 Ohio St. 588, 32 N.E. 600.

A surety is entitled to reimbursement and lien. Tidd v. Bloch (Ohio Cir. 1904) 16 Ohio C.D. 113, 4 Ohio C.C.N.S. 216.

6. Judgment liens and court decrees

Where there is a judgment lien upon a widow's real estate, and subsequently she asserts a homestead claim and occupies the property as such until her death, giving a mortgage on the property during such occupancy, in a suit by her administrator to sell the land for the payment of debts, the judgment lien has priority over the mortgage lien. Smith v. Phillips (Ohio Com.Pl. 1907) 18 Ohio Dec. 429, 5 Ohio N.P.(N.S.) 502, reversed 82 Ohio St. 388, 92 N.E. 1122, 7 Ohio Law Rep. 618.

Before a probate court can make the necessary order for an entry of a release and satisfaction of mortgage the court must first follow the procedures of RC 2127.18 and determine the equities among the parties and the priorities of liens on the subject real estate prior to its sale. In re Estate of Marquis, No. L-97-1453, 1998 WL 769786 (6th Dist Ct App, Lucas, 11–6–98).

A decree for alimony that was a lien on the decedent's property at his death continues afterwards, and the estate descended subject to the lien although no execution had been issued; such a lien has priority from the day it was rendered. Webster v Dennis, 4 CC 313, 2 CD 566 (Hamilton 1890).

7. Subrogation

Where heirs of an estate give new mortgages in substitution for old mortgages securing and continuing an indebtedness incurred by the decedent, such mortgages will be subrogated to the rights of the prior liens. Jacobs v. Jacobs (Ohio Prob. 1897) 7 Ohio Dec. 486. Executors And Administrators ⇐ 264(1).

2127.19 Release of liens

When an action to obtain authority to sell real estate is determined by the probate court, the probate judge shall make the necessary order for an entry of release and satisfaction of all mortgages and other liens upon the real estate except such mortgage as is assumed by the purchaser. The executor, administrator, or guardian shall thereupon enter such release and satisfaction, together with a memorandum of the title of the case, the character of the proceedings, and the volume and page of record where recorded, upon the record of such mortgage, judgment, or other lien in the office where it appears as matter of record. If the executor, administrator, or guardian fails to enter such release and satisfaction, the court may, on the application of an interested party, enter such release and satisfaction and tax in his cost bill the fee provided by law for entering such release and satisfaction, and a fee of twenty-five cents to the court.

(1953 H 1, eff. 10–1–53; GC 10510–22)

Historical and Statutory Notes

Pre–1953 H 1 Amendments: 114 v 455

Library References

Executors and Administrators ⇐ 402.
Guardian and Ward ⇐ 108, 114.
Mental Health ⇐ 271, 273.
Westlaw Topic Nos. 162, 196, 257A.
C.J.S. Executors and Administrators § 685.

Research References

Encyclopedias

OH Jur. 3d Decedents' Estates § 1549, Disposition of Liens and Other Prior Rights; Generally—Entry of Release and Satisfaction of Liens.

OH Jur. 3d Guardian & Ward § 158, Order Authorizing Sale—Release and Satisfaction of Liens.

Treatises and Practice Aids

Carlin, Baldwin's Ohio Practice, Merrick-Rippner Probate Law § 2:56, Sale of Land—Hearing and Order Granting Authority to Sell.

Carlin, Baldwin's Ohio Practice, Merrick-Rippner Probate Law § 2:59, Sale of Land—Distribution of Proceeds.

Carlin, Baldwin's Ohio Practice, Merrick-Rippner Probate Law § 92:12, Sale of Land Subject to Encumbrances—Release and Satisfaction of Liens Against Real Property.

Carlin, Baldwin's Ohio Practice, Merrick-Rippner Probate Law § 92:24, Application to Require Court to Satisfy Lien—Form.

Carlin, Baldwin's Ohio Practice, Merrick-Rippner Probate Law § 92:25, Certificate of Satisfaction and Cancellation of Lien—Form.

Carlin, Baldwin's Ohio Practice, Merrick-Rippner Probate Law § 96:16, Entry Confirming Sale, Ordering Deed and Distribution—Form.

Carlin, Baldwin's Ohio Practice, Merrick-Rippner Probate Law § 96:17, Entry Confirming Sale, Ordering Deed and Distribution Where Entire Interest in Real Estate Sold—Form.

Carlin, Baldwin's Ohio Practice, Merrick-Rippner Probate Law § 97:14, Land Sale by Guardian—Liens Against Property to be Sold.

Kuehnle and Levey, Ohio Real Estate Law and Practice § 11:12, Ohio Property Tax Liens—General Taxes—Proceeds of Judicial Sale Insufficient to Pay All Taxes.

Kuehnle and Levey, Ohio Real Estate Law and Practice § 53:22, Land Sales—Interests Subject to Sale by Fiduciaries—Sale Free of Mortgage.

Notes of Decisions

Fees 1
Lien priorities 3
Taxes 2

---

1. Fees

When a mortgage or lien is released or satisfied by court order, pursuant to RC 2127.19, and a marginal entry is made upon the records of the county recorder as required in said section, the fee to be charged for such marginal entry is that set forth in RC 317.32(G). 1960 OAG 1770.

2. Taxes

Notwithstanding RC 2127.19, where the proceeds of a probate sale of real estate to pay debts are insufficient to completely cover the amount owing for unpaid taxes, penalties and interest, a lien remains on the land for the unpaid balance. Marini v. Roach (Stark 1976) 54 Ohio App.2d 114, 375 N.E.2d 808, 8 O.O.3d 212.

3. Lien priorities

Before a probate court can make the necessary order for an entry of a release and satisfaction of mortgage the court must first follow the procedures of RC 2127.18 and determine the equities among the parties and the priorities of liens on the subject real estate prior to its sale. In re Estate of Marquis, No. L-97-1453, 1998 WL 769786 (6th Dist Ct App, Lucas, 11-6-98).

2127.20 Sale subject to mortgage

The probate court, with the consent of the mortgagee, may authorize the sale of lands subject to mortgage, but the giving of any such consent shall release the estate of the decedent or ward should a deficit later appear.

(129 v 7, eff. 10-5-61; 1953 H 1; GC 10510-23)

Historical and Statutory Notes

Pre-1953 H 1 Amendments: 114 v 456

Library References

Executors and Administrators ⚖329(1), 385.
Guardian and Ward ⚖112.
Mental Health ⚖275.
Westlaw Topic Nos. 162, 196, 257A.
C.J.S. Executors and Administrators §§ 595, 670.

Research References

Encyclopedias

OH Jur. 3d Decedents' Estates § 1548, Disposition of Liens and Other Prior Rights; Generally.
OH Jur. 3d Guardian & Ward § 158, Order Authorizing Sale—Release and Satisfaction of Liens.

Treatises and Practice Aids

Carlin, Baldwin's Ohio Practice, Merrick-Rippner Probate Law § 2:56, Sale of Land—Hearing and Order Granting Authority to Sell.
Carlin, Baldwin's Ohio Practice, Merrick-Rippner Probate Law § 92:10, Sale of Land Subject to Encumbrances—Mortgage.
Carlin, Baldwin's Ohio Practice, Merrick-Rippner Probate Law § 92:21, Answer and Cross-Claim of Mortgagee—Form.
Carlin, Baldwin's Ohio Practice, Merrick-Rippner Probate Law § 92:22, Consent of Mortgagee—Form.
Carlin, Baldwin's Ohio Practice, Merrick-Rippner Probate Law § 95:16, Price—Property Subject to Mortgage.
Carlin, Baldwin's Ohio Practice, Merrick-Rippner Probate Law § 95:20, Application for Order of Private Sale and Allowance of Real Estate Commission—Form.
Carlin, Baldwin's Ohio Practice, Merrick-Rippner Probate Law § 97:14, Land Sale by Guardian—Liens Against Property to be Sold.
Kuehnle and Levey, Ohio Real Estate Law and Practice § 53:24, Land Sales—Interests Subject to Sale by Fiduciaries—Sale Subject to Mortgage.

2127.21 Petition of guardian to have land laid out in town lots

If a guardian's complaint in an action to obtain authority to sell real estate seeks to have land laid out in town lots, and the court finds it to the advantage of the ward, it shall authorize the survey and platting of the land as provided by law. Upon subsequent return of the survey and plat, the court, if it approves it, shall authorize the guardian on behalf of his ward to sign, seal, and acknowledge the plat in that behalf for record.

(1975 S 145, eff. 1-1-76; 1953 H 1; GC 10510-24)

Historical and Statutory Notes

Pre-1953 H 1 Amendments: 114 v 456

Cross References

Plats, Ch 711

Library References

Guardian and Ward ⚖28, 95.
Westlaw Topic No. 196.

Research References

Encyclopedias

OH Jur. 3d Guardian & Ward § 152, Hearing and Determination of Necessity of Sale.

Treatises and Practice Aids

Carlin, Baldwin's Ohio Practice, Merrick-Rippner Probate Law § 97:3, Land Sale by Guardian—Platting.

Notes of Decisions

Appraisal of land 1
Federal court jurisdiction 2

1. Appraisal of land

A judgment debtor should apply to the sheriff to have his appraisement and sale in parcels, since an appraisement and sale of the whole property by the sheriff will not be set aside on the opinion of witnesses that the property would bring more if parceled into lots. Hartshorne v Reeder, 3 D Repr 109, 3 Gaz 245 (DC, Hamilton 1859). Judicial Sales ⚖ 6

2. Federal court jurisdiction

Federal court has jurisdiction to set aside a sale of an infant's land if fraudulently made. Arrowsmith v. Gleason (U.S.Ohio 1889) 9 S.Ct. 237, 129 U.S. 86, 32 L.Ed. 630.

APPRAISEMENT; BOND; SALE

2127.22 Appraisement may be dispensed with; new appraisement; appraisers

If an appraisement of the real estate is contained in the inventory required of an executor or administrator by section 2115.02 of the Revised Code, and of a guardian by section 2111.14 of the Revised Code, the probate court may order a sale in accordance with the appraisement, or order a new appraisement. If a new appraisement is not ordered, the value set forth in the inventory shall be the appraised value of the real estate. If the court orders a new appraisement, the value returned shall be the appraised value of the real estate.

If the interest of the deceased or ward in the real estate is fractional and undivided, and if a party requests and the court orders the entire interest in the real estate to be sold, a new appraisement of the entire interest in the real estate shall be ordered.

If the relief requested is granted and new appraisement is ordered, the court shall appoint one, or on request of the executor, administrator, or guardian, not exceeding three judicious and disinterested persons of the vicinity, not next of kin of the complainant, to appraise the real estate in whole and in parcels at its true value in money. Where the real estate lies in two or more counties the court may appoint appraisers in any or all of the counties in which the real estate or a part of it is situated.

(1975 S 145, eff. 1-1-76; 1970 S 185; 1953 H 1; GC 10510-25, 10510-26)

Historical and Statutory Notes

Pre-1953 H 1 Amendments: 119 v 394, § 1; 114 v 456

Cross References

Duties of appraisers of real estate of ward, 2111.30

Library References

Executors and Administrators ⚖═353.
Guardian and Ward ⚖═93.
Mental Health ⚖═264.
Westlaw Topic Nos. 162, 196, 257A.
C.J.S. Executors and Administrators § 624.

Research References

Encyclopedias

OH Jur. 3d Decedents' Estates § 1539, Determination of Sale Price; Appraisement.
OH Jur. 3d Decedents' Estates § 1540, Determination of Sale Price; Appraisement—Appointment and Compensation of Appraisers.
OH Jur. 3d Guardian & Ward § 154, Appraisement of Property; Appointment and Removal of Appraisers.

Treatises and Practice Aids

Carlin, Baldwin's Ohio Practice, Merrick-Rippner Probate Law § 2:56, Sale of Land—Hearing and Order Granting Authority to Sell.
Carlin, Baldwin's Ohio Practice, Merrick-Rippner Probate Law § 92:3, Property Subject to Sale—Fractional Interests in Real Property.
Carlin, Baldwin's Ohio Practice, Merrick-Rippner Probate Law § 93:1, Ordering Appraisal of Real Property.
Carlin, Baldwin's Ohio Practice, Merrick-Rippner Probate Law § 93:2, Appraisers—Appointment, Compensation, Removal.
Carlin, Baldwin's Ohio Practice, Merrick-Rippner Probate Law § 93:3, Appraisers—Report.
Carlin, Baldwin's Ohio Practice, Merrick-Rippner Probate Law § 93:4, Order to Appraiser—Form.
Carlin, Baldwin's Ohio Practice, Merrick-Rippner Probate Law § 93:5, Report of Appraiser—Form.
Carlin, Baldwin's Ohio Practice, Merrick-Rippner Probate Law § 93:6, Entry Confirming Appraisal and Ordering Additional Bond—Form.
Carlin, Baldwin's Ohio Practice, Merrick-Rippner Probate Law § 93:7, Entry Dispensing With New Appraisal and Ordering Additional Bond—Form.
Carlin, Baldwin's Ohio Practice, Merrick-Rippner Probate Law § 93:8, Motion to Set Appraisal Aside—Form.
Carlin, Baldwin's Ohio Practice, Merrick-Rippner Probate Law § 94:1, Bond of Fiduciary Before Sale of Land.
Carlin, Baldwin's Ohio Practice, Merrick-Rippner Probate Law § 91:48, Entry Authorizing Sale of Real Estate and Appraisal—Form.
Carlin, Baldwin's Ohio Practice, Merrick-Rippner Probate Law § 91:51, Entry Granting Complaint and Ordering Appraisal of Entire Interest—Form.
Carlin, Baldwin's Ohio Practice, Merrick-Rippner Probate Law § 95:20, Application for Order of Private Sale and Allowance of Real Estate Commission—Form.
Carlin, Baldwin's Ohio Practice, Merrick-Rippner Probate Law § 95:22, Entry Partially Granting Application for Private Sale and Ordering Additional Bond—Form.
Carlin, Baldwin's Ohio Practice, Merrick-Rippner Probate Law § 95:23, Entry Approving Bond and Authorizing Private Sale and Allowing a Real Estate Commission—Form.
Carlin, Baldwin's Ohio Practice, Merrick-Rippner Probate Law § 95:24, Entry Dispensing With Additional Bond and Authorizing Private Sale and Allowing Real Estate Commission—Form.
Carlin, Baldwin's Ohio Practice, Merrick-Rippner Probate Law § 97:15, Land Sale by Guardian—Appraisal of Property to be Sold.

Notes of Decisions

Dower 1
Sheriff's report 2

1. Dower

Where a mortgagee stands by and permits a widow's dower to be assigned, he is afterwards barred from foreclosing on the part set off to her. Affleck's Adm'r v. Snodgrass's Adm'r (Ohio 1858) 8 Ohio St. 234.

2. Sheriff's report

A sheriff's report of appraisement, advertisement and sale may be disproved on material facts not legally required to be stated, such as appraisal on "actual view," in an action to set aside a sheriff's sale on execution. Creditors v. Search (Ohio Com.Pl. 1861) 3 West. L. Monthly 319.

2127.23   Duties of appraisers

The appraisers appointed under section 2127.22 of the Revised Code shall agree to truly and impartially appraise the real estate at its fair cash value upon actual view and to perform the duties required of them by the order of the court. The appraisement shall be signed by the appraisers, and the officer to whom it is issued shall make return of it to the court for confirmation.

(1992 H 427, eff. 10–8–92; 1953 H 1; GC 10510–27)

Historical and Statutory Notes

Pre–1953 H 1 Amendments: 114 v 456

Cross References

Notary public may administer oaths, 147.07
Oath defined, 1.59
Oath includes affirmation; form of oath, 3.20, 3.21

Library References

Executors and Administrators ⚖═353.
Guardian and Ward ⚖═93.
Mental Health ⚖═264.
Westlaw Topic Nos. 162, 196, 257A.
C.J.S. Executors and Administrators § 624.

Research References

Encyclopedias

OH Jur. 3d Decedents' Estates § 1541, Determination of Sale Price; Appraisement—Duties of Appraisers; Return.
OH Jur. 3d Guardian & Ward § 154, Appraisement of Property; Appointment and Removal of Appraisers.

Treatises and Practice Aids

Carlin, Baldwin's Ohio Practice, Merrick-Rippner Probate Law § 93:3, Appraisers—Report.

2127.24   Vacancy in appraisers

When a person appointed by the court under section 2127.22 of the Revised Code as an appraiser fails to discharge his duties, the probate judge on his own motion or on the motion of the executor, administrator, or guardian may appoint another appraiser.

(1953 H 1, eff. 10–1–53; GC 10510–28)

Historical and Statutory Notes

Pre–1953 H 1 Amendments: 114 v 456

Library References

Executors and Administrators ⚖═353.
Guardian and Ward ⚖═93.

Mental Health ⟳263.
Westlaw Topic Nos. 162, 196, 257A.
C.J.S. Executors and Administrators § 624.

Research References

Encyclopedias

OH Jur. 3d Decedents' Estates § 1540, Determination of Sale Price; Appraisement—Appointment and Compensation of Appraisers.

OH Jur. 3d Guardian & Ward § 154, Appraisement of Property; Appointment and Removal of Appraisers.

Treatises and Practice Aids

Carlin, Baldwin's Ohio Practice, Merrick-Rippner Probate Law § 93:2, Appraisers—Appointment, Compensation, Removal.

Notes of Decisions

Binding report 1

1. Binding report

Where one of three appraisers wants to alter a partition made and finally erases his name from the report, the action of the remaining majority is binding, as the report need not be unanimous. Nichols v. Balser (Ohio Cir. 1885) 1 Ohio C.D. 29.

2127.25 Compensation of appraisers

Appraisers appointed under section 2127.22 of the Revised Code shall each be paid such compensation as the court thinks proper for services performed by them.

(1953 H 1, eff. 10–1–53; GC 10510–29)

Historical and Statutory Notes

Pre–1953 H 1 Amendments: 114 v 457

Library References

Executors and Administrators ⟳353, 401.
Guardian and Ward ⟳93, 114.
Mental Health ⟳264, 273.
Westlaw Topic Nos. 162, 196, 257A.
C.J.S. Executors and Administrators §§ 624, 684.

Research References

Encyclopedias

OH Jur. 3d Decedents' Estates § 1540, Determination of Sale Price; Appraisement—Appointment and Compensation of Appraisers.

OH Jur. 3d Guardian & Ward § 154, Appraisement of Property; Appointment and Removal of Appraisers.

Treatises and Practice Aids

Carlin, Baldwin's Ohio Practice, Merrick-Rippner Probate Law § 93:2, Appraisers—Appointment, Compensation, Removal.

Notes of Decisions

Dower 1
Homestead allowance 3
Minor 2

1. Dower

A divorced wife not in the wrong may have dower assigned, though the lands have been sold by the administrator. Arnold v. Donaldson (Ohio 1888) 46 Ohio St. 73, 20 W.L.B. 431, 18 N.E. 540.

Where the dower interest of a widow is manifest, it will be protected, though she may not have filed an answer. McDonald v. Aten (Ohio 1853) 1 Ohio St. 293.

In application of the amount of the dower interest and a homestead exemption to the satisfaction of a mortgage in which husband and wife joined, resort should first be had to the amount of homestead where wife, claiming dower, joined in the mortgage simply as surety. Stoehr v. Moerlein Brewing Co. (Ohio Cir. 1905) 17 Ohio C.D. 330, 2 Ohio Law Rep. 449.

Where a will gives the widow a life estate in one-third of the property and directs a sale to pay debts, a sale by the administrator under order of the court to sell subject to dower passes title to the whole estate notwithstanding the widow's election to take under the will. Hamilton v. Stewart (Ohio Com.Pl. 1907) 18 Ohio Dec. 130, 5 Ohio N.P.(N.S.) 553, affirmed 80 Ohio St. 740, 89 N.E. 1120, 7 Ohio Law Rep. 85.

2. Minor

In order to set aside a homestead for the widow in the lands of a deceased debtor, there must also be an unmarried minor child composing a part of decedent's family at the time of his death; when the minor child comes of age, the administrator may sell the premises so set aside to pay debts still remaining. Taylor v. Thorn (Ohio 1876) 29 Ohio St. 569.

3. Homestead allowance

A widow has a right to have the homestead set off in an action to sell land to pay debts. Bliss v. Fuhrman (Ohio Cir. 1892) 3 Ohio C.D. 416.

A widow whose husband was not the owner of a homestead is not entitled to an allowance in lieu of a homestead out of his estate. Wolverton v. Paddock (Ohio Cir. 1888) 2 Ohio C.D. 279. Exemptions ⟳ 30

2127.27 Additional bond before sale

Upon the return and approval of the appraisement provided for by section 2127.22 of the Revised Code, the court shall require the executor, administrator, or guardian to execute a bond with two or more personal sureties, or one or more corporate sureties, whose qualifications shall be those provided by section 2109.17 of the Revised Code. Such bond shall be payable to the state in an amount which the court deems sufficient, having regard to the amount of real estate to be sold, its appraised value, the amount of the original bond given by the executor, administrator, or guardian, and the distribution to be made of the proceeds arising from the sale, and such bond shall be conditioned for the faithful discharge of his duties and the payment of, and accounting for, all moneys arising from such sale according to law. Such bond shall be additional to that given by the executor, administrator, or guardian at the time of his appointment. If the court finds the amount of the original bond given by the executor, administrator, or guardian is sufficient, having regard for the amount of real estate to be sold, its appraised value, and the distribution to be made of the proceeds arising from the sale, the giving of additional bond may be dispensed with by order of the court. Such bond shall be given in the court from which the executor, administrator, or guardian received his appointment.

If the action to obtain authority to sell real estate is pending in another court, the latter shall proceed no further until there is filed therein a certificate from the court wherein the executor, administrator, or guardian received his appointment, under its seal, that such bond has been given or that the original bond is sufficient. This section does not prevent the court in an action to sell real estate from ordering the sale of such real estate without bond in cases where the testator had provided by his will that the executor need not give bond.

(1953 H 1, eff. 10–1–53; GC 10510–31)

Historical and Statutory Notes

Pre–1953 H 1 Amendments: 123 v 460; 117 v 545, § 1; 114 v 457

Cross References

Surviving spouse may purchase property, 2106.16

Library References

Executors and Administrators ⚖351.
Guardian and Ward ⚖92.
Mental Health ⚖258.1.
Westlaw Topic Nos. 162, 196, 257A.
C.J.S. Executors and Administrators § 630.

Research References

Encyclopedias

OH Jur. 3d Decedents' Estates § 1542, Requirement of Additional Bond by Executor or Administrator.
OH Jur. 3d Fiduciaries § 183, New or Additional Bond—for Sale of Realty.
OH Jur. 3d Fiduciaries § 198, Personal.
OH Jur. 3d Fiduciaries § 199, Corporate.
OH Jur. 3d Guardian & Ward § 155, Additional Bond for Guardian.

Treatises and Practice Aids

Carlin, Baldwin's Ohio Practice, Merrick-Rippner Probate Law § 2:56, Sale of Land—Hearing and Order Granting Authority to Sell.
Carlin, Baldwin's Ohio Practice, Merrick-Rippner Probate Law § 93:7, Entry Dispensing With New Appraisal and Ordering Additional Bond—Form.
Carlin, Baldwin's Ohio Practice, Merrick-Rippner Probate Law § 93:9, Additional Bond in Land Sale Proceedings—Form.
Carlin, Baldwin's Ohio Practice, Merrick-Rippner Probate Law § 94:1, Bond of Fiduciary Before Sale of Land.
Carlin, Baldwin's Ohio Practice, Merrick-Rippner Probate Law § 93:10, Certificate from Former Court of Fiduciary's Bond—Form.
Carlin, Baldwin's Ohio Practice, Merrick-Rippner Probate Law § 95:20, Application for Order of Private Sale and Allowance of Real Estate Commission—Form.
Carlin, Baldwin's Ohio Practice, Merrick-Rippner Probate Law § 95:22, Entry Partially Granting Application for Private Sale and Ordering Additional Bond—Form.
Carlin, Baldwin's Ohio Practice, Merrick-Rippner Probate Law § 95:23, Entry Approving Bond and Authorizing Private Sale and Allowing a Real Estate Commission—Form.
Carlin, Baldwin's Ohio Practice, Merrick-Rippner Probate Law § 95:24, Entry Dispensing With Additional Bond and Authorizing Private Sale and Allowing Real Estate Commission—Form.
Carlin, Baldwin's Ohio Practice, Merrick-Rippner Probate Law § 97:16, Land Sale by Guardian—Additional Bond of Guardian.

Notes of Decisions

Court's power 3
Death of ward 2
Liability of sureties 1
Number of sureties 4

---

1. Liability of sureties

Sureties on a guardian's additional bond are not liable beyond the terms of the bond, although the guardian commingles the ward's money with money from other sources for which he fails to account. McWhinney v. Swisher (Ohio 1898) 58 Ohio St. 378, 39 W.L.B. 402, 50 N.E. 812.

Where proceeds of real estate are exceeded by general payments made by the guardian from commingled funds, sureties are liable for all proceeds of the land. McWhinney v. Swisher (Ohio 1898) 58 Ohio St. 378, 39 W.L.B. 402, 50 N.E. 812.

Where an administrator gives a bond when appointed, and an additional bond on sale of real estate, all the sureties on both bonds are equally liable for the proceeds of the sale. Kehnast v. Daum (Ohio Com.Pl. 1897) 6 Ohio Dec. 401, 4 Ohio N.P. 366, affirmed 9 Ohio C.D. 867.

2. Death of ward

Where a ward dies pending an appeal from an action ordering property of the ward sold and a new appraisement made, the guardianship terminates and the appeal is moot. Becker v. Becker (Summit 1952) 125 N.E.2d 563, 69 Ohio Law Abs. 414.

3. Court's power

The court's failing to require a new bond, though erroneous, does not render the proceedings void. Arrowsmith v. Harmoning (Ohio 1884) 42 Ohio St. 254, affirmed 6 S.Ct. 1023, 118 U.S. 194, 30 L.Ed. 243.

Stipulation that law as finally held in one case tried shall be conclusive as to matters in cases not yet tried, except as to matters of fact on which issue may be joined therein, does not preclude either party, after one case has been finally disposed of, from raising other issues of fact by proper pleadings, on leave of court. Swisher v. McWhinney (Ohio 1901) 64 Ohio St. 343, 45 W.L.B. 355, 60 N.E. 565. Stipulations ⚖ 18(5)

The court has power to demand conditions in bond beyond the requirements of the statute, and such conditions cannot be limited by the terms of the statute under which it is given. The amount recoverable under such bond is not fixed by the sum realized from the sale, and reinvestment of such sum under order of the court does not relieve the surety, if the fund is not finally accounted for. Huntington v Globe Indemnity Co, 6 Abs 99, 27 NS(NS) 12 (CP, Franklin 1927).

4. Number of sureties

Under 1 Swan & C. Rev. St. Ohio, requiring a guardian on the sale of the ward's realty to execute a bond "with sufficient freehold sureties," the bond is not void because it has but one surety. Arrowsmith v. Gleason (U.S.Ohio 1889) 9 S.Ct. 237, 129 U.S. 86, 32 L.Ed. 630. Guardian And Ward ⚖ 92

2127.28 Expense of sale

The probate court may, after notice to all parties in interest, allow a real estate commission in an action to sell real estate by an executor, administrator, or guardian, but an allowance shall be passed upon by the court prior to the sale.

The court may allow payment for certificate or abstract of title or policy of title insurance in connection with the sale of any land by an executor, administrator, or guardian.

(1975 S 145, eff. 1–1–76; 1953 H 1; GC 10510–32, 10510–33)

Historical and Statutory Notes

Pre–1953 H 1 Amendments: 114 v 457

Library References

Executors and Administrators ⚖401.
Guardian and Ward ⚖114.
Mental Health ⚖273.
Westlaw Topic Nos. 162, 196, 257A.
C.J.S. Executors and Administrators § 684.

Research References

Encyclopedias

OH Jur. 3d Decedents' Estates § 1598, Real Estate Commission; Auctioneer's Fees.
OH Jur. 3d Decedents' Estates § 1599, Title Documents and Title Insurance.
OH Jur. 3d Guardian & Ward § 163, Sale Price; Expense of Sale.

Treatises and Practice Aids

Carlin, Baldwin's Ohio Practice, Merrick-Rippner Probate Law § 2:56, Sale of Land—Hearing and Order Granting Authority to Sell.
Carlin, Baldwin's Ohio Practice, Merrick-Rippner Probate Law § 95:7, Private Sale—Procedure.
Carlin, Baldwin's Ohio Practice, Merrick-Rippner Probate Law § 91:55, Application to Employ Real Estate Broker—Form.
Carlin, Baldwin's Ohio Practice, Merrick-Rippner Probate Law § 91:56, Order Fixing Time for Hearing on Application to Employ Real Estate Broker—Form.
Carlin, Baldwin's Ohio Practice, Merrick-Rippner Probate Law § 91:57, Consent of Beneficiaries to Employment of Real Estate Broker—Form.
Carlin, Baldwin's Ohio Practice, Merrick-Rippner Probate Law § 91:58, Order Authorizing Employment of Real Estate Broker—Form.

Carlin, Baldwin's Ohio Practice, Merrick-Rippner Probate Law § 95:20, Application for Order of Private Sale and Allowance of Real Estate Commission—Form.

Carlin, Baldwin's Ohio Practice, Merrick-Rippner Probate Law § 95:22, Entry Partially Granting Application for Private Sale and Ordering Additional Bond—Form.

Carlin, Baldwin's Ohio Practice, Merrick-Rippner Probate Law § 95:23, Entry Approving Bond and Authorizing Private Sale and Allowing a Real Estate Commission—Form.

Carlin, Baldwin's Ohio Practice, Merrick-Rippner Probate Law § 95:24, Entry Dispensing With Additional Bond and Authorizing Private Sale and Allowing Real Estate Commission—Form.

Carlin, Baldwin's Ohio Practice, Merrick-Rippner Probate Law § 95:28, Application to Fix Price and Sell at Private Sale and for Real Estate Commission—Form.

Carlin, Baldwin's Ohio Practice, Merrick-Rippner Probate Law § 96:11, Expenses of Sale—Real Estate Commission.

Carlin, Baldwin's Ohio Practice, Merrick-Rippner Probate Law § 97:20, Land Sale by Guardian—Fees and Expenses.

Notes of Decisions

Attorney's fees 1

1. Attorney's fees

Neither attorney's fees of the administrator in an action by him to sell real estate to pay debts, general costs of administration, nor premiums due a surety company on his bonds are included in the costs of the sale under this section. Sherman v. Millard (Ohio Cir. 1904) 17 Ohio C.D. 175, 6 Ohio C.C.N.S. 338.

2127.29 Order of sale

When the bond required by section 2127.27 of the Revised Code is filed and approved by the court, it shall order the sale of the real estate included in the complaint set forth in section 2127.10 of the Revised Code, or the part of the real estate it deems necessary for the interest of all parties concerned. If the complaint alleges that it is necessary to sell part of the real estate, and that by the partial sale the residue of the estate, or a specific part of it, would be greatly injured, the court, if it so finds, may order a sale of the whole estate.

(1975 S 145, eff. 1–1–76; 125 v 903; 1953 H 1; GC 10510–34)

Historical and Statutory Notes

Pre–1953 H 1 Amendments: 114 v 458

Library References

Executors and Administrators ⟐329(1), 345.1.
Guardian and Ward ⟐79, 90.
Mental Health ⟐262, 267.
Westlaw Topic Nos. 162, 196, 257A.
C.J.S. Executors and Administrators §§ 595, 618.

Research References

Encyclopedias

OH Jur. 3d Decedents' Estates § 1477, Personalty as Primary Fund.
OH Jur. 3d Decedents' Estates § 1501, Determination of Particular Property or Quantity to be Sold.
OH Jur. 3d Decedents' Estates § 1543, Order of Sale, Generally.
OH Jur. 3d Decedents' Estates § 1544, Order of Sale, Generally—Contents of Order.
OH Jur. 3d Guardian & Ward § 156, Order Authorizing Sale.

Treatises and Practice Aids

Carlin, Baldwin's Ohio Practice, Merrick-Rippner Probate Law § 2:56, Sale of Land—Hearing and Order Granting Authority to Sell.

Carlin, Baldwin's Ohio Practice, Merrick-Rippner Probate Law § 92:1, Property Subject to Sale—General Rule.

Carlin, Baldwin's Ohio Practice, Merrick-Rippner Probate Law § 95:1, Order of Sale—Necessity.

Carlin, Baldwin's Ohio Practice, Merrick-Rippner Probate Law § 95:2, Order of Sale—Real Property Interest to be Sold.

Carlin, Baldwin's Ohio Practice, Merrick-Rippner Probate Law § 95:4, Public Sale—Statutory Provisions.

Kuehnle and Levey, Ohio Real Estate Law and Practice § 53:25, Land Sales—Interests Subject to Sale by Fiduciaries—Entire Tract Ordered Sold Despite Complaint for Sale of Only Part.

Notes of Decisions

Appeal 2
Necessity of sale 5
Procedural issues 6
Proof and record 1
Purchasers' rights 3
Repeal of law 4

1. Proof and record

An order of sale will not be reversed for want of a journal entry showing that the facts stated in the petition were found to be true, as it will be presumed that the judgment was based on proper proof. Sidener v. Hawes (Ohio 1882) 37 Ohio St. 532. Executors And Administrators ⟐ 346

An order to sell land made but not entered upon the record cannot be proved by parol. Newcomb's Lessee v. Smith (Ohio 1832) 5 Ohio 447.

Where administrators of an estate make a sale of the decedent's real estate to pay his debts without an order of sale by the court on the record, such sale is void. Goforth's Lessee v. Longworth (Ohio 1829) 4 Ohio 129, 19 Am.Dec. 588.

An order of sale made subsequent to a sale cannot be given in evidence to support such prior sale. Ludlow's Heirs' Lessee v. Park (Ohio 1829) 4 Ohio 5.

Under 1 Swan & C. Rev. St. Ohio, requiring a guardian on the sale of the ward's realty to execute a bond "with sufficient freehold sureties," the bond is not void because it has but one surety. Arrowsmith v. Gleason (U.S.Ohio 1889) 9 S.Ct. 237, 129 U.S. 86, 32 L.Ed. 630. Guardian And Ward ⟐ 92

An order of sale is essential to a title under an administrator's deed and should be entered on the journal, as marking "allowed" on a petition to sell, by an associate judge, is not sufficient. Newcomb's Lessee v Smith, W 208 (Hamilton 1833).

2. Appeal

An order of the common pleas court for the sale of land pursuant to a petition under the statute by an administrator for the sale of lands for the payment of debts is not appealable. Steinbarger's Adm'r v. Steinbarger (Ohio 1850) 19 Ohio 106.

Where a ward dies pending an appeal from an action ordering property of the ward sold and a new appraisement made, the guardianship terminates and the appeal is moot. Becker v. Becker (Summit 1952) 125 N.E.2d 563, 69 Ohio Law Abs. 414.

3. Purchasers' rights

A purchaser who loses title can set up no equity by reason of the appropriation of his purchase money to pay the debts of decedent. Beall v. Price (Ohio 1844) 13 Ohio 368, 42 Am.Dec. 204.

Purchase money paid to an administrator cannot be recovered where the sale is inoperative and the heir recovers the land. Nowler v. Coit (Ohio 1824) 1 Ohio 519, 13 Am.Dec. 640.

Misdescription of property in administratrix's sale, by fraction of foot, corrected on purchaser's motion, would not justify setting aside otherwise proper sale. Watson v. Watson (Hamilton 1927) 24 Ohio App. 45, 156 N.E. 241. Executors And Administrators ⟐ 379

Executor directed by probate court to sell lands to pay debts may sue for wrongful destruction of market value of such premises, where it appears that rights of creditor will be prejudiced thereby, in view of constitutional provisions that person for injury done him in land or goods shall have remedy by due course of law. Clark v. McClain Fire Brick Co. (Ohio 1919) 100 Ohio St. 110, 125 N.E. 877, 17 Ohio Law Rep. 154, 17 Ohio Law

Rep. 164. Constitutional Law ⇨ 321; Executors And Administrators ⇨ 129(1)

Unless there is authority given in the will or in the order issued by the court for the sale of the lands, the executor cannot bind the decedent's estate by a verbal promise to indemnify the purchaser against encumbrances or defects in title. Arnold v. Donaldson (Ohio 1888) 46 Ohio St. 73, 20 W.L.B. 431, 18 N.E. 540. Executors And Administrators ⇨ 388(4)

4. Repeal of law

An order of sale made before the law authorizing it was repealed, but not executed until afterwards, will not support the sale. Ludlow's Heirs Lessee v. Wade (Ohio 1832) 5 Ohio 494.

Where administrators were ordered by the court to sell real estate and before the sale was made the law allowing such an order was repealed, the power of the administrators to sell terminated with the law's repeal; thus, a sale made by such administrators after the repeal was void. Bank of Hamilton v. Dudley's Lessee (U.S.Ohio 1829) 27 U.S. 492, 2 Pet. 492, 7 L.Ed. 496.

5. Necessity of sale

An intestate's real estate may only be sold by an administrator to pay debts upon the express order of the court after it has ascertained the necessity of such sale. Avery v. Pugh (Ohio 1839) 9 Ohio 67.

Probate court had authority, pursuant to a complaint filed by estate administrator, to order that decedent's real property be sold to pay decedent's debts, even if decedent expressed a wish that the real property be divided among certain designated heirs, where the personalty belonging to the estate was insufficient to pay decedent's debts. Rossi v. Visnich (Ohio App. 11 Dist., Trumbull, 03-17-2006) No. 2005-T-0039, 2006-Ohio-1266, 2006 WL 687994, Unreported, appeal not allowed 110 Ohio St.3d 1441, 852 N.E.2d 189, 2006-Ohio-3862. Executors And Administrators ⇨ 325

Probate court's order requiring decedent's real property to be sold by sealed bidding with a requirement that the high bidder close within 30 days was not arbitrary; interested parties had been bidding on the property for a year prior to probate court's order, high bidder had abundant time to secure financing, high bidder did not object to estate administrator's motion to resolve the sale by sealed bids or the condition that sale close within 30 days, and high bidder did not file a request with the probate court for an extension of time to close. Rossi v. Visnich (Ohio App. 11 Dist., Trumbull, 03-17-2006) No. 2005-T-0039, 2006-Ohio-1266, 2006 WL 687994, Unreported. Executors And Administrators ⇨ 364

Action does not lie by the administrator to sell real estate to pay a mortgage debt upon it where the personal assets of the estate are sufficient to pay the unsecured debts, and the sale of the real estate is not desired by the mortgagee or by the heirs. In re Marhoover's Estate (Ohio Com.Pl. 1919) 30 Ohio Dec. 6, 22 Ohio NP(NS) 46.

These sections intended to place strict limits upon sales and prevent same except when necessary. Kummer v Lapp, 1 NP(NS) 209, 13 D 491 (CP, Franklin 1903).

6. Procedural issues

The court is to settle priorities of liens and order sale of land free therefrom. Stone v. Strong (Ohio 1884) 42 Ohio St. 53.

The decree of a Virginia court for the sale of lands in Ohio is inoperative. Price v. Johnston (Ohio 1853) 1 Ohio St. 390.

A bill in chancery will not lie to set aside a sale because it was made without order of court as there is an adequate remedy at law. Mawhorter v. Armstrong (Ohio 1847) 16 Ohio 188. Ejectment ⇨ 9(3); Equity ⇨ 43; Executors And Administrators ⇨ 380(2)

A court after its jurisdiction has been withdrawn by legislation cannot by nunc pro tunc order correct mistakes or errors committed while it possessed jurisdiction. Ludlow's Heirs v. Johnston (Ohio 1828) 3 Ohio 553, 17 Am.Dec. 609.

Where an order for the sale of a decedent's real estate for the payment of debts has been made and the widow's allowance and dower set off to her, and no error was prosecuted or appeal taken from it, such order cannot be collaterally attacked by exception to the widow's account as administratrix of the estate. In re Hess' Estate (Ohio Cir. 1911) 23 Ohio C.D. 449, 14 Ohio C.C.(N.S.) 463. Executors And Administrators ⇨ 194(6); Homestead ⇨ 150(2)

Sale of a part of the tract may be made, though the petition prays for the sale of the whole tract. Ewing v. Higby (Ohio 1835) 7 Ohio 198, PT. I.

2127.30 Order of sale when an equitable estate is included

If the order of sale set forth in section 2127.29 of the Revised Code includes real estate in which the ward or the estate has an equitable interest only, the court may make an order for the appraisement and sale of such equitable estate free from dower, for the indemnity of the estate against any claim for purchase money, and for payment of the value of such dower in money, as the court deems equitable, having regard for the rights of all parties in interest.

(1953 H 1, eff. 10–1–53; GC 10510–35)

Historical and Statutory Notes

Pre–1953 H 1 Amendments: 114 v 458

Library References

Executors and Administrators ⇨345.
Guardian and Ward ⇨90.
Mental Health ⇨267.
Westlaw Topic Nos. 162, 196, 257A.
C.J.S. Executors and Administrators §§ 605 to 608, 618.

Research References

Encyclopedias

OH Jur. 3d Decedents' Estates § 1544, Order of Sale, Generally—Contents of Order.
OH Jur. 3d Decedents' Estates § 1550, Disposition of Liens and Other Prior Rights; Generally—Spouse's Dower Rights.
OH Jur. 3d Family Law § 177, Proceeding to Sell Realty for Payment of Decedent's Debts.
OH Jur. 3d Guardian & Ward § 156, Order Authorizing Sale.

Treatises and Practice Aids

Carlin, Baldwin's Ohio Practice, Merrick-Rippner Probate Law § 95:2, Order of Sale—Real Property Interest to be Sold.

Notes of Decisions

Heirs' interests 3
Personal contracts 2
Trusts 1

---

1. Trusts

A conveyance in trust on condition for a reconveyance creates an equitable estate that may be sold to pay debts. Biggs v. Bickel (Ohio 1861) 12 Ohio St. 49.

2. Personal contracts

Personal representative may perform or rescind personal contracts of the intestate subject to the approval of the court. Gray v. Hawkins's Adm'rx (Ohio 1858) 8 Ohio St. 449, 72 Am.Dec. 600.

Where an administrator for the benefit of the estate cancels an unexecuted contract, equity will not set it up again upon the request of the heirs. Howard v Babcock, 7 O 359 (1836).

3. Heirs' interests

Equity in lands passes to the heirs and may be sold by the personal representative of the deceased for the payment of the estate's debts. Avery's Lessee v. Dufrees (Ohio 1839) 9 Ohio 145.

2127.31 Persons interested may give bond to prevent sale

An order to sell the real property of a decedent shall not be granted in an action by an executor or administrator, if, after the action is commenced and before the order of sale is granted, any person interested in the estate gives bond to the executor or administrator in a sum with sureties approved by the probate court, conditioned to pay all debts and legacies found due from the estate, the charges of administration, and the allowance for support to the surviving spouse, minor children, or surviving spouse and minor children of the decedent as provided in section 2106.13 of the Revised Code, insofar as the personal property of the decedent is insufficient. If the bond is not given until after the order of sale is granted, and the executor or administrator in reliance on the bond abates the action, the bond shall be binding upon the obligors, and may be enforced as though given prior to the granting of the order of sale.

(1990 H 346, eff. 5–31–90; 1975 S 145; 1953 H 1; GC 10510–36)

Uncodified Law

1990 H 346, § 3, eff. 5–31–90, reads, in part: (A) Sections 1 and 2 of this act shall apply only to the estates of decedents who die on or after the effective date of this act.

Historical and Statutory Notes

Pre–1953 H 1 Amendments: 114 v 458

Library References

Executors and Administrators ⇨331.
Westlaw Topic No. 162.
C.J.S. Executors and Administrators § 600.
Baldwin's Ohio Legislative Service, 1990 Laws of Ohio, H 346—LSC Analysis, p 5–87

Research References

Encyclopedias

OH Jur. 3d Cotenancy & Partition § 50, Effect of Rights of Decedent's Creditors—Avoidance of Sale to Pay Decedent's Debts.
OH Jur. 3d Decedents' Estates § 1499, Right of Interested Persons to Prevent Sale by Giving Bond.

Treatises and Practice Aids

Carlin, Baldwin's Ohio Practice, Merrick-Rippner Probate Law § 90:8, Authority for Land Sale Action—Insufficient Personal Property to Pay Debts.
Carlin, Baldwin's Ohio Practice, Merrick-Rippner Probate Law § 94:2, Bond of Interested Person to Prevent Sale.
Carlin, Baldwin's Ohio Practice, Merrick-Rippner Probate Law § 94:3, Bond to Prevent Sale—Form.
Carlin, Baldwin's Ohio Practice, Merrick-Rippner Probate Law § 94:4, Entry Approving Bond and Staying Sale—Form.
Carlin, Baldwin's Ohio Practice, Merrick-Rippner Probate Law § 2:121, Administration of Decedent's Estate—Checklist.
Kuehnle and Levey, Ohio Real Estate Law and Practice § 52:24, Statutory Fiduciary Sales—Partition of Decedent's Real Estate.

Notes of Decisions

Bond requirements 2
Dower 4
Partition 1
Rents 3

---

1. Partition

Where heir brought an action to partition real estate more than one year after death of decedent from whom estate came, action was properly dismissed where plaintiff in partition failed to give bond as provided in this section. Retterer v. Retterer (Marion 1935) 32 N.E.2d 513, 20 Ohio Law Abs. 393, 4 O.O. 333.

Heirs at law can prevent a sale of real estate for the payment of debts and have a partition only by giving bond for the payment of debts, etc., as provided by GC 10785 (Repealed). Stout v. Stout (Ohio 1910) 82 Ohio St. 358, 92 N.E. 465, 137 Am.St.Rep. 785, 8 Ohio Law Rep. 118. Executors And Administrators ⇨ 331

An action for partition cannot be maintained within one year unless the debts are secured by bond. Smith v. Montag (Ohio Super. 1894) 1 Ohio Dec. 224, 32 W.L.B. 153.

2. Bond requirements

A bond not in strict conformity to the statute, on account of being executed before the order of sale, is binding. Davisson v. Burgess (Ohio 1876) 31 Ohio St. 78.

3. Rents

Where testator gave, devised and bequeathed to certain individuals "the monies realized from sale of" certain properties, the rents received from such properties prior to sale passed to the residuary legatee. In re Anderson's Estate (Franklin 1956) 141 N.E.2d 478, 74 Ohio Law Abs. 549.

4. Dower

Where a widow with a dower interest gave bond under this section, and paid to the administrator the amount of all claims, she is entitled to stand in place of administrator with respect to a lien against real estate of decedent. Corey v. Hayes (Ohio Cir. 1896) 7 Ohio C.D. 272.

2127.32 Public or private sale

The real estate included in the court's order of sale, as provided in section 2127.29 of the Revised Code, shall be sold either in whole or in parcels at public auction at the door of the courthouse in the county in which the order of sale was granted, or at another place, as the court directs, and the order shall fix the place, day, and hour of sale. If it appears to be more for the interest of the ward or the estate to sell the real estate at private sale, the court may authorize the complainant to sell it either in whole or in parcels. If an order for private sale is issued, it shall be returned by the complainant. Upon motion and showing of a person interested in the proceeds of the sale, filed after thirty days from the date of the order, the court may require the complainant to return the order, if the premises have not been sold. Thereupon, the court may order the real estate to be sold at public sale.

If upon showing of any person interested, the court finds that it will be to the interest of the ward or the estate, it may order a reappraisement and sale in parcels.

If the sale is to be public, the executor, administrator, or guardian must give notice of the time and place of the sale by advertisement at least three weeks successively in a newspaper published in the county where the lands are situated.

(1977 H 42, eff. 10–7–77; 1975 S 145; 1953 H 1; GC 10510–37, 10510–38)

Historical and Statutory Notes

Pre–1953 H 1 Amendments: 114 v 458, 459

Cross References

Notice by newspaper publication, standards, 7.11 to 7.15

Library References

Executors and Administrators ⇨363.
Guardian and Ward ⇨97.
Mental Health ⇨258.1.
Westlaw Topic Nos. 162, 196, 257A.
C.J.S. Executors and Administrators § 633.

SALE OF LANDS

2127.32
Note 3

Research References

Encyclopedias

OH Jur. 3d Decedents' Estates § 1544, Order of Sale, Generally—Contents of Order.
OH Jur. 3d Decedents' Estates § 1553, Notice of Sale.
OH Jur. 3d Decedents' Estates § 1554, Place of Sale.
OH Jur. 3d Decedents' Estates § 1555, Sale as a Whole or in Parcels.
OH Jur. 3d Decedents' Estates § 1562, Return Where Private Sale Ordered.
OH Jur. 3d Guardian & Ward § 160, Generally; Terms of Sale.
OH Jur. 3d Guardian & Ward § 161, Type of Sale; Public.
OH Jur. 3d Guardian & Ward § 162, Type of Sale; Public—Private.

Treatises and Practice Aids

Carlin, Baldwin's Ohio Practice, Merrick-Rippner Probate Law § 2:57, Sale of Land—Public or Private Sale.
Carlin, Baldwin's Ohio Practice, Merrick-Rippner Probate Law § 90:8, Authority for Land Sale Action—Insufficient Personal Property to Pay Debts.
Carlin, Baldwin's Ohio Practice, Merrick-Rippner Probate Law § 95:4, Public Sale—Statutory Provisions.
Carlin, Baldwin's Ohio Practice, Merrick-Rippner Probate Law § 95:5, Public Sale—Notice.
Carlin, Baldwin's Ohio Practice, Merrick-Rippner Probate Law § 95:6, Private Sale—Statutory Provisions.
Carlin, Baldwin's Ohio Practice, Merrick-Rippner Probate Law § 95:7, Private Sale—Procedure.
Carlin, Baldwin's Ohio Practice, Merrick-Rippner Probate Law § 2:121, Administration of Decedent's Estate—Checklist.
Carlin, Baldwin's Ohio Practice, Merrick-Rippner Probate Law § 91:50, Complaint for Authority to Sell Real Estate, and for Order of Private Sale—Form.
Carlin, Baldwin's Ohio Practice, Merrick-Rippner Probate Law § 95:14, Price—Minimum—Private Sale.
Carlin, Baldwin's Ohio Practice, Merrick-Rippner Probate Law § 95:19, Entry Authorizing Private Sale—Where No Written Application for Private Sale or Notice on Private Sale is Required—Form.
Carlin, Baldwin's Ohio Practice, Merrick-Rippner Probate Law § 95:20, Application for Order of Private Sale and Allowance of Real Estate Commission—Form.
Carlin, Baldwin's Ohio Practice, Merrick-Rippner Probate Law § 95:21, Entry Authorizing Sale of Real Estate at Private Sale—Form.
Carlin, Baldwin's Ohio Practice, Merrick-Rippner Probate Law § 95:22, Entry Partially Granting Application for Private Sale and Ordering Additional Bond—Form.
Carlin, Baldwin's Ohio Practice, Merrick-Rippner Probate Law § 95:23, Entry Approving Bond and Authorizing Private Sale and Allowing a Real Estate Commission—Form.
Carlin, Baldwin's Ohio Practice, Merrick-Rippner Probate Law § 95:24, Entry Dispensing With Additional Bond and Authorizing Private Sale and Allowing Real Estate Commission—Form.
Carlin, Baldwin's Ohio Practice, Merrick-Rippner Probate Law § 95:25, Order of Private Sale—Form.
Carlin, Baldwin's Ohio Practice, Merrick-Rippner Probate Law § 95:26, Report of Private Sale; Statement—Form.
Carlin, Baldwin's Ohio Practice, Merrick-Rippner Probate Law § 95:27, Motion to Require Fiduciary to Return Order for Private Sale—Form.
Carlin, Baldwin's Ohio Practice, Merrick-Rippner Probate Law § 95:30, Entry Authorizing Public Sale—Form.
Carlin, Baldwin's Ohio Practice, Merrick-Rippner Probate Law § 95:31, Order for Public Sale—Form.
Carlin, Baldwin's Ohio Practice, Merrick-Rippner Probate Law § 95:32, Notice of Public Sale—Form.
Carlin, Baldwin's Ohio Practice, Merrick-Rippner Probate Law § 95:33, Report of Public Sale—Form.

Notes of Decisions

Appraiser purchase 4
Covenants 6
Manner of sale 5
Notice of sale 2
Place of sale 3

Self–dealing by fiduciary 1

1. Self–dealing by fiduciary

An administrator cannot act as agent for others in purchasing at his own sale with a view of making profit therefrom. Piatt v. Longworth's Devisees (Ohio 1875) 27 Ohio St. 159.

Where an administrator procures a third party to purchase and convey in trust for the use of the administrator's wife and children, the transaction is void. Riddle v. Roll (Ohio 1874) 24 Ohio St. 572.

To guard against the uncertainty and hazard of attempting to prove unfairness in a purchase by the administrator, the cestui que trusts may come into court without showing actual fraud and have the property resold. Barrington v. Alexander (Ohio 1856) 6 Ohio St. 189.

Where an administrator has enjoyed the land under a sale made by himself an accounting of the improvements made and rents received will be ordered and the balance retained for the use of the estate. Barrington v. Alexander (Ohio 1856) 6 Ohio St. 189.

Acquisition by the administrator raises an appearance of unfairness, and the sale may be set aside on the application of the cestui que trust. Barrington v. Alexander (Ohio 1856) 6 Ohio St. 189.

An administrator cannot purchase at his own sale. Barrington v. Alexander (Ohio 1856) 6 Ohio St. 189.

The fiduciary relation of the administrator to the land is not terminated by sale but continues until full payment of the purchase price and delivery of proper deeds. Barrington v. Alexander (Ohio 1856) 6 Ohio St. 189.

If an administrator purchases at his own sale, and the property remained in his hands or that of his vendee with notice, the sale may be set aside. Sheldon's Lessee v. Newton (Ohio 1854) 3 Ohio St. 494.

Where an infant purchases for the administrator, and conveys to him, he cannot disaffirm on arriving at full age. Sheldon's Lessee v. Newton (Ohio 1854) 3 Ohio St. 494.

Where after purchasing at his own sale, the administrator sells to a third person, he will be held to account to the heirs with interest. Glass v. Greathouse (Ohio 1851) 20 Ohio 503.

Where an administrator purchases at his own sale, he is held to have purchased in trust for the heirs. Glass v. Greathouse (Ohio 1851) 20 Ohio 503.

The rule is the same, whether the administrator purchases directly or through another for his benefit. Glass v. Greathouse (Ohio 1851) 20 Ohio 503.

Where the administrator of an estate buys the testator's land from a purchaser at the sale conducted according to this section and charges himself with the purchase price of such lands in his account as administrator, such transaction is void and a beneficiary is not estopped by lapse of time to compel a resale of the lands. Caldwell v. Caldwell (Ohio 1888) 45 Ohio St. 512, 19 W.L.B. 185, 15 N.E. 297.

2. Notice of sale

The court may refuse to confirm a sale if notice was published in a paper not in general circulation in the county. Craig, Adm'x v. Fox (Ohio 1847) 16 Ohio 563.

Title of a purchaser cannot be defeated by showing that no legal notice of the sale was given. Stall's Lessee v. Macalester (Ohio 1839) 9 Ohio 19.

Where, in a proceeding by an administrator to sell land for the payment of debts, a public sale was ordered by the court, held and confirmed, and the purchaser received his deed, such sale was not set aside on exceptions thereafter filed on the ground that this section was not complied with in that twenty-eight days had not elapsed from the first publication of notice to the date of sale. Richcreek v. Clark (Coshocton 1939) 64 Ohio App. 305, 28 N.E.2d 670, 18 O.O. 118. Executors And Administrators ⇒ 379

3. Place of sale

The provision as to where the sale shall be made is directory only and not mandatory; and where the order of sale is silent and the executor sells the property at auction on the premises, the purchaser takes a good title. Smiley v. Cook (Ohio Prob. 1907) 8 Ohio N.P.(N.S.) 191, 52 W.L.B. 156, 4 Ohio Law Rep. 737, affirmed 79 Ohio St. 452, 87 N.E. 1131, 6 Ohio Law Rep. 565.

2127.32
Note 3

A public sale by executors need not be held at court house, as the provisions as to place of sale in RS 6161 are directory only, and not mandatory. Smiley v. Cook (Ohio Prob. 1907) 8 Ohio N.P.(N.S.) 191, 52 W.L.B. 156, 4 Ohio Law Rep. 737, affirmed 79 Ohio St. 452, 87 N.E. 1131, 6 Ohio Law Rep. 565.

4. Appraiser purchase

A purchase by an appraiser is voidable but not void. Terrill v. Auchauer (Ohio 1862) 14 Ohio St. 80.

Purchase by an appraiser of lands appraised by him and sold by an administrator will be set aside at the instance of the heirs, and fullness of price and absence of fraud will not avoid this rule. Armstrong v. Huston's Heirs (Ohio 1838) 8 Ohio 552.

Where an appraiser of lands of a decedent buys such land at a sheriff's sale, unknown to the judgment debtor, and undertakes to prevent others from bidding at such sale, causing the price for the land to be less, the sale can be set aside and a new sale ordered on petition of the judgment debtor, even though the purchase money has been paid and the deed delivered. Hurst v Fisher, 46 B 19 (OS Unrep 1901).

5. Manner of sale

In sales of land by an administrator, sheriff, or guardian, the land may be sold in parcels or in one entire tract. Stall's Lessee v. Macalester (Ohio 1839) 9 Ohio 19.

Where a sole devisee appointed as executor sells as devisee lands of the estate at private sale, he must account for the full value thereof if necessary for the payment of the testator's debts, regardless of whether the sale was for less or full value. Hocking Valley R. Co. v. White (Ohio 1913) 87 Ohio St. 413, 101 N.E. 354, 10 Ohio Law Rep. 611, Am.Ann.Cas. 1914A, 190. Executors And Administrators ⇐ 40

A sheriff's report of appraisement, advertisement and sale may be disproved on material facts not legally required to be stated, such as appraisal on "actual view," in an action to set aside a sheriff's sale on execution. Creditors v. Search (Ohio Com.Pl. 1861) 3 West. L. Monthly 319.

In conducting a judicial sale of real estate at public sale an administrator may employ an auctioneer for a fee when such employment is authorized or approved by the court, and such auctioneer must be a licensed auctioneer. 1957 OAG 969.

6. Covenants

In a deed of conveyance of real estate containing full covenants of seizin and warranty where the grantor names herself "G. L., administratrix of S. M. L.," and subscribes the same as "G. L., administratrix of S. M. L.'s estate," but in the covenanting part of the deed she is named G. L. simply, and the deed contains no reference to any order of court authorizing a sale of real estate of an intestate, in an action for breach of covenants of seizin and warranty the covenants are prima facie the covenants of G. L., in her individual capacity. Lockwood v. Gilson (Ohio 1861) 12 Ohio St. 526. Covenants ⇐ 30; Executors And Administrators ⇐ 391

2127.33 Price at which real estate may be sold

Where the sale authorized by a court as provided in section 2127.32 of the Revised Code is private, the real estate shall not be sold for less than the appraised value. When the sale is at public auction the real estate if improved shall not be sold for less than two thirds of the appraised value, or if not improved, for less than one half of the appraised value. In private sales if no sale has been effected after one bona fide effort to sell under this section, or if in public sales the land remains unsold for want of bidders when offered pursuant to advertisement, the court may fix the price for which such real estate may be sold or may set aside the appraisement and order a new appraisement. If such new appraisement does not exceed five hundred dollars, and upon the first offer thereunder at public sale there are no bids, then upon the motion of any party interested the court may order the real estate to be readvertised and sold at public auction to the highest bidder.

(125 v 903, eff. 10–1–53; 1953 H 1; GC 10510–39)

Historical and Statutory Notes

Pre–1953 H 1 Amendments: 114 v 459

Library References

Executors and Administrators ⇐ 364.
Guardian and Ward ⇐ 98.
Mental Health ⇐ 258.1.
Westlaw Topic Nos. 162, 196, 257A.
C.J.S. Executors and Administrators § 635.

Research References

Encyclopedias

OH Jur. 3d Decedents' Estates § 1559, Price for Which Property May be Sold.
OH Jur. 3d Guardian & Ward § 163, Sale Price; Expense of Sale.

Treatises and Practice Aids

Carlin, Baldwin's Ohio Practice, Merrick-Rippner Probate Law § 2:57, Sale of Land—Public or Private Sale.
Carlin, Baldwin's Ohio Practice, Merrick-Rippner Probate Law § 95:6, Private Sale—Statutory Provisions.
Carlin, Baldwin's Ohio Practice, Merrick-Rippner Probate Law § 95:13, Price—Court's Role in Setting.
Carlin, Baldwin's Ohio Practice, Merrick-Rippner Probate Law § 95:14, Price—Minimum—Private Sale.
Carlin, Baldwin's Ohio Practice, Merrick-Rippner Probate Law § 95:15, Price—Minimum—Public Sale.
Carlin, Baldwin's Ohio Practice, Merrick-Rippner Probate Law § 95:16, Price—Property Subject to Mortgage.
Carlin, Baldwin's Ohio Practice, Merrick-Rippner Probate Law § 95:28, Application to Fix Price and Sell at Private Sale and for Real Estate Commission—Form.
Carlin, Baldwin's Ohio Practice, Merrick-Rippner Probate Law § 95:29, Entry Granting Application to Fix Price and Sell at Private Sale and Real Estate Commission—Form.
Carlin, Baldwin's Ohio Practice, Merrick-Rippner Probate Law § 95:34, Motion to Sell Real Estate to Highest Bidder—Form.
Kuehnle and Levey, Ohio Real Estate Law and Practice § 53:24, Land Sales—Interests Subject to Sale by Fiduciaries—Sale Subject to Mortgage.

Notes of Decisions

Charge against executor 1
Self–dealing by fiduciary 4
Title 3
Voidable sale 2

---

1. Charge against executor

Where an executor in bad faith sells his testator's lands for manifestly less than their true value under a testamentary power to sell land to pay debts, he should be charged with the difference between such inadequate price and the true value of the lands, on exception to his account in probate court. Brown v. Reed (Ohio 1897) 56 Ohio St. 264, 37 W.L.B. 324, 46 N.E. 982.

2. Voidable sale

Sale by administrator of real estate to his wife, who was only bidder, at two-thirds of the appraised value, held voidable on suit of general creditors under the facts disclosed by the record. Gahanna Bank Co. v. Miesse (Franklin 1931) 41 Ohio App. 316, 181 N.E. 31, 11 Ohio Law Abs. 26. Executors And Administrators ⇐ 365

3. Title

Where lands were erroneously sold by an administrator for less than the appraised value and the court thereafter confirmed the sale, such sale does not constitute a flaw in the title of a bona fide purchaser. Pierson v. Merritt (Ohio Com.Pl. 1956) 134 N.E.2d 591, 73 Ohio Law Abs. 431, 4 O.O.2d 425.

4. Self–dealing by fiduciary

Administrator, executor, or other trustee may not profit directly or indirectly from his own sale. Gahanna Bank Co. v. Miesse (Franklin 1931) 41 Ohio App. 316, 181 N.E. 31, 11 Ohio Law Abs. 26. Executors And Administrators ⟸ 365

2127.34 Terms of sale

The order for the sale of real estate, granted by the probate court in an action by an executor, administrator, or guardian, shall prescribe the terms of the sale, and payment of the purchase money, either in whole or in part, for cash, or on deferred payments. In the sales by executors or administrators, deferred payments shall not exceed two years with interest.

(1975 S 145, eff. 1–1–76; 1953 H 1; GC 10510–40)

Historical and Statutory Notes

Pre–1953 H 1 Amendments: 114 v 459

Library References

Executors and Administrators ⟸ 364.
Guardian and Ward ⟸ 98.
Mental Health ⟸ 258.1.
Westlaw Topic Nos. 162, 196, 257A.
C.J.S. Executors and Administrators § 635.

Research References

Encyclopedias

OH Jur. 3d Decedents' Estates § 1558, Terms of Sale.
OH Jur. 3d Guardian & Ward § 160, Generally; Terms of Sale.

Treatises and Practice Aids

Carlin, Baldwin's Ohio Practice, Merrick-Rippner Probate Law § 2:56, Sale of Land—Hearing and Order Granting Authority to Sell.
Carlin, Baldwin's Ohio Practice, Merrick-Rippner Probate Law § 95:18, Terms of Sale.
Carlin, Baldwin's Ohio Practice, Merrick-Rippner Probate Law § 97:18, Land Sale by Guardian—Terms.

Notes of Decisions

Court's power   1

---

1. Court's power

Probate court, under section, is without power to order or confirm sale of real estate by executor, where terms of such sale were part cash and balance other real and personal property. Binns v. Isabel (Franklin 1943) 72 Ohio App. 222, 51 N.E.2d 501, 39 Ohio Law Abs. 237, 27 O.O. 87. Executors And Administrators ⟸ 137

2127.35 Confirmation of sale; deed

An executor, administrator, or guardian shall make return of his proceedings under the order for the sale of real estate granted by the probate court. The court, after careful examination, if satisfied that the sale has in all respects been legally made, shall confirm the sale, and order the executor, administrator, or guardian to make a deed to the purchaser.

The deed shall be received in all courts as prima-facie evidence that the executor, administrator, or guardian in all respects observed the direction of the court, and complied with the requirements of the law, and shall convey the interest in the real estate directed to be sold by the court, and shall vest title to the interest in the purchaser as if conveyed by the deceased in his lifetime, or by the ward free from disability, and by the owners of the remaining interests in the real estate.

(1975 S 145, eff. 1–1–76; 1953 H 1; GC 10510–41, 10510–44)

Historical and Statutory Notes

Pre–1953 H 1 Amendments: 119 v 394, § 1; 114 v 459

Cross References

Deed of fiduciary, form, 5302.09

Library References

Executors and Administrators ⟸ 374 to 375, 397.
Guardian and Ward ⟸ 102 to 103, 111.
Mental Health ⟸ 268 to 269.
Westlaw Topic Nos. 162, 196, 257A.
C.J.S. Executors and Administrators §§ 643 to 644, 681 to 682.

Research References

Encyclopedias

OH Jur. 3d Decedents' Estates § 1544, Order of Sale, Generally—Contents of Order.
OH Jur. 3d Decedents' Estates § 1585, Execution and Construction of Deed.
OH Jur. 3d Decedents' Estates § 1586, Effect of Deed.
OH Jur. 3d Equity § 51, Legal Effect of Unperformed Decree.
OH Jur. 3d Guardian & Ward § 164, Confirmation of Sale; Deed.

Treatises and Practice Aids

Carlin, Baldwin's Ohio Practice, Merrick-Rippner Probate Law § 2:58, Sale of Land—Confirmation of Sale.
Carlin, Baldwin's Ohio Practice, Merrick-Rippner Probate Law § 96:1, Confirmation of Sale—Introduction.
Carlin, Baldwin's Ohio Practice, Merrick-Rippner Probate Law § 96:2, Confirmation of Sale—Sufficiency.
Carlin, Baldwin's Ohio Practice, Merrick-Rippner Probate Law § 96:5, Deed of Fiduciary.
Carlin, Baldwin's Ohio Practice, Merrick-Rippner Probate Law § 95:33, Report of Public Sale—Form.
Carlin, Baldwin's Ohio Practice, Merrick-Rippner Probate Law § 96:16, Entry Confirming Sale, Ordering Deed and Distribution—Form.
Carlin, Baldwin's Ohio Practice, Merrick-Rippner Probate Law § 96:17, Entry Confirming Sale, Ordering Deed and Distribution Where Entire Interest in Real Estate Sold—Form.
Carlin, Baldwin's Ohio Practice, Merrick-Rippner Probate Law § 96:18, Fiduciary's Deed Under Private Sale—Form.
Carlin, Baldwin's Ohio Practice, Merrick-Rippner Probate Law § 96:19, Fiduciary's Deed Under Public Sale—Form.
Carlin, Baldwin's Ohio Practice, Merrick-Rippner Probate Law § 96:20, Writ of Possession—Form.
Carlin, Baldwin's Ohio Practice, Merrick-Rippner Probate Law § 96:21, Entry Referring Action to Torrens Examiner—Form.
Carlin, Baldwin's Ohio Practice, Merrick-Rippner Probate Law § 96:22, Entry Approving Report of Torrens Examiner—Form.
Carlin, Baldwin's Ohio Practice, Merrick-Rippner Probate Law § 97:17, Land Sale by Guardian—Deed.
Kuehnle and Levey, Ohio Real Estate Law and Practice § 8:6, Deed of Executor, Administrator, or Guardian as Evidence of Regularity of Proceedings.
Kuehnle and Levey, Ohio Real Estate Law and Practice § 21:8, Covenants—Covenants in Fiduciary Deed.
Kuehnle and Levey, Ohio Real Estate Law and Practice § 7:29, Public Records—Deed of Executor, Administrator, or Guardian as Evidence of Regularity of Proceedings.
Kuehnle and Levey, Ohio Real Estate Law and Practice § 20:62, Conveyancing—Warranties—Fiduciary Deed.

Notes of Decisions

Administrator's powers   6
Dower   1
Priority of liens   7
Procedural issues   5
Sheriff's sale   2
Title   4

Warranties 3

1. Dower

B. died testate leaving land incumbered by a mortgage for his debt, made by himself and wife, who survived him, she duly elected to take under the law and not under the will, and when the land was sold upon a proper petition of the administrator with the will annexed the proceeds added to the personalty made a sum large enough to pay all debts (including the mortgage), the statutory allowance for one year, the costs of administering the estate, dower in the entire proceeds of the land, and leave a surplus for the devisees; the widow, as against the devisees, is entitled to dower in the entire proceeds of the land. Kling v. Ballentine (Ohio 1883) 40 Ohio St. 391. Dower And Curtesy ⚖ 23

A purchaser of lands of a decedent who has had the dower interest of the divorced wife of the decedent set off from his land cannot maintain an action to recover back a portion of the purchase price to compensate him for the loss sustained by reason of the assignment of dower since the rule caveat emptor is applicable. Arnold v. Donaldson (Ohio 1888) 46 Ohio St. 73, 20 W.L.B. 431, 18 N.E. 540.

Where the wife joins her husband in a mortgage releasing dower, a sale of land by the administrator of her husband conveys an unincumbered title to the purchaser. St. Clair v Morris, 9 O 16 (1839).

2. Sheriff's sale

A sheriff's deed relates back to the sheriff's sale, and is operative from that time as a conveyance to pass whatever interest the judgment debtor had in the lands at the time of the levy. Boyd's Lessee v. Longworth (Ohio 1842) 11 Ohio 235. Execution ⚖ 321; Judicial Sales ⚖ 61

A sale by sheriff excludes all warranty, and where a judgment creditor purchases land upon his own execution and thereafter discovers a defect in title, the sale will not be set aside absent fraud. Vattier v. Lytle's Ex'rs (Ohio 1834) 6 Ohio 477.

Deeds should not be executed by the sheriff until an examination of his proceedings is made and approved by the court, and an order for execution entered on the journal. Curtis' Lessee v. Norton (Ohio 1824) 1 Ohio 278.

Even though growing grapes are not sown annually, they are emblements and are not embraced in the appraisement in judicial sales of real estate, and do not pass to the purchaser of the land at the judicial sale. Mason v Lemmon, 3 NP 116, 4 D 322 (CP, Ottawa 1896), affirmed by 56 OS 793, 49 NE 1113 (1897).

Where real estate is sold at a judicial sale, it does not become complete until the deed is executed and delivered, but when such deed is finally executed and delivered, it relates back to the day of sale. In re Harper's Estate (Ohio Prob. 1927) 26 Ohio NP(NS) 431.

Where an appraiser of lands of a decedent buys such land at a sheriff's sale, unknown to the judgment debtor, and undertakes to prevent others from bidding at such sale, causing the price for the land to be less, the sale can be set aside and a new sale ordered on petition of the judgment debtor, even though the purchase money has been paid and the deed delivered. Hurst v Fisher, 46 B 19 (OS Unrep 1901).

3. Warranties

Where an administrator deeds with covenants of warranty, the covenants were his in his individual capacity. Lockwood v. Gilson (Ohio 1861) 12 Ohio St. 526.

4. Title

As sale without warranty does not render the estate liable for false representations as to title. Dunlap v. Robinson (Ohio 1861) 12 Ohio St. 530.

Title of a purchaser is not divested by a reversal of the order of sale. Irwin v. Jeffers (Ohio 1854) 3 Ohio St. 389. Appeal And Error ⚖ 1180(3); Executors And Administrators ⚖ 358(3)

An heir who assents to a void Virginia decree and sale of Ohio lands and who acts as commissioner to carry it into execution passes his own title in equity. Beall v. Price (Ohio 1844) 13 Ohio 368, 42 Am.Dec. 204.

Where lands were erroneously sold by an administrator for less than the appraised value and the court thereafter confirmed the sale, such sale does not constitute a flaw in the title of a bona fide purchaser. Pierson v. Merritt (Ohio Com.Pl. 1956) 134 N.E.2d 591, 73 Ohio Law Abs. 431, 4 O.O.2d 425.

5. Procedural issues

The probate court cannot order sale subject to liens. Stone v. Strong (Ohio 1884) 42 Ohio St. 53.

In case of an executed contract of sale by executors of the property of their testator, the purchaser making no offer or attempt to rescind the contract, the purchaser, in an action by the executors as such for the recovery of the purchase money, can not avail himself of false and fraudulent representations made by the executors at the time of the sale, in respect to its subject matter, either as a defense, or by way of recoupment, or counterclaim; his remedy, if any, is against the executors personally. Westfall v. Dungan (Ohio 1863) 14 Ohio St. 276. Executors And Administrators ⚖ 146; Vendor And Purchaser ⚖ 305

In case of an executed contract of sale by executors, the purchaser making no attempt to rescind the contract, in an action for the purchase money, the defendant cannot set up fraudulent representations as a defense as his remedy is against the executor personally. Westfall v. Dungan (Ohio 1863) 14 Ohio St. 276. Executors And Administrators ⚖ 146; Vendor And Purchaser ⚖ 305

Where the statutes authorizing an order of sale is repealed after the order is made, a nunc pro tunc order will not give it effect. Ludlow's Heirs Lessee v. Wade (Ohio 1832) 5 Ohio 494.

The power to sell land to pay debts is strictly a legal power, and if sale is made, the question is triable at law, and after having there been decided that no authority to sell existed, equity cannot set it up. Lieby v. Ludlow's Heirs (Ohio 1831) 4 Ohio 469.

A purchaser acquires no lien by paying the purchase money if the sale is set aside. Lieby v. Ludlow's Heirs (Ohio 1831) 4 Ohio 469.

A conveyance made under a general order to an executor authorizing him to make a deed is void, and equity cannot make the deed good. Tiernan v. Beam (Ohio 1826) 2 Ohio 383, 15 Am.Dec. 557.

Where no order is entered by the probate court in its journal confirming the sale of the intestate's land for the payment of debts, although such order had been made, the probate court may enter the confirmation order nunc pro tunc, and may receive the testimony of witnesses who have personal knowledge on the subject in determining whether judicial action was taken. Jacks v. Adamson (Ohio 1897) 56 Ohio St. 397, 37 W.L.B. 377, 47 N.E. 48, 60 Am.St.Rep. 749.

Where an administrator makes a sale of his decedent's lands that for irregularity passes no title, a judgment creditor of the decedent with a subsisting lien against his real estate may proceed by scire facias against the heirs and purchasers in possession to revive the judgment and to have execution awarded against the lands. Miami Exporting Co. v. Halley's Heirs (Ohio 1835) 7 Ohio 11, PT. I.

6. Administrator's powers

The administration act of 1840, and the amendatory act of April 12, 1858 (S. & C. 622), give a full adversary character to the petition of an administrator for authority to sell lands for the payment of debts. Therefore the lien of a mortgagee who is not made a party to such petition remains unaffected by the order of sale and the proceedings thereunder. Holloway v. Stuart (Ohio 1869) 19 Ohio St. 472. Executors And Administrators ⚖ 335

Failure by administratrix of father's estate to provide assurances to son's proposed lender that money lent to son would go to estate in exchange for clear title to real property was not a breach of settlement agreement between son and estate, even though settlement agreement obligated administratrix to cooperate in the final disposition of the estate; settlement agreement stated that son had option to purchase the property and intended to sign purchase agreement, but did not require administratrix to cooperate in the sale of the property, and only probate court could give the requested assurances. Wilhelm v. Foster (Ohio App. 7 Dist., Mahoning, 11-02-2004) No. 03 MA 29, 2004-Ohio-5928, 2004 WL 2521404, Unreported, appeal not allowed 105 Ohio St.3d 1470, 824 N.E.2d 540, 2005-Ohio-1186. Executors And Administrators ⚖ 515

Where the administrator after sale, and before payment of purchase money obtains a deed to himself from the purchaser assuming the obligation to pay for the land the transaction is void. Caldwell v. Caldwell (Ohio 1888) 45 Ohio St. 512, 19 W.L.B. 185, 15 N.E. 297.

Where an administrator's deed contains no words of perpetuity, although the parties contemplated the creation of an entire legal fee simple, if the power was given and the execution was defective, the mistake will be aided in equity. Piatt v. St. Clair's Heirs (Ohio 1836) 7 Ohio 165, PT. II.

An administrator does not vitiate the conveyance by attaching trusts intended for the benefit of heirs and creditors. Piatt v. St. Clair's Heirs (Ohio 1836) 7 Ohio 165, PT. II.

Where an administrator has sold under order of court he may convey directly to the assignee of the purchaser. Ewing v. Higby (Ohio 1835) 7 Ohio 198, PT. I.

7. Priority of liens

In proceedings by an executor or administrator for the sale of real estate to pay debts where the same is encumbered by mortgages or other liens, the court is to settle the priorities among lien-holders and order a sale free from such liens, and when such proceedings are in the probate court, it is not authorized to make an order to sell the same subject to the mortgage or other liens. Stone v. Strong (Ohio 1884) 42 Ohio St. 53.

2127.36 Security for deferred payments

The order for the sale of real estate granted in an action by an executor, administrator, or guardian shall require that before the delivery of the deed the deferred installments of the purchase money be secured by mortgage on the real estate sold, and mortgage notes bearing interest at a rate approved by the probate court. If after the sale is made, and before delivery of deed, the purchaser offers to pay the full amount of the purchase money in cash, the court may order that it be accepted, if for the best interest of the estate or the ward, and direct its distribution.

The court in such an order may also direct the sale, without recourse, of any or all of the notes taken for deferred payments, if for the best interest of the estate or the ward, at not less than their face value with accrued interest, and direct the distribution of the proceeds.

(1975 S 145, eff. 1–1–76; 1953 H 1; GC 10510–42, 10510–43)

Historical and Statutory Notes

Pre–1953 H 1 Amendments: 122 v H 191; 114 v 459

Library References

Executors and Administrators ⇌398.
Guardian and Ward ⇌112.
Mental Health ⇌275.
Westlaw Topic Nos. 162, 196, 257A.
C.J.S. Executors and Administrators § 323.

Research References

Encyclopedias

OH Jur. 3d Decedents' Estates § 1484, Property Subject to Sale—Promissory Notes and Mortgage Securing the Notes.
OH Jur. 3d Decedents' Estates § 1560, Security for Deferred Payments.
OH Jur. 3d Guardian & Ward § 160, Generally; Terms of Sale.

Treatises and Practice Aids

Carlin, Baldwin's Ohio Practice, Merrick-Rippner Probate Law § 73:18, Deed of Fiduciary Under Power of Sale in Will—Form.
Carlin, Baldwin's Ohio Practice, Merrick-Rippner Probate Law § 95:18, Terms of Sale.
Carlin, Baldwin's Ohio Practice, Merrick-Rippner Probate Law § 96:23, Mortgage to Secure Deferred Payments—Form.
Carlin, Baldwin's Ohio Practice, Merrick-Rippner Probate Law § 97:18, Land Sale by Guardian—Terms.

Notes of Decisions

Bona fide purchaser 1
Resale 2
Void sale 3

---

1. Bona fide purchaser

Where an administrator sells land to a person by order of court, taking notes and mortgages in partial payment therefor, and sells such notes to an innocent purchaser and then converts the proceeds to his own use, the purchaser is not responsible and takes good title. Jelke v. Goldsmith (Ohio 1895) 52 Ohio St. 499, 33 W.L.B. 193, 40 N.E. 167, 49 Am.St.Rep. 730, 2 Ohio Leg. N. 430.

2. Resale

A beneficiary, interested in distribution, may apply for an order of resale. Caldwell v. Caldwell (Ohio 1888) 45 Ohio St. 512, 19 W.L.B. 185, 15 N.E. 297.

3. Void sale

Purchase money paid to an administrator cannot be recovered of the heir where the sale is inoperative and the heir recovers the land. Nowler v. Coit (Ohio 1824) 1 Ohio 519, 13 Am.Dec. 640.

2127.37 Compensation of executor, administrator, or guardian

When an action to sell real estate is prosecuted by an executor or administrator he shall be allowed the compensation provided by law, by the probate court from which his letters issued. When such action is by a guardian, his duties and obligations therein shall be considered by the court appointing him in awarding such compensation as the court deems reasonable.

(1953 H 1, eff. 10–1–53; GC 10510–45)

Historical and Statutory Notes

Pre–1953 H 1 Amendments: 114 v 460

Library References

Executors and Administrators ⇌495(0.5), 495(1), 495(5).
Guardian and Ward ⇌151.
Mental Health ⇌182.
Westlaw Topic Nos. 162, 196, 257A.
C.J.S. Executors and Administrators § 821.

Research References

Encyclopedias

OH Jur. 3d Decedents' Estates § 1595, Commissions of Executor or Administrator.
OH Jur. 3d Decedents' Estates § 1596, Commissions of Executor or Administrator—Amount and Computation.

Treatises and Practice Aids

Carlin, Baldwin's Ohio Practice, Merrick-Rippner Probate Law § 80:2, Commissions—Computation of Allowance.
Carlin, Baldwin's Ohio Practice, Merrick-Rippner Probate Law § 80:3, Commissions—Determination of Compensation Other Than by Percentage.
Carlin, Baldwin's Ohio Practice, Merrick-Rippner Probate Law § 96:9, Distribution of Proceeds—Method.
Carlin, Baldwin's Ohio Practice, Merrick-Rippner Probate Law § 96:12, Expenses of Sale—Compensation of Executor or Administrator.
Carlin, Baldwin's Ohio Practice, Merrick-Rippner Probate Law § 97:20, Land Sale by Guardian—Fees and Expenses.

Law Review and Journal Commentaries

Ten Questions Arising in Settlement of Executor's Accounts, Harry Lewis Deibel. 31 Ohio L Rep 7 (January 30, 1930).

Notes of Decisions

Computation 1

Entitlement to payment   2

---

1. Computation

RS 6165 and RS 6188 should be construed together in computing the administrator's percentage. (See also Mutual Aid Bldg & Loan Co v Gashe, 56 OS 273, 46 NE 985 (1897).) Stone v. Strong (Ohio 1884) 42 Ohio St. 53.

Where there are personal assets it is wrong to graduate the percentage on the proceeds of the real estate without regard to the personal estate; the higher rate should first be applied to the personal estate. Stone v. Strong (Ohio 1884) 42 Ohio St. 53.

2. Entitlement to payment

The percentage of the executor is to be paid for selling the lands, before paying liens. Stone v. Strong (Ohio 1884) 42 Ohio St. 53.

Where a mortgagee becomes a purchaser, the administrator is not entitled to a percentage on the money required to pay the mortgage. Stone v. Strong (Ohio 1884) 42 Ohio St. 53.

Even if there be unfaithful administration of an estate, it will not deprive the executor or administrator of a right to compensation for his services, so far as they have been beneficial to the persons interested in the estate. Campbell v. McCormick (Ohio Cir. 1886) 1 Ohio C.D. 281. Executors And Administrators ☞ 500

2127.38 Distribution of proceeds of sale

The sale price of real estate sold following an action by an executor, administrator, or guardian shall be applied and distributed as follows:

(A) To discharge the costs and expenses of the sale, including reasonable fees to be fixed by the probate court for services performed by attorneys for the fiduciary in connection with the sale, and compensation, if any, to the fiduciary for his services in connection with the sale as the court may fix, which costs, expenses, fees, and compensation shall be paid prior to any liens upon the real estate sold [1] and notwithstanding the purchase of the real estate by a lien holder;

(B) To the payment of taxes, interest, penalties, and assessments then due against the real estate, and to the payment of mortgages and judgments against the ward or deceased person, according to their respective priorities of lien, so far as they operated as a lien on the real estate of the deceased at the time of the sale, or on the estate of the ward at the time of the sale, which shall be apportioned and determined by the court, or on reference to a master, or otherwise;

(C) In the case of an executor or administrator, the remaining proceeds of sale shall be applied as follows:

(1) To the payment of legacies with which the real estate of the deceased was charged, if the action is to sell real estate to pay legacies;

(2) To discharge the claims and debts of the estate in the order provided by law.

Whether the executor or administrator was appointed in this state or elsewhere, the surplus of the proceeds of sale must be considered for all purposes as real estate, and be disposed of accordingly.

(1982 H 379, eff. 9–21–82; 1975 S 145; 131 v S 25; 1953 H 1; GC 10510–46)

[1] Prior and current versions differ although no amendment to this punctuation was indicated in 1982 H 379; "sold" appeared as "sold," in 1975 S 145.

Historical and Statutory Notes

Pre–1953 H 1 Amendments: 116 v 385; 114 v 460

Library References

Executors and Administrators ☞400.
Guardian and Ward ☞114.
Mental Health ☞273.
Westlaw Topic Nos. 162, 196, 257A.
C.J.S. Executors and Administrators § 684.

Research References

Encyclopedias

OH Jur. 3d Decedents' Estates § 1582, Rights in Relation to Taxes.
OH Jur. 3d Decedents' Estates § 1590, Generally; Statutory Order.
OH Jur. 3d Decedents' Estates § 1594, Attorneys' Fees.
OH Jur. 3d Decedents' Estates § 1595, Commissions of Executor or Administrator.
OH Jur. 3d Decedents' Estates § 1597, Commissions of Executor or Administrator—Priority.
OH Jur. 3d Decedents' Estates § 1604, Treatment of Surplus as Realty.
OH Jur. 3d Judgments § 239, Effect of Death of Judgment Debtor.
OH Jur. 3d Judicial Sales § 64, Effect of Owner's Death Pending Sale.
OH Jur. 3d Taxation § 183, Payment Out of Proceeds of Sale by Executor or Other Fiduciary.

Treatises and Practice Aids

Carlin, Baldwin's Ohio Practice, Merrick-Rippner Probate Law § 2:59, Sale of Land—Distribution of Proceeds.
Carlin, Baldwin's Ohio Practice, Merrick-Rippner Probate Law § 80:2, Commissions—Computation of Allowance.
Carlin, Baldwin's Ohio Practice, Merrick-Rippner Probate Law § 80:3, Commissions—Determination of Compensation Other Than by Percentage.
Carlin, Baldwin's Ohio Practice, Merrick-Rippner Probate Law § 93:2, Appraisers—Appointment, Compensation, Removal.
Carlin, Baldwin's Ohio Practice, Merrick-Rippner Probate Law § 96:6, Distribution of Proceeds—Statutory Scheme.
Carlin, Baldwin's Ohio Practice, Merrick-Rippner Probate Law § 96:8, Distribution of Proceeds—Nature.
Carlin, Baldwin's Ohio Practice, Merrick-Rippner Probate Law § 96:9, Distribution of Proceeds—Method.
Carlin, Baldwin's Ohio Practice, Merrick-Rippner Probate Law § 80:15, Attorney Fees—Allowed.
Carlin, Baldwin's Ohio Practice, Merrick-Rippner Probate Law § 91:14, Land Sale—Not to Pay for Real Estate Taxes.
Carlin, Baldwin's Ohio Practice, Merrick-Rippner Probate Law § 92:12, Sale of Land Subject to Encumbrances—Release and Satisfaction of Liens Against Real Property.
Carlin, Baldwin's Ohio Practice, Merrick-Rippner Probate Law § 96:12, Expenses of Sale—Compensation of Executor or Administrator.
Carlin, Baldwin's Ohio Practice, Merrick-Rippner Probate Law § 96:13, Expenses of Sale—Attorney Fees.
Carlin, Baldwin's Ohio Practice, Merrick-Rippner Probate Law § 96:14, Taxes.
Carlin, Baldwin's Ohio Practice, Merrick-Rippner Probate Law § 96:15, Mortgages, Judgments, and Liens.
Carlin, Baldwin's Ohio Practice, Merrick-Rippner Probate Law § 97:19, Land Sale by Guardian—Proceeds.
Carlin, Baldwin's Ohio Practice, Merrick-Rippner Probate Law § 97:20, Land Sale by Guardian—Fees and Expenses.
Kuehnle and Levey, Ohio Real Estate Law and Practice § 52:14, Statutory Fiduciary Sales—Validity of Mortgages and Judgment Liens—Date of Debtor's Death or Date of Sale.

Notes of Decisions

Assessments and taxes   10
Constitutional issues   1
Executor's duties   7
Fiduciary and attorney fees   3
Nature of surplus: realty versus personalty   4
Procedural issues   9
Purchasers' rights and duties   2
Rights of judgment creditors   5
Rights of mortgagees   6

Widow 8

1. Constitutional issues

Under provisions of O Const Art IV, § 6, court of appeals, in an appeal on questions of law from a judgment of probate court, is without jurisdiction to retry the issues of fact and substitute its judgment for that of the probate court awarding a lump sum judgment to an administrator for statutory compensation and for services in connection with sale of land ordered to be made by court; the court of appeals may not modify such judgment on the weight of the evidence and render final judgment for such modified amount, but may reverse judgment of probate court and remand cause to that court for further proceedings. In re Murnan's Estate (Ohio 1949) 151 Ohio St. 529, 87 N.E.2d 84, 39 O.O. 333. Courts ⚖ 202(5)

Section is a valid legislative enactment and, being remedial in nature, does not impair the obligation of contracts or violate the constitutional provision against retroactive laws, even though real estate is sold for less than the adjudged lien against the property. Flory v. Cripps (Licking 1936) 55 Ohio App. 510, 9 N.E.2d 925, 24 Ohio Law Abs. 469, 9 O.O. 177.

Section, relative to the sale of lands by executors and administrators, providing that a commission to the executor or administrator for his administration and reasonable attorney fees "shall be paid prior to any liens upon the real estate sold and notwithstanding the purchase of such real estate by a lienholder," is constitutional although the lienholder receives less than the sum due on the sale on a mortgage executed prior to its effective date. Bruin v. Leveline (Butler 1936) 55 Ohio App. 339, 9 N.E.2d 895, 24 Ohio Law Abs. 412, 9 O.O. 80.

The provisions of this section are not violative of constitutional guaranties of due process, equal protection of the law or the inviolability of contracts. Flory v. Cripps (Ohio 1937) 132 Ohio St. 487, 9 N.E.2d 500, 8 O.O. 484.

2. Purchasers' rights and duties

Upon a judicial sale of lands for the satisfaction of a judgment or decree against the owner, the proceeds of sale can not without his consent be applied in discharge of the claim of a prior purchaser of the same premises at tax sale, where such purchaser is a stranger to the decree or order under which the judicial sale is made. Ketcham v. Fitch (Ohio 1862) 13 Ohio St. 201. Execution ⚖ 324; Judicial Sales ⚖ 62

Where a sale of land for the payment of debts is in conformity with the requirements of the statute, the purchaser takes the land discharged of all creditors' liens, and the priorities given by such liens are transferred by statute to the fund arising from the sale of lands; the purchaser is not responsible for the administrator's application of such fund. Defrees v. Greenham (Ohio 1860) 11 Ohio St. 486. Executors And Administrators ⚖ 385

A purchaser of the legal title having notice takes subject to a trust. Stiver v. Stiver's Heirs (Ohio 1837) 8 Ohio 217.

The purchaser holds the land discharged of all liens, the proceeds of the land being subject thereto. Bank of Muskingum v. Carpenter's Adm'rs (Ohio 1835) 7 Ohio 21, PT. I, 28 Am.Dec. 616.

Where installments of street assessments stand unsatisfied on the tax duplicate, they should be paid out of the proceeds of a sale by administrators, executors or guardians; and where such assessments are not yet due and payable they remain a lien upon the real estate in the hands of the purchaser, and he has no right to have such unmatured assessments paid out of the proceeds of the sale. (See also Hoglan v Cohan, 30 OS 436 (1877).) Makley v. Whitmore (Ohio 1900) 61 Ohio St. 587, 43 W.L.B. 187, 56 N.E. 461.

3. Fiduciary and attorney fees

Administrator and his attorney may claim their fee from proceeds of sale of real estate to prejudice of mortgagee in an action to sell real estate in probate court to pay decedents debts and property is sold at public auction to a person other than mortgagee for a sum less than enough to pay mortgage in full. Federal Land Bank of Louisville v. McClain (Greene 1935) 20 Ohio Law Abs. 550.

The proceeds from the sale of mortgaged real estate sold by an administrator in the proceeding to settle an estate, cannot be charged with the commission for making the sale, and the lien of the mortgages reduced by that amount, where the sale was for less than the face of the mortgage with interest and necessary expenses, and there is personalty from which the commission can be paid. Lakes v. Lakes (Butler 1933) 15 Ohio Law Abs. 275, 39 Ohio Law Rep. 25.

By amendment to this section, reasonable attorney's fees were included in costs and expenses in proceedings for sale of real estate to pay debts, and are to be taxed as a part of the court costs. Griffith v. Ohio State Bank (Fayette 1932) 13 Ohio Law Abs. 211, 37 Ohio Law Rep. 353.

By virtue of the provisions of section, the probate court has exclusive jurisdiction to fix compensation due a fiduciary for his services, and to fix fees for services performed by attorneys for the fiduciary, in connection with the sale of lands ordered by the court to be made by such fiduciary. In re Murnan's Estate (Ohio 1949) 151 Ohio St. 529, 87 N.E.2d 84, 39 O.O. 333. Courts ⚖ 202(5)

Under the provisions of section as amended, reasonable compensation and fees to be fixed by the court for services performed by the fiduciary and by his attorneys in connection with the sale of real estate to pay debts may be allowed as a part of the costs in the proceeding and paid prior to any liens upon the real estate sold, even though a lien holder was the purchaser thereof, and at a price less than his lien thereon. Flory v. Cripps (Ohio 1937) 132 Ohio St. 487, 9 N.E.2d 500, 8 O.O. 484. Executors And Administrators ⚖ 401

The commission for the service of an executor or administrator in the sale of real estate and attorney fees for services performed for such fiduciary therein may be computed only upon and paid out of "the money arising from the sale of such real estate." State ex rel. Fulton v. Griffith (Ohio 1933) 127 Ohio St. 161, 187 N.E. 121, 38 Ohio Law Rep. 479.

Where land is sold by an administrator to pay the debts of the decedent, fees of the attorney filing such proceedings are not entitled to priority over mortgages, where the property was bought in by the mortgagees for sums insufficient to discharge mortgage claims, taxes, penalties and interest, nor is the claim for such fees superior to that of the compensation of the administrator of the estate. Fulton v. Griffith (Ohio Com.Pl. 1932) 29 Ohio NP(NS) 435, 11 Ohio Law Abs. 673.

When real estate is sold by the fiduciary through a court other than that from which letters issued, and a mortgagee purchases the property for less than the mortgage debt, before receiving his instrument of conveyance from the fiduciary the mortgagee must pay the costs and expenses of the sale, including such compensation for the fiduciary as the court through which the sale is had shall deem warranted and fix, and the fixing of such amount is within the sound discretion of the court, and is not determined by the commission schedule established by GC 10509–192 (RC 2113.35). West v. Child (Ohio Prob. 1939) 5 Ohio Supp. 85, 30 Ohio Law Abs. 231, 16 O.O. 31. Executors And Administrators ⚖ 368; Executors And Administrators ⚖ 496(1)

Probate court has exclusive jurisdiction in making order for allowance of attorney's fees from estate assets. In re Whinery's Estate (Ohio Com.Pl. 1938) 4 Ohio Supp. 387, 26 Ohio Law Abs. 347, 11 O.O. 96.

As to the distribution of costs, commissions, and attorney fees among the lienholders and creditors, the lienholders should contribute ratably thereto on the ground that the attorney's fees were rendered in part for their benefit. Alms & Doepke v Fitton, 9 CC 255, 6 CD 415 (Butler 1888).

4. Nature of surplus: realty versus personalty

The surplus proceeds of sale of real estate is to be considered real estate, and the widow is not entitled to any part thereof as one of the distributees of personal estate. Griswold v. Frink (Ohio 1871) 22 Ohio St. 79. Executors And Administrators ⚖ 404

Where real estate is sold to pay debts and thereafter a posthumous child is born, which dies intestate the proceeds are to be regarded as real estate of the first decedent and as personal estate of the child. Pence v. Pence's Adm'r (Ohio 1860) 11 Ohio St. 290.

Land directed to be sold and converted into money is treated as a personal estate. (See also Collier v Collier's Executors, 3 OS 369 (1854).) Ferguson v. Stuart's Ex'rs (Ohio 1846) 14 Ohio 140.

Where a sole devisee appointed as executor sells lands as devisee, the proceeds come into his hands as executor; and, where the personal estate is insufficient, he must apply such proceeds to the payment of testator's debts. Hocking Valley R. Co. v. White (Ohio 1913) 87 Ohio St. 413, 101 N.E. 354, 10 Ohio Law Rep. 611, Am.Ann.Cas. 1914A, 190. Executors And Administrators ⚖ 40

The balance left from a sale of real estate to pay debts is real and not personal property and goes by descent to the heirs. Kling v. Bordner (Ohio 1901) 65 Ohio St. 86, 46 W.L.B. 180, 61 N.E. 148.

5. Rights of judgment creditors

In proceedings by an executor or administrator for the sale of real estate to pay debts where the same is encumbered by mortgages or other liens, the court is to settle the priorities among lien-holders and order a sale free from such liens, and when such proceedings are in the probate court, it is not authorized to make an order to sell the same subject to the mortgage or other liens. Stone v. Strong (Ohio 1884) 42 Ohio St. 53.

A judgment in personam against a decedent on which execution had not been made during his lifetime and under which no specific lien on real estate was acquired cannot be revived and enforced against the heirs; the judgment creditor cannot obtain a preference over other creditors of the estate and must obtain satisfaction of the judgment through the administrator in the normal course of administration. Miller v. Taylor (Ohio 1876) 29 Ohio St. 257.

The allowance of the claim of a judgment creditor by the personal representative of debtor is not requisite to the judgment creditor's right to share in the proceeds of the sale of land on which the judgment was a lien. Ambrose v. Byrne (Ohio 1899) 61 Ohio St. 146, 42 W.L.B. 360, 55 N.E. 408.

The widow's allowance does not take precedence, upon sale of real estate, over judgment liens. (See also Webster v Dennis, 4 CC 313, 2 CD 567 (Hamilton 1890).) Jones v. Allen (Ohio Com.Pl. 1898) 8 Ohio Dec. 338, 6 Ohio N.P. 518.

A judgment creditor of a devisee is not a lienholder within GC 10780 (Repealed), as to parties to sell to pay debts, and he is not a necessary party; his remedy is under this section. Kummer v Lapp, 1 NP(NS) 209, 13 D 491 (CP, Franklin 1903).

6. Rights of mortgagees

Where the will gives power to an executor to sell lands to pay debts and the holder of the mortgage agrees with the executor that the latter shall sell the land, which he does, but fails to pay the mortgage, the mortgagee has a specific interest in the purchase money and a like interest in other assets. Western Reserve Bank v. McIntire (Ohio 1884) 40 Ohio St. 528.

The lien of a mortgagee who is not made a party remains unaffected by an order for sale and the proceedings thereunder. Holloway v. Stuart (Ohio 1869) 19 Ohio St. 472.

Administrator and his attorney may claim their fee from proceeds of sale of real estate to prejudice of mortgagee in an action to sell real estate in probate court to pay decedents debts and property is sold at public auction to a person other than mortgagee for a sum less than enough to pay mortgage in full. Federal Land Bank of Louisville v. McClain (Greene 1935) 20 Ohio Law Abs. 550.

The proceeds from the sale of mortgaged real estate sold by an administrator in the proceeding to settle an estate, cannot be charged with the commission for making the sale, and the lien of the mortgages reduced by that amount, where the sale was for less than the face of the mortgage with interest and necessary expenses, and there is personalty from which the commission can be paid. Lakes v. Lakes (Butler 1933) 15 Ohio Law Abs. 275, 39 Ohio Law Rep. 25.

In distributing proceeds from decedent's estate, mortgage indebtedness shall be paid from proceeds of sale of real estate before payment of funeral expenses. In re Estate of Cogan (App. 8 Dist., 10-06-1997) 123 Ohio App.3d 186, 703 N.E.2d 858, dismissed, jurisdictional motion overruled 81 Ohio St.3d 1442, 690 N.E.2d 14. Executors And Administrators 261

When, in the administration of his estate it becomes necessary to sell the real estate of a decedent to pay debts, the statutes authorizing such sale provide that the mortgage indebtedness thereon shall be paid from the proceeds of sale before payment therefrom of funeral expenses. Nolan v. Kroll (Erie 1930) 37 Ohio App. 350, 174 N.E. 750, 8 Ohio Law Abs. 676, 33 Ohio Law Rep. 222. Executors And Administrators 402

Where land is sold by an administrator to pay the debts of the decedent, fees of the attorney filing such proceedings are not entitled to priority over mortgages, where the property was bought in by the mortgagees for sums insufficient to discharge mortgage claims, taxes, penalties and interest, nor is the claim for such fees superior to that of the compensation of the administrator of the estate. Fulton v. Griffith (Ohio Com.Pl. 1932) 29 Ohio NP(NS) 435, 11 Ohio Law Abs. 673.

When real estate is sold by the fiduciary through a court other than that from which letters issued, and a mortgagee purchases the property for less than the mortgage debt, before receiving his instrument of conveyance from the fiduciary the mortgagee must pay the costs and expenses of the sale, including such compensation for the fiduciary as the court through which the sale is had shall deem warranted and fix, and the fixing of such amount is within the sound discretion of the court, and is not determined by the commission schedule established by GC 10509–192 (RC 2113.35). West v. Child (Ohio Prob. 1939) 5 Ohio Supp. 85, 30 Ohio Law Abs. 231, 16 O.O. 31. Executors And Administrators 368; Executors And Administrators 496(1)

7. Executor's duties

The executor is accountable for everything he receives notwithstanding an attempt to become a receiver in a different character. Stiver v. Stiver's Heirs (Ohio 1837) 8 Ohio 217.

Statute requiring executor of decedent's estate to obtain legatees' written consent before selling real estate does not apply to estates of decedents who die testate. In re Estate of Cogan (App. 8 Dist., 10-06-1997) 123 Ohio App.3d 186, 703 N.E.2d 858, dismissed, jurisdictional motion overruled 81 Ohio St.3d 1442, 690 N.E.2d 14. Executors And Administrators 138(1)

Under RC 2127.38 proceeds of land sale proceeding of guardian must be held and finally distributed in same manner as would have been done had there been no sale, but such proceedings are subject to bear proportionate part of expenses of supporting the ward. Guerra v. Guerra (Ohio Com.Pl. 1970) 25 Ohio Misc. 1, 265 N.E.2d 818, 54 O.O.2d 14. Mental Health 273

The exercise of a power to sell real estate by executors upon a finding that the personal property is insufficient to pay the debts of the estate does not effect an equitable conversion of the real estate to personalty. Burroughs v. Raymond (Ohio Prob. 1951) 112 N.E.2d 82, 65 Ohio Law Abs. 108, 50 O.O. 169.

Where an executor purchases real estate belonging to his decedent's estate at his own sale, he is entitled, in stating his account, to credits for moneys paid out for taxes, repairs and improvements, but the allowance for improvement must not exceed the value added to the land. In re Estate of Wilds, 50 B 384 (Prob, Warren 1905).

8. Widow

A will and codicil are to be taken and construed together as parts of one and the same instrument and the intent of the testator gathered from the whole, and a codicil will not be held to revoke the dispositions of a will further than is clearly expressed or necessarily to be inferred from it; therefore, a bequest to the wife of a testator of one-third of his real and personal property, directed to be sold and converted into money by his executors is not impliedly revoked by a codicil which reserves from sale a part of such real property until her death, and secures to her the use of it during her life. Collier v. Collier's Ex'rs (Ohio 1854) 3 Ohio St. 369.

Where the undevised portion of realty, together with the personalty, is sufficient to pay debts, the portions devised should be exonerated from contribution to pay debts and widow cannot claim undevised portion as heir. Gilson v. Gilson (Ohio Cir. 1907) 20 Ohio C.D. 322, 11 Ohio C.C.N.S. 49.

The distribution of the fund arising from the sale of lands upon which the widow gave a mortgage after her husband's death shall be in accordance with the provisions of RS 6090, as the widow's allowance is a debt of the estate and the mortgage does not become a lien on it. Neeley v Neeley, 1 NP(NS) 97, 48 WLB 929 (Prob 1903).

9. Procedural issues

Statute respecting application of proceeds of sale of land to pay decedent's debts, and statute respecting order of paying debts, must be construed together. Nolan v. Kroll (Erie 1930) 37 Ohio App. 350, 174 N.E. 750, 8 Ohio Law Abs. 676, 33 Ohio Law Rep. 222. Executors And Administrators 403; Statutes 223.2(12)

A judgment reversing the order of distribution should specifically indicate what judgment the probate court should render, and prescribe how distribution shall be made. Sherman v. Millard (Ohio Cir. 1904) 17 Ohio C.D. 175, 6 Ohio C.C.N.S. 338.

10. Assessments and taxes

Installments of assessments for public improvements should be collected the same as other taxes, and in case of a judicial sale of real estate, or a sale by administrators, executors, guardians, or trustees, made after the last day of September in any year, such installments as stand unsatisfied upon such duplicate should be paid out of the proceeds of such sale, as required by RS 2854 (See. GC 5690 to 5693) regulating payment of taxes on land sold at judicial sales. Makley v. Whitmore (Ohio 1900) 61 Ohio St. 587, 43 W.L.B. 187, 56 N.E. 461. Executors And Administrators ⚖ 400; Guardian And Ward ⚖ 114; Judicial Sales ⚖ 62; Municipal Corporations ⚖ 587; Trusts ⚖ 202

2127.39 When proceeds of sale marshaled in conformity with will

When an action to sell real estate is brought by an executor or administrator with the will annexed, if in the last will of the deceased there is a disposition of his estate for the payment of debts, or a provision that may require or induce the probate court to marshal the assets differently from the way the law otherwise would prescribe, such devises, or parts of the will, shall be set forth in the complaint, and a copy of the will exhibited to the court, whereupon the court shall marshal the proceeds of the sale accordingly, so far as it can be done consistently with the rights of creditors.

(1975 S 145, eff. 1–1–76; 1953 H 1; GC 10510–47)

Historical and Statutory Notes

Pre–1953 H 1 Amendments: 114 v 461

Library References

Executors and Administrators ⚖400.
Westlaw Topic No. 162.
C.J.S. Executors and Administrators § 684.

Research References

Encyclopedias
OH Jur. 3d Decedents' Estates § 1535, Practice and Procedure, Generally—Complaint.
OH Jur. 3d Decedents' Estates § 1591, Effect of Specific Provisions in Will.

Treatises and Practice Aids
Kuehnle and Levey, Ohio Real Estate Law and Practice § 53:37, Land Sales—Venue—Service—Testamentary Direction for Discharge of Debts.

FRAUDULENT CONVEYANCES

2127.40 Sale by executor or administrator of real estate fraudulently transferred by decedent

When an action is brought by an executor or administrator to sell real estate to pay debts, the real estate subject to sale shall include all rights and interests in lands, tenements, and hereditaments transferred by the decedent in his lifetime with intent to defraud his creditors, except that lands fraudulently transferred cannot be taken from any person who purchased them for a valuable consideration, in good faith, and without knowledge of the fraud. No claim to such lands shall be made unless within four years next after the decease of the grantor.

If real estate fraudulently transferred is to be included in such an action, the executor or administrator, either before or at the same time, may commence a civil action in the court of common pleas in the county in which the real estate is situated to recover possession of it, or, in his action for its sale, he may allege the fraud and have the fraudulent transfer avoided. But when the real estate is included in the complaint before the recovery of possession by the executor or administrator, the action shall be brought in the court of common pleas in the county in which the real estate is situated.

(1990 H 506, eff. 9–28–90; 1975 S 145; 1953 H 1; GC 10510–49, 10510–50)

Historical and Statutory Notes

Pre–1953 H 1 Amendments: 114 v 461

Library References

Executors and Administrators ⚖329(1).
Westlaw Topic No. 162.
C.J.S. Executors and Administrators § 595.

Research References

Encyclopedias
OH Jur. 3d Decedents' Estates § 1276, Voidable Transfers—Conveyances in Fraud of Creditors.
OH Jur. 3d Decedents' Estates § 1504, Lands Fraudulently Conveyed by Decedent.
OH Jur. 3d Decedents' Estates § 1529, Time Within Which Action Must be Brought.
OH Jur. 3d Decedents' Estates § 1765, Action to Set Aside Fraudulent Transfers.
OH Jur. 3d Decedents' Estates § 1766, Action to Set Aside Fraudulent Transfers—Jurisdiction.
OH Jur. 3d Decedents' Estates § 1823, Action to Set Aside Fraudulent Conveyances.

Treatises and Practice Aids
Blackford, Baldwin's Ohio Practice Business Organizations § 16:12, Free Transferability of Shares.
Carlin, Baldwin's Ohio Practice, Merrick-Rippner Probate Law § 92:6, Property Not Subject to Sale.
Carlin, Baldwin's Ohio Practice, Merrick-Rippner Probate Law § 92:7, Sale of Land Fraudulently Conveyed.
Carlin, Baldwin's Ohio Practice, Merrick-Rippner Probate Law § 90:13, Land Sale Action—Jurisdiction of Probate Court.
Kuehnle and Levey, Ohio Real Estate Law and Practice § 53:26, Land Sales—Interests Subject to Sale by Fiduciaries—Fraudulently Conveyed Lands.

Notes of Decisions

Action to recover assets   1
Action to set aside conveyance   4
Common pleas court jurisdiction   6
Family member transfers   2
Parties with right of action   5
Probate court jurisdiction   7
Procedural issues   3

---

1. Action to recover assets

An action by an administrator to recover personal property transferred by intestate to defraud creditors cannot be maintained. Benjamin v. Le Baron's Adm'r. (Ohio 1846) 15 Ohio 517.

An administrator may maintain an action against a fraudulent grantee to recover the value of land sold to an innocent purchaser. Doney v. Clark (Ohio 1896) 55 Ohio St. 294, 36 W.L.B. 320, 45 N.E. 316.

An equity receiver of insolvent company may recover assets fraudulently transferred. Sayle v Guarantee Savings & Loan Co, 2 CC(NS) 401, 15 CD 503 (Cuyahoga 1903), affirmed by 72 OS 639, 76 NE 1125 (1905).

2. Family member transfers

A court will not pronounce a conveyance from a husband to his wife in consideration of a release of her inchoate right to dower fraudulent from the fact that the wife insisted upon and received an amount greater than her dower if the facts do not show mala fides in her or her husband, since contingent dower rights are so uncertain and difficult to compute. Singree v. Welch (Ohio 1877) 32 Ohio St. 320.

2127.40
Note 2

Evidence held to show that father, who had paid for lots purchased by deceased daughter, and had taken her note for the amount, was her creditor and had the right to sue to set aside her conveyance as in fraud of creditors. Hause v. Coblentz (Williams 1926) 22 Ohio App. 17, 153 N.E. 255, 4 Ohio Law Abs. 350, 4 Ohio Law Abs. 730.

Decedent's conveyance to daughter a few months before death for consideration of $1, of lots which she had borrowed money to purchase, was constructively fraudulent as against creditors, and should be set aside, where she had no other property. Hause v. Coblentz (Williams 1926) 22 Ohio App. 17, 153 N.E. 255, 4 Ohio Law Abs. 350, 4 Ohio Law Abs. 730. Executors And Administrators ☞ 423; Fraudulent Conveyances ☞ 96(1)

3. Procedural issues

In proceedings to sell lands to pay debts, an answer of a guardian ad litem alleging ignorance of the matters and asking that his wards be protected is in effect a general denial. Wood v. Butler (Ohio 1872) 23 Ohio St. 520.

An order of the probate court for sale of lands upon its judgment setting aside a fraudulent conveyance may be impeached in a collateral proceeding to recover the land. Spoors v Coen, 44 OS 497, 9 NE 132 (1886). Courts ☞ 200.5

A petition by an administrator to sell lands of the decedent to pay debts and to sell land fraudulently conveyed by him is not an action at law or a suit in equity, but a statutory proceeding not appealable to the district court. Webster v. Ballard (Ohio Dist. 1879) 2 Cleve. Law Rep. 137.

An averment that there is no personal property sufficient to pay the decedent's debts is imperative under RS 6136 to RS 6141, and this requirement is not dispensed with by an allegation that the land in question had been fraudulently conveyed by the decedent. Baen v. Weller (Ohio Com.Pl. 1901) 12 Ohio Dec. 128.

Power to sell lands conveyed by the deceased to defraud creditors is wholly derived from statutory law. Longley v. Sewell (Ohio Com.Pl. 1895) 4 Ohio Dec. 1, 2 Ohio N.P. 376.

4. Action to set aside conveyance

Lands fraudulently conveyed but in possession of grantor cannot be sold unless the conveyance is set aside under this section. Spoors v Coen, 44 OS 497, 9 NE 132 (1886).

An administrator cannot set aside a fraudulent conveyance for the benefit of estate or heirs at law, but may for creditors. Jones v. Lehman (Ohio Com.Pl. 1905) 15 Ohio Dec. 541.

An administrator may bring ejectment or he may in one action seek to avoid the fraudulent conveyance and ask a sale of the land. Longley v. Sewell (Ohio Com.Pl. 1895) 4 Ohio Dec. 1, 2 Ohio N.P. 376.

An administrator cannot set aside the conveyance in common pleas court and then proceed in probate court to sell the land. Longley v. Sewell (Ohio Com.Pl. 1895) 4 Ohio Dec. 1, 2 Ohio N.P. 376.

5. Parties with right of action

Where a debtor conveys land to a creditor to sell to pay a debt and dies, his personal representatives should proceed and sell the land if not sold by the creditor. Craig v. Jennings (Ohio 1876) 31 Ohio St. 84.

Where a chattel mortgage is declared void, and the mortgagor dies possessed of the mortgaged property, it becomes assets in the hands of the administrator and he should defend his possession against the mortgagee, though the mortgage was valid against the mortgagor. Kilbourne v. Fay (Ohio 1876) 29 Ohio St. 264, 23 Am.Rep. 741.

An allowance to widow and children is a debt of the estate authorizing the sale of lands for its payment. Allen v. Allen's Adm'r (Ohio 1868) 18 Ohio St. 234.

Creditor of decedent can bring action to set aside latter's conveyance in fraud of creditors, since former GC 10777 (RC 2127.40) does not give executor or administrator exclusive power to bring such action. Hause v. Coblentz (Williams 1926) 22 Ohio App. 17, 153 N.E. 255, 4 Ohio Law Abs. 350, 4 Ohio Law Abs. 730.

The administrator of an insolvent estate is a trustee for the creditor of his decedent with respect to lands conveyed to defraud the creditor. Doney v. Clark (Ohio 1896) 55 Ohio St. 294, 36 W.L.B. 320, 45 N.E. 316.

A conveyance by the debtor to defraud creditors cannot be questioned by personal representatives unless the property is actually needed to pay debts. McCall v. Pixley (Ohio 1891) 48 Ohio St. 379, 25 W.L.B. 417, 27 N.E. 887.

Lands conveyed to defraud creditors though in the possession of grantor's administrator may be sold to pay debts. Spoors v Coen, 44 OS 497, 9 NE 132 (1886).

The administrator's right to proceed to subject property fraudulently conveyed by decedent to pay debts is not exclusive and the creditors have a right to prosecute such action. Hoffman v. Kiefer (Ohio Cir. 1899) 10 Ohio C.D. 304.

6. Common pleas court jurisdiction

The petition to sell land to pay debts may include land to which the decedent never held title but purchased in the name of another with intent to defraud creditors if the action is in the common pleas having general equity powers. Beebe v. Canda (Ohio Cir. 1911) 28 Ohio C.D. 582, 18 Ohio C.C.N.S. 104.

When an action in common pleas court is pending to sell land the probate court has no jurisdiction. Longley v. Sewell (Ohio Com.Pl. 1895) 4 Ohio Dec. 1, 2 Ohio N.P. 376.

7. Probate court jurisdiction

Where an action is prosecuted by a creditor the court will not take administration out of probate court, but assets reached will be placed in the hands of administrator. Hoffman v. Kiefer (Ohio Cir. 1899) 10 Ohio C.D. 304. Executors And Administrators ☞ 57

After a conveyance by intestate has been set aside in common pleas, the probate court may order the land sold to pay debts. Lowman v. Sewall (Ohio Cir. 1898) 9 Ohio C.D. 177.

Where conveyances have been declared fraudulent in common pleas court, the administrator may apply to the probate court to sell the land to pay debts. Lowman v. Sewall (Ohio Cir. 1898) 9 Ohio C.D. 177.

PARTITION

2127.41 Proceeds arising from partition of real estate may be reached by the executor or administrator

If, after the institution of proceedings for the partition of the real property of a decedent, it is found that the assets in the hands of the executor or administrator probably are insufficient to pay the debts of the estate, together with the allowance for support of the surviving spouse, minor children, or surviving spouse and minor children as provided in section 2106.13 of the Revised Code, the expenses of administration, and the legacies that are a charge upon the real property, the executor or administrator shall make a written statement to the probate court of the assets, indebtedness, expenses, and legacies, and the court forthwith shall ascertain the amount necessary to pay the debts, expenses, and legacies and give a certificate of the amount to the executor or administrator.

The executor or administrator then shall present the certificate to the court in which the proceedings for partition are or have been pending, and, on his motion, the court shall order the amount named in the certificate to be paid over to the executor or administrator out of the proceeds of the sale of the premises, if thereafter they are sold or already have been sold. This section does not prohibit an executor or administrator from proceeding to sell real property belonging to the estate for the payment of debts or legacies, although it has been sold on partition or otherwise, or the proceeds of the sale have been fully distributed.

(1990 H 346, eff. 5–31–90; 1975 S 145; 1953 H 1; GC 10510–51, 10510–52)

Uncodified Law

1990 H 346, § 3, eff. 5–31–90, reads, in part: (A) Sections 1 and 2 of this act shall apply only to the estates of decedents who die on or after the effective date of this act.

Historical and Statutory Notes

Pre–1953 H 1 Amendments: 114 v 462

Cross References

Partition, Ch 5307

Library References

Executors and Administrators ⟨key⟩403, 414.
Westlaw Topic No. 162.
C.J.S. Executors and Administrators §§ 684, 700.
    Baldwin's Ohio Legislative Service, 1990 Laws of Ohio, H 346—LSC Analysis, p 5–87

Research References

Encyclopedias
  OH Jur. 3d Decedents' Estates § 1505, Land Partitioned or to be Partitioned.
  OH Jur. 3d Decedents' Estates § 1506, Land Partitioned or to be Partitioned—Certification of Indebtedness and Legacies in Partition Proceedings.

Treatises and Practice Aids
Carlin, Baldwin's Ohio Practice, Merrick-Rippner Probate Law § 73:17, Entry Directing Sheriff to Pay Executor Proceeds of Partition Action—Form.
Carlin, Baldwin's Ohio Practice, Merrick-Rippner Probate Law § 90:12, Land Sale and Action in Partition Distinguished.
Carlin, Baldwin's Ohio Practice, Merrick-Rippner Probate Law § 92:26, Application for Certificate of Indebtedness With Statement of Assets, Debts, Expenses, and Legacies—Form.
Carlin, Baldwin's Ohio Practice, Merrick-Rippner Probate Law § 92:27, Entry Authorizing Certificate of Indebtedness—Form.
Carlin, Baldwin's Ohio Practice, Merrick-Rippner Probate Law § 92:28, Certificate of Indebtedness—Form.
Carlin, Baldwin's Ohio Practice, Merrick-Rippner Probate Law § 92:29, Motion to Require Proceeds from Partition Suit to be Paid to Administrator—Form.
Kuehnle and Levey, Ohio Real Estate Law and Practice § 51:5, Partition—Persons Entitled to Partition—Devisees, Next of Kin, Fiduciaries.
Kuehnle and Levey, Ohio Real Estate Law and Practice § 52:24, Statutory Fiduciary Sales—Partition of Decedent's Real Estate.

Notes of Decisions

Administrator's right of sale 1
Election of remedies 2
Probate court's power 3
Procedural issues 4

---

1. Administrator's right of sale

Where an administrator of a decedent's estate is made a defendant in an action for partition brought by one of the heirs and answers that it is necessary to sell such property for the payment of debts of the decedent, such administrator is entitled to an order of sale, and the statutes of limitations have no application in favor of the heirs as they hold title subject to the right of the administrator to sell the land for that purpose. Lafferty v. Shinn (Ohio 1882) 38 Ohio St. 46.

An administrator is entitled to an order of sale of so much of the real estate as may be necessary to pay debts, although the real estate may have been partitioned among the heirs and sold and conveyed by them. Faran v. Robinson (Ohio 1867) 17 Ohio St. 242, 93 Am.Dec. 617.

Where, after the administrator of an estate has made a settlement he believes to be final and all the personal estate of the decedent has been exhausted, a judgment is recovered against the administrator on a liability contracted by the intestate, the administrator is entitled to an order for the sale of enough of the decedent's land to pay the judgment even though such land has been partitioned among the heirs and sold by them. Faran v. Robinson (Ohio 1867) 17 Ohio St. 242, 93 Am.Dec. 617.

Right of administrator to sell to pay debts is superior to right of heirs at law to have partition. Stout v. Stout (Ohio 1910) 82 Ohio St. 358, 92 N.E. 465, 137 Am.St.Rep. 785, 8 Ohio Law Rep. 118. Executors And Administrators ⟨key⟩ 323; Executors And Administrators ⟨key⟩ 338

A suit in partition does not prevent a sale by the administrator to pay debts. Myers v. Myers (Ohio Cir. 1907) 19 Ohio C.D. 396, 9 Ohio C.C.N.S. 449.

Where real estate is sold to pay debts and by mistake part of the debts are overlooked, the real estate sold remains liable. In re Estate of Cavagna (Ohio Com.Pl. 1901) 11 Ohio Dec. 725, 8 Ohio N.P. 557.

2. Election of remedies

Where the personal property of a deceased person is insufficient to pay debts of the estate, and partition proceedings are instituted in the court of common pleas for the partition of decedent's real property, the executor or administrator of the estate of such decedent may elect either to bring an action in the probate court to sell the real property to pay debts, or to secure and file a certificate in the court in which the partition proceedings are pending. Burrier v. Kiefer (Crawford 1951) 90 Ohio App. 571, 107 N.E.2d 565, 48 O.O. 210.

Administrator of decedent may either bring action to sell real estate to pay debts or secure and file certificate in partition proceedings as provided in GC 10510–51 and 10510–52 (RC 2127.41) and in case he elects to file action for the sale of the real estate to pay debts, such action supplants an action in partition. Retterer v. Retterer (Marion 1935) 32 N.E.2d 513, 20 Ohio Law Abs. 393, 4 O.O. 333.

The widow may furnish the funds to pay the debts and come into court and be reimbursed. Corey v. Hayes (Ohio Cir. 1896) 7 Ohio C.D. 272.

3. Probate court's power

On settlement of a final account it is not the duty of the probate judge to provide for the payment of claims which no creditor is asserting. Cox v. John (Ohio 1877) 32 Ohio St. 532.

The probate court cannot compel the dismissal and termination of an action in partition after the common pleas court has acquired full and complete jurisdiction of said partition action and has made and issued a valid order of sale. Child v. Snyder (Ohio Com.Pl. 1962) 181 N.E.2d 315, 88 Ohio Law Abs. 401, 20 O.O.2d 432. Courts ⟨key⟩ 475(6)

4. Procedural issues

Provisions of GC 10510–51 and 10510–52 (RC 2127.41) for the appropriation to the payment of debts, of proceeds arising from sales in partition proceedings where deficiency of assets is found to exist do not supplant provisions of GC 10510–2 (RC 2127.02), requiring an administrator as soon as he ascertains that the personal property in his hands is not sufficient to pay all debts, to commence a civil action in the probate court or the court of common pleas for authority to sell real estate. Retterer v. Retterer (Marion 1935) 32 N.E.2d 513, 20 Ohio Law Abs. 393, 4 O.O. 333. Executors And Administrators ⟨key⟩ 356

A partition suit is appealable. Elstner v. Fisher (Ohio Cir. 1892) 5 Ohio C.D. 597.

The journal entry will be set aside where the executor's statement does not show all the assets and indebtedness of estate. In re De Serisy's Estate (Ohio Com.Pl. 1901) 11 Ohio Dec. 666, 8 Ohio N.P. 694.

Heirs should have notice of a partition under this section. In re De Serisy's Estate (Ohio Com.Pl. 1901) 11 Ohio Dec. 666, 8 Ohio N.P. 694.

NONRESIDENTS

2127.42 Sale of the lands of foreign wards

Wards living out of this state and owning lands within it are entitled to the benefit of sections 2127.01 to 2127.43 of the Revised Code. Complaints for the sale of real estate by guardians of such wards shall be filed in the county in which the land is situated, or if situated in two or more counties, then in one of the counties in which a part of it is situated. Additional security shall be required from such guardians, when deemed necessary by the probate court of the county in which the complaints are filed.

(1975 S 145, eff. 1–1–76; 1953 H 1; GC 10510–48)

Historical and Statutory Notes

Pre–1953 H 1 Amendments: 114 v 461

Cross References

Guardian for nonresident, 2111.37
Sale of lands of foreign wards, 2111.44

Library References

Guardian and Ward ⚖169.
Mental Health ⚖196.
Westlaw Topic Nos. 196, 257A.

Research References

Encyclopedias

OH Jur. 3d Guardian & Ward § 145, Property Subject to Sale—Property of Nonresident or Foreign Ward.
OH Jur. 3d Guardian & Ward § 146, Generally; Jurisdiction and Venue.
OH Jur. 3d Guardian & Ward § 155, Additional Bond for Guardian.

Treatises and Practice Aids

Carlin, Baldwin's Ohio Practice, Merrick-Rippner Probate Law § 97:22, Land Sale by Guardian—Nonresident Guardian.
Kuehnle and Levey, Ohio Real Estate Law and Practice § 52:3, Statutory Fiduciary Sales—21 Statutory Proceedings.
Kuehnle and Levey, Ohio Real Estate Law and Practice § 52:19, Statutory Fiduciary Sales—Action to Sell by Guardian for Ward Living Outside Ohio.

2127.43 Sale of real estate by trustees of nonresidents

Chapter 2127. of the Revised Code extends to an action brought by the trustee of a nonresident minor or mentally ill or deficient person to sell the real estate of the ward.

(1975 S 145, eff. 1–1–76; 1953 H 1; GC 10510–53)

Historical and Statutory Notes

Pre–1953 H 1 Amendments: 114 v 462

Library References

Guardian and Ward ⚖169.
Mental Health ⚖196.
Westlaw Topic Nos. 196, 257A.

Research References

Encyclopedias

OH Jur. 3d Decedents' Estates § 1718, Proceedings for Sale of Real Estate.
OH Jur. 3d Guardian & Ward § 145, Property Subject to Sale—Property of Nonresident or Foreign Ward.
OH Jur. 3d Guardian & Ward § 146, Generally; Jurisdiction and Venue.

Forms

Ohio Forms Legal and Business § 24:394, Payment of Debts—Order of Sale of Realty.

Treatises and Practice Aids

Carlin, Baldwin's Ohio Practice, Merrick-Rippner Probate Law § 97:21, Land Sale by Guardian—Nonresident Ward.
Kuehnle and Levey, Ohio Real Estate Law and Practice § 52:3, Statutory Fiduciary Sales—21 Statutory Proceedings.
Kuehnle and Levey, Ohio Real Estate Law and Practice § 52:21, Statutory Fiduciary Sales—Action by Trustee to Sell Trust Property.

CHAPTER 2129

ANCILLARY ADMINISTRATION

PRELIMINARY PROVISIONS

Section
2129.01 Record of extracounty and extrastate proceedings
2129.02 Proceedings by nonresident executor or administrator to bar creditor's claims
2129.03 Delivery of personal property and payment of debts to nonresident executor or administrator

ANCILLARY ADMINISTRATION

2129.04 Ancillary administration
2129.05 Foreign wills
2129.06 Will made outside the United States
2129.07 Proceedings to admit foreign will to record
2129.08 Appointment
2129.10 Procedure
2129.11 No domiciliary administration
2129.12 Presentation of claims
2129.13 Sale of real estate
2129.14 Sale requested by domiciliary executor or administrator
2129.15 Certificate of assets and liabilities
2129.16 Property not to be sold
2129.17 Transcript to be filed
2129.18 Determination of heirship
2129.19 Application for certificate of transfer
2129.20 Payments to ancillary administrator
2129.21 Bona fide purchaser protected
2129.22 Estate discharged by payment
2129.23 Distribution
2129.24 Fees

FOREIGN EXECUTOR OR ADMINISTRATOR

2129.25 Foreign executor or administrator may be authorized to sell real estate
2129.26 Bond

Section
TRUSTS UNDER FOREIGN WILL

2129.27 Trusts created by foreign will
2129.28 Trustee's bond
2129.29 Trustee appointed by a foreign court
2129.30 Probate court may appoint a trustee under a foreign will

PRELIMINARY PROVISIONS

2129.01 Record of extracounty and extrastate proceedings

The authenticated record of any extracounty or extrastate administration proceedings filed in the probate court shall be admitted to record, docketed, and indexed in the same manner as local administration proceedings.

(1953 H 1, eff. 10–1–53; GC 10511–1)

Historical and Statutory Notes

Pre–1953 H 1 Amendments: 114 v 462

Library References

Executors and Administrators ⚖517, 521.
Westlaw Topic No. 162.
C.J.S. Executors and Administrators §§ 915, 927.

Research References

Encyclopedias

OH Jur. 3d Decedents' Estates § 1716, Record of Administration Proceedings.

ANCILLARY ADMINISTRATION

Treatises and Practice Aids

Kuehnle and Levey, Ohio Real Estate Law and Practice § 10:51, Rights of Heirs When Owner Dies Resident Out of County, Preserving Marketability.

Notes of Decisions

Ancillary administration   1

1. Ancillary administration

Administration of estates has no extraterritorial operation, and the ancillary administration of an estate is concerned solely with the real and personal property of the decedent located within the territorial limits of the state in which ancillary administration is granted. In re Kelley's Estate (Hancock 1940) 68 Ohio App. 51, 34 N.E.2d 34, 33 Ohio Law Abs. 258, 22 O.O. 158. Executors And Administrators ⚖ 519(1).

2129.02 Proceedings by nonresident executor or administrator to bar creditor's claims

When letters of administration or letters testamentary have been granted in any state other than this state, in any territory or possession of the United States, or in any foreign country, as to the estate of a deceased resident of that state, territory, possession, or country, and when no ancillary administration proceedings have been commenced in this state, the person to whom the letters of appointment were granted may file an authenticated copy of them in the probate court of any county of this state in which is located real estate of the decedent.

The claim of any creditor of such a decedent shall be subject to section 2117.06 of the Revised Code. The person filing such letters in the probate court may accelerate the bar against claims against the estate established by that section, by giving written notice to a potential claimant that identifies the decedent by name, states the date of the death of the decedent, identifies the court, states its mailing address, and informs the potential claimant that any claims he may have against the estate are required to be presented to the court within the earlier of thirty days after receipt of the notice by the potential claimant or one year after the date of the death of the decedent. A claim of that potential claimant that is not presented to the court within the earlier of thirty days after receipt of the notice by the potential claimant or one year after the date of the death of the decedent is forever barred as a possible lien upon the real estate of the decedent in this state. If, at the expiration of that period, any such claim has been filed and remains unpaid after reasonable notice of the claim to the nonresident executor or administrator, ancillary administration proceedings as to the estate may be had forthwith.

(1990 H 346, eff. 5–31–90; 1987 H 21; 1953 H 1; GC 10511–2)

Uncodified Law

1990 H 346, § 3, eff. 5–31–90, reads, in part: (A) Sections 1 and 2 of this act shall apply only to the estates of decedents who die on or after the effective date of this act.

1987 H 21, § 3, eff. 10–20–87, reads: Sections 2113.03 and 2129.02 of the Revised Code, as amended by this act, apply only to the estates of decedents who die on or after the effective date of this act.

Historical and Statutory Notes

Pre–1953 H 1 Amendments: 114 v 462

Cross References

Newspaper of general circulation defined, 7.12

Library References

Executors and Administrators ⚖521, 522.
Westlaw Topic No. 162.
C.J.S. Executors and Administrators §§ 927 to 928.

Baldwin's Ohio Legislative Service, 1990 Laws of Ohio, H 346—LSC Analysis, p 5–87

Research References

Encyclopedias

OH Jur. 3d Decedents' Estates § 884, Where Intestate was Not a Resident of Ohio.
OH Jur. 3d Decedents' Estates § 1713, Filing of Copy of Letters of Appointment of Foreign Representative.
OH Jur. 3d Decedents' Estates § 1714, Presentation, Payment, or Bar of Claims of Creditors.
OH Jur. 3d Decedents' Estates § 1728, When Ancillary Administration is Necessary or Available, Generally.

Treatises and Practice Aids

Carlin, Baldwin's Ohio Practice, Merrick-Rippner Probate Law § 84:29, Creditor's Claims—Statute of Limitations.

Notes of Decisions

Revival of action   2
Statute of limitations   1

1. Statute of limitations

Where, following an automobile accident upon an Ohio highway, a nonresident defendant dies after an action has been commenced against him pursuant to RC 2703.20, if there has been no administration in Ohio, the time limitation of RC 2311.31 and RC 2117.06 has not commenced to run, and under RC 2311.25 and RC 2703.20 the pending action may be revived any time before judgment against the nonresident decedent's executor or administrator appointed in another state. Kibbey v. Mercer (Scioto 1967) 11 Ohio App.2d 51, 228 N.E.2d 337, 40 O.O.2d 223. Abatement And Revival ⚖ 74(1).

Where an authenticated copy of letters of appointment of the executor of the estate of a deceased nonresident is filed in a probate court in this state in accordance with section, the filing in such court of a claim against such estate within six months from the filing of the copy of the letters, is within time and is not governed by GC 10509–133 (RC 2117.12), which provides that suit on a claim must be brought within two months after such claim is disallowed. Foulks v. Talbott (Crawford 1943) 74 Ohio App. 281, 58 N.E.2d 790, 29 O.O. 434. Executors And Administrators ⚖ 521

Where there is no evidence a nonresident decedent's estate received notice of a revived judgment against the decedent within six months of filing letters testamentary, and where the estate published a notice to creditors in compliance with RC 2129.02, a claim against the estate filed more than six months from the date an application to admit to record authenticated copy of will and to bar creditors is filed will be forever barred as untimely. In re Estate of Dindot, No. 11–93–1 (3d Dist Ct App, Paulding, 6–4–93).

2. Revival of action

Where an action, arising out of an automobile accident or collision occurring in Ohio, has been commenced in Ohio against a nonresident defendant operator or owner who has become amenable to RC 2703.20, if the defendant dies thereafter, the Ohio court has jurisdiction to revive and continue said action against his executor or administrator whose letters of administration have been issued in another state. Kibbey v. Mercer (Scioto 1967) 11 Ohio App.2d 51, 228 N.E.2d 337, 40 O.O.2d 223.

2129.03 Delivery of personal property and payment of debts to nonresident executor or administrator

The money, debts, and other personal property located in Ohio belonging to a nonresident decedent may be delivered to the nonresident executor or administrator without further liability to the estate, provided the person delivering such money, debts, or other personal property has no knowledge of ancillary proceedings being had or having been had in Ohio.

(125 v 903, eff. 10–1–53; 1953 H 1; GC 10511–3)

Historical and Statutory Notes

Pre–1953 H 1 Amendments: 114 v 463

Library References

Executors and Administrators ⚖519(1), 521, 522.
Westlaw Topic No. 162.
C.J.S. Executors and Administrators §§ 924, 927 to 928.

Research References

Encyclopedias

OH Jur. 3d Decedents' Estates § 1715, Payment or Delivery of Personalty to Foreign Representative.

Treatises and Practice Aids

Restatement (2d) of Conflicts § 322, When Delivery of Chattel to Executor or Administrator Operates as Quittance.

Restatement (2d) of Conflicts § 329, When Payment to Foreign Executor or Administrator of Claim Not Represented by Negotiable Instrument Operates as Quittance.

ANCILLARY ADMINISTRATION

2129.04 Ancillary administration

When a nonresident decedent leaves property in Ohio, ancillary administration proceedings may be had upon application of any interested person in any county in Ohio in which is located property of the decedent, or in which a debtor of such decedent resides. Such applicant may or may not be a creditor of the estate. The ancillary administration first granted shall extend to all the estate of the deceased within the state, and shall exclude the jurisdiction of any other court.

(1953 H 1, eff. 10–1–53; GC 10511–4)

Historical and Statutory Notes

Pre–1953 H 1 Amendments: 114 v 463

Cross References

Falsification, 2921.13
Foreign guardians, sale of lands of foreign ward, 2111.39 to 2111.44

Library References

Executors and Administrators ⚖518(1), 518(3).
Westlaw Topic No. 162.
C.J.S. Executors and Administrators § 916.

Research References

Encyclopedias

OH Jur. 3d Decedents' Estates § 884, Where Intestate was Not a Resident of Ohio.

OH Jur. 3d Decedents' Estates § 1062, Wills Admitted in Another State or Territory—Who May Apply for Recordation.

OH Jur. 3d Decedents' Estates § 1730, When Ancillary Administration is Necessary or Available, Generally—Existence of Property Within the Jurisdiction as Prerequisite.

OH Jur. 3d Decedents' Estates § 1732, Who May Apply for Ancillary Administration.

OH Jur. 3d Decedents' Estates § 1734, Jurisdiction.

Treatises and Practice Aids

Carlin, Baldwin's Ohio Practice, Merrick-Rippner Probate Law § 3:13, Jurisdiction of Probate Court—Scope—Exclusive and Concurrent Jurisdiction.

Carlin, Baldwin's Ohio Practice, Merrick-Rippner Probate Law § 68:4, Letters of Administration—Specific Qualifications of Administrators—Residency Requirement.

Notes of Decisions

Appointment and duties 4
Final account 5
Jurisdiction 6
Nonresident creditors, legatees and distributees 2
Procedural issues 1
Property right 3

---

1. Procedural issues

When an injured party has brought an action in Ohio against an insured nonresident tortfeasor for damages arising out of an automobile collision, and service has been made upon said tortfeasor who dies during the pendency of such action, the injured party is an interested party who can apply for ancillary administration of said nonresident's estate under RC 2129.04. In re McQueen's Estate (Ohio Prob. 1963) 4 Ohio Misc. 65, 210 N.E.2d 157, 32 O.O.2d 210.

After the death of a nonresident operator of a motor vehicle the provisions for substituted service do not authorize such service upon the nonresident personal representative of the deceased nonresident operator. In re Wilcox' Estate (Vinton 1955) 137 N.E.2d 301, 73 Ohio Law Abs. 571, 60 O.O. 232.

Notice to next of kin or other parties interested is not required under RS 6013. In re McCreight (Ohio Prob. 1895) 9 Ohio Dec. 450, 6 Ohio N.P. 479.

The proof required as to whether the applicant is a creditor is such that the court is satisfied there is a strong possibility the applicant can so prove. In re McCreight (Ohio Prob. 1895) 9 Ohio Dec. 450, 6 Ohio N.P. 479.

A motion to set aside such appointment, filed within a reasonably short time after it is made, by one having had notice, should be considered by the court. In re McCreight (Ohio Prob. 1895) 9 Ohio Dec. 450, 6 Ohio N.P. 479. Executors And Administrators ⚖ 32(2)

Lis pendens does not apply in proceedings under RS 6013. In re Worthington's Estate (Ohio Prob. 1896) 4 Ohio Dec. 381.

Where there is no record of the hearing overruling a motion to set aside the appointment of ancillary administrator on the grounds that such administrator is not an interested party, the probate court's decision is presumed to be valid. In re Estate of LeMay, No. 82 CA 18 (4th Dist Ct App, Pickaway, 7–1–83).

2. Nonresident creditors, legatees and distributees

A bill in equity to subject the real estate of a decedent in Ohio, where the heirs and representatives reside in another state and where no letters of administration have been taken in Ohio, cannot be sustained, unless the foreign creditor takes out letters of administration in Ohio. Bustard v. Dabney (Ohio 1829) 4 Ohio 68.

Unless expressly otherwise provided, the rights of creditors, legatees and distributees who are not residents of the state in which the ancillary administration is granted are not the subject of adjudication in the ancillary administration. In re Kelley's Estate (Hancock 1940) 68 Ohio App. 51, 34 N.E.2d 34, 33 Ohio Law Abs. 258, 22 O.O. 158. Executors And Administrators ⚖ 522; Executors And Administrators ⚖ 523

3. Property right

The protection afforded to a decedent under a policy of insurance for indemnity or against liability, dependent upon the establishment of a liability against him or his estate, constitutes property to support ancillary administration proceeding under RC 2129.04, although the decedent leaves no other estate to be administered in Ohio. In re McQueen's Estate (Ohio Prob. 1963) 4 Ohio Misc. 65, 210 N.E.2d 157, 32 O.O.2d 210.

That a deceased nonresident operator of a motor vehicle was involved in an accident in a particular county does not bring into existence any property right in his liability insurance to justify appointment in such county of an ancillary administrator. In re Wilcox' Estate (Vinton 1955) 137 N.E.2d 301, 73 Ohio Law Abs. 571, 60 O.O. 232.

A claim for wrongful death of Pennsylvania motorist who was killed in collision with train in Ohio, was not "property" within meaning of Ohio statute authorizing the appointment of an ancillary administrator in Ohio for the estate of a nonresident decedent who dies leaving property in Ohio, and hence the appointment of an ancillary administrator in Ohio was improper and would be dissolved on the application of an interested party. In re Walker's Estate (Columbiana 1940) 36 N.E.2d 800. Executors And Administrators ⚖ 518(2)

Right of action for wrongful death does not arise during the lifetime of the deceased, and is in no sense property of the decedent and, therefore, could not be the basis for appointing ancillary administrator in county wherein death occurred. In re Walker's Estate (Ohio Prob. 1939) 6 Ohio Supp. 324, 34 Ohio Law Abs. 246, 21 O.O. 220, affirmed 36 N.E.2d 800.

4. Appointment and duties

Administrators of an estate in Ohio who are residents of a different state may be sued in Ohio. Williams' Adm'rs v. Welton's Adm'r (Ohio 1876) 28 Ohio St. 451.

An attorney who neither has a claim against a nonresident decedent nor represents any persons who do, is not eligible to apply for ancillary administration. In re Wilcox' Estate (Vinton 1955) 137 N.E.2d 301, 73 Ohio Law Abs. 571, 60 O.O. 232.

The power of an administrator or executor over the estate of the decedent emanates from the laws of the state where he receives his appointment and is confined to the territory of such state. In re Crawford (Ohio 1903) 68 Ohio St. 58, 48 W.L.B. 492, 67 N.E. 156, 96 Am.St.Rep. 648, 1 Ohio Law Rep. 91. Executors And Administrators ⊜ 519(1)

Where a decedent is, at the time of his death, a resident of another state, administration must be ancillary and funds in the hands of an administrator here are properly ordered turned over to an administrator appointed in the other state. Meswald v. Marks (Ohio Cir. 1899) 10 Ohio C.D. 355.

An appointment made under RS 6013 cannot be collaterally attacked. In re McCreight (Ohio Prob. 1895) 9 Ohio Dec. 450, 6 Ohio N.P. 479.

In order to appoint ancillary administration, the decedent must have been, at the time of his death, a nonresident of this state and been engaged in business in this state. In re McCreight (Ohio Prob. 1895) 9 Ohio Dec. 450, 6 Ohio N.P. 479.

The duties of an ancillary administrator are to collect the proceeds and property of the estate, make application of them to the payment of the debts proved against the estate, and this having been done, to pay the surplus into the court granting administration for the benefit of the estate of the decedent in the state where he resided at the time of his death; he has no duty here as in some states to pay legatees according to the law of the domicile of the decedent. In re Estate of Wood, 27 NP(NS) 323 (CP, Montgomery 1928).

5. Final account

The final account of distribution made by an administrator, appointed upon the estate of a nonresident of this state, approved by the probate court, and ordered to be recorded, is no bar to an action brought to compel distribution according to the law of the decedent's domicile, when the distribution actually made and approved does not conform to such law. Swearingen v. Morris (Ohio 1863) 14 Ohio St. 424. Executors And Administrators ⊜ 523

Unless expressly otherwise provided, ancillary administration is subservient only to the rights of creditors, legatees and distributees of a nonresident decedent, who are resident within the state where it is granted; and the residuum is transmissible to the court of the foreign state granting ancillary administration only when a final account has been settled in a proper tribunal where the ancillary administration is granted. In re Kelley's Estate (Hancock 1940) 68 Ohio App. 51, 34 N.E.2d 34, 33 Ohio Law Abs. 258, 22 O.O. 158. Executors And Administrators ⊜ 519(1)

6. Jurisdiction

The probate court has constitutional jurisdiction to issue letters of administration upon the estates of all those having a legal domicile in Ohio, and statutory jurisdiction under former GC 10604 (RC 2113.01, RC 2129.04) to issue such letters on the estates of inhabitants not domiciled in Ohio, and additional statutory jurisdiction under former GC 10625 (RC 2129.04) over those having no residence of any kind in Ohio, but possessed of property therein. Hill v. Blumenberg (Ohio App. 4 Dist. 1924) 19 Ohio App. 404.

Probate court's jurisdiction to proceed with the administration of an intestate nonresident decedent's estate extended only to the decedent's Ohio property. State ex rel. Lee v. Trumbull County Probate Court (Ohio, 10-14-1998) 83 Ohio St.3d 369, 700 N.E.2d 4, 1998-Ohio-51, on remand 1999 WL 744032. Courts ⊜ 200.7

Jurisdiction attaches upon the filing of a petition for appointment in a probate court, and remains in the court until final completion of administration, and is exclusive of every other probate court in this state. In re Worthington's Estate (Ohio Prob. 1896) 4 Ohio Dec. 381.

2129.05 Foreign wills

Authenticated copies of wills, executed and proved according to the laws of any state or territory of the United States, relative to property in this state, may be admitted to record in the probate court of a county where a part of such property is situated. Such authenticated copies, so recorded, shall be as valid as wills made in this state.

When such a will, or authenticated copy, is admitted to record, a copy thereof, with the copy of the order to record it annexed thereto, certified by the probate judge under the seal of his court, may be filed and recorded in the office of the probate judge of any other county where a part of such property is situated, and it shall be as effectual as the authenticated copy of such will would be if approved and admitted to record by the court.

(1953 H 1, eff. 10–1–53; GC 10511–5, 10511–6)

Historical and Statutory Notes

Pre–1953 H 1 Amendments: 114 v 463

Comparative Laws

Ill.—ILCS 755 5/7–1.
Ind.—West's A.I.C. 29–1–7–25.
Iowa—I.C.A. § 633.495 et seq.
Ky.—Baldwin's KRS 394.150
Mass.—M.G.L.A. c. 192, § 9.
Mich.—M.C.L.A. § 600.2936.
N.D.—NDCC 30.1–24–01 et seq.
N.Y.—McKinney's EPTL 3–5.1.
Ore.—ORS 113.065.
Pa.—20 Pa.C.S.A. § 3136.
Tex.—V.A.T.S. Probate Code § 95.
W.Va.—Code, 41–5–13.

Cross References

Will not admitted to record ineffectual, 2107.61
Wills, sale of land by executor's successor, 2107.59

Library References

Wills ⊜245, 347.
Westlaw Topic No. 409.
C.J.S. Wills §§ 517, 734.

Research References

Encyclopedias

OH Jur. 3d Conflict of Laws § 40, Formal Validity.
OH Jur. 3d Conflict of Laws § 41, Essential Validity.
OH Jur. 3d Decedents' Estates § 1060, Wills Admitted in Another State or Territory.
OH Jur. 3d Decedents' Estates § 1065, Wills Admitted in Another State or Territory—Admission to Record in Other Counties.
OH Jur. 3d Decedents' Estates § 1607, Exercise of Power by Coexecutors and Successors.

Forms

Ohio Forms Legal and Business § 24:3, Conflict of Law Considerations.

Treatises and Practice Aids

Carlin, Baldwin's Ohio Practice, Merrick-Rippner Probate Law § 35:4, Jurisdiction as Between States.

Carlin, Baldwin's Ohio Practice, Merrick-Rippner Probate Law § 21:27, Rights of Surviving Spouse to Make Election—Effect of Ancillary Administration on Right of Election.

Carlin, Baldwin's Ohio Practice, Merrick-Rippner Probate Law § 90:16, Application to Admit to Record Authenticated Copy of Foreign Will—Form.

Carlin, Baldwin's Ohio Practice, Merrick-Rippner Probate Law § 90:17, Entry Admitting Foreign Will to Probate—Form.

Carlin, Baldwin's Ohio Practice, Merrick-Rippner Probate Law § 90:18, Certificate of Authenticated Copy of Will—Form.

Kuehnle and Levey, Ohio Real Estate Law and Practice § 10:51, Rights of Heirs When Owner Dies Resident Out of County, Preserving Marketability.

Restatement (2d) of Property, Don. Trans. § 33.1, Meaning of a Will.

Notes of Decisions

Choice of laws, compliance 2
Domicile 3
Procedural issues 1
Recording 4

---

1. Procedural issues

The neglect of a devisee to cause a known will to be admitted to probate within three years, whereby the devise lapses, refers to the original probate in a foreign state, and not to the admission to record of an authenticated copy of the probated will. Carpenter v. Denoon (Ohio 1876) 29 Ohio St. 379.

The requirement of notice by publication of the application to admit a foreign will to record in Ohio does not apply to wills executed and admitted to probate in a sister state. Carpenter v. Denoon (Ohio 1876) 29 Ohio St. 379.

No proceeding shall be had in this state to contest a foreign will executed and proved according to the foreign law relative to property in this state. Jones v. Robinson (Ohio 1867) 17 Ohio St. 171. Wills ⚖ 223

A will made in another state takes effect from the death of the testator, and not from the date of its registry in Ohio. Hall's Lessee v. Ashby & Craven (Ohio 1839) 9 Ohio 96, 34 Am.Dec. 424. Wills ⚖ 434

An order of a common pleas court finding and establishing the contents of a lost will is not reviewable upon petition in error. Roth v. Siefert (Ohio 1908) 77 Ohio St. 417, 83 N.E. 611, 5 Ohio Law Rep. 565. Wills ⚖ 356

An application for admission of a will probated in another state is ex parte, and is not a bar to a second application on other proof. Barr v. Closterman (Ohio Cir. 1888) 2 Ohio C.D. 251, affirmed.

The admission of a foreign will to record in this state and the giving of bond here relate back and give validity to notice and suit by a trust company for recovery of compensation for land held in trust and unlawfully taken by a railroad company. Union Sav. Bank & Trust Co. v. Baltimore & O.S.W.R. Co. (Ohio Insolv. 1908) 7 Ohio NP(NS) 497, 53 W.L.B. 450.

2. Choice of laws, compliance

The laws of Ohio govern in the construction of a foreign will disposing of lands situated in this state. Jennings v. Jennings (Ohio 1871) 21 Ohio St. 56.

A will made in another state, valid in the place where made but not in the forms required by the laws of Ohio, passes no property in Ohio. Meese v. Keefe (Ohio 1841) 10 Ohio 362. Wills ⚖ 70

Where an authenticated copy of a will, executed and proved according to the laws of the state of the decedent's domicile, has been admitted to record pursuant to RC 2129.05, and where it is not established that the widow who was domiciled in that state had claimed anything under that will or otherwise elected to take thereunder and where the testator owned real estate in Ohio at his death, such widow has the right, with respect to that Ohio real estate, to elect not to take under the testator's will but to take under the Ohio statute of descent and distribution, even though no such election is permitted by the law of the state of the testator's domicile at death. Pfau v. Moseley (Ohio 1966) 9 Ohio St.2d 13, 222 N.E.2d 639, 38 O.O.2d 8. Wills ⚖ 778

A foreign will not provable under the laws of a sister state cannot be admitted here. Barr v. Closterman (Ohio Cir. 1887) 1 Ohio C.D. 546, affirmed.

A person claiming under a will proved in one state cannot sue for property of a testator in another state unless the will is proved in the latter state; Ohio law must be complied with in order to give the will the same validity and effect as if it was made in Ohio. Kerr v. Moon's Devisees (U.S.Ohio 1824) 22 U.S. 565, 6 L.Ed. 161, 9 Wheat. 565. Executors And Administrators ⚖ 6; Executors And Administrators ⚖ 518(1)

3. Domicile

The will of a person whose domicile, at the time of his death, is in this state, is properly admitted to original probate at the place of such domicile, without regard to where the will was made, or where such person died. Converse v. Starr (Ohio 1872) 23 Ohio St. 491. Wills ⚖ 249

Where the testator at the time of his death is domiciled in Ohio, Ohio law governs the determination of the validity of the will, and a will first proved in a sister state cannot be properly admitted to record in Ohio absent such determination here. Manuel v. Manuel (Ohio 1862) 13 Ohio St. 458.

4. Recording

A will devising land in Ohio executed in a sister state according to the laws of that state is good in Ohio when properly authenticated and recorded in the county where the lands lie. Bailey v. Bailey (Ohio 1837) 8 Ohio 239.

A will made in a sister state, though proved and recorded in that state, must be recorded in Ohio before title to land vests in the devisee. Wilson's Ex'rs v. Tappan (Ohio 1833) 6 Ohio 172. Wills ⚖ 434

A record showing proof of a foreign will in a sister state cannot be impeached collaterally. Barr v. Closterman (Ohio Cir. 1887) 1 Ohio C.D. 546, affirmed.

2129.06 Will made outside the United States

A will executed, proved, and allowed in a country other than the United States and territories thereof, according to the laws of such foreign state or country, may be allowed and admitted to record in this state in the manner and for the purpose mentioned in sections 2129.07 to 2129.30, inclusive, of the Revised Code.

(1953 H 1, eff. 10–1–53; GC 10511–7)

Historical and Statutory Notes

Pre–1953 H 1 Amendments: 114 v 464

Cross References

Will not admitted to record ineffectual, 2107.61

Library References

Wills ⚖245, 347.
Westlaw Topic No. 409.
C.J.S. Wills §§ 517, 734.

Research References

Encyclopedias

OH Jur. 3d Conflict of Laws § 40, Formal Validity.
OH Jur. 3d Decedents' Estates § 1068, Wills Admitted in Another Country.

Forms

Ohio Forms Legal and Business § 24:3, Conflict of Law Considerations.

Treatises and Practice Aids

Carlin, Baldwin's Ohio Practice, Merrick-Rippner Probate Law § 3:13, Jurisdiction of Probate Court—Scope—Exclusive and Concurrent Jurisdiction.

Kuehnle and Levey, Ohio Real Estate Law and Practice § 10:51, Rights of Heirs When Owner Dies Resident Out of County, Preserving Marketability.

Notes of Decisions

Full faith and credit 1

---

1. Full faith and credit

Ohio need not give full faith and credit to wills proved and allowed in foreign countries. State ex rel. Lee v. Trumbull County Probate Court (Ohio, 10-14-1998) 83 Ohio St.3d 369, 700 N.E.2d 4, 1998-Ohio-51, on remand 1999 WL 744032. Judgment ⚖ 830.1

2129.07 Proceedings to admit foreign will to record

(A) An authenticated copy of a will executed, proved, and allowed in a country other than the United States and territories of the United States, and the probate of that will shall be produced by the executor, or by a person interested in the will, to the probate court of the county in which there is any estate upon which the will may operate. The court then shall continue the application to admit it to probate for two months. Notice of the filing of the application shall be given to all persons interested in the will, in a public newspaper published in or in general circulation in the county in which the application is made, at least three weeks consecutively. The first publication shall be at least forty days before the time set for the final hearing of the application. If, on the final hearing, it appears to the court that the instrument ought to be allowed in this state, it shall order the copy to be filed and recorded. The will, and the probate and record of it, then shall have the same effect as if the will originally had been proved and allowed in that court.

(B) This section does not give effect to the will of an alien different from that which it would have had if originally proved and allowed in this state.

(C) When the copy of the will has been filed and recorded, and when no ancillary administration proceedings have been had or are being had in this state, sections 2106.01 to 2106.08 of the Revised Code, relating to the election of a surviving spouse, shall apply the same as in the case of resident decedents, except that an election under section 2106.01 of the Revised Code shall not be made subject to division (E) of that section, but instead shall be made at any time after the death of a decedent but not later than six months after the recording of the copy of the will.

(1990 H 346, eff. 5–31–90; 1977 H 42; 125 v 903; 1953 H 1; GC 10511–8, 10511–9)

Uncodified Law

1990 H 346, § 3, eff. 5–31–90, reads, in part: (A) Sections 1 and 2 of this act shall apply only to the estates of decedents who die on or after the effective date of this act.

Historical and Statutory Notes

Pre–1953 H 1 Amendments: 114 v 464

Cross References

Newspaper of general circulation defined, 7.12

Library References

Wills ⇐245, 347.
Westlaw Topic No. 409.
C.J.S. Wills §§ 517, 734.
    Baldwin's Ohio Legislative Service, 1990 Laws of Ohio, H 346—LSC Analysis, p 5–87

Research References

Encyclopedias
OH Jur. 3d Conflict of Laws § 40, Formal Validity.
OH Jur. 3d Decedents' Estates § 758, Election Under Foreign Will.
OH Jur. 3d Decedents' Estates § 1068, Wills Admitted in Another Country.

Forms
Ohio Forms Legal and Business § 24:3, Conflict of Law Considerations.

Treatises and Practice Aids
Carlin, Baldwin's Ohio Practice, Merrick-Rippner Probate Law § 3:13, Jurisdiction of Probate Court—Scope—Exclusive and Concurrent Jurisdiction.
Carlin, Baldwin's Ohio Practice, Merrick-Rippner Probate Law § 90:19, Motion to Admit Will to Record—Foreign Country—Form.
Carlin, Baldwin's Ohio Practice, Merrick-Rippner Probate Law § 90:20, Entry Setting for Hearing and Ordering Notice—Form.
Carlin, Baldwin's Ohio Practice, Merrick-Rippner Probate Law § 90:21, Notice by Publication—Form.
Carlin, Baldwin's Ohio Practice, Merrick-Rippner Probate Law § 90:22, Entry Admitting Foreign Will to Probate—Form.
Kuehnle and Levey, Ohio Real Estate Law and Practice § 10:51, Rights of Heirs When Owner Dies Resident Out of County, Preserving Marketability.

Notes of Decisions

Full faith and credit   3
Notice   2
Surviving spouse   1

---

1. Surviving spouse

Where an authenticated copy of a will, executed and proved according to the laws of the state of the decedent's domicile, has been admitted to record pursuant to RC 2129.05, and where it is not established that the widow who was domiciled in that state had claimed anything under that will or otherwise elected to take thereunder and where the testator owned real estate in Ohio at his death, such widow has the right, with respect to that Ohio real estate, to elect not to take under the testator's will but to take under the Ohio statute of descent and distribution, even though no such election is permitted by the law of the state of the testator's domicile at death. Pfau v. Moseley (Ohio 1966) 9 Ohio St.2d 13, 222 N.E.2d 639, 38 O.O.2d 8. Wills ⇐ 778

2. Notice

The requirement of notice by publication of the application to admit a foreign will to record in Ohio does not apply to wills executed and admitted to probate in a sister state. Carpenter v. Denoon (Ohio 1876) 29 Ohio St. 379.

3. Full faith and credit

Ohio need not give full faith and credit to wills proved and allowed in foreign countries. State ex rel. Lee v. Trumbull County Probate Court (Ohio, 10-14-1998) 83 Ohio St.3d 369, 700 N.E.2d 4, 1998-Ohio-51, on remand 1999 WL 744032. Judgment ⇐ 830.1

2129.08 Appointment

(A) After an authenticated copy of the will of a nonresident decedent has been allowed and admitted to record as provided in this chapter, and after there has been filed in the probate court a complete exemplification of the record of the grant of the domiciliary letters of appointment and of any other records of the court of domiciliary administration that the court requires, the court shall appoint as the ancillary administrator the person named in the will, or nominated in accordance with any power of nomination conferred in the will, as general executor of the decedent's estate or as executor of the portion of the decedent's estate located in this state, provided that the person makes application and qualifies under division (B)(2) of section 2109.21 of the Revised Code and in all other respects as required by law. If the testator in the will naming or providing for the nomination of that executor orders or requests that bond not be given by him, bond shall not be required unless, for sufficient reason, the court requires it.

(B) If a nonresident decedent died intestate, or failed to designate in his will any person qualified to act as ancillary administrator or to confer in the will a power to nominate a person as an executor as described in division (A) of this section, or if the will of a nonresident decedent conferred such a power but no person qualified to act as ancillary administrator was nominated, the court shall appoint in such capacity some suitable person who is a resident of the county including, but not limited to, a creditor of the estate.

(C) An ancillary administrator, acting as to the estate of a testate decedent that is located in this state, may sell and convey the real and personal property by virtue of the will as executors or administrators with the will annexed may do.

(D) No person shall be appointed as an ancillary administrator of the estate of a nonresident presumed decedent that is located in this state, except after Chapter 2121. of the Revised Code, relative to the appointment of an ancillary administrator, has been complied with.

(1990 H 346, eff. 5–31–90; 1974 S 349; 125 v 903; 1953 H 1; GC 10511–10)

Uncodified Law

1990 H 346, § 3, eff. 5–31–90, reads, in part: (A) Sections 1 and 2 of this act shall apply only to the estates of decedents who die on or after the effective date of this act.

Historical and Statutory Notes

Pre–1953 H 1 Amendments: 114 v 464

Cross References

Nonresident appointed as ancillary administrator, 2109.21

Library References

Executors and Administrators ⟜518(1), 518(3).
Westlaw Topic No. 162.
C.J.S. Executors and Administrators § 916.
  Baldwin's Ohio Legislative Service, 1990 Laws of Ohio, H 346—LSC Analysis, p 5–87

Research References

Encyclopedias

  OH Jur. 3d Decedents' Estates § 1068, Wills Admitted in Another Country.
  OH Jur. 3d Decedents' Estates § 1733, Who May be Appointed.
  OH Jur. 3d Decedents' Estates § 1735, Appointment.
  OH Jur. 3d Decedents' Estates § 1736, Appointment in Case of Nonresident Presumed Decedent.
  OH Jur. 3d Decedents' Estates § 1743, Sale of Real or Personal Property.
  OH Jur. 3d Fiduciaries § 186, Dispensing With Bond.

Treatises and Practice Aids

  Carlin, Baldwin's Ohio Practice, Merrick-Rippner Probate Law § 2:15, Appointment of Fiduciary—Appointment of Executor or Administrator.
  Carlin, Baldwin's Ohio Practice, Merrick-Rippner Probate Law § 57:5, Removal of Fiduciary—Grounds—Nonresidency of Fiduciary.
  Carlin, Baldwin's Ohio Practice, Merrick-Rippner Probate Law § 68:4, Letters of Administration—Specific Qualifications of Administrators—Residency Requirement.
  Carlin, Baldwin's Ohio Practice, Merrick-Rippner Probate Law § 90:4, Persons Entitled to Bring Land Sale Actions—Foreign Executor or Administrator.
  Carlin, Baldwin's Ohio Practice, Merrick-Rippner Probate Law § 2:121, Administration of Decedent's Estate—Checklist.
  Carlin, Baldwin's Ohio Practice, Merrick-Rippner Probate Law § 30:34, Drafting a Will—Appointment of Executor, Alternate Executor; Ancillary Administrator.
  Carlin, Baldwin's Ohio Practice, Merrick-Rippner Probate Law § 68:18, Letters Testamentary—Letters of Administration With the Will Annexed.
  Carlin, Baldwin's Ohio Practice, Merrick-Rippner Probate Law § 68:24, Letters Testamentary—Qualifications for Executors—Residency Requirement.
  Carlin, Baldwin's Ohio Practice, Merrick-Rippner Probate Law § 68:42, Application for Authority to Administer Estate—Form.
  Carlin, Baldwin's Ohio Practice, Merrick-Rippner Probate Law § 68:43, Supplemental Application for Ancillary Administration—Form.
  Carlin, Baldwin's Ohio Practice, Merrick-Rippner Probate Law § 90:23, Application for Letters of Ancillary Administration—Form.

2129.10 Procedure

Except as otherwise provided in this chapter, the procedure in ancillary administration shall be the same as in the administration of the estates of resident decedents.

(1990 H 346, eff. 5–31–90; 125 v 411, 903; 1953 H 1; GC 10511–12)

Uncodified Law

1990 H 346, § 3, eff. 5–31–90, reads, in part: (A) Sections 1 and 2 of this act shall apply only to the estates of decedents who die on or after the effective date of this act.

Historical and Statutory Notes

Pre–1953 H 1 Amendments: 114 v 465

Library References

Executors and Administrators ⟜519(1).
Westlaw Topic No. 162.
C.J.S. Executors and Administrators § 924.
  Baldwin's Ohio Legislative Service, 1990 Laws of Ohio, H 346—LSC Analysis, p 5–87

Research References

Encyclopedias

  OH Jur. 3d Decedents' Estates § 1738, General Statutory Rule as to Powers and Duties.

Notes of Decisions

Insolvent estate 1
Surviving spouse 2

---

1. Insolvent estate

In the payment of unsecured claims allowed in an Ohio ancillary administration of a wholly insolvent estate, such administrator shall consider the total of the available assets in the hands of the domiciliary administrator and those in his own hands, and also the total of the unsecured claims allowed by the domiciliary administrator and those allowed in Ohio. In re Hirsch's Estate (Ohio 1946) 146 Ohio St. 393, 66 N.E.2d 636, 164 A.L.R. 761, 32 O.O. 445. Executors And Administrators ⟜ 522

In order to receive payment from funds in the hands of an ancillary administrator in Ohio of a nonresident decedent's insolvent estate all creditors, both resident and nonresident of Ohio, are required to file and prove their claims in accordance with the Ohio statutes. In re Hirsch's Estate (Hamilton 1945) 76 Ohio App. 69, 63 N.E.2d 174, 43 Ohio Law Abs. 493, 31 O.O. 386, reversed 146 Ohio St. 393, 66 N.E.2d 636, 164 A.L.R. 761, 32 O.O. 445. Executors And Administrators ⟜ 521

2. Surviving spouse

A year's allowance should be set off to a nonresident surviving spouse in the local estate of a nonresident decedent where the state of her residence does not make provision for widows and children. In re Weatherhead's Estate (Ohio Prob. 1956) 137 N.E.2d 315, 73 Ohio Law Abs. 524. Executors And Administrators ⟜ 181

A surviving spouse though a nonresident is entitled to have set off to her the property deemed exempt from administration provided for by statute in effect at the time her husband died. In re Weatherhead's Estate (Ohio Prob. 1956) 137 N.E.2d 315, 73 Ohio Law Abs. 524.

2129.11 No domiciliary administration

If no domiciliary administration has been commenced, the ancillary administrator shall proceed with the administration in Ohio as though the decedent had been a resident of Ohio at the time of his death.

(125 v 903, eff. 10–1–53; 1953 H 1; GC 10511–13)

Historical and Statutory Notes

Pre–1953 H 1 Amendments: 114 v 465

Library References

Executors and Administrators ⇔519(1).
Westlaw Topic No. 162.
C.J.S. Executors and Administrators § 924.

Research References

Encyclopedias

OH Jur. 3d Decedents' Estates § 1738, General Statutory Rule as to Powers and Duties.

Treatises and Practice Aids

Carlin, Baldwin's Ohio Practice, Merrick-Rippner Probate Law § 68:4, Letters of Administration—Specific Qualifications of Administrators—Residency Requirement.

Notes of Decisions

Choice of laws 1
Surviving spouse 2

1. Choice of laws

In an original ancillary administration in Ohio, the Ohio probate law, including the statute of descent and distribution is applied. Darrow v. Fifth Third Union Trust Co. (Ohio Com.Pl. 1954) 139 N.E.2d 112, 78 Ohio Law Abs. 303, 1 O.O.2d 104.

2. Surviving spouse

The surviving spouse of a testatrix, both of whom were American citizens, domiciled in a foreign country at the time of her death, at which time she owned personal property located in Ohio, where the sole original administration of her estate was being administered in a probate court, is entitled to elect to take under the law rather than under her will. In re Gould's Estate (Ohio Prob. 1956) 140 N.E.2d 793, 75 Ohio Law Abs. 289, 1 O.O.2d 366, affirmed 140 N.E.2d 801, 75 Ohio Law Abs. 298, 1 O.O.2d 372.

2129.12 Presentation of claims

Creditors having claims against the estate of a nonresident decedent shall file them with the ancillary administrator who is appointed in accordance with sections 2109.21 and 2129.08 of the Revised Code, within the time and in the manner provided by sections 2117.06 and 2117.07 of the Revised Code.

(1990 H 346, eff. 5–31–90; 1953 H 1; GC 10511–14)

Uncodified Law

1990 H 346, § 3, eff. 5–31–90, reads, in part: (A) Sections 1 and 2 of this act shall apply only to the estates of decedents who die on or after the effective date of this act.

Historical and Statutory Notes

Pre–1953 H 1 Amendments: 114 v 465

Library References

Executors and Administrators ⇔521.
Westlaw Topic No. 162.
C.J.S. Executors and Administrators § 927.
Baldwin's Ohio Legislative Service, 1990 Laws of Ohio, H 346—LSC Analysis, p 5–87.

Research References

Encyclopedias

OH Jur. 3d Decedents' Estates § 1741, Presentation and Payment of Creditors' Claims.

Notes of Decisions

Insolvent estate 1
Nonresident creditors 4
Residue 2
Revival of action 3

1. Insolvent estate

In the payment of unsecured claims allowed in an Ohio ancillary administration of a wholly insolvent estate, such administrator shall consider the total of the available assets in the hands of the domiciliary administrator and those in his own hands, and also the total of the unsecured claims allowed by the domiciliary administrator and those allowed in Ohio. In re Hirsch's Estate (Ohio 1946) 146 Ohio St. 393, 66 N.E.2d 636, 164 A.L.R. 761, 32 O.O. 445. Executors And Administrators ⇔ 522.

In order to receive payment from funds in the hands of an ancillary administrator in Ohio of a nonresident decedent's insolvent estate, all creditors, both resident and nonresident of Ohio, are required to file and prove their claims in accordance with the Ohio statutes. In re Hirsch's Estate (Hamilton 1945) 76 Ohio App. 69, 63 N.E.2d 174, 43 Ohio Law Abs. 493, 31 O.O. 386, reversed 146 Ohio St. 393, 66 N.E.2d 636, 164 A.L.R. 761, 32 O.O. 445. Executors And Administrators ⇔ 521

2. Residue

RC 2129.23 provides that when the expenses of ancillary administration of a nonresident decedent's estate, including attorney's fees as is allowed by the probate court, all public charges and taxes, and all claims of creditors presented have been paid, any residue of the personal estate and the proceeds of any real estate sold for the payment of debts shall be distributed by the ancillary administrator, with the approval of the court, to the domiciliary administrator or executor, or if the court orders, to the persons entitled thereto. In re Radu's Estate (Cuyahoga 1973) 35 Ohio App.2d 187, 301 N.E.2d 263, 64 O.O.2d 293.

3. Revival of action

Where an action, arising out of an automobile accident or collision occurring in Ohio, has been commenced in Ohio against a nonresident defendant operator or owner who has become amenable to RC 2703.20, if the defendant dies thereafter, the Ohio court has jurisdiction to revive and continue said action against his executor or administrator whose letters of administration have been issued in another state. Kibbey v. Mercer (Scioto 1967) 11 Ohio App.2d 51, 228 N.E.2d 337, 40 O.O.2d 223.

Where, following an automobile accident upon an Ohio highway, a nonresident defendant dies after an action has been commenced against him pursuant to RC 2703.20, if there has been no administration in Ohio, the time limitation of RC 2311.31 and RC 2117.06 has not commenced to run, and under RC 2311.25 and RC 2703.20 the pending action may be revived any time before judgment against the nonresident decedent's executor or administrator appointed in another state. Kibbey v. Mercer (Scioto 1967) 11 Ohio App.2d 51, 228 N.E.2d 337, 40 O.O.2d 223. Abatement And Revival ⇔ 74(1)

4. Nonresident creditors

Rights of creditors who are nonresidents of state of ancillary administration are not subject to adjudication in ancillary administration. In re Kelley's Estate (Hancock 1940) 68 Ohio App. 51, 34 N.E.2d 34, 33 Ohio Law Abs. 258, 22 O.O. 158. Executors And Administrators ⇔ 522; Executors And Administrators ⇔ 523

2129.13 Sale of real estate

If an ancillary administrator finds that the personal property of the nonresident decedent in Ohio is not sufficient to pay the expenses of administration, public rates and taxes, and other valid claims which have been presented, he shall proceed to sell as much of the real estate of the decedent located in this state as is necessary to pay such debts. The procedure shall be the same as in sales of real estate in administration proceedings relating to the estates of resident decedents under sections 2127.01 to 2127.43, inclusive, of the Revised Code.

(125 v 903, eff. 10–1–53; 1953 H 1; GC 10511–15)

Historical and Statutory Notes

Pre–1953 H 1 Amendments: 114 v 465

Library References

Executors and Administrators ⚖519(2), 520.
Westlaw Topic No. 162.
C.J.S. Executors and Administrators §§ 924 to 926.

Research References

Encyclopedias

OH Jur. 3d Decedents' Estates § 1743, Sale of Real or Personal Property.

Treatises and Practice Aids

Carlin, Baldwin's Ohio Practice, Merrick-Rippner Probate Law § 90:2, Persons Entitled to Bring Land Sale Actions—Other Parties.

Carlin, Baldwin's Ohio Practice, Merrick-Rippner Probate Law § 90:5, Persons Entitled to Bring Land Sale Actions—Ancillary Administrator.

Kuehnle and Levey, Ohio Real Estate Law and Practice § 52:3, Statutory Fiduciary Sales—21 Statutory Proceedings.

Restatement (2d) of Conflicts § 334, Where Land May be Administered.

2129.14 Sale requested by domiciliary executor or administrator

A domiciliary executor or administrator of a nonresident decedent may file in the probate court by which the ancillary administrator was appointed information showing that it will be necessary to sell Ohio real estate of the decedent to pay debts and legacies, and the court may thereupon authorize the ancillary administrator to sell such part or all of such real estate as is necessary. The ancillary administrator shall proceed to sell such real estate in the manner provided by section 2129.13 of the Revised Code.

(1953 H 1, eff. 10–1–53; GC 10511–16)

Historical and Statutory Notes

Pre–1953 H 1 Amendments: 114 v 466

Library References

Executors and Administrators ⚖520.
Westlaw Topic No. 162.
C.J.S. Executors and Administrators § 926.

Research References

Encyclopedias

OH Jur. 3d Decedents' Estates § 1744, Sale of Real or Personal Property—Upon Request of Domiciliary Executor or Administrator.

Treatises and Practice Aids

Carlin, Baldwin's Ohio Practice, Merrick-Rippner Probate Law § 90:2, Persons Entitled to Bring Land Sale Actions—Other Parties.

Carlin, Baldwin's Ohio Practice, Merrick-Rippner Probate Law § 90:5, Persons Entitled to Bring Land Sale Actions—Ancillary Administrator.

Notes of Decisions

Jurisdiction 1

---

1. Jurisdiction

Upon compliance by a domiciliary executor with provisions of section, any probate court in this state, by which an ancillary administrator has been appointed in conformity with law, has jurisdiction to order administrator to sell Ohio real property of which deceased died seized to pay debts and legacies. Crabbe v. Lingo (Ohio 1946) 146 Ohio St. 489, 67 N.E.2d 1, 32 O.O. 561. Executors And Administrators ⚖ 520

2129.15 Certificate of assets and liabilities

Within five months after his appointment the ancillary administrator of a nonresident decedent shall forward to the domiciliary administrator, if any, of such decedent, if the name and address of such domiciliary administrator are known, a certificate showing all assets of the estate in this state and all debts and liabilities including estimated expenses of administration. If the name and address of such domiciliary administrator are not known, such certificate shall be forwarded to the next of kin of the deceased whose names and addresses are known and to the court having jurisdiction in estate matters in the county in which the decedent resided at the time of his death.

(125 v 903, eff. 10–1–53; 1953 H 1; GC 10511–17)

Historical and Statutory Notes

Pre–1953 H 1 Amendments: 114 v 466

Library References

Executors and Administrators ⚖519(1), 521.
Westlaw Topic No. 162.
C.J.S. Executors and Administrators §§ 924, 927.

Research References

Encyclopedias

OH Jur. 3d Decedents' Estates § 1747, Duty to File: Certificate of Assets and Liabilities.

Treatises and Practice Aids

Carlin, Baldwin's Ohio Practice, Merrick-Rippner Probate Law § 90:24, Certificate of Assets and Liabilities—Form.

2129.16 Property not to be sold

An ancillary administrator shall not sell property of a nonresident decedent if the domiciliary administrator or executor, or any other person having an interest in the estate, within thirty days after the forwarding of the certificate of assets and liabilities required by section 2129.15 of the Revised Code pays to the ancillary administrator a sum sufficient to pay all expenses of administration, public rates and charges, and creditors' claims filed in the state, or secures the payment of such sum to the satisfaction of the probate court. The domiciliary administrator or executor, or any other person having an interest in the estate, may likewise prevent the sale of any part of such property by paying, or securing to the satisfaction of the court the payment of, the appraised value of the property withheld from sale.

(125 v 903, eff. 10–1–53; 1953 H 1; GC 10511–18)

Historical and Statutory Notes

Pre–1953 H 1 Amendments: 114 v 466

Library References

Executors and Administrators ⚖519(2), 520.
Westlaw Topic No. 162.
C.J.S. Executors and Administrators §§ 924 to 926.

Research References

Encyclopedias

OH Jur. 3d Decedents' Estates § 1746, When Property Not to be Sold.

2129.17 Transcript to be filed

An ancillary administrator shall file in the probate court of every county in Ohio in which real estate of the nonresident decedent is located a certified copy of the records in the court of his appointment which affect the title to such real estate.

(125 v 903, eff. 10–1–53; 1953 H 1; GC 10511–19)

Historical and Statutory Notes

Pre–1953 H 1 Amendments: 114 v 466

Library References

Executors and Administrators ☞519(1).
Westlaw Topic No. 162.
C.J.S. Executors and Administrators § 924.

Research References

Encyclopedias

OH Jur. 3d Decedents' Estates § 1748, Duty to File: Certificate of Assets and Liabilities—Application for Certificate of Transfer and Transcript of Records.

2129.18 Determination of heirship

Whenever property of a nonresident decedent as to whose estate ancillary administration proceedings are being had in Ohio passes by the laws of intestate succession or under a will to a beneficiary not named therein, proceedings may be had to determine the persons entitled to such property in the same manner as in the estates of resident decedents under sections 2123.01 to 2123.07, inclusive, of the Revised Code. The ancillary administrator shall file a certified copy of such finding in the probate court in every county in Ohio in which real estate of the decedent is located. Such administrator shall procure and file in the court for the information of the court a certified copy of any determination of heirship relative to such decedent's estate made in the state of the domiciliary administration.

(125 v 903, eff. 10–1–53; 1953 H 1; GC 10511–20)

Historical and Statutory Notes

Pre–1953 H 1 Amendments: 116 v 385; 114 v 466

Cross References

Determination of rights or legal relations, 2721.05
Recording will in each county property situated, 2107.21, 2129.05

Library References

Descent and Distribution ☞71(1).
Westlaw Topic No. 124.
C.J.S. Descent and Distribution §§ 77, 82.

Research References

Encyclopedias

OH Jur. 3d Decedents' Estates § 198, When Special Proceedings Lie.
OH Jur. 3d Decedents' Estates § 206, Findings and Order—Copies to be Filed by Ancillary Administrator.

Treatises and Practice Aids

Klein, Darling, & Terez, Baldwin's Ohio Practice Civil Practice § 73:5, Probate Division--Service and Filing of Pleadings and Papers Subsequent to the Original Complaint.

Notes of Decisions

Evidence 2
Foreign decree 1

---

1. Foreign decree

Special legislation authorizing apportionment of certain allowed exemptions in assessing Ohio tax on succession of Ohio property from a nonresident decedent did not authorize the deduction of all or proportionate part of the estate's debts, costs of administration or federal estate tax from appraised value of Ohio realty passing under residuary clause of nonresident's will where will authorized the executor to sell, lease, mortgage or otherwise dispose of the Ohio realty and where the estate contains sufficient personalty to pay the debts, taxes and costs. In re Packard's Estate (Ohio 1963) 174 Ohio St. 349, 189 N.E.2d 434, 22 O.O.2d 409. Taxation ☞ 3355; Taxation ☞ 3356

RC 2129.18 places upon the ancillary administrator of a nonresident decedent's estate the mandatory duty to procure and file in the court where the ancillary administration is being had "for the information of the court a certified copy of any determination of heirship relative to such decedent's estate made in the state of the domiciliary administration." Howells v. Limbeck (Wayne 1960) 114 Ohio App. 129, 180 N.E.2d 624, 18 O.O.2d 449, affirmed 172 Ohio St. 297, 175 N.E.2d 517, 87 A.L.R.2d 1269, 16 O.O.2d 68. Executors And Administrators ☞ 523

An Ohio court is not in error in according full faith and credit to a valid decree of a Florida court of competent jurisdiction holding that an illegitimate son is the sole and only heir of his deceased father and as such entitled to receive the father's entire estate, real, personal and mixed, wheresoever situated. Howells v. Limbeck (Ohio 1961) 172 Ohio St. 297, 175 N.E.2d 517, 87 A.L.R.2d 1269, 16 O.O.2d 68. Judgment ☞ 822(3)

Under statute relating to distribution of residuum of ancillary estate, where all of legatees to whom distribution of residuum of ancillary estate was ordered made were legatees of specific bequests made payable to them out of proceeds of realty located in state, probate court was vested with authority to order ancillary administrator to make payment of respective legacies direct to legatees, if, taking into consideration status of whole estate of decedent, wherever situated, as to assets and liabilities, equitable principles of law of Ohio applicable to application and distribution of assets of decedent's estate, and particularly the equitable principle that creditors are entitled to priority of payment out of assets of an estate before legatees and distributees warranted the making of such order. In re Kelley's Estate (Hancock 1940) 68 Ohio App. 51, 34 N.E.2d 34, 33 Ohio Law Abs. 258, 22 O.O. 158. Executors And Administrators ☞ 523

2. Evidence

In an action in Ohio by the ancillary administrator of a nonresident decedent's estate to determine the heirs to whom Ohio property of the estate should pass, a copy of the petition for letters of administration of such estate filed in a state other than Ohio, a copy of the order appointing the administrator, and a copy of the letters of administration are admissible to establish, such matters being in issue, the domicile of the decedent, the appointment of the administrator, and the basis for the ancillary administration in Ohio. Howells v. Limbeck (Wayne 1960) 114 Ohio App. 129, 180 N.E.2d 624, 18 O.O.2d 449, affirmed 172 Ohio St. 297, 175 N.E.2d 517, 87 A.L.R.2d 1269, 16 O.O.2d 68. Executors And Administrators ☞ 524(3)

2129.19 Application for certificate of transfer

Prior to filing his final account, an ancillary administrator shall file in the probate court an application for a certificate of transfer as to the real estate of the nonresident decedent situated in Ohio, in the same manner as in the administration of the estates of resident decedents under section 2113.61 of the Revised Code.

(125 v 903, eff. 10–1–53; 1953 H 1; GC 10511–21)

Historical and Statutory Notes

Pre–1953 H 1 Amendments: 116 v 385; 114 v 467

Library References

Executors and Administrators ☞523, 526.
Westlaw Topic No. 162.
C.J.S. Executors and Administrators §§ 929 to 930, 934 to 935.

Research References

Encyclopedias

OH Jur. 3d Decedents' Estates § 1748, Duty to File: Certificate of Assets and Liabilities—Application for Certificate of Transfer and Transcript of Records.

2129.20 Payments to ancillary administrator

Any person indebted to the estate of a nonresident decedent or holding property belonging thereto may pay such indebtedness or deliver such property to the ancillary administrator when appointed, and shall thereupon be discharged from further liability to said estate.

(1953 H 1, eff. 10–1–53; GC 10511–22)

Historical and Statutory Notes

Pre–1953 H 1 Amendments: 114 v 467

Library References

Executors and Administrators ⚖519(1).
Westlaw Topic No. 162.
C.J.S. Executors and Administrators § 924.

Research References

Encyclopedias

OH Jur. 3d Decedents' Estates § 1742, Payment of Debts to Ancillary Administrator.

2129.21 Bona fide purchaser protected

The bona fide purchaser of real or personal property sold as provided by law by an ancillary administrator shall take the title free from all obligations of the estate.

(125 v 903, eff. 10–1–53; 1953 H 1; GC 10511–23)

Historical and Statutory Notes

Pre–1953 H 1 Amendments: 114 v 467

Library References

Executors and Administrators ⚖519(2), 520.
Westlaw Topic No. 162.
C.J.S. Executors and Administrators §§ 924 to 926.

Research References

Encyclopedias

OH Jur. 3d Decedents' Estates § 1745, Sale of Real or Personal Property—Protection of Bona Fide Purchaser.

2129.22 Estate discharged by payment

When an ancillary administrator has paid a claim against the estate of a nonresident decedent, such estate shall be fully discharged of all liability therefor.

(125 v 903, eff. 10–1–53; 1953 H 1; GC 10511–24)

Historical and Statutory Notes

Pre–1953 H 1 Amendments: 114 v 467

Library References

Executors and Administrators ⚖522.
Westlaw Topic No. 162.
C.J.S. Executors and Administrators § 928.

Research References

Encyclopedias

OH Jur. 3d Decedents' Estates § 1741, Presentation and Payment of Creditors' Claims.

2129.23 Distribution

When the expense of the ancillary administration of a nonresident decedent's estate, including such attorney's fee as is allowed by the probate court, all public charges and taxes, and all claims of creditors presented as provided in section 2129.12 of the Revised Code, have been paid, any residue of the personal estate and the proceeds of any real estate sold for the payment of debts shall be distributed by the ancillary administrator as follows:

(A) With the approval of the court such residue may be delivered to the domiciliary administrator or executor.

(B) If the court orders, such residue shall be delivered to the persons entitled thereto.

(1953 H 1, eff. 10–1–53; GC 10511–25)

Historical and Statutory Notes

Pre–1953 H 1 Amendments: 114 v 467

Library References

Executors and Administrators ⚖523.
Westlaw Topic No. 162.
C.J.S. Executors and Administrators §§ 929 to 930.

Research References

Encyclopedias

OH Jur. 3d Decedents' Estates § 1749, Transmission or Distribution of Assets.

Treatises and Practice Aids

Restatement (2d) of Conflicts § 364, How Court of Administration Will Dispose of Balance.

Notes of Decisions

Court authority, limits 5
Direct distribution 6
Insolvent estate 3
Limitation of distribution 4
Priority of distribution 2
Succession tax 1

---

1. Succession tax

RC 5731.10 requires the apportionment of the exemptions allowed by RC 5731.09 but not the debts, including federal estate taxes and costs of administration, in assessing the Ohio tax on the succession from a nonresident decedent to Ohio property. In re Packard's Estate (Ohio 1963) 174 Ohio St. 349, 189 N.E.2d 434, 22 O.O.2d 409.

Where the executor of an estate may sell, lease, mortgage or otherwise dispose of any properties, real or personal, included in the residuary clause of the will of a nonresident decedent, and at the time of the decedent's death the property situated in Ohio is realty, the succession to which is subject to the Ohio succession tax, the debts, including federal estate taxes and costs of administration, should not be deducted in whole or on a proportionate basis from the appraised value of such realty in assessing the succession tax if there is sufficient personalty in such estate to pay such debts, taxes and costs. In re Packard's Estate (Ohio 1963) 174 Ohio St. 349, 189 N.E.2d 434, 22 O.O.2d 409.

2. Priority of distribution

RC 2129.23 provides that when the expenses of ancillary administration of a nonresident decedent's estate, including attorney's fees as is allowed by the probate court, all public charges and taxes, and all claims of creditors presented have been paid, any residue of the personal estate and the proceeds of any real estate sold for the payment of debts shall be distributed by the ancillary administrator, with the approval of the court, to the domiciliary administrator or executor, or if the court orders, to the persons entitled thereto. In re Radu's Estate (Cuyahoga 1973) 35 Ohio App.2d 187, 301 N.E.2d 263, 64 O.O.2d 293.

Because of the Ohio statutes, the equitable doctrine of pro rata payment to all creditors has no application in Ohio. In re Hirsch's Estate (Hamilton 1945) 76 Ohio App. 69, 63 N.E.2d 174, 43 Ohio Law Abs. 493, 31 O.O. 386, reversed 146 Ohio St. 393, 66 N.E.2d 636, 164 A.L.R. 761, 32 O.O. 445.

Section requires funds in hands of ancillary administrator of nonresident decedent's insolvent estate, after payment of expenses of ancillary administration including attorney fees, public charges and taxes, to be applied to the payment of all creditors' claims, duly presented and proven to the ancillary administrator, in accordance with the Ohio priority statute, before remission of any part thereof to the domiciliary administrator or the persons entitled thereto. In re Hirsch's Estate (Hamilton 1945) 76 Ohio App. 69, 63 N.E.2d 174, 43 Ohio Law Abs. 493, 31 O.O. 386, reversed 146 Ohio St. 393, 66 N.E.2d 636, 164 A.L.R. 761, 32 O.O. 445. Executors And Administrators 522

3. Insolvent estate

In the payment of unsecured claims allowed in an Ohio ancillary administration of a wholly insolvent estate, such administrator shall consider the total of the available assets in the hands of the domiciliary administrator and those in his own hands, and also the total of the unsecured claims allowed by the domiciliary administrator and those allowed in Ohio. In re Hirsch's Estate (Ohio 1946) 146 Ohio St. 393, 66 N.E.2d 636, 164 A.L.R. 761, 32 O.O. 445. Executors And Administrators 522

4. Limitation of distribution

RC 2129.23(B) places no restriction or limitation on persons entitled to the residue in ancillary administration, so that after payments of expenses, taxes, and debts, the probate court may, in its discretion, order the residue of the personal estate and the proceeds of any real estate sold for the payments of debts, distributed to heirs or legatees, whether resident in Ohio or not, and without limitation to bequests of specific property. In re Radu's Estate (Cuyahoga 1973) 35 Ohio App.2d 187, 301 N.E.2d 263, 64 O.O.2d 293. Executors And Administrators 523

5. Court authority, limits

A probate court of this state has no authority to order rejection of claims of domiciliary executor of another state, or to order ancillary administrator to require domiciliary executor to present his claims under GC 10509–112 (RC 2117.06), for rejection or allowance, or to make adjudication of rejection or allowance of these claims a condition precedent to distribution to named beneficiaries, or to order such distribution without regard to whether funds in hands of ancillary administrator are required by domiciliary administration to pay claims of domiciliary executor. In re Kelley's Estate (Hancock 1940) 68 Ohio App. 51, 34 N.E.2d 34, 33 Ohio Law Abs. 258, 22 O.O. 158.

Section confers discretion upon probate court, in ancillary administration, to order residuum of personal estate and proceeds of sale of real estate, remaining after payment of expenses of administration, public charges and taxes and all claims of resident creditors, to be distributed to legatees and distributees of specific property in this state, but court, in making such order, must take into consideration status of whole estate, wherever situated, as to assets and liabilities, with particular regard to principle that creditors are entitled to priority of payment out of assets of estate before legatees and distributees. In re Kelley's Estate (Hancock 1940) 68 Ohio App. 51, 34 N.E.2d 34, 33 Ohio Law Abs. 258, 22 O.O. 158.

6. Direct distribution

This section makes it within discretion of probate court as to whether ancillary administrator makes distribution direct, or returns funds in its hands to domiciliary administrator. Knight v. Burdsal (Ohio Com.Pl. 1937) 2 Ohio Supp. 375, 24 Ohio Law Abs. 28, 8 O.O. 363. Executors And Administrators 523

Where no domiciliary executor or administrator has been appointed, the court may order the ancillary administrator to make distribution directly to the persons entitled thereto. Mastics v Kiraly, 93 Abs 193, 196 NE(2d) 712 (Prob, Cuyahoga 1964).

2129.24 Fees

Probate judges, county recorders, and county auditors shall for services required by sections 2129.01 to 2129.30, inclusive, of the Revised Code, charge and collect the same fees as for similar services in the administration of the estates of resident decedents.

(1953 H 1, eff. 10–1–53; GC 10511–26)

Historical and Statutory Notes

Pre–1953 H 1 Amendments: 114 v 467

Library References

Executors and Administrators ⚖519(1), 520, 522, 524(3), 526.
Westlaw Topic No. 162.
C.J.S. Executors and Administrators §§ 924, 926, 928, 931, 934 to 935.

Research References

Encyclopedias
OH Jur. 3d Decedents' Estates § 1731, Fees.

FOREIGN EXECUTOR OR ADMINISTRATOR

2129.25 Foreign executor or administrator may be authorized to sell real estate

When an executor or administrator is appointed in any other state, territory, or foreign country for the estate of a person dying out of this state, and no executor or administrator thereon is appointed in this state, the foreign executor or administrator may file an authenticated copy of his appointment in the probate court of any county in which there is real estate of the deceased, together with an authenticated copy of the will. After filing such copies, he may be authorized, under an order of the court, to sell real estate for the payment of debts or legacies and charges of administration, in the manner prescribed in sections 2127.01 to 2127.43, inclusive, of the Revised Code.

(1953 H 1, eff. 10–1–53; GC 10511–27)

Historical and Statutory Notes

Pre–1953 H 1 Amendments: 114 v 468

Cross References

Sale of lands, Ch 2127

Library References

Executors and Administrators ⚖519(2), 520.
Westlaw Topic No. 162.
C.J.S. Executors and Administrators §§ 924 to 926.

Research References

Encyclopedias
OH Jur. 3d Decedents' Estates § 1718, Proceedings for Sale of Real Estate.

Treatises and Practice Aids
Carlin, Baldwin's Ohio Practice, Merrick-Rippner Probate Law § 90:2, Persons Entitled to Bring Land Sale Actions—Other Parties.
Carlin, Baldwin's Ohio Practice, Merrick-Rippner Probate Law § 90:4, Persons Entitled to Bring Land Sale Actions—Foreign Executor or Administrator.

Notes of Decisions

Foreign decree 1

Letters of administration 2

1. Foreign decree

A decree of a foreign court for the sale of lands lying in Ohio is entirely inoperative to transfer or affect any interest of the owner, either legal or equitable. Price v. Johnston (Ohio 1853) 1 Ohio St. 390.

Judicial proceedings in another state cannot affect interests in lands in this state. Blake's Lessee v. Davis (Ohio 1851) 20 Ohio 231.

Where a void decree is made in a court of a foreign state for the sale of Ohio lands, an heir who assents to the decree and the sale and acts as commissioner to carry it into execution passes his own title in equity. Beall v. Price (Ohio 1844) 13 Ohio 368, 42 Am.Dec. 204.

An order of a court of a foreign state compelling the sale by an administrator of land in this state is void; purchase money paid at such a sale cannot be recovered of the heirs, but taxes paid by such purchaser will be refunded. Nowler v. Coit (Ohio 1824) 1 Ohio 519, 13 Am.Dec. 640.

2. Letters of administration

A bill in equity to subject the real estate of a decedent in Ohio, where the heirs and representatives reside in another state and where no letters of administration have been taken in Ohio, cannot be sustained, unless the foreign creditor takes out letters of administration in Ohio. Bustard v. Dabney (Ohio 1829) 4 Ohio 68.

2129.26 Bond

When it appears to the probate court granting the order of sale set forth in section 2129.25 of the Revised Code that the foreign executor or administrator is bound with sufficient surety in the state or country in which he was appointed to account for the proceeds of such sale, for the payment of debts or legacies, and for charges of administration, and an authenticated copy of such bond is filed in court, no further bond for that purpose shall be required of him. When the court finds that such bond is insufficient, before making such sale, such foreign executor or administrator must give bond to this state with two or more sufficient sureties, conditioned to account for and dispose of such proceeds for the payment of the debts or legacies of the deceased and the charges of administration according to the laws of the state or country in which he was appointed.

When such foreign executor or administrator is authorized by order of the court to sell more than is necessary for the payment of debts, legacies, and charges of administration, before making the sale, he shall give bond with two or more sufficient sureties to this state, conditioned to account before the court for all the proceeds of the sale that remain and to dispose of such proceeds after payment of such debts, legacies, and charges.

(1953 H 1, eff. 10–1–53; GC 10511–28, 10511–29)

Historical and Statutory Notes

Pre–1953 H 1 Amendments: 114 v 468

Cross References

Bond of fiduciary, 2109.04 to 2109.20

Library References

Executors and Administrators ⇌520.
Westlaw Topic No. 162.
C.J.S. Executors and Administrators § 926.

Research References

Encyclopedias

OH Jur. 3d Fiduciaries § 183, New or Additional Bond—for Sale of Realty.

Treatises and Practice Aids

Carlin, Baldwin's Ohio Practice, Merrick-Rippner Probate Law § 90:2, Persons Entitled to Bring Land Sale Actions—Other Parties.

Notes of Decisions

Liability 1

1. Liability

Securities of an administrator are liable on their bond for the proceeds of lands sold by the administrator under an order of court for the payment of debts. Wade v. Graham (Ohio 1829) 4 Ohio 126.

TRUSTS UNDER FOREIGN WILL

2129.27 Trusts created by foreign will

Trusts created by a will made out of this state and relating to lands situated herein may be executed as provided in sections 2129.28 to 2129.30, inclusive, of the Revised Code, after the will is admitted to record in this state.

(1953 H 1, eff. 10–1–53; GC 10511–30)

Historical and Statutory Notes

Pre–1953 H 1 Amendments: 114 v 468

Library References

Trusts ⇌271.
Westlaw Topic No. 390.
C.J.S. Trusts §§ 318 to 320.

Research References

Encyclopedias

OH Jur. 3d Conflict of Laws § 38, Testamentary Trusts—Administration.

OH Jur. 3d Fiduciaries § 179, Bond Requirement for Testamentary Trust.

OH Jur. 3d Trusts § 173, Nonresidents—Nonresident Named in Foreign Will.

Treatises and Practice Aids

Kuehnle and Levey, Ohio Real Estate Law and Practice § 52:21, Statutory Fiduciary Sales—Action by Trustee to Sell Trust Property.

Notes of Decisions

Recovery of trust assets 1

1. Recovery of trust assets

The admission of a foreign will to record in this state and the giving of bond here relate back and give validity to notice and suit by a trust company for recovery of compensation for land held in trust and unlawfully taken by a railroad company. Union Sav. Bank & Trust Co. v. Baltimore & O.S.W.R. Co. (Ohio Insolv. 1908) 7 Ohio NP(NS) 497, 53 W.L.B. 450.

2129.28 Trustee's bond

If a trustee is named in a foreign will which creates a trust relating to lands situated in this state, such trustee may execute the trust upon giving bond to the state in such sum and with such sureties as the probate court of the county in which such lands or a part thereof are situated approves, conditioned to discharge with fidelity the trust reposed in him. If the testator in the will naming the trustee orders or requests that bond be not given by him, bond shall not be required, unless for sufficient cause the court requires it.

(1953 H 1, eff. 10–1–53; GC 10511–31)

Historical and Statutory Notes

Pre–1953 H 1 Amendments: 114 v 468

Cross References

Bond of fiduciary, 2109.04 to 2109.20

Library References

Trusts ⚖161.
Westlaw Topic No. 390.
C.J.S. Trusts § 302.

Research References

Encyclopedias

OH Jur. 3d Fiduciaries § 186, Dispensing With Bond.
OH Jur. 3d Trusts § 173, Nonresidents—Nonresident Named in Foreign Will.

Treatises and Practice Aids

Bogert - the Law of Trusts and Trustees § 151, Oath, Bond, and Letters of Trusteeship.

2129.29 Trustee appointed by a foreign court

If a trustee has been appointed under a foreign will which creates a trust relating to lands situated in this state by a foreign court according to the laws of the foreign jurisdiction, he may execute the trust upon giving bond as provided in section 2129.28 of the Revised Code, and after satisfying the probate court of the county in which such lands or a part of them are situated, by an authenticated record of his appointment, that he has been appointed trustee to execute the trust.

(1953 H 1, eff. 10–1–53; GC 10511–32)

Historical and Statutory Notes

Pre–1953 H 1 Amendments: 114 v 469

Library References

Trusts ⚖161, 270.
Westlaw Topic No. 390.
C.J.S. Trusts §§ 302, 321 to 324, 330 to 331.

Research References

Encyclopedias

OH Jur. 3d Fiduciaries § 186, Dispensing With Bond.
OH Jur. 3d Trusts § 173, Nonresidents—Nonresident Named in Foreign Will.

2129.30 Probate court may appoint a trustee under a foreign will

When necessary, the probate court of the county where the property affected by the trust is situated, on application by petition of the parties interested, may appoint a trustee to carry into effect a trust created by a foreign will. Such trustee, before entering upon his trust, must give bond with such security and in such amount as the court directs.

(1953 H 1, eff. 10–1–53; GC 10511–33)

Historical and Statutory Notes

Pre–1953 H 1 Amendments: 114 v 469

Library References

Trusts ⚖160(1).
Westlaw Topic No. 390.
C.J.S. Trusts §§ 295 to 296.

Research References

Encyclopedias

OH Jur. 3d Conflict of Laws § 38, Testamentary Trusts—Administration.
OH Jur. 3d Fiduciaries § 179, Bond Requirement for Testamentary Trust.
OH Jur. 3d Trusts § 173, Nonresidents—Nonresident Named in Foreign Will.

Treatises and Practice Aids

Kuehnle and Levey, Ohio Real Estate Law and Practice § 10:51, Rights of Heirs When Owner Dies Resident Out of County, Preserving Marketability.

CHAPTER 2131

MISCELLANEOUS

Section
2131.01 Present values for estate tax purposes used as present values for probate matters
2131.02 Legal disability defined

FUTURE INTERESTS

2131.04 Expectant estates descendible, devisable and alienable
2131.05 Validity of remainders
2131.06 When expectant estates defeated
2131.07 Estate in fee simple may be made defeasible

RULE AGAINST PERPETUITIES

2131.08 Statute against perpetuities
2131.09 Exemption of certain trusts

DEPOSITS PAYABLE ON DEATH

2131.10 Any natural person, entity, or organization may be beneficiary of P.O.D. account
2131.11 Release and discharge upon payment

Section

TRANSFER OF MOTOR VEHICLE, WATERCRAFT, OR OUTBOARD MOTOR ON DEATH

2131.12 Joint ownership with right of survivorship of motor vehicle, watercraft, or outboard motor
2131.13 Designation of motor vehicle, watercraft, or outboard motor in beneficiary form

DEPOSIT OF SECURITIES HELD BY FIDUCIARY

2131.21 Fiduciary may deposit securities in federal reserve bank, clearing corporation, or securities depository; procedures

2131.01 Present values for estate tax purposes used as present values for probate matters

Present values for probate matters shall be the values determined for Ohio estate tax purposes pursuant to division (B) of section 5731.01 of the Revised Code.

(1999 H 59, eff. 10–29–99)

Historical and Statutory Notes

Ed. Note: Former 2131.01 repealed by 1999 H 59, eff. 10–29–99; 1953 H 1, eff. 10–1–53; GC 10512–1.

Pre–1953 H 1 Amendments: 114 v 469

Library References

Internal Revenue ⇐4183.10.
Taxation ⇐895(1).
Westlaw Topic Nos. 220, 371.
C.J.S. Internal Revenue §§ 519 to 520, 524.
C.J.S. Taxation §§ 1900 to 1901, 1904 to 1905, 1909, 1941, 1943 to 1944.

Research References

Encyclopedias

OH Jur. 3d Family Law § 178, Partition Action.

Treatises and Practice Aids

Carlin, Baldwin's Ohio Practice, Merrick-Rippner Probate Law § 64:78, Application of Guardian for Sale of Dower Interest—Form.

Carlin, Baldwin's Ohio Practice, Merrick-Rippner Probate Law § 91:47, Complaint of Guardian for Authority to Sell Real Estate—Form.

Carlin, Baldwin's Ohio Practice, Merrick-Rippner Probate Law § 91:48, Entry Authorizing Sale of Real Estate and Appraisal—Form.

Carlin, Baldwin's Ohio Practice, Merrick-Rippner Probate Law § 91:49, Complaint for Authority to Sell Entire Interest in Real Estate—Form.

Carlin, Baldwin's Ohio Practice, Merrick-Rippner Probate Law § 91:51, Entry Granting Complaint and Ordering Appraisal of Entire Interest—Form.

Carlin, Baldwin's Ohio Practice, Merrick-Rippner Probate Law § 92:16, Dower—Computation of Interest.

Carlin, Baldwin's Ohio Practice, Merrick-Rippner Probate Law § 92:17, Dower—Interest Subject to Debts.

Carlin, Baldwin's Ohio Practice, Merrick-Rippner Probate Law § 92:19, Dower—Sale of Land Subject to Interest.

Carlin, Baldwin's Ohio Practice, Merrick-Rippner Probate Law § 92:23, Answer of Spouse—Form.

Carlin, Baldwin's Ohio Practice, Merrick-Rippner Probate Law § 95:21, Entry Authorizing Sale of Real Estate at Private Sale—Form.

Carlin, Baldwin's Ohio Practice, Merrick-Rippner Probate Law § 96:16, Entry Confirming Sale, Ordering Deed and Distribution—Form.

Carlin, Baldwin's Ohio Practice, Merrick-Rippner Probate Law § 96:17, Entry Confirming Sale, Ordering Deed and Distribution Where Entire Interest in Real Estate Sold—Form.

Kuehnle and Levey, Ohio Real Estate Law and Practice § 9:4, Incohate Right of Dower of Person Not a Party to Contract of Sale.

Kuehnle and Levey, Ohio Real Estate Law and Practice § 51:6, Partition—Spouse of Co-Tenant as Necessary Party.

Kuehnle and Levey, Ohio Real Estate Law and Practice § 38:15, Foreclosure—Sheriff's Sales—Distribution—Dower.

Notes of Decisions

Ed. Note: *This section contains annotations from former RC 2131.01.*

Dower 1
Life tenancy 2
Personal injury 3
Remainders 4

---

1. Dower

The value of a wife's contingent right to dower can be ascertained by reference to tables of recognized authority on mortality, in connection with the state of health and constitutional vigor of the wife and her husband. Unger v. Leiter (Ohio 1877) 32 Ohio St. 210.

The present value of one's right to dower depends largely on the length of one's life, which can be approximately ascertained by the use of mathematical mortality tables. Black's Adm'r v. Kuhlman (Ohio 1876) 30 Ohio St. 196.

The contingent right of a wife, during her husband's life, to be endowed of his real estate at his death, is property having a substantial value that may be ascertained with reasonable certainty from established tables of mortality, aided by evidence respecting the state of health and constitutional vigor of the husband and wife respectively. Mandel v. McClave (Ohio 1889) 46 Ohio St. 407, 22 W.L.B. 267, 22 N.E. 290, 15 Am.St.Rep. 627. Dower And Curtesy ⇐ 32

A wife's contingent right of dower is to be ascertained in the entire proceeds of a sale of land, from tables of mortality, aided by evidence respecting the state of health and constitutional vigor of the husband and wife respectively. Moerlein Brewing Co. v. Westmeier (Ohio Cir. 1890) 2 Ohio C.D. 555.

2. Life tenancy

Where lands are sold pursuant to RC 5303.21 and both life tenants are shown to enjoy excellent health, the value of their shares should be determined by application of the statutory six per cent formula and the factor determined by reference to the mortality table prescribed by RC 2131.01 for the age of the younger life tenant, with the resulting percentage of the net sales proceeds to be distributed equally between such life tenants; the balance should be placed in trust to be accumulated until the death of the surviving life tenant and then distributed among the remaindermen as provided by the court under the will and applicable statutes. Henderson v. Henderson (Ohio Com.Pl. 1968) 15 Ohio Misc. 276, 237 N.E.2d 336, 44 O.O.2d 463.

Where the probate court fixes the value of a life estate and remainder based on the actuarial value on the date of death, it may not subsequently adjust the values based on the actual duration of the life estate and order a refund. In re Hough's Estate (Ohio Prob. 1958) 152 N.E.2d 561, 78 Ohio Law Abs. 238. Taxation ⇐ 3358

3. Personal injury

In an action against a saloon keeper by a wife for selling liquor to her husband after notice not to sell, where the husband due to intoxication had his limbs amputated after they were frozen, the Carlisle mortality tables were admissible in evidence. Wasmer v. Rawlins (Ohio 1901) 64 Ohio St. 585, 46 W.L.B. 147, 61 N.E. 1150. Damages ⇐ 167; Evidence ⇐ 364

4. Remainders

Where testamentary gift is given in form of remainder or other future interest, value of gift, for purposes of mortmain statute, is "present value" of interest as of date of testator's death. In re Roberts' Estate (Wood 1980) 1 Ohio App.3d 15, 437 N.E.2d 1205, 1 O.B.R. 80. Wills ⇐ 15

2131.02 Legal disability defined

"Legal disability" as used in Chapters 2101., 2103., 2105., 2107., 2109., 2111., 2113., 2115., 2117., 2119., 2121., 2123., 2125., 2127., 2129., and 2131. of the Revised Code includes the following:

(A) Persons under the age of eighteen years;

(B) Persons of unsound mind;

(C) Persons in captivity;

(D) Persons under guardianship of the person and estate, or either.

(1973 S 1, eff. 1–1–74; 1953 H 1; GC 10512–2)

Historical and Statutory Notes

Pre-1953 H 1 Amendments: 114 v 469

Cross References

Age of majority, 3109.01

Library References

Convicts ⚖=1.
Guardian and Ward ⚖=1.
Infants ⚖=1.
Limitation of Actions ⚖=70 to 75.
Mental Health ⚖=104, 331.
Westlaw Topic Nos. 196, 211, 241, 257A, 98.
C.J.S. Convicts §§ 2 to 3.
C.J.S. Infants §§ 2 to 4.
C.J.S. Limitations of Actions §§ 105 to 106, 110 to 118.
C.J.S. Mental Health §§ 111, 209.

Research References

Encyclopedias

OH Jur. 3d Decedents' Estates § 1117, Statutory Time Limitation, Generally—for Persons Under a Disability.
OH Jur. 3d Guardian & Ward § 3, Nature of Guardian Ward Relationship.

Forms

Ohio Jurisprudence Pleading and Practice Forms § 22:8, Capacity of Minors and Incompetent Persons.

Treatises and Practice Aids

Carlin, Baldwin's Ohio Practice, Merrick-Rippner Probate Law § 38:2, Will Contests—Statutory Provisions.
Carlin, Baldwin's Ohio Practice, Merrick-Rippner Probate Law § 38:4, Will Contests—Interested Persons.
Carlin, Baldwin's Ohio Practice, Merrick-Rippner Probate Law § 61:1, Legal Disability—Introduction.
Carlin, Baldwin's Ohio Practice, Merrick-Rippner Probate Law § 61:2, Legal Disability—Person Under the Age of 18.
Carlin, Baldwin's Ohio Practice, Merrick-Rippner Probate Law § 61:4, Legal Disability—Person in Captivity.
Carlin, Baldwin's Ohio Practice, Merrick-Rippner Probate Law § 61:5, Legal Disability—Person Under Guardianship of Person or Estate.
Carlin, Baldwin's Ohio Practice, Merrick-Rippner Probate Law § 21:36, Rights of Surviving Spouse to Make Election—One Under Legal Disability—Discretion of Probate Court in Making Election.
Kuehnle and Levey, Ohio Real Estate Law and Practice § 20:18, Conveyancing—Grantors—Capacity—Individuals—Minors and Persons Incarcerated.

Notes of Decisions

Captivity 3
Guardianship 5
Mental incapacity 2
Minority 1
Time limit, reinstatement 4

1. Minority

Great-grandchildren of a decedent who are not legatees under the will are not "persons interested" in the will for purposes of bringing a will contest action under RC 2107.71; therefore, the fact that the great-grandchildren of decedent are under the legal disability of minority does not toll the four-month statute of limitations for filing a will contest, since the great-grandchildren have no standing to file such suit. Mayfield v. Herderick (Franklin 1986) 33 Ohio App.3d 44, 514 N.E.2d 441.

2. Mental incapacity

RC 5123.57 does not apply as a defense to a party to an action on a contract until such party establishes by credible evidence an adjudication of mental incapacity and a lawful commitment to a state institution by a probate court. Elder v. Baker (Cuyahoga 1962) 115 Ohio App. 372, 180 N.E.2d 858, 20 O.O.2d 448.

A person committed to a mental hospital for mental incompetency is of unsound mind within the definition of legal disability contained in RC 2117.07 and RC 2131.02, and under RC 5123.57 such mental incompetency continues until it is finally dissolved by an order of court; and a person legally a person of unsound mind (even though not necessarily so in fact) during a part of the four-month period who, during such period, is, by proper application on order of court, legally restored to mental competency, may be allowed to present a late claim, such legal disability of a person as an individual being attributable to such person as a "claimant" under RC 2117.07. In re Wyckoff's Estate (Licking 1958) 105 Ohio App. 212, 152 N.E.2d 141, 6 O.O.2d 42.

3. Captivity

A person confined in a county jail is a person in captivity as defined in this section. In re Gogan's Estate (Cuyahoga 1951) 108 N.E.2d 170, 63 Ohio Law Abs. 69.

Where claimant was confined in hospital for basilar skull fracture and broken femur and for a period of six to eight weeks suffered from mental confusion, was kept under sedatives for extended period and was administered hypnotic drugs for three to four weeks, claimant was under a "legal disability" within statute authorizing presentment of claim against estate to administrator thereof after four months if claimant was subject to any "legal disability" during any part of such period. In re Price's Estate (Darke 1949) 87 Ohio App. 23, 93 N.E.2d 769, 42 O.O. 272. Executors And Administrators ⚖= 225(6)

4. Time limit, reinstatement

Neither death nor the inability to sue due to a delay in the appointment of a legal representative is a "legal disability" under RC 2131.02 for purposes of tolling the four-month statute of limitations found in RC 2107.76 for bringing a will contest action under RC 2107.71. Mayfield v. Herderick (Franklin 1986) 33 Ohio App.3d 44, 514 N.E.2d 441.

The definition of "legal disability" in RC 2131.02 is not for use in connection with the tolling statute, RC 2305.16. Seguin v. Gallo (Cuyahoga 1985) 21 Ohio App.3d 163, 486 N.E.2d 1270, 21 O.B.R. 174.

A probate court is guilty of an abuse of discretion in refusing a claimant the right to file a claim with an executor after the expiration of the four-month time limit when such refusal to allow the claim to be filed prevents the revivor of an action pending against the executor's decedent in the court of common pleas, where the uncontradicted evidence establishes that the claimant was under a legal disability. In re Fuller's Estate (Medina 1960) 112 Ohio App. 25, 174 N.E.2d 613, 15 O.O.2d 378.

Physical aches and pains, headaches, dizziness and inability to walk around or drive an automobile are not legal excuses for failure to comply with the statutory provisions for the presentation of claims against an estate, and where such claimant for the four-month period following the appointment of the administrator was able to and did go about and look into his business and affairs, he was not under legal disability. In re Christman's Estate (Crawford 1955) 100 Ohio App. 133, 136 N.E.2d 80, 60 O.O. 129.

GC 10509–134 (RC 2117.07) and this section must be construed in pari materia. In re Gogan's Estate (Cuyahoga 1951) 108 N.E.2d 170, 63 Ohio Law Abs. 69.

It is an abuse of discretion for a probate court to refuse to permit a claimant to file an alleged claim with an administrator more than four months after the latter's appointment where there is a clear showing of legal disability on the claimant's part. In re Gogan's Estate (Cuyahoga 1951) 108 N.E.2d 170, 63 Ohio Law Abs. 69.

In order to be entitled to relief asked for in a petition to reinstate barred claims, creditor must plead one of the following allegations: first: that claimant was under "legal disability," as provided by this section; second: that creditor was absent from state for greater portion of the four months period immediately following appointment of executor or administrator, and had no notice of the death of debtor or appointment of a fiduciary; third: that claimant's rights had been prejudiced by fraud or misrepresentation occasioned by the conduct of the executor or administrator. In re Dudley's Estate (Ohio Prob. 1937) 2 Ohio Supp. 95, 23 Ohio Law Abs. 522, 8 O.O. 404. Executors And Administrators ⚖= 233

5. Guardianship

Alleged mental competence of ward was irrelevant to question of validity of fees and expenses related to ward's attorney's challenge to guardianship.

2131.02
Note 5

In re Guardianship of Allen (Ohio 1990) 50 Ohio St.3d 142, 552 N.E.2d 934, rehearing denied 51 Ohio St.3d 705, 555 N.E.2d 322. Mental Health ⚖ 159

Children committed by a juvenile court to a county department of welfare pursuant to RC Ch 2151, either permanently or temporarily, remain the responsibility of the department until they reach the age of twenty-one, unless the court, upon a proper application, terminates the order of commission at an earlier date. OAG 75–035.

FUTURE INTERESTS

2131.04 Expectant estates descendible, devisable and alienable

Remainders, whether vested or contingent, executory interests, and other expectant estates are descendible, devisable, and alienable in the same manner as estates in possession.

(1953 H 1, eff. 10–1–53; GC 10512–4)

Historical and Statutory Notes

Pre–1953 H 1 Amendments: 114 v 470

Cross References

Sale of entailed and other estates, 5303.21

Library References

Descent and Distribution ⚖ 17.
Wills ⚖ 7.
Westlaw Topic Nos. 124, 409.
C.J.S. Descent and Distribution § 22.
C.J.S. Wills §§ 53, 58, 63 to 64, 68.

Research References

Encyclopedias

OH Jur. 3d Decedents' Estates § 65, Future and Contingent Interests and Estates.
OH Jur. 3d Decedents' Estates § 66, Future and Contingent Interests and Estates—Remainders and Reversions.
OH Jur. 3d Decedents' Estates § 67, Future and Contingent Interests and Estates—Possibilities of Reverter and Rights of Re-Entry.
OH Jur. 3d Decedents' Estates § 129, Release of Expectancy.
OH Jur. 3d Decedents' Estates § 274, Expectancies, Executory Interests, Remainders, and Reversionary Interests.
OH Jur. 3d Estates, Pwrs., & Restrnts. on Alienat. § 85, Breach of Condition Subsequent; Forfeiture of Estate.
OH Jur. 3d Estates, Pwrs., & Restrnts. on Alienat. § 91, Possibilities of Reverter and Rights of Reentry for Condition Broken—Alienability.
OH Jur. 3d Estates, Pwrs., & Restrnts. on Alienat. § 94, Decreasing Significance of Technical Distinctions.
OH Jur. 3d Estates, Pwrs., & Restrnts. on Alienat. § 124, Right to Transfer Remainders.
OH Jur. 3d Estates, Pwrs., & Restrnts. on Alienat. § 130, Transfer.

Forms

Am. Jur. Pl. & Pr. Forms Estates § 2, 2.

Treatises and Practice Aids

Carlin, Baldwin's Ohio Practice, Merrick-Rippner Probate Law § 10:1, Expectant Estates—Statutory Provision.

Law Review and Journal Commentaries

Ohio Dynasty Trusts: Where are We Now? Craig F. Frederickson, 12 Prob L J Ohio 104 (July/August 2002).

Reversionary restrictions, Charles C. White. 14 U Cin L Rev 524 (November 1940).

Rule Against Perpetuity—The Case for Exemption of Trusts or The Repeal of the Rule, Gerald P. Moran and Craig F. Frederickson. 6 Prob L J Ohio 10 (September/October 1995).

'Tis a Gift to be Simple: The Need for a New Definition of "Future Interest" for Gift Tax Purposes, Jeffrey G. Sherman. 55 U Cin L Rev 585 (1987).

Notes of Decisions

Contingent remainders 2
Fee tails 3
Possibility of reverter 5
Procedural issues 4
Spendthrift trust 6
Vested remainders 1

---

1. Vested remainders

Estate of trust beneficiary who survived settlor but died before distribution of trust's real property was entitled to beneficiary's share of trust's real property, pursuant to trust instrument that granted beneficiary life estate in most of the property then ordered distribution to settlor's three children, including beneficiary, even though provision authorizing distribution to the issue of beneficiaries who predeceased settlor did not apply; beneficiary's remainder interest vested when he survived settlor and was descendible and devisable, and settlor did not manifest an intent that only living beneficiaries receive distribution of trust property. McCoy v. Witzleb (Ohio App. 2 Dist., Greene, 12-16-2005) No. 2005 CA 25, 2005-Ohio-6678, 2005 WL 3454689, Unreported. Trusts ⚖ 140(3)

Under GC 8573 (RC 2105.01, RC 2105.06) as it existed in 1912 the vesting of property in the brothers and sisters of an intestate upon the death of his relict was postponed until the death of such relict. Green v. Shough (Fayette 1958) 158 N.E.2d 736, 80 Ohio Law Abs. 248.

Where a testator devised to his son for life with a remainder to his grandchildren, the grandchildren's interest vested on the death of the testator, and the interest of a grandchild who died intestate during the life of the life tenant passed under the law of descent and distribution. Hoppes v. American Nat. Red Cross (Ohio Com.Pl. 1955) 128 N.E.2d 851, 71 Ohio Law Abs. 259.

Where a life estate is devised to testator's wife "so long as she remains my widow," and the remainder is left equally to testator's two children, the children take vested remainders in fee, subject to the interest of the widow, which remainders may be alienated or mortgaged. Eastman v. Sohl (Franklin 1940) 66 Ohio App. 383, 34 N.E.2d 291, 33 Ohio Law Abs. 160, 20 O.O. 305. Life Estates ⚖ 3; Wills ⚖ 634(1)

"Remainder" is "vested" where there is present fixed right to future enjoyment. Simpson v. Welsh (Knox 1932) 44 Ohio App. 115, 184 N.E. 242, 13 Ohio Law Abs. 714. Wills ⚖ 634(1)

Under Ohio law, "life estate" is freehold estate, not an estate of inheritance, whereby tenant holds property for his or her own life, or for lives of one or more other persons, with fee then vesting in one or more remainderman upon death of the life-in-being. In re Sargent (Bkrtcy. N.D.Ohio, 01-04-2006) 337 B.R. 661. Life Estates ⚖ 1

2. Contingent remainders

Where separation agreement embodied in divorce decree mandates insurance coverage and unambiguously designates purpose for which insurance proceeds are to be used by certain beneficiaries, constructive trust for that designated purpose is appropriate remedy to ensure that proceeds are used for the purpose intended under the agreement; moreover, insured party or policy owner has contingent right to dispose of any proceeds not used by beneficiaries in accordance with agreement's express purpose. Aetna Life Ins. Co. v. Hussey (Ohio 1992) 63 Ohio St.3d 640, 590 N.E.2d 724, decision clarified on rehearing 64 Ohio St.3d 1207, 595 N.E.2d 942. Insurance ⚖ 3481(1); Trusts ⚖ 103(3)

The interest of the beneficiary of a spendthrift trust can be reached by the wife and dependent children of the beneficiary, and where the beneficiary has not come into enjoyment of the interest, the court will reserve jurisdiction until he does. O'Connor v. O'Connor (Ohio Com.Pl. 1957) 141 N.E.2d 691, 75 Ohio Law Abs. 420, 3 O.O.2d 186.

"Remainder" is "contingent" which comes into enjoyment or possession on happening of some uncertain event. Simpson v. Welsh (Knox 1932) 44 Ohio App. 115, 184 N.E. 242, 13 Ohio Law Abs. 714. Wills ⚖ 634(1)

A remainder to a son following a life estate in the mother is vested in interest though contingent as to amount where the mother has the right to use principal as well as interest for her support; the son's interest therefore falls within the "real and personal" property of a husband that a decree for alimony may be charged to under RS 5699, subject to the right of the widow. Min Young v. Min Young (Ohio 1890) 47 Ohio St. 501, 24 W.L.B. 260, 25 N.E. 168.

3. Fee tails

The common-law fee tail estate exists in Ohio and the statutory enactment of December 17, 1811 (10 Ohio Laws 7), now embodied in RC 2131.08, which converted estates tail into fees simple in the issue of the first donee in tail, did not change the nature of the estate in the donee in tail from an inheritable estate to an estate for life, but merely restricted the entailment to the immediate issue of such donee. Long v. Long (Ohio 1976) 45 Ohio St.2d 165, 343 N.E.2d 100, 74 O.O.2d 287.

There remains in the grantor of a fee tail estate a reversion in fee simple expectant upon the failure of a stated condition, which reversion is a descendible, devisable and alienable estate, which, if otherwise undisposed of, passes upon the death of the grantor by descent to his heirs then living. Long v. Long (Ohio 1976) 45 Ohio St.2d 165, 343 N.E.2d 100, 74 O.O.2d 287. Descent And Distribution ⚖ 17

4. Procedural issues

Former husband had a vested interest to $20,000 in estate of third person which was capable of being a gift to his former wife; former husband was an heir, as well as executor of the estate, and third person was deceased at the time of the attempted gift (Per opinion of McFarland, J., with two judges concurring in the result). Bobo v. Stansberry (Ohio App. 4 Dist., 07-29-2005) 162 Ohio App.3d 565, 834 N.E.2d 373, 2005-Ohio-3928. Gifts ⚖ 27

RC 2131.04 codified the existing common law. Schneider v. Dorr (Ohio Prob. 1965) 3 Ohio Misc. 103, 210 N.E.2d 311, 32 O.O.2d 391.

Equitable or beneficial ownership or interest in securities is alienable and may be conveyed. Moore v. Foresman (Ohio 1962) 172 Ohio St. 559, 179 N.E.2d 349, 18 O.O.2d 123. Property ⚖ 11

In an action to determine title to real property, the remaindermen who will take a fee simple upon the death of the life tenant are proper parties to be joined as plaintiffs, and a determination of their interest is res judicata. Scott v. Wilson (Fayette 1955) 136 N.E.2d 282, 73 Ohio Law Abs. 85.

Where there is a distribution of stock in kind to one of the two remaindermen, prior to the termination of the widow's life estate, consented to by the probate court and all interested parties, and, subsequently, at the end of the life estate there is not sufficient personalty remaining to give a like amount to the other remainderman under the will, such other remainderman, in an action to partition the real estate, is entitled to a lien on the proceeds of the sale in partition up to the amount advanced to the first remainderman, before the fund so obtained shall be divided equally between them; but, where the transfer of the real estate to the persons named in the will has been ordered by the court to be made on the tax duplicate and where the certificate of transfer has been issued and recorded, the lien of such other remainderman is inferior to the liens of creditors against the interest of such first remainderman. Eastman v. Sohl (Franklin 1940) 66 Ohio App. 383, 34 N.E.2d 291, 33 Ohio Law Abs. 160, 20 O.O. 305.

Future interests are expressly made transmissible by this section. Joseph Schonthal Co. v. Village of Sylvania (Lucas 1938) 60 Ohio App. 407, 21 N.E.2d 1008, 14 O.O. 471.

"Estate in remainder" is estate limited to take effect in possession immediately after expiration of prior estate created at same time by same instrument. Simpson v. Welsh (Knox 1932) 44 Ohio App. 115, 184 N.E. 242, 13 Ohio Law Abs. 714. Remainders ⚖ 1

Under Ohio law, remainderman interests are fully alienable. In re Sargent (Bkrtcy.N.D.Ohio, 01-04-2006) 337 B.R. 661. Remainders ⚖ 14

5. Possibility of reverter

A possibility of reverter is alienable. Willis v. Hannah (Ohio Com.Pl. 1966) 9 Ohio Misc. 221, 224 N.E.2d 769, 38 O.O.2d 396. Deeds ⚖ 156

Where property is conveyed for highway purposes with the grantor retaining a possibility of reverter, a conveyance of the adjoining property thereafter with an exception of such property contained therein is not sufficient to retain the possibility of reverter in the grantor. Willis v. Hannah (Ohio Com.Pl. 1966) 9 Ohio Misc. 221, 224 N.E.2d 769, 38 O.O.2d 396.

RC 2131.04 permits a contract to convey, or the actual conveyance, of a possibility of reverter before a right of re-entry is exercised or before an estate is automatically terminated through breach of condition which delimits the duration of the estate. P C K Properties, Inc. v. City of Cuyahoga Falls (Summit 1960) 112 Ohio App. 492, 176 N.E.2d 441, 16 O.O.2d 378.

An inter vivos trust which reserves to the trustor the income for life and an absolute power to revoke during his lifetime with a remainder over at his death, creates in the remainderman a vested interest subject to defeasance by the exercise of the power to revoke, which may be bequeathed by the remainderman, the legatee taking such interest subject only to the same limitations and possibility of defeasance as were imposed upon the interest held by the testator. First Nat. Bank of Cincinnati v. Tenney (Ohio 1956) 165 Ohio St. 513, 138 N.E.2d 15, 61 A.L.R.2d 470, 60 O.O. 481. Trusts ⚖ 140(3)

6. Spendthrift trust

Trust which provided that trustee would distribute the property outright to the beneficiary unless he were insolvent, had filed a petition of bankruptcy, or would not personally enjoy the property and which made the trust discretionary in those situations, with the beneficiary entitled to outright distribution of the trust when all those conditions ceased to exist, was a "spendthrift trust." Scott v. Bank One Trust Co., N.A. (Ohio 1991) 62 Ohio St.3d 39, 577 N.E.2d 1077. Trusts ⚖ 28

2131.05 Validity of remainders

A remainder valid in its creation shall not be defeated by the determination of the precedent estate before the happening of the contingency on which the remainder was limited to take effect. Should such contingency afterwards happen, the remainder shall take effect in the same manner and to the same extent as if the precedent estate had continued to the same period.

(1953 H 1, eff. 10–1–53; GC 10512–5)

Historical and Statutory Notes

Pre–1953 H 1 Amendments: 114 v 470

Library References

Remainders ⚖3.
Westlaw Topic No. 333.
C.J.S. Estates §§ 70 to 71, 77.

Research References

Encyclopedias

OH Jur. 3d Estates, Pwrs., & Restrnts. on Alienat. § 94, Decreasing Significance of Technical Distinctions.
OH Jur. 3d Estates, Pwrs., & Restrnts. on Alienat. § 96, Necessity and Character of Particular Estate.

Law Review and Journal Commentaries

Ohio Dynasty Trusts: Where are We Now? Craig F. Frederickson, 12 Prob L J Ohio 104 (July/August 2002).

Rule Against Perpetuity—The Case for Exemption of Trusts or The Repeal of the Rule, Gerald P. Moran and Craig F. Frederickson. 6 Prob L J Ohio 10 (September/October 1995).

Notes of Decisions

Contingent remainder   2
Limitation of estate   1
Settlement   3

---

1. Limitation of estate

What would otherwise be an estate is not a mere possibility of an estate because it may terminate by its own limitation before another estate is provided to arise. Cleveland Trust Co. v. McQuade (Cuyahoga 1957) 106 Ohio App. 237, 142 N.E.2d 249, 76 Ohio Law Abs. 324, 6 O.O.2d 493.

A devise to one when he arrives at a given age—the intermediate estate being devised to another—vests on the death of the testator, and is not defeated by the death of the devisee before the specified age. Cleveland Trust Co. v. McQuade (Cuyahoga 1957) 106 Ohio App. 237, 142 N.E.2d 249, 76 Ohio Law Abs. 324, 6 O.O.2d 493.

2. Contingent remainder

A provision in a will that upon the death of eight named persons the trust shall terminate and the principal and accumulated income shall be paid over and delivered to the various named residuary beneficiaries, if they survive, creates a contingent interest in such remaindermen. Cleveland Trust Co. v. McQuade (Cuyahoga 1957) 106 Ohio App. 237, 142 N.E.2d 249, 76 Ohio Law Abs. 324, 6 O.O.2d 493.

3. Settlement

The proper court may, under appropriate circumstances, approve a valid compromise agreement in which the beneficiary of a spendthrift testamentary trust releases her rights in the trust as part of an overall settlement of the will contest and in consideration of other payments made to her or for her benefit, when there is a genuine will contest pending; when the payment is made to one who is properly contesting the validity of the will; when the payment to the contestant (and the contestant's reciprocal surrender of her interest in the spendthrift trust) is reasonably necessary in order to protect the interest of the other beneficiaries in the will, which might be lost in the event that the will was wholly upset; and when the settlement appears by its terms to be fair and equitable. Central Nat. Bank of Cleveland v. Eells (Ohio Prob. 1965) 5 Ohio Misc. 187, 215 N.E.2d 77, 33 O.O.2d 418. Wills ⚖ 740(2)

2131.06 When expectant estates defeated

An expectant estate cannot be defeated or barred by any transfer or other act of the owner of the intermediate or precedent estate, nor by any destruction of such precedent estate by disseizen [sic.], forfeiture, surrender, merger, or otherwise; but an expectant estate may be defeated in any manner which the party creating such estate, in the creation thereof, has provided for or authorized. An expectant estate thus liable to be defeated shall not, on that ground, be adjudged void in its creation.

(1953 H 1, eff. 10–1–53; GC 10512–6)

Historical and Statutory Notes

Pre–1953 H 1 Amendments: 114 v 470

Library References

Life Estates ⚖ 4.
Remainders ⚖ 9, 10.
Westlaw Topic Nos. 240, 333.
C.J.S. Estates §§ 59, 88, 129, 152.

Research References

Encyclopedias

OH Jur. 3d Estates, Pwrs., & Restrnts. on Alienat. § 94, Decreasing Significance of Technical Distinctions.

Notes of Decisions

Release 1

1. Release

The proper court may, under appropriate circumstances, approve a valid compromise agreement in which the beneficiary of a spendthrift testamentary trust releases her rights in the trust as part of an overall settlement of the will contest and in consideration of other payments made to her or for her benefit, when there is a genuine will contest pending; when the payment is made to one who is properly contesting the validity of the will; when the payment to the contestant (and the contestant's reciprocal surrender of her interest in the spendthrift trust) is reasonably necessary in order to protect the interest of the other beneficiaries in the will, which might be lost in the event that the will was wholly upset; and when the settlement appears by its terms to be fair and equitable. Central Nat. Bank of Cleveland v. Eells (Ohio Prob. 1965) 5 Ohio Misc. 187, 215 N.E.2d 77, 33 O.O.2d 418. Wills ⚖ 740(2)

An estate tail cannot be enlarged into an estate in fee simple absolute through the release by the original donor of his possibility of reversion to the donee in tail. Guida v. Thompson (Ohio Com.Pl. 1957) 160 N.E.2d 153, 80 Ohio Law Abs. 148.

2131.07 Estate in fee simple may be made defeasible

An estate in fee simple may be made defeasible upon the death of the holder thereof without having conveyed or devised the same, and the limitation over upon such event shall be a valid future interest. For the purpose of involuntary alienation, such a defeasible fee is a fee simple absolute.

(1953 H 1, eff. 10–1–53; GC 10512–7)

Historical and Statutory Notes

Pre–1953 H 1 Amendments: 114 v 470

Library References

Deeds ⚖ 125.
Estates in Property ⚖ 5.
Wills ⚖ 541, 602.
Westlaw Topic Nos. 120, 154, 409.
C.J.S. Deeds § 246.
C.J.S. Estates § 9.
C.J.S. Wills §§ 1029, 1033 to 1051, 1242 to 1257.

Research References

Encyclopedias

OH Jur. 3d Estates, Pwrs., & Restrnts. on Alienat. § 133, Particular Provisions Creating Executory Interests—Limitations Over on Failure to Convey or Devise.

OH Jur. 3d Estates, Pwrs., & Restrnts. on Alienat. § 134, Particular Provisions Creating Executory Interests—Limitations Over of Property Remaining at Death.

Law Review and Journal Commentaries

Life Estate or Fee?, Charles C. White. 1 U Cin L Rev 405 (November 1927).

Life Estate or Fee? A Sequel, Charles C. White. 6 U Cin L Rev 429 (November 1932).

Notes of Decisions

Fee simple 2
Life estate with vested remainder 3
Limitations 1

---

1. Limitations

RC 2131.07 applies only to realty. In re Knickel's Will (Ohio Prob. 1961) 185 N.E.2d 93, 89 Ohio Law Abs. 135.

A fee simple estate cannot be made defeasible even under this section unless the words of the instrument devising such estate indicate the specific real property upon which the limitation is intended. Sweigert v Sweigert, 55 Abs 442, 89 NE(2d) 686 (App, Cuyahoga 1949).

2. Fee simple

A residuary gift to testator's widow "absolutely and in fee simple" to be held for her by a trustee, with a provision for a disposition after her death, constitutes an absolute gift to her. Koval's Estate v. Koval (Ohio Prob. 1966) 8 Ohio Misc. 206, 221 N.E.2d 490, 37 O.O.2d 265.

Where testatrix in one item of her will gave her husband absolutely all of her property real and personal and in next item of her will provided that upon the husband's death all of his property shall become the property of their son absolutely and forever, the husband received a fee simple title and the following item was of no effect whatsoever as it was an attempt by testatrix to execute a will for her husband, nor can the latter item of the will be deemed an attempt to make the fee simple estate defeasible, as even under GC 10512–7 (RC 2131.07) the instrument must indicate the specific property upon which the limitation is intended. Sweigert v Sweigert, 55 Abs 442, 89 NE(2d) 686 (App, Cuyahoga 1949).

3. Life estate with vested remainder

The following provision: "the balance of my estate, including the farm, I give to W. After she is through with the farm it is to go to the Masonic Home", created a life estate with a vested remainder. In re Knickel's Will (Ohio Prob. 1961) 185 N.E.2d 93, 89 Ohio Law Abs. 135. Wills ⚖ 614(2); Wills ⚖ 634(3)

RULE AGAINST PERPETUITIES

2131.08 Statute against perpetuities

(A) Subject to sections 1746.14, 1747.09, and 2131.09 of the Revised Code, no interest in real or personal property shall be good unless it must vest, if at all, not later than twenty-one years after a life or lives in being at the creation of the interest. All estates given in tail, by deed or will, in lands or tenements lying within this state shall be and remain an absolute estate in fee simple to the issue of the first donee in tail. It is the intention by the adoption of this section to make effective in this state what is generally known as the common law rule against perpetuities, except as set forth in divisions (B) and (C) of this section.

(B) For the purposes of this section and subject to sections 1746.14, 1747.09, and 2131.09 of the Revised Code, the time of the creation of an interest in real or personal property subject to a power reserved by the grantor to revoke or terminate the interest shall be the time at which the reserved power expires by reason of the death of the grantor, by release of the power, or otherwise.

(C) Any interest in real or personal property that would violate the rule against perpetuities, under division (A) of this section, shall be reformed, within the limits of the rule, to approximate most closely the intention of the creator of the interest. In determining whether an interest would violate the rule and in reforming an interest, the period of perpetuities shall be measured by actual rather than possible events.

(D) Divisions (B) and (C) of this section shall be effective with respect to interests in real or personal property created by wills of decedents dying after December 31, 1967, with respect to interests in real or personal property created by inter vivos instruments executed after December 31, 1967, and with respect to interests in real or personal property created by inter vivos instruments executed on or before December 31, 1967, that by reason of division (B) of this section will be treated as interests created after December 31, 1967. Divisions (B) and (C) of this section shall be effective with respect to interests in real or personal property created by the exercise of a power of appointment if divisions (B) and (C) of this section apply to the instrument that exercises the power, whether or not divisions (B) and (C) of this section apply to the instrument that creates the power.

(1998 H 701, eff. 3–22–99; 1980 S 317, eff. 3–23–81; 132 v S 13; 1953 H 1; GC 10512–8)

Uncodified Law

1998 H 701, § 3, eff. 3–22–99, reads:

If, on the effective date of this act, a trust meets all of the following conditions, it is not subject to this act until January 1, 2000:

(A) The trust assets are invested and managed by a non-corporate trustee.

(B) The trust cannot be terminated by the grantor.

(C) The value of the trust, as of December 31, 1998, is less than $100,000.

Historical and Statutory Notes

Pre–1953 H 1 Amendments: 114 v 470

Amendment Note: 1998 H 701 inserted "Subject to sections 1746.14, 1747.09, and 2131.09 of the Revised Code," in division (A); inserted "and subject to sections 1746.14, 1747.09, and 2131.09 of the Revised Code" in division (B); and made other nonsubstantive changes.

OSBA Probate and Trust Law Section

1980:

The need for the amendment of Section 2131.08 of the Revised Code is to prevent the Internal Revenue Service from taxing, under the generation-skipping transfer tax provisions of the Tax Reform Act of 1976, the exercise of a special power of appointment after April 30, 1976 which was created under an irrevocable trust prior to that date (which trusts have been excluded from such tax under the grandfather provisions of the Act). The grandfather provisions apply to such trusts so long as the exercise of the special power does not result in the creation of any estate or interest which postpones or suspends the vesting of any estate or interest in the trust property for a period ascertainable without regard to the creation of the trust.

The last sentence of R. C. 2131.08 presently reads as follows: "An interest in real or personal property which comes into effect through the exercise of a power of appointment shall be regarded as having been created by the instrument exercising the power rather than the instrument which created the power."

It is the concern of the Board of Governors that this wording, unless amended, will be used by the Internal Revenue Service to tax the exercise of special powers of appointment under irrevocable trusts in existence prior to April 30, 1976, even though it is the intent of the Act to exempt such trusts. The suggested amendment clarifies the distinction between the point at which such trusts are created and the point at which powers created by them are exercised. This will assure that the many irrevocable trusts created in Ohio prior to April 30, 1976, will benefit from the grandfather provisions of the Tax Reform Act of 1976.

1967:

The Committee proposes two legislative changes to the existing statute *neither of which has any effect on the period which the statute now requires for the vesting of property interests.*

The first proposed change, which would be Paragraph (B) of the revised statute, helps to clarify a point which is now unclear under Ohio law. Neither case nor statutory law in Ohio now furnishes an answer to the question: When does the period for measuring the rule begin to run when the creator of the interest has reserved the right to revoke or terminate the interest? The question is of importance particularly for revocable, inter vivos trusts (or "insurance trusts"). The person establishing such a trust usually reserves the power to revoke the trust during his lifetime and, in the typical case, the trust contains only life insurance policies or a small amount of cash during the creator's lifetime and the bulk of his estate is "poured over" into the trust at the time of his death under provisions of his Will. Under present circumstances, because of the uncertainty of Ohio law, the attorney must consider the possibility that the rule might begin to run from the date of execution of such a trust, rather than the date of the creator's death (when the power to revoke would normally be relinquished). This has handicapped the use of such trusts in Ohio. The authorities seem agreed that "(T)he policy underlying the rule against perpetuities... is not violated if that period is taken to begin at the time of the settlor's death, rather than at the time when the trust was actually created." Vol. 1 *Scott on Trusts,* Sec. 62.10 (1). This has been established as the rule in other jurisdictions, in some instances by statute and in other instances by case law. The proposal, Paragraph (B), is similar to Section 179–a, New York Real Property Law, adopted by the State of New York effective April 12, 1960.

The second proposed change which would be Paragraph (C) of the revised statute, is designed to avoid the harsh consequences of the common law rule when applied to interests which, perhaps for a very technical reason, would now be found to have violated the rule. The impetus to reform the rule has come from many members of the bench and bar, and a growing number of states have enacted or are in the process of enacting new legislation. The principal advocate for reform, Professor W. Barton Leach, has stated the case succinctly and well in his recent article entitled "Perpetuities: The Nutshell Revisited" appearing in the March, 1965, edition of the *Harvard Law Review,* 78 HLR 973.

Paragraph (C) would be operative in two situations. First, it would permit a court to look at the events taking place after the interest was created and which exist at the time of the litigation, and then determine whether or not the interest in fact violates the rule. This is usually called the "wait and see" doctrine. It would reverse the present requirement that if there is any possibility, no matter how remote, that the interest *might* fail at the time the interest is created, then the entire interest *must* fail—notwithstanding that subsequent events might clearly establish the impossibility that the interest could in fact vest beyond the period of the rule.

In addition, if the interest would violate the rule even after considering subsequent events, in such case, the court is given authority to reform the interest within the period permitted by the rule. This is often called the "*cy pres*" doctrine, and is similar to the principle well known to attorneys which permits a court to reform a charitable trust in cases where the purposes for which the trust was originally established can no longer be carried out.

The following example illustrates the application of both parts of proposed Paragraph (C): A testator establishes in his Will a trust providing for the payment of income to his son for life, and upon his son's death, the income is to be payable to his son's children. Each of the son's children is to receive his or her share of the principal of the trust if he or she attains the age of 25. Under present Ohio law the trust would violate the rule because of the possibility that the son could have additional children after the death of the testator and the interests created might not vest within lives in being at the testator's death and twenty-one years. Under the proposed legislation, the validity of the trust would not be determined until the son's death. If at that time it is found that all of the son's children were born *before* the testator's death, or if all of them are over 4 years of age at the son's death, the trust would not violate the rule. (This is the application of the "wait and see" portion of the proposed Paragraph (C).) If, however, at the son's death there is a child who is then under the age of 4 years who was not living at the time of the testator's death, the court would reform the trust so that it terminated no later than twenty-one years after the son's death. (This is the application of the "*cy pres*" doctrine.) Thus, it can be seen that (1) in many cases the interest created will in fact vest within the required period of the rule and, (2) in cases where the interest will vest beyond the required period, the court is permitted to reform the trust, in the manner which will best carry out the testator's interest, but which requires that it terminate within the period of the rule.

Paragraph (C) of the proposed statute is the form advocated by Professor Leach, "Perpetuities: The Nutshell Revisited," *supra*, and similar forms of the statute have already been adopted by the states of Vermont and Kentucky.

Cross References

Sale of entailed and other estates, 5303.21

Library References

Perpetuities ⟜1.
Westlaw Topic No. 298.
C.J.S. Perpetuities §§ 10 to 15, 18, 20 to 24, 35.

Research References

Encyclopedias

OH Jur. 3d Charities § 7, Perpetuities and Restraints on Alienation.
OH Jur. 3d Estates, Pwrs., & Restrnts. on Alienat. § 35, Estate of Donee in Tail.
OH Jur. 3d Estates, Pwrs., & Restrnts. on Alienat. § 37, Interest of Issue of Donee in Tail.
OH Jur. 3d Estates, Pwrs., & Restrnts. on Alienat. § 38, Interest of Issue of Donee in Tail—Alienability of Interest of Issue During Life of Donee in Tail.
OH Jur. 3d Estates, Pwrs., & Restrnts. on Alienat. § 200, Ohio Perpetuities Legislation.
OH Jur. 3d Estates, Pwrs., & Restrnts. on Alienat. § 201, Application of Former Statute.
OH Jur. 3d Estates, Pwrs., & Restrnts. on Alienat. § 206, Common-Law Rule Applicable.
OH Jur. 3d Estates, Pwrs., & Restrnts. on Alienat. § 213, When Period Begins.
OH Jur. 3d Estates, Pwrs., & Restrnts. on Alienat. § 214, Rule as Referring to Time Rather Than Persons.
OH Jur. 3d Estates, Pwrs., & Restrnts. on Alienat. § 215, Rule as Referring to Remoteness of Vesting.
OH Jur. 3d Estates, Pwrs., & Restrnts. on Alienat. § 225, Generally; Wait-And-See Approach.
OH Jur. 3d Estates, Pwrs., & Restrnts. on Alienat. § 226, Cy Pres Reformation.
OH Jur. 3d Estates, Pwrs., & Restrnts. on Alienat. § 227, Effective Date.
OH Jur. 3d Estates, Pwrs., & Restrnts. on Alienat. § 228, Effective Date—Effect of Reserved Power to Revoke.
OH Jur. 3d Estates, Pwrs., & Restrnts. on Alienat. § 229, Effective Date—Effect of Exercise of Power of Appointment.
OH Jur. 3d Estates, Pwrs., & Restrnts. on Alienat. § 230, Realty and Personalty.
OH Jur. 3d Estates, Pwrs., & Restrnts. on Alienat. § 242, Duration of Trust.

Forms

Ohio Forms Legal and Business § 1B:2, Form Drafting Principles—in General.
Ohio Forms Legal and Business § 2:67, Introduction.
Ohio Forms Legal and Business § 25:53, Irrevocable Trusts—Husband and Wife as Grantors—Income to Children for Life—Remainder to Descendants.
Ohio Forms Legal and Business § 24:748, No Beneficiary to Take Any Interest in Violation of Rule Against Perpetuities.
Ohio Forms Legal and Business § 25:355, Division of Irrevocable Trust—Provision for After-Born Children.
Ohio Forms and Transactions KP 30.04, Common Disaster and Presumed Order of Death.
Ohio Forms and Transactions KP 30.20, Rule Against Perpetuities.

Treatises and Practice Aids

Carlin, Baldwin's Ohio Practice, Merrick-Rippner Probate Law § 10:3, Expectant Estates—Descendible and Devisable.
Carlin, Baldwin's Ohio Practice, Merrick-Rippner Probate Law § 16:1, Statutory Provisions.
Carlin, Baldwin's Ohio Practice, Merrick-Rippner Probate Law § 32:2, Charitable Bequests—Doctrines of Cy Pres and Deviation.
Carlin, Baldwin's Ohio Practice, Merrick-Rippner Probate Law § 45:1, Rule Against Perpetuities—Statutory Expression—Vesting of Estate.
Carlin, Baldwin's Ohio Practice, Merrick-Rippner Probate Law § 45:2, Rule Against Perpetuities—Statutory Expression—Fee Tail Estate.
Carlin, Baldwin's Ohio Practice, Merrick-Rippner Probate Law § 45:3, Rule Against Perpetuities—Statutory Expression—Intent of Statute.
Carlin, Baldwin's Ohio Practice, Merrick-Rippner Probate Law § 45:4, Rule Against Perpetuities—Statutory Expression—Construction of Time of Creation of Interest.
Carlin, Baldwin's Ohio Practice, Merrick-Rippner Probate Law § 45:5, Rule Against Perpetuities—Statutory Expression—Reformation of Interests.
Carlin, Baldwin's Ohio Practice, Merrick-Rippner Probate Law § 45:6, Rule Against Perpetuities—Statutory Expression—Effective Date and Powers of Appointment.
Carlin, Baldwin's Ohio Practice, Merrick-Rippner Probate Law § 45:7, Rule Against Perpetuities—Statutory Expression—Ohio State Bar Association, Probate and Trust Law Section Comment on Amendments Effective January 1, 1968.
Carlin, Baldwin's Ohio Practice, Merrick-Rippner Probate Law § 45:9, Rule Against Perpetuities—Application to Powers of Appointment.
Carlin, Baldwin's Ohio Practice, Merrick-Rippner Probate Law § 43:11, Construing a Will—Liberal Construction—Introduction.
Carlin, Baldwin's Ohio Practice, Merrick-Rippner Probate Law § 43:25, Construing a Will—Words and Phrases—Heirs or Children.
Carlin, Baldwin's Ohio Practice, Merrick-Rippner Probate Law § 43:26, Construing a Will—Words and Phrases—Issue.
Carlin, Baldwin's Ohio Practice, Merrick-Rippner Probate Law § 43:43, Construing a Will—Apportionment of Estate—Construing a Fee Simple—When a Fee Simple Passes.
Carlin, Baldwin's Ohio Practice, Merrick-Rippner Probate Law § 45:10, Rule Against Perpetuities—Application to Estates.
Carlin, Baldwin's Ohio Practice, Merrick-Rippner Probate Law § 45:11, Rule Against Perpetuities—Application to Trusts.
Carlin, Baldwin's Ohio Practice, Merrick-Rippner Probate Law § 45:13, Rule Against Perpetuities—Effect.
Carlin, Baldwin's Ohio Practice, Merrick-Rippner Probate Law § 45:14, Rule Against Perpetuities—Dynasty Trusts.
Bogert - the Law of Trusts and Trustees § 213, The Rule Against Perpetuities—Remoteness of Vesting.
Bogert - the Law of Trusts and Trustees § 214, The Rule Against Perpetuities—History and Status of Rule in the Several States.
Bogert - the Law of Trusts and Trustees § 219, Statutory Limits Upon Suspension of Power of Alienation.

Kuehnle and Levey, Ohio Real Estate Law and Practice § 3:2, Estates—Fee Tail—Ohio Law.

Kuehnle and Levey, Ohio Real Estate Law and Practice § 4:3, The Rule Against Perpetuities—Statement of the Common Law and Ohio Rule.

Kuehnle and Levey, Ohio Real Estate Law and Practice § 4:21, Ohio's Rule Against Perpetuities—"Wait and See".

Kuehnle and Levey, Ohio Real Estate Law and Practice § 4:22, Ohio's Rule Against Perpetuities—Doctrine of Cy Pres.

Kuehnle and Levey, Ohio Real Estate Law and Practice § 4:23, Ohio's Rule Against Perpetuities—Charitable Exception.

Kuehnle and Levey, Ohio Real Estate Law and Practice § 4:25, Ohio's Rule Against Perpetuities—Commencement of the Rule Against Perpetuities Period.

Kuehnle and Levey, Ohio Real Estate Law and Practice § 29:23, Common Elements—Granting Easements Across the Common Elements.

Restatement (2d) of Property, Don. Trans. § 1.1, Period of the Rule Against Perpetuities in Donative Transfers.

Restatement (2d) of Property, Don. Trans. § 1.2, When the Period of the Rule Against Perpetuities Begins to Run With Respect to Donative Transfers.

Restatement (2d) of Property, Don. Trans. § 1.4, The Vesting Requirement With Respect to Donative Transfers.

Restatement (2d) of Property, Don. Trans. § 1.5, Consequences of the Failure of an Interest Under the Rule Against Perpetuities in a Donative Transfer.

Restatement (2d) of Property, Don. Trans. § 30.1, Rule in Shelley's Case.

Restatement (3d) Property (Wills & Don. Trans.) § 12.2, Modifying Donative Documents to Achieve Donor's Tax Objectives.

Law Review and Journal Commentaries

Applicability of Common Law Conflicts of Interest Principles to the Non–Ohio Grantor Who Seeks to Create an Ohio Dynasty Trust, Karen M. Moore. 10 Prob L J Ohio 33 (January/February 2000).

Application of the Rule Against Perpetuities to Powers of Appointment: Ohio Style, C. Terry Johnson and Frank B. Williams, III. 5 U Dayton L Rev 39 (Winter 1980).

Drafting Trust Instruments, Robert P. Goldman. 5 U Cin L Rev 172 (March 1931).

Drafting Trust Instruments Revisited, Robert P. Goldman. 36 U Cin L Rev 650 (Fall 1967).

The Dynasty Trust is Here!, Craig F. Frederickson. 9 Prob L J Ohio 41 (January/February 1999).

How To Do A Perpetuities Problem, John Makdisi. 36 Clev St L Rev 95 (1987–88).

Is the Dynasty Trust Here? Almost, Craig F. Frederickson. 7 Prob L J Ohio 53 (May/June 1997).

Ohio Dynasty Trusts: Where are We Now? Craig F. Frederickson, 12 Prob L J Ohio 104 (July/August 2002).

Perpetual Dynasty Trusts: One of the Most Powerful Tools in the Estate Planner's Arsenal, Comment. 32 Akron L Rev 747 (1999).

Perpetuities Literacy for the 21st Century, Robert J. Lynn. 50 Ohio St L J 220 (1989).

The Rule Against Perpetuities and the Generation–Skipping Tax: Do We Need Both?, Leonard Levin and Michael Mulroney. 35 Vill L Rev 333 (1990).

The Rule Against Perpetuities as Applied to Living Trusts and Living Life Insurance Trusts, Earl F. Morris. 11 U Cin L Rev 327 (May 1937).

Rule Against Perpetuity—The Case for Exemption of Trusts or The Repeal of the Rule, Gerald P. Moran and Craig F. Frederickson. 6 Prob L J Ohio 10 (September/October 1995).

Teaching the Rule Against Perpetuities in First Year Property, Robert J. Hopperton. 31 U Tol L Rev 55 (Fall 1999).

Trusteed Capital vs Trade and Industry, Robert M. Ochiltree. 18 A B A J 538 (August 1932).

Notes of Decisions

Constitutional issues 1
Fee tail 3
Immediate issue 6
Legal effect; reformation 4
Life in being 5
Procedure; vesting 2
Property interest not violative of rule 7
Statutory application 8

---

1. Constitutional issues

S & C 550 and acts amendatory thereto are not unconstitutional as to estates vesting after the passage of those acts. Oyler v. Scanlan (Ohio 1877) 33 Ohio St. 308.

The statute to restrict the entailment of estates, S & C 550, is not a prejudicial interference with vested rights nor beyond legitimate legislative power. Pollock v. Speidel (Ohio 1875) 27 Ohio St. 86.

There is no constitutional prohibition against applying the 1967 statute against perpetuities, RC 2131.08, to a power of appointment granted before that date. Dollar Sav. & Trust Co. v. First Nat. Bank of Boston (Ohio Com.Pl. 1972) 32 Ohio Misc. 81, 285 N.E.2d 768, 61 O.O.2d 134. Perpetuities ⇔ 3

2. Procedure; vesting

In an action to determine the validity of a will it is not the duty of the court to pass upon whether provisions of the will violate the act to restrain the entailment of estates, which is a matter for subsequent determination after it has been determined whether the writing is the last will of the testator. Mears v. Mears (Ohio 1864) 15 Ohio St. 90.

A deed dated November 30, 1962, purporting to convey land in trust "for and during the natural lifetime of the grantor herein or until December 1, 1990, whichever later occurs" is invalid to create any expectant estates in said land because not within the rule against perpetuities. Eisenmann v. Eisenmann (Ohio Com.Pl. 1976) 52 Ohio Misc. 119, 370 N.E.2d 788, 6 O.O.3d 449. Perpetuities ⇔ 4(15.1)

A trust agreement which provides that the share of a daughter, who receives monthly payments for life, shall, at her death, vest in the then surviving lineal descendants of such daughter, per stirpes, does not violate the rule against perpetuities. Vinson v. First Trust & Sav. Bank (Ohio Com.Pl. 1974) 44 Ohio Misc. 97, 339 N.E.2d 670, 73 O.O.2d 489. Perpetuities ⇔ 4(15.1)

Where a testator bequeaths money in trust for a charitable corporation to be organized after his death for the purpose of accomplishing certain charitable purposes, the gift is valid although it is possible that the corporation might not be organized within the period of the rule against perpetuities, and the court will direct that the property be conveyed to the corporation if it is organized within a reasonable time, and if not so organized, will frame a scheme for the application of the property to the designated charitable purposes and direct that it be administered under the doctrine of cy pres. Rice v. Stanley (Ohio 1975) 42 Ohio St.2d 209, 327 N.E.2d 774, 71 O.O.2d 205.

In applying the rule against perpetuities, the test of vesting is not whether the beneficial enjoyment of the proceeds of the estate will arise within the period of the lives in being plus twenty-one years, but, whether, within such period it becomes certain that the interest is unconditional and will reach fruition in the future. Third Nat. Bank & Trust Co. v. Eaton (Montgomery 1972) 33 Ohio App.2d 264, 294 N.E.2d 247, 62 O.O.2d 379. Perpetuities ⇔ 4(3)

Where a charitable gift vests, a direction for accumulation, being for the management of the fund and not of the essence of the gift, will not, even if invalid, affect the validity of the gift. Third Nat. Bank & Trust Co. v. Eaton (Montgomery 1972) 33 Ohio App.2d 264, 294 N.E.2d 247, 62 O.O.2d 379. Perpetuities ⇔ 9(7)

The last sentence of RC 2131.08(D) applies only to the effective date of the 1967 amendment and its purpose was not to establish a general starting time for all powers of appointment; it does not change the Ohio common law rule that the perpetuities period of an interest derived from the exercise of a general testamentary power of appointment is measured from the time of the creation of the power and not from its exercise. Dollar Sav. & Trust Co. v. First Nat. Bank of Boston (Ohio Com.Pl. 1972) 32 Ohio Misc. 81, 285 N.E.2d 768, 61 O.O.2d 134.

Where testator's will provided that a trust created thereunder should cease and determine upon the death of all the issue of his children, such bequest violated the rule against perpetuities. Large v. National City Bank of Cleveland (Ohio Prob. 1960) 170 N.E.2d 309, 85 Ohio Law Abs. 11, 14 O.O.2d 100.

Will by which testatrix left her estate to a designated person in trust with almost unlimited power to manage, control and dispose of both income and principal, and to pay or expend from time to time such sums as she deems necessary for the benefit of certain named beneficiaries, "until my grandson, M, shall, or would if he lived so long, attain the age of thirty years"; and upon disposition of the principal the trust to that extent to terminate; and in case the trust shall not be wholly disposed of under the foregoing provisions, such part not disposed of shall vest in equal shares in such of certain named beneficiaries "as shall be living when my grandson, M, shall, or would if he lived so long, attain the age of thirty years and the trust shall cease and determine," does not violate the rule against perpetuities. Finkbeiner v. Finkbeiner (Hamilton 1959) 111 Ohio App. 64, 165 N.E.2d 825, 13 O.O.2d 424.

The period for testing the validity of an exercise of a general testamentary power of appointment under the common-law rule against perpetuities is measured from the time of the creation of the power and not from its exercise. Cleveland Trust Co. v. McQuade (Cuyahoga 1957) 106 Ohio App. 237, 142 N.E.2d 249, 76 Ohio Law Abs. 324, 6 O.O.2d 493. Perpetuities ☞ 4(20)

As applied to a general power of appointment exercisable only by will, the period of the rule against perpetuities is computed from the time of the exercise of the power rather than from the date of its creation. Cleveland Trust Co. v. McQuade (Ohio Prob. 1955) 133 N.E.2d 664, 72 Ohio Law Abs. 120, reversed 106 Ohio App. 237, 142 N.E.2d 249, 76 Ohio Law Abs. 324, 6 O.O.2d 493.

Where a will provides for the establishment of a trust the assets of which are to be selected by the executor, the trust comes into existence upon the appointment of the executor and relates back to the date of the testator's death, and the title of the beneficiary vests immediately and is not conditional upon the selection of specific property. Braun v. Central Trust Co. (Ohio App. 1 Dist. 1952) 92 Ohio App. 110, 109 N.E.2d 476, 49 O.O. 249.

Where a testator gives to a trustee approximately one-half of his property for a marital deduction trust, the half to be selected by the executor, the legal title of the trustee is not contingent upon the death of the testator as a springing or shifting executory interest, but is vested, only the identification of the specific property being postponed. Braun v. Central Trust Co (Ohio Com.Pl. 1951) 104 N.E.2d 480, 62 Ohio Law Abs. 127, 46 O.O. 198, affirmed 92 Ohio App. 110, 109 N.E.2d 476, 49 O.O. 249.

Under a will which creates a trust for benefit of one person for life, then for the use of others until their marriage or death, and then "the trust to be continued... and... one-half of the annual income of said trust fund" to be paid to a charity, the gift to the charity does not violate rule against perpetuities as equitable estate vests in the charity immediately upon transfer of legal title to trustee. Schreiner v. Cincinnati Altenheim (Hamilton 1939) 61 Ohio App. 344, 22 N.E.2d 587, 29 Ohio Law Abs. 249, 15 O.O. 228. Perpetuities ☞ 8(3)

The right to make a will is limited by RS 4200 which limits the granting of estates to the immediate issue of a person in being at the time of the testator's death. Phillips v. Herron (Ohio 1896) 55 Ohio St. 478, 37 W.L.B. 48, 45 N.E. 720.

This section does not render void a devise to the testator's grandchildren, possession of which is to be postponed until they reach the age of thirty years and is then to vest only on condition that they qualify as distributees by measuring up to a designated standard of character and habits. Sager v. Byrer (Ohio Com.Pl. 1921) 24 Ohio N.P.N.S. 129.

A devise to a trustee to pay income to a beneficiary for life and at his decease to his children for life, with a fee to their children, is void because of the perpetuity, as the beneficiary might have a child after the testator's death and thus the vesting be suspended for more than lives in being plus twenty-one years after, and since void as to one of a class it is void as to all. Dayton v. Phillips (Ohio Super. 1892) 28 W.L.B. 327.

Under a will giving testator's property to trustees, to hold during the lives of testator's daughter and two grandchildren, and to pay the income in equal shares to them, with provision that, if the daughter shall remarry and die leaving issue by a future marriage while either of the two grandchildren survive, the income should be, during the continuance of the trust, equally divided among all the children of testator's daughter, the children living when that contingency happened did not constitute a fixed class entitled to the property, since it was not then to be finally distributed, so that the share of one of those children who died leaving a son is to be paid to the son during the continuance of the trust. Dahlgren v. Pierce (C.C.A.6 (Ohio) 1921) 270 F. 507, appeal dismissed 41 S.Ct. 534, 256 U.S. 682, 65 L.Ed. 1170, certiorari denied 41 S.Ct. 534, 256 U.S. 692, 65 L.Ed. 1174. Wills ☞ 682(1)

A testamentary trust providing for fixed yearly payments to the testator's children to continue to be paid yearly to the lineal descendants of such children, surviving at the time of the children's deaths, violates the rule against perpetuities, as such yearly payments could vest more than twenty-one years after the deaths of the testator's children, who are the lives in being for purposes of the rule. Crow v Kistler, No. 25–CA–87 (5th Dist Ct App, Fairfield, 12–2–87).

3. Fee tail

The statute to restrict the entailment of real estate, S & C 550, does not change the nature of the estate in the first donee in tail from an inheritable estate to an estate for life merely. Harkness v. Corning (Ohio 1873) 24 Ohio St. 416.

Where lands are conveyed by deed "to A, the heirs of his body, and assigns, forever," the grantee takes an estate tail. Pollock v. Speidel (Ohio 1867) 17 Ohio St. 439. Deeds ☞ 127(1); Estates In Property ☞ 12

The first donee in tail cannot by a sale and conveyance in fee simple bar the entail or deprive his issue of the right of succession to the inheritance. Pollock v. Speidel (Ohio 1867) 17 Ohio St. 439.

The common law fee tail estate exists in Ohio and the statutory enactment of December 17, 1811 (10 Ohio Laws 7), now embodied in RC 2131.08, which converted estates tail into fees simple in the issue of the first donee in tail, did not change the nature of the estate in the donee in tail from an inheritable estate to an estate for life, but merely restricted the entailment to the immediate issue of such donee. Long v. Long (Ohio 1976) 45 Ohio St.2d 165, 343 N.E.2d 100, 74 O.O.2d 287.

There remains in the grantor of a fee tail estate a reversion in fee simple expectant upon the failure of a stated condition, which reversion is a descendible, devisable and alienable estate, which, if otherwise undisposed of, passes upon the death of the grantor by descent to his heirs then living. Long v. Long (Ohio 1976) 45 Ohio St.2d 165, 343 N.E.2d 100, 74 O.O.2d 287. Descent And Distribution ☞ 17

Characteristics of title of tenants in tail are such that they cannot have an estate in property which will endure beyond their lifetime if their issue assert their rights. Guida v. Thompson (Ohio Com.Pl. 1957) 160 N.E.2d 153, 80 Ohio Law Abs. 148. Estates In Property ☞ 12

An estate tail cannot be enlarged into an estate in fee simple absolute through the release by the original donor of his possibility of reversion to the donee in tail. Guida v. Thompson (Ohio Com.Pl. 1957) 160 N.E.2d 153, 80 Ohio Law Abs. 148.

Where no remainderman was named in nor any executory interest limited by deed conveying land to grantor's son in fee tail for life of first taker only and son thereafter reconveyed land in fee simple to father who in turn reconveyed in fee simple to son, and son died without issue following death of father testate without specific mention or devise of such land, son died seized of a fee simple estate in such land, since no person living was entitled to contest rights acquired by father as transferee of first donee in tail under conveyance in fee simple. Hoppes v. American Nat. Red Cross (Ohio Com.Pl. 1955) 128 N.E.2d 851, 71 Ohio Law Abs. 259. Estates In Property ☞ 12

Under deed to grantee and the heirs of his body, grantee was the first donee in tail of the estate and held an 'estate in fee tail' and had full enjoyment of all the rights and subject to all the disabilities incident to that species of estates, and on his death the right of entry accrued to the issue of his body, and their estate immediately became an absolute estate in fee simple. In re Jones' Estate (Van Wert 1943) 64 N.E.2d 609, 44 Ohio Law Abs. 339. Deeds ☞ 127(1)

Will providing for distribution after deaths of life tenants to their bodily heirs in fee simple does not to create an estate tail in that words in fee simple are inconsistent with usual form of limitation in estate tail to bodily heirs. Pollock v. Brayton (Hamilton 1924) 28 Ohio App. 172, 162 N.E. 608, 6 Ohio Law Abs. 616.

Under Rev.St. 1908, § 4200 (See GC 10512–8) providing that an estate given in tail shall be an absolute estate in fee simple to the issue of the first donee in tail, the issue of the donee in tail during the life of such donee has no estate or interest in the lands entailed which he can alienate. Dungan v. Kline (Ohio 1910) 81 Ohio St. 371, 90 N.E. 938, 7 Ohio Law Rep. 578. Estates In Property ☞ 12

Under RS 4200, the issue of a donee in tail, during the life of such donee, has no estate or interest in the lands entailed which he can alienate. Dungan v. Kline (Ohio 1910) 81 Ohio St. 371, 90 N.E. 938, 7 Ohio Law Rep. 578.

A devise to a son "and his heirs to the third generation" is an entailment within the meaning of RC 4200, and under this section the son takes a life estate and his heirs an absolute estate in fee simple. Naylor v. Loomis (Ohio Cir. 1894) 6 Ohio C.D. 41, 2 Ohio Dec. 114, dismissed. Estates In Property 12; Wills 607(2)

RC 4200 does not enlarge the estate of the first donee in tail, but operates only after the estate reaches the issue. Richardson v. Cincinnati Union Stockyard Co. (Ohio Super. 1901) 11 Ohio Dec. 367, 8 Ohio N.P. 213.

There is no attempt to create a perpetuity in violation of Gen.Code § 8622 (repealed 1932. See § 10512–8), by a will giving to A., living at time of execution of the will and death of testator, certain lands for life, and after his death to the heirs of his body, part to be possessed by him on arriving at majority, and the balance after that event and the death of testator's wife, the wife being given the use and occupation till such times. In re Youtsey (S.D.Ohio 1916) 260 F. 423, 15 Ohio Law Rep. 125. Perpetuities 4(10); Wills 614(6.1)

Under this section, if a will creates a fee tail, the interest of the first donee is not a mere life estate, but his children do not take the fee-simple title till his death, when the estate tail is enlarged into an absolute estate in fee simple. A deed by a child of the donee conveys no estate if the grantor dies before the donee, leaving issue surviving. In re Youtsey (S.D.Ohio 1916) 260 F. 423, 15 Ohio Law Rep. 125. Wills 607(2)

Where a testator devised lands to his children for their natural life, directing that on their death the property should go to the heirs of their body, but if any should die without leaving heirs of their body, the lands, subject to the rights of curtesy or dower of the spouses of such children, should revert back and be divided equally between those living or their heirs per stirpes, a son of the testator did not take an estate in fee, but his estate ended with his life and his issue took in fee simple. Youtsey v. Niswonger (C.C.A.6 (Ohio) 1918) 258 F. 16, 169 C.C.A. 154. Wills 607(1)

4. Legal effect; reformation

Under a devise to a testator's sister's children N, J, and W, for life, then to their issue for life and so on to their issue for life as far as S & C 550 allows, where N dies leaving an illegitimate daughter, W dies leaving a daughter who dies without leaving surviving parents or issue, and J still lives with issue, the property goes to N, J, and W, for life, with remainder for life in the issue of each in being at the date of the will, but in those born later a remainder in tail. Gibson v. McNeely (Ohio 1860) 11 Ohio St. 131.

Where a testator gives property to two daughters and two grandsons for life and provides that the portion in which each of them enjoys a life estate shall descend and pass absolutely in fee simple respectively to the children of each lawfully begotten or to the children or child lawfully begotten of such child or children, the words "or to the children or child" designate persons who might be living at the death of the tenants for life. Stevenson v. Evans (Ohio 1859) 10 Ohio St. 307.

Where a grantor conveys land to the state and reserves a possibility of reverter by specifying that the land be used for an insane asylum, but fails to include language about succession or perpetuity, the possibility of reverter terminates on the death of the grantor; heirs of the grantor will not thereafter be entitled to quiet title in the land when the state ceases using it for the asylum. Burk v. State (Cuyahoga 1992) 79 Ohio App.3d 573, 607 N.E.2d 911, dismissed, jurisdictional motion overruled 65 Ohio St.3d 1431, 600 N.E.2d 675, rehearing denied 65 Ohio St.3d 1467, 602 N.E.2d 1175.

A testamentary trust for the establishment of an annual harness horse stake race is not for a charitable purpose and does not create a valid charitable trust; therefore the doctrine of cy pres does not apply to the trust, and the trust violates RC 2131.08, the rule against perpetuities. Barton v. Parrott (Ohio Com.Pl. 1984) 25 Ohio Misc.2d 8, 495 N.E.2d 973, 25 O.B.R. 229, affirmed.

The Cy-pres doctrine did not apply to uphold the validity of a trust, where there was no valid charitable trust and settlor did not exhibit general charitable intent; a horse race to perpetuate the memory of the decedent's daughter cannot, by any stretch of the imagination, be termed "charitable," as the horse race is created to benefit a small or finite class of persons and not the general community, this provision establishes a sporting event and not the facilities for a sporting event, and certainly gambling cannot be considered charitable and profits paid to private owners and trainers cannot be said to inure to the benefit of the general community or be for a charitable purpose. Barton v. Parrott (Ohio Com.Pl. 1984) 25 Ohio Misc.2d 8, 495 N.E.2d 973, 25 O.B.R. 229, affirmed.

RC 2131.08, as amended effective October 24, 1967, does not apply to authorize reform of any inter-vivos conveyance (deed) executed before December 31, 1967 (invalid as not within the rule against perpetuities), except those wherein the grantor reserved a power to revoke or terminate such interest or such a power expired "by reason of the death of the grantor or by release of the power or otherwise." Eisenmann v. Eisenmann (Ohio Com.Pl. 1976) 52 Ohio Misc. 119, 370 N.E.2d 788, 6 O.O.3d 449. Perpetuities 3

Before the validity and enforceability of an agreement, containing no duration period, not to sell or partition realty will be sustained, sufficient evidence must exist therein of the purpose for the restraint to permit a determination of a duration reasonably necessary to accomplish such purpose. Raisch v. Schuster (Hamilton 1975) 47 Ohio App.2d 98, 352 N.E.2d 657, 1 O.O.3d 202. Perpetuities 6(1)

Where property is deeded by a mother to her son for life, and then to the heirs of his body, and if he die without heirs of his body, the remainder to revert to the grantor, if living, and if not living, then the remainder to the grantor's heirs at law, it is incumbent upon the widow of the grantee-son, in an action to have quieted her title to such premises, to prove by a preponderance of the evidence that upon the death of the grantee-son without having had issue he had an absolute estate in fee simple in such premises which could pass to her as his heir or which could pass to her under the provisions of his will, i.e., that the grantor-mother had not successfully conveyed or devised away the reversion. Kohler v. Ichler (Hardin 1961) 116 Ohio App. 16, 186 N.E.2d 202, 21 O.O.2d 221. Quieting Title 44(3)

Where a testator bequeaths the residue of his estate to a trustee and by separate, identical provisions directs the trustee to make monthly payments of $200 to each of five sons "during his lifetime and after his death the said payments of $200 each month shall continue and be paid to his issue, per stirpes," until the trust fund has been depleted, the provisions for later generations not in being at the time of the testator's death or within twenty-one years thereafter are invalid as violative of the rule against perpetuities, but such partial invalidity of the attempted dispositions will not invalidate the balance of such dispositions where it is evident that the general purpose of the testator was to create a trust primarily for the benefit of his five sons and only secondarily for the issue of such sons. Gwinner v. Schoeny (Hamilton 1960) 111 Ohio App. 177, 171 N.E.2d 728, 13 O.O.2d 389.

Invalidity of certain bequests under rule against perpetuities did not invalidate other gifts in series. Cleveland Trust Co. v. McQuade (Cuyahoga 1957) 106 Ohio App. 237, 142 N.E.2d 249, 76 Ohio Law Abs. 324, 6 O.O.2d 493.

Where trust gave donee a general power to appoint by will only, the period of the rule against perpetuities was to be computed from date and power was exercised by donee, and would not be related back to the creation of such special power by the trust and to its date. Cleveland Trust Co. v. McQuade (Ohio Prob. 1955) 133 N.E.2d 664, 72 Ohio Law Abs. 120, reversed 106 Ohio App. 237, 142 N.E.2d 249, 76 Ohio Law Abs. 324, 6 O.O.2d 493. Perpetuities 4(20)

Where a testator provided in his will as follows: "item third; I give and bequeath my dog, Trixie, to Florence Hand of Wooster, Ohio, and I direct my executor to deposit... the sum of $1000 to be used by him to pay Florence Hand at the rate of 75 cents per day for the keep and care of my dog as long as it shall live...," such bequest does not, by the terms of the creating instrument, violate the rule against perpetuities. In re Searight's Estate (Wayne 1950) 87 Ohio App. 417, 95 N.E.2d 779, 43 O.O. 169.

Statute has supplanted the common-law rule that a bequest for the permanent care of the settlor's cemetery grave or family lot violated the rule against perpetuities, and under the statute such trusts are valid. Heinlein v. Elyria Sav. & Trust Co. (Lorain 1945) 75 Ohio App. 353, 62 N.E.2d 284, 31 O.O. 123.

Where a grantor conveys property to a municipal corporation, and municipality in turn donates property to a railway, such attempted acquisition of property by municipality for purpose of donating it is void and title remains in grantor who may convey good title to a subsequent grantee. Joseph Schonthal Co. v. Village of Sylvania (Lucas 1938) 60 Ohio App. 407, 21 N.E.2d 1008, 14 O.O. 471.

Limitations over to a municipal corporation, after conveying to a grantee "for the purpose of a power house, machine shop or car barns" but "when said land, if ever, is not used" for named purposes then to municipality, are not void as violating former statute governing perpetuities, and where such conveyances were made in 1900 and 1901, validity of limitations over to a municipal corporation is governed by former GC 8622 (RC 2131.08), in effect at that time, and not by law, in effect when purpose is abandoned, or by common-law rule against perpetuities. Joseph Schonthal Co. v. Village of Sylvania (Lucas 1938) 60 Ohio App. 407, 21 N.E.2d 1008, 14 O.O. 471.

Note 4

Where land is devised to one in trust to divide the land among the children of the testator and to pay them the rents, but on the death of a child his share is to go to his issue, forever, the issue will take a fee discharged of the trust. Lindsay v. Zanoni (Ohio Cir. 1892) 3 Ohio C.D. 544.

"Heirs of the body" in a devise to a testatrix's son of the undivided one-half in certain real estate, "to have and to hold the said property for his life, and the remainder over at his death to the heirs of his body, their heirs and assigns forever share and share alike," but in no event to be sold or partitioned until the youngest of his sons attains his majority, intends that the children of said son take the fee thereof and not an estate tail. Poor v. Hart (Ohio Com.Pl. 1910) 21 Ohio Dec. 260, 11 Ohio N.P.(N.S.) 49, affirmed 84 Ohio St. 489, 95 N.E. 1149, 9 Ohio Law Rep. 96. Wills ⇔ 614(6.1)

Where the owner in fee conveys lands to his son during his natural life and then to pass exclusively to the heirs of his own body in fee simple forever, provided the son does not sell and convey said premises before his death, the title passes to the purchaser; in case of the reconveyance to the father in fee simple and then to the son's wife, the wife takes the estate in fee. Aikin v. Spellman (Ohio Com.Pl. 1897) 6 Ohio Dec. 409, 4 Ohio N.P. 297. Estates In Property ⇔ 12

A devise not too remote may be legal and a part of that same devise illegal if too remote. Hatch v. Hatch (Ohio Com.Pl. 1893) 1 Ohio Dec. 270, 31 W.L.B. 57.

A devise to children in trust and to their issue absolutely gives a fee to the issue discharged of the trust. Dayton v. Phillips (Ohio Super. 1892) 28 W.L.B. 327.

Under S & C 550, a devise of a vested remainder to grandchildren of the testator, with an executory devise over of the share of any grandchild, who shall have died leaving children before the coming of age of the youngest grandchild, to the children of such deceased grandchild, is valid, so far at least as concerns the grandchildren, though born after the testator's death. McArthur v. Scott (U.S.Ohio 1885) 5 S.Ct. 652, 113 U.S. 340, 28 L.Ed. 1015.

5. Life in being

A child in utero at the death of the testator is in being as to RS 4200. Phillips v. Herron (Ohio 1896) 55 Ohio St. 478, 37 W.L.B. 48, 45 N.E. 720. Perpetuities ⇔ 1

A child en ventre sa mere at the time of the testator's death will be considered as then living, since it is to his interest to be so considered. Dayton v. Phillips (Ohio Super. 1892) 28 W.L.B. 327.

Under Ohio law, provision of warranty deed granting right of first refusal to a corporation and its shareholders did not violate the Rule Against Perpetuities, despite possibility that new shareholders would continue to purchase stock in corporation; at the time right was granted, all shareholders were readily identifiable, and statutory period had not yet expired. Tiger, Inc. v. Time Warner Entertainment Co., L.P. (N.D.Ohio, 11-13-1998) 26 F.Supp.2d 1011. Perpetuities ⇔ 4(1)

6. Immediate issue

"Immediate issue" only includes the children of persons in being, but "immediate descendants" includes remote lineal descendants if living at the death of the person in being when the will was made. Turley v. Turley (Ohio 1860) 11 Ohio St. 173.

Where a tenant for life, in fee simple and then a limitation over, "should die without leaving any heirs lawfully begotten of their or either of their bodies," the latter words are to be construed with reference to the former, and the heirs of the body intended by the testator are the children of the tenant for life designated in the prior limitation. Stevenson v. Evans (Ohio 1859) 10 Ohio St. 307.

RS 4200 inhibits only devises to persons who are in fact more remote than the immediate issue of persons in being at the death of the testator. Phillips v. Herron (Ohio 1896) 55 Ohio St. 478, 37 W.L.B. 48, 45 N.E. 720.

The right to make a will is limited by RS 4200 which limits the granting of estates to the immediate issue of a person in being at the time of the testator's death. Phillips v. Herron (Ohio 1896) 55 Ohio St. 478, 37 W.L.B. 48, 45 N.E. 720.

Under the statute of Ohio of December 17, 1811 providing that no estate in lands "shall be given or granted by deed or will to any person or persons, but such as are in being, or to the immediate issue or descendants of such as are in being, at the time of making such deed or will," a devise of a vested remainder to grandchildren of the testator, with an executory devise over of the share of any grandchild who shall have died leaving children before the coming of age of the youngest grandchild, to the children of such deceased grandchild, is valid, so far, at least, as concerns the grandchildren, though born after the testator's death. McArthur v. Scott (U.S.Ohio 1885) 5 S.Ct. 652, 113 U.S. 340, 28 L.Ed. 1015. Perpetuities ⇔ 4(5); Wills ⇔ 497(7)

Time for determining immediacy of descendants descendants under perpetuities statute is date of vesting (Gen Code Ohio, ec. 8622). Time for determining immediacy of issue of descendants of persons in being at time of making will, under Gen Code Ohio, Sec. 8622, relating to perpetuities, held to be date of vesting, and not date of death of life tenant, whose issue and descendants and their heirs were entitled to distribution of remainder under will. Von Overbeck v. Dahlgren (C.C.A.6 (Ohio) 1928) 28 F.2d 936.

7. Property interest not violative of rule

In determining the application of the rule against perpetuities, a court should look at the actual events and then determine whether the interest in fact violates the rule. Hamilton Cty. Bd. of Commrs. v. Cincinnati (Ohio App. 1 Dist., 09-26-2003) 154 Ohio App.3d 504, 797 N.E.2d 1027, 2003-Ohio-5089, appeal not allowed 101 Ohio St.3d 1424, 802 N.E.2d 154, 2004-Ohio-123. Perpetuities ⇔ 4(1)

Right of first refusal or preemptive right with respect to real property was personal to grantee and had to vest, if at all, within his lifetime, and thus, preemptive right did not violate rule against perpetuities. Stratman v. Sheetz (Hamilton 1989) 60 Ohio App.3d 71, 573 N.E.2d 776. Perpetuities ⇔ 4(3)

A preemptive right to purchase property that is personal to the grantee and does not extend beyond his lifetime does not violate the rule against perpetuities; to determine if the right is personal to the grantee the court must look to the contract language exclusively and focus on whether it states that the right extends to either party's heir or assigns or indicates in some other fashion that the contract is meant to be binding beyond either party's life. Stratman v. Sheetz (Hamilton 1989) 60 Ohio App.3d 71, 573 N.E.2d 776.

An option to purchase land is valid as part of a long-term lease of that land and does not offend the rule against perpetuities. Quarto Mining Co. v. Litman (Ohio 1975) 42 Ohio St.2d 73, 326 N.E.2d 676, 71 O.O.2d 58, certiorari denied 96 S.Ct. 128, 423 U.S. 866, 46 L.Ed.2d 96. Landlord And Tenant ⇔ 92(1); Perpetuities ⇔ 4(1)

A land purchase option which is appurtenant to a mineral estate and is limited to the necessary and reasonable use of the overlying surface estate for the exercise of mining rights, is a vested part of the mineral estate and is not void as a restraint upon alienation, although unlimited in time. Quarto Mining Co. v. Litman (Ohio 1975) 42 Ohio St.2d 73, 326 N.E.2d 676, 71 O.O.2d 58, certiorari denied 96 S.Ct. 128, 423 U.S. 866, 46 L.Ed.2d 96. Perpetuities ⇔ 6(1)

Former section does not apply to a bequest of the income from lands and tenements devised in trust, nor the payment of such income to the child of a grandson born after testator's death. Dahlgren v. Pierce (C.C.A.6 (Ohio) 1921) 270 F. 507, appeal dismissed 41 S.Ct. 534, 256 U.S. 682, 65 L.Ed. 1170, certiorari denied 41 S.Ct. 534, 256 U.S. 692, 65 L.Ed. 1174.

There is no attempt to create a perpetuity in violation of this section by a will giving to A, living at the time of execution of the will and death of testator, certain lands for life, and after his death to the heirs of his body, part to be possessed by him on arriving at majority, and the balance after that event and the death of testator's wife, the wife being given the use and occupation till such times. In re Youtsey (S.D.Ohio 1916) 260 F. 423, 15 Ohio Law Rep. 125. Perpetuities ⇔ 4(10); Wills ⇔ 614(6.1)

Rule against perpetuities has no application to unlimited option for purchase of corporate stock. Warner & Swasey Co. v. Rusterholz (D.Minn. 1941) 41 F.Supp. 498, 22 O.O. 114.

8. Statutory application

A right of first refusal in the sale of property is subject to the statute against perpetuities. Hamilton Cty. Bd. of Commrs. v. Cincinnati (Ohio App. 1 Dist., 09-26-2003) 154 Ohio App.3d 504, 797 N.E.2d 1027, 2003-Ohio-5089, appeal not allowed 101 Ohio St.3d 1424, 802 N.E.2d 154, 2004-Ohio-123. Perpetuities ⇔ 4(1)

Provision of a subdivision's declaration of restrictions that gave a right of first refusal to "the lot owner to the right and left" of any lot owner wishing to sell his lot was void under a former codification of the rule against perpetuities; right was not personal and was of unlimited duration.

Schafer v. Deszcz (Ohio App. 6 Dist., 05-09-1997) 120 Ohio App.3d 410, 698 N.E.2d 60, appeal not allowed 79 Ohio St.3d 1509, 684 N.E.2d 91. Perpetuities ☞ 6(1)

Common-law rule against perpetuities was abrogated in Ohio in 1812 and was not effective from that time until enactment of this section in 1932, which re-adopted the rule. Joseph Schonthal Co. v. Village of Sylvania (Lucas 1938) 60 Ohio App. 407, 21 N.E.2d 1008, 14 O.O. 471. Perpetuities ☞ 3

Former GC 8622 (RC 2131.08), governing perpetuities, applied to municipal corporations as well as to persons. Joseph Schonthal Co. v. Village of Sylvania (Lucas 1938) 60 Ohio App. 407, 21 N.E.2d 1008, 14 O.O. 471.

RC 4200 does not apply to a charitable bequest. O'Neal v. Caulfield (Ohio Com.Pl. 1898) 8 Ohio Dec. 248, 5 Ohio N.P. 149. Charities ☞ 4; Perpetuities ☞ 8(1)

The rule against perpetuities applies to property interest, not to contractual obligations such as insurance policies. Doyle v. Massachusetts Mut. Life Ins. Co. (C.A.6 (Ky.) 1967) 377 F.2d 19, 41 O.O.2d 348.

2131.09 Exemption of certain trusts

(A) A trust of real or personal property created by an employer as part of a stock bonus plan, pension plan, disability or death benefit plan, or profit-sharing plan, for the benefit of some or all of the employees, to which contributions are made by the employer or employees, or both, for the purpose of distributing to the employees or their beneficiaries the earnings or the principal, or both earnings and principal, of the fund so held in trust is not invalid as violating the rule against perpetuities, any other existing law against perpetuities, or any law restricting or limiting the duration of trusts; but the trust may continue for the time that is necessary to accomplish the purposes for which it was created.

The income arising from any trust within the classifications mentioned in this division may be accumulated in accordance with the terms of the trust for as long a time as is necessary to accomplish the purposes for which the trust was created, notwithstanding any law limiting the period during which trust income may be accumulated.

No rule of law against perpetuities or the suspension of the power of alienation of the title to property invalidates any trust within the classifications mentioned in this division unless the trust is terminated by decree of a court in a suit instituted within two years after June 25, 1951.

(B)(1) No rule of law against perpetuities or suspension of the power of alienation of the title to property, any other existing law against perpetuities, or any law restricting or limiting the duration of trusts shall apply with respect to any interest in real or personal property held in trust if the instrument creating the trust specifically states that the rule against perpetuities or the provisions of division (B) of section 2131.08 of the Revised Code shall not apply to the trust and if either the trustee of the trust has unlimited power to sell all trust assets or if one or more persons, one of whom may be the trustee, has the unlimited power to terminate the entire trust.

(2) Division (B) of this section shall apply to the interpretation of a testamentary or inter vivos trust instrument that creates an interest in real or personal property in relation to which one or more of the following conditions applies:

(a) The testamentary or inter vivos trust is executed in this state.

(b) The sole trustee or one of the trustees is domiciled in this state.

(c) The testamentary or inter vivos trust is administered in this state or the situs of a substantial portion of the assets subject to the testamentary portion of the testamentary or inter vivos trust is in this state, even though some part or all of those assets are physically deposited for safekeeping in a state other than this state.

(d) The instrument creating the testamentary or inter vivos trust states that the law of this state is to apply.

(3) Division (B) of this section shall be effective with respect to all of the following:

(a) An interest in real or personal property in trust created by wills of decedents dying on or after the effective date of this amendment;

(b) An interest in real or personal property created by an inter vivos or testamentary trust instrument executed on or after the effective date of this amendment;

(c) An interest in real or personal property in trust created by the exercise of a general power of appointment on or after the effective date of this amendment.

(4) Division (B) of this section shall not apply to the exercise of a power of appointment other than a general power of appointment.

(C) For purposes of this section, "general power of appointment" means a power that is exercisable in favor of the individual possessing the power, the person's estate, the person's creditors, or the creditors of the person's estate.

(1998 H 701, eff. 3–22–99; 1953 H 1, eff. 10–1–53; GC 10512–8a)

Uncodified Law

1998 H 701, § 3: See Uncodified Law under 2131.08.

Historical and Statutory Notes

Pre–1953 H 1 Amendments: 124 v S 42

Amendment Note: 1998 H 701 rewrote this section, which prior thereto read:

"A trust of real or personal property created by an employer as part of a stock bonus plan, pension plan, disability or death benefit plan, or profit-sharing plan, for the benefit of some or all of the employees, to which contributions are made by such employer or employees, or both, for the purpose of distributing to such employees or their beneficiaries the earnings or the principal, or both earnings and principal, of the fund so held in trust, is not invalid as violating the rule against perpetuities, any other existing law against perpetuities, or any law restricting or limiting the duration of trusts; but such trust may continue for such time as is necessary to accomplish the purposes for which it was created.

"The income arising from any trust within the classifications mentioned in this section may be accumulated in accordance with the terms of such trust for as long a time as is necessary to accomplish the purposes for which the same was created, notwithstanding any law limiting the period during which trust income may be accumulated.

"No rule of law against perpetuities or the suspension of the power of alienation of the title to property invalidates any such trust unless such trust is terminated by decree of a court in a suit instituted within two years after June 25, 1951."

Library References

Perpetuities ☞7(2).
Westlaw Topic No. 298.
C.J.S. Perpetuities § 65.

Research References

Encyclopedias

OH Jur. 3d Decedents' Estates § 1370, Personal Liability of Representative for Attorneys' Fees—Whether Charged to General Estate or Apportioned.
OH Jur. 3d Estates, Pwrs., & Restrnts. on Alienat. § 243, Exempted Trusts.
OH Jur. 3d Trusts § 129, Accumulation.

Forms

Ohio Forms and Transactions KP 30.20, Rule Against Perpetuities.

Treatises and Practice Aids

Carlin, Baldwin's Ohio Practice, Merrick-Rippner Probate Law § 45:1, Rule Against Perpetuities—Statutory Expression—Vesting of Estate.

Carlin, Baldwin's Ohio Practice, Merrick-Rippner Probate Law § 45:14, Rule Against Perpetuities—Dynasty Trusts.

Bogert - the Law of Trusts and Trustees § 342, The Rule Against Remoteness of Vesting.

Kuehnle and Levey, Ohio Real Estate Law and Practice § 4:1, The Rule Against Perpetuities—History.

Kuehnle and Levey, Ohio Real Estate Law and Practice § 4:3, The Rule Against Perpetuities—Statement of the Common Law and Ohio Rule.

Kuehnle and Levey, Ohio Real Estate Law and Practice § 2:14, Estates—Fee Simple Absolute—Restraints Upon Alienation—Trusts.

Kuehnle and Levey, Ohio Real Estate Law and Practice § 4:24, Ohio's Rule Against Perpetuities—Perpetual Trusts—Pension and Dynasty.

Kuehnle and Levey, Ohio Real Estate Law and Practice § 4:25, Ohio's Rule Against Perpetuities—Commencement of the Rule Against Perpetuities Period.

Restatement (2d) of Property, Don. Trans. § 1.6, Charitable Gifts.

Law Review and Journal Commentaries

Applicability of Common Law Conflicts of Interest Principles to the Non–Ohio Grantor Who Seeks to Create an Ohio Dynasty Trust, Karen M. Moore. 10 Prob L J Ohio 33 (January/February 2000).

The Dynasty Trust is Here!, Craig F. Frederickson. 9 Prob L J Ohio 41 (January/February 1999).

Effective Use of Powers of Appointment: Tools of Flexibility, Robert K. Lease. 9 Prob L J Ohio 82 (May/June 1999).

Is the Dynasty Trust Here? Almost, Craig F. Frederickson. 7 Prob L J Ohio 53 (May/June 1997).

Ohio Dynasty Trusts: Where are We Now? Craig F. Frederickson, 12 Prob L J Ohio 104 (July/August 2002).

Perpetual Dynasty Trusts: One of the Most Powerful Tools in the Estate Planner's Arsenal, Comment. 32 Akron L Rev 747 (1999).

Perpetuities Literacy for the 21st Century, Robert J. Lynn. 50 Ohio St L J 220 (1989).

Teaching the Rule Against Perpetuities in First Year Property, Robert J. Hopperton. 31 U Tol L Rev 55 (Fall 1999).

Notes of Decisions

Purpose 1

---

1. Purpose

Where all beneficiaries to a trust agree to terminate such trust, the trial court may properly refuse to terminate on the grounds that letting the trust run for its designated fifteen years is a material purpose yet to be accomplished. In re Complaint to Terminate Trust of Grant, No. CA–6122 (5th Dist Ct App, Stark, 9–26–83).

DEPOSITS PAYABLE ON DEATH

2131.10 Any natural person, entity, or organization may be beneficiary of P.O.D. account

A natural person, adult or minor, referred to in sections 2131.10 and 2131.11 of the Revised Code as the owner, may enter into a written contract with any bank, building and loan or savings and loan association, credit union, or society for savings, authorized to receive money on an investment share certificate, share account, deposit, or stock deposit, and transacting business in this state, whereby the proceeds of the owner's investment share certificate, share account, deposit, or stock deposit may be made payable on the death of the owner to another person or to any entity or organization, referred to in such sections as the beneficiary, notwithstanding any provisions to the contrary in Chapter 2107. of the Revised Code. In creating such accounts, "payable on death" or "payable on the death of" may be abbreviated to "P.O.D."

Every contract of an investment share certificate, share account, deposit, or stock deposit authorized by this section shall be deemed to contain a right on the part of the owner during the owner's lifetime both to withdraw the proceeds of such investment share certificate, share account, deposit, or stock deposit, in whole or in part, as though no beneficiary has been named, and to designate a change in beneficiary. The interest of the beneficiary shall be deemed not to vest until the death of the owner.

No change in the designation of the beneficiary shall be valid unless executed in the form and manner prescribed by the bank, building and loan or savings and loan association, credit union, or society for savings.

(2000 H 313, eff. 8–29–00; 1984 H 348, eff. 9–20–84; 130 v H 1; 129 v 245)

Uncodified Law

2002 H 509, § 3, eff. 3–14–03, reads:

No liability shall arise against any one of the following that, prior to the effective date of this section, authorized or was otherwise responsible for a distribution or other payment or a transfer of property that is inconsistent with division (A)(3) of section 3107.15 of the Revised Code, as amended by this act:

(1) A fiduciary under a trust instrument, will, or other document;

(2) A bank, savings and loan association, credit union, or society for savings, in connection with written contracts described in sections 2131.10 and 2131.11 of the Revised Code;

(3) A registering entity, as defined in division (H) of section 1709.01 of the Revised Code, for a transfer-on-death made pursuant to Chapter 1709. of the Revised Code.

Historical and Statutory Notes

Amendment Note: 2000 H 313 deleted "natural" after "death of the owner to another"; and made changes to reflect gender neutral language.

Cross References

Banks, deposits payable on death, 1109.07

Library References

Banks and Banking ⚖129, 301(5).
Building and Loan Associations ⚖40.
Westlaw Topic Nos. 52, 66.
C.J.S. Banks and Banking §§ 269 to 270, 280, 327, 608, 610 to 612, 618.
C.J.S. Building and Loan Associations, Savings and Loan Associations, and Credit Unions §§ 66 to 67, 71 to 79.

Research References

Encyclopedias

7 Am. Jur. Proof of Facts 2d 311, Ownership of Bank Deposit Made in the Names of Two or More Persons.

7 Am. Jur. Proof of Facts 2d 375, Gift of Fund on Deposit in Bank Account.

OH Jur. 3d Banks & Financial Institutions § 185, Withdrawal of Proceeds; Change of Beneficiary and Registration.

OH Jur. 3d Banks & Financial Institutions § 586, Payable-On-Death Accounts.

OH Jur. 3d Decedents' Estates § 68, Joint Estates; Pod Accounts.

OH Jur. 3d Decedents' Estates § 270, Interests that Terminate at Death; Pod Accounts.

Treatises and Practice Aids

Carlin, Baldwin's Ohio Practice, Merrick-Rippner Probate Law § 2:6, Identification of Assets.

Carlin, Baldwin's Ohio Practice, Merrick-Rippner Probate Law § 27:2, Testamentary Formalities—Compliance With Statute.

Carlin, Baldwin's Ohio Practice, Merrick-Rippner Probate Law § 33:7, Trusts—Beneficiary of Payable on Death Account.

Carlin, Baldwin's Ohio Practice, Merrick-Rippner Probate Law § 79:7, Inventory—Exclusion of Nonprobate Assets.

Carlin, Baldwin's Ohio Practice, Merrick-Rippner Probate Law § 14:18, Payable on Death Accounts.

Carlin, Baldwin's Ohio Practice, Merrick-Rippner Probate Law § 2:121, Administration of Decedent's Estate—Checklist.

Carlin, Baldwin's Ohio Practice, Merrick-Rippner Probate Law § 2:122, Administration of Decedent's Estate—Release—Checklist.

Bogert - the Law of Trusts and Trustees § 47, Creation of a Trust of a Savings Account--Joint Accounts.

Law Review and Journal Commentaries

POD Bank Accounts, Robert M. Brucken. 10 Prob L J Ohio 74 (May/June 2000).

Special Purpose Bank Accounts, Gregory W. Klucher. 12 Lake Legal Views 6 (February 1989).

Types of bank accounts. Ohio B Ass'n Serv Letter, Commercial Law Edition, Sept, 1965.

Notes of Decisions

Artificial persons 1
Change of beneficiary 4
Grantor's retained interest 6
Pledge 2
Procedural issues 5
Survivor's interest 3

---

1. Artificial persons

RC 2131.10 as enacted in 1961 did not permit artificial persons to be beneficiaries of accounts payable on death, but the present version of the statute does as amended by 1984 H 348, eff. 9–20–84, notwithstanding the fact the legislative summary stated the amendment was meant to merely "clarify" the law. Estate of Kinsey v. Janes (Franklin 1992) 82 Ohio App.3d 822, 613 N.E.2d 686.

Each time certificates of deposit are renewed, they are governed by statutes in effect at the time of renewal; consequently, a payable-on-death provision designating an artificial person as a beneficiary is valid where the certificate was renewed after 1984. Estate of Kinsey v. Janes (Franklin 1992) 82 Ohio App.3d 822, 613 N.E.2d 686.

The amendment of RC 2131.10 by 1984 H 348, eff. 9–20–84, allowing the naming of artificial persons as beneficiaries of payable-on-death bank accounts, is prospective in its effect; nevertheless, where a depositor designated an artificial person as a beneficiary before the amendment and left the designation unchanged for five years after the amendment without expressly redesignating the artificial person as beneficiary, it will be held that the depositor's decision to leave the original designation intact after the amendment effectively reaffirmed it. Estate of Kinsey v. Janes (Franklin 1992) 82 Ohio App.3d 822, 613 N.E.2d 686.

A corporation may not be the beneficiary of a payable on death account. Powell v. City Nat. Bank & Trust Co. (Franklin 1981) 2 Ohio App.3d 1, 440 N.E.2d 560, 2 O.B.R. 1.

The general assembly did not create an unreasonable and arbitrary classification when it permitted only natural persons to be the beneficiaries of "POD" accounts. Powell v. City Nat. Bank & Trust Co. (Franklin 1981) 2 Ohio App.3d 1, 440 N.E.2d 560, 2 O.B.R. 1.

2. Pledge

The lifetime owner of a payable-on-death certificate of deposit ("P.O.D. C.D.") has a complete present interest in the account and may withdraw its proceeds, change the beneficiary, or pledge the P.O.D. C.D. as collateral for a loan; upon the owner's death, the beneficiary's interest vests, and if the owner has pledged the P.O.D. C.D. as collateral, the beneficiary is entitled to only an encumbered interest in the P.O.D. C.D. proceeds. Jamison v. Soc. Natl. Bank (Ohio 1993) 66 Ohio St.3d 201, 611 N.E.2d 307. Banks And Banking ⚖ 152; Secured Transactions ⚖ 166

Where an owner of payable on death certificates of deposit pledges them for security on a bank loan and the loan becomes in default after her death, the bank may apply the certificates to the debt and is only liable for the surplus to the named beneficiary; the fund from the certificates does not go into the estate. In re Estate of Gullett (Ohio Com.Pl. 1987) 36 Ohio Misc.2d 8, 521 N.E.2d 14.

3. Survivor's interest

Parent of minor beneficiaries of payment-on-death (POD) certificates did not have standing to bring suit on children's behalf against deceased depositor's estate and bank to challenge the liquidation of POD account by depositor's guardian 13 months before depositor's death; beneficiaries' legal interest did not vest until depositor's death. Ferguson v. Walsh (Ohio App. 10 Dist., Franklin, 08-26-2003) No. 02AP-1231, 2003-Ohio-4504, 2003 WL 22006833, Unreported. Banks And Banking ⚖ 129; Banks And Banking ⚖ 221; Executors And Administrators ⚖ 55

Return annuities were nonprobate assets that were not to be included in decedent's probate estate; return annuities purchased by deceased in which he named children as death beneficiaries were similar to life insurance policies for purposes of estate planning and probate. Adams v. Adams (Ohio App. 12 Dist., Warren, 07-14-2003) No. CA2002-09-087, 2003-Ohio-3703, 2003 WL 21638002, Unreported. Executors And Administrators ⚖ 46

Deceased husband did not violate wife's right to receive a distributive share of his estate by purchasing certain annuities and naming his children as beneficiaries; the fact that annuities were purchased by deceased husband while he was married did not necessarily mean that annuities were purchased with marital assets, and thus, wife was not entitled to a distributive share of annuities. Adams v. Adams (Ohio App. 12 Dist., Warren, 07-14-2003) No. CA2002-09-087, 2003-Ohio-3703, 2003 WL 21638002, Unreported. Executors And Administrators ⚖ 46

Assets in payable on death (POD) account belonged to beneficiary, rather than to estate of account owner, although assets were generated solely by owner, and beneficiary, as holder of power of attorney, opened account by transferring assets from certificate of deposit (CD) account with right of survivorship in the name of owner and beneficiary, where there was no evidence of fraud, duress, undue influence, or lack of mental capacity on part of owner, owner intended to give beneficiary survivorship interest in CD account, and beneficiary conferred no benefit upon himself by depositing assets from CD account into POD account. In re Estate of Platt (Ohio App. 11 Dist., 06-28-2002) 148 Ohio App.3d 132, 772 N.E.2d 198, 2002-Ohio-3382. Banks And Banking ⚖ 129

Sums remaining on deposit at the death of a party to a joint and survivorship account belong to the surviving party against the estate of the decedent unless there is clear and convincing evidence of a different intent at the time of creation. Witt v. Ward (Preble 1989) 60 Ohio App.3d 21, 573 N.E.2d 201, motion overruled 43 Ohio St.3d 712, 541 N.E.2d 78. Joint Tenancy ⚖ 12

A beneficiary to a payable-on-death account has a vested enforceable interest in the proceeds of the account at the time of the depositor's death; thus, where a bank pays the proceeds of a payable-on-death account to an estate creditor under a facially valid probate court order, genuine issues of material fact exist as to whether the bank breached its contract with the depositor and whether the bank violated its duty of good faith and reasonable care in failing to discover the existence of a beneficiary to the account. Taylor v. First Nat. Bank of Cincinnati (Hamilton 1986) 31 Ohio App.3d 49, 508 N.E.2d 1006, 31 O.B.R. 88.

In payable-on-death account, depositor owner retains both legal and equitable interests in account, and interest of "beneficiary" in such account does not vest until death of owner. Friedrich v. BancOhio Nat. Bank (Madison 1984) 14 Ohio App.3d 247, 470 N.E.2d 467, 53 A.L.R.4th 1285, 14 O.B.R. 276. Wills ⚖ 89

A lease agreement executed by two parties as co-lessees for a safe deposit box, which agreement provides that such co-lessees are joint tenants with right of survivorship, is a contract vesting inter vivos a present and equal joint interest in such co-lessees, and where the evidence of decedent's intention confirms the written provisions of the contract, then upon the death of one of the co-lessees the survivor becomes the absolute owner of the entire contents of the box by the operative provisions of that contract. Steinhauser v. Repko (Ohio 1972) 30 Ohio St.2d 262, 285 N.E.2d 55, 59 O.O.2d 334. Joint Tenancy ⚖ 6

A lease agreement executed by two parties as co-lessees for a safe deposit box, which agreement provides that such co-lessees are joint tenants with right of survivorship, raises a rebuttable presumption that the parties to the agreement have a present, equal joint interest in the res, and, in the absence of any evidence, that presumption is sufficient, as a matter of law, to sustain a judgment declaring the survivor the absolute owner of the entire contents of the box. Steinhauser v. Repko (Ohio 1972) 30 Ohio St.2d 262, 285 N.E.2d 55, 59 O.O.2d 334. Joint Tenancy ⚖ 6

Where decedent placed currency in safe deposit box which was rented from bank pursuant to lease agreement signed by decedent and his sister-in-law as "joint tenants with right of survivorship," which agreement also recited that all property placed in such box was declared to be joint property of both lessees and upon death of either passes to survivor, and only testimony concerning statements of decedent made at time such arrangement was made confirmed his intention to establish right of survivorship, it is effective to vest title in such survivor upon his death. Steinhauser v. Repko (Mahoning 1971) 28 Ohio App.2d 251, 277 N.E.2d 73, 57 O.O.2d 374, affirmed 30 Ohio St.2d 262, 285 N.E.2d 55, 59 O.O.2d 334. Joint Tenancy ⊂⇒ 6

Where a natural adult person enters into a contract with his bank, depositing therein various sums of money in savings accounts, payable on death to certain named individuals, such savings accounts, upon the death of the depositor, are, by such statute, expressly exempt from the statute of wills. In re Tonsic's Estate (Summit 1968) 13 Ohio App.2d 195, 235 N.E.2d 239, 42 O.O.2d 341. Wills ⊂⇒ 88(2)

4. Change of beneficiary

In a payable on death (POD) bank account, the owner retains sole ownership and only he may withdraw the proceeds or change the named beneficiary during his lifetime, whereas, a joint account with a right of survivorship belongs to all the parties during their lifetimes. In re Estate of Platt (Ohio App. 11 Dist., 06-28-2002) 148 Ohio App.3d 132, 772 N.E.2d 198, 2002-Ohio-3382. Banks And Banking ⊂⇒ 129; Joint Tenancy ⊂⇒ 8

An incompetent for whom a guardian has been appointed may change the beneficiary designation of payable on death (P.O.D.) accounts as such designations are in the manner of testamentary dispositions and a guardian has no authority to make testamentary dispositions on behalf of a ward. Witt v. Ward (Preble 1989) 60 Ohio App.3d 21, 573 N.E.2d 201, motion overruled 43 Ohio St.3d 712, 541 N.E.2d 78.

The change of a beneficiary on a payable on death account is not a sale, gift, conveyance, or encumbrance of the account within the meaning of RC 2111.04. Ogilvie v. Kehr (Fairfield 1988) 39 Ohio App.3d 170, 530 N.E.2d 957.

A payable on death (P.O.D.) account created under RC 2131.10 is one where funds are made payable upon the death of the owner to another without the documents having complied with the formalities of the statute of wills, and the funds involved do not become part of the decedent's estate; in a P.O.D. account the owner retains sole ownership of the account, only he may withdraw the proceeds or change the beneficiary during his lifetime, and the beneficiary's interest does not vest until the death of the owner. Eger v. Eger (Cuyahoga 1974) 39 Ohio App.2d 14, 314 N.E.2d 394, 68 O.O.2d 150.

Where husband and wife open a joint account with a right of survivorship and wife authorizes the bank to change the name of her deceased husband and replace it with her sister's name, upon the husband's death, the account passes to the sister by virtue of her right of survivorship where a name on the account is changed and its designation as a joint account with right of survivorship is unchanged. The Trumbull Savings & Loan Co. v. Vaccar (Ohio App. 11 Dist., Trumbull, 11-21-2001) No. 2000-T-0101, 2001-Ohio-8810, 2001 WL 1497205, Unreported, appeal not allowed 94 Ohio St.3d 1507, 764 N.E.2d 1037.

5. Procedural issues

Parent of minor beneficiaries of payment-on-death (POD) certificates filed her motion for leave to amend complaint against deceased depositor's estate and bank ten months after re-filing of complaint in second county and sixteen months after filing of original complaint, and thus motion was untimely filed and subject to denial; motion was filed after deadline for dispositive motions and four months before trial, and amendment would prejudice bank. Ferguson v. Walsh (Ohio App. 10 Dist., Franklin, 08-26-2003) No. 02AP-1231, 2003-Ohio-4504, 2003 WL 22006833, Unreported. Pleading ⊂⇒ 245(1)

Bank owed no duty to former beneficiaries of payment-on-death (POD) certificates liquidated prior to death of depositor unless bank was shown to have acted in bad faith, and thus procedures for closing POD account before depositor's death were followed properly, such that liquidation of accounts was not wrongful, even though bank did not ascertain and inform guardian status of accounts prior to liquidation; bank received letter of guardian's appointment, guardian requested a record of all accounts held by bank, guardian acted within her powers in withdrawing funds from POD accounts, and depositor was permitted by statute to close account. Ferguson v. Walsh (Ohio App. 10 Dist., Franklin, 08-26-2003) No. 02AP-1231, 2003-Ohio-4504, 2003 WL 22006833, Unreported. Banks And Banking ⊂⇒ 129; Banks And Banking ⊂⇒ 133

Payable-on-death (P.O.D.) account was valid, even though depositor had not signed signature card and statutes require "written contract" in order to establish valid P.O.D. account; assistant branch manager's testimony that she had bank's authority to mark "Okay, too hard for customer to sign" in place required for depositor's signature and that both bank and depositor intended to open such account established requisite meeting of the minds to form contract establishing valid P.O.D. account. Giurbino v. Giurbino (Ohio App. 8 Dist., 08-02-1993) 89 Ohio App.3d 646, 626 N.E.2d 1017, motion overruled 68 Ohio St.3d 1421, 624 N.E.2d 195. Banks And Banking ⊂⇒ 129

A certificate of deposit does not constitute the writing required by RC 2131.10 to create a P.O.D. account. Witt v. Ward (Preble 1989) 60 Ohio App.3d 21, 573 N.E.2d 201, motion overruled 43 Ohio St.3d 712, 541 N.E.2d 78.

The owner of a payable on death savings account opened pursuant to RC 2131.10 may designate more than one person as a beneficiary of the account. Wingate v. Hordge (Ohio 1979) 60 Ohio St.2d 55, 396 N.E.2d 770, 14 O.O.3d 212.

6. Grantor's retained interest

In a payable on death (POD) bank account, the depositor of the funds retains both the legal and equitable interest on the account; the beneficiary's interest does not vest until the death of the owner. In re Estate of Platt (Ohio App. 11 Dist., 06-28-2002) 148 Ohio App.3d 132, 772 N.E.2d 198, 2002-Ohio-3382. Banks And Banking ⊂⇒ 129

By reserving power of revocation, settlor retains right to reinvest himself with legal title to trust res at some point in future, but power of revocation does not give settlor same ownership interest in trust res as that which depositor retains upon creating payable-on-death account. Friedrich v. BancOhio Nat. Bank (Madison 1984) 14 Ohio App.3d 247, 470 N.E.2d 467, 53 A.L.R.4th 1285, 14 O.B.R. 276. Trusts ⊂⇒ 59(2)

2131.11 Release and discharge upon payment

When an investment share certificate, share account, deposit, or stock deposit is made, in any bank, building and loan or savings and loan association, credit union, or society for savings, payable to the owner during his lifetime, and to another on his death, such investment share certificate, share account, deposit, or stock deposit or any part thereof or any interest or dividend thereon, may be paid to the owner during his lifetime, and on his death such investment share certificate, share account, deposit, or stock deposit or any part thereof or any interest or dividend thereon, may be paid to the designated beneficiary, and the receipt of acquittance of the person paid is a sufficient release and discharge of the bank, building and loan or savings and loan association, credit union, or society for savings for any payment so made.

(129 v 245, eff. 7–25–61)

Uncodified Law

2002 H 509, § 3: See Uncodified Law under 2131.10.

Cross References

Banks, deposits payable on death, 1109.07

Library References

Banks and Banking ⊂⇒133, 301(5), 305.
Building and Loan Associations ⊂⇒40.
Westlaw Topic Nos. 52, 66.
C.J.S. Banks and Banking §§ 269 to 270, 280, 326, 328 to 329, 331, 342, 347 to 348, 399, 608, 610 to 612, 615 to 616, 618.
C.J.S. Building and Loan Associations, Savings and Loan Associations, and Credit Unions §§ 66 to 67, 71 to 79.

Research References

Encyclopedias

7 Am. Jur. Proof of Facts 2d 311, Ownership of Bank Deposit Made in the Names of Two or More Persons.
OH Jur. 3d Banks & Financial Institutions § 188, Payment by Financial Institution as Releasing It.

MISCELLANEOUS

Treatises and Practice Aids

Carlin, Baldwin's Ohio Practice, Merrick-Rippner Probate Law § 2:6, Identification of Assets.

Carlin, Baldwin's Ohio Practice, Merrick-Rippner Probate Law § 27:2, Testamentary Formalities—Compliance With Statute.

Carlin, Baldwin's Ohio Practice, Merrick-Rippner Probate Law § 79:7, Inventory—Exclusion of Nonprobate Assets.

Carlin, Baldwin's Ohio Practice, Merrick-Rippner Probate Law § 14:18, Payable on Death Accounts.

Carlin, Baldwin's Ohio Practice, Merrick-Rippner Probate Law § 2:121, Administration of Decedent's Estate—Checklist.

Carlin, Baldwin's Ohio Practice, Merrick-Rippner Probate Law § 2:122, Administration of Decedent's Estate—Release—Checklist.

Bogert - the Law of Trusts and Trustees § 47, Creation of a Trust of a Savings Account--Joint Accounts.

Notes of Decisions

Natural persons as beneficiaries 1
Presumptions and evidence 2

1. Natural persons as beneficiaries

A corporation may not be the beneficiary of a payable on death account. Powell v. City Nat. Bank & Trust Co. (Franklin 1981) 2 Ohio App.3d 1, 440 N.E.2d 560, 2 O.B.R. 1.

The general assembly did not create an unreasonable and arbitrary classification when it permitted only natural persons to be the beneficiaries of "POD" accounts. Powell v. City Nat. Bank & Trust Co. (Franklin 1981) 2 Ohio App.3d 1, 440 N.E.2d 560, 2 O.B.R. 1.

2. Presumptions and evidence

Bank's failure to discover that beneficiary existed for payable-on-death account and was entitled to proceeds raised genuine issue of fact whether bank violated duty of good faith and reasonable care when it paid account proceeds to estate creditor, even though bank relied on facially valid probate court order. Taylor v. First Nat. Bank of Cincinnati (Hamilton 1986) 31 Ohio App.3d 49, 508 N.E.2d 1006, 31 O.B.R. 88. Judgment ⊕ 181(17)

A lease agreement executed by two parties as co-lessees for a safe deposit box, which agreement provides that such co-lessees are joint tenants with right of survivorship, is a contract vesting inter vivos a present and equal joint interest in such co-lessees, and where the evidence of decedent's intention confirms the written provisions of the contract, then upon the death of one of the co-lessees the survivor becomes the absolute owner of the entire contents of the box by the operative provisions of that contract. Steinhauser v. Repko (Ohio 1972) 30 Ohio St.2d 262, 285 N.E.2d 55, 59 O.O.2d 334. Joint Tenancy ⊕ 6

A lease agreement executed by two parties as co-lessees for a safe deposit box, which agreement provides that such co-lessees are joint tenants with right of survivorship, raises a rebuttable presumption that the parties to the agreement have a present, equal joint interest in the res, and, in the absence of any evidence, that presumption is sufficient, as a matter of law, to sustain a judgment declaring the survivor the absolute owner of the entire contents of the box. Steinhauser v. Repko (Ohio 1972) 30 Ohio St.2d 262, 285 N.E.2d 55, 59 O.O.2d 334. Joint Tenancy ⊕ 6

Where decedent placed currency in safe deposit box which was rented from bank pursuant to lease agreement signed by decedent and his sister-in-law as "joint tenants with right of survivorship," which agreement also recited that all property placed in such box was declared to be joint property of both lessees and upon death of either passes to survivor, and only testimony concerning statements of decedent made at time such arrangement was made confirmed his intention to establish right of survivorship, it is effective to vest title in such survivor upon his death. Repko v. Repko (Mahoning 1971) 28 Ohio App.2d 251, 277 N.E.2d 73, 57 O.O.2d 374, affirmed 30 Ohio St.2d 262, 285 N.E.2d 55, 59 O.O.2d 334. Joint Tenancy ⊕ 6

Where a natural adult person enters into a contract with his bank, depositing therein various sums of money in savings accounts, payable on death to certain named individuals, such savings accounts, upon the death of the depositor, are, by such statute, expressly exempt from the statute of wills. In re Tonsic's Estate (Summit 1968) 13 Ohio App.2d 195, 235 N.E.2d 239, 42 O.O.2d 341. Wills ⊕ 88(2)

TRANSFER OF MOTOR VEHICLE, WATERCRAFT, OR OUTBOARD MOTOR ON DEATH

2131.12 Joint ownership with right of survivorship of motor vehicle, watercraft, or outboard motor

(A) As used in this section:

(1) "Motor vehicle" has the same meaning as in section 4505.01 of the Revised Code.

(2) "Joint ownership with right of survivorship" means a form of ownership of a motor vehicle, watercraft, or outboard motor that is established pursuant to this section and pursuant to which the entire interest in the motor vehicle, watercraft, or outboard motor is held by two persons for their joint lives and thereafter by the survivor of them.

(3) "Watercraft" has the same meaning as in division (A) of section 1548.01 of the Revised Code.

(B)(1) Any two persons may establish in accordance with this section joint ownership with right of survivorship in a motor vehicle or in a watercraft or outboard motor for which a certificate of title is required under Chapter 1548. of the Revised Code.

(2) If two persons wish to establish joint ownership with right of survivorship in a motor vehicle or in a watercraft or outboard motor that is required to be titled under Chapter 1548. of the Revised Code, they may make a joint application for a certificate of title under section 4505.06 or 1548.07 of the Revised Code, as applicable.

(C) If two persons have established in a certificate of title joint ownership with right of survivorship in a motor vehicle or a watercraft or outboard motor that is required to be titled under Chapter 1548. of the Revised Code, and if one of those persons dies, the interest of the deceased person in the motor vehicle, watercraft, or outboard motor shall pass to the survivor of them upon transfer of title to the motor vehicle or watercraft or outboard motor in accordance with section 4505.10 or 1548.11 of the Revised Code. The motor vehicle, watercraft, or outboard motor shall not be considered an estate asset and shall not be included and stated in the estate inventory.

(2002 H 345, eff. 7–23–02)

Historical and Statutory Notes

Ed. Note: 2131.12 is former 2106.17, recodified by 2002 H 345, eff. 7–23–02; 1994 H 458, eff. 7–20–94.

Cross References

Boats and watercraft, joint ownership with right of survivorship, 1547.54, 1548.071, 1548.08
Certificates of title, application, 1548.07
Motor vehicle, application for certificate of title, 4505.06
Motor vehicle, certificate of title, application, 4906.06
Motor vehicle, certificate of title, ownership changed by operation of law, 4505.10
Motor vehicle, transfer of ownership and registration, 4503.12
Motor vehicles, joint ownership with right of survivorship, 4503.12
Odometer tampering, transfer defined, 4549.41
Surviving spouse, right to automobile of decedent, 2106.18
Watercraft or outboard motor, certificate of title, issuance to transfer-on-death beneficiary, 1548.11
Watercraft or outboard motor, contents of certificate of title, 1548.08
Watercraft or outboard motor, joint ownership with right of survivorship, 1548.071
Watercraft or outboard motor, registration, 1547.54

Library References

Joint Tenancy ⊕6.
Westlaw Topic No. 226.
C.J.S. Joint Tenancy §§ 3 to 5, 7, 10, 19 to 20, 36.

Research References

Encyclopedias

OH Jur. 3d Automobiles & Other Vehicles § 42, Transfer of Ownership and Registration—Death of Owner.

OH Jur. 3d Automobiles & Other Vehicles § 62, Application for Certificate—Place of Filing.

OH Jur. 3d Automobiles & Other Vehicles § 67, Change of Ownership by Operation of Law.

OH Jur. 3d Boats, Ships, & Shipping § 8, Certificate of Title; Manufacturer's or Importer's Certificate—Application and Issuance.

OH Jur. 3d Boats, Ships, & Shipping § 9, Certificate of Title; Manufacturer's or Importer's Certificate—Assignment; Change of Ownership by Operation of Law; Surrender and Cancellation.

OH Jur. 3d Decedents' Estates § 119, Under the Statute of Descent and Distribution—Motor Vehicles and Boats.

OH Jur. 3d Decedents' Estates § 1677, Right to Automobiles and Boats.

Treatises and Practice Aids

Carlin, Baldwin's Ohio Practice, Merrick-Rippner Probate Law § 15:6, Descent and Distribution—Surviving Spouse—in General.

Carlin, Baldwin's Ohio Practice, Merrick-Rippner Probate Law § 2:21, Inventory and Appraisal—Decedent's Automobiles to Spouse, or Motor Vehicle, Boat or Outboard Motor to Surviving Joint Owner.

Carlin, Baldwin's Ohio Practice, Merrick-Rippner Probate Law § 2:22, Inventory and Appraisal—Family Allowance.

Carlin, Baldwin's Ohio Practice, Merrick-Rippner Probate Law § 2:38, Elective Rights of Surviving Spouse—Election to Take Under Law or Under the Will—Elective Share of Surviving Spouse Against the Will.

Carlin, Baldwin's Ohio Practice, Merrick-Rippner Probate Law § 21:5, Rights of Surviving Spouse to Make Election—Statutory Provisions—Effect.

Carlin, Baldwin's Ohio Practice, Merrick-Rippner Probate Law § 89:4, Payment of Debts—Order of Payment.

Carlin, Baldwin's Ohio Practice, Merrick-Rippner Probate Law § 2:107, Distribution of Assets—Transfer of Titles to Motor Vehicles, Boat or Outboard Motor.

Carlin, Baldwin's Ohio Practice, Merrick-Rippner Probate Law § 2:121, Administration of Decedent's Estate—Checklist.

Carlin, Baldwin's Ohio Practice, Merrick-Rippner Probate Law § 2:122, Administration of Decedent's Estate—Release—Checklist.

Carlin, Baldwin's Ohio Practice, Merrick-Rippner Probate Law § 21:19, Rights of Surviving Spouse to Make Election—Effect of Election—Generally.

Carlin, Baldwin's Ohio Practice, Merrick-Rippner Probate Law § 21:62, Rights of Surviving Spouse—Purchase of Other Property at Appraised Value.

Carlin, Baldwin's Ohio Practice, Merrick-Rippner Probate Law § 21:77, Rights of Surviving Spouse—Right to Receive Motor Vehicles, Boat or Outboard Motor—Automobile or Truck Owned by Decedent.

Carlin, Baldwin's Ohio Practice, Merrick-Rippner Probate Law § 21:78, Rights of Surviving Spouse—Right to Receive Motor Vehicles, Boat or Outboard Motor—Motor Vehicle, Boat or Motor Owned Jointly With Right of Survivorship.

Carlin, Baldwin's Ohio Practice, Merrick-Rippner Probate Law § 30:23, Drafting a Will—Surviving Spouse—Bequest in Lieu of Statutory Rights.

Carlin, Baldwin's Ohio Practice, Merrick-Rippner Probate Law § 30:25, Drafting a Will—Surviving Spouse—Disinheritance of Spouse.

Carlin, Baldwin's Ohio Practice, Merrick-Rippner Probate Law § 30:88, Automobile, Specific Bequest; Provision If There is More Than One—Form.

Carlin, Baldwin's Ohio Practice, Merrick-Rippner Probate Law § 75:14, Transfer of Automobiles to Surviving Spouse.

Carlin, Baldwin's Ohio Practice, Merrick-Rippner Probate Law § 75:16, Transfer of Motor Vehicle, Watercraft or Outboard Motor to Surviving Joint Owner.

Carlin, Baldwin's Ohio Practice, Merrick-Rippner Probate Law § 75:17, Other Transfers of Automobiles, Watercraft and Outboard Motor.

2131.13 Designation of motor vehicle, watercraft, or outboard motor in beneficiary form

(A) As used in this section:

(1) "Designate or designation in beneficiary form" means to designate, or the designation of, a motor vehicle, watercraft, or outboard motor in a certificate of title that indicates the present owner of the motor vehicle, watercraft, or outboard motor and the intention of the present owner with respect to the transfer of ownership on the present owner's death by designating one or more persons as the beneficiary or beneficiaries who will become the owner or owners of the motor vehicle, watercraft, or outboard motor upon the death of the present owner.

(2) "Motor vehicle" has the same meaning as in section 4505.01 of the Revised Code.

(3) "Person" means an individual, a corporation, an organization, or other legal entity.

(4) "Transfer-on-death beneficiary or beneficiaries" means a person or persons specified in a certificate of title of a motor vehicle, watercraft, or outboard motor who will become the owner or owners of the motor vehicle, watercraft, or outboard motor upon the death of the present owner of the motor vehicle, watercraft, or outboard motor.

(5) "Watercraft" has the same meaning as in section 1548.01 of the Revised Code.

(B) An individual whose certificate of title of a motor vehicle, watercraft, or outboard motor shows sole ownership by that individual may make an application for a certificate of title under section 1548.07 or 4505.06 of the Revised Code to designate that motor vehicle, watercraft, or outboard motor in beneficiary form pursuant to this section.

(C)(1) A motor vehicle, watercraft, or outboard motor is designated in beneficiary form if the certificate of title of the motor vehicle, watercraft, or outboard motor includes the name or names of the transfer-on-death beneficiary or beneficiaries.

(2) The designation of a motor vehicle, watercraft, or outboard motor in beneficiary form is not required to be supported by consideration, and the certificate of title in which the designation is made is not required to be delivered to the transfer-on-death beneficiary or beneficiaries in order for the designation in beneficiary form to be effective.

(D) The designation of a motor vehicle, watercraft, or outboard motor in beneficiary form may be shown in the certificate of title by the words "transfer-on-death" or the abbreviation "TOD" after the name of the owner of a motor vehicle, watercraft, or outboard motor and before the name or names of the transfer-on-death beneficiary or beneficiaries.

(E) The designation of a transfer-on-death beneficiary or beneficiaries on a certificate of title has no effect on the ownership of a motor vehicle, watercraft, or outboard motor until the death of the owner of the motor vehicle, watercraft, or outboard motor. The owner of a motor vehicle, watercraft, or outboard motor may cancel or change the designation of a transfer-on-death beneficiary or beneficiaries on a certificate of title at any time without the consent of the transfer-on-death beneficiary or beneficiaries by making an application for a certificate of title under section 1548.07 or 4505.06 of the Revised Code.

(F)(1) Upon the death of the owner of a motor vehicle, watercraft, or outboard motor designated in beneficiary form, the ownership of the motor vehicle, watercraft, or outboard motor shall pass to the transfer-on-death beneficiary or beneficiaries who survive the owner upon transfer of title to the motor vehicle, watercraft, or outboard motor in accordance with section 1548.11 or 4505.10 of the Revised Code. The transfer-on-death beneficiary or beneficiaries who survive the owner may apply for a certificate of title to the motor vehicle, watercraft, or outboard motor upon submitting proof of the death of the owner of the motor vehicle, watercraft, or outboard motor.

(2) If no transfer-on-death beneficiary or beneficiaries survive the owner of a motor vehicle, watercraft, or outboard motor, the

motor vehicle, watercraft, or outboard motor shall be included in the probate estate of the deceased owner.

(G)(1) Any transfer of a motor vehicle, watercraft, or outboard motor to a transfer-on-death beneficiary or beneficiaries that results from a designation of the motor vehicle, watercraft, or outboard motor in beneficiary form is not testamentary.

(2) This section does not limit the rights of any creditor of the owner of a motor vehicle, watercraft, or outboard motor against any transfer-on-death beneficiary or beneficiaries or other transferees of the motor vehicle, watercraft, or outboard motor under other laws of this state.

(H)(1) This section shall be known and may be cited as the "Transfer-on-Death of Motor Vehicle, Watercraft, or Outboard Motor Statute."

(2) Divisions (A) to (H) of this section shall be liberally construed and applied to promote their underlying purposes and policy.

(3) Unless displaced by particular provisions of divisions (A) to (H) of this section, the principles of law and equity supplement the provisions of those divisions.

(2002 H 345, eff. 7–23–02)

Cross References

Disclaimer of succession to property, 1339.68
Motor vehicle, application for certificate of title, 4505.06
Motor vehicle, certificate of title, application, 4906.06
Motor vehicle, certificate of title, ownership changed by operation of law, 4505.10
Motor vehicle, transfer of ownership and registration, 4503.12
Surviving spouse, right to automobile of decedent, 2106.18
Watercraft or outboard motor, certificate of title, inclusion of transfer-on-death provision, 1548.072
Watercraft or outboard motor, certificate of title, issuance to transfer-on-death beneficiary, 1548.11
Watercraft or outboard motor, contents of certificate of title, 1548.08

Library References

Joint Tenancy ⚖6.
Westlaw Topic No. 226.
C.J.S. Joint Tenancy §§ 3 to 5, 7, 10, 19 to 20, 36.

Research References

Encyclopedias

OH Jur. 3d Automobiles & Other Vehicles § 41, Transfer of Ownership and Registration.
OH Jur. 3d Automobiles & Other Vehicles § 42, Transfer of Ownership and Registration—Death of Owner.
OH Jur. 3d Automobiles & Other Vehicles § 57, Delivery of Certificate on Transfer of Vehicle—Contents of Certificate.
OH Jur. 3d Automobiles & Other Vehicles § 62, Application for Certificate—Place of Filing.
OH Jur. 3d Automobiles & Other Vehicles § 67, Change of Ownership by Operation of Law.
OH Jur. 3d Boats, Ships, & Shipping § 8, Certificate of Title; Manufacturer's or Importer's Certificate—Application and Issuance.
OH Jur. 3d Boats, Ships, & Shipping § 9, Certificate of Title; Manufacturer's or Importer's Certificate—Assignment; Change of Ownership by Operation of Law; Surrender and Cancellation.
OH Jur. 3d Decedents' Estates § 119, Under the Statute of Descent and Distribution—Motor Vehicles and Boats.
OH Jur. 3d Decedents' Estates § 191, Disclaiming or Renouncing Succession to Property.
OH Jur. 3d Decedents' Estates § 731, Disclaimer Instrument—Filing and Recording.
OH Jur. 3d Decedents' Estates § 1677, Right to Automobiles and Boats.

Forms

Ohio Forms Legal and Business § 24:981, Renunciation or Disclaimer of Devise or Bequest in Will.

Treatises and Practice Aids

Carlin, Baldwin's Ohio Practice, Merrick-Rippner Probate Law § 15:6, Descent and Distribution—Surviving Spouse—in General.
Carlin, Baldwin's Ohio Practice, Merrick-Rippner Probate Law § 2:21, Inventory and Appraisal—Decedent's Automobiles to Spouse, or Motor Vehicle, Boat or Outboard Motor to Surviving Joint Owner.
Carlin, Baldwin's Ohio Practice, Merrick-Rippner Probate Law § 2:22, Inventory and Appraisal—Family Allowance.
Carlin, Baldwin's Ohio Practice, Merrick-Rippner Probate Law § 2:38, Elective Rights of Surviving Spouse—Election to Take Under Law or Under the Will—Elective Share of Surviving Spouse Against the Will.
Carlin, Baldwin's Ohio Practice, Merrick-Rippner Probate Law § 21:5, Rights of Surviving Spouse to Make Election—Statutory Provisions—Effect.
Carlin, Baldwin's Ohio Practice, Merrick-Rippner Probate Law § 79:7, Inventory—Exclusion of Nonprobate Assets.
Carlin, Baldwin's Ohio Practice, Merrick-Rippner Probate Law § 89:4, Payment of Debts—Order of Payment.
Carlin, Baldwin's Ohio Practice, Merrick-Rippner Probate Law § 11:14, Delivery of Disclaimer Instrument—Interest Disclaimed—Nontestamentary Instrument.
Carlin, Baldwin's Ohio Practice, Merrick-Rippner Probate Law § 14:21, Transfer-On-Death for Motor Vehicles, Watercraft, And Outboard Motors.
Carlin, Baldwin's Ohio Practice, Merrick-Rippner Probate Law § 2:107, Distribution of Assets—Transfer of Titles to Motor Vehicles, Boat or Outboard Motor.
Carlin, Baldwin's Ohio Practice, Merrick-Rippner Probate Law § 2:121, Administration of Decedent's Estate—Checklist.
Carlin, Baldwin's Ohio Practice, Merrick-Rippner Probate Law § 2:122, Administration of Decedent's Estate—Release—Checklist.
Carlin, Baldwin's Ohio Practice, Merrick-Rippner Probate Law § 21:19, Rights of Surviving Spouse to Make Election—Effect of Election—Generally.
Carlin, Baldwin's Ohio Practice, Merrick-Rippner Probate Law § 21:62, Rights of Surviving Spouse—Purchase of Other Property at Appraised Value.
Carlin, Baldwin's Ohio Practice, Merrick-Rippner Probate Law § 21:77, Rights of Surviving Spouse—Right to Receive Motor Vehicles, Boat or Outboard Motor—Automobile or Truck Owned by Decedent.
Carlin, Baldwin's Ohio Practice, Merrick-Rippner Probate Law § 21:78, Rights of Surviving Spouse—Right to Receive Motor Vehicles, Boat or Outboard Motor—Motor Vehicle, Boat or Motor Owned Jointly With Right of Survivorship.
Carlin, Baldwin's Ohio Practice, Merrick-Rippner Probate Law § 21:79, Rights of Surviving Spouse—Right to Receive Motor Vehicles, Boat or Outboard Motor—Watercraft or Outboard Motor Owned by Decedent.
Carlin, Baldwin's Ohio Practice, Merrick-Rippner Probate Law § 30:23, Drafting a Will—Surviving Spouse—Bequest in Lieu of Statutory Rights.
Carlin, Baldwin's Ohio Practice, Merrick-Rippner Probate Law § 30:25, Drafting a Will—Surviving Spouse—Disinheritance of Spouse.
Carlin, Baldwin's Ohio Practice, Merrick-Rippner Probate Law § 30:88, Automobile, Specific Bequest; Provision If There is More Than One—Form.
Carlin, Baldwin's Ohio Practice, Merrick-Rippner Probate Law § 75:14, Transfer of Automobiles to Surviving Spouse.
Carlin, Baldwin's Ohio Practice, Merrick-Rippner Probate Law § 75:16, Transfer of Motor Vehicle, Watercraft or Outboard Motor to Surviving Joint Owner.
Carlin, Baldwin's Ohio Practice, Merrick-Rippner Probate Law § 75:17, Other Transfers of Automobiles, Watercraft and Outboard Motor.

Law Review and Journal Commentaries

Transfer on Death of Motor Vehicles, Watercraft or Outboard Motors. J. MacAlpine Smith, 12 Prob L J Ohio 81 (May/June 2002).

DEPOSIT OF SECURITIES HELD BY FIDUCIARY

2131.21 Fiduciary may deposit securities in federal reserve bank, clearing corporation, or securities depository; procedures

Any person holding securities in a fiduciary capacity, or any state bank, trust company, or national bank, any of which is holding securities as a custodian, managing agent, or custodian for a fiduciary, is authorized to deposit or arrange for the deposit of the securities in a federal reserve bank, a clearing corporation, or a securities depository. When the securities are so deposited, certificates representing securities of the same class of the same issuer may be merged and held in bulk in the name of the nominee of the federal reserve bank, clearing corporation, or securities depository with any other such securities deposited in the federal reserve bank, clearing corporation, or securities depository by any person, regardless of the ownership of the securities, and certificates of small denomination may be merged into one or more certificates of larger denomination. The records of the fiduciary and the records of a state bank, trust company, or national bank acting as custodian, managing agent, or custodian for a fiduciary shall at all times show the name of the party for whose account the securities are so deposited. Title to the securities may be transferred by bookkeeping entry on the books of the federal reserve bank, clearing corporation, or securities depository without physical delivery of certificates representing the securities. A state bank, trust company, or national bank depositing securities pursuant to this section shall be subject to the rules as, in the case of state chartered institutions, the superintendent of banks or state bank commissioner of another state, and in the case of national banking associations, the comptroller of the currency, may issue. A state bank, trust company, or national bank, acting as custodian for a fiduciary, shall, on demand by the fiduciary, certify in writing to the fiduciary the securities so deposited by the state bank, trust company, or national bank in the federal reserve bank, clearing corporation, or securities depository for the account of the fiduciary. A fiduciary shall, on demand by any party to a judicial proceeding for the settlement of the fiduciary's account, or on demand by the attorney for such a party, certify in writing to the party the securities deposited by the fiduciary in the federal reserve bank, clearing corporation, or securities depository.

This section shall apply to any fiduciary holding securities in its fiduciary capacity, and to any state bank, trust company, or national bank holding securities as a custodian, managing agent, or custodian for a fiduciary, or who thereafter may act, regardless of the date of the agreement, instrument, or court order by which it is appointed, and regardless of whether or not the fiduciary, custodian, managing agent, or custodian for a fiduciary owns capital stock of the clearing corporation or securities depository.

(1975 S 145, eff. 1–1–76)

Legislative Service Commission

1975:

This new section would authorize any person holding securities in a fiduciary capacity to place the securities in a Federal Reserve Bank, a Clearing Corporation, or other securities depository and would authorize the Bank, Corporation, or other depository to merge securities so deposited with others it holds of the same class, subject to appropriate record-keeping requirements.

Cross References

Accounts of fiduciaries, 2109.30
Clearing corporation, defined, 1308.01
Recordkeeping and separation of trust property, 5808.10

Library References

Banks and Banking ⚖123, 356.
Deposits and Escrows ⚖2, 12.
Executors and Administrators ⚖102.
Trusts ⚖217.1.
Westlaw Topic Nos. 122A, 162, 390, 52.
C.J.S. Banks and Banking §§ 383, 652 to 658.
C.J.S. Depositaries § 2.
C.J.S. Escrows § 4.
C.J.S. Executors and Administrators §§ 223 to 225.
C.J.S. Trusts §§ 482 to 484, 486, 488 to 490, 504 to 505.

Research References

Encyclopedias

OH Jur. 3d Decedents' Estates § 1667, Contents and Designation of Accounts.
OH Jur. 3d Fiduciaries § 64, Fiduciary's Rights as Security Holder—Deposit of Securities.
OH Jur. 3d Fiduciaries § 260, Examination of Fiduciary; Exhibiting Securities and Passbooks.

Treatises and Practice Aids

Carlin, Baldwin's Ohio Practice, Merrick-Rippner Probate Law § 54:6, Fiduciary Accounts—Exhibition of Assets.
Carlin, Baldwin's Ohio Practice, Merrick-Rippner Probate Law § 54:42, Certificate of Depository—Form.
Bogert - the Law of Trusts and Trustees § 596, Duty to Earmark and Separate Trust Property.

CHAPTER 2133

MODIFIED UNIFORM RIGHTS OF THE TERMINALLY ILL ACT AND THE DNR IDENTIFICATION AND DO–NOT–RESUSCITATE ORDER LAW

LIVING WILLS

Section	
2133.01	Definitions
2133.02	Execution of declaration; witnesses; refusal to comply with declaration
2133.03	Requirements for declaration to become operative; priority of declaration
2133.04	Revocation of declaration
2133.05	Records; notice requirements; objections; complaints
2133.06	Patients able to make informed decisions; pregnant declarants
2133.07	Printed form of declaration
2133.08	Withholding or withdrawal of life-sustaining treatment
2133.09	Withholding or withdrawal of nutrition or hydration
2133.10	Transfer of patient to physician or facility complying with declaration
2133.11	Immunities
2133.12	Death not deemed suicide or homicide; effect of declaration on insurance and annuities; rights not affected; euthanasia not authorized; comfort care
2133.13	Presumption of validity of declaration
2133.14	Effect of foreign declaration
2133.15	Effect of declaration executed prior to effective date of act
2133.16	Instrument of gift other than will

Section

DO NOT RESUSCITATE ORDERS

2133.21 Definitions
2133.211 Actions by nurse practitioners or nurse specialists authorized
2133.22 Criminal and civil immunities
2133.23 Compliance with DNR identification; transfer of person to different physician or facility; notice of DNR identification
2133.24 Death not deemed suicide or homicide; effect of DNR identification on insurance and annuities; rights not affected
2133.25 Rulemaking powers; advisory committee
2133.26 Violations

Comparative Laws
Uniform Rights of the Terminally Ill Act
Table of Jurisdictions Wherein Act Has Been Adopted.

For text of Uniform Act, and variation notes and annotation materials for adopting jurisdictions, see Uniform Laws Annotated, Master Edition, Volume 9C.

Jurisdiction	Statutory Citation
Montana	MCA 50-9-101 to 50-9-206.
Nevada	N.R.S. 449.535 to 449.690.
Oklahoma	63 Okl.St.Ann. § 3101.1 to 3101.16.
Rhode Island	Gen.Laws 1956, § 23-4.11-1 to 23-4.11-15.
Virgin Islands	19 V.I.C. § 185 to 200.

Uncodified Law

1998 H 354, § 3, eff. 7-9-98, amended 1991 S 1, § 3, to read:

Chapter 2133. of the Revised Code, as amended by this act, shall be entitled the Modified Uniform Rights of the Terminally Ill Act and the DNR Identification and Do–Not–Resuscitate Order Law.

Cross References

Commercial driver's license applications, 4507.06
Driver's license applications, 4506.07
Identification card applications, 4507.51

Law Review and Journal Commentaries

Attorneys On Bioethics Committees: Unwelcome Menace or Valuable Asset?, Randall B. Bateman. 9 J L & Health 247 (1994–95).

The Constitutional Right To Suicide, The Quality of Life, And The "Slippery-Slope": An Explicit Reply To Lingering Concerns, Dr. G. Steven Neeley. 28 Akron L Rev 53 (Summer 1994).

Ethical and Legal Issues in the Individual's Right to Die, Robert L. Risley. 20 Ohio N U L Rev 597 (1994).

The Health Care Proxy and the Narrative of Death, Steven I. Friedland. 10 J L & Health 95 (1995–96).

Incompetents and the Right to Die: In Search of Consistent Meaningful Standards, Mark Strasser. 83 Ky L J 733 (1994–95).

Law Reform, Essay. (Ed. note: Discussion of right to die, assisted suicide and California uniform model Death With Dignity Act). 20 Ohio N U L Rev 729 (1994).

The Legal Response to Assisted Suicide, Comment. 20 Ohio N U L Rev 673 (1994).

Medical Self–Determination: A Call for Uniformity, Comment. 31 Duq L Rev 87 (Fall 1992).

Ohio advanced directives (Ed. Note: Living wills and powers of attorney for health care are among the topics discussed). Ellen K. Meehan and Michael J. Meehan, 16 Prob L J Ohio 82 (January/February 2006).

Ohio's Living Will Legislation—Are We Finally Getting the Right to Die?, Wayne A. Jenkins. 1 Prob L J Ohio 125 (July/August 1991).

Punishing Assisted Suicide: Where Legislators Should Fear to Tread. 20 Ohio N U L Rev 647 (1994).

Refusing, Withdrawing, or Withholding Medical Treatment in Ohio, Peter N. Cultice. 5 Health L J Ohio 53 (May/June 1994).

The Right of the Dying to Refuse Life Prolonging Medical Procedures: The Evolving Importance of State Constitutions, Thomas Clark Marks, Jr. and Rebecca C. Morgan. 18 Ohio N U L Rev 467 (1992).

The Right to Refuse Medical Treatment in Ohio After Cruzan: The Need for a Comprehensive Legislative Solution, Thomas J. Onusko and Patricia Casey Cuthbertson. 5 J L & Health 35 (1990–91).

Wrongful Living: A Sequel. 68 Clev B J 10 (May 1997).

LIVING WILLS

2133.01 Definitions

Unless the context otherwise requires, as used in sections 2133.01 to 2133.15 of the Revised Code:

(A) "Adult" means an individual who is eighteen years of age or older.

(B) "Attending physician" means the physician to whom a declarant or other patient, or the family of a declarant or other patient, has assigned primary responsibility for the treatment or care of the declarant or other patient, or, if the responsibility has not been assigned, the physician who has accepted that responsibility.

(C) "Comfort care" means any of the following:

(1) Nutrition when administered to diminish the pain or discomfort of a declarant or other patient, but not to postpone the declarant's or other patient's death;

(2) Hydration when administered to diminish the pain or discomfort of a declarant or other patient, but not to postpone the declarant's or other patient's death;

(3) Any other medical or nursing procedure, treatment, intervention, or other measure that is taken to diminish the pain or discomfort of a declarant or other patient, but not to postpone the declarant's or other patient's death.

(D) "Consulting physician" means a physician who, in conjunction with the attending physician of a declarant or other patient, makes one or more determinations that are required to be made by the attending physician, or to be made by the attending physician and one other physician, by an applicable provision of this chapter, to a reasonable degree of medical certainty and in accordance with reasonable medical standards.

(E) "Declarant" means any adult who has executed a declaration in accordance with section 2133.02 of the Revised Code.

(F) "Declaration" means a written document executed in accordance with section 2133.02 of the Revised Code.

(G) "Durable power of attorney for health care" means a document created pursuant to sections 1337.11 to 1337.17 of the Revised Code.

(H) "Guardian" means a person appointed by a probate court pursuant to Chapter 2111. of the Revised Code to have the care and management of the person of an incompetent.

(I) "Health care facility" means any of the following:

(1) A hospital;

(2) A hospice care program or other institution that specializes in comfort care of patients in a terminal condition or in a permanently unconscious state;

(3) A nursing home or residential care facility, as defined in section 3721.01 of the Revised Code;

(4) A home health agency and any residential facility where a person is receiving care under the direction of a home health agency;

(5) An intermediate care facility for the mentally retarded.

(J) "Health care personnel" means physicians, nurses, physician assistants, emergency medical technicians-basic, emergency medical technicians-intermediate, emergency medical technicians-paramedic, medical technicians, dietitians, other authorized persons acting under the direction of an attending physician, and administrators of health care facilities.

(K) "Home health agency" has the same meaning as in section 3701.881 of the Revised Code.

(L) "Hospice care program" has the same meaning as in section 3712.01 of the Revised Code.

(M) "Hospital" has the same meanings as in sections 2108.01, 3701.01, and 5122.01 of the Revised Code.

(N) "Hydration" means fluids that are artificially or technologically administered.

(O) "Incompetent" has the same meaning as in section 2111.01 of the Revised Code.

(P) "Intermediate care facility for the mentally retarded" has the same meaning as in section 5111.20 of the Revised Code.

(Q) "Life–sustaining treatment" means any medical procedure, treatment, intervention, or other measure that, when administered to a qualified patient or other patient, will serve principally to prolong the process of dying.

(R) "Nurse" means a person who is licensed to practice nursing as a registered nurse or to practice practical nursing as a licensed practical nurse pursuant to Chapter 4723. of the Revised Code.

(S) "Nursing home" has the same meaning as in section 3721.01 of the Revised Code.

(T) "Nutrition" means sustenance that is artificially or technologically administered.

(U) "Permanently unconscious state" means a state of permanent unconsciousness in a declarant or other patient that, to a reasonable degree of medical certainty as determined in accordance with reasonable medical standards by the declarant's or other patient's attending physician and one other physician who has examined the declarant or other patient, is characterized by both of the following:

(1) Irreversible unawareness of one's being and environment.

(2) Total loss of cerebral cortical functioning, resulting in the declarant or other patient having no capacity to experience pain or suffering.

(V) "Person" has the same meaning as in section 1.59 of the Revised Code and additionally includes political subdivisions and governmental agencies, boards, commissions, departments, institutions, offices, and other instrumentalities.

(W) "Physician" means a person who is authorized under Chapter 4731. of the Revised Code to practice medicine and surgery or osteopathic medicine and surgery.

(X) "Political subdivision" and "state" have the same meanings as in section 2744.01 of the Revised Code.

(Y) "Professional disciplinary action" means action taken by the board or other entity that regulates the professional conduct of health care personnel, including the state medical board and the board of nursing.

(Z) "Qualified patient" means an adult who has executed a declaration and has been determined to be in a terminal condition or in a permanently unconscious state.

(AA) "Terminal condition" means an irreversible, incurable, and untreatable condition caused by disease, illness, or injury from which, to a reasonable degree of medical certainty as determined in accordance with reasonable medical standards by a declarant's or other patient's attending physician and one other physician who has examined the declarant or other patient, both of the following apply:

(1) There can be no recovery.

(2) Death is likely to occur within a relatively short time if life-sustaining treatment is not administered.

(BB) "Tort action" means a civil action for damages for injury, death, or loss to person or property, other than a civil action for damages for breach of a contract or another agreement between persons.

(2003 H 95, eff. 9–26–03; 1998 H 354, eff. 7–9–98; 1995 S 143, eff. 3–5–96; 1995 S 150, eff. 11–24–95; 1991 S 1, eff. 10–10–91)

Historical and Statutory Notes

Amendment Note: 2003 H 95 substituted "3701.881" for "3701.88" in division (K).

Amendment Note: 1998 H 354 added references to residential care facilities in division (I); and made other nonsubstantive changes.

Amendment Note: 1995 S 143 substituted "physician assistants" for "physician's assistants" in division (J).

Amendment Note: 1995 S 150 substituted "technicians-basic" for "technicians-ambulance" and "emergency medical technicians-intermediate" for "advanced emergency medical technicians-ambulance" in division (J); substituted "authorized under Chapter 4731. of the Revised Code" for "licensed" and "and" for "or", and deleted "pursuant to Chapter 4731. of the Revised Code, or a person who otherwise is authorized to practice medicine or surgery or osteopathic medicine and surgery in this state" from division (W); and made changes to reflect gender neutral language and other nonsubstantive changes.

Cross References

Assisting suicide; activities not proscribed as, 3795.03
Durable power of attorney for health care, declaration defined, 1337.12

Library References

Health ⚖=916.
Westlaw Topic No. 198H.
Baldwin's Ohio Legislative Service, 1991 Laws of Ohio, S 1—LSC Analysis, p 5–250

Research References

Encyclopedias

40 Am. Jur. Proof of Facts 3d 287, Proof of Basis for Refusal or Discontinuance of Life-Sustaining Treatment on Behalf of Incapacitated Person.
63 Am. Jur. Trials 1, Decisionmaking at the End of Life.
OH Jur. 3d Agency & Independent Contractors § 46, Effect of a Do Not Resuscitate Declaration or Identification.
OH Jur. 3d Cemeteries & Dead Bodies § 74, Manner of Making Anatomical Gift—by Declarant Under Modified Uniform Rights of the Terminally Ill Act.
OH Jur. 3d Cemeteries & Dead Bodies § 76, Amendment or Revocation of Anatomical Gift.
OH Jur. 3d Death § 24, Generally; Declarant's Rights.

Forms

Ohio Forms Legal and Business § 12B:19, Declaration Regarding Medical Treatment in the Case of Terminal Illness or Permanent Unconsciousness.
Ohio Forms and Transactions KP 24.06, Durable Power of Attorney for Health Care.
Ohio Forms and Transactions KP 30.23, Living Will, or Health Care Declaration.

Treatises and Practice Aids

Carlin, Baldwin's Ohio Practice, Merrick-Rippner Probate Law § 60:31, Power of Attorney for Health Care—Withholding or Withdrawing Life-Support Measures or Other Care—Terminal Condition; Permanently Unconscious State.
Carlin, Baldwin's Ohio Practice, Merrick-Rippner Probate Law § 60:32, Power of Attorney for Health Care—Withholding or Withdrawing Life-Support Measures or Other Care—Comfort Care; Nutrition and Hydration.
Carlin, Baldwin's Ohio Practice, Merrick-Rippner Probate Law § 60:35.20, Declaration of Anatomical Gift.

Law Review and Journal Commentaries

Estate planning techniques for nontraditional couples. Susan L. Racey, 14 Prob L J Ohio 57 (January/February 2004).

Euphemistic Codes and Tell-Tale Hearts: Humane Assistance in End-of-Life Cases. George P. Smith, 11, 10 Health Matrix: J Law-Medicine 175 (Summer 2000).

Living Wills: The Right to Refuse Life Sustaining Medical Treatment—A Right Without a Remedy?, Maggie J. Randall Robb. 23 U Dayton L Rev 169 (Fall 1997).

Planning Ahead: Proper Implementation and Execution of Advance Directives, Bryan B. Johnson and Tristan A. McCormick. 17 Ohio Law 14 (September/October 2003).

Redrafting Ohio's Advance Directive Laws, Susan R. Martyn, et al. 26 Akron L Rev 229 (Fall 1992).

Saying Yes Or No To Life—Sustaining Treatment, Who Decides? In Ohio: The Patient, Family, And Physician, Comment. 21 Cap U L Rev 647 (Spring 1992).

S.B. 1: A Hospital Attorney's Perspective, Paul A. Greve, Jr. 3 Health L J Ohio 145 (May/June 1992).

A Womb of My Own: A Moral Evaluation of Ohio's Treatment of Pregnant Patients With Living Wills, Comment. 45 Case W Res L Rev 351 (Fall 1994).

2133.02 Execution of declaration; witnesses; refusal to comply with declaration

(A)(1) An adult who is of sound mind voluntarily may execute at any time a declaration governing the use or continuation, or the withholding or withdrawal, of life-sustaining treatment. The declaration shall be signed at the end by the declarant or by another individual at the direction of the declarant, state the date of its execution, and either be witnessed as described in division (B)(1) of this section or be acknowledged by the declarant in accordance with division (B)(2) of this section. The declaration may include a designation by the declarant of one or more persons who are to be notified by the declarant's attending physician at any time that life-sustaining treatment would be withheld or withdrawn pursuant to the declaration. The declaration may include a specific authorization for the use or continuation or the withholding or withdrawal of CPR, but the failure to include a specific authorization for the withholding or withdrawal of CPR does not preclude the withholding or withdrawal of CPR in accordance with sections 2133.01 to 2133.15 or sections 2133.21 to 2133.26 of the Revised Code.

(2) Depending upon whether the declarant intends the declaration to apply when the declarant is in a terminal condition, in a permanently unconscious state, or in either a terminal condition or a permanently unconscious state, the declarant's declaration shall use either or both of the terms "terminal condition" and "permanently unconscious state" and shall define or otherwise explain those terms in a manner that is substantially consistent with the provisions of section 2133.01 of the Revised Code.

(3)(a) If a declarant who has authorized the withholding or withdrawal of life-sustaining treatment intends that the declarant's attending physician withhold or withdraw nutrition or hydration when the declarant is in a permanently unconscious state and when the nutrition and hydration will not or no longer will serve to provide comfort to the declarant or alleviate the declarant's pain, then the declarant shall authorize the declarant's attending physician to withhold or withdraw nutrition or hydration when the declarant is in the permanently unconscious state by doing both of the following in the declaration:

(i) Including a statement in capital letters or other conspicuous type, including, but not limited to, a different font, bigger type, or boldface type, that the declarant's attending physician may withhold or withdraw nutrition and hydration if the declarant is in a permanently unconscious state and if the declarant's attending physician and at least one other physician who has examined the declarant determine, to a reasonable degree of medical certainty and in accordance with reasonable medical standards, that nutrition or hydration will not or no longer will serve to provide comfort to the declarant or alleviate the declarant's pain, or checking or otherwise marking a box or line that is adjacent to a similar statement on a printed form of a declaration;

(ii) Placing the declarant's initials or signature underneath or adjacent to the statement, check, or other mark described in division (A)(3)(a)(i) of this section.

(b) Division (A)(3)(a) of this section does not apply to the extent that a declaration authorizes the withholding or withdrawal of life-sustaining treatment when a declarant is in a terminal condition. The provisions of division (E) of section 2133.12 of the Revised Code pertaining to comfort care shall apply to a declarant in a terminal condition.

(B)(1) If witnessed for purposes of division (A) of this section, a declaration shall be witnessed by two individuals as described in this division in whose presence the declarant, or another individual at the direction of the declarant, signed the declaration. The witnesses to a declaration shall be adults who are not related to the declarant by blood, marriage, or adoption, who are not the attending physician of the declarant, and who are not the administrator of any nursing home in which the declarant is receiving care. Each witness shall subscribe the witness' signature after the signature of the declarant or other individual at the direction of the declarant and, by doing so, attest to the witness' belief that the declarant appears to be of sound mind and not under or subject to duress, fraud, or undue influence. The signatures of the declarant or other individual at the direction of the declarant under division (A) of this section and of the witnesses under this division are not required to appear on the same page of the declaration.

(2) If acknowledged for purposes of division (A) of this section, a declaration shall be acknowledged before a notary public, who shall make the certification described in section 147.53 of the Revised Code and also shall attest that the declarant appears to be of sound mind and not under or subject to duress, fraud, or undue influence.

(C) An attending physician, or other health care personnel acting under the direction of an attending physician, who is furnished a copy of a declaration shall make it a part of the declarant's medical record and, when section 2133.05 of the Revised Code is applicable, also shall comply with that section.

(D)(1) Subject to division (D)(2) of this section, an attending physician of a declarant or a health care facility in which a declarant is confined may refuse to comply or allow compliance with the declarant's declaration on the basis of a matter of conscience or on another basis. An employee or agent of an attending physician of a declarant or of a health care facility in which a declarant is confined may refuse to comply with the declarant's declaration on the basis of a matter of conscience.

(2) If an attending physician of a declarant or a health care facility in which a declarant is confined is not willing or not able to comply or allow compliance with the declarant's declaration, the physician or facility promptly shall so advise the declarant and comply with the provisions of section 2133.10 of the Revised Code, or, if the declaration has become operative as described in division (A) of section 2133.03 of the Revised Code, shall comply with the provisions of section 2133.10 of the Revised Code.

(E) As used in this section, "CPR" has the same meaning as in section 2133.21 of the Revised Code.

(2000 H 494, eff. 3–15–01; 1998 H 354, eff. 7–9–98; 1991 S 1, eff. 10–10–91)

Historical and Statutory Notes

Amendment Note: 2000 H 494 deleted "in capital letters" before "in a manner" in division (A)(2); inserted "or other conspicuous type, including, but not limited to, a different font, bigger type, or boldface type," in division (A)(3)(a)(i); and substituted "after the signature of the declarant or other individual" for "on the declaration" and added the fourth sentence in division (B)(1).

Amendment Note: 1998 H 354 added the fourth sentence in division (A)(1); added division (E); and made changes to reflect gender neutral language and other nonsubstantive changes.

Cross References

Anatomical gifts, instrument of gift, 2108.04

Library References

Health ⇔916.
Westlaw Topic No. 198H.
Baldwin's Ohio Legislative Service, 1991 Laws of Ohio, S 1—LSC Analysis, p 5–250

Research References

Encyclopedias

40 Am. Jur. Proof of Facts 3d 287, Proof of Basis for Refusal or Discontinuance of Life-Sustaining Treatment on Behalf of Incapacitated Person.

63 Am. Jur. Trials 1, Decisionmaking at the End of Life.

OH Jur. 3d Agency & Independent Contractors § 46, Effect of a Do Not Resuscitate Declaration or Identification.

OH Jur. 3d Cemeteries & Dead Bodies § 74, Manner of Making Anatomical Gift—by Declarant Under Modified Uniform Rights of the Terminally Ill Act.

OH Jur. 3d Counties, Townships, & Municipal Corp. § 162, Recording of Instruments.

OH Jur. 3d Death § 24, Generally; Declarant's Rights.

OH Jur. 3d Death § 32, Withholding or Withdrawal of Life-Sustaining Treatment.

OH Jur. 3d Death § 33, Withholding or Withdrawal of Nutrition or Hydration.

OH Jur. 3d Records & Recording § 66, Record Books.

Forms

Ohio Forms Legal and Business § 12B:19, Declaration Regarding Medical Treatment in the Case of Terminal Illness or Permanent Unconsciousness.

Ohio Forms Legal and Business § 24:380.30, Anatomical Gift by Next of Kin or Other Authorized Person.

Ohio Forms and Transactions F 30.29, Health Care Declaration (Living Will).

Ohio Forms and Transactions F 30.30, Health Care Declaration (Living Will, Alternate Form).

Ohio Forms and Transactions KP 24.06, Durable Power of Attorney for Health Care.

Ohio Forms and Transactions KP 30.23, Living Will, or Health Care Declaration.

Treatises and Practice Aids

Carlin, Baldwin's Ohio Practice, Merrick-Rippner Probate Law § 60:16, Power of Attorney for Health Care—Ohio Legislation.

Carlin, Baldwin's Ohio Practice, Merrick-Rippner Probate Law § 60:19, Power of Attorney for Health Care—Health Care Declaration.

Carlin, Baldwin's Ohio Practice, Merrick-Rippner Probate Law § 60:20, Power of Attorney for Health Care—Who May Execute Health Care Instrument.

Carlin, Baldwin's Ohio Practice, Merrick-Rippner Probate Law § 60:24, Power of Attorney for Health Care—Formal Execution Requirements.

Carlin, Baldwin's Ohio Practice, Merrick-Rippner Probate Law § 60:31, Power of Attorney for Health Care—Withholding or Withdrawing Life-Support Measures or Other Care—Terminal Condition; Permanently Unconscious State.

Carlin, Baldwin's Ohio Practice, Merrick-Rippner Probate Law § 60:32, Power of Attorney for Health Care—Withholding or Withdrawing Life-Support Measures or Other Care—Comfort Care; Nutrition and Hydration.

Carlin, Baldwin's Ohio Practice, Merrick-Rippner Probate Law § 60:35, Do-Not-Resuscitate Order.

Carlin, Baldwin's Ohio Practice, Merrick-Rippner Probate Law § 60:35.20, Declaration of Anatomical Gift.

Law Review and Journal Commentaries

Anderson v. St. Francis-St. George Hospital: Wrongful Living from an American and Jewish Legal Perspective, Daniel Pollack, Chaim Steinmetz, and Vicki Lens. 45 Clev St L Rev 621 (1997).

Directing Health Care Choices, William M. Todd. 5 Ohio Law 10 (September/October 1991).

End of Life Issues and Ohio's Do Not Resuscitate Law. David A. Dennis, 11 Prob L J Ohio 75 (May/June 2001).

Euphemistic Codes and Tell-Tale Hearts: Humane Assistance in End-of-Life Cases. George P. Smith, 11, 10 Health Matrix: J Law-Medicine 175 (Summer 2000).

Incompetents and the Right to Die: In Search of Consistent Meaningful Standards, Mark Strasser. 83 Ky L J 733 (1994–95).

A New Predicament for Physicians: The Concept of Medical Futility, the Physician's Obligation to Render Inappropriate Treatment, and the Interplay of the Medical Standard of Care, Eric M. Levine. 9 J L & Health 69 (1994–95).

Patient Autonomy and State Intervention: Reexamining the State's Purported Interest, Dr. G. Steven Neeley. 19 N Ky L Rev 235 (1992).

The Patient Self-Determination Act: Patients Need To Be Informed Of Their Right To Make Health–Care Choices, Gregory S. French. 5 Ohio Law 14 (September/October 1991).

Planning Ahead: Proper Implementation and Execution of Advance Directives, Bryan B. Johnson and Tristan A. McCormick. 17 Ohio Law 14 (September/October 2003).

The Right to Die: Who Really Makes the Decision?, Comment. 96 Dick L Rev 649 (Summer 1992).

Someone To Watch Over Me: Medical Decision–Making For Hopelessly Ill Incompetent Adult Patients, Note. 24 Akron L Rev 639 (Spring 1991).

A Time To Live, A Time To Die, Note. 24 Akron L Rev 699 (Spring 1991).

"Wrongful Living": Resuscitation As Tortious Interference With A Patient's Right to Give Informed Refusal, William C. Knapp and Fred Hamilton. 19 N Ky L Rev 253 (1992).

Notes of Decisions

Federal law 1
Nonconsensual treatment 2
Spousal consent 3

---

1. Federal law

"Nutrition and hydration" and "life sustaining treatment" are addressed separately in Modified Uniform Rights of the Terminally Ill Act and, for purposes of living will, each must be referred to specifically. In re Biersack (Ohio App. 3 Dist., Mercer, 12-06-2004) No. 10-04-03, 2004-Ohio-6491, 2004 WL 2785963, Unreported. Health ⇔ 916

2. Nonconsensual treatment

In proceeding in which guardian of ward, who has not made advance directive or prepared living will and who currently is or has been in permanently unconscious state for immediately preceding 12 months, seeks court order allowing attending physician to withdraw nutrition and hydration from ward, each physician should testify to his opinion that other physician in matter is qualified, by reason of advanced education or training in one of three categories prescribed by statute, to make findings and provide opinions about ward which are required by statute. In re Biersack (Ohio App. 3 Dist., Mercer, 12-06-2004) No. 10-04-03, 2004-Ohio-6491, 2004 WL 2785963, Unreported. Health ⇔ 926

Reversal of guardian of patient's consent to the use or continuation of life-sustaining treatment for patient in intensive care was warranted; patient signed a declaration regarding the use of life-sustaining treatment after nursing home discussed the form in the context of patient having a heart attack and did not discuss patient's option if he had a terminal illness or was in a permanent unconscious state, son of patient established that the use of life-sustaining treatment was not consistent with the previously expressed intentions of patient, and patient was in a terminal state.

Carpenter v. Mason (Ohio Com.Pl., 11-26-2003) 126 Ohio Misc.2d 17, 800 N.E.2d 404, 2003-Ohio-6490. Health ⇐ 916

Cardiologist and nurse did not commit medical battery on patient by administering life-sustaining treatment, even though patient had living will stating that such treatment should not be administered if he was in terminal condition, where cardiologist and nurse were not aware of patient's "refusal" of treatment as expressed in living will, patient had signed consent form for treatment when he entered hospital, attending physician entered orders allowing life support in emergency situations, and emergency situation occurred. Allore v. Flower Hosp. (Ohio App. 6 Dist., 06-27-1997) 121 Ohio App.3d 229, 699 N.E.2d 560, appeal not allowed 80 Ohio St.3d 1437, 685 N.E.2d 546. Health ⇐ 915

Cardiologist and nurse did not commit malpractice by administering life-prolonging medical treatment to patient, notwithstanding fact that patient's living will stated that such treatment was not to be administered, where nurse informed patient's treating physician of emergency situation, when he failed to respond, nurse contacted cardiologist, who ordered intubation and ventilation, nurse and cardiologist did not have knowledge of living will, and there was expert testimony that cardiologist and nurse complied with applicable standards of care. Allore v. Flower Hosp. (Ohio App. 6 Dist., 06-27-1997) 121 Ohio App.3d 229, 699 N.E.2d 560, appeal not allowed 80 Ohio St.3d 1437, 685 N.E.2d 546. Evidence ⇐ 571(3); Health ⇐ 916

There is no cause of action for wrongful prolongation of life. Allore v. Flower Hosp. (Ohio App. 6 Dist., 06-27-1997) 121 Ohio App.3d 229, 699 N.E.2d 560, appeal not allowed 80 Ohio St.3d 1437, 685 N.E.2d 546. Health ⇐ 914

Patient's estate could not recover damages incurred due to the prolongation of patient's life in medical battery action based on wrongful administration of life sustaining treatment. Allore v. Flower Hosp. (Ohio App. 6 Dist., 06-27-1997) 121 Ohio App.3d 229, 699 N.E.2d 560, appeal not allowed 80 Ohio St.3d 1437, 685 N.E.2d 546. Health ⇐ 928

Nonconsensual medical treatment that prolongs a person's life may be a battery for which plaintiff would be entitled to some relief; however, when nonconsensual treatment is harmless or beneficial, damages for wrongful act are nominal only, not actual. Anderson v. St. Francis–St. George Hosp. (Hamilton 1992) 83 Ohio App.3d 221, 614 N.E.2d 841, motion to certify overruled 66 Ohio St.3d 1459, 610 N.E.2d 423. Assault And Battery ⇐ 2; Assault And Battery ⇐ 37

Prolonging of patient's life by resuscitating him after he suffered ventricular fibrillation was not wrongful living; life is not a compensable harm. Anderson v. St. Francis–St. George Hosp. (Hamilton 1992) 83 Ohio App.3d 221, 614 N.E.2d 841, motion to certify overruled 66 Ohio St.3d 1459, 610 N.E.2d 423. Health ⇐ 917

3. Spousal consent

Spouse, individually and without intervention of court, and without appointment of guardian, has authority to discontinue life-sustaining treatment. In re Guardianship of McInnis (Ohio Prob. 1991) 61 Ohio Misc.2d 790, 584 N.E.2d 1389. Health ⇐ 915

2133.03 Requirements for declaration to become operative; priority of declaration

(A)(1) A declaration becomes operative when it is communicated to the attending physician of the declarant, the attending physician and one other physician who examines the declarant determine that the declarant is in a terminal condition or in a permanently unconscious state, whichever is addressed in the declaration, the applicable requirements of divisions (A)(2) and (3) of this section are satisfied, and the attending physician determines that the declarant no longer is able to make informed decisions regarding the administration of life-sustaining treatment. When the declaration becomes operative, the attending physician and health care facilities shall act in accordance with its provisions or comply with the provisions of section 2133.10 of the Revised Code.

(2) In order for a declaration to become operative in connection with a declarant who is in a permanently unconscious state, the consulting physician associated with the determination that the declarant is in the permanently unconscious state shall be a physician who, by virtue of advanced education or training, of a practice limited to particular diseases, illnesses, injuries, therapies, or branches of medicine or surgery or osteopathic medicine and surgery, of certification as a specialist in a particular branch of medicine or surgery or osteopathic medicine and surgery, or of experience acquired in the practice of medicine or surgery or osteopathic medicine and surgery, is qualified to determine whether the declarant is in a permanently unconscious state.

(3) In order for a declaration to become operative in connection with a declarant who is in a terminal condition or in a permanently unconscious state, the attending physician of the declarant shall determine, in good faith, to a reasonable degree of medical certainty, and in accordance with reasonable medical standards, that there is no reasonable possibility that the declarant will regain the capacity to make informed decisions regarding the administration of life-sustaining treatment.

(B)(1)(a) A declaration supersedes any general consent to treatment form signed by or on behalf of the declarant prior to, upon, or after the declarant's admission to a health care facility to the extent there is a conflict between the declaration and the form, even if the form is signed after the execution of the declaration. To the extent that the provisions of a declaration and a general consent to treatment form do not conflict, both documents shall govern the use or continuation, or the withholding or withdrawal, of life-sustaining treatment and other medical or nursing procedures, treatments, interventions, or other measures in connection with the declarant. Division (B)(1)(a) of this section does not apply if a declaration is revoked pursuant to section 2133.04 of the Revised Code after the signing of a general consent to treatment form.

(b) A declaration supersedes a DNR identification, as defined in section 2133.21 of the Revised Code, of the declarant that is based upon a prior inconsistent declaration of the declarant or that is based upon a do-not-resuscitate order, as defined in section 2133.21 of the Revised Code, that a physician has issued for the declarant and that is inconsistent with the declaration.

(2) If a declarant has both a valid durable power of attorney for health care and a valid declaration, the declaration supersedes the durable power of attorney for health care to the extent that the provisions of the documents would conflict if the declarant should be in a terminal condition or in a permanently unconscious state. Division (B)(2) of this section does not apply if the declarant revokes the declaration pursuant to section 2133.04 of the Revised Code.

(1998 H 354, eff. 7–9–98; 1991 S 1, eff. 10–10–91)

Historical and Statutory Notes

Amendment Note: 1998 H 354 designated division (B)(1)(a); added division (B)(1)(b); and made other nonsubstantive changes.

Cross References

Durable power of attorney for health care, effect of existence of living will, 1337.12

Library References

Health ⇐916.
Westlaw Topic No. 198H.
   Baldwin's Ohio Legislative Service, 1991 Laws of Ohio, S 1—LSC Analysis, p 5–250

Research References

Encyclopedias
   OH Jur. 3d Death § 29, When Declaration Becomes Operative.

Forms
Ohio Forms and Transactions F 30.29, Health Care Declaration (Living Will).
Ohio Forms and Transactions KP 24.06, Durable Power of Attorney for Health Care.

Ohio Forms and Transactions KP 30.23, Living Will, or Health Care Declaration.

Treatises and Practice Aids

Carlin, Baldwin's Ohio Practice, Merrick-Rippner Probate Law § 60:21, Power of Attorney for Health Care—Health Care Declaration to Govern in Case of Conflict.

Carlin, Baldwin's Ohio Practice, Merrick-Rippner Probate Law § 60:22, Power of Attorney for Health Care—When Instruments Effective.

Carlin, Baldwin's Ohio Practice, Merrick-Rippner Probate Law § 60:31, Power of Attorney for Health Care—Withholding or Withdrawing Life-Support Measures or Other Care—Terminal Condition; Permanently Unconscious State.

Carlin, Baldwin's Ohio Practice, Merrick-Rippner Probate Law § 60:35, Do-Not-Resuscitate Order.

Law Review and Journal Commentaries

Euphemistic Codes and Tell-Tale Hearts: Humane Assistance in End-of-Life Cases. George P. Smith, 11, 10 Health Matrix: J Law-Medicine 175 (Summer 2000).

Notes of Decisions

Communication 1

1. **Communication**

Damages relating to prolongation of a patient's life are not recoverable in Ohio and any recovery on plaintiff's medical claim is limited to those damages from battery which likewise are not recoverable where there is no fact issue as to implied consent of a patient to intubation and ventilation and (1) no evidence suggests that hospital personnel are aware of the patient's refusal of treatment as expressed in his living will and durable power of attorney for health care; (2) the patient signs a consent form for treatment when he is admitted to the hospital; (3) the attending physician enters orders allowing life support measures in an emergency situation; and (4) an emergency occurs. Allore v. Flower Hosp. (Ohio App. 6 Dist., 06-27-1997) 121 Ohio App.3d 229, 699 N.E.2d 560, appeal not allowed 80 Ohio St.3d 1437, 685 N.E.2d 546.

2133.04 Revocation of declaration

(A) A declarant may revoke a declaration at any time and in any manner. The revocation shall be effective when the declarant expresses his intention to revoke the declaration, except that, if the declarant made his attending physician aware of the declaration, the revocation shall be effective upon its communication to the attending physician of the declarant by the declarant himself, a witness to the revocation, or other health care personnel to whom the revocation is communicated by such a witness. Absent actual knowledge to the contrary, the attending physician of a declarant and other health care personnel who are informed of the revocation of a declaration by an alleged witness may rely on the information and act in accordance with the revocation.

(B) Upon the communication as described in division (A) of this section to the attending physician of a declarant of the fact that his declaration has been revoked, the attending physician or other health care personnel acting under the direction of the attending physician shall make the fact a part of the declarant's medical record.

(1991 S 1, eff. 10–10–91)

Library References

Health ⚖916.
Westlaw Topic No. 198H.
  Baldwin's Ohio Legislative Service, 1991 Laws of Ohio, S 1—LSC Analysis, p 5–250

Research References

Encyclopedias

63 Am. Jur. Trials 1, Decisionmaking at the End of Life.
OH Jur. 3d Death § 25, Revocation of Declaration.

Forms

Ohio Forms Legal and Business § 12B:19, Declaration Regarding Medical Treatment in the Case of Terminal Illness or Permanent Unconsciousness.

Treatises and Practice Aids

Carlin, Baldwin's Ohio Practice, Merrick-Rippner Probate Law § 60:23, Power of Attorney for Health Care—Expiration; Revocation.

Law Review and Journal Commentaries

Euphemistic Codes and Tell-Tale Hearts: Humane Assistance in End-of-Life Cases. George P. Smith, 11, 10 Health Matrix: J Law-Medicine 175 (Summer 2000).

Planning Ahead: Proper Implementation and Execution of Advance Directives, Bryan B. Johnson and Tristan A. McCormick. 17 Ohio Law 14 (September/October 2003).

2133.05 Records; notice requirements; objections; complaints

(A) If the attending physician of a declarant and one other physician who examines the declarant determine that he is in a terminal condition or in a permanently unconscious state, whichever is addressed in the declaration, if the attending physician additionally determines that the declarant no longer is able to make informed decisions regarding the administration of life-sustaining treatment for himself and that there is no reasonable possibility that the declarant will regain the capacity to make those informed decisions for himself, and if the attending physician is aware of the existence of the declarant's declaration, then the attending physician shall do all of the following:

(1) Record the determinations, together with the terms of the declaration or any copy of the declaration acquired as described in division (C) of section 2133.02 of the Revised Code, in the declarant's medical record;

(2)(a) Make a good faith effort, and use reasonable diligence, to notify either of the following of the determinations:

(i) If the declarant designated in his declaration one or more persons to be notified at any time that life-sustaining treatment would be withheld or withdrawn pursuant to the declaration, that person or those persons;

(ii) If division (A)(2)(a)(i) of this section is not applicable, the appropriate individual or individuals, in accordance with the following descending order of priority: if any, the guardian of the declarant, but this division does not permit or require, and shall not be construed as permitting or requiring, the appointment of a guardian for the declarant; the declarant's spouse; the declarant's adult children who are available within a reasonable period of time for consultation with the declarant's attending physician; the declarant's parents; or an adult sibling of the declarant or, if there is more than one adult sibling, a majority of the declarant's adult siblings who are available within a reasonable period of time for such consultation.

(b) The attending physician shall record in the declarant's medical record the names of the individual or individuals notified pursuant to division (A)(2)(a) of this section and the manner of notification.

(c) If, despite making a good faith effort, and despite using reasonable diligence, to notify the appropriate individual or individuals described in division (A)(2)(a) of this section, the attending physician cannot notify the individual or individuals of the determinations because the individual or individuals are deceased, cannot be located, or cannot be notified for some other reason, then the requirements of divisions (A)(2)(a) and (b) and (3) of this section and, except as provided in division (B)(1)(b) of this section, the provisions of division (B) of this section shall not apply in connection with the declarant and his declaration. However, the attending physician shall record in the declarant's medical record information pertaining to the reason for the failure to provide the requisite notices and information pertaining to the nature of the good faith effort and reasonable diligence used.

(3) Afford time for the individual or individuals notified in accordance with division (A)(2) of this section to object in the manner described in division (B)(1)(a) of this section.

(B)(1)(a) Within forty-eight hours after receipt of a notice pursuant to division (A)(2) of this section, any individual so notified shall advise the attending physician of the declarant whether he objects on a basis specified in division (B)(2)(c) of this section. If an objection as described in that division is communicated to the attending physician, then, within two business days after the communication, the individual shall file a complaint as described in division (B)(2) of this section in the probate court of the county in which the declarant is located. If the individual fails to so file a complaint, his objections as described in division (B)(2)(c) of this section shall be considered to be void.

(b) Within forty-eight hours after a person described in division (A)(2)(a)(i) of this section or a priority individual or any member of a priority class of individuals described in division (A)(2)(a)(ii) of this section receives a notice pursuant to division (A)(2) of this section or within forty-eight hours after information pertaining to an unnotified person described in division (A)(2)(a)(i) of this section or an unnotified priority individual or unnotified priority class of individuals described in division (A)(2)(a)(ii) of this section is recorded in a declarant's medical record pursuant to division (A)(2)(c) of this section, either of the following shall advise the attending physician of the declarant whether he or they object on a basis specified in division (B)(2)(c) of this section:

(i) If a person described in division (A)(2)(a)(i) of this section was notified pursuant to division (A)(2) of this section or was the subject of a recordation under division (A)(2)(c) of this section, then the objection shall be communicated by the individual or a majority of the individuals in either of the first two classes of individuals that pertain to the declarant in the descending order of priority set forth in division (A)(2)(a)(ii) of this section.

(ii) If an individual or individuals in the descending order of priority set forth in division (A)(2)(a)(ii) of this section were notified pursuant to division (A)(2) of this section or were the subject of a recordation under division (A)(2)(c) of this section, then the objection shall be communicated by the individual or a majority of the individuals in the next class of individuals that pertains to the declarant in the descending order of priority set forth in division (A)(2)(a)(ii) of this section.

If an objection as described in division (B)(2)(c) of this section is communicated to the attending physician in accordance with division (B)(1)(b)(i) or (ii) of this section, then, within two business days after the communication, the objecting individual or majority shall file a complaint as described in division (B)(2) of this section in the probate court of the county in which the declarant is located. If the objecting individual or majority fails to file a complaint, his or their objections as described in division (B)(2)(c) of this section shall be considered to be void.

(2) A complaint of an individual that is filed in accordance with division (B)(1)(a) of this section or of an individual or majority of individuals that is filed in accordance with division (B)(1)(b) of this section shall satisfy all of the following:

(a) Name any health care facility in which the declarant is confined;

(b) Name the declarant, his attending physician, and the consulting physician associated with the determination that the declarant is in a terminal condition or in a permanently unconscious state, whichever is addressed in the declaration;

(c) Indicate whether the plaintiff or plaintiffs object on one or more of the following bases:

(i) To the attending physician's and consulting physician's determinations that the declarant is in a terminal condition or in a permanently unconscious state, whichever is addressed in the declaration;

(ii) To the attending physician's determination that the declarant no longer is able to make informed decisions regarding the administration of life-sustaining treatment;

(iii) To the attending physician's determination that there is no reasonable possibility that the declarant will regain the capacity to make informed decisions regarding the administration of life-sustaining treatment;

(iv) That the course of action proposed to be undertaken by the attending physician is not authorized by the declarant's declaration;

(v) That the declaration was executed when the declarant was not of sound mind or was under or subject to duress, fraud, or undue influence;

(vi) That the declaration otherwise does not substantially comply with this chapter.

(d) Request the probate court to issue one of the following types of orders:

(i) An order to the attending physician to reevaluate, in light of the court proceedings, the determination that the declarant is in a terminal condition or in a permanently unconscious state, whichever is addressed in the declaration, the determination that the declarant no longer is able to make informed decisions regarding the administration of life-sustaining treatment, the determination that there is no reasonable possibility that the declarant will regain the capacity to make those informed decisions, or the course of action proposed to be undertaken;

(ii) An order invalidating the declaration because it was executed when the declarant was not of sound mind or was under or subject to duress, fraud, or undue influence, or because it otherwise does not substantially comply with this chapter;

(e) Be accompanied by an affidavit of the plaintiff or plaintiffs that includes averments relative to whether he is an individual or they are individuals as described in division (A)(2)(a)(i) or (ii) of this section and to the factual basis for his or their objections;

(f) Name any individuals who were notified by the attending physician in accordance with division (A)(2)(a) of this section and who are not joining in the complaint as plaintiffs;

(g) Name, in the caption of the complaint, as defendants the attending physician of the declarant, the consulting physician associated with the determination that the declarant is in a terminal condition or in a permanently unconscious state, whichever is addressed in the declaration, any health care facility in which the declarant is confined, and any individuals who were notified by the attending physician in accordance with division (A)(2)(a) of this section and who are not joining in the complaint as plaintiffs.

(3) Notwithstanding any contrary provision of the Revised Code or of the Rules of Civil Procedure, the state and persons other than an objecting individual as described in division (B)(1)(a) of this section, other than an objecting individual or majority of individuals as described in division (B)(2)(b)(i) or (ii) of this section, and other than persons described in division (B)(2)(g) of this section are prohibited from commencing a civil action under this section and from joining or being joined as parties to an action commenced under this section, including joining by way of intervention.

(4)(a) A probate court in which a complaint as described in division (B)(2) of this section is filed within the period specified in division (B)(1)(a) or (b) of this section shall conduct a hearing on the complaint after a copy of the complaint and a notice of the hearing have been served upon the defendants. The clerk of the probate court in which the complaint is filed shall cause the complaint and the notice of the hearing to be so served in accordance with the Rules of Civil Procedure, which service shall be made, if possible, within three days after the filing of the complaint. The hearing shall be conducted at the earliest possible time, but no later than the third business day after such service has been completed. Immediately following the hearing, the court shall enter on its journal its determination whether a requested order will be issued.

(b) If the declarant's declaration authorized the use or continuation of life-sustaining treatment should he be in a terminal condition or in a permanently unconscious state and if the plaintiff or plaintiffs requested a reevaluation order to the attending physician of the declarant as described in division (B)(2)(d)(i) of this section, the court shall issue the reevaluation order only if it finds that the plaintiff or plaintiffs have established a factual basis for the objection or objections involved by clear and convincing evidence, to a reasonable degree of medical certainty, and in accordance with reasonable medical standards.

(c) If the declarant's declaration authorized the withholding or withdrawal of life-sustaining treatment should he be in a terminal condition or in a permanently unconscious state and if the plaintiff or plaintiffs requested a reevaluation order to the attending physician of the declarant as described in division (B)(2)(d)(i) of this section, the court shall issue the reevaluation order only if it finds that the plaintiff or plaintiffs have established a factual basis for the objection or objections involved by a preponderance of the evidence, to a reasonable degree of medical certainty, and in accordance with reasonable medical standards.

(d) If the plaintiff or plaintiffs requested an invalidation order as described in division (B)(2)(d)(ii) of this section, the court shall issue the order only if it finds that the plaintiff or plaintiffs have established a factual basis for the objection or objections involved by clear and convincing evidence.

(e) If the court issues a reevaluation order to the declarant's attending physician pursuant to division (B)(4)(b) or (c) of this section, then the attending physician shall make the requisite reevaluation. If, after doing so, the attending physician again determines that the declarant is in a terminal condition or in a permanently unconscious state, that the declarant no longer is able to make informed decisions regarding the administration of life-sustaining treatment, that there is no reasonable possibility that the declarant will regain the capacity to make those informed decisions, or that he would undertake the same proposed course of action, then he shall notify the court in writing of the determination and comply with the provisions of section 2133.10 of the Revised Code.

(1991 S 1, eff. 10–10–91)

Cross References

Probate court jurisdiction, 2101.24

Library References

Health ⚖ 916.
Westlaw Topic No. 198H.
   Baldwin's Ohio Legislative Service, 1991 Laws of Ohio, S 1—LSC Analysis, p 5–250

Research References

Encyclopedias

  OH Jur. 3d Death § 30, Records and Notice Requirements; Objections and Complaints.
  OH Jur. 3d Malpractice § 99, Under Statute Regarding Patients' Advance Directives; Generally.

Treatises and Practice Aids

Carlin, Baldwin's Ohio Practice, Merrick-Rippner Probate Law § 60:30, Power of Attorney for Health Care—Withholding or Withdrawing Life-Support Measures or Other Care—Notice.

Carlin, Baldwin's Ohio Practice, Merrick-Rippner Probate Law § 60:34, Power of Attorney for Health Care—Withholding or Withdrawing Life-Support Measures or Other Care—Objections to Health Care Decisions; Probate Court Proceedings.

Law Review and Journal Commentaries

Euphemistic Codes and Tell-Tale Hearts: Humane Assistance in End-of-Life Cases. George P. Smith, 11, 10 Health Matrix: J Law-Medicine 175 (Summer 2000).

Planning Ahead: Proper Implementation and Execution of Advance Directives, Bryan B. Johnson and Tristan A. McCormick. 17 Ohio Law 14 (September/October 2003).

S.B. 1: A Hospital Attorney's Perspective, Paul A. Greve, Jr. 2 Prob L J Ohio 93 (May/June 1992).

2133.06 Patients able to make informed decisions; pregnant declarants

(A) As long as a qualified patient is able to make informed decisions regarding the administration of life-sustaining treatment, he may continue to do so.

(B) Life–sustaining treatment shall not be withheld or withdrawn from a declarant pursuant to a declaration if she is pregnant and if the withholding or withdrawal of the treatment would terminate the pregnancy, unless the declarant's attending physician and one other physician who has examined the declarant determine, to a reasonable degree of medical certainty and in accordance with reasonable medical standards, that the fetus would not be born alive.

(1991 S 1, eff. 10–10–91)

Library References

Health ⚖ 913.
Westlaw Topic No. 198H.
   Baldwin's Ohio Legislative Service, 1991 Laws of Ohio, S 1—LSC Analysis, p 5–250

Research References

Encyclopedias

  63 Am. Jur. Trials 1, Decisionmaking at the End of Life.
  OH Jur. 3d Death § 24, Generally; Declarant's Rights.
  OH Jur. 3d Death § 31, Effect of Pregnancy.

Forms

Ohio Forms and Transactions F 30.29, Health Care Declaration (Living Will).

Treatises and Practice Aids

Carlin, Baldwin's Ohio Practice, Merrick-Rippner Probate Law § 60:33, Power of Attorney for Health Care—Withholding or Withdrawing Life-Support Measures or Other Care—Pregnant Patient.

Law Review and Journal Commentaries

A Womb of My Own: A Moral Evaluation of Ohio's Treatment of Pregnant Patients With Living Wills, Comment. 45 Case W Res L Rev 351 (Fall 1994).

2133.07 Printed form of declaration

(A) A printed form of a declaration may be sold or otherwise distributed in this state for use by adults who are not advised by an attorney. By use of a printed form of that nature, a declarant may authorize the use or continuation, or the withholding or withdrawal, of life-sustaining treatment should the declarant be in a terminal condition, a permanently unconscious state, or either a terminal condition or a permanently unconscious state, may authorize the withholding or withdrawal of nutrition or hydration should the declarant be in a permanently unconscious state as described in division (A)(3)(a) of section 2133.02 of the Revised Code, and may designate one or more persons who are to be notified by the declarant's attending physician at any time that life-sustaining treatment would be withheld or withdrawn pursuant to the declaration. The printed form shall not be used as an instrument for granting any other type of authority or for making any other type of designation, except that the printed form may be used as a DNR identification if the declarant specifies on the form that the declarant wishes to use it as a DNR identification and except as provided in division (B) of this section.

(B) A printed form of a declaration under division (A) of this section shall include, before the signature of the declarant or another individual at the direction of the declarant, statements that conform substantially to the following form:

"ANATOMICAL GIFT (optional)

Upon my death, the following are my directions regarding donation of all or part of my body:

In the hope that I may help others upon my death, I hereby give the following body parts:

....
....

for any purpose authorized by law: transplantation, therapy, research, or education.

If I do not indicate a desire to donate all or part of my body by filling in the lines above, no presumption is created about my desire to make or refuse to make an anatomical gift."

(C)(1) A printed form of a declaration under division (A) of this section shall include, as a separate page or as a portion of a page that can be detached from the declaration, a donor registry enrollment form that permits the donor to be included in the donor registry created under section 2108.18 of the Revised Code.

(2) The donor registry enrollment form shall conform substantially to the following form:

"DONOR REGISTRY ENROLLMENT
FORM (optional)

To register for the Donor Registry, please complete this form and send it to the Ohio Bureau of Motor Vehicles. This form must be signed by two witnesses. If the donor is under age eighteen, one witness must be the donor's parent or legal guardian.

... Please include me in the donor registry.

... Please remove me from the donor registry.

Full Name (please print) ....
Mailing address ....
....
....
Phone .... Date of Birth ....
Driver License or ID Card No. ....
Social Security No. ....

... On my death, I make an anatomical gift of my organs, tissues, and eyes for any purpose authorized by law.

OR

... On my death, I make an anatomical gift of the following specified organs, tissues, or eyes for any purposes indicated below.

....
....
....

Purposes:

... Any purpose authorized by law

... Transplantation

... Therapy

... Research

... Education

... Advancement of medical science

... Advancement of dental science

....
Signature of donor registrant   Date
....
Witness signature
....
Witness signature"

(D) As used in this section:

(1) "Anatomical gift" has the same meaning as in section 2108.01 of the Revised Code.

(2) "DNR identification" has the same meaning as in section 2133.21 of the Revised Code.

(2004 H 392, eff. 12–15–04; 1998 H 354, eff. 7–9–98; 1991 S 1, eff. 10–10–91)

Uncodified Law

2004 H 392, § 4, eff. 9–16–04, reads:

The amendments made by this act to section 2133.07 of the Revised Code do not affect an otherwise valid declaration governing the use, continuation, withholding, or withdrawal of life-sustaining treatment that was executed before the effective date of section 2133.07 of the Revised Code as amended by this act.

Historical and Statutory Notes

Amendment Note: 2004 H 392 rewrote this section, which prior thereto read:

"A printed form of a declaration may be sold or otherwise distributed in this state for use by adults who are not advised by an attorney. By use of a printed form of that nature, a declarant may authorize the use or continuation, or the withholding or withdrawal, of life-sustaining treatment should the declarant be in a terminal condition, a permanently unconscious state, or either a terminal condition or a permanently unconscious state, may authorize the withholding or withdrawal of nutrition or hydration should the declarant be in a permanently unconscious state as described in division (A)(3)(a) of section 2133.02 of the Revised Code, and may designate one or more persons who are to be notified by the declarant's attending physician at any time that life-sustaining treatment would be withheld or withdrawn pursuant to the declaration. The printed form shall not be used as an instrument for granting any other type of authority or for making any other type of designation, except that the printed form may be used as a DNR identification if the declarant specifies on the form that the declarant wishes to use it as a DNR identification."

Amendment Note: 1998 H 354 inserted ", except that the printed form may be used as a DNR identification if the declarant specifies on the form that the declarant wishes to use it as a DNR identification" at the end of the first paragraph; added the second paragraph; and made changes to reflect gender neutral language and other nonsubstantive changes.

Cross References

Anatomical gifts, forms of document of gift, 2108.10
Forms, distribution by county recorder, 317.41

Library References

Health ☞916.
Westlaw Topic No. 198H.
    Baldwin's Ohio Legislative Service, 1991 Laws of Ohio, S 1—LSC Analysis, p 5–250

Research References

Encyclopedias

OH Jur. 3d Cemeteries & Dead Bodies § 74, Manner of Making Anatomical Gift—by Declarant Under Modified Uniform Rights of the Terminally Ill Act.

Forms

Ohio Forms and Transactions F 30.29, Health Care Declaration (Living Will).

Treatises and Practice Aids

Carlin, Baldwin's Ohio Practice, Merrick-Rippner Probate Law § 60:35.20, Declaration of Anatomical Gift.

2133.08 Withholding or withdrawal of life-sustaining treatment

(A)(1) If written consent to the withholding or withdrawal of life-sustaining treatment, witnessed by two individuals who satisfy the witness eligibility criteria set forth in division (B)(1) of section 2133.02 of the Revised Code, is given by the appropriate individual or individuals as specified in division (B) of this section to the attending physician of a patient who is an adult, and if all of the following apply in connection with the patient, then, subject to section 2133.09 of the Revised Code, his attending physician may withhold or withdraw the life-sustaining treatment:

(a) The attending physician and one other physician who examines the patient determine, in good faith, to a reasonable degree of medical certainty, and in accordance with reasonable medical standards, that the patient is in a terminal condition or the patient currently is and for at least the immediately preceding twelve months has been in a permanently unconscious state, and the attending physician additionally determines, in good faith, to a reasonable degree of medical certainty, and in accordance with reasonable medical standards, that the patient no longer is able to make informed decisions regarding the administration of life-sustaining treatment and that there is no reasonable possibility that the patient will regain the capacity to make those informed decisions.

(b) The patient does not have a declaration that addresses his intent should he be determined to be in a terminal condition or in a permanently unconscious state, whichever applies, or a durable power of attorney for health care, or has a document that purports to be such a declaration or durable power of attorney for health care but that document is not legally effective.

(c) The consent of the appropriate individual or individuals is given after consultation with the patient's attending physician and after receipt of information from the patient's attending physician or a consulting physician that is sufficient to satisfy the requirements of informed consent.

(d) The appropriate individual or individuals who give a consent are of sound mind and voluntarily give the consent.

(e) If a consent would be given under division (B)(3) of this section, the attending physician made a good faith effort, and used reasonable diligence, to notify the patient's adult children who are available within a reasonable period of time for consultation as described in division (A)(1)(c) of this section.

(2) The consulting physician under division (A)(1)(a) of this section associated with a patient allegedly in a permanently unconscious state shall be a physician who, by virtue of advanced education or training, of a practice limited to particular diseases, illnesses, injuries, therapies, or branches of medicine or surgery or osteopathic medicine and surgery, of certification as a specialist in a particular branch of medicine or surgery or osteopathic medicine and surgery, or of experience acquired in the practice of medicine or surgery or osteopathic medicine and surgery, is qualified to determine whether the patient currently is and for at least the immediately preceding twelve months has been in a permanently unconscious state.

(B) For purposes of division (A) of this section, a consent to withhold or withdraw life-sustaining treatment may be given by the appropriate individual or individuals, in accordance with the following descending order of priority:

(1) If any, the guardian of the patient. This division does not permit or require, and shall not be construed as permitting or requiring, the appointment of a guardian for the patient.

(2) The patient's spouse;

(3) An adult child of the patient or, if there is more than one adult child, a majority of the patient's adult children who are available within a reasonable period of time for consultation with the patient's attending physician;

(4) The patient's parents;

(5) An adult sibling of the patient or, if there is more than one adult sibling, a majority of the patient's adult siblings who are available within a reasonable period of time for such consultation;

(6) The nearest adult who is not described in divisions (B)(1) to (5) of this section, who is related to the patient by blood or adoption, and who is available within a reasonable period of time for such consultation.

(C) If an appropriate individual or class of individuals entitled to decide under division (B) of this section whether or not to consent to the withholding or withdrawal of life-sustaining treatment for a patient is not available within a reasonable period of time for such consultation and competent to so decide, or declines to so decide, then the next priority individual or class of individuals specified in that division is authorized to make the decision. However, an equal division in a priority class of individuals under that division does not authorize the next class of individuals specified in that division to make the decision. If an equal division in a priority class of individuals under that division occurs, no written consent to the withholding or withdrawal of life-sustaining treatment from the patient can be given pursuant to this section.

(D)(1) A decision to consent pursuant to this section to the use or continuation, or the withholding or withdrawal, of life-sustaining treatment for a patient shall be made in good faith.

(2) Except as provided in division (D)(4) of this section, if the patient previously expressed his intention with respect to the use or continuation, or the withholding or withdrawal, of life-sustaining treatment should he subsequently be in a terminal condition or in a permanently unconscious state, whichever applies, and no longer able to make informed decisions regarding the administration of life-sustaining treatment, a consent given pursuant to this section shall be valid only if it is consistent with that previously expressed intention.

(3) Except as provided in division (D)(4) of this section, if the patient did not previously express his intention with respect to the use or continuation, or the withholding or withdrawal, of life-sustaining treatment should he subsequently be in a terminal condition or in a permanently unconscious state, whichever applies, and no longer able to make informed decisions regarding the administration of life-sustaining treatment, a consent given pursuant to this section shall be valid only if it is consistent with the type of informed consent decision that the patient would have made if he previously had expressed his intention with respect to the use or continuation, or the withholding or withdrawal, of life-sustaining treatment should he subsequently be in a terminal condition or in a permanently unconscious state, whichever applies, and no longer able to make informed decisions regarding the administration of life-sustaining treatment, as inferred from the lifestyle and character of the patient, and from any other evidence of the desires of the patient, prior to his becoming no longer able to make informed decisions regarding the administration of life-sustaining treatment. The Rules of Evidence shall not be binding for purposes of this division.

(4)(a) The attending physician of the patient, and other health care personnel acting under the direction of the attending physician, who do not have actual knowledge of a previously expressed intention as described in division (D)(2) of this section or who do not have actual knowledge that the patient would have made a different type of informed consent decision under the circumstances described in division (D)(3) of this section, may rely on a consent given in accordance with this section unless a probate court decides differently under division (E) of this section.

(b) The immunity conferred by division (C)(1) of section 2133.11 of the Revised Code is not forfeited by an individual who gives a consent to the use or continuation, or the withholding or withdrawal, of life-sustaining treatment for a patient under division (B) of this section if the individual gives the consent in good faith and without actual knowledge, at the time of giving the consent, of either a contrary previously expressed intention of the patient, or a previously expressed intention of the patient, as described in division (D)(2) of this section, that is revealed to the individual subsequent to the time of giving the consent.

(E)(1) Within forty-eight hours after a priority individual or class of individuals gives a consent pursuant to this section to the use or continuation, or the withholding or withdrawal, of life-sustaining treatment and communicates the consent to the patient's attending physician, any individual described in divisions (B)(1) to (5) of this section who objects to the application of this section to the patient shall advise the attending physician of the grounds for the objection. If an objection is so communicated to the attending physician, then, within two business days after that communication, the objecting individual shall file a complaint against the priority individual or class of individuals, the patient's attending physician, and the consulting physician associated with the determination that the patient is in a terminal condition or that the patient currently is and for at least the immediately preceding twelve months has been in a permanently unconscious state, in the probate court of the county in which the patient is located for the issuance of an order reversing the consent of the priority individual or class of individuals. If the objecting individual fails to so file a complaint, his objections shall be considered to be void.

A probate court in which a complaint is filed in accordance with this division shall conduct a hearing on the complaint after a copy of the complaint and a notice of the hearing have been served upon the defendants. The clerk of the probate court in which the complaint is filed shall cause the complaint and the notice of the hearing to be so served in accordance with the Rules of Civil Procedure, which service shall be made, if possible, within three days after the filing of the complaint. The hearing shall be conducted at the earliest possible time, but no later than the third business day after such service has been completed. Immediately following the hearing, the court shall enter on its journal its determination whether the decision of the priority individual or class of individuals to consent to the use or continuation, or the withholding or withdrawal, of life-sustaining treatment in connection with the patient will be confirmed or reversed.

(2) If the decision of the priority individual or class of individuals was to consent to the use or continuation of life-sustaining treatment in connection with the patient, the court only may reverse that consent if the objecting individual establishes, by clear and convincing evidence and, if applicable, to a reasonable degree of medical certainty and in accordance with reasonable medical standards, one or more of the following:

(a) The patient is able to make informed decisions regarding the administration of life-sustaining treatment.

(b) The patient has a legally effective declaration that addresses his intent should he be determined to be in a terminal condition or in a permanently unconscious state, whichever applies, or a legally effective durable power of attorney for health care.

(c) The decision to use or continue life-sustaining treatment is not consistent with the previously expressed intention of the patient as described in division (D)(2) of this section.

(d) The decision to use or continue life-sustaining treatment is not consistent with the type of informed consent decision that the patient would have made if he previously had expressed his intention with respect to the use or continuation, or the withholding or withdrawal, of life-sustaining treatment should he subsequently be in a terminal condition or in a permanently unconscious state, whichever applies, and no longer able to make informed decisions regarding the administration of life-sustaining treatment as described in division (D)(3) of this section.

(e) The decision of the priority individual or class of individuals was not made after consultation with the patient's attending physician and after receipt of information from the patient's attending physician or a consulting physician that is sufficient to satisfy the requirements of informed consent.

(f) The priority individual, or any member of the priority class of individuals, who made the decision to use or continue life-sustaining treatment was not of sound mind or did not voluntarily make the decision.

(g) If the decision of a priority class of individuals under division (B)(3) of this section is involved, the patient's attending physician did not make a good faith effort, and use reasonable diligence, to notify the patient's adult children who were available within a reasonable period of time for consultation as described in division (A)(1)(c) of this section.

(h) The decision of the priority individual or class of individuals otherwise was made in a manner that does not comply with this section.

(3) If the decision of the priority individual or class of individuals was to consent to the withholding or withdrawal of life-sustaining treatment in connection with the patient, the court only may reverse that consent if the objecting individual establishes, by a preponderance of the evidence and, if applicable, to a reasonable degree of medical certainty and in accordance with reasonable medical standards, one or more of the following:

(a) The patient is not in a terminal condition, the patient is not in a permanently unconscious state, or the patient has not been in a permanently unconscious state for at least the immediately preceding twelve months.

(b) The patient is able to make informed decisions regarding the administration of life-sustaining treatment.

(c) There is a reasonable possibility that the patient will regain the capacity to make informed decisions regarding the administration of life-sustaining treatment.

(d) The patient has a legally effective declaration that addresses his intent should he be determined to be in a terminal condition or in a permanently unconscious state, whichever applies, or a legally effective durable power of attorney for health care.

(e) The decision to withhold or withdraw life-sustaining treatment is not consistent with the previously expressed intention of the patient as described in division (D)(2) of this section.

(f) The decision to withhold or withdraw life-sustaining treatment is not consistent with the type of informed consent decision that the patient would have made if he previously had expressed his intention with respect to the use or continuation, or the withholding or withdrawal, of life-sustaining treatment should he subsequently be in a terminal condition or in a permanently unconscious state, whichever applies, and no longer able to make informed decisions regarding the administration of life-sustaining treatment as described in division (D)(3) of this section.

(g) The decision of the priority individual or class of individuals was not made after consultation with the patient's attending physician and after receipt of information from the patient's attending physician or a consulting physician that is sufficient to satisfy the requirements of informed consent.

(h) The priority individual, or any member of the priority class of individuals, who made the decision to withhold or withdraw life-sustaining treatment was not of sound mind or did not voluntarily make the decision.

(i) If the decision of a priority class of individuals under division (B)(3) of this section is involved, the patient's attending physician did not make a good faith effort, and use reasonable diligence, to notify the patient's adult children who were available within a reasonable period of time for consultation as described in division (A)(1)(c) of this section.

(j) The decision of the priority individual or class of individuals otherwise was made in a manner that does not comply with this section.

(4) Notwithstanding any contrary provision of the Revised Code or of the Rules of Civil Procedure, the state and persons other than individuals described in divisions (B)(1) to (5) of this section are prohibited from filing a complaint under division (E) of this section and from joining or being joined as parties to a hearing conducted under division (E) of this section, including joining by way of intervention.

(F) A valid consent given in accordance with this section supersedes any general consent to treatment form signed by or on behalf of the patient prior to, upon, or after his admission to a health care facility to the extent there is a conflict between the consent and the form.

(G) Life–sustaining treatment shall not be withheld or withdrawn from a patient pursuant to a consent given in accordance with this section if she is pregnant and if the withholding or withdrawal of the treatment would terminate the pregnancy, unless the patient's attending physician and one other physician who has examined the patient determine, to a reasonable degree of medical certainty and in accordance with reasonable medical standards, that the fetus would not be born alive.

(1991 S 1, eff. 10–10–91)

Cross References

Probate court jurisdiction, 2101.24

Library References

Health ☞916.
Westlaw Topic No. 198H.

Baldwin's Ohio Legislative Service, 1991 Laws of Ohio, S 1—LSC Analysis, p 5–250

Research References

Encyclopedias

40 Am. Jur. Proof of Facts 3d 287, Proof of Basis for Refusal or Discontinuance of Life-Sustaining Treatment on Behalf of Incapacitated Person.

63 Am. Jur. Trials 1, Decisionmaking at the End of Life.

OH Jur. 3d Death § 26, Immunity.

OH Jur. 3d Death § 32, Withholding or Withdrawal of Life-Sustaining Treatment.

OH Jur. 3d Death § 33, Withholding or Withdrawal of Nutrition or Hydration.

OH Jur. 3d Malpractice § 99, Under Statute Regarding Patients' Advance Directives; Generally.

Forms

Ohio Forms and Transactions KP 24.06, Durable Power of Attorney for Health Care.

Ohio Forms and Transactions KP 30.23, Living Will, or Health Care Declaration.

Treatises and Practice Aids

Carlin, Baldwin's Ohio Practice, Merrick-Rippner Probate Law § 62:5, Appointment of Guardian—Definitions—Limited Guardian.

Carlin, Baldwin's Ohio Practice, Merrick-Rippner Probate Law § 64:8, Powers and Duties of Guardian—Ward's Person—Discretionary Acts—Medical Care/Removal of Nutrition and Hydration.

Carlin, Baldwin's Ohio Practice, Merrick-Rippner Probate Law § 67:7, Alternatives to Guardianship—Adult Wards.

Carlin, Baldwin's Ohio Practice, Merrick-Rippner Probate Law § 60:27, Power of Attorney for Health Care—Decision in Absence of Valid Health Care Instrument; Probate Court Proceedings.

Carlin, Baldwin's Ohio Practice, Merrick-Rippner Probate Law § 62:43, Guardianship Proceedings—Who May Serve—Life Support Cases.

Carlin, Baldwin's Ohio Practice, Merrick-Rippner Probate Law § 62:60, Limited Guardianship.

Carlin, Baldwin's Ohio Practice, Merrick-Rippner Probate Law § 62:61, Interim Guardianship.

Carlin, Baldwin's Ohio Practice, Merrick-Rippner Probate Law § 62:62, Emergency Guardianship.

Carlin, Baldwin's Ohio Practice, Merrick-Rippner Probate Law § 62:66, Appellate Standard of Review—Discretion of Court.

Law Review and Journal Commentaries

Absence of living will can turn into a nightmare, Mark S. Reckman. 13 Ohio Law 18 (November/December 1999).

Anderson v. St. Francis–St. George Hospital: Wrongful Living from an American and Jewish Legal Perspective, Daniel Pollack, Chaim Steinmetz, and Vicki Lens. 45 Clev St L Rev 621 (1997).

Euphemistic Codes and Tell-Tale Hearts: Humane Assistance in End-of-Life Cases. George P. Smith, 11, 10 Health Matrix: J Law-Medicine 175 (Summer 2000).

The Health Care Proxy and the Narrative of Death, Steven I. Friedland. 10 J L & Health 95 (1995–96).

The New Durable Power of Attorney for Health Care and Living Will Under Am. Sub. S.B.1, Hon. Fred V. Skok. 15 Lake Legal Views 1 (February 1992).

Redrafting Ohio's Advance Directive Laws, Susan R. Martyn, et al. 26 Akron L Rev 229 (Fall 1992).

Notes of Decisions

Emergency situation 2
Infants 3
Nonconsensual treatment 1

---

1. Nonconsensual treatment

In proceeding in which co-guardians of comatose ward sought court order allowing attending physician to withdraw nutrition and hydration from ward, who had not made advance directive or prepared living will, consulting physician's opinion was not in conformity with statutory requirements, where opinion was not sworn testimony, it was not clear whether consulting physician's independent examination of ward was physical examination of ward herself or independent review of ward's medical records, there was no evidence of consulting physician's education or training, and consulting physician merely affirmed attending physician's opinion and did not specifically set out his own opinion. In re Biersack (Ohio App. 3 Dist., Mercer, 12-06-2004) No. 10-04-03, 2004-Ohio-6491, 2004 WL 2785963, Unreported. Health ☞ 926

Opinions and conclusions of physician should be presented by personal in-court testimony in proceeding in which guardian of ward, who has not made advance directive or prepared living will and who currently is or has been in permanently unconscious state for immediately preceding 12 months, seeks court order allowing attending physician to withdraw nutrition and hydration from ward. In re Biersack (Ohio App. 3 Dist., Mercer, 12-06-2004) No. 10-04-03, 2004-Ohio-6491, 2004 WL 2785963, Unreported. Health ☞ 926

In proceeding in which guardian of ward, who has not made advance directive or prepared living will and who currently is or has been in permanently unconscious state for immediately preceding 12 months, seeks court order allowing attending physician to withdraw nutrition and hydration from ward, consulting physician's opinion should be more than conclusory adoption of attending physician's opinion; instead, consulting physician's opinion should be independently stated and, ideally, should include reasons upon which it is based. In re Biersack (Ohio App. 3 Dist., Mercer, 12-06-2004) No. 10-04-03, 2004-Ohio-6491, 2004 WL 2785963, Unreported. Health ☞ 926

Reversal of guardian of patient's consent to the use or continuation of life-sustaining treatment for patient in intensive care was warranted; patient signed a declaration regarding the use of life-sustaining treatment after nursing home discussed the form in the context of patient having a heart attack and did not discuss patient's option if he had a terminal illness or was in a permanent unconscious state, son of patient established that the use of life-sustaining treatment was not consistent with the previously expressed intentions of patient, and patient was in a terminal state. Carpenter v. Mason (Ohio Com.Pl., 11-26-2003) 126 Ohio Misc.2d 17, 800 N.E.2d 404, 2003-Ohio-6490. Health ☞ 916

Nonconsensual medical treatment that prolongs a person's life may be a battery for which plaintiff would be entitled to some relief; however, when nonconsensual treatment is harmless or beneficial, damages for wrongful act are nominal only, not actual. Anderson v. St. Francis–St. George Hosp. (Hamilton 1992) 83 Ohio App.3d 221, 614 N.E.2d 841, motion to certify overruled 66 Ohio St.3d 1459, 610 N.E.2d 423. Assault And Battery 2; Assault And Battery 37.

Prolonging of patient's life by resuscitating him after he suffered ventricular fibrillation was not wrongful living; life is not a compensable harm. Anderson v. St. Francis–St. George Hosp. (Hamilton 1992) 83 Ohio App.3d 221, 614 N.E.2d 841, motion to certify overruled 66 Ohio St.3d 1459, 610 N.E.2d 423. Health 917.

2. Emergency situation

The statutes governing living wills and durable powers of attorney for health care do not provide for the application of those documents when a rescue squad is acting in an emergency situation and without the direction of an individual's attending physician. OAG 93–062.

Existing statutes and case law do not expressly authorize a member of a rescue squad, acting in an emergency situation and without the direction of a physician, to honor the request of a relative of a resident of a rest home to provide no extraordinary care to the resident. OAG 93–062.

3. Infants

The Uniform Rights of the Terminally Ill Act, which explicitly authorizes the removal of life-sustaining treatment from adults, does not authorize the removal of life-sustaining treatment from infants. (Per Lundberg Stratton, J., with two Justices concurring and three Justices concurring separately.) In re Guardianship of Stein (Ohio, 12-30-2004) 105 Ohio St.3d 30, 821 N.E.2d 1008, 2004-Ohio-7114. Health 915.

2133.09 Withholding or withdrawal of nutrition or hydration

(A) The attending physician of a patient who is an adult and who currently is and for at least the immediately preceding twelve months has been in a permanently unconscious state may withhold or withdraw nutrition and hydration in connection with the patient only if all of the following apply:

(1) Written consent to the withholding or withdrawal of life-sustaining treatment in connection with the patient has been given by an appropriate individual or individuals in accordance with section 2133.08 of the Revised Code, and divisions (A)(1)(a) to (e) and (2) of that section have been satisfied.

(2) A probate court has not reversed the consent to the withholding or withdrawal of life-sustaining treatment in connection with the patient pursuant to division (E) of section 2133.08 of the Revised Code.

(3) The attending physician of the patient and one other physician as described in division (A)(2) of section 2133.08 of the Revised Code who examines the patient determine, in good faith, to a reasonable degree of medical certainty, and in accordance with reasonable medical standards, that nutrition and hydration will not or no longer will provide comfort or alleviate pain in connection with the patient.

(4) Written consent to the withholding or withdrawal of nutrition and hydration in connection with the patient, witnessed by two individuals who satisfy the witness eligibility criteria set forth in division (B)(1) of section 2133.02 of the Revised Code, is given to the attending physician of the patient by an appropriate individual or individuals as specified in division (B) of section 2133.08 of the Revised Code.

(5) The written consent to the withholding or withdrawal of the nutrition and hydration in connection with the patient is given in accordance with division (B) of this section.

(6) The probate court of the county in which the patient is located issues an order to withhold or withdraw the nutrition and hydration in connection with the patient pursuant to division (C) of this section.

(B)(1) A decision to consent pursuant to this section to the withholding or withdrawal of nutrition and hydration in connection with a patient shall be made in good faith.

(2) Except as provided in division (B)(4) of this section, if the patient previously expressed his intention with respect to the use or continuation, or the withholding or withdrawal, of nutrition and hydration should he subsequently be in a permanently unconscious state and no longer able to make informed decisions regarding the administration of nutrition and hydration, a consent given pursuant to this section shall be valid only if it is consistent with that previously expressed intention.

(3) Except as provided in division (B)(4) of this section, if the patient did not previously express his intention with respect to the use or continuation, or the withholding or withdrawal, of nutrition and hyrdation [sic.] should he subsequently be in a permanently unconscious state and no longer able to make informed decisions regarding the administration of nutrition and hydration, a consent given pursuant to this section shall be valid only if it is consistent with the type of informed consent decision that the patient would have made if he previously had expressed his intention with respect to the use or continuation, or the withholding or withdrawal, of nutrition and hydration should he subsequently be in a permanently unconscious state and no longer able to make informed decisions regarding the administration of nutrition and hydration, as inferred from the lifestyle and character of the patient, and from any other evidence of the desires of the patient, prior to his becoming no longer able to make informed decisions regarding the administration of nutrition and hydration. The Rules of Evidence shall not be binding for purposes of this division.

(4)(a) The attending physician of the patient, and other health care personnel acting under the direction of the attending physician, who do not have actual knowledge of a previously expressed intention as described in division (B)(2) of this section or who do not have actual knowledge that the patient would have made a different type of informed consent decision under the circumstances described in division (B)(3) of this section, may rely on a consent given in accordance with this section unless a probate court decides differently under division (C) of this section.

(b) The immunity conferred by division (C)(2) of section 2133.11 of the Revised Code is not forfeited by an individual who gives a consent to the withholding or withdrawal of nutrition and hydration in connection with a patient under division (A)(4) of this section if the individual gives the consent in good faith and without actual knowledge, at the time of giving the consent, of either a contrary previously expressed intention of the patient, or a previously expressed intention of the patient, as described in divison [sic.] (B)(2) of this section, that is revealed to the individual subsequent to the time of giving the consent.

(C)(1) Prior to the withholding or withdrawal of nutrition and hydration in connection with a patient pursuant to this section, the priority individual or class of individuals that consented to the withholding or withdrawal of the nutrition and hydration shall apply to the probate court of the county in which the patient is located for the issuance of an order that authorizes the attending physician of the patient to commence the withholding or withdrawal of the nutrition and hydration in connection with the patient. Upon the filing of the application, the clerk of the probate court shall schedule a hearing on it and cause a copy of it and a notice of the hearing to be served in accordance with the Rules of Civil Procedure upon the applicant, the attending physician, the consulting physician associated with the determination that nutrition and hydration will not or no longer will provide comfort or alleviate pain in connection with the patient, and the individuals described in divisions (B)(1) to (5) of section 2133.08 of the Revised Code who are not applicants, which service shall be made, if possible, within three days after the filing of the application. The hearing shall be conducted at the earliest possible time, but no sooner than the thirtieth business day, and no later than the sixtieth business day, after such service has been completed.

At the hearing, any individual described in divisions (B)(1) to (5) of section 2133.08 of the Revised Code who is not an applicant and who disagrees with the decision of the priority individual or class of individuals to consent to the withholding or withdrawal of nutrition and hydration in connection with the patient shall be permitted to testify and present evidence relative to the use or continuation of nutrition and hydration in connection with the patient. Immediately following the hearing, the court shall enter on its journal its determination whether the requested order will be issued.

(2) The court shall issue an order that authorizes the patient's attending physician to commence the withholding or withdrawal of nutrition and hydration in connection with the patient only if the applicants establish, by clear and convincing evidence, to a reasonable degree of medical certainty, and in accordance with reasonable medical standards, all of the following:

(a) The patient currently is and for at least the immediately preceding twelve months has been in a permanently unconscious state.

(b) The patient no longer is able to make informed decisions regarding the administration of life-sustaining treatment.

(c) There is no reasonable possibility that the patient will regain the capacity to make informed decisions regarding the administration of life-sustaining treatment.

(d) The conditions specified in divisions (A)(1) to (4) of this section have been satisfied.

(e) The decision to withhold or withdraw nutrition and hydration in connection with the patient is consistent with the previously expressed intention of the patient as described in division (B)(2) of this section or is consistent with the type of informed consent decision that the patient would have made if he previously had expressed his intention with respect to the use or continuation, or the withholding or withdrawal, of nutrition and hydration should he subsequently be in a permanently unconscious state and no longer able to make informed decisions regarding the administration of nutrition and hydration as described in division (B)(3) of this section.

(3) Notwithstanding any contrary provision of the Revised Code or of the Rules of Civil Procedure, the state and persons other than individuals described in division (A)(4) of this section or in divisions (B)(1) to (5) of section 2133.08 of the Revised Code and other than the attending physician and consulting physician associated with the determination that nutrition and hydration will not or no longer will provide comfort or alleviate pain in connection with the patient are prohibited from filing an application under this division and from joining or being joined as parties to a hearing conducted under this division, including joining by way of intervention.

(D) A valid consent given in accordance with this section supersedes any general consent to treatment form signed by or on behalf of the patient prior to, upon, or after his admission to a health care facility to the extent there is a conflict between the consent and the form.

(1991 S 1, eff. 10–10–91)

Cross References

Probate court jurisdiction, 2101.24

Library References

Health ⚖=913.
Westlaw Topic No. 198H.

Baldwin's Ohio Legislative Service, 1991 Laws of Ohio, S 1—LSC Analysis, p 5–250

Research References

Encyclopedias

OH Jur. 3d Death § 26, Immunity.
OH Jur. 3d Death § 32, Withholding or Withdrawal of Life-Sustaining Treatment.
OH Jur. 3d Death § 33, Withholding or Withdrawal of Nutrition or Hydration.
OH Jur. 3d Malpractice § 99, Under Statute Regarding Patients' Advance Directives; Generally.

Forms

Ohio Forms and Transactions KP 24.06, Durable Power of Attorney for Health Care.
Ohio Forms and Transactions KP 30.23, Living Will, or Health Care Declaration.

Treatises and Practice Aids

Carlin, Baldwin's Ohio Practice, Merrick-Rippner Probate Law § 3:11, Jurisdiction of Probate Court—Subject Matter—Specific Areas—Removal of Life Support.
Carlin, Baldwin's Ohio Practice, Merrick-Rippner Probate Law § 60:27, Power of Attorney for Health Care—Decision in Absence of Valid Health Care Instrument; Probate Court Proceedings.
Carlin, Baldwin's Ohio Practice, Merrick-Rippner Probate Law § 60:29, Power of Attorney for Health Care—Withholding or Withdrawing Life-Support Measures or Other Care.
Carlin, Baldwin's Ohio Practice, Merrick-Rippner Probate Law § 60:32, Power of Attorney for Health Care—Withholding or Withdrawing Life-Support Measures or Other Care—Comfort Care; Nutrition and Hydration.
Carlin, Baldwin's Ohio Practice, Merrick-Rippner Probate Law § 60:34, Power of Attorney for Health Care—Withholding or Withdrawing Life-Support Measures or Other Care—Objections to Health Care Decisions; Probate Court Proceedings.
Carlin, Baldwin's Ohio Practice, Merrick-Rippner Probate Law § 62:43, Guardianship Proceedings—Who May Serve—Life Support Cases.

Law Review and Journal Commentaries

Barriers to forgoing nutrition and hydration in nursing homes, Alan Meisel. 21 Am J L & Med 335 (1995).

The "Non-Declarant" in a PVS: Adventures in Ohio's Legal Wonderland, Gere B. Fulton. 20 Ohio N U L Rev 571 (1994).

Redrafting Ohio's Advance Directive Laws, Susan R. Martyn, et al. 26 Akron L Rev 229 (Fall 1992).

S.B. 1: A Hospital Attorney's Perspective, Paul A. Greve, Jr. 2 Prob L J Ohio 93 (May/June 1992).

Notes of Decisions

Burden of proof 3
Court's power 4
Federal law 1
Minors 2

---

1. Federal law

"Nutrition and hydration" and "life sustaining treatment" are addressed separately in Modified Uniform Rights of the Terminally Ill Act and, for purposes of living will, each must be referred to specifically. In re Biersack (Ohio App. 3 Dist., Mercer, 12-06-2004) No. 10-04-03, 2004-Ohio-6491, 2004 WL 2785963, Unreported. Health ⚖= 916

2. Minors

RC 2133.09 applies to adults and is not binding where a decision involves removing nutrition and hydration from a minor. In re Guardianship of Myers (Ohio Com.Pl. 1993) 62 Ohio Misc.2d 763, 610 N.E.2d 663.

3. Burden of proof

In proceeding in which guardian of ward, who has not made advance directive or prepared living will and who currently is or has been in permanently unconscious state for immediately preceding 12 months, seeks court order allowing attending physician to withdraw nutrition and hydration from ward, testimony of each physician must, at least, encompass the following to meet clear and convincing evidence standard: physician's education, training, and experience; physician's history and experience with patient; fact that physician personally examined patient; and opinions required by statute. In re Biersack (Ohio App. 3 Dist., Mercer, 12-06-2004) No. 10-04-03, 2004-Ohio-6491, 2004 WL 2785963, Unreported. Health ⚖ 926

In proceeding in which co-guardians of comatose ward sought court order allowing attending physician to withdraw nutrition and hydration from ward, who had not made advance directive or prepared living will, consulting physician's opinion was not in conformity with statutory requirements, where opinion was not sworn testimony, it was not clear whether consulting physician's independent examination of ward was physical examination of ward herself or independent review of ward's medical records, there was no evidence of consulting physician's education or training, and consulting physician merely affirmed attending physician's opinion and did not specifically set out his own opinion. In re Biersack (Ohio App. 3 Dist., Mercer, 12-06-2004) No. 10-04-03, 2004-Ohio-6491, 2004 WL 2785963, Unreported. Health ⚖ 926

In proceeding in which co-guardians of comatose ward sought court order allowing attending physician to withdraw nutrition and hydration from ward, who had not made advance directive or prepared living will, clear and convincing evidence supported inference that withdrawing nutrition and hydration was consistent with ward's wishes; ward's children gave uncontradicted testimony indicating that ward had expressed intent never to be "kept alive by machine or any type of life support" and stated that ward would not want to live in vegetative state. In re Biersack (Ohio App. 3 Dist., Mercer, 12-06-2004) No. 10-04-03, 2004-Ohio-6491, 2004 WL 2785963, Unreported. Health ⚖ 926

Opinions and conclusions of physician should be presented by personal in-court testimony in proceeding in which guardian of ward, who has not made advance directive or prepared living will and who currently is or has been in permanently unconscious state for immediately preceding 12 months, seeks court order allowing attending physician to withdraw nutrition and hydration from ward. In re Biersack (Ohio App. 3 Dist., Mercer, 12-06-2004) No. 10-04-03, 2004-Ohio-6491, 2004 WL 2785963, Unreported. Health ⚖ 926

4. Court's power

A probate court is empowered to authorize the withdrawal of nutrition and hydration to a person in a chronic vegetative state, as the state's interests do not outweigh those of the person, and the withdrawal of nutrition and hydration in such a case is consistent with the canons of medical ethics. In re Guardianship of Crum (Ohio Prob. 1991) 61 Ohio Misc.2d 596, 580 N.E.2d 876.

2133.10 Transfer of patient to physician or facility complying with declaration

(A) An attending physician who, or a health care facility in which a qualified patient or other patient is confined that, is not willing or is not able to comply or allow compliance with a declaration of a qualified patient, with a consent given in accordance with section 2133.08 or 2133.09 of the Revised Code, with any probate court order issued pursuant to section 2133.05, 2133.08, or 2133.09 of the Revised Code, or with any other applicable provision of sections 2133.01 to 2133.15 of the Revised Code shall not prevent or attempt to prevent, or unreasonably delay or attempt to unreasonably delay, the transfer of the qualified patient or other patient to the care of a physician who, or a health care facility that, is willing and able to so comply or allow compliance.

(B) If a declaration provides for the use or continuation of life-sustaining treatment should its declarant subsequently be in a terminal condition or in a permanently unconscious state, if a consent decision of a priority individual or class of individuals under section 2133.08 of the Revised Code is to use or continue life-sustaining treatment in connection with a patient described in that section, or if a probate court issues a reevaluation order pursuant to section 2133.05 or 2133.08 of the Revised Code that is intended to result in the use or continuation of life-sustaining treatment in connection with a qualified patient or other patient, then the attending physician of the qualified patient or other patient who, or health care facility in which the qualified patient or other patient is confined that, is not willing or is not able to comply or allow compliance with the declaration, consent decision, or reevaluation order shall use or continue the life-sustaining treatment or cause it to be used or continued until a transfer as described in division (A) of this section is made.

(1998 H 354, eff. 7–9–98; 1991 S 1, eff. 10–10–91)

Historical and Statutory Notes

Amendment Note: 1998 H 354 substituted "sections 2133.01 to 2133.15 of the Revised Code" for "this chapter" in division (A); and made other nonsubstantive changes.

Library References

Health ⚖915, 916.
Westlaw Topic No. 198H.
Baldwin's Ohio Legislative Service, 1991 Laws of Ohio, S 1—LSC Analysis, p 5–250

Research References

Encyclopedias

63 Am. Jur. Trials 1, Decisionmaking at the End of Life.
OH Jur. 3d Physicians, Surgeons & Other Healers § 211, Terminally Ill Patients.

Law Review and Journal Commentaries

Planning Ahead: Proper Implementation and Execution of Advance Directives, Bryan B. Johnson and Tristan A. McCormick. 17 Ohio Law 14 (September/October 2003).

2133.11 Immunities

(A) Subject to division (D) of this section, an attending physician, consulting physician, health care facility, and health care personnel acting under the direction of an attending physician are not subject to criminal prosecution, are not liable in damages in a tort or other civil action, and are not subject to professional disciplinary action for any of the following:

(1) Giving effect to a declaration, if the physician, facility, or personnel gives effect to the declaration in good faith and does not have actual knowledge that the declaration has been revoked or does not substantially comply with this chapter;

(2) Giving effect to a consent under the circumstances described in section 2133.08 of the Revised Code, if the physician, facility, or personnel gives effect to the consent in good faith and does not have actual knowledge that the consent is invalid under that section and if a probate court has not issued an order reversing the consent pursuant to division (E) of that section;

(3) Giving effect to a consent under the circumstances described in section 2133.09 of the Revised Code, if the physician, facility, or personnel gives effect to the consent in good faith and does not have actual knowledge that the consent is invalid under that section and if the appropriate probate court has issued an order authorizing the withholding or withdrawal of nutrition and hydration in connection with the patient in question;

(4) Refusing to or not being able to comply or allow compliance with a declaration of a qualified patient, with a consent given in accordance with section 2133.08 or 2133.09 of the Revised Code, with a probate court order issued pursuant to section 2133.05, 2133.08, or 2133.09 of the Revised Code, or with another applicable provision of this chapter, if the refusal or inability to comply or allow compliance is in good faith, provided that, in the case of an attending physician or health care facility, whichever of the following apply are satisfied:

(a) The attending physician or health care facility does not prevent or attempt to prevent, or unreasonably delay or attempt to unreasonably delay, the transfer of the qualified patient or other patient to the care of a physician who, or a health care facility that, is willing and able to so comply or allow compliance.

(b) If the declaration of the qualified patient provided for the use or continuation of life-sustaining treatment should the declarant subsequently be in a terminal condition or in a permanently unconscious state, if the consent decision of a priority individual or class of individuals under section 2133.08 of the Revised Code was to use or continue life-sustaining treatment in connection with the patient described in that section, or if the probate court issued a reevaluation order pursuant to section 2133.05 or 2133.08 of the Revised Code that was intended to result in the use or continuation of life-sustaining treatment in connection with the qualified patient or other patient, the attending physician or health care facility used or continued the life-sustaining treatment or caused it to be used or continued until a transfer as described in division (A)(4)(a) of this section was made.

(5) Making determinations other than those described in division (B) of this section, or otherwise acting under this chapter, if the determinations or other actions are made in good faith and in accordance with reasonable medical standards;

(6) Prescribing, dispensing, administering, or causing to be administered any particular medical procedure, treatment, intervention, or other measure to a qualified patient or other patient, including, but not limited to, prescribing, personally furnishing, administering, or causing to be administered by judicious titration or in another manner any form of medication, for the purpose of diminishing the qualified patient's or other patient's pain or discomfort and not for the purpose of postponing or causing the qualified patient's or other patient's death, even though the medical procedure, treatment, intervention, or other measure may appear to hasten or increase the risk of the patient's death, if the attending physician so prescribing, dispensing, administering, or causing to be administered or the health care personnel acting under the direction of the attending physician so dispensing, administering, or causing to be administered are carrying out in good faith the responsibility to provide comfort care described in division (E)(1) of section 2133.12 of the Revised Code.

(B) Subject to division (D) of this section, an attending or consulting physician is not subject to criminal prosecution, is not liable in damages in a tort or other civil action, and is not subject to professional disciplinary action if the physician makes any of the following determinations in good faith, to a reasonable degree of medical certainty, and in accordance with reasonable medical standards:

(1) A determination that a declarant or a patient as described in section 2133.08 of the Revised Code is in a terminal condition;

(2) A determination that a declarant is in a permanently unconscious state;

(3) A determination that a patient as described in section 2133.08 of the Revised Code currently is and for at least the immediately preceding twelve months has been in a permanently unconscious state;

(4) A determination that a declarant or a patient as described in section 2133.08 of the Revised Code no longer is able to make informed decisions regarding the administration of life-sustaining treatment;

(5) A determination that there is no reasonable possibility that a declarant or a patient as described in section 2133.08 of the Revised Code will regain the capacity to make informed decisions regarding the administration of life-sustaining treatment;

(6) A determination that nutrition or hydration will not or no longer will provide comfort or alleviate pain in connection with a patient as described in section 2133.09 of the Revised Code.

(C)(1) Subject to division (D) of this section, an individual who is authorized to give a consent to the use or continuation, or the withholding or withdrawal, of life-sustaining treatment under division (B) of section 2133.08 of the Revised Code and who makes the decision in good faith is not subject to criminal prosecution, is not liable in damages in a tort or other civil action, and is not subject to professional disciplinary action in connection with that decision.

(2) Subject to division (D) of this section, an individual who is authorized to give a consent to the withholding or withdrawal of nutrition and hydration in connection with a patient under division (A)(4) of section 2133.09 of the Revised Code and who gives the consent in good faith is not subject to criminal prosecution, is not liable in damages in a tort or other civil action, and is not subject to professional disciplinary action in connection with that consent.

(D) This section does not grant an immunity from criminal or civil liability or from professional disciplinary action to health care personnel for actions that are outside the scope of their authority.

(1998 S 66, eff. 7–22–98; 1994 H 343, eff. 7–22–94; 1991 S 1, eff. 10–10–91)

Historical and Statutory Notes

Amendment Note: 1998 S 66 substituted "personally furnishing" for "dispensing" in division (A)(6); and made changes to reflect gender neutral language.

Amendment Note: 1994 H 343 added division (A)(6).

Library References

Health ⚖204, 916.
Homicide ⚖765.
Suicide ⚖3.
Westlaw Topic Nos. 198H, 203, 368.
C.J.S. Suicide §§ 8 to 12.
  Baldwin's Ohio Legislative Service, 1991 Laws of Ohio, S 1—LSC Analysis, p 5–250

Research References

Encyclopedias
63 Am. Jur. Trials 1, Decisionmaking at the End of Life.
OH Jur. 3d Death § 26, Immunity.
OH Jur. 3d Malpractice § 99, Under Statute Regarding Patients' Advance Directives; Generally.
OH Jur. 3d Malpractice § 100, Under Statute Regarding Patients' Advance Directives; Generally—Determinations by Physician.

Forms
Ohio Forms and Transactions KP 30.23, Living Will, or Health Care Declaration.

Treatises and Practice Aids
Carlin, Baldwin's Ohio Practice, Merrick-Rippner Probate Law § 60:27, Power of Attorney for Health Care—Decision in Absence of Valid Health Care Instrument; Probate Court Proceedings.

Law Review and Journal Commentaries

New Statutory Guideline for Treating Patients Who Are Permanently Unconscious or Suffering from a Terminal Condition, K. Ann Zimmerman and Jane Pine Wood. 6 Health L J Ohio 11 (July/August 1994).

"Wrongful Living": Resuscitation As Tortious Interference With A Patient's Right to Give Informed Refusal, William C. Knapp and Fred Hamilton. 19 N Ky L Rev 253 (1992).

2133.12 Death not deemed suicide or homicide; effect of declaration on insurance and annuities; rights not affected; euthanasia not authorized; comfort care

(A) The death of a qualified patient or other patient resulting from the withholding or withdrawal of life-sustaining treatment in accordance with sections 2133.01 to 2133.15 of the Revised Code does not constitute for any purpose a suicide, aggravated murder, murder, or any other homicide offense.

(B)(1) The execution of a declaration shall not do either of the following:

(a) Affect the sale, procurement, issuance, or renewal of any policy of life insurance or annuity, notwithstanding any term of a policy or annuity to the contrary;

(b) Be deemed to modify or invalidate the terms of any policy of life insurance or annuity that is in effect on October 10, 1991.

(2) Notwithstanding any term of a policy of life insurance or annuity to the contrary, the withholding or withdrawal of life-sustaining treatment from an insured, qualified patient or other patient in accordance with sections 2133.01 to 2133.15 of the Revised Code shall not impair or invalidate any policy of life insurance or annuity.

(3) Notwithstanding any term of a policy or plan to the contrary, the use or continuation, or the withholding or withdrawal, of life-sustaining treatment from an insured, qualified patient or other patient in accordance with sections 2133.01 to 2133.15 of the Revised Code shall not impair or invalidate any policy of health insurance or any health care benefit plan.

(4) No physician, health care facility, other health care provider, person authorized to engage in the business of insurance in this state under Title XXXIX of the Revised Code, health insuring corporation, other health care plan, legal entity that is self-insured and provides benefits to its employees or members, or other person shall require any individual to execute or refrain from executing a declaration, or shall require an individual to revoke or refrain from revoking a declaration, as a condition of being insured or of receiving health care benefits or services.

(C)(1) Sections 2133.01 to 2133.15 of the Revised Code do not create any presumption concerning the intention of an individual who has revoked or has not executed a declaration with respect to the use or continuation, or the withholding or withdrawal, of life-sustaining treatment if the individual should be in a terminal condition or in a permanently unconscious state at any time.

(2) Sections 2133.01 to 2133.15 of the Revised Code do not affect the right of a qualified patient or other patient to make informed decisions regarding the use or continuation, or the withholding or withdrawal, of life-sustaining treatment as long as the qualified patient or other patient is able to make those decisions.

(3) Sections 2133.01 to 2133.15 of the Revised Code do not require a physician, other health care personnel, or a health care facility to take action that is contrary to reasonable medical standards.

(4) Sections 2133.01 to 2133.15 of the Revised Code and, if applicable, a declaration do not affect or limit the authority of a physician or a health care facility to provide or not to provide life-sustaining treatment to a person in accordance with reasonable medical standards applicable in an emergency situation.

(D) Nothing in sections 2133.01 to 2133.15 of the Revised Code condones, authorizes, or approves of mercy killing, assisted suicide, or euthanasia.

(E)(1) Sections 2133.01 to 2133.15 of the Revised Code do not affect the responsibility of the attending physician of a qualified patient or other patient, or other health care personnel acting under the direction of the patient's attending physician, to provide comfort care to the patient. Nothing in sections 2133.01 to 2133.15 of the Revised Code precludes the attending physician of a qualified patient or other patient who carries out the responsibility to provide comfort care to the patient in good faith and while acting within the scope of the attending physician's authority from prescribing, dispensing, administering, or causing to be administered any particular medical procedure, treatment, intervention, or other measure to the patient, including, but not limited to, prescribing, personally furnishing, administering, or causing to be administered by judicious titration or in another manner any form of medication, for the purpose of diminishing the qualified patient's or other patient's pain or discomfort and not for the purpose of postponing or causing the qualified patient's or other patient's death, even though the medical procedure, treatment, intervention, or other measure may appear to hasten or increase the risk of the patient's death. Nothing in sections 2133.01 to 2133.15 of the Revised Code precludes health care personnel acting under the direction of the patient's attending physician who carry out the responsibility to provide comfort care to the patient in good faith and while acting within the scope of their authority from dispensing, administering, or causing to be administered any particular medical procedure, treatment, intervention, or other measure to the patient, including, but not limited to, personally furnishing, administering, or causing to be administered by judicious titration or in another manner any form of medication, for the purpose of diminishing the qualified patient's or other patient's pain or discomfort and not for the purpose of postponing or causing the qualified patient's or other patient's death, even though the medical procedure, treatment, intervention, or other measure may appear to hasten or increase the risk of the patient's death.

(2)(a) If, at any time, a person described in division (A)(2)(a)(i) of section 2133.05 of the Revised Code or the individual or a majority of the individuals in either of the first two classes of individuals that pertain to a declarant in the descending order of priority set forth in division (A)(2)(a)(ii) of section 2133.05 of the Revised Code believes in good faith that both of the following circumstances apply, the person or the individual or majority of individuals in either of the first two classes of individuals may commence an action in the probate court of the county in which a declarant who is in a terminal condition or permanently unconscious state is located for the issuance of an order mandating the use or continuation of comfort care in connection with the declarant in a manner that is consistent with division (E)(1) of this section:

(i) Comfort care is not being used or continued in connection with the declarant.

(ii) The withholding or withdrawal of the comfort care is contrary to division (E)(1) of this section.

(b) If a declarant did not designate in the declarant's declaration a person as described in division (A)(2)(a)(i) of section 2133.05 of the Revised Code and if, at any time, a priority individual or any member of a priority class of individuals under division (A)(2)(a)(ii) of section 2133.05 of the Revised Code or, at any time, the individual or a majority of the individuals in the next class of individuals that pertains to the declarant in the descending order of priority set forth in that division believes in good faith that both of the following circumstances apply, the priority individual, the member of the priority class of individuals, or the individual or majority of individuals in the next class of individuals that pertains to the declarant may commence an action in the probate court of the county in which a declarant who is in a terminal condition or permanently unconscious state is located for the issuance of an order mandating the use or continuation of comfort care in connection with the declarant in a manner that is consistent with division (E)(1) of this section:

(i) Comfort care is not being used or continued in connection with the declarant.

(ii) The withholding or withdrawal of the comfort care is contrary to division (E)(1) of this section.

(c) If, at any time, a priority individual or any member of a priority class of individuals under division (B) of section 2133.08 of the Revised Code or, at any time, the individual or a majority of the individuals in the next class of individuals that pertains to the patient in the descending order of priority set forth in that division believes in good faith that both of the following circumstances apply, the priority individual, the member of the priority class of individuals, or the individual or majority of individuals in the next class of individuals that pertains to the patient may commence an action in the probate court of the county in which a patient as described in division (A) of section 2133.08 of the Revised Code is located for the issuance of an order mandating the use or continuation of comfort care in connection with the patient in a manner that is consistent with division (E)(1) of this section:

(i) Comfort care is not being used or continued in connection with the patient.

(ii) The withholding or withdrawal of the comfort care is contrary to division (E)(1) of this section.

(1998 S 66, eff. 7–22–98; 1998 H 354, eff. 7–9–98; 1997 S 67, eff. 6–4–97; 1994 H 343, eff. 7–22–94; 1991 S 1, eff. 10–10–91)

Historical and Statutory Notes

Ed. Note: A special endorsement by the Legislative Service Commission states, "Comparison of these amendments [1998 S 66, eff. 7–22–98 and 1998 H 354, eff. 7–9–98] in pursuance of section 1.52 of the Revised Code discloses that they are not irreconcilable so that they are required by that section to be harmonized to give effect to each amendment." In recognition of this rule of construction, changes made by 1998 S 66, eff. 7–22–98, and 1998 H 354, eff. 7–9–98, have been incorporated in the above amendment. See *Baldwin's Ohio Legislative Service Annotated*, 1998, pages 4/L–590 and 3/L–466, or the OH–LEGIS or OH–LEGIS–OLD database on Westlaw, for original versions of these Acts.

Amendment Note: 1998 S 66 substituted "personally furnishing" for "dispensing" twice in division (E)(1).

Amendment Note: 1998 H 354 substituted "sections 2133.01 to 2133.15 of the Revised Code" for "this chapter" and "Sections 2133.01 to 2133.15 of the Revised Code" for "This chapter" throughout; and made other nonsubstantive changes.

Amendment Note: 1997 S 67 added language in division (B)(4) pertaining to health insuring corporations; deleted references to medical care corporations and health maintenance organization from the same division; and made changes to reflect gender neutral language.

Amendment Note: 1994 H 343 substituted "October 10, 1991" for "the effective date fo this section" in division (B)(1)(b); and rewrote division (E)(1), which previously read:

"(E)(1) This chapter does not affect, and shall not be construed as affecting, the responsibility of the attending physician of a qualified patient or other patient, or other health care personnel authorized to do so, to provide comfort care to the patient."

Cross References

Probate court jurisdiction, 2101.24

Library References

Health ⚖ 916.
Homicide ⚖ 565, 765.
Insurance ⚖ 2434(1), 2436, 2456, 2457(1).
Suicide ⚖ 1, 3.
Westlaw Topic Nos. 198H, 203, 217, 368.
C.J.S. Insurance §§ 53, 55, 427, 989, 1172, 1178.
C.J.S. Suicide §§ 2 to 5, 8 to 12.
Baldwin's Ohio Legislative Service, 1991 Laws of Ohio, S 1—LSC Analysis, p 5–250

Research References

Encyclopedias

63 Am. Jur. Trials 1, Decisionmaking at the End of Life.
OH Jur. 3d Death § 26, Immunity.
OH Jur. 3d Death § 27, Effect on Insurance.
OH Jur. 3d Malpractice § 99, Under Statute Regarding Patients' Advance Directives; Generally.

Treatises and Practice Aids

Carlin, Baldwin's Ohio Practice, Merrick-Rippner Probate Law § 60:32, Power of Attorney for Health Care—Withholding or Withdrawing Life-Support Measures or Other Care—Comfort Care; Nutrition and Hydration.

Law Review and Journal Commentaries

Ancient Answers to Modern Questions: Death, Dying, and Organ Transplants—A Jewish Law Perspective, Stephen J. Merber. 11 J L & Health 13 (1996–1997).

Anderson v. St. Francis–St. George Hospital: Wrongful Living from an American and Jewish Legal Perspective, Daniel Pollack, Chaim Steinmetz, and Vicki Lens. 45 Clev St L Rev 621 (1997).

The Constitution Provides No Right to be Killed, Jason A. Lief. 19 Nat'l L J A20 (August 26, 1996).

Euphemistic Codes and Tell-Tale Hearts: Humane Assistance in End-of-Life Cases. George P. Smith, 11, 10 Health Matrix: J Law-Medicine 175 (Summer 2000).

New Statutory Guideline for Treating Patients Who Are Permanently Unconscious or Suffering from a Terminal Condition, K. Ann Zimmerman and Jane Pine Wood. 6 Health L J Ohio 11 (July/August 1994).

The "Non-Declarant" in a PVS: Adventures in Ohio's Legal Wonderland, Gere B. Fulton. 20 Ohio N U L Rev 571 (1994).

Ohio's DNR Law: How Does It Differ from Advance Directive and How Will It Affect Your Practice, Renee M. Mallett. 15 Ohio Law 10 (January/February 2001).

Physician–Assisted Suicide—Michigan's Temporary Solution, George J. Annas. 20 Ohio N U L Rev 561 (1994).

Physician–Assisted Suicide: The Supreme Court's Wary Rejection, Henry J. Bourguignon, Susan R. Martyn. 31 U Tol L Rev 253 (Winter 2000).

Respect for Life in Bioethical Dilemmas—The Case of Physician-Assisted Suicide, John A. Robertson. 45 Clev St L Rev 329 (1997).

Was this Term Historic? Maybe, Say Some, but None of its Big Rulings was Seen as a True Landmark, Marcia Coyle. (Ed. note: Assisted suicide denied: no constitutionally protected liberty interest in physician-assisted suicide.) 19 Nat'l L J B5 (August 11, 1997).

Notes of Decisions

Constitutional issues 2
Nonconsensual treatment 1

---

1. Nonconsensual treatment

Nonconsensual medical treatment that prolongs a person's life may be a battery for which plaintiff would be entitled to some relief; however, when nonconsensual treatment is harmless or beneficial, damages for wrongful act are nominal only, not actual. Anderson v. St. Francis–St. George Hosp. (Hamilton 1992) 83 Ohio App.3d 221, 614 N.E.2d 841, motion to certify overruled 66 Ohio St.3d 1459, 610 N.E.2d 423. Assault And Battery ⚖ 2; Assault And Battery ⚖ 37

Prolonging of patient's life by resuscitating him after he suffered ventricular fibrillation was not wrongful living; life is not a compensable harm. Anderson v. St. Francis–St. George Hosp. (Hamilton 1992) 83 Ohio App.3d 221, 614 N.E.2d 841, motion to certify overruled 66 Ohio St.3d 1459, 610 N.E.2d 423. Health ⚖ 917

2. Constitutional issues

Due process, assisted suicide ban, liberty rights, rational relationship to government interests. Washington v. Glucksberg (U.S.Wash., 06-26-1997) 117 S.Ct. 2258, 521 U.S. 702, 138 L.Ed.2d 772, concurring opinion 117 S.Ct. 2302, 521 U.S. 702, 138 L.Ed.2d 772, on remand 122 F.3d 1262.

Any violation of petitioner's Sixth Amendment right to counsel occurring when police officers, who had obtained counsel's permission to conduct polygraph examination in counsel's absence, took petitioner to investigator's office after exam to inform him that test showed he had not been truthful and then took volunteered statement from him, was harmless, and thus did not warrant federal habeas relief, notwithstanding crucial nature of statement, in which petitioner admitted for first time that he had assisted supposed suicide victim in inflicting first gunshot wound, where petitioner had admitted in other statements inflicting second shot by himself, and both shots were deemed cause of death by pathologist, who could not state whether first shot would have been fatal without second; evidence presented no more than possibility that post-polygraph statement contributed to murder verdict. Mitzel v. Tate (C.A.6 (Ohio), 10-05-2001) 267 F.3d 524, certiorari denied 122 S.Ct. 1384, 535 U.S. 966, 152 L.Ed.2d 375. Habeas Corpus ⚖ 490(3)

Under Ohio law, aiding and abetting a suicide is not a crime. Mitzel v. Tate (C.A.6 (Ohio), 10-05-2001) 267 F.3d 524, certiorari denied 122 S.Ct. 1384, 535 U.S. 966, 152 L.Ed.2d 375. Suicide ⇐ 3

2133.13 Presumption of validity of declaration

In the absence of actual knowledge to the contrary and if acting in good faith, an attending or consulting physician, other health care personnel, and health care facilities may assume that a declaration complies with sections 2133.01 to 2133.15 of the Revised Code and is valid.

(1998 H 354, eff. 7–9–98; 1991 S 1, eff. 10–10–91)

Historical and Statutory Notes

Amendment Note: 1998 H 354 substituted "sections 2133.01 to 2133.15 of the Revised Code" for "this chapter [.]"

Library References

Health ⇐ 916.
Westlaw Topic No. 198H.
Baldwin's Ohio Legislative Service, 1991 Laws of Ohio, S 1—LSC Analysis, p 5–250

Research References

Encyclopedias
OH Jur. 3d Death § 24, Generally; Declarant's Rights.

Law Review and Journal Commentaries

Living Wills: The Right to Refuse Life Sustaining Medical Treatment—A Right Without a Remedy?, Maggie J. Randall Robb. 23 U Dayton L Rev 169 (Fall 1997).

2133.14 Effect of foreign declaration

A declaration executed under the law of another state in compliance with that law or in substantial compliance with sections 2133.01 to 2133.15 of the Revised Code shall be considered to be valid for purposes of sections 2133.01 to 2133.15 of the Revised Code.

(1998 H 354, eff. 7–9–98; 1991 S 1, eff. 10–10–91)

Historical and Statutory Notes

Amendment Note: 1998 H 354 substituted "sections 2133.01 to 2133.15 of the Revised Code" for "this chapter" twice.

Library References

Health ⇐ 916.
Westlaw Topic No. 198H.
Baldwin's Ohio Legislative Service, 1991 Laws of Ohio, S 1—LSC Analysis, p 5–250

Research References

Encyclopedias
63 Am. Jur. Trials 1, Decisionmaking at the End of Life.
OH Jur. 3d Death § 24, Generally; Declarant's Rights.

Treatises and Practice Aids
Carlin, Baldwin's Ohio Practice, Merrick-Rippner Probate Law § 60:28, Power of Attorney for Health Care—Instruments Executed Under Law of Another State or Former Law.

2133.15 Effect of declaration executed prior to effective date of act

(A) Sections 2133.01 to 2133.15 of the Revised Code apply to any written document that was executed anywhere prior to October 10, 1991, that voluntarily was so executed by an adult who was of sound mind, that was signed by the adult or by another individual at the direction of the adult, that was or was not witnessed or acknowledged before a notary public as described in division (B) of section 2133.02 of the Revised Code, and that specifies the adult's intention with respect to the use or continuation, or the withholding or withdrawal, of life-sustaining treatment if the adult is at any time in a terminal condition, in a permanently unconscious state, or in either a terminal condition or a permanently unconscious state, if the adult is at that time no longer able to make informed decisions regarding the administration of life-sustaining treatment, and if at that time there is no reasonable possibility that the adult will regain the capacity to make those informed decisions. The document shall be considered to be a declaration, shall be given effect as if it had been executed on or after October 10, 1991, in accordance with sections 2133.01 to 2133.15 of the Revised Code, and, except as otherwise provided in division (B) of this section, shall be subject to all provisions of sections 2133.01 to 2133.15 of the Revised Code pertaining to declarations.

(B)(1) If a declaration as described in division (A) of this section does not state that, or does not contain a checked or marked box or line adjacent to a statement indicating that, the declarant authorizes the declarant's attending physician to withhold or withdraw nutrition or hydration when the declarant is in a permanently unconscious state and when the declarant's attending physician and at least one other physician who has examined the declarant determine, to a reasonable degree of medical certainty and in accordance with reasonable medical standards, that nutrition or hydration will not or no longer will serve to provide comfort to the declarant or alleviate the declarant's pain, then, if the declaration becomes operative under section 2133.03 of the Revised Code because the declarant is in a permanently unconscious state, the attending physician of the declarant shall apply to the probate court of the county in which the declarant is located for the issuance of an order whether or not the attending physician is required to provide the declarant with nutrition and hydration for as long as the declarant is in the permanently unconscious state. Upon the filing of the application, the clerk of the probate court shall schedule a hearing on it and cause a copy of it and a notice of the hearing to be served in accordance with the Rules of Civil Procedure upon the attending physician and the individuals described in divisions (B)(1) to (5) of section 2133.08 of the Revised Code, which service shall be made, if possible, within three days after the filing of the application. The hearing shall be conducted at the earliest possible time, but no sooner than the thirtieth business day, and no later than the sixtieth business day, after that service has been completed.

(2) At the hearing, the attending physician and any individual described in divisions (B)(1) to (5) of section 2133.08 of the Revised Code shall be permitted to testify and present evidence relative to the use or continuation, or the withholding or withdrawal, of nutrition and hydration for as long as the declarant is in the permanently unconscious state. Immediately following the hearing, the court shall enter on its journal its determination, based on the evidence presented by all of the parties at the hearing on the application and subject to division (B)(3) of this section, whether or not the attending physician is required to provide the declarant with nutrition and hydration for as long as the declarant is in the permanently unconscious state.

(3) The court shall issue an order that authorizes the declarant's attending physician to commence the withholding or withdrawal of nutrition and hydration in connection with the declarant only if the applicant establishes, by clear and convincing evidence, that the order would be consistent with one of the following:

(a) The declarant's previously expressed intention with respect to the use or continuation, or the withholding or withdrawal, of nutrition and hydration should the declarant subsequently be in a permanently unconscious state and no longer able to make informed decisions regarding the administration of nutrition and hydration;

(b) In the absence of a previously expressed intention of that nature, the type of informed consent decision that the declarant would have made if the declarant had expressed the declarant's intention with respect to the use or continuation, or the withholding or withdrawal, of nutrition and hydration should the declarant subsequently be in a permanently unconscious state and no longer able to make informed decisions regarding the administration of nutrition and hydration, as inferred from the lifestyle and character of the declarant, and from any other evidence of the declarant's desires, prior to the declarant becoming no longer able to make informed decisions regarding the administration of nutrition and hydration. The Rules of Evidence shall not be binding for purposes of this division.

(4) Notwithstanding any contrary provision of the Revised Code or of the Rules of Civil Procedure, the state and persons other than individuals described in divisions (B)(1) to (5) of section 2133.08 of the Revised Code and other than the attending physician of the declarant are prohibited from filing an application under division (B) of this section and from joining or being joined as parties to a hearing conducted under division (B) of this section, including joining by way of intervention.

(1998 H 354, eff. 7–9–98; 1991 S 1, eff. 10–10–91)

Historical and Statutory Notes

Amendment Note: 1998 H 354 substituted "Sections 2133.01 to 2133.15 of the Revised Code" for "This chapter", "sections 2133.01 to 2133.15 of the Revised Code" for "this chapter", and "October 10, 1991" for "the effective date of this section" throughout; and made changes to reflect gender neutral language and other nonsubstantive changes.

Cross References

Probate court jurisdiction, 2101.24

Library References

Health ⇐902, 916.
Westlaw Topic No. 198H.
Baldwin's Ohio Legislative Service, 1991 Laws of Ohio, S 1—LSC Analysis, p 5–250

Research References

Encyclopedias
40 Am. Jur. Proof of Facts 3d 287, Proof of Basis for Refusal or Discontinuance of Life-Sustaining Treatment on Behalf of Incapacitated Person.
63 Am. Jur. Trials 1, Decisionmaking at the End of Life.

Forms
Ohio Forms and Transactions KP 24.06, Durable Power of Attorney for Health Care.
Ohio Forms and Transactions KP 30.23, Living Will, or Health Care Declaration.

Law Review and Journal Commentaries

Redrafting Ohio's Advance Directive Laws, Susan R. Martyn, et al. 26 Akron L Rev 229 (Fall 1992).

2133.16 Instrument of gift other than will

(A) As used in this section:

(1) "Anatomical gift" and "donor" have the same meanings as in section 2108.01 of the Revised Code.

(2) "Declarant" and "declaration" have the same meanings as in section 2133.01 of the Revised Code.

(B) A declarant may make an anatomical gift of all or part of the declarant's body by specifying the intent of the declarant to make the anatomical gift in a space provided in the declaration. All of the following apply to a declaration that specifies the intent of the declarant to make an anatomical gift:

(1) The declaration serves as a document other than a will in which a declarant makes an anatomical gift as provided in divisions (B)(1) and (3) of section 2108.04 of the Revised Code.

(2) The declaration is considered as having satisfied the requirements specified in divisions (B)(1) and (3) of section 2108.04 of the Revised Code to make an anatomical gift by a document other than a will.

(3) The declaration is subject to sections 2108.01 to 2108.12 of the Revised Code to the extent that the declaration specifies the intent of the declarant to make an anatomical gift.

(C) A declarant who makes an anatomical gift in the manner described in division (B) of this section may amend the anatomical gift under the circumstances and by any of the means provided in division (A) of section 2108.06 of the Revised Code.

(D) A declarant who makes an anatomical gift in the manner described in division (B) of this section may revoke the anatomical gift under the circumstances and by any of the means provided in division (A) of section 2108.06 of the Revised Code or by cancellation of the declarant's intent to make the anatomical gift as specified in the declaration.

(E) A declarant may refuse to make an anatomical gift of all or part of the declarant's body by specifying the intent of the declarant to refuse to make the anatomical gift in a space provided in the declaration.

(F) Nothing in this section requires a declarant to make, amend, or refuse to make an anatomical gift in a space provided in a declaration or otherwise limits a declarant from making, amending, or refusing to make an anatomical gift. The failure of a declarant to indicate in the space provided in the declaration the intent of the declarant to make an anatomical gift or to refuse to make an anatomical gift does not create a presumption of the intent of the declarant in regard to the matter of making or refusing to make an anatomical gift.

(2004 H 392, eff. 9–16–04)

Cross References

Anatomical gifts, forms of document of gift, 2108.10

Library References

Dead Bodies ⇐1.
Westlaw Topic No. 116.
C.J.S. Dead Bodies §§ 1 to 3.

Research References

Encyclopedias
OH Jur. 3d Cemeteries & Dead Bodies § 74, Manner of Making Anatomical Gift—by Declarant Under Modified Uniform Rights of the Terminally Ill Act.
OH Jur. 3d Cemeteries & Dead Bodies § 76, Amendment or Revocation of Anatomical Gift.

Forms
Ohio Forms Legal and Business § 24:380.30, Anatomical Gift by Next of Kin or Other Authorized Person.

Treatises and Practice Aids
Carlin, Baldwin's Ohio Practice, Merrick-Rippner Probate Law § 60:35.20, Declaration of Anatomical Gift.

DO NOT RESUSCITATE ORDERS

2133.21 Definitions

As used in sections 2133.21 to 2133.26 of the Revised Code, unless the context clearly requires otherwise:

(A) "Attending physician" means the physician to whom a person, or the family of a person, has assigned primary responsibility for the treatment or care of the person or, if the person or the person's family has not assigned that responsibility, the physician who has accepted that responsibility.

(B) "Declaration," "health care facility," "life–sustaining treatment," "physician," "professional disciplinary action," and "tort action" have the same meanings as in section 2133.01 of the Revised Code.

(C) "DNR identification" means a standardized identification card, form, necklace, or bracelet that is of uniform size and design, that has been approved by the department of health pursuant to section 2133.25 of the Revised Code, and that signifies either of the following:

(1) That the person who is named on and possesses the card, form, necklace, or bracelet has executed a declaration that authorizes the withholding or withdrawal of CPR and that has not been revoked pursuant to section 2133.04 of the Revised Code;

(2) That the attending physician of the person who is named on and possesses the card, form, necklace, or bracelet has issued a current do-not-resuscitate order, in accordance with the do-not-resuscitate protocol adopted by the department of health pursuant to section 2133.25 of the Revised Code, for that person and has documented the grounds for the order in that person's medical record.

(D) "Do–not–resuscitate order" means a directive issued by a physician that identifies a person and specifies that CPR should not be administered to the person so identified.

(E) "Do–not–resuscitate protocol" means the standardized method of procedure for the withholding of CPR by physicians, emergency medical service personnel, and health care facilities that is adopted in the rules of the department of health pursuant to section 2133.25 of the Revised Code.

(F) "Emergency medical services personnel" means paid or volunteer firefighters, law enforcement officers, first responders, emergency medical technicians-basic, emergency medical technicians-intermediate, emergency medical technicians-paramedic, medical technicians, or other emergency services personnel acting within the ordinary course of their profession.

(G) "CPR" means cardiopulmonary resuscitation or a component of cardiopulmonary resuscitation, but it does not include clearing a person's airway for a purpose other than as a component of CPR.

(1998 H 354, eff. 7–9–98)

Cross References

Durable power of attorney for health care, do-not-resuscitate order and DNR identification defined, 1337.12

Library References

Health ⇔916.
Westlaw Topic No. 198H.

Research References

Encyclopedias

OH Jur. 3d Agency & Independent Contractors § 46, Effect of a Do Not Resuscitate Declaration or Identification.

OH Jur. 3d Malpractice § 99, Under Statute Regarding Patients' Advance Directives; Generally.

OH Jur. 3d Malpractice § 103, Under Statute Regarding Patients' Advance Directives; Generally—Emergency Medical Services Personnel.

OH Jur. 3d Malpractice § 104, Under Statute Regarding Patients' Advance Directives; Generally—Certified Nurse Practitioner or Clinical Nurse Specialist.

Forms

Ohio Forms and Transactions KP 24.06, Durable Power of Attorney for Health Care.

Treatises and Practice Aids

Katz, Giannelli, Blair and Lipton, Baldwin's Ohio Practice, Criminal Law, § 108:6, Disorderly Conduct.

Carlin, Baldwin's Ohio Practice, Merrick-Rippner Probate Law § 60:35, Do-Not-Resuscitate Order.

Law Review and Journal Commentaries

Do not resuscitate decision-making: Ohio's Do Not Resuscitate Law should be amended to include a mature minor's right to initiate a DNR order. Note, 17 J L & Health 359 (2002–03).

Ohio's DNR Law: How Does It Differ from Advance Directive and How Will It Affect Your Practice, Renee M. Mallett. 15 Ohio Law 10 (January/February 2001).

2133.211 Actions by nurse practitioners or nurse specialists authorized

A person who holds a certificate of authority to practice as a certified nurse practitioner or clinical nurse specialist issued under section 4723.42 of the Revised Code may take any action that may be taken by an attending physician under sections 2133.21 to 2133.26 of the Revised Code and has the immunity provided by section 2133.22 of the Revised Code if the action is taken pursuant to a standard care arrangement with a collaborating physician.

(1998 H 354, eff. 7–9–98)

Library References

Health ⇔916.
Westlaw Topic No. 198H.

Research References

Encyclopedias

OH Jur. 3d Malpractice § 104, Under Statute Regarding Patients' Advance Directives; Generally—Certified Nurse Practitioner or Clinical Nurse Specialist.

2133.22 Criminal and civil immunities

(A)(1) None of the following are subject to criminal prosecution, to liability in damages in a tort or other civil action for injury, death, or loss to person or property, or to professional disciplinary action arising out of or relating to the withholding or withdrawal of CPR from a person after DNR identification is discovered in the person's possession and reasonable efforts have been made to determine that the person in possession of the DNR identification is the person named on the DNR identification:

(a) A physician who causes the withholding or withdrawal of CPR from the person possessing the DNR identification;

(b) A person who participates under the direction of or with the authorization of a physician in the withholding or withdrawal of CPR from the person possessing the DNR identification;

(c) Any emergency medical services personnel who cause or participate in the withholding or withdrawal of CPR from the person possessing the DNR identification.

(2) None of the following are subject to criminal prosecution, to liability in damages in a tort or other civil action for injury, death, or loss to person or property, or to professional disciplinary action arising out of or relating to the withholding or withdrawal of CPR from a person in a health care facility after DNR identification is discovered in the person's possession and reasonable efforts have been made to determine that the person in possession of the DNR identification is the person named on the DNR identification or a do-not-resuscitate order is issued for the person:

(a) The health care facility or the administrator of the health care facility;

(b) A physician who causes the withholding or withdrawal of CPR from the person possessing the DNR identification or for whom the do-not-resuscitate order has been issued;

(c) Any person who works for the health care facility as an employee, contractor, or volunteer and who participates under the direction of or with the authorization of a physician in the withholding or withdrawal of CPR from the person possessing the DNR identification;

(d) Any person who works for the health care facility as an employee, contractor, or volunteer and who participates under the direction of or with the authorization of a physician in the withholding or withdrawal of CPR from the person for whom the do-not-resuscitate order has been issued.

(3) If, after DNR identification is discovered in the possession of a person, the person makes an oral or written request to receive CPR, any person who provides CPR pursuant to the request, any health care facility in which CPR is provided, and the administrator of any health care facility in which CPR is provided are not subject to criminal prosecution as a result of the provision of the CPR, are not liable in damages in a tort or other civil action for injury, death, or loss to person or property that arises out of or is related to the provision of the CPR, and are not subject to professional disciplinary action as a result of the provision of the CPR.

(B) Divisions (A)(1), (A)(2), and (C) of this section do not apply when CPR is withheld or withdrawn from a person who possesses DNR identification or for whom a do-not-resuscitate order has been issued unless the withholding or withdrawal is in accordance with the do-not-resuscitate protocol.

(C) Any emergency medical services personnel who comply with a do-not-resuscitate order issued by a physician and any individuals who work for a health care facility as employees, contractors, or volunteers and who comply with a do-not-resuscitate order issued by a physician are not subject to liability in damages in a civil action for injury, death, or loss to person or property that arises out of or is related to compliance with the order, are not subject to criminal prosecution as a result of compliance with the order, and are not subject to professional disciplinary action as a result of compliance with the order.

In an emergency situation, emergency medical services personnel and emergency department personnel are not required to search a person to determine if the person possesses DNR identification. If a person possesses DNR identification, if emergency medical services personnel or emergency department personnel provide CPR to the person in an emergency situation, and if, at that time, the personnel do not know and do not have reasonable cause to believe that the person possesses DNR identification, the emergency medical services personnel and emergency department personnel are not subject to criminal prosecution as a result of the provision of the CPR, are not liable in damages in a tort or other civil action for injury, death, or loss to person or property that arises out of or is related to the provision of the CPR, and are not subject to professional disciplinary action as a result of the provision of the CPR.

(D) Nothing in sections 2133.21 to 2133.26 of the Revised Code or the do-not-resuscitate protocol grants immunity to a physician for issuing a do-not-resuscitate order that is contrary to reasonable medical standards or that the physician knows or has reason to know is contrary to the wishes of the patient or of a person who is lawfully authorized to make informed medical decisions on the patient's behalf.

(1998 H 354, eff. 7–9–98)

Library References

Health ⚖204, 916.
Homicide ⚖765.
Suicide ⚖3.
Westlaw Topic Nos. 198H, 203, 368.
C.J.S. Suicide §§ 8 to 12.

Research References

Encyclopedias

OH Jur. 3d Death § 28, Do-Not-Resuscitate Procedures.
OH Jur. 3d Malpractice § 99, Under Statute Regarding Patients' Advance Directives; Generally.
OH Jur. 3d Malpractice § 101, Under Statute Regarding Patients' Advance Directives; Generally—Withholding or Withdrawal of Cardiopulmonary Resuscitation.
OH Jur. 3d Malpractice § 102, Under Statute Regarding Patients' Advance Directives; Generally—Request by Person With Dnr Identification to Receive Cardiopulmonary Resuscitation.
OH Jur. 3d Malpractice § 103, Under Statute Regarding Patients' Advance Directives; Generally—Emergency Medical Services Personnel.
OH Jur. 3d Malpractice § 104, Under Statute Regarding Patients' Advance Directives; Generally—Certified Nurse Practitioner or Clinical Nurse Specialist.

Law Review and Journal Commentaries

Ohio's DNR Law: How Does It Differ from Advance Directive and How Will It Affect Your Practice, Renee M. Mallett. 15 Ohio Law 10 (January/February 2001).

2133.23 Compliance with DNR identification; transfer of person to different physician or facility; notice of DNR identification

(A) If emergency medical services personnel, other than physicians, are presented with DNR identification possessed by a person or are presented with a written do-not-resuscitate order for a person or if a physician directly issues to emergency medical services personnel, other than physicians, an oral do-not-resuscitate order for a person, the emergency medical services personnel shall comply with the do-not-resuscitate protocol for the person. If an oral do-not-resuscitate order is issued by a physician who is not present at the scene, the emergency medical services personnel shall verify the physician's identity.

(B) If a person possesses DNR identification and if the person's attending physician or the health care facility in which the person is located is unwilling or unable to comply with the do-not-resuscitate protocol for the person, the attending physician or the health care facility shall not prevent or attempt to prevent, or unreasonably delay or attempt to delay, the transfer of the person to a different physician who will follow the protocol or to a different health care facility in which the protocol will be followed.

(C) If a person who possesses DNR identification or for whom a current do-not-resuscitate order has been issued is being transferred from one health care facility to another, before or at the time of the transfer, the transferring health care facility shall notify the receiving health care facility and the persons transporting the person of the existence of the DNR identification or the order. If a current do-not-resuscitate order was issued orally, it shall be reduced to writing before the time of the transfer. The DNR identification or the order shall accompany the person to the receiving health care facility and shall remain in effect unless it is revoked or unless, in the case of a do-not-resuscitate order, the order no longer is current.

(1998 H 354, eff. 7–9–98)

Cross References

Prohibition: 2133.26

Library References

Health ⚖916.
Westlaw Topic No. 198H.

Law Review and Journal Commentaries

Do not resuscitate decision-making: Ohio's Do Not Resuscitate Law should be amended to include a mature minor's right to initiate a DNR order. Note, 17 J L & Health 359 (2002–03).

Ohio's DNR Law: How Does It Differ from Advance Directive and How Will It Affect Your Practice, Renee M. Mallett. 15 Ohio Law 10 (January/February 2001).

2133.24 Death not deemed suicide or homicide; effect of DNR identification on insurance and annuities; rights not affected

(A) The death of a person resulting from the withholding or withdrawal of CPR for the person pursuant to the do-not-resuscitate protocol and in the circumstances described in section 2133.22 of the Revised Code or in accordance with division (A) of section 2133.23 of the Revised Code does not constitute for any purpose a suicide, aggravated murder, murder, or any other homicide.

(B)(1) If a person possesses DNR identification or if a current do-not-resuscitate order has been issued for a person, the possession or order shall not do either of the following:

(a) Affect in any manner the sale, procurement, issuance, or renewal of a policy of life insurance or annuity, notwithstanding any term of a policy or annuity to the contrary;

(b) Be deemed to modify in any manner or invalidate the terms of any policy of life insurance or annuity that is in effect on the effective date of this section.

(2) Notwithstanding any term of a policy of life insurance or annuity to the contrary, the withholding or withdrawal of CPR from a person who is insured or covered under the policy or annuity and who possesses DNR identification or for whom a current do-not-resuscitate order has been issued, in accordance with sections 2133.21 to 2133.26 of the Revised Code, shall not impair or invalidate any policy of life insurance or annuity.

(3) Notwithstanding any term of a policy or plan to the contrary, neither of the following shall impair or invalidate any policy of health insurance or other health care benefit plan:

(a) The withholding or withdrawal in accordance with sections 2133.21 to 2133.26 of the Revised Code of CPR from a person who is insured or covered under the policy or plan and who possesses DNR identification or for whom a current do-not-resuscitate order has been issued;

(b) The provision in accordance with sections 2133.21 to 2133.26 of the Revised Code of CPR to a person of the nature described in division (B)(3)(a) of this section.

(4) No physician, health care facility, other health care provider, person authorized to engage in the business of insurance in this state under Title XXXIX of the Revised Code, health insuring corporation, other health care benefit plan, legal entity that is self-insured and provides benefits to its employees or members, or other person shall require an individual to possess DNR identification, or shall require an individual to revoke or refrain from possessing DNR identification, as a condition of being insured or of receiving health care benefits or services.

(C)(1) Sections 2133.21 to 2133.26 of the Revised Code do not create any presumption concerning the intent of an individual who does not possess DNR identification with respect to the use, withholding, or withdrawal of CPR.

(2) Sections 2133.21 to 2133.26 of the Revised Code do not affect the right of a person to make informed decisions regarding the use, withholding, or withdrawal of CPR for the person as long as the person is able to make those decisions.

(3) Sections 2133.21 to 2133.26 of the Revised Code are in addition to and independent of, and do not limit, impair, or supersede, any right or responsibility that a person has to effect the withholding or withdrawal of life-sustaining treatment to another pursuant to sections 2133.01 to 2133.15 of the Revised Code or in any other lawful manner.

(D) Nothing in sections 2133.21 to 2133.26 of the Revised Code condones, authorizes, or approves of mercy killing, assisted suicide, or euthanasia.

(1998 H 354, eff. 7–9–98)

Library References

Health ⚖916.
Homicide ⚖565, 765.
Insurance ⚖2434(1), 2436, 2456, 2457(1).
Suicide ⚖1, 3.
Westlaw Topic Nos. 198H, 203, 217, 368.
C.J.S. Insurance §§ 53, 55, 427, 989, 1172, 1178.
C.J.S. Suicide §§ 2 to 5, 8 to 12.

Law Review and Journal Commentaries

Respect for Life in Bioethical Dilemmas—The Case of Physician–Assisted Suicide, John A. Robertson. 45 Clev St L Rev 329 (1997).

2133.25 Rulemaking powers; advisory committee

(A) The department of health, by rule adopted pursuant to Chapter 119. of the Revised Code, shall adopt a standardized method of procedure for the withholding of CPR by physicians, emergency medical services personnel, and health care facilities in accordance with sections 2133.21 to 2133.26 of the Revised Code. The standardized method shall specify criteria for determining when a do-not-resuscitate order issued by a physician is current. The standardized method so adopted shall be the "do-not-resuscitate protocol" for purposes of sections 2133.21 to 2133.26 of the Revised Code. The department also shall approve one or more standard forms of DNR identification to be used throughout this state.

(B) The department of health shall adopt rules in accordance with Chapter 119. of the Revised Code for the administration of sections 2133.21 to 2133.26 of the Revised Code.

(C) The department of health shall appoint an advisory committee to advise the department in the development of rules under this section. The advisory committee shall include, but shall not be limited to, representatives of each of the following organizations:

(1) The association for hospitals and health systems (OHA);

(2) The Ohio state medical association;

(3) The Ohio chapter of the American college of emergency physicians;

(4) The Ohio hospice organization;

(5) The Ohio council for home care;

(6) The Ohio health care association;

(7) The Ohio ambulance association;

(8) The Ohio medical directors association;

(9) The Ohio association of emergency medical services;

(10) The bioethics network of Ohio;

(11) The Ohio nurses association;

(12) The Ohio academy of nursing homes;

(13) The Ohio association of professional firefighters;

(14) The department of mental retardation and developmental disabilities;

(15) The Ohio osteopathic association;

(16) The association of Ohio philanthropic homes, housing and services for the aging;

(17) The catholic conference of Ohio;

(18) The department of aging;

(19) The department of mental health;

(20) The Ohio private residential association;

(21) The northern Ohio fire fighters association.

(1998 H 354, eff. 7–9–98)

Ohio Administrative Code References

Attending physician, or CNP or CNS as provided in rule 3701–62–02 of the Administrative Code, or health care facility unwilling or unable to comply with DNR protocol, OAC 3701–62–08
Authority of certified nurse practitioners and clinical nurse specialists, OAC 3701–62–02
Compliance with DNR protocol not homicide or suicide, OAC 3701–62–11
Definitions, OAC 3701–62–01
Do-not-resuscitate identification, OAC 3701–62–04
Do-not-resuscitate protocol, OAC 3701–62–05
Effect of DNR identification or order on insurance, OAC 3701–62–12
Emergency medical services personnel; compliance with DNR protocol, OAC 3701–62–07
Immunity from criminal prosecution, civil liability, and professional disciplinary action, OAC 3701–62–03
Individual rights not abrogated, OAC 3701–62–13
Prohibitions, OAC 3701–62–14
Relationship of DNR orders and identification with declarations and durable powers of attorney for health care, OAC 3701–62–10
Revocation of DNR identification or DNR order, OAC 3701–62–06
Transfer of person between health care facilities; forwarding of DNR order, OAC 3701–62–09

Library References

Health ⚖︎194, 913.
Westlaw Topic No. 198H.

Research References

Encyclopedias

OH Jur. 3d Death § 28, Do-Not-Resuscitate Procedures.
OH Jur. 3d Malpractice § 99, Under Statute Regarding Patients' Advance Directives; Generally.

Law Review and Journal Commentaries

Ohio's DNR Law: How Does It Differ from Advance Directive and How Will It Affect Your Practice, Renee M. Mallett. 15 Ohio Law 10 (January/February 2001).

2133.26 Violations

(A)(1) No physician shall purposely prevent or attempt to prevent, or delay or unreasonably attempt to delay, the transfer of a patient in violation of division (B) of section 2133.23 of the Revised Code.

(2) No person shall purposely conceal, cancel, deface, or obliterate the DNR identification of another person without the consent of the other person.

(3) No person shall purposely falsify or forge a revocation of a declaration that is the basis of the DNR identification of another person or purposely falsify or forge an order of a physician that purports to supersede a do-not-resuscitate order issued for another person.

(4) No person shall purposely falsify or forge the DNR identification of another person with the intent to cause the use, withholding, or withdrawal of CPR for the other person.

(5) No person who has personal knowledge that another person has revoked a declaration that is the basis of the other person's DNR identification or personal knowledge that a physician has issued an order that supersedes a do-not-resuscitate order that the physician issued for another person shall purposely conceal or withhold that personal knowledge with the intent to cause the use, withholding, or withdrawal of CPR for the other person.

(B)(1) Whoever violates division (A)(1) or (5) of this section is guilty of a misdemeanor of the third degree.

(2) Whoever violates division (A)(2), (3), or (4) of this section is guilty of a misdemeanor of the first degree.

(1998 H 354, eff. 7–9–98)

Library References

Health ⚖︎975.
Westlaw Topic No. 198H.

Research References

Encyclopedias

OH Jur. 3d Cemeteries & Dead Bodies § 74, Manner of Making Anatomical Gift—by Declarant Under Modified Uniform Rights of the Terminally Ill Act.
OH Jur. 3d Cemeteries & Dead Bodies § 76, Amendment or Revocation of Anatomical Gift.
OH Jur. 3d Death § 24, Generally; Declarant's Rights.
OH Jur. 3d Death § 28, Do-Not-Resuscitate Procedures.
OH Jur. 3d Malpractice § 99, Under Statute Regarding Patients' Advance Directives; Generally.
OH Jur. 3d Malpractice § 104, Under Statute Regarding Patients' Advance Directives; Generally—Certified Nurse Practitioner or Clinical Nurse Specialist.

Treatises and Practice Aids

Carlin, Baldwin's Ohio Practice, Merrick-Rippner Probate Law § 60:35, Do-Not-Resuscitate Order.

CHAPTER 2135

DECLARATIONS FOR MENTAL HEALTH TREATMENT

Section	
2135.01	Definitions
2135.02	Execution of declaration governing mental health treatment
2135.03	Validity; revocation; renewal
2135.04	Operation of declaration
2135.05	Designation of proxy
2135.06	Validity of declaration
2135.07	Provider unwilling to comply with declaration
2135.08	Liability of proxy
2135.09	Revocation
2135.10	Liability of care provider
2135.11	Prohibited conduct
2135.12	Priority of declarations
2135.13	Dispute resolution; appointment of proxy
2135.14	Form

2135.01 Definitions

As used in sections 2135.01 to 2135.14 of the Revised Code:

(A) "Adult" means a person who is eighteen years of age or older.

(B) "Capacity to consent to mental health treatment decisions" means the functional ability to understand information about the risks of, benefits of, and alternatives to the proposed mental health treatment, to rationally use that information, to appreciate how that information applies to the declarant, and to express a choice about the proposed treatment.

(C) "Declarant" means an adult who has executed a declaration for mental health treatment in accordance with this chapter.

(D) "Declaration for mental health treatment" or "declaration" means a written document declaring preferences or instructions regarding mental health treatment executed in accordance with this chapter.

(E) "Designated physician" means the physician the declarant has named in a declaration for mental health treatment and has assigned the primary responsibility for the declarant's mental health treatment or, if the declarant has not so named a physician, the physician who has accepted that responsibility.

(F) "Guardian" means a person appointed by a probate court pursuant to Chapter 2111. of the Revised Code to have the care and management of the person of an incompetent.

(G) "Health care" means any care, treatment, service, or procedure to maintain, diagnose, or treat an individual's physical or mental condition or physical or mental health.

(H) "Health care facility" has the same meaning as in section 1337.11 of the Revised Code.

(I) "Incompetent" has the same meaning as in section 2111.01 of the Revised Code.

(J) "Informed consent" means consent voluntarily given by a person after a sufficient explanation and disclosure of the subject matter involved to enable that person to have a general understanding of the nature, purpose, and goal of the treatment or procedures, including the substantial risks and hazards inherent in the proposed treatment or procedures and any alternative treatment or procedures, and to make a knowing health care decision without coercion or undue influence.

(K) "Medical record" means any document or combination of documents that pertains to a declarant's medical history, diagnosis, prognosis, or medical condition and that is generated and maintained in the process of the declarant's health care.

(L) "Mental health treatment" means any care, treatment, service, or procedure to maintain, diagnose, or treat an individual's mental condition or mental health, including, but not limited to, electroconvulsive or other convulsive treatment, treatment of mental illness with medication, and admission to and retention in a health care facility.

(M) "Mental health treatment decision" means informed consent, refusal to give informed consent, or withdrawal of informed consent to mental health treatment.

(N) "Mental health treatment provider" means physicians, physician assistants, psychologists, licensed independent social workers, licensed professional clinical counselors, and psychiatric nurses.

(O) "Physician" means a person who is authorized under Chapter 4731. of the Revised Code to practice medicine and surgery or osteopathic medicine and surgery.

(P) "Professional disciplinary action" means action taken by the board or other entity that regulates the professional conduct of health care personnel, including, but not limited to, the state medical board, the state board of psychology, and the state board of nursing.

(Q) "Proxy" means an adult designated to make mental health treatment decisions for a declarant under a valid declaration for mental health treatment.

(R) "Psychiatric nurse" means a registered nurse who holds a master's degree or doctorate in nursing with a specialization in psychiatric nursing.

(S) "Psychiatrist" has the same meaning as in section 5122.01 of the Revised Code.

(T) "Psychologist" has the same meaning as in section 4732.01 of the Revised Code.

(U) "Registered nurse" has the same meaning as in section 4723.01 of the Revised Code.

(V) "Tort action" means a civil action for damages for injury, death, or loss to person or property, other than a civil action for damages for a breach of contract or another agreement between persons.

(2003 H 72, eff. 10–29–03)

Research References

Encyclopedias

OH Jur. 3d Agency & Independent Contractors § 44, Generally; Expiration.

Treatises and Practice Aids

Carlin, Baldwin's Ohio Practice, Merrick-Rippner Probate Law § 67:7, Alternatives to Guardianship—Adult Wards.

Carlin, Baldwin's Ohio Practice, Merrick-Rippner Probate Law § 60:16, Power of Attorney for Health Care—Ohio Legislation.

Carlin, Baldwin's Ohio Practice, Merrick-Rippner Probate Law § 60:19, Power of Attorney for Health Care—Health Care Declaration.

Carlin, Baldwin's Ohio Practice, Merrick-Rippner Probate Law § 60:23, Power of Attorney for Health Care—Expiration; Revocation.

Carlin, Baldwin's Ohio Practice, Merrick-Rippner Probate Law § 60:32, Power of Attorney for Health Care—Withholding or Withdrawing Life-Support Measures or Other Care—Comfort Care; Nutrition and Hydration.

Carlin, Baldwin's Ohio Practice, Merrick-Rippner Probate Law § 60:35.30, Declaration for Mental Health Treatment.

2135.02 Execution of declaration governing mental health treatment

(A) An adult who has the capacity to consent to mental health treatment decisions voluntarily may execute at any time a declaration governing the use or continuation, or the withholding or withdrawal, of mental health treatment. The declaration shall be signed at the end by the declarant, state the date of its execution, and either be witnessed or be acknowledged in accordance with section 2135.06 of the Revised Code. The declaration may include a designation by the declarant of a person to act as a proxy to make decisions regarding mental health treatment pursuant to the declaration, and, if the declaration includes a designation of a proxy, the declaration shall be signed at the end by the designated proxy. The declarant may also specifically designate in the declaration an alternate proxy to act in that role if the original proxy is unable or unwilling to act at any time, and, if the declaration includes a designation of an alternate proxy, the declaration shall be signed at the end by the designated alternate proxy. The declarant may name in the declaration a physician and assign the physician the primary responsibility for the declarant's mental health treatment. The declaration may include a specific authorization for the use or continuation, or the withholding or withdrawal, of mental health treatment.

(B) A mental health treatment provider or a health care facility providing services to a declarant shall continue to obtain the declarant's informed consent to all mental health treatment decisions if the declarant has the capacity to consent to mental health treatment decisions.

(2003 H 72, eff. 10–29–03)

Library References

Health ⇔912.
Mental Health ⇔51.15.
Westlaw Topic Nos. 198H, 257A.
C.J.S. Mental Health §§ 86 to 87.

Research References

Encyclopedias

OH Jur. 3d Agency & Independent Contractors § 33, Creation Formalities.

OH Jur. 3d Agency & Independent Contractors § 44, Generally; Expiration.

Treatises and Practice Aids

Carlin, Baldwin's Ohio Practice, Merrick-Rippner Probate Law § 60:35.40, Declaration for Mental Health Treatment—Capacity and Formalities of Execution.

Carlin, Baldwin's Ohio Practice, Merrick-Rippner Probate Law § 60:35.50, Declaration for Mental Health Treatment—Designation of a Proxy.

Carlin, Baldwin's Ohio Practice, Merrick-Rippner Probate Law § 60:35.60, Declaration for Mental Health Treatment—Withholding or Withdrawal of Treatment.

2135.03 Validity; revocation; renewal

(A) Except as otherwise provided in this division and subject to division (C) of this section, a declaration for mental health treatment remains valid and effective for three years after its execution unless it is properly revoked. A declaration for mental health treatment may become operative as provided in section 2135.04 of the Revised Code. If the declaration becomes operative, the authority of a proxy named in the declaration continues in effect as long as the declaration designating the proxy is in effect or until the proxy has withdrawn. If a declaration for mental health treatment has become operative and is in effect at the expiration of three years after its execution, the declaration remains effective until the declarant has the capacity to consent to mental health treatment decisions. If a declaration for mental health treatment has not become operative at the expiration of three years after its execution, the declaration may be renewed as provided in division (C)(1) of this section or remains effective as provided in division (C)(2) of this section.

(B) A valid declaration may be revoked in accordance with section 2135.09 of the Revised Code or renewed in accordance with division (C)(1) of this section, but it shall not otherwise be altered or amended after it has been executed. A properly executed declaration is not revoked or invalidated by an alteration of or amendment to the declaration. Any alteration of or amendment to the declaration is not a part of the declaration.

(C)(1) A declarant may renew a declaration once, extending the validity of the document for an additional three-year period from the date of the renewal, by repeating the procedures set forth in section 2135.06 of the Revised Code, if the declarant has included in the declaration a specific authorization for the use or continuation, or the withholding or withdrawal, of mental health treatment, and the declarant makes no change with respect to that authorization. A declarant shall not make any changes to any term or provision of the declaration when renewing under division (C)(1) of this section.

(2) A declaration for mental health treatment that has not become operative at the expiration of three years after its execution remains effective if both of the following apply:

(a) The declaration designates a proxy or an alternate proxy.

(b) The declarant does not include in the declaration a specific authorization for the use or continuation, or the witholding[1] or withdrawal, of mental health treatment.

(2003 H 72, eff. 10–29–03)

[1] So in original; 2003 H 72.

Library References

Health ⇔912.
Mental Health ⇔51.15.
Westlaw Topic Nos. 198H, 257A.
C.J.S. Mental Health §§ 86 to 87.

Research References

Encyclopedias

OH Jur. 3d Agency & Independent Contractors § 39, Termination or Revocation of Authority.

OH Jur. 3d Agency & Independent Contractors § 44, Generally; Expiration.

OH Jur. 3d Agency & Independent Contractors § 51, Expiration and Revocation.

Treatises and Practice Aids

Carlin, Baldwin's Ohio Practice, Merrick-Rippner Probate Law § 60:35.70, Declaration for Mental Health Treatment—Time Limit.

2135.04 Operation of declaration

(A) A declaration becomes operative when both of the following apply:

(1) The declaration is communicated to a mental health treatment provider of the declarant.

(2) The designated physician or a psychiatrist, and one other mental health treatment provider, who examine the declarant determine that the declarant does not have the capacity to consent to mental health treatment decisions. At least one of the two persons who make this determination shall not currently be involved in the declarant's treatment at the time of the determination. If a designated physician is named in the declaration and is not one of the two persons who make this determination, then the psychiatrist who makes the determination in lieu of the designated physician shall make a good faith effort to consult with the designated physician as soon as practicable.

(B) A mental health treatment provider for a declarant or a health care facility providing services to a declarant shall make a declaration part of the declarant's medical record and shall note in that record when the declaration is operative.

(C) A mental health treatment provider for a declarant or a health care facility providing services to a declarant shall act in accordance with an operative declaration of the declarant consistent with reasonable medical practice, the availability of treatments requested, and applicable law. The mental health treatment provider or the health care facility shall continue to act in accordance with an operative declaration until the declarant has the capacity to consent to mental health treatment decisions.

(D) An operative declaration of a declarant supersedes any general consent to treatment form signed by the declarant prior to, upon, or after the declarant's admission to a health care facility to the extent there is a conflict between the declaration and the form, even if the declarant signs the form after the execution of the declaration. To the extent that the provisions of a declarant's declaration and a general consent to treatment form signed by the declarant do not conflict, both documents shall govern the use or continuation, or the withholding or withdrawal, of mental health treatment for the declarant. This division does not apply if a declarant revokes a declaration after the declarant signs a general consent to treatment form.

(2003 H 72, eff. 10–29–03)

Library References

Health ⇔912.
Mental Health ⇔51.15.
Westlaw Topic Nos. 198H, 257A.
C.J.S. Mental Health §§ 86 to 87.

Research References

Encyclopedias

OH Jur. 3d Agency & Independent Contractors § 33, Creation Formalities.

OH Jur. 3d Agency & Independent Contractors § 44, Generally; Expiration.

Treatises and Practice Aids

Carlin, Baldwin's Ohio Practice, Merrick-Rippner Probate Law § 60:35.90, Declaration for Mental Health Treatment—Other Provisions as to Operation of the Declaration.

2135.05 Designation of proxy

(A) A declaration may designate an adult to act as a proxy to make decisions about the mental health treatment of the declarant and may designate an adult as an alternate proxy as described in section 2135.02 of the Revised Code. A proxy designated to make decisions about mental health treatment may make decisions about mental health treatment on behalf of the declarant only when the declaration has become operative. The decisions of the proxy regarding the mental health treatment of the declarant must be consistent with desires the declarant has expressed in the declaration.

(B) The following persons may not serve as a proxy for a declarant:

(1) The declarant's mental health treatment provider, or an employee of the declarant's mental health treatment provider;

(2) The owner, operator, or employee of a health care facility in which the declarant is a patient receiving its services or a resident.

(C) Divisions (B)(1) and (2) of this section do not apply if the declarant and proxy are related by blood, marriage, or adoption.

(D) A proxy may withdraw from a declaration prior to the declaration becoming operative by giving notice to the declarant. If the declaration is operative, a proxy may withdraw by giving written notice to the declarant's mental health treatment provider or the health care facility providing services to the declarant. The mental health treatment provider or the health care facility shall note the withdrawal of a proxy as part of the declarant's medical record.

(2003 H 72, eff. 10-29-03)

Library References

Health ☞912.
Mental Health ☞34, 51.15.
Westlaw Topic Nos. 198H, 257A.
C.J.S. Mental Health §§ 47, 86 to 87.

Research References

Encyclopedias

OH Jur. 3d Agency & Independent Contractors § 33, Creation Formalities.

OH Jur. 3d Agency & Independent Contractors § 59, Required Form of Durable Power of Attorney for Health Care.

Treatises and Practice Aids

Carlin, Baldwin's Ohio Practice, Merrick-Rippner Probate Law § 3:2, Jurisdiction of Probate Court—Statutory.

Carlin, Baldwin's Ohio Practice, Merrick-Rippner Probate Law § 60:35.80, Declaration of Mental Health Treatment—Probate Court Jurisdiction.

Carlin, Baldwin's Ohio Practice, Merrick-Rippner Probate Law § 60:35.90, Declaration for Mental Health Treatment—Other Provisions as to Operation of the Declaration.

2135.06 Validity of declaration

(A) A declaration for mental health treatment is valid only if it is signed by the declarant, states the date of its execution, and is either witnessed by two adults or acknowledged before a notary public.

If a proxy, or a proxy and an alternate proxy, have been designated in the declaration, then each proxy also shall sign the declaration, and the signature of each proxy shall be either witnessed by two adults or acknowledged before a notary public, except that, notwithstanding these requirements, both of the following apply:

(1) No declaration shall be invalid or be held invalid because a proxy has not signed the declaration.

(2) If a proxy has not signed the declaration, or if the signature of a proxy named in a valid declaration is not either witnessed by two adults or acknowledged before a notary public, then the designation of the proxy is invalid, but the declaration is not invalid because of the absence of a witnessed or acknowledged signature of a proxy.

(B) If witnessed for purposes of this section, a declaration shall be witnessed by two individuals as described in this division in whose presence the declarant and each designated proxy signs the declaration. Each witness shall subscribe the witness' signature after the signature of the declarant and, by doing so, attest to the witness' belief that the declarant appears to be of sound mind and not under or subject to duress, fraud, or undue influence. The signatures of the declarant and any proxy under this section and of the witnesses under this division are not required to appear on the same page of the declaration.

(C) If acknowledged for purposes of this section, a declaration shall be acknowledged before a notary public, who shall make the certification described in section 147.53 of the Revised Code and also shall attest that the declarant and each designated proxy appear to be of sound mind and not under or subject to duress, fraud, or undue influence.

(D) The following may not serve as a witness to the signing of a declarant's declaration:

(1) The declarant's mental health treatment provider or a relative or employee of the declarant's mental health treatment provider;

(2) The owner, the operator, or a relative or employee of an owner or operator of a health care facility in which the declarant is a patient receiving its services or a resident;

(3) A person related to the declarant by blood, marriage, or adoption;

(4) A person named as a proxy in the declarant's declaration.

(2003 H 72, eff. 10-29-03)

Library References

Health ☞912.
Mental Health ☞51.15.
Westlaw Topic Nos. 198H, 257A.
C.J.S. Mental Health §§ 86 to 87.

Research References

Encyclopedias

OH Jur. 3d Agency & Independent Contractors § 33, Creation Formalities.

OH Jur. 3d Agency & Independent Contractors § 59, Required Form of Durable Power of Attorney for Health Care.

Treatises and Practice Aids

Carlin, Baldwin's Ohio Practice, Merrick-Rippner Probate Law § 60:35.40, Declaration for Mental Health Treatment—Capacity and Formalities of Execution.

Carlin, Baldwin's Ohio Practice, Merrick-Rippner Probate Law § 60:35.90, Declaration for Mental Health Treatment—Other Provisions as to Operation of the Declaration.

2135.07 Provider unwilling to comply with declaration

(A) If a mental health treatment provider of a declarant or a health care facility providing services to a declarant is unwilling at any time to comply with the declarant's declaration, the mental health treatment provider or health care facility promptly shall notify the declarant and any proxy and document the notification in the declarant's medical record. The mental health treatment provider or health care facility that is unwilling to comply with the declarant's declaration shall not prevent or attempt to prevent, or unreasonably delay or attempt to unreasonably delay, the transfer of the declarant to the care of a mental health treatment provider or a health care facility that is willing and able to comply or allow compliance with the declarant's declaration.

(B) The mental health treatment provider of a declarant or a health care facility providing services to a declarant may subject the declarant to treatment in a manner contrary to the declarant's expressed wishes only if either of the following applies:

(1) The declarant has been committed as a patient under Chapter 2945. or 5122. of the Revised Code, and, if the court knows of the declaration, the committing court acknowledges the existence of the declaration and specifically orders treatment in a manner contrary to the declaration.

(2) An emergency situation endangers the life or health of the declarant or others.

(2003 H 72, eff. 10–29–03)

Library References

Health ⟐912.
Mental Health ⟐51.15.
Westlaw Topic Nos. 198H, 257A.
C.J.S. Mental Health §§ 86 to 87.

Research References

Encyclopedias

OH Jur. 3d Agency & Independent Contractors § 57, Refusal to Comply With Instructions.
OH Jur. 3d Hosp. & Related Facil.; Hlth. Care Pro. § 111, Rights, Generally.
OH Jur. 3d Incompetent Persons § 65, Treatment.

Treatises and Practice Aids

Carlin, Baldwin's Ohio Practice, Merrick-Rippner Probate Law § 60:35.90, Declaration for Mental Health Treatment—Other Provisions as to Operation of the Declaration.

2135.08 Liability of proxy

(A) The proxy under a declaration is not, as a result of acting in that capacity, personally liable for the cost of treatment provided to the declarant. Except to the extent the right is limited by the declaration or any federal law, a proxy has the same right as the declarant to receive information regarding the proposed mental health treatment of the declarant and to receive, review, and consent to disclosure of the declarant's medical records relating to that treatment. This right of access does not waive any evidentiary privilege.

(B) In exercising authority under a declaration, the proxy has a duty to act consistently with the desires of the declarant as expressed in the declaration. If the declarant's desires are not expressed in the declaration, the proxy has a duty to act in what the proxy in good faith believes to be the best interests of the declarant.

(C) A proxy is not subject to criminal prosecution, tort or other civil liability for injury, death, or loss to person or property, or professional disciplinary action for an action taken in good faith under a declaration for mental health treatment.

(2003 H 72, eff. 10–29–03)

Library References

Health ⟐912.
Mental Health ⟐34, 51.15, 476.
Westlaw Topic Nos. 198H, 257A.
C.J.S. Mental Health §§ 47, 86 to 87, 256 to 257.

Research References

Encyclopedias

OH Jur. 3d Agency & Independent Contractors § 43, Liability of Attorney in Fact; Fiduciary Relationship.
OH Jur. 3d Agency & Independent Contractors § 62, Extent of Authority.
OH Jur. 3d Incompetent Persons § 17, Liability of Persons Assisting in Hospitalization or Discharge.
OH Jur. 3d Incompetent Persons § 68, Consent to Treatment.

Treatises and Practice Aids

Carlin, Baldwin's Ohio Practice, Merrick-Rippner Probate Law § 60:35.90, Declaration for Mental Health Treatment—Other Provisions as to Operation of the Declaration.

2135.09 Revocation

(A) A declarant may revoke a declaration at any time the declarant has the capacity to consent to mental health treatment decisions. Any revocation of a declaration by a declarant shall be in writing, signed by the declarant, and dated. The revocation shall be effective upon its communication to the mental health treatment provider of the declarant or the health care facility providing services to the declarant. If the declaration is operative, then the declarant may revoke the declaration after a designated physician or a psychiatrist, and one other mental health treatment provider, who examine the declarant determine that the declarant has the capacity to consent to mental health treatment decisions.

(B) Upon the declarant's revocation of a declaration, the mental health treatment provider or the health care facility shall make the revocation a part of the declarant's medical record.

(C) A valid declaration for mental health treatment revokes a prior, valid declaration for mental health treatment.

(D) The probate judge of the county in which the declarant is located may revoke a declaration if the judge appoints a guardian for the declarant and specifically orders the revocation of the declaration.

(2003 H 72, eff. 10–29–03)

Library References

Health ⟐912.
Mental Health ⟐51.15.
Westlaw Topic Nos. 198H, 257A.
C.J.S. Mental Health §§ 86 to 87.

Research References

Encyclopedias

OH Jur. 3d Agency & Independent Contractors § 39, Termination or Revocation of Authority.
OH Jur. 3d Agency & Independent Contractors § 51, Expiration and Revocation.
OH Jur. 3d Incompetent Persons § 68, Consent to Treatment.

Treatises and Practice Aids

Carlin, Baldwin's Ohio Practice, Merrick-Rippner Probate Law § 60:35.90, Declaration for Mental Health Treatment—Other Provisions as to Operation of the Declaration.

2135.10 Liability of care provider

A mental health treatment provider of a declarant, a health care facility providing services to a declarant, or other authorized persons acting under the direction of either a mental health treatment provider of a declarant or a health care facility providing services to a declarant who administer or do not administer mental health treatment according to and in good faith reliance upon the validity of the declarant's declaration are not subject to criminal prosecution, are not liable in tort or other civil damages for injury, death, or loss to person or property, and are not subject to professional disciplinary action resulting from a subsequent finding of a declaration's invalidity.

(2003 H 72, eff. 10-29-03)

Library References

Health ⚖︎912.
Mental Health ⚖︎51.15, 475.1.
Westlaw Topic Nos. 198H, 257A.
C.J.S. Mental Health §§ 86 to 87, 256 to 257.

Research References

Encyclopedias
OH Jur. 3d Agency & Independent Contractors § 52, Immunity for Actions Taken Pursuant to Power; Attending Physician.
OH Jur. 3d Agency & Independent Contractors § 53, Immunity of Consulting Physician; Other Health Care Personnel and Employees.
OH Jur. 3d Agency & Independent Contractors § 54, Immunity of Health Care Facility and Attorney in Fact.
OH Jur. 3d Incompetent Persons § 17, Liability of Persons Assisting in Hospitalization or Discharge.

2135.11 Prohibited conduct

No person shall require an individual to execute or to refrain from executing a declaration as a criterion for insurance, as a condition for receiving mental health treatment or health care, or as a condition of admission to or discharge from a health care facility.

(2003 H 72, eff. 10-29-03)

Library References

Health ⚖︎912.
Mental Health ⚖︎51.15.
Westlaw Topic Nos. 198H, 257A.
C.J.S. Mental Health §§ 86 to 87.

Research References

Encyclopedias
OH Jur. 3d Agency & Independent Contractors § 56, Freedom to Create or Decline.

2135.12 Priority of declarations

(A) A declaration executed in accordance with this chapter shall not supersede a valid declaration governing the use or continuation, or the withholding or withdrawal, of life-sustaining treatment executed under Chapter 2133. of the Revised Code.

(B) A declaration executed in accordance with this chapter does not revoke a valid durable power of attorney for health care created under Chapter 1337. of the Revised Code, but a declaration so executed shall supersede the designation of an attorney in fact made in a valid health care power of attorney under Chapter 1337. of the Revised Code with respect to the mental health treatment of the declarant. The designation of an attorney in fact in a valid health care power of attorney under Chapter 1337. of the Revised Code shall remain effective in all other respects.

(2003 H 72, eff. 10-29-03)

Library References

Health ⚖︎912, 915 to 916.
Mental Health ⚖︎51.15.
Westlaw Topic Nos. 198H, 257A.
C.J.S. Mental Health §§ 86 to 87.

Research References

Encyclopedias
OH Jur. 3d Agency & Independent Contractors § 39, Termination or Revocation of Authority.
OH Jur. 3d Agency & Independent Contractors § 46, Effect of a Do Not Resuscitate Declaration or Identification.
OH Jur. 3d Agency & Independent Contractors § 47, Extent of Authority, Generally.
OH Jur. 3d Agency & Independent Contractors § 51, Expiration and Revocation.

Treatises and Practice Aids
Carlin, Baldwin's Ohio Practice, Merrick-Rippner Probate Law § 60:19, Power of Attorney for Health Care—Health Care Declaration.
Carlin, Baldwin's Ohio Practice, Merrick-Rippner Probate Law § 60:29, Power of Attorney for Health Care—Withholding or Withdrawing Life-Support Measures or Other Care.

2135.13 Dispute resolution; appointment of proxy

(A) A person who opposes any decision arising under this chapter may make an application opposing the decision to the probate division of the court of common pleas of the county in which the declarant is located or in which the declaration was either witnessed or acknowledged as described in this chapter.

(B) If a declarant has not named any proxies in the declaration, or if all the named proxies have withdrawn or are unable or unwilling to act at a time when the declaration has become operative, then the physician who has the primary responsibility for treating the declarant may petition the probate division of the court of common pleas of the county in which the declarant is located to appoint a person to act as a proxy. If the judge of the probate division of the court of common pleas finds it to be in the best interest of the declarant, then the court shall appoint a person to serve as a proxy for the declarant while the declaration is effective. The person so appointed shall be a person who is eligible to serve as a proxy as determined under section 2135.05 of the Revised Code.

(2003 H 72, eff. 10-29-03)

Library References

Health ⚖︎912.
Mental Health ⚖︎51.15.
Westlaw Topic Nos. 198H, 257A.
C.J.S. Mental Health §§ 86 to 87.

Research References

Encyclopedias
OH Jur. 3d Agency & Independent Contractors § 58, Refusal to Comply With Instructions—Objection to Health Care Decision; Court Order.
OH Jur. 3d Incompetent Persons § 65, Treatment.

Treatises and Practice Aids
Carlin, Baldwin's Ohio Practice, Merrick-Rippner Probate Law § 3:2, Jurisdiction of Probate Court—Statutory.
Carlin, Baldwin's Ohio Practice, Merrick-Rippner Probate Law § 60:35.80, Declaration of Mental Health Treatment—Probate Court Jurisdiction.

2135.14 Form

A printed form of a declaration may be sold or otherwise distributed in this state for use by adults who are not advised by an attorney. By use of a printed form of that nature, a declarant may consent or refuse to consent to mental health treatment and may designate a proxy to make mental health treatment decisions in accordance with this chapter. The printed form shall not be used as an instrument for granting any other type of authority or for making any other type of designation, including those declarations that may be made under Chapter 2133. of the Revised Code or designations made under Chapter 1337. of the Revised Code.

(2003 H 72, eff. 10–29–03)

Library References

Health ⛭912.
Mental Health ⛭51.15.
Westlaw Topic Nos. 198H, 257A.
C.J.S. Mental Health §§ 86 to 87.

Research References

Encyclopedias

OH Jur. 3d Agency & Independent Contractors § 17, Mode of Creation; Form of Appointment.

OH Jur. 3d Agency & Independent Contractors § 33, Creation Formalities.

OH Jur. 3d Agency & Independent Contractors § 44, Generally; Expiration.

OH Jur. 3d Agency & Independent Contractors § 59, Required Form of Durable Power of Attorney for Health Care.

Treatises and Practice Aids

Carlin, Baldwin's Ohio Practice, Merrick-Rippner Probate Law § 67:7, Alternatives to Guardianship—Adult Wards.

Carlin, Baldwin's Ohio Practice, Merrick-Rippner Probate Law § 60:35.30, Declaration for Mental Health Treatment.

Carlin, Baldwin's Ohio Practice, Merrick-Rippner Probate Law § 60:35.90, Declaration for Mental Health Treatment—Other Provisions as to Operation of the Declaration.

CHAPTER 2151

JUVENILE COURTS—GENERAL PROVISIONS

CONSTRUCTION; DEFINITIONS

Section	
2151.01	Construction; purpose
2151.011	Definitions
2151.022	"Unruly child" defined
2151.03	"Neglected child" defined
2151.031	"Abused child" defined
2151.04	"Dependent child" defined
2151.05	Child without proper parental care
2151.06	Residence or legal settlement

ADMINISTRATION, OFFICIALS, AND JURISDICTION

Section	
2151.07	Creation and powers of juvenile court; assignment of judge
2151.08	Juvenile court in Hamilton county
2151.09	Separate building and site may be purchased or leased
2151.10	Appropriation for expenses of the court and maintenance of children; hearing; action in court of appeals; limitation of contempt power
2151.12	Clerk; judge as clerk; bond
2151.13	Employees; compensation; bond
2151.14	Duties and powers of probation department; records; command assistance; notice to victim of accused sex offender's communicable disease; order to provide copies of records
2151.141	Requests for copies of records
2151.142	Confidentiality of residential addresses; exceptions
2151.15	Powers and duties vested in county department of probation
2151.151	Juvenile court may contract for services to children on probation
2151.152	Agreement to reimburse juvenile court for foster care maintenance costs and associated administrative and training costs
2151.16	Referees; powers and duties
2151.17	Rules governing practice and procedure
2151.18	Records of cases; annual report
2151.19	Summons; expense
2151.20	Seal of court; dimensions
2151.21	Jurisdiction in contempt
2151.211	Employee's attendance at proceeding; employer may not penalize
2151.22	Terms of court; sessions
2151.23	Jurisdiction of juvenile court; orders for child support
2151.231	Action for child support order
2151.232	Action for child support order before acknowledgment becomes final
2151.24	Separate room for hearings

PRACTICE AND PROCEDURE

Section	
2151.27	Complaint
2151.271	Transfer to juvenile court of another county
2151.28	Summons
2151.281	Guardian ad litem
2151.282	Court appointed special advocate/guardian ad litem study committee
2151.29	Service of summons
2151.30	Issuance of warrant
2151.31	Apprehension, custody, and detention
2151.311	Procedure upon apprehension
2151.312	Place of detention
2151.313	Fingerprinting or photographing child in an investigation
2151.314	Detention hearing
2151.32	Selection of custodian
2151.33	Temporary care; emergency medical treatment; reimbursement
2151.331	Detention in certified foster home; arrangement for temporary care; alternative diversion programs

HEARING AND DISPOSITION

Section	
2151.35	Hearing procedure; findings; record
2151.352	Right to counsel
2151.353	Disposition of abused, neglected, or dependent child
2151.354	Disposition of unruly child; driver's license suspension; habitual truants
2151.355	Expunged or sealed records defined
2151.356	Criteria for sealing records; notice
2151.357	Effect of sealed records; retention; limited disclosure
2151.358	Expungement of sealed records
2151.359	Control of conduct of parent, guardian, or custodian; contempt
2151.3510	Notice of intended dispositional order
2151.3514	Orders requiring alcohol and drug addiction assessment, treatment, and testing of parents or caregivers
2151.3515	Definitions
2151.3516	Persons authorized to take possession of deserted child
2151.3517	Duties of persons taking possession of deserted child
2151.3518	Duties of public children services agencies
2151.3519	Emergency hearings; adjudications
2151.3520	Temporary custody orders
2151.3521	Deserted child treated as neglected child

JUVENILE COURTS—GENERAL PROVISIONS   Ch 2151

Section	
2151.3522	Case plans, investigations, administrative reviews, and services
2151.3523	Immunity from criminal liability; exceptions
2151.3524	Anonymity of parent; exceptions
2151.3525	Completion of medical information forms by parents
2151.3526	Refusal of parents to accept written materials
2151.3527	Coercion prohibited
2151.3528	DNA testing of parents
2151.3529	Medical information forms; written materials
2151.3530	Distribution of forms and materials by job and family services department
2151.36	Support of child
2151.361	Payment for care, support, maintenance, and education of child
2151.362	Cost of education
2151.37	Institution receiving children required to make report
2151.38	Temporary nature of dispositional orders
2151.39	Placement of children from other states
2151.40	Cooperation with court

GENERAL PROVISIONS

2151.412	Case plans
2151.413	Motion for permanent custody
2151.414	Procedures upon motion
2151.415	Motions for dispositional orders; procedure
2151.416	Administrative review of case plans
2151.417	Review by court issuing dispositional orders
2151.419	Hearings on efforts of agencies to prevent removal of children from homes
2151.42	Modification or termination of dispositional order
2151.421	Persons required to report injury or neglect; procedures on receipt of report
2151.422	Investigations concerning children in domestic violence or homeless shelters; services; custody; confidentiality of information
2151.423	Confidential information disclosure
2151.424	Notice of dispositional hearings

CHILDREN'S ADVOCACY CENTERS

2151.425	Definitions
2151.426	Children's advocacy center; memorandum of understanding with other entities regarding child abuse
2151.427	Multidisciplinary team; members; powers and duties
2151.428	Interagency agreements relating to child abuse

ADULT CASES

2151.43	Charges against adults; defendant bound over to grand jury
2151.44	Complaint after hearing
2151.49	Suspension of sentence
2151.50	Forfeiture of bond
2151.52	Appeals on questions of law
2151.53	Physical and mental examinations; records of examination; expenses

FEES AND COSTS

2151.54	Fees and costs; waiver
2151.541	Additional fees for computer services

PLACEMENT OF CHILDREN IN FOSTER HOMES OUTSIDE COUNTIES OF RESIDENCE

2151.55	Persons entitled to oral communication of intended placement
2151.551	Requirements of oral communication of intended placement
2151.552	Time for provision of written information
2151.553	School district procedures for receiving information
2151.554	Provision of written information to juvenile court

INTERSTATE COMPACT ON JUVENILES

2151.56	Interstate compact on juveniles
2151.57	Compact administrator; powers and duties
2151.58	Supplementary agreements
2151.59	Discharge of financial obligations
2151.60	Enforcement by agencies of state and subdivisions
2151.61	Additional article

FACILITIES FOR TRAINING, TREATMENT, AND REHABILITATION OF JUVENILES

2151.65	Facilities for treatment of juveniles; joint boards; admission
2151.651	Application for financial assistance for acquisition or construction of facilities
2151.653	Program of education; teachers
2151.654	Agreements for admission of children from counties not maintaining facilities
2151.655	County taxing authority may submit securities issue to electors for support of schools, detention homes, forestry camps, or other facilities; permissible agreements to pay costs of permanent improvements of districts
2151.66	Annual tax assessments
2151.67	Receipt and use of gifts, grants, devises, bequests and public moneys
2151.68	Board of trustees
2151.69	Board meetings; compensation
2151.70	Appointment of superintendent; bond; compensation; duties
2151.71	Operation of facilities
2151.72	Selection of site for district facility
2151.73	Apportionment of trustees; executive committee
2151.74	Removal of trustee
2151.75	Interim duties of trustees; trustees fund; reports
2151.76	Authority for choice, construction, and furnishing of district facility
2151.77	Capital and current expenses of district
2151.78	Withdrawal of county from district; continuity of district tax levy
2151.79	Designation of fiscal officer of district; duties of county auditors
2151.80	Expenses of members of boards of county commissioners

MISCELLANEOUS PROVISIONS

2151.85	Minor female's complaint for abortion; hearing; appeal
2151.86	Criminal records check; disqualification from employment
2151.861	Random sampling of registered child day camps; effect of noncompliance relating to criminal records check

PENALTIES

2151.99	Penalties

Publisher's Note: Until 1968, when the Modern Courts Amendment to the Ohio Constitution was adopted, Ohio court procedure was governed entirely by statute and case law. The Modern Courts Amendment required the Supreme Court of Ohio, subject to the approval of the General Assembly, to "prescribe rules governing practice and procedure in all courts of the state." Rules of practice and procedure are the Civil, Criminal, Appellate, and Juvenile Rules, Rules of the Court of Claims, and the Ohio Rules of Evidence. Pursuant to Ohio Constitution Article IV, Section 5(B), such rules "shall not abridge, enlarge, or modify any substantive right," and " [a]ll laws in conflict with such rules shall be of no further force or effect." Provisions of Chapter 2151 should be read with this in mind.

Uncodified Law

2000 S 179, § 10, eff. 4-9-01, reads:

The General Assembly hereby states its intention to do the following in the remainder of the 123rd General Assembly and in the 124th General Assembly:

(A) Address the issue of competency in juvenile proceedings and its various aspects;

(B) Review and continue to support the RECLAIM Ohio program and the alternative schools program;

(C) Review and address the anticipated costs of implementing this act.

1997 H 215, § 163, eff. 6–30–97, reads:

The General Assembly hereby requests that the Supreme Court adopt, pursuant to its authority under Ohio Constitution, Article IV, Section 5, rules governing procedure in juvenile courts of the state that address the placement of children in foster homes in a county other than the county in which the child resided at the time of the removal.

Comparative Laws

Ariz.—A.R.S. § 8-201 et seq.
Minn.—M.S.A. § 260.011 et seq.
N.D.—NDCC 27–20–01 et seq.
Va.—Code 1950, § 16.1–226 et seq.
Wyo.—Wyo.Stat.Ann., § 14–6–201.

Cross References

Adoption, search of putative father registry prior to adoption, exemptions, 3107.064
Affidavit of disqualification for prejudice filed against judge, powers pending resolution, 2701.03
Birth parent or sibling's request for assistance in finding adoptee's name by adoption, requirements, 3107.49
Common pleas courts; probate and other divisions; jurisdiction, O Const Art IV §4
County children services boards, powers and duties, 5153.16
County public children services agencies, emergency assistance and funding, 5153.165
Courts of record, premature judgment deemed clerical error, 2701.18
Curfew for persons under eighteen, 307.71
Cuyahoga county juvenile court, jurisdiction and powers, 2153.16
Deception to obtain matter harmful to juveniles, 2907.33
Department of youth services, powers and duties, 5139.04
Factors to consider in felony sentencing, 2929.12
Guardianship of mentally retarded minors, 5123.93
Job and family services department, payments for services to children, 5101.14
Humane societies, protection of children, 1717.14
Judges of the division of domestic relations, certain counties; juvenile court powers, 2301.03
Judicial power vested in courts, O Const Art IV §1
Juvenile court jurisdiction over juvenile capital facilities, 307.021
Minor employees, conditions on employment, 4109.08
Parent convicted of killing other parent, termination of custody order deemed new complaint for institutional custody, 3109.46
Rules of criminal procedure; scope, applicability, construction, exceptions, Crim R 1
Rules of juvenile procedure, Juv R 1 to 48
School pupils, withdrawal, habitual absence, suspension, or expulsion from school, notice to juvenile court judge, 3321.13
Townships, curfews for minors, violators, 505.89
Transfer of child to foster care facility, 5139.39
Transfer of children to correctional medical center, 5139.06
Trial, magistrate courts, applicability to juveniles, 2938.02
Visitation rights, juvenile court powers not limited, 3109.051, 3109.11, 3109.12
When consent not required for adoption, 3107.07
Youth commission, powers with respect to children, 5139.05

Ohio Administrative Code References

Authority to assume and retain custody of a child, OAC 5101:2–42–04

Law Review and Journal Commentaries

An Answer to the Challenge of Kent, Daniels W. McLean. 53 A B A J 456 (May 1967).

Basic Juvenile Delinquency Practice In Ohio, John P. Mahaffey. 7 Ohio Law 8 (January/February 1993).

A Brief History of Ohio Gang Trends—Changes in Legislation as a Result of Gangs and Successful Prevention Methods, Linda M. Schmidt. 10 Baldwin's Ohio Sch L J 69 (November/December 1998).

Capital Punishment of Children in Ohio: "They'd Never Send a Boy of Seventeen to the Chair in Ohio Would They?", Victor L. Streib. 18 Akron L Rev 51 (Summer 1984).

Evidence in Cuyahoga County Juvenile Court, Elaine J. Columbro. 10 Clev–Marshall L Rev 524 (September 1961).

The History of Juvenile Law Reform in Ohio Since *Gault*, Robert W. Willey. 12 Ohio N U L Rev 469 (1985).

In re Gault, Juvenile Courts and Lawyers, Norman Lefstein. 53 A B A J 811 (September 1967).

In Search of Affirmative Duties Toward Children Under a Post–Deshaney Constitution, Comment. 139 U Pa L Rev 227 (November 1990).

Is Ohio Juvenile Justice Still Serving Its Purpose?, Comment. 29 Akron L Rev 335 (Winter 1996).

Is The Separation Of Powers Doctrine Accountable For The Foster Care Drift Of Ohio Children? A Judicial Perspective Of Amended House Bill 279, A Proposal To Change Juvenile Court Procedures Regarding The Neglected, Dependent, And Abused Children In The Care And Custody Removed From Familial Home, Hon. Gerald E. Radcliffe. 14 Ohio N U L Rev 179 (1987).

The Juvenile Court—A Court of Law, Walter G. Whitlatch. 18 Case W Res L Rev 1239 (May 1967).

The Juvenile Court: Effective Justice or Benevolent Despotism?, Bertram Polow. 53 A B A J 31 (January 1967).

Juvenile Court: "Neglected Child" of the Judiciary, Hon. Albert A. Woldman. 37 Clev B J 257 (September 1966).

Juvenile Court: Time for Change, Charles Auerbach. 37 Clev B J 179 (June 1966).

Juvenile Delinquency, Hon. Richard L. Davis. (Ed. note: Observations from twenty-two years on the bench concerning the decline of family values as delinquency's cause.) 14 Ohio N U L Rev 195 (1987).

Juvenile Delinquent and Unruly Proceedings in Ohio: Unconstitutional Adjudications, Note. 24 Clev St L Rev 602 (1975).

The Kent Case and the Juvenile Court: A Challenge to Lawyers, Robert Gardner. 52 A B A J 923 (October 1966).

A Legal Look at Juvenile Court, Paul W. Alexander. 27 Clev B J 171 (August 1956).

Post-disposition Treatment and Recidivism in the Juvenile Court: Towards Justice for All, Elyce Zenoff Ferster and Thomas Courtless. 11 J Fam L 683 (1972).

Reconstructing Section Five Of The Fourteenth Amendment To Assist Impoverished Children, James Wilson. 38 Clev St L Rev 391 (1990).

Rights of Children: The Legal Vacuum, Lois G. Forer. 55 A B A J 1151 (December 1969).

Role of the Attorney in Juvenile Court, Julian Greenspun. 18 Clev St L Rev 599 (September 1969).

Symposium: Juvenile Justice Reform, A Critical Perspective. 39 Ohio St L J 239 (1978).

A Synopsis of Ohio Juvenile Court Law, Don J. Young, Jr. 31 U Cin L Rev 131 (Spring 1962).

"Unusual" Punishment: The Domestic Effects of International Norms Restricting the Application of the Death Penalty, Joan F. Hartman. 52 U Cin L Rev 655 (1983).

A way out of Juvenile Delinquency, Roman C. Pucinski. 54 A B A J 33 (January 1968).

CONSTRUCTION; DEFINITIONS

2151.01 Construction; purpose

The sections in Chapter 2151. of the Revised Code, with the exception of those sections providing for the criminal prosecution of adults, shall be liberally interpreted and construed so as to effectuate the following purposes:

(A) To provide for the care, protection, and mental and physical development of children subject to Chapter 2151. of the Revised Code, whenever possible, in a family environment, separating the child from the child's parents only when necessary for the child's welfare or in the interests of public safety;

(B) To provide judicial procedures through which Chapters 2151. and 2152. of the Revised Code are executed and enforced, and in which the parties are assured of a fair hearing, and their constitutional and other legal rights are recognized and enforced.

(2000 S 179, § 3, eff. 1–1–02; 1969 H 320, eff. 11–19–69)

Historical and Statutory Notes

Ed. Note: Former 2151.01 repealed by 1969 H 320, eff. 11–19–69; 1953 H 1; GC 1639–1; see now 2151.011 for provisions analogous to former 2151.01.

Pre–1953 H 1 Amendments: 121 v 557

Amendment Note: 2000 S 179, § 3, eff. 1–1–02, rewrote this section, which prior thereto read:

"The sections in Chapter 2151. of the Revised Code, with the exception of those sections providing for the criminal prosecution of adults, shall be liberally interpreted and construed so as to effectuate the following purposes:

"(A) To provide for the care, protection, and mental and physical development of children subject to Chapter 2151. of the Revised Code;

"(B) To protect the public interest in removing the consequences of criminal behavior and the taint of criminality from children committing delinquent acts and to substitute therefor a program of supervision, care, and rehabilitation;

"(C) To achieve the foregoing purposes, whenever possible, in a family environment, separating the child from its parents only when necessary for his welfare or in the interests of public safety;

"(D) To provide judicial procedures through which Chapter 2151. of the Revised Code is executed and enforced, and in which the parties are assured of a fair hearing, and their constitutional and other legal rights are recognized and enforced."

Cross References

Applicability and construction, Juv R 1
Authority of grandparent to execute caretaker authorization certificate, 3109.65.
Grandparents, form and content of power of attorney, 3109.53
Hearing, notice, de novo review, 3109.77
Intake, Juv R 9
Judges of the court of domestic relations, juvenile court responsibility, 2301.03
Judges of the divisions of domestic relations, 2301.03
Power of attorney, conditions determining execution of power by one or both parents, 3109.56
Power of attorney, notice to nonresidential parent and guardian, 3109.55.
Waiver of rights, Juv R 3

Ohio Administrative Code References

Definition of terms for the implementation of the "Comprehensive Assessment and Planning Model - Interim Solution" and statewide automated child welfare database, OAC 5101:2–1–01.1

Research References

Encyclopedias

OH Jur. 3d Constitutional Law § 506, Other Particular Rights.
OH Jur. 3d Courts & Judges § 18, Courts of Common Pleas—Juvenile Division and Juvenile Courts.
OH Jur. 3d Criminal Law § 3242, Community Control Sanction.
OH Jur. 3d Family Law § 1518, Correctional Service—After-Care Services.
OH Jur. 3d Family Law § 1531, Construction of Statutes.
OH Jur. 3d Family Law § 1655, Right to Attend; Public or Private Hearing.

Forms

Ohio Jurisprudence Pleading and Practice Forms § 96:29, Adoption Period.

Treatises and Practice Aids

Carlin, Baldwin's Ohio Practice, Merrick-Rippner Probate Law § 104:3, Juvenile Court—Purpose and Function.
Carlin, Baldwin's Ohio Practice, Merrick-Rippner Probate Law § 104:4, Juvenile Court—Constitutional Issues.
Carlin, Baldwin's Ohio Practice, Merrick-Rippner Probate Law § 106:4, Juvenile Court Jurisdiction—Delinquent Child—Non-Criminal Nature of Delinquency Proceedings.
Carlin, Baldwin's Ohio Practice, Merrick-Rippner Probate Law § 107:1, Intake.
Carlin, Baldwin's Ohio Practice, Merrick-Rippner Probate Law § 107:73, Alternatives for Disposition of Juvenile Cases.
Carlin, Baldwin's Ohio Practice, Merrick-Rippner Probate Law § 107:78, Disposition of Abused, Neglected, or Dependent Child—Temporary Custody.
Carlin, Baldwin's Ohio Practice, Merrick-Rippner Probate Law § 107:80, Disposition of Abused, Neglected, or Dependent Child—Permanent Custody.
Carlin, Baldwin's Ohio Practice, Merrick-Rippner Probate Law § 107:84, Disposition of Delinquent Children—Prior to January 1, 2002.
Carlin, Baldwin's Ohio Practice, Merrick-Rippner Probate Law § 108:10, Juvenile Court—Criminal Jurisdiction—Criminal Trial of Adults: Rules and Procedures.
Carlin, Baldwin's Ohio Practice, Merrick-Rippner Probate Law § 108:12, Juvenile Court—Criminal Jurisdiction—Sentencing and Punishment of Convicted Adults.
Carlin, Baldwin's Ohio Practice, Merrick-Rippner Probate Law § 108:26, Juvenile Court—Parentage Act—Applicability of Civil Rules to Paternity Proceedings.
Carlin, Baldwin's Ohio Practice, Merrick-Rippner Probate Law § 107:116, Juvenile Court Records—Expungement.
Giannelli & Yeomans, Ohio Juvenile Law § 1:7, Juvenile Code.
Giannelli & Yeomans, Ohio Juvenile Law § 4:1, Introduction.
Giannelli & Yeomans, Ohio Juvenile Law § 10:3, Dependency—Homeless, Destitute or Without Adequate Care.
Giannelli & Yeomans, Ohio Juvenile Law § 15:3, Diversion, Youth Services Grant.
Giannelli & Yeomans, Ohio Juvenile Law § 30:2, General Principles for Abuse, Neglect and Dependency Dispositions.
Giannelli & Yeomans, Ohio Juvenile Law § 30:6, Temporary Custody.
Giannelli & Yeomans, Ohio Juvenile Law § 30:8, Permanent Custody—Defined.
Giannelli & Yeomans, Ohio Juvenile Law § 31:8, Implementation of Case Plan.
Giannelli & Yeomans, Ohio Juvenile Law § 35:4, Expungement and Sealing.

Law Review and Journal Commentaries

Children in Limbo in Ohio: Permanency Planning and the State of the Law, John Paul Christoff. 16 Cap U L Rev 1 (Fall 1986).

Notes of Decisions

Ed. Note: *This section contains annotations from former RC 2151.55.*

Care, protection, mental development 3
Constitutional issues 1
Procedural issues 2
Public policy 6
Removal from parents 4
Suitability of parents 5

---

1. Constitutional issues

On juvenile delinquent's claim that his equal protection right was violated based on fact that trial court was statutorily required at original sentencing proceeding to give adult criminal offenders notice of sentence that would be imposed for violation of community control but that trial court was not required at original sentencing proceeding to give juvenile delinquents notice of sentence that would be imposed for probation violation, juvenile failed to establish that juvenile delinquents and adult criminal offenders are similarly situated; although juvenile delinquency laws feature inherently criminal aspects, Ohio Supreme Court has recognized that overriding purpose of juvenile system is to provide for care and protection of children, and United States Supreme Court has recognized that constitution does not mandate elimination of all differences in treatment of juveniles. In re Estes (Ohio App. 4 Dist., Washington, 09-24-2004) No. 04CA11, 2004-Ohio-5163, 2004 WL 2260510, Unreported. Constitutional Law ⚖ 242.1(4); Infants ⚖ 132

Note 1

Not requiring trial court at original sentencing proceeding to give juvenile delinquent notice of sentence that would be imposed for violation of community control, but statutorily requiring trial court at original sentencing proceeding to give adult criminal offenders notice of sentence that would be imposed for violation of community control, was rationally related to legitimate government objective of protecting and caring for children and providing court with flexibility that is hallmark of juvenile justice system, and thus, juvenile's equal protection right was not violated. In re Estes (Ohio App. 4 Dist., Washington, 09-24-2004) No. 04CA11, 2004-Ohio-5163, 2004 WL 2260510, Unreported. Constitutional Law ⚖ 242.1(4); Infants ⚖ 132

Community-control condition imposed on defendant convicted of fifth-degree felony domestic violence against his adult cohabitant, directing defendant to have no contact with his children for four years, was statutorily and constitutionally impermissible, especially in absence of any evidence that defendant had ever been convicted of abusing his children or that instant offense occurred in front of children; effect of order was to terminate defendant's parental rights without due process, and defendant was not given opportunity to respond to information in victim impact statement alleging that he had previously whipped his child. State v. Sturgeon (Ohio App. 1 Dist., 09-22-2000) 138 Ohio App.3d 882, 742 N.E.2d 730. Sentencing And Punishment ⚖ 1971(2)

Traditional interests of confidentiality and rehabilitation prevent the public from having a qualified constitutional right of access to juvenile delinquency proceedings. State ex rel. Plain Dealer Publishing Co. v. Geauga Cty. Court of Common Pleas, Juv. Div. (Ohio, 08-11-2000) 90 Ohio St.3d 79, 734 N.E.2d 1214, 2000-Ohio-35. Constitutional Law ⚖ 90.1(3); Constitutional Law ⚖ 328

News media did not have qualified constitutional right of access to delinquency proceedings involving juvenile charged in connection with murder and robbery, including proceedings on motion to transfer case to adult court. State ex rel. Plain Dealer Publishing Co. v. Geauga Cty. Court of Common Pleas, Juv. Div. (Ohio, 08-11-2000) 90 Ohio St.3d 79, 734 N.E.2d 1214, 2000-Ohio-35. Constitutional Law ⚖ 90.1(3); Constitutional Law ⚖ 328; Infants ⚖ 203

Proceedings in juvenile court to determine if a child is abused, neglected, or dependent, or to determine custody of a minor child, are neither presumptively open nor presumptively closed to the public, and the juvenile court may restrict public access to the proceedings if the court finds, after hearing evidence and argument on the issue, that there exists a reasonable and substantial basis for believing that public access could harm the child or endanger the fairness of the adjudication, and the potential for harm outweighs the benefits of public access. In re T.R. (Ohio 1990) 52 Ohio St.3d 6, 556 N.E.2d 439, certiorari denied 111 S.Ct. 386, 498 U.S. 958, 112 L.Ed.2d 396. Infants ⚖ 172; Infants ⚖ 203

The prosecution of a twelve-year-old girl as a delinquent based on a charge of complicity to commit rape violates RC Ch 2151, Juv R 9(A), local court intake policy, public policy, and due process of law where such prosecution arises from an incident of three children "playing doctor," with the adjudicated delinquent directing a five-year-old boy to drop his pants and place his penis in a five-year-old girl's mouth in order to take her temperature, because no offense was actually committed and the failure to raise the issue of the constitutionality of applying the rape statute to children under the age of thirteen does not preclude consideration of the constitutional challenge on appeal. In re M.D. (Ohio 1988) 38 Ohio St.3d 149, 527 N.E.2d 286.

The matter of unlawful search and seizure under of US Const Am 4 applies to juveniles. In re Morris (Ohio Com.Pl. 1971) 29 Ohio Misc. 71, 278 N.E.2d 701, 58 O.O.2d 126.

The Akron city ordinances requiring parental consent, informed consent, a 24–hour waiting period, and disposal of fetal remains are unconstitutional. City of Akron v. Akron Center for Reproductive Health, Inc. (U.S.Ohio 1983) 103 S.Ct. 2481, 462 U.S. 416, 76 L.Ed.2d 687, on remand 604 F.Supp. 1268, on remand 604 F.Supp. 1275.

Married high school students may not by reason thereof be excluded from extracurricular activities. Davis v. Meek (N.D.Ohio 1972) 32 Ohio Misc. 43, 344 F.Supp. 298, 61 O.O.2d 65. Schools ⚖ 172

2. Procedural issues

Extending permanent custody proceedings so that county could present newly discovered evidence was consistent with juvenile code's purpose to provide for the care, protection, and mental and physical development of children, where evidence exposed fact that father had lied to county when he told county that he had no other children, when, in fact, he had another son who resided with him, allegedly had been victim of sexual abuse perpetrated by father and father's brother, and was also a perpetrator of sexual abuse. In re Sullivan (Ohio App. 12 Dist., Butler, 01-21-2003) No. CA2002-03-061, 2003-Ohio-195, 2003 WL 138665, Unreported. Infants ⚖ 207

Trial court was required to conduct in camera inspection of defendant's anger management counseling records before ordering disclosure to plaintiff during discovery in civil action relating to altercation, to determine whether the records were medical or psychiatric documents, so that physician-patient privilege generally would apply during discovery, except if the records were related causally or historically to physical or mental injuries relevant to the issues in the civil action, or whether the records were counseling records from mental health professionals who were not physicians, so that counselor-patient privilege generally would apply during discovery, except if defendant voluntarily testified or if the treatment was ordered in a juvenile court proceeding. Folmar v. Griffin (Ohio App. 5 Dist., 04-07-2006) 166 Ohio App.3d 154, 849 N.E.2d 324, 2006-Ohio-1849. Witnesses ⚖ 223

Res judicata does not prohibit the litigation of issues relevant to a motion for permanent custody of a child even though the same or similar issues may have been considered in a prior action. In re Ament (Ohio App. 12 Dist., 04-23-2001) 142 Ohio App.3d 302, 755 N.E.2d 448, appeal not allowed 92 Ohio St.3d 1431, 749 N.E.2d 757. Child Custody ⚖ 400

"Clear and convincing evidence" is that which will produce in the trier of fact a firm belief or conviction as to the facts sought to be established. In re Ament (Ohio App. 12 Dist., 04-23-2001) 142 Ohio App.3d 302, 755 N.E.2d 448, appeal not allowed 92 Ohio St.3d 1431, 749 N.E.2d 757. Evidence ⚖ 596(1)

On review, judicial decisions to terminate parental rights receive careful scrutiny and the permanent removal of a child from his or her family may be condoned only where there is demonstrated an incapacity on the part of the parent to provide adequate parental care, not because better parental care can be provided by foster parents or adoptive parents. In re Stacey S. (Ohio App. 6 Dist., 12-30-1999) 136 Ohio App.3d 503, 737 N.E.2d 92, 1999-Ohio-989. Infants ⚖ 248.1; Infants ⚖ 254

The juvenile court is entitled to review the appropriateness of filing a complaint against a ten-year old boy for rape and to dismiss the complaint because it would not further the policies of the state. In re Smith (Hamilton 1992) 80 Ohio App.3d 502, 609 N.E.2d 1281, dismissed, jurisdictional motion overruled 65 Ohio St.3d 1441, 600 N.E.2d 683.

A proceeding upon a complaint charging a child as a juvenile traffic offender is neither criminal nor civil. In re C. (Ohio Com.Pl. 1975) 43 Ohio Misc. 98, 334 N.E.2d 545, 72 O.O.2d 421. Infants ⚖ 194.1

The language, "all fines collected from or moneys arising from bonds forfeited by persons apprehended or arrested by state highway patrolmen," appearing in RC 5503.04, includes such fines or moneys when they are collected in probate and juvenile courts. An action in a juvenile court may be considered a "prosecution" for purposes of RC 5503.04. OAG 87–023.

Judge of juvenile court may not commit child who has been found to be delinquent child, or juvenile traffic offender, to county jail upon failure, refusal, or inability of such child to pay fine and court costs. OAG 70–143.

3. Care, protection, mental development

There is no evidence of negligent supervision in a personal injury accident brought by a motorcyclist against the parents of a child who is riding his friend's bicycle and enters the same intersection as the motorcyclist when the bicycle brakes fail, where shortly before the accident, the parents (1) give the child strict instructions to stop and look before crossing the road, (2) observe the child ride in their yard and conclude he has no difficulty with the bicycle, and (3) exert reasonable control over their child's conduct by way of instructions, restrictions, and limited permission. Bertok v. Rohloff (Ohio App. 6 Dist., Ottawa, 11-17-1995) No. OT-95-032, 1995 WL 680030, Unreported.

Order of disposition in juvenile case is matter within court's discretion, and while objective of juvenile system is rehabilitation rather than punishment, juvenile justice system is purely statutory creation and may contain punitive elements. State v. Matha (Ohio App. 9 Dist., 12-13-1995) 107 Ohio App.3d 756, 669 N.E.2d 504. Infants ⚖ 223.1

A juvenile charged with committing criminal mischief by failing to stop his friend from putting superglue on a gerbil in a pet store would not have been provided with the necessary care, protection, and mental development contemplated by RC 2151.01 if the trial court had simply dismissed his case because the juvenile claimed no wrongdoing. In re Corcoran (Geauga 1990) 68 Ohio App.3d 213, 587 N.E.2d 957, dismissed 56 Ohio St.3d 702, 564 N.E.2d 703.

The statutory law of arrest does not apply to special statutory proceedings in the juvenile court which are civil in nature and have for their purpose the securing for each child under the jurisdiction of the juvenile court such care, guidance and control... as will best serve the child's welfare. In re L——(Ohio Juv. 1963) 194 N.E.2d 797, 92 Ohio Law Abs. 475, 25 O.O.2d 369.

4. Removal from parents

Parents of minor children who do not bring their children into court pursuant to a court order are not guilty of contempt where the children's whereabouts are unknown to the parents and no evidence suggests that the parents are able to comply with the court's order. State v. Hershberger (Wayne 1959) 168 N.E.2d 12, 83 Ohio Law Abs. 63.

Where a juvenile court found that a child was neglected, and committed such child to the temporary custody of the local child welfare board, the parents of such child could be punished for contempt for passively resisting such order. (Amish school attendance case.) State v. Hershberger (Ohio Juv. 1958) 150 N.E.2d 671, 77 Ohio Law Abs. 487, reversed 168 N.E.2d 12, 83 Ohio Law Abs. 63.

Under Ohio law, unless matters of public safety are involved, a child alleged to be abused, neglected, or dependent may be removed from his home by court order only upon a judicial determination that continuation in the home would be contrary to the child's best interest. OAG 87–105.

The Ohio youth commission may pursuant to RC 5139.281 adopt a rule requiring the separation of an adjudicated delinquent where extraordinary circumstances make such separation necessary for the care, treatment or training of such youth, or where necessary to insure the safety of that youth, or any other youth in the detention home. OAG 77–006.

5. Suitability of parents

While best interest of child is primary standard to be applied to custody issue arising in dependency proceeding, suitable parents have paramount right to custody; before divesting parent of this right and awarding custody to nonparent, court must determine whether preponderance of evidence shows that parent abandoned child, that parent contractually relinquished custody of child, that parent has become totally incapable of supporting or caring for child or that award of custody to parent would be detrimental to child. In re Pryor (Athens 1993) 86 Ohio App.3d 327, 620 N.E.2d 973. Infants ⟐ 154.1; Infants ⟐ 177; Infants ⟐ 180

Although primary consideration in disposition of all children's cases is best interests and welfare of child, considerations of parental rights and suitability and any detriment from custody award must also be factored into "best interest" equation. In re Pryor (Athens 1993) 86 Ohio App.3d 327, 620 N.E.2d 973. Child Custody ⟐ 77

6. Public policy

Public policy to ensure accountability and compel respect for court orders did not warrant judicial exception to the legislatively imposed limits on juvenile court jurisdiction to the age of twenty-one years. In re R.K. (Ohio App. 8 Dist., Cuyahoga, 12-16-2004) No. 84948, 2004-Ohio-6918, 2004 WL 2931013, Unreported, appeal not allowed 105 Ohio St.3d 1561, 828 N.E.2d 117, 2005-Ohio-2447. Infants ⟐ 196

2151.011   Definitions

(A) As used in the Revised Code:

(1) "Juvenile court" means whichever of the following is applicable that has jurisdiction under this chapter and Chapter 2152. of the Revised Code:

(a) The division of the court of common pleas specified in section 2101.022 or 2301.03 of the Revised Code as having jurisdiction under this chapter and Chapter 2152. of the Revised Code or as being the juvenile division or the juvenile division combined with one or more other divisions;

(b) The juvenile court of Cuyahoga county or Hamilton county that is separately and independently created by section 2151.08 or Chapter 2153. of the Revised Code and that has jurisdiction under this chapter and Chapter 2152. of the Revised Code;

(c) If division (A)(1)(a) or (b) of this section does not apply, the probate division of the court of common pleas.

(2) "Juvenile judge" means a judge of a court having jurisdiction under this chapter.

(3) "Private child placing agency" means any association, as defined in section 5103.02 of the Revised Code, that is certified under section 5103.03 of the Revised Code to accept temporary, permanent, or legal custody of children and place the children for either foster care or adoption.

(4) "Private noncustodial agency" means any person, organization, association, or society certified by the department of job and family services that does not accept temporary or permanent legal custody of children, that is privately operated in this state, and that does one or more of the following:

(a) Receives and cares for children for two or more consecutive weeks;

(b) Participates in the placement of children in certified foster homes;

(c) Provides adoption services in conjunction with a public children services agency or private child placing agency.

(B) As used in this chapter:

(1) "Adequate parental care" means the provision by a child's parent or parents, guardian, or custodian of adequate food, clothing, and shelter to ensure the child's health and physical safety and the provision by a child's parent or parents of specialized services warranted by the child's physical or mental needs.

(2) "Adult" means an individual who is eighteen years of age or older.

(3) "Agreement for temporary custody" means a voluntary agreement authorized by section 5103.15 of the Revised Code that transfers the temporary custody of a child to a public children services agency or a private child placing agency.

(4) "Certified foster home" means a foster home, as defined in section 5103.02 of the Revised Code, certified under section 5103.03 of the Revised Code.

(5) "Child" means a person who is under eighteen years of age, except that the juvenile court has jurisdiction over any person who is adjudicated an unruly child prior to attaining eighteen years of age until the person attains twenty-one years of age, and, for purposes of that jurisdiction related to that adjudication, a person who is so adjudicated an unruly child shall be deemed a "child" until the person attains twenty-one years of age.

(6) "Child day camp," "child care," "child day-care center," "part-time child day-care center," "type A family day-care home," "certified type B family day-care home," "type B home," "administrator of a child day-care center," "administrator of a type A family day-care home," "in-home aide," and "authorized provider" have the same meanings as in section 5104.01 of the Revised Code.

(7) "Child care provider" means an individual who is a child-care staff member or administrator of a child day-care center, a type A family day-care home, or a type B family day-care home, or an in-home aide or an individual who is licensed, is regulated, is approved, operates under the direction of, or otherwise is certified by the department of job and family services, department of mental retardation and developmental disabilities, or the early childhood programs of the department of education.

(8) "Chronic truant" has the same meaning as in section 2152.02 of the Revised Code.

(9) "Commit" means to vest custody as ordered by the court.

(10) "Counseling" includes both of the following:

(a) General counseling services performed by a public children services agency or shelter for victims of domestic violence to assist a child, a child's parents, and a child's siblings in alleviating identified problems that may cause or have caused the child to be an abused, neglected, or dependent child.

(b) Psychiatric or psychological therapeutic counseling services provided to correct or alleviate any mental or emotional illness or disorder and performed by a licensed psychiatrist, licensed psychologist, or a person licensed under Chapter 4757. of the Revised Code to engage in social work or professional counseling.

(11) "Custodian" means a person who has legal custody of a child or a public children services agency or private child placing agency that has permanent, temporary, or legal custody of a child.

(12) "Delinquent child" has the same meaning as in section 2152.02 of the Revised Code.

(13) "Detention" means the temporary care of children pending court adjudication or disposition, or execution of a court order, in a public or private facility designed to physically restrict the movement and activities of children.

(14) "Developmental disability" has the same meaning as in section 5123.01 of the Revised Code.

(15) "Foster caregiver" has the same meaning as in section 5103.02 of the Revised Code.

(16) "Guardian" means a person, association, or corporation that is granted authority by a probate court pursuant to Chapter 2111. of the Revised Code to exercise parental rights over a child to the extent provided in the court's order and subject to the residual parental rights of the child's parents.

(17) "Habitual truant" means any child of compulsory school age who is absent without legitimate excuse for absence from the public school the child is supposed to attend for five or more consecutive school days, seven or more school days in one school month, or twelve or more school days in a school year.

(18) "Juvenile traffic offender" has the same meaning as in section 2152.02 of the Revised Code.

(19) "Legal custody" means a legal status that vests in the custodian the right to have physical care and control of the child and to determine where and with whom the child shall live, and the right and duty to protect, train, and discipline the child and to provide the child with food, shelter, education, and medical care, all subject to any residual parental rights, privileges, and responsibilities. An individual granted legal custody shall exercise the rights and responsibilities personally unless otherwise authorized by any section of the Revised Code or by the court.

(20) A "legitimate excuse for absence from the public school the child is supposed to attend" includes, but is not limited to, any of the following:

(a) The fact that the child in question has enrolled in and is attending another public or nonpublic school in this or another state;

(b) The fact that the child in question is excused from attendance at school for any of the reasons specified in section 3321.04 of the Revised Code;

(c) The fact that the child in question has received an age and schooling certificate in accordance with section 3331.01 of the Revised Code.

(21) "Mental illness" and "mentally ill person subject to hospitalization by court order" have the same meanings as in section 5122.01 of the Revised Code.

(22) "Mental injury" means any behavioral, cognitive, emotional, or mental disorder in a child caused by an act or omission that is described in section 2919.22 of the Revised Code and is committed by the parent or other person responsible for the child's care.

(23) "Mentally retarded person" has the same meaning as in section 5123.01 of the Revised Code.

(24) "Nonsecure care, supervision, or training" means care, supervision, or training of a child in a facility that does not confine or prevent movement of the child within the facility or from the facility.

(25) "Of compulsory school age" has the same meaning as in section 3321.01 of the Revised Code.

(26) "Organization" means any institution, public, semipublic, or private, and any private association, society, or agency located or operating in the state, incorporated or unincorporated, having among its functions the furnishing of protective services or care for children, or the placement of children in certified foster homes or elsewhere.

(27) "Out-of-home care" means detention facilities, shelter facilities, certified children's crisis care facilities, certified foster homes, placement in a prospective adoptive home prior to the issuance of a final decree of adoption, organizations, certified organizations, child day-care centers, type A family day-care homes, child care provided by type B family day-care home providers and by in-home aides, group home providers, group homes, institutions, state institutions, residential facilities, residential care facilities, residential camps, day camps, public schools, chartered nonpublic schools, educational service centers, hospitals, and medical clinics that are responsible for the care, physical custody, or control of children.

(28) "Out-of-home care child abuse" means any of the following when committed by a person responsible for the care of a child in out-of-home care:

(a) Engaging in sexual activity with a child in the person's care;

(b) Denial to a child, as a means of punishment, of proper or necessary subsistence, education, medical care, or other care necessary for a child's health;

(c) Use of restraint procedures on a child that cause injury or pain;

(d) Administration of prescription drugs or psychotropic medication to the child without the written approval and ongoing supervision of a licensed physician;

(e) Commission of any act, other than by accidental means, that results in any injury to or death of the child in out-of-home care or commission of any act by accidental means that results in an injury to or death of a child in out-of-home care and that is at variance with the history given of the injury or death.

(29) "Out-of-home care child neglect" means any of the following when committed by a person responsible for the care of a child in out-of-home care:

(a) Failure to provide reasonable supervision according to the standards of care appropriate to the age, mental and physical condition, or other special needs of the child;

(b) Failure to provide reasonable supervision according to the standards of care appropriate to the age, mental and physical condition, or other special needs of the child, that results in sexual or physical abuse of the child by any person;

(c) Failure to develop a process for all of the following:

(i) Administration of prescription drugs or psychotropic drugs for the child;

(ii) Assuring that the instructions of the licensed physician who prescribed a drug for the child are followed;

(iii) Reporting to the licensed physician who prescribed the drug all unfavorable or dangerous side effects from the use of the drug.

(d) Failure to provide proper or necessary subsistence, education, medical care, or other individualized care necessary for the health or well-being of the child;

(e) Confinement of the child to a locked room without monitoring by staff;

(f) Failure to provide ongoing security for all prescription and nonprescription medication;

(g) Isolation of a child for a period of time when there is substantial risk that the isolation, if continued, will impair or retard the mental health or physical well-being of the child.

(30) "Permanent custody" means a legal status that vests in a public children services agency or a private child placing agency, all parental rights, duties, and obligations, including the right to consent to adoption, and divests the natural parents or adoptive parents of all parental rights, privileges, and obligations, including all residual rights and obligations.

(31) "Permanent surrender" means the act of the parents or, if a child has only one parent, of the parent of a child, by a voluntary agreement authorized by section 5103.15 of the Revised Code, to transfer the permanent custody of the child to a public children services agency or a private child placing agency.

(32) "Person" means an individual, association, corporation, or partnership and the state or any of its political subdivisions, departments, or agencies.

(33) "Person responsible for a child's care in out-of-home care" means any of the following:

(a) Any foster caregiver, in-home aide, or provider;

(b) Any administrator, employee, or agent of any of the following: a public or private detention facility; shelter facility; certified children's crisis care facility; organization; certified organization; child day-care center; type A family day-care home; certified type B family day-care home; group home; institution; state institution; residential facility; residential care facility; residential camp; day camp; school district; community school; chartered nonpublic school; educational service center; hospital; or medical clinic;

(c) Any person who supervises or coaches children as part of an extracurricular activity sponsored by a school district, public school, or chartered nonpublic school;

(d) Any other person who performs a similar function with respect to, or has a similar relationship to, children.

(34) "Physically impaired" means having one or more of the following conditions that substantially limit one or more of the individual's major life activities, including self-care, receptive and expressive language, learning, mobility, and self-direction:

(a) A substantial impairment of vision, speech, or hearing;

(b) A congenital orthopedic impairment;

(c) An orthopedic impairment caused by disease, rheumatic fever or any other similar chronic or acute health problem, or amputation or another similar cause.

(35) "Placement for adoption" means the arrangement by a public children services agency or a private child placing agency with a person for the care and adoption by that person of a child of whom the agency has permanent custody.

(36) "Placement in foster care" means the arrangement by a public children services agency or a private child placing agency for the out-of-home care of a child of whom the agency has temporary custody or permanent custody.

(37) "Planned permanent living arrangement" means an order of a juvenile court pursuant to which both of the following apply:

(a) The court gives legal custody of a child to a public children services agency or a private child placing agency without the termination of parental rights.

(b) The order permits the agency to make an appropriate placement of the child and to enter into a written agreement with a foster care provider or with another person or agency with whom the child is placed.

(38) "Practice of social work" and "practice of professional counseling" have the same meanings as in section 4757.01 of the Revised Code.

(39) "Sanction, service, or condition" means a sanction, service, or condition created by court order following an adjudication that a child is an unruly child that is described in division (A)(4) of section 2152.19 of the Revised Code.

(40) "Protective supervision" means an order of disposition pursuant to which the court permits an abused, neglected, dependent, or unruly child to remain in the custody of the child's parents, guardian, or custodian and stay in the child's home, subject to any conditions and limitations upon the child, the child's parents, guardian, or custodian, or any other person that the court prescribes, including supervision as directed by the court for the protection of the child.

(41) "Psychiatrist" has the same meaning as in section 5122.01 of the Revised Code.

(42) "Psychologist" has the same meaning as in section 4732.01 of the Revised Code.

(43) "Residential camp" means a program in which the care, physical custody, or control of children is accepted overnight for recreational or recreational and educational purposes.

(44) "Residential care facility" means an institution, residence, or facility that is licensed by the department of mental health under section 5119.22 of the Revised Code and that provides care for a child.

(45) "Residential facility" means a home or facility that is licensed by the department of mental retardation and developmental disabilities under section 5123.19 of the Revised Code and in which a child with a developmental disability resides.

(46) "Residual parental rights, privileges, and responsibilities" means those rights, privileges, and responsibilities remaining with the natural parent after the transfer of legal custody of the child, including, but not necessarily limited to, the privilege of reasonable visitation, consent to adoption, the privilege to determine the child's religious affiliation, and the responsibility for support.

(47) "School day" means the school day established by the state board of education pursuant to section 3313.48 of the Revised Code.

(48) "School month" and "school year" have the same meanings as in section 3313.62 of the Revised Code.

(49) "Secure correctional facility" means a facility under the direction of the department of youth services that is designed to physically restrict the movement and activities of children and used for the placement of children after adjudication and disposition.

(50) "Sexual activity" has the same meaning as in section 2907.01 of the Revised Code.

(51) "Shelter" means the temporary care of children in physically unrestricted facilities pending court adjudication or disposition.

(52) "Shelter for victims of domestic violence" has the same meaning as in section 3113.33 of the Revised Code.

(53) "Temporary custody" means legal custody of a child who is removed from the child's home, which custody may be terminated at any time at the discretion of the court or, if the legal custody is granted in an agreement for temporary custody, by the person who executed the agreement.

(C) For the purposes of this chapter, a child shall be presumed abandoned when the parents of the child have failed to visit or maintain contact with the child for more than ninety days, regardless of whether the parents resume contact with the child after that period of ninety days.

(2006 S 238, eff. 9–21–06; 2004 H 11, eff. 5–18–05; 2004 H 106, eff. 9–16–04; 2002 H 400, eff. 4–3–03; 2000 S 179, § 3, eff. 1–1–02; 2000 H 332, eff. 1–1–01; 2000 H 448, eff. 10–5–00; 2000 S 181, eff. 9–4–00; 1999 H 470, eff. 7–1–00; 1998 H 484, eff. 3–18–99; 1998 S 212, eff. 9–30–98; 1997 H 408, eff. 10–1–97; 1996 S 223, eff. 3–18–97; 1996 H 124, eff. 3–31–97; 1996 H 265, eff. 3–3–97; 1996 H 274, § 4, eff. 8–8–96; 1996 H 274, § 1, eff. 8–8–96; 1995 S 2, eff. 7–1–96; 1995 H 1, eff. 1–1–96; 1994 H 715, eff. 7–22–94; 1993 S 21, eff. 10–29–93; 1993 H 152, eff. 7–1–93; 1992 H 356; 1991 H 155; 1990 H 38; 1989 H 257; 1988 H 403)

Uncodified Law

1996 H 445, § 3: See Uncodified Law under 2151.14.

1995 H 1, § 3, eff. 1–1–96, reads in part: (B) The General Assembly hereby declares that its purpose in enacting the language in division (B) of section 2151.011 and divisions (B) and (C) of section 2151.26 of the Revised Code that exists on and after the effective date of this act is to overrule the holding in **State v. Adams** (1982), 69 Ohio St. 2d 120, regarding the effect of binding a child over for trial as an adult.

Historical and Statutory Notes

Ed. Note: Former 2151.011 repealed by 1988 H 403, eff. 1–1–89; 1988 S 89, H 399; 1986 H 428; 1983 S 210; 1981 H 440; 1980 H 695; 1969 H 320.

Ed. Note: Former 2151.011 contained provisions analogous to former 2151.01 repealed by 1969 H 320, eff. 11–19–69.

Amendment Note: 2006 S 238 rewrote this section. See *Baldwin's Ohio Legislative Service Annotated*, 2006, page 3/L–1552, or the OH–LEGIS or OH–LEGIS–OLD database on WESTLAW, for prior version of this section.

Amendment Note: 2004 H 11 substituted "'child care'" for "'child day care'" in divisions (B)(6), (B)(7), and "child care" for "day care" in division (B)(27).

Amendment Note: 2004 H 106 inserted "public schools, chartered nonpublic schools, educational service centers," in division (B)(27); "school district; community school; chartered nonpublic school; educational service center;" in division (B)(32)(a); "Any person who supervises or coaches children as part of an extracurricular activity sponsored by a school district, public school, or chartered nonpublic school;" in division (B)(32)(c); and redesignated former (B)(32)(c) as new division (B)(32)(d).

Amendment Note: 2002 H 400 substituted "(4)" for "(3)" in division (B)(38).

Amendment Note: 2000 S 179, § 3, eff. 1–1–02, rewrote this section. See *Baldwin's Ohio Legislative Service Annotated*, 2000, page 11/L–3601, or the OH–LEGIS or OH–LEGIS–OLD database on Westlaw, for prior version of this section.

Amendment Note: 2000 H 332 substituted "under" for "pursuant to" in division (A)(3) and "certified" for "family" in division (A)(4)(b); deleted former divisions (B)(4), (B)(14), (B)15 and (B)(27); redesignated former divisions (B)(5) to (B)(46) as new divisions (B)(4) to (B)(43); deleted "family" before "foster" twice and substituted "as defined in section 5103.02 of the Revised Code, certified" for "operated by persons holding a certificate in force, issued" in new division (B)(4); substituted "(5)" for "(6)" throughout new division (B)(5); deleted "foster homes" after "shelter facilities" in former division (B)(23); and added new division (B)(29). Prior to deletion former divisions (B)(4), (B)(14), (B)15 and (B)(27) read:

"(4) 'Babysitting care' means care provided for a child while the parents, guardian, or legal custodian of the child are temporarily away.

"(14) 'Family foster home' means a private residence in which children are received apart from their parents, guardian, or legal custodian by an individual for hire, gain, or reward for nonsecure care, supervision, or training twenty four hours a day. 'Family foster home' does not include babysitting care provided for a child in the home of a person other then the home of the parents, guardian, or legal custodian of the child.

"(15) 'Foster home' means a family home in which any child is received apart from the child's parents for care, supervision, or training

"(27) 'Planned permanent living arrangement' means an order of a juvenile court pursuant to which both of the following apply:

"(a) The court gives legal custody of a child to a public children services agency or a private child placing agency without the termination of parental rights.

"(b) The order permits the agency to make an appropriate placement of the child and to enter into a written agreement with a foster care provider or with another person or agency with whom the child is placed."

Amendment Note: 2000 H 448 substituted "certified" for "family" in division (A)(4)(b); deleted former divisions (B)(4), (B)(14), (B)(27); redesignated former divisions (B)(5) to (B)(46) as new divisions (B)(4) to (B)(44); rewrote former division (B)(5); substituted "(5)" for "(6)" throughout new division (B)(5); rewrote former division (B)(15); inserted "certified" in new division (20); deleted "foster homes" in new division (B)(21); substituted "caregiver" for "parent" in new division (B)(26); and added new division (B)(30). Prior to deletion or amendment, division (B)(4), (B)(5), (B)(14), (B)(15) and (B)(27) read:

"(4) 'Babysitting care' means care provided for a child while the parents, guardian, or legal custodian of the child are temporarily away.

"(5) 'Certified family foster home' means a family foster home operated by persons holding a certificate in force, issued under section 5103.03 of the Revised Code.

"(14) 'Family foster home' means a private residence in which children are received apart from their parents, guardian, or legal custodian by an individual for hire, gain, or reward for nonsecure care, supervision, or training twenty-four hours a day. 'Family foster home' does not include babysitting care provided for a child in the home of a person other than the home of the parents, guardian, or legal custodian of the child.

"(15) 'Foster home' means a family home in which any child is received apart from the child's parents for care, supervision, or training.

"(27) 'Planned permanent living arrangement' means an order of a juvenile court pursuant to which both of the following apply:

"(a) The court gives legal custody of a child to a public children services agency or a private child placing agency without the termination of parental rights.

"(b) The order permits the agency to make an appropriate placement of the child and to enter into a written agreement with a foster care provider or with another person or agency with whom the child is placed."

Amendment Note: 2000 S 181 added new division (B)(9); redesignated former divisions (B)(9) through (B)(16) as new divisions (B)(10) through (B)(17); added new division (B)(18); redesignated former divisions (B)(17) and (B)(18) as new divisions (B)(19) and (B)(20); added new division (B)(20); redesignated former divisions (B)(18) through (B)(21) as new divisions (B)(21) through (B)(24); added new division (B)(25); redesignated former divisions (B)(22) through (B)(41) as new divisions (B)(26) through (B)(45); added new divisions (B)(46) and (B)(47); and redesignated former divisions (B)(42) through (B)(46) as new divisions (B)(48) through (B)(52).

Amendment Note: 1999 H 470 substituted "section 5103.03" for "sections 5103.03 to 5103.05" in division (A)(3); and substituted "job and family" for "human" in division (A)(4).

Amendment Note: 1998 S 212 substituted "mentally" for "mental" in division (B)(19); substituted "in foster care" for "for adoption" in division (B)(32); and rewrote division (B)(38), which prior to amendment read:

"(38) 'Residential camp' means a public or private facility that engages or accepts the care, physical custody, or control of children during summer months and that is licensed, regulated, approved, operated under the direction of, or otherwise certified by the department of health for the American camping association."

Amendment Note: 1998 H 484 deleted former division (B)(18); redesignated former division (B)(19) through (B)(27) as new divisions (B)(18) through (B)(26); and added new division (B)(27). Prior to deletion, former division (B)(18) read:

"(18) "Long–term foster care" means an order of a juvenile court pursuant to which both of the following apply:

"(a) Legal custody of a child is given to a public children services agency or a private child placing agency without the termination of parental rights.

"(b) The agency is permitted to make an appropriate placement of the child and to enter into a written long-term foster care agreement with a foster care provider or with another person or agency with whom the child is placed."

Amendment Note: 1997 H 408 rewrote this section; see *Baldwin's Ohio Legislative Service Annotated*, 1997, p 7/L–764, or the OH–LEGIS or OH–LEGIS–OLD database on Westlaw, for text of previous version.

Amendment Note: 1996 S 223 rewrote division (B)(29); deleted former divisions (B)(33) and (B)(34); redesignated former divisions (B)(35) through (B)(52) as divisions (B)(33) through (B)(50); substituted "Practice of social work" for "Social work" in division (B)(33); and made other nonsubstantive changes. Prior to amendment, division (B)(29), and former divisions (B)(33) and (B)(34), read, respectively:

"(29) 'Therapeutic counseling' means psychiatric or psychological services performed by a licensed psychiatrist or psychologist, a licensed or certified social worker, or licensed professional counselor to correct or alleviate any mental or emotional handicap or disorder of a person."

"(33) 'Social worker' means any person who is licensed or certified under Chapter 4757. of the Revised Code to engage in social work.

"(34) 'Licensed professional counselor' means any person who is licensed under Chapter 4757. of the Revised Code to engage in the practice of professional counseling."

Amendment Note: 1996 H 124 rewrote division (B)(1), which prior thereto read:

"(1)(a) 'Child' means a person who is under eighteen years of age, except that any person who violates a federal or state law or municipal ordinance prior to attaining eighteen years of age shall be deemed a "child" irrespective of that person's age at the time the complaint is filed or the hearing on the complaint is held and except that any person whose case is transferred for criminal prosecution pursuant to division (B) or (C) of section 2151.26 of the Revised Code and subsequently is convicted in that case shall after the transfer be deemed not to be a child in any of the following cases:

"(i) The transferred case;

"(ii) A case in which the person is alleged to have committed prior to the transfer an act that would be an offense if committed by an adult;

"(iii) A case in which the person is alleged to have committed subsequent to the transfer an act that would be an offense if committed by an adult.

"(b) Divisions (B)(1)(a)(ii) and (iii) of this section apply to a case regardless of whether the prior or subsequent act that is alleged in the case and that would be an offense if committed by an adult allegedly was committed in the same county in which the case was transferred or in another county and regardless of whether the complaint in the case involved was filed in the same county in which the case was transferred or in another county. Division (B)(1)(a)(ii) of this section applies to a case only when the prior act alleged in the case has not been disposed of by a juvenile court or trial court."

Amendment Note: 1996 H 265 rewrote division (B)(3); and added division (B)(55). Prior to amendment, division (B)(3) read:

"(3) 'Detention' means the temporary care of children in restricted facilities pending court adjudication or disposition."

Amendment Note: 1996 H 274, § 1, eff. 8–8–96, inserted "family" before "foster home operated by" in division (B)(6); substituted "illness" for "handicap" in division (B)(29); substituted "children" for "no more than five children, or in which all the children in a sibling group," in division (B)(48); added divisions (B)(53), (B)(54), and (C); and made changes to reflect gender neutral language.

Amendment Note: 1996 H 274, § 4, eff. 8–8–96, harmonized the versions of this section as amended by 1995 S 2, § 1, eff. 7–1–96, and 1996 H 274, § 1, eff. 8–8–96; and deleted division (C), which prior thereto read:

"(C) This is an interim section effective until July 1, 1996."

Amendment Note: 1995 S 2 deleted ", an aggravated felony of the first or second degree," from and inserted ", or third" in division (B)(1); and made changes to reflect gender neutral language.

Amendment Note: 1995 H 1 rewrote division (B)(1); and made changes to reflect gender neutral language and other nonsubstantive changes. Prior to amendment, division (B)(1) read:

"(1) "Child" means a person who is under the age of eighteen years, except that any person who violates a federal or state law or municipal ordinance prior to attaining eighteen years of age shall be deemed a "child" irrespective of his age at the time the complaint is filed or the hearing on the complaint is held and except that any person whose case is transferred for criminal prosecution pursuant to section 2151.26 of the Revised Code and is subsequently convicted in that case shall after the transfer be deemed not to be a child in any case in which he is alleged to have committed an act that if committed by an adult would constitute murder or aggravated murder, an aggravated felony of the first or second degree, or a felony of the first or second degree."

Amendment Note: 1993 H 152 inserted "family", changed "permit" to "certificate", and changed a reference to sections 5103.03 to 5103.05 to a reference to section 5103.03, in division (B)(6); deleted former division (B)(7); redesignated former divisions (B)(8) through (50) as divisions (B)(7) through (49), respectively; deleted "approved foster care," prior to "placement" in division (B)(41); and added divisions (B)(50) through (B)(54). Prior to amendment, division (B)(7) read:

"(7) 'Approved foster care' means facilities approved by the department of youth services under section 5139.37 of the Revised Code."

Amendment Note: 1993 S 21 deleted "and 'mentally retarded person subject to institutionalization by court order' have" from division (B)(20); substituted "5123.01" for "5123.19" in division (B)(44); removed former divisions (B)(46) and (47), which duplicated divisions (B)(21) and (20), respectively; and redesignated former divisions (B)(48) through (50) as divisions (B)(46) through (48), respectively.

Amendment Note: 1994 H 715 corrected the designations of divisions (B)(45) through (B)(52); and rewrote division (B)(50), which previously read:

"(52) 'Private noncustodial agency' means any person, organization, association, or society certified by the department of human services that does not accept temporary or permanent legal custody of children, that is privately operated in the state, that receives and cares for children for two or more consecutive weeks, and that participates in the placement of children in family foster homes or provides adoption services in conjunction with a public children services agency or private child placing agency."

Cross References

Additional definitions applicable to juvenile courts, Juv R 2
Body piercing and tattooing, custodian defined, 3730.01
Disability assistance, annual report of number of children requiring services from children services agency due to denial of, 5115.012
Foster parent or relative wanting to adopt child, permanent custody defined, 5103.161
Job and family services department, agreements to make payments to encourage adoptive placement of children with agencies, permanent custody defined, 5103.12
Infant hearing-impairment screening, custodian defined, 3701.503
Judges of the court of domestic relations, juvenile court responsibility, 2301.03
Juvenile court jurisdiction over juvenile capital facilities, 307.021
Obstructing justice, adult and child defined, 2921.32
Permanent exclusion of pupils, out-of-home care defined, 3313.662
Permanent exclusion of pupils, out-of-home care and legal custody defined, 3301.121, 3313.662
Power of attorney, certain pending actions prohibiting creation, 3109.58
Procedure under Criminal Rules, exceptions, Crim R 1
Sex offender registration, notification of public children services agency, 2950.11
Social administration division, private child placing agency, private noncustodial agency, public children services agency, and treatment foster home defined, 5103.02
Voyeurism, babysitting care defined, 2907.08

Ohio Administrative Code References

Definition of terms for the implementation of the "Comprehensive Assessment and Planning Model - Interim Solution" and statewide automated child welfare database, OAC 5101:2–1–01.1
Department of public welfare, social services, eligibility of child for subsidized adoption, OAC 5101:2–44–05

Library References

Baldwin's Ohio Legislative Service, 1988 Laws of Ohio, S 89—LSC Analysis, p 5–571

Research References

Encyclopedias

OH Jur. 3d Courts & Judges § 3, Judge.
OH Jur. 3d Courts & Judges § 18, Courts of Common Pleas—Juvenile Division and Juvenile Courts.
OH Jur. 3d Criminal Law § 2012, Effect of Juvenile Court; Transfers to Juvenile Court.
OH Jur. 3d Family Law § 570, Jurisdiction of Juvenile Court.
OH Jur. 3d Family Law § 1485, "Child".
OH Jur. 3d Family Law § 1486, "Child"—Significance of Age at Time of Offense.
OH Jur. 3d Family Law § 1487, "Delinquent Child".
OH Jur. 3d Family Law § 1490, "Neglected Child".
OH Jur. 3d Family Law § 1491, "Neglected Child"—Culpable Act by Parents.
OH Jur. 3d Family Law § 1500, Relating to Persons.
OH Jur. 3d Family Law § 1501, Relating to Control and Care.
OH Jur. 3d Family Law § 1502, Relating to Facilities.
OH Jur. 3d Family Law § 1503, Relating to Procedure.
OH Jur. 3d Family Law § 1535, Definitions.
OH Jur. 3d Family Law § 1565, Order of Transfer; Resumption of Jurisdiction by Juvenile Court.
OH Jur. 3d Family Law § 1626, Right Under Juvenile Court Law and Rules.
OH Jur. 3d Family Law § 1696, Commitment to Youth Commission.
OH Jur. 3d Family Law § 1706, Modification or Vacation of Order.
OH Jur. 3d Schools, Universities, & Colleges § 286, Excuses for Nonattendance.

Forms

Ohio Forms Legal and Business § 28:17, Introduction.

Ohio Jurisprudence Pleading and Practice Forms § 2:25, Powers and Duties Via Particular Courts—Juvenile Division.

Ohio Jurisprudence Pleading and Practice Forms § 96:1, Definitions.

Treatises and Practice Aids

Sowald & Morganstern, Baldwin's Ohio Practice Domestic Relations Law § 15:51, Award to Third Party—by Parents' Agreement.

Carlin, Baldwin's Ohio Practice, Merrick-Rippner Probate Law § 105:8, Juvenile Court—Age Jurisdiction.

Carlin, Baldwin's Ohio Practice, Merrick-Rippner Probate Law § 105:9, Juvenile Court—Waiver of Jurisdiction.

Carlin, Baldwin's Ohio Practice, Merrick-Rippner Probate Law § 106:1, Juvenile Court Jurisdiction—Delinquent Child—Definition: Evidence of Delinquency.

Carlin, Baldwin's Ohio Practice, Merrick-Rippner Probate Law § 106:8, Juvenile Court Jurisdiction—Unruly Child—Definition: Evidence of Unruliness.

Carlin, Baldwin's Ohio Practice, Merrick-Rippner Probate Law § 108:1, Juvenile Court—Criminal Jurisdiction.

Carlin, Baldwin's Ohio Practice, Merrick-Rippner Probate Law § 105:10, Juvenile Court—Duration and Termination of Jurisdiction.

Carlin, Baldwin's Ohio Practice, Merrick-Rippner Probate Law § 106:11, Juvenile Court Jurisdiction—Neglected Child—Definition: Evidence of Neglect.

Carlin, Baldwin's Ohio Practice, Merrick-Rippner Probate Law § 106:14, Juvenile Court Jurisdiction—Dependent Child—Definition: Evidence of Dependency.

Carlin, Baldwin's Ohio Practice, Merrick-Rippner Probate Law § 106:17, Juvenile Court Jurisdiction—Abused Child—Definition: Evidence of Abuse.

Carlin, Baldwin's Ohio Practice, Merrick-Rippner Probate Law § 107:70, Authority of Criminal Court Over Children.

Carlin, Baldwin's Ohio Practice, Merrick-Rippner Probate Law § 107:74, Reasonable Efforts Determination.

Carlin, Baldwin's Ohio Practice, Merrick-Rippner Probate Law § 107:76, Disposition of Abused, Neglected, or Dependent Child—Types of Orders Court May Make.

Carlin, Baldwin's Ohio Practice, Merrick-Rippner Probate Law § 107:77, Disposition of Abused, Neglected, or Dependent Child—Protective Supervision.

Carlin, Baldwin's Ohio Practice, Merrick-Rippner Probate Law § 107:78, Disposition of Abused, Neglected, or Dependent Child—Temporary Custody.

Carlin, Baldwin's Ohio Practice, Merrick-Rippner Probate Law § 107:79, Disposition of Abused, Neglected, or Dependent Child—Legal Custody.

Carlin, Baldwin's Ohio Practice, Merrick-Rippner Probate Law § 107:80, Disposition of Abused, Neglected, or Dependent Child—Permanent Custody.

Carlin, Baldwin's Ohio Practice, Merrick-Rippner Probate Law § 107:82, Disposition of Abused, Neglected, or Dependent Child—Planned Permanent Living Arrangement.

Carlin, Baldwin's Ohio Practice, Merrick-Rippner Probate Law § 107:84, Disposition of Delinquent Children—Prior to January 1, 2002.

Carlin, Baldwin's Ohio Practice, Merrick-Rippner Probate Law § 107:105, Commitment of Delinquent Children to the Custody of Department of Youth Services, Effective January 1, 2002.

Adrine & Ruden, Ohio Domestic Violence Law § 9:8, Relationships Covered—Parents and Children.

Adrine & Ruden, Ohio Domestic Violence Law § 12:11, Court Enforcement of Civil Protection Orders—Related Substantive Concerns.

Giannelli & Yeomans, Ohio Juvenile Law § 1:7, Juvenile Code.

Giannelli & Yeomans, Ohio Juvenile Law § 2:2, Age Jurisdiction.

Giannelli & Yeomans, Ohio Juvenile Law § 2:3, Child Subject to Adult Prosecution.

Giannelli & Yeomans, Ohio Juvenile Law § 4:5, Truancy.

Giannelli & Yeomans, Ohio Juvenile Law § 8:4, Unruly—Truancy.

Giannelli & Yeomans, Ohio Juvenile Law § 9:5, Neglect—Abandonment.

Giannelli & Yeomans, Ohio Juvenile Law § 9:6, Neglect—Inadequate Care Due to Parental Fault.

Giannelli & Yeomans, Ohio Juvenile Law § 10:2, Dependent Child Defined.

Giannelli & Yeomans, Ohio Juvenile Law § 19:2, Place of Detention.

Giannelli & Yeomans, Ohio Juvenile Law § 19:7, Time Requirements.

Giannelli & Yeomans, Ohio Juvenile Law § 22:4, Improper Transfer; Lack of Jurisdiction.

Giannelli & Yeomans, Ohio Juvenile Law § 27:8, Probation.

Giannelli & Yeomans, Ohio Juvenile Law § 28:6, Commitment to Juvenile Facility.

Giannelli & Yeomans, Ohio Juvenile Law § 28:8, Revocation of Probationary Operator's License.

Giannelli & Yeomans, Ohio Juvenile Law § 30:5, Protective Supervision.

Giannelli & Yeomans, Ohio Juvenile Law § 30:6, Temporary Custody.

Giannelli & Yeomans, Ohio Juvenile Law § 30:7, Legal Custody.

Giannelli & Yeomans, Ohio Juvenile Law § 30:8, Permanent Custody—Defined.

Giannelli & Yeomans, Ohio Juvenile Law § 31:6, Findings.

Giannelli & Yeomans, Ohio Juvenile Law § 32:2, Jurisdiction Over Parents and Others.

Giannelli & Yeomans, Ohio Juvenile Law § 33:4, Abuse, Neglect, and Dependency Proceedings.

Giannelli & Yeomans, Ohio Juvenile Law § 33:9, Department of Youth Services.

Giannelli & Yeomans, Ohio Juvenile Law § 9:10, Neglect—Physical or Mental Injury Due to Omissions.

Giannelli & Yeomans, Ohio Juvenile Law § 9:11, Neglect—Out-Of-Home Care Neglect.

Giannelli & Yeomans, Ohio Juvenile Law § 9:15, Abused Child—Physical or Mental Injury Exhibited.

Giannelli & Yeomans, Ohio Juvenile Law § 9:17, Abused Child—Out-Of-Home Abuse.

Giannelli & Yeomans, Ohio Juvenile Law App. D, Appendix D. Glossary.

Giannelli & Yeomans, Ohio Juvenile Law § 22:22, Transfer of Jurisdiction.

Giannelli & Yeomans, Ohio Juvenile Law § 25:14, Reasonable Efforts Determination; Abuse, Neglect & Dependency.

Giannelli & Yeomans, Ohio Juvenile Law § 30:10, Permanent Custody—Parental Placement Within Reasonable Time.

Giannelli & Yeomans, Ohio Juvenile Law § 30:13, Planned Permanent Living Arrangement.

Gotherman, Babbit and Lang, Baldwin's Ohio Practice, Local Government Law—Municipal, § 27:5, Courts Having Jurisdiction Over Municipal Offenses.

Hastings, Manoloff, Sheeran, & Stype, Ohio School Law § 23:2, Admission Requirements and Tuition Liability-Statutory Requirements in General.

Hastings, Manoloff, Sheeran, & Stype, Ohio School Law § 20:15, Duty to Enforce School Attendance.

Hastings, Manoloff, Sheeran, & Stype, Ohio School Law § 20:19, Enforcement Procedures-Investigation.

Hastings, Manoloff, Sheeran, & Stype, Ohio School Law § 20:48, Warning to Child (Non-Attendance).

Hastings, Manoloff, Sheeran, & Stype, Ohio School Law § 20:50, Notice and Warning to Parent or Guardian or Other Person in Charge of Child (With Return of Service).

Hastings, Manoloff, Sheeran, & Stype, Ohio School Law § 24:11, Duty to Report Suspected Child Abuse or Neglect-Definition of Child Abuse.

Hastings, Manoloff, Sheeran, & Stype, Ohio School Law § 24:12, Duty to Report Suspected Child Abuse or Neglect-Definition of Child Neglect.

Law Review and Journal Commentaries

Implications of the United States Ratification of the United Nations Convention on the Rights of the Child: Civil Rights, the Constitution, and the Family, Note. (Ed. note: The author discusses damaging effects of the Treaty, which has not been ratified by the United States, on parental rights and the well-being of children.) 42 Clev St L Rev 675 (1994).

The Liberty Interests of Foster Parents and the Future of Foster Care, Comment. 63 U Cin L Rev 403 (1994).

Notes of Decisions

Ed. Note: *This section contains annotations from former RC 2151.01.*

Abandonment, presumption 11
Adult facility 7
Child defined 6
Constitutional issues 1
Custody defined 2
"Detention," construed 10
Foster homes 8
Jurisdiction of juvenile court 4
Parents' rights and duties 5
Placement defined 12
Procedural issues 3
Sovereign immunity 9

1. **Constitutional issues**

Court of Appeals declined to address merits of mother's claim that statute governing child abandonment unconstitutionally shifted burden of proving non-abandonment to the parent, where mother failed to direct Court to a single instance in record in which trial court relied upon statutory section and actually shifted burden to mother, and claim was based on erroneous premise that trial court's finding of abandonment was based solely on time period when mother allegedly believed her visitation rights had been revoked. (Per Evans, J., with two judges concurring in judgment only.) In re Fennell (Ohio App. 4 Dist., Athens, 09-26-2002) No. 02CA17, 2002-Ohio-6151, 2002 WL 31521504, Unreported. Infants ⇐ 241

Mother waived her appellate argument that statute which created a presumption of parental abandonment if the parent did not visit with or maintain contact with a child for ninety days violated mother's procedural and substantive due process rights, in child dependency proceeding, where mother failed to argue that the statute was unconstitutional during the trial court proceedings. In re Barnhart (Ohio App. 4 Dist., Athens, 10-30-2002) No. 02CA20, 2002-Ohio-6023, 2002 WL 31455949, Unreported. Infants ⇐ 243

Statute requiring child's parents to demonstrate a change in circumstances for either the child or the maternal grandparents, who had been granted legal custody of child adjudicated abused and dependent, in order for court to modify custody, violated parents' right to due process and, as such, was unconstitutional; grandparents had only legal custody of child, which was non-permanent custody award, fact that trial court awarded parents supervised visitation with child and ordered them to pay child support to grandparents indicated that grandparents' custody of child was only temporary, and grandparents repeatedly stated that they did not view their custody of child as permanent. In re James (Ohio App. 1 Dist., 09-16-2005) 163 Ohio App.3d 442, 839 N.E.2d 39, 2005-Ohio-4847, appeal allowed 108 Ohio St.3d 1413, 841 N.E.2d 318, 2006-Ohio-179. Infants ⇐ 132

Statutory amendments that subjected a person 21 years of age or older to criminal prosecution, regardless of age at time of alleged offense and without any necessity of bindover proceeding in juvenile court, did not impair any vested rights of defendant who was 15 at time of charged aggravated murder and thus could constitutionally be retroactively applied to him; even under law in effect at time of offense, defendant was subject to criminal prosecution if juvenile court made certain determinations, and amendments merely removed procedural prerequisite of a juvenile-court proceeding. State v. Walls (Ohio, 10-09-2002) 96 Ohio St.3d 437, 775 N.E.2d 829, 2002-Ohio-5059, reconsideration denied 97 Ohio St.3d 1461, 778 N.E.2d 1052, 2002-Ohio-6248, habeas corpus denied 2006 WL 293750. Constitutional Law ⇐ 190; Infants ⇐ 152

As retroactively applied to defendant who was 15 years old at time of charged aggravated murder, statutory amendments that subjected a person 21 years of age or older to criminal prosecution in general division of court of common pleas, regardless of age at time of alleged offense and without any necessity of a bindover proceeding in juvenile court, did not retroactively criminalize defendant's conduct so as to violate Ex Post Facto Clause. State v. Walls (Ohio, 10-09-2002) 96 Ohio St.3d 437, 775 N.E.2d 829, 2002-Ohio-5059, reconsideration denied 97 Ohio St.3d 1461, 778 N.E.2d 1052, 2002-Ohio-6248, habeas corpus denied 2006 WL 293750. Constitutional Law ⇐ 200; Infants ⇐ 152

For ex post facto purposes, application to 29–year–old defendant, who was 15 at time of charged aggravated murder, of statute that subjected a person 21 years of age or older to criminal prosecution in general division of court of common pleas, regardless of age at time of alleged offense and without any necessity of a bindover proceeding in juvenile court, did not increase defendant's available punishment in any manner other than a speculative and attenuated one; even applying the law in effect at time of alleged offense, juvenile court would have had virtually no discretion to retain jurisdiction in defendant's case because of his mature age. State v. Walls (Ohio, 10-09-2002) 96 Ohio St.3d 437, 775 N.E.2d 829, 2002-Ohio-5059, reconsideration denied 97 Ohio St.3d 1461, 778 N.E.2d 1052, 2002-Ohio-6248, habeas corpus denied 2006 WL 293750. Constitutional Law ⇐ 203; Infants ⇐ 152

General Assembly expressly intended that statutory amendments effectively removing anyone over 21 years of age at time of apprehension from the jurisdiction of juvenile court, regardless of date on which the person allegedly committed the offense, have retroactive application. State v. Walls (Ohio, 10-09-2002) 96 Ohio St.3d 437, 775 N.E.2d 829, 2002-Ohio-5059, reconsideration denied 97 Ohio St.3d 1461, 778 N.E.2d 1052, 2002-Ohio-6248, habeas corpus denied 2006 WL 293750. Infants ⇐ 132

Probation, imposed following adjudication of juvenile as delinquent, is not "sentence" or punishment for double jeopardy purposes, but is merely legal status allowing juvenile to remain with his family while under supervision of court. In re Bracewell (Ohio App. 1 Dist., 04-17-1998) 126 Ohio App.3d 133, 709 N.E.2d 938, dismissed, appeal not allowed 82 Ohio St.3d 1481, 696 N.E.2d 1087. Double Jeopardy ⇐ 33

Reinstatement of commitment order with respect to juvenile adjudicated delinquent by reason of acts which, if committed by adult, would have constituted third-degree felony of carrying concealed weapon, was within juvenile court's continuing jurisdiction over juvenile to make appropriate dispositional orders and was not constitutionally impermissible double punishment; goal of reinstatement of commitment order was juvenile's protection and rehabilitation, in light of his parents' inability to ensure his compliance with law following his release from official probation. In re Bracewell (Ohio App. 1 Dist., 04-17-1998) 126 Ohio App.3d 133, 709 N.E.2d 938, dismissed, appeal not allowed 82 Ohio St.3d 1481, 696 N.E.2d 1087. Double Jeopardy ⇐ 33

Miranda warnings were not required, in light of police officers' need to assess situation and concern for public safety, before officers asked juvenile, who was running from park, to stop and explain what was going on, where officers were responding to complaint of possible gunshots being fired; further, it was responsible for police to inquire what further knowledge juvenile might have after he responded that "some guy set that thing off over there," and that "it was a bomb thing." In re Travis (Ohio App. 10 Dist., 04-30-1996) 110 Ohio App.3d 684, 675 N.E.2d 36. Infants ⇐ 174; Infants ⇐ 192

Speedy trial statutes applicable to adults in criminal proceedings did not apply to juvenile who was charged with being juvenile traffic offender. In re Washburn (Wyandot 1990) 70 Ohio App.3d 178, 590 N.E.2d 855. Infants ⇐ 204

Natural parents have a constitutionally-protected liberty interest in the care and custody of their children. In re Barker (Ohio App. 12 Dist., Butler, 07-29-2002) No. CA2001-12-293, 2002-Ohio-3871, 2002 WL 1758378, Unreported. Constitutional Law ⇐ 274(5)

2. **Custody defined**

A newborn baby who tests positive for cocaine and shows signs of cocaine withdrawal is "neglected" where prenatal fault can be assigned to the mother who (1) tests positive for cocaine at the hospital, (2) admits to alcohol usage during her pregnancy, and (3) claims the last time she smoked crack cocaine was two weeks prior to giving birth; and where the mother unexpectedly gives birth at home and calls for medical assistance which transports her and the baby to the hospital she is custodian of the child as defined by RC 2151.011(B)(17) and removal of the child to the department of human services is warranted. In re Crawford (Ohio App. 5 Dist., Stark, 02-01-1999) No. 1998CA00194, 1999 WL 100377, Unreported.

Mother who had custody of children pursuant to divorce decree could decide that children would live in mother's residence with mother's current husband even though mother and husband had separated and mother had moved out; statute allowed legal custodian to determine where and with whom child would live. Palmer v. Harrold (Ohio App. 2 Dist., 03-17-1995) 101 Ohio App.3d 732, 656 N.E.2d 708. Child Custody ⇐ 100

While stepparent relationship, without more, does not confer any rights or impose any duties, situation may be different where stepparent has taken children into his home; stepparent who receives stepchildren into his home and educates and supports them stands in loco parentis and is liable for children's support. Palmer v. Harrold (Ohio App. 2 Dist., 03-17-1995) 101 Ohio App.3d 732, 656 N.E.2d 708. Child Support ⇐ 30

Once a child has been found to be "dependent" as defined in RC 2151.04, the "best interests" of the child are the primary consideration in determining whether an award of permanent custody is justified pursuant to RC 2151.353(D). In re Cunningham (Ohio 1979) 59 Ohio St.2d 100, 391 N.E.2d 1034, 13 O.O.3d 78. Infants 222

The meaning of the term "permanent custody" as used in RC 5153.16(B) is the same as defined in RC 2151.011(B)(12), and thus legal transfer of permanent custody of a child to a board or county department that has assumed the administration of child welfare is contingent upon consent to the transfer by the juvenile court. Angle v. Children's Services Division, Holmes County Welfare Dept. (Ohio 1980) 63 Ohio St.2d 227, 407 N.E.2d 524, 17 O.O.3d 140.

For purposes of RC 3313.64, "legal or permanent custody" may be established by a court order, or by evidence of the transfer of temporary custody without a court order in accordance with RC 5103.15. The temporary placement of a child with persons related by blood or marriage in accordance with RC 5103.16(A) does not affect the legal custody of the child for purposes of RC 3313.64(B)(2)(a). A notarized statement that is prepared by the court-designated custodial parent and purports to grant temporary custody of a child to a relative is not an "agreement for temporary custody," as that term is defined in RC 2151.011(B)(17), and does not operate to transfer legal custody for purposes of RC 3313.64(B)(2)(a). OAG 95-032.

Children committed by a juvenile court to a county department of welfare pursuant to RC Ch 2151, either permanently or temporarily, remain the responsibility of the department until they reach the age of twenty-one, unless the court, upon a proper application, terminates the order of commission at an earlier date. OAG 75-035.

As used in RC 4507.07, "custody" refers to any relationship in which a person stands in loco parentis to a minor, whether or not that person has legal custody of the minor. OAG 72-087.

For purposes of RC 4507.07 the parents of a minor who have abandoned the minor for a period of six years are not considered as having custody of such minor, provided the intent to abandon and actual abandonment are clear. OAG 72-087.

3. Procedural issues

The trial court limitation of testimony concerning child's relationship with her mother to events from the time child was three years old was not an abuse of discretion, in child dependency proceeding; child was five years old when paternal grandmother filed a dependency complaint, and the court refused to hear testimony about events in the distant past. In re Brown (Ohio App. 2 Dist., Darke, 06-23-2006) No. 1676, 2006-Ohio-3189, 2006 WL 1719277, Unreported. Infants 207

Because the presumption set forth in statute providing a child is presumed abandoned when the parents of the child have failed to visit or maintain contact with the child for more than 90 days is in derogation of the natural rights of parents, the Court of Appeals construes it narrowly as a rebuttable presumption, rather than expansively, as an irrebuttable presumption. In re Custody of C.E. (Ohio App. 2 Dist., Champaign, 11-04-2005) No. 2005-CA-11, 2005-Ohio-5913, 2005 WL 2978538, Unreported. Child Custody 454

Trial court's denial of father's second request for a continuance of permanent custody hearing was not an abuse of discretion; father was granted a continuance at the first permanent custody hearing to consult with appointed counsel, father sought a second continuance to obtain new counsel, father asserted that he needed a continuance until he was released from jail and was able to find a job and "get me some money and get me a lawyer," and the court indicated that members from father's attorney's office were "in this court all of the time and I know that they do a very good job for their clients." In re Bailey Children (Ohio App. 5 Dist., Stark, 06-13-2005) No. 2004 CA 00386, 2005-Ohio-2981, 2005 WL 1400026, Unreported. Infants 204

Evidence supported finding that biological father "abandoned" child, as grounds for terminating parental rights, where father failed to visit or provide for child's support for more than 90 days. In re Cravens (Ohio App. 3 Dist., Defiance, 05-10-2004) No. 4-03-48, 2004-Ohio-2356, 2004 WL 1049142, Unreported. Infants 157

Grandparents were not prejudiced by denial of motion to intervene in dependency proceedings involving grandson; grandparents were not parties to juvenile proceeding under juvenile rule governing such proceedings, and there was no showing that grandparents had legally protectable interest in custody or visitation or that they acted in loco parentis with respect to child. In re Goff (Ohio App. 11 Dist., Portage, 12-12-2003) No. 2001-P-0144, 2003-Ohio-6768, 2003 WL 22952808, Unreported. Infants 200

An appointment to act as guardian ad litem (GAL) for a child in neglect proceedings does not constitute an appointment to act as the children's lawyer without an express appointment also to act as such. In re Clark (Ohio App. 8 Dist., 01-29-2001) 141 Ohio App.3d 55, 749 N.E.2d 833, 2001-Ohio-4126. Infants 205

Failure to appoint counsel for children in neglect proceedings in which their permanent custody was granted to county Department of Child and Family Services' (DCFS) was reversible error; governing statute provided that lawyer must be provided for child not represented by his parent, guardian, or custodian, guardian ad litem (GAL) appointed for children was not their "guardian" within meaning of that statute because GAL was not authorized to "exercise parental rights" over children, GAL was not expressly appointed to act as children's lawyer, neither mother nor father could be considered as representing children here, as they and their lawyers represented their own interests, and DCFS' prosecution of permanent custody complaint could not be considered direct representation of children, as DCFS sought permanent custody and argued solely for that result. In re Clark (Ohio App. 8 Dist., 01-29-2001) 141 Ohio App.3d 55, 749 N.E.2d 833, 2001-Ohio-4126. Infants 205; Infants 253

Court of Common Pleas never adequately determined that juvenile was probation violator after date on which it continued his probation; court in judgment entry neither identified condition allegedly violated, nor "found" juvenile had violated condition. In re Edwards (Ohio App. 8 Dist., 12-23-1996) 117 Ohio App.3d 108, 690 N.E.2d 22. Infants 230.1

Juvenile court lacked jurisdiction to hear and determine child support complaint filed after child had reached age of majority. In re Livingston (Ohio App. 8 Dist., 11-18-1996) 115 Ohio App.3d 613, 685 N.E.2d 1285. Child Support 103

Trial court could adjudicate claim that defendant had committed act of delinquency involving offenses committed at age 16, even though defendant had not appeared at hearings and was not taken into custody until he was over 21 years of age. In re J.B. (Ohio Com.Pl., 06-13-1995) 71 Ohio Misc.2d 63, 654 N.E.2d 216. Infants 196

Conduct of a child is not measured by same rules that apply to adult; measure of care required of boy is that degree of care which boy of ordinary care and prudence of same age, capacity, education and experience is accustomed to exercise for his own safety under same or similar circumstances. Siders v. Reynoldsburg School Dist. (Ohio App. 10 Dist., 12-13-1994) 99 Ohio App.3d 173, 650 N.E.2d 150. Infants 61

In a juvenile court proceeding brought by the welfare department for permanent custody, the juvenile court need not consider the parents' pending application in the probate court for approval of adoption placements, nor must it stay its proceedings in favor of the probate court. In re Palmer (Ohio 1984) 12 Ohio St.3d 194, 465 N.E.2d 1312, 12 O.B.R. 259, certiorari denied 105 S.Ct. 918, 469 U.S. 1162, 83 L.Ed.2d 930.

4. Jurisdiction of juvenile court

Juvenile court had subject matter jurisdiction in proceedings for juvenile's adjudication as delinquent, where complaint alleged juvenile to be a delinquent child. In re C.W. (Ohio App. 12 Dist., Butler, 08-01-2005) No. CA2004-12-312, 2005-Ohio-3905, 2005 WL 1799317, Unreported. Infants 196

Evidence supported finding that father received adequate service of process regarding permanent custody hearing, where father was personally served with the motion for permanent custody at the first permanent custody hearing, and father was again served with the motion by certified mail. In re Bailey Children (Ohio App. 5 Dist., Stark, 06-13-2005) No. 2004 CA 00386, 2005-Ohio-2981, 2005 WL 1400026, Unreported. Infants 198

Court of Common Pleas had subject matter jurisdiction to try defendant on charges of aggravated murder, murder, and aggravated robbery, even though defendant was a juvenile at time of offenses; juvenile court held bindover hearing and relinquished jurisdiction to common pleas court after defendant was charged with burglary arising out of the same events, and second bindover proceeding was not required after murder and robbery charges were filed. State v. Burrell (Ohio App. 1 Dist., Hamilton, 01-07-2005) No. C-030803, 2005-Ohio-34, 2005 WL 27469, Unreported, appeal not allowed 105 Ohio St.3d 1546, 827 N.E.2d 328, 2005-Ohio-2188. Infants 68.7(3)

Trial court had jurisdiction to hear and determine merits of nonmarital child's request for retroactive child support against mother in parentage action, even though child was emancipated; juvenile court had jurisdiction over a parentage action, and the court could consider a claim for support after it determined parentage. Elzey v. Springer (Ohio App. 12 Dist., Fayette, 03-22-2004) No. CA2003-04-005, 2004-Ohio-1373, 2004 WL 549805, Unreported. Children Out-of-wedlock 36

Juvenile waived all but plain error in trial court's alleged failure to establish jurisdiction over him in delinquency proceeding, where juvenile did not raise that objection below. In re Ball (Ohio App. 3 Dist., Allen, 01-30-2003) No. 1-02-72, 2003-Ohio-395, 2003 WL 193519, Unreported. Infants ⇔ 243

Trial court established proper jurisdiction in juvenile delinquency proceeding by eliciting testimony by subject of proceeding, at preliminary hearing, that he was 16 years old and by making a finding in judgment entry of commitment that subject of proceeding was born on a particular date and was therefore a juvenile. In re Ball (Ohio App. 3 Dist., Allen, 01-30-2003) No. 1-02-72, 2003-Ohio-395, 2003 WL 193519, Unreported. Infants ⇔ 196

A juvenile court is without authority to order a delinquent child to serve a term of incarceration in an adult correctional facility or to place him on adult probation even though he is chronologically an adult when "sentenced" and was sixteen when the incidents giving rise to the complaint took place. Matter of Campbell (Ohio App. 11 Dist., Lake, 06-27-1997) No. 96-L-133, 1997 WL 401546, Unreported.

Statutes applying to juvenile courts, when viewed as a whole, demonstrate that the legislature does not intend to confer jurisdiction on a juvenile court over a person who is now over twenty-one years of age for acts committed when legally a child. In Matter of Jay I. (Ohio App. 6 Dist., Wood, 10-13-1995) No. WD-94-115, 1995 WL 604613, Unreported.

Court of common pleas lacked subject matter jurisdiction to convict 17-year-old defendant of grand theft and, thus, judgment of conviction against him was void ab initio; since defendant was child under statute and was never bound over by juvenile court, juvenile court retained exclusive jurisdiction over defendant's case. State v. Wilson (Ohio, 08-09-1995) 73 Ohio St.3d 40, 652 N.E.2d 196, 1995-Ohio-217. Infants ⇔ 68.5

A juvenile court has no jurisdiction to rule on a delinquency complaint alleging rape where the complaint is filed after the alleged delinquent has reached the age of twenty-one, even though the fact that the alleged offense was committed before the juvenile's fifteenth birthday precludes the relinquishment of jurisdiction to an adult court. In re C. (Ohio Com.Pl. 1991) 61 Ohio Misc.2d 610, 580 N.E.2d 1182.

Where a child, as defined by RC 2151.011(B), who has been adjudicated a delinquent leaves the jurisdiction of the juvenile court so that such court cannot dispose of his case until he is over twenty-one years of age, he is an adult within the meaning of RC 2151.011. In re Cox (Mahoning 1973) 36 Ohio App.2d 65, 301 N.E.2d 907, 65 O.O.2d 51. Infants ⇔ 152

After the effective date of GC 1639–1 (RC 2151.01) et seq., in all counties of Ohio not having a juvenile court or division of domestic relations, all juvenile jurisdiction is reposed in a juvenile court within the probate court of such county. 1937 OAG 871.

5. Parents' rights and duties

Evidence supported trial court's determination that placing minor child in the legal custody of his paternal grandmother was in his best interest, following dependent child adjudication; mother had taken very few steps to remedy the problems that led to child's removal, mother had problems with cocaine abuse, alcohol dependence, and opiate abuse, she had not been attending drug and alcohol counseling, nor had she been consistent in submitting urine samples for drug screening, and grandmother testified that, if the trial court placed child in her legal custody, she was willing to be responsible for him until he reached the age of 18. In re K.K. (Ohio App. 9 Dist., Summit, 06-22-2005) No. 22352, 2005-Ohio-3112, 2005 WL 1460317, Unreported, appeal allowed 107 Ohio St.3d 1407, 836 N.E.2d 1228, 2005-Ohio-5859, affirmed 109 Ohio St.3d 206, 846 N.E.2d 853, 2006-Ohio-2184. Infants ⇔ 222

Clear and convincing evidence supported trial court order in dependency proceeding granting legal custody of child, who had been adjudicated neglected, to child's father and his new wife; child was clean and well-taken care of by father and his new wife, father facilitated mother's visitation with child in Ohio by transporting child from his home in Kentucky, mother sporadically applied the parenting concepts that she learned in parenting classes, she continued to be ineffective at disciplining her children, and she failed to demonstrate that she was able to independently care for her children and protect them from future harm. In re Fulton (Ohio App. 12 Dist., Butler, 11-10-2003) No. CA2002-09-236, 2003-Ohio-5984, 2003 WL 22522895, Unreported. Infants ⇔ 222

Child placing agency, in permanent custody hearing involving dependent child, was not prejudiced by trial court's placing child in legal custody of father and in ordering protective supervision of child; clear and convincing evidence supported finding that granting agency permanent custody of child was not in child's best interests. In re J. H. (Ohio App. 9 Dist., Summit, 10-22-2003) No. 21575, 2003-Ohio-5611, 2003 WL 22399693, Unreported. Infants ⇔ 253

Mother had a legal duty to support child, even though paternal grandmother had legal custody of child and there was no court order for child support; statutes provided that a parent had a legal duty to support their child and that the duty survived an order of legal custody, and grandmother expressed an interest in receiving child support from mother and father of child. In re Placement for Adoption Of C.E.T (Ohio App. 2 Dist., Montgomery, 07-11-2003) No. 19566, 2003-Ohio-3783, 2003 WL 21658682, Unreported. Child Support ⇔ 32

Evidence supported finding that children were neglected; home had no electricity and cold weather was approaching, home lacked food, younger child lacked supervision, and mother refused to accept and follow advice which was precipitating factor in failing of neglect complaint. In re Browne Children (Ohio App. 5 Dist., Stark, 07-07-2003) No. 2003CA00027, 2003-Ohio-3637, 2003 WL 21546103, Unreported. Infants ⇔ 156

Evidence supported trial court's finding in termination proceedings that mother did not fail to contact her children for more than ninety days, thus supporting finding that children were not abandoned; although mother's whereabouts were unknown to the county, mother testified that she continued to see children while they were living with their paternal grandparents, and mother said she wrote to her children every month. In re N.B. (Ohio App. 8 Dist., Cuyahoga, 07-10-2003) No. 81392, 2003-Ohio-3656, 2003 WL 21545142, Unreported, appeal not allowed 100 Ohio St.3d 1425, 797 N.E.2d 93, 2003-Ohio-5232. Infants ⇔ 180

Judgment entry in divorce proceeding transferring custody of children to their paternal grandmother and grandmother's husband did not terminate mother's support obligation, where entry did not specifically state that mother was relieved of her duty to support her children. In re Minich (Ohio App. 11 Dist., Trumbull, 05-30-2003) No. 2003-T-0010, No. 2003-T-0011, 2003-Ohio-2817, 2003 WL 21263874, Unreported. Child Custody ⇔ 531(1); Child Support ⇔ 394

An award of legal custody of a child does not divest parents of their residual parental rights, privileges, and responsibilities. In re C.R. (Ohio, 03-29-2006) 108 Ohio St.3d 369, 843 N.E.2d 1188, 2006-Ohio-1191, reconsideration denied 109 Ohio St.3d 1483, 847 N.E.2d 1227, 2006-Ohio-2466. Parent And Child ⇔ 2.5

Neglect statute was intended to reach situation in which small children are left alone with no adult supervision; although statute defines "adequate parental care" as involving only provision of adequate food, clothing and shelter, shelter encompasses situations involving lack of parental supervision that present danger to child's health and physical safety. In re Zeiser (Ohio App. 11 Dist., 03-26-1999) 133 Ohio App.3d 338, 728 N.E.2d 10, appeal not allowed 86 Ohio St.3d 1437, 713 N.E.2d 1049. Infants ⇔ 156

State intervention for parental neglect in leaving children home alone is not limited to situations in which house contains an undue danger or dangerous condition, such as a gun. In re Zeiser (Ohio App. 11 Dist., 03-26-1999) 133 Ohio App.3d 338, 728 N.E.2d 10, appeal not allowed 86 Ohio St.3d 1437, 713 N.E.2d 1049. Infants ⇔ 156

It constitutes neglect per se to allow a six-year-old child to be left alone for two entire days per week on a regular basis and to be regularly left at other times under the supervision of his eight-year-old sibling. In re Zeiser (Ohio App. 11 Dist., 03-26-1999) 133 Ohio App.3d 338, 728 N.E.2d 10, appeal not allowed 86 Ohio St.3d 1437, 713 N.E.2d 1049. Infants ⇔ 156

Mother engaged in neglect through lack of parental supervision with respect to eight-year-old boy by allowing him to be babysitter for six-year-old brother on regular daily basis for intervals of two hours plus. In re Zeiser (Ohio App. 11 Dist., 03-26-1999) 133 Ohio App.3d 338, 728 N.E.2d 10, appeal not allowed 86 Ohio St.3d 1437, 713 N.E.2d 1049. Infants ⇔ 156

Clear and convincing evidence supported determination that single mother was guilty of "neglect" for leaving her six- and eight-year-old sons unsupervised for two hours each day in late afternoon and for leaving six-year-old son at home entirely alone for two days each week, notwithstanding evidence that boys were very bright, mature and responsible for their ages, testimony by day care director that boys could be left alone for a few hours occasionally, mother's provision of extensive instructions regarding boys' activities in her absence, and guardian ad litem's recommendation that court not find neglect, given pattern, regularity and length of unsupervised periods and mother's failure to acknowledge inherent dangers of the situation, indicating that situation would continue. In re Zeiser (Ohio App. 11 Dist., 03-26-1999) 133 Ohio App.3d 338, 728 N.E.2d 10, appeal not allowed 86 Ohio St.3d 1437, 713 N.E.2d 1049. Infants ⇔ 179

Result of order vacating county agency's permanent custody of children adjudicated neglected and giving legal custody of children to adoptive parent of their older sibling was to restore biological parents' residual rights to children, including biological parents' ability to consent to children's adoption. In re Hitchcock (Ohio App. 8 Dist., 11-21-1996) 120 Ohio App.3d 88, 696 N.E.2d 1090, stay granted 77 Ohio St.3d 1462, 672 N.E.2d 1119, stay denied 77 Ohio St.3d 1502, 673 N.E.2d 921, motion to vacate stay denied 77 Ohio St.3d 1521, 674 N.E.2d 373, appeal allowed 78 Ohio St.3d 1455, 677 N.E.2d 815, appeal dismissed as improvidently allowed 81 Ohio St.3d 1222, 689 N.E.2d 43, 1998-Ohio-653, stay denied 81 Ohio St.3d 1469, 690 N.E.2d 1288, stay denied 81 Ohio St.3d 1476, 691 N.E.2d 294. Infants ⇐ 231

Child's biological parents retain residual rights upon court's grant of legal custody to another, including privilege of reasonable visitation, consent to adoption, privilege to determine child's religious affiliation, and responsibility for support. In re Hitchcock (Ohio App. 8 Dist., 11-21-1996) 120 Ohio App.3d 88, 696 N.E.2d 1090, stay granted 77 Ohio St.3d 1462, 672 N.E.2d 1119, stay denied 77 Ohio St.3d 1502, 673 N.E.2d 921, motion to vacate stay denied 77 Ohio St.3d 1521, 674 N.E.2d 373, appeal allowed 78 Ohio St.3d 1455, 677 N.E.2d 815, appeal dismissed as improvidently allowed 81 Ohio St.3d 1222, 689 N.E.2d 43, 1998-Ohio-653, stay denied 81 Ohio St.3d 1469, 690 N.E.2d 1288, stay denied 81 Ohio St.3d 1476, 691 N.E.2d 294. Child Custody ⇐ 575; Child Custody ⇐ 578

Natural mother's alleged ignorance of law requiring her to support child was not justifiable cause for nonsupport of child, for purposes of mother's right to object to adoption of child. In re Adoption of Kuhlmann (Ohio App. 1 Dist., 12-07-1994) 99 Ohio App.3d 44, 649 N.E.2d 1279. Adoption ⇐ 7.4(6)

Parental obligation to support child is not excused by temporary custody of child being lodged with another. In re Adoption of Kuhlmann (Ohio App. 1 Dist., 12-07-1994) 99 Ohio App.3d 44, 649 N.E.2d 1279. Child Support ⇐ 32

Juvenile court had authority to hold parents of delinquent who, ten days before his eighteenth birthday, broke into high school and set it on fire responsible for his support until the age of 21, as he was a "child" within meaning of applicable statute. In re Hinko (Cuyahoga 1992) 84 Ohio App.3d 89, 616 N.E.2d 515. Infants ⇐ 228(2)

Residual parental rights, privileges, and responsibilities, including the responsibility of support, remained with parents notwithstanding juvenile court's order committing their child to Youth Development Center. In re Hinko (Cuyahoga 1992) 84 Ohio App.3d 89, 616 N.E.2d 515. Infants ⇐ 228(2)

An agreement by a parent with the county board or welfare department for permanent surrender of a child prior to consent of the juvenile court is not only revocable by the parent prior to consent of the juvenile court, but such revocation operates to dissolve the offer to surrender, and the public agency's continued retention of the child and refusal to return the child to the parent is illegal and gives rise to an action in habeas corpus. Angle v. Children's Services Division, Holmes County Welfare Dept. (Ohio 1980) 63 Ohio St.2d 227, 407 N.E.2d 524, 17 O.O.3d 140. Habeas Corpus ⇐ 536; Infants ⇐ 222

In a RC 2151.23(A)(2) child custody proceeding between a parent and a nonparent, the hearing officer may not award custody to the nonparent without first making a finding of parental unsuitability—that is, without first determining that a preponderance of the evidence shows that the parent abandoned the child, that the parent contractually relinquished custody of the child, that the parent has become totally incapable of supporting or caring for the child, or that an award of custody to the parent would be detrimental to the child. In re Perales (Ohio 1977) 52 Ohio St.2d 89, 369 N.E.2d 1047, 6 O.O.3d 293. Child Custody ⇐ 42

Where a juvenile court grants the temporary custody of a minor child, with the consent of his parents, to a nonrelative after the father had unrestricted custody pursuant to a divorce decree, RC 3109.04(B) and RC 3109.04(C), as effective September 23, 1974, are not applicable to prevent the court's consideration of a motion filed by the father, in the same court, for the restoration of custody. Leininger v. Leininger (Fulton 1975) 48 Ohio App.2d 21, 355 N.E.2d 508, 2 O.O.3d 15. Child Custody ⇐ 6; Child Custody ⇐ 578

It is not absolutely necessary for parents to have physical control or legal custody of a child for that child to be neglected as to them; a child may be adjudicated a neglected child where the parents have failed to meet their obligations related to their residual rights under RC 2151.011. In re Luke, No. 83–CA–09 (5th Dist Ct App, Coshocton, 1–13–84).

6. Child defined

Order granting temporary custody of child to paternal grandmother was not an abuse of discretion, in child dependency case; mother and father were both low functioning, mother had severe anger control problems and lacked parenting skills, and mother and father had only been provided with limited services. In re Haywood (Ohio App. 3 Dist., Allen, 07-03-2003) No. 1-02-97, 2003-Ohio-3518, 2003 WL 21511308, Unreported. Infants ⇐ 192

Child may have reached the age of 18 at the time of a juvenile disposition and still be deemed a "child" for purposes of the juvenile code, as the applicable statute does not expressly exclude such a finding. In re Hennessey (Ohio App. 3 Dist., 09-13-2001) 146 Ohio App.3d 743, 768 N.E.2d 663, 2001-Ohio-2267, appeal not allowed 94 Ohio St.3d 1431, 761 N.E.2d 47. Infants ⇐ 222

Juvenile who was 17 years of age at time he committed vehicular manslaughter forming basis of his adjudication, but was to turn 18 years old 38 days into his 90–day confinement was statutory "child" for purposes of disposition or sentencing, and court was limited to dispositional alternatives available in sentencing juveniles. In re Hennessey (Ohio App. 3 Dist., 09-13-2001) 146 Ohio App.3d 743, 768 N.E.2d 663, 2001-Ohio-2267, appeal not allowed 94 Ohio St.3d 1431, 761 N.E.2d 47. Infants ⇐ 223.1

Defendant was an adult, subject to municipal court jurisdiction, when acts of criminal mischief and petit theft were committed on defendant's 18th birthday but six hours before anniversary of defendant's birth time; age of majority was reached at 12:01 a.m. on defendant's birthday. State v. Clark (Stark 1993) 84 Ohio App.3d 789, 618 N.E.2d 257. Time ⇐ 4; Time ⇐ 11

RC 2151.011(B)(1) provides for a statutory definition of a "child" which includes any person who violates any law whether federal, state or municipal ordinance prior to attaining eighteen years of age irrespective of his age at the time the complaint is filed or hearing had thereon. In re Cox (Mahoning 1973) 36 Ohio App.2d 65, 301 N.E.2d 907, 65 O.O.2d 51. Infants ⇐ 152

A child of kindergarten age is included within the meaning of the word "child" as used in RC 2151.357. OAG 72–099.

7. Adult facility

Where a child, as defined in RC 2151.011(B)(1), who has been adjudicated a delinquent beyond a reasonable doubt leaves the jurisdiction of the juvenile court so that such court cannot dispose of his case, the juvenile court has authority under RC 2151.355(I) to treat such person as an adult and to impose upon such person the penalty prescribed in the statute he violated and which constituted the basis for the adjudication of delinquency. In re Cox (Mahoning 1973) 36 Ohio App.2d 65, 301 N.E.2d 907, 65 O.O.2d 51. Infants ⇐ 223.1

A person shall be considered eighteen years of age for purposes of determining whether the person is a minor or has reached the age of majority at 12:01 a.m. on the date of birth, not the exact hour and minute of birth eighteen years later; thus, a person born at 9:20 a.m. on August 26, 1974 and charged with committing criminal acts between 3:14 a.m. and 3:30 a.m. on August 26, 1992 is an adult subject to the jurisdiction of a court of common pleas. State v Clark, No. CA-9194, 1993 WL 218320 (5th Dist Ct App, Stark, 6-1-93).

If the county adult detention facility is designed with a space which is enclosed on all sides, that is distinct, set apart and disconnected so that no child over the age of fifteen placed in that space will come in contact or communication with any adult convicted of or arrested for a crime, and the public interest and safety require the detention of such child when a delinquent detention facility is not available, the use of such adult facility is authorized. OAG 70–015.

8. Foster homes

A person who receives farm property as a result of a devise cannot be considered a foster child of the decedent for special tax valuation purposes where the person claiming to be the foster child never resided with the decedent, was not adopted by the decedent, and where the decedent had no control over the purported foster child but the child received gifts and affection from the decedent and provided assistance to the decedent and was very close to the decedent for over fifty years. In re Estate of Cummins (Ohio Com.Pl. 1991) 61 Ohio Misc.2d 579, 580 N.E.2d 866.

Pursuant to RC 2151.418, a home that constitutes a "foster home" or "family foster home," as those terms are defined in RC 2151.011(B), is a permitted use in all zoning districts in which residential uses are permitted, and no township zoning regulation may require a conditional permit or any other special exception certification for any such home. OAG 96–009.

When a county children services board has temporary care and custody of a child who resides in a residential care facility operated by the board, that board has legal custody of the child and, pursuant to RC 2151.011(B)(9), has the right and duty to provide the child with education, subject to any residual parental rights, privileges, and responsibilities; the board cannot, however, select for the child a school district other than the district in which the residential care facility is located. OAG 94–070.

Foster home is not educational facility within meaning of RC 2151.357 and section has no application to foster home. OAG 70–166.

9. Sovereign immunity

Statutory prohibitions against criminal child endangerment and wrongful death did not expressly impose liability upon county or its employee and did not limit county's or employee's sovereign immunity from liability for death to child that occurred during fishing trip sponsored by county child services agency for children in its custody. Colling v. Franklin Cty. Children Serv. (Franklin 1993) 89 Ohio App.3d 245, 624 N.E.2d 230, dismissed, jurisdictional motion overruled 67 Ohio St.3d 1511, 622 N.E.2d 658, rehearing denied 68 Ohio St.3d 1431, 624 N.E.2d 1067. Counties ⚖ 146

10. "Detention," construed

Juvenile's placement in treatment and rehabilitation facilities before placement in the Department of Youth Services (DYS) did not amount to a detention for which juvenile was entitled to credit against time served at DYS, unless: (1) juvenile was held at a rehabilitation or treatment facility while awaiting the final adjudication or disposition of the original delinquency complaint; (2) juvenile was held in one of those facilities after an order of commitment to DYS was made but before the order was executed by his or her transfer to the custody of DYS; or (3) juvenile was held in one of these facilities while awaiting the final disposition of an alleged probation violation. In re Thomas (Ohio, 10-15-2003) 100 Ohio St.3d 89, 796 N.E.2d 908, 2003-Ohio-5162. Infants ⚖ 223.1

Time spent in rehabilitation center while on probation was not detention within meaning of statute providing for credit against sentence for time held in detention, and thus juvenile was not entitled to credit against 18 month sentence for nine months spent in juvenile rehabilitation center. In re Henderson (Ohio App. 12 Dist., Butler, 06-03-2002) No. CA2001-07-162, No. CA2001-09-228, 2002-Ohio-2575, 2002 WL 1160073, Unreported. Infants ⚖ 225

11. Abandonment, presumption

Once trial court had determined mother had not abandoned her children and was not otherwise unsuitable for custody, analysis of the best interests of the children became immaterial in her action to regain custody, which had temporarily been granted to the children's grandparents. In re Custody of C.E. (Ohio App. 2 Dist., Champaign, 11-04-2005) No. 2005-CA-11, 2005-Ohio-5913, 2005 WL 2978938, Unreported. Child Custody ⚖ 554

Mother presented sufficient evidence to overcome the rebuttable presumption she had "abandoned" her children when she failed to visit or maintain contact with the children for a period exceeding 90 days in her action to regain custody, which had been temporarily granted to the children's grandparents; evidence indicated that mother avoided contact with children for four months in order to avoid a substantial possibility that her location could have been communicated to her husband, who had physically abused her, and grandmother testified she did not think mother intended to abandon her children. In re Custody of C.E. (Ohio App. 2 Dist., Champaign, 11-04-2005) No. 2005-CA-11, 2005-Ohio-5913, 2005 WL 2978938, Unreported. Child Custody ⚖ 641

County's motion for permanent custody gave father notice that trial court could terminate his parental rights to children if it found that he had abandoned them; motion alleged that children had been abandoned, that father had complied with no case plan objectives, and that he had not maintained contact with children for period in excess of 90 days. In re Vann (Ohio App. 5 Dist., Stark, 08-22-2005) No. 2005-CA-00127, 2005-Ohio-4398, 2005 WL 2045442, Unreported. Infants ⚖ 197

Trial court's finding that father abandoned his children was not against the manifest weight of the evidence; father was aware that his children had been removed from mother's care, he made no attempt to contact mother or the county department of job and family services to determine the status of the children, he had no contact with the children for more than 90 days, and he admitted that he did not provide financial support for the children. In re Bailey Children (Ohio App. 5 Dist., Stark, 06-13-2005) No. 2004 CA 00386, 2005-Ohio-2981, 2005 WL 1400026, Unreported. Infants ⚖ 157

Finding that mother abandoned child, as grounds for terminating parental rights, was supported by evidence that, at time of permanent custody hearing, mother had not visited child for more than eight months and that attempts by Children Services Board to contact mother to make visitation arrangements were unsuccessful. In re B.C.M. (Ohio App. 9 Dist., Lorain, 04-20-2005) No. 05CA0001, 2005-Ohio-1818, 2005 WL 901210, Unreported. Infants ⚖ 157

The magistrate's finding that mother abandoned child was not supported by clear and convincing evidence, during termination of parental rights proceeding; mother called child weekly for over six months after child was initially under father's care, mother later called child once every month, mother wrote to child, mother sought visitation with child three times and was denied visitation each time, and mother had one visit with child in the presence of child's therapist. In re Anderson (Ohio App. 11 Dist., Trumbull, 09-30-2004) No. 2004-T-0059, 2004-Ohio-5298, 2004 WL 2804824, Unreported. Infants ⚖ 157

Finding that grant of permanent custody of children to their aunt and uncle, rather than legal custody, was in best interests of children was supported by testimony of social worker that children were well adjusted to their placement with aunt and uncle and did not have a bond with their parents and that aunt and uncle wished to adopt children but were not interested in a legal custody arrangement, by custodial history of children which showed that they had been in custody for twelve months, and by fact that father had legally abandoned the children. In re R.H. (Ohio App. 8 Dist., Cuyahoga, 10-28-2004) No. 84051, 2004-Ohio-5734, 2004 WL 2425831, Unreported. Infants ⚖ 222

Evidence supported juvenile court's determination that child was abandoned, thus supporting grant of permanent custody of child to county; parents had not visited with or sent cards or gifts to child for the 15 months he had been in agency's temporary care, agency mailed calendars to parents listing the dates available for visitation, and father stopped at agency and called by telephone but did not inquire about or arrange visitation. In re L.D. (Ohio App. 12 Dist., Clinton, 08-02-2004) No. CA2004-03-007, 2004-Ohio-4000, 2004 WL 1717680, Unreported. Infants ⚖ 157

Father failed to rebut statutory presumption that he abandoned child by having no contact with child for over 90 days, for purpose of proceeding in which permanent child custody was granted to department of job and family services, where father conceded that he did not have contact with child for more than 90 days and merely made reference to sending letters to his attorney to let her know that he was still interested in child. In re Wright (Ohio App. 5 Dist., Stark, 03-08-2004) No. 2003CA00347, 2004-Ohio-1094, 2004 WL 434036, Unreported. Infants ⚖ 180

Assuming that mother was told she was denied visitation with child, such fact did not overcome finding that child was neglected and dependent based on abandonment; such an order only addressed visitation and would not have prevented a mother from calling or sending letters or cards to her son, and there was ample evidence in the record to support a finding of abandonment. (Per Evans, J., with two judges concurring in judgment only.) In re Fennell (Ohio App. 4 Dist., Athens, 09-26-2002) No. 02CA17, 2002-Ohio-6151, 2002 WL 31521504, Unreported. Infants ⚖ 157

Competent, credible evidence supported finding that child was neglected and dependent based on abandonment; mother failed to pay child support since child was placed with county children services, mother failed to attend a single scheduled visitation for three-month period and mother's subsequent visitation was sporadic, and mother made no contact whatsoever with child for more than a year. (Per Evans, J., with two judges concurring in judgment only.) In re Fennell (Ohio App. 4 Dist., Athens, 09-26-2002) No. 02CA17, 2002-Ohio-6151, 2002 WL 31521504, Unreported. Infants ⚖ 157

Competent, credible evidence supported decision to grant grandmother legal custody of child; record indicated that mother did not attend custody hearings, during one hearing she was gambling in Las Vegas, mother did not contribute to support of child, had very little contact with child and failed to follow through with supervised visitations. In re Allen (Ohio App. 5 Dist., Delaware, 10-10-2002) No. 02CAF06028, 2002-Ohio-5555, 2002 WL 31312392, Unreported. Child Custody ⚖ 279; Child Custody ⚖ 281

12. Placement defined

Definition of "placement," for purposes of statute providing that parent's consent to child's adoption was not required when parent had failed to communication with child, without justifiable cause, for over one year immediately preceding child's placement in home of adoption petitioner, could not be taken from juvenile statute defining "placement for adoption," as juvenile statute explicitly provided definitions of terms used in juvenile delinquency, abuse, dependency, and neglect cases. In re Adoption of G.W. (Ohio App. 9 Dist., Lorain, 03-23-2005) No. 04CA008609, 2005-Ohio-1274, 2005 WL 663002, Unreported. Adoption ⇔ 7.4(1)

2151.022 "Unruly child" defined

As used in this chapter, "unruly child" includes any of the following:

(A) Any child who does not submit to the reasonable control of the child's parents, teachers, guardian, or custodian, by reason of being wayward or habitually disobedient;

(B) Any child who is an habitual truant from school and who previously has not been adjudicated an unruly child for being an habitual truant;

(C) Any child who behaves in a manner as to injure or endanger the child's own health or morals or the health or morals of others;

(D) Any child who violates a law, other than division (C) of section 2907.39, division (A) of section 2923.211, division (C)(1) or (D) of section 2925.55, or section 2151.87 of the Revised Code, that is applicable only to a child.

(2006 H 23, eff. 8–17–06; 2006 S 53, eff. 5–17–06; 2000 S 179, § 3, eff. 1–1–02; 2000 S 218, eff. 3–15–01; 2000 S 181, eff. 9–4–00; 1995 H 4, eff. 11–9–95; 1969 H 320, eff. 11–19–69)

Uncodified Law

1995 H 4, § 3: See *Baldwin's Ohio Revised Code Annotated*, Uncodified Law under 2151.02.

Historical and Statutory Notes

Ed. Note: The legal review and technical services staff of the Legislative Service Commission has issued an opinion regarding the treatment of multiple amendments. The opinion is neither legally authoritative nor binding, but is provided as a general indication that the amendments of the several acts [2006 H 23, eff. 8–17–06 and 2006 S 53, eff. 5–17–06] may be harmonized pursuant to the rule of construction contained in R.C. 1.52(B) requiring all amendments be given effect if they can reasonably be put into simultaneous operation. See *Baldwin's Ohio Legislative Service Annotated*, 2006, pages 3/L–1243 and 1/L–220, or the OH-LEGIS or OH-LEGIS-OLD database on Westlaw, for original versions of these Acts.

Amendment Note: 2006 H 23 inserted "division (C) of section 2907.39," in division (D).

Amendment Note: 2006 S 53 inserted ", division (C)(1) or (D) of section 2925.55," in division (D).

Amendment Note: 2000 S 179, § 3, eff. 1–1–02, rewrote this section, which prior thereto read:

"As used in this chapter, 'unruly child' includes any of the following:

"(A) Any child who does not subject the child's self to the reasonable control of the child's parents, teachers, guardian, or custodian, by reason of being wayward or habitually disobedient;

"(B) Any child who is persistently truant from home;

"(C) Any child who is an habitual truant from school and who previously has not been adjudicated an unruly child for being an habitual truant;

"(D) Any child who so deports the child's self as to injure or endanger the child's own health or morals or the health or morals of others;

"(E) Any child who attempts to enter the marriage relation in any state without the consent of the child's parents, custodian, or legal guardian or other legal authority;

"(F) Any child who is found in a disreputable place, visits or patronizes a place prohibited by law, or associates with vagrant, vicious, criminal, notorious, or immoral persons;

"(G) Any child who engages in an occupation prohibited by law or is in a situation dangerous to life or limb or injurious to the child's own health or morals or the health or morals of others;

"(H) Any child who violates a law, other than division (A) of section 2923.211 of the Revised Code, that is applicable only to a child."

Amendment Note: 2000 S 218 inserted "or section 2151.87" in division (H).

Amendment Note: 2000 S 181 substituted "persistently" for "an habitual", and deleted "or school" from the end of, division (B); added new division (C); redesignated former divisions (C) through (G) as new divisions (D) through (H); and made changes to reflect gender neutral language.

Amendment Note: 1995 H 4 substituted "this chapter" for "sections 2151.01 to 2151.54, inclusive, of the Revised Code" and "of the following:" for "child" in the first paragraph; substituted "Any child who" for "Who" in divisions (A) through (F); added "the health or morals of" to divisions (C) and (F); rewrote division (G), which formerly read "Who has violated a law applicable only to a child."; and made changes to reflect gender neutral language and other nonsubstantive changes throughout.

Cross References

Contributing to unruliness or delinquency, 2919.24
Right to counsel, guardian ad litem, Juv R 4
Standards of operation and construction for facilities for rehabilitation of delinquent juveniles, 5139.27
Waiver of rights, Juv R 3
Youth services department, unruly child defined, 5139.01

Library References

Infants ⇔ 151.
Westlaw Topic No. 211.
C.J.S. Infants §§ 31, 33, 41, 62.

Research References

Encyclopedias

OH Jur. 3d Criminal Law § 861, What Constitutes Contributing to Unruliness.
OH Jur. 3d Family Law § 1489, "Unruly Child".
OH Jur. 3d Family Law § 1500, Relating to Persons.
OH Jur. 3d Family Law § 1735, Adult Acts Punishable in Juvenile Court.
OH Jur. 3d Family Law § 1748, Instructions to Jury.

Treatises and Practice Aids

Katz, Giannelli, Blair and Lipton, Baldwin's Ohio Practice, Criminal Law, § 105:16, Deception to Obtain Material Harmful to Juveniles.
Katz, Giannelli, Blair and Lipton, Baldwin's Ohio Practice, Criminal Law, § 109:14, Contributing to Unruliness or Delinquency.
Carlin, Baldwin's Ohio Practice, Merrick-Rippner Probate Law § 106:8, Juvenile Court Jurisdiction—Unruly Child—Definition: Evidence of Unruliness.
Carlin, Baldwin's Ohio Practice, Merrick-Rippner Probate Law § 108:2, Juvenile Court—Criminal Jurisdiction—Contributing to Dependency, Neglect, Unruliness, or Delinquency.
Carlin, Baldwin's Ohio Practice, Merrick-Rippner Probate Law § 107:25, Juvenile Detention and Shelter Care—Grounds for Detention or Shelter Care.
Carlin, Baldwin's Ohio Practice, Merrick-Rippner Probate Law § 107:137, Complaint, Unruly Child—Form.
Giannelli & Yeomans, Ohio Juvenile Law § 4:4, Ohio Penal Law.
Giannelli & Yeomans, Ohio Juvenile Law § 4:6, Court Order Violations.
Giannelli & Yeomans, Ohio Juvenile Law § 8:1, Introduction.
Giannelli & Yeomans, Ohio Juvenile Law § 8:2, Unruly Child Defined.
Giannelli & Yeomans, Ohio Juvenile Law § 8:3, Unruly—Wayward or Habitually Disobedient.
Giannelli & Yeomans, Ohio Juvenile Law § 8:4, Unruly—Truancy.
Giannelli & Yeomans, Ohio Juvenile Law § 8:5, Unruly—Endangering Conduct.
Giannelli & Yeomans, Ohio Juvenile Law § 8:7, Unruly—Miscellaneous Conduct.
Giannelli & Yeomans, Ohio Juvenile Law § 9:7, Neglect—Subsistence, Education & Medical Care.
Hastings, Manoloff, Sheeran, & Stype, Ohio School Law § 25:2, Statutory Standards for Student Conduct.
Hastings, Manoloff, Sheeran, & Stype, Ohio School Law § 20:19, Enforcement Procedures-Investigation.
Hastings, Manoloff, Sheeran, & Stype, Ohio School Law § 24:27, Contributing to the Delinquency or Unruliness of a Minor.

Law Review and Journal Commentaries

Due Process in Ohio for the Delinquent and Unruly Child, Max Kravitz. 2 Cap U L Rev 53 (1973).

"Families with Service Needs":—The Newest Euphemism?, Stanley Z. Fisher. 18 J Fam L 1 (1979–80).

Juvenile Delinquent and Unruly Proceedings in Ohio: Unconstitutional Adjudications, Note. 24 Clev St L Rev 602 (1975).

Manipulated by *Miranda*: A Critical Analysis of Bright Lines and Voluntary Confessions Under *United States v. Dickerson*, Casenote. 68 U Cin L Rev 555 (Winter 2000).

The Right to Remain Silent: The Use of Pre–Arrest Silence in *United States v. Oplinger*, 150 F.3d 1061 (5th Cir. 1998), Casenote. 68 U Cin L Rev 505 (Winter 2000).

Status Offenders and Juvenile Court: A Proposal for Revamping Jurisdiction, Comment. 42 Ohio St L J 1005 (1981).

Notes of Decisions

Acts not prohibited 4
Constitutional issues 1
Evidence 2
Juvenile detention facility 3
Procedural issues 5

---

1. Constitutional issues

Prior to juvenile's admission to habitual truancy charge, trial court failed to adequately advise juvenile of his constitutional rights and of consequences of his admission and also failed to sufficiently ascertain whether juvenile's purported waiver of counsel was made knowingly and voluntarily; there was no indication in record that trial court ever made determination concerning juvenile's indigency or advised juvenile that he had right to appointed counsel based on his indigency; trial court had merely asked juvenile whether it could be assumed that juvenile wished to proceed without attorney since juvenile was there without attorney, and trial court had not advised juvenile of purpose of hearing, possible penalties for alleged truancy violation, ramifications of admission to charge or of juvenile's rights to remain silent, offer evidence, cross-examine witnesses and have record made of proceedings. In re Kimble (Ohio App. 3 Dist., 09-25-1996) 114 Ohio App.3d 136, 682 N.E.2d 1066. Infants ⇐ 199; Infants ⇐ 205

A defendant's due process rights are violated when the original charge against him of underage consumption of alcohol is amended at the close of trial to charge him with unruliness, where he is found not guilty of the original charge. State v. Aller (Lucas 1992) 82 Ohio App.3d 9, 610 N.E.2d 1170.

Parents who intentionally keep their child from attending school due to religious beliefs but do not obtain an exemption may be convicted under RC 2919.24 for contributing to the unruliness of a minor as truancy is included as a definition of an unruly child, RC 2151.022(B). State v. Wood (Lucas 1989) 63 Ohio App.3d 855, 580 N.E.2d 484, dismissed 48 Ohio St.3d 704, 549 N.E.2d 1190, certiorari denied 110 S.Ct. 3279, 497 U.S. 1028, 111 L.Ed.2d 788.

Former RC 2151.41 (see now RC 2919.24) and 2151.022(C) are not unconstitutionally vague, since they convey sufficiently definite warnings as to proscribed conduct when measured by common understanding and practices. State v. Garfield (Geauga 1986) 34 Ohio App.3d 300, 518 N.E.2d 568. Criminal Law ⇐ 13.1(1)

2. Evidence

Conviction for contributing to unruliness of child was not against manifest weight of evidence; state provided evidence of sexual activity between defendant, who was adult, and victim, who was 12 years old. State v. Chewning (Ohio App. 12 Dist., Clermont, 12-13-2004) No. CA2004-01-002, No. CA2004-01-003, 2004-Ohio-6661, 2004 WL 2849222, Unreported, appeal not allowed 105 Ohio St.3d 1544, 827 N.E.2d 327, 2005-Ohio-2188, reconsideration granted 106 Ohio St.3d 1465, 830 N.E.2d 1171, 2005-Ohio-3490, reversed in part 109 Ohio St.3d 313, 847 N.E.2d 1174, 2006-Ohio-2109. Infants ⇐ 13

Testimony of alleged victim's high school classmate that she witnessed juvenile grab victim's breast during change of classes, together with testimony of school officials indicating that juvenile admitted to having grabbed victim's breast, was sufficient to support juvenile's adjudication as unruly by reason of conduct endangering his health or morals or health or morals of others. In re Felton (Ohio App. 3 Dist., 12-19-1997) 124 Ohio App.3d 500, 706 N.E.2d 809, dismissed, appeal not allowed 81 Ohio St.3d 1497, 691 N.E.2d 1058. Infants ⇐ 175.1

Juvenile's adjudication as unruly by reason of conduct endangering his health or morals or health or morals of others did not require testimony of juvenile, or of victim of his conduct, concerning effect of his conduct on his, or her, health or morals, where sufficient evidence in record indicated that juvenile's conduct in grabbing victim's breast in presence of others was potentially damaging to morals of other students present. In re Felton (Ohio App. 3 Dist., 12-19-1997) 124 Ohio App.3d 500, 706 N.E.2d 809, dismissed, appeal not allowed 81 Ohio St.3d 1497, 691 N.E.2d 1058. Infants ⇐ 175.1

A minor's mere presence at a party where other minors are drinking alcohol does not constitute conduct likely to injure himself or others; such presence does not support a finding of unruliness. State v. Aller (Lucas 1992) 82 Ohio App.3d 9, 610 N.E.2d 1170.

Evidence supported conviction of defendant for acting in way tending to cause child to become unruly or delinquent; defendant permitted children of mixed sexes aged 14 to 16 to play strip poker and to streak if they lost the game and enforced agreed streaking on part of losers, although defendant testified that he did not tell children to play cards, tell them what kind of cards to play, or make them take any action which they had not discussed. State v. Ellis (Greene 1989) 64 Ohio App.3d 158, 580 N.E.2d 1112, motion overruled 47 Ohio St.3d 703, 547 N.E.2d 991. Infants ⇐ 20

A single act of consensual sexual relations between an eighteen-year-old defendant and a seventeen-year-old minor that results in the minor's absence from school does not, without other injury to the health or morals of the minor, support a conviction for contributing to the unruliness of a minor. State v Linzy, No. 92–CA–49 (5th Dist Ct App, Richland, 2–5–93).

3. Juvenile detention facility

In accordance with RC 5119.64 et seq., juvenile runaways who are apprehended by law enforcement officials may not be placed in juvenile detention facilities even though suitable shelter is unavailable; however, if such a youth is determined to be a delinquent child as defined in RC 2151.02, an unruly child as defined in RC 2151.022, or a juvenile traffic offender as defined in RC 2151.021, he may be processed through the juvenile justice system and placed in a juvenile detention facility. OAG 77–063.

4. Acts not prohibited

A sixteen year old boy cannot be held responsible as a delinquent for a violation of RC 2905.03. In re J. P. (Ohio Com.Pl. 1972) 32 Ohio Misc. 5, 287 N.E.2d 926, 61 O.O.2d 24.

A board of education may enact a regulation designating areas within a school building where students shall be permitted to smoke as long as the board of education determines it is not injurious to the health or morals of the students. OAG 74–095.

5. Procedural issues

The act of intercourse whether consensual or nonconsensual is an intentional act for which coverage is excluded under homeowners' and watercraft insurance policies where the insureds give permission to their seventeen-year-old son to stay overnight on the family's boat and he engages in sexual intercourse with a friend who is fourteen and who suffers the physical and psychological harm which could reasonably be expected from the encounter; in addition, a claim brought by the girl's parents for negligent supervision related to the presence of alcoholic beverages on the boat is not covered where the complaint states the son intentionally and willfully served the girl alcoholic beverages to "lower her defenses." Noftz v. Ernsberger (Ohio App. 6 Dist., 01-16-1998) 125 Ohio App.3d 376, 708 N.E.2d 760, appeal not allowed 81 Ohio St.3d 1527, 692 N.E.2d 1027.

County agency to which juveniles were committed was not a party to proceeding in which juveniles were determined to be unruly minors and could not appeal from that determination. In re Blakey (Franklin 1989) 65 Ohio App.3d 341, 583 N.E.2d 1343. Infants ⇐ 242

2151.03 "Neglected child" defined

(A) As used in this chapter, "neglected child" includes any child:

(1) Who is abandoned by the child's parents, guardian, or custodian;

(2) Who lacks adequate parental care because of the faults or habits of the child's parents, guardian, or custodian;

(3) Whose parents, guardian, or custodian neglects the child or refuses to provide proper or necessary subsistence, education, medical or surgical care or treatment, or other care necessary for the child's health, morals, or well being;

(4) Whose parents, guardian, or custodian neglects the child or refuses to provide the special care made necessary by the child's mental condition;

(5) Whose parents, legal guardian, or custodian have placed or attempted to place the child in violation of sections 5103.16 and 5103.17 of the Revised Code;

(6) Who, because of the omission of the child's parents, guardian, or custodian, suffers physical or mental injury that harms or threatens to harm the child's health or welfare;

(7) Who is subjected to out-of-home care child neglect.

(B) Nothing in this chapter shall be construed as subjecting a parent, guardian, or custodian of a child to criminal liability when, solely in the practice of religious beliefs, the parent, guardian, or custodian fails to provide adequate medical or surgical care or treatment for the child. This division does not abrogate or limit any person's responsibility under section 2151.421 of the Revised Code to report child abuse that is known or reasonably suspected or believed to have occurred, child neglect that is known or reasonably suspected or believed to have occurred, and children who are known to face or are reasonably suspected or believed to be facing a threat of suffering abuse or neglect and does not preclude any exercise of the authority of the state, any political subdivision, or any court to ensure that medical or surgical care or treatment is provided to a child when the child's health requires the provision of medical or surgical care or treatment.

(2006 S 17, eff. 8–3–06; 1996 H 274, eff. 8–8–96; 1989 H 257, eff. 8–3–89; 1969 H 320; 1953 H 1; GC 1639–3)

Uncodified Law

2006 S 17, § 5, eff. 8–3–06, reads:

If any provision of a section of the Revised Code as amended or enacted by this act or the application of the provision to any person or circumstance is held invalid, the invalidity does not affect other provisions or applications of the section or related sections that can be given effect without the invalid provision or application, and to this end the provisions are severable.

Historical and Statutory Notes

Pre–1953 H 1 Amendments: 117 v 520

Amendment Note: 2006 S 17 rewrote the second sentence of division (B), which prior thereto read:

"This division does not abrogate or limit any person's responsibility under section 2151.421 of the Revised Code to report known or suspected child abuse, known or suspected child neglect, and children who are known to face or are suspected of facing a threat of suffering abuse or neglect and does not preclude any exercise of the authority of the state, any political subdivision, or any court to ensure that medical or surgical care or treatment is provided to a child when the child's health requires the provision of medical or surgical care or treatment."

Amendment Note: 1996 H 274 substituted "adequate" for "proper" in division (A)(2); and made changes to reflect gender neutral language and other nonsubstantive changes.

Cross References

Duty of husband to support family, wife to assist, duration of duty to support, 3103.03
False report of child abuse or neglect, 2921.14
Nonsupport of dependents, 2919.21
Right to counsel, guardian ad litem, Juv R 4
Shared parenting, neglected child defined, 3109.04
Taking into custody, Juv R 6
Visitation rights, effect of finding child neglected, 3109.051
Waiver of rights, Juv R 3

Library References

Infants ⟠156.
Westlaw Topic No. 211.
C.J.S. Infants §§ 31, 33 to 50, 55, 62.

Research References

Encyclopedias

OH Jur. 3d Appellate Review § 90, Child Custody.
OH Jur. 3d Criminal Law § 1073, Contributing to Child's Dependency or Neglect.
OH Jur. 3d Criminal Law § 2012, Effect of Juvenile Court; Transfers to Juvenile Court.
OH Jur. 3d Family Law § 1490, "Neglected Child".
OH Jur. 3d Family Law § 1491, "Neglected Child"—Culpable Act by Parents.
OH Jur. 3d Family Law § 1500, Relating to Persons.
OH Jur. 3d Family Law § 1544, on Certification from Another Court.
OH Jur. 3d Family Law § 1664, on Request for Permanent Custody—Factors to be Considered.
OH Jur. 3d Family Law § 1665, to Make Temporary Commitment Permanent.
OH Jur. 3d Family Law § 1735, Adult Acts Punishable in Juvenile Court.
OH Jur. 3d Family Law § 1746, Evidence and Witnesses—Weight of Evidence; Degree of Proof.

Treatises and Practice Aids

Katz, Giannelli, Blair and Lipton, Baldwin's Ohio Practice, Criminal Law, § 110:9, False Report of Child Abuse.
Katz, Giannelli, Blair and Lipton, Baldwin's Ohio Practice, Criminal Law, § 109:10, Nonsupport.
Carlin, Baldwin's Ohio Practice, Merrick-Rippner Probate Law § 105:7, Juvenile Court—Attachment of Jurisdiction.
Carlin, Baldwin's Ohio Practice, Merrick-Rippner Probate Law § 98:15, Adoption—Types of Placement—Agency Adoptions—Through Juvenile Court.
Carlin, Baldwin's Ohio Practice, Merrick-Rippner Probate Law § 98:23, Adoption—Illegal Placement.
Carlin, Baldwin's Ohio Practice, Merrick-Rippner Probate Law § 106:11, Juvenile Court Jurisdiction—Neglected Child—Definition: Evidence of Neglect.
Carlin, Baldwin's Ohio Practice, Merrick-Rippner Probate Law § 106:17, Juvenile Court Jurisdiction—Abused Child—Definition: Evidence of Abuse.
Carlin, Baldwin's Ohio Practice, Merrick-Rippner Probate Law § 107:80, Disposition of Abused, Neglected, or Dependent Child—Permanent Custody.
Carlin, Baldwin's Ohio Practice, Merrick-Rippner Probate Law § 108:16, Juvenile Court—Habeas Corpus Involving Child Custody.
Carlin, Baldwin's Ohio Practice, Merrick-Rippner Probate Law § 107:138, Complaint, Abused, Neglected, or Dependent Child—Form.
Adrine & Ruden, Ohio Domestic Violence Law § 8:6, Parents and Children.
Giannelli & Yeomans, Ohio Juvenile Law § 2:6, Common Law Infancy Defense.
Giannelli & Yeomans, Ohio Juvenile Law § 9:2, Parental Rights.
Giannelli & Yeomans, Ohio Juvenile Law § 9:3, Time of Neglect.
Giannelli & Yeomans, Ohio Juvenile Law § 9:4, Neglected Child Defined.
Giannelli & Yeomans, Ohio Juvenile Law § 9:6, Neglect—Inadequate Care Due to Parental Fault.
Giannelli & Yeomans, Ohio Juvenile Law § 9:7, Neglect—Subsistence, Education & Medical Care.
Giannelli & Yeomans, Ohio Juvenile Law § 9:8, Neglect—Special Care for Child's Mental Condition.
Giannelli & Yeomans, Ohio Juvenile Law § 9:9, Neglect—Illegal Placement.
Giannelli & Yeomans, Ohio Juvenile Law § 9:10, Neglect—Physical or Mental Injury Due to Omissions.

Giannelli & Yeomans, Ohio Juvenile Law § 9:11, Neglect—Out-Of-Home Care Neglect.

Giannelli & Yeomans, Ohio Juvenile Law § 9:12, Abused Child Defined.

Giannelli & Yeomans, Ohio Juvenile Law § 9:15, Abused Child—Physical or Mental Injury Exhibited.

Giannelli & Yeomans, Ohio Juvenile Law § 9:16, Abused Child—Physical or Mental Injury Due to Parents.

Giannelli & Yeomans, Ohio Juvenile Law § 9:17, Abused Child—Out-Of-Home Abuse.

Giannelli & Yeomans, Ohio Juvenile Law § 16:17, Objections to Complaints.

Giannelli & Yeomans, Ohio Juvenile Law § 30:10, Permanent Custody—Parental Placement Within Reasonable Time.

Hastings, Manoloff, Sheeran, & Stype, Ohio School Law § 24:12, Duty to Report Suspected Child Abuse or Neglect-Definition of Child Neglect.

Law Review and Journal Commentaries

Blood Transfusions and Elective Surgery: a Custodial Function of an Ohio Juvenile Court, M. J. Zaremski. 23 Clev St L Rev 231 (Spring 1974).

Child Maltreatment: An Overview of Current Approaches, Note. 18 J Fam L 115 (1979–80).

Drug–Using Families And Child Protection: Results Of A Study And Implications For Change, Wendy Chaukin, et al. 54 U Pitt L Rev 295 (Fall 1992).

Prosecution Of Mothers Of Drug–Exposed Babies: Constitutional And Criminal Theory, Doretta Massardo McGinnis. 139 U Pa L Rev 505 (December 1990).

The Use of Juvenile Court Jurisdiction and Restraining Authority to Address the Problem of Maternal Drug Abuse in Ohio, Deborah A. Wainey. 18 Ohio N U L Rev 611 (1991).

When Children Die as a Result of Religious Practices, Note. 51 Ohio St L J 1429 (1990).

Notes of Decisions

Abandonment 4
Constitutional issues, religious beliefs exception 1
Evidence of neglect 2
Jurisdiction 7
Parental rights and unification 6
Procedural issues 3
School attendance 5

---

1. Constitutional issues, religious beliefs exception

Plaintiff children, through their father, had standing to bring action challenging constitutionality of "spiritual/religious" exemptions of child endangerment statute; threatened injury was real, particularly in that several children in state had already died because they were denied adequate medical care due to their parents' religious beliefs, children claimed that, absent religious exemption, child endangerment statute would protect them, as it did all other children, and children's threatened injury would subside if court found that statute was unconstitutional. Children's Healthcare is a Legal Duty, Inc. v. Deters (S.D.Ohio, 07-12-1995) 894 F.Supp. 1129, reversed 92 F.3d 1412, rehearing and suggestion for rehearing en banc denied, certiorari denied 117 S.Ct. 1082, 519 U.S. 1149, 137 L.Ed.2d 217. Constitutional Law ⇔ 42.1(1)

Child endangerment statute was self-enforcing and, thus, if portion of statute was unconstitutional, problem of revoking that portion rested with Attorney General and, thus, Attorney General was proper party in action challenging constitutionality of "spiritual/religious" exemptions. Children's Healthcare is a Legal Duty, Inc. v. Deters (S.D.Ohio, 07-12-1995) 894 F.Supp. 1129, reversed 92 F.3d 1412, rehearing and suggestion for rehearing en banc denied, certiorari denied 117 S.Ct. 1082, 519 U.S. 1149, 137 L.Ed.2d 217. Constitutional Law ⇔ 44.1

Plaintiffs challenging constitutionality of "spiritual/religious" exemptions of child endangerment statute sought prospective declaratory relief, which was not barred by Eleventh Amendment. Children's Healthcare is a Legal Duty, Inc. v. Deters (S.D.Ohio, 07-12-1995) 894 F.Supp. 1129, reversed 92 F.3d 1412, rehearing and suggestion for rehearing en banc denied, certiorari denied 117 S.Ct. 1082, 519 U.S. 1149, 137 L.Ed.2d 217. Federal Courts ⇔ 272

2. Evidence of neglect

Juvenile court's adjudication of parents' three minor children as dependent and neglected was unsupported by clear and convincing evidence, despite allegations of severe domestic violence between the parents; county agency presented no evidence that the parents' actions constituted or caused the children any neglect as defined by applicable statute, there was virtually no evidence presented regarding the children and how they were being cared for, and record was devoid of evidence that the environment that parents provided for their children was unsafe, apart from one admission by mother, testified to by one caseworker, that the children were present during an unknown number of episodes of domestic violence between the parents. In re Alexander C. (Ohio App. 6 Dist., 11-18-2005) 164 Ohio App.3d 540, 843 N.E.2d 211, 2005-Ohio-6134. Infants ⇔ 179

Clear and convincing evidence supported conclusion that county had had temporary custody of mother's children for 16 months of a consecutive 22 months period, and, as such, county was required to file motion for permanent custody of children. In re Donell F. (Ohio App. 6 Dist., Lucas, 08-12-2005) No. L-04-1308, 2005-Ohio-4175, 2005 WL 1926512, Unreported. Infants ⇔ 178

Father demonstrated lack of commitment to children, as basis for adjudication that children were either neglected or dependent, for purposes of granting County Job and Family Services custody of children; father was perpetrator of violence against one of children, he utilized corporal punishment, and he refused to address his anger management issues and lack of parenting skills. In re Green (Ohio App. 5 Dist., Tuscarawas, 06-23-2005) No. 2005AP010007, No. 2005AP020008, 2005-Ohio-3308, 2005 WL 1523855, Unreported. Infants ⇔ 156

Sufficient evidence supported findings of neglect and dependency, in proceeding in which mother's parental rights were terminated and permanent custody was awarded to county children services board; children had no stable residence for nearly a year, there was not a sufficient amount of food consistently in their home, children were subjected to domestic violence between their mother and stepfather, their mother and stepfather continually used marijuana and crack cocaine and drank beer, and children were witnesses to their mother's attempted suicide. In re Brittany W. (Ohio App. 6 Dist., Lucas, 06-24-2005) No. L-04-1202, 2005-Ohio-3201, 2005 WL 1492028, Unreported. Infants ⇔ 156

Clear and convincing evidence supported finding of child's neglect and dependency, in termination of parental rights proceeding; evidence showed that mother received no prenatal care and that child tested positive for illegal drugs at the time of his birth. In re Barnhart (Ohio App. 4 Dist., Athens, 05-26-2005) No. 05CA8, 2005-Ohio-2692, 2005 WL 1283675, Unreported. Infants ⇔ 156

Father's conduct and parenting methods threatened health and welfare of children, as required to support determination that children were abused, neglected and dependent; father, a former military man, had unreasonable expectations with respect to children's schoolwork, father whipped children multiple times with belt to extent that children sustained long-lasting bruises and welts, some of blows were inflicted while child was required to remain sitting in "P.O.W. position" with hands behind his back, and father believed that his form of discipline was reasonable form of corporal punishment. In re Mercer (Ohio App. 10 Dist., Franklin, 04-21-2005) No. 04AP-422, 2005-Ohio-1845, 2005 WL 914671, Unreported, appeal not allowed 106 Ohio St.3d 1534, 835 N.E.2d 383, 2005-Ohio-5146. Infants ⇔ 156

Clear and convincing evidence supported finding that mother's two children were dependent; the children were left with a babysitter who was unaware that older child had left apartment and was unable to provide needed medication to younger child, and drugs and drug paraphernalia were found within access of older child. In re Bierley (Ohio App. 5 Dist., Tuscarawas, 01-24-2005) No. 2004-AP-07-0049, 2005-Ohio-331, 2005 WL 217025, Unreported. Infants ⇔ 156

Clear and convincing evidence supported finding that mother's children were neglected; the children were left with a babysitter, older child was found wandering naked in the street, when police went to residence after finding older child babysitter stated he had fallen asleep and did not know that older child was missing, and babysitter stated he was not instructed on how to give younger child his medication. In re Bierley (Ohio App. 5 Dist., Tuscarawas, 01-24-2005) No. 2004-AP-07-0049, 2005-Ohio-331, 2005 WL 217025, Unreported. Infants ⇔ 156

Trial court could not find that clear and convincing evidence supported grandmother's allegation that grandson was abused, neglected, or dependent; although grandmother was concerned for grandson's welfare and health, evidence adduced by grandmother to support her complaints regarding mother's care of child was not credible. In re Forrest (Ohio

App. 4 Dist., Athens, 08-05-2004) No. 04CA104CA1, 2004-Ohio-4189, 2004 WL 1778436, Unreported. Infants ☞ 179

In child neglect proceeding, County Department of Jobs and Family Services failed to present clear and convincing proof that mother's children lacked adequate parental care as a result of her faults or habits; there was no showing that children had ever been deprived of adequate food or clothing, none of school children on school field trip were ever actually subjected to sole parental supervision of mother who was intoxicated on the day of field trip, and mother's child did not even attend field trip, so she could not be considered neglected as result of mother's behavior on field trip, and mother provided children with adequate supervision following school. In re C.M. (Ohio App. 12 Dist., Brown, 05-10-2004) No. CA2003-02-003, No. CA2003-02-004, 2004-Ohio-2294, 2004 WL 1040677, Unreported. Infants ☞ 179

In child neglect proceeding, County Department of Jobs and Family Services proved by clear and convincing evidence that mother was intoxicated at child's school field trip, despite fact that no field sobriety test was administered to mother; teacher testified that she had been around people who have been intoxicated and was able to recognize the signs, and her testimony left little doubt that mother arrived intoxicated at the field trip, and trial court was free to give little or no weight to the fact that teacher did not smell alcoholic beverage on mother at the time of their confrontation. In re C.M. (Ohio App. 12 Dist., Brown, 05-10-2004) No. CA2003-02-003, No. CA2003-02-004, 2004-Ohio-2294, 2004 WL 1040677, Unreported. Infants ☞ 179

Former husband's complaint against former wife alleging dependency and neglect of parties' children failed to adequately set forth particular facts upon which allegations were based and contained no notice concerning evidence against which wife would have to defend; while husband claimed children would be molested and wife would flee should children be returned to her custody, these were general conclusory claims unsupported by particular facts, and husband's only specific claim, that children were not functioning at appropriate level, did not fall within definition of dependency, neglect, or abuse. Louck v. Louck (Ohio App. 3 Dist., Marion, 11-10-2003) No. 9-03-35, 2003-Ohio-5999, 2003 WL 22533679, Unreported. Infants ☞ 197

Evidence supported finding in child protection proceedings that child was neglected; child did not consistently attend counseling proceedings when child was returned to mother, child's progress in counseling deteriorated when returned to mother, child's behavior was out of control when she stayed with mother, condition of mother's home was cluttered and unsanitary, child had numerous hygiene issues, child suffered from gingivitis, and child needed structure and routine. In re Lewis (Ohio App. 4 Dist., Athens, 09-25-2003) No. 03CA12, 2003-Ohio-5262, 2003 WL 22267129, Unreported. Infants ☞ 156

Evidence supported finding that children were neglected; home had no electricity and cold weather was approaching, home lacked food, younger child lacked supervision, and mother refused to accept and follow advice which was precipitating factor in failing of neglect complaint. In re Browne Children (Ohio App. 5 Dist., Stark, 07-07-2003) No. 2003CA00027, 2003-Ohio-3637, 2003 WL 21546103, Unreported. Infants ☞ 156

Evidence was sufficient to support finding that mother provided inadequate care to 3-month-old infant, as would support finding that infant was neglected; although mother sought medical care for infant, child was diagnosed with failure to thrive and mother failed to follow up with an orthopedic surgeon regarding a hip dislocation, at time of removal infant was severely underweight, pale, and listless, yet after infant's removal she gained weight and was developmentally on-track for her age, mother and grandmother, who apparently lived in the home, were resistant to advice and assistance, medical and otherwise, mother did not receive any prenatal care, and home was not fit for an infant, in that boards with exposed nails were on floor, excessive clutter, exposed plumbing, problem with sewer pipes, and a foul odor existed in home, and little food was in cupboards. In re Goff (Ohio App. 11 Dist., Ashtabula, 04-04-2003) No. 2002-A-0038, 2003-Ohio-1744, 2003 WL 1793063, Unreported. Infants ☞ 156; Infants ☞ 159

Clear and convincing evidence supported the juvenile court finding that children were neglected and dependent, in child dependency proceeding; father failed to comply with programs or toxicology screenings requested by the county jobs and family services, and he did not attend any programs on his own. In re Harris (Ohio App. 1 Dist., Hamilton, 02-14-2003) No. C-020512, 2003-Ohio-672, 2003 WL 327996, Unreported. Infants ☞ 156

Mother's alleged decision in context of neglect proceeding not to voluntarily comply with provision of case plan prohibiting contact between children and individual with whom mother was romantically involved did not, in and of itself, prove by clear and convincing evidence an omission by mother that caused physical or mental injury or threatened to harm children's health or welfare. In re Locker (Ohio App. 5 Dist., Tuscarawas, 11-06-2002) No. 2002AP020011, 2002-Ohio-6124, 2002 WL 31518192, Unreported. Infants ☞ 156

Neglect allegation against mother, arising from automobile accident in which children were not wearing seatbelts, was not supported by clear and convincing evidence; there was no showing the failure to wear seatbelts caused children's injuries and no indication that any failure to wear seatbelts violated statute requiring that children of certain ages and weights be secured in child restraint systems or statute requiring that front seat passengers wear safety belt. In re Locker (Ohio App. 5 Dist., Tuscarawas, 11-06-2002) No. 2002AP020011, 2002-Ohio-6124, 2002 WL 31518192, Unreported. Infants ☞ 179

Neglect allegation arising from mother's alleged violation of a "no contact" order was not supported by clear and convincing evidence; order on which case worker based allegation prohibited individual with whom mother had been romantically involved from being in her residence, and that individual was not in residence as of the time of the filing of neglect complaint through dates of adjudicatory hearing. In re Locker (Ohio App. 5 Dist., Tuscarawas, 11-06-2002) No. 2002AP020011, 2002-Ohio-6124, 2002 WL 31518192, Unreported. Infants ☞ 156

Clear and convincing evidence supported finding that child was a neglected and dependent child, in dependency proceeding; mother had been incarcerated four times since child's birth, her mental health issues interfered with her ability to parent, she failed to address child's developmental delays and behavioral problems, she provided no financial support for child, she failed to provide child with a stable home, and she attempted to commit suicide in child's presence. In re Barnhart (Ohio App. 4 Dist., Athens, 10-30-2002) No. 02CA20, 2002-Ohio-6023, 2002 WL 31455949, Unreported. Infants ☞ 155; Infants ☞ 157; Infants ☞ 158

Clear and convincing evidence that turbulent relationship between child's parents created an environment which threatened the physical and emotional well-being of child supported finding that child was dependent and neglected, for purposes of termination of father's parental rights. In re Jehosephat W. (Ohio App. 6 Dist., Lucas, 10-11-2002) No. L-01-1505, 2002-Ohio-5503, 2002 WL 31270290, Unreported. Infants ☞ 179

Though mother did not strictly comply with the Children Services Board's safety plan, as provided under RC 2151.412(B)(2), the determination of child neglect was not supported by clear and convincing evidence, where mother has steady employment, adequate financial resources, and where children services worker observed that mother properly clothed, fed, and cared for child, as well as had a well-maintained home with all belongings for the child. In re Tate (Ohio App. 9 Dist., Summit, 09-12-2001) No. 20417, 2001 WL 1044084, Unreported.

Juvenile court's finding that a particular child is neglected and dependent is not supported by clear and convincing evidence where the mother obtains adequate parental care for the child during the time she is unable to provide that care personally by voluntarily taking him to his paternal grandparents who in turn provide adequate parental care. Johnson v. Johnson (Ohio App. 10 Dist., Franklin, 03-22-2001) No. 00AP-691, 2001 WL 277272, Unreported.

A newborn baby who tests positive for cocaine and shows signs of cocaine withdrawal is "neglected" where prenatal fault can be assigned to the mother who (1) tests positive for cocaine at the hospital, (2) admits to alcohol usage during her pregnancy, and (3) claims the last time she smoked crack cocaine was two weeks prior to giving birth; and where the mother unexpectedly gives birth at home and calls for medical assistance which transports her and the baby to the hospital she is custodian of the child as defined by RC 2151.011(B)(17) and removal of the child to the department of human services is warranted. In re Crawford (Ohio App. 5 Dist., Stark, 02-01-1999) No. 1998CA00194, 1999 WL 100377, Unreported.

Evidence was insufficient to support finding that father's two children were neglected; mother voluntarily relinquished control of the children to maternal grandparents prior to entering drug rehabilitation, and grandparents provided children with proper parental care. In re Stoll (Ohio App. 3 Dist., 01-30-2006) 165 Ohio App.3d 226, 845 N.E.2d 581, 2006-Ohio-346. Infants ☞ 156

Neglect statute was intended to reach situation in which small children are left alone with no adult supervision; although statute defines "adequate parental care" as involving only provision of adequate food, clothing and shelter, shelter encompasses situations involving lack of parental supervision that present danger to child's health and physical safety. In re Zeiser (Ohio App. 11 Dist., 03-26-1999) 133 Ohio App.3d 338, 728 N.E.2d 10, appeal not allowed 86 Ohio St.3d 1437, 713 N.E.2d 1049. Infants ☞ 156

State intervention for parental neglect in leaving children home alone is not limited to situations in which house contains an undue danger or dangerous condition, such as a gun. In re Zeiser (Ohio App. 11 Dist., 03-26-1999) 133 Ohio App.3d 338, 728 N.E.2d 10, appeal not allowed 86 Ohio St.3d 1437, 713 N.E.2d 1049. Infants ⇔ 156

It constitutes neglect per se to allow a six-year-old child to be left alone for two entire days per week on a regular basis and to be regularly left at other times under the supervision of his eight-year-old sibling. In re Zeiser (Ohio App. 11 Dist., 03-26-1999) 133 Ohio App.3d 338, 728 N.E.2d 10, appeal not allowed 86 Ohio St.3d 1437, 713 N.E.2d 1049. Infants ⇔ 156

Mother engaged in neglect through lack of parental supervision with respect to eight-year-old boy by allowing him to be babysitter for six-year-old brother on regular daily basis for intervals of two hours plus. In re Zeiser (Ohio App. 11 Dist., 03-26-1999) 133 Ohio App.3d 338, 728 N.E.2d 10, appeal not allowed 86 Ohio St.3d 1437, 713 N.E.2d 1049. Infants ⇔ 156

Clear and convincing evidence supported determination that single mother was guilty of "neglect" for leaving her six- and eight-year-old sons unsupervised for two hours each day in late afternoon and for leaving six-year-old son at home entirely alone for two days each week, notwithstanding evidence that boys were very bright, mature and responsible for their ages, testimony by day care director that boys could be left alone for a few hours occasionally, mother's provision of extensive instructions regarding boys' activities in her absence, and guardian ad litem's recommendation that court not find neglect, given pattern, regularity and length of unsupervised periods and mother's failure to acknowledge inherent dangers of the situation, indicating that situation would continue. In re Zeiser (Ohio App. 11 Dist., 03-26-1999) 133 Ohio App.3d 338, 728 N.E.2d 10, appeal not allowed 86 Ohio St.3d 1437, 713 N.E.2d 1049. Infants ⇔ 179

A six and an eight-year-old, regardless of intelligence, maturity, or social adjustment are too young to be left alone for an entire day or on a regular basis for hours at a time. In re Zeiser (Ohio App. 11 Dist., 03-26-1999) 133 Ohio App.3d 338, 728 N.E.2d 10, appeal not allowed 86 Ohio St.3d 1437, 713 N.E.2d 1049.

Parent's voluntary act of temporarily placing child with responsible relative is indicator of proper parental care, and does not support finding that parent is at fault; therefore, under such circumstances, care furnished by relative can be imputed to parent such that child is not neglected child. In re Riddle (Ohio, 07-23-1997) 79 Ohio St.3d 259, 680 N.E.2d 1227, 1997-Ohio-391. Infants ⇔ 156

Parents' complaint alleging that child suffered neglect while in foster care should not have been dismissed even though complaint incorrectly cited dependency statute, rather than child neglect statute, where complaint demonstrated good faith effort to comply with rules, and adequately notified opposing party of the claim; thus, dismissal of complaint would be reversed and cause remanded to allow parents opportunity to cure the defect. In re Fetters (Ohio App. 12 Dist., 04-22-1996) 110 Ohio App.3d 483, 674 N.E.2d 766, on reconsideration 1996 WL 280739. Infants ⇔ 17

Finding that children were neglected was supported by evidence that parents demonstrated poor child-care skills, as documented by their inability to maintain their home in clear and hazard-free manner, the constant filth of the children, and parents' inability to supervise the children. In re Meyer (Ohio App. 3 Dist., 10-25-1994) 98 Ohio App.3d 189, 648 N.E.2d 52, corrected. Infants ⇔ 179

A child who has been beaten so severely over time with a belt and a paddle as to cause extensive bruising is beyond reasonable punishment and is abused within the meaning of the law and properly removed from the mother's custody. In re Schuerman (Paulding 1991) 74 Ohio App.3d 528, 599 N.E.2d 728.

A court errs in adjudicating a child neglected absent a finding that a parent is guilty of, or aware of, abuse of his child. In re Webb (Hamilton 1989) 64 Ohio App.3d 280, 581 N.E.2d 570, dismissed, jurisdictional motion overruled 48 Ohio St.3d 704, 549 N.E.2d 1191.

Children services board failed to show that child who had bruises on her arm caused by her stepmother was neglected where, although stepmother had consumed some alcohol, she was not intoxicated and, although stepmother did strike child with sole of tennis shoe, bruises on child's arms were result of her being grabbed by stepmother when child balked at changing her clothes. In re Wall (Wayne 1989) 60 Ohio App.3d 6, 572 N.E.2d 248. Infants ⇔ 156

The burden to show that a child is neglected is upon the party making the allegation; neglect is not shown where the child's bruises, forming the basis of the neglect charge, are the result of the child's stepmother, not a party to the action, grabbing the child after the child refused to change her clothes. In re Wall (Wayne 1989) 60 Ohio App.3d 6, 572 N.E.2d 248.

Unlike a finding of neglect under RC 2151.03, which requires proof that the parents were willfully at fault in abandoning or neglecting the children or refusing to perform their parental duties, a finding of dependency under RC 2151.04 must be grounded on whether the children are receiving proper care and support. The focus is on the condition of the children, not the fault of the parents. In re Bibb (Hamilton 1980) 70 Ohio App.2d 117, 435 N.E.2d 96, 24 O.O.3d 159. Infants ⇔ 154.1

In the absence of evidence showing a detrimental impact upon the children, the fact that the mother is living with a boyfriend in their presence will not justify a finding that the children are neglected or dependent. In re Burrell (Ohio 1979) 58 Ohio St.2d 37, 388 N.E.2d 738, 12 O.O.3d 43.

The custody of an illegitimate child will not be taken from the mother and awarded to the father merely upon the basis that the wife has contracted an interracial marriage. In re H. (Ohio Com.Pl. 1973) 37 Ohio Misc. 123, 305 N.E.2d 815, 66 O.O.2d 178, 66 O.O.2d 368.

Where 16-year-old unwed mother of two-day-old baby was an incorrigible child who had been sexually promiscuous and had no visible means of supporting herself or infant, mother had previously been in a foster home where she was unruly and disobedient, mother sought to take baby into grandparents' home but grandparents were unable to give either financial or emotional assistance to either mother or baby and welfare department had refused to approve aid for child in mother's home, conditions and environment of child were such as to warrant the state, in the interest of the child, in assuming his guardianship. In re East (Ohio Com.Pl. 1972) 32 Ohio Misc. 65, 288 N.E.2d 343, 61 O.O.2d 38, 61 O.O.2d 108. Infants ⇔ 154.1

Juvenile court cannot deprive mother of adulterine bastard of the custody of such child, in absence of evidence to warrant finding that such mother is unfit or that such child is dependent or neglected within purview of law or that best interests of child require such action. In re Gutman (Hamilton 1969) 22 Ohio App.2d 125, 259 N.E.2d 128, 51 O.O.2d 252. Children Out-of-wedlock ⇔ 20.1

In a proceeding in the juvenile court, instituted by the filing of a complaint under RC 2151.27, a finding by the court that a child is "neglected," in that it "lacked proper parental care because of the faults and habits of his parents" and "dependent," in that its "condition and environment... is such as to warrant the court... in assuming his guardianship" must be based on evidence with respect to whether the child was receiving proper parental care in a proper environment in its home at the time of the hearing. In re Minton (Darke 1960) 112 Ohio App. 361, 176 N.E.2d 252, 16 O.O.2d 283. Infants ⇔ 156

On the evidence, children of parents to whom adultery was a normal course of life, who were selfish and childish far beyond any reasonable limits, and whose ideas of proper upbringing were to tell the children how vile each other had been, were both neglected and dependent. In re Douglas (Ohio Juv. 1959) 164 N.E.2d 475, 82 Ohio Law Abs. 170, 11 O.O.2d 340. Infants ⇔ 156

The determination of the lack of proper parental care because of the faults or habits of a parent as a basis for finding that a child is neglected must be made as of the time of the hearing on the charge of neglect. In re Kronjaeger (Ohio 1957) 166 Ohio St. 172, 140 N.E.2d 773, 1 O.O.2d 459. Infants ⇔ 210

Evidence of the confinement of a mother of minor children in a state hospital by reason of mental illness, during which confinement she had no funds with which to support the children and during which she was unaware of their whereabouts is not sufficient evidence to support a finding by the juvenile court that such children are "neglected" within the meaning of RC 2151.03. In re Masters (Ohio 1956) 165 Ohio St. 503, 137 N.E.2d 752, 60 O.O. 474.

Division of child welfare granted custody of minor children upon ground children's return to mother and maternal relatives would not serve the best interests of the children. In re Zerick, 129 NE(2d) 661, 74 Abs 525, 57 OO 331 (Juv. 1955).

In a prosecution for contributing to the neglect or dependency of a minor child, the admission in evidence of the record of a separate proceeding in the same court, involving the same acts of misconduct and adjudicating the child to be a neglected and dependent child, is not erroneous. State v. Griffin (Champaign 1952) 93 Ohio App. 299, 106 N.E.2d 668, 63 Ohio Law Abs. 122, 51 O.O. 47. Criminal Law ⇔ 429(2); Criminal Law ⇔ 1169.1(2.1)

In a prosecution for contributing to the neglect or dependency of a minor child the record of a separate proceeding adjudicating the child to be a neglected and dependent child, and the testimony of the child's mother that she and the defendant engaged in acts of illicit sexual relations in the presence of the child, is sufficient competent evidence to prove the child to be a neglected or dependent child. State v. Griffin (Champaign 1952) 93 Ohio App. 299, 106 N.E.2d 668, 63 Ohio Law Abs. 122, 51 O.O. 47.

In order to sustain a judgment finding the natural child of legally married parents, living together in an established home, in a respectable community, to be a neglected child under this section, the evidence must show that any fault of the parents occurring in the past is at the time of the hearing of such charge effective to render such parents unfit and unsuitable to have the custody and care of such child, and that they are then at such time, by reason of such fault, incapable of extending to such child proper parental care. In re Hock (Hamilton 1947) 88 N.E.2d 597, 55 Ohio Law Abs. 73, appeal dismissed 149 Ohio St. 460, 78 N.E.2d 901, 37 O.O. 125. Infants ⇐ 156

In a proceeding under GC 1639–1 (RC 2151.01) et seq., on a complaint charging that a child is neglected, evidence of immoral conduct of the father may be introduced to show that the child lacked proper parental care under this section, although such acts occurred prior to the effective date of such sections. In re Hayes (Franklin 1939) 62 Ohio App. 289, 23 N.E.2d 956, 30 Ohio Law Abs. 568, 16 O.O. 10. Infants ⇐ 207

Department store's ban on breast-feeding in public areas did not prevent mothers from providing necessary subsistence to their infant children in violation of Ohio law, and thus did not tortiously interfere with mothers' alleged right to breast-feed; interruption of single feeding did not prevent provision of necessary subsistence, store did not prevent mothers from bottle-feeding their children anywhere in store, and store did not prevent mothers from breast-feeding outside of public areas. Derungs v. Wal-Mart Stores, Inc. (S.D.Ohio, 03-05-2001) 162 F.Supp.2d 861, affirmed 374 F.3d 428. Torts ⇐ 200; Torts ⇐ 6

Father's allegation that mother neglected child was not supported by clear and convincing evidence; testimony revealed that mother placed child in father's care after she was involved in a serious accident and that she went to her parent's out-of-state residence to recuperate, which did not show that child was abandoned or that he lacked adequate care. In re Henry (Ohio App. 11 Dist., Lake, 08-30-2002) No. 2001-L-115, 2002-Ohio-4513, 2002 WL 2022737, Unreported. Infants ⇐ 157

Clear and convincing evidence supported finding that because of acts of mother, children suffered physical or mental injury which threatened to harm their health or welfare, where mother admitted to social worker that she over disciplined children, daughter had scar on face from incident where mother threw her down, daughter testified that mother slapped her at least every three days, sometimes for no reason at all, younger daughter testified that mother pulled her, and her older sister's, hair, mother's sister testified that mother would often smack children across face and use derogatory language towards them, mother's other sister testified that mother would grab children by shoulders and shake them in violent way, and, while mother disputed hitting children on daily basis, she admitted striking children across their faces and that she made girls get out of car and walk behind it as she drove down street. In re Kimble (Ohio App. 7 Dist., Harrison, 05-15-2002) No. 99 517 CA, 2002-Ohio-2409, 2002 WL 1065977, Unreported. Infants ⇐ 179

Placement of an illegitimate child for adoption and subsequent withdrawal of consent thereto by the mother does not of itself warrant a finding that the child is neglected. In re O——(Ohio Juv. 1964) 199 N.E.2d 765, 95 Ohio Law Abs. 101, 28 O.O.2d 165.

The term "child neglect" as used in RC 2151.421 applies to children without proper parental care or guardianship as defined by RC 2151.05. OAG 78–038.

Custodian's punishment of 11-year-old child by beating him with a belt created a substantial risk of serious physical harm, as required to find child an abused minor child in child protection proceeding, where punishment resulted in deep bruising with pain that was acute enough to wake child from sleep during the night. In re Horton (Ohio App. 10 Dist., Franklin, 11-23-2004) No. 03AP-1181, 2004-Ohio-6249, 2004 WL 2674562, Unreported. Infants ⇐ 156

3. Procedural issues

Mother's right against self-incrimination was not violated in child dependency proceeding when she was allegedly required to admit that she believed her son was sexually abused; the case plan adopted by the parties did not require mother to admit or believe that son was sexually abused. In re Krems (Ohio App. 11 Dist., Geauga, 05-14-2004) No. 2003-G-2534, 2004-Ohio-2446, 2004 WL 1086869, Unreported. Infants ⇐ 207

Although dependency case focuses on condition or environment of child, and not on fault, neglect case does require inquiry into faults or habits of caregiver and requires ultimate finding that child lacks proper or adequate parental care due to those faults or habits. In re Riddle (Ohio, 07-23-1997) 79 Ohio St.3d 259, 680 N.E.2d 1227, 1997-Ohio-391. Infants ⇐ 156

Fault of parent, guardian, or custodian is relevant to neglect adjudication. In re Riddle (Ohio, 07-23-1997) 79 Ohio St.3d 259, 680 N.E.2d 1227, 1997-Ohio-391. Infants ⇐ 156

Because paternal grandparents were caring for child pursuant to agreement initiated by caseworker, rather than pursuant to voluntary informal agreement initiated by child's parent, child could be adjudicated as neglected, notwithstanding fact that he was receiving adequate care from paternal grandparents. In re Riddle (Ohio, 07-23-1997) 79 Ohio St.3d 259, 680 N.E.2d 1227, 1997-Ohio-391. Infants ⇐ 156

Neglect/dependency complaint should not be filed as substitute for custody action on behalf of other relatives of neglected or dependent child. In re Riddle (Ohio, 07-23-1997) 79 Ohio St.3d 259, 680 N.E.2d 1227, 1997-Ohio-391. Infants ⇐ 191

Where a complaint alleges that a child is neglected or dependent within the meaning of RC 2151.03(B) and RC 2151.04(A), RC 2151.04(B), and RC 2151.04(C), the child's mother is not prohibited by Juv R 29(D)(2) from taking part in the adjudicatory hearing by the fact that she entered a plea of "admitted" to the allegations in the complaint. In re Sims (Preble 1983) 13 Ohio App.3d 37, 468 N.E.2d 111, 13 O.B.R. 40.

In actions brought pursuant to RC 2151.27 and RC 2151.03, the state's primary objective is not to decide conflicting claims to custody; its objective is to determine if a child is receiving proper parental care, and if that care is being provided by a relative pursuant to an agreement initiated by the child's parent, then the child is not a neglected child. In re Reese (Franklin 1982) 4 Ohio App.3d 59, 446 N.E.2d 482, 4 O.B.R. 109. Infants ⇐ 156

Before the court may consider what disposition should be made of children for their best interest and welfare, there must first be an adjudication that said children are neglected or dependent, and where neglect and dependency existed at the time of the filing of the complaint, but said cause was not prosecuted further until more than four years afterwards and the conditions of the parents had changed sufficiently that evidence was lacking to establish neglect or dependency at the time of the hearing, said complaint must be dismissed. In re Burkhart (Ohio Juv. 1968) 15 Ohio Misc. 170, 239 N.E.2d 772, 44 O.O.2d 329.

An allegation in a motion filed in juvenile court seeking to have that court "determine and award the future care and custody" of a child that "neither parent is a suitable person to have the care and custody of said child" does not constitute a charge that such child is "neglected" or "dependent" and is not sufficiently definite to constitute the "complaint" necessitated by RC 2151.27. Union County Child Welfare Bd. v. Parker (Union 1964) 7 Ohio App.2d 79, 218 N.E.2d 757, 36 O.O.2d 162. Infants ⇐ 197

A juvenile court order finding children to be "neglected" and committing them to permanent custody of a child welfare board for ultimate adoption is a final appealable order. In re Masters (Ohio 1956) 165 Ohio St. 503, 137 N.E.2d 752, 60 O.O. 474.

In a prosecution for contributing to the neglect or dependency of a minor child, a failure of the court to give the statutory definition of "neglected child" or "dependent child" is an error of omission, and does not constitute reversible error unless the court's attention was seasonably called to the omission and specific instructions requested and refused. State v. Griffin (Champaign 1952) 93 Ohio App. 299, 106 N.E.2d 668, 63 Ohio Law Abs. 122, 51 O.O. 47.

In a prosecution for contributing to the neglect or dependency of a minor child it is not a prerequisite that the child be adjudicated as a neglected, dependent or delinquent child in a separate proceeding before a charge of contributing toward such neglect, dependency or delinquency of such child can be maintained. State v. Griffin (Champaign 1952) 93 Ohio App. 299, 106 N.E.2d 668, 63 Ohio Law Abs. 122, 51 O.O. 47. Infants ⇐ 13

The court of appeals may review upon appeal on questions of law final judgment of the division of domestic relations of the court of common pleas, entered in a proceeding to determine the status of a minor, alleged to be a "neglected child" under this section. In re Hock (Hamilton 1947) 88 N.E.2d 597, 55 Ohio Law Abs. 73, appeal dismissed 149 Ohio St. 460, 78 N.E.2d 901, 37 O.O. 125. Infants ⇐ 242

In child neglect case, any error was harmless in juvenile court's allowing mother to invoke her Fifth Amendment right against self-incrimination through her attorney's objection, even though the more appropriate method would have been for mother to take the witness stand and invoke the right. In re Henry (Ohio App. 11 Dist., Lake, 08-30-2002) No. 2001-L-115, 2002-Ohio-4513, 2002 WL 2022737, Unreported. Infants ⇐ 253

Juvenile court, after dismissing father's child neglect complaint for lack of evidence, could properly issue a nunc pro tunc entry vacating prior interim order that granted father temporary custody. In re Henry (Ohio App. 11 Dist., Lake, 08-30-2002) No. 2001-L-115, 2002-Ohio-4513, 2002 WL 2022737, Unreported. Infants 230.1

4. Abandonment

Assuming that mother was told she was denied visitation with child, such fact did not overcome finding that child was neglected and dependent based on abandonment; such an order only addressed visitation and would not have prevented a mother from calling or sending letters or cards to her son, and there was ample evidence in the record to support a finding of abandonment. (Per Evans, J., with two judges concurring in judgment only.) In re Fennell (Ohio App. 4 Dist., Athens, 09-26-2002) No. 02CA17, 2002-Ohio-6151, 2002 WL 31521504, Unreported. Infants 157

Competent, credible evidence supported finding that child was neglected and dependent based on abandonment; mother failed to pay child support since child was placed with county children services, mother failed to attend a single scheduled visitation for three-month period and mother's subsequent visitation was sporadic, and mother made no contact whatsoever with child for more than a year. (Per Evans, J., with two judges concurring in judgment only.) In re Fennell (Ohio App. 4 Dist., Athens, 09-26-2002) No. 02CA17, 2002-Ohio-6151, 2002 WL 31521504, Unreported. Infants 157

A parent, to be barred from the right to custody of his minor children on the ground of abandonment, must either have relinquished his right to custody by express agreement or have forfeited his right because of unfavorable circumstances clearly detrimental to the welfare of the children such as would constitute dependency or neglect under the juvenile court act, and the mere placing of minor children in a children's home by a parent does not, of itself, constitute evidence of relinquishment of the right to custody or abandonment of such minor children. Gallagher v. Gallagher (Henry 1962) 115 Ohio App. 453, 185 N.E.2d 571, 21 O.O.2d 74.

To constitute "abandonment" of a child there must be a willful leaving of a child by his parent, with an intention of causing perpetual separation; to constitute "neglect," there must be a willful or indifferent disregard of the duty owed by a parent to his child. In re Kronjaeger (Ohio 1957) 166 Ohio St. 172, 140 N.E.2d 773, 1 O.O.2d 459. Infants 157

5. School attendance

Proceedings declaring a child neglected by the juvenile court of another county do not prevent a child from thereafter becoming a school resident in a county to which he moves with his family. In re Laricchiuta (Preble 1968) 16 Ohio App.2d 164, 243 N.E.2d 111, 45 O.O.2d 456.

The school board of the district in which a child has a school residence at the time of his placement in another district must pay his tuition, whether such placement was by order of court or by the child welfare board in whose care the parent had voluntarily left him, and subsequent proceedings by the juvenile court declaring such child neglected will not end the obligation of the district of his school residence to continue paying his tuition. In re Laricchiuta (Preble 1968) 16 Ohio App.2d 164, 243 N.E.2d 111, 45 O.O.2d 456.

Where the father of a minor child endeavors to send such child to a proper public school but such child is excluded because he has not been vaccinated, and where there is no showing that the father has prevented vaccination of such child, such child is not a neglected child within this section. State v. Dunham (Ohio 1950) 154 Ohio St. 63, 93 N.E.2d 286, 42 O.O. 133. Infants 13

6. Parental rights and unification

County social worker's alleged conduct in thwarting parents' attempts to have children returned to parents' home, after children were removed due to unsanitary conditions, and in effectively denying parents prompt hearing on children's placement did not rise to the level of conscience-shocking behavior, and thus did not support substantive due process claim. Smith v. Williams-Ash (C.A.6 (Ohio), 12-06-2005) No. 04-4547, 173 Fed.Appx. 363, 2005 WL 3304101, Unreported. Infants 17

County social worker should have known that her alleged conduct in thwarting parents' attempts to have children returned to parents' home, after children were removed due to unsanitary conditions, and in effectively denying parents prompt hearing on children's placement had effect of violating parents' clearly established rights to procedural due process by involuntarily depriving parents of physical custody of children, and therefore qualified immunity did not apply to preclude social worker's liability under §§ 1983. Smith v. Williams-Ash (C.A.6 (Ohio), 12-06-2005) No. 04-4547, 173 Fed.Appx. 363, 2005 WL 3304101, Unreported. Civil Rights 1376(4)

Allegations that parents whose children were removed from home by county social worker were not allowed to recover children after safety plan providing for children's placement with friends had been initiated, despite parents' best efforts to do so, that continued deprivation of children was involuntary, and that parents were effectively denied prompt hearing on children's placement supported claim against social worker for violating parents' procedural due process rights. Smith v. Williams-Ash (C.A.6 (Ohio), 12-06-2005) No. 04-4547, 173 Fed.Appx. 363, 2005 WL 3304101, Unreported. Infants 17

A parent's primary rights to the care and custody of a child are rights that must be protected, and parental custody will be terminated only when necessary for the mental and physical development of the child. In re Bibb (Hamilton 1980) 70 Ohio App.2d 117, 435 N.E.2d 96, 24 O.O.3d 159. Infants 155

Where children are adjudged neglected under RC 2151.03 and committed to the temporary custody of a social agency, the agency should plan for the rehabilitation and reunification of the children with their family, and the court should insist that the agency make a conscientious effort to bring the plan to fruition before considering the alternative of adoptive placement. In re M. (Ohio Com.Pl. 1979) 65 Ohio Misc. 7, 416 N.E.2d 669, 18 O.O.3d 283, 19 O.O.3d 112. Infants 231

7. Jurisdiction

The juvenile court has the authority to hear and determine the case of a "neglected child" notwithstanding the fact that the child is at the time within the continuing jurisdiction of the common pleas court by virtue of a divorce decree. In re L. (Ohio Juv. 1967) 12 Ohio Misc. 251, 231 N.E.2d 253, 41 O.O.2d 341. Courts 475(15)

The juvenile court is given original jurisdiction in a proper proceeding to determine the right of custody of any child where such child is not a ward of another court, and it is not necessary in the exercise of such jurisdiction that the juvenile court first determine that such child is a dependent, neglected or delinquent child. In re Lorok (Cuyahoga 1952) 93 Ohio App. 251, 114 N.E.2d 65, 51 O.O. 10. Child Custody 920

2151.031 "Abused child" defined

As used in this chapter, an "abused child" includes any child who:

(A) Is the victim of "sexual activity" as defined under Chapter 2907. of the Revised Code, where such activity would constitute an offense under that chapter, except that the court need not find that any person has been convicted of the offense in order to find that the child is an abused child;

(B) Is endangered as defined in section 2919.22 of the Revised Code, except that the court need not find that any person has been convicted under that section in order to find that the child is an abused child;

(C) Exhibits evidence of any physical or mental injury or death, inflicted other than by accidental means, or an injury or death which is at variance with the history given of it. Except as provided in division (D) of this section, a child exhibiting evidence of corporal punishment or other physical disciplinary measure by a parent, guardian, custodian, person having custody or control, or person in loco parentis of a child is not an abused child under this division if the measure is not prohibited under section 2919.22 of the Revised Code.

(D) Because of the acts of his parents, guardian, or custodian, suffers physical or mental injury that harms or threatens to harm the child's health or welfare.

(E) Is subjected to out-of-home care child abuse.

(1989 H 257, eff. 8–3–89; 1988 S 89; 1975 H 85)

Cross References

Domestic violence, defined, 3113.31
Endangering children (child abuse), 2919.22
Failure to report a felony, including child abuse, 2921.22

False report of child abuse or neglect, 2921.14
Prevention of child abuse and child neglect, 3109.13 to 3109.18
Requirement to report child abuse, 2151.421
Sexual activity, defined, 2907.01
Shared parenting, abused child defined, 3109.04
Visitation rights, effect of finding child abused, 3109.051

Ohio Administrative Code References

Definition of terms for the implementation of the "Comprehensive Assessment and Planning Model - Interim Solution" and statewide automated child welfare database, OAC 5101:2–1–01.1

Library References

Infants ⚯156.
Westlaw Topic No. 211.
C.J.S. Infants §§ 31, 33 to 50, 55, 62.
    Baldwin's Ohio Legislative Service, 1988 Laws of Ohio, S 89—LSC Analysis, p 5–571

Research References

ALR Library

20 ALR 5th 534, Parent's Use of Drugs as Factor in Award of Custody of Children, Visitation Rights, or Termination of Parental Rights.

Encyclopedias

2 Am. Jur. Proof of Facts 2d 365, Child Abuse--The Battered Child Syndrome.
OH Jur. 3d Family Law § 1492, "Abused Child".
OH Jur. 3d Family Law § 1500, Relating to Persons.
OH Jur. 3d Family Law § 1664, on Request for Permanent Custody—Factors to be Considered.
OH Jur. 3d Family Law § 1735, Adult Acts Punishable in Juvenile Court.

Treatises and Practice Aids

Katz, Giannelli, Blair and Lipton, Baldwin's Ohio Practice, Criminal Law, § 110:9, False Report of Child Abuse.
Katz, Giannelli, Blair and Lipton, Baldwin's Ohio Practice, Criminal Law, § 109:11, Child Endangerment.
Sowald & Morganstern, Baldwin's Ohio Practice Domestic Relations Law § 5:5, Civil Proceeding—Jurisdiction, Venue.
Sowald & Morganstern, Baldwin's Ohio Practice Domestic Relations Law § 37:8, Exceptions to Confidentiality—Reporting Statutes—Child Abuse.
Carlin, Baldwin's Ohio Practice, Merrick-Rippner Probate Law § 106:17, Juvenile Court Jurisdiction—Abused Child—Definition: Evidence of Abuse.
Carlin, Baldwin's Ohio Practice, Merrick-Rippner Probate Law § 107:80, Disposition of Abused, Neglected, or Dependent Child—Permanent Custody.
Carlin, Baldwin's Ohio Practice, Merrick-Rippner Probate Law § 107:138, Complaint, Abused, Neglected, or Dependent Child—Form.
Adrine & Ruden, Ohio Domestic Violence Law § 8:3, Statutory Elements of Domestic Violence Under RC 3113.31(A)(1)(a).
Adrine & Ruden, Ohio Domestic Violence Law § 8:5, Statutory Elements of Domestic Violence Under RC 3113.31(A)(1)(C).
Adrine & Ruden, Ohio Domestic Violence Law § 8:6, Parents and Children.
Adrine & Ruden, Ohio Domestic Violence Law § 13:6, Law Enforcement Policies and Procedures.
Adrine & Ruden, Ohio Domestic Violence Law § 11:15, Remedies—Orders Allocating Parental Rights and Responsibilities.
Giannelli & Yeomans, Ohio Juvenile Law § 9:2, Parental Rights.
Giannelli & Yeomans, Ohio Juvenile Law § 9:7, Neglect—Subsistence, Education & Medical Care.
Giannelli & Yeomans, Ohio Juvenile Law § 9:10, Neglect—Physical or Mental Injury Due to Omissions.
Giannelli & Yeomans, Ohio Juvenile Law § 9:11, Neglect—Out-Of-Home Care Neglect.
Giannelli & Yeomans, Ohio Juvenile Law § 9:12, Abused Child Defined.
Giannelli & Yeomans, Ohio Juvenile Law § 9:13, Abused Child—Sexual Victim.
Giannelli & Yeomans, Ohio Juvenile Law § 9:14, Abused Child—Child Endangerment.
Giannelli & Yeomans, Ohio Juvenile Law § 9:15, Abused Child—Physical or Mental Injury Exhibited.
Giannelli & Yeomans, Ohio Juvenile Law § 9:16, Abused Child—Physical or Mental Injury Due to Parents.
Giannelli & Yeomans, Ohio Juvenile Law § 9:17, Abused Child—Out-Of-Home Abuse.
Giannelli & Yeomans, Ohio Juvenile Law § 30:10, Permanent Custody—Parental Placement Within Reasonable Time.
Hastings, Manoloff, Sheeran, & Stype, Ohio School Law § 24:11, Duty to Report Suspected Child Abuse or Neglect-Definition of Child Abuse.

Law Review and Journal Commentaries

Abused Children: The Supreme Court Considers The Due Process Right To Protection, Note. 29 J Fam L 679 (May 1991).

Child Maltreatment: An Overview of Current Approaches, Note. 18 J Fam L 115 (1979–80).

Children And Cults: A Practical Guide, Susan Linda. 29 J Fam L 591 (May 1991).

Criminalizing Poor Parenting Skills As A Means To Contain Violence By And Against Children, S. Randall Humm. 139 U Pa L Rev 1123 (April 1991).

Fetal Abuse: Culpable Behavior By Pregnant Women Or Parental Immunity?, George P. Smith, II. 3 J L & Health 223 (1988–89).

Fundamentally Speaking: Application of Ohio's Domestic Violence Laws in Parental Discipline Cases—A Parental Perspective, Richard Garner. 30 U Tol L Rev 1 (Fall 1998).

Honor thy father and mother?—The unintended consequences of Ohio's domestic violence preferred arrest policy on Ohio's parents, Richard M. Garner. 11 Ohio Law 12 (January/February 1997).

Interviewing Child Victims/Witnesses, Mary A. Lentz. 9 Baldwin's Ohio Sch L J 25 (July/August 1997).

Legal implications of drug use during pregnancy, William A. Kurtz. 1 Prob L J Ohio 66 (January/February 1991).

The Legal Response to Child Abuse: In the Best Interest of Children?, John E. B. Myers. 24 J Fam L 149 (1985–86).

Physicians and Maternal–Fetal Conflicts: Duties, Rights and Responsibilities, James J. Nocon. 5 J L & Health 1 (1990–91).

Prosecution Of Mothers Of Drug–Exposed Babies: Constitutional And Criminal Theory, Doretta Massardo McGinnis. 139 U Pa L Rev 505 (December 1990).

Understanding Faith: When Religious Parents Decline Conventional Medical Treatment for Their Children, Note. 45 Case W Res L Rev 891 (Spring 1995).

The Use of Juvenile Court Jurisdiction and Restraining Authority to Address the Problem of Maternal Drug Abuse in Ohio, Deborah A. Wainey. 18 Ohio N U L Rev 611 (1991).

The Voice of a Child: Independent Legal Representation of Children in Private Custody Disputes When Sexual Abuse Is Alleged, Kerin S. Bischoff. 138 U Pa L Rev 1383 (May 1990).

Notes of Decisions

Constitutional issues   1
Corporal punishment   3
Discovery rule   4
False allegations effect   5
Grounds for finding of abuse   2
Sentencing   6

---

1. Constitutional issues

Father's allegation that state social services agency and agency employees maliciously pursued allegations of child abuse, with knowledge that allegations were unfounded, in attempt to coerce father to surrender custody of his daughter, did not rise to level of substantive due process violation, absent allegation that father and daughter were detained or physically abused in any manner. Roe v. Franklin Cty. (Ohio App. 10 Dist., 03-12-1996) 109 Ohio App.3d 772, 673 N.E.2d 172, appeal not allowed 77 Ohio St.3d 1415, 670 N.E.2d 1003. Constitutional Law ⇐ 274(5); Infants ⇐ 17

Father's allegations that state social services agency and agency employees filed child abuse complaint in juvenile court without probable cause was insufficient to state claim for malicious civil prosecution, absent allegation that defendants seized person or property of father or his daughter. Roe v. Franklin Cty. (Ohio App. 10 Dist., 03-12-1996) 109 Ohio App.3d 772, 673 N.E.2d 172, appeal not allowed 77 Ohio St.3d 1415, 670 N.E.2d 1003. Malicious Prosecution ⇐ 11

Confrontation rights are inapplicable in dependency and neglect proceedings in juvenile courts. In re Burchfield (Athens 1988) 51 Ohio App.3d 148, 555 N.E.2d 325. Infants ⇐ 207

The use of two-way closed circuit television for the testimony of a child in a civil abuse, neglect, or dependency hearing does not violate the confrontation rights of the parents or due process. In re Burchfield (Athens 1988) 51 Ohio App.3d 148, 555 N.E.2d 325. Constitutional Law ⇐ 314; Infants ⇐ 207; Trial ⇐ 38; Witnesses ⇐ 228

Allowing victim-witness advocate to sit next to minor during his testimony at trial in child protection proceeding to determine whether he was an abused child did not violate his custodian's right to equal protection under the law. In re Horton (Ohio App. 10 Dist., Franklin, 11-23-2004) No. 03AP-1181, 2004-Ohio-6249, 2004 WL 2674562, Unreported. Constitutional Law ⇐ 225.1; Infants ⇐ 207

2. Grounds for finding of abuse

Trial court's finding that child was an abused and dependent child was not against the manifest weight of the evidence, despite lack of physical evidence; child complained of sexual abuse to a teacher, child told social workers that father had sexually abused her and spanked her with an extension cord and a belt, child's allegations of abuse were consistent, and child indicated that she needed to be kept safe from father. In re A.R. (Ohio App. 9 Dist., Summit, 03-31-2006) No. 22836, 2006-Ohio-1548, 2006 WL 825400, Unreported. Infants ⇐ 179

Trial court's grant of temporary custody of children to county child protection agency was not against the manifest weight of the evidence; decision was based on testimony of doctor who examined younger child and opined that his injuries were caused by abuse, testimony of investigator with the protective unit to mother's admission she may have bruised child, and recommendation of the guardian ad litem. In re Butcher (Ohio App. 5 Dist., Tuscarawas, 07-25-2005) No. 2005 AP 05 0031, 2005-Ohio-3827, 2005 WL 1785116, Unreported. Infants ⇐ 175.1

Finding that children were abused was supported by the evidence, thus supporting grant of temporary custody of children to county child protection agency; doctor who examined child opined that child's bruise injuries were caused by abuse, investigator with protective unit testified that mother admitted that she may have bruised child, and guardian ad litem recommended grant of temporary custody of child to agency. In re Butcher (Ohio App. 5 Dist., Tuscarawas, 07-25-2005) No. 2005 AP 05 0032, 2005-Ohio-3816, 2005 WL 1785072, Unreported. Infants ⇐ 179

Trial court could not find that clear and convincing evidence supported grandmother's allegation that grandson was abused, neglected, or dependent; although grandmother was concerned for grandson's welfare and health, evidence adduced by grandmother to support her complaints regarding mother's care of child was not credible. In re Forrest (Ohio App. 4 Dist., Athens, 08-05-2004) No. 04CA104CA1, 2004-Ohio-4189, 2004 WL 1778436, Unreported. Infants ⇐ 179

Clear and convincing evidence supported finding at permanent custody proceeding that two of parents' children were abused; evidence was presented concerning one child's sexualized and aggressive behaviors, including fondling herself, asking other children if they wanted to pull her pants down, and attempting to urinate on others, and other child, at the age of six, tested positive for a sexually transmitted disease. In re Wilkinson (Ohio App. 1 Dist., Hamilton, 08-06-2004) No. C-040182, No. C-040203, No. C-040282, 2004-Ohio-4107, 2004 WL 1752821, Unreported, appeal not allowed 104 Ohio St.3d 1410, 818 N.E.2d 711, 2004-Ohio-6364. Infants ⇐ 179

Former husband's complaint against former wife alleging dependency and neglect of parties' children failed to adequately set forth particular facts upon which allegations were based and contained no notice concerning evidence against which wife would have to defend; while husband claimed children would be molested and wife would flee should children be returned to her custody, these were general conclusory claims unsupported by particular facts, and husband's only specific claim, that children were not functioning at appropriate level, did not fall within definition of dependency, neglect, or abuse. Louck v. Louck (Ohio App. 3 Dist., Marion, 11-10-2003) No. 9-03-35, 2003-Ohio-5999, 2003 WL 22533679, Unreported. Infants ⇐ 197

Clear and convincing evidence supported finding in dependency proceeding that father's youngest child was abused; uncontroverted expert testimony was given from physician that child's injury was inflicted, rather than accidental, and physician further testified that child's injury was at variance with the history given by father, and father failed to refute this testimony. In re Anthony (Ohio App. 11 Dist., Ashtabula, 10-24-2003) No. 2002-A-0096, 2003-Ohio-5712, 2003 WL 22429035, Unreported. Infants ⇐ 179

Trial court's determination that step-child was abused child did not amount to plain error; counselor and caseworker testified that step-child and child said that father hit step-child in mouth and punched step-child's leg, counselor and caseworker observed bruising on step-child, and father admitted that he hit step-child on back of head and on mouth. In re Youngerman (Ohio App. 2 Dist., Miami, 10-10-2003) No. 2002 CA 61, 2003-Ohio-5397, 2003 WL 22318106, Unreported. Infants ⇐ 243

Domestic violence civil protection order properly was entered against ex-wife; doctor testified that case involved fictitious disorder by proxy on behalf of ex-wife, and this fictitious disorder by proxy involved deliberate production or feigning of physical or psychological signs or symptoms in children who were under doctor's care, ex-wife had permitted absenteeism from school and undermined children's relationship with, and alienated them from, ex-husband, ex-wife interfered with child's psychological treatment, and child's medical condition dramatically deteriorated while solely in ex-wife's care. Schottenstein v. Schottenstein (Ohio App. 10 Dist., Franklin, 09-23-2003) No. 02AP-842, 2003-Ohio-5032, 2003 WL 22176786, Unreported. Breach Of The Peace ⇐ 17; Breach Of The Peace ⇐ 20

Evidence in juvenile proceeding to determine if child was abused, neglected, or dependent supported trial court's finding of no abuse by father, despite mother's claim that child had been sexually abused by father; child psychologist testified child denied any vaginal touching by father and summarized that her evaluation was inconclusive as to sexual abuse, and guardian ad litem testified that meetings with mother and her parents consisted of almost exclusively negative comments about father. In re Lennon (Ohio App. 5 Dist., Stark, 05-19-2003) No. 2002CA00373, 2003-Ohio-2645, 2003 WL 21185947, Unreported. Infants ⇐ 179

Trial court's refusal to admit testimony from physician, regarding statements on the mechanisms of shaken baby syndrome a second physician made at a seminar, was not an abuse of discretion, in prosecution for child endangerment; physician admitted that there was a debate in the medical community regarding the cause of the injuries suffered by infant victim. State v. Howard (Ohio App. 12 Dist., Butler, 04-21-2003) No. CA2002-02-040, 2003-Ohio-2006, 2003 WL 1906410, Unreported, appeal not allowed 99 Ohio St.3d 1470, 791 N.E.2d 984, 2003-Ohio-3669, reconsideration denied 99 Ohio St.3d 1548, 795 N.E.2d 685, 2003-Ohio-4671, appeal not allowed 100 Ohio St.3d 1485, 798 N.E.2d 1093, 2003-Ohio-5992. Infants ⇐ 20

Record failed to support any finding that step-mother by force or threat of force placed her step-daughter in fear of imminent serious physical harm or that the child was in danger of further domestic violence in hearing brought by child's mother for a domestic violence civil protection order; although mother testified that her daughter was afraid of her father and stepmother, there was nothing in the record to support a finding that the step-mother would intentionally or recklessly harm the child or abuse her. Sepesi v. Goris (Ohio App. 6 Dist., Wood, 03-31-2003) No. WD-02-028, 2003-Ohio-1622, 2003 WL 1702505, Unreported. Breach Of The Peace ⇐ 20

Evidence failed to support finding that child, who was injured by step-mother's conduct in tipping child out of her chair, was victim of abuse as basis for a domestic violence civil protection order; when step-mother first tipped the chair to force the child from sitting on her feet, the child was not harmed, and nothing in the record indicated that the step-mother, by tipping the chair a second time, intended to injure the child. Sepesi v. Goris (Ohio App. 6 Dist., Wood, 03-31-2003) No. WD-02-028, 2003-Ohio-1622, 2003 WL 1702505, Unreported. Breach Of The Peace ⇐ 17

The fact that a child was hospitalized after a traumatic visit with his father, a self-proclaimed Reverend, that his father caused his nightmares by telling him Jesus was hiding in the closet of his foster mother's house, and that the child explained to his psychiatrist he was a "bad child" and as evidence pointed to the cigarette burns on his arm were all clear and convincing evidence that the child was the victim of "abuse" as defined by RC 2151.031(C) and (D). In re Sowell (Ohio App. 8 Dist., Cuyahoga, 06-07-2001) No. 78444, 2001 WL 664120, Unreported.

A petition for domestic violence is granted for acts which result in child abuse and a temporary order is enforced against the mother to protect the child from further domestic violence where (1) the child's fractured forearm injury is at variance with the account provided by the mother, (2) there is improper care and hygiene including constant exposure to filth and grime, and (3) there is an inordinate amount of minor physical injuries while in the care of the mother and a babysitter who was hired by the mother. Tischler v. Vahcic (Ohio App. 8 Dist., Cuyahoga, 11-16-1995) No. 68053, 1995 WL 680928, Unreported.

Out of court statements made by defendant's child to police that defendant struck the child with a belt were inadmissible as hearsay, and therefore, there was no admissible evidence that defendant caused injury to her children in trial on child endangering and domestic violence charges. Newburgh Hts. v. Cole (Ohio App. 8 Dist., 05-18-2006) 166 Ohio App.3d 826, 853 N.E.2d 689, 2006-Ohio-2463. Infants ⇐ 20

A newborn child, whose toxicology screen yielded a positive test result for an illegal drug due to prenatal maternal drug abuse, was per se an "abused child" for purposes of civil child abuse statute. In re Baby Boy Blackshear (Ohio, 10-25-2000) 90 Ohio St.3d 197, 736 N.E.2d 462, 2000-Ohio-173. Infants ⇐ 156

Within the parent-child relationship, explicit threats or displays of force are not necessary to prove sexual abuse. State v. Netherland (Ohio App. 1 Dist., 02-08-1999) 132 Ohio App.3d 252, 724 N.E.2d 1182, dismissed, appeal not allowed 85 Ohio St.3d 1496, 710 N.E.2d 716. Infants ⇐ 13

A physician may testify as to the statements given by allegedly abused children to a clinical social worker that he considered in his determination whether the children were sexually abused where the testifying physician has physically examined the children, and reviews both the social history and physical findings in forming an overall "clinical impression" of whether the child has been sexually abused. In re Webb (Hamilton 1989) 64 Ohio App.3d 280, 581 N.E.2d 570, dismissed, jurisdictional motion overruled 48 Ohio St.3d 704, 549 N.E.2d 1191.

A finding that a child is an abused child under RC 2151.031 does not require a specific finding of parental or custodial fault; rather the focus is on the child's condition and whether the child is a victim, regardless of who is responsible. In re Pitts (Knox 1987) 38 Ohio App.3d 1, 525 N.E.2d 814.

A child may be found "abused" for purposes of RC 2151.031 on the basis of the mother's heroin addiction before the child's birth. In re Ruiz (Ohio Com.Pl. 1986) 27 Ohio Misc.2d 31, 500 N.E.2d 935, 27 O.B.R. 350.

A viable unborn child is a "child" for purposes of RC 2151.031. In re Ruiz (Ohio Com.Pl. 1986) 27 Ohio Misc.2d 31, 500 N.E.2d 935, 27 O.B.R. 350.

The trial court's finding of child abuse and dependency was supported by the evidence; physician trained in performing sexual assault examinations testified that she examined child and that child genitalia revealed redness that "was more than I expect, normally," wife testified that child told her that father put his finger in her vagina, and social worker testified that child told her that father placed his finger in her vagina. In re Rossantelli (Ohio App. 5 Dist., Delaware, 05-13-2002) No. 01CAF12072, 2002-Ohio-2525, 2002 WL 999301, Unreported. Infants ⇐ 179

Evidence was not sufficient to find that act of mother's fiancee, which consisted of biting child on cheek, was an act that created a risk of substantial or serious physical harm, and thus, did not support finding that child was an abused child; record did not contain any evidence that acute pain from bite resulted of any lasting duration to result in substantial suffering, or that pain from bite lasted for an extended period of time or was intractable. In re Miles (Ohio App. 9 Dist., Wayne, 05-22-2002) No. 01CA0054, 2002-Ohio-2438, 2002 WL 1065704, Unreported, appeal not allowed 96 Ohio St.3d 1514, 775 N.E.2d 856, 2002-Ohio-4950. Infants ⇐ 179

3. Corporal punishment

Father's conduct and parenting methods threatened health and welfare of children, as required to support determination that children were abused, neglected and dependent; father, a former military man, had unreasonable expectations with respect to children's schoolwork, father whipped children multiple times with belt to extent that children sustained long-lasting bruises and welts, some of blows were inflicted while child was required to remain sitting in "P.O.W. position" with hands behind his back, and father believed that his form of discipline was reasonable form of corporal punishment. In re Mercer (Ohio App. 10 Dist., Franklin, 04-21-2005) No. 04AP-422, 2005-Ohio-1845, 2005 WL 914671, Unreported. Infants ⇐ 156

Custodian's punishment of 11-year-old child by beating him with a belt was excessive, as required to find child an abused minor child in child protection proceeding, where it was precipitated by dispute over homework log. In re Horton (Ohio App. 10 Dist., Franklin, 11-23-2004) No. 03AP-1181, 2004-Ohio-6249, 2004 WL 2674562, Unreported. Infants ⇐ 156

Testimony regarding degree of difference between African-American community and majority community with respect to attitudes toward corporal punishment was inadmissible at trial in child protection proceeding to determine whether minor was an abused child. In re Horton (Ohio App. 10 Dist., Franklin, 11-23-2004) No. 03AP-1181, 2004-Ohio-6249, 2004 WL 2674562, Unreported. Infants ⇐ 173.1

There was competent credible evidence to show that child suffered from acute pain of lasting duration, to support finding that child was abused; doctor testified that multiple bruises found on child's body were from one to five days old, were not in typical locations of common toddler bruises, and were in the outline of a hand. In re K.B. (Ohio App. 9 Dist., Summit, 07-16-2003) No. 21365, 2003-Ohio-3784, 2003 WL 21658319, Unreported. Infants ⇐ 179

A parent may use corporal punishment as a method of discipline without violating the domestic-violence statute as long as the discipline is proper and reasonable under the circumstances. State v. Adaranijo (Ohio App. 1 Dist., 07-18-2003) 153 Ohio App.3d 266, 792 N.E.2d 1138, 2003-Ohio-3822, appeal not allowed 100 Ohio St.3d 1486, 798 N.E.2d 1094, 2003-Ohio-5992. Assault And Battery ⇐ 64; Parent And Child ⇐ 2.5

Swatting nine-year-old with a paddle was unwarranted and clearly excessive but did not create a substantial risk of "serious physical harm," and, therefore, child was not an "abused child" within meaning of statute prohibiting unwarranted and excessive corporal punishment or physical discipline that creates substantial risk of serious physical harm to child, where child suffered bruise and welt but was not in great pain, did not have trouble sitting or walking, and was not left with a scar. Clark v. Clark (Ohio App. 12 Dist., 09-23-1996) 114 Ohio App.3d 558, 683 N.E.2d 800. Infants ⇐ 156

Law not only prohibits parent from violating his or her duties of care, protection and support, but also prohibits parent from administering to child under 18 years of age corporal punishment which is excessive and which creates substantial risk of serious harm to child. In re Schuerman (Paulding 1991) 74 Ohio App.3d 528, 599 N.E.2d 728. Infants ⇐ 13; Infants ⇐ 15

Evidence was sufficient to support finding that it was in the best interest of children to grant permanent custody of the children to the county department of jobs and family services; evidence indicated suspected past incidents of abuse, child's sister told police that her brother received a lot of spankings, photograph showed that child had sustained a blackened eye, a swollen, injured hand and grotesquely red, swollen and bruised buttocks, with much broken skin, and, although mother admitted that she struck her child "ten to fifteen times" with a shoe, in the end, she both denied her culpability for the abuse and refused to submit to agency's order that she obtain help for her anger, parenting and self-control issues. In re C.F. (Ohio App. 8 Dist., Cuyahoga, 08-22-2002) No. 80371, 2002-Ohio-4286, 2002 WL 1938611, Unreported. Infants ⇐ 222

The children's trust fund board does not have the authority to prohibit schools or school districts which allow corporal punishment from receiving funds from the children's trust fund. OAG 89–053.

Trial court's failure to admit belt used to beat 11-year-old child at trial to determine whether he was an abused child did not constitute plain error, given that defendant in proceeding failed to subpoena the evidence or to make any attempt to arrange for the evidence to be present at trial. In re Horton (Ohio App. 10 Dist., Franklin, 11-23-2004) No. 03AP-1181, 2004-Ohio-6249, 2004 WL 2674562, Unreported. Infants ⇐ 243

4. Discovery rule

The mere fact a plaintiff is unaware of the full extent of the psychological injuries suffered as a result of childhood sexual abuse until ten years after reaching the age of majority is insufficient to toll the statute of limitations under the "discovery rule" where the plaintiff is at all times cognizant of being sexually abused and there is no evidence the plaintiff had completely repressed any memory of childhood sexual abuse until adulthood. Stewart v Kennedy, No. C-920152, 1993 WL 368967 (1st Dist Ct App, Hamilton, 9-22-93), reversed by 70 Ohio St.3d 536 (1994).

Complainant's cause of action asserting tort claims against Catholic archdiocese, its archbishop, and individual priest alleging that priest had abused him when he was a minor accrued, and two-year statute of limitations began to run, on date complainant reached age of majority, as, at time of alleged abuse, complainant knew identity of perpetrator, he knew the employer of the perpetrator, and he was fully aware of the fact that a battery had occurred; abrogating, *Cramer v. Archdiocese of Cincinnati*, 158 Ohio App.3d 110, 814 N.E.2d 97. Doe v. Archdiocese of Cincinnati (Ohio, 05-31-2006) 109 Ohio St.3d 491, 849 N.E.2d 268, 2006-Ohio-2625. Limitation Of Actions ⇐ 95(4.1)

A minor who is the victim of sexual abuse has two years from the date he or she reaches the age of majority to assert any claims against the employer of the perpetrator arising from the sexual abuse when at the time of the abuse, the victim knows the identity of the perpetrator, the employer of the perpetrator, and that a battery has occurred. Doe v. Archdiocese of Cincinnati (Ohio, 05-31-2006) 109 Ohio St.3d 491, 849 N.E.2d 268, 2006-Ohio-2625. Limitation Of Actions ⚖ 95(4.1)

Discovery rule, under which statute of limitations begins to run when plaintiff discovers or, through exercise of reasonable diligence, should have discovered possible cause of action did not apply to toll two-year statute of limitations applicable to complainant's cause of action asserting tort claims against Catholic archdiocese, its archbishop, and priest alleging that priest had abused him when he was a minor, as, at time injury allegedly occurred, complainant knew he was injured, knew the perpetrator, and knew the employer of the perpetrator, such that he was on notice to investigate possible tortious conduct of the archbishop and the archdiocese. Doe v. Archdiocese of Cincinnati (Ohio, 05-31-2006) 109 Ohio St.3d 491, 849 N.E.2d 268, 2006-Ohio-2625. Limitation Of Actions ⚖ 95(4.1)

Complainant's claim against Catholic archdiocese under Corrupt Activities Act stemming from priest's alleged sexual abuse of complainant when complainant was a minor accrued, and five-year statute of limitations began to run at the very latest when complainant reached the age of majority. Doe v. Archdiocese of Cincinnati (Ohio, 05-31-2006) 109 Ohio St.3d 491, 849 N.E.2d 268, 2006-Ohio-2625. Limitation Of Actions ⚖ 72(1)

Incarcerated father did not have due process right to attend permanent custody hearing regarding abused and neglected child; father was represented by counsel at hearing, counsel presented the testimony of mother and cross-examined witnesses, and father could have provided testimony by deposition. In re Maciulewicz (Ohio App. 11 Dist., Ashtabula, 09-13-2002) No. 2002-A-0046, 2002-Ohio-4820, 2002 WL 31053851, Unreported. Constitutional Law ⚖ 274(5); Infants ⚖ 203

5. False allegations effect

Father's allegations that social services agency and agency employees published false statements regarding father having sexually abused his daughter when they filed complaint to that effect in juvenile court, that father suffered public humiliation when his name was placed on "central registry" and that false statements were published maliciously were sufficient to state defamation claim. Roe v. Franklin Cty. (Ohio App. 10 Dist., 03-12-1996) 109 Ohio App.3d 772, 673 N.E.2d 172, appeal not allowed 77 Ohio St.3d 1415, 670 N.E.2d 1003. Libel And Slander ⚖ 7(16)

Father's allegations that social services agency and agency employees maliciously pursued claim that father sexually abused his daughter, knowing that claim was unfounded, for purpose of coercing father to give up custody of daughter, and father suffered humiliation, embarrassment and physical and mental suffering as result of such conduct, did not allege type of serious mental anguish required to state claim for intentional infliction of emotional distress. Roe v. Franklin Cty. (Ohio App. 10 Dist., 03-12-1996) 109 Ohio App.3d 772, 673 N.E.2d 172, appeal not allowed 77 Ohio St.3d 1415, 670 N.E.2d 1003. Damages ⚖ 57.25(2)

6. Sentencing

Trial court adequately considered all of the required statutory factors, made all required findings, and stated its reasons for making such findings when it imposed maximum and consecutive sentences for child endangering and involuntary manslaughter; trial court discussed defendant's criminal history and prior adjudications, his failure to respond favorably to past sanctions, his history of drug and alcohol abuse, his refusal to seek treatment for such abuse, his lack of remorse at the time of the offense, his relationship to the victim, the age of the victim, and the amount of physical harm to the victim. State v. Daniels (Ohio App. 3 Dist., Putnam, 04-25-2005) No. 12-04-07, 2005-Ohio-1920, 2005 WL 941019, Unreported. Sentencing And Punishment ⚖ 373

Defendant's maximum consecutive sentences for child endangering and involuntary manslaughter did not violate *Blakely v. Washington*; *Blakely* did not apply to Ohio's sentencing scheme. State v. Daniels (Ohio App. 3 Dist., Putnam, 04-25-2005) No. 12-04-07, 2005-Ohio-1920, 2005 WL 941019, Unreported. Sentencing And Punishment ⚖ 11

2151.04 "Dependent child" defined

As used in this chapter, "dependent child" means any child:

(A) Who is homeless or destitute or without adequate parental care, through no fault of the child's parents, guardian, or custodian;

(B) Who lacks adequate parental care by reason of the mental or physical condition of the child's parents, guardian, or custodian;

(C) Whose condition or environment is such as to warrant the state, in the interests of the child, in assuming the child's guardianship;

(D) To whom both of the following apply:

(1) The child is residing in a household in which a parent, guardian, custodian, or other member of the household committed an act that was the basis for an adjudication that a sibling of the child or any other child who resides in the household is an abused, neglected, or dependent child.

(2) Because of the circumstances surrounding the abuse, neglect, or dependency of the sibling or other child and the other conditions in the household of the child, the child is in danger of being abused or neglected by that parent, guardian, custodian, or member of the household.

(1996 H 274, eff. 8–8–96; 1988 S 89, eff. 1–1–89; 1969 H 320; 129 v 1778; 1953 H 1; GC 1639–4)

Historical and Statutory Notes

Pre–1953 H 1 Amendments: 117 v 520, § 1

Amendment Note: 1996 H 274 rewrote the section, which prior thereto read:

"As used in this chapter, "dependent child" includes any child:

"(A) Who is homeless or destitute or without proper care or support, through no fault of his parents, guardian, or custodian;

"(B) Who lacks proper care or support by reason of the mental or physical condition of his parents, guardian, or custodian;

"(C) Whose condition or environment is such as to warrant the state, in the interests of the child, in assuming his guardianship;

"(D) To whom both of the following apply:

"(1) He is residing in a household in which a parent, guardian, custodian, or other member of the household has abused or neglected a sibling of the child;

"(2) Because of the circumstances surrounding the abuse or neglect of the sibling and the other conditions in the household of the child, the child is in danger of being abused or neglected by that parent, guardian, custodian, or member of the household."

Cross References

Nonsupport of dependents, 2919.21
School attendance, juvenile court proceedings, 3321.22
Taking into custody, Juv R 6

Library References

Infants ⚖154.1 to 159.
Westlaw Topic No. 211.
C.J.S. Infants §§ 31, 33 to 50, 55, 62.
    Baldwin's Ohio Legislative Service, 1988 Laws of Ohio, S 89—LSC Analysis, p 5–571

Research References

ALR Library
21 ALR 5th 248, Power of Court or Other Public Agency to Order Medical Treatment Over Parental Religious Objections for Child Whose Life is Not Immediately Endangered.

Encyclopedias
  OH Jur. 3d Appellate Review § 90, Child Custody.
  OH Jur. 3d Criminal Law § 1073, Contributing to Child's Dependency or Neglect.
  OH Jur. 3d Family Law § 1495, Jurisdictional Issues.

OH Jur. 3d Family Law § 1497, Factors to be Considered in Determining Dependency.
OH Jur. 3d Family Law § 1500, Relating to Persons.
OH Jur. 3d Family Law § 1735, Adult Acts Punishable in Juvenile Court.
OH Jur. 3d Family Law § 1746, Evidence and Witnesses—Weight of Evidence; Degree of Proof.
OH Jur. 3d Habeas Corpus & Post Convict. Remedies § 3, Restrictions on Scope or Availability of Remedy; Strict Compliance With Statutory Procedures; Effect of Adequate Remedy at Law.

Treatises and Practice Aids

Katz, Giannelli, Blair and Lipton, Baldwin's Ohio Practice, Criminal Law, § 109:10, Nonsupport.
Carlin, Baldwin's Ohio Practice, Merrick-Rippner Probate Law § 105:7, Juvenile Court—Attachment of Jurisdiction.
Carlin, Baldwin's Ohio Practice, Merrick-Rippner Probate Law § 108:2, Juvenile Court—Criminal Jurisdiction—Contributing to Dependency, Neglect, Unruliness, or Delinquency.
Carlin, Baldwin's Ohio Practice, Merrick-Rippner Probate Law § 101:28, Judicial Hearings—Hearing Procedures.
Carlin, Baldwin's Ohio Practice, Merrick-Rippner Probate Law § 106:14, Juvenile Court Jurisdiction—Dependent Child—Definition: Evidence of Dependency.
Carlin, Baldwin's Ohio Practice, Merrick-Rippner Probate Law § 106:17, Juvenile Court Jurisdiction—Abused Child—Definition: Evidence of Abuse.
Carlin, Baldwin's Ohio Practice, Merrick-Rippner Probate Law § 107:74, Reasonable Efforts Determination.
Carlin, Baldwin's Ohio Practice, Merrick-Rippner Probate Law § 108:16, Juvenile Court—Habeas Corpus Involving Child Custody.
Carlin, Baldwin's Ohio Practice, Merrick-Rippner Probate Law § 107:138, Complaint, Abused, Neglected, or Dependent Child—Form.
Giannelli & Yeomans, Ohio Juvenile Law § 9:2, Parental Rights.
Giannelli & Yeomans, Ohio Juvenile Law § 9:3, Time of Neglect.
Giannelli & Yeomans, Ohio Juvenile Law § 9:6, Neglect—Inadequate Care Due to Parental Fault.
Giannelli & Yeomans, Ohio Juvenile Law § 9:8, Neglect—Special Care for Child's Mental Condition.
Giannelli & Yeomans, Ohio Juvenile Law § 10:2, Dependent Child Defined.
Giannelli & Yeomans, Ohio Juvenile Law § 10:3, Dependency—Homeless, Destitute or Without Adequate Care.
Giannelli & Yeomans, Ohio Juvenile Law § 10:4, Dependency—Inadequate Care Due to Parents' Mental or Physical Condition.
Giannelli & Yeomans, Ohio Juvenile Law § 10:5, Dependency—Detrimental Condition or Environment.
Giannelli & Yeomans, Ohio Juvenile Law § 10:6, Dependency—Danger of Abuse of Neglect.
Giannelli & Yeomans, Ohio Juvenile Law § 21:6, Social History Report.
Giannelli & Yeomans, Ohio Juvenile Law § 9:12, Abused Child Defined.
Giannelli & Yeomans, Ohio Juvenile Law § 9:15, Abused Child—Physical or Mental Injury Exhibited.
Giannelli & Yeomans, Ohio Juvenile Law § 16:12, Dependency Complaints.
Giannelli & Yeomans, Ohio Juvenile Law § 16:17, Objections to Complaints.
Giannelli & Yeomans, Ohio Juvenile Law § 23:13, Burden of Proof.

Law Review and Journal Commentaries

Children And Cults: A Practical Guide, Susan Linda. 29 J Fam L 591 (May 1991).
The Effect of Custodial Parents' Sexual Conduct in Dependency Determinations: In re Burrell, Note. 40 Ohio St L J 1017 (1979).

Notes of Decisions

Condition or environment 4
Constitutional issues 1
Evidence 2
Illegitimate child 6
Jurisdiction 8
Medical treatment 7
Parental fault or unfitness 5
Parental rights and responsibilities 9
Procedure 3

---

1. Constitutional issues

Mother's right against self-incrimination was not violated in child dependency proceeding when she was allegedly required to admit that she believed her son was sexually abused; the case plan adopted by the parties did not require mother to admit or believe that son was sexually abused. In re Krems (Ohio App. 11 Dist., Geauga, 05-14-2004) No. 2003-G-2534, 2004-Ohio-2446, 2004 WL 1086869, Unreported. Infants ⇐ 207

Because a parent has a fundamental liberty interest in the custody of his or her child, this important legal right is protected by law and, thus, comes within the purview of a substantial right. In re Stoll (Ohio App. 3 Dist., 01-30-2006) 165 Ohio App.3d 226, 845 N.E.2d 581, 2006-Ohio-346. Constitutional Law ⇐ 274(5)

Confrontation rights are inapplicable in dependency and neglect proceedings in juvenile courts. In re Burchfield (Athens 1988) 51 Ohio App.3d 148, 555 N.E.2d 325. Infants ⇐ 207

The use of two-way closed circuit television for the testimony of a child in a civil abuse, neglect, or dependency hearing does not violate the confrontation rights of the parents or due process. In re Burchfield (Athens 1988) 51 Ohio App.3d 148, 555 N.E.2d 325. Constitutional Law ⇐ 314; Infants ⇐ 207; Trial ⇐ 38; Witnesses ⇐ 228

RC 2151.04(C) is not unconstitutionally vague. In re Barzak (Trumbull 1985) 24 Ohio App.3d 180, 493 N.E.2d 1011, 24 O.B.R. 270.

Obligation of court to consider best interests of children serves to protect them from emotionally unstable and fanatically misguided custodial parents, whether parents' behavior is religiously motivated or otherwise, while simultaneously safeguarding parents' fundamental constitutional freedom to raise their children as they deem proper. Birch v. Birch (Ohio 1984) 11 Ohio St.3d 85, 463 N.E.2d 1254, 11 O.B.R. 327. Child Custody ⇐ 76

RC 2151.04 is constitutional. In re Williams (Hamilton 1982) 7 Ohio App.3d 324, 455 N.E.2d 1027, 7 O.B.R. 421.

The "interests of the child" standard of RC 2151.04(C) is not so vague as to run afoul of the Due Process Clause of US Const Am 14. Lesher v. Lavrich (N.D.Ohio 1984) 632 F.Supp. 77, affirmed 784 F.2d 193.

2. Evidence

Clear and convincing evidence supported juvenile court's adjudication of parents' minor child as dependent, on statutory grounds relating to prior sibling abuse; child was residing, and would reside if she were returned to the home, in a household where a parent previously committed an act that was the basis for an adjudication of abuse regarding a sibling of child. In re E.R. (Ohio App. 9 Dist., Medina, 09-18-2006) No. 05CA0108-M, 2006-Ohio-4816, 2006 WL 2661046, Unreported. Infants ⇐ 156

Clear and convincing evidence supported juvenile court's adjudication of parents' minor child as dependent, on statutory grounds that the child's condition or environment was such as to warrant the state, in the interests of the child, in assuming the child's guardianship; hospitalized child's attending physician initially diagnosed child with major depression, single episode, with severe and psychotic features, two additional evaluations confirmed his diagnosis, he said he was struck by the child's homicidal and suicidal preoccupation, along with a command auditory hallucination, i.e., voices telling her to kill herself or her parents, child's perception was that she had been mistreated and scape-goated by her family, and visits by family or any discussion of returning home spurred outbursts of emotional or physically violent behavior in child. In re E.R. (Ohio App. 9 Dist., Medina, 09-18-2006) No. 05CA0108-M, 2006-Ohio-4816, 2006 WL 2661046, Unreported. Infants ⇐ 155

Evidence supported trial court's finding that minor was dependent child, although minor did not witness father's excessive drinking or incident in which father stabbed father's fiancee, and although father's actions did not have specific adverse effect on minor; father was sole party legally responsible for minor's care, father's behavior could have detrimental effect on minor, and father did not make arrangements for minor's care after stabbing incident. In re A.P. (Ohio App. 12 Dist., Butler, 05-30-2006) No. CA2005-10-425, 2006-Ohio-2717, 2006 WL 1493313, Unreported. Infants ⇐ 154.1

Trial court's finding that child was an abused and dependent child was not against the manifest weight of the evidence, despite lack of physical evidence; child complained of sexual abuse to a teacher, child told social workers that father had sexually abused her and spanked her with an extension cord and a belt, child's allegations of abuse were consistent, and child indicated that she needed to be kept safe from father. In re A.R. (Ohio App. 9 Dist., Summit, 03-31-2006) No. 22836, 2006-Ohio-1548, 2006 WL 825400, Unreported. Infants ⇐ 179

Juvenile court's adjudication of parents' three minor children as dependent and neglected was unsupported by clear and convincing evidence, despite allegations of severe domestic violence between the parents; county agency presented no evidence that the parents' actions constituted or caused the children any neglect as defined by applicable statute, there was virtually no evidence presented regarding the children and how they were being cared for, and record was devoid of evidence that the environment that parents provided for their children was unsafe, apart from one admission by mother, testified to by one caseworker, that the children were present during an unknown number of episodes of domestic violence between the parents. In re Alexander C. (Ohio App. 6 Dist., 11-18-2005) 164 Ohio App.3d 540, 843 N.E.2d 211, 2005-Ohio-6134. Infants ⇐ 179

Trial court's grant of temporary custody of children to county child protection agency was not against the manifest weight of the evidence; decision was based on testimony of doctor who examined younger child and opined that his injuries were caused by abuse, testimony of investigator with the protective unit to mother's admission she may have bruised child, and recommendation of the guardian ad litem. In re Butcher (Ohio App. 5 Dist., Tuscarawas, 07-25-2005) No. 2005 AP 05 0031, 2005-Ohio-3827, 2005 WL 1785116, Unreported. Infants ⇐ 175.1

Credible evidence supported the court's finding of dependency; mother admitted that she told incarcerated father that she was considering killing herself and the children, social worker testified that mother gave guarded answers during evaluation, minimized the seriousness of the questions posed, and lacked a credible support network, mother told father and sheriff's deputy that she was depressed, and mother had attempted suicide in the past. In re Ohm (Ohio App. 4 Dist., Hocking, 07-01-2005) No. 05CA1, 2005-Ohio-3500, 2005 WL 1595245, Unreported. Infants ⇐ 181

Evidence of emotional harm to children from their environment was insufficient to warrant their adjudication as dependent on that basis, where no competent evidence established that children were emotionally harmed, no basis existed for finding that children's home environment was not providing children with adequate care or support, evidence established that family home was well kept and that children appeared to be appropriately dressed and fed, testimony established that mother's actions toward two children were reasonable and appropriate punishment, and no evidence supported mother's testimony that she did not believe father was taking his medication. In re Holzwart (Ohio App. 3 Dist., Seneca, 04-04-2005) No. 13-04-32, No. 13-04-40, No. 13-04-33, No. 13-04-34, 2005-Ohio-1602, 2005 WL 742842, Unreported. Infants ⇐ 179

Trial court could not find that clear and convincing evidence supported grandmother's allegation that grandson was abused, neglected, or dependent; although grandmother was concerned for grandson's welfare and health, evidence adduced by grandmother to support her complaints regarding mother's care of child was not credible. In re Forrest (Ohio App. 4 Dist., Athens, 08-05-2004) No. 04CA104CA1, 2004-Ohio-4189, 2004 WL 1778436, Unreported. Infants ⇐ 179

Adjudicating adopted child a dependent and abused child was not against manifest weight of evidence; although there was no physical evidence of sexual abuse by father and father denied such abuse, child testified that sexual abuse occurred, mother corroborated child's testimony that father watched pornographic movies, and caseworkers indicated that child's testimony was virtually identical to description of abuse child gave to caseworkers. In re Moonshower (Ohio App. 3 Dist., Van, 08-02-2004) No. 15-04-04, No. 15-04-05, 2004-Ohio-4024, 2004 WL 1718180, Unreported. Infants ⇐ 179

Mere fact that unrelated infant whom mother was babysitting in her home may have been injured while under mother's care on a particular evening, which evidence was sketchy at best, did not constitute clear and convincing evidence that mother's children were at risk, as required to support determination that mother's own children were dependent, absent any evidence regarding mother's children or how they were being cared for. In re A.C. (Ohio App. 9 Dist., Wayne, 06-23-2004) No. 03CA0054, No. 03CA0053, No. 03CA0055, 2004-Ohio-3248, 2004 WL 1397624, Unreported. Infants ⇐ 156

Evidence supported juvenile court's adjudication of infant as a dependent child; father smoked marijuana in presence of mother and child on the day of child's birth, nurse testified that mother failed to feed child for several hours, mother placed adult-sized pillow in child's bassinet, parents had lost custody of four older children because of substance abuse and parents' unwillingness to rectify housing and employment instability, parents had not demonstrated ability to maintain stable residence, and parents had insufficient income to meet monthly expenses. In re Christian (Ohio App. 4 Dist., Athens, 06-15-2004) No. 04CA10, 2004-Ohio-3146, 2004 WL 1367399, Unreported. Infants ⇐ 156

County Department of Jobs and Family Services failed to set forth clear and convincing evidence that mother's children were dependent; none of school children on school field trip were ever actually subjected to sole parental supervision of mother who was intoxicated on the day of field trip, and mother's child did not even attend field trip, so she could not be considered dependent as result of mother's behavior on field trip. In re C.M. (Ohio App. 12 Dist., Brown, 05-10-2004) No. CA2003-02-003, No. CA2003-02-004, 2004-Ohio-2294, 2004 WL 1040677, Unreported. Infants ⇐ 179

Evidence supported finding that developmentally delayed child of minor mother was a dependent child; mother's residence was unstable, mother admitted that she could not care for child on her own, child's father was committed to youth detention facility, mother was unemployed, mother had not financially supported child while child was in care of paternal grandmother, and social worker did not think mother would be able to handle special services and time required for child's special needs. In re Malone (Ohio App. 10 Dist., Franklin, 12-30-2003) No. 03AP-489, 2003-Ohio-7156, 2003 WL 23024377, Unreported, appeal not allowed 102 Ohio St.3d 1423, 807 N.E.2d 367, 2004-Ohio-2003. Infants ⇐ 177

Trial court finding that child was a dependent child was not against the sufficiency of the evidence; mother had a history of being unable to provide for her children and for being unable to provide adequate housing, mother was unemployed, psychological testing of mother indicated a lack of efficacy and a lack of independence, and, at the hearing on mother's objections to dependency finding, the court found out that mother had moved out of the state and had not been in contact with child or inquired about child's welfare. In re Barker (Ohio App. 5 Dist., Stark, 11-24-2003) No. 03-CA-279, 2003-Ohio-6406, 2003 WL 22843907, Unreported. Infants ⇐ 155; Infants ⇐ 157; Infants ⇐ 158

Clear and convincing evidence supported finding that father's oldest child was dependent; child's younger sibling was an abused child, physician testified that there were concerns for child remaining in the household because of child's behavior and the disciplinary methods utilized on her, and nature and extent of younger sibling's injury clearly indicated that any child residing in the household would have been in danger of abuse if he or she were to remain in the household. In re Anthony (Ohio App. 11 Dist., Ashtabula, 10-24-2003) No. 2002-A-0096, 2003-Ohio-5712, 2003 WL 22429035, Unreported. Infants ⇐ 179

Trial court's determination that child was dependent child did not amount to plain error, where counselor and caseworker testified that stepchild and child reported that father hit child, father admitted that he struck child in mouth, and child and step-child reported that father verbally abused them and that father's use of alcohol was stimulant to his abusive behavior. In re Youngerman (Ohio App. 2 Dist., Miami, 10-10-2003) No. 2002 CA 61, 2003-Ohio-5397, 2003 WL 22318106, Unreported. Infants ⇐ 243

Trial court finding of dependency was not against the manifest weight of the evidence; mother and father's parental rights to child's older siblings had been involuntarily terminated, parents had mental health issues, they allowed dangerous individuals to stay in their home, witness testified that parents would require help at least 16 hours per day to care for children, father had not sought treatment for his emotional or alcohol problems, and father had fears that he would sexually molest child. In re D.B. (Ohio App. 9 Dist., Medina, 08-27-2003) No. 03CA0015-M, No. 03CA0018-M, 2003-Ohio-4526, 2003 WL 22015445, Unreported. Infants ⇐ 156; Infants ⇐ 158

Clear and convincing evidence supported the juvenile court finding that children were neglected and dependent, in child dependency proceeding; father failed to comply with programs or toxicology screenings requested by the county jobs and family services, and he did not attend any programs on his own. In re Harris (Ohio App. 1 Dist., Hamilton, 02-14-2003) No. C-020512, 2003-Ohio-672, 2003 WL 327996, Unreported. Infants ⇐ 156

Assuming that mother was told she was denied visitation with child, such fact did not overcome finding that child was neglected and dependent based on abandonment; such an order only addressed visitation and would not have prevented a mother from calling or sending letters or cards to her son, and there was ample evidence in the record to support a finding of abandonment. (Per Evans, J., with two judges concurring in judgment only.) In re Fennell (Ohio App. 4 Dist., Athens, 09-26-2002) No. 02CA17, 2002-Ohio-6151, 2002 WL 31521504, Unreported. Infants ⇐ 157

Competent, credible evidence supported finding that child was neglected and dependent based on abandonment; mother failed to pay child support since child was placed with county children services, mother failed to attend a single scheduled visitation for three-month period and mother's subsequent visitation was sporadic, and mother made no contact whatsoever with child for more than a year. (Per Evans, J., with two judges concurring in judgment only.) In re Fennell (Ohio App. 4 Dist., Athens, 09-26-2002) No. 02CA17, 2002-Ohio-6151, 2002 WL 31521504, Unreported. Infants ⚖ 157

Past truancy of minor children, which resulted in adjudications of unruliness and court sanctions, did not provide a basis for a finding of dependency, where there was no allegation in dependency complaint that children had violated any of those sanctions or that mother had, in any way, created an environment in which children continued to be truant. In re Locker (Ohio App. 5 Dist., Tuscarawas, 11-06-2002) No. 2002AP020011, 2002-Ohio-6124, 2002 WL 31518192, Unreported. Infants ⚖ 159

Clear and convincing evidence supported finding that child was a neglected and dependent child, in dependency proceeding; mother had been incarcerated four times since child's birth, her mental health issues interfered with her ability to parent, she failed to address child's developmental delays and behavioral problems, she provided no financial support for child, she failed to provide child with a stable home, and she attempted to commit suicide in child's presence. In re Barnhart (Ohio App. 4 Dist., Athens, 10-30-2002) No. 02CA20, 2002-Ohio-6023, 2002 WL 31455949, Unreported. Infants ⚖ 155; Infants ⚖ 157; Infants ⚖ 158

Clear and convincing evidence that turbulent relationship between child's parents created an environment which threatened the physical and emotional well-being of child supported finding that child was dependent and neglected, for purposes of termination of father's parental rights. In re Jehosphat W. (Ohio App. 6 Dist., Lucas, 10-11-2002) No. L-01-1505, 2002-Ohio-5503, 2002 WL 31270290, Unreported. Infants ⚖ 179

Juvenile court's finding that a particular child is neglected and dependent is not supported by clear and convincing evidence where the mother obtains adequate parental care for the child during the time she is unable to provide that care personally by voluntarily taking him to his paternal grandparents who in turn provide adequate parental care. Johnson v. Johnson (Ohio App. 10 Dist., Franklin, 03-22-2001) No. 00AP-691, 2001 WL 277272, Unreported.

Clear and convincing evidence supported conclusion that children were dependent; father left children, the oldest of whom was 16, home alone and informed police that he would not be returning for at least a couple of days, father's home was dirty, carpets were soiled, two bedrooms were occupied by 18 puppies and two dogs, and father admitted to smoking cigarettes in the home in spite of fact that he was also using an oxygen tank. In re Colaner Children (Ohio App. 5 Dist., 05-02-2006) 166 Ohio App.3d 355, 850 N.E.2d 794, 2006-Ohio-2404. Infants ⚖ 157

Evidence was insufficient to support finding that father's two children were dependent children; mother voluntarily relinquished control of the children to maternal grandparents prior to entering drug rehabilitation, and the children had been receiving proper care and support from grandparents. In re Stoll (Ohio App. 3 Dist., 01-30-2006) 165 Ohio App.3d 226, 845 N.E.2d 581, 2006-Ohio-346. Infants ⚖ 154.1

The determination that a child is a dependent child requires no showing of fault on each parent's part, but focuses specifically on the child's situation to determine whether the child is without proper or adequate care or support. In re Stoll (Ohio App. 3 Dist., 01-30-2006) 165 Ohio App.3d 226, 845 N.E.2d 581, 2006-Ohio-346. Infants ⚖ 154.1

While children which mother left with their grandmother may have been neglected, they were not dependent, since they were not homeless, destitute, without proper care or without support. In re Tikyra A. (Ohio App. 6 Dist., 05-12-1995) 103 Ohio App.3d 452, 659 N.E.2d 867. Infants ⚖ 156

Dependency of child must be established by clear and convincing evidence. In re Brodbeck (Ohio App. 3 Dist., 10-19-1994) 97 Ohio App.3d 652, 647 N.E.2d 240. Infants ⚖ 177

A trial court, having found instances of past abuse of a sibling, does not abuse its discretion in finding a child to be dependent and in danger of abuse or neglect. In re Schuerman (Paulding 1991) 74 Ohio App.3d 528, 599 N.E.2d 728.

A finding that a child is a dependent child under RC 2151.04 does not require a specific finding of parental or custodial fault; rather the focus is on the child's condition and whether the child is a victim, regardless of who is responsible. In re Pitts (Knox 1987) 38 Ohio App.3d 1, 525 N.E.2d 814.

Dependency of a child at the time of a hearing on dependency may be established by evidence of conditions existing several months before the filing of the complaint if there is no evidence of a substantial change in circumstances to warrant a conclusion that the child is no longer dependent. In re Smart (Franklin 1984) 21 Ohio App.3d 31, 486 N.E.2d 147, 21 O.B.R. 33. Infants ⚖ 177

On the evidence, despite the strong maternal attachments and instincts, and the well-intentioned concern of grandparents, infant's best interests would be served by the child being placed in the permanent custody of the county welfare department for adoption-placement. In re Baby Girl S. (Ohio Com.Pl. 1972) 32 Ohio Misc. 217, 290 N.E.2d 925, 61 O.O.2d 439.

Where 15-year-old girl had had numerous acts of sexual intercourse with different men, had failed to respond to reasonable control and discipline of her mother, had committed felony and had family situation of financial and emotional instability, child born of girl was a "dependent child," even though child had never been in custody of mother. In re Turner (Ohio Com.Pl. 1967) 229 N.E.2d 764. Infants ⚖ 154.1

Court is not justified in finding a child dependent unless the evidence brings it within this section. In re Hayes (Franklin 1939) 62 Ohio App. 289, 23 N.E.2d 956, 30 Ohio Law Abs. 568, 16 O.O. 10.

Under this section, a child is "dependent," where it is not being provided with an education substantially equivalent to the education provided by the common schools even though the child has been excluded from the public schools for failure to be vaccinated in obedience to an order of the board of education. In re Hargy (Ohio Com.Pl. 1920) 32 Ohio Dec. 8, 23 Ohio N.P.(N.S.) 129.

Trial court and magistrate could rely on psychological assessment of mother prepared more than a year before dependency hearing; court and magistrate considered assessment only in relation to older child, court had ongoing jurisdiction, and assessment was corroborated by other evidence. In re Williams (Ohio App. 10 Dist., Franklin, 06-11-2002) No. 01AP-867, No. 01AP-868, 2002-Ohio-2902, 2002 WL 1275514, Unreported. Infants ⚖ 208

Evidence supported finding that foster mother was suitable legal custodian of birth mother's daughter; evidence showed that child was attached to foster parents, that they provided a stable home, that they were receptive to visits by birth mother, and that they were relatives in a position to encourage family contact. In re Williams (Ohio App. 10 Dist., Franklin, 06-11-2002) No. 01AP-867, No. 01AP-868, 2002-Ohio-2902, 2002 WL 1275514, Unreported. Infants ⚖ 226

Finding that child was dependent was supported by mother's stipulation to dependency and by evidence that father was incarcerated and was not scheduled to be released for five years. In re Cassidy (Ohio App. 5 Dist., Stark, 06-10-2002) No. 2001CA00278, 2002-Ohio-2897, 2002 WL 1299786, Unreported. Infants ⚖ 179

No person or parent can give his consent to a finding of "dependency" for a child, but the requirements of this section must be found to exist. In re Hobson, 44 Abs 86, 62 NE(2d) 510 86 (App, Franklin 1945).

3. Procedure

To support defendants' conviction for contributing to nonsupport of dependents the state need only prove that the parents had contributed to their children becoming dependent at the time stated in the complaint; as such the state is not required to show that the children were dependent or neglected at the time of trial. State v. Frazier (Ohio App. 2 Dist., Montgomery, 09-13-1996) No. 15273, No. 15274, 1996 WL 517271, Unreported.

A juvenile court commits plain error in terminating the rights of a child's custodian where the court sua sponte takes judicial notice of a prior case involving the child and his custodian in addition to ruling the child dependent and neglected based upon unsworn admissions of the child's mother that are not within her personal knowledge and do not constitute testimony. In Matter of Erin N. (Ohio App. 6 Dist., Erie, 04-12-1996) No. E-95-029, 1996 WL 168626, Unreported.

Mother was not entitled to extraordinary relief in habeas corpus to compel county children services executive director to release her dependent child from its temporary custody, as she had adequate legal remedies in the ordinary course of law to raise her claims; mother could have objected to magistrate's decision, raised issues regarding sufficiency of dependency complaint or constitutionality of child dependency statute in any subsequent hearing in case, or appealed any adverse judgment by the juvenile court. Rammage v. Saros (Ohio, 12-13-2002) 97 Ohio St.3d 430, 780 N.E.2d 278, 2002-Ohio-6669. Habeas Corpus ⚖ 280

County department of human services was not required to have custody of child for twelve consecutive months prior to filing motion for permanent custody, where department filed original complaint alleging child to be a dependent child and requesting permanent custody of child as the first disposition and temporary custody as the alternative disposition. In re Ament (Ohio App. 12 Dist., 04-23-2001) 142 Ohio App.3d 302, 755 N.E.2d 448, appeal not allowed 92 Ohio St.3d 1431, 749 N.E.2d 757. Infants ⚖ 193

Trial court was not required to readjudicate children as dependent prior to awarding permanent custody of children to county department of human services, where court had previously adjudicated children as dependent when it committed them to temporary custody of department, and children remained in protective supervision after they were returned to parents. In re Ament (Ohio App. 12 Dist., 04-23-2001) 142 Ohio App.3d 302, 755 N.E.2d 448, appeal not allowed 92 Ohio St.3d 1431, 749 N.E.2d 757. Infants ⇔ 210

Trial judge lacked authority to take judicial notice of previous adjudication and journal entry to establish abuse and dependency of children in instant case; entry at issue was result of another proceeding which had different case numbers and separate dockets. In re Knotts (Ohio App. 3 Dist., 02-12-1996) 109 Ohio App.3d 267, 671 N.E.2d 1357. Infants ⇔ 171

Where journal entry of prior adjudication of children as abused or dependent was not admitted as part of record, it was error for trial court to conclude by clear and convincing evidence that children were abused or dependent. In re Knotts (Ohio App. 3 Dist., 02-12-1996) 109 Ohio App.3d 267, 671 N.E.2d 1357. Infants ⇔ 179

Incidents that occurred after first adjudication of dependency may be basis for second adjudication of dependency, though children are not in mother's custody during that time; prospective finding of dependency is appropriate where children have not been in custody of mother, but circumstances demonstrate that to allow mother to have custody of her children would threaten their life and safety. In re Pieper Children (Preble 1993) 85 Ohio App.3d 318, 619 N.E.2d 1059. Infants ⇔ 154.1

Standard of review of determination that children are dependent is whether sufficient, credible evidence exists to support trial court's adjudication. In re Pieper Children (Preble 1993) 85 Ohio App.3d 318, 619 N.E.2d 1059. Infants ⇔ 252

A sexually abused 21-day-old infant is properly adjudicated dependent. In re Webb (Hamilton 1989) 64 Ohio App.3d 280, 581 N.E.2d 570, dismissed, jurisdictional motion overruled 48 Ohio St.3d 704, 549 N.E.2d 1191.

Where a complaint alleges that a child is neglected or dependent within the meaning of RC 2151.03(B) and RC 2151.04(A), RC 2151.04(B), and RC 2151.04(C), the child's mother is not prohibited by Juv R 29(D)(2) from taking part in the adjudicatory hearing by the fact that she entered a plea of "admitted" to the allegations in the complaint. In re Sims (Preble 1983) 13 Ohio App.3d 37, 468 N.E.2d 111, 13 O.B.R. 40.

The determination of whether or not a child is "dependent," as defined in RC 2151.04, must be made as of the time of the hearing on the complaint, and a determination that a child is not a "dependent child" at one time is no bar to a later determination that the child is then "dependent." In re Justice (Clinton 1978) 59 Ohio App.2d 78, 392 N.E.2d 897, 13 O.O.3d 139. Infants ⇔ 154.1; Infants ⇔ 281

Once a child has been found to be "dependent" as defined in RC 2151.04, the "best interests" of the child are the primary consideration in determining whether an award of permanent custody is justified pursuant to RC 2151.353(D). In re Cunningham (Ohio 1979) 59 Ohio St.2d 100, 391 N.E.2d 1034, 13 O.O.3d 78. Infants ⇔ 222

The issue of whether a child is a dependent child is to be determined as of "on or about the date specified in the complaint," and need not be determined as of the time of the hearing. In re Baby Girl S. (Ohio Com.Pl. 1972) 32 Ohio Misc. 217, 290 N.E.2d 925, 61 O.O.2d 439.

Before the court may consider what disposition should be made of children for their best interest and welfare, there must first be an adjudication that said children are neglected or dependent, and where neglect and dependency existed at the time of the filing of the complaint, but said cause was not prosecuted further until more than four years afterwards and the conditions of the parents had changed sufficiently that evidence was lacking to establish neglect or dependency at the time of the hearing, said complaint must be dismissed. In re Burkhart (Ohio Juv. 1968) 15 Ohio Misc. 170, 239 N.E.2d 772, 44 O.O.2d 329.

An allegation in a motion filed in juvenile court seeking to have that court "determine and award the future care and custody" of a child that "neither parent is a suitable person to have the care and custody of said child" does not constitute a charge that such child is "neglected" or "dependent" and is not sufficiently definite to constitute the "complaint" necessitated by RC 2151.27. Union County Child Welfare Bd. v. Parker (Union 1964) 7 Ohio App.2d 79, 218 N.E.2d 757, 36 O.O.2d 162. Infants ⇔ 197

A judicial determination that a child is "dependent" pursuant to RC 2151.04 must be based on evidence as to conditions at the time of the hearing held therefor. In re Darst (Franklin 1963) 117 Ohio App. 374, 192 N.E.2d 287, 24 O.O.2d 144. Infants ⇔ 154.1

The provisions of RC 2151.04 which define the grounds upon which a child can be found to be "dependent," limit the extent of the juvenile court's authority to remove children from a parent, guardian or custodian, and place them under control of the state. In re Darst (Franklin 1963) 117 Ohio App. 374, 192 N.E.2d 287, 24 O.O.2d 144. Infants ⇔ 154.1

RC 5103.16 and RC 2151.04 effect by implication a partial repeal of RC 3107.08, and by such sections it is required that the parents of a child apply to the probate court for placement of the child for adoption prior to the placement. In re Boyd's Adoption (Ohio Prob. 1962) 185 N.E.2d 331, 89 Ohio Law Abs. 202.

In an action to determine that a minor is a dependent child, a mere allegation of dependency in the complaint is sufficient, although the court must find that the condition was due to no fault of the parent, guardian, or custodian. In re Duncan (Preble 1951) 107 Ohio App.2d 256, 62 Ohio Law Abs. 173.

In a prosecution for contributing to the neglect or dependency of a minor child, a failure of the court to give the statutory definition of "neglected child" or "dependent child" is an error of omission, and does not constitute reversible error unless the court's attention was seasonably called to the omission and specific instructions requested and refused. State v. Griffin (Champaign 1952) 93 Ohio App. 299, 106 N.E.2d 668, 63 Ohio Law Abs. 122, 51 O.O. 47.

In a prosecution for contributing to the neglect or dependency of a minor child it is not a prerequisite that the child be adjudicated as a neglected, dependent or delinquent child in a separate proceeding before a charge of contributing toward such neglect, dependency or delinquency of such child can be maintained. State v. Griffin (Champaign 1952) 93 Ohio App. 299, 106 N.E.2d 668, 63 Ohio Law Abs. 122, 51 O.O. 47. Infants ⇔ 13

Affidavit charging that accused contributed to dependency of minor child without charging that minor was a dependent child as defined in this section, does not charge an offense under laws of Ohio. State v. Krauss (Auglaize 1945) 81 Ohio App. 453, 80 N.E.2d 164, 37 O.O. 282. Infants ⇔ 20

Parents waived any right to argue, on appeal from disposition of permanent custody of their child to county, that they were not to blame for death of another of their children or that they would pose no threat to subject child, where prior to permanent custody hearing, each parent orally stipulated to an adjudication of dependency and initialed a written entry to that effect, and trial judge fully explained consequences of stipulation at time parents agreed to such adjudication. In re Rivas (Ohio App. 9 Dist., Lorain, 07-24-2002) No. 02CA007989, 2002-Ohio-3747, 2002 WL 1626663, Unreported. Infants ⇔ 243

Order that father have no contact with minor daughter, as contained in judgment declaring daughter to be dependent, was not abuse of discretion, where father was incarcerated based on charges of gross sexual imposition upon minor boys, and daughter had not yet undergone an evaluation to determine any potential abuse she might have endured from father. In re Cassidy (Ohio App. 5 Dist., Stark, 06-10-2002) No. 2001CA00278, 2002-Ohio-2897, 2002 WL 1299786, Unreported. Infants ⇔ 222

To declare a child of an allegedly mentally ill parent dependent, it is necessary to prove not only the parent's mental incapacity, but also that the child lacks proper care because of the mental incapacity. In re H——— (Ohio Juv. 1963) 192 N.E.2d 683, 92 Ohio Law Abs. 436, 24 O.O.2d 334.

4. Condition or environment

Adjudication of child as prospectively dependent was not against manifest weight of the evidence, pursuant to statute permitting juvenile court to find child prospectively dependent based on parents' custodial history; mother's parental rights had been involuntarily terminated with respect to four of her children, father had been convicted of child endangering based on incident in which he shook his child by another woman, causing severe injuries to that child, mother lived with father, relied on him for support of herself and child, and evidenced an intent to marry him, and thus permitted the presence of a known child abuser in the child's home. In re W.C. (Ohio App. 9 Dist., Summit, 06-15-2005) No. 22356, 2005-Ohio-2968, 2005 WL 1398843, Unreported. Infants ⇔ 156

Mother's previous involvement with men who were domestically violent to her and verbally abusive to her children and her current relationship with a man who been involved in incidents of domestic violence which resulted in his own parental rights being involuntarily terminated supported a finding of dependency. In re Hurst (Ohio App. 3 Dist., Seneca, 10-14-2003) No. 13-03-27, 2003-Ohio-5460, 2003 WL 22336087, Unreported. Infants ⇔ 156

Note 4

Evidence was sufficient to support finding that 16-year-old was a dependent child; home situation was unstable and not improving, rather, home showed signs of increased problems, including physical and verbal abuse by mother and brother, parents and child saw no hope of improving situation absent some type of intervention, and it would have been in child's best interest to be removed from her home until the parties could begin to work on their problems. In re Day (Ohio App. 12 Dist., Clermont, 07-07-2003) No. CA2002-09-073, 2003-Ohio-3544, 2003 WL 21517343, Unreported. Infants 155

Domestic violence between mother and an individual, previously convicted of felony child endangering, who had resided with mother and her children was not sufficient basis for a finding in dependency proceeding that children's condition or environment warranted state's assumption of guardianship, where at the time of the filing of dependency complaint and at time of adjudicatory hearing that individual had left the home, and there was no testimony that he had ever returned to the home except for the time when it burned down. In re Locker (Ohio App. 5 Dist., Tuscarawas, 11-06-2002) No. 2002AP020011, 2002-Ohio-6124, 2002 WL 31518192, Unreported. Infants 154.1

Record did not support a finding in dependency proceeding concerning presence of animal feces in the home; one of the children who were subject of dependency proceeding testified that he was responsible for cleaning up messes resulting when children's puppy relieved itself on floor, and both social worker and art therapist testified they did not consider animal feces a problem in the home. In re Locker (Ohio App. 5 Dist., Tuscarawas, 11-06-2002) No. 2002AP020011, 2002-Ohio-6124, 2002 WL 31518192, Unreported. Infants 179

Minor children were not dependent based on homelessness, though mother's mobile home had been destroyed by fire at the time dependency complaint was filed, where mother immediately arranged for shelter for herself and for the children. In re Locker (Ohio App. 5 Dist., Tuscarawas, 11-06-2002) No. 2002AP020011, 2002-Ohio-6124, 2002 WL 31518192, Unreported. Infants 156

Trial court did not base its decision that children were not dependent because of mother's poverty but because of living conditions where evidence indicated that large pool of sewage was located underneath trailer, trash was piled up around trailer, unprotected wiring was hanging at level easily accessible to child, there was testimony that second trailer in better condition was parked on parents' property but was not being used, that conditions in home had declined, and that parents disregarded offer of assistance and recommendations to improve conditions. In re Brodbeck (Ohio App. 3 Dist., 10-19-1994) 97 Ohio App.3d 652, 647 N.E.2d 240. Infants 154.1

Finding children dependent must be grounded on whether children are receiving proper care and support; therefore, determination must be based on children and their conditions, not parents' deficiencies. In re Brodbeck (Ohio App. 3 Dist., 10-19-1994) 97 Ohio App.3d 652, 647 N.E.2d 240. Infants 154.1

Testimony that mother had planned to stage separation from father, whose parental rights had been terminated, in order to mislead court into returning custody of children to her, that father was seen at mother's residence several times after claimed separation, that father's current mail was found in trash container near mother's residence, and that father's address was same as mother's address on her hospital admission forms amounted to clear and convincing evidence that mother would expose her children to potentially abusive environment such that her children were "dependent," because children were being subjected to potentially abusive environment and because abusive and neglectful parent would be residing in home with children he had previously abused and neglected. In re Pieper Children (Preble 1993) 85 Ohio App.3d 318, 619 N.E.2d 1059. Infants 179

A child need not be placed in a particular environment before a court can determine that such environment is unhealthy or unsafe since the unfitness of a parent, guardian, or custodian can be predicted by past history. In re Bishop (Ashland 1987) 36 Ohio App.3d 123, 521 N.E.2d 838.

Even though a child has never been in the custody of its natural parents, it may be a dependent child within the meaning of RC 2151.04(C) if the condition or environment in which the child would live if found not dependent would warrant the state, in the interests of the child, in assuming guardianship. In re Smart (Franklin 1984) 21 Ohio App.3d 31, 486 N.E.2d 147, 21 O.B.R. 33.

Where the state can make a showing, by clear and convincing evidence, that the "environment" or "condition" into which a newborn baby would enter upon leaving the hospital would threaten the child's health and safety, the state may intervene to have the child declared a "dependent child" under RC 2151.04. In re Campbell (Butler 1983) 13 Ohio App.3d 34, 468 N.E.2d 93, 13 O.B.R. 36. Infants 177

The crux of a dependency action is the condition or environment of the child, not the culpable acts of the parents. In re East (Ohio Com.Pl. 1972) 32 Ohio Misc. 65, 288 N.E.2d 343, 61 O.O.2d 38, 61 O.O.2d 108. Infants 154.1

The state's interest under RC 2151.04 arises only if there is no one meeting the obligations of care, support and custody which are owed to a child by a parent, and the fact that relatives other than a parent are providing such care and support is immaterial to the determination of whether a child is a "dependent child" within the purview of such section. In re Darst (Franklin 1963) 117 Ohio App. 374, 192 N.E.2d 287, 24 O.O.2d 144.

In a proceeding in the juvenile court, instituted by the filing of a complaint under RC 2151.27, a finding by the court that a child is "neglected," in that it "lacked proper parental care because of the faults and habits of his parents," and "dependent," in that its "condition and environment… is such as to warrant the court… in assuming his guardianship" must be based on evidence with respect to whether the child was receiving proper parental care in a proper environment in its home at the time of the hearing. In re Minton (Darke 1960) 112 Ohio App. 361, 176 N.E.2d 252, 16 O.O.2d 283. Infants 156

Evidence was sufficient to support finding, by clear and convincing evidence, that child was dependent; mother had anger issues and threatened violence against Children's Services Unit (CSU), mother continued to have relationship with father who may have caused severe injuries, including numerous fractures and chronic subdural hematomas, to child's older sibling, and mother lost custody of her two other children for failure to follow requirements of CSU's case plans. In re Crow (Ohio App. 2 Dist., Darke, 06-28-2002) No. 1566, 2002-Ohio-3282, 2002 WL 1393618, Unreported. Infants 177

Evidence supported finding that mother's two younger children were in danger of being abused or neglected, where court found that two older children had been abused, older siblings testified that younger siblings had been slapped and had derogatory language directed at them, and circumstances in household created danger that younger children would be abused in future. In re Kimble (Ohio App. 7 Dist., Harrison, 05-15-2002) No. 99 517 CA, 2002-Ohio-2409, 2002 WL 1065977, Unreported. Infants 179

Under former GC 1645 (RC 2151.04) a child may be dependent (1) if its home, by the neglect of its parents, is an unfit place for it to be and (2) if its environment is such as to warrant the state, in the interest of the child, to assume its guardianship. In re Decker (Ohio Juv. 1930) 28 Ohio NP(NS) 433.

5. Parental fault or unfitness

Evidence was insufficient to support child's adjudication as dependent on the basis that child lacked adequate parental care by reason of mental or physical condition of child's mother; while physician testified that mother suffered from an adjustment disorder, depression, and anxiety, he did not state that her mental condition affected her ability to parent child. In re Walling (Ohio App. 1 Dist., Hamilton, 02-24-2006) No. C-050646, 2006-Ohio-810, 2006 WL 445981, Unreported. Infants 181

Evidence was insufficient to support child's adjudication as dependent on the basis that child's condition or environment was such as to warrant the State, in the interests of the child, in assuming the child's guardianship; while county department of jobs and family services and child's guardian ad litem urged that harm be presumed to child because of mother's failure to abide by protective orders that directed mother to partake in counseling, to submit to weekly urine tests, and to attend Alcoholics Anonymous or Narcotics Anonymous meetings, such harm could not be inferred, and department presented no evidence demonstrating how mother's failure to comply with such orders were harmful to child. In re Walling (Ohio App. 1 Dist., Hamilton, 02-24-2006) No. C-050646, 2006-Ohio-810, 2006 WL 445981, Unreported. Infants 181

Mother failed to articulate clearly her constitutional challenge to statute allowing trial court to find child prospectively dependent based on parents' custodial history, as necessary for Court of Appeals to consider it on appeal from dependency adjudication, as mother failed to allege sufficient facts to demonstrate how juvenile court's application of statute infringed upon her parenting choices and protected freedoms. In re W.C. (Ohio App. 9 Dist., Summit, 06-15-2005) No. 22356, 2005-Ohio-2968, 2005 WL 1398843, Unreported. Infants 241

Evidence supported adjudication of child as dependent, even though child had never resided with mother; mother had been unable to keep a suitable clean home environment without supervision at time her three oldest children had been removed from her care, and, since that time, county had received referrals involving same sanitation and environmental concerns that existed in mother's home at time children were removed from her care. In re Cazad (Ohio App. 4 Dist., Lawrence, 05-09-2005) No. 04CA36, 2005-Ohio-2574, 2005 WL 1228386, Unreported. Infants ⇔ 156

Father's conduct and parenting methods threatened health and welfare of children, as required to support determination that children were abused, neglected and dependent; father, a former military man, had unreasonable expectations with respect to children's schoolwork, father whipped children multiple times with belt to extent that children sustained long-lasting bruises and welts, some of blows were inflicted while child was required to remain sitting in "P.O.W. position" with hands behind his back, and father believed that his form of discipline was reasonable form of corporal punishment. In re Mercer (Ohio App. 10 Dist., Franklin, 04-21-2005) No. 04AP-422, 2005-Ohio-1845, 2005 WL 914671, Unreported, appeal not allowed 106 Ohio St.3d 1534, 835 N.E.2d 383, 2005-Ohio-5146. Infants ⇔ 156

Clear and convincing evidence supported juvenile court's determination that children's conditions and their environment warranted the State's assumption of guardianship, and thus, dependency adjudication was warranted; children's paternal grandmother regularly and willingly left the children in the unsupervised care of their legal father, who was a known sexual offender, the older three children had severe psychological issues due to past abuse, and the parents and grandmother were unable to acknowledge or appropriately deal with the children's issues. In re Wilkinson (Ohio App. 1 Dist., Hamilton, 08-06-2004) No. C-040182, No. C-040203, No. C-040282, 2004-Ohio-4107, 2004 WL 1752821, Unreported, appeal not allowed 104 Ohio St.3d 1410, 818 N.E.2d 711, 2004-Ohio-6364. Infants ⇔ 156

Even if juvenile court erred in considering evidence of mother's positive marijuana screen at the time of child's birth, such error was harmless in proceedings to determine whether child was a dependent child; mother admitted that father and his family smoked marijuana in her presence on the day she gave birth, revealing mother's unwillingness to remove herself and child from a harmful situation, and revealing father's continued drug use and failure to protect child. In re Christian (Ohio App. 4 Dist., Athens, 06-15-2004) No. 04CA10, 2004-Ohio-3146, 2004 WL 1367399, Unreported. Infants ⇔ 253

Finding that children were not receiving proper care and that their environment had the potential for an adverse impact, warranting a determination of dependency, was supported by evidence that mother had admitted to violently shaking her child after becoming frustrated and to having violent fantasies about hurting the child. In re Hauenstein (Ohio App. 3 Dist., Hancock, 06-07-2004) No. 5-03-38, No. 5-03-39, 2004-Ohio-2915, 2004 WL 1238288, Unreported. Infants ⇔ 156

Juvenile court was not required to make a separate finding of parental unsuitability before awarding legal custody of children to paternal cousin of mother; children were adjudicated dependent based on the lack of an adequate environment, and if a child lacked an adequate environment it followed that an award of custody to parent would be detrimental to child. In re Gales (Ohio App. 10 Dist., Franklin, 11-25-2003) No. 03AP-445, No. 03AP-446, 2003-Ohio-6309, 2003 WL 22785029, Unreported. Infants ⇔ 210

Former husband's complaint against former wife alleging dependency and neglect of parties' children failed to adequately set forth particular facts upon which allegations were based and contained no notice concerning evidence against which wife would have to defend; while husband claimed children would be molested and wife would flee should children be returned to her custody, these were general conclusory claims unsupported by particular facts, and husband's only specific claim, that children were not functioning at appropriate level, did not fall within definition of dependency, neglect, or abuse. Louck v. Louck (Ohio App. 3 Dist., Marion, 11-10-2003) No. 9-03-35, 2003-Ohio-5999, 2003 WL 22533679, Unreported. Infants ⇔ 197

Mother's diagnosis of depression, her failure to follow a treatment regimen that included medication, and her repeated placing of herself and children in situations involving adult males where they were victims of domestic violence and/or verbal abuse was sufficient evidence to conclude that the children lacked adequate parental care by reason of mental condition of their mother. In re Hurst (Ohio App. 3 Dist., Seneca, 10-14-2003) No. 13-03-27, 2003-Ohio-5460, 2003 WL 22336087, Unreported. Infants ⇔ 158

Competent and credible evidence supported trial court award of permanent custody of child to county children services; child had been in the temporary custody of children services for at least 12 months of the 22 months before the hearing, child was not bonded to parents, child thrived in foster care but regressed when he had extended visitation with parents, and parents failed to continuously maintain a clean and safe home. In re Riley (Ohio App. 4 Dist., Washington, 07-25-2003) No. 03CA16, 2003-Ohio-4108, 2003 WL 21783368, Unreported. Infants ⇔ 155; Infants ⇔ 156

Trial court erred in finding four children dependent based upon mother's admission to use of marijuana, where county failed to show that mother's marijuana use affected her supervision or home environment of her children in some negative way; no one had witnessed mother exhibiting symptoms of drug use, or marijuana or drug paraphernalia in the home, no evidence was presented as to amount of drug owned or used by mother, or how drug may have impaired her parenting ability, children's home environment suggested that there were no basic problems with mother's parenting, in that she apparently worked to support her children, her rent was paid up to date, home was furnished and had working appliances and utilities, children appeared happy and well cared for, were clean, healthy, attended school, and were apparently good students. In re R.S. (Ohio App. 9 Dist., Summit, 03-31-2003) No. 21177, 2003-Ohio-1594, 2003 WL 1689595, Unreported. Infants ⇔ 156

The determination that a child is dependent requires no showing of fault on the parent's part; instead, the focus is solely upon the child's situation to determine whether the child is without proper or adequate care or support. In re Ament (Ohio App. 12 Dist., 04-23-2001) 142 Ohio App.3d 302, 755 N.E.2d 448, appeal not allowed 92 Ohio St.3d 1431, 749 N.E.2d 757. Infants ⇔ 156

When a child is receiving proper care pursuant to an arrangement initiated by the parent with a caregiver, the child is not a "dependent child." In re Ament (Ohio App. 12 Dist., 04-23-2001) 142 Ohio App.3d 302, 755 N.E.2d 448, appeal not allowed 92 Ohio St.3d 1431, 749 N.E.2d 757. Infants ⇔ 156

Evidence that mother left child in care of child's maternal grandmother without any arrangement or agreement after being asked to leave grandmother's home, did not have a permanent place for her or her children to live, attempted to commit suicide, and was sentenced to complete a lock-down drug treatment program, was sufficient to support determination that child was a "dependent child." In re Ament (Ohio App. 12 Dist., 04-23-2001) 142 Ohio App.3d 302, 755 N.E.2d 448, appeal not allowed 92 Ohio St.3d 1431, 749 N.E.2d 757. Infants ⇔ 179

Since fault, parental or otherwise, is not an issue in dependency inquiry, such that focus is exclusively on child's situation, child who is receiving proper care pursuant to arrangement initiated by parent with caregiver is not dependent child. In re Riddle (Ohio, 07-23-1997) 79 Ohio St.3d 259, 680 N.E.2d 1227, 1997-Ohio-391. Infants ⇔ 154.1

Children are properly determined to be dependent or neglected where a newborn infant's urine tests positive for cocaine and is born to a mother who has consumed cocaine one to five times daily for a period of more than one and one-half years and the mother expresses an unwillingness to care for a two-year-old child; a child may be declared dependent if its prospective environment would be threatening to its health or well-being. In re Massengill (Lucas 1991) 76 Ohio App.3d 220, 601 N.E.2d 206.

A minor is correctly judged "dependent" where the record reveals that the mother's mental illness, repeated hospitalization for that illness, and persistent failure to follow prescribed drug therapy interfere with her ability to provide proper care and support for the minor under RC 2151.04 and 2151.05. In re Brown (Hamilton 1989) 60 Ohio App.3d 136, 573 N.E.2d 1217. Infants ⇔ 181

When parents refuse necessary medical treatment for their child in the belief, based on religious faith, that the treatment is not necessary, a juvenile court may find the child dependent as defined by RC 2151.04(C), place the child in temporary custody of a hospital, and order the necessary medical treatment. In re Willmann (Hamilton 1986) 24 Ohio App.3d 191, 493 N.E.2d 1380, 24 O.B.R. 313.

A child may properly be found dependent within the meaning of RC 2151.04(B) on the basis of its mother's emotional status, immaturity, inconsistent living arrangements, and inability to provide the child with basic needs. In re Green (Montgomery 1984) 18 Ohio App.3d 43, 480 N.E.2d 492, 18 O.B.R. 155.

Unlike a finding of neglect under RC 2151.03, which requires proof that the parents were willfully at fault in abandoning or neglecting the children or refusing to perform their parental duties, a finding of dependency under RC 2151.04 must be grounded on whether the children are receiving proper care and support. The focus is on the condition of the children, not the fault of the parents. In re Bibb (Hamilton 1980) 70 Ohio App.2d 117, 435 N.E.2d 96, 24 O.O.3d 159. Infants ⇔ 154.1

Note 5

Where the evidence shows that to return a child to her natural parent would be clearly detrimental to the child, such child is a "dependent child" under RC 2151.04(C) and the court is authorized to commit the child permanently to the children's services board under RC 2151.353(D), even though the parent might be capable of giving proper care and support to other children. In re Justice (Clinton 1978) 59 Ohio App.2d 78, 392 N.E.2d 897, 13 O.O.3d 139. Infants ⇨ 154.1; Infants ⇨ 155

In the absence of evidence showing a detrimental impact upon the children, the fact that the mother is living with a boyfriend in their presence will not justify a finding that the children are neglected or dependent. In re Burrell (Ohio 1979) 58 Ohio St.2d 37, 388 N.E.2d 738, 12 O.O.3d 43.

As to mother, infant was a dependent child in that the mother was physically, emotionally, and financially unable to care and provide for an infant, and the fact that she has not had the child in her physical custody and control does not preclude the court from such finding. In re Baby Girl S. (Ohio Com.Pl. 1972) 32 Ohio Misc. 217, 290 N.E.2d 925, 61 O.O.2d 439.

The crux of a neglect action is the commission of culpable acts by the parents of the child. In re East (Ohio Com.Pl. 1972) 32 Ohio Misc. 65, 288 N.E.2d 343, 61 O.O.2d 38, 61 O.O.2d 108. Infants ⇨ 154.1

The unfitness of the mother may be a factor in adjudging that the child's condition or environment is such as to warrant the state in the interests of the child in assuming his guardianship. In re East (Ohio Com.Pl. 1972) 32 Ohio Misc. 65, 288 N.E.2d 343, 61 O.O.2d 38, 61 O.O.2d 108. Infants ⇨ 158

Finding a mother unfit to have custody of her child is not a necessary condition precedent to an adjudication that the child is dependent. In re East (Ohio Com.Pl. 1972) 32 Ohio Misc. 65, 288 N.E.2d 343, 61 O.O.2d 38, 61 O.O.2d 108. Infants ⇨ 158

A child born to a fifteen-year-old girl who has a substantial record of delinquency, including numerous acts of sexual intercourse with different men; failure to respond to the reasonable control and discipline of her mother; has an eighth-grade education, and attempts to enter into a ceremonial marriage in Florida—prior to her pregnancy by a man other than her "husband"; and is also a delinquent child by the commission of a felony, where the father of the child is a married man, and the "husband" of the mother is currently serving a sentence in the Florida state penitentiary, and where the mother's family situation is financially and emotionally unstable, is a "dependent child," even though the child has never been in the custody of the natural mother. In re Turner (Ohio Com.Pl. 1967) 12 Ohio Misc. 171, 231 N.E.2d 502, 41 O.O.2d 264. Infants ⇨ 154.1

On the evidence, children of parents to whom adultery was a normal course of life, who were selfish and childish far beyond any reasonable limits, and whose ideas of proper upbringing were to tell the children how vile each other had been, were both neglected and dependent. In re Douglas (Ohio Juv. 1959) 164 N.E.2d 475, 82 Ohio Law Abs. 170, 11 O.O.2d 340. Infants ⇨ 156

In a prosecution for contributing to the neglect or dependency of a minor child the record of a separate proceeding adjudicating the child to be a neglected and dependent child, and the testimony of the child's mother that she and the defendant engaged in acts of illicit sexual relations in the presence of the child, is sufficient competent evidence to prove the child to be a neglected or dependent child. State v. Griffin (Champaign 1952) 93 Ohio App. 299, 106 N.E.2d 668, 63 Ohio Law Abs. 122, 51 O.O. 47.

Minor is not "dependent," within juvenile act, merely because she is daughter of divorced parents. Sonnenberg v. State (Franklin 1931) 40 Ohio App. 475, 178 N.E. 855, 10 Ohio Law Abs. 271. Infants ⇨ 154.1

Evidence supported finding that mother's son was dependent; evidence showed that mother lacked even rudimentary parenting skills, treated son harshly and irrationally, became easily upset, and had a history of severe mental illness. In re Williams (Ohio App. 10 Dist., Franklin, 06-11-2002) No. 01AP-867, No. 01AP-868, 2002-Ohio-2902, 2002 WL 1275514, Unreported. Infants ⇨ 181

Adjudication of dependency was supported by competent and credible evidence that mother was intoxicated while she was pushing child in a stroller at 4 a.m., that she was engaged in an altercation with her boyfriend, that she screamed and summoned police, that boyfriend was holding mother, and that boyfriend's blood was found on child. In re Payne (Ohio App. 12 Dist., Clinton, 05-28-2002) No. CA2001-08-027, 2002-Ohio-2603, 2002 WL 1063361, Unreported. Infants ⇨ 177

6. Illegitimate child

Fact that child is illegitimate would not constitute child as dependent child under this section. Smith v. Privette & State (Franklin 1932) 13 Ohio Law Abs. 291.

Juvenile court cannot deprive mother of adulterine bastard of the custody of such child, in absence of evidence to warrant finding that such mother is unfit or that such child is dependent or neglected within purview of law or that best interests of child require such action. In re Gutman (Hamilton 1969) 22 Ohio App.2d 125, 259 N.E.2d 128, 51 O.O.2d 252. Children Out-of-wedlock ⇨ 20.1

The children of a woman who has had a series of illegitimate children may be found to be dependent children. In re Dake (Ohio Juv. 1961) 180 N.E.2d 646, 87 Ohio Law Abs. 483.

7. Medical treatment

Father waived appellate consideration of his contention, in dependency adjudication proceedings, that state was not entitled to regulate mother's election to take medications during her pregnancy, and of his claim of prosecutorial misconduct, by failing to raise such contention and claim before trial court. In re F.S. (Ohio App. 9 Dist., Summit, 08-10-2005) No. 22437, 2005-Ohio-4085, 2005 WL 1876160, Unreported. Infants ⇨ 243

Evidence was sufficient to support children's adjudication as dependent; evidence established both parents' lack of parenting ability, mother's continued use of contraindicated prescription medication during pregnancy and failure to see that children received suggested medical care, history of referrals to county Children Services Board (CSB) related to family violence and drug use, and older child's significant absences from preschool, interfering with her speech therapy classes. In re F.S. (Ohio App. 9 Dist., Summit, 08-10-2005) No. 22437, 2005-Ohio-4085, 2005 WL 1876160, Unreported. Infants ⇨ 159

Clear and convincing evidence supported finding of child's neglect and dependency, in termination of parental rights proceeding; evidence showed that mother received no prenatal care and that child tested positive for illegal drugs at the time of his birth. In re Barnhart (Ohio App. 4 Dist., Athens, 05-26-2005) No. 05CA8, 2005-Ohio-2692, 2005 WL 1283675, Unreported. Infants ⇨ 156

A sexually active minor diagnosed with acute gonorrhea who refuses medical treatment on religious grounds is properly adjudicated a dependent child, and the state may compel the juvenile to submit to medical treatment for the contagious and potentially life-threatening disease even though it would violate the juvenile's religious beliefs, since his refusal also subjects other members of the community to the disease. In re J.J. (Butler 1990) 64 Ohio App.3d 806, 582 N.E.2d 1138.

The parent of a child adjudicated dependent due to his refusal to seek medical treatment of a venereal disease may be ordered to pay the costs of court-ordered treatment of the venereal disease. In re J.J. (Butler 1990) 64 Ohio App.3d 806, 582 N.E.2d 1138.

8. Jurisdiction

A complaint under Juv R 10 and RC 2151.27 alleging that a child is dependent must state the essential facts which bring the proceeding within the jurisdiction of the court. In re Hunt (Ohio 1976) 46 Ohio St.2d 378, 348 N.E.2d 727, 75 O.O.2d 450. Infants ⇨ 197

An Ohio juvenile court, in a dependency proceeding pursuant to RC 2151.27 et seq., has no jurisdiction to interfere with a mother's legal custody of her children in the absence of proof and a finding of unfitness of such parent merely for the purpose of releasing such children to the officers of the court of a foreign state, and the court need not give full faith and credit to a Michigan decree where that decree was obtained by the husband in an ex parte custody determination, subsequent to a divorce decree, in which the Michigan court had no personal jurisdiction over the nonresident wife. In re Messner (Huron 1969) 19 Ohio App.2d 33, 249 N.E.2d 532, 48 O.O.2d 31.

Where a decree of guardianship of a minor Ohio resident is made in the state where the child has a technical domicile without personal service on either the child or the person with whom the child lives, it is not entitled to such full faith and credit as would nullify the prior appointment of a guardian for the child by the probate court in the county of his residence, since the child's residence will suffice to confer jurisdiction even though domicile may be elsewhere. In re Fore (Ohio 1958) 168 Ohio St. 363, 155 N.E.2d 194, 7 O.O.2d 127, appeal dismissed, certiorari denied 79 S.Ct. 878, 359 U.S. 313, 3 L.Ed.2d 831. Judgment ⇨ 818(2)

Where both parents of a child were killed in a common disaster in France and the maternal aunt brought such child to Ohio, and a paternal grandparent has obtained the right of "tutorship" from a Louisiana court in the parish of the grandmother and hence the child domicile, the Ohio courts have no authority to grant letters of guardianship to the maternal aunt. Petition of Fore (Cuyahoga 1958) 151 N.E.2d 777, 79 Ohio Law Abs. 15, reversed 168 Ohio St. 363, 155 N.E.2d 194, 7 O.O.2d 127, appeal dismissed, certiorari denied 79 S.Ct. 878, 359 U.S. 313, 3 L.Ed.2d 831.

The juvenile court is given original jurisdiction in a proper proceeding to determine the right of custody of any child where such child is not a ward of another court, and it is not necessary in the exercise of such jurisdiction that the juvenile court first determine that such child is a dependent, neglected or delinquent child. In re Lorok (Cuyahoga 1952) 93 Ohio App. 251, 114 N.E.2d 65, 51 O.O. 10. Child Custody ⇌ 920

The legislature having defined a dependent child and provided a special court proceeding for determining such dependency, the power must be exercised by the court only within the jurisdiction granted. In re Konneker (Summit 1929) 30 Ohio App. 502, 165 N.E. 850, 7 Ohio Law Abs. 137.

Before a court can make any disposition of children, they must be brought under its jurisdiction by an adjudication of dependency as defined in RC 2151.04. In re H——— (Ohio Juv. 1963) 192 N.E.2d 683, 92 Ohio Law Abs. 436, 24 O.O.2d 334.

9. Parental rights and responsibilities

Allegations that parents whose children were removed from home by county social worker were not allowed to recover children after safety plan providing for children's placement with friends had been initiated, despite parents' best efforts to do so, that continued deprivation of children was involuntary, and that parents were effectively denied prompt hearing on children's placement supported claim against social worker for violating parents' procedural due process rights. Smith v. Williams-Ash (C.A.6 (Ohio), 12-06-2005) No. 04-4547, 173 Fed.Appx. 363, 2005 WL 3304101, Unreported. Infants ⇌ 17

County social worker should have known that her alleged conduct in thwarting parents' attempts to have children returned to parents' home, after children were removed due to unsanitary conditions, and in effectively denying parents prompt hearing on children's placement had effect of violating parents' clearly established rights to procedural due process by involuntarily depriving parents of physical custody of children, and therefore qualified immunity did not apply to preclude social worker's liability under §§ 1983. Smith v. Williams-Ash (C.A.6 (Ohio), 12-06-2005) No. 04-4547, 173 Fed.Appx. 363, 2005 WL 3304101, Unreported. Civil Rights ⇌ 1376(4)

County social worker's alleged conduct in thwarting parents' attempts to have children returned to parents' home, after children were removed due to unsanitary conditions, and in effectively denying parents prompt hearing on children's placement did not rise to the level of conscience-shocking behavior, and thus did not support substantive due process claim. Smith v. Williams-Ash (C.A.6 (Ohio), 12-06-2005) No. 04-4547, 173 Fed.Appx. 363, 2005 WL 3304101, Unreported. Infants ⇌ 17

RC 2151.353, permitting the state to receive permanent custody of a "dependent child" whose parent is jailed, does not conflict with RC 3107.07; where the child is a "dependent child" under RC 2151.04 the state has authority to obtain permanent custody under RC 2151.353, and once parental rights have been terminated under RC Ch 2151, it is provided by RC 3107.06(D) that this parent's consent to adoption is no longer necessary. In re Dillard (Montgomery 1988) 48 Ohio App.3d 263, 549 N.E.2d 213.

A finding of dependency under RC 2151.04 is warranted where the mother of the child has relinquished her parental rights by execution of a permanent surrender and neither the natural father nor the mother's husband has any interest in caring for the child. In re Infant Female Luallen (Hamilton 1985) 27 Ohio App.3d 29, 499 N.E.2d 358, 27 O.B.R. 30.

A parent's primary rights to the care and custody of a child are rights that must be protected, and permanent custody will be terminated only when necessary for the mental and physical development of the child. In re Bibb (Hamilton 1980) 70 Ohio App.2d 117, 435 N.E.2d 96, 24 O.O.3d 159. Infants ⇌ 155

In a dependency action, where the child's condition or environment warrant it, the child may be removed from the custody of the mother, and it is not necessary that she first be given the opportunity to prove that she can properly care for said child. In re East (Ohio Com.Pl. 1972) 32 Ohio Misc. 65, 288 N.E.2d 343, 61 O.O.2d 38, 61 O.O.2d 108. Infants ⇌ 154.1

In an action commenced by a county welfare department requesting permanent custody of appellant's minor child and termination of parental rights pursuant to RC 2151.353(A)(4), it was error for the trial court to base its determination upon statements of appellant's attorney who was appointed by the court both as personal counsel for the appellant and guardian ad litem for the child. In re Johnson, No. C–810516 (1st Dist Ct App, Hamilton, 4–28–82).

A stepparent is generally not liable for the support, care, maintenance and education of a minor stepchild as if it were his own child. 1925 OAG 2450.

2151.05 Child without proper parental care

Under sections 2151.01 to 2151.54 of the Revised Code, a child whose home is filthy and unsanitary; whose parents, stepparents, guardian, or custodian permit him to become dependent, neglected, abused, or delinquent; whose parents, stepparents, guardian, or custodian, when able, refuse or neglect to provide him with necessary care, support, medical attention, and educational facilities; or whose parents, stepparents, guardian, or custodian fail to subject such child to necessary discipline is without proper parental care or guardianship.

(1975 H 85, eff. 11–28–75; 1953 H 1; GC 1639–5)

Historical and Statutory Notes

Pre–1953 H 1 Amendments: 117 v 520, § 1

Cross References

Taking into custody, Juv R 6

Library References

Infants ⇌156.
Westlaw Topic No. 211.
C.J.S. Infants §§ 31, 33 to 50, 55, 62.

Research References

Encyclopedias

OH Jur. 3d Family Law § 1493, "Child Without Proper Parental Care or Guardianship".

Treatises and Practice Aids

Carlin, Baldwin's Ohio Practice, Merrick-Rippner Probate Law § 108:1, Juvenile Court—Criminal Jurisdiction.

Carlin, Baldwin's Ohio Practice, Merrick-Rippner Probate Law § 106:11, Juvenile Court Jurisdiction—Neglected Child—Definition: Evidence of Neglect.

Carlin, Baldwin's Ohio Practice, Merrick-Rippner Probate Law § 106:14, Juvenile Court Jurisdiction—Dependent Child—Definition: Evidence of Dependency.

Giannelli & Yeomans, Ohio Juvenile Law § 9:6, Neglect—Inadequate Care Due to Parental Fault.

Law Review and Journal Commentaries

Are All Murderers Unfit Parents?: Defining "Depravity" in the Illinois Adoption Act, Kenneth Frederick Berg. 20 J Fam L 415 (1981–82).

Fetal Abuse: Culpable Behavior By Pregnant Women Or Parental Immunity?, George P. Smith, II. 3 J L & Health 223 (1988–89).

In re Barzak: Access to Children Services Board Files, David Hazelkorn. 19 Akron L Rev 237 (Fall 1985).

When Children Die as a Result of Religious Practices, Note. 51 Ohio St L J 1429 (1990).

Notes of Decisions

Best interest of child 4
Claims against parent 6
Jurisdiction 3
Parental rights 2
Purpose of statute 5

Unfitness of parent   1

1. Unfitness of parent

Evidence supported finding that children were neglected; home had no electricity and cold weather was approaching, home lacked food, younger child lacked supervision, and mother refused to accept and follow advice which was precipitating factor in failing of neglect complaint. In re Browne Children (Ohio App. 5 Dist., Stark, 07-07-2003) No. 2003CA00027, 2003-Ohio-3637, 2003 WL 21546103, Unreported. Infants ⚖ 156

Clear and convincing evidence supported conclusion that children were dependent; father left children, the oldest of whom was 16, home alone and informed police that he would not be returning for at least a couple of days, father's home was dirty, carpets were soiled, two bedrooms were occupied by 18 puppies and two dogs, and father admitted to smoking cigarettes in the home in spite of fact that he was also using an oxygen tank. In re Colaner Children (Ohio App. 5 Dist., 05-02-2006) 166 Ohio App.3d 355, 850 N.E.2d 794, 2006-Ohio-2404. Infants ⚖ 157

Parent's voluntary act of temporarily placing child with responsible relative is indicator of proper parental care, and does not support finding that parent is at fault; therefore, under such circumstances, care furnished by relative can be imputed to parent such that child is not neglected child. In re Riddle (Ohio, 07-23-1997) 79 Ohio St.3d 259, 680 N.E.2d 1227, 1997-Ohio-391. Infants ⚖ 156

Decision in earlier proceeding to terminate parental rights that evidence was insufficient as matter of law to support finding that mother had neglected children did not bar, pursuant to doctrine of res judicata, subsequent decision that children were dependent, based upon father's adjudicated abuse and neglect and mother's subsequent conduct to extent that it subjected children to possibility of further abuse by father. In re Pieper Children (Preble 1993) 85 Ohio App.3d 318, 619 N.E.2d 1059. Infants ⚖ 232

A minor is correctly judged "dependent" where the record reveals that the mother's mental illness, repeated hospitalization for that illness, and persistent failure to follow prescribed drug therapy interfere with her ability to provide proper care and support for the minor under RC 2151.04 and 2151.05. In re Brown (Hamilton 1989) 60 Ohio App.3d 136, 573 N.E.2d 1217. Infants ⚖ 181

Juvenile court cannot deprive mother of adulterine bastard of the custody of such child, in absence of evidence to warrant finding that such mother is unfit or that such child is dependent or neglected within purview of law or that best interests of child require such action. In re Gutman (Hamilton 1969) 22 Ohio App.2d 125, 259 N.E.2d 128, 51 O.O.2d 252. Children Out-of-wedlock ⚖ 20.1

Where a minor child was entrusted to friends because the mother was unfit, and the father subsequently remarried and reclaimed the child, a court may not award custody under GC 8005–4 (RC 3109.04) to any person other than the father except upon a finding of the father's unfitness. Garabrandt v. Garabrandt (Ohio Com.Pl. 1953) 114 N.E.2d 919, 65 Ohio Law Abs. 380, 51 O.O. 319.

To declare a child of an allegedly mentally ill parent dependent, it is necessary to prove not only the parent's mental incapacity, but also that the child lacks proper care because of the mental incapacity. In re H——— (Ohio Juv. 1963) 192 N.E.2d 683, 92 Ohio Law Abs. 436, 24 O.O.2d 334.

2. Parental rights

County social worker's alleged conduct in thwarting parents' attempts to have children returned to parents' home, after children were removed due to unsanitary conditions, and in effectively denying parents prompt hearing on children's placement did not rise to the level of conscience-shocking behavior, and thus did not support substantive due process claim. Smith v. Williams-Ash (C.A.6 (Ohio), 12-06-2005) No. 04-4547, 173 Fed.Appx. 363, 2005 WL 3304101, Unreported. Infants ⚖ 17

County social worker should have known that her alleged conduct in thwarting parents' attempts to have children returned to parents' home, after children were removed due to unsanitary conditions, and in effectively denying parents prompt hearing on children's placement had effect of violating parents' clearly established rights to procedural due process by involuntarily depriving parents of physical custody of children, and therefore qualified immunity did not apply to preclude social worker's liability under §§ 1983. Smith v. Williams-Ash (C.A.6 (Ohio), 12-06-2005) No. 04-4547, 173 Fed.Appx. 363, 2005 WL 3304101, Unreported. Civil Rights ⚖ 1376(4)

Allegations that parents whose children were removed from home by county social worker were not allowed to recover children after safety plan providing for children's placement with friends had been initiated, despite parents' best efforts to do so, that continued deprivation of children was involuntary, and that parents were effectively denied prompt hearing on children's placement supported claim against social worker for violating parents' procedural due process rights. Smith v. Williams-Ash (C.A.6 (Ohio), 12-06-2005) No. 04-4547, 173 Fed.Appx. 363, 2005 WL 3304101, Unreported. Infants ⚖ 17

Parent's right to raise his or her children is basic civil right. In re Awkal (Ohio App. 8 Dist., 06-27-1994) 95 Ohio App.3d 309, 642 N.E.2d 424. Civil Rights ⚖ 1057

Although parents have right of restraint over their children and duty of correcting and punishing them for misbehavior, such punishment must be reasonable and not exceed bounds of moderation and inflict cruel punishment. Murray v. Murray (Cuyahoga 1993) 89 Ohio App.3d 141, 623 N.E.2d 1236. Infants ⚖ 15; Parent And Child ⚖ 2.5

Parents have a right to the custody of their children, and the fact that someone may think that the children can be reared better by someone else is no justification for judicial interference. In re Konneker (Summit 1929) 30 Ohio App. 502, 165 N.E. 850, 7 Ohio Law Abs. 137.

The provisions of this chapter generally apply to a stepparent in the same manner as to a real parent, providing said application is consistent with the intent of said chapter. 1925 OAG 2450.

3. Jurisdiction

The word "parent" may mean one or both parents, and it is not necessary that both or either of the parents be present in court to give juvenile court jurisdiction to make legal commitment of a child for permanent transfer of guardianship to a certified institution or agency. 1925 OAG 2451.

4. Best interest of child

Division of child welfare granted custody of minor children upon ground children's return to mother, and custody by maternal relatives would not serve the best interests of the children. In re Zerick, 129 NE(2d) 661, 74 Abs 525, 57 OO 331 (Juv. 1955).

5. Purpose of statute

The juvenile statutes are designed primarily for the protection of dependent and reformation of delinquent children and must be given a liberal construction. In re Decker (Ohio Juv. 1930) 28 Ohio NP(NS) 433.

The term "child neglect" as used in RC 2151.421 applies to children without proper parental care or guardianship as defined by RC 2151.05. OAG 78–038.

6. Claims against parent

Complaint filed in child dependency proceeding, alleging that condition and environment of children were such as to warrant intervention in children's temporary care and custody, put father on notice that issues regarding children's environment would be litigated so as to permit testimony concerning allegations of sexual abuse made by father and children against mother's husband and possibility that father might be programming children to make such allegations. In re Colaner Children (Ohio App. 5 Dist., 05-02-2006) 166 Ohio App.3d 355, 850 N.E.2d 794, 2006-Ohio-2404. Infants ⚖ 197

Conviction for disorderly conduct, on basis of defendant's exclaiming that he was going to bash his stepdaughter's head in and his throwing telephone in stepdaughter's direction, was against weight of evidence, where evidence indicated act was independent of statement, stepdaughter did not believe either that he was trying to hit her or that he would be violent with her, and defendant raised his voice in light of stepdaughter's breaking house rules, and without any physical harm, discipline meted out fell within established parameters of proper and reasonable parental discipline. State v. Holzwart (Ohio App. 3 Dist., 01-28-2003) 151 Ohio App.3d 417, 784 N.E.2d 192, 2003-Ohio-345. Disorderly Conduct ⚖ 9

Only prohibition against a parent disciplining his or her own child is that parent may not cause physical harm, or an injury defined as the invasion of any legally protected interest of another. State v. Holzwart (Ohio App. 3 Dist., 01-28-2003) 151 Ohio App.3d 417, 784 N.E.2d 192, 2003-Ohio-345. Parent And Child ⚖ 2.5

A child does not have any legally protected interest which is invaded by proper and reasonable parental discipline. State v. Holzwart (Ohio App. 3 Dist., 01-28-2003) 151 Ohio App.3d 417, 784 N.E.2d 192, 2003-Ohio-345. Parent And Child ⇔ 2.5

Parental immunity no longer serves as bar to children's claims against their parents. Murray v. Murray (Cuyahoga 1993) 89 Ohio App.3d 141, 623 N.E.2d 1236. Parent And Child ⇔ 11

Stepparents, like natural parents, will be held accountable for their actions with respect to children. Murray v. Murray (Cuyahoga 1993) 89 Ohio App.3d 141, 623 N.E.2d 1236. Parent And Child ⇔ 14

Punishment of child which exceeds boundaries of reasonable corporal punishment by parents may lay basis for claims of assault and battery. Murray v. Murray (Cuyahoga 1993) 89 Ohio App.3d 141, 623 N.E.2d 1236. Assault And Battery ⇔ 2

2151.06 Residence or legal settlement

Under sections 2151.01 to 2151.54, inclusive, of the Revised Code, a child has the same residence or legal settlement as his parents, legal guardian of his person, or his custodian who stands in the relation of loco parentis.

(1953 H 1, eff. 10–1–53; GC 1639–6)

Historical and Statutory Notes

Pre–1953 H 1 Amendments: 121 v 557; 117 v 520

Library References

Domicile ⇔1.
Infants ⇔73, 196.
Westlaw Topic Nos. 135, 211.
C.J.S. Domicile §§ 2 to 3, 5, 11.
C.J.S. Infants §§ 41, 53 to 54, 220.

Research References

Encyclopedias
OH Jur. 3d Domicil § 10, Domicil by Operation of Law.

Treatises and Practice Aids
Giannelli & Yeomans, Ohio Juvenile Law § 17:2, Proper Venue.
Giannelli & Yeomans, Ohio Juvenile Law § 17:4, Transfer of Venue.
Giannelli & Yeomans, Ohio Juvenile Law App. D, Appendix D. Glossary.

Notes of Decisions

Legal settlement 2
Parental residence 3
Procedural issues 4
Residence of child 1

---

1. Residence of child

Even if father had a duty to supervise his 47-year-old son, son's actions in running into a pedestrian entering a store as son left the store through a door marked "entrance" were not foreseeable by the father, and therefore such duty was not breached, even if father was aware that son had become violent in the past when he failed take prescribed medication for his mental illness, where son was taking his medication at the time of the run-in, and son's behavior at the time of the run-in was not disruptive. Shirdon v. Houston (Ohio App. 2 Dist., Montgomery, 09-01-2006) No. 21529, 2006-Ohio-4521, 2006 WL 2522394, Unreported. Parent And Child ⇔ 13.5(4)

Father did not have a "special relationship" with his 47-year-old son as would create a duty to supervise his son so to prevent son from running into a pedestrian who was entering a store as son exited the store through a door marked "entrance," even though father was aware of son's past disruptive behavior and of son's past failures to take medication for mental illness; son lived in separate dwelling from father, father never affirmatively accepted responsibility for son's care, son was never adjudicated incompetent, and father had never assumed the role of son's guardian. Shirdon v. Houston (Ohio App. 2 Dist., Montgomery, 09-01-2006) No. 21529, 2006-Ohio-4521, 2006 WL 2522394, Unreported. Parent And Child ⇔ 13.5(4)

Transfer of a permanent custody hearing from the county where the children have been found to be neglected and dependent and are the subjects of a temporary custody order to the county in which the children's parents currently reside is improper as the residency of the children, not the parents, controls jurisdiction. In re Smith (Lucas 1990) 64 Ohio App.3d 773, 582 N.E.2d 1117.

In order for juvenile court to have jurisdiction to declare a child to be dependent, it must be shown that either the residence of the child is in the county or the acts constituting neglect or dependency occurred in the county. State ex rel. Burchett v. Juvenile Court for Scioto County (Scioto 1962) 194 N.E.2d 912, 92 Ohio Law Abs. 357, 28 O.O.2d 116.

2. Legal settlement

A child has, for the purposes of the sections enumerated in RC 2151.06, the same residence or legal settlement as his custodian who stands in the relation of loco parentis, and in such a case a child may acquire a legal settlement otherwise than in accordance with the definition of legal settlement provided in RC 5113.05. 1956 OAG 7008.

The term "legal settlement," as used in RC Ch 2151, with respect to parents, guardians, or persons standing in the relation of loco parentis of children within the jurisdiction of the juvenile court, has reference to that term as defined in RC 5113.05. 1956 OAG 7008.

When a juvenile court terminates its jurisdiction over a child, said child immediately acquires a legal settlement in the county of residence of the parents, surviving parent, sole parent, parent having custody awarded by a court having jurisdiction, or guardian of the person of such minor. 1953 OAG 2656.

An illegitimate child born and abandoned in a county other than that of legal settlement of the mother retains the legal settlement of its mother; county of legal settlement is responsible for its support. 1937 OAG 891.

3. Parental residence

Forum county was proper venue in child custody dispute as both custodian in loco parentis and natural father of child were residents of that county, even though child's mother resided in another county. Ackerman v. Lucas County Children Services Bd. (Lucas 1989) 49 Ohio App.3d 14, 550 N.E.2d 549. Infants ⇔ 196

Military personnel based in Ohio, as well as their wives and children, who intend to return to their home state, are nonresidents and may operate a motor vehicle in Ohio without obtaining an Ohio operator's license, provided they are legally and properly licensed in the state of their residence. OAG 66–074.

4. Procedural issues

Where an affidavit was filed charging that children were neglected and dependent and the mother unfit, and such children were taken into custody by the county welfare department at a time when the mother and children were residents of the county, the juvenile court had jurisdiction of such proceedings even though citation was not served on the mother until after her removal to another county. In re Goshorn (Ohio Juv. 1959) 167 N.E.2d 148, 82 Ohio Law Abs. 599.

Where a decree of guardianship of a minor Ohio resident is made in the state where the child has a technical domicile without personal service on either the child or the person with whom the child lives, it is not entitled to such full faith and credit as would nullify the prior appointment of a guardian for the child by the probate court in the county of his residence, since the child's residence will suffice to confer jurisdiction even though domicile may be elsewhere. In re Fore (Ohio 1958) 168 Ohio St. 363, 155 N.E.2d 194, 7 O.O.2d 127, appeal dismissed, certiorari denied 79 S.Ct. 878, 359 U.S. 313, 3 L.Ed.2d 831. Judgment ⇔ 818(2)

Where both parents of a child were killed in a common disaster in France and the maternal aunt brought such child to Ohio, and a paternal grandparent has obtained the right of "tutorship" from a Louisiana court in the parish of the grandmother and hence the child domicile, the Ohio courts have no authority to grant letters of guardianship to the maternal aunt. Petition of Fore (Cuyahoga 1958) 151 N.E.2d 777, 79 Ohio Law Abs. 15, reversed 168 Ohio St. 363, 155 N.E.2d 194, 7 O.O.2d 127, appeal dismissed, certiorari denied 79 S.Ct. 878, 359 U.S. 313, 3 L.Ed.2d 831.

ADMINISTRATION, OFFICIALS, AND JURISDICTION

2151.07 Creation and powers of juvenile court; assignment of judge

The juvenile court is a court of record within the court of common pleas. The juvenile court has and shall exercise the powers and jurisdiction conferred in Chapters 2151. and 2152. of the Revised Code.

Whenever the juvenile judge of the juvenile court is sick, is absent from the county, or is unable to attend court, or the volume of cases pending in court necessitates it, upon the request of the administrative juvenile judge, the presiding judge of the court of common pleas pursuant to division (DD) of section 2301.03 of the Revised Code shall assign a judge of any division of the court of common pleas of the county to act in the juvenile judge's place or in conjunction with the juvenile judge. If no judge of the court of common pleas is available for that purpose, the chief justice of the supreme court shall assign a judge of the court of common pleas, a juvenile judge, or a probate judge from a different county to act in the place of that juvenile judge or in conjunction with that juvenile judge. The assigned judge shall receive the compensation and expenses for so serving that is provided by law for judges assigned to hold court in courts of common pleas.

(2003 H 86, eff. 11–13–03; 2003 H 26, eff. 8–8–03; 2001 H 11, § 3, eff. 1–1–02; 2000 S 179, § 3, eff. 1–1–02; 1972 H 574, eff. 6–29–72; 1969 H 320; 127 v 847; 1953 H 1; GC 1639–7)

Historical and Statutory Notes

Ed. Note: Guidelines for Assignment of Judges were announced by the Chief Justice of the Ohio Supreme Court on 5-24-88, and revised 2-25-94 and 3-25-94, but not adopted as rules pursuant to O Const Art IV, §5. For the full text, see 37 OS(3d) xxxix, 61 OBar A–2 (6–13–88), and 69 OS(3d) xcix, 67 OBar xiii (4–18–94).

Pre–1953 H 1 Amendments: 122 v S 50

Amendment Note: 2003 H 86 substituted "(DD)" for "(CC)" in the second paragraph.

Amendment Note: 2003 H 26 substituted "(CC)" for "(BB)" in the second paragraph of the section.

Amendment Note: 2001 H 11, § 3 substituted "(BB)" for "(AA)".

Amendment Note: 2000 S 179, § 3, eff. 1–1–02, rewrote this section, which prior thereto read:

"The juvenile court is a court of record and within the division of domestic relations or probate of the court of common pleas, except that the juvenile courts of Cuyahoga county and Hamilton county shall be separate divisions of the court of common pleas. The juvenile court has and shall exercise the powers and jurisdiction conferred in sections 2151.01 to 2151.99 of the Revised Code.

"Whenever the juvenile judge of the juvenile court is absent from the county, or is unable to attend court, or the volume of cases pending in court necessitates it, upon the request of said judge, the presiding judge of the court of common pleas shall assign a judge of the court of common pleas of the county to act in his place or in conjunction with him. If no such judge is available for said purpose, the chief justice of the supreme court shall assign a judge of the court of common pleas, a juvenile judge, or a probate judge from some other county to act in the place of such judge or in conjunction with him, who shall receive such compensation and expenses for his services as is provided by law for judges assigned to hold court in courts of common pleas."

Cross References

Compensation and expenses of judges holding court outside county of residence, 141.07
Cuyahoga county juvenile court administrative judge shall be clerk of court, may appoint deputies and clerks, bonds, 2153.08

Library References

Courts ⇔50, 70, 174.
Westlaw Topic No. 106.
C.J.S. Courts §§ 106, 123.

Research References

Encyclopedias

OH Jur. 3d Courts & Judges § 14, Courts of Common Pleas.
OH Jur. 3d Courts & Judges § 18, Courts of Common Pleas—Juvenile Division and Juvenile Courts.
OH Jur. 3d Courts & Judges § 71, Assignment of Judges.
OH Jur. 3d Courts & Judges § 104, Courts of Common Pleas and Divisions.
OH Jur. 3d Courts & Judges § 105, Juvenile Division.

Forms

Ohio Jurisprudence Pleading and Practice Forms § 2:8, Courts of Common Pleas—Juvenile Division.
Ohio Jurisprudence Pleading and Practice Forms § 2:25, Powers and Duties Via Particular Courts—Juvenile Division.
Ohio Jurisprudence Pleading and Practice Forms § 5:40, Divisions of the Common Pleas Courts—Generally.

Treatises and Practice Aids

Carlin, Baldwin's Ohio Practice, Merrick-Rippner Probate Law § 104:20, Affidavit for Disqualification of Judge—Form.
Giannelli & Yeomans, Ohio Juvenile Law § 34:2, Types of Cases.
Gotherman, Babbit and Lang, Baldwin's Ohio Practice, Local Government Law—Municipal, § 27:5, Courts Having Jurisdiction Over Municipal Offenses.

Notes of Decisions

Constitutional issues 1
Court's duty to juvenile 7
Judges 3
Jurisdiction 5
Nature of juvenile court 2
Parents' duty 4
Relation to other statutes 6

---

1. Constitutional issues

The general assembly has constitutional authority to assign a probate judge to perform the duties of a judge of the court of common pleas. (Ed. note: But see O Const Art IV, § 5(A)(3).) In re Ely's Trust Estate (Ohio 1964) 176 Ohio St. 311, 199 N.E.2d 746, 27 O.O.2d 236.

Whether county social workers who receive complaints of child abuse, yet take no steps to remove the child from the custody of a parent who eventually injures him severely, have violated a duty of protection owed to the child is a question to be answered by each state's law of torts, not by the federal constitution. DeShaney v. Winnebago County Dept. of Social Services (U.S.Wis. 1989) 109 S.Ct. 998, 489 U.S. 189, 103 L.Ed.2d 249.

A court is not a "person" within the meaning of 42 USC 1983 and consequently cannot be sued under that law; such an attempt at a suit is to be distinguished from a suit against an individual judge performing unconstitutional acts. Foster v. Walsh (C.A.6 (Ohio) 1988) 864 F.2d 416.

2. Nature of juvenile court

Juvenile court has the power to limit parental rights. State v. Sturgeon (Ohio App. 1 Dist., 09-22-2000) 138 Ohio App.3d 882, 742 N.E.2d 730. Infants ⇔ 155

No "separate and independent Juvenile Court" has ever been created in Lucas county, the tribunal authorized to administer code relating to juveniles being the court of common pleas, division of domestic relations, and not the "Juvenile Court." Burke v. Burke (Lucas 1945) 76 Ohio App. 431, 64 N.E.2d 683, 32 O.O. 176. Child Custody ⇔ 920

The discretion of the juvenile court as to the care of a delinquent or neglected child is judicial, to be exercised in good faith and in the interest of the child, upon evidence introduced. State ex rel. Tailford v. Bristline (Ohio 1917) 96 Ohio St. 581, 119 N.E. 138, 15 Ohio Law Rep. 191. Infants ⇔ 222

A juvenile court may exercise its power to punish for contempt, conduct proceedings under RC Chapter 2152 to adjudicate the juvenile a delinquent child, or conduct probation revocation proceedings to compel a juvenile who is on some form of probation supervision imposed by a juvenile court pursuant to RC 2152.19(A)(4) to comply with a court order that requires the juvenile to submit to a DNA specimen collection procedure under RC 2152.74(B)(3). OAG 05–037.

The juvenile court is a court of record. OAG 68–123.

The juvenile court is now a part of a division of the court of common pleas and subject to the requirement that it provide a court reporter for its proceedings if so requested. OAG 68–123.

Where an agreement has been entered into pursuant to GC 3070–17 (RC 335.16), such fact does not divert courts of jurisdiction over offenses described in GC 1639–46 (RC 2151.42), GC 13008 (RC 3113.01) and GC 13012 (RC 3116.06), and parent may be held criminally liable for failure to support a minor child as provided in said sections; juvenile courts have no jurisdiction of felonies, nor over offenses described in GC 13008 (RC 3113.01) and GC 13012 (RC 3113.06). 1946 OAG 1100.

Juvenile court created within a probate court under this section is subject to GC 3056–2 (RC 3375.52), requiring payment to trustees of a county law library association of certain moneys therein specified collected by a probate court. 1939 OAG 1478.

3. Judges

Where the former judge of a juvenile-probate court found a minor child to be dependent and neglected but failed to journalize the entry, a successor judge may enter a nunc pro tunc entry in conformity therewith. In re Howell (Ohio Juv. 1956) 140 N.E.2d 347, 74 Ohio Law Abs. 217.

Judges and other court officers are absolutely immune from suit on claims arising out of their performance of judicial or quasi-judicial functions, but not from suits that arise out of other conduct. Holloway v. Brush (C.A.6 (Ohio), 07-31-2000) 220 F.3d 767. Judges ☞ 36; Officers And Public Employees ☞ 114

The official seeking absolute immunity bears the burden of showing that immunity is justified in light of the function she was performing. Holloway v. Brush (C.A.6 (Ohio), 07-31-2000) 220 F.3d 767. Officers And Public Employees ☞ 114

Term "elected state officials," as used in RC 145.381(A), applies to governor, lieutenant governor, secretary of state, auditor of state, treasurer of state, attorney general, members of general assembly, and members of supreme court, court of appeals, court of common pleas, probate court and juvenile court. OAG 71–075.

The office of probate and juvenile judge is incompatible with the office of county court judge. 1957 OAG 880.

A judge of the court of common pleas may not proceed to hear and pronounce sentence on an adult guilty of acting in a way tending to cause the delinquency of a minor, except under such circumstances as are provided in paragraph two of this section of the juvenile court code. 1950 OAG 1901.

A judge of the court exercising the powers and jurisdiction conferred by this chapter is limited to advising and recommending the need of a detention home and the extent of the facilities required to fulfill that need; such advice and recommendation is a prerequisite to the exercise of the mandatory duty imposed upon the county commissioners to provide a detention home by GC 1639–22 (RC 2151.34). 1949 OAG 1231.

4. Parents' duty

Parents of minor children who do not bring their children into court pursuant to a court order are not guilty of contempt where the children's whereabouts are unknown to the parents and no evidence suggests that the parents are able to comply with the court's order. State v. Hershberger (Wayne 1959) 168 N.E.2d 12, 83 Ohio Law Abs. 63.

Where a juvenile court found that a child was neglected, and committed such child to the temporary custody of the local child welfare board, the parents of such child could be punished for contempt for passively resisting such order. (Amish school attendance case.) State v. Hershberger (Ohio Juv. 1958) 150 N.E.2d 671, 77 Ohio Law Abs. 487, reversed 168 N.E.2d 12, 83 Ohio Law Abs. 63.

5. Jurisdiction

Statutes applying to juvenile courts, when viewed as a whole, demonstrate that the legislature does not intend to confer jurisdiction on a juvenile court over a person who is now over twenty-one years of age for acts committed when legally a child. In Matter of Jay I. (Ohio App. 6 Dist., Wood, 10-13-1995) No. WD-94-115, 1995 WL 604613, Unreported.

The grant of original jurisdiction, by RC 2151.23(A)(3), to juvenile courts in habeas corpus action involving the custody of minors is exclusive only as between juvenile courts and those courts given general habeas corpus jurisdiction by RC 2725.02. In re Black (Ohio 1973) 36 Ohio St.2d 124, 304 N.E.2d 394, 65 O.O.2d 308. Courts ☞ 472.1

The juvenile court is given original jurisdiction in a proper proceeding to determine the right of custody of any child where such child is not a ward of another court, and it is not necessary in the exercise of such jurisdiction that the juvenile court first determine that such child is a dependent, neglected or delinquent child. In re Lorok (Cuyahoga 1952) 93 Ohio App. 251, 114 N.E.2d 65, 51 O.O. 10. Child Custody ☞ 920

Under former GC 1639 (RC 2151.23) et seq., the commission of a felony by a minor constitutes him a delinquent and authorizes such court to take charge of him as a delinquent, but does not relieve him of the consequences of his crime, or abridge the right of the grand jury to indict him, or of the common pleas court to try him, where the juvenile court does not acquire jurisdiction of him for the delinquency before the common pleas court acquires jurisdiction of him for the crime. Gerak v. State (Cuyahoga 1920) 22 Ohio App. 357, 153 N.E. 902, 5 Ohio Law Abs. 761. Infants ☞ 68.5

In the sense that violation of law by a minor constitutes delinquency, as defined by former GC 1644 (RC 2151.02), the juvenile court has jurisdiction of any crime committed by an infant. State v. Klingenberger (Ohio 1925) 113 Ohio St. 418, 149 N.E. 395, 3 Ohio Law Abs. 675, 23 Ohio Law Rep. 588.

Juvenile courts or probate courts acting as such under GC 1639–1 (RC 2151.01) et seq. are courts of record, and their jurisdiction over a child, having attached, is conclusive and cannot be assailed by any other court in an independent proceeding; hence, an order as to the child in a subsequent divorce case between the parents is void. Children's Home of Marion County v. Fetter (Ohio 1914) 90 Ohio St. 110, 106 N.E. 761, 11 Ohio Law Rep. 518. Courts ☞ 198

Only in the absence of subject matter jurisdiction are judicial actors devoid of the shield of immunity. Holloway v. Brush (C.A.6 (Ohio), 07-31-2000) 220 F.3d 767. Judges ☞ 36

Under former GC 1639 (RC 2151.23), GC 1647 (RC 2151.27) and GC 1681 (RC 2151.26), transfer by court of common pleas of felony case against minor to court of domestic relations merely gives latter court information and authority to act thereon. State ex rel. Brown v. Hoffman (Hamilton 1926) 23 Ohio App. 348, 155 N.E. 499, 5 Ohio Law Abs. 6.

When a girl commits an act of delinquency before arriving at the age of eighteen, and the complaint is not filed or hearing held until after said child arrives at the age of eighteen years, the juvenile court has jurisdiction to hear and dispose of such complaint, except that GC 2101 (RC 5141.31) prohibits the commitment of such child to the girls industrial school if, at the time of such hearing, she has arrived at the age of eighteen years. 1945 OAG 247.

A probate court may take jurisdiction of a child who is found to be in the county of which such court has jurisdiction under facts and circumstances which constitute truancy, irrespective of the school to which such child is assigned; ordinarily the county of the child's residence will be the county in which such delinquency occurs, although it is possible for such child to be delinquent in another for the same cause. 1930 OAG 1843.

Pursuant to RC 2301.03(G), a judge of the Richland county court of common pleas, division of domestic relations, exercises the powers and jurisdiction conferred in RC Ch 2151 and serves as Richland county juvenile judge. OAG 95–026.

6. Relation to other statutes

In prosecution for contributing to the delinquency of female child, the initial fact to be proven is prior delinquency, for without this defendant could not have contributed and would be entitled to be discharged; the record of the child's conviction for delinquency is properly in evidence. Fisher v. State (Ohio 1911) 84 Ohio St. 360, 95 N.E. 908, 9 Ohio Law Rep. 129.

Although Ohio participates in the Juvenile Justice and Delinquency Act, 42 USC 5601 to 5751, and is paid federal funds for conforming to its provisions, a juvenile who alleges a participating state's failure to so conform does not have a cause of action in district court. Doe v. McFaul (N.D.Ohio 1984) 599 F.Supp. 1421.

7. Court's duty to juvenile

Evidence did not support juvenile's assertion that juvenile court personnel failed in duty owed to him in proceedings by which he was adjudicated delinquent, thereby violating his constitutional rights to due process and equal protection of laws; transcripts of hearings, together with reports submitted to juvenile court, demonstrated caring and diligent attitude toward appellant on parts of his children's services providers, including his probation officers, and record revealed juvenile was given several opportunities to learn positive behaviors, but simply refused to do so. In re R.M. (Ohio App. 8 Dist., Cuyahoga, 02-27-2003) No. 81085, 2003-Ohio-872, 2003 WL 549904, Unreported. Constitutional Law ⇐ 242.1(4); Constitutional Law ⇐ 255(4); Infants ⇐ 17

2151.08 Juvenile court in Hamilton county

In Hamilton county, the powers and jurisdiction of the juvenile court as conferred by Chapters 2151. and 2152. of the Revised Code shall be exercised by the judge of the court of common pleas whose term begins on January 1, 1957, and that judge's successors and by the judge of the court of common pleas whose term begins on February 14, 1967, and that judge's successors as provided by section 2301.03 of the Revised Code. This conferral of powers and jurisdiction on the specified judges shall be deemed a creation of a separately and independently created and established juvenile court in Hamilton county, Ohio. The specified judges shall serve in each and every position where the statutes permit or require a juvenile judge to serve.

(2000 S 179, § 3, eff. 1–1–02; 131 v H 165, eff. 11–16–65; 127 v 84)

Historical and Statutory Notes

Ed. Note: Former 2151.08 repealed by 126 v 778, eff. 10–11–55; 1953 H 1; GC 1639–8.

Pre–1953 H 1 Amendments: 117 v S 20, § 1

Amendment Note: 2000 S 179, § 3, eff. 1–1–02, added the reference to Chapter 2152; and made changes to reflect gender neutral language and other nonsubstantive changes.

Library References

Courts ⇐ 50, 70, 174.
Westlaw Topic No. 106.
C.J.S. Courts §§ 106, 123.

Research References

Encyclopedias

OH Jur. 3d Courts & Judges § 18, Courts of Common Pleas—Juvenile Division and Juvenile Courts.
OH Jur. 3d Family Law § 1535, Definitions.

Forms

Ohio Jurisprudence Pleading and Practice Forms § 2:25, Powers and Duties Via Particular Courts—Juvenile Division.
Ohio Jurisprudence Pleading and Practice Forms § 5:40, Divisions of the Common Pleas Courts—Generally.

Notes of Decisions

Judge's duty 1

---

1. Judge's duty

The judge of the juvenile court of Hamilton county is not the clerk of his own court, when exercising the powers and jurisdictions conferred in RC 2151.01 to RC 2151.54, and mandamus will not lie to require him to exhibit to the attorneys representing a minor charged with a crime "all books, records, papers, [and] dockets... in all cases and proceedings involving" such minor. State ex rel. Hibbard v. Hoffman (Hamilton 1955) 101 Ohio App. 547, 137 N.E.2d 606, 1 O.O.2d 454.

2151.09 Separate building and site may be purchased or leased

Upon the advice and recommendation of the juvenile judge, the board of county commissioners may provide by purchase, lease, or otherwise a separate building and site to be known as "the juvenile court" at a convenient location within the county which shall be appropriately constructed, arranged, furnished, and maintained for the convenient and efficient transaction of the business of the court and all parts thereof and its employees, including adequate facilities to be used as laboratories, dispensaries, or clinics for the use of scientific specialists connected with the court.

(1953 H 1, eff. 10–1–53; GC 1639–15)

Historical and Statutory Notes

Pre–1953 H 1 Amendments: 117 v 520, § 1

Library References

Courts ⇐ 72, 74.
Westlaw Topic No. 106.
C.J.S. Courts § 121.

Research References

Encyclopedias

OH Jur. 3d Counties, Townships, & Municipal Corp. § 221, Courthouses.
OH Jur. 3d Family Law § 1536, Terms, Sessions, and Places of Court.

2151.10 Appropriation for expenses of the court and maintenance of children; hearing; action in court of appeals; limitation of contempt power

The juvenile judge shall annually submit a written request for an appropriation to the board of county commissioners that shall set forth estimated administrative expenses of the juvenile court that the judge considers reasonably necessary for the operation of the court, including reasonably necessary expenses of the judge and such officers and employees as the judge may designate in attending conferences at which juvenile or welfare problems are discussed, and such sum each year as will provide for the maintenance and operation of the detention facility, the care, maintenance, education, and support of neglected, abused, dependent, and delinquent children, other than children eligible to participate in the Ohio works first program established under Chapter 5107. of the Revised Code, and for necessary orthopedic, surgical, and medical treatment, and special care as may be ordered by the court for any neglected, abused, dependent, or delinquent children. The board shall conduct a public hearing with respect to the written request submitted by the judge and shall appropriate such sum of money each year as it determines, after conducting the public hearing and considering the written request of the judge, is reasonably necessary to meet all the administrative expenses of the court. All disbursements from such appropriations shall be upon specifically itemized vouchers, certified to by the judge.

If the judge considers the appropriation made by the board pursuant to this section insufficient to meet all the administrative expenses of the court, the judge shall commence an action under Chapter 2731. of the Revised Code in the court of appeals for the judicial district for a determination of the duty of the board of county commissioners to appropriate the amount of money in dispute. The court of appeals shall give priority to the action filed by the juvenile judge over all cases pending on its docket. The burden shall be on the juvenile judge to prove that the appropriation requested is reasonably necessary to meet all administrative expenses of the court. If, prior to the filing of an action under Chapter 2731. of the Revised Code or during the pendency of the action, the judge exercises the judge's contempt power in order to obtain the sum of money in dispute, the judge shall not order the imprisonment of any member of the board of county commissioners notwithstanding sections 2705.02 to 2705.06 of the Revised Code.

(2000 S 179, § 3, eff. 1–1–02; 1997 H 408, eff. 10–1–97; 1979 S 63, eff. 7–26–79; 1975 H 85; 1953 H 1; GC 1639–57)

Historical and Statutory Notes

Pre–1953 H 1 Amendments: 121 v 557; 119 v 731; 117 v 520

Amendment Note: 2000 S 179, § 3, eff. 1–1–02, substituted "facility" for "home" in the first paragraph.

Amendment Note: 1997 H 408 substituted "eligible to participate in the Ohio works first program established under Chapter 5107." for "entitled to aid under sections 5107.01 to 5107.16" in the first paragraph; and made changes to reflect gender neutral language.

Cross References

Board of county commissioners, appropriation for court of common pleas; juvenile court excepted, 307.01
Judicial and court fund, tax levy, 5707.02

Library References

Counties ⬩162.
Westlaw Topic No. 104.
C.J.S. Counties § 199.

Research References

Encyclopedias

OH Jur. 3d Family Law § 1542, Expenses.
OH Jur. 3d Family Law § 1725, Transportation; Extradition.

Treatises and Practice Aids

Carlin, Baldwin's Ohio Practice, Merrick-Rippner Probate Law § 104:13, Juvenile Court—Appropriations.

Carlin, Baldwin's Ohio Practice, Merrick-Rippner Probate Law § 107:73, Alternatives for Disposition of Juvenile Cases.

Notes of Decisions

Administrative expenses 5
Competing demands, availability of funds 4
Constitutional issues 1
Enforcement of appropriation 2
Excessive appropriation 3
Travel expenses 6

1. Constitutional issues

That portion of RC 2101.11(B), containing language substantially identical to that in RC 2151.10 is unconstitutional. State ex rel. Johnston v. Taulbee (Ohio 1981) 66 Ohio St.2d 417, 423 N.E.2d 80, 20 O.O.3d 361.

That portion of RC 2101.11(B), containing language substantially identical to that in RC 2151.10 is unconstitutional. State ex rel. Slaby v. Summit County Council (Summit 1983) 7 Ohio App.3d 199, 454 N.E.2d 1379, 7 O.B.R. 258.

2. Enforcement of appropriation

County Board of Commissioners, which added $170,400 to juvenile court budget in 1991, more than fully complied with judgment ordering board to appropriate $182,996.96 for juvenile court salaries, where Board had already been credited $49,151 toward such amount for unemployment compensation payments. State ex rel. Lake Cty. Bd. of Commrs. v. Weaver (Ohio 1993) 67 Ohio St.3d 160, 616 N.E.2d 890, rehearing denied 67 Ohio St.3d 1457, 619 N.E.2d 424. Mandamus ⬩ 185

A writ of mandamus to compel a county board of commissioners to appropriate funds requested, but not allocated, for a juvenile court's 1990 operating expenses will be allowed where the commissioners fail to show that the juvenile court's 1990 budget order was unreasonable or unnecessary; the fact that county revenues from 1990 have already been appropriated does not relieve the commissioners from their mandatory duty to fund the reasonable and necessary expenses of the court for as long as those needs exist, even if the needs carry over into succeeding budget years. State, ex rel. Weaver, v. Lake Cty. Bd. of Commrs. (Ohio 1991) 62 Ohio St.3d 204, 580 N.E.2d 1090.

Mandamus actions for court appropriations are not necessarily moot if not resolved prior to the end of the budget year, but rather relief in the case must be impossible to grant; to prove impossibility requires at least a showing that the court's reasonable and necessary expenses could not be funded without taking money from other county offices and rendering them unable to perform their statutory duties. State, ex rel. Weaver, v. Lake Cty. Bd. of Commrs. (Ohio 1991) 62 Ohio St.3d 204, 580 N.E.2d 1090.

Pursuant to RC 2151.10 it is for the juvenile court judge to determine the fiscal needs of the court, and the board of commissioners may not substitute its judgment by refusing to appropriate the amount requested by the judge. When the board does refuse to perform its duty, the juvenile judge may seek to enforce his order by way of mandamus, or by proceedings in contempt. In re Appropriation for Juvenile and Probate Division for 1979 (Ohio 1980) 62 Ohio St.2d 99, 403 N.E.2d 974, 16 O.O.3d 104. Counties ⬩ 162

Where the basic function of a court, whether named in the constitution or established in pursuance of provisions of the constitution, is impeded by a failure or refusal of the body responsible to provide a necessary appropriation, that court possesses the inherent power to order such appropriation and to enforce its order by contempt proceedings. State ex rel. Edwards v. Murray (Ohio 1976) 48 Ohio St.2d 303, 358 N.E.2d 577, 2 O.O.3d 446. Mandamus ⬩ 141; Mandamus ⬩ 185

When a board of county commissioners fails to appropriate funds for the use of the juvenile court in the maintenance and support of a dependent child, the juvenile court may not order the county auditor to issue a warrant for such purpose, but the court may proceed against the board of county commissioners to compel it to appropriate the necessary funds. 1962 OAG 3489.

When an individual charged with a felony in this state or a child charged with juvenile delinquency in this state is arrested and detained by the officers of another state and is returned without the issuance of a requisition by the governor, the fees charged by the officers of such other state may not be paid under the provisions of RC 307.50 or RC 2151.45, but in the case of an individual charged with a felony the county commissioners of the county which sought his return and to which he is returned may, under RC 2335.10, pay to the officers of such other state the fees charged by such officers, and in the case of a child charged with juvenile delinquency in this state the fees charged by the officers of such other state may be paid from the funds appropriated under RC 2151.10. 1956 OAG 7308.

3. Excessive appropriation

Although some measured increases in salaries in all categories of court personnel would have been reasonable and were necessary to retain quality of employees currently in county court of common pleas, overall budget submitted by court of common pleas relative to court personnel was unreasonable and unnecessary in that, in many categories, level of increases was at, or greater than, highest level of compensation provided in other counties, and increases were attempted to be accomplished in one year. State ex rel. Britt v. Board of County Com'rs, Franklin County (Ohio 1985) 18 Ohio St.3d 1, 480 N.E.2d 77, 18 O.B.R. 1. Counties ⬩ 137

Amount requested by juvenile court judge was not unreasonable and excessive merely because such amount was five times the amount appropriated in prior years. State ex rel. Moorehead v. Reed (Ohio 1964) 177 Ohio St. 4, 201 N.E.2d 594, 28 O.O.2d 409.

4. Competing demands, availability of funds

County Board of Commissioners' payment of $49,151 for unemployment compensation in 1989 was required to be deducted from $182,996.96 Board was being compelled to pay for juvenile court's 1989 salary expenses. State ex rel. Lake Cty. Bd. of Commrs. v. Weaver (Ohio 1993) 67 Ohio St.3d 160, 616 N.E.2d 890, rehearing denied 67 Ohio St.3d 1457, 619 N.E.2d 424. Counties ⬩ 137

Board of county commissioners failed to sustain their burden of proving that budget requests submitted by common pleas courts were both unreasonable and unnecessary and, hence, the board abused its discretion in appropriating lesser amounts; courts must not be held hostage to competing interests when, in their discretionary power, they have submitted budgetary requests that are reasonable and necessary. State ex rel.

Rudes v. Rofkar (Ohio 1984) 15 Ohio St.3d 69, 472 N.E.2d 354, 15 O.B.R. 163. Counties ⇔ 162

Court's modification of budget was within its discretion, and county's claim of governmental hardship, while relevant to a determination of reasonableness and necessity, was not solely determinative of the issue. State ex rel. Arbaugh v. Richland County Bd. of Com'rs (Ohio 1984) 14 Ohio St.3d 5, 470 N.E.2d 880, 14 O.B.R. 311. Counties ⇔ 137

Under RC 2151.10, it is the mandatory duty of board of county commissioners to appropriate annually a sum of money sufficient to meet all administrative expenses of juvenile court of its county regardless of competing demands made upon such board by other branches of county government, and inasmuch as determination of such necessary annual administrative expenses lies solely within sound discretion of juvenile court judge, board of county commissioners has no authority to substitute its judgment for that of juvenile court judge by appropriating an amount less than that requested. State ex rel. Milligan v. Freeman (Ohio 1972) 31 Ohio St.2d 13, 285 N.E.2d 352, 60 O.O.2d 7.

A board of county commissioners has a duty to appropriate funds requested by a juvenile court, so long as such funds are reasonable and necessary to the court's administration of its business, whether or not the program for which such funds are requested is a "traditional" juvenile court program. OAG 05–028.

RC 2151.10 imposes an absolute duty upon the board of county commissioners to appropriate an amount equal to that which is reasonably requested by a juvenile court judge, and that duty is unaffected by the availability or unavailability of unanticipated or unappropriated funds. OAG 68–094.

5. Administrative expenses

County board of commissioners was not entitled to writ of prohibition to prevent juvenile court judge from operating court under salary schedule contained in judge's journal entry; because it was judge's function to direct operation of his court, prohibiting judge from operating court under salary schedule would have permitted county board of commissioners to control operation of court even though judge was conducting court's business in lawful manner. State ex rel. Lake County Bd. of Com'rs v. Hoose (Ohio 1991) 58 Ohio St.3d 220, 569 N.E.2d 1046, rehearing denied 60 Ohio St.3d 705, 573 N.E.2d 673, subsequent mandamus proceeding 67 Ohio St.3d 160, 616 N.E.2d 890, rehearing denied 67 Ohio St.3d 1457, 619 N.E.2d 424. Prohibition ⇔ 5(2)

Under RC 2151.10 determination of the necessary annual administrative expenses of the juvenile court lies solely within the sound discretion of the juvenile judge, and the board of county commissioners has no authority to substitute its judgment for that of the juvenile judge by appropriating an amount less than that requested. State ex rel. Foster v. Board of County Com'rs of Lucas County (Ohio 1968) 16 Ohio St.2d 89, 242 N.E.2d 884, 45 O.O.2d 442.

As used in RC 2101.11 and RC 2151.10, "administrative expenses" of the juvenile and probate courts, respectively, include expenses of office equipment, stationery and supplies. State ex rel. Ray v. South (Ohio 1964) 176 Ohio St. 241, 198 N.E.2d 919, 27 O.O.2d 133.

The provisions of GC 10501–5 (RC 2101.11), requiring county commissioners to appropriate such sums of money each year as will meet all the administrative expense of probate court which the judge thereof deems necessary are mandatory and it is the duty of such county commissioners to make appropriations for such purposes accordingly. State ex rel. Motter v. Atkinson (Ohio 1945) 146 Ohio St. 11, 63 N.E.2d 440, 31 O.O. 472.

A board of county commissioners has no authority to impose upon a juvenile court a charge for rental of space for the court's operations, whether such space is in the courthouse or in another county building. OAG 05–028.

The juvenile judge can require the board of county commissioners to provide the juvenile judge with a telephone service option not provided to other county offices only if the provision of the service option is reasonable and necessary for the proper administration of the court. If the board of county commissioners opposes the provision of the service option, the board has the burden of demonstrating that the requested service option is unreasonable or unnecessary for the proper administration of the court's business. Whether a particular service option is reasonable and necessary is a question of fact to be decided on a case-by-case basis. OAG 98–005.

A juvenile court may, upon finding that a child is neglected, dependent, or delinquent, commit the child to any person or institution meeting the requirements of RC 5103.02 and RC 5103.03 even though a county child welfare board exists and could provide care and support for the child. The board of county commissioners has a duty to appropriate each year such sum as will provide the court with necessary funds for the care, maintenance, education, and support of neglected, dependent, and delinquent children. 1962 OAG 3489.

6. Travel expenses

A board of county commissioners has no authority to approve or disapprove the travel expenses of a juvenile court judge. OAG 97–012.

When a requisition for extradition has been issued by the governor, all expenses incurred in effecting the return of the accused must be reimbursed from the county treasury pursuant to either RC 307.50 or RC 2151.45, with the exception of fees paid to the officers of the foreign state, and any necessary travel expenses up to ten cents a mile, which must be paid out of the state treasury pursuant to RC 2963.22. OAG 72–105.

2151.12 Clerk; judge as clerk; bond

(A) Except as otherwise provided in this division, whenever a court of common pleas, division of domestic relations, exercises the powers and jurisdictions conferred in Chapters 2151. and 2152. of the Revised Code, the judge or judges of that division or, if applicable, the judge of that division who specifically is designated by section 2301.03 of the Revised Code as being responsible for administering sections 2151.13, 2151.16, 2151.17, 2151.18, and 2152.71 of the Revised Code shall be the clerk of the court for all records filed with the court pursuant to Chapter 2151. or 2152. of the Revised Code or pursuant to any other section of the Revised Code that requires documents to be filed with a juvenile judge or a juvenile court. If, in a division of domestic relations of a court of common pleas that exercises the powers and jurisdiction conferred in Chapters 2151. and 2152. of the Revised Code, the judge of the division, both judges in a two-judge division, or a majority of the judges in a division with three or more judges and the clerk of the court of common pleas agree in an agreement that is signed by the agreeing judge or judges and the clerk and entered into formally in the journal of the court, the clerk of courts of common pleas shall keep the records filed with the court pursuant to Chapter 2151. or 2152. of the Revised Code or pursuant to any other section of the Revised Code that requires documents to be filed with a juvenile judge or a juvenile court.

Whenever the juvenile judge, or a majority of the juvenile judges of a multi-judge juvenile division, of a court of common pleas, juvenile division, and the clerk of the court of common pleas agree in an agreement that is signed by the judge and the clerk and entered formally in the journal of the court, the clerks of courts of common pleas shall keep the records of those courts. In all other cases, the juvenile judge shall be the clerk of the judge's own court.

(B) In counties in which the juvenile judge is clerk of the judge's own court, before entering upon the duties of office as the clerk, the judge shall execute and file with the county treasurer a bond in a sum to be determined by the board of county commissioners, with sufficient surety to be approved by the board, conditioned for the faithful performance of duties as clerk. The bond shall be given for the benefit of the county, the state, or any person who may suffer loss by reason of a default in any of the conditions of the bond.

(2000 S 179, § 3, eff. 1–1–02; 1996 H 423, eff. 10–31–96; 1977 S 336, eff. 3–3–78; 1953 H 1; GC 1639–17)

Historical and Statutory Notes

Pre–1953 H 1 Amendments: 117 v 520, § 1

Amendment Note: 2000 S 179, § 3, eff. 1–1–02, added references to Chapter 2152 throughout; inserted "and 2152.71" in the first paragraph; and made other nonsubstantive changes.

Amendment Note: 1996 H 423 rewrote this section, which prior thereto read:

"Whenever the courts of common pleas, division of domestic relations, exercise the powers and jurisdictions conferred in sections 2151.01 to

2151.54 of the Revised Code, or whenever the juvenile judge, or a majority of the juvenile judges of a multi-judge juvenile division, of a court of common pleas, juvenile division and the clerk of the court of common pleas agree in an agreement that is signed by the judge and the clerk and entered formally in the journal of the court, the clerks of courts of common pleas shall keep the records of such courts. In all other cases, the juvenile judge shall be the clerk of his own court.

"In counties in which the juvenile judge is clerk of his own court, before entering upon the duties of his office as such clerk, he shall execute and file with the county treasurer a bond in a sum to be determined by the board of county commissioners, with sufficient surety to be approved by the board, conditioned for the faithful performance of his duties as clerk. The bond shall be given for the benefit of the county, the state, or any person who may suffer loss by reason of a default in any of the conditions of the bond."

Library References

Clerks of Courts ⚖69.
Infants ⚖133.
Westlaw Topic Nos. 211, 79.
C.J.S. Courts § 252.
C.J.S. Infants §§ 57, 69 to 85.

Research References

Encyclopedias

OH Jur. 3d Courts & Judges § 38, Official Bond.
OH Jur. 3d Courts & Judges § 188, Official Bonds.
OH Jur. 3d Family Law § 1540, Court Personnel.

Treatises and Practice Aids

Carlin, Baldwin's Ohio Practice, Merrick-Rippner Probate Law § 104:14, Juvenile Court—Clerk.

Carlin, Baldwin's Ohio Practice, Merrick-Rippner Probate Law § 104:21, Bond of Juvenile Court Judge—Form.

Carlin, Baldwin's Ohio Practice, Merrick-Rippner Probate Law § 107:66, Discretionary Transfer.

Giannelli & Yeomans, Ohio Juvenile Law § 15:2, Intake.

Notes of Decisions

Blanket bond 2
Clerk's duties 3
Judge as clerk 1

---

1. Judge as clerk

Administrative judge who signed notation journalizing permanent custody judgment entry was acting ex officio as a clerk and, thus, filing and journalization notation on judgment entry was not a manifestation of another judge's intent to succeed to judgment of judge who had been suspended from the practice of law after signing judgment entry. In re Hlavsa (Ohio App. 8 Dist., 10-30-2000) 139 Ohio App.3d 871, 745 N.E.2d 1144. Child Custody ⚖ 521

Affidavit from the chief deputy clerk of juvenile division indicating that voiding permanent custody judgment entry that was not journalized until after the signing judge had been suspended from the practice of law would affect a number of pending cases by same judge was not part of record below and, thus, would not be considered by Court of Appeals. In re Hlavsa (Ohio App. 8 Dist., 10-30-2000) 139 Ohio App.3d 871, 745 N.E.2d 1144. Child Custody ⚖ 915

The judge of the juvenile court of Hamilton county is not the clerk of his own court, when exercising the powers and jurisdictions conferred in RC 2151.01 to RC 2151.54, and mandamus will not lie to require him to exhibit to the attorneys representing a minor charged with a crime "all books, records, papers, [and] dockets... in all cases and proceedings involving" such minor. State ex rel. Hibbard v. Hoffman (Hamilton 1955) 101 Ohio App. 547, 137 N.E.2d 606, 1 O.O.2d 454.

When, as in Richland county, the court of common pleas, division of domestic relations, exercises the powers and jurisdiction of a juvenile court, existing law does not permit any arrangement under which the juvenile judge serves as clerk of the juvenile court. OAG 95–026.

2. Blanket bond

Assuming that the requirement can be fulfilled which calls for a bond to be filed with a certain official, all officers, deputies, clerks, assistants, bookkeepers and employees of the offices of a political subdivision who are required to file a bond, and who may be properly covered by a blanket bond, may be covered under the same blanket bond. OAG 65–087.

3. Clerk's duties

Because the Richland County Court of Common Pleas, division of domestic relations, exercises the powers and jurisdiction of a juvenile court, the clerk of the Richland County Court of Common Pleas is required by RC 2151.12 to keep the juvenile court records. OAG 95–026.

2151.13 Employees; compensation; bond

The juvenile judge may appoint such bailiffs, probation officers, and other employees as are necessary and may designate their titles and fix their duties, compensation, and expense allowances. The juvenile court may by entry on its journal authorize any deputy clerk to administer oaths when necessary in the discharge of his duties. Such employees shall serve during the pleasure of the judge.

The compensation and expenses of all employees and the salary and expenses of the judge shall be paid in semimonthly installments by the county treasurer from the money appropriated for the operation of the court, upon the warrant of the county auditor, certified to by the judge.

The judge may require any employee to give bond in the sum of not less than one thousand dollars, conditioned for the honest and faithful performance of his duties. The sureties on such bonds shall be approved in the manner provided by section 2151.12 of the Revised Code. The judge shall not be personally liable for the default, misfeasance, or nonfeasance of any employee from whom a bond has been required.

(1953 H 1, eff. 10–1–53; GC 1639–18)

Historical and Statutory Notes

Pre–1953 H 1 Amendments: 121 v 557; 117 v 520

Cross References

Judges of the court of domestic relations, juvenile court responsibility, 2301.03
Peace officer training, 109.73 et seq.

Library References

Courts ⚖55, 58.
Westlaw Topic No. 106.
C.J.S. Courts §§ 107 to 109.

Research References

Encyclopedias

OH Jur. 3d Cvl. Servants & Pub. Officers & Employ. § 44, Officers Who May Place Employees in Unclassified Service.
OH Jur. 3d Courts & Judges § 112, Insurance; Liability for Acts of Subordinates.
OH Jur. 3d Courts & Judges § 188, Official Bonds.
OH Jur. 3d Courts & Judges § 199, Salaries.
OH Jur. 3d Family Law § 1540, Court Personnel.

Treatises and Practice Aids

Carlin, Baldwin's Ohio Practice, Merrick-Rippner Probate Law § 104:16, Juvenile Court—Employees.

Carlin, Baldwin's Ohio Practice, Merrick-Rippner Probate Law § 104:22, Oath of Juvenile Court Judge—Form.

Carlin, Baldwin's Ohio Practice, Merrick-Rippner Probate Law § 104:23, Bond of Deputy Clerk—Form.

Carlin, Baldwin's Ohio Practice, Merrick-Rippner Probate Law § 104:24, Oath of Office—Deputy Clerk or Probation Officer—Form.

Carlin, Baldwin's Ohio Practice, Merrick-Rippner Probate Law § 104:25, Itemized Voucher for Compensation, Necessary Expenses and Cost of Transportation—Form.

Carlin, Baldwin's Ohio Practice, Merrick-Rippner Probate Law § 107:41, Prehearing Procedures in Juvenile Court—Temporary Orders Pending Hearing.

Carlin, Baldwin's Ohio Practice, Merrick-Rippner Probate Law § 107:43, Scheduling Juvenile Court Hearing.

Carlin, Baldwin's Ohio Practice, Merrick-Rippner Probate Law § 107:47, Adjudicatory Hearings—Hearing Without a Jury.

Carlin, Baldwin's Ohio Practice, Merrick-Rippner Probate Law § 107:102, Serious Youthful Offenders, Effective January 1, 2002.

Giannelli & Yeomans, Ohio Juvenile Law § 5:9, Procedural Rights.

Giannelli & Yeomans, Ohio Juvenile Law § 15:2, Intake.

Giannelli & Yeomans, Ohio Juvenile Law § 16:6, Oath Requirement.

Notes of Decisions

Civil service 4
Compatibility of offices 3
Constitutional issues 1
Hiring and compensation 5
Termination 2

1. Constitutional issues

This section is not contra to O Const Art XV, § 10. State ex rel. Haskins v. Tyroler (Athens 1939) 63 Ohio App. 88, 25 N.E.2d 309, 16 O.O. 378, affirmed 137 Ohio St. 24, 27 N.E.2d 931, 17 O.O. 335.

2. Termination

County human rights commission patently lacked jurisdiction over appeal by unclassified juvenile court employees, who had been discharged by judge of juvenile court division, so that judge was entitled to writ of prohibition barring commission from exercising jurisdiction even though commission had not yet ruled on jurisdictional issue; commission conceded that it lacked jurisdiction over appeals by unclassified employees, and its own rules defined juvenile court employees as unclassified. State ex rel. Hunter v. Summit County Human Resource Com'n (Ohio, 04-22-1998) 81 Ohio St.3d 450, 692 N.E.2d 185, 1998-Ohio-614. Prohibition ⟶ 10(2)

Full-time juvenile court employees working part time at a juvenile detention center may be terminated from their part-time employment by the administrative judge of a juvenile court notwithstanding oral promises of continued employment that may have been made by the superintendent of the juvenile detention facility, as the terms of employment at juvenile detention facilities are governed by statute, not the doctrine of employment at will. Abbott v. Stepanik (Cuyahoga 1990) 64 Ohio App.3d 719, 582 N.E.2d 1082, dismissed, jurisdictional motion overruled 50 Ohio St.3d 717, 553 N.E.2d 1364.

County visitor appointed from a civil service eligible list by a juvenile court judge may be dismissed at the latter's discretion under this section. State ex rel. Haskins v. Tyroler (Athens 1939) 63 Ohio App. 88, 25 N.E.2d 309, 16 O.O. 378, affirmed 137 Ohio St. 24, 27 N.E.2d 931, 17 O.O. 335. Officers And Public Employees ⟶ 69.4

A state judge firing a court employee such as a probation officer is not absolutely immune to a damage suit under 42 USC 1983 claiming sex discrimination, because a personnel decision is an administrative act rather than an act of judging that is protected from suit; whether the judge enjoys qualified immunity is a matter not now before the court. Forrester v. White (U.S.Ill. 1988) 108 S.Ct. 538, 484 U.S. 219, 98 L.Ed.2d 555, on remand 846 F.2d 29.

3. Compatibility of offices

The offices of township trustee and juvenile probation officer are compatible. OAG 73-035.

There is no incompatibility in the offices of probation officer in the juvenile court and executive secretary of the child welfare board, in the same county. 1951 OAG 961.

Positions of probation officer of a juvenile court and relief administrator of a city are not in themselves incompatible and may be held by one person at the same time, unless it is physically impossible to faithfully and efficiently discharge the duties of both positions. 1941 OAG 3410.

The offices of a member of the county board of education and probation officer appointed under former GC 1662-(RC 2151.13) are incompatible. 1933 OAG 1926.

4. Civil service

Employees within the court of common pleas, division of domestic relations, are unclassified civil service employees. OAG 76-031.

Person employed within a juvenile court as chief probation officer, who also acts as county visitor for aid to dependent children, serves under this section, and is within the unclassified civil service of Ohio. 1939 OAG 1123.

Juvenile court code expressly takes out of the classified service of the civil service the employees and officers mentioned in this section, who must be appointed by the juvenile judge and hold their positions subject to his pleasure. 1937 OAG 1190.

5. Hiring and compensation

An administrative judge of the juvenile division of a court of common pleas is not authorized to enter into an employment agreement with employees of the court. Malone v. Court of Common Pleas of Cuyahoga County (Ohio 1976) 45 Ohio St.2d 245, 344 N.E.2d 126, 74 O.O.2d 413. Courts ⟶ 55

County juvenile center employees appointed by the juvenile court under RC 2151.13 and 2153.08 serve at the pleasure of the court, are not "public employees" for purposes of RC 4117.01(C) and have no right to hold a representation election; the fact they are appointed as deputy clerks to administer oaths does not make them employees of the clerk. Service Employees International Union, Local 47 v SERB, 1996 SERB 4-39 (CP, Franklin, 7-10-95).

A juvenile judge may fix as the expense allowance of a bailiff, probation officer, or other employee appointed under that section a fixed sum to be paid periodically, provided that the amount paid shall never exceed the amount of actual compensable expense incurred in that period. 1958 OAG 2208.

GC 1639-18 (RC 2151.13) and GC 1639-57 (RC 2151.10) are mandatory as to appropriations for compensation of a chief probation officer and the administrative expenses of the court in connection with these statutes; the county commissioners must appropriate money for such purposes from the date act becomes effective. 1937 OAG 1246.

Under former GC 1662 (RC 2151.13) a probate judge could not fix the compensation of employees under such section in an amount in excess of the aggregate fixed by the county commissioners for such purposes. 1932 OAG 4045.

2151.14 Duties and powers of probation department; records; command assistance; notice to victim of accused sex offender's communicable disease; order to provide copies of records

(A) The chief probation officer, under the direction of the juvenile judge, shall have charge of the work of the probation department. The department shall make any investigations that the judge directs, keep a written record of the investigations, and submit the record to the judge or deal with them as the judge directs. The department shall furnish to any person placed on community control a statement of the conditions of community control and shall instruct the person regarding them. The department shall keep informed concerning the conduct and condition of each person under its supervision and shall report on their conduct and condition to the judge as the judge directs. Each probation officer shall use all suitable methods to aid persons on community control and to bring about improvement in their conduct and condition. The department shall keep full records of its work, keep accurate and complete accounts of money collected from persons under its supervision, give receipts for the money, and make reports on the money as the judge directs.

(B) Except as provided in this division or in division (C) or (D) of this section, the reports and records of the department shall be considered confidential information and shall not be made public. If an officer is preparing pursuant to section 2947.06 or 2951.03 of the Revised Code or Criminal Rule 32.2 a presentence investigation report pertaining to a person, the department shall make available to the officer, for use in preparing the report, any reports and records it possesses regarding any adjudications of that person as a delinquent child or regarding the dispositions made relative to those adjudications. A probation officer may serve the process of the court within or without the county, make arrests without warrant upon reasonable information or upon view of the violation of this chapter or Chapter 2152. of the Revised Code, detain the person arrested pending the issuance of a warrant, and perform any other duties, incident to the office, that the judge directs. All sheriffs, deputy sheriffs, constables, marshals, deputy marshals, chiefs of police, municipal corporation and township police officers, and other peace officers shall render assistance to probation officers in the performance of their duties when requested to do so by any probation officer.

(C) When a complaint has been filed alleging that a child is delinquent by reason of having committed an act that would constitute a violation of section 2907.02, 2907.03, 2907.05, or 2907.06 of the Revised Code if committed by an adult and the arresting authority, a court, or a probation officer discovers that the child or a person whom the child caused to engage in sexual activity, as defined in section 2907.01 of the Revised Code, has a communicable disease, the arresting authority, court, or probation officer immediately shall notify the victim of the delinquent act of the nature of the disease.

(D)(1) In accordance with division (D)(2) of this section, subject to the limitation specified in division (D)(4) of this section, and in connection with a disposition pursuant to section 2151.354 of the Revised Code when a child has been found to be an unruly child, a disposition pursuant to sections 2152.19 and 2152.20 of the Revised Code when a child has been found to be a delinquent child, or a disposition pursuant to sections 2152.20 and 2152.21 of the Revised Code when a child has been found to be a juvenile traffic offender, the court may issue an order requiring boards of education, governing bodies of chartered nonpublic schools, public children services agencies, private child placing agencies, probation departments, law enforcement agencies, and prosecuting attorneys that have records related to the child in question to provide copies of one or more specified records, or specified information in one or more specified records, that the individual or entity has with respect to the child to any of the following individuals or entities that request the records in accordance with division (D)(3)(a) of this section:

(a) The child;

(b) The attorney or guardian ad litem of the child;

(c) A parent, guardian, or custodian of the child;

(d) A prosecuting attorney;

(e) A board of education of a public school district;

(f) A probation department of a juvenile court;

(g) A public children services agency or private child placing agency that has custody of the child, is providing services to the child or the child's family, or is preparing a social history or performing any other function for the juvenile court;

(h) The department of youth services when the department has custody of the child or is performing any services for the child that are required by the juvenile court or by statute;

(i) The individual in control of a juvenile detention or rehabilitation facility to which the child has been committed;

(j) An employee of the juvenile court that found the child to be an unruly child, a delinquent child, or a juvenile traffic offender;

(k) Any other entity that has custody of the child or is providing treatment, rehabilitation, or other services for the child pursuant to a court order, statutory requirement, or other arrangement.

(2) Any individual or entity listed in divisions (D)(1)(a) to (k) of this section may file a motion with the court that requests the court to issue an order as described in division (D)(1) of this section. If such a motion is filed, the court shall conduct a hearing on it. If at the hearing the movant demonstrates a need for one or more specified records, or for information in one or more specified records, related to the child in question and additionally demonstrates the relevance of the information sought to be obtained from those records, and if the court determines that the limitation specified in division (D)(4) of this section does not preclude the provision of a specified record or specified information to the movant, then the court may issue an order to a designated individual or entity to provide the movant with copies of one or more specified records or with specified information contained in one or more specified records.

(3)(a) Any individual or entity that is authorized by an order issued pursuant to division (D)(1) of this section to obtain copies of one or more specified records, or specified information, related to a particular child may file a written request for copies of the records or for the information with any individual or entity required by the order to provide copies of the records or the information. The request shall be in writing, describe the type of records or the information requested, explain the need for the records or the information, and be accompanied by a copy of the order.

(b) If an individual or entity that is required by an order issued pursuant to division (D)(1) of this section to provide one or more specified records, or specified information, related to a child receives a written request for the records or information in accordance with division (D)(3)(a) of this section, the individual or entity immediately shall comply with the request to the extent it is able to do so, unless the individual or entity determines that it is unable to comply with the request because it is prohibited by law from doing so, or unless the requesting individual or entity does not have authority to obtain the requested records or information. If the individual or entity determines that it is unable to comply with the request, it shall file a motion with the court that issued the order requesting the court to determine the extent to which it is required to comply with the request for records or information. Upon the filing of the motion, the court immediately shall hold a hearing on the motion, determine the extent to which the movant is required to comply with the request for records or information, and issue findings of fact and conclusions of law in support of its determination. The determination of the court shall be final. If the court determines that the movant is required to comply with the request for records or information, it shall identify the specific records or information that must be supplied to the individual or entity that requested the records or information.

(c) If an individual or entity is required to provide copies of one or more specified records pursuant to division (D) of this section, the individual or entity may charge a fee for the copies that does not exceed the cost of supplying them.

(4) Division (D) of this section does not require, authorize, or permit the dissemination of any records or any information contained in any records if the dissemination of the records or information generally is prohibited by any provision of the Revised Code and a specific provision of the Revised Code does not specifically authorize or permit the dissemination of the records or information pursuant to division (D) of this section.

(2002 H 247, eff. 5–30–02; 2000 S 179, § 3, eff. 1–1–02; 2000 H 442, eff. 10–17–00; 1996 H 445, eff. 9–3–96; 1990 S 258, eff. 8–22–90; 1986 H 468; 1953 H 1; GC 1639–19)

Uncodified Law

1996 H 445, § 3, eff. 9-3-96, reads:

(A) When a complaint is filed alleging that a child is a delinquent child for committing felonious sexual penetration in violation of former section

2907.12 of the Revised Code and the arresting authority, a court, or a probation officer discovers that the child or a person whom the child caused to engage in sexual activity has a communicable disease, the arresting authority, court, or probation officer shall notify the victim of the delinquent act of the nature of the disease in accordance with division (C) of section 2151.14 of the Revised Code.

As used in division (A) of Section 3 of this act:

(1) "Child" has the same meaning as in section 2151.011 of the Revised Code.

(2) "Delinquent child" has the same meaning as in section 2151.02 of the Revised Code.

(3) "Sexual activity" has the same meaning as in section 2907.01 of the Revised Code.

(B) If a child is adjudicated a delinquent child for violating any provision of former section 2907.12 of the Revised Code other than division (A)(1)(b) of that section when the insertion involved was consensual and when the victim of the violation of division (A)(1)(b) of that section was older than the delinquent child, was the same age as the delinquent child, or was less that three years younger than the delinquent child, the juvenile court with jurisdiction over the child may commit the child to the legal custody of the department of youth services pursuant to division (A)(5)(a) of section 2151.355 of the Revised Code, as amended by this act, and all provisions of the Revised Code that apply to a disposition otherwise imposed pursuant to division (A)(5)(a) of section 2151.355 of the Revised Code, as amended by this act, apply to a disposition imposed in accordance with division (B) of Section 3 of this act.

As used in division (B) of Section 3 of this act:

(1) "Child" and "legal custody" have the same meanings as in section 2151.011 of the Revised Code.

(2) "Delinquent child" has the same meaning as in section 2151.02 of the Revised Code.

(C) Section 2151.3511 of the Revised Code, as amended by this act, applies to a proceeding in juvenile court involving a complaint in which a child is charged with committing an act that if committed by an adult would be felonious sexual penetration in violation of former section 2907.12 of the Revised Code and in which an alleged victim of the act was a child who was under eleven years of age when the complaint was filed.

As used in division (C) of Section 3 of this act, "child" has the same meaning as in section 2151.011 of the Revised Code.

(D) Division (E) of section 2743.62 of the Revised Code applies to a claim for an award of reparations arising out of the commission of felonious sexual penetration in violation of former section 2907.12 of the Revised Code.

(E) Section 2907.11 of the Revised Code, as amended by this act, applies to a prosecution for felonious sexual penetration committed in violation of former section 2907.12 of the Revised Code.

(F) Division (A) of section 2907.28 and sections 2907.29 and 2907.30 of the Revised Code, as amended by this act, apply to a victim of felonious sexual penetration committed in violation of former section 2907.12 of the Revised Code.

(G) Sections 2907.41 and 2945.49 of the Revised Code, as amended by this act, apply to a trial or other proceeding involving a charge of felonious sexual penetration in violation of former section 2907.12 of the Revised Code in which an alleged victim of the offense was a child who was under eleven years of age when the complaint, indictment, or information was filed relative to the trial or other proceeding.

(H) Divisions (B) and (C) of section 2937.11 of the Revised Code, as amended by this act, apply to a case involving an alleged commission of the offense of felonious sexual penetration in violation of former section 2907.12 of the Revised Code.

(I) Notwithstanding section 2967.13 of the Revised Code, as amended by this act, a prisoner serving a term of imprisonment for life for committing the offense of felonious sexual penetration in violation of former section 2907.12 of the Revised Code becomes eligible for parole after serving a term of ten full years' imprisonment.

(J) Notwithstanding section 2967.18 of the Revised Code, as amended by this act, no reduction of sentence pursuant to division (B)(1) of section 2967.18 of the Revised Code shall be given to a person who is serving a term of imprisonment for the commission of felonious sexual penetration in violation of former section 2907.12 of the Revised Code.

Historical and Statutory Notes

Pre–1953 H 1 Amendments: 117 v 520, § 1

Amendment Note: 2002 H 247 inserted "this division or in" before "division (C)" in the first sentence of division (B); added the second sentence of division (B); and substituted "2152.20" for "2156.20" in division (D)(1).

Amendment Note: 2000 S 179, § 3, eff. 1–1–02, substituted "community control" for "probation" three times in division (A); inserted "or Chapter 2152. of the Revised Code" in division (B); and substituted "sections 2152.19 and 2152.20" for "section 2151.355" and "sections 2152.20 and 2152.21" for "section 2151.356" in the introductory paragraph in division (D)(1).

Amendment Note: 2000 H 442 deleted "2907.04," after "2907.03" in division (C).

Amendment Note: 1996 H 445 removed a reference to section 2907.12 from division (C); and made changes to reflect gender neutral language and other nonsubstantive changes.

Cross References

Bureau of aftercare services, contract with county agency, 5139.18
Dispositional hearing, Juv R 34
Limits on public access to records concerning pupils, 3319.321
Personal information systems, applicability of chapter, 1347.04
Presentence investigation reports, mandatory consideration of certain information, 2951.03
Process: service, Juv R 16
Social history, physical and mental examinations, custody investigation, Juv R 32
Subpoena, Juv R 17

Library References

Courts ⇌55.
Infants ⇌17, 131, 133.
Westlaw Topic Nos. 106, 211.
C.J.S. Courts §§ 107 to 109.
C.J.S. Infants §§ 8 to 9, 31, 33, 41 to 54, 57, 69 to 85.
Baldwin's Ohio Legislative Service, 1990 Laws of Ohio, S 258—LSC Analysis, p 5–954

Research References

Encyclopedias

OH Jur. 3d Family Law § 1541, Probation Department.
OH Jur. 3d Family Law § 1658, Restrictions on Use.
OH Jur. 3d Family Law § 1680, Record.

Treatises and Practice Aids

Carlin, Baldwin's Ohio Practice, Merrick-Rippner Probate Law § 107:61, Adjudicatory Hearings—Notice to Victims of Crime of Right to Recover Damages and Victim-Impact Statements.
Carlin, Baldwin's Ohio Practice, Merrick-Rippner Probate Law § 107:84, Disposition of Delinquent Children—Prior to January 1, 2002.
Carlin, Baldwin's Ohio Practice, Merrick-Rippner Probate Law § 107:104, Requests to Invoke Adult Portion of Serious Youthful Offender Disposition, Effective January 1, 2002.
Carlin, Baldwin's Ohio Practice, Merrick-Rippner Probate Law § 107:114, Juvenile Court Records—Confidentiality.
Giannelli & Yeomans, Ohio Juvenile Law § 21:2, Scope of Discovery; Rule 24.
Giannelli & Yeomans, Ohio Juvenile Law § 21:6, Social History Report.
Giannelli & Yeomans, Ohio Juvenile Law § 27:8, Probation.
Giannelli & Yeomans, Ohio Juvenile Law § 32:3, Responsibilities to Victims and Others.
Giannelli & Yeomans, Ohio Juvenile Law § 35:2, Confidentiality Requirement.
Giannelli & Yeomans, Ohio Juvenile Law § 25:13, Judgment & Records.

Law Review and Journal Commentaries

The Existing Confidentiality Privileges as Applied to Rape Victims, Note. 5 J L & Health 101 (1990–91).

Notes of Decisions

Compatibility of offices 4
Constitutional issues 1
Court records 3
Enforcement officers 2

1. Constitutional issues

Dissemination of social histories, compiled by probation officers in connection with juvenile proceedings, to social and religious agencies did not violate any federal constitutional right of privacy. J. P. v. DeSanti (C.A.6 (Ohio) 1981) 653 F.2d 1080. Constitutional Law ⇨ 82(7); Infants ⇨ 133

2. Enforcement officers

Juvenile's release from probation is not rendered a nullity by fact that court's jurisdiction over him does not terminate by reason thereof, as release from probation releases juvenile from supervision of probation officer and from any other condition of probation that was placed on him; juvenile court has authority to require juvenile placed on probation to undergo counseling or satisfy other conditions, and probation in general carries with it duty to report to probation officer and provide whatever information probation officer requests. In re Bracewell (Ohio App. 1 Dist., 04-17-1998) 126 Ohio App.3d 133, 709 N.E.2d 938, dismissed, appeal not allowed 82 Ohio St.3d 1481, 696 N.E.2d 1087. Infants ⇨ 225

Under RC 2151.14 and RC 2151.31 it is the manifest duty of enforcement officers to cooperate with and assist the juvenile authorities in the performance of their duties when such officers are specifically requested to do so by the juvenile authorities; such officers may avoid liability in an action for false imprisonment by showing that they were justified in the detention or restraint of the juvenile made under the specific direction and order of the juvenile authorities. Garland v. Dustman (Portage 1969) 19 Ohio App.2d 292, 251 N.E.2d 153, 48 O.O.2d 408. False Imprisonment ⇨ 11; Infants ⇨ 192

Trial court's finding in termination of parental rights case that father failed to remedy problems that caused child's removal despite children's services agency's diligent efforts to assist him, as factor to determine whether child could be returned to father within reasonable period of time, was not supported by clear and convincing evidence; state acquired temporary custody because child was exposed to cocaine in utero and that abuse was caused by the mother, father complied with drug assessment requirement of case plan and attended parenting class in order to remedy source of child's removal, and six- month period of agency assistance fell short of a diligent effort. In re Willis (Ohio App. 3 Dist., Allen, 09-20-2002) No. 1-02-17, 2002-Ohio-4942, 2002 WL 31114983, Unreported. Infants ⇨ 155

In termination of parental rights case, trial court's finding, that father demonstrated a lack of commitment toward child by failing to regularly support, visit, or communicate with her, as factor to determine whether child could be returned to father within reasonable period of time, was not supported by clear and convincing evidence; caseworkers provided conflicting testimony on the number of visits that father attended, and father's failure to attend every visit did not demonstrate a total lack of commitment, in that he missed visits because he had to work or because child was in an unsuitable condition for visitation, and although visitation ended with father's incarceration, he continually wrote letters inquiring as to child's well being. In re Willis (Ohio App. 3 Dist., Allen, 09-20-2002) No. 1-02-17, 2002-Ohio-4942, 2002 WL 31114983, Unreported. Infants ⇨ 155

3. Court records

Application to the juvenile court was not only mechanism for obtaining confidential juvenile court records; rather, proper procedure for determining discoverability of confidential juvenile records required trial court to conduct in camera inspection to determine: (1) whether the records were necessary and relevant to the pending action; (2) whether good cause had been shown by the person seeking disclosure; and (3) whether their admission outweighed the statutory confidentiality considerations. Grantz v. Discovery For Youth (Ohio App. 12 Dist., Butler, 02-22-2005) No. CA2004-09-216, No. CA2004-09-217, 2005-Ohio-680, 2005 WL 406211, Unreported. Records ⇨ 32

Good cause was demonstrated to release juvenile court records in action brought by tutor who was raped by juvenile placed in independent living facility and tutor's husband against county, its placement contractor, and facility owner, among others, for their alleged negligent supervision and placement of juvenile, where juvenile and his parent executed waivers permitting tutor and husband to access records. Grantz v. Discovery For Youth (Ohio App. 12 Dist., Butler, 02-22-2005) No. CA2004-09-216, No. CA2004-09-217, 2005-Ohio-680, 2005 WL 406211, Unreported. Records ⇨ 32

Although Ohio law generally protects a minor from exposure of his acts in another judicial forum, RC 2151.35(G) does not prohibit cross-examination, in a criminal trial, of defendant or defendant's witnesses concerning prior juvenile record, where defendant's evidence attempts to establish his good character. State v. Hale (Franklin 1969) 21 Ohio App.2d 207, 256 N.E.2d 239, 50 O.O.2d 340.

The provisions of 2151.14 that "the reports and records of the [probation] department [of the juvenile court] shall be considered confidential information and shall not be made public," apply only to the probation department of the juvenile court and have no application to cases where juvenile delinquents have been sentenced and committed to a state institution. State v. Sherow (Gallia 1956) 101 Ohio App. 169, 138 N.E.2d 444, 1 O.O.2d 100. Constitutional Law ⇨ 70.1(7.1); Infants ⇨ 68.1

The judge of the juvenile court of Hamilton county is not the clerk of his own court, when exercising the powers and jurisdictions conferred in RC 2151.01 to RC 2151.54, and mandamus will not lie to require him to exhibit to the attorneys representing a minor charged with a crime "all books, records, papers, [and] dockets in all cases and proceedings involving" such minor. State ex rel. Hibbard v. Hoffman (Hamilton 1955) 101 Ohio App. 547, 137 N.E.2d 606, 1 O.O.2d 454.

Pursuant to Juv R 32(B), 37(B) and RC 2151.14, juvenile court records, the records of social, mental, and physical examinations pursuant to court order, and records of the juvenile court probation department are not public records under RC 149.43. OAG 90–101.

4. Compatibility of offices

Trial court order awarding permanent custody of child to county department of children and family services was not against the manifest weight of the evidence; mother failed to attend parenting classes, classes on domestic violence, or attend a psychological evaluation, mother failed to seek treatment for substance abuse, father failed to complete parenting classes, attend periodic drug screenings, or complete a drug and alcohol assessment, both parents failed to regularly visit child, and child was thriving in his current environment. In re I.M. (Ohio App. 8 Dist., Cuyahoga, 12-24-2003) No. 82669, No. 82695, 2003-Ohio-7069, 2003 WL 23010024, Unreported. Infants ⇨ 222

The offices of township trustee and juvenile probation officer are compatible. OAG 73–035.

The duties of the office of chief of police are incompatible with those of a probation officer, and the same person is not entitled to receive compensation for both offices. 1922 OAG p 108.

2151.141 Requests for copies of records

(A) If a complaint filed with respect to a child pursuant to section 2151.27 of the Revised Code alleges that a child is an abused, neglected, or dependent child, any individual or entity that is listed in divisions (D)(1)(a) to (k) of section 2151.14 of the Revised Code and that is investigating whether the child is an abused, neglected, or dependent child, has custody of the child, is preparing a social history for the child, or is providing any services for the child may request any board of education, governing body of a chartered nonpublic school, public children services agency, private child placing agency, probation department, law enforcement agency, or prosecuting attorney that has any records related to the child to provide the individual or entity with a copy of the records. The request shall be in writing, describe the type of records requested, explain the need for the records, be accompanied by a copy of the complaint, and describe the relationship of the requesting individual or entity to the child. The individual or entity shall provide a copy of the request to the child in question, the attorney or guardian ad litem of the child, and the parent, guardian, or custodian of the child.

(B)(1) Any board of education, governing body of a chartered nonpublic school, public children services agency, private child placing agency, probation department, law enforcement agency, or prosecuting attorney that has any records related to a child who is the subject of a complaint as described in division (A) of this section and that receives a request for a copy of the records pursuant to division (A) of this section shall comply with the request, unless the individual or entity determines that it is unable to do so because it is prohibited by law from complying with the request, the request does not comply with division (A) of this section, or a complaint as described in division (A) of this section has not been filed with respect to the child who is the subject of the requested records. If the individual or entity determines that it is unable to comply with the request, it shall file a motion with the court in which the complaint as described in division (A) of this section was filed or was alleged to have been filed requesting the court to determine the extent to which it is required to comply with the request for records. Upon the filing of the motion, the court immediately shall hold a hearing on the motion, determine the extent to which the movant is required to comply with the request for records, and issue findings of fact and conclusions of law in support of its determination. The determination of the court shall be final. If the court determines that the movant is required to comply with the request for records, it shall identify the specific records that must be supplied to the individual or entity that requested them.

(2) In addition to or in lieu of the motion described in division (B)(1) of this section, a law enforcement agency or prosecuting attorney that receives a request for a copy of records pursuant to division (A) of this section may file a motion for a protective order as described in this division with the court in which the complaint as described in division (A) of this section was filed or alleged to have been filed. Upon the filing of a motion of that nature, the court shall conduct a hearing on the motion. If at the hearing the law enforcement agency or prosecuting attorney demonstrates that any of the following applies and if, after considering the purposes for which the records were requested pursuant to division (A) of this section, the best interest of the child, and any demonstrated need to prevent specific information in the records from being disclosed, the court determines that the issuance of a protective order is necessary, then the court shall issue a protective order that appropriately limits the disclosure of one or more specified records or specified information in one or more specified records:

(a) The records or information in the records relate to a case in which the child is alleged to be a delinquent child or a case in which a child is transferred for trial as an adult pursuant to section 2152.12 of the Revised Code and Juvenile Rule 30, and the adjudication hearing in the case, the trial in the case, or other disposition of the case has not been concluded.

(b) The records in question, or the records containing the information in question, are confidential law enforcement investigatory records, as defined in section 149.43 of the Revised Code.

(c) The records or information in the records relate to a case in which the child is or was alleged to be a delinquent child or to a case in which a child is or was transferred for trial as an adult pursuant to section 2152.12 of the Revised Code and Juvenile Rule 30; another case is pending against any child or any adult in which the child is alleged to be a delinquent child, the child is so transferred for trial as an adult, or the adult is alleged to be a criminal offender; the allegations in the case to which the records or information relate and the allegations in the other case are based on the same act or transaction, are based on two or more connected transactions or constitute parts of a common scheme or plan, or are part of a course of criminal conduct; and the adjudication hearing in, trial in, or other disposition of the other case has not been concluded.

(C) If an individual or entity is required to provide copies of records pursuant to this section, the individual or entity may charge a fee for the copies that does not exceed the cost of supplying them.

(D) This section does not require, authorize, or permit the dissemination of any records or any information contained in any records if the dissemination of the records or information generally is prohibited by section 2151.142 or another section of the Revised Code and a waiver as described in division (B)(1) of section 2151.142 of the Revised Code or a specific provision of the Revised Code does not specifically authorize or permit the dissemination of the records or information pursuant to this section.

(2000 S 179, § 3, eff. 1–1–02; 2000 H 412, eff. 4–10–01; 1990 S 258, eff. 8–22–90)

Historical and Statutory Notes

Ed. Note: A special endorsement by the Legislative Service Commission states, "Comparison of these amendments [2000 S 179, § 3, eff. 1–1–02 and 2000 H 412, eff. 4–10–01] in pursuance of section 1.52 of the Revised Code discloses that they are not irreconcilable so that they are required by that section to be harmonized to give effect to each amendment." In recognition of this rule of construction, changes made by 2000 S 179, § 3, eff. 1–1–02 and 2000 H 412, eff. 4–10–01, have been incorporated in the above amendment. See *Baldwin's Ohio Legislative Service Annotated*, 2000, pages 11/L–3610 and 11/L–3174, or the OH–LEGIS or OH–LEGIS–OLD database on Westlaw, for original versions of these Acts.

Amendment Note: 2000 S 179, § 3, eff. 1–1–02, substituted "transferred" for "bound over" and "2152.12" for "2151.26" throughout divisions (B)(2)(a) and (B)(2)(c).

Amendment Note: 2000 H 412 inserted "of that nature" in division (B)(2); deleted "shall not be construed to require, authorize, or permit, and," before "does not require, authorize, or permit"; substituted "section 2151.142 or another section" for "any provision," and inserted "waiver as described in division (B)(1) of section 2151.142 of the Revised Code or a" in division (D); and made other nonsubstantive changes.

Cross References

Limits on public access to records concerning pupils, 3319.321
Personal information systems, applicability of chapter, 1347.04

Library References

Infants ⟶ 133.
Westlaw Topic No. 211.
C.J.S. Infants §§ 57, 69 to 85.
Baldwin's Ohio Legislative Service, 1990 Laws of Ohio, S 258—LSC Analysis, p 5–954

Research References

Encyclopedias

OH Jur. 3d Appellate Review § 49, Orders Granting or Denying a Provisional Remedy.

Treatises and Practice Aids

Giannelli & Yeomans, Ohio Juvenile Law § 21:2, Scope of Discovery; Rule 24.

Giannelli & Yeomans, Ohio Juvenile Law § 21:6, Social History Report.

Giannelli & Yeomans, Ohio Juvenile Law § 35:2, Confidentiality Requirement.

Giannelli & Yeomans, Ohio Juvenile Law § 25:13, Judgment & Records.

Notes of Decisions

Procedure 2
Sealing records 1

---

1. Sealing records

Records of a county children services board investigation made pursuant to RC 5153.17 and 2151.141 are "official records" within the ambit of the sealing provisions of RC 2953.52; the trial court should weigh the privacy interests of the person seeking to seal the official records against the legitimate needs of the agency in maintaining those records. State v. S.R. (Ohio 1992) 63 Ohio St.3d 590, 589 N.E.2d 1319. Criminal Law ⟶ 1226(3.1)

2. Procedure

In context of a criminal prosecution, records of a children services agency must be made available to the trial court for an in camera inspection, notwithstanding privilege protecting such records. Chambers v. Chambers (Ohio App. 8 Dist., 04-03-2000) 137 Ohio App.3d 355, 738 N.E.2d 834, dismissed, appeal not allowed 89 Ohio St.3d 1454, 731 N.E.2d 1141. Infants ⇌ 133

Orders in which trial court denied requests by county and various county entities, which had been sued after minor was sexually abused by her father, for protective orders barring disclosure of any county records relating to minor, while constituting final orders within meaning of statute, were not appealable, where trial court did not make determination that there was no just reason for delay on any of judgment entries concerning denial of motions for protective order. Chambers v. Chambers (Ohio App. 8 Dist., 04-03-2000) 137 Ohio App.3d 355, 738 N.E.2d 834, dismissed, appeal not allowed 89 Ohio St.3d 1454, 731 N.E.2d 1141. Infants ⇌ 133

Pursuant to RC 2151.141, when a complaint alleging abuse, neglect, or dependency of a child is filed under RC 2151.27, a request directed to a public children services agency or the prosecuting attorney for "any records related to the child" must be granted or denied by following the procedures set forth in RC 2151.141. OAG 91–003.

2151.142 Confidentiality of residential addresses; exceptions

(A) As used in this section, "public record" and "journalist" have the same meanings as in section 149.43 of the Revised Code.

(B) Both of the following apply to the residential address of each officer or employee of a public children services agency or a private child placing agency who performs official responsibilities or duties described in section 2151.14, 2151.141, 2151.33, 2151.353, 2151.412, 2151.413, 2151.414, 2151.415, 2151.416, 2151.417, or 2151.421 or another section of the Revised Code and to the residential address of persons related to that officer or employee by consanguinity or affinity:

(1) Other officers and employees of a public children services agency, private child placing agency, juvenile court, or law enforcement agency shall consider those residential addresses to be confidential information. The officer or employee of the public children services agency or private child placing agency may waive the confidentiality of those residential addresses by giving express permission for their disclosure to other officers or employees of a public children services agency, private child placing agency, juvenile court, or law enforcement agency.

(2) To the extent that those residential addresses are contained in public records kept by a public children services agency, private child placing agency, juvenile court, or law enforcement agency, they shall not be considered to be information that is subject to inspection or copying as part of a public record under section 149.43 of the Revised Code.

(C) Except as provided in division (D) of this section, in the absence of a waiver as described in division (B)(1) of this section, no officer or employee of a public children services agency, private child placing agency, juvenile court, or law enforcement agency shall disclose the residential address of an officer or employee of a public children services agency or private child placing agency, or the residential address of a person related to that officer or employee by consanguinity or affinity, that is confidential information under division (B)(1) of this section to any person, when the disclosing officer or employee knows that the person is or may be a subject of an investigation, interview, examination, criminal case, other case, or other matter with which the officer or employee to whom the residential address relates currently is or has been associated.

(D) If, on or after the effective date of this section, a journalist requests a public children services agency, private child placing agency, juvenile court, or law enforcement agency to disclose a residential address that is confidential information under division (B)(1) of this section, the agency or juvenile court shall disclose to the journalist the residential address if all of the following apply:

(1) The request is in writing, is signed by the journalist, includes the journalist's name and title, and includes the name and address of the journalist's employer.

(2) The request states that disclosure of the residential address would be in the public interest.

(3) The request adequately identifies the person whose residential address is requested.

(4) The public children services agency, private child placing agency, juvenile court, or law enforcement agency receiving the request is one of the following:

(a) The agency or juvenile court with which the official in question serves or with which the employee in question is employed;

(b) The agency or juvenile court that has custody of the records of the agency with which the official in question serves or with which the employee in question is employed.

(2000 H 412, eff. 4–10–01)

Library References

Infants ⇌133.
Westlaw Topic No. 211.
C.J.S. Infants §§ 57, 69 to 85.

2151.15 Powers and duties vested in county department of probation

When a county department of probation has been established in the county and the juvenile judge does not establish a probation department within the juvenile court as provided in section 2151.14 of the Revised Code, all powers and duties of the probation department provided for in sections 2151.01 to 2151.54, inclusive, of the Revised Code, shall vest in and be imposed upon such county department of probation.

In counties in which a county department of probation has been or is hereafter established the judge may transfer to such department all or any part of the powers and duties of his own probation department; provided that all juvenile cases shall be handled within a county department of probation exclusively by an officer or division separate and distinct from the officers or division handling adult cases.

(1953 H 1, eff. 10–1–53; GC 1639–20)

Historical and Statutory Notes

Pre–1953 H 1 Amendments: 121 v 557; 117 v 520

Cross References

Advertising for children for adoption or foster homes forbidden, 5103.17
Bureau of aftercare services, contract with county agency, 5139.18

Library References

Courts ⇌55.
Infants ⇌225.
Westlaw Topic Nos. 106, 211.
C.J.S. Courts §§ 107 to 109.
C.J.S. Infants §§ 57, 69 to 85.

Research References

Encyclopedias

OH Jur. 3d Family Law § 1541, Probation Department.

2151.151 Juvenile court may contract for services to children on probation

(A) The juvenile judge may contract with any agency, association, or organization, which may be of a public or private, or profit or nonprofit nature, or with any individual for the provision of supervisory or other services to children placed on probation who are under the custody and supervision of the juvenile court.

(B) The juvenile judges of two or more adjoining or neighboring counties may join together for purposes of contracting with any agency, association, or organization, which may be of a public or private, or profit or nonprofit nature, or with any individual for the provision of supervisory or other services to children placed on probation who are under the custody and supervision of the juvenile court of any of the counties that joins [sic.] together.

(1981 H 440, eff. 11–23–81)

Ohio Administrative Code References

Community corrections facilities—fiscal rules and procedures, OAC Ch 5139–63
Community juvenile corrections facilities program—rules and procedures, OAC Ch 5139–61

Library References

Courts ⚖=55.
Infants ⚖=17, 225.
Westlaw Topic Nos. 106, 211.
C.J.S. Courts §§ 107 to 109.
C.J.S. Infants §§ 8 to 9, 57, 69 to 85.

Research References

Encyclopedias

OH Jur. 3d Family Law § 1537, Powers and Duties.

Treatises and Practice Aids

Carlin, Baldwin's Ohio Practice, Merrick-Rippner Probate Law § 104:19, Juvenile Facilities—Participation With Service Providers.

2151.152 Agreement to reimburse juvenile court for foster care maintenance costs and associated administrative and training costs

The juvenile judge may enter into an agreement with the department of job and family services pursuant to section 5101.11 of the Revised Code for the purpose of reimbursing the court for foster care maintenance costs and associated administrative and training costs incurred on behalf of a child eligible for payments under Title IV–E of the "Social Security Act," 94 Stat. 501, 42 U.S.C.A. 670 (1980) and who is in the temporary or permanent custody of the court or subject to a disposition issued under division (A)(5) of section 2151.354 or division (A)(7) (a)(ii) or (A)(8) of section 2152.19 of the Revised Code. The agreement shall govern the responsibilities and duties the court shall perform in providing services to the child.

(2002 H 400, eff. 4–3–03; 2001 H 57, eff. 2–19–02; 1999 H 471, eff. 7–1–00; 1996 H 274, eff. 8–8–96)

Historical and Statutory Notes

Amendment Note: 2002 H 400 substituted "(7)" for "(6)" and "(8)" for "(7)".

Amendment Note: 2001 H 57 rewrote this section, which prior thereto read:

"The juvenile judge may enter into an agreement with the department of job and family services pursuant to section 5101.11 of the Revised Code for the purpose of reimbursing the court for foster care maintenance costs and administrative and training costs incurred on behalf of a child eligible for payments under Title IV–E of the 'Social Security Act,' 94 Stat. 501, 42 U.S.C.A. 670 (1980). The agreement shall govern the responsibilities and duties the court shall perform in providing services to the child."

Amendment Note: 1999 H 471 substituted "job and family" for "human".

Library References

Infants ⚖=228(1).
Westlaw Topic No. 211.
C.J.S. Infants §§ 41, 53 to 54, 57, 69 to 85.
Baldwin's Ohio Legislative Service, 1996 H 274—LSC Analysis, p 5/L–697

Research References

Encyclopedias

OH Jur. 3d Family Law § 1542, Expenses.

Law Review and Journal Commentaries

Symposium: The Implications of Welfare Reform for Children. 60 Ohio St L J 1177 (1999).

2151.16 Referees; powers and duties

The juvenile judge may appoint and fix the compensation of referees who shall have the usual power of masters in chancery cases, provided, in all such cases submitted to them by the juvenile court, they shall hear the testimony of witnesses and certify to the judge their findings upon the case submitted to them, together with their recommendation as to the judgment or order to be made in the case in question. The court, after notice to the parties in the case of the presentation of such findings and recommendation, may make the order recommended by the referee, or any other order in the judgment of the court required by the findings of the referee, or may hear additional testimony, or may set aside said findings and hear the case anew. In appointing a referee for the trial of females, a female referee shall be appointed where possible.

(1953 H 1, eff. 10–1–53; GC 1639–21)

Historical and Statutory Notes

Pre–1953 H 1 Amendments: 117 v 520, § 1

Cross References

Advertising for children for adoption or foster homes forbidden, 5103.17
Judges of the court of domestic relations, juvenile court responsibility, 2301.03
Referees, Juv R 40

Library References

Infants ⚖=206.
Westlaw Topic No. 211.
C.J.S. Infants §§ 62, 68.

Research References

Encyclopedias

OH Jur. 3d Family Law § 1540, Court Personnel.
OH Jur. 3d Family Law § 1647, Proceedings Before Referee; Powers and Duties.
OH Jur. 3d Family Law § 1650, Report of Referee.
OH Jur. 3d Family Law § 1651, Report of Referee—Draft Report; Stipulations and Objections.
OH Jur. 3d Family Law § 1432.1, Agreement for Temporary Custody—Children Under Six Months Old—Voluntary Delivery of Newborn.

Treatises and Practice Aids

Carlin, Baldwin's Ohio Practice, Merrick-Rippner Probate Law § 107:49, Adjudicatory Hearings—Conduct of Hearing by Magistrate.
Carlin, Baldwin's Ohio Practice, Merrick-Rippner Probate Law § 107:119, Custody Review Proceedings—Semiannual Administrative Review.

Carlin, Baldwin's Ohio Practice, Merrick-Rippner Probate Law § 107:179, Findings and Decision of Magistrate; Child Placed on Probation; Approval by Judge—Form.

Giannelli & Yeomans, Ohio Juvenile Law § 20:4, Required Hearings.

Giannelli & Yeomans, Ohio Juvenile Law § 24:1, Introduction.

Giannelli & Yeomans, Ohio Juvenile Law § 24:2, Qualifications.

Notes of Decisions

Adults 3
Findings and recommendations 2
Procedural issues 1

1. Procedural issues

An evidentiary hearing before the juvenile court judge after a hearing before a juvenile court referee is not mandatory. In re Stall (Ohio 1973) 36 Ohio St.2d 139, 304 N.E.2d 596, 65 O.O.2d 338.

Juvenile court is not required to provide, at state expense, bill of exceptions in custody proceeding, especially absent a demand for taking of testimony by court reporter. In re Gutman (Hamilton 1969) 22 Ohio App.2d 125, 259 N.E.2d 128, 51 O.O.2d 252. Child Custody ⚖ 905

A referee of the juvenile court appointed pursuant to this section has functions and duties similar to those of a master commissioner appointed pursuant to GC 11487 (RC 2315.38) et seq. De Ville v. De Ville (Lucas 1949) 87 Ohio App. 220, 94 N.E.2d 474, 42 O.O. 423. Courts ⚖ 176

Notice required by this section to be given to parties must be in writing. In re Hobson, 44 Abs 86, 62 NE(2d) 510 (App 1945).

2. Findings and recommendations

Disposition of juvenile for gross sexual imposition, which permanently committed juvenile to the Department of Youth Services with a minimum stay of six months, was not an abuse of discretion; sex assessment of juvenile revealed that he had no empathy for the victim, he attempted to manipulate the tests given, and that he was at high risk to reoffend, juvenile refused to admit any wrongdoing and thought that the assessment was a waste of time. In re Hoyle (Ohio App. 5 Dist., Stark, 12-23-2002) No. 2002CA00266, 2002-Ohio-7212, 2002 WL 31874994, Unreported. Infants ⚖ 223.1

The action of juvenile court in postponing hearing on matter submitted to referee who failed to file findings and recommendations and in rectifying such deficiency by taking additional testimony and, thereafter, rendering decision constitutes substantial compliance with RC 2151.16. In re Gutman (Hamilton 1969) 22 Ohio App.2d 125, 259 N.E.2d 128, 51 O.O.2d 252.

While the juvenile court has authority to appoint a referee with power of masters in chancery to hear a case and report his findings and recommendations to the judge, there is no such authority with reference to an investigating counselor, and the action and report of such counselor is ex parte and does not constitute the hearing of "additional testimony" by the judge under such statute. Dolgin v. Dolgin (Lucas 1965) 1 Ohio App.2d 430, 205 N.E.2d 106, 30 O.O.2d 435.

A judgment of the juvenile court in the form of journalized recommendations of the referee is not rendered invalid because it was not immediately signed by the judge. Allstate Ins. Co. v. Cook (C.A.6 (Ohio) 1963) 324 F.2d 752, 26 O.O.2d 192.

African–American former court referee, who was appointed by elected judge, was policy making appointee that was not subject to Ohio's civil service laws, and thus referee was not an "employee" for purposes of Title VII race discrimination claim. Dyer v. Radcliffe (S.D.Ohio, 03-30-2001) 169 F.Supp.2d 770. Civil Rights ⚖ 1116(3)

3. Adults

A juvenile judge has no authority to commit the trial of a criminal charge against an adult to a referee, and any proceedings so committed are null and void. State v. Eddington (Marion 1976) 52 Ohio App.2d 312, 369 N.E.2d 1054, 6 O.O.3d 317. Criminal Law ⚖ 254.1

2151.17 Rules governing practice and procedure

Except as otherwise provided by rules promulgated by the supreme court, the juvenile court may prescribe rules regulating the docketing and hearing of causes, motions, and demurrers, and such other matters as are necessary for the orderly conduct of its business and the prevention of delay, and for the government of its officers and employees, including their conduct, duties, hours, expenses, leaves of absence, and vacations.

(1969 H 320, eff. 11–19–69; 1953 H 1; GC 1639–11)

Historical and Statutory Notes

Pre–1953 H 1 Amendments: 121 v 557; 117 v 520

Cross References

Judges of the court of domestic relations, juvenile court responsibility, 2301.03
Procedure not otherwise specified, Juv R 45
Rules of civil procedure; scope, applicability, construction, exceptions, Civ R 1

Library References

Courts ⚖ 176.
Infants ⚖ 194.1.
Westlaw Topic Nos. 106, 211.
C.J.S. Infants §§ 41 to 50, 54.

Research References

Encyclopedias

OH Jur. 3d Family Law § 1538, Powers and Duties—Rules as to Practice and Procedure.
OH Jur. 3d Family Law § 1540, Court Personnel.

Forms

Ohio Jurisprudence Pleading and Practice Forms § 2:8, Courts of Common Pleas—Juvenile Division.

Treatises and Practice Aids

Carlin, Baldwin's Ohio Practice, Merrick-Rippner Probate Law § 107:50, Adjudicatory Hearings—Applicability of Rules of Court.

Notes of Decisions

Constitutional issues 1
Employees 3
Governing rules 2

1. Constitutional issues

The matter of unlawful search and seizure under US Const Am 4 applies to juveniles. In re Morris (Ohio Com.Pl. 1971) 29 Ohio Misc. 71, 278 N.E.2d 701, 58 O.O.2d 126.

2. Governing rules

The Ohio Rules of Civil Procedure do not apply to a custody proceeding in the juvenile division of a court of common pleas; rather, such proceedings are governed by the Ohio Rules of Juvenile Procedure. Squires v. Squires (Preble 1983) 12 Ohio App.3d 138, 468 N.E.2d 73, 12 O.B.R. 460. Infants ⚖ 191

3. Employees

An administrative judge of the juvenile division of a court of common pleas is not authorized to enter into an employment agreement with employees of the court. Malone v. Court of Common Pleas of Cuyahoga County (Ohio 1976) 45 Ohio St.2d 245, 344 N.E.2d 126, 74 O.O.2d 413. Courts ⚖ 55

2151.18 Records of cases; annual report

(A) The juvenile court shall maintain records of all official cases brought before it, including, but not limited to, an appearance docket, a journal, and records of the type required by division (A)(2) of section 2151.35 of the Revised Code. The parents, guardian, or other custodian of any child affected, if living, or the nearest of kin of the child, if the parents would be entitled to inspect the records but are deceased, may inspect these records, either in person or by counsel, during the hours in which the court is open.

(B) Not later than June of each year, the court shall prepare an annual report covering the preceding calendar year showing the number and kinds of cases that have come before it, the disposition of the cases, and any other data pertaining to the work of the court that the juvenile judge directs. The court shall file copies of the report with the board of county commissioners. With the approval of the board, the court may print or cause to be printed copies of the report for distribution to persons and agencies interested in the court or community program for dependent, neglected, abused, or delinquent children and juvenile traffic offenders. The court shall include the number of copies ordered printed and the estimated cost of each printed copy on each copy of the report printed for distribution.

(2002 H 393, eff. 7–5–02; 2000 S 179, § 3, eff. 1–1–02)

Historical and Statutory Notes

Ed. Note: Former 2151.18 amended and recodified as 2152.71 by 2000 S 179, § 3, eff. 1–1–02; 2000 S 181, eff. 9–4–00; 1999 H 3, eff. 11–22–99; 1998 H 2, eff. 1–1–99; 1996 H 124, eff. 3–31–97; 1995 H 1, eff. 1–1–96; 1993 H 152, eff. 7–1–93; 1990 S 268; 1984 S 5; 1981 H 440; 1979 H 394; 1975 H 85; 127 v 547; 1953 H 1; GC 1639–13.

Pre–1953 H 1 Amendments: 123 v 367; 121 v 557; 117 v 520

Amendment Note: 2002 H 393 added the last sentence to division (A).

Library References

Courts ⚖113.
Infants ⚖133.
Westlaw Topic Nos. 106, 211.
C.J.S. Courts §§ 179, 181.
C.J.S. Infants §§ 57, 69 to 85.

Research References

Encyclopedias

OH Jur. 3d Actions § 82, Record of Appearance.
OH Jur. 3d Courts & Judges § 205, Records of Court Judgments and Proceedings, and Miscellaneous Records Prescribed by Statute.
OH Jur. 3d Courts & Judges § 207, Dockets.
OH Jur. 3d Family Law § 1539, Powers and Duties—Records and Reports.
OH Jur. 3d Family Law § 1540, Court Personnel.

Forms

Ohio Jurisprudence Pleading and Practice Forms § 10:2, Record of Appearance.

Treatises and Practice Aids

Carlin, Baldwin's Ohio Practice, Merrick-Rippner Probate Law § 106:1, Juvenile Court Jurisdiction—Delinquent Child—Definition: Evidence of Delinquency.
Carlin, Baldwin's Ohio Practice, Merrick-Rippner Probate Law § 107:1, Intake.
Carlin, Baldwin's Ohio Practice, Merrick-Rippner Probate Law § 107:86, Disposition of Delinquent Children—Previous Convictions—Prior to January 1, 2002.
Carlin, Baldwin's Ohio Practice, Merrick-Rippner Probate Law § 107:114, Juvenile Court Records—Confidentiality.
Carlin, Baldwin's Ohio Practice, Merrick-Rippner Probate Law § 107:115, Juvenile Court Records—Statistical.
Giannelli & Yeomans, Ohio Juvenile Law § 15:2, Intake.
Giannelli & Yeomans, Ohio Juvenile Law § 35:2, Confidentiality Requirement.

2151.19 Summons; expense

The summons, warrants, citations, subpoenas, and other writs of the juvenile court may issue to a probation officer of any such court or to the sheriff of any county or any marshal, constable, or police officer, and the provisions of law relating to the subpoenaing of witnesses in other cases shall apply in so far as they are applicable.

When a summons, warrant, citation, subpoena, or other writ is issued to any such officer, other than a probation officer, the expense in serving the same shall be paid by the county, township, or municipal corporation in the manner prescribed for the payment of sheriffs, deputies, assistants, and other employees.

(1953 H 1, eff. 10–1–53; GC 1639–52, 1639–53)

Historical and Statutory Notes

Pre–1953 H 1 Amendments: 117 v 520, § 1

Cross References

Process, issuance, form, Juv R 15
Right to compulsory process to obtain witnesses, O Const Art I §10

Library References

Infants ⚖198, 207, 212.
Sheriffs and Constables ⚖68.
Westlaw Topic Nos. 211, 353.
C.J.S. Infants §§ 50, 57, 62 to 67, 69 to 85.
C.J.S. Sheriffs and Constables § 504.

Research References

Encyclopedias

OH Jur. 3d Family Law § 1719, Service; Witness Fees.

Treatises and Practice Aids

Carlin, Baldwin's Ohio Practice, Merrick-Rippner Probate Law § 107:90, Disposition Orders for Delinquent Children, Effective January 1, 2002.

Notes of Decisions

Expenses 1
Service 2

---

1. Expenses

In juvenile court cases in which the Ohio Rules of Juvenile Procedure apply, Juv R 17(B) grants a juvenile court the authority to tax as costs and collect from a party the fees of the county sheriff in serving subpoenas issued by the court and the fees of witnesses subpoenaed by the court; however, pursuant to RC 2151.54, such fees may not be taxed as costs and collected by a juvenile court in cases of delinquent, unruly, dependent, abused, or neglected children except when specifically ordered by the court. OAG 98–021.

Expenses incurred by a county sheriff in serving summonses, warrants, citations, subpoenas, writs, and other papers issued by a juvenile court in connection with cases filed therein shall, pursuant to RC 2151.19, be paid out of the monthly allowance made available therefor by a board of county commissioners under RC 325.07; such expenses shall not be taxed and collected by the juvenile court as fees or costs under RC 2151.54. OAG 89–086, clarified by OAG 98–021.

2. Service

Adjudication in criminal case that complaint is insufficient to charge an offense is not conclusive on officer serving the process in an action for false imprisonment against him. Brinkman v. Drolesbaugh (Ohio 1918) 97 Ohio St. 171, 119 N.E. 451, 15 Ohio Law Rep. 555. False Imprisonment ⚖7(5)

Sheriff is required to serve summons, notices, and subpoenas which are directed to him by juvenile court, and whether juvenile court requests summons, notices or subpoenas to be served personally or to be delivered by registered or certified mail, sheriff's office is legally required to serve them in accordance with such directions of juvenile court; if person to be served is out of state and his address is known, service of summons may be made by sheriff by delivering copy to him personally or mailing copy to him by registered or certified mail. OAG 70–130.

2151.20 Seal of court; dimensions

Juvenile courts within the probate court shall have a seal which shall consist of the coat of arms of the state within a circle one and one-fourth inches in diameter and shall be surrounded by the words "juvenile court _____ county."

The seal of other courts exercising the powers and jurisdiction conferred in sections 2151.01 to 2151.54, inclusive, of the Revised Code, shall be attached to all writs and processes.

(132 v H 164, eff. 12–15–67; 1953 H 1; GC 1639–9)

Historical and Statutory Notes

Pre–1953 H 1 Amendments: 117 v 520, § 1

Research References

Encyclopedias
OH Jur. 3d Family Law § 1537, Powers and Duties.

2151.21 Jurisdiction in contempt

The juvenile court has the same jurisdiction in contempt as courts of common pleas.

(1953 H 1, eff. 10–1–53; GC 1639–10)

Historical and Statutory Notes

Pre–1953 H 1 Amendments: 117 v 520, § 1

Cross References

Contempt of court, Ch 2705

Library References

Contempt ☞35.
Westlaw Topic No. 93.
C.J.S. Contempt §§ 51, 59.

Research References

Encyclopedias
OH Jur. 3d Family Law § 1545, Contempt.
OH Jur. 3d Family Law § 1689, Juvenile Traffic Offender.

Treatises and Practice Aids
Carlin, Baldwin's Ohio Practice, Merrick-Rippner Probate Law § 107:127, Contempt of Court in Juvenile Proceedings.
Giannelli & Yeomans, Ohio Juvenile Law § 18:3, Summons: Contents and Form.
Giannelli & Yeomans, Ohio Juvenile Law § 28:4, Community Control and Probation.
Giannelli & Yeomans, Ohio Juvenile Law § 32:2, Jurisdiction Over Parents and Others.
Giannelli & Yeomans, Ohio Juvenile Law § 33:8, Contempt.

Notes of Decisions

Parents' duties 1

1. Parents' duties

Determination of civil, rather than criminal, contempt for mother's violation of court order requiring mother to ensure that her son complied with state school attendance rules was appropriate as sanction was intended to coerce mother to act in compliance with a court order, not to punish her for an offense to the court. In re M.B. (Ohio App. 6 Dist., Huron, 09-03-2004) No. H-03-042, 2004-Ohio-4672, 2004 WL 1949418, Unreported. Contempt ☞ 20

It was not inappropriate to impose civil contempt sanction on mother for failing to comply with order requiring her to ensure that her child complied with state school attendance rules, although she alleged that at time of hearing her son had been placed in temporary custody of Department of Job & Family Services which rendered her compliance with order moot, where son was not permanently removed from mother's care, and Department was required to work toward eventual reunification of mother and child. In re M.B. (Ohio App. 6 Dist., Huron, 09-03-2004) No. H-03-042, 2004-Ohio-4672, 2004 WL 1949418, Unreported. Contempt ☞ 48

Trial court, in delinquency proceeding, had authority to initiate contempt proceedings against juvenile's mother based on a violation of order that required mother to attend parenting classes, even though a stay of execution of such order on was issued next day; stay of execution only dealt with juvenile's ninety-day sentence to juvenile detention center, and thus order to attend parenting classes was still in effect at all times. In re Cunningham (Ohio App. 7 Dist., Harrison, 10-18-2002) No. 02-537-CA, 2002-Ohio-5875, 2002 WL 31412256, Unreported. Contempt ☞ 22

The issue of whether, under equal protection analysis, an individual suffering from battered child syndrome should be permitted to present expert testimony to assist the trier of fact in determining the subjective element of a claim of self-defense is a question worthy of Supreme Court review. State v. Nemeth (Ohio App. 7 Dist., Jefferson, 03-19-1997) No. 95-JE-32, 1997 WL 150649, Unreported.

Where questions directed toward mother at deposition in child dependency proceeding were found by trial court to be material and relevant to issue of case, where court order directed that mother answer such questions, and where mother was granted transactional immunity so that she could testify as to treatment of child, trial court's finding of contempt for mother's refusal to answer questions at deposition was supported by weight of evidence. In re Poth (Huron 1981) 2 Ohio App.3d 361, 442 N.E.2d 105, 2 O.B.R. 417. Pretrial Procedure ☞ 227

Where the evidence indicates that the whereabouts of their children are unknown to parents, the parents may not be found guilty of contempt for failure to produce the children in court in accordance with its order. State v. Hershberger (Wayne 1959) 168 N.E.2d 13, 83 Ohio Law Abs. 62.

In proceeding for determination of custody of neglected child, statutory requirements were met when child was in fact represented by counsel, and parents who had several weeks in which to obtain counsel but failed to do so could not avoid punishment for contempt in failing to produce child on ground that they did not have benefit of counsel. State v. Hershberger (Ohio Juv. 1958) 150 N.E.2d 671, 77 Ohio Law Abs. 487, reversed 168 N.E.2d 12, 83 Ohio Law Abs. 63. Contempt ☞ 61(1); Infants ☞ 205

2151.211 Employee's attendance at proceeding; employer may not penalize

No employer shall discharge or terminate from employment, threaten to discharge or terminate from employment, or otherwise punish or penalize any employee because of time lost from regular employment as a result of the employee's attendance at any proceeding pursuant to a subpoena under this chapter or Chapter 2152. of the Revised Code. This section generally does not require and shall not be construed to require an employer to pay an employee for time lost as a result of attendance at any proceeding under either chapter. However, if an employee is subpoenaed to appear at a proceeding under either chapter and the proceeding pertains to an offense against the employer or an offense involving the employee during the course of the employee's employment, the employer shall not decrease or withhold the employee's pay for any time lost as a result of compliance with the subpoena. Any employer who knowingly violates this section is in contempt of court.

(2000 S 179, § 3, eff. 1–1–02; 1984 S 172, eff. 9–26–84)

Historical and Statutory Notes

Amendment Note: 2000 S 179, § 3, eff. 1–1–02, substituted "under this chapter or Chapter 2152. of the Revised Code" for "in a delinquency case" in the first sentence; substituted "under either chapter" for "in a delinquency case" in the second and third sentences; and made changes to reflect gender neutral language.

Cross References

Victim's rights pamphlet, publication and distribution, 109.42

Library References

Labor and Employment ⚖️818.
Westlaw Topic No. 231H.

Research References

Treatises and Practice Aids

Carlin, Baldwin's Ohio Practice, Merrick-Rippner Probate Law § 107:127, Contempt of Court in Juvenile Proceedings.

Employment Coordinator Benefits § 14:37, Ohio.

2151.22 Terms of court; sessions

The term of any juvenile or domestic relations court, whether a division of the court of common pleas or an independent court, is one calendar year. All actions and other business pending at the expiration of any term of court is automatically continued without further order. The judge may adjourn court or continue any case whenever, in his opinion, such continuance is warranted.

Sessions of the court may be held at such places throughout the county as the judge shall from time to time determine.

(1976 H 390, eff. 8-6-76; 1953 H 1; GC 1639-12)

Historical and Statutory Notes

Pre-1953 H 1 Amendments: 117 v 520, § 1

Library References

Courts ⚖️63, 75.
Westlaw Topic No. 106.
C.J.S. Courts §§ 111 to 113, 120.

Research References

Encyclopedias

OH Jur. 3d Family Law § 1536, Terms, Sessions, and Places of Court.

Treatises and Practice Aids

Carlin, Baldwin's Ohio Practice, Merrick-Rippner Probate Law § 104:12, Juvenile Court—Term.

Giannelli & Yeomans, Ohio Juvenile Law § 33:2, Motions.

2151.23 Jurisdiction of juvenile court; orders for child support

(A) The juvenile court has exclusive original jurisdiction under the Revised Code as follows:

(1) Concerning any child who on or about the date specified in the complaint, indictment, or information is alleged to have violated section 2151.87 of the Revised Code or an order issued under that section or to be a juvenile traffic offender or a delinquent, unruly, abused, neglected, or dependent child and, based on and in relation to the allegation pertaining to the child, concerning the parent, guardian, or other person having care of a child who is alleged to be an unruly or delinquent child for being an habitual or chronic truant;

(2) Subject to divisions (G) and (V) of section 2301.03 of the Revised Code, to determine the custody of any child not a ward of another court of this state;

(3) To hear and determine any application for a writ of habeas corpus involving the custody of a child;

(4) To exercise the powers and jurisdiction given the probate division of the court of common pleas in Chapter 5122. of the Revised Code, if the court has probable cause to believe that a child otherwise within the jurisdiction of the court is a mentally ill person subject to hospitalization by court order, as defined in section 5122.01 of the Revised Code;

(5) To hear and determine all criminal cases charging adults with the violation of any section of this chapter;

(6) To hear and determine all criminal cases in which an adult is charged with a violation of division (C) of section 2919.21, division (B)(1) of section 2919.22, section 2919.222, division (B) of section 2919.23, or section 2919.24 of the Revised Code, provided the charge is not included in an indictment that also charges the alleged adult offender with the commission of a felony arising out of the same actions that are the basis of the alleged violation of division (C) of section 2919.21, division (B)(1) of section 2919.22, section 2919.222, division (B) of section 2919.23, or section 2919.24 of the Revised Code;

(7) Under the interstate compact on juveniles in section 2151.56 of the Revised Code;

(8) Concerning any child who is to be taken into custody pursuant to section 2151.31 of the Revised Code, upon being notified of the intent to take the child into custody and the reasons for taking the child into custody;

(9) To hear and determine requests for the extension of temporary custody agreements, and requests for court approval of permanent custody agreements, that are filed pursuant to section 5103.15 of the Revised Code;

(10) To hear and determine applications for consent to marry pursuant to section 3101.04 of the Revised Code;

(11) Subject to divisions (G) and (V) of section 2301.03 of the Revised Code, to hear and determine a request for an order for the support of any child if the request is not ancillary to an action for divorce, dissolution of marriage, annulment, or legal separation, a criminal or civil action involving an allegation of domestic violence, or an action for support brought under Chapter 3115. of the Revised Code;

(12) Concerning an action commenced under section 121.38 of the Revised Code;

(13) To hear and determine violations of section 3321.38 of the Revised Code;

(14) To exercise jurisdiction and authority over the parent, guardian, or other person having care of a child alleged to be a delinquent child, unruly child, or juvenile traffic offender, based on and in relation to the allegation pertaining to the child;

(15) To conduct the hearings, and to make the determinations, adjudications, and orders authorized or required under sections 2152.82 to 2152.85 and Chapter 2950. of the Revised Code regarding a child who has been adjudicated a delinquent child and to refer the duties conferred upon the juvenile court judge under sections 2152.82 to 2152.85 and Chapter 2950. of the Revised Code to magistrates appointed by the juvenile court judge in accordance with Juvenile Rule 40.

(B) Except as provided in divisions (G) and (I) of section 2301.03 of the Revised Code, the juvenile court has original jurisdiction under the Revised Code:

(1) To hear and determine all cases of misdemeanors charging adults with any act or omission with respect to any child, which act or omission is a violation of any state law or any municipal ordinance;

(2) To determine the paternity of any child alleged to have been born out of wedlock pursuant to sections 3111.01 to 3111.18 of the Revised Code;

(3) Under the uniform interstate family support act in Chapter 3115. of the Revised Code;

(4) To hear and determine an application for an order for the support of any child, if the child is not a ward of another court of this state;

(5) To hear and determine an action commenced under section 3111.28 of the Revised Code;

(6) To hear and determine a motion filed under section 3119.961 of the Revised Code;

(7) To receive filings under section 3109.74 of the Revised Code, and to hear and determine actions arising under sections 3109.51 to 3109.80 of the Revised Code.

(8) To enforce an order for the return of a child made under the Hague Convention on the Civil Aspects of International Child Abduction pursuant to section 3127.32 of the Revised Code;

(9) To grant any relief normally available under the laws of this state to enforce a child custody determination made by a court of another state and registered in accordance with section 3127.35 of the Revised Code.

(C) The juvenile court, except as to juvenile courts that are a separate division of the court of common pleas or a separate and independent juvenile court, has jurisdiction to hear, determine, and make a record of any action for divorce or legal separation that involves the custody or care of children and that is filed in the court of common pleas and certified by the court of common pleas with all the papers filed in the action to the juvenile court for trial, provided that no certification of that nature shall be made to any juvenile court unless the consent of the juvenile judge first is obtained. After a certification of that nature is made and consent is obtained, the juvenile court shall proceed as if the action originally had been begun in that court, except as to awards for spousal support or support due and unpaid at the time of certification, over which the juvenile court has no jurisdiction.

(D) The juvenile court, except as provided in divisions (G) and (I) of section 2301.03 of the Revised Code, has jurisdiction to hear and determine all matters as to custody and support of children duly certified by the court of common pleas to the juvenile court after a divorce decree has been granted, including jurisdiction to modify the judgment and decree of the court of common pleas as the same relate to the custody and support of children.

(E) The juvenile court, except as provided in divisions (G) and (I) of section 2301.03 of the Revised Code, has jurisdiction to hear and determine the case of any child certified to the court by any court of competent jurisdiction if the child comes within the jurisdiction of the juvenile court as defined by this section.

(F)(1) The juvenile court shall exercise its jurisdiction in child custody matters in accordance with sections 3109.04, 3127.01 to 3127.53, and 5103.20 to 5103.22 of the Revised Code.

(2) The juvenile court shall exercise its jurisdiction in child support matters in accordance with section 3109.05 of the Revised Code.

(G) Any juvenile court that makes or modifies an order for child support shall comply with Chapters 3119., 3121., 3123., and 3125. of the Revised Code. If any person required to pay child support under an order made by a juvenile court on or after April 15, 1985, or modified on or after December 1, 1986, is found in contempt of court for failure to make support payments under the order, the court that makes the finding, in addition to any other penalty or remedy imposed, shall assess all court costs arising out of the contempt proceeding against the person and require the person to pay any reasonable attorney's fees of any adverse party, as determined by the court, that arose in relation to the act of contempt.

(H) If a child who is charged with an act that would be an offense if committed by an adult was fourteen years of age or older and under eighteen years of age at the time of the alleged act and if the case is transferred for criminal prosecution pursuant to section 2152.12 of the Revised Code, the juvenile court does not have jurisdiction to hear or determine the case subsequent to the transfer. The court to which the case is transferred for criminal prosecution pursuant to that section has jurisdiction subsequent to the transfer to hear and determine the case in the same manner as if the case originally had been commenced in that court, including, but not limited to, jurisdiction to accept a plea of guilty or another plea authorized by Criminal Rule 11 or another section of the Revised Code and jurisdiction to accept a verdict and to enter a judgment of conviction pursuant to the Rules of Criminal Procedure against the child for the commission of the offense that was the basis of the transfer of the case for criminal prosecution, whether the conviction is for the same degree or a lesser degree of the offense charged, for the commission of a lesser-included offense, or for the commission of another offense that is different from the offense charged.

(I) If a person under eighteen years of age allegedly commits an act that would be a felony if committed by an adult and if the person is not taken into custody or apprehended for that act until after the person attains twenty-one years of age, the juvenile court does not have jurisdiction to hear or determine any portion of the case charging the person with committing that act. In those circumstances, divisions (A) and (B) of section 2152.12 of the Revised Code do not apply regarding the act, and the case charging the person with committing the act shall be a criminal prosecution commenced and heard in the appropriate court having jurisdiction of the offense as if the person had been eighteen years of age or older when the person committed the act. All proceedings pertaining to the act shall be within the jurisdiction of the court having jurisdiction of the offense, and that court has all the authority and duties in the case that it has in other criminal cases in that court.

(2006 S 238, eff. 9–21–06; 2004 S 185, eff. 4–11–05; 2004 H 38, eff. 6–17–04; 2001 S 3, eff. 1–1–02; 2000 S 179, § 3, eff. 1–1–02; 2000 S 180, eff. 3–22–01; 2000 S 218, eff. 3–15–01; 2000 H 583, eff. 6–14–00; 2000 S 181, eff. 9–4–00; 1997 H 352, eff. 1–1–98; 1997 H 215, eff. 6–30–97; 1996 H 124, eff. 3–31–97; 1996 H 377, eff. 10–17–96; 1996 S 269, eff. 7–1–96; 1996 H 274, eff. 8–8–96; 1995 H 1, eff. 1–1–96; 1993 H 173, eff. 12–31–93; 1993 S 21; 1992 S 10; 1990 S 3, H 514, S 258, H 591; 1988 S 89; 1986 H 428, H 509, H 476; 1984 H 614; 1983 H 93; 1982 H 515; 1981 H 1; 1977 S 135; 1976 H 244; 1975 H 85; 1970 H 931; 1969 H 320)

Historical and Statutory Notes

Ed. Note: Former RC 2151.23 repealed by 1969 H 320, eff. 11–19–69; 130 v S 187; 127 v 547; 1953 H 1; GC 1639–16.

Ed. Note: Former RC 2151.23(G)(2) related to the duration of child support orders beyond the child's eighteenth birthday. See now RC 3119.86 for provisions analogous to former RC 2151.23(G)(2).

Pre–1953 H 1 Amendments: 121 v 557; 117 v 520

Amendment Note: 2006 S 238 substituted "5103.22" for "5103.28" in division (F)(1).

Amendment Note: 2004 S 185 added divisions (B)(7) through (B)(9); substituted "3127.01" for "3109.21" and "3127.53" for "3109.36" in division (F)(1); and made other nonsubstantive changes.

Amendment Note: 2004 H 38 inserted "divisions (G) and" in divisions (A)(2), (A)(11), (B), (D), and (E).

Amendment Note: 2001 S 3 added new division (A)(15).

Amendment Note: 2000 S 179 inserted ", indictment, or information" in division (A)(1); substituted "2152.12" for "2151.26" in division (H); substituted "divisions (A) and (B) of section 2152.12" for "divisions (B) and (C) of section 2151.26" in division (I); and made corrective internal numbering changes and other nonsubstantive changes.

Amendment Note: 2000 S 180 redesignated divisions (A)(14) and (A)(15) as (A)(13) and (A)(14); substituted "3111.18" for "3111.19" in division (B)(2) and "3111.28" for "5101.34" in division (B)(5); inserted new division (B)(6); rewrote division (G); and made other nonsubstantive amendments. Prior to amendment division (G) read:

"(G)(1) Each order for child support made or modified by a juvenile court shall include as part of the order a general provision, as described in division (A)(1) of section 3113.21 of the Revised Code, requiring the withholding or deduction of income or assets of the obligor under the order as described in division (D) of section 3113.21 of the Revised Code, or another type of appropriate requirement as described in division (D)(3), (D)(4), or (H) of that section, to ensure that withholding or deduction from the income or assets of the obligor is available from the commencement of the support order for collection of the support and of any arrearages that occur; a statement requiring all parties to the order to notify the child support enforcement agency in writing of their current mailing address, current residence address, current residence telephone number, and current driver's license number, and any changes to that information; and a notice that the requirement to notify the child support enforcement agency of all changes to that information continues until further notice from the court. Any juvenile court that makes or modifies an order for child support shall comply with sections 3113.21 to 3113.219 of the Revised Code. If any person required to pay child support under an order made by a juvenile court on or after April 15, 1985, or modified on or after December 1, 1986, is found in contempt of court for failure to make support payments under the order, the court that makes the finding, in addition to any other penalty or remedy imposed, shall assess all court costs arising out of the contempt proceeding against the person and require the person to pay any reasonable attorney's fees of any adverse party, as determined by the court, that arose in relation to the act of contempt.

"(2) Notwithstanding section 3109.01 of the Revised Code, if a juvenile court issues a child support order under this chapter, the order shall remain in effect beyond the child's eighteenth birthday as long as the child continuously attends on a full-time basis any recognized and accredited high school or the order provides that the duty of support of the child continues beyond the child's eighteenth birthday. Except in cases in which the order provides that the duty of support continues for any period after the child reaches nineteen years of age the order shall not remain in effect after the child reaches nineteen years of age. Any parent ordered to pay support under a child support order issued under this chapter shall continue to pay support under the order, including during seasonal vacation periods, until the order terminates."

Amendment Note: 2000 S 218 inserted "have violated section 2151.87 of the Revised Code or an order issued under that section or to" in division (A)(1); and made corrective internal numbering changes.

Amendment Note: 2000 H 583 deleted former division (A)(13); inserted "except as provided in division (I) of section 2301.03 of the Revised Code," in divisions (B), (D), and (E); and made other nonsubstantive changes. Prior to deletion, former division (A)(13) read:

"(13) Concerning an action commenced under section 2151.55 of the Revised Code."

Amendment Note: 2000 S 181 inserted "and, based on and in relation to the allegation pertaining to the child, concerning the parent, guardian, or other person having care of a child who is alleged to be an unruly or delinquent child for being an habitual or chronic truant" in division (A)(1); inserted "section 2919.222," twice in division (A)(6); and added divisions (A)(14) and (A)(15).

Amendment Note: 1997 H 352 substituted "uniform interstate family support act" for "uniform reciprocal enforcement of support act" in division (B)(3); added division (B)(5); deleted "on or after December 31, 1993," before "shall include", substituted "income" for "wages" twice and "(D)(3), (D)(4)" for "(D)(6), (D)(7)", inserted "current residence telephone number, current driver's license number,", and deleted "on or after April 12, 1990," before "shall comply", in division (G)(1); inserted "or the order provides that the duty of support of the child continues beyond the child's eighteenth birthday" and added the second sentence in division (G)(2); and made other nonsubstantive changes.

Amendment Note: 1997 H 215 added division (A)(13).

Amendment Note: 1996 H 124 removed the designation of division (H)(1); deleted former division (H)(2); and added division (I). Prior to deletion, former division (H)(2) read:

"(2) The department of rehabilitation and correction shall house an inmate who is fourteen years of age or older and under eighteen years of age in a housing unit in a state correctional institution separate from inmates who are eighteen years of age or older, if the inmate who is under eighteen years of age observes the rules and regulations of the institution and does not otherwise create a security risk by being housed separately. When an inmate attains eighteen years of age, the department may house the inmate with the adult population of the state correctional institution. If the department receives too few inmates who are under eighteen years of age to fill a housing unit in the state correctional institution separate from inmates who are eighteen years of age or older, the department also may assign to the housing unit inmates who are eighteen years of age or older and under twenty-one years of age."

Amendment Note: 1996 H 377 inserted "as follows" in the introductory paragraph of division (A); inserted "Subject to division (V) of section 2301.03 of the Revised Code," in divisions (A)(2) and (A)(11); and made other nonsubstantive changes.

Amendment Note: 1996 S 269 changed statutory references from section 2919.21(B) to 2919.21(C) throughout in division (A)(6).

Amendment Note: 1996 H 274 added division (A)(12).

Amendment Note: 1995 H 1 added division (H); and made other nonsubstantive changes.

Amendment Note: 1993 S 21 removed a reference to Chapter 5123 in, and deleted "or a mentally retarded person subject to institutionalization by court order, as defined in section 5123.01 of the Revised Code" from the end of, division (A)(4).

Amendment Note: 1993 H 173 rewrote division (G)(1) before the first semi-colon, which previously read:

"(G)(1) Each order for child support made or modified by a juvenile court on or after December 1, 1986, shall be accompanied by one or more orders described in division (D) or (H) of section 3113.21 of the Revised Code, whichever is appropriate under the requirements of that section".

Cross References

Custody of minor children, 3109.03, 3109.04
Duty of parents to support children of unemancipated minor children, 3109.19
Failure to send child to school, 3321.38
Interfering with action to issue or modify support order, 2919.231
Marriage, method of consent, 3101.02
Minor female's complaint for abortion, juvenile court to hear, 2151.85
Nonsupport of dependents, 2919.21
Paternity proceedings, jurisdiction of courts, 3111.06
Placing of children, 5103.16
Rules of procedure do not affect jurisdiction, Juv R 44
Scope of rules, Juv R 1
Uniform Interstate Family Support Act, venue of actions, 3115.56

Library References

Child Support ⇐173.
Courts ⇐175.
Habeas Corpus ⇐614.
Infants ⇐196.
Westlaw Topic Nos. 106, 197, 211, 76E.
C.J.S. Infants §§ 41, 53 to 54.
C.J.S. Parent and Child §§ 206, 211.

Baldwin's Ohio Legislative Service, 1988 Laws of Ohio, S 89—LSC Analysis, p 5–571; 1990 Laws of Ohio, S 258—LSC Analysis, p 5–954, H 591—LSC Analysis, p 5–576

Research References

ALR Library

102 ALR 5th 525, Criminal Jurisdiction of Municipal or Other Local Court.

87 ALR 5th 361, Liability of Father for Retroactive Child Support on Judicial Determination of Paternity.

80 ALR 5th 1, Child Custody and Visitation Rights Arising from Same-Sex Relationship.

74 ALR 5th 453, Juvenile's Guilty or No Contest Plea in Adult Court as Waiver of Defects in Transfer or Certification Proceedings.

39 ALR 5th 103, Propriety of Exclusion of Press or Other Media Representatives from Civil Trial.

Encyclopedias

OH Jur. 3d Constitutional Law § 503, Liberty.
OH Jur. 3d Criminal Law § 582, Application to Criminal Statutes.
OH Jur. 3d Criminal Law § 583, Application to Criminal Statutes—Types of Ex Post Facto Laws; Exception.
OH Jur. 3d Criminal Law § 2012, Effect of Juvenile Court; Transfers to Juvenile Court.
OH Jur. 3d Criminal Law § 2013, Transfers from Juvenile Court for Criminal Prosecution; Relinquishment of Jurisdiction.
OH Jur. 3d Criminal Law § 3447, Generally; Constitutionality.
OH Jur. 3d Family Law § 106, Corporate Stock.
OH Jur. 3d Family Law § 570, Jurisdiction of Juvenile Court.
OH Jur. 3d Family Law § 571, Jurisdiction of Juvenile Court—Certification to Juvenile Court.
OH Jur. 3d Family Law § 803, Custody Decrees; Generally—Jurisdiction to Award Custody.
OH Jur. 3d Family Law § 812, Custody Decrees; Generally.
OH Jur. 3d Family Law § 935, Dismissal.

OH Jur. 3d Family Law § 973, Jurisdiction.
OH Jur. 3d Family Law § 1002, Application of Res Judicata.
OH Jur. 3d Family Law § 1058, Relinquishment of Custody and Control to Other Parent.
OH Jur. 3d Family Law § 1105, Determining Child's Best Interest.
OH Jur. 3d Family Law § 1165, Effect of Child's Emancipation.
OH Jur. 3d Family Law § 1201, Minimum Child Support Order.
OH Jur. 3d Family Law § 1222, Interfering With Action to Issue or Modify Support Order.
OH Jur. 3d Family Law § 1301, Hearing to Determine Withholding or Deduction Requirements.
OH Jur. 3d Family Law § 1306, Upon Agency's Receipt of Notice.
OH Jur. 3d Family Law § 1308, Reissuance Upon Change in Obligor's Status.
OH Jur. 3d Family Law § 1421, Adoption by Relatives.
OH Jur. 3d Family Law § 1495, Jurisdictional Issues.
OH Jur. 3d Family Law § 1544, on Certification from Another Court.
OH Jur. 3d Family Law § 1545, Contempt.
OH Jur. 3d Family Law § 1547, Juvenile Traffic Offenders.
OH Jur. 3d Family Law § 1549, Delinquent, Unruly, Abused, Neglected, or Dependent Children.
OH Jur. 3d Family Law § 1550, Child Custody.
OH Jur. 3d Family Law § 1551, Child Custody—Habeas Corpus Involving Custody.
OH Jur. 3d Family Law § 1552, Mentally Ill or Retarded Children.
OH Jur. 3d Family Law § 1553, Adults Charged With Violating Juvenile Court Law.
OH Jur. 3d Family Law § 1555, Generally—Adult Misdemeanors Affecting Children.
OH Jur. 3d Family Law § 1557, on Certification from Common Pleas.
OH Jur. 3d Family Law § 1558, on Certification from Common Pleas—After Termination of Marriage.
OH Jur. 3d Family Law § 1565, Order of Transfer; Resumption of Jurisdiction by Juvenile Court.
OH Jur. 3d Family Law § 1571, Apprehension—Release on Bail.
OH Jur. 3d Family Law § 1590, Who May File Complaint.
OH Jur. 3d Family Law § 1624, Waiver of Child's Rights; Double Jeopardy.
OH Jur. 3d Family Law § 1662, on Request for Permanent Custody.
OH Jur. 3d Family Law § 1693, Permanent Custody.
OH Jur. 3d Family Law § 1704, Effect on Court's Jurisdiction of Child's Commitment to Public Agency.
OH Jur. 3d Family Law § 1709, Revocation of Probation on Hearing—Detention During Proceeding.
OH Jur. 3d Family Law § 1735, Adult Acts Punishable in Juvenile Court.
OH Jur. 3d Family Law § 1736, Adult Acts Punishable in Juvenile Court—Failure to Report Child Abuse.
OH Jur. 3d Family Law § 1737, Adult Acts Punishable in Juvenile Court—Failure to Follow Procedures for Fingerprinting and Photographing Children Involved in Crimes.
OH Jur. 3d Family Law § 1739, Commencement of Proceedings.
OH Jur. 3d Habeas Corpus & Post Convict. Remedies § 40, Jurisdiction, Generally.

Forms

Ohio Forms Legal and Business § 28:43, Introduction.
Ohio Jurisprudence Pleading and Practice Forms § 2:8, Courts of Common Pleas—Juvenile Division.
Ohio Jurisprudence Pleading and Practice Forms § 111:36, Support Obligee—Notify Court of Any Changes.

Treatises and Practice Aids

Katz, Giannelli, Blair and Lipton, Baldwin's Ohio Practice, Criminal Law, § 91:6, Infancy.
Katz, Giannelli, Blair and Lipton, Baldwin's Ohio Practice, Criminal Law, § 128:1, Introduction.
Katz, Giannelli, Blair and Lipton, Baldwin's Ohio Practice, Criminal Law, § 109:10, Nonsupport.
Katz, Giannelli, Blair and Lipton, Baldwin's Ohio Practice, Criminal Law, § 109:13, Interfering With Support Actions.
Sowald & Morganstern, Baldwin's Ohio Practice Domestic Relations Law § 3:8, Jurisdiction and Venue.
Sowald & Morganstern, Baldwin's Ohio Practice Domestic Relations Law § 15:1, Allocating Parental Rights.
Sowald & Morganstern, Baldwin's Ohio Practice Domestic Relations Law § 17:2, UCCJA—Applicability.
Sowald & Morganstern, Baldwin's Ohio Practice Domestic Relations Law § 19:2, Jurisdiction Over Child Support.
Sowald & Morganstern, Baldwin's Ohio Practice Domestic Relations Law § 21:3, Parenting Time—Jurisdiction—in General.
Sowald & Morganstern, Baldwin's Ohio Practice Domestic Relations Law § 22:6, Establishing Parentage—Rescission After Final Acknowledgment.
Sowald & Morganstern, Baldwin's Ohio Practice Domestic Relations Law § 3:13, Judicial Parentage Action—Presumptions of Parentage—Creating.
Sowald & Morganstern, Baldwin's Ohio Practice Domestic Relations Law § 3:39, Effect of Judgment—Child Support—Other Remedies.
Sowald & Morganstern, Baldwin's Ohio Practice Domestic Relations Law § 3:59, Complaint for Custody, Support, and Visitation—Form.
Sowald & Morganstern, Baldwin's Ohio Practice Domestic Relations Law § 7:19, Relief Incident to Annulment—Children of an Annulled Marriage—Child Support and Custody.
Sowald & Morganstern, Baldwin's Ohio Practice Domestic Relations Law § 15:52, Award to Third Party—by the Court.
Sowald & Morganstern, Baldwin's Ohio Practice Domestic Relations Law § 15:72, Custody in Juvenile Court Proceedings.
Sowald & Morganstern, Baldwin's Ohio Practice Domestic Relations Law § 17:15, UCCJA—Registration of Custody Decrees and Enforcement.
Sowald & Morganstern, Baldwin's Ohio Practice Domestic Relations Law § 21:31, Habeas Corpus.
Sowald & Morganstern, Baldwin's Ohio Practice Domestic Relations Law § 23:27, Uifsa—in General.
Sowald & Morganstern, Baldwin's Ohio Practice Domestic Relations Law § 27:32, Jurisdiction Over Children.
Sowald & Morganstern, Baldwin's Ohio Practice Domestic Relations Law § 3:38.50, Effect of Judgment--Child Support--Past Care--Claim Brought After Child is Emancipated.
Carlin, Baldwin's Ohio Practice, Merrick-Rippner Probate Law § 3:5, Jurisdiction of Probate Court—Subject Matter—Specific Areas—Fiduciaries.
Carlin, Baldwin's Ohio Practice, Merrick-Rippner Probate Law § 19:2, Legitimation—Procedure—Acknowledgment of Paternity.
Carlin, Baldwin's Ohio Practice, Merrick-Rippner Probate Law § 19:6, Uniform Parentage Act—Jurisdiction of Action to Determine Father-Child Relationship.
Carlin, Baldwin's Ohio Practice, Merrick-Rippner Probate Law § 98:3, Adoption—Jurisdiction.
Carlin, Baldwin's Ohio Practice, Merrick-Rippner Probate Law § 105:1, Juvenile Court—Exclusive Original Jurisdiction.
Carlin, Baldwin's Ohio Practice, Merrick-Rippner Probate Law § 105:2, Juvenile Court—Original Jurisdiction.
Carlin, Baldwin's Ohio Practice, Merrick-Rippner Probate Law § 105:3, Juvenile Court—Divorce or Alimony Involving Care or Custody of Children.
Carlin, Baldwin's Ohio Practice, Merrick-Rippner Probate Law § 105:4, Juvenile Court—Custody and Support of Children: Certified from Common Pleas Court.
Carlin, Baldwin's Ohio Practice, Merrick-Rippner Probate Law § 105:5, Juvenile Court—Case Certified by Court of Competent Jurisdiction.
Carlin, Baldwin's Ohio Practice, Merrick-Rippner Probate Law § 105:6, Juvenile Court—Probate Powers.
Carlin, Baldwin's Ohio Practice, Merrick-Rippner Probate Law § 105:7, Juvenile Court—Attachment of Jurisdiction.
Carlin, Baldwin's Ohio Practice, Merrick-Rippner Probate Law § 105:8, Juvenile Court—Age Jurisdiction.
Carlin, Baldwin's Ohio Practice, Merrick-Rippner Probate Law § 105:9, Juvenile Court—Waiver of Jurisdiction.
Carlin, Baldwin's Ohio Practice, Merrick-Rippner Probate Law § 107:2, Types of Complaints.
Carlin, Baldwin's Ohio Practice, Merrick-Rippner Probate Law § 108:1, Juvenile Court—Criminal Jurisdiction.
Carlin, Baldwin's Ohio Practice, Merrick-Rippner Probate Law § 108:2, Juvenile Court—Criminal Jurisdiction—Contributing to Dependency, Neglect, Unruliness, or Delinquency.
Carlin, Baldwin's Ohio Practice, Merrick-Rippner Probate Law § 108:3, Juvenile Court—Criminal Jurisdiction—Proceedings for Nonsupport.
Carlin, Baldwin's Ohio Practice, Merrick-Rippner Probate Law § 62:59, Appointment of Guardian of a Minor—Custody Issues—Termination.

Carlin, Baldwin's Ohio Practice, Merrick-Rippner Probate Law § 101:22, Judicial Hospitalization—Jurisdiction—Noncriminal Cases.

Carlin, Baldwin's Ohio Practice, Merrick-Rippner Probate Law § 105:10, Juvenile Court—Duration and Termination of Jurisdiction.

Carlin, Baldwin's Ohio Practice, Merrick-Rippner Probate Law § 105:11, Juvenile Court—Certification from Common Pleas Court.

Carlin, Baldwin's Ohio Practice, Merrick-Rippner Probate Law § 105:13, Juvenile Court—Authority Following Certification.

Carlin, Baldwin's Ohio Practice, Merrick-Rippner Probate Law § 105:14, Juvenile Court—Jurisdiction Over the Enforcement of Child Support Orders.

Carlin, Baldwin's Ohio Practice, Merrick-Rippner Probate Law § 106:19, Juvenile Court Jurisdiction—Mentally Ill or Mentally Retarded Child.

Carlin, Baldwin's Ohio Practice, Merrick-Rippner Probate Law § 107:88, Adult Sentence for Juvenile.

Carlin, Baldwin's Ohio Practice, Merrick-Rippner Probate Law § 108:13, Juvenile Court—Jurisdiction Over Child Custody Matters—Determination of Custody.

Carlin, Baldwin's Ohio Practice, Merrick-Rippner Probate Law § 108:14, Juvenile Court—Modification of Decree Allocating Parental Rights and Responsibilities for Care of Children.

Carlin, Baldwin's Ohio Practice, Merrick-Rippner Probate Law § 108:15, Juvenile Court—Visitation Right of Noncustodial Parent and Others.

Carlin, Baldwin's Ohio Practice, Merrick-Rippner Probate Law § 108:16, Juvenile Court—Habeas Corpus Involving Child Custody.

Carlin, Baldwin's Ohio Practice, Merrick-Rippner Probate Law § 108:17, Juvenile Court—Uniform Child Custody Jurisdiction Act.

Carlin, Baldwin's Ohio Practice, Merrick-Rippner Probate Law § 108:20, Juvenile Court—Parentage Act—Jurisdiction and Venue.

Carlin, Baldwin's Ohio Practice, Merrick-Rippner Probate Law § 108:22, Juvenile Court—Parentage Act—Presumption of Paternity.

Carlin, Baldwin's Ohio Practice, Merrick-Rippner Probate Law § 108:23, Juvenile Court—Parentage Act—Parties in Parentage Action.

Carlin, Baldwin's Ohio Practice, Merrick-Rippner Probate Law § 108:26, Juvenile Court—Parentage Act—Applicability of Civil Rules to Paternity Proceedings.

Carlin, Baldwin's Ohio Practice, Merrick-Rippner Probate Law § 108:31, Juvenile Court—Parentage Act—Continuing Jurisdiction to Modify or Revoke Judgment.

Carlin, Baldwin's Ohio Practice, Merrick-Rippner Probate Law § 108:34, Juvenile Court—Civil Support Proceedings—Liability for Child Support.

Carlin, Baldwin's Ohio Practice, Merrick-Rippner Probate Law § 108:38, Juvenile Court—Civil Support Proceedings—Remedies for Failure to Comply With Support Order.

Carlin, Baldwin's Ohio Practice, Merrick-Rippner Probate Law § 108:41, Juvenile Court—Parental Responsibility—Destructive Acts of Children.

Carlin, Baldwin's Ohio Practice, Merrick-Rippner Probate Law § 107:117, Proceedings After Judgment—Continuing Jurisdiction of Juvenile Court.

Carlin, Baldwin's Ohio Practice, Merrick-Rippner Probate Law § 107:118, Modification of Dispositional Orders in Abuse, Neglect, and Dependency Proceedings.

Carlin, Baldwin's Ohio Practice, Merrick-Rippner Probate Law § 107:121, Custody Review Hearing—Revocation of Probation or Parole.

Carlin, Baldwin's Ohio Practice, Merrick-Rippner Probate Law § 107:133, Complaint for an Order of Support and for Custody—Form.

Carlin, Baldwin's Ohio Practice, Merrick-Rippner Probate Law § 107:134, Request for Support Order—Form.

Carlin, Baldwin's Ohio Practice, Merrick-Rippner Probate Law § 107:139, Motion to Certify Case to Juvenile Court—Form.

Carlin, Baldwin's Ohio Practice, Merrick-Rippner Probate Law § 107:140, Consent to Certification—Form.

Carlin, Baldwin's Ohio Practice, Merrick-Rippner Probate Law § 107:177, Order for Support and Custody—Form.

Hennenberg & Reinhart, Ohio Criminal Defense Motions F 15.12, Miscellaneous Motions-Petition for Writ of Habeas Corpus-Supplemental Memorandum-Single Judge Without Jurisdiction to Accept Plea in Capital Case.

Hennenberg & Reinhart, Ohio Criminal Defense Motions F 15.13, Supplemental Memorandum in Support of State Habeas Petition-Miscellaneous Motions.

Adrine & Ruden, Ohio Domestic Violence Law § 9:8, Relationships Covered—Parents and Children.

Adrine & Ruden, Ohio Domestic Violence Law § 14:5, Ohio's Legislative Response to Domestic Violence.

Adrine & Ruden, Ohio Domestic Violence Law § 12:11, Court Enforcement of Civil Protection Orders—Related Substantive Concerns.

Giannelli & Yeomans, Ohio Juvenile Law § 2:3, Child Subject to Adult Prosecution.

Giannelli & Yeomans, Ohio Juvenile Law § 3:2, Exclusive Original Jurisdiction.

Giannelli & Yeomans, Ohio Juvenile Law § 3:3, Concurrent Jurisdiction.

Giannelli & Yeomans, Ohio Juvenile Law § 9:3, Time of Neglect.

Giannelli & Yeomans, Ohio Juvenile Law § 9:5, Neglect—Abandonment.

Giannelli & Yeomans, Ohio Juvenile Law § 9:7, Neglect—Subsistence, Education & Medical Care.

Giannelli & Yeomans, Ohio Juvenile Law § 11:2, Jurisdiction for Custody Agreements.

Giannelli & Yeomans, Ohio Juvenile Law § 12:2, Jurisdictional Requirements.

Giannelli & Yeomans, Ohio Juvenile Law § 13:2, Jurisdictional Requirements.

Giannelli & Yeomans, Ohio Juvenile Law § 15:6, Family & Children First Council—Dispute Resolution Process.

Giannelli & Yeomans, Ohio Juvenile Law § 19:7, Time Requirements.

Giannelli & Yeomans, Ohio Juvenile Law § 22:4, Improper Transfer; Lack of Jurisdiction.

Giannelli & Yeomans, Ohio Juvenile Law § 32:2, Jurisdiction Over Parents and Others.

Giannelli & Yeomans, Ohio Juvenile Law § 34:4, Final Order Requirement.

Giannelli & Yeomans, Ohio Juvenile Law § 35:4, Expungement and Sealing.

Giannelli & Yeomans, Ohio Juvenile Law § 9:16, Abused Child—Physical or Mental Injury Due to Parents.

Giannelli & Yeomans, Ohio Juvenile Law § 16:13, Custody Proceedings; Required Information.

Giannelli & Yeomans, Ohio Juvenile Law § 16:15, Certification or Transfer from Another Court.

Giannelli & Yeomans, Ohio Juvenile Law § 16:17, Objections to Complaints.

Giannelli & Yeomans, Ohio Juvenile Law § 27:18, "Catch-All" Provision.

Giannelli & Yeomans, Ohio Juvenile Law § 30:11, Permanent Custody—"Best Interest" Factors.

Giannelli & Yeomans, Ohio Juvenile Law § 34:11, Effect on Further Juvenile Court Proceedings.

Giannelli & Yeomans, Ohio Juvenile Law § 34:12, Habeas Corpus.

Gotherman, Babbit and Lang, Baldwin's Ohio Practice, Local Government Law—Municipal, § 27:5, Courts Having Jurisdiction Over Municipal Offenses.

Law Review and Journal Commentaries

The Custody Contest Between a Parent and a Nonparent, Don C. Bolsinger. 2 Domestic Rel J Ohio 51 (July/August 1990).

Jurisdiction Under Ohio's Uniform Child Custody Jurisdiction Act, Pamela J. MacAdams. 3 Domestic Rel J Ohio 125 (September/October 1991).

Keeping Kids Out of Court. (Ed. note: Arbitration of custody disputes, but courts reserve the right to review awards.) 19 Nat'l L J B8 (May 5, 1997).

The Law of Adoption in Ohio, Beverly E. Sylvester. 2 Cap U L Rev 23 (1973).

Legal implications of drug use during pregnancy, William A. Kurtz. 1 Prob L J Ohio 66 (January/February 1991).

Navigating Between Scylla and Charybdis: Ohio's Efforts to Protect Children Without Eviscerating the Rights of Criminal Defendants–Evidentiary Considerations and the Rebirth of Confrontation Clause Analysis in Child Abuse Cases, Myrna S. Raeder. 25 U Tol L Rev 43 (1994).

The Relevance of Psychological and Psychiatric Studies to the Future Development of the Laws Governing the Settlement of Inter-parental Child Custody Disputes, Adrian Bradbrook. 11 J Fam L 557 (1972).

A Surrogacy Agreement that Could Have and Should Have Been Enforced: *R.R. v. M.H.*, 689 N.E.2d 790 (Mass. 1998), Note. 24 U Dayton L Rev 513 (Spring 1999).

Notes of Decisions

Adoption proceeding, effect   18
Age of child   11
Commitment   14
Concurrent jurisdiction   15
Constitutional issues   1
Criminal charges against adults   7
Custody   4
Delinquent   17
Dependent, defined   3
Divorce   12
Exclusive original jurisdiction   2
Foreign order   16
Liability of government officials   19
Medical treatment   13
Mentally ill or retarded child   6
Paternity   8
Procedural issues   10
Support orders   9
Writ of habeas corpus   5

---

1. Constitutional issues

Statutory provisions requiring reunification plans in cases of dependency, neglect and abuse involving a state agency, but not in private custody cases, did not implicate due process and equal protection rights of parents who voluntarily relinquished custody of their child to custodian, where private custody proceedings did not implicate potential for institutional indifference or need to reduce inattentiveness and inaction on part of state child welfare agencies toward children in their custody, and proceedings instituted by state to terminate or limit parental rights and cases in which parents forfeited their parental rights did not involve persons similarly situated. In re Bailey (Ohio App. 1 Dist., Hamilton, 06-17-2005) No. C-040014, No. C-040479, 2005-Ohio-3039, 2005 WL 1413269, Unreported, appeal not allowed 107 Ohio St.3d 1423, 837 N.E.2d 1208, 2005-Ohio-6124. Constitutional Law ⟐ 274(5)

Trial court did not abuse its discretion by finding mother to be unsuitable custodian for children, and thus award of custody to maternal grandmother did not violate mother's constitutional interest in the custody of her children; evidence established that grandmother was primary caregiver for two years prior to filing petition for custody, mother was bi-polar and had obsessive compulsive disorder, mother frequently changed residences and was unemployed for over a year and a half until shortly before hearing on grandmother's petition, and mother married a man she soon discovered was abusive and unsafe to be around the children. In re Hamblett (Ohio App. 3 Dist., Van, 02-14-2005) No. 15-04-11, No. 15-04-12, 2005-Ohio-550, 2005 WL 334451, Unreported. Child Custody ⟐ 279

Mother did not have constitutional right to effective assistance of counsel in proceeding between mother and grandmother for custody of mother's two children, even though custody proceeding arose from dependency action filed by Children's Services Board, where Board had terminated its protective supervision involvement in case. In re Mahley (Ohio App. 5 Dist., Guernsey, 04-05-2004) No. 03 CA 23, 2004-Ohio-1772, 2004 WL 740003, Unreported. Child Custody ⟐ 500; Infants ⟐ 232

Trying defendant as an adult for an offense which he allegedly committed while still a juvenile did not violate constitutional guarantee of fundamental fairness. State v. Schaar (Ohio App. 5 Dist., Stark, 03-30-2004) No. 2003CA00129, 2004-Ohio-1631, 2004 WL 626815, Unreported. Infants ⟐ 68.5

Statute governing custody determinations arising out of divorce action was inapplicable, and trial court appropriately considered statutory requirements for other custody determinations in deciding to modify custody of nonmarital child, which had originally been awarded to maternal grandparents, in favor of biological father; since original placement father had married, obtained employment, cleared support arrearage, and attended parenting and anger classes, trial court considered such factors sufficient changes in circumstances to warrant custody reconsideration, and trial court was bound by Constitutional imperatives preferring natural parent in raising of child absent certain factors. In re Hollowell (Ohio App. 5 Dist., Stark, 11-18-2002) No. 2002CA00127, 2002-Ohio-6405, 2002 WL 31649171, Unreported. Children Out-of-wedlock ⟐ 20.10

Juvenile court's continued exercise of jurisdiction over juvenile regarding his parole violation in delinquency matter, when the parole violation was committed by juvenile when he was 19, was not an act of discrimination treating juvenile differently from other adults, but, rather, an act recognizing juvenile's ongoing status as a juvenile; pursuant to statute, juvenile court retained jurisdiction over the juvenile, who was adjudicated delinquent prior to age of 18, until he turned 21. In re Gillespie (Ohio App. 10 Dist., 12-19-2002) 150 Ohio App.3d 502, 782 N.E.2d 140, 2002-Ohio-7025, appeal not allowed 98 Ohio St.3d 1513, 786 N.E.2d 63, 2003-Ohio-1572. Infants ⟐ 281

Juvenile court's continued exercise of jurisdiction over juvenile in delinquency matter, after juvenile committed parole violation when he was 19 years old, did not arbitrarily or capriciously deny juvenile's right to bail in violation of due process, although common pleas court had released juvenile on bail on the adult charges underlying parole violation while juvenile court revoked juvenile's parole and returned him to custody; common pleas court's exercise of power over juvenile with respect to adult charges did not eviscerate juvenile court's coexisting power to hold juvenile pursuant to his parole violation, and juvenile had no absolute constitutional right to bail as a juvenile. In re Gillespie (Ohio App. 10 Dist., 12-19-2002) 150 Ohio App.3d 502, 782 N.E.2d 140, 2002-Ohio-7025, appeal not allowed 98 Ohio St.3d 1513, 786 N.E.2d 63, 2003-Ohio-1572. Constitutional Law ⟐ 255(4); Infants ⟐ 281

Juvenile, who was adjudicated delinquent before the age of 18 and then committed parole violation at age 19, was not similarly situated to adults convicted of a crime, and thus juvenile court's decision to hold juvenile in custody pursuant to his parole violation, even though common pleas court had released juvenile on bail with respect to the adult criminal charges underlying the parole violation, did not violate equal protection guarantees. In re Gillespie (Ohio App. 10 Dist., 12-19-2002) 150 Ohio App.3d 502, 782 N.E.2d 140, 2002-Ohio-7025, appeal not allowed 98 Ohio St.3d 1513, 786 N.E.2d 63, 2003-Ohio-1572. Constitutional Law ⟐ 242.1(4); Infants ⟐ 281

Within the framework of the governing statutes, the overriding principle in custody cases between a parent and nonparent is that natural parents have a fundamental liberty interest in the care, custody, and management of their children; this interest is protected by the Due Process Clause of the Fourteenth Amendment to the United States Constitution and by Due Process Clause of Ohio Constitution. In re Hockstok (Ohio, 12-27-2002) 98 Ohio St.3d 238, 781 N.E.2d 971, 2002-Ohio-7208, modified 98 Ohio St.3d 1476, 784 N.E.2d 709, 2003-Ohio-980. Child Custody ⟐ 42; Constitutional Law ⟐ 274(5)

Statutory amendments that subjected a person 21 years of age or older to criminal prosecution, regardless of age at time of alleged offense and without any necessity of bindover proceeding in juvenile court, did not impair any vested rights of defendant who was 15 at time of charged aggravated murder and thus could constitutionally be retroactively applied to him; even under law in effect at time of offense, defendant was subject to criminal prosecution if juvenile court made certain determinations, and amendments merely removed procedural prerequisite of a juvenile-court proceeding. State v. Walls (Ohio, 10-09-2002) 96 Ohio St.3d 437, 775 N.E.2d 829, 2002-Ohio-5059, reconsideration denied 97 Ohio St.3d 1461, 778 N.E.2d 1052, 2002-Ohio-6248, habeas corpus denied 2006 WL 293750. Constitutional Law ⟐ 190; Infants ⟐ 152

As retroactively applied to defendant who was 15 years old at time of charged aggravated murder, statutory amendments that subjected a person 21 years of age or older to criminal prosecution in general division of court of common pleas, regardless of age at time of alleged offense and without any necessity of a bindover proceeding in juvenile court, did not retroactively criminalize defendant's conduct so as to violate Ex Post Facto Clause. State v. Walls (Ohio, 10-09-2002) 96 Ohio St.3d 437, 775 N.E.2d 829, 2002-Ohio-5059, reconsideration denied 97 Ohio St.3d 1461, 778 N.E.2d 1052, 2002-Ohio-6248, habeas corpus denied 2006 WL 293750. Constitutional Law ⟐ 200; Infants ⟐ 152

For ex post facto purposes, application to 29-year-old defendant, who was 15 at time of charged aggravated murder, of statute that subjected a person 21 years of age or older to criminal prosecution in general division of court of common pleas, regardless of age at time of alleged offense and without any necessity of a bindover proceeding in juvenile court, did not increase defendant's available punishment in any manner other than a speculative and attenuated one; even applying the law in effect at time of alleged offense, juvenile court would have had virtually no discretion to retain jurisdiction in defendant's case because of his mature age. State v. Walls (Ohio, 10-09-2002) 96 Ohio St.3d 437, 775 N.E.2d 829, 2002-Ohio-

5059, reconsideration denied 97 Ohio St.3d 1461, 778 N.E.2d 1052, 2002-Ohio-6248, habeas corpus denied 2006 WL 293750. Constitutional Law ⇐ 203; Infants ⇐ 152

General Assembly expressly intended that statutory amendments effectively removing anyone over 21 years of age at time of apprehension from the jurisdiction of juvenile court, regardless of date on which the person allegedly committed the offense, have retroactive application. State v. Walls (Ohio, 10-09-2002) 96 Ohio St.3d 437, 775 N.E.2d 829, 2002-Ohio-5059, reconsideration denied 97 Ohio St.3d 1461, 778 N.E.2d 1052, 2002-Ohio-6248, habeas corpus denied 2006 WL 293750. Infants ⇐ 132

Father in custody dispute with children's maternal uncle, which fell within statute allowing award of custody to relative other than parent when in best interest of child, was not similarly situated to parent involved in custody dispute under statute establishing jurisdiction of juvenile courts over various matters, which required explicit finding of unsuitability before awarding custody to any nonparent, as opposed to only relatives, and father's right to equal protection of law was therefore not violated by lack of explicit finding of unsuitability in connection with award of custody to maternal uncle. Baker v. Baker (Ohio App. 9 Dist., 08-21-1996) 113 Ohio App.3d 805, 682 N.E.2d 661, appeal not allowed 77 Ohio St.3d 1525, 674 N.E.2d 376. Constitutional Law ⇐ 225.1; Child Custody ⇐ 42

Trial court did not abuse its discretion in ordering gag order in consolidated dependency and custody proceedings, involving child born to surrogate mother, even though public had interest in studying potential pitfalls of surrogacy contracts, and even though the trial judge was an elected official, and even though media had legitimate interests, where evidence showed that mother was engaged in a campaign to intensify media coverage of the custody dispute, unrebutted expert testimony of doctor was that intensive coverage of custody disputes is detrimental to children, and sensationalist tone of some media coverage indicated that there was a basis for believing that public access could psychologically harm the child. In re T.R. (Ohio 1990) 52 Ohio St.3d 6, 556 N.E.2d 439, certiorari denied 111 S.Ct. 386, 498 U.S. 958, 112 L.Ed.2d 396. Injunction ⇐ 94

Where a petition is filed which states a proper cause of action for a writ of habeas corpus, and there is no plain and adequate remedy in the ordinary course of the law, O Const Art IV, § 2 and O Const Art IV, § 3, respectively, require the Supreme Court and the court of appeals to exercise their original jurisdiction in habeas corpus; and in such a case, these courts cannot refuse to exercise that original jurisdiction under the doctrine of forum non conveniens. Hughes v. Scaffide (Ohio 1978) 53 Ohio St.2d 85, 372 N.E.2d 598, 7 O.O.3d 175. Habeas Corpus ⇐ 613

Delinquency proceedings in juvenile court do not require indictment or trial by jury under US Const Am 5, US Const Am 6, and US Const Am 14 or under O Const Art I, § 5 and O Const Art I, § 10. In re Agler (Ohio 1969) 19 Ohio St.2d 70, 249 N.E.2d 808, 48 O.O.2d 85.

Where petitioner invokes the Full Faith and Credit Clause of US Const Art IV, § 1 in the US Supreme Court to challenge a state court's interpretation of the Uniform Child Custody Jurisdiction Act, but fails to raise the constitutional claim in the state courts, thus precluding the state supreme court from ruling on the federal issue, a writ of certiorari will be dismissed for want of jurisdiction. Webb v. Webb (U.S.Ga. 1981) 101 S.Ct. 1889, 451 U.S. 493, 68 L.Ed.2d 392.

Dissemination of social histories, compiled by probation officers in connection with juvenile proceedings, to social and religious agencies did not violate any federal constitutional right of privacy. J. P. v. DeSanti (C.A.6 (Ohio) 1981) 653 F.2d 1080. Constitutional Law ⇐ 82(7); Infants ⇐ 133

2. Exclusive original jurisdiction

Municipal court lacked subject matter jurisdiction to prosecute defendant for contributing to unruliness or delinquency of child, under statute that conferred exclusive jurisdiction to juvenile court over prosecution of adult offenders charged with offense, and indictment did not include felony charges for conduct arising from same behavior. State v. King (Ohio App. 3 Dist., Van, 11-21-2005) No. 15-05-02, No. 15-05-03, 2005-Ohio-6174, 2005 WL 3111939, Unreported. Infants ⇐ 18

Trial court had jurisdiction to adjudicate abuse complaint involving child who was deceased and had no siblings; child's status as an abuse victim had profound implications for the future of her family and the children within that family, and the technicality of child's death did not rob those children of the protection afforded them simply because child was an only child at the time of her death. In re Darling (Ohio App. 9 Dist., Wayne, 12-31-2003) No. 03CA0023, 2003-Ohio-7184, 2003 WL 23094930, Unreported. Infants ⇐ 196

Child became a ward of the Coshocton County Juvenile Court when that court granted legal custody of child to custodians and specifically retained jurisdiction, and thus, Tuscarawas County Juvenile Court lacked jurisdiction to rule on Tuscarawas County's motion for permanent custody of child. In re Frenz (Ohio App. 5 Dist., Tuscarawas, 07-10-2003) No. 2003AP030025, No. 2003AP040027, 2003-Ohio-3653, 2003 WL 21545125, Unreported, appeal not allowed 99 Ohio St.3d 1547, 795 N.E.2d 684, 2003-Ohio-4671. Infants ⇐ 196

Habeas corpus was not available as a remedy to mother seeking to challenge award of permanent custody of her three children to county, where juvenile court possessed the necessary basic jurisdiction to determine whether the children were dependent, mother possessed an adequate remedy at law through a direct appeal of custody order, and mother failed to cite any extreme circumstances which would require issuance of a habeas writ. C.F. v. Cuyahoga County Dept. of Human/Childrens's Service (Ohio App. 8 Dist., Cuyahoga, 01-27-2003) No. 81886, 2003-Ohio-439, 2003 WL 194895, Unreported. Habeas Corpus ⇐ 280

Jurisdiction of juvenile court is fixed generally by this section which pertains particularly to dependency and delinquency actions; "The Juvenile Court shall have jurisdiction to proceed therein as in original cases," has reference to cases involving custody and support of minor children growing out of divorce actions, and has no application to this section. Metz v. Metz (Franklin 1934) 17 Ohio Law Abs. 531.

Juvenile courts have exclusive initial subject matter jurisdiction over any case involving a person alleged to be delinquent for having committed, when younger than 18 years of age, an act that would constitute a felony if committed by an adult. State v. Mock (Ohio Com.Pl., 09-26-2005) 136 Ohio Misc.2d 21, 846 N.E.2d 108, 2005-Ohio-7142. Infants ⇐ 196

Court of Common Pleas had subject matter jurisdiction to hear defendant's case, following his bind-over from juvenile division, as juvenile division, in its bind-over entry, specifically stated that it found probable cause and that defendant was 17 years of age at time of conduct charged, and juvenile division went on to explain factors it considered in making its determination that defendant was not amenable to care or rehabilitation in the juvenile system, in compliance with provisions of statute and rule governing transfer of cases from juvenile court. State v. Mock (Ohio Com.Pl., 09-26-2005) 136 Ohio Misc.2d 21, 846 N.E.2d 108, 2005-Ohio-7142. Infants ⇐ 68.7(4)

The juvenile court had jurisdiction to determine whether a petition for shared custody was in the best interests of the children, where an unmarried mother was living with a same-sex partner. In re Bonfield (Ohio, 08-28-2002) 96 Ohio St.3d 218, 773 N.E.2d 507, 2002-Ohio-4182, opinion superseded on reconsideration 97 Ohio St.3d 387, 780 N.E.2d 241, 2002-Ohio-6660. Child Custody ⇐ 404

The juvenile court has jurisdiction to determine the custody of any child not a ward of another court, even though the court has not first found the child to be delinquent, neglected, or dependent. In re Bonfield (Ohio, 08-28-2002) 96 Ohio St.3d 218, 773 N.E.2d 507, 2002-Ohio-4182, opinion superseded on reconsideration 97 Ohio St.3d 387, 780 N.E.2d 241, 2002-Ohio-6660. Child Custody ⇐ 404

Juvenile court had subject matter jurisdiction over juvenile delinquency proceeding in which complaint alleged juvenile appellant to be a delinquent child. In re Burton S. (Ohio App. 6 Dist., 12-17-1999) 136 Ohio App.3d 386, 736 N.E.2d 928. Infants ⇐ 196

Juvenile courts have exclusive initial subject-matter jurisdiction over any case involving person alleged to be delinquent for having committed, when younger than 18 years of age, act which would constitute felony if committed by adult. State v. Golphin (Ohio, 04-29-1998) 81 Ohio St.3d 543, 692 N.E.2d 608, 1998-Ohio-336. Infants ⇐ 68.5

Existence of juvenile court and scope of its jurisdiction are subject to authority and discretion of General Assembly. In re Writ of Habeas Corpus for Baker (Ohio App. 10 Dist., 12-05-1996) 116 Ohio App.3d 580, 688 N.E.2d 1068, cause dismissed 78 Ohio St.3d 1443, 677 N.E.2d 354. Courts ⇐ 175

Court of common pleas has jurisdiction to determine paternity of child born out of wedlock in conjunction with wrongful death claim; juvenile court's jurisdiction over such issues is not exclusive. Brookbank v. Gray (Ohio, 01-17-1996) 74 Ohio St.3d 279, 658 N.E.2d 724, 1996-Ohio-135. Children Out-of-wedlock ⇐ 36; Courts ⇐ 472.1

Court of common pleas lacked subject matter jurisdiction to convict 17-year-old defendant of grand theft and, thus, judgment of conviction against him was void ab initio; since defendant was child under statute and was never bound over by juvenile court, juvenile court retained exclusive jurisdiction over defendant's case. State v. Wilson (Ohio, 08-09-1995) 73 Ohio St.3d 40, 652 N.E.2d 196, 1995-Ohio-217. Infants ⇐ 68.5

Exclusive subject matter jurisdiction of juvenile court cannot be waived; abrogating *Tillman*, 585 N.E.2d 550, 66 Ohio App.3d 464. State v. Wilson (Ohio, 08-09-1995) 73 Ohio St.3d 40, 652 N.E.2d 196, 1995-Ohio-217. Infants ⇐ 68.5

Common pleas court of which children were wards had jurisdiction to adjudicate complaint in neglect and dependency, even though parents and their children resided in another county when complaint was filed. In re Meyer (Ohio App. 3 Dist., 10-25-1994) 98 Ohio App.3d 189, 648 N.E.2d 52, corrected. Infants ⇐ 196

Juvenile court had exclusive jurisdiction over children once complaints which alleged that they were dependent, neglected and abused children were filed. In re Doe Children (Ohio App. 6 Dist., 02-11-1994) 93 Ohio App.3d 134, 637 N.E.2d 977, cause dismissed 69 Ohio St.3d 1481, 634 N.E.2d 1027. Infants ⇐ 196

Under statute limiting juvenile court's jurisdiction to those matters "duly certified," default in the certification process may preclude juvenile court's subject matter jurisdiction over child custody case. In re Whaley (Athens 1993) 86 Ohio App.3d 304, 620 N.E.2d 954. Courts ⇐ 487(1)

Trial court properly exercised in personam jurisdiction over nonresident mother by virtue of her tortious failure to support her two minor children residing in Ohio. Wayne Cty. Bur. of Support v. Wolfe (Wayne 1991) 71 Ohio App.3d 765, 595 N.E.2d 421. Courts ⇐ 12(2.25)

Once a probate court terminates a guardianship, the subject of the terminated guardianship ceases to be a ward of the court and the juvenile court then has exclusive jurisdiction to determine custody of the minor. In re Guardianship of Harrison (Hamilton 1989) 60 Ohio App.3d 19, 572 N.E.2d 855, motion overruled 47 Ohio St.3d 708, 547 N.E.2d 992. Courts ⇐ 472.1; Guardian And Ward ⇐ 25

While juvenile court entered order granting temporary custody of minor child to county welfare department of social services upon adjudging minor child to be dependent child, when juvenile court terminated order and returned minor child to mother, jurisdiction of juvenile court ceased, so that when grandmother of minor child applied to probate court to become child's guardian, probate court acquired exclusive jurisdiction over ward and guardian, and juvenile court was without jurisdiction to grant custody over ward to another person until guardianship had been terminated. In re Miller (Cuyahoga 1986) 33 Ohio App.3d 224, 515 N.E.2d 635. Courts ⇐ 475(6)

In exercising its jurisdiction under RC 2151.23(A)(2) to determine custody of children, a juvenile court must rely on the standards in RC 3109.04. In re Brazell (Ohio Com.Pl. 1986) 27 Ohio Misc.2d 7, 499 N.E.2d 925, 27 O.B.R. 68.

A juvenile court which obtains jurisdiction over and enters orders regarding the custody and support of children retains continuing and exclusive jurisdiction over such matters, and its attempted transfer of jurisdiction to a domestic relations court is a nullity. Hardesty v. Hardesty (Franklin 1984) 16 Ohio App.3d 56, 474 N.E.2d 368, 16 O.B.R. 59. Courts ⇐ 475(1)

The juvenile court has exclusive original jurisdiction, pursuant to RC 2151.23(A), concerning any child who is alleged in a proper complaint to be neglected, and the court does not lose jurisdiction by failing to adhere to the time limits set forth in Juv R 29(A) and Juv R 34(A). Linger v. Weiss (Ohio 1979) 57 Ohio St.2d 97, 386 N.E.2d 1354, 11 O.O.3d 281, certiorari denied 100 S.Ct. 128, 444 U.S. 862, 62 L.Ed.2d 83.

Under RC 2151.23(A), the juvenile court has exclusive original jurisdiction in applications for a writ of habeas corpus involving custody of a child and is thereby empowered to determine custody in such proceeding. In re Wright (Ohio Com.Pl. 1977) 52 Ohio Misc. 4, 367 N.E.2d 931, 6 O.O.3d 31.

The physical presence of a child within the geography of the court empowers the juvenile court to determine its custody, provided it is not a ward of another court. In re Wolfe (Ohio Juv. 1962) 187 N.E.2d 658, 91 Ohio Law Abs. 167, 26 O.O.2d 274.

RC 2151.23 excludes action by any other court not explicitly given jurisdiction. Hartshorne v. Hartshorne (Columbiana 1959) 185 N.E.2d 329, 89 Ohio Law Abs. 243.

The juvenile court of the county in which acts constituting neglect or dependency of a minor child occur has jurisdiction over complaints concerning such child whether or not the parent or minor child was a nonresident of such county. In re Belk (Crawford 1954) 97 Ohio App. 114, 123 N.E.2d 757, 55 O.O. 330. Infants ⇐ 196

The juvenile court is invested with original jurisdiction to determine the custody of any child not a ward of another court, and in order to determine such right of custody, it is not necessary for the court to find first that such child is delinquent, neglected, dependent, crippled, or otherwise physically handicapped. In re Torok (Ohio 1954) 161 Ohio St. 585, 120 N.E.2d 307, 53 O.O. 433.

The juvenile court is given original jurisdiction in a proper proceeding to determine the right of custody of any child where such child is not a ward of another court, and it is not necessary in the exercise of such jurisdiction that the juvenile court first determine that such child is a dependent, neglected or delinquent child. In re Lorok (Cuyahoga 1952) 93 Ohio App. 251, 114 N.E.2d 65, 51 O.O. 10. Child Custody ⇐ 920

This section, relative to jurisdiction of probate court to determine custody of minors, is a grant, and not a limitation, of jurisdiction. McFadden v. Kendall (Auglaize 1946) 81 Ohio App. 107, 77 N.E.2d 625, 36 O.O. 414. Child Custody ⇐ 920

Juvenile court was not deprived of jurisdiction, based on existence of previously pending divorce case, over complaint alleging that children were abused, neglected, and dependent, as juvenile court had exclusive original jurisdiction over any child alleged to be abused, neglected, or dependent, and court had exclusive original jurisdiction to determine custody of child not a ward of another court in state. In re Kimble (Ohio App. 7 Dist., Harrison, 05-15-2002) No. 99 517 CA, 2002-Ohio-2409, 2002 WL 1065977, Unreported. Infants ⇐ 196

Pursuant to RC 2151.23(A), the Probate and Juvenile Division of the Muskingum County Court of Common Pleas has exclusive original jurisdiction to issue orders of support in cases brought under RC 2151.27 to RC 2151.331, including orders complying with RC 2151.33(B)(2)(a). The language of RC 2301.03(AA) establishing the powers and duties of the judge of the Domestic Relations Division of the Muskingum County Court of Common Pleas does not modify or restrict the exclusive original jurisdiction of the juvenile court in this regard. OAG 05–003.

When a juvenile court terminates its jurisdiction over a child, said child immediately acquires a legal settlement in the county of residence of the parents, surviving parent, sole parent, parent having custody awarded by a court having jurisdiction, or guardian of the person of such minor. 1953 OAG 2656.

3. Dependent, defined

Statute pertaining to modification of custody awards has no application where parent is seeking to extinguish award of temporary custody to nonparent in order to re-establish custody of child. In re Custody of Carpenter (Greene 1987) 41 Ohio App.3d 182, 534 N.E.2d 1216. Child Custody ⇐ 550

Determination that child was neglected and award of custody to child's mother could not stand where trial court relied on evidence of father's past alcohol problems, other times child had been taken from father in other jurisdictions and father's hospitalization, but there was no testimony showing that any of those "faults" existed at date of complaint. In re Sims (Preble 1983) 13 Ohio App.3d 37, 468 N.E.2d 111, 13 O.B.R. 40. Infants ⇐ 177

The determination of whether or not a child is "dependent," as defined in RC 2151.04, must be made as of the time of the hearing on the complaint, and a determination that a child is not a "dependent child" at one time is no bar to a later determination that the child is then "dependent." In re Justice (Clinton 1978) 59 Ohio App.2d 78, 392 N.E.2d 897, 13 O.O.3d 139. Infants ⇐ 154.1; Infants ⇐ 281

The issue of whether a child is a dependent child is to be determined as of "on or about the date specified in the complaint," and need not be determined as of the time of the hearing. In re Baby Girl S. (Ohio Com.Pl. 1972) 32 Ohio Misc. 217, 290 N.E.2d 925, 61 O.O.2d 439.

Modification of order of common pleas court in divorce case, affecting custody of minor, cannot be accomplished by dependency proceeding in juvenile court to which divorce case is certified, unless dependency be charged and proven. Sonnenberg v. State (Franklin 1931) 40 Ohio App. 475, 178 N.E. 855, 10 Ohio Law Abs. 271. Child Custody ⇐ 609; Child Custody ⇐ 601

Common pleas court has, in a divorce action, complete jurisdiction over dependent children when jurisdiction of the juvenile court over "dependent" children has been terminated under GC 1639–35 (RC 2151.38), but common pleas court may, under GC 1639–16 (RC 2151.23), transfer said jurisdiction to the juvenile court. 1938 OAG 3356.

When a juvenile court acquires jurisdiction over a dependent child the jurisdiction continues until the child becomes twenty-one years of age; the county in which such court is situated is responsible for its support. 1937 OAG 891.

A juvenile court has jurisdiction to declare any child dependent which is found within the county under facts and circumstances constituting dependency; the legal residence of the child, its parents, or those standing in loco parentis does not determine the jurisdiction of the court. The county in which such court assumes jurisdiction and declares such child to be dependent will be responsible for the support of such child. (See also 1929 OAG 755). 1935 OAG 4172.

4. Custody

The best interest test, rather than the parental suitability test, applied to child custody modification proceeding involving father and maternal grandmother, where father, mother, and grandmother had previously entered into a shared parenting/joint custody agreement, the custody agreement was adopted by the court and constituted an original child custody determination, and father consented to the agreement. In re DeLucia v. West (Ohio App. 7 Dist., Mahoning, 12-21-2005) No. 05-MA-5, 2005-Ohio-6933, 2005 WL 3536486, Unreported. Child Custody ⇐ 571

Evidence was sufficient to support parental-unsuitability determination to sustain order granting foster parents legal custody of child; foster parents maintained working farm and provided home for four other foster children, as well as their own six children, foster mother held nursing degree, and, by time of termination proceedings, child was in second grade and participating in activities, whereas mother had not obtained high school diploma or equivalent certification, and, prior to moving to live with foster parents, child was five and one-half years of age, but was not toilet-trained, lacked daily living skills, and had an IQ in the well below average range. In re Fout (Ohio App. 5 Dist., Delaware, 08-19-2005) No. 04 CA-F 05036, 2005-Ohio-4344, 2005 WL 2002259, Unreported. Infants ⇐ 230.1

Domestic relations court lacked jurisdiction to determine custody and make custody orders in parties' divorce decree, where county initiated neglect proceedings in juvenile court regarding parties' minor child while divorce proceedings were pending, and juvenile court had exclusive original jurisdiction to determine custody of the child, including child support obligations and allocation of parental rights and responsibilities. Ryan v. Ryan (Ohio App. 8 Dist., Cuyahoga, 08-11-2005) No. 85506, 2005-Ohio-4166, 2005 WL 1926497, Unreported. Infants ⇐ 196

Deceased mother's surviving husband, to whom mother was married at time she gave birth to child, failed to establish that biological father, to whom court awarded custody on mother's death, was an unsuitable parent; biological father began having visitation with child when child was two years old and child knew who biological father was, biological father provided adequate care for child during visits, child had own bedroom at biological father's house and was exposed to his extended family, and biological father had steady and sufficient income and made adequate arrangements for child care in his absence. Lorence v. Goeller (Ohio App. 9 Dist., Lorain, 06-01-2005) No. CIV.A. 04CA008556, 2005-Ohio-2678, 2005 WL 1283713, Unreported. Children Out-of-wedlock ⇐ 20.3

Trial court that awarded custody of minor child to biological father rather than deceased mother's surviving husband, to whom mother was married at time she gave birth to child, applied proper standard in considering biological father's suitability as a parent, despite surviving husband's contention that court required a finding that placement with biological father would be "devastating" rather than merely "detrimental" to child; trial court repeatedly phrased its inquiry in terms of whether detriment to child warranted divesting biological father of his parental rights. Lorence v. Goeller (Ohio App. 9 Dist., Lorain, 06-01-2005) No. CIV.A. 04CA008556, 2005-Ohio-2678, 2005 WL 1283713, Unreported. Children Out-of-wedlock ⇐ 20.3

Evidence of mother's parental unsuitability was sufficient to support award of custody of child to child's paternal grandmother; mother coached child to report that child's father was sex offender and would commit offenses against child, mother's allegations of sexual abuse were unsubstantiated and were detrimental to child, child had significant knowledge of sexual behavior and terminology, counselor who opined that mother should have custody testified that his recommendation had been based solely on information received from mother, and other witnesses, including guardian ad litem, owner of day care center, and child's father were concerned for child's health while in mother's custody. In re Manweiler (Ohio App. 11 Dist., Ashtabula, 05-27-2005) No. 2003-A-0032, 2005-Ohio-2657, 2005 WL 1272227, Unreported. Child Custody ⇐ 279

Trial court abused its discretion by terminating mother's parental rights to her children and awarding custody of children to paternal grandparents, where there was no evidence to support trial court's finding that mother was incapable of caring for children, or that continued custody with mother would be detrimental to children, as would establish that mother was unsuitable parent. In re Keylor (Ohio App. 7 Dist., Monroe, 03-30-2005) No. 04 MO 02, 2005-Ohio-1661, 2005 WL 775890, Unreported, stay granted 106 Ohio St.3d 1410, 830 N.E.2d 344, 2005-Ohio-3154, appeal not allowed 106 Ohio St.3d 1506, 833 N.E.2d 1249, 2005-Ohio-4605. Infants ⇐ 222

Evidence supported juvenile court's decision to award custody of mother's three children to relatives; although mother completed her case plan and followed through with the services provided for her, mother's abuse of alcohol and drugs suggested that mother's progress was not permanent, and children's fathers and guardian ad litem recommended that relatives take custody of children. In re Joemiyde L. (Ohio App. 6 Dist., Lucas, 02-11-2005) No. L-04-1109, No. L-04-1110, 2005-Ohio-537, 2005 WL 327193, Unreported. Infants ⇐ 222

Trial court was required to consider whether shared parenting plan proposed by cohabiting, same sex partners was in the best interest of child, in light of evidence of benefits from having two caregivers, legally responsible for child's welfare, as well as evaluation conducted by clinical psychologist concluding that both partners were effective parents, committed to child's well being. In re J.D.M. (Ohio App. 12 Dist., Warren, 10-11-2004) No. CA2003-11-113, No. CA2004-04-035, No. CA2004-04-040, 2004-Ohio-5409, 2004 WL 2272063, Unreported. Children Out-of-wedlock ⇐ 20.3

In proceeding on petition of cohabiting, same sex partners for shared custody of child, trial court was required to make a conclusive finding as to who was child's mother and which partner was assuming parental rights. In re J.D.M. (Ohio App. 12 Dist., Warren, 10-11-2004) No. CA2003-11-113, No. CA2004-04-035, No. CA2004-04-040, 2004-Ohio-5409, 2004 WL 2272063, Unreported. Children Out-of-wedlock ⇐ 20.4

Lack of a present controversy between cohabiting, same sex partners was not an impediment to consideration of petition seeking entry of shared custody agreement for child. In re J.D.M. (Ohio App. 12 Dist., Warren, 10-11-2004) No. CA2003-11-113, No. CA2004-04-035, No. CA2004-04-040, 2004-Ohio-5409, 2004 WL 2272063, Unreported. Children Out-of-wedlock ⇐ 20.4

Juvenile court was required to determine that child's father, as the natural parent of child, was unsuitable to have custody of child before awarding legal custody to child's maternal aunt and uncle, in juvenile court case in which child's maternal aunt and uncle, her paternal grandmother, and her father all moved for legal custody after the County Department of Children and Family Services obtained emergency custody of child from child's mother. In re C.R. (Ohio App. 8 Dist., Cuyahoga, 08-26-2004) No. 82891, 2004-Ohio-4465, 2004 WL 1899219, Unreported, stay granted 104 Ohio St.3d 1443, 819 N.E.2d 1125, 2004-Ohio-7119, motion to certify allowed 105 Ohio St.3d 1436, 822 N.E.2d 809, 2005-Ohio-531, certified question answered 108 Ohio St.3d 369, 843 N.E.2d 1188, 2006-Ohio-1191, reconsideration denied 109 Ohio St.3d 1483, 847 N.E.2d 1227, 2006-Ohio-2466. Infants ⇐ 222

Even if trial court erred in child custody dispute between maternal grandmother and aunt and paternal uncle and aunt by applying statute governing modification of existing decree allocating parental rights and responsibilities, rather than statute applicable to custody disputes between nonparents, no prejudice resulted, where court ultimately addressed best interest of orphaned children and considered appropriate statutory factors. In re R.N. (Ohio App. 10 Dist., Franklin, 08-24-2004) No. 04AP-130, 2004-Ohio-4420, 2004 WL 1879061, Unreported. Child Custody ⇐ 923(1); Child Custody ⇐ 923(5)

Statutory "best interest of the child" standard, not *Perales* "parental suitability" standard, governed custody dispute between parent and nonparent, where case arose from complaint filed by children's services agency alleging that children were "dependent children," not from a private custody dispute. In re Trowbridge (Ohio App. 10 Dist., Franklin, 05-25-2004) No. 03AP-405, No. 03AP-406, 2004-Ohio-2645, 2004 WL 1152934, Unreported. Infants ⇐ 222

Statutory grant of exclusive original jurisdiction to juvenile court to determine "custody" did not give juvenile court subject matter jurisdiction over visitation cases and, therefore, juvenile court lacked subject matter jurisdiction of maternal grandmother's motion for visitation with grandchild, notwithstanding death of child's mother; presence of a "disrupting precipitating event" under *Gibson* in the form of mother's death went to merits of motion and not to jurisdiction. In re Burrows (Ohio App. 3 Dist., Seneca, 05-24-2004) No. 13-04-03, No. 13-04-04, 2004-Ohio-2619, 2004 WL 1147067, Unreported. Child Custody ⇐ 404

Evidence supported juvenile court's return to mother of legal custody of child in temporary placement with paternal great-grandmother pursuant to agreement for dismissal of child neglect charge; mother had ability to care for child's special needs, mother had extensive family support, mother had stable home, drug use was a problem in great-grandmother's home, and great-grandmother had not always ensured that child was tended as required. In re E. B. (Ohio App. 9 Dist., Summit, 05-05-2004) No. 21823, 2004-Ohio-2250, 2004 WL 950622, Unreported. Infants ⇐ 231

Finding of parental unsuitability or unfitness was required before trial court could award legal custody of mother's two children to children's grandmother, even though custody proceeding arose from dependency action filed by Children's Services Board, where Board had terminated its protective supervision involvement in case. In re Mahley (Ohio App. 5 Dist., Guernsey, 04-05-2004) No. 03 CA 23, 2004-Ohio-1772, 2004 WL 740003, Unreported. Child Custody ⟐ 279; Infants ⟐ 232

Trial court had jurisdiction in child custody proceedings to proceed on child's grandmother's motions to show cause and find child's mother in contempt of the prior court orders, despite fact that mother was not personally served with orders, where journal entry indicated that mother was present with her attorney at contempt hearing and waived service of process on motions to show cause which had been set for hearing. In re S.M. (Ohio App. 8 Dist., Cuyahoga, 03-18-2004) No. 81566, 2004-Ohio-1243, 2004 WL 527925, Unreported. Child Custody ⟐ 859

Trial court was not required to find that mother was unsuitable before awarding legal custody of her children to relatives, in child dependency proceeding; statute requiring a finding of parental unfitness before awarding custody to a nonparent applied to private custody matters between presumptively fit parents and nonparents, and mother's children had previously been adjudicated dependent. In re T. W. (Ohio App. 9 Dist., Summit, 12-31-2003) No. 21594, 2003-Ohio-7185, 2003 WL 23094939, Unreported. Infants ⟐ 222

Trial court decision to grant the county children services board's motion for legal custody of mother's four children and to deny mother's motion for a six-month extension of temporary custody was not against the manifest weight of the evidence; clinical psychologist testified that she did not believe that the children had been supervised by mother in the past, counselor testified that mother's attendance at drug and alcohol counseling was inconsistent and she had tested positive for marijuana, and caseworker testified that mother had a history of being homeless. In re T. W. (Ohio App. 9 Dist., Summit, 12-31-2003) No. 21594, 2003-Ohio-7185, 2003 WL 23094939, Unreported. Infants ⟐ 179

Trial court did not abuse its discretion in awarding custody of child to father, even though father had a history of mental illness, and drug and alcohol abuse, where father was medication-compliant, his court-ordered drug screen result was negative, and father's psychiatrist testified and reported no barriers to his ability to take care of child. Simmons v. Willett (Ohio App. 5 Dist., Morgan, 07-08-2003) No. 02 CA 8, 2003-Ohio-3677, 2003 WL 21569718, Unreported. Child Custody ⟐ 60; Child Custody ⟐ 62; Child Custody ⟐ 469

Trial court was not required to journalize case plan for minor children in its dispositional order granting legal custody of children to children's paternal grandparents rather than to mother, since court did not adjudicate children as abused, neglected, or dependent, and court presumably granted custody pursuant to statute governing custody disputes between parent and nonparent. Ives v. Ives (Ohio App. 9 Dist., Lorain, 07-02-2003) No. 02CA008176, 2003-Ohio-3505, 2003 WL 21508795, Unreported. Child Custody ⟐ 511

Credible and competent evidence existed to support trial court's finding that continued custody with mother would have been detrimental to minor children, as would support trial court's award of legal custody of children to children's paternal grandparents; evidence indicated that mother had repeated and violent outbursts, mother engaged in harassing and threatening behavior, mother threatened children's father, and one child was severely behind in immunizations. Ives v. Ives (Ohio App. 9 Dist., Lorain, 07-02-2003) No. 02CA008176, 2003-Ohio-3505, 2003 WL 21508795, Unreported. Child Custody ⟐ 473

Action between mother and paternal grandparents of minor children concerning legal custody of children fell within coverage of statute involving custody disputes between parent and non-parent, not statute governing custody determinations involving divorcing parties, and thus trial court was required to examine parental unsuitability before custody could be awarded to nonparent. Ives v. Ives (Ohio App. 9 Dist., Lorain, 07-02-2003) No. 02CA008176, 2003-Ohio-3505, 2003 WL 21508795, Unreported. Child Custody ⟐ 279

Minor children's paternal grandparents were not required to have been granted intervenor status in order to assert petition for legal custody of children, since any person had statutory right to file complaint regarding children who appeared to be abused, neglected, or dependent, and juvenile court had exclusive jurisdiction over dispute. Ives v. Ives (Ohio App. 9 Dist., Lorain, 07-02-2003) No. 02CA008176, 2003-Ohio-3505, 2003 WL 21508795, Unreported. Child Custody ⟐ 404; Child Custody ⟐ 409

Mother allowed trial court to acquire personal jurisdiction over her for permanent custody hearing, even though mother argued she was not properly served with notice of hearing, where mother voluntarily attended, and participated in, permanent custody hearing, and she raised no claim at that time that trial court lacked personal jurisdiction. In re B.B. (Ohio App. 9 Dist., Summit, 06-25-2003) No. 21447, 2003-Ohio-3314, 2003 WL 21459019, Unreported. Infants ⟐ 196

Evidence supported findings that mother contractually relinquished custody of minor child and that awarding custody to mother would be detrimental to child, and thus trial court did not abuse its discretion in determining that mother was unsuitable parent and awarding custody of child to paternal grandparents; except for a brief period when mother was primary caretaker, paternal grandparents or maternal grandmother had always been primary caretaker, mother voluntarily placed minor child in child's paternal grandparents' custody and intended for grandparents to raise child, mother consistently placed her own needs above those of child, mother's visitation of child was sporadic, and child wanted to continue to live with paternal grandparents. In re Galan (Ohio App. 3 Dist., Seneca, 03-19-2003) No. 13-02-44, 2003-Ohio-1298, 2003 WL 1239715, Unreported. Child Custody ⟐ 279

Trial court finding that mother was unsuitable to maintain custody of child, and grant of custody to maternal aunt, was not an abuse of discretion; father of child did not object to aunt maintaining custody of child, aunt and aunt's girlfriend testified that mother over-disciplined child, mother gave aunt temporary custody of child after she attempted suicide, and, after aunt retrieved child from mother following an incident of physical violence, mother did not file for custody or terminate the prior temporary custody agreement. In re Exline (Ohio App. 7 Dist., Columbiana, 02-26-2003) No. 02 CO 24, 2003-Ohio-929, 2003 WL 685520, Unreported. Child Custody ⟐ 271

Trial court had right to reach a final decision upon custody of parties' children, even though juvenile court also obtained custody jurisdiction post-divorce via county's filing of a dependency motion, where juvenile court subsequently abandoned its jurisdiction over the children. Bland v. Bland (Ohio App. 9 Dist., Summit, 02-26-2003) No. 21228, 2003-Ohio-828, 2003 WL 470180, Unreported. Child Custody ⟐ 404

Parental suitability, rather than best interest, applies as threshold determination in a proceeding for custody between a parent and nonparent; best interest standard is premised on idea that both parents in a divorce-related custody dispute are suitable, and thus, child's best interest becomes only relevant consideration in dispute between parents, which cannot be said in a dispute between a parent and a nonparent. In re Daily (Ohio App. 4 Dist., Athens, 02-12-2003) No. 02CA31, 2003-Ohio-787, 2003 WL 368105, Unreported. Child Custody ⟐ 42; Child Custody ⟐ 76

In evaluating great-grandmother's motion for custody of infant, in proceedings on county's complaint in dependency and neglect and motion for permanent custody, court was not required to have subject matter jurisdiction over infant's mother, a 15-year-old chronic run-away, whose parental rights as to infant had been terminated, to consider as part of the best interests evaluation the possible effects of fact that great-grandmother was also legal custodian of mother, including risk that mother would return and take the infant and flee. In re Tammy M. (Ohio App. 6 Dist., Lucas, 01-31-2003) No. L-02-1108, 2003-Ohio-492, 2003 WL 220596, Unreported. Infants ⟐ 222

Trial court properly found that mother was unsuitable and that detriment would occur to child if mother was to have custody, and thus child's maternal grandmother was entitled to be awarded residential and legal custody of child in grandmother's third-party action, although mother had clean, two-bedroom apartment and mother was gainfully employed full-time, since mother had not participated in any school conferences, mother had not met child's teacher, mother's relationship with child had deteriorated in six months prior to hearing, and mother had violated conditions of probation following release from jail. Creamer v. Stone (Ohio App. 5 Dist., Delaware, 12-18-2002) No. 02CA-F-08-039, 2002-Ohio-7047, 2002 WL 31837888, Unreported. Child Custody ⟐ 279

Juvenile court had subject matter jurisdiction over underlying action brought by father to allocate parental rights and responsibilities and obtain legal custody of his child, and also had authority to include prospective adoptive parents as parties in underlying action. Callahan v. Court of Common Pleas of Pickaway County (Ohio App. 4 Dist., Pickaway, 09-26-2002) No. 02CA4, 2002-Ohio-5418, 2002 WL 31248607, Unreported. Child Custody ⟐ 404; Child Custody ⟐ 409

Exclusion as the father through genetic testing constitutes clear and convincing evidence that overcomes the presumption of paternity created under RC 3111.03 and where the defendant is excluded as the father there is no minor issue of the marriage and RC 3109.04 no longer provides the court of common pleas with subject matter jurisdiction to make a ruling on custody; instead the issue of custody becomes subject matter exclusive to the juvenile court pursuant to RC 2151.23, and consequently, the "best interest of the child" standard in determining custody does not apply.

Thompson v. Thompson (Ohio App. 4 Dist., Highland, 08-10-1995) No. 94CA859, 1995 WL 481480, Unreported.

The juvenile court in Ohio does not have jurisdiction to determine custody of a child who lived in Virginia the past two years and is not physically present in Ohio during pendency of the action. Rupert v. Landis (Ohio App. 7 Dist., Jefferson, 03-22-1995) No. 93-J-27, 1995 WL 138911, Unreported.

Juvenile court lacked jurisdiction to grant custody of child to private child-placing agency, as juvenile court in another county had granted legal custody of child to county and retained jurisdiction, such that child became a ward of that court. Adoption Link, Inc. v. Suver (Ohio, 12-27-2006) 112 Ohio St.3d 166, 858 N.E.2d 424, 2006-Ohio-6528. Infants ⇐ 232

Action involving the permanent custody of child following a complaint alleging neglect is within the subject-matter jurisdiction of the juvenile court. In re J.J. (Ohio, 11-08-2006) 111 Ohio St.3d 205, 855 N.E.2d 851, 2006-Ohio-5484. Infants ⇐ 196

When a juvenile court adjudicates a child to be abused, neglected, or dependent, it has no duty to make a separate finding at the dispositional hearing that a noncustodial parent is unsuitable before awarding legal custody to a nonparent. In re C.R. (Ohio, 03-29-2006) 108 Ohio St.3d 369, 843 N.E.2d 1188, 2006-Ohio-1191, reconsideration denied 109 Ohio St.3d 1483, 847 N.E.2d 1227, 2006-Ohio-2466. Infants ⇐ 222

Evidence supported trial court's finding in custody proceeding that paternal grandmother had violated court order by not returning child to mother, and thus violation of order was evidence to support finding it was not in child's best interests for grandmother to have custody and that shared parenting arrangement between biological parents should be terminated; several periods of time existed that grandmother had physical custody in clear violation of the court order for child to be with mother. Vance v. Vance (Ohio App. 2 Dist., 01-24-2003) 151 Ohio App.3d 391, 784 N.E.2d 172, 2003-Ohio-310. Child Custody ⇐ 473

Trial court, in overruling paternal grandmother's objections to court order that vacated prior order giving grandmother temporary custody of child, did not abuse its discretion in not awarding custody to paternal grandmother, even though grandmother alleged she was child's primary caretaker and primary attachment figure; physician testified that even if grandmother were the primary attachment figure for child, child would have been able to establish another primary attachment figure without significant trauma. Vance v. Vance (Ohio App. 2 Dist., 01-24-2003) 151 Ohio App.3d 391, 784 N.E.2d 172, 2003-Ohio-310. Child Custody ⇐ 473

Trial court did not abuse its discretion in custody proceeding involving biological parents and paternal grandmother, in finding that physician's testimony, that mother was a suitable parent and awarding custody to mother would not be detrimental to child, was credible and persuasive; physician had interviewed all of the parties in the matter and had conducted a thorough report and evaluation of the custody situation. Vance v. Vance (Ohio App. 2 Dist., 01-24-2003) 151 Ohio App.3d 391, 784 N.E.2d 172, 2003-Ohio-310. Child Custody ⇐ 473

Evidence supported finding in custody proceeding involving biological parents and paternal grandmother that shared parenting agreement between biological parents be terminated and that mother be granted sole custody of child. Vance v. Vance (Ohio App. 2 Dist., 01-24-2003) 151 Ohio App.3d 391, 784 N.E.2d 172, 2003-Ohio-310. Child Custody ⇐ 473

Trial court, in determining whether paternal grandmother should be granted custody of child, properly applied standard of whether a preponderance of the evidence supported finding that child's biological parents abandoned child, contractually relinquished custody, and demonstrated a total inability to provide care or support for child, or were otherwise unsuitable. Vance v. Vance (Ohio App. 2 Dist., 01-24-2003) 151 Ohio App.3d 391, 784 N.E.2d 172, 2003-Ohio-310. Child Custody ⇐ 279

Trial court did not abuse its discretion in custody proceeding involving biological parents and paternal grandmother, in finding that physician's testimony, that mother was a suitable parent and awarding custody to mother would not be detrimental to child, was credible and persuasive; physician had interviewed all of the parties in the matter and had conducted a thorough report and evaluation of the custody situation. Vance v. Vance (Ohio App. 2 Dist., 01-24-2003) 151 Ohio App.3d 391, 784 N.E.2d 172, 2003-Ohio-310. Child Custody ⇐ 473

Evidence supported finding in custody proceeding involving biological parents and paternal grandmother that shared parenting agreement between biological parents be terminated and that mother be granted sole custody of child. Vance v. Vance (Ohio App. 2 Dist., 01-24-2003) 151 Ohio App.3d 391, 784 N.E.2d 172, 2003-Ohio-310. Child Custody ⇐ 473

Juvenile court had jurisdiction to determine whether petition for shared custody was in best interests of subject children, where children's unmarried mother cohabited with same-sex partner. In re Bonfield (Ohio, 12-13-2002) 97 Ohio St.3d 387, 780 N.E.2d 241, 2002-Ohio-6660. Child Custody ⇐ 404

Juvenile court has jurisdiction to determine the custody of any child not a ward of another court, even though the court has not first found the child to be delinquent, neglected, or dependent. In re Bonfield (Ohio, 12-13-2002) 97 Ohio St.3d 387, 780 N.E.2d 241, 2002-Ohio-6660. Child Custody ⇐ 404

Juvenile court may adjudicate custodial claims brought by persons considered nonparents at law. In re Bonfield (Ohio, 12-13-2002) 97 Ohio St.3d 387, 780 N.E.2d 241, 2002-Ohio-6660. Child Custody ⇐ 409

When making a custody decision, the best interest of the child standard is to be applied. In re Brown (Ohio App. 12 Dist., 04-02-2001) 142 Ohio App.3d 193, 755 N.E.2d 365. Child Custody ⇐ 76

Competent, credible evidence supported the determination that granting custody to maternal grandmother was in the children's best interest; mother had a history of substance abuse, mother had only recently initiated rehabilitative serves, mother failed to comply with major portions of her case plan, mother had been convicted of child endangerment based on one of her children overdosing on medication, mother was under the threat of eviction, and the guardian ad litem recommended that the children remain with their maternal grandmother. In re Brown (Ohio App. 12 Dist., 04-02-2001) 142 Ohio App.3d 193, 755 N.E.2d 365. Child Custody ⇐ 473

A trial court's child custody decision will not be reversed absent an abuse of discretion. In re Brown (Ohio App. 12 Dist., 04-02-2001) 142 Ohio App.3d 193, 755 N.E.2d 365. Child Custody ⇐ 921(1)

Opinion testimony regarding mother's ability to care for and nurture her children, and the prospects for reunification with her children was not admissible in child dependency and custody proceeding; the opinion testimony of one witness was too remote in time to be relevant since he had not interacted with the family in over six months, and the other witness had only worked with treating mother's depression and possessed no knowledge of whether mother would be a good candidate for reunification with her children. In re Brown (Ohio App. 12 Dist., 04-02-2001) 142 Ohio App.3d 193, 755 N.E.2d 365. Infants ⇐ 173.1

Following death of mother to whom trial court had awarded custody in divorce proceeding, dispute over custody of children between father and children's maternal uncle fell within coverage of statute allowing custody to be awarded to relative other than parent "when it is in the best interest of the child," rather than under statute establishing jurisdiction of juvenile courts to determine custody of child not ward of another court of state. Baker v. Baker (Ohio App. 9 Dist., 08-21-1996) 113 Ohio App.3d 805, 682 N.E.2d 661, appeal not allowed 77 Ohio St.3d 1525, 674 N.E.2d 376. Child Custody ⇐ 271; Child Custody ⇐ 405

"Unsuitability" of parent to have custody of child does not necessarily connote any moral or character weakness, but rather, is designed to indicate that contractual relinquishment of custody, abandonment, complete inability to provide care or support, or that parental custody would be detrimental to child, has been proved by preponderance of evidence. Baker v. Baker (Ohio App. 9 Dist., 08-21-1996) 113 Ohio App.3d 805, 682 N.E.2d 661, appeal not allowed 77 Ohio St.3d 1525, 674 N.E.2d 376. Child Custody ⇐ 465

Mother, rather than paternal grandmother, was entitled to custody of child, absent showing, by a preponderance of evidence, that returning child to mother would be detrimental to child. In re Porter (Ohio App. 3 Dist., 08-19-1996) 113 Ohio App.3d 580, 681 N.E.2d 954. Child Custody ⇐ 579

Mother did not contractually relinquish her right to custody, and therefore, best interest test, rather than Perales unsuitability test, applied in dispute with paternal grandmother, where mother agreed to give paternal grandmother temporary, rather than permanent, custody, even though temporary custody period lasted six years. In re Porter (Ohio App. 3 Dist., 08-19-1996) 113 Ohio App.3d 580, 681 N.E.2d 954. Child Custody ⇐ 574; Child Custody ⇐ 579

Discretion which trial court enjoys in custody matters should be accorded utmost respect, given nature of proceeding and impact court's determination will have on lives of parties concerned. Reynolds v. Goll (Ohio, 03-04-1996) 75 Ohio St.3d 121, 661 N.E.2d 1008, 1996-Ohio-153. Child Custody ⇐ 7; Child Custody ⇐ 921(1)

In custody matters, reviewing court should be guided by presumption that trial court's findings were indeed correct. Reynolds v. Goll (Ohio, 03-04-1996) 75 Ohio St.3d 121, 661 N.E.2d 1008, 1996-Ohio-153. Child Custody ⇐ 920

In balancing interests of both parent and child, right of custody by biological parents is not absolute and can be forfeited. Reynolds v. Goll

(Ohio, 03-04-1996) 75 Ohio St.3d 121, 661 N.E.2d 1008, 1996-Ohio-153. Child Custody ⇌ 22

Parents may be denied custody of child only if preponderance of the evidence indicates abandonment, contractual relinquishment of custody, total inability to provide care or support, or that parent is otherwise unsuitable, that is, award of custody would be detrimental to child. Reynolds v. Goll (Ohio, 03-04-1996) 75 Ohio St.3d 121, 661 N.E.2d 1008, 1996-Ohio-153. Child Custody ⇌ 42; Child Custody ⇌ 465

Evidence supported trial court's decision that it was in best interests of 11-year-old child to remain with nonparents who had cared for her since she was a week old; guardian ad litem, court investigator and psychologist all testified that nonparents should be granted custody with liberal visitation by biological father. Reynolds v. Goll (Ohio, 03-04-1996) 75 Ohio St.3d 121, 661 N.E.2d 1008, 1996-Ohio-153. Child Custody ⇌ 468

Juvenile court was without subject matter jurisdiction to approve a permanent surrender of custody of child to mother's relatives, as permanent surrender can only be granted to public children services agency or private child placing agency. State ex rel. Lunsford v. Buck (Meigs 1993) 88 Ohio App.3d 425, 623 N.E.2d 1356. Infants ⇌ 196

Because RC 2151.23 is a jurisdictional statute without any substantive law test, the common-law parental-suitability test is to be applied when a non-parent seeks custody of a child; the "best-interest" test of RC 3109.04 applies only to divorce-custody proceedings. Reynolds v. Goll (Lorain 1992) 80 Ohio App.3d 494, 609 N.E.2d 1276.

Where the natural father placed his infant daughter in the care of nonrelatives during and after the natural mother's protracted final illness, that father's paramount right to custody may be terminated only upon a finding of unsuitability. Reynolds v. Goll (Lorain 1992) 80 Ohio App.3d 494, 609 N.E.2d 1276.

The complaint of a grandparent seeking only visitation with a grandchild may not be determined by the juvenile court pursuant to its authority to determine the "custody" of children under RC 2151.23(A)(2). In re Gibson (Ohio 1991) 61 Ohio St.3d 168, 573 N.E.2d 1074. Child Custody ⇌ 404

Rule of the United States Supreme Court in *Santosky* that a state seeking to sever completely and irrevocably the rights of parents in their natural children must support its allegations by at least clear and convincing evidence does not affect a temporary custody determination and does not modify Ohio law requiring proof by clear and convincing evidence in proceedings to terminate parental rights. Reynolds v. Ross County Children's Services Agency (Ohio 1983) 5 Ohio St.3d 27, 448 N.E.2d 816, 5 O.B.R. 87. Infants ⇌ 177; Infants ⇌ 178

In a child custody dispute between the parent of a child and a nonparent brought under RC 3109.04, a suitable parent has a paramount right to custody so long as such custody is not detrimental to the child. Thrasher v. Thrasher (Summit 1981) 3 Ohio App.3d 210, 444 N.E.2d 431, 3 O.B.R. 240. Child Custody ⇌ 42

When the alleged natural father of an illegitimate child, who has participated in the nurturing process of the child, files a complaint seeking custody of the child under RC 2151.23(A)(2), and the mother admits that he is the natural father of the child, the natural father has equality of standing with the mother with respect to the custody of the child, and the court shall determine which parent shall have the legal custody of the child, taking into account what would be in the best interests of the child. In re Byrd (Ohio 1981) 66 Ohio St.2d 334, 421 N.E.2d 1284, 20 O.O.3d 309. Children Out-of-wedlock ⇌ 20.4

When a petitioner has improperly retained custody of a child after a visit or other temporary relinquishment of physical custody by the person entitled thereto, the court may decline to exercise its jurisdiction if this is just and proper under the circumstances in accordance with RC 3109.26(B). Matter of Potter (Ohio Com.Pl. 1978) 56 Ohio Misc. 17, 377 N.E.2d 536, 10 O.O.3d 214. Child Custody ⇌ 725

The custody of an illegitimate child will not be taken from the mother and awarded to the father merely upon the basis that the wife has contracted an interracial marriage. In re H. (Ohio Com.Pl. 1973) 37 Ohio Misc. 123, 305 N.E.2d 815, 66 O.O.2d 178, 66 O.O.2d 368.

RC 3109.04 is applicable to a proceeding for change of custody under the Juvenile Court Act. In re Custody of Smelser (Ohio Com.Pl. 1969) 22 Ohio Misc. 41, 257 N.E.2d 769, 51 O.O.2d 31, 51 O.O.2d 75.

Upon hearing of a motion for change of custody of a child now fifteen years old previously granted to the father, the expression of the child of the preference to live with his mother is a sufficient change in conditions to require consideration of the motion, and the child's preference between parents should be a major factor in the determination of what will be in his best interest. In re Custody of Smelser (Ohio Com.Pl. 1969) 22 Ohio Misc. 41, 257 N.E.2d 769, 51 O.O.2d 31, 51 O.O.2d 75.

Except when the question of custody is incidental to the separation of parents, their right to custody cannot be taken away unless the grounds as recognized by statute, in general that the child is dependent, neglected or delinquent or that the parent is unfit, are present to support a proper exercise of the police power. Holderle v. Holderle (Franklin 1967) 11 Ohio App.2d 148, 229 N.E.2d 79, 40 O.O.2d 305. Child Custody ⇌ 8

Each of the three subsections under paragraph (A) of RC 2151.23 is independent of the other, and it is not necessary that the juvenile court first determine that the children are delinquent or neglected, etc., before making an award of their custody. In re Wolfe (Ohio Juv. 1962) 187 N.E.2d 658, 91 Ohio Law Abs. 167, 26 O.O.2d 274. Infants ⇌ 196

Where a juvenile court has awarded the county welfare department permanent custody of a minor, the probate court is without authority to grant letters of guardianship in such case. In re Guardianship of Brinegar (Ohio Prob. 1959) 160 N.E.2d 589, 81 Ohio Law Abs. 158. Courts ⇌ 475(6)

Where child is properly charged with being a delinquent, neglected, or dependent child, and is proven to be such, juvenile court is a special and exclusive tribunal for determining issue of such child's care, custody and control. McFadden v. Kendall (Auglaize 1946) 81 Ohio App. 107, 77 N.E.2d 625, 36 O.O. 414. Courts ⇌ 475(15)

Evidence supported finding that father relinquished his right to custody of his minor children because he was an unsuitable parent, thus supporting trial court's decision to grant custody of minor children to their adult sibling rather than to father; report of guardian ad litem (GAL) stated that father was verbally and physically abusive, minor children testified that they were afraid of father, adult sibling testified that father had beaten him when he was younger, and friend of family testified that father was not equipped to care for one of the children who had cerebral palsy. In re Medure (Ohio App. 7 Dist., Columbiana, 09-18-2002) No. 01 CO 3, 2002-Ohio-5035, 2002 WL 31114919, Unreported. Child Custody ⇌ 469

Petitioner, who allegedly had resided with biological mother and acted as child's co-custodian for several years, was not the natural or adoptive parent of child to be deemed a parent within meaning of statutory section governing the best interests of child test used in child custody cases, and thus, was not entitled to award of parental rights under statute giving juvenile courts exclusive jurisdiction to determine custody of child who is not a ward of another court of state. In re Jones (Ohio App. 2 Dist., Miami, 05-10-2002) No. 2000 CA 56, 2002-Ohio-2279, 2002 WL 940195, Unreported. Child Custody ⇌ 274

An Ohio juvenile court properly exercises discretion in declining to exercise jurisdiction over a custody and abuse complaint and instead defers to Kentucky under the Uniform Child Custody Jurisdiction Act (UCCJA) where jurisdiction of the Kentucky court is invoked by filing of the action for divorce and child custody in Kentucky which has substantial evidence concerning the child. Johnson v Montgomery County Children's Services, No. 16020, 1997 WL 102015 (2d Dist Ct App, Montgomery, 3–7–97).

Where a mother grants voluntary temporary custody to an infant's paternal grandparents, the proper standard to be used by the court in determining an award of custody upon the filing of a petition by the mother is the fitness of the mother, not the best interests of the child standard in RC 3109.04(B). In re Curry, No. 89AP-550 (10th Dist Ct App, Franklin, 11–21–89).

Where jurisdiction over custody matters concerning a minor child was certified to the juvenile court, the probate court has jurisdiction to hear adoption proceedings where such minor child was not placed in custody of the juvenile court and there were no pending proceedings in said court concerning custody. In re Adoption of Bailey, No. L–82–358 (6th Dist Ct App, Lucas, 4–15–83).

Any person has standing to bring an action for child custody under RC 2151.23; such a person need not be a parent, need not have established paternity and need not have legitimized the child. Harris v Hopper, No. L–81–187 (6th Dist Ct App, Lucas, 1–15–82).

Where a child is placed for adoption and the mother's consent is subsequently withdrawn, a certification of the case to the juvenile court upon dismissal of the petition does not of itself give the juvenile court jurisdiction to determine the child's custody. In re O——(Ohio Juv. 1964) 199 N.E.2d 765, 95 Ohio Law Abs. 101, 28 O.O.2d 165.

Where the mother of an infant child is placed in jail and there are no relatives or friends to care for such infant, it should be placed in the custody of the juvenile court. 1931 OAG 3756.

5. Writ of habeas corpus

A juvenile court adjudication of abuse, neglect, or dependency is a determination about the care and condition of a child and implicitly involves a determination of the unsuitability of the child's custodial and/or noncustodial parents. In re C.R. (Ohio, 03-29-2006) 108 Ohio St.3d 369, 843 N.E.2d 1188, 2006-Ohio-1191, reconsideration denied 109 Ohio St.3d 1483, 847 N.E.2d 1227, 2006-Ohio-2466. Infants ⇔ 210

Juvenile court did not patently and unambiguously lack jurisdiction to grant permanent custody of child to county children's services (CCS) and, thus, mother had an adequate remedy at law by her previous unsuccessful appeal, precluding habeas corpus relief; notwithstanding failure to appear, mother had notice of proceeding and was represented by counsel, and any ineffectiveness of counsel was due to mother's failure to communicate with counsel prior to hearing. Ross v. Saros (Ohio, 08-20-2003) 99 Ohio St.3d 412, 792 N.E.2d 1126, 2003-Ohio-4128. Habeas Corpus ⇔ 280

Because the single issue on habeas corpus is the legality of the custody, natural mother is entitled to custody of the children unless it be determined in a juvenile proceeding that the best interests of the children dictate otherwise. In re Haws (Cuyahoga 1977) 64 Ohio App.2d 168, 411 N.E.2d 802, 18 O.O.3d 123.

Before a court can deny a mother's habeas corpus petition for custody of her child, it is necessary that she be found an unfit parent and that such finding result from a hearing at which the parties are accorded due process. In re Gossette (Ohio 1975) 42 Ohio St.2d 143, 326 N.E.2d 675, 71 O.O.2d 117.

The grant of original jurisdiction, by RC 2151.23(A)(3), to juvenile courts in habeas corpus action involving the custody of minors is exclusive only as between juvenile courts and those courts given general habeas corpus jurisdiction by RC 2725.02. In re Black (Ohio 1973) 36 Ohio St.2d 124, 304 N.E.2d 394, 65 O.O.2d 308. Courts ⇔ 472.1

A court of appeals has jurisdiction to entertain a petition for a writ of habeas corpus involving the custody of a child. In re Black (Ohio 1973) 36 Ohio St.2d 124, 304 N.E.2d 394, 65 O.O.2d 308. Habeas Corpus ⇔ 614(1)

A juvenile who submits without challenge to the jurisdiction of a municipal court cannot thereafter secure release in a habeas corpus action on the ground that the judgment and sentence of a municipal court is void for want of jurisdiction. Hemphill v. Johnson (Montgomery 1972) 31 Ohio App.2d 241, 287 N.E.2d 828, 60 O.O.2d 404. Habeas Corpus ⇔ 535

Where juvenile court assumes jurisdiction in habeas corpus proceeding relating to rights of parent to custody of his children, it may exercise such further powers as are necessary to complete resolution of entire issue, including retention of continuing jurisdiction to make further orders, although petition for writ of habeas corpus is denied. Baker v. Rose (Ohio Com.Pl. 1970) 28 Ohio Misc. 200, 270 N.E.2d 678, 57 O.O.2d 57, 57 O.O.2d 351.

Habeas corpus in a court of competent jurisdiction as prescribed in RC Ch 2725 is the proper proceeding to raise the question of rightful custody of minor children, where it is alleged that the restraint is illegal, or where a parent or other person claims that he or she has been unlawfully deprived of custody of a minor child; as part of such proceedings, the best interests and welfare of the child is a primary question and determining factor, and all other matters must yield accordingly, including the comity existing between states. In re Messner (Huron 1969) 19 Ohio App.2d 33, 249 N.E.2d 532, 48 O.O.2d 31.

Habeas corpus will not lie where a child has been adjudicated a neglected and dependent child and committed by a juvenile court. Byington v. Byington (Ohio 1964) 175 Ohio St. 513, 196 N.E.2d 588, 26 O.O.2d 176.

Where a juvenile court has acquired jurisdiction over the question of custody of a child, the court of common pleas may not thereafter inquire into such custody in a habeas corpus proceeding. In re Ruth (Ohio Com.Pl. 1961) 176 N.E.2d 187, 88 Ohio Law Abs. 1, 16 O.O.2d 408.

An action for a writ of habeas corpus brought by the rightful custodian of a child is a legal action separate from a custody proceeding and should be given its own number by the clerk of the juvenile court; a request for the writ mistakenly filed in the custody proceeding may be granted, however, without prejudice to the noncustodial parent. In re Scarso, No. 1230 (11th Dist Ct App, Lake, 3-7-86).

6. Mentally ill or retarded child

A juvenile court has authority to order the mental retardation and developmental disabilities department to serve as guardian for a mentally retarded child without the consent of the agency. In re Brown (Hamilton 1988) 43 Ohio App.3d 212, 540 N.E.2d 317.

The juvenile court acts beyond the scope of its jurisdiction when it orders the Ohio department of mental health to pay the cost of care of a child placed in a private, non-public psychiatric hospital. In re Hamil (Ohio 1982) 69 Ohio St.2d 97, 431 N.E.2d 317, 23 O.O.3d 151. Infants ⇔ 228(1)

Where the juvenile court, after a proper hearing, determines that a minor requires state institutional care and guardianship and commits the minor to the care and custody of the department of mental hygiene and correction, the director of mental hygiene and correction is under a clear legal duty to accept the minor as a ward of the department, and the department becomes vested with the exclusive guardianship of such minor. State ex rel. Schwartz v. Haines (Ohio 1962) 172 Ohio St. 572, 179 N.E.2d 46, 18 O.O.2d 130.

7. Criminal charges against adults

Court of common pleas, rather than juvenile court, had exclusive jurisdiction over the prosecution of defendant, even though defendant allegedly committed charged offense while still a juvenile; defendant was apprehended, arrested, and prosecuted after his 21st birthday. State v. Schaar (Ohio App. 5 Dist., Stark, 03-30-2004) No. 2003CA00129, 2004-Ohio-1631, 2004 WL 626815, Unreported. Infants ⇔ 68.5

Legislature plainly intended by language "misdemeanors against minors" in this section to refer to offense against minor mentioned in former GC 1655 (RC 2151.42) as well as offenses under other enumerated sections of code and acts done to minors. (See also Baker v State, 15 Abs 505 (App, Summit 1933).) Baker v. State (Summit 1935) 19 Ohio Law Abs. 126.

Juvenile court had jurisdiction to try plaintiff in error on affidavit charging him with failing to support his minor child. (See also Baker v State, 15 Abs 505 (App, Summit 1933).) Baker v. State (Summit 1935) 19 Ohio Law Abs. 126. Criminal Law ⇔ 87

RC 2151.23 does not confer exclusive jurisdiction over cases of adults charged with violations of RC Ch 2907 for activity which might also constitute a violation of RC Ch 2151, where no violation of RC Ch 2151 is charged. Peck v. Marshall (Ohio 1986) 22 Ohio St.3d 78, 488 N.E.2d 870, 22 O.B.R. 94.

The juvenile court has exclusive original jurisdiction to hear and determine all criminal cases charging an adult with a violation of RC 2151.41. State v. Moore (Fulton 1978) 62 Ohio App.2d 86, 404 N.E.2d 174, 16 O.O.3d 183.

Amendment of RC 2151.23, adopted effective November 19, 1969, deprives municipal court of any jurisdiction to hear and determine any criminal case charging adult with violation of any section of RC Ch 2151. State v. Sanchez (Defiance 1970) 22 Ohio App.2d 145, 259 N.E.2d 139, 51 O.O.2d 292.

A parent, chargeable with the support of a child, who fails to obtain public relief because of an unwillingness to work out relief slips is guilty of a failure to provide subsistence for such child. State v. Earich (Ohio Juv. 1961) 176 N.E.2d 191, 86 Ohio Law Abs. 90, 19 O.O.2d 39.

Where defendant is charged in a juvenile court on charges of contributing to the delinquency of a minor, the juvenile judge, upon finding reason to believe that a felony has been committed, may bind defendant over to the grand jury without placing him in double jeopardy. Grear v. Maxwell (C.A.6 (Ohio) 1966) 8 Ohio Misc. 210, 355 F.2d 991, 35 O.O.2d 333, 37 O.O.2d 268, certiorari denied 86 S.Ct. 1580, 384 U.S. 957, 16 L.Ed.2d 552, rehearing denied 87 S.Ct. 27, 385 U.S. 893, 17 L.Ed.2d 127.

A juvenile court does not have exclusive original jurisdiction over adults charged with crimes against juveniles under RC Ch 2907. State ex rel. McMinn v. Whitfield (Ohio 1986) 27 Ohio St.3d 4, 500 N.E.2d 875, 27 O.B.R. 75.

Under former GC 1642 (RC 2151.23), juvenile court does not deal with crimes; its jurisdiction is limited to delinquent, neglected and dependent minors under age of eighteen. State ex rel. Brown v. Hoffman (Hamilton 1926) 23 Ohio App. 348, 155 N.E. 499, 5 Ohio Law Abs. 6.

The court of common pleas and municipal courts have jurisdiction in offenses involving adults, concurrent with that of the juvenile court, arising under RC 2151.41 or RC 2151.42. 1958 OAG 2016.

Where an agreement has been entered into pursuant to GC 3070-17 (RC 335.16), such fact does not divert courts of jurisdiction over offenses described in GC 1639-46 (RC 2151.42), GC 13008 (RC 3113.01) and GC 13012 (RC 3113.06), and parent may be held criminally liable for failure to support a minor child as provided in said sections; juvenile courts have no jurisdiction of felonies, nor over offenses described in GC 13008 (RC 3113.01) and GC 13012 (RC 3113.06). 1946 OAG 1100.

A probate court may exercise jurisdiction over prosecutions for nonsupport and contributing to the delinquency of a minor, without the filing of an information by the prosecuting attorney. 1932 OAG 4154.

8. Paternity

Child who was born after his mother divorced her former husband was "alleged to have been born out of wedlock," and thus juvenile court had jurisdiction over child's paternity action, where former husband alleged that he was not child's biological father during the divorce proceedings, and divorce decree stated that child was not parties' child. Fitzpatrick v. Fitzpatrick (Ohio App. 12 Dist., 03-02-1998) 126 Ohio App.3d 476, 710 N.E.2d 778, dismissed, appeal not allowed 82 Ohio St.3d 1441, 695 N.E.2d 264. Children Out-of-wedlock ⚖ 36

Juvenile division had jurisdiction over child's paternity action filed after mother's paternity action was dismissed with prejudice by general division and before alleged father filed motion to reopen the action in the general division. Payne v. Cartee (Ohio App. 4 Dist., 06-10-1996) 111 Ohio App.3d 580, 676 N.E.2d 946, appeal not allowed 77 Ohio St.3d 1482, 673 N.E.2d 143. Children Out-of-wedlock ⚖ 36

Juvenile court did not abuse its discretion in denying alleged father's motion for a new trial of paternity action based on new evidence relating to defense of res judicata, where, because of lack of privity between mother and son, doctrine of res judicata did not apply. Payne v. Cartee (Ohio App. 4 Dist., 06-10-1996) 111 Ohio App.3d 580, 676 N.E.2d 946, appeal not allowed 77 Ohio St.3d 1482, 673 N.E.2d 143. Children Out-of-wedlock ⚖ 62

General division of Common Pleas Court exhausted its exclusive jurisdiction over paternity action by dismissing action with prejudice, and, therefore, juvenile division had concurrent jurisdiction over child's later filed paternity action against same alleged father. Payne v. Cartee (Ohio App. 4 Dist., 06-10-1996) 111 Ohio App.3d 580, 676 N.E.2d 946, appeal not allowed 77 Ohio St.3d 1482, 673 N.E.2d 143. Courts ⚖ 50

Juvenile court did not abuse its discretion by permitting mother to proceed as child's next friend in his paternity action, where such action was prosecuted solely on son's behalf, there was no showing that she might fail to vigorously pursue child's action, and guardian ad litem was appointed three days after determination that alleged father was, in fact, child's father. Payne v. Cartee (Ohio App. 4 Dist., 06-10-1996) 111 Ohio App.3d 580, 676 N.E.2d 946, appeal not allowed 77 Ohio St.3d 1482, 673 N.E.2d 143. Infants ⚖ 81

Juvenile courts have original jurisdiction over parentage actions. State ex rel. Willacy v. Smith (Ohio, 03-19-1997) 78 Ohio St.3d 47, 676 N.E.2d 109, 1997-Ohio-244. Children Out-of-wedlock ⚖ 36

Putative father would not be allowed, three years after judgment finding him to be child's father, which adjudication he had originally sought, to dismiss complaint or to have genetic testing done to determine whether he was biological father, notwithstanding physician's statement in affidavit that it was highly unlikely that plaintiff could be child's father; there would be no current benefit to child to change her position as plaintiff's daughter, procedural rule did not contemplate dismissal of action, at plaintiff's request, three years after rendering of final appealable order in plaintiff's favor, and plaintiff had failed to request genetic testing when he could have properly done so, at which time request would have been granted. Frederick v. Alltop (Ohio Com.Pl., 05-16-1996) 80 Ohio Misc.2d 13, 672 N.E.2d 1123. Children Out-of-wedlock ⚖ 68

A juvenile court's original jurisdiction over parentage actions does not exclude the jurisdiction of a court of common pleas. Standifer v. Arwood (Warren 1984) 17 Ohio App.3d 241, 479 N.E.2d 304, 17 O.B.R. 508.

Public policy does not compel rejection of a proposed witness in a paternity action when such witness is the child whose paternity is under inquiry. Philpot v. Williams (Hamilton 1983) 8 Ohio App.3d 241, 456 N.E.2d 1315, 8 O.B.R. 314.

There is a distinction between a "putative" father and a father who has been adjudicated as such by his own admission, in that a father adjudicated as such by his own admission has legal standing to seek custody of his illegitimate child against the world, including the mother. In re Wright (Ohio Com.Pl. 1977) 52 Ohio Misc. 4, 367 N.E.2d 931, 6 O.O.3d 31.

The mother of an illegitimate child has a right of custody that is superior to that of the putative father. In re H. (Ohio Com.Pl. 1973) 37 Ohio Misc. 123, 305 N.E.2d 815, 66 O.O.2d 178, 66 O.O.2d 368.

Jurisdiction is conferred by this section on the juvenile court to determine the paternity of a child born out of wedlock and to provide for its support. Knox v. Covrett (Ottawa 1949) 85 Ohio App. 524, 89 N.E.2d 610, 40 O.O. 437. Children Out-of-wedlock ⚖ 36

Where child is properly charged with being a delinquent, neglected, or dependent child, and is proven to be such, juvenile court is a special and exclusive tribunal for determining issue of such child's care, custody and control. McFadden v. Kendall (Auglaize 1946) 81 Ohio App. 107, 77 N.E.2d 625, 36 O.O. 414. Courts ⚖ 475(15)

Acknowledgment of paternity by husband of child's biological mother did not make him legal father of child, for purposes of resolving custody dispute between husband and child's maternal aunt and uncle following mother's death, where husband admitted that he was not biological father of child and implicitly admitted that he was aware of such fact when he acknowledged paternity. Biggs v. Balosky (Ohio App. 9 Dist., Medina, 07-31-2002) No. 3280-M, 2002-Ohio-3859, 2002 WL 1766603, Unreported. Child Custody ⚖ 274; Children Out-of-wedlock ⚖ 12

9. Support orders

Mother, the non-residential parent, could not be held in contempt of court for failure to pay certain of children's expenses, where trial court, in calculating amount due, had not considered credits due mother for child support payments made to father while mother had physical custody of children. Johnson v. Johnson (Ohio App. 3 Dist., Union, 12-15-2003) No. 14-03-32, 2003-Ohio-6710, 2003 WL 22939480, Unreported. Child Support ⚖ 444

Noncustodial unwed father substantially complied with child support orders, even though he was $1,982.13 in arrears, where he consistently paid support obligation through county support enforcement agency, arrearages accrued during periods in which he was laid off, and he was presently reducing arrearage through regular deductions from his paycheck. In re Seitz (Ohio App. 11 Dist., Trumbull, 09-26-2003) No. 2002-T-0097, 2003-Ohio-5218, 2003 WL 22234850, Unreported. Children Out-of-wedlock ⚖ 69(7)

Where domestic relations court has previously entered child support order in divorce case and child who is beneficiary of that support order is subsequently found to be delinquent in juvenile court, domestic relations court and juvenile court have concurrent jurisdiction to entertain motions regarding that support order. Machaterre v. Looker (Ohio App. 6 Dist., Lucas, 01-17-2003) No. L-02-1155, 2003-Ohio-220, 2003 WL 139772, Unreported. Child Support ⚖ 173

A trial court does not err by ordering a father to pay a lump sum support arrearage directly to his daughter after her emancipation where the request for support is properly made prior to the child's emancipation and the motion for support arises out of a court's disposition of unruly charges filed by the father which results in termination of the father's previous status as residential parent; therefore, the father as the non-custodial parent remains responsible for the child's financial support. In re Hollaender (Ohio App. 12 Dist., Warren, 06-19-2000) No. CA99-08-092, 2000 WL 783070, Unreported.

Juvenile court had jurisdiction to try plaintiff in error on affidavit charging him with failing to support his minor child. (See also Baker v State, 15 Abs 505 (1933).) Baker v. State (Summit 1935) 19 Ohio Law Abs. 126. Criminal Law ⚖ 87

Even though juvenile court had adjudicated dependency action involving children, domestic relations court properly enforced its own valid orders concerning child support in contempt proceedings against father; domestic relations court had determined issues relating to child support since initial action, and juvenile court did not attempt to exercise jurisdiction over child support issues. State ex rel. Clermont Cty. Dept. of Human Serv. v. Walsson (Ohio App. 12 Dist., 12-26-1995) 108 Ohio App.3d 125, 670 N.E.2d 287, dismissed, appeal not allowed 76 Ohio St.3d 1405, 666 N.E.2d 565. Child Support ⚖ 470

Juvenile court, in determining paternity, had jurisdiction to decide state's action for aid furnished by state for support and medical expenses of children born out-of-wedlock. Brightwell v. Easter (Ohio App. 9 Dist., 03-09-1994) 93 Ohio App.3d 425, 638 N.E.2d 1067. Social Security And Public Welfare ⚖ 194.19

A juvenile court does not have jurisdiction to entertain a complaint filed by a county human services department against a child's natural father to establish child support and for reimbursement of ADC payments made to the child's grandmother who had been appointed guardian by a probate court. Lake Cty. Dept. of Human Serv. v. Adams (Lake 1992) 82 Ohio App.3d 494, 612 N.E.2d 766.

Juvenile courts have jurisdiction to hear and determine support order applications as long as the child is not a ward of another court under RC

2151.23
Note 9

2151.23. Lake Cty. Dept. of Human Serv. v. Adams (Lake 1992) 82 Ohio App.3d 494, 612 N.E.2d 766.

In any case where a court of common pleas has made an award of custody or an order for support, or both, of minor children, that court may certify the case to the juvenile court of any county in the state for further proceedings. Pylant v. Pylant (Huron 1978) 61 Ohio App.2d 247, 401 N.E.2d 940, 15 O.O.3d 407. Courts ⇐ 483

Where an original child support order was for a total sum on behalf of four children and did not designate a specific amount for each child, and thereafter one child was emancipated and the custody of a second child was transferred from the wife to the husband, the court, in its discretion, may modify the prior order retroactively, and such modification, if any, need not be made on a pro rata basis. Asztalos v. Fortney (Lucas 1975) 48 Ohio App.2d 66, 355 N.E.2d 517, 2 O.O.3d 45. Child Support ⇐ 236; Child Support ⇐ 364

A parent, chargeable with the support of a child, who fails to obtain public relief because of an unwillingness to work out relief slips is guilty of a failure to provide subsistence for such child. State v. Earich (Ohio Juv. 1961) 176 N.E.2d 191, 86 Ohio Law Abs. 90, 19 O.O.2d 39.

When the question of custody only comes before a court, under the authority granted in RC 2151.23(A)(2), that court has jurisdiction to include in the award of custody an order for the support of such child. Kolody v. Kolody (Summit 1960) 110 Ohio App. 260, 169 N.E.2d 34, 13 O.O.2d 25.

Juvenile court has no authority to render a money judgment, but it does have authority to order a parent to pay for the support of his minor children, and can enforce such an order by use of a jail sentence as punishment. Snyder v. Snyder (Ohio Juv. 1940) 5 Ohio Supp. 222, 32 Ohio Law Abs. 28, 18 O.O. 69.

10. Procedural issues

Father's concession, both at trial and in his appellate brief, that child was dependent as of date alleged in complaint, due to father's incarceration, was dispositive with respect to trial court's finding that child was dependent; dependency determination was properly made considering child's circumstances as of date alleged in complaint, as required by statute. In re S.H. (Ohio App. 12 Dist., Butler, 09-26-2005) No. CA2005-01-007, 2005-Ohio-5047, 2005 WL 2335320, Unreported. Infants ⇐ 241

The state is required by statute to prove the dependency of a child at the time alleged in the complaint. In re S.H. (Ohio App. 12 Dist., Butler, 09-26-2005) No. CA2005-01-007, 2005-Ohio-5047, 2005 WL 2335320, Unreported. Infants ⇐ 197

Even if trial court erred when it excluded testimony of maternal grandmother of children adjudicated dependent, that children were always appropriately cared for while in mother's custody prior to intervention by child services agency, error was harmless in child protection proceeding on motions to modify custody in light of extensive evidence regarding mother's unsuitability as parent at time of custody modification hearing. In re Mick (Ohio App. 4 Dist., Washington, 09-07-2005) No. 05CA23, 2005-Ohio-4951, 2005 WL 2293577, Unreported. Infants ⇐ 253

Probative value of testimony of maternal grandmother of children adjudicated dependent, that children were always appropriately cared for while in mother's custody prior to intervention by child services agency, was very low, and thus evidence could be excluded in child protection proceeding on motions to modify custody; testimony mother may have been suitable parent to children at one time did not negate extensive evidence that mother was not currently fit to parent her children. In re Mick (Ohio App. 4 Dist., Washington, 09-07-2005) No. 05CA23, 2005-Ohio-4951, 2005 WL 2293577, Unreported. Infants ⇐ 173.1

Parents who voluntarily relinquished custody of their child to custodian without intervention of any state agency were not entitled to reunification plan. In re Bailey (Ohio App. 1 Dist., Hamilton, 06-17-2005) No. C-040014, No. C-040479, 2005-Ohio-3039, 2005 WL 1413269, Unreported, appeal not allowed 107 Ohio St.3d 1423, 837 N.E.2d 1208, 2005-Ohio-6124. Infants ⇐ 155

Mother, who was found to be an unsuitable parent before custody of daughter was awarded to paternal grandparents, was not entitled to another unsuitability determination on her custody modification petition; best-interest-of-the-child standard would be used for custody modification petition. Shargo v. Gregory (Ohio App. 11 Dist., Trumbull, 06-30-2004) No. 2003-T-0058, 2004-Ohio-3512, 2004 WL 1486940, Unreported. Child Custody ⇐ 579

Father was not entitled to writ of prohibition to prevent juvenile court judge from conducting a permanent custody hearing involving one child;

PROBATE LAWS & RULES ANNOTATED

the judge had statutory authority to conduct a permanent custody hearing, the father appealed award of permanent custody to the county department, and the legal remedy providing adequate relief foreclosed the extraordinary remedy in prohibition. Wells v. Costine (Ohio App. 7 Dist., Belmont, 02-04-2004) No. 03 BE 51, 2004-Ohio-563, 2004 WL 234716, Unreported. Prohibition ⇐ 3(2)

Both magistrate and trial court were justified in awarding former wife monthly child support award based only upon evidence presented at final divorce hearing that former husband did not attend. Clemons v. Clemons (Ohio App. 4 Dist., Athens, 11-17-2003) No. 03CA5, 2003-Ohio-6210, 2003 WL 22762722, Unreported. Child Support ⇐ 199

Child support obligee's motion for retroactive child support for period before marriage to obligor was not ancillary to a divorce proceeding and thus was properly maintained within juvenile court's jurisdiction that was originally invoked by county child support enforcement agency's original complaint to set child support, since motion was filed prior to any proceedings being commenced in domestic relations court and concerned period of time prior to parties' marriage. Thelmond H.S. v. Angela L.S. (Ohio App. 6 Dist., Lucas, 02-14-2003) No. L-02-1172, 2003-Ohio-685, 2003 WL 329167, Unreported. Child Support ⇐ 173

In order for a reviewing court to find that an abuse of discretion in awarding child custody occurred, there must be an indication in the record that the trial court had an unreasonable, arbitrary or unconscionable attitude in its handling of the case. In re Brown (Ohio App. 12 Dist., 04-02-2001) 142 Ohio App.3d 193, 755 N.E.2d 365. Child Custody ⇐ 921(1)

The discretion granted to the trial court in child custody matters should be accorded the utmost respect given the nature of the proceedings and the impact the court's determination will have on the lives of the parties concerned. In re Brown (Ohio App. 12 Dist., 04-02-2001) 142 Ohio App.3d 193, 755 N.E.2d 365. Child Custody ⇐ 921(1)

Juvenile court abused its discretion in admitting results of polygraph examinations of juvenile and his mother in juvenile delinquency proceeding, pursuant to stipulation of the parties, and then failing to consider that evidence. In re Burton S. (Ohio App. 6 Dist., 12-17-1999) 136 Ohio App.3d 386, 736 N.E.2d 928. Infants ⇐ 208

Juvenile court's error in admitting results of polygraph examinations of juvenile and his mother and then failing to consider that evidence was not harmless in juvenile delinquency proceeding, where central issue of the magistrate's decision to adjudicate the juvenile to be delinquent was credibility of juvenile and his mother. In re Burton S. (Ohio App. 6 Dist., 12-17-1999) 136 Ohio App.3d 386, 736 N.E.2d 928. Infants ⇐ 253

Mother's complaint in parentage action sufficiently alleged that child was "born out of wedlock," as required by statute, where complaint alleged that child's conception and birth resulted from mother's affair with putative father. Nwabara v. Willacy (Ohio App. 8 Dist., 08-09-1999) 135 Ohio App.3d 120, 733 N.E.2d 267, dismissed, appeal not allowed 87 Ohio St.3d 1451, 719 N.E.2d 967. Children Out-of-wedlock ⇐ 41

Mother's alleged failure to disclose to putative father identity of her DNA expert and to provide putative father with expert's detailed report prior to trial neither surprised putative father nor substantially harmed or prejudiced him in his cross-examination of expert, where mother and putative father had jointly selected expert to perform DNA tests prior to trial, and where putative father admitted in his answer that he had agreed to take DNA test and had seen results of that testing that indicated that he was child's likely father. Nwabara v. Willacy (Ohio App. 8 Dist., 08-09-1999) 135 Ohio App.3d 120, 733 N.E.2d 267, dismissed, appeal not allowed 87 Ohio St.3d 1451, 719 N.E.2d 967. Children Out-of-wedlock ⇐ 45

Res judicata did not bar former wife's child, who was found in divorce decree to be illegitimate, from bringing parentage action in juvenile court; child was not party to divorce action, and child was not in privity with former wife. Fitzpatrick v. Fitzpatrick (Ohio App. 12 Dist., 03-02-1998) 126 Ohio App.3d 476, 710 N.E.2d 778, dismissed, appeal not allowed 82 Ohio St.3d 1441, 695 N.E.2d 264. Children Out-of-wedlock ⇐ 33

Evidence that nonparent would be better custodian is insufficient to overcome presumption in favor of parent; rather, nonparent must demonstrate by preponderance of the evidence that parent is unsuitable. In re Porter (Ohio App. 3 Dist., 08-19-1996) 113 Ohio App.3d 580, 681 N.E.2d 954. Child Custody ⇐ 510; Child Custody ⇐ 468

Postjudgment appeal was adequate remedy at law in juvenile court parentage action, precluding putative father from challenging juvenile court's exercise of subject matter jurisdiction by seeking writ of prohibition or mandamus, absent patent and unambiguous lack of jurisdiction, despite numerous interlocutory orders and alleged absence of mechanism to guarantee reimbursement of putative father's temporary child support payments. State ex rel. Willacy v. Smith (Ohio, 03-19-1997) 78 Ohio St.3d

47, 676 N.E.2d 109, 1997-Ohio-244. Mandamus ⟜ 4(4); Prohibition ⟜ 3(3)

Jurisdiction was not patently and unambiguously lacking in juvenile court parentage action brought by natural mother against child's putative father, barring putative father's mandamus and prohibition action challenging juvenile court's subject matter jurisdiction, although mother was married to another man at time child was born; mother's complaint sufficiently alleged that child was born out of wedlock by stating that his conception and birth resulted from her affair with putative father, giving juvenile court basic statutory jurisdiction to proceed. State ex rel. Willacy v. Smith (Ohio, 03-19-1997) 78 Ohio St.3d 47, 676 N.E.2d 109, 1997-Ohio-244. Mandamus ⟜ 31; Prohibition ⟜ 5(3)

Juvenile court had jurisdiction in contempt; thus, challenge to juvenile court's holding juvenile witness in direct contempt, and sentencing her to 30 days, had to be made by appeal, and not by petition for habeas corpus. State ex rel. Frazer v. Administrator/Director, Juvenile Court Detention Home (Ohio App. 8 Dist., 11-03-1995) 107 Ohio App.3d 245, 668 N.E.2d 546. Contempt ⟜ 66(1); Habeas Corpus ⟜ 289

County child support enforcement agency (CSEA) had standing, as collecting agent of Department of Human Services (DHS), to bring action in juvenile court to determine child support and to make determination of reimbursement for amount of support already provided by DHS to children of mothers receiving public assistance who had assigned their rights to child support to DHS; even if statute authorizing only parent, guardian, or custodian of child to bring action in juvenile court requesting child support order did not authorize state to bring such action, Juvenile Rules of Procedure giving state or its agencies standing to file complaint to order child support payments controlled over statute. State ex rel. Lamier v. Lamier (Ohio App. 8 Dist., 09-05-1995) 105 Ohio App.3d 797, 664 N.E.2d 1384. Child Support ⟜ 179

Any error by juvenile court in vacating its prior allowance of writ of habeas corpus for return of children to mother could have been raised on appeal and, therefore, mother was precluded from seeking extraordinary relief from juvenile court's decision in mandamus and procedendo. State ex rel. Fogle v. Steiner (Ohio, 12-06-1995) 74 Ohio St.3d 158, 656 N.E.2d 1288, 1995-Ohio-278. Courts ⟜ 207.1; Mandamus ⟜ 4(1)

Although juvenile division of Court of Common Pleas did find that Cuyahoga County Department of Children and Family Services (CCDCFS) fraudulently misrepresented adopted child's condition prior to adoption, action by parents was dependency action, with regard to support, rather than fraud action, and thus, action was within jurisdiction of juvenile court. In re Robert S. (Ohio App. 6 Dist., 12-09-1994) 98 Ohio App.3d 84, 647 N.E.2d 869. Infants ⟜ 196

When a juvenile court makes a custody determination under RC 2151.23 and 2151.353, it must do so in accordance with RC 3109.04. In re Poling (Ohio 1992) 64 Ohio St.3d 211, 594 N.E.2d 589.

Noncustodial parent was not entitled to writ of prohibition directed at juvenile court with regard to order compelling parent to respond to interrogatories concerning her financial status and recommendation by referee of juvenile court that she should be held in contempt for refusing to answer the interrogatories, considering that juvenile court had original jurisdiction under Uniform Reciprocal Enforcement of Support Act, and that if court were to uphold referee's recommendation and find parent in contempt, parent would have right to appeal such finding, and thus she had available an adequate remedy in ordinary course of the law. Manrow v. Court of Common Pleas of Lucas County, Juvenile Div. (Ohio 1985) 20 Ohio St.3d 37, 485 N.E.2d 713, 20 O.B.R. 285. Prohibition ⟜ 3(3); Prohibition ⟜ 5(3)

A RC 2151.23(A)(3) action does not need to comply with RC 2151.27 and RC 2151.23, as the latter sections clearly apply to neglect, abuse, and dependency hearings provided for in RC 2151.23(A)(1). In re Perales (Ohio 1977) 52 Ohio St.2d 89, 369 N.E.2d 1047, 6 O.O.3d 293.

RC 2151.23(A)(1) and RC 2151.23(A)(2) are independent grants of jurisdiction to the juvenile court; subsection (A)(2) does not modify the power granted by subsection (A)(1). James v. Child Welfare Bd. (Summit 1967) 9 Ohio App.2d 299, 224 N.E.2d 358, 38 O.O.2d 347.

Each of the three subsections under paragraph (A) of RC 2151.23 is independent of the other, and it is not necessary that the juvenile court first determine that the children are delinquent or neglected, etc., before making an award of their custody. In re Wolfe (Ohio Juv. 1962) 187 N.E.2d 658, 91 Ohio Law Abs. 167, 26 O.O.2d 274. Infants ⟜ 196

RC 3105.20 does not deny the court of common pleas in any matter concerning domestic relations the exercise of "its full equity powers and jurisdiction," but there must be a statutory basis upon which to exercise those powers before they may be put into execution. Haynie v. Haynie (Summit 1958) 108 Ohio App. 342, 161 N.E.2d 549, 9 O.O.2d 301, affirmed 169 Ohio St. 467, 159 N.E.2d 765, 8 O.O.2d 476. Courts ⟜ 472.5

Except in those instances specified in GC 8004-6 (RC 3107.06), a probate court had no power to make a final decree or interlocutory order of adoption of a child where it affirmatively appears that there was not filed with the court a written consent to the adoption by the living mother of such child; the requirement of such consent was not dispensed with in an instance where a juvenile court had previously made a valid determination that such child was "neglected." In re Ramsey (Ohio 1956) 164 Ohio St. 567, 132 N.E.2d 469, 58 O.O. 431.

Where judge of Franklin County Court of Common Pleas, division of domestic relations, signs an entry of order in juvenile court case merely with his name and term, "Judge" thereafter, and heading of entry does not have designation "Juvenile Branch," the Court of Appeals will take judicial notice of fact that such judge, by this section, also exercises powers of judge of juvenile court, and will assume that entry was signed by judge in latter capacity, and that order was properly and judicially entered. Harlor v. Harlor (Franklin 1946) 79 Ohio App. 504, 65 N.E.2d 512, 35 O.O. 310.

Jurisdiction over the person may always be waived, even by a minor. In re Evans (Richland 1941) 67 Ohio App. 66, 35 N.E.2d 887, 21 O.O. 93. Criminal Law ⟜ 105

Act 96 v 314, creating juvenile courts and establishing procedure therein, is not void for lack of definiteness in stating the offenses therein proscribed. Travis v. State (Ohio Cir. 1909) 21 Ohio C.D. 492, 12 Ohio C.C.(N.S.) 374, affirmed 82 Ohio St. 439, 92 N.E. 1125, 8 Ohio Law Rep. 91.

The trial court had the authority to accept defendant's guilty pleas on charges of aggravated burglary and aggravated robbery, where those charges were derived from the charged act of aggravated murder that was the basis of the transfer from juvenile court. State v. White (Ohio App. 7 Dist., Jefferson, 09-26-2002) No. 01-JE-3, 2002-Ohio-5226, 2002 WL 31169182, Unreported, appeal not allowed 98 Ohio St.3d 1425, 782 N.E.2d 78, 2003-Ohio-259, motion for delayed appeal denied 99 Ohio St.3d 1433, 789 N.E.2d 1116, 2003-Ohio-2902. Criminal Law ⟜ 273(1)

Juvenile court abused its discretion in modifying delinquency adjudication for robbery to misdemeanor theft after disposition, where rule cited by juvenile for amendment of pleading did not authorize the court to amend the complaint after the juvenile's adjudication and disposition, and no other rule authorized juvenile court to modify the adjudication. In re Harris (Ohio App. 11 Dist., Portage, 07-26-2002) No. 2001-P-0177, 2002-Ohio-3848, 2002 WL 1752261, Unreported. Infants ⟜ 230.1

A juvenile court may not enter summary judgment in a dependency action, as the Juvenile Rules contain no provision for summary judgments. In re Morgan, No. 90–CA–13 (5th Dist Ct App, Knox, 10–25–90).

Where a child is placed for adoption and the mother's consent is subsequently withdrawn, a certification of the case to the juvenile court upon dismissal of the petition does not of itself give the juvenile court jurisdiction to determine the child's custody. In re O—— (Ohio Juv. 1964) 199 N.E.2d 765, 95 Ohio Law Abs. 101, 28 O.O.2d 165.

A stepparent is generally not liable for minor stepchild in the same manner as his own child; this chapter generally applies to a stepparent in the same manner as to a real parent, providing said application is consistent with the intent of said chapter. 1925 OAG 2450.

11. Age of child

When a juvenile is adjudicated delinquent before age 18 and then commits offense qualifying as parole violation between the ages of 18 and 21, separate jurisdiction of juvenile court and common pleas court may coexist according to classifications of "adult" and "juvenile," and divergent dispositions of those courts may also exist. In re Gillespie (Ohio App. 10 Dist., 12-19-2002) 150 Ohio App.3d 502, 782 N.E.2d 140, 2002-Ohio-7025, appeal not allowed 98 Ohio St.3d 1513, 786 N.E.2d 63, 2003-Ohio-1572. Infants ⟜ 281

Juvenile court lacked jurisdiction to hear and determine child support complaint filed after child had reached age of majority. In re Livingston (Ohio App. 8 Dist., 11-18-1996) 115 Ohio App.3d 613, 685 N.E.2d 1285. Child Support ⟜ 103

Juvenile court could suspend juvenile offender's driver's license only until offender's eighteenth birthday, regardless of status of restitution order, absent finding that offender had failed to comply with orders of court and that his operation of motor vehicle constituted danger to himself and others. State v. Minix (Ohio App. 4 Dist., 02-24-1995) 101 Ohio App.3d 380, 655 N.E.2d 789. Automobiles ⟜ 144.2(8)

Note 11

While juvenile court may generally order restitution from offending juvenile driver, court is not statutorily permitted to use restitution order to suspend juvenile's driver's license beyond that time proscribed by statute, i.e., juvenile's eighteenth birthday, absent application of statute that requires finding that juvenile has failed to comply with orders of court and that his operation of motor vehicle constitutes danger to himself and others. State v. Minix (Ohio App. 4 Dist., 02-24-1995) 101 Ohio App.3d 380, 655 N.E.2d 789. Automobiles ⇐ 144.2(8)

Proof beyond a reasonable doubt of a defendant's majority is established by (1) introduction of the results of a bone marrow examination determining the defendant's age as at least eighteen years, (2) prior adult criminal prosecutions establishing the defendant's majority, and (3) the defendant's use for at least five years of the now-disputed birthdate establishing his majority, notwithstanding the facts that his mother gave immigration authorities a birthdate which would make the defendant a minor and that the defendant makes a self-serving reassertion of the birthdate memorialized in the immigration documents despite his earlier repudiation of that date. State v. Neguse (Franklin 1991) 71 Ohio App.3d 596, 594 N.E.2d 1116.

A juvenile court has no jurisdiction over the person and body of an adult pregnant woman so as to control her personal life for the benefit and protection of her unborn child. Cox v. Court of Common Pleas of Franklin County, Div. of Domestic Relations, Juvenile Branch (Franklin 1988) 42 Ohio App.3d 171, 537 N.E.2d 721.

Writ of habeas corpus will not be granted to release from the state reformatory a minor who stated his age to be nineteen years, when in fact he was but seventeen years, and thereafter was indicted, pleaded guilty and was convicted in the common pleas court on a criminal charge. In re Evans (Richland 1941) 67 Ohio App. 66, 35 N.E.2d 887, 21 O.O. 93. Habeas Corpus ⇐ 535

The juvenile court has exclusive jurisdiction over minors under eighteen years old, former GC 1642 (RC 2151.23), charged with crime, whether misdemeanor or felony, former GC 1644 (RC 2151.02). State v. Joiner (Ohio Com.Pl. 1917) 28 Ohio Dec. 199, 20 Ohio N.P.N.S. 313.

A juvenile court lacks jurisdiction to compel a pregnant woman over the age of eighteen to take action for the alleged benefit of her unborn child; thus, a writ of prohibition ordering the court to cease the exercise of juvenile court jurisdiction over the pregnant mother in a dependency and neglect action will be issued. Cox v Franklin County Common Pleas Court, Domestic Div, Juvenile Branch, No. 88AP–856 (10th Dist Ct App, Franklin, 12–13–88).

When a girl commits an act or acts of delinquency before arriving at the age of eighteen years, and the complaint is not filed or hearing held until after said child arrives at the age of eighteen years, the juvenile court has jurisdiction to hear and dispose of such complaint, the same as if the complaint and hearing were held before such child arrived at the age of eighteen years, except that GC 2101 (RC 5141.31) prohibits the commitment of such child to the girls industrial school if, at the time of such hearing, she has arrived at the age of eighteen years. 1945 OAG 247.

The jurisdiction of a juvenile court to commit a crippled child to the division of charities is limited by the provisions of former GC 1642 (RC 2151.23) and to children under eighteen years. 1933 OAG 1047.

12. Divorce

Juvenile court's exercise of jurisdiction over child custody and abuse complaint filed by mother and grandmother was subject to terms of Uniform Child Custody Jurisdiction Act (UCCJA), given that there was pending divorce and custody proceeding in Kentucky. In re Simons (Ohio App. 2 Dist., 03-07-1997) 118 Ohio App.3d 622, 693 N.E.2d 1111. Child Custody ⇐ 748

Pursuant to RC 2151.23(A), the juvenile court has jurisdiction to determine the custody of a child alleged to be abused, neglected, or dependent, when that child is not the ward of any court in this state; this jurisdiction includes children subject to a divorce decree granting custody pursuant to RC 3109.04. In re Poling (Ohio 1992) 64 Ohio St.3d 211, 594 N.E.2d 589. Infants ⇐ 196

Where a court, having acquired jurisdiction over a child by virtue of a divorce action between the child's parents, certifies the matter of the child's custody to a juvenile court, the consent of the juvenile court having been first obtained, the juvenile court has exclusive jurisdiction over the child's custody by virtue of RC 3109.06 and RC 2151.23(D) and a finding of unfitness of the parents or that there is no suitable relative to have custody is not a necessary prerequisite to such certification, and while such certification shall be deemed to be the complaint in the juvenile court, it does not constitute a complaint in the juvenile court that such child is dependent or neglected and those dispositions provided for under RC 2151.353, RC 2151.354, and RC 2151.355 are not applicable to the disposition of such a child, disposition thereof being subject to and controlled by RC 3109.04. In re Height (Van Wert 1975) 47 Ohio App.2d 203, 353 N.E.2d 887, 1 O.O.3d 279. Courts ⇐ 472.1

Where the jurisdiction of the juvenile court has been invoked by the arrest of a father of minor children on a charge of nonsupport filed by the mother, and upon trial the father pleads guilty and is sentenced, which sentence is suspended and the defendant put on probation, the condition of the probation being that the defendant will pay a specified sum weekly for support, the minor children thereby become wards of the juvenile court and the subject of their support and the power to enforce the condition of probation is exclusively in that court until each child has reached the age of eighteen years, so that if the mother thereafter files a petition for divorce in the common pleas court and a divorce is granted to her, the common pleas court is without jurisdiction to deal with the custody and support of the minor children or to entertain an action filed by the mother against the father for alleged delinquencies in the weekly payments ordered as a condition of probation by the juvenile court, and the manner of enforcing such order of the juvenile court is to seek, by motion filed in the juvenile court, a revocation of the order of probation and to enforce against him the penalty of the judgment. Anderson v. Anderson (Cuyahoga 1965) 4 Ohio App.2d 90, 212 N.E.2d 643, 33 O.O.2d 145.

A juvenile court which acquires jurisdiction of a minor child of persons who are subsequently divorced has exclusive jurisdiction of such minor, and the common pleas court wherein such divorce is granted has no jurisdiction to make any order respecting the custody of such child. Patton v. Patton (Muskingum 1963) 1 Ohio App.2d 1, 203 N.E.2d 662, 30 O.O.2d 49.

Where a neglected child proceeding is instituted in the juvenile court by a parent of such child, and a divorce action is later instituted by such parent, the juvenile court has exclusive original jurisdiction to determine whether the child is neglected, the power to determine his custody and the authority to place the child with a relative. In re Small (Darke 1960) 114 Ohio App. 248, 181 N.E.2d 503, 19 O.O.2d 128.

Where a plaintiff is denied a divorce because of her own wrongful conduct, even though the evidence established grounds for divorce against the defendant, the court thereby loses jurisdiction to make an order respecting the future custody of a minor child; therefore, the action of the court ordering the custody of a minor child of the parties to be confided to the defendant is without statutory authority and is a nullity. Cowgill v. Cowgill (Highland 1960) 172 N.E.2d 721, 85 Ohio Law Abs. 185, 17 O.O.2d 138. Child Custody ⇐ 328

In a divorce action a court has jurisdiction to award custody of minor children even though no divorce is granted. Cowgill v. Cowgill (Ohio Com.Pl. 1960) 171 N.E.2d 769, 84 Ohio Law Abs. 406, reversed 172 N.E.2d 721, 85 Ohio Law Abs. 185, 17 O.O.2d 138.

Where the court of common pleas in a divorce action dismisses the action for insufficient evidence and without making a determination on the merits, it lacks the power and authority to certify the question of the custody of the minor child of the parties to the juvenile court, and the juvenile court is without power to accept such question. Haynie v. Haynie (Ohio 1959) 169 Ohio St. 467, 159 N.E.2d 765, 8 O.O.2d 476. Child Custody ⇐ 328

A common pleas court has no jurisdiction to make any order respecting the care and custody or visitation with minor children unless in the prayer of the petition the plaintiff asks for a divorce or alimony. Crum v. Howard (Ohio Com.Pl. 1956) 137 N.E.2d 654, 73 Ohio Law Abs. 111, 1 O.O.2d 399. Child Custody ⇐ 404

Jurisdiction over minors acquired by common pleas court in divorce action is continuing and, as between parties to divorce action, no other court may affect custody of such minors. McFadden v. Kendall (Auglaize 1946) 81 Ohio App. 107, 77 N.E.2d 625, 36 O.O. 414. Courts ⇐ 475(15); Child Custody ⇐ 404

Juvenile court to which divorce case is certified by common pleas court is charged with knowledge of existing orders affecting minor's custody. Sonnenberg v. State (Franklin 1931) 40 Ohio App. 475, 178 N.E. 855, 10 Ohio Law Abs. 271. Child Custody ⇐ 454

Order of common pleas court in divorce case affecting custody of minor is effective until reversed or modified, although case relating to minor is transferred to juvenile court. Sonnenberg v. State (Franklin 1931) 40 Ohio App. 475, 178 N.E. 855, 10 Ohio Law Abs. 271. Child Custody ⇐ 523; Child Custody ⇐ 531(1)

Where divorce case affecting minor's custody is certified to juvenile court, one desiring modification of order of common pleas court affecting child's custody may file motion in juvenile court. Sonnenberg v. State

(Franklin 1931) 40 Ohio App. 475, 178 N.E. 855, 10 Ohio Law Abs. 271. Child Custody ⇐ 601

A domestic relations court has jurisdiction under RC 3105.21(B) to determine custody despite dismissal of a divorce action for lack of prosecution. State ex rel. Easterday v. Zieba (Ohio 1991) 58 Ohio St.3d 251, 569 N.E.2d 1028.

13. Medical treatment

A juvenile court acts beyond the scope of its jurisdiction when it orders the mental health department and the regional consortium for children to pay the costs of a delinquent child's private psychiatric care. In re Hoodlet (Athens 1991) 72 Ohio App.3d 115, 593 N.E.2d 478. Infants ⇐ 228(1)

Where a child has been permanently committed to a child welfare board by order of juvenile court, such board may properly consent to medical and surgical treatment of such child; where a child has been temporarily so committed, the child remains ward of juvenile court, and such court may properly consent to medical and surgical treatment of such child. 1951 OAG 898.

Where a child is being cared for by a county welfare department or board of child welfare by agreement with the parents or guardian of such child, only such parents or guardian may properly consent to medical or surgical treatment of such child. 1951 OAG 898.

14. Commitment

Juvenile courts have exclusive original jurisdiction over adjudicated delinquents, and a juvenile court judge may impose consecutive commitment orders; moreover, if the juvenile perpetrates what would be a third-degree felony if committed by an adult, such as safecracking, under RC 2151.355 the court may make "any further disposition" it deems proper; therefore, this statute need not expressly confer jurisdiction for the court to order consecutive commitment terms for subsequent delinquent acts. In re Samkas (Cuyahoga 1992) 80 Ohio App.3d 240, 608 N.E.2d 1172, dismissed, jurisdictional motion overruled 65 Ohio St.3d 1431, 600 N.E.2d 676.

Judge of juvenile court may not commit child who has been found to be delinquent child or juvenile traffic offender, to county jail upon failure, refusal, or inability of such child to pay fine and court costs. OAG 70–143.

Where a juvenile court commits a child to the boys industrial school, the jurisdiction of the court over the child ceases, and the fact that the court may have attempted to put a condition upon the release of the child, such as making restitution for damages, does not affect the exclusive power of the school and the department of mental hygiene and correction to release the child for satisfactory behavior and progress in training. The department may so release the child regardless of whether or not such condition has been fulfilled. 1962 OAG 3461.

A minor under eighteen years of age who, after having been admitted to either boys industrial school or girls industrial school under commitment by a juvenile court, escapes therefrom and flees to another state may not be returned to this state under provisions of Uniform Extradition Act. 1946 OAG 1378.

15. Concurrent jurisdiction

Filing of juvenile court complaint alleging child was neglected or dependent child did not divest probate court of jurisdiction to issue letters of guardianship over child but, rather, probate court and juvenile court retained concurrent jurisdiction as to child, where guardianship application was filed first-in-time, and the juvenile court had yet to adjudicate child neglected or dependent or enter dispositional order at time guardianship letters issued. In re Guardianship of Pierce (Ohio App. 4 Dist., Ross, 07-22-2003) No. 03CA2712, 2003-Ohio-3997, 2003 WL 21715997, Unreported. Courts ⇐ 472.1; Infants ⇐ 196

Trial court and juvenile court maintained concurrent jurisdiction to determine custody of children, where custody of minor children was initially decided in a divorce decree, thus, trial court retained continuing jurisdiction over any matters relating to the custody of the children, yet juvenile court obtained jurisdiction over custody matters post-divorce, once county filed a complaint alleging children to be dependent. Bland v. Bland (Ohio App. 9 Dist., Summit, 02-26-2003) No. 21228, 2003-Ohio-828, 2003 WL 470180, Unreported. Child Custody ⇐ 404; Infants ⇐ 196

Forfeiture proceedings are applicable to juveniles, and juvenile courts have jurisdiction to hear and decide forfeiture matters, in light of statute providing that forfeiture division should be liberally construed to give effect to legislative intent enacting division that forfeiture and contraband provisions apply to property possessed, or possessed and owned, by persons under 18 years of age in the same manner as those provisions apply to property possessed, or possessed and owned, by adults. In re Harman (Ohio Com.Pl., 03-11-1994) 63 Ohio Misc.2d 529, 635 N.E.2d 96. Forfeitures ⇐ 1; Forfeitures ⇐ 5

Juvenile court has concurrent jurisdiction with domestic relations court in ordering child support. Albertson v. Ryder (Lake 1993) 85 Ohio App.3d 765, 621 N.E.2d 480. Courts ⇐ 472.1

RC 2151.23(A) confers concurrent jurisdiction on an Ohio court where a court of another state has previously assumed and exercised jurisdiction pursuant to RC 3109.21 to RC 3109.36. Squires v. Squires (Preble 1983) 12 Ohio App.3d 138, 468 N.E.2d 73, 12 O.B.R. 460.

Both the court of appeals and juvenile court have original jurisdiction in habeas corpus. In re Haws (Cuyahoga 1977) 64 Ohio App.2d 168, 411 N.E.2d 802, 18 O.O.3d 123. Courts ⇐ 472.1; Courts ⇐ 472.2

The juvenile and general divisions of a court of common pleas possess concurrent jurisdiction over a juvenile accused of a crime, and the juvenile division has not been divested of personal jurisdiction over one whose disposition is returned to it after the accused initially waived his right to be judged in that tribunal. State ex rel. Leis v. Black (Hamilton 1975) 45 Ohio App.2d 191, 341 N.E.2d 853, 74 O.O.2d 270. Infants ⇐ 68.5

Juvenile court code, GC 1639–1 (RC 2151.01) et seq., does not make the jurisdiction of the juvenile court exclusive throughout since it vests jurisdiction over the infant, not the crime. In re Evans (Richland 1941) 67 Ohio App. 66, 35 N.E.2d 887, 21 O.O. 93. Criminal Law ⇐ 100(3)

16. Foreign order

An Ohio juvenile court may not assume original jurisdiction if custody has been finally adjudicated in another state, and no request for decree modification has been made since the authority to enforce is different from the authority to modify, and the juvenile court is required to determine the enforcement issue under the applicable law and not conduct a hearing to expand its decision to include modification. In re McClurg (Butler 1992) 78 Ohio App.3d 465, 605 N.E.2d 418, dismissed, jurisdictional motion overruled 64 Ohio St.3d 1429, 594 N.E.2d 971. Child Custody ⇐ 779

The finding by another state court that a child is neglected and dependent is entitled to recognition in Ohio if the requirements of RC 3109.30(B) are met. Squires v. Squires (Preble 1983) 12 Ohio App.3d 138, 468 N.E.2d 73, 12 O.B.R. 460.

In appropriate circumstances, a court, in the "interest of the child," may exercise limited jurisdiction to enforce an original custody decree of a sister state to which it gives full faith and credit. Matter of Potter (Ohio Com.Pl. 1978) 56 Ohio Misc. 17, 377 N.E.2d 536, 10 O.O.3d 214. Judgment ⇐ 823

The mere showing by a petitioner who wrongfully retains custody that he now provides a better environment for a child as opposed to the party granted custody under the original out of state decree does not, per se, meet the "best interest" standard set forth in the Uniform Child Custody Jurisdiction Act. Matter of Potter (Ohio Com.Pl. 1978) 56 Ohio Misc. 17, 377 N.E.2d 536, 10 O.O.3d 214. Child Custody ⇐ 731

An Ohio juvenile court, in a dependency proceeding pursuant to RC 2151.27 et seq., has no jurisdiction to interfere with a mother's legal custody of her children in the absence of proof and a finding of unfitness of such parent merely for the purpose of releasing such children to the officers of the court of a foreign state, and the court need not give full faith and credit to a Michigan decree where that decree was obtained by the husband in an ex parte custody determination, subsequent to a divorce decree, in which the Michigan court had no personal jurisdiction over the nonresident wife. In re Messner (Huron 1969) 19 Ohio App.2d 33, 249 N.E.2d 532, 48 O.O.2d 31.

The right to custody of a minor child, the duty to support and the right of a parent to reasonable visitation may, where the interest of the child requires it, be determined or altered by a court of this state in whose jurisdiction the child may be, even though a court of another state has determined the right to custody, and in determining such matters it is not required to find that the child is delinquent, neglected, dependent, crippled, or otherwise physically handicapped. Bain v. Rose (Franklin 1957) 103 Ohio App. 297, 145 N.E.2d 319, 3 O.O.2d 326. Child Custody ⇐ 732

After divorce without specific award of custody of children, application for change of custody should be made to the court rendering the decree, and no jurisdiction is acquired by a writ of habeas corpus issuing from another court. Ex parte Crist (Ohio 1913) 89 Ohio St. 33, 105 N.E. 71, 11 Ohio Law Rep. 295. Courts ⇐ 475(15); Child Custody ⇐ 601; Habeas Corpus ⇐ 636

Note 16

The amendment of RC 2151.23(F) to include RC 3109.04 does not mandate a pure "best interests" approach to the question of in which forum it is more appropriate to resolve a custody dispute between a parent in a foreign state and a nonparent having temporary custody in Ohio; the superior interest of natural parents in the custody of their children makes it more appropriate to defer the decision of whether the parent's custody is in the child's best interest to the court of the parent's state. Spencer v Pryor, No. CA–85–01–002 (12th Dist Ct App, Preble, 7–22–85).

If a child is not the ward of any other court, trial court has jurisdiction over custody proceedings where the trial court's state has been the child's home state within six months before commencement of the proceeding, the child has developed significant connections with the state by virtue of the former residence, and the plaintiff, who acknowledges that he is the child's natural father, resides in the state. Harris v Hopper, No. L–81–187 (6th Dist Ct App, Lucas, 1–15–82).

17. Delinquent

Juvenile court had subject matter jurisdiction in proceedings for juvenile's adjudication as delinquent, where complaint alleged juvenile to be a delinquent child. In re C.W. (Ohio App. 12 Dist., Butler, 08-01-2005) No. CA2004-12-312, 2005-Ohio-3905, 2005 WL 1799317, Unreported. Infants ⇐ 196

Juvenile court's jurisdiction concerning any child who on or about date specified in complaint is alleged to be delinquent child is continuing and may be invoked at any time by motion before juvenile court. In re Bracewell (Ohio App. 1 Dist., 04-17-1998) 126 Ohio App.3d 133, 709 N.E.2d 938, dismissed, appeal not allowed 82 Ohio St.3d 1481, 696 N.E.2d 1087. Infants ⇐ 230.1

Juvenile court's jurisdiction to reinstate order of commitment upon juvenile adjudicated delinquent by reason of acts which, if committed by adult, would have constituted third-degree felony of carrying concealed weapon, continued after juvenile was released from official probation; at dispositional hearing, order of commitment was stayed, and juvenile was informed that he would not have to appear before court again unless he got himself into some "more difficulty" or violated his probation. In re Bracewell (Ohio App. 1 Dist., 04-17-1998) 126 Ohio App.3d 133, 709 N.E.2d 938, dismissed, appeal not allowed 82 Ohio St.3d 1481, 696 N.E.2d 1087. Infants ⇐ 230.1

Absent proper bindover procedure pursuant to statute, juvenile court has exclusive subject matter jurisdiction over any case concerning child who is alleged to be delinquent. State v. Wilson (Ohio, 08-09-1995) 73 Ohio St.3d 40, 652 N.E.2d 196, 1995-Ohio-217. Infants ⇐ 68.5

Although the statutes relating to juvenile delinquency contemplate that more than one act of delinquency occurring in the same time reference may be the predicate for more than one complaint and, upon trial, for more than one finding of delinquency, the plural findings that a child is a delinquent child constitute a finding of a single legal status existing at that point of time and permit one disposition common to all the complaints and findings of delinquency, or permit a disposition for each finding based on a single complaint which must be consistent with and not mutually exclusive of the disposition for each other finding made pursuant to some other complaint. In re Bolden (Allen 1973) 37 Ohio App.2d 7, 306 N.E.2d 166, 66 O.O.2d 26. Infants ⇐ 210

The state of Ohio has the burden of proof in the prosecution of a delinquency complaint to establish the jurisdiction of the juvenile court over the person of the "child." State v. Mendenhall (Lake 1969) 21 Ohio App.2d 135, 255 N.E.2d 307, 50 O.O.2d 227.

Juvenile court has jurisdiction on arrest of minor on complaint charging delinquency, though citation has not been issued to parent or guardian. State ex rel. Heth v. Moloney (Ohio 1933) 126 Ohio St. 526, 186 N.E. 362. Child Custody ⇐ 920

Where a delinquent child has become a ward of the juvenile court and has been committed, it may vacate or modify its original order, or make further orders in the case. State ex rel. Tailford v. Bristline (Ohio 1917) 96 Ohio St. 581, 119 N.E. 138, 15 Ohio Law Rep. 191. Infants ⇐ 230.1

Where the Ohio statute required a full investigation of the facts underlying a charge of delinquency and a finding of delinquency that the accused had committed acts in violation of Ohio law, jeopardy attached at a hearing at which accused was bound over for trial as an adult. Sims v. Engle (C.A.6 (Ohio) 1980) 619 F.2d 598, certiorari denied 101 S.Ct. 1403, 450 U.S. 936, 67 L.Ed.2d 372.

The juvenile court may not take jurisdiction of minor children where jurisdiction of common pleas court has attached in a divorce proceeding unless the minor child is charged with being delinquent. 1924 OAG 1993.

18. Adoption proceeding, effect

Continuing jurisdiction of juvenile court is not jurisdictional bar to adoption proceedings in probate court; probate court may exercise its jurisdiction in adoption proceedings while juvenile court has continuing jurisdiction over custody, and adoption hearing can go forth in probate court even if juvenile court may not agree with specific adoption. In re Hitchcock (Ohio App. 8 Dist., 11-21-1996) 120 Ohio App.3d 88, 696 N.E.2d 1090, stay granted 77 Ohio St.3d 1462, 672 N.E.2d 1119, stay denied 77 Ohio St.3d 1502, 673 N.E.2d 921, motion to vacate stay denied 77 Ohio St.3d 1521, 674 N.E.2d 373, appeal allowed 78 Ohio St.3d 1455, 677 N.E.2d 815, appeal dismissed as improvidently allowed 81 Ohio St.3d 1222, 689 N.E.2d 43, 1998-Ohio-653, stay denied 81 Ohio St.3d 1469, 690 N.E.2d 1288, stay denied 81 Ohio St.3d 1476, 691 N.E.2d 294. Adoption ⇐ 10; Infants ⇐ 230.1

19. Liability of government officials

Allegations that parents whose children were removed from home by county social worker were not allowed to recover children after safety plan providing for children's placement with friends had been initiated, despite parents' best efforts to do so, that continued deprivation of children was involuntary, and that parents were effectively denied prompt hearing on children's placement supported claim against social worker for violating parents' procedural due process rights. Smith v. Williams-Ash (C.A.6 (Ohio), 12-06-2005) No. 04-4547, 173 Fed.Appx. 363, 2005 WL 3304101, Unreported. Infants ⇐ 17

County social worker should have known that her alleged conduct in thwarting parents' attempts to have children returned to parents' home, after children were removed due to unsanitary conditions, and in effectively denying parents prompt hearing on children's placement had effect of violating parents' clearly established rights to procedural due process by involuntarily depriving parents of physical custody of children, and therefore qualified immunity did not apply to preclude social worker's liability under §§ 1983. Smith v. Williams-Ash (C.A.6 (Ohio), 12-06-2005) No. 04-4547, 173 Fed.Appx. 363, 2005 WL 3304101, Unreported. Civil Rights ⇐ 1376(4)

County social worker's alleged conduct in thwarting parents' attempts to have children returned to parents' home, after children were removed due to unsanitary conditions, and in effectively denying parents prompt hearing on children's placement did not rise to the level of conscience-shocking behavior, and thus did not support substantive due process claim. Smith v. Williams-Ash (C.A.6 (Ohio), 12-06-2005) No. 04-4547, 173 Fed.Appx. 363, 2005 WL 3304101, Unreported. Infants ⇐ 17

2151.231 Action for child support order

The parent, guardian, or custodian of a child, the person with whom a child resides, or the child support enforcement agency of the county in which the child, parent, guardian, or custodian of the child resides may bring an action in a juvenile court or other court with jurisdiction under section 2101.022 or 2301.03 of the Revised Code under this section requesting the court to issue an order requiring a parent of the child to pay an amount for the support of the child without regard to the marital status of the child's parents. No action may be brought under this section against a person presumed to be the parent of a child based on an acknowledgment of paternity that has not yet become final under former section 3111.211 or 5101.314 or section 2151.232, 3111.25, or 3111.821 of the Revised Code.

The parties to an action under this section may raise the issue of the existence or nonexistence of a parent-child relationship, unless a final and enforceable determination of the issue has been made with respect to the parties pursuant to Chapter 3111. of the Revised Code or an acknowledgment of paternity signed by the child's parents has become final pursuant to former section 3111.211 or 5101.314 or section 2151.232, 3111.25, or 3111.821 of the Revised Code. If a complaint is filed under this section and an issue concerning the existence or nonexistence of a parent-child relationship is raised, the court shall treat the action as an action pursuant to sections 3111.01 to 3111.18 of the Revised Code. An order issued in an action under this section does not preclude a party to the action from bringing a subsequent action pursuant to sections 3111.01 to 3111.18 of the Revised Code if the issue concerning the existence or nonexistence of the parent-child relationship was not determined with respect to the party pursuant to a proceeding under this section, a proceeding under Chapter 3111. of the Revised Code, or an acknowledgment of paternity that has become final under former section 3111.211 or 5101.314 or section 2151.232, 3111.25, or 3111.821 of the Revised Code. An order issued pursuant to this section shall remain effective until an order is issued pursuant to sections 3111.01 to 3111.18 of the Revised Code that a parent-child relationship does not exist between the alleged father of the child and the child or until the occurrence of an event described in section 3119.88 of the Revised Code that would require the order to terminate.

The court, in accordance with sections 3119.29 to 3119.56 of the Revised Code, shall include in each support order made under this section the requirement that one or both of the parents provide for the health care needs of the child to the satisfaction of the court.

(2002 H 657, eff. 12–13–02; 2000 S 180, eff. 3–22–01; 1997 H 352, eff. 1–1–98; 1996 H 710, § 7, eff. 6–11–96; 1995 H 167, eff. 6–11–96; 1992 S 10, eff. 7–15–92)

Uncodified Law

1996 H 710, § 15, eff. 6–11–96, reads, in part:

(A) The amendments to sections 2151.231, 2301.34, 2301.35, 2301.351, 2301.358, 2705.02, 3111.20, 3111.21, 3111.22, 3111.23, 3111.241, 3111.242, 3111.27, 3111.28, 3111.99, 3113.21, 3113.214, 3113.215, 3113.99, 4723.07, and 4723.09 of the Revised Code by Sub. H.B. 167 of the 121st General Assembly take effect, and their existing interim versions are correspondingly repealed, on the date this act takes effect and not on November 15, 1996 [.]

Historical and Statutory Notes

Ed. Note: The effective date of the amendment of this section by 1995 H 167 was changed from 11–15–96 to 6–11–96 by 1996 H 710, § 7, eff. 6–11–96.

Amendment Note: 2002 H 657 substituted "3119.29" for "3119.30" and "3119.56" for "3119.58" in the last paragraph of the section.

Amendment Note: 2000 S 180 rewrote this section, which prior thereto read:

"The parent, guardian, or custodian of a child, the person with whom a child resides, or the child support enforcement agency of the county in which the child, parent, guardian, or custodian of the child resides may bring an action in a juvenile court under this section requesting the court to issue an order requiring a parent of the child to pay an amount for the support of the child without regard to the marital status of the child's parents.

"The parties to an action under this section may raise the issue of the existence or nonexistence of a parent-child relationship, unless a final and enforceable determination of the issue has been made with respect to the parties pursuant to Chapter 3111. of the Revised Code or an acknowledgment of paternity signed by the child's parents has become final pursuant to section 2151.232, 3111.211, or 5101.314 of the Revised Code. If a complaint is filed under this section and an issue concerning the existence or nonexistence of a parent-child relationship is raised, the court shall treat the action as an action pursuant to sections 3111.01 to 3111.19 of the Revised Code. An order issued in an action under this section does not preclude a party to the action from bringing a subsequent action pursuant to sections 3111.01 to 3111.19 of the Revised Code if the issue concerning the existence or nonexistence of the parent-child relationship was not determined with respect to the party pursuant to a proceeding under this section, a proceeding under Chapter 3111. of the Revised Code, or an acknowledgment of paternity that has become final under section 2151.232, 3111.211, or 5101.314 of the Revised Code. An order issued pursuant to this section shall remain effective until an order is issued pursuant to sections 3111.01 to 3111.19 of the Revised Code that a parent-child relationship does not exist between the alleged father of the child and the child or until the occurrence of an event described in division (G)(4)(a) of section 3113.21 of the Revised Code that would require the order to terminate.

"The court, in accordance with section 3113.217 of the Revised Code, shall include in each support order made under this section the requirement that one or both of the parents provide for the health care needs of the child to the satisfaction of the court."

Amendment Note: 1997 H 352 inserted "or an acknowledgment of paternity signed by the child's parents has become final pursuant to section 2151.232, 3111.211, or 5101.314 of the Revised Code" and "pursuant to a proceeding under this section, a proceeding under Chapter 3111. of the Revised Code, or an acknowledgment of paternity that has become final under section 2151.232, 3111.211, or 5101.314 of the Revised Code" in the second paragraph; and added the third paragraph.

Amendment Note: 1995 H 167 inserted ", the person with whom a child resides, or the child support enforcement agency of the county in which the child, parent, guardian, or custodian of the child resides" in the first paragraph; and added the second paragraph.

Cross References

Child support orders, penalties, child support order defined, 3113.99
Interfering with action to issue or modify support order, 2919.231
Nonsupport of dependents, court costs and attorney fees, 2919.21
Parental duty of support, 3111.20
Review of administrative child support orders, 3111.27
Support orders, withholding or deduction requirements and notices, 3113.21

Ohio Administrative Code References

Administrative support order, OAC 5101:12–45–05.3
Objecting to the administrative support order, OAC 5101:12–45–05.4

Library References

Child Support ⚖173, 178.
Westlaw Topic No. 76E.
C.J.S. Parent and Child §§ 206, 211.

Research References

Encyclopedias

OH Jur. 3d Family Law § 973, Jurisdiction.
OH Jur. 3d Family Law § 1002, Application of Res Judicata.
OH Jur. 3d Family Law § 1039, Request for Administrative Order.
OH Jur. 3d Family Law § 1046, Modification by Agency.
OH Jur. 3d Family Law § 1201, Minimum Child Support Order.
OH Jur. 3d Family Law § 1222, Interfering With Action to Issue or Modify Support Order.
OH Jur. 3d Family Law § 1308, Reissuance Upon Change in Obligor's Status.

Treatises and Practice Aids

Klein, Darling, & Terez, Baldwin's Ohio Practice Civil Practice § 8:14, Affirmative Defenses.
Katz, Giannelli, Blair and Lipton, Baldwin's Ohio Practice, Criminal Law, § 109:13, Interfering With Support Actions.
Sowald & Morganstern, Baldwin's Ohio Practice Domestic Relations Law § 3:2, Administrative Determination of Parentage—Purpose.
Sowald & Morganstern, Baldwin's Ohio Practice Domestic Relations Law § 3:4, Administrative Determination of Parentage—Acknowledgment, Support Order, and Birth Record.
Sowald & Morganstern, Baldwin's Ohio Practice Domestic Relations Law § 3:5, Administrative Determination of Parentage—No Acknowledgment and Support Order.
Sowald & Morganstern, Baldwin's Ohio Practice Domestic Relations Law § 3:8, Jurisdiction and Venue.
Sowald & Morganstern, Baldwin's Ohio Practice Domestic Relations Law § 19:2, Jurisdiction Over Child Support.
Sowald & Morganstern, Baldwin's Ohio Practice Domestic Relations Law § 22:7, Establishing Support Order.
Sowald & Morganstern, Baldwin's Ohio Practice Domestic Relations Law § 22:16, Support Modification—Review of Administrative Support Orders.
Sowald & Morganstern, Baldwin's Ohio Practice Domestic Relations Law § 22:20, Role of Csea Attorneys and Party Status of Csea.
Sowald & Morganstern, Baldwin's Ohio Practice Domestic Relations Law § 23:14, In-State Remedies—in General.
Sowald & Morganstern, Baldwin's Ohio Practice Domestic Relations Law § 23:16, In-State Remedies—Determination of Support.
Carlin, Baldwin's Ohio Practice, Merrick-Rippner Probate Law § 19:2, Legitimation—Procedure—Acknowledgment of Paternity.

Carlin, Baldwin's Ohio Practice, Merrick-Rippner Probate Law § 19:6, Uniform Parentage Act—Jurisdiction of Action to Determine Father-Child Relationship.

Carlin, Baldwin's Ohio Practice, Merrick-Rippner Probate Law § 105:6, Juvenile Court—Probate Powers.

Carlin, Baldwin's Ohio Practice, Merrick-Rippner Probate Law § 108:1, Juvenile Court—Criminal Jurisdiction.

Carlin, Baldwin's Ohio Practice, Merrick-Rippner Probate Law § 19:10, Uniform Parentage Act—Procedure in Action to Determine Father-Child Relationship.

Carlin, Baldwin's Ohio Practice, Merrick-Rippner Probate Law § 108:13, Juvenile Court—Jurisdiction Over Child Custody Matters—Determination of Custody.

Carlin, Baldwin's Ohio Practice, Merrick-Rippner Probate Law § 108:20, Juvenile Court—Parentage Act—Jurisdiction and Venue.

Carlin, Baldwin's Ohio Practice, Merrick-Rippner Probate Law § 108:33, Juvenile Court—Parentage Act—Administrative Support Orders.

Carlin, Baldwin's Ohio Practice, Merrick-Rippner Probate Law § 108:34, Juvenile Court—Civil Support Proceedings—Liability for Child Support.

Carlin, Baldwin's Ohio Practice, Merrick-Rippner Probate Law § 107:134, Request for Support Order—Form.

Law Review and Journal Commentaries

The Presumption of Paternity in Child Support Cases: A Triumph of Law over Biology, Comment. 70 U Cin L Rev 1151 (Spring 2002).

Notes of Decisions

Child support enforcement agency assistance 1
Procedural issues 2
Retroactive awards 3

---

1. Child support enforcement agency assistance

Rules of Juvenile Procedure authorizing state or its agencies to file complaint in juvenile court to order child support payments was not inconsistent with statute authorizing only parent, guardian, or custodian of child to bring action in juvenile court requesting child support order, where statute, although specifying that parent, guardian, or custodian could bring support action, neither expressly authorized nor excluded state from bringing such action. State ex rel. Lamier v. Lamier (Ohio App. 8 Dist., 09-05-1995) 105 Ohio App.3d 797, 664 N.E.2d 1384. Child Support ⚖ 179

County child support enforcement agency (CSEA), as division of Department of Human Services (DHS), was obliged to collect support paid by DHS and, thus, had real interest necessary for standing to bring action seeking child support order for mothers receiving public assistance. State ex rel. Lamier v. Lamier (Ohio App. 8 Dist., 09-05-1995) 105 Ohio App.3d 797, 664 N.E.2d 1384. Child Support ⚖ 179

Ruling that county support enforcement agency lacked standing to bring action for child support in own name when relator and husband were married, did not dispute parentage, and did not receive public assistance did not unconstitutionally deny relator use of agency's services or undermine relator's right to support. In re Owens (Ohio App. 8 Dist., 07-05-1994) 104 Ohio App.3d 201, 661 N.E.2d 765, appeal allowed 71 Ohio St.3d 1422, 642 N.E.2d 387, appeal dismissed as improvidently allowed 74 Ohio St.3d 1280, 658 N.E.2d 304, 1996-Ohio-273. Child Support ⚖ 179

County support enforcement agency lacked statutory authority to bring action in its own name against relator's husband for child support when relator and husband were married, did not dispute parentage, and did not receive public assistance; two statutory exceptions permitting agency to bring action in its own name, when probate court enters acknowledgement of paternity upon its journal and when father voluntarily signs birth certificate as informant pursuant to statute, did not apply. In re Owens (Ohio App. 8 Dist., 07-05-1994) 104 Ohio App.3d 201, 661 N.E.2d 765, appeal allowed 71 Ohio St.3d 1422, 642 N.E.2d 387, appeal dismissed as improvidently allowed 74 Ohio St.3d 1280, 658 N.E.2d 304, 1996-Ohio-273. Child Support ⚖ 179

Trial court's dismissal of child support enforcement agency as party in five child support actions where parentage was established through administrative proceedings violated equal protection clauses of State and Federal Constitutions; statutory scheme, which permits agency to be party in support actions where parentage is established through probate court and where parents are on public assistance, but which does not specifically permit agency to be party when parentage is established through administrative proceedings, did not have rational basis, since enforcement agency can only effectuate its duty to protect best interests of child and public fisc by being joined as party in all child support enforcement actions. Cuyahoga Cty. Support Enforcement Agency v. Lozada (Ohio App. 8 Dist., 07-10-1995) 102 Ohio App.3d 442, 657 N.E.2d 372. Constitutional Law ⚖ 249(4); Child Support ⚖ 473

It is a violation of the equal protection clauses of the United States and Ohio constitutions to allow the aid and support of the child support enforcement agency in an action for child support brought by parents who have established their parentage through the probate court and residential parents who are on public assistance while denying the aid and support of the child support enforcement agency to parents who have established their parentage through the administrative process. Cuyahoga County Support Enforcement Agency v Lozada, Nos. 67463+, 1995 WL 386965 (8th Dist Ct App, Cuyahoga, 6-29-95).

Dismissal of the child support enforcement agency (CSEA) as a party in an action for child support under RC 3111.21 via RC 2151.231 violates the Ohio and federal Equal Protection Clauses when a similarly situated residential parent who legitimizes a child through probate court is entitled to have the CSEA advocate for a proper child support order in the juvenile court under RC 3111.20, by way of RC 2151.231. Cuyahoga County Support Enforcement Agency v Lozada, No. 67463+, 1995 WL 386965 (8th Dist Ct App, Cuyahoga, 6-29-95).

2. Procedural issues

Juvenile court had jurisdiction to hear motion by children's guardian seeking child support from children's mother, where guardian was statutorily empowered to bring such action. In re Lefever (Ohio App. 5 Dist., Muskingum, 12-15-2004) No. CT2004-0005, 2004-Ohio-6857, 2004 WL 2958348, Unreported. Guardian And Ward ⚖ 123

Holding oral hearing and receiving additional evidence before ruling on ex-husband's objections to magistrate's decision in child support proceeding was not abuse of trial court's discretion, even though ex-husband failed to present trial court with transcript of prior hearing before magistrate or affidavit of evidence to support his objections. Weitzel v. Way (Ohio App. 9 Dist., Summit, 12-17-2003) No. 21539, 2003-Ohio-6822, 2003 WL 22956521, Unreported. Child Support ⚖ 211

Father's signing of consent form to allow adoption of child, and failure to pay child support for seven years after consent to adoption, did not bar enforcement of child support payments after consent when adoption never took place, on a theory of absolution or laches, where there was no credible evidence in record of an agreement that would absolve father of his child support duties, and mother attempted to enforce child support obligation through two letters to father. Porter v. Ferrall (Ohio App. 11 Dist., Portage, 12-12-2003) No. 2002-P-0109, 2003-Ohio-6685, 2003 WL 22931383, Unreported. Child Support ⚖ 451; Child Support ⚖ 452

Child support order could not be administratively set, nor adopted by the court, on behalf of a caretaker who did not have legal custody of child. Tuscarawas County CSEA v. Sanders (Ohio App. 5 Dist., Tuscarawas, 10-15-2003) No. 2003AP030020, 2003-Ohio-5624, 2003 WL 22400729, Unreported. Child Support ⚖ 189

Doctrine of res judicata did not bar putative father's attempt, in context of mother's action for child support, to disestablish his paternity of children, where support statute specifically precluded doctrine as bar to subsequent paternity action. Crago v. Kinzie (Ohio Com.Pl., 06-01-2000) 106 Ohio Misc.2d 51, 733 N.E.2d 1219. Children Out-of-wedlock ⚖ 33

3. Retroactive awards

While a court is not required in every instance to make modifications to child support awards retroactive, a court must have a valid reason, consistent with law and equity, when it chooses not to do so. Zamos v. Zamos (Ohio App. 11 Dist., Portage, 05-07-2004) No. 2002-P-0085, 2004-Ohio-2310, 2004 WL 1043673, Unreported, appeal not allowed 103 Ohio St.3d 1463, 815 N.E.2d 679, 2004-Ohio-5056. Child Support ⚖ 364

Father was entitled to recover child support from mother from date their child began residing with him, rather than later date that he was awarded formal custody of the child. Zamos v. Zamos (Ohio App. 11 Dist., Portage, 05-07-2004) No. 2002-P-0085, 2004-Ohio-2310, 2004 WL 1043673, Unreported, appeal not allowed 103 Ohio St.3d 1463, 815 N.E.2d 679, 2004-Ohio-5056. Child Support ⚖ 150

2151.232 Action for child support order before acknowledgment becomes final

If an acknowledgment has been filed and entered into the birth registry pursuant to section 3111.24 of the Revised Code but has not yet become final, either parent who signed the acknowledgment may bring an action in the juvenile court or other court with jurisdiction under section 2101.022 or 2301.03 of the Revised Code under this section requesting that the court issue an order requiring a parent of the child to pay an amount for the support of the child in accordance with Chapters 3119., 3121., 3123., and 3125. of the Revised Code.

The parties to an action under this section may raise the issue of the existence or nonexistence of a parent-child relationship. If an action is commenced pursuant to this section and the issue of the existence or nonexistence of a parent-child relationship is raised, the court shall treat the action as an action commenced pursuant to sections 3111.01 to 3111.18 of the Revised Code. If the issue is raised, the court shall promptly notify the office of child support in the department of job and family services that it is conducting proceedings in compliance with sections 3111.01 to 3111.18 of the Revised Code. On receipt of the notice by the office, the acknowledgment of paternity signed by the parties and filed pursuant to section 3111.23 of the Revised Code shall be considered rescinded.

If the parties do not raise the issue of the existence or nonexistence of a parent-child relationship in the action and an order is issued pursuant to this section prior to the date the acknowledgment filed and entered on the birth registry becomes final, the acknowledgment shall be considered final as of the date of the issuance of the order. An order issued pursuant to this section shall not affect an acknowledgment that becomes final pursuant to section 3111.25 of the Revised Code prior to the issuance of the order.

(2000 S 180, eff. 3-22-01; 1999 H 471, eff. 7-1-00; 1997 H 352, eff. 1-1-98)

Historical and Statutory Notes

Amendment Note: 2000 S 180 rewrote this section, which prior thereto read:

"If an acknowledgment has been filed and entered into the birth registry pursuant to section 5101.314 of the Revised Code but has not yet become final, either parent who signed the acknowledgment may bring an action in the juvenile court under this section requesting that the court issue an order requiring a parent of the child to pay an amount for the support of the child in accordance with sections 3113.21 to 3113.219 of the Revised Code.

"The parties to an action under this section may raise the issue of the existence or nonexistence of a parent-child relationship. If an action is commenced pursuant to this section and the issue of the existence or nonexistence of a parent-child relationship is raised, the court shall treat the action as an action commenced pursuant to sections 3111.01 to 3111.19 of the Revised Code. If the issue is raised, the court shall promptly notify the division of child support in the department of job and family services that it is conducting proceedings in compliance with sections 3111.01 to 3111.19 of the Revised Code. On receipt of the notice by the division, the acknowledgment of paternity signed by the parties and filed pursuant to section 5101.314 of the Revised Code shall be considered rescinded.

"If the parties do not raise the issue of the existence or nonexistence of a parent-child relationship in the action and an order is issued pursuant to this section prior to the date the acknowledgment filed and entered on the birth registry under section 5101.314 of the Revised Code becomes final, the acknowledgment shall be considered final as of the date of the issuance of the order. An order issued pursuant to this section shall not affect an acknowledgment that becomes final pursuant to section 5101.314 of the Revised Code prior to the issuance of the order."

Amendment Note: 1999 H 471 substituted "job and family" for "human" in the second paragraph.

Cross References

Adoption, consents required, 3107.06
Adoption, exception to requirement of search of putative father registry, 3107.064
Child support orders, penalties, child support order defined, 3113.99
Duty of parents to support children of unemancipated minor children, complaints regarding, 3109.19
Filing of birth certificate upon acknowledgement of paternity, 3705.09
Interfering with action to issue or modify support order, 2919.231
Nonsupport of dependents, court costs and attorney fees, 2919.21
Parental duty of support, raising issue of existence of parent-child relationship, 3111.20
Parental duty of support, when arising, 3103.031
Presumptions regarding father-child relationship, 3111.03
Visitation rights of grandparents and other relatives, complaints for, 3109.12

Library References

Children Out-of-Wedlock ⚖34 to 35.
Westlaw Topic No. 76H.
C.J.S. Children Out-of-Wedlock §§ 46, 49, 85 to 90.

Research References

Encyclopedias

OH Jur. 3d Family Law § 892, Birth Record of Legitimated Child.
OH Jur. 3d Family Law § 965, Statutory Presumptions.
OH Jur. 3d Family Law § 973, Jurisdiction.
OH Jur. 3d Family Law § 1000, Review of Support Orders and Judgments.
OH Jur. 3d Family Law § 1038, Child Support Action in Juvenile Court.
OH Jur. 3d Family Law § 1039, Request for Administrative Order.
OH Jur. 3d Family Law § 1201, Minimum Child Support Order.
OH Jur. 3d Family Law § 1222, Interfering With Action to Issue or Modify Support Order.
OH Jur. 3d Family Law § 908.1, Putative Father Registry.
OH Jur. 3d Family Law § 1031.1, Rescission of Acknowledgment of Paternity.

Forms

Ohio Jurisprudence Pleading and Practice Forms § 96:9, Putative Father Registry.
Ohio Jurisprudence Pleading and Practice Forms § 111:6, Presumptions.
Ohio Jurisprudence Pleading and Practice Forms § 96:11, Consent Required.

Treatises and Practice Aids

Sowald & Morganstern, Baldwin's Ohio Practice Domestic Relations Law § 18:7, Visitation by Third Parties in Domestic Relations Actions.
Sowald & Morganstern, Baldwin's Ohio Practice Domestic Relations Law § 19:3, Support Obligations—in General.
Sowald & Morganstern, Baldwin's Ohio Practice Domestic Relations Law § 21:2, Parenting Time—Establishing Visitation Order.
Carlin, Baldwin's Ohio Practice, Merrick-Rippner Probate Law § 19:1, Legitimation—Statutory Provisions.
Carlin, Baldwin's Ohio Practice, Merrick-Rippner Probate Law § 19:2, Legitimation—Procedure—Acknowledgment of Paternity.
Carlin, Baldwin's Ohio Practice, Merrick-Rippner Probate Law § 19:4, Legitimation—Historical Provisions.
Carlin, Baldwin's Ohio Practice, Merrick-Rippner Probate Law § 19:6, Uniform Parentage Act—Jurisdiction of Action to Determine Father-Child Relationship.
Carlin, Baldwin's Ohio Practice, Merrick-Rippner Probate Law § 19:7, Uniform Parentage Act—Presumptions.
Carlin, Baldwin's Ohio Practice, Merrick-Rippner Probate Law § 108:3, Juvenile Court—Criminal Jurisdiction—Proceedings for Nonsupport.
Carlin, Baldwin's Ohio Practice, Merrick-Rippner Probate Law § 19:10, Uniform Parentage Act—Procedure in Action to Determine Father-Child Relationship.
Carlin, Baldwin's Ohio Practice, Merrick-Rippner Probate Law § 98:30, Adoption—Statutorily Required Consent.
Carlin, Baldwin's Ohio Practice, Merrick-Rippner Probate Law § 98:31, Adoption—Parties Giving Consent—Biological Parents.

Carlin, Baldwin's Ohio Practice, Merrick-Rippner Probate Law § 98:32, Adoption—Parties Giving Consent—Putative Father.

Carlin, Baldwin's Ohio Practice, Merrick-Rippner Probate Law § 98:34, Adoption—Parties Giving Consent—Agency.

Carlin, Baldwin's Ohio Practice, Merrick-Rippner Probate Law § 98:38, Adoption—Consent Not Required—Statutory Scheme.

Carlin, Baldwin's Ohio Practice, Merrick-Rippner Probate Law § 98:49, Adoption—Interlocutory and Final Orders.

Carlin, Baldwin's Ohio Practice, Merrick-Rippner Probate Law § 108:13, Juvenile Court—Jurisdiction Over Child Custody Matters—Determination of Custody.

Carlin, Baldwin's Ohio Practice, Merrick-Rippner Probate Law § 108:20, Juvenile Court—Parentage Act—Jurisdiction and Venue.

Carlin, Baldwin's Ohio Practice, Merrick-Rippner Probate Law § 108:22, Juvenile Court—Parentage Act—Presumption of Paternity.

Carlin, Baldwin's Ohio Practice, Merrick-Rippner Probate Law § 108:24, Juvenile Court—Parentage Act—Genetic Tests, Fees, and Costs.

Carlin, Baldwin's Ohio Practice, Merrick-Rippner Probate Law § 108:26, Juvenile Court—Parentage Act—Applicability of Civil Rules to Paternity Proceedings.

Carlin, Baldwin's Ohio Practice, Merrick-Rippner Probate Law § 108:31, Juvenile Court—Parentage Act—Continuing Jurisdiction to Modify or Revoke Judgment.

Carlin, Baldwin's Ohio Practice, Merrick-Rippner Probate Law § 108:34, Juvenile Court—Civil Support Proceedings—Liability for Child Support.

Law Review and Journal Commentaries

Acknowledgement of Paternity—Changes in Statutes and Forms, Angela G. Carlin. 10 Prob L J Ohio 10 (September/October 1999).

2151.24 Separate room for hearings

(A) Except as provided in division (B) of this section, the board of county commissioners shall provide a special room not used for the trial of criminal or adult cases, when available, for the hearing of the cases of dependent, neglected, abused, and delinquent children.

(B) Division (A) of this section does not apply to the case of an alleged delinquent child when the case is one in which the prosecuting attorney seeks a serious youthful offender disposition under section 2152.13 of the Revised Code.

(2000 S 179, § 3, eff. 1–1–02; 1975 H 85, eff. 11–28–75; 1953 H 1; GC 1639–14)

Historical and Statutory Notes

Pre–1953 H 1 Amendments: 117 v 520, § 1

Amendment Note: 2000 S 179 designated division (A) and inserted "Except as provided in division (B) of this section," therein; and added division (B).

Library References

Courts ⚖︎72, 74.
Westlaw Topic No. 106.
C.J.S. Courts § 121.

Research References

Encyclopedias

OH Jur. 3d Family Law § 1536, Terms, Sessions, and Places of Court.

Treatises and Practice Aids

Carlin, Baldwin's Ohio Practice, Merrick-Rippner Probate Law § 107:52, Adjudicatory Hearings—Confidentiality of Juvenile Court Proceedings.

Giannelli & Yeomans, Ohio Juvenile Law § 5:1, Introduction.

PRACTICE AND PROCEDURE

2151.27 Complaint

(A)(1) Subject to division (A)(2) of this section, any person having knowledge of a child who appears to have violated section 2151.87 of the Revised Code or to be a juvenile traffic offender or to be an unruly, abused, neglected, or dependent child may file a sworn complaint with respect to that child in the juvenile court of the county in which the child has a residence or legal settlement or in which the violation, unruliness, abuse, neglect, or dependency allegedly occurred. If an alleged abused, neglected, or dependent child is taken into custody pursuant to division (D) of section 2151.31 of the Revised Code or is taken into custody pursuant to division (A) of section 2151.31 of the Revised Code without the filing of a complaint and placed into shelter care pursuant to division (C) of that section, a sworn complaint shall be filed with respect to the child before the end of the next day after the day on which the child was taken into custody. The sworn complaint may be upon information and belief, and, in addition to the allegation that the child committed the violation or is an unruly, abused, neglected, or dependent child, the complaint shall allege the particular facts upon which the allegation that the child committed the violation or is an unruly, abused, neglected, or dependent child is based.

(2) Any person having knowledge of a child who appears to be an unruly child for being an habitual truant may file a sworn complaint with respect to that child and the parent, guardian, or other person having care of the child in the juvenile court of the county in which the child has a residence or legal settlement or in which the child is supposed to attend public school. The sworn complaint may be upon information and belief and shall contain the following allegations:

(a) That the child is an unruly child for being an habitual truant and, in addition, the particular facts upon which that allegation is based;

(b) That the parent, guardian, or other person having care of the child has failed to cause the child's attendance at school in violation of section 3321.38 of the Revised Code and, in addition, the particular facts upon which that allegation is based.

(B) If a child, before arriving at the age of eighteen years, allegedly commits an act for which the child may be adjudicated an unruly child and if the specific complaint alleging the act is not filed or a hearing on that specific complaint is not held until after the child arrives at the age of eighteen years, the court has jurisdiction to hear and dispose of the complaint as if the complaint were filed and the hearing held before the child arrived at the age of eighteen years.

(C) If the complainant in a case in which a child is alleged to be an abused, neglected, or dependent child desires permanent custody of the child or children, temporary custody of the child or children, whether as the preferred or an alternative disposition, or the placement of the child in a planned permanent living arrangement, the complaint shall contain a prayer specifically requesting permanent custody, temporary custody, or the placement of the child in a planned permanent living arrangement.

(D) Any person with standing under applicable law may file a complaint for the determination of any other matter over which the juvenile court is given jurisdiction by section 2151.23 of the Revised Code. The complaint shall be filed in the county in which the child who is the subject of the complaint is found or was last known to be found.

(E) A public children services agency, acting pursuant to a complaint or an action on a complaint filed under this section, is not subject to the requirements of section 3127.23 of the Revised Code.

(F) Upon the filing of a complaint alleging that a child is an unruly child, the court may hold the complaint in abeyance pending the child's successful completion of actions that constitute a method to divert the child from the juvenile court system. The method may be adopted by a county pursuant to divisions (D) and (E) of section 121.37 of the Revised Code or it may be another method that the court considers satisfactory. If the child completes the actions to the court's satisfaction, the court may dismiss the complaint. If the child fails to complete the actions to the court's satisfaction, the court may consider the complaint.

(2004 S 185, eff. 4-11-05; 2001 H 57, eff. 2-19-02; 2000 S 179, § 3, eff. 1-1-02; 2000 S 218, eff. 3-15-01; 2000 S 181, eff. 9-4-00; 1998 H 484, eff. 3-18-99; 1996 H 445, eff. 9-3-96; 1996 H 274, § 4, eff. 8-8-96; 1996 H 274, § 1, eff. 8-8-96; 1995 S 2, eff. 7-1-96; 1992 H 154, eff. 7-31-92; 1988 S 89; 1984 S 5; 1975 H 85; 1969 H 320)

Historical and Statutory Notes

Ed. Note: Former RC 2151.27 repealed by 1969 H 320, eff. 11-19-69; 127 v 547; 1953 H 1; GC 1639-23.

Pre-1953 H 1 Amendments: 121 v 557; 117 v 520

Amendment Note: 2004 S 185 substituted "3127.23" for "3109.27 in division (E).

Amendment Note: 2001 H 57 added new division (F).

Amendment Note: 2000 S 179 rewrote this section, which prior thereto read:

"(A)(1) Subject to division (A)(2) of this section, any person having knowledge of a child who appears to be a juvenile traffic offender or to be a delinquent, unruly, abused, neglected, or dependent child may file a sworn complaint with respect to that child in the juvenile court of the county in which the child has a residence or legal settlement or in which the traffic offense, delinquency, unruliness, abuse, neglect, or dependency allegedly occurred. If an alleged abused, neglected, or dependent child is taken into custody pursuant to division (D) of section 2151.31 of the Revised Code or is taken into custody pursuant to division (A) of section 2151.31 of the Revised Code without the filing of a complaint and placed into shelter care pursuant to division (C) of that section, a sworn complaint shall be filed with respect to the child before the end of the next day after the day on which the child was taken into custody. The sworn complaint may be upon information and belief, and, in addition to the allegation that the child is a delinquent, unruly, abused, neglected, or dependent child or a juvenile traffic offender, the complaint shall allege the particular facts upon which the allegation that the child is a delinquent, unruly, abused, neglected, or dependent child or a juvenile traffic offender is based.

"(2) Any person having knowledge of a child who appears to be an unruly or delinquent child for being an habitual or chronic truant may file a sworn complaint with respect to that child and the parent, guardian, or other person having care of the child in the juvenile court of the county in which the child has a residence or legal settlement or in which the child is supposed to attend public school. The sworn complaint may be upon information and belief and shall contain the following allegations:

"(a) That the child is an unruly child for being an habitual truant or the child is a delinquent child for being a chronic truant or an habitual truant who previously has been adjudicated an unruly child for being an habitual truant and, in addition, the particular facts upon which that allegation is based;

"(b) That the parent, guardian, or other person having care of the child has failed to cause the child's attendance at school in violation of section 3321.38 of the Revised Code and, in addition, the particular facts upon which that allegation is based.

"(B) If a child, before arriving at the age of eighteen years, allegedly commits an act for which the child may be adjudicated a delinquent child, an unruly child, or a juvenile traffic offender and if the specific complaint alleging the act is not filed or a hearing on that specific complaint is not held until after the child arrives at the age of eighteen years, the court has jurisdiction to hear and dispose of the complaint as if the complaint were filed and the hearing held before the child arrived at the age of eighteen years.

"(C) If the complainant in a case in which a child is alleged to be an abused, neglected, or dependent child desires permanent custody of the child or children, temporary custody of the child or children, whether as the preferred or an alternative disposition, or the placement of the child in a planned permanent living arrangement, the complaint shall contain a prayer specifically requesting permanent custody, temporary custody, or the placement of the child in a planned permanent living arrangement.

"(D) For purposes of the record to be maintained by the clerk under division (B) of section 2151.18 of the Revised Code, when a complaint is filed that alleges that a child is a delinquent child, the court shall determine if the victim of the alleged delinquent act was sixty-five years of age or older or permanently and totally disabled at the time of the alleged commission of the act.

"(E) Any person with standing under applicable law may file a complaint for the determination of any other matter over which the juvenile court is given jurisdiction by section 2151.23 of the Revised Code. The complaint shall be filed in the county in which the child who is the subject of the complaint is found or was last known to be found.

"(F) Within ten days after the filing of a complaint, the court shall give written notice of the filing of the complaint and of the substance of the complaint to the superintendent of a city, local, exempted village, or joint vocational school district if the complaint alleges that a child committed an act that would be a criminal offense if committed by an adult, that the child was sixteen years of age or older at the time of the commission of the alleged act, and that the alleged act is any of the following:

"(1) A violation of section 2923.122 of the Revised Code that relates to property owned or controlled by, or to an activity held under the auspices of, the board of education of that school district;

"(2) A violation of section 2923.12 of the Revised Code, of a substantially similar municipal ordinance, or of section 2925.03 of the Revised Code that was committed on property owned or controlled by, or at an activity held under the auspices of, the board of education of that school district;

"(3) A violation of section 2925.11 of the Revised Code that was committed on property owned or controlled by, or at an activity held under the auspices of, the board of education of that school district, other than a violation of that section that would be a minor drug possession offense, as defined in section 2925.01 of the Revised Code, if committed by an adult;

"(4) A violation of section 2903.01, 2903.02, 2903.03, 2903.04, 2903.11, 2903.12, 2907.02, or 2907.05 of the Revised Code, or a violation of former section 2907.12 of the Revised Code, that was committed on property owned or controlled by, or at an activity held under the auspices of, the board of education of that school district, if the victim at the time of the commission of the alleged act was an employee of the board of education of that school district.

"(5) Complicity in any violation described in division (F)(1), (2), (3), or (4) of this section that was alleged to have been committed in the manner described in division (F)(1), (2), (3), or (4) of this section, regardless of whether the act of complicity was committed on property owned or controlled by, or at an activity held under the auspices of, the board of education of that school district.

"(G) A public children services agency, acting pursuant to a complaint or an action on a complaint filed under this section, is not subject to the requirements of section 3109.27 of the Revised Code."

Amendment Note: 2000 S 218 inserted "have violated section 2151.87 of the Revised Code or to", "violation," and "committed the violation or" twice, in division (A)(1).

Amendment Note: 2000 S 181 designated division (A)(1) and inserted "Subject to division (A)(2) of this section," therein; and added division (A)(2).

Amendment Note: 1998 H 484 substituted "a planned permanent living arrangement" for "long-term foster care" twice in division (C).

Amendment Note: 1996 H 445 changed a reference to section 2907.12 to the reference to former section 2907.12 in division (F)(4); and made other nonsubstantive changes.

Amendment Note: 1996 H 274, § 4, eff. 8-8-96, harmonized the versions of this section as amended by 1995 S 2, § 1, eff. 7-1-96, and 1996 H 274, § 1, eff. 8-8-96; and deleted division (H), which prior thereto read:

"(H) This is an interim section effective until July 1, 1996."

Amendment Note: 1996 H 274, § 1, eff. 8-8-96, deleted "business" after "next" in division (A); added divisions (G) and (H); and made changes to reflect gender neutral language.

Amendment Note: 1995 S 2 substituted "adjudicated" for "adjudged" in division (B); deleted "division (A)(1), (4), (5), (6), (7), (9), or (10) of" before "section 2925.03" in division (F)(2); added division (F)(3); redesignated former divisions (F)(3) and (F)(4) as divisions (F)(4) and (F)(5); inserted "or (4)" twice in division (F)(5); and made changes to reflect gender neutral language and other nonsubstantive changes.

Cross References

Complaint, Juv R 10
Extension of expulsion of pupils, 3313.66
Minor, diversion program, 4301.69
Parent convicted of killing other parent, termination of custody order deemed new complaint for institutional custody, 3109.46
Placing of child in institution, agency filing complaint and case plan, 5103.15
Power of attorney or caretaker authorization affidavit, hearing, notice, de novo review, 3109.77

Ohio Administrative Code References

Obtaining permanent custody: termination of parental rights, OAC 5101:2–42–95

Library References

Infants ⇐197.
Westlaw Topic No. 211.
C.J.S. Infants § 55.
Baldwin's Ohio Legislative Service, 1988 Laws of Ohio, S 89—LSC Analysis, p 5–571

Research References

Encyclopedias

OH Jur. 3d Criminal Law § 432, Nature and Seriousness of Offense as Affecting Right of Accused.
OH Jur. 3d Criminal Law § 1585, Jury and Jury Selection.
OH Jur. 3d Criminal Law § 2609, Computation of Amount of Fine for Jury Trial.
OH Jur. 3d Family Law § 1138, Information to be Included in Pleading or Affidavit.
OH Jur. 3d Family Law § 1486, "Child"—Significance of Age at Time of Offense.
OH Jur. 3d Family Law § 1542, Expenses.
OH Jur. 3d Family Law § 1550, Child Custody.
OH Jur. 3d Family Law § 1576, Detention Hearing; Notice.
OH Jur. 3d Family Law § 1586, County in Which to File Complaint.
OH Jur. 3d Family Law § 1590, Who May File Complaint.
OH Jur. 3d Family Law § 1595, Permanent Custody.
OH Jur. 3d Family Law § 1601, Prehearing Motions—Motion to Release Child.
OH Jur. 3d Family Law § 1684, Conclusiveness; Collateral Attack—Where Proceedings Are Void.
OH Jur. 3d Family Law § 1744, Trial by Jury.

Forms

Ohio Jurisprudence Pleading and Practice Forms § 96:43, Temporary and Permanent Custody.

Treatises and Practice Aids

Katz, Giannelli, Blair and Lipton, Baldwin's Ohio Practice, Criminal Law, § 62:3, Ohio Law.
Katz, Giannelli, Blair and Lipton, Baldwin's Ohio Practice, Criminal Law, § 35:11, Juvenile Cases.
Carlin, Baldwin's Ohio Practice, Merrick-Rippner Probate Law § 104:5, Juvenile Courts—Constitutional Issues—Right to Notice, Counsel, and Trial.
Carlin, Baldwin's Ohio Practice, Merrick-Rippner Probate Law § 105:8, Juvenile Court—Age Jurisdiction.
Carlin, Baldwin's Ohio Practice, Merrick-Rippner Probate Law § 107:2, Types of Complaints.
Carlin, Baldwin's Ohio Practice, Merrick-Rippner Probate Law § 107:3, Contents of Juvenile Complaint—Facts Establishing Jurisdiction.
Carlin, Baldwin's Ohio Practice, Merrick-Rippner Probate Law § 107:4, Contents of Juvenile Complaint—Prayer for Disposition.
Carlin, Baldwin's Ohio Practice, Merrick-Rippner Probate Law § 107:5, Time for Filing Complaint.
Carlin, Baldwin's Ohio Practice, Merrick-Rippner Probate Law § 107:7, Jurisdiction and Venue for Juvenile Proceedings.
Carlin, Baldwin's Ohio Practice, Merrick-Rippner Probate Law § 107:8, Notice to School Officials.
Carlin, Baldwin's Ohio Practice, Merrick-Rippner Probate Law § 105:13, Juvenile Court—Authority Following Certification.
Carlin, Baldwin's Ohio Practice, Merrick-Rippner Probate Law § 107:50, Adjudicatory Hearings—Applicability of Rules of Court.
Carlin, Baldwin's Ohio Practice, Merrick-Rippner Probate Law § 107:84, Disposition of Delinquent Children—Prior to January 1, 2002.
Carlin, Baldwin's Ohio Practice, Merrick-Rippner Probate Law § 108:16, Juvenile Court—Habeas Corpus Involving Child Custody.
Carlin, Baldwin's Ohio Practice, Merrick-Rippner Probate Law § 107:136, Complaint, Delinquent Child—Form.
Carlin, Baldwin's Ohio Practice, Merrick-Rippner Probate Law § 107:137, Complaint, Unruly Child—Form.
Carlin, Baldwin's Ohio Practice, Merrick-Rippner Probate Law § 107:138, Complaint, Abused, Neglected, or Dependent Child—Form.
Giannelli & Yeomans, Ohio Juvenile Law § 2:2, Age Jurisdiction.
Giannelli & Yeomans, Ohio Juvenile Law § 14:3, Custody, Arrests & Stops.
Giannelli & Yeomans, Ohio Juvenile Law § 15:2, Intake.
Giannelli & Yeomans, Ohio Juvenile Law § 16:1, Introduction.
Giannelli & Yeomans, Ohio Juvenile Law § 16:2, Standing to File Complaint.
Giannelli & Yeomans, Ohio Juvenile Law § 16:3, Basis for Complaint.
Giannelli & Yeomans, Ohio Juvenile Law § 16:4, Time Requirements—Custody; Detention.
Giannelli & Yeomans, Ohio Juvenile Law § 16:6, Oath Requirement.
Giannelli & Yeomans, Ohio Juvenile Law § 16:7, Content of Complaint; Designating Type of Case.
Giannelli & Yeomans, Ohio Juvenile Law § 16:8, Delinquency Complaints.
Giannelli & Yeomans, Ohio Juvenile Law § 17:2, Proper Venue.
Giannelli & Yeomans, Ohio Juvenile Law § 18:2, Issuance of Summons: Proper Parties.
Giannelli & Yeomans, Ohio Juvenile Law § 18:4, Summons: Methods of Service.
Giannelli & Yeomans, Ohio Juvenile Law § 31:2, Filing of Motion.
Giannelli & Yeomans, Ohio Juvenile Law § 16:10, Unruly Complaints.
Giannelli & Yeomans, Ohio Juvenile Law § 16:11, Neglect & Abuse Complaints.
Giannelli & Yeomans, Ohio Juvenile Law § 16:12, Dependency Complaints.
Giannelli & Yeomans, Ohio Juvenile Law § 16:13, Custody Proceedings; Required Information.
Giannelli & Yeomans, Ohio Juvenile Law § 16:14, Permanent & Temporary Custody Complaints; Planned Permanent Living Arrangements.
Giannelli & Yeomans, Ohio Juvenile Law § 16:15, Certification or Transfer from Another Court.
Giannelli & Yeomans, Ohio Juvenile Law § 16:17, Objections to Complaints.
Hastings, Manoloff, Sheeran, & Stype, Ohio School Law § 20:20, Enforcement Procedures-Consequences.

Law Review and Journal Commentaries

Faith–Healing And Religious–Treatment Exemptions To Child–Endangerment Laws: Should Parental Religious Practices Excuse The Failure To Provide Necessary Medical Care To Children?, Comment. 13 U Dayton L Rev 79 (Fall 1987).

Interviewing Child Victims/Witnesses, Mary A. Lentz. 9 Baldwin's Ohio Sch L J 25 (July/August 1997).

Privacy, Dangerousness and Counselors, Steven R. Smith. 15 J L & Educ 121 (Winter 1986).

Notes of Decisions

Finding that child is neglected or dependent 3
Jurisdiction 2
Procedural issues 4
Sufficiency of complaint 1

---

1. Sufficiency of complaint

Child dependency complaint filed by the county department of children and family services was sufficient to put father on notice of the issues and did not deprive father of due process; complaint alleged that child was born while mother tested positive for drugs, mother's drug problem prevented her from caring for child, mother had other children that were not in her custody, mother failed to comply with her agency caseplan, father failed to provide care or support for child, and complaint sought an award of permanent custody to county department of children and family services. In re I.M. (Ohio App. 8 Dist., Cuyahoga, 12-24-2003) No. 82669, No. 82695, 2003-Ohio-7069, 2003 WL 23010024, Unreported. Infants 197

Former husband's complaint against former wife alleging dependency and neglect of parties' children failed to adequately set forth particular facts upon which allegations were based and contained no notice concerning evidence against which wife would have to defend; while husband claimed children would be molested and wife would flee should children be returned to her custody, these were general conclusory claims unsupported by particular facts, and husband's only specific claim, that children were not functioning at appropriate level, did not fall within definition of dependency, neglect, or abuse. Louck v. Louck (Ohio App. 3 Dist., Marion, 11-10-2003) No. 9-03-35, 2003-Ohio-5999, 2003 WL 22533679, Unreported. Infants 197

Maternal aunt and uncle lacked standing to seek modification of placement of children, who were returned to custodial paternal grandmother at conclusion of neglect proceeding against her, notwithstanding apparently mistaken adjudication of neglect against children's parents rather than grandmother, where aunt and uncle were not parties to proceeding and were not made so by temporary emergency placement of children in their custody pending proceeding; however, aunt and uncle were not without recourse, as they could themselves bring a neglect proceeding against grandmother based on new information and obtain legal custody thereby. In re Crowder (Ohio App. 8 Dist., Cuyahoga, 10-03-2002) No. 80738, 2002-Ohio-5347, 2002 WL 31195430, Unreported. Infants 230.1

Under this section it is sufficient in affidavit to set out that child is dependent or delinquent, but where affiant sets out particular wherein it is claimed that child is dependent, and it is insufficient to constitute dependency, court does not have jurisdiction. Smith v. Privette & State (Franklin 1932) 13 Ohio Law Abs. 291.

A complaint filed with the juvenile court in a child abuse case must be made under oath and contain the facts of the abuse or neglect, sections of the Ohio Revised Code that have been violated, names and addresses of the parents, and a prayer for custody which must specifically indicate permanent custody, temporary custody, or long-term foster care. In re Dukes (Summit 1991) 81 Ohio App.3d 145, 610 N.E.2d 513, motion overruled 63 Ohio St.3d 1411, 585 N.E.2d 835.

A complaint to terminate parental custody in juvenile court is sufficient if the allegations therein notify the opposing party of the nature of the claim against her even if no specific facts or dates are mentioned. In re Pieper Children (Preble 1991) 74 Ohio App.3d 714, 600 N.E.2d 317, dismissed, jurisdictional motion overruled 66 Ohio St.3d 1410, 607 N.E.2d 9.

Although a complaining witness may refer to one or more particular statutes as being violated by a child, a juvenile court may find a violation of another statute and determine that the accused is a delinquent child. In re Burgess (Preble 1984) 13 Ohio App.3d 374, 469 N.E.2d 967, 13 O.B.R. 456. Infants 210

Complaint alleging that child is dependent must state essential facts which bring proceeding within jurisdiction of juvenile court because juvenile court, being court of limited jurisdiction, must be able to ascertain at early stage of proceeding whether or not it has jurisdiction over subject matter of claim. In re Sims (Preble 1983) 13 Ohio App.3d 37, 468 N.E.2d 111, 13 O.B.R. 40. Infants 197

A complaint under Juv R 10 and RC 2151.27 alleging that a child is dependent must state the essential facts which bring the proceeding within the jurisdiction of the court. In re Hunt (Ohio 1976) 46 Ohio St.2d 378, 348 N.E.2d 727, 75 O.O.2d 450. Infants 197

An allegation in a motion filed in juvenile court seeking to have that court "determine and award the future care and custody" of a child that "neither parent is a suitable person to have the care and custody of said child" does not constitute a charge that such child is "neglected" or "dependent" and is not sufficiently definite to constitute the "complaint" necessitated by RC 2151.27. Union County Child Welfare Bd. v. Parker (Union 1964) 7 Ohio App.2d 79, 218 N.E.2d 757, 36 O.O.2d 162. Infants 197

A certification by a common pleas court of its record to the juvenile court constitutes a filing of a complaint within the meaning of RC 2151.27. Hartshorne v. Hartshorne (Columbiana 1959) 185 N.E.2d 329, 89 Ohio Law Abs. 243.

In an action to determine that a minor is a dependent child, a mere allegation of dependency in the complaint is sufficient, although the court must find that the condition was due to no fault of the parent, guardian, or custodian. In re Duncan (Preble 1951) 107 N.E.2d 256, 62 Ohio Law Abs. 173.

The certification of a cause from the probate court to the juvenile court does not constitute a complaint against the parents that the child who is the subject of the adoption proceedings is a dependent, delinquent or neglected child, and a judgment by the juvenile court finding that such child is a dependent child, made without the filing of a complaint against the parents, is void ab initio for lack of jurisdiction. State ex rel. Clark v. Allaman (Ohio 1950) 154 Ohio St. 296, 95 N.E.2d 753, 43 O.O. 190.

Complaint filed under GC 1639–23 (RC 2151.27), which alleges that a child under twenty months of age is dependent is sufficiently definite. In re Anteau (Lucas 1941) 67 Ohio App. 117, 36 N.E.2d 47, 21 O.O. 129.

A complaint under this section, is sufficient if complainant defines child's dependent condition in words of statute without setting out details. In re Hayes (Franklin 1939) 62 Ohio App. 289, 23 N.E.2d 956, 30 Ohio Law Abs. 568, 16 O.O. 10.

In an action to remove a child from her mother's custody, the mere allegation that such child is dependent, where the complaint fails to state the essential facts upon which the allegation of dependency is based and which allegations bring the proceeding within the jurisdiction of the court, such complaint is insufficient to confer jurisdiction upon the trial court. In re Baker, No. 6–81–12 (3d Dist Ct App, Hardin, 7–14–82).

Under former GC 1647 (RC 2151.27), a complaint alleging the dependency of a child was sufficiently definite without designating any of the various facts of dependency, and when a child was alleged to be dependent, a juvenile court had authority to receive evidence on all matters pertaining to that question. In re Decker (Ohio Juv. 1930) 28 Ohio NP(NS) 433.

2. Jurisdiction

Juvenile court had jurisdiction to address paternal grandmother's complaint, which alleged that child was dependent; grandmother filed her complaint under statute that allowed any person who had knowledge that a child appeared to be dependent child to file a sworn complaint in juvenile court, and statute allowed the person who filed such a complaint to request temporary custody of the child, which grandmother did. In re Brown (Ohio App. 2 Dist., Darke, 06-23-2006) No. 1676, 2006-Ohio-3189, 2006 WL 1719277, Unreported. Infants 196

Trial court did not lack jurisdiction to preside over dependency proceedings based on father's claim that children were living in Pennsylvania and that he was not living in county where dependency complaint was filed, where complaint was filed in county where father's legal residence was listed and at which address father was receiving welfare benefits, and alleged acts constituting neglect or dependency occurred in county where complaint was filed. In re McLean (Ohio App. 11 Dist., Trumbull, 05-25-2005) No. 2005-T-0018, 2005-Ohio-2576, 2005 WL 1231614, Unreported. Infants 196

Where, subsequent to the filing of a notice of appeal from an alleged erroneous denial of custody in a habeas corpus proceeding by a parent seeking, on the basis of a valid Oregon permanent custody degree, immediate return of his minor children, the parent confers personal jurisdiction over himself upon an Ohio court which originally granted his wife a divorce from him upon service of publication only and made no order respecting custody of their minor children because the children were with him out of the state; the Ohio divorce court having both parties and the minor children before it generally and without reservation is fully empowered to adjudicate the issue of custody of the minor children under RC 3105.061, and the appeal from the judgment denying custody in the habeas corpus proceeding is moot. Thompson v. McNeely (Richland 1969) 21 Ohio App.2d 5, 254 N.E.2d 368, 50 O.O.2d 9.

An Ohio juvenile court, in a dependency proceeding pursuant to RC 2151.27 et seq., has no jurisdiction to interfere with a mother's legal custody of her children in the absence of proof and a finding of unfitness of such parent merely for the purpose of releasing such children to the officers of the court of a foreign state, and the court need not give full faith and credit to a Michigan decree where that decree was obtained by the husband in an ex parte custody determination, subsequent to a divorce decree, in which the Michigan court had no personal jurisdiction over the nonresident wife. In re Messner (Huron 1969) 19 Ohio App.2d 33, 249 N.E.2d 532, 48 O.O.2d 31.

The juvenile court has the authority to hear and determine the case of a "neglected child" notwithstanding the fact that the child is at the time within the continuing jurisdiction of the common pleas court by virtue of a divorce decree. In re L. (Ohio Juv. 1967) 12 Ohio Misc. 251, 231 N.E.2d 253, 41 O.O.2d 341. Courts ⇒ 475(15)

In order for a juvenile court to have jurisdiction to declare a child to be dependent, it must be shown either that the residence of the child is in the county or that the acts constituting neglect or dependency occurred in the county. State ex rel. Burchett v. Juvenile Court for Scioto County (Scioto 1962) 194 N.E.2d 912, 92 Ohio Law Abs. 357, 28 O.O.2d 116.

Where a neglected child proceeding is instituted in the juvenile court by a parent of such child, and a divorce action is later instituted by such parent, the juvenile court has exclusive original jurisdiction to determine whether the child is neglected, the power to determine his custody and the authority to place the child with a relative. In re Small (Darke 1960) 114 Ohio App. 248, 181 N.E.2d 503, 19 O.O.2d 128.

Where a juvenile court in the jurisdiction in which an offender resides waives jurisdiction so that the offender will be tried by a common pleas court, such defendant is entitled to a trial in the county where the offense occurred. In re Davis (Ohio Juv. 1961) 179 N.E.2d 198, 87 Ohio Law Abs. 222, 22 O.O.2d 108.

Where an affidavit was filed charging that children were neglected and dependent and the mother unfit, and such children were taken into custody by the county welfare department at a time when the mother and children were residents of the county, the juvenile court had jurisdiction of such proceedings even though citation was not served on the mother until after her removal to another county. In re Goshorn (Ohio Juv. 1959) 167 N.E.2d 148, 82 Ohio Law Abs. 599.

The juvenile court of the county in which acts constituting neglect or dependency of a minor child occur has jurisdiction over complaints concerning such child whether or not the parent or minor child was a nonresident of such county. In re Belk (Crawford 1954) 97 Ohio App. 114, 123 N.E.2d 757, 55 O.O. 330. Infants ⇒ 196

The juvenile court is given original jurisdiction in a proper proceeding to determine the right of custody of any child where such child is not a ward of another court, and it is not necessary in the exercise of such jurisdiction that the juvenile court first determine that such child is a dependent, neglected or delinquent child. In re Lorok (Cuyahoga 1952) 93 Ohio App. 251, 114 N.E.2d 65, 51 O.O. 10. Child Custody ⇒ 920

Juvenile court has no jurisdiction to adjudicate a child as a dependent child until after filing of a complaint charging such dependency and notice given to the parent or parents. State ex rel. Clark v. Allaman (Montgomery 1950) 87 Ohio App. 101, 90 N.E.2d 394, 57 Ohio Law Abs. 17, 42 O.O. 330, affirmed 154 Ohio St. 296, 95 N.E.2d 753, 43 O.O. 190.

Where an affidavit is filed in support of a motion for a new trial, alleging that the child was a neglected child within the meaning of this section, on which charges a hearing was had, the juvenile court has jurisdiction in such matter and may grant a motion for new trial. State ex rel. Sparto v. Williams (Darke 1949) 86 Ohio App. 377, 86 N.E.2d 501, 55 Ohio Law Abs. 341, 41 O.O. 474.

Pursuant to RC 2151.23(A), the Probate and Juvenile Division of the Muskingum County Court of Common Pleas has exclusive original jurisdiction to issue orders of support in cases brought under RC 2151.27 to RC 2151.331, including orders complying with RC 2151.33(B)(2)(a). The language of RC 2301.03(AA) establishing the powers and duties of the judge of the Domestic Relations Division of the Muskingum County Court of Common Pleas does not modify or restrict the exclusive original jurisdiction of the juvenile court in this regard. OAG 05–003.

3. Finding that child is neglected or dependent

Juvenile court's finding that a particular child is neglected and dependent is not supported by clear and convincing evidence where the mother obtains adequate parental care for the child during the time she is unable to provide that care personally by voluntarily taking him to his paternal grandparents who in turn provide adequate parental care. Johnson v. Johnson (Ohio App. 10 Dist., Franklin, 03-22-2001) No. 00AP-691, 2001 WL 277272, Unreported.

Decision of trier of fact relating to adjudication of children as neglected or dependent will not be overturned as against manifest weight of the evidence, so long as record contains competent credible evidence by which trial court could have formed firm belief or conviction that the essential statutory elements for neglect or dependency have been established. In re S. (Ohio App. 6 Dist., 03-31-1995) 102 Ohio App.3d 338, 657 N.E.2d 307. Infants ⇒ 252

Trial court acted within its discretion in adjudicating children neglected and dependent in spite of arguably improper admission of hearsay testimony concerning alleged sexual abuse of children by parents; ample evidence from occurrence witnesses alone supported court's determination, and court clearly demonstrated its ability to sort out admissible and inadmissible evidence when it declined to find that children were abused. In re S. (Ohio App. 6 Dist., 03-31-1995) 102 Ohio App.3d 338, 657 N.E.2d 307. Infants ⇒ 179

In actions brought pursuant to RC 2151.27 and RC 2151.03, the state's primary objective is not to decide conflicting claims to custody; its objective is to determine if a child is receiving proper parental care, and if that care is being provided by a relative pursuant to an agreement initiated by the child's parent, then the child is not a neglected child. In re Reese (Franklin 1982) 4 Ohio App.3d 59, 446 N.E.2d 482, 4 O.B.R. 109. Infants ⇒ 156

Proceedings declaring a child neglected by the juvenile court of another county do not prevent a child from thereafter becoming a school resident in a county to which he moves with his family. In re Laricchiuta (Preble 1968) 16 Ohio App.2d 164, 243 N.E.2d 111, 45 O.O.2d 456.

The school board of the district in which a child has a school residence at the time of his placement in another district must pay his tuition, whether such placement was by order of court or by the child welfare board in whose care the parent had voluntarily left him, and subsequent proceedings by the juvenile court declaring such child neglected will not end the obligation of the district of its school residence to continue paying his tuition. In re Laricchiuta (Preble 1968) 16 Ohio App.2d 164, 243 N.E.2d 111, 45 O.O.2d 456.

An application for a writ of habeas corpus will be denied where a complaint is duly filed in the county of legal residence, pursuant to RC 2151.27, charging a child with being a dependent or neglected child, notwithstanding the court of common pleas of another county in this state, as a result of a divorce action there heard, gave custody of the child to the mother, who subsequently moved with the child to the county where the affidavit of dependency and neglect was filed. James v. Child Welfare Bd. (Summit 1967) 9 Ohio App.2d 299, 224 N.E.2d 358, 38 O.O.2d 347.

Proceedings wherein the juvenile court determines in response to such motion that such child is a neglected and dependent child and orders such child placed in the temporary custody of the county welfare board are void ab initio for want of a complaint filed as prescribed by RC 2151.27 and such proceedings cannot be the foundation for a determination of dependency or neglect necessary to support an order awarding custody of such child. Union County Child Welfare Bd. v. Parker (Union 1964) 7 Ohio App.2d 79, 218 N.E.2d 757, 36 O.O.2d 162. Infants ⇒ 197

In an appeal on questions of law from a judgment in a neglected-child proceeding, the court of appeals may not substitute its judgment for that of the trial court as to what order of custody would be for the best interest of the child. In re Small (Darke 1960) 114 Ohio App. 248, 181 N.E.2d 503, 19 O.O.2d 128.

RC 3109.04 is not applicable to a neglected-child proceeding under RC 2151.27. In re Small (Darke 1960) 114 Ohio App. 248, 181 N.E.2d 503, 19 O.O.2d 128.

In a proceeding in the juvenile court instituted by the filing of a complaint under RC 2151.27, a finding by the court that a child is "neglected," in that it "lacked proper parental care because of the faults and habits of his parents," and "dependent," in that its "condition and environment... is such as to warrant the court... in assuming his guardianship" must be based on evidence with respect to whether the child was receiving proper parental care in a proper environment in its home at the time of the hearing. In re Minton (Darke 1960) 112 Ohio App. 361, 176 N.E.2d 252, 16 O.O.2d 283. Infants ⇒ 156

A proceeding instituted in the juvenile court under RC 2151.27 may not be used by the complainant either to force an adoption or as a substitute for an adoption proceeding. In re Minton (Darke 1960) 112 Ohio App. 361, 176 N.E.2d 252, 16 O.O.2d 283. Infants ⇒ 131

In complaint under this section, that a child of separated parents is dependent, a judgment of common pleas court that the child is dependent and awarding its custody to its father "until further order of the court," is a final order from which appeal to the Court of Appeals may be taken. In re Anteau (Lucas 1941) 67 Ohio App. 117, 36 N.E.2d 47, 21 O.O. 129.

Evidence was sufficient to support adjudication of delinquency based on finding that juvenile endangered children; evidence established that juvenile knew her roommate was a violent person, that he abused juvenile's daughter in juvenile's presence, that juvenile allowed her roommate to babysit her daughter, and that juvenile's daughter suffered numerous fractures while in his care. In re Coia (Ohio App. 2 Dist., Miami, 05-31-2002) No. 2001CA58, 2002-Ohio-2697, 2002 WL 1096077, Unreported. Infants ⇒ 176

Where a mother stipulates that the allegations in a dependency complaint are true, with the exception of the allegation that she cannot care for the child, the court may have sufficient support for a finding of dependency, with no need for evidence of dependency. In re Ware, No. 79–03243 (8th Dist Ct App, Cuyahoga, 7–17–80).

Placement of an illegitimate child for adoption and subsequent withdrawal of consent thereto by the mother does not of itself warrant a finding that the child is neglected. In re O——(Ohio Juv. 1964) 199 N.E.2d 765, 95 Ohio Law Abs. 101, 28 O.O.2d 165.

Trial court erred in entering order making minor child a ward of the court because of his dependency and placing him permanently for adoption without giving mother who signed affidavit of dependency written notice of referee's findings and recommendation on which such order was based, regardless of whether referee told mother what such findings and recommendation would be. In re Hobson, 62 NE(2d) 510, 44 Abs 86 (App 1945).

4. Procedural issues

Trial court could consider evidence concerning custody evaluations of mother, father and paternal grandmother and consider child's wishes regarding whether she wanted to live with grandmother, in dependency proceeding; grandmother initiated the dependency action by filing a complaint that alleged child was a dependent child, and grandmother sought custody of child. In re Brown (Ohio App. 2 Dist., Darke, 06-23-2006) No. 1676, 2006-Ohio-3189, 2006 WL 1719277, Unreported. Infants ⚖ 222

Mother did not have standing on appeal to challenge trial court's jurisdiction over putative father in child protection proceedings; one could not challenge an error committed against a non-appealing party, and there was no evidence that putative father was actual father. In re D.H. (Ohio App. 8 Dist., Cuyahoga, 12-04-2003) No. 82533, 2003-Ohio-6478, 2003 WL 22861922, Unreported. Infants ⚖ 242

Minor children's paternal grandparents were not required to have been granted intervenor status in order to assert petition for legal custody of children, since any person had statutory right to file complaint regarding children who appeared to be abused, neglected, or dependent, and juvenile court had exclusive jurisdiction over dispute. Ives v. Ives (Ohio App. 9 Dist., Lorain, 07-02-2003) No. 02CA008176, 2003-Ohio-3505, 2003 WL 21508795, Unreported. Child Custody ⚖ 404; Child Custody ⚖ 409

Trial court lacked authority to place children in a Planned Permanent Living Arrangement (PPLA) as an alternative to terminating father's parental rights; there was no evidence to suggest that father or county department of children and family services sought a PPLA, and there was no evidence presented to establish any of the other statutory requirements necessary for court to place children in a PPLA. (Per O'Donnell, J., with two judges concurring in judgment only). In re Harlston (Ohio App. 8 Dist., Cuyahoga, 01-23-2003) No. 80672, 2003-Ohio-282, 2003 WL 152939, Unreported, appeal not allowed 98 Ohio St.3d 1492, 785 N.E.2d 474, 2003-Ohio-1189. Infants ⚖ 226

Action of social services agency and agency employees in pursuing child abuse allegations against father was "under color of state law" for purposes of father's civil rights claim, where agency and employees acted pursuant to state child abuse reporting statute. Roe v. Franklin Cty. (Ohio App. 10 Dist., 03-12-1996) 109 Ohio App.3d 772, 673 N.E.2d 172, appeal not allowed 77 Ohio St.3d 1415, 670 N.E.2d 1003. Civil Rights ⚖ 1326(1)

Trial court acted within its discretion in refusing to allow children to be called as witnesses in dependency and neglect proceeding; court gave extensive consideration to issue and conducted in camera examinations, and in the end, determined that calling children was not in their best interests. In re S. (Ohio App. 6 Dist., 03-31-1995) 102 Ohio App.3d 338, 657 N.E.2d 307. Infants ⚖ 207

Objection that evidence introduced into adjudicatory hearing on issue of neglect or dependency is "dispositional," is not proper objection; rather, objection should focus on whether the evidence is relevant to child's alleged abuse, neglect, or dependency. In re S. (Ohio App. 6 Dist., 03-31-1995) 102 Ohio App.3d 338, 657 N.E.2d 307. Infants ⚖ 207

Parents were not prejudiced by admission of hearsay testimony regarding child abuse in dependency and neglect proceeding, where parents prevailed on issue of abuse. In re S. (Ohio App. 6 Dist., 03-31-1995) 102 Ohio App.3d 338, 657 N.E.2d 307. Infants ⚖ 253

Where public children services agency did not have requisite grant of temporary custody, instead of filing postdispositional motion for permanent custody, agency should have sought grant of temporary custody by asking court to modify its disposition terminating agency's grant of temporary custody or by filing a new complaint based on more recent allegations of abuse or on dependency theory. In re Miller (Ohio App. 2 Dist., 02-15-1995) 101 Ohio App.3d 199, 655 N.E.2d 252. Infants ⚖ 230.1

Where complaint was filed alleging that child was dependent and/or neglected, rule requiring that party who enters admission waive his rights to challenge witnesses and evidence against him, to remain silent and to introduce evidence at adjudicatory hearing did not prohibit child's mother from participating in adjudicatory hearing just because she entered plea of "admitted" to allegations in complaint. In re Sims (Preble 1983) 13 Ohio App.3d 37, 468 N.E.2d 111, 13 O.B.R. 40. Infants ⚖ 199

A RC 2151.23(A)(3) action does not need to comply with RC 2151.27 and RC 2151.23, as the latter sections clearly apply to neglect, abuse, and dependency hearings provided for in RC 2151.23(A)(1). In re Perales (Ohio 1977) 52 Ohio St.2d 89, 369 N.E.2d 1047, 6 O.O.3d 293.

A minor detained on delinquency charges is not charged with an offense and hence is not entitled to release on bail. State ex rel. Peaks v. Allaman (Montgomery 1952) 115 N.E.2d 849, 66 Ohio Law Abs. 403, 51 O.O. 321.

Whether county social workers who receive complaints of child abuse, yet take no steps to remove the child from the custody of a parent who eventually injures him severely, have violated a duty of protection owed to the child is a question to be answered by each state's law of torts, not by the federal constitution. DeShaney v. Winnebago County Dept. of Social Services (U.S.Wis. 1989) 109 S.Ct. 998, 489 U.S. 189, 103 L.Ed.2d 249.

Under former GC 1639 (RC 2151.23), GC 1647 (RC 2151.27) and GC 1681 (RC 2151.26), transfer by court of common pleas of felony case against minor to court of domestic relations merely gives latter court information and authority to act thereon. State ex rel. Brown v. Hoffman (Hamilton 1926) 23 Ohio App. 348, 155 N.E. 499, 5 Ohio Law Abs. 6.

Where a complaint for dependency is filed, an unknown father must be served by publication; even an apparently unconcerned putative father is entitled to notice by publication, and the mother's statement that she does not know who the father is does not justify dispensing with the notice. In re Ware, No. 79–03243 (8th Dist Ct App, Cuyahoga, 7–17–80).

Pursuant to RC 2151.141, when a complaint alleging abuse, neglect, or dependency of a child is filed under RC 2151.27, a request directed to a public children services agency or the prosecuting attorney for "any records related to the child" must be granted or denied by following the procedures set forth in RC 2151.141. OAG 91–003.

2151.271 Transfer to juvenile court of another county

Except in a case in which the child is alleged to be a serious youthful offender under section 2152.13 of the Revised Code, if the child resides in a county of the state and the proceeding is commenced in a juvenile court of another county, that court, on its own motion or a motion of a party, may transfer the proceeding to the county of the child's residence upon the filing of the complaint or after the adjudicatory, or dispositional hearing, for such further proceeding as required. The court of the child's residence shall then proceed as if the original complaint had been filed in that court. Transfer may also be made if the residence of the child changes. The proceeding shall be so transferred if other proceedings involving the child are pending in the juvenile court of the county of the child's residence.

Whenever a case is transferred to the county of the child's residence and it appears to the court of that county that the interests of justice and the convenience of the parties requires that the adjudicatory hearing be had in the county in which the complaint was filed, the court may return the proceeding to the county in which the complaint was filed for the purpose of the adjudicatory hearing. The court may thereafter proceed as to the transfer to the county of the child's legal residence as provided in this section.

Certified copies of all legal and social records pertaining to the case shall accompany the transfer.

(2000 S 179, § 3, eff. 1–1–02; 1969 H 320, eff. 11–19–69)

Historical and Statutory Notes

Amendment Note: 2000 S 179, § 3, eff. 1-1-02, inserted "Except in a case in which the child is alleged to be a serious youthful offender under section 2152.13 of the Revised Code," in the first paragraph; and made changes to reflect gender neutral language and other nonsubstantive changes.

Cross References

Complaint, Juv R 10
Transfer to another county, Juv R 11

Library References

Courts ⚖486, 488(1).
Infants ⚖196.
Westlaw Topic Nos. 106, 211.
C.J.S. Courts §§ 194, 199 to 202.
C.J.S. Infants §§ 41, 53 to 54.

Research References

Encyclopedias

OH Jur. 3d Family Law § 1587, Transfer to County of Residence.
OH Jur. 3d Family Law § 1588, Transfer to County of Residence—Adjudicatory Hearing in County Where Complaint Filed.

Treatises and Practice Aids

Carlin, Baldwin's Ohio Practice, Merrick-Rippner Probate Law § 107:7, Jurisdiction and Venue for Juvenile Proceedings.
Giannelli & Yeomans, Ohio Juvenile Law § 3:2, Exclusive Original Jurisdiction.
Giannelli & Yeomans, Ohio Juvenile Law § 5:4, Syo Venue.
Giannelli & Yeomans, Ohio Juvenile Law § 17:2, Proper Venue.
Giannelli & Yeomans, Ohio Juvenile Law § 17:4, Transfer of Venue.

Notes of Decisions

Collateral decisions 3
Court authority 2
Mandatory transfer 4
Residence 1

---

1. Residence

Although parents and children had moved to Paulding County before complaint in neglect and dependency was filed, Defiance County common pleas court did not abuse its discretion in denying parents' motion to dismiss case, noting that alleged incidents of neglect occurred while children resided in Defiance County and that majority of witnesses resided in Defiance County. In re Meyer (Ohio App. 3 Dist., 10-25-1994) 98 Ohio App.3d 189, 648 N.E.2d 52, corrected. Infants ⚖ 196

Transfer of a permanent custody hearing from the county where the children have been found to be neglected and dependent and are the subjects of a temporary custody order to the county in which the children's parents currently reside is improper as the residency of the children, not the parents, controls jurisdiction. In re Smith (Lucas 1990) 64 Ohio App.3d 773, 582 N.E.2d 1117.

2. Court authority

Venue was proper in permanent custody hearing; county agency's complaint was filed in same county in which children were removed from their home. In re S.V. (Ohio App. 9 Dist., Summit, 10-13-2004) No. 22116, 2004-Ohio-5445, 2004 WL 2292825, Unreported. Infants ⚖ 196

Proper venue for child custody dispute was a matter within discretion of trial court where no other proceedings were pending in juvenile court of county of child's legal residence. Ackerman v. Lucas County Children Services Bd. (Lucas 1989) 49 Ohio App.3d 14, 550 N.E.2d 549. Infants ⚖ 196

The trial court exceeded its authority by attempting both to impose a fine and transfer the matter to another jurisdiction. In re Sekulich (Ohio 1981) 65 Ohio St.2d 13, 417 N.E.2d 1014, 19 O.O.3d 192.

3. Collateral decisions

A juvenile court's erroneous transfer of a custodial proceeding subsequent to a dependency and neglect adjudication, but before a dispositional hearing, does not render subsequent collateral decisions by the receiving court null and void. In re Smith (Lucas 1990) 64 Ohio App.3d 773, 582 N.E.2d 1117.

4. Mandatory transfer

Trial court was not required to transfer dependency case to county which had previously instigated investigation at request of Children Services, where complaint in other county had been dismissed on grounds father and children were not residing in that county prior to Children Services filing complaint in instant case. In re McLean (Ohio App. 11 Dist., Trumbull, 05-25-2005) No. 2005-T-0018, 2005-Ohio-2576, 2005 WL 1231614, Unreported. Infants ⚖ 196

Transfer of abused child case to county where child legally resided and matters were pending was mandatory despite court's failure to complete an adjudicatory hearing; child's parents resided in other county, and that county's children and family services agency held emergency temporary custody of the child pursuant to an order of the juvenile court. In re Don B. (Ohio App. 6 Dist., Huron, 03-21-2003) No. H-02-033, 2003-Ohio-1400, 2003 WL 1448059, Unreported. Venue ⚖ 45

Where a case is pending against a juvenile in a foreign county, such case must be transferred to the juvenile's home county, if, at any time prior to dispositional order, proceedings against the juvenile are pending in his home county. Furthermore, such mandatory transfer may not be avoided by the foreign county through the use of a bindover proceeding. State v Payne, No. 81–CA–22 (4th Dist Ct App, Pickaway, 7–28–82).

2151.28 Summons

(A) No later than seventy-two hours after the complaint is filed, the court shall fix a time for an adjudicatory hearing. The court shall conduct the adjudicatory hearing within one of the following periods of time:

(1) Subject to division (C) of section 2152.13 of the Revised Code and division (A)(3) of this section, if the complaint alleged that the child violated section 2151.87 of the Revised Code or is a delinquent or unruly child or a juvenile traffic offender, the adjudicatory hearing shall be held and may be continued in accordance with the Juvenile Rules.

(2) If the complaint alleged that the child is an abused, neglected, or dependent child, the adjudicatory hearing shall be held no later than thirty days after the complaint is filed, except that, for good cause shown, the court may continue the adjudicatory hearing for either of the following periods of time:

(a) For ten days beyond the thirty-day deadline to allow any party to obtain counsel;

(b) For a reasonable period of time beyond the thirty-day deadline to obtain service on all parties or any necessary evaluation, except that the adjudicatory hearing shall not be held later than sixty days after the date on which the complaint was filed.

(3) If the child who is the subject of the complaint is in detention and is charged with violating a section of the Revised Code that may be violated by an adult, the hearing shall be held not later than fifteen days after the filing of the complaint. Upon a showing of good cause, the adjudicatory hearing may be continued and detention extended.

(B) At an adjudicatory hearing held pursuant to division (A)(2) of this section, the court, in addition to determining whether the child is an abused, neglected, or dependent child, shall determine whether the child should remain or be placed in shelter care until the dispositional hearing. When the court makes the shelter care determination, all of the following apply:

(1) The court shall determine whether there are any relatives of the child who are willing to be temporary custodians of the child. If any relative is willing to be a temporary custodian, the child otherwise would remain or be placed in shelter care, and the appointment is appropriate, the court shall appoint the

relative as temporary custodian of the child, unless the court appoints another relative as custodian. If it determines that the appointment of a relative as custodian would not be appropriate, it shall issue a written opinion setting forth the reasons for its determination and give a copy of the opinion to all parties and the guardian ad litem of the child.

The court's consideration of a relative for appointment as a temporary custodian does not make that relative a party to the proceedings.

(2) The court shall comply with section 2151.419 of the Revised Code.

(3) The court shall schedule the date for the dispositional hearing to be held pursuant to section 2151.35 of the Revised Code. The parents of the child have a right to be represented by counsel; however, in no case shall the dispositional hearing be held later than ninety days after the date on which the complaint was filed.

(C)(1) The court shall direct the issuance of a summons directed to the child except as provided by this section, the parents, guardian, custodian, or other person with whom the child may be, and any other persons that appear to the court to be proper or necessary parties to the proceedings, requiring them to appear before the court at the time fixed to answer the allegations of the complaint. The summons shall contain the name and telephone number of the court employee designated by the court pursuant to section 2151.314 of the Revised Code to arrange for the prompt appointment of counsel for indigent persons. A child alleged to be an abused, neglected, or dependent child shall not be summoned unless the court so directs. A summons issued for a child who is under fourteen years of age and who is alleged to be a delinquent child, unruly child, or a juvenile traffic offender shall be served on the parent, guardian, or custodian of the child in the child's behalf.

If the person who has physical custody of the child, or with whom the child resides, is other than the parent or guardian, then the parents and guardian also shall be summoned. A copy of the complaint shall accompany the summons.

(2) In lieu of appearing before the court at the time fixed in the summons and prior to the date fixed for appearance in the summons, a child who is alleged to have violated section 2151.87 of the Revised Code and that child's parent, guardian, or custodian may sign a waiver of appearance before the clerk of the juvenile court and pay a fine of one hundred dollars. If the child and that child's parent, guardian, or custodian do not waive the court appearance, the court shall proceed with the adjudicatory hearing as provided in this section.

(D) If the complaint contains a prayer for permanent custody, temporary custody, whether as the preferred or an alternative disposition, or a planned permanent living arrangement in a case involving an alleged abused, neglected, or dependent child, the summons served on the parents shall contain as is appropriate an explanation that the granting of permanent custody permanently divests the parents of their parental rights and privileges, an explanation that an adjudication that the child is an abused, neglected, or dependent child may result in an order of temporary custody that will cause the removal of the child from their legal custody until the court terminates the order of temporary custody or permanently divests the parents of their parental rights, or an explanation that the issuance of an order for a planned permanent living arrangement will cause the removal of the child from the legal custody of the parents if any of the conditions listed in divisions (A)(5)(a) to (c) of section 2151.353 of the Revised Code are found to exist.

(E)(1) Except as otherwise provided in division (E)(2) of this section, the court may endorse upon the summons an order directing the parents, guardian, or other person with whom the child may be to appear personally at the hearing and directing the person having the physical custody or control of the child to bring the child to the hearing.

(2) In cases in which the complaint alleges that a child is an unruly or delinquent child for being an habitual or chronic truant and that the parent, guardian, or other person having care of the child has failed to cause the child's attendance at school, the court shall endorse upon the summons an order directing the parent, guardian, or other person having care of the child to appear personally at the hearing and directing the person having the physical custody or control of the child to bring the child to the hearing.

(F)(1) The summons shall contain a statement advising that any party is entitled to counsel in the proceedings and that the court will appoint counsel or designate a county public defender or joint county public defender to provide legal representation if the party is indigent.

(2) In cases in which the complaint alleges a child to be an abused, neglected, or dependent child and no hearing has been conducted pursuant to division (A) of section 2151.314 of the Revised Code with respect to the child or a parent, guardian, or custodian of the child does not attend the hearing, the summons also shall contain a statement advising that a case plan may be prepared for the child, the general requirements usually contained in case plans, and the possible consequences of failure to comply with a journalized case plan.

(G) If it appears from an affidavit filed or from sworn testimony before the court that the conduct, condition, or surroundings of the child are endangering the child's health or welfare or those of others, that the child may abscond or be removed from the jurisdiction of the court, or that the child will not be brought to the court, notwithstanding the service of the summons, the court may endorse upon the summons an order that a law enforcement officer serve the summons and take the child into immediate custody and bring the child forthwith to the court.

(H) A party, other than the child, may waive service of summons by written stipulation.

(I) Before any temporary commitment is made permanent, the court shall fix a time for hearing in accordance with section 2151.414 of the Revised Code and shall cause notice by summons to be served upon the parent or guardian of the child and the guardian ad litem of the child, or published, as provided in section 2151.29 of the Revised Code. The summons shall contain an explanation that the granting of permanent custody permanently divests the parents of their parental rights and privileges.

(J) Any person whose presence is considered necessary and who is not summoned may be subpoenaed to appear and testify at the hearing. Anyone summoned or subpoenaed to appear who fails to do so may be punished, as in other cases in the court of common pleas, for contempt of court. Persons subpoenaed shall be paid the same witness fees as are allowed in the court of common pleas.

(K) The failure of the court to hold an adjudicatory hearing within any time period set forth in division (A)(2) of this section does not affect the ability of the court to issue any order under this chapter and does not provide any basis for attacking the jurisdiction of the court or the validity of any order of the court.

(L) If the court, at an adjudicatory hearing held pursuant to division (A) of this section upon a complaint alleging that a child is an abused, neglected, dependent, delinquent, or unruly child or a juvenile traffic offender, determines that the child is a dependent child, the court shall incorporate that determination into written findings of fact and conclusions of law and enter those findings of fact and conclusions of law in the record of the case. The court shall include in those findings of fact and conclusions of law specific findings as to the existence of any danger to the child and any underlying family problems that are the basis for the court's determination that the child is a dependent child.

(2002 H 393, eff. 7–5–02; 2002 H 180, eff. 5–16–02; 2000 S 179, § 3, eff. 1–1–02; 2000 S 218, eff. 3–15–01; 2000 S 181, eff. 9–4–00; 1998 H 484, eff. 3–18–99; 1996 H 274, eff. 8–8–96; 1996 H 419, eff. 9–18–96; 1988 S 89, eff. 1–1–89; 1975 H 164, H 85; 1969 H 320)

Uncodified Law

2002 H 180, § 3, eff. 5–16–02, reads, in part:

The General Assembly hereby requests the Supreme Court to promptly modify Rule 29 of the Rules of Juvenile Procedure pursuant to its authority under the Ohio Constitution to make that rule consistent with the amendments of this act to section 2151.28 of the Revised Code.

Historical and Statutory Notes

Ed. Note: Former 2151.28 repealed by 1969 H 320, eff. 11–19–69; 1953 H 1; GC 1639–24.

Pre–1953 H 1 Amendments: 121 v 557; 117 v 520

Amendment Note: 2002 H 393 substituted "(C)" for "(D)" in division (A)(1).

Amendment Note: 2002 H 180 inserted "and division (A)(3) of this section" after "Revised Code" in division (A)(1); and added new division (A)(3).

Amendment Note: 2000 S 179, § 3, eff. 1–1–02, inserted "Subject to division (D) of section 2152.13 of the Revised Code," in division (A)(1).

Amendment Note: 2000 S 218 inserted "violated section 2151.87 of the Revised Code or" in division (A)(1); designated division (C)(1); and added division (C)(2).

Amendment Note: 2000 S 181 designated division (E)(1) and inserted "Except as otherwise provided in division (E)(2) of this section," therein; and added division (E)(2).

Amendment Note: 1998 H 484 substituted "comply with" for "make the determination and issue the written finding of facts required by" in division (B)(2); substituted "a planned permanent living arrangement" for "long-term foster care" twice in division (D); and made other nonsubstantive changes.

Amendment Note: 1996 H 274 substituted "No later than seventy-two hours after the complaint is filed" for "After the complaint has been filed" in the first paragraph in division (A); designated division (F)(1); and added division (F)(2).

Amendment Note: 1996 H 419 added division (L) and made changes to reflect gender neutral language throughout.

Cross References

Adjudicatory hearing, Juv R 29
Definitions, Juv R 2
Learnfare program, requirements for participation, 5107.281
Process, issuance, form, Juv R 15
Process, service, Juv R 16
Right to counsel, O Const Art I §10
Subpoena, Juv R 17
Taking into custody, Juv R 6

Library References

Infants ⚖198.
Westlaw Topic No. 211.
  Baldwin's Ohio Legislative Service, 1988 Laws of Ohio, S 89—LSC Analysis, p 5–571

Research References

Encyclopedias

OH Jur. 3d Family Law § 1545, Contempt.
OH Jur. 3d Family Law § 1610, Form and Contents.
OH Jur. 3d Family Law § 1611, Form and Contents—Orders Endorsed on Summons.
OH Jur. 3d Family Law § 1612, Summons for Hearing to Make Temporary Commitment Permanent.
OH Jur. 3d Family Law § 1613, Service; Proof of Service.
OH Jur. 3d Family Law § 1614, Waiver of Notice or Service.
OH Jur. 3d Family Law § 1620, to Compel Attendance at Hearing.
OH Jur. 3d Family Law § 1654, Determination of Reasonable Efforts.
OH Jur. 3d Family Law § 1661, Advisement and Findings at Commencement of Hearing.
OH Jur. 3d Family Law § 1663, on Request for Permanent Custody—on Motion of Agency.
OH Jur. 3d Family Law § 1665, to Make Temporary Commitment Permanent.
OH Jur. 3d Family Law § 1678, Generally—Placement of Child Until Dispositional Hearing.
OH Jur. 3d Family Law § 1719, Service; Witness Fees.

Forms

Ohio Jurisprudence Pleading and Practice Forms § 96:43, Temporary and Permanent Custody.

Treatises and Practice Aids

Klein, Darling, & Terez, Baldwin's Ohio Practice Civil Practice § 52:4, Findings by the Court--Findings of Fact Required by Statute.
Katz, Giannelli, Blair and Lipton, Baldwin's Ohio Practice, Criminal Law, § 61:10, Out-Of-State Witnesses.
Giannelli and Snyder, Baldwin's Ohio Practice, Evidence, § 804.8, Unavailability: Unable to Procure Testimony.
Carlin, Baldwin's Ohio Practice, Merrick-Rippner Probate Law § 107:9, Parties to Proceedings.
Carlin, Baldwin's Ohio Practice, Merrick-Rippner Probate Law § 107:10, Contents and Issuance of Summons.
Carlin, Baldwin's Ohio Practice, Merrick-Rippner Probate Law § 107:26, Detention Prior to Hearing.
Carlin, Baldwin's Ohio Practice, Merrick-Rippner Probate Law § 107:43, Scheduling Juvenile Court Hearing.
Carlin, Baldwin's Ohio Practice, Merrick-Rippner Probate Law § 107:56, Adjudicatory Hearings—Attendance of Parties at Hearing.
Carlin, Baldwin's Ohio Practice, Merrick-Rippner Probate Law § 107:72, Dispositional Hearings—Procedure.
Carlin, Baldwin's Ohio Practice, Merrick-Rippner Probate Law § 107:74, Reasonable Efforts Determination.
Carlin, Baldwin's Ohio Practice, Merrick-Rippner Probate Law § 107:122, Appeals—Juvenile Court Judgments—Determination of Neglect, Dependency, Unruliness, Abuse, or Delinquency.
Carlin, Baldwin's Ohio Practice, Merrick-Rippner Probate Law § 107:127, Contempt of Court in Juvenile Proceedings.
Carlin, Baldwin's Ohio Practice, Merrick-Rippner Probate Law § 107:161, Summons to Parents, Guardian, or Person With Whom Child May be—Form.
Carlin, Baldwin's Ohio Practice, Merrick-Rippner Probate Law § 107:162, Precipe for Subpoena—Form.
Carlin, Baldwin's Ohio Practice, Merrick-Rippner Probate Law § 107:163, Subpoena—Form.
Carlin, Baldwin's Ohio Practice, Merrick-Rippner Probate Law § 107:164, Waiver of Service of Summons—Form.
Giannelli & Yeomans, Ohio Juvenile Law § 14:3, Custody, Arrests & Stops.
Giannelli & Yeomans, Ohio Juvenile Law § 18:2, Issuance of Summons: Proper Parties.
Giannelli & Yeomans, Ohio Juvenile Law § 18:3, Summons: Contents and Form.
Giannelli & Yeomans, Ohio Juvenile Law § 18:4, Summons: Methods of Service.
Giannelli & Yeomans, Ohio Juvenile Law § 18:5, Waiver of Summons Requirements.
Giannelli & Yeomans, Ohio Juvenile Law § 19:6, Standard for Detention.
Giannelli & Yeomans, Ohio Juvenile Law § 19:7, Time Requirements.
Giannelli & Yeomans, Ohio Juvenile Law § 20:6, Time Requirements.
Giannelli & Yeomans, Ohio Juvenile Law § 23:3, Right to Counsel.
Giannelli & Yeomans, Ohio Juvenile Law § 25:4, Time Requirements.
Giannelli & Yeomans, Ohio Juvenile Law § 31:2, Filing of Motion.
Giannelli & Yeomans, Ohio Juvenile Law § 31:6, Findings.
Giannelli & Yeomans, Ohio Juvenile Law § 33:8, Contempt.
Giannelli & Yeomans, Ohio Juvenile Law § 23:29, Speedy Trial.
Giannelli & Yeomans, Ohio Juvenile Law § 25:14, Reasonable Efforts Determination; Abuse, Neglect & Dependency.
Giannelli & Yeomans, Ohio Juvenile Law § 30:11, Permanent Custody—"Best Interest" Factors.

Hastings, Manoloff, Sheeran, & Stype, Ohio School Law § 20:20, Enforcement Procedures-Consequences.

Law Review and Journal Commentaries

Do Juveniles Facing Civil Commitment Have a Right to Counsel? A Therapeutic Jurisprudence Brief. Bruce J. Winick and Ginger Lerner-Wren, 71 U Cin L Rev 115 (Fall 2002).

Due Process in Ohio for the Delinquent and Unruly Child, Max Kravitz. 2 Cap U L Rev 53 (1973).

Notes of Decisions

Constitutional issues 1
Jurisdiction 6
Notice; parties 2
Parents' responsibility 5
Procedural issues 3
Right to counsel 4

---

1. Constitutional issues

The Akron city ordinances requiring parental consent, informed consent, a 24-hour waiting period, and disposal of fetal remains are unconstitutional. City of Akron v. Akron Center for Reproductive Health, Inc. (U.S.Ohio 1983) 103 S.Ct. 2481, 462 U.S. 416, 76 L.Ed.2d 687, on remand 604 F.Supp. 1268, on remand 604 F.Supp. 1275.

Where the Ohio statute required a full investigation of the facts underlying a charge of delinquency and a finding of delinquency that the accused had committed acts in violation of Ohio law, jeopardy attached at a hearing at which accused was bound over for trial as an adult. Sims v. Engle (C.A.6 (Ohio) 1980) 619 F.2d 598, certiorari denied 101 S.Ct. 1403, 450 U.S. 936, 67 L.Ed.2d 372.

Any construction of RC 2151.354 that would allow commitment of an "unruly" child to the legal custody of the Ohio youth commission would be a violation of due process of law, and therefore an improper construction. OAG 72–071.

2. Notice; parties

Statutory notice requirements of juvenile delinquency proceeding were met by providing juvenile's guardian with notice, instead of juvenile's father, where juvenile was in permanent custody and had a guardian who was not his father. State v. D.M. (Ohio App. 8 Dist., Cuyahoga, 06-19-2003) No. 81641, 2003-Ohio-3228, 2003 WL 21419595, Unreported. Infants 198

Trial court was without jurisdiction to accept juvenile's admission to aggravated robbery offense and adjudicate him as delinquent, where notice regarding juvenile delinquency proceedings was not given to juvenile's parents. In re Brunner (Ohio App. 4 Dist., Scioto, 03-10-2003) No. 02CA2865, 2003-Ohio-2590, 2003 WL 21152500, Unreported. Infants 198

Mother who executed voluntary surrender of her parental rights was not a necessary party entitled to notice when dependency complaint was filed, as she was presumed to know consequences of surrender of child. In re Infant Female Luallen (Hamilton 1985) 27 Ohio App.3d 29, 499 N.E.2d 358, 27 O.B.R. 30. Infants 172; Infants 198

Juvenile court jurisdiction to consent to an agreement surrendering permanent custody of a minor to a county children services board, pursuant to RC 5103.15 and RC 5153.16(B), is not dependent upon service of process on the child and his parents as provided for in RC 2151.28, nor upon appointment of a guardian ad litem as provided for in RC 2151.281. In re Miller (Ohio 1980) 61 Ohio St.2d 184, 399 N.E.2d 1262, 15 O.O.3d 211. Infants 222

A father is a party to proceedings in a juvenile court in which his children are found to be neglected and in which temporary custody is given to the mother; he is also a party to a subsequent proceeding in the same court modifying such temporary custody order and is entitled to appear in an appeal from such order and to move to dismiss such appeal. In re Rule (Crawford 1963) 1 Ohio App.2d 57, 203 N.E.2d 501, 30 O.O.2d 76.

Where the mother of an illegitimate child was served with notice of a hearing on the motion of a county child welfare board for permanent custody of the child, and then married the father, who acknowledged paternity, and said father and mother appeared together at the hearing, the father could not thereafter complain that he had no notice of said hearing.

Mobley v. Allaman (Ohio Prob. 1961) 184 N.E.2d 707, 89 Ohio Law Abs. 473.

Under this section, the parents of a minor child or children are entitled to notice, actual or constructive, in a proceeding instituted in the juvenile court upon a complaint of dependency of such children; without such notice, jurisdiction of the court does not attach and a judgment of commitment in proceeding is void. In re Corey (Ohio 1945) 145 Ohio St. 413, 61 N.E.2d 892, 31 O.O. 35. Infants 198

Mother's voluntary appearance at and participation in hearing on question of child's dependency held waiver by mother of statutory notice of proceeding (GC §1648). Ex parte Province (Ohio 1933) 127 Ohio St. 333, 188 N.E. 550, 39 Ohio Law Rep. 651. Infants 198

Under this section, a juvenile court may either issue a citation, requiring a minor charged with being dependent, neglected or delinquent and its parents or guardian or other person to appear, or the judge may in the first instance issue a warrant for the arrest of such minor. State ex rel. Heth v. Moloney (Ohio 1933) 126 Ohio St. 526, 186 N.E. 362.

Where warrant was issued requiring infant daughter to be produced in court, and subpoena was issued for mother, and mother appeared at hearing, the mother, under former GC 1648 (RC 2151.28), received due notice in dependency proceeding against daughter. Ex parte Cunningham (Hamilton 1927) 27 Ohio App. 306, 160 N.E. 733, 6 Ohio Law Abs. 374.

Juvenile court judgment permanently committing illegitimate child may be attacked for want of jurisdiction because of fraud in constructive notice to mother, whose whereabouts were falsely stated as unknown. Lewis v. Reed (Ohio 1927) 117 Ohio St. 152, 157 N.E. 897, 5 Ohio Law Abs. 420, 25 Ohio Law Rep. 386. Infants 232

Where complaint was filed in juvenile court alleging dependency of child, and where mother and reputed father were beyond state, and custody was in orphan asylum, publication of citation under former GC 1647 (RC 2151.27) and GC 1648 (RC 2151.28), was sufficient, even though affidavit that citation could not be served on parents was not filed. In re Veselich (Cuyahoga 1926) 22 Ohio App. 528, 154 N.E. 55, 5 Ohio Law Abs. 277. Infants 198

Pleading provisions of Ohio parental notification of abortion statute, pursuant to which juvenile court was allowed to consider both minor's maturity and allegation that notification of parent was not in minor's best interest only if minor filed one of three different types of complaints, and could otherwise consider only whether minor was sufficiently mature to make informed decision or whether notification was in her best interest, violated due process. Akron Center for Reproductive Health v. Slaby (C.A.6 (Ohio) 1988) 854 F.2d 852, probable jurisdiction noted 109 S.Ct. 3239, 492 U.S. 916, 106 L.Ed.2d 586, reversed 110 S.Ct. 2972, 497 U.S. 502, 111 L.Ed.2d 405, on remand 911 F.2d 731, on remand 911 F.2d 733. Abortion And Birth Control 1.30; Constitutional Law 274(5)

Regular legal notice by service of process on the parent is an indispensable prerequisite to jurisdiction of juvenile court to make commitment of a minor child in delinquency cases. Ex parte Flickinger (Ohio Com.Pl. 1940) 5 Ohio Supp. 252, 33 Ohio Law Abs. 8, 20 O.O. 224.

Where a complaint alleges that a minor is unruly, failure to serve notice on the non-custodial parent of such minor renders the court without jurisdiction to declare the minor unruly. In re Koogle, Nos. CA–82–68 and CA–82–93 (2d Dist Ct App, Greene, 6–16–83).

Both the existing juvenile code and the juvenile rules require a hearing before a temporary commitment to the Ohio youth commission can be made permanent, which hearing requires the presence of the youth involved. OAG 72–071.

Sheriff is required to serve summons, notices, and subpoenas which are directed to him by juvenile court, and whether juvenile court requests summons, notices or subpoenas to be served personally or to be delivered by registered or certified mail, sheriff's office is legally required to serve them in accordance with such directions of juvenile court; if person to be served is out of state and his address is known, service of summons may be made by sheriff by delivering copy to him personally or mailing copy to him by registered or certified mail. OAG 70–130.

A new citation to the parents or guardian is not necessary at the time a juvenile judge wishes to change a temporary order to a permanent one. 1925 OAG 2451.

3. Procedural issues

Mother waived any objection to the untimeliness of the adjudicatory and dispositional hearings, in child dependency proceeding, where mother did not raise the issue of the timeliness of the hearings until more than a year and a half after the 90-day deadline passed for the dispositional hearing, and she continued to participate in the case well beyond the 90-day deadline for the dispositional hearing. In re Brown (Ohio App. 2 Dist., Darke, 06-23-2006) No. 1676, 2006-Ohio-3189, 2006 WL 1719277, Unreported. Infants ⟲ 204

Father's motion to dismiss dependency proceeding on basis of failure to hold adjudication and dispositional hearings within statutory time periods failed to comply with juvenile rule governing filing deadline for all prehearing motions; motion was filed on day of hearing. In re A.P. (Ohio App. 12 Dist., Butler, 05-30-2006) No. CA2005-10-425, 2006-Ohio-2717, 2006 WL 1493313, Unreported. Infants ⟲ 204

Father implicitly waived his right to adjudication hearing and dispositional hearing within applicable statutory time periods in dependency proceeding; father's attorney was aware that hearing date was after expiration of applicable statutory time periods, yet agreed to that date at pretrial hearing, father did not take issue with hearing date at pretrial hearing, and father did not move for dismissal when it became his right to do so, but rather waited until day of adjudication hearing to raise issue. In re A.P. (Ohio App. 12 Dist., Butler, 05-30-2006) No. CA2005-10-425, 2006-Ohio-2717, 2006 WL 1493313, Unreported. Infants ⟲ 204

Child's biological mother waived complaint to holding of dispositional hearing in child dependency proceedings more than 90 days after dependency complaint, as she did not file timely motion to dismiss complaint. In re Jessica M. B. (Ohio App. 6 Dist., Ottawa, 03-05-2004) No. OT-03-022, 2004-Ohio-1040, 2004 WL 413307, Unreported. Infants ⟲ 243

Although the 349 days that had passed between time county holding three children in temporary custody filed motion for permanent custody and hearing on motion was unreasonable, time nonetheless established relevant 12-month time period that children were in county's custody to support its permanent custody case. In re Fricke (Ohio App. 3 Dist., Allen, 03-11-2003) No. 1-02-75, No. 1-02-76, No. 1-02-77, 2003-Ohio-1116, 2003 WL 952173, Unreported. Infants ⟲ 155

Dispositional hearing on county's complaint that three children were dependent did not follow statutory requirements, where hearing was held 125 days after county filed complaint; statute required that such hearing was to be conducted within 90 days of complaint. In re Fricke (Ohio App. 3 Dist., Allen, 03-11-2003) No. 1-02-75, No. 1-02-76, No. 1-02-77, 2003-Ohio-1116, 2003 WL 952173, Unreported. Infants ⟲ 204

Mother was entitled to adjudicatory hearing on her complaint alleging that father abused child and seeking order to protect child; trial court was not permitted to dismiss complaint without first conducting adjudicatory hearing. In re Robinson (Ohio App. 5 Dist., Perry, 11-02-2002) No. 02CA7, 2002-Ohio-6020, 2002 WL 31458237, Unreported. Breach Of The Peace ⟲ 20

Trial court did not err in denying grandfather's motion to intervene in temporary custody action involving his granddaughter since RC 2151.28(B)(1), which allows consideration of a relative as temporary custodian, does not require making that relative a party to the proceedings. In re Thomas, No. 16077, 1993 WL 141597 (9th Dist Ct App, Summit, 4–28–93).

An order modifying a previously-entered temporary custody order, which was made in disposition of a finding that a child is neglected, constitutes a final appealable order. In re Rule (Crawford 1963) 1 Ohio App.2d 57, 203 N.E.2d 501, 30 O.O.2d 76.

RC 2151.28 and RC 2151.31 do not require a hearing as a condition precedent to the taking of a child into custody, pursuant to order of a juvenile court, during pendency of an action in such court. In re Jones (Allen 1961) 114 Ohio App. 319, 182 N.E.2d 631, 19 O.O.2d 286. Infants ⟲ 192

The words "other person having custody of such child," as used in former GC 1648 (RC 2151.28) meant a person having custody created by operation of law or awarded to such person by judicial order, judgment, or decree. Rarey v. Schmidt (Ohio 1926) 115 Ohio St. 518, 154 N.E. 914, 5 Ohio Law Abs. 12, 25 Ohio Law Rep. 134.

In complaint under former GC 1647 (RC 2151.27) and GC 1648 (RC 2151.28), alleging dependency of child, paramount duty of juvenile court is conservation of child's interests. In re Veselich (Cuyahoga 1926) 22 Ohio App. 528, 154 N.E. 55, 5 Ohio Law Abs. 277. Infants ⟲ 194.1

Where a case against a delinquent under Juvenile Act arose in the juvenile court, the validity of Gen.Code Ohio, § 1659 (repealed 1937. See § 1639–29), providing for the transfer of proceedings to the juvenile court from a justice of the peace or the police court, will not be considered. Ex parte Januszewski (S.D.Ohio 1911) 196 F. 123, 10 Ohio Law Rep. 151. Constitutional Law ⟲ 46(1); Infants ⟲ 132

Habeas corpus relief was not available from decision of the juvenile court awarding temporary custody of father's children to county, which had alleged that one child was neglected; juvenile court had jurisdiction to make the award of temporary custody under applicable statutes, appeal provided an adequate remedy, and alleged errors actually attacked findings of the court. Rothacker v. McCafferty (Ohio App. 8 Dist., Cuyahoga, 09-19-2002) No. 81427, 2002-Ohio-4927, 2002 WL 31087671, Unreported. Habeas Corpus ⟲ 289; Habeas Corpus ⟲ 536

Parents are considered to be necessary parties to any proceeding concerning their child and must be served. In re Jordan (Ohio App. 11 Dist., Trumbull, 05-31-2002) No. 2001-T-0067, 2002-Ohio-2820, 2002 WL 1173654, Unreported. Infants ⟲ 200

Juvenile court lacked jurisdiction to proceed with delinquency proceedings, absent any indication that statutory notice was given to juvenile's mother or grandmother, especially given that juvenile mother was one of the victims of juvenile's alleged assaults and grandmother had custody of juvenile. In re Jordan (Ohio App. 11 Dist., Trumbull, 05-31-2002) No. 2001-T-0067, 2002-Ohio-2820, 2002 WL 1173654, Unreported. Infants ⟲ 196

Where a juvenile was arrested for felonious assault, and the juvenile court failed to hold a detention hearing within seventy-two hours and an adjudicatory hearing within ten days after detention, the juvenile court shall dismiss the complaint without prejudice. State v Newton, No. F–82–17 (6th Dist Ct App, Fulton, 6–10–83).

4. Right to counsel

Petition for writ of habeas corpus alleging that mother had wrongfully been deprived of custody of children at custody hearing at which she was not represented by counsel stated a claim for relief. In re Brown (Ohio 1973) 35 Ohio St.2d 9, 298 N.E.2d 579, 64 O.O.2d 5. Habeas Corpus ⟲ 744

Where a minor is found unruly, the trial court committed error in failing to advise the non-custodial parent of such minor of his right to counsel during the proceedings. In re Koogle, Nos. CA–82–68 and CA–82–93 (2d Dist Ct App, Greene, 6–16–83).

5. Parents' responsibility

Parents of minor children who do not bring their children into court pursuant to a court order are not guilty of contempt where the children's whereabouts are unknown to the parents and no evidence suggests that the parents are able to comply with the court's order. State v. Hershberger (Wayne 1959) 168 N.E.2d 12, 83 Ohio Law Abs. 63.

Where parents passively resisted an order of the juvenile court, both could be held for contempt, not just the husband. State v. Hershberger (Ohio Juv. 1958) 150 N.E.2d 671, 77 Ohio Law Abs. 487, reversed 168 N.E.2d 12, 83 Ohio Law Abs. 63.

Where a juvenile court found that a child was neglected, and committed such child to the temporary custody of the local child welfare board, the parents of such child could be punished for contempt for passively resisting such order. (Amish school attendance case.) State v. Hershberger (Ohio Juv. 1958) 150 N.E.2d 671, 77 Ohio Law Abs. 487, reversed 168 N.E.2d 12, 83 Ohio Law Abs. 63.

Juvenile court by issuing warrant under former GC 1648 (RC 2151.28) for parent of minor children on charge of neglect, but failing to issue warrant for children, acquired jurisdiction of parent only, and court of common pleas in subsequent divorce action between parents had jurisdiction over children in order of custody and support. Pesta v. Pesta (Cuyahoga 1944) 68 N.E.2d 234, 45 Ohio Law Abs. 631.

Foster parents of a minor child have no right to intervene either at the adjudicatory or dispositional stage of a dependency or neglect proceeding involving said child. In re Palmer, No. CA–6026 (5th Dist Ct App, Stark, 4–12–83).

6. Jurisdiction

Notice to the parent is not a condition precedent to jurisdiction of the juvenile court under former GC 1648 (RC 2151.28) over a dependent child; parent not cited required to seek his remedy in the court of which the minor is a ward, it having an exclusive and continuing jurisdiction, not resort to habeas corpus in another court. Bleier v. Crouse (Ohio App. 1 Dist. 1920) 13 Ohio App. 69, 31 Ohio C.A. 453.

A failure to hold a dispositional hearing within ninety days of the filing of a complaint in a child protection matter does not divest the court of the jurisdiction to enter dispositional orders. In re Don B. (Ohio App. 6 Dist., Huron, 03-21-2003) No. H-02-033, 2003-Ohio-1400, 2003 WL 1448059, Unreported. Infants ⟲ 204

Where the father of a child is named as a defendant in a divorce proceeding and is properly served, the court has jurisdiction to find the child to be a dependent child and to place it in a foster home. In re McCoy (Franklin 1954) 135 N.E.2d 638, 72 Ohio Law Abs. 519.

Juvenile court has no jurisdiction to adjudicate a child as dependent until after filing of a complaint charging such dependency and notice given to the parent or parents. State ex rel. Clark v. Allaman (Montgomery 1950) 87 Ohio App. 101, 90 N.E.2d 394, 57 Ohio Law Abs. 17, 42 O.O. 330, affirmed 154 Ohio St. 296, 95 N.E.2d 753, 43 O.O. 190.

In case of arrest of a minor, upon a warrant issued by a juvenile court arising out of a complaint charging such minor with delinquency, the juvenile court has jurisdiction of the proceedings even though a citation has not been issued to the parents, guardian or other person having custody and control of such child, or with whom it may be. State ex rel. Heth v. Moloney (Ohio 1933) 126 Ohio St. 526, 186 N.E. 362.

2151.281 Guardian ad litem

(A) The court shall appoint a guardian ad litem, subject to rules adopted by the supreme court, to protect the interest of a child in any proceeding concerning an alleged or adjudicated delinquent child or unruly child when either of the following applies:

(1) The child has no parent, guardian, or legal custodian.

(2) The court finds that there is a conflict of interest between the child and the child's parent, guardian, or legal custodian.

(B)(1) The court shall appoint a guardian ad litem, subject to rules adopted by the supreme court, to protect the interest of a child in any proceeding concerning an alleged abused or neglected child and in any proceeding held pursuant to section 2151.414 of the Revised Code. The guardian ad litem so appointed shall not be the attorney responsible for presenting the evidence alleging that the child is an abused or neglected child and shall not be an employee of any party in the proceeding.

(2) The guardian ad litem appointed for an alleged or adjudicated abused or neglected child may bring a civil action against any person who is required by division (A)(1) or (4) of section 2151.421 of the Revised Code to file a report of child abuse or child neglect that is known or reasonably suspected or believed to have occurred if that person knows, or has reasonable cause to suspect or believe based on facts that would cause a reasonable person in a similar position to suspect or believe, as applicable, that the child for whom the guardian ad litem is appointed is the subject of child abuse or child neglect and does not file the required report and if the child suffers any injury or harm as a result of the child abuse or child neglect that is known or reasonable suspected or believed to have occurred or suffers additional injury or harm after the failure to file the report.

(C) In any proceeding concerning an alleged or adjudicated delinquent, unruly, abused, neglected, or dependent child in which the parent appears to be mentally incompetent or is under eighteen years of age, the court shall appoint a guardian ad litem to protect the interest of that parent.

(D) The court shall require the guardian ad litem to faithfully discharge the guardian ad litem's duties and, upon the guardian ad litem's failure to faithfully discharge the guardian ad litem's duties, shall discharge the guardian ad litem and appoint another guardian ad litem. The court may fix the compensation for the service of the guardian ad litem, which compensation shall be paid from the treasury of the county, subject to rules adopted by the supreme court.

(E) A parent who is eighteen years of age or older and not mentally incompetent shall be deemed sui juris for the purpose of any proceeding relative to a child of the parent who is alleged or adjudicated to be an abused, neglected, or dependent child.

(F) In any case in which a parent of a child alleged or adjudicated to be an abused, neglected, or dependent child is under eighteen years of age, the parents of that parent shall be summoned to appear at any hearing respecting the child, who is alleged or adjudicated to be an abused, neglected, or dependent child.

(G) In any case involving an alleged or adjudicated abused or neglected child or an agreement for the voluntary surrender of temporary or permanent custody of a child that is made in accordance with section 5103.15 of the Revised Code, the court shall appoint the guardian ad litem in each case as soon as possible after the complaint is filed, the request for an extension of the temporary custody agreement is filed with the court, or the request for court approval of the permanent custody agreement is filed. In any case involving an alleged dependent child in which the parent of the child appears to be mentally incompetent or is under eighteen years of age, there is a conflict of interest between the child and the child's parents, guardian, or custodian, or the court believes that the parent of the child is not capable of representing the best interest of the child, the court shall appoint a guardian ad litem for the child. The guardian ad litem or the guardian ad litem's replacement shall continue to serve until any of the following occur:

(1) The complaint is dismissed or the request for an extension of a temporary custody agreement or for court approval of the permanent custody agreement is withdrawn or denied;

(2) All dispositional orders relative to the child have terminated;

(3) The legal custody of the child is granted to a relative of the child, or to another person;

(4) The child is placed in an adoptive home or, at the court's discretion, a final decree of adoption is issued with respect to the child;

(5) The child reaches the age of eighteen if the child is not mentally retarded, developmentally disabled, or physically impaired or the child reaches the age of twenty-one if the child is mentally retarded, developmentally disabled, or physically impaired;

(6) The guardian ad litem resigns or is removed by the court and a replacement is appointed by the court.

If a guardian ad litem ceases to serve a child pursuant to division (G)(4) of this section and the petition for adoption with respect to the child is denied or withdrawn prior to the issuance of a final decree of adoption or prior to the date an interlocutory order of adoption becomes final, the juvenile court shall reappoint a guardian ad litem for that child. The public children services agency or private child placing agency with permanent custody of the child shall notify the juvenile court if the petition for adoption is denied or withdrawn.

(H) If the guardian ad litem for an alleged or adjudicated abused, neglected, or dependent child is an attorney admitted to the practice of law in this state, the guardian ad litem also may serve as counsel to the ward. Until the supreme court adopts rules regarding service as a guardian ad litem that regulate conflicts between a person's role as guardian ad litem and as counsel, if a person is serving as guardian ad litem and counsel for a child and either that person or the court finds that a conflict may exist between the person's roles as guardian ad litem and as counsel, the court shall relieve the person of duties as guardian ad litem and appoint someone else as guardian ad litem for the child. If the court appoints a person who is not an attorney admitted to the practice of law in this state to be a guardian ad litem, the court also may appoint an attorney admitted to the practice of law in this state to serve as counsel for the guardian ad litem.

(I) The guardian ad litem for an alleged or adjudicated abused, neglected, or dependent child shall perform whatever functions are necessary to protect the best interest of the child, including, but not limited to, investigation, mediation, monitoring court proceedings, and monitoring the services provided the child by the public children services agency or private child placing agency that has temporary or permanent custody of the child, and shall file any motions and other court papers that are in the best interest of the child.

The guardian ad litem shall be given notice of all hearings, administrative reviews, and other proceedings in the same manner as notice is given to parties to the action.

(J)(1) When the court appoints a guardian ad litem pursuant to this section, it shall appoint a qualified volunteer or court appointed special advocate whenever one is available and the appointment is appropriate.

(2) Upon request, the department of job and family services shall provide for the training of volunteer guardians ad litem.

(2006 S 238, eff. 9–21–06; 2006 S 17, eff. 8–3–06; 1999 H 471, eff. 7–1–00; 1996 H 274, eff. 8–8–96; 1996 H 419, eff. 9–18–96; 1988 S 89, eff. 1–1–89; 1986 H 529; 1984 S 321; 1980 H 695; 1975 H 85; 1969 H 320)

Uncodified Law

2006 S 17 § 5: See Uncodified Law under RC 2151.03.

1996 H 274, § 12, eff. 8–8–96, reads: Section 2151.281 of the Revised Code as amended by this act shall take effect the earliest time permitted by law, but division (G)(4) and the last unnumbered paragraph of division (G) of the section as amended or added by Am. Sub. H.B. 419 of the 121st General Assembly shall not be applied until the later of the earliest time permitted by law or September 18, 1996.

Historical and Statutory Notes

Ed. Note: The legal review and technical services staff of the Legislative Service Commission has issued an opinion regarding the treatment of multiple amendments. The opinion is neither legally authoritative nor binding, but is provided as a general indication that the amendments of the several acts [2006 S 238, eff. 9–21–06 and 2006 S 17, eff. 8–3–06] may be harmonized pursuant to the rule of construction contained in R.C. 1.52(B) requiring all amendments be given effect if they can reasonably be put into simultaneous operation. See *Baldwin's Ohio Legislative Service Annotated*, 2006, pages 3/L–1559 and 2/L–1129, or the OH-LEGIS or OH-LEGIS-OLD database on Westlaw, for original versions of these Acts.

Amendment Note: 2006 S 238 inserted ", subject to rules adopted by the supreme court," in the introductory paragraph of division (A), division (B)(1), and division (D); substituted "Until the supreme court adopts rules regarding service as a guardian ad litem that regulate conflicts between a person's role as guardian ad litem and as counsel, if" for "If" in the second sentence of division (H); and inserted "or court appointed special advocate" in division (J)(2).

Amendment Note: 2006 S 17 rewrote division (B)(2), which prior thereto read:

"(2) The guardian ad litem appointed for an alleged or adjudicated abused or neglected child may bring a civil action against any person, who is required by division (A)(1) of section 2151.421 of the Revised Code to file a report of known or suspected child abuse or child neglect, if that person knows or suspects that the child for whom the guardian ad litem is appointed is the subject of child abuse or child neglect and does not file the required report and if the child suffers any injury or harm as a result of the known or suspected child abuse or child neglect or suffers additional injury or harm after the failure to file the report."

Amendment Note: 1999 H 471 substituted "job and family" for "human" in division (J)(2).

Amendment Note: 1996 H 274 inserted "either of the following applies" in the first paragraph of division (A); inserted "any injury or harm as a result of the known or suspected child abuse or child neglect or suffers" in division (B)(2); substituted "retarded, developmentally disabled, or physically impaired" for "or physically handicapped" twice in division (G)(5); deleted "guardian," after "mediation," in the first paragraph in division (I); deleted former division (K); and made other nonsubstantive changes. Prior to amendment, former division (K) read:

"(K) A guardian ad litem appointed pursuant to this section on or after the effective date of this amendment may be compensated an amount not exceeding four hundred dollars for the appointment."

Amendment Note: 1996 H 419 substituted "The child is placed in an adoptive home or, at the court's discretion, a" for "A" at the beginning of division (G)(4); added the second and third sentences to division (G)(6); added division (K); and made changes to reflect gender neutral language throughout.

Cross References

Competency of child as witness, submission of questions to determine, 2317.01
Persons required to report injury or neglect, 2151.421
Right to counsel, guardian ad litem, Juv R 4
Waiver of rights, Juv R 3

Library References

Infants ⇐205.
Westlaw Topic No. 211.
C.J.S. Infants §§ 50, 62 to 67.
   Baldwin's Ohio Legislative Service, 1988 Laws of Ohio, S 89—LSC Analysis, p 5–571

Research References

Encyclopedias

OH Jur. 3d Alternative Dispute Resolution § 201, Mediation by Guardians Ad Litem.
OH Jur. 3d Family Law § 1082, Determination of Preference.
OH Jur. 3d Family Law § 1626, Right Under Juvenile Court Law and Rules.
OH Jur. 3d Family Law § 1630, for Abused, Neglected or Dependent Child.
OH Jur. 3d Family Law § 1631, Withdrawal or Discharge of Guardian Ad Litem.
OH Jur. 3d Family Law § 1722, Guardian Ad Litem.
OH Jur. 3d Family Law § 1629.5, in Delinquency Proceedings.

Forms

Ohio Jurisprudence Pleading and Practice Forms § 96:43, Temporary and Permanent Custody.

Treatises and Practice Aids

Klein, Darling, & Terez, Baldwin's Ohio Practice Civil Practice § 24:8, Intervention of Right--Statutory Intervention of Right--"A Statute of This State Confers an Unconditional Right to Intervene".
Sowald & Morganstern, Baldwin's Ohio Practice Domestic Relations Law § 15:64, Guardian Ad Litem—Conflict of Interest.
Carlin, Baldwin's Ohio Practice, Merrick-Rippner Probate Law § 107:9, Parties to Proceedings.
Carlin, Baldwin's Ohio Practice, Merrick-Rippner Probate Law § 107:45, Adjudicatory Hearings—Parties' Right to Counsel.
Carlin, Baldwin's Ohio Practice, Merrick-Rippner Probate Law § 107:46, Adjudicatory Hearings—Child's Right to Guardian Ad Litem.
Carlin, Baldwin's Ohio Practice, Merrick-Rippner Probate Law § 108:13, Juvenile Court—Jurisdiction Over Child Custody Matters—Determination of Custody.
Carlin, Baldwin's Ohio Practice, Merrick-Rippner Probate Law § 108:31, Juvenile Court—Parentage Act—Continuing Jurisdiction to Modify or Revoke Judgment.
Giannelli & Yeomans, Ohio Juvenile Law § 1:8, Rules of Juvenile Procedure.
Giannelli & Yeomans, Ohio Juvenile Law § 3:3, Concurrent Jurisdiction.
Giannelli & Yeomans, Ohio Juvenile Law § 23:6, Guardian Ad Litem.
Giannelli & Yeomans, Ohio Juvenile Law App. D, Appendix D. Glossary.

Law Review and Journal Commentaries

Between A Rock And A Hard Place: Michigan Social Worker Liability For Child Abuse Investigations After *Achterhof v. Selvaggio*, Note. 22 U Tol L Rev 455 (Winter 1991).

Guardians Ad Litem For Child Victims In Criminal Proceedings, Mark Hardin. 25 J Fam L 687 (1986–87).

The Voice of a Child: Independent Legal Representation of Children in Private Custody Disputes When Sexual Abuse Is Alleged, Kerin S. Bischoff. 138 U Pa L Rev 1383 (May 1990).

Notes of Decisions

Abuse 2

Appointment 3, 4
    Child's action regarding paternity 3
    When mandatory 4
Child's action regarding paternity, appointment 3
Compatibility of offices 5
Conflict of interest between child and parent, guardian, or custodian 6
Constitutional issues 1
County custody 7
Dependency 8
Duty of guardian 9
Fees 10
Immunity 11
When mandatory, appointment 4

---

1. Constitutional issues

Untimely filing of report of guardian ad litem, in proceedings for termination of mother's parental rights, depriving mother of opportunity to cross-examine guardian ad litem, did not require complete reversal of termination of mother's parental rights, where due process violation was singular and capable of being cured by remand for evidentiary hearing. (Per Westcott Rice, J., with one judge concurring in result only.) In re Kangas (Ohio App. 11 Dist., Ashtabula, 06-30-2006) No. 2006-A-0010, 2006-Ohio-3433, 2006 WL 1817069, Unreported. Infants ⇔ 254

Appointment of a guardian ad litem in juvenile cases is mandatory as opposed to the discretionary appointment in domestic relations cases and due process mandates that a party shall have adequate notice of a proposed action as well as an opportunity to be heard; therefore, in a dependency action a trial court errs in granting the motion of the guardian ad litem for attorney fees without affording the father of the child notice and an opportunity to be heard. In Matter of Marquez (Ohio App. 11 Dist., Geauga, 11-22-1996) No. 96-G-1976, 1996 WL 702461, Unreported.

Complaint to terminate parental rights claiming that children were neglected and dependent, which included facts showing that both physical and sexual abuse were believed to be at issue, was sufficient to allege that children were 'abused," such that children had right to appointed counsel. In re Stacey S. (Ohio App. 6 Dist., 12-30-1999) 136 Ohio App.3d 503, 737 N.E.2d 92, 1999-Ohio-989. Infants ⇔ 197; Infants ⇔ 205

Appointment of guardian ad litem and attorney for the guardian ad litem was not sufficient to satisfy children's right to counsel in action to terminate parental rights. In re Stacey S. (Ohio App. 6 Dist., 12-30-1999) 136 Ohio App.3d 503, 737 N.E.2d 92, 1999-Ohio-989. Infants ⇔ 205

Juvenile court was required to appoint counsel to represent child in custody dispute between former spouses, where court was aware that child's wishes as to custody were different from those of his appointed guardian ad litem, and where guardian ad litem, while an attorney, was not specifically appointed to act as child's attorney. In re Janie M. (Ohio App. 6 Dist., 02-05-1999) 131 Ohio App.3d 637, 723 N.E.2d 191. Infants ⇔ 90

Father was not denied due process in custody determination by trial court's appointment of counsel for guardian ad litem without affording father an opportunity to be heard, where guardian ad litem was to be subjected to cross-examination. Rife v. Morgan (Ohio App. 2 Dist., 10-18-1995) 106 Ohio App.3d 843, 667 N.E.2d 450. Constitutional Law ⇔ 274(5); Child Custody ⇔ 500

Father was not denied a fair trial in custody determination by trial court's refusal to permit his child to be cross-examined during evidentiary hearing, where remand from previous appeal of trial court's award of custody to maternal grandparents was limited to requiring trial court to allow cross-examination of guardian ad litem. Rife v. Morgan (Ohio App. 2 Dist., 10-18-1995) 106 Ohio App.3d 843, 667 N.E.2d 450. Child Custody ⇔ 924

Father in custody proceeding was not prejudiced by trial court's failure to rule on motions to allow newly discovered evidence and for finding of contempt against child's maternal grandmother, and thus was not denied a fair trial, where trial court recognized that it had not yet ruled upon motions and matter had been remanded to trial court from earlier appeal only for purpose of allowing father to cross-examine guardian ad litem. Rife v. Morgan (Ohio App. 2 Dist., 10-18-1995) 106 Ohio App.3d 843, 667 N.E.2d 450. Child Custody ⇔ 923(1)

Father in custody proceeding was not prejudiced by trial court's implicit overruling of father's motion to remove guardian ad litem for child, and thus was not denied a fair trial, where father did not explain how he was prejudiced and matter had been remanded to trial court from earlier appeal only for purpose of allowing father to cross-examine guardian ad litem. Rife v. Morgan (Ohio App. 2 Dist., 10-18-1995) 106 Ohio App.3d 843, 667 N.E.2d 450. Child Custody ⇔ 923(1)

Father in custody proceeding was not prejudiced by trial court's failure to rule on pro se motions for findings of contempt against school, social worker, and children's home after remand from earlier appeal to allow father opportunity to cross-examine guardian ad litem, and thus was not denied a fair trial, where father did not explain how he was prejudiced, motions did not implicate limited purpose of remand, and there was no reason to conclude that trial court would not eventually rule on motions. Rife v. Morgan (Ohio App. 2 Dist., 10-18-1995) 106 Ohio App.3d 843, 667 N.E.2d 450. Child Custody ⇔ 923(1)

Father who lost custody of his child was not denied a fair trial or equal protection by trial court's failure to obtain complete record of prior proceedings to resolve authenticity objection to report used by father's counsel on cross-examination of guardian ad litem, where father's counsel convinced trial court that document was authentic and counsel was allowed to use report. Rife v. Morgan (Ohio App. 2 Dist., 10-18-1995) 106 Ohio App.3d 843, 667 N.E.2d 450. Evidence ⇔ 382; Constitutional Law ⇔ 249(5); Constitutional Law ⇔ 311

When an attorney is appointed guardian ad litem and is also appointed to represent the person, the attorney's first and highest duty is to represent his client within the bounds of the law and therefore, where a trial court in a change of custody proceeding, allows a guardian ad litem to act as the children's attorney it denies the children proper representation of counsel in the protection of their wishes to live with their father which requires the trial court's judgment to be reversed and the cause remanded for a new trial. Bawidamann v. Bawidamann (Montgomery 1989) 63 Ohio App.3d 691, 580 N.E.2d 15.

Due process is not denied to the parent of a severely abused child by a court holding a temporary custody hearing ex parte under Juv R 13 without appointing a guardian ad litem under RC 2151.281. Parker v. Children Services Bd. of Trumbull County (Trumbull 1984) 21 Ohio App.3d 115, 487 N.E.2d 341, 21 O.B.R. 123.

Appointment of the guardian ad litem for the children as counsel for child did not violate child's constitutional right to counsel, in termination of parental rights proceeding; there was no conflict of interest between counsel's roles as guardian ad litem and as attorney for child since the children both expressed a desire to remain with their foster mother. In re Legg (Ohio App. 8 Dist., Cuyahoga, 09-05-2002) No. 80542, No. 80543, 2002-Ohio-4582, 2002 WL 2027290, Unreported. Infants ⇔ 205

2. Abuse

Effect upon validity of guardian ad litem's report of her inability to provide name of emergency room physician who told her that child was dehydrated or to provide report of diagnosis was for trial court to determine in custody proceeding, and there was no abuse of trial court's discretion in according this lack of information little significance. Rife v. Morgan (Ohio App. 2 Dist., 10-18-1995) 106 Ohio App.3d 843, 667 N.E.2d 450. Child Custody ⇔ 467

RC 2151.281, providing for appointment of a guardian ad litem to protect a child's interests in an abuse proceeding, is inapplicable where no abuse charges are filed against the noncustodial parent and the custodial parent moves to terminate visitation on grounds that abuse by the noncustodial parent occurred. Truitt v. Truitt (Preble 1989) 65 Ohio App.3d 126, 583 N.E.2d 331. Infants ⇔ 78(1); Infants ⇔ 205

3. Appointment—Child's action regarding paternity

Court determining whether to permit child to bring his or her own action to seek or challenge adjudication of paternity should consider appointment of guardian ad litem to aid in determining child's best interests. Leguillon v. Leguillon (Ohio App. 12 Dist., 01-12-1998) 124 Ohio App.3d 757, 707 N.E.2d 571. Infants ⇔ 78(1)

4. —— When mandatory, appointment

Trial court in child protection proceedings was required to determine, prior to permanent custody proceedings, whether subject child was capable of expressing opinion regarding her custody, and whether such opinion was consistent with guardian ad litem's recommendation that mother's parental rights be terminated, by expressly appointing child's guardian ad litem as child's counsel. (Per Westcott Rice, J., with one judge concurring in result only.) In re Kangas (Ohio App. 11 Dist., Ashtabula, 06-30-2006) No. 2006-A-0010, 2006-Ohio-3433, 2006 WL 1817069, Unreported. Infants ⇔ 207

Juvenile court abused its discretion by failing to appoint a guardian ad litem or further inquire into whether a guardian ad litem was necessary during delinquency proceeding in which juvenile was charged with felonious assault, domestic violence, and being an unruly child, where record demonstrated at least the strong possibility of a conflict between juvenile and his father, the victim. In re Cook (Ohio App. 11 Dist., Ashtabula, 09-30-2005) No. 2003-A-0132, 2005-Ohio-5288, 2005 WL 2416615, Unreported. Infants ⇐ 205

Juvenile court abused its discretion during delinquency proceeding by failing to appoint a guardian ad litem or to make further inquiry into whether a guardian ad litem was necessary, in light of father's statements against juvenile's penal interest. In re Bostwick (Ohio App. 4 Dist., Ross, 09-26-2005) No. 05CA2820, 2005-Ohio-5123, 2005 WL 2374933, Unreported. Infants ⇐ 205

Mother failed to demonstrate that trial court committed plain error by failing to appoint her guardian ad litem (GAL) and that her trial counsel was ineffective for failing to request that GAL be appointed on her behalf, in proceeding terminating parental rights; there was nothing in record to indicate extent to which, if at all, mother's mental health issues impeded her ability to understand and participate in proceedings, record demonstrated that mother appeared to understand nature of proceedings, and there was nothing to suggest that mother appeared incompetent at time she voluntarily relinquished her parental rights. In re D.C.H. (Ohio App. 9 Dist., Summit, 08-17-2005) No. 22648, 2005-Ohio-4257, 2005 WL 1962963, Unreported. Infants ⇐ 243

Guardian ad litem adequately performed her statutory duty to protect the best interest of child, during dependency proceeding, where guardian ad litem visited mother and father's home, she observed visitations between parents and child, she met with parents, she met with child's foster mother, and she reviewed county children services records from mother's prior dependency cases. In re West (Ohio App. 4 Dist., Athens, 06-10-2005) No. 05CA4, 2005-Ohio-2977, 2005 WL 1400029, Unreported. Infants ⇐ 205

Mother was not prejudiced by trial court's failure to appoint guardian ad litem for her, in permanent custody proceeding in which children had been removed from mother's custody; appointment of guardian ad litem would not have remedied mother's failure to comply with her case plan and would not have improved her parenting abilities or changed fact that children had special needs, and mother was adequately protected because she had been represented by counsel throughout dispositional hearing. In re McHugh Children (Ohio App. 5 Dist., Licking, 05-05-2005) No. 2004CA00091, 2005-Ohio-2345, 2005 WL 1125334, Unreported. Infants ⇐ 253

Appointment of guardian ad litem was required for juvenile accused of rape for performing fellatio on his seven-year-old step-brother, where juvenile's victims in previous episodes of physical and sexual acting out were also family members, and juvenile's parents testified for prosecution and recommended that juvenile be placed in Department of Youth Services (DYS). In re Wilson (Ohio App. 4 Dist., Washington, 12-22-2004) No. 04CA26, 2004-Ohio-7276, 2004 WL 3090235, Unreported. Infants ⇐ 205

Trial court committed prejudicial error in failing to appoint guardian ad litem for juvenile accused of raping family member and whose parents testified for prosecution and recommended that juvenile be placed in Department of Youth Services (DYS), even though juvenile was represented by competent counsel; task of guardian ad litem and attorney could conflict, and no one testified on juvenile's behalf at adjudicatory hearing. In re Wilson (Ohio App. 4 Dist., Washington, 12-22-2004) No. 04CA26, 2004-Ohio-7276, 2004 WL 3090235, Unreported. Infants ⇐ 253

Trial court's failure to appoint guardian ad litem for mother at child dependency hearing did not constitute plain error; although mother appeared to be mentally incompetent, mother was represented by appointed counsel throughout proceeding, and appointment of guardian ad litem would not have remedied mother's failure to comply with case plan or improved her parenting abilities, which resulted in termination of her parental rights. In re Amber G. & Josie G. (Ohio App. 6 Dist., Lucas, 10-22-2004) No. L-04-1091, 2004-Ohio-5665, 2004 WL 2384453, Unreported. Infants ⇐ 243

Mother waived all but plain error with respect to claim that trial court erred by failing to appoint guardian ad litem for mother at child dependency hearing, where, in trial court, mother never requested appointment of guardian ad litem or questioned failure of court to appoint guardian ad litem. In re Amber G. & Josie G. (Ohio App. 6 Dist., Lucas, 10-22-2004) No. L-04-1091, 2004-Ohio-5665, 2004 WL 2384453, Unreported. Infants ⇐ 243

Mother was not entitled to guardian ad litem in proceeding to grant custody of her children to children's services agency; nothing in record suggested that mother appeared incompetent at any of the proceedings, psychologist was unable to conclude that mother suffered from any mental illness, and testified that mother had no history of psychosis and appeared cooperative, lucid, and goal-oriented, and neither mother nor her attorney indicated that guardian ad litem be appointed, or that mother's mental competence was issue. In re K.P. (Ohio App. 8 Dist., Cuyahoga, 03-25-2004) No. 82709, 2004-Ohio-1448, 2004 WL 583867, Unreported, as amended nunc pro tunc, stay denied 102 Ohio St.3d 1457, 809 N.E.2d 31, 2004-Ohio-2569, appeal not allowed 102 Ohio St.3d 1473, 809 N.E.2d 1159, 2004-Ohio-2830. Infants ⇐ 205

Statute governing appointment of guardian ad litem for children in cases involving an alleged delinquent or unruly child, an alleged abused or neglected child, or a motion for permanent custody, did not apply to hearing on motion seeking visitation rights. Putthoff v. Thompson (Ohio App. 2 Dist., Clark, 01-09-2004) No. 2003CA19, 2004-Ohio-76, 2004 WL 41563, Unreported. Infants ⇐ 205

The trial court's failure to appoint counsel for child, other than an attorney who was acting as child's guardian ad litem, did not constitute reversible error, in proceeding to obtain a planned permanent living arrangement (PPLA) order for child; there was no conflict between the wishes of child and the recommendation of guardian ad litem for child. In re Holt (Ohio App. 10 Dist., Franklin, 10-21-2003) No. 03AP-355, 2003-Ohio-5580, 2003 WL 22390048, Unreported. Infants ⇐ 253

Trial court was required to appoint a guardian ad litem for children in termination of parental rights case, whereas the court was not likewise required to appoint counsel to represent them. In re Alfrey (Ohio App. 2 Dist., Clark, 02-07-2003) No. 01CA0083, 2003-Ohio-608, 2003 WL 262587, Unreported. Infants ⇐ 205

Mother was entitled to have guardian ad litem appointed for child, where mother filed complaint alleging father abused child; court was statutorily obligated to appoint guardian ad litem for child alleged to be abused. In re Robinson (Ohio App. 5 Dist., Perry, 11-02-2002) No. 02CA7, 2002-Ohio-6020, 2002 WL 31458237, Unreported. Infants ⇐ 78(1)

Failure to appoint guardian at litem for juvenile or at least inquire further into whether guardian ad litem was necessary was reversible error in delinquency proceedings after juvenile's grandfather, his legal guardian, informed court that he had recently filed unruly charge against juvenile, thereby suggesting strong possibility of conflict of interest, particularly where grandfather apparently acted for purpose of ascertaining status of this additional charge rather than out of concern for juvenile's best interests, as evidenced by his refusal to explain circumstances surrounding charge. In re Spradlin (Ohio App. 4 Dist., 12-01-2000) 140 Ohio App.3d 402, 747 N.E.2d 877, 2000-Ohio-2003. Infants ⇐ 253

Absent express dual appointment, courts should not presume dual appointment when appointed guardian ad litem for indigent child is also an attorney, as roles of guardian ad litem and attorney are different. In re Janie M. (Ohio App. 6 Dist., 02-05-1999) 131 Ohio App.3d 637, 723 N.E.2d 191. Infants ⇐ 205

Failure of court to appoint guardian ad litem for juvenile, when such appointment is required under applicable rule or statute, constitutes reversible error. In re Sappington (Ohio App. 2 Dist., 10-31-1997) 123 Ohio App.3d 448, 704 N.E.2d 339. Infants ⇐ 205; Infants ⇐ 253

5. Compatibility of offices

Type of conflict of interest between parent and juvenile triggering court's statutory obligation to appoint guardian ad litem is different from conflict between roles of attorney and guardian ad litem, and is more apparent in dependency, neglect, and abuse proceedings than in delinquency cases. In re Howard (Ohio App. 1 Dist., 04-16-1997) 119 Ohio App.3d 201, 695 N.E.2d 1. Infants ⇐ 78(1)

The position of county personnel officer is compatible with the position of court appointed volunteer of a juvenile court. OAG 91–067.

6. Conflict of interest between child and parent, guardian, or custodian

The juvenile court was not required to appoint a guardian ad litem for juvenile, in delinquency proceeding, even though juvenile alleged a conflict of interest existed between him and his parents; mother appeared with juvenile at each of the hearings, and mother spoke on juvenile's behalf at the dispositional hearing and urged the court not to commit juvenile to the Department of Youth Services (DYS). In re Smith (Ohio App. 3 Dist., Union, 06-05-2006) No. 14-05-33, 2006-Ohio-2788, 2006 WL 1519688, Unreported. Infants ⇐ 205

Attorney was permitted to act as guardian ad litem and as attorney for mother and father's ten children, in termination of parental rights proceeding; there was no evidence that the children expressed strong desires or interests that were inconsistent with the recommendations of the guardian ad litem, and when the guardian ad litem reported that one child had expressed an interest in living with a relative the court made an inquiry and determined that the child was not serious and was more concerned about staying in contact with her siblings. In re Hilyard (Ohio App. 4 Dist., Vinton, 04-13-2006) No. 05CA600, No. 05CA603, No. 05CA607, No. 05CA601, No. 05CA604, No. 05CA608, No. 05CA602, No. 05CA606, No. 05CA609, 2006-Ohio-1965, 2006 WL   Infants ⚮ 205

The trial court's failure to appoint a separate attorney for child was not error, during dependency proceedings; an attorney was appointed as guardian ad litem for child, attorney acted as guardian ad litem for child and as counsel for child, and there was no evidence of a conflict of interest between the desires of child and the guardian ad litem's recommendations. In re P.S. (Ohio App. 8 Dist., Cuyahoga, 08-11-2005) No. 85917, 2005-Ohio-4157, 2005 WL 1926042, Unreported. Infants ⚮ 205

Children's guardian ad litem's prior representation of mother's husband's ex-wife in domestic violence case did not constitute improper conflict of interest in proceedings to determine whether to grant permanent custody of mother's two children to county agency; facts of husband's domestic violence incident were before the court, guardian ad litem's position taken in prior representation was not inconsistent with his current position regarding husband, and any confidential information gained through prior representation would be covered under attorney/client privilege. In re Morgan (Ohio App. 3 Dist., Marion, 08-02-2004) No. 9-04-02, No. 9-04-03, 2004-Ohio-4018, 2004 WL 1717934, Unreported. Infants ⚮ 205

Removing attorney retained by ex-wife to represent child in proceeding to modify parental rights and determine child support was not abuse of discretion, where trial court had previously appointed lawyer to serve both as child's guardian ad litem and as child's attorney and nothing in record indicated that trial court or lawyer thought conflict existed in lawyer assuming both roles. Jennings-Harder v. Yarmesch (Ohio App. 8 Dist., Cuyahoga, 07-29-2004) No. 83984, 2004-Ohio-3960, 2004 WL 1688538, Unreported. Infants ⚮ 90

The trial court's failure to appoint a guardian ad litem for juvenile when a conflict of interest existed between juvenile and his parents constituted reversible error; the victim of juvenile's crime was his half-sister, juvenile's stepfather informed the court at juvenile's arraignment that they did not want juvenile to return to their home, juvenile's mother informed the court that she did not feel that she could make choices that were in juvenile's best interest, and juvenile was not represented by counsel at his probation revocation hearing. In re K.J.F. (Ohio App. 2 Dist., Clark, 01-23-2004) No. 2003 CA 41, 2004-Ohio-263, 2004 WL 102847, Unreported. Infants ⚮ 205; Infants ⚮ 253

Although juvenile was appointed a guardian ad litem based on juvenile's conflict of interest with his father, juvenile failed to show he was prejudiced by failure of guardian ad litem to appear for trial, and thus defendant was not entitled to reversal of delinquency determination; juvenile was represented by counsel throughout the course of proceedings, defendant's father made no recommendation to the court, and there was no basis to believe that outcome of proceedings would have changed if guardian ad litem had been present during trial. In re J.A. (Ohio App. 8 Dist., Cuyahoga, 01-08-2004) No. 82608, 2004-Ohio-48, 2004 WL 35755, Unreported. Infants ⚮ 205; Infants ⚮ 253

Magistrate's failure to appoint guardian ad litem in delinquency proceeding, despite fact that minor's mother requested treatment for minor, while minor desired commitment to Department of Youth Services, was not plain error; transcript of proceeding revealed no anger or tension between minor and mother, which may have necessitated appointment of guardian ad litem. In re Harper (Ohio App. 2 Dist., Montgomery, 12-12-2003) No. 19948, 2003-Ohio-6666, 2003 WL 22927248, Unreported. Infants ⚮ 243

Evidence was sufficient to show that father of children subject of custody dispute engaged in menacing by stalking children's guardian ad litem, as required to justify anti-stalking civil protection order preventing father from coming within two blocks or 300 yards of guardian ad litem, even though father never threatened violence or committed physical violence against guardian ad litem; in approximately 40-45 encounters with guardian ad litem, father yelled and called guardian vulgar names, he drove vehicle towards guardian ad litem at least three times in what appeared to be attempts to run guardian down, and on two occasions he sat and gazed at guardian ad litem with hostile stare. Wallace v. Masten (Ohio App. 4 Dist., Hocking, 02-11-2003) No. 02CA13, 2003-Ohio-1081, 2003 WL 927600, Unreported, appeal not allowed 99 Ohio St.3d 1437, 789 N.E.2d 1118, 2003-Ohio-2902. Extortion And Threats ⚮ 25.1

No conflict of interest existed with respect to guardian ad litem representing interests of oldest child, as well as other children, and, as such, children were not each entitled to appointment of separate guardian ad litem, in proceeding in which county child protection agency sought permanent custody of children; professional clinical counselor indicated that oldest child had symptoms of reactive attachment disorder, and that if he was returned to his family, he might become a danger to himself and/or his family members, and, as such, it was not in either oldest child's or other children's interest to be reunited. In re Lopez (Ohio App. 3 Dist., 05-08-2006) 166 Ohio App.3d 688, 852 N.E.2d 1266, 2006-Ohio-2251. Infants ⚮ 205

Trial court committed reversible error when it failed to appoint guardian ad litem on behalf of juvenile, who had been adjudicated delinquent, at show-cause hearing that state brought against juvenile for failing to follow all terms and conditions of treatment at Youth Treatment Center (YTC); although juvenile's mother was present at court proceedings, as one of juvenile's victims, and as custodian of another of juvenile's victims, interests of juvenile's mother were in conflict with interests of juvenile. In re William B. (Ohio App. 6 Dist., 08-26-2005) 163 Ohio App.3d 201, 837 N.E.2d 414, 2005-Ohio-4428. Infants ⚮ 253

When a guardian ad litem who is also appointed as the juvenile's attorney in a proceeding for the termination of parental rights recommends a disposition that conflicts with the juvenile's wishes, the juvenile court must appoint independent counsel to represent the child. In re Williams (Ohio, 04-14-2004) 101 Ohio St.3d 398, 805 N.E.2d 1110, 2004-Ohio-1500. Infants ⚮ 205

Guardian ad litem can, in some situations, serve a dual role, in a proceeding for the termination of parental rights, as both the guardian ad litem and the juvenile's attorney, and thereby fulfill the juvenile's right to counsel, provided there has been an express dual appointment by the juvenile court. In re Williams (Ohio, 04-14-2004) 101 Ohio St.3d 398, 805 N.E.2d 1110, 2004-Ohio-1500. Infants ⚮ 205

Appointment of attorney for guardian ad litem as the substitute guardian ad litem in parental rights termination proceeding did not satisfy children's right to counsel, even though attorney claimed she performed as counsel to children, where court failed to make finding that there was no conflict between the attorney's dual roles as guardian ad litem and attorney for children and suggestions were raised during dispositional hearing that a conflict did exist. In re Stacey S. (Ohio App. 6 Dist., 12-30-1999) 136 Ohio App.3d 503, 737 N.E.2d 92, 1999-Ohio-989. Infants ⚮ 205

Strong possibility of conflict of interest between juvenile involved in delinquency adjudication proceeding and his father, who represented him in such proceeding, mandated appointment of guardian ad litem for juvenile; juvenile's parents had previously brought him before juvenile court on domestic violence charge, and father attempted to persuade juvenile court to act in manner which may have been against juvenile's interests and persuaded juvenile not to exercise his statutory right to attorney. In re Sappington (Ohio App. 2 Dist., 10-31-1997) 123 Ohio App.3d 448, 704 N.E.2d 339. Infants ⚮ 205

Court is not statutorily required to appoint guardian ad litem for juvenile in every case in which juvenile's parent speaks against juvenile's penal interest in dispositional hearing; however, such conduct on part of parent raises colorable claim of conflict of interest between parent and child and requires thorough inquiry. In re Howard (Ohio App. 1 Dist., 04-16-1997) 119 Ohio App.3d 201, 695 N.E.2d 1. Infants ⚮ 78(1)

Comments made by mother of juvenile subjected to delinquency proceeding, indicating her belief that juvenile would be better off in custody of Department of Youth Services than in his then-current placement, did not evidence conflict of interest triggering court's statutory obligation to appoint guardian ad litem for juvenile; mother's belief that she was acting in juvenile's best interest was validated by testimony from representative from juvenile's then-current placement, juvenile's rights were adequately protected, and all information necessary was before court. In re Howard (Ohio App. 1 Dist., 04-16-1997) 119 Ohio App.3d 201, 695 N.E.2d 1. Infants ⚮ 78(1)

Lawyer may, in proper circumstances, take on duties of both counsel for juvenile subjected to delinquency proceeding and juvenile's guardian ad litem; however, as lawyer's role is to represent client zealously within boundaries of law, and guardian's role is to investigate juvenile's situation and ask court to do what is in juvenile's best interest, duties of counsel and guardian may conflict to extent rendering lawyer incapable of performing both functions. In re Howard (Ohio App. 1 Dist., 04-16-1997) 119 Ohio App.3d 201, 695 N.E.2d 1. Infants ⚮ 205

Juvenile court was required to appoint guardian ad litem to protect rights and interests of juvenile in delinquency proceeding involving rape charge, where only person who appeared on juvenile's behalf was his mother, and juvenile's mother was also mother of nine-year-old victim in case. In re Miller (Ohio App. 2 Dist., 04-04-1997) 119 Ohio App.3d 52, 694 N.E.2d 500. Infants ⇐ 78(1)

Appointment of guardian ad litem (GAL) did not constitute an appointment to act as child's attorney in proceeding on father's motion which sought custody of child; there was no evidence of a dual appointment, such as mention on judgment entry that GAL was also acting as child's attorney or inclusion of an attorney number on documents bearing signature of GAL. Sabrina J. v Robbin C, No. L–00–1374, 2002–Ohio–2691, 2002 WL 1303148 (6th Dist Ct App, Lucas, 5–31–02).

7. County custody

Trial court's acceptance of guardian ad litem's supplemental report and recommendation that grandmother be granted custody of mother's children, which was submitted one month after trial on petition by Department of Children and Family Services for permanent custody of children, was abuse of discretion, where recommendation was accepted without allowing parties to cross-examine guardian ad litem regarding her report and recommendations. In re D.D. (Ohio App. 8 Dist., Cuyahoga, 08-12-2004) No. 83537, 2004-Ohio-4243, 2004 WL 1797186, Unreported. Infants ⇐ 208

Trial court's failure to reference guardian ad litem's recommendation against grant of permanent child custody to county department of children's services was not abuse of discretion in proceeding in which court granted permanent custody of dependent children to department, where guardian ad litem also stated that he could not recommend that children be returned to mother. In re Yeager (Ohio App. 5 Dist., Fairfield, 03-25-2004) No. 03CA49, No. 03CA52, No. 03CA50, No. 03CA53, 2004-Ohio-1560, 2004 WL 625285, Unreported. Infants ⇐ 208

Juvenile court jurisdiction to consent to an agreement surrendering permanent custody of a minor to a county children services board, pursuant to RC 5103.15 and RC 5153.16(B), is not dependent upon service of process on the child and his parents as provided for in RC 2151.28, nor upon appointment of a guardian ad litem as provided for in RC 2151.281. In re Miller (Ohio 1980) 61 Ohio St.2d 184, 399 N.E.2d 1262, 15 O.O.3d 211. Infants ⇐ 222

8. Dependency

Guardian ad litem appointed for mother during dependency proceeding by reason of mother's diminished mental capacity lacked authority to consent to waiver of mother's fundamental constitutional rights, and guardian's indication that there was no objection to finding of dependency based upon complaint did not satisfy or lessen magistrate's obligation to ascertain that mother's waiver of her rights was knowing, intelligent and voluntary. In re Etter (Ohio App. 1 Dist., 06-12-1998) 134 Ohio App.3d 484, 731 N.E.2d 694. Infants ⇐ 205

RC 2151.281 does not require appointment of a guardian ad litem in a dependency case. In re Barzak (Trumbull 1985) 24 Ohio App.3d 180, 493 N.E.2d 1011, 24 O.B.R. 270. Infants ⇐ 205

9. Duty of guardian

When conducting investigation in connection with proceeding to modify child support, guardian ad litem acted unreasonably when he directed all financial inquiries solely at father. Jarvis v. Witter (Ohio App. 8 Dist., Cuyahoga, 12-09-2004) No. 84128, 2004-Ohio-6628, 2004 WL 2830789, Unreported. Child Support ⇐ 328

When conducting investigation in connection with proceeding to modify child support, guardian ad litem did not act unreasonably in visiting father's residence and hiring expert to ascertain father's finances and gross income. Jarvis v. Witter (Ohio App. 8 Dist., Cuyahoga, 12-09-2004) No. 84128, 2004-Ohio-6628, 2004 WL 2830789, Unreported. Child Support ⇐ 328

Juvenile court was not required to follow guardian ad litem's recommendation during termination of parental rights proceeding. In re Keaton (Ohio App. 4 Dist., Ross, 11-19-2004) No. 04CA2785, No. 04CA2788, 2004-Ohio-6210, 2004 WL 2650249, Unreported. Infants ⇐ 208

Children's guardian ad litem made independent investigation in termination of parental rights proceeding; although mother contended guardian ad litem merely summarized agency record, guardian ad litem's report revealed that she based report on review of agency files, observations of parents and children, visits to foster home, and participation in court hearings and reviews. In re Sanders Children (Ohio App. 5 Dist., Tuscarawas, 10-29-2004) No. 2004 AP 08 0057, 2004-Ohio-5878, 2004 WL 2497028, Unreported. Infants ⇐ 155; Infants ⇐ 205

Children's guardian ad litem is not required to address in guardian ad litem's report each statutory factor for determining whether it is in children's best interest to terminate parental rights. In re Sanders Children (Ohio App. 5 Dist., Tuscarawas, 10-29-2004) No. 2004 AP 08 0057, 2004-Ohio-5878, 2004 WL 2497028, Unreported. Infants ⇐ 155; Infants ⇐ 205

Children's guardian ad litem addressed in her report statutory factors for determining whether it was in children's best interest to terminate parental rights, even though guardian ad litem did not specifically identify statute, where guardian ad litem indicated that children were young and could not verbalize their wishes, that parents had not visited one child, length of time children were placed in foster care, that parents were doing well in foster care, and that termination of parental rights was recommended. In re Sanders Children (Ohio App. 5 Dist., Tuscarawas, 10-29-2004) No. 2004 AP 08 0057, 2004-Ohio-5878, 2004 WL 2497028, Unreported. Infants ⇐ 155; Infants ⇐ 205

Guardian ad litem properly discharged her duties in termination of parental rights action; guardian testified it was not possible for her to interview a child 2½ months old, guardian further testified she had met with the foster care providers at the prior hearing and discussed the medical concerns of the child and talked about the feedings and basic needs of the child, and guardian was very familiar with mother and her prior history. In re Gaugler (Ohio App. 5 Dist., Stark, 08-02-2004) No. 2004-CA-00114, 2004-Ohio-4114, 2004 WL 1753368, Unreported. Infants ⇐ 205

Guardian ad litem (GAL) complied with duties required of him in termination of parental rights proceeding, where GAL was familiar with family, read documents provided to him, and attended court hearings. In re Andy-Jones (Ohio App. 10 Dist., Franklin, 06-24-2004) No. 03AP-1167, No. 03AP-1231, 2004-Ohio-3312, 2004 WL 1405319, Unreported, stay denied 103 Ohio St.3d 1425, 814 N.E.2d 489, 2004-Ohio-4524, appeal not allowed 103 Ohio St.3d 1429, 814 N.E.2d 491, 2004-Ohio-4524, appeal not allowed 103 Ohio St.3d 1465, 815 N.E.2d 680, 2004-Ohio-5056. Infants ⇐ 205

Trial court error, if any, in allowing the guardian ad litem, who was not a licensed attorney, to question witnesses at termination of parental rights hearing did not constitute plain error; mother failed to establish that the guardian ad litems' questioning of witnesses seriously affected the fairness, integrity, or public reputation of the judicial process. In re Curry (Ohio App. 4 Dist., Washington, 02-11-2004) No. 03CA51, 2004-Ohio-750, 2004 WL 307476, Unreported. Infants ⇐ 243

Guardian ad litem who filed petition to adjudicate child neglected was statutorily prohibited from representing both State and child in subsequent hearing on petition; although nothing prevented guardian from filing complaint alleging that child was neglected, guardian was required to step aside upon commencement of hearing on complaint, in which proceeding duty fell on children services agency to investigate situation and, if necessary, prosecute complaint. In re Kheirkhah (Ohio App. 11 Dist., Lake, 02-06-2004) No. 2002-L-128, 2004-Ohio-521, 2004 WL 231495, Unreported. Infants ⇐ 205

On remand of termination of parental rights case, trial court did not abuse its discretion in ordering the guardian ad litem to submit a supplemental report addressing child's wishes as to grant of permanent custody to County Jobs and Family Services; County did not have burden of proving what child's wishes were regarding her custody, obligation to provide statement on that point was on guardian ad litem, and thus, this was not situation in which party who had burden of proof on particular issue was given second chance to establish the necessary facts. In re Salsgiver (Ohio App. 11 Dist., Geauga, 03-13-2003) No. 2002-G-2477, 2003-Ohio-1206, 2003 WL 1193784, Unreported. Infants ⇐ 254

The trial court abused its discretion when it failed to appoint a guardian ad litem for juvenile, during delinquency proceeding charging juvenile with kidnapping, where juvenile and his legal guardians exhibited a conflict of interest since juvenile's victim was the daughter of his legal guardians, guardians refused to hire an attorney for juvenile, and guardians requested that the court institutionalize juvenile. In re Slider (Ohio App. 4 Dist., 03-23-2005) 160 Ohio App.3d 159, 826 N.E.2d 356, 2005-Ohio-1457. Infants ⇐ 205

Permitting mother's counsel to withdraw from proceedings to terminate mother's parental rights was neither error nor an abuse of discretion; mother abducted child from foster parents' home in violation of existing court orders and voluntarily absconded from the court's jurisdiction to China, choosing not to contact either her counsel or the court, counsel advised the court that she did not know what her client wanted her to do and therefore could not zealously represent her client, and the Juvenile Court Rules authorized mother's guardian ad litem, also an attorney, to serve as her counsel. In re Zhang (Ohio App. 8 Dist., 06-10-1999) 135

Ohio App.3d 350, 734 N.E.2d 379, dismissed, appeal not allowed 87 Ohio St.3d 1417, 717 N.E.2d 1105, reconsideration stricken 87 Ohio St.3d 1437, 719 N.E.2d 2. Infants ⇐ 205

Purpose of guardian ad litem is to secure for juvenile or incompetent person proper defense or adequate protection of his or her rights. In re Etter (Ohio App. 1 Dist., 06-12-1998) 134 Ohio App.3d 484, 731 N.E.2d 694. Infants ⇐ 85; Mental Health ⇐ 179

Guardian ad litem is considered officer of court, and must be distinguished from general guardian who has general care and control of person. In re Etter (Ohio App. 1 Dist., 06-12-1998) 134 Ohio App.3d 484, 731 N.E.2d 694. Infants ⇐ 205

In action to terminate parental rights, guardian ad litem's report was hearsay and could not be considered evidence, where report was not submitted under oath and guardian did not testify and was not subjected to direct or cross-examination. Matter of Duncan/Walker Children (Ohio App. 5 Dist., 03-18-1996) 109 Ohio App.3d 841, 673 N.E.2d 217. Infants ⇐ 174

Since guardian ad litem was not counsel for ward in action to terminate parental rights, guardian had no authority to file findings of fact and conclusions of law, and court should not have ordered guardian to do so. Matter of Duncan/Walker Children (Ohio App. 5 Dist., 03-18-1996) 109 Ohio App.3d 841, 673 N.E.2d 217. Infants ⇐ 210

Father had no justiciable concern in whether trial court discharged guardian ad litem after determination was made to maintain custody with maternal grandparents. Rife v. Morgan (Ohio App. 2 Dist., 10-18-1995) 106 Ohio App.3d 843, 667 N.E.2d 450. Child Custody ⇐ 903

Appellate court, on appeal after remand to allow father in custody proceeding to cross-examine guardian ad litem, would not address argument by father that trial court had denied him a fair trial by withholding the record of its discussions with child; discussion appeared to be germane to prior appeal from court's original judgment, and any problem with securing record should have been addressed during pendency of prior appeal. Rife v. Morgan (Ohio App. 2 Dist., 10-18-1995) 106 Ohio App.3d 843, 667 N.E.2d 450. Child Custody ⇐ 907

Juvenile court's appointment of juvenile's grandmother as guardian ad litem in delinquency proceeding was error, where grandmother did not protect juvenile's interests, damaged his credibility and recommended a stiff penalty. In re Johnson (Ohio App. 1 Dist., 08-23-1995) 106 Ohio App.3d 38, 665 N.E.2d 247. Infants ⇐ 205

Guardian ad litem appointed for child has no duty whatsoever to protect parental interests in retaining child custody. In re Pryor (Athens 1993) 86 Ohio App.3d 327, 620 N.E.2d 973. Infants ⇐ 205

Actions taken by children's guardian ad litem in dependency proceeding were not inadequate; any hearsay in guardian ad litem's report was not fatal. In re Pryor (Athens 1993) 86 Ohio App.3d 327, 620 N.E.2d 973. Infants ⇐ 205

On parents' appeal of order granting permanent custody of their children to county children services board, parents had standing to assert that there was direct conflict between attorney's dual roles as guardian ad litem and attorney for children; interests of parents and at least five of their children were aligned, as they all sought reunification of family, and thus, any error prejudicial to children's interest in reunification was similarly prejudicial to parents' interest. In re Smith (Ottawa 1991) 77 Ohio App.3d 1, 601 N.E.2d 45. Infants ⇐ 200

Where attorney is appointed to represent person and is also appointed guardian ad litem for such person, his first and highest duty is to zealously represent client within bounds of law and to champion client's cause; if attorney feels there is conflict between role as attorney and role as guardian, he should petition court for order allowing him to withdraw as guardian, and court should not hesitate to grant such request. In re Baby Girl Baxter (Ohio 1985) 17 Ohio St.3d 229, 479 N.E.2d 257, 17 O.B.R. 469. Infants ⇐ 205

Catholic Social Service is not a person within RC 2151.281 so that an award of permanent custody to CSS does not terminate the association of the guardian ad litem at that point in the proceedings, but when CSS places the child in a home and a person is given legal custody of the child, the services of the guardian ad litem are extinguished. In re Moran, Nos. C–020904+, 1994 WL 123683 (1st Dist Ct App, 4–13–94).

10. Fees

Minor defendant in tort action is responsible for paying fee of court-appointed guardian ad litem. Thatcher v. Fields (Ohio App. 10 Dist., 01-30-1997) 118 Ohio App.3d 63, 691 N.E.2d 1103. Infants ⇐ 116

Trial court had no authority to shift, to party that prevailed on his tort claims against minor defendant, the responsibility for paying fee of guardian ad litem appointed to represent minor defendant's interests in tort action. Thatcher v. Fields (Ohio App. 10 Dist., 01-30-1997) 118 Ohio App.3d 63, 691 N.E.2d 1103. Infants ⇐ 116

Attorney's work as guardian ad litem for children in custody dispute between former husband and former wife could be compensated at hourly rate of $100, although attorney was compensated at same hourly rate for his legal work. Robbins v. Ginese (Ohio App. 8 Dist., 03-07-1994) 93 Ohio App.3d 370, 638 N.E.2d 627, motion overruled 69 Ohio St.3d 1490, 635 N.E.2d 44. Guardian And Ward ⇐ 150

Trial court has discretion whether to employ lodestar method to compute fees for guardian ad litem. Robbins v. Ginese (Ohio App. 8 Dist., 03-07-1994) 93 Ohio App.3d 370, 638 N.E.2d 627, motion overruled 69 Ohio St.3d 1490, 635 N.E.2d 44. Guardian And Ward ⇐ 150

Indigent mother was not liable for her indigent minor's guardian ad litem fees, where trial court in civil suit for fire damages to apartment found minor responsible for damages, but not mother; fees were properly chargeable to minor as court costs. Nationwide Mut. Ins. Co. v. Wymer (Franklin 1986) 33 Ohio App.3d 318, 515 N.E.2d 987. Infants ⇐ 116

Ex-wife's obligation for one half of fees awarded to guardian ad litem appointed to represent child in custody proceedings in which there were allegations of sexual abuse was nondischargeable, as being in nature of obligation for child's "support"; services provided by guardian, including review of police reports, home visitation with child's father and attendance at proceedings in which custody and visitation issues were addressed, were necessary for support of child. In re Lever (Bkrtcy.N.D.Ohio, 10-18-1991) 174 B.R. 936. Bankruptcy ⇐ 3365(10)

11. Immunity

Guardian ad litem, who had been appointed by court to represent children during divorce proceedings, was entitled to absolute immunity in negligence action brought by children's father. Penn v. McMonagle (Huron 1990) 60 Ohio App.3d 149, 573 N.E.2d 1234, motion overruled 58 Ohio St.3d 704, 569 N.E.2d 512. Infants ⇐ 85

2151.282 Court appointed special advocate/guardian ad litem study committee

(A) There is hereby created the Ohio court appointed special advocate/ guardian ad litem (CASA/GAL) study committee consisting of five members. One member shall be a representative of the Ohio court appointed special advocate/ guardian ad litem association appointed by the governor and shall be the chairperson of the committee. One member shall be a member of the Ohio juvenile judges association, appointed by the president of the senate. One member shall be a member of the Ohio state bar association appointed by the speaker of the house of representatives. One member shall be a representative of the office of the state public defender appointed by the minority leader of the senate. One member shall be a representative of the Ohio county commissioner's association appointed by the minority leader of the house of representatives. The members of the committee shall be appointed within sixty days after the effective date of this section. The committee shall do all of the following:

(1) Compile available public data associated with state and local costs of advocating on behalf of children who have been found to be abused, neglected, or dependent children;

(2) Examine the costs in counties that have established and operated an Ohio CASA/GAL association program, and the costs in counties that utilize the county public defender, joint county public defender, or court-appointed counsel, to advocate on behalf of children who have been found to be abused, neglected, or dependent children;

(3) Analyze the total cost of advocating on behalf of children who have been found to be abused, neglected, or dependent children on a per county basis and a per child served basis;

(4) Analyze the cost benefit of having an Ohio CASA/GAL association versus utilizing the county public defender, joint county public defender, or court-appointed counsel to advocate

on behalf of children who have been found to be abused, neglected, or dependent children;

(5) Analyze the advocacy services provided to abused children, neglected children, or dependent children by Ohio CASA/GAL association programs versus the advocacy services provided to abused, neglected, or dependent children by county public defenders, joint county public defenders, or court-appointed counsel.

(B) The Ohio CASA/GAL association shall provide staff for the Ohio CASA/GAL study committee and shall pay for any expenses incurred by the study committee. The study committee shall meet within thirty days after the appointment of the members to the study committee.

(C) The Ohio CASA/GAL study committee shall prepare a report containing all relevant data and information that division (A) of this section requires the study committee to compile, examine, and analyze. The Ohio CASA/GAL study committee shall deliver a final copy of the report to the governor, the speaker of the house of representatives, and the president of the senate on or before July 1, 2007.

(2005 H 66, eff. 9–29–05)

2151.29 Service of summons

Service of summons, notices, and subpoenas, prescribed by section 2151.28 of the Revised Code, shall be made by delivering a copy to the person summoned, notified, or subpoenaed, or by leaving a copy at the person's usual place of residence. If the juvenile judge is satisfied that such service is impracticable, the juvenile judge may order service by registered or certified mail. If the person to be served is without the state but the person can be found or the person's address is known, or the person's whereabouts or address can with reasonable diligence be ascertained, service of the summons may be made by delivering a copy to the person personally or mailing a copy to the person by registered or certified mail.

Whenever it appears by affidavit that after reasonable effort the person to be served with summons cannot be found or the person's post-office address ascertained, whether the person is within or without a state, the clerk shall publish such summons once in a newspaper of general circulation throughout the county. The summons shall state the substance and the time and place of the hearing, which shall be held at least one week later than the date of the publication. A copy of the summons and the complaint, indictment, or information shall be sent by registered or certified mail to the last known address of the person summoned unless it is shown by affidavit that a reasonable effort has been made, without success, to obtain such address.

A copy of the advertisement, the summons, and the complaint, indictment, or information, accompanied by the certificate of the clerk that such publication has been made and that the summons and the complaint, indictment, or information have been mailed as required by this section, is sufficient evidence of publication and mailing. When a period of one week from the time of publication has elapsed, the juvenile court shall have full jurisdiction to deal with such child as provided by sections 2151.01 to 2151.99 of the Revised Code.

(2000 S 179, § 3, eff. 1–1–02; 1969 H 320, eff. 11–19–69)

Historical and Statutory Notes

Ed. Note: Former 2151.29 repealed by 1969 H 320, eff. 11–19–69; 1953 H 1; GC 1639–25.

Pre–1953 H 1 Amendments: 121 v 557; 117 v 520

Amendment Note: 2000 S 179, § 3, eff. 1–1–02, inserted ", indictment, or information" throughout the section; and made changes to reflect gender neutral language and other nonsubstantive changes.

Cross References

Process, service, Juv R 16
Subpoena, Juv R 17

Library References

Infants ⚖=198.
Westlaw Topic No. 211.

Research References

Encyclopedias

OH Jur. 3d Family Law § 1612, Summons for Hearing to Make Temporary Commitment Permanent.
OH Jur. 3d Process § 58, Reasonable Diligence Requirement and Affidavit.

Treatises and Practice Aids

Klein, Darling, & Terez, Baldwin's Ohio Practice Civil Practice § 4.4:2, Process: Service by Publication--Service by Publication Authorized by Law--In General.
Katz, Giannelli, Blair and Lipton, Baldwin's Ohio Practice, Criminal Law, § 61:10, Out-Of-State Witnesses.
Giannelli and Snyder, Baldwin's Ohio Practice, Evidence, § 804.8, Unavailability: Unable to Procure Testimony.
Carlin, Baldwin's Ohio Practice, Merrick-Rippner Probate Law § 107:165, Affidavit for Service by Publication—Form.
Carlin, Baldwin's Ohio Practice, Merrick-Rippner Probate Law § 107:166, Summons on Parents, Guardian, or Custodian by Publication—Form.
Giannelli & Yeomans, Ohio Juvenile Law § 18:4, Summons: Methods of Service.

Notes of Decisions

Constitutional issues 1
Notice to parents 3
Procedural issues 4
Representation by counsel 2

---

1. Constitutional issues

The Akron city ordinances requiring parental consent, informed consent, a 24–hour waiting period, and disposal of fetal remains are unconstitutional. City of Akron v. Akron Center for Reproductive Health, Inc. (U.S.Ohio 1983) 103 S.Ct. 2481, 462 U.S. 416, 76 L.Ed.2d 687, on remand 604 F.Supp. 1268, on remand 604 F.Supp. 1275.

2. Representation by counsel

Petition for writ of habeas corpus alleging that mother had wrongfully been deprived of custody of children at custody hearing at which she was not represented by counsel stated a claim for relief. In re Brown (Ohio 1973) 35 Ohio St.2d 9, 298 N.E.2d 579, 64 O.O.2d 5. Habeas Corpus ⚖ 744

Where only notice given mother of hearing to change child's temporary commitment to a permanent one was served on mother within an hour before such hearing and she had no opportunity to either prepare for such hearing or to engage counsel to represent her, such notice is insufficient in law and an order for permanent custody made at such hearing is void for want of jurisdiction of court in making it, even though mother was present at hearing; attack made upon it by an application for a writ of habeas corpus is proper even though judgment appears to be regular and valid upon its face. In re Frinzl (Ohio 1949) 152 Ohio St. 164, 87 N.E.2d 583, 39 O.O. 456.

3. Notice to parents

Evidence supported finding that notice of permanent custody hearing was served upon mother; record included certified mail receipts demonstrating that mother was served, and she acknowledged receipt of the summons for the permanent custody hearing. In re D.P. (Ohio App. 8 Dist., Cuyahoga, 03-02-2006) No. 86271, No. 86272, 2006-Ohio-937, 2006 WL 496058, Unreported. Infants ⚖ 198

Father received adequate notice of the permanent custody hearing for children; father was personally served at the initial shelter care hearing with a summons and a copy of the permanent custody complaint, the complaint set forth the dates of the pretrial, trial, and subsequent review dates, and father was present at the pretrial hearing. In re Zurfley/Chatman/Black Children (Ohio App. 5 Dist., Stark, 02-13-2006) No. 2005CA00217, 2006-Ohio-683, 2006 WL 337366, Unreported. Infants ⇐ 198

Failure to provide notice to father of trial date in permanent custody proceeding for his child violated father's right to due process, despite fact that he had previously appeared for a pretrial conference. In re Th.W. (Ohio App. 8 Dist., Cuyahoga, 06-09-2005) No. 85278, 2005-Ohio-2852, 2005 WL 1364742, Unreported. Infants ⇐ 198

Mother received adequate notice of final hearing in permanent custody case involving dependent children; mother was personally served with notice of the hearing, she failed to attend the hearing, her attorney informed her of the date of the final permanent custody hearing, and she failed to attend that hearing. In re Keith Lee P. (Ohio App. 6 Dist., Lucas, 04-16-2004) No. L-03-1266, 2004-Ohio-1976, 2004 WL 835989, Unreported. Infants ⇐ 198

Trial court did not have jurisdiction to award permanent custody of child to Department of Children and Family Services, even though mother had notice of preliminary hearing, where service was not attempted on mother in regards to trial. In re D.H. (Ohio App. 8 Dist., Cuyahoga, 12-04-2003) No. 82533, 2003-Ohio-6478, 2003 WL 22861922, Unreported. Infants ⇐ 198

Minor mother's legal guardian received sufficient notice of temporary custody hearing to provide court with jurisdiction in matter, even though mother claimed no notice was provided, where notice was endorsed and left at guardian's residence. In re D.H. (Ohio App. 8 Dist., Cuyahoga, 12-04-2003) No. 82533, 2003-Ohio-6478, 2003 WL 22861922, Unreported. Infants ⇐ 198

Mother received proper notice of motion filed by county department of children and family services seeking permanent custody of dependent child; record indicated that mother was personally served with notice some six months after filing of motion to modify temporary custody and seven months prior to the hearing for permanent custody. In re R.K. (Ohio App. 8 Dist., Cuyahoga, 11-26-2003) No. 82374, 2003-Ohio-6333, 2003 WL 22804937, Unreported. Infants ⇐ 198

Father waived on appeal in termination of parental rights proceeding issue of whether trial court lacked jurisdiction to enter order awarding permanent custody of children to county department of children and family services, based on his allegation that court did not provide proper notice to mother of proceedings, as he failed to raise issue in trial court. (Per O'Donnell, J., with two judges concurring in judgment only). In re Harlston (Ohio App. 8 Dist., Cuyahoga, 01-23-2003) No. 80672, 2003-Ohio-282, 2003 WL 152939, Unreported, appeal not allowed 98 Ohio St.3d 1492, 785 N.E.2d 474, 2003-Ohio-1189. Infants ⇐ 243

Mother's absence at termination of parental rights hearing did not prejudice father's rights; not only was there no evidence that mother would have been awarded custody of children, but mother was in agreement with permanent custody of children being awarded to county department of children and family services. (Per O'Donnell, J., with two judges concurring in judgment only). In re Harlston (Ohio App. 8 Dist., Cuyahoga, 01-23-2003) No. 80672, 2003-Ohio-282, 2003 WL 152939, Unreported, appeal not allowed 98 Ohio St.3d 1492, 785 N.E.2d 474, 2003-Ohio-1189. Infants ⇐ 253

Where county department of human services failed to serve notice of permanent custody hearing on father by personal service pursuant to RC 2151.29 or by certified or registered mail at judge's discretion, court was without jurisdiction to order permanent custody of children despite father's presence at hearing. Matter of McCurdy (Ohio App. 5 Dist., Morrow, 12-13-1993) No. 786, 1993 WL 544430, Unreported.

Service by publication is proper in a case in which a county children's services board files a motion for permanent custody of a mother's children where the board adequately establishes that it exercised reasonable diligence in attempting to locate the mother; the mother's history of sporadic contact coupled with her inability to obtain stable housing, ten addresses within one year, or provide the board with an address to send notices made it extremely impractical, if not impossible, to serve the mother in any other manner than by publication. In re Cowling (Summit 1991) 72 Ohio App.3d 499, 595 N.E.2d 470. Infants ⇐ 198

Juvenile court is without jurisdiction to make permanent a temporary commitment of child unless notice of time and place of hearing is served on parent or guardian either by delivering a copy to the person to be notified, by leaving a copy at his usual place of residence, by service by registered mail, or by publication, as provided by this section; such notice must be served sufficiently in advance of hearing to allow reasonable time to obtain counsel and prepare for participation in such hearing. In re Frinzl (Ohio 1949) 152 Ohio St. 164, 87 N.E.2d 583, 39 O.O. 456. Infants ⇐ 198

Under GC 1648 (RC 2151.28), the mother of an illegitimate child is entitled to notice, actual or constructive, of proceedings upon a complaint of dependency instituted in the juvenile court in reference to such child; until notice of such proceedings has been given to the mother, the jurisdiction of the juvenile court does not attach and a judgment of permanent commitment rendered in such dependency proceeding is void. Lewis v. Reed (Ohio 1927) 117 Ohio St. 152, 157 N.E. 897, 5 Ohio Law Abs. 420, 25 Ohio Law Rep. 386.

Where a minor child has neither legal guardian nor custodian other than a parent, and the residence of the parent is known, service, actual or constructive, must be had upon such parent before a juvenile court has jurisdiction to declare such child a dependent child. Rarey v. Schmidt (Ohio 1926) 115 Ohio St. 518, 154 N.E. 914, 5 Ohio Law Abs. 12, 25 Ohio Law Rep. 134.

Knowledge by a mother that her girl was being held and that a complaint might or even probably would be made against her was not sufficient to meet the requirements of this section. Ex parte Flickinger (Ohio Com.Pl. 1940) 5 Ohio Supp. 252, 33 Ohio Law Abs. 8, 20 O.O. 224.

4. Procedural issues

Service by publication, in child protection proceedings, was not rendered defective when affidavit incorrectly listed affiant, where affidavit contained a statement by the notary certifying that content was sworn to and it was subscribed in her presence. In re D.H. (Ohio App. 8 Dist., Cuyahoga, 12-04-2003) No. 82533, 2003-Ohio-6478, 2003 WL 22861922, Unreported. Infants ⇐ 198

Failure of service of publication pursuant to Juvenile Procedure Rule 16 to include last known address of juvenile's mother or summary statement of object of complaint, which sought permanent custody of juvenile, rendered service of process defective. In re Wilson (Huron 1984) 21 Ohio App.3d 36, 486 N.E.2d 152, 21 O.B.R. 38. Infants ⇐ 198

The matters required to be shown under former GC 1648 (RC 2151.28) as a prerequisite to notice by publication of proceedings as to dependency of minor children were jurisdictional; in such case an attack upon a judgment for fraud in its procurement is direct, and is permitted, notwithstanding that the judgment questioned may appear on its face regular and valid. Lewis v. Reed (Ohio 1927) 117 Ohio St. 152, 157 N.E. 897, 5 Ohio Law Abs. 420, 25 Ohio Law Rep. 386.

An order of a juvenile court declaring a minor child to be a dependent child and awarding its custody to a stranger, obtained without service upon the parent, the guardian, or a person having the custody of such child by operation of law or awarded by a judicial order, judgment, or decree, confers upon such stranger no power to consent to the adoption of such child by any one. Rarey v. Schmidt (Ohio 1926) 115 Ohio St. 518, 154 N.E. 914, 5 Ohio Law Abs. 12, 25 Ohio Law Rep. 134.

Sheriff is required to serve summons, notices, and subpoenas which are directed to him by juvenile court, and whether juvenile court requests summons, notices or subpoenas to be served personally or to be delivered by registered or certified mail, sheriff's office is legally required to serve them in accordance with such directions of juvenile court; if person to be served is out of state and his address is known, service of summons may be made by sheriff by delivering copy to him personally or mailing copy to him by registered or certified mail. OAG 70-130.

2151.30 Issuance of warrant

In any case when it is made to appear to the juvenile judge that the service of a citation under section 2151.29 of the Revised Code will be ineffectual or the welfare of the child requires that he be brought forthwith into the custody of the juvenile court, a warrant may be issued against the parent, custodian, or guardian, or against the child himself.

(1953 H 1, eff. 10–1–53; GC 1639–26)

Historical and Statutory Notes

Pre–1953 H 1 Amendments: 117 v 520, § 1

Cross References

Process, issuance, form, Juv R 15
Process, service, Juv R 16

Library References

Infants ⚖︎192.
Westlaw Topic No. 211.
C.J.S. Infants §§ 41, 53 to 55.

Research References

Treatises and Practice Aids

Carlin, Baldwin's Ohio Practice, Merrick-Rippner Probate Law § 107:167, Warrant for Arrest of Child or Custodian—Form.

Notes of Decisions

Constitutional issues 1

1. Constitutional issues

Where the Ohio statute required a full investigation of the facts underlying a charge of delinquency and a finding of delinquency that the accused had committed acts in violation of Ohio law, jeopardy attached at a hearing at which accused was bound over for trial as an adult. Sims v. Engle (C.A.6 (Ohio) 1980) 619 F.2d 598, certiorari denied 101 S.Ct. 1403, 450 U.S. 936, 67 L.Ed.2d 372.

2151.31 Apprehension, custody, and detention

(A) A child may be taken into custody in any of the following ways:

(1) Pursuant to an order of the court under this chapter or pursuant to an order of the court upon a motion filed pursuant to division (B) of section 2930.05 of the Revised Code;

(2) Pursuant to the laws of arrest;

(3) By a law enforcement officer or duly authorized officer of the court when any of the following conditions are present:

(a) There are reasonable grounds to believe that the child is suffering from illness or injury and is not receiving proper care, as described in section 2151.03 of the Revised Code, and the child's removal is necessary to prevent immediate or threatened physical or emotional harm;

(b) There are reasonable grounds to believe that the child is in immediate danger from the child's surroundings and that the child's removal is necessary to prevent immediate or threatened physical or emotional harm;

(c) There are reasonable grounds to believe that a parent, guardian, custodian, or other household member of the child's household has abused or neglected another child in the household and to believe that the child is in danger of immediate or threatened physical or emotional harm from that person.

(4) By an enforcement official, as defined in section 4109.01 of the Revised Code, under the circumstances set forth in section 4109.08 of the Revised Code;

(5) By a law enforcement officer or duly authorized officer of the court when there are reasonable grounds to believe that the child has run away from the child's parents, guardian, or other custodian;

(6) By a law enforcement officer or duly authorized officer of the court when any of the following apply:

(a) There are reasonable grounds to believe that the conduct, conditions, or surroundings of the child are endangering the health, welfare, or safety of the child.

(b) A complaint has been filed with respect to the child under section 2151.27 or 2152.021 of the Revised Code or the child has been indicted under division (A) of section 2152.13 of the Revised Code or charged by information as described in that section and there are reasonable grounds to believe that the child may abscond or be removed from the jurisdiction of the court.

(c) The child is required to appear in court and there are reasonable grounds to believe that the child will not be brought before the court when required.

(d) There are reasonable grounds to believe that the child committed a delinquent act and that taking the child into custody is necessary to protect the public interest and safety.

(B)(1) The taking of a child into custody is not and shall not be deemed an arrest except for the purpose of determining its validity under the constitution of this state or of the United States.

(2) Except as provided in division (C) of section 2151.311 of the Revised Code, a child taken into custody shall not be held in any state correctional institution, county, multicounty, or municipal jail or workhouse, or any other place where any adult convicted of crime, under arrest, or charged with crime is held.

(C)(1) Except as provided in division (C)(2) of this section, a child taken into custody shall not be confined in a place of juvenile detention or placed in shelter care prior to the implementation of the court's final order of disposition, unless detention or shelter care is required to protect the child from immediate or threatened physical or emotional harm, because the child is a danger or threat to one or more other persons and is charged with violating a section of the Revised Code that may be violated by an adult, because the child may abscond or be removed from the jurisdiction of the court, because the child has no parents, guardian, or custodian or other person able to provide supervision and care for the child and return the child to the court when required, or because an order for placement of the child in detention or shelter care has been made by the court pursuant to this chapter.

(2) A child alleged to be a delinquent child who is taken into custody may be confined in a place of juvenile detention prior to the implementation of the court's final order of disposition if the confinement is authorized under section 2152.04 of the Revised Code or if the child is alleged to be a serious youthful offender under section 2152.13 of the Revised Code and is not released on bond.

(D) Upon receipt of notice from a person that the person intends to take an alleged abused, neglected, or dependent child into custody pursuant to division (A)(3) of this section, a juvenile judge or a designated referee may grant by telephone an ex parte emergency order authorizing the taking of the child into custody if there is probable cause to believe that any of the conditions set forth in divisions (A)(3)(a) to (c) of this section are present. The judge or referee shall journalize any ex parte emergency order issued pursuant to this division. If an order is issued pursuant to this division and the child is taken into custody pursuant to the order, a sworn complaint shall be filed with respect to the child before the end of the next business day after the day on which the child is taken into custody and a hearing shall be held pursuant to division (E) of this section and the Juvenile Rules. A juvenile judge or referee shall not grant an emergency order by telephone pursuant to this division until after the judge or referee determines that reasonable efforts have been made to notify the parents, guardian, or custodian of the child that the child may be placed into shelter care and of the reasons for placing the child into shelter care, except that, if the requirement for notification would jeopardize the physical or emotional safety of the child or result in the child being removed from the court's jurisdiction, the judge or referee may issue the order for taking the child into custody and placing the child into shelter care prior to giving notice to the parents, guardian, or custodian of the child.

(E) If a judge or referee pursuant to division (D) of this section issues an ex parte emergency order for taking a child into custody, the court shall hold a hearing to determine whether there is probable cause for the emergency order. The hearing shall be held before the end of the next business day after the day on which the emergency order is issued, except that it shall not be held later than seventy-two hours after the emergency order is issued.

If the court determines at the hearing that there is not probable cause for the issuance of the emergency order issued pursuant to division (D) of this section, it shall order the child released to the custody of the child's parents, guardian, or custodian. If the court determines at the hearing that there is probable cause for the issuance of the emergency order issued pursuant to division (D) of this section, the court shall do all of the following:

(1) Ensure that a complaint is filed or has been filed;

(2) Comply with section 2151.419 of the Revised Code;

(3) Hold a hearing pursuant to section 2151.314 of the Revised Code to determine if the child should remain in shelter care.

(F) If the court determines at the hearing held pursuant to division (E) of this section that there is probable cause to believe that the child is an abused child, as defined in division (A) of section 2151.031 of the Revised Code, the court may do any of the following:

(1) Upon the motion of any party, the guardian ad litem, the prosecuting attorney, or an employee of the public children services agency, or its own motion, issue reasonable protective orders with respect to the interviewing or deposition of the child;

(2) Order that the child's testimony be videotaped for preservation of the testimony for possible use in any other proceedings in the case;

(3) Set any additional conditions with respect to the child or the case involving the child that are in the best interest of the child.

(G) This section is not intended, and shall not be construed, to prevent any person from taking a child into custody, if taking the child into custody is necessary in an emergency to prevent the physical injury, emotional harm, or neglect of the child.

(2002 H 180, eff. 5–16–02; 2000 S 179, § 3, eff. 1–1–02; 1999 H 3, eff. 11–22–99; 1999 H 176, eff. 10–29–99; 1998 H 484, eff. 3–18–99; 1997 H 408, eff. 10–1–97; 1994 H 571, eff. 10–6–94; 1989 H 166, eff. 2–14–90; 1988 S 89; 1978 H 883; 1969 H 320)

Uncodified Law

2002 H 180, § 3, eff. 5–16–02, reads, in part:

The General Assembly further requests the Supreme Court to promptly modify Rule 7 of the Rules of Juvenile Procedure pursuant to its authority under the Ohio Constitution to make that rule consistent with the amendments of this act to section 2151.31 of the Revised Code.

Historical and Statutory Notes

Ed. Note: Former 2151.31 repealed by 1969 H 320, eff. 11–19–69; 1953 H 1; GC 1639–27.

Pre–1953 H 1 Amendments: 121 v 557; 117 v 520

Amendment Note: 2002 H 180 inserted "because the child is a danger or threat to one or more other persons and is charged with violating a section of the Revised Code that may be violated by an adult" in division (C)(1).

Amendment Note: 2000 S 179, § 3, eff. 1–1–02, inserted "or 2152.021" and "or the child has been indicted under division (A) of section 2152.13 of the Revised Code or charged by information as described in that section" in division (A)(6)(b); added division (A)(6)(d); designated division (C)(1) and inserted "Except as provided in division (C)(2) of this section," therein; and added division (C)(2).

Amendment Note: 1999 H 3 inserted "or pursuant to an order of the court upon a motion filed pursuant to division (B) of section 2930.05 of the Revised Code" in division (A)(1).

Amendment Note: 1999 H 176 added new division (E)(2); redesignated former division (E)(2) as division (E)(3); and made other nonsubstantive changes.

Amendment Note: 1998 H 484 deleted former division (E)(3); and made other nonsubstantive changes. Prior to deletion, former division (E)(3) read:

"(3) At the hearing held pursuant to section 2151.314 of the Revised Code, make the determination and issue the written finding of facts required by section 2151.419 of the Revised Code."

Amendment Note: 1997 H 408 substituted "public children services agency" for "children services board or the county department of human services exercising the children services function" in division (F)(1); and made changes to reflect gender neutral language.

Amendment Note: 1994 H 571 substituted "correctional" for "penal or reformatory" in division (B)(2).

Cross References

Caretaker authorization affidavit not permitted when certain proceedings are pending, 3109.68
Detention and shelter care, Juv R 7
Delinquent children, information provided to foster caregivers regarding, 2152.72
Power of attorney, certain pending actions prohibiting creation, 3109.58
Taking into custody, Juv R 6
Youth services department, taking into custody child violating supervised release from, 5139.52

Ohio Administrative Code References

Emergency removal and placement of the Indian child, OAC 5101:2–42–57

Library References

Infants ⇐68.3, 192.
Westlaw Topic No. 211.
C.J.S. Infants §§ 41, 53 to 55, 198 to 207.
Baldwin's Ohio Legislative Service, 1988 Laws of Ohio, S 89—LSC Analysis, p 5–571

Research References

Encyclopedias

14 Am. Jur. Trials 619, Juvenile Court Proceedings.
OH Jur. 3d Family Law § 1569, Ex Parte Order for Detention.
OH Jur. 3d Family Law § 1570, Apprehension.
OH Jur. 3d Family Law § 1571, Apprehension—Release on Bail.
OH Jur. 3d Family Law § 1579, Detention Hearing; Notice—Rehearing.
OH Jur. 3d Family Law § 1590, Who May File Complaint.
OH Jur. 3d Family Law § 1654, Determination of Reasonable Efforts.
OH Jur. 3d Family Law § 1704, Effect on Court's Jurisdiction of Child's Commitment to Public Agency.
OH Jur. 3d Family Law § 1709, Revocation of Probation on Hearing—Detention During Proceeding.

Forms

Ohio Jurisprudence Pleading and Practice Forms § 2:8, Courts of Common Pleas—Juvenile Division.

Treatises and Practice Aids

Klein, Darling, & Terez, Baldwin's Ohio Practice Civil Practice § 52:4, Findings by the Court--Findings of Fact Required by Statute.
Carlin, Baldwin's Ohio Practice, Merrick-Rippner Probate Law § 104:9, Juvenile Court—Constitutional Issues—Pretrial Preventive Detention of Juveniles.
Carlin, Baldwin's Ohio Practice, Merrick-Rippner Probate Law § 105:1, Juvenile Court—Exclusive Original Jurisdiction.
Carlin, Baldwin's Ohio Practice, Merrick-Rippner Probate Law § 107:5, Time for Filing Complaint.
Carlin, Baldwin's Ohio Practice, Merrick-Rippner Probate Law § 107:13, Issuance of Warrant.
Carlin, Baldwin's Ohio Practice, Merrick-Rippner Probate Law § 107:25, Juvenile Detention and Shelter Care—Grounds for Detention or Shelter Care.
Carlin, Baldwin's Ohio Practice, Merrick-Rippner Probate Law § 107:26, Detention Prior to Hearing.
Carlin, Baldwin's Ohio Practice, Merrick-Rippner Probate Law § 107:41, Prehearing Procedures in Juvenile Court—Temporary Orders Pending Hearing.
Carlin, Baldwin's Ohio Practice, Merrick-Rippner Probate Law § 107:49, Adjudicatory Hearings—Conduct of Hearing by Magistrate.

Carlin, Baldwin's Ohio Practice, Merrick-Rippner Probate Law § 107:74, Reasonable Efforts Determination.

Carlin, Baldwin's Ohio Practice, Merrick-Rippner Probate Law § 107:152, Motion for Temporary Custody Pending Hearing—Form.

Giannelli & Yeomans, Ohio Juvenile Law § 14:3, Custody, Arrests & Stops.

Giannelli & Yeomans, Ohio Juvenile Law § 16:4, Time Requirements—Custody; Detention.

Giannelli & Yeomans, Ohio Juvenile Law § 19:1, Introduction.

Giannelli & Yeomans, Ohio Juvenile Law § 19:3, Admissions Officer.

Giannelli & Yeomans, Ohio Juvenile Law § 19:6, Standard for Detention.

Giannelli & Yeomans, Ohio Juvenile Law § 19:9, Bail.

Giannelli & Yeomans, Ohio Juvenile Law § 20:4, Required Hearings.

Giannelli & Yeomans, Ohio Juvenile Law § 20:6, Time Requirements.

Giannelli & Yeomans, Ohio Juvenile Law § 25:14, Reasonable Efforts Determination; Abuse, Neglect & Dependency.

Notes of Decisions

Ed. Note: This section contains annotations from former RC 2151.31.

Constitutional issues 1
Custody 3
Detention 2
Procedural issues 4
Welfare of child 5

1. Constitutional issues

Juvenile court's continued exercise of jurisdiction over juvenile regarding his parole violation in delinquency matter, when the parole violation was committed by juvenile when he was 19, was not an act of discrimination treating juvenile differently from other adults, but, rather, an act recognizing juvenile's ongoing status as a juvenile; pursuant to statute, juvenile court retained jurisdiction over the juvenile, who was adjudicated delinquent prior to age of 18, until he turned 21. In re Gillespie (Ohio App. 10 Dist., 12-19-2002) 150 Ohio App.3d 502, 782 N.E.2d 140, 2002-Ohio-7025, appeal not allowed 98 Ohio St.3d 1513, 786 N.E.2d 63, 2003-Ohio-1572. Infants ⚖ 281

Juvenile court's continued exercise of jurisdiction over juvenile in delinquency matter, after juvenile committed parole violation when he was 19 years old, did not arbitrarily or capriciously deny juvenile's right to bail in violation of due process, although common pleas court had released juvenile on bail on the adult charges underlying parole violation while juvenile court revoked juvenile's parole and returned him to custody; common pleas court's exercise of power over juvenile with respect to adult charges did not eviscerate juvenile court's coexisting power to hold juvenile pursuant to his parole violation, and juvenile had no absolute constitutional right to bail as a juvenile. In re Gillespie (Ohio App. 10 Dist., 12-19-2002) 150 Ohio App.3d 502, 782 N.E.2d 140, 2002-Ohio-7025, appeal not allowed 98 Ohio St.3d 1513, 786 N.E.2d 63, 2003-Ohio-1572. Constitutional Law ⚖ 255(4); Infants ⚖ 281

In delinquency matter, a juvenile is not entitled to indictment by grand jury, to a public trial, or to trial by jury. In re Gillespie (Ohio App. 10 Dist., 12-19-2002) 150 Ohio App.3d 502, 782 N.E.2d 140, 2002-Ohio-7025, appeal not allowed 98 Ohio St.3d 1513, 786 N.E.2d 63, 2003-Ohio-1572. Infants ⚖ 197; Infants ⚖ 203; Jury ⚖ 19.5

The Confrontation Clause of US Const Am 6 does not guarantee criminal defendants an absolute right to meet face-to-face at trial with witnesses against them but may be satisfied without physical confrontation if denial of confrontation is necessary to further an important public policy and the testimony's reliability is otherwise assured; a state interest in protecting child witnesses from the trauma of testifying in child abuse cases, where shown necessary in a particular case, justifies a procedure whereby the child, prosecutor, and defense counsel withdraw to another room where the child is examined and cross-examined while judge, jury, and defendant remain in the courtroom where the testimony is displayed by television and the defendant is able to communicate electronically with his counsel. (Ed. note: Maryland statute construed in light of federal constitution.) Maryland v. Craig (U.S.Md. 1990) 110 S.Ct. 3157, 497 U.S. 836, 111 L.Ed.2d 666, on remand 322 Md. 418, 588 A.2d 328.

Where the Ohio statute required a full investigation of the facts underlying a charge of delinquency and a finding of delinquency that the accused had committed acts in violation of Ohio law, jeopardy attached at a hearing at which accused was bound over for trial as an adult. Sims v. Engle (C.A.6 (Ohio) 1980) 619 F.2d 598, certiorari denied 101 S.Ct. 1403, 450 U.S. 936, 67 L.Ed.2d 372.

Federal district court lacked jurisdiction over suit against county officials, seeking declaration that arrest and deprivation of custody over children violated his constitutional rights. Hughes v. Hamann (C.A.6 (Ohio), 10-25-2001) No. 00-4132, 23 Fed.Appx. 337, 2001 WL 1356143, Unreported. Federal Courts ⚖ 8

Abstention doctrine precluded federal court from assuming jurisdiction over suit by father, against county officials, claiming that removal of children from his custody violated his constitutional rights; state custody proceedings were ongoing, important state interests were implicated, and claims sought to be brought in federal court could be raised in state proceedings. Hughes v. Hamann (C.A.6 (Ohio), 10-25-2001) No. 00-4132, 23 Fed.Appx. 337, 2001 WL 1356143, Unreported. Federal Courts ⚖ 47.1

Where a fourteen-year-old minor, without counsel, made a statement to police implicating herself in setting a fire which killed her father, and the court psychologist testified that such minor was of average intelligence, the minor's statement is properly admitted into evidence where the minor had waived her Miranda rights and during the course of such statement the minor answered intelligently, coherently, and gave no indication of undue influence. In re Hawkins, No. 3430 (9th Dist Ct App, Lorain, 5–11–83).

2. Detention

Under RC 2151.14 and RC 2151.31 it is the manifest duty of enforcement officers to cooperate with and assist the juvenile authorities in the performance of their duties when such officers are specifically requested to do so by the juvenile authorities; such officers may avoid liability in an action for false imprisonment by showing that they were justified in the detention or restraint of the juvenile made under the specific direction and order of the juvenile authorities. Garland v. Dustman (Portage 1969) 19 Ohio App.2d 292, 251 N.E.2d 153, 48 O.O.2d 408. False Imprisonment ⚖ 11; Infants ⚖ 192

Where police apprehended a fourteen-year-old minor for questioning following a fire, police may properly question such minor at the police station before delivering her to a place of detention or bringing her to court. In re Hawkins, No. 3430 (9th Dist Ct App, Lorain, 5–11–83).

A minor detained on delinquency charges is not charged with an offense and hence is not entitled to release on bail. State ex rel. Peaks v. Allaman (Montgomery 1952) 115 N.E.2d 849, 66 Ohio Law Abs. 403, 51 O.O. 321.

If a peace officer determines that the detention or shelter care of a child appears to be required as provided in RC 2151.31(C) and Juv R 7(A), the peace officer is required by RC 2151.311(A) and Juv R 7(B) to bring the child to the court or deliver the child to a place of detention or shelter care designated by the court. A peace officer who determines that the detention or shelter care of a child appears to be required may contact the juvenile court by telephone to determine the place of detention or shelter care to which to deliver the child. OAG 96–061.

A law enforcement official may hold a runaway juvenile against his will, provided his detention or care is required to protect the person or property of others or those of the child, or because the child may abscond or be removed from the jurisdiction of the court, or because he has no parents, guardian or custodian or other person able to provide supervision and care for him. OAG 77–063.

3. Custody

Under Ohio law, unless matters of public safety are involved, a child alleged to be abused, neglected, or dependent may be removed from his home by court order only upon a judicial determination that continuation in the home would be contrary to the child's best interest. OAG 87–105.

4. Procedural issues

Although trial court granted ex parte order of temporary custody pursuant to statute providing only the means, and not the authority, for ordering a child into custody, trial court's subsequent journal entry on reaffirmation of temporary order made clear that it was acting pursuant to appropriate authorizing statute and, therefore, agency had authority to make, and trial court had authority to grant, motion for permanent custody under separate subsection of latter statute. In re Van Atta (Ohio App. 3 Dist., Hancock, 08-15-2005) No. 5-05-03, 2005-Ohio-4182, 2005 WL 1939418, Unreported. Infants ⚖ 192

When a juvenile is adjudicated delinquent before age 18 and then commits offense qualifying as parole violation between the ages of 18 and

21, separate jurisdiction of juvenile court and common pleas court may coexist according to classifications of "adult" and "juvenile," and divergent dispositions of those courts may also exist. In re Gillespie (Ohio App. 10 Dist., 12-19-2002) 150 Ohio App.3d 502, 782 N.E.2d 140, 2002-Ohio-7025, appeal not allowed 98 Ohio St.3d 1513, 786 N.E.2d 63, 2003-Ohio-1572. Infants ⟳ 281

Genuine issues of material fact existed as to whether child, whose grandmother was at the scene, needed to be arrested for jaywalking for her own safety, whether officer acted with malicious purpose, in bad faith, or in a wanton or reckless manner in making the arrest, and whether probable cause existed for arrest, precluding summary judgment in favor of officer, on immunity grounds, as to state law claims, including false arrest; jaywalking is an offense except where crossroads are an unreasonable distance apart, and officer testified that there are no crosswalks nearby. Hicks v. Leffler (Ohio App. 10 Dist., 04-24-1997) 119 Ohio App.3d 424, 695 N.E.2d 777. Judgment ⟳ 185.3(1)

Statutes setting forth responsibilities of children's services agency with regard to temporary orders, ex parte orders, and case plans allow for considerable breadth in agency's discretion, i.e., to treat some cases as criminal matters involving sanctions and to treat other cases as social matters amenable to social services intervention. Rich v. Erie Cty. Dept. of Human Resources (Ohio App. 6 Dist., 08-25-1995) 106 Ohio App.3d 88, 665 N.E.2d 278, dismissed, appeal not allowed 74 Ohio St.3d 1498, 659 N.E.2d 314. Infants ⟳ 17

A minor charged with a felony who fails to object to the jurisdiction of the common pleas court by a plea in abatement because of his age waives his right to object. Harris v. Alvis (Franklin 1950) 104 N.E.2d 182, 61 Ohio Law Abs. 311.

The statutory law of arrest does not apply to special statutory proceedings in the juvenile court which are civil in nature and have for their purpose the securing for each child under the jurisdiction of the juvenile court such care, guidance and control as will best serve the child's welfare. In re L——(Ohio Juv. 1963) 194 N.E.2d 797, 92 Ohio Law Abs. 475, 25 O.O.2d 369.

5. Welfare of child

Juvenile's liberty interest may, in appropriate circumstance, be subordinated to state's parens patriae interest in preserving and promoting welfare of child. Schall v. Martin (U.S.N.Y. 1984) 104 S.Ct. 2403, 467 U.S. 253, 81 L.Ed.2d 207. Infants ⟳ 151

2151.311 Procedure upon apprehension

(A) A person taking a child into custody shall, with all reasonable speed and in accordance with division (C) of this section, either:

(1) Release the child to the child's parents, guardian, or other custodian, unless the child's detention or shelter care appears to be warranted or required as provided in section 2151.31 of the Revised Code;

(2) Bring the child to the court or deliver the child to a place of detention or shelter care designated by the court and promptly give notice thereof, together with a statement of the reason for taking the child into custody, to a parent, guardian, or other custodian and to the court.

(B) If a parent, guardian, or other custodian fails, when requested by the court, to bring the child before the court as provided by this section, the court may issue its warrant directing that the child be taken into custody and brought before the court.

(C)(1) Before taking any action required by division (A) of this section, a person taking a child into custody may hold the child for processing purposes in a county, multicounty, or municipal jail or workhouse, or other place where an adult convicted of crime, under arrest, or charged with crime is held for either of the following periods of time:

(a) For a period not to exceed six hours, if all of the following apply:

(i) The child is alleged to be a delinquent child for the commission of an act that would be a felony if committed by an adult;

(ii) The child remains beyond the range of touch of all adult detainees;

(iii) The child is visually supervised by jail or workhouse personnel at all times during the detention;

(iv) The child is not handcuffed or otherwise physically secured to a stationary object during the detention.

(b) For a period not to exceed three hours, if all of the following apply:

(i) The child is alleged to be a delinquent child for the commission of an act that would be a misdemeanor if committed by an adult, is alleged to be a delinquent child for being a chronic truant or an habitual truant who previously has been adjudicated an unruly child for being an habitual truant, or is alleged to be an unruly child or a juvenile traffic offender;

(ii) The child remains beyond the range of touch of all adult detainees;

(iii) The child is visually supervised by jail or workhouse personnel at all times during the detention;

(iv) The child is not handcuffed or otherwise physically secured to a stationary object during the detention.

(2) If a child has been transferred to an adult court for prosecution for the alleged commission of a criminal offense, subsequent to the transfer, the child may be held as described in division (F) of section 2152.26 or division (B) of section 5120.16 of the Revised Code.

(D) As used in division (C)(1) of this section, "processing purposes" means all of the following:

(1) Fingerprinting, photographing, or fingerprinting and photographing the child in a secure area of the facility;

(2) Interrogating the child, contacting the child's parent or guardian, arranging for placement of the child, or arranging for transfer or transferring the child, while holding the child in a nonsecure area of the facility.

(2000 S 179, § 3, eff. 1–1–02; 2000 S 181, eff. 9–4–00; 1996 H 124, eff. 3–31–97; 1996 H 480, eff. 10–16–96; 1994 H 571, eff. 10–6–94; 1989 H 166, eff. 2–14–90; 1972 S 445; 1970 H 931; 1969 H 320)

Historical and Statutory Notes

Amendment Note: 2000 S 179, § 3, eff. 1–1–02, substituted "2152.26" for "2151.312" in division (C)(2).

Amendment Note: 2000 S 181 inserted ", is alleged to be a delinquent child for being a chronic truant or an habitual truant who previously has been adjudicated an unruly child for being an habitual truant," in division (C)(1)(b)(i); and substituted "(F)" for "(C)" in division (C)(2).

Amendment Note: 1996 H 124 rewrote division (C)(2), which prior thereto read:

"(2) If a child has been transferred to an adult court for prosecution for the alleged commission of a criminal offense, subsequent to the transfer, the child may be held as described in division (C) of section 2151.312 of the Revised Code or, if that division does not apply, may be held in a state correctional institution or other place where an adult convicted of crime, under arrest, or charged with crime is held."

Amendment Note: 1996 H 480 rewrote the section, which prior thereto read:

"(A) A person taking a child into custody shall, with all reasonable speed and in accordance with division (C) of this section, either:

"(1) Release the child to his parents, guardian, or other custodian, unless his detention or shelter care appears to be warranted or required as provided in section 2151.31 of the Revised Code;

"(2) Bring the child to the court or deliver him to a place of detention or shelter care designated by the court and promptly give notice thereof, together with a statement of the reason for taking the child into custody, to a parent, guardian, or other custodian and to the court.

"(B) If a parent, guardian, or other custodian fails, when requested by the court, to bring the child before the court as provided by this section, the court may issue its warrant directing that the child be taken into custody and brought before the court.

"(C)(1) Before taking any action required by division (A) of this section, a person taking a child into custody may hold the child for processing purposes in a county, multicounty, or municipal jail or workhouse, or other place where an adult convicted of crime, under arrest, or charged with crime is held for either of the following periods of time:

"(a) For a period not to exceed six hours, if all of the following apply:

"(i) The child is alleged to be a delinquent child for the commission of an act that would be a felony if committed by an adult;

"(ii) The detention is in a room totally separate and removed by both sight and sound from all adult detainees;

"(iii) The child is supervised at all times during the detention.

"(b) For a period not to exceed three hours, if all of the following apply:

"(i) The child is alleged to be a delinquent child for the commission of an act that would be a misdemeanor if committed by an adult or is alleged to be an unruly child or a juvenile traffic offender;

"(ii) The detention is in a room totally separate and removed by both sight and sound from all adult detainees;

"(iii) The child is supervised at all times during the detention.

"(2) If a child has been transferred to an adult court for prosecution for the alleged commission of a criminal offense, the child is convicted of a criminal offense, and sentence is imposed upon the child subsequent to the conviction, the child, during the period of time that he is subject to that sentence and for any action related to that sentence, may be held in a state correctional institution or other place where an adult convicted of crime, under arrest, or charged with crime is held."

Amendment Note: 1994 H 571 substituted "correctional" for "penal institution, reformatory" in division (C)(2).

Cross References

Confinement of minors in county, multicounty, or municipal jails, 341.11
Detention and shelter care, release to parents, procedure, Juv R 7

Library References

Infants ⚖ 68.3, 192.
Westlaw Topic No. 211.
C.J.S. Infants §§ 41, 53 to 55, 198 to 207.

Research References

Encyclopedias
OH Jur. 3d Family Law § 1570, Apprehension.
OH Jur. 3d Family Law § 1574, Delivery of Child to Shelter or Detention Facility.
OH Jur. 3d Family Law § 1581, Alleged Delinquent or Unruly Child or Juvenile Traffic Offender.
OH Jur. 3d Family Law § 1583, Alleged Neglected, Abused, or Dependent Child.
OH Jur. 3d Penal & Correctional Institutions § 94, Separation of Prisoners.

Treatises and Practice Aids
Carlin, Baldwin's Ohio Practice, Merrick-Rippner Probate Law § 107:25, Juvenile Detention and Shelter Care—Grounds for Detention or Shelter Care.
Carlin, Baldwin's Ohio Practice, Merrick-Rippner Probate Law § 107:27, Detention Separate from Adult Detainees.
Carlin, Baldwin's Ohio Practice, Merrick-Rippner Probate Law § 107:29, Admission and Release from Detention.
Carlin, Baldwin's Ohio Practice, Merrick-Rippner Probate Law § 107:152, Motion for Temporary Custody Pending Hearing—Form.
Carlin, Baldwin's Ohio Practice, Merrick-Rippner Probate Law § 107:169, Written Promise of Parent to Bring Child to Court—Form.
Giannelli & Yeomans, Ohio Juvenile Law § 19:2, Place of Detention.

Notes of Decisions

Confessions 3
Constitutional issues 1
Delay 2
Detention or shelter 4
Release from custody 5

---

1. Constitutional issues

The matter of unlawful search and seizure under the US Const Am 4 applies to juveniles. In re Morris (Ohio Com.Pl. 1971) 29 Ohio Misc. 71, 278 N.E.2d 701, 58 O.O.2d 126.

2. Delay

The delay in turning over to a juvenile detention facility a seventeen-year-old juvenile murder defendant who for twelve hours after being taken into custody is held in the police station narcotics unit, with one hand cuffed to a chair, and without food, sleep, or the presence of his parents, does not constitute an unreasonable delay in violation of the "all reasonable speed" requirement of RC 2151.311 and does not render his custodial statement inadmissible. State v. Bobo (Cuyahoga 1989) 65 Ohio App.3d 685, 585 N.E.2d 429, dismissed, jurisdictional motion overruled 50 Ohio St.3d 714, 553 N.E.2d 1363.

Where police apprehended a fourteen-year-old minor for questioning following a fire, police may properly question such minor at the police station before delivering her to a place of detention or bringing her to court. In re Hawkins, No. 3430 (9th Dist Ct App, Lorain, 5–11–83).

3. Confessions

In determining whether juvenile's confession is voluntary, court should consider juvenile's age, educational and cultural background, worldly maturity, and prior experiences with police procedures and arrest, in addition to those factors considered in evaluating whether adult's confession was coerced. In re Travis (Ohio App. 10 Dist., 04-30-1996) 110 Ohio App.3d 684, 675 N.E.2d 36. Infants ⚖ 174.

Juvenile's statement was not rendered involuntary by fact that investigator may have informed juvenile's mother that he had power to arrest juvenile, where investigator explained juvenile's constitutional rights to him and to his mother, both understood nature of the rights, nothing suggested that juvenile was mentally or physically incapable or incompetent to make written statement, mother was present, length and intensity of investigation were limited, and there were no inducements or threats. In re Travis (Ohio App. 10 Dist., 04-30-1996) 110 Ohio App.3d 684, 675 N.E.2d 36. Infants ⚖ 174; Infants ⚖ 192.

A juvenile defendant's confession is not rendered involuntary where he is taken to a police station instead of to a juvenile court or other juvenile detention center as required by RC 2151.311. State v Dickens, No. 12967 (9th Dist Ct App, Summit, 9–23–87).

Where a fourteen-year-old minor, without counsel, made a statement to police implicating herself in setting a fire which killed her father, and the court psychologist testified that such minor was of average intelligence, the minor's statement is properly admitted into evidence where the minor had waived her Miranda rights and during the course of such statement the minor answered intelligently, coherently, and gave no indication of undue influence. In re Hawkins, No. 3430 (9th Dist Ct App, Lorain, 5–11–83).

4. Detention or shelter

If a peace officer determines that the detention or shelter care of a child appears to be required as provided in RC 2151.31(C) and Juv R 7(A), the peace officer is required by RC 2151.311(A) and Juv R 7(B) to bring the child to the court or deliver the child to a place of detention or shelter care designated by the court. A peace officer who determines that the detention or shelter care of a child appears to be required may contact the juvenile court by telephone to determine the place of detention or shelter care to which to deliver the child. OAG 96–061.

5. Release from custody

RC 2151.311(A)(1), 2151.314(A), and Juv R 7(B) do not authorize the release of a child to the peace officer who took the child into custody. OAG 96–061.

2151.312 Place of detention

(A) A child alleged to be or adjudicated an unruly child may be held only in the following places:

(1) A certified family foster home or a home approved by the court;

(2) A facility operated by a certified child welfare agency;

(3) Any other suitable place designated by the court.

(B)(1) Except as provided under division (C)(1) of section 2151.311 of the Revised Code, a child alleged to be or adjudicated a neglected child, an abused child, a dependent child, or an unruly child may not be held in any of the following facilities:

(a) A state correctional institution, county, multicounty, or municipal jail or workhouse, or other place in which an adult convicted of a crime, under arrest, or charged with a crime is held;

(b) A secure correctional facility.

(2) Except as provided under sections 2151.26 to 2151.61 of the Revised Code and division (B)(3) of this section, a child alleged to be or adjudicated an unruly child may not be held for more than twenty-four hours in a detention facility. A child alleged to be or adjudicated a neglected child, an abused child, or a dependent child shall not be held in a detention facility.

(3) A child who is alleged to be or adjudicated an unruly child and who is taken into custody on a Saturday, Sunday, or legal holiday, as listed in section 1.14 of the Revised Code, may be held in a detention facility until the next succeeding day that is not a Saturday, Sunday, or legal holiday.

(2000 S 179, § 3, eff. 1–1–02)

Historical and Statutory Notes

Ed. Note: Former 2151.312 amended and recodified as 2152.26 by 2000 S 179, § 3, eff. 1–1–02; 2000 H 332, eff. 1–1–01; 2000 H 448, eff. 10–5–00; 2000 S 181, eff. 9–4–00; 1997 H 1, eff. 7–1–98; 1996 H 124, eff. 3–31–97; 1996 H 265, eff. 3–3–97; 1994 H 571, eff. 10–6–94; 1993 H 152, eff. 7–1–93; 1992 S 331; 1989 H 166; 1981 H 440; 1975 H 85; 1969 H 320.

Library References

Infants ⚖=192, 222, 226.
Westlaw Topic No. 211.
C.J.S. Adoption of Persons § 10.
C.J.S. Infants §§ 41, 53 to 55, 57, 69 to 85.

Research References

Encyclopedias

OH Jur. 3d Family Law § 695, Involuntary Dismissal.
OH Jur. 3d Family Law § 1581, Alleged Delinquent or Unruly Child or Juvenile Traffic Offender.
OH Jur. 3d Family Law § 1582, Alleged Delinquent or Unruly Child or Juvenile Traffic Offender—Transfer of Child Upon Transfer of Case for Criminal Prosecution.
OH Jur. 3d Family Law § 1583, Alleged Neglected, Abused, or Dependent Child.
OH Jur. 3d Family Law § 1688, Unruly Child.

Treatises and Practice Aids

Carlin, Baldwin's Ohio Practice, Merrick-Rippner Probate Law § 107:27, Detention Separate from Adult Detainees.
Carlin, Baldwin's Ohio Practice, Merrick-Rippner Probate Law § 107:28, Children Subject to Detention.
Carlin, Baldwin's Ohio Practice, Merrick-Rippner Probate Law § 107:29, Admission and Release from Detention.
Giannelli & Yeomans, Ohio Juvenile Law § 19:2, Place of Detention.
Giannelli & Yeomans, Ohio Juvenile Law § 19:7, Time Requirements.
Giannelli & Yeomans, Ohio Juvenile Law § 28:6, Commitment to Juvenile Facility.
Giannelli & Yeomans, Ohio Juvenile Law § 29:3, Unruly—Delinquency Dispositions.
Giannelli & Yeomans, Ohio Juvenile Law § 22:22, Transfer of Jurisdiction.
Giannelli & Yeomans, Ohio Juvenile Law § 27:18, "Catch-All" Provision.

2151.313 Fingerprinting or photographing child in an investigation

(A)(1) Except as provided in division (A)(2) of this section and in sections 109.57, 109.60, and 109.61 of the Revised Code, no child shall be fingerprinted or photographed in the investigation of any violation of law without the consent of the juvenile judge.

(2) Subject to division (A)(3) of this section, a law enforcement officer may fingerprint and photograph a child without the consent of the juvenile judge when the child is arrested or otherwise taken into custody for the commission of an act that would be an offense, other than a traffic offense or a minor misdemeanor, if committed by an adult, and there is probable cause to believe that the child may have been involved in the commission of the act. A law enforcement officer who takes fingerprints or photographs of a child under division (A)(2) of this section immediately shall inform the juvenile court that the fingerprints or photographs were taken and shall provide the court with the identity of the child, the number of fingerprints and photographs taken, and the name and address of each person who has custody and control of the fingerprints or photographs or copies of the fingerprints or photographs.

(3) This section does not apply to a child to whom either of the following applies:

(a) The child has been arrested or otherwise taken into custody for committing, or has been adjudicated a delinquent child for committing, an act that would be a felony if committed by an adult or has been convicted of or pleaded guilty to committing a felony.

(b) There is probable cause to believe that the child may have committed an act that would be a felony if committed by an adult.

(B)(1) Subject to divisions (B)(4), (5), and (6) of this section, all fingerprints and photographs of a child obtained or taken under division (A)(1) or (2) of this section, and any records of the arrest or custody of the child that was the basis for the taking of the fingerprints or photographs, initially may be retained only until the expiration of thirty days after the date taken, except that the court may limit the initial retention of fingerprints and photographs of a child obtained under division (A)(1) of this section to a shorter period of time and except that, if the child is adjudicated a delinquent child for the commission of an act described in division (B)(3) of this section or is convicted of or pleads guilty to a criminal offense for the commission of an act described in division (B)(3) of this section, the fingerprints and photographs, and the records of the arrest or custody of the child that was the basis for the taking of the fingerprints and photographs, shall be retained in accordance with division (B)(3) of this section. During the initial period of retention, the fingerprints and photographs of a child, copies of the fingerprints and photographs, and records of the arrest or custody of the child shall be used or released only in accordance with division (C) of this section. At the expiration of the initial period for which fingerprints and photographs of a child, copies of fingerprints and photographs of a child, and records of the arrest or custody of a child may be retained under this division, if no complaint, indictment, or information is pending against the child in relation to the act for which the fingerprints and photographs originally were obtained or taken and if the child has neither been adjudicated a delinquent child for the commission of that act nor been convicted of or pleaded guilty to a criminal offense based on that act subsequent to a transfer of the child's case for criminal prosecution pursuant to section 2152.12 of the Revised Code, the fingerprints and photographs of the child, all copies of the fingerprints and photographs, and all records of the arrest or custody of the child that was the basis of the taking of the fingerprints and photographs shall be removed from the file and delivered to the juvenile court.

(2) If, at the expiration of the initial period of retention set forth in division (B)(1) of this section, a complaint, indictment, or information is pending against the child in relation to the act for which the fingerprints and photographs originally were obtained or the child either has been adjudicated a delinquent child for the commission of an act other than an act described in division (B)(3) of this section or has been convicted of or pleaded guilty to a criminal offense for the commission of an act other than an act described in division (B)(3) of this section subsequent to transfer of the child's case, the fingerprints and photographs of the child, copies of the fingerprints and photographs, and the records of the arrest or custody of the child that was the basis of the taking of the fingerprints and photographs may further be retained, subject to division (B)(4) of this section, until the earlier of the expiration of two years after the date on which the fingerprints or photographs were taken or the child attains eighteen years of age, except that, if the child is adjudicated a delinquent child for the commission of an act described in division (B)(3) of this section or is convicted of or pleads guilty to a criminal offense for the commission of an act described in division (B)(3) of this section, the fingerprints and photographs, and the records of the arrest or custody of the child that was the basis for the taking of the fingerprints and photographs, shall be retained in accordance with division (B)(3) of this section.

Except as otherwise provided in division (B)(3) of this section, during this additional period of retention, the fingerprints and photographs of a child, copies of the fingerprints and photographs of a child, and records of the arrest or custody of a child shall be used or released only in accordance with division (C) of this section. At the expiration of the additional period, if no complaint, indictment, or information is pending against the child in relation to the act for which the fingerprints originally were obtained or taken or in relation to another act for which the fingerprints were used as authorized by division (C) of this section and that would be a felony if committed by an adult, the fingerprints of the child, all copies of the fingerprints, and all records of the arrest or custody of the child that was the basis of the taking of the fingerprints shall be removed from the file and delivered to the juvenile court, and, if no complaint, indictment, or information is pending against the child concerning the act for which the photographs originally were obtained or taken or concerning an act that would be a felony if committed by an adult, the photographs and all copies of the photographs, and, if no fingerprints were taken at the time the photographs were taken, all records of the arrest or custody that was the basis of the taking of the photographs shall be removed from the file and delivered to the juvenile court. In either case, if, at the expiration of the applicable additional period, such a complaint, indictment, or information is pending against the child, the photographs and copies of the photographs of the child, or the fingerprints and copies of the fingerprints of the child, whichever is applicable, and the records of the arrest or custody of the child may be retained, subject to division (B)(4) of this section, until final disposition of the complaint, indictment, or information, and, upon final disposition of the complaint, indictment, or information, they shall be removed from the file and delivered to the juvenile court, except that, if the child is adjudicated a delinquent child for the commission of an act described in division (B)(3) of this section or is convicted of or pleads guilty to a criminal offense for the commission of an act described in division (B)(3) of this section, the fingerprints and photographs, and the records of the arrest or custody of the child that was the basis for the taking of the fingerprints and photographs, shall be retained in accordance with division (B)(3) of this section.

(3) If a child is adjudicated a delinquent child for violating section 2923.42 of the Revised Code or for committing an act that would be a misdemeanor offense of violence if committed by an adult, or is convicted of or pleads guilty to a violation of section 2923.42 of the Revised Code, a misdemeanor offense of violence, or a violation of an existing or former municipal ordinance or law of this state, another state, or the United States that is substantially equivalent to section 2923.42 of the Revised Code or any misdemeanor offense of violence, both of the following apply:

(a) Originals and copies of fingerprints and photographs of the child obtained or taken under division (A)(1) of this section, and any records of the arrest or custody that was the basis for the taking of the fingerprints or photographs, may be retained for the period of time specified by the juvenile judge in that judge's grant of consent for the taking of the fingerprints or photographs. Upon the expiration of the specified period, all originals and copies of the fingerprints, photographs, and records shall be delivered to the juvenile court or otherwise disposed of in accordance with any instructions specified by the juvenile judge in that judge's grant of consent. During the period of retention of the photographs and records, all originals and copies of them shall be retained in a file separate and apart from all photographs taken of adults. During the period of retention of the fingerprints, all originals and copies of them may be maintained in the files of fingerprints taken of adults. If the juvenile judge who grants consent for the taking of fingerprints and photographs under division (A)(1) of this section does not specify a period of retention in that judge's grant of consent, originals and copies of the fingerprints, photographs, and records may be retained in accordance with this section as if the fingerprints and photographs had been taken under division (A)(2) of this section.

(b) Originals and copies of fingerprints and photographs taken under division (A)(2) of this section, and any records of the arrest or custody that was the basis for the taking of the fingerprints or photographs, may be retained for the period of time and in the manner specified in division (B)(3)(b) of this section. Prior to the child's attainment of eighteen years of age, all originals and copies of the photographs and records shall be retained and shall be kept in a file separate and apart from all photographs taken of adults. During the period of retention of the fingerprints, all originals and copies of them may be maintained in the files of fingerprints taken of adults. Upon the child's attainment of eighteen years of age, all originals and copies of the fingerprints, photographs, and records shall be disposed of as follows:

(i) If the juvenile judge issues or previously has issued an order that specifies a manner of disposition of the originals and copies of the fingerprints, photographs, and records, they shall be delivered to the juvenile court or otherwise disposed of in accordance with the order.

(ii) If the juvenile judge does not issue and has not previously issued an order that specifies a manner of disposition of the originals and copies of the fingerprints not maintained in adult files, photographs, and records, the law enforcement agency, in its discretion, either shall remove all originals and copies of them from the file in which they had been maintained and transfer them to the files that are used for the retention of fingerprints and photographs taken of adults who are arrested for, otherwise taken into custody for, or under investigation for the commission of a criminal offense or shall remove them from the file in which they had been maintained and deliver them to the juvenile court. If the originals and copies of any fingerprints of a child who attains eighteen years of age are maintained in the files of fingerprints taken of adults or if pursuant to division (B)(3)(b)(ii) of this section the agency transfers the originals and copies of any fingerprints not maintained in adult files, photographs, or records to the files that are used for the retention of fingerprints and photographs taken of adults who are arrested for, otherwise taken into custody for, or under investigation for the commission of a criminal offense, the originals and copies of the fingerprints, photographs, and records may be maintained, used, and released after they are maintained in the adult files or after the transfer as if the fingerprints and photographs had been taken of, and as if the records pertained to, an adult who was arrested for, otherwise taken into custody for, or under investigation for the commission of a criminal offense.

(4) If a sealing or expungement order issued under sections 2151.356 to 2151.358 of the Revised Code requires the sealing or destruction of any fingerprints or photographs of a child obtained or taken under division (A)(1) or (2) of this section or of the records of an arrest or custody of a child that was the basis of the taking of the fingerprints or photographs prior to the expiration of any period for which they otherwise could be retained under division (B)(1), (2), or (3) of this section, the fingerprints, photographs, and arrest or custody records that are subject to the order and all copies of the fingerprints, photographs, and arrest or custody records shall be sealed or destroyed in accordance with the order.

(5) All fingerprints of a child, photographs of a child, records of an arrest or custody of a child, and copies delivered to a juvenile court in accordance with division (B)(1), (2), or (3) of this section shall be destroyed by the court, provided that, if a complaint is filed against the child in relation to any act to which the records pertain, the court shall maintain all records of an arrest or custody of a child so delivered for at least three years after the final disposition of the case or after the case becomes inactive.

(6)(a) All photographs of a child and records of an arrest or custody of a child retained pursuant to division (B) of this section and not delivered to a juvenile court shall be kept in a file separate and apart from fingerprints, photographs, and records of an arrest or custody of an adult. All fingerprints of a child retained pursuant to division (B) of this section and not delivered to a juvenile court may be maintained in the files of fingerprints taken of adults.

(b) If a child who is the subject of photographs or fingerprints is adjudicated a delinquent child for the commission of an act that would be an offense, other than a traffic offense or a minor misdemeanor, if committed by an adult or is convicted of or pleads guilty to a criminal offense, other than a traffic offense or a minor misdemeanor, all fingerprints not maintained in the files of fingerprints taken of adults and all photographs of the child, and all records of the arrest or custody of the child that is the basis of the taking of the fingerprints or photographs, that are retained pursuant to division (B) of this section and not delivered to a juvenile court shall be kept in a file separate and apart from fingerprints, photographs, and arrest and custody records of children who have not been adjudicated a delinquent child for the commission of an act that would be an offense, other than a traffic offense or a minor misdemeanor, if committed by an adult and have not been convicted of or pleaded guilty to a criminal offense other than a traffic offense or a minor misdemeanor.

(C) Until they are delivered to the juvenile court or sealed, transferred in accordance with division (B)(3)(b) of this section, or destroyed pursuant to a sealing or expungement order, the originals and copies of fingerprints and photographs of a child that are obtained or taken pursuant to division (A)(1) or (2) of this section, and the records of the arrest or custody of the child that was the basis of the taking of the fingerprints or photographs, shall be used or released only as follows:

(1) During the initial thirty-day period of retention, originals and copies of fingerprints and photographs of a child, and records of the arrest or custody of a child, shall be used, prior to the filing of a complaint or information against or the obtaining of an indictment of the child in relation to the act for which the fingerprints and photographs were originally obtained or taken, only for the investigation of that act and shall be released, prior to the filing of the complaint, only to a court that would have jurisdiction of the child's case under this chapter. Subsequent to the filing of a complaint or information or the obtaining of an indictment, originals and copies of fingerprints and photographs of a child, and records of the arrest or custody of a child, shall be used or released during the initial thirty-day period of retention only as provided in division (C)(2)(a), (b), or (c) of this section.

(2) Originals and copies of fingerprints and photographs of a child, and records of the arrest or custody of a child, that are retained beyond the initial thirty-day period of retention subsequent to the filing of a complaint or information or the obtaining of an indictment, a delinquent child adjudication, or a conviction of or guilty plea to a criminal offense shall be used or released only as follows:

(a) Originals and copies of photographs of a child, and, if no fingerprints were taken at the time the photographs were taken, records of the arrest or custody of the child that was the basis of the taking of the photographs, may be used only as follows:

(i) They may be used for the investigation of the act for which they originally were obtained or taken; if the child who is the subject of the photographs is a suspect in the investigation, for the investigation of any act that would be an offense if committed by an adult; and for arresting or bringing the child into custody.

(ii) If the child who is the subject of the photographs is adjudicated a delinquent child for the commission of an act that would be a felony if committed by an adult or is convicted of or pleads guilty to a criminal offense that is a felony as a result of the arrest or custody that was the basis of the taking of the photographs, a law enforcement officer may use the photographs for a photo line-up conducted as part of the investigation of any act that would be a felony if committed by an adult, whether or not the child who is the subject of the photographs is a suspect in the investigation.

(b) Originals and copies of fingerprints of a child, and records of the arrest or custody of the child that was the basis of the taking of the fingerprints, may be used only for the investigation of the act for which they originally were obtained or taken; if a child is a suspect in the investigation, for the investigation of another act that would be an offense if committed by an adult; and for arresting or bringing the child into custody.

(c) Originals and copies of fingerprints, photographs, and records of the arrest or custody that was the basis of the taking of the fingerprints or photographs shall be released only to the following:

(i) Law enforcement officers of this state or a political subdivision of this state, upon notification to the juvenile court of the name and address of the law enforcement officer or agency to whom or to which they will be released;

(ii) A court that has jurisdiction of the child's case under Chapters 2151. and 2152. of the Revised Code or subsequent to a transfer of the child's case for criminal prosecution pursuant to section 2152.12 of the Revised Code.

(D) No person shall knowingly do any of the following:

(1) Fingerprint or photograph a child in the investigation of any violation of law other than as provided in division (A)(1) or (2) of this section or in sections 109.57, 109.60, and 109.61 of the Revised Code;

(2) Retain fingerprints or photographs of a child obtained or taken under division (A)(1) or (2) of this section, copies of fingerprints or photographs of that nature, or records of the arrest or custody that was the basis of the taking of fingerprints or photographs of that nature other than in accordance with division (B) of this section;

(3) Use or release fingerprints or photographs of a child obtained or taken under division (A)(1) or (2) of this section, copies of fingerprints or photographs of that nature, or records of the arrest or custody that was the basis of the taking of fingerprints or photographs of that nature other than in accordance with division (B) or (C) of this section.

(2006 H 137, eff. 10-9-06; 2000 S 179, § 3, eff. 1-1-02; 2000 S 181, eff. 9-4-00; 1998 H 2, eff. 1-1-99; 1996 H 124, eff. 3-31-97; 1996 H 445, eff. 9-3-96; 1995 H 1, eff. 1-1-96; 1992 H 198, eff. 10-6-92; 1984 H 258; 1977 H 315; 1973 S 1; 1969 H 320)

Historical and Statutory Notes

Amendment Note: 2006 H 137 substituted "agaist" with "against" in division (B)(2) and substituted "section" with "sections 2151.356 to" in division (B)(4).

Amendment Note: 2000 S 179, § 3, eff. 1–1–02, added references to indictments and informations throughout the section; substituted "2152.12" for "2151.26" in divisions (B)(1) and (C)(2)(c)(ii); and added the reference to Chapter 2152 in division (C)(2)(c)(ii).

Amendment Note: 2000 S 181 inserted ", provided that, if a complaint is filed against the child in relation to any act to which the records pertain, the court shall maintain all records of an arrest or custody of a child so delivered for at least three years after the final disposition of the case or after the case becomes inactive" in division (B)(5); and made other nonsubstantive changes.

Amendment Note: 1998 H 2 substituted "an offense, other than a traffic offense or a minor misdemeanor," for "a felony" in division (A)(2); rewrote divisions (A)(3) and (B)(3); substituted "an offense, other than a traffic offense or a minor misdemeanor," for "a felony" and "other than a traffic offense or a minor misdemeanor" for "that is a felony" twice each in division (B)(6)(b); deleted "No later than ninety days after a law enforcement officer uses the photographs in a photo line up, the officer shall return them to the file from which the officer obtained them." from the end of division (C)(2)(a)(ii); and made other nonsubstantive changes. Prior to amendment, divisions (A)(3) and (B)(3) read:

"(3) This section does not apply to a child who is fourteen years of age or older and under eighteen years of age and to whom either of the following applies:

"(a) The child has been arrested or otherwise taken into custody for committing, has been adjudicated a delinquent child for committing, or has been convicted of or pleaded guilty to committing a designated delinquent act or juvenile offense, as defined in section 109.57 of the Revised Code.

"(b) There is probable cause to believe that the child may have committed a designated delinquent act or juvenile offense, as defined in section 109.57 of the Revised Code."

"(3) If a child is adjudicated a delinquent child for the commission of an act in violation of, or is convicted of or pleads guilty to a criminal offense for the commission of an act that is a violation of, section 2903.01, 2903.02, 2903.03, 2903.04, 2903.11, 2903.12, 2903.13, 2903.21, 2903.22, 2905.01, 2905.02, 2905.11, 2907.02, 2907.03, 2907.05, 2909.02, 2909.03, 2911.01, 2911.02, 2911.11, 2911.12, 2911.13, 2921.34, or 2921.35 of the Revised Code, section 2913.02 of the Revised Code involving the theft of a motor vehicle, former section 2907.12 of the Revised Code, or an existing or former municipal ordinance or law of this state, another state, or the United States that is substantially equivalent to any of those sections, both of the following apply [.]"

Amendment Note: 1996 H 124 rewrote division (A)(3), which prior thereto read:

"(3) This section does not apply to a child who is fourteen years of age or older and under eighteen years of age and who has been arrested or otherwise taken into custody for committing an act that is a category one offense or a category two offense, as defined in section 2151.26 of the Revised Code, has been adjudicated a delinquent child for committing an act that is a category one offense or a category two offense, has been convicted of or pleaded guilty to a category one offense or a category two offense, or is a child with respect to whom there is probable cause to believe that the child may have committed an act that is a category one offense or a category two offense."

Amendment Note: 1996 H 445 changed a reference to section 2907.12 to the reference to former section 2907.12 in the first paragraph in division (B)(3).

Amendment Note: 1995 H 1 inserted "and in sections 109.57, 109.60, and 109.61 of the Revised Code" in division (A)(1); added "Subject to division (A)(3) of this section," at the beginning of division (A)(2); added division (A)(3); inserted "or in sections 109.57, 109.60, or 109.61 of the Revised Code" in division (D)(1); and made changes to reflect gender neutral language and other nonsubstantive changes.

Cross References

Penalty: 2151.99
Duties of the superintendent of the bureau of criminal investigation, 109.57

Library References

Infants ⚖68.3, 133, 192.
Westlaw Topic No. 211.
C.J.S. Infants §§ 41, 53 to 55, 57, 69 to 85, 198 to 207.

Research References

Encyclopedias

OH Jur. 3d Family Law § 1572, Fingerprints and Photographs of Children.

OH Jur. 3d Family Law § 1573, Fingerprints and Photographs of Children—Retention, Removal, and Destruction.

OH Jur. 3d Family Law § 1737, Adult Acts Punishable in Juvenile Court—Failure to Follow Procedures for Fingerprinting and Photographing Children Involved in Crimes.

OH Jur. 3d Family Law § 1749, Sentence and Punishment.

Treatises and Practice Aids

Baldwin's Ohio Handbook Series—Trial Handbook § 14:5, Privilege Against Self-Incrimination—Inspection of Person of Accused or Witness.

Carlin, Baldwin's Ohio Practice, Merrick-Rippner Probate Law § 108:1, Juvenile Court—Criminal Jurisdiction.

Carlin, Baldwin's Ohio Practice, Merrick-Rippner Probate Law § 108:9, Juvenile Court—Criminal Jurisdiction—Assignment of Case for Disposition.

Carlin, Baldwin's Ohio Practice, Merrick-Rippner Probate Law § 107:21, Fingerprints and Photographs of Juveniles—Necessity for Judicial Consent.

Carlin, Baldwin's Ohio Practice, Merrick-Rippner Probate Law § 107:22, Fingerprints and Photographs of Juveniles—Disposition.

Carlin, Baldwin's Ohio Practice, Merrick-Rippner Probate Law § 107:23, Expungement of Arrest Records.

Carlin, Baldwin's Ohio Practice, Merrick-Rippner Probate Law § 107:24, Use and Release of Juvenile Records.

Carlin, Baldwin's Ohio Practice, Merrick-Rippner Probate Law § 107:83, Motion for Permanent Custody of Abused, Neglected, or Dependent Child.

Carlin, Baldwin's Ohio Practice, Merrick-Rippner Probate Law § 107:154, Motion for Consent to Fingerprint or Photograph—Form.

Carlin, Baldwin's Ohio Practice, Merrick-Rippner Probate Law § 107:155, Order Granting Consent to Fingerprint or Photograph—Form.

Giannelli & Yeomans, Ohio Juvenile Law § 35:2, Confidentiality Requirement.

Giannelli & Yeomans, Ohio Juvenile Law § 35:4, Expungement and Sealing.

Giannelli & Yeomans, Ohio Juvenile Law § 14:15, Fingerprints & Photographs.

Law Review and Journal Commentaries

Civil Procedure: Ohio Foregoes Probable Cause on Order for Obtaining Nontestimonial Evidence from a Juvenile—In re Order Requiring Fingerprinting of a Juvenile, Note. 15 U Dayton L Rev 289 (Winter 1990).

Preventing Violence in Ohio's Schools, Comment. 33 Akron L Rev 311 (2000).

Notes of Decisions

Ed. Note: This section contains annotations from former RC 2151.31.

Admissibility of evidence 1
Less than probable cause needed 3
Use of records 2

---

1. Admissibility of evidence

RC 2151.313 does not require the exclusion by a trial court of fingerprint evidence obtained in violation thereof. State v. Davis (Ohio 1978) 56 Ohio St.2d 51, 381 N.E.2d 641, 10 O.O.3d 87. Criminal Law ⚖ 394.1(1)

Where testimony is offered for the purpose of identifying the accused as the perpetrator of a crime but such is based in part on illegally obtained evidence, it will not be excluded if the totality of circumstances manifests an effective identification apart from and independent of the tainted procedure. State v. Jones (Hamilton 1976) 49 Ohio App.2d 170, 359 N.E.2d 1386, 3 O.O.3d 222. Criminal Law ⊂⊃ 394.1(3)

The purpose of RC 2151.31 is not to determine the admissibility into evidence of a child's fingerprints, but rather to conform to the theory that juvenile proceedings are not criminal in nature. State v. Carder (Ohio 1966) 9 Ohio St.2d 1, 222 N.E.2d 620, 38 O.O.2d 1.

2. Use of records

If, pursuant to RC 2151.313, a law enforcement officer or other authorized person takes fingerprints or photographs of a juvenile arrested or taken into custody, the fingerprints, photographs, and other records relating to that arrest or custody of the juvenile are not public records. OAG 90–101.

Where no fingerprints or photographs of a juvenile have been taken in connection with a first-time drug or alcohol offense, a law enforcement agency may share with other law enforcement agencies or local schools personal information regarding such offenses by a juvenile, as the law enforcement agency deems such sharing appropriate to carry out its duties and to promote the goals of RC Ch 2151, including the prevention and control of juvenile delinquency. OAG 87–010.

If a law enforcement officer or other authorized person takes photographs and fingerprints of a juvenile taken into custody for a first-time drug or alcohol offense, records of that custody and of the photographs and fingerprints may be disclosed only as permitted by RC 2151.313. OAG 87–010.

Police officers may not forward fingerprints of juveniles to the state bureau of criminal identification, and may not procure and file for record the fingerprints of juveniles who are in any place of confinement under a commitment by a juvenile court on a charge of delinquency. 1952 OAG 1771.

3. Less than probable cause needed

RC 2151.313(A)(1) permits a juvenile court judge to order fingerprinting of a juvenile not in custody or under arrest without a finding of probable cause, when the juvenile court judge determines: (1) there is an articulable and specific basis in fact for suspecting criminal activity; (2) the intrusion is justified by substantial law enforcement interests; and (3) the intrusion is limited in scope, purpose, and duration. In re Order Requiring Fingerprinting of a Juvenile (Ohio 1989) 42 Ohio St.3d 124, 537 N.E.2d 1286, certiorari denied 110 S.Ct. 165, 493 U.S. 857, 107 L.Ed.2d 122. Infants ⊂⊃ 192

A juvenile court may order the fingerprinting of a juvenile suspected of involvement in a series of pipe bomb explosions pursuant to RC 2151.313(A)(1), even though such suspicion is less than the probable cause necessary for arrest or search. In re Order Requiring Fingerprinting of a Juvenile (Ohio 1989) 42 Ohio St.3d 124, 537 N.E.2d 1286, certiorari denied 110 S.Ct. 165, 493 U.S. 857, 107 L.Ed.2d 122.

2151.314 Detention hearing

(A) When a child is brought before the court or delivered to a place of detention or shelter care designated by the court, the intake or other authorized officer of the court shall immediately make an investigation and shall release the child unless it appears that the child's detention or shelter care is warranted or required under section 2151.31 of the Revised Code.

If the child is not so released, a complaint under section 2151.27 or 2152.021 or an information under section 2152.13 of the Revised Code shall be filed or an indictment under division (B) of section 2152.13 of the Revised Code shall be sought and an informal detention or shelter care hearing held promptly, not later than seventy-two hours after the child is placed in detention or shelter care, to determine whether detention or shelter care is required. Reasonable oral or written notice of the time, place, and purpose of the detention or shelter care hearing shall be given to the child and, if they can be found, to the child's parents, guardian, or custodian. In cases in which the complaint alleges a child to be an abused, neglected, or dependent child, the notice given the parents, guardian, or custodian shall inform them that a case plan may be prepared for the child, the general requirements usually contained in case plans, and the possible consequences of the failure to comply with a journalized case plan.

Prior to the hearing, the court shall inform the parties of their right to counsel and to appointed counsel or to the services of the county public defender or joint county public defender, if they are indigent, of the child's right to remain silent with respect to any allegation of delinquency, and of the name and telephone number of a court employee who can be contacted during the normal business hours of the court to arrange for the prompt appointment of counsel for any party who is indigent. Unless it appears from the hearing that the child's detention or shelter care is required under the provisions of section 2151.31 of the Revised Code, the court shall order the child's release as provided by section 2151.311 of the Revised Code. If a parent, guardian, or custodian has not been so notified and did not appear or waive appearance at the hearing, upon the filing of an affidavit stating these facts, the court shall rehear the matter without unnecessary delay.

(B) When the court conducts a hearing pursuant to division (A) of this section, all of the following apply:

(1) The court shall determine whether an alleged abused, neglected, or dependent child should remain or be placed in shelter care;

(2) The court shall determine whether there are any relatives of the child who are willing to be temporary custodians of the child. If any relative is willing to be a temporary custodian, the child would otherwise be placed or retained in shelter care, and the appointment is appropriate, the court shall appoint the relative as temporary custodian of the child, unless the court appoints another relative as temporary custodian. If it determines that the appointment of a relative as custodian would not be appropriate, it shall issue a written opinion setting forth the reasons for its determination and give a copy of the opinion to all parties and to the guardian ad litem of the child.

The court's consideration of a relative for appointment as a temporary custodian does not make that relative a party to the proceedings.

(3) The court shall comply with section 2151.419 of the Revised Code.

(C) If a child is in shelter care following the filing of a complaint pursuant to section 2151.27 or 2152.021 of the Revised Code, the filing of an information, or the obtaining of an indictment or following a hearing held pursuant to division (A) of this section, any party, including the public children services agency, and the guardian ad litem of the child may file a motion with the court requesting that the child be released from shelter care. The motion shall state the reasons why the child should be released from shelter care and, if a hearing has been held pursuant to division (A) of this section, any changes in the situation of the child or the parents, guardian, or custodian of the child that have occurred since that hearing and that justify the release of the child from shelter care. Upon the filing of the motion, the court shall hold a hearing in the same manner as under division (A) of this section.

(D) Each juvenile court shall designate at least one court employee to assist persons who are indigent in obtaining appointed counsel. The court shall include in each notice given pursuant to division (A) or (C) of this section and in each summons served upon a party pursuant to this chapter, the name and telephone number at which each designated employee can be contacted during the normal business hours of the court to arrange for prompt appointment of counsel for indigent persons.

(2002 H 393, eff. 7–5–02; 2000 S 179, § 3, eff. 1–1–02; 1999 H 176, eff. 10–29–99; 1998 H 484, eff. 3–18–99; 1996 H 274, eff. 8–8–96; 1988 S 89, eff. 1–1–89; 1975 H 164; 1969 H 320)

Historical and Statutory Notes

Amendment Note: 2002 H 393 substituted "(B)" for "(C)" in the second paragraph of division (A).

Amendment Note: 2000 S 179, § 3, eff. 1–1–02, inserted "or 2152.021 or an information under section 2152.13" and "or an indictment under division (C) of section 2152.13 of the Revised Code shall be sought" in the first paragraph in division (A); inserted "or 2152.021" and ", the filing of an information, or the obtaining of an indictment" in division (C); and inserted "at least" and substituted "each" for "the" in division (D).

Amendment Note: 1999 H 176 added division (B)(3); and made other nonsubstantive changes.

Amendment Note: 1998 H 484 deleted former division (B)(3); and made other nonsubstantive changes. Prior to deletion, former division (B)(3) read:

"(3) The court shall make the determination and issue the written finding of facts required by section 2151.419 of the Revised Code."

Amendment Note: 1996 H 274 added the third sentence in the second paragraph in division (A); inserted ", including the public children services agency," in division (C); and made changes to reflect gender neutral language.

Cross References

Caretaker authorization affidavit not permitted when certain proceedings are pending, 3109.68
Detention and shelter care, release to parents, hearing, Juv R 7
Power of attorney, certain pending actions prohibiting creation, 3109.58.
Temporary disposition, Juv R 13

Library References

Infants ⚖68.3, 192, 203.
Westlaw Topic No. 211.
C.J.S. Infants §§ 41 to 55, 62 to 67, 198 to 207.
    Baldwin's Ohio Legislative Service, 1988 Laws of Ohio, S 89—LSC Analysis, p 5–571

Research References

Encyclopedias

OH Jur. 3d Family Law § 1574, Delivery of Child to Shelter or Detention Facility.
OH Jur. 3d Family Law § 1576, Detention Hearing; Notice.
OH Jur. 3d Family Law § 1577, Detention Hearing; Notice—Conduct of Hearing.
OH Jur. 3d Family Law § 1578, Detention Hearing; Notice—Evidence and Order.
OH Jur. 3d Family Law § 1579, Detention Hearing; Notice—Rehearing.
OH Jur. 3d Family Law § 1601, Prehearing Motions—Motion to Release Child.
OH Jur. 3d Family Law § 1610, Form and Contents.
OH Jur. 3d Family Law § 1626, Right Under Juvenile Court Law and Rules.
OH Jur. 3d Family Law § 1654, Determination of Reasonable Efforts.

Treatises and Practice Aids

Klein, Darling, & Terez, Baldwin's Ohio Practice Civil Practice § 52:4, Findings by the Court--Findings of Fact Required by Statute.
Carlin, Baldwin's Ohio Practice, Merrick-Rippner Probate Law § 107:5, Time for Filing Complaint.
Carlin, Baldwin's Ohio Practice, Merrick-Rippner Probate Law § 107:9, Parties to Proceedings.
Carlin, Baldwin's Ohio Practice, Merrick-Rippner Probate Law § 107:30, Detention Hearing.
Carlin, Baldwin's Ohio Practice, Merrick-Rippner Probate Law § 107:42, Prehearing Motions in Juvenile Court.
Carlin, Baldwin's Ohio Practice, Merrick-Rippner Probate Law § 107:74, Reasonable Efforts Determination.
Carlin, Baldwin's Ohio Practice, Merrick-Rippner Probate Law § 107:75, Case Plans.
Carlin, Baldwin's Ohio Practice, Merrick-Rippner Probate Law § 107:172, Order Following Detention Hearing—Form.
Giannelli & Yeomans, Ohio Juvenile Law § 1:8, Rules of Juvenile Procedure.
Giannelli & Yeomans, Ohio Juvenile Law § 16:4, Time Requirements—Custody; Detention.
Giannelli & Yeomans, Ohio Juvenile Law § 18:2, Issuance of Summons: Proper Parties.
Giannelli & Yeomans, Ohio Juvenile Law § 18:3, Summons: Contents and Form.
Giannelli & Yeomans, Ohio Juvenile Law § 19:4, Detention Hearing: Notice.
Giannelli & Yeomans, Ohio Juvenile Law § 19:5, Detention Hearing.
Giannelli & Yeomans, Ohio Juvenile Law § 19:6, Standard for Detention.
Giannelli & Yeomans, Ohio Juvenile Law § 19:7, Time Requirements.
Giannelli & Yeomans, Ohio Juvenile Law § 19:8, Motions for Release.
Giannelli & Yeomans, Ohio Juvenile Law § 19:9, Bail.
Giannelli & Yeomans, Ohio Juvenile Law § 25:14, Reasonable Efforts Determination; Abuse, Neglect & Dependency.

Law Review and Journal Commentaries

Children in Limbo in Ohio: Permanency Planning and the State of the Law, John Paul Christoff. 16 Cap U L Rev 1 (Fall 1986).

Notes of Decisions

Ed. Note: This section contains annotations from former RC 2151.31.

Admissibility of evidence   1
Child service agency   4
Commitment   2
Public access   6
Release from custody   5
Transcript, media request   7
Waiver of notice   3

---

1. Admissibility of evidence

A voluntary confession to the perpetration of murder obtained from a sixteen-and-three-fourths-year-old high school junior, which confession was made before indictment and while the accused was detained for investigation, is admissible in evidence (1) where the accused had been allowed to consult with an attorney prior to being questioned, (2) where the accused first was advised that he did not have to talk, (3) where the accused, when told that his parents and another attorney were there and waiting to see him, stated that he did not want to see them, and (4) where there is no showing that the confession was obtained by inquisitorial processes. State v. Carder (Fairfield 1965) 3 Ohio App.2d 381, 210 N.E.2d 714, 32 O.O.2d 524, affirmed 9 Ohio St.2d 1, 222 N.E.2d 620, 38 O.O.2d 1.

A voluntary confession to the perpetration of murder, obtained from a seventeen-year-old high school senior, which confession was made before indictment on said charge and while the accused was under arrest for a misdemeanor, is admissible in evidence (1) where the accused was first advised that "he would not be compelled to give a statement... if he wanted to give a statement it would be by his own free will and that statement would be used for or against him in court"; (2) where the accused was further advised that "he could secure the services of an attorney"; and (3) where there is no showing that the confession was obtained by inquisitorial processes, without the procedural safeguards of due process, and by such compulsion that the confession is irreconcilable with the possession of mental freedom. State v. Stewart (Summit 1963) 120 Ohio App. 199, 201 N.E.2d 793, 29 O.O.2d 4, affirmed 176 Ohio St. 156, 198 N.E.2d 439, 27 O.O.2d 42, certiorari denied 85 S.Ct. 443, 379 U.S. 947, 13 L.Ed.2d 544.

2. Commitment

Trial court error in failing to inform father of the possible consequences of failing to comply with his caseplan did not prejudice father, in child dependency proceeding; caseplan and each amendment thereto stated that father was required to comply with the plan's requirements, protective service worker testified that she told father that he had to comply with the service plan, counsel was appointed for father, father made an attempt to follow his service plan, and the county department of job and family services motion for permanent custody stated that it sought custody based on father's failure to comply with his service plan. In re Moore (Ohio App. 3 Dist., 08-11-2003) 153 Ohio App.3d 641, 795 N.E.2d 149, 2003-Ohio-4250. Infants ⚖ 253

Commitment of a fifteen year old to a state institution pursuant to RC 2151.26 for purpose of examination is not an act for which a writ of prohibition will issue. State ex rel. Harris v. Common Pleas Court, Division of Probate and Juvenile (Ross 1970) 25 Ohio App.2d 78, 266 N.E.2d 589, 54 O.O.2d 115.

3. Waiver of notice

Child's biological mother waived complaint to holding of dispositional hearing in child dependency proceedings more than 90 days after dependency complaint, as she did not file timely motion to dismiss complaint. In re Jessica M. B. (Ohio App. 6 Dist., Ottawa, 03-05-2004) No. OT-03-022, 2004-Ohio-1040, 2004 WL 413307, Unreported. Infants ⚖ 243

When a mother voluntarily appears at and participates in a hearing in which the dependency of the child is considered, she waives all prior notice of proceedings upon such complaint of dependency to which she was entitled under the statute. Ex parte Province (Ohio 1933) 127 Ohio St. 333, 188 N.E. 550, 39 Ohio Law Rep. 651.

4. Child service agency

Trial court error in failing to inform father of the possible consequences of failing to comply with his caseplan did not prejudice father, in child dependency proceeding; caseplan and each amendment thereto stated that father was required to comply with the plan's requirements, protective service worker testified that she told father that he had to comply with the service plan, counsel was appointed for father, father made an attempt to follow his service plan, and the county department of job and family services motion for permanent custody stated that it sought custody based on father's failure to comply with his service plan. In re Moore (Ohio App. 3 Dist., 08-11-2003) 153 Ohio App.3d 641, 795 N.E.2d 149, 2003-Ohio-4250. Infants ⚖ 253

RC 2151.314 does not apply where parents voluntarily give temporary custody of child to a children services agency; no hearing within seventy-two hours is necessary. In re Pachin (Montgomery 1988) 50 Ohio App.3d 44, 552 N.E.2d 655, cause dismissed 39 Ohio St.3d 720, 534 N.E.2d 350.

5. Release from custody

RC 2151.311(A)(1), 2151.314(A), and Juv R 7(B) do not authorize the release of a child to the peace officer who took the child into custody. OAG 96–061.

6. Public access

Order by juvenile court judge's court administrator and chief probation counselor to close courthouse to the media during detention hearing was not justified and erroneously denied newspaper access to a public building. State ex rel. Dispatch Printing Co. v. Louden (Ohio, 02-14-2001) 91 Ohio St.3d 61, 741 N.E.2d 517, 2001-Ohio-268. Infants ⚖ 203

7. Transcript, media request

Supreme Court would sua sponte convert newspaper's request for a writ of prohibition, which sought to compel juvenile court judge to provide newspaper with a complete, unredacted copy of transcript of detention hearing, to a request for a writ of mandamus; writ of mandamus was the appropriate writ to compel requested relief, principal issue would have be argued the same way under either a mandamus or prohibition theory, and judge did not contend that requested relief was inappropriate because it was improperly styled as being in prohibition. State ex rel. Dispatch Printing Co. v. Louden (Ohio, 02-14-2001) 91 Ohio St.3d 61, 741 N.E.2d 517, 2001-Ohio-268. Mandamus ⚖ 154(2)

Juvenile court judge's providing newspaper with a redacted copy of transcript from detention hearing involving juvenile who was charged with a delinquency count of kidnapping did not render moot newspaper's prohibition claim, which sought to vacate closure of detention hearing, to prevent judge from closing further proceedings unless all requirements of notice, hearing, and findings had been fulfilled, and to order judge to provide a complete transcript of detention hearing; judge continued to refuse to give newspaper a complete, unredacted copy of transcript, and there was a reasonable expectation that, absent a writ providing requested relief, judge would again close further proceedings. State ex rel. Dispatch Printing Co. v. Louden (Ohio, 02-14-2001) 91 Ohio St.3d 61, 741 N.E.2d 517, 2001-Ohio-268. Prohibition ⚖ 13

2151.32 Selection of custodian

In placing a child under any guardianship or custody other than that of its parent, the juvenile court shall, when practicable, select a person or an institution or agency governed by persons of like religious faith as that of the parents of such child, or in case of a difference in the religious faith of the parents, then of the religious faith of the child, or if the religious faith of the child is not ascertained, then of either of the parents.

(1953 H 1, eff. 10–1–53; GC 1639–33)

Historical and Statutory Notes

Pre–1953 H 1 Amendments: 117 v 520, § 1

Library References

Infants ⚖ 222, 226.
Westlaw Topic No. 211.
C.J.S. Adoption of Persons § 10.
C.J.S. Infants §§ 57, 69 to 85.

Research References

Encyclopedias

OH Jur. 3d Family Law § 1686, Discretion of Court—Religion as Factor in Selecting Custodian.

OH Jur. 3d Guardian & Ward § 30, Priority of Relatives; Effect of Parent's Religion.

Treatises and Practice Aids

Carlin, Baldwin's Ohio Practice, Merrick-Rippner Probate Law § 107:73, Alternatives for Disposition of Juvenile Cases.

Giannelli & Yeomans, Ohio Juvenile Law § 30:2, General Principles for Abuse, Neglect and Dependency Dispositions.

2151.33 Temporary care; emergency medical treatment; reimbursement

(A) Pending hearing of a complaint filed under section 2151.27 of the Revised Code or a motion filed or made under division (B) of this section and the service of citations, the juvenile court may make any temporary disposition of any child that it considers necessary to protect the best interest of the child and that can be made pursuant to division (B) of this section. Upon the certificate of one or more reputable practicing physicians, the court may summarily provide for emergency medical and surgical treatment that appears to be immediately necessary to preserve the health and well-being of any child concerning whom a complaint or an application for care has been filed, pending the service of a citation upon the child's parents, guardian, or custodian. The court may order the parents, guardian, or custodian, if the court finds the parents, guardian, or custodian able to do so, to reimburse the court for the expense involved in providing the emergency medical or surgical treatment. Any person who disobeys the order for reimbursement may be adjudged in contempt of court and punished accordingly.

If the emergency medical or surgical treatment is furnished to a child who is found at the hearing to be a nonresident of the county in which the court is located and if the expense of the medical or surgical treatment cannot be recovered from the parents, legal guardian, or custodian of the child, the board of county commissioners of the county in which the child has a legal settlement shall reimburse the court for the reasonable cost of the emergency medical or surgical treatment out of its general fund.

(B)(1) After a complaint, petition, writ, or other document initiating a case dealing with an alleged or adjudicated abused, neglected, or dependent child is filed and upon the filing or making of a motion pursuant to division (C) of this section, the court, prior to the final disposition of the case, may issue any of the following temporary orders to protect the best interest of the child:

(a) An order granting temporary custody of the child to a particular party;

(b) An order for the taking of the child into custody pursuant to section 2151.31 of the Revised Code pending the outcome of the adjudicatory and dispositional hearings;

(c) An order granting, limiting, or eliminating parenting time or visitation rights with respect to the child;

(d) An order requiring a party to vacate a residence that will be lawfully occupied by the child;

(e) An order requiring a party to attend an appropriate counseling program that is reasonably available to that party;

(f) Any other order that restrains or otherwise controls the conduct of any party which conduct would not be in the best interest of the child.

(2) Prior to the final disposition of a case subject to division (B)(1) of this section, the court shall do both of the following:

(a) Issue an order pursuant to Chapters 3119. to 3125. of the Revised Code requiring the parents, guardian, or person charged with the child's support to pay support for the child.

(b) Issue an order requiring the parents, guardian, or person charged with the child's support to continue to maintain any health insurance coverage for the child that existed at the time of the filing of the complaint, petition, writ, or other document, or to obtain health insurance coverage in accordance with sections 3119.29 to 3119.56 of the Revised Code.

(C)(1) A court may issue an order pursuant to division (B) of this section upon its own motion or if a party files a written motion or makes an oral motion requesting the issuance of the order and stating the reasons for it. Any notice sent by the court as a result of a motion pursuant to this division shall contain a notice that any party to a juvenile proceeding has the right to be represented by counsel and to have appointed counsel if the person is indigent.

(2) If a child is taken into custody pursuant to section 2151.31 of the Revised Code and placed in shelter care, the public children services agency or private child placing agency with which the child is placed in shelter care shall file or make a motion as described in division (C)(1) of this section before the end of the next day immediately after the date on which the child was taken into custody and, at a minimum, shall request an order for temporary custody under division (B)(1)(a) of this section.

(3) A court that issues an order pursuant to division (B)(1)(b) of this section shall comply with section 2151.419 of the Revised Code.

(D) The court may grant an ex parte order upon its own motion or a motion filed or made pursuant to division (C) of this section requesting such an order if it appears to the court that the best interest and the welfare of the child require that the court issue the order immediately. The court, if acting on its own motion, or the person requesting the granting of an ex parte order, to the extent possible, shall give notice of its intent or of the request to the parents, guardian, or custodian of the child who is the subject of the request. If the court issues an ex parte order, the court shall hold a hearing to review the order within seventy-two hours after it is issued or before the end of the next day after the day on which it is issued, whichever occurs first. The court shall give written notice of the hearing to all parties to the action and shall appoint a guardian ad litem for the child prior to the hearing.

The written notice shall be given by all means that are reasonably likely to result in the party receiving actual notice and shall include all of the following:

(1) The date, time, and location of the hearing;

(2) The issues to be addressed at the hearing;

(3) A statement that every party to the hearing has a right to counsel and to court-appointed counsel, if the party is indigent;

(4) The name, telephone number, and address of the person requesting the order;

(5) A copy of the order, except when it is not possible to obtain it because of the exigent circumstances in the case.

If the court does not grant an ex parte order pursuant to a motion filed or made pursuant to division (C) of this section or its own motion, the court shall hold a shelter care hearing on the motion within ten days after the motion is filed. The court shall give notice of the hearing to all affected parties in the same manner as set forth in the Juvenile Rules.

(E) The court, pending the outcome of the adjudicatory and dispositional hearings, shall not issue an order granting temporary custody of a child to a public children services agency or private child placing agency pursuant to this section, unless the court determines and specifically states in the order that the continued residence of the child in the child's current home will be contrary to the child's best interest and welfare and the court complies with section 2151.419 of the Revised Code.

(F) Each public children services agency and private child placing agency that receives temporary custody of a child pursuant to this section shall maintain in the child's case record written documentation that it has placed the child, to the extent that it is consistent with the best interest, welfare, and special needs of the child, in the most family-like setting available and in close proximity to the home of the parents, custodian, or guardian of the child.

(G) For good cause shown, any court order that is issued pursuant to this section may be reviewed by the court at any time upon motion of any party to the action or upon the motion of the court.

(2002 H 657, eff. 12–13–02; 2000 S 180, eff. 3–22–01; 1999 H 176, eff. 10–29–99; 1998 H 484, eff. 3–18–99; 1997 H 352, eff. 1–1–98; 1996 H 274, eff. 8–8–96; 1988 S 89, eff. 1–1–89; 1953 H 1; GC 1639–28)

Historical and Statutory Notes

Pre–1953 H 1 Amendments: 121 v 557; 119 v 731; 117 v 520

Amendment Note: 2002 H 657 substituted "3119.29" for "3119.30" and "3119.56" for "3119.58" in division (B)(2)(b).

Amendment Note: 2000 S 180 substituted "Chapters 3119. to 3125." for "sections 3113.21 to 3113.219" in division (B)(2)(a) and "sections 3119.30 to 3119.58" for "section 3113.217" in division (B)(2)(b).

Amendment Note: 1999 H 176 added division (B)(3); and inserted "and the court complies with section 2151.419 of the Revised Code" in division (E).

Amendment Note: 1998 H 484 deleted former division (C)(3); deleted "and makes the determination and issues the written finding of facts required by section 2151.419 of the Revised Code" from the end of division (E); and made other nonsubstantive changes. Prior to deletion, former division (C)(3) read:

"(3) Any court that issues an order pursuant to division (B)(1)(b) of this section shall make the determination and issue the written finding of facts required by section 2151.419 of the Revised Code."

Amendment Note: 1997 H 352 substituted "in accordance with" for "pursuant to" in division (B)(2)(b).

Amendment Note: 1996 H 274 rewrote divisions (B) and (C) and the first paragraph in division (D); inserted "or its own motion" in the final paragraph in division (D); and made changes to reflect gender neutral language. Prior to amendment, divisions (B) and (C) and the first paragraph in division (D) read:

"(B) After a complaint, petition, writ, or other document initiating a case dealing with an alleged or adjudicated abused, neglected, or dependent child is filed and upon the filing or making of a motion pursuant to division (C) of this section, the court, prior to the final disposition of the case, may issue any of the following temporary orders to protect the best interest of the child:

"(1) An order granting temporary custody of the child to a particular party;

"(2) An order for the taking of the child into custody pursuant to section 2151.31 of the Revised Code pending the outcome of the adjudicatory and dispositional hearings;

"(3) An order granting, limiting, or eliminating visitation rights with respect to the child;

"(4) An order for the payment of child support for the child and the continued maintenance of any medical, surgical, or hospital policies of insurance for the child that existed at the time of the filing of the complaint, petition, writ, or other document;

"(5) An order requiring a party to vacate a residence that will be lawfully occupied by the child;

"(6) An order requiring a party to attend an appropriate counseling program that is reasonably available to that party;

"(7) Any other order that restrains or otherwise controls the conduct of any party which conduct would not be in the best interest of the child.

"(C)(1) A court may issue an order pursuant to division (B) of this section only if a party files a written motion or makes an oral motion requesting the issuance of the order and stating the reasons for it. Any notice sent by the court as a result of the filing or making of a motion pursuant to this division shall contain a notice that any party to a juvenile proceeding has the right to be represented by counsel and to have counsel appointed for him if he is an indigent person.

"(2) If a child is taken into custody pursuant to section 2151.31 of the Revised Code and placed in shelter care, the public children services agency or private child placing agency with which the child is placed in shelter care shall file or make a motion as described in division (C)(1) of this section before the end of the next business day immediately after the date on which the child was taken into custody and, at a minimum, shall request an order for temporary custody under division (B)(1)(a) of this section.

"(3) Any court that issues an order pursuant to division (B)(2) of this section shall make the determination and issue the written finding of facts required by section 2151.419 of the Revised Code.

"(D) If a motion filed or made pursuant to division (C) of this section requests the issuance of an ex parte order, the court may grant an ex parte order if it appears to the court that the best interest and the welfare of the child require that the court issue the order immediately. The person requesting the granting of an ex parte order, to the extent possible, shall give notice of the request to the parents, guardian, or custodian of the child who is the subject of the request. If the court issues the requested ex parte order, the court shall hold a hearing to review the order within seventy-two hours after it is issued or before the end of the next business day after the day on which it is issued, whichever occurs first. The court shall give written notice of the hearing to all parties to the action and shall appoint a guardian ad litem for the child prior to the hearing."

Cross References

Caretaker authorization affidavit not permitted when certain proceedings are pending, 3109.68
Foster caregivers, information regarding delinquent children provided to, 2152.72
Interfering with action to issue or modify support order, 2919.231
Nonsupport of dependents, 2919.21
Power of attorney, certain pending actions prohibiting creation, 3109.58
Social history, physical and mental examinations, custody investigation, Juv R 32
Temporary disposition, emergency medical and surgical treatment, Juv R 13

Ohio Administrative Code References

Protective supervision by PCSAs and PCPAS, OAC 5101:2–39–30
Protective supervision by PCSAs, OAC 5101:2–38–02

Library References

Infants ⚖192, 228.
Westlaw Topic No. 211.
C.J.S. Infants §§ 41, 53 to 55, 57, 69 to 85.
Baldwin's Ohio Legislative Service, 1988 Laws of Ohio, S 89—LSC Analysis, p 5–571

Research References

Encyclopedias

OH Jur. 3d Family Law § 1308, Reissuance Upon Change in Obligor's Status.
OH Jur. 3d Family Law § 1430, Agreement for Temporary Custody.
OH Jur. 3d Family Law § 1596, Habeas Corpus.
OH Jur. 3d Family Law § 1633, Emergency Medical Care.
OH Jur. 3d Family Law § 1634, Procedure.
OH Jur. 3d Family Law § 1635, Ex Parte Orders.
OH Jur. 3d Family Law § 1654, Determination of Reasonable Efforts.
OH Jur. 3d Family Law § 1724, Physicians, Psychologists, and Psychiatrists—Emergency Medical Treatment.

Treatises and Practice Aids

Klein, Darling, & Terez, Baldwin's Ohio Practice Civil Practice § 52:4, Findings by the Court--Findings of Fact Required by Statute.
Carlin, Baldwin's Ohio Practice, Merrick-Rippner Probate Law § 107:41, Prehearing Procedures in Juvenile Court—Temporary Orders Pending Hearing.
Carlin, Baldwin's Ohio Practice, Merrick-Rippner Probate Law § 107:74, Reasonable Efforts Determination.
Carlin, Baldwin's Ohio Practice, Merrick-Rippner Probate Law § 107:76, Disposition of Abused, Neglected, or Dependent Child—Types of Orders Court May Make.
Carlin, Baldwin's Ohio Practice, Merrick-Rippner Probate Law § 107:78, Disposition of Abused, Neglected, or Dependent Child—Temporary Custody.
Carlin, Baldwin's Ohio Practice, Merrick-Rippner Probate Law § 108:22, Juvenile Court—Parentage Act—Presumption of Paternity.
Carlin, Baldwin's Ohio Practice, Merrick-Rippner Probate Law § 107:152, Motion for Temporary Custody Pending Hearing—Form.
Carlin, Baldwin's Ohio Practice, Merrick-Rippner Probate Law § 107:153, Order Granting Temporary Custody Pending Hearing—Form.
Giannelli & Yeomans, Ohio Juvenile Law § 9:7, Neglect—Subsistence, Education & Medical Care.
Giannelli & Yeomans, Ohio Juvenile Law § 20:2, Temporary Care Orders.
Giannelli & Yeomans, Ohio Juvenile Law § 20:3, Emergency Medical Orders.
Giannelli & Yeomans, Ohio Juvenile Law § 20:5, Notice of Hearing.
Giannelli & Yeomans, Ohio Juvenile Law § 20:6, Time Requirements.
Giannelli & Yeomans, Ohio Juvenile Law § 30:3, Costs of Dispositions.
Giannelli & Yeomans, Ohio Juvenile Law § 30:4, Dispositional Alternatives for Abuse, Neglect or Dependency.
Giannelli & Yeomans, Ohio Juvenile Law § 32:2, Jurisdiction Over Parents and Others.
Giannelli & Yeomans, Ohio Juvenile Law § 25:14, Reasonable Efforts Determination; Abuse, Neglect & Dependency.

Law Review and Journal Commentaries

Emergency Custody in Domestic Relations Court: A Proposed Procedural and Substantive Litmus Test, Hon. V. Michael Brigner. 49 Dayton B Briefs 19 (December 1999).

Faith–Healing And Religious–Treatment Exemptions To Child–Endangerment Laws: Should Parental Religious Practices Excuse The Failure To Provide Necessary Medical Care To Children?, Comment. 13 U Dayton L Rev 79 (Fall 1987).

Notes of Decisions

Medical treatment 1
Removal from home 3
Temporary order 2

---

1. Medical treatment

Juvenile court properly authorized hospital to administer blood transfusions to child over religious objections of parents. In re Clark (Ohio Com.Pl. 1962) 185 N.E.2d 128, 90 Ohio Law Abs. 21, 21 O.O.2d 86.

Civil rights action to challenge statutes which provided exceptions from prosecution for those who fail to provide adequate care for children because they treat physical or mental illness or defects in children by spiritual means only did not allege any action or threat of action by defendant Attorney General, and therefore *Ex parte Young* exception to Eleventh Amendment immunity of state officials did not apply; also, plaintiffs did not seek to enjoin enforcement of allegedly unconstitutional statute as was required for immunity exception. Children's Healthcare is a Legal Duty, Inc. v. Deters (C.A.6 (Ohio), 08-05-1996) 92 F.3d 1412, rehearing and suggestion for rehearing en banc denied, certiorari denied 117 S.Ct. 1082, 519 U.S. 1149, 137 L.Ed.2d 217. Federal Courts ⚖ 269; Federal Courts ⚖ 272

When a complaint or application for care concerning a child has been filed with the juvenile court, such court may, pending service of a citation on the child's parents, guardian or custodian, order the provision of emergency medical or surgical treatment. 1951 OAG 898.

2. **Temporary order**

Juvenile court's repeated failures to comply with procedural and substantive requirements regarding emergency temporary custody orders were not of sufficient merit to require extraordinary remedy of habeas corpus, where complaint alleged that private child-placing agency had child voluntarily placed with it, where father allegedly testified that he was unable to care for child, and where complaint alleged that father was unfit because of alcoholism and substance abuse. Howard v. Catholic Social Serv. of Cuyahoga Cty., Inc. (Ohio, 08-31-1994) 70 Ohio St.3d 141, 637 N.E.2d 890, 1994-Ohio-219, reconsideration denied 70 Ohio St.3d 1457, 639 N.E.2d 796. Habeas Corpus ⊂⊃ 532(2)

RC 2151.412 and RC 2151.414 do not apply where a request for permanent custody is made by a welfare department and a temporary custody order is issued under RC 2151.33 pending a hearing on the request. In re Covert (Seneca 1984) 17 Ohio App.3d 122, 477 N.E.2d 678, 17 O.B.R. 185.

Grant of custodian's "emergency" motion to suspend visitation between parents and child was not an ex parte emergency order, for purposes of statute setting forth procedures to be followed in issuing such orders, where motion was heard with child's parents present. In re Bailey (Ohio App. 1 Dist., Hamilton, 07-26-2002) No. C-010015, No. C-010186, 2002-Ohio-3801, 2002 WL 1724030, Unreported, appeal not allowed 97 Ohio St.3d 1483, 780 N.E.2d 287, 2002-Ohio-6866. Child Custody ⊂⊃ 659

Pursuant to RC 2151.23(A), the Probate and Juvenile Division of the Muskingum County Court of Common Pleas has exclusive original jurisdiction to issue orders of support in cases brought under RC 2151.27 to RC 2151.331, including orders complying with RC 2151.33(B)(2)(a). The language of RC 2301.03(AA) establishing the powers and duties of the judge of the Domestic Relations Division of the Muskingum County Court of Common Pleas does not modify or restrict the exclusive original jurisdiction of the juvenile court in this regard. OAG 05–003.

3. **Removal from home**

Under Ohio law, unless matters of public safety are involved, a child alleged to be abused, neglected, or dependent may be removed from his home by court order only upon a judicial determination that continuation in the home would be contrary to the child's best interest. OAG 87–105.

2151.331 Detention in certified foster home; arrangement for temporary care; alternative diversion programs

A child alleged to be or adjudicated an abused, neglected, dependent, or unruly child or a juvenile traffic offender may be detained after a complaint is filed in a certified foster home for a period not exceeding sixty days or until the final disposition of the case, whichever comes first. The court also may arrange with a public children services agency or private child placing agency to receive, or with a private noncustodial agency for temporary care of, the child within the jurisdiction of the court. A child alleged to be or adjudicated an unruly child also may be assigned to an alternative diversion program established by the court for a period not exceeding sixty days after a complaint is filed or until final disposition of the case, whichever comes first.

If the court arranges for the board of a child temporarily detained in a certified foster home or arranges for the board of a child through a private child placing agency, the board of county commissioners shall pay a reasonable sum, which the court shall fix, for the board of the child. In order to have certified foster homes available for service, an agreed monthly subsidy may be paid in addition to a fixed rate per day for care of a child actually residing in the certified foster home.

(2000 H 332, eff. 1–1–01; 2000 H 448, eff. 10–5–00; 1996 H 265, eff. 3–3–97)

Historical and Statutory Notes

Ed. Note: The amendment of this section by 2000 H 332, eff. 1–1–01, and 2000 H 448, eff. 10–5–00, was identical. See *Baldwin's Ohio Legislative Service Annotated*, 2000, pages 6/L–2155 and 6/L–2219, or the OH–LEGIS or OH–LEGIS–OLD database on Westlaw, for original versions of these Acts.

Amendment Note: 2000 H 332 deleted "family" before "foster home" throughout the section.

Amendment Note: 2000 H 448 deleted "family" after "certified" throughout the section.

Library References

Infants ⊂⊃192, 228(1).
Westlaw Topic No. 211.
C.J.S. Infants §§ 41, 53 to 55, 57, 69 to 85.

Research References

Treatises and Practice Aids
Giannelli & Yeomans, Ohio Juvenile Law § 19:2, Place of Detention.

Notes of Decisions

Jurisdiction 1

---

1. **Jurisdiction**

Pursuant to RC 2151.23(A), the Probate and Juvenile Division of the Muskingum County Court of Common Pleas has exclusive original jurisdiction to issue orders of support in cases brought under RC 2151.27 to RC 2151.331, including orders complying with RC 2151.33(B)(2)(a). The language of RC 2301.03(AA) establishing the powers and duties of the judge of the Domestic Relations Division of the Muskingum County Court of Common Pleas does not modify or restrict the exclusive original jurisdiction of the juvenile court in this regard. OAG 05–003.

HEARING AND DISPOSITION

2151.35 Hearing procedure; findings; record

(A)(1) Except as otherwise provided by division (A)(3) of this section or in section 2152.13 of the Revised Code, the juvenile court may conduct its hearings in an informal manner and may adjourn its hearings from time to time. The court may exclude the general public from its hearings in a particular case if the court holds a separate hearing to determine whether that exclusion is appropriate. If the court decides that exclusion of the general public is appropriate, the court still may admit to a particular hearing or all of the hearings relating to a particular case those persons who have a direct interest in the case and those who demonstrate that their need for access outweighs the interest in keeping the hearing closed.

Except cases involving children who are alleged to be unruly or delinquent children for being habitual or chronic truants and except as otherwise provided in section 2152.13 of the Revised Code, all cases involving children shall be heard separately and apart from the trial of cases against adults. The court may excuse the attendance of the child at the hearing in cases involving abused, neglected, or dependent children. The court shall hear and determine all cases of children without a jury, except cases involving serious youthful offenders under section 2152.13 of the Revised Code.

If a complaint alleges a child to be a delinquent child, unruly child, or juvenile traffic offender, the court shall require the parent, guardian, or custodian of the child to attend all proceedings of the court regarding the child. If a parent, guardian, or custodian fails to so attend, the court may find the parent, guardian, or custodian in contempt.

If the court finds from clear and convincing evidence that the child violated section 2151.87 of the Revised Code, the court shall proceed in accordance with divisions (F) and (G) of that section.

If the court at the adjudicatory hearing finds from clear and convincing evidence that the child is an abused, neglected, or dependent child, the court shall proceed, in accordance with division (B) of this section, to hold a dispositional hearing and hear the evidence as to the proper disposition to be made under section 2151.353 of the Revised Code. If the court at the adjudicatory hearing finds beyond a reasonable doubt that the child is a delinquent or unruly child or a juvenile traffic offender, the court shall proceed immediately, or at a postponed hearing, to hear the evidence as to the proper disposition to be made under section 2151.354 or Chapter 2152. of the Revised Code. If the court at the adjudicatory hearing finds beyond a reasonable doubt that the child is an unruly child for being an habitual truant, or that the child is an unruly child for being an habitual truant and that the parent, guardian, or other person having care of the child has failed to cause the child's attendance at school in violation of section 3321.38 of the Revised Code, the court shall proceed to hold a hearing to hear the evidence as to the proper disposition to be made in regard to the child under division (C)(1) of section 2151.354 of the Revised Code and the proper action to take in regard to the parent, guardian, or other person having care of the child under division (C)(2) of section 2151.354 of the Revised Code. If the court at the adjudicatory hearing finds beyond a reasonable doubt that the child is a delinquent child for being a chronic truant or for being an habitual truant who previously has been adjudicated an unruly child for being an habitual truant, or that the child is a delinquent child for either of those reasons and the parent, guardian, or other person having care of the child has failed to cause the child's attendance at school in violation of section 3321.38 of the Revised Code, the court shall proceed to hold a hearing to hear the evidence as to the proper disposition to be made in regard to the child under division (A)(7) (a) of section 2152.19 of the Revised Code and the proper action to take in regard to the parent, guardian, or other person having care of the child under division (A)(7) (b) of section 2152.19 of the Revised Code.

If the court does not find the child to have violated section 2151.87 of the Revised Code or to be an abused, neglected, dependent, delinquent, or unruly child or a juvenile traffic offender, it shall order that the case be dismissed and that the child be discharged from any detention or restriction theretofore ordered.

(2) A record of all testimony and other oral proceedings in juvenile court shall be made in all proceedings that are held pursuant to section 2151.414 of the Revised Code or in which an order of disposition may be made pursuant to division (A)(4) of section 2151.353 of the Revised Code, and shall be made upon request in any other proceedings. The record shall be made as provided in section 2301.20 of the Revised Code.

(3) The authority of a juvenile court to exclude the general public from its hearings that is provided by division (A)(1) of this section does not limit or affect any right of a victim of a crime or delinquent act, or of a victim's representative, under Chapter 2930. of the Revised Code.

(B)(1) If the court at an adjudicatory hearing determines that a child is an abused, neglected, or dependent child, the court shall not issue a dispositional order until after the court holds a separate dispositional hearing. The court may hold the dispositional hearing for an adjudicated abused, neglected, or dependent child immediately after the adjudicatory hearing if all parties were served prior to the adjudicatory hearing with all documents required for the dispositional hearing. The dispositional hearing may not be held more than thirty days after the adjudicatory hearing is held. The court, upon the request of any party or the guardian ad litem of the child, may continue a dispositional hearing for a reasonable time not to exceed the time limits set forth in this division to enable a party to obtain or consult counsel. The dispositional hearing shall not be held more than ninety days after the date on which the complaint in the case was filed.

If the dispositional hearing is not held within the period of time required by this division, the court, on its own motion or the motion of any party or the guardian ad litem of the child, shall dismiss the complaint without prejudice.

(2) The dispositional hearing shall be conducted in accordance with all of the following:

(a) The judge or referee who presided at the adjudicatory hearing shall preside, if possible, at the dispositional hearing;

(b) The court may admit any evidence that is material and relevant, including, but not limited to, hearsay, opinion, and documentary evidence;

(c) Medical examiners and each investigator who prepared a social history shall not be cross-examined, except upon consent of the parties, for good cause shown, or as the court in its discretion may direct. Any party may offer evidence supplementing, explaining, or disputing any information contained in the social history or other reports that may be used by the court in determining disposition.

(3) After the conclusion of the dispositional hearing, the court shall enter an appropriate judgment within seven days and shall schedule the date for the hearing to be held pursuant to section 2151.415 of the Revised Code. The court may make any order of disposition that is set forth in section 2151.353 of the Revised Code. A copy of the judgment shall be given to each party and to the child's guardian ad litem. If the judgment is conditional, the order shall state the conditions of the judgment. If the child is not returned to the child's own home, the court shall determine which school district shall bear the cost of the child's education and shall comply with section 2151.36 of the Revised Code.

(4) As part of its dispositional order, the court may issue any order described in division (B) of section 2151.33 of the Revised Code.

(C) The court shall give all parties to the action and the child's guardian ad litem notice of the adjudicatory and dispositional hearings in accordance with the Juvenile Rules.

(D) If the court issues an order pursuant to division (A)(4) of section 2151.353 of the Revised Code committing a child to the permanent custody of a public children services agency or a private child placing agency, the parents of the child whose parental rights were terminated cease to be parties to the action upon the issuance of the order. This division is not intended to eliminate or restrict any right of the parents to appeal the permanent custody order issued pursuant to division (A)(4) of section 2151.353 of the Revised Code.

(E) Each juvenile court shall schedule its hearings in accordance with the time requirements of this chapter.

(F) In cases regarding abused, neglected, or dependent children, the court may admit any statement of a child that the court determines to be excluded by the hearsay rule if the proponent of the statement informs the adverse party of the proponent's intention to offer the statement and of the particulars of the statement, including the name of the declarant, sufficiently in advance of the hearing to provide the party with a fair opportunity to prepare to challenge, respond to, or defend against the statement, and the court determines all of the following:

(1) The statement has circumstantial guarantees of trustworthiness;

(2) The statement is offered as evidence of a material fact;

(3) The statement is more probative on the point for which it is offered than any other evidence that the proponent can procure through reasonable efforts;

(4) The general purposes of the evidence rules and the interests of justice will best be served by the admission of the statement into evidence.

(G) If a child is alleged to be an abused child, the court may order that the testimony of the child be taken by deposition. On motion of the prosecuting attorney, guardian ad litem, or any party, or in its own discretion, the court may order that the deposition be videotaped. Any deposition taken under this division shall be taken with a judge or referee present.

If a deposition taken under this division is intended to be offered as evidence at the hearing, it shall be filed with the court. Part or all of the deposition is admissible in evidence if counsel for all parties had an opportunity and similar motive at the time of the taking of the deposition to develop the testimony by direct, cross, or redirect examination and the judge determines that there is reasonable cause to believe that if the child were to testify in person at the hearing, the child would experience emotional trauma as a result of participating at the hearing.

(2002 H 400, eff. 4–3–03; 2000 S 179, § 3, eff. 1–1–02; 2000 S 179, § 1, eff. 4–9–01; 2000 S 218, eff. 3–15–01; 2000 S 181, eff. 9–4–00; 1996 H 124, eff. 3–31–97; 1996 H 274, eff. 8–8–96; 1995 H 1, eff. 1–1–96; 1988 S 89, eff. 1–1–89; 1980 H 695; 1975 H 85; 1969 H 320)

Historical and Statutory Notes

Ed. Note: Former 2151.35 repealed by 1969 H 320, eff. 11–19–69; 1969 S 49; 132 v S 278; 130 v H 299, H 879; 127 v 547; 125 v 324; 1953 H 1; GC 1639–30; see now 2151.352 for provisions analogous to former 2151.35.

Pre–1953 H 1 Amendments: 121 v 557; 119 v 731; 117 v 520

Amendment Note: 2002 H 400 substituted "(7)" for "(6)" twice in the last sentence of the fifth paragraph of division (A).

Amendment Note: 2000 S 179, § 3, eff. 1–1–02, rewrote division (A), which prior thereto read:

"(A)(1) The juvenile court may conduct its hearings in an informal manner and may adjourn its hearings from time to time. In the hearing of any case, the general public may be excluded and only those persons admitted who have a direct interest in the case.

"Except cases involving children who are alleged to be unruly or delinquent children for being habitual or chronic truants, all cases involving children shall be heard separately and apart from the trial of cases against adults. The court may excuse the attendance of the child at the hearing in cases involving abused, neglected, or dependent children. The court shall hear and determine all cases of children without a jury.

"If a complaint alleges a child to be a delinquent child, unruly child, or juvenile traffic offender, the court shall require the parent, guardian, or custodian of the child to attend all proceedings of the court regarding the child. If a parent, guardian, or custodian fails to so attend, the court may find the parent, guardian, or custodian in contempt.

"If the court at the adjudicatory hearing finds from clear and convincing evidence that the child is an abused, neglected, or dependent child, the court shall proceed, in accordance with division (B) of this section, to hold a dispositional hearing and hear the evidence as to the proper disposition to be made under section 2151.353 of the Revised Code. If the court at the adjudicatory hearing finds beyond a reasonable doubt that the child is a delinquent or unruly child or a juvenile traffic offender, the court shall proceed immediately, or at a postponed hearing, to hear the evidence as to the proper disposition to be made under sections 2151.352 to 2151.355 of the Revised Code. If the court at the adjudicatory hearing finds beyond a reasonable doubt that the child is an unruly child for being an habitual truant, or that the child is an unruly child for being an habitual truant and that the parent, guardian, or other person having care of the child has failed to cause the child's attendance at school in violation of section 3321.38 of the Revised Code, the court shall proceed to hold a hearing to hear the evidence as to the proper disposition to be made in regard to the child under division (C)(1) of section 2151.354 of the Revised Code and the proper action to take in regard to the parent, guardian, or other person having care of the child under division (C)(2) of section 2151.354 of the Revised Code. If the court at the adjudicatory hearing finds beyond a reasonable doubt that the child is a delinquent child for being a chronic truant or for being an habitual truant who previously has been adjudicated an unruly child for being an habitual truant, or that the child is a delinquent child for either of those reasons and the parent, guardian, or other person having care of the child has failed to cause the child's attendance at school in violation of section 3321.38 of the Revised Code, the court shall proceed to hold a hearing to hear the evidence as to the proper disposition to be made in regard to the child under division (A)(24)(a) of section 2151.355 of the Revised Code and the proper action to take in regard to the parent, guardian, or other person having care of the child under division (A)(24)(b) of section 2151.355 of the Revised Code.

"If the court does not find the child to be an abused, neglected, dependent, delinquent, or unruly child or a juvenile traffic offender, it shall order that the complaint be dismissed and that the child be discharged from any detention or restriction theretofore ordered.

"(2) A record of all testimony and other oral proceedings in juvenile court shall be made in all proceedings that are held pursuant to section 2151.414 of the Revised Code or in which an order of disposition may be made pursuant to division (A)(4) of section 2151.353 of the Revised Code, and shall be made upon request in any other proceedings. The record shall be made as provided in section 2301.20 of the Revised Code."

Amendment Note: 2000 S 179, § 1, eff. 4–9–01, deleted ", except that section 2151.47 of the Revised Code shall apply in cases involving a complaint that jointly alleges that a child is an unruly or delinquent child for being an habitual or chronic truant and that a parent, guardian, or other person having care of the child failed to cause the child's attendance at school" from the end of the second paragraph in division (A)(1).

Amendment Note: 2000 S 218 added the fourth paragraph in division (A)(1); and inserted "have violated section 2151.87 of the Revised Code or to" in the sixth paragraph in division (A)(1).

Amendment Note: 2000 S 181 designated and rewrote division (A)(1); and designated division (A)(2). Prior to designation and amendment, division (A)(1) read:

"(A) The juvenile court may conduct its hearings in an informal manner and may adjourn its hearings from time to time. In the hearing of any case, the general public may be excluded and only those persons admitted who have a direct interest in the case.

"All cases involving children shall be heard separately and apart from the trial of cases against adults. The court may excuse the attendance of the child at the hearing in cases involving abused, neglected, or dependent children. The court shall hear and determine all cases of children without a jury.

"If the court at the adjudicatory hearing finds from clear and convincing evidence that the child is an abused, neglected, or dependent child, the court shall proceed, in accordance with division (B) of this section, to hold a dispositional hearing and hear the evidence as to the proper disposition to be made under section 2151.353 of the Revised Code. If the court at the adjudicatory hearing finds beyond a reasonable doubt that the child is a delinquent or unruly child or a juvenile traffic offender, the court shall proceed immediately, or at a postponed hearing, to hear the evidence as to the proper disposition to be made under sections 2151.352 to 2151.355 of the Revised Code. If the court does not find the child to be an abused, neglected, dependent, delinquent, or unruly child or a juvenile traffic offender, it shall order that the complaint be dismissed and that the child be discharged from any detention or restriction theretofore ordered."

Amendment Note: 1996 H 124 deleted former division (H), which read:

"(H)(1) Before accepting from an alleged delinquent child a plea of guilty or no contest to the commission of an act that is a category one or category two offense, the court shall inform the child of the possible length of commitment to the legal custody of the department of youth services to which the child could be subject under section 2151.26 of the Revised Code.

"(2) As used in division (H) of this section, 'category one offense' and 'category two offense' have the same meanings as in section 2151.26 of the Revised Code."

Amendment Note: 1996 H 274 rewrote the second sentence in the first paragraph in division (B)(1); added the third sentence in the first paragraph in division (B)(1); and substituted "shall comply with section 2151.36 of the Revised Code" for "may fix an amount of support to be paid by the responsible parent or to be paid from public funds" in division (B)(3). Prior to amendment, the second sentence in the first paragraph in division (B)(1) read:

"The dispositional hearing for an adjudicated abused, neglected, or dependent child shall be held at least one day but not more than thirty days after the adjudicatory hearing is held, except that the dispositional hearing may be held immediately after the adjudicatory hearing if all parties were served prior to the adjudicatory hearing with all documents required for the dispositional hearing and all parties consent to the dispositional hearing being held immediately after the adjudicatory hearing."

Amendment Note: 1995 H 1 added division (H); and made changes to reflect gender neutral language and other nonsubstantive changes.

Cross References

Adjudicatory hearing, Juv R 29
Child sex offense victims, deposition, 2152.81
Disposition of child committed to youth services department, 5139.06
Hearings, Juv R 27
Juvenile court proceedings for truancy, 3321.22
Recordings of proceedings, Juv R 37
Trial by jury, O Const Art I, § 5
Waiver of rights, Juv R 3

Library References

Infants ☞173, 203 to 204, 210, 221, 246.
Westlaw Topic No. 211.
C.J.S. Infants §§ 50, 57 to 86.
Baldwin's Ohio Legislative Service, 1988 Laws of Ohio, S 89—LSC Analysis, p 5–571

Research References

ALR Library
39 ALR 5th 103, Propriety of Exclusion of Press or Other Media Representatives from Civil Trial.

Encyclopedias
OH Jur. 3d Constitutional Law § 519, Evidence, Argument, and Witnesses.
OH Jur. 3d Courts & Judges § 18, Courts of Common Pleas—Juvenile Division and Juvenile Courts.
OH Jur. 3d Evidence & Witnesses § 253, Statements of Children With Respect to Sexual or Physical Abuse as Hearsay.
OH Jur. 3d Family Law § 1489, "Unruly Child".
OH Jur. 3d Family Law § 1539, Powers and Duties—Records and Reports.
OH Jur. 3d Family Law § 1595, Permanent Custody.
OH Jur. 3d Family Law § 1655, Right to Attend; Public or Private Hearing.
OH Jur. 3d Family Law § 1656, Right to Jury Trial.
OH Jur. 3d Family Law § 1668, Initial Procedure—on Admission.
OH Jur. 3d Family Law § 1670, Required Degree of Proof.
OH Jur. 3d Family Law § 1672, Testimony of Child.
OH Jur. 3d Family Law § 1674, Hearsay.
OH Jur. 3d Family Law § 1678, Generally—Placement of Child Until Dispositional Hearing.
OH Jur. 3d Family Law § 1681, Conduct of Hearing; Advisement of Rights.
OH Jur. 3d Family Law § 1693, Permanent Custody.

Forms
Ohio Jurisprudence Pleading and Practice Forms § 63:1, Introduction.

Treatises and Practice Aids
Baldwin's Ohio Handbook Series—Trial Handbook § 4:1, Criminal Procedure; in General.
Baldwin's Ohio Handbook Series—Trial Handbook § 26:30, Hearsay Exception—Declarant Unavailable—Child Abuse.
Klein, Darling, & Terez, Baldwin's Ohio Practice Civil Practice § 1:26, Civ. R. 1(C)(1): Upon Appeal to Review Any Judgment, Order, or Ruling--Appeals in Supreme Court--Role of Revised Code Provisions Purporting to Control Application of Civil Rules.
Klein, Darling, & Terez, Baldwin's Ohio Practice Civil Practice § 1:29, Civ. R. 1(C)(1): Upon Appeal to Review Any Judgment, Order, or Ruling--Appeals in Courts of Appeals--Role of Revised Code Provisions Purporting to Control Application of Civil...
Klein, Darling, & Terez, Baldwin's Ohio Practice Civil Practice § 1:32, Civ. R. 1(C)(1): Upon Appeal to Review Any Judgment, Order, or Ruling--Appeals to Common Pleas Courts from Decisions of Governmental Entities--Role of Revised Code Provisions Purporting to...
Katz, Giannelli, Blair and Lipton, Baldwin's Ohio Practice, Criminal Law, § 1:6, Ohio Rules of Criminal Procedure.
Katz, Giannelli, Blair and Lipton, Baldwin's Ohio Practice, Criminal Law, § 66:3, Juvenile Proceedings—Closure.
Giannelli and Snyder, Baldwin's Ohio Practice, Evidence, R 807, Hearsay Exceptions; Child Statements in Abuse Cases.
Giannelli and Snyder, Baldwin's Ohio Practice, Evidence, § 102.5, Substance & Procedure.
Giannelli and Snyder, Baldwin's Ohio Practice, Evidence, § 402.5, Ohio Statutes.
Giannelli and Snyder, Baldwin's Ohio Practice, Evidence, § 802.5, Ohio Statutes.
Giannelli and Snyder, Baldwin's Ohio Practice, Evidence, § 807.1, Introduction.
Giannelli and Snyder, Baldwin's Ohio Practice, Evidence, § 807.3, History of Rule.
Carlin, Baldwin's Ohio Practice, Merrick-Rippner Probate Law § 104:1, Juvenile Court—Introduction.
Carlin, Baldwin's Ohio Practice, Merrick-Rippner Probate Law § 104:5, Juvenile Courts—Constitutional Issues—Right to Notice, Counsel, and Trial.
Carlin, Baldwin's Ohio Practice, Merrick-Rippner Probate Law § 105:7, Juvenile Court—Attachment of Jurisdiction.
Carlin, Baldwin's Ohio Practice, Merrick-Rippner Probate Law § 106:2, Juvenile Court Jurisdiction—Delinquent Child—Quantum of Proof in Delinquency Hearings.
Carlin, Baldwin's Ohio Practice, Merrick-Rippner Probate Law § 106:9, Juvenile Court Jurisdiction—Unruly Child—Quantum of Proof in Unruly Child Hearing.
Carlin, Baldwin's Ohio Practice, Merrick-Rippner Probate Law § 107:1, Intake.
Carlin, Baldwin's Ohio Practice, Merrick-Rippner Probate Law § 107:9, Parties to Proceedings.
Carlin, Baldwin's Ohio Practice, Merrick-Rippner Probate Law § 106:12, Juvenile Court Jurisdiction—Neglected Child—Quantum of Proof in Neglect Hearings.
Carlin, Baldwin's Ohio Practice, Merrick-Rippner Probate Law § 106:15, Juvenile Court Jurisdiction—Dependent Child—Quantum of Proof in Dependency Hearings.
Carlin, Baldwin's Ohio Practice, Merrick-Rippner Probate Law § 106:18, Juvenile Court Jurisdiction—Abused Child—Quantum of Proof in Abuse Hearings.
Carlin, Baldwin's Ohio Practice, Merrick-Rippner Probate Law § 107:10, Contents and Issuance of Summons.
Carlin, Baldwin's Ohio Practice, Merrick-Rippner Probate Law § 107:40, Testimony of Child in Child Abuse Proceedings.
Carlin, Baldwin's Ohio Practice, Merrick-Rippner Probate Law § 107:43, Scheduling Juvenile Court Hearing.
Carlin, Baldwin's Ohio Practice, Merrick-Rippner Probate Law § 107:47, Adjudicatory Hearings—Hearing Without a Jury.
Carlin, Baldwin's Ohio Practice, Merrick-Rippner Probate Law § 107:50, Adjudicatory Hearings—Applicability of Rules of Court.
Carlin, Baldwin's Ohio Practice, Merrick-Rippner Probate Law § 107:52, Adjudicatory Hearings—Confidentiality of Juvenile Court Proceedings.
Carlin, Baldwin's Ohio Practice, Merrick-Rippner Probate Law § 107:56, Adjudicatory Hearings—Attendance of Parties at Hearing.
Carlin, Baldwin's Ohio Practice, Merrick-Rippner Probate Law § 107:57, Adjudicatory Hearings—Admission or Denial of Complaint.
Carlin, Baldwin's Ohio Practice, Merrick-Rippner Probate Law § 107:59, Adjudicatory Hearings—Proof Beyond a Reasonable Doubt.
Carlin, Baldwin's Ohio Practice, Merrick-Rippner Probate Law § 107:60, Adjudicatory Hearings—Right to Transcript of Proceedings.
Carlin, Baldwin's Ohio Practice, Merrick-Rippner Probate Law § 107:72, Dispositional Hearings—Procedure.
Carlin, Baldwin's Ohio Practice, Merrick-Rippner Probate Law § 107:76, Disposition of Abused, Neglected, or Dependent Child—Types of Orders Court May Make.
Carlin, Baldwin's Ohio Practice, Merrick-Rippner Probate Law § 107:78, Disposition of Abused, Neglected, or Dependent Child—Temporary Custody.
Carlin, Baldwin's Ohio Practice, Merrick-Rippner Probate Law § 107:115, Juvenile Court Records—Statistical.
Carlin, Baldwin's Ohio Practice, Merrick-Rippner Probate Law § 107:173, Order Adjudging Child Dependent, Neglected, or Abused—Form.

Carlin, Baldwin's Ohio Practice, Merrick-Rippner Probate Law § 107:174, Order Committing Child to Temporary Custody of Public or Private Agency or Foster Care—Form.

Carlin, Baldwin's Ohio Practice, Merrick-Rippner Probate Law § 107:175, Order Committing Child to Permanent Custody of Public or Private Agency—Form.

Carlin, Baldwin's Ohio Practice, Merrick-Rippner Probate Law § 107:176, Order Placing Child in Planned Permanent Living Arrangement—Form.

Giannelli & Yeomans, Ohio Juvenile Law § 9:3, Time of Neglect.

Giannelli & Yeomans, Ohio Juvenile Law § 15:2, Intake.

Giannelli & Yeomans, Ohio Juvenile Law § 16:5, Parental Identification.

Giannelli & Yeomans, Ohio Juvenile Law § 18:2, Issuance of Summons: Proper Parties.

Giannelli & Yeomans, Ohio Juvenile Law § 20:6, Time Requirements.

Giannelli & Yeomans, Ohio Juvenile Law § 21:4, Depositions.

Giannelli & Yeomans, Ohio Juvenile Law § 23:1, Introduction.

Giannelli & Yeomans, Ohio Juvenile Law § 23:9, Uncontested Cases.

Giannelli & Yeomans, Ohio Juvenile Law § 25:2, Bifurcated Hearings.

Giannelli & Yeomans, Ohio Juvenile Law § 25:3, Judge or Magistrate.

Giannelli & Yeomans, Ohio Juvenile Law § 25:4, Time Requirements.

Giannelli & Yeomans, Ohio Juvenile Law § 25:8, Burden of Proof.

Giannelli & Yeomans, Ohio Juvenile Law § 25:9, Evidence.

Giannelli & Yeomans, Ohio Juvenile Law § 30:3, Costs of Dispositions.

Giannelli & Yeomans, Ohio Juvenile Law § 30:4, Dispositional Alternatives for Abuse, Neglect or Dependency.

Giannelli & Yeomans, Ohio Juvenile Law § 30:6, Temporary Custody.

Giannelli & Yeomans, Ohio Juvenile Law § 31:2, Filing of Motion.

Giannelli & Yeomans, Ohio Juvenile Law § 32:2, Jurisdiction Over Parents and Others.

Giannelli & Yeomans, Ohio Juvenile Law § 33:6, Revocation of Probation.

Giannelli & Yeomans, Ohio Juvenile Law § 34:4, Final Order Requirement.

Giannelli & Yeomans, Ohio Juvenile Law § 34:9, Right to Transcript.

Giannelli & Yeomans, Ohio Juvenile Law § 35:2, Confidentiality Requirement.

Giannelli & Yeomans, Ohio Juvenile Law § 22:19, Public Hearing; Victims; Gag Orders.

Giannelli & Yeomans, Ohio Juvenile Law § 23:10, Jury Trials.

Giannelli & Yeomans, Ohio Juvenile Law § 23:11, Public Trials; Gag Orders.

Giannelli & Yeomans, Ohio Juvenile Law § 23:13, Burden of Proof.

Giannelli & Yeomans, Ohio Juvenile Law § 23:16, Evidence—Hearsay.

Giannelli & Yeomans, Ohio Juvenile Law § 23:23, Confrontation—Face-To-Face Confrontation.

Giannelli & Yeomans, Ohio Juvenile Law § 23:24, Confrontation—Cross-Examination.

Giannelli & Yeomans, Ohio Juvenile Law § 23:30, Right to a Transcript.

Giannelli & Yeomans, Ohio Juvenile Law § 23:32, Juvenile & Adult Cases; Truancy.

Giannelli & Yeomans, Ohio Juvenile Law § 25:10, Social History & Medical Examinations.

Giannelli & Yeomans, Ohio Juvenile Law § 25:12, Transcripts.

Giannelli & Yeomans, Ohio Juvenile Law § 25:13, Judgment & Records.

Giannelli & Yeomans, Ohio Juvenile Law § 30:11, Permanent Custody—"Best Interest" Factors.

Law Review and Journal Commentaries

Confidentiality of Juvenile Court Proceedings, William A. Kurtz. 1 Prob L J Ohio 115 (May/June 1991).

Due Process in Ohio for the Delinquent and Unruly Child, Max Kravitz. 2 Cap U L Rev 53 (1973).

The Effect of the Double Jeopardy Clause on Juvenile Proceedings, James G. Carr. 6 U Tol L Rev 1 (Fall 1974).

In re T.R.: Not In Front of the Children, Bill Dickhaut. I Ky Children's Rts J 10 (July 1991).

Judge's Column, Hon. William W. Weaver. (Ed. note: Judge Weaver discusses children's testimony in abuse cases). 17 Lake Legal Views 1 (July 1994).

Juvenile Delinquent and Unruly Proceedings in Ohio: Unconstitutional Adjudications, Note. 24 Clev St L Rev 602 (1975).

Representing Abused and Neglected Children: When Protecting Children Means Seeking the Dismissal of Court Proceedings, Douglas J. Besharov. 20 J Fam L 217 (1981–82).

Notes of Decisions

Adult facilities 4
Best interest of child 9
Constitutional issues 1
Evidence and testimony 6
Procedural issues 7
Public access 3
Representation by counsel 5
Separate hearings 2
Time limit for filing report 8

---

1. Constitutional issues

Juvenile's counsel was not ineffective by failing to request a second competency evaluation; while physician's final conclusion as to juvenile's competency was mixed, there was sufficient evidence that juvenile's deficiencies in understanding nature of proceedings before him could be compensated for by special measures allowed by juvenile court. In re Stone (Ohio App. 12 Dist., Clinton, 06-16-2003) No. CA2002-09-035, 2003-Ohio-3071, 2003 WL 21373156, Unreported, appeal not allowed 100 Ohio St.3d 1432, 797 N.E.2d 512, 2003-Ohio-5396. Infants ⚖ 205

A judgment of delinquency against a sixth grader is void based upon a municipal ordinance that is unconstitutionally vague in prohibiting the disruption, disturbance or interference of school activity without specifying what constitutes such behavior; as a result a charge may be filed for something as minor as throwing a spitball to something as serious as assaulting a school employee with no reasonably clear guidelines to prevent official arbitrariness or discrimination in its enforcement. In re Williams (Ohio App. 5 Dist., Stark, 02-22-2000) No. 1999CA00128, 2000 WL 222033, Unreported.

Juvenile procedure rule that no public use shall be made by any person of any juvenile court record must yield when it impinges on the public's due process right to a meaningful hearing on a motion to close proceedings. State ex rel. Plain Dealer Publishing Co. v. Floyd (Ohio, 08-30-2006) 111 Ohio St.3d 56, 855 N.E.2d 35, 2006-Ohio-4437. Infants ⚖ 203

If a parent expresses uncertainty or misunderstandings about his or her decision to waive parental rights, the trial court's acceptance of the waiver is improper. In re Terrence (Ohio App. 6 Dist., 07-13-2005) 162 Ohio App.3d 229, 833 N.E.2d 306, 2005-Ohio-3600. Infants ⚖ 199

While a full colloquy for admissions on disposition is not required by statute or rule governing juvenile proceedings, fundamental due process requires that when a parent is waiving the fundamental right to care for and have custody of a child, the trial court must have a meaningful dialogue with that parent to be certain that the consent is truly voluntary. In re Terrence (Ohio App. 6 Dist., 07-13-2005) 162 Ohio App.3d 229, 833 N.E.2d 306, 2005-Ohio-3600. Infants ⚖ 199

Mother whose children were subjects of county's motion for permanent custody had statutory right to rebut guardian ad litem's unsworn testimony concerning suitability of placement with mother's sister and condition of her home, as these matters were not contained in guardian ad litem's written report and were not previously addressed by sister in her earlier testimony; thus, refusal to permit such rebuttal evidence violated due process. In re Sadiku (Ohio App. 9 Dist., 11-22-2000) 139 Ohio App.3d 263, 743 N.E.2d 507. Constitutional Law ⚖ 274(5); Infants ⚖ 207

The right of parents to raise their children is basic and essential, protected by due process of law. In re Sadiku (Ohio App. 9 Dist., 11-22-2000) 139 Ohio App.3d 263, 743 N.E.2d 507. Constitutional Law ⚖ 274(5)

Due process requires "fundamentally fair procedures" when a state attempts to terminate parental rights. In re Sadiku (Ohio App. 9 Dist., 11-22-2000) 139 Ohio App.3d 263, 743 N.E.2d 507. Constitutional Law ⚖ 274(5)

Delay of 28 months between trial on county agency's filing of motion for permanent custody on ground that children were dependent and issuance of judgment denied mother her basic right to due process, where one of trial court's major factual findings was not supported by evidence in record, and there was nothing in judgment which indicated that court had independent recollection of evidence offered. In re Omosun Children (Ohio App. 11 Dist., 10-16-1995) 106 Ohio App.3d 813, 667 N.E.2d 431. Constitutional Law ⇔ 274(5); Infants ⇔ 193

Twenty-eight months of limbo in juvenile dispositional hearing is a per se due process violation, barring extraordinary circumstances. In re Omosun Children (Ohio App. 11 Dist., 10-16-1995) 106 Ohio App.3d 813, 667 N.E.2d 431. Constitutional Law ⇔ 274(5); Infants ⇔ 204

Statute requiring dispositional hearings to be held within 90 days of filing of complaint in child custody cases involving abused or neglected children did not require dismissal without prejudice of child custody case in which dispositional hearing was begun, but not completed, within 90 days of filing of complaint; any other conclusion would have been contrary to legislative intent to expedite hearings in child-custody cases, frustrated judicial process, and arguably amounted to withdrawal of due process rights of parties, particularly those of child. In re Brown (Ohio App. 2 Dist., 08-03-1994) 96 Ohio App.3d 306, 644 N.E.2d 1117. Infants ⇔ 204

Juvenile court committed reversible error in forcing parent to testify in dependency proceeding over her assertion of her Fifth Amendment privilege against self-incrimination; right to refrain from testifying against oneself attaches to dependency action in juvenile court, and testimony elicited from parent in such proceeding could open door for potential prosecution, at minimum, for child endangering. In re Billman (Ohio App. 8 Dist., 11-22-1993) 92 Ohio App.3d 279, 634 N.E.2d 1050, dismissed, jurisdictional motion overruled 69 Ohio St.3d 1409, 629 N.E.2d 1370. Infants ⇔ 253; Witnesses ⇔ 293.5

Public had First Amendment right of access to probable cause hearing in juvenile delinquency case and to parts of amenability hearing involving prior juvenile record, but public had no right of access to portions of amenability hearing involving information about child's psychological, social, and family histories. In re N.H. (Ohio Com.Pl., 06-09-1992) 63 Ohio Misc.2d 285, 626 N.E.2d 697. Constitutional Law ⇔ 90.1(3); Infants ⇔ 203

Statute establishing admissibility of otherwise inadmissible hearsay statements by child who is subject of abuse, neglect, or dependency proceeding is inconsistent with evidentiary rules dealing with hearsay and has no force and effect; subject matter of statute was already covered by hearsay rule and various hearsay exceptions. In re Coy (Ohio 1993) 67 Ohio St.3d 215, 616 N.E.2d 1105. Courts ⇔ 85(1)

Illegal seizure of digital pager from juvenile suspected of giving refuge to fugitive drug dealer did not taint evidence which underlay her adjudication for obstructing justice; police lawfully seized Western Union receipt indicating that juvenile had wired fugitive $4,000 at his request, during search incident to arrest, and juvenile's admission that she wired money to fugitive logically flowed from seizure of receipt, rather than from illegal search that produced digital pager. In re Smalley (Cuyahoga 1989) 62 Ohio App.3d 435, 575 N.E.2d 1198. Infants ⇔ 174

The use of two-way closed circuit television for the testimony of a child in a civil abuse, neglect, or dependency hearing does not violate the confrontation rights of the parents or due process. In re Burchfield (Athens 1988) 51 Ohio App.3d 148, 555 N.E.2d 325. Constitutional Law ⇔ 314; Infants ⇔ 207; Trial ⇔ 38; Witnesses ⇔ 228

Delinquency proceedings in juvenile court do not require indictment or trial by jury under US Const Am 5, US Const Am 6, US Const Am 14, or under O Const Art I, § 5 and O Const Art I, § 10. In re Agler (Ohio 1969) 19 Ohio St.2d 70, 249 N.E.2d 808, 48 O.O.2d 85. Infants ⇔ 197; Jury ⇔ 19.5

Where a juvenile has received the following essentials of due process and fair treatment, (1) written notice of the specific charge or factual allegations, given to the juvenile and his parents or guardian sufficiently in advance of the hearing to permit preparation; (2) notification to the juvenile and his parents of the juvenile's right to be represented by counsel retained by them, or, if they are unable to afford counsel, that counsel will be appointed to represent the juvenile; (3) application of the constitutional privileges against self-incrimination; and (4), absent a valid confession, a determination of delinquency and an order of commitment based only on sworn testimony subjected to the opportunity for cross-examination in accordance with constitutional requirements, such juvenile has not been deprived of due process under either the Constitution of the United States or the Constitution of the State of Ohio. In re Baker (Hocking 1969) 18 Ohio App.2d 276, 248 N.E.2d 620, 47 O.O.2d 411.

Proceedings in a juvenile court are not criminal in nature, and a minor charged with delinquency in a juvenile court is not prosecuted for a criminal offense; and the constitutional rights of such minor with respect to self- incrimination are not invaded by compelling such minor to testify. State v. Shardell (Cuyahoga 1958) 107 Ohio App. 338, 153 N.E.2d 510, 79 Ohio Law Abs. 534, 8 O.O.2d 262.

Despite asserted state interest in protecting anonymity of juvenile offenders in order to further rehabilitation, West Virginia statute violated First and Fourteenth Amendments by making it a crime for newspaper to publish, without written approval of juvenile court, name of any youth charged as a juvenile offender, where name was lawfully obtained by monitoring police band radio frequency and interviewing eyewitnesses; even assuming statute served a state interest of the highest order, it did not accomplish its stated purpose where it did not restrict publication by electronic media or any form of publication except "newspapers." Smith v. Daily Mail Pub. Co. (U.S.W.Va. 1979) 99 S.Ct. 2667, 443 U.S. 97, 61 L.Ed.2d 399. Constitutional Law ⇔ 90.1(3); Infants ⇔ 132; Infants ⇔ 12(9)

Even though state statute provided for closed juvenile hearings unless specifically open to the public by court order, and even though there was no explicit order opening hearing on delinquency petition, where members of the press were present with full knowledge of the presiding judge, the prosecutor, and the defense counsel, where no objection was made to presence of the press or to the photographing of the juvenile, and where there was no evidence that newspapers acquired information unlawfully or without the state's implicit approval, the name and picture of the juvenile were in the public domain and order which precluded the press from publishing the name or picture violated First and Fourteenth Amendments. Oklahoma Pub. Co. v. District Court In and For Oklahoma County (U.S.Okl. 1977) 97 S.Ct. 1045, 430 U.S. 308, 51 L.Ed.2d 355. Constitutional Law ⇔ 90.1(3); Constitutional Law ⇔ 274.1(2.1); Infants ⇔ 203

Defendant, who was prosecuted for grand larceny and burglary, was denied his constitutional right of confrontation of witnesses in state trial where he was precluded by protective order from cross-examining key prosecution witness to show that witness was on probation following an adjudication of juvenile delinquency, notwithstanding state statutory policy of protecting the anonymity of juvenile offenders; defendant had right to attempt to show that prosecution witness was biased because of his vulnerable status. Davis v. Alaska (U.S.Alaska 1974) 94 S.Ct. 1105, 415 U.S. 308, 39 L.Ed.2d 347. Criminal Law ⇔ 662.7

Juvenile court proceeding is not a "criminal prosecution" within meaning and reach of Sixth Amendment guaranteeing right to an impartial jury in all criminal prosecutions. McKeiver v. Pennsylvania (U.S.Pa. 1971) 91 S.Ct. 1976, 403 U.S. 528, 29 L.Ed.2d 647. Jury ⇔ 19.5

Where the Ohio statute required a full investigation of the facts underlying a charge of delinquency and a finding of delinquency that the accused had committed acts in violation of Ohio law, jeopardy attached at a hearing at which accused was bound over for trial as an adult. Sims v. Engle (C.A.6 (Ohio) 1980) 619 F.2d 598, certiorari denied 101 S.Ct. 1403, 450 U.S. 936, 67 L.Ed.2d 372.

Ohio Juvenile Act is not unconstitutional because it does not provide for jury trial. Ex parte Januszewski (S.D.Ohio 1911) 196 F. 123, 10 Ohio Law Rep. 151. Infants ⇔ 132; Jury ⇔ 10

Parents' claim against juvenile court and court officers challenging procedure used in preliminary hearing in neglect proceeding would not be dismissed with prejudice for mootness, since issue was capable of repetition yet evaded review, where length of time between preliminary hearing and hearing on merits would be too short to litigate claim, and parents were likely to encounter same procedure if child were returned, given family's history with county department of children services. Meyers v. Franklin County Court of Common Pleas (C.A.6 (Ohio), 08-07-2001) No. 99-4411, 23 Fed.Appx. 201, 2001 WL 1298942, Unreported, on subsequent appeal 81 Fed.Appx. 49, 2003 WL 22718238. Federal Courts ⇔ 13

State courts provided parents of minor child with opportunity to present their constitutional challenge to procedure juvenile court used in granting temporary custody of child to county agency, and thus District Court's abstention from parents' action under 1983 against juvenile court and court officials was warranted under the Younger abstention doctrine, where parents consented to temporary custody order. Meyers v. Franklin County Court of Common Pleas (C.A.6 (Ohio), 08-07-2001) No. 99-4411, 23 Fed.Appx. 201, 2001 WL 1298942, Unreported, on subsequent appeal 81 Fed.Appx. 49, 2003 WL 22718238. Federal Courts ⇔ 48

Federal court abstention under the Younger abstention doctrine is generally appropriate in matters of family relations such as child custody. Meyers v. Franklin County Court of Common Pleas (C.A.6 (Ohio), 08-07-2001) No. 99-4411, 23 Fed.Appx. 201, 2001 WL 1298942, Unreported, on subsequent appeal 81 Fed.Appx. 49, 2003 WL 22718238. Federal Courts ⇔ 47.1

Where a defendant and his wife were coerced to appear at an interview by a social worker threatening to remove their child from the home if they refuse to comply, and the interview was physically and verbally dominated by a police officer 6' 5" in height and weighing 330 pounds, it was reasonable for a defendant to believe he was not free to leave without creating serious consequences to his family even though the defendant was told he was free to leave; therefore, since no Miranda warnings were given, the suppression of defendant's statements at the interview was proper. State v Brown, No. 92WD098, 1993 WL 452096 (6th Dist Ct App, Wood, 11–5–93).

Any construction of RC 2151.354 that would allow commitment of an "unruly" child to the legal custody of the Ohio youth commission would be a violation of due process of law, and therefore an improper construction. OAG 72–071.

2. Separate hearings

The trial court committed reversible error when it failed to conduct separate adjudicatory and dispositional hearings, during child dependency proceedings; the parties were not served with all documents required for the dispositional hearing before the adjudicatory hearing, as required to conduct a dispositional hearing immediately after an adjudicatory hearing, and counsel for father twice objected to the court's failure to hold separate hearings. In re Monroe (Ohio App. 7 Dist., Belmont, 09-17-2004) No. 03 BE 50, 2004-Ohio-4988, 2004 WL 2334358, Unreported. Infants ⇐ 253

Dismissal of dependency complaint was warranted, where the Court of Appeals reversed the dependency finding based on the trial court's failure to conduct separate adjudicatory and dispositional hearings, a statute required that a dispositional order be entered within 90 days after the complaint was filed, and father filed a motion to dismiss the complaint on the 91st day due to the court's failure to conduct separate adjudicatory and dispositional hearings. In re Monroe (Ohio App. 7 Dist., Belmont, 09-17-2004) No. 03 BE 50, 2004-Ohio-4988, 2004 WL 2334358, Unreported. Infants ⇐ 202

The requirement of RC 2151.414(A) that a court conduct a hearing to determine whether termination of parental rights is in the child's best interest does not mandate two hearings; upon a motion under RC 2151.413 to convert temporary custody to permanent custody, the court need hold only one hearing, which will be adjudicatory in its procedural nature. In re Hopkins (Hocking 1992) 78 Ohio App.3d 92, 603 N.E.2d 1138. Infants ⇐ 203

In proceedings where parental rights are subject to termination, it is reversible error not to provide separate adjudicatory and dispositional hearings as required by RC 2151.35, Juv R 29(F)(2)(a), and Juv R 34. In re Baby Girl Baxter (Ohio 1985) 17 Ohio St.3d 229, 479 N.E.2d 257, 17 O.B.R. 469.

Where in a juvenile court proceeding the testimony of a codefendant is going to be a material part of the state's case and a motion for a separate hearing is made, the motion should generally be granted. In re Allen (Franklin 1967) 10 Ohio App.2d 120, 226 N.E.2d 135, 39 O.O.2d 200. Criminal Law ⇐ 622.7(7)

3. Public access

The press should not be expected to camp out in the hallway in order to ascertain whether evidentiary proceedings are being conducted in chambers on motions for closure of juvenile delinquency proceedings; instead, representatives of the press and general public must be given the opportunity to be heard on the question of exclusion. State ex rel. Plain Dealer Publishing Co. v. Floyd (Ohio, 08-30-2006) 111 Ohio St.3d 56, 855 N.E.2d 35, 2006-Ohio-4437. Infants ⇐ 203

Closure of delinquency proceedings for 17–year–old charged with aggravated murder, aggravated attempted murder, and aggravated robbery was abuse of discretion; public interest in proceedings outweighed bare assertion by juvenile's attorney that permitting access would not be in juvenile's best interest, in view of juvenile's near-adult age at time of alleged offenses, minimal likelihood that probable cause hearing would disclose confidential information, gravity of offenses, and fact that juvenile would be subject to mandatory bindover to adult court if probable cause was found. State ex rel. Plain Dealer Publishing Co. v. Geauga Cty. Court of Common Pleas, Juv. Div. (Ohio, 08-11-2000) 90 Ohio St.3d 79, 734 N.E.2d 1214, 2000-Ohio-35. Infants ⇐ 203

Decision to close juvenile proceedings to general public will be upheld unless juvenile court abused its discretion. State ex rel. Plain Dealer Publishing Co. v. Geauga Cty. Court of Common Pleas, Juv. Div. (Ohio, 08-11-2000) 90 Ohio St.3d 79, 734 N.E.2d 1214, 2000-Ohio-35. Infants ⇐ 251

Juvenile delinquency proceeding has different rules from criminal trial; juvenile court hears and determines all cases without jury and can conduct its hearings in informal manner, and general public may be excluded from juvenile court hearing. In re Good (Ohio App. 12 Dist., 02-24-1997) 118 Ohio App.3d 371, 692 N.E.2d 1072, dismissed, appeal not allowed 79 Ohio St.3d 1418, 680 N.E.2d 156. Infants ⇐ 195

Summary denial of motion for closure in juvenile proceeding was improper where there was severe physical injury to young child, nature of injury and information provided by child's two sisters gave rise to inference that evidence might be offered which, if made public, would be psychologically damaging to all three children, media had already expressed interest in case, no parties objected to closure hearing, and trial court relied on incorrect presumption in favor of public proceeding. In re Joanne M. (Ohio App. 6 Dist., 05-12-1995) 103 Ohio App.3d 447, 659 N.E.2d 864. Infants ⇐ 203

In determining whether to summarily deny motion for closure without a hearing, any presumption in favor of public proceeding in abuse, neglect, dependency, or custody proceeding is erroneous. In re Joanne M. (Ohio App. 6 Dist., 05-12-1995) 103 Ohio App.3d 447, 659 N.E.2d 864. Infants ⇐ 203

Summary denial of motion for closure in juvenile proceeding may not be disturbed unless trial court's attitude in reaching its judgment was unreasonable, arbitrary, or unconscionable. In re Joanne M. (Ohio App. 6 Dist., 05-12-1995) 103 Ohio App.3d 447, 659 N.E.2d 864. Infants ⇐ 248.1

Since juvenile proceedings to determine if child is abused, neglected, or dependent or to determine custody of minor child are neither presumptively open nor presumptively closed to public, juvenile court may restrict public access to those proceedings if it finds, after hearing evidence and argument on issue, that there exists reasonable and substantial basis for believing that public access could harm child or endanger fairness of adjudication, and that potential for harm outweighs benefits of public access. State ex rel. Scripps Howard Broadcasting Co. v. Cuyahoga Cty. Court of Common Pleas, Juv. Div. (Ohio, 07-13-1995) 73 Ohio St.3d 19, 652 N.E.2d 179. Constitutional Law ⇐ 90.1(3); Constitutional Law ⇐ 328

Juvenile court proceedings in delinquency cases are not presumed to be opened or closed; rather, in each case juvenile court must weigh competing interests for and against public access. In re N.H. (Ohio Com.Pl., 06-09-1992) 63 Ohio Misc.2d 285, 626 N.E.2d 697. Infants ⇐ 203

Proceedings in juvenile court to determine if a child is abused, neglected, or dependent, or to determine custody of a minor child, are neither presumptively open nor presumptively closed to the public; the juvenile court may restrict public access to these proceedings pursuant to Juv R 27 and RC 2151.35 if the court finds, after hearing evidence and argument on the issue, that (1) there exists a reasonable and substantial basis for believing that public access could harm the child or endanger the fairness of the adjudication and, (2) the potential for harm outweighs the benefits of public access. In re T.R. (Ohio 1990) 52 Ohio St.3d 6, 556 N.E.2d 439, certiorari denied 111 S.Ct. 386, 498 U.S. 958, 112 L.Ed.2d 396. Infants ⇐ 172; Infants ⇐ 203

It is within the discretion of a juvenile court judge to determine whether or not to close from the general public a hearing on the transfer of jurisdiction from the juvenile division to the court of common pleas, and thus a writ of prohibition to prevent the judge from conducting an open hearing will not lie. State ex rel. Fyffe v. Pierce (Ohio 1988) 40 Ohio St.3d 8, 531 N.E.2d 673.

4. Adult facilities

Juveniles adjudicated as delinquent for commission of act which if committed by adult would be felony may be committed by court to custody of department of mental hygiene and correction for purpose of training and rehabilitation only, in which case custody of such juveniles must be completely separate and apart from and free of any contact with adult convicts, but if such custody of such juveniles is, in fact, not for training and rehabilitation or is a commingling with adult convicts, such defalcation is administrative matter and should not invalidate nor affect an otherwise valid commitment or power to commit. In re Tsesmilles (Columbiana 1970) 24 Ohio App.2d 153, 265 N.E.2d 308, 53 O.O.2d 363. Infants ⇐ 223.1

The commitment of a juvenile to the Ohio state reformatory by a juvenile court under the provisions of former RC 2151.35(E) is prejudicially erroneous where the evidence fails to establish that the acts committed by the juvenile were such that they would constitute a felony if committed by an adult. In re Baker (Ohio 1969) 20 Ohio St.2d 142, 254 N.E.2d 363, 49 O.O.2d 473.

5. Representation by counsel

Approval by the court of the permanent surrender of a child is purely an administrative matter, and not in the nature of an adversary proceeding;

the court has no duty to advise the mother of her right to counsel or to appoint a lawyer for her in the event of indigency. In re K. (Ohio Juv. 1969) 31 Ohio Misc. 218, 282 N.E.2d 370, 60 O.O.2d 134, 60 O.O.2d 388.

In order to sustain commitment of a juvenile offender to a state institution in a delinquency proceeding, where such commitment will deprive the child of his liberty, the alleged delinquent must have been afforded representation by counsel, appointed at state expense in case of indigency. In re Agler (Ohio 1969) 19 Ohio St.2d 70, 249 N.E.2d 808, 48 O.O.2d 85. Infants ⇐ 205

Habeas corpus will not lie based upon an allegation of denial of counsel to a juvenile adjudicated delinquent inasmuch as a right of appeal to the Court of Appeals exists in such cases. In re Piazza (Ohio 1966) 7 Ohio St.2d 102, 218 N.E.2d 459, 36 O.O.2d 84.

6. Evidence and testimony

Credible evidence supported the court's finding of dependency; mother admitted that she told incarcerated father that she was considering killing herself and the children, social worker testified that mother gave guarded answers during evaluation, minimized the seriousness of the questions posed, and lacked a credible support network, mother told father and sheriff's deputy that she was depressed, and mother had attempted suicide in the past. In re Ohm (Ohio App. 4 Dist., Hocking, 07-01-2005) No. 05CA1, 2005-Ohio-3500, 2005 WL 1595245, Unreported. Infants ⇐ 181

Adjudication of delinquency based on knowingly causing a fire was against the manifest weight of the evidence; the State presented an improbable timeline that required juvenile to collect kerosene lamps from other rooms, return to her room and empty them on smoldering fire, grab her telephone, place an emergency call, and then walk outside the house within a span of 60-120 seconds, arson investigator never framed his opinions on the origins of the fire in terms of a reasonable degree of professional certainty, his conclusions were based on assumption that other witnesses proved to be false, and stepmother indicated that she awoke to crackling noises and her dogs barking, which would indicate an advanced fire. In re Horton (Ohio App. 4 Dist., Adams, 07-06-2005) No. 04CA794, 2005-Ohio-3502, 2005 WL 1595241, Unreported. Infants ⇐ 176

Evidence presented during delinquency proceeding was sufficient to support finding that juvenile "knowingly" caused fire in her room; juvenile repeatedly went in and out of her home before the fire, she placed several personal belongings, including make-up, a stereo, and clothing, in her stepmother's car before the fire, expert witness testified that the fire was not accidental in origin and kerosene lamps re-ignited the fire, stepmother testified that juvenile was the only person in the room when the fire started and that she had removed several kerosene lamps from the closet adjoining a wall in juvenile's room several weeks before the fire. In re Horton (Ohio App. 4 Dist., Adams, 07-06-2005) No. 04CA794, 2005-Ohio-3502, 2005 WL 1595241, Unreported. Infants ⇐ 176

Clear and convincing evidence supported finding of child's neglect and dependency, in termination of parental rights proceeding; evidence showed that mother received no prenatal care and that child tested positive for illegal drugs at the time of his birth. In re Barnhart (Ohio App. 4 Dist., Athens, 05-26-2005) No. 05CA8, 2005-Ohio-2692, 2005 WL 1283675, Unreported. Infants ⇐ 156

Father's complaint that no evidence was presented to support magistrate's alleged determination, in context of dependency proceedings, that child's sibling continued to display extreme emotional problems "as result of residing in household with [mother] and [father]" constituted misstatement of trial court's stated concern that abuse would continue to occur in home, and no where on page pointed to by father was there discussion of sibling's emotional problems as result of living in home. In re Hortsmann (Ohio App. 5 Dist., Tuscarawas, 04-29-2005) No. 2005AP020016, 2005-Ohio-2168, 2005 WL 1038856, Unreported. Infants ⇐ 241

Evidence supported adjudication of dependency; in companion case, child's half sibling had been adjudicated abused, and mother and father had only supervised visits with two other children, abuse on half-sibling was based on diagnosis of Munchausen Syndrome by Proxy perpetuated by mother, mother and father had abandoned children for periods of seven to eight hours, children were to taken to doctors for no reason and for unnecessary surgery, and neither mother or father acknowledged concerns. In re Hortsmann (Ohio App. 5 Dist., Tuscarawas, 04-29-2005) No. 2005AP020016, 2005-Ohio-2168, 2005 WL 1038856, Unreported. Infants ⇐ 156

Juvenile's adjudication as a delinquent child as a result of committing gross sexual imposition was not against the manifest weight of the evidence; witnesses testified that juvenile admitted putting five-year old victim's penis in his mouth, officer testified that juvenile admitted inappropriately touching and kissing victim, victim's mother testified that victim's behavior changed following the incident, and there was no innocent explanation for juvenile's placement of his mouth on the victim's mouth, chest, and penis. In re Higginbotham (Ohio App. 4 Dist., Lawrence, 10-27-2004) No. 04CA26, 2004-Ohio-6004, 2004 WL 2569446, Unreported. Infants ⇐ 176

Evidence presented at juvenile's probation revocation hearing was sufficient to support finding that juvenile violated the terms of his probation; counsel for juvenile admitted the violation. In re A.B. (Ohio App. 9 Dist., Wayne, 09-08-2004) No. 04CA0017, No. 04CA0018, 2004-Ohio-4724, 2004 WL 1969355, Unreported. Infants ⇐ 225

Trial court could not find that clear and convincing evidence supported grandmother's allegation that grandson was abused, neglected, or dependent; although grandmother was concerned for grandson's welfare and health, evidence adduced by grandmother to support her complaints regarding mother's care of child was not credible. In re Forrest (Ohio App. 4 Dist., Athens, 08-05-2004) No. 04CA104CA1, 2004-Ohio-4189, 2004 WL 1778436, Unreported. Infants ⇐ 179

Relying on testimony of employees of Athens County Children Services (ACCS) was proper in proceeding in which grandmother claimed that grandson was abused, neglected, and dependent child; even if ACCS did not strictly follow administrative procedures, ACCS investigated grandmother's complaint, fact that grandmother disagreed with findings of ACCS did not mean that ACCS's investigation was unreliable, independent agencies reviewed grandmother's allegations and found them meritless, and employees' testimony was not biased. In re Forrest (Ohio App. 4 Dist., Athens, 08-05-2004) No. 04CA104CA1, 2004-Ohio-4189, 2004 WL 1778436, Unreported. Infants ⇐ 179

Trial court addressed grandmother's allegation that grandson was neglected and dependent child, where court specifically stated in judgment entry that allegation of neglect and dependency remained unproven. In re Forrest (Ohio App. 4 Dist., Athens, 08-05-2004) No. 04CA104CA1, 2004-Ohio-4189, 2004 WL 1778436, Unreported. Infants ⇐ 210

Finding that children were not receiving proper care and that their environment had the potential for an adverse impact, warranting a determination of dependency, was supported by evidence that mother had admitted to violently shaking her child after becoming frustrated and to having violent fantasies about hurting the child. In re Hauenstein (Ohio App. 3 Dist., Hancock, 06-07-2004) No. 5-03-38, No. 5-03-39, 2004-Ohio-2915, 2004 WL 1238288, Unreported. Infants ⇐ 156

Trial court finding that child was a dependent child was not against the sufficiency of the evidence; mother had a history of being unable to provide for her children and for being unable to provide adequate housing, mother was unemployed, psychological testing of mother indicated a lack of efficacy and a lack of independence, and, at the hearing on mother's objections to dependency finding, the court found out that mother had moved out of the state and had not been in contact with child or inquired about child's welfare. In re Barker (Ohio App. 5 Dist., Stark, 11-24-2003) No. 03-CA-279, 2003-Ohio-6406, 2003 WL 22843907, Unreported. Infants ⇐ 155; Infants ⇐ 157; Infants ⇐ 158

Evidence supported finding that children were neglected; home had no electricity and cold weather was approaching, home lacked food, younger child lacked supervision, and mother refused to accept and follow advice which was precipitating factor in failing of neglect complaint. In re Browne Children (Ohio App. 5 Dist., Stark, 07-07-2003) No. 2003CA00027, 2003-Ohio-3637, 2003 WL 21546103, Unreported. Infants ⇐ 156

Trial court's denial of grandmother's motion to intervene in dependency proceeding involving her two grandchildren was not an abuse of discretion; evidence was insufficient to establish grandmother's role in the lives of her grandchildren rose to the level of in loco parentis. In re The Cunningham Children (Ohio App. 5 Dist., Stark, 06-16-2003) No. 2003CA00042, No. 2003CA00090, 2003-Ohio-3176, 2003 WL 21398883, Unreported. Infants ⇐ 200

Clear and convincing evidence supported determination that child could not be placed with father within reasonable time, for purposes of award of permanent custody to county children services board; record showed father failed to complete programs for substance abuse and domestic violence, and that he did not secure permanent housing, but continued to reside in the homes of various women. In re S.S. (Ohio App. 2 Dist., Montgomery, 01-24-2003) No. 19406, 2003-Ohio-319, 2003 WL 164598, Unreported. Infants ⇐ 178

Adjudication of delinquency for assault was not against manifest weight of evidence, even if victim had threatened juvenile in past; eyewitnesses testified that victim approached juvenile from behind and tapped juvenile on shoulder and that juvenile then punched victim in face and had friends hold victim down to kick her, and victim's provocative words and threats, by themselves, did not justify assault. In re Morton (Ohio App. 7 Dist., Belmont, 05-21-2002) No. 01-BA-29, 2002-Ohio-2648, 2002 WL 32832637, Unreported. Infants ⇐ 176

Evidence supported finding that mother demonstrated lack of commitment toward minor child, for purposes of dependency proceeding; at time of hearing, mother remained unemployed and did not have her own residence, and report of guardian ad litem demonstrated that mother did not believe that child's father had harmed other children and that mother elected to pursue a relationship with father, despite fact that guardian had informed mother that she might be able to provide appropriate parenting for child if she demonstrated improvement through concentrated therapy. In re Llewellyn (Ohio App. 5 Dist., Fairfield, 12-18-2002) No. 2002CA51, 2002-Ohio-7188, 2002 WL 32005260, Unreported. Infants ⇐ 155; Infants ⇐ 156

Rules of Evidence applied at motion for permanent custody of dependent child. In re Ashley E.D. (Ohio App. 6 Dist., Huron, 11-15-2002) No. H-02-025, 2002-Ohio-6238, 2002 WL 31529030, Unreported. Infants ⇐ 173.1

Clear and convincing evidence supported finding that child was a neglected and dependent child, in dependency proceeding; mother had been incarcerated four times since child's birth, her mental health issues interfered with her ability to parent, she failed to address child's developmental delays and behavioral problems, she provided no financial support for child, she failed to provide child with a stable home, and she attempted to commit suicide in child's presence. In re Barnhart (Ohio App. 4 Dist., Athens, 10-30-2002) No. 02CA20, 2002-Ohio-6023, 2002 WL 31455949, Unreported. Infants ⇐ 155; Infants ⇐ 157; Infants ⇐ 158

Clear and convincing evidence that turbulent relationship between child's parents created an environment which threatened the physical and emotional well-being of child supported finding that child was dependent and neglected, for purposes of termination of father's parental rights. In re Jehosephat W. (Ohio App. 6 Dist., Lucas, 10-11-2002) No. L-01-1505, 2002-Ohio-5503, 2002 WL 31270290, Unreported. Infants ⇐ 179

Juvenile court's finding that a particular child is neglected and dependent is not supported by clear and convincing evidence where the mother obtains adequate parental care for the child during the time she is unable to provide that care personally by voluntarily taking him to his paternal grandparents who in turn provide adequate parental care. Johnson v. Johnson (Ohio App. 10 Dist., Franklin, 03-22-2001) No. 00AP-691, 2001 WL 277272, Unreported.

Evidence was insufficient to support finding that father's two children were dependent children; mother voluntarily relinquished control of the children to maternal grandparents prior to entering drug rehabilitation, and the children had been receiving proper care and support from grandparents. In re Stoll (Ohio App. 3 Dist., 01-30-2006) 165 Ohio App.3d 226, 845 N.E.2d 581, 2006-Ohio-346. Infants ⇐ 154.1

Admission of ten exhibits by stipulation of the parties was not an abuse of discretion, at permanent custody hearing, even though father was not represented by counsel at the hearing; prosecutor briefly went over all of the exhibits with father, the trial court explained to father that by stipulating to the exhibits the court could use them in determining whether to grant county department of job and family services permanent custody of child, father was offered the choice of stipulating to the exhibits or hearing all of the evidence, and father was adamant about not hearing the evidence against him. In re Moore (Ohio App. 3 Dist., 08-11-2003) 153 Ohio App.3d 641, 795 N.E.2d 149, 2003-Ohio-4250. Stipulations ⇐ 18(6)

The proper scope of rebuttal testimony in a parental rights termination case lies within the sound discretion of the trial court. In re Sadiku (Ohio App. 9 Dist., 11-22-2000) 139 Ohio App.3d 263, 743 N.E.2d 507. Infants ⇐ 207

A trial court's decision regarding the scope of rebuttal testimony in a parental rights termination case will not be reversed unless the trial court's decision was unreasonable, arbitrary, or unconscionable. In re Sadiku (Ohio App. 9 Dist., 11-22-2000) 139 Ohio App.3d 263, 743 N.E.2d 507. Infants ⇐ 252

A six and an eight-year-old, regardless of intelligence, maturity, or social adjustment are too young to be left alone for an entire day or on a regular basis for hours at a time. In re Zeiser (Ohio App. 11 Dist., 03-26-1999) 133 Ohio App.3d 338, 728 N.E.2d 10, appeal not allowed 86 Ohio St.3d 1437, 713 N.E.2d 1049.

"Evidence," for purposes of statute providing that juvenile court at dispositional hearing may admit any evidence that is material and relevant, contemplates sworn testimony, despite informal nature of such hearing. In re Ramsey Children (Ohio App. 5 Dist., 03-27-1995) 102 Ohio App.3d 168, 656 N.E.2d 1311. Infants ⇐ 173.1

Fact of child's dependency must be proven by clear and convincing evidence. In re Pieper Children (Preble 1993) 85 Ohio App.3d 318, 619 N.E.2d 1059. Infants ⇐ 178

Hearsay exception exists for permanent custody hearings allowing admission of out-of-court statements by allegedly abused children of tender years, even if statements were not made to medical personnel, if statement was made to qualified expert in abuse who has independent evidence of physical or emotional abuse of child, if child has no apparent motive for fabricating statement and child is unavailable after good-faith effort to produce child in court. In re Brofford (Franklin 1992) 83 Ohio App.3d 869, 615 N.E.2d 1120. Infants ⇐ 174

Although there was sufficient evidence to support finding that permanent commitment and termination of parental rights were in children's best interest, hearsay statements of child abuse, not admissible under any exception, were so inflammatory that admitting hearsay was reversible error. In re Brofford (Franklin 1992) 83 Ohio App.3d 869, 615 N.E.2d 1120. Infants ⇐ 174; Infants ⇐ 253

Even if the admission of a child's hearsay statements in a juvenile court adjudication hearing implicates the Confrontation Clause, the parents' rights are not violated where the hearsay statements are admissible under the hearsay exception rules as statements made to a doctor for purposes of a medical diagnosis and statements made to a police officer which go to the child's state of mind and physical condition, where the child is unavailable to testify on his own behalf. In re Dukes (Summit 1991) 81 Ohio App.3d 145, 610 N.E.2d 513, motion overruled 63 Ohio St.3d 1411, 585 N.E.2d 835.

Clear and convincing evidence supported proof of newborn infant's dependency; infant was born while mother was incarcerated in prison on a sentence of life imprisonment, for which she was not eligible for parole for 14 years, mother admitted she could not keep child at women's reformatory, her husband at the time of birth abandoned the family, the natural father of the child, who was also serving a life imprisonment term, had taken no formal steps to acknowledge his paternity of the infant, and the proposed placement with relatives was not advisable in light of the severe overcrowding and poverty conditions which continued to exist within the relatives' household. In re Bishop (Ashland 1987) 36 Ohio App.3d 123, 521 N.E.2d 838. Infants ⇐ 177

In proceeding seeking temporary custody of a child who is alleged to be a dependent child, responsibility of the reviewing court is to determine whether juvenile court had before it evidence sufficient to convince a reasonable mind, clearly, certainly, and convincingly, that the minor child was a dependent child as defined in the statute and whether the dispositional order of the juvenile court was supported by a preponderance of the evidence. In re Willmann (Hamilton 1986) 24 Ohio App.3d 191, 493 N.E.2d 1380, 24 O.B.R. 313. Infants ⇐ 252

In a hearing to determine whether a child is dependent, hearsay evidence contained in a social history report may not be used as evidence of the truth of the complaint, although, pursuant to Juv R 32(A)(3), the report may be used to clarify allegations of the complaint. In re Barzak (Trumbull 1985) 24 Ohio App.3d 180, 493 N.E.2d 1011, 24 O.B.R. 270.

Although trial court in action seeking determination of dependency and neglect and an order of permanent custody of a child erred by allowing psychiatrist to testify as to privileged communications made to him by mother, by allowing psychologist to testify as to privileged communications made to him by father and by allowing social worker employed by psychologist to testify regarding privileged communications by both parents, error was not reversible where parents closely cross-examined challenged witnesses and additional evidence by other witnesses was offered tending to prove the same things as to parents' mental condition as did challenged testimony. In re Decker (Van Wert 1984) 20 Ohio App.3d 203, 485 N.E.2d 751, 20 O.B.R. 248. Infants ⇐ 253

Indigent parent in custody hearing who had right to and obtained free court-ordered psychological evaluation could not subsequently limit disclosure of adverse results of that testing where the court order granting the evaluation did not limit purpose of report solely for parent's defense, but rather it was ordered for purpose of assisting court in determining parent's capability of resuming responsibility for the children. In re Green (Montgomery 1984) 18 Ohio App.3d 43, 480 N.E.2d 492, 18 O.B.R. 155. Infants ⇐ 208

Juv R 10(B) is not meant to force a complainant to state every fact surrounding every incident described in the complaint, and therefore, in proving its case in a neglect and dependency proceeding, the state need not limit its proof to the habits and faults of the custodial parent that are actually listed in the complaint. In re Sims (Preble 1983) 13 Ohio App.3d 37, 468 N.E.2d 111, 13 O.B.R. 40.

The fact of dependency must be proved by clear and convincing evidence. In re Bibb (Hamilton 1980) 70 Ohio App.2d 117, 435 N.E.2d 96, 24 O.O.3d 159.

In a hearing conducted pursuant to RC 2151.35 in which the welfare department seeks to take permanent custody of children from their natural parents, the welfare department has the burden to plead and prove by clear and convincing evidence that the children are presently neglected or dependent. In re Fassinger (Cuyahoga 1974) 43 Ohio App.2d 89, 334 N.E.2d 5, 72 O.O.2d 292, affirmed 42 Ohio St.2d 505, 330 N.E.2d 431, 71 O.O.2d 503. Infants ⚖ 197

Although Ohio law generally protects a minor from exposure of his acts in another judicial forum, RC 2151.35(G) does not prohibit cross-examination, in a criminal trial, of defendant or defendant's witnesses concerning prior juvenile record, where defendant's evidence attempts to establish his good character. State v. Hale (Franklin 1969) 21 Ohio App.2d 207, 256 N.E.2d 239, 50 O.O.2d 340.

Where the defense introduces character evidence to the effect that the defendant had never been in any kind of trouble and where the trial court disallows cross-examination of defendant's witnesses on the subject of prior juvenile court involvement, the introduction of a juvenile record to rebut such evidence is not prejudicial error. State v. Hale (Franklin 1969) 21 Ohio App.2d 207, 256 N.E.2d 239, 50 O.O.2d 340.

Any adjudication of delinquency must be supported by clear and convincing evidence. In re Agler (Ohio 1969) 19 Ohio St.2d 70, 249 N.E.2d 808, 48 O.O.2d 85. Infants ⚖ 176

Proof of possession, use, or control by a juvenile of a hallucinogen is sufficient evidence upon which a juvenile court can find such juvenile a delinquent under Ch 2151. In re Baker (Hocking 1969) 18 Ohio App.2d 276, 248 N.E.2d 620, 47 O.O.2d 411.

Proceedings in a juvenile court are civil in nature, the customary rules of evidence governing civil actions must be followed, and hearsay evidence is not admissible; and a mere preponderance of the evidence is sufficient to warrant a determination that a minor is a delinquent, even though such determination involves a finding that a criminal statute has been violated by such minor. State v. Shardell (Cuyahoga 1958) 107 Ohio App. 338, 153 N.E.2d 510, 79 Ohio Law Abs. 534, 8 O.O.2d 262.

Juvenile convictions are inadmissible as evidence and may not be used to enhance punishment. Workman v. Cardwell (N.D.Ohio 1972) 31 Ohio Misc. 99, 338 F.Supp. 893, 60 O.O.2d 187, 60 O.O.2d 250, affirmed in part, vacated in part 471 F.2d 909, certiorari denied 93 S.Ct. 2748, 412 U.S. 932, 37 L.Ed.2d 161, certiorari denied 93 S.Ct. 2762, 412 U.S. 932, 37 L.Ed.2d 161.

Child's status as dependent child was established by clear and convincing evidence; woman who had legal custody of child placed child with married couple who were virtual strangers and woman's friend testified that child was bruised and had black eyes and that woman said she was going to send child back. In re Bradford (Ohio App. 10 Dist., Franklin, 08-08-2002) No. 01AP-1151, 2002-Ohio-4013, 2002 WL 1813406, Unreported, appeal not allowed 97 Ohio St.3d 1470, 779 N.E.2d 236, 2002-Ohio-6347. Infants ⚖ 177

The trial court's finding of child abuse and dependency was supported by the evidence; physician trained in performing sexual assault examinations testified that she examined child and that child genitalia revealed redness that "was more than I expect, normally," wife testified that child told her that father put his finger in her vagina, and social worker testified that child told her that father placed his finger in her vagina. In re Rossantelli (Ohio App. 5 Dist., Delaware, 05-13-2002) No. 01CAF12072, 2002-Ohio-2525, 2002 WL 999301, Unreported. Infants ⚖ 179

The finding of emotional trauma to a child if forced to testify may be made after the child is deposed, but before admission at trial. In re Collier, No. CA91–07–124+ (12th Dist Ct App, Butler, 9–21–92).

Where a mother took her child voluntarily to children's services on a temporary basis until the mother found housing, a subsequent order granting the children's services permanent custody based on evidence that the mother had a domestic spat with her husband, did poorly on a psychological test, refused counseling and had a cluttered home is not sustained by the manifest weight of the evidence. Howser v Ashtabula County Children's Services Bd, No. 1134 (11th Dist Ct App, Ashtabula, 9–19–83).

Where a mother stipulates that the allegations in a dependency complaint are true, with the exception of the allegation that she cannot care for the child, the court may have sufficient support for a finding of dependency, with no need for evidence of dependency. In re Ware, No. 79–03243 (8th Dist Ct App, Cuyahoga, 7–17–80).

7. Procedural issues

Father's appellate claim, that juvenile court should have considered his motion to terminate public children services agency's temporary custody of unruly child or in the alternative held an adjudicatory hearing on the issue of child abuse, was moot, where the juvenile court magistrate had terminated the temporary custody 11 days after father filed his motion, even if such termination of temporary custody did not relieve father from paying for the care child had received while in temporary custody of agency. In re Kidd (Ohio App. 11 Dist., Lake, 12-27-2002) No. 2001-L-039, 2002-Ohio-7264, 2002 WL 31886759, Unreported. Infants ⚖ 248.1

Hearing on motion for permanent custody of dependent child was dispositional, rather than adjudicatory. In re Ashley E.D. (Ohio App. 6 Dist., Huron, 11-15-2002) No. H-02-025, 2002-Ohio-6238, 2002 WL 31529030, Unreported. Infants ⚖ 203

Writ of mandamus would issue to compel juvenile court to release transcript of amenability hearing to determine whether juvenile should be tried as adult for murder after juvenile court denied juvenile's motion to close proceedings but refused to allow media to attend hearing after juvenile's mother testified. State ex rel. Plain Dealer Publishing Co. v. Floyd (Ohio, 08-30-2006) 111 Ohio St.3d 56, 855 N.E.2d 35, 2006-Ohio-4437. Mandamus ⚖ 60

Writ of mandamus would not issue to compel juvenile court to release transcript of arraignment hearing in delinquency proceedings based on court's failure to conduct evidentiary hearing to determine whether closure of hearing was appropriate when no party had filed motion to close proceedings; rather, mandamus would issue to compel juvenile court to conduct closure hearing, and then, if court decided that closure was unwarranted, to release transcript. State ex rel. Plain Dealer Publishing Co. v. Floyd (Ohio, 08-30-2006) 111 Ohio St.3d 56, 855 N.E.2d 35, 2006-Ohio-4437. Mandamus ⚖ 60

When a party requests that the juvenile court proceeding be closed, but the court fails to hold an appropriate evidentiary hearing and make the required findings before closing the proceeding, a person or entity successfully challenging that practice is not automatically entitled to release of the transcript of the improperly closed proceeding; instead, the party challenging the improper closure is entitled to a writ of mandamus to compel the juvenile court judge to conduct the closure hearing that should have been held in order to determine if release of the transcript is warranted, and, if the judge decides that the proceeding should not have been closed, the transcript should be released. State ex rel. Plain Dealer Publishing Co. v. Floyd (Ohio, 08-30-2006) 111 Ohio St.3d 56, 855 N.E.2d 35, 2006-Ohio-4437. Mandamus ⚖ 60

Statutory mandate to dismiss juvenile matter if dispositional hearing is not held within 90 days of date complaint was filed is mandatory, not discretionary. In re Olah (Ohio App. 9 Dist., 08-24-2000) 142 Ohio App.3d 176, 754 N.E.2d 1271, motion to certify allowed 90 Ohio St.3d 1491, 739 N.E.2d 816, appeal allowed 90 Ohio St.3d 1493, 739 N.E.2d 817, cause dismissed 93 Ohio St.3d 1404, 753 N.E.2d 208. Infants ⚖ 204

County children services' complaint for temporary custody of minor was statutorily required to be dismissed, where dispositional hearing was held some five months after date complaint was filed, rather than within mandated 90 days of filing. In re Olah (Ohio App. 9 Dist., 08-24-2000) 142 Ohio App.3d 176, 754 N.E.2d 1271, motion to certify allowed 90 Ohio St.3d 1491, 739 N.E.2d 816, appeal allowed 90 Ohio St.3d 1493, 739 N.E.2d 817, cause dismissed 93 Ohio St.3d 1404, 753 N.E.2d 208. Infants ⚖ 204

Party seeking closure of juvenile proceedings bears burden of proof on relevant factors. State ex rel. Plain Dealer Publishing Co. v. Geauga Cty. Court of Common Pleas, Juv. Div. (Ohio, 08-11-2000) 90 Ohio St.3d 79, 734 N.E.2d 1214, 2000-Ohio-35. Infants ⚖ 172

Seven-day time limit for entering judgment after conclusion of dispositional hearing for children adjudicated abused, neglected, or dependent is directory, not mandatory, and failure to comply with it will not deprive a court of jurisdiction. In re Davis (Ohio, 03-03-1999) 84 Ohio St.3d 520, 705 N.E.2d 1219, 1999-Ohio-419. Infants ⚖ 204

When juvenile court delays its ruling for more than seven days following the conclusion of dispositional hearing on an agency's motion for permanent child custody filed prior to September 18, 1996, violation of that time constraint serves as justification for seeking a writ of procedendo. In re Davis (Ohio, 03-03-1999) 84 Ohio St.3d 520, 705 N.E.2d 1219, 1999-Ohio-419. Infants ⚖ 204

Parents were estopped from complaining on appeal that they were prejudiced when juvenile court did not rule on agency's petition for permanent custody of children until seventeen months after conclusion of dispositional hearing, where parents failed to seek writ of procedendo after seven-day deadline for issuance of judgment following hearing had passed.

In re Davis (Ohio, 03-03-1999) 84 Ohio St.3d 520, 705 N.E.2d 1219, 1999-Ohio-419. Infants ⇐ 232; Infants ⇐ 243

Children's Services Board's (CSB) filing of five successive complaints seeking permanent custody of child, followed by dismissal without prejudice in four of those cases, did not constitute harassment prejudicial to child's father; statute required dismissal without prejudice when no hearing was held within 90 days of filing of complaint and it was "unthinkable" that welfare and interests of child could be abandoned with prejudice. In re Brown (Ohio App. 2 Dist., 08-03-1994) 96 Ohio App.3d 306, 644 N.E.2d 1117. Infants ⇐ 204; Infants ⇐ 253

Juvenile court possessed jurisdiction to consider third dependency complaint and, therefore, only nonjurisdictional issues were involved in habeas corpus petition wherein father alleged that he was entitled to immediate custody of child, as prior dismissals of dependency complaints were without prejudice because dispositional hearings were not held within specified 90-day period. Howard v. Catholic Social Serv. of Cuyahoga Cty., Inc. (Ohio, 08-31-1994) 70 Ohio St.3d 141, 637 N.E.2d 890, 1994-Ohio-219, reconsideration denied 70 Ohio St.3d 1457, 639 N.E.2d 796. Habeas Corpus ⇐ 532(1)

In absence of motion by mother for transcript of oral proceedings on her motion to reopen custody cases of her two children, and to recover legal custody of those children, no transcript was required; it was not matter determining permanent custody, but only motion to change legal custody. In re Wright (Montgomery 1993) 88 Ohio App.3d 539, 624 N.E.2d 347. Child Custody ⇐ 907

Mother had standing in dependency proceeding to raise only those issues which affected her own legal interests. In re Pryor (Athens 1993) 86 Ohio App.3d 327, 620 N.E.2d 973. Infants ⇐ 200

Any error in failure of county children's services to participate in hearings on dependency petition was waived, where no objection was raised. In re Pryor (Athens 1993) 86 Ohio App.3d 327, 620 N.E.2d 973. Infants ⇐ 243

An order of emergency shelter care pending adjudication is not such an award of temporary custody as to trigger the provisions of RC 2151.413 requiring an agency granted temporary custody of a child to wait six months before seeking to convert the temporary placement to permanent custody; thus, a trial court does not err in entertaining a motion for permanent custody filed two months after an order of emergency shelter care is issued. In re Massengill (Lucas 1991) 76 Ohio App.3d 220, 601 N.E.2d 206.

Juvenile failed to show that he was prejudiced by juvenile court's refusal to conduct informal proceedings, rather than formal court proceedings, on charges of criminal mischief. In re Corcoran (Geauga 1990) 68 Ohio App.3d 213, 587 N.E.2d 957, dismissed 56 Ohio St.3d 702, 564 N.E.2d 703. Infants ⇐ 253

Although a finding of dependency may be made only upon the presentation of clear and convincing evidence, if the parties agree to waive such a hearing and stipulate to certain facts, then Juv R 29(D) must be fully complied with and the facts set forth in the record must sufficiently support a finding of dependency. Elmer v. Lucas County Children Services Bd. (Lucas 1987) 36 Ohio App.3d 241, 523 N.E.2d 540.

An agreement by a parent with the welfare department for permanent surrender of a child prior to consent of the juvenile court is not only revocable by the parent prior to consent of the juvenile court, but such revocation also operates to dissolve the offer to surrender. In re Williams (Hamilton 1982) 7 Ohio App.3d 324, 455 N.E.2d 1027, 7 O.B.R. 421. Infants ⇐ 157

The mere allegation in a motion filed by the county welfare department that "it would appear to be in the best interest of said minors that they be placed permanently for adoption" does not state grounds under which a juvenile court may lawfully take permanent custody of children from their natural parents. In re Fassinger (Cuyahoga 1974) 43 Ohio App.2d 89, 334 N.E.2d 5, 72 O.O.2d 292, affirmed 42 Ohio St.2d 505, 330 N.E.2d 431, 71 O.O.2d 503. Infants ⇐ 197

RC 3109.04 is applicable to a proceeding for change of custody under the Juvenile Court Act. In re Custody of Smelser (Ohio Com.Pl. 1969) 22 Ohio Misc. 41, 257 N.E.2d 769, 51 O.O.2d 31, 51 O.O.2d 75.

An Ohio juvenile court, in a dependency proceeding pursuant to RC 2151.27 et seq., has no jurisdiction to interfere with a mother's legal custody of her children in the absence of proof and a finding of unfitness of such parent merely for the purpose of releasing such children to the officers of the court of a foreign state, and the court need not give full faith and credit to a Michigan decree where that decree was obtained by the husband in an ex parte custody determination, subsequent to a divorce decree, in which the Michigan court had no personal jurisdiction over the nonresident wife. In re Messner (Huron 1969) 19 Ohio App.2d 33, 249 N.E.2d 532, 48 O.O.2d 31.

Where a juvenile court in the jurisdiction in which an offender resides waives jurisdiction so that the offender will be tried by a common pleas court, such defendant is entitled to a trial in the county where the offense occurred. In re Davis (Ohio Juv. 1961) 179 N.E.2d 198, 87 Ohio Law Abs. 222, 22 O.O.2d 108.

Under Ohio law, no conflicting dispositions arose from juvenile's adjudication as a juvenile for same incident that led to adult conviction, where juvenile disposition was vacated. Robertson v. Morgan (C.A.6 (Ohio), 09-14-2000) 227 F.3d 589, rehearing denied. Infants ⇐ 232

Requirement that dispositional hearing for children adjudicated as abused, neglected, or dependent be held within 90 days of adjudication was not jurisdictional, and thus parent waived time limit by failing to request dismissal of complaint asserting neglect based on 90-day time limit and by expressly waiving all time requirements on the record. In re Kimble (Ohio App. 7 Dist., Harrison, 05-15-2002) No. 99 517 CA, 2002-Ohio-2409, 2002 WL 1065977, Unreported. Infants ⇐ 222

Juvenile's admission to two probation violations stemmed from conditions of probation placed upon him for the original delinquency complaint for attempted gross sexual imposition and, thus, any time served for such violations were connected to delinquent child complaint, such that juvenile was entitled to credit for time served while awaiting his hearing for his first probation violation. In re Ringo (Ohio App. 3 Dist., Crawford, 03-19-2002) No. 3-01-25, 2002-Ohio-1218, 2002 WL 418968, Unreported. Infants ⇐ 225

Parent's request for transcript at state expense in permanent child custody action may be denied if juvenile court finds that party has adequate financial means to obtain transcript. State ex rel. Howard v. Ferreri (Ohio 1994) 70 Ohio St.3d 587, 639 N.E.2d 1189.

Indigent, noncustodial parent is not entitled to transcript of custody proceedings in which temporary custody is given to other parent; right to transcript applies only to state-instituted permanent custody cases. State ex rel. Howard v. Ferreri (Ohio 1994) 70 Ohio St.3d 587, 639 N.E.2d 1189.

Indigent father established clear legal right to access to files in case involving private agency's permanent custody proceedings and corresponding clear legal duty on part of agency to provide access, and thus was entitled to issuance of writ of mandamus to compel access in light of lack of any adequate legal remedy given the juvenile court's refusal to provide access. State ex rel. Howard v Ferreri (Ohio 1994) 70 Ohio St.3d 587, 639 N.E.2d 1189.

RC 2151.35(B)(2) does not require that the same referee who presided at an adjudicatory hearing preside at the dispositional hearing; a court does not err in ordering another referee to preside at the dispositional hearing where the original referee has been appointed to the juvenile bench and, although originally agreeing to preside as judge at the dispositional hearing, orders that a referee preside upon the parent's motion for continuance. Hood v Hood, No. 14957 (9th Dist Ct App, Summit, 7-3-91).

Both the existing juvenile code and the juvenile rules require a hearing before a temporary commitment to the Ohio youth commission can be made permanent, which hearing requires the presence of the youth involved. OAG 72-071.

8. Time limit for filing report

Mother waived any objection to the untimeliness of the adjudicatory and dispositional hearings, in child dependency proceeding, where mother did not raise the issue of the timeliness of the hearings until more than a year and a half after the 90-day deadline passed for the dispositional hearing, and she continued to participate in the case well beyond the 90-day deadline for the dispositional hearing. In re Brown (Ohio App. 2 Dist., Darke, 06-23-2006) No. 1676, 2006-Ohio-3189, 2006 WL 1719277, Unreported. Infants ⇐ 204

Trial court committed prejudicial error in granting custody of child to Children's Services Bureau over father's objection where referee who held dispositional hearing in case never filed any written report or recommendation and trial court issued dispositional order 11 months later with no opportunity for child's father to consider or challenge evidence. In re Brown (Ohio App. 2 Dist., 08-03-1994) 96 Ohio App.3d 306, 644 N.E.2d 1117. Infants ⇐ 203; Infants ⇐ 208; Infants ⇐ 253

While the seven-day requirement for filing a report is mandatory in a custody action, a trial court's failure to comply with the rule is not ground for reversal of its decision to terminate parental custody since the proper remedy would be for the complaining party to file a writ of procedendo compelling the court to finalize the decision. In re Galloway (Lucas 1991) 77 Ohio App.3d 61, 601 N.E.2d 83, motion overruled 62 Ohio St.3d 1503, 583 N.E.2d 974, denial of post-conviction relief affirmed.

The seven day time requirement of RC 2151.35(B)(3) and Juv R 34(C) is mandatory and must be applied as such and it may not be relaxed or eliminated. In re Fleming (Lucas 1991) 76 Ohio App.3d 30, 600 N.E.2d 1112.

The seven day rule of RC 2151.35(B)(3) and Juv R 34(C) can be applied consistently with Juv R 40(D), which (1) mandates the preparation and filing of findings of fact and recommendations by the referee; (2) provides an allowance of fourteen days from the filing of the referee's report for the filing of objections by the parties; and (3) provides for a hearing on the objections; when the dispositional hearing is conducted before a referee, the referee has seven days from the time the case becomes decisional in which to issue his findings of fact and recommendations and at the expiration of the fourteen day period for filing objections, if no objections are filed, the case is decisional and the trial court has seven days to issue its final judgment; however, if objections are filed pursuant to Juv R 40 and a hearing is held, the judge has seven days from the conclusion of the hearing to enter his final judgment. In re Fleming (Lucas 1991) 76 Ohio App.3d 30, 600 N.E.2d 1112.

In a proceeding to terminate a father's parental rights, a trial court's failure to comply with RC 2151.35(B)(3) and Juv R 34(C), which requires judgment to be entered within seven days of dispositional hearings, does not (1) result in a denial of the father's due process rights; (2) deprive the court of jurisdiction to enter a final determination; or (3) require reversal of the court's final judgment. In re Fleming (Lucas 1991) 76 Ohio App.3d 30, 600 N.E.2d 1112. Constitutional Law 274(5); Infants 221; Infants 254

The proper remedy in cases where a trial court fails to meet the seven day requirement imposed by RC 2151.35(B)(3) and/or Juv R 34(C) is for counsel for the parents or county children services board to file, on expiration of the seven day time period, a petition for a writ of procedendo with the court of appeals requesting the court to direct the trial court to comply immediately with those requirements and proceed to final judgment. In re Fleming (Lucas 1991) 76 Ohio App.3d 30, 600 N.E.2d 1112. Courts 207.1

A party waives the right to seek dismissal of an abuse petition based on the court's failure to conduct a dispositional hearing within ninety days of the filing of the complaint where the party first seeks a continuance after the ninety-day limit and, upon its denial, subsequently moves for dismissal of the complaint. In re Kutzli (Paulding 1991) 71 Ohio App.3d 843, 595 N.E.2d 1026.

Although RC 2151.35(B)(3) and Juv R 34(C) require that final judgment in the dispositional phase of an institutional child custody action be rendered within seven days of the dispositional hearing, failure to render judgment within seven days does not require reversal of the judgment ultimately rendered; procedendo is the proper remedy to compel a court to comply with the time limits. Galloway v Lucas County Children Services Bd, No. L–90–197 (6th Dist Ct App, Lucas, 9–6–91).

9. Best interest of child

Evidence supported adjudication of dependency; child's half-sibling had been adjudicated dependent based on incident of abuse, mother took children to doctors for no reason and for unnecessary surgery, mother and father had abandoned children in home for seven to eight hours and had no food in house, and neither mother nor father had yet recognized or acknowledged concerns involving care of children. In re Hortsmann (Ohio App. 5 Dist., Tuscarawas, 04-29-2005) No. 2005AP020015, 2005-Ohio-2172, 2005 WL 1038857, Unreported. Infants 156

Any error by juvenile court or guardian ad litem in not specifically probing into minor children's wishes was essentially harmless in permanent custody proceeding, based upon the children's lack of maturity in conjunction with the overwhelming evidence supporting the court's findings that the children's best interests were to be served by awarding custody to county agency. In re Lane (Ohio App. 3 Dist., Marion, 06-01-2004) No. 9-03-61, No. 9-03-62, 2004-Ohio-2798, 2004 WL 1192087, Unreported. Infants 253

Child placing agency, in permanent custody hearing involving dependent child, was not prejudiced by trial court's act of terminating mother's parental rights, where mother voluntarily surrendered her parental rights to the child, trial court found that mother's parental rights were terminated, and mother had not appealed from that judgment. In re J. H. (Ohio App. 9 Dist., Summit, 10-22-2003) No. 21575, 2003-Ohio-5611, 2003 WL 22399693, Unreported. Infants 253

A proposed settlement of child support and custody disputes was not in the best interests of the child; the former husband was five-and-one-half years delinquent in child support, and the former wife waived a major portion of the court-ordered entitlements for the benefit of the child. In re Contemnor Caron (Ohio Com.Pl., 04-27-2000) 110 Ohio Misc.2d 58, 744 N.E.2d 787. Child Custody 35; Child Support 44

The best interests of a child demand that the father pay to the mother, for the benefit of the child, all monies and expenses previously ordered by the court. In re Contemnor Caron (Ohio Com.Pl., 04-27-2000) 110 Ohio Misc.2d 58, 744 N.E.2d 787. Child Support 430

A parent's primary rights to the care and custody of a child are rights that must be protected, and parental custody will be terminated only when necessary for the mental and physical development of the child. In re Bibb (Hamilton 1980) 70 Ohio App.2d 117, 435 N.E.2d 96, 24 O.O.3d 159. Infants 155

Where a natural parent moves to terminate temporary custody in another based on a previous finding of dependency, the parent's present suitability and fitness for the role of parent must be considered in the context of the child's best interests. In re Christopher (Morrow 1977) 54 Ohio App.2d 137, 376 N.E.2d 603, 8 O.O.3d 271.

Evidence supported trial court's dispositional ruling granting custody of children who were adjudicated abused and dependent to their father and requiring supervised visitation by mother, where Department of Human Services recommended that children be placed with father, home study of father's residence was favorable, older children consistently indicated that they wished to remain at father's house, and family members and caseworker testified to positive changes in children since they had been in father's custody. In re Kimble (Ohio App. 7 Dist., Harrison, 05-15-2002) No. 99 517 CA, 2002-Ohio-2409, 2002 WL 1065977, Unreported. Infants 222

Where a court determines that a child is a neglected child, it commits reversible error when it proceeds to make dispositional rulings without first holding a disposition hearing to determine the child's best interests. In re Manjarrez, No. 4–86–11 (3d Dist Ct App, Defiance, 3–7–89).

2151.352 Right to counsel

A child, the child's parents or custodian, or any other person in loco parentis of the child is entitled to representation by legal counsel at all stages of the proceedings under this chapter or Chapter 2152. of the Revised Code. If, as an indigent person, a party is unable to employ counsel, the party is entitled to have counsel provided for the person pursuant to Chapter 120. of the Revised Code except in civil matters in which the juvenile court is exercising jurisdiction pursuant to division (A)(2), (3), (9), (10), (11), (12), or (13); (B)(2), (3), (4), (5), or (6); (C); (D); or (F)(1) or (2) of section 2151.23 of the Revised Code. If a party appears without counsel, the court shall ascertain whether the party knows of the party's right to counsel and of the party's right to be provided with counsel if the party is an indigent person. The court may continue the case to enable a party to obtain counsel, to be represented by the county public defender or the joint county public defender, or to be appointed counsel upon request pursuant to Chapter 120. of the Revised Code. Counsel must be provided for a child not represented by the child's parent, guardian, or custodian. If the interests of two or more such parties conflict, separate counsel shall be provided for each of them.

Section 2935.14 of the Revised Code applies to any child taken into custody. The parents, custodian, or guardian of such child, and any attorney at law representing them or the child, shall be entitled to visit such child at any reasonable time, be present at any hearing involving the child, and be given reasonable notice of such hearing.

Any report or part thereof concerning such child, which is used in the hearing and is pertinent thereto, shall for good cause shown be made available to any attorney at law representing such child and to any attorney at law representing the parents, custodian, or guardian of such child, upon written request prior to any hearing involving such child.

(2005 H 66, eff. 9–29–05; 2000 S 179, § 3, eff. 1–1–02; 1975 H 164, eff. 1–13–76; 1969 H 320)

Historical and Statutory Notes

Publisher's Note: This section appears in the main volume as partially vetoed by 2003 H 95. The full section veto contained in the purpose and amending and enacting clauses of 2003 H 95, however, supersedes the partial veto contained in the body of the act. As a result, the amendment of this section by 2003 H 95 has been removed to reflect the full veto by the governor of those provisions.

Ed. Note: 2151.352 contains provisions analogous to former 2151.35 repealed by 1969 H 320, eff. 11–19–69.

Amendment Note: 2005 H 66 rewrote the first paragraph of this section, which prior thereto read:

"A child, or the child's parents, custodian, or other person in loco parentis of such child is entitled to representation by legal counsel at all stages of the proceedings under this chapter or Chapter 2152. of the Revised Code and if, as an indigent person, any such person is unable to employ counsel, to have counsel provided for the person pursuant to Chapter 120. of the Revised Code. If a party appears without counsel, the court shall ascertain whether the party knows of the party's right to counsel and of the party's right to be provided with counsel if the party is an indigent person. The court may continue the case to enable a party to obtain counsel or to be represented by the county public defender or the joint county public defender and shall provide counsel upon request pursuant to Chapter 120. of the Revised Code. Counsel must be provided for a child not represented by the child's parent, guardian, or custodian. If the interests of two or more such parties conflict, separate counsel shall be provided for each of them."

Amendment Note: 2000 S 179, § 3, eff. 1–1–02, inserted "under this chapter or Chapter 2152. of the Revised Code" in the first paragraph; and made changes to reflect gender neutral language and other nonsubstantive changes.

Cross References

Adjudicatory hearing, court to state right to counsel, Juv R 29
Right to counsel, O Const Art I §10
Right to counsel, guardian ad litem, procedure, Juv R 4
Social history, physical and mental examinations, custody investigation, availability of reports to counsel, Juv R 32
Waiver of rights, Juv R 3

Library References

Infants ⇐205.
Westlaw Topic No. 211.
C.J.S. Infants §§ 50, 62 to 67.

Research References

ALR Library

101 ALR 5th 351, Validity and Efficacy of Minor's Waiver of Right to Counsel--Cases Decided Since Application of Gault, 387 U.S. 1, 87 S. Ct. 1428, 18 L. Ed. 2d 527 (1967).

Encyclopedias

OH Jur. 3d Family Law § 1082, Determination of Preference.
OH Jur. 3d Family Law § 1575, Delivery of Child to Shelter or Detention Facility—Telephone and Visitation Rights.
OH Jur. 3d Family Law § 1626, Right Under Juvenile Court Law and Rules.
OH Jur. 3d Family Law § 1627, Procedure to Obtain Counsel.
OH Jur. 3d Family Law § 1628, Appearance by and Withdrawal of Counsel.
OH Jur. 3d Family Law § 1638, Order for Social History or Physical or Mental Examination—Availability and Use of Results.
OH Jur. 3d Family Law § 1655, Right to Attend; Public or Private Hearing.
OH Jur. 3d Family Law § 1681, Conduct of Hearing; Advisement of Rights.
OH Jur. 3d Family Law § 1628.1, Ineffective Assistance of Counsel.
OH Jur. 3d Family Law § 1628.5, Waiver of Counsel.

Treatises and Practice Aids

Sowald & Morganstern, Baldwin's Ohio Practice Domestic Relations Law § 15:63, Guardian Ad Litem—Procedure.
Sowald & Morganstern, Baldwin's Ohio Practice Domestic Relations Law § 15:64, Guardian Ad Litem—Conflict of Interest.

Carlin, Baldwin's Ohio Practice, Merrick-Rippner Probate Law § 104:5, Juvenile Courts—Constitutional Issues—Right to Notice, Counsel, and Trial.
Carlin, Baldwin's Ohio Practice, Merrick-Rippner Probate Law § 107:9, Parties to Proceedings.
Carlin, Baldwin's Ohio Practice, Merrick-Rippner Probate Law § 107:33, Restricting And/Or Enforcing Discovery.
Carlin, Baldwin's Ohio Practice, Merrick-Rippner Probate Law § 107:36, Use of Social History and Investigation Report.
Carlin, Baldwin's Ohio Practice, Merrick-Rippner Probate Law § 107:45, Adjudicatory Hearings—Parties' Right to Counsel.
Carlin, Baldwin's Ohio Practice, Merrick-Rippner Probate Law § 107:55, Adjudicatory Hearings—Procedure at Adjudicatory Hearing.
Carlin, Baldwin's Ohio Practice, Merrick-Rippner Probate Law § 107:56, Adjudicatory Hearings—Attendance of Parties at Hearing.
Carlin, Baldwin's Ohio Practice, Merrick-Rippner Probate Law § 107:80, Disposition of Abused, Neglected, or Dependent Child—Permanent Custody.
Carlin, Baldwin's Ohio Practice, Merrick-Rippner Probate Law § 107:81, Disposition of Abused, Neglected, or Dependent Child—Permanent Custody—Best Interest Determination Factors.
Carlin, Baldwin's Ohio Practice, Merrick-Rippner Probate Law § 108:13, Juvenile Court—Jurisdiction Over Child Custody Matters—Determination of Custody.
Carlin, Baldwin's Ohio Practice, Merrick-Rippner Probate Law § 108:25, Juvenile Court—Parentage Act—Right to Counsel for Indigent Paternity Defendant.
Carlin, Baldwin's Ohio Practice, Merrick-Rippner Probate Law § 108:31, Juvenile Court—Parentage Act—Continuing Jurisdiction to Modify or Revoke Judgment.
Giannelli & Yeomans, Ohio Juvenile Law § 21:2, Scope of Discovery; Rule 24.
Giannelli & Yeomans, Ohio Juvenile Law § 21:6, Social History Report.
Giannelli & Yeomans, Ohio Juvenile Law § 23:3, Right to Counsel.
Giannelli & Yeomans, Ohio Juvenile Law § 23:4, Waiver of Right to Counsel.
Giannelli & Yeomans, Ohio Juvenile Law § 23:5, Ineffective Assistance of Counsel.
Giannelli & Yeomans, Ohio Juvenile Law § 25:7, Advisement of Rights.
Giannelli & Yeomans, Ohio Juvenile Law § 35:2, Confidentiality Requirement.
Giannelli & Yeomans, Ohio Juvenile Law § 19:10, Rights While Detained.
Giannelli & Yeomans, Ohio Juvenile Law § 22:11, Right to Counsel.
Giannelli & Yeomans, Ohio Juvenile Law § 22:15, Access to Reports & Discovery.
Giannelli & Yeomans, Ohio Juvenile Law § 23:11, Public Trials; Gag Orders.

Law Review and Journal Commentaries

The Criminal Defense Lawyer in the Juvenile Justice System, David A. Harris. 26 U Tol L Rev 751 (Summer 1995).

Do Juveniles Facing Civil Commitment Have a Right to Counsel? A Therapeutic Jurisprudence Brief. Bruce J. Winick and Ginger Lerner-Wren, 71 U Cin L Rev 115 (Fall 2002).

Manipulated by *Miranda*: A Critical Analysis of Bright Lines and Voluntary Confessions Under *United States v. Dickerson*, Casenote. 68 U Cin L Rev 555 (Winter 2000).

The Representation of Juveniles Before the Court: A Look into the Past and the Future, Note. 31 Case W Res L Rev 580 (Spring 1981).

The Right to Remain Silent: The Use of Pre–Arrest Silence in *United States v. Oplinger*, 150 F.3d 1061 (5th Cir. 1998), Casenote. 68 U Cin L Rev 505 (Winter 2000).

Notes of Decisions

Ed. Note: This section contains annotations from former RC 2151.31 and RC 2151.35.

Admissibility of confession 7
Advising of rights 3
Appointment of counsel 2
Counsel not required 5
Custodian 10
Ineffective assistance 6

Non–parent in loco parentis, right to counsel 9
Parents' right to counsel 1
Procedural matters 8
Testimony and evidence 4

1. **Parents' right to counsel**

Mother had right to assistance of counsel in dependency proceeding in which county jobs and family services sought permanent custody of child; state and federal constitutions' guarantees of due process and equal protection of the law required that indigent parents be provided with counsel in actions instituted by the state to force the permanent, involuntary termination of parental rights, and mother had statutory right to representation at all stages of proceedings. In re Walling (Ohio App. 1 Dist., Hamilton, 04-01-2005) No. C-040745, 2005-Ohio-1558, 2005 WL 736665, Unreported. Infants 205

Indigent father had legal right to appointed counsel in his attempt to obtain visitation rights to his child born out of wedlock. Hatton v. Ankney (Ohio App. 3 Dist., Defiance, 03-21-2005) No. 4-04-26, 2005-Ohio-1252, 2005 WL 638441, Unreported. Children Out-of-wedlock 57

Magistrate erred in conducting hearing on father's motion to modify allocation of parental rights and responsibilities, which father brought following finding in paternity proceeding that he was child's natural father, without first informing mother of her statutory right to counsel or asking mother whether she wished to waive this right; magistrate further erred by conducting hearing despite mother's obvious unpreparedness and desire for counsel. Christopher W. v. Roxanne G. (Ohio App. 6 Dist., Lucas, 10-15-2004) No. L-03-1259, 2004-Ohio-5510, 2004 WL 2320336, Unreported. Children Out-of-wedlock 20.10

Mother did not have constitutional right to effective assistance of counsel in proceeding between mother and grandmother for custody of mother's two children, even though custody proceeding arose from dependency action filed by Children's Services Board, where Board had terminated its protective supervision involvement in case. In re Mahley (Ohio App. 5 Dist., Guernsey, 04-05-2004) No. 03 CA 23, 2004-Ohio-1772, 2004 WL 740003, Unreported. Child Custody 500; Infants 232

Mother's failure to cooperate with appointed counsel and court constituted waiver of her right to counsel in termination of parental rights proceeding; mother did not appear at disposition hearing in spite of receiving notice, counsel made continued attempts to contact mother without success, caseworker had not had recent contact with mother, other evidence showed that mother was disinterested in welfare of child since birth, and court permitted counsel to withdraw. In re Savanah M. (Ohio App. 6 Dist., Lucas, 10-31-2003) No. L-03-1112, 2003-Ohio-5855, 2003 WL 22462478, Unreported. Infants 205

Mother waived her right to the appointment of counsel at the hearing on a planned permanent living arrangement (PPLA) for teenage child; mother was served with a copy of the PPLA motion, notice of the hearing, and summons six days before the hearing, mother failed to contact the court to request appointment of counsel or appear at the hearing and request counsel, and mother had enough time to contact an attorney who had previously been appointed to represent her in proceeding involving child and explain the situation to him. In re Holt (Ohio App. 10 Dist., Franklin, 10-21-2003) No. 03AP-355, 2003-Ohio-5580, 2003 WL 22390048, Unreported. Infants 205

Incarcerated father had not been formally adjudicated indigent, for purposes of child support arrearage proceedings, and thus his right to appointed counsel had not been triggered. Jones v. Bowens (Ohio App. 11 Dist., Ashtabula, 09-26-2003) No. 2002-A-0034, 2003-Ohio-5224, 2003 WL 22235372, Unreported, appeal not allowed 101 Ohio St.3d 1423, 802 N.E.2d 154, 2004-Ohio-123. Child Support 491

Fact that incarcerated father did not face jail time was not a proper basis for denying him appointed counsel in child support arrearage proceedings. Jones v. Bowens (Ohio App. 11 Dist., Ashtabula, 09-26-2003) No. 2002-A-0034, 2003-Ohio-5224, 2003 WL 22235372, Unreported, appeal not allowed 101 Ohio St.3d 1423, 802 N.E.2d 154, 2004-Ohio-123. Child Support 491

Father failed to establish that he was prejudiced by his trial counsel's alleged failure to be more involved in the parental rights termination hearing, counsel's representation of mother and father and the same time, and counsel's failure to arrange for father's presence at the hearing; none of counsel's alleged deficiencies affected the outcome at trial. In re Joseph P. (Ohio App. 6 Dist., Lucas, 05-02-2003) No. L-02-1385, 2003-Ohio-2217, 2003 WL 2007268, Unreported. Infants 205

Juvenile court commits reversible error when it violates a parent's statutory right to be represented by counsel at a dispositional hearing to modify temporary custody of her son to long term foster care by failing to advise the parent of her right to counsel and her right to appointed counsel if she is indigent. In re Lander (Ohio App. 12 Dist., Butler, 06-26-2000) No. CA99-05-096, 2000 WL 819775, Unreported.

Parents were denied their statutory right to counsel in termination of parental rights proceedings, where father was never represented, mother's counsel withdrew at dispositional hearing for lack of contact with mother, and hearing continued ex parte. In re Alyssa C. (Ohio App. 6 Dist., 05-23-2003) 153 Ohio App.3d 10, 790 N.E.2d 803, 2003-Ohio-2673. Infants 205

Trial court committed reversible error in allowing father's attorney to withdraw at outset of dispositional hearing regarding termination of father's rights to minor child, on basis of father's tardiness at hearing and alleged failure to cooperate with attorney beforehand, where statute provided that parents were entitled to representation by legal counsel at all stages of such proceedings, father's attorney did not make requisite good cause showing to withdraw, from ethical perspective, attorney could not withdraw from employment until attorney had taken reasonable steps to avoid foreseeable prejudice to rights of client, and father could not have been deemed to have waived right to counsel. In re M.L.R. (Ohio App. 8 Dist., 10-31-2002) 150 Ohio App.3d 39, 779 N.E.2d 772, 2002-Ohio-5958. Infants 205; Infants 253

State and federal constitutional guarantees of due process and equal protection require that indigent parents be provided with counsel and transcript in actions for permanent, involuntary termination of parental rights; parties are afforded every procedural and substantive protection allowed by law because termination of parental rights is family law equivalent of death penalty in criminal case. In re Hitchcock (Ohio App. 8 Dist., 11-21-1996) 120 Ohio App.3d 88, 696 N.E.2d 1090, stay granted 77 Ohio St.3d 1462, 672 N.E.2d 1119, stay denied 77 Ohio St.3d 1502, 673 N.E.2d 921, motion to vacate stay denied 77 Ohio St.3d 1521, 674 N.E.2d 373, appeal allowed 78 Ohio St.3d 1455, 677 N.E.2d 815, appeal dismissed as improvidently allowed 81 Ohio St.3d 1222, 689 N.E.2d 43, 1998-Ohio-653, stay denied 81 Ohio St.3d 1469, 690 N.E.2d 1288, stay denied 81 Ohio St.3d 1476, 691 N.E.2d 294. Constitutional Law 225.1; Constitutional Law 274(5)

Under plain language of statute affording right to counsel at juvenile proceedings in general, indigent children, parents, custodians, or other persons in loco parentis are entitled to appointed counsel in all juvenile proceedings. State ex rel. Asberry v. Payne (Ohio, 05-20-1998) 82 Ohio St.3d 44, 693 N.E.2d 794, 1998-Ohio-596. Infants 205

Mother was not denied her statutory right to counsel at shelter care and adjudicatory hearings at which her children were placed into long-term foster care; she was served by certified mail with copy of complaint, and she failed to contact public defender's office to ask that they represent her. In re Ramsey Children (Ohio App. 5 Dist., 03-27-1995) 102 Ohio App.3d 168, 656 N.E.2d 1311. Infants 205

Indigent father was entitled to have counsel appointed to represent him on custody and visitation issues in child support action under statute and juvenile court rule; both rule and statute guarantee right to appointed counsel for all indigent parties in juvenile court proceedings, father, being natural father and parent of children, was a party to juvenile court proceeding under juvenile court rules, and father was indigent as defined in rules. McKinney v. McClure (Ohio App. 12 Dist., 03-27-1995) 102 Ohio App.3d 165, 656 N.E.2d 1310. Children Out-of-wedlock 20.4

Two-part test for ineffective assistance of counsel used in criminal cases is equally applicable in actions by state to force permanent, involuntary termination of parental rights. Jones v. Lucas County Children Services Bd. (Lucas 1988) 46 Ohio App.3d 85, 546 N.E.2d 471. Infants 205

In actions instituted by the state to force the permanent, involuntary termination of parental rights, the United States and Ohio Constitutions' guarantees of due process and equal protection of the law require that indigent parents be provided with counsel and a transcript at public expense for appeals as of right. State ex rel. Heller v. Miller (Ohio 1980) 61 Ohio St.2d 6, 399 N.E.2d 66, 15 O.O.3d 3. Constitutional Law 242.1(4); Constitutional Law 255(4)

An indigent mother seeking to regain custody of her son from a non-parent after the child has been adjudged to be dependent or neglected is entitled to appointed counsel and is prejudiced by the denial of such representation. Wright v Smith, No. 1475 (4th Dist Ct App, Ross, 1–19–89).

Where the natural parent of minor children was not represented by counsel during neglect, dependency and temporary custody proceedings but was represented by counsel at the parental rights termination and permanent custody proceedings, such parent is barred from bringing a habeas corpus action more than one year after the final decrees of adoption were issued for the minor children. Beard v Williams County Dept of Social Services, No. WMS–83–3 (6th Dist Ct App, Williams, 7–15–83).

2. **Appointment of counsel**

Juvenile did not have statutory right to appointed counsel in delinquency adjudication proceedings, where both juvenile and his mother chose to waive counsel. In re Spears (Ohio App. 5 Dist., Licking, 04-17-2006) No. 2005-CA-93, 2006-Ohio-1920, 2006 WL 1011201, Unreported. Infants ⚖ 205

Trial court was not required to appoint independent legal counsel to represent child in proceeding in which court granted permanent custody of child to county department of children and family services; there were no express or implied conflicts barring guardian ad litem (GAL) from serving as child's attorney, as he recommended disposition which was not in conflict with wishes of child. In re K.M. (Ohio App. 8 Dist., Cuyahoga, 07-14-2005) No. 85647, 2005-Ohio-3594, 2005 WL 1654569, Unreported, appeal not allowed 106 Ohio St.3d 1537, 835 N.E.2d 385, 2005-Ohio-5146. Infants ⚖ 205

Grandmother whose minor daughter gave birth to child who was adjudicated dependent was not entitled to appointed counsel at dispositional hearing for the child, and thus trial court that appointed counsel for grandmother could permit such appointed counsel to withdraw at outset of the dispositional hearing, even though grandmother was party to the proceeding by virtue of her daughter's minor status, where there was no evidence that grandmother was ever a custodian of child or acted in loco parentis with respect to child. In re Denisha Michelle T. (Ohio App. 6 Dist., Lucas, 03-11-2005) No. L-04-1236, 2005-Ohio-1032, 2005 WL 567121, Unreported. Infants ⚖ 205

Trial court was not required to appoint separate attorney and guardian ad litem to represent child in child dependency proceeding, as there was no evidence to establish that conflict existed with respect to attorney's performance as child's guardian ad litem and attorney. In re Miller (Ohio App. 5 Dist., Licking, 02-24-2005) No. 04 CA 32, 2005-Ohio-856, 2005 WL 469260, Unreported. Infants ⚖ 205

Juvenile court's procedures in obtaining juvenile's waiver of right to counsel and admission to probation violation violated juvenile's rights to counsel and due process in probation revocation proceedings; court had minimal discussion with juvenile regarding his right to counsel and no discussion with juvenile's father, juvenile's decision to admit violation was made without counsel and after consultation with his father, juvenile's father's interests were adverse to juvenile's given that father acknowledged he could not control juvenile's behavior and father was not opposed to juvenile court's involvement, juvenile court never answered juvenile's main concern as to how long he would be committed to Department of Youth Services (DYS), trial court never explained that consecutive minimum sentences would need to be served before any release for good behavior, and trial court's explanation of rights was misleading. In re Poland (Ohio App. 5 Dist., Licking, 10-15-2004) No. 04CA18, 2004-Ohio-5693, 2004 WL 2391813, Unreported. Constitutional Law ⚖ 255(4); Infants ⚖ 225

Trial court in child dependency proceedings committed plain error in allowing appointed counsel for child to withdraw and the guardian ad litem to act in the dual capacity of guardian and advocate for child, where there was no evidence presented to the trial court regarding child's wishes for placement, such that it was possible that separately assigned counsel would have advocated differently on behalf of child than did guardian ad litem. In re T.M., III (Ohio App. 8 Dist., Cuyahoga, 09-30-2004) No. 83933, 2004-Ohio-5222, 2004 WL 2340654, Unreported. Infants ⚖ 243

Statute, providing that counsel must be appointed for child not represented by his parent, did not require appointment of counsel in delinquency proceeding related to probation violation, where parents were present with juvenile to counsel and advise him and parents supported juvenile. In re Estes (Ohio App. 4 Dist., Washington, 09-24-2004) No. 04CA11, 2004-Ohio-5163, 2004 WL 2260510, Unreported. Infants ⚖ 205

Trial court was required to conduct investigation into whether dependent children were entitled to independent counsel in proceeding to determine their permanent custodian; guardian ad litem (GAL) who had been appointed for children was not a lawyer, and thus there was no possibility of court appointing him to represent children as their attorney, and, in GAL's report to court, in which he recommended that permanent custody of children be awarded to county, he made no mention of having talked with children about their feelings as to their permanent custodian, and whether children needed counsel was not discernable from record, given that, while court interviewed one child and was able to obtain some input from him as to his feelings about his mother, court failed to interview other child. In re Moore (Ohio App. 7 Dist., 08-24-2004) 158 Ohio App.3d 679, 821 N.E.2d 1039, 2004-Ohio-4544, supplemented 2005-Ohio-136, 2005 WL 78754. Infants ⚖ 205

Juvenile rule providing that, when complaint alleged that child was an abused child, court had to appoint attorney to represent interests of child, with respect to proceedings to determine permanent custodian for child, did not preclude appointment of independent counsel to represent children who had been adjudicated dependent rather than as abused. In re Moore (Ohio App. 7 Dist., 08-24-2004) 158 Ohio App.3d 679, 821 N.E.2d 1039, 2004-Ohio-4544, supplemented 2005-Ohio-136, 2005 WL 78754. Infants ⚖ 205

Mother did not waive on appeal issue of whether trial court should have appointed independent counsel for dependent children, in proceeding to determine whether county department of job and family services should be granted permanent custody of children, though mother did not raise issue in trial court; it would have been unfair to deny children their due process rights because mother failed to raise issue for children. In re Moore (Ohio App. 7 Dist., 08-24-2004) 158 Ohio App.3d 679, 821 N.E.2d 1039, 2004-Ohio-4544, supplemented 2005-Ohio-136, 2005 WL 78754. Infants ⚖ 243

Supreme Court decision in *In re Williams* that, pursuant to statute governing right to counsel in juvenile cases and juvenile rules, child who was subject of juvenile court proceeding to terminate parental rights was a party to that proceeding and, thus, was entitled to independent counsel in certain circumstances, had retroactive effect and applied to mother's case, in which permanent custody of her dependent children was being determined; *Williams* decision had been foreshadowed, and applying *Williams* decision retroactively would not produce injustice or hardship. In re Moore (Ohio App. 7 Dist., 08-24-2004) 158 Ohio App.3d 679, 821 N.E.2d 1039, 2004-Ohio-4544, supplemented 2005-Ohio-136, 2005 WL 78754. Courts ⚖ 100(1)

Mother waived her appellate argument that the trial court erred when it failed to appoint independent legal representation for child, during termination of parental rights proceeding, where mother failed to request the appointment of independent legal counsel for child and never objected to the trial court's failure to appoint independent legal counsel for child. In re Wright (Ohio App. 10 Dist., Franklin, 08-03-2004) No. 04AP-435, 2004-Ohio-4045, 2004 WL 1729881, Unreported. Infants ⚖ 243

Juvenile court's colloquy with 13-year-old juvenile, in which the court simply asked if juvenile had any questions and asked whether juvenile wanted to be represented by a lawyer in the juvenile delinquency proceeding, did not establish that juvenile knowingly waived his right to counsel before admitting to committing acts constituting burglary. In A.C. (Ohio App. 8 Dist., Cuyahoga, 10-16-2003) No. 82289, 2003-Ohio-5496, 2003 WL 22351114, Unreported. Infants ⚖ 199

Failing to appoint counsel to represent children in termination of parental rights proceeding involving allegations of child abuse was harmless error, where allegations of abuse were dismissed by agreement of parties and court attempted to determine each child's wishes by conducting in camera interview. In re Joshua B. (Ohio App. 6 Dist., Sandusky, 06-13-2003) No. S-02-018, No. S-02-021, No. S-02-019, No. S-02-020, 2003-Ohio-3096, 2003 WL 21384883, Unreported. Infants ⚖ 253

Trial court erred in failing to appoint counsel to represent children in termination of parental rights proceeding involving allegations of child abuse. In re Joshua B. (Ohio App. 6 Dist., Sandusky, 06-13-2003) No. S-02-018, No. S-02-021, No. S-02-019, No. S-02-020, 2003-Ohio-3096, 2003 WL 21384883, Unreported. Infants ⚖ 205

Indigent dependent children were parties to termination of parental rights proceeding who had right to appointed counsel upon being name in complaints. In re Emery (Ohio App. 4 Dist., Lawrence, 04-25-2003) No. 02CA40, 2003-Ohio-2206, 2003 WL 2003811, Unreported. Infants ⚖ 205

Trial court was required to appoint a guardian ad litem for children in termination of parental rights case, whereas the court was not likewise required to appoint counsel to represent them. In re Alfrey (Ohio App. 2 Dist., Clark, 02-07-2003) No. 01CA0083, 2003-Ohio-608, 2003 WL 262587, Unreported. Infants ⚖ 205

Trial court erred in failing to consider indigent child's level of maturity and whether his repeated desire for reunification with his mother required appointment of counsel to represent child's interest in whether to terminate mother's parental rights, even though guardian ad litem had been appointed for child, where guardian ad litem recommended termination of mother's rights, and conflict existed between guardian's recommendation and child's stated desire to stay with his mother. In re Williams (Ohio App. 11 Dist., Geauga, 11-29-2002) No. 2002-G-2454, No. 2002-G-2459, 2002-Ohio-6588, 2002 WL 31716777, Unreported, stay granted 98 Ohio

St.3d 1408, 781 N.E.2d 1017, 2003-Ohio-60, appeal not allowed 98 Ohio St.3d 1425, 782 N.E.2d 79, 2003-Ohio-259. Infants ⬳ 205

Allegedly abused child was entitled to have counsel appointed to represent his interests in dependency proceedings. (Per O'Neill, P.J., with one judge concurring in judgment only.) In re Calvin, Anthony, Alyshia (Ohio App. 11 Dist., Geauga, 11-22-2002) No. 2001-G-2379, 2002-Ohio-6468, 2002 WL 31663562, Unreported, stay granted 98 Ohio St.3d 1459, 783 N.E.2d 518, 2003-Ohio-644, appeal not allowed 98 Ohio St.3d 1513, 786 N.E.2d 63, 2003-Ohio-1572. Infants ⬳ 205

Trial court's failure to inquire as to appointment of counsel for mother in father's proceeding to modify shared parenting plan was harmless error, where, at trial, mother admitted that she made too much money to be considered indigent, and thus, mother would not have been entitled to appointment of counsel. In re Lemon (Ohio App. 5 Dist., Stark, 11-12-2002) No. 2002 CA 00098, 2002-Ohio-6263, 2002 WL 31546216, Unreported. Child Custody ⬳ 923(4)

Juvenile court's conduct of dispositional hearing in delinquency proceedings in absence of juvenile's counsel, and without obtaining waiver of counsel from juvenile, violated juvenile's constitutional right to counsel and to due process of law. In re B.M.S. (Ohio App. 2 Dist., 03-03-2006) 165 Ohio App.3d 609, 847 N.E.2d 506, 2006-Ohio-981. Infants ⬳ 205

Juvenile court should have appointed juvenile, who had been adjudicated delinquent, counsel to protect his constitutional rights at show-cause hearing that state brought against him for failing to follow all terms and conditions of treatment at Youth Treatment Center (YTC); although state argued court was not required to appoint counsel for juvenile since he was represented by his mother at court proceedings, sufficient evidence demonstrated that, as one of juvenile's victims and custodian of another of juvenile's victims, juvenile's mother may have had interests adverse to juvenile's best interests and therefore was unable to fully represent his interests. In re William B. (Ohio App. 6 Dist., 08-26-2005) 163 Ohio App.3d 201, 837 N.E.2d 414, 2005-Ohio-4428. Infants ⬳ 205

Where a parent in proceeding to terminate parental rights fails to maintain contact with counsel, fails to appear for scheduled hearings despite receiving notice of such, and fails to cooperate with counsel and the court, the court may infer that the parent has waived his or her right to counsel and may grant counsel's request to withdraw. In re C.H. (Ohio App. 3 Dist., 08-15-2005) 162 Ohio App.3d 602, 834 N.E.2d 401, 2005-Ohio-4183. Infants ⬳ 205

Mother waived her right to counsel in proceeding to terminate mother's parental rights; mother failed to maintain contact with and to cooperate with counsel, mother failed to appear at scheduled hearings even though she was present at hearing when county department of jobs and family services initially filed complaint alleging dependency, and counsel sent one letter and made numerous phone calls in attempt to contact mother. In re C.H. (Ohio App. 3 Dist., 08-15-2005) 162 Ohio App.3d 602, 834 N.E.2d 401, 2005-Ohio-4183. Infants ⬳ 205

Trial court's failure to appoint separate counsel to represent eldest child was erroneous, in termination of parental rights proceeding involving four siblings; during course of proceedings, eldest child changed her mind and expressed desire to reside with father, wishes of three other children did not change, which meant that eldest child and her siblings had inconsistent interests, and, when asked about potential conflict, children's attorney stated that it would be difficult for her to advocate eldest child's position. In re Sherman (Ohio App. 3 Dist., 07-05-2005) 162 Ohio App.3d 73, 832 N.E.2d 797, 2005-Ohio-3444, opinion vacated on reconsideration 2005-Ohio-5888, 2005 WL 2933064. Infants ⬳ 205

Supreme Court decision in In re Williams that, pursuant to statute governing right to counsel in juvenile cases and juvenile rules, child who was subject of juvenile court proceeding to terminate parental rights was a party to that proceeding and, thus, was entitled to independent counsel in certain circumstances, had retroactive effect and applied to mother's case, in which permanent custody of her dependent children was being determined; Williams decision had been foreshadowed, and applying Williams decision retroactively would not produce injustice or hardship. In re Moore (Ohio App. 7 Dist., 08-24-2004) 158 Ohio App.3d 679, 821 N.E.2d 1039, 2004-Ohio-4544, supplemented 2005-Ohio-136, 2005 WL 78754. Courts ⬳ 100(1)

Juvenile has a right to counsel in a proceeding to terminate parental rights, based on the juvenile's status as a party to the proceeding; courts should make a determination, on a case-by-case basis, whether the child actually needs independent counsel, taking into account the maturity of the child and the possibility of the child's guardian ad litem being appointed to represent the child. In re Williams (Ohio, 04-14-2004) 101 Ohio St.3d 398, 805 N.E.2d 1110, 2004-Ohio-1500. Infants ⬳ 205

Child who was subject of juvenile court proceeding to terminate parental rights was party to that proceeding, and entitled to independent counsel; abrogating In re Alfrey, Clark App. No. 01CA0083, 2003-Ohio-608, 2003 WL 262587. In re Williams (Ohio, 04-14-2004) 101 Ohio St.3d 398, 805 N.E.2d 1110, 2004-Ohio-1500. Infants ⬳ 200; Infants ⬳ 205

Father's waiver of counsel was made knowingly, voluntarily, and intelligently, at permanent custody hearing; father originally established his indigency and was appointed counsel, father terminated appointed counsel and signed a document indicating that he would retain his own counsel, notice of permanent custody hearing stated that all parties were entitled to a lawyer, father failed to reapply for a determination of his indigent status, father appeared at the permanent custody hearing and informed the court that he was ready to proceed pro se, and father never requested appointment of counsel. In re Moore (Ohio App. 3 Dist., 08-11-2003) 153 Ohio App.3d 641, 795 N.E.2d 149, 2003-Ohio-4250. Infants ⬳ 205

Juvenile was entitled to representation by counsel in adjudication for vandalism and criminal trespass, where juvenile did not waive his right to counsel, and conviction on charges could result in juvenile having his liberty curtailed. In re Johnston (Ohio App. 11 Dist., 04-30-2001) 142 Ohio App.3d 314, 755 N.E.2d 457. Infants ⬳ 205

An appointment to act as guardian ad litem (GAL) for a child in neglect proceedings does not constitute an appointment to act as the children's lawyer without an express appointment also to act as such. In re Clark (Ohio App. 8 Dist., 01-29-2001) 141 Ohio App.3d 55, 749 N.E.2d 833, 2001-Ohio-4126. Infants ⬳ 205

Failure to appoint counsel for children in neglect proceedings in which their permanent custody was granted to county Department of Child and Family Services' (DCFS) was reversible error; governing statute provided that lawyer must be provided for child not represented by his parent, guardian, or custodian, guardian ad litem (GAL) appointed for children was not their "guardian" within meaning of that statute because GAL was not authorized to "exercise parental rights" over children, GAL was not expressly appointed to act as children's lawyer, neither mother nor father could be considered as representing children here, as they and their lawyers represented their own interests, and DCFS' prosecution of permanent custody complaint could not be considered direct representation of children, as DCFS sought permanent custody and argued solely for that result. In re Clark (Ohio App. 8 Dist., 01-29-2001) 141 Ohio App.3d 55, 749 N.E.2d 833, 2001-Ohio-4126. Infants ⬳ 205; Infants ⬳ 253

Juvenile court was required to appoint counsel to represent child in custody dispute between former spouses, where court was aware that child's wishes as to custody were different from those of his appointed guardian ad litem, and where guardian ad litem, while an attorney, was not specifically appointed to act as child's attorney. In re Janie M. (Ohio App. 6 Dist., 02-05-1999) 131 Ohio App.3d 637, 723 N.E.2d 191. Infants ⬳ 90

Indigent children are entitled to appointed counsel in all juvenile court proceedings. In re Janie M. (Ohio App. 6 Dist., 02-05-1999) 131 Ohio App.3d 637, 723 N.E.2d 191. Infants ⬳ 205

Child is entitled to counsel at all stages of juvenile proceedings. In re Solis (Ohio App. 8 Dist., 12-22-1997) 124 Ohio App.3d 547, 706 N.E.2d 839. Infants ⬳ 205

Juvenile adjudicated delinquent and provisionally placed in foster care was entitled to counsel at dispositional hearing, as provisional placement was not equivalent of probation and dispositional hearing was not equivalent of probation revocation hearing. In re Solis (Ohio App. 8 Dist., 12-22-1997) 124 Ohio App.3d 547, 706 N.E.2d 839. Infants ⬳ 205

Even if juvenile adjudicated delinquent was improperly denied counsel at dispositional hearing, such denial did not mandate or permit reversal of underlying adjudication, where juvenile's counsel was present at adjudication hearing. In re Solis (Ohio App. 8 Dist., 12-22-1997) 124 Ohio App.3d 547, 706 N.E.2d 839. Infants ⬳ 254

Juvenile's right to representation by attorney in delinquency adjudication proceeding is one recognized by statute. In re Sappington (Ohio App. 2 Dist., 10-31-1997) 123 Ohio App.3d 448, 704 N.E.2d 339. Infants ⬳ 205

Under statutes involving right to counsel for indigent persons, phrase "pursuant to Chapter 120. of the Revised Code" in one statute does not limit circumstances in which a person is entitled to appointed counsel at juvenile proceedings, and instead phrase incorporates statutory procedures to provide that appointed counsel. State ex rel. Asberry v. Payne (Ohio, 05-20-1998) 82 Ohio St.3d 44, 693 N.E.2d 794, 1998-Ohio-596. Trial ⬳ 21

Ohio provides a statutory right to appointed counsel that goes beyond constitutional requirements. State ex rel. Asberry v. Payne (Ohio, 05-20-1998) 82 Ohio St.3d 44, 693 N.E.2d 794, 1998-Ohio-596. Trial ⬳ 21

There is no material difference with respect to constitutional right to counsel between adult and juvenile proceedings. In re East (Ohio App. 8 Dist., 07-17-1995) 105 Ohio App.3d 221, 663 N.E.2d 983, dismissed, appeal not allowed 74 Ohio St.3d 1482, 657 N.E.2d 1375. Infants ⊜ 205

Right to appointed counsel for indigent parties applies to all matters properly brought before juvenile court, including custody and visitation issues. McKinney v. McClure (Ohio App. 12 Dist., 03-27-1995) 102 Ohio App.3d 165, 656 N.E.2d 1310. Child Custody ⊜ 500

Failing to appoint separate counsel for mother in proceeding granting permanent custody of her and her husband's minor children to county department of human services was not erroneous where record was void of any evidence to establish that mother and father were going to separate, dissolve their marriage, or that they did not plan to raise their family together, record showed that counsel had represented couple in previous matters, that counsel had previously given couple the option of requesting alternate counsel, but they had not wanted to do so, and neither parent appeared at initial hearing. In re Brodbeck (Ohio App. 3 Dist., 10-19-1994) 97 Ohio App.3d 652, 647 N.E.2d 240. Infants ⊜ 205

Indigent parent was entitled to writ of mandamus commanding juvenile court judge to appoint counsel for her in child custody action commenced by her; parent had a clear legal right to relief prayed for, judge was under clear legal duty to appoint counsel for mother, and mother had no plain and adequate remedy in the ordinary course of law. State ex rel. Lunsford v. Buck (Meigs 1993) 88 Ohio App.3d 425, 623 N.E.2d 1356. Mandamus ⊜ 29

Mother who attended hearing on stepmother's motion to obtain custody of her child suffered no prejudice from alleged lack of appointed counsel or lack of notice that custody of her child would be at issue in proceeding; despite mother's assertions that she did not realize that hearing involved motion for change of custody, record of hearing contained ample indications that it included custody motion. In re Whaley (Athens 1993) 86 Ohio App.3d 304, 620 N.E.2d 954. Child Custody ⊜ 907

Because decision to appoint or refuse to appoint attorney to represent indigent clients in juvenile court rests entirely in judge's discretion, court administrator, county board of commissioners, and juvenile court could not be held responsible for any damages suffered by attorney by removal of his name from court appointment list. Eichenberger v. Petree (Franklin 1992) 76 Ohio App.3d 779, 603 N.E.2d 366, motion overruled 64 Ohio St.3d 1409, 592 N.E.2d 846. Counties ⊜ 59; Courts ⊜ 55; Judges ⊜ 36

In order to sustain commitment of a juvenile offender to a state institution in a delinquency proceeding, where such commitment will deprive the child of his liberty, the alleged delinquent must have been afforded representation by counsel, appointed at state expense in case of indigency. In re Agler (Ohio 1969) 19 Ohio St.2d 70, 249 N.E.2d 808, 48 O.O.2d 85. Infants ⊜ 205

Failure to appoint counsel for indigent parents in proceeding for termination of parental status did not deprive parent of due process in light of circumstances which included that petition contained no allegations upon which criminal charges could be based, no expert witnesses testified, case presented no specially troublesome points of law, and presence of counsel could not have made a determinative difference for petitioner; such decision does not imply that appointment of counsel is other than enlightened and wise. Lassiter v. Department of Social Services of Durham County, N. C. (U.S.N.C. 1981) 101 S.Ct. 2153, 452 U.S. 18, 68 L.Ed.2d 640, rehearing denied 102 S.Ct. 889, 453 U.S. 927, 69 L.Ed.2d 1023. Constitutional Law ⊜ 274(5)

Appointment of the guardian ad litem for the children as counsel for child did not violate child's constitutional right to counsel, in termination of parental rights proceeding; there was no conflict of interest between counsel's roles as guardian ad litem and as attorney for child since the children both expressed a desire to remain with their foster mother. In re Legg (Ohio App. 8 Dist., Cuyahoga, 09-05-2002) No. 80542, No. 80543, 2002-Ohio-4582, 2002 WL 2027290, Unreported. Infants ⊜ 205

Father and minor child were entitled to appointment of counsel to represent them at hearing on father's motion which sought custody of child. Sabrina J. v. Robbin C. (Ohio App. 6 Dist., Lucas, 05-31-2002) No. L-00-1374, 2002-Ohio-2691, 2002 WL 1303148, Unreported. Child Custody ⊜ 416; Infants ⊜ 205

RC 120.33(B) does not impose a clear legal duty upon a judge to appoint as counsel of record the attorney personally selected by an indigent party. State ex rel. Butler v. Demis (Ohio 1981) 66 Ohio St.2d 123, 420 N.E.2d 116, 20 O.O.3d 121.

Appointment of guardian ad litem (GAL) did not constitute an appointment to act as child's attorney in proceeding on father's motion which sought custody of child; there was no evidence of a dual appointment, such as mention on judgment entry that GAL was also acting as child's attorney or inclusion of an attorney number on documents bearing signature of GAL. Sabrina J. v Robbin C, No. L-00-1374, 2002-Ohio-2691, 2002 WL 1303148 (6th Dist Ct App, Lucas, 5-31-02).

An indigent child is entitled pursuant to RC 2151.352 and Juv R 4(A) to be represented by the county public defender in all juvenile court proceedings pertaining to a complaint alleging the child to be a juvenile traffic offender, regardless of whether the outcome of the proceeding could result in a loss of liberty, except when the right to counsel is waived or the juvenile court pursuant to RC 120.16(E) appoints counsel other than the county public defender or allows an indigent child to select his own personal counsel to represent him. OAG 97-040.

Pursuant to RC 2151.352, a child, his parents, custodian, or other persons in loco parentis, if indigent, is entitled to be represented in all juvenile proceedings by a public defender in accordance with the comprehensive system set forth in RC Ch 120, regardless of whether the outcome of the proceeding could result in a loss of liberty. OAG 84-023, approved and followed by OAG 97-040.

3. Advising of rights

Evidence was insufficient to establish that juvenile waived his right to counsel at the adjudicatory hearing or at the sexual predator classification hearing; at the adjudicatory hearing juvenile was never advised that he had the right to the assistance of legal counsel in connection with the hearing, he was never afforded the opportunity to request the assistance of counsel, and he never waived his right to counsel, and, at the sexual predator classification hearing, the court elicited a waiver from juvenile's mother but did not ascertain whether juvenile was willing to waive his right to counsel. In re C.A.C. (Ohio App. 2 Dist., Clark, 08-04-2006) No. 2005-CA-134, No. 2005-CA-135, 2006-Ohio-4003, 2006 WL 2219570, Unreported. Infants ⊜ 227(2)

Juvenile's constitutional right to counsel was violated during delinquency proceeding; juvenile indicated that he wanted an attorney at his arraignment, and there was no further discussion, either at the arraignment, or thereafter, of the matter of juvenile's legal representation. In re R.B. (Ohio App. 2 Dist., 01-13-2006) 2006-Ohio-264, 2006 WL 172367. Infants ⊜ 205

Defendant, who was convicted of burglary and committed to Department of Youth Services, did not validly waive his right to counsel; at adjudication hearing, trial court made no mention of counsel issue and merely asked whether defendant was ready to proceed, record was devoid of any evidence that court explained defendant's rights to him with respect to obtaining counsel, there was no evidence that defendant waived his right to counsel at any point prior to or during trial, and record did not disclose any attempt on part of court to explain defendant's right to counsel or waiver of that right at any time. In re L.E.P. (Ohio App. 2 Dist., Clark, 09-02-2005) No. 2004 CA 85, 2005-Ohio-4600, 2005 WL 2107854, Unreported. Criminal Law ⊜ 641.4(4)

Record did not support finding that juvenile was represented by counsel at time of his commitment and sexual predator classification hearing that was held subsequent to juvenile's guilty plea to gross sexual imposition, even though trial court made two references to counsel and argument was made on juvenile's behalf urging the court not to impose a sexual predator classification; review of the record revealed that juvenile's probation officer argued in juvenile's defense, record indicated trial court's reference to "counsel" related to probation officer and the argument he made on juvenile's behalf, and transcript of the proceedings did not mention the name of defense counsel. In re C.F. (Ohio App. 8 Dist., Cuyahoga, 05-05-2005) No. 84434, 2005-Ohio-2190, 2005 WL 1048126, Unreported. Infants ⊜ 205

Trial court failed to conduct a sufficient inquiry with juvenile during delinquency proceeding to determine whether juvenile knowingly, intelligently, and voluntarily waived her right to counsel; colloquy did not establish whether juvenile understood the nature of the right to counsel that she would be waiving, and there was no indication the trial court considered factors such as the juvenile's age, emotional stability, mental capacity, and prior criminal experience in making its determination. In re Kindred (Ohio App. 5 Dist., Licking, 07-02-2004) No. 04CA7, 2004-Ohio-3647, 2004 WL 1534135, Unreported. Infants ⊜ 205

The trial court's failure to comply with the statutory requirement that it inform parents of their right to counsel, and the right to appointed counsel if indigent, at the initial permanent custody hearing did not warrant reversal of order granting permanent custody of child to county children services; mother did not appear at the permanent custody hearing. In re Williams (Ohio App. 10 Dist., Franklin, 02-12-2004) No. 03AP-1007, 2004-Ohio-678, 2004 WL 285560, Unreported. Infants ⊜ 253

Juvenile did not validly waive her right to counsel in delinquency proceeding; while juvenile court orally informed juvenile that she had a right to an attorney at date in which juvenile was not admit or deny guilt to delinquency charge, trial court made no mention of the counsel issue at adjudication hearing and merely asked whether juvenile was ready to proceed, and juvenile court never inquired whether juvenile was waiving her right to counsel. In re Bays (Ohio App. 2 Dist., Greene, 03-14-2003) No. 2002-CA-52, No. 2002-CA-56, 2003-Ohio-1256, 2003 WL 1193787, Unreported. Infants 205

Juvenile's waiver of right to counsel at probation violation hearing was not voluntary, knowing, and intelligent, where trial court did not engage juvenile in meaningful discussion to determine whether juvenile understood rights she was waiving. In re Vaughters (Ohio App. 8 Dist., Cuyahoga, 10-24-2002) No. 80650, 2002-Ohio-5843, 2002 WL 31401623, Unreported. Infants 205

A trial court does not fulfill its duty to ascertain whether a juvenile knows of his right to be provided with counsel if he is indigent simply by asking the juvenile if he has received a copy of the statement of rights and whether he has any questions about those rights where (1) the statement of rights is two pages in length, (2) single-spaced, and (3) the right of counsel if indigent is not stated until near the top of the second page; under such circumstances, the juvenile even with a parent present, is likely to sign a form he has not fully read or does not fully understand while at the same time telling a judge otherwise. In re Shane (Ohio App. 2 Dist., Darke, 01-26-2001) No. 1523, 2001 WL 62550, Unreported.

Statute requiring counsel to be provided for juvenile not represented by the juvenile's parent, guardian, or custodian did not mean that participation by juvenile's father at adjudication hearing obviated juvenile's constitutional right to counsel in delinquency proceeding; no statute could override juvenile's constitutional right to counsel, and statute instead served purpose of assuring that juvenile's waiver of the right to counsel was knowing and voluntary. In re R.B. (Ohio App. 2 Dist., 01-13-2006) 166 Ohio App.3d 626, 852 N.E.2d 1219, 2006-Ohio-264. Infants 205

Juvenile, who had been adjudicated delinquent, did not knowingly, intelligently, and voluntarily waive his right to counsel, at show-cause hearing that state brought against juvenile for failing to follow all terms and conditions of treatment at Youth Treatment Center (YTC); juvenile was advised that in order to be afforded his constitutional rights, he would have to deny charges levied against him, juvenile had right to counsel at every stage of juvenile proceeding, including disposition, and statute governing right to counsel did not differentiate between juvenile who denied charge and juvenile who admitted charge. In re William B. (Ohio App. 6 Dist., 08-26-2005) 163 Ohio App.3d 201, 837 N.E.2d 414, 2005-Ohio-4428. Infants 205

Juvenile court magistrate's judgment entry, indicating only a finding that "subject child, after first being advised of all procedural and constitutional rights, including the right to counsel and a continuance herein, asserts said rights and ADMITS the allegations as they appear in the complaint," did not establish under the federal and state due process clauses a valid waiver of counsel or that the admission was voluntarily, knowingly, and intelligently made. In re Royal (Ohio App. 7 Dist., 03-01-1999) 132 Ohio App.3d 496, 725 N.E.2d 685. Constitutional Law 43(1); Infants 199; Infants 205

Juvenile court's limited inquiry at dispositional hearing and 14-year-old juvenile's limited responses, including court's asking whether juvenile recalled the rights explained to him at adjudicatory hearing and juvenile's response, "Um-hum," were insufficient to establish valid admission or valid waiver of right to counsel under the federal and state due process clauses. In re Royal (Ohio App. 7 Dist., 03-01-1999) 132 Ohio App.3d 496, 725 N.E.2d 685. Constitutional Law 43(1); Infants 199; Infants 205

Trial court failed to adequately advise juvenile of her right to counsel, where court did not conduct any meaningful colloquy with juvenile, made most of its remarks to juvenile's mother, who had filed unruly child complaint, and addressed child directly only briefly, almost as an afterthought. In re Rogers (Ohio App. 9 Dist., 12-10-1997) 124 Ohio App.3d 392, 706 N.E.2d 390. Infants 205

Magistrate who presided over arraignment in juvenile proceeding failed to adequately inform juvenile of her right to counsel; magistrate discussed right to counsel only in terms of representation if she were to proceed to trial, and gave explanation of right to counsel that was confusing, if not misleading, and could have led juvenile to believe that she was not entitled to counsel while deciding whether to admit or deny complaint. In re Doyle (App. 2 Dist., 10-03-1997) 122 Ohio App.3d 767, 702 N.E.2d 970. Infants 205

A juvenile does not knowingly and intelligently waive her right to counsel (1) in absence of any examination by the court regarding such right in deciding whether to admit or deny the complaint, (2) where the complaint states that the juvenile is a delinquent child by reason of committing an act that would constitute complicity to receiving stolen property if she were an adult, and (3) where the magistrate fails to ascertain whether the juvenile understands the charge against her or the possible length of any commitment in the custody of the Department of Youth Services. In re Doyle (App. 2 Dist., 10-03-1997) 122 Ohio App.3d 767, 702 N.E.2d 970.

Prior to juvenile's admission to habitual truancy charge, trial court failed to adequately advise juvenile of his constitutional rights and of consequences of his admission and also failed to sufficiently ascertain whether juvenile's purported waiver of counsel was made knowingly and voluntarily; there was no indication in record that trial court ever made determination concerning juvenile's indigency or advised juvenile that he had right to appointed counsel based on his indigency; trial court had merely asked juvenile whether it could be assumed that juvenile wished to proceed without attorney since juvenile was there without attorney, and trial court had not advised juvenile of purpose of hearing, possible penalties for alleged truancy violation, ramifications of admission to charge or of juvenile's rights to remain silent, offer evidence, cross-examine witnesses and have record made of proceedings. In re Kimble (Ohio App. 3 Dist., 09-25-1996) 114 Ohio App.3d 136, 682 N.E.2d 1066. Infants 199; Infants 205

Trial court accepted 13-year-old juvenile's waiver of counsel without proper assurances that waiver was knowing, intelligent and voluntary; referee gave basic explanation to juvenile on his right to counsel at initial hearing and adjudicatory hearing, and asked juvenile to sign waiver form, but failed to inquire into any circumstances that would demonstrate that juvenile knowingly, intelligently, and voluntarily waived his right to counsel, and trial judge did not address subject of right to counsel at dispositional hearing. In re Johnson (Ohio App. 1 Dist., 08-23-1995) 106 Ohio App.3d 38, 665 N.E.2d 247. Infants 205

Since juvenile was advised of his right to counsel and waived it when he entered his admission to robbery charge, it was not necessary for court to again advise juvenile of his right at disposition hearing. In re East (Ohio App. 8 Dist., 07-17-1995) 105 Ohio App.3d 221, 663 N.E.2d 983, dismissed, appeal not allowed 74 Ohio St.3d 1482, 657 N.E.2d 1375. Infants 203

Fact that juvenile's mother signed waiver of counsel form did not amount to waiver of juvenile's right to counsel, but fact that mother was present when waiver took place indicated that waiver was voluntary and knowing. In re East (Ohio App. 8 Dist., 07-17-1995) 105 Ohio App.3d 221, 663 N.E.2d 983, dismissed, appeal not allowed 74 Ohio St.3d 1482, 657 N.E.2d 1375. Infants 205

Parents should not have been ordered to pay bill prepared by Public Defender's Office for representation of their son in delinquency proceedings, where, at no time prior to dispositional hearing did court address parents, inform them of their status as parties to action, or advise them of their right to counsel. In re Hinko (Cuyahoga 1992) 84 Ohio App.3d 89, 616 N.E.2d 515. Infants 205

Unless the record establishes that a juvenile court advised a defendant of indigents' right to appointed counsel and that all claims of indigency were determined, there is a violation of the juvenile's statutory right to counsel requiring vacation of his conviction. In re Kriak (Medina 1986) 30 Ohio App.3d 83, 506 N.E.2d 556, 30 O.B.R. 140.

When a juvenile in custody asks to have his probation officer present, the question does not constitute a request for an attorney and subsequent statements by the juvenile are not taken in violation of the rule in Miranda v Arizona. (Ed. note: California law construed in light of federal constitution.) Fare v. Michael C. (U.S.Cal. 1979) 99 S.Ct. 2560, 442 U.S. 707, 61 L.Ed.2d 197, rehearing denied 100 S.Ct. 186, 444 U.S. 887, 62 L.Ed.2d 121.

Where a fifteen-year-old boy is arrested on a murder charge and questioned from midnight to five a.m. by relays of policemen without the benefit of counsel or friends to advise him, the fact that he is formally advised of his constitutional rights just before he signed a confession typed by the police does not alter the result that the boy's constitutional due process right had been violated, and such a confession is not admissible against him. Haley v. State of Ohio (U.S.Ohio 1948) 68 S.Ct. 302, 332 U.S. 596, 92 L.Ed. 224, 36 O.O. 530.

Colloquy prior to juvenile's admission of delinquency allegations, in which trial court informed juvenile that she had the right to an attorney and that one would be appointed for her if she could not afford one, asked whether juvenile wished to have an attorney, and was told "no" by juvenile, was not sufficient to establish a knowing, voluntary, and intelligent waiver of juvenile's right to counsel. In re K.J. (Ohio App. 8 Dist., Cuyahoga, 05-23-2002) No. 79612, No. 79940, 2002-Ohio-2615, 2002 WL 1041818, Unreported. Infants 174

Where a minor is found unruly, the trial court committed error in failing to advise the non-custodial parent of such minor of his right to counsel during the proceedings. In re Koogle, Nos. CA–82–68 and CA–82–93 (2d Dist Ct App, Greene, 6–16–83).

4. Testimony and evidence

Attorney was permitted to act as guardian ad litem and as attorney for mother and father's ten children, in termination of parental rights proceeding; there was no evidence that the children expressed strong desires or interests that were inconsistent with the recommendations of the guardian ad litem, and when the guardian ad litem reported that one child had expressed an interest in living with a relative the court made an inquiry and determined that the child was not serious and was more concerned about staying in contact with her siblings. In re Hilyard (Ohio App. 4 Dist., Vinton, 04-13-2006) No. 05CA600, No. 05CA603, No. 05CA607, No. 05CA601, No. 05CA604, No. 05CA608, No. 05CA602, No. 05CA606, No. 05CA609, 2006-Ohio-1965, 2006 WL   Infants ⇒ 205

Even assuming that testimony of protective services supervisor for county children's services agency, that child's maternal grandmother told on-call social worker and supervisor that she was upset that she could not have custody of child and that "she was just going to 'go' over and just take him," was inadmissible hearsay, any deficient performance of father's counsel in failing to object at the shelter care hearing was not prejudicial; court was not bound by formal rules of evidence at the hearing, and there was abundant evidence establishing that father's relatives were no longer able to care for child and that child should be placed in foster care. In re Wingo (Ohio App. 4 Dist., 06-01-2001) 143 Ohio App.3d 652, 758 N.E.2d 780, 2001-Ohio-2477.   Infants ⇒ 173.1; Infants ⇒ 253

Even assuming father's counsel provided deficient performance by failing to object that testimony of protective services supervisor for county children's services agency involved events and statements outside her personal knowledge, father was not prejudiced at hearing on agency's motion to terminate parental rights; much of the information was also testified to by other witnesses who had firsthand knowledge of events. In re Wingo (Ohio App. 4 Dist., 06-01-2001) 143 Ohio App.3d 652, 758 N.E.2d 780, 2001-Ohio-2477.   Infants ⇒ 205; Infants ⇒ 253

If parents of a juvenile who is the subject of delinquency hearing in juvenile court are to testify at that hearing, exclusion by judge of parents from courtroom under an order for separation of witnesses until they have testified is not prejudicial, where the juvenile is represented by counsel during hearing. State v. Ostrowski (Ohio 1972) 30 Ohio St.2d 34, 282 N.E.2d 359, 59 O.O.2d 62, certiorari denied 93 S.Ct. 130, 409 U.S. 890, 34 L.Ed.2d 147.   Infants ⇒ 207

Fact that minor was compelled to testify in juvenile delinquency proceedings instituted against him resulting in judgment that minor was a juvenile delinquent did not violate his constitutional rights against self-incriminations, since juvenile delinquency proceeding was not criminal in nature even though it might have involved violation of state criminal statute. State v. Shardell (Cuyahoga 1958) 107 Ohio App. 338, 153 N.E.2d 510, 79 Ohio Law Abs. 534, 8 O.O.2d 262.   Witnesses ⇒ 293.5

5. Counsel not required

Dependent children were not deprived right to counsel in proceedings to terminate father's parental rights when guardians ad litem were appointed to also act as counsel for children, where there was no showing of either implied or actual conflict of interest in acting as their guardian ad litem or as counsel. In re McLean (Ohio App. 11 Dist., Trumbull, 05-25-2005) No. 2005-T-0018, 2005-Ohio-2576, 2005 WL 1231614, Unreported, appeal not allowed 106 Ohio St.3d 1510, 833 N.E.2d 1251, 2005-Ohio-4605.   Infants ⇒ 205

Trial court was not required to conduct independent examination as to whether children should have been appointed separate counsel in proceedings to terminate mother's and father's parental rights based on initial ambivalence by children regarding their wishes for placement; guardian ad litem subsequently determined that children expressed adamant desire to remain with foster family, and such wishes were not in conflict with those of guardian ad litem. In re Miller (Ohio App. 10 Dist., Franklin, 03-03-2005) No. 04AP-783, 2005-Ohio-897, 2005 WL 488396, Unreported, appeal not allowed 106 Ohio St.3d 1463, 830 N.E.2d 1170, 2005-Ohio-3490.   Infants ⇒ 205

Trial court in child dependency proceedings did not commit plain error in allowing appointed counsel for child to withdraw and the guardian ad litem to act in the dual capacity of guardian and advocate for child; child wished to remain with foster parents, such that there would have been no conflict between what counsel would have advocated for him and the recommendation of permanent placement for child made by the guardian ad litem. In re T.M., III (Ohio App. 8 Dist., Cuyahoga, 09-30-2004) No. 83933, 2004-Ohio-5222, 2004 WL 2340654, Unreported.   Infants ⇒ 243

Juvenile knowingly, voluntarily, and intelligently waived right to counsel at delinquency proceeding related to probation violation, where juvenile was 17 years old, possessed above-average intelligence, had extensive experience with juvenile court system, had his parents present to assist him, was advised of charge and possible punishments, was advised of right to counsel, and indicated that he did not want counsel to represent him. In re Estes (Ohio App. 4 Dist., Washington, 09-24-2004) No. 04CA11, 2004-Ohio-5163, 2004 WL 2260510, Unreported.   Infants ⇒ 205

Circumstances did not warrant appointment of independent counsel to represent minor children in permanent custody proceeding; juvenile court was made aware of child's possible desire to be placed with his mother though his mother's testimony and testimony from caseworker. In re Lane (Ohio App. 3 Dist., Marion, 06-01-2004) No. 9-03-61, No. 9-03-62, 2004-Ohio-2798, 2004 WL 1192087, Unreported.   Infants ⇒ 205

Trial court was not required to appoint an attorney to represent children in a termination of parental rights case, where children were not parties to action, and mother's position concerning custody of children were exactly aligned with children's position, in that both mother and children wanted mother to retain custody. In re Alfrey (Ohio App. 2 Dist., Clark, 02-07-2003) No. 01CA0083, 2003-Ohio-608, 2003 WL 262587, Unreported.   Infants ⇒ 205

A conflict between the recommendation of the guardian ad litem in termination proceedings and the desires of children did not require the court to appoint counsel to represent them. In re Alfrey (Ohio App. 2 Dist., Clark, 02-07-2003) No. 01CA0083, 2003-Ohio-608, 2003 WL 262587, Unreported.   Infants ⇒ 205

Alleged failure to appoint an attorney to represent father in termination proceedings did not so prejudice mother that she had standing to prosecute claim on appeal, where father was present and available to be called as a witness at proceeding. In re Alfrey (Ohio App. 2 Dist., Clark, 02-07-2003) No. 01CA0083, 2003-Ohio-608, 2003 WL 262587, Unreported.   Infants ⇒ 242

There is no constitutional right to appointment of counsel for indigent parents in a hearing on a complaint by a county social services department for temporary custody of allegedly neglected children. In re Miller (Ohio 1984) 12 Ohio St.3d 40, 465 N.E.2d 397, 12 O.B.R. 35.

O Const Art I, § 10, US Const Am 5, and US Const Am 6, being applicable only to the rights of accused persons charged with criminal offenses, do not apply to, or require the appointment of counsel in, a delinquent-child proceeding in the juvenile court. Cope v. Campbell (Ohio 1964) 175 Ohio St. 475, 196 N.E.2d 457, 26 O.O.2d 88.

6. Ineffective assistance

In proceeding in which county children services sought permanent custody of children, failure of mother's counsel to obtain an expert witness to rebut testimony of psychologist who testified on behalf of county did not result in prejudice to mother, and thus could not amount to ineffective assistance. In re Ohler (Ohio App. 4 Dist., Hocking, 03-24-2005) No. 04CA8, 2005-Ohio-1583, 2005 WL 737580, Unreported.   Infants ⇒ 205

Mother in permanent custody proceedings failed to show prejudice resulting from trial counsel's failure to object to admission of testimony regarding criminal history of the man she was supposedly dating during time immediately preceding trial, and thus such failure was not ineffective assistance of counsel; testimony was wholly disregarded by magistrate, who based his recommendation on facts relating to mother's choices, not those of her boyfriend. In re Brooks (Ohio App. 10 Dist., Franklin, 07-22-2004) No. 04AP-164, No. 04AP-201, No. 04AP-202, No. 04AP-165, 2004-Ohio-3887, 2004 WL 1631760, Unreported, appeal not allowed 103 Ohio St.3d 1495, 816 N.E.2d 1081, 2004-Ohio-5605.   Infants ⇒ 205

Mother in permanent custody proceedings failed to show deficient assistance in trial counsel's failure to object to presence in the courtroom of caseworker-witness designated to represent county at trial, and thus such failure was not ineffective assistance of counsel; there was no suggestion that caseworker-witness interfered with the proceedings or that her presence had any effect on the testimony of other witnesses. In re Brooks (Ohio App. 10 Dist., Franklin, 07-22-2004) No. 04AP-164, No. 04AP-201, No. 04AP-202, No. 04AP-165, 2004-Ohio-3887, 2004 WL 1631760, Unreported, appeal not allowed 103 Ohio St.3d 1495, 816 N.E.2d 1081, 2004-Ohio-5605.   Infants ⇒ 205

Mother in permanent custody proceedings failed to show deficient assistance in trial counsel's failure to cross-examine guardian ad litem, and thus such failure was not ineffective assistance of counsel; decision may have been strategic, given that guardian ad litem strongly supported termination of parental rights. In re Brooks (Ohio App. 10 Dist., Franklin, 07-22-2004) No. 04AP-164, No. 04AP-201, No. 04AP-202, No. 04AP-165, 2004-Ohio-3887, 2004 WL 1631760, Unreported, appeal not allowed 103 Ohio St.3d 1495, 816 N.E.2d 1081, 2004-Ohio-5605. Infants ⇔ 205

Mother in permanent custody proceedings failed to show prejudice resulting from trial counsel's failure to submit more detailed objections to magistrate's decision, and thus such failure was not ineffective assistance of counsel; although counsel was warned to file more specific objections in the future, trial court proceeded to fully address issues related to applicable best interest factors. In re Brooks (Ohio App. 10 Dist., Franklin, 07-22-2004) No. 04AP-164, No. 04AP-201, No. 04AP-202, No. 04AP-165, 2004-Ohio-3887, 2004 WL 1631760, Unreported, appeal not allowed 103 Ohio St.3d 1495, 816 N.E.2d 1081, 2004-Ohio-5605. Infants ⇔ 205

Parents did not establish that failure of their counsel to object to allegedly damaging testimony of witnesses constituted ineffective assistance in termination of parental rights proceeding, where parents failed to argue basis upon which counsel could have objected and, even if witnesses' testimony was damaging, remainder of evidence was more than sufficient to support termination of parental rights. In re Andy-Jones (Ohio App. 10 Dist., Franklin, 06-24-2004) No. 03AP-1167, No. 03AP-1231, 2004-Ohio-3312, 2004 WL 1405319, Unreported, stay denied 103 Ohio St.3d 1425, 814 N.E.2d 489, 2004-Ohio-4524, appeal not allowed 103 Ohio St.3d 1429, 814 N.E.2d 491, 2004-Ohio-4524, appeal not allowed 103 Ohio St.3d 1465, 815 N.E.2d 680, 2004-Ohio-5056. Infants ⇔ 205

Failure of counsel for parents to raise claim that Franklin County Children Services (FCCS) failed to comply with ADA in developing case plan related to dependent child did not constitute ineffective assistance in termination of parental rights proceeding, where there was no evidence to support finding that father had disability protected by ADA. In re Andy-Jones (Ohio App. 10 Dist., Franklin, 06-24-2004) No. 03AP-1167, No. 03AP-1231, 2004-Ohio-3312, 2004 WL 1405319, Unreported, stay denied 103 Ohio St.3d 1425, 814 N.E.2d 489, 2004-Ohio-4524, appeal not allowed 103 Ohio St.3d 1429, 814 N.E.2d 491, 2004-Ohio-4524, appeal not allowed 103 Ohio St.3d 1465, 815 N.E.2d 680, 2004-Ohio-5056. Infants ⇔ 205

Failure of counsel for parents to challenge constitutionality of statutes applicable in termination of parental rights proceeding did not constitute ineffective assistance, where courts had previously found statutes to be constitutional and there was no reasonable probability that result of proceeding would have been different had counsel challenged statutes. In re Andy-Jones (Ohio App. 10 Dist., Franklin, 06-24-2004) No. 03AP-1167, No. 03AP-1231, 2004-Ohio-3312, 2004 WL 1405319, Unreported, stay denied 103 Ohio St.3d 1425, 814 N.E.2d 489, 2004-Ohio-4524, appeal not allowed 103 Ohio St.3d 1429, 814 N.E.2d 491, 2004-Ohio-4524, appeal not allowed 103 Ohio St.3d 1465, 815 N.E.2d 680, 2004-Ohio-5056. Infants ⇔ 205

Counsel's failure to object when guardian ad litem for the children questioned witnesses during termination of parental rights hearing did not constitute ineffective assistance; mother failed to overcome the strong presumption that counsel's failure to object was reasonable trial strategy, and mother failed to establish that counsel's failure to object to the questioning by guardian ad litem prejudiced mother or affected the outcome of trial. In re Curry (Ohio App. 4 Dist., Washington, 02-11-2004) No. 03CA51, 2004-Ohio-750, 2004 WL 307476, Unreported. Infants ⇔ 205

Father's counsel in child support hearing as to nonmarital child was not ineffective for failing to raise the defense of laches in mother's action for child support that occurred six years after the child's birth; father's claim that he would have conducted his financial affairs differently had he known that he would be subject to a child support order did not amount to a showing of material prejudice as required for laches, and thus, there was not a reasonable probability that the juvenile court's decision on child support would have been different had the laches defense been raised. Newbauer v. Bertrand (Ohio App. 12 Dist., Clermont, 09-29-2003) No. CA2002-09-074, 2003-Ohio-5109, 2003 WL 22227372, Unreported. Children Out-of-wedlock ⇔ 67

Father's counsel in child support hearing as to nonmarital child was not ineffective for failing to introduce documentation of father's alleged support of child over the years, where it was not clear from the record that any such documentation existed. Newbauer v. Bertrand (Ohio App. 12 Dist., Clermont, 09-29-2003) No. CA2002-09-074, 2003-Ohio-5109, 2003 WL 22227372, Unreported. Children Out-of-wedlock ⇔ 67

Father's counsel at termination of parental rights hearing was not ineffective for failing to ask questions on cross examination or present witnesses; failing to question witnesses on cross examination and choosing not to present witnesses fell within realm of trial strategy, and father failed to demonstrate how counsel's alleged deficient performance affected outcome of proceedings. In re Riley (Ohio App. 4 Dist., Washington, 07-25-2003) No. 03CA19, 2003-Ohio-4109, 2003 WL 21783373, Unreported. Infants ⇔ 205

Comments made by counsel during dispositional hearing, in which counsel stated that father worked intermittently and father "claims a lot of things," did not prejudice father, and could not amount to ineffective assistance; the comments were offhand comments, they did not demonstrate that counsel did not zealously represent father, and they did not affect the trial court's decision to grant permanent custody. In re Moore (Ohio App. 3 Dist., 08-11-2003) 153 Ohio App.3d 641, 795 N.E.2d 149, 2003-Ohio-4250. Infants ⇔ 205

Counsel's withdrawal of his motion for contempt and objections did not prejudice defendant, and thus could not amount to ineffective assistance, in child dependency proceeding; counsel withdrew his motion and objections after father indicated that he wanted to surrender permanent custody of child to county department of job and family services. In re Moore (Ohio App. 3 Dist., 08-11-2003) 153 Ohio App.3d 641, 795 N.E.2d 149, 2003-Ohio-4250. Infants ⇔ 205

Comments made by counsel during dispositional hearing, in which counsel stated that father worked intermittently and father "claims a lot of things," did not prejudice father, and could not amount to ineffective assistance; the comments were offhand comments, they did not demonstrate that counsel did not zealously represent father, and they did not affect the trial court's decision to grant permanent custody. In re Moore (Ohio App. 3 Dist., 08-11-2003) 153 Ohio App.3d 641, 795 N.E.2d 149, 2003-Ohio-4250. Infants ⇔ 205

Counsel's withdrawal of his motion for contempt and objections did not prejudice defendant, and thus could not amount to ineffective assistance, in child dependency proceeding; counsel withdrew his motion and objections after father indicated that he wanted to surrender permanent custody of child to county department of job and family services. In re Moore (Ohio App. 3 Dist., 08-11-2003) 153 Ohio App.3d 641, 795 N.E.2d 149, 2003-Ohio-4250. Infants ⇔ 205

Juvenile court did not patently and unambiguously lack jurisdiction to grant permanent custody of child to county children's services (CCS) and, thus, mother had an adequate remedy at law by her previous unsuccessful appeal, precluding habeas corpus relief; notwithstanding failure to appear, mother had notice of proceeding and was represented by counsel, and any ineffectiveness of counsel was due to mother's failure to communicate with counsel prior to hearing. Ross v. Saros (Ohio, 08-20-2003) 99 Ohio St.3d 412, 792 N.E.2d 1126, 2003-Ohio-4128. Habeas Corpus ⇔ 280

For purposes of ineffective assistance claim, minor mother and her parents did not make necessary showing that mother was prejudiced, in dependency proceeding that culminated in judgment terminating mother's parental rights to infant child, by failure of mother's counsel to appear at a pretrial hearing, where counsel made unsuccessful request for continuance of pretrial hearing, and all information shared at hearing was to be shared with mother's counsel. In re Baby Girl Doe (Ohio App. 6 Dist., 08-30-2002) 149 Ohio App.3d 717, 778 N.E.2d 1053, 2002-Ohio-4470, appeal not allowed 97 Ohio St.3d 1425, 777 N.E.2d 278, 2002-Ohio-5820. Infants ⇔ 205

Where the proceeding contemplates the loss of parents' essential and basic civil rights to raise their children, the test for ineffective assistance of counsel used in criminal cases is equally applicable to actions seeking to force the permanent, involuntary termination of parental custody. In re Baby Girl Doe (Ohio App. 6 Dist., 08-30-2002) 149 Ohio App.3d 717, 778 N.E.2d 1053, 2002-Ohio-4470, appeal not allowed 97 Ohio St.3d 1425, 777 N.E.2d 278, 2002-Ohio-5820. Infants ⇔ 205

Assuming that father's counsel provided deficient performance by failing to submit written argument to court regarding whether child was dependent child and by failing to appear at the hearing extending temporary custody, father was not prejudiced; at that juncture of the case, county children's services agency was attempting to reunify child with mother and place him with a relative until such goal could be accomplished, father had expressed no desire to gain custody of child, and child's relatives were either not interested in custody or were considered improper placements by agency. In re Wingo (Ohio App. 4 Dist., 06-01-2001) 143 Ohio App.3d 652, 758 N.E.2d 780, 2001-Ohio-2477. Infants ⇔ 205; Infants ⇔ 253

Where proceeding contemplates loss of parents' essential and basic civil rights to raise their children, test for ineffective assistance of counsel used in criminal cases is equally applicable to actions seeking to force permanent, involuntary termination of parental custody. In re Heston (Ohio App. 1 Dist., 09-18-1998) 129 Ohio App.3d 825, 719 N.E.2d 93. Infants ⇔ 205

Statutory right to counsel in child protection proceedings includes right to effective assistance of counsel. In re Heston (Ohio App. 1 Dist., 09-18-1998) 129 Ohio App.3d 825, 719 N.E.2d 93. Infants ⇔ 205

Counsel's performance in representing mother in proceeding granting permanent custody of her and her husband's minor children to county department of human services was not deficient and counsel was not obligated to withdraw due to conflict and, thus, mother was not denied effective assistance of counsel where record was void of any evidence to establish that mother and father were going to separate, dissolve their marriage, or that they did not plan to raise their family together, counsel addressed effort made by mother and father, children's relationship with them, importance of family unit, mother's actions in applying for financial assistance and faithfulness in going to doctor appointments, and counsel had mother testify regarding visits with children and her feelings regarding custody. In re Brodbeck (Ohio App. 3 Dist., 10-19-1994) 97 Ohio App.3d 652, 647 N.E.2d 240. Infants 205

To establish ineffective assistance of counsel in proceeding for permanent, involuntary termination of parental rights, parent first must show that counsel's performance was deficient, requiring showing that counsel made errors so serious that counsel was not functioning as counsel guaranteed parent by the Sixth Amendment; second, parent must show that the deficient performance prejudiced the defense, requiring showing that counsel's errors were so serious as to deprive parent of a fair trial, a trial whose result is reliable. In re Brodbeck (Ohio App. 3 Dist., 10-19-1994) 97 Ohio App.3d 652, 647 N.E.2d 240. Infants 205

An appointed counsel's failure to object to lack of jurisdiction for failure of the trial court to comply with the statutory mandate of RC 2151.353 is so fundamental a failure that the natural mother as a consequence does not receive the required effective assistance of counsel at her hearing to terminate her parental rights and grant custody to the county department of human services. In re Travis Children (Stark 1992) 80 Ohio App.3d 620, 609 N.E.2d 1356.

Failure of an incarcerated parent to prove that having his children visit him in prison is in the children's best interest results in denial of the motion for visitation; counsel's failure to present any evidence in support of his own motion constitutes a deficient performance where counsel has an obligation to at least have his client testify on this issue, not to merely refer the court to the client to explain his position in a non-testimonial fashion. In re Lenz (Ohio App. 3 Dist., Seneca, 08-29-2001) No. 13-01-05, 2001-Ohio-2132, 2001 WL 991029, Unreported.

7. Admissibility of confession

Neither juvenile's waiver of counsel nor his admission to charges against him were made in a knowing manner, for purposes of delinquency proceedings, where juvenile was never informed of nature of charges against him, trial court made no mention of possible defenses or mitigating circumstances that related to juvenile's situation, and juvenile was not informed that if he admitted to the charges he would be losing certain rights associated with trial. In re Styer (Ohio App. 3 Dist., Union, 11-19-2002) No. 14-02-12, 2002-Ohio-6273, 2002 WL 31555992, Unreported. Infants 199; Infants 205

Three minors, suspected of murder, were apprehended; prior to their being taken before any court and before any charges were filed against them, signed confessions were obtained from each of them; they were then taken before juvenile court which conducted investigation, and nature of crime being apparent, cases were referred to common pleas court where accused were indicted, tried and convicted; in each instance confession obtained was used against one making it, in both juvenile court and court of common pleas; held: confessions were admissible in evidence, even though accused were not taken immediately before juvenile court as directed by this section; fact that confessions were used in juvenile court, did not render them inadmissible in court of common pleas under GC 1639–30 (RC 2151.35) because there was but one case or proceeding. (Ed. note: See 19 OS(2d) 70, 249 NE(2d) 808 (1969), In re Agler, for prevailing opinion on juvenile rights.) State v. Lowder (Stark 1946) 79 Ohio App. 237, 72 N.E.2d 785, 34 O.O. 568, appeal dismissed 147 Ohio St. 340, 70 N.E.2d 905, 34 O.O. 249, certiorari granted 67 S.Ct. 1728, 331 U.S. 803, 91 L.Ed. 1826, reversed 68 S.Ct. 302, 332 U.S. 596, 92 L.Ed. 224, 36 O.O. 530, appeal dismissed 147 Ohio St. 530, 72 N.E.2d 102, 34 O.O. 423, appeal dismissed 147 Ohio St. 531, 72 N.E.2d 81, 34 O.O. 423, appeal dismissed 151 Ohio St. 80, 84 N.E.2d 217, 38 O.O. 531, certiorari denied 69 S.Ct. 1501, 337 U.S. 945, 93 L.Ed. 1748.

8. Procedural matters

Juvenile court was required to hold in-camera interview of child to determine whether conflict existed between guardian ad litem's recommended disposition and child's wishes, such that appointment of separate counsel for child was required, in child protection proceeding in which county sought permanent custody of child; potential conflict between guardian ad litem's recommended disposition of adoption and child's wishes to maintain some contact with her father could not be avoided by guardian ad litem's mere expression of child's wishes to trial court. In re H.R. (Ohio App. 2 Dist., Montgomery, 03-31-2006) No. 21274, 2006-Ohio-1595, 2006 WL 827385, Unreported. Infants 205

Trial court had the duty to interview three-year-old child who was the subject of a termination of parental rights proceeding to determine if she wanted to live with her mother, which would require appointment of independent counsel, where guardian ad litem recommended that parental rights be terminated, but child's older sister had told the guardian ad litem she and her sister wanted to live with their mother. In re Wylie (Ohio App. 2 Dist., Greene, 12-14-2004) No. 2004CA0054, 2004-Ohio-7243, 2004 WL 3561213, Unreported. Infants 207

Adjudicated father of child lacked standing to request that mother's attorney be disqualified in child support proceeding, based on alleged conflict of interest stemming from fact that mother's attorney had represented her former husband in divorce action; mother's former husband was not a party to support action in which issue of disqualification had been raised, record did not show that mother's attorney had ever represented putative father, and mother's former husband was only person who could raise potential conflict of interest and ask for disqualification of mother's attorney. Dawn G. v. Michael L.G. (Ohio App. 6 Dist., Huron, 09-17-2004) No. H-04-007, 2004-Ohio-4920, 2004 WL 2072466, Unreported. Attorney And Client 21.20; Children Out-of-wedlock 57

Mother had standing on appeal to assert her children's right to attorney in proceedings on county Department of Child and Family Services' (DCFS) petition for permanent custody of mother's children. In re Clark (Ohio App. 8 Dist., 01-29-2001) 141 Ohio App.3d 55, 749 N.E.2d 833, 2001-Ohio-4126. Infants 242

In applying totality-of-the-circumstances test to waiver of counsel by juveniles, courts must give close scrutiny to factors such as juvenile's age, emotional stability, mental capacity, and prior criminal experience. In re Johnson (Ohio App. 1 Dist., 08-23-1995) 106 Ohio App.3d 38, 665 N.E.2d 247. Infants 205

Referee's report/journal entry and supplemental report, stating that juvenile was advised of his right to counsel and he chose to waive this right, were adequate to show juvenile's waiver of his right to counsel, absent request for transcript of admission hearing. In re East (Ohio App. 8 Dist., 07-17-1995) 105 Ohio App.3d 221, 663 N.E.2d 983, dismissed, appeal not allowed 74 Ohio St.3d 1482, 657 N.E.2d 1375. Infants 246

Although rule is generally move expansive than statute governing discovery in juvenile delinquency proceedings, nature of proceedings for which discovery is sought is relevant in determining extent to which discovery will be granted under rule. In re Doss (Ohio Com.Pl., 05-11-1994) 65 Ohio Misc.2d 8, 640 N.E.2d 618. Infants 201

Habeas corpus will not lie based upon an allegation of denial of counsel to a juvenile adjudicated delinquent inasmuch as a right of appeal to the Court of Appeals exists in such case. In re Piazza (Ohio 1966) 7 Ohio St.2d 102, 218 N.E.2d 459, 36 O.O.2d 84.

9. Non–parent in loco parentis, right to counsel

For grandmother who cared for child for years to be entitled to writ of mandamus to compel appointment of counsel for her in her juvenile court custody proceeding, grandmother must establish that she has a clear legal right to the appointment of counsel, that juvenile court judge has a clear legal duty to appoint counsel for her, and that she has no adequate remedy in the ordinary course of law. State ex rel. Asberry v. Payne (Ohio, 05-20-1998) 82 Ohio St.3d 44, 693 N.E.2d 794, 1998-Ohio-596. Mandamus 3(3); Mandamus 32

Grandmother, who had cared for child for years and who trial court recognized as indigent party to custody proceeding and in loco parentis to child, had a clear legal right to appointment of counsel in juvenile court custody proceeding, there was corresponding clear legal duty on judge's part to appoint counsel, and grandmother lacked adequate remedy in the ordinary course of law to challenge judge's refusal to appoint her counsel; thus, grandmother was entitled to writ of mandamus to compel judge to appoint counsel to her in custody proceeding. State ex rel. Asberry v. Payne (Ohio, 05-20-1998) 82 Ohio St.3d 44, 693 N.E.2d 794, 1998-Ohio-596. Mandamus 3(3); Mandamus 32

10. Custodian

Social worker from residential facility in whose custody juvenile had been committed was a "custodian" for purposes of statute requiring that counsel be provided for child not represented by parent, guardian, or custodian. In re Smith (Ohio App. 8 Dist., 03-26-2001) 142 Ohio App.3d 16, 753 N.E.2d 930. Infants 205

Custodian's advice that juvenile admit to the charges if true, or deny them if false, did not indicate that custodian did not have juvenile's best interests in mind sufficient to require that juvenile be automatically appointed counsel. In re Smith (Ohio App. 8 Dist., 03-26-2001) 142 Ohio App.3d 16, 753 N.E.2d 930. Infants ⊙— 205

Fundamental liberty interest of natural parents in care, custody and management of their child does not evaporate simply because they have not been model parents or have lost temporary custody of their child to State. Santosky v. Kramer (U.S.N.Y. 1982) 102 S.Ct. 1388, 455 U.S. 745, 71 L.Ed.2d 599, on remand 89 A.D.2d 738, 453 N.Y.S.2d 942. Child Custody ⊙— 42; Child Custody ⊙— 68

2151.353 Disposition of abused, neglected, or dependent child

(A) If a child is adjudicated an abused, neglected, or dependent child, the court may make any of the following orders of disposition:

(1) Place the child in protective supervision;

(2) Commit the child to the temporary custody of a public children services agency, a private child placing agency, either parent, a relative residing within or outside the state, or a probation officer for placement in a certified foster home, or in any other home approved by the court;

(3) Award legal custody of the child to either parent or to any other person who, prior to the dispositional hearing, files a motion requesting legal custody of the child or is identified as a proposed legal custodian in a complaint or motion filed prior to the dispositional hearing by any party to the proceedings. A person identified in a complaint or motion filed by a party to the proceedings as a proposed legal custodian shall be awarded legal custody of the child only if the person identified signs a statement of understanding for legal custody that contains at least the following provisions:

(a) That it is the intent of the person to become the legal custodian of the child and the person is able to assume legal responsibility for the care and supervision of the child;

(b) That the person understands that legal custody of the child in question is intended to be permanent in nature and that the person will be responsible as the custodian for the child until the child reaches the age of majority. Responsibility as custodian for the child shall continue beyond the age of majority if, at the time the child reaches the age of majority, the child is pursuing a diploma granted by the board of education or other governing authority, successful completion of the curriculum of any high school, successful completion of an individualized education program developed for the student by any high school, or an age and schooling certificate. Responsibility beyond the age of majority shall terminate when the child ceases to continuously pursue such an education, completes such an education, or is excused from such an education under standards adopted by the state board of education, whichever occurs first.

(c) That the parents of the child have residual parental rights, privileges, and responsibilities, including, but not limited to, the privilege of reasonable visitation, consent to adoption, the privilege to determine the child's religious affiliation, and the responsibility for support;

(d) That the person understands that the person must be present in court for the dispositional hearing in order to affirm the person's intention to become legal custodian, to affirm that the person understands the effect of the custodianship before the court, and to answer any questions that the court or any parties to the case may have.

(4) Commit the child to the permanent custody of a public children services agency or private child placing agency, if the court determines in accordance with division (E) of section 2151.414 of the Revised Code that the child cannot be placed with one of the child's parents within a reasonable time or should not be placed with either parent and determines in accordance with division (D) of section 2151.414 of the Revised Code that the permanent commitment is in the best interest of the child. If the court grants permanent custody under this division, the court, upon the request of any party, shall file a written opinion setting forth its findings of fact and conclusions of law in relation to the proceeding.

(5) Place the child in a planned permanent living arrangement with a public children services agency or private child placing agency, if a public children services agency or private child placing agency requests the court to place the child in a planned permanent living arrangement and if the court finds, by clear and convincing evidence, that a planned permanent living arrangement is in the best interest of the child and that one of the following exists:

(a) The child, because of physical, mental, or psychological problems or needs, is unable to function in a family-like setting and must remain in residential or institutional care.

(b) The parents of the child have significant physical, mental, or psychological problems and are unable to care for the child because of those problems, adoption is not in the best interest of the child, as determined in accordance with division (D) of section 2151.414 of the Revised Code, and the child retains a significant and positive relationship with a parent or relative.

(c) The child is sixteen years of age or older, has been counseled on the permanent placement options available to the child, is unwilling to accept or unable to adapt to a permanent placement, and is in an agency program preparing the child for independent living.

(6) Order the removal from the child's home until further order of the court of the person who committed abuse as described in section 2151.031 of the Revised Code against the child, who caused or allowed the child to suffer neglect as described in section 2151.03 of the Revised Code, or who is the parent, guardian, or custodian of a child who is adjudicated a dependent child and order any person not to have contact with the child or the child's siblings.

(B) No order for permanent custody or temporary custody of a child or the placement of a child in a planned permanent living arrangement shall be made pursuant to this section unless the complaint alleging the abuse, neglect, or dependency contains a prayer requesting permanent custody, temporary custody, or the placement of the child in a planned permanent living arrangement as desired, the summons served on the parents of the child contains as is appropriate a full explanation that the granting of an order for permanent custody permanently divests them of their parental rights, a full explanation that an adjudication that the child is an abused, neglected, or dependent child may result in an order of temporary custody that will cause the removal of the child from their legal custody until the court terminates the order of temporary custody or permanently divests the parents of their parental rights, or a full explanation that the granting of an order for a planned permanent living arrangement will result in the removal of the child from their legal custody if any of the conditions listed in divisions (A)(5)(a) to (c) of this section are found to exist, and the summons served on the parents contains a full explanation of their right to be represented by counsel and to have counsel appointed pursuant to Chapter 120. of the Revised Code if they are indigent.

If after making disposition as authorized by division (A)(2) of this section, a motion is filed that requests permanent custody of the child, the court may grant permanent custody of the child to the movant in accordance with section 2151.414 of the Revised Code.

(C) If the court issues an order for protective supervision pursuant to division (A)(1) of this section, the court may place any reasonable restrictions upon the child, the child's parents, guardian, or custodian, or any other person, including, but not limited to, any of the following:

(1) Order a party, within forty-eight hours after the issuance of the order, to vacate the child's home indefinitely or for a specified period of time;

(2) Order a party, a parent of the child, or a physical custodian of the child to prevent any particular person from having contact with the child;

(3) Issue an order restraining or otherwise controlling the conduct of any person which conduct would not be in the best interest of the child.

(D) As part of its dispositional order, the court shall journalize a case plan for the child. The journalized case plan shall not be changed except as provided in section 2151.412 of the Revised Code.

(E)(1) The court shall retain jurisdiction over any child for whom the court issues an order of disposition pursuant to division (A) of this section or pursuant to section 2151.414 or 2151.415 of the Revised Code until the child attains the age of eighteen years if the child is not mentally retarded, developmentally disabled, or physically impaired, the child attains the age of twenty-one years if the child is mentally retarded, developmentally disabled, or physically impaired, or the child is adopted and a final decree of adoption is issued, except that the court may retain jurisdiction over the child and continue any order of disposition under division (A) of this section or under section 2151.414 or 2151.415 of the Revised Code for a specified period of time to enable the child to graduate from high school or vocational school. The court shall make an entry continuing its jurisdiction under this division in the journal.

(2) Any public children services agency, any private child placing agency, the department of job and family services, or any party, other than any parent whose parental rights with respect to the child have been terminated pursuant to an order issued under division (A)(4) of this section, by filing a motion with the court, may at any time request the court to modify or terminate any order of disposition issued pursuant to division (A) of this section or section 2151.414 or 2151.415 of the Revised Code. The court shall hold a hearing upon the motion as if the hearing were the original dispositional hearing and shall give all parties to the action and the guardian ad litem notice of the hearing pursuant to the Juvenile Rules. If applicable, the court shall comply with section 2151.42 of the Revised Code.

(F) Any temporary custody order issued pursuant to division (A) of this section shall terminate one year after the earlier of the date on which the complaint in the case was filed or the child was first placed into shelter care, except that, upon the filing of a motion pursuant to section 2151.415 of the Revised Code, the temporary custody order shall continue and not terminate until the court issues a dispositional order under that section.

(G)(1) No later than one year after the earlier of the date the complaint in the case was filed or the child was first placed in shelter care, a party may ask the court to extend an order for protective supervision for six months or to terminate the order. A party requesting extension or termination of the order shall file a written request for the extension or termination with the court and give notice of the proposed extension or termination in writing before the end of the day after the day of filing it to all parties and the child's guardian ad litem. If a public children services agency or private child placing agency requests termination of the order, the agency shall file a written status report setting out the facts supporting termination of the order at the time it files the request with the court. If no party requests extension or termination of the order, the court shall notify the parties that the court will extend the order for six months or terminate it and that it may do so without a hearing unless one of the parties requests a hearing. All parties and the guardian ad litem shall have seven days from the date a notice is sent pursuant to this division to object to and request a hearing on the proposed extension or termination.

(a) If it receives a timely request for a hearing, the court shall schedule a hearing to be held no later than thirty days after the request is received by the court. The court shall give notice of the date, time, and location of the hearing to all parties and the guardian ad litem. At the hearing, the court shall determine whether extension or termination of the order is in the child's best interest. If termination is in the child's best interest, the court shall terminate the order. If extension is in the child's best interest, the court shall extend the order for six months.

(b) If it does not receive a timely request for a hearing, the court may extend the order for six months or terminate it without a hearing and shall journalize the order of extension or termination not later than fourteen days after receiving the request for extension or termination or after the date the court notifies the parties that it will extend or terminate the order. If the court does not extend or terminate the order, it shall schedule a hearing to be held no later than thirty days after the expiration of the applicable fourteen-day time period and give notice of the date, time, and location of the hearing to all parties and the child's guardian ad litem. At the hearing, the court shall determine whether extension or termination of the order is in the child's best interest. If termination is in the child's best interest, the court shall terminate the order. If extension is in the child's best interest, the court shall issue an order extending the order for protective supervision six months.

(2) If the court grants an extension of the order for protective supervision pursuant to division (G)(1) of this section, a party may, prior to termination of the extension, file with the court a request for an additional extension of six months or for termination of the order. The court and the parties shall comply with division (G)(1) of this section with respect to extending or terminating the order.

(3) If a court grants an extension pursuant to division (G)(2) of this section, the court shall terminate the order for protective supervision at the end of the extension.

(H) The court shall not issue a dispositional order pursuant to division (A) of this section that removes a child from the child's home unless the court complies with section 2151.419 of the Revised Code and includes in the dispositional order the findings of fact required by that section.

(I) If a motion or application for an order described in division (A)(6) of this section is made, the court shall not issue the order unless, prior to the issuance of the order, it provides to the person all of the following:

(1) Notice and a copy of the motion or application;

(2) The grounds for the motion or application;

(3) An opportunity to present evidence and witnesses at a hearing regarding the motion or application;

(4) An opportunity to be represented by counsel at the hearing.

(J) The jurisdiction of the court shall terminate one year after the date of the award or, if the court takes any further action in the matter subsequent to the award, the date of the latest further action subsequent to the award, if the court awards legal custody of a child to either of the following:

(1) A legal custodian who, at the time of the award of legal custody, resides in a county of this state other than the county in which the court is located;

(2) A legal custodian who resides in the county in which the court is located at the time of the award of legal custody, but moves to a different county of this state prior to one year after the date of the award or, if the court takes any further action in the matter subsequent to the award, one year after the date of the latest further action subsequent to the award.

The court in the county in which the legal custodian resides then shall have jurisdiction in the matter.

(2006 S 238, eff. 9–21–06; 2004 S 185, eff. 4–11–05; 2000 H 332, eff. 1–1–01; 2000 H 448, eff. 10–5–00; 1999 H 471, eff. 7–1–00; 1998 H 484, eff. 3–18–99; 1996 H 265, eff. 3–3–97; 1996 H 274, eff. 8–8–96; 1996 H 419, eff. 9–18–96; 1993 H 152, eff. 7–1–93; 1988 S 89; 1986 H 428; 1981 H 440; 1980 H 695; 1975 H 85; 1969 H 320)

Historical and Statutory Notes

Amendment Note: 2006 S 238 inserted "or is identified as a proposed legal custodian in a complaint or motion filed prior to the dispositional hearing by any party to the proceedings.", added the second sentence, and added divisions (a) through (d) in division (A); and made other nonsubstantive changes.

Amendment Note: 2004 S 185 inserted a comma after "home" in division (A)(2).

Amendment Note: 2000 H 332 deleted "family" before "foster home" in division (A)(2); and inserted "years" twice in division (E)(1).

Amendment Note: 2000 H 448 deleted "family" after "certified" in division (A)(2).

Amendment Note: 1999 H 471 substituted "job and family" for "human" in division (E)(2).

Amendment Note: 1998 H 484 substituted "a planned permanent living arrangement" for "long-term foster care" throughout division (A)(5) and (B); added the third sentence in division (E)(2); substituted "complies with" for "makes the determination required by" in division (H); and made other nonsubstantive changes.

Amendment Note: 1996 H 265 inserted "or in any other home approved by the court" in division (A)(2).

Amendment Note: 1996 H 274 added division (A)(6); substituted "retarded, developmentally disabled, or physically impaired" for "or physically handicapped" twice in division (E)(1); deleted former division (G); added divisions (G), (I), and (J); and made changes to reflect gender neutral language. Prior to amendment, former division (G) read:

"(G) Any order for protective supervision issued pursuant to division (A)(1) of this section shall terminate one year after the earlier of the date on which the complaint in the case was filed or the child was first placed into shelter care, unless the public children services agency or private child placing agency that prepared the child's case plan files a motion with the court requesting the extension for a period of up to six months of the original dispositional order or the extension of a previously granted extension for an additional period of up to six months. Upon the filing of the motion and the court's giving notice of the date, time, and location of the hearing to all parties and the guardian ad litem, the court shall hold a hearing on the motion. If the court determines at the hearing that the extension of the original dispositional order or of any previously granted extension is in the best interest of the child, the court shall issue an order extending the original dispositional order or previously granted extension for an additional period of up to six months.

"At any time after the court issues an order extending an original order for protective supervision issued under division (A)(1) of this section or a previously granted extension, the agency that filed the motion requesting the extension may request the court to terminate the dispositional order, and the court, upon receipt of the motion, shall terminate the dispositional order."

Amendment Note: 1996 H 419 made changes to reflect gender neutral language throughout, and made other nonsubstantive changes.

Amendment Note: 1993 H 152 inserted "family" in, and deleted "or approved foster care" from the end of division (A)(2); and inserted "family" in division (A)(5).

Cross References

Adjudicatory hearing, Juv R 29
Child care, persons prohibited from employment, statements, 5104.09
Day-care facilities, certain persons not to be employed by, 5104.09
Dispositional hearing, procedure, Juv R 34
Lists of prospective adoptive children and parents, 5103.16
Services for children with special needs, 5153.163

Ohio Administrative Code References

Protective supervision by PCSAs and PCPAs, OAC 5101:2–39–30
Protective supervision by PCSAs, OAC 5101:2–38–02

Library References

Infants ⊙=222, 226, 230.
Westlaw Topic No. 211.
C.J.S. Adoption of Persons § 10.
C.J.S. Infants §§ 57, 69 to 85.

Baldwin's Ohio Legislative Service, 1996 H 274—LSC Analysis, p 5/L–697
Baldwin's Ohio Legislative Service, 1988 Laws of Ohio, S 89—LSC Analysis, p 5–571

Research References

Encyclopedias

OH Jur. 3d Appellate Review § 90, Child Custody.
OH Jur. 3d Family Law § 1166, Effect of Child's Mental or Physical Disability.
OH Jur. 3d Family Law § 1424, Listing of Children and Persons Wishing to Adopt.
OH Jur. 3d Family Law § 1496, Procedure.
OH Jur. 3d Family Law § 1544, on Certification from Another Court.
OH Jur. 3d Family Law § 1550, Child Custody.
OH Jur. 3d Family Law § 1602, Prehearing Motions—Motion for Order of Disposition.
OH Jur. 3d Family Law § 1610, Form and Contents.
OH Jur. 3d Family Law § 1654, Determination of Reasonable Efforts.
OH Jur. 3d Family Law § 1662, on Request for Permanent Custody.
OH Jur. 3d Family Law § 1663, on Request for Permanent Custody—on Motion of Agency.
OH Jur. 3d Family Law § 1664, on Request for Permanent Custody—Factors to be Considered.
OH Jur. 3d Family Law § 1685, Discretion of Court.
OH Jur. 3d Family Law § 1692, Protective Supervision.
OH Jur. 3d Family Law § 1693, Permanent Custody.
OH Jur. 3d Family Law § 1694, Long-Term Foster Care.
OH Jur. 3d Family Law § 1703, Generally; Continuing Jurisdiction.
OH Jur. 3d Family Law § 1704, Effect on Court's Jurisdiction of Child's Commitment to Public Agency.
OH Jur. 3d Family Law § 1706, Modification or Vacation of Order.
OH Jur. 3d Family Law § 1711, Review Hearing.
OH Jur. 3d Family Law § 1432.1, Agreement for Temporary Custody—Children Under Six Months Old—Voluntary Delivery of Newborn.

Forms

Ohio Jurisprudence Pleading and Practice Forms § 96:43, Temporary and Permanent Custody.

Treatises and Practice Aids

Klein, Darling, & Terez, Baldwin's Ohio Practice Civil Practice § 52:4, Findings by the Court--Findings of Fact Required by Statute.
Klein, Darling, & Terez, Baldwin's Ohio Practice Civil Practice § 24:12, Intervention of Right--Nonstatutory Intervention of Right--"The Applicant Claims an Interest Relating to the Property or Transaction Which is the Subject of the Action"--Interest...
Klein, Darling, & Terez, Baldwin's Ohio Practice Civil Practice § 24:19, Permissive Intervention--Statutory Permissive Intervention--"A Statute of This State Confers a Conditional Right to Intervene".
Sowald & Morganstern, Baldwin's Ohio Practice Domestic Relations Law § 15:72, Custody in Juvenile Court Proceedings.
Carlin, Baldwin's Ohio Practice, Merrick-Rippner Probate Law § 105:7, Juvenile Court—Attachment of Jurisdiction.
Carlin, Baldwin's Ohio Practice, Merrick-Rippner Probate Law § 107:4, Contents of Juvenile Complaint—Prayer for Disposition.
Carlin, Baldwin's Ohio Practice, Merrick-Rippner Probate Law § 98:15, Adoption—Types of Placement—Agency Adoptions—Through Juvenile Court.
Carlin, Baldwin's Ohio Practice, Merrick-Rippner Probate Law § 98:20, Adoption—Types of Placement—Agency Adoptions—Lists of Prospective Adoptive Children and Parents.
Carlin, Baldwin's Ohio Practice, Merrick-Rippner Probate Law § 98:23, Adoption—Illegal Placement.

Carlin, Baldwin's Ohio Practice, Merrick-Rippner Probate Law § 98:41, Adoption—Consent Not Required—Parent Who Has Relinquished Rights.

Carlin, Baldwin's Ohio Practice, Merrick-Rippner Probate Law § 101:63, Miscellaneous Provisions—Children.

Carlin, Baldwin's Ohio Practice, Merrick-Rippner Probate Law § 106:10, Juvenile Court Jurisdiction—Neglected Child—Introduction.

Carlin, Baldwin's Ohio Practice, Merrick-Rippner Probate Law § 107:10, Contents and Issuance of Summons.

Carlin, Baldwin's Ohio Practice, Merrick-Rippner Probate Law § 107:72, Dispositional Hearings—Procedure.

Carlin, Baldwin's Ohio Practice, Merrick-Rippner Probate Law § 107:73, Alternatives for Disposition of Juvenile Cases.

Carlin, Baldwin's Ohio Practice, Merrick-Rippner Probate Law § 107:74, Reasonable Efforts Determination.

Carlin, Baldwin's Ohio Practice, Merrick-Rippner Probate Law § 107:75, Case Plans.

Carlin, Baldwin's Ohio Practice, Merrick-Rippner Probate Law § 107:76, Disposition of Abused, Neglected, or Dependent Child—Types of Orders Court May Make.

Carlin, Baldwin's Ohio Practice, Merrick-Rippner Probate Law § 107:77, Disposition of Abused, Neglected, or Dependent Child—Protective Supervision.

Carlin, Baldwin's Ohio Practice, Merrick-Rippner Probate Law § 107:78, Disposition of Abused, Neglected, or Dependent Child—Temporary Custody.

Carlin, Baldwin's Ohio Practice, Merrick-Rippner Probate Law § 107:79, Disposition of Abused, Neglected, or Dependent Child—Legal Custody.

Carlin, Baldwin's Ohio Practice, Merrick-Rippner Probate Law § 107:80, Disposition of Abused, Neglected, or Dependent Child—Permanent Custody.

Carlin, Baldwin's Ohio Practice, Merrick-Rippner Probate Law § 107:81, Disposition of Abused, Neglected, or Dependent Child—Permanent Custody—Best Interest Determination Factors.

Carlin, Baldwin's Ohio Practice, Merrick-Rippner Probate Law § 107:82, Disposition of Abused, Neglected, or Dependent Child—Planned Permanent Living Arrangement.

Carlin, Baldwin's Ohio Practice, Merrick-Rippner Probate Law § 107:83, Motion for Permanent Custody of Abused, Neglected, or Dependent Child.

Carlin, Baldwin's Ohio Practice, Merrick-Rippner Probate Law § 107:84, Disposition of Delinquent Children—Prior to January 1, 2002.

Carlin, Baldwin's Ohio Practice, Merrick-Rippner Probate Law § 107:90, Disposition Orders for Delinquent Children, Effective January 1, 2002.

Carlin, Baldwin's Ohio Practice, Merrick-Rippner Probate Law § 108:13, Juvenile Court—Jurisdiction Over Child Custody Matters—Determination of Custody.

Carlin, Baldwin's Ohio Practice, Merrick-Rippner Probate Law § 107:112, Disposition of Unruly Children—Permissive.

Carlin, Baldwin's Ohio Practice, Merrick-Rippner Probate Law § 107:118, Modification of Dispositional Orders in Abuse, Neglect, and Dependency Proceedings.

Carlin, Baldwin's Ohio Practice, Merrick-Rippner Probate Law § 107:120, Custody Review Hearing—Juvenile Court Dispositional Review.

Carlin, Baldwin's Ohio Practice, Merrick-Rippner Probate Law § 107:121, Custody Review Hearing—Revocation of Probation or Parole.

Carlin, Baldwin's Ohio Practice, Merrick-Rippner Probate Law § 107:161, Summons to Parents, Guardian, or Person With Whom Child May be—Form.

Carlin, Baldwin's Ohio Practice, Merrick-Rippner Probate Law § 107:174, Order Committing Child to Temporary Custody of Public or Private Agency or Foster Care—Form.

Carlin, Baldwin's Ohio Practice, Merrick-Rippner Probate Law § 107:175, Order Committing Child to Permanent Custody of Public or Private Agency—Form.

Carlin, Baldwin's Ohio Practice, Merrick-Rippner Probate Law § 107:176, Order Placing Child in Planned Permanent Living Arrangement—Form.

Giannelli & Yeomans, Ohio Juvenile Law § 1:7, Juvenile Code.

Giannelli & Yeomans, Ohio Juvenile Law § 2:2, Age Jurisdiction.

Giannelli & Yeomans, Ohio Juvenile Law § 9:3, Time of Neglect.

Giannelli & Yeomans, Ohio Juvenile Law § 10:2, Dependent Child Defined.

Giannelli & Yeomans, Ohio Juvenile Law § 11:2, Jurisdiction for Custody Agreements.

Giannelli & Yeomans, Ohio Juvenile Law § 16:5, Parental Identification.

Giannelli & Yeomans, Ohio Juvenile Law § 18:3, Summons: Contents and Form.

Giannelli & Yeomans, Ohio Juvenile Law § 23:5, Ineffective Assistance of Counsel.

Giannelli & Yeomans, Ohio Juvenile Law § 25:2, Bifurcated Hearings.

Giannelli & Yeomans, Ohio Juvenile Law § 25:8, Burden of Proof.

Giannelli & Yeomans, Ohio Juvenile Law § 26:4, Court Approval; Journalization.

Giannelli & Yeomans, Ohio Juvenile Law § 27:5, Child Protective Services.

Giannelli & Yeomans, Ohio Juvenile Law § 29:2, Unruly—Dispositional Alternatives.

Giannelli & Yeomans, Ohio Juvenile Law § 30:4, Dispositional Alternatives for Abuse, Neglect or Dependency.

Giannelli & Yeomans, Ohio Juvenile Law § 30:5, Protective Supervision.

Giannelli & Yeomans, Ohio Juvenile Law § 30:6, Temporary Custody.

Giannelli & Yeomans, Ohio Juvenile Law § 30:7, Legal Custody.

Giannelli & Yeomans, Ohio Juvenile Law § 30:8, Permanent Custody—Defined.

Giannelli & Yeomans, Ohio Juvenile Law § 31:1, Introduction.

Giannelli & Yeomans, Ohio Juvenile Law § 31:2, Filing of Motion.

Giannelli & Yeomans, Ohio Juvenile Law § 31:8, Implementation of Case Plan.

Giannelli & Yeomans, Ohio Juvenile Law § 31:9, Effect on Parental Rights.

Giannelli & Yeomans, Ohio Juvenile Law § 32:2, Jurisdiction Over Parents and Others.

Giannelli & Yeomans, Ohio Juvenile Law § 33:4, Abuse, Neglect, and Dependency Proceedings.

Giannelli & Yeomans, Ohio Juvenile Law § 33:5, Other Proceedings.

Giannelli & Yeomans, Ohio Juvenile Law § 34:4, Final Order Requirement.

Giannelli & Yeomans, Ohio Juvenile Law § 34:9, Right to Transcript.

Giannelli & Yeomans, Ohio Juvenile Law § 16:14, Permanent & Temporary Custody Complaints; Planned Permanent Living Arrangements.

Giannelli & Yeomans, Ohio Juvenile Law § 16:15, Certification or Transfer from Another Court.

Giannelli & Yeomans, Ohio Juvenile Law § 23:30, Right to a Transcript.

Giannelli & Yeomans, Ohio Juvenile Law § 25:12, Transcripts.

Giannelli & Yeomans, Ohio Juvenile Law § 25:14, Reasonable Efforts Determination; Abuse, Neglect & Dependency.

Giannelli & Yeomans, Ohio Juvenile Law § 30:10, Permanent Custody—Parental Placement Within Reasonable Time.

Giannelli & Yeomans, Ohio Juvenile Law § 30:12, Permanent Custody—Procedural Issues.

Giannelli & Yeomans, Ohio Juvenile Law § 30:13, Planned Permanent Living Arrangement.

Giannelli & Yeomans, Ohio Juvenile Law § 33:11, Child Custody Agency Commitment—Juvenile Court Dispositional Review.

Law Review and Journal Commentaries

Dissolving Family Relations: Termination of Parent–Child Relations—An Overview, Jacqueline Y. Parker. 11 U Dayton L Rev 555 (Summer 1986).

The Legal Response to Child Abuse: In the Best Interest of Children?, John E. B. Myers. 24 J Fam L 149 (1985–86).

A New Issue In Foster–Parenting—Gays, Note. 25 J Fam L 577 (1986–87).

Preventing Foster Care Placement; Supportive Services in the Home, Nancy S. Erickson. 19 J Fam L 569 (1980–81).

State v. Parent Termination of Parental Rights: Contradictory Actions by the Ohio Legislature and the Ohio Supreme Court in 1996, Keith Wiens. 26 Cap U L Rev 673 (1997).

Notes of Decisions

Ed. Note: This section contains annotations from former RC 2151.35.

Bifurcated hearings 12
Constitutional issues 1
County custody and duties 7
Divorce 8
Evidence 6
Foster care 9
Notice; parties 4
Parental rights and responsibilities 11
Permanent order 3
Procedural issues 5
Reunification 10
Temporary order 2

---

1. Constitutional issues

Court of Appeals lacked jurisdiction to consider mother's claim that she was deprived of her right to effective assistance of counsel during dependency hearing, where no appeal was taken from that hearing; present appeal concerned trial court's judgment granting permanent custody of mother's three minor children to the Children Services Board (CSB). In re Calvert Children (Ohio App. 5 Dist., Guernsey, 10-24-2005) No. 05-CA-19, No. 05-CA-20, 2005-Ohio-5653, 2005 WL 2746329, Unreported. Infants 248.1

Foster mother was allowed to file motions and present evidence in dependency case, and foster mother's involvement in case did not violate father's due process rights; foster mother was a party to the case after her motion for child custody was consolidated with the county department of job and family services' dependency case, and mother of child consented to foster mother having custody of child. In re Narwrocki (Ohio App. 5 Dist., Stark, 08-09-2004) No. 2004-CA-00028, 2004-Ohio-4208, 2004 WL 1784525, Unreported. Constitutional Law 274(5); Infants 200

Mother did not have constitutional right to effective assistance of counsel in proceeding between mother and grandmother for custody of mother's two children, even though custody proceeding arose from dependency action filed by Children's Services Board, where Board had terminated its protective supervision involvement in case. In re Mahley (Ohio App. 5 Dist., Guernsey, 04-05-2004) No. 03 CA 23, 2004-Ohio-1772, 2004 WL 740003, Unreported. Child Custody 500; Infants 232

Child dependency complaint filed by the county department of children and family services was sufficient to put father on notice of the issues and did not deprive father of due process; complaint alleged that child was born while mother tested positive for drugs, mother's drug problem prevented her from caring for child, mother had other children that were not in her custody, mother failed to comply with her agency caseplan, father failed to provide care or support for child, and complaint sought an award of permanent custody to county department of children and family services. In re I.M. (Ohio App. 8 Dist., Cuyahoga, 12-24-2003) No. 82669, No. 82695, 2003-Ohio-7069, 2003 WL 23010024, Unreported. Infants 197

Defense counsel's act of making mother stipulate to issue of dependency in dependency hearing concerning mother's two children did not constitute ineffective assistance; magistrate at dependency proceeding went through an extended colloquy with mother at hearing to assure that mother wanted to stipulate to the dependency of her children, and mother responded repeatedly that she did. In re Anisha N. (Ohio App. 6 Dist., Lucas, 05-09-2003) No. L-02-1370, 2003-Ohio-2356, 2003 WL 21040311, Unreported. Infants 205

Defense counsel did not render ineffective assistance by failing to meet with mother outside of scheduled court hearing dates regarding mother's children who were found to be dependent and subject to permanent custody of county children's services agency; record showed that defense counsel attempted to contact mother on a number of occasions, but mother did not respond, and record showed that mother skipped meetings set up by her caseworker where her attorney was present. In re Anisha N. (Ohio App. 6 Dist., Lucas, 05-09-2003) No. L-02-1370, 2003-Ohio-2356, 2003 WL 21040311, Unreported. Infants 205

Mother of dependent children was entitled to assert children's right to counsel in termination of parental rights proceeding, where both mother and children desired reunification. In re Emery (Ohio App. 4 Dist., Lawrence, 04-25-2003) No. 02CA40, 2003-Ohio-2206, 2003 WL 2003811, Unreported. Infants 200

Mother's procedural due process rights as guaranteed by US Const 14th amendment and O Const Art I § 16 were violated when juvenile court granted guardian ad litem's oral motion to award paternal grandmother legal custody of minor child without first requiring that, prior to the hearing, a written motion be filed by the paternal grandmother, as required by RC 2151.353(A)(3), or by the agency, as required by RC 2151.415(A)(3). In re Fleming, No. 63911, 1993 WL 277186 (8th Dist Ct App, Cuyahoga, 7–22-93).

Defendant was coerced and in custody during interview at Department of Human Services (DHS) and, therefore, was entitled to be informed of his constitutional rights under *Miranda* where DHS social worker told defendant that his child would be removed from home if defendant did not attend interview and coercive methods of interrogation employed by police officer during interview created in-custody, police-dominated atmosphere. State v. Brown (Ohio App. 6 Dist., 11-05-1993) 91 Ohio App.3d 427, 632 N.E.2d 970, dismissed, jurisdictional motion overruled 68 Ohio St.3d 1471, 628 N.E.2d 1390. Criminal Law 412.2(2)

RC 2151.353 is constitutional. In re Williams (Hamilton 1982) 7 Ohio App.3d 324, 455 N.E.2d 1027, 7 O.B.R. 421.

A mother with custody of her child under a juvenile court order that imposes extensive conditions cannot invoke the privilege against self-incrimination under US Const Am 5 to resist a later court order to produce the child; the fact that she can comply with the order through the unadorned act of producing the child does not necessarily deprive her of the privilege, since the act of complying may itself testify to the existence, possession, or authenticity of the thing produced, but in this case invocation of the privilege would interfere with the effective working of the state's regulation of custody of juveniles needing assistance, which is a purpose unrelated to the enforcement of criminal laws; the mother here, moreover, accepted the obligation to permit inspection when she took responsibility under the custody order. (Ed. note: Maryland procedures construed in light of federal constitution.) Baltimore City Dept. of Social Services v. Bouknight (U.S.Md. 1990) 110 S.Ct. 900, 493 U.S. 549, 107 L.Ed.2d 992.

Any construction of RC 2151.354 that would allow commitment of an "unruly" child to the legal custody of the Ohio youth commission would be a violation of due process of law, and therefore an improper construction. OAG 72–071.

2. Temporary order

Temporary custody of children in the care of a children's services agency is limited to a period of two years. In re D.J. (Ohio App. 2 Dist., Montgomery, 12-01-2006) No. 21666, 2006-Ohio-6304, 2006 WL 3462142, Unreported. Infants 226

Relatives who were named by mother as alternatives for placement of children during parental rights termination proceeding were not suitable options for placement, and thus, trial court was under no obligation to grant mother's request; first individual was only marginally interested in obtaining custody of the boys, and stated that she did not want to disrupt their current placement if it would cause stress to the boys, and second individual had criminal history and health problems. In re Bowers (Ohio App. 7 Dist., Mahoning, 08-18-2005) No. 04 MA 216, 2005-Ohio-4376, 2005 WL 2033100, Unreported. Infants 222

Trial court's grant of temporary custody of children to county child protection agency was not against the manifest weight of the evidence; decision was based on testimony of doctor who examined younger child and opined that his injuries were caused by abuse, testimony of investigator with the protective unit to mother's admission she may have bruised child, and recommendation of the guardian ad litem. In re Butcher (Ohio App. 5 Dist., Tuscarawas, 07-25-2005) No. 2005 AP 05 0031, 2005-Ohio-3827, 2005 WL 1785116, Unreported. Infants 175.1

Judgment entry following detention-shelter care hearing involving child did not constitute dependency adjudication, which was necessary step in process for county to gain permanent custody of child; trial court stated during hearing that proceedings were not "a hearing where...the dependency issue is being argued," but was hearing to determine whether county had sufficient evidence to base initial finding of dependency to remove child from mother's custody, evidence introduced at hearing did not support dependency determination, and trial court had granted ex parte order granting temporary emergency custody of child to county, thus indicating that hearing was that statutorily required to review ex parte order. In re Nibert (Ohio App. 4 Dist., Gallia, 05-24-2005) No. 04CA15, 2005-Ohio-2797, 2005 WL 1332019, Unreported. Infants 222

Minor's appeal from decision continuing her temporary custody with foster family was rendered moot, where minor reached age 18 while appeal was pending, and Juvenile Division of Court of Common Pleas lost jurisdiction over her. In re M. (Ohio App. 6 Dist., Wood, 07-16-2004) No. WD-03-092, 2004-Ohio-3798, 2004 WL 1595006, Unreported. Infants ⇐ 247

Determination in child dependency case that children's "best interest" warranted change in temporary custody from their great-aunt to one child's paternal grandparents was not arbitrary, unconscionable or unreasonable; children had been removed from great-aunt's home due to a lack of medical attention, which resulted in one child's hospitalization for bilateral pneumonia, and, while child was hospitalized, it was discovered that she had bruises all over her body and she tested positive for opiates, and social worker testified that she conducted a home study of the grandparents and determined that they were "loving individuals" that could provide "the best placement for the children." In re Allen (Ohio App. 5 Dist., Delaware, 06-01-2004) No. 03CAF08041, 2004-Ohio-2911, 2004 WL 1240506, Unreported. Infants ⇐ 230.1

Finding in dependency proceeding, that temporary removal of children to mother's parents was in their best interests, was supported by evidence that mother had violently shaken child after becoming frustrated and that mother had fantasies about causing the child further harm. In re Hauenstein (Ohio App. 3 Dist., Hancock, 06-07-2004) No. 5-03-38, No. 5-03-39, 2004-Ohio-2915, 2004 WL 1238288, Unreported. Infants ⇐ 156

Trial court order granting children services temporary custody of mother's two children was not an abuse of discretion; mother was a heavy prescription drug user, she had been arrested four times in the past three years, she missed several counseling appointments and was terminated from services, and she refused to comply with the case management plan. In re Barnosky (Ohio App. 4 Dist., Athens, 03-09-2004) No. 03CA32, 2004-Ohio-1127, 2004 WL 444527, Unreported. Infants ⇐ 154.1

Evidence supported finding, following determination that developmentally delayed child of minor mother was a dependent child, that child should be temporarily placed in custody of paternal grandmother; child had lived with grandmother most of his life, grandmother was committed to caring for child and taking him to all the special services he required, child had bonded with grandmother's family, and mother conceded that grandmother did well in caring for child. In re Malone (Ohio App. 10 Dist., Franklin, 12-30-2003) No. 03AP-489, 2003-Ohio-7156, 2003 WL 23024377, Unreported, appeal not allowed 102 Ohio St.3d 1423, 807 N.E.2d 367, 2004-Ohio-2003. Infants ⇐ 222

Trial court was authorized to extend temporary custody of children with County Department of Child and Family Services, even though such extension meant that children would be in temporary custody more than two years beyond limit set forth in statute governing disposition of abused, neglected, or dependent children, given that problems that led to the original temporary custody order remained unresolved; mother still needed to secure appropriate housing and maintain sobriety, and county had failed to meet its burden of proof on its motion to modify temporary custody to permanent custody. In re N.B. (Ohio App. 8 Dist., Cuyahoga, 07-10-2003) No. 81392, 2003-Ohio-3656, 2003 WL 21545142, Unreported, appeal not allowed 100 Ohio St.3d 1425, 797 N.E.2d 93, 2003-Ohio-5232. Infants ⇐ 230.1

Removing 16-year-old who was adjudicated dependent from her parents' home on a temporary basis, until the parents and child could have gotten to a point where restoring the relationship was possible, was not an abuse of discretion, where court found that reasonable efforts were made to prevent the need for placement and/or make it possible for child to return home, but current situation was "contentious" and "not working," and parents and child needed intervention to get to a point at which they could have received counseling and begin to work on their problems. In re Day (Ohio App. 12 Dist., Clermont, 07-07-2003) No. CA2002-09-073, 2003-Ohio-3544, 2003 WL 21517343, Unreported. Infants ⇐ 222

Order granting temporary custody of child to paternal grandmother was not an abuse of discretion, in child dependency case; mother and father were both low functioning, mother had severe anger control problems and lacked parenting skills, and mother and father had only been provided with limited services. In re Haywood (Ohio App. 3 Dist., Allen, 07-03-2003) No. 1-02-97, 2003-Ohio-3518, 2003 WL 21511308, Unreported. Infants ⇐ 192

A juvenile court does not lose jurisdiction to enter dispositional orders upon technical termination of temporary custody due to the expiration of the sunset date, especially where the problems that led to removal are unresolved. In re Hess (Ohio App. 7 Dist., Jefferson, 03-21-2003) No. 02 JE 37, 2003-Ohio-1429, 2003 WL 1465190, Unreported. Infants ⇐ 192

Juvenile court's judgment entry awarding temporary custody of stepson to county children services agency and ordering protective supervision of the remaining children was not a final appealable order at time of entry, where judgment entry contained no adjudication of dependency or neglect. (Per O'Neill, P.J., with one judge concurring in judgment only.) In re Calvin, Anthony, Alyshia (Ohio App. 11 Dist., Geauga, 11-22-2002) No. 2001-G-2379, 2002-Ohio-6468, 2002 WL 31663562, Unreported, stay granted 98 Ohio St.3d 1459, 783 N.E.2d 518, 2003-Ohio-644, appeal not allowed 98 Ohio St.3d 1513, 786 N.E.2d 63, 2003-Ohio-1572. Infants ⇐ 242

An adjudication that a child is neglected or dependent followed by a disposition awarding temporary custody to a public children services agency pursuant to RC 2151.353(A)(2) constitutes a final appealable order by which the agency is made a party with standing to appeal the matter below. In re Surdel (Ohio App. 9 Dist., Lorain, 05-12-1999) No. 98CA007172, 1999 WL 312380, Unreported.

Juvenile court lacked authority to place children in permanent planned living arrangement (PPLA) after grant of temporary custody to county Children Services Board (CSB), where CSB did not request such placement and placement in PPLA ran counter to legislative intent to provide permanency for children in foster care. In re A.B. (Ohio, 09-06-2006) 110 Ohio St.3d 230, 852 N.E.2d 1187, 2006-Ohio-4359. Infants ⇐ 226

Statutory time periods for grant of temporary custody of child to public children's services agency and extension of temporary custody are mandatory, and failure to comply results in loss of authority by trial court to make any order as to custody of child until that authority has been reinvoked by filing of a new complaint. In re Omosun Children (Ohio App. 11 Dist., 10-16-1995) 106 Ohio App.3d 813, 667 N.E.2d 431. Infants ⇐ 193

If failure to render final dispositional order in dependency proceeding within required statutory two-year period can be attributed to existence of extenuating circumstances, it is not necessary for public children's services agency to give custody of child back to parents prior to filing of new complaint, i.e., agency's temporary custody of child can be continuous throughout entire period, and only instance in which child must be returned to parents is when failure of juvenile court and agency to comply with two-year limit cannot be explained by extenuating circumstances and purpose of filing new complaint is simply to circumvent statutory requirement. In re Omosun Children (Ohio App. 11 Dist., 10-16-1995) 106 Ohio App.3d 813, 667 N.E.2d 431. Infants ⇐ 222

Adjudication by juvenile court that child is neglected or dependent followed by disposition awarding temporary custody to public children services agency is final appealable order. In re Shaeffer Children (Van Wert 1993) 85 Ohio App.3d 683, 621 N.E.2d 426, dismissed, jurisdictional motion overruled 67 Ohio St.3d 1451, 619 N.E.2d 419. Infants ⇐ 242

Trial court's determination of whether protective supervision of children should be extended because of best interest of children is within its discretion. In re Collier (Athens 1993) 85 Ohio App.3d 232, 619 N.E.2d 503. Infants ⇐ 230.1

Term "any" in statute, providing that "any" order for protective supervision of child shall terminate upon earlier of one year after date on which complaint was filed or child was first placed in shelter care, unless agency files motion requesting extension for period of up to six months of original dispositional order or extension of previously granted extension for additional period of up to six months, means that there can be indefinite number of extensions of protective supervision orders. In re Collier (Athens 1993) 85 Ohio App.3d 232, 619 N.E.2d 503. Infants ⇐ 230.1

A minor parent's due process rights are not violated by the application the six-month to two-year time frame for reunification of a parent and child on the ground that because minor parents often lack social and emotional maturity necessary to rear a child, the time frame is arbitrary since the six-month to two-year time frame is tightly drawn to attain only the state's interest in the future well being of the child, which dictates that the child not wait any longer than is necessary for parents to assume their rightful responsibilities. In re McCrary (Madison 1991) 75 Ohio App.3d 601, 600 N.E.2d 347, dismissed, jurisdictional motion overruled 64 Ohio St.3d 1427, 594 N.E.2d 969. Constitutional Law ⇐ 274(5); Infants ⇐ 132

A trial court has sufficient evidence to order that a child be placed in temporary custody with the human services department where it is uncontradicted that the mother is a diabetic and had numerous hypoglycemic reactions wherein she tended to be confused and hungry and eventually lost consciousness if proper care was not taken, resulting in the child having to take care of his mother which caused him to lose sleep and miss school, and affected his grades. In re Ward (Defiance 1992) 75 Ohio App.3d 377, 599 N.E.2d 431.

RC 2151.353(F)'s one-year limitation on a temporary custody order begins to run from the date the human services department's request for temporary custody of a child is made rather than from the filing date of the original complaint. In re Ward (Defiance 1992) 75 Ohio App.3d 377, 599 N.E.2d 431. Infants ⇐ 222

A mother's petition for a writ of habeas corpus filed in the court of appeals in response to a trial court's order granting temporary custody of her two minor children to a county children's services board is properly denied where the mother has an adequate remedy at law through appeal. McNeal v. Miami Cty. Children's Services Bd. (Ohio 1992) 64 Ohio St.3d 208, 594 N.E.2d 587.

The order of a juvenile court modifying a temporary custody order is a final appealable order. In re Smith (Lucas 1989) 61 Ohio App.3d 788, 573 N.E.2d 1170, reconsideration denied.

An adjudication by a juvenile court that a child is "neglected" or "dependent" as defined in RC Ch 2151, followed by a disposition awarding temporary custody to a public children services agency pursuant to RC 2151.353(A)(2), constitutes a "final order" within the meaning of RC 2505.02 and is appealable to the court of appeals pursuant to RC 2501.02. In re Murray (Ohio 1990) 52 Ohio St.3d 155, 556 N.E.2d 1169, on remand. Infants 242

A journal entry of a jury verdict finding a child's stepfather guilty of endangering children pursuant to RC 2919.22 is admissible in an action to place temporary custody and care of the child with a county department of human services. In re Boyce (Medina 1987) 37 Ohio App.3d 105, 523 N.E.2d 900.

When parents refuse necessary medical treatment for their child in the belief, based on religious faith, that the treatment is not necessary, a juvenile court may find the child dependent as defined by RC 2151.04(C), place the child in temporary custody of a hospital, and order the necessary medical treatment. In re Willmann (Hamilton 1986) 24 Ohio App.3d 191, 493 N.E.2d 1380, 24 O.B.R. 313.

Where an allegedly neglected, dependent, or abused child is committed to the temporary, emergency custody of a children services board after a shelter care hearing under Juv R 7, the court need not order a reunification plan where it has not finally adjudged and disposed of the matter under RC 2151.353. In re Moloney (Ohio 1986) 24 Ohio St.3d 22, 492 N.E.2d 805, 24 O.B.R. 18.

Neither a parents' voluntary surrender of a child to the custody of a children's services institute nor an appellate stay maintaining such custody constitutes a temporary commitment that invokes the requirement of a comprehensive unification plan. In re Smart (Franklin 1984) 21 Ohio App.3d 31, 486 N.E.2d 147, 21 O.B.R. 33.

Where a natural parent moves to terminate temporary custody in another based on a previous finding of dependency, the parent's present suitability and fitness for the role of parent must be considered in the context of the child's best interests. In re Christopher (Morrow 1977) 54 Ohio App.2d 137, 376 N.E.2d 603, 8 O.O.3d 271.

A juvenile court loses authority to make orders concerning custody of a child by a department of human services, and the child is returned to the parents, upon expiration of the thirty-day deadline for DHS to file a motion to extend or to modify temporary custody, that is, thirty days prior to the one-year statutory termination date set forth in RC 2151.353. In re White, No. CA–9461, 1994 WL 66881 (5th Dist Ct App, Stark, 2–14–94).

A comprehensive reunification plan need be prepared only when a child is committed to the temporary custody of the department of public welfare under RC 2151.353(A)(2) or RC 2151.353(A)(3); this is the plain meaning of RC 2151.412(C), which does not, it follows, require preparation of a plan when a temporary custody order is based on Juv R 13(A) and Juv R 13(D). In re Koballa, Nos. 48417 and 48480 (8th Dist Ct App, Cuyahoga, 1–24–85).

If a juvenile court commits to the temporary custody of a public children services agency a child who has been adjudicated to be unruly or delinquent pursuant to RC 2151.354(A)(1) or RC 2152.19(A)(1), respectively, the duration of the temporary custody order is subject to the time limitations set forth in RC 2151.353(F) and RC 2151.415. OAG 03–004.

A juvenile court retains jurisdiction over a child who has been adjudicated to be unruly or delinquent until the child attains twenty-one years of age, and may continue to make dispositional orders with respect to the child until that time, regardless of whether the court's order of temporary custody has expired under the time limitations set forth in RC 2151.353(F) and RC 2151.415. OAG 03–004.

3. Permanent order

Trial court's grant of permanent custody of child to county department of children and family services was not an abuse of discretion; child had been in custody of department for at least 12 months of a consecutive 22 month period, mother had continuously failed to substantially remedy underlying conditions that prompted child's removal from her home, mother could not provide adequate, permanent home for child, child was thriving in her foster home, and foster parent was willing to adopt child, yet still allow mother to be involved in child's life. In re T.W. (Ohio App. 8 Dist., Cuyahoga, 10-13-2005) No. 85845, 2005-Ohio-5446, 2005 WL 2600663, Unreported, appeal not allowed 108 Ohio St.3d 1418, 841 N.E.2d 321, 2006-Ohio-179, reconsideration denied 108 Ohio St.3d 1513, 844 N.E.2d 857, 2006-Ohio-1329. Infants 155

Awarding county children services agency permanent custody of child, rather than placing child in the care of either of his parents or his maternal grandmother, was in the child's best interest, where child had well-established relationship with foster family, he did not inquire about his parents or comment upon their absence, grandmother had previously lost custody of her children to children services agency, grandmother stated that her fiancee probably had a criminal record, and grandmother failed her home inspection and made no effort to challenge or remedy the failure. In re Poke (Ohio App. 4 Dist., Lawrence, 09-23-2005) No. 05CA15, 2005-Ohio-5226, 2005 WL 2403893, Unreported. Infants 222

Evidence supported award of permanent custody of children to county; although children loved mother and desired to remain with her, she had violated no contact order, moved boyfriend into her trailer that had past domestic violence issues and sexual abuse allegation, and had violated her safety plan. In re Aaron F. (Ohio App. 6 Dist., Lucas, 12-30-2004) No. L-04-1156, 2004-Ohio-7152, 2004 WL 3017288, Unreported. Infants 156

In termination of parental rights proceeding, juvenile court was not required to consider placing parent's two minor children with father's parents before granting the Department of Job and Family Services (DJFS) permanent custody of the children. In re Keaton (Ohio App. 4 Dist., Ross, 11-19-2004) No. 04CA2785, No. 04CA2788, 2004-Ohio-6210, 2004 WL 2650249, Unreported. Infants 222

Statute allowing court to commit an abused, neglected, or dependent child to the permanent custody of a public children services agency under certain circumstances did not apply to case that was tried on county children services agency's motion to modify temporary custody to permanent custody. In re J.L. (Ohio App. 8 Dist., Cuyahoga, 11-10-2004) No. 84368, 2004-Ohio-6024, 2004 WL 2578874, Unreported, appeal not allowed 104 Ohio St.3d 1463, 821 N.E.2d 578, 2005-Ohio-204. Infants 230.1

Mother failed to establish that her four children should have been placed in planned permanent living arrangement (PPLA), rather than in permanent custody with county agency, where neither mother, guardian ad litem, nor county agency requested or argued for a PPLA, nor did court suggest an alternative disposition. In re B.N. (Ohio App. 8 Dist., Cuyahoga, 08-26-2004) No. 83704, 2004-Ohio-4469, 2004 WL 1902115, Unreported. Infants 226

Finding that it was in best interest of dependent children to grant permanent custody to County Children Services Board was not abuse of discretion, where children had been in Board's temporary custody for over three and one-half years, children needed secure placement, mother's witnesses had never met children or seen mother interact with children, and caseworker and guardian ad litem who had most contact with mother and children recommended that permanent custody be granted to Board. In re Bicanovsky (Ohio App. 7 Dist., Mahoning, 06-10-2004) No. 04-MA-5, 2004-Ohio-3034, 2004 WL 1321900, Unreported. Infants 222

Juvenile court's judgment provided proper reason for placing dependent child in permanent planned living arrangement (PPLA), as required by statute, where judgment explicitly stated that mother suffered from physical and psychological problems for which mother failed to obtain appropriate treatment and that such problems rendered mother unable to care for child. In re M. B. (Ohio App. 9 Dist., Summit, 05-26-2004) No. 21812, 2004-Ohio-2666, 2004 WL 1160170, Unreported. Infants 210

Evidence was sufficient to support finding that placing dependent child in permanent planned living arrangement (PPLA) was in child's best interest; caseworker stated that child was removed from mother's home due to concerns about mother's mental health and drinking, caseworker indicated that child was afraid of mother, caseworker said that mother had not substantially complied with case plan, psychologist indicated mother did not have necessary parenting skills, and father testified that mother had mental health issues and had attempted suicide. In re M. B. (Ohio App. 9 Dist., Summit, 05-26-2004) No. 21812, 2004-Ohio-2666, 2004 WL 1160170, Unreported. Infants 226

Denying mother's motion for legal custody of dependent children, placing first child in permanent planned living arrangement (PPLA), and placing second child in legal custody of father was not against manifest weight of evidence; caseworker stated that first child was removed from mother's home due to concerns about mother's mental health and drinking, caseworker indicated that first child was afraid of mother and that second child wanted to live with father, caseworker said that mother had not substantially complied with case plan, psychologist indicated mother did not have necessary parenting skills, and father testified that mother had mental health issues and had attempted suicide. In re M. B. (Ohio App. 9

Dist., Summit, 05-26-2004) No. 21812, 2004-Ohio-2666, 2004 WL 1160170, Unreported. Infants ⇐ 222; Infants ⇐ 226

Record supported magistrate's conclusion that dependent children's great aunt and great grandmother were not suitable custodians for children, for purpose of proceeding in which county children's services board filed motion for permanent custody; aunt was only interested in custody of one child, great grandmother was only interested in custody of same child, and mother alleged that great grandmother sexually abused that child. In re Paris (Ohio App. 11 Dist., Ashtabula, 04-16-2004) No. 2003-A-0133, No. 2003-A-0134, 2004-Ohio-1962, 2004 WL 833594, Unreported. Infants ⇐ 222

Magistrate's conclusion that grant of permanent custody to county children's services board was in best interest of dependent children was supported by relevant statutory factors; magistrate indicated that guardian ad litem concluded that it was in children's best interest to grant board's motion for permanent custody, that child stated that she wanted to stay in foster home, that children had made significant developmental advances following removal from parents' home, and that children needed secure permanent placement. In re Paris (Ohio App. 11 Dist., Ashtabula, 04-16-2004) No. 2003-A-0133, No. 2003-A-0134, 2004-Ohio-1962, 2004 WL 833594, Unreported. Infants ⇐ 210

Magistrate's determination that children could not be placed with either parent within reasonable time or should not be placed with either parent, and thus, that permanent custody of children should be granted to county children's services board was sufficiently detailed and not against manifest weight of evidence; magistrate indicated that parents' home was filthy, that children were not properly supervised, that children were ill but had not had prescriptions filled, and that parents had not completed case plans. In re Paris (Ohio App. 11 Dist., Ashtabula, 04-16-2004) No. 2003-A-0133, No. 2003-A-0134, 2004-Ohio-1962, 2004 WL 833594, Unreported. Infants ⇐ 178; Infants ⇐ 179; Infants ⇐ 210

Trial court could not have ordered planned permanent living arrangement for mother's children, in lieu of granting children's services agency permanent custody of children, since agency never requested planned permanent living arrangement, but always sought permanent custody of five of the children, and grant of legal custody of sixth child to her biological father. In re K.P. (Ohio App. 8 Dist., Cuyahoga, 03-25-2004) No. 82709, 2004-Ohio-1448, 2004 WL 583867, Unreported, as amended nunc pro tunc, stay denied 102 Ohio St.3d 1457, 809 N.E.2d 31, 2004-Ohio-2569, appeal not allowed 102 Ohio St.3d 1473, 809 N.E.2d 1159, 2004-Ohio-2830. Infants ⇐ 226

Trial court did not abuse its discretion, in hearing on motion by county children's services (CCS) seeking permanent custody of child who had previously been adjudicated dependent, by placing child in a planned permanent living arrangement (PPLA) rather than awarding CCS permanent custody; there was evidence that there was no prospective adopting family, that current foster parents had special training in dealing with child's attachment disorder and that removal of child from foster home could result in child having feelings of rejection and abandonment, such evidence supported trial court's finding that an order of permanent custody was not in child's best interest, such evidence also indicated that child would be unable to function in a family-like setting, which was required for a PPLA placement, and a foster home could qualify as "residential care," which was also a requirement for a PPLA placement. In re Priser (Ohio App. 2 Dist., Montgomery, 03-19-2004) No. 19861, 2004-Ohio-1315, 2004 WL 541124, Unreported. Infants ⇐ 226

Trial court's failure to file findings and conclusions in support of its judgment granting permanent custody of children to county department of jobs and family services necessitated remand. In re McCune/Warnken Children (Ohio App. 5 Dist., Stark, 01-20-2004) No. 2003CA00359, 2004-Ohio-293, 2004 WL 113483, Unreported. Infants ⇐ 210; Infants ⇐ 254

Trial court's failure to grant grandmother's motion for new dispositional hearing in child dependency proceedings was not plain error; grandmother had entered evidence and testified in permanent custody hearing as to her desire and ability to care for the children on a permanent basis, and magistrate and trial court determined, based on all the evidence, that it was in best interests of children to grant permanent custody to county agency. In re McCann (Ohio App. 12 Dist., Clermont, 01-26-2004) No. CA2003-02-017, 2004-Ohio-283, 2004 WL 111644, Unreported. Infants ⇐ 243

Award of permanent custody of dependent child to county children services board was not against the manifest weight of the evidence; child had been in county custody for over four years and parents had not shown significant progress toward reunification, visitation between father and child had not been frequent enough to establish and maintain a meaningful parent-child relationship, and child was in need of permanent placement but neither parent was a suitable placement, nor were there any relatives with whom child could be placed. In re T.S. (Ohio App. 9 Dist., Summit, 01-07-2004) No. 21743, No. 21740, 2004-Ohio-32, 2004 WL 32650, Unreported. Infants ⇐ 155

The trial court's failure to order a planned permanent living arrangement (PPLA) for child was not an abuse of discretion, in dependency proceeding where permanent custody of child was awarded to county department of children and family services; there was no evidence that adoption was not in child's best interests, mother never sought an alternative disposition in the trial court, and there was no evidence that a PPLA would be in child's best interests. In re I.M. (Ohio App. 8 Dist., Cuyahoga, 12-24-2003) No. 82669, No. 82695, 2003-Ohio-7069, 2003 WL 23010024, Unreported. Infants ⇐ 222

County Children Services never requested the placement of child in a planned permanent living arrangement (PPLA) as required by child protection statute, and thus order granting child's placement in PPLA was to be vacated and the matter remanded for a new dispositional hearing. In re McKee (Ohio App. 5 Dist., Muskingum, 10-31-2003) No. CT2003-0027, 2003-Ohio-5925, 2003 WL 22511361, Unreported. Infants ⇐ 254

Trial court order granting paternal aunt and uncle legal custody of children in a custody proceeding incident to a dependency action was not an abuse of discretion, even though children were bonded to their foster parents; aunt and uncle had a positive home study and were willing to do whatever was necessary to care for the children, and children were bonded to grandmother. In re Mitchell (Ohio App. 11 Dist., Lake, 08-01-2003) No. 2002-L-078, No. 2002-L-079, 2003-Ohio-4102, 2003 WL 21782611, Unreported. Child Custody ⇐ 271; Infants ⇐ 230.1

Mother's decision to agree to have her child placed in a planned permanent living arrangement (PPLA) was informed and voluntary; trial judge asked mother whether she was making such decision of her own free will and mother answered in the affirmative, and county department of children and family services did not make any guarantees or promises that child would be reunited with extended family. In re D.B. (Ohio App. 8 Dist., Cuyahoga, 07-03-2003) No. 81421, 2003-Ohio-3521, 2003 WL 21511310, Unreported. Infants ⇐ 226

The trial court was not required to make an explicit finding of parental unsuitability before it granted legal custody of child to maternal aunt and uncle, in child dependency proceeding; trial court implicitly made a parental unsuitability finding when it determined that child was dependent. In re Reeher (Ohio App. 7 Dist., Belmont, 06-30-2003) No. 02-BE-38, 2003-Ohio-3470, 2003 WL 21500180, Unreported. Infants ⇐ 210

Clear and convincing evidence supported finding that award of permanent custody of mother's two children to county children's services agency was in children's best interests; both children had been under temporary custody of agency for over 12 consecutive months, agency put into action a reasonable caseplan for both the mother and father but both parents failed to comply, mother failed to sever herself from the abusive relationship she was in, neither parent attempted to visit their children over two years, and both mother and father failed to address the pervasive issues of physical and mental abuse in their household. In re Anisha N. (Ohio App. 6 Dist., Lucas, 05-09-2003) No. L-02-1370, 2003-Ohio-2356, 2003 WL 21040311, Unreported. Infants ⇐ 155

Trial court properly determined that granting permanent custody of children to Franklin County Children Services (FCCS) was in children's best interest and that children could not be placed with either parent within reasonable amount of time; parents were incarcerated for six years for child endangerment and children were bonded with caregivers. In re Kramer (Ohio App. 10 Dist., Franklin, 05-06-2003) No. 02AP-1038, No. 02AP-1039, 2003-Ohio-2277, 2003 WL 21007196, Unreported. Infants ⇐ 155

Clear and convincing evidence supported trial court's decision to award permanent custody of dependent child to county social services board; mother's parental rights to eight other children and father's parental rights to one other child had recently been terminated and parents had ongoing volatile relationship. In re Alizah W. (Ohio App. 6 Dist., Lucas, 04-25-2003) No. L-02-1333, 2003-Ohio-2133, 2003 WL 1962379, Unreported. Infants ⇐ 155

Placement of mother's six children in permanent custody of county children's services board was in best interest of children; mother failed to comply with case plan requiring her to obtain high school graduation equivalent degree (GED), to secure stable employment, and to complete budgeting classes, children suffered numerous psychological and learning disabilities and required security and structure, and mother refused to acknowledge problems with herself or her family that contributed to necessity to remove children from home. In re Adams (Ohio App. 2 Dist., Miami, 02-07-2003) No. 2002 CA 45, 2003-Ohio-618, 2003 WL 264357, Unreported. Infants ⇐ 155

Trial court acted within its discretion in terminating all visitation between mother, who, as sole living parent, was serving 14-year sentence, and her children, and in directing Department of Jobs and Family Services to file for permanent custody, following its finding of dependency and award of temporary custody to Department; children's counselor and caseworker recommended termination of visitation, temporary foster father testified children were traumatized after visiting mother in jail and never asked for her, and there was lack of probability of mother's release in near future. McDonald v. McDonald (Ohio App. 5 Dist., Delaware, 01-30-2003) No. 02CAF11051, 2003-Ohio-543, 2003 WL 245660, Unreported. Infants ⇐ 175.1

Clear and convincing evidence supported determination that child could not be placed with father within reasonable time, for purposes of award of permanent custody to county children services board; record showed father failed to complete programs for substance abuse and domestic violence, and that he did not secure permanent housing, but continued to reside in the homes of various women. In re S.S. (Ohio App. 2 Dist., Montgomery, 01-24-2003) No. 19406, 2003-Ohio-319, 2003 WL 164598, Unreported. Infants ⇐ 178

Trial court, in permanency hearing, abused its discretion in requiring State to arrange an open adoption prior to awarding permanent custody; State was required to include in the case plan a specific plan to seek an adoptive family for the child and to prepare the child for adoption, but was not required to set forth an exact plan for adoption until permanent custody was granted. In re Muldrew (Ohio App. 2 Dist., Montgomery, 12-27-2002) No. 19469, 2002-Ohio-7288, 2002 WL 31888158, Unreported. Infants ⇐ 222

Order awarding county children's services permanent custody of mother and father's children, rather than placing the children in a planned permanent living arrangement (PPLA), was not an abuse of discretion; a court could only order a PPLA placement if a public children services agency or a private child placing agency requested that disposition, county children's services did not request PPLA placement, and competent evidence established that granting permanent placement with county children's services was in the best interests of the children. In re Clever (Ohio App. 2 Dist., Montgomery, 10-18-2002) No. 19298, No. 19299, 2002-Ohio-5588, 2002 WL 31341602, Unreported. Infants ⇐ 226

Trial court order granting permanent custody of mother's and father's children to county children's services was not against the manifest weight of the evidence, even though both parents had completed all of their child dependency caseplan objectives; evidence established that both parents were at risk of relapse, and physician testified that father's ability to parent was conditioned on father's ability to stay drug free. In re Clever (Ohio App. 2 Dist., Montgomery, 10-18-2002) No. 19298, No. 19299, 2002-Ohio-5588, 2002 WL 31341602, Unreported. Infants ⇐ 178

Intellectual limitations which render a father unable to adequately parent his two developmentally delayed children and which jeopardize chances for a lifelong recovery from alcohol dependency is sufficient evidence upon which a court could base its decision to terminate parental rights. Matter of McKean (Ohio App. 3 Dist., Allen, 04-22-1998) No. 1-97-46, No. 1-97-47, 1998 WL 229793, Unreported, motion for delayed appeal denied 230 F.3d 1377.

A mother who shows no therapeutic improvement after attending six months of psychological counseling according to a case plan instituted after her daughter is sexually abused allegedly by the mother's husband, and who is unwilling to admit that her daughter was even abused at all despite contrary medical evidence and her daughter's own statements, is ill-equipped to protect her daughter from further possible abuse and the permanent termination of custody of her daughter is justified and supported by the manifest weight of the evidence. Matter of Misty B. (Ohio App. 6 Dist., Lucas, 08-18-1995) No. L-94-213, 1995 WL 490965, Unreported.

Statutes applying to permanent custody proceedings did not apply in child dependency proceeding in which maternal grandparents sought legal custody of children, as trial court did not grant permanent custody of children to public children services agency or private child placing agency, but, instead, granted grandparents legal custody of children. In re Sean T. (Ohio App. 6 Dist., 10-28-2005) 164 Ohio App.3d 218, 841 N.E.2d 838, 2005-Ohio-5739. Infants ⇐ 222

Statute governing modification or termination of custody order regarding dependent child, not statute governing disposition of dependent child, applied to motion for permanent custody that was filed by county children services board (CSB); motion did not concern initial dispositional order following adjudication of dependency, but instead concerned modification of temporary-custody order after first six-month extension. In re A.S. (Ohio App. 9 Dist., 10-05-2005) 163 Ohio App.3d 647, 839 N.E.2d 972,

2005-Ohio-5309, reversed 2009 WL 728, motion to certify allowed 108 Ohio St.3d 1410, 841 N.E.2d 315, 2006-Ohio-179. Infants ⇐ 230.1

Juvenile court did not patently and unambiguously lack jurisdiction to grant permanent custody of child to county children's services (CCS) and, thus, mother had an adequate remedy at law by her previous unsuccessful appeal, precluding habeas corpus relief; notwithstanding failure to appear, mother had notice of proceeding and was represented by counsel, and any ineffectiveness of counsel was due to mother's failure to communicate with counsel prior to hearing. Ross v. Saros (Ohio, 08-20-2003) 99 Ohio St.3d 412, 792 N.E.2d 1126, 2003-Ohio-4128. Habeas Corpus ⇐ 280

County department of human services was not required to have custody of child for twelve consecutive months prior to filing motion for permanent custody, where department filed original complaint alleging child to be a dependent child and requesting permanent custody of child as the first disposition and temporary custody as the alternative disposition. In re Ament (Ohio App. 12 Dist., 04-23-2001) 142 Ohio App.3d 302, 755 N.E.2d 448, appeal not allowed 92 Ohio St.3d 1431, 749 N.E.2d 757. Infants ⇐ 193

Trial court was not required to readjudicate children as dependent prior to awarding permanent custody of children to county department of human services, where court had previously adjudicated children as dependent when it committed them to temporary custody of department, and children remained in protective supervision after they were returned to parents. In re Ament (Ohio App. 12 Dist., 04-23-2001) 142 Ohio App.3d 302, 755 N.E.2d 448, appeal not allowed 92 Ohio St.3d 1431, 749 N.E.2d 757. Infants ⇐ 210

Mother waived her contention that juvenile court lacked authority to extend, sua sponte, agency's temporary custody of four siblings, two of whom had been adjudicated neglected and two of whom had been adjudicated dependent, where extension was final appealable order and mother failed to appeal therefrom. In re Nice (Ohio App. 7 Dist., 03-20-2001) 141 Ohio App.3d 445, 751 N.E.2d 552, 2001-Ohio-3214. Infants ⇐ 242

Willingness of a relative to care for a child does not alter what a court considers in determining permanent custody in a dependency proceeding. In re Patterson (Ohio App. 9 Dist., 09-01-1999) 134 Ohio App.3d 119, 730 N.E.2d 439. Infants ⇐ 155

Motion for permanent custody was never filed and, thus, order for permanent custody was improper; while hearing was repeatedly described by judge as hearing on motion for permanent custody, and was referred to as such in his journal entry, both form and substance of complaints clearly sought adjudication that children were abused, neglected or dependent, and finding or adjudication of abuse, neglect or dependency was prerequisite to order of permanent custody. In re Knotts (Ohio App. 3 Dist., 02-12-1996) 109 Ohio App.3d 267, 671 N.E.2d 1357. Infants ⇐ 197

In proceeding in which county children services board sought permanent custody of children as dependent, neglected and abused children, juvenile court had jurisdiction over children from dates of original adjudications of each child, and it would continue to have jurisdiction until each child reached age of 18. In re Doe Children (Ohio App. 6 Dist., 02-11-1994) 93 Ohio App.3d 134, 637 N.E.2d 977, cause dismissed 69 Ohio St.3d 1481, 634 N.E.2d 1027. Infants ⇐ 152; Infants ⇐ 196

To terminate parental rights in natural child, where child is neither abandoned nor orphaned, juvenile court must find by clear and convincing evidence both that grant of permanent custody to petitioning agency is in best interest of child and that child cannot or should not be placed with either parent within reasonable time. In re Higby (Wayne 1992) 81 Ohio App.3d 466, 611 N.E.2d 403. Infants ⇐ 155

Permanent custody should be granted at an initial disposition hearing in an action under RC 2151.353(A)(4) only in extreme situations where reunification is not possible. In re Pachin (Montgomery 1988) 50 Ohio App.3d 44, 552 N.E.2d 655, cause dismissed 39 Ohio St.3d 720, 534 N.E.2d 350. Infants ⇐ 222

RC 2151.353, permitting the state to receive permanent custody of a "dependent child" whose parent is jailed, does not conflict with RC 3107.07; where the child is a "dependent child" under RC 2151.04 the state has authority to obtain permanent custody under RC 2151.353, and once parental rights have been terminated under RC Ch 2151, it is provided by RC 3107.06(D) that this parent's consent to adoption is no longer necessary. In re Dillard (Montgomery 1988) 48 Ohio App.3d 263, 549 N.E.2d 213.

Substantial evidence that children are unwashed, not suitably clothed, and living in an unkempt house is sufficient to support an order under RC 2151.353 committing the children to the permanent custody of the county welfare department where two years of county assistance with basic housekeeping produced only a temporary improvement in household cleanliness. In re Covert (Seneca 1984) 17 Ohio App.3d 122, 477 N.E.2d 678, 17 O.B.R. 185.

When a case concerning a child is transferred or certified from another court, such certification does not constitute a complaint in the juvenile court such that a child is neglected, dependent, or abused, and those dispositions provided for under RC 2151.353 pertaining to neglected, dependent, or abused children, including an award of permanent custody to a county welfare department which has assumed the administration of child welfare, are not applicable to such a child, disposition thereof being subject to and controlled by RC 3109.04. In re Snider (Defiance 1984) 14 Ohio App.3d 353, 471 N.E.2d 516, 14 O.B.R. 420. Infants ⇔ 197; Infants ⇔ 222

In a juvenile court proceeding brought by the welfare department for permanent custody, the juvenile court need not consider the parents' pending application in the probate court for approval of adoption placements, nor must it stay its proceedings in favor of the probate court. In re Palmer (Ohio 1984) 12 Ohio St.3d 194, 465 N.E.2d 1312, 12 O.B.R. 259, certiorari denied 105 S.Ct. 918, 469 U.S. 1162, 83 L.Ed.2d 930.

Where the evidence shows that to return a child to her natural parent would be clearly detrimental to the child, such child is a "dependent child" under RC 2151.04(C) and the court is authorized to commit the child permanently to the children's services board under RC 2151.353(D), even though the parent might be capable of giving proper care and support to other children. In re Justice (Clinton 1978) 59 Ohio App.2d 78, 392 N.E.2d 897, 13 O.O.3d 139. Infants ⇔ 154.1; Infants ⇔ 155

Once a child has been found to be "dependent" as defined in RC 2151.04, the "best interests" of the child are the primary consideration in determining whether an award of permanent custody is justified pursuant to RC 2151.353(D). In re Cunningham (Ohio 1979) 59 Ohio St.2d 100, 391 N.E.2d 1034, 13 O.O.3d 78. Infants ⇔ 222

An adjudication of dependency made in a temporary custody hearing does not constitute legal grounds for granting permanent custody of minor children to the welfare department where over twenty-two months have elapsed between the temporary and permanent custody hearings, and where custody had been returned to the natural parents in the interim period between the temporary and permanent custody hearings; the granting of permanent custody under such circumstances requires a contemporaneous finding of dependency. In re Fassinger (Cuyahoga 1974) 43 Ohio App.2d 89, 334 N.E.2d 5, 72 O.O.2d 292, affirmed 42 Ohio St.2d 505, 330 N.E.2d 431, 71 O.O.2d 503. Infants ⇔ 222

The mere allegation in a motion filed by the county welfare department that "it would appear to be in the best interest of said minors that they be placed permanently for adoption" does not state grounds under which a juvenile court may lawfully take permanent custody of children from their natural parents. In re Fassinger (Cuyahoga 1974) 43 Ohio App.2d 89, 334 N.E.2d 5, 72 O.O.2d 292, affirmed 42 Ohio St.2d 505, 330 N.E.2d 431, 71 O.O.2d 503. Infants ⇔ 197

Under RC 2151.353, the filing of a complaint containing a prayer requesting permanent custody of minor children, sufficiently apprising the parents of the grounds upon which the order is to be based, and the service of summons upon the parents, explaining that the granting of such an order permanently divests them of their parental rights, are prerequisite to a valid adjudication that a child is neglected or dependent for the purpose of obtaining an order for permanent custody divesting parental rights. In re Fassinger (Ohio 1975) 42 Ohio St.2d 505, 330 N.E.2d 431, 71 O.O.2d 503.

On the evidence, despite the strong maternal attachments and instincts, and the well-intentioned concern of grandparents, infant's best interests would be served by the child being placed in the permanent custody of the county welfare department for adoption-placement. In re Baby Girl S. (Ohio Com.Pl. 1972) 32 Ohio Misc. 217, 290 N.E.2d 925, 61 O.O.2d 439.

Private child placement agency which requested permanent custody of child acted within statutory authority to institute permanent custody proceedings, for purposes of showing that custody proceedings were under state authority, as necessary for indigent parent challenging action to have right to free transcript. State ex rel. Howard v. Ferreri (Ohio 1994) 70 Ohio St.3d 587, 639 N.E.2d 1189.

Under RC 2151.353, a court may award permanent custody of a dependent or neglected child to specific agencies enumerated in the statute; therefore, an award of permanent custody to a relative of a child is void for lack of jurisdiction. Fronk v Arison, No. 1167 (11th Dist Ct App, Ashtabula, 10–26–84).

Where the mother of a minor child voluntarily placed such child in the temporary custody of a children services board, the trial court may properly grant permanent custody to such board where during the two years following the initial placement the mother was arrested five times for offenses including soliciting and petty theft, was terminated from three jobs, and testimony by the social worker assigned to her case indicated that the mother did not comply with any terms of a court approved reunification plan. Drushal v Drushal, No. 10955 (9th Dist Ct App, Summit, 4–20–83).

Where the trial court determines that it is in the best interest of a minor child to terminate parental rights permanently, the trial court may grant permanent custody to a county children services board without first granting temporary custody. In re Hollins, No. CA–703 (5th Dist Ct App, Guernsey, 3–29–83).

A child welfare board may not legally request support payments from parents who have voluntarily surrendered their children to the board under permanent surrender, nor from parents whose children have been taken from them permanently by the courts. OAG 66–148.

4. Notice; parties

Failure to provide notice to father of trial date in permanent custody proceeding for his child violated father's right to due process, despite fact that he had previously appeared for a pretrial conference. In re Th.W. (Ohio App. 8 Dist., Cuyahoga, 06-09-2005) No. 85241, No. 85278, 2005-Ohio-2852, 2005 WL 1364742, Unreported. Infants ⇔ 198

The Common Pleas Court had jurisdiction to grant permanent custody of mother's two children to the county job and family services agency, even though notice to mother of the dispositional hearing was returned undeliverable; mother appeared with counsel at an earlier shelter-care hearing, at the shelter-care hearing the trial court noted the date of the adjudicatory hearing, counsel for mother appeared at the dispositional hearing, and neither mother or her counsel objected to the notice provided to mother. In re Billingsley (Ohio App. 3 Dist., Putnam, 01-28-2003) No. 12-02-07, No. 12-02-08, 2003-Ohio-344, 2003 WL 178661, Unreported. Infants ⇔ 198

An adjudication that child was unruly, followed by a disposition awarding temporary custody to a public children services agency, constituted a final, appealable order. In re Kidd (Ohio App. 11 Dist., Lake, 12-27-2002) No. 2001-L-039, 2002-Ohio-7264, 2002 WL 31886759, Unreported. Infants ⇔ 242

Trial court's failure to follow procedural notice requirements of statute governing disposition of dependent children did not necessitate reversal of decision that child was abandoned and that child's grandmother should have custody of child, following previous decision finding child dependent and granting temporary custody to grandmother; mother was aware of potential custodians, received adequate notice of trial court's intention to review custody issue and participated in hearings. In re Allen (Ohio App. 5 Dist., Delaware, 10-10-2002) No. 02CAF06028, 2002-Ohio-5555, 2002 WL 31312392, Unreported. Child Custody ⇔ 280

Juvenile court was not required to schedule and notice separate hearing on extension of temporary custody of children following hearing on state's petition for permanent and legal custody, where agency had not requested extension of temporary custody, and where evidence at hearing on permanent and legal custody persuaded court that factors for extending temporary custody existed; mother was on notice, as result of prior hearing, that state wished to permanently terminate her parental rights with regard to two children and give legal custody of the other two children to a relative, and had opportunity to be heard on propriety of such dispositions. In re Nice (Ohio App. 7 Dist., 03-20-2001) 141 Ohio App.3d 445, 751 N.E.2d 552, 2001-Ohio-3214. Infants ⇔ 230.1

Where an agency requests an extension of temporary custody or the court wishes to extend temporary custody sua sponte where no other proceedings are occurring in the case, then the parent is entitled to notice and a hearing on the extension. In re Nice (Ohio App. 7 Dist., 03-20-2001) 141 Ohio App.3d 445, 751 N.E.2d 552, 2001-Ohio-3214. Infants ⇔ 230.1

Foster parents had sufficient notice of issues to be addressed in post-dispositional custody proceeding, and sufficient opportunity to present evidence and witnesses, to permit them effectively to oppose adoptive parents' motion for legal custody; trial court repeatedly stated that proceeding was one for custody review, and foster parents' opposition to motion for legal custody indicated their awareness of issue concerning whether legal custody should be given to adoptive parents. In re Hitchcock (Ohio App. 8 Dist., 11-21-1996) 120 Ohio App.3d 88, 696 N.E.2d 1090, stay granted 77 Ohio St.3d 1462, 672 N.E.2d 1119, stay denied 77 Ohio St.3d 1502, 673 N.E.2d 921, motion to vacate stay denied 77 Ohio St.3d 1521, 674 N.E.2d 373, appeal allowed 78 Ohio St.3d 1455, 677 N.E.2d 815, appeal dismissed as improvidently allowed 81 Ohio St.3d 1222, 689 N.E.2d 43, 1998-Ohio-653, stay denied 81 Ohio St.3d 1469, 690 N.E.2d 1288, stay denied 81 Ohio St.3d 1476, 691 N.E.2d 294. Infants ⇔ 230.1

While statute regarding dispositional review hearings does not list a child's legal custodian at the time review hearing is ordered as an "interested party" entitled to notice of the review hearing, the list is not exhaustive. In re Bowman (Ohio App. 9 Dist., 03-08-1995) 101 Ohio App.3d 599, 656 N.E.2d 355. Infants ⇐ 230.1

Grandmother became an "interested party," entitled to notice of dispositional hearing, when court awarded her legal custody of dependent child. In re Bowman (Ohio App. 9 Dist., 03-08-1995) 101 Ohio App.3d 599, 656 N.E.2d 355. Infants ⇐ 230.1

Joinder of grandparents granted visitation as part of an emergency shelter care placement is not required as they do not have standing to intervene in a permanent custody action. In re Massengill (Lucas 1991) 76 Ohio App.3d 220, 601 N.E.2d 206.

The limitation in RC 2151.353 merely provides that the trial court may not award custody of a child to a nonparent who has not sought custody before the hearing resulting in the award; it does not preclude a foster parent from seeking review of a disposition. In re Moorehead (Montgomery 1991) 75 Ohio App.3d 711, 600 N.E.2d 778.

Foster parents of a dependent child are proper parties to seek review of a dispositional judgment concerning placement of the foster child in their care. In re Moorehead (Montgomery 1991) 75 Ohio App.3d 711, 600 N.E.2d 778.

Failure to serve a parent with a summons in a permanent custody action does not require dismissal of the action where the parent has actual notice of the action and has been served with a complaint. In re Webb (Hamilton 1989) 64 Ohio App.3d 280, 581 N.E.2d 570, dismissed, jurisdictional motion overruled 48 Ohio St.3d 704, 549 N.E.2d 1191.

A summons in a permanent custody proceeding that clearly explains that granting permanent custody to a children services agency will divest the parents of their parental rights suffices to satisfy the requirements set forth in RC 2151.353(B). In re Pachin (Montgomery 1988) 50 Ohio App.3d 44, 552 N.E.2d 655, cause dismissed 39 Ohio St.3d 720, 534 N.E.2d 350. Constitutional Law ⇐ 274(5); Infants ⇐ 198

A reference in a summons to the associated complaint does not comply with the requirement of RC 2151.353(B) that the summons contain a full explanation of the effects of the granting of an order for permanent custody and an explanation of the parents' rights. In re Wilson (Huron 1984) 21 Ohio App.3d 36, 486 N.E.2d 152, 21 O.B.R. 38.

A properly served summons containing the "full explanation" required by RC 2151.353(B) must be accompanied by a copy of the complaint, amended or not, if the complaint seeks, temporarily or permanently, to divest a parent of his parental rights. In re Wilson (Huron 1984) 21 Ohio App.3d 36, 486 N.E.2d 152, 21 O.B.R. 38.

A father is a party to proceedings in a juvenile court in which his children are found to be neglected and in which temporary custody is given to the mother; he is also a party to a subsequent proceeding in the same court modifying such temporary custody order and is entitled to appear in an appeal from such order and to move to dismiss such appeal. In re Rule (Crawford 1963) 1 Ohio App.2d 57, 203 N.E.2d 501, 30 O.O.2d 76.

Except in those instances specified in GC 8004–6 (RC 3107.06), a probate court had no power to make a final decree or interlocutory order of adoption of a child where it affirmatively appears that there was not filed with the court a written consent to the adoption by the living mother of such child; the requirement of such a consent was not dispensed with in an instance where a juvenile court had previously made a valid determination that such child was "neglected." In re Ramsey (Ohio 1956) 164 Ohio St. 567, 132 N.E.2d 469, 58 O.O. 431.

The county welfare department, when removing children from a natural parent, must give notice to the parents prior to or at the time of removal stating reasons for removal, and must give parents a full opportunity to present witnesses at a hearing at which they may be represented by retained counsel; such hearing must be held before a neutral hearing officer, who is to state in writing the decision reached and reasons therefor. Doe v. Staples (C.A.6 (Ohio) 1983) 706 F.2d 985, rehearing denied 717 F.2d 953, certiorari denied 104 S.Ct. 1301, 465 U.S. 1033, 79 L.Ed.2d 701. Constitutional Law ⇐ 274(5)

Fact that neither maternal grandmother nor purported father filed motions for legal custody of mother's children did not preclude trial court from awarding legal custody of mother's daughter to grandmother and legal custody of her son to his purported father, in dependency proceeding, as mother was provided with adequate notice of the possibility of legal custody, was afforded with opportunities to be heard, and actively participated in proceedings. In re Callier (Ohio App. 12 Dist., Brown, 05-20-2002) No. CA2001-04-006, No. CA2001-04-007, 2002-Ohio-2406, 2002 WL 1010081, Unreported. Infants ⇐ 222

Where a complaint for dependency is filed, an unknown father must be served by publication; even an apparently unconcerned putative father is entitled to notice by publication, and the mother's statement that she does not know who the father is does not justify dispensing with the notice. In re Ware, No. 79–03243 (8th Dist Ct App, Cuyahoga, 7–17–80).

5. Procedural issues

The trial court limitation of testimony concerning child's relationship with her mother to events from the time child was three years old was not an abuse of discretion, in child dependency proceeding; child was five years old when paternal grandmother filed a dependency complaint, and the court refused to hear testimony about events in the distant past. In re Brown (Ohio App. 2 Dist., Darke, 06-23-2006) No. 1676, 2006-Ohio-3189, 2006 WL 1719277, Unreported. Infants ⇐ 207

Trial court was not required to include a case plan in its dispositional order, in child dependency proceeding; paternal grandmother filed a complaint that alleged child was a dependent child, and a children services agency did not file a complaint and did not provide services to child. In re Brown (Ohio App. 2 Dist., Darke, 06-23-2006) No. 1676, 2006-Ohio-3189, 2006 WL 1719277, Unreported. Infants ⇐ 222

Juvenile court had jurisdiction to address paternal grandmother's complaint, which alleged that child was dependent; grandmother filed her complaint under statute that allowed any person who had knowledge that a child appeared to be dependent child to file a sworn complaint in juvenile court, and statute allowed the person who filed such a complaint to request temporary custody of the child, which grandmother did. In re Brown (Ohio App. 2 Dist., Darke, 06-23-2006) No. 1676, 2006-Ohio-3189, 2006 WL 1719277, Unreported. Infants ⇐ 196

The trial court was not required to consider father's brother as a placement option for children, during dependency proceeding, where neither father nor his brother filed a motion requesting legal custody of the children prior to the disposition hearing. In re Zurfley/Chatman/Black Children (Ohio App. 5 Dist., Stark, 02-13-2006) No. 2005CA00217, 2006-Ohio-683, 2006 WL 337366, Unreported. Infants ⇐ 222

Trial court was not required to make finding of mother's parental unfitness at disposition stage of dependency proceedings as prerequisite to transfer of legal custody of children to grandmother. In re D.R. (Ohio App. 12 Dist., Butler, 01-30-2006) No. CA2005-06-150, No. CA2005-06-151, 2006-Ohio-340, 2006 WL 216642, Unreported. Infants ⇐ 210

Court of Appeals lacked jurisdiction to consider parents' claims that the juvenile court erred in accepting their admissions during dependency hearing, where no appeal was taken from that hearing; present appeal concerned trial court's judgment granting permanent custody of parents' three minor children to the Children Services Board (CSB). In re Calvert Children (Ohio App. 5 Dist., Guernsey, 10-24-2005) No. 05-CA-19, No. 05-CA-20, 2005-Ohio-5653, 2005 WL 2746329, Unreported. Infants ⇐ 248.1

Child's mother had standing to challenge the trial court's denial of maternal grandmother's motion for custody of child in action by county children services agency for permanent custody of child that county alleged was neglected and dependant, even though grandmother did not appeal the denial of her motion; mother's interests were aligned with grandmother's and the denial of grandmother's motion prejudiced mother. In re Poke (Ohio App. 4 Dist., Lawrence, 09-23-2005) No. 05CA15, 2005-Ohio-5226, 2005 WL 2403893, Unreported. Infants ⇐ 242

Although trial court granted ex parte order of temporary custody pursuant to statute providing only the means, and not the authority, for ordering a child into custody, trial court's subsequent journal entry on reaffirmation of temporary order made clear that it was acting pursuant to appropriate authorizing statute and, therefore, agency had authority to make, and trial court had authority to grant, motion for permanent custody under separate subsection of latter statute. In re Van Atta (Ohio App. 3 Dist., Hancock, 08-15-2005) No. 5-05-03, 2005-Ohio-4182, 2005 WL 1939418, Unreported. Infants ⇐ 192

Expert witness was not required in child protection proceedings for trial court to determine that mother could not provide adequate supervision of child; issue of whether a parent can provide adequate supervision of child is a subject matter within comprehension of a lay person. In re Nolen (Ohio App. 3 Dist., Crawford, 06-20-2005) No. 3-04-20, 2005-Ohio-3075, 2005 WL 1421777, Unreported. Infants ⇐ 179

Once trial court was divested of subject matter jurisdiction over matters relating to custody of child after one-year period following entry of order granting legal custody to child's great aunt and uncle had lapsed, it was not "a court that had jurisdiction to make parenting determination related to child" under Uniform Child Custody Jurisdiction Act. In re N.W. (Ohio

App. 8 Dist., Cuyahoga, 05-19-2005) No. 85468, 2005-Ohio-2466, 2005 WL 1190728, Unreported. Children Out-of-wedlock ⇔ 20.13

Guardian ad litem's filing of motion to dismiss on morning of hearing on biological father's motion to modify custody did not waive claim that trial court lacked subject matter jurisdiction over father's motion that was brought more than one year after custody was awarded to child's great aunt and uncle who resided in different county at time of order. In re N.W. (Ohio App. 8 Dist., Cuyahoga, 05-19-2005) No. 85468, 2005-Ohio-2466, 2005 WL 1190728, Unreported. Children Out-of-wedlock ⇔ 20.10

Trial court lacked subject matter jurisdiction over biological father's motion to modify custody that was filed more than one year after trial court awarded custody of child to child's great aunt and uncle who resided in different county at time of order. In re N.W. (Ohio App. 8 Dist., Cuyahoga, 05-19-2005) No. 85468, 2005-Ohio-2466, 2005 WL 1190728, Unreported. Children Out-of-wedlock ⇔ 20.10

Motion for legal custody of child filed by child's paternal aunt after dispositional hearing in child protection proceedings was timely, where aunt was granted leave to intervene by trial court and was therefore entitled to seek modification of original dispositional ruling. In Matter of Mouser (Ohio App. 3 Dist., Logan, 05-09-2005) No. 8-04-34, 2005-Ohio-2244, 2005 WL 1077532, Unreported. Infants ⇔ 230.1

Attorney purportedly retained by minor child in child protection proceedings had no standing to appeal trial court's determination that child was a dependent minor and granting temporary custody to child protection agency, where trial court refused to allow attorney to enter his appearance, attorney did not serve as guardian ad litem and was not a person specifically designated by the court, and attorney had no immediate and pecuniary interest in the subject matter. In re Elliot (Ohio App. 10 Dist., Franklin, 05-05-2005) No. 03AP-1280, 2005-Ohio-2195, 2005 WL 1055798, Unreported, appeal not allowed 106 Ohio St.3d 1536, 835 N.E.2d 384, 2005-Ohio-5146, reconsideration denied 107 Ohio St.3d 1685, 839 N.E.2d 405, 2005-Ohio-6480. Infants ⇔ 242

Admission of disputed testimony, even if testimony was hearsay, was not plain error in proceeding in which trial court awarded permanent custody of child to county department of children and family services; mother offered nothing which demonstrated that court relied on testimony in rendering its final verdict or that mother was prejudiced by testimony, and there was nothing in record that overcame presumption that judge disregarded any evidence that was not properly before her. In re D.W. (Ohio App. 8 Dist., Cuyahoga, 04-21-2005) No. 84547, 2005-Ohio-1867, 2005 WL 926991, Unreported. Infants ⇔ 243

Trial court was not required to enter finding of parental unsuitability to support order denying mother's motion to modify prior dispositional order awarding custody of her dependent daughter to child's great aunt, when, in previous dependency proceeding, the trial court had already determined that the child was abused, dependent, or neglected, and trial court correctly applied the best-interests test, supported by competent evidence in the record. In re Allah (Ohio App. 1 Dist., Hamilton, 03-18-2005) No. C-040239, 2005-Ohio-1182, 2005 WL 627795, Unreported. Infants ⇔ 230.1

Oral motion by guardian ad litem at dispositional hearing in child protection proceedings, seeking award of custody of subject child to child's maternal aunt, was insufficient basis upon which to award custody, where no motion for custody was filed by aunt or on her behalf prior to dispositional hearing, trial record contained no indication that child's mother consented to such award of custody, and mother's counsel explicitly argued against and objected to custody order on grounds that no motion for legal custody had been filed as required by statute. In re C.T. (Ohio App. 8 Dist., Cuyahoga, 03-03-2005) No. 84648, 2005-Ohio-887, 2005 WL 488914, Unreported. Infants ⇔ 222

Trial court erred in overruling mother's objections to magistrate's recommendation, that child be placed into planned permanent living arrangement, without first reviewing transcript from hearing. In re Wheeler (Ohio App. 5 Dist., Muskingum, 01-14-2005) No. CT 2004-0037, 2005-Ohio-220, 2005 WL 121717, Unreported. Infants ⇔ 203

Passing of two-year statutory time period during which trial court could issue temporary custody orders and extensions of temporary custody orders with respect to dependent child did not divest juvenile court of jurisdiction to enter dispositional order granting permanent custody to county children services board; portion of delay arose from fact that appeal was taken from dependency adjudication and prior permanent custody award, and statute provides that juvenile court retains jurisdiction over dependent children to ensure their safety and proper treatment until they become adults. In re M.B. (Ohio App. 9 Dist., Summit, 10-27-2004) No. 22103, 2004-Ohio-5686, 2004 WL 2390987, Unreported. Infants ⇔ 196

Granting children services board (CSB) new trial based on allegedly newly discovered evidence was abuse of discretion in proceeding in which CSB sought permanent custody of neglected children, where proffered evidence of events that occurred after hearing on CSB's motion for permanent custody was not newly discovered evidence as those facts were not in existence at time of first trial and had no relevance to question of whether parental rights should have been terminated as of time of first trial. In re S.S. (Ohio App. 9 Dist., Wayne, 10-06-2004) No. C.A. 04CA0032, 2004-Ohio-5371, 2004 WL 2244094, Unreported. Infants ⇔ 211

Trial court's acceptance of guardian ad litem's supplemental report and recommendation that grandmother be granted custody of mother's children, which was submitted one month after trial on petition by Department of Children and Family Services for permanent custody of children, was abuse of discretion, where recommendation was accepted without allowing parties to cross-examine guardian ad litem regarding her report and recommendations. In re D.D. (Ohio App. 8 Dist., Cuyahoga, 08-12-2004) No. 83537, 2004-Ohio-4243, 2004 WL 1797186, Unreported. Infants ⇔ 208

The trial court was not required to make a finding of parental unfitness or find a change in circumstances prior to granting legal custody of child to foster parent; an unfitness finding was not required in a dependency, neglect or abuse case, and dependency, neglect and abuse cases were governed by the best interests of the child standard, not by a change in circumstances standard. In re Narwrocki (Ohio App. 5 Dist., Stark, 08-09-2004) No. 2004-CA-00028, 2004-Ohio-4208, 2004 WL 1784525, Unreported. Infants ⇔ 226

Mother appealing decision of juvenile court granting permanent custody of daughter to county agency could not challenge prior determination that daughter was a dependent child, where mother failed to timely appeal neglect and dependency adjudication. In re K.M. (Ohio App. 12 Dist., Butler, 08-09-2004) No. CA2004-02-052, 2004-Ohio-4152, 2004 WL 1765462, Unreported. Infants ⇔ 248.1

Trial court applied the appropriate legal standard to determine legal custody of child, during child dependency proceeding; father filed a motion for an order allocating parental rights and responsibilities, and the trial court considered the best interests of the child. In re Rosier Lemmon (Ohio App. 5 Dist., Stark, 03-15-2004) No. 2003 CA 00306, 2004-Ohio-1290, 2004 WL 540299, Unreported. Child Custody ⇔ 76; Infants ⇔ 222

Father was not entitled to writ of prohibition to prevent juvenile court judge from conducting a permanent custody hearing involving one child; the judge had statutory authority to conduct a permanent custody hearing, the father appealed award of permanent custody to the county department, and the legal remedy providing adequate relief foreclosed the extraordinary remedy in prohibition. Wells v. Costine (Ohio App. 7 Dist., Belmont, 02-04-2004) No. 03 BE 51, 2004-Ohio-563, 2004 WL 234716, Unreported. Prohibition ⇔ 3(2)

Grandmother waived for appeal issue of whether she was entitled to grant of her motion for new dispositional hearing in child dependency proceedings, where grandmother failed to object to magistrate's denial of her motion. In re McCann (Ohio App. 12 Dist., Clermont, 01-26-2004) No. CA2003-02-017, 2004-Ohio-283, 2004 WL 111644, Unreported. Infants ⇔ 243

In ordering that child be removed from mother's care and enter planned permanent living arrangement, trial court failed to address required statutory factors, warranting remand with instruction that court make statutorily required findings; court made findings required to grant state permanent custody of child, and such findings were not same as those required for imposing planned permanent living arrangement. In re C.R. (Ohio App. 8 Dist., Cuyahoga, 01-15-2004) No. 81485, 2004-Ohio-131, 2004 WL 63623, Unreported. Infants ⇔ 210; Infants ⇔ 254

Fact that scientific tests had established father's paternity did not constitute change in circumstances as would justify modification or termination of order granting legal custody of child to her aunt in dependency proceeding. In re Osberry (Ohio App. 3 Dist., Allen, 10-14-2003) No. 1-03-26, 2003-Ohio-5462, 2003 WL 22336115, Unreported. Infants ⇔ 231

Following adjudication of child as dependent and neglected and award of temporary custody of child to aunt, which was later converted to one of legal custody, proper standard for trial court to apply in considering father's motion for legal custody was standard for amending dispositional order; consequently, trial court was required to consider whether it was in the best interest of child to return her to father. In re Osberry (Ohio App. 3 Dist., Allen, 10-14-2003) No. 1-03-26, 2003-Ohio-5462, 2003 WL 22336115, Unreported. Infants ⇔ 231

Juvenile court lacked jurisdiction over father's motion to set aside termination of parental rights judgment; child had been adopted, and thus jurisdiction lay within the probate court. In re Phillips (Ohio App. 12

Dist., Butler, 09-29-2003) No. CA2003-03-062, 2003-Ohio-5107, 2003 WL 22227364, Unreported. Infants ⇐ 196

Trial court was not required to journalize case plan for minor children in its dispositional order granting legal custody of children to children's paternal grandparents rather than to mother, since court did not adjudicate children as abused, neglected, or dependent, and court presumably granted custody pursuant to statute governing custody disputes between parent and nonparent. Ives v. Ives (Ohio App. 9 Dist., Lorain, 07-02-2003) No. 02CA008176, 2003-Ohio-3505, 2003 WL 21508795, Unreported. Child Custody ⇐ 511

Planned Permanent Living Arrangement (PPLA) was not available option for dependent child, in dependency proceeding; child's therapist testified that he was able to function in family-like setting and did not require residential or institutional care, mother did not present any evidence that she had physical, mental or psychological problems that would render her unable to care for child, and child was only 13 years old at the time of disposition hearing. In re Beasley (Ohio App. 4 Dist., Scioto, 05-28-2003) No. 03CA2874, 2003-Ohio-2857, 2003 WL 21278912, Unreported, motion for delayed appeal denied 99 Ohio St.3d 1466, 791 N.E.2d 982, 2003-Ohio-3669, appeal not allowed 99 Ohio St.3d 1515, 792 N.E.2d 201, 2003-Ohio-3957. Infants ⇐ 226

Court of Appeals would not consider issue of whether trial court erred when it adjudicated child to be dependent, in termination of parental rights proceeding, as father failed to timely file an appeal from order adjudicating child to be dependent. In re Rinaldi (Ohio App. 3 Dist., Allen, 05-19-2003) No. 1-02-74, 2003-Ohio-2562, 2003 WL 21142907, Unreported, appeal not allowed 99 Ohio St.3d 1461, 791 N.E.2d 978, 2003-Ohio-3717. Infants ⇐ 244.1

Allowing dependency proceeding involving mother's children to be dismissed and refiled by county children's services agency, including filing of new complaint seeking permanent custody, was not counter to mandate of prior appellate decision finding record insufficient to prove dependency. In re Anisha N. (Ohio App. 6 Dist., Lucas, 05-09-2003) No. L-02-1370, 2003-Ohio-2356, 2003 WL 21040311, Unreported. Infants ⇐ 254

Parents were entitled to continuance of hearing determining care and custody of their children, where parents' counsel was detained in another court on an unrelated case, counsel had been given the impression by prosecution that matter was going to be dismissed, and counsel had notified court that he was unavoidably detained in another court. In re K.D. (Ohio App. 8 Dist., Cuyahoga, 04-10-2003) No. 81843, 2003-Ohio-1847, 2003 WL 1849225, Unreported. Infants ⇐ 204

Passing of the statutory time period, or "sunset date," pursuant to statute governing disposition of abused, neglected, or dependent children, does not divest juvenile courts of jurisdiction to enter dispositional orders. M.W. v. A.W. (Ohio App. 8 Dist., Cuyahoga, 02-27-2003) No. 81518, 2003-Ohio-877, 2003 WL 549961, Unreported. Infants ⇐ 196

Mother waived for appeal issue of juvenile court's 13-month delay before ruling on State's motion for permanent custody, where mother failed to petition at trial level for writ of procedendo to compel execution of court's statutory duty to promptly resolve the matter. M.W. v. A.W. (Ohio App. 8 Dist., Cuyahoga, 02-27-2003) No. 81518, 2003-Ohio-877, 2003 WL 549961, Unreported. Infants ⇐ 241

Time limitations within statute governing disposition of abused, neglected, or dependent children are directory rather than mandatory due to fact that they exist for the assurance of a prompt resolution of child custody matters rather than as a jurisdictional prerequisite to custody determinations. M.W. v. A.W. (Ohio App. 8 Dist., Cuyahoga, 02-27-2003) No. 81518, 2003-Ohio-877, 2003 WL 549961, Unreported. Infants ⇐ 196; Infants ⇐ 222

Although child's great-grandmother was legal custodian of child's 15-year-old mother, great-grandmother did not hold any legally protectable interest in child's care and custody, and thus, she had no legal right to participate in proceedings on county's complaint in dependency and neglect and motion for permanent custody. In re Tammy M. (Ohio App. 6 Dist., Lucas, 01-31-2003) No. L-02-1108, 2003-Ohio-492, 2003 WL 220596, Unreported. Infants ⇐ 200

In evaluating great-grandmother's motion for custody of infant, in proceedings on county's complaint in dependency and neglect and motion for permanent custody, court was not required to have subject matter jurisdiction over infant's mother, a 15-year-old chronic run-away, whose parental rights as to infant had been terminated, to consider as part of the best interests evaluation the possible effects of fact that great-grandmother was also legal custodian of mother, including risk that mother would return and take the infant and flee. In re Tammy M. (Ohio App. 6 Dist., Lucas, 01-31-2003) No. L-02-1108, 2003-Ohio-492, 2003 WL 220596, Unreported. Infants ⇐ 222

Juvenile waived all but plain error in trial court's alleged failure to establish jurisdiction over him in delinquency proceeding, where juvenile did not raise that objection below. In re Ball (Ohio App. 3 Dist., Allen, 01-30-2003) No. 1-02-72, 2003-Ohio-395, 2003 WL 193519, Unreported. Infants ⇐ 243

Trial court established proper jurisdiction in juvenile delinquency proceeding by eliciting testimony by subject of proceeding, at preliminary hearing, that he was 16 years old and by making a finding in judgment entry of commitment that subject of proceeding was born on a particular date and was therefore a juvenile. In re Ball (Ohio App. 3 Dist., Allen, 01-30-2003) No. 1-02-72, 2003-Ohio-395, 2003 WL 193519, Unreported. Infants ⇐ 196

Trial court lacked authority to place children in a Planned Permanent Living Arrangement (PPLA) as an alternative to terminating father's parental rights; there was no evidence to suggest that father or county department of children and family services sought a PPLA, and there was no evidence presented to establish any of the other statutory requirements necessary for court to place children in a PPLA. (Per O'Donnell, J., with two judges concurring in judgment only). In re Harlston (Ohio App. 8 Dist., Cuyahoga, 01-23-2003) No. 80672, 2003-Ohio-282, 2003 WL 152939, Unreported, appeal not allowed 98 Ohio St.3d 1492, 785 N.E.2d 474, 2003-Ohio-1189. Infants ⇐ 226

Statute allowing the juvenile court to review at any time the placement or custody arrangement for an abused child did not apply to juvenile court's order placing unruly child in temporary custody of public children services agency, even if custody was awarded based on allegations of child abuse, where father was never charged with child abuse and child was not adjudicated as abused child. In re Kidd (Ohio App. 11 Dist., Lake, 12-27-2002) No. 2001-L-039, 2002-Ohio-7264, 2002 WL 31886759, Unreported. Infants ⇐ 192

Juvenile court had the authority, once it had adjudicated child to be an unruly child, to award temporary custody to public children services agency without first making additional findings the child was abused, neglected, or dependent. In re Kidd (Ohio App. 11 Dist., Lake, 12-27-2002) No. 2001-L-039, 2002-Ohio-7264, 2002 WL 31886759, Unreported. Infants ⇐ 192

Court of Appeals could consider father's appeal from juvenile court's order adjudicating child as unruly and awarding temporary custody to public children services agency, though such order was a final appealable order which father did not timely appeal, where such order was only a partial final judgment and father timely appealed from the juvenile court order disposing of the remaining claims. In re Kidd (Ohio App. 11 Dist., Lake, 12-27-2002) No. 2001-L-039, 2002-Ohio-7264, 2002 WL 31886759, Unreported. Infants ⇐ 244.1

Mother's appeal of trial court judgment that found her child dependent was proper, where trial court's adjudication of dependency and disposition of temporary custody constituted a final appealable order. In re Hennen (Ohio App. 11 Dist., Trumbull, 12-27-2002) No. 2002-T-0028, 2002-Ohio-7282, 2002 WL 31886716, Unreported. Infants ⇐ 242

Father's motion for legal custody of child, whose custody had been placed with county children services board (CCSB) on allegations of abuse by mother's boyfriend, was facially inadequate, and thus dismissal of motion was warranted, in dependency proceeding on CCSB's motion to terminate public custody and return child to mother; motion failed to state why father was requesting custody, beyond fact that statute governing disposition of abused, neglected, or dependent child permitted him to do so, and mere recitation of statutory language did not satisfy rule requiring that motion filed with juvenile court state with particularity grounds upon which it was made. In re Marhefka (Ohio App. 11 Dist., Ashtabula, 12-20-2002) No. 2001-A-0065, 2002-Ohio-7123, 2002 WL 31862685, Unreported. Infants ⇐ 231

Fact that parents in permanent custody proceedings were not afforded opportunity to cross-examine guardian ad litem did not constitute plain error, where trial court did not rely heavily on guardian's report, but noted in its decision that guardian had filed a report documenting her lengthy involvement in the case and that guardian recommended granting permanent custody to the County Children Services Board, trial court's decision detailed extensive testimony it relied upon, and vast majority of information in guardian's report was testified to at trial by persons who gave information to guardian. In re Tyas (Ohio App. 12 Dist., Clinton, 12-09-2002) No. CA2002-02-010, 2002-Ohio-6679, 2002 WL 31740248, Unreported. Infants ⇐ 243

Order adjudging the children to be abused and placing them in county's temporary custody was a final, appealable order at point at which order was journalized, and thus, the Court of Appeals was without jurisdiction to consider issue that trial court erred in accepting, on county's original complaint for temporary custody, father's admission that his children were abused, where father failed to appeal temporary custody order within 30 days from journalization. In re M.Z. (Ohio App. 8 Dist., Cuyahoga, 12-05-2002) No. 80799, 2002-Ohio-6634, 2002 WL 31722231, Unreported. Infants ⇐ 248.1

Although county's motion for permanent custody of seven children was not decided until more than two years after the filing of the original complaint, the lower court did not err in failing to grant the father's motion to dismiss, since the trial court retained continuing jurisdiction for further dispositional orders necessary for the protection of the children. In re M.Z. (Ohio App. 8 Dist., Cuyahoga, 12-05-2002) No. 80799, 2002-Ohio-6634, 2002 WL 31722231, Unreported. Infants ⇐ 202

Hearing on motion for permanent custody of dependent child was dispositional, rather than adjudicatory. In re Ashley E.D. (Ohio App. 6 Dist., Huron, 11-15-2002) No. H-02-025, 2002-Ohio-6238, 2002 WL 31529030, Unreported. Infants ⇐ 203

Maternal aunt and uncle lacked standing to seek modification of placement of children, who were returned to custodial paternal grandmother at conclusion of neglect proceeding against her, notwithstanding apparently mistaken adjudication of neglect against children's parents rather than grandmother, where aunt and uncle were not parties to proceeding and were not made so by temporary emergency placement of children in their custody pending proceeding; however, aunt and uncle were not without recourse, as they could themselves bring a neglect proceeding against grandmother based on new information and obtain legal custody thereby. In re Crowder (Ohio App. 8 Dist., Cuyahoga, 10-03-2002) No. 80738, 2002-Ohio-5347, 2002 WL 31195430, Unreported. Infants ⇐ 230.1

Temporary custody statute, providing for temporary custody order to terminate one year after the earlier of the date on which the complaint in the case was filed or the child was first placed into shelter care, was inapplicable to entitle maternal aunt and uncle to hearing on termination of their temporary custody of children, who had been placed with them on emergency basis pending neglect proceeding against children's custodial paternal grandmother, where statute by its terms was restricted to cases in which there had been no disposition or the child was placed in shelter care, and return of custody of allegedly neglected children to grandmother disposed of proceeding; return of custody was final action on neglect complaint against grandmother. In re Crowder (Ohio App. 8 Dist., Cuyahoga, 10-03-2002) No. 80738, 2002-Ohio-5347, 2002 WL 31195430, Unreported. Infants ⇐ 203

The juvenile court loses jurisdiction over children and cannot enter judgment granting permanent custody to the Department of Human Services where the DHS has been involved with the family in an out-of-home protective supervision setting longer than a year. Matter of Farrar (Ohio App. 5 Dist., Guernsey, 06-23-1995) No. 94CA20, 1995 WL 495471, Unreported, appeal allowed 73 Ohio St.3d 1452, 654 N.E.2d 988, reversed 76 Ohio St.3d 632, 669 N.E.2d 1140, 1996-Ohio-45.

After a public children services agency or private child placing agency is granted temporary custody of a child and files a motion for permanent custody, a juvenile court does not have the authority to place the child in a planned permanent living arrangement (PPLA) when the agency does not request this disposition. In re A.B. (Ohio, 09-06-2006) 110 Ohio St.3d 230, 852 N.E.2d 1187, 2006-Ohio-4359. Infants ⇐ 226

Juvenile rule allowing "any person" to file for custody of a child did not override express statutory language precluding natural parent who lost permanent custody of child from filing nonparent custody petition, where right to file petition for custody was substantive right not subject to abridgment, enlargement, or modification by court rules. In re McBride (Ohio, 07-19-2006) 110 Ohio St.3d 19, 850 N.E.2d 43, 2006-Ohio-3454. Infants ⇐ 231

Mother who lost permanent custody of child was statutorily barred from filing petition for custody of child as nonparent, where mother's nonparent custody petition was filed with same case number used in amended complaint of abuse, neglect, and dependency that resulted in termination of her parental rights, and statute providing for modification or termination of dispositional orders specifically excluded as parties any parent whose parental rights with respect to the child have been terminated. In re McBride (Ohio, 07-19-2006) 110 Ohio St.3d 19, 850 N.E.2d 43, 2006-Ohio-3454. Infants ⇐ 231

Compliance with procedural requirements set forth in statute and rule providing that, if a child is adjudicated an abused, neglected, or dependent child, the court may award legal custody of the child to either parent or to any person who, prior to the dispositional hearing, files a motion requesting legal custody of the child is mandatory. In re L.R.T. (Ohio App. 12 Dist., 01-23-2006) 165 Ohio App.3d 77, 844 N.E.2d 914, 2006-Ohio-207. Infants ⇐ 222

Trial court erred as a matter of law in awarding custody of dependent and neglected child to child's great-aunt when child's great-aunt had failed to file a motion for legal custody before the dispositional hearing; any person who sought an award of legal custody of a child had to file a motion, prior to the dispositional hearing, requesting such custody; abrogating In re Callier, 2002 WL 1010081 (Ohio App. 12 Dist.) In re L.R.T. (Ohio App. 12 Dist., 01-23-2006) 165 Ohio App.3d 77, 844 N.E.2d 914, 2006-Ohio-207. Infants ⇐ 222

A trial court is not required to make a finding of parental unfitness before granting to a nonparent custody of a child adjudicated dependent or neglected. In re Alexander C. (Ohio App. 6 Dist., 11-18-2005) 164 Ohio App.3d 540, 843 N.E.2d 211, 2005-Ohio-6134. Infants ⇐ 210

At dispositional hearing in child dependency proceeding, trial court should have considered both grandmother's motion for legal custody of dependent child and mother's motion for return of custody based on best interest standard, without requiring grandmother to establish that mother was unsuitable before her motion would be considered. In re D.R. (Ohio App. 9 Dist., 06-04-2003) 153 Ohio App.3d 156, 792 N.E.2d 203, 2003-Ohio-2852. Infants ⇐ 222; Infants ⇐ 231

Assuming that temporary custody of four siblings, two of whom had been adjudicated neglected and two of whom had been adjudicated dependent, technically terminated and sunset date passed due to combination of state's failure to request extension of temporary custody and lack of separate hearing on propriety of extension, juvenile court maintained jurisdiction to rule on subsequent requests for permanent and legal custody, and its rulings on such requests therefore rendered moot mother's challenge on appeal to juvenile court's jurisdiction to grant extension of temporary custody. In re Nice (Ohio App. 7 Dist., 03-20-2001) 141 Ohio App.3d 445, 751 N.E.2d 552, 2001-Ohio-3214. Infants ⇐ 196; Infants ⇐ 247

On appeal from a trial court's determination that grant of permanent custody of a child to an agency applying for such custody is in the child's best interests, a reviewing court must determine whether the trial court complied with statutory requirements and whether there was sufficient evidence to support a finding by clear and convincing evidence that one or more statutory factors precluding that child's return to one or both parents exist. In re Nicholas H. (Ohio App. 6 Dist., 05-05-2000) 137 Ohio App.3d 442, 738 N.E.2d 896. Infants ⇐ 252

Trial court was not authorized to grant legal custody of children to their father's brother and sister-in-law, where brother and sister-in-law did not file a motion for legal custody prior to dispositional hearing. In re Perez (Ohio App. 9 Dist., 11-03-1999) 135 Ohio App.3d 494, 734 N.E.2d 858. Child Custody ⇐ 271

Juvenile court was not required, prior to awarding permanent custody of child to county agency in proceeding to terminate mother's parental rights, to find by clear and convincing evidence that child's maternal grandmother was an unsuitable placement option. In re Patterson (Ohio App. 9 Dist., 09-01-1999) 134 Ohio App.3d 119, 730 N.E.2d 439. Infants ⇐ 178

Where complaint involving parents' children was filed before effective date of amended statute allowing for only two extensions of protective supervision of abused, neglected or dependent children, application of such amended statute to parents' case would be retroactive, rather than prospective, though motion for extension of protective supervision was filed after effective date of amended statute; specific events mentioned in amended statute took place before its effective date, and none of specified events occurred after the amendment. In re Carroll (Ohio App. 2 Dist., 11-07-1997) 124 Ohio App.3d 51, 705 N.E.2d 402. Infants ⇐ 132

Amended statute allowing for only two extensions of protective supervision of abused, neglected or dependent children could not apply retroactively to case in which complaint was filed against parents before amended statute's effective date, where General Assembly did not specify that the amendments would apply retroactively. In re Carroll (Ohio App. 2 Dist., 11-07-1997) 124 Ohio App.3d 51, 705 N.E.2d 402. Infants ⇐ 132

Juvenile court order vacating county agency's permanent custody of children adjudicated neglected and giving legal custody of children to adoptive parents of their older sibling was in effect denial of foster parents' adoption petition and as such exceeded that court's jurisdiction; previous termination of biological parents' parental rights left no one with capacity to consent to children's adoption once agency's permanent custody was vacated. In re Hitchcock (Ohio App. 8 Dist., 11-21-1996) 120 Ohio App.3d 88, 696 N.E.2d 1090, stay granted 77 Ohio St.3d 1462, 672 N.E.2d 1119, stay denied 77 Ohio St.3d 1502, 673 N.E.2d 921, motion to vacate stay denied 77 Ohio St.3d 1521, 674 N.E.2d 373, appeal allowed 78 Ohio St.3d 1455, 677 N.E.2d 815, appeal dismissed as improvidently allowed 81 Ohio St.3d 1222, 689 N.E.2d 43, 1998-Ohio-653, stay denied 81 Ohio St.3d 1469, 690 N.E.2d 1288, stay denied 81 Ohio St.3d 1476, 691 N.E.2d 294. Infants ⇐ 226

No new finding of dependency is required based upon circumstances of current placement of child before trial court may consider motion to modify or change dispositional order, as juvenile court retains jurisdiction following initial dispositional hearing until child reaches age of majority or is adopted, and may therefore hold additional hearings sua sponte or on motion of any party to reconsider original order. In re Hitchcock (Ohio App. 8 Dist., 11-21-1996) 120 Ohio App.3d 88, 696 N.E.2d 1090, stay granted 77 Ohio St.3d 1462, 672 N.E.2d 1119, stay denied 77 Ohio St.3d 1502, 673 N.E.2d 921, motion to vacate stay denied 77 Ohio St.3d 1521, 674 N.E.2d 373, appeal allowed 78 Ohio St.3d 1455, 677 N.E.2d 815, appeal dismissed as improvidently allowed 81 Ohio St.3d 1222, 689 N.E.2d 43, 1998-Ohio-653, stay denied 81 Ohio St.3d 1469, 690 N.E.2d 1288, stay denied 81 Ohio St.3d 1476, 691 N.E.2d 294. Infants ⚖ 230.1

Foster parents of child adjudicated neglected had standing to appeal from order terminating county agency's permanent custody of child and child's younger sibling and granting legal custody to adoptive parents of children's elder sibling; foster parents had been permitted to intervene in placement of children with adoptive parents of elder sibling and sought to adopt both children, and trial court's order effectively precluded their adoption petition from being heard. In re Hitchcock (Ohio App. 8 Dist., 11-21-1996) 120 Ohio App.3d 88, 696 N.E.2d 1090, stay granted 77 Ohio St.3d 1462, 672 N.E.2d 1119, stay denied 77 Ohio St.3d 1502, 673 N.E.2d 921, motion to vacate stay denied 77 Ohio St.3d 1521, 674 N.E.2d 373, appeal allowed 78 Ohio St.3d 1455, 677 N.E.2d 815, appeal dismissed as improvidently allowed 81 Ohio St.3d 1222, 689 N.E.2d 43, 1998-Ohio-653, stay denied 81 Ohio St.3d 1469, 690 N.E.2d 1288, stay denied 81 Ohio St.3d 1476, 691 N.E.2d 294. Infants ⚖ 242

Biological mother of children adjudicated dependent and subsequently adopted by foster family was not entitled to writ of habeas corpus returning custody of children to her, where mother did not establish that immediate return of custody of children to her would be in the children's best interest, and she possessed an adequate legal remedy in the ordinary course of law through being served with copy of the amended complaint for permanent custody in proceedings in juvenile court on remand from Court of Appeals' earlier reversal of permanent custody order for defective service on mother. Holloway v. Clermont County Dept. of Human Services (Ohio, 10-22-1997) 80 Ohio St.3d 128, 684 N.E.2d 1217, 1997-Ohio-131. Habeas Corpus ⚖ 536

With respect to statute providing that temporary custody order shall terminate one year after the earlier of the date on which the complaint in the case was filed or the child was first placed into shelter care, passing of sunset date does not divest juvenile courts of jurisdiction to enter dispositional orders. Holloway v. Clermont County Dept. of Human Services (Ohio, 10-22-1997) 80 Ohio St.3d 128, 684 N.E.2d 1217, 1997-Ohio-131. Infants ⚖ 222

Permanent custody of child may be granted to children services agency if court determines, upon consideration of statutory grounds, that children cannot or should not be placed with their parents. In re Shanequa H. (Ohio App. 6 Dist., 02-02-1996) 109 Ohio App.3d 142, 671 N.E.2d 1113. Infants ⚖ 155

Juvenile courts retain jurisdiction to issue dispositional order, even though statutory requirement that motion to continue original temporary custody order be filed within one year has not been fulfilled, provided that problems leading to original grant of temporary custody have not been resolved or sufficiently mitigated. In re Young Children (Ohio, 10-09-1996) 76 Ohio St.3d 632, 669 N.E.2d 1140, 1996-Ohio-45. Infants ⚖ 196; Infants ⚖ 197

New one-year limit for filing motion to continue original temporary custody order applies when new complaint is filed based on past facts discovered subsequent to original complaint or upon subsequent facts; new filing is not merely refiling of original complaint. In re Young Children (Ohio, 10-09-1996) 76 Ohio St.3d 632, 669 N.E.2d 1140, 1996-Ohio-45. Infants ⚖ 196; Infants ⚖ 197

Juvenile courts retained jurisdiction to decide untimely dispositional motions and, thus, juvenile courts were required to determine whether problems leading to original grant of temporary custody had been resolved or sufficiently mitigated when temporary custody order expired. In re Young Children (Ohio, 10-09-1996) 76 Ohio St.3d 632, 669 N.E.2d 1140, 1996-Ohio-45. Infants ⚖ 196; Infants ⚖ 197

Juvenile court could take action with respect to legal custody of dependent child, even though no motion had been filed by a party in interest requesting a modification of child's legal custody arrangement. In re Bowman (Ohio App. 9 Dist., 03-08-1995) 101 Ohio App.3d 599, 656 N.E.2d 355. Infants ⚖ 230.1

While statute requires juvenile court to review dispositional order if any party files motion requesting modification or termination of order, statute and rule additionally allow juvenile court to review child's placement or custody arrangement at any time. In re Bowman (Ohio App. 9 Dist., 03-08-1995) 101 Ohio App.3d 599, 656 N.E.2d 355. Infants ⚖ 230.1

Where public children services agency did not have requisite grant of temporary custody, instead of filing postdispositional motion for permanent custody, agency should have sought grant of temporary custody by asking court to modify its disposition terminating agency's grant of temporary custody or by filing a new complaint based on more recent allegations of abuse or on dependency theory. In re Miller (Ohio App. 2 Dist., 02-15-1995) 101 Ohio App.3d 199, 655 N.E.2d 252. Infants ⚖ 230.1

Public children services agency did not have standing to bring postdispositional motion for permanent custody of child after its grant of temporary custody of child was terminated and it had only protective supervision of child. In re Miller (Ohio App. 2 Dist., 02-15-1995) 101 Ohio App.3d 199, 655 N.E.2d 252. Infants ⚖ 200

In order for public children services agency to file motion for permanent custody of child previously adjudicated as abused, neglected or dependent, it must have current temporary custody of that child pursuant to order of disposition. In re Miller (Ohio App. 2 Dist., 02-15-1995) 101 Ohio App.3d 199, 655 N.E.2d 252. Infants ⚖ 230.1

Failing to order long-term foster care for children, including continued visitation between mother and children, was not erroneous where county department of human services did not request such placement, as required by statute. In re Brodbeck (Ohio App. 3 Dist., 10-19-1994) 97 Ohio App.3d 652, 647 N.E.2d 240. Infants ⚖ 222

Notwithstanding statute which establishes that juvenile court retains jurisdiction over any child for whom court issues order of disposition, juvenile court proceedings do not divest probate court of jurisdiction over adoptions. State ex rel. Hitchcock v. Cuyahoga Cty. Court of Common Pleas, Probate Div. (Ohio App. 8 Dist., 10-07-1994) 97 Ohio App.3d 600, 647 N.E.2d 208. Courts ⚖ 472.4(8)

Prospective adoptive parents were not entitled to writ of prohibition to prevent juvenile court judge from going forward with neglect proceeding while ordering that adoption proceedings be held in abeyance; judge's going forward in neglect proceeding was not unauthorized by law. State ex rel. Cuyahoga Cty. Dept. of Children & Family Serv. v. Ferreri (Ohio App. 8 Dist., 09-26-1994) 96 Ohio App.3d 660, 645 N.E.2d 837. Prohibition ⚖ 10(2)

Father's 18-year-old daughter was "physically handicapped" as result of diabetes such that juvenile court could, after adjudicating daughter to be unruly child and placing her on probation and in foster home, retain jurisdiction and order father to maintain medical coverage for daughter until she was 21. In re Kessler (Ohio App. 6 Dist., 09-17-1993) 90 Ohio App.3d 231, 628 N.E.2d 153, motion overruled 68 Ohio St.3d 1437, 625 N.E.2d 625. Infants ⚖ 228(2)

Father failed to file timely appeal of juvenile court's adjudication that his two minor children were dependent children where he filed his appeal more than one year after adjudicatory hearing on dependency issue and nearly one year after order awarding temporary custody to public children services agency. In re Shaeffer Children (Van Wert 1993) 85 Ohio App.3d 683, 621 N.E.2d 426, dismissed, jurisdictional motion overruled 67 Ohio St.3d 1451, 619 N.E.2d 419. Infants ⚖ 244.1

While there is no statutory mandate that factors for determining best interest of child in custody disputes arising from divorce actions be considered in custody proceedings incident to dependency action, juvenile courts should consider totality of circumstances, including those factors, to extent they are applicable. In re Pryor (Athens 1993) 86 Ohio App.3d 327, 620 N.E.2d 973. Infants ⚖ 154.1

County children services' second motion to extend order of protective supervision for children should not have been denied since second extension motion was filed prior to expiration of six-month extension obtained by first motion. In re Collier (Athens 1993) 85 Ohio App.3d 232, 619 N.E.2d 503. Infants ⚖ 230.1

County children services was not precluded from filing motion requesting second extension of child protective supervision orders by plain language of statute providing that any order for protective supervision shall terminate upon earlier of one year after date on which complaint was filed or child was first placed in shelter care, unless agency files motion requesting extension for period of up to six months of original dispositional order or extension of previously granted extension for additional period of up to six months. In re Collier (Athens 1993) 85 Ohio App.3d 232, 619 N.E.2d 503. Infants ⚖ 230.1

The county department of human services loses jurisdiction over neglected children, and cannot grant permanent custody to the department, where the "sunset" date lapsed before the ruling on the department's motion for permanent custody, which is improperly filed less than thirty days prior to the "sunset" date. In re Travis Children (Stark 1992) 80 Ohio App.3d 620, 609 N.E.2d 1356.

When a juvenile court makes a custody determination under RC 2151.23 and 2151.353, it must do so in accordance with RC 3109.04. In re Poling (Ohio 1992) 64 Ohio St.3d 211, 594 N.E.2d 589.

RC 2151.353, permitting the state to receive permanent custody of a "dependent child" whose parent is jailed, does not conflict with RC 3107.07; where the child is a "dependent child" under RC 2151.04 the state has authority to obtain permanent custody under RC 2151.353, and once parental rights have been terminated under RC Ch 2151, it is provided by RC 3107.06(D) that this parent's consent to adoption is no longer necessary. In re Dillard (Montgomery 1988) 48 Ohio App.3d 263, 549 N.E.2d 213.

Welfare department's motion for permanent custody of two children which contained allegations that children were dependent due to lack of proper care and support, and which contained several allegations of fact which demonstrated children's dependency, sufficiently apprised natural mother whose parental rights were terminated on grounds upon which permanent commitment proceedings were based, notwithstanding welfare department's incorrect citation to repealed statute. In re Covin (Hamilton 1982) 8 Ohio App.3d 139, 456 N.E.2d 520, 8 O.B.R. 196. Infants ⚖ 197

RC 3107.06 does not mandate that the ongoing jurisdiction of a Kentucky juvenile court bars the issuance of an adoption order by the probate division of an Ohio court of common pleas. In re Johnson (Hamilton 1978) 56 Ohio App.2d 265, 382 N.E.2d 1176, 10 O.O.3d 278.

A RC 2151.23(A)(3) action does not need to comply with RC 2151.27 and RC 2151.23, as the latter sections clearly apply to neglect, abuse, and dependency hearings provided for in RC 2151.23(A)(1). In re Perales (Ohio 1977) 52 Ohio St.2d 89, 369 N.E.2d 1047, 6 O.O.3d 293.

An order modifying a previously entered temporary custody order, which was made in disposition of a finding that a child is neglected, constitutes a final appealable order. In re Rule (Crawford 1963) 1 Ohio App.2d 57, 203 N.E.2d 501, 30 O.O.2d 76.

Juvenile court's termination of father's parental rights without explicitly granting permanent child custody to Jefferson County Children Services Board (JCCSB) constituted ultra vires act, given that act is not provided for by statute. In re Sims (Ohio App. 7 Dist., Jefferson, 06-28-2002) No. 02-JE-2, 2002-Ohio-3458, 2002 WL 1483889, Unreported. Infants ⚖ 221

Acceptance, custody, and placement of dependent, abused, or neglected children by private child care agency was traditional governmental function subject to comprehensive regulatory scheme promulgated by state, and, thus, permanent custody actions were in effect "instituted by the state" for purposes of indigent father's request for free transcript of proceedings. State ex rel. Howard v. Ferreri (Ohio 1994) 70 Ohio St.3d 587, 639 N.E.2d 1189.

RC 2151.413 is inapplicable where a juvenile court acts on a complaint that seeks permanent commitment of a dependent child pursuant to RC 2151.353(A)(4). In re Stanton, No. C–830501 (1st Dist Ct App, Hamilton, 6–20–84).

The trial court's failure to make findings of fact and conclusions of law following a grant of permanent custody of a minor child to a county children services board does not constitute prejudicial error where the parties agree generally to the facts of the case. In re Hollins, No. CA–703 (5th Dist Ct App, Guernsey, 3–29–83).

In an action commenced by a county welfare department requesting permanent custody of appellant's minor child and termination of parental rights pursuant to RC 2151.353(A)(4), it was error for the trial court to base its determination upon statements of appellant's attorney who was appointed by the court both as personal counsel for the appellant and guardian ad litem for the child. In re Johnson, No. C–810516 (1st Dist Ct App, Hamilton, 4–28–82).

6. Evidence

Evidence supported finding that mother and father's relatives were not suitable placements for their ten children, in termination of parental rights proceeding; grandmother moved frequently, did not maintain a stable residence, had a small residence, and her visits with the children were chaotic, and aunt had four children, allowed her oldest son to live with her mother, earned approximately $25,000 per year as a bus driver, lived in a three-bedroom house, and her husband was unable to work due to a seizure disorder. In re Hilyard (Ohio App. 4 Dist., Vinton, 04-13-2006) No. 05CA600, No. 05CA603, No. 05CA607, No. 05CA601, No. 05CA604, No. 05CA608, No. 05CA602, No. 05CA606, No. 05CA609, 2006-Ohio-1965, 2006 WL Infants ⚖ 222

Competent evidence supported the trial court's finding that adoption, rather than placement in a planned permanent living arrangement, was in the best interest of the children; mother suffered from significant physical, mental, or psychological problems that interfered with her ability to parent her children, and case worker for the children and guardian ad litem presented evidence that adoption of the children was possible and that their need for stability was critical. In re Laigle (Ohio App. 5 Dist., Stark, 02-21-2006) No. 2005-CA-00264, 2006-Ohio-829, 2006 WL 438702, Unreported. Infants ⚖ 175.1

Transfer of legal custody of mother's children to paternal grandmother, in context of dependency and neglect proceedings, was in best interests of children; mother had unresolved mental health issues, children had resided with grandmother for over two years, children had special needs and were involved with therapy which grandmother was working with, behavior problems of children were exacerbated following visitation with mother, and grandmother had provided stable home for children. In re D.R. (Ohio App. 12 Dist., Butler, 01-30-2006) No. CA2005-06-150, No. CA2005-06-151, 2006-Ohio-340, 2006 WL 216642, Unreported. Infants ⚖ 222

Clear and convincing evidence supported juvenile court's decision to terminate mother's and father's parental rights with regard to their three minor children and award permanent custody of the children to the Children Services Board (CSB); each parent was mentally retarded with an I.Q. of only 55, both parents suffered from alcohol problems, father had a personality disorder, and the two oldest children expressed a preference for foster care. In re Calvert Children (Ohio App. 5 Dist., Guernsey, 10-24-2005) No. 05-CA-19, No. 05-CA-20, 2005-Ohio-5653, 2005 WL 2746329, Unreported. Infants ⚖ 158

Evidence supported trial court's determination that grant of legal custody of child to paternal aunt was in best interests of child; mother failed to achieve any of the objectives listed in the case plan, mother lacked appropriate parenting skills, mother was unable to obtain stable housing, and mother failed to seek full-time employment and reliable transportation. In re Nolen (Ohio App. 3 Dist., Crawford, 06-20-2005) No. 3-04-20, 2005-Ohio-3075, 2005 WL 1421777, Unreported. Infants ⚖ 155

Sufficient evidence supported trial court's finding that permanent custody was in best interest of child, as would support court's decision to award permanent custody of child to county department of children and family services; child had been in custody of department since her birth and had never lived with mother, child's relationship with mother was "nonexistent," and grant of permanent custody was necessary for child to achieve a legally secure permanent placement. In re D.W. (Ohio App. 8 Dist., Cuyahoga, 04-21-2005) No. 84547, 2005-Ohio-1867, 2005 WL 926991, Unreported. Infants ⚖ 155

Sufficient evidence supported trial court's finding that child could not or should not be placed with either parent in reasonable time, as would support court's decision to award permanent custody of child to county department of children and family services; parents had failed, for over six months, to remedy conditions that had caused child to be placed outside home, and mother had failed to provide basic necessities for child, had failed to visit or communicate with her, and had shown an unwillingness to provide adequate permanent home for her. In re D.W. (Ohio App. 8 Dist., Cuyahoga, 04-21-2005) No. 84547, 2005-Ohio-1867, 2005 WL 926991, Unreported. Infants ⚖ 157

Trial court's decision that grant of permanent custody of children to county child protection agency was in best interests of children was not against the manifest weight of the evidence; children referred to foster family as their family, children had been in agency custody for over three years, children were adoptable, mother refused to believe child's allegations of sexual abuse against her husband, and mother had previously had other children removed from her care based on similar allegations. In re Moore (Ohio App. 7 Dist., Belmont, 01-05-2005) No. 04-BE-9, 2005-Ohio-136, 2005 WL 78754, Unreported. Infants ⚖ 156

Finding that award of legal custody of dependant infant to paternal aunt and uncle, rather than to paternal grandfather who already had custody of older sibling, would be in best interest of infant was not abuse of discretion; though both parties presented good and viable options for placement, grandfather's smoking risked aggravation of infant's pre-asthmatic condition, and aunt and uncle appeared to have more realistic understanding of infant's developmental levels. In re M.S. (Ohio App. 9 Dist., Summit, 01-05-2005) No. 22158, 2005-Ohio-10, 2005 WL 19441, Unreported. Infants ⚖ 222

Grant of permanent custody of child to county child protection agency was not against the manifest weight of the evidence; mother suffered moderate mental retardation and was unable to parent safely, and mother's parenting ability was not subject to improvement. In re Keiondre S. (Ohio App. 6 Dist., Lucas, 11-24-2004) No. L-04-1025, 2004-Ohio-6316, 2004 WL 2690668, Unreported. Infants ⚖ 158

Substantial evidence supported trial court's rejection of planned permanent living arrangement (PPLA) as alternative to awarding permanent custody of dependent child to county children services agency; there was no evidence that child was unable to function in family-like setting, child was not 16 years of age or older, putative father did not suffer from drug addiction problem that made him unable to care for child, and adoption was in child's best interest. In re C.S. (Ohio App. 2 Dist., Montgomery, 10-22-2004) No. 20379, 2004-Ohio-5810, 2004 WL 2445238, Unreported. Infants ⇌ 226

Clear and convincing evidence supported finding that child could not be placed with mother within a reasonable time, in support of termination of parental rights; child was in need of legally secure placement, and mother's parental rights to ten of her other children had been terminated. In re Jared C. (Ohio App. 6 Dist., Lucas, 09-17-2004) No. L-04-1016, 2004-Ohio-4922, 2004 WL 2334313, Unreported. Infants ⇌ 155

Clear and convincing evidence supported trial court's determination that it was in infant child's best interest to be permanently placed in custody of Department of Job and Family Services (DJFS), and that child should not be placed with either of his parents; child, like his older sister, tested positive for cocaine at birth, father's identity was unknown, mother suffered from apparent drug addiction and abandoned court-ordered drug rehabilitation, mother violated her probation several times, and child, in the meantime, had established a bond with his foster parents, who not only enjoyed custody of child's older sister, but were in the process of adopting her, with plans to adopt child thereafter. In re M.C. (Ohio App. 12 Dist., Madison, 09-07-2004) No. CA2004-04-008, 2004-Ohio-4782, 2004 WL 2003714, Unreported. Infants ⇌ 155; Infants ⇌ 156

Father's due process rights were not violated when the trial court held termination of parental rights hearing even though incarcerated father was not present in the courtroom; father was represented by an attorney, the attorney entered into evidence a letter written by father, father's brother and sister testified on his behalf at the hearing, a full record was made of the proceeding, and any additional testimony father wanted to submit could have been presented by deposition. In re Jesse P. (Ohio App. 6 Dist., Lucas, 07-16-2004) No. L-04-1028, 2004-Ohio-3801, 2004 WL 1595103, Unreported. Constitutional Law ⇌ 274(5); Infants ⇌ 203

Clear and convincing evidence supported trial court order granting permanent custody of children to county children's services; father failed to complete anger management classes, parent classes, and domestic violence classes, father's supervised visits with the children were cancelled due to father's failure to appear for visitation, when father was not incarcerated he did not visit the children, he failed to acknowledge holidays of the birthdays of the children, and it was in the best interests of the children to be adopted by maternal grandparents. In re Jesse P. (Ohio App. 6 Dist., Lucas, 07-16-2004) No. L-04-1028, 2004-Ohio-3801, 2004 WL 1595103, Unreported. Infants ⇌ 155; Infants ⇌ 157

The trial court's failure to order child to be placed in a planned permanent living arrangement was not an abuse of discretion; after mother completed a parenting class, she continued to blame child for being removed from her custody, and guardian ad litem supported the award of custody to the State. In re R.N. (Ohio App. 8 Dist., Cuyahoga, 05-20-2004) No. 83121, 2004-Ohio-2560, 2004 WL 1118825, Unreported. Infants ⇌ 226

Granting legal custody of child, who had been adjudicated a dependent child, to her paternal grandmother, rather than mother, was in the child's best interest; child did not always want to visit mother and usually exhibited some behavioral problems upon her return from visiting mother, child developed rash while in mother's care despite numerous discussions and written instructions to mother regarding how to keep the rash from occurring or to properly treat rash, and child was well-adjusted in her grandmother's home. In re A.W.-G. (Ohio App. 12 Dist., Butler, 05-10-2004) No. CA2003-04-099, 2004-Ohio-2298, 2004 WL 1040696, Unreported. Infants ⇌ 222

Preponderance of the evidence, as opposed to clear and convincing evidence, was appropriate standard for granting legal custody of child to paternal grandmother in dependency proceeding; clear and convincing evidence was standard in permanent custody proceeding, legal custody where parental rights were not terminated was not as drastic a remedy as permanent custody, and mother retained residual parental rights, such as visitation. In re A.W.-G. (Ohio App. 12 Dist., Butler, 05-10-2004) No. CA2003-04-099, 2004-Ohio-2298, 2004 WL 1040696, Unreported. Infants ⇌ 222

County Department of Jobs and Family Services failed to set forth clear and convincing evidence that mother's children were dependent; none of school children on school field trip were ever actually subjected to sole parental supervision of mother who was intoxicated on the day of field trip, and mother's child did not even attend field trip, so she could not be considered dependent as result of mother's behavior on field trip. In re C.M. (Ohio App. 12 Dist., Brown, 05-10-2004) No. CA2003-02-003, No. CA2003-02-004, 2004-Ohio-2294, 2004 WL 1040677, Unreported. Infants ⇌ 179

In child neglect proceeding, County Department of Jobs and Family Services failed to present clear and convincing proof that mother's children lacked adequate parental care as a result of her faults or habits; there was no showing that children had ever been deprived of adequate food or clothing, none of school children on school field trip were ever actually subjected to sole parental supervision of mother who was intoxicated on the day of field trip, and mother's child did not even attend field trip, so she could not be considered neglected as result of mother's behavior on field trip, and mother provided children with adequate supervision following school. In re C.M. (Ohio App. 12 Dist., Brown, 05-10-2004) No. CA2003-02-003, No. CA2003-02-004, 2004-Ohio-2294, 2004 WL 1040677, Unreported. Infants ⇌ 179

Children's best interests warranted termination of mother's parental rights and placement of children in permanent custody of Children Services Board (CSB); mother was unable to provide stable home for children due to long history of abusing alcohol and crack cocaine, children missed a lot of school during periods when mother was using drugs, and children were living in same foster home, had adjusted to living there, and seemed to be happy. In re J.O. (Ohio App. 9 Dist., Wayne, 04-28-2004) No. 03CA0076, 2004-Ohio-2121, 2004 WL 894571, Unreported. Infants ⇌ 155; Infants ⇌ 159

There was clear and convincing evidence that it was in best interest of child to grant permanent custody to county children services; although mother had regularly visited child and made efforts towards reunification, caseworkers and guardian ad litem testified that mother had not eliminated conditions which led to child's removal on permanent basis, that mother's marriage to man convicted of gross sexual imposition after being warned not to associate with him posed danger to child, and that child wished to remain with her foster parent and was afraid to return to mother, and foster mother had expressed desire to adopt child. In re Reese (Ohio App. 10 Dist., Franklin, 02-26-2004) No. 03AP-1072, 2004-Ohio-854, 2004 WL 350927, Unreported. Infants ⇌ 155; Infants ⇌ 156

Evidence supported order granting permanent custody of children to county children's service agency; neither parent fully complied with their caseplan or addressed issues of domestic violence or drug and alcohol abuse, the parents did not have stable housing and were living with paternal grandparents, children were physically and sexually abused while in parental custody, both children expressed fear at the idea of living with parents, and during visitation parents threatened to physically harm children if they made allegations of abuse against half-brother. In re Foucht (Ohio App. 2 Dist., Montgomery, 02-06-2004) No. 19930, 2004-Ohio-456, 2004 WL 225458, Unreported. Infants ⇌ 155; Infants ⇌ 156

Evidence in shelter care hearing supported trial court's finding that award of legal custody of child to father, rather than mother, was in child's best interest; case manager testified that drugs had been sold at mother's home, that domestic violence had occurred in child's presence, that child had not begun to learn age appropriate skills, that child flourished in father's custody, that child had become attached to father, that mother had only recently begun to apply herself to attempt to complete her case plan, father testified to child's growth under his care, and mother testified that she had been diagnosed as bipolar, had been charged with writing bad checks, and with possession of illegal drugs. In re Law (Ohio App. 5 Dist., Tuscarawas, 01-09-2004) No. 2003AP0645, 2004-Ohio-117, 2004 WL 60485, Unreported. Infants ⇌ 231

Planned permanent living arrangement with public children services agency or private child placing agency, rather than permanent custody, was not in best interests of children, despite guardian ad litem's request; counselors and assessing psychologist determined it was in best interest of children to stay in foster care, children would not be available for adoption if county did not receive permanent custody, children were functioning well in family-like setting in the foster home, there was no evidence that mother had any significant physical, medical or psychological problems which impaired her caring for children, evidence did not show that adoption was not in children's best interest, and, although counselors testified that children loved their mother, they were afraid of her and did not want to live with her. In re M.H. (Ohio App. 8 Dist., Cuyahoga, 12-24-2003) No. 81893, 2003-Ohio-7053, 2003 WL 23009016, Unreported. Infants ⇌ 222

Trial court finding that it was in the best interest of the children to award legal custody of children to paternal cousin of mother was not an abuse of discretion; mother provided little financial assistance to children during the three years they were not in her custody, she failed to attend any counseling sessions, she missed more than half of the random drug screenings, mother was not concerned with the abuse of child, even though child's claim of physical abuse was substantiated, children had become more outgoing while under the care of cousin, father of one child was opposed to returning children to mother, and social worker believed that it was in the best interest of children to remain with cousin. In re Gales (Ohio App. 10 Dist., Franklin, 11-25-2003) No. 03AP-445, No. 03AP-446, 2003-Ohio-6309, 2003 WL 22785029, Unreported. Infants ⬩ 155; Infants ⬩ 156; Infants ⬩ 157; Infants ⬩ 222

Evidence was insufficient to support trial court finding that mother's mental retardation was so severe that mother was unable to provide child with an adequate home within one year, in termination of parental rights proceeding; there was no evidence that mother's mental deficiencies were so severe that she could not provide a home for child within one year, mother's psychologist recommended reunification as long as certain treatment conditions were satisfied, mother had previously lived on her own and paid her own bills, and child's counselor did not recommend termination of parental rights. In re Jordan (Ohio App. 2 Dist., Clark, 11-14-2003) No. 02CA0092, 2003-Ohio-6071, 2003 WL 22681603, Unreported. Infants ⬩ 181

Clear and convincing evidence supported trial court order in dependency proceeding granting legal custody of child, who had been adjudicated neglected, to child's father and his new wife; child was clean and well-taken care of by father and his new wife, father facilitated mother's visitation with child in Ohio by transporting child from his home in Kentucky, mother sporadically applied the parenting concepts that she learned in parenting classes, she continued to be ineffective at disciplining her children, and she failed to demonstrate that she was able to independently care for her children and protect them from future harm. In re Fulton (Ohio App. 12 Dist., Butler, 11-10-2003) No. CA2002-09-236, 2003-Ohio-5984, 2003 WL 22532895, Unreported. Infants ⬩ 222

Evidence supported finding that child could not be placed with parent within a reasonable time, in support of termination of mother's parental rights; mother was incarcerated when county children services filed its motion for permanent custody of child, and, even if mother was released early for good behavior, she still would not be released until more than 18 months had passed from the date children services filed its motion for permanent custody. In re V. S. (Ohio App. 9 Dist., Lorain, 10-22-2003) No. 03CA008273, 2003-Ohio-5612, 2003 WL 22399705, Unreported. Infants ⬩ 155

Evidence supported finding that change in custody to award legal custody to child's father after child had been adjudicated as dependent and neglected and placed in custody of her aunt would not be in child's best interest, given that child had had limited contact with her father, she had lived for an extended period of time with her aunt, as well as her half-siblings and cousins, and father and his paramour, who was to be primary caretaker of child, had previously had children removed from their care by County Children's Services Board. In re Osberry (Ohio App. 3 Dist., Allen, 10-14-2003) No. 1-03-26, 2003-Ohio-5462, 2003 WL 22336115, Unreported. Infants ⬩ 231

Evidence supported finding that grant of permanent custody of child to county children services board was in child's best interest; mother's parental rights to five other children had been terminated, father's parental rights to two other children had been terminated, and parents failed to complete case plan services offered to them by children services board. In re Kristiana B. (Ohio App. 6 Dist., Lucas, 10-03-2003) No. L-03-1060, 2003-Ohio-5268, 2003 WL 22272068, Unreported. Infants ⬩ 155

Evidence supported trial court finding that mother failed to substantially comply with the requirements of her caseplan, in child dependency proceeding; mother failed to provide documentation of full-time employment, she admitted that she lied about employment at a previous hearing, she failed to maintain stable and permanent housing and lived in a shelter, an acceptable apartment, and then her mother's residence during the pendency of the case, she missed drug screens, and she missed almost half of her scheduled visits with child. In re James (Ohio App. 10 Dist., Franklin, 09-30-2003) No. 03AP-373, 2003-Ohio-5208, 2003 WL 22232965, Unreported. Infants ⬩ 155

Trial court's findings that child could not and should not be placed with mother within reasonable time and that it was in best interest of child to grant permanent custody to county department of jobs and family services were not against the manifest weight and sufficiency of the evidence in proceeding to terminate mother's parental rights; evidence indicated that mother refused to comply with the case plan relative to child, mother refused to accept copy of case plan from caseworker, and mother failed to rectify problems that caused removal of her two other children, which included mental health and anger management issues, domestic violence, and her lack of parenting skills. In re Foster (Ohio App. 5 Dist., Stark, 09-22-2003) No. 2003CA0236, 2003-Ohio-5053, 2003 WL 22204489, Unreported. Infants ⬩ 155; Infants ⬩ 158

Trial court, prior to ordering that child be placed in planned permanent living arrangement (PPLA), found that mother had neglected child and that child would be unable to function in a family-like setting; trial court had previously adjudicated child neglected, and substantial evidence demonstrated that the child was not receiving the necessary medical care and was at physical risk, and that such physical risk involved a severe life-threatening liver problem that hindered the child's ability to function in a typical family setting. In re D.B. (Ohio App. 8 Dist., Cuyahoga, 07-03-2003) No. 81421, 2003-Ohio-3521, 2003 WL 21511310, Unreported. Infants ⬩ 210

Juvenile court's decision to grant maternal grandfather and step-grandmother legal custody of dependent children was against manifest weight of evidence; home study did not recommend such placement and caseworker did not investigate grandfather's prior criminal conviction or records from time grandfather and step-grandmother were foster parents of other children, during which allegations of sexual abuse were made. In re K.A. (Ohio App. 9 Dist., Lorain, 05-21-2003) No. 02CA008162, 2003-Ohio-2635, 2003 WL 21185955, Unreported. Infants ⬩ 208

Evidence was sufficient to support finding that child could not have been placed with father within a reasonable time or should not have been placed with him, as would support award of permanent custody to county; father's paternity was established when child was eight years old and, after child had been taken into temporary custody of county, case plan required that he attend parenting classes, obtain a drug and alcohol assessment, and submit to a psychological evaluation, and, while he started such objectives, he never completed them, or requested visitation, while father saw child at church, they did not speak or interact, father had never had custody of or provided care to child, father had an extensive criminal arrest record on attempted rape, domestic violence, aggravated burglary, and drug and alcohol charges, child never wanted a relationship with her father, and was stable and happy in her current placement which wanted to adopt her. In re Honaker (Ohio App. 5 Dist., Richland, 05-07-2003) No. 03CA10, No. 03CA11, 2003-Ohio-2407, 2003 WL 21060699, Unreported. Infants ⬩ 155

Evidence was sufficient to support finding that children could not be placed with father within a reasonable time, in child dependency proceeding; father withdrew from chemical dependency treatment programs and refused to participate in toxicology screenings, evidence suggested that father had relapsed and was abusing drugs, and father had a history of drug abuse. In re Harris (Ohio App. 1 Dist., Hamilton, 02-14-2003) No. C-020512, 2003-Ohio-672, 2003 WL 327996, Unreported. Infants ⬩ 155

Evidence supported finding that granting permanent custody of mother's two children to the county job and family services agency would be in the best interest of the children; while children were in agency custody, warrants were issued for the arrest of their parents, both parents fled from the state, after both parents were arrested mother was sentenced to serve a four year and nine months sentence for attempted manufacturing of drugs, mother never provided any support for the children or assisted the agency in developing a caseplan, and while mother was out of state she made no attempts to contact her children. In re Billingsley (Ohio App. 3 Dist., Putnam, 01-28-2003) No. 12-02-07, No. 12-02-08, 2003-Ohio-344, 2003 WL 178661, Unreported. Infants ⬩ 157

Substantial evidence supported termination of mother's parental rights and award of permanent custody of children to county department of job and family services; mother admitted that she failed to complete parenting program or to undergo counseling, and mother was early into three-year prison sentence for child endangering. In re Mastache Children (Ohio App. 5 Dist., Stark, 01-21-2003) No. 2002CA00360, 2003-Ohio-260, 2003 WL 157330, Unreported. Infants ⬩ 156

Clear and convincing evidence supported termination of father's parental rights; children had been in custody of county department of children and family services for over three years, father failed to follow and complete his proposed case plan which ordered him to participate in substance abuse treatment and stay drug free, submit to random drug tests, complete parenting classes, and maintain stable employment, father demonstrated a lack of commitment toward children by failing to regularly support, visit, or communicate with them when able to do so, and he was unable to provide food, clothing, shelter, and other basic necessities for children. (Per O'Donnell, J., with two judges concurring in judgment only). In re Harlston (Ohio App. 8 Dist., Cuyahoga, 01-23-2003) No. 80672, 2003-Ohio-282, 2003 WL 152939, Unreported, appeal not allowed 98 Ohio St.3d 1492, 785 N.E.2d 474, 2003-Ohio-1189. Infants ⬩ 155; Infants ⬩ 157

Clear and convincing evidence supported finding that removal of child from father's custody and granting county permanent custody was in child's best interest; although father loved daughter, daughter had bonded with foster family, family was interested in adopting her, father lied about using drugs and about existence of son who had perpetrated sexual abuse, and father had difficulty controlling anger, lacked ability to independently parent, and was responsible for sexual abuse of daughter's half-sister. In re Sullivan (Ohio App. 12 Dist., Butler, 01-21-2003) No. CA2002-03-061, 2003-Ohio-195, 2003 WL 138665, Unreported. Infants ⟐ 155

Evidence was not sufficient in permanency hearing to justify placing children in a planned permanent living arrangement (PPLA) based on grandmother's inability to care for children due to significant, physical, mental, or psychological problems; evidence indicated that children's grandmother was able to care for the children, but did not wish to do so, and grandmother made no attempt in her brief to argue that significant physical, mental, or psychological problems rendered her unable to care for the children. In re Muldrew (Ohio App. 2 Dist., Montgomery, 12-27-2002) No. 19469, 2002-Ohio-7288, 2002 WL 31888158, Unreported. Infants ⟐ 226

Evidence supported conclusion that child, whose custody had been placed with county children services board (CCSB) on allegations of abuse by mother's boyfriend, would be safe in mother's care, on CCSB's motion to terminate public custody and return child to mother; guardian ad litem's report was far from an unqualified endorsement of mother's parenting skills, particularly in view of guardian's statement that she was not convinced mother would adequately protect child, but guardian's recommendation of a shared parenting plan indicated that guardian did, in fact, believe that child would be safe in mother's care, mother had complied with her case plan, and CCSB was of opinion that child would be safe in mother's custody. In re Marhefka (Ohio App. 11 Dist., Ashtabula, 12-20-2002) No. 2001-A-0065, 2002-Ohio-7123, 2002 WL 31862685, Unreported. Infants ⟐ 231

Mother's ongoing criminal legal problems (some involving dishonesty), her failure to provide stable housing, and her failure to financially support her children constituted clear and convincing evidence that county agency should be awarded permanent custody of dependent child. In re Ashley E.D. (Ohio App. 6 Dist., Huron, 11-15-2002) No. H-02-025, 2002-Ohio-6238, 2002 WL 31529030, Unreported. Infants ⟐ 155; Infants ⟐ 157

Rules of Evidence applied at motion for permanent custody of dependent child. In re Ashley E.D. (Ohio App. 6 Dist., Huron, 11-15-2002) No. H-02-025, 2002-Ohio-6238, 2002 WL 31529030, Unreported. Infants ⟐ 173.1

Decision of juvenile court to grant legal custody of the two children who were subjects of dependency proceeding to mother, and to require that father's visitation with one of the children be supervised, was not abuse of discretion, where father had been convicted of child endangerment and was incarcerated, and juvenile court found father to be the perpetrator of abuse against child subject of supervised visitation. In re Howard (Ohio App. 12 Dist., Butler, 10-07-2002) No. CA2001-11-264, No. CA2001-12-281, No. CA2001-12-282, 2002-Ohio-5451, 2002 WL 31255755, Unreported. Child Custody ⟐ 58; Child Custody ⟐ 61; Child Custody ⟐ 217

A department of human services "running record" of a particular case is not a business record for purposes of Evid R 803(6) as it is replete with "double hearsay" and entries not properly identified by the employees who made the entries or under whose supervision they were made, and the admission of the "running record" into evidence at an adjudicatory permanent custody hearing constitutes prejudicial error requiring a reversal of a termination of parental rights. In re Workman, No. 92AP080055, 1993 WL 222843 (5th Dist Ct App, Tuscarawas, 6–14–93).

Hearsay evidence was admissible at dispositional hearing in child dependency proceeding. In re Sean T. (Ohio App. 6 Dist., 10-28-2005) 164 Ohio App.3d 218, 841 N.E.2d 838, 2005-Ohio-5739. Infants ⟐ 174

Trial court's finding that awarding custody of children to mother would be detrimental to children was supported by preponderance of the evidence, in child dependency proceeding in which legal custody of children had been awarded to maternal grandparents; at time of trial, mother had been living apart from children for over two years, mother's financial situation was precarious, and mother's home, which was eight-hour drive from grandparents' home, had not been approved as appropriate placement for children after three home studies. In re Sean T. (Ohio App. 6 Dist., 10-28-2005) 164 Ohio App.3d 218, 841 N.E.2d 838, 2005-Ohio-5739. Infants ⟐ 222

Although it is not required that a psychiatric expert be appointed in every permanent-custody child dependency proceeding, where a parent's mental health is made an issue and a parent makes a timely request for such assistance, the assistance of a court-appointed psychiatric expert is mandated by the Federal Constitution. In re Sherman (Ohio App. 3 Dist., 07-05-2005) 162 Ohio App.3d 73, 832 N.E.2d 797, 2005-Ohio-3444, opinion vacated on reconsideration 2005-Ohio-5888, 2005 WL 2933064. Infants ⟐ 212

Guardian ad litem's report was inadmissible, in termination of parental rights proceeding, as it was based largely on hearsay; report was based on guardian ad litem's interviews with various individuals involved in case, it was also based on numerous reports, most of which had never been entered into evidence, and several of those to whom guardian ad litem spoke and whose statements provided basis for her report did not testify. In re Sherman (Ohio App. 3 Dist., 07-05-2005) 162 Ohio App.3d 73, 832 N.E.2d 797, 2005-Ohio-3444, opinion vacated on reconsideration 2005-Ohio-5888, 2005 WL 2933064. Infants ⟐ 173.1

Any error in admission of children's hearsay statements to psychologist or social worker did not rise to level of plain error, in termination of parental rights proceeding, as record did not indicate that trial court had relied upon these statements in reaching its conclusion, and record provided ample evidence other than these statements that supported trial court's conclusions. In re Sherman (Ohio App. 3 Dist., 07-05-2005) 162 Ohio App.3d 73, 832 N.E.2d 797, 2005-Ohio-3444, opinion vacated on reconsideration 2005-Ohio-5888, 2005 WL 2933064. Infants ⟐ 243

Clear and convincing evidence supported trial court's finding, in granting permanent custody of infant child to county children services agency, that birth parents demonstrated a lack of commitment to child, where trial court found that minor mother and her parents did not visit child or inquire about her well-being, that father visited child when his college was not in session until his commitment to swim team's optional out-of-state training became more important, and that birth parents' joint motion for consent to third party, private adoption further showed a desire not to obtain custody. In re Baby Girl Doe (Ohio App. 6 Dist., 08-30-2002) 149 Ohio App.3d 717, 778 N.E.2d 1053, 2002-Ohio-4470, appeal not allowed 97 Ohio St.3d 1425, 777 N.E.2d 278, 2002-Ohio-5820. Infants ⟐ 222

Evidence supported trial court's conclusion in dependency proceeding that three-month-old infant's best interest would be served by granting permanent custody to county children services agency, as opposed to moving infant from her foster home to father's home, where both caseworker and guardian ad litem (GAL) testified that the baby had bonded with her foster family and that the foster family was a prospective adoptive family, and GAL testified that the baby's best interest would be served by granting permanent custody to agency for purposes of adoption. In re Baby Girl Doe (Ohio App. 6 Dist., 08-30-2002) 149 Ohio App.3d 717, 778 N.E.2d 1053, 2002-Ohio-4470, appeal not allowed 97 Ohio St.3d 1425, 777 N.E.2d 278, 2002-Ohio-5820. Infants ⟐ 222

Trial court's grant of permanent custody of child to county Department of Children and Family Services (DCFS) was not against manifest weight of the evidence; child was removed from parental home following diagnosis of non-organic failure to thrive, parents repeatedly failed to comply with requirements of case plan by missing appointments and by failing to incorporate lessons of parenting classes, child had to be placed in specialized home because of her health, parents were uninvolved in child's medical appointments, neither parent accepted responsibility for child's condition, and child was bonded to her foster parents rather than to her biological parents. In re Washington (Ohio App. 8 Dist., 05-21-2001) 143 Ohio App.3d 576, 758 N.E.2d 724. Infants ⟐ 252

Sufficient evidence supported court's finding that four minor siblings qualified for a planned permanent living arrangement and were unable to function in a family-like setting, even though the siblings were doing well in their foster home; the foster parents were trained in dealing with the siblings' emotional and behavioral problems, unlike the typical adoptive home. In re Tanker (Ohio App. 8 Dist., 04-02-2001) 142 Ohio App.3d 159, 754 N.E.2d 813. Infants ⟐ 226

Sufficient evidence supported finding by trial court that four minor siblings maintained a positive relationship with their parents, even though the parents were unable to provide for the siblings due to the parents' own physical and mental problems or needs, and, thus, siblings did not qualify for planned permanent living arrangement; parents were attending parenting classes and maintained regular visitation when allowed to do so. In re Tanker (Ohio App. 8 Dist., 04-02-2001) 142 Ohio App.3d 159, 754 N.E.2d 813. Infants ⟐ 226

Circumstantial evidence in child protection proceedings demonstrated that mother's husband caused children's injuries; husband's testimony that one child's brain injuries were caused when he dropped child while bathing him was contradicted by medical testimony that child's injuries were caused by inflicted shaken baby syndrome, as well as by husband's statement to his counselor that child's injuries resulted when "someone got frustrated," and husband originally attributed the other child's broken ribs to his attempt to administer cardio-pulmonary resuscitation (CPR), but subsequently stated that child's five-year-old sister had attempted to administer CPR. In re Nice (Ohio App. 7 Dist., 03-20-2001) 141 Ohio App.3d 445, 751 N.E.2d 552, 2001-Ohio-3214. Infants ⟐ 179

Award to agency of permanent custody of child previously adjudicated dependent and neglected was demonstrated by clear and convincing evidence to be in child's best interests; child had suffered from nonorganic failure to thrive while in mother's care, and mother's psychologist, psychiatrist and caseworkers testified that mother suffered from major depression, lacked parenting skills, failed to accept any responsibility for removal of her children from her custody, refused to participate in parenting classes or allow home visits, discontinued medication prescribed for her depression, and remained in relationship with child's alleged father despite history of domestic violence. In re Nicholas H. (Ohio App. 6 Dist., 05-05-2000) 137 Ohio App.3d 442, 738 N.E.2d 896. Infants ⇐ 178

Determination not to grant permanent custody of four-year-old child to maternal grandmother, but instead to award permanent custody to county agency, was not abuse of discretion in proceeding to terminate mother's parental rights; there was evidence grandmother was unable to provide necessary level of care because she worked 40 hours a week, grandmother was unable to articulate specific child care plans, and there was testimony grandmother had allowed mother to remove child from grandmother's home after he had been placed there by agency. In re Patterson (Ohio App. 9 Dist., 09-01-1999) 134 Ohio App.3d 119, 730 N.E.2d 439. Infants ⇐ 222

Trial court in dependency proceeding correctly applied "best interest" of child standard in awarding custody of child to biological father rather than stepfather, absent any indication that biological father had abandoned child, contractually relinquished her custody or had become totally incapable of caring for her. In re Pryor (Athens 1993) 86 Ohio App.3d 327, 620 N.E.2d 973. Infants ⇐ 222

Award in dependency proceeding of legal custody of children to their natural father, subject to order of protective supervision, was supported by sufficient evidence, showing that mother's brother had precipitated a number of violent episodes at father's home. In re Pryor (Athens 1993) 86 Ohio App.3d 327, 620 N.E.2d 973. Infants ⇐ 177

Award in dependency proceeding of custody of child to her natural father, rather than mother and stepfather, was supported by sufficient evidence; although clinical psychologist testified to fact that it would be traumatic to split up child from her half-sisters, he also opined that it would be equally traumatic for daughter to remain with stepfather in a continuing atmosphere of violence. In re Pryor (Athens 1993) 86 Ohio App.3d 327, 620 N.E.2d 973. Infants ⇐ 177

At dispositional hearing in which permanent custody of parents' children was granted to county children services board, court properly allowed uncorroborated allegations of sexual conduct between parents and children through hearsay testimony of children's therapist; since focus of dispositional phase of neglect or dependency matter is future care and best interest of child, testimony relative to child's home environment and parental care is material and relevant to case. In re Smith (Ottawa 1991) 77 Ohio App.3d 1, 601 N.E.2d 45. Infants ⇐ 174

Hearsay statements made by a child sexual abuse victim are admissible in an action to terminate parental custody when there is a showing of particular guarantees of trustworthiness such as the child's explicit knowledge of sexual terms and sensuality of behavior. In re Pieper Children (Preble 1991) 74 Ohio App.3d 714, 600 N.E.2d 317, dismissed, jurisdictional motion overruled 66 Ohio St.3d 1410, 607 N.E.2d 9.

Competent, credible evidence supported trial court's findings, in support of determination to commit permanent custody of abused children to county department of human resources, that children could not be placed with parents within reasonable time or should not be placed with either parent, that permanent commitment was in best interests of children, and that reasonable efforts had been made to make it possible for children to return home; there was evidence that mother had consistently denied occurrence of any sexual abuse of children by their father, and that, after father was sent to prison pursuant to gross sexual imposition convictions, mother took up residence with person who previously had been convicted of child molestation. In re Kutzli (Paulding 1991) 71 Ohio App.3d 843, 595 N.E.2d 1026. Infants ⇐ 179

Evidence of the ability and suitability of a foster parent as an adoptive parent is properly considered in the disposition phase of a dependency action. In re Webb (Hamilton 1989) 64 Ohio App.3d 280, 581 N.E.2d 570, dismissed, jurisdictional motion overruled 48 Ohio St.3d 704, 549 N.E.2d 1191.

There was clear and convincing evidence that biological father, who was brother of mother's husband, was unfit parent and that it was in best interest of children to terminate his parental rights, where there was evidence, inter alia, that biological father used belt to discipline children while babysitting for them and used belt to discipline his fiancee's children, that he did not have sufficient income to support the children, and that he had severe emotional problems. Garabrandt v. Lucas County Children Services Bd. (Lucas 1988) 47 Ohio App.3d 119, 547 N.E.2d 997. Infants ⇐ 178

Generally, when proceeding under RC 2151.353(A)(4), the court must find by clear and convincing evidence that the behavior of the parents has created an environment which is having an adverse impact on the child and that such environment will continue. Elmer v. Lucas County Children Services Bd. (Lucas 1987) 36 Ohio App.3d 241, 523 N.E.2d 540. Infants ⇐ 177

A party who seeks to modify a dispositional custody order must show by clear and convincing evidence that the modification serves the best interests of the child. In re Patterson (Madison 1984) 16 Ohio App.3d 214, 475 N.E.2d 160, 16 O.B.R. 229.

A child born to a fifteen-year-old girl who has a substantial record of delinquency, including numerous acts of sexual intercourse with different men; failure to respond to the reasonable control and discipline of her mother; has an eighth-grade education, and attempts to enter into a ceremonial marriage in Florida—prior to her pregnancy by a man other than her "husband"; and is also a delinquent child by the commission of a felony, where the father of the child is a married man, and the "husband" of the mother is currently serving a sentence in the Florida state penitentiary, and where the mother's family situation is financially and emotionally unstable, is a "dependent child," even though the child has never been in the custody of the natural mother. In re Turner (Ohio Com.Pl. 1967) 12 Ohio Misc. 171, 231 N.E.2d 502, 41 O.O.2d 264. Infants ⇐ 154.1

The authority granted a juvenile court in RC 2151.35 to make certain specified dispositions and commitments of children in matters before it can be exercised by such court only if the child before it is found to be a juvenile traffic offender or is delinquent, neglected or dependent. In re Darst (Franklin 1963) 117 Ohio App. 374, 192 N.E.2d 287, 24 O.O.2d 144.

In a proceeding in the juvenile court, instituted by the filing of a complaint under RC 2151.27, a finding by the court that a child is "neglected," in that it "lacked proper parental care because of the faults and habits of his parents" and "dependent," in that its "condition and environment... is such as to warrant the court... in assuming his guardianship" must be based on evidence with respect to whether the child was receiving proper parental care in a proper environment in its home at the time of the hearing. In re Minton (Darke 1960) 112 Ohio App. 361, 176 N.E.2d 252, 16 O.O.2d 283. Infants ⇐ 156

Trial court's determination that grant of permanent custody to county was in child's best interest was not supported by substantial amount of credible and competent evidence; although child had bonded with foster family, testimony indicated that mother had been in full compliance with her case plan, attended substance abuse programs, had maintained sobriety for over two years, obtained suitable housing, obtained a full-time job, maintained regular over-night visits with child, and mother and child had bonded very well. In re Gill (Ohio App. 8 Dist., Cuyahoga, 06-27-2002) No. 79640, 2002-Ohio-3242, 2002 WL 1397156, Unreported, appeal not allowed 96 Ohio St.3d 1517, 775 N.E.2d 858, 2002-Ohio-4950. Infants ⇐ 222

Evidence supported trial court's dispositional ruling granting custody of children who were adjudicated abused and dependent to their father and requiring supervised visitation by mother, where Department of Human Services recommended that children be placed with father, home study of father's residence was favorable, older children consistently indicated that they wished to remain at father's house, and family members and caseworker testified to positive changes in children since they had been in father's custody. In re Kimble (Ohio App. 7 Dist., Harrison, 05-15-2002) No. 99 517 CA, 2002-Ohio-2409, 2002 WL 1065977, Unreported. Infants ⇐ 222

Award of legal custody of mother's daughter to maternal grandmother and of mother's son to his purported father were in children's best interests, in dependency proceeding; grandmother had had custody of daughter since inception of proceedings, father had established relationship with child, had weekend visits with him, and was attending counseling sessions with child, child's psychologist noted in his report that father and child were "well-bonded," and mother changed residences numerous times during case, domestic disturbances were occurring between mother and her male companion, and three psychological evaluations indicated that mother had borderline personality disorder. In re Callier (Ohio App. 12 Dist., Brown, 05-20-2002) No. CA2001-04-006, No. CA2001-04-007, 2002-Ohio-2406, 2002 WL 1010081, Unreported. Infants ⇐ 222

Denial of the motion to place child in the home of his maternal aunt was not an abuse of discretion, in termination of parental rights proceeding; maternal aunt was 24–years–old and was a single mother with four children of her own, mother's previous involvement with her children when they had been placed with relatives had led to the termination of both of those placements, and aunt had only visited child once and there was no evidence of bonding or a positive relationship between child and aunt. In re Pittman (Ohio App. 9 Dist., Summit, 05-08-2002) No. 20894, 2002-Ohio-2208, 2002 WL 987852, Unreported. Infants ⇐ 251

Trial court did not abuse its discretion in denying mother's motion to award legal custody of children, who had been adjudicated dependent, to maternal great-aunt, where, if custody were granted, great-aunt's household would consist of seven people, including five children, great-aunt worked third shift, children's mother was in great-aunt's custody as teenager, and it was at this time she began abusing alcohol and using illegal drugs, and great-aunt had had custody of mother's younger siblings, but returned them to Children Services Board custody when they refused to follow her rules or attend school. In re Robinson (Ohio App. 9 Dist., Summit, 04-03-2002) No. 20826, 2002-Ohio-1504, 2002 WL 501149, Unreported. Child Custody ⇐ 271

In an adjudicatory hearing to convert temporary custody of a minor to permanent custody pursuant to Juv R 2(1), the trial court erred in admitting into evidence reports of a child welfare agency where no foundation was laid to admit such report as a business records exception or public records exception to hearsay. In re Knipp, No. 1388 (4th Dist Ct App, Scioto, 3–28–83).

7. County custody and duties

Trial court was not required to make record of its in camera interview with child, in proceeding in which permanent custody of child was granted to county department of children and family services; although department made request for in camera interview, at no time did any party request that interview be recorded, and, given the lack of such a request, court did not violate any procedural requirements pursuant to juvenile rule governing recording of proceedings. In re T.W. (Ohio App. 8 Dist., Cuyahoga, 10-13-2005) No. 85845, 2005-Ohio-5446, 2005 WL 2600663, Unreported, appeal not allowed 108 Ohio St.3d 1418, 841 N.E.2d 321, 2006-Ohio-179, reconsideration denied 108 Ohio St.3d 1513, 844 N.E.2d 857, 2006-Ohio-1329. Infants ⇐ 207

County department of children and family services made good-faith effort to implement reunification plan, in proceeding in which permanent custody of child was granted to department; department's motion for permanent custody only came after it had previously filed two extensions to maintain temporary custody in an effort to assist mother in her reunification efforts, and there was ample proof in the record to show that department social worker repeatedly made efforts to aid and help mother with her substance abuse issues, and thus, efforts satisfied good faith effort requirement imposed on department. In re T.W. (Ohio App. 8 Dist., Cuyahoga, 10-13-2005) No. 85845, 2005-Ohio-5446, 2005 WL 2600663, Unreported, appeal not allowed 108 Ohio St.3d 1418, 841 N.E.2d 321, 2006-Ohio-179, reconsideration denied 108 Ohio St.3d 1513, 844 N.E.2d 857, 2006-Ohio-1329. Infants ⇐ 155

Sufficient evidence supported finding that placement of children with grandmother, even if she had filed motion for legal custody, would not be in best interests of children, in proceeding in which permanent custody of children was awarded to county department of children and family services; social worker testified that department had received 12 referrals for abuse, neglect, and dependency against grandmother, three other adults and one child already resided in grandmother's four-bedroom home, and grandmother worked full time and did not have adequate day care plans for children. In re A.D. (Ohio App. 8 Dist., Cuyahoga, 10-13-2005) No. 85648, 2005-Ohio-5441, 2005 WL 2600638, Unreported. Infants ⇐ 222

Trial court was without authority to grant custody of children to grandmother in proceeding in which permanent custody of children was awarded to county department of children and family services, where grandmother did not file motion requesting legal custody of children. In re A.D. (Ohio App. 8 Dist., Cuyahoga, 10-13-2005) No. 85648, 2005-Ohio-5441, 2005 WL 2600638, Unreported. Infants ⇐ 197

Trial court was not required to consider placing children with relative prior to granting permanent custody to county department of children and family services. In re A.D. (Ohio App. 8 Dist., Cuyahoga, 10-13-2005) No. 85648, 2005-Ohio-5441, 2005 WL 2600638, Unreported. Infants ⇐ 155

Placing child into planned permanent living arrangement of county was in child's best interest; child had been in custody of county for more than 12 of last 22 months, child could not be placed with mother within reasonable time due to mother's drug addiction and failure to complete case plan, and, although child stated she wished to maintain relationship with mother, she preferred to remain with foster parents. In re Wheeler (Ohio App. 5 Dist., Muskingum, 07-11-2005) No. CT 2005-0015, 2005-Ohio-3613, 2005 WL 1661981, Unreported. Infants ⇐ 226

County Jobs and Family Services made reasonable attempts to reunify children with mother and father prior to seeking permanent custody of children; County developed case plan to reunify mother and father with children in previous case which involved parenting and anger management and which required mother to protect children from father, but mother re-established relationship with father when children were returned to her, mother made no attempt to contact County for assistance or guidance, father failed to complete case plan and continued to use corporal punishment with children, father admitted repeated use of drugs, and his pattern fit profile of aggressive partner in relationship. In re Green (Ohio App. 5 Dist., Tuscarawas, 06-23-2005) No. 2005AP010007, No. 2005AP020008, 2005-Ohio-3308, 2005 WL 1523855, Unreported. Infants ⇐ 155

Finding that child could not be placed with either parent within a reasonable amount of time or should not be placed with the parent was not necessary to support grant of permanent custody of child to county child protection agency, where child had been in the agency's temporary custody for well over twelve consecutive months prior to the permanent custody hearing. In re Smith (Ohio App. 3 Dist., Marion, 01-18-2005) No. 9-04-35, 2005-Ohio-149, 2005 WL 91639, Unreported. Infants ⇐ 210

Trial court could not place children in planned permanent living arrangement (PPLA) as requested by mother, instead of awarding county permanent custody, where county department of children and family services did not request or argue for a PPLA and the court did not suggest an alternative disposition. In re A.B. (Ohio App. 8 Dist., Cuyahoga, 11-04-2004) No. 83971, 2004-Ohio-5862, 2004 WL 2491677, Unreported. Infants ⇐ 226

Finding in dependency proceeding, that county had fulfilled its duty to reasonably attempt to avoid the removal of the children from their home, was supported by evidence that it had been involved with mother through protective day care, two detailed safety assessments, and counseling. In re Hauenstein (Ohio App. 3 Dist., Hancock, 06-07-2004) No. 5-03-38, No. 5-03-39, 2004-Ohio-2915, 2004 WL 1238288, Unreported. Infants ⇐ 154.1

Where appellant, caretaker of child for first two years of child's life, turned out not to be child's biological father, and appellant's father had been accused of past sexual abuse, trial court properly adopted referee's report recommending temporary custody of child be granted to children services, since RC 2151.353 does not mandate that custody be granted in any particular order. In re Balazy, No. 92CA005491, 1993 WL 164790 (9th Dist Ct App, Lorain, 5–19–93).

Trial court had authority to consider dispositional option of planned permanent living arrangement (PPLA) when deciding whether to terminate mother's parental rights and grant permanent custody to county children services board (CSB), even though CSB never requested PPLA option; court, not CSB, had authority to make ultimate decision about disposition, statute governing initial disposition did not apply since court was considering modifying temporary-custody order after first six-month extension, and PPLA was one of dispositional alternatives available to court. In re A.S. (Ohio App. 9 Dist., 10-05-2005) 163 Ohio App.3d 647, 839 N.E.2d 972, 2005-Ohio-5309, reversed 2009 WL 728, motion to certify allowed 108 Ohio St.3d 1410, 841 N.E.2d 315, 2006-Ohio-179. Infants ⇐ 230.1

A juvenile court exceeds its power under RC 2151.353 in awarding custody of a child to a county mental health board where it fails to comply with judicial commitment proceedings and the board does not request custody of the child; for the juvenile court to make a determination that the child is mentally ill subject to hospitalization and to commit her to the custody of the board under RC Ch 5122, the juvenile court's jurisdiction must be invoked by following the procedures specified in RC 5122.11 through 5122.15, and since jurisdiction was invoked under RC Ch 2151, the court was empowered only to make a determination as to the child's status as a dependent child and to place her accordingly under RC 2151.353. In re Shott (Warren 1991) 75 Ohio App.3d 270, 599 N.E.2d 363.

RC 2151.355(A)(9) does not authorize the juvenile court to exercise unlimited discretion in sentencing a delinquent child, and there is no authority for it to commit a delinquent juvenile to a jail for adult offenders, absent a finding that housing in an appropriate juvenile facility is unavailable, or that the public safety and protection so require. State v. Grady (Cuyahoga 1981) 3 Ohio App.3d 174, 444 N.E.2d 51, 3 O.B.R. 199.

In a hearing conducted pursuant to RC 2151.35 in which the welfare department seeks to take permanent custody of children from their natural parents, the welfare department has the burden to plead and prove by clear and convincing evidence that the children are presently neglected or dependent. In re Fassinger (Cuyahoga 1974) 43 Ohio App.2d 89, 334 N.E.2d 5, 72 O.O.2d 292, affirmed 42 Ohio St.2d 505, 330 N.E.2d 431, 71 O.O.2d 503. Infants ⇐ 197

Whether county social workers who receive complaints of child abuse, yet take no steps to remove the child from the custody of a parent who eventually injures him severely, have violated a duty of protection owed to the child is a question to be answered by each state's law of torts, not by the federal constitution. DeShaney v. Winnebago County Dept. of Social Services (U.S.Wis. 1989) 109 S.Ct. 998, 489 U.S. 189, 103 L.Ed.2d 249.

States are "encouraged" by 42 USC 627(b)(3) to employ a "preventive service program" before removing allegedly neglected or dependent children from an adult's custody, but the fact that Ohio does not have such a program is no basis for a federal suit under 42 USC 1983 to nullify a state judgment of neglect and dependency brought by an adult relieved of custody. Lesher v. Lavrich (C.A.6 (Ohio) 1986) 784 F.2d 193.

Where the government has custody of a child, dependency may be found despite the fact that the child is thus receiving adequate care. In re Luke, No. 83–CA–09 (5th Dist Ct App, Coshocton, 1–13–84).

If a juvenile court, in making disposition of an unruly or delinquent child pursuant to RC 2151.354 or RC 2151.355, places the child into the temporary custody of the county department of human services in accordance with RC 2151.353 and the department provides services to that child, the county department of human services is required to develop and file with the court a case plan pursuant to RC 2151.412 and to hold semiannual reviews of the case plan pursuant to RC 2151.416. OAG 99–041.

If a juvenile court, in making disposition of an unruly or delinquent child pursuant to RC 2151.354 or RC 2151.355, places the child into the temporary custody of the county department of human services in accordance with RC 2151.353, the juvenile court is required to hold periodic reviews pursuant to RC 2151.417 and Juv R 36(A). OAG 99–041.

Both the existing juvenile code and the Juvenile Rules require a hearing before a temporary commitment to the Ohio youth commission can be made permanent, which hearing requires the presence of the youth involved. OAG 72–071.

The placement or detention of delinquent, dependent, neglected children, or juvenile traffic offenders, is upon final disposition of the juvenile court and does not include placement in a detention home provided under RC 2151.34. 1963 OAG 553; overruled to the extent that it is inconsistent with OAG 80–101.

A juvenile court may, upon finding that a child is neglected, dependent, or delinquent, commit the child to any person or institution meeting the requirements of RC 5103.02 and RC 5103.03, even though a county child welfare board exists and could provide care and support for the child. The board of county commissioners has a duty to appropriate each year such sum as will provide the court with necessary funds for the care, maintenance, education, and support of neglected, dependent, and delinquent children. 1962 OAG 3489.

Where a child has been permanently committed to a child welfare board by order of the juvenile court, such board may properly consent to medical and surgical treatment of such child; where a child has been temporarily so committed, the child remains a ward of juvenile court, and such court may properly consent to medical and surgical treatment of such child. 1951 OAG 898.

The juvenile court under this section may commit children directly to a district children's home. 1950 OAG 2529.

A public or approved private agency, institution or association having as its object the care of dependent and neglected children, may transfer custody of a child committed to its care by a juvenile court, or surrendered to it by parents or guardians, to another such public or approved private agency, institution or association under a written agreement prescribed and furnished by the division of charities, department of public welfare. 1939 OAG 1322.

8. Divorce

Where a court, having acquired jurisdiction over a child by virtue of a divorce action between the child's parents, certifies the matter of the child's custody to a juvenile court, the consent of the juvenile court having been first obtained, the juvenile court has exclusive jurisdiction over the child's custody by virtue of RC 3109.06 and RC 2151.23(D) and a finding of unfitness of the parents or that there is no suitable relative to have custody is not a necessary prerequisite to such certification, and while such certification shall be deemed to be the complaint in the juvenile court, it does not constitute a complaint in the juvenile court that such child is dependent or neglected and those dispositions provided for under RC 2151.353, RC 2151.354, and RC 2151.355 are not applicable to the disposition of such a child, disposition thereof being subject to and controlled by RC 3109.04. In re Height (Van Wert 1975) 47 Ohio App.2d 203, 353 N.E.2d 887, 1 O.O.3d 279. Courts ⟸ 472.1

The juvenile court has the authority to hear and determine the case of a "neglected child" notwithstanding the fact that the child is at the time within the continuing jurisdiction of the common pleas court by virtue of a divorce decree. In re L. (Ohio Juv. 1967) 12 Ohio Misc. 251, 231 N.E.2d 253, 41 O.O.2d 341. Courts ⟸ 475(15)

Where a neglected child proceeding is instituted in the juvenile court by a parent of such child, and a divorce action is later instituted by such parent, the juvenile court has exclusive original jurisdiction to determine whether the child is neglected, the power to determine his custody and the authority to place the child with a relative. In re Small (Darke 1960) 114 Ohio App. 248, 181 N.E.2d 503, 19 O.O.2d 128.

9. Foster care

Clear and convincing evidence supported trial court's determination that child with Down Syndrome was not capable of living in a family-like setting and therefore that planned permanent living arrangement was in his best interest; there was evidence that child had profound disability with severe attendant health problems which made it difficult to place him in an ordinary adoptive household, that current foster mother had specialized training that enabled her to care appropriately for child, and that current family was willing to continue as a long-term foster family for child. Miller v. Greene Cty. Children's Serv. Bd. (Ohio App. 2 Dist., 08-05-2005) 162 Ohio App.3d 416, 833 N.E.2d 805, 2005-Ohio-4035. Infants ⟸ 226

Clear and convincing evidence supported trial court's finding, in awarding permanent custody of infant child to county children services agency, that seriousness of abuse or neglect made placement with birth parents a threat to child's safety, where child had been found in tightly tied plastic bag in trash dumpster with her umbilical cord wrapped around her neck and was admitted to hospital with hypothermia. In re Baby Girl Doe (Ohio App. 6 Dist., 08-30-2002) 149 Ohio App.3d 717, 778 N.E.2d 1053, 2002-Ohio-4470, appeal not allowed 97 Ohio St.3d 1425, 777 N.E.2d 278, 2002-Ohio-5820. Infants ⟸ 222

In action to terminate parental rights, trial court had authority to grant long-term foster care, even though juvenile complaint prayed for permanent custody rather than foster care. Matter of Duncan/Walker Children (Ohio App. 5 Dist., 03-18-1996) 109 Ohio App.3d 841, 673 N.E.2d 217. Infants ⟸ 197

The Adoption and Assistance Welfare Act of 1980, 42 USC 671, does not give its beneficiaries any private right of action enforceable under 42 USC 1983 or create any implied cause of action on their behalf by giving federally collected funds to states for certain foster care and adoption services if they agree that their subdivisions shall make "reasonable efforts" to prevent removal of children from their families and facilitate reunification after children have been removed. Suter v. Artist M. (U.S.Ill. 1992) 112 S.Ct. 1360, 503 U.S. 347, 118 L.Ed.2d 1, on remand 968 F.2d 1218.

A trial court does not err in failing to place a child in long-term foster care under RC 2151.353 pursuant to a county children services agency's RC 2151.413 motion for permanent custody where it grants such permanent custody to the agency; long–term foster care only becomes an alternative, by operation of RC 2151.415, where the motion for permanent custody is denied. In re McDaniel, No. 92–CA–359 (4th Dist Ct App, Adams, 2–11–93).

Juvenile court is empowered to commit a child to a foster home and to make such terms respecting such commitment as may be proper and suitable under the circumstances. 1941 OAG 3353.

10. Reunification

County, which filed original complaint for permanent custody of mother's children, was not required to formulate reunification plan. In re Aaron F. (Ohio App. 6 Dist., Lucas, 12-30-2004) No. L-04-1156, 2004-Ohio-7152, 2004 WL 3017288, Unreported. Infants ⟸ 155

Trial court was under no obligation to file and implement a reunification plan prior to entering final judgment terminating mother's parental rights and awarding Department of Job and Family Services (DJFS) permanent custody of mother's infant child who, like his older sister, had tested positive for cocaine at birth, since any reunification plan would have been futile, as demonstrated by mother's continued drug abuse, abandonment of drug rehabilitation, and several probation violations. In re M.C. (Ohio App. 12 Dist., Madison, 09-07-2004) No. CA2004-04-008, 2004-Ohio-4782, 2004 WL 2003714, Unreported. Infants ⟸ 155

Trial court properly refused to award permanent custody to children's maternal grandmother in action brought by county children services to terminate parental rights of children's mother, although grandmother stated that she loved the children and could provide a safe, comfortable home for them, where grandmother was convicted of child endangering for whipping mother with belt when mother was a teenager, friends whom grandmother invited into her home sexually and physically abused mother when mother was a child, and one of children at issue was removed from grandmother's home after initial placement with her due to child stating that grandmother called her names and hit her. In re Zorns (Ohio App. 10 Dist., Franklin, 10-23-2003) No. 02AP-1297, No. 02AP-1298, 2003-Ohio-5664, 2003 WL 22415613, Unreported, appeal not allowed 100 Ohio St.3d 1547, 800 N.E.2d 752, 2003-Ohio-6879. Infants ⇐ 222

Mother failed to establish that the county job and family services agency failed to offer mother services designed to reunify her and the children; when the agency initially took custody, mother refused to cooperate with the agency in developing a caseplan, later mother fled out of state and her whereabouts were unknown or she was incarcerated, and, when mother was told how to arrange for visitation with the children, she failed to do so. In re Billingsley (Ohio App. 3 Dist., Putnam, 01-28-2003) No. 12-02-07, No. 12-02-08, 2003-Ohio-344, 2003 WL 178661, Unreported. Infants ⇐ 155

Sufficient evidence supported finding that county children services board made reasonable attempt to reunify father and child; record indicated that board assisted father to meet goals of his case plan, and that board investigated possibility of placement with other relatives, but no evidence was presented to indicate that any relative wanted to, or could, assume custody of child. In re S.S. (Ohio App. 2 Dist., Montgomery, 01-24-2003) No. 19406, 2003-Ohio-319, 2003 WL 164598, Unreported. Infants ⇐ 178

A county children services agency failed to make a good faith effort to reunify a child with his father and failed to meet its burden of showing the child could not be placed with his father within a reasonable time where (1) although the father had no contact with his son for a number of years, he was unable to do so because the mother refused to allow him to see his son and moved so he would not know where the son lived; (2) the record is devoid of any proof that an award of permanent custody to the children services agency would facilitate adoption, especially since the child is aggressive and assaultive and has been relocated to many foster homes and hospitalized several times; (3) the children services agency never filed or attempted to implement a reunification plan for father and son, and had begun to implement its plan to obtain permanent custody and appeared reluctant to abandon or suspend that plan; (4) instead of facilitating any opportunity for the son to get to know his father, the children services agency may have hindered the father's attempts to contact or visit the child in the last six months; and (5) there is no evidence that the father could not provide a suitable home for the son upon completion of a case plan, and the father said he would do "whatever it takes" to reunify with his son. In re Forrest (Ohio App. 10 Dist., Franklin, 07-30-1996) No. 96APF02-211, 1996 WL 434180, Unreported.

County children services agency was not required to attempt reunification of child with birth parents in proceeding in which it sought original permanent custody of child. In re Baby Girl Doe (Ohio App. 6 Dist., 08-30-2002) 149 Ohio App.3d 717, 778 N.E.2d 1053, 2002-Ohio-4470, appeal not allowed 97 Ohio St.3d 1425, 777 N.E.2d 278, 2002-Ohio-5820. Infants ⇐ 155

County children services agency was not required to attempt reunification of child with birth parents in proceeding in which it sought original permanent custody of child. In re Baby Girl Doe (Ohio App. 6 Dist., 08-30-2002) 149 Ohio App.3d 717, 778 N.E.2d 1053, 2002-Ohio-4470, appeal not allowed 97 Ohio St.3d 1425, 777 N.E.2d 278, 2002-Ohio-5820. Infants ⇐ 155

Permanent custody of child will be awarded at initial disposition hearing only under extreme situations where reunification is not possible. In re Miller (Ohio App. 2 Dist., 02-15-1995) 101 Ohio App.3d 199, 655 N.E.2d 252. Infants ⇐ 226

Permanent termination of parental rights without an attempt at reunification is proper where the father of abused children refuses to acknowledge evidence of their abuse. In re Webb (Hamilton 1989) 64 Ohio App.3d 280, 581 N.E.2d 570, dismissed, jurisdictional motion overruled 48 Ohio St.3d 704, 549 N.E.2d 1191.

Evidence relating to natural mother's past parenting history and her inability to comply with prior reunification plans regarding her other children was relevant to juvenile court's determination of whether to commit one of her children to permanent custody of Department of Human Services. In re Brown (Hamilton 1989) 60 Ohio App.3d 136, 573 N.E.2d 1217. Infants ⇐ 173.1

In the absence of a good faith effort to reunite a child with its parents and of evidence that such an effort would be futile, it is an abuse of discretion to determine, under RC 2151.353(A)(4), that the child would continue to be without adequate parental care if a reunification plan were prepared. In re Smart (Franklin 1984) 21 Ohio App.3d 31, 486 N.E.2d 147, 21 O.B.R. 33.

Under R.C. §2151.412(A), which requires that, if court commits dependent child to temporary custody of welfare department, parent, relative or probation officer or commits child to temporary custody of authorized institution pursuant to R.C. §2151.353(A)(2, 3), welfare department must submit initial plan to reunite family, juvenile court was not required to order reunification plan, where it committed child to permanent custody of welfare department pursuant to R.C. §2151.353(A)(4). In re Baby Girl Baxter (Ohio 1985) 17 Ohio St.3d 229, 479 N.E.2d 257, 17 O.B.R. 469. Infants ⇐ 222

Whenever a dependent child is placed temporarily with someone other than a parent, a reunification plan should be developed; further, when a child is placed with a relative pursuant to RC 2151.353(A)(2), a reunification plan, though not required by RC 2151.412, should be prepared by the court or a court-appointed agency. In re Patterson (Madison 1984) 16 Ohio App.3d 214, 475 N.E.2d 160, 16 O.B.R. 229.

Minor's best interests did not require reunification plan with her mother prior to termination of parental rights for adoption where mother had failed in the past to follow through on similar plans. In re Ball (Lucas 1982) 5 Ohio App.3d 56, 449 N.E.2d 490, 5 O.B.R. 152. Infants ⇐ 155

11. Parental rights and responsibilities

Evidence supported finding that granting permanent custody of children to county department of job and family services, rather that placing the children in a planned permanent living arrangement, was in the best interests of the children; guardian ad litem report indicated that father's daughter wanted a "fresh start" in a family setting, both children understood the difference between foster placement and permanent placement and expressed a desire to be part of a family rather than in foster care, and daughter would be 19 years old and son would be 17 years old when father was eligible for his first parole hearing. In re Lenix (Ohio App. 5 Dist., Ashland, 03-17-2006) No. 05-COA-039, 2006-Ohio-1294, 2006 WL 700953, Unreported. Infants ⇐ 226

County social worker's alleged conduct in thwarting parents' attempts to have children returned to parents' home, after children were removed due to unsanitary conditions, and in effectively denying parents prompt hearing on children's placement did not rise to the level of conscience-shocking behavior, and thus did not support substantive due process claim. Smith v. Williams-Ash (C.A.6 (Ohio), 12-06-2005) No. 04-4547, 173 Fed.Appx. 363, 2005 WL 3304101, Unreported. Infants ⇐ 17

County social worker should have known that her alleged conduct in thwarting parents' attempts to have children returned to parents' home, after children were removed due to unsanitary conditions, and in effectively denying parents prompt hearing on children's placement had effect of violating parents' clearly established rights to procedural due process by involuntarily depriving parents of physical custody of children, and therefore qualified immunity did not apply to preclude social worker's liability under §§ 1983. Smith v. Williams-Ash (C.A.6 (Ohio), 12-06-2005) No. 04-4547, 173 Fed.Appx. 363, 2005 WL 3304101, Unreported. Civil Rights ⇐ 1376(4)

Allegations that parents whose children were removed from home by county social worker were not allowed to recover children after safety plan providing for children's placement with friends had been initiated, despite parents' best efforts to do so, that continued deprivation of children was involuntary, and that parents were effectively denied prompt hearing on children's placement supported claim against social worker for violating parents' procedural due process rights. Smith v. Williams-Ash (C.A.6 (Ohio), 12-06-2005) No. 04-4547, 173 Fed.Appx. 363, 2005 WL 3304101, Unreported. Infants ⇐ 17

Trial court had the authority to place mother's minor child in the legal custody of his paternal grandmother, following dependent child adjudication, even though grandmother did not herself file a motion for legal custody; Children Services Board (CSB) was permitted to file the motion on grandmother's behalf. In re K.K. (Ohio App. 9 Dist., Summit, 06-22-2005) No. 22352, 2005-Ohio-3112, 2005 WL 1460317, Unreported, appeal allowed 107 Ohio St.3d 1407, 836 N.E.2d 1228, 2005-Ohio-5859, affirmed 109 Ohio St.3d 206, 846 N.E.2d 853, 2006-Ohio-2184. Infants ⇐ 222

Maternal grandmother lacked standing to challenge juvenile court's award of permanent custody of children to county department of children and family services, as she was not biological parent to any of the children, and she failed to file motion to request legal custody of children during course of dependency and neglect proceedings, as required by statute. In re Th.W. (Ohio App. 8 Dist., Cuyahoga, 06-09-2005) No. 85241, No. 85278, 2005-Ohio-2852, 2005 WL 1364742, Unreported. Infants ⇐ 242

Evidence was sufficient to establish that best interests of mother's children were served by granting legal custody of one child to foster parents, and extending temporary custody of other child to County Children's Services Board (CCSB); 31-year-old mother had IQ of 80, with mental age of a 12- to 13-year-old, and had nine children, none in her custody, with at least four different fathers, and mother testified that she had no relationship with relatives or fathers. In re C.H. (Ohio App. 2 Dist., Montgomery, 04-08-2005) No. 20634, 2005-Ohio-1711, 2005 WL 844965, Unreported. Infants ⇐ 230.1

The county department of children and family services complaint for permanent custody adequately notified that he may be divested of his parental rights, in child dependency proceeding; notice served on father fully explained that if the court granted the order of permanent custody it would permanently divest father of his parental rights. In re I.M. (Ohio App. 8 Dist., Cuyahoga, 12-24-2003) No. 82669, No. 82695, 2003-Ohio-7069, 2003 WL 23010024, Unreported. Infants ⇐ 197

Adjudication of out-of-wedlock child as dependent and neglected implied parental unfitness, and thus trial court was not required to determine father's suitability as parent prior to awarding legal custody to child's aunt, even though mother allegedly misrepresented nonparentage to the father, who as a result had no contact with child prior to award, the basis for dependency was the mother's drug habit, and father's paternity was not confirmed until after the award. In re Osberry (Ohio App. 3 Dist., Allen, 10-14-2003) No. 1-03-26, 2003-Ohio-5462, 2003 WL 22336115, Unreported. Infants ⇐ 222

Trial court in legal custody proceeding was not required to give child's father a parental unsuitability determination before awarding custody of child, who has been adjudicated neglected, to maternal grandmother. In re C.F. (Ohio App. 8 Dist., Cuyahoga, 06-19-2003) No. 82107, 2003-Ohio-3260, 2003 WL 21434769, Unreported. Child Custody ⇐ 276

Trial court's refusal to conduct second in camera interview of eldest child was not abuse of discretion, in termination of parental rights proceeding involving four children; subsequent to child's first in camera interview, she indicated that she wanted to speak with trial judge again because she had changed her mind and now wanted to reside with her father, but trial spoke with child's attorney and accepted attorney's representation that child now wanted to reside with father. In re Sherman (Ohio App. 3 Dist., 07-05-2005) 162 Ohio App.3d 73, 832 N.E.2d 797, 2005-Ohio-3444, opinion vacated on reconsideration 2005-Ohio-5888, 2005 WL 2933064. Infants ⇐ 207

A sentence of thirty days in jail was warranted for criminal contempt by a former husband for failing to pay child support for several years. In re Contemnor Caron (Ohio Com.Pl., 04-27-2000) 110 Ohio Misc.2d 58, 744 N.E.2d 787. Child Support ⇐ 444

A proposed settlement of child support and custody disputes was not in the best interests of the child; the former husband was five-and-one-half years delinquent in child support, and the former wife waived a major portion of the court-ordered entitlements for the benefit of the child. In re Contemnor Caron (Ohio Com.Pl., 04-27-2000) 110 Ohio Misc.2d 58, 744 N.E.2d 787. Child Custody ⇐ 35; Child Support ⇐ 44

The best interests of a child demand that the father pay to the mother, for the benefit of the child, all monies and expenses previously ordered by the court. In re Contemnor Caron (Ohio Com.Pl., 04-27-2000) 110 Ohio Misc.2d 58, 744 N.E.2d 787. Child Support ⇐ 430

Former husband was required to comply with child support orders until paternity claim was resolved. In re Contemnor Caron (Ohio Com.Pl., 04-27-2000) 110 Ohio Misc.2d 58, 744 N.E.2d 787. Child Support ⇐ 375

Statute defining handicapped child for purposes of determining child's eligibility for special education could not serve as basis for juvenile court's exercise of jurisdiction to order father to maintain medical coverage for 18-year-old daughter until she was 21. In re Kessler (Ohio App. 6 Dist., 09-17-1993) 90 Ohio App.3d 231, 628 N.E.2d 153, motion overruled 68 Ohio St.3d 1437, 625 N.E.2d 625. Infants ⇐ 228(2)

Father should not have been required to undergo therapy as sex offender as condition of visiting his child where there was no finding that he had abused her. In re Sarah H. (Butler 1993) 86 Ohio App.3d 455, 621 N.E.2d 545. Infants ⇐ 221

In parental custody proceedings incident to dependency action, juvenile court had authority to award custody of children to their natural father, subject to order of protective supervision; court was not restricted from both awarding custody and issuing protective supervision order. In re Pryor (Athens 1993) 86 Ohio App.3d 327, 620 N.E.2d 973. Infants ⇐ 221; Infants ⇐ 222

Rights afforded parents relating to orders of temporary custody R.C. §2151.353(C) could be waived. Parker v. Children Services Bd. of Trumbull County (Trumbull 1984) 21 Ohio App.3d 115, 487 N.E.2d 341, 21 O.B.R. 123. Infants ⇐ 192

In a hearing concerning the dependency of a child, the trial court need not consider the desires of the mother with regard to its placement prior to a permanent commitment with a county agency. In re Baumgartner (Franklin 1976) 50 Ohio App.2d 37, 361 N.E.2d 501, 4 O.O.3d 22.

Where a juvenile court found that a child was neglected and committed such child to the temporary custody of the local child welfare board, the parents of such child could be punished for contempt for passively resisting such order. (Amish school attendance case.) State v. Hershberger (Ohio Juv. 1958) 150 N.E.2d 671, 77 Ohio Law Abs. 487, reversed 168 N.E.2d 12, 83 Ohio Law Abs. 63.

Trial court properly ordered father to continue carrying eighteen-year-old daughter on health insurance policy, where daughter was diabetic, daughter was ruled unruly, RC 2151.353(E)(1) allows court to retain jurisdiction over "physically handicapped" unruly child until age of 21 years, and Code of Federal Regulations for implementation of Americans With Disabilities Act of 1990 considers diabetes a physical impairment qualifying as a disability. In re Kessler, No. H–92–27, 1993 WL 356941 (6th Dist Ct App, Huron, 9–17–93).

Where a juvenile is adjudged delinquent for possession of marijuana and drug paraphernalia and his father admits to using and intending to continue using marijuana, the court may order the father to undergo urinalysis as a condition of the juvenile sentence. In re Dague, No. 87–CA–12 (5th Dist Ct App, Delaware, 10–22–87).

It is not absolutely necessary for parents to have physical control or legal custody of a child for that child to be neglected as to them; a child may be adjudicated a neglected child where the parents have failed to meet their obligations related to their residual rights under RC 2151.011. In re Luke, No. 83–CA–09 (5th Dist Ct App, Coshocton, 1–13–84).

Relatives or grandparents are not included within the meaning of "parents" as that term is used in RC 2151.353(A)(4). In re Smith, No. 83–CA–8 (5th Dist Ct App, Coshocton, 1–12–84).

12. Bifurcated hearings

When permanent custody of allegedly abused child is sought at hearing at which only dispositional option is determination to grant or deny motion for permanent custody, bifurcation is not required; determination to grant motion required showing by clear and convincing evidence that permanent commitment is in child's best interest and that child cannot be placed with parents within reasonable time or should not be placed with parents. In re Brofford (Franklin 1992) 83 Ohio App.3d 869, 615 N.E.2d 1120. Infants ⇐ 179; Infants ⇐ 203

Bifurcation is required where permanent custody of allegedly abused child is sought at initial disposition. In re Brofford (Franklin 1992) 83 Ohio App.3d 869, 615 N.E.2d 1120. Infants ⇐ 203

RC 2151.353 requires that hearings on dependency, neglect, and abuse be bifurcated into separate adjudicatory and dispositional hearings because the issues raised and the procedures used at each hearing differ; thus, the trial court must focus on whether the child has been proven to be dependent, neglected, or abused during the adjudicatory phase of the proceedings, and must not allow dispositional issues to dominate the determination of dependency, neglect, or abuse. In re Pitts (Knox 1987) 38 Ohio App.3d 1, 525 N.E.2d 814.

2151.354 Disposition of unruly child; driver's license suspension; habitual truants

(A) If the child is adjudicated an unruly child, the court may:

(1) Make any of the dispositions authorized under section 2151.353 of the Revised Code;

(2) Place the child on community control under any sanctions, services, and conditions that the court prescribes, as described in division (A)(4) of section 2152.19 of the Revised Code, provided that, if the court imposes a period of community service upon the child, the period of community service shall not exceed one hundred seventy-five hours;

(3) Suspend the driver's license, probationary driver's license, or temporary instruction permit issued to the child for a period of time prescribed by the court and suspend the registration of all motor vehicles registered in the name of the child for a period of time prescribed by the court. A child whose license or permit is so suspended is ineligible for issuance of a license or permit during the period of suspension. At the end of the period of suspension, the child shall not be reissued a license or permit until the child has paid any applicable reinstatement fee and complied with all requirements governing license reinstatement.

(4) Commit the child to the temporary or permanent custody of the court;

(5) Make any further disposition the court finds proper that is consistent with sections 2151.312 and 2151.56 to 2151.61 of the Revised Code;

(6) If, after making a disposition under division (A)(1), (2), or (3) of this section, the court finds upon further hearing that the child is not amenable to treatment or rehabilitation under that disposition, make a disposition otherwise authorized under divisions (A)(1), (4), (5), and (8) of section 2152.19 of the Revised Code that is consistent with sections 2151.312 and 2151.56 to 2151.61 of the Revised Code.

(B) If a child is adjudicated an unruly child for committing any act that, if committed by an adult, would be a drug abuse offense, as defined in section 2925.01 of the Revised Code, or a violation of division (B) of section 2917.11 of the Revised Code, in addition to imposing, in its discretion, any other order of disposition authorized by this section, the court shall do both of the following:

(1) Require the child to participate in a drug abuse or alcohol abuse counseling program;

(2) Suspend the temporary instruction permit, probationary driver's license, or driver's license issued to the child for a period of time prescribed by the court. The court, in its discretion, may terminate the suspension if the child attends and satisfactorily completes a drug abuse or alcohol abuse education, intervention, or treatment program specified by the court. During the time the child is attending a program as described in this division, the court shall retain the child's temporary instruction permit, probationary driver's license, or driver's license, and the court shall return the permit or license if it terminates the suspension.

(C)(1) If a child is adjudicated an unruly child for being an habitual truant, in addition to or in lieu of imposing any other order of disposition authorized by this section, the court may do any of the following:

(a) Order the board of education of the child's school district or the governing board of the educational service center in the child's school district to require the child to attend an alternative school if an alternative school has been established pursuant to section 3313.533 of the Revised Code in the school district in which the child is entitled to attend school;

(b) Require the child to participate in any academic program or community service program;

(c) Require the child to participate in a drug abuse or alcohol abuse counseling program;

(d) Require that the child receive appropriate medical or psychological treatment or counseling;

(e) Make any other order that the court finds proper to address the child's habitual truancy, including an order requiring the child to not be absent without legitimate excuse from the public school the child is supposed to attend for five or more consecutive days, seven or more school days in one school month, or twelve or more school days in a school year and including an order requiring the child to participate in a truancy prevention mediation program.

(2) If a child is adjudicated an unruly child for being an habitual truant and the court determines that the parent, guardian, or other person having care of the child has failed to cause the child's attendance at school in violation of section 3321.38 of the Revised Code, in addition to any order of disposition authorized by this section, all of the following apply:

(a) The court may require the parent, guardian, or other person having care of the child to participate in any community service program, preferably a community service program that requires the involvement of the parent, guardian, or other person having care of the child in the school attended by the child.

(b) The court may require the parent, guardian, or other person having care of the child to participate in a truancy prevention mediation program.

(c) The court shall warn the parent, guardian, or other person having care of the child that any subsequent adjudication of the child as an unruly or delinquent child for being an habitual or chronic truant may result in a criminal charge against the parent, guardian, or other person having care of the child for a violation of division (C) of section 2919.21 or section 2919.24 of the Revised Code.

(2002 H 400, § 4, eff. 1–1–04; 2002 H 400, § 1, eff. 4–3–03; 2002 S 123, eff. 1–1–04; 2002 H 393, eff. 7–5–02; 2001 H 57, eff. 2–19–02; 2000 S 179, § 3, eff. 1–1–02; 2000 S 181, eff. 9–4–00; 1997 S 35, eff. 1–1–99; 1996 H 265, eff. 3–3–97; 1996 H 274, eff. 8–8–96; 1992 H 154, eff. 7–31–92; 1990 S 258, S 131; 1989 H 381, H 330, H 329; 1988 H 643; 1969 H 320)

Historical and Statutory Notes

Amendment Note: 2002 H 400 changed "(A)(3)" to "(A)(4)" in division (A)(2); and changed "(A)(1), (3), (4), and (7)" to "(A)(1), (4), (5), and (8)" in division (A)(6).

Amendment Note: 2002 S 123 rewrote divisions (A) and (B) of this section, which prior thereto read:

"(A) If the child is adjudicated an unruly child, the court may:

"(1) Make any of the dispositions authorized under section 2151.353 of the Revised Code;

"(2) Place the child on community control under any sanctions, services, and conditions that the court prescribes, as described in division (A)(3) of section 2152.19 of the Revised Code, provided that, if the court imposes a period of community service upon the child, the period of community service shall not exceed one hundred seventy-five hours;

"(3) Suspend or revoke the driver's license, probationary driver's license, or temporary instruction permit issued to the child and suspend or revoke the registration of all motor vehicles registered in the name of the child. A child whose license or permit is so suspended or revoked is ineligible for issuance of a license or permit during the period of suspension or revocation. At the end of the period of suspension or revocation, the child shall not be reissued a license or permit until the child has paid any applicable reinstatement fee and complied with all requirements governing license reinstatement.

"(4) Commit the child to the temporary or permanent custody of the court;

"(5) Make any further disposition the court finds proper that is consistent with sections 2151.312 and 2151.56 to 2151.61 of the Revised Code;

"(6) If, after making a disposition under division (A)(1), (2), or (3) of this section, the court finds upon further hearing that the child is not amenable to treatment or rehabilitation under that disposition, make a disposition otherwise authorized under divisions (A)(1), (3), (4), and (7) of section 2152.19 of the Revised Code that is consistent with sections 2151.312 and 2151.56 to 2151.61 of the Revised Code.

"(B) If a child is adjudicated an unruly child for committing any act that, if committed by an adult, would be a drug abuse offense, as defined in section 2925.01 of the Revised Code, or a violation of division (B) of section 2917.11 of the Revised Code, then, in addition to imposing, in its discretion, any other order of disposition authorized by this section, the court shall do both of the following:

"(1) Require the child to participate in a drug abuse or alcohol abuse counseling program;

"(2) Suspend or revoke the temporary instruction permit, probationary driver's license, or driver's license issued to the child for a period of time prescribed by the court or, at the discretion of the court, until the child attends and satisfactorily completes a drug abuse or alcohol abuse education, intervention, or treatment program specified by the court. During the time the child is attending the program, the court shall retain any temporary instruction permit, probationary driver's license, or driver's license issued to the child and shall return the permit or license when the child satisfactorily completes the program."

Amendment Note: 2002 H 393 inserted ", provided that, if the court imposes a period of community service upon the child, the period of community service shall not exceed one hundred seventy-five hours;" in division (A)(2).

Amendment Note: 2001 H 57 inserted new division (A)(5), redesignated former division (A)(5) as new division (A)(6); and rewrote new division (A)(6), which as former division (A)(5) read:

"If, after making a disposition under division (A)(1), (2), or (3) of this section, the court finds upon further hearing that the child is not amenable to treatment or rehabilitation under that disposition, make a disposition otherwise authorized under divisions (A)(1), (3), (4) and (7) of section 2152.19 of the Revised Code, except that the child may not be committed to or placed in a secure correctional facility, and commitment to or placement in a detention facility may not exceed twenty-four hours unless authorized by division (C)(3) of section 2151.312 or sections 2151.56 to 2151.61 of the Revised Code."

Amendment Note: 2000 S 179, § 3, eff. 1–1–02, substituted "community control" for "probation" and inserted "sanctions, services, and" and "as described in division (A) of section 2152.19 of the Revised Code" in division (A)(2); and substituted "divisions (A)(1), (3), (4), and (7) of section 2152.19" for "divisions (A)(1), (2), and (A)(8) to (12) of section 2151.355", "facility" for "home", and "division (B)(3)" for "division (C)(3)", in division (A)(5).

Amendment Note: 2000 S 181 substituted "(A)(8) to (12)" for "(A)(7) to (11)" in division (A)(5); and added division (C).

Amendment Note: 1997 S 35 inserted "probationary driver's license, or temporary instruction permit" and added the second and third sentences in division (A)(3); rewrote division (B)(2); and made other nonsubstantive changes. Prior to amendment, division (B)(2) read:

"(2) Suspend or revoke the temporary instruction permit or probationary operator's license issued to the child until the child attains the age of eighteen years or, at the discretion of the court, attends and satisfactorily completes a drug abuse or alcohol abuse education, intervention, or treatment program specified by the court. During the time the child is attending the program, the court shall retain any temporary instruction permit or probationary license issued to the child and shall return the permit or license when the child satisfactorily completes the program."

Amendment Note: 1996 H 265 substituted "(A)(1), (2), and (A)(7) to (11)" for "(A)(1) to (3) and (A)(6) to (10)" and inserted ", except that the child may not be committed to or placed in a secure correctional facility, and commitment to or placement in a detention home may not exceed twenty-four hours unless authorized by division (C)(3) of section 2151.312 or sections 2151.56 to 2151.61 of the Revised Code" in division (A)(5).

Amendment Note: 1996 H 274 added division (A)(4); and redesignated former division (A)(4) as division (A)(5).

Cross References

Adjudicatory hearing, Juv R 29
Deception to obtain matter harmful to juveniles, 2907.33
Dispositional hearing, procedure, Juv R 34
Foster caregivers, information regarding delinquent children provided to, 2152.72
Registrar of motor vehicles, revocation of probationary driver's license, 4507.162

Library References

Automobiles ⇐144.
Infants ⇐222, 227(1).
Westlaw Topic Nos. 211, 48A.
C.J.S. Infants §§ 41, 53 to 54, 57, 69 to 85.
C.J.S. Motor Vehicles §§ 290 to 408.
    Baldwin's Ohio Legislative Service, 1990 Laws of Ohio, S 258—LSC Analysis, p 5–954

Research References

Encyclopedias

OH Jur. 3d Family Law § 1688, Unruly Child.
OH Jur. 3d Family Law § 1690, Restraining Conduct of Party.

Treatises and Practice Aids

Sowald & Morganstern, Baldwin's Ohio Practice Domestic Relations Law § 15:72, Custody in Juvenile Court Proceedings.
Carlin, Baldwin's Ohio Practice, Merrick-Rippner Probate Law § 104:19, Juvenile Facilities—Participation With Service Providers.
Carlin, Baldwin's Ohio Practice, Merrick-Rippner Probate Law § 107:111, Disposition of Unruly Children—Mandatory.
Carlin, Baldwin's Ohio Practice, Merrick-Rippner Probate Law § 107:112, Disposition of Unruly Children—Permissive.
Carlin, Baldwin's Ohio Practice, Merrick-Rippner Probate Law § 107:113, Juvenile Court's Authority Over Parents.
Painter, Ohio Driving Under the Influence § 12:45, Juvenile and "Underage" Offenders—Generally.
Giannelli & Yeomans, Ohio Juvenile Law § 4:6, Court Order Violations.
Giannelli & Yeomans, Ohio Juvenile Law § 11:2, Jurisdiction for Custody Agreements.
Giannelli & Yeomans, Ohio Juvenile Law § 19:2, Place of Detention.
Giannelli & Yeomans, Ohio Juvenile Law § 29:1, Introduction.
Giannelli & Yeomans, Ohio Juvenile Law § 29:2, Unruly—Dispositional Alternatives.
Giannelli & Yeomans, Ohio Juvenile Law § 29:3, Unruly—Delinquency Dispositions.
Giannelli & Yeomans, Ohio Juvenile Law § 29:4, Unruly—Drug & Alcohol Cases.
Giannelli & Yeomans, Ohio Juvenile Law § 29:5, Unruly—Truancy Cases.
Giannelli & Yeomans, Ohio Juvenile Law § 16:14, Permanent & Temporary Custody Complaints; Planned Permanent Living Arrangements.
Giannelli & Yeomans, Ohio Juvenile Law § 16:15, Certification or Transfer from Another Court.
Hastings, Manoloff, Sheeran, & Stype, Ohio School Law § 20:20, Enforcement Procedures-Consequences.

Law Review and Journal Commentaries

Curfew Laws, Freedom of Movement, and the Rights of Juveniles, Note. 50 Case W Res L Rev 681 (Spring 2000).

"Families with Service Needs":—The Newest Euphemism?, Stanley Z. Fisher. 18 J Fam L 1 (1979–80).

Notes of Decisions

Constitutional issues   1
Jurisdiction   2
Procedural issues   3

---

1. Constitutional issues

Any construction of RC 2151.354 that would allow commitment of an "unruly" child to the legal custody of the Ohio youth commission would be a violation of due process of law, and therefore an improper construction. OAG 72–071.

2. Jurisdiction

Statute allowing the juvenile court to review at any time the placement or custody arrangement for an abused child did not apply to juvenile court's order placing unruly child in temporary custody of public children services agency, even if custody was awarded based on allegations of child abuse, where father was never charged with child abuse and child was not adjudicated as abused child. In re Kidd (Ohio App. 11 Dist., Lake, 12-27-2002) No. 2001-L-039, 2002-Ohio-7264, 2002 WL 31886759, Unreported. Infants ⇐ 192

Father's 18–year–old daughter was "physically handicapped" as result of diabetes such that juvenile court could, after adjudicating daughter to be unruly child and placing her on probation and in foster home, retain jurisdiction and order father to maintain medical coverage for daughter until she was 21. In re Kessler (Ohio App. 6 Dist., 09-17-1993) 90 Ohio App.3d 231, 628 N.E.2d 153, motion overruled 68 Ohio St.3d 1437, 625 N.E.2d 625. Infants ⇐ 228(2)

Where a court, having acquired jurisdiction over a child by virtue of a divorce action between the child's parents, certifies the matter of the child's custody to a juvenile court, the consent of the juvenile court having been first obtained, the juvenile court has exclusive jurisdiction over the child's custody by virtue of RC 3109.06 and RC 2151.23(D) and a finding of unfitness of the parents or that there is no suitable relative to have custody is not a necessary prerequisite to such certification, and while such certification shall be deemed to be the complaint in the juvenile court, it does not constitute a complaint in the juvenile court that such child is dependent or neglected and those dispositions provided for under RC 2151.353, RC 2151.354, and RC 2151.355 are not applicable to the disposition of such a child, disposition thereof being subject to and controlled by RC 3109.04. In re Height (Van Wert 1975) 47 Ohio App.2d 203, 353 N.E.2d 887, 1 O.O.3d 279. Courts ☞ 472.1

A juvenile court retains jurisdiction over a child who has been adjudicated to be unruly or delinquent until the child attains twenty-one years of age, and may continue to make dispositional orders with respect to the child until that time, regardless of whether the court's order of temporary custody has expired under the time limitations set forth in RC 2151.353(F) and RC 2151.415. OAG 03-004.

3. Procedural issues

Juvenile court had the authority, once it had adjudicated child to be an unruly child, to award temporary custody to public children services agency without first making additional findings the child was abused, neglected, or dependent. In re Kidd (Ohio App. 11 Dist., Lake, 12-27-2002) No. 2001-L-039, 2002-Ohio-7264, 2002 WL 31886759, Unreported. Infants ☞ 192

Juvenile adjudicated as unruly child, based on violation of city curfew ordinance, could not be sentenced to five days of detention without further hearing to determine whether juvenile was amenable to treatment or rehabilitation, even if sentence was suspended. In re Osman (Ohio App. 11 Dist., 04-22-1996) 109 Ohio App.3d 731, 672 N.E.2d 1114. Infants ☞ 223.1

A county children services agency may not appeal an order of a juvenile court finding two minors to be unruly because of habitual truancy and committing them to the agency's custody, as the agency is not a party to the litigation under Juv R 2(16). In re Blakey (Franklin 1989) 65 Ohio App.3d 341, 583 N.E.2d 1343.

If a juvenile court commits to the temporary custody of a public children services agency a child who has been adjudicated to be unruly or delinquent pursuant to RC 2151.354(A)(1) or RC 2152.19(A)(1), respectively, the duration of the temporary custody order is subject to the time limitations set forth in RC 2151.353(F) and RC 2151.415. OAG 03-004.

If a juvenile court, in making disposition of an unruly or delinquent child pursuant to RC 2151.354 or RC 2151.355, places the child into the temporary custody of the county department of human services in accordance with RC 2151.353 and the department provides services to that child, the county department of human services is required to develop and file with the court a case plan pursuant to RC 2151.412 and to hold semiannual reviews of the case plan pursuant to RC 2151.416. OAG 99-041.

If a juvenile court, in making disposition of an unruly or delinquent child pursuant to RC 2151.354 or RC 2151.355, places the child into the temporary custody of the county department of human services in accordance with RC 2151.353, the juvenile court is required to hold periodic reviews pursuant to RC 2151.417 and Juv R 36(A). OAG 99-041.

Both the existing juvenile code and the juvenile rules require a hearing before a temporary commitment to the Ohio youth commission can be made permanent, which hearing requires the presence of the youth involved. OAG 72-071.

2151.355 Expunged or sealed records defined

As used in sections 2151.356 to 2151.358 of the Revised Code:

(A) "Expunge" means to destroy, delete, and erase a record, as appropriate for the record's physical or electronic form or characteristic, so that the record is permanently irretrievable.

(B) "Seal a record" means to remove a record from the main file of similar records and to secure it in a separate file that contains only sealed records accessible only to the juvenile court.

(2006 H 137, eff. 10–9–06)

Uncodified Law

2002 H 130, § 4, eff. 4–7–03, reads:

The amendment of section 2151.355 of the Revised Code is not intended to supersede the earlier repeal, with delayed effective date, of that section.

2001 S 3, § 5, eff. 10–26–01, reads:

Section 2152.19 of the Revised Code, as presented in this act, includes matter that was amended into former section 2151.355 of the Revised Code by Am. Sub. S.B. 181 of the 123rd General Assembly. Paragraphs of former section 2151.355 of the Revised Code containing S.B. 181 amendments were transferred to section 2152.19 of the Revised Code by Am. Sub. S.B. 179 of the 123rd General Assembly as part of its general revision of the juvenile sentencing laws. The General Assembly, applying the principle stated in division (B) of section 1.52 of the Revised Code that amendments are to be harmonized if reasonably capable of simultaneous operation, finds that the version of section 2152.19 of the Revised Code presented in this act is the resulting version of the section in effect prior to the effective date of the section as presented in this act.

1996 H 445, § 3: See Uncodified Law under 2151.14.

1995 H 1, § 3, eff. 1–1–96, reads in part: (A) The General Assembly hereby declares that its purpose in enacting the language of division (A)(2) of section 2151.18 and division (D)(2) of section 2151.355 of the Revised Code that exists on and after the effective date of this act is to recognize the holding of the Supreme Court in *In re Russell* (1984), 12 Ohio St. 3d 304.

1995 H 4, § 3: See *Baldwin's Ohio Revised Code Annotated*, Uncodified Law under 2151.02.

1990 H 51, § 3, eff. 11–8–90, reads: This act does not apply to any criminal sentence or dispositional order imposed prior to the effective date of this act, which sentence or dispositional order requires an offender or delinquent child to serve a period of time restricted to his home or any other specified premises for specified periods of time and requires the offender or delinquent child to be monitored by some type of electronic monitoring device, unless the court that imposed the sentence or dispositional order modifies the sentence or dispositional order and specifically makes the provisions of this act applicable to the criminal sentence or dispositional order.

Historical and Statutory Notes

Ed. Note: Former RC 2151.355 repealed by 2000 S 179, § 4, eff. 1–1–02; 2002 H 130, eff. 4–7–03; 2000 S 222, eff. 3–22–01; 2000 S 181, eff. 9–4–00; 1999 H 3, eff. 11–22–99; 1998 H 526, § 4, eff. 1–1–99; 1998 H 526, § 1, eff. 9–1–98; 1998 H 2, eff. 1–1–99; 1997 S 35, eff. 1–1–99; 1997 H 1, eff. 7–1–98; 1997 H 215, § 7, eff. 9–30–97; 1997 H 215, § 1, eff. 9–29–97; 1996 H 124, eff. 9–30–97; 1996 S 269, eff. 7–1–96; 1996 H 445, eff. 9–3–96; 1996 H 274, § 4, eff. 8–8–96; 1996 H 274, § 1, eff. 8–8–96; 1995 S 2, eff. 7–1–96; 1995 H 1, eff. 1–1–96; 1995 H 4, eff. 11–9–95; 1994 H 571, eff. 10–6–94; 1992 H 725, eff. 4–16–93; 1992 S 331, H 154; 1990 S 258, H 51, H 266, H 513, S 131; 1989 H 166, H 381, H 330, H 329; 1988 H 643; 1983 S 210; 1982 H 209; 1981 H 440; 1978 H 565, S 119; 1977 H 1; 1976 H 1196; 1974 H 1067; 1973 S 324; 1972 H 494; 1970 H 931; 1969 H 320. See now 2152.18, 2152.19 and 2152.20 for provisions analogous to former 2151.355.

Research References

Encyclopedias

OH Jur. 3d Criminal Law § 2013, Transfers from Juvenile Court for Criminal Prosecution; Relinquishment of Jurisdiction.

OH Jur. 3d Family Law § 695, Involuntary Dismissal.

OH Jur. 3d Family Law § 1515, Powers.

OH Jur. 3d Family Law § 1548, Juvenile Traffic Offenders—Orders of Disposition.

OH Jur. 3d Family Law § 1549, Delinquent, Unruly, Abused, Neglected, or Dependent Children.

OH Jur. 3d Family Law § 1685, Discretion of Court.

OH Jur. 3d Family Law § 1689, Juvenile Traffic Offender.

OH Jur. 3d Family Law § 1690, Restraining Conduct of Party.

OH Jur. 3d Family Law § 1696, Commitment to Youth Commission.

OH Jur. 3d Family Law § 1697, Notification of Victims.

OH Jur. 3d Family Law § 1698, Victim Impact Statement.

OH Jur. 3d Family Law § 1705, Effect on Court's Jurisdiction of Child's Commitment to Public Agency—Commitment to Youth Commission.

OH Jur. 3d Family Law § 1708, Revocation of Probation on Hearing.

OH Jur. 3d Penal & Correctional Institutions § 77, Examination and Classification of Inmates—Classification of Children Committed to Department of Youth Services.

Treatises and Practice Aids

Sowald & Morganstern, Baldwin's Ohio Practice Domestic Relations Law § 15:72, Custody in Juvenile Court Proceedings.

Carlin, Baldwin's Ohio Practice, Merrick-Rippner Probate Law § 105:9, Juvenile Court—Waiver of Jurisdiction.

Carlin, Baldwin's Ohio Practice, Merrick-Rippner Probate Law § 106:1, Juvenile Court Jurisdiction—Delinquent Child—Definition: Evidence of Delinquency.

Carlin, Baldwin's Ohio Practice, Merrick-Rippner Probate Law § 107:61, Adjudicatory Hearings—Notice to Victims of Crime of Right to Recover Damages and Victim-Impact Statements.

Carlin, Baldwin's Ohio Practice, Merrick-Rippner Probate Law § 107:84, Disposition of Delinquent Children—Prior to January 1, 2002.

Carlin, Baldwin's Ohio Practice, Merrick-Rippner Probate Law § 107:85, Disposition of Delinquent Children—Mandatory Dispositions—Prior to January 1, 2002.

Carlin, Baldwin's Ohio Practice, Merrick-Rippner Probate Law § 107:86, Disposition of Delinquent Children—Previous Convictions—Prior to January 1, 2002.

Carlin, Baldwin's Ohio Practice, Merrick-Rippner Probate Law § 107:87, Disposition of Delinquent Children—Further Disposition of Delinquent Children—Prior to January 1, 2002.

Carlin, Baldwin's Ohio Practice, Merrick-Rippner Probate Law § 107:88, Adult Sentence for Juvenile.

Carlin, Baldwin's Ohio Practice, Merrick-Rippner Probate Law § 107:89, Custody of Department of Youth Services.

Carlin, Baldwin's Ohio Practice, Merrick-Rippner Probate Law § 108:41, Juvenile Court—Parental Responsibility—Destructive Acts of Children.

Carlin, Baldwin's Ohio Practice, Merrick-Rippner Probate Law § 108:45, Juvenile Court—Parental Responsibility—Search of Residence and Property.

Carlin, Baldwin's Ohio Practice, Merrick-Rippner Probate Law § 107:112, Disposition of Unruly Children—Permissive.

Carlin, Baldwin's Ohio Practice, Merrick-Rippner Probate Law § 107:113, Juvenile Court's Authority Over Parents.

Carlin, Baldwin's Ohio Practice, Merrick-Rippner Probate Law § 107:115, Juvenile Court Records—Statistical.

Carlin, Baldwin's Ohio Practice, Merrick-Rippner Probate Law § 107:121, Custody Review Hearing—Revocation of Probation or Parole.

Carlin, Baldwin's Ohio Practice, Merrick-Rippner Probate Law § 107:130, Forfeiture Proceedings.

Carlin, Baldwin's Ohio Practice, Merrick-Rippner Probate Law § 107:179, Findings and Decision of Magistrate; Child Placed on Probation; Approval by Judge—Form.

Carlin, Baldwin's Ohio Practice, Merrick-Rippner Probate Law § 107:182, Order of Commitment of Delinquent Child to Department of Youth Services Under RC 2151.355(A)(6)—Murder or Aggravated Murder—Form.

Carlin, Baldwin's Ohio Practice, Merrick-Rippner Probate Law § 107:183, Order Committing Delinquent Child to Department of Youth Services Under RC 2151.355(A)(4) or (5)—Form.

Giannelli & Yeomans, Ohio Juvenile Law § 1:7, Juvenile Code.

Giannelli & Yeomans, Ohio Juvenile Law § 4:4, Ohio Penal Law.

Giannelli & Yeomans, Ohio Juvenile Law § 4:6, Court Order Violations.

Giannelli & Yeomans, Ohio Juvenile Law § 11:2, Jurisdiction for Custody Agreements.

Giannelli & Yeomans, Ohio Juvenile Law § 13:5, Hearing.

Giannelli & Yeomans, Ohio Juvenile Law § 19:2, Place of Detention.

Giannelli & Yeomans, Ohio Juvenile Law § 23:9, Uncontested Cases.

Giannelli & Yeomans, Ohio Juvenile Law § 27:1, Introduction.

Giannelli & Yeomans, Ohio Juvenile Law § 27:3, Department of Youth Services Commitment.

Giannelli & Yeomans, Ohio Juvenile Law § 27:5, Child Protective Services.

Giannelli & Yeomans, Ohio Juvenile Law § 27:7, Community Control Sanctions.

Giannelli & Yeomans, Ohio Juvenile Law § 27:8, Probation.

Giannelli & Yeomans, Ohio Juvenile Law § 27:9, Drug & Alcohol Dispositions.

Giannelli & Yeomans, Ohio Juvenile Law § 28:5, Restitution.

Giannelli & Yeomans, Ohio Juvenile Law § 29:3, Unruly—Delinquency Dispositions.

Giannelli & Yeomans, Ohio Juvenile Law § 34:4, Final Order Requirement.

Giannelli & Yeomans, Ohio Juvenile Law § 16:14, Permanent & Temporary Custody Complaints; Planned Permanent Living Arrangements.

Giannelli & Yeomans, Ohio Juvenile Law § 16:15, Certification or Transfer from Another Court.

Giannelli & Yeomans, Ohio Juvenile Law § 27:10, House Arrest & Electronic Monitoring.

Giannelli & Yeomans, Ohio Juvenile Law § 27:13, Restitution.

Giannelli & Yeomans, Ohio Juvenile Law § 27:18, "Catch-All" Provision.

Giannelli & Yeomans, Ohio Juvenile Law § 27:19, Plural Dispositions.

Gotherman, Babbit and Lang, Baldwin's Ohio Practice, Local Government Law—Municipal, § 32:8, Defenses and Immunities.

2151.356 Criteria for sealing records; notice

(A) The records of a case in which a person was adjudicated a delinquent child for committing a violation of section 2903.01, 2903.02, 2907.02, 2907.03, or 2907.05 of the Revised Code shall not be sealed under this section.

(B)(1) The juvenile court shall promptly order the immediate sealing of records pertaining to a juvenile in any of the following circumstances:

(a) If the court receives a record from a public office or agency under division (B)(2) of this section;

(b) If a person was brought before or referred to the court for allegedly committing a delinquent or unruly act and the case was resolved without the filing of a complaint against the person with respect to that act pursuant to section 2151.27 of the Revised Code;

(c) If a person was charged with violating division (E)(1) of section 4301.69 of the Revised Code and the person has successfully completed a diversion program under division (E)(2)(a) of section 4301.69 of the Revised Code with respect to that charge;

(d) If a complaint was filed against a person alleging that the person was a delinquent child, an unruly child, or a juvenile traffic offender and the court dismisses the complaint after a trial on the merits of the case or finds the person not to be a delinquent child, an unruly child, or a juvenile traffic offender;

(e) Notwithstanding division (C) of this section and subject to section 2151.358 of the Revised Code, if a person has been adjudicated an unruly child, that person has attained eighteen years of age, and the person is not under the jurisdiction of the court in relation to a complaint alleging the person to be a delinquent child.

(2) The appropriate public office or agency shall immediately deliver all original records at that public office or agency pertaining to a juvenile to the court, if the person was arrested or taken into custody for allegedly committing a delinquent or unruly act, no complaint was filed against the person with respect to the commission of the act pursuant to section 2151.27 of the Revised Code, and the person was not brought before or referred to the court for the commission of the act. The records delivered to the court as required under this division shall not include fingerprints, DNA specimens, and DNA records described under division (A)(3) of section 2151.357 of the Revised Code.

(C)(1) The juvenile court shall consider the sealing of records pertaining to a juvenile upon the court's own motion or upon the application of a person if the person has been adjudicated a delinquent child for committing an act other than a violation of section 2903.01, 2903.02, 2907.02, 2907.03, or 2907.05 of the Revised Code, an unruly child, or a juvenile traffic offender and if, at the time of the motion or application, the person is not under the jurisdiction of the court in relation to a complaint alleging the person to be a delinquent child. The motion or application may be made at any time after two years after the later of the following:

(a) The termination of any order made by the court in relation to the adjudication;

(b) The unconditional discharge of the person from the department of youth services with respect to a dispositional order made in relation to the adjudication or from an institution or facility to which the person was committed pursuant to a dispositional order made in relation to the adjudication.

(2) In making the determination whether to seal records pursuant to division (C)(1) of this section, all of the following apply:

(a) The court may require a person filing an application under division (C)(1) of this section to submit any relevant documentation to support the application.

(b) The court may cause an investigation to be made to determine if the person who is the subject of the proceedings has been rehabilitated to a satisfactory degree.

(c) The court shall promptly notify the prosecuting attorney of any proceedings to seal records initiated pursuant to division (C)(1) of this section.

(d)(i) The prosecuting attorney may file a response with the court within thirty days of receiving notice of the sealing proceedings.

(ii) If the prosecuting attorney does not file a response with the court or if the prosecuting attorney files a response but indicates that the prosecuting attorney does not object to the sealing of the records, the court may order the records of the person that are under consideration to be sealed without conducting a hearing on the motion or application. If the court decides in its discretion to conduct a hearing on the motion or application, the court shall conduct the hearing within thirty days after making that decision and shall give notice, by regular mail, of the date, time, and location of the hearing to the prosecuting attorney and to the person who is the subject of the records under consideration.

(iii) If the prosecuting attorney files a response with the court that indicates that the prosecuting attorney objects to the sealing of the records, the court shall conduct a hearing on the motion or application within thirty days after the court receives the response. The court shall give notice, by regular mail, of the date, time, and location of the hearing to the prosecuting attorney and to the person who is the subject of the records under consideration.

(e) After conducting a hearing in accordance with division (C)(2)(d) of this section or after due consideration when a hearing is not conducted, except as provided in division (B)(1)(c) of this section, the court may order the records of the person that are the subject of the motion or application to be sealed if it finds that the person has been rehabilitated to a satisfactory degree. In determining whether the person has been rehabilitated to a satisfactory degree, the court may consider all of the following:

(i) The age of the person;

(ii) The nature of the case;

(iii) The cessation or continuation of delinquent, unruly, or criminal behavior;

(iv) The education and employment history of the person;

(v) Any other circumstances that may relate to the rehabilitation of the person who is the subject of the records under consideration.

(D)(1)(a) The juvenile court shall provide verbal notice to a person whose records are sealed under division (B) of this section, if that person is present in the court at the time the court issues a sealing order, that explains what sealing a record means, states that the person may apply to have those records expunged under section 2151.358 of the Revised Code, and explains what expunging a record means.

(b) The juvenile court shall provide written notice to a person whose records are sealed under division (B) of this section by regular mail to the person's last known address, if that person is not present in the court at the time the court issues a sealing order and if the court does not seal the person's record upon the court's own motion, that explains what sealing a record means, states that the person may apply to have those records expunged under section 2151.358 of the Revised Code, and explains what expunging a record means.

(2) Upon final disposition of a case in which a person has been adjudicated a delinquent child for committing an act other than a violation of section 2903.01, 2903.02, 2907.02, 2907.03, or 2907.05 of the Revised Code, an unruly child, or a juvenile traffic offender, the juvenile court shall provide written notice to the person that does all of the following:

(a) States that the person may apply to the court for an order to seal the record;

(b) Explains what sealing a record means;

(c) States that the person may apply to the court for an order to expunge the record under section 2151.358 of the Revised Code;

(d) Explains what expunging a record means.

(3) The department of youth services and any other institution or facility that unconditionally discharges a person who has been adjudicated a delinquent child, an unruly child, or a juvenile traffic offender shall immediately give notice of the discharge to the court that committed the person. The court shall note the date of discharge on a separate record of discharges of those natures.

(2006 H 137, eff. 10–9–06)

Historical and Statutory Notes

Ed. Note: Former RC 2151.356 amended and recodified as RC 2152.21 by 2000 S 179, § 3, eff. 1–1–02; 2000 S 181, eff. 9–4–00; 1998 H 2, eff. 1–1–99; 1997 S 35, eff. 1–1–99; 1996 H 265, eff. 3–3–97; 1995 H 1, eff. 1–1–96; 1992 S 98, eff. 11–12–92; 1992 H 154, H 118; 1990 S 131; 1989 H 381, H 330, H 329; 1988 H 643; 1986 H 428, S 54; 1977 H 222, H 1; 1970 H 931; 1969 H 320.

Cross References

Information provided to foster caregivers or prospective adoptive parents regarding delinquent children, psychological examination, 2152.72
Sale to underage persons, restrictions relating to public and private places and accommodations, 4301.69

Research References

Encyclopedias

OH Jur. 3d Family Law § 1547, Juvenile Traffic Offenders.
OH Jur. 3d Family Law § 1548, Juvenile Traffic Offenders—Orders of Disposition.
OH Jur. 3d Family Law § 1689, Juvenile Traffic Offender.

Treatises and Practice Aids

Carlin, Baldwin's Ohio Practice, Merrick-Rippner Probate Law § 107:106, Disposition of Juvenile Traffic Offender—Mandatory.
Carlin, Baldwin's Ohio Practice, Merrick-Rippner Probate Law § 107:107, Disposition of Juvenile Traffic Offender—Permissive.
Carlin, Baldwin's Ohio Practice, Merrick-Rippner Probate Law § 107:109, Disposition of Juvenile Traffic Offender—Violations of Seat Belt Law.
Giannelli & Yeomans, Ohio Juvenile Law § 28:2, Suspension or Revocation.
Giannelli & Yeomans, Ohio Juvenile Law § 28:4, Community Control and Probation.
Giannelli & Yeomans, Ohio Juvenile Law § 28:5, Restitution.
Giannelli & Yeomans, Ohio Juvenile Law § 28:8, Revocation of Probationary Operator's License.
Giannelli & Yeomans, Ohio Juvenile Law § 27:13, Restitution.
Giannelli & Yeomans, Ohio Juvenile Law § 28:10, Imposition of Adult Penalties.

2151.357 Effect of sealed records; retention; limited disclosure

(A) If the court orders the records of a person sealed pursuant to section 2151.356 of the Revised Code, the person who is subject of the order properly may, and the court shall, reply that no record exists with respect to the person upon any inquiry in the matter, and the court, except as provided in division (D) of this section, shall do all of the following:

(1) Order that the proceedings in a case described in divisions (B) and (C) of section 2151.356 of the Revised Code be deemed never to have occurred;

(2) Except as provided in division (C) of this section, delete all index references to the case and the person so that the references are permanently irretrievable;

(3) Order that all original records of the case maintained by any public office or agency, except fingerprints held by a law enforcement agency, DNA specimens collected pursuant to section 2152.74 of the Revised Code, and DNA records derived from DNA specimens pursuant to section 109.573 of the Revised Code, be delivered to the court;

(4) Order each public office or agency, upon the delivering of records to the court under division (A)(3) of this section, to expunge remaining records of the case that are the subject of the sealing order that are maintained by that public office or agency, except fingerprints, DNA specimens, and DNA records described under division (A)(3) of this section;

(5) Send notice of the order to seal to any public office or agency that the court has reason to believe may have a record of the sealed record;

(6) Seal all of the records delivered to the court under division (A)(3) of this section, in a separate file in which only sealed records are maintained.

(B) Except as provided in division (D) of this section, an order to seal under section 2151.356 of the Revised Code applies to every public office or agency that has a record relating to the case, regardless of whether it receives notice of the hearing on the sealing of the record or a copy of the order. Except as provided in division (D) of this section, upon the written request of a person whose record has been sealed and the presentation of a copy of the order and compliance with division (A)(3) of this section, a public office or agency shall expunge its record relating to the case, except a record of the adjudication or arrest or taking into custody that is maintained for compiling statistical data and that does not contain any reference to the person who is the subject of the order.

(C) The court that maintains sealed records pursuant to this section may maintain a manual or computerized index of the sealed records and shall make the index available only for the purposes set forth in division (E) of this section.

(1) Each entry regarding a sealed record in the index of sealed records shall contain all of the following:

(a) The name of the person who is the subject of the sealed record;

(b) An alphanumeric identifier relating to the person who is the subject of the sealed record;

(c) The word "sealed";

(d) The name of the court that has custody of the sealed record.

(2) Any entry regarding a sealed record in the index of sealed records shall not contain either of the following:

(a) The social security number of the person who is subject of the sealed record;

(b) The name or a description of the act committed.

(D) Notwithstanding any provision of this section that requires otherwise, a board of education of a city, local, exempted village, or joint vocational school district that maintains records of an individual who has been permanently excluded under sections 3301.121 and 3313.662 of the Revised Code is permitted to maintain records regarding an adjudication that the individual is a delinquent child that was used as the basis for the individual's permanent exclusion, regardless of a court order to seal the record. An order issued under section 2151.356 of the Revised Code to seal the record of an adjudication that an individual is a delinquent child does not revoke the adjudication order of the superintendent of public instruction to permanently exclude the individual who is the subject of the sealing order. An order to seal the record of an adjudication that an individual is a delinquent child may be presented to a district superintendent as evidence to support the contention that the superintendent should recommend that the permanent exclusion of the individual who is the subject of the sealing order be revoked. Except as otherwise authorized by this division and sections 3301.121 and 3313.662 of the Revised Code, any school employee in possession of or having access to the sealed adjudication records of an individual that were the basis of a permanent exclusion of the individual is subject to division (F) of this section.

(E) Inspection of records that have been ordered sealed under section 2151.356 of the Revised Code may be made only by the following persons or for the following purposes:

(1) By the court;

(2) If the records in question pertain to an act that would be an offense of violence that would be a felony if committed by an adult, by any law enforcement officer or any prosecutor, or the assistants of a law enforcement officer or prosecutor, for any valid law enforcement or prosecutorial purpose;

(3) Upon application by the person who is the subject of the sealed records, by the person that is named in that application;

(4) If the records in question pertain to an alleged violation of division (E)(1) of section 4301.69 of the Revised Code, by any law enforcement officer or any prosecutor, or the assistants of a law enforcement officer or prosecutor, for the purpose of determining whether the person is eligible for diversion under division (E)(2) of section 4301.69 of the Revised Code;

(5) At the request of a party in a civil action that is based on a case the records for which are the subject of a sealing order issued under section 2151.356 of the Revised Code, as needed for the civil action. The party also may copy the records as needed for the civil action. The sealed records shall be used solely in the civil action and are otherwise confidential and subject to the provisions of this section.

(F) No officer or employee of the state or any of its political subdivisions shall knowingly release, disseminate, or make available for any purpose involving employment, bonding, licensing, or education to any person or to any department, agency, or other instrumentality of the state or of any of its political subdivisions any information or other data concerning any arrest, taking into custody, complaint, indictment, information, trial, hearing, adjudication, or correctional supervision, the records of which have been sealed pursuant to section 2151.356 of the Revised Code and the release, dissemination, or making available of which is not expressly permitted by this section. Whoever violates this division is guilty of divulging confidential information, a misdemeanor of the fourth degree.

(G) In any application for employment, license, or other right or privilege, any appearance as a witness, or any other inquiry, a person may not be questioned with respect to any arrest or taking into custody for which the records were sealed. If an inquiry is made in violation of this division, the person may respond as if the sealed arrest or taking into custody did not occur, and the person shall not be subject to any adverse action because of the arrest or taking into custody or the response.

(H) The judgment rendered by the court under this chapter shall not impose any of the civil disabilities ordinarily imposed by conviction of a crime in that the child is not a criminal by reason of the adjudication, and no child shall be charged with or convicted of a crime in any court except as provided by this chapter. The disposition of a child under the judgment rendered or any evidence given in court shall not operate to disqualify a child in any future civil service examination, appointment, or application. Evidence of a judgment rendered and the disposition of a child under the judgment is not admissible to impeach the credibility of the child in any action or proceeding. Otherwise, the disposition of a child under the judgment rendered or any evidence given in court is admissible as evidence for or against the child in any action or proceeding in any court in accordance with the Rules of Evidence and also may be considered by any court as to the matter of sentence or to the granting of probation, and a court may consider the judgment rendered and the disposition of a child under that judgment for purposes of determining whether the child, for a future criminal conviction or guilty plea, is a repeat violent offender, as defined in section 2929.01 of the Revised Code.

(2006 H 137, eff. 10–9–06)

Historical and Statutory Notes

Ed. Note: Former RC 2151.357 recodified as RC 2151.362 by 2006 H 137, eff. 10–9–06; 2006 H 530, eff. 6–30–06; 2000 S 179, § 3, eff. 1–1–02; 1995 H 117, eff. 6–30–95; 1981 S 140, eff. 7–1–81; 1970 S 518; 1969 H 320.

Cross References

Required terms of contracts, comprehensive plans, void contracts, 3314.03
Statewide education management information system, rules, guidelines, reports, 3301.0714

Research References

Encyclopedias

OH Jur. 3d Family Law § 1718, Cost of Education.

Treatises and Practice Aids

Carlin, Baldwin's Ohio Practice, Merrick-Rippner Probate Law § 107:73, Alternatives for Disposition of Juvenile Cases.

Carlin, Baldwin's Ohio Practice, Merrick-Rippner Probate Law § 107:174, Order Committing Child to Temporary Custody of Public or Private Agency or Foster Care—Form.

Carlin, Baldwin's Ohio Practice, Merrick-Rippner Probate Law § 107:175, Order Committing Child to Permanent Custody of Public or Private Agency—Form.

Carlin, Baldwin's Ohio Practice, Merrick-Rippner Probate Law § 107:176, Order Placing Child in Planned Permanent Living Arrangement—Form.

Giannelli & Yeomans, Ohio Juvenile Law § 30:3, Costs of Dispositions.

Giannelli & Yeomans, Ohio Juvenile Law § 19:11, Detention Facilities.

Hastings, Manoloff, Sheeran, & Stype, Ohio School Law § 23:2, Admission Requirements and Tuition Liability-Statutory Requirements in General.

Hastings, Manoloff, Sheeran, & Stype, Ohio School Law § 23:3, Admission Requirements and Tuition Liability-Determining Residence.

2151.358 Expungement of sealed records

(A) The juvenile court shall expunge all records sealed under section 2151.356 of the Revised Code five years after the court issues a sealing order or upon the twenty-third birthday of the person who is the subject of the sealing order, whichever date is earlier.

(B) Notwithstanding division (A) of this section, upon application by the person who has had a record sealed under section 2151.356 of the Revised Code, the juvenile court may expunge a record sealed under section 2151.356 of the Revised Code. In making the determination whether to expunge records, all of the following apply:

(1) The court may require a person filing an application for expungement to submit any relevant documentation to support the application.

(2) The court may cause an investigation to be made to determine if the person who is the subject of the proceedings has been rehabilitated to a satisfactory degree.

(3) The court shall promptly notify the prosecuting attorney of any proceedings to expunge records.

(4)(a) The prosecuting attorney may file a response with the court within thirty days of receiving notice of the expungement proceedings.

(b) If the prosecuting attorney does not file a response with the court or if the prosecuting attorney files a response but indicates that the prosecuting attorney does not object to the expungement of the records, the court may order the records of the person that are under consideration to be expunged without conducting a hearing on the application. If the court decides in its discretion to conduct a hearing on the application, the court shall conduct the hearing within thirty days after making that decision and shall give notice, by regular mail, of the date, time, and location of the hearing to the prosecuting attorney and to the person who is the subject of the records under consideration.

(c) If the prosecuting attorney files a response with the court that indicates that the prosecuting attorney objects to the expungement of the records, the court shall conduct a hearing on the application within thirty days after the court receives the response. The court shall give notice, by regular mail, of the date, time, and location of the hearing to the prosecuting attorney and to the person who is the subject of the records under consideration.

(5) After conducting a hearing in accordance with division (B)(4) of this section or after due consideration when a hearing is not conducted, the court may order the records of the person that are the subject of the application to be expunged if it finds that the person has been rehabilitated to a satisfactory degree. In determining whether the person has been rehabilitated to a satisfactory degree, the court may consider all of the following:

(a) The age of the person;

(b) The nature of the case;

(c) The cessation or continuation of delinquent, unruly, or criminal behavior;

(d) The education and employment history of the person;

(e) Any other circumstances that may relate to the rehabilitation of the person who is the subject of the records under consideration.

(C) If the juvenile court is notified by any party in a civil action that a civil action has been filed based on a case the records for which are the subject of a sealing order, the juvenile court shall not expunge a record sealed under section 2151.356 of the Revised Code until the civil action has been resolved and is not subject to further appellate review, at which time the records shall be expunged pursuant to division (A) of this section.

(D) After the records have been expunged, the person who is the subject of the expunged records properly may, and the court shall, reply that no record exists with respect to the person upon any inquiry in the matter.

(2006 H 137, eff. 10–9–06)

Uncodified Law

1999 H 121, § 3: See *Baldwin's Ohio Revised Code Annotated*, Uncodified Law under Ch 3314.

1995 H 1, § 3, eff. 1–1–96, reads, in part: (C) The amendments made by this act to section 2151.358 of the Revised Code apply to persons who were adjudicated juvenile traffic offenders or charged with being juvenile traffic offenders prior to the effective date of this act, regardless of their age on that date. A person who was adjudicated a juvenile traffic offender or charged with being a juvenile traffic offender prior to the effective date of this act may file an application in accordance with division (D) or (F) of section 2151.358 of the Revised Code on or after the effective date of this act for the sealing of the record of the person's adjudication as a juvenile traffic offender or the expungement of the record of the case in which the person was adjudicated not guilty of being a juvenile traffic offender or the charges of being a juvenile traffic offender were dismissed, and the juvenile court involved shall proceed with a hearing on the application in accordance with division (D) or (F) of that section. A juvenile court is not required to send the notice described in division (C)(1)(b) of section 2151.358 of the Revised Code to a person who was adjudicated a juvenile traffic offender prior to the effective date of this act if, on the effective date of this act, more than ninety days has expired after the expiration of the two-year period described in division (C)(1) of section 2151.358 of the Revised Code.

Historical and Statutory Notes

Ed. Note: Former RC 2151.358 repealed by 2006 H 137, eff. 10-9-06; 2002 H 17, eff. 10-11-02; 2000 S 179, § 3, eff. 1-1-02; 2000 S 181, eff. 9-4-00; 1995 S 2, eff. 7-1-96; 1995 H 1, eff. 1-1-96; 1992 H 154, eff. 7-31-92; 1991 H 27; 1984 H 37; 1981 H 440; 1977 H 315; 1969 H 320.

Comparative Laws

Ariz.—A.R.S. § 8-247.
Conn.—C.G.S.A. § 46b-146.
Ga.—O.C.G.A. § 15-11-61.
Idaho—I.C. § 16-1816A.
Ind.—West's A.I.C. 31-6-8-2.
Mo.—V.A.M.S. § 211.321.
Tex.—V.T.C.A. Family Code § 51.16.
W.Va.—Code, 49-5-17.

Cross References

Advising child of right to expungement, Juv R 34
Community schools, required terms of contracts, 3314.03
Education management information system, collection and reporting of data, 3301.0714
Expungement in adult cases, 2953.31 to 2953.55
Foster caregivers, information regarding delinquent children provided to, 2152.72

Library References

Infants ⚖133.
Westlaw Topic No. 211.
C.J.S. Infants §§ 57, 69 to 85.

Research References

Encyclopedias

OH Jur. 3d Criminal Law § 2960, Evidence of Defendant's Juvenile Court Proceedings.
OH Jur. 3d Criminal Law § 3447, Generally; Constitutionality.
OH Jur. 3d Evidence & Witnesses § 856, Juvenile Adjudications.
OH Jur. 3d Family Law § 1659, Restrictions on Use—in Other Proceedings.
OH Jur. 3d Family Law § 1713, Order to Seal or Expunge.

Treatises and Practice Aids

Baldwin's Ohio Handbook Series—Trial Handbook § 12:10, Prior Conviction—Juvenile Delinquency Adjudication.
Giannelli and Snyder, Baldwin's Ohio Practice, Evidence, R 501, General Rule.
Giannelli and Snyder, Baldwin's Ohio Practice, Evidence, R 609, Impeachment by Evidence of Conviction of Crime.
Giannelli and Snyder, Baldwin's Ohio Practice, Evidence, § 501.4, Ohio Statutory Privileges.
Giannelli and Snyder, Baldwin's Ohio Practice, Evidence, § 404.25, Related Issues.
Giannelli and Snyder, Baldwin's Ohio Practice, Evidence, § 609.11, Pardon, Annulment & Expungement.
Giannelli and Snyder, Baldwin's Ohio Practice, Evidence, § 609.12, Juvenile Adjudications: in General.
Giannelli and Snyder, Baldwin's Ohio Practice, Evidence, § 609.13, Juvenile Adjudications: Other Theories of Admissibility.
1 Giannelli and Snyder, Baldwin's Ohio Practice, Evidence, Index, Index.
Carlin, Baldwin's Ohio Practice, Merrick-Rippner Probate Law § 22:5, Necessity for Conviction; Common Law Forfeiture.
Carlin, Baldwin's Ohio Practice, Merrick-Rippner Probate Law § 106:4, Juvenile Court Jurisdiction—Delinquent Child—Non-Criminal Nature of Delinquency Proceedings.
Carlin, Baldwin's Ohio Practice, Merrick-Rippner Probate Law § 107:22, Fingerprints and Photographs of Juveniles—Disposition.
Carlin, Baldwin's Ohio Practice, Merrick-Rippner Probate Law § 107:51, Adjudicatory Hearings—Applicability of Rules of Evidence.
Carlin, Baldwin's Ohio Practice, Merrick-Rippner Probate Law § 107:52, Adjudicatory Hearings—Confidentiality of Juvenile Court Proceedings.
Carlin, Baldwin's Ohio Practice, Merrick-Rippner Probate Law § 107:114, Juvenile Court Records—Confidentiality.
Carlin, Baldwin's Ohio Practice, Merrick-Rippner Probate Law § 107:116, Juvenile Court Records—Expungement.
Carlin, Baldwin's Ohio Practice, Merrick-Rippner Probate Law § 107:158, Motion for Expungement of Record—Form.
Carlin, Baldwin's Ohio Practice, Merrick-Rippner Probate Law § 107:159, Order Expunging Record—Form.
Employment Coordinator Employment Practices § 33:25, Ohio.
Giannelli & Yeomans, Ohio Juvenile Law § 2:2, Age Jurisdiction.
Giannelli & Yeomans, Ohio Juvenile Law § 35:2, Confidentiality Requirement.
Giannelli & Yeomans, Ohio Juvenile Law § 35:3, Non-Juvenile Court Proceedings.
Giannelli & Yeomans, Ohio Juvenile Law § 35:4, Expungement and Sealing.
Giannelli & Yeomans, Ohio Juvenile Law App. D, Appendix D. Glossary.
Giannelli & Yeomans, Ohio Juvenile Law § 23:20, Evidence—Impeachment.
Giannelli & Yeomans, Ohio Juvenile Law § 28:10, Imposition of Adult Penalties.
Gotherman, Babbit and Lang, Baldwin's Ohio Practice, Local Government Law—Municipal, § 28:45, Suspension of Driving Privilege.
Hastings, Manoloff, Sheeran, & Stype, Ohio School Law § 3:12, Powers and Duties of State Board of Education-Statewide Education Management Information System.
Hastings, Manoloff, Sheeran, & Stype, Ohio School Law § 25:18, Suspension and Expulsion-Permanent Exclusion for Certain Offenses.

Law Review and Journal Commentaries

Due Process in Ohio for the Delinquent and Unruly Child, Max Kravitz. 2 Cap U L Rev 53 (1973).

Notes of Decisions

Ed. Note: This section contains annotations from former RC 2151.35 and 2151.358.

Admissibility of evidence 1
Expungement 5
Prior conviction 2
Prior juvenile adjudication 3
Witnesses and testimony 4

---

1. Admissibility of evidence

Defendant's suggested cross-examination of juvenile, seeking to elicit from juvenile that she had been under a curfew and electronic monitoring imposed by juvenile court, was nothing more than a general attack on juvenile's credibility and, as such, was prohibited in prosecution for pandering sexually oriented matter involving a minor. State v. Braxton (Ohio App. 10 Dist., Franklin, 05-05-2005) No. 04AP-725, 2005-Ohio-2198, 2005 WL 1055819, Unreported. Witnesses ⚖ 345(9)

Trial court's ruling precluding any testimony regarding fact that alleged victim's brother had been adjudicated a juvenile offender did not deny defendant opportunity to fully testify on his own behalf, in prosecution for attempted rape and gross sexual imposition; defendant was permitted to testify about his own participation in family counseling, and only testimony trial court prohibited was that which dealt with brother, a non-testifying juvenile offender, which testimony would have been irrelevant to defense and impermissible under statute and by rule. State v. Webber (Ohio App. 9 Dist., Lorain, 09-01-2004) No. 01CA007837, 2004-Ohio-4579, 2004 WL 1933212, Unreported. Criminal Law ⚖ 338(4); Witnesses ⚖ 345(9)

Defendant was not precluded from fully cross-examining alleged victim by trial court's ruling that defendant could not question victim about adjudication of victim's brother as juvenile offender, and thus defendant's right to confrontation was not violated, in prosecution for attempted rape and gross sexual imposition; testimony regarding brother, a non-testifying juvenile offender, was irrelevant to defense, and information as to brother's status as delinquent was inadmissible under statute and by rule, and trial court did not preclude defendant from asking victim questions about his own participation in counseling and access to counselor at time defendant's sexual abuse allegedly occurred. State v. Webber (Ohio App. 9 Dist., Lorain, 09-01-2004) No. 01CA007837, 2004-Ohio-4579, 2004 WL 1933212, Unreported. Criminal Law ⚖ 662.7

Juvenile court records regarding juvenile diver's proceeding in which he had been accused of perpetrating an offense of a sexual nature upon another person exceeded matters relevant to defenses of other diver's parent in action by diver's father for defamation, invasion of privacy, and other claims, and thus trial court erred by conducting in camera inspection of records and releasing some documents; juvenile court recommendations and dispositions could not support parent's defense that allegations that diver was a "convicted sex offender" and had been "convicted of sexual crimes" were true. Roe ex rel. Roe v. Heap (Ohio App. 10 Dist., Franklin, 05-11-2004) No. 03AP-586, 2004-Ohio-2504, 2004 WL 1109849, Unreported, appeal not allowed 103 Ohio St.3d 1464, 815 N.E.2d 679, 2004-Ohio-5056. Infants ⚖ 133; Pretrial Procedure ⚖ 389; Pretrial Procedure ⚖ 411

A child's status as an unruly child is not an element of the offense of contributing to the unruliness of a child and is not relevant at trial for such a purpose; thus, a defendant is not prejudiced at trial by the trial court's restriction of a child's juvenile records for that purpose. State v. Lukens (Franklin 1990) 66 Ohio App.3d 794, 586 N.E.2d 1099, motion to certify overruled 55 Ohio St.3d 713, 563 N.E.2d 722. Infants ⚖ 20; Infants ⚖ 133

Under RC 2151.358(H), testimony, documents, or exhibits presented as evidence against a juvenile in a juvenile proceeding are inadmissible against the juvenile in any other criminal case or criminal proceeding except one in which the same underlying alleged crime is being adjudicated. State v. Shedrick (Ohio 1991) 61 Ohio St.3d 331, 574 N.E.2d 1065.

Under RC 2151.358(H), testimony, documents, or exhibits presented as evidence against a juvenile in a juvenile proceeding are inadmissible against the juvenile in any other case or proceeding. State v. Shedrick (Ohio 1991) 59 Ohio St.3d 146, 572 N.E.2d 59, on rehearing 61 Ohio St.3d 331, 574 N.E.2d 1065. Criminal Law ⚖ 385; Evidence ⚖ 148

When a child admits the allegations of a juvenile complaint for rape, evidence of the acts which underlie the allegations are inadmissible against the child in a subsequent case or proceeding for rape, except as provided in RC 2151.358. State v. Hall (Cuyahoga 1989) 57 Ohio App.3d 144, 567 N.E.2d 305, motion overruled 42 Ohio St.3d 714, 538 N.E.2d 1065. Criminal Law ⚖ 369.1

RC 2151.358 does not prohibit the use of records pertaining to traffic violations, kept pursuant to RC 4507.40, in a driver's license revocation hearing conducted after the accused has attained majority. Gebell v. Dollison (Clermont 1978) 57 Ohio App.2d 198, 386 N.E.2d 845, 9 O.O.3d 23, 11 O.O.3d 187. Infants ⚖ 133

Although the general assembly may enact legislation to effectuate its policy of protecting the confidentiality of juvenile records, such enactments may not impinge upon the right of a defendant in a criminal case to present all available, relevant and probative evidence which is pertinent to a specific and material aspect of his defense. State v. Cox (Ohio 1975) 42 Ohio St.2d 200, 327 N.E.2d 639, 71 O.O.2d 186. Criminal Law ⚖ 338(1)

2. Prior conviction

Defendant failed to establish trial court erred in preventing him from impeaching witness's credibility with a previous criminal incident; it was not established whether excluded evidence related to a criminal conviction, juvenile adjudication, or mere criminal allegations. State v. Hines (Ohio App. 8 Dist., Cuyahoga, 09-30-2004) No. 83485, 2004-Ohio-5206, 2004 WL 2340167, Unreported, appeal not allowed 105 Ohio St.3d 1452, 823 N.E.2d 457, 2005-Ohio-763, motion to reopen denied 2005-Ohio-3129, 2005 WL 1484017, appeal not allowed 106 Ohio St.3d 1537, 835 N.E.2d 384, 2005-Ohio-5146. Witnesses ⚖ 345(1); Witnesses ⚖ 345(9)

Previous adjudication of juvenile delinquency, which was based on sexually oriented offense, did not qualify as prior conviction for purposes of determining whether defendant was habitual sex offender; statute that permitted juvenile delinquency adjudications to be used in considering crime to be charged or sentence to be imposed was inapplicable, as classification as sexual offender was neither criminal crime nor sentence. State v. Prether (Ohio App. 2 Dist., 01-05-2001) 141 Ohio App.3d 6, 749 N.E.2d 796. Mental Health ⚖ 454

Evidence of acts by a defendant, which is otherwise admissible under RC 2945.59 and which does not constitute part of a disposition or evidence given in court, is not barred by RC 2151.358, even though the evidence tends to show the commission of another crime by the defendant when a juvenile. State v. Bayless (Ohio 1976) 48 Ohio St.2d 73, 357 N.E.2d 1035, 2 O.O.3d 249, vacated 98 S.Ct. 3135, 438 U.S. 911, 57 L.Ed.2d 1155.

3. Prior juvenile adjudication

True purpose of defendant's desired use of a witness's juvenile record in defendant's murder trial was to present other acts evidence, rather than to show bias, and thus, records were inadmissible, where defendant sought to advance his defense theory that witness was true perpetrator and committed crime in conformity of past behavior. State v. Winston (Ohio App. 8 Dist., Cuyahoga, 02-06-2003) No. 81436, 2003-Ohio-561, 2003 WL 253716, Unreported, withdrawn and superseded 2003-Ohio-653, 2003 WL 302416, appeal not allowed 99 Ohio St.3d 1453, 790 N.E.2d 1218, 2003-Ohio-3396. Witnesses ⚖ 345(9); Witnesses ⚖ 374(1)

Trial court did not abuse its discretion in denying application to seal juvenile records of individual who had been adjudicated a delinquent, pursuant to admission, for having committed involuntary manslaughter and aggravated burglary, where individual had vacillated between admitting and denying responsibility for his role in victim's death, at hearing on application individual claimed he was given a "bum rap" and accused prosecution and defense counsel of misconduct, psychologist's report indicated that individual went to great lengths to avoid accepting responsibility for his actions, and individual had done nothing after his discharge to further his education. In re Anspach (Ohio App. 2 Dist., 01-28-2000) 136 Ohio App.3d 535, 737 N.E.2d 115. Infants ⚖ 133

An earlier adjudication that the defendant was a juvenile traffic offender violating RC 4511.19(A) is not a "conviction" under RC 4511.99(A)(2); therefore, an adult convicted of violating RC 4511.19(A) cannot have his penalty enhanced pursuant to RC 4511.99(A)(2) because of the earlier juvenile adjudication. However, the sentencing court can consider the juvenile adjudication when it sentences the adult in accordance with RC 2151.358(H). State v. Blogna (Stark 1990) 60 Ohio App.3d 141, 573 N.E.2d 1223.

A prior rape adjudication should not be admitted in a rape prosecution where neither sentencing nor probation is involved; cross–examination of the juvenile about the inadmissible prior conviction is not prejudicial, however, where the judge is aware of it from the amenability hearing on the prosecutor's motion to bind the boy over for trial as an adult, there is no jury trial before laypersons, and the judge says that he put the adjudication out of his mind. In re Johnson (Cuyahoga 1989) 61 Ohio App.3d 544, 573 N.E.2d 184.

A prior adjudication of delinquency based on petty theft is admissible as a prior conviction to enhance the degree of a theft offense. In re Hayes (Franklin 1986) 29 Ohio App.3d 162, 504 N.E.2d 491, 29 O.B.R. 191. Infants ⚖ 223.1

Because RC 2151.358(H) declares that a judgment of delinquency neither imposes any of the civil disabilities imposed by a conviction nor renders the child a criminal, a child found delinquent by reason of having purposely killed his father is not disqualified by RC 2105.19 from taking under his father's will. In re Estate of Birt (Ohio Com.Pl. 1983) 18 Ohio Misc.2d 7, 481 N.E.2d 1387, 18 O.B.R. 407.

Evidence of a juvenile delinquency adjudication cannot be used to impeach the witness' general credibility, but it may be used in a case to expose a possible bias by the witness. State v. White (Cuyahoga 1982) 6 Ohio App.3d 1, 451 N.E.2d 533, 6 O.B.R. 23.

A proceeding upon a complaint charging a child as a juvenile traffic offender is neither criminal nor civil. In re C. (Ohio Com.Pl. 1975) 43 Ohio Misc. 98, 334 N.E.2d 545, 72 O.O.2d 421. Infants ⚖ 194.1

A minor, tried and found guilty by a juvenile court on a charge of auto theft, is neither charged with a crime nor convicted of a felony, and the judgment rendered therein is not admissible as evidence against him in any other case or proceeding in any other court. Beatty v. Riegel (Montgomery 1961) 115 Ohio App. 448, 185 N.E.2d 555, 21 O.O.2d 71. Infants ⚖ 68.1

It is prejudicial error to permit examination of a witness in a negligence action as to convictions and imprisonments with respect to law violations committed in another state, where charges for the offenses involved were heard and disposed of by a juvenile court of such state and, under the laws of such state, denominating a child a criminal because of the adjudication of a juvenile court and denominating such an adjudication a conviction, are expressly forbidden. Mason v. Klaserner (Franklin 1961) 114 Ohio App. 171, 180 N.E.2d 870, 19 O.O.2d 24. Appeal And Error ⚖ 1048(6); Witnesses ⚖ 345(1)

Note 3

When defendant in criminal case is permitted to introduce evidence of his life history, he waives this section, and may be cross-examined with reference to the disposition of any charge preferred against him as a juvenile. State v. Marinski (Ohio 1942) 139 Ohio St. 559, 41 N.E.2d 387, 23 O.O. 50.

Adjudication as a juvenile traffic offender for drunk driving cannot be considered a prior conviction for purposes of sentence enhancement as RC 2151.358 states that such an adjudication is not a conviction and RC 4511.99(A)(2) speaks of convictions only. State v Blogna, No. CA–7880 (5th Dist Ct App, Stark, 1–8–90).

Where defense counsel attempts in cross-examination to use the state witness's prior juvenile record for impeachment, the trial court properly refused to allow such cross-examination under Evid R 609(D) and RC 2151.358(H). State v Mann, No. 1074 (11th Dist Ct App, Ashtabula, 5–28–82).

4. Witnesses and testimony

Where a witness has testified in a juvenile proceeding, RC 2151.358(H) prohibits that witness from giving essentially the same testimony in any other criminal case or criminal proceeding. State v. Shedrick (Ohio 1991) 61 Ohio St.3d 331, 574 N.E.2d 1065.

Where a witness has testified in a juvenile proceeding, RC 2151.358(H) prohibits that witness from giving essentially the same testimony in any other case or proceeding. State v. Shedrick (Ohio 1991) 59 Ohio St.3d 146, 572 N.E.2d 59, on rehearing 61 Ohio St.3d 331, 574 N.E.2d 1065.

The testimony of a witness which is not essentially the same as that given in the prior juvenile proceeding is not barred from admission in a subsequent case or proceeding. State v. Shedrick (Ohio 1991) 59 Ohio St.3d 146, 572 N.E.2d 59, on rehearing 61 Ohio St.3d 331, 574 N.E.2d 1065. Criminal Law ⇔ 385; Evidence ⇔ 148

On a supplemental action to collect from a defendant insurance company on a judgment rendered against a minor for injuries in an auto accident, testimony received in the juvenile court in an action against the minor is admissible. Bingham v. Hartman (Columbiana 1961) 181 N.E.2d 721, 88 Ohio Law Abs. 126.

5. Expungement

Statements by parent of diving club member that other diver had been "convicted of sexual crimes" and was a "convicted sexual offender" were not substantially true, although magistrate had recommended that diver be adjudicated delinquent for assault and gross sexual imposition; juvenile justice system did not contemplate convictions, purpose of juvenile system was rehabilitation rather than punishment, magistrate's recommendation was not a decision, and diver was never adjudicated delinquent as to sexual offense but rather entered Alford plea to one count of disorderly conduct. Roe ex rel. Roe v. Heap (Ohio App. 10 Dist., Franklin, 05-11-2004) No. 03AP-586, 2004-Ohio-2504, 2004 WL 1109849, Unreported, appeal not allowed 103 Ohio St.3d 1464, 815 N.E.2d 679, 2004-Ohio-5056. Libel And Slander ⇔ 55

A civil suit charging a clerk of courts with negligence for failure to notify a local police department that a juvenile record has been expunged pursuant to RC 2151.358 will not lie, as this is not one of the clerk's statutory duties listed in RC 2303.08. Zajac v Vivo, No. 87 CA 135 (7th Dist Ct App, Mahoning, 12–22–88).

Pursuant to RC 2953.321, RC 2953.54, and RC 2151.358, a county sheriff may not disclose to the public information in an investigatory work product report that pertains to a case the records of which have been ordered sealed or expunged pursuant to RC 2953.31-.61 or RC 2151.358, but the sheriff must disclose information in the report that relates to a defendant, suspect, or juvenile offender who has not had this information ordered sealed or expunged, unless one of the exceptions set forth in RC 149.43(A) applies to the information. OAG 03–025.

When a record of the adjudication or arrest of a juvenile has been ordered sealed or expunged pursuant to RC 2151.358, such record is not a public record. OAG 90–101.

2151.359 Control of conduct of parent, guardian, or custodian; contempt

(A)(1) In any proceeding in which a child has been adjudicated an unruly, abused, neglected, or dependent child, on the application of a party, or on the court's own motion, the court may make an order restraining or otherwise controlling the conduct of any parent, guardian, or other custodian in the relationship of that individual to the child if the court finds that an order of that type is necessary to do either of the following:

(a) Control any conduct or relationship that will be detrimental or harmful to the child.

(b) Control any conduct or relationship that will tend to defeat the execution of the order of disposition made or to be made.

(2) The court shall give due notice of the application or motion under division (A) of this section, the grounds for the application or motion, and an opportunity to be heard to the person against whom an order under this division is directed. The order may include a requirement that the child's parent, guardian, or other custodian enter into a recognizance with sufficient surety, conditioned upon the faithful discharge of any conditions or control required by the court.

(B) The authority to make an order under division (A) of this section and any order made under that authority is in addition to the authority to make an order pursuant to division (C)(2) of section 2151.354 or division (A)(7)(b) of section 2152.19 of the Revised Code and to any order made under either division.

(C) A person's failure to comply with any order made by the court under this section is contempt of court under Chapter 2705. of the Revised Code.

(2002 H 400, eff. 4–3–03; 2000 S 179, § 3, eff. 1–1–02; 2000 S 181, eff. 9–4–00; 1975 H 85, eff. 11–28–75; 1969 H 320)

Historical and Statutory Notes

Amendment Note: 2002 H 400 substituted "(7)" for "(6)" in division (B).

Amendment Note: 2000 S 179, § 3, eff. 1–1–02, rewrote this section, which prior thereto read:

"(A)(1) In any proceeding in which a child has been adjudicated a delinquent, unruly, abused, neglected, or dependent child, on the application of a party, or on the court's own motion, the court may make an order restraining or otherwise controlling the conduct of any parent, guardian, or other custodian in the relationship of that individual to the child if the court finds both of the following:

"(a) An order of that nature is necessary to control any conduct or relationship that will be detrimental or harmful to the child.

"(b) That conduct or relationship will tend to defeat the execution of the order of disposition made or to be made.

"(2) The court shall give due notice of the application or motion, the grounds for the application or motion, and an opportunity to be heard to the person against whom an order under this division is directed.

"(B) The authority to make an order under division (A) of this section and any order made under that authority is in addition to the authority to make an order pursuant to division (C)(2) of section 2151.354 or division (A)(24)(b) of section 2151.355 of the Revised Code and to any order made under either division."

Amendment Note: 2000 S 181 rewrote this section, which prior thereto read:

"In any proceeding wherein a child has been adjudged delinquent, unruly, abused, neglected, or dependent, on the application of a party, or the court's own motion, the court may make an order restraining or otherwise controlling the conduct of any parent, guardian, or other custodian in the relationship of such individual to the child if the court finds that such an order is necessary to:

"(A) Control any conduct or relationship that will be detrimental or harmful to the child;

"(B) Where such conduct or relationship will tend to defeat the execution of the order of disposition made or to be made.

"Due notice of the application or motion and the grounds therefor, and an opportunity to be heard shall be given to the person against whom such order is directed."

Cross References

Dispositional hearing, Juv R 34

Temporary disposition, Juv R 13

Library References

Infants ⚙=221.
Westlaw Topic No. 211.
C.J.S. Infants §§ 57, 69 to 85.

Research References

Encyclopedias

OH Jur. 3d Family Law § 1690, Restraining Conduct of Party.

Treatises and Practice Aids

Carlin, Baldwin's Ohio Practice, Merrick-Rippner Probate Law § 64:17, Powers and Duties of Guardian—Special Matters Relating to Minor Wards—Liability for Acts of Minor.

Carlin, Baldwin's Ohio Practice, Merrick-Rippner Probate Law § 107:28, Children Subject to Detention.

Carlin, Baldwin's Ohio Practice, Merrick-Rippner Probate Law § 107:73, Alternatives for Disposition of Juvenile Cases.

Carlin, Baldwin's Ohio Practice, Merrick-Rippner Probate Law § 107:113, Juvenile Court's Authority Over Parents.

Carlin, Baldwin's Ohio Practice, Merrick-Rippner Probate Law § 107:127, Contempt of Court in Juvenile Proceedings.

Giannelli & Yeomans, Ohio Juvenile Law § 30:6, Temporary Custody.

Giannelli & Yeomans, Ohio Juvenile Law § 32:2, Jurisdiction Over Parents and Others.

Notes of Decisions

Best interests of child   3
Constitutional issues   1
Parents' rights and responsibilities   2

---

1. Constitutional issues

To extent court's orders in dependency proceeding limited contacts between mother and father, whose parental rights had been terminated, they were in derogation of fundamental right of marriage and had to be narrowly tailored to serve their purpose. In re Pieper Children (Preble 1993) 85 Ohio App.3d 318, 619 N.E.2d 1059. Constitutional Law ⚙= 274(5); Infants ⚙= 221

Dispositional order prohibiting mother from having any contact or communication with father, whose parental rights had been terminated, and requiring her to report any contacts which did occur, was not necessary to serve best interests of children, determined to be dependent, as their interests could be accommodated by more narrowly tailored provision that protected them from contact with father but did not infringe upon mother's marital rights; thus, order would be modified to require mother not to have contact or communication with father and not to permit any contact or communication between father and children while children were in her physical presence or custody. In re Pieper Children (Preble 1993) 85 Ohio App.3d 318, 619 N.E.2d 1059. Infants ⚙= 221

The US Constitution does not compel states to provide their citizens with any "protective services" even if state officers are aware of a particular person's predicament or have expressed an intention to help him; a state has a duty to protect someone from certain harms under the Due Process Clause of the Fourteenth Amendment only after it has limited his own freedom to act by imprisonment, commitment to an institution, or similar restraints on his personal liberty. DeShaney v. Winnebago County Dept. of Social Services (U.S.Wis. 1989) 109 S.Ct. 998, 489 U.S. 189, 103 L.Ed.2d 249.

2. Parents' rights and responsibilities

Trial court, in delinquency proceeding, had authority to initiate contempt proceedings against juvenile's mother based on a violation of order that required mother to attend parenting classes, even though a stay of execution of such order on was issued next day; stay of execution only dealt with juvenile's ninety-day sentence to juvenile detention center, and thus order to attend parenting classes was still in effect at all times. In re Cunningham (Ohio App. 7 Dist., Harrison, 10-18-2002) No. 02-537-CA, 2002-Ohio-5875, 2002 WL 31412256, Unreported. Contempt ⚙= 22

Dispositional order in dependency proceeding requiring mother to provide county agency with confidentiality waiver concerning any medical treatment was appropriate to ensure that visitation take place only while mother was taking medication to control symptoms of bipolar disorder and to ensure that mother was not using illicit drugs. In re Pieper Children (Preble 1993) 85 Ohio App.3d 318, 619 N.E.2d 1059. Infants ⚙= 221

Dispositional order entered in dependency proceeding requiring mother to cooperate in drug testing, to ensure that she was taking medication and not using illicit drugs, did not subject mother to standardless, discretionary, and unlimited testing; provisions of case plan and amendments ordered by court indicated that blood or urine screening was to be performed on monthly basis to monitor mother's lithium level and to check for presence of illicit drugs. In re Pieper Children (Preble 1993) 85 Ohio App.3d 318, 619 N.E.2d 1059. Infants ⚙= 221

A juvenile court has no jurisdiction over the person and body of an adult pregnant woman so as to control her personal life for the benefit and protection of her unborn child. Cox v. Court of Common Pleas of Franklin County, Div. of Domestic Relations, Juvenile Branch (Franklin 1988) 42 Ohio App.3d 171, 537 N.E.2d 721.

The county welfare department, when removing children from a natural parent, must give notice to the parents prior to or at the time of removal stating reasons for removal, and must give parents a full opportunity to present witnesses at a hearing at which they may be represented by retained counsel, and such hearing must be held before a neutral hearing officer, who is to state in writing the decision reached and reasons therefor. Doe v. Staples (C.A.6 (Ohio) 1983) 706 F.2d 985, rehearing denied 717 F.2d 953, certiorari denied 104 S.Ct. 1301, 465 U.S. 1033, 79 L.Ed.2d 701. Constitutional Law ⚙= 274(5)

Magistrate, when deciding to award legal custody of neglected and dependent child to paternal grandparents, was not required to establish a specific visitation schedule; parent only requested unsupervised visitation and did not request a specific visitation schedule, and magistrate reasonably decided to let grandparents determine specifics of parent's supervised visitation, given that they facilitated visitation in the past and were willing to do so in the future. In re Farrow (Ohio App. 10 Dist., Franklin, 06-25-2002) No. 01AP-837, 2002-Ohio-3237, 2002 WL 1377798, Unreported. Infants ⚙= 222

Where a juvenile is adjudged delinquent for possession of marijuana and drug paraphernalia and his father admits to using and intending to continue using marijuana, the court may order the father to undergo urinalysis as a condition of the juvenile sentence. In re Dague, No. 87-CA-12 (5th Dist Ct App, Delaware, 10-22-87).

The father of a juvenile adjudged delinquent is a party as defined in Juv R 2(16) and is subject to orders of the court. In re Dague, No. 87-CA-12 (5th Dist Ct App, Delaware, 10-22-87).

3. Best interests of child

On the evidence, despite the strong maternal attachments and instincts, and the well intentioned concern of grandparents, infant's best interests would be served by the child being placed in the permanent custody of the county welfare department for adoption-placement. In re Baby Girl S. (Ohio Com.Pl. 1972) 32 Ohio Misc. 217, 290 N.E.2d 925, 61 O.O.2d 439.

2151.3510 Notice of intended dispositional order

Before a juvenile court issues an order of disposition pursuant to division (A)(1) of section 2151.354 or 2152.19 of the Revised Code committing an unruly or delinquent child to the custody of a public children services agency, it shall give the agency notice in the manner prescribed by the Juvenile Rules of the intended dispositional order.

(2000 S 179, § 3, eff. 1–1–02; 1996 H 274, eff. 8–8–96; 1991 H 298, eff. 7–26–91)

Historical and Statutory Notes

Amendment Note: 2000 S 179, § 3, eff. 1–1–02, substituted "2152.19" for "2151.355".

Amendment Note: 1996 H 274 deleted "temporary or permanent" before "custody".

Library References

Infants ⚙=198, 223.1, 226.
Westlaw Topic No. 211.

C.J.S. Adoption of Persons § 10.
C.J.S. Infants §§ 57, 69 to 85.

Research References

Treatises and Practice Aids

Carlin, Baldwin's Ohio Practice, Merrick-Rippner Probate Law § 107:84, Disposition of Delinquent Children—Prior to January 1, 2002.

Giannelli & Yeomans, Ohio Juvenile Law § 27:5, Child Protective Services.

Notes of Decisions

Constitutional issues 1

1. Constitutional issues

Trial court, by issuing orders granting custody of delinquent juvenile to county department of job and family services and requiring department to be financially responsible for juvenile without notice, violated department's right to due process; department had no opportunity to be heard with respect either to custody or financial matters. In re Roberson (Ohio App. 5 Dist., Stark, 09-13-2004) No. 2003CA00393, 2004-Ohio-4996, 2004 WL 2260687, Unreported. Constitutional Law ⚖ 255(4); Infants ⚖ 198

2151.3514 Orders requiring alcohol and drug addiction assessment, treatment, and testing of parents or caregivers

(A) As used in this section:

(1) "Alcohol and drug addiction program" has the same meaning as in section 3793.01 of the Revised Code;

(2) "Chemical dependency" means either of the following:

(a) The chronic and habitual use of alcoholic beverages to the extent that the user no longer can control the use of alcohol or endangers the user's health, safety, or welfare or that of others;

(b) The use of a drug of abuse to the extent that the user becomes physically or psychologically dependent on the drug or endangers the user's health, safety, or welfare or that of others.

(3) "Drug of abuse" has the same meaning as in section 3719.011 of the Revised Code.

(4) "Medicaid" means the program established under Chapter 5111. of the Revised Code.

(B) If the juvenile court issues an order of temporary custody or protective supervision under division (A) of section 2151.353 of the Revised Code with respect to a child adjudicated to be an abused, neglected, or dependent child and the alcohol or other drug addiction of a parent or other caregiver of the child was the basis for the adjudication of abuse, neglect, or dependency, the court shall issue an order requiring the parent or other caregiver to submit to an assessment and, if needed, treatment from an alcohol and drug addiction program certified by the department of alcohol and drug addiction services. The court may order the parent or other caregiver to submit to alcohol or other drug testing during, after, or both during and after, the treatment. The court shall send any order issued pursuant to this division to the public children services agency that serves the county in which the court is located for use as described in section 340.15 of the Revised Code.

(C) Any order requiring alcohol or other drug testing that is issued pursuant to division (B) of this section shall require one alcohol or other drug test to be conducted each month during a period of twelve consecutive months beginning the month immediately following the month in which the order for alcohol or other drug testing is issued. Arrangements for administering the alcohol or other drug tests, as well as funding the costs of the tests, shall be locally determined in accordance with sections 340.033 and 340.15 of the Revised Code. If a parent or other caregiver required to submit to alcohol or other drug tests under this section is not a recipient of medicaid, the agency that refers the parent or caregiver for the tests may require the parent or caregiver to reimburse the agency for the cost of conducting the tests.

(D) The certified alcohol and drug addiction program that conducts any alcohol or other drug tests ordered in accordance with divisions (B) and (C) of this section shall send the results of the tests, along with the program's recommendations as to the benefits of continued treatment, to the court and to the public children services agency providing services to the involved family, according to federal regulations set forth in 42 C.F.R. Part 2, and division (B) of section 340.15 of the Revised Code. The court shall consider the results and the recommendations sent to it under this division in any adjudication or review by the court, according to section 2151.353, 2151.414, or 2151.419 of the Revised Code.

(1998 H 484, eff. 3–18–99)

Library References

Infants ⚖ 192, 221.
Westlaw Topic No. 211.
C.J.S. Infants §§ 41, 53 to 55, 57, 69 to 85.

Research References

Encyclopedias

OH Jur. 3d Family Law § 1692, Protective Supervision.

Treatises and Practice Aids

Carlin, Baldwin's Ohio Practice, Merrick-Rippner Probate Law § 107:77, Disposition of Abused, Neglected, or Dependent Child—Protective Supervision.

Carlin, Baldwin's Ohio Practice, Merrick-Rippner Probate Law § 107:78, Disposition of Abused, Neglected, or Dependent Child—Temporary Custody.

Giannelli & Yeomans, Ohio Juvenile Law § 30:14, Jurisdiction Over Parents.

2151.3515 Definitions

As used in sections 2151.3515 to 2151.3530 of the Revised Code:

(A) "Deserted child" means a child whose parent has voluntarily delivered the child to an emergency medical service worker, peace officer, or hospital employee without expressing an intent to return for the child.

(B) "Emergency medical service organization," "emergency medical technician–basic," "emergency medical technician–intermediate," "first responder," and "paramedic" have the same meanings as in section 4765.01 of the Revised Code.

(C) "Emergency medical service worker" means a first responder, emergency medical technician-basic, emergency medical technician-intermediate, or paramedic.

(D) "Hospital" has the same meaning as in section 3727.01 of the Revised Code.

(E) "Hospital employee" means any of the following persons:

(1) A physician who has been granted privileges to practice at the hospital;

(2) A nurse, physician assistant, or nursing assistant employed by the hospital;

(3) An authorized person employed by the hospital who is acting under the direction of a physician described in division (E)(1) of this section.

(F) "Law enforcement agency" means an organization or entity made up of peace officers.

(G) "Nurse" means a person who is licensed under Chapter 4723. of the Revised Code to practice as a registered nurse or licensed practical nurse.

(H) "Nursing assistant" means a person designated by a hospital as a nurse aide or nursing assistant whose job is to aid nurses, physicians, and physician assistants in the performance of their duties.

(I) "Peace officer" means a sheriff, deputy sheriff, constable, police officer of a township or joint township police district, marshal, deputy marshal, municipal police officer, or a state highway patrol trooper.

(J) "Physician" and "physician assistant" have the same meanings as in section 4730.01 of the Revised Code.

(2000 H 660, eff. 4–9–01)

2151.3516 Persons authorized to take possession of deserted child

The following persons, while acting in an official capacity, shall take possession of a child who is seventy-two hours old or younger if that child's parent has voluntarily delivered the child to that person without the parent expressing an intent to return for the child:

(A) A peace officer on behalf of the law enforcement agency that employs the officer;

(B) A hospital employee on behalf of the hospital that has granted the person privilege to practice at the hospital or that employs the person;

(C) An emergency medical service worker on behalf of the emergency medical service organization that employs the worker or for which the worker provides services.

(2000 H 660, eff. 4–9–01)

Ohio Administrative Code References

PCSA requirements for conducting a specialized assessment/investigation, OAC 5101:2–36–04

Library References

Adoption ⚖7.3, 7.4(1).
Health ⚖258.
Westlaw Topic Nos. 17, 198H.
C.J.S. Adoption of Persons §§ 51 to 70.

Research References

Encyclopedias
OH Jur. 3d Family Law § 1432.1, Agreement for Temporary Custody—Children Under Six Months Old—Voluntary Delivery of Newborn.

2151.3517 Duties of persons taking possession of deserted child

(A) On taking possession of a child pursuant to section 2151.3516 of the Revised Code, a law enforcement agency, hospital, or emergency medical service organization shall do all the following:

(1) Perform any act necessary to protect the child's health or safety;

(2) Notify the public children services agency of the county in which the agency, hospital, or organization is located that the child has been taken into possession;

(3) If possible, make available to the parent who delivered the child forms developed under section 2151.3529 of the Revised Code that are designed to gather medical information concerning the child and the child's parents;

(4) If possible, make available to the parent who delivered the child written materials developed under section 2151.3529 of the Revised Code that describe services available to assist parents and newborns;

(5) If the child has suffered a physical or mental wound, injury, disability, or condition of a nature that reasonably indicates abuse or neglect of the child, attempt to identify and pursue the person who delivered the child.

(B) An emergency medical service worker who takes possession of a child shall, in addition to any act performed under division (A)(1) of this section, perform any medical service the worker is authorized to perform that is necessary to protect the physical health or safety of the child.

(2000 H 660, eff. 4–9–01)

Library References

Adoption ⚖7.3, 7.4(1).
Health ⚖258.
Westlaw Topic Nos. 17, 198H.
C.J.S. Adoption of Persons §§ 51 to 70.

Research References

Encyclopedias
OH Jur. 3d Family Law § 1432.1, Agreement for Temporary Custody—Children Under Six Months Old—Voluntary Delivery of Newborn.

2151.3518 Duties of public children services agencies

On receipt of a notice given pursuant to section 2151.3517 of the Revised Code that an emergency medical service organization, a law enforcement agency, or hospital has taken possession of a child and in accordance with rules of the department of job and family services, a public children services agency shall do all of the following:

(A) Consider the child to be in need of public care and protective services;

(B) Accept and take emergency temporary custody of the child;

(C) Provide temporary emergency care for the child, without agreement or commitment;

(D) Make an investigation concerning the child;

(E) File a motion with the juvenile court of the county in which the agency is located requesting that the court grant temporary custody of the child to the agency or to a private child placing agency;

(F) Provide any care for the child that the public children services agency considers to be in the best interest of the child, including placing the child in shelter care;

(G) Provide any care and perform any duties that are required of public children services agencies under section 5153.16 of the Revised Code;

(H) Prepare and keep written records of the investigation of the child, of the care and treatment afforded the child, and any other records required by the department of job and family services.

(2000 H 660, eff. 4–9–01)

Ohio Administrative Code References

Intake and screening procedures for child abuse, neglect, dependency and family in need of services reports; and information and/or referral intakes, OAC 5101:2–36–01
PCSA requirements for a deserted child assessment/investigation, OAC 5101:2–36–06
PCSA requirements for a deserted child investigation, OAC 5101:2–34–321
PCSA requirements for conducting third party assessment/investigations, OAC 5101:2–36–08

PCSA requirements for intra-familial child abuse and/or neglect assessment/investigations, OAC 5101:2-36-03

Library References

Infants ⚖17.
Westlaw Topic No. 211.
C.J.S. Infants §§ 8 to 9.

Research References

Encyclopedias

OH Jur. 3d Family Law § 1432.1, Agreement for Temporary Custody—Children Under Six Months Old—Voluntary Delivery of Newborn.

2151.3519 Emergency hearings; adjudications

When a public children services agency files a motion pursuant to division (E) of section 2151.3518 of the Revised Code, the juvenile court shall hold an emergency hearing as soon as possible to determine whether the child is a deserted child. The court is required to give notice to the parents of the child only if the court has knowledge of the names of the parents. If the court determines at the initial hearing or at any other hearing that a child is a deserted child, the court shall adjudicate the child a deserted child and enter its findings in the record of the case.

(2000 H 660, eff. 4–9–01)

Library References

Adoption ⚖7.3, 7.4(1).
Infants ⚖157, 204.
Westlaw Topic Nos. 17, 211.
C.J.S. Adoption of Persons §§ 51 to 70.
C.J.S. Infants §§ 31, 33 to 50, 55, 62 to 67.

Research References

Encyclopedias

OH Jur. 3d Family Law § 1432.1, Agreement for Temporary Custody—Children Under Six Months Old—Voluntary Delivery of Newborn.

2151.3520 Temporary custody orders

If a juvenile court adjudicates a child a deserted child, the court shall commit the child to the temporary custody of a public children services agency or a private child placing agency. The court shall consider the order committing the child to the temporary custody of the agency to be an order of disposition issued under division (A)(2) of section 2151.353 of the Revised Code with respect to a child adjudicated a neglected child.

(2000 H 660, eff. 4–9–01)

Library References

Adoption ⚖7.3, 7.4(1).
Infants ⚖157, 192.
Westlaw Topic Nos. 17, 211.
C.J.S. Adoption of Persons §§ 51 to 70.
C.J.S. Infants §§ 31, 33 to 55, 62.

Research References

Encyclopedias

OH Jur. 3d Family Law § 1432.1, Agreement for Temporary Custody—Children Under Six Months Old—Voluntary Delivery of Newborn.

2151.3521 Deserted child treated as neglected child

A court that issues an order pursuant to section 2151.3520 of the Revised Code shall treat the child who is the subject of the order the same as a child adjudicated a neglected child when performing duties under Chapter 2151. of the Revised Code with respect to the child, except that there is a rebuttable presumption that it is not in the child's best interest to return the child to the natural parents.

(2000 H 660, eff. 4–9–01)

Library References

Adoption ⚖7.3, 7.4(1).
Infants ⚖157, 172, 231.
Westlaw Topic Nos. 17, 211.
C.J.S. Adoption of Persons §§ 10, 51 to 70.
C.J.S. Infants §§ 31, 33 to 50, 55, 57 to 62, 69 to 85.

Research References

Encyclopedias

OH Jur. 3d Family Law § 1432.1, Agreement for Temporary Custody—Children Under Six Months Old—Voluntary Delivery of Newborn.

2151.3522 Case plans, investigations, administrative reviews, and services

A public children services agency or private child placing agency that receives temporary custody of a child adjudicated a deserted child shall prepare case plans, conduct investigations, conduct periodic administrative reviews of case plans, and provide services for the deserted child as if the child were adjudicated a neglected child and shall follow the same procedures under this chapter in performing those functions as if the deserted child was a neglected child.

(2000 H 660, eff. 4–9–01)

Ohio Administrative Code References

PCPA case plan for children in custody or under court-ordered protective supervision, OAC 5101:2-39-10
PCSA case plan for children in custody or under court-ordered protective supervision, OAC 5101:2-39-08.1

Library References

Adoption ⚖7.3, 7.4(1).
Infants ⚖17, 192.
Westlaw Topic Nos. 17, 211.
C.J.S. Adoption of Persons §§ 51 to 70.
C.J.S. Infants §§ 8 to 9, 41, 53 to 55.

Research References

Encyclopedias

OH Jur. 3d Family Law § 1432.1, Agreement for Temporary Custody—Children Under Six Months Old—Voluntary Delivery of Newborn.

2151.3523 Immunity from criminal liability; exceptions

(A) A parent does not commit a criminal offense under the laws of this state and shall not be subject to criminal prosecution in this state for the act of voluntarily delivering a child under section 2151.3516 of the Revised Code.

(B) A person who delivers or attempts to deliver a child who has suffered any physical or mental wound, injury, disability, or condition of a nature that reasonably indicates abuse or neglect of the child is not immune from civil or criminal liability for abuse or neglect.

(C) A person or governmental entity that takes possession of a child pursuant to section 2151.3516 of the Revised Code or takes emergency temporary custody of and provides temporary emergency care for a child pursuant to section 2151.3518 of the Revised Code is immune from any civil liability that might otherwise be incurred or imposed as a result of these actions, unless the person or entity has acted in bad faith or with malicious purpose. The immunity provided by this division does not apply if the person or governmental entity has immunity from civil liability under section 9.86, 2744.02, or 2744.03 of the Revised Code for the action in question.

(D) A person or governmental entity that takes possession of a child pursuant to section 2151.3516 of the Revised Code or takes emergency temporary custody of and provides temporary emergency care for a child pursuant to section 2151.3518 of the Revised Code is immune from any criminal liability that might otherwise be incurred or imposed as a result of these actions, unless the person or entity has acted in bad faith or with malicious purpose.

(E) Divisions (C) and (D) of this section do not create a new cause of action or substantive legal right against a person or governmental entity, and do not affect any immunities from civil liability or defenses established by another section of the Revised Code or available at common law, to which a person or governmental entity may be entitled under circumstances not covered by this section.

(2000 H 660, eff. 4–9–01)

Library References

Adoption ⚖7.3, 7.4(1).
Child Support ⚖650.
Infants ⚖13, 17, 157.
Westlaw Topic Nos. 17, 211, 76E.
C.J.S. Adoption of Persons §§ 51 to 70.
C.J.S. Infants §§ 5, 8 to 9, 31, 33 to 50, 55, 62, 92 to 93.
C.J.S. Parent and Child §§ 174, 237, 359 to 362, 364 to 365.

Research References

Encyclopedias

OH Jur. 3d Family Law § 1432.1, Agreement for Temporary Custody—Children Under Six Months Old—Voluntary Delivery of Newborn.

2151.3524 Anonymity of parent; exceptions

(A) A parent who voluntarily delivers a child under section 2151.3516 of the Revised Code has the absolute right to remain anonymous. The anonymity of a parent who voluntarily delivers a child does not affect any duty imposed under sections 2151.3516 or 2151.3517 of the Revised Code. A parent who voluntarily delivers a child may leave the place at which the parent delivers the child at any time after the delivery of the child.

(B) Notwithstanding division (A) of this section, a parent who delivers or attempts to deliver a child who has suffered any physical or mental wound, injury, disability, or condition of a nature that reasonably indicates abuse or neglect of the child does not have the right to remain anonymous and may be subject to arrest pursuant to Chapter 2935. of the Revised Code.

(2000 H 660, eff. 4–9–01)

Library References

Adoption ⚖7.3, 7.4(1).
Health ⚖257.
Infants ⚖133, 157.
Westlaw Topic Nos. 17, 198H, 211.
C.J.S. Adoption of Persons §§ 51 to 70.
C.J.S. Infants §§ 31, 33 to 50, 55, 57, 62, 69 to 85.

Research References

Encyclopedias

OH Jur. 3d Family Law § 1432.1, Agreement for Temporary Custody—Children Under Six Months Old—Voluntary Delivery of Newborn.

2151.3525 Completion of medical information forms by parents

A parent who voluntarily delivers a child under section 2151.3516 of the Revised Code may complete all or any part of the medical information forms the parent receives under division (A)(3) of section 2151.3517 of the Revised Code. The parent may deliver the fully or partially completed forms at the same time as delivering the child or at a later time. The parent is not required to complete all or any part of the forms.

(2000 H 660, eff. 4–9–01)

Library References

Adoption ⚖7.3, 7.4(1).
Health ⚖257, 575.
Infants ⚖11.5.
Westlaw Topic Nos. 17, 198H, 211.
C.J.S. Adoption of Persons §§ 51 to 70.

2151.3526 Refusal of parents to accept written materials

A parent who voluntarily delivers a child under section 2151.3516 of the Revised Code may refuse to accept the materials made available under division (A)(4) of section 2151.3517 of the Revised Code.

(2000 H 660, eff. 4–9–01)

Library References

Adoption ⚖7.3, 7.4(1).
Health ⚖906, 911.
Infants ⚖11.5.
Westlaw Topic Nos. 17, 198H, 211.
C.J.S. Adoption of Persons §§ 51 to 70.

2151.3527 Coercion prohibited

(A) No person described in section 2151.3516 of the Revised Code shall do the following with respect to a parent who voluntarily delivers a child under that section:

(1) Coerce or otherwise try to force the parent into revealing the identity of the child's parents;

(2) Pursue or follow the parent after the parent leaves the place at which the child was delivered;

(3) Coerce or otherwise try to force the parent not to desert the child;

(4) Coerce or otherwise try to force the parent to complete all or any part of the medical information forms received under division (A)(3) of section 2151.3517 of the Revised Code;

(5) Coerce or otherwise try to force the parent to accept the materials made available under division (A)(4) of section 2151.3517 of the Revised Code.

(B) Divisions (A)(1) and (2) of this section do not apply to a person who delivers or attempts to deliver a child who has suffered any physical or mental wound, injury, disability, or condition of a nature that reasonably indicates abuse or neglect of the child.

(2000 H 660, eff. 4–9–01)

Library References

Adoption ⚖7.3, 7.4(1).
Health ⚖257, 575, 906, 911, 984.
Westlaw Topic Nos. 17, 198H.

C.J.S. Adoption of Persons §§ 51 to 70.

Research References

Encyclopedias

OH Jur. 3d Family Law § 1432.1, Agreement for Temporary Custody—Children Under Six Months Old—Voluntary Delivery of Newborn.

2151.3528 DNA testing of parents

If a child is adjudicated a deserted child and a person indicates to the court that the person is the parent of the child and that the person seeks to be reunited with the child, the court that adjudicated the child shall require the person, at the person's expense, to submit to a DNA test to verify that the person is a parent of the child.

(2000 H 660, eff. 4–9–01)

Library References

Infants ⚖201.
Westlaw Topic No. 211.
C.J.S. Infants §§ 41, 53 to 54.

Research References

Encyclopedias

OH Jur. 3d Family Law § 1432.1, Agreement for Temporary Custody—Children Under Six Months Old—Voluntary Delivery of Newborn.

2151.3529 Medical information forms; written materials

(A) The director of job and family services shall promulgate forms designed to gather pertinent medical information concerning a deserted child and the child's parents. The forms shall clearly and unambiguously state on each page that the information requested is to facilitate medical care for the child, that the forms may be fully or partially completed or left blank, that completing the forms or parts of the forms is completely voluntary, and that no adverse legal consequence will result from failure to complete any part of the forms.

(B) The director shall promulgate written materials to be given to the parents of a child delivered pursuant to section 2151.3516 of the Revised Code. The materials shall describe services available to assist parents and newborns and shall include information directly relevant to situations that might cause parents to desert a child and information on the procedures for a person to follow in order to reunite with a child the person delivered under section 2151.3516 of the Revised Code, including notice that the person will be required to submit to a DNA test, at that person's expense, to prove that the person is the parent of the child.

(C) If the department of job and family services determines that money in the putative father registry fund created under section 2101.16 of the Revised Code is more than is needed for its duties related to the putative father registry, the department may use surplus moneys in the fund for costs related to the development and publication of forms and materials promulgated pursuant to divisions (A) and (B) of this section.

(2003 H 95, eff. 6–26–03; 2000 H 660, eff. 4–9–01)

Historical and Statutory Notes

Amendment Note: 2003 H 95 added division (C).

Cross References

Probate court; fees; cost of investigations; advance deposit, 2101.16.

Library References

Adoption ⚖7.3, 7.4(1).
Health ⚖257, 575, 906.
Infants ⚖17.
States ⚖127.
Westlaw Topic Nos. 17, 198H, 211, 360.
C.J.S. Adoption of Persons §§ 51 to 70.
C.J.S. Infants §§ 8 to 9.
C.J.S. States § 228.

2151.3530 Distribution of forms and materials by job and family services department

(A) The director of job and family services shall distribute the medical information forms and written materials promulgated under section 2151.3529 of the Revised Code to entities permitted to receive a deserted child, to public children services agencies, and to other public or private agencies that, in the discretion of the director, are best able to disseminate the forms and materials to the persons who are most in need of the forms and materials.

(B) If the department of job and family services determines that money in the putative father registry fund created under section 2101.16 of the Revised Code is more than is needed to perform its duties related to the putative father registry, the department may use surplus moneys in the fund for costs related to the distribution of forms and materials pursuant to this section.

(2003 H 95, eff. 6–26–03; 2000 H 660, eff. 4–9–01)

Historical and Statutory Notes

Amendment Note: 2003 H 95 designated the language of the former section as Division (A); and added Division (B).

Cross References

Probate court; fees; cost of investigations; advance deposit, 2101.16.

Library References

Infants ⚖17.
Westlaw Topic No. 211.
C.J.S. Infants §§ 8 to 9.

Notes of Decisions

Constitutional issues   1

---

1. Constitutional issues

Action challenging constitutionality of state Desertion of Child Under 72 Hours Old Act (DCA), which allows for voluntary surrender of newborn to "safe haven," while surrendering parent retains anonymity and is protected from criminal prosecution, was not rare and extraordinary case that would give rise to application of public right exception to traditional standing rule, and thus action was subject to dismissal for lack of jurisdiction, because public citizen bringing action failed to allege any concrete interest threatened by law. Smith v. Hayes (Ohio App. 10 Dist., Franklin, 06-14-2005) No. 04AP-1321, 2005-Ohio-2961, 2005 WL 1394779, Unreported. Constitutional Law ⚖42.3(2)

2151.36 Support of child

Except as provided in section 2151.361 of the Revised Code, when a child has been committed as provided by this chapter or Chapter 2152. of the Revised Code, the juvenile court shall issue an order pursuant to Chapters 3119., 3121., 3123., and 3125. of the Revised Code requiring that the parent, guardian, or person charged with the child's support pay for the care, support, maintenance, and education of the child. The juvenile court shall order that the parents, guardian, or person pay for the expenses involved in providing orthopedic, medical, or surgical treatment for, or for special care of, the child, enter a judgment for the amount due, and enforce the judgment by execution as in the court of common pleas.

Any expenses incurred for the care, support, maintenance, education, orthopedic, medical, or surgical treatment, and special care of a child who has a legal settlement in another county shall be at the expense of the county of legal settlement if the consent of the juvenile judge of the county of legal settlement is first obtained. When the consent is obtained, the board of county commissioners of the county in which the child has a legal settlement shall reimburse the committing court for the expenses out of its general fund. If the department of job and family services considers it to be in the best interest of any delinquent, dependent, unruly, abused, or neglected child who has a legal settlement in a foreign state or country that the child be returned to the state or country of legal settlement, the juvenile court may commit the child to the department for the child's return to that state or country.

Any expenses ordered by the court for the care, support, maintenance, education, orthopedic, medical, or surgical treatment, or special care of a dependent, neglected, abused, unruly, or delinquent child or of a juvenile traffic offender under this chapter or Chapter 2152. of the Revised Code, except the part of the expense that may be paid by the state or federal government or paid by the parents, guardians, or person charged with the child's support pursuant to this section, shall be paid from the county treasury upon specifically itemized vouchers, certified to by the judge. The court shall not be responsible for any expenses resulting from the commitment of children to any home, public children services agency, private child placing agency, or other institution, association, or agency, unless the court authorized the expenses at the time of commitment.

(2001 S 27, § 3, eff. 3–15–02; 2001 S 27, § 1, eff. 3–15–02; 2000 S 179, § 3, eff. 1–1–02; 2000 S 180, eff. 3–22–01; 1999 H 471, eff. 7–1–00; 1996 H 274, eff. 8–8–96; 1988 S 89, eff. 1–1–89; 1986 H 428; 1975 H 85; 1969 S 49, H 320; 1953 H 1; GC 1639–34)

Historical and Statutory Notes

Pre–1953 H 1 Amendments: 121 v 557; 119 v 731; 117 v 520

Amendment Note: 2001 S 27, § 1 and 3 substituted "Except as provided in section 2151.361 of the Revised Code, when" for "When" at the beginning of the section; and deleted "sections" after "order pursuant to" in the first sentence.

Amendment Note: 2000 S 179, § 3, eff. 1–1–02, inserted "or Chapter 2152. of the Revised Code" in the first and third paragraphs.

Amendment Note: 2000 S 180 substituted "Chapters 3119., 3121., 3123., and 3125." for "3113.21 to 3113.219" in the first paragraph.

Amendment Note: 1999 H 471 substituted "job and family" for "human" in the second paragraph.

Amendment Note: 1996 H 274 rewrote the section, which prior thereto read:

"When a child has been committed as provided by this chapter, the juvenile court may make an examination regarding the income of the parents, guardian, or person charged with the child's support, and may then order that the parent, guardian, or person pay for the care, maintenance, and education of the child and for expenses involved in providing orthopedic, medical or surgical treatment for, or special care of, the child. The court may enter judgment for the money due and enforce the judgment by execution as in the court of common pleas.

"Any expenses incurred for the care, support, maintenance, education, medical or surgical treatment, special care of a child, who has a legal settlement in another county, shall be at the expense of the county of legal settlement, if the consent of the juvenile judge of the county of legal settlement is first obtained. When the consent is obtained, the board of county commissioners of the county in which the child has a legal settlement shall reimburse the committing court for the expense out of its general fund. If the department of human services considers it to be in the best interest of any delinquent, dependent, unruly, abused, or neglected child who has a legal settlement in a foreign state or country, that the child be returned to the state or country of legal settlement, the child may be committed to the department for the return.

"Any expense ordered by the court for the care, maintenance, and education of dependent, neglected, abused, unruly, or delinquent children, or for orthopedic, medical or surgical treatment, or special care of such children under this chapter, except the part of the expense as may be paid by the state or federal government, shall be paid from the county treasury upon specifically itemized vouchers, certified to by the judge. The court shall not be responsible for any expense resulting from the commitment of children to any home, public children services agency, private child placing agency, or other institution, association, or agency, unless such expense has been authorized by the court at the time of commitment."

Cross References

Duty of husband to support family, wife to assist, 3103.03
Interfering with action to issue or modify support order, 2919.231

Library References

Infants ⚖=228, 279.
Westlaw Topic No. 211.
C.J.S. Infants §§ 41, 53 to 54, 57, 69 to 85, 278.
Baldwin's Ohio Legislative Service, 1988 Laws of Ohio, S 89—LSC Analysis, p 5–571

Research References

Encyclopedias

OH Jur. 3d Family Law § 1201, Minimum Child Support Order.
OH Jur. 3d Family Law § 1222, Interfering With Action to Issue or Modify Support Order.
OH Jur. 3d Family Law § 1301, Hearing to Determine Withholding or Deduction Requirements.
OH Jur. 3d Family Law § 1308, Reissuance Upon Change in Obligor's Status.
OH Jur. 3d Family Law § 1489, "Unruly Child".
OH Jur. 3d Family Law § 1545, Contempt.
OH Jur. 3d Family Law § 1710, Return of Child to Another State or Country.
OH Jur. 3d Family Law § 1715, Expenses of Committed Children; Liability of Parent or Guardian.
OH Jur. 3d Family Law § 1716, Expenses of Committed Children; Liability of Parent or Guardian—Liability of County of Legal Settlement.
OH Jur. 3d Family Law § 1717, Expenses of Committed Children; Liability of Parent or Guardian—Payment by County.

Treatises and Practice Aids

Katz, Giannelli, Blair and Lipton, Baldwin's Ohio Practice, Criminal Law, § 109:13, Interfering With Support Actions.
Sowald & Morganstern, Baldwin's Ohio Practice Domestic Relations Law § 22:7, Establishing Support Order.
Carlin, Baldwin's Ohio Practice, Merrick-Rippner Probate Law § 108:1, Juvenile Court—Criminal Jurisdiction.
Carlin, Baldwin's Ohio Practice, Merrick-Rippner Probate Law § 106:19, Juvenile Court Jurisdiction—Mentally Ill or Mentally Retarded Child.
Carlin, Baldwin's Ohio Practice, Merrick-Rippner Probate Law § 107:73, Alternatives for Disposition of Juvenile Cases.
Carlin, Baldwin's Ohio Practice, Merrick-Rippner Probate Law § 107:76, Disposition of Abused, Neglected, or Dependent Child—Types of Orders Court May Make.
Carlin, Baldwin's Ohio Practice, Merrick-Rippner Probate Law § 108:22, Juvenile Court—Parentage Act—Presumption of Paternity.
Carlin, Baldwin's Ohio Practice, Merrick-Rippner Probate Law § 108:34, Juvenile Court—Civil Support Proceedings—Liability for Child Support.
Giannelli & Yeomans, Ohio Juvenile Law § 30:3, Costs of Dispositions.
Giannelli & Yeomans, Ohio Juvenile Law § 32:2, Jurisdiction Over Parents and Others.

Notes of Decisions

County liability 3
Jurisdiction and court authority 5
Legal settlement 4
Parental responsibility 2

Private school or institution   1

1. Private school or institution

The youth services department is not required to pay the full costs of placing a juvenile parole violator in a private, out-of-state school where the juvenile court exceeds its authority by ordering the child to be sent to the private school; thus, since the expense was neither authorized by statute nor did the department elect to pay the expense, the cost must be assessed to the county treasury. In re Sanders (Cuyahoga 1991) 72 Ohio App.3d 655, 595 N.E.2d 974, motion overruled 61 Ohio St.3d 1422, 574 N.E.2d 1093.

Juvenile court acted beyond scope of its jurisdiction when it ordered Department of Mental Health and regional consortium for children to pay costs of care of juvenile placed in private, nonpublic mental health facility. In re Hoodlet (Athens 1991) 72 Ohio App.3d 115, 593 N.E.2d 478. Infants ☞ 228(1)

A juvenile court lacks the statutory authority to require the state department of mental health to pay the psychiatric costs associated with the care of a child who is placed in a private psychiatric institution; RC Ch 2151 and 2151.36 provide that the expense of the psychiatric treatment of a child in a private institution must be borne by the county treasury. In re Lozano (Cuyahoga 1990) 66 Ohio App.3d 583, 585 N.E.2d 889. Mental Health ☞ 78.1

When a juvenile court commits a delinquent child to an out-of-state private residential facility pursuant to RC 2151.355, the cost of educating the child is paid with funds from the state subsidy provided in RC 2151.357; if such subsidy is insufficient, any remaining educational expense is to be paid by the court as provided in RC 2151.36. OAG 89-006.

Where a juvenile court commits a child to a specialized school in another state, the court must itself pay expenses occasioned by the commitment and authorized by the court at the time of commitment, which expenses are paid out of funds appropriated to the court by the board of county commissioners under RC 2151.10. The court may order the parents, guardian, or person charged with the child's support to reimburse the court for such payments. 1962 OAG 2938.

In a county in which there is a county children's home, the county commissioners have no authority to pay to the children's bureau, which is a private agency, the board of neglected and dependent children who have been adjudged by the juvenile court as county dependents. 1934 OAG 3700.

When the juvenile court permanently committed child to a private institution under former GC 1653 (RC 2151.35 and RC 2151.36), said child became the ward of said private institution and the trustees thereof, guardian of the person of said child. 1929 OAG 1038.

2. Parental responsibility

Father was not entitled to have his child support obligation suspended while he was incarcerated; statute required a parent to provide child support for a child that had been adjudicated delinquent, as father's child had, and incarceration did not constitute a change in circumstances that warranted modification of child support. In re Pease (Ohio App. 3 Dist., Mercer, 06-05-2006) No. 10-05-21, 2006-Ohio-2785, 2006 WL 1519685, Unreported. Child Support ☞ 375

Trial court properly ordered parents to pay child support to the state, where their child had been adjudicated dependent and removed from the home. In re Day (Ohio App. 12 Dist., Clermont, 07-07-2003) No. CA2002-09-073, 2003-Ohio-3544, 2003 WL 21517343, Unreported. Infants ☞ 228(2)

Where domestic relations court has previously entered child support order in divorce case and child who is beneficiary of that support order is subsequently found to be delinquent in juvenile court, domestic relations court and juvenile court have concurrent jurisdiction to entertain motions regarding that support order. Machaterre v. Looker (Ohio App. 6 Dist., Lucas, 01-17-2003) No. L-02-1155, 2003-Ohio-220, 2003 WL 139572, Unreported. Child Support ☞ 173

Father's appellate claim, that juvenile court should have considered his motion to terminate public children services agency's temporary custody of unruly child or in the alternative held an adjudicatory hearing on the issue of child abuse, was moot, where the juvenile court magistrate had terminated the temporary custody 11 days after father filed his motion, even if such termination of temporary custody did not relieve father from paying for the care child had received while in temporary custody of agency. In re Kidd (Ohio App. 11 Dist., Lake, 12-27-2002) No. 2001-L-039, 2002-Ohio-7264, 2002 WL 31886759, Unreported. Infants ☞ 248.1

In a dependency and neglect proceeding involving three children who were hospitalized for psychological treatment, the juvenile court abuses its discretion by ordering the county children services agency to pay the balance of the children's medical bills without first requiring the parents to demonstrate their ability to pay for the medical expenses in light of the fact that the father is a physician and makes a substantial income. In re Rosser Children (Ohio App. 9 Dist., Summit, 06-14-1995) No. 16911, 1995 WL 353720, Unreported.

Residual parental rights, privileges, and responsibilities, including the responsibility of support, remained with parents notwithstanding juvenile court's order committing their child to Youth Development Center. In re Hinko (Cuyahoga 1992) 84 Ohio App.3d 89, 616 N.E.2d 515. Infants ☞ 228(2)

In absence of statutory provision to the contrary, duty of parent to support child ends when child reaches the age of majority. In re Hinko (Cuyahoga 1992) 84 Ohio App.3d 89, 616 N.E.2d 515. Child Support ☞ 390

The parents of an adjudicated delinquent may be ordered to continue to support their child in custodial care until he attains the age of twenty-one. In re Hinko, No. 61394 (8th Dist Ct App, Cuyahoga, 11–19–92).

Where a minor has been placed in a children's home, the trial court erred in ordering such minor's parent to pay for the expenses of such placement without considering the parent's income. In re Koogle, Nos. CA–82–68 and CA–82–93 (2d Dist Ct App, Greene, 6–16–83).

Where a temporary commitment is made of a dependent child to the division of charities, such child should be kept in readiness for return to the parent or guardian upon order of the court. 1932 OAG 4883.

3. County liability

Authorization of the juvenile court at time of commitment is a condition precedent to the accrual of liability against the county for expenses resulting from the commitment of children to any institution. City of Cleveland v. Gorman (Cuyahoga 1949) 87 Ohio App. 36, 89 N.E.2d 605, 55 Ohio Law Abs. 410, 42 O.O. 278.

A committing juvenile court may, at the time of commitment, obligate the county for such expenses as are authorized and approved by the judge of the juvenile court for the care of delinquent child committed to the department of mental hygiene and correction for placement in a private family home or institution operating under such rules and regulations as are adopted by the department. 1956 OAG 7007.

While duty rests upon board of education where juvenile detention home is located to employ and provide such teachers and incidental facilities as are necessary to furnish instruction to children confined in home, board of education may recover from county commissioners the cost and expense involved. 1946 OAG 1200.

Department of public welfare is required to accept "when able to do so" child committed by juvenile court under authority of former section to department of public welfare for transportation to home of said child's legal settlement, but lack of available funds to carry on such activity would render department of public welfare unable "to do so." 1938 OAG 2391.

Unless a dependent child was committed to an institution designated by GC 1639–34 (RC 2151.36) or a family home as therein provided, and in conformity with the juvenile court code, no payment for the care and board of such child was authorized. 1937 OAG 983.

By virtue of former GC 1653 (RC 2151.35 and RC 2151.36), even though a county child welfare board has been established in a particular county, the judge of the juvenile court of such county, if there is no county children's home in the county, may commit dependent children to a county children's home in another county, and county commissioners of the county from which they are committed are required to pay for their care if they have a legal settlement in the county from which they were committed. 1934 OAG 2759.

When the commitment of a minor to a children's home is temporary and is terminated by subsequent orders of the juvenile court with no further commitment, the trustees of such children's home are no longer obligated to provide for the care and support of such minors. 1934 OAG 2388.

Former GC 1653 (RC 2151.35 and RC 2151.36) while authorizing commitments by the juvenile court of dependent and neglected children to the care of suitable private individuals, made no provision for payment by the county commissioners for the board of such committed children. 1922 OAG p 148.

4. Legal settlement

The term "legal settlement," as used in RC Ch 2151, with respect to parents, guardians, or persons standing in the relation of loco parentis of children within the jurisdiction of the juvenile court, has reference to that term as defined in RC 5113.05. 1956 OAG 7008.

A child has, for the purposes of the sections enumerated in RC 2151.06, the same residence or legal settlement as his custodian who stands in the relation of loco parentis, and in such a case a child may acquire legal settlement otherwise than in accordance with the definition of legal settlement provided in RC 5113.05. 1956 OAG 7008.

The term "legal settlement" as used in RC 2151.36 has reference to that term as defined in RC 5113.05. 1956 OAG 6542.

The extension of aid to crippled children does not constitute poor relief as such term is used in the definition of legal settlement; where a crippled child has been committed to the division of social administration for care by the juvenile court of a county in which such child does not have legal settlement, the division of social administration is authorized to meet the expense of such care from funds allocated from the federal children's bureau to the state of Ohio for the care of crippled children; in the event that such child has, or subsequently acquires, legal settlement in a county other than the county from which commitment was ordered, the county of legal settlement can be charged with the expense thus incurred only after the consent of the juvenile court of the county of legal settlement has been obtained. In such case, the committing court should, in the ordinary case, certify such case to the juvenile court of such other county for further proceedings; following such certification, and until the juvenile court of such other county otherwise orders, the division of social administration may continue to extend care to such child under the original order of commitment, and the cost of such care must be borne by the county of legal settlement. 1952 OAG 1839.

5. Jurisdiction and court authority

Juvenile court had authority to hold parents of delinquent who, ten days before his eighteenth birthday, broke into high school and set it on fire responsible for his support until the age of 21, as he was a "child" within meaning of applicable statute. In re Hinko (Cuyahoga 1992) 84 Ohio App.3d 89, 616 N.E.2d 515. Infants ⚖ 228(2)

A court of the county in which the mother was originally committed to the girls industrial school, such county being the legal residence of the mother, has jurisdiction to commit her illegitimate child born in another county. 1933 OAG 1397.

A juvenile court has jurisdiction to declare any child a dependent which is found within the county under facts and circumstances constituting dependency; the county in which such court assumes jurisdiction and declares such child to be dependent will be responsible for the support of such child. 1933 OAG 1397.

A juvenile court has no authority to make a permanent order of separation of a child from its parents, or in the case of an illegitimate child, from its mother, and follow the same with a temporary commitment to the division of charities. 1932 OAG 4883.

Where a child is born to a feeble-minded mother while she is out of the institution for feeble-minded on a trial visit in a county other than Franklin and other than the county from which said mother was committed and such child is now in the institution with the mother, juvenile court of county in which child was born has no jurisdiction over said child. 1930 OAG 2236.

A juvenile court does not have jurisdiction to make commitments of children under former GC 1653 (RC 2151.35 and RC 2151.36) unless service, either actual or constructive, is first had on the father of such child or on the person having the custody of such child. 1929 OAG 281.

2151.361 Payment for care, support, maintenance, and education of child

(A) If the parents of a child enter into an agreement with a public children services agency or private child placing agency to place the child into the temporary custody of the agency or the child is committed as provided by this chapter, the juvenile court, at its discretion, may issue an order pursuant to Chapters 3119., 3121., 3123., and 3125. of the Revised Code requiring that the parents pay for the care, support, maintenance, and education of the child if the parents adopted the child.

(B) When determining whether to issue an order under division (A) of this section, the juvenile court shall consider all pertinent issues, including, but not limited to, all of the following:

(1) The ability of the parents to pay for the care, support, maintenance, and education of the child;

(2) The chances for reunification of the parents and child;

(3) Whether issuing the order will encourage the reunification of the parents and child or undermine that reunification;

(4) Whether the problem underlying the agreement to place the child into temporary custody existed prior to the parents' adoption of the child and whether the parents were informed of the problem prior to that adoption;

(5) Whether the problem underlying the agreement to place the child into temporary custody began after the parents' adoption of the child;

(6) Whether the parents have contributed to the child's problems;

(7) Whether the parents are part of the solution to the child's problems.

(2001 S 27, eff. 3–15–02)

Cross References

Interfering with action to issue or modify support order, 2919.231

Library References

Infants ⚖ 228.
Westlaw Topic No. 211.
C.J.S. Infants §§ 41, 53 to 54, 57, 69 to 85.

Research References

Encyclopedias

OH Jur. 3d Family Law § 1222, Interfering With Action to Issue or Modify Support Order.
OH Jur. 3d Family Law § 1715, Expenses of Committed Children; Liability of Parent or Guardian.
OH Jur. 3d Family Law § 1717, Expenses of Committed Children; Liability of Parent or Guardian—Payment by County.

Treatises and Practice Aids

Carlin, Baldwin's Ohio Practice, Merrick-Rippner Probate Law § 108:34, Juvenile Court—Civil Support Proceedings—Liability for Child Support.

Notes of Decisions

Adoptive parent duties 1

1. Adoptive parent duties

Trial court's decision not to order child support payments from adoptive parents, sought by county that assumed custody of child after adoption failed, was not unconscionable or unreasonable; court's decision detailed its significant concern that it not create a "chilling effect" on future adoptions of children with behavioral problems, court feared that compelling child support payments from adoptive parents posed risk of discouraging future adoptions, and court was within its proper scope of discretion in heavily weighing serious public policy concerns in tendering its decision. Wood Cty. Dept. of Job & Family Serv. v. Pete F. (Ohio App. 6 Dist., Wood, 11-10-2005) No. WD-05-023, 2005-Ohio-6006, 2005 WL 3008904, Unreported. Infants ⚖ 228(1)

2151.362 Cost of education

(A)(1) In the manner prescribed by division (C)(1) or (2) of section 3313.64 of the Revised Code, as applicable, the court, at the time of making any order that removes a child from the child's own home or that vests legal or permanent custody of the child in a person other than the child's parent or a government agency, shall determine the school district that is to bear the cost of educating the child. The court shall make the determination a part of the order that provides for the child's placement or commitment. That school district shall bear the cost of educating the child unless and until the court modifies its order pursuant to division (A)(2) of this section.

(2) If, while the child is in the custody of a person other than the child's parent or a government agency, the department of education notifies the court that the place of residence of the child's parent has changed since the court issued its initial order, the court may modify its order to name a different school district to bear the cost of educating the child. The department may submit the notice to the court upon receipt, from the school district initially ordered to bear the cost of educating the child, of evidence acceptable to the department that the residence of the child's parent has changed since the court issued its initial order. In the notice to the court, the department shall recommend to the court whether a different district should be ordered to bear the cost of educating the child and, if so, which district should be so ordered. The department shall recommend to the court the district in which the child's parent currently resides or, if the parent's residence is not known, the district in which the parent's last known residence is located. If the department cannot determine any Ohio district in which the parent currently resides or has resided, the school district designated in the initial court order shall continue to bear the cost of educating the child.

The court may consider the content of a notice by the department of education under division (A)(2) of this section as conclusive evidence as to which school district should bear the cost of educating the child and may amend its order accordingly.

(B) Whenever a child is placed in a detention facility established under section 2152.41 of the Revised Code or a juvenile facility established under section 2151.65 of the Revised Code, the child's school district as determined by the court shall pay the cost of educating the child based on the per capita cost of the educational facility within the detention home or juvenile facility.

(C) Whenever a child is placed by the court in a private institution, school, or residential treatment center or any other private facility, the state shall pay to the court a subsidy to help defray the expense of educating the child in an amount equal to the product of the daily per capita educational cost of the private facility, as determined pursuant to this section, and the number of days the child resides at the private facility, provided that the subsidy shall not exceed twenty-five hundred dollars per year per child. The daily per capita educational cost of a private facility shall be determined by dividing the actual program cost of the private facility or twenty-five hundred dollars, whichever is less, by three hundred sixty-five days or by three hundred sixty-six days for years that include February twenty-ninth. The state shall pay seventy-five per cent of the total subsidy for each year quarterly to the court. The state may adjust the remaining twenty-five per cent of the total subsidy to be paid to the court for each year to an amount that is less than twenty-five per cent of the total subsidy for that year based upon the availability of funds appropriated to the department of education for the purpose of subsidizing courts that place a child in a private institution, school, or residential treatment center or any other private facility and shall pay that adjusted amount to the court at the end of the year.

(2006 H 137, eff. 10–9–06)

Historical and Statutory Notes

Ed. Note: RC 2151.362 is former RC 2151.357, recodified by 2006 H 137, eff. 10–9–06; 2006 H 530, eff. 6–30–06; 2000 S 179, § 3, eff. 1–1–02; 1995 H 117, eff. 6–30–95; 1981 S 140, eff. 7–1–81; 1970 S 518; 1969 H 320.

Amendment Note: 2006 H 530 designated divisions (A)(1), (B), and (C); inserted "(1) or" and "as applicable," in the first sentence of division (A)(1); added the last sentence in division (A)(1); and added division (A)(2).

Amendment Note: 2000 S 179, § 3, eff. 1–1–02, substituted "facility" for "home" and "2152.42" for "2151.34" in the second paragraph.

Amendment Note: 1995 H 117 rewrote this section, which previously read:

"In the manner prescribed by division (C)(2) of section 3313.64 of the Revised Code, the court shall, at the time of making any order that removes a child from his own home or that vests legal or permanent custody of the child in a person or government agency other than his parent, determine the school district that is to bear the cost of educating the child. Such determination shall be made a part of the order that provides for the child's placement or commitment.

"Whenever a child is placed in a detention home established under section 2151.34 of the Revised Code or a juvenile facility established under section 2151.65 of the Revised Code, his school district as determined by the court shall pay the cost of educating the child based on the per capita cost of the educational facility within such detention home or juvenile facility. Whenever a child is placed by the court in a private institution, school, residential treatment center, or other private facility, the state shall pay to the court a subsidy to help defray the expense of educating the child in an amount equal to the product of the daily per capita educational cost of such facility and the number of days the child resides at the facility, provided that such subsidy shall not exceed five hundred dollars per year. The subsidy shall be paid quarterly to the court."

Cross References

Boards of education, residency for attendance purposes, acceptance of certain tuition requirements, enforcement, 3313.64
Definitions, residency for attendance purposes, acceptance of certain tuition requirements, tuition waivers, enforcement, 3313.64
Dispositional hearing, Juv R 34
Education of handicapped children, definitions, 3323.01
Permanent exclusion of pupils, revocation, probationary admission, 3313.662

Library References

Infants ⇔222, 223.1, 279.
Schools ⇔87.
Westlaw Topic Nos. 211, 345.
C.J.S. Infants §§ 57, 69 to 85, 278.
C.J.S. Schools and School Districts § 452.

Notes of Decisions

Ed. Note: *This section contains annotations from former RC 2151.35 and 2151.357.*

County custody 2
Out of state or district 3
Persons and facilities included 4
Residence of family 1

---

1. Residence of family

Statutes applicable to assignment of responsibility for educational costs of handicapped child did not apply to special education student, where whereabouts of student's father were unknown at time custody of student was awarded to Department of Job and Family Services, and student's mother was known at that time to be living in Missouri, outside purview of orders of Ohio courts. In re Zachariah T. (Ohio App. 6 Dist., Wood, 05-20-2005) No. WD-04-059, 2005-Ohio-2488, 2005 WL 1201213, Unreported. Schools ⇔ 87

Statute specifically directing juvenile court that vests legal custody of child in government agency to determine, as part of its placement order, school district that is to bear cost of educating child and to make this determination in accordance with statute that requires child's tuition to be paid by district in which child's parent resided at time the court removed child from home unless custody was vested in agency at earlier time, governed payment of tuition costs for handicapped child whose mother moved to another district shortly after child's removal from home, even though another section of statute, which dealt specifically with responsibility for tuition costs of handicapped children, would have assigned responsibility to district of mother's new residence. In re Humerick (Ohio App. 2 Dist., 03-10-2000) 137 Ohio App.3d 45, 738 N.E.2d 31. Schools ⇔ 159

A mother's continuing receipt of aid to dependent children from one county after moving to another does not prevent her children from becoming school residents of a district in the county to which she moved with them. In re Laricchiuta (Preble 1968) 16 Ohio App.2d 164, 243 N.E.2d 111, 45 O.O.2d 456. Schools ⇐ 159

Proceedings declaring a child neglected by the juvenile court of another county do not prevent a child from thereafter becoming a school resident in a county to which he moves with his family. In re Laricchiuta (Preble 1968) 16 Ohio App.2d 164, 243 N.E.2d 111, 45 O.O.2d 456.

For school attendance purposes a child becomes a resident in a school district as soon as he acquires any kind of home in that district, whether or not that particular home is permanent or temporary in nature, and whether or not schools are in session at the time he acquires such home. In re Sheard (Ohio Juv. 1959) 163 N.E.2d 86, 82 Ohio Law Abs. 259. Schools ⇐ 153

RC 2151.357 and 3313.64(C)(2) are applicable in determining which school district bears the cost of educating a child who moves during juvenile court proceedings; pursuant to RC 3313.64(C)(2)(a), the school district in which the child's family resided at the time the child was removed from his home and the time the court vested permanent custody in the youth services must pay the cost of educating the child. Christman v Washington Court House, No. CA–85–04–006 (12th Dist Ct App, Fayette, 1–31–86).

When a child who does not receive special education is admitted to school pursuant to RC 3313.64(B)(2)(a) because the child is in the legal custody of a person other than the child's natural or adoptive parent, when the child's parents reside outside Ohio, and when RC 3313.64(C)(2)(d) does not apply, then tuition is paid by the school district determined pursuant to RC 3313.64(C)(2)(a) to (c)—that is, by the district in which the child's parent resided when the court removed the child from his home or vested legal custody in the person, whichever occurred first; if that residence is unknown, by the district in which the child resided when he was removed from his home or placed in legal custody, whichever occurred first; or by the district determined by the court as required by RC 2151.357. If no district is determined pursuant to these provisions, then the district that has admitted the child must bear the cost of educating the child. The district may seek reimbursement from an out-of-state source pursuant to any contracts or other legal arrangements that may exist. OAG 94–033.

2. County custody

When a child is placed in the permanent custody of the youth services department, the court shall determine the school district responsible for the costs of educating the child as provided by RC 2151.357; Juv R 34(C) is not inconsistent with RC 2151.357, and gives the court no discretion to determine such school district in any other manner. Christman v. Washington Court House (Fayette 1986) 30 Ohio App.3d 228, 507 N.E.2d 384, 30 O.B.R. 386.

The school board of the district in which a child has a school residence at the time of his placement in another district must pay his tuition, whether such placement was by order of court or by the child welfare board in whose care the parent had voluntarily left him, and subsequent proceedings by the juvenile court declaring such child neglected will not end the obligation of the district of his school residence to continue paying his tuition. In re Laricchiuta (Preble 1968) 16 Ohio App.2d 164, 243 N.E.2d 111, 45 O.O.2d 456.

A court that commits a child to the custody of the youth services department is required to determine which school district shall bear the cost of educating the child. OAG 88–023.

RC 2151.357 does not require the school district of residence of a child placed in a detention home by a juvenile court to pay the cost of nonacademic summer activities provided for the child by the detention home. OAG 85–028.

Pursuant to RC 2151.357, when a child is placed in a detention home established under RC 2151.34, the child's school district as determined by the court is responsible for paying the cost of the education of the child. OAG 80–101.

If the juvenile court, pursuant to RC 2151.357, removes a child of kindergarten age from the home of its parents and places it under the custody of a welfare agency, and that agency then places the child in a kindergarten program in a school district other than that of the child's parents, RC 5153.16(D) places the responsibility for payment of the tuition on the welfare agency. OAG 72–099.

When a county child welfare board assumes control of a school age child and such child is placed by the board in the county children's home or in a foster home, the child's district of school residence prior to the board's assumption of control must pay tuition to another school district in which the child subsequently attends school. OAG 66–077.

Under RC 2151.35 the juvenile court "shall, at time of placing the child, determine which school district must bear the cost of educating the child while he is residing at such place as the court directs." 1963 OAG 553; overruled to the extent that it is inconsistent with OAG 80–101.

3. Out of state or district

School system in which legal guardian of juvenile adjudicated delinquent resided was statutorily responsible for costs of juvenile's education while juvenile was in state custody. In re Zachariah T. (Ohio App. 6 Dist., Wood, 05-20-2005) No. WD-04-059, 2005-Ohio-2488, 2005 WL 1201213, Unreported. Schools ⇐ 87

It is not inequitable to require a school district to pay the tuition of a child who does not attend its district and whose parents do not reside within its boundaries. Matter of Fetters (Ohio App. 12 Dist., Preble, 03-09-1998) No. CA97-08-022, 1998 WL 102997, Unreported.

When a juvenile court commits a neglected child to the temporary custody of a children services board, RC 2151.357 requires the court to determine, in the manner prescribed by RC 3313.64(C)(2), the school district that is to bear the cost of educating the child. Where the children services board, retaining legal custody of the child, places the child to live with a relative in another state party to the interstate compact on the placement of children, RC 5103.20, Art V(A) imposes upon the children services board, as the sending agency, the financial responsibility for assuring payment to the receiving state of the cost of the child's out-of-state public school tuition. In the absence of statutory direction as to the manner in which payment for the receiving state's tuition will be made by the responsible school district, as determined in the manner prescribed by RC 3313.64(C)(2), the juvenile court may, in the exercise of its discretion, direct the manner in which payment will be made. OAG 89–092.

When a juvenile court commits a delinquent child to an out-of-state private residential facility pursuant to RC 2151.355, the cost of educating the child is paid with funds from the state subsidy provided in RC 2151.357; if such subsidy is insufficient, any remaining educational expense is to be paid by the court as provided in RC 2151.36. OAG 89–006.

If a welfare agency has placed a child in a kindergarten program outside the district of the residence of the child's parents, the parents will be responsible for the tuition if they are able to pay; if they are not able to pay, the welfare agency will be responsible for the tuition, even if the board of education of the parents' residence has made no provision for a kindergarten program. OAG 72–099.

4. Persons and facilities included

A child of kindergarten age is included within the meaning of the word "child" as used in RC 2151.357. OAG 72–099.

Foster home is not educational facility within meaning of RC 2151.357 and section has no application to foster home. OAG 70–166.

2151.37 Institution receiving children required to make report

At any time the juvenile judge may require from an association receiving or desiring to receive children, such reports, information, and statements as he deems necessary. He may at any time require from an association or institution reports, information, or statements concerning any child committed to it by such judge under sections 2151.01 to 2151.54, inclusive, of the Revised Code.

(1953 H 1, eff. 10–1–53; GC 1639–36)

Historical and Statutory Notes

Pre–1953 H 1 Amendments: 117 v 520, § 1

Library References

Infants ⇐ 17, 226, 271.
Westlaw Topic No. 211.
C.J.S. Adoption of Persons § 10.
C.J.S. Infants §§ 8 to 9, 57, 70 to 77, 271.

Research References

Encyclopedias

OH Jur. 3d Family Law § 1537, Powers and Duties.

Law Review and Journal Commentaries

Rethinking The Relationship Between Juvenile Courts And Treatment Agencies—An Administrative Law Approach, Leslie J. Harris. 28 J Fam L 217 (1990).

2151.38 Temporary nature of dispositional orders

Subject to sections 2151.353 and 2151.412 to 2151.421 of the Revised Code, and any other provision of law that specifies a different duration for a dispositional order, all dispositional orders made by the court under this chapter shall be temporary and shall continue for a period that is designated by the court in its order, until terminated or modified by the court or until the child attains twenty-one years of age.

(2002 H 393, eff. 7–5–02; 2000 S 179, § 3, eff. 1–1–02; 1999 H 3, eff. 11–22–99; 1998 H 526, eff. 9–1–98; 1997 H 1, eff. 7–1–98; 1996 H 124, eff. 3–31–97; 1995 H 1, eff. 1–1–96; 1994 H 314, eff. 9–29–94; 1994 H 715, eff. 7–22–94; 1993 H 152, eff. 7–1–93; 1992 S 241; 1988 S 89; 1986 H 428; 1983 H 291; 1981 H 440, H 1; 1980 H 695; 1969 H 320, S 49; 130 v H 299; 1953 H 1; GC 1639–35)

Historical and Statutory Notes

Pre–1953 H 1 Amendments: 121 v 557; 117 v 520

Amendment Note: 2002 H 393 rewrote the section which prior thereto read:

"(A) Subject to sections 2151.353 and 2151.412 to 2151.421 of the Revised Code, and any other provision of law that specifies a different duration for a dispositional order, all dispositional orders made by the court under this chapter shall be temporary and shall continue for a period that is designated by the court in its order, until terminated or modified by the court or until the child attains twenty-one years of age.

"The release authority of the department of youth services shall not release the child from institutional care or institutional care in a secure facility and as a result shall not discharge the child or order the child's release on supervised release prior to the expiration of the prescribed minimum period of institutionalization or institutionalization in a secure facility or prior to the child's attainment of twenty-one years of age, whichever is applicable under the order of commitment."

Amendment Note: 2000 S 179, § 3, eff. 1–1–02, rewrote this section. See *Baldwin's Ohio Legislative Service Annotated*, 2000, page 11/L–3635, or the OH–LEGIS or OH–LEGIS–OLD database on Westlaw, for prior version of this section.

Amendment Note: 1999 H 3 rewrote divisions (B)(2) and (C)(2); and deleted "treatment" before "plan" in division (E)(4). Prior to amendment, divisions (B)(2) and (C)(2) read:

"(2) If a court schedules a hearing under division (B)(1) of this section to determine whether a child should be granted a judicial release, it may order the department to deliver the child to the court on the date set for the hearing and may order the department to present to the court a report on the child's progress in the institution to which the child was committed and recommendations for terms and conditions of supervision of the child by the court after release. The court may conduct the hearing without the child being present. The court shall determine at the hearing whether the child should be granted a judicial release from institutionalization or institutionalization in a secure facility. If the court approves the judicial release, the court shall order its staff to prepare a written treatment and rehabilitation plan for the child that may include any terms and conditions of the child's release that were recommended by the department and approved by the court. The committing court shall send the juvenile court of the county in which the child is placed a copy of the recommended plan and the terms and conditions set by the committing court. The court of the county in which the child is placed may adopt the recommended terms and conditions set by the committing court as an order of the court and may add any additional consistent terms and conditions it considers appropriate. If a child is granted a judicial release, the judicial release discharges the child from the custody of the department of youth services."

"(2) If a court schedules a hearing under division (C)(1) of this section to determine whether a child committed to the department should be granted an early release, it may order the department to deliver the child to the court on the date set for the hearing and shall order the department to present to the court at that time a treatment plan for the child's post-institutional care. The court may conduct the hearing without the child being present. The court shall determine at the hearing whether the child should be granted an early release from institutionalization or institutionalization in a secure facility. If the court approves the early release, the department shall prepare a written treatment and rehabilitation plan for the child pursuant to division (E) of this section that shall include the terms and conditions of the child's release. It shall send the committing court and the juvenile court of the county in which the child is placed a copy of the plan and the terms and conditions that it fixed. The court of the county in which the child is placed may adopt the terms and conditions set by the department as an order of the court and may add any additional consistent terms and conditions it considers appropriate, provided that the court may not add any term or condition that decreases the level or degree of supervision specified by the department in its plan, that substantially increases the financial burden of supervision that will be experienced by the department, or that alters the placement specified by the department in its plan. If the court of the county in which the child is placed adds to the department's plan any additional terms and conditions, it shall enter those additional terms and conditions in its journal and shall send to the department a copy of the journal entry of the additional terms and conditions."

Amendment Note: 1998 H 526 deleted "the most serious act for" after "prescribed minimum term for" in divisions (B)(1) and (C)(1); added the seventh sentence in division (B)92); added division (C)(3); inserted ", and, if the child was released under division (C) of this section, divisions (A) to (E) of section 5139.52 of the Revised Code apply regarding the child", and deleted "specialized supervised release" before "revocation program" twice, in division (D); and made other nonsubstantive changes.

Amendment Note: 1997 H 1 rewrote this section; see *Baldwin's Ohio Legislative Service Annotated*, 1997, page 9/L–2444, or the OH–LEGIS or OH–LEGIS–OLD database on Westlaw, for text of previous version.

Amendment Note: 1996 H 124 substituted "dispositional order" for "commitment" and "dispositional orders" for "commitments" in division (A); and made changes to reflect gender neutral language.

Amendment Note: 1995 H 1 added the third sentence in division (A); designated division (B)(1)(a) and inserted "in division (B)(1)(b) and (c) of this section and" twice and "or institutionalization in a secure facility" therein; added divisions (B)(1)(b) and (B)(1)(c); inserted "if it desires to release a child committed to it pursuant to division (A)(7) of that section from institutional care in a secure facility prior to the expiration of the period of commitment required to be imposed by that division and prior to the expiration of the prescribed minimum period of institutionalization or institutionalization in a secure facility under division (A)(4) or (5) of that section if either of those divisions applies or prior to the child's attainment of twenty-one years of age if division (A)(6) of that section applies, or if it desires to release a child committed to it under the circumstances described in division (B)(1)(c) of this section prior to the expiration of the prescribed minimum periods or prescribed periods of institutionalization or institutionalization in a secure facility described in that division" in division (B)(2)(a); substituted "as described in division (B)(1)(a), (b), or (c) of this section" for "whichever is applicable, prior to the expiration of the prescribed minimum period of institutionalization or prior to the child's attainment of the age of twenty-one years, whichever is applicable" in division (B)(2)(b); inserted "or prescribed period" in division (B)(2)(c); and made changes to reflect gender neutral language and other nonsubstantive changes.

Amendment Note: 1994 H 314 added ", or shall reject the request by journal entry without conducting a hearing" at the end of division (B)(2)(a).

Amendment Note: 1994 H 715 deleted a reference to section 5139.38 from division (A).

Amendment Note: 1993 H 152 added references to section 5139.38 throughout divisions (A), (B)(1), and (B)(2)(a); and added "or until the child successfully completes a specialized parole revocation program of a duration of not less than thirty days operated either by the department or by an entity with whom the department has contracted to provide a specialized parole revocation program" at the end of divisions (B) and (C).

Cross References

Commitment of child to department of youth services, 5139.05 to 5139.10
Commitment of child to youth services department, permanent assignment defined, 5139.05
Department of youth services as legal custodian, release and placement defined, 5139.01
Department of youth services, early releases in emergency overcrowding condition, 5139.20
Duties of the department of youth services to reduce and control delinquency, 5139.11
Interference with custody, 2919.23
Victims' rights pamphlet, contents, 109.42
Youth services department, placement of released children, applicability, 5139.18

Library References

Infants ⟲ 222, 226, 230, 278.
Westlaw Topic No. 211.
C.J.S. Adoption of Persons § 10.
C.J.S. Infants §§ 57, 69 to 85, 198, 206 to 213, 277.
   Baldwin's Ohio Legislative Service, 1988 Laws of Ohio, S 89—LSC Analysis, p 5–571

Research References

Encyclopedias

OH Jur. 3d Family Law § 1517, Correctional Service—Children Committed to Commission.
OH Jur. 3d Family Law § 1571, Apprehension—Release on Bail.
OH Jur. 3d Family Law § 1704, Effect on Court's Jurisdiction of Child's Commitment to Public Agency.
OH Jur. 3d Family Law § 1705, Effect on Court's Jurisdiction of Child's Commitment to Public Agency—Commitment to Youth Commission.
OH Jur. 3d Family Law § 1708, Revocation of Probation on Hearing.
OH Jur. 3d Family Law § 1709, Revocation of Probation on Hearing—Detention During Proceeding.

Forms

Ohio Jurisprudence Pleading and Practice Forms § 96:43, Temporary and Permanent Custody.

Treatises and Practice Aids

Klein, Darling, & Terez, Baldwin's Ohio Practice Civil Practice § 1:72, Civ. R. 1(C)(7): All Other Special Statutory Proceedings--Matters Held to be Other Special Statutory Proceedings--Dependency Action (RC 2151.353).
Carlin, Baldwin's Ohio Practice, Merrick-Rippner Probate Law § 105:10, Juvenile Court—Duration and Termination of Jurisdiction.
Carlin, Baldwin's Ohio Practice, Merrick-Rippner Probate Law § 107:31, Bail.
Carlin, Baldwin's Ohio Practice, Merrick-Rippner Probate Law § 107:73, Alternatives for Disposition of Juvenile Cases.
Carlin, Baldwin's Ohio Practice, Merrick-Rippner Probate Law § 107:89, Custody of Department of Youth Services.
Carlin, Baldwin's Ohio Practice, Merrick-Rippner Probate Law § 107:121, Custody Review Hearing—Revocation of Probation or Parole.
Carlin, Baldwin's Ohio Practice, Merrick-Rippner Probate Law § 107:184, Terms and Conditions of Child's Release from Department of Youth Services—Form.
Carlin, Baldwin's Ohio Practice, Merrick-Rippner Probate Law § 107:185, Order Committing Child to Department of Youth Services Upon Parole Revocation—Form.
Giannelli & Yeomans, Ohio Juvenile Law § 2:3, Child Subject to Adult Prosecution.
Giannelli & Yeomans, Ohio Juvenile Law § 27:3, Department of Youth Services Commitment.
Giannelli & Yeomans, Ohio Juvenile Law § 33:5, Other Proceedings.

Law Review and Journal Commentaries

Children Born Out Of Wedlock And Nonsupport—Valid Statutory Grounds For Termination Of Parental Rights?, Note. 25 J Fam L 755 (1986–87).

Irreconcilable Differences: When Children Sue Their Parents For "Divorce", Note. 32 J Fam L 67 (Winter 1994).

A New Issue In Foster–Parenting—Gays, Note. 25 J Fam L 577 (1986–87).

Rethinking The Relationship Between Juvenile Courts And Treatment Agencies—An Administrative Law Approach, Leslie J. Harris. 28 J Fam L 217 (1990).

Notes of Decisions

Age of ward 5
Constitutional issues 1
Credit for time served 9
Early release 8
Foster home 7
Jurisdiction 3
Notice; consent 4
Procedure; evidence 2
Schooling 6

---

1. Constitutional issues

Juvenile court's continued exercise of jurisdiction over juvenile regarding his parole violation in delinquency matter, when the parole violation was committed by juvenile when he was 19, was not an act of discrimination treating juvenile differently from other adults, but, rather, an act recognizing juvenile's ongoing status as a juvenile; pursuant to statute, juvenile court retained jurisdiction over the juvenile, who was adjudicated delinquent prior to age of 18, until he turned 21. In re Gillespie (Ohio App. 10 Dist., 12-19-2002) 150 Ohio App.3d 502, 782 N.E.2d 140, 2002-Ohio-7025, appeal not allowed 98 Ohio St.3d 1513, 786 N.E.2d 63, 2003-Ohio-1572. Infants ⟲ 281

Juvenile court's continued exercise of jurisdiction over juvenile in delinquency matter, after juvenile committed parole violation when he was 19 years old, did not arbitrarily or capriciously deny juvenile's right to bail in violation of due process, although common pleas court had released juvenile on bail on the adult charges underlying parole violation while juvenile court revoked juvenile's parole and returned him to custody; common pleas court's exercise of power over juvenile with respect to adult charges did not eviscerate juvenile court's coexisting power to hold juvenile pursuant to his parole violation, and juvenile had no absolute constitutional right to bail as a juvenile. In re Gillespie (Ohio App. 10 Dist., 12-19-2002) 150 Ohio App.3d 502, 782 N.E.2d 140, 2002-Ohio-7025, appeal not allowed 98 Ohio St.3d 1513, 786 N.E.2d 63, 2003-Ohio-1572. Constitutional Law ⟲ 255(4); Infants ⟲ 281

Revocation of juvenile's probation violated due process notice rights, where juvenile was unrepresented by counsel and neither transcript of dispositional hearing, docket, nor judgment entry of disposition mentioned a probation violation or informed juvenile of the condition of probation that he was alleged to have violated, and juvenile court made no finding that juvenile violated a probation condition. In re Royal (Ohio App. 7 Dist., 03-01-1999) 132 Ohio App.3d 496, 725 N.E.2d 685. Constitutional Law ⟲ 255(4); Infants ⟲ 225

Trial court violated due process in revoking juvenile's parole following juvenile's admission to habitual truancy charge, where juvenile had never received any type of notice concerning issue of possible parole violation until after his parole had been revoked. In re Kimble (Ohio App. 3 Dist., 09-25-1996) 114 Ohio App.3d 136, 682 N.E.2d 1066. Constitutional Law ⟲ 255(4); Infants ⟲ 230.1

Due process standards applicable to adult parole revocation hearings apply to juvenile parole revocation proceedings. In re Kimble (Ohio App. 3 Dist., 09-25-1996) 114 Ohio App.3d 136, 682 N.E.2d 1066. Constitutional Law ⟲ 255(4)

Mother's due process rights were not denied when she was not transported from prison to appear at hearing on motion to terminate custody of child, where mother was incarcerated for death of her older child, mother was represented by counsel, full record was made of proceedings, mother took no steps to present testimony by alternative means, and government's interest in meeting child's best interests and in minimizing risk and expense of transporting prisoners outweighed mother's interest in appearing. In re Sprague (Ohio App. 12 Dist., 08-05-1996) 113 Ohio App.3d 274, 680 N.E.2d 1041. Constitutional Law ⟲ 272(2); Constitutional Law ⟲ 274(5); Convicts ⟲ 6

RC 2151.38 is constitutional. State v. Clevenger (Clinton 1969) 19 Ohio App.2d 306, 251 N.E.2d 159, 48 O.O.2d 416.

2. Procedure; evidence

Where an adjudged delinquent is confined as an adult in an adult jail while waiting for his dispositional hearing, the provisions of RC 2967.15, granting credit for time served, should be applied. In re Smith (Butler 1986) 32 Ohio App.3d 82, 513 N.E.2d 1387.

In a hearing for revocation of parole under RC 2151.38(C), a juvenile's due process rights are satisfied by a hearing where (1) notice is given, (2) representation by counsel is allowed, and (3) an opportunity to present evidence is given; the lack of opportunity to cross-examine witnesses violates no due process right when the revocation is premised on previously admitted violations. In re Long (Franklin 1985) 24 Ohio App.3d 32, 492 N.E.2d 878, 24 O.B.R. 55.

Juvenile court consent to an agreement surrendering permanent custody of a child to a county children services board, pursuant to RC 5103.15 and RC 5153.16(B), is not an adversary proceeding, nor is such judicial consent a "commitment" of the child into the board's custody for purposes of RC 2151.38. In re Miller (Ohio 1980) 61 Ohio St.2d 184, 399 N.E.2d 1262, 15 O.O.3d 211. Infants ⚖ 230.1

RC 2151.38 is not applicable to, nor does it bar the filing of, a motion to vacate the required judicial consent to an agreement surrendering permanent custody of a child to a county children services board pursuant to RC 5103.15 and RC 5153.16(B). In re Miller (Ohio 1980) 61 Ohio St.2d 184, 399 N.E.2d 1262, 15 O.O.3d 211. Infants ⚖ 222

It is an abuse of discretion for the juvenile court under RC 2151.26 to recognize a fourteen year old youth to appear before the common pleas court when the evidence is insufficient to support a finding that he is other than a fit subject for rehabilitation under the provisions of the juvenile code, and insufficient to support a finding that recognizing him to common pleas court is necessary as a protection to the public. (See also In re Whittington, 13 App(2d) 11, 233 NE(2d) 333 (1967); vacated by 391 US 341, 88 SCt 1507, 20 LEd(2d) 625 (1968).) In re Whittington (Fairfield 1969) 17 Ohio App.2d 164, 245 N.E.2d 364, 46 O.O.2d 237. Infants ⚖ 68.7(2)

Where the former judge of a juvenile-probate court found a minor child to be dependent and neglected but failed to journalize the entry, a successor judge may enter a nunc pro tunc entry in conformity therewith. In re Howell (Ohio Juv. 1956) 140 N.E.2d 347, 74 Ohio Law Abs. 217.

Where the Ohio statute required a full investigation of the facts underlying a charge of delinquency and a finding of delinquency that the accused had committed acts in violation of Ohio law, jeopardy attached at a hearing at which accused was bound over for trial as an adult. Sims v. Engle (C.A.6 (Ohio) 1980) 619 F.2d 598, certiorari denied 101 S.Ct. 1403, 450 U.S. 936, 67 L.Ed.2d 372.

For purposes of a home furlough for a child committed to the legal custody of the youth services department for institutionalization under RC 2151.355(A)(4) or (5), said department may not allow the child to leave prior to the expiration of the minimum statutory commitment period without approval of the committing court pursuant to RC 2151.38(B); approval of the court is not required after expiration of that period and the department may allow the child to leave in accordance with RC 2151.38(C) and 5139.06. OAG 88–062.

The department of mental hygiene and correction has the exclusive guardianship of delinquent children committed to it by a juvenile court, and such guardianship may not be transferred to the division of social administration, department of public welfare, merely with the consent of the committing court, but such guardianship continues until the commitment order expires or is terminated upon application to the committing court. 1956 OAG 7007.

Dependent children, temporarily committed by the juvenile court to the care and custody of the board of state charities under the provisions of former GC 1672 (RC 2151.38), may in turn be placed temporarily in the home of a mother or parent by said board under the provisions of GC 1352–3 (RC 5103.06) for no more than twelve months, subject to the court's approval. 1922 OAG p 125.

3. Jurisdiction

In a divorce and alimony proceeding in the common pleas court in which the status of husband and wife is not changed, the court is without jurisdiction to annul or modify a decree previously made by the juvenile court awarding custody of a minor child and providing for its support. Partington v. Partington (Ohio App. 2 Dist. 1923) 18 Ohio App. 432.

Absent a specific statute that extends jurisdiction beyond the age of twenty-one years, juvenile court's jurisdiction over previously entered orders is limited to the age of twenty-one years. In re R.K. (Ohio App. 8 Dist., Cuyahoga, 12-16-2004) No. 84948, 2004-Ohio-6918, 2004 WL 2931013, Unreported, appeal not allowed 105 Ohio St.3d 1561, 828 N.E.2d 117, 2005-Ohio-2447. Infants ⚖ 230.1

Juvenile court did not have authority to impose indefinite driving suspensions beyond juvenile traffic offender's twenty-first birthday. In re R.K. (Ohio App. 8 Dist., Cuyahoga, 12-16-2004) No. 84948, 2004-Ohio-6918, 2004 WL 2931013, Unreported, appeal not allowed 105 Ohio St.3d 1561, 828 N.E.2d 117, 2005-Ohio-2447. Infants ⚖ 223.1

Under former GC 1643 (RC 2151.38), except as therein expressly provided, the juvenile court has continuing jurisdiction of a dependent child after having once acquired jurisdiction by service of citation and notice upon the parent, and adjudication of dependency; a new citation to parent or guardian is not necessary at time the court wishes to change temporary order to permanent one. Conti v. Shriner (Crawford 1939) 30 Ohio Law Abs. 193. Infants ⚖ 198; Infants ⚖ 230.1

When a juvenile is adjudicated delinquent before age 18 and then commits offense qualifying as parole violation between the ages of 18 and 21, separate jurisdiction of juvenile court and common pleas court may coexist according to classifications of "adult" and "juvenile," and divergent dispositions of those courts may also exist. In re Gillespie (Ohio App. 10 Dist., 12-19-2002) 150 Ohio App.3d 502, 782 N.E.2d 140, 2002-Ohio-7025, appeal not allowed 98 Ohio St.3d 1513, 786 N.E.2d 63, 2003-Ohio-1572. Infants ⚖ 281

Where a minor child is committed to the permanent custody of a county child welfare board, the juvenile court has no further jurisdiction over such child. In re Howell (Ohio Juv. 1956) 140 N.E.2d 347, 74 Ohio Law Abs. 217.

Trial court lacked jurisdiction to recalculate detention credit for juvenile, where it had already entered order of commitment. In re Tomecko (Ohio App. 9 Dist., Lorain, 07-24-2002) No. 02CA007981, 2002-Ohio-3749, 2002 WL 1628797, Unreported, appeal not allowed 97 Ohio St.3d 1483, 780 N.E.2d 287, 2002-Ohio-6866. Infants ⚖ 196

A juvenile court's order committing a delinquent does not divest the court of jurisdiction to order restitution where the orders are not inconsistent. In re Wood, No. 9–84–44 (3d Dist Ct App, Marion, 4–14–86).

Jurisdiction of juvenile court over "dependent" child terminated by proper entry in accordance with this section. 1938 OAG 3356.

Where the juvenile court of county assumes jurisdiction over an illegitimate child and subsequently relinquishes such jurisdiction, former GC 1643 (RC 2151.38) did not bar the juvenile court of county where child and mother have established a residence from assuming jurisdiction over the child under facts and circumstances constituting dependency. 1929 OAG 1090.

When a juvenile court takes jurisdiction of dependent children and commits them to the county children's home, their status therein will not be affected by change of the residence of their parents. 1928 OAG 2941.

4. Notice; consent

Except in those instances specified in GC 8004–6 (RC 3107.06), a probate court had no power to make a final decree or interlocutory order of adoption of a child where it affirmatively appears that there was not filed with the court a written consent to the adoption by the living mother of such child; the requirement of such a consent was not dispensed with in an instance where a juvenile court had previously made a valid determination that such child was "neglected." In re Ramsey (Ohio 1956) 164 Ohio St. 567, 132 N.E.2d 469, 58 O.O. 431.

The word "parent" may mean one or both parents, and it is not necessary that both or either of the parents be present in court in order to give the juvenile court jurisdiction to make legal commitment of a child for permanent transfer of guardianship to a certified institution or agency. 1925 OAG 2451.

New citation to parents or guardian is not necessary when juvenile judge wishes to change a temporary order to a permanent one. 1925 OAG 2451.

5. Age of ward

Where an adjudicated delinquent child becomes twenty-one years of age during the pendency of appeal from his adjudication, all jurisdiction of the juvenile court terminates by operation of RC 2151.38 so that the court has no authority even to vacate its previous order of commitment, which was suspended by an appellate court. In re J. F. (Ohio Juv. 1968) 17 Ohio Misc. 40, 242 N.E.2d 604, 46 O.O.2d 49.

The juvenile court has jurisdiction to require the father of a child whose custody had been given to the mother in a divorce decree to support said child after he has reached his eighteenth birthday, but before he attains the age of twenty-one years, where such continued support beyond the age of eighteen is intended for the purpose of a college education for said child. Calogeras v. Calogeras (Ohio Juv. 1959) 163 N.E.2d 713, 82 Ohio Law Abs. 438, 10 O.O.2d 441.

Under this section, when a child under eighteen comes into the custody of the juvenile court by warrant and arrest, such child continues, for purposes of discipline and protection, a ward of the court until age of twenty-one, and this is true even though court has not adjudicated such complaint prior to the time that the minor becomes eighteen years of age. State ex rel. Heth v. Moloney (Ohio 1933) 126 Ohio St. 526, 186 N.E. 362.

For purposes of a home furlough for a child committed to the legal custody of the youth services department for institutionalization under RC 2151.355(A)(6), the department may not allow the child to leave before his attainment of the age of twenty-one years without approval of the committing court pursuant to RC 2151.38(B). OAG 88–062.

Children committed by a juvenile court to a county department of welfare pursuant to RC Ch 2151, either permanently or temporarily, remain the responsibility of the department until they reach the age of twenty-one, unless the court, upon a proper application, terminates the order of commission at an earlier date. OAG 75–035.

When under this section, minor is committed to permanent care and guardianship of the department of public welfare, jurisdiction of the juvenile court over such child ceases at time of commitment, and it is the duty of such department to care for, supervise and otherwise look after such child until child attains the age of twenty-one years, even though child enlists in the army or navy or marries with the consent of the department. 1940 OAG 2959.

A juvenile court having found that a male child over sixteen years of age was delinquent, such child, having been made a ward of the juvenile court, remains such until attaining the age of twenty-one, and jurisdiction of court over said male delinquent continues until such time, even though he has been committed to the Ohio state reformatory. 1935 OAG 4865.

The board of parole has no jurisdiction to release on parole or otherwise a male delinquent who has been committed to the Ohio state reformatory by a juvenile court; release may only be by committing juvenile court any time before child reaches age of twenty-one. 1935 OAG 4865.

When either a boy or girl is temporarily committed to the children's home by the juvenile court, their marriage at the age of nineteen, while in the custody of the trustees of the children's home, does not affect the jurisdiction of the juvenile court over them. 1934 OAG 3160.

Where a juvenile court has taken jurisdiction of a dependent child, the change of the residence of the father does not divest the court of its jurisdiction which continues until the child is twenty-one unless terminated by permanent commitment. 1930 OAG 1690.

If a child has become a ward of the juvenile court before the age of eighteen and has been committed temporarily before that age, the juvenile court has power to recommit the child after it attains the age of eighteen years. 1925 OAG 2451.

Dependent girls committed by the juvenile court to the permanent care and custody of the board of state charities come under the sole and exclusive guardianship of such board, and such board shall, in the absence of any proceedings for their legal adoption, retain their guardianship until they reach eighteen. 1920 OAG p 1009.

Dependent girls committed by the juvenile court to the temporary care and custody of the board of state charities, remain under the legal control and guardianship of the court until they attain the age of twenty-one, should such commitment endure that long. 1920 OAG p 1009.

6. Schooling

A juvenile court is prohibited from placing a child under the legal custody of the youth services department in a specific school since the department, and not the court, has the right to determine where and with whom a juvenile should be placed; thus, a trial court's order requiring the youth services department to place a juvenile parole violator at a specific private, out-of-state school is erroneous. In re Sanders (Cuyahoga 1991) 72 Ohio App.3d 655, 595 N.E.2d 974, motion overruled 61 Ohio St.3d 1422, 574 N.E.2d 1093.

The youth services department is not required to pay the full costs of placing a juvenile parole violator in a private, out-of-state school where the juvenile court exceeds its authority by ordering the child to be sent to the private school; thus, since the expense was neither authorized by statute nor did the department elect to pay the expense, the cost must be assessed to the county treasury. In re Sanders (Cuyahoga 1991) 72 Ohio App.3d 655, 595 N.E.2d 974, motion overruled 61 Ohio St.3d 1422, 574 N.E.2d 1093.

Where a juvenile court commits a child to the boys industrial school, the jurisdiction of the court over the child ceases, and the fact that the court may have attempted to put a condition upon the release of the child, such as making restitution for damages, does not affect the exclusive power of the school and the department of mental hygiene and correction to release the child for satisfactory behavior and progress in training. The department may so release the child regardless of whether or not such condition had been fulfilled. 1962 OAG 3461.

Where a juvenile court commits a child to a specialized school in another state, the court must itself pay expenses occasioned by the commitment and authorized by the court at the time of commitment, which expenses are paid out of funds appropriated to the court by the board of county commissioners under RC 2151.10. The court may order the parents, guardian, or person charged with the child's support to reimburse the court for such payments. 1962 OAG 2938.

Children who are inmates of a county children's home, and at the time of placement in the home were not school residents of the district in which such home is located, should be admitted to the schools in the district where the home is located, at the expense of their respective school districts in which they were school residents at the time of placement, notwithstanding the status of the children as to temporary or permanent custody by the county welfare board. 1959 OAG 092.

7. Foster home

"Foster home," as the term is used in Ohio law, means a family home where persons maintaining the home rear a child or children of another as their own child or children. 1941 OAG 3353.

8. Early release

The decision whether to grant a request for early release lies within the court's discretionary power to strike a desired balance between the goals of confining the juvenile for purposes of rehabilitation and the release of the juvenile to society once satisfactory progress has been made toward rehabilitation. In re Howard (Ohio App. 7 Dist., 10-29-2002) 150 Ohio App.3d 1, 778 N.E.2d 1106, 2002-Ohio-6004. Infants ⚖ 223.1

Under the former version of statute governing early release from a term of commitment, a juvenile is eligible for early release after serving more than one-half of the prescribed minimum term of commitment and there is no exception for terms of commitment a juvenile is serving on a firearm specification. In re Howard (Ohio App. 7 Dist., 10-29-2002) 150 Ohio App.3d 1, 778 N.E.2d 1106, 2002-Ohio-6004. Infants ⚖ 223.1

A juvenile court has no authority pursuant to RC 2151.38(B) or 2151.38(C) to release a child committed to the youth services department under RC 2151.355(A)(4) to 2151.355(A)(6) for institutional care after expiration of the applicable minimum period of institutionalization. The effect of RC 2151.38(A), therefore, is that the juvenile court's jurisdiction to release a child terminates when the child has completed the minimum period of institutionalization. OAG 93–079.

If a request for early release is made pursuant to one of the procedures specified in RC 2151.38(B) prior to expiration of the minimum period of institutionalization imposed under RC 2151.355(A)(4) to 2151.355(A)(6), and the hearing is rescheduled or continued beyond the expiration of the minimum period of institutionalization, the juvenile court does not acquire or retain jurisdiction to grant an early release after that date. The court's jurisdiction over releases after the minimum period of confinement is limited to that set out in RC 2151.38(C). OAG 93–079.

If a juvenile court schedules an early release hearing pursuant to RC 2151.38(B) after expiration of the applicable minimum period of institutionalization imposed under RC 2151.355(A)(4) to 2151.355(A)(6) and orders the youth services department to deliver the child for the hearing and to present a treatment plan for post-institutional care as described in RC 2151.38(B)(2)(c), the youth services department should raise the issue of lack of jurisdiction by motion in that proceeding. OAG 93–079.

9. Credit for time served

Juvenile was entitled to a credit of 51 days served at the department of youth services (DYS) against his subsequent commitment for felony robbery and felony failure to comply with order of a police officer, where the delinquent allegation that the juvenile had violated parole by failing to report to his probation officer was based not on a separate a criminal offense bringing with it a separate sentence but, rather, was still connected with the original delinquency action. In re Mills (Ohio App. 5 Dist., Richland, 05-02-2002) No. 01 CA 96, 2002-Ohio-2503, 2002 WL 925270, Unreported. Infants ⇐ 223.1.

2151.39 Placement of children from other states

No person, association or agency, public or private, of another state, incorporated or otherwise, shall place a child in a family home or with an agency or institution within the boundaries of this state, either for temporary or permanent care or custody or for adoption, unless such person or association has furnished the department of job and family services with a medical and social history of the child, pertinent information about the family, agency, association, or institution in this state with whom the sending party desires to place the child, and any other information or financial guaranty required by the department to determine whether the proposed placement will meet the needs of the child. The department may require the party desiring the placement to agree to promptly receive and remove from the state a child brought into the state whose placement has not proven satisfactorily responsive to the needs of the child at any time until the child is adopted, reaches majority, becomes self-supporting or is discharged with the concurrence of the department. All placements proposed to be made in this state by a party located in a state which is a party to the interstate compact on the placement of children shall be made according to the provisions of sections 5103.20 to 5103.22 of the Revised Code.

(2006 S 238, eff. 9–21–06; 1999 H 471, eff. 7–1–00; 1986 H 428, eff. 12–23–86; 1975 H 247; 126 v 1165; 1953 H 1; GC 1639–37)

Historical and Statutory Notes

Pre–1953 H 1 Amendments: 117 v 520, § 1

Amendment Note: 2006 S 238 substituted "5103.22" for "5103.28" in the last sentence.

Amendment Note: 1999 H 471 substituted "job and family" for "human".

Cross References

Placing of children, 5103.16
Social administration division, enforcement by job and family services department, 5103.14

Ohio Administrative Code References

Agency and court interstate placement requirements, OAC 5101:2–42–21
Interstate placements of children into or from Ohio, foreign-born children, OAC 5101:2–42–20 to 5101:2–42–22

Library References

Infants ⇐229.
Westlaw Topic No. 211.
C.J.S. Infants §§ 57, 69 to 85.

Research References

Encyclopedias
OH Jur. 3d Family Law § 1524, Administrator.

Forms
Ohio Jurisprudence Pleading and Practice Forms § 96:2, Introduction.

Treatises and Practice Aids
Carlin, Baldwin's Ohio Practice, Merrick-Rippner Probate Law § 98:6, Adoption—Parties—Who May be Adopted—Foreign Child.
Carlin, Baldwin's Ohio Practice, Merrick-Rippner Probate Law § 107:128, Interstate Compacts.
Giannelli & Yeomans, Ohio Juvenile Law § 36:2, Interstate Compact on Juveniles.

Law Review and Journal Commentaries

Child Welfare—Outside the Interstate Compact on the Placement of Children—Placement of a Child with a Natural Parent, McComb v Wambaugh, Comment. 37 Vill L Rev 896 (1992).

Notes of Decisions

Certification 2
Interstate compact 1

---

1. Interstate compact

County failed to make a reasonable effort to reunify a mother and her daughter, and thus, reversal of trial court's judgment awarding permanent custody of daughter to county was required, even though county determined that mother failed to comply with her case plan, where mother, who had moved to a neighboring state while daughter was under temporary custody of county, requested that daughter be transferred to custody of neighboring state, no evidence suggested that neighboring state would not have accepted transfer, transfer would have been possible under the Interstate Compact on the Placement of Children, and county apparently ignored facts that mother had difficulty traveling back to state to be with her daughter and comply with her case plan, attainment of goals of case plan may have been enhanced by a transfer, and a transfer may have been a viable option. In re Secrest (Ohio App. 2 Dist., Montgomery, 12-20-2002) No. 19377, 2002-Ohio-7096, 2002 WL 31846268, Unreported. Infants ⇐ 155

Montgomery County Child Services (MCCS) failed to make reasonable effort to reunify family before seeking permanent custody of child and termination of mother's parental rights, where MCCS failed to give serious consideration to possibility of transferring temporary custody of children to state where mother's new residence was located, even though it appeared transfer would be possible under Interstate Compact on Placement of Children; decision of MCCS not to transfer case was based on fact that mother had not completed case plan set by MCCS. In re Erin Secrest (Ohio App. 2 Dist., Montgomery, 12-20-2002) No. 19378, 2002-Ohio-7094, 2002 WL 31846262, Unreported. Infants ⇐ 155

RC 2151.39 is not applicable to the acceptance of a juvenile delinquent by the Ohio compact administrator pursuant to RC 2151.56 to RC 2151.61. 1959 OAG 758.

2. Certification

The department of public welfare could under GC 1352–1 (RC 5103.03) investigate and certify a child-caring organization incorporated under the laws of another state and desirous of placing children in private homes in the state of Ohio so long as it first complied with this section. 1922 OAG p 517.

2151.40 Cooperation with court

Every county, township, or municipal official or department, including the prosecuting attorney, shall render all assistance and co-operation within his jurisdictional power which may further the objects of sections 2151.01 to 2151.54 of the Revised Code. All institutions or agencies to which the juvenile court sends any child shall give to the court or to any officer appointed by it such information concerning such child as said court or officer requires. The court may seek the co-operation of all societies or organizations having for their object the protection or aid of children.

On the request of the judge, when the child is represented by an attorney, or when a trial is requested the prosecuting attorney shall assist the court in presenting the evidence at any hearing or proceeding concerning an alleged or adjudicated delinquent, unruly, abused, neglected, or dependent child or juvenile traffic offender.

(1975 H 85, eff. 11–28–75; 1969 H 320; 1953 H 1; GC 1639–55)

Historical and Statutory Notes

Pre–1953 H 1 Amendments: 117 v 520, § 1

Cross References

Adjudicatory hearing, Juv R 29

Library References

District and Prosecuting Attorneys ⚖8 to 9.
Infants ⚖17.
Westlaw Topic Nos. 131, 211.
C.J.S. District and Prosecuting Attorneys §§ 20 to 21, 29 to 31.
C.J.S. Infants §§ 8 to 9.

Research References

Encyclopedias

OH Jur. 3d Family Law § 1567, Requirement of Cooperation With Juvenile Court.

Treatises and Practice Aids

Carlin, Baldwin's Ohio Practice, Merrick-Rippner Probate Law § 104:15, Juvenile Court—Prosecuting Attorney's Role.

Carlin, Baldwin's Ohio Practice, Merrick-Rippner Probate Law § 107:48, Adjudicatory Hearings—Prosecuting Attorney's Assistance at Hearing.

Giannelli & Yeomans, Ohio Juvenile Law § 18:2, Issuance of Summons: Proper Parties.

Giannelli & Yeomans, Ohio Juvenile Law § 35:2, Confidentiality Requirement.

Law Review and Journal Commentaries

Access to "Confidential" Welfare Records in the Course of Child Protection Proceedings, Stephen Levine. 14 J Fam L 535 (1975–76).

Notes of Decisions

Police 1

---

1. Police

Conviction for contributing to delinquency of minor by owner of restaurant for serving liquor to fifteen-year-old girl accompanied by police officers reversed upon ground evidence was inadmissible because means of procuring it improper and upon ground that the defendant, acting upon orders of police officers, did not commit any delinquency. State v. Miclau (Cuyahoga 1957) 104 Ohio App. 347, 140 N.E.2d 596, 5 O.O.2d 36, affirmed 167 Ohio St. 38, 146 N.E.2d 293, 4 O.O.2d 6.

GENERAL PROVISIONS

2151.412 Case plans

(A) Each public children services agency and private child placing agency shall prepare and maintain a case plan for any child to whom the agency is providing services and to whom any of the following applies:

(1) The agency filed a complaint pursuant to section 2151.27 of the Revised Code alleging that the child is an abused, neglected, or dependent child;

(2) The agency has temporary or permanent custody of the child;

(3) The child is living at home subject to an order for protective supervision;

(4) The child is in a planned permanent living arrangement.

Except as provided by division (A)(2) of section 5103.153 of the Revised Code, a private child placing agency providing services to a child who is the subject of a voluntary permanent custody surrender agreement entered into under division (B)(2) of section 5103.15 of the Revised Code is not required to prepare and maintain a case plan for that child.

(B)(1) The director of job and family services shall adopt rules pursuant to Chapter 119. of the Revised Code setting forth the content and format of case plans required by division (A) of this section and establishing procedures for developing, implementing, and changing the case plans. The rules shall at a minimum comply with the requirements of Title IV–E of the "Social Security Act," 94 Stat. 501, 42 U.S.C. 671 (1980), as amended.

(2) The director of job and family services shall adopt rules pursuant to Chapter 119. of the Revised Code requiring public children services agencies and private child placing agencies to maintain case plans for children and their families who are receiving services in their homes from the agencies and for whom case plans are not required by division (A) of this section. The agencies shall maintain case plans as required by those rules; however, the case plans shall not be subject to any other provision of this section except as specifically required by the rules.

(C) Each public children services agency and private child placing agency that is required by division (A) of this section to maintain a case plan shall file the case plan with the court prior to the child's adjudicatory hearing but no later than thirty days after the earlier of the date on which the complaint in the case was filed or the child was first placed into shelter care. If the agency does not have sufficient information prior to the adjudicatory hearing to complete any part of the case plan, the agency shall specify in the case plan the additional information necessary to complete each part of the case plan and the steps that will be taken to obtain that information. All parts of the case plan shall be completed by the earlier of thirty days after the adjudicatory hearing or the date of the dispositional hearing for the child.

(D) Any agency that is required by division (A) of this section to prepare a case plan shall attempt to obtain an agreement among all parties, including, but not limited to, the parents, guardian, or custodian of the child and the guardian ad litem of the child regarding the content of the case plan. If all parties agree to the content of the case plan and the court approves it, the court shall journalize it as part of its dispositional order. If the agency cannot obtain an agreement upon the contents of the case plan or the court does not approve it, the parties shall present evidence on the contents of the case plan at the dispositional hearing. The court, based upon the evidence presented at the dispositional hearing and the best interest of the child, shall determine the contents of the case plan and journalize it as part of the dispositional order for the child.

(E)(1) All parties, including the parents, guardian, or custodian of the child, are bound by the terms of the journalized case plan. A party that fails to comply with the terms of the journalized case plan may be held in contempt of court.

(2) Any party may propose a change to a substantive part of the case plan, including, but not limited to, the child's placement and the visitation rights of any party. A party proposing a change to the case plan shall file the proposed change with the court and give notice of the proposed change in writing before the end of the day after the day of filing it to all parties and the child's guardian ad litem. All parties and the guardian ad litem shall have seven days from the date the notice is sent to object to and request a hearing on the proposed change.

(a) If it receives a timely request for a hearing, the court shall schedule a hearing pursuant to section 2151.417 of the Revised Code to be held no later than thirty days after the request is received by the court. The court shall give notice of the date, time, and location of the hearing to all parties and the guardian ad litem. The agency may implement the proposed change after the hearing, if the court approves it. The agency shall not implement the proposed change unless it is approved by the court.

(b) If it does not receive a timely request for a hearing, the court may approve the proposed change without a hearing. If the court approves the proposed change without a hearing, it shall journalize the case plan with the change not later than fourteen days after the change is filed with the court. If the court does not approve the proposed change to the case plan, it shall schedule a hearing to be held pursuant to section 2151.417 of the Revised Code no later than thirty days after the expiration of the fourteen-day time period and give notice of the date, time, and location of the hearing to all parties and the guardian ad litem of the child. If, despite the requirements of division (E)(2) of this section, the court neither approves and journalizes the proposed change nor conducts a hearing, the agency may implement the proposed change not earlier than fifteen days after it is submitted to the court.

(3) If an agency has reasonable cause to believe that a child is suffering from illness or injury and is not receiving proper care and that an appropriate change in the child's case plan is necessary to prevent immediate or threatened physical or emotional harm, to believe that a child is in immediate danger from the child's surroundings and that an immediate change in the child's case plan is necessary to prevent immediate or threatened physical or emotional harm to the child, or to believe that a parent, guardian, custodian, or other member of the child's household has abused or neglected the child and that the child is in danger of immediate or threatened physical or emotional harm from that person unless the agency makes an appropriate change in the child's case plan, it may implement the change without prior agreement or a court hearing and, before the end of the next day after the change is made, give all parties, the guardian ad litem of the child, and the court notice of the change. Before the end of the third day after implementing the change in the case plan, the agency shall file a statement of the change with the court and give notice of the filing accompanied by a copy of the statement to all parties and the guardian ad litem. All parties and the guardian ad litem shall have ten days from the date the notice is sent to object to and request a hearing on the change.

(a) If it receives a timely request for a hearing, the court shall schedule a hearing pursuant to section 2151.417 of the Revised Code to be held no later than thirty days after the request is received by the court. The court shall give notice of the date, time, and location of the hearing to all parties and the guardian ad litem. The agency shall continue to administer the case plan with the change after the hearing, if the court approves the change. If the court does not approve the change, the court shall make appropriate changes to the case plan and shall journalize the case plan.

(b) If it does not receive a timely request for a hearing, the court may approve the change without a hearing. If the court approves the change without a hearing, it shall journalize the case plan with the change within fourteen days after receipt of the change. If the court does not approve the change to the case plan, it shall schedule a hearing under section 2151.417 of the Revised Code to be held no later than thirty days after the expiration of the fourteen-day time period and give notice of the date, time, and location of the hearing to all parties and the guardian ad litem of the child.

(F)(1) All case plans for children in temporary custody shall have the following general goals:

(a) Consistent with the best interest and special needs of the child, to achieve a safe out-of-home placement in the least restrictive, most family-like setting available and in close proximity to the home from which the child was removed or the home in which the child will be permanently placed;

(b) To eliminate with all due speed the need for the out-of-home placement so that the child can safely return home.

(2) The director of job and family services shall adopt rules pursuant to Chapter 119. of the Revised Code setting forth the general goals of case plans for children subject to dispositional orders for protective supervision, a planned permanent living arrangement, or permanent custody.

(G) In the agency's development of a case plan and the court's review of the case plan, the child's health and safety shall be the paramount concern. The agency and the court shall be guided by the following general priorities:

(1) A child who is residing with or can be placed with the child's parents within a reasonable time should remain in their legal custody even if an order of protective supervision is required for a reasonable period of time;

(2) If both parents of the child have abandoned the child, have relinquished custody of the child, have become incapable of supporting or caring for the child even with reasonable assistance, or have a detrimental effect on the health, safety, and best interest of the child, the child should be placed in the legal custody of a suitable member of the child's extended family;

(3) If a child described in division (G)(2) of this section has no suitable member of the child's extended family to accept legal custody, the child should be placed in the legal custody of a suitable nonrelative who shall be made a party to the proceedings after being given legal custody of the child;

(4) If the child has no suitable member of the child's extended family to accept legal custody of the child and no suitable nonrelative is available to accept legal custody of the child and, if the child temporarily cannot or should not be placed with the child's parents, guardian, or custodian, the child should be placed in the temporary custody of a public children services agency or a private child placing agency;

(5) If the child cannot be placed with either of the child's parents within a reasonable period of time or should not be placed with either, if no suitable member of the child's extended family or suitable nonrelative is available to accept legal custody of the child, and if the agency has a reasonable expectation of placing the child for adoption, the child should be committed to the permanent custody of the public children services agency or private child placing agency;

(6) If the child is to be placed for adoption or foster care, the placement shall not be delayed or denied on the basis of the child's or adoptive or foster family's race, color, or national origin.

(H) The case plan for a child in temporary custody shall include at a minimum the following requirements if the child is or has been the victim of abuse or neglect or if the child witnessed the commission in the child's household of abuse or neglect against a sibling of the child, a parent of the child, or any other person in the child's household:

(1) A requirement that the child's parents, guardian, or custodian participate in mandatory counseling;

(2) A requirement that the child's parents, guardian, or custodian participate in any supportive services that are required by or provided pursuant to the child's case plan.

(I) A case plan may include, as a supplement, a plan for locating a permanent family placement. The supplement shall not be considered part of the case plan for purposes of division (D) of this section.

(1999 H 471, eff. 7–1–00; 1998 H 484, eff. 3–18–99; 1996 H 274, eff. 8–8–96; 1996 H 419, eff. 9–18–96; 1988 H 403, eff. 1–1–89)

Uncodified Law

1988 S 89, § 4: See Uncodified Law under 2151.414.

Historical and Statutory Notes

Ed. Note: Former 2151.412 repealed by 1988 H 403, eff. 1–1–89; 1988 S 89. Prior 2151.412 repealed by 1988 S 89, eff. 1–1–89; 1988 H 399; 1986 H 428; 1980 H 695.

Amendment Note: 1999 H 471 substituted "director of job and family services" for "department of human services" in divisions (B)(1), (B)(2), and (F)(2).

Amendment Note: 1998 H 484 substituted "a planned permanent living arrangement" for "long-term foster care" in divisions (A)(4) and (F)(2); inserted "safe" in division (F)(1)(a); rewrote division (F)(1)(b); inserted "child's health and safety shall be the paramount concern. The" in the first paragraph in division (G); deleted "solely" after "denied" in division (G)(6); added division (I); and made other nonsubstantive changes. Prior to amendment, division (F)(1)(b) read:

"(b) To do either of the following:

"(i) With all due speed eliminate the need for the out-of-home placement so that the child can return home;

"(ii) If return to the child's home is not imminent and desirable, develop and implement an alternative permanent living arrangement for the child."

Amendment Note: 1996 H 274 rewrote division (E), which prior thereto read:

"(E)(1) All parties are bound by the terms of the journalized case plan.

"(2) No party shall change a substantive part of the case plan, including, but not limited to, the child's placement and the visitation rights of any party, unless the proposed change has been approved by all parties and the guardian ad litem. The proposed change shall be submitted to the court within seven days of approval. If the court approves the proposed change, it shall journalize the case plan with the change within fourteen days after receipt of the proposed change. The agency may implement the proposed change fourteen days after it is submitted to the court for approval, unless the court schedules a hearing under section 2151.417 of the Revised Code to consider the proposed change. If the court does not approve the proposed change to the case plan, it shall schedule a hearing under section 2151.417 of the Revised Code to be held no later than thirty days after the expiration of the fourteen-day time period and give notice of the date, time, and location of the hearing to all parties and the guardian ad litem of the child. The agency shall not implement any proposed change to a case plan pursuant to this division, unless the proposed change has been approved by the court or the court has failed to either approve and journalize the proposed change or schedule a hearing pursuant to section 2151.417 of the Revised Code on the proposed change within fourteen days after the proposed change was submitted to the court.

"(3) If an agency has reasonable cause to believe that a child is suffering from illness or injury and is not receiving proper care and that an appropriate change in the child's case plan is necessary to prevent immediate or threatened physical or emotional harm, to believe that a child is in immediate danger from the child's surroundings and that an immediate change in the child's case plan is necessary to prevent immediate or threatened physical or emotional harm to the child, or to believe that a parent, guardian, custodian, or other member of the child's household has abused or neglected the child and that the child is in danger of immediate or threatened physical or emotional harm from that person unless the agency makes an appropriate change in the child's case plan, it may implement the change without prior agreement or a court hearing and, before the end of the next business day after the change is made, give all parties, the guardian ad litem of the child, and the court notice of the change. If the agency, within seven days after implementing the change pursuant to this division, can obtain an agreement on the change to the case plan that is signed by all parties and the child's guardian ad litem, it shall immediately file the change with the court. If the court approves the change, it shall journalize the case plan with the change within fourteen days after receipt of the change. If the court does not approve the change to the case plan, it shall schedule a hearing under section 2151.417 of the Revised Code to be held no later than thirty days after the expiration of the fourteen-day time period and give notice of the date, time, and location of the hearing to all parties and the guardian ad litem of the child. If the agency cannot obtain the approval of all parties and the child's guardian ad litem to a change to the case plan, it shall request the court to schedule a hearing under section 2151.417 of the Revised Code to consider the change. The court shall schedule the requested hearing to be held within fourteen days after the request and give notice of the date, time, and location of the hearing to all parties and the guardian ad litem of the child."

Amendment Note: 1996 H 419 added the second sentence to division (A)(4); added division (G)(6); made changes to reflect gender neutral language throughout; and made other nonsubstantive changes.

Cross References

Child day-care, protective day-care defined, 5104.01
Foster caregivers, information regarding delinquent children provided to, 2152.72
Ohio works first program, eligibility, 5107.10
Placing of child in institution, agency filing complaint and case plan, 5103.15
Review hearing of adoption agreement, case plan, 5103.153

Ohio Administrative Code References

Children services, definition of terms, OAC 5101:2–1–01
Child's education and health information, OAC 5101:2–38–08
Child's education and health information, OAC 5101:2–39–08.2
Definition of terms for the implementation of the "Comprehensive Assessment and Planning Model - Interim Solution" and statewide automated child welfare database, OAC 5101:2–1–01.1
Emergency removal of a child from an out-of-home care setting, OAC 5101:2–39–03
PCPA and PNA case plans and administrative case reviews for direct placements, OAC 5101:2–5–34
PCPA case plan for children in custody or under court-ordered protective supervision, OAC 5101:2–39–08.1, OAC 5101:2–5101:2–39–10
PCSA case plan for children in custody or under protective supervision, OAC 5101:2–38–05
Public children services agency case plan, OAC 5101:2–39–07 to 5101:2–39–081, 5101:2–39–10
Removal of a child from his own home, OAC 5101:2–39–01, OAC 5101:2–39–12
Requirements for PCSA case plan for in-home supportive services without court order, OAC 5101:2–38–01
Supportive services for prevention of placement, reunification and life skills, OAC 5101:2–40–02
Supportive services, OAC 5101:2–39–07

Library References

Infants ⚖ 17, 155.
Westlaw Topic No. 211.
C.J.S. Infants §§ 8 to 9, 31, 33 to 50, 55, 62.
    Baldwin's Ohio Legislative Service, 1996 H 274—LSC Analysis, p 5/L-697
    Baldwin's Ohio Legislative Service, 1988 Laws of Ohio, S 89—LSC Analysis, p 5–571

Research References

Encyclopedias

OH Jur. 3d Family Law § 1427, Content, Format, and Agreement.
OH Jur. 3d Family Law § 1428, Changes to Case Plan.
OH Jur. 3d Family Law § 1434, Court Approval.
OH Jur. 3d Family Law § 1654, Determination of Reasonable Efforts.
OH Jur. 3d Family Law § 1664, on Request for Permanent Custody—Factors to be Considered.
OH Jur. 3d Family Law § 1700, Factors to be Considered in Making Plan.
OH Jur. 3d Family Law § 1702, Rules to be Adopted.
OH Jur. 3d Public Welfare § 49, Eligibility.

Forms

Ohio Jurisprudence Pleading and Practice Forms § 96:28, Permanent Custody Surrender Agreement—Review Hearing.
Ohio Jurisprudence Pleading and Practice Forms § 96:43, Temporary and Permanent Custody.

Treatises and Practice Aids

Sowald & Morganstern, Baldwin's Ohio Practice Domestic Relations Law § 37:12, Privileged Communication—Criteria for Privilege.
Sowald & Morganstern, Baldwin's Ohio Practice Domestic Relations Law § 37:23, Privileged Communication—Voluntary Factor.
Carlin, Baldwin's Ohio Practice, Merrick-Rippner Probate Law § 98:8, Adoption—Suitability of Adoptive Parents—Best Interests of Child.
Carlin, Baldwin's Ohio Practice, Merrick-Rippner Probate Law § 98:11, Adoption—Suitability of Adopted Parents—Religion.
Carlin, Baldwin's Ohio Practice, Merrick-Rippner Probate Law § 98:17, Adoption—Types of Placement—Agency Adoptions—Timing of Review.
Carlin, Baldwin's Ohio Practice, Merrick-Rippner Probate Law § 107:54, Adjudicatory Hearings—Applicability of Physician-Patient Privilege.
Carlin, Baldwin's Ohio Practice, Merrick-Rippner Probate Law § 107:73, Alternatives for Disposition of Juvenile Cases.
Carlin, Baldwin's Ohio Practice, Merrick-Rippner Probate Law § 107:74, Reasonable Efforts Determination.
Carlin, Baldwin's Ohio Practice, Merrick-Rippner Probate Law § 107:75, Case Plans.

Carlin, Baldwin's Ohio Practice, Merrick-Rippner Probate Law § 107:80, Disposition of Abused, Neglected, or Dependent Child—Permanent Custody.

Carlin, Baldwin's Ohio Practice, Merrick-Rippner Probate Law § 108:13, Juvenile Court—Jurisdiction Over Child Custody Matters—Determination of Custody.

Carlin, Baldwin's Ohio Practice, Merrick-Rippner Probate Law § 107:119, Custody Review Proceedings—Semiannual Administrative Review.

Carlin, Baldwin's Ohio Practice, Merrick-Rippner Probate Law § 107:175, Order Committing Child to Permanent Custody of Public or Private Agency—Form.

Adrine & Ruden, Ohio Domestic Violence Law § 16:5, Conclusion.

Giannelli & Yeomans, Ohio Juvenile Law § 1:7, Juvenile Code.

Giannelli & Yeomans, Ohio Juvenile Law § 11:4, Extension of Temporary Custody Agreements.

Giannelli & Yeomans, Ohio Juvenile Law § 26:2, Requirements.

Giannelli & Yeomans, Ohio Juvenile Law § 26:3, Time Requirements for Case Plans.

Giannelli & Yeomans, Ohio Juvenile Law § 26:4, Court Approval; Journalization.

Giannelli & Yeomans, Ohio Juvenile Law § 26:5, Case Plan Amendments.

Giannelli & Yeomans, Ohio Juvenile Law § 26:6, Goals & Priorities.

Giannelli & Yeomans, Ohio Juvenile Law § 26:7, Due Process.

Giannelli & Yeomans, Ohio Juvenile Law § 27:5, Child Protective Services.

Giannelli & Yeomans, Ohio Juvenile Law § 31:2, Filing of Motion.

Giannelli & Yeomans, Ohio Juvenile Law § 31:7, Foster Parents as "Psychological Parents".

Giannelli & Yeomans, Ohio Juvenile Law § 33:8, Contempt.

Giannelli & Yeomans, Ohio Juvenile Law § 34:4, Final Order Requirement.

Giannelli & Yeomans, Ohio Juvenile Law § 25:14, Reasonable Efforts Determination; Abuse, Neglect & Dependency.

Giannelli & Yeomans, Ohio Juvenile Law § 30:10, Permanent Custody—Parental Placement Within Reasonable Time.

Giannelli & Yeomans, Ohio Juvenile Law § 33:10, Child Custody Agency Commitment—Semiannual Administrative Review.

Law Review and Journal Commentaries

Reunification Planning for Children in Custody of Ohio's Children Services Boards: What Does the Law Require?, Norma Blank. 16 Akron L Rev 681 (Spring 1983).

Notes of Decisions

Constitutional issues 1
Evidence and testimony 2
Procedural issues 5
Reunification plan not required 4
Reunification plan required 3

---

1. Constitutional issues

Father, whose children were placed in temporary custody of county children's services board after children were found to be abused, did not have his Fifth Amendment right against self-incrimination violated by the inclusion of case plan requirement that he participate in a sexual offender group treatment program without an offer of immunity, even though father claimed such treatment required him to admit he sexually abused his daughter; significant evidence supported claim that father sexually abused his daughter, including facts stipulated by father, and trial court's subsequent decision to terminate father's parental rights was not based solely on father's failure to attend treatment sessions. In re A.D. (Ohio App. 9 Dist., Summit, 09-30-2005) No. 22668, 2005-Ohio-5183, 2005 WL 2400960, Unreported. Infants ⇐ 155

Statutory provisions requiring reunification plans in cases of dependency, neglect and abuse involving a state agency, but not in private custody cases, did not implicate due process and equal protection rights of parents who voluntarily relinquished custody of their child to custodian, where private custody proceedings did not implicate potential for institutional indifference or need to reduce inattentiveness and inaction on part of state child welfare agencies toward children in their custody, and proceedings instituted by state to terminate or limit parental rights and cases in which parents forfeited their parental rights did not involve persons similarly situated. In re Bailey (Ohio App. 1 Dist., Hamilton, 06-17-2005) No. C-040014, No. C-040479, 2005-Ohio-3039, 2005 WL 1413269, Unreported. Constitutional Law ⇐ 274(5)

Mother of dependent children did not waive right to assert children's right to counsel in termination of parental rights proceeding, where mother filed motion raising issue of counsel one week after guardian ad litem (GAL) interviewed children and they indicated desire to reunify. In re Emery (Ohio App. 4 Dist., Lawrence, 04-25-2003) No. 02CA40, 2003-Ohio-2206, 2003 WL 2003811, Unreported. Infants ⇐ 200

Implicit, and potent, penalty for parent's failure to satisfy the requirements of a particular case plan is the loss of a parent's fundamental liberty right to the care, custody, and management of his or her child. In re Amanda W. (Ohio App. 6 Dist., 11-21-1997) 124 Ohio App.3d 136, 705 N.E.2d 724. Infants ⇐ 155

Clear and convincing evidence did not support juvenile court's finding that child could not be placed with her parents within reasonable time or should be placed with parents, as required to sustain judgment granting permanent custody of child to children services agency, where only area in which parents did not comply with reunification case plan was their failure to admit that father sexually abused child, but that condition of plan violated parents' Fifth Amendment privilege against self-incrimination. In re Amanda W. (Ohio App. 6 Dist., 11-21-1997) 124 Ohio App.3d 136, 705 N.E.2d 724. Infants ⇐ 178

In an appeal by the county children's services bureau which obtained custody of allegedly neglected children, a statute which affects substantive rather than remedial rights by terminating custody after one year violates the constitution by placing additional burdens upon a previous judicial decision and will not apply retroactively to the action. In re Smith (Ottawa 1991) 77 Ohio App.3d 1, 601 N.E.2d 45.

Due process of law is not denied to an unidentified natural parent by a children's services board that divests him of parental rights without first proving a comprehensive reunification plan where he did not step forward voluntarily and identify himself as the parent of the abused, neglected, or dependent children and ask that he be reunited with them; at the same time, however, an agency that is made aware before the court grants it permanent custody of a child, by means of a paternity suit or otherwise, that a previously unidentified individual is the child's natural parent, the agency must recognize this fact and include this parent as a party to the permanent custody proceedings. Garabrandt v. Lucas County Children Services Bd. (Lucas 1988) 47 Ohio App.3d 119, 547 N.E.2d 997. Constitutional Law ⇐ 274(5); Infants ⇐ 155; Infants ⇐ 200

The Due Process Clause of US Const Am 14 does not require states to carry out a reunification plan before a final adjudication of abuse or dependency; RC 2151.412 is thus not unconstitutional on its face. Lesher v. Lavrich (N.D.Ohio 1984) 632 F.Supp. 77, affirmed 784 F.2d 193.

2. Evidence and testimony

Evidence supported finding that mother and father's relatives were not suitable placements for their ten children, in termination of parental rights proceeding; grandmother moved frequently, did not maintain a stable residence, had a small residence, and her visits with the children were chaotic, and aunt had four children, allowed her oldest son to live with her mother, earned approximately $25,000 per year as a bus driver, lived in a three-bedroom house, and her husband was unable to work due to a seizure disorder. In re Hilyard (Ohio App. 4 Dist., Vinton, 04-13-2006) No. 05CA600, No. 05CA603, No. 05CA607, No. 05CA601, No. 05CA604, No. 05CA608, No. 05CA602, No. 05CA606, No. 05CA609, 2006-Ohio-1965, 2006 WL Infants ⇐ 222

Relatives who were named by mother as alternatives for placement of children during parental rights termination proceeding were not suitable options for placement, and thus, trial court was under no obligation to grant mother's request; first individual was only marginally interested in obtaining custody of the boys, and stated that she did not want to disrupt their current placement if it would cause stress to the boys, and second individual had criminal history and health problems. In re Bowers (Ohio App. 7 Dist., Mahoning, 08-18-2005) No. 04 MA 216, 2005-Ohio-4376, 2005 WL 2033100, Unreported. Infants ⇐ 222

Parents who voluntarily relinquished custody of their child to custodian without intervention of any state agency were not entitled to reunification plan. In re Bailey (Ohio App. 1 Dist., Hamilton, 06-17-2005) No. C-040014, No. C-040479, 2005-Ohio-3039, 2005 WL 1413269, Unreported. Infants ⇐ 155

County Children Services made reasonable attempts toward reunification with mother, as prerequisite to termination of mother's parental rights, despite unilateral suspension of visitation by county without seeking statutory amendment to case plan; county was authorized by court order to modify visitation as necessary, temporary suspension of visitation was necessary to allow mother time to recover from contagious illness, reinstatement of visitation was contingent on mother providing letter from physician that she was no longer contagious, county provided mother with medicine to treat illness, which mother refused to take, and county provided mother with substantial assistance, including financial support, referrals for drug and mental health counseling, and other assistance. In re Townsend (Ohio App. 4 Dist., Athens, 05-09-2005) No. 04CA46, 2005-Ohio-2473, 2005 WL 1190706, Unreported. Infants ⇔ 155

Case plan adopted by court in context of dependency proceedings for child that did not specifically include father was not reversible error; case plan for child was "pretty much same case plan" as in dependency and abuse cases involving siblings, and father was included in those case plans. In re Hortsmann (Ohio App. 5 Dist., Tuscarawas, 04-29-2005) No. 2005AP020016, 2005-Ohio-2168, 2005 WL 1038856, Unreported. Infants ⇔ 253

Evidence in termination of parental rights proceeding supported juvenile court's finding that granting the Department of Job and Family Services (DJFS) permanent custody of parent's two minor children, instead of granting father's parents legal custody of the children, served the children's best interests; father's parents had previously returned the children to the DJFS, stating that they could not deal with the children's mother. In re Keaton (Ohio App. 4 Dist., Ross, 11-19-2004) No. 04CA2785, No. 04CA2788, 2004-Ohio-6210, 2004 WL 2650249, Unreported. Infants ⇔ 222

Clear and convincing evidence supported trial court's determination that it was in infant child's best interest to be permanently placed in custody of Department of Job and Family Services (DJFS), and that child should not be placed with either of his parents; child, like his older sister, tested positive for cocaine at birth, father's identity was unknown, mother suffered from apparent drug addiction and abandoned court-ordered drug rehabilitation, mother violated her probation several times, and child, in the meantime, had established a bond with his foster parents, who not only enjoyed custody of child's older sister, but were in the process of adopting her, with plans to adopt child thereafter. In re M.C. (Ohio App. 12 Dist., Madison, 09-07-2004) No. CA2004-04-008, 2004-Ohio-4782, 2004 WL 2003714, Unreported. Infants ⇔ 155; Infants ⇔ 156

Mother challenging grant of permanent custody of children to county agency failed to establish that agency failed to make reasonable efforts to return children to mother's custody; mother failed to cite authority supporting her claim that agency had duty to provide public housing, mother's admitted marijuana use disqualified mother from public housing, agency was not entity responsible for determining participation in public housing, and mother bore ultimate responsibility for insuring that she satisfied requirements for eligibility. In re K. (Ohio App. 8 Dist., Cuyahoga, 09-02-2004) No. 83410, 2004-Ohio-4629, 2004 WL 1946141, Unreported. Infants ⇔ 155; Infants ⇔ 241

Order denying motion for change of custody of dependent child from family services agency to child's maternal grandmother when mother's parental rights were terminated was not abuse of discretion; grandmother had history of sexual abuse and domestic violence, grandmother was not employed and moved constantly, and grandmother had long history of involvement with Department of Job and Family Services. In re Cohoon (Ohio App. 5 Dist., Stark, 08-17-2004) No. 2004CA00072, 2004-Ohio-4430, 2004 WL 1879672, Unreported. Infants ⇔ 230.1

Blood relative of mother's adoptive parent was not an appropriate placement for child in termination of parental rights action; relative's husband had criminal conviction, there was no available space for child in relative's home, relative testified that she would encourage contact between mother, who had substance abuse problem, and the child, and guardian ad litem expressed concern because she believed it was not safe for mother to have access to the child. In re Gaugler (Ohio App. 5 Dist., Stark, 08-02-2004) No. 2004-CA-00114, 2004-Ohio-4114, 2004 WL 1753368, Unreported. Infants ⇔ 222

Evidence in termination of parental rights proceeding supported finding that Geauga County Job and Family Services (GCJFS) used reasonable case planning and diligent efforts to assist parents to remedy problems that caused dependent children to be placed outside their home; case plan, which included counseling, chemical dependency assessments, and employment program, was designed to remedy parents' domestic violence, drug use, and unstable home. In re Ross (Ohio App. 11 Dist., Geauga, 07-09-2004) No. 2003-G-2549, 2004-Ohio-3689, 2004 WL 1559781, Unreported, appeal not allowed 103 Ohio St.3d 1429, 814 N.E.2d 491, 2004-Ohio-4524. Infants ⇔ 155

Finding that mother demonstrated lack of commitment to dependent children by failing to work toward completion of case plan was not abuse of discretion in termination of parental rights proceeding, where mother failed to receive counseling, to complete chemical dependency assessment, and to have stable home, and fact that mother loved and visited children did not preclude finding that mother demonstrated lack of commitment to case plan. In re Ross (Ohio App. 11 Dist., Geauga, 07-07-2004) No. 2003-G-2551, 2004-Ohio-3684, 2004 WL 1559742, Unreported. Infants ⇔ 155

Trial court's failure to grant custody of child to maternal grandmother was not an abuse of discretion, in child dependency proceeding; physician who conducted a psychological evaluation of grandmother testified that grandmother was not appropriate for custody or placement due to mental health concerns, he recommended that grandmother receive psychiatric/psychotherapy treatment, and he diagnosed grandmother with psycho-agitation. In re Lisbon (Ohio App. 5 Dist., Stark, 01-12-2004) No. 2003CA00318, 2004-Ohio-126, 2004 WL 67256, Unreported. Infants ⇔ 222

Evidence supported trial court's placement of child in the permanent custody of County Job & Family Services, rather than placement with grandmother; grandmother could not alter her environment in a permanent manner to allow child to flourish, although grandmother made diligent efforts to follow all recommendations of her case plan, she was unable to apply that knowledge in a practical manner, and grandmother's history demonstrated her inability to protect minor children from inappropriate individuals. Swisher v. Tuscarawas County Job & Family Services (Ohio App. 5 Dist., Tuscarawas, 12-05-2003) No. 2003AP080060, No. 2003AP080066, 2003-Ohio-7317, 2003 WL 23269346, Unreported, appeal not allowed 101 Ohio St.3d 1453, 803 N.E.2d 401, 2004-Ohio-462. Infants ⇔ 222

In proceedings to terminate father's parental rights, trial court did not abuse its discretion in denying father's motion for change of legal custody to children's grandmother; trial court stated children's need for permanency and its concerns relative to achieving that goal if children services agency did not receive permanent custody. In re Cunningham Children (Ohio App. 5 Dist., Stark, 05-27-2003) No. 2003CA00054, 2003-Ohio-2805, 2003 WL 21260017, Unreported. Infants ⇔ 222

Placement of mother's six children in permanent custody of county children's services board was in best interest of children; mother failed to comply with case plan requiring her to obtain high school graduation equivalent degree (GED), to secure stable employment, and to complete budgeting classes, children suffered numerous psychological and learning disabilities and required security and structure, and mother refused to acknowledge problems with herself or her family that contributed to necessity to remove children from home. In re Adams (Ohio App. 2 Dist., Miami, 02-07-2003) No. 2002 CA 45, 2003-Ohio-618, 2003 WL 264357, Unreported. Infants ⇔ 155

Clear and convincing evidence supported determination that child could not be placed with father within reasonable time, for purposes of award of permanent custody to county children services board; record showed father failed to complete programs for substance abuse and domestic violence, and that he did not secure permanent housing, but continued to reside in the homes of various women. In re S.S. (Ohio App. 2 Dist., Montgomery, 01-24-2003) No. 19406, 2003-Ohio-319, 2003 WL 164598, Unreported. Infants ⇔ 178

Sufficient evidence supported finding that county children services board made reasonable attempt to reunify father and child; record indicated that board assisted father to meet goals of his case plan, and that board investigated possibility of placement with other relatives, but no evidence was presented to indicate that any relative wanted to, or could, assume custody of child. In re S.S. (Ohio App. 2 Dist., Montgomery, 01-24-2003) No. 19406, 2003-Ohio-319, 2003 WL 164598, Unreported. Infants ⇔ 178

As between home schooling or public school multi-handicapped special education programs, public schooling would better meet the special needs of children who are both physically and mentally handicapped where a home setting would lack (1) access to speech therapists as well as occupational and physical therapists and adaptive physical education instructors, (2) the opportunity to interact with peers and observe age appropriate activities and behaviors, and (3) the opportunity to set children on a course of competition with their handicapped peers which can instill in them a motivation toward better performance and greater achievement that will ultimately work to their benefit. In Matter of Carroll (Ohio App. 2 Dist., Greene, 09-20-1996) No. 95-CA-62, 1996 WL 535302, Unreported, dismissed, appeal not allowed 77 Ohio St.3d 1543, 674 N.E.2d 1183.

The admission or exclusion of relevant evidence is left to the sound discretion of the trial court. In re Brown (Ohio App. 12 Dist., 04-02-2001) 142 Ohio App.3d 193, 755 N.E.2d 365. Trial ⇔ 43

Juvenile court properly considered failure of mother's husband to comply with case plan as factor in determining whether to grant permanent custody of children adjudicated neglected to agency, despite fact that husband did not contest termination of his parental rights, where mother's husband resided with mother and had been responsible for abuse leading to neglect adjudication, and mother refused to admit that injuries to children were anything other than accidental or that her husband still had anger control problems. In re Nice (Ohio App. 7 Dist., 03-20-2001) 141 Ohio App.3d 445, 751 N.E.2d 552, 2001-Ohio-3214. Infants ☞ 179

A board of county commissioners and a county human services department do not act with malice, wantonness, or willfulness in possibly underfunding and understaffing an agency charged with protecting children's welfare and in returning a child to her father's care following her removal from his care due to neglect, and the child dies from repeated beatings inflicted by the father, as the agency was unaware of any physical danger to the child or the father's violent propensity prior to the child's death. Jackson v. Butler Cty. Bd. of Cty. Commrs. (Butler 1991) 76 Ohio App.3d 448, 602 N.E.2d 363, motion overruled 63 Ohio St.3d 1463, 590 N.E.2d 757.

A journal entry of a jury verdict finding a child's stepfather guilty of endangering children pursuant to RC 2919.22 is admissible in an action to place temporary custody and care of the child with a county department of human services. In re Boyce (Medina 1987) 37 Ohio App.3d 105, 523 N.E.2d 900.

A comprehensive reunification plan must include "regular and frequent visitation and communication or other contact between the parents and child" under normal circumstances; however, a juvenile court may in its discretion deny visitation where the testimony of therapists and psychologists and the child's own wishes justify such denial. In re Jones (Cuyahoga 1985) 29 Ohio App.3d 176, 504 N.E.2d 719, 29 O.B.R. 206.

3. Reunification plan required

County Children Services made reasonable efforts to reunify child with mother and father prior to termination of parental rights; parents were provided with visitation, parenting instruction, financial assistance, and case management. In re West (Ohio App. 4 Dist., Athens, 06-10-2005) No. 05CA6, 2005-Ohio-2978, 2005 WL 1400031, Unreported. Infants ☞ 155

Evidence supported finding that the county department of children and family services made reasonable efforts to reunify mother and her children, in child dependency proceeding; the department made referrals for parenting education classes, domestic violence counseling, mental health counseling, and drug and alcohol assessments, mother failed to utilize the mental health services, she failed to regularly support, visit, or communicate with the children, and mother failed to maintain stable housing. In re La.B. (Ohio App. 8 Dist., Cuyahoga, 12-18-2003) No. 81981, 2003-Ohio-6852, 2003 WL 22966171, Unreported, stay denied 101 Ohio St.3d 1453, 803 N.E.2d 401, 2004-Ohio-462, cause dismissed 101 Ohio St.3d 1458, 803 N.E.2d 830, 2004-Ohio-703, reconsideration granted 101 Ohio St.3d 1482, 805 N.E.2d 534, 2004-Ohio-1398, appeal not allowed 102 Ohio St.3d 1445, 808 N.E.2d 397, 2004-Ohio-2263. Infants ☞ 178

Mother's failure to remedy problem that initially caused her children to be placed outside the home, i.e., on two occasions when she was out of town she left children with friend who may have abused them, was not established by clear and convincing evidence, as element for terminating her parental rights; case plan offered aspirational goal that mother would learn to protect her children from all harm and would not expose them to offenders who had hurt them in the past, action plan for meeting the goal was parenting classes, mother completed parenting classes, but practical test of mother's skill never occurred because children were not returned to her custody after she completed parenting classes. In re Alexis K. (Ohio App. 6 Dist., 03-24-2005) 160 Ohio App.3d 32, 825 N.E.2d 1148, 2005-Ohio-1380. Infants ☞ 155

The adoption and journalization of a case plan by the trial court is mandatory in a case where a children services agency is granted temporary custody. In re Brown (Ohio App. 12 Dist., 04-02-2001) 142 Ohio App.3d 193, 755 N.E.2d 365. Infants ☞ 210

There was no plain error in trial court's requiring mother to attend counseling classes within state, as part of plan to reunify her with her children, despite fact that mother currently resided in another bordering state; crossing state line to nearby community for counseling was not shown to be hardship or matter beyond authority of lower court to require. In re Pieper Children (Preble 1993) 85 Ohio App.3d 318, 619 N.E.2d 1059. Infants ☞ 243

Whenever a dependent child is placed temporarily with someone other than a parent, a reunification plan should be developed; further, when a child is placed with a relative pursuant to RC 2151.353(A)(2), a reunification plan, though not required by RC 2151.412, should be prepared by the court or a court-appointed agency. In re Patterson (Madison 1984) 16 Ohio App.3d 214, 475 N.E.2d 160, 16 O.B.R. 229.

Where a non-custodial parent has maintained a continuing interest in his child's welfare, RC 2151.412(C) places a mandatory burden on a social welfare agency that is seeking permanent custody of the child for adoptive placement to prepare a comprehensive reunification plan for that parent. In re Ball (Lucas 1982) 5 Ohio App.3d 56, 449 N.E.2d 490, 5 O.B.R. 152.

Trial court erred by ordering continued temporary custody to children services agency without requiring that agency file and maintain a new case plan that included reunification with mother as a goal. In re Ware (Ohio App. 2 Dist., Montgomery, 09-06-2002) No. 19302, 2002-Ohio-4686, 2002 WL 31002612, Unreported, opinion modified on reconsideration 2002-Ohio-6086, 2002 WL 31492584. Infants ☞ 222

Where children's services does not submit a comprehensive reunification plan within sixty days as required by RC 2151.412(C) but a parent fails to appear at a dispositional hearing and at its continuance does not object to the plan, and there is no showing of prejudice based on a later submission of the plan, there is no error in an award of permanent custody to the agency. In re Wolbaugh, No. 3–87–7 (3d Dist Ct App, Crawford, 10–31–88).

A comprehensive reunification plan need be prepared only when a child is committed to the temporary custody of the department of public welfare under RC 2151.353(A)(2) or RC 2151.353(A)(3); this is the plain meaning of RC 2151.412(C), which does not, it follows, require preparation of a plan when a temporary custody order is based on Juv R 13(A) and Juv R 13(D). In re Koballa, Nos. 48417 and 48480 (8th Dist Ct App, Cuyahoga, 1–24–85).

4. Reunification plan not required

Trial court was not required to include a case plan in its dispositional order, in child dependency proceeding; paternal grandmother filed a complaint that alleged child was a dependent child, and a children services agency did not file a complaint and did not provide services to child. In re Brown (Ohio App. 2 Dist., Darke, 06-23-2006) No. 1676, 2006-Ohio-3189, 2006 WL 1719277, Unreported. Infants ☞ 222

In termination of parental rights proceeding, juvenile court was not required to consider placing parent's two minor children with father's parents before granting the Department of Job and Family Services (DJFS) permanent custody of the children. In re Keaton (Ohio App. 4 Dist., Ross, 11-19-2004) No. 04CA2785, No. 04CA2788, 2004-Ohio-6210, 2004 WL 2650249, Unreported. Infants ☞ 222

Department of Job and Family Services (DJFS) made reasonable efforts to reunify father's two minor children with him prior to seeking permanent custody of the children; DJFS developed a case plan that included the father, it attempted to locate him and to communicate with him, but father failed to communicate with the DJFS regarding the case plan. In re Keaton (Ohio App. 4 Dist., Ross, 11-19-2004) No. 04CA2785, No. 04CA2788, 2004-Ohio-6210, 2004 WL 2650249, Unreported. Infants ☞ 155

Trial court was under no obligation to file and implement a reunification plan prior to entering final judgment terminating mother's parental rights and awarding Department of Job and Family Services (DJFS) permanent custody of mother's infant child who, like his older sister, had tested positive for cocaine at birth, since any reunification plan would have been futile, as demonstrated by mother's continued drug abuse, abandonment of drug rehabilitation, and several probation violations. In re M.C. (Ohio App. 12 Dist., Madison, 09-07-2004) No. CA2004-04-008, 2004-Ohio-4782, 2004 WL 2003714, Unreported. Infants ☞ 155

Child's best interests were served by juvenile court's terminating father's parental rights and awarding permanent custody to Children Services Board; father had been incarcerated since child was born, child and father had never met, and father's own testimony was that he would not be prepared to provide a home for child for approximately five years due to his incarceration. In re T.K. (Ohio App. 9 Dist., Wayne, 05-21-2003) No. 03CA0006, 2003-Ohio-2634, 2003 WL 21185949, Unreported. Infants ☞ 157

Case plan statute requiring an abused, neglected, or dependent child to be placed in the legal custody of a suitable member of the child's extended family, as well as statute giving preference for placement with family members, did not apply to require placement of child with his maternal grandmother, where grandmother chose not to be considered for permanent custody of the child when approached for same by the county department of job and family services. In re Hoffman (Ohio App. 5 Dist.,

Stark, 03-03-2003) No. 2002CA0419, No. 2002CA0422, 2003-Ohio-1241, 2003 WL 1193770, Unreported. Infants ⇐ 222

Trial court was not required to maintain or establish a reunification plan for a mother to regain custody of her six-year-old son, where the county was no longer involved in the matter and was no longer providing any services to mother, no other private entity was providing services, and mother did not challenge court's order dismissing the county's involvement. In re Timberlake (Ohio App. 10 Dist., Franklin, 03-13-2003) No. 02AP-792, 2003-Ohio-1183, 2003 WL 1094078, Unreported. Infants ⇐ 231

Mother failed to establish that the county job and family services agency failed to offer mother services designed to reunify her and the children; when the agency initially took custody, mother refused to cooperate with the agency in developing a caseplan, later mother fled out of state and her whereabouts were unknown or she was incarcerated, and, when mother was told how to arrange for visitation with the children, she failed to do so. In re Billingsley (Ohio App. 3 Dist., Putnam, 01-28-2003) No. 12-02-07, No. 12-02-08, 2003-Ohio-344, 2003 WL 178661, Unreported. Infants ⇐ 155

Evidence was sufficient to support finding that county made reasonable efforts to reunify mother with her three children prior to termination of her parental rights; county designed a case plan for parents to follow, made referrals for parents to engage in parenting class, assisted parents in engaging in development of living skills program, and while mother tried to comply reunification requirements, being intellectually challenged with an overall IQ of 55, mother required assistance of a co-parent, father was ordered to complete a substance abuse program, yet failed to do so, and failed every one of his urine screens, and while mother had also asked court to consider her brother as a co-parent, brother falsified his answers to a substance abuse evaluation by stating that there was no history of family alcohol abuse and he had never thought of suicide, and brother needed to address anger management and anxiety issues before being able to parent. In re Moore (Ohio App. 12 Dist., Butler, 01-06-2003) No. CA2002-03-065, No. CA2002-04-076, 2003-Ohio-9, 2003 WL 40746, Unreported. Infants ⇐ 155

County children services agency was not required to attempt reunification of child with birth parents in proceeding in which it sought original permanent custody of child. In re Baby Girl Doe (Ohio App. 6 Dist., 08-30-2002) 149 Ohio App.3d 717, 778 N.E.2d 1053, 2002-Ohio-4470, appeal not allowed 97 Ohio St.3d 1425, 777 N.E.2d 278, 2002-Ohio-5820. Infants ⇐ 155

County children services agency was not required to attempt reunification of child with birth parents in proceeding in which it sought original permanent custody of child. In re Baby Girl Doe (Ohio App. 6 Dist., 08-30-2002) 149 Ohio App.3d 717, 778 N.E.2d 1053, 2002-Ohio-4470, appeal not allowed 97 Ohio St.3d 1425, 777 N.E.2d 278, 2002-Ohio-5820. Infants ⇐ 155

Statute setting forth guidelines for county agency's development and court's review of case plans for dependent children did not require trial court to consider placing legal custody of children with one of father's relatives in rendering its decision to place children in permanent custody of county agency. In re Hiatt (Adams 1993) 86 Ohio App.3d 716, 621 N.E.2d 1222. Infants ⇐ 222

Where parents voluntarily enter a temporary custody arrangement with a children services agency and the agency's original request was for permanent custody, the requirements for initial and comprehensive reunification plans under RC 2151.412 are not applicable. In re Pachin (Montgomery 1988) 50 Ohio App.3d 44, 552 N.E.2d 655, cause dismissed 39 Ohio St.3d 720, 534 N.E.2d 350.

There is no need to implement a comprehensive reunification plan where the circumstances are such that to do so would be futile. Elmer v. Lucas County Children Services Bd. (Lucas 1987) 36 Ohio App.3d 241, 523 N.E.2d 540.

Where an allegedly neglected, dependent, or abused child is committed to the temporary, emergency custody of a children services board after a shelter care hearing under Juv R 7, the court need not order a reunification plan where it has not finally adjudged and disposed of the matter under RC 2151.353. In re Moloney (Ohio 1986) 24 Ohio St.3d 22, 492 N.E.2d 805, 24 O.B.R. 18.

Neither a parents' voluntary surrender of a child to the custody of a children's services institute nor an appellate stay maintaining such custody constitutes a temporary commitment that invokes the requirement of a comprehensive unification plan. In re Smart (Franklin 1984) 21 Ohio App.3d 31, 486 N.E.2d 147, 21 O.B.R. 33.

RC 2151.412 does not require a juvenile court to order a reunification plan when it grants permanent custody of a child to a welfare department pursuant to RC 2151.353(A)(4). In re Baby Girl Baxter (Ohio 1985) 17 Ohio St.3d 229, 479 N.E.2d 257, 17 O.B.R. 469.

The comprehensive reunification plan required by 1980 H 695, § 3, eff. 10–24–80, to be included in the second annual review made of a child who is in temporary custody upon the effective date of the act, is not required when the board files a motion for permanent custody of a child before the occurrence of the second annual review. In re Smith (Greene 1982) 7 Ohio App.3d 75, 454 N.E.2d 171, 7 O.B.R. 88.

Where the trial court determines that it is in the best interest of a minor child to terminate parental rights permanently, the trial court may grant permanent custody to a county children services board without first granting temporary custody. In re Hollins, No. CA–703 (5th Dist Ct App, Guernsey, 3–29–83).

5. Procedural issues

Trial court was not required to exhaust every possible option for placing mother's twin boys with a family member prior to choosing some other option, namely, permanent placement with County Children Services Board (MCCSB). In re Bowers (Ohio App. 7 Dist., Mahoning, 08-18-2005) No. 04 MA 216, 2005-Ohio-4376, 2005 WL 2033100, Unreported. Infants ⇐ 222

County Children Services' unilateral suspension of mother's telephone visitation with children in order to force compliance with mandatory drug screens without having followed statutory procedures for amending case plan did not warrant reversal of order terminating mother's parental rights, in view of trial court's findings that county made substantial efforts to prevent continued removal of children from mother's home, and that mother failed to comply with case plan. In re Townsend (Ohio App. 4 Dist., Athens, 05-09-2005) No. 04CA46, 2005-Ohio-2473, 2005 WL 1190706, Unreported. Infants ⇐ 253

County's failure to timely file case plan, as required by statute, did not render its efforts to reunify family unreasonable, in child dependency proceeding, as father had not demonstrated any prejudicial effect by county's late filing of plan. In re Miller (Ohio App. 5 Dist., Licking, 02-24-2005) No. 04 CA 32, 2005-Ohio-856, 2005 WL 469260, Unreported. Infants ⇐ 155

Father waived on appeal issue of whether trial court had erred in determining that county had made reasonable efforts to reunify family, given county's failure to timely file copy of case plan, as required by statute, as father failed to raise issue at trial court level in child dependency proceeding. In re Miller (Ohio App. 5 Dist., Licking, 02-24-2005) No. 04 CA 32, 2005-Ohio-856, 2005 WL 469260, Unreported. Infants ⇐ 243

Statutory language indicating a preference for awarding custody of a child who has been removed from his or her biological parents to a relative before a non-relative is precatory, not mandatory. In re Halstead (Ohio App. 7 Dist., Columbiana, 01-27-2005) No. 04 CO 37, 2005-Ohio-403, 2005 WL 289576, Unreported. Infants ⇐ 222

Factor, applicable when parent has placed child at substantial risk of harm two or more times due to alcohol or drug abuse and has rejected treatment two or more times or refused to participate in further treatment two or more times after a case plan, was inapplicable to mother challenging determination that grant of permanent custody of child to county agency was in best interests of child, although mother's case plan required her to be assessed for drug use, where there was no recommendation for treatment and no dispositional order requiring treatment. In re K. (Ohio App. 8 Dist., Cuyahoga, 09-02-2004) No. 83410, 2004-Ohio-4629, 2004 WL 1946141, Unreported. Infants ⇐ 155

Failing to grant mother extension of time to complete reunification process with dependent children was not abuse of discretion in termination of parental rights proceeding, where evidence showed pattern of neglect by mother which resulted from her drug use and inability to maintain stable employment. In re Ross (Ohio App. 11 Dist., Geauga, 07-09-2004) No. 2003-G-2549, 2004-Ohio-3689, 2004 WL 1559781, Unreported, appeal not allowed 103 Ohio St.3d 1429, 814 N.E.2d 491, 2004-Ohio-4524. Infants ⇐ 230.1

Agency is not required to file an adoption plan before permanent custody is granted. In re McCann (Ohio App. 12 Dist., Clermont, 01-26-2004) No. CA2003-02-017, 2004-Ohio-283, 2004 WL 111644, Unreported. Infants ⇐ 226

Mother in dependency proceedings failed to show she was prejudiced by failure of county children services to file case plan prior to adjudicatory hearing; there was no evidence to demonstrate lack of action on behalf of county children services, any lack of action on behalf of county children services was not the result of any error by magistrate or trial court, and trial counsel's failure to raise issue with regard to such failure may have

Note 5

been result of strategy to avoid further delays. In re Malone (Ohio App. 10 Dist., Franklin, 12-30-2003) No. 03AP-489, 2003-Ohio-7156, 2003 WL 23024377, Unreported, appeal not allowed 102 Ohio St.3d 1423, 807 N.E.2d 367, 2004-Ohio-2003. Infants ⚖ 191

Statute establishing priorities to guide children services agency's development of case plan does not require trial court to act in a specific manner, but rather suggests criteria to be considered in making its decision regarding case plan goals. In re Cunningham Children (Ohio App. 5 Dist., Stark, 05-27-2003) No. 2003CA00054, 2003-Ohio-2805, 2003 WL 21260017, Unreported. Infants ⚖ 155

Hearing on mother's motion to dismiss/rehear termination of parental rights case due to conflict between children's desire to reunify and guardian ad litem's (GAL's) recommendation against reunification was deficient, warranting remand for proper hearing on issue, where court failed to make inquiries to determine whether actual conflict existed, considering children's maturity and ability to understand proceeding. In re Emery (Ohio App. 4 Dist., Lawrence, 04-25-2003) No. 02CA40, 2003-Ohio-2206, 2003 WL 2003811, Unreported. Infants ⚖ 202; Infants ⚖ 211; Infants ⚖ 254

Trial court lacked authority to place children in a Planned Permanent Living Arrangement (PPLA) as an alternative to terminating father's parental rights; there was no evidence to suggest that father or county department of children and family services sought a PPLA, and there was no evidence presented to establish any of the other statutory requirements necessary for court to place children in a PPLA. (Per O'Donnell, J., with two judges concurring in judgment only). In re Harlston (Ohio App. 8 Dist., Cuyahoga, 01-23-2003) No. 80672, 2003-Ohio-282, 2003 WL 152939, Unreported, appeal not allowed 98 Ohio St.3d 1492, 785 N.E.2d 474, 2003-Ohio-1189. Infants ⚖ 226

Errors which arise during the course of proceedings are waived unless brought to the attention of the trial court at a time when they can be remedied. In re Brown (Ohio App. 12 Dist., 04-02-2001) 142 Ohio App.3d 193, 755 N.E.2d 365. Appeal And Error ⚖ 230

The trial court's error in failing to journalize mother's case plan after her dependency case was transferred from another county was harmless, in child dependency and custody proceeding; case plan created by previous county was followed when case was transferred to a new county, and the case plan was attached to the predispositional summary provided to the trial court. In re Brown (Ohio App. 12 Dist., 04-02-2001) 142 Ohio App.3d 193, 755 N.E.2d 365. Infants ⚖ 253

Mother was given adequate time to comply with second case plan, developed following extension of temporary custody of children with agency and approved by the court one month prior to hearing on agency's motion for permanent custody, where such plan was substantially identical to plan originally developed upon removal of children from her custody two years previously and neither mother nor mother's husband took any steps to comply with original plan until after agency filed its motion for permanent custody. In re Nice (Ohio App. 7 Dist., 03-20-2001) 141 Ohio App.3d 445, 751 N.E.2d 552, 2001-Ohio-3214. Infants ⚖ 155

Statute allowing court to proceed in contempt for violation of a journalized case plan specifically applied only to parties involved in cases of abuse, neglect or dependency, temporary or permanent custody, protective supervision, or long-term foster care, and did not authorize juvenile court to proceed in contempt against juvenile previously adjudicated delinquent for alleged failure to complete court-ordered treatment program. In re Nowak (Ohio App. 11 Dist., 04-26-1999) 133 Ohio App.3d 396, 728 N.E.2d 411. Infants ⚖ 191

Mother's challenge to location of counseling classes that she would be required to attend as part of plan to reunify her with her children was waived by her failure to object to alleged error in trial court. In re Pieper Children (Preble 1993) 85 Ohio App.3d 318, 619 N.E.2d 1059. Infants ⚖ 243

RC 2151.412 and RC 2151.414 do not apply where a request for permanent custody is made by a welfare department and a temporary custody order is issued under RC 2151.33 pending a hearing on the request. In re Covert (Seneca 1984) 17 Ohio App.3d 122, 477 N.E.2d 678, 17 O.B.R. 185.

Although 42 USC 627(b)(3) provides that the amount of federal tax money granted to states for child welfare programs will be reduced unless the state has a "replacement preventive service program," the statute is a mere funding provision and creates no federal "right" to such a reunification program. Lesher v. Lavrich (N.D.Ohio 1984) 632 F.Supp. 77, affirmed 784 F.2d 193.

Mother was not prejudiced by children services agency's failure to file a case plan when it refiled a complaint for permanent custody and failure to serve mother with such plan, where mother obtained a copy of plan prior to hearing. In re Ware (Ohio App. 2 Dist., Montgomery, 09-06-2002) No. 19302, 2002-Ohio-4686, 2002 WL 31002612, Unreported, opinion modified on reconsideration 2002-Ohio-6086, 2002 WL 31492584. Infants ⚖ 253

Where an initial plan is instituted after children's services is awarded emergency temporary custody, the child is later found neglected, and after a dispositional hearing, awarding temporary custody to children's services, the court's journal entry awarding custody summarizes the requirements under the plan but does not specifically state them as such, there is substantial compliance with RC 2151.412(A). In re Wolbaugh, No. 3–87–7 (3d Dist Ct App, Crawford, 10–31–88).

RC 2151.412(C) requires a court to provide a copy of the reunification plan to all parties and give them seven days to object before the court may approve the plan. In re Becker, No. 3301 (11th Dist Ct App, Trumbull, 3–9–84).

Where the court filed an initial plan the day after entry of its amended decree and stated that it was amending the decree to incorporate the plan, the requirements of RC 2151.412(A) were met. In re Becker, No. 3301 (11th Dist Ct App, Trumbull, 3–9–84).

If a juvenile court, in making disposition of an unruly or delinquent child pursuant to RC 2151.354 or RC 2151.355, places the child into the temporary custody of the county department of human services in accordance with RC 2151.353 and the department provides services to that child, the county department of human services is required to develop and file with the court a case plan pursuant to RC 2151.412 and to hold semiannual reviews of the case plan pursuant to RC 2151.416. OAG 99–041.

2151.413 Motion for permanent custody

(A) A public children services agency or private child placing agency that, pursuant to an order of disposition under division (A)(2) of section 2151.353 of the Revised Code or under any version of section 2151.353 of the Revised Code that existed prior to January 1, 1989, is granted temporary custody of a child who is not abandoned or orphaned may file a motion in the court that made the disposition of the child requesting permanent custody of the child.

(B) A public children services agency or private child placing agency that, pursuant to an order of disposition under division (A)(2) of section 2151.353 of the Revised Code or under any version of section 2151.353 of the Revised Code that existed prior to January 1, 1989, is granted temporary custody of a child who is orphaned may file a motion in the court that made the disposition of the child requesting permanent custody of the child whenever it can show that no relative of the child is able to take legal custody of the child.

(C) A public children services agency or private child placing agency that, pursuant to an order of disposition under division (A)(5) of section 2151.353 of the Revised Code, places a child in a planned permanent living arrangement may file a motion in the court that made the disposition of the child requesting permanent custody of the child.

(D)(1) Except as provided in division (D)(3) of this section, if a child has been in the temporary custody of one or more public children services agencies or private child placing agencies for twelve or more months of a consecutive twenty-two month period ending on or after March 18, 1999, the agency with custody shall file a motion requesting permanent custody of the child. The motion shall be filed in the court that issued the current order of temporary custody. For the purposes of this division, a child shall be considered to have entered the temporary custody of an agency on the earlier of the date the child is adjudicated pursuant to section 2151.28 of the Revised Code or the date that is sixty days after the removal of the child from home.

(2) Except as provided in division (D)(3) of this section, if a court makes a determination pursuant to division (A)(2) of section 2151.419 of the Revised Code, the public children services agency or private child placing agency required to develop the permanency plan for the child under division (K) of section 2151.417 of the Revised Code shall file a motion in the court that

made the determination requesting permanent custody of the child.

(3) An agency shall not file a motion for permanent custody under division (D)(1) or (2) of this section if any of the following apply:

(a) The agency documents in the case plan or permanency plan a compelling reason that permanent custody is not in the best interest of the child.

(b) If reasonable efforts to return the child to the child's home are required under section 2151.419 of the Revised Code, the agency has not provided the services required by the case plan to the parents of the child or the child to ensure the safe return of the child to the child's home.

(c) The agency has been granted permanent custody of the child.

(d) The child has been returned home pursuant to court order in accordance with division (A)(3) of section 2151.419 of the Revised Code.

(E) Any agency that files a motion for permanent custody under this section shall include in the case plan of the child who is the subject of the motion, a specific plan of the agency's actions to seek an adoptive family for the child and to prepare the child for adoption.

(F) The department of job and family services may adopt rules pursuant to Chapter 119. of the Revised Code that set forth the time frames for case reviews and for filing a motion requesting permanent custody under division (D)(1) of this section.

(1999 H 471, eff. 7–1–00; 1999 H 176, eff. 10–29–99; 1998 H 484, eff. 3–18–99; 1996 H 419, eff. 9–18–96; 1988 S 89, eff. 1–1–89; 1980 H 695)

Historical and Statutory Notes

Amendment Note: 1999 H 471 substituted "job and family" for "human" in division (F).

Amendment Note: 1999 H 176 rewrote division (D)(1); and made other nonsubstantive changes. Prior to amendment, division (D)(1) read:

"(D)(1) Except as provided in division (D)(3) of this section, if a child has been in temporary custody for twelve or more months of a consecutive twenty-two month period ending on or after the effective date of this amendment pursuant to an order of disposition that was issued under division (A)(2) of section 2151.353 of the Revised Code or pursuant to an order that extends temporary custody and was issued prior to the effective date of this amendment under division (D) of section 2151.415 of the Revised Code, the public children services agency or private child placing agency with custody shall file a motion requesting permanent custody of the child. The motion shall be filed in the court that issued the order of disposition."

Amendment Note: 1998 H 484 rewrote this section, which prior thereto read:

"(A) A public children services agency or private child placing agency that, pursuant to an order of disposition under division (A)(2) of section 2151.353 of the Revised Code or under any version of section 2151.353 of the Revised Code that existed prior to January 1, 1989, is granted temporary custody of a child who is not abandoned or orphaned or of an abandoned child whose parents have been located may file a motion in the court that made the disposition of the child requesting permanent custody of the child.

"(B) A public children services agency or private child placing agency that, pursuant to an order of disposition under division (A)(2) of section 2151.353 of the Revised Code or under any version of section 2151.353 of the Revised Code that existed prior to January 1, 1989, is granted temporary custody of a child who is abandoned or orphaned may file a motion in the court that made the disposition of the child requesting permanent custody of the child, if the child is abandoned, whenever it can show the court that the parents cannot be located and, if the child is orphaned, whenever it can show that no relative of the child is able to take legal custody of the child.

"(C) A public children services agency or private child placing agency that, pursuant to an order of disposition under division (A)(5) of section 2151.353 of the Revised Code, places a child in long-term foster care may file a motion in the court that made the disposition of the child requesting permanent custody of the child.

"(D) Any agency that files a motion for permanent custody under this section shall include in the case plan of the child who is the subject of the motion, a specific plan of the agency's actions to seek an adoptive family for the child and to prepare the child for adoption."

Amendment Note: 1996 H 419 substituted "January 1, 1989" for "the effective date of this amendment" in divisions (A) and (B); deleted "if a period of at least six months has elapsed since the order of temporary custody was issued or the initial filing of the case plan with the court if the child is an abandoned child whose parents have been located" from the end of division (A); added division (C); and redesignated former division (C) as (D).

Ohio Administrative Code References

Extension of "Agreement for Temporary Custody of Child" (JFS 01645), OAC 5101:2–42–07

Obtaining permanent custody: termination of parental rights, OAC 5101:2–42–95

Library References

Infants ⚖17, 155 to 159, 197, 200.

Westlaw Topic No. 211.

C.J.S. Infants §§ 8 to 9, 31, 33 to 55, 62.

Baldwin's Ohio Legislative Service, 1988 Laws of Ohio, S 89—LSC Analysis, p 5–571

Research References

Encyclopedias

OH Jur. 3d Family Law § 1413, Care of Dependent, Neglected, or Delinquent Children.

OH Jur. 3d Family Law § 1602, Prehearing Motions—Motion for Order of Disposition.

OH Jur. 3d Family Law § 1612, Summons for Hearing to Make Temporary Commitment Permanent.

OH Jur. 3d Family Law § 1663, on Request for Permanent Custody—on Motion of Agency.

OH Jur. 3d Family Law § 1693, Permanent Custody.

Forms

Ohio Jurisprudence Pleading and Practice Forms § 96:43, Temporary and Permanent Custody.

Treatises and Practice Aids

Carlin, Baldwin's Ohio Practice, Merrick-Rippner Probate Law § 107:78, Disposition of Abused, Neglected, or Dependent Child—Temporary Custody.

Carlin, Baldwin's Ohio Practice, Merrick-Rippner Probate Law § 107:80, Disposition of Abused, Neglected, or Dependent Child—Permanent Custody.

Carlin, Baldwin's Ohio Practice, Merrick-Rippner Probate Law § 107:83, Motion for Permanent Custody of Abused, Neglected, or Dependent Child.

Giannelli & Yeomans, Ohio Juvenile Law § 1:7, Juvenile Code.

Giannelli & Yeomans, Ohio Juvenile Law § 30:6, Temporary Custody.

Giannelli & Yeomans, Ohio Juvenile Law § 31:1, Introduction.

Giannelli & Yeomans, Ohio Juvenile Law § 31:2, Filing of Motion.

Giannelli & Yeomans, Ohio Juvenile Law § 31:6, Findings.

Giannelli & Yeomans, Ohio Juvenile Law § 16:14, Permanent & Temporary Custody Complaints; Planned Permanent Living Arrangements.

Giannelli & Yeomans, Ohio Juvenile Law § 25:14, Reasonable Efforts Determination; Abuse, Neglect & Dependency.

Notes of Decisions

Constitutional issues 1
Foster care 2
Requirements for permanent custody 4

Time limitation 3

1. Constitutional issues

Failure of counsel for parents to challenge constitutionality of statutes applicable in termination of parental rights proceeding did not constitute ineffective assistance, where courts had previously found statutes to be constitutional and there was no reasonable probability that result of proceeding would have been different had counsel challenged statutes. In re Andy-Jones (Ohio App. 10 Dist., Franklin, 06-24-2004) No. 03AP-1167, No. 03AP-1231, 2004-Ohio-3312, 2004 WL 1405319, Unreported, stay denied 103 Ohio St.3d 1425, 814 N.E.2d 489, 2004-Ohio-4524, appeal not allowed 103 Ohio St.3d 1429, 814 N.E.2d 491, 2004-Ohio-4524, appeal not allowed 103 Ohio St.3d 1465, 815 N.E.2d 680, 2004-Ohio-5056. Infants ⊗ 205

Court of Appeals would decline to address parents' claim that statutes relating to termination of parental rights were unconstitutional, where parents failed in trial court to challenge constitutionality of statutes. In re Andy-Jones (Ohio App. 10 Dist., Franklin, 06-24-2004) No. 03AP-1167, No. 03AP-1231, 2004-Ohio-3312, 2004 WL 1405319, Unreported, stay denied 103 Ohio St.3d 1425, 814 N.E.2d 489, 2004-Ohio-4524, appeal not allowed 103 Ohio St.3d 1429, 814 N.E.2d 491, 2004-Ohio-4524, appeal not allowed 103 Ohio St.3d 1465, 815 N.E.2d 680, 2004-Ohio-5056. Infants ⊗ 243

2. Foster care

Trial court lacked authority to place children in a Planned Permanent Living Arrangement (PPLA) as an alternative to terminating father's parental rights; there was no evidence to suggest that father or county department of children and family services sought a PPLA, and there was no evidence presented to establish any of the other statutory requirements necessary for court to place children in a PPLA. (Per O'Donnell, J., with two judges concurring in judgment only). In re Harlston (Ohio App. 8 Dist., Cuyahoga, 01-23-2003) No. 80672, 2003-Ohio-282, 2003 WL 152939, Unreported, appeal not allowed 98 Ohio St.3d 1492, 785 N.E.2d 474, 2003-Ohio-1189. Infants ⊗ 226

The Adoption and Assistance Welfare Act of 1980, 42 USC 671, does not give its beneficiaries any private right of action enforceable under 42 USC 1983 or create any implied cause of action on their behalf by giving federally collected funds to states for certain foster care and adoption services if they agree that their subdivisions shall make "reasonable efforts" to prevent removal of children from their families and facilitate reunification after children have been removed. Suter v. Artist M. (U.S.Ill. 1992) 112 S.Ct. 1360, 503 U.S. 347, 118 L.Ed.2d 1, on remand 968 F.2d 1218.

A trial court does not err in failing to place a child in long-term foster care under RC 2151.353 pursuant to a county children services agency's RC 2151.413 motion for permanent custody where it grants such permanent custody to the agency; long–term foster care only becomes an alternative, by operation of RC 2151.415, where the motion for permanent custody is denied. In re McDaniel, No. 92–CA–359 (4th Dist Ct App, Adams, 2–11–93).

3. Time limitation

Time that passed between filing of motion for permanent custody and permanent custody hearing could not be counted toward 12 month period of previous 22 months that child must have been in temporary custody of county agency for permanent custody to be granted to agency. In re Arnold (Ohio App. 3 Dist., Allen, 03-28-2005) No. 1-04-71, No. 1-04-72, No. 1-04-73, 2005-Ohio-1418, 2005 WL 696844, Unreported. Infants ⊗ 222

Children's best interest would be served by awarding Job and Family Services (JFS) permanent custody of children; vocational rehabilitation counselor who specifically counseled deaf individuals to help them find employment worked with mother who was deaf, mother lacked skills necessary to provide adequate food and clothing for children, children were often dirty, mother did not discipline children, JFS provided mother with numerous services, and children had been in JFS's temporary custody for twelve or more months of a consecutive twenty-two month period and could not or should not be placed with mother within a reasonable time. In re Berkley (Ohio App. 4 Dist., Pickaway, 09-03-2004) No. 04CA12, No. 04CA13, No. 04CA14, 2004-Ohio-4797, 2004 WL 2009421, Unreported. Infants ⊗ 155; Infants ⊗ 156

A juvenile court errs when it overrules a parent's motion to dismiss an order granting permanent custody to a children services agency when the motion for permanent custody is filed less than six months after granting temporary custody. In re James (Ohio App. 9 Dist., Summit, 07-23-1997) No. 18159, 1997 WL 423039, Unreported.

When juvenile court delays its ruling for more than seven days following the conclusion of dispositional hearing on an agency's motion for permanent child custody filed prior to September 18, 1996, violation of that time constraint serves as justification for seeking a writ of procedendo. In re Davis (Ohio, 03-03-1999) 84 Ohio St.3d 520, 705 N.E.2d 1219, 1999-Ohio-419. Infants ⊗ 204

Parents were estopped from complaining on appeal that they were prejudiced when juvenile court did not rule on agency's petition for permanent custody of children until seventeen months after conclusion of dispositional hearing, where parents failed to seek writ of procedendo after seven-day deadline for issuance of judgment following hearing had passed. In re Davis (Ohio, 03-03-1999) 84 Ohio St.3d 520, 705 N.E.2d 1219, 1999-Ohio-419. Infants ⊗ 232; Infants ⊗ 243

Statutory amendment eliminating requirement that children services agency must have had temporary custody of child for at least six months immediately preceding the filing of motion for permanent custody did not apply to motion for permanent custody of children filed by County Department of Human Services (CDHS) that accrued prior to effective date of amendment. In re Brenna E. (Ohio App. 6 Dist., 11-21-1997) 124 Ohio App.3d 143, 705 N.E.2d 728. Infants ⊗ 132

Child services agency had standing to file second motion for permanent custody of child, even though child had not been in temporary custody of agency for the six months immediately preceding filing of motion, where agency filed first motion at time when child had been in temporary custody well in excess of six months, but agency relinquished temporary custody to relative in attempt for more permanent placement instead of following through with motion, second motion was filed one month after temporary custody was reestablished, child had been in "state of limbo" for nearly four years at that time, child was never returned to custody of mother, and conditions that led to his removal from home had not been remedied. Lorain Cty. Children Serv. v. Keene (Ohio App. 9 Dist., 03-05-1997) 118 Ohio App.3d 535, 693 N.E.2d 833. Infants ⊗ 230.1

Purpose of requirement of six-month delay between granting of temporary emergency custody to children services agency and agency's ability to move for permanent custody was to give parents an adequate opportunity to rectify the problems which initially forced the child into temporary custody. In re Hayes (Ohio, 06-18-1997) 79 Ohio St.3d 46, 679 N.E.2d 680, reconsideration denied 79 Ohio St.3d 1492, 683 N.E.2d 793. Infants ⊗ 155

An order of emergency shelter care pending adjudication is not such an award of temporary custody as to trigger the provisions of RC 2151.413 requiring an agency granted temporary custody of a child to wait six months before seeking to convert the temporary placement to permanent custody; thus, a trial court does not err in entertaining a motion for permanent custody filed two months after an order of emergency shelter care is issued. In re Massengill (Lucas 1991) 76 Ohio App.3d 220, 601 N.E.2d 206.

Motions for permanent custody and the termination of parental rights pursuant to RC 2151.413 may only be filed after at least six months have elapsed since the temporary custody order was issued, and a judgment granting permanent custody to the human services department is in error. In re Bogan Children, No. CA–8919 (5th Dist Ct App, Stark, 1–4–93).

Where the county human services department obtains temporary custody of minor children, and three months later files a motion for permanent custody, the six-month minimum waiting period mandated by RC 2151.413(A) has not been met and the award of permanent custody will be reversed. In re Bogan Children, No. CA–8919 (5th Dist Ct App, Stark, 1–4–93).

The six-month limitations period for a county board to convert temporary custody into permanent custody under RC 2151.413(A) is not applicable where the grant of temporary custody was not pursuant to an order of disposition and where the request for permanent custody is by amended complaint rather than by motion. Stanford v Lucas County Children Services Bd, No. L–86–137 (6th Dist Ct App, Lucas, 3–20–87).

4. Requirements for permanent custody

Clear and convincing evidence supported conclusion that county had had temporary custody of mother's children for 16 months of a consecutive 22 months period, and, as such, county was required to file motion for permanent custody of children. In re Donell F. (Ohio App. 6 Dist., Lucas, 08-12-2005) No. L-04-1308, 2005-Ohio-4175, 2005 WL 1926512, Unreported. Infants ⊗ 178

Clear and convincing evidence supported trial court's determination that award of permanent custody of children to county children services was in children's best interest; children had been in custody of county child services for 12 or more months of consecutive 22-month period, parents had failed to substantially remedy conditions causing children to be placed outside home, parents had demonstrated lack of commitment toward children by failing to regularly support or visit them, parents were unwilling to provide basic necessities for children, and parents continued to use drugs after children had been removed from home. In re Briazanna G. (Ohio App. 6 Dist., Lucas, 06-24-2005) No. L-04-1366, 2005-Ohio-3206, 2005 WL 1492034, Unreported. Infants ⇐ 155

Reasonable efforts requirement did not apply in child protection proceedings in which motion for permanent custody was filed by county children's services agency pursuant to statute governing placement of children who cannot be placed with relatives, are abandoned or orphaned, or have been in temporary custody of public or private agencies for more than 12 months out of 22-month period. In re S.P. (Ohio App. 12 Dist., Butler, 03-14-2005) No. CA2004-10-255, 2005-Ohio-1079, 2005 WL 578976, Unreported. Infants ⇐ 155

Trial court was not required to describe services county had provided to father in effort to reunify family in its findings of fact, in child dependency proceeding in which county had filed motion for permanent custody of child, as requirement for such findings contained in statute governing hearings on efforts of agencies to prevent removal of children from homes did not apply to motions for permanent custody. In re Miller (Ohio App. 5 Dist., Licking, 02-24-2005) No. 04 CA 32, 2005-Ohio-856, 2005 WL 469260, Unreported. Infants ⇐ 210

Statute requiring county agency to make reasonable efforts to prevent child's removal or to make it possible for child to return home with parent did not apply to agency's motion seeking permanent custody of child. In re T.T. (Ohio App. 12 Dist., Butler, 01-24-2005) No. CA2004-07-175, No. CA2004-08-198, 2005-Ohio-240, 2005 WL 123948, Unreported. Infants ⇐ 155

Procedures necessary to implement an agreement surrendering permanent custody of a child are not applicable when a juvenile court considers a child protection agency's motion for permanent custody of child. In re Gordon (Ohio App. 3 Dist., Hancock, 11-08-2004) No. 5-04-22, No. 5-04-23, 2004-Ohio-5889, 2004 WL 2496513, Unreported. Infants ⇐ 194.1

Statute requiring county agency to make reasonable efforts to prevent child's removal or to make it possible for child to return home with parent did not apply to agency's motion seeking permanent custody of child. In re A.C. (Ohio App. 12 Dist., Clermont, 10-18-2004) No. CA2004-05-041, 2004-Ohio-5531, 2004 WL 2340127, Unreported. Infants ⇐ 155

County Children Services Board (CSB) was excepted from requirement to make reasonable efforts to reunite parents with their child before permanent custody could be awarded to agency; parents had previously had their parental rights terminated with respect to child's siblings. In re Richardson (Ohio App. 5 Dist., Guernsey, 04-27-2004) No. 04 CA 02, 2004-Ohio-2170, 2004 WL 911316, Unreported. Infants ⇐ 155

Evidence failed to establish that it was in the best interest of the children to grant county children services permanent custody; father underwent substance abuse counseling, was employed, and had modest housing for himself and the children, the children expressed love for father, and the trial court determined that father deserved a chance to have his own caseplan, since the previous caseplan was designed for mother and father and the parents had divorced, and chance to see if he could reunify with his children. In re Cunningham (Ohio App. 4 Dist., Athens, 02-17-2004) No. 03CA26, 2004-Ohio-787, 2004 WL 323339, Unreported. Infants ⇐ 155

The trial court was not required to find that the county department of children and family services made reasonable efforts to reunify mother with her children prior to terminating parental rights; the county department of children and family services' motion for permanent custody was filed pursuant to statute. In re La.B. (Ohio App. 8 Dist., Cuyahoga, 12-18-2003) No. 81981, 2003-Ohio-6852, 2003 WL 22966171, Unreported, stay denied 101 Ohio St.3d 1453, 803 N.E.2d 401, 2004-Ohio-462, cause dismissed 101 Ohio St.3d 1458, 803 N.E.2d 830, 2004-Ohio-703, reconsideration granted 101 Ohio St.3d 1482, 805 N.E.2d 534, 2004-Ohio-1398, appeal not allowed 102 Ohio St.3d 1445, 808 N.E.2d 397, 2004-Ohio-2263. Infants ⇐ 210

Trial court had jurisdiction to hear motion filed by county children services seeking permanent custody of dependent children, where county children services was granted temporary custody prior to seeking permanent custody, county children services filed motion for permanent custody in court that made finding of temporary custody, and children were not orphaned or abandoned. In re Brooks (Ohio App. 10 Dist., Franklin, 10-07-2003) No. 03AP-282, No. 03AP-442, 2003-Ohio-5348, 2003 WL 22290239, Unreported. Infants ⇐ 196

Clear and convincing evidence supported trial court finding that granting permanent custody of children to the county children's service board was in the best interest of the children; the children had been under the care of the county for at least 12 of the prior 22 months, mother allowed the children to steal, use alcohol, and observe mother using alcohol, older child did not want to continue to visit mother, older child's behavior improved greatly while he lived with foster family, older child had been removed from mother's custody previously, visits with mother caused both children to regress in their behaviors, and mother previously lost custody to a sibling of the children. In re Large (Ohio App. 4 Dist., Hocking, 09-29-2003) No. 03CA9, No. 03CA10, 2003-Ohio-5275, 2003 WL 22272817, Unreported. Infants ⇐ 155; Infants ⇐ 156

Clear and convincing evidence was presented to establish that awarding Sandusky County Department of Jobs and Family Services permanent custody of children was in children's best interest; mother's homelessness and unstable relationships reflected pattern of behavior that mother was either unwilling or unable to correct. In re Joshua B. (Ohio App. 6 Dist., Sandusky, 06-13-2003) No. S-02-018, No. S-02-021, No. S-02-019, No. S-02-020, 2003-Ohio-3096, 2003 WL 21384883, Unreported. Infants ⇐ 155

Analysis of whether reasonable efforts were made to reunify mother and children was not required in determining whether to grant motion by Cuyahoga County Department of Children and Family Services (CCDCFS) to modify temporary custody of children to permanent custody. In re C.N. (Ohio App. 8 Dist., Cuyahoga, 04-24-2003) No. 81813, 2003-Ohio-2048, 2003 WL 1924648, Unreported. Infants ⇐ 230.1

Evidence supported finding that county agency that had been awarded emergency temporary custody of three minor children made diligent efforts to help parents achieve reunification, and thus trial court did not abuse its discretion in awarding permanent custody to agency based on parents' continuous and repeated failure to substantially remedy problems that had caused children to be placed outside of home; parents failed to present any evidence supporting their claims to be learning disabled, and licensed professional counselor, caseworker, parent educator, and intake therapist who worked with parents all believed that parents' conduct reflected a lack of motivation or devotion, as opposed to any cognitive or learning deficiencies. In re Leveck (Ohio App. 3 Dist., Hancock, 03-18-2003) No. 5-02-52, No. 5-02-53, No. 5-02-54, 2003-Ohio-1269, 2003 WL 1205082, Unreported. Infants ⇐ 178

Trial court, in permanency hearing, abused its discretion in requiring State to arrange an open adoption prior to awarding permanent custody; State was required to include in the case plan a specific plan to seek an adoptive family for the child and to prepare the child for adoption, but was not required to set forth an exact plan for adoption until permanent custody was granted. In re Muldrew (Ohio App. 2 Dist., Montgomery, 12-27-2002) No. 19469, 2002-Ohio-7288, 2002 WL 31888158, Unreported. Infants ⇐ 222

The juvenile court errs in permitting the county department of children and family services to orally amend its complaint for temporary custody to one which seeks permanent custody on the day of trial since the department has only been granted emergency temporary custody, and the court should proceed on the motion for temporary custody and provide the parents with an opportunity to prepare for a permanent custody hearing. In re Vandivner (Ohio App. 8 Dist., Cuyahoga, 02-22-2001) No. 77963, No. 77966, No. 77964, No. 77965, 2001 WL 175542, Unreported.

Until at least constructive notice is given to the parents, the jurisdiction of the juvenile court does not attach, making any judgment of permanent custody to the state void. In re Starkey (Ohio App. 7 Dist., 12-11-2002) 150 Ohio App.3d 612, 782 N.E.2d 665, 2002-Ohio-6892. Infants ⇐ 198

County department of human services met requirements for filing motion for permanent custody of children, where children remained in custody of department for sixteen consecutive months before trial court returned them to mother and her husband, children remained under protective custody for approximately seven months before trial court returned them to temporary custody of department, and children were in department's temporary custody at time department filed its motion for permanent custody. In re Ament (Ohio App. 12 Dist., 04-23-2001) 142 Ohio App.3d 302, 755 N.E.2d 448, appeal not allowed 92 Ohio St.3d 1431, 749 N.E.2d 757. Infants ⇐ 193

Sufficient evidence supported finding that mother failed, continuously and repeatedly for more than six months, to remedy conditions causing two children to be placed outside home, for purposes of child services agency's motion for permanent custody, even though mother claimed she had demonstrated ability to care for her youngest child and was working on reunification with a fourth child, where caseworker testified that mother did not have ability to care for more than one child at a time, mother made only minimal progress toward reunification with two removed children, and guardian ad litem testified that he believed mother would be overwhelmed if reunited with removed children. Lorain Cty. Children Serv. v. Keene (Ohio App. 9 Dist., 03-05-1997) 118 Ohio App.3d 535, 693 N.E.2d 833. Infants ⇐ 178

Former statute required that children services agency seeking permanent custody of child must have had temporary custody of child for at least six months immediately preceding the filing of motion for permanent custody. In re Hayes (Ohio, 06-18-1997) 79 Ohio St.3d 46, 679 N.E.2d 680, reconsideration denied 79 Ohio St.3d 1492, 683 N.E.2d 793. Infants ⇐ 155

Under former statute, children services agency was not permitted to move for permanent custody of child in its temporary emergency custody, though over six months had elapsed since child had initially been placed in agency's temporary custody, where child had not been in agency's continuous custody in the six months immediately preceding the filing of motion. In re Hayes (Ohio, 06-18-1997) 79 Ohio St.3d 46, 679 N.E.2d 680, reconsideration denied 79 Ohio St.3d 1492, 683 N.E.2d 793. Infants ⇐ 155

Former statutes concerning motions by children services agency for permanent custody of child, when read in pari materia, indicated legislature's intent that agency have current temporary custody when moving for permanent custody. In re Hayes (Ohio, 06-18-1997) 79 Ohio St.3d 46, 679 N.E.2d 680, reconsideration denied 79 Ohio St.3d 1492, 683 N.E.2d 793. Infants ⇐ 155

Public children services agency did not have standing to bring postdispositional motion for permanent custody of child after its grant of temporary custody of child was terminated and it had only protective supervision of child. In re Miller (Ohio App. 2 Dist., 02-15-1995) 101 Ohio App.3d 199, 655 N.E.2d 252. Infants ⇐ 200

In order for public children services agency to file motion for permanent custody of child previously adjudicated as abused, neglected or dependent, it must have current temporary custody of that child pursuant to order of disposition. In re Miller (Ohio App. 2 Dist., 02-15-1995) 101 Ohio App.3d 199, 655 N.E.2d 252. Infants ⇐ 230.1

Public children services agency that has had temporary custody of child for at least six months may file motion requesting permanent custody. In re Awkal (Ohio App. 8 Dist., 06-27-1994) 95 Ohio App.3d 309, 642 N.E.2d 424. Infants ⇐ 197

The comprehensive reunification plan required by 1980 H 695, § 3, eff. 10–24–80, to be included in the second annual review made of a child who is in temporary custody upon the effective date of the act, is not required when the board files a motion for permanent custody of a child before the occurrence of the second annual review. In re Smith (Greene 1982) 7 Ohio App.3d 75, 454 N.E.2d 171, 7 O.B.R. 88.

RC 2151.413 is inapplicable where a juvenile court acts on a complaint that seeks permanent commitment of a dependent child pursuant to RC 2151.353(A)(4). In re Stanton, No. C–830501 (1st Dist Ct App, Hamilton, 6–20–84).

Where the trial court determines that it is in the best interest of a minor child to terminate parental rights permanently, the trial court may grant permanent custody to a county children services board without first granting temporary custody. In re Hollins, No. CA–703 (5th Dist Ct App, Guernsey, 3–29–83).

2151.414 Procedures upon motion

(A)(1) Upon the filing of a motion pursuant to section 2151.413 of the Revised Code for permanent custody of a child, the court shall schedule a hearing and give notice of the filing of the motion and of the hearing, in accordance with section 2151.29 of the Revised Code, to all parties to the action and to the child's guardian ad litem. The notice also shall contain a full explanation that the granting of permanent custody permanently divests the parents of their parental rights, a full explanation of their right to be represented by counsel and to have counsel appointed pursuant to Chapter 120. of the Revised Code if they are indigent, and the name and telephone number of the court employee designated by the court pursuant to section 2151.314 of the Revised Code to arrange for the prompt appointment of counsel for indigent persons.

The court shall conduct a hearing in accordance with section 2151.35 of the Revised Code to determine if it is in the best interest of the child to permanently terminate parental rights and grant permanent custody to the agency that filed the motion. The adjudication that the child is an abused, neglected, or dependent child and any dispositional order that has been issued in the case under section 2151.353 of the Revised Code pursuant to the adjudication shall not be readjudicated at the hearing and shall not be affected by a denial of the motion for permanent custody.

(2) The court shall hold the hearing scheduled pursuant to division (A)(1) of this section not later than one hundred twenty days after the agency files the motion for permanent custody, except that, for good cause shown, the court may continue the hearing for a reasonable period of time beyond the one-hundred-twenty-day deadline. The court shall issue an order that grants, denies, or otherwise disposes of the motion for permanent custody, and journalize the order, not later than two hundred days after the agency files the motion.

If a motion is made under division (D)(2) of section 2151.413 of the Revised Code and no dispositional hearing has been held in the case, the court may hear the motion in the dispositional hearing required by division (B) of section 2151.35 of the Revised Code. If the court issues an order pursuant to section 2151.353 of the Revised Code granting permanent custody of the child to the agency, the court shall immediately dismiss the motion made under division (D)(2) of section 2151.413 of the Revised Code.

The failure of the court to comply with the time periods set forth in division (A)(2) of this section does not affect the authority of the court to issue any order under this chapter and does not provide any basis for attacking the jurisdiction of the court or the validity of any order of the court.

(B)(1) Except as provided in division (B)(2) of this section, the court may grant permanent custody of a child to a movant if the court determines at the hearing held pursuant to division (A) of this section, by clear and convincing evidence, that it is in the best interest of the child to grant permanent custody of the child to the agency that filed the motion for permanent custody and that any of the following apply:

(a) The child is not abandoned or orphaned or has not been in the temporary custody of one or more public children services agencies or private child placing agencies for twelve or more months of a consecutive twenty-two month period ending on or after March 18, 1999, and the child cannot be placed with either of the child's parents within a reasonable time or should not be placed with the child's parents.

(b) The child is abandoned.

(c) The child is orphaned, and there are no relatives of the child who are able to take permanent custody.

(d) The child has been in the temporary custody of one or more public children services agencies or private child placing agencies for twelve or more months of a consecutive twenty-two month period ending on or after March 18, 1999.

For the purposes of division (B)(1) of this section, a child shall be considered to have entered the temporary custody of an agency on the earlier of the date the child is adjudicated pursuant to section 2151.28 of the Revised Code or the date that is sixty days after the removal of the child from home.

(2) With respect to a motion made pursuant to division (D)(2) of section 2151.413 of the Revised Code, the court shall grant permanent custody of the child to the movant if the court determines in accordance with division (E) of this section that the child cannot be placed with one of the child's parents within a reasonable time or should not be placed with either parent and determines in accordance with division (D) of this section that permanent custody is in the child's best interest.

(C) In making the determinations required by this section or division (A)(4) of section 2151.353 of the Revised Code, a court shall not consider the effect the granting of permanent custody to the agency would have upon any parent of the child. A written report of the guardian ad litem of the child shall be submitted to the court prior to or at the time of the hearing held pursuant to division (A) of this section or section 2151.35 of the Revised Code but shall not be submitted under oath.

If the court grants permanent custody of a child to a movant under this division, the court, upon the request of any party, shall file a written opinion setting forth its findings of fact and conclusions of law in relation to the proceeding. The court shall not deny an agency's motion for permanent custody solely because the agency failed to implement any particular aspect of the child's case plan.

(D) In determining the best interest of a child at a hearing held pursuant to division (A) of this section or for the purposes of division (A)(4) or (5) of section 2151.353 or division (C) of section 2151.415 of the Revised Code, the court shall consider all relevant factors, including, but not limited to, the following:

(1) The interaction and interrelationship of the child with the child's parents, siblings, relatives, foster caregivers and out-of-home providers, and any other person who may significantly affect the child;

(2) The wishes of the child, as expressed directly by the child or through the child's guardian ad litem, with due regard for the maturity of the child;

(3) The custodial history of the child, including whether the child has been in the temporary custody of one or more public children services agencies or private child placing agencies for twelve or more months of a consecutive twenty-two month period ending on or after March 18, 1999;

(4) The child's need for a legally secure permanent placement and whether that type of placement can be achieved without a grant of permanent custody to the agency;

(5) Whether any of the factors in divisions (E)(7) to (11) of this section apply in relation to the parents and child.

For the purposes of this division, a child shall be considered to have entered the temporary custody of an agency on the earlier of the date the child is adjudicated pursuant to section 2151.28 of the Revised Code or the date that is sixty days after the removal of the child from home.

(E) In determining at a hearing held pursuant to division (A) of this section or for the purposes of division (A)(4) of section 2151.353 of the Revised Code whether a child cannot be placed with either parent within a reasonable period of time or should not be placed with the parents, the court shall consider all relevant evidence. If the court determines, by clear and convincing evidence, at a hearing held pursuant to division (A) of this section or for the purposes of division (A)(4) of section 2151.353 of the Revised Code that one or more of the following exist as to each of the child's parents, the court shall enter a finding that the child cannot be placed with either parent within a reasonable time or should not be placed with either parent:

(1) Following the placement of the child outside the child's home and notwithstanding reasonable case planning and diligent efforts by the agency to assist the parents to remedy the problems that initially caused the child to be placed outside the home, the parent has failed continuously and repeatedly to substantially remedy the conditions causing the child to be placed outside the child's home. In determining whether the parents have substantially remedied those conditions, the court shall consider parental utilization of medical, psychiatric, psychological, and other social and rehabilitative services and material resources that were made available to the parents for the purpose of changing parental conduct to allow them to resume and maintain parental duties.

(2) Chronic mental illness, chronic emotional illness, mental retardation, physical disability, or chemical dependency of the parent that is so severe that it makes the parent unable to provide an adequate permanent home for the child at the present time and, as anticipated, within one year after the court holds the hearing pursuant to division (A) of this section or for the purposes of division (A)(4) of section 2151.353 of the Revised Code;

(3) The parent committed any abuse as described in section 2151.031 of the Revised Code against the child, caused the child to suffer any neglect as described in section 2151.03 of the Revised Code, or allowed the child to suffer any neglect as described in section 2151.03 of the Revised Code between the date that the original complaint alleging abuse or neglect was filed and the date of the filing of the motion for permanent custody;

(4) The parent has demonstrated a lack of commitment toward the child by failing to regularly support, visit, or communicate with the child when able to do so, or by other actions showing an unwillingness to provide an adequate permanent home for the child;

(5) The parent is incarcerated for an offense committed against the child or a sibling of the child;

(6) The parent has been convicted of or pleaded guilty to an offense under division (A) or (C) of section 2919.22 or under section 2903.16, 2903.21, 2903.34, 2905.01, 2905.02, 2905.03, 2905.04, 2905.05, 2907.07, 2907.08, 2907.09, 2907.12, 2907.21, 2907.22, 2907.23, 2907.25, 2907.31, 2907.32, 2907.321, 2907.322, 2907.323, 2911.01, 2911.02, 2911.11, 2911.12, 2919.12, 2919.24, 2919.25, 2923.12, 2923.13, 2923.161, 2925.02, or 3716.11 of the Revised Code and the child or a sibling of the child was a victim of the offense or the parent has been convicted of or pleaded guilty to an offense under section 2903.04 of the Revised Code, a sibling of the child was the victim of the offense, and the parent who committed the offense poses an ongoing danger to the child or a sibling of the child.

(7) The parent has been convicted of or pleaded guilty to one of the following:

(a) An offense under section 2903.01, 2903.02, or 2903.03 of the Revised Code or under an existing or former law of this state, any other state, or the United States that is substantially equivalent to an offense described in those sections and the victim of the offense was a sibling of the child or the victim was another child who lived in the parent's household at the time of the offense;

(b) An offense under section 2903.11, 2903.12, or 2903.13 of the Revised Code or under an existing or former law of this state, any other state, or the United States that is substantially equivalent to an offense described in those sections and the victim of the offense is the child, a sibling of the child, or another child who lived in the parent's household at the time of the offense;

(c) An offense under division (B)(2) of section 2919.22 of the Revised Code or under an existing or former law of this state, any other state, or the United States that is substantially equivalent to the offense described in that section and the child, a sibling of the child, or another child who lived in the parent's household at the time of the offense is the victim of the offense;

(d) An offense under section 2907.02, 2907.03, 2907.04, 2907.05, or 2907.06 of the Revised Code or under an existing or former law of this state, any other state, or the United States that is substantially equivalent to an offense described in those sections and the victim of the offense is the child, a sibling of the child, or another child who lived in the parent's household at the time of the offense;

(e) A conspiracy or attempt to commit, or complicity in committing, an offense described in division (E)(7)(a) or (d) of this section.

(8) The parent has repeatedly withheld medical treatment or food from the child when the parent has the means to provide the treatment or food, and, in the case of withheld medical treatment, the parent withheld it for a purpose other than to treat the physical or mental illness or defect of the child by spiritual means

through prayer alone in accordance with the tenets of a recognized religious body.

(9) The parent has placed the child at substantial risk of harm two or more times due to alcohol or drug abuse and has rejected treatment two or more times or refused to participate in further treatment two or more times after a case plan issued pursuant to section 2151.412 of the Revised Code requiring treatment of the parent was journalized as part of a dispositional order issued with respect to the child or an order was issued by any other court requiring treatment of the parent.

(10) The parent has abandoned the child.

(11) The parent has had parental rights involuntarily terminated pursuant to this section or section 2151.353 or 2151.415 of the Revised Code with respect to a sibling of the child.

(12) The parent is incarcerated at the time of the filing of the motion for permanent custody or the dispositional hearing of the child and will not be available to care for the child for at least eighteen months after the filing of the motion for permanent custody or the dispositional hearing.

(13) The parent is repeatedly incarcerated, and the repeated incarceration prevents the parent from providing care for the child.

(14) The parent for any reason is unwilling to provide food, clothing, shelter, and other basic necessities for the child or to prevent the child from suffering physical, emotional, or sexual abuse or physical, emotional, or mental neglect.

(15) The parent has committed abuse as described in section 2151.031 of the Revised Code against the child or caused or allowed the child to suffer neglect as described in section 2151.03 of the Revised Code, and the court determines that the seriousness, nature, or likelihood of recurrence of the abuse or neglect makes the child's placement with the child's parent a threat to the child's safety.

(16) Any other factor the court considers relevant.

(F) The parents of a child for whom the court has issued an order granting permanent custody pursuant to this section, upon the issuance of the order, cease to be parties to the action. This division is not intended to eliminate or restrict any right of the parents to appeal the granting of permanent custody of their child to a movant pursuant to this section.

(2000 H 448, eff. 10–5–00; 1999 H 176, eff. 10–29–99; 1998 H 484, eff. 3–18–99; 1996 H 274, eff. 8–8–96; 1996 H 419, eff. 9–18–96; 1988 S 89, eff. 1–1–89; 1980 H 695)

Uncodified Law

1988 S 89, § 4, eff. 1–1–89, reads:

If a child is in the permanent custody of a public children services agency or private child placing agency on the effective date of this act, both of the following apply:

(A) The agency shall do both of the following:

(1) Prepare and file with the court a case plan for the child in accordance with section 2151.412 of the Revised Code, as enacted by this act, on or before July 1, 1989, and, after the case plan is prepared and filed with the court, comply with all provisions of section 2151.412 of the Revised Code, as enacted by this act.

(2) Conduct an administrative review of the child's case plan in accordance with section 2151.416 of the Revised Code, as renumbered and amended by this act, on or before the sixth month after the court conducts its first review hearing as required by division (B) of this section and continue to conduct administrative reviews of the child's case plan no later than every six months in accordance with that section until the child attains the age of eighteen if the child is not mentally or physically handicapped, the child attains the age of twenty-one if the child is mentally or physically handicapped, the child is adopted and a final decree of adoption is issued, or the court otherwise terminates the custody arrangement.

(B) The court with jurisdiction over the child shall conduct its first review hearing in accordance with division (C) of section 2151.417 of the Revised Code to review the child's case plan after the case plan is filed pursuant to division (A)(1) of this section and on or before July 1, 1989, and shall continue to hold review hearings no later than every twelve months in accordance with division (C) of section 2151.417 of the Revised Code until the child attains the age of eighteen if the child is not mentally or physically handicapped, the child attains the age of twenty-one if the child is mentally or physically handicapped, the child is adopted and a final decree of adoption is issued, or the court otherwise terminates the custody arrangement.

Historical and Statutory Notes

Ed. Note: Per In re Vickers Children, 14 App(3d) 201, 14 OBR 228, 470 NE(2d) 438 (Butler 1983), 2151.414 is in conflict with Juvenile Rule 29 and 34.

Amendment Note: 2000 H 448 substituted "caregivers'" for "parents'" in division (D)(1); and inserted "this section or" and deleted "2151.414" after "2151.353" in division (E)(11).

Amendment Note: 1999 H 176 rewrote divisions (B)(1)(a), (B)(1)(d), and (D)(3); substituted "(11)" for "(12)" in division (D)(5); and added the final paragraph in division (D). Prior to amendment, divisions (B)(1)(a), (B)(1)(d), and (D)(3) read:

"(a) The child is not abandoned or orphaned or has not been in the temporary custody of a public children services agency or private child placing agency under one or more separate orders of disposition issued under section 2151.353 or 2151.415 of the Revised Code for twelve or more months of a consecutive twenty-two month period ending on or after the effective date of this amendment, and the child cannot be placed with either of the child's parents within a reasonable time or should not be placed with the child's parents.

"(d) The child has been in the temporary custody of a public children services agency or private child placing agency under one or more separate orders of disposition issued under section 2151.353 of the Revised Code for twelve or more months of a consecutive twenty-two month period ending on or after the effective date of this amendment.

"(3) The custodial history of the child, including whether the child has been in the temporary custody of a public children services agency or private child placing agency under one or more separate orders of disposition issued under section 2151.353 or 2151.415 of the Revised Code for twelve or more months of a consecutive twenty-two month period ending on or after the effective date of this amendment;"

Amendment Note: 1998 H 484 rewrote this section, which prior thereto read:

"(A)(1) Upon the filing of a motion pursuant to section 2151.413 of the Revised Code for permanent custody of a child by a public children services agency or private child placing agency that has temporary custody of the child or has placed the child in long-term foster care, the court shall schedule a hearing and give notice of the filing of the motion and of the hearing, in accordance with section 2151.29 of the Revised Code, to all parties to the action and to the child's guardian ad litem. The notice also shall contain a full explanation that the granting of permanent custody permanently divests the parents of their parental rights, a full explanation of their right to be represented by counsel and to have counsel appointed pursuant to Chapter 120. of the Revised Code if they are indigent, and the name and telephone number of the court employee designated by the court pursuant to section 2151.314 of the Revised Code to arrange for the prompt appointment of counsel for indigent persons.

"The court shall conduct a hearing in accordance with section 2151.35 of the Revised Code to determine if it is in the best interest of the child to permanently terminate parental rights and grant permanent custody to the agency that filed the motion. The adjudication that the child is an abused, neglected, or dependent child and the grant of temporary custody to the agency that filed the motion or placement into long-term foster care shall not be readjudicated at the hearing and shall not be affected by a denial of the motion for permanent custody.

"(2) The court shall hold the hearing scheduled pursuant to division (A)(1) of this section not later than one hundred twenty days after the agency files the motion for permanent custody, except that, for good cause shown, the court may continue the hearing for a reasonable period of time beyond the one-hundred-twenty-day deadline. The court shall issue an order that grants, denies, or otherwise disposes of the motion for permanent custody, and journalize the order, not later than two hundred days after the agency files the motion.

"The failure of the court to comply with the time periods set forth in division (A)(2) of this section does not affect the authority of the court to issue any order under this chapter and does not provide any basis for attacking the jurisdiction of the court or the validity of any order of the court.

"(B) The court may grant permanent custody of a child to a movant if the court determines at the hearing held pursuant to division (A) of this section, by clear and convincing evidence, that it is in the best interest of the child to grant permanent custody of the child to the agency that filed the motion for permanent custody and that any of the following apply:

"(1) The child is not abandoned or orphaned and the child cannot be placed with either of the child's parents within a reasonable time or should not be placed with the child's parents;

"(2) The child is abandoned and the parents cannot be located;

"(3) The child is orphaned and there are no relatives of the child who are able to take permanent custody.

"(C) In making the determinations required by this section or division (A)(4) of section 2151.353 of the Revised Code, a court shall not consider the effect the granting of permanent custody to the agency would have upon any parent of the child. A written report of the guardian ad litem of the child shall be submitted to the court prior to or at the time of the hearing held pursuant to division (A) of this section or section 2151.35 of the Revised Code but shall not be submitted under oath.

"If the court grants permanent custody of a child to a movant under this division, the court, upon the request of any party, shall file a written opinion setting forth its findings of fact and conclusions of law in relation to the proceeding. The court shall not deny an agency's motion for permanent custody solely because the agency failed to implement any particular aspect of the child's case plan.

"(D) In determining the best interest of a child at a hearing held pursuant to division (A) of this section or for the purposes of division (A)(4) or (5) of section 2151.353 or division (C) of section 2151.415 of the Revised Code, the court shall consider all relevant factors, including, but not limited to, the following:

"(1) The interaction and interrelationship of the child with the child's parents, siblings, relatives, foster parents and out-of-home providers, and any other person who may significantly affect the child;

"(2) The wishes of the child, as expressed directly by the child or through the child's guardian ad litem, with due regard for the maturity of the child;

"(3) The custodial history of the child;

"(4) The child's need for a legally secure permanent placement and whether that type of placement can be achieved without a grant of permanent custody to the agency.

"(E) In determining at a hearing held pursuant to division (A) of this section or for the purposes of division (A)(4) of section 2151.353 of the Revised Code whether a child cannot be placed with either parent within a reasonable period of time or should not be placed with the parents, the court shall consider all relevant evidence. If the court determines, by clear and convincing evidence, at a hearing held pursuant to division (A) of this section or for the purposes of division (A)(4) of section 2151.353 of the Revised Code that one or more of the following exist as to each of the child's parents, the court shall enter a finding that the child cannot be placed with either parent within a reasonable time or should not be placed with either parent:

"(1) Following the placement of the child outside the child's home and notwithstanding reasonable case planning and diligent efforts by the agency to assist the parents to remedy the problems that initially caused the child to be placed outside the home, the parent has failed continuously and repeatedly to substantially remedy the conditions causing the child to be placed outside the child's home. In determining whether the parents have substantially remedied those conditions, the court shall consider parental utilization of medical, psychiatric, psychological, and other social and rehabilitative services and material resources that were made available to the parents for the purpose of changing parental conduct to allow them to resume and maintain parental duties.

"(2) Chronic mental illness, chronic emotional illness, mental retardation, physical disability, or chemical dependency of the parent that is so severe that it makes the parent unable to provide an adequate permanent home for the child at the present time and, as anticipated, within one year after the court holds the hearing pursuant to division (A) of this section or for the purposes of division (A)(4) of section 2151.353 of the Revised Code;

"(3) The parent committed any abuse as described in section 2151.031 of the Revised Code against the child, caused the child to suffer any neglect as described in section 2151.03 of the Revised Code, or allowed the child to suffer any neglect as described in section 2151.03 of the Revised Code between the date that the original complaint alleging abuse or neglect was filed and the date of the filing of the motion for permanent custody;

"(4) The parent has demonstrated a lack of commitment toward the child by failing to regularly support, visit, or communicate with the child when able to do so, or by other actions showing an unwillingness to provide an adequate permanent home for the child;

"(5) The parent is incarcerated for an offense committed against the child or a sibling of the child;

"(6) The parent violated section 2903.11, 2903.12, 2903.13, 2903.16, 2903.21, 2903.34, 2905.01, 2905.02, 2905.03, 2905.04, 2905.05, 2907.02, 2907.03, 2907.04, 2907.05, 2907.06, 2907.07, 2907.08, 2907.09, 2907.12, 2907.21, 2907.22, 2907.23, 2907.25, 2907.31, 2907.32, 2907.321, 2907.322, 2907.323, 2911.01, 2911.02, 2911.11, 2911.12, 2919.12, 2919.22, 2919.24, 2919.25, 2923.12, 2923.13, 2923.161, 2925.02, or 3716.11 of the Revised Code and the child or a sibling of the child was a victim of the violation or the parent violated section 2903.01, 2903.02, 2903.03, or 2903.04 of the Revised Code, a sibling of the child was the victim of the violation, and the parent who committed the violation poses an ongoing danger to the child or a sibling of the child.

"(7) The parent is incarcerated at the time of the filing of the motion for permanent custody or the dispositional hearing of the child and will not be available to care for the child for at least eighteen months after the filing of the motion for permanent custody or the dispositional hearing;

"(8) The parent is repeatedly incarcerated and the repeated incarceration prevents the parent from providing care for the child;

"(9) The parent for any reason is unwilling to provide food, clothing, shelter, and other basic necessities for the child or to prevent the child from suffering physical, emotional, or sexual abuse or physical, emotional, or mental neglect;

"(10) The parent has committed abuse as described in section 2151.031 of the Revised Code against the child or caused or allowed the child to suffer neglect as described in section 2151.03 of the Revised Code and the court determines that the seriousness, nature, or likelihood of recurrence of the abuse or neglect makes the child's placement with the child's parent a threat to the child's safety;

"(11) The parent committed abuse as described in section 2151.031 of the Revised Code against the child or caused or allowed the child to suffer neglect as described in section 2151.03 of the Revised Code and a sibling of the child previously has been permanently removed from the home of the child's parents because the parent abused or neglected the sibling.

"(12) Any other factor the court considers relevant.

"(F) The parents of a child for whom the court has issued an order granting permanent custody pursuant to this section, upon the issuance of the order, cease to be parties to the action. This division is not intended to eliminate or restrict any right of the parents to appeal the granting of permanent custody of their child to a movant pursuant to this section."

Amendment Note: 1996 H 274 rewrote the first paragraph in division (E); and added division (E)(12). Prior to amendment, the first paragraph in division (E) read:

"(E) In determining at a hearing held pursuant to division (A) of this section or for the purposes of division (A)(4) of section 2151.353 of the Revised Code whether a child cannot be placed with either of the child's parents within a reasonable period of time or should not be placed with the child's parents, the court shall make its findings based upon all relevant evidence, including evidence of the circumstances described in divisions (E)(1) to (11) of this section. If the court determines, by clear and convincing evidence, at a hearing held pursuant to division (A) of this section or for the purposes of division (A)(4) of section 2151.353 of the Revised Code, that the child cannot be placed with either of the child's parents within a reasonable time or should not be placed with the child's parents, the court shall enter a finding to that effect. Factors the court shall consider include the following and any other factor the court considers relevant:"

Amendment Note: 1996 H 419 rewrote this section, which previously read:

"(A) Upon the filing of a motion pursuant to section 2151.413 of the Revised Code for permanent custody of a child by a public children services agency or private child placing agency that has temporary custody of the child, the court shall schedule a hearing and give notice of the filing of the motion and of the hearing, in accordance with section 2151.29 of the Revised Code, to all parties to the action and to the child's guardian ad litem. The notice also shall contain a full explanation that the granting of permanent custody permanently divests the parents of their parental rights, a full explanation of their right to be represented by counsel and to have counsel appointed pursuant to Chapter 120. of the Revised Code if they are indigent, and the name and telephone number of the court employee designated by the court pursuant to section 2151.314 of the Revised Code to arrange for the prompt appointment of counsel for indigent persons. The court shall conduct a hearing in accordance with section 2151.35 of the Revised Code to determine if it is in the best interest of the child to permanently terminate parental rights and grant permanent custody to the agency that filed the motion. The adjudication that the child is an abused, neglected, or dependent child and the grant of temporary custody to the agency that filed the motion shall not be readjudicated at the hearing and shall not be affected by a denial of the motion for permanent custody.

"(B) The court may grant permanent custody of a child to a movant if the court determines at the hearing held pursuant to division (A) of this section, by clear and convincing evidence, that it is in the best interest of the child to grant permanent custody of the child to the agency that filed the motion for permanent custody and that any of the following apply:

"(1) The child is not abandoned or orphaned and the child cannot be placed with either of his parents within a reasonable time or should not be placed with his parents;

"(2) The child is abandoned and the parents cannot be located;

"(3) The child is orphaned and there are no relatives of the child who are able to take permanent custody.

"(C) In making the determinations required by this section or division (A)(4) of section 2151.353 of the Revised Code, a court shall not consider the effect the granting of permanent custody to the agency would have upon any parent of the child. A written report of the guardian ad litem of the child shall be submitted to the court prior to or at the time of the hearing held pursuant to division (A) of this section or section 2151.35 of the Revised Code but shall not be submitted under oath.

"If the court grants permanent custody of a child to a movant under this division, the court, upon the request of any party, shall file a written opinion setting forth its findings of fact and conclusions of law in relation to the proceeding. The court shall not deny an agency's motion for permanent custody solely because the agency failed to implement any particular aspect of the child's case plan.

"(D) In determining the best interest of a child at a hearing held pursuant to division (A) of this section or for the purposes of division (A)(4) of section 2151.353 of the Revised Code, the court shall consider all relevant factors, including, but not limited to, the following:

"(1) The reasonable probability of the child being adopted, whether an adoptive placement would positively benefit the child, and whether a grant of permanent custody would facilitate an adoption;

"(2) The interaction and interrelationship of the child with his parents, siblings, relatives, foster parents and out-of-home providers, and any other person who may significantly affect the child;

"(3) The wishes of the child, as expressed directly by the child or through his guardian ad litem, with due regard for the maturity of the child;

"(4) The custodial history of the child;

"(5) The child's need for a legally secure permanent placement and whether that type of placement can be achieved without a grant of permanent custody to the agency.

"(E) In determining at a hearing held pursuant to division (A) of this section or for the purposes of division (A)(4) of section 2151.353 of the Revised Code whether a child cannot be placed with either of his parents within a reasonable period of time or should not be placed with his parents, the court shall consider all relevant evidence. If the court determines, by clear and convincing evidence, at a hearing held pursuant to division (A) of this section or for the purposes of division (A)(4) of section 2151.353 of the Revised Code that one or more of the following exist as to each of the child's parents, the court shall enter a finding that the child cannot be placed with either of his parents within a reasonable time or should not be placed with his parents:

"(1) Following the placement of the child outside his home and notwithstanding reasonable case planning and diligent efforts by the agency to assist the parents to remedy the problems that initially caused the child to be placed outside the home, the parent has failed continuously and repeatedly for a period of six months or more to substantially remedy the conditions causing the child to be placed outside his home. In determining whether the parents have substantially remedied those conditions, the court shall consider parental utilization of medical, psychiatric, psychological, and other social and rehabilitative services and material resources that were made available to the parents for the purpose of changing parental conduct to allow them to resume and maintain parental duties.

"(2) The severe and chronic mental illness, severe and chronic emotional illness, severe mental retardation, severe physical disability, or chemical dependency of the parent makes the parent unable to provide an adequate permanent home for the child at the present time and in the forseeable [sic] future;

"(3) The parent committed any abuse as described in section 2151.031 of the Revised Code against the child, caused the child to suffer any neglect as described in section 2151.03 of the Revised Code, or allowed the child to suffer any neglect as described in section 2151.03 of the Revised Code between the date that the original complaint alleging abuse or neglect was filed and the date of the filing of the motion for permanent custody;

"(4) The parent has demonstrated a lack of commitment toward the child by failing to regularly support, visit, or communicate with the child when able to do so, or by other actions showing an unwillingness to provide an adequate permanent home for the child;

"(5) The parent is incarcerated for an offense committed against the child or a sibling of the child;

"(6) The parent is incarcerated at the time of the filing of the motion for permanent custody or the dispositional hearing of the child and will not be available to care for the child for at least eighteen months after the filing of the motion for permanent custody or the dispositional hearing;

"(7) The parent is repeatedly incarcerated and the repeated incarceration prevents the parent from providing care for the child;

"(8) The parent for any reason is unwilling to provide food, clothing, shelter, and other basic necessities for the child or to prevent the child from suffering physical, emotional, or sexual abuse or physical, emotional, or mental neglect.

"(F) The parents of a child for whom the court has issued an order granting permanent custody pursuant to this section, upon the issuance of the order, cease to be parties to the action. This division is not intended to eliminate or restrict any right of the parents to appeal the granting of permanent custody of their child to a movant pursuant to this section."

Cross References

Adjudicatory hearing, Juv R 29
Dispositional hearing, Juv R 34

Ohio Administrative Code References

Obtaining permanent custody: termination of parental rights, OAC 5101:2–42–95

Library References

Infants ⚖191 to 212.
Westlaw Topic No. 211.
C.J.S. Infants §§ 41 to 55, 57 to 85.
Baldwin's Ohio Legislative Service, 1988 Laws of Ohio, S 89—LSC Analysis, p 5–571

Research References

ALR Library

113 ALR 5th 349, Parents' Mental Illness or Mental Deficiency as Ground for Termination of Parental Rights--General Considerations.

20 ALR 5th 534, Parent's Use of Drugs as Factor in Award of Custody of Children, Visitation Rights, or Termination of Parental Rights.

Encyclopedias

OH Jur. 3d Constitutional Law § 341, Fourteenth Amendment; Due Process of Law—Equal Protection of the Laws.

OH Jur. 3d Constitutional Law § 476, Distinction Between Retrospective or Retroactive and Ex Post Facto Laws.

OH Jur. 3d Constitutional Law § 487, What Legislation Specifically Relates to the Remedy.

OH Jur. 3d Constitutional Law § 506, Other Particular Rights.

OH Jur. 3d Family Law § 1499, Evidentiary Standards.

OH Jur. 3d Family Law § 1612, Summons for Hearing to Make Temporary Commitment Permanent.

OH Jur. 3d Family Law § 1626, Right Under Juvenile Court Law and Rules.

OH Jur. 3d Family Law § 1630, for Abused, Neglected or Dependent Child.
OH Jur. 3d Family Law § 1654, Determination of Reasonable Efforts.
OH Jur. 3d Family Law § 1655, Right to Attend; Public or Private Hearing.
OH Jur. 3d Family Law § 1663, on Request for Permanent Custody—on Motion of Agency.
OH Jur. 3d Family Law § 1664, on Request for Permanent Custody—Factors to be Considered.
OH Jur. 3d Family Law § 1670, Required Degree of Proof.
OH Jur. 3d Family Law § 1681, Conduct of Hearing; Advisement of Rights.
OH Jur. 3d Family Law § 1693, Permanent Custody.
OH Jur. 3d Family Law § 1694, Long-Term Foster Care.
OH Jur. 3d Family Law § 1711, Review Hearing.
OH Jur. 3d Family Law § 1676.5, Sufficiency.

Forms

Ohio Jurisprudence Pleading and Practice Forms § 96:43, Temporary and Permanent Custody.

Treatises and Practice Aids

Klein, Darling, & Terez, Baldwin's Ohio Practice Civil Practice § 52:4, Findings by the Court--Findings of Fact Required by Statute.
Carlin, Baldwin's Ohio Practice, Merrick-Rippner Probate Law § 107:10, Contents and Issuance of Summons.
Carlin, Baldwin's Ohio Practice, Merrick-Rippner Probate Law § 107:46, Adjudicatory Hearings—Child's Right to Guardian Ad Litem.
Carlin, Baldwin's Ohio Practice, Merrick-Rippner Probate Law § 107:60, Adjudicatory Hearings—Right to Transcript of Proceedings.
Carlin, Baldwin's Ohio Practice, Merrick-Rippner Probate Law § 107:72, Dispositional Hearings—Procedure.
Carlin, Baldwin's Ohio Practice, Merrick-Rippner Probate Law § 107:74, Reasonable Efforts Determination.
Carlin, Baldwin's Ohio Practice, Merrick-Rippner Probate Law § 107:75, Case Plans.
Carlin, Baldwin's Ohio Practice, Merrick-Rippner Probate Law § 107:78, Disposition of Abused, Neglected, or Dependent Child—Temporary Custody.
Carlin, Baldwin's Ohio Practice, Merrick-Rippner Probate Law § 107:79, Disposition of Abused, Neglected, or Dependent Child—Legal Custody.
Carlin, Baldwin's Ohio Practice, Merrick-Rippner Probate Law § 107:80, Disposition of Abused, Neglected, or Dependent Child—Permanent Custody.
Carlin, Baldwin's Ohio Practice, Merrick-Rippner Probate Law § 107:81, Disposition of Abused, Neglected, or Dependent Child—Permanent Custody—Best Interest Determination Factors.
Carlin, Baldwin's Ohio Practice, Merrick-Rippner Probate Law § 107:82, Disposition of Abused, Neglected, or Dependent Child—Planned Permanent Living Arrangement.
Carlin, Baldwin's Ohio Practice, Merrick-Rippner Probate Law § 107:83, Motion for Permanent Custody of Abused, Neglected, or Dependent Child.
Carlin, Baldwin's Ohio Practice, Merrick-Rippner Probate Law § 107:119, Custody Review Proceedings—Semiannual Administrative Review.
Carlin, Baldwin's Ohio Practice, Merrick-Rippner Probate Law § 107:120, Custody Review Hearing—Juvenile Court Dispositional Review.
Carlin, Baldwin's Ohio Practice, Merrick-Rippner Probate Law § 107:175, Order Committing Child to Permanent Custody of Public or Private Agency—Form.
Giannelli & Yeomans, Ohio Juvenile Law § 1:7, Juvenile Code.
Giannelli & Yeomans, Ohio Juvenile Law § 16:5, Parental Identification.
Giannelli & Yeomans, Ohio Juvenile Law § 18:2, Issuance of Summons: Proper Parties.
Giannelli & Yeomans, Ohio Juvenile Law § 18:3, Summons: Contents and Form.
Giannelli & Yeomans, Ohio Juvenile Law § 23:6, Guardian Ad Litem.
Giannelli & Yeomans, Ohio Juvenile Law § 30:6, Temporary Custody.
Giannelli & Yeomans, Ohio Juvenile Law § 30:8, Permanent Custody—Defined.
Giannelli & Yeomans, Ohio Juvenile Law § 30:9, Permanent Custody—Requirements.
Giannelli & Yeomans, Ohio Juvenile Law § 31:2, Filing of Motion.
Giannelli & Yeomans, Ohio Juvenile Law § 31:3, Time Requirements for Permanent Custody Motions.
Giannelli & Yeomans, Ohio Juvenile Law § 31:4, Hearings on Permanent Custody Motions.
Giannelli & Yeomans, Ohio Juvenile Law § 31:5, Evidence.
Giannelli & Yeomans, Ohio Juvenile Law § 31:6, Findings.
Giannelli & Yeomans, Ohio Juvenile Law § 31:8, Implementation of Case Plan.
Giannelli & Yeomans, Ohio Juvenile Law § 31:9, Effect on Parental Rights.
Giannelli & Yeomans, Ohio Juvenile Law § 34:9, Right to Transcript.
Giannelli & Yeomans, Ohio Juvenile Law § 23:13, Burden of Proof.
Giannelli & Yeomans, Ohio Juvenile Law § 23:24, Confrontation—Cross-Examination.
Giannelli & Yeomans, Ohio Juvenile Law § 23:30, Right to a Transcript.
Giannelli & Yeomans, Ohio Juvenile Law § 25:12, Transcripts.
Giannelli & Yeomans, Ohio Juvenile Law § 25:14, Reasonable Efforts Determination; Abuse, Neglect & Dependency.
Giannelli & Yeomans, Ohio Juvenile Law § 30:10, Permanent Custody—Parental Placement Within Reasonable Time.
Giannelli & Yeomans, Ohio Juvenile Law § 30:11, Permanent Custody—"Best Interest" Factors.
Giannelli & Yeomans, Ohio Juvenile Law § 30:12, Permanent Custody—Procedural Issues.
Giannelli & Yeomans, Ohio Juvenile Law § 33:10, Child Custody Agency Commitment—Semiannual Administrative Review.
Giannelli & Yeomans, Ohio Juvenile Law § 33:11, Child Custody Agency Commitment—Juvenile Court Dispositional Review.

Law Review and Journal Commentaries

Improving Child Welfare Practice Through Improvements In Attorney-Social Worker Relationships, Paul Johnson and Katharine Cahn. 54 U Pitt L Rev 229 (Fall 1992).

Inclusion Of The Reasonable Efforts Requirement In Termination Of Parental Rights Statutes: Punishing The Child For The Failures Of The State Child Welfare System, David J. Herring. 54 U Pitt L Rev 139 (Fall 1992).

A Response To Elimination Of The Reasonable Efforts Required Prior To Termination Of Parental Rights Status, Hon. Patrick R. Tamilia. 54 U Pitt L Rev 211 (Fall 1992).

Reunification Planning for Children in Custody of Ohio's Children Services Boards: What Does the Law Require?, Norma Blank. 16 Akron L Rev 681 (Spring 1983).

The Right to Counsel for Indigent Parents in Termination Proceedings: A Critical Analysis of Lassiter v. Department of Social Services, Note. 21 J Fam L 83 (1982–83).

State v. Parent Termination of Parental Rights: Contradictory Actions by the Ohio Legislature and the Ohio Supreme Court in 1996, Keith Wiens. 26 Cap U L Rev 673 (1997).

When a Hearing Is Not a Hearing: Irrebuttable Presumptions and Termination of Parental Rights Based on Status, Philip J. Prygoski. 44 U Pitt L Rev 879 (Summer 1983).

Notes of Decisions

Adequate parental care, factors 5
Best interests of child 10, 11
    Multiple siblings 10
    Permanent custody to county 11
Children's services agency duties 6
Constitutional issues 1
Evidence 3
Federal civil rights liability or 42 USC 1983 8
Grandparent visitation 9
Hearings 7
Multiple siblings, best interests of child 10
Permanent custody to county, best interests of child 11
Procedural issues 2
Representation by counsel 4

Review 12

1. Constitutional issues

Failure to afford mother opportunity to cross-examine guardian ad litem or present evidence in rebuttal of guardian's untimely-filed report in proceedings for termination of mother's parental rights violated mother's right to substantive due process of law, and required remand for evidentiary hearing. (Per Westcott Rice, J., with one judge concurring in result only.) In re Kangas (Ohio App. 11 Dist., Ashtabula, 06-30-2006) No. 2006-A-0010, 2006-Ohio-3433, 2006 WL 1817069, Unreported. Infants ⚖ 207

Failure of mother's counsel in proceedings for termination of parental rights to request appointment of independent counsel for subject child did not prejudice mother and did not amount to ineffective assistance requiring reversal of termination, where child's right to counsel could not be waived by mother's failure to assert it, and any appointed counsel would have been required to advocate in favor of child's expressed wish that mother's parental rights be terminated. (Per Westcott Rice, J., with one judge concurring in result only.) In re Kangas (Ohio App. 11 Dist., Ashtabula, 06-30-2006) No. 2006-A-0010, 2006-Ohio-3433, 2006 WL 1817069, Unreported. Infants ⚖ 205

Mother's due process rights were not violated when trial court proceeded with permanent custody hearing in her absence; at the time of the permanent custody hearing, mother was incarcerated, had not completed drug treatment, had not completed parenting class, was not employed, and was not prepared to provide a home for her children. In re D.P. (Ohio App. 8 Dist., Cuyahoga, 03-02-2006) No. 86271, No. 86272, 2006-Ohio-937, 2006 WL 496058, Unreported. Infants ⚖ 203

The exception to the mootness doctrine for a debatable constitutional question did not apply to father's appeal of the trial court's denial of his objections to magistrate's decision, which found clear and convincing evidence that child was a neglected and dependent child; the potential constitutional issue of the magistrate denial of father's right to counsel at child's adjudication hearing was addressed and resolved by the trial court when it noted at the commencement of the adjudicatory hearing that father had a right to appointed counsel at the adjudicatory hearing and that the court would appoint counsel to represent him despite any contrary advisement by the magistrate. In re L.W. (Ohio App. 10 Dist., Franklin, 02-14-2006) No. 05AP-317, 2006-Ohio-644, 2006 WL 330089, Unreported, appeal not allowed 109 Ohio St.3d 1497, 848 N.E.2d 859, 2006-Ohio-2762. Infants ⚖ 247

Trial court failed to follow basic procedural safeguards mandated within permanent custody statute and basic constitutional due process requirements of both state and federal constitutions, in proceeding to terminate parental rights; mother was denied proper notice of complaint and hearing, was denied recitation of her rights, was denied proper participation in proceedings, and was denied continuance of permanent custody hearing, mother's failure to attend hearing was not voluntary, but based upon her incarceration, and mother was not appointed counsel during hearing for neglect and dependency. In re Sheffey (Ohio App. 11 Dist., 02-10-2006) 2006-Ohio-619, 2006 WL 319350. Infants ⚖ 191

In permanent custody case, neither county agency nor trial court infringed upon mother's right to marriage or association by prohibiting father from having contact with children as a result of his propensity for domestic violence; case plan merely required mother to "not allow" contact between father and children, and agency indicated it did not prohibit contact between mother and father, only that mother communicate honestly about her contact with father. In re Janson (Ohio App. 11 Dist., Geauga, 12-16-2005) No. 2005-G-2657, 2005-Ohio-6713, 2005 WL 3476624, Unreported. Infants ⚖ 222

Order allowing county to call father to testify as if on cross-examination did not violate father's Fifth Amendment right against self-incrimination, in proceedings to terminate father's parental rights; father testified of his own free will, father never invoked Fifth Amendment, father never asserted that he was subject to prosecution for any crime, and no testimony was elicited from father regarding alleged sexual abuse of child's sister. In re A.S. (Ohio App. 10 Dist., Franklin, 10-18-2005) No. 05AP-351, No. 05AP-352, 2005-Ohio-5492, 2005 WL 2650108, Unreported. Infants ⚖ 207

Children's independent counsel was not deficient during permanent custody proceeding, despite mother's claim that counsel failed to advocate against an award of permanent custody to Children Services Board (CSB); counsel met with the children, questioned witnesses at trial, and called the guardian ad litem to the stand. In re Spears (Ohio App. 5 Dist., Fairfield, 08-22-2005) No. 05CA7, No. 05CA10, No. 05CA8, No. 05CA9, 2005-Ohio-4498, 2005 WL 2077940, Unreported. Infants ⚖ 205

Mother waived her privilege against self-incrimination during permanent custody proceeding by freely answering questions pertaining to her drug use before consulting with her attorney and invoking her Fifth Amendment rights. In re Spears (Ohio App. 5 Dist., Fairfield, 08-22-2005) No. 05CA7, No. 05CA10, No. 05CA8, No. 05CA9, 2005-Ohio-4498, 2005 WL 2077940, Unreported. Infants ⚖ 207

Alleged failure of father's counsel to have father's family members present at permanent custody hearing to testify that county had never contacted any of them regarding placement of children with them did not prejudice father, and, as such, was not ineffective assistance; to demonstrate prejudice, father was required to show that, if county had investigated suitability of his father and/or sister, court would have awarded custody of children to one of them rather than to county, but juvenile statute did not require award of legal custody of children to a relative rather than to county, and where relative did not come forward prior to dispositional hearing, court had discretion to award custody to a non-family member or to county. In re Vann (Ohio App. 5 Dist., Stark, 08-22-2005) No. 2005-CA-00127, 2005-Ohio-4398, 2005 WL 2045442, Unreported. Infants ⚖ 205

Even if mother's counsel discussed negative aspects of mother's parenting abilities in his closing argument, she was not prejudiced thereby, and, as such, counsel did not render ineffective assistance in this regard, in termination of parental rights proceeding; closing arguments did not constitute evidence, and nothing in record indicated that trial court considered anything other than evidence offered at trial in deciding to terminate mother's parental rights. In re Donell F. (Ohio App. 6 Dist., Lucas, 08-12-2005) No. L-04-1308, 2005-Ohio-4175, 2005 WL 1926512, Unreported. Infants ⚖ 205

Alleged failure of mother's counsel to present testimony as to number and success of mother's visits with children while they were in temporary custody of county was not deficient performance, and, thus, was not ineffective assistance, in termination of parental rights proceeding; it was undisputed that mother had "disappeared" for several months after temporary custody was awarded to county and that she did not visit her children for eight months during this period, and witness for mother testified that, after mother's return, she had gone with mother every week for visitation with children, which she described as "normal." In re Donell F. (Ohio App. 6 Dist., Lucas, 08-12-2005) No. L-04-1308, 2005-Ohio-4175, 2005 WL 1926512, Unreported. Infants ⚖ 205

Failure of mother's counsel to call more than one witness to attest to mother's progress on completion of goals enumerated in her case plan did not prejudice mother, and, as such, was not ineffective assistance, in termination of parental rights proceeding; fact that mother had completed, albeit belatedly, most of the services outlined in her case plan was admitted at trial by the county. In re Donell F. (Ohio App. 6 Dist., Lucas, 08-12-2005) No. L-04-1308, 2005-Ohio-4175, 2005 WL 1926512, Unreported. Infants ⚖ 205

Failure of father's counsel to seek opportunity for father, who was incarcerated, to participate in dispositional aspect of permanent custody hearing, did not prejudice father, and thus did not amount to ineffective assistance, in dependency and neglect proceeding; father did little or nothing to take advantage of his opportunity to visit or otherwise reunify with child during periods of non-incarceration, nor did he comply with numerous provisions of his case plan, and, thus, father failed to show a reasonable probability that outcome of proceeding would have been different had such steps been taken. In re Roberts (Ohio App. 5 Dist., Guernsey, 06-08-2005) No. 04 CA 23, 2005-Ohio-2842, 2005 WL 1364610, Unreported. Infants ⚖ 205

Mother's stipulation agreeing to termination of her parental rights to child was not voluntary and knowing, in violation of her due process rights, as trial court failed to comply with procedural safeguards set forth in rule governing such stipulations; trial court addressed mother personally but failed to determine whether she understood nature of allegations against her and whether she was aware of consequences of stipulation, and trial court failed to advise mother that, by entering into stipulation, she was waiving her rights to challenge witnesses and evidence against her, to introduce evidence at adjudicatory hearing, and to remain silent should she so choose. In re Rock Children (Ohio App. 5 Dist., Stark, 05-23-2005) No. 2004CA00358, 2005-Ohio-2572, 2005 WL 1228036, Unreported. Infants ⚖ 199

Probate court violated mother's due process rights by granting the adoption petition; during pendency of mother's appeal of order granting permanent custody of child to county social services agency and terminating mother's parental rights, trial court overruled both agency's and mother's motions to vacate adoption decree, thereby, in essence, divesting mother of her right to appeal underlying permanent custody award. In re Adoption of V.N.M. (Ohio App. 5 Dist., Licking, 05-23-2005) No.

04CA109, 2005-Ohio-2555, 2005 WL 1208855, Unreported. Infants ⇐ 244.1

Father waived appellate review of claim that he was deprived of his constitutional right to due process by the alleged failure of county social service agency to make a reasonable effort to reunify him with minor child, where father did not raise a state or federal due process error at the trial court level. In re Greathouse (Ohio App. 5 Dist., Fairfield, 05-18-2005) No. 04 CA 57, 2005-Ohio-2553, 2005 WL 1208850, Unreported. Infants ⇐ 243

Statutory provision providing for grant of permanent child custody to public children services agency based on fact that child has been in temporary custody of one or more such agency for 12 or more months of consecutive 22 month period is constitutional. In re Unger Children (Ohio App. 5 Dist., Coshocton, 05-12-2005) No. 04 CA 6, 2005-Ohio-2414, 2005 WL 1163915, Unreported. Infants ⇐ 132

Mother failed to establish prejudice, as required to prove claim of ineffective assistance of counsel, based on counsel's failure to present evidence of her compliance with her case plan objectives, during proceeding on county agency's motion for permanent custody; trial court found the children had been in the temporary custody of the agency for more than 12 of the last 22 months, and thus, the agency was not required to present evidence regarding whether the children could be returned within a reasonable amount of time. In re Langford (Ohio App. 5 Dist., Stark, 05-09-2005) No. 2004CA00349, 2005-Ohio-2304, 2005 WL 1111220, Unreported. Infants ⇐ 205

Statute permitting termination of parental rights when child has been in temporary custody of one or more public children service agencies or private child placing agencies for 12 or more months of consecutive 22 month period, was not unconstitutional as applied to mother, and thus did not violate due process provisions of Federal and State Constitutions; mother had numerous opportunities and sufficient time to demonstrate her parental fitness and ability to care for child, and record did not support mother's contention that child remained in substitute care for significant period of time due to circumstances beyond her control or solely under the control of county children services agency. In re Bray (Ohio App. 10 Dist., Franklin, 03-31-2005) No. 04AP-842, 2005-Ohio-1540, 2005 WL 737401, Unreported, appeal not allowed 105 Ohio St.3d 1564, 828 N.E.2d 118, 2005-Ohio-2447. Infants ⇐ 155

Statute permitting termination of parental rights when child has been in temporary custody of one or more public children services agencies or private child placing agencies for 12 or more months of consecutive 22 month period, was not unconstitutional on its face, and thus, did not violate due process provisions of Federal and State Constitutions. In re Bray (Ohio App. 10 Dist., Franklin, 03-31-2005) No. 04AP-842, 2005-Ohio-1540, 2005 WL 737401, Unreported. Infants ⇐ 132

Appointed trial counsel's failure to ask trial judge to recuse herself in county proceeding to obtain permanent custody of child after judge disclosed that she had briefly spoken to foster mother at a party was not a breach of an essential duty and was not ineffective assistance of counsel, where judge appeared to fully disclose the length and content of her interaction, and there was no indication that her interaction somehow affected her decision in matter. In re M.W. (Ohio App. 8 Dist., Cuyahoga, 03-24-2005) No. 83390, 2005-Ohio-1302, 2005 WL 678111, Unreported. Infants ⇐ 205

Mother's mental health issues were not determinative factor in court's decision to grant agency permanent custody of children, and thus, due process did not require court to appoint psychiatric expert to assist mother in her defense. In re M.W. (Ohio App. 8 Dist., Cuyahoga, 03-24-2005) No. 83409, 2005-Ohio-1305, 2005 WL 678109, Unreported. Infants ⇐ 212

Father was not denied due process in termination of parental rights proceedings by magistrate's refusal to take additional testimony apart from "updates" regarding father's progress with case plan; magistrate indicated at prior hearing that he would not take additional testimony, father's counsel acquiesced in magistrate's proposal, magistrate heard summaries from everyone involved in the case, father's positive testimony would not erase the elements of the case plan that counsel admitted father failed to complete, father indicated that he had nothing to say for himself when asked, and father had been expressly warned that failure to comply with case plan would result in termination of parental rights. In re M.B. (Ohio App. 10 Dist., Franklin, 03-08-2005) No. 04AP755, 2005-Ohio-986, 2005 WL 534904, Unreported. Infants ⇐ 207

Mother in termination of parental rights proceedings failed to establish ineffective assistance of counsel due to counsel's alleged failure to effectively cross-examine guardian ad litem on his reasoning for his recommendation; trial counsel acted within the wide range of acceptable professional assistance, and mother failed to show that alleged errors were sufficient to undermine confidence in trial court's decision. In re Smith (Ohio App. 3 Dist., Marion, 01-18-2005) No. 9-04-35, 2005-Ohio-149, 2005 WL 91639, Unreported. Infants ⇐ 205

Trial counsel did not provide ineffective assistance in termination of parental rights proceeding, despite challenge to counsel's failure during first phase of hearing to present rebuttal evidence regarding mother's compliance with case plan objectives, where children were found to have been in temporary custody of department of job and family services for more than 12 out of last 22 months such that trial court was not required to make finding that children could not be returned to mother within reasonable time and could proceed to second phase of hearing, which addressed children's best interest. In re Hayes/Reichenbach Children (Ohio App. 5 Dist., Stark, 12-13-2004) No. 2004CA00278, 2004-Ohio-6751, 2004 WL 2896008, Unreported. Infants ⇐ 205

Father waived right to claim on appeal that statute providing for termination of parental rights if child has been in temporary custody of public children services agency for 12 or more months of consecutive 22-month period is unconstitutional, where father failed to raise claim in trial court. In re Hinkle (Ohio App. 10 Dist., Franklin, 11-16-2004) No. 04AP-509, No. 04AP-510, 2004-Ohio-6071, 2004 WL 2591221, Unreported. Infants ⇐ 243

Mother failed to prove that she was denied effective assistance of counsel during termination of parental rights proceeding, despite contention that her attorney failed to explain the importance of testifying on her own behalf; record failed to reveal why mother elected not to testify or what, if anything, she could have said to bolster her case if she had testified. In re T.P. (Ohio App. 2 Dist., Montgomery, 10-29-2004) No. 20604, 2004-Ohio-5835, 2004 WL 2453304, Unreported. Infants ⇐ 205

Putative father failed to establish that he was denied effective assistance of counsel in termination of parental rights proceeding, where, even if counsel had informed trial court that putative father wished to be reunited with son, there was no reasonable probability that court would not have granted permanent custody to county children services agency as there was ample evidence that putative father failed to meet requirements of case plan, including that putative father did not cooperate in paternity testing process and did not offer financial support for child. In re C.S. (Ohio App. 2 Dist., Montgomery, 10-22-2004) No. 20379, 2004-Ohio-5810, 2004 WL 2445238, Unreported. Infants ⇐ 205

Putative father was not denied due process with respect to service of notice of termination of parental rights proceeding, where putative father was served with certified mail notice, putative father did not claim certified mail, and trial court sent notice by regular mail, which was not returned to court. In re C.S. (Ohio App. 2 Dist., Montgomery, 10-22-2004) No. 20379, 2004-Ohio-5810, 2004 WL 2445238, Unreported. Constitutional Law ⇐ 274(5); Infants ⇐ 198

Incarcerated mother's due process rights were not violated by trial court's decision, in proceedings to determine if permanent custody of children should be awarded to county agency, to deny mother's request to continue adjudicatory/dispositional hearing until her attendance could be secured; mother was represented by counsel at all stages of proceedings, and court was aware that mother was being held without bond in another county on very serious charges. In re G.C. & M.C. (Ohio App. 8 Dist., Cuyahoga, 10-21-2004) No. 83994, 2004-Ohio-5607, 2004 WL 2367243, Unreported. Constitutional Law ⇐ 274(5); Infants ⇐ 204

Mother failed to demonstrate ineffective assistance of counsel in permanent custody proceedings in trial counsel's alleged failure to object to hearsay statements; there was an abundance of evidence to support trial court's decision to terminate parental rights, even absent hearsay evidence. In re S.V. (Ohio App. 9 Dist., Summit, 10-13-2004) No. 22116, 2004-Ohio-5445, 2004 WL 2292825, Unreported. Infants ⇐ 205

The failure of counsel for father to advise father of his Fifth Amendment right to remain silent did not prejudice father, during termination of parental rights proceeding, and therefore did not constitute ineffective assistance; father's admissions that he failed to follow court orders and that he had prior problems with local law enforcement were not "self-incriminating," evidence of father's criminal court records was admitted as State's exhibits, and other witnesses testified as to father's failure to complete parenting classes. In re Dixon (Ohio App. 5 Dist., Stark, 10-04-2004) No. 2004CA00134, 2004-Ohio-5361, 2004 WL 2260572, Unreported. Infants ⇐ 205

Failing to hold new hearing on permanent custody of children after Court of Appeals reversed finding that children had been in custody of children services board (CSB) for 12 of past 22 months and remanded custody issue to trial court did not deny father due process, where, in original motion for permanent custody, CSB alleged alternate factor for granting CSB permanent custody that children could not or should not be placed with parent because parent failed to substantially remedy conditions that caused children to be placed outside home, and father was heard on such allegation, cross-examined witness, and offered evidence. In re T.G. (Ohio App. 9 Dist., Wayne, 09-29-2004) No. 04CA0040, 2004-Ohio-5173, 2004 WL 2244123, Unreported. Constitutional Law ⚖ 274(5); Infants ⚖ 254

Statute providing for termination of parental rights when child had been in temporary custody of children service agency for 12 or more months of consecutive 22 month period did not deprive mother of due process. In re K. (Ohio App. 8 Dist., Cuyahoga, 09-02-2004) No. 83410, 2004-Ohio-4629, 2004 WL 1946141, Unreported. Constitutional Law ⚖ 274(5); Infants ⚖ 132

Mother challenging grant of permanent custody of children to county agency waived for appeal issue of whether statute governing permanent custody proceedings was unconstitutional, where mother failed to raise constitutional claim in trial court. In re K. (Ohio App. 8 Dist., Cuyahoga, 09-02-2004) No. 83410, 2004-Ohio-4629, 2004 WL 1946141, Unreported. Infants ⚖ 243

Denying mother's request to call her child as witness in best interest phase of proceeding in which department of job and family services sought permanent custody of children did not violate mother's due process rights, where children's guardian ad litem, social worker assigned to family, and children's counselor testified as to children's wishes to return to their mother. In re Sunderman/Daniels Children Minor Children (Ohio App. 5 Dist., Stark, 08-30-2004) No. 2004CA00093, 2004-Ohio-4608, 2004 WL 1941061, Unreported. Constitutional Law ⚖ 274(5); Infants ⚖ 207

Denying mother opportunity to present testimony of witness, who was subpoenaed by both mother and department of job and family services but who did not appear, did not violate mother's due process rights in proceeding on department's motion for permanent custody of dependent children, where mother did not show that she was prejudiced as mother did not contest trial court's finding that children had been in department's custody for 12 of last 22 months and grant of permanent custody could be based on such finding. In re Sunderman/Daniels Children Minor Children (Ohio App. 5 Dist., Stark, 08-30-2004) No. 2004CA00093, 2004-Ohio-4608, 2004 WL 1941061, Unreported. Constitutional Law ⚖ 274(5); Infants ⚖ 207

Statutory subsection providing for grant of permanent child custody to public children services agency based on fact that child has been in temporary custody of one or more such agency for 12 or more months of consecutive 22 month period is constitutional. In re Villaneuva/Hampton Children (Ohio App. 5 Dist., Stark, 08-30-2004) No. 2004CA00120, 2004-Ohio-4609, 2004 WL 1933504, Unreported, appeal not allowed 104 Ohio St.3d 1441, 819 N.E.2d 1124, 2004-Ohio-7033. Infants ⚖ 132

Trial court's acceptance of guardian ad litem's supplemental report and recommendation that grandmother be granted custody of mother's children, which was submitted one month after trial on petition by Department of Children and Family Services for permanent custody of children, was abuse of discretion, where recommendation was accepted without allowing parties to cross-examine guardian ad litem regarding her report and recommendations. In re D.D. (Ohio App. 8 Dist., Cuyahoga, 08-12-2004) No. 83537, 2004-Ohio-4243, 2004 WL 1797186, Unreported. Infants ⚖ 208

Statute providing for termination of parental rights when child has been in temporary custody of one or more public children service agencies or private child placing agencies for 12 or more months of consecutive 22 month period was not unconstitutional as applied to mother; roughly 18 months elapsed between the time that mother's case plan was first adopted and the date of commencement of trial on the permanent custody motion, such period was adequate to permit mother to demonstrate parental fitness, and county did not control mother and her actions such that it effectively foreclosed her ability to demonstrate suitability as a parent. In re Brooks (Ohio App. 10 Dist., Franklin, 07-22-2004) No. 04AP-164, No. 04AP-201, No. 04AP-202, No. 04AP-165, 2004-Ohio-3887, 2004 WL 1631760, Unreported, appeal not allowed 103 Ohio St.3d 1495, 816 N.E.2d 1081, 2004-Ohio-5605. Infants ⚖ 132

Clear and convincing evidence supported trial court order granting permanent custody of children to county children's services; father failed to complete anger management classes, parent classes, and domestic violence classes, father's supervised visits with the children were cancelled due to father's failure to appear for visitation, when father was not incarcerated he did not visit the children, he failed to acknowledge holidays or the birthdays of the children, and it was in the best interests of the children to be adopted by maternal grandparents. In re Jesse P. (Ohio App. 6 Dist., Lucas, 07-16-2004) No. L-04-1028, 2004-Ohio-3801, 2004 WL 1595103, Unreported. Infants ⚖ 155; Infants ⚖ 157

Father's due process rights were not violated when the trial court held termination of parental rights hearing even though incarcerated father was not present in the courtroom; father was represented by an attorney, the attorney entered into evidence a letter written by father, father's brother and sister testified on his behalf at the hearing, a full record was made of the proceeding, and any additional testimony father wanted to submit could have been presented by deposition. In re Jesse P. (Ohio App. 6 Dist., Lucas, 07-16-2004) No. L-04-1028, 2004-Ohio-3801, 2004 WL 1595103, Unreported. Constitutional Law ⚖ 274(5); Infants ⚖ 203

Mother failed to establish that her appointed counsel provided ineffective assistance in termination of parental rights proceeding, where mother merely alleged that requiring mother to proceed with counsel with whom she had not been in direct communication for lengthy period of time and with whom she did not have trust relationship denied mother constitutional rights, mother presented no specific facts to support argument, and transcript revealed that mother was more than adequately represented by counsel and that no prejudice occurred. In re Baby Girl Elliott (Ohio App. 12 Dist., Butler, 07-06-2004) No. CA2003-10-256, 2004-Ohio-3539, 2004 WL 1485858, Unreported. Infants ⚖ 205

Failure of counsel for parents to challenge constitutionality of statutes applicable in termination of parental rights proceeding did not constitute ineffective assistance, where courts had previously found statutes to be constitutional and there was no reasonable probability that result of proceeding would have been different had counsel challenged statutes. In re Andy-Jones (Ohio App. 10 Dist., Franklin, 06-24-2004) No. 03AP-1167, No. 03AP-1231, 2004-Ohio-3312, 2004 WL 1405319, Unreported, stay denied 103 Ohio St.3d 1425, 814 N.E.2d 489, 2004-Ohio-4524, appeal not allowed 103 Ohio St.3d 1429, 814 N.E.2d 491, 2004-Ohio-4524, appeal not allowed 103 Ohio St.3d 1465, 815 N.E.2d 680, 2004-Ohio-5056. Infants ⚖ 205

Court of Appeals would decline to address parents' claim that statutes relating to termination of parental rights were unconstitutional, where parents failed in trial court to challenge constitutionality of statutes. In re Andy-Jones (Ohio App. 10 Dist., Franklin, 06-24-2004) No. 03AP-1167, No. 03AP-1231, 2004-Ohio-3312, 2004 WL 1405319, Unreported, stay denied 103 Ohio St.3d 1425, 814 N.E.2d 489, 2004-Ohio-4524, appeal not allowed 103 Ohio St.3d 1429, 814 N.E.2d 491, 2004-Ohio-4524, appeal not allowed 103 Ohio St.3d 1465, 815 N.E.2d 680, 2004-Ohio-5056. Infants ⚖ 243

Court of Appeals would decline to address mother's constitutional challenge to statutory subsection providing that trial court may grant permanent custody to public children services agency if child has been in temporary custody of agency for 12 or more months of consecutive 22-month period, where trial court did not rely on subsection in granting permanent custody to agency. In re Merryman/Wilson Children (Ohio App. 5 Dist., Stark, 06-14-2004) No. 2004 CA 00056, No. 2004 CA 00071, 2004-Ohio-3174, 2004 WL 1376278, Unreported. Infants ⚖ 248.1

Granting permanent custody of dependent children to County Children Services Board did not violate mother's equal protection rights; although mother claimed decision was based on her mental illness, mother's mental illness was only one factor considered, and decision was based on fact that children were in Board's custody for more that 12 months of consecutive 22-month period and that it was in children's best interest to grant permanent custody to Board. In re Bicanovsky (Ohio App. 7 Dist., Mahoning, 06-10-2004) No. 04-MA-5, 2004-Ohio-3034, 2004 WL 1321900, Unreported. Constitutional Law ⚖ 225.1; Infants ⚖ 222

Mother waived for appellate review claim that termination of parental rights statute imposes a statutory presumption of parental unfitness if trial court finds that a child has been in the temporary custody of the Children Services Board (CSB) for 12 or more months of a 22-month period and violates a parent's substantive and procedural due process rights, where mother did not raise this constitutional challenge in the trial court. In re K. S. (Ohio App. 9 Dist., Summit, 05-26-2004) No. 21913, 2004-Ohio-2660, 2004 WL 1160031, Unreported. Infants ⚖ 243

Failure of counsel for mother to object to the allegedly improper notice to mother of the final permanent custody hearing was reasonable trial strategy, and therefore could not amount to ineffective assistance; mother received personal notice of the original trial date and constructive notice, from counsel, of the final hearing date, and thus counsel was aware that mother received proper notice of the hearing and ethically could not object to the notice. In re Keith Lee P. (Ohio App. 6 Dist., Lucas, 04-16-2004) No. L-03-1266, 2004-Ohio-1976, 2004 WL 835989, Unreported. Infants ⚖ 205

Statute providing for termination of parental rights when child had been in temporary custody of children service agency for 12 or more months of consecutive 22 month period did not deprive parent of due process; parent had 12 months to demonstrate that he was fit to care for child. In re Gomer (Ohio App. 3 Dist., Wyandot, 04-05-2004) No. 16-03-19, No. 16-03-20, No. 16-03-21, 2004-Ohio-1723, 2004 WL 722978, Unreported, appeal not allowed 102 Ohio St.3d 1473, 809 N.E.2d 1159, 2004-Ohio-2830. Constitutional Law ⇔ 274(5); Infants ⇔ 132

Court of Appeals would not address argument by mother, in termination of parental rights proceeding, that portions of statutes related to the termination of parental rights were unconstitutional, where mother entered no objection in the juvenile court to the constitutionality of the statutes. In Re P. C. (Ohio App. 9 Dist., Summit, 03-17-2004) No. 21734, No. 21739, 2004-Ohio-1230, 2004 WL 509368, Unreported. Infants ⇔ 243

Failure to grant indigent mother's motion for appointment of psychological expert witness at State's expense, after granting Children Services Board's (CSB) motion that mother be evaluated by forensic psychologist, thereby making mother's mental health critical issue in parental termination proceeding, violated mother's due process rights; CSB expert's report and testimony regarding mother's mental health were central reasons why trial court granted CSB's motion for permanent custody, mother's mental health directly impacted trial court's conclusion that she was unfit to parent, and mother could not challenge testimony since trial court denied her request for similarly qualified expert. In re Elliott (Ohio App. 7 Dist., Jefferson, 01-26-2004) No. 03JE30, No. 03JE33, 2004-Ohio-388, 2004 WL 187413, Unreported. Constitutional Law ⇔ 274(5); Infants ⇔ 212

The trial court's failure to sua sponte order a mental health examination of mother to aid in her defense of the county department of children and family services' effort to obtain permanent custody of child did not violate mother's due process rights; the department was awarded permanent custody due to mother's failure to remedy the conditions that caused the removal of child, and mother's mental health issues were not the determinative factor in the court's decision. In re J.D. (Ohio App. 8 Dist., Cuyahoga, 01-29-2004) No. 82898, 2004-Ohio-358, 2004 WL 170338, Unreported. Constitutional Law ⇔ 274(5); Infants ⇔ 208

Court of Appeals would not consider mother's claim on appeal that child protection statute was unconstitutional, where it did not appear that trial court relied on statute in placing child in the permanent custody of County Job & Family Services. Swisher v. Tuscarawas County Job & Family Services (Ohio App. 5 Dist., Tuscarawas, 12-05-2003) No. 2003AP080060, No. 2003AP080066, 2003-Ohio-7317, 2003 WL 23269346, Unreported, appeal not allowed 101 Ohio St.3d 1453, 803 N.E.2d 401, 2004-Ohio-462. Infants ⇔ 248.1

Child protection statute did not apply to grandmother, but rather to biological parents, and thus grandmother did not have standing to challenge whether statute was constitutional. Swisher v. Tuscarawas County Job & Family Services (Ohio App. 5 Dist., Tuscarawas, 12-05-2003) No. 2003AP080060, No. 2003AP080066, 2003-Ohio-7317, 2003 WL 23269346, Unreported, appeal not allowed 101 Ohio St.3d 1453, 803 N.E.2d 401, 2004-Ohio-462. Constitutional Law ⇔ 42.1(1)

Whatever the nature of the evidence regarding "real reason" children were removed from foster parents, failure of County Children Services and guardian ad litem to disclose information did not deprive father of his right to a fair trial in custody proceeding, in light of overwhelming evidence presented by County Children Services germane to best interest factors. In re Damron (Ohio App. 10 Dist., Franklin, 10-30-2003) No. 03AP-419, 2003-Ohio-5810, 2003 WL 22455693, Unreported. Infants ⇔ 201

Mother's claim that her counsel rendered ineffective assistance in permanent custody hearing was rendered moot, where remand was required for trial to issue findings addressing statutory factors used to determine whether termination of mother's parental rights as in best interests of the children. In re Brooks (Ohio App. 10 Dist., Franklin, 10-07-2003) No. 03AP-282, No. 03AP-442, 2003-Ohio-5348, 2003 WL 22290239, Unreported. Infants ⇔ 248.1

The trial court's failure to adjudicate county children services' motion for permanent custody of child within the time frame provided by statute did not prejudice mother or violate due process; mother agreed to or requested several of the continuances, and the length of the delay allowed mother further opportunity to comply with her caseplan and be reunited with child. In re James (Ohio App. 10 Dist., Franklin, 09-30-2003) No. 03AP-373, 2003-Ohio-5208, 2003 WL 22232965, Unreported. Infants ⇔ 253

Mother's mental health in termination of parental rights case was not predominant issue and did not ultimately become determinative issue in court's permanent custody analysis, and thus due process did not mandate appointment of psychiatric expert to assist mother in her defense; court's award of permanent custody to county agency was based on mother's continuous and repeated failure to substantially remedy conditions causing children to be placed outside home, and on fact that she had had parental rights involuntarily terminated with respect to sibling of children. In re B.G. (Ohio App. 8 Dist., Cuyahoga, 06-19-2003) No. 81982, 2003-Ohio-3256, 2003 WL 21434172, Unreported, appeal not allowed 99 Ohio St.3d 1547, 795 N.E.2d 684, 2003-Ohio-4671. Constitutional Law ⇔ 274(5); Infants ⇔ 212

Mother received adequate statutory notice of proceedings to terminate parental rights, insofar as notice provided that any party was entitled to counsel in proceedings and that counsel would be appointed for indigent party upon request, mother appeared at hearing with counsel, notice explained legal effects of termination of parental rights, and notice provided name and number of court personnel to be contacted. In re Shumate (Ohio App. 5 Dist., Muskingum, 04-29-2003) No. CT2002-0051, No. CT2002-0054, No. CT2002-0052, No. CT2002-0053, 2003-Ohio-2509, 2003 WL 21130058, Unreported. Infants ⇔ 198

Father, whose parental rights were terminated, failed to establish ineffective assistance of counsel; even if unknown witnesses had been called to testify as to children's best interest, it was mere speculation how these witnesses would have testified and, assuming counsel did not scrutinize guardian ad litem's report, father failed to explain how scrutinizing report would have altered result of case. In re Kramer (Ohio App. 10 Dist., Franklin, 05-06-2003) No. 02AP-1038, No. 02AP-1039, 2003-Ohio-2277, 2003 WL 21007196, Unreported. Infants ⇔ 205

Statute providing for termination of parental rights when child has been in temporary custody of one or more public children service agencies or private child placing agencies for 12 or more months of consecutive 22 month period does not deprive mother of due process; although mother contended statute does not require finding that parent is unsuitable or unfit to care for child, statute contains implicit presumption that parent is unsuitable or unfit based on prior reasons given for placing child in temporary custody of agencies and parent is not denied fundamentally fair procedures as parent has 12 months to demonstrate ability to reunify and that she is fit to care for child. In re Workman (Ohio App. 4 Dist., Vinton, 04-03-2003) No. 02CA574, 2003-Ohio-2220, 2003 WL 2012574, Unreported. Constitutional Law ⇔ 274(5); Infants ⇔ 132

Father's due process rights were not violated by the trial court's failure to convey him from prison to allow father to be present during termination of parental rights hearing; father was represented by counsel at the hearing, a full record of the hearing was made, and father could have presented his evidence through deposition. U.S.C.A. Const.Amend. 14. In re Joseph P. (Ohio App. 6 Dist., Lucas, 05-02-2003) No. L-02-1385, 2003-Ohio-2217, 2003 WL 2007268, Unreported. Constitutional Law ⇔ 274(5); Convicts ⇔ 6; Infants ⇔ 203

Denial of mother's motion for a continuance of the permanent custody hearing in child protection matter based on mother's unexplained absence did not deprive mother of due process; mother's counsel's inability to explain to trial court why mother was absent indicated that mother's absence was voluntary, and child protection agency asserted that it would be prejudiced by any continuance because of the difficulty in securing the presence of the professional witnesses. In re Kutcher (Ohio App. 7 Dist., Belmont, 03-14-2003) No. 02 BE 58, 2003-Ohio-1235, 2003 WL 1194147, Unreported. Constitutional Law ⇔ 274(5); Infants ⇔ 204

Trial court's ex parte consideration of guardian ad litem's supplemental report submitted after the termination of parental rights case had been remanded to determine child's "best interests" violated mother's right to due process; while mother may have been somewhat lackadaisical because she never requested opportunity to submit new evidence in response to the report, an additional hearing was required so that mother could indicate whether she wanted to present new evidence in regard to the supplemental report and cross-examine the guardian ad litem on the report's contents. In re Salsgiver (Ohio App. 11 Dist., Geauga, 03-13-2003) No. 2002-G-2478, 2003-Ohio-1203, 2003 WL 1193789, Unreported. Constitutional Law ⇔ 274(5); Infants ⇔ 208

Although father's actions in termination of parental rights case were somewhat lackadaisical, trial court was required to schedule an additional hearing so that father could indicate whether he wanted to present new evidence in regard to guardian ad litem's supplemental report which addressed child's wishes as to custody and to cross-examine the guardian ad litem on the report's contents, and, since such an opportunity was not afforded to father, trial court violated father's rights to due process by considering the supplemental report ex parte. In re Salsgiver (Ohio App. 11 Dist., Geauga, 03-13-2003) No. 2002-G-2477, 2003-Ohio-1206, 2003 WL 1193784, Unreported. Constitutional Law ⇔ 274(5); Infants ⇔ 203

In order to afford father his complete right to due process in termination of parental rights case, the trial court, on remand, was required to hold an additional evidentiary hearing in which father had the opportunity to cross-examine the guardian ad litem on both his original and supplemental reports and to present any new evidence in response to the contents of the guardian ad litem's supplemental report, and, after the completion of this hearing, the trial court was required to issue new factual findings on the "best interests" question and render a new final decision on the motion for permanent custody filed by County Jobs and Family Services. In re Salsgiver (Ohio App. 11 Dist., Geauga, 03-13-2003) No. 2002-G-2477, 2003-Ohio-1206, 2003 WL 1193784, Unreported. Constitutional Law ⇨ 274(5); Infants ⇨ 254

Father's constitutional right to due process was not violated due to fact that trial court did not appoint counsel to represent him in proceedings related to county's motion for permanent custody of his two sons, where record did not reflect that father was indigent, and, at dispositional hearing, which was last hearing for which father appeared, father was referred to the public defender and given a contact number. In re Whipple Children (Ohio App. 5 Dist., Stark, 03-10-2003) No. 2002CA00406, 2003-Ohio-1101, 2003 WL 950448, Unreported. Constitutional Law ⇨ 274(5); Infants ⇨ 205

Decision of mother's counsel not to call expert witness to rebut testimony of expert witness presented by County Children Services Board (Board) in permanent custody proceeding was reasonable trial strategy and, therefore, was not ineffective assistance of counsel; counsel effectively cross-examined Board's expert and elicited information favorable to mother. In re Spillman (Ohio App. 12 Dist., Clinton, 02-18-2003) No. CA2002-06-028, 2003-Ohio-713, 2003 WL 352477, Unreported. Infants ⇨ 205

Evidence supported trial court's finding that child could not, and should not, be returned to custody of her mother within reasonable time with respect to determining whether mother's parental rights should be terminated; case manager for Department of Job and Family Services testified that mother had not demonstrated she had acquired and maintained stable housing, had failed to pursue counseling, and had not been assessed regarding substance abuse, and case worker testified there had been past incidents of domestic violence, and mother had become threatening and aggressive with staff at Job and Family Services. In re Berry (Ohio App. 5 Dist., Tuscarawas, 01-13-2003) No. 2002AP090075, 2003-Ohio-149, 2003 WL 124843, Unreported. Infants ⇨ 155

The failure of counsel for mother and father to timely object to the admission of the guardian ad litem's report, which contained confidential statements made by father during mediation, did not prejudice mother and father, and thus did not amount to ineffective assistance; the trial court removed the report from the casefile after counsel made the court aware of the contents of the report at the adjudication and disposition hearing, the trial judge stated that he had not reviewed the report, and mother and father failed to include the transcript of the adjudication hearing to allow the Court of Appeal to review objections from the hearing. In re Miriah W. (Ohio App. 6 Dist., Lucas, 11-22-2002) No. L-02-1182, 2002-Ohio-6361, 2002 WL 31630758, Unreported. Infants ⇨ 205

The Court of Appeals could not address mother's appellate argument which challenged the constitutionality of the statute which allowed for the establishment of the unsuitability of a parent by the fact that the child had been in the temporary custody of county child services for 12 consecutive months during the 22 months preceding the dependency hearing, where mother raised the argument for the first time on appeal. In re C.F. (Ohio App. 9 Dist., Lorain, 11-13-2002) No. 02CA008084, 2002-Ohio-6113, 2002 WL 31513423, Unreported. Infants ⇨ 243

Mother waived for appellate review challenge to constitutionality of statute which allowed for establishment of unsuitability of a parent by the fact that child had been in temporary custody of county child services for 12 consecutive months during 22 months preceding dependency hearing, where mother raised argument for first time on appeal. In re C.F. (Ohio App. 9 Dist., Lorain, 11-13-2002) No. 02CA008084, 2002-Ohio-6113, 2002 WL 31513423, Unreported. Infants ⇨ 243

A parent's constitutionally protected liberty interest in the care and custody of their children is not violated where a parent's past alcoholism, lack of family support and repeated incarceration for multiple convictions involving violence support a finding that the grant of permanent custody to a county children services board is in the best interest of the child. In re Huddleston (Ohio App. 12 Dist., Clinton, 08-23-1999) No. CA99-01-003, 1999 WL 636492, Unreported.

Although a trial court does not err in overruling an incarcerated parent's motion to be present at a permanent custody hearing, and the incarcerated parent is represented by counsel at the permanent custody hearing, due process requires that the parent be afforded some other means of presenting his testimony such as by deposition and where the court fails to provide such alternative means of presenting the incarcerated parent's testimony, the termination of parental rights will be reversed and remanded. In re Elliot, No. 92 CA 34, 1993 WL 268846 (4th Dist Ct App, Lawrence, 6-25-93).

Mother's due process rights were violated, in suit by county agency to obtain permanent custody of neglected child, when the trial court refused to allow mother to call relatives, who were considered for possible placement of child, to testify at hearing to modify child's disposition, though relatives did not file motion for custody; the parties had notice that relatives were possible custodians for child in advance of the hearing since the court had previously ordered the county job and family services to conduct a home study of relatives, the court had ordered visitation between child and relatives, and the hearing had been continued to provide child with an opportunity to spend more time with relatives, and the trial court permitted job and family services to present lengthy testimony concerning the appropriateness of relatives as a placement alternative at the hearing. In re Beatty (Ohio App. 5 Dist., 07-14-2006) 2006-Ohio-3698, 2006 WL 2022213. Infants ⇨ 230.1

A parent's right to raise his or her children is an essential and basic civil right. In re Sheffey (Ohio App. 11 Dist., 02-10-2006) 167 Ohio App.3d 141, 854 N.E.2d 508, 2006-Ohio-619. Parent And Child ⇨ 1

When the state initiates a permanent-custody proceeding, parents must be provided with fundamentally fair procedures in accordance with the due process provisions under the Fourteenth Amendment and the Ohio Constitution. In re Sheffey (Ohio App. 11 Dist., 02-10-2006) 167 Ohio App.3d 141, 854 N.E.2d 508, 2006-Ohio-619. Constitutional Law ⇨ 274(5)

In lieu of appearance of parent at hearing on permanent custody of child, the court may make other accommodations so that the parent can witness and participate in the hearing, guaranteeing the parent's rights to due process, confrontation of witnesses, and participation in the hearing. In re Sheffey (Ohio App. 11 Dist., 02-10-2006) 167 Ohio App.3d 141, 854 N.E.2d 508, 2006-Ohio-619. Infants ⇨ 207

A parent has a right to be present at a hearing regarding permanent custody of child. In re Sheffey (Ohio App. 11 Dist., 02-10-2006) 167 Ohio App.3d 141, 854 N.E.2d 508, 2006-Ohio-619. Infants ⇨ 203

Mother had statutory right to be present at and/or participate in hearing on neglect and dependency of her child. In re Sheffey (Ohio App. 11 Dist., 02-10-2006) 167 Ohio App.3d 141, 854 N.E.2d 508, 2006-Ohio-619. Infants ⇨ 203

Trial court failed to follow basic procedural safeguards mandated within permanent custody statute and basic constitutional due process requirements of both state and federal constitutions, in proceeding to terminate parental rights; mother was denied proper notice of complaint and hearing, was denied recitation of her rights, was denied proper participation in proceedings, and was denied continuance of permanent custody hearing, mother's failure to attend hearing was not voluntary, but based upon her incarceration, and mother was not appointed counsel during hearing for neglect and dependency. In re Sheffey (Ohio App. 11 Dist., 02-10-2006) 167 Ohio App.3d 141, 854 N.E.2d 508, 2006-Ohio-619. Infants ⇨ 191

The fundamental liberty interest of natural parents in the care, custody, and management of their child, as protected by due process, does not evaporate simply because they have not been model parents or have lost temporary custody of their child to the state. In re Sheffey (Ohio App. 11 Dist., 02-10-2006) 167 Ohio App.3d 141, 854 N.E.2d 508, 2006-Ohio-619. Constitutional Law ⇨ 274(5)

The trial court's consideration of new evidence at termination of parental rights hearing on remand, without allowing other parties to present new evidence, violated due process; the new evidence presented included an opinion by expert that mother was not capable of caring for child, the magistrate relied on that testimony in support of order terminating mother's parental rights, and mother was prohibited from presenting any evidence to rebut the new evidence presented by expert. In re Walker (Ohio App. 11 Dist., 07-22-2005) 162 Ohio App.3d 303, 833 N.E.2d 362, 2005-Ohio-3773, on subsequent appeal 2006-Ohio-739, 2006 WL 389596, appeal allowed 109 Ohio St.3d 1506, 849 N.E.2d 1027, 2006-Ohio-2998. Infants ⇨ 254

Permanent termination of parental rights has been described as the family law equivalent of the death penalty in a criminal case; therefore, parents must be afforded every procedural and substantive protection the law allows. In re Walker (Ohio App. 11 Dist., 07-22-2005) 162 Ohio App.3d 303, 833 N.E.2d 362, 2005-Ohio-3773, on subsequent appeal 2006-Ohio-739, 2006 WL 389596, appeal allowed 109 Ohio St.3d 1506, 849 N.E.2d 1027, 2006-Ohio-2998. Infants ⇨ 194.1

Parents who are suitable persons maintain a paramount right to custody of their minor children. In re Alexis K. (Ohio App. 6 Dist., 03-24-2005) 160 Ohio App.3d 32, 825 N.E.2d 1148, 2005-Ohio-1380. Child Custody ⇨ 42

The inviolability of the parent-child relationship finds protection in the Due Process Clause, the Equal Protection Clause, and the Ninth Amendment. In re Alexis K. (Ohio App. 6 Dist., 03-24-2005) 160 Ohio App.3d 32, 825 N.E.2d 1148, 2005-Ohio-1380. Constitutional Law ⇨ 82(10); Constitutional Law ⇨ 225.1; Constitutional Law ⇨ 274(5)

Evidence that county children's services agency, which sought to terminate father's parental rights, conducted home study of child's paternal grandmother and determined child should not be placed there because of substantiated allegation of physical abuse, allegations of grandmother's alcohol abuse, and grandmother's medical concerns arising from car accident, and that agency could not complete home study of father's maternal grandmother because grandmother could not provide required economic information, established agency's efforts to place child with African American relatives, so that agency did not violate father's equal protection and due process rights by allegedly failing to consider keeping the light-complected child with African American relatives. In re Wingo (Ohio App. 4 Dist., 06-01-2001) 143 Ohio App.3d 652, 758 N.E.2d 780, 2001-Ohio-2477. Constitutional Law 215.2; Constitutional Law 274(5); Infants 178

Evidence that caseworker from county children's services agency told father's maternal grandmother, who had not seen child since shortly after his birth, that child was white and blue-eyed did not establish that agency, which sought to terminate father's parental rights, preferred to keep the light-complected child with his white foster family rather than with father's African American family, in alleged violation of father's equal protection and due process rights. In re Wingo (Ohio App. 4 Dist., 06-01-2001) 143 Ohio App.3d 652, 758 N.E.2d 780, 2001-Ohio-2477. Constitutional Law 215.2; Constitutional Law 274(5); Infants 178

Mother received constitutionally effective assistance of counsel in proceeding for termination of her parental rights, despite counsel's line of questioning of her tending to suggest that she sought out domestic violence and lacked commitment to her children; counsel vigorously cross-examined state's witnesses, attempted to establish that mother's continuing relationship with father was not unusual and did not necessarily need to be terminated, challenged domestic violence program's method of evaluating client's degree of success as well as its overall success rate, and elicited beneficial facts and testimony from other witnesses. In re Glenn (Ohio App. 8 Dist., 10-30-2000) 139 Ohio App.3d 105, 742 N.E.2d 1210. Infants 205

Amendment to permanent custody statute, changing methods and procedure by which court was to determine whether parental rights were to be terminated, was not ex post facto law as applied to motion for permanent custody filed before amendment's effective date, as statute in question was not a criminal statute. In re Rodgers (Ohio App. 12 Dist., 06-05-2000) 138 Ohio App.3d 510, 741 N.E.2d 901. Infants 132

Amendment to permanent custody statute, which changed only the methods and procedure by which court was to determine whether parental rights were to be terminated, was remedial in nature, and thus its application to a motion for permanent custody filed before amendment's effective date did not violate State Constitution's prohibition against retroactive laws. In re Rodgers (Ohio App. 12 Dist., 06-05-2000) 138 Ohio App.3d 510, 741 N.E.2d 901. Constitutional Law 191; Infants 132

Because a parent's constitutionally protected liberty interest is at stake in a permanent custody case, due process requires the state to prove by clear and convincing evidence that applicable statutory standards have been met. In re Rodgers (Ohio App. 12 Dist., 06-05-2000) 138 Ohio App.3d 510, 741 N.E.2d 901. Constitutional Law 274(5)

Conduct of parents' counsel in child protection proceeding did not deprive parents of substantial or procedural right rendering trial fundamentally unfair, and therefore did not amount to ineffective assistance; parents stipulated to truthfulness of allegations that children were victims of sexual and physical abuse, children continued to report abuse, children's guardian ad litem cross-examined caseworkers, testimony of child psychiatrist and psychologists concerning continuing harm to children went largely unrebutted, and at least three defense witnesses were called. In re Heston (Ohio App. 1 Dist., 09-18-1998) 129 Ohio App.3d 825, 719 N.E.2d 93. Infants 205

Clear and convincing evidence did not support juvenile court's finding that child could not be placed with her parents within reasonable time or should be placed with parents, as required to sustain judgment granting permanent custody of child to children services agency, where only area in which parents did not comply with reunification case plan was their failure to admit that father sexually abused child, but that condition of plan violated parents' Fifth Amendment privilege against self-incrimination. In re Amanda W. (Ohio App. 6 Dist., 11-21-1997) 124 Ohio App.3d 136, 705 N.E.2d 724. Infants 178

Right to raise a child is an essential and basic civil right; therefore, parents facing permanent termination of parental rights must be afforded every procedural and substantive protection the law allows. In re Hayes (Ohio, 06-18-1997) 79 Ohio St.3d 46, 679 N.E.2d 680, reconsideration denied 79 Ohio St.3d 1492, 683 N.E.2d 793. Infants 194.1

Parents' constitutional rights with respect to custody of children could not be abridged by a cursory judgment which simply stated, that while each individual act of parents may not warrant granting of permanent custody to county, totality of acts and pattern of parents' behavior over three-year period more than satisfied court that permanent custody requirements had been met. In re Brown (Ohio App. 3 Dist., 11-02-1994) 98 Ohio App.3d 337, 648 N.E.2d 576. Infants 221

Because clear and convincing evidence standard must be met before permanent custody of children is granted to county and parental rights terminated, permanent custody hearing should be adjudicatory and not dispositional hearing; hearsay will not be admissible in adjudicatory proceedings unless exception is applicable. In re Brofford (Franklin 1992) 83 Ohio App.3d 869, 615 N.E.2d 1120. Infants 173.1; Infants 203

The test for ineffective assistance of counsel used in criminal cases is applicable in actions to terminate parental rights. Jones v. Lucas County Children Services Bd. (Lucas 1988) 46 Ohio App.3d 85, 546 N.E.2d 471. Infants 205

The standard of proof by clear and convincing evidence set forth by RC 2151.414 is constitutional; O Const Art I, § 1 does not require proof beyond a reasonable doubt to terminate parental rights. In re Schmidt (Ohio 1986) 25 Ohio St.3d 331, 496 N.E.2d 952, 25 O.B.R. 386.

Mother failed to establish that her court appointed counsel during termination of parental rights proceeding was ineffective due to counsel's alleged failure to advise her of the implications of terminating her parental rights to child; during discussion with the court mother responded that she understood that if the agency was granted permanent custody of child she would no longer be considered the child's mother, that she would have no right to visit with child, and stated that "permanent custody is where I won't have no rights to her whatsoever" and "I will not see her, no contact, no nothing." In re Helton (Ohio App. 3 Dist., Hardin, 04-18-2002) No. 6-01-07, 2002-Ohio-1765, 2002 WL 596117, Unreported. Infants 205

2. Procedural issues

Father's waiver of right to permanent custody hearing and agreement to county children's services board being granted permanent custody of children was not knowing, given repeated referrals to continued correspondence between father and children following grant of permanent custody to board, and mention of visitation between father and children after board was granted permanent custody of children, both of which were likely to have been confusing to father's understanding that he was giving up all rights to his children. In re D.R. (Ohio App. 2 Dist., Miami, 07-07-2006) No. 2005 CA 10, No. 2006 CA 7, 2006-Ohio-3513, 2006 WL 1868314, Unreported. Infants 199

Trial court's denial of mother's motion for continuance of proceeding for termination of her parental rights was not arbitrary, unreasonable or unconscionable, and was not abuse of discretion, where mother failed to establish that her absence at hearing was unavoidable; mother alleged that she was "tired," "weak," and "nervous" on scheduled hearing date, provided no evidence that such conditions were debilitating, did not inform her attorney or court that she would not be present at hearing until after hearing was scheduled to begin, and made no post-hearing attempts to further justify her absence or submit evidence. (Per Westcott Rice, J., with one judge concurring in result only.) In re Kangas (Ohio App. 11 Dist., Ashtabula, 06-30-2006) No. 2006-A-0010, 2006-Ohio-3433, 2006 WL 1817069, Unreported. Infants 204

Mother's claims of error with respect to constitutionality of termination of parental rights statutes, sufficiency of evidence to support termination of her parental rights, and agency's alleged failure to use reasonable efforts to reunite mother with children were rendered moot by reviewing court's finding that trial court lacked statutory authority to terminate mother's parental rights. In re A.C. (Ohio App. 9 Dist., Summit, 06-30-2006) No. 23090, 2006-Ohio-3337, 2006 WL 1789853, Unreported. Infants 248.1

Trial court erred in denying mother's motion for six-month extension of temporary custody in regard to all three children who were subjects of proceeding for termination of parental rights, where denial was based upon trial court's misunderstanding as to amount of time two of the three children had been in temporary custody. In re A.C. (Ohio App. 9 Dist., Summit, 06-30-2006) No. 23090, 2006-Ohio-3337, 2006 WL 1789853, Unreported. Infants 230.1

Trial court lacked statutory authority to terminate mother's parental rights to two children, where children had been in custody of agency for only 352 days during relevant 22-month period, and court made no additional findings as to those children on first prong of permanent custody statutory test. In re A.C. (Ohio App. 9 Dist., Summit, 06-30-2006) No. 23090, 2006-Ohio-3337, 2006 WL 1789853, Unreported. Infants 210

In considering the custodial history of a child when making a determination as to whether granting permanent custody of the child to the county is in the child's best interests, the time that is attributable to an appeal of the initial permanent custody order should not be held against the parents, as they should not be penalized for pursuing their appellate rights. In re E.T. (Ohio App. 9 Dist., Summit, 05-17-2006) No. 23017, 2006-Ohio-2413, 2006 WL 1329653, Unreported. Infants ⟲ 155

Stepfather of neglected child, who had two other children with child's mother and was participating in a county children's services board caseplan to reunite him with his children, was not entitled to the same procedural protections as child's biological parents during dependency and termination of parental rights proceeding; no statute granted an unrelated individual the same legal status as a biological or adoptive parent, and stepfather was child's legal custodian, not an adoptive parent. In re Kenny B. (Ohio App. 6 Dist., Lucas, 03-03-2006) No. L-05-1227, 2006-Ohio-968, 2006 WL 513958, Unreported. Infants ⟲ 191

Evidence supported finding that notice of permanent custody hearing was served upon mother; record included certified mail receipts demonstrating that mother was served, and she acknowledged receipt of the summons for the permanent custody hearing. In re D.P. (Ohio App. 8 Dist., Cuyahoga, 03-02-2006) No. 86271, No. 86272, 2006-Ohio-937, 2006 WL 496058, Unreported. Infants ⟲ 198

Magistrate, prior to terminating mother's parental rights and granting permanent custody of child to county department of jobs and family services, was required to consider the wishes of child as expressed directly by child or through child's guardian ad litem, even though guardian ad litem cited parts of mother's testimony as evidence that child was too young to be able to express his wishes; testimony by mother constituted inadmissible hearsay and did not fulfill requirement that trial court take a child's wishes into consideration prior to terminating parental rights. In re Walling (Ohio App. 1 Dist., Hamilton, 02-24-2006) No. C-050646, 2006-Ohio-810, 2006 WL 445981, Unreported. Infants ⟲ 210

Factors in support of maternal grandparent of child remaining as a party outweighed those calling for her removal, in proceeding in which county children services board sought permanent custody of child; grandmother was significantly and actively involved in proceedings up to point board's motion to remove her was filed, and potential prejudice to mother and child weighed heavily in favor of keeping grandmother as a party to proceeding, since mother allegedly had developmental difficulties, court joined foster parents as parties to proceeding, and mother was facing permanent custody proceeding from the very beginning. In re Walker (Ohio App. 11 Dist., Ashtabula, 02-17-2006) No. 2005-A-0067, 2006-Ohio-739, 2006 WL 389596, Unreported, appeal allowed 109 Ohio St.3d 1506, 849 N.E.2d 1027, 2006-Ohio-2998. Infants ⟲ 200

Trial court abused its discretion in removing maternal grandmother of child as a party in proceeding in which county children services board sought permanent custody of child; court removed grandparents, who were opposed to granting of board's motion for permanent custody, and added foster parents, who were in favor of granting board's motion, court provided no reasoning in support of decision, and collective nature of court's decisions regarding grandparents and foster parents was arbitrary. In re Walker (Ohio App. 11 Dist., Ashtabula, 02-17-2006) No. 2005-A-0067, 2006-Ohio-739, 2006 WL 389596, Unreported, appeal allowed 109 Ohio St.3d 1506, 849 N.E.2d 1027, 2006-Ohio-2998. Infants ⟲ 200

Burden fell on county children services board, as party seeking to remove grandparents of child from proceeding in which board sought permanent custody of child, to demonstrate why grandparents should no longer be parties; juvenile rules deemed inclusion of grandparents mandatory when respective parent was less than 18 years old, mother was 15 years old at time of child's birth, and, since grandparents were already parties, they had vested interest in proceedings. In re Walker (Ohio App. 11 Dist., Ashtabula, 02-17-2006) No. 2005-A-0067, 2006-Ohio-739, 2006 WL 389596, Unreported, appeal allowed 109 Ohio St.3d 1506, 849 N.E.2d 1027, 2006-Ohio-2998. Infants ⟲ 200

Following mother's eighteenth birthday, any party could file motion with juvenile court to remove grandparents of mother's child as parties in proceeding in which county children services board sought permanent custody of mother's child; although grandparents were necessary parties to proceeding prior to mother's eighteenth birthday, they remained discretionary parties following mother's eighteenth birthday. In re Walker (Ohio App. 11 Dist., Ashtabula, 02-17-2006) No. 2005-A-0067, 2006-Ohio-739, 2006 WL 389596, Unreported, appeal allowed 109 Ohio St.3d 1506, 849 N.E.2d 1027, 2006-Ohio-2998. Infants ⟲ 200

The trial court did not commit plain error when it permitted counsel for county children services to elicit hearsay testimony from caseworker concerning the dependency referral call made by hospital social workers to children services intake worker, during termination of parental rights proceeding; the presumption that counsel had a good-faith basis for the questions applied, since father did not challenge the questions at trial, and the record contained non-hearsay evidence in support of her testimony. In re H.M.S. (Ohio App. 10 Dist., Franklin, 02-16-2006) No. 05AP-613, 2006-Ohio-701, 2006 WL 350211, Unreported. Infants ⟲ 250

The trial court did not commit plain error when it permitted counsel for county children services to question father regarding whether a children services investigator found rails for a crib at parents' home were not attached, whether hospital staff reported that parents did not have supplies for child, and whether parenting-class counselors indicated that it was unsafe for child to reside in parents' home, during termination of parental rights proceeding; none of the allegations posed in counsel's questions were cited by the court in rendering its decision, and the presumption that counsel had a good-faith basis for the questions applied, since father did not challenge the questions at trial. In re H.M.S. (Ohio App. 10 Dist., Franklin, 02-16-2006) No. 05AP-613, 2006-Ohio-701, 2006 WL 350211, Unreported. Infants ⟲ 250

Father received adequate notice of the permanent custody hearing for children; father was personally served at the initial shelter care hearing with a summons and a copy of the permanent custody complaint, the complaint set forth the dates of the pretrial, trial, and subsequent review dates, and father was present at the pretrial hearing. In re Zurfley/Chatman/Black Children (Ohio App. 5 Dist., Stark, 02-13-2006) No. 2005CA00217, 2006-Ohio-683, 2006 WL 337366, Unreported. Infants ⟲ 198

Statute that suspended a lawsuit at the death of either party did not apply to except father's appeal of the trial court's denial of his objections to magistrate's decision, which found clear and convincing evidence that child was a neglected and dependent child, from the doctrine of mootness; the action abated with child's death since her death accomplished the primary objectives of the neglect case, and the neglect case was not one that could proceed with a substituted party. In re L.W. (Ohio App. 10 Dist., Franklin, 02-14-2006) No. 05AP-317, 2006-Ohio-644, 2006 WL 330089, Unreported, appeal not allowed 109 Ohio St.3d 1497, 848 N.E.2d 859, 2006-Ohio-2762. Infants ⟲ 247

Dismissal of father's appeal of the trial court's denial of his objections to magistrate's decision, which found clear and convincing evidence that child was a neglected and dependent child, was warranted; father's appeal was rendered moot by child's death. In re L.W. (Ohio App. 10 Dist., Franklin, 02-14-2006) No. 05AP-317, 2006-Ohio-644, 2006 WL 330089, Unreported, appeal not allowed 109 Ohio St.3d 1497, 848 N.E.2d 859, 2006-Ohio-2762. Infants ⟲ 247

The trial court's denial of mother and father's motion for a six-month extension of temporary custody was an abuse of discretion, in child dependency proceeding, where the trial court erroneously determined that mother and father's children had been in the temporary custody of county children services board (CSB) for more than 12 of the previous 22 months, when actually the children had been in the custody of CSB for less than nine months when the motion for permanent custody was filed. In re E.T. (Ohio App. 9 Dist., Summit, 11-16-2005) No. 22720, 2005-Ohio-6087, 2005 WL 3050991, Unreported. Infants ⟲ 230.1

Foster mother's failure to conclusively decide, as of date of permanent custody hearing, whether she wished to adopt subject child did not provide ground for reversal of decision granting permanent custody of child to child services agency and terminating parents' parental rights; adoption into a secure, safe environment, whether it be with foster mother or any other family, cannot take place without agency first gaining permanent custody of child. R.C. 2151.414(D), (D)(4). In re A.S. (Ohio App. 10 Dist., Franklin, 10-18-2005) No. 05AP-351, No. 05AP-352, 2005-Ohio-5492, 2005 WL 2650108, Unreported. Infants ⟲ 253

Trial court was not required to make record of its in camera interview with child, in proceeding in which permanent custody of child was granted to county department of children and family services; although department made request for in camera interview, at no time did any party request that interview be recorded, and, given the lack of such a request, court did not violate any procedural requirements pursuant to juvenile rule governing recording of proceedings. In re T.W. (Ohio App. 8 Dist., Cuyahoga, 10-13-2005) No. 85845, 2005-Ohio-5446, 2005 WL 2600663, Unreported, appeal not allowed 108 Ohio St.3d 1418, 841 N.E.2d 321, 2006-Ohio-179, reconsideration denied 108 Ohio St.3d 1513, 844 N.E.2d 857, 2006-Ohio-1329. Infants ⟲ 207

Father had no standing to challenge trial court's grant of permanent custody of child to county department of children and family services; father did not allege to be putative father of child, and father was named as a party only for other two children. In re A.D. (Ohio App. 8 Dist., Cuyahoga, 10-13-2005) No. 85648, 2005-Ohio-5441, 2005 WL 2600638, Unreported. Infants ⟲ 242

Mother challenging termination of parental rights waived any error based on guardian ad litem's alleged failure to timely file reports, where mother failed to object at trial regarding the submission of the guardian ad litem's report. In re Di.R. (Ohio App. 8 Dist., Cuyahoga, 10-06-2005) No. 85765, No. 85766, 2005-Ohio-5346, 2005 WL 2471033, Unreported. Infants 243

Mother challenging termination of her parental rights was barred from alleging trial court errors in prior stages of child protection proceedings, where trial court's prior order of adjudication and order extending original temporary custody order were final and appealable. In re Di.R. (Ohio App. 8 Dist., Cuyahoga, 10-06-2005) No. 85765, No. 85766, 2005-Ohio-5346, 2005 WL 2471033, Unreported. Infants 232

Guardian ad litem's failure to file reports prior to trial in termination of parental rights proceedings did not constitute plain error; mother not only acquiesced in decision to proceed with testimony in the absence of a formally-filed report, but encouraged magistrate to permit guardian ad litem to hear trial testimony before submitting his written report, and guardian ad litem relied only on previously-introduced evidence in making his written recommendation. In re K.W. (Ohio App. 8 Dist., Cuyahoga, 10-06-2005) No. 86275, 2005-Ohio-5351, 2005 WL 2471014, Unreported. Infants 243

Child's mother had standing to challenge the trial court's denial of maternal grandmother's motion for custody of child in action by county children services agency for permanent custody of child that county alleged was neglected and dependant, even though grandmother did not appeal the denial of her motion; mother's interests were aligned with grandmother's and the denial of grandmother's motion prejudiced mother. In re Poke (Ohio App. 4 Dist., Lawrence, 09-23-2005) No. 05CA15, 2005-Ohio-5226, 2005 WL 2403893, Unreported. Infants 242

Mother was afforded sufficient time to comply with her case plan prior to trial court's entry of order relieving county Children Services Board (CSB) of any further obligation to make reasonable efforts toward reunification, where mother failed to make any progress on any aspect of her case plan during three months prior to CSB's motion for permanent custody; mother failed to keep appointment for mental health assessment, secure stable, independent housing, complete substance abuse assessment, complete parenting assessment, or attend any visitations other than single family meeting. In re G.B. (Ohio App. 9 Dist., Summit, 08-31-2005) No. 22628, 2005-Ohio-4540, 2005 WL 2087826, Unreported. Infants 155

Mother's unsupported contention that trial court erred in terminating her parental rights because she was not afforded sufficient time to comply with objectives of her case plan or to demonstrate that she was capable of and willing to complete her case plan was insufficient to warrant reversal of termination of her parental rights. In re G.B. (Ohio App. 9 Dist., Summit, 08-31-2005) No. 22628, 2005-Ohio-4540, 2005 WL 2087826, Unreported. Infants 241

Any error in trial court's finding, in child protection proceeding, that child's mother had failed to remedy problems which had led to child's removal form her custody was harmless, where trial court's findings as to three other grounds for concluding that child could not or should not be placed with mother were unchallenged. In re G.B. (Ohio App. 9 Dist., Summit, 08-31-2005) No. 22628, 2005-Ohio-4540, 2005 WL 2087826, Unreported. Infants 253

Father lacked standing to assert negligence or professional malpractice against his child's psychologist for making custody recommendation in mother's favor, regardless of whether he had retained and paid for psychologist's counseling services in the past; absent physician-patient relationship between himself and psychologist, father was not entitled to recover damages for injuries based on psychologist's duty owed strictly to the minor child. Silvers v. Bardenstein (Ohio App. 8 Dist., Cuyahoga, 08-18-2005) No. 85971, 2005-Ohio-4309, 2005 WL 1994941, Unreported. Health 750

Trial court's failure to inquire into wishes of dependent children during permanent custody proceeding constituted reversible error; while one child may have been too young to express his opinions about placement, the other child, who was five years old at the time of the hearing, was arguably capable of expressing his wishes, and guardian ad litem did not specifically address children's wishes. In re T.V. (Ohio App. 10 Dist., Franklin, 08-18-2005) No. 04AP-1159, No. 04AP-1160, 2005-Ohio-4280, 2005 WL 1983962, Unreported. Infants 253

Trial court's failure to align all of its factual findings with statutory factors supporting termination of parental rights did not require reversal of termination of mother's parental rights. In re Donell F. (Ohio App. 6 Dist., Lucas, 08-12-2005) No. L-04-1308, 2005-Ohio-4175, 2005 WL 1926512, Unreported. Infants 253

Testimony of intake specialist and certified chemical dependency counselor, early childhood supervisor, counselor and chemical dependency facilitator, and case manager was admissible in proceeding in which trial court granted permanent custody of child to county department of job and family services, where testimony was not covered by privilege governing communications between provider of treatment and patient-client. In re Patfield (Ohio App. 11 Dist., Lake, 07-18-2005) No. 2005-L-007, 2005-Ohio-3769, 2005 WL 1714185, Unreported, appeal not allowed 106 Ohio St.3d 1548, 835 N.E.2d 728, 2005-Ohio-5343. Infants 207

Father was not prejudiced by filing of report of guardian ad litem (GAL) on day of hearing, in proceeding in which permanent custody of child was awarded to county children services board; pursuant to statute, GAL could file report on day of hearing, and GAL took stand and was available for cross-examination. In re Woods (Ohio App. 5 Dist., Muskingum, 07-07-2005) No. CT2005-0011, 2005-Ohio-3561, 2005 WL 1645614, Unreported. Infants 253

Trial court did not abuse its discretion in refusing to grant mother's motion for continuance prior to commencement of trial, in custody proceeding involving parties' out-of-wedlock child; mother had failed to contact her counsel until shortly before trial, which made it more difficult for her counsel to prepare, but any weaknesses in mother's case were result of her own failure to contact counsel earlier, and delay would be undeserved hardship for father. In re Jump (Ohio App. 5 Dist., Holmes, 06-15-2005) No. 04CA011, 2005-Ohio-3287, 2005 WL 1519297, Unreported. Children Out-of-wedlock 20.4

Trial court is not required to list factors or conditions it found applicable before making its determination that dependent child cannot be placed with either parent or that grant of permanent custody of child to county child protection agency is in that child's best interest; as long as the record reveals that the trial court considered the factors, despite its failure to specifically discuss each one on the record, appellate court will find no reversible error. In re S.B. (Ohio App. 8 Dist., Cuyahoga, 06-23-2005) No. 85560, 2005-Ohio-3163, 2005 WL 1490128, Unreported. Infants 246

Any error in admitting results of father's independent polygraph examination during proceeding on county agency's motion requesting an award of permanent custody of child did not give rise to plain error; it was undisputed that agency required father to undergo a sex offender assessment and to take part in a sex offender counseling program, and completion of that program required the participant to submit to a polygraph examination. In re G.B. (Ohio App. 10 Dist., Franklin, 06-23-2005) No. 04AP-1024, 2005-Ohio-3141, 2005 WL 1476884, Unreported. Infants 243

Trial court in child protection proceedings could properly consider child's grandmother's opinion of her own supervision of children in courthouse in determining credibility of grandmother's testimony that mother adequately supervised child. In re Nolen (Ohio App. 3 Dist., Crawford, 06-20-2005) No. 3-04-20, 2005-Ohio-3075, 2005 WL 1421777, Unreported. Infants 179

Mother's motion seeking relief, on grounds of fraud, from juvenile court judgment granting permanent custody of children to county child protection agency was untimely, where motion was filed 17 months after the trial court journalized its permanent custody entry. In re M.H. (Ohio App. 8 Dist., Cuyahoga, 06-09-2005) No. 85308, 2005-Ohio-2854, 2005 WL 1364962, Unreported. Infants 230.1

Mother had standing to assert on appeal that trial court had erred in finding that it was not in child's best interests to be placed with father, in termination of parental rights proceeding; statute specifically required trial court to find that child could not be placed with either parent within reasonable time or should not be placed with either parent, and thus mother's residual parental rights were affected by termination of father's parental rights. In re Cazad (Ohio App. 4 Dist., Lawrence, 05-09-2005) No. 04CA36, 2005-Ohio-2574, 2005 WL 1228386, Unreported. Infants 242

Mother's cohabitant, who had lived with mother on and off over the course of 23 years, lacked standing to challenge trial court's judgment granting permanent custody of mother's child to Children Services Board (CSB), where cohabitant was not child's biological father, he did not have any legal relationship to the child, and he had never moved for legal custody of the child. In re J.O. (Ohio App. 9 Dist., Summit, 05-18-2005) No. 22510, 2005-Ohio-2399, 2005 WL 1162976, Unreported. Infants 242

Father appealing determination that his minor children were neglected and dependent did not have standing to appeal order denying the children's grandmother's motion to intervene in child protection proceedings. In re Lloyd (Ohio App. 5 Dist., Tuscarawas, 05-11-2005) No. 2005 AP 01 0003, 2005-Ohio-2380, 2005 WL 1152596, Unreported. Infants 242

Dependency portion of child protection complaint, stating that "[t]he condition and environment of the . . . children is such, that in their best interest, the state is warranted in intervening in their temporary care and custody" was sufficient to put father on notice that issues regarding the children's environment would be litigated before the trial court, and thus determination that children were neglected and dependent was properly based in part on unsanitary condition of family residence. In re Lloyd (Ohio App. 5 Dist., Tuscarawas, 05-11-2005) No. 2005 AP 01 0003, 2005-Ohio-2380, 2005 WL 1152596, Unreported. Infants ⇐ 197

Trial court was not required to make a finding that children could not have been returned to mother within a reasonable time, in proceedings on county's motion for permanent custody of children, where court found that children had been in temporary custody of county for more than 12 out of last 22 months. In re Lewis/Louk Children (Ohio App. 5 Dist., Stark, 05-03-2005) No. 2004CA00373, 2005-Ohio-2344, 2005 WL 1125339, Unreported. Infants ⇐ 210

Sufficient evidence supported finding that father had had his parental rights terminated with respect to child's sibling, in termination of parental rights proceeding; judgment entry terminating father's and mother's parental rights as to child's sibling was admitted as trial exhibit, and father did not dispute that he was sibling's parent. In re Danielle E. (Ohio App. 6 Dist., Lucas, 05-13-2005) No. L-04-1339, 2005-Ohio-2349, 2005 WL 1125322, Unreported. Infants ⇐ 178

Mother failed to establish that prior dependency proceedings were terminated in her favor, as required to establish her claim of malicious prosecution against county children services board and its employees; mother's children were adjudicated dependent, the adjudication was affirmed on appeal, and father obtained custody of the children. Doe v. Trumbull Cty. Children Servs. Bd. (Ohio App. 11 Dist., Trumbull, 05-06-2005) No. 2004-T-0034, 2005-Ohio-2260, 2005 WL 1075785, Unreported. Malicious Prosecution ⇐ 34

Admission of disputed testimony, even if testimony was hearsay, was not plain error in proceeding in which trial court awarded permanent custody of child to county department of children and family services; mother offered nothing which demonstrated that court relied on testimony in rendering its final verdict or that mother was prejudiced by testimony, and there was nothing in record that overcame presumption that judge disregarded any evidence that was not properly before her. In re D.W. (Ohio App. 8 Dist., Cuyahoga, 04-21-2005) No. 84547, 2005-Ohio-1867, 2005 WL 926991, Unreported. Infants ⇐ 243

Magistrate lacked authority to refer child protection proceeding to visiting judge, especially without judicial approval from sitting judge assigned to case. In re S.J. (Ohio App. 8 Dist., Cuyahoga, 04-21-2005) No. 84410, 2005-Ohio-1854, 2005 WL 914692, Unreported. Judges ⇐ 25(1)

Trial court's citation to the wrong statute in its order terminating mother's parental rights to her son did not warrant reversal of court's decision. In re Na'eem A. (Ohio App. 6 Dist., Lucas, 04-08-2005) No. L-04-1259, No. L-04-1260, 2005-Ohio-1679, 2005 WL 791448, Unreported. Infants ⇐ 253

Father lacked standing to raise challenge on appeal that juvenile court erred by granting Children Services Board's motion for permanent custody because it should have placed his two minor children in the legal custody of their paternal grandfather; father's challenge was limited to whether the court improperly terminated his parental rights. In re E.C. (Ohio App. 9 Dist., Summit, 04-06-2005) No. 22355, 2005-Ohio-1633, 2005 WL 767099, Unreported. Infants ⇐ 242

Circumstances under which trial court conducted in-camera interview of child for purpose of determining child's wishes, in action in which County Children Services Board (CCSB) sought permanent custody of child for purpose of adoption, did not constitute noncompliance with juvenile procedural rule governing discovery in parental rights termination proceedings, since child was not called to testify as a witness under oath on behalf of CCSB, but was rather summoned by trial court, sua sponte. In re Ratliff (Ohio App. 10 Dist., Franklin, 03-24-2005) No. 04AP-803, 2005-Ohio-1301, 2005 WL 675798, Unreported, appeal not allowed 106 Ohio St.3d 1417, 830 N.E.2d 348, 2005-Ohio-3154. Infants ⇐ 207

Failure of trial court to dispose of child protection agency's motion for permanent custody within the time period set forth in statute did not provide a basis for attacking the validity of the judgment. In re B.L. (Ohio App. 10 Dist., Franklin, 03-17-2005) No. 04AP-1108, 2005-Ohio-1151, 2005 WL 615642, Unreported, stay denied 105 Ohio St.3d 1553, 828 N.E.2d 110, 2005-Ohio-2424, appeal not allowed 105 Ohio St.3d 1564, 828 N.E.2d 118, 2005-Ohio-2447, appeal not allowed 106 Ohio St.3d 1417, 830 N.E.2d 348, 2005-Ohio-3154, reconsideration denied 106 Ohio St.3d 1511, 833 N.E.2d 1251, 2005-Ohio-4605, certiorari denied 126 S.Ct. 443, 163 L.Ed.2d 337, rehearing denied, rehearing denied 126 S.Ct. 726, 163 L.Ed.2d 623. Infants ⇐ 221

Court of Appeals would not address on appeal in child dependency proceeding assignments of error in father's brief contained in those pages of brief that exceeded page limit under rule. In re Miller (Ohio App. 5 Dist., Licking, 02-24-2005) No. 04 CA 32, 2005-Ohio-856, 2005 WL 469260, Unreported. Infants ⇐ 241

Trial court error, if any, in failing to discuss the best interest factor that required to court to determine if any of the factors listed in different subsection of statute, that pertained to parental criminal convictions, a parent's withholding of food or medical treatment, a parent's abandonment of child, or a parent's placement of child at substantial risk of harm due to alcohol or drug abuse, was not prejudicial, and thus did not warrant reversal of order granting permanent custody of mother's children to county children's services board; none of the factors applied to mother. In re Hershberger & Smith (Ohio App. 3 Dist., Allen, 02-07-2005) No. 1-04-55, No. 1-04-61, 2005-Ohio-429, 2005 WL 280356, Unreported. Infants ⇐ 253

Trial court was not required to specifically discuss in its judgment entry each of the five statutory factors for determining whether a grant of permanent custody is in child's best interest to comply with statute; trial court was only required to indicate on the record that all of the statutory best interest factors were considered. In re Hershberger & Smith (Ohio App. 3 Dist., Allen, 02-07-2005) No. 1-04-55, No. 1-04-61, 2005-Ohio-429, 2005 WL 280356, Unreported. Infants ⇐ 210

Mother in termination of parental rights proceedings did not have standing on appeal to challenge trial court's failure to place the children in the legal custody of their maternal grandmother; mother's challenge was limited to whether the trial court improperly terminated her parental rights. In re C.D. (Ohio App. 9 Dist., Summit, 01-19-2005) No. 22250, 2005-Ohio-158, 2005 WL 100783, Unreported. Infants ⇐ 242

Denial of paternal grandfather's motion to intervene in permanent custody proceeding, following adjudication of infant as dependent, was not abuse of discretion; infant had been living with foster parents, and grandfather's only interactions with infant had consisted of occasional visits. In re M.S. (Ohio App. 9 Dist., Summit, 01-05-2005) No. 22158, 2005-Ohio-10, 2005 WL 19441, Unreported. Infants ⇐ 200

County's failure to initially notify child's biological father of proceeding did not deprive court of jurisdiction to terminate parental rights; mother did not notify county that presumed father might not be biological father until day of hearing, service by publication on biological father was accomplished, and biological father never appeared. In re D.P. (Ohio App. 9 Dist., Summit, 12-30-2004) No. 22257, 2004-Ohio-7173, 2004 WL 3017312, Unreported. Infants ⇐ 198

Use of separate orders to terminate parental rights and place child in county's permanent custody, though not best practice, was not reversible error absent showing of prejudice. In re D.P. (Ohio App. 9 Dist., Summit, 12-30-2004) No. 22257, 2004-Ohio-7173, 2004 WL 3017312, Unreported. Infants ⇐ 253

Evidence in child protection proceedings was sufficient to support trial court's finding that subject child had been in agency custody for statutorily required period prior to hearing on agency's motion for permanent custody, where record indicated that hearing on motion for permanent custody was conducted more than one year after child was first adjudicated neglected. In re Adams (Ohio App. 3 Dist., Seneca, 12-27-2004) No. 13-04-27, 2004-Ohio-7039, 2004 WL 2980493, Unreported. Infants ⇐ 204

Denying mother's request for continuance of permanent child custody hearing based on mother's alleged temporary incompetency was not abuse of discretion in termination of parental rights proceeding; although mother had previously been found incompetent to stand trial in unrelated criminal case, mother waited until day of hearing to seek continuance, statute under which mother was referred for treatment in criminal case permitted treatment for up to one year such that child could have remained in custodial limbo for additional year if court had granted continuance, mother was represented by two competent attorneys and had guardian ad litem appointed to represent her interests, and mother's alleged incompetence did not affect issue of whether maternal aunt was suitable custodian for child. In re A.U. (Ohio App. 2 Dist., Montgomery, 11-19-2004) No. 20583, No. 20585, 2004-Ohio-6219, 2004 WL 2659137, Unreported. Infants ⇐ 204

Juvenile court was not required to follow guardian ad litem's recommendation during termination of parental rights proceeding. In re Keaton (Ohio App. 4 Dist., Ross, 11-19-2004) No. 04CA2785, No. 04CA2788, 2004-Ohio-6210, 2004 WL 2650249, Unreported. Infants ⇐ 208

While trial judge's comment after father's initial testimony indicating judge thought motion filed by Franklin County Children Services (FCCS) for permanent custody of dependent children should be granted may have been made prematurely and was inappropriate, comment did rise to decision on motion or taint judge's analysis of motion, where judge adduced all relevant evidence prior to making official decision on motion, did not bar further testimony after making comment, and correctly applied statutory guidelines before ruling on motion. In re Hinkle (Ohio App. 10 Dist., Franklin, 11-16-2004) No. 04AP-509, No. 04AP-510, 2004-Ohio-6071, 2004 WL 2591221, Unreported. Infants ⇐ 203

Even if testimony of children's treating therapist should not have been admitted at proceeding on county children services agency's motion to modify temporary custody to permanent custody because she was not on agency's witness list, admission of this testimony was not reversible error, since trial court did not rely on this testimony in making its decision. In re J.L. (Ohio App. 8 Dist., Cuyahoga, 11-10-2004) No. 84368, 2004-Ohio-6024, 2004 WL 2578874, Unreported, appeal not allowed 104 Ohio St.3d 1463, 821 N.E.2d 578, 2005-Ohio-204. Infants ⇐ 253

Where children had been in temporary custody of county children services agency for more than 12 out of 22 consecutive months when trial on agency's motion to modify temporary custody to permanent custody commenced, trial court was not required to make a finding that the children could not or should not be placed with either parent before moving on to the best interest determination. In re J.L. (Ohio App. 8 Dist., Cuyahoga, 11-10-2004) No. 84368, 2004-Ohio-6024, 2004 WL 2578874, Unreported, appeal not allowed 104 Ohio St.3d 1463, 821 N.E.2d 578, 2005-Ohio-204. Infants ⇐ 230.1

Where children had been in temporary custody of county children services agency for more than 12 out of 22 consecutive months when trial on agency's motion to modify temporary custody to permanent custody commenced, trial court was not required to find that reasonable case planning and diligent efforts to achieve reunification were used by agency before granting permanent custody to agency. In re J.L. (Ohio App. 8 Dist., Cuyahoga, 11-10-2004) No. 84368, 2004-Ohio-6024, 2004 WL 2578874, Unreported, appeal not allowed 104 Ohio St.3d 1463, 821 N.E.2d 578, 2005-Ohio-204. Infants ⇐ 230.1

Trial court considered in termination of parental rights proceeding wishes of children with due regard to their maturity and as expressed by guardian ad litem, as required by statute, where court stated that it considered all statutory factors in reaching its conclusion that it was in children's best interest for permanent custody to be granted to county job and family services. In re Sanders Children (Ohio App. 5 Dist., Tuscarawas, 10-29-2004) No. 2004 AP 08 0057, 2004-Ohio-5878, 2004 WL 2497028, Unreported. Infants ⇐ 155

Following father's stipulation that agency's evidence satisfied agency's burden of proving by clear and convincing evidence that permanent custody was in the best interests of the child and that the child could not be placed with parents within a reasonable time, burden of production shifted to father to rebut agency's evidence by producing evidence sufficient to negate or counteract agency's evidence and convince the court that the clear and convincing standard had not been met. In re Gordon (Ohio App. 3 Dist., Hancock, 11-08-2004) No. 5-04-22, No. 5-04-23, 2004-Ohio-5889, 2004 WL 2496513, Unreported. Infants ⇐ 172

Putative father lacked standing to object on appeal to magistrate's refusal to continue at mother's request hearing in termination of parental rights proceeding. In re C.S. (Ohio App. 2 Dist., Montgomery, 10-22-2004) No. 20379, 2004-Ohio-5810, 2004 WL 2445238, Unreported. Infants ⇐ 242

Trial court, which permitted foster mother to testify despite ruling that county agency could not use witness to prove its allegations due to agency's failure to list foster mother as a witness, did not abuse its discretion in refusing to allow cross-examination of foster mother in proceedings to determine if permanent custody of children should be awarded to county agency; although better practice would have been to permit cross-examination, trial court permitted foster mother to testify so as show concern for foster parents' participation in proceedings, and trial court expressly stated that it would only consider testimony about how the children were doing in their current placement. In re G.C. & M.C. (Ohio App. 8 Dist., Cuyahoga, 10-21-2004) No. 83994, 2004-Ohio-5607, 2004 WL 2367243, Unreported. Infants ⇐ 207

Trial court in child dependency proceedings committed plain error in allowing appointed counsel for child to withdraw and the guardian ad litem to act in the dual capacity of guardian and advocate for child, where there was no evidence presented to the trial court regarding child's wishes for placement, such that it was possible that separately assigned counsel would have advocated differently on behalf of child than did guardian ad litem. In re T.M., III (Ohio App. 8 Dist., Cuyahoga, 09-30-2004) No. 83933, 2004-Ohio-5222, 2004 WL 2340654, Unreported. Infants ⇐ 243

Trial court in child dependency proceedings did not commit plain error in allowing appointed counsel for child to withdraw and the guardian ad litem to act in the dual capacity of guardian and advocate for child; child wished to remain with foster parents, such that there would have been no conflict between what counsel would have advocated for him and the recommendation of permanent placement for child made by the guardian ad litem. In re T.M., III (Ohio App. 8 Dist., Cuyahoga, 09-30-2004) No. 83933, 2004-Ohio-5222, 2004 WL 2340654, Unreported. Infants ⇐ 243

Mother challenging grant of permanent custody of children to county agency waived for appeal issue of whether juvenile court erred in allowing appointed counsel for the children to withdraw and the guardian ad litem to act in the dual capacity of guardian and advocate for the children, where mother specifically stated that she had no objection to the withdrawal. In re T.M., III (Ohio App. 8 Dist., Cuyahoga, 09-30-2004) No. 83933, 2004-Ohio-5222, 2004 WL 2340654, Unreported. Infants ⇐ 248.1

Mother waived for appeal issue of whether juvenile court erred in admitting alleged hearsay evidence in hearing to determine whether to grant permanent custody of children to county agency, where mother failed to object to alleged inadmissible hearsay. In re T.M., III (Ohio App. 8 Dist., Cuyahoga, 09-30-2004) No. 83933, 2004-Ohio-5222, 2004 WL 2340654, Unreported. Infants ⇐ 243

Trial court acted within its discretion in considering county agency's motion for permanent custody of child before considering father's motion seeking visitation with child; agency sought permanent custody only after child had been in their custody for more than a year after he had been born, and decision to consider motion for permanent custody first allowed court to determine whether it was appropriate to grant permanent custody of child to agency or to attempt to unify father with child. In re A.C. (Ohio App. 12 Dist., Clermont, 10-18-2004) No. CA2004-05-041, 2004-Ohio-5531, 2004 WL 2340127, Unreported. Infants ⇐ 203

Trial court was not required to conduct in-camera interview with minor children in permanent custody proceedings initiated by county agency; guardian ad litem represented desires of children to court, and children were afraid of mother and did not wish to come to court to express their desires about placement. In re S.V. (Ohio App. 9 Dist., Summit, 10-13-2004) No. 22116, 2004-Ohio-5445, 2004 WL 2292825, Unreported. Infants ⇐ 207

Res judicata doctrine precluded father, whose parental rights were terminated, from raising on second appeal claims that guardian ad litem failed to express children's wishes and that case plan failed to provide services to address reason for children's removal, where such claims did not relate to any action taken by trial court on remand, but instead pertained to original permanent custody hearing, and claims could have raised on first appeal, but were not. In re T.G. (Ohio App. 9 Dist., Wayne, 09-29-2004) No. 04CA0040, 2004-Ohio-5173, 2004 WL 2244123, Unreported. Infants ⇐ 232

Mother challenging grant of permanent custody of children to county agency waived for appeal issue of whether trial court erred in finding that reasonable efforts were made to return children to mother's custody, where mother failed to raise claim in trial court. In re K. (Ohio App. 8 Dist., Cuyahoga, 09-02-2004) No. 83410, 2004-Ohio-4629, 2004 WL 1946141, Unreported. Infants ⇐ 243

Mother's claim on appeal from grant of permanent child custody to department of job and family services that trial court erred when it found that children could not or should not be placed with mother within reasonable time was moot, where trial court made alternative finding that children had been in department's custody for 12 of last 22 months, mother did not challenge alternative finding, and alternative finding, by itself, supported grant of permanent custody to department. In re Sunderman/Daniels Children Minor Children (Ohio App. 5 Dist., Stark, 08-30-2004) No. 2004CA00093, 2004-Ohio-4608, 2004 WL 1941061, Unreported. Infants ⇐ 248.1

Father's challenge on appeal to trial court's underlying finding that children were abandoned failed to set forth proper challenge to trial court's ultimate grant of permanent child custody to department of job and family services, where trial court's grant of permanent custody was based on statutory subsection addressing abandonment and statutory subsection addressing prior placement of children in department's temporary custody for specified time period, father failed to challenge trial court's finding based on latter subsection, and trial court could properly have moved to next step of analyzing best interest of children based only on trial court's finding based on latter unchallenged subsection. In re Villanueva/Hampton Children Dependant Children (Ohio App. 5 Dist., Stark, 08-30-2004) No. 2004CA00126, 2004-Ohio-4610, 2004 WL 1933542, Unreported. Infants ⇐ 241

Mother failed to show that trial court did not consider statutory best interest factors before awarding permanent child custody to department of job and family services; that court's findings and conclusions did not mention testimony of most of mother's witnesses did not equate with finding that court failed to consider statutory factors and court was not statutorily required to list such factors or conditions it found applicable before making custody determination. In re Villaneuva/Hampton Children (Ohio App. 5 Dist., Stark, 08-30-2004) No. 2004CA00120, 2004-Ohio-4609, 2004 WL 1933504, Unreported, appeal not allowed 104 Ohio St.3d 1441, 819 N.E.2d 1124, 2004-Ohio-7033. Infants ⇐ 210

Better practice for courts, with respect to statute setting forth specific permanent custody factors for courts to consider, in determining whether dependent child could be placed with a parent within a reasonable time or should not be placed with a parent, is for trial court to indicate specific factor or factors upon which it relied in reaching its determination. In re S. C. (Ohio App. 9 Dist., Lorain, 09-01-2004) No. 04CA008469, 2004-Ohio-4570, 2004 WL 1932854, Unreported. Infants ⇐ 210

Child had not been in temporary custody of agency for at least 12 of the prior 22 months, as required for permanent custody, where child had been adjudicated dependent only nine months before county children services agency moved for permanent custody. In re S. C. (Ohio App. 9 Dist., Lorain, 09-01-2004) No. 04CA008469, 2004-Ohio-4570, 2004 WL 1932854, Unreported. Infants ⇐ 155

Grandmother's letter to court requesting legal custody of mother's children was not substantive equivalent of motion to intervene, and thus, trial court's consideration of letter as basis for granting grandmother custody of mother's children was abuse of discretion, in proceedings brought by Department of Children and Family Services for permanent custody of children; letter was not in form of motion as required, letter was not served on any of parties involved, grandmother was never made party to proceedings, and she did not testify at trial. In re D.D. (Ohio App. 8 Dist., Cuyahoga, 08-12-2004) No. 83537, 2004-Ohio-4243, 2004 WL 1797186, Unreported. Infants ⇐ 200

Mother appealing decision of juvenile court granting permanent custody of daughter to county agency could not challenge prior determination that daughter was a dependent child, where mother failed to timely appeal neglect and dependency adjudication. In re K.M. (Ohio App. 12 Dist., Butler, 08-09-2004) No. CA2004-02-052, 2004-Ohio-4152, 2004 WL 1765462, Unreported. Infants ⇐ 248.1

The Court of Appeals would not address father's appellate argument that claimed that the trial court erred when it admitted documents, reports, and testimony from psychologist who examined parents, during termination of parental rights proceeding, where the Court of Appeals addressed the same argument from father during father's appeal from the order terminating his parental rights to child's sibling. In re Kaylee P. (Ohio App. 6 Dist., Fulton, 07-16-2004) No. F-04-011, 2004-Ohio-3807, 2004 WL 1595702, Unreported. Infants ⇐ 254

Failing to grant mother extension of time to complete reunification process with dependent children was not abuse of discretion in termination of parental rights proceeding, where evidence showed pattern of neglect by mother which resulted from her drug use and inability to maintain stable employment. In re Ross (Ohio App. 11 Dist., Geauga, 07-07-2004) No. 2003-G-2551, 2004-Ohio-3684, 2004 WL 1559742, Unreported. Infants ⇐ 230.1

The trial court abused its discretion in adopting magistrate's decision in support of terminating parental rights and granting permanent custody of children to county children services board, where the magistrate failed to discuss all five factors listed in statute to determine whether termination of parental rights was n the best interests of the children. In re Bentley (Ohio App. 11 Dist., Ashtabula, 06-30-2004) No. 2004-A-0010, 2004-Ohio-3513, 2004 WL 1486948, Unreported. Infants ⇐ 206

Trial court's refusal in termination of parental rights proceeding to remove magistrate, guardian ad litem, and Court Appointed Special Advocate (CASA) assigned to case was not abuse of discretion, where record did not suggest any prejudice on part of magistrate, guardian ad litem, or CASA simply because they were involved in prior termination of parental rights proceeding involving sibling of dependent child at issue in instant proceeding. In re Baby Girl Elliott (Ohio App. 12 Dist., Butler, 07-06-2004) No. CA2003-10-256, 2004-Ohio-3539, 2004 WL 1485858, Unreported. Infants ⇐ 205; Justices Of The Peace ⇐ 57(1)

County Department of Job and Family Services (DJFS) was not required to demonstrate that minor could not be placed with other relative, such as grandmother, in action to terminate father's parental rights and grant permanent custody to DJFS; determination that minor could not be placed with other relative was to be made by trial court, grandmother had never expressed interest in having custody of child, and child had been unsuccessfully placed with other relatives. In re Brown (Ohio App. 11 Dist., Lake, 06-21-2004) No. 2004-L-027, 2004-Ohio-3337, 2004 WL 1433674, Unreported. Infants ⇐ 155

Whether department of job and family services made reasonable efforts to reunify mother and dependent and neglected children, as part of analysis as to whether children could not be placed with mother within reasonable time or should not be placed with mother, did not need to be resolved in proceeding in which department sought permanent custody of children, where it was undisputed that children were in department's temporary custody for 12 months or more of consecutive 22 month period, which provided alternative statutory basis for granting department permanent custody. In re Katrina T. (Ohio App. 6 Dist., Sandusky, 06-18-2004) No. S-03-024, 2004-Ohio-3164, 2004 WL 1368324, Unreported. Infants ⇐ 208

Denial of motion for continuance made by father's counsel at start of final permanent custody hearing, due to father's absence, was justified; counsel could not explain to trial court why father was absent, father never attended any scheduled review hearings, and at no time after having been served with notice of trial did father contact his attorney, resulting in attorney's withdrawal from case. In re Gibby (Ohio App. 5 Dist., Fairfield, 05-24-2004) No. 2003-CA-93, 2004-Ohio-2708, 2004 WL 1171698, Unreported. Infants ⇐ 204

Dismissal of mother's appeal of child custody order in dependency proceeding was warranted; judgment was not a final appealable order since it did not dispose of all claims, rights and liabilities of the parties. In re Nichols (Ohio App. 4 Dist., Washington, 04-09-2004) No. 03CA41, 2004-Ohio-2026, 2004 WL 868364, Unreported. Infants ⇐ 242; Infants ⇐ 247

Record failed to support finding that minor child was in temporary custody of Children Services Board (CSB) for more than 12 months prior to CSB's filing of motion for permanent custody, and thus, trial court erred in relying on this ground in granting permanent custody of child to CSB. In re C.W. (Ohio App. 9 Dist., Summit, 04-21-2004) No. 21809, No. 21811, 2004-Ohio-1987, 2004 WL 840124, Unreported, motion to certify allowed 102 Ohio St.3d 1481, 810 N.E.2d 966, 2004-Ohio-3069, affirmed 104 Ohio St.3d 163, 818 N.E.2d 1176, 2004-Ohio-6411. Infants ⇐ 178

Guardian ad litem assigned to children did not fulfill his purpose by failing to file a report prior to commencement of hearing on motion for permanent custody by County Department of Job and Family Services; guardian had been involved in action for six years, but alleged he was unable to give any opinion regarding permanent custody until he heard evidence at hearing, even though report was to be based on guardian's experience rather than on evidence produced at hearing. In re Ridenour (Ohio App. 11 Dist., Lake, 04-16-2004) No. 2003-L-146, No. 2003-L-147, No. 2003-L-148, 2004-Ohio-1958, 2004 WL 834579, Unreported. Infants ⇐ 205

Trial court did not abuse its discretion by considering father's decision not to testify and refute testimony at termination of parental rights hearing; father failed to present evidence that his alleged temper problems had been addressed, or that refuted claims that he declined additional visitation with child and that he and child did not share a bond. In re Gomer (Ohio App. 3 Dist., Wyandot, 04-05-2004) No. 16-03-19, No. 16-03-20, No. 16-03-21, 2004-Ohio-1723, 2004 WL 722978, Unreported, appeal not allowed 102 Ohio St.3d 1473, 809 N.E.2d 1159, 2004-Ohio-2830. Infants ⇐ 210

Father was not entitled to continuance in termination of parental rights proceeding in order to have hearing to qualify psychologist as expert; trial court questioned father's counsel at length as to reasons for continuance and as to any possible prejudice that might result from proceeding as scheduled, and determined that father's concerns about psychologist's qualifications could be addressed during trial. In re Lauren P. (Ohio App. 6 Dist., Lucas, 03-31-2004) No. L-03-1252, 2004-Ohio-1656, 2004 WL 628659, Unreported. Infants ⇐ 204

Although trial court's failure to make explicit finding that granting permanent custody of dependent and neglected child to county children services board would have amounted to reversible error, Court of Appeals would not address this issue, where parents did not raise issue when appealing from termination of their parental rights. In re T.O. (Ohio App. 9 Dist., Summit, 03-31-2004) No. 2185821868, 2004-Ohio-1605, 2004 WL 625816, Unreported. Infants ⇐ 248.1

There was no evidence that trial court harbored any bias or prejudice against mother in proceeding depriving mother of custody of her children, based on its question regarding what permanency plan was for children; trial court fulfilled its duty regarding child service's agency's reasonable efforts to finalize permanency plan so that children would still be eligible for federal funding while in foster care. In re K.P. (Ohio App. 8 Dist., Cuyahoga, 03-25-2004) No. 82709, 2004-Ohio-1448, 2004 WL 583867, Unreported, as amended nunc pro tunc, stay denied 102 Ohio St.3d 1457, 809 N.E.2d 31, 2004-Ohio-2569, appeal not allowed 102 Ohio St.3d 1473, 809 N.E.2d 1159, 2004-Ohio-2830. Infants ⇐ 203

Order granting permanent custody of children to county department of job and family services, rather than placing children in long-term foster care, was proper; neither child expressed a desire to reside with parents, and older child expressed a desire to be adopted by his foster parents. In re Bradley John B. (Ohio App. 6 Dist., Huron, 03-19-2004) No. H-03-037, No. H-03-041, 2004-Ohio-1328, 2004 WL 541028, Unreported. Infants ⇌ 226

Given that trial court found that child was abandoned, court was not required to determine whether department of job and family services used reasonable efforts to reunify child with parents or whether child could not or should not be placed with either parent within reasonable time before granting department permanent child custody. In re Wright (Ohio App. 5 Dist., Stark, 03-08-2004) No. 2003CA00347, 2004-Ohio-1094, 2004 WL 434036, Unreported. Infants ⇌ 155

Trial court decision, coupled with the transcript of the permanent custody hearing and the transcript from the court's in camera interview with the children, formed an adequate basis for appellate review of order denying county children services' motion for permanent custody, and thus the denial of children services' request for findings of fact and conclusions of law was proper. In re Cunningham (Ohio App. 4 Dist., Athens, 02-17-2004) No. 03CA26, 2004-Ohio-787, 2004 WL 323339, Unreported. Infants ⇌ 210

Remand of permanent custody proceeding was required, where trial court, prior to terminating mother's parental rights and awarding county children services board permanent custody of dependent child, did not make requisite statutory finding that granting county permanent custody of child was in child's best interests. In re M.B. (Ohio App. 9 Dist., Summit, 02-11-2004) No. 21760, 2004-Ohio-597, 2004 WL 239924, Unreported. Infants ⇌ 210; Infants ⇌ 254

Evidence supported finding that father knowingly, voluntarily, and intelligently waived his right to contest the permanent custody proceeding involving his children; father initialed each of his rights on the parental stipulation to permanent custody form, the stipulation listed all of father's rights, and the trial court questioned father as to whether he understood the nature of the proceedings and the effect of the proceedings. In re Foresha/Kinkel Children (Ohio App. 5 Dist., Stark, 02-09-2004) No. 2003CA00364, 2004-Ohio-578, 2004 WL 237987, Unreported. Infants ⇌ 199

Guardian ad litem who filed petition to adjudicate child neglected was statutorily prohibited from representing both State and child in subsequent hearing on petition; although nothing prevented guardian from filing complaint alleging that child was neglected, guardian was required to step aside upon commencement of hearing on complaint, in which proceeding duty fell on children services agency to investigate situation and, if necessary, prosecute complaint. In re Kheirkhah (Ohio App. 11 Dist., Lake, 02-06-2004) No. 2002-L-128, 2004-Ohio-521, 2004 WL 231495, Unreported. Infants ⇌ 205

Trial court order which required father to submit to a modified sex offender evaluation, even though father had not been convicted of a sex offense, was not an abuse of discretion, in child dependency proceeding; psychologist recommended the evaluation. In re Foucht (Ohio App. 2 Dist., Montgomery, 02-06-2004) No. 19930, 2004-Ohio-456, 2004 WL 225458, Unreported. Infants ⇌ 208

Trial court was under no obligation to make finding as to whether child could or could not be placed with either parent within reasonable amount of time, in support of its determination in parental termination proceeding, since child had been in temporary custody of Children Services Board for 12 or more months of consecutive 22-month period, a circumstance recognized by termination statute as relieving moving agency from its duty to make such showing. In re Elliott (Ohio App. 7 Dist., Jefferson, 01-26-2004) No. 03JE30, No. 03JE33, 2004-Ohio-388, 2004 WL 187413, Unreported. Infants ⇌ 210

Father waived his appellate argument that the complaint for permanent custody failed to set forth allegations in compliance with statute, in child dependency proceeding, where father failed to object to the sufficiency of the complaint until ten months after he was first served with the summons and complaint. In re I.M. (Ohio App. 8 Dist., Cuyahoga, 12-24-2003) No. 82669, No. 82695, 2003-Ohio-7069, 2003 WL 23010024, Unreported. Infants ⇌ 243

Report of guardian ad litem was properly submitted to trial court prior to or at time of permanent custody hearing regarding dependent child, where report was made part of the trial exhibits. In re R.K. (Ohio App. 8 Dist., Cuyahoga, 11-26-2003) No. 82374, 2003-Ohio-6333, 2003 WL 22804937, Unreported. Infants ⇌ 208

Mother received proper notice of motion filed by county department of children and family services seeking permanent custody of dependent child; record indicated that mother was personally served with notice some six months after filing of motion to modify temporary custody and seven months prior to the hearing for permanent custody. In re R.K. (Ohio App. 8 Dist., Cuyahoga, 11-26-2003) No. 82374, 2003-Ohio-6333, 2003 WL 22804937, Unreported. Infants ⇌ 198

Father lacked standing to raise the appellate argument that the trial court erred when it denied his motion for a stay of child dependency proceeding pending the outcome of father's parents (child's paternal grandparents) appeal of the denial of their motion to intervene in child dependency proceeding; the denial of the motion to intervene did not affect father's rights. In re Goff (Ohio App. 11 Dist., Portage, 11-14-2003) No. 2003-P-0069, 2003-Ohio-6089, 2003 WL 22697970, Unreported. Infants ⇌ 242

Paternal grandparents of allegedly dependent child, who was born to underage mother who allegedly was artificially inseminated by step-father, were not entitled to stay of motion for permanent custody of child that was filed by county department of job and family services while grandparents were appealing denial of motion to intervene in proceeding concerning temporary custody of child; child had need for secure permanent placement, and grandparents were not prejudiced because grandparents' presence or absence would not have affected trial court's finding to terminate father's parental rights. In re Goff (Ohio App. 11 Dist., Portage, 11-14-2003) No. 2003-P-0068, 2003-Ohio-6087, 2003 WL 22697969, Unreported. Infants ⇌ 244.1

Child placing agency, in permanent custody hearing involving dependent child, was not prejudiced by trial court's placing child in legal custody of father and in ordering protective supervision of child; clear and convincing evidence supported finding that granting agency permanent custody of child was not in child's best interests. In re J. H. (Ohio App. 9 Dist., Summit, 10-22-2003) No. 21575, 2003-Ohio-5611, 2003 WL 22399693, Unreported. Infants ⇌ 253

Claim of child placing agency, in permanent custody hearing involving dependent child, that trial court utilized the wrong legal test for permanent custody when it declared that agency failed to establish that father was unfit or unable to provide a suitable home for the child, was rendered moot, where agency failed to establish that granting agency permanent custody of child was in child's best interests. In re J. H. (Ohio App. 9 Dist., Summit, 10-22-2003) No. 21575, 2003-Ohio-5611, 2003 WL 22399693, Unreported. Infants ⇌ 248.1

Any temporary custody awarded to the Department of Job and Family Services had not lapsed when department sought to terminate mother's parental rights and obtain permanent custody, given that trial court continued temporary custody upon department's filing of permanent custody motion until permanent custody issue could be resolved. In re Robinson (Ohio App. 2 Dist., Clark, 10-17-2003) No. 2002-CA-83, No. 2002-CA-84, No. 2002-CA-85, 2003-Ohio-5528, 2003 WL 22359657, Unreported. Infants ⇌ 192

Trial court's failure to consider wishes of dependent children in permanent custody proceeding constituted reversible error; while one child may have been too young to express her wishes concerning her placement, the other four children were capable of communicating such wishes, and guardian ad litem did not specifically address children's wishes. In re Swisher (Ohio App. 10 Dist., Franklin, 10-14-2003) No. 02AP-1408, No. 02AP-1409, 2003-Ohio-5446, 2003 WL 22331995, Unreported. Infants ⇌ 203; Infants ⇌ 253

Father lacked standing to challenge the trial court's refusal to allow paternal uncle, who was not a party to appeal, to participate in child dependency proceeding. In re Conn (Ohio App. 10 Dist., Franklin, 10-07-2003) No. 03AP-348, No. 03AP-349, No. 03AP-372, 2003-Ohio-5344, 2003 WL 22290217, Unreported. Infants ⇌ 242

Calculation of how many days parents' children had been in temporary custody of child services agency began on date children were adjudicated dependent, rather than date they were removed from parents' home, and thus children were in agency's temporary custody for approximately 17 months of prior 22 months, satisfying statutory requirements for grant of permanent custody to agency. In re Sessoms (Ohio App. 12 Dist., Butler, 10-06-2003) No. CA2002-11-280, 2003-Ohio-5281, 2003 WL 22283495, Unreported. Infants ⇌ 155

County children's services' complaint was sufficient to put mother on notice of essential facts underlying the claim of dependency, because complaint alleged that same issues which led to earlier removal of son from home, caused agency to fear for safety and well-being of daughter. In re Estepp (Ohio App. 5 Dist., Fairfield, 09-24-2003) No. 03-CA-11, 2003-Ohio-5084, 2003 WL 22208743, Unreported. Infants ⇌ 197

Mother lacked standing to raise the appellate argument that the county children services board prevented father from participating in his caseplan unless he violated his right against self-incrimination, in child dependency proceeding, where father did not appeal the trial court order terminating parental rights, and mother failed to show that she was aggrieved by the alleged actions of the board. In re Cornett (Ohio App. 12 Dist., Warren, 09-11-2003) No. CA2003-03-034, 2003-Ohio-4871, 2003 WL 22118857, Unreported. Infants ⇌ 242

Trial court had sufficient grounds for denying mother's motion for continuance during permanent custody hearing; mother had already twice moved to continue the permanent custody hearing, and more than two years had expired since Children Services Board (CSB) had filed initial complaints for temporary custody of children. In re L.A. (Ohio App. 9 Dist., Summit, 09-10-2003) No. 21531, 2003-Ohio-4790, 2003 WL 22093456, Unreported. Infants ⇌ 204

Trial court error, if any, in accepting judgment entries from county job and family services that failed to comply with the local rules did not prejudice mother, in termination of parental rights case; mother failed to detail any of the alleged misrepresentations of fact contained in the journal entries. In re J.B. (Ohio App. 9 Dist., Medina, 09-10-2003) No. 03CA0024-M, No. 03CA0025-M, 2003-Ohio-4786, 2003 WL 22093226, Unreported. Infants ⇌ 253

The trial court's failure to discuss the wishes of the children when determining whether termination of parental rights was in the best interests of the children was prejudicial error and warranted reversal of termination of parental rights order; a guardian ad litem had been appointed to represent the three children, and the guardian ad litem filed a report and made recommendations. In re Meyer (Ohio App. 11 Dist., Ashtabula, 08-22-2003) No. 2003-A-0065, 2003-Ohio-4605, 2003 WL 22038691, Unreported. Infants ⇌ 210; Infants ⇌ 253

Allowing guardian ad litem to file her written report eight days after permanent custody hearing was not error, where court stated at hearing that it would not make any judgment in matter until report was submitted, guardian ad litem voiced her concerns orally at hearing, court invited mother to question guardian ad litem during hearing, and mother declined invitation. In re Johns (Ohio App. 5 Dist., Stark, 07-07-2003) No. 2003CA00146, 2003-Ohio-3621, 2003 WL 21540772, Unreported. Infants ⇌ 208

The trial court's failure to consider child's desire to reside with mother prejudiced mother, in permanent custody proceeding, and warranted remand for a new hearing; child had a right to be represented by counsel at the hearing, counsel for child had a duty to advocate for child's position, and mother was entitled to cross-examine the supplemental evidence concerning child's wishes. In re Williams (Ohio App. 11 Dist., Geauga, 07-03-2003) No. 2003-G-2498, No. 2003-G-2499, 2003-Ohio-3550, 2003 WL 21517986, Unreported, stay granted 99 Ohio St.3d 1526, 793 N.E.2d 496, 2003-Ohio-4303, motion to certify allowed 99 Ohio St.3d 1540, 795 N.E.2d 680, 2003-Ohio-4671, appeal not allowed 99 Ohio St.3d 1547, 795 N.E.2d 684, 2003-Ohio-4671, affirmed 101 Ohio St.3d 398, 805 N.E.2d 1110, 2004-Ohio-1500. Infants ⇌ 205; Infants ⇌ 207; Infants ⇌ 253; Infants ⇌ 254

Trial court did not abuse its discretion in awarding permanent custody of children to Children Services Board (CSB), where children had been in temporary custody of CSB for more than 12 of past 22 months, and evidence supported finding that it was in best interests of children to be placed in permanent custody of CSB; children were in need of permanent placement and mother could not provide such placement at current time, or in near future, because of her failure to complete drug treatment program, and follow through with recommended treatment for depression. In re B.B. (Ohio App. 9 Dist., Summit, 06-25-2003) No. 21447, 2003-Ohio-3314, 2003 WL 21459019, Unreported. Infants ⇌ 155; Infants ⇌ 158; Infants ⇌ 178

Trial court was required to set forth, in judgment entry following dispositional hearing awarding permanent custody of children to county children services agency, its specific factual findings regarding individual factors under statute on determining best interests of children, where parents requested findings of fact and conclusions of law; journal entry lacked factual findings related to children's interaction and relationship with parents, siblings, and foster parents, and also failed to discuss children's wishes regarding custody. In re Myers (Ohio App. 4 Dist., Athens, 05-23-2003) No. 02CA50, 2003-Ohio-2776, 2003 WL 21246432, Unreported. Infants ⇌ 210

Even if trial court erred in finding that father had failed continuously and repeatedly to substantially remedy conditions that caused child to be placed outside child's home, given that, while child was removed from mother's home, she was not removed from father's care, such error was harmless, in termination of parental rights proceeding, as trial court also listed other relevant factors in terminating father's parental rights, such as his prior convictions and his inability to control his anger. In re Rinaldi (Ohio App. 3 Dist., Allen, 05-19-2003) No. 1-02-74, 2003-Ohio-2562, 2003 WL 21142907, Unreported, appeal not allowed 99 Ohio St.3d 1461, 791 N.E.2d 978, 2003-Ohio-3717. Infants ⇌ 253

Mother waived claim that trial court failed to require submission of written guardian ad litem report prior to permanent custody hearing to terminate her parental rights, where she failed to raise issue at hearing. In re Shumate (Ohio App. 5 Dist., Muskingum, 04-29-2003) No. CT2002-0051, No. CT2002-0054, No. CT2002-0052, No. CT2002-0053, 2003-Ohio-2509, 2003 WL 21130058, Unreported. Infants ⇌ 243

Mother waived claim on appeal that notice of parental termination hearing was defective, where she failed to raise issue of notice with trial court. In re Shumate (Ohio App. 5 Dist., Muskingum, 04-29-2003) No. CT2002-0051, No. CT2002-0054, No. CT2002-0052, No. CT2002-0053, 2003-Ohio-2509, 2003 WL 21130058, Unreported. Infants ⇌ 243

Summons notifying mother of permanent custody proceedings involving her eight-year-old daughter met statutory requirements, in that it notified mother of date, time, and place of hearing, identified child at issue, and noticed mother of failure to appear, right to counsel and case plan, and consequences of permanent custody. In re Honaker (Ohio App. 5 Dist., Richland, 05-07-2003) No. 03CA10, No. 03CA11, 2003-Ohio-2407, 2003 WL 21060699, Unreported. Infants ⇌ 198

Father was entitled to relief from permanent custody order, even though father was served with notice of the hearing by publication; the prosecutor's office had notice that father was incarcerated in county prior to the permanent custody hearing, the prosecutor's office represented the county children services board at the permanent custody hearing, and father learned of the permanent custody hearing a few weeks after it occurred. In re Schutte (Ohio App. 12 Dist., Clinton, 05-12-2003) No. CA2002-11-042, 2003-Ohio-2371, 2003 WL 21054760, Unreported. Infants ⇌ 230.1

Written report of guardian ad litem was properly submitted in termination of parental rights proceeding, where report was time stamped on same day that magistrate's decision was filed. In re Kramer (Ohio App. 10 Dist., Franklin, 05-06-2003) No. 02AP-1038, No. 02AP-1039, 2003-Ohio-2277, 2003 WL 21007196, Unreported. Infants ⇌ 208

The trial court's failure to dispose of the county children's services motion for permanent custody within 120 days after the motion was filed, as required by statute, did not invalidate the judgment terminating father's parental rights; even though statute required the court to dispose of a motion for permanent custody of a child within 20 days, the statute further stated that the failure to dispose of the motion within the statutory time limits did not affect the validity of the judgment entered. In re Joseph P. (Ohio App. 6 Dist., Lucas, 05-02-2003) No. L-02-1385, 2003-Ohio-2217, 2003 WL 2007268, Unreported. Infants ⇌ 221

Upon grant of county children services board's motion to terminate father's parental rights, trial court was not required to list reasons for termination in the judgment entry. In re Hess (Ohio App. 7 Dist., Jefferson, 03-21-2003) No. 02 JE 37, 2003-Ohio-1429, 2003 WL 1465190, Unreported. Infants ⇌ 210

Trial court erred by failing to consider child's wishes on matter of permanent custody, though trial court found that child was not sufficiently mature to express her own wishes about the permanent custody issue, given that the court failed to make a finding about child's wishes as expressed by the guardian ad litem through his opinion as to child's best interests. In re Salsgiver (Ohio App. 11 Dist., Geauga, 03-13-2003) No. 2002-G-2478, 2003-Ohio-1203, 2003 WL 1193789, Unreported. Infants ⇌ 210

Filing of guardian ad litem's report after the completion of proceeding to terminate parental rights does not violate statute requiring a written report of the child's guardian ad litem to be submitted to the trial court prior to or at the time of the hearing if the parties are given a full opportunity to submit evidence or arguments as to the report; purpose of requirement is to give the parties an opportunity to rebut any assertion contained in the report. In re Salsgiver (Ohio App. 11 Dist., Geauga, 03-13-2003) No. 2002-G-2478, 2003-Ohio-1203, 2003 WL 1193789, Unreported. Infants ⇌ 208

Guardian ad litem's failure to address the minor child's wishes on custody issue in initial child protection proceeding before case was appealed and remanded could not stop trial court on remand from ordering guardian to submit supplemental report, for purposes of rendering a final decision on merits of county agency's motion for permanent custody; agency could not control whether the guardian ad litem had addressed child's wishes in his original report, and thus, ordering supplemental report did not give the agency a second chance to establish the necessary facts. In re Salsgiver (Ohio App. 11 Dist., Geauga, 03-13-2003) No. 2002-G-2478, 2003-Ohio-1203, 2003 WL 1193789, Unreported. Infants ⇌ 254

On remand of termination of parental rights case, trial court did not abuse its discretion in ordering the guardian ad litem to submit a supplemental report addressing child's wishes as to grant of permanent custody to County Jobs and Family Services; County did not have burden of proving what child's wishes were regarding her custody, obligation to provide statement on that point was on guardian ad litem, and thus, this was not situation in which party who had burden of proof on particular issue was given second chance to establish the necessary facts. In re Salsgiver (Ohio App. 11 Dist., Geauga, 03-13-2003) No. 2002-G-2477, 2003-Ohio-1206, 2003 WL 1193784, Unreported. Infants ⊙→ 254

In termination of parental rights case, if the trial court could not make a finding concerning the child's wishes as to whether permanent custody should be granted to County Jobs and Family Services, because child was not sufficiently mature to express her own wishes about permanent custody issue, court had to make a specific finding about child's wishes as expressed by the guardian ad litem through his opinion as to child's best interests. In re Salsgiver (Ohio App. 11 Dist., Geauga, 03-13-2003) No. 2002-G-2477, 2003-Ohio-1206, 2003 WL 1193784, Unreported. Infants ⊙→ 210

Doctrine of res judicata barred maternal relatives' motion to intervene, motion for custody, and motion for visitation of child involved in child protection matter, where relatives had failed to appeal denial of first motion, and second motion was attempt to relitigate same issues. In re Hoffman (Ohio App. 5 Dist., Stark, 03-03-2003) No. 2002CA0419, No. 2002CA0422, 2003-Ohio-1241, 2003 WL 1193770, Unreported. Infants ⊙→ 232

Failure to comply with statutory requirement that hearing on county's motion for permanent custody of three children was to be held within 120 days of filing of motion did not affect validity of trial court's judgment awarding permanent custody to county. In re Fricke (Ohio App. 3 Dist., Allen, 03-11-2003) No. 1-02-75, No. 1-02-76, No. 1-02-77, 2003-Ohio-1116, 2003 WL 952173, Unreported. Infants ⊙→ 204

Even if trial court erred in permanency hearing in finding that mother's children could not be returned to her within a reasonable time, or should not be placed with her, county children services was still entitled to award of physical custody of children, where mother failed to attack award of permanent custody to county children services based on fact that children had been in temporary custody of one or more public children services agencies or private child agencies for 12 or more months of a consecutive 22 month period. In re Llewellyn (Ohio App. 5 Dist., Fairfield, 03-10-2003) No. 02CA10, No. 02CA11, No. 02CA12, 2003-Ohio-1102, 2003 WL 951481, Unreported. Infants ⊙→ 222

In proceedings on county's motion for permanent custody, trial court was not required to make a finding that children could not have been returned to father within a reasonable time, and county was able to proceed directly to best interests portion of hearing, where court found that children had been in temporary custody of county for more than 12 out of last 22 months. In re Whipple Children (Ohio App. 5 Dist., Stark, 03-10-2003) No. 2002CA00406, 2003-Ohio-1101, 2003 WL 950448, Unreported. Infants ⊙→ 203; Infants ⊙→ 210

Affidavit verifying that father was served notice of county's motion for permanent custody by publication was timely filed, where docketing statement and the file stamp on affidavit reflected that affidavit was filed 26 days prior to hearing. In re Whipple Children (Ohio App. 5 Dist., Stark, 03-10-2003) No. 2002CA00406, 2003-Ohio-1101, 2003 WL 950448, Unreported. Infants ⊙→ 198

Serving notice of county's motion for permanent custody upon father via publication was not insufficient on grounds that address of juvenile court within publication was incorrect, even though the notice identified the court building as being the "Citizens Savings Building," yet the savings bank was no longer the primary tenant of building, where juvenile court was still located in such building, and street address and location of court room remained correct within publication. In re Whipple Children (Ohio App. 5 Dist., Stark, 03-10-2003) No. 2002CA00406, 2003-Ohio-1101, 2003 WL 950448, Unreported. Infants ⊙→ 198

Although child's paternal grandmother was not a party in permanent custody action, she had standing to appeal award of permanent custody to State, where the trial court permitted her to testify at the permanent custody hearing and considered her request for custody of child. In re P.P. (Ohio App. 2 Dist., Montgomery, 03-07-2003) No. 19582, 2003-Ohio-1051, 2003 WL 863568, Unreported. Infants ⊙→ 242

Grandmother involved in termination of parental rights proceeding waived argument on appeal that statute governing procedures upon filing of motion for permanent child custody was unconstitutional, where issue was not raised at the trial court even though issue was apparent at time. In re Walker (Ohio App. 11 Dist., Ashtabula, 02-24-2003) No. 2002-A-0087, 2003-Ohio-798, 2003 WL 473987, Unreported. Infants ⊙→ 243

Trial court was precluded from adopting the magistrate's decision awarding permanent custody of minor child to the county children services board that did not consider each of the five statutory factors for determining whether a grant of permanent custody was in child's best interest; although the magistrate reviewed the child's custodial and procedural history, the magistrate failed to discuss the child's interaction and interrelationship with her mother prior to being temporarily placed in a foster home, there was no discussion of the guardian ad litem's recommendation regarding the custody of the child, and there were no findings with respect to child's need for a legally secure placement or whether that type of placement could be achieved without a grant of permanent custody to the county. In re Smith (Ohio App. 11 Dist., Ashtabula, 02-24-2003) No. 2002-A-0098, 2003-Ohio-800, 2003 WL 470198, Unreported. Infants ⊙→ 206

Failure of trial court to allow mother to cross-examine guardian ad litem in permanent custody proceeding was not harmless error, where guardian ad litem's report contained evidence that was not submitted or testified to at hearing, including statements made by children to guardian, as well as conclusions and opinions of guardian regarding issues bearing on mother's ability to parent. In re Spillman (Ohio App. 12 Dist., Clinton, 02-18-2003) No. CA2002-06-028, 2003-Ohio-713, 2003 WL 352477, Unreported. Infants ⊙→ 207; Infants ⊙→ 253

Order limiting scope of mother's discovery with respect to guardian ad litem did not deprive mother of right to prepare for trial, in proceedings to place mother's children in permanent custody of county children's services board; mother's discovery requests were overly broad and went beyond scope of allowable discovery, mother did not bring any discrepancies in guardian ad litem's information to court's attention, and mother never called guardian ad litem to testify at hearing. In re Adams (Ohio App. 2 Dist., Miami, 02-07-2003) No. 2002 CA 45, 2003-Ohio-618, 2003 WL 264357, Unreported. Infants ⊙→ 201

Mother waived any possible claims of inadequacy of notice of county's motions for permanent custody, where she was represented by counsel who filed motions prior to trial and signed continuance forms for a change in trial dates. In re Thompson (Ohio App. 10 Dist., Franklin, 02-06-2003) No. 02AP-557, No. 02AP-558, 2003-Ohio-580, 2003 WL 257413, Unreported, appeal not allowed 98 Ohio St.3d 1515, 786 N.E.2d 64, 2003-Ohio-1572, certiorari denied 124 S.Ct. 185, 540 U.S. 866, 157 L.Ed.2d 121. Infants ⊙→ 198

Although child's great-grandmother was legal custodian of child's 15-year-old mother, great-grandmother did not hold any legally protectable interest in child's care and custody, and thus, she had no legal right to participate in proceedings on county's complaint in dependency and neglect and motion for permanent custody. In re Tammy M. (Ohio App. 6 Dist., Lucas, 01-31-2003) No. L-02-1108, 2003-Ohio-492, 2003 WL 220596, Unreported. Infants ⊙→ 200

In evaluating great-grandmother's motion for custody of infant, in proceedings on county's complaint in dependency and neglect and motion for permanent custody, court was not required to have subject matter jurisdiction over infant's mother, a 15-year-old chronic run-away, whose parental rights as to infant had been terminated, to consider as part of the best interests evaluation the possible effects of fact that great-grandmother was also legal custodian of mother, including risk that mother would return and take the infant and flee. In re Tammy M. (Ohio App. 6 Dist., Lucas, 01-31-2003) No. L-02-1108, 2003-Ohio-492, 2003 WL 220596, Unreported. Infants ⊙→ 222

The Common Pleas Court had jurisdiction to grant permanent custody of mother's two children to the county job and family services agency, even though notice to mother of the dispositional hearing was returned undeliverable; mother appeared with counsel at an earlier shelter-care hearing, at the shelter-care hearing the trial court noted the date of the adjudicatory hearing, counsel for mother appeared at the dispositional hearing, and neither mother or her counsel objected to the notice provided to mother. In re Billingsley (Ohio App. 3 Dist., Putnam, 01-28-2003) No. 12-02-07, No. 12-02-08, 2003-Ohio-344, 2003 WL 178661, Unreported. Infants ⊙→ 198

Trial court lacked authority to place children in a Planned Permanent Living Arrangement (PPLA) as an alternative to terminating father's parental rights; there was no evidence to suggest that father or county department of children and family services sought a PPLA, and there was no evidence presented to establish any of the other statutory requirements necessary for court to place children in a PPLA. (Per O'Donnell, J., with two judges concurring in judgment only). In re Harlston (Ohio App. 8 Dist., Cuyahoga, 01-23-2003) No. 80672, 2003-Ohio-282, 2003 WL 152939, Unreported, appeal not allowed 98 Ohio St.3d 1492, 785 N.E.2d 474, 2003-Ohio-1189. Infants ⊙→ 226

Father waived on appeal in termination of parental rights proceeding issue of whether trial court lacked jurisdiction to enter order awarding permanent custody of children to county department of children and family services, based on his allegation that court did not provide proper notice to mother of proceedings, as he failed to raise issue in trial court. (Per O'Donnell, J., with two judges concurring in judgment only). In re Harlston (Ohio App. 8 Dist., Cuyahoga, 01-23-2003) No. 80672, 2003-

Mother's absence at termination of parental rights hearing did not prejudice father's rights; not only was there no evidence that mother would have been awarded custody of children, but mother was in agreement with permanent custody of children being awarded to county department of children and family services. (Per O'Donnell, J., with two judges concurring in judgment only). In re Harlston (Ohio App. 8 Dist., Cuyahoga, 01-23-2003) No. 80672, 2003-Ohio-282, 2003 WL 152939, Unreported, appeal not allowed 98 Ohio St.3d 1492, 785 N.E.2d 474, 2003-Ohio-1189. Infants ⚖ 253

The trial court's adoption of the magistrate's decision to terminate mother's parental rights was an abuse of discretion, where the magistrate failed to specifically discuss each of the five factors listed in statute to determine whether termination was in the best interests of the children. In re Kelley (Ohio App. 11 Dist., Ashtabula, 01-17-2003) No. 2002-A-0088, 2003-Ohio-194, 2003 WL 139283, Unreported. Infants ⚖ 206

New evidence discovered by county was relevant and material to permanent custody proceedings relating to child who was removed from father's home, as would support juvenile court's decision to extend proceedings so that county could present such evidence; father, who sought custody of child, lied when he told county that he had no other children, when, in fact, he had another son who resided with him, allegedly had been victim of sexual abuse perpetrated by father and father's brother, and was also a perpetrator of sexual abuse. In re Sullivan (Ohio App. 12 Dist., Butler, 01-21-2003) No. CA2002-03-061, 2003-Ohio-195, 2003 WL 138665, Unreported. Infants ⚖ 207

County should not have discovered new evidence prior to filing its motion to extend permanent custody proceedings based upon such evidence, as would support juvenile court's decision to extend proceedings, where father concealed information from county that he had another son who resided with him, had perpetrated sexual abuse, and had alleged that he was the victim of sexual abuse perpetrated by father and father's brother, by specifically stating to county that he had no other children. In re Sullivan (Ohio App. 12 Dist., Butler, 01-21-2003) No. CA2002-03-061, 2003-Ohio-195, 2003 WL 138665, Unreported. Infants ⚖ 207

Extending permanent custody proceedings so that county could present newly discovered evidence was consistent with juvenile code's purpose to provide for the care, protection, and mental and physical development of children, where evidence exposed fact that father had lied to county when he told county that he had no other children, when, in fact, he had another son who resided with him, allegedly had been victim of sexual abuse perpetrated by father and father's brother, and was also a perpetrator of sexual abuse. In re Sullivan (Ohio App. 12 Dist., Butler, 01-21-2003) No. CA2002-03-061, 2003-Ohio-195, 2003 WL 138665, Unreported. Infants ⚖ 207

Juvenile court had the power to grant permanent custody to county, where it found by clear and convincing evidence that it was in child's best interest for county to take permanent custody, and child had been in the temporary custody of the county for well over 12 months in a consecutive 22-month period. In re Sullivan (Ohio App. 12 Dist., Butler, 01-21-2003) No. CA2002-03-061, 2003-Ohio-195, 2003 WL 138665, Unreported. Infants ⚖ 222

Trial court's act of allowing conservator for both mother and child to testify to child's best interests at permanency hearing did not result in prejudice to mother, even though mother claimed such constituted a conflict of interest; any statutory duty on the part of the conservator existed when she was acting in capacity of making medical or other decisions on behalf of mother or child and conservator, and conservator was not performing such a role when she testified as a witness at permanency hearing. In re J.J. (Ohio App. 9 Dist., Summit, 12-31-2002) No. 21226, 2002-Ohio-7330, 2002 WL 31890708, Unreported. Infants ⚖ 253

Mother moved for nunc pro tunc order, jointly with county Children Services Board, to correct trial court's omission of award of permanent custody of child to board in its order terminating mother's parental rights, and thus could not now complain that nunc pro tunc entry was in error. In re Amonte A. (Ohio App. 6 Dist., Lucas, 12-20-2002) No. L-02-1280, 2002-Ohio-7103, 2002 WL 31846314, Unreported. Infants ⚖ 248.1

While trial court's judgment entry terminating mother's parental rights erred for lacking language awarding permanent custody of child to county Children Services Board, omission was corrected by nunc pro tunc order, for which mother and board jointly moved, which awarded permanent custody of child to board. In re Amonte A. (Ohio App. 6 Dist., Lucas, 12-20-2002) No. L-02-1280, 2002-Ohio-7103, 2002 WL 31846314, Unreported. Infants ⚖ 222

Fact that parents in permanent custody proceedings were not afforded opportunity to cross-examine guardian ad litem did not constitute plain error, where trial court did not rely heavily on guardian's report, but noted in its decision that guardian had filed a report documenting her lengthy involvement in the case and that guardian recommended granting permanent custody to the County Children Services Board, trial court's decision detailed extensive testimony it relied upon, and vast majority of information in guardian's report was testified to at trial by persons who gave information to guardian. In re Tyas (Ohio App. 12 Dist., Clinton, 12-09-2002) No. CA2002-02-010, 2002-Ohio-6679, 2002 WL 31740248, Unreported. Infants ⚖ 243

Trial court, prior to finding child dependent and granting county children services permanent custody, complied with statutory requirement that it determine that child could not be placed with one of child's parents within a reasonable time or should not be placed with either parent; court specifically examined subdivisions of the statute. In re Barnhart (Ohio App. 4 Dist., Athens, 10-30-2002) No. 02CA21, 2002-Ohio-6024, 2002 WL 31455952, Unreported. Infants ⚖ 210

In proceeding to determine whether child victim was an abused and dependent child, decision to allow witness to act as victim's support person during victim's in camera testimony was not unreasonable, arbitrary, or unconscionable, and was in victim's best interest; witness's direct testimony was completed before she acted as a support person for victim, and she was given a detailed admonition prior to victim's testimony. In re Morris (Ohio App. 12 Dist., Butler, 10-28-2002) No. CA2002-03-054, 2002-Ohio-5881, 2002 WL 31414557, Unreported. Infants ⚖ 207

A seven-year-old child is capable of sharing his own opinion about his placement in a hearing on a motion for permanent custody by a county children services agency. In re Williams (Ohio App. 10 Dist., Franklin, 03-20-2001) No. 00AP-973, 2001 WL 266886, Unreported, on subsequent appeal 2002-Ohio-7205, 2002 WL 31870153.

A trial court is under no obligation to consider whether a grandparent of the child would be a fit parent before it could consider whether there was clear and convincing evidence to show that the child's best interest would be met by granting permanent custody to the county agency. In re Leonard (Ohio App. 12 Dist., Butler, 04-28-1997) No. CA96-08-146, 1997 WL 208137, Unreported.

A juvenile court's permanent placement of a minor child with a county children services board is against the manifest weight of the evidence where the record on appeal is silent as to (1) the conditions which caused the child to be initially placed outside the home, (2) the case plan of the board or the mother's actions relative to a case plan, and (3) the reason why it is not in the best interest of the child to be in the care, custody or control of the mother. Matter of Mesko (Ohio App. 7 Dist., Belmont, 04-24-1997) No. 95 BA 32, 1997 WL 205279, Unreported.

The trial court errs in failing to inform the parent of her rights to remain silent, to cross-examine witnesses, and to offer evidence at the adjudicatory hearing and in granting permanent custody when no guardian ad litem's report is filed with the court. Matter of Eplin (Ohio App. 5 Dist., Stark, 06-29-1995) No. 94 CA 0311, 1995 WL 495451, Unreported.

Divesting a father of parental rights is error where (1) the children's services board fails to timely include the father in a case plan and does not provide him with a minimally adequate direction or opportunity regarding his rehabilitation as a parent, (2) the trial court fails to find that reunification would have been futile as required by RC 2151.419, and (3) the court improperly denies the father's motion for a continuance before the guardian ad litem submits a written report as mandated by RC 2151.414(C). In re Richard, Laqueeda, Shennell & Dominique (Ohio App. 2 Dist., Montgomery, 12-14-1994) No. 14140, No. 14200, 1994 WL 702071, Unreported.

Where foster parents move to intervene prior to a dispositional hearing, a trial court's grant of the motion to intervene does not constitute an abuse of discretion where the trial court correctly states the intervention of the foster parents does not change the state's burden of proof in seeking to permanently remove a child from her natural parents and where neither the foster parents nor their attorney participate in any part of the dispositional hearing. In re Kapp, No. 13-93-9, 1993 WL 415446 (3d Dist Ct App, Seneca, 10-14-93).

Foster parents who have cared for a child for most of the child's life and are the child's "psychological parents" have standing to appeal from the denial of a motion to intervene in a permanent custody action. In re Rundio, No. 92-CA-35, 1993 WL 379512 (4th Dist Ct App, Pickaway, 9-8-93).

A trial court's award of permanent custody of a child to a children's services agency instead of granting legal custody to foster parents or continuing placement with the foster parents pending the adoption of the child is not error where both the foster parents and another couple who have already adopted the child's siblings seek to adopt the child and where no final determination as to the child's adoption has been made because to continue placement with the foster parents would make it difficult to impossible to assess the possibility of adoption by the other couple. In re Rundio, No. 92-CA-35, 1993 WL 379512 (4th Dist Ct App, Pickaway, 9-8-93).

The denial of a motion to intervene in an action for permanent custody filed by foster parents of a child does not constitute an abuse of discretion where the foster parents were allowed to participate in the dispositional hearing in the presentation of evidence and cross-examination of witnesses. In re Rundio, No. 92 CA 35, 1993 WL 379512 (4th Dist Ct App, Pickaway, 9–8–93).

After child's death, exception to the mootness doctrine for a debatable constitutional question did not apply to father's appeal from trial court's denial of his objections to magistrate's decision, which found clear and convincing evidence that the child was a neglected and dependent child; unresolved constitutional question was ordinarily taken only by the highest court of the state, and the potential constitutional issue of the magistrate's denial of father's right to counsel at the adjudicatory hearing was addressed and resolved by the trial court at its hearing on father's objections. In re L.W. (Ohio App. 10 Dist., 02-14-2006) 2006-Ohio-644, 2006 WL 330089. Infants 247

Child's death rendered moot the issues raised in father's objections to magistrate's decision, which found clear and convincing evidence that child was neglected and dependent, such that dismissal of father's appeal from the denial of those objections was warranted. In re L.W. (Ohio App. 10 Dist., 02-14-2006) 2006-Ohio-644, 2006 WL 330089. Infants 247

Statutes applying to permanent custody proceedings did not apply in child dependency proceeding in which maternal grandparents sought legal custody of children, as trial court did not grant permanent custody of children to public children services agency or private child placing agency, but, instead, granted grandparents legal custody of children. In re Sean T. (Ohio App. 6 Dist., 10-28-2005) 164 Ohio App.3d 218, 841 N.E.2d 838, 2005-Ohio-5739. Infants 222

A prior adjudication of permanent custody does not result in a de facto termination of parental rights. In re Sheffey (Ohio App. 11 Dist., 02-10-2006) 167 Ohio App.3d 141, 854 N.E.2d 508, 2006-Ohio-619. Infants 232

Mother who lost permanent custody of child was statutorily barred from filing petition for custody of child as nonparent, where mother's nonparent custody petition was filed with same case number used in amended complaint of abuse, neglect, and dependency that resulted in termination of her parental rights, and statute providing for modification or termination of dispositional orders specifically excluded as parties any parent whose parental rights with respect to the child have been terminated. In re McBride (Ohio, 07-19-2006) 110 Ohio St.3d 19, 850 N.E.2d 43, 2006-Ohio-3454. Infants 231

Juvenile rule allowing "any person" to file for custody of a child did not override express statutory language precluding natural parent who lost permanent custody of child from filing nonparent custody petition, where right to file petition for custody was substantive right not subject to abridgment, enlargement, or modification by court rules. In re McBride (Ohio, 07-19-2006) 110 Ohio St.3d 19, 850 N.E.2d 43, 2006-Ohio-3454. Infants 231

Mother and maternal grandmother adequately preserved for appellate review their claim that the trial court erred during hearing on remand following appeal of termination of parental rights decision when it considered new evidence without allowing all of the parties to present additional evidence; the nature of the evidence mother sought to present, to rebut the new testimony of expert at hearing on remand, was evident from discussions between counsel and the magistrate, and the magistrate ruled that mother and grandmother were prohibited from offering any new evidence during remand hearing. In re Walker (Ohio App. 11 Dist., 07-22-2005) 162 Ohio App.3d 303, 833 N.E.2d 362, 2005-Ohio-3773, on subsequent appeal 2006-Ohio-739, 2006 WL 389596, appeal allowed 109 Ohio St.3d 1506, 849 N.E.2d 1027, 2006-Ohio-2998. Infants 243

Mother's consent to termination of her parental rights to child was not knowing and voluntary; when first asked whether she was there to give up custody of her child, she twice said, "I don't want to," she also said she felt she had no other choice, rather than that she believed the choice she was making was in her child's best interest, after 45 minutes, with three separate off-the-record discussions, mother eventually acquiesced verbally in relinquishment of her rights, and mother's responses, together with length of time it took to convince her to consent demonstrated that mother's waiver of her rights to custody of her child was made under duress at best, or was coerced at worst. In re Terrence (Ohio App. 6 Dist., 07-13-2005) 162 Ohio App.3d 229, 833 N.E.2d 306, 2005-Ohio-3600. Infants 199

Father waived his appellate argument that the permanent custody statutory provision that provided for transfer of permanent custody of child if the child has been in the temporary custody of one or more public children services agencies or private child placing agencies for twelve or more months of a consecutive twenty-two month period was unconstitutional, where father failed to raise the issue in the trial court. In re Stillman (Ohio App. 11 Dist., 11-19-2003) 155 Ohio App.3d 333, 801 N.E.2d 475, 2003-Ohio-6228, appeal not allowed 101 Ohio St.3d 1425, 802 N.E.2d 155, 2004-Ohio-123. Infants 243

County department of human services was not required to have custody of child for twelve consecutive months prior to filing motion for permanent custody, where department filed original complaint alleging child to be a dependent child and requesting permanent custody of child as the first disposition and temporary custody as the alternative disposition. In re Ament (Ohio App. 12 Dist., 04-23-2001) 142 Ohio App.3d 302, 755 N.E.2d 448, appeal not allowed 92 Ohio St.3d 1431, 749 N.E.2d 757. Infants 193

A trial court should apply the version of the statute in effect at the time that the motion for permanent custody was filed when ruling upon a motion for permanent custody. In re Ament (Ohio App. 12 Dist., 04-23-2001) 142 Ohio App.3d 302, 755 N.E.2d 448, appeal not allowed 92 Ohio St.3d 1431, 749 N.E.2d 757. Infants 132

An appellate court's inquiry into a trial court's determination of dependency is limited to whether sufficient credible evidence exists to support the trial court's determination. In re Ament (Ohio App. 12 Dist., 04-23-2001) 142 Ohio App.3d 302, 755 N.E.2d 448, appeal not allowed 92 Ohio St.3d 1431, 749 N.E.2d 757. Infants 252

Assuming that temporary custody of four siblings, two of whom had been adjudicated neglected and two of whom had been adjudicated dependent, technically terminated and sunset date passed due to combination of state's failure to request extension of temporary custody and lack of separate hearing on propriety of extension, juvenile court maintained jurisdiction to rule on subsequent requests for permanent and legal custody, and its rulings on such requests therefore rendered moot mother's challenge on appeal to juvenile court's jurisdiction to grant extension of temporary custody. In re Nice (Ohio App. 7 Dist., 03-20-2001) 141 Ohio App.3d 445, 751 N.E.2d 552, 2001-Ohio-3214. Infants 196; Infants 247

For the purpose of the statute governing an award of permanent custody, a child is considered to have entered temporary custody on the earlier of the date of adjudication or 60 days after the child's removal. In re Nice (Ohio App. 7 Dist., 03-20-2001) 141 Ohio App.3d 445, 751 N.E.2d 552, 2001-Ohio-3214. Infants 222

On appeal from a trial court's determination that grant of permanent custody of a child to an agency applying for such custody is in the child's best interests, a reviewing court must determine whether the trial court complied with statutory requirements and whether there was sufficient evidence to support a finding by clear and convincing evidence that one or more statutory factors precluding that child's return to one or both parents exist. In re Nicholas H. (Ohio App. 6 Dist., 05-05-2000) 137 Ohio App.3d 442, 738 N.E.2d 896. Infants 252

Before any court may consider whether a child's best interests may be served by permanent removal from his or her family, there must be first a demonstration that the parents are "unfit." In re Stacey S. (Ohio App. 6 Dist., 12-30-1999) 136 Ohio App.3d 503, 737 N.E.2d 92, 1999-Ohio-989. Infants 155

Mother could not be compelled to disclose communications between herself and her physician, licensed psychologist, or licensed counselor or social worker, made by her in course of treatment ordered as part of reunification plan in action for dependency and neglect; none of the applicable privilege statutes made provision for in-court disclosure of confidential information on basis that treatment or service received by patient or client was involuntary in nature, ordered as part of journalized case plan, or was necessary or relevant to determination of permanent custody. In re Wieland (Ohio, 09-06-2000) 89 Ohio St.3d 535, 733 N.E.2d 1127, 2000-Ohio-233. Witnesses 208(2); Witnesses 214.5

Juvenile court was not required, prior to awarding permanent custody of child to county agency in proceeding to terminate mother's parental rights, to find by clear and convincing evidence that child's maternal grandmother was an unsuitable placement option. In re Patterson (Ohio App. 9 Dist., 09-01-1999) 134 Ohio App.3d 119, 730 N.E.2d 439. Infants 178

When juvenile court delays its ruling for more than seven days following the conclusion of dispositional hearing on an agency's motion for permanent child custody filed prior to September 18, 1996, violation of that time constraint serves as justification for seeking a writ of procedendo. In re Davis (Ohio, 03-03-1999) 84 Ohio St.3d 520, 705 N.E.2d 1219, 1999-Ohio-419. Infants ⇐ 204

Parents were estopped from complaining on appeal that they were prejudiced when juvenile court did not rule on agency's petition for permanent custody of children until seventeen months after conclusion of dispositional hearing, where parents failed to seek writ of procedendo after seven-day deadline for issuance of judgment following hearing had passed. In re Davis (Ohio, 03-03-1999) 84 Ohio St.3d 520, 705 N.E.2d 1219, 1999-Ohio-419. Infants ⇐ 232; Infants ⇐ 243

Child services agency had standing to file second motion for permanent custody of child, even though child had not been in temporary custody of agency for the six months immediately preceding filing of motion, where agency filed first motion at time when child had been in temporary custody well in excess of six months, but agency relinquished temporary custody to relative in attempt for more permanent placement instead of following through with motion, second motion was filed one month after temporary custody was reestablished, child had been in "state of limbo" for nearly four years at that time, child was never returned to custody of mother, and conditions that led to his removal from home had not been remedied. Lorain Cty. Children Serv. v. Keene (Ohio App. 9 Dist., 03-05-1997) 118 Ohio App.3d 535, 693 N.E.2d 833. Infants ⇐ 230.1

Child welfare agency has burden of establishing statutory antecedents for terminating parental rights. In re Shanequa H. (Ohio App. 6 Dist., 02-02-1996) 109 Ohio App.3d 142, 671 N.E.2d 1113. Infants ⇐ 172

For purpose of termination of parental rights proceeding, judicial reaction should be no greater than warranted and judicial response should be least intrusive available; each child is and should be treated as individual. In re William S. (Ohio, 03-04-1996) 75 Ohio St.3d 95, 661 N.E.2d 738, 1996-Ohio-182. Infants ⇐ 155

In order for public children services agency to file motion for permanent custody of child previously adjudicated as abused, neglected or dependent, it must have current temporary custody of that child pursuant to order of disposition. In re Miller (Ohio App. 2 Dist., 02-15-1995) 101 Ohio App.3d 199, 655 N.E.2d 252. Infants ⇐ 230.1

In contested dependency cases, juvenile court is required to find by clear and convincing evidence that grant of permanent custody/termination of parental rights is in best interests of child, and that child cannot be placed with either parent within reasonable time or should not be placed with parents. In re Makuch (Ohio App. 9 Dist., 02-08-1995) 101 Ohio App.3d 45, 654 N.E.2d 1331. Infants ⇐ 178

If court has determined that child cannot or should not be placed with parents within reasonable time, before court can determine that it is in the best interests of the child to be permanently placed with county, court must consider all relevant evidence and find, by clear and convincing evidence, that one of the eight statutory conditions exists that would prohibit placement of the child with one of its parents. In re Brown (Ohio App. 3 Dist., 11-02-1994) 98 Ohio App.3d 337, 648 N.E.2d 576. Infants ⇐ 178

Permanent custody determination must be supported by "clear and convincing evidence," which is more than mere preponderance of the evidence and requires that petitioner prove each of its allegations, clearly and convincingly, producing in the mind of the trier of facts a firm belief or conviction as to the facts sought to be established. In re Brown (Ohio App. 3 Dist., 11-02-1994) 98 Ohio App.3d 337, 648 N.E.2d 576. Infants ⇐ 178

Trial court may grant motion for permanent custody if it determines by clear and convincing evidence, after a child has been found to be neglected, dependent, or abused, that it is in the child's best interest to grant the movant permanent custody and either that the child cannot be placed with either of his parents, or the parents cannot be located, if the child is abandoned, or there are no relatives of the child able to take permanent custody, if the child is orphaned. In re Brown (Ohio App. 3 Dist., 11-02-1994) 98 Ohio App.3d 337, 648 N.E.2d 576. Infants ⇐ 179; Infants ⇐ 180

It was error to terminate parental rights of mother who was never given notice of the hearing wherein the child was adjudged dependent. In re Brown (Ohio App. 3 Dist., 11-02-1994) 98 Ohio App.3d 337, 648 N.E.2d 576. Infants ⇐ 198

Before awarding permanent custody to county, court must not only find by clear and convincing evidence that certain criteria have been met, court must state those findings on the record, so that it is clear to all parties that the decision is supported by the facts. In re Brown (Ohio App. 3 Dist., 11-02-1994) 98 Ohio App.3d 337, 648 N.E.2d 576. Infants ⇐ 210

When committing child to permanent custody, trial court must adhere to statutory mandates. In re Brodbeck (Ohio App. 3 Dist., 10-19-1994) 97 Ohio App.3d 652, 647 N.E.2d 240. Infants ⇐ 155

Statutory provisions governing child custody matters are to be liberally construed to provide for care, protection and mental and physical development of children, in a family environment when possible, separating child from parents only when necessary for his or her welfare. In re Wise (Ohio App. 9 Dist., 08-31-1994) 96 Ohio App.3d 619, 645 N.E.2d 812. Child Custody ⇐ 3; Infants ⇐ 132

On appeal from order terminating parental rights, court must determine from record whether juvenile court, as trier of fact, had sufficient evidence to satisfy clear and convincing evidence standard; judgment will not be reversed if supported by sufficient credible evidence. In re Wise (Ohio App. 9 Dist., 08-31-1994) 96 Ohio App.3d 619, 645 N.E.2d 812. Infants ⇐ 252

Both best interest determination and determination that child could not be placed with either parent in motion for permanent custody focus on child, not parent. In re Awkal (Ohio App. 8 Dist., 06-27-1994) 95 Ohio App.3d 309, 642 N.E.2d 424. Infants ⇐ 155

Discretion enjoyed by juvenile court in determining whether order of permanent custody is in best interests of child should be accorded utmost respect, given nature of proceeding and impact court's determination will have on lives of parties concerned. In re Awkal (Ohio App. 8 Dist., 06-27-1994) 95 Ohio App.3d 309, 642 N.E.2d 424. Infants ⇐ 155

Clear and convincing evidence established that children could not be placed with either of their parents within reasonable time, supporting granting of permanent custody to county children services board as dependent, neglected and abused children; therefore, trial court acted unreasonably and in abuse of its discretion by modifying its award of permanent custody to award of temporary custody. In re Doe Children (Ohio App. 6 Dist., 02-11-1994) 93 Ohio App.3d 134, 637 N.E.2d 977, cause dismissed 69 Ohio St.3d 1481, 634 N.E.2d 1027. Infants ⇐ 230.1

Guardian ad litem satisfied statutory requirement that report be submitted "at the time of the hearing" where he submitted his report to court just prior to end of permanent custody hearing, where he read report into record in open court, at close of evidence but prior to closing arguments. In re Shaeffer Children (Van Wert 1993) 85 Ohio App.3d 683, 621 N.E.2d 426, dismissed, jurisdictional motion overruled 67 Ohio St.3d 1451, 619 N.E.2d 419. Infants ⇐ 208

Award of temporary custody for shelter care pending adjudication is not such an "award of temporary custody" as to prevent agency from filing for permanent custody for statutory six-month period; rather, agency may seek permanent custody at any time, and complaint will relate back as though it had sought permanent custody in the first instance. In re Massengill (Lucas 1991) 76 Ohio App.3d 220, 601 N.E.2d 206. Infants ⇐ 155

Service by publication is proper in a case in which a county children's services board files a motion for permanent custody of a mother's children where the board adequately establishes that it exercised reasonable diligence in attempting to locate the mother; the mother's history of sporadic contact coupled with her inability to obtain stable housing, ten addresses within one year, or provide the board with an address to send notices made it extremely impractical, if not impossible, to serve the mother in any other manner than by publication. In re Cowling (Summit 1991) 72 Ohio App.3d 499, 595 N.E.2d 470. Infants ⇐ 198

Transfer of a permanent custody hearing from the county where the children have been found to be neglected and dependent and are the subjects of a temporary custody order to the county in which the children's parents currently reside is improper as the residency of the children, not the parents, controls jurisdiction. In re Smith (Lucas 1990) 64 Ohio App.3d 773, 582 N.E.2d 1117.

The family reunification law set forth in RC 2151.414 has no relevance and does not apply to motions for a change of custody under RC 3109.04; RC 2151.414 is limited to matters pertaining to a motion for permanent custody of a child by a county department, board, or certified organization that has temporary custody of the child. Miller v. Miller (Ohio 1988) 37 Ohio St.3d 71, 523 N.E.2d 846, clarification denied 43 Ohio St.3d 710, 540 N.E.2d 728.

A parent who has voluntarily surrendered her parental rights to a certified private agency, in accordance with RC 5103.15, is not a necessary party entitled to notice when a dependency complaint is later filed. In re Infant Female Luallen (Hamilton 1985) 27 Ohio App.3d 29, 499 N.E.2d 358, 27 O.B.R. 30. Infants ⇐ 172; Infants ⇐ 198

RC 2151.412 and RC 2151.414 do not apply where a request for permanent custody is made by a welfare department and a temporary custody order is issued under RC 2151.33 pending a hearing on the request. In re Covert (Seneca 1984) 17 Ohio App.3d 122, 477 N.E.2d 678, 17 O.B.R. 185.

Under statute, permanent child custody creates status which divests natural parents or adoptive parents of any and all parental rights, privileges and obligations, including all residual rights and obligations, and where county welfare department filed motion in juvenile court for permanent custody and court found that permanent custody was appropriate under circumstances of particular case, and, all due process safeguards having been followed, whatever residual rights parent might have held prior to such determination were properly divested. In re Palmer (Ohio 1984) 12 Ohio St.3d 194, 465 N.E.2d 1312, 12 O.B.R. 259, certiorari denied 105 S.Ct. 918, 469 U.S. 1162, 83 L.Ed.2d 930. Infants ⚖ 232

The determination to be made by the juvenile court during a hearing upon a motion for permanent custody should be included within the court's findings of fact and conclusions of law, if they were requested by any of the parties pursuant to RC 2151.414(B), but do not need to be listed in the judgment entry. In re Covin (Hamilton 1982) 8 Ohio App.3d 139, 456 N.E.2d 520, 8 O.B.R. 196.

An agreement by a parent with the welfare department for permanent surrender of a child prior to consent of the juvenile court is not only revocable by the parent prior to consent of the juvenile court, but such revocation also operates to dissolve the offer to surrender. In re Williams (Hamilton 1982) 7 Ohio App.3d 324, 455 N.E.2d 1027, 7 O.B.R. 421. Infants ⚖ 157

The comprehensive reunification plan required by 1980 H 695, § 3, eff. 10–24–80, to be included in the second annual review made of a child who is in temporary custody upon the effective date of the act, is not required when the board files a motion for permanent custody of a child before the occurrence of the second annual review. In re Smith (Greene 1982) 7 Ohio App.3d 75, 454 N.E.2d 171, 7 O.B.R. 88.

Jurisdiction to consider collateral challenges to a state court judgment, which involuntarily terminated parental rights, is not conferred upon federal courts by habeas corpus statute. Lehman v. Lycoming County Children's Services Agency (U.S.Pa. 1982) 102 S.Ct. 3231, 458 U.S. 502, 73 L.Ed.2d 928.

Trial court's judgment terminating father's parental rights and awarding permanent custody to public agency was facially defective on ground mandatory findings were not made, and thus Court of Appeals would reverse and remand for entry of those findings; trial court stated that clear and convincing evidence supported existence of three statutory factors necessary to award custody to agency, but statute was amended to list four factors and it was unclear as to which factor the court was referring. In re Belanger (Ohio App. 11 Dist., Ashtabula, 09-20-2002) No. 2002-A-0047, 2002-Ohio-4956, 2002 WL 31107545, Unreported. Infants ⚖ 210; Infants ⚖ 254

Error, if any, in determining that mother failed to substantially comply with case plan in order to be reunited with her dependent children was harmless, given clear and convincing evidence that she failed to remedy situation that caused children's removal from home because they were home alone, and that children would still be neglected and dependent if they were returned to her, as she had no means of providing housing for them, and there was no indication of when, if ever, mother was going to be able to support her children. In re Cather (Ohio App. 11 Dist., Portage, 08-30-2002) No. 2002-P-0014, No. 2002-P-0015, No. 2002-P-0016, 2002-Ohio-4519, 2002 WL 2022964, Unreported. Infants ⚖ 253

Trial court was not required to make findings that mother's dependent children could not be placed with either parent within a reasonable amount of time or that the children should not be placed with either parent, given its finding, based on uncontested evidence that the children had been in the custody of public children services agency for nearly two years, that children have been in the custody of the agency for twelve or more months in a twenty-two month period. In re Cather (Ohio App. 11 Dist., Portage, 08-30-2002) No. 2002-P-0014, No. 2002-P-0015, No. 2002-P-0016, 2002-Ohio-4519, 2002 WL 2022964, Unreported. Infants ⚖ 210

Amendment of complaint from temporary to that of permanent custody on day of adjudicatory hearing in child abuse/neglect proceeding did not prejudice mother, where it was clear that mother had a meaningful, complete opportunity to contest the amended permanent custody complaint, and her attorney's objection to the amendment was not premised on anything to do with the amendment, but was actually a discovery objection affecting completely different issues; all parties were reminded at outset of every single hearing that case involved county department of children and family services's request for permanent custody of all mother's children, mother was served with a complaint specifically encaptioned as a complaint seeking permanent custody, and agency had been granted temporary custody at the pre-dispositional custody hearing. In re C.F. (Ohio App. 8 Dist., Cuyahoga, 08-22-2002) No. 80371, 2002-Ohio-4286, 2002 WL 1938611, Unreported. Infants ⚖ 197; Infants ⚖ 253

Trial court's failure, in order terminating father's parental rights and awarding permanent custody of child to county job and family services agency, to discuss child's wishes expressed through her guardian ad litem in determining child's best interest, was prejudicial error. In re Salsgiver (Ohio App. 11 Dist., Geauga, 07-22-2002) No. 2002-G-2412, 2002-Ohio-3713, 2002 WL 1627231, Unreported. Infants ⚖ 221; Infants ⚖ 253

Trial court's denial of mother's motion for continuance of hearing on permanent placement of her three dependent or abused children was not an abuse of discretion; mother had been forbidden by her parole officer from attending the hearing, mother had three more months to serve in prison, children had "languished" in foster care placement with relatives for more than a year, mother's potential testimony at the hearing was essentially uncontested, and mother's primary motivation for seeking a continuance was to gain additional time to complete her case plan. In re Campbell/Spicer Children (Ohio App. 5 Dist., Stark, 07-15-2002) No. 2002CA00056, 2002-Ohio-3696, 2002 WL 1585840, Unreported. Infants ⚖ 251

Juvenile court's termination of father's parental rights without explicitly granting permanent child custody to Jefferson County Children Services Board (JCCSB) constituted ultra vires act, given that act is not provided for by statute. In re Sims (Ohio App. 7 Dist., Jefferson, 06-28-2002) No. 02-JE-2, 2002-Ohio-3458, 2002 WL 1483889, Unreported. Infants ⚖ 221

Mother did not waive her right to challenge sufficiency of the evidence against her by failing to raise issue in first appeal of order terminating her parental rights; issue regarding sufficiency of evidence would have been premature in first appeal, which challenged trial court's failure to acquire jurisdiction over children's father. In re Stephens (Ohio App. 7 Dist., Columbiana, 06-05-2002) No. 2001 CO 56, 2002-Ohio-3057, 2002 WL 1376240, Unreported. Infants ⚖ 243

Court was not required to determine, on petition of county Department of Children and Family Services (DCFS) to modify its temporary custody of child to permanent custody, that child could not or should not be placed with either parent within a reasonable time, where child had been in temporary custody of one or more public children services agencies for more than 12 of the last 22 months. In re M.H. (Ohio App. 8 Dist., Cuyahoga, 06-13-2002) No. 80620, 2002-Ohio-2968, 2002 WL 1307426, Unreported. Infants ⚖ 230.1

The right to raise a child is an essential and paramount civil right, and before that right may be terminated, the juvenile court must afford the parent every procedural and substantive protection the law allows. In re Kinney (Ohio App. 1 Dist., Hamilton, 05-10-2002) No. C-020067, 2002-Ohio-2310, 2002 WL 950266, Unreported. Infants ⚖ 155; Parent And Child ⚖ 2.5

Remand of trial court order, which granted county children services permanent custody of mother's three children, was required for the court to issue findings addressing the statutory factors to determine the best interests of the children, where the court's order was deficient on its face due to the trial court's failure to conduct a best interests of the child determination on the record. In re Strong (Ohio App. 10 Dist., Franklin, 05-09-2002) No. 01AP-1418, No. 01AP-1419, 2002-Ohio-2247, 2002 WL 926813, Unreported. Infants ⚖ 254

Incarceration does not toll the six month time period set forth in RC 2151.414(E); thus, where mother made no steps toward substantially remedying conditions which caused findings of dependency in her children during statutory period, permanent custody of children to children's services is affirmed. In re Nolan, No. 92 C.A.–109, 1993 WL 327681 (7th Dist Ct App, Mahoning, 8–24–93).

The trial court's failure to make findings of fact and conclusions of law following a grant of permanent custody of a minor child to a county children services board does not constitute prejudicial error where the parties agree generally to the facts of the case. In re Hollins, No. CA–703 (5th Dist Ct App, Guernsey, 3–29–83).

3. Evidence

Evidence during permanent custody proceeding supported juvenile court's finding that mother's 19-month-old child could not be placed with mother within a reasonable period of time; case has been pending for nearly two years and mother has not yet progressed to the point of being able to exercise unsupervised visitation. In re C.E. (Ohio App. 12 Dist., Butler, 09-18-2006) No. CA2006-01-015, No. CA2006-02-024, 2006-Ohio-4827, 2006 WL 2663464, Unreported. Infants ⚖ 155

Mother's claim that evidence was insufficient to support termination of her parental rights was rendered moot by reviewing court's determination that mother was entitled to evidentiary hearing to permit her to cross-examine guardian ad litem concerning guardian's late-submitted report and to present evidence in rebuttal. (Per Westcott Rice, J., with one judge concurring in result only.) In re Kangas (Ohio App. 11 Dist., Ashtabula, 06-30-2006) No. 2006-A-0010, 2006-Ohio-3433, 2006 WL 1817069, Unreported. Infants ⇐ 248.1

Trial court's wholesale adoption in its judgment entry in proceeding for termination of parental rights of written closing argument of agency did not evince failure to consider evidence before it, where judgment of termination was supported by evidence before the court. (Per Westcott Rice, J., with one judge concurring in result only.) In re Kangas (Ohio App. 11 Dist., Ashtabula, 06-30-2006) No. 2006-A-0010, 2006-Ohio-3433, 2006 WL 1817069, Unreported. Infants ⇐ 210

Trial court's finding, in proceeding for termination of mother's parental rights, that mother had abandoned child was not invalidated by court's erroneous statement in judgment entry that mother had attended one-third of possible visitations with child, where additional evidence in record supported such finding, including evidence that mother failed to exercise visitation after particular date, failed to take opportunity to contact child at home of child's legal guardian, and failed to remedy conditions preventing child's return. (Per Westcott Rice, J., with one judge concurring in result only.) In re Kangas (Ohio App. 11 Dist., Ashtabula, 06-30-2006) No. 2006-A-0010, 2006-Ohio-3433, 2006 WL 1817069, Unreported. Infants ⇐ 210

Juvenile court abused its discretion when it failed to grant permanent custody of mother's oldest child to county agency pursuant to its motion for permanent custody; juvenile court expressed its concern regarding the safety of mother's children since she was residing with known felons, and, although at nine years of age child may have been able to feed and bathe herself, there was no competent and credible evidence in the record that she would have been able to protect herself from the known felons that mother had residing in her residence. In re Jones (Ohio App. 5 Dist., Guernsey, 06-29-2006) No. 06 CA 9, 2006-Ohio-3363, 2006 WL 1793249, Unreported. Infants ⇐ 155

Juvenile court's judgment terminating mother's parental rights as to her two younger children was not against the manifest weight of the evidence; attempts at reunification with the children were unsuccessful, the children needed a safe and secure environment and mother demonstrated an unwillingness to work with professionals in order to provide such an environment, and, although the children may have been bonded with mother, evidence established that they thrived while in the care of foster parents. In re Jones (Ohio App. 5 Dist., Guernsey, 06-29-2006) No. 06 CA 9, 2006-Ohio-3363, 2006 WL 1793249, Unreported. Infants ⇐ 155

Evidence in termination of parental rights action did not support finding that mother was "unwilling" to provide adequate housing for children, although mother was unsuccessful in obtaining satisfactory housing; evidence established that anything mother could afford was unacceptable to the county department of job and family services, while anything acceptable to the department was out of mother's price range, and mother had maintained her employment, followed her case plan, kept in touch with her children, and sought out housing in order to keep her family together, but had not found adequate housing. In re Cassandra (Ohio App. 6 Dist., Wood, 06-02-2006) No. WD-05-097, 2006-Ohio-2767, 2006 WL 1516408, Unreported. Infants ⇐ 156

Evidence did not support conclusion that termination of mother's parental rights was in children's best interests; mother's visits with children were consistent, affectionate, and appropriate, seven-year-old child was very attached and bonded to mother and wanted to return to her care, and mother testified that she would separate from father, who had been convicted of child endangering, in order to keep her children. In re E.T. (Ohio App. 9 Dist., Summit, 05-17-2006) No. 23017, 2006-Ohio-2413, 2006 WL 1329653, Unreported. Infants ⇐ 156

Evidence supported conclusion that termination of father's parental rights was in children's best interests; children's relationship with father was contentious, oldest child told guardian ad litem that father was "mean," father was aggressive with children, and father had been convicted of child endangering. In re E.T. (Ohio App. 9 Dist., Summit, 05-17-2006) No. 23017, 2006-Ohio-2413, 2006 WL 1329653, Unreported. Infants ⇐ 156

Evidence failed to clearly and convincingly support conclusion that children could not be placed with mother within a reasonable time or should not be placed with her, which, in turn, did not support termination of mother's parental rights; there was no evidence that mother ever caused harm to children or that she was present when father did so, there were only positive statements regarding her handling of even the difficult behavior of child who had symptoms of attention deficit hyperactivity disorder (ADHD), mother's only mental health diagnosis was an adjustment disorder stemming from removal of children, and she had adequate housing for herself and for children. In re E.T. (Ohio App. 9 Dist., Summit, 05-17-2006) No. 23017, 2006-Ohio-2413, 2006 WL 1329653, Unreported. Infants ⇐ 158

Trial court error in admitting guardian ad litem's report and considering it as substantive evidence, in termination of parental rights proceeding, was harmless and did not unfairly prejudice father; the court only referred to the guardian ad litem's report when it referred to the wishes of the four oldest children, and other admissible evidence supported the court's order terminating parental rights. In re Hilyard (Ohio App. 4 Dist., Vinton, 04-13-2006) No. 05CA600, No. 05CA603, No. 05CA607, No. 05CA601, No. 05CA604, No. 05CA608, No. 05CA602, No. 05CA606, No. 05CA609, 2006-Ohio-1965, 2006 WL Infants ⇐ 253

Trial court's determination during permanent custody proceeding that children could not be placed with mother within a reasonable time was supported by clear and convincing evidence; at the time of the permanent custody hearing, mother was incarcerated, and she had failed continuously and repeatedly to substantially remedy the conditions causing the children to be removed from the home. In re D.P. (Ohio App. 8 Dist., Cuyahoga, 03-02-2006) No. 86271, No. 86272, 2006-Ohio-937, 2006 WL 496058, Unreported. Infants ⇐ 155

Sufficient evidence in permanent custody proceeding commenced by county children services board supported conclusion that child could not be placed with mother within a reasonable period of time or should not be placed with mother, on basis that mother failed continuously and repeatedly to substantially remedy conditions that caused child to be placed outside the home; mother's three older children had been placed in permanent custody of board due at least in part, to mother's relationship with child's father, who was a registered sex offender, and mother appeared to have little insight on how to protect child from potentially dangerous situations. In re King (Ohio App. 5 Dist., Fairfield, 02-15-2006) No. 05 CA 77, 2006-Ohio-781, 2006 WL 401598, Unreported. Infants ⇐ 156

Trial court did not rely upon improper evidence concerning mother's criminal record and children's custody in making its finding of dependency; mother, testifying on her own behalf, admitted to convictions or guilty pleas to fraud, forgery, and domestic violence, and admitted that her children were in custody of their fathers, and court would have been remiss in failing to consider self-admitted evidence concerning mother's past conduct, which impacted upon her ability to provide appropriate environment and home for children. In re Elliott (Ohio App. 11 Dist., Ashtabula, 02-17-2006) No. 2005-A-0018, 2006-Ohio-738, 2006 WL 389595, Unreported. Infants ⇐ 210

Record failed to reveal clear and convincing evidence in support of trial court's determination that it was in children's best interests to terminate mother's parental rights and grant permanent custody of children to county agency; there was ample testimony from agency's witnesses regarding the strong bond between children and mother, the court made no finding as to why placement with mother could not be achieved, mother had maintained stable employment and housing for some six months prior to the permanent custody hearing, and she maintained a regular visitation schedule pursuant to her case plan. In re Janson (Ohio App. 11 Dist., Geauga, 12-16-2005) No. 2005-G-2657, 2005-Ohio-6713, 2005 WL 3476624, Unreported. Infants ⇐ 210

Record failed to reveal clear and convincing evidence in support of trial court's determination that it was children's best interests to terminate mother's parental rights and grant permanent custody of children to county agency; there was ample testimony from agency's witnesses regarding the strong bond between children and mother, the court made no finding as to why placement with mother could not be achieved, mother had maintained stable employment and housing for some six months prior to the permanent custody hearing, and she maintained a regular visitation schedule pursuant to her case plan. In re Janson (Ohio App. 11 Dist., Geauga, 12-16-2005) No. 2005-G-2656, 2005-Ohio-6712, 2005 WL 3476623, Unreported. Infants ⇐ 155

Trial court's finding that mother's children had been in the temporary custody of county agency for more than 12 months of the 22 months immediately preceding the filing of agency's permanent custody motion was supported by clear and convincing evidence; thus, court did not have to engage in an explicit finding of "unfitness." In re Janson (Ohio App. 11 Dist., Geauga, 12-16-2005) No. 2005-G-2656, 2005-Ohio-6712, 2005 WL 3476623, Unreported. Infants ⇐ 210

Evidence was insufficient to support award of permanent custody of children to county children services board (CSB), where the trial court miscalculated the amount of time the children had been in the custody of CSB and erroneously relied on the fact that the children had been in the custody of CSB for at least 12 of the previous 22 months to support termination of parental rights, even though the children had been in CSB custody for nine months when the motion for permanent custody was filed, and the trial court made no additional findings that would support termination. In re E.T. (Ohio App. 9 Dist., Summit, 11-16-2005) No. 22720, 2005-Ohio-6087, 2005 WL 3050991, Unreported. Infants ⇐ 155

Clear and convincing evidence established that mother was unable to function as a parent, so as to support trial court's award of permanent custody of two children to county department of job and family services; mother had IQ of 61, mother was unable to use information from parenting class in a novel situation or apply it abstractly, mother had to be instructed on proper handling of her baby despite it being her sixth child, mother expressed opinion that it would be proper to teach a seven-year-old about oral sex, and mother had no insight into her disabilities and did not realize that she was seven months pregnant. In re Kinkel Children (Ohio App. 5 Dist., Stark, 10-31-2005) No. 2005CA00158, 2005-Ohio-5950, 2005 WL 2995128, Unreported. Infants ⇐ 158

Trial court did not abuse its discretion in considering report of guardian ad litem (GAL), irrespective of the hearsay contained therein, in termination of parental rights proceeding, where GAL testified at hearing and was available for cross-examination by both parties. In re Sherman (Ohio App. 3 Dist., Hancock, 11-07-2005) No. 05-04-47, No. 05-04-48, No. 05-04-49, 2005-Ohio-5888, 2005 WL 2933064, Unreported. Infants ⇐ 208

Trial court's admission of report of psychologist, which was based on inadmissible hearsay evidence, was reversible error, in termination of parental rights proceeding; court considered report, and statements in it which were based on hearsay testimony, in reaching its conclusions. In re Sherman (Ohio App. 3 Dist., Hancock, 11-07-2005) No. 05-04-47, No. 05-04-48, No. 05-04-49, 2005-Ohio-5888, 2005 WL 2933064, Unreported. Infants ⇐ 253

Psychologist's report, which stated that psychologist had relied upon reports of others and was based upon not only psychologist's own observations, but also on observations of others, did not meet requirements of rule of evidence requiring that facts or data in particular case upon which expert based opinion or inference be those perceived by him or admitted in evidence at hearing, and thus, should have been excluded in termination of parental rights proceeding; reports on which psychologist based his report were not admitted into evidence and contained numerous accounts of statements and actions not perceived by him personally. In re Sherman (Ohio App. 3 Dist., Hancock, 11-07-2005) No. 05-04-47, No. 05-04-48, No. 05-04-49, 2005-Ohio-5888, 2005 WL 2933064, Unreported. Infants ⇐ 173.1

Any error in admission of children's hearsay statements to psychologist or social worker did not rise to level of plain error, in termination of parental rights proceeding; record did not indicate that trial court had relied upon statements in reaching its conclusion, and record provided ample evidence, other than direct statements of children, which could support trial court's conclusions. In re Sherman (Ohio App. 3 Dist., Hancock, 11-07-2005) No. 05-04-47, No. 05-04-48, No. 05-04-49, 2005-Ohio-5888, 2005 WL 2933064, Unreported. Infants ⇐ 243

Clear and convincing evidence supported juvenile court's decision to terminate mother's and father's parental rights with regard to their three minor children and award permanent custody of the children to the Children Services Board (CSB); each parent was mentally retarded with an I.Q. of only 55, both parents suffered from alcohol problems, father had a personality disorder, and the two oldest children expressed a preference for foster care. In re Calvert Children (Ohio App. 5 Dist., Guernsey, 10-24-2005) No. 05-CA-19, No. 05-CA-20, 2005-Ohio-5653, 2005 WL 2746329, Unreported. Infants ⇐ 158

Juvenile court's finding, as grounds for termination of parental rights, that minor child could not or should not be placed with mother in a reasonable period of time was not against the manifest weight or sufficiency of the evidence; court found mother had not completed her case plan, and, despite marginal compliance with some aspects of the case plan, the exact problems which led to the initial removal remained in existence, and the court further found that, by continuing her relationship with abusive individual, mother placed her needs above child's needs, and subjected the child to "at-risk" individuals. In re Summerfield (Ohio App. 5 Dist., Stark, 10-17-2005) No. 2005CA00139, 2005-Ohio-5523, 2005 WL 2660536, Unreported. Infants ⇐ 156

Trial court's grant of permanent custody of child to county department of children and family services was not an abuse of discretion; child had been in custody of department for at least 12 months of a consecutive 22 month period, mother had continuously failed to substantially remedy underlying conditions that prompted child's removal from her home, mother could not provide adequate, permanent home for child, child was thriving in her foster home, and foster parent was willing to adopt child, yet still allow mother to be involved in child's life. In re T.W. (Ohio App. 8 Dist., Cuyahoga, 10-13-2005) No. 85845, 2005-Ohio-5446, 2005 WL 2600663, Unreported, appeal not allowed 108 Ohio St.3d 1418, 841 N.E.2d 321, 2006-Ohio-179, reconsideration denied 108 Ohio St.3d 1513, 844 N.E.2d 857, 2006-Ohio-1329. Infants ⇐ 155

Trial court did not abuse its discretion with regard to use of report of guardian ad litem (GAL) and father's right to cross-examine GAL, in proceeding in which permanent custody of children was awarded to county department of children and family services; court's decision would not have been different had GAL been cross-examined, there was ample evidence to support court's decision absent GAL's report, and court did not refuse to allow father to cross-examine GAL. In re A.D. (Ohio App. 8 Dist., Cuyahoga, 10-13-2005) No. 85648, 2005-Ohio-5441, 2005 WL 2600638, Unreported. Infants ⇐ 208

Evidence supported termination of mother's parental rights and grant of permanent custody of mother's four children to county child protection agency; although mother was making progress with regard to her mental illness, children had been in custody of a public children services agency for 12 or more months of a consecutive 22–month period, older children did not wish to return to mother's custody, youngest child was not bonded to mother, and there was no evidence mother would be able to care for her children in the near future. In re Di.R. (Ohio App. 8 Dist., Cuyahoga, 10-06-2005) No. 85765, No. 85766, 2005-Ohio-5346, 2005 WL 2471033, Unreported. Infants ⇐ 158

Evidence was sufficient to support trial court's finding, in proceeding for termination of mother's parental rights, that termination was in child's best interest; mother never developed relationship with child or maintained any bond with her, mother had had parental rights terminated as to seven of her children, mother's husband had been convicted of gross sexual imposition in regard to child's sibling and adjudicated sexually oriented offender, mother had been convicted of child endangerment and was incarcerated at time of permanent custody hearing, child was attached to her foster parents and thriving in foster care, and no suitable friend or family member was available to assume custody. In re G.B. (Ohio App. 9 Dist., Summit, 08-31-2005) No. 22628, 2005-Ohio-4540, 2005 WL 2087826, Unreported. Infants ⇐ 156

Evidence that individual named as child's biological father on child's birth certificate failed to support child and failed to remedy problems requiring child's removal from his custody was sufficient to support trial court's finding that child could not or should not be placed with such individual within reasonable time, as required for termination of his parental rights. In re G.B. (Ohio App. 9 Dist., Summit, 08-31-2005) No. 22628, 2005-Ohio-4540, 2005 WL 2087826, Unreported. Infants ⇐ 157

Evidence that husband of child's mother had abandoned child, had been convicted of gross sexual imposition as to a sibling of the child, and had his parental rights involuntarily terminated as to two siblings of child was sufficient to support trial court's finding that child could not or should not be placed with him within reasonable time, as required for termination of his parental rights. In re G.B. (Ohio App. 9 Dist., Summit, 08-31-2005) No. 22628, 2005-Ohio-4540, 2005 WL 2087826, Unreported. Infants ⇐ 157

Evidence that child's mother failed to remedy any of the problems which necessitated child's removal, failed to visit with, support, or plan permanent home for child, had her parental rights terminated as to all seven of child's siblings, and had been convicted of child endangering as to one of child's siblings was sufficient to support trial court's finding that child could not or should not be placed with mother within reasonable time, as required for termination of mother's parental rights. In re G.B. (Ohio App. 9 Dist., Summit, 08-31-2005) No. 22628, 2005-Ohio-4540, 2005 WL 2087826, Unreported. Infants ⇐ 156

Evidence was sufficient to support conclusion that child's placement in custody of his maternal aunt was in child's best interest; aunt testified that child was making progress in school and had made many friends there, and that she had attempted to maintain contact between child and his father's family and was willing to facilitate appropriate visits, aunt was approved by agency as long-term placement and lived with her fiancee, both were employed and had no other children, and father had history of unemployment, drug use, and violence, did not admit that he had problems as parent, and had made little progress toward remedying conditions that had led to child's removal from his home. In re A.A. (Ohio App. 9 Dist., Summit, 08-31-2005) No. 22644, 2005-Ohio-4539, 2005 WL 2087823, Unreported. Infants ⇐ 222

Determination that children could not or should not be placed with mother at time of termination of parental rights proceeding or within a reasonable period of time was not against manifest weight of the evidence; initial concerns that had necessitated removal of children from mother's custody had not been remedied, and, despite mother's efforts, she was unable to independently care for children due to her lack of mental ability.

In re Tucke (Ohio App. 5 Dist., Stark, 08-22-2005) No. 2005CA00077, 2005-Ohio-4409, 2005 WL 2045454, Unreported. Infants ⇌ 158

County's motion for permanent custody gave father notice that trial court could terminate his parental rights to children if it found that he had abandoned them; motion alleged that children had been abandoned, that father had complied with no case plan objectives, and that he had not maintained contact with children for period in excess of 90 days. In re Vann (Ohio App. 5 Dist., Stark, 08-22-2005) No. 2005-CA-00127, 2005-Ohio-4398, 2005 WL 2045442, Unreported. Infants ⇌ 197

Evidence supported trial court's grant of permanent custody of mother's four children to county child protection agency; mother failed to substantially remedy the conditions that necessitated removal, children had been in the temporary custody of the state for more than twelve of a consecutive twenty-two-month period, mother's boyfriend was a registered sex offender and had lied in connection with child protection proceedings, mother could not protect children from her overbearing boyfriend, children were doing well in foster care together, mother discontinued counseling contrary to terms of case plan, and mother refused home investigation. In re Brown (Ohio App. 7 Dist., Columbiana, 08-16-2005) No. 04 CO 59, 2005-Ohio-4374, 2005 WL 2033241, Unreported. Infants ⇌ 156

Clear and convincing evidence supported juvenile court's finding that a grant of permanent custody to Franklin County Children Services (FCCS) was in dependent child's best interest, despite mother's recent efforts at stabilizing her life; child had been in the temporary custody of FCCS for at least 12 months of a consecutive 22–month period prior to FCCS's motion for permanent custody, mother had been in and out of jail for several years, she failed to attend semi-annual reviews of child's case plan, and child had bonded with his foster family. In re S.S. (Ohio App. 10 Dist., Franklin, 08-18-2005) No. 05AP-204, 2005-Ohio-4282, 2005 WL 1983963, Unreported. Infants ⇌ 157

Clear and convincing evidence supported order granting county department of children and family services permanent custody of child; child had been in the custody of the department for almost three years when the custody hearing occurred, father had abandoned child, mother refused to allow a parent aide into her home, she failed to attend out-patient drug treatment, she tested positive for marijuana, she failed to find stable and clean housing, she failed to find steady employment, and she failed to consistently attend child's medical and therapy appointments. In re P.S. (Ohio App. 8 Dist., Cuyahoga, 08-11-2005) No. 85917, 2005-Ohio-4157, 2005 WL 1926042, Unreported. Infants ⇌ 157

Evidence of mother's unfitness to parent was sufficient to support termination of her parental rights; although mother completed portions of her case plan, she failed to complete majority of case plan requirements, mother could not provide secure environment for the children, had not participated in individual counseling as recommended, had not maintained stable employment or housing, and continued to lack understanding of critical parenting skills. In re S.B. (Ohio App. 12 Dist., Butler, 07-25-2005) No. CA2004-12-305, No. CA2004-12-308, No. CA2004-12-306, No. CA2004-12-307, 2005-Ohio-3889, 2005 WL 1798271, Unreported. Infants ⇌ 155

Clear and convincing evidence supported termination of mother's and father's parental rights to children; mother and father had failed continuously and repeatedly to substantially remedy conditions that led to children's removal from their custody, neither father nor mother had completed their case plans, mother continued to see father despite requirement that she terminate contact with him due to history of domestic violence, another child born to mother in another state had been removed from her custody, and authorities in that state had moved for immediate permanent custody of that child. In re Rhyan B. (Ohio App. 6 Dist., Lucas, 07-29-2005) No. L-05-1023, 2005-Ohio-3867, 2005 WL 1793724, Unreported. Infants ⇌ 156

Evidence supported conclusion that county made reasonable efforts to reunify mother and father with children, in termination of parental rights proceeding; county developed case plan designed to help mother and father deal with issues of domestic violence, anger management, alcohol abuse, and lack of parenting skills, caseworker assigned to family attempted regular contact with both parents but was hampered by mother's frequent changes of residence and father's failure to visit children regularly and remain in contact with county, and caseworker repeatedly attempted to impress upon mother importance of not only completing services but putting to use skills she learned. In re Rhyan B. (Ohio App. 6 Dist., Lucas, 07-29-2005) No. L-05-1023, 2005-Ohio-3867, 2005 WL 1793724, Unreported. Infants ⇌ 155

Sufficient evidence supported award of permanent custody of child to county department of job and family services; child had been in temporary custody of county for more than 12 months of a consecutive 22 month period, father had not made enough progress with his case plan to justify reunification as a realistic possibility, father did not address his emotional and alcohol problems, and father failed to show that award of permanent custody of child to county was not in child's best interests. In re Patfield (Ohio App. 11 Dist., Lake, 07-18-2005) No. 2005-L-006, 2005-Ohio-3768, 2005 WL 1714186, Unreported, appeal not allowed 106 Ohio St.3d 1548, 835 N.E.2d 728, 2005-Ohio-5343. Infants ⇌ 178

Sufficient evidence supported trial court's decision to grant permanent custody of child to county department of job and family services; child had been in temporary custody of department for more than 12 of consecutive 22 month period, mother had not made enough progress with her case plan to justify conclusion that reunification could be realistic possibility, although department made efforts to assist mother in correcting problems that caused child's removal from home, mother did not resolve her emotional and alcohol problems, and mother failed to show that giving permanent custody to department would not be in best interest of child. In re Patfield (Ohio App. 11 Dist., Lake, 07-18-2005) No. 2005-L-007, 2005-Ohio-3769, 2005 WL 1714185, Unreported, appeal not allowed 106 Ohio St.3d 1548, 835 N.E.2d 728, 2005-Ohio-5343. Infants ⇌ 155

Trial court's error, if any, in admitting testimony of intake specialist and certified chemical dependency counselor, early childhood supervisor, counselor and chemical dependency facilitator, and case manager was harmless, in proceeding in which trial court granted permanent custody of child to county department of job and family services, where there was other testimony, which also included mother's own statement, that demonstrated mother's lack of desire to address her continued substance addiction and inability to maintain a stable environment. In re Patfield (Ohio App. 11 Dist., Lake, 07-18-2005) No. 2005-L-007, 2005-Ohio-3769, 2005 WL 1714185, Unreported, appeal not allowed 106 Ohio St.3d 1548, 835 N.E.2d 728, 2005-Ohio-5343. Infants ⇌ 253

Trial court's award of permanent custody of child to county children services board was not against manifest weight of evidence; on day before hearing, father tested positive for cocaine, during six months prior to hearing father had been unavailable, out of state or in jail, father had no involvement with case plan or agency, father had extensive criminal history, during times he was not in jail father purposely remained unavailable, and child had been in foster care since being released from hospital, child did not have a bond with father, and foster family wished to adopt child. In re Woods (Ohio App. 5 Dist., Muskingum, 07-07-2005) No. CT2005-0011, 2005-Ohio-3561, 2005 WL 1645614, Unreported. Infants ⇌ 157

Trial court's finding that children could not or should not be placed with mother within reasonable time, as basis for terminating parental rights, was supported by evidence that mother resumed relationship with father who had physically abused one of children, mother suffered from severe depression and dependent personality disorder, mother lacked insight into her own behavior and defendant father's use of corporal punishment, and mental health prognosis was very guarded at best. In re Green (Ohio App. 5 Dist., Tuscarawas, 06-23-2005) No. 2005AP010007, No. 2005AP020008, 2005-Ohio-3308, 2005 WL 1523855, Unreported. Infants ⇌ 158

Statute and juvenile rule imposing duties on trial court in regard to shelter care hearings did not impose duties relative to permanent custody hearings. In re Speaks (Ohio App. 5 Dist., Licking, 06-20-2005) No. 2004 CA 0090, 2005-Ohio-3526, 2005 WL 1503572, Unreported, appeal not allowed 107 Ohio St.3d 1423, 837 N.E.2d 1208, 2005-Ohio-6124. Infants ⇌ 203

Juvenile court's judgment dismissing county agency's motion for permanent custody of child was not against the manifest weight of the evidence; testimony indicated that there was a loving and bonded relationship between child and her father, child indicated she wished to return to her father, child's foster parents were not in a position to adopt her, and father completed most, if not all, of the requirements in his case plan. In re G.B. (Ohio App. 10 Dist., Franklin, 06-23-2005) No. 04AP-1024, 2005-Ohio-3141, 2005 WL 1476884, Unreported. Infants ⇌ 155

Juvenile court was not required to consider, during proceeding on county agency's motion requesting an award of permanent custody of child, fact that father had previously had another child placed for adoption in another state; evidence indicated that father was unaware that the child had been placed for adoption by child's mother. In re G.B. (Ohio App. 10 Dist., Franklin, 06-23-2005) No. 04AP-1024, 2005-Ohio-3141, 2005 WL 1476884, Unreported. Infants ⇌ 155

Termination of mother's and father's parental rights was in child's best interest; child had bonded with foster family, neither mother nor father demonstrated adequate parenting skills, child had been in custody of Children Services since birth, placement of child with mother, father or relative would not provide child with legally secure permanent placement, and father had not played any role in life of other child. In re West (Ohio

App. 4 Dist., Athens, 06-10-2005) No. 05CA6, 2005-Ohio-2978, 2005 WL 1400031, Unreported. Infants ⇔ 155

Child could not be returned to either mother or father within reasonable time, as grounds for terminating their parental rights; mother had parental rights involuntarily terminated with respect to two other children and did not visit other child who was in custody of relative, parents were unable and unwilling to provide adequate home for child, mother refused to work, father lived with his own mother who had long history with County Children Services, and father did not show any commitment toward his other child and demonstrated inability to care for child during visits. In re West (Ohio App. 4 Dist., Athens, 06-10-2005) No. 05CA6, 2005-Ohio-2978, 2005 WL 1400031, Unreported. Infants ⇔ 156

Evidence was sufficient to support trial court's findings that reunification was not in child's best interests, in parental rights termination proceeding; child had no history of a relationship with his biological parents, child was doing well in foster care, family that had already adopted some of child's siblings were considering adopting him, child was too young to express his wishes, County Children Services (ACCS) had custody of child since birth, father was not married to mother, father and mother smoked marijuana together and were frequently surrounded by relatives who used illegal drugs, father's income was less than $10,000 per year, and evidence tended to show that father had sexually abused one, perhaps two, of mother's children. In re Barnhart (Ohio App. 4 Dist., Athens, 05-26-2005) No. 05CA8, 2005-Ohio-2692, 2005 WL 1283675, Unreported. Infants ⇔ 155

Termination of father's parental rights was in best interests of children; children had been in custody of Children Services for more than 12 months of last 22 months since adjudication of dependency, children could not be returned to father within reasonable time in that father had failed to remedy conditions that warranted removal of children from home, father failed to pay any child support and maintained no income, all children had special developmental needs and required dependable transportation for medical appointments, therapy, and special education, children were doing well with foster parents, and children needed legally secure, permanent placement. In re McLean (Ohio App. 11 Dist., Trumbull, 05-25-2005) No. 2005-T-0018, 2005-Ohio-2576, 2005 WL 1231614, Unreported, appeal not allowed 106 Ohio St.3d 1510, 833 N.E.2d 1251, 2005-Ohio-4605. Infants ⇔ 157

Evidence supported conclusion that placement of child with father was not in child's best interests, in termination of parental rights proceeding; statute provided that a parent's rights had to be terminated if parent had had parental rights involuntarily terminated with respect to sibling of child, and evidence indicated that father had had three children removed from his care and his parental rights to those children involuntarily terminated. In re Cazad (Ohio App. 4 Dist., Lawrence, 05-09-2005) No. 04CA36, 2005-Ohio-2574, 2005 WL 1228386, Unreported. Infants ⇔ 155

Evidence supported conclusion that child could not or should not be placed with mother within a reasonable time, because she had failed to remedy conditions that led to removal of her three oldest children from her care, in termination of parental rights proceeding; county had offered mother case plans in prior cases, which mother had not successfully completed, and caseworker testified concerning his home visits with mother prior to removal of her three oldest children from her care and mother's inability to keep a safe and suitable home environment absent supervision. In re Cazad (Ohio App. 4 Dist., Lawrence, 05-09-2005) No. 04CA36, 2005-Ohio-2574, 2005 WL 1228386, Unreported. Infants ⇔ 156

Finding that minor child could not be placed with mother within a reasonable time or should not be placed with mother was not against manifest weight of evidence that mother suffered from alcohol and marijuana dependency, depressive disorder, and dependent personality disorder, that mother was in relationships with five different men, not including child's father, who had lengthy history of acts of domestic violence against mother, that mother was arrested for disorderly conduct, and that she violated court orders. In re Greathouse (Ohio App. 5 Dist., Fairfield, 05-12-2005) No. 04 CA 56, 2005-Ohio-2552, 2005 WL 1208851, Unreported. Infants ⇔ 158

Evidence of father's dependency, influence upon him of other persons engaging in drug or alcohol abuse, his domestic violence history, and his lack of consistent contact with minor child supported finding that child could not be placed with father within a reasonable time or should not be placed with him. In re Greathouse (Ohio App. 5 Dist., Fairfield, 05-18-2005) No. 04 CA 57, 2005-Ohio-2553, 2005 WL 1208850, Unreported. Infants ⇔ 157

Evidence supported finding that mother's children were neglected and dependent; agency employee testified to condition of children's residence and to appearance of children at time of their removal, and various witnesses testified regarding their observations as to the care and discipline of the children. In re Lloyd (Ohio App. 5 Dist., Tuscarawas, 05-11-2005)

No. 2005 AP 01 0006, 2005-Ohio-2379, 2005 WL 1152788, Unreported. Infants ⇔ 179

Evidence in child protection proceedings supported trial court's finding that father's minor children were neglected and dependent; social worker testified that family residence was unsanitary and smelled of urine and feces, and multiple witnesses testified regarding their observations of the family. In re Lloyd (Ohio App. 5 Dist., Tuscarawas, 05-11-2005) No. 2005 AP 01 0003, 2005-Ohio-2380, 2005 WL 1152596, Unreported. Infants ⇔ 179

Trial court's consideration of father's repeated problems with chemical dependency, his criminal history, his obligations to his other children, and that his new job would require his attention over long period of time in concluding that child could not be placed with father within reasonable time, was appropriate, in termination of parental rights proceeding. In re Danielle E. (Ohio App. 6 Dist., Lucas, 05-13-2005) No. L-04-1339, 2005-Ohio-2349, 2005 WL 1125322, Unreported. Infants ⇔ 155

Sufficient evidence supported trial court's finding that child could not or should not be placed with either parent in reasonable time, as would support court's decision to award permanent custody of child to county department of children and family services; parents had failed, for over six months, to remedy conditions that had caused child to be placed outside home, and mother had failed to provide basic necessities for child, had failed to visit or communicate with her, and had shown an unwillingness to provide adequate permanent home for her. In re D.W. (Ohio App. 8 Dist., Cuyahoga, 04-21-2005) No. 84547, 2005-Ohio-1867, 2005 WL 926991, Unreported. Infants ⇔ 157

Termination of mother's parental rights was in best interest of child; mother admitted having cocaine addiction she had not taken any action to resolve, mother had minimal interaction with child during child's first few months following birth, child had no relationship with siblings and mother took no steps to establish relationship with siblings, and child had been living with foster parents since birth and had bonded with foster family. In re B.C.M. (Ohio App. 9 Dist., Lorain, 04-20-2005) No. 05CA0001, 2005-Ohio-1818, 2005 WL 901210, Unreported. Infants ⇔ 155

Children services was entitled to permanent custody of child and termination of mother's parental rights was warranted, where mother continuously failed to complete her case plan services after her daughter was removed, she failed to follow through with drug treatment program, and she failed to re-engage in domestic violence services. In re Na'eem A. (Ohio App. 6 Dist., Lucas, 04-08-2005) No. L-04-1259, No. L-04-1260, 2005-Ohio-1679, 2005 WL 791448, Unreported. Infants ⇔ 155

Evidence in termination of parental rights proceeding supported juvenile court's finding that father's two minor children could not be placed with a parent within a reasonable time or should not be placed with a parent; father had been sentenced to a three-year prison term on drug charges and, at the time of the permanent custody hearing, he had served less than one year of that term. In re E.C. (Ohio App. 9 Dist., Summit, 04-06-2005) No. 22355, 2005-Ohio-1633, 2005 WL 767099, Unreported. Infants ⇔ 157

Evidence in termination of parental rights proceeding supported juvenile court's finding that children could not be placed with a parent within a reasonable time or should not be placed with a parent; child's father did not participate in any case planning efforts directed towards improving his parenting skills or addressing substance abuse problems, and his temper was volatile and served to escalate the temper of child's mother, and mother suffered from major depression and intermittent explosive disorder, she had numerous convictions for violent offenses and currently had an outstanding arrest warrant, and she failed to comply with court-ordered counseling and prescribed medications. In re I.K. (Ohio App. 9 Dist., Summit, 04-06-2005) No. 22424, 2005-Ohio-1634, 2005 WL 767093, Unreported. Infants ⇔ 158

Clear and convincing evidence that mother was not making progress on her case plan was sufficient to support finding that children could not be placed with mother within reasonable time and should not be placed with mother, as required to support termination of mother's parental rights; mother never progressed to unsupervised visitation, due to agency's concerns for children's safety, expert testified that mother could not adequately parent children, and mother failed to make sustained progress in working with caseworkers and family therapy professionals, was not taking necessary medication, and did not cooperate in reunification process. In re Capasso (Ohio App. 3 Dist., Hancock, 04-04-2005) No. 5-04-36, No. 5-04-39, No. 5-04-37, No. 5-04-38, 2005-Ohio-1601, 2005 WL 742847, Unreported. Infants ⇔ 178

Clear and convincing evidence supported conclusion that termination of mother's parental rights was in child's best interests; child, who had many special needs, had bonded with his foster parents, mother failed to failed to take necessary initiative to establish a bond and parental relationship with child, despite opportunities available to educate herself about child's daily lifestyle and activities, mother had not taken sufficient steps to reinsert herself into child's life and learn what it would take to care for his many special needs, and mother lacked independent housing, transportation, and employment, all of which demonstrated her lack of ability to care for child's intensive, ongoing needs. In re Bray (Ohio App. 10 Dist., Franklin, 03-31-2005) No. 04AP-842, 2005-Ohio-1540, 2005 WL 737401, Unreported, appeal not allowed 105 Ohio St.3d 1564, 828 N.E.2d 118, 2005-Ohio-2447. Infants ⚖ 179

Trial court's decision not to award legal custody of child to her paternal aunt was not abuse of discretion, in child dependency proceeding in which county sought permanent custody of child; there was concern that aunt might permit contact between child and her father, such that child's placement with aunt was not in child's best interests, and guardian ad litem recommended that child's maternal grandmother petition for adoption of child, as grandmother had provided care for child for a significant portion of child's life. In re Miller (Ohio App. 5 Dist., Licking, 02-24-2005) No. 04 CA 32, 2005-Ohio-856, 2005 WL 469260, Unreported. Infants ⚖ 222

Clear and convincing evidence supported conclusion that child could not be reunified with father within a reasonable period of time, in child dependency proceeding in which county sought permanent custody of child; father was incarcerated for offense he committed against child's sibling, and, due to father's failure to remedy problems that had initially caused child to be removed from his custody, he needed long-term substance abuse and anger management counseling. In re Miller (Ohio App. 5 Dist., Licking, 02-24-2005) No. 04 CA 32, 2005-Ohio-856, 2005 WL 469260, Unreported. Infants ⚖ 157

Clear and convincing evidence supported conclusion that father had failed to remedy conditions that had caused child's removal from his custody, in child dependency proceeding in which county sought permanent custody of child; father failed to complete inpatient drug and alcohol treatment programs, as required by his case plan, he had continued to abuse alcohol, and he had been physically abusive to child's sibling, which had resulted in his incarceration for felony domestic violence. In re Miller (Ohio App. 5 Dist., Licking, 02-24-2005) No. 04 CA 32, 2005-Ohio-856, 2005 WL 469260, Unreported. Infants ⚖ 156

Lack of evidence in record concerning child's wishes as to custody, including absence of such evidence in guardian ad litem's report, required remand for guardian ad litem to meet with child and discuss child's wishes, after which trial court was to consider child's wishes and render new decision regarding child's best interests, in child dependency proceeding in which trial court had granted county's request for permanent custody of child. In re Miller (Ohio App. 5 Dist., Licking, 02-24-2005) No. 04 CA 32, 2005-Ohio-856, 2005 WL 469260, Unreported. Infants ⚖ 254

Evidence supported juvenile court's decision to grant foster parents' motion for legal custody of child who had been found dependent and removed from his biological parents' care, despite competing motion from child's paternal uncle and aunt; child was very young and had been in the foster parents' care since he was first placed in temporary custody, child had not established a relationship with uncle and aunt, and child had developed a strong bond with foster parents. In re Halstead (Ohio App. 7 Dist., Columbiana, 01-27-2005) No. 04 CO 37, 2005-Ohio-403, 2005 WL 289576, Unreported. Infants ⚖ 230.1

Conclusion that mother was unsuitable to maintain custody of child was supported by competent and credible evidence in child protection proceeding, including evidence that 11-week-old baby had 21 fractures, of which some could have been two to three weeks old, and that mother was either involved in child's injuries or suffered from narcissistic personality disorder which allowed her to create a fantasy that nothing was wrong with baby, because she wished to maintain her relationship with man who injured baby. In re Volheim (Ohio App. 5 Dist., Fairfield, 01-31-2005) No. 2004-CA-53, 2005-Ohio-369, 2005 WL 267651, Unreported. Infants ⚖ 158

Findings in child protection proceeding that child could not be placed with mother within a reasonable time and should not be placed with her were not contrary to the weight of the evidence; psychologist who evaluated mother declined to set a specific time period for her therapy, but indicated it would take a substantial amount of time to deal with her personality disorders. In re Volheim (Ohio App. 5 Dist., Fairfield, 01-31-2005) No. 2004-CA-53, 2005-Ohio-369, 2005 WL 267651, Unreported. Infants ⚖ 178

Finding in child protection proceeding that mother had failed to protect her child was supported by evidence that 11-week old-baby had numerous bruises, some of which were old, 21 fractures, of which some could have been two to three weeks old, and testimony of psychologist and representative of Children's Services expressing serious concerns that mother had to have known about the injuries and had not reported them earlier. In re Volheim (Ohio App. 5 Dist., Fairfield, 01-31-2005) No. 2004-CA-53, 2005-Ohio-369, 2005 WL 267651, Unreported. Infants ⚖ 156

Credible evidence supported finding that no suitable relative was available to take custody of children, even though mother argued that grandmother was available for placement; grandmother had a felony conviction for assault, she had a history of involvement with county jobs and family services, and she indicated that she had no particular concerns with the situation which resulted in removal of the children. In re Bierley (Ohio App. 5 Dist., Tuscarawas, 01-24-2005) No. 2004-AP-07-0049, 2005-Ohio-331, 2005 WL 217025, Unreported. Infants ⚖ 222

Trial court was required to articulate what other factor it deemed relevant as grounds for terminating mother's and father's parental rights under statutory "catchall" finding that child cannot or should not be reunited with parents "for any other factor." In re Delfino M. (Ohio App. 6 Dist., Lucas, 01-28-2005) No. L-04-1010, No. L-04-1009, 2005-Ohio-320, 2005 WL 195488, Unreported. Infants ⚖ 210

Evidence supported finding that it was in best interest of three-year-old daughter, who had been in county's temporary custody for at least 12 of past 22 months, to terminate father's parental rights; father was unwilling to leave violent, substance-abusing mother in order to protect child. In re T.T. (Ohio App. 12 Dist., Butler, 01-24-2005) No. CA2004-07-175, No. CA2004-08-198, 2005-Ohio-240, 2005 WL 123948, Unreported. Infants ⚖ 156

Evidence supported finding that mother failed continuously and repeatedly to substantially remedy the conditions that had caused her five children to be placed outside the home, thus supporting grant of permanent custody of children to county child protection agency; children had been removed from home due to mother's drug abuse and her inability to provide a safe and stable home, mother continued to test positive for alcohol and several different drugs, mother failed to submit urine samples as required, mother never completed a drug treatment program, mother had problems with domestic violence and sexual abuse, and mother was incarcerated for felony child endangering. In re C.D. (Ohio App. 9 Dist., Summit, 01-19-2005) No. 22250, 2005-Ohio-158, 2005 WL 100783, Unreported. Infants ⚖ 156

Evidence supported trial court's finding that grant of permanent custody of child to county child protection agency was in best interests of child, thus supporting termination of parental rights; trial court considered the interaction and interrelationship of child with mother as well as the family with whom child was currently living, mother had lost custody of her other children, child was too young to express his wishes, child was in need of legally permanent placement, and mother had history of noncompliance with her medications for treatment of bipolar disorder. In re Smith (Ohio App. 3 Dist., Marion, 01-18-2005) No. 9-04-35, 2005-Ohio-149, 2005 WL 91639, Unreported. Infants ⚖ 158

Trial court's decision that grant of permanent custody of children to county child protection agency was in best interests of children was not against the manifest weight of the evidence; children referred to foster family as their family, children had been in agency custody for over three years, children were adoptable, mother refused to believe child's allegations of sexual abuse against her husband, and mother had previously had other children removed from her care based on similar allegations. In re Moore (Ohio App. 7 Dist., Belmont, 01-05-2005) No. 04-BE-9, 2005-Ohio-136, 2005 WL 78754, Unreported. Infants ⚖ 156

Award of legal custody of dependent infant to paternal aunt and uncle was supported by evidence they were motivated to provide home for infant, their home seemed appropriate with adequate space to accommodate infant, and they both expressed love and concern for infant. In re M.S. (Ohio App. 9 Dist., Summit, 01-05-2005) No. 22158, 2005-Ohio-10, 2005 WL 19441, Unreported. Infants ⚖ 222

Finding that award of legal custody of dependant infant to paternal aunt and uncle, rather than to paternal grandfather who already had custody of older sibling, would be in best interest of infant was not abuse of discretion; though both parties presented good and viable options for placement, grandfather's smoking risked aggravation of infant's pre-asthmatic condition, and aunt and uncle appeared to have more realistic understanding of infant's developmental levels. In re M.S. (Ohio App. 9 Dist., Summit, 01-05-2005) No. 22158, 2005-Ohio-10, 2005 WL 19441, Unreported. Infants ⚖ 222

Clear and convincing evidence established that it was in child's best interest to terminate mother's parental rights, despite guardian ad litem's recommendation to the contrary; record demonstrated that mother was unable to provide safe and sanitary housing for her child, she failed to comply with the goal of maintaining a regular income, she continually blamed the Children Services Board for child's removal, and she failed to cooperate with her caseworker. In re Goff (Ohio App. 11 Dist., Ashtabula, 12-23-2004) No. 2004-A-0051, 2004-Ohio-7235, 2004 WL 3090218, Unreported, appeal not allowed 105 Ohio St.3d 1473, 824 N.E.2d 542, 2005-Ohio-1186. Infants ⚖ 208

Evidence of a dispositional review hearing judgment entry, which concerned child's half-brother, was relevant for purposes of mother's termination of parental rights proceeding; document was probative of mother's progress in developing parenting skills and because it indicated that mother was ordered to take a second set of parenting classes. In re Goff (Ohio App. 11 Dist., Ashtabula, 12-23-2004) No. 2004-A-0051, 2004-Ohio-7235, 2004 WL 3090218, Unreported, appeal not allowed 105 Ohio St.3d 1473, 824 N.E.2d 542, 2005-Ohio-1186. Infants ⚖ 173.1

Finding that termination of mother's parental rights was in best interest of nearly eight-year-old special-needs daughter was supported by evidence of mother's lack of parenting skills and continued relationship with child's alleged sex abuser, deterioration of child's behavior when returned to mother from foster care, and child's needs for permanency and stability in her life. In re D.P. (Ohio App. 9 Dist., Summit, 12-30-2004) No. 22257, 2004-Ohio-7173, 2004 WL 3017312, Unreported. Infants ⚖ 156

Trial court's finding that termination of mother's parental rights and award of permanent custody to county children services agency was in her children's best interests was supported by testimony of guardian ad litem, as well as evidence that children had thrived in foster home and that their foster parents wanted to adopt them. In re Waliyyudden (Ohio App. 6 Dist., Lucas, 12-23-2004) No. L-04-1174, No. L-04-1182, 2004-Ohio-7076, 2004 WL 2984030, Unreported. Infants ⚖ 178

Trial court's finding that children could not be placed with mother within a reasonable time, warranting termination of her parental rights and award of permanent custody to county children services agency, was supported by mother's failure to remedy the conditions that led to the children's removal by securing adequate and safe housing. In re Waliyyudden (Ohio App. 6 Dist., Lucas, 12-23-2004) No. L-04-1174, No. L-04-1182, 2004-Ohio-7076, 2004 WL 2984030, Unreported. Infants ⚖ 156

Trial court's finding that children could not be placed with mother within a reasonable time, warranting termination of her parental rights and award of permanent custody to county children services agency, was supported by mother's refusal to comply with terms of her probation, which demonstrated a lack of commitment toward her children. In re Waliyyudden (Ohio App. 6 Dist., Lucas, 12-23-2004) No. L-04-1174, No. L-04-1182, 2004-Ohio-7076, 2004 WL 2984030, Unreported. Infants ⚖ 155

Trial court's decision that best interests of children would be served by termination of father's parental rights was supported by testimony of caseworker that children were doing well in their placement with relatives and relatives would like to adopt them, and children's bonding with father would be difficult to ascertain as he had only visited with children three times in thirteen months. In re Brown Children (Ohio App. 5 Dist., Stark, 12-16-2004) No. 2004CA00301, 2004-Ohio-6971, 2004 WL 2939008, Unreported. Infants ⚖ 178

Trial court's decision to terminate father's parental rights because children could not or should not be placed with father was supported by evidence that father had drug problem and used cocaine, he did not complete his case plan, he only visited children three times in 13 months, and both urine samples, provided over 13-month period, tested positive for cocaine. In re Brown Children (Ohio App. 5 Dist., Stark, 12-16-2004) No. 2004CA00301, 2004-Ohio-6971, 2004 WL 2939008, Unreported. Infants ⚖ 155

Some competent, credible evidence supported trial court's finding in termination of parental rights proceeding that dependent child could not or should not be placed with mother within reasonable time; mother had substantial history of drug and alcohol abuse that she failed to address through counseling, did not attend most scheduled visitation with child, and failed to remedy conditions, including alcohol use and mother's abuse by live-in boyfriend, that caused continued removal of child from home. In re Marano (Ohio App. 4 Dist., Athens, 12-09-2004) No. 04CA30, 2004-Ohio-6826, 2004 WL 2913586, Unreported. Infants ⚖ 155

Therapist's testimony regarding mother's alleged compliance with case plan was irrelevant in portion of permanent child custody hearing addressing best interest of children. In re Hayes/Reichenbach Children (Ohio App. 5 Dist., Stark, 12-13-2004) No. 2004CA00278, 2004-Ohio-6751, 2004 WL 2896008, Unreported. Infants ⚖ 173.1

Trial court's determination that it was in children's best interests to terminate father's parental rights and grant permanent custody to county child services agency was supported by evidence that father continued to use drugs, stopped attending counseling, was evicted from his home, had begun dating young pregnant woman, and relied upon his girlfriend's mother for housing. In re Cunningham (Ohio App. 4 Dist., Athens, 12-06-2004) No. 04CA39, 2004-Ohio-6568, 2004 WL 2809829, Unreported. Infants ⚖ 155

Trial court's determination that it was in children's best interests to terminate father's parental rights was not against the manifest weight of the evidence, even though all of the children's counselors were equivocal on this issue. In re Cunningham (Ohio App. 4 Dist., Athens, 12-06-2004) No. 04CA39, 2004-Ohio-6568, 2004 WL 2809829, Unreported. Infants ⚖ 178

Clear and convincing evidence supported the magistrate's finding that mother was unwilling to prevent child from suffering emotional or mental neglect, in support of termination of parental rights; mother had the time to move to state, find a job, and engage in counseling with the objective of re-establishing a relationship with child, but refused to move to state, and mother failed to engage in therapeutic visitation with child, even though this was the only way in which mother could interact with child without damaging child emotionally. In re Anderson (Ohio App. 11 Dist., Trumbull, 09-30-2004) No. 2004-T-0059, 2004-Ohio-5298, 2004 WL 2804824, Unreported. Infants ⚖ 156

Clear and convincing evidence supported the magistrate's finding that mother failed to substantially comply with her caseplan, in support of termination of parental rights; mother failed to maintain stable housing and moved eight times in eight years, she currently lived in a mobile home on a relative's property, she was in arrears in her child support obligation, she failed to present any evidence that she engaged in independent counseling to prepare her for joint counseling with child, and she failed to obtain approval for her drug and alcohol assessment and her psychological evaluation. In re Anderson (Ohio App. 11 Dist., Trumbull, 09-30-2004) No. 2004-T-0059, 2004-Ohio-5298, 2004 WL 2804824, Unreported. Infants ⚖ 155

Clear and convincing evidence supported finding that county children services board made diligent efforts to aid parents in their efforts to substantially remedy the problems that initially caused the children to be placed outside of the home, during termination proceeding; the board developed several caseplans for mother, mother was offered substance abuse counseling, mental health services, stable housing, visitation with the children, and bus tokens for transportation, and father was incarcerated during the entire dependency proceedings. In re Matthew R.A. (Ohio App. 6 Dist., Lucas, 12-03-2004) No. L-04-1088, No. L-04-1104, 2004-Ohio-6470, 2004 WL 2785530, Unreported. Infants ⚖ 155

Clear and convincing evidence supported finding that it was in the best interests of the children to award permanent custody to the county children services board, during termination proceeding; all six children received counseling, the children were placed with siblings in two foster homes, the children all liked their foster homes, the foster parents of the children expressed a desire to adopt the children, at the time of the permanent custody hearing the children had been in the custody of the board for two years, and the guardian ad litems for the children recommended awarding permanent custody to the board. In re Matthew R.A. (Ohio App. 6 Dist., Lucas, 12-03-2004) No. L-04-1088, No. L-04-1104, 2004-Ohio-6470, 2004 WL 2785530, Unreported. Infants ⚖ 155; Infants ⚖ 208

Order terminating parental rights was not against the manifest weight of the evidence; clear and convincing evidence showed that the children could not be placed with their parents within a reasonable time or should not be placed with either parent, mother failed to regularly support, visit or communicate with her children, both parents failed to maintain an adequate permanent home for the children, father was incarcerated when the permanent custody motion was filed and would not be able to provide for the children for more than 18 months after the motion was filed, and both parents were repeatedly incarcerated. In re Matthew R.A. (Ohio App. 6 Dist., Lucas, 12-03-2004) No. L-04-1088, No. L-04-1104, 2004-Ohio-6470, 2004 WL 2785530, Unreported. Infants ⚖ 156; Infants ⚖ 157

Statutory factor of children's wishes did not weigh against termination of mother's parental rights; although children did not testify as to their wishes, guardian ad litem testified that children would like to live with mother if they could go back to functioning household, and other evidence supported conclusion that mother's home was not functioning, safe, and stable. In re D.M. Children (Ohio App. 9 Dist., Summit, 12-01-2004) No. 22206, 2004-Ohio-6369, 2004 WL 2715922, Unreported. Infants ⚖ 155

Statutory factor of children's custodial history did not weigh against termination of mother's parental rights, where, during course of last ten years, children were in board's temporary custody four times for total of nearly four years. In re D.M. Children (Ohio App. 9 Dist., Summit, 12-01-2004) No. 22206, 2004-Ohio-6369, 2004 WL 2715922, Unreported. Infants ⚖ 155

Statutory factor of interaction of children with parents and siblings did not weigh against termination of mother's parental rights; although there was bond between mother and children, caseworker was concerned that children took over parenting role in family, children were doing well in foster placements, and foster parents affirmed they would encourage contact between children. In re D.M. Children (Ohio App. 9 Dist.,

Summit, 12-01-2004) No. 22206, 2004-Ohio-6369, 2004 WL 2715922, Unreported. Infants ⇔ 155

Statutory factor of children's need for legally secure placement did not weigh against termination of mother's parental rights, where children had long history of instability due to mother's alcoholism, mother lacked emotional stability to handle children in her home, mother failed to complete parenting classes, mother was terminated from substance abuse programs for non-compliance, it would be detrimental to children to be returned to mother and removed again in future, and children benefited from being in foster care. In re D.M. Children (Ohio App. 9 Dist., Summit, 12-01-2004) No. 22206, 2004-Ohio-6369, 2004 WL 2715922, Unreported. Infants ⇔ 155

Decision to grant permanent custody of child to county children services board was supported by clear and convincing evidence that removed child was bonded and had a relationship with her sister and foster mother, little progress was made from time child's sister was removed regarding parents obtaining services that would improve their situation, other children had been removed, parents' prior history showed a complete inability to follow through, complete and apply services provided for in previous case plans, and parents failed to attend visits with child. In re A.S. (Ohio App. 12 Dist., Butler, 11-29-2004) No. CA2004-07-182, No. CA2004-08-185, 2004-Ohio-6323, 2004 WL 2698408, Unreported. Infants ⇔ 155; Infants ⇔ 157

Clear and convincing evidence supported decision that permanent placement of children with county children services board was in children's best interests; as of date of hearing, children had been in temporary custody of board for 12 or more months of a consecutive 22-month period, there appeared to be no bond of any kind with father, children were bonded with each other and with foster parents, guardian ad litem recommended permanent placement, both parents had failed to complete significant portions of case plan services, and mother had failed to consistently attend visitations. In re D.R. (Ohio App. 12 Dist., Butler, 11-29-2004) No. CA2004-07-171, 2004-Ohio-6322, 2004 WL 2698406, Unreported. Infants ⇔ 155; Infants ⇔ 208

There was clear and convincing evidence that dependent children should not be returned to their parents, as required for permanent placement of children with county children services board; father had not completed case plan services and had not contacted board for two years, although mother had completed some case plan services she failed to fulfill her obligations under plan, she refused recommended treatment for her characherological depression, she failed to demonstrate an ability to maintain stable employment and housing, and both parents failed to consistently take advantage of scheduled visitations. In re D.R. (Ohio App. 12 Dist., Butler, 11-29-2004) No. CA2004-07-171, 2004-Ohio-6322, 2004 WL 2698406, Unreported. Infants ⇔ 155; Infants ⇔ 158

Grant of permanent custody of child to county child protection agency was not against the manifest weight of the evidence; mother suffered moderate mental retardation and was unable to parent safely, and mother's parenting ability was not subject to improvement. In re Keiondre S. (Ohio App. 6 Dist., Lucas, 11-24-2004) No. L-04-1025, 2004-Ohio-6316, 2004 WL 2690668, Unreported. Infants ⇔ 158

Evidence was sufficient to support trial court's conclusion that awarding permanent custody of child to county children services, rather than to maternal aunt, was in child's best interest; aunt severed contact with child after keeping child for approximately three months, aunt did not seek custody until after she learned that permanent custody hearing would be held, child had been in custody of county children services for well over one year and needed legally secure permanent placement, and aunt's child was abusive to child at issue during time that child at issue resided with aunt. In re A.U. (Ohio App. 2 Dist., Montgomery, 11-19-2004) No. 20583, No. 20585, 2004-Ohio-6219, 2004 WL 2659137, Unreported. Infants ⇔ 178

Clear and convincing evidence supported trial court's finding in termination of parental rights proceeding that dependent children could not be placed with mother within reasonable time; mother demonstrated lack of commitment toward children by failing to regularly support or visit with children and mother did not complete any requirements of case plan. In re Carr (Ohio App. 5 Dist., Stark, 11-15-2004) No. 2004-CA-00256, 2004-Ohio-6144, 2004 WL 2635596, Unreported. Infants ⇔ 178

Sufficient, competent and credible evidence supported trial court's finding that it was in best interest of dependent children to grant permanent custody to county department of job and family services; foster-to-adopt family was interested in providing permanent home for children, children were adoptable, mother visited children semi-regularly, and harm done by severing bond between mother and children was outweighed by benefit of insuring that children had safe, stable, and permanent home. In re Carr (Ohio App. 5 Dist., Stark, 11-15-2004) No. 2004-CA-00256, 2004-Ohio-6144, 2004 WL 2635596, Unreported. Infants ⇔ 178

Evidence in permanent custody proceeding supported trial court's finding that mother's minor child could not or should not be placed with mother within a reasonable time; mother demonstrated an unwillingness to provide an adequate permanent home for child, she initially requested to surrender child, and she stated that she could not "handle" child. In re Lilley (Ohio App. 4 Dist., Lawrence, 11-09-2004) No. 04CA22, 2004-Ohio-6156, 2004 WL 2631490, Unreported. Infants ⇔ 155

Evidence in termination of parental rights proceeding supported finding that the Department of Job and Family Services put forth good faith and diligent efforts to reunify family, but that mother had failed to substantially remedy the conditions which originally caused her two minor children to be removed from the home; mother continued to test positive for illegal substances throughout the pendency of her case, she did not keep the department apprised of her most recent address, and her counsel was unable to locate her or have contact with her. In re Robinson/ Brooks Children (Ohio App. 5 Dist., Stark, 11-15-2004) No. 2004-CA-00094, 2004-Ohio-6142, 2004 WL 2616425, Unreported. Infants ⇔ 155

Evidence in termination of parental rights proceeding supported trial court's finding that mother's two minor children could not and should not be placed with her within the foreseeable future; mother continued to test positive for illegal substances throughout the pendency of her case, she did not keep the department apprised of her most recent address, and her counsel was unable to locate her or have contact with her. In re Robinson/ Brooks Children (Ohio App. 5 Dist., Stark, 11-15-2004) No. 2004-CA-00094, 2004-Ohio-6142, 2004 WL 2616425, Unreported. Infants ⇔ 155

Evidence did not support trial court's finding that termination of father's parental rights and placement of child in permanent custody of county agency was in child's best interests; although guardian ad litem concluded permanent custody was in child's best interest and there was testimony that father's relationship with mother was not good for child, evidence regarding father's compliance with case plan was vague, father's sister stated that father visited child regularly and that child was bonded to father, there was no admissible evidence that child had observed any violence between father and mother, there was nothing to indicate that guardian ad litem ever observed father and child together, guardian ad litem did not explain her testimony that child needed a "clean break," and evidence established that there was a relative available who was suitable for long-term placement. In re A.A. (Ohio App. 9 Dist., Summit, 11-10-2004) No. 22196, 2004-Ohio-5955, 2004 WL 2535416, Unreported. Infants ⇔ 178

Some competent, credible evidence supported trial court's finding in termination of parental rights proceeding that children could not be placed with mother within reasonable time and should not be placed with mother; despite reasonable case planning and diligent efforts to assist mother, mother continuously and repeatedly failed to substantially remedy conditions that caused children to be placed outside home and mother did not complete case plan. In re Sanders Children (Ohio App. 5 Dist., Tuscarawas, 10-29-2004) No. 2004 AP 08 0057, 2004-Ohio-5878, 2004 WL 2497028, Unreported. Infants ⇔ 178

Some competent, credible evidence supported trial court's finding that granting permanent child custody to county job and family services was in children's best interest; children were placed in foster home that would consider adopting them, child's delays and aggression had improved since he was in foster home, mother had unrealistic expectations about children's behavior considering their ages, and mother previously stated that she did not want child. In re Sanders Children (Ohio App. 5 Dist., Tuscarawas, 10-29-2004) No. 2004 AP 08 0057, 2004-Ohio-5878, 2004 WL 2497028, Unreported. Infants ⇔ 178

Evidence supported juvenile court's finding that children could not be safely placed in parents' home within a reasonable time, thus supporting grant of permanent custody of child to county child protection agency, despite evidence that parents had substantially complied with case plans; parent educator and case worker testified they did not believe parents were competent to adequately care for children without supervision, and that children could not be safely returned to their home within a reasonable time. In re Gordon (Ohio App. 3 Dist., Hancock, 11-08-2004) No. 5-04-22, No. 5-04-23, 2004-Ohio-5889, 2004 WL 2496513, Unreported. Infants ⇔ 178

Clear and convincing evidence supported determination that grant of permanent custody of children to county department of children and family services was in children's best interests; mother had a long history with the county agency of removal of her three children at various times, children had lived together in a foster home since their removal, all of the children had developed a close bond with their foster family and were developing normally for their age, and guardian ad litem recommended that permanent custody be granted. In re A.B. (Ohio App. 8 Dist., Cuyahoga, 11-04-2004) No. 83971, 2004-Ohio-5862, 2004 WL 2491677, Unreported. Infants ⇔ 155; Infants ⇔ 208

Evidence supported determination that children could not be placed with a parent within a reasonable time, a determination required for award of permanent custody of children to county; trial court found that mother had failed continuously and repeatedly to substantially remedy conditions causing children to be removed, mother had a chronic mental illness which prevented her from providing adequate parental care now or in the foreseeable future, and father had demonstrated a lack of commitment toward children. In re A.B. (Ohio App. 8 Dist., Cuyahoga, 11-04-2004) No. 83971, 2004-Ohio-5862, 2004 WL 2491677, Unreported. Infants ⇔ 155; Infants ⇔ 158

Clear and convincing evidence supported determination that mother failed to meet the requirements of her case plan, despite being given ample opportunity to do so, and that termination of her parental rights was in the best interest of her two minor children; mother refused to allow caseworker inside her home, caseworker detected smell of alcohol on mother while she was visiting her children, she underwent a urinalysis and tested positive for alcohol consumption, she failed to attend chemical dependency treatment, and she failed to maintain regular visitation with her children, appearing for only 53 percent of 125 weekly visits. In re T.P. (Ohio App. 2 Dist., Montgomery, 10-29-2004) No. 20604, 2004-Ohio-5835, 2004 WL 2453304, Unreported. Infants ⇔ 155

Trial court was justified in finding that mother's two minor children could not be returned to her within a reasonable time, in termination of parental rights proceeding; mother failed to remedy all of the conditions that caused the removal of her children and she failed to maintain regular visitation with her children, appearing for only 53 percent of 125 weekly visits. In re T.P. (Ohio App. 2 Dist., Montgomery, 10-29-2004) No. 20604, 2004-Ohio-5835, 2004 WL 2453304, Unreported. Infants ⇔ 155

Substantial evidence supported trial court's decision to award permanent custody of dependent child to county children services agency; mother and putative father failed continuously and repeatedly for six months or more to substantially remedy conditions causing child to be placed outside home, putative father demonstrated lack of commitment to child by failing to assist in establishment of his paternity of child and to regularly support and visit child, child could not be placed with either mother or putative father within reasonable time as mother and putative father had not even attempted to complete case plan and had not visited child in over one year, and permanent commitment of child to county children services agency was in child's best interest. In re C.S. (Ohio App. 2 Dist., Montgomery, 10-22-2004) No. 20379, 2004-Ohio-5810, 2004 WL 2445238, Unreported. Infants ⇔ 155; Infants ⇔ 157

Trial court's findings that six children in foster care could not be placed with mother within a reasonable period of time and that granting permanent custody to county was in their best interests were supported by evidence that mother chose to pursue relationship with alleged sex offender, thus putting her children at risk, allowed her children to have contact with this man despite court's no-contact order, and failed to fully address her own past sexual abuse, as well as evidence that children, who needed permanency and stability, had thrived in foster care. In re Pernell C. (Ohio App. 6 Dist., Lucas, 11-01-2004) No. L-04-1007, 2004-Ohio-5791, 2004 WL 2438968, Unreported. Infants ⇔ 155; Infants ⇔ 156; Infants ⇔ 158

Trial court's decision to grant permanent custody of children to county was supported by father's own testimony that he did not have a permanent residence, he had not been drug tested since his previous positive drug test shortly after children were removed from home two years earlier, and he had failed to support or regularly visit children. In re R.H. (Ohio App. 8 Dist., Cuyahoga, 10-28-2004) No. 84051, 2004-Ohio-5734, 2004 WL 2425831, Unreported. Infants ⇔ 155; Infants ⇔ 157

Finding that grant of permanent custody of children to their aunt and uncle, rather than legal custody, was in best interests of children was supported by testimony of social worker that children were well adjusted to their placement with aunt and uncle and did not have a bond with their parents and that aunt and uncle wished to adopt children but were not interested in a legal custody arrangement, by custodial history of children which showed that they had been in custody for twelve months, and by fact that father had legally abandoned the children. In re R.H. (Ohio App. 8 Dist., Cuyahoga, 10-28-2004) No. 84051, 2004-Ohio-5734, 2004 WL 2425831, Unreported. Infants ⇔ 222

County children services board failed to establish by clear and convincing evidence that granting permanent custody of dependent child to board was in child's best interest; although caseworker and guardian ad litem believed child should be placed in board's permanent custody, there was no basis for concluding that alcohol or drug abuse was current issue for mother, counselors indicated mother's diagnosis of mental health disorder did not prohibit her from being able to parent, visitation went well, and child relationship with her siblings. In re M.B. (Ohio App. 9 Dist., Summit, 10-27-2004) No. 22103, 2004-Ohio-5686, 2004 WL 2390987, Unreported. Infants ⇔ 155; Infants ⇔ 158

Mother challenging grant of permanent custody of children to county agency failed to demonstrate prejudice arising out of any error in trial court's admission of alleged hearsay evidence; mother argued only that hearsay had the "possibility" of tainting the court's perception of her ability to parent her children, and no evidence in the record overcame presumption that judge disregarded any evidence that was not properly before her. In re T.M., III (Ohio App. 8 Dist., Cuyahoga, 09-30-2004) No. 83933, 2004-Ohio-5222, 2004 WL 2340654, Unreported. Infants ⇔ 253

Clear and convincing evidence supported finding that child could not be placed with mother within a reasonable time, in support of termination of parental rights; child was in need of legally secure placement, and mother's parental rights to ten of her other children had been terminated. In re Jared C. (Ohio App. 6 Dist., Lucas, 09-17-2004) No. L-04-1016, 2004-Ohio-4922, 2004 WL 2334313, Unreported. Infants ⇔ 155

Evidence supported juvenile court's finding that mother failed to substantially remedy the conditions that caused the children to be placed outside the home, thus supporting decision to grant permanent custody of children to county agency; although mother completed parenting classes, mother did not supervise or discipline her children, children had mental health and learning problems requiring structure and predictability during visits, mother failed to accept criticism, mother tested positive for drug use, mother failed to submit to drug screens and pled guilty to drug offenses, and mother continued to associate with other drug users. In re S.V. (Ohio App. 9 Dist., Summit, 10-13-2004) No. 22116, 2004-Ohio-5445, 2004 WL 2292825, Unreported. Infants ⇔ 155; Infants ⇔ 156

Evidence supported trial court's finding in state's proceeding to obtain permanent custody that dependent children cannot or should not be placed with mother of children or with father of one of the children; evidence indicated that reunification of children with mother after mother's release from prison could not be considered due to mother's failure to undergo psychological evaluations, mother failed to take necessary steps to educate herself regarding one child's medical treatments, father was serving eight-year prison sentence for child endangering, and both fathers had abandoned children. In re K.W. (Ohio App. 12 Dist., Butler, 10-11-2004) No. CA2003-11-289, No. CA2003-11-291, 2004-Ohio-5406, 2004 WL 2272064, Unreported. Infants ⇔ 155; Infants ⇔ 157; Infants ⇔ 159

Evidence supported trial court's finding that it was in dependent children's best interest that permanent custody of children be awarded to government agency; evidence indicated that father of one child was unknown and had never come forward, father of other child had no contact with either child after conviction for child endangering, mother failed to demonstrate ability to protect children from future harm, and children had bonded with foster parents. In re K.W. (Ohio App. 12 Dist., Butler, 10-11-2004) No. CA2003-11-289, No. CA2003-11-291, 2004-Ohio-5406, 2004 WL 2272064, Unreported. Infants ⇔ 155; Infants ⇔ 157

Determination that termination of father's parental rights was in child's best interest was not against manifest weight of the evidence; child had developed bond with cousin, with whom she had been placed approximately six weeks after her birth, no bond existed between child and father, who had only visited child on two occasions, child had been distant with her mother at prior visit, and child's cousin was interested in adopting her. In re Flanagan (Ohio App. 5 Dist., Stark, 10-01-2004) No. 2004CA00181, 2004-Ohio-5343, 2004 WL 2260677, Unreported. Infants ⇔ 155

Evidence supported denial of father's motion to change legal custody of his child, who had been adjudicated as dependent and neglected, from county department of job and family services to child's great-grandmother; great grandmother was 69 years old, she already had legal custody of two of her great-grandchildren, ages two and three, she had previously indicated that she could not care for child because she already had her hands full caring for other children, and great-grandmother admitted that she had never seen child. In re Flanagan (Ohio App. 5 Dist., Stark, 10-01-2004) No. 2004CA00181, 2004-Ohio-5343, 2004 WL 2260677, Unreported. Infants ⇔ 230.1

Trial court's finding that children could not or should not be placed with mother was not against the manifest weight of the evidence in termination of parental rights proceeding; children had been in the custody of Stark County Department of Jobs and Family Services for 12 of the last 22 consecutive months, and the children could not be placed with either parent at that time or within a reasonable period of time. In re Heldt/Woodson Children (Ohio App. 5 Dist., Stark, 09-27-2004) No. 2004CA00191, 2004-Ohio-5188, 2004 WL 2260574, Unreported. Infants ⇔ 155

Evidence supported finding that termination of parental rights was in the best interests of the children; experts testified that mother had unreasonable expectations for her children and got angry and frustrated when the children failed her, mother failed to supervise the children and did not provide any structure to their lives, she was unable to control the children without resorting to physically grabbing, pulling, or restraining the children, the children were thriving in their foster home, and their behavior had improved. In re Sparks (Ohio App. 3 Dist., Hancock, 10-04-2004) No. 5-04-16, No. 5-04-19, No. 5-04-17, No. 5-04-18, 2004-Ohio-5353, 2004 WL 2258178, Unreported. Infants ⇐ 155; Infants ⇐ 156

Evidence supported finding that the children could not be placed with either parent within a reasonable time, in support of termination of parental rights; father told social services workers that he was unable to care for the children, and forensic psychologist who interviewed mother testified that mother had a long history of psychological treatment, that it was difficult to treat mother due to her co-morbidity, that mother's multiple psychological difficulties made it difficult for her to have a relationship with her children, and that mother's situation would probably be the same six months in the future. In re Sparks (Ohio App. 3 Dist., Hancock, 10-04-2004) No. 5-04-16, No. 5-04-19, No. 5-04-17, No. 5-04-18, 2004-Ohio-5353, 2004 WL 2258178, Unreported. Infants ⇐ 155; Infants ⇐ 158

In finding that dependent child could not or should not be placed with parents, trial court erred by relying on statutory factor that parents showed unwillingness to provide adequate permanent home for child; although father was occasionally reluctant to hold child and mother may not have pursued employment vigorously, parents attended visitation regularly, mother interacted well with child, father had two jobs, and mother walked three miles to take child to his first medical examination and obtain formula for him. In re B.E.M. (Ohio App. 9 Dist., Wayne, 09-22-2004) No. 04CA0028, 2004-Ohio-4959, 2004 WL 2244246, Unreported. Infants ⇐ 231

In finding that dependent child could not or should not be placed with parents, trial court properly relied on statutory factor that parents suffered from chronic mental health issues that precluded them from offering proper care for child, where psychological evaluations of parents revealed that mother had major depressive disorder, dependent personality disorder, and avoidant personality disorder and that father had major depressive disorder and personality disorder with prominent dependent and avoidant traits and that, although such conditions were treatable, neither parent was consistent in seeking treatment. In re B.E.M. (Ohio App. 9 Dist., Wayne, 09-22-2004) No. 04CA0028, 2004-Ohio-4959, 2004 WL 2244246, Unreported. Infants ⇐ 231

In finding that dependent child could not or should not be placed with parents, trial court properly relied on statutory factor that parents had their parental rights terminated as to child's siblings, where mother had her parental rights involuntarily terminated as to five of her children and father had his parental rights involuntarily terminated as to three of his children. In re B.E.M. (Ohio App. 9 Dist., Wayne, 09-22-2004) No. 04CA0028, 2004-Ohio-4959, 2004 WL 2244246, Unreported. Infants ⇐ 231

Error in relying on statutory factor that parents failed to remedy conditions that caused dependent child's removal from parents' home to support finding that child could not or should not be placed with parents was harmless, where other statutory factors were established, including that parents had their parental rights terminated as to child's siblings and that parents suffered from chronic mental health issues that precluded them from offering proper care for child. In re B.E.M. (Ohio App. 9 Dist., Wayne, 09-22-2004) No. 04CA0028, 2004-Ohio-4959, 2004 WL 2244246, Unreported. Infants ⇐ 253

It was in the best interest of children to terminate mother's parental rights and to place children in the permanent custody of County Children's Services; mother was victim of domestic violence at the hands of father, mother associated herself with other questionable individuals, mother was pregnant by an individual who was a schizophrenic and did not regularly take his medication and was not good with small children, mother had involved herself with a church whose members expected her to cough until she vomited to rid herself of demons, and mother refused to address her own mental health issues. In re Lyons Children (Ohio App. 5 Dist., Fairfield, 09-07-2004) No. 2004CA3, No. 2004CA4, 2004-Ohio-4813, 2004 WL 2029211, Unreported. Infants ⇐ 155; Infants ⇐ 156; Infants ⇐ 158

Deaf mother was not entitled to additional opportunities to demonstrate adequate parenting skills in termination of parental rights action; children had been in temporary custody of Job and Family Services (JFS) for twelve or more months of a consecutive twenty-two-month period and could not be placed with mother within a reasonable time, mother had had a number of years to demonstrate her parenting abilities, numerous resources had been provided to mother, including case planning, counseling, budgeting, meal preparation, and learning to shop for nutritious food within budget, and over 30 different agencies were involved in helping mother. In re Berkley (Ohio App. 4 Dist., Pickaway, 09-03-2004) No. 04CA12, No. 04CA13, No. 04CA14, 2004-Ohio-4797, 2004 WL 2009421, Unreported. Infants ⇐ 230.1

Children's best interest would be served by awarding Job and Family Services (JFS) permanent custody of children; vocational rehabilitation counselor who specifically counseled deaf individuals to help them find employment worked with mother who was deaf, mother lacked skills necessary to provide adequate food and clothing for children, children were often dirty, mother did not discipline children, JFS provided mother with numerous services, and children had been in JFS's temporary custody for twelve or more months of a consecutive twenty-two month period and could not or should not be placed with mother within a reasonable time. In re Berkley (Ohio App. 4 Dist., Pickaway, 09-03-2004) No. 04CA12, No. 04CA13, No. 04CA14, 2004-Ohio-4797, 2004 WL 2009421, Unreported. Infants ⇐ 155; Infants ⇐ 156

Evidence supported grant of permanent custody of mother's two children to county agency; children had been in the temporary custody of agency for over 12 months of a consecutive 22 month period, children had been living with foster mother for more than two years, developmentally-delayed children were making progress out of mother's custody, foster mother was interested in adopting children, children required permanency, mother was unable to sustain suitable housing, mother failed to take steps to obtain public housing, and mother failed to keep appointments with social workers for home visits. In re K. (Ohio App. 8 Dist., Cuyahoga, 09-02-2004) No. 83410, 2004-Ohio-4629, 2004 WL 1946141, Unreported. Infants ⇐ 155

Evidence supported trial court's finding that granting permanent custody of dependent children to department of job and family services was in children's best interests; therapist concluded that children should not be returned to mother, guardian ad litem concluded that granting permanent custody to department was in children's best interests, and children continued to be beaten by mother, despite mother's completion of various services and department's involvement with children. In re Villanueva/Hampton Children (Ohio App. 5 Dist., Stark, 08-30-2004) No. 2004CA00120, 2004-Ohio-4609, 2004 WL 1933504, Unreported, appeal not allowed 104 Ohio St.3d 1441, 819 N.E.2d 1124, 2004-Ohio-7033. Infants ⇐ 156; Infants ⇐ 178

Weight of the evidence supported conclusion that it was in best interests of dependent child that she be placed in permanent custody of county children services agency, which was necessary prerequisite to termination of mother's parental rights; mother attended less than half of the scheduled visitations between herself and child, mother had little to no relationship with her other four children and had continued abusing drugs and alcohol while they were in her custody, child had good relationship with her foster mother and foster brother, and, while in foster care, child made good strides in her development, and child needed stability in her life, particularly given that she was developmentally delayed. In re S. C. (Ohio App. 9 Dist., Lorain, 09-01-2004) No. 04CA008469, 2004-Ohio-4570, 2004 WL 1932854, Unreported. Infants ⇐ 155; Infants ⇐ 156; Infants ⇐ 157

Weight of the evidence supported finding that dependent child could not be placed with either parent within reasonable time or should not be placed with either parent, as necessary to support termination of mother's parental rights; mother failed to demonstrate sustained effort necessary to complete drug and alcohol treatment to resolve her addiction issues, she failed to complete psychological evaluation until her participation in program in which she had been enrolled at time of hearing, she failed to participate in therapy regarding anger issues and coping skills, and she had sporadic visitation record with child, as well as criminal convictions. In re S. C. (Ohio App. 9 Dist., Lorain, 09-01-2004) No. 04CA008469, 2004-Ohio-4570, 2004 WL 1932854, Unreported. Infants ⇐ 155; Infants ⇐ 157

Evidence supported juvenile court's determination that permanent custody was in the best interest of mother's children; three of mother's children had previously been removed from her care, children had bonded with paternal grandmother, paternal grandmother expressed interest in adopting children, mother was often late or failed to show up for visitation with children, mother failed to remedy conditions causing children to be removed from home, and mother failed to obtain stable employment or address mental health issues. In re B.N. (Ohio App. 8 Dist., Cuyahoga, 08-26-2004) No. 83704, 2004-Ohio-4469, 2004 WL 1902115, Unreported. Infants ⇐ 155; Infants ⇐ 158

Evidence supported trial court finding that child could not or should not be returned to parents, in support of termination of parental rights; mother failed to take anger management classes as required under her caseplan, she stopped taking her medication and continued to be involved in physical and verbal outbursts with others, and father planned on leaving child alone with mother while he worked 60 to 70 hours per week. In re M.L.J. (Ohio App. 10 Dist., Franklin, 08-19-2004) No. 04AP-152, 2004-Ohio-4358, 2004 WL 1853547, Unreported, appeal not allowed 103 Ohio St.3d 1528, 817 N.E.2d 410, 2004-Ohio-5852. Infants ⇐ 155; Infants ⇐ 156; Infants ⇐ 158

Trial court award of permanent custody of child to department of job and family services was not against the manifest weight of the evidence; mother did not complete a program regarding domestic violence issues, she was unable to maintain stable employment and housing, the department had permanent custody of another of mother's children, psychologist stated that mother lacked initiative and had difficulty accepting responsibility for her actions, and child was in a foster home with her half-sister and the foster parents wanted to adopt both children. In re Keen (Ohio App. 5 Dist., Stark, 08-09-2004) No. 2004CA00125, 2004-Ohio-4211, 2004 WL 1789632, Unreported. Infants ⇐ 155

Trial court's determination during termination of parental rights proceeding that children could not have been placed with their mother within a reasonable time was supported by clear and convincing evidence; mother demonstrated a lack of commitment toward the children by failing to regularly support, visit, or communicate with them, the children had lived with their paternal grandparents for over two years, mother was incarcerated at the time of trial, and she had a severe and chronic drug addiction. In re A.P. (Ohio App. 8 Dist., Cuyahoga, 08-05-2004) No. 83220, 2004-Ohio-4080, 2004 WL 1752941, Unreported. Infants ⇐ 157

Clear and convincing evidence supported trial court's determination that award of permanent custody to the Department of Children and Family Services was in children's best interest; children had lived with their paternal grandparents for over two years and were doing well, grandparents had expressed an interest in adopting the children, mother was incarcerated at the time of trial, and she had a severe and chronic drug addiction. In re A.P. (Ohio App. 8 Dist., Cuyahoga, 08-05-2004) No. 83220, 2004-Ohio-4080, 2004 WL 1752941, Unreported. Infants ⇐ 155; Infants ⇐ 157

Juvenile court's finding that award of permanent custody of children to the Hamilton County Jobs and Family Services was in children's best interest was supported by clear and convincing evidence; children's paternal grandmother regularly and willingly left the children in the unsupervised care of their legal father, who was a known sexual offender, several experts testified that the older three children had severe psychological issues due to past sexual abuse, and the parents and grandmother were unable to acknowledge or appropriately deal with the children's issues. In re Wilkinson (Ohio App. 1 Dist., Hamilton, 08-06-2004) No. C-040182, No. C-040203, No. C-040282, 2004-Ohio-4107, 2004 WL 1752821, Unreported, appeal not allowed 104 Ohio St.3d 1410, 818 N.E.2d 711, 2004-Ohio-6364. Infants ⇐ 156

The trial court's failure to conduct an in camera interview with four-year-old child to determine child's level of maturity was not an abuse of discretion, during termination of parental rights proceeding; both the guardian ad litem and the caseworker testified that child was too young to express his desires regarding placement, and caseworker stated that child called his foster mom "mom" and called his mother by her first name. In re Wright (Ohio App. 10 Dist., Franklin, 08-03-2004) No. 04AP-435, 2004-Ohio-4045, 2004 WL 1729881, Unreported. Infants ⇐ 207

Evidence supported trial court's finding that reunification of child and mother could not take place within a reasonable time, thus supporting termination of parental rights and grant of permanent custody of child to county agency; mother failed to ensure follow-up care when child failed hearing test, mother had parental rights terminated as to three other children, mother had history of criminal offenses and drug use, and mother failed to exercise visitation rights with child. In re Burton (Ohio App. 3 Dist., Mercer, 08-02-2004) No. 10-04-01, 2004-Ohio-4021, 2004 WL 1718166, Unreported, appeal not allowed 103 Ohio St.3d 1495, 816 N.E.2d 1081, 2004-Ohio-5605. Infants ⇐ 155; Infants ⇐ 157; Infants ⇐ 159

Evidence supported trial court's finding that reunification of child and father could not take place within a reasonable time, thus supporting termination of parental rights and grant of permanent custody of child to county agency; father had been incarcerated since before child was born and would be incarcerated for 18 months following dispositional hearing, at which time child would be two and one-half years old. In re Burton (Ohio App. 3 Dist., Mercer, 08-02-2004) No. 10-04-01, 2004-Ohio-4021, 2004 WL 1718166, Unreported, appeal not allowed 103 Ohio St.3d 1495, 816 N.E.2d 1081, 2004-Ohio-5605. Infants ⇐ 157

Evidence that mother's husband had been involved in domestic violence incident with his ex-wife was relevant and admissible in proceedings to determine whether to grant permanent custody of mother's two children to county agency; husband was a factor in children's lives because he was married to mother. In re Morgan (Ohio App. 3 Dist., Marion, 08-02-2004) No. 9-04-02, No. 9-04-03, 2004-Ohio-4018, 2004 WL 1717934, Unreported. Infants ⇐ 173.1

Evidence supported juvenile court's determination that child was abandoned, thus supporting grant of permanent custody of child to county; parents had not visited with or sent cards or gifts to child for the 15 months he had been in agency's temporary care, agency mailed calendars to parents listing the dates available for visitation, and father stopped at agency and called by telephone but did not inquire about or arrange visitation. In re L.D. (Ohio App. 12 Dist., Clinton, 08-02-2004) No. CA2004-03-007, 2004-Ohio-4000, 2004 WL 1717680, Unreported. Infants ⇐ 157

In determining whether permanent custody of child should be granted to county, juvenile court was not required to determine whether parents had remedied the conditions which caused removal of child, where ground for granting custody to county was that child had been in temporary custody for at least 12 months of a consecutive 22–month period. In re L.D. (Ohio App. 12 Dist., Clinton, 08-02-2004) No. CA2004-03-007, 2004-Ohio-4000, 2004 WL 1717680, Unreported. Infants ⇐ 210

Trial court's decision granting permanent custody of children to the Lucas County Children Services (LCCS) was supported by some competent, credible evidence and, therefore, was not against manifest weight of the evidence; mother had continuously and repeatedly failed to substantially remedy the problems which prompted the removal of children, mother was not scheduled to complete drug treatment program for another four to five months, assuming she remained fully compliant, mother had no housing, and she still had not had her mental health assessment. In re Denzel M. (Ohio App. 6 Dist., Lucas, 07-30-2004) No. L-03-1337, 2004-Ohio-3982, 2004 WL 1698086, Unreported. Infants ⇐ 155

Clear and convincing evidence supported trial court's finding that children could not or should not be placed with parents within reasonable time, such that their parental rights should be terminated; at time of first evaluation, child who was 5 1/2 years old was functioning at three-year-old level regarding her fine motor skills, child was functioning at five-year, six-month level concerning her fine motor skills after six months in foster care, children ate with their hands, rather than utensils, at time children were placed in foster care, and parents demonstrated lack of commitment towards children and failed to provide adequate home for children. In re Kitana (Ohio App. 5 Dist., Tuscarawas, 07-23-2004) No. 2004-AP-03-0024, 2004-Ohio-3963, 2004 WL 1688560, Unreported. Infants ⇐ 156

Out-of-court statements by children regarding their fears or wishes for placement were admissible against mother in permanent custody proceedings as statements of then-existing state of mind. In re Brooks (Ohio App. 10 Dist., Franklin, 07-22-2004) No. 04AP-164, No. 04AP-201, No. 04AP-202, No. 04AP-165, 2004-Ohio-3887, 2004 WL 1631760, Unreported, appeal not allowed 103 Ohio St.3d 1495, 816 N.E.2d 1081, 2004-Ohio-5605. Infants ⇐ 174

Trial court in permanent custody proceedings was not required to hold new evidentiary hearing on remand from appellate court, where appellate court did not expressly require that trial court conduct new trial, and decision by trial court not to take new evidence was not inconsistent with appellate decision. In re Brooks (Ohio App. 10 Dist., Franklin, 07-22-2004) No. 04AP-164, No. 04AP-201, No. 04AP-202, No. 04AP-165, 2004-Ohio-3887, 2004 WL 1631760, Unreported, appeal not allowed 103 Ohio St.3d 1495, 816 N.E.2d 1081, 2004-Ohio-5605. Infants ⇐ 254

Opinion testimony of caseworkers regarding relationship between mother and her children was admissible in permanent custody proceedings; witnesses' opinions were rationally based upon their perceptions and experience with individuals involved, and their opinions were directly relevant to issues before the court. In re Brooks (Ohio App. 10 Dist., Franklin, 07-22-2004) No. 04AP-164, No. 04AP-201, No. 04AP-202, No. 04AP-165, 2004-Ohio-3887, 2004 WL 1631760, Unreported, appeal not allowed 103 Ohio St.3d 1495, 816 N.E.2d 1081, 2004-Ohio-5605. Infants ⇐ 173.1

Evidence supported finding that grant to county of permanent custody of children, who had been in custody of county agency for almost three years, was in children's best interest; mother failed to distance herself from children's sexually abusive father, children feared father, mother lied about continued relationship with father, children had positive relationship with foster parents, children wished to be adopted, mother failed to complete drug treatment programs, and children needed legally secure placement. In re Johnson (Ohio App. 10 Dist., Franklin, 07-22-2004) No. 03AP-1264, 2004-Ohio-3886, 2004 WL 1631756, Unreported, appeal not allowed 103 Ohio St.3d 1465, 815 N.E.2d 680, 2004-Ohio-5056, reconsideration denied 104 Ohio St.3d 1412, 818 N.E.2d 712, 2004-Ohio-6364. Infants ⇐ 155; Infants ⇐ 156

Evidence was sufficient to support termination of mother's parental rights to child; child had been in the custody of county department of job and family services for 23 months at the time of the termination of parental rights hearing, and permanent custody of child's younger sibling had previously been granted to county children services board. In re Kaylee P. (Ohio App. 6 Dist., Fulton, 07-16-2004) No. F-04-011, 2004-Ohio-3807, 2004 WL 1595702, Unreported. Infants ⚖ 155

Finding that mother demonstrated lack of commitment to dependent children by failing to work toward completion of case plan was not abuse of discretion in termination of parental rights proceeding, where mother failed to receive counseling, to complete chemical dependency assessment, and to have stable home; fact that mother loved and visited children did not preclude finding that mother demonstrated lack of commitment to case plan. In re Ross (Ohio App. 11 Dist., Geauga, 07-09-2004) No. 2003-G-2549, 2004-Ohio-3689, 2004 WL 1559781, Unreported, appeal not allowed 103 Ohio St.3d 1429, 814 N.E.2d 491, 2004-Ohio-4524. Infants ⚖ 155

Finding that mother continuously and repeatedly failed to substantially remedy conditions causing dependent children to be placed outside her home, including mother's drug use and lack of stable home, was not abuse of discretion in termination of parental rights proceeding, where mother failed to receive counseling, did not complete chemical dependency assessment, repeatedly tested positive for drugs, and failed to maintain stable home. In re Ross (Ohio App. 11 Dist., Geauga, 07-09-2004) No. 2003-G-2549, 2004-Ohio-3689, 2004 WL 1559781, Unreported, appeal not allowed 103 Ohio St.3d 1429, 814 N.E.2d 491, 2004-Ohio-4524. Infants ⚖ 155

Trial court's judgment granting permanent custody of dependent children to county department of job and family services was not against the manifest weight of the evidence; evidence indicated that father, despite reasonable case planning and the diligent efforts of department, continuously and repeatedly failed to remedy the conditions causing children to be placed in the temporary custody of department, and that father failed to maintain contact with children. In re Thompson (Ohio App. 11 Dist., Portage, 07-07-2004) No. 2004-P-0023, No. 2004-P-0024, 2004-Ohio-3686, 2004 WL 1559747, Unreported. Infants ⚖ 155; Infants ⚖ 157

Evidence supported finding in proceeding on motion for permanent custody of dependent children that father had abandoned children; social worker testified that father had no contact with the children for a period of six months. In re Thompson (Ohio App. 11 Dist., Portage, 07-07-2004) No. 2004-P-0023, No. 2004-P-0024, 2004-Ohio-3686, 2004 WL 1559747, Unreported. Infants ⚖ 157

Evidence was sufficient to support finding in proceeding on motion for permanent custody of dependent children that children had been in custody of county department of job and family services for longer than twelve months of a twenty-two month consecutive period; testimony and exhibits admitted at custody hearing showed that department was granted temporary custody of the twins on particular date and filed motion for permanent custody fifteen months later, and that at no time during such period did department relinquish temporary custody of the children. In re Thompson (Ohio App. 11 Dist., Portage, 07-07-2004) No. 2004-P-0023, No. 2004-P-0024, 2004-Ohio-3686, 2004 WL 1559747, Unreported. Infants ⚖ 155

Finding that mother continuously and repeatedly failed to substantially remedy conditions causing dependent children to be placed outside her home, including mother's drug use and lack of stable home, was not abuse of discretion in termination of parental rights proceeding, where mother failed to receive counseling, did not complete chemical dependency assessment, repeatedly tested positive for drugs, and failed to maintain stable home. In re Ross (Ohio App. 11 Dist., Geauga, 07-07-2004) No. 2003-G-2551, 2004-Ohio-3684, 2004 WL 1559742, Unreported. Infants ⚖ 155

Failing to grant mother extension of time to complete reunification process with dependent children was not abuse of discretion in termination of parental rights proceeding, where evidence showed pattern of neglect by mother which resulted from her drug use and inability to maintain stable employment. In re Ross (Ohio App. 11 Dist., Geauga, 07-09-2004) No. 2003-G-2550, 2004-Ohio-3680, 2004 WL 1559729, Unreported, appeal not allowed 103 Ohio St.3d 1481, 816 N.E.2d 256, 2004-Ohio-5405. Infants ⚖ 230.1

Evidence in termination of parental rights proceeding supported finding that Geauga County Job and Family Services (GCJFS) used reasonable case planning and diligent efforts to assist parents to remedy problems that caused dependent children to be placed outside their home; case plan, which included counseling, chemical dependency assessments, and employment program, was designed to remedy parents' domestic violence, drug use, and unstable home. In re Ross (Ohio App. 11 Dist., Geauga, 07-09-2004) No. 2003-G-2550, 2004-Ohio-3680, 2004 WL 1559729, Unreported, appeal not allowed 103 Ohio St.3d 1481, 816 N.E.2d 256, 2004-Ohio-5405. Infants ⚖ 155

Finding that mother was chemically dependent and that her dependency was so severe that it made her unable to provide adequate home for dependent children was not abuse of discretion in termination of parental rights proceeding, where mother, who denied drug use, repeatedly tested positive for drugs and was arrested for drug possession; expert testimony was not required to establish chemical dependency. In re Ross (Ohio App. 11 Dist., Geauga, 07-09-2004) No. 2003-G-2550, 2004-Ohio-3680, 2004 WL 1559729, Unreported, appeal not allowed 103 Ohio St.3d 1481, 816 N.E.2d 256, 2004-Ohio-5405. Infants ⚖ 155; Infants ⚖ 178

Finding that mother continuously and repeatedly failed to substantially remedy conditions causing dependent children to be placed outside her home, including mother's drug use and lack of stable home, was not abuse of discretion in termination of parental rights proceeding, where mother failed to receive counseling, did not complete chemical dependency assessment, repeatedly tested positive for drugs, and failed to maintain stable home. In re Ross (Ohio App. 11 Dist., Geauga, 07-09-2004) No. 2003-G-2550, 2004-Ohio-3680, 2004 WL 1559729, Unreported, appeal not allowed 103 Ohio St.3d 1481, 816 N.E.2d 256, 2004-Ohio-5405. Infants ⚖ 155

Clear and convincing evidence supported finding that granting permanent custody of father's children to county children services was in the best interests of the children, in support of terminating parental rights; father committed various criminal acts and was incarcerated on lengthy prison sentences, the presence of the children did not deter father from committing crimes in the past, father had no plan for employment or housing, and father required psychotropic medications but claimed to have no knowledge of or interest in knowing his diagnosis. In re Bailey (Ohio App. 4 Dist., Athens, 06-07-2004) No. 04CA11, 2004-Ohio-3628, 2004 WL 1531917, Unreported. Infants ⚖ 155; Infants ⚖ 157; Infants ⚖ 158

In termination of parental rights proceeding related to dependent child, trial court was statutorily required to consider prior termination of mother's parental rights related to second child and circumstances surrounding such prior termination of mother's parental rights, where such circumstances were highly relevant in that mother had same problems with both children, despite repeated efforts by children services board to remedy situation. In re Baby Girl Elliott (Ohio App. 12 Dist., Butler, 07-06-2004) No. CA2003-10-256, 2004-Ohio-3539, 2004 WL 1485858, Unreported. Infants ⚖ 210

Evidence overwhelmingly supported trial court's decision awarding permanent custody of children to the Department of Children and Family Services (DCFS); mother could not hold job, could not medically care for children, and could not provide a stable environment for them, much less for herself, children's guardian ad litem repeatedly recommended that court award permanent custody to DCFS, permanent custody was in best interest of children, and not only had mother failed to sufficiently comply with case plan, but she had continually offered excuses for her failure to do so, and had neglected her children to point that children now suffered permanent hearing loss. In re T.S. (Ohio App. 8 Dist., Cuyahoga, 07-01-2004) No. 83100, No. 83101, 2004-Ohio-3475, 2004 WL 1472032, Unreported. Infants ⚖ 155; Infants ⚖ 159

Clear and convincing evidence supported trial court's finding that child could not be placed with father within reasonable time, or should not be placed with father, in termination of parental rights proceeding; father was in custody at time county Department of Job and Family Services (DJFS) filed for permanent custody, father had served only eight years of 15 year sentence, mere possibility of parole was too speculative for court to find that child could be placed with incarcerated parent within reasonable time, and fact father had been convicted of gross sexual imposition involving child who resided with father was evidence that child should not be placed with father. In re Brown (Ohio App. 11 Dist., Lake, 06-21-2004) No. 2004-L-027, 2004-Ohio-3337, 2004 WL 1433674, Unreported. Infants ⚖ 155

Finding that dependent child could not or should not be placed with father within reasonable time was not against manifest weight of evidence; father failed to comply with case plan, had dirty home, and allowed uncle, who was alleged to have abused another child, to reside in his home. In re Merryman/Wilson Children (Ohio App. 5 Dist., Stark, 06-14-2004) No. 2004 CA 00056, No. 2004 CA 00071, 2004-Ohio-3174, 2004 WL 1376278, Unreported. Infants ⚖ 155; Infants ⚖ 156

In proceeding in which department of job and family services sought permanent custody of dependent and neglected children, evidence supported finding that children were abandoned, where mother did not visit or have any contact with children for period of more than 90 days and, while there was testimony offered that mother called caseworker and left message that she wanted to visit children, it was undisputed that mother did not leave telephone number where she could be reached and did not appear for scheduled visitations. In re Katrina T. (Ohio App. 6 Dist., Sandusky, 06-18-2004) No. S-03-024, 2004-Ohio-3164, 2004 WL 1368324, Unreported. Infants ⚖ 157

Evidence supported finding that termination of father's parental rights was in the best interest of the children; children had long-term custody of the State, children were in need to a secure, permanent placement, children were young and were "very adoptable," relative placement had failed, and parents demonstrated a lack of commitment to the children. In re H.E.R. (Ohio App. 2 Dist., Darke, 06-18-2004) No. 1631, 2004-Ohio-3138, 2004 WL 1366098, Unreported. Infants ⇐ 157

Evidence supported finding that the State would not be able to return father's children to father's custody within a reasonable amount of time, in support of order terminating parental rights; father had been convicted of three felony counts of domestic violence while the children were removed from his custody, father failed to attend anger management classes or court-ordered psychological counseling, he had been unemployed for six months, and he relied on his parents for support. In re H.E.R. (Ohio App. 2 Dist., Darke, 06-18-2004) No. 1631, 2004-Ohio-3138, 2004 WL 1366098, Unreported. Infants ⇐ 157

Evidence supported juvenile court's finding that child could not be placed with father within a reasonable time, thus warranting termination of father's parental rights; father failed to obtain employment while his case plan was pending, he also failed to obtain independent housing, he continued to reside with his father, who refused to permit Department of Job and Family Services officials to enter the residence to determine whether the housing was suitable for a young child, and he did not attend any counseling sessions prior to the motion for permanent custody. In re Miller (Ohio App. 3 Dist., Auglaize, 06-14-2004) No. 2-04-02, 2004-Ohio-3023, 2004 WL 1302250, Unreported. Infants ⇐ 155

Trial court's determination that a legally secure permanent placement for child could not be achieved without a grant of permanent custody to county was supported by evidence that mother would not be able to parent child in the foreseeable future, that father never had any contact with child, and that no other relative sought custody. In re King (Ohio App. 11 Dist., Lake, 06-04-2004) No. 2004-L-013, 2004-Ohio-2919, 2004 WL 1238377, Unreported. Infants ⇐ 155

Trial court's determination that mother failed to avail herself of necessary services and visitation opportunities, warranting the grant of permanent custody of child to county, was supported by evidence that mother continuously failed to complete drug treatment program. In re King (Ohio App. 11 Dist., Lake, 06-04-2004) No. 2004-L-013, 2004-Ohio-2919, 2004 WL 1238377, Unreported. Infants ⇐ 155

Evidence supported finding that mother's children could not be placed with her within a reasonable time or should not be placed with her, in support of termination of parental rights; mother continued to live with boyfriend with whom she had numerous altercations and with whom she overdosed following an argument, she failed to seek counseling for three months following her overdose, she missed visits with the children, and she was unemployed during the two years that county children services board was involved with the family. In re Archer (Ohio App. 3 Dist., Allen, 06-07-2004) No. 1-03-89, No. 1-03-90, 2004-Ohio-2916, 2004 WL 1238306, Unreported. Infants ⇐ 155; Infants ⇐ 158

Evidence was sufficient to support trial court's finding that termination of father's parental rights was in child's best interest; during father's scheduled visitation with child he would either sleep or not interact with child, he demonstrated difficulty in controlling his anger and an inability to cope with stress, he had made four suicide attempts, he was bulimic, he had been to jail on four separate occasions, and his only means of support was Social Security. In re Hollon (Ohio App. 5 Dist., Fairfield, 05-27-2004) No. 03CA85, No. 03CA88, No. 03CA89, 2004-Ohio-2866, 2004 WL 1233582, Unreported. Infants ⇐ 155; Infants ⇐ 157; Infants ⇐ 158

Evidence was sufficient to support trial court's finding that termination of parental rights was in children's best interest; mother had severe cognitive limitations and her intelligence was in the lower five percent of the population, evidence indicated that it was probable that she would make decisions that would be inappropriate or risky for her children, mother was very resistant to discussing and learning appropriate parenting skills, she demonstrated a lack of insight concerning her children's needs, and she did not have the ability to provide children with stable housing. In re Hollon (Ohio App. 5 Dist., Fairfield, 05-27-2004) No. 03CA85, No. 03CA88, No. 03CA89, 2004-Ohio-2866, 2004 WL 1233582, Unreported. Infants ⇐ 155; Infants ⇐ 158

Termination of mother's parental rights was in best interest of children; mother suffered from depression, sometimes severe, mother had attempted suicide on at least two occasions, mother failed to comply with therapy requirements or parenting classes, mother did not submit to urinalysis as ordered, mother informed trial court at hearing that she did not use illegal drugs but then tested positive for cocaine immediately thereafter, and children had bonded with foster parent and were doing well. In re McCune/Warnken Children (Ohio App. 5 Dist., Stark, 06-01-2004) No. 2004CA00083, 2004-Ohio-2826, 2004 WL 1202760, Unreported. Infants ⇐ 155; Infants ⇐ 158

Clear and convincing evidence supported juvenile court's finding that grant of permanent custody of mother's two minor children to county agency was in the children's best interest; children had been in foster care for 15 consecutive months prior to the permanent custody hearing, mother failed to regularly visit or communicate with her children, and she failed to begin working on her case plan until agency's request for permanent custody had been filed. In re Lane (Ohio App. 3 Dist., Marion, 06-01-2004) No. 9-03-61, No. 9-03-62, 2004-Ohio-2798, 2004 WL 1192087, Unreported. Infants ⇐ 222

Decision to terminate mother's parental rights to her minor child and place child in permanent custody of Children Services Board (CSB) was not supported by clear and convincing evidence, even though caseworker and guardian ad litem expressed view that permanent custody in CSB was in child's best interest; much of delay and time spent without visitation was attributed to CSB and lack of cooperation by foster family, child was happy to see her mother despite length of time that child has been out of mother's care, child's caregiver was not interested in adopting child and permanent home has not been located, and clinical counselor who spent greatest amount of time working with child and mother believed that termination of parental rights would be harmful to child. In re K. S. (Ohio App. 9 Dist., Summit, 05-26-2004) No. 21913, 2004-Ohio-2660, 2004 WL 1160031, Unreported. Infants ⇐ 179

Evidence supported finding that child could not be placed with mother within a reasonable period of time, in dependency proceeding; mother was evicted, following repeated warnings from her landlord, for allowing prostitutes and drug users to use her apartment, mother received food stamps and social security income to live on each month, mother's gas was turned off at the time of the permanent custody hearing, and mother was diagnosed with chronic paranoid schizophrenia, a psychotic disorder characterized by auditory hallucinations, and difficulty with thought processing and her physician stated that she was failing to comply with her treatment plan. In re R.N. (Ohio App. 8 Dist., Cuyahoga, 05-20-2004) No. 83121, 2004-Ohio-2560, 2004 WL 1118825, Unreported. Infants ⇐ 155; Infants ⇐ 158

Sufficient evidence supported finding that terminating mother's parental rights was in the best interests of her minor son; mother had failed for two years to complete any of the elements of her case plan, particularly treatment for her addiction to drugs and alcohol, son required daily breathing treatments, which mother could not provide, and son had a strong bond with his foster mother, who was interested in adopting him. In re E.S. (Ohio App. 10 Dist., Franklin, 05-20-2004) No. 03AP-869, 2004-Ohio-2572, 2004 WL 1118689, Unreported. Infants ⇐ 155; Infants ⇐ 159

Evidence supported trial court's finding that grant of permanent custody to county Children Services Board (CSB) was in minor children's best interests, so as to support termination of mother's parental rights, where mother refused to address her drug problem and had mental health issues that impeded her ability to parent children, guardian ad litem testified that he did not observe normal parent-child bonding and that children were thriving in foster care, mother had not begun to address most serious problems that threatened her family, there were no relatives or friends willing to care for children, and mother's parental rights to her older children had been previously terminated. In re J.G. (Ohio App. 9 Dist., Summit, 05-19-2004) No. 21944, 2004-Ohio-2513, 2004 WL 1103971, Unreported. Infants ⇐ 155; Infants ⇐ 158

Clear and convincing evidence supported juvenile court's determination in termination of parental rights proceeding that child could not be placed with mother within reasonable period of time and should not be placed with mother; mother only obtained employment for one month during implementation of case plan, mother was not actively searching for employment, mother's failure to obtain regular employment perpetuated her inability to provide stable home environment, and mother had long history of unwillingness or inability to provide for herself and child. In re Krems (Ohio App. 11 Dist., Geauga, 05-14-2004) No. 2003-G-2535, 2004-Ohio-2449, 2004 WL 1086974, Unreported. Infants ⇐ 155

Sufficient evidence supported termination of mother's parental rights to minor son; although mother was not abusive, son was victimized by mother's neglect and inability to care for him, son had been in county's custody for more than 12 months of a consecutive 22-month period, and mother had failed to obtain employment or provide son with a stable home environment. In re Krems (Ohio App. 11 Dist., Geauga, 05-14-2004) No. 2003-G-2534, 2004-Ohio-2446, 2004 WL 1086869, Unreported. Infants ⇐ 155; Infants ⇐ 156

Evidence supported finding that maternal grandmother was not a "suitable" relative to assume custody of children and that award of permanent custody to county children services board was in the best interests of children; grandmother was in relationship that involved domestic violence, children had head lice and other conditions needing medical attention, grandmother permitted children to have contact with convicted sex offender, grandmother's husband sold drugs and had grandmother and her children help him sell drugs, and grandmother had serious limitations in her ability to use good judgment in providing care for children. In re Brewer (Ohio App. 2 Dist., Greene, 05-14-2004) No. 2003 CA 88, 2004-Ohio-2417, 2004 WL 1073757, Unreported. Infants ⇐ 222

Order granting permanent custody of two children to county department of job and family services was not against the manifest weight of the evidence; both children had special needs and required a structured environment that mother and step-father could not provide, and the children had improved academically and behaviorally after they were removed from mother and step-father. In re Caine (Ohio App. 5 Dist., Licking, 05-06-2004) No. 2003-CA-00118, 2004-Ohio-2270, 2004 WL 1047414, Unreported. Infants ⇐ 155

Trial court was not required to determine whether department of job and family services used reasonable efforts to reunify or whether child could not or should not be placed with either parent within a reasonable time, in child dependency proceeding; trial court found that mother had abandoned child, and mother did not challenge abandonment finding on appeal. In re Bender (Ohio App. 5 Dist., Stark, 05-03-2004) No. 2004CA00015, 2004-Ohio-2268, 2004 WL 1047411, Unreported. Infants ⇐ 210

Order granting permanent custody of children to county department of job and family services was not against the manifest weight of the evidence; mother failed to meet the medical needs of the children, mother and her husband allowed others to reside with them in violation of their caseplan, mother was often unable to meet her own medical needs, she did not understand the special needs of her children, and the health of the children improved while they were in foster care. In re Caine (Ohio App. 5 Dist., Licking, 05-06-2004) No. 03-CA-115, 2004-Ohio-2326, 2004 WL 1045467, Unreported, appeal not allowed 102 Ohio St.3d 1534, 811 N.E.2d 1152, 2004-Ohio-3580. Infants ⇐ 155; Infants ⇐ 159

Evidence supported order granting permanent custody of child to county children services board; father was recently released from prison, father was incarcerated for stabbing mother's boyfriend, and child had a no contact order against father based on a substantiated allegation of sexual abuse by father. In re Kaylee T. (Ohio App. 6 Dist., Lucas, 05-04-2004) No. L-03-1320, 2004-Ohio-2227, 2004 WL 941779, Unreported. Infants ⇐ 155; Infants ⇐ 156

Evidence supported award of permanent custody of child to agency, even though counselor opined that parents could care for child if they worked together; parents had previously had their parental rights terminated with respect to child's siblings, parents demonstrated inability to care for child alone, and parents could not be expected to be jointly present at all times. In re Richardson (Ohio App. 5 Dist., Guernsey, 04-27-2004) No. 04 CA 02, 2004-Ohio-2170, 2004 WL 911316, Unreported. Infants ⇐ 155

Evidence supported finding that granting permanent custody of children to county children services board was in the best interests of the children; children had been in the custody of children services board for over 12 of the last 22 months, mother of the children was deceased and the alleged fathers of the children had no contact with them, maternal grandmother told the court that she could not care for the children on a full-time basis, and the Juvenile Court recommended an open adoption to allow maternal grandmother to maintain contact with the children. In re Muldrew (Ohio App. 2 Dist., Montgomery, 04-23-2004) No. 19966, 2004-Ohio-2044, 2004 WL 870427, Unreported. Infants ⇐ 155; Infants ⇐ 157

Trial court's finding that children could or should not be placed with their parents within a reasonable time was unnecessary in termination of parental rights action, as court only needed to determine that granting County Department of Job and Family Services custody was in best interests of children and that children were in county's temporary custody for 12 or more months of a consecutive 22-month period. In re Ridenour (Ohio App. 11 Dist., Lake, 04-16-2004) No. 2003-L-146, No. 2003-L-147, No. 2003-L-148, 2004-Ohio-1958, 2004 WL 834579, Unreported. Infants ⇐ 210

Court could not rely on the testimony of child's caseworker as evidence of child's wishes regarding his custody in termination of parental rights action, as statute restricted court to considering wishes "as expressed directly by the child or through the child's guardian ad litem." In re Ridenour (Ohio App. 11 Dist., Lake, 04-16-2004) No. 2003-L-146, No. 2003-L-147, No. 2003-L-148, 2004-Ohio-1958, 2004 WL 834579, Unreported. Infants ⇐ 210

Trial court was not required to discuss alternatives such as planned permanent living arrangement when considering children's need for legally secure placement in termination of parental rights proceeding, although permanent living arrangement was discussed at hearing, where court discussed at length children's need for secure placement, court found that mother had not been able to properly parent children at any time and discussed reasons she had been unable to do so. In re Ridenour (Ohio App. 11 Dist., Lake, 04-16-2004) No. 2003-L-146, No. 2003-L-147, No. 2003-L-148, 2004-Ohio-1958, 2004 WL 834579, Unreported. Infants ⇐ 210

Trial court properly considered mother's relationship with children when considering whether to terminate parental rights; court's judgment entry discussed at length mother's efforts to care for her children and noted that the failure of those efforts "does not detract from the clear evidence that she deeply loves them," and court could not comment on other interaction due to fact that children had been separated from mother for 17 months. In re Ridenour (Ohio App. 11 Dist., Lake, 04-16-2004) No. 2003-L-146, No. 2003-L-147, No. 2003-L-148, 2004-Ohio-1958, 2004 WL 834579, Unreported. Infants ⇐ 210

Record supported magistrate's conclusion that dependent children's great aunt and great grandmother were not suitable custodians for children, for purpose of proceeding in which county children's services board filed motion for permanent custody; aunt was only interested in custody of one child, great grandmother was only interested in custody of same child, and mother alleged that great grandmother sexually abused that child. In re Paris (Ohio App. 11 Dist., Ashtabula, 04-16-2004) No. 2003-A-0133, No. 2003-A-0134, 2004-Ohio-1962, 2004 WL 833594, Unreported. Infants ⇐ 222

Magistrate's determination that children could not be placed with either parent within reasonable time or should not be placed with either parent, and thus, that permanent custody of children should be granted to county children's services board was sufficiently detailed and not against manifest weight of evidence; magistrate indicated that parents' home was filthy, that children were not properly supervised, that children were ill but had not had prescriptions filled, and that parents had not completed case plans. In re Paris (Ohio App. 11 Dist., Ashtabula, 04-16-2004) No. 2003-A-0133, No. 2003-A-0134, 2004-Ohio-1962, 2004 WL 833594, Unreported. Infants ⇐ 178; Infants ⇐ 179; Infants ⇐ 210

Psychologist's testimony did not constitute hearsay, for purpose of proceeding in which county children's services board filed motion for permanent custody of dependent children; although parents alleged psychologist's testimony referred to collateral sources used by psychologist in making her recommendation, psychologist testified that her opinions were based on her interviews of parents and parents' test scores and psychologist stated that she did not rely on collateral sources as basis for her opinion. In re Paris (Ohio App. 11 Dist., Ashtabula, 04-16-2004) No. 2003-A-0133, No. 2003-A-0134, 2004-Ohio-1962, 2004 WL 833594, Unreported. Infants ⇐ 174

Evidence supported trial court's decision terminating mother's parental rights and granting county Department of Job and Family Services permanent custody of children found to be neglected or dependent; mother failed to comply with requirements of approved case plan in that she failed to complete parenting program, failed to attend recommended outpatient substance abuse treatment sessions, and, although she did obtain housing one month prior to hearing, she was unavailable for home call by social service worker, mother moved and did not visit children for several months, and evidence showed that children could not be placed with mother or father within reasonable time, children were together with foster family interested in adopting them, and it was in children's best interest to be provided stable home environment which could only be available through permanent custody. In re Ragland Children (Ohio App. 5 Dist., Stark, 04-12-2004) No. 2004CA004, 2004-Ohio-1872, 2004 WL 772211, Unreported. Infants ⇐ 155; Infants ⇐ 157

Evidence was sufficient to support trial court's conclusion that best interests of child previously adjudicated abused would be served by terminating mother's parental rights, despite foster mother's professed inability to adopt child due to her own age and health problems and child's Downs Syndrome, where child was high-functioning and adoptable, and where foster mother wanted child to remain in her care until adoptive home could be found for him and was willing to assist in child's transition from her home into new home. In re Robinson (Ohio App. 5 Dist., Stark, 04-05-2004) No. 2004-CA-00003, 2004-Ohio-1776, 2004 WL 744880, Unreported. Infants ⇐ 155

Trial court finding that child could not be placed with mother and that the best interests of child would be served by granting permanent custody to county department of job and family services was not against the manifest weight of the evidence; child had been in the department's custody for 18 months, child was two years old and had no developmental, behavioral, or medical problems, child resided in a foster home with a sibling, child's foster parents wanted to adopt her, and evidence established that child was more bonded to her foster mother than to mother. In re Adams (Ohio App. 5 Dist., Stark, 04-06-2004) No. 2003CA00441, 2004-Ohio-1770, 2004 WL 740002, Unreported. Infants ⟜ 155

There was clear and convincing evidence that children could not be placed with one of their parents within reasonable time and that permanent commitment was in best interest of children, to support termination of parental rights; at least one of the children suffered severe abuse from mother's husband, the seriousness of which mother downplayed, mother sought to blame everyone but herself for children being in custody of county Department of Job and Family Services, mother did not accept responsibility for her failure to protect her children, mother exhibited instability and lack of coping skills, and children were doing well in home of foster family, who expressed interested in adopting them. In re Gomer (Ohio App. 3 Dist., Wyandot, 04-05-2004) No. 16-03-19, No. 16-03-20, No. 16-03-21, 2004-Ohio-1723, 2004 WL 722978, Unreported, appeal not allowed 102 Ohio St.3d 1473, 809 N.E.2d 1159, 2004-Ohio-2830. Infants ⟜ 155; Infants ⟜ 156

Father waived any argument on appeal as to psychologist testifying as expert in proceeding to terminate parents' parental rights, since father did not object at trial to psychologist testifying, but stated that he simply wanted witness to be qualified as an expert and for all facts upon which psychologist relied to be admitted into evidence. In re Lauren P. (Ohio App. 6 Dist., Lucas, 03-31-2004) No. L-03-1252, 2004-Ohio-1656, 2004 WL 628659, Unreported. Infants ⟜ 243

Granting county children services permanent custody of dependent and neglected child was not against manifest weight of evidence; although mother regularly visited child, caseworker testified that there was little bond between mother and child and that mother did not take mature approach to parenting, therapist testified that mother was financially and emotionally unstable, mother violated terms of probation, and mother failed to complete case plan. In re V.Y. (Ohio App. 9 Dist., Lorain, 03-31-2004) No. 03CA008404, 2004-Ohio-1606, 2004 WL 625935, Unreported. Infants ⟜ 155

Competent, credible evidence supported finding that granting permanent custody to county department of children's services was in dependent children's best interests; mother had little bond with one child and stated in front of that child that she would choose other child if she could only have one child, there was little interaction between mother and children during visitation, and mother prioritized her relationships over children's needs. In re Yeager (Ohio App. 5 Dist., Fairfield, 03-25-2004) No. 03CA49, No. 03CA52, No. 03CA50, No. 03CA53, 2004-Ohio-1560, 2004 WL 625285, Unreported. Infants ⟜ 155; Infants ⟜ 156

Competent, credible evidence supported finding that granting permanent custody to county department of children's services was in dependent children's best interests; father had problems with alcohol, father's bond with one child had weakened, father did not have bond with other child, and father had dependent personality disorder and, at times, allowed his relationship with mother to take priority over his children. In re Yeager (Ohio App. 5 Dist., Fairfield, 03-25-2004) No. 03CA49, No. 03CA52, No. 03CA50, No. 03CA53, 2004-Ohio-1560, 2004 WL 625285, Unreported. Infants ⟜ 155; Infants ⟜ 158

Evidence was sufficient to establish, in dependency proceeding involving two children, that awarding county department of jobs and family services permanent custody was not in the best interest of the children; there was evidence that mother made enough progress with her case plan such that reunification was a realistic possibility, mother's clinical psychologist testified, that though it was unlikely for mother to adequately parent children within the foreseeable future the presence of a spouse might impact that opinion, mother was married and living with her husband, mother's clinical counselor testified that mother had developed a better sense of how to manage her stress so that she could plan for what her children needed, there was evidence that children retained a positive relationship with mother, mother's husband had steady employment, and mother's husband had substantially complied with his case plan objectives. In re Cutright (Ohio App. 11 Dist., Portage, 03-29-2004) No. 2003-P-0081, 2004-Ohio-1524, 2004 WL 605172, Unreported. Infants ⟜ 155

Awarding permanent custody of mother's children to children's services agency, rather than ordering a planned permanent living arrangement, was not against manifest weight of evidence; there was evidence that interaction between mother and children was abnormal during visits, mother admitted that her relationship with two of the children had deteriorated, children did not want to live with mother, children were in placement for 12 or more months of consecutive 22-month period, trial court found that children could or should not be placed with mother, and mother's husband was convicted of child endangering as to three of the children. In re K.P. (Ohio App. 8 Dist., Cuyahoga, 03-25-2004) No. 82709, 2004-Ohio-1448, 2004 WL 583867, Unreported, as amended nunc pro tunc, stay denied 102 Ohio St.3d 1457, 809 N.E.2d 31, 2004-Ohio-2569, appeal not allowed 102 Ohio St.3d 1473, 809 N.E.2d 1159, 2004-Ohio-2830. Infants ⟜ 226

Trial court did not abuse its discretion, in hearing on motion by county children's services (CCS) seeking permanent custody of child who had previously been adjudicated dependent, by placing child in a planned permanent living arrangement (PPLA) rather than awarding CCS permanent custody; there was evidence that there was no prospective adopting family, that current foster parents had special training in dealing with child's attachment disorder and that removal of child from foster home could result in child having feelings of rejection and abandonment, such evidence supported trial court's finding that an order of permanent custody was not in child's best interest, such evidence also indicated that child would be unable to function in a family-like setting, which was required for a PPLA placement, and a foster home could qualify as "residential care," which was also a requirement for a PPLA placement. In re Priser (Ohio App. 2 Dist., Montgomery, 03-19-2004) No. 19861, 2004-Ohio-1315, 2004 WL 541124, Unreported. Infants ⟜ 226

Clear and convincing evidence supported finding that granting permanent custody of children to county department of job and family services was in the best interests of the children; it took parents nearly two years to begin individual counseling, even though it was ordered in the original caseplan, neither child expressed a desire to reside with parents, and father admitted he could not handle the children and that the children were doing better now than they ever had before. In re Bradley John B. (Ohio App. 6 Dist., Huron, 03-19-2004) No. H-03-037, No. H-03-041, 2004-Ohio-1328, 2004 WL 541028, Unreported. Infants ⟜ 155

Even if trial court improperly admitted witness testimony in termination of parental rights proceedings, that county children services board had received complaints about mother, such error was harmless; magistrate did not rely on complaints in reaching decision to terminate parental rights, and other sufficient evidence supported magistrate's decision. In re Joiner (Ohio App. 11 Dist., Ashtabula, 03-12-2004) No. 2003-A-0110, 2004-Ohio-1158, 2004 WL 473260, Unreported, appeal not allowed 102 Ohio St.3d 1425, 807 N.E.2d 368, 2004-Ohio-2003. Infants ⟜ 253

Witness testimony in termination of parental rights proceedings, that county children services board had received complaints about mother, did not constitute inadmissible hearsay, given that testimony was not offered to prove truth of the complaints, but offered to prove that agency had received complaints; witness gave general examples of typical complaints he received, but did not testify regarding the nature of the complaints he received about mother. In re Joiner (Ohio App. 11 Dist., Ashtabula, 03-12-2004) No. 2003-A-0110, 2004-Ohio-1158, 2004 WL 473260, Unreported, appeal not allowed 102 Ohio St.3d 1425, 807 N.E.2d 368, 2004-Ohio-2003. Infants ⟜ 174

Any error in trial court's admission of county children services board's referral report in termination of parental rights proceedings under business records exception to hearsay rule was harmless, where concerns raised in report were testified to by other witnesses. In re Joiner (Ohio App. 11 Dist., Ashtabula, 03-12-2004) No. 2003-A-0110, 2004-Ohio-1158, 2004 WL 473260, Unreported, appeal not allowed 102 Ohio St.3d 1425, 807 N.E.2d 368, 2004-Ohio-2003. Infants ⟜ 253

County children services board's referral report was admissible in termination of parental rights proceedings under business records exception to hearsay rule; witness testified regarding the procedure of creating the report and that the report was kept in the normal course of business, and it was the agency's regular practice to make such a report. In re Joiner (Ohio App. 11 Dist., Ashtabula, 03-12-2004) No. 2003-A-0110, 2004-Ohio-1158, 2004 WL 473260, Unreported, appeal not allowed 102 Ohio St.3d 1425, 807 N.E.2d 368, 2004-Ohio-2003. Infants ⟜ 173.1

Competent, credible evidence supported trial court's finding that awarding permanent custody of neglected child to department of job and family services was in child's best interest; child had limited interaction with father due to father's imprisonment and child was bonded to foster parents, who also cared for child's siblings. In re Wright (Ohio App. 5 Dist., Stark, 03-08-2004) No. 2003CA00347, 2004-Ohio-1094, 2004 WL 434036, Unreported. Infants ⟜ 155

Evidence supported trial court finding that child's need for legally secure placement could not be achieved without granting permanent custody of child to children services; no relative sought custody of child during the pendency of the case, and maternal grandmother's failing health prevented her from assisting mother with the care of child. In re Boring Myers (Ohio App. 4 Dist., Athens, 03-04-2004) No. 03CA333, 2004-Ohio-1065, 2004 WL 432228, Unreported. Infants ⟜ 155

Evidence supported trial court finding, in support of its "reasonable efforts" finding, that mother failed to clean her home to a degree required for in-home visits with child, in child dependency proceeding; caseworker testified that children services assisted mother twice to help mother get her home sanitary, that they helped mother clear paths from room to room, that they filled a dumpster with debris, that the cleaning days made only minimal progress towards making the home safe for child, and that mother refused to allow children services to inspect her home. In re Boring Myers (Ohio App. 4 Dist., Athens, 03-04-2004) No. 03CA333, 2004-Ohio-1065, 2004 WL 432228, Unreported. Infants ⚖ 178

Clear and convincing evidence supported finding that mother was diagnosed with schizotypal personality disorder marked by paranoia and psychosis, in child dependency case; psychologist testified that she performed a psychological evaluation of mother, that she diagnosed mother with schizotypal personality, which is a long-standing personality disorder characterized by difficulties in thinking and eccentricities of behavior, and that mother indicated she could not think clearly when she was with child. In re Boring Myers (Ohio App. 4 Dist., Athens, 03-04-2004) No. 03CA333, 2004-Ohio-1065, 2004 WL 432228, Unreported. Infants ⚖ 181

Evidence failed to establish that it was in the best interest of the children to grant county children services permanent custody; father underwent substance abuse counseling, was employed, and had modest housing for himself and the children, the children expressed love for father, and the trial court determined that father deserved a chance to have his own caseplan, since the previous caseplan was designed for mother and father and the parents had divorced, and chance to see if he could reunify with his children. In re Cunningham (Ohio App. 4 Dist., Athens, 02-17-2004) No. 03CA26, 2004-Ohio-787, 2004 WL 323339, Unreported. Infants ⚖ 155

Evidence supported finding that granting permanent custody of three children to county children services was in the best interests of the children; mother's mental disability prevented her from being able to address the developmental delays of the children or appropriately interact with the children, guardian ad litem recommended granting permanent custody to children services, children thrived while in foster care, and mother was unable to retain information learned regarding how to maintain a safe home and how to address the developmental delays of the children. In re Curry (Ohio App. 4 Dist., Washington, 02-11-2004) No. 03CA51, 2004-Ohio-750, 2004 WL 307476, Unreported. Infants ⚖ 158

Evidence supported finding that granting permanent custody of children to the county department of children and family services was in the best interests of the children; the children had not seen father since their removal and they did not request to see him, father physically and emotionally abused the children, the behavior of the children had improved since their removal from the home, social worker testified that father failed to benefit from services, and father continued to believe that the actions of the children caused their removal. In re D.B. (Ohio App. 8 Dist., Cuyahoga, 02-12-2004) No. 82450, 2004-Ohio-625, 2004 WL 253468, Unreported, as amended nunc pro tunc, appeal not allowed 102 Ohio St.3d 1449, 808 N.E.2d 399, 2004-Ohio-2263. Infants ⚖ 155; Infants ⚖ 156

Trial court properly found, in proceedings for termination of father's parental rights, that father had been repeatedly incarcerated, where father's incarceration for driving under suspension and drug possession and his subsequent prison sentence for community control violation were separate incarcerations, and father admitted to at least two periods of incarceration. In re Myers (Ohio App. 3 Dist., Seneca, 02-09-2004) No. 13-03-61, No. 13-03-65, No. 13-03-64, No. 13-03-63, No. 13-03-62, 2004-Ohio-539, 2004 WL 231796, Unreported. Infants ⚖ 157; Infants ⚖ 180

Evidence that children had been in temporary custody of agency for over one year at time of termination hearing, that father had failed to follow his case plans, and that father had shown lack of commitment to children was sufficient to support termination of father's parental rights. In re Myers (Ohio App. 3 Dist., Seneca, 02-09-2004) No. 13-03-61, No. 13-03-65, No. 13-03-64, No. 13-03-63, No. 13-03-62, 2004-Ohio-539, 2004 WL 231796, Unreported. Infants ⚖ 155

Evidence that father had failed to attempt to communicate with his children for more than a year prior to termination hearing was sufficient to support trial court's finding that father had demonstrated lack of commitment to children. In re Myers (Ohio App. 3 Dist., Seneca, 02-09-2004) No. 13-03-61, No. 13-03-65, No. 13-03-64, No. 13-03-63, No. 13-03-62, 2004-Ohio-539, 2004 WL 231796, Unreported. Infants ⚖ 180

Trial court did not abuse its discretion, in proceeding for termination of father's parental rights, in finding that for more than two years father had failed to remedy circumstances causing children's removal from the home, even though he was given numerous opportunities to do so; father failed to seek treatment for his chemical dependency or to complete parenting and anger management classes called for in his case plans, and only enrolled in anger management class and self-esteem class at prison three weeks prior to termination hearing. In re Myers (Ohio App. 3 Dist., Seneca, 02-09-2004) No. 13-03-61, No. 13-03-65, No. 13-03-64, No. 13-03-63, No. 13-03-62, 2004-Ohio-539, 2004 WL 231796, Unreported. Infants ⚖ 155

Passage of more than one year between children's most recent removal from parental home and agency's filing of motion for permanent custody, without more, was sufficient to support termination of father's parental rights. In re Myers (Ohio App. 3 Dist., Seneca, 02-09-2004) No. 13-03-61, No. 13-03-65, No. 13-03-64, No. 13-03-63, No. 13-03-62, 2004-Ohio-539, 2004 WL 231796, Unreported. Infants ⚖ 155

Clear and convincing evidence supported finding that child could not be placed with either parent within reasonable time, despite trial court's error in finding that child had been in the temporary custody of county Department of Job and Family Services: Children's Protective Services Unit (CPSU) for 12 or more months of consecutive 22 month period; prior involuntary termination of parents' parental rights over child's siblings supported finding that child could not be placed with either parent within reasonable time. In re Jackson (Ohio App. 3 Dist., Hancock, 02-09-2004) No. 5-03-25, 2004-Ohio-542, 2004 WL 231513, Unreported. Infants ⚖ 155

There was sufficient evidence that it was in child's best interests to be placed in permanent custody of county Department of Job and Family Services: Children's Protective Services Unit (CPSU), and that child could not be placed with either parent within reasonable time, to support award of permanent custody to CPSU; child had been in temporary custody of CPSU since a few days after birth, there was testimony regarding child's immediate need for permanent placement and inability of her parents to provide her with adequate living environment, and parents previously had their parental rights of child's siblings involuntarily terminated. In re Jackson (Ohio App. 3 Dist., Hancock, 02-09-2004) No. 5-03-25, 2004-Ohio-542, 2004 WL 231513, Unreported. Infants ⚖ 155

Child's best interests warranted termination of father's parental rights and placement of child in permanent custody of county children services; there was no specific evidence of continuing relationship between child and other family members, child had been in foster care for one year by time of permanent custody hearing, father had relapsed into drug use during period when he was responsible for child, he had lost his job, became homeless, and was convicted of offense of unlawful sexual conduct with minor, and child's mother had no contact with child and her whereabouts were unknown. In re R. K. (Ohio App. 9 Dist., Lorain, 02-04-2004) No. 03CA008360, 2004-Ohio-439, 2004 WL 200002, Unreported. Infants ⚖ 155

Evidence in parental rights termination proceeding failed to support finding that child could not be placed with mother within reasonable time or should not be placed with her; although mother may not have made good choices in such matters as dropping out of high school, quitting job, and failing to keep appointments with service providers, she was appropriate, affectionate, and loving to child, she was employed at time of proceeding, she had enrolled in GED program at community college, and her father testified that he was able to provide home for mother and child if necessary. In re M. W. (Ohio App. 9 Dist., Lorain, 02-04-2004) No. 03CA008342, 2004-Ohio-438, 2004 WL 199962, Unreported. Infants ⚖ 155

Evidence supported finding that child could not be placed with mother within a reasonable time, in support of order granting permanent custody of child to county children's services; mother left for France while child was in foster care and did not provide adequate emergency contacts, child's psychological and emotional problems would require years of treatment, mother was unwilling to work with social service agencies or follow through with recommendations from the guardian ad litem, and mother intended to reunite child with child's older brother, even though child's brother physically abused her and there was an allegation that he had sexually abused her. In re Nibert (Ohio App. 4 Dist., Gallia, 01-22-2004) No. 03CA19, 2004-Ohio-429, 2004 WL 193862, Unreported. Infants ⚖ 155

Trial court's judgment granting permanent custody of child to Department of Job and Family Services was supported by clear and convincing evidence; child was born while mother was incarcerated, mother was unwilling or unable to overcome her drug addiction and, consequently, was unable to stay out of jail for any length of time, mother had no contact with child in spite of fact that she was afforded visitation rights, and child had a strong bond with his foster family and his sister who was also in the same foster home. In re King (Ohio App. 11 Dist., Lake, 01-27-2004) No. 2003-L-101, 2004-Ohio-386, 2004 WL 187150, Unreported, appeal not allowed 101 Ohio St.3d 1491, 805 N.E.2d 541, 2004-Ohio-1293. Infants ⚖ 155; Infants ⚖ 157

Evidence was sufficient to support finding that placing child with county children services agency was in child's best interests, thus supporting grant of permanent custody to agency; there was evidence child had been with the same foster parents for well over a year, that they had bonded, and that foster parents wished to adopt child, child's guardian ad litem recommended to the court that permanent custody be granted to agency, and there was evidence that mother had not satisfied case plan requirements and could not be reunited with child within a reasonable time. In re Nelson (Ohio App. 2 Dist., Montgomery, 01-23-2004) No. 19991, 2004-Ohio-268, 2004 WL 103021, Unreported. Infants ⇐ 155

Evidence was sufficient to support finding that mother's relative was not a suitable legal guardian for child who was in temporary custody of county children services agency, thus supporting grant of permanent custody to agency, although relative was licensed day care worker and had raised four children of her own; relative twice informed social worker that she would be unable to take child, social worker testified that relative had no relationship with daughter, and social worker could not verify relative's income level or housing. In re Nelson (Ohio App. 2 Dist., Montgomery, 01-23-2004) No. 19991, 2004-Ohio-268, 2004 WL 103021, Unreported. Infants ⇐ 155

Evidence was sufficient to support finding that placement with mother's great-aunt was not in best interests of child who was in temporary custody of county children services agency, thus supporting grant of permanent custody to agency, although great-aunt had raised two children, had foster care license, and had taken many foster children into her care; there was evidence great-aunt did not visit with child more than 15 minutes per week, despite permitted two hours of visitation, and did not increase visitation once she quit second job, there was evidence child was burned while in great-aunt's care, and there was evidence great-aunt had not helped mother meet case plan goals as required by case plan. In re Nelson (Ohio App. 2 Dist., Montgomery, 01-23-2004) No. 19991, 2004-Ohio-268, 2004 WL 103021, Unreported. Infants ⇐ 155

Evidence was sufficient to support finding that child who was in temporary custody of county children services agency could not be placed with mother in a reasonable time, thus supporting grant of permanent custody to agency; doctor testified he did not believe mother could independently parent child, there was substantial evidence mother was given ample opportunity to complete case plan yet failed to do so, and there was evidence that mother lacked necessary parenting skills and had not made reasonable effort to obtain necessary skills. In re Nelson (Ohio App. 2 Dist., Montgomery, 01-23-2004) No. 19991, 2004-Ohio-268, 2004 WL 103021, Unreported. Infants ⇐ 181

Evidence supported trial court finding that child could not or should not be placed with father within a reasonable period of time, in support of termination of father's parental rights; father failed to participate in any reunification services, he allowed his child support obligation to go into arrears and at one time owed over $1,000.00 on his $50.00 per month support obligation, his visits with child were sporadic, and he maintained throughout the hearing that he did not want custody of child and that he only wanted to prevent his parental rights from being terminated. In re Kierra D. (Ohio App. 6 Dist., Lucas, 01-22-2004) No. L-03-1164, 2004-Ohio-277, 2004 WL 102939, Unreported. Infants ⇐ 155; Infants ⇐ 157

Evidence supported juvenile court's determination that child could not be placed with mother within a reasonable time, thus supporting termination of parental rights and award of permanent custody of child to county department of family services; mother was a minor who showed lack of initiative and motivation in learning parenting skills and in actively caring for her child, mother required assistance from adults in caring for child and was not capable of parenting on her own, and maternal grandmother was unable to provide family support mother would require to appropriately parent and care for child. In re Crystal S. (Ohio App. 6 Dist., Sandusky, 01-14-2004) No. S-03-001, 2004-Ohio-219, 2004 WL 89190, Unreported. Infants ⇐ 155

Evidence supported finding that child could not or should not be placed with mother within a reasonable period of time, for purposes of permanent custody determination in child dependency proceeding; mother failed to attend substance abuse treatment, provide urine samples for drug testing, attend parenting classes, maintain employment, or find suitable housing, as required by her caseplan, mother was incarcerated in another state on drug charges, prior to her incarceration mother's contact with child was sporadic, and physician recommended that mother undergo a year of psychotherapy and psychiatric consult to help stabilize her. In re Lisbon (Ohio App. 5 Dist., Stark, 01-12-2004) No. 2003CA00318, 2004-Ohio-126, 2004 WL 67256, Unreported. Infants ⇐ 155

Mother was not prejudiced by guardian ad litem's failure to file report with court, in proceeding to grant permanent custody of child to county Department of Children and Family Services (CCDCFS); record showed guardian ad litem testified at hearing and recommended permanent custody be granted to CCDCFS, and there was ample evidence to support ruling without guardian ad litem's written recommendation. In re R.C. (Ohio App. 8 Dist., Cuyahoga, 12-23-2003) No. 82453, 2003-Ohio-7062, 2003 WL 23009947, Unreported. Infants ⇐ 205

Even if any alleged hearsay, regarding sexual abuse of children by older brother, in permanent custody hearing, were eliminated, trial court did not base its determination that county should have permanent custody of children on finding, and sufficient evidence supported determination; court also cited children's fear of their mother, her failure to recognize their special needs, her tardiness in attending hearing, and her failure to attend to their medical needs. In re M.H. (Ohio App. 8 Dist., Cuyahoga, 12-24-2003) No. 81893, 2003-Ohio-7053, 2003 WL 23009016, Unreported. Infants ⇐ 222

Clear and convincing evidence supported finding that children could not be reunited with their mother in reasonable period of time; evidence indicated that mother failed to cooperate in family counseling, which county required for reunification, mother refused to consider possibility that children were telling truth about their teenage brother's abusing them, because children were living in fear of sexual assault, mother did not provided adequate permanent home and demonstrated that she was unwilling to prevent further abuse, and mother failed to recognize children's special needs. In re M.H. (Ohio App. 8 Dist., Cuyahoga, 12-24-2003) No. 81893, 2003-Ohio-7053, 2003 WL 23009016, Unreported. Infants ⇐ 222

Overwhelming evidence supported finding that granting permanent custody of children to county was in best interest of children; evidence showed children had positive relationship with their foster mother and were afraid of their mother and teenage brother, they told guardian ad litem that they wished to stay in foster home, they were in need of stable environment where their special needs would be addressed and had lived in foster home for over two years, they had never learned to brush their teeth, their vaccinations were not up to dad, and mother failed to recognize or acknowledge their need for medication. In re M.H. (Ohio App. 8 Dist., Cuyahoga, 12-24-2003) No. 81893, 2003-Ohio-7053, 2003 WL 23009016, Unreported. Infants ⇐ 222

Evidence supported trial court finding that mother's children could not be reunited with her in the near future and that granting permanent custody of the children to the county department of children and family services was in the best interests of the children; mother failed to benefit from parenting programs, she smoked in front of the twins even though she knew that they had respiratory problems, she spent money on herself and her boyfriend even though the twins did not have suitable car seats or diapers, she failed to keep appointments or take medication designed to address her mental illness, and experts testified that mother suffered from severe depression with psychotic features. In re C.H. (Ohio App. 8 Dist., Cuyahoga, 12-18-2003) No. 82258, No. 82852, 2003-Ohio-6854, 2003 WL 22966248, Unreported. Infants ⇐ 156; Infants ⇐ 158

Evidence supported trial court finding that granting permanent custody of child to county department of children and family services was in child's best interests, in child dependency proceeding; child had been in the department's temporary custody for over three years, expert testified that child's primary bond was with her foster family, child stated that she did not want to visit mother and that she wanted to stay with her foster family, mother failed to take her medications, and mother failed to comply with the requirements of her caseplan. In re C.H. (Ohio App. 8 Dist., Cuyahoga, 12-18-2003) No. 82258, No. 82852, 2003-Ohio-6854, 2003 WL 22966248, Unreported. Infants ⇐ 155; Infants ⇐ 158

Evidence supported trial court's determination that it was in child's best interest to terminate mother's parental rights, even though mother had made some progress; at a certain point mother ceased her efforts to comply with case plan, mother ceased meeting with her counselor and did not maintain scheduled home visits with her caseworkers, mother suffered from alcohol dependency, mother had not yet sought assistance with anger management, and mother did not contact income maintenance worker, failed to secure consistent employment, and did not take steps to reinstate her driver's license. In re Salsgiver (Ohio App. 11 Dist., Geauga, 11-26-2003) No. 2003-G-2517, 2003-Ohio-6412, 2003 WL 22844229, Unreported. Infants ⇐ 155

Findings of fact and conclusions of law supported decision to grant permanent custody to agency and terminate father's parental rights; findings indicated father failed to remedy conditions which led to removal of children from his custody, that his residence was insufficient to house children, and that children were developing strong relationships with former foster family which was being considered as adoptive placement, and conclusions indicated that agency had made significant attempts to prevent children's removal from home, and that an award of permanent custody would serve children's best interests. In re Kincer (Ohio App. 5 Dist., Licking, 11-24-2003) No. 03-CA-43, 2003-Ohio-6356, 2003 WL 22828046, Unreported. Infants ⇐ 155

Evidence in child protection proceeding was sufficient to support trial court's finding that award of permanent custody of children to paternal grandparents was in children's best interests; children had been in agency's temporary custody for approximately one and one-half years, paternal grandparents were interested in adopting both children, children were doing well under their care and were bonded with each other and with grandparents, grandparents maintained safe, secure and loving home for both children, and mother frequently did not visit with children when given opportunity to do so. In re Hull (Ohio App. 5 Dist., Stark, 11-17-2003) No. 2003CA00241, 2003-Ohio-6352, 2003 WL 22827944, Unreported. Infants ⇐ 222

Evidence in child protection proceeding was sufficient to support trial court's finding that children could not or should not be placed with mother within reasonable time, as required to support termination of mother's parental rights; mother failed to attend individual and joint counseling as required by her case plan, failed to complete substance abuse programs required by her case plan and as condition of her parole, and had repeated incarcerations that prevented her from being able to care for children. In re Hull (Ohio App. 5 Dist., Stark, 11-17-2003) No. 2003CA00241, 2003-Ohio-6352, 2003 WL 22827944, Unreported. Infants ⇐ 155; Infants ⇐ 157

Evidence in child protection proceeding that children had been in temporary custody of agency for 12 or more of past 22 months was sufficient, without more, to support termination of mother's parental rights and grant of permanent custody to paternal grandparents. In re Hull (Ohio App. 5 Dist., Stark, 11-17-2003) No. 2003CA00241, 2003-Ohio-6352, 2003 WL 22827944, Unreported. Infants ⇐ 155

Evidence supported finding that awarding county department of children and family services permanent custody of dependent child was in child's best interests; record indicated that guardian ad litem witnessed little affection between child and mother, no affirmative expression was given by child that child wanted to return to mother, and parenting program coordinator testified that child had "absolutely completely" bonded with her foster family. In re R.K. (Ohio App. 8 Dist., Cuyahoga, 11-26-2003) No. 82374, 2003-Ohio-6333, 2003 WL 22804937, Unreported. Infants ⇐ 155

Clear and convincing evidence existed that dependent child had been in temporary custody of county department of children and family services for twelve or more months of a consecutive twenty-two month period, as required for child to be placed in permanent custody of department; record indicated that child had been removed from mother's home on particular date and remained in custody of department for over two years. In re R.K. (Ohio App. 8 Dist., Cuyahoga, 11-26-2003) No. 82374, 2003-Ohio-6333, 2003 WL 22804937, Unreported. Infants ⇐ 178

Mother's compliance with reunification plan, without more, did not entitle her to regain custody of her dependent children. In re West (Ohio App. 4 Dist., Athens, 11-19-2003) No. 03CA20, 2003-Ohio-6299, 2003 WL 22769711, Unreported. Infants ⇐ 231

Evidence supported finding that termination of mother's parental rights was in best interests of her dependent children; mother introduced a string of men into children's lives, including a man who beat her in front of children and two men who had been convicted of sexually molesting children, mother had dependent personality disorder and cognitive limitations which created ongoing difficulties in putting her children's needs before her own, meeting children's developmental needs, and creating a stable environment, children wished for adoption rather than reunification with mother, children had diagnosed mental, emotional, and medical problems that required special care, and children had been in custody of children services agency for more than 12 of a consecutive 22-month period. In re West (Ohio App. 4 Dist., Athens, 11-19-2003) No. 03CA20, 2003-Ohio-6299, 2003 WL 22769711, Unreported. Infants ⇐ 155; Infants ⇐ 156; Infants ⇐ 158

Clear and convincing evidence supported conclusion that award of permanent custody of children to Department of Job and Family Services was in children's best interests, in child dependency proceeding; at time of hearing, mother was attempting to live in apartment, but was not residing there, she had lived in a shelter several times, but, during her most recent stay in shelter, she had been asked to leave because she would not comply with its rules, she had been unable to hold a stable job, and, at time of hearing, she was sharing hotel room with former drug addict. In re Tiffany Y. (Ohio App. 6 Dist., Sandusky, 11-12-2003) No. S-03-004, 2003-Ohio-6203, 2003 WL 22740848, Unreported. Infants ⇐ 222

Evidence supported finding that permanent custody with family services agency was in child's best interests; court-appointed special advocate stated that parents failed to follow through with case plan services and had done little to ensure return of child, child was doing well in foster placement, and father failed to complete anger management class required by his case plan. In re Julia G. (Ohio App. 6 Dist., Sandusky, 11-12-2003) No. S-02-031, No. S-02-034, No. S-03-005, No. S-02-033, 2003-Ohio-6196, 2003 WL 22736473, Unreported. Infants ⇐ 155

Trial court, in granting motion for permanent custody with family services agency, properly considered children's best interests with regard to children's need for a legally secure permanent placement; trial court considered voluminous evidence as to children's relationships with parents and, in particular, parents' demonstrated abilities to care for the children over the two years that the agency was involved. In re Julia G. (Ohio App. 6 Dist., Sandusky, 11-12-2003) No. S-02-031, No. S-02-034, No. S-03-005, No. S-02-033, 2003-Ohio-6196, 2003 WL 22736473, Unreported. Infants ⇐ 155

Clear and convincing evidence supported trial court decision to grant permanent custody of children to county children services, based on finding that the children could not be placed with mother within a reasonable time; mother failed to maintain a drug-free lifestyle or provide a stable home for the children, the court determined that mother's chemical dependency was severe and prevented her from providing an adequate permanent home for the children within one year of the permanent custody hearing, and while incarcerated mother chose to communicate with her husband but not with the children. In re Anderson (Ohio App. 4 Dist., Athens, 11-12-2003) No. 03CA17, 2003-Ohio-6154, 2003 WL 22718864, Unreported. Infants ⇐ 155; Infants ⇐ 157

Competent evidence supported trial court decision to grant legal custody of child to maternal great-grandmother, rather than child's prior legal custodian; legal custodian never had a psychiatric evaluation, she never finished a drug or alcohol treatment plan, she failed to attend an alcohol support group until nine months after child was removed from her care, child interacted well with maternal grandmother and the four other children in her home, and grandmother had a good relationship with custodian and planned to maintain a relationship between child and custodian. In re Rowe (Ohio App. 10 Dist., Franklin, 11-13-2003) No. 03AP-111, 2003-Ohio-6062, 2003 WL 22682063, Unreported. Infants ⇐ 222

Evidence was insufficient to support finding that mother failed to remedy the conditions that caused child to be placed outside of the home, in termination of parental rights proceeding; child was removed after mother was convicted of child endangerment involving her sister's child, there was no evidence that mother intended to watch her sister's children again, mother complied with her caseplan by completing a drug and alcohol assessment, attending individual counseling, completing a parenting court, completing a psychological evaluation, and attending visitation, and the maternal grandmother and step-grandfather were willing to assist mother in raising child. In re Jordan (Ohio App. 2 Dist., Clark, 11-14-2003) No. 02CA0092, 2003-Ohio-6071, 2003 WL 22681603, Unreported. Infants ⇐ 156

Evidence was insufficient to support trial court finding that mother's mental retardation was so severe that mother was unable to provide child with an adequate home within one year, in termination of parental rights proceeding; there was no evidence that mother's mental deficiencies were so severe that she could not provide a home for child within one year, mother's psychologist recommended reunification as long as certain treatment conditions were satisfied, mother had previously lived on her own and paid her own bills, and child's counselor did not recommend termination of parental rights. In re Jordan (Ohio App. 2 Dist., Clark, 11-14-2003) No. 02CA0092, 2003-Ohio-6071, 2003 WL 22681603, Unreported. Infants ⇐ 181

Determination that minor child's best interests would be served by granting permanent custody to Department of Jobs and Family Services was not against manifest weight of evidence; although child and mother were bonded to some degree, testimony showed that bond between child and foster mother was greater, caseworker testified that child needed a stable, loving environment which mother was not able to provide, and guardian ad litem recommended that permanent custody be granted to Department of Jobs and Family Services. In re Wilcoxen (Ohio App. 5 Dist., Stark, 11-03-2003) No. 2003-CA-00221, 2003-Ohio-6046, 2003 WL 22674661, Unreported. Infants ⇐ 178

Clear and convincing evidence supported trial court decision to grant permanent custody of child to county children services board; child had been in the custody of the board for more than 12 of the last consecutive 22 months, mother sporadically visited child, she refused to participate in court-ordered services, she lacked stable housing or stable employment, her parental rights had previously been terminated to child's half-sibling, child was very bonded to her foster family and was extremely bonded to her half-sibling, who resided in the same foster home, and foster family was interested in adopting child. In re Ebenschweiger (Ohio App. 12 Dist., Butler, 11-10-2003) No. CA2003-04-080, 2003-Ohio-5990, 2003 WL 22533124, Unreported. Infants ⇐ 155; Infants ⇐ 157

Evidence supported finding that parents failed to substantially remedy the condition that caused child's removal, in child dependency proceeding; father attended six hours of parenting classes and mother attended 16 hours of parenting classes out of the 46 hours of parenting classes that were offered, parent educator and caseworker both testified that there was no increase in the quality of parents' visits with child, and parents cleaned their house but also allowed a sexual predator and a man they met through a "dirty chat room" to reside in the residence. In re Thomas (Ohio App. 3 Dist., Hancock, 11-03-2003) No. 5-03-08, 2003-Ohio-5885, 2003 WL 22474843, Unreported. Infants ⇔ 155; Infants ⇔ 156

Clear and convincing evidence supported trial court finding that it was in child's best interest to grant permanent custody to county children services board; father failed to complete a drug evaluation and individual counseling required by his caseplan, father moved numerous times after child's birth and many of the places where father lived were unsafe for child, father had ten jobs in two years and his longest term of employment was for three or four months, father missed many visitation meetings with child, and child had severe developmental delays and a behavior disorder. In re Baby Girl Elliott (Ohio App. 12 Dist., Butler, 11-03-2003) No. CA2003-04-096, 2003-Ohio-5876, 2003 WL 22470168, Unreported. Infants ⇔ 155

Caseworker's testimony that father often hit children with a belt in order to control their behavior, that father told caseworker that he felt it was appropriate for him to use a belt and he intended to continue to do so, that children had bonded with their foster parents, and guardian ad litem's recommendation that County Children Services be granted permanent custody was credible evidence supporting determination that children's best interests were served by placing them in permanent custody of County Children Services. In re Damron (Ohio App. 10 Dist., Franklin, 10-30-2003) No. 03AP-419, 2003-Ohio-5810, 2003 WL 22455693, Unreported. Infants ⇔ 179

Evidence was sufficient to support finding that granting county job and family services permanent custody of dependent children was in childrens' best interests; testimony was given that children had adverse reactions when seeing mother in public and that a potential adoptive home was being pursued for the children, guardian ad litem recommended that permanent custody be granted to county job and family services, evidence indicated that childrens' behavior had improved substantially since they have been in foster care and that the children had not been negatively affected by a lack of contact with their mother. In re Blunt (Ohio App. 5 Dist., Tuscarawas, 10-17-2003) No. 2003AP 07 0053, No. 2003AP 07 0055, 2003-Ohio-5646, 2003 WL 22413723, Unreported. Infants ⇔ 178; Infants ⇔ 208

Evidence supported finding in permanent custody hearing that dependent children could not or should not be placed with either mother or father within a reasonable time; testimony was adduced that mother had failed to secure stable housing and that she continued to have contact with her husband, who had a history of domestic violence, evidence indicated that mother had difficulty providing appropriate parenting to her children due to her mental health problems, and evidence indicated that father was unable to address his child's special needs and failed to become involved in his child's counseling. In re Blunt (Ohio App. 5 Dist., Tuscarawas, 10-17-2003) No. 2003AP 07 0053, No. 2003AP 07 0055, 2003-Ohio-5646, 2003 WL 22413723, Unreported. Infants ⇔ 178; Infants ⇔ 179; Infants ⇔ 181

Child placing agency failed to establish by clear and convincing evidence that granting agency permanent custody of dependent child was in child's best interests; visitation supervisor reported that visits between child and father had progressed well and that child appeared more comfortable with father, father had completed many parenting classes and had been eager to improve his parenting skills, shortcomings in father's ability to parent arose more from the fact that he had not had child with him for any extended periods, and such was not due to father's fault but rather agency's reluctance to reunify father and child, and father had achieved a plan that allowed him to provide a permanent and secure placement for his son. In re J. H. (Ohio App. 9 Dist., Summit, 10-22-2003) No. 21575, 2003-Ohio-5611, 2003 WL 22399693, Unreported. Infants ⇔ 155

Trial court order awarding wife the marital residence was not an abuse of discretion, in divorce proceeding; wife was allowed to purchase the marital home if she paid husband his share of the marital equity, wife owned the house before the parties were married, the children were familiar with the residence, and wife was named residential parent of the children. Stan v. Stan (Ohio App. 12 Dist., Preble, 10-20-2003) No. CA2003-01-001, 2003-Ohio-5540, 2003 WL 22382973, Unreported. Divorce ⇔ 252.5(1); Divorce ⇔ 252.5(2)

Property distribution was not an abuse of discretion in divorce proceeding; there was no evidence in record regarding marital items that wife allegedly took from marital residence when parties separated, award of children's play items and appliances to wife was reasonable since she was to be residential parent, record only contained wife's list of property and failed to contain any list from husband, and court equalized property and debt distribution so that wife would have no claim to any of husband's retirement account. Stan v. Stan (Ohio App. 12 Dist., Preble, 10-20-2003) No. CA2003-01-001, 2003-Ohio-5540, 2003 WL 22382973, Unreported. Divorce ⇔ 252.2; Divorce ⇔ 252.3(1); Divorce ⇔ 252.3(4)

Decision to award Department of Job and Family Services permanent custody of mother's children was supported by manifest weight of evidence; contrary to case plan requirements, mother failed to complete recommended counseling, failed to obtain safe and stable housing, failed to obtain employment, failed to address concerns of prior abuse of her daughter, and did not consistently followed through with recommendations of parenting instructors and counselors, and children were appropriately growing, maturing, and developing in foster care. In re Robinson (Ohio App. 2 Dist., Clark, 10-17-2003) No. 2002-CA-83, No. 2002-CA-84, No. 2002-CA-85, 2003-Ohio-5528, 2003 WL 22359657, Unreported. Infants ⇔ 155

Clear and convincing evidence supported trial court order granting permanent custody of children to county children services, in child dependency proceeding; the children had been in the custody of children services for 12 or more months of a consecutive 22 month period, mother failed to participate in a drug treatment plan, develop adequate parenting skills, avoid relationships with violent men, or set up a stable home for the children, and she failed to remedy the conditions that resulted in removal of the children. In re Conn (Ohio App. 10 Dist., Franklin, 10-07-2003) No. 03AP-348, No. 03AP-349, No. 03AP-372, 2003-Ohio-5344, 2003 WL 22290217, Unreported. Infants ⇔ 155

Record contained sufficient evidence that children had been in custody of child services agency for 12 or more months of consecutive 22–month period and that children could not be placed with either parent, to support permanent placement of children with agency; children had been in agency's temporary custody for 17 of the previous 22 months, and parents failed to acknowledge or address readily apparent domestic violence issues. In re Sessoms (Ohio App. 12 Dist., Butler, 10-06-2003) No. CA2002-11-280, 2003-Ohio-5281, 2003 WL 22283495, Unreported. Infants ⇔ 155

Clear and convincing evidence supported trial court finding that granting permanent custody of children to the county children's service board was in the best interest of the children; the children had been under the care of the county for at least 12 of the prior 22 months, mother allowed the children to steal, use alcohol, and observe mother using alcohol, older child did not want to continue to visit mother, older child's behavior improved greatly while he lived with foster family, older child had been removed from mother's custody previously, visits with mother caused both children to regress in their behaviors, and mother previously lost custody to a sibling of the children. In re Large (Ohio App. 4 Dist., Hocking, 09-29-2003) No. 03CA9, No. 03CA10, 2003-Ohio-5275, 2003 WL 22272817, Unreported. Infants ⇔ 155; Infants ⇔ 156

Evidence supported trial court's finding that child could not be placed with either parent, for purposes of order awarding permanent custody to county children services agency; father abandoned child, mother was unwilling to provide an adequate permanent home, testimony indicated that child's clothes were filthy and poorly fitted, that mother repeatedly neglected to take child to counseling appointments, and that child's behavior regressed during time she lived with mother, and mother neglected child. In re Lewis (Ohio App. 4 Dist., Athens, 09-25-2003) No. 03CA12, 2003-Ohio-5262, 2003 WL 22267129, Unreported. Infants ⇔ 156; Infants ⇔ 157; Infants ⇔ 159

Trial court's decision, combined with the transcript of the adjudication and disposition hearings, and the transcript of the trial court's in camera interview with child, formed an adequate basis for the trial court's ruling granting permanent custody of child to county children services agency, and for appellate review, and separate findings of fact were not required, notwithstanding mother's specific request for those findings, where trial court stated in its decision that mother had failed to utilize services and resources made available to her, that mother had failed to change her conduct as a parent, that child's medical, psychological, emotional, and education needs were not met by mother, that her mother demonstrated a lack of commitment, that father had abandoned child, and that mother provided inadequate nutrition to child. In re Lewis (Ohio App. 4 Dist., Athens, 09-25-2003) No. 03CA12, 2003-Ohio-5262, 2003 WL 22267129, Unreported. Infants ⇔ 210

Evidence supported trial court finding that mother failed to substantially comply with the requirements of her caseplan, in child dependency proceeding; mother failed to provide documentation of full-time employment, she admitted that she lied about employment at a previous hearing, she failed to maintain stable and permanent housing and lived in a shelter, an acceptable apartment, and then her mother's residence during the pendency of the case, she missed drug screens, and she missed almost half of her scheduled visits with child. In re James (Ohio App. 10 Dist., Franklin, 09-30-2003) No. 03AP-373, 2003-Ohio-5208, 2003 WL 22232965, Unreported. Infants ⇔ 155

Trial court order terminating mother and father's parental rights to children was not against the manifest weight of the evidence; pediatrician testified that child had various developmental delays, psychiatrist testified that mother had chronic mental health issues and was diagnosed as bipolar mixed with borderline personality disorder, after developmentally delayed child was removed from the care of parents he improved, and caseworker testified that parents failed to follow their caseplan and were inconsistent with their visitation. In re Richardson (Ohio App. 5 Dist., Guernsey, 09-26-2003) No. 03CA16, 2003-Ohio-5164, 2003 WL 22232643, Unreported. Infants ⟳ 178; Infants ⟳ 181

Father failed to prove his allegation that the trial court found, in support of order terminating father's parental rights, that father had previously had his parental rights terminated to a sibling of the children; trial court order specifically stated that mother had previously had her parental rights terminated to a sibling of the children, and order did not support termination of father's parental rights on those grounds. In re Richardson (Ohio App. 5 Dist., Guernsey, 09-26-2003) No. 03CA16, 2003-Ohio-5164, 2003 WL 22232643, Unreported. Infants ⟳ 210

Evidence supported finding in dependency proceeding that awarding permanent custody of two minor children to county children services board was in children's best interest; mother had long history of substance abuse problems that were cause of children's removal, mother had consistently been unable to complete drug treatment programs, there was evidence that children immediately needed legally secure placement, and both children had been in foster care for majority of their lives. In re Mercurio (Ohio App. 12 Dist., Butler, 09-29-2003) No. CA2003-05-109, 2003-Ohio-5108, 2003 WL 22227367, Unreported. Infants ⟳ 155

Evidence that mother missed numerous scheduled appointments with parent educator, had difficulty understanding how her parenting affected her children, and that mother's immaturity made it extremely difficult for her to provide for her children's emotional needs supported finding that daughter could not be placed with her within a reasonable time. In re Estepp (Ohio App. 5 Dist., Fairfield, 09-24-2003) No. 03-CA-11, 2003-Ohio-5084, 2003 WL 22208743, Unreported. Infants ⟳ 155

Evidence that mother did not bond with infant daughter, refused to continue feeding her after she spit up, and failed to grasp importance of bonding with child supported finding that awarding permanent custody of daughter to county children's services board was in child's best interest. In re Estepp (Ohio App. 5 Dist., Fairfield, 09-24-2003) No. 03-CA-11, 2003-Ohio-5084, 2003 WL 22208743, Unreported. Infants ⟳ 155

Trial court's findings that child could not and should not be placed with mother within reasonable time and that it was in best interest of child to grant permanent custody to county department of jobs and family services were not against the manifest weight and sufficiency of the evidence in proceeding to terminate mother's parental rights; evidence indicated that mother refused to comply with the case plan relative to child, mother refused to accept copy of case plan from caseworker, and mother failed to rectify problems that caused removal of her two other children, which included mental health and anger management issues, domestic violence, and her lack of parenting skills. In re Foster (Ohio App. 5 Dist., Stark, 09-22-2003) No. 2003CA0236, 2003-Ohio-5053, 2003 WL 22204489, Unreported. Infants ⟳ 155; Infants ⟳ 158

Evidence was insufficient to support finding that termination of mother's parental rights as to 18-month-old was in child's best interests, and thus, termination was reversible error; county focused almost exclusively on mother's failure to comply with case plan, ignoring other best interests factors, witnesses testified on mother's behalf that she and daughter were bonded and had a great relationship, while county alleged visitation problems in petition, it did not present evidence of problems at hearing, guardian ad litem testified that termination was not in child's best interests and that more visitation should be granted to mother, and county did not present evidence regarding child's need to for legally secure permanent placement. In re C.M. (Ohio App. 9 Dist., Summit, 09-24-2003) No. 21372, 2003-Ohio-5040, 2003 WL 22187268, Unreported. Infants ⟳ 178; Infants ⟳ 252

Clear and convincing evidence supported trial court order terminating mother's parental rights to child; child was in the custody of county department of job and family services for 12 months of a consecutive 22 month period, mother moved out of state and only visited child once in a 225 day period, mother did not make any additional attempt to contact child, mother's parental rights were terminated to a sibling of child, child was bonded to her foster parents and called them "mommy" and "daddy," and psychologist testified that mother suffered from a personality disorder. In re Cornell (Ohio App. 11 Dist., Portage, 09-16-2003) No. 2003-P-0054, 2003-Ohio-5007, 2003 WL 22171435, Unreported. Infants ⟳ 157; Infants ⟳ 158

Clear and convincing evidence supported finding that mother's failure to comply with case plan requirements demonstrated her lack of commitment to her dependent children, and thus, granting of permanent custody of children to county children's services board was in children's best interests;
mother failed to comply with requirement that she obtain and maintain stable housing, mother failed to comply with requirement that she obtain and maintain sufficient employment, and mother was required to attend counseling and managed only to complete one session. In re A.F. (Ohio App. 2 Dist., Miami, 09-19-2003) No. 2003-CA-10, 2003-Ohio-4981, 2003 WL 22149657, Unreported. Infants ⟳ 155

Order granting permanent custody of mother's youngest child to county department of jobs and family services was not against the manifest weight of the evidence; youngest child was injured and required therapy, mother was ordered by the court to attend child's therapy at least once per month, and mother only attended three of child's therapy sessions in approximately two years. In re Hawkins Children (Ohio App. 5 Dist., Stark, 09-15-2003) No. 2003CA00152, 2003-Ohio-4899, 2003 WL 22129533, Unreported. Infants ⟳ 157

The trial court's failure to conduct an in camera interview with the children did not deprive parents of a fair trial, in child dependency proceeding; guardian ad litem report and the testimony from two psychologists adequately represented the wishes of the children. In re Beresh Children (Ohio App. 5 Dist., Stark, 09-15-2003) No. 2003CA00089, 2003-Ohio-4898, 2003 WL 22128799, Unreported, appeal not allowed 100 Ohio St.3d 1510, 799 N.E.2d 187, 2003-Ohio-6161. Infants ⟳ 207

Trial court order granting permanent custody of mother and father's two youngest children to county department of job and family services was not against the manifest weight of the evidence; department had been involved with family numerous times over the past 15 years, daughter's older brother was convicted of sexually abusing her, older brother resided in the family home, children referred to past physical abuse by parents and sexual abuse by all older brothers, psychologist diagnosed son with adjustment disorder and post-traumatic stress disorder, and second psychologist testified that visits with parents impaired the emotional, social, and academic functioning of the children. In re Beresh Children (Ohio App. 5 Dist., Stark, 09-15-2003) No. 2003CA00089, 2003-Ohio-4898, 2003 WL 22128799, Unreported, appeal not allowed 100 Ohio St.3d 1510, 799 N.E.2d 187, 2003-Ohio-6161. Infants ⟳ 156

Clear and convincing evidence supported finding that it was in child's best interests to grant county children services board custody of child; mother relapsed and began abusing drugs, she was unemployed and homeless, she refused to attend counseling or submit to a drug test, child was bonded with his foster family, and child was in need of a secure and stable placement. In re Cornett (Ohio App. 12 Dist., Warren, 09-11-2003) No. CA2003-03-034, 2003-Ohio-4871, 2003 WL 22118857, Unreported. Infants ⟳ 155; Infants ⟳ 156

Clear and convincing evidence supported finding that it was in the best interests of the children to grant permanent custody to county job and family services; mother only attended 30 of 86 visits with the children, during the five month period before the hearing mother did not visit the children, the two and three year old children had resided out of mother's home for 12 months before the permanency hearing occurred, mother admitted that she was out drinking and partying with friends five to seven days per week while her children were removed from her custody, and mother did not work on the anger management, educational, or counseling goals of her case plan. In re J.B. (Ohio App. 9 Dist., Medina, 09-10-2003) No. 03CA0024-M, No. 03CA0025-M, 2003-Ohio-4786, 2003 WL 22093226, Unreported. Infants ⟳ 155; Infants ⟳ 157

Evidence was insufficient to support finding that granting permanent custody of child to the county children services board was in child's best interest, in termination of parental rights proceeding; mother's delay in obtaining services resulted from delay in receiving financial assistance from state agencies to help with the services, mother had been attending sex offender treatment and individual counseling since she obtained financial assistance, she attended alcohol support groups regularly, she was employed, she stayed in regular contact with child, and child informed the court he wanted to live with his mother. In re Bounds (Ohio App. 3 Dist., Allen, 09-08-2003) No. 1-03-11, 2003-Ohio-4733, 2003 WL 22071460, Unreported. Infants ⟳ 155; Infants ⟳ 158

Trial court order terminating mother's parental rights to her three children was not an abuse of discretion; the children were in agency placement for more than 12 of the last 22 consecutive months before the termination hearing, the children had done well in their foster care placement and had shown marked improvement in their self-esteem and social skills, and no relatives were available or approved for possible placement. In re Sarah S. (Ohio App. 6 Dist., Erie, 08-11-2003) No. E-02-052, No. E-02-053, No. E-02-054, 2003-Ohio-4730, 2003 WL 22070505, Unreported. Infants ⟳ 155

Evidence was sufficient to support finding that awarding permanent custody of child to county was in child's best interests; mother suffered from severe and chronic brain damage, mental illness, and alcohol abuse, child suffered from post-traumatic stress disorder, anxiety disorders, attention deficit hyperactivity disorder, and developmental delays, psychologist opined that returning child to mother's care was inappropriate, guardian ad litem recommended county as permanent custodian, child did not want to return to mother, lacked meaningful relationship with mother or any sibling, was in a safe and nurturing foster home environment, and wanted to be adopted by foster family. Campbell v. Richland County Children Services Bd. (Ohio App. 5 Dist., Richland, 08-20-2003) No. 2003CA0059, 2003-Ohio-4535, 2003 WL 22017251, Unreported. Infants ⇔ 155; Infants ⇔ 158

Evidence was sufficient to support finding that mother's mental illness rendered her unable to provide an adequate permanent home for child at present, and, as anticipated, within one year of permanent custody hearing, and conditions leading to removal, to wit, mother's illness and alcohol abuse, remained present and insurmountable, as would support awarding permanent custody of child to county; mother had dementia secondary to brain trauma and severe loss of intelligence, memory, and orientation, she had a history of treatment struggles, impulsivity, and alcohol abuse problems, and both mother's psychiatrist and physician felt that mother was unable to care for child who had special needs. Campbell v. Richland County Children Services Bd. (Ohio App. 5 Dist., Richland, 08-20-2003) No. 2003CA0059, 2003-Ohio-4535, 2003 WL 22017251, Unreported. Infants ⇔ 158

Clear and convincing evidence supported trial court finding that it was in the best interests of the children to grant permanent custody of mother's two children to the county children services board; mother had a history of drug abuse, the children had health concerns, they were bonded with their foster family, and mother had previously received services and had relapsed after she had reunified with the children. In re Marlow (Ohio App. 12 Dist., Butler, 08-25-2003) No. CA2003-03-065, 2003-Ohio-4456, 2003 WL 21998633, Unreported. Infants ⇔ 155

Evidence was insufficient to establish that it was in the best interests of the children to grant legal custody of the children to the county children services board or that parents could not provide a legally secure home for the children; there was a bond between parents and the children, parents interacted appropriately with the children, parents did not drive and their failure to attend some counseling and visitation sessions were due to transportation problems, the board provided little transportation assistance to parents, parents maintained an acceptable home environment, and parents complied with parts of their case plan. In re Knuckles (Ohio App. 12 Dist., Butler, 08-21-2003) No. CA2003-01-004, No. CA2003-01-005, 2003-Ohio-4418, 2003 WL 21991581, Unreported. Infants ⇔ 155

Clear and convincing evidence supported finding that awarding permanent custody of child to county agency thereby terminating mother's parental rights was in child's best interests; mother missed half of scheduled visits with child over four months prior to hearing, child was doing well in foster placement, guardian ad litem recommended custody be awarded to agency, and expressed concern about mother missing drug screens and mental health appointments and child's safety if left in mother's care, mother's residence did not have room for a crib, mother was unable to put child's needs ahead of her own, and child had been in agency's custody from age of eight months up to hearing 14 months later. In re C. P. (Ohio App. 9 Dist., Summit, 08-20-2003) No. 21523, 2003-Ohio-4387, 2003 WL 21976125, Unreported. Infants ⇔ 155; Infants ⇔ 157; Infants ⇔ 208

Mother failed to substantially comply with her case plan, which failure supported awarding permanent custody of her child to county and terminating her parental rights; mother missed nearly half of her mental health counseling sessions, failed to submit to drug screens, missed several visitations with child, and poorly complied with individual and group drug counseling sessions. In re C. P. (Ohio App. 9 Dist., Summit, 08-20-2003) No. 21523, 2003-Ohio-4387, 2003 WL 21976125, Unreported. Infants ⇔ 155

Clear and convincing evidence supported finding that child could not have been placed with mother within a reasonable time or should not have been placed with mother due to mother's chronic and severe mental illness and chemical dependency, as would support awarding permanent custody of child to county agency and terminating mother's rights; mother suffered from hallucinations, delusions, and "acting out" types of personality disorders, she had two recent hospitalizations due to inability to care for herself, lost her housing, missed nearly 50% of her mental health counseling sessions, and had been sporadic with drug counseling and visitation with child. In re C. P. (Ohio App. 9 Dist., Summit, 08-20-2003) No. 21523, 2003-Ohio-4387, 2003 WL 21976125, Unreported. Infants ⇔ 158

Evidence supported court's finding that dependent child could not be reunited with mother within reasonable time, in termination of parental rights proceeding; mother had significant cognitive limitations and dependent personality disorder, she was unable to manage her anger, was socially detached and unable to protect herself, and she could not maintain stable home, as required in her case plan. In re Duvall (Ohio App. 5 Dist., Fairfield, 08-14-2003) No. 03-CA-10, 2003-Ohio-4313, 2003 WL 21949717, Unreported. Infants ⇔ 158

Evidence supported finding that termination of mother's parental rights was in child's best interest; child was in protective custody for at least 12 months in consecutive 22 month period, mother had negative interaction with child during visitation, and child thrived in protective custody after being placed in stable environment. In re Duvall (Ohio App. 5 Dist., Fairfield, 08-14-2003) No. 03-CA-10, 2003-Ohio-4313, 2003 WL 21949717, Unreported. Infants ⇔ 155

Ample competent and credible evidence supported trial court's decision that awarding County Children Services permanent custody of child was in child's best interest, where child had not bonded with parents, child thrived in foster care but regressed when allowed to have extended visits with his parents, and parents failed to demonstrate that they were capable of or willing to provide child with a stable and nurturing home where the child could have flourished. In re Riley (Ohio App. 4 Dist., Washington, 07-25-2003) No. 03CA19, 2003-Ohio-4109, 2003 WL 21783373, Unreported. Infants ⇔ 155

Trial court erred in granting county permanent custody of infant, predicated on mother's past failures with case plans, without affording her time to successfully complete current plan; county gave mother only three months to complete plan, mother had been in residential treatment since birth of child, all of her urine drops had been negative, she was unable to attend parenting classes as required by plan while in treatment, she completed a psychological evaluation as required, and, while psychologist did not recommend permanent custody, he did recommend completion of case plan and counseling for eight months, which was impossible to complete within time allotted by county, mother was excluded from work program while in treatment, but, as required, applied for Section 8 housing and looked into other housing assistance programs, contacted Planned Parenthood regarding birth control options, attended visits with the child pursuant to visitation policy, and her behavior had been appropriate. In re Johns (Ohio App. 5 Dist., Stark, 07-07-2003) No. 2003CA00146, 2003-Ohio-3621, 2003 WL 21540772, Unreported. Infants ⇔ 155

Trial court finding that children could not be placed with mother within a reasonable period of time was not supported by the manifest weight of the evidence, in child dependency proceeding; mother was participating in counseling and her housing was stable, removal of older child from mother's custody had a detrimental effect on child, mother had divorced father and was not involved in a romantic relationship, and mother had been seeing her psychiatrist and her major depression and personality disorder had been stabilized through medication. In re Williams (Ohio App. 11 Dist., Geauga, 07-03-2003) No. 2003-G-2498, No. 2003-G-2499, 2003-Ohio-3550, 2003 WL 21517986, Unreported, stay granted 99 Ohio St.3d 1526, 793 N.E.2d 496, 2003-Ohio-4303, motion to certify allowed 99 Ohio St.3d 1540, 795 N.E.2d 680, 2003-Ohio-4671, appeal not allowed 99 Ohio St.3d 1547, 795 N.E.2d 684, 2003-Ohio-4671, affirmed 101 Ohio St.3d 398, 805 N.E.2d 1110, 2004-Ohio-1500. Infants ⇔ 155; Infants ⇔ 158

Evidence supported trial court's order, awarding permanent custody of children to Children Services Board after parents entered into stipulation of permanent custody with Board, even though parents had second thoughts regarding stipulation; once parties indicated their intentions to enter into stipulation, there was no need for hearing on agency's efforts toward reunification and whether custody should be awarded to Board, parents were informed there would be no guarantee of visitation, and transcript otherwise indicated that parents' interests were adequately served. In re Diane M. (Ohio App. 6 Dist., Lucas, 06-30-2003) No. L-02-1397, 2003-Ohio-3450, 2003 WL 21500033, Unreported. Infants ⇔ 199

Clear and convincing evidence supported finding that awarding children county services agency permanent custody of child, who had been previously adjudicated delinquent, was in child's best interests; evidence revealed that child had some history of committing sex offenses against other children, mother adamantly refused to allow the child to return to her home absent a "written guarantee" that he would not re-offend, and child had been in custody of county children services agency for over two years. In re Beasley (Ohio App. 4 Dist., Scioto, 06-25-2003) No. 03CA2881, 2003-Ohio-3462, 2003 WL 21500016, Unreported. Infants ⇔ 155

Clear and convincing evidence supported finding in neglect and dependency proceeding that it was in minor children's best interest to be permanently placed in custody of county children services board; there was testimony that children were not cared for by mother and had been in and out of board's custody, that they had currently been in board's custody for more than a 12-month period, that mother was serving two consecutive 18-month jail sentences, that the children needed permanency, and that another county had found that maternal grandparents' home was not a viable placement. In re Schueler (Ohio App. 12 Dist., Butler, 06-30-2003)

No. CA2002-12-320, 2003-Ohio-3443, 2003 WL 21496722, Unreported. Infants ⇐ 178

Evidence supported trial court's finding that award of permanent custody of mother's children to Department of Jobs and Family Services was in children's best interest; children were placed in licensed foster homes, children were doing well in homes and each home was willing and able to adopt children, children suffered from no physical delays, and mother had strained relationship with children. In re Lowry/Owens Children (Ohio App. 5 Dist., Stark, 06-16-2003) No. 2003CA00105, 2003-Ohio-3166, 2003 WL 21398970, Unreported. Infants ⇐ 155

Evidence supported trial court's finding, in awarding permanent custody of mother's children to Department of Jobs and Family Services, that children would not be placed with mother in a reasonable time; social worker testified that mother was unemployed and having trouble providing sufficient housing, mother refused to comply with request for urine sample to test for marijuana use, mother had trouble interacting with children, and mother refused recommended therapy. In re Lowry/Owens Children (Ohio App. 5 Dist., Stark, 06-16-2003) No. 2003CA00105, 2003-Ohio-3166, 2003 WL 21398970, Unreported. Infants ⇐ 155

Clear and convincing evidence was presented to establish that awarding Sandusky County Department of Jobs and Family Services permanent custody of children was in children's best interest; mother's homelessness and unstable relationships reflected pattern of behavior that mother was either unwilling or unable to correct. In re Joshua B. (Ohio App. 6 Dist., Sandusky, 06-13-2003) No. S-02-018, No. S-02-021, No. S-02-019, No. S-02-020, 2003-Ohio-3096, 2003 WL 21384883, Unreported. Infants ⇐ 155

Finding that permanent custody was in child's best interest was not against the manifest weight of the evidence, where supervised visits between parents and child had been problematic, mother attempted to provide age-inappropriate food and drink to child and handled child roughly, father became agitated and defensive when staff from Department of Jobs and Family Services offered suggestions, and child displayed stronger bond with foster parents. In re Matuszczak (Ohio App. 5 Dist., Stark, 06-02-2003) No. 2003CA000100, 2003-Ohio-2892, 2003 WL 21290901, Unreported. Infants ⇐ 155

Evidence that both parents had prior involuntary terminations of parental rights, that mother had been terminated from substance abuse treatment for non-compliance, and that father was not in compliance with the mental health services or substance abuse treatment recommended to him, and had not established paternity, supported finding that child could not be placed with either parent within a reasonable time. In re Matuszczak (Ohio App. 5 Dist., Stark, 06-02-2003) No. 2003CA000100, 2003-Ohio-2892, 2003 WL 21290901, Unreported. Infants ⇐ 155

Competent, credible evidence supported grant of permanent custody of dependent child to county children services board; mother repeatedly stated her intention never to allow child to return home and refused to participate in counseling geared toward reunification, which indicated that child could not be placed with mother within a reasonable time, and grant of permanent custody to board was in child's best interests, given child's confusion due to mother telling him that board forced her to send him away from home, and that child had been in board's custody for over 40 consecutive months. In re Beasley (Ohio App. 4 Dist., Scioto, 05-28-2003) No. 03CA2874, 2003-Ohio-2857, 2003 WL 21278912, Unreported, motion for delayed appeal denied 99 Ohio St.3d 1466, 791 N.E.2d 982, 2003-Ohio-3669, appeal not allowed 99 Ohio St.3d 1515, 792 N.E.2d 201, 2003-Ohio-3957. Infants ⇐ 155

Evidence in proceeding for termination of father's parental rights was sufficient to support conclusion that granting permanent custody of child to county Children's Services Board was in child's best interest; although father complied with his case plan, he had mental capacity of an eleven or twelve year old, exercised poor judgment in caring for child, slept much of day due to depression, and displayed difficulty with anger management, and child had special needs, which went significantly beyond those of an average child. In re McKinley (Ohio App. 2 Dist., Montgomery, 05-30-2003) No. CIV.A. 19716, 2003-Ohio-2828, 2003 WL 21267264, Unreported. Infants ⇐ 155; Infants ⇐ 158

In proceedings to terminate father's parental rights, trial court's findings that children could not and should not be placed with father within a reasonable time and that it was in the best interest of the children to grant permanent custody to children services agency were not against the manifest weight of the evidence; father made almost no attempt to comply with case plan, father tested positive for cocaine and would not attend treatment program, father was unemployed, and father admitted he was an unfit parent. In re Cunningham Children (Ohio App. 5 Dist., Stark, 05-27-2003) No. 2003CA00054, 2003-Ohio-2805, 2003 WL 21260017, Unreported. Infants ⇐ 155

Evidence supported finding that the county department of job and family services put forth good faith and diligent efforts to rehabilitate the family situation, in child dependency proceeding; mother admitted that she terminated contact with her caseworker, mother's visitation with her children was terminated due to mother's behavior, and mother refused to follow her medication regime for her mental illness. In re Hatfield Children (Ohio App. 5 Dist., Stark, 05-27-2003) No. 2003CA00085, 2003-Ohio-2798, 2003 WL 21260016, Unreported. Infants ⇐ 155

Evidence supported finding that the children could not be placed with mother within a reasonable time, and it was in the best interests of the children to grant permanent custody to the county department of job and family services; mother failed to take medication for mental illness, she failed to undergo a psychological evaluation, she did not maintain stable housing, and mother's visitation with the children was terminated due to her violent behavior. In re Hatfield Children (Ohio App. 5 Dist., Stark, 05-27-2003) No. 2003CA00085, 2003-Ohio-2798, 2003 WL 21260016, Unreported. Infants ⇐ 158

Competent, credible evidence supported trial court's finding in permanent custody hearing that children's guardian ad litem supported awarding permanent custody of children to county children services agency, even though guardian ad litem's report did not use phrase "permanent custody," where trial court's journal entries indicated dispositional hearing was permanent custody hearing, guardian ad litem's report referred to proceeding as permanent custody hearing, and report stated that guardian ad litem could not support return of children to family. In re Myers (Ohio App. 4 Dist., Athens, 05-23-2003) No. 02CA50, 2003-Ohio-2776, 2003 WL 21246432, Unreported. Infants ⇐ 178

Evidence supported finding that children should not be placed with their parents, for purposes of dependency proceeding; deplorable condition of parents' home persisted on and off over course of county children services board's eight-year involvement with children, and testimony indicated that parents were not only unwilling to meet basic home cleanliness standards, but they were also unable to meet personal hygiene standards established by court for themselves and their children. In re Kuhn (Ohio App. 3 Dist., Crawford, 05-28-2003) No. 3-02-47, No. 3-02-48, No. 3-02-49, 2003-Ohio-2710, 2003 WL 21221328, Unreported. Infants ⇐ 156

Decision to grant permanent custody of mother's three children to Department of Job and Family Services was not against manifest weight of evidence; mother failed to comply with any of the eight requirements contained in her case plan. In re Dunaway (Ohio App. 5 Dist., Licking, 05-19-2003) No. 03 CA 14, 2003-Ohio-2572, 2003 WL 21152503, Unreported. Infants ⇐ 155

Evidence supported trial court's conclusion that father's counselor, who addressed anger management issues with father, had nothing further to offer that would change father's behavior, in termination of parental rights proceeding; counselor testified that, for father to be more successful with controlling his anger, he needed to take more responsibility with regard to his behavior when he was angry, and that, while father had made improvements and understood how his angry reactions would be perceived by others, he did not necessarily feel that his type of reaction was wrong. In re Rinaldi (Ohio App. 3 Dist., Allen, 05-19-2003) No. 1-02-74, 2003-Ohio-2562, 2003 WL 21142907, Unreported, appeal not allowed 99 Ohio St.3d 1461, 791 N.E.2d 978, 2003-Ohio-3717. Infants ⇐ 178

Clear and convincing evidence supported conclusion that termination of father's parental rights and grant of permanent custody of child to county children's services board was in child's best interest; at time of termination hearing, child had been in temporary custody of board for 12 or more months, child's need for legally secure placement could not be achieved without grant of permanent custody to board, father had convictions for child endangering and domestic violence, and child was at risk due to father's inability to control his anger. In re Rinaldi (Ohio App. 3 Dist., Allen, 05-19-2003) No. 1-02-74, 2003-Ohio-2562, 2003 WL 21142907, Unreported, appeal not allowed 99 Ohio St.3d 1461, 791 N.E.2d 978, 2003-Ohio-3717. Infants ⇐ 155; Infants ⇐ 156

Clear and convincing evidence supported finding that award of permanent custody of mother's two children to county children's services agency was in children's best interests; both children had been under temporary custody of agency for over 12 consecutive months, agency put into action a reasonable caseplan for both the mother and father but both parents failed to comply, mother failed to sever herself from the abusive relationship she was in, neither parent attempted to visit their children over two years, and both mother and father failed to address the pervasive issues of physical and mental abuse in their household. In re Anisha N. (Ohio App. 6 Dist., Lucas, 05-09-2003) No. L-02-1370, 2003-Ohio-2356, 2003 WL 21040311, Unreported. Infants ⇐ 155

Substantial competent and credible evidence supported trial court's determination that best interests of dependent children would be served by awarding Vinton County Department of Job and Family Services permanent custody of children; children had been in Department's temporary custody for at least 12 of prior 22 months, children had behavior problems that required highly structured environment and close supervision, father's living arrangement hampered his ability to provide structured and monitored environment, and father minimized children's problems. In re Workman (Ohio App. 4 Dist., Vinton, 04-30-2000) No. 02CA576, 2003-Ohio-2221, 2003 WL 2012576, Unreported. Infants ⇐ 155

Clear and convincing evidence supported trial court finding that placing child in the permanent custody of county children's services was proper; father had sporadic contact with child, father was incarcerated and would not be available for at least 18 months, father was frequently incarcerated, child was in a stable home with his grandparents and siblings, grandparents desired to adopt child, and father failed to comply with his caseplan. In re Joseph P. (Ohio App. 6 Dist., Lucas, 05-02-2003) No. L-02-1385, 2003-Ohio-2217, 2003 WL 2007268, Unreported. Infants ⇐ 155; Infants ⇐ 157

Evidence supported trial court's decision committing the child to the permanent custody of Franklin County Children Services (FCCS) for the purposes of adoption; parents had not substantially complied with the reunification plan, verbal abuse seemed to continue without improvement, prolonging foster care for too lengthy a time was undesirable, and there was no evidence of a strong bond between the child and her parents. In re Johnson (Ohio App. 10 Dist., Franklin, 05-01-2003) No. 02AP-845, No. 02AP-857, 2003-Ohio-2186, 2003 WL 1994780, Unreported. Infants ⇐ 155

Trial court order granting permanent custody of mother's three children to the county department of family services was not against the manifest weight of the evidence; despite assistance from family services mother and father lost their subsidized housing, they had an unstable marriage, father failed to attend an alcoholic support group, they were unable to keep their home clean, and they were unable to maintain utilities consistently. In re Simpson (Ohio App. 5 Dist., Licking, 04-24-2003) No. 2003-CA-00006, 2003-Ohio-2040, 2003 WL 1930320, Unreported. Infants ⇐ 155; Infants ⇐ 156

Competent and credible evidence supported juvenile court's determination that granting permanent custody of children to Cuyahoga County Department of Children and Family Services (CCDCFS) was in children's best interest; children were placed outside home for extended period, mother had history of substance abuse and repeated incarceration, and guardian ad litem stated that children were happy with foster parents. In re C.N. (Ohio App. 8 Dist., Cuyahoga, 04-24-2003) No. 81813, 2003-Ohio-2048, 2003 WL 1924648, Unreported. Infants ⇐ 155

Since children were in temporary custody of Cuyahoga County Department of Children and Family Services (CCDCFS) for 12 or more months of consecutive 22-month period, it was unnecessary for juvenile court in determining whether to grant permanent custody of children to CCDCFS to analyze whether children could be placed with their parents within reasonable time or whether parents failed to remedy conditions causing children's removal. In re C.N. (Ohio App. 8 Dist., Cuyahoga, 04-24-2003) No. 81813, 2003-Ohio-2048, 2003 WL 1924648, Unreported. Infants ⇐ 155

Some competent, credible evidence existed to support trial court's finding that county children services made sufficient reasonable efforts to reunite mother with child, in proceeding to terminate mother's parental rights; evidence indicated that caseworkers developed case plan with mother, mother failed to monitor child's water intake despite reminders from caseworkers, caseworkers provided gas vouchers and scheduled child's doctor appointments at mother's request, and mother was non-compliant with case plan. In re Mourey (Ohio App. 4 Dist., Athens, 04-08-2003) No. 02CA48, 2003-Ohio-1870, 2003 WL 1869911, Unreported. Infants ⇐ 155

Some competent, credible evidence existed to support trial court's finding that neither mother nor mother's parent was able to provide secure placement for child, and thus trial court properly found that child's best interests would be served by granting permanent custody to county children services; evidence indicated that mother frequently failed to attend visitation with child and refused to take prescribed medication for her schizophrenia, mother's parent had been unable to raise her own children without losing at least temporary custody of them to children services agencies, and parent's husband had committed domestic violence against her on three occasions and had allegedly given drug-laced marijuana cigarette to mother. In re Mourey (Ohio App. 4 Dist., Athens, 04-08-2003) No. 02CA48, 2003-Ohio-1870, 2003 WL 1869911, Unreported. Infants ⇐ 155

Clear and convincing evidence supported finding that was in children's best interests that father's parental rights be terminated and custody of children be granted to county children services board; father had had no contact with children for more than two years, father's visitation with children was terminated after he failed to regularly appear for visits and children were upset and reluctant to visit with him, physician diagnosed father as mildly mentally retarded and afflicted with intermittent explosive disorder, and physician expressed concern that father's cognitive limitations could result in difficulty assisting the children with their educational needs, medical issues and daily functioning. In re Hugle (Ohio App. 12 Dist., Butler, 04-07-2003) No. CA2002-10-254, 2003-Ohio-1772, 2003 WL 1795591, Unreported. Infants ⇐ 157; Infants ⇐ 158

Judgment entry that granted permanent custody of child to county agency in dependency proceeding technically complied with requirement of discussing child's wishes when determining child's best interests by stating that child was only three-and-a-half years old, that efforts by guardian ad litem to determine child's wishes were unsuccessful, and that child was either unable or unwilling to express her wishes regarding issue of permanent custody, but entry should have mentioned statement in guardian ad litem's report that child had indicated desire to live with foster mother. In re Hill (Ohio App. 11 Dist., Geauga, 04-04-2003) No. 2002-G-2486, 2003-Ohio-1748, 2003 WL 1792958, Unreported. Infants ⇐ 210

Clear and convincing evidence supported a finding in dependency proceeding that it was in minor child's best interest to grant permanent custody to county agency; while child and mother were together five days a week and trial court found that granting permanent custody to agency would be emotionally devastating, court also found it highly likely that child would have to be removed again if placed with mother, and evidence of mother's continuing verbal disputes with child's father and of filthy manner in which mother maintained home showed an inability to provide safe, wholesome environment. In re Hill (Ohio App. 11 Dist., Geauga, 04-04-2003) No. 2002-G-2486, 2003-Ohio-1748, 2003 WL 1792958, Unreported. Infants ⇐ 156

Clear and convincing evidence supported a finding, on motion by county agency in dependency proceeding for permanent custody of minor child, that agency used reasonable case planning and made diligent efforts to assist mother in remedying problems that led to child's removal from mother's home; goal of case plans was reunification, social workers provided mother with access to counseling, parent aides, parenting classes, day care assistance, and other services, and case aide testified that she reviewed problem areas with mother after visiting home. In re Hill (Ohio App. 11 Dist., Geauga, 04-04-2003) No. 2002-G-2486, 2003-Ohio-1748, 2003 WL 1792958, Unreported. Infants ⇐ 155

Clear and convincing evidence supported a finding, on county agency's motion in dependency proceeding for permanent custody of minor child, that child could not be placed in mother's home within reasonable time because mother had not substantially remedied conditions that caused child's removal; mother was still co-dependent on child's father with whom mother had engaged in violent arguments in child's presence, she failed to respond to child's emotional cues, and she left sewing pins and needles scattered on her floor and failed to remove pets that caused unsanitary conditions in home. In re Hill (Ohio App. 11 Dist., Geauga, 04-04-2003) No. 2002-G-2486, 2003-Ohio-1748, 2003 WL 1792958, Unreported. Infants ⇐ 156

Termination of mother's parental rights to her five children was not against the manifest weight of the evidence; mother had been convicted of child endangering involving her children, mother was convicted and incarcerated for assault of her oldest child, and mother's chronic mental and emotional illness was so severe that she was unable to provide an adequate home for the children. In re Hurt (Ohio App. 5 Dist., Richland, 04-01-2003) No. 2002CA0079, 2003-Ohio-1713, 2003 WL 1756120, Unreported. Infants ⇐ 156; Infants ⇐ 158

Clear and convincing evidence supported trial court's finding that minor child's mother, despite case planning and diligent efforts by the county children services agency to assist her to remedy the problems that caused the child to be placed outside the home, had continuously and repeatedly failed to substantially remedy the conditions causing the child to be placed outside his home, and thus, permanent placement of child with the agency was in child's best interests; although trial court did not make all the statutory findings necessary to terminate mother's parental rights, there was no evidence to rebut trial court's findings, mother, herself a minor and subject of the county children services agency, was absent without leave (AWOL) and clearly and willfully abandoned the child to pursue her own misguided interests, and it was clear that mother's parents would not provide adequate care for the child. In re Telson (Ohio App. 10 Dist., Franklin, 03-31-2003) No. 02AP-851, 2003-Ohio-1656, 2003 WL 1701430, Unreported. Infants ⇐ 157

Clear and convincing evidence supported finding that permanent custody of dependent child with county child protection agency, rather than with his natural parents, was in best interests of the child, where child had been in agency's temporary custody for 12 or more months of a consecutive 22-month period, and child's interaction and relationship with his natural parents caused him to regress, while interaction and relationship with his foster parents resulted in child beginning to act his age. In re Nicholas Bruce Lee R. (Ohio App. 6 Dist., Huron, 03-13-2003) No. H-02-053, 2003-Ohio-1414, 2003 WL 1487341, Unreported. Infants ⇒ 155

Evidence supported trial court's determination to terminate father's parental rights and grant permanent custody to county children services board; child was in father's care when it suffered injury caused by shaking and blunt force trauma, medical expert testified that the child's injuries were definitely abusive, father failed to refrain from abusing alcohol as required by case plan, and father had pled guilty to child endangering charge. In re Hess (Ohio App. 7 Dist., Jefferson, 03-21-2003) No. 02 JE 37, 2003-Ohio-1429, 2003 WL 1465190, Unreported. Infants ⇒ 156

Evidence supported finding that county agency that had been awarded emergency temporary custody of three minor children made diligent efforts to help parents achieve reunification, and thus trial court did not abuse its discretion in awarding permanent custody to agency based on parents' continuous and repeated failure to substantially remedy problems that had caused children to be placed outside of home; parents failed to present any evidence supporting their claims to be learning disabled, and licensed professional counselor, caseworker, parent educator, and intake therapist who worked with parents all believed that parents' conduct reflected a lack of motivation or devotion, as opposed to any cognitive or learning deficiencies. In re Leveck (Ohio App. 3 Dist., Hancock, 03-18-2003) No. 5-02-52, No. 5-02-53, No. 5-02-54, 2003-Ohio-1269, 2003 WL 1205082, Unreported. Infants ⇒ 178

Factual findings supported award of permanent custody of mother's three children to county children services; of the last 49 months, two of mother's children had been in the temporary custody of county children services for approximately 32 months, mother's third child had been in temporary custody of county children services for 20 months of her 45 months of her life, and evidence was given that mother failed to attend all of the recommended parenting classes, causing her case to be closed due to non-compliance. In re Llewellyn (Ohio App. 5 Dist., Fairfield, 03-10-2003) No. 02CA10, No. 02CA11, No. 02CA12, 2003-Ohio-1102, 2003 WL 951481, Unreported. Infants ⇒ 155

Evidence was sufficient to support finding that granting permanent custody to county was in two boys' best interest; boys had been placed together, had been in their current placement for 18 months prior to custody hearing, were bonded to each other, were on track educationally, did not suffer from any physiological, psychological, or developmental disabilities, responded very well to their placement, and had a positive male mentor figure in their lives, one boy stated he was angry at his parents for allowing situation to reach this point and wanted to stay in current placement, boys were bonded with foster family, and parents visited children inconsistently, which was detrimental to the boys. In re Whipple Children (Ohio App. 5 Dist., Stark, 03-10-2003) No. 2002CA00406, 2003-Ohio-1101, 2003 WL 950448, Unreported. Infants ⇒ 155

Testimony of county social worker, that the children were removed 18 months prior to permanent custody hearing, and had been in county's continuous custody since removal, was sufficient to support finding that children had been in temporary custody of county for 12 of the last 22 months, as would support award of permanent custody to county. In re Whipple Children (Ohio App. 5 Dist., Stark, 03-10-2003) No. 2002CA00406, 2003-Ohio-1101, 2003 WL 950448, Unreported. Infants ⇒ 155

Evidence was sufficient to show that termination of parents' rights as to their two sons was in sons' best interest; sons had been in foster care for over 15 months, one son had a behavior problem and functioned best when in a highly structured environment, parents had a history of being unable to retain employment, housing, or otherwise provide structure for sons, and had no plans as to how to change situation, although sons enjoyed and looked forward to visits with parents, during visits sons were late to and misbehaved at school, were dirty, wore same clothing, and were not given their medications, parents' rights as to another son had been terminated, and their daughter was no longer in their custody, and numerous services were offered to family throughout several years yet parents were persistently unable to support children or themselves. In re Gambrel (Ohio App. 3 Dist., Logan, 03-07-2003) No. 8-02-32, No. 8-02-33, 2003-Ohio-1025, 2003 WL 832278, Unreported. Infants ⇒ 155; Infants ⇒ 156; Infants ⇒ 159

Clear and convincing evidence supported finding in dependency proceeding that it was in child's best interest to grant permanent custody to county agency; while court recognized child's bond with mother, it also considered child's wishes to be adopted by his foster parents and his custodial history of numerous removals from mother's home based on her mental health problems and found that child could not obtain the legally secure permanent placement he needed without a grant of permanent custody to agency. In re Slocum (Ohio App. 11 Dist., Portage, 02-28-2003) No. 2002-P-0112, 2003-Ohio-925, 2003 WL 679254, Unreported. Infants ⇒ 155; Infants ⇒ 158

Clear and convincing evidence supported trial court's finding, in granting permanent custody of child to county agency in dependency proceeding, that child could not be placed with mother within reasonable period of time; mother suffered from chronic mental illness, including bipolar affective disorder, that made her unable to provide adequate permanent home for child, and testimony of social worker who had been assigned to child's case indicated that mother had not complied with case plan objectives and had stopped attending individual and family therapy sessions. In re Slocum (Ohio App. 11 Dist., Portage, 02-28-2003) No. 2002-P-0112, 2003-Ohio-925, 2003 WL 679254, Unreported. Infants ⇒ 155; Infants ⇒ 158

Evidence was sufficient to support finding that termination of mother's parental rights as to her newborn daughter was in infant's best interest; evidence included fact that mother's parental rights as to three older children had been terminated, she remained a transient, depending upon and residing with others in locations unfit for children, she failed to maintain suitable employment, lacked a driver's license, owed nearly $3,000 in child support arrearages, remained dependent upon child's father despite having a protection order against him, failed to complete or learn from parenting, domestic violence, or other counseling, rarely visited child, and hid her pregnancy with infant in case from county, infant's foster mother had custody of mother's two-year-old since she was three days old, had provided a safe, nurturing, stable, and healthy home for her for more than two years, and desired to adopt both children. In re Cook (Ohio App. 3 Dist., Seneca, 02-27-2003) No. 13-02-29, 2003-Ohio-868, 2003 WL 548484, Unreported. Infants ⇒ 155; Infants ⇒ 156; Infants ⇒ 157

County seeking permanent custody of newborn made reasonable effort toward reunification of mother and father with their two-year-old daughter, even though they were not required to do so, as would support termination of their parental rights as to newborn in this separate case; although mother complained of a series of phone calls that were unreturned by county, county testified that at time mother made calls at issue, she resided in another state, significant periods of time existed wherein neither parent contacted the agency, father refused to provide his address and phone number to county, county returned nearly all phone calls and made repeated follow-up calls when a parent requested visitation or other assistance, and several caseworkers and counselors attempted to assist parents in satisfying case plan. In re Cook (Ohio App. 3 Dist., Seneca, 02-27-2003) No. 13-02-29, 2003-Ohio-868, 2003 WL 548484, Unreported. Infants ⇒ 155

Evidence was sufficient to support finding that termination of father's rights as to two-year-old was best interest of the child; evidence included fact that father's rights had been terminated as to his four-year-old son, father had history of belligerent, threatening, and abusive behavior toward child's mother, family services caseworkers, and others, he had been convicted of domestic violence and aggravated rioting, had two civil protection orders against him, owed more than $4,000 in child support arrearages, was unemployed during most of proceedings, failed to obtain visitation, and failed to complete parenting, domestic violence, or anger management counseling, even though he was aware that case plan so required, and child's foster mother had provided a safe, nurturing, stable, and healthy home for child since she was three days old and wished to adopt child as well as father's newborn daughter. In re Cook (Ohio App. 3 Dist., Seneca, 02-27-2003) No. 13-02-27, 2003-Ohio-865, 2003 WL 547630, Unreported. Infants ⇒ 155; Infants ⇒ 156; Infants ⇒ 157

County made a reasonable effort toward reunification of mother and father with their two-year-old daughter, as would support termination of parties' parental rights; although mother complained of a series of phone calls that were unreturned by county, county testified that at time mother made calls at issue, she resided in another state, significant periods of time existed wherein neither parent contacted the agency, father refused to provide his address and phone number to county, county returned nearly all phone calls, and made repeated follow-up calls when a parent requested visitation or other assistance, and several caseworkers and counselors attempted to assist parents in satisfying case plan. In re Cook (Ohio App. 3 Dist., Seneca, 02-27-2003) No. 13-02-27, 2003-Ohio-865, 2003 WL 547630, Unreported. Infants ⇒ 155

Trial court's refusal to allow legal guardian of mother to cross-examine witnesses and present evidence at the permanent custody hearing in termination of parental rights proceeding did not violate due process; as prospective adoptive parent, the guardian had no role in adjudicatory phase, which was to determine whether mother's parental rights would be terminated, and as the mother's legal guardian, the guardian's interests in the dispositional phase stemmed directly from the mother's interests, which were adequately represented, as she was represented by counsel, was appointed an attorney guardian ad litem, and had her parents and their counsel present. In re Walker (Ohio App. 11 Dist., Ashtabula, 02-24-2003) No. 2002-A-0090, 2003-Ohio-795, 2003 WL 474280, Unreported. Constitutional Law ⚖ 274(5); Infants ⚖ 207

Evidence was sufficient to support finding that termination of mother's rights as to her three children were in the children's best interest; although mother completed a parenting class after the children's removal, she failed to protect her children from effects of domestic violence, as mother continued to live with her boyfriend even though a no contact order was in place between boyfriend and children, mother failed to complete counseling for victims of domestic abuse, motions for permanent custody were extended twice to allow mother more time to work on reunification plan, but she did nothing to mitigate problems which led to children's removal, mother failed to significantly contribute to the care or support of children, and made no progress on her reunification plan. In re McLaughlin Children (Ohio App. 5 Dist., Stark, 02-18-2003) No. 2002-CA-00316, 2003-Ohio-761, 2003 WL 360649, Unreported. Infants ⚖ 155; Infants ⚖ 156

Finding that permanent commitment of the children was in their best interest was not contrary to the manifest weight of the evidence, in child dependency proceeding; father refused to participate in chemical dependency treatment, a sex offender assessment, or an updated psychological evaluation, father stated that he "grew weary" of the screenings and programs and simply stopped going, father refused to address his substance abuse problems, there was no evidence that the children desired to live with father, and the children appeared to thrive in foster care. In re Harris (Ohio App. 1 Dist., Hamilton, 02-14-2003) No. C-020512, 2003-Ohio-672, 2003 WL 327996, Unreported. Infants ⚖ 155

Reports by a foster care agency caseworker were inadmissible in hearing on county's motion for permanent custody of three children, where reports were a record of caseworker's impressions as an observer of the children's welfare and of their interaction with their foster family, were not a reliable source of information regarding county's position in matter, were incorrect and confusing, and did not contain any specific recommendation by agency caseworker regarding whether parental rights should have been terminated. In re Thompson (Ohio App. 10 Dist., Franklin, 02-06-2003) No. 02AP-557, No. 02AP-558, 2003-Ohio-580, 2003 WL 257413, Unreported, appeal not allowed 98 Ohio St.3d 1515, 786 N.E.2d 64, 2003-Ohio-1572, certiorari denied 124 S.Ct. 185, 540 U.S. 866, 157 L.Ed.2d 121. Infants ⚖ 173.1

Evidence was sufficient to support finding that grant of permanent custody of mother's three children to county was in children's best interest; children had been in county's custody for over two years, mother failed to obtain psychiatric, psychological, and other services as required by her case plan, her chronic and severe mental illness required re-occurring hospitalization and made her unable to provide an adequate permanent home, she demonstrated lack of commitment to children in that she visited less than half of time that she could have visited, she was frequently late to those visits, during visits she failed to demonstrate affection, and she frequently requested to leave early, children were not bonded with mother, and children were bonded with each other and with foster family, which was able to adopt them. In re Thompson (Ohio App. 10 Dist., Franklin, 02-06-2003) No. 02AP-557, No. 02AP-558, 2003-Ohio-580, 2003 WL 257413, Unreported, appeal not allowed 98 Ohio St.3d 1515, 786 N.E.2d 64, 2003-Ohio-1572, certiorari denied 124 S.Ct. 185, 540 U.S. 866, 157 L.Ed.2d 121. Infants ⚖ 158

Evidence supported finding that granting permanent custody of mother's two children to the county job and family services agency would be in the best interest of the children; while children were in agency custody, warrants were issued for the arrest of their parents, both parents fled from the state, after both parents were arrested mother was sentenced to serve a four year and nine months sentence for attempted manufacturing of drugs, mother never provided any support for the children or assisted the agency in developing a caseplan, and while mother was out of state she made no attempts to contact her children. In re Billingsley (Ohio App. 3 Dist., Putnam, 01-28-2003) No. 12-02-07, No. 12-02-08, 2003-Ohio-344, 2003 WL 178661, Unreported. Infants ⚖ 157

Clear and convincing evidence supported determination that child could not be placed with father within reasonable time, for purposes of award of permanent custody to county children services board; record showed father failed to complete programs for substance abuse and domestic violence, and that he did not secure permanent housing, but continued to reside in the homes of various women. In re S.S. (Ohio App. 2 Dist., Montgomery, 01-24-2003) No. 19406, 2003-Ohio-319, 2003 WL 164598, Unreported. Infants ⚖ 178

Sufficient evidence supported finding that awarding custody of child to county children services board was in child's best interests; record indicated that child had good relationship with foster parents, and that foster parents wished to adopt child and her brother. In re S.S. (Ohio App. 2 Dist., Montgomery, 01-24-2003) No. 19406, 2003-Ohio-319, 2003 WL 164598, Unreported. Infants ⚖ 178

Substantial evidence supported termination of mother's parental rights and award of permanent custody of children to county department of job and family services; mother admitted that she failed to complete parenting program or to undergo counseling, and mother was early into three-year prison sentence for child endangering. In re Mastache Children (Ohio App. 5 Dist., Stark, 01-21-2003) No. 2002CA00360, 2003-Ohio-260, 2003 WL 157330, Unreported. Infants ⚖ 156

Clear and convincing evidence supported termination of father's parental rights; children had been in custody of county department of children and family services for over three years, father failed to follow and complete his proposed case plan which ordered him to participate in substance abuse treatment and stay drug free, submit to random drug tests, complete parenting classes, and maintain stable employment, father demonstrated a lack of commitment toward children by failing to regularly support, visit, or communicate with them when able to do so, and he was unable to provide food, clothing, shelter, and other basic necessities for children. (Per O'Donnell, J., with two judges concurring in judgment only). In re Harlston (Ohio App. 8 Dist., Cuyahoga, 01-23-2003) No. 80672, 2003-Ohio-282, 2003 WL 152939, Unreported, appeal not allowed 98 Ohio St.3d 1492, 785 N.E.2d 474, 2003-Ohio-1189. Infants ⚖ 155; Infants ⚖ 157

Evidence that children required a legally secure placement that termination of parental rights would facilitate was sufficient to support finding that termination was in children's best interests, where guardian ad litem, case workers, and psychiatrist reported positive change in children's behavior since being in foster care and that children were thriving in that environment. In re Gang (Ohio App. 12 Dist., Warren, 01-21-2003) No. CA2002-04-032, No. CA2002-04-033, 2003-Ohio-197, 2003 WL 138676, Unreported. Infants ⚖ 155

Trial court did not err in determining that clear and convincing evidence supported finding that children could not be returned to parents' custody in termination of parental rights proceeding, even though parents' treating psychiatrist testified that parents were doing the best they could with uncontrollable child with severe behavioral problems, where another psychiatrist testified that behavioral problems arose from stressful environment of living with parents, and that testimony was supported by testimony of case workers, foster parents, and guardian ad litem who all testified to child's remarkable behavioral progress since being in foster care. In re Gang (Ohio App. 12 Dist., Warren, 01-21-2003) No. CA2002-04-032, No. CA2002-04-033, 2003-Ohio-197, 2003 WL 138676, Unreported. Infants ⚖ 178

Clear and convincing evidence supported finding that removal of child from father's custody and granting county permanent custody was in child's best interest; although father loved daughter, daughter had bonded with foster family, family was interested in adopting her, father lied about using drugs and about existence of son who had perpetrated sexual abuse, and father had difficulty controlling anger, lacked ability to independently parent, and was responsible for sexual abuse of daughter's half-sister. In re Sullivan (Ohio App. 12 Dist., Butler, 01-21-2003) No. CA2002-03-061, 2003-Ohio-195, 2003 WL 138665, Unreported. Infants ⚖ 155

Trial court's finding that a grant of permanent custody to the Department of Job and Family Services would be in the best interest of dependent child was not against the manifest weight of evidence; although the foster family was not interested in adopting the child, a one-year old, who, evidently, was slightly advanced and communicated well, there was evidence that the child was an adoptable child, who had no trouble bonding to substitute care givers, but he was not significantly bonded to his mother, and that the harm done by severing that bond was outweighed by the benefit of adoption. In re Alexander (Ohio App. 5 Dist., Stark, 01-13-2003) No. 2002CA00342, 2003-Ohio-136, 2003 WL 125070, Unreported. Infants ⚖ 155

Evidence was sufficient to support trial court order terminating father's parental rights; mother and father engaged in domestic violence in front of the children, and father denied that he had an anger management problem. In re Crystal C. (Ohio App. 6 Dist., Lucas, 03-01-2002) No. L-01-1336, 2003-Ohio-4414, 2002 WL 32143494, Unreported. Infants ⚖ 155

Evidence was sufficient to support trial court order terminating mother's parental rights; father sexually abused his two oldest daughters, mother, who did not have a high school diploma, home-schooled the children, when removed all of the children were performing two or more grade levels below normal for their age, mother and boyfriend engaged in domestic violence in front of the children, mother failed to provide the children with proper medical or dental care, and mother's behaviors continued even after she had attended parenting classes and therapy. In re Crystal C. (Ohio App. 6 Dist., Lucas, 03-01-2002) No. L-01-1336, 2003-Ohio-4414, 2002 WL 32143494, Unreported. Infants ⚖ 156; Infants ⚖ 159

Evidence was sufficient to support finding that granting permanent custody to county children services board was in child's best interests, and thus supported termination of mother's parental rights; interaction between mother and child was described by mother's medical conservator as being "like two children interacting," several witnesses explained that mother did not set appropriate limits for child and did not make appropriate choices for her, several witnesses testified that mother did not have the ability to care for child without assistance, and many witnesses explained how mother interfered with the work of the service providers. In re J.J. (Ohio App. 9 Dist., Summit, 12-31-2002) No. 21226, 2002-Ohio-7330, 2002 WL 31890708, Unreported. Infants ⇒ 178

Trial court decision granting permanent custody of child to the county department of jobs and family services was not against the manifest weight of the evidence, even though father complied with all of his caseplan requirements; psychologist testified that defendant had antisocial personality disorder, was cold and hostile, had no ability to relate to human beings, and had no ability to empathize or understand another person's feelings, licensed social worker presented a similar diagnosis of father and said he was untreatable, and licensed professional counsel recommended that father not be given responsibility for children. In re Mraz (Ohio App. 12 Dist., Brown, 12-30-2002) No. CA2002-05-011, No. CA2002-07-014, 2002-Ohio-7278, 2002 WL 31883343, Unreported. Infants ⇒ 181

Clear and convincing evidence supported award of permanent custody of child to county children services; child had been in the temporary custody of county children services for three and a half years when it moved for permanent custody, child stated that it would be "okay" if he never saw father again and was adopted, father admitted that he was not bonded with child, child was bonded to his prospective adoptive parents, and father had relapses of alcohol abuse and numerous incarcerations. In re Williams (Ohio App. 10 Dist., Franklin, 12-24-2002) No. 02AP-924, 2002-Ohio-7205, 2002 WL 31870153, Unreported. Infants ⇒ 155

Remand was required in permanency proceeding to enter findings of fact and conclusions of law proper in form in relation to record, where transcript of proceedings before magistrate and trial court did not indicate what evidence was relied upon to make finding that granting of permanent custody to county children's services board was in children's best interests. In re McColloch (Ohio App. 2 Dist., Greene, 12-20-2002) No. 02CA39, No. 02CA40, 2002-Ohio-7097, 2002 WL 31846270, Unreported, opinion after remand 2003-Ohio-5739, 2003 WL 22429293. Infants ⇒ 254

Trial court's grant of permanent custody of mother's children to Job and Family Services was not against manifest weight of evidence; mother failed to successfully complete case plan after three years, she attended only fifty percent of her parenting classes and her counseling sessions, she stopped attending her counseling sessions six months prior to permanent custody hearing, and she was unable to maintain employment. In re Willis (Ohio App. 5 Dist., Coshocton, 12-18-2002) No. 02 CA 14, 2002-Ohio-7054, 2002 WL 31838530, Unreported. Infants ⇒ 155

Clear and convincing evidence supported the trial court determination that granting permanent custody of child to county children services board was in child's best interest; child had been in foster care since birth, child had been with the same foster family for 14 months and had bonded with family, mother stopped visiting child due to fear that she would be arrested on an outstanding warrant if she attended, mother had a history of substance abuse and relapses after treatment, all of mother's other children were in the care of others, mother was incarcerated, and child's guardian ad litem strongly advocated the permanent custody motion. In re Rucker (Ohio App. 12 Dist., Butler, 12-16-2002) No. CA2002-05-126, 2002-Ohio-6878, 2002 WL 31797533, Unreported. Infants ⇒ 155; Infants ⇒ 157

Testimony of social worker that child had little bonding with either parent and she believed it was in the best interest of the child to place him with Department of Job and Family Services so he could have permanency, along with recommendation of guardian ad litem that permanent custody be granted to Department was some competent, credible evidence supporting determination that granting custody to Department was in child's best interest. In re DeWalt (Ohio App. 5 Dist., Stark, 12-09-2002) No. 2002CA00282, 2002-Ohio-6849, 2002 WL 31771227, Unreported. Infants ⇒ 178

Mother's failure to complete case plan and continuing, unresolved mental health and substance abuse issues that put child at risk was some competent, credible evidence supporting determination that child could not be returned to mother within a reasonable period of time. In re DeWalt (Ohio App. 5 Dist., Stark, 12-09-2002) No. 2002CA00282, 2002-Ohio-6849, 2002 WL 31771227, Unreported. Infants ⇒ 155

Finding that terminating father's parental rights was in best interest of children was established by clear and convincing evidence that, despite reasonable efforts to reunify children with father and prolonged length of time afforded to correct on-going concerns of county children's services board, father continued to be unable to provide a secure, stable residence for children. In re Cook, Alleged Dependent Child (Ohio App. 3 Dist., Allen, 12-11-2002) No. 1-02-47, No. 1-02-48, No. 1-02-49, 2002-Ohio-6771, 2002 WL 31758704, Unreported. Infants ⇒ 155

Evidence was sufficient to support finding that it was in the best interests of father's seven children that permanent custody be awarded to county; father was incarcerated for raping and molesting his children, mother voluntarily relinquished her parental rights, and, although paternal grandmother had good intentions in wanting to care for the children, the children did not wish to live with her, but wished to remain with their current caregivers, and grandmother lacked the resources to provide for them. In re M.Z. (Ohio App. 8 Dist., Cuyahoga, 12-05-2002) No. 80799, 2002-Ohio-6634, 2002 WL 31722231, Unreported. Infants ⇒ 155; Infants ⇒ 156

Clear and convincing evidence supported finding that father's seven children could not or should not have been returned to father within a reasonable time, as would support termination of his parental rights; father had pled guilty to the rape and molestation of his children, for which he was serving two life sentences in addition to two five-year sentences and an eight-year sentence, and county attempted to implement a case plan, but plan was interrupted when father was taken into custody. In re M.Z. (Ohio App. 8 Dist., Cuyahoga, 12-05-2002) No. 80799, 2002-Ohio-6634, 2002 WL 31722231, Unreported. Infants ⇒ 155; Infants ⇒ 156; Infants ⇒ 157

Father did not meet burden of showing that testimony of instructors for his court-ordered parenting programs concerning his improved parenting skills would have changed outcome of trial terminating his parental rights, as required to establish that counsel was ineffective for failing to subpoena instructors, where case plan required successful completion of such programs, and father admitted that he attended only four or five sessions. In re Penley (Ohio App. 5 Dist., Stark, 11-25-2002) No. 2002CA00236, No. 2002CA00252, 2002-Ohio-6551, 2002 WL 31689357, Unreported. Infants ⇒ 205

Father did not meet burden of showing that a motion for change of custody of his dependent children to their paternal great uncle would have changed outcome of trial terminating his parental rights and granting permanent custody to county, as required to establish that counsel was ineffective for failing to file motion, where paternal great uncle testified at trial concerning his interest in obtaining custody. In re Penley (Ohio App. 5 Dist., Stark, 11-25-2002) No. 2002CA00236, No. 2002CA00252, 2002-Ohio-6551, 2002 WL 31689357, Unreported. Infants ⇒ 205

Evidence supported trial court's decision in termination proceeding not to grant permanent custody of child to his paternal great uncle; uncle testified that he already cared for four children in his home, two of which had special needs, and that he allowed father to have contact with three of the minor children who were subject child's siblings. In re Penley (Ohio App. 5 Dist., Stark, 11-25-2002) No. 2002CA00236, No. 2002CA00252, 2002-Ohio-6551, 2002 WL 31689357, Unreported. Infants ⇒ 175.1

Trial court could terminate parents' rights and grant permanent custody of child to county agency without finding that child could not or should not be placed with mother or father within a reasonable time, where child had been in agency's temporary custody for 12 or more months of a consecutive 22-month period. In re Penley (Ohio App. 5 Dist., Stark, 11-25-2002) No. 2002CA00236, No. 2002CA00252, 2002-Ohio-6551, 2002 WL 31689357, Unreported. Infants ⇒ 210

Clear and convincing evidence supported finding that permanent placement in custody of county Child Services Board was in child's best interests; there was evidence that father was incarcerated and had not seen child since his birth, that child had bonded with foster family, that child had complicated medical needs for which foster family had received medical training, that father was unaware of those medical needs, that county had made efforts to prevent need for removal, and that father did not participate in lives of his other children. In re Cleckley (Ohio App. 12 Dist., Butler, 12-02-2002) No. CA2002-05-104, No. CA2002-05-134, 2002-Ohio-6518, 2002 WL 31682220, Unreported. Infants ⇒ 178

Clear and convincing evidence supported best interest finding that mother failed to consistently comply with court ordered case plan, was unable to secure a suitable home environment, and lacked patience and knowledge for care of special needs child, so as to warrant termination of mother's parental rights. In re Butts (Ohio App. 3 Dist., Logan, 11-27-2002) No. 8-02-18, 2002-Ohio-6485, 2002 WL 31667234, Unreported. Infants ⇒ 178

Clear and convincing evidence supported termination of mother's and father's parental rights; father had been convicted of manslaughter involving a sibling of child, and mother had lost permanent custody of a sibling of child. In re Miriah W. (Ohio App. 6 Dist., Lucas, 11-22-2002) No. L-

02-1182, 2002-Ohio-6361, 2002 WL 31630758, Unreported. Infants ⇐ 155; Infants ⇐ 156

Rules of Evidence applied at motion for permanent custody of dependent child. In re Ashley E.D. (Ohio App. 6 Dist., Huron, 11-15-2002) No. H-02-025, 2002-Ohio-6238, 2002 WL 31529030, Unreported. Infants ⇐ 173.1

Lay opinions of social workers and dependent child's guardian ad litem were admissible on motion for permanent custody on issue of whether child's best interest was served by granting permanent custody to county department of jobs and family services. In re Ashley E.D. (Ohio App. 6 Dist., Huron, 11-15-2002) No. H-02-025, 2002-Ohio-6238, 2002 WL 31529030, Unreported. Infants ⇐ 173.1

Any error in admitting father's testimony was harmless at motion for permanent custody of dependent child, as there was more than sufficient evidence absent father's testimony to support trial court's findings. In re Ashley E.D. (Ohio App. 6 Dist., Huron, 11-15-2002) No. H-02-025, 2002-Ohio-6238, 2002 WL 31529030, Unreported. Infants ⇐ 253

Mother's ongoing criminal legal problems (some involving dishonesty), her failure to provide stable housing, and her failure to financially support her children constituted clear and convincing evidence that county agency should be awarded permanent custody of dependent child. In re Ashley E.D. (Ohio App. 6 Dist., Huron, 11-15-2002) No. H-02-025, 2002-Ohio-6238, 2002 WL 31529030, Unreported. Infants ⇐ 155; Infants ⇐ 157

Evidence supported finding that it was in the children's best interests to grant permanent custody of the children to county children services, in termination of parental rights proceeding; mother's interaction with her children at visitation was not alway appropriate, mother did not participate in the counseling sessions for the children, mother exerted little effort toward reunification with the children, and the behavior of the children had improved while in foster care. In re C.F. (Ohio App. 9 Dist., Lorain, 11-13-2002) No. 02CA008084, 2002-Ohio-6113, 2002 WL 31513423, Unreported. Infants ⇐ 155

Evidence supported finding that mother failed to substantially remedy the conditions that caused the removal of her children, in support of termination of mother's parental rights; mother's caseworker testified that he had met or called mother at least 40 times to discuss her failure to follow through with treatment, mother completed an alcohol treatment plan only because it was required as a part of her incarceration, and mother failed to take parenting classes, or secure employment or housing, as required by her caseplan. In re C.F. (Ohio App. 9 Dist., Lorain, 11-13-2002) No. 02CA008084, 2002-Ohio-6113, 2002 WL 31513423, Unreported. Infants ⇐ 155

Evidence supported finding that it was in children's best interests to grant permanent custody to county children services and terminate mother's parental rights; mother's interaction with her children at visitation was not always appropriate, mother did not participate in counseling sessions for children, mother exerted little effort toward reunification, and behavior of children had improved while in foster care. In re C.F. (Ohio App. 9 Dist., Lorain, 11-13-2002) No. 02CA008084, 2002-Ohio-6113, 2002 WL 31513423, Unreported. Infants ⇐ 155

Trial court decision to grant permanent custody of mother's two children to the county department of jobs and family services was not against the manifest weight of the evidence; mother's oldest child did not undergo a sexual assessment as ordered in mother's caseplan, mother had difficulty maintaining housing due to the behavior of her three resident children and her paramour, mother did not believe that her husband and oldest son sexually abused child, and mother was often unable to control the behavior of her three resident children. In re Williamson (Ohio App. 5 Dist., Tuscarawas, 11-01-2002) No. 2002AP060050, 2002-Ohio-6069, 2002 WL 31492278, Unreported. Infants ⇐ 155; Infants ⇐ 156

Evidence supported finding that children could not be placed with mother within a reasonable time, and thus supported termination of mother's parental rights and grant of permanent custody to county agency; evidence indicated that mother had not followed through with several attempts to treat her mental problems and had not completed parenting classes. In re Howard (Ohio App. 8 Dist., Cuyahoga, 10-24-2002) No. 78573, 2002-Ohio-5818, 2002 WL 31398668, Unreported. Infants ⇐ 155

Clear and convincing evidence supported finding that termination of mother's parental rights and granting of permanent custody to county agency was in the children's best interest; evidence indicated that mother's mental state remained questionable in light of her refusal to follow through with treatment, and mother failed to overcome evidence that she did suffer from schizophrenia that existed apart from her auditory hallucinations. In re Howard (Ohio App. 8 Dist., Cuyahoga, 10-24-2002) No. 78573, 2002-Ohio-5818, 2002 WL 31398668, Unreported. Infants ⇐ 181

Evidence clearly and convincingly supported trial court's decision to terminate mother's parental rights and award permanent custody of child to Job and Family Services; mother had history of alcohol abuse and abuse towards other people, she abused alcohol in her child's presence, transported him in a vehicle while under the influence of alcohol, failed to comply with her court-ordered case plan, and housed child in potentially dangerous dwellings. In re Palladino (Ohio App. 11 Dist., Geauga, 10-18-2002) No. 2002-G-2445, 2002-Ohio-5606, 2002 WL 31356652, Unreported. Infants ⇐ 155; Infants ⇐ 156

Clear and convincing evidence supported finding that granting permanent custody of the children to county children's services was in the childrens' best interests; children were bonded with each other, their parents, and their foster parents, female child expressed concern over returning to live with her parents, and children had been in the custody of county children's services for at least 12 of the 22 months before the hearing. In re Clever (Ohio App. 2 Dist., Montgomery, 10-18-2002) No. 19298, No. 19299, 2002-Ohio-5588, 2002 WL 31341602, Unreported. Infants ⇐ 155

Competent, credible evidence supported finding that child was dependent child and that permanent custody of child was properly granted to county Department of Job and Family Services; record indicated mother functioned at nine-year-old level, had schizophrenia, was unable to maintain stable housing, was resistant to following her medication regime, and had minimal parenting skills. In re Fazio (Ohio App. 5 Dist., Licking, 10-11-2002) No. 2002CA0057, 2002-Ohio-5554, 2002 WL 31312276, Unreported. Infants ⇐ 158

Clear and convincing evidence supported determination that it was in child's best interest for county children services board to be awarded permanent custody of him; mother's bond to child was not strong, while he had developed a significant bond with his foster parents and was thriving in their care, mother failed to complete any portion of her case plan, mother displayed a marked lack of interest in child by failing to exercise her visitation rights, and child's guardian ad litem strongly recommended that permanent custody be granted to the board. In re Marsh (Ohio App. 12 Dist., Warren, 08-05-2002) No. CA2002-02-015, 2002-Ohio-3982, 2002 WL 1791132, Unreported. Infants ⇐ 155; Infants ⇐ 157

Evidence was sufficient to support termination of parental rights; there was evidence of problems in the home, including marital discord, intellectual, physical, and psychological impairment, safety of the home, child's delinquency, and parents' economic resources, that parents made little or no progress under case plan and refused to cooperate with Department of Health Services, that parents demonstrated a lack of commitment to children, that placement with relatives had been unsuccessful due to parents' belligerent behavior, and that parents were unemployed and did not maintain their home. In re Hayes (Ohio App. 5 Dist., Tuscarawas, 04-19-2002) No. 2001AP110099, No. 2001AP110098, 2002-Ohio-2446, 2002 WL 819216, Unreported. Infants ⇐ 155; Infants ⇐ 156; Infants ⇐ 158

In considering rights of parents as well as needs of children the state fails to prove its burden that parental rights should be terminated where the factor of drug addiction and rehabilitation is used by the trial court as justification for granting an agency permanent custody and there is no evidence to indicate that the mother is a drug addict or that she has to go through rehabilitation. In re Aughburns (Ohio App. 8 Dist., Cuyahoga, 04-09-2001) No. 78572, 2001 WL 370503, Unreported.

A court's finding that a mother is unwilling or unable to provide food, clothing, and shelter for her child is unreasonable in light of (1) the mother's minority when her baby is born and being thrown out of her home, (2) the mother and child having to leave the foster home where they are placed in order to meet the provision of the case plan requiring the mother to secure independent housing, and (3) custody of the child by the department of human services since birth. In re Mays (Ohio App. 5 Dist., Stark, 05-17-1999) No. 98-CA-0293, 1999 WL 333351, Unreported.

Intellectual limitations which render a father unable to adequately parent his two developmentally delayed children and which jeopardize chances for a lifelong recovery from alcohol dependency is sufficient evidence upon which a court could base its decision to terminate parental rights. Matter of McKean (Ohio App. 3 Dist., Allen, 04-22-1998) No. 1-97-46, No. 1-97-47, 1998 WL 229793, Unreported, motion for delayed appeal denied 230 F.3d 1377.

A young mother's lack of commitment to her child mandates a finding that the child should not be returned to his mother's custody and that granting permanent custody to the agency would free the child for adoption and a legally secure future in light of (1) the mother's infrequent visits to her son while in the custody of the children services board, (2) her lack of parenting skills when she is with her son despite "consistent counseling and daily advice and instruction from her foster parent," (3) the mother's statement that parenting "overwhelmed" her, and (4) the fact that at age eighteen she voluntarily left the custody and care of the agency as well as her son. In re Gallatin (Ohio App. 9 Dist., Wayne, 04-16-1997) No. 96CA0059, 1997 WL 193683, Unreported.

Award of permanent custody to the county department of human services is in children's best interest where a parent's repeated incarceration prevents him from providing care for the children on a permanent basis and there is failure to achieve the overall level of stability required to suggest reunification even where the parent obtains an apartment and employment prior to his latest incarceration. In Matter of Eberle (Ohio App. 12 Dist., Clermont, 12-02-1996) No. CA96-03-032, 1996 WL 688761, Unreported.

Permanent custody to a Catholic social services agency as well as the court's conclusion that a father is not a suitable parent to take custody is sufficiently based upon (1) failure to obtain appropriate housing and consistent employment, (2) chronic chemical dependency, (3) choosing to spend for himself money available for support, and (4) a history of domestic violence and abuse. Mary Beth v. Howard (Ohio App. 8 Dist., Cuyahoga, 10-12-1995) No. 67995, 1995 WL 601110, Unreported, dismissed, appeal not allowed 75 Ohio St.3d 1448, 663 N.E.2d 330.

A mother is fit to regain custody of children where the issues include the mother's willingness and ability to protect them from the husband's sexual abuse and the mother's ability to financially support her children and (1) she acts to sever her relationship with her husband, and the only contact involves uninvited telephone calls; (2) she files for divorce and applies for a protective order to prevent any further contact; and (3) there is marked improvement in attendance at group and individual counseling; in regard to financial support, the consequences of failure to "support" a child in a termination of parental rights action are less than consequences in a child support action and the mother in this case who subsists on $100 per month general assistance, works briefly for minimum wage, and uses part of her earnings to pay for parenting classes does not demonstrate a failure to support so egregious or as to demonstrate an unwillingness to provide a home for her children. Matter of Sara H. (Ohio App. 6 Dist., Lucas, 12-16-1994) No. L-94-116, 1994 WL 700629, Unreported.

Absent clear and convincing evidence that reasonable efforts to return a child to a parent would be futile due to the unsuitability or unfitness of the parent, a children services board's failure to include a parent in its comprehensive reunification plan in contravention of RC 2151.414 is erroneous and a termination of parental rights will be reversed and remanded. In re Stevens, No. 13523, 1993 WL 265130 (2d Dist Ct App, Montgomery, 7–16–93).

Trial court's finding that awarding custody of children to mother would be detrimental to children was supported by preponderance of the evidence, in child dependency proceeding in which legal custody of children had been awarded to maternal grandparents; at time of trial, mother had been living apart from children for over two years, mother's financial situation was precarious, and mother's home, which was eight-hour drive from grandparents' home, had not been approved as appropriate placement for children after three home studies. In re Sean T. (Ohio App. 6 Dist., 10-28-2005) 164 Ohio App.3d 218, 841 N.E.2d 838, 2005-Ohio-5739. Infants ⇐ 222

Evidence supported trial court's finding that terminating mother's parental rights and granting permanent custody to county children services board (CSB) was not in dependent child's best interest, although mother was mentally ill and unable to care for child, and although child was very comfortable in foster parents' home; evidence indicated that mother remained bonded to child, visitation between mother and child had always been very positive, and there was less drastic permanent placement that would ensure that child stayed with foster family and would allow child to continue to have visits with mother. In re A.S. (Ohio App. 9 Dist., 10-05-2005) 163 Ohio App.3d 647, 839 N.E.2d 972, 2005-Ohio-5309, reversed 2009 WL 728, motion to certify allowed 108 Ohio St.3d 1410, 841 N.E.2d 315, 2006-Ohio-179. Infants ⇐ 158

Clear and convincing evidence supported grant of permanent custody of children to county child protection agency; while there was some evidence that mother and father had taken steps to comply with case plan, there was significant evidence that both parents remained unable to provide structure and stability their children needed, children were removed from parents' home due to poor decision-making of parents, and there was evidence that parents continued to make poor decisions. In re Lopez (Ohio App. 3 Dist., 05-08-2006) 166 Ohio App.3d 688, 852 N.E.2d 1266, 2006-Ohio-2251. Infants ⇐ 179

Finding that five-year-old child was too young to express her wishes regarding custody was not supported by clear and convincing evidence, in proceeding in which county child protection agency sought permanent custody of child; child was arguably capable of expressing her wishes, although there was some indication that child might have been sexually abused when she was younger, there was no evidence that child had any developmental delays or lacked the maturity to express her wishes, and no one testified as to level of child's maturity. In re Lopez (Ohio App. 3 Dist., 05-08-2006) 166 Ohio App.3d 688, 852 N.E.2d 1266, 2006-Ohio-2251. Infants ⇐ 207

Existence of chronic mental or emotional illness so severe that it made mother unable to provide adequate permanent home for children was not established by clear and convincing evidence, as element for terminating parental rights; while psychologist testified that mother suffered from generalized anxiety disorder and personality disorder, there was no evidence of causative relationship between such conditions and mother's difficulty in maintaining adequate home, and psychologist testified that mother's anxiety was easily treatable with medication. In re Alexis K. (Ohio App. 6 Dist., 03-24-2005) 160 Ohio App.3d 32, 825 N.E.2d 1148, 2005-Ohio-1380. Infants ⇐ 158

Trial court was not required to make a specific finding of parental unfitness prior to terminating father's parental rights to child, where father's parental rights were terminated based on child having been in the temporary custody of county children services board for more than 12 months of a consecutive 22 month period; once the court made the 12-month finding, it was only required to determine whether the grant of permanent custody was in child's best interest, and the 12-month finding implicitly presumed that the parent was unable, unsuitable, or unfit to care for the child. In re Stillman (Ohio App. 11 Dist., 11-19-2003) 155 Ohio App.3d 333, 801 N.E.2d 475, 2003-Ohio-6228, appeal not allowed 101 Ohio St.3d 1425, 802 N.E.2d 155, 2004-Ohio-123. Infants ⇐ 210

Clear and convincing evidence supported trial court's finding, in granting permanent custody of infant child to county children services agency, that birth parents demonstrated a lack of commitment to child, where trial court found that minor mother and her parents did not visit child or inquire about her well-being, that father visited child when his college was not in session until his commitment to swim team's optional out-of-state training became more important, and that birth parents' joint motion for consent to third party, private adoption further showed a desire not to obtain custody. In re Baby Girl Doe (Ohio App. 6 Dist., 08-30-2002) 149 Ohio App.3d 717, 778 N.E.2d 1053, 2002-Ohio-4470, appeal not allowed 97 Ohio St.3d 1425, 777 N.E.2d 278, 2002-Ohio-5820. Infants ⇐ 222

Evidence supported trial court's conclusion in dependency proceeding that three-month-old infant's best interest would be served by granting permanent custody to county children services agency, as opposed to moving infant from her foster home to father's home, where both caseworker and guardian ad litem (GAL) testified that the baby had bonded with her foster family and that the foster family was a prospective adoptive family, and GAL testified that the baby's best interest would be served by granting permanent custody to agency for purposes of adoption. In re Baby Girl Doe (Ohio App. 6 Dist., 08-30-2002) 149 Ohio App.3d 717, 778 N.E.2d 1053, 2002-Ohio-4470, appeal not allowed 97 Ohio St.3d 1425, 777 N.E.2d 278, 2002-Ohio-5820. Infants ⇐ 222

Clear and convincing evidence supported trial court's finding, in awarding permanent custody of infant child to county children services agency, that seriousness of abuse or neglect made placement with birth parents a threat to child's safety, where child had been found in tightly tied plastic bag in trash dumpster with her umbilical cord wrapped around her neck and was admitted to hospital with hypothermia. In re Baby Girl Doe (Ohio App. 6 Dist., 08-30-2002) 149 Ohio App.3d 717, 778 N.E.2d 1053, 2002-Ohio-4470, appeal not allowed 97 Ohio St.3d 1425, 777 N.E.2d 278, 2002-Ohio-5820. Infants ⇐ 222

In a neglect case, the juvenile court may proceed to find neglect at the adjudication stage upon the admission of the parent charged; no other evidence is required, even when the standard is clear and convincing evidence. In re Lakes (Ohio App. 2 Dist., 08-02-2002) 149 Ohio App.3d 128, 776 N.E.2d 510, 2002-Ohio-3917. Infants ⇐ 179

At the dispositional stage of a neglect case, evidence other than the parent's admission is required to determine whether a particular placement is in the child's best interest. In re Lakes (Ohio App. 2 Dist., 08-02-2002) 149 Ohio App.3d 128, 776 N.E.2d 510, 2002-Ohio-3917. Infants ⇐ 179

In dispositional hearing related to permanent custody of neglected children, trial court was not required to engage in colloquy with mother similar to that required at adjudicatory hearing in determining whether mother knowingly, intelligently, and voluntarily relinquished custody of children. In re Lakes (Ohio App. 2 Dist., 08-02-2002) 149 Ohio App.3d 128, 776 N.E.2d 510, 2002-Ohio-3917. Infants ⇐ 203

In a permanent custody proceeding in which the guardian ad litem's report will be a factor in the trial court's decision, parties to the proceeding have the right to cross-examine the guardian ad litem concerning the contents of the report and the basis for a custody recommendation; abrogating In re Fox, 2000 WL 1420276. In re Hoffman (Ohio, 10-23-

2002) 97 Ohio St.3d 92, 776 N.E.2d 485, 2002-Ohio-5368, on subsequent appeal 2003-Ohio-1241, 2003 WL 1193770. Infants ⇐ 207

Trial court's decision granting permanent custody of father's children to county children services board was not against manifest weight of the evidence; in approximately 18 months, father had yet to complete case plan goals of becoming financially able to support himself and his children and being able to provide safe and stable home for children, father could not provide court an explanation of where he would live in event he would get custody of children or even overnight visits, as he was living in motel room, and father's case worker testified that he had not seen father demonstrate effective parenting. In re Mack (Ohio App. 3 Dist., 08-15-2002) 148 Ohio App.3d 626, 774 N.E.2d 1243, 2002-Ohio-4161. Infants ⇐ 178

Even assuming that testimony of protective services supervisor for county children's services agency, that child's maternal grandmother told on-call social worker and supervisor that she was upset that she could not have custody of child and that "she was just going to 'go' over and just take him," was inadmissible hearsay, any deficient performance of father's counsel in failing to object at the shelter care hearing was not prejudicial; court was not bound by formal rules of evidence at the hearing, and there was abundant evidence establishing that father's relatives were no longer able to care for child and that child should be placed in foster care. In re Wingo (Ohio App. 4 Dist., 06-01-2001) 143 Ohio App.3d 652, 758 N.E.2d 780, 2001-Ohio-2477. Infants ⇐ 173.1; Infants ⇐ 253

A finding that a child cannot be placed with either parent within a reasonable period of time or should not be placed with the parents, in a proceeding to terminate parental rights and grant permanent custody to children's services agency, does not require that each and every condition listed in the statute exist before the trial court may terminate parental rights; the trial court may make its decision based solely on the existence of one of the conditions. In re Wingo (Ohio App. 4 Dist., 06-01-2001) 143 Ohio App.3d 652, 758 N.E.2d 780, 2001-Ohio-2477. Infants ⇐ 155

Evidence that father had only one visit with child before county children's services agency filed motion for permanent custody, he did not complete parenting classes, his personal and home life were unstable, and he had not displayed an ability to meet child's basic needs or provided any support or maintained his own home, supported termination of father's parental rights and award of permanent custody to agency. In re Wingo (Ohio App. 4 Dist., 06-01-2001) 143 Ohio App.3d 652, 758 N.E.2d 780, 2001-Ohio-2477. Infants ⇐ 178

Evidence that mother canceled or failed to appear for 36 out of 45 scheduled visits with child during nine-month period in which child was in foster care, that mother stated she could not handle the child and he "got on her nerves," that during visits mother failed to have diapers for child and she transported child in vehicle without car seat, and that mother strayed from her case plan and would "party" instead of providing for child, established that child could not be placed with mother, in proceeding to terminate father's parental rights and grant permanent custody to county children's services agency. In re Wingo (Ohio App. 4 Dist., 06-01-2001) 143 Ohio App.3d 652, 758 N.E.2d 780, 2001-Ohio-2477. Infants ⇐ 178

Sufficient evidence supported court's finding that four minor siblings qualified for a planned permanent living arrangement and were unable to function in a family-like setting, even though the siblings were doing well in their foster home; the foster parents were trained in dealing with the siblings' emotional and behavioral problems, unlike the typical adoptive home. In re Tanker (Ohio App. 8 Dist., 04-02-2001) 142 Ohio App.3d 159, 754 N.E.2d 813. Infants ⇐ 226

Sufficient evidence supported finding by trial court that four minor siblings maintained a positive relationship with their parents, even though the parents were unable to provide for the siblings due to the parents' own physical and mental problems or needs, and, thus, siblings did not qualify for planned permanent living arrangement; parents were attending parenting classes and maintained regular visitation when allowed to do so. In re Tanker (Ohio App. 8 Dist., 04-02-2001) 142 Ohio App.3d 159, 754 N.E.2d 813. Infants ⇐ 226

Trial court's standard of review of a petition for legal custody not involving a termination of parental rights is not clear and convincing evidence, as it is in a permanent custody proceeding, but is merely preponderance of the evidence; legal custody where parental rights are not terminated is not as drastic a remedy as permanent custody. In re Nice (Ohio App. 7 Dist., 03-20-2001) 141 Ohio App.3d 445, 751 N.E.2d 552, 2001-Ohio-3214. Child Custody ⇐ 914

Clear and convincing evidence in child protection proceedings established that permanent custody of children previously adjudicated neglected was in children's best interests; mother and her husband failed to comply with their case plans, mother refused to acknowledge her husband's abuse of the children and his problem with anger control, injuries inflicted upon children by mother's husband had been severe, and children had been in agency's temporary custody for more than 12 months. In re Nice (Ohio App. 7 Dist., 03-20-2001) 141 Ohio App.3d 445, 751 N.E.2d 552, 2001-Ohio-3214. Infants ⇐ 178

Preponderance of the evidence supported juvenile court's award of legal custody of children adjudicated dependent to their paternal grandmother; guardian ad litem recommended that legal custody be given to grandmother, children's father had no objection to such arrangement, mother's husband had not completed recommended anger management counseling, children's twin siblings had been abused, mother refused to acknowledge that abuse had occurred, and evidence offered without objection established that children were in fear of their mother's husband due to inappropriate physical contact and that mother had characterized such contact as "just playing." In re Nice (Ohio App. 7 Dist., 03-20-2001) 141 Ohio App.3d 445, 751 N.E.2d 552, 2001-Ohio-3214. Infants ⇐ 179

Admission, in proceedings on petition for permanent custody of two siblings, of evidence that would have been admissible to support adjudication of neglect had such adjudication not been entered with parental consent, did not amount to statutorily prohibited readjudication of neglect. In re Nice (Ohio App. 7 Dist., 03-20-2001) 141 Ohio App.3d 445, 751 N.E.2d 552, 2001-Ohio-3214. Infants ⇐ 207

Juvenile court properly considered evidence of shaken baby syndrome in ruling on state's petition for permanent custody of children, as relevant to issue of whether it was in children's best interests to be returned to possible perpetrator of injuries. In re Nice (Ohio App. 7 Dist., 03-20-2001) 141 Ohio App.3d 445, 751 N.E.2d 552, 2001-Ohio-3214. Infants ⇐ 207

Any error in juvenile court's finding, in proceedings on agency's second motion for permanent custody of children adjudicated neglected, that children could or should not be returned to either parent within reasonable time, was harmless, where clear and convincing evidence demonstrating that children had been in agency's temporary custody for more than 12 months was sufficient to support award of permanent custody to agency. In re Nice (Ohio App. 7 Dist., 03-20-2001) 141 Ohio App.3d 445, 751 N.E.2d 552, 2001-Ohio-3214. Infants ⇐ 253

Evidence in proceeding for termination of parental rights was sufficient to support conclusion that granting permanent custody of children to county Department of Children and Family Services (DCFS) was in children's best interest and that children could not and should not be placed with either parent within reasonable time; parents maintained continuing and abusive relationship, mother's pattern of behavior suggested her intent to continue her relationship with father upon his release from jail, and father exhibited pattern of violence toward women, was incarcerated and had history of repeated incarcerations. In re Glenn (Ohio App. 8 Dist., 10-30-2000) 139 Ohio App.3d 105, 742 N.E.2d 1210. Infants ⇐ 178

Evidence of parents' failure to rectify conditions which led to children's adjudication as neglected and their temporary placement with county Department of Children and Family Services (DCFS) was sufficient to support finding that children could not be placed with either parent within a reasonable time. In re Glenn (Ohio App. 8 Dist., 10-30-2000) 139 Ohio App.3d 105, 742 N.E.2d 1210. Infants ⇐ 179

Evidence in proceeding for termination of parental rights supported magistrate's conclusion that award of permanent custody of child to agency was in child's best interests; child had at time of hearing spent almost half of his life in foster care and enjoyed good relationship with his foster parent, child and his biological mother were not close, and mother was often unprepared for her visits with child and had problems setting limits for him during her visits. In re Campbell (Ohio App. 10 Dist., 06-08-2000) 138 Ohio App.3d 786, 742 N.E.2d 663, appeal not allowed 89 Ohio St.3d 1470, 732 N.E.2d 1001, reconsideration granted 90 Ohio St.3d 1420, 735 N.E.2d 457, appeal dismissed as improvidently allowed 91 Ohio St.3d 1202, 740 N.E.2d 1103, 2001-Ohio-230. Infants ⇐ 178

Evidence in proceeding for termination of parental rights supported magistrate's conclusion that secure environment for child would only be achieved through permanent termination of mother's parental rights; mother failed to complete her case plan, which called for her to obtain employment and housing stability, despite substantial assistance. In re Campbell (Ohio App. 10 Dist., 06-08-2000) 138 Ohio App.3d 786, 742 N.E.2d 663, appeal not allowed 89 Ohio St.3d 1470, 732 N.E.2d 1001, reconsideration granted 90 Ohio St.3d 1420, 735 N.E.2d 457, appeal dismissed as improvidently allowed 91 Ohio St.3d 1202, 740 N.E.2d 1103, 2001-Ohio-230. Infants ⇐ 178

Evidence of mother's failure to substantially remedy conditions which caused her child to be placed in foster care, under circumstances evincing a lack of commitment to child, was sufficient to support magistrate's conclusion that child could or should not be placed with mother; although at time of hearing mother had begun a job and had entered into apartment lease, she had history of starting new jobs which would last for only a month or two and had been employed at new job for only two days, had not paid her first month's rent on apartment, had obtained apartment lease only the week before the hearing despite having had two years to do so, and missed many appointments with counselors. In re Campbell (Ohio App. 10 Dist., 06-08-2000) 138 Ohio App.3d 786, 742 N.E.2d 663, appeal not allowed 89 Ohio St.3d 1470, 732 N.E.2d 1001, reconsideration granted 90 Ohio St.3d 1420, 735 N.E.2d 457, appeal dismissed as improvidently allowed 91 Ohio St.3d 1202, 740 N.E.2d 1103, 2001-Ohio-230. Infants ⇐ 178

Decision to grant permanent custody to county agency of child who was previously adjudicated dependent was supported, under governing statute, by evidence that child's mother failed to comply with case plan requiring drug testing as condition of visitation and failed to finish counseling sessions, that father failed to meet any requirements of case plan, that child had strong attachment to foster family and foster family wished to adopt him, and that child had been in agency's care under court order for 12 or more months of a consecutive 22–month period. In re Rodgers (Ohio App. 12 Dist., 06-05-2000) 138 Ohio App.3d 510, 741 N.E.2d 901. Infants ⇐ 178

Award to agency of permanent custody of child previously adjudicated dependent and neglected was demonstrated by clear and convincing evidence to be in child's best interests; child had suffered from nonorganic failure to thrive while in mother's care, and mother's psychologist, psychiatrist and caseworkers testified that mother suffered from major depression, lacked parenting skills, failed to accept any responsibility for removal of her children from her custody, refused to participate in parenting classes or allow home visits, discontinued medication prescribed for her depression, and remained in relationship with child's alleged father despite history of domestic violence. In re Nicholas H. (Ohio App. 6 Dist., 05-05-2000) 137 Ohio App.3d 442, 738 N.E.2d 896. Infants ⇐ 178

Evidence in parental rights termination proceeding did not support trial court's finding that parents had demonstrated lack of commitment to children by showing an unwillingness to provide an adequate permanent home for the children, where parents were purchasing the home in which the family lived, the house desperately needed repairs, repairs were under way when the children were taken from the home and county children's service agency refused to allow the children to return to the home until certain repairs were made, and house was brought into sufficient compliance to return the children there. In re Stacey S. (Ohio App. 6 Dist., 12-30-1999) 136 Ohio App.3d 503, 737 N.E.2d 92, 1999-Ohio-989. Infants ⇐ 178

Evidence supported trial court's finding in parental rights termination proceeding that father and mother failed to remedy condition which caused the children to be removed from the home, that father was obscene, defiant, and uncooperative and mother did not stop him, where evidence showed that father's bizarre behavior continued, mother was unable to restrain father's behavior, and father refused to avail himself of the services offered by children's services agency. In re Stacey S. (Ohio App. 6 Dist., 12-30-1999) 136 Ohio App.3d 503, 737 N.E.2d 92, 1999-Ohio-989. Infants ⇐ 178

Determination not to grant permanent custody of four-year-old child to maternal grandmother, but instead to award permanent custody to county agency, was not abuse of discretion in proceeding to terminate mother's parental rights; there was evidence grandmother was unable to provide necessary level of care because she worked 40 hours a week, grandmother was unable to articulate specific child care plans, and there was testimony grandmother had allowed mother to remove child from grandmother's home after he had been placed there by agency. In re Patterson (Ohio App. 9 Dist., 09-01-1999) 134 Ohio App.3d 119, 730 N.E.2d 439. Infants ⇐ 222

Clear and convincing evidence supported a finding in dependency proceeding that terminating mother's parental rights over four-year-old child and awarding permanent custody to county agency was in child's best interest; child had bonded with foster family, guardian ad litem recommended placement with agency, child had been out of mother's custody for over twelve months and was making significant progress in therapy, and child's special health and educational needs arising from Down's syndrome made a legally secure permanent placement desirable. In re Patterson (Ohio App. 9 Dist., 09-01-1999) 134 Ohio App.3d 119, 730 N.E.2d 439. Infants ⇐ 178

Clear and convincing evidence supported a finding in termination of parental rights proceeding that mother had failed to substantially remedy conditions that caused removal of child from home; compliance with case plan's requirement that mother transport child to medical appointments was inconsistent, mother failed to attend counseling regularly, and she missed most of the days on which she was scheduled to participate in child's schooling. In re Patterson (Ohio App. 9 Dist., 09-01-1999) 134 Ohio App.3d 119, 730 N.E.2d 439. Infants ⇐ 178

Clear and convincing evidence supported a finding in termination of parental rights proceeding that mother showed lack of commitment toward child by a failure to visit him regularly; mother missed 53 of 82 scheduled visits over a six-month period even though visitation schedule was changed in order to accommodate her schedule, she often showed up late or brought child home early when she did show up, and she attributed missed visitations to work schedule and car problems. In re Patterson (Ohio App. 9 Dist., 09-01-1999) 134 Ohio App.3d 119, 730 N.E.2d 439. Infants ⇐ 178

Evidence that parents had failed, despite over 18 months of intervention by county Department of Human Services (DHS), to remedy home situation in which two of their children had been physically and sexually abused by older siblings and another relative, to the point where they could adequately provide care and protection for abused children, was clear and convincing, and sufficient to support award of permanent custody of children to DHS. In re Heston (Ohio App. 1 Dist., 09-18-1998) 129 Ohio App.3d 825, 719 N.E.2d 93. Infants ⇐ 181

Juvenile court can terminate parental rights and grant permanent custody to children services agency on grounds that child cannot be placed with either parent within reasonable time or should not be placed with parents, under statute allowing for termination of parental rights, only if court finds clear and convincing evidence that one or more of statutorily enumerated factors exists. In re Amanda W. (Ohio App. 6 Dist., 11-21-1997) 124 Ohio App.3d 136, 705 N.E.2d 724. Infants ⇐ 178

Sufficient evidence supported trial court's finding that child was dependent and award of permanent custody to County Children Services Board, where physicians testified that child was in danger due to mother's repeated presentation of him for unnecessary medical care with symptoms fabricated by mother, expert testified that mother had personality disorders that interfered with her ability to parent effectively, and there was evidence that mother did not modify her inappropriate behavior with child even though offered suggestions. In re Dylan C. (Ohio App. 6 Dist., 06-27-1997) 121 Ohio App.3d 115, 699 N.E.2d 107. Infants ⇐ 181

Permanent custody hearing is adjudicatory, and reliance upon inadmissible hearsay evidence is prejudicial error. Matter of Duncan/Walker Children (Ohio App. 5 Dist., 03-18-1996) 109 Ohio App.3d 841, 673 N.E.2d 217. Infants ⇐ 174; Infants ⇐ 203; Infants ⇐ 253

Permanent custody of child may not be granted to human services agency on grounds that child cannot be placed with either parent within reasonable time or should not be placed with parents, under statute allowing for termination of parental rights, unless trial court finds clear and convincing evidence that one or more of eight factors enumerated in statute exists; court has no discretion to make finding based on other factors. In re William S. (Ohio, 03-04-1996) 75 Ohio St.3d 95, 661 N.E.2d 738, 1996-Ohio-182. Infants ⇐ 178

Trial court's finding that mother failed for period of years after children's removal from home to remedy conditions which prompted removal was not supported by clear and convincing evidence and thus did not support termination of parental rights; cigarette burns on one child's toes prompted removal of children and mother's roommate, who apparently caused burns, no longer resided with mother. In re William S. (Ohio, 03-04-1996) 75 Ohio St.3d 95, 661 N.E.2d 738, 1996-Ohio-182. Infants ⇐ 178

Determination that termination of biological mother's parental rights was in best interests of infant was supported by evidence that efforts at reunification of mother and child had been aborted due to lack of mother's emotional stability and hospitalization for major depression, and that child had low to normal development, no contact with sibling, little bonding with mother, and had been in foster care since age of six weeks. In re Makuch (Ohio App. 9 Dist., 02-08-1995) 101 Ohio App.3d 45, 654 N.E.2d 1331. Infants ⇐ 181

Award of permanent custody to child services board was not error, where clear and convincing evidence supported juvenile court's findings that parents' three children could not be placed with either parent within reasonable time, and that award of permanent custody to board was in children's best interest; mother suffered from chronic depression and severe emotional instability, had history of alcohol and narcotics abuse and had prior child endangering conviction, father was chronic drug-abuser, had criminal history and was living in out-of-state trailer with woman and two other children, and both parents had failed to comply with reunification plan. In re Egbert Children (Ohio App. 12 Dist., 12-27-1994) 99 Ohio App.3d 492, 651 N.E.2d 38. Infants ⇐ 222

Mother's contention that juvenile court erred in failing to place her three children in long-term foster care was rendered moot by Court of Appeals' conclusion that clear and convincing evidence supported award of permanent custody to child services board. In re Egbert Children (Ohio App. 12 Dist., 12-27-1994) 99 Ohio App.3d 492, 651 N.E.2d 38. Infants ⚖ 248.1

Error in admitting testimony of mother's treating psychiatrist in connection with petition to place custody with county required reversal where there was no other evidence concerning the mother's competency to care for the child which would have supported the decision that there was clear and convincing evidence the child could not or should not be placed with her mother. In re Brown (Ohio App. 3 Dist., 11-02-1994) 98 Ohio App.3d 337, 648 N.E.2d 576. Infants ⚖ 253

Determination to grant permanent custody of children to human services agency must be supported by "clear and convincing evidence," defined as that measure or degree of proof which is more than mere preponderance of the evidence, but not to extent of such certainty as is required beyond reasonable doubt in criminal cases, and which will provide in mind of trier of fact a firm belief or conviction as to facts sought to be established. In re Meyer (Ohio App. 3 Dist., 10-25-1994) 98 Ohio App.3d 189, 648 N.E.2d 52, corrected. Infants ⚖ 178

Trial court's award of permanent custody of six children to human services agency was supported by evidence that children were extremely dirty and had poor personal hygiene, substantial testimony that family's residence was extremely filthy, untidy and hazardous for small children, and record revealing that parents were unable to follow case plan. In re Meyer (Ohio App. 3 Dist., 10-25-1994) 98 Ohio App.3d 189, 648 N.E.2d 52, corrected. Infants ⚖ 178

Evidence supported determination that permanent commitment of children to county department of human services was in the best interests of the children; there were no suitable relatives, even though there was little probability that two older children would be adopted, custodial history and need for secure placement outweighed that factor, there was high probability of adoption of youngest child, and testimony revealed positive aspects of foster care placement and progress children had made since being placed there. In re Brodbeck (Ohio App. 3 Dist., 10-19-1994) 97 Ohio App.3d 652, 647 N.E.2d 240. Infants ⚖ 178

In parental rights termination proceeding, evidence supported finding that mother failed continuously for period of six months to remedy situation that caused daughter to be placed with social services agency and conclusion that permanent placement with foster mother was in best interest of child; 11 months after case plan was approved, mother had not completed training with visiting nurse, had not completed alcohol assessment, had not made arrangements for sitter, had not completed training on apnea monitor and made no effort to begin her psychological evaluation as required by plan. In re Wise (Ohio App. 9 Dist., 08-31-1994) 96 Ohio App.3d 619, 645 N.E.2d 812. Infants ⚖ 178

In parental rights termination proceeding, sufficient evidence supported finding that child could not be placed with mother within reasonable time; mother failed to visit daughter for over three months prior to hearing and did not contact foster mother by phone to inquire about child, she failed to complete case plan activity despite knowledge that social services agency would be seeking permanent custody of daughter if she failed to provide environment in which child's needs could be met, and she testified at hearing she did not believe she could yet meet 16—month-old child's medical needs. In re Wise (Ohio App. 9 Dist., 08-31-1994) 96 Ohio App.3d 619, 645 N.E.2d 812. Infants ⚖ 178

Juvenile court did not abuse its discretion in granting permanent custody of child to County Department of Children and Family Services after her father fatally shot her mother and had been sentenced to death, where social worker and child psychologist testified that order of permanent custody rather than legal custody was within child's best interests so that she could be adopted by her maternal uncle and his wife, and her guardian ad litem recommended permanent custody based on his observations of child with her maternal uncle and his wife. In re Awkal (Ohio App. 8 Dist., 06-27-1994) 95 Ohio App.3d 309, 642 N.E.2d 424. Infants ⚖ 155

Court may grant motion for permanent custody if it determines, by clear and convincing evidence, that permanent custody is in best interests of child, and child cannot be placed with either of his or her parents within reasonable period of time or should not be placed with them. In re Awkal (Ohio App. 8 Dist., 06-27-1994) 95 Ohio App.3d 309, 642 N.E.2d 424. Infants ⚖ 155; Infants ⚖ 178

Trial court's decision not to grant legal custody of children to father's relatives and instead to grant permanent custody to county agency was supported by some competent, credible evidence, including evidence that one of the three relatives failed to file motion requesting legal custody, another relative had criminal conviction for complicity in theft and forgery, other relative had similar charges dismissed after she paid restitution, and neither relative protected stepchild from abuse, although they were aware of abuse. In re Hiatt (Adams 1993) 86 Ohio App.3d 716, 621 N.E.2d 1222. Infants ⚖ 175.1

Competent, credible evidence supported placement of children in permanent custody of public children services agency; children were present on perhaps two occasions when father sexually molested their stepsister, father's and mother's kidnapping of stepsister resulted in uprooting of children as well, and during supervised visits with mother, one child was moody and the other became more physically aggressive. In re Hiatt (Adams 1993) 86 Ohio App.3d 716, 621 N.E.2d 1222. Infants ⚖ 179

Court may grant permanent custody if court determines by clear and convincing evidence that it is in best interest of children to grant permanent custody and if children cannot be placed with either parent within reasonable time or should not be placed with their parents. In re Brofford (Franklin 1992) 83 Ohio App.3d 869, 615 N.E.2d 1120. Infants ⚖ 155

Hearsay testimony concerning statements made by children to caseworker and psychologist regarding sexual abuse were not admissible at permanent custody hearing as statements did not fall within any exceptions to hearsay exclusion; statements were not asserted against parties admitting them, and foundation required to satisfy excited utterance exception was not established. In re Brofford (Franklin 1992) 83 Ohio App.3d 869, 615 N.E.2d 1120. Infants ⚖ 174

To terminate parental rights in natural child, where child is neither abandoned nor orphaned, juvenile court must find by clear and convincing evidence both that grant of permanent custody to petitioning agency is in best interest of child and that child cannot or should not be placed with either parent within reasonable time. In re Higby (Wayne 1992) 81 Ohio App.3d 466, 611 N.E.2d 403. Infants ⚖ 155

Inclusion of eight conditions in parental rights termination statute for court to consider in determining whether child can or should be placed with his parent eliminated trial court's discretion to decide that child could be placed with his parent when any one of eight conditions existed as to that parent, but did not require court to find that child could be placed with parent in absence of those eight conditions. In re Higby (Wayne 1992) 81 Ohio App.3d 466, 611 N.E.2d 403. Infants ⚖ 155

A trial court does not err in granting permanent custody of four minors to a county children services board after the mother fails to comply with a reunification plan and, over a nine-month period, the mother was involved in illegal activities, abused alcohol, missed twelve of fourteen scheduled visitations with the children, was incarcerated three times, had a violent temper, and failed to establish a permanent residence; evidence was sufficient to justify permanent termination of parental rights in the best interest of the children. In re Grant (Lorain 1991) 81 Ohio App.3d 59, 610 N.E.2d 460.

A court does not err in finding a children's services board made a good faith effort to implement a comprehensive reunification plan, and that a cocaine-addicted infant could not be placed with his parents within a reasonable length of time where the mother repeatedly failed to attend skills and psychological evaluation sessions, and where the father continued to use illicit drugs which resulted in numerous incarcerations and absences from sessions. In re Weaver (Butler 1992) 79 Ohio App.3d 59, 606 N.E.2d 1011.

A trial court's judgment permanently terminating a mother and father's parental rights and granting custody to a county children services board is supported by clear and convincing evidence which meets the standard of proof required by RC 2151.414. In re Fleming (Lucas 1991) 76 Ohio App.3d 30, 600 N.E.2d 1112.

In a parental termination proceeding, a trial court's determination that the child could not be placed with its mother within a reasonable time is supported by clear and convincing evidence that the mother demonstrated a lack of commitment toward her child; the mother's sporadic and irregular visits, which over an eight-month period totalled one weekend and four hours, indicates a lax and cavalier attitude on her part to regain custody of her child, and the mother showed an unwillingness to provide a permanent home for her child. In re McCrary (Madison 1991) 75 Ohio App.3d 601, 600 N.E.2d 347, dismissed, jurisdictional motion overruled 64 Ohio St.3d 1427, 594 N.E.2d 969.

A trial court commits reversible error in limiting evidence of adequate parental care to acts occurring prior to the filing of a motion for permanent custody. In re Foust (Crawford 1989) 57 Ohio App.3d 149, 567 N.E.2d 1042.

An award of permanent custody of two children to a children's services board is proper when (1) the mother suffers from a personality disorder requiring years of intense psychotherapy to overcome, (2) tests have shown no substantial improvement in her condition for two years, and (3) she lacks motivation and fails to establish goals for treatment while the children are in the temporary custody of the children's services board. In re Ison (Wayne 1989) 47 Ohio App.3d 103, 547 N.E.2d 420. Infants ⇐ 181

Before a trial court may terminate parental rights and grant permanent custody to a children's services board, RC 2151.414(A) requires the trial court to determine that (1) the board has made a good faith effort to implement the initial and subsequent reunification plans, (2) the parents have acted so as to leave the child without adequate parental care and they will continue to do so in the near future, and (3) it is in the best interests of the child to permanently terminate parental rights. In re Lay (Wayne 1987) 43 Ohio App.3d 78, 539 N.E.2d 664. Infants ⇐ 155

In the adjudicatory phase of a hearing pursuant to RC 2151.414, the issue is whether the parent has so acted that the child is without adequate parental care, and evidence as to the best interests of the child is inadmissible; however, admission of such evidence may be harmless when the evidence against the parent is overwhelming. In re Vickers Children (Butler 1983) 14 Ohio App.3d 201, 470 N.E.2d 438, 14 O.B.R. 228.

Although hearsay is inadmissible in adversarial juvenile court proceedings in which a parent may lose custody of his child, since a judge is the trier of fact, admission of hearsay is not prejudicial unless it is shown that such evidence was relied on by the judge in making his decision. In re Vickers Children (Butler 1983) 14 Ohio App.3d 201, 470 N.E.2d 438, 14 O.B.R. 228.

Evidence supported trial court's decision to award custody to child's half brother on ground that it was in child's best interest; testimony indicated that child markedly improved at school while living with half-brother, his attendance and his dealings with other students were indicia that he had more potential to thrive in half-brother's home, and child expressed to his guardian ad litem that he desired to remain in half-brother's custody. In re Rayl (Ohio App. 7 Dist., Belmont, 09-25-2002) No. 00-BA-55, 2002-Ohio-5176, 2002 WL 31160587, Unreported. Child Custody ⇐ 778

Clear and convincing evidence supported finding that father could not provide an adequate permanent home for child within one year of the permanent custody hearing; father had been diagnosed with schizoaffective disorder, his current diagnosis was adjustment disorder with anxiety and substance abuse in remission, psychologist testified that father would likely struggle with the "demands of adulthood from a cognitive standpoint," father's sole source of income was Social Security benefits for his mental illness, and therapist testified that father had difficulty handling finances, household matters, and medication needs. In re Shirkey (Ohio App. 12 Dist., Warren, 09-30-2002) No. CA2002-03-032, 2002-Ohio-5146, 2002 WL 31158059, Unreported. Infants ⇐ 178

Evidence was sufficient to support finding that termination of mother's parental rights and grant of permanent custody to county agency was in best interest of two special needs children; evidence included that children had been placed in foster care on multiple occasions, for past 19 months, children had been living with foster family who ensured that children received needed care and who wished to adopt them, mother failed to provide the children with a stable environment due to her continuing and episodic mental and physical breakdowns, mother's health needs forced 10-year-old to assume a parental role, guardian ad litem concluded that it was in the children's best interest that county be granted permanent custody, and court's in camera interview with children also supported this position. In re Cabanas (Ohio App. 12 Dist., Butler, 09-30-2002) No. CA2002-03-059, 2002-Ohio-5140, 2002 WL 31155124, Unreported. Infants ⇐ 178

Trial court sufficiently considered wishes of the children in its determination that grant of permanent custody to county agency was in the children's best interest; although all four children retained a bond with their natural parents, children had lived together in one foster home for two and one-half years and a strong bond existed between children and foster parents, two youngest children had stronger bond with foster parents than with natural parents, children were assimilated in the community of foster parents, and expressed their wishes to remain in foster care and not return to natural parents. In re Bowers (Ohio App. 10 Dist., Franklin, 09-26-2002) No. 02AP-347, No. 02AP-379, 2002-Ohio-5084, 2002 WL 31124026, Unreported, appeal not allowed 97 Ohio St.3d 1471, 779 N.E.2d 237, 2002-Ohio-6347, reconsideration denied 97 Ohio St.3d 1497, 780 N.E.2d 601, 2002-Ohio-7200. Infants ⇐ 222

Evidence was sufficient to find that the award of permanent custody of four siblings to county agency and termination of natural parents' rights to children was in children's best interest; both natural parents failed to complete provisions of their case plan which required that each parent obtain drug and alcohol treatment, demonstrate sobriety, submit to random urine screens, obtain adequate housing and employment, and demonstrate ability to provide adequate food, clothing and shelter to children, parents failed to support or regularly visit children, children had been living together with same foster parents for two and one-half years, two youngest children had stronger bond with foster parents than natural parents, and children expressed desire to remain in foster care. In re Bowers (Ohio App. 10 Dist., Franklin, 09-26-2002) No. 02AP-347, No. 02AP-379, 2002-Ohio-5084, 2002 WL 31124026, Unreported, appeal not allowed 97 Ohio St.3d 1471, 779 N.E.2d 237, 2002-Ohio-6347, reconsideration denied 97 Ohio St.3d 1497, 780 N.E.2d 601, 2002-Ohio-7200. Infants ⇐ 155

Evidence supported trial court's finding in termination of parental rights case that child could not be placed with mother within a reasonable time; evidence established that mother had an IQ of 68, indicating mild mental retardation, mother was minimally self supporting but she required supervision, guidance, and assistance, especially with stressful situations, mother also suffered from a passive aggressive personality disorder, which featured a pervasive pattern of negative attitudes and passive resistance to demands of adequate performances, mother was unable to maintain adequate income and stable housing, and child had a seizure disorder and symptoms of cerebral palsy and mother's ability to properly meet child's special needs was limited. In re Bair (Ohio App. 5 Dist., Richland, 09-10-2002) No. 02CA13, 2002-Ohio-5053, 2002 WL 31116692, Unreported. Infants ⇐ 158

Clear and convincing evidence supported trial court's finding in termination of parental rights case that it was in the best interest of the child to award public agency permanent custody; evidence showed that mother had no contact with the child for the first 15 months that she was in foster care and that in the two preceding years she either was not informed that child was being physically abused or did nothing about it, child's counselor opined that it was better for child to remain with foster family, custodial history demonstrated the child had not lived with mother for over three and one-half years, and the negligible relationship between mother and child belied mother's assertion that she could provide a legally secure placement. In re T.B. (Ohio App. 9 Dist., Summit, 09-25-2002) No. 21124, 2002-Ohio-5036, 2002 WL 31114995, Unreported. Infants ⇐ 178

In termination of parental rights case, child's counselor had foundational requirements of personal perception and observation that were necessary to provide opinion that it was in child's best interest to award permanent custody to public agency; counselor never met mother and spoke to her only once on the telephone, but she counseled child for over one year and diagnosed her to be a victim of neglect, and based on that experience she could reasonably conclude that mother "did not have what it takes" to be a good parent. In re T.B. (Ohio App. 9 Dist., Summit, 09-25-2002) No. 21124, 2002-Ohio-5036, 2002 WL 31114995, Unreported. Infants ⇐ 205

Clear and convincing evidence supported placing mother's two children in the permanent custody of county children services board; both children had been in and out of foster care throughout their lives, mother had gone more than ten months without seeing the children before resuming visits, mother did not exhibit a typical parent-child bond with children, although mother had completed drug and alcohol abuse treatment, mother had undergone treatment so many times before without any measurable degree of success, mother had pled guilty to child endangering and had her parental rights with regard to two older children terminated, and children's guardian ad litem strongly advocated that the permanent custody motion be granted. In re Johnson (Ohio App. 12 Dist., Butler, 09-09-2002) No. CA2002-02-035, 2002-Ohio-4708, 2002 WL 31008818, Unreported. Infants ⇐ 178

Clear and convincing evidence supported finding that termination of mother and father's parental rights was in the best interests of the children; the children were afraid of father, the children expressed a desire to remain with their foster mother, the children had been in the custody of the county department of children and family services for 12 or more months of a consecutive 22 month period, mother and father failed to provide an adequate home for the children and often could not provide the children with basic necessities, and mother and father had both pled guilty to child endangerment. In re Legg (Ohio App. 8 Dist., Cuyahoga, 09-05-2002) No. 80542, No. 80543, 2002-Ohio-4582, 2002 WL 2027290, Unreported. Infants ⇐ 155; Infants ⇐ 178

Ample evidence existed to support trial court's judgment that it was in dependent child's best interest to terminate his father's parental rights and to grant permanent custody to county children services; evidence indicated that father consistently failed to obtain adequate housing, attend parenting classes, successfully complete substance-abuse treatment, and gain full-time employment. In re Graham (Ohio App. 4 Dist., Athens, 08-02-2002) No. 01CA57, 2002-Ohio-4411, 2002 WL 1978881, Unreported. Infants ⇐ 155

Evidence was sufficient to support finding that it was in the best interest of children to grant permanent custody of the children to the county department of jobs and family services; evidence indicated suspected past incidents of abuse, child's sister told police that her brother received a lot of spankings, photograph showed that child had sustained a blackened eye, a swollen, injured hand and grotesquely red, swollen and bruised buttocks, with much broken skin, and, although mother admitted that she struck her child "ten to fifteen times" with a shoe, in the end, she both denied her culpability for the abuse and refused to submit to agency's order that she obtain help for her anger, parenting and self-control issues. In re C.F. (Ohio App. 8 Dist., Cuyahoga, 08-22-2002) No. 80371, 2002-Ohio-4286, 2002 WL 1938611, Unreported. Infants ⇌ 222

Evidence supported termination of mother's parental rights and placement of children with the state; evidence showed that mother was an alcoholic, which exacerbated domestic violence with her boyfriend, in which children became involved, that boyfriend sexually abused one child, and that father could not be found. In re Heintz (Ohio App. 3 Dist., Logan, 08-07-2002) No. 8-02-01, No. 8-02-04, No. 8-02-02, No. 8-02-03, 2002-Ohio-4004, 2002 WL 1801772, Unreported. Infants ⇌ 178

Clear and convincing evidence established that granting permanent custody of dependent child to county children services agency was in four-year-old child's best interests; child had lived with foster family for the last 19 months, play therapist testified that foster mother was able to meet child's special needs and responded appropriately to him, child gained weight while with foster family and had bonded with them, foster mother testified that child was improving in areas where he had shown developmental delays and expressed her interest in adopting him, father had not completed high school, he already had special needs child with his wife, and he was not viewed by any of the medical experts as having the skills necessary for child's special needs. In re Andrew B. (Ohio App. 6 Dist., Lucas, 08-02-2002) No. L-01-1440, 2002-Ohio-3977, 2002 WL 1788485, Unreported. Infants ⇌ 226

Clear and convincing evidence supported award of permanent custody of four neglected and dependent children to county children services board; biological mother's scheduled release from prison was more than two years away and she could face further prison time on theft and child endangering charges, board's caseworker testified that placement with relatives was not possible and that one child's foster family was willing to adopt all four children, mother had been unable to maintain stable environment and to refrain from criminal activity despite board's past and present attempts to provide services to her, and child and family therapist testified that lack of permanency was a major problem for the children and that the younger two girls had no recollection of their mother and were at critical attachment stage. In re Steele (Ohio App. 12 Dist., Butler, 07-29-2002) No. CA2002-01-011, 2002-Ohio-3872, 2002 WL 1758391, Unreported. Infants ⇌ 178

Clear and convincing evidence supported juvenile court's conclusion that it was in children's best interests to award permanent custody to county children services board, thereby terminating mother's parental rights; both mother and father pleaded guilty to child endangering, father was declared a sexual predator after he was convicted of raping children's half-sister, children's counselor testified that children were sexually abused by their father and that mother knew of the abuse, and witnesses testified that children's learning and behavioral problems improved after their placement with foster parents. In re Selina and Joseph (Ohio App. 9 Dist., Summit, 07-31-2002) No. 20940, 2002-Ohio-3866, 2002 WL 1758707, Unreported. Infants ⇌ 178

In proceeding for termination of parental rights, trial court erred by failing to consider mother's relationship and interaction with child, and child's wishes as expressed by guardian ad litem. In re Salsgiver (Ohio App. 11 Dist., Geauga, 07-22-2002) No. 2002-G-2411, 2002-Ohio-3712, 2002 WL 1627395, Unreported. Infants ⇌ 155

Clear and convincing evidence supported juvenile court's findings, which were made as basis to terminate parental rights and award permanent custody of child to public services agency, that child was in agency's temporary custody for sufficient time period and that parent showed an unwillingness to provide an adequate permanent home; parent's lack of commitment was shown by evidence that she failed to visit child on a regular basis when she was able to do so, parent did not support child by obtaining and maintaining a job, and parent did not find suitable housing for herself and the child, and it was undisputed that child was in agency's temporary custody for 12 or more months of a consecutive 22 month period. In re Miqueal M. (Ohio App. 6 Dist., Lucas, 06-28-2002) No. L-02-1020, 2002-Ohio-3417, 2002 WL 1438664, Unreported. Infants ⇌ 178

Given evidence that mother repeatedly failed to comply with her case plan by failing to acquire proper housing, not completing parenting classes or drug treatment, and continuing to use drugs, trial court did not lose its way in concluding that terminating mother's parental rights and granting permanent custody to county children service bureau was in children's best interest. In re Brown (Ohio App. 9 Dist., Summit, 07-03-2002) No. 21004, 2002-Ohio-3405, 2002 WL 1454025, Unreported. Infants ⇌ 222

Evidence supported granting custody of mother's two children to county children's services board; evidence showed that mother had weak bond with children, who had bonded with foster parents, mother had difficulty watching both children at the same time, there were no beds for the children in mother's home, mother did not complete significant parts of her case plan, and guardian ad litem strongly recommended permanent state custody. In re Meadows (Ohio App. 12 Dist., Warren, 06-24-2002) No. CA2001-11-096, 2002-Ohio-3168, 2002 WL 1358701, Unreported. Infants ⇌ 177

Findings that children had been abandoned and that children had been in custody of county department of jobs and family services for 12 or more months of consecutive 22 month period were not contradictory, but were alternate grounds upon which to base grant of permanent custody of children with department, in termination of parental rights proceeding; finding that children were abandoned was sufficient in and of itself under statute to base grant of permanent custody, but court also made finding that children had been in custody of department for 12 or more months of consecutive 22 month period. In re Tolley (Ohio App. 5 Dist., Stark, 06-17-2002) No. 2002CA102, 2002-Ohio-3094, 2002 WL 1343292, Unreported. Infants ⇌ 180

Grant of permanent custody of children to county department of jobs and family services and termination of mother's parental rights based on finding that children could not be placed with mother within reasonable time was not against manifest weight of the evidence; mother's home was extremely dirty and in general disarray, children's older brother had sexually abused children, mother did not pay child support, nor did she provide support to children of any sort, department had not viewed mother's current home, but mother had not requested home study, mother had pattern of living with several adults in small home or trailer, and children did not wish to have contact with mother. In re Tolley (Ohio App. 5 Dist., Stark, 06-17-2002) No. 2002CA102, 2002-Ohio-3094, 2002 WL 1343292, Unreported. Infants ⇌ 222

Finding that grant of permanent custody of children to county department of jobs and family services was in their best interests was supported by evidence; there was no significant bonding between mother and children, there were no relatives with which children could be placed, social worker testified that she did not believe that mother could meet children's emotional needs for a permanent home, and that mother had not expressed commitment to provide for children, and children expressed desire to be adopted. In re Tolley (Ohio App. 5 Dist., Stark, 06-17-2002) No. 2002CA102, 2002-Ohio-3094, 2002 WL 1343292, Unreported. Infants ⇌ 222

Evidence in proceeding to terminate mother's parental rights supported finding that mother failed to substantially remedy the problems which caused son to be removed from her custody, and that son could not be placed in her custody within a reasonable amount of time; two caseworkers testified that her compliance with case plan was minimal and had deteriorated over time, and that she tested positive for marijuana on two occasions just prior to the hearing. In re Heatherly (Ohio App. 9 Dist., Summit, 06-19-2002) No. 20925, 2002-Ohio-3028, 2002 WL 1363711, Unreported. Infants ⇌ 178

Alleged error of trial court, in finding that county agency that brought dependency and neglect proceeding made good faith effort to reunify children with their parents, did not invalidate determination in judgment terminating parental rights that children could not be placed with parents within a reasonable time; trial court also found two other applicable statutory factors, each of which by itself required determination that children could not be placed with parents within a reasonable time. In re Chianna C. (Ohio App. 6 Dist., Lucas, 06-07-2002) No. L-02-1019, 2002-Ohio-2800, 2002 WL 1303212, Unreported. Infants ⇌ 155

Trial court finding that child had been in an out-of-home placement for 12 of the last 24 months, when the statute required a finding that child had been in an out-of-home placement for 12 of the prior 22 months was harmless error, in child dependency proceeding; mother conceded that the State had established that child had been in an out-of-home placement for 12 of the past 22 months. In re Borders (Ohio App. 12 Dist., Brown, 05-28-2002) No. CA2001-10-017, 2002-Ohio-2578, 2002 WL 1058119, Unreported. Infants ⇌ 253

A trial court errs in finding that a child could not be placed with either parent within a reasonable period of time where there is no indication in the record that there was ever any attempt to serve the child's father with notice of the permanent custody proceedings; in the absence of any evidence concerning the father the trial court could not have found that the child could not be placed with his father. In re Kincaid (Ohio App. 4 Dist., Lawrence, 10-27-2000) No. 00CA3, 2000-Ohio-2005, 2000-Ohio-2017, 2000 WL 1683456, Unreported.

Where a trial court enters a finding pursuant to RC 2151.414(E) that a child cannot be placed with either parent within a reasonable period of time, the court improperly circumvents the statute by then granting legal custody of the child to the foster parent of the child's mother (also a minor). In re Mayle, Nos. 76739 and 77165, 2000 WL 1038189 (8th Dist Ct App, Cuyahoga, 7–27–00).

Permanent custody of a child is properly awarded to a county children services agency where the home of the natural parents is dirty and unhealthy because, among other factors, of lack of running water or a well, and where diligent efforts were made to engage in "reasonable care planning" with the parents. In re McDaniel, No. 92–CA–359 (4th Dist Ct App, Adams, 2–11–93).

Evidence that a minor child was sexually exploited by the mother, that family lived in an unsuitable residence lacking heat, water, and electricity, and that the minor child had not been attending school, constituted overwhelming evidence of inadequate care in light of the factors listed in RC 2151.414(A)(2). Stanford v Lucas County Children Services Bd, No. L–86–137 (6th Dist Ct App, Lucas, 3–20–87).

Termination of parental rights is against the manifest weight of evidence where the parents have substantially complied with a comprehensive reunification plan. In re Lash, No. S–83–16 (6th Dist Ct App, Sandusky, 4–20–84).

Where a mother took her child voluntarily to children's services on a temporary basis until the mother found housing, a subsequent order granting the children's services permanent custody based on evidence that the mother had a domestic spat with her husband, did poorly on a psychological test, refused counseling and had a cluttered home is not sustained by the manifest weight of the evidence. Howser v Ashtabula County Children's Services Bd, No. 1134 (11th Dist Ct App, Ashtabula, 9–19–83).

In an action for permanent custody, where the mother has been convicted of several theft offenses but claims to have "learned her lesson," the court must give the mother the benefit of the doubt and deny permanent custody to the welfare department. In re Groves, 13 OBR 77 (CP, Fayette 1983).

Finding that mother's parental rights to her six children should be terminated and permanent custody granted to county children services agency was not against the manifest weight of the evidence, where children had been in agency's custody for 12 out of 22 consecutive months, mother had failed to complete her case plan and was unable to provide for the children's basic needs, children were doing well in foster care, and mother had failed to engage in individual counseling relative to the children's disclosure of sexual abuse. In re J.L. (Ohio App. 8 Dist., Cuyahoga, 11-10-2004) No. 84368, 2004-Ohio-6024, 2004 WL 2578874, Unreported, appeal not allowed 104 Ohio St.3d 1463, 821 N.E.2d 578, 2005-Ohio-204. Infants ⇐ 155

4. Representation by counsel

Magistrate's failure to consider the wishes of child as expressed directly by child or through child's guardian ad litem prior to terminating mother's parental rights and granting permanent custody of child to county department of jobs and family services constituted reversible error; without knowing child's wishes, trial court could not determine if independent counsel for child was necessary. In re Walling (Ohio App. 1 Dist., Hamilton, 02-24-2006) No. C-050646, 2006-Ohio-810, 2006 WL 445981, Unreported. Infants ⇐ 253

Trial court was obligated to conduct second in camera interview to determine whether eldest child needed independent counsel, in termination of parental rights proceeding involving four children; appointed counsel for children was unsure of eldest child's interests and could not adequately represent her if eldest child desired to live with her father, since then her interests were adverse to her sisters' interests, and thus, in camera interview was necessary to discover whether eldest child's interests were in conflict with her sisters' interests. In re Sherman (Ohio App. 3 Dist., Hancock, 11-07-2005) No. 05-04-47, No. 05-04-48, No. 05-04-49, 2005-Ohio-5888, 2005 WL 2933064, Unreported. Infants ⇐ 205

Trial court was not required to appoint separate counsel for children, in termination of parental rights proceeding, as recommendations of children's guardian ad litem were consistent with wishes of children to remain with their foster families and, if possible, to be adopted by them, as expressed to her by children and as expressed by children directly to trial court at in camera review. In re Amber L. (Ohio App. 6 Dist., Williams, 08-12-2005) No. 20230034, No. 20230035, No. 20230336, 2005-Ohio-4172, 2005 WL 1926515, Unreported. Infants ⇐ 205

Father could not be viewed as having waived his right to counsel, and thus trial court committed plain error in allowing father's counsel to withdraw her representation immediately prior to dispositional hearing at which father's parental rights were terminated; trial court could not have reasonably concluded that failure of counsel's communication with father resulted in inability of counsel to ascertain father's wishes because it was counsel who informed court that it was father's desire to have custody of child. In re Tyler S. (Ohio App. 6 Dist., Lucas, 03-18-2005) No. L-04-1294, 2005-Ohio-1225, 2005 WL 635029, Unreported. Infants ⇐ 243

Any error in trial court's failure to appoint counsel to represent dependent child prior to hearing before magistrate in termination of parental rights proceeding was waived, where counsel, who was appointed to represent child before trial court adopted magistrate's recommendations, did not object to magistrate's recommendations for reason that child did not have counsel at hearing, as presumably counsel believed child's guardian ad litem adequately protected child's interest at that hearing. In re C.S. (Ohio App. 2 Dist., Montgomery, 10-22-2004) No. 20379, 2004-Ohio-5810, 2004 WL 2445238, Unreported. Infants ⇐ 243

Appointment of separate counsel for mother's four-year-old child was not warranted in proceedings to determine if permanent custody of child should be awarded to county agency; although child expressed desire to "see" her mother, child also stated to her guardian ad litem that she wanted to live with the foster mother, and any inconsistency only underscored the lack of cognitive maturity necessary for appointment of independent counsel. In re G.C. & M.C. (Ohio App. 8 Dist., Cuyahoga, 10-21-2004) No. 83994, 2004-Ohio-5607, 2004 WL 2367243, Unreported. Infants ⇐ 205

Children in proceedings brought by county agency seeking permanent custody were not entitled to independent legal counsel, despite claim that separately assigned attorney would have advocated for housing for children, a right seemingly of constitutional importance that the guardian ad litem allegedly failed to protect; four-year-old children exhibiting delayed speech and language development were unlikely to possess or be able to express their wishes for housing, and any perceived dereliction of duty on the part of agency in satisfying children's basic needs should have been addressed by caregiver's counsel. In re K. (Ohio App. 8 Dist., Cuyahoga, 09-02-2004) No. 83410, 2004-Ohio-4629, 2004 WL 1946141, Unreported. Infants ⇐ 205

Mother waived her appellate argument that the trial court erred when it failed to appoint independent legal representation for child, during termination of parental rights proceeding, where mother failed to request the appointment of independent legal counsel for child and never objected to the trial court's failure to appoint independent legal counsel for child. In re Wright (Ohio App. 10 Dist., Franklin, 08-03-2004) No. 04AP-435, 2004-Ohio-4045, 2004 WL 1729881, Unreported. Infants ⇐ 243

Any error in trial court failure to directly probe wishes of mother's two children regarding custody, for purposes of determining whether they should be appointed separate counsel in permanent custody proceedings, was harmless; testimony established that children desired not to be returned to their mother's custody, and abundant evidence supported trial court's findings that children's best interests were served by awarding permanent custody to county. In re Brooks (Ohio App. 10 Dist., Franklin, 07-22-2004) No. 04AP-164, No. 04AP-201, No. 04AP-202, No. 04AP-165, 2004-Ohio-3887, 2004 WL 1631760, Unreported, appeal not allowed 103 Ohio St.3d 1495, 816 N.E.2d 1081, 2004-Ohio-5605. Infants ⇐ 253

Trial court was not required to appoint separate counsel for each of mother's two children in permanent custody proceedings; although guardian ad litem never told trial court what the children's wishes were with regard to placement, there was no evidence demonstrating that children's wishes were incongruent with recommendation of guardian ad litem that permanent custody be awarded to county, credible evidence showed that neither child wished to return to custody of mother, and abundant evidence established that award of permanent custody to county was in best interests of children. In re Brooks (Ohio App. 10 Dist., Franklin, 07-22-2004) No. 04AP-164, No. 04AP-201, No. 04AP-202, No. 04AP-165, 2004-Ohio-3887, 2004 WL 1631760, Unreported, appeal not allowed 103 Ohio St.3d 1495, 816 N.E.2d 1081, 2004-Ohio-5605. Infants ⇐ 205

Trial court's failure to provide independent counsel for mother's children was not plain error in proceedings to determine whether permanent custody of mother's three dependent children should be granted to county agency; mother stated no objection to withdrawal of counsel for children and did not object to the procedure outlined by the court if circumstances necessitated appointment of counsel later in the proceedings, and interests of the children, who wished to be adopted, were not aligned with mother but were consistent with guardian ad litem. In re Johnson (Ohio App. 10 Dist., Franklin, 07-22-2004) No. 03AP-1264, 2004-Ohio-3886, 2004 WL 1631756, Unreported, appeal not allowed 103 Ohio St.3d 1465, 815 N.E.2d 680, 2004-Ohio-5056, reconsideration denied 104 Ohio St.3d 1412, 818 N.E.2d 712, 2004-Ohio-6364. Infants ⇐ 243

Mother, challenging county's effort seeking permanent custody of her three dependent children, waived issue of whether trial court was required to provide independent counsel for her children; mother stated no objection to the withdrawal of counsel for children and did not object to the procedure outlined by the court if circumstances necessitated appointment of counsel later in the proceedings. In re Johnson (Ohio App. 10 Dist., Franklin, 07-22-2004) No. 03AP-1264, 2004-Ohio-3886, 2004 WL 1631756, Unreported, appeal not allowed 103 Ohio St.3d 1465, 815 N.E.2d 680, 2004-Ohio-5056, reconsideration denied 104 Ohio St.3d 1412, 818 N.E.2d 712, 2004-Ohio-6364. Infants 243

Denying attorney's request to withdraw as counsel for mother in termination of parental rights proceeding was not abuse of discretion, where attorney was mother's third appointed counsel and there was no indication that mother would be able to obtain counsel before hearing date. In re Baby Girl Elliott (Ohio App. 12 Dist., Butler, 07-06-2004) No. CA2003-10-256, 2004-Ohio-3539, 2004 WL 1485858, Unreported. Infants 205

Children were entitled to counsel in termination of parental rights hearing to advocate for their wishes regarding custody, where court did not appoint counsel for the children, did not expressly appoint the guardian ad litem to act as their counsel, and did not make any determination as to whether any of the children lacked the maturity to benefit from the appointment of counsel, and there was no evidence regarding wishes and/or level of maturity of two of the children on which the court could have made any decision regarding the appointment of counsel. In re Ridenour (Ohio App. 11 Dist., Lake, 04-16-2004) No. 2003-L-146, No. 2003-L-147, No. 2003-L-148, 2004-Ohio-1958, 2004 WL 834579, Unreported. Infants 205

Trial court denial of county department of job and family services' motion for permanent custody of child was not an abuse of discretion and was in the best interests of the children; mother's clinical counselor testified that mother developed a better sense of how to manage her stress, child's therapist testified that mother and father attended some sessions with child and that mother's parenting ability had improved, mother had completed a parenting class, secured suitable housing, and was in counseling, and mother and the children were bonded to each other. In re Snow (Ohio App. 11 Dist., Portage, 03-29-2004) No. 2003-P-0080, 2004-Ohio-1519, 2004 WL 605151, Unreported. Infants 178

Mother of dependent children was entitled to assert children's right to counsel in termination of parental rights proceeding, where both mother and children desired reunification. In re Emery (Ohio App. 4 Dist., Lawrence, 04-25-2003) No. 02CA40, 2003-Ohio-2206, 2003 WL 2003811, Unreported. Infants 200

Father waived his right to counsel in termination of parental rights proceedings, and thus, trial court did not err in granting father's counsel's motion to withdraw, where father had demonstrated a disinterest in matter from beginning, in that father failed to meet objectives of his case plan to regain custody, failed to cooperate with the court, had not communicated with his attorney since his last appearance in court six months prior to termination, which appearance was a hearing on county's motion for change in disposition to allow county to file for permanent custody wherein father agreed that county should seek permanent custody of his daughters. In re Rachal G. (Ohio App. 6 Dist., Lucas, 03-07-2003) No. L-02-1306, 2003-Ohio-1041, 2003 WL 863556, Unreported. Infants 205

Trial court erred in failing to consider indigent child's level of maturity and whether his repeated desire for reunification with his mother required appointment of counsel to represent child's interest in whether to terminate mother's parental rights, even though guardian ad litem had been appointed for child, where guardian ad litem recommended termination of mother's rights, and conflict existed between guardian's recommendation and child's stated desire to stay with his mother. In re Williams (Ohio App. 11 Dist., Geauga, 11-29-2002) No. 2002-G-2454, No. 2002-G-2459, 2002-Ohio-6588, 2002 WL 31716777, Unreported, stay granted 98 Ohio St.3d 1408, 781 N.E.2d 1017, 2003-Ohio-60, appeal not allowed 98 Ohio St.3d 1425, 782 N.E.2d 79, 2003-Ohio-259. Infants 205

Hearing on termination of parental rights could continue despite counsel's withdrawal due to lack of contact with parents and parents' subsequent lack of legal representation; parents stated at hearing they did not object to counsel's withdrawal, lawyer was the fifth attorney appointed for parents, who had asked that the first four be dismissed, parents had not cooperated with any of their attorneys, and parents told court that attorneys were nasty and wanted to lie and that they did not need people like that involved with their case. In re Hayes (Ohio App. 5 Dist., Tuscarawas, 04-19-2002) No. 2001AP110099, No. 2001AP110098, 2002-Ohio-2446, 2002 WL 819216, Unreported. Infants 205

Mother who claimed ineffective assistance of counsel was not prejudiced by counsel's failure to request separate counsel for children in county's permanent custody proceeding and counsel's failure to cross-examine guardian ad litem on the contents of her report recommending permanent custody to county jobs and family services agency; independent counsel for the children was not warranted, and outcome of the hearing would not have been different with any additional cross-examination of the guardian ad litem. In re Graham (Ohio App. 1 Dist., 06-23-2006) 167 Ohio App.3d 284, 854 N.E.2d 1126, 2006-Ohio-3170. Infants 205

Children were not entitled to independent legal counsel, in proceeding in which county child protection agency sought permanent custody of children; two of children were represented by the same attorney, but there was no evidence that their interests conflicted, and, youngest child was only two years old, and was incapable of expressing his wishes. In re Lopez (Ohio App. 3 Dist., 05-08-2006) 166 Ohio App.3d 688, 852 N.E.2d 1266, 2006-Ohio-2251. Infants 205

Assuming that mother's counsel was derelict in failing to timely move for appointment of new counsel due to conflict of interest and in failing to follow up on motion, mother did not show prejudice, and thus, mother could not establish ineffective assistance of counsel in proceeding for permanent custody of dependent children; Montgomery County Children Services (MCCS) proved its case by clear and convincing evidence and nothing in record suggested any viable objections. In re Lakes (Ohio App. 2 Dist., 08-02-2002) 149 Ohio App.3d 128, 776 N.E.2d 510, 2002-Ohio-3917. Infants 205

If the defendant, in seeking appointment of new counsel, alleges facts which, if true, would require relief, the trial court must inquire into the defendant's complaint and make the inquiry part of the record; the inquiry may be brief and minimal, but it must be made if the allegations are sufficiently specific. In re Lakes (Ohio App. 2 Dist., 08-02-2002) 149 Ohio App.3d 128, 776 N.E.2d 510, 2002-Ohio-3917. Criminal Law 641.10(2)

Even assuming father's counsel provided deficient performance by failing to object that testimony of protective services supervisor for county children's services agency involved events and statements outside her personal knowledge, father was not prejudiced at hearing on agency's motion to terminate parental rights; much of the information was also testified to by other witnesses who had firsthand knowledge of events. In re Wingo (Ohio App. 4 Dist., 06-01-2001) 143 Ohio App.3d 652, 758 N.E.2d 780, 2001-Ohio-2477. Infants 205; Infants 253

Assuming that father's counsel provided deficient performance by failing to submit written argument to court regarding whether child was dependent child and by failing to appear at the hearing extending temporary custody, father was not prejudiced; at that juncture of the case, county children's services agency was attempting to reunify child with mother and place him with a relative until such goal could be accomplished, father had expressed no desire to gain custody of child, and child's relatives were either not interested in custody or were considered improper placements by agency. In re Wingo (Ohio App. 4 Dist., 06-01-2001) 143 Ohio App.3d 652, 758 N.E.2d 780, 2001-Ohio-2477. Infants 205; Infants 253

For attorney to act as guardian ad litem and attorney for ward, there must be dual appointment, and finding that no conflict exists. Matter of Duncan/Walker Children (Ohio App. 5 Dist., 03-18-1996) 109 Ohio App.3d 841, 673 N.E.2d 217. Attorney And Client 21.5(1); Infants 81

Court of Appeals would grant father's attorney's motion to withdraw as counsel following his filing of *Anders* brief, and would dismiss as wholly frivolous father's appeal from award of permanent custody of his three children to child services board, notwithstanding that attorney failed to list any possible errors that might arguably support the appeal, where Court examined record and found no error prejudicial to father's rights in proceedings before juvenile court. In re Egbert Children (Ohio App. 12 Dist., 12-27-1994) 99 Ohio App.3d 492, 651 N.E.2d 38. Attorney And Client 76(1); Infants 247

In parental rights termination proceeding, mother was not denied effective assistance of appointed counsel despite her claims that counsel failed to meet with her until day before hearing, that no discovery was conducted and that no witnesses other than mother were called; there was no evidence that failure of attorney to meet with mother sooner was caused by attorney, particularly in light of mother's demonstrated communication problems with social services agency, child's foster mother, health officials and her own daughter, and there was no evidence that witnesses were available or that discovery would have led to facts pertinent to action. In re Wise (Ohio App. 9 Dist., 08-31-1994) 96 Ohio App.3d 619, 645 N.E.2d 812. Infants 205

Mother whose parental rights were terminated failed to show that she was denied effective assistance of counsel by counsel's failure to forcefully pursue option in foster care; when mother testified at hearing, she indicated she was comfortable with idea of foster mother adopting child and that she thought adoption by foster mother would be best for the child, particularly when considered in light of circumstances of case. In re Wise (Ohio App. 9 Dist., 08-31-1994) 96 Ohio App.3d 619, 645 N.E.2d 812. Infants 205

Defendant was coerced and in custody during interview at Department of Human Services (DHS) and, therefore, was entitled to be informed of his constitutional rights under *Miranda* where DHS social worker told defendant that his child would be removed from home if defendant did not attend interview and coercive methods of interrogation employed by police officer during interview created in-custody, police-dominated atmosphere. State v. Brown (Ohio App. 6 Dist., 11-05-1993) 91 Ohio App.3d 427, 632 N.E.2d 970, dismissed, jurisdictional motion overruled 68 Ohio St.3d 1471, 628 N.E.2d 1390. Criminal Law ⇔ 412.2(2)

The test for ineffective assistance of counsel used in criminal cases is applicable in actions to terminate parental rights. Jones v. Lucas County Children Services Bd. (Lucas 1988) 46 Ohio App.3d 85, 546 N.E.2d 471. Infants ⇔ 205

Failure to advise mother that she had a right to appointed counsel in child abuse and neglect proceeding if she were indigent did not prejudice mother; fact that mother had retained counsel negated the statutory notice requirement. In re C.F. (Ohio App. 8 Dist., Cuyahoga, 08-22-2002) No. 80371, 2002-Ohio-4286, 2002 WL 1938611, Unreported. Infants ⇔ 253

Where the natural parent of minor children was not represented by counsel during neglect, dependency and temporary custody proceedings but was represented by counsel at the parental rights termination and permanent custody proceedings, such parent is barred from bringing a habeas corpus action more than one year after the final decrees of adoption were issued for the minor children. Beard v Williams County Dept of Social Services, No. WMS–83–3 (6th Dist Ct App, Williams, 7–15–83).

5. Adequate parental care, factors

Evidence during permanent custody proceeding supported juvenile court's finding that father could not adequately parent his child; father refused to undergo a psychological evaluation even though he knew why he needed to be evaluated, father, age 38, had never lived alone, had never worked until he started working for fast food restaurant, had never done a budget, and let grandmother take care of the household budget and monthly bills, he was never forthcoming during the proceedings as to his parenting experience and ability, and he was vague as to how he would take care of child if he were the child's custodial parent and working full time. In re C.E. (Ohio App. 12 Dist., Butler, 09-18-2006) No. CA2006-01-015, No. CA2006-02-024, 2006-Ohio-4827, 2006 WL 2663464, Unreported. Infants ⇔ 155

Trial court error in finding that father would be incarcerated for four more years, and thus would be unable to care for his children for at least 18 months after the filing of the motion for permanent custody, was harmless, during termination of parental rights proceeding, where the court found that children could not be placed with father within a reasonable time or should not be placed with father. In re Jason S. (Ohio App. 6 Dist., Lucas, 02-17-2006) No. L-05-1264, 2006-Ohio-726, 2006 WL 367104, Unreported. Infants ⇔ 253

The trial court's failure to award custody of father's children to father's brother was not an abuse of discretion, during termination of parental rights proceeding; family service worker testified that the department of job and family services denied brother's home study based on concerns about whether brother and his girlfriend could care for and meet the needs of the children since brother and girlfriend both worked full time jobs, with girlfriend working two or three jobs at a time, and that the commitment from brother and his girlfriend was "extremely concerning." In re Zurfley/Chatman/Black Children (Ohio App. 5 Dist., Stark, 02-13-2006) No. 2005CA00217, 2006-Ohio-683, 2006 WL 337366, Unreported. Infants ⇔ 175.1

Competent and credible evidence supported trial court's finding that children could not be placed with either parent within reasonable time or should not be placed with either parent, and would support court's decision to terminate parents' parental rights; on separate occasions children had been injured in home, and, although abuse was not linked to parents, parents were unable to explain how injuries occurred, parents had not remedied condition which caused children to be removed from home, and parents had demonstrated unwillingness to provide adequate permanent home and prevent neglect. In re Daniel D. (Ohio App. 6 Dist., Lucas, 10-14-2005) No. L-04-1363, 2005-Ohio-5457, 2005 WL 2600425, Unreported. Infants ⇔ 156

For purposes of determining whether mother substantially complied with terms of her case plan in child protection proceedings, mother's testimony that she expected to live in home recently purchased by individual listed on child's birth certificate as child's father was insufficient to demonstrate that she had secured stable, independent housing, where such individual was facing criminal charges for receiving stolen property, had outstanding arrest warrant, had failed to visit child or comply with any of his own case plan requirements, and failed to attend permanent custody hearing. In re G.B. (Ohio App. 9 Dist., Summit, 08-31-2005) No. 22628, 2005-Ohio-4540, 2005 WL 2087826, Unreported. Infants ⇔ 179

For purposes of determining whether mother substantially complied with terms of her case plan in child protection proceedings, mother's incarceration or expressed fear of arrest on outstanding warrant should she attend scheduled visitation with her child were insufficient justifications for missed visitation. In re G.B. (Ohio App. 9 Dist., Summit, 08-31-2005) No. 22628, 2005-Ohio-4540, 2005 WL 2087826, Unreported. Infants ⇔ 155

Clear and convincing evidence supported conclusion that child could not be placed with his mother or father within a reasonable time, or should not be placed with them, in termination of parental rights proceeding; child had no connection with his father, father had no interest in being part of child's life, mother had made no progress in treatment of her borderline personality disorder and resisted taking her medication, and psychologist who performed psychological evaluation on mother testified that within reasonable degree of psychological certainty mother could not adequately parent child, and that there was nothing county could do that could facilitate child's return to mother's care. In re Van Atta (Ohio App. 3 Dist., Hancock, 08-15-2005) No. 5-05-03, 2005-Ohio-4182, 2005 WL 1939418, Unreported. Infants ⇔ 158

Sufficient evidence supported conclusion that mother's repeated incarcerations prevented her from providing adequate care for her children, in termination of parental rights proceeding; mother was a career criminal, who had spent significant amounts of time in incarceration as result of her offenses, at time county filed permanent custody motion she had spent 12 of prior 24 months in incarceration, and mother acknowledged her continued inability to comply with terms and conditions of her probation. In re Amber L. (Ohio App. 6 Dist., Williams, 08-12-2005) No. 20230034, No. 20230035, No. 20230336, 2005-Ohio-4172, 2005 WL 1926515, Unreported. Infants ⇔ 157

Evidence supported conclusion that mother failed to pay county child support for her children, despite her ability to do so, in termination of parental rights proceeding; mother's child support obligation was $116 per month for each of three children at issue, mother admitted she was not paying any child support, and evidence demonstrated that her monthly family income amounted to more than $2,500 per month. In re Amber L. (Ohio App. 6 Dist., Williams, 08-12-2005) No. 20230034, No. 20230035, No. 20230336, 2005-Ohio-4172, 2005 WL 1926515, Unreported. Infants ⇔ 157

Evidence did not support conclusion that mother's mental health disorders were so severe as to render her incapable of providing an adequate, stable home for her children, in termination of parental rights proceeding; psychologist did opine that, left untreated, mother, who suffered from borderline personality disorder, was likely to repeat same patterns of behavior without a lot of insight into or understanding about causes of that behavior, but there was no specific discussion of what those behavior patterns might be or how they might impact mother's ability to care for her children. In re Amber L. (Ohio App. 6 Dist., Williams, 08-12-2005) No. 20230034, No. 20230035, No. 20230336, 2005-Ohio-4172, 2005 WL 1926515, Unreported. Infants ⇔ 181

Record established clear and convincing evidence that mother had failed to substantially remedy circumstances that resulted in removal of her children, in proceeding in which court terminated mother's parental rights and granted permanent custody of children to county child services board; mother failed to address her various mental health issues via psychological counseling, mother failed to obtain housing or stable employment, and, although mother had taken step toward recovery by enrolling in residential program, there was no indication mother had remedied her substance abuse problem. In re Phillips (Ohio App. 11 Dist., Ashtabula, 07-22-2005) No. 2005-A-0020, 2005-Ohio-3774, 2005 WL 1714181, Unreported. Infants ⇔ 158

Trial court properly found that children could not be placed with mother in a reasonable amount of time, in proceeding in which court terminated mother's parental rights and granted permanent custody of children to county child services board; evidence affirmatively established that mother had demonstrated a lack of commitment to her children, as she had failed to communicate or visit with children for approximately nine months. In re Phillips (Ohio App. 11 Dist., Ashtabula, 07-22-2005) No. 2005-A-0020, 2005-Ohio-3774, 2005 WL 1714181, Unreported. Infants ⇔ 157

Trial court properly found that children had been abandoned, in proceeding in which court terminated mother's parental rights and granted permanent custody of children to county child services board; upon mother's own admission at hearing, there was approximately a nine-month period during which she had no contact or visitation with children, well beyond statutory 90-day period, and there was no evidence that would rebut presumption that mother abandoned her children. In re Phillips (Ohio App. 11 Dist., Ashtabula, 07-22-2005) No. 2005-A-0020, 2005-Ohio-3774, 2005 WL 1714181, Unreported. Infants ⇔ 180

Evidence supported trial court's finding that children could not or should not be placed with mother within a reasonable period of time, thus supporting grant of permanent custody of children to county child protection agency; mother failed continuously and repeatedly to substantially remedy the conditions which led to the removal, mother showed inability and/or unwillingness to work toward reunification, mother failed to complete any aspect of case plan, and mother had previously lost permanent custody of one child and surrendered custody of another child. In re Zink (Ohio App. 5 Dist., Licking, 07-05-2005) No. 2004CA0081, No. 2004CA00106, 2005-Ohio-3460, 2005 WL 1579312, Unreported. Infants ⇔ 155

Evidence in termination of parental rights proceeding supported juvenile court's finding that child could not be placed with father within a reasonable period of time; father had been convicted of numerous crimes, including domestic violence against a child, and he was mildly mentally retarded with strong propensities toward a number of personality disorders. In re Spangler (Ohio App. 3 Dist., Hardin, 07-05-2005) No. 6-04-15, 2005-Ohio-3450, 2005 WL 1545777, Unreported. Infants ⇔ 158

Termination of mother's parental rights was in child's best interests; mother's incarceration precluded her from providing adequate and permanent home for child, and child had progressed in foster care and had opportunity to be adopted in a foster home where he had bonded with the parent, an opportunity that would be lost absent termination of parental rights. In re J.Z. (Ohio App. 10 Dist., Franklin, 06-28-2005) No. 05AP-8, 2005-Ohio-3285, 2005 WL 1515395, Unreported. Infants ⇔ 157

Sufficient evidence supported conclusion that child could not or should not be returned to his parents, in termination of parental rights proceeding; mother would not be available to child for more than 18 months after motion for permanent custody was filed, due to her incarceration, mother failed to remedy conditions which led to child being placed in county's custody, given that she failed to successfully complete any of the significant elements of her case plan, and neither child's putative father nor child's maternal grandmother were suitable placements for child. In re J.Z. (Ohio App. 10 Dist., Franklin, 06-28-2005) No. 05AP-8, 2005-Ohio-3285, 2005 WL 1515395, Unreported. Infants ⇔ 157

Sufficient evidence supported trial court's decision that it was in best interests of children that permanent custody of children be granted to county department of job and family services; although children had strong bond with mother, social worker assigned to case testified that children also had strong bond with foster parents and grandparents with whom they had been placed, and record showed that children had been in custody of department for over 15 consecutive months at time of hearing, and that mother committed felony for which she was serving prison sentence. In re Speaks (Ohio App. 5 Dist., Licking, 06-20-2005) No. 2004 CA 0090, 2005-Ohio-3526, 2005 WL 1503572, Unreported, appeal not allowed 107 Ohio St.3d 1423, 837 N.E.2d 1208, 2005-Ohio-6124. Infants ⇔ 157

Sufficient evidence supported trial court's finding that it was in children's best interest for county children services board to be awarded permanent custody of children; despite mother's efforts to seek counseling and educational training, mother failed to follow through with recommendations that she seek further drug rehabilitative services or psychological assistance, mother's efforts with respect to meeting children's needs did not negate fact that children were denied stable housing, and mother continued to regularly use crack cocaine on top of medication she was prescribed for her bipolar diagnosis. In re Brittany W. (Ohio App. 6 Dist., Lucas, 06-24-2005) No. L-04-1202, 2005-Ohio-3201, 2005 WL 1492028, Unreported. Infants ⇔ 158

Evidence supported trial court's determination that placing minor child in the legal custody of his paternal grandmother was in his best interest, following dependent child adjudication; mother had taken very few steps to remedy the problems that led to child's removal, mother had problems with cocaine abuse, alcohol dependence, and opiate abuse, she had not been attending drug and alcohol counseling, nor had she been consistent in submitting urine samples for drug screening, and grandmother testified that, if the trial court placed child in her legal custody, she was willing to be responsible for him until he reached the age of 18. In re K.K. (Ohio App. 9 Dist., Summit, 06-22-2005) No. 22352, 2005-Ohio-3112, 2005 WL 1460317, Unreported, appeal allowed 107 Ohio St.3d 1407, 836 N.E.2d 1228, 2005-Ohio-5859, affirmed 109 Ohio St.3d 206, 846 N.E.2d 853, 2006-Ohio-2184. Infants ⇔ 222

Evidence supported finding that child could not be placed with mother, in support of order awarding permanent custody of child to county children services; mother's parental rights had previously been terminated to two of her other children, mother's oldest child was in the custody of a relative, mother and father lived in a two-bedroom apartment with father's mother, and mother was able to be employed but remained unemployed. In re West (Ohio App. 4 Dist., Athens, 06-10-2005) No. 05CA4, 2005-Ohio-2977, 2005 WL 1400029, Unreported. Infants ⇔ 155

Evidence supported finding that child could not be placed with father, in support of order awarding permanent custody of child to county children services; father and mother lived in a two-bedroom apartment with father's mother, father's mother had a long history with county children services, father was unemployed, father did not visit his other son regularly, and mother of father's older son testified that when father returned son after visits son was dirty and had behavior issues. In re West (Ohio App. 4 Dist., Athens, 06-10-2005) No. 05CA4, 2005-Ohio-2977, 2005 WL 1400029, Unreported. Infants ⇔ 155

Clear and convincing evidence supported conclusion that termination of mother's parental rights was in child's best interests; mother had voluntarily admitted herself for psychiatric hospitalization when she became afraid of physically harming child, she was diagnosed with depression and borderline personality disorder, child was unable to crawl at ten months of age because mother reported that she did not allow him to play on floor, while mother and child lived in father's home home lacked adequate plumbing and raw sewage had backed up into basement, and mother admitted she had not taken her prescribed medication for her mental illness for previous eight months. In re Erich L. (Ohio App. 6 Dist., Lucas, 06-10-2005) No. L-04-1340, 2005-Ohio-2945, 2005 WL 1389086, Unreported. Infants ⇔ 158

Juvenile court's determination to terminate mother's parental rights to her minor child was supported by clear and convincing evidence; mother continued to place her child in the home of a convicted child molester, who refused to seek any counseling for his behavior. In re D.B. (Ohio App. 2 Dist., Montgomery, 04-29-2005) No. 20577, 2005-Ohio-2016, 2005 WL 994591, Unreported. Infants ⇔ 179

Trial court abused its discretion by terminating mother's parental rights to her children and awarding custody of children to paternal grandparents, where there was no evidence to support trial court's finding that mother was incapable of caring for children, or that continued custody with mother would be detrimental to children, as would establish that mother was unsuitable parent. In re Keylor (Ohio App. 7 Dist., Monroe, 03-30-2005) No. 04 MO 02, 2005-Ohio-1661, 2005 WL 775890, Unreported, stay granted 106 Ohio St.3d 1410, 830 N.E.2d 344, 2005-Ohio-3154, appeal not allowed 106 Ohio St.3d 1506, 833 N.E.2d 1249, 2005-Ohio-4605. Infants ⇔ 222

Trial court finding that awarding permanent custody of children to county children services board, and denying mother's motion for a six month extension of temporary custody, was in the best interests of the children was not against the manifest weight of the evidence; mother was an alcoholic, she participated in numerous alcohol programs and continuously relapsed into alcohol use, she failed to comply with requests for drug screens, she had a pattern of associating with convicted felons and substance abusers with whom she had volatile relationships, during the pendency of the case mother was involved in six domestic violence incidents involving at least three different men, guardian ad litem testified that she believed granting permanent custody to the board was in the best interests of the children, children were attached to their foster family, and foster parents were interested in adopting children. In re A.W. (Ohio App. 9 Dist., Summit, 03-30-2005) No. 22401, 2005-Ohio-1465, 2005 WL 711919, Unreported. Infants ⇔ 222

Termination of mother's parental rights was in children's best interest, where children were doing well in foster placement and in school, children's behavior deteriorated before and after visitation with mother, children wished to be adopted by their respective foster parents, children had been in agency's temporary custody for over four years at time of hearing, mother was unable or unwilling to keep children's father out of her home despite allegations of physical and sexual abuse which had formed basis for dependency adjudication, mother refused to believe such allegations, and mother failed to maintain drug-free home as required by her case plan. In re Faulk (Ohio App. 7 Dist., Columbiana, 03-18-2005) No. 04-CO-36, 2005-Ohio-1352, 2005 WL 678581, Unreported. Infants ⇔ 155

Love and affection flowing between parent and child is not a factor trial court must consider in making a decision regarding permanent custody. In re B.L. (Ohio App. 10 Dist., Franklin, 03-17-2005) No. 04AP-1108, 2005-Ohio-1151, 2005 WL 615642, Unreported, stay denied 105 Ohio St.3d 1553, 828 N.E.2d 110, 2005-Ohio-2424, appeal not allowed 105 Ohio St.3d 1564, 828 N.E.2d 118, 2005-Ohio-2447, appeal not allowed 106 Ohio St.3d 1417, 830 N.E.2d 348, 2005-Ohio-3154, reconsideration denied 106 Ohio St.3d 1511, 833 N.E.2d 1251, 2005-Ohio-4605, certiorari denied 126 S.Ct. 443, 163 L.Ed.2d 337, rehearing denied, rehearing denied 126 S.Ct. 726, 163 L.Ed.2d 623. Infants ⇔ 155

2151.414
Note 5

In proceedings to determine permanent custody of child, trial court may properly consider the interaction of the child with his parents, siblings, relatives, foster caregivers, and any other persons who may affect the child; child's relationships are relevant to best interests of child. In re B.L. (Ohio App. 10 Dist., Franklin, 03-17-2005) No. 04AP-1108, 2005-Ohio-1151, 2005 WL 615642, Unreported, stay denied 105 Ohio St.3d 1553, 828 N.E.2d 110, 2005-Ohio-2424, appeal not allowed 105 Ohio St.3d 1564, 828 N.E.2d 118, 2005-Ohio-2447, appeal not allowed 106 Ohio St.3d 1417, 830 N.E.2d 348, 2005-Ohio-3154, reconsideration denied 106 Ohio St.3d 1511, 833 N.E.2d 1251, 2005-Ohio-4605, certiorari denied 126 S.Ct. 443, 163 L.Ed.2d 337, rehearing denied, rehearing denied 126 S.Ct. 726, 163 L.Ed.2d 623. Infants ⇔ 155

Trial court's decision to grant permanent custody of child to the Department of Job and Family Services was not against the manifest weight of the evidence; mother was incarcerated and unable to care for the child for a period in excess of 18 months beyond the date of the permanent custody hearing, and father did not appear for the hearing, had not provided any support or financial assistance to the child, and had not completed any of the case plan objectives, and was also wanted on outstanding felony arrest warrants. In re Silva (Ohio App. 5 Dist., Stark, 02-14-2005) No. 2004CA00294, 2005-Ohio-631, 2005 WL 375460, Unreported. Infants ⇔ 157

Magistrate's determination in termination of parental rights proceeding that child's grandmother and maternal uncle were not appropriate to assume the care and custody of child was supported by clear and convincing evidence; condition of grandmother's residence was part of the reason for child's removal, and uncle did not retain counsel to assist in filing for custody and has not arranged for an interstate home study, and he had only seen the child once since birth. In re Goff (Ohio App. 11 Dist., Ashtabula, 12-23-2004) No. 2004-A-0051, 2004-Ohio-7235, 2004 WL 3090218, Unreported, appeal not allowed 105 Ohio St.3d 1473, 824 N.E.2d 542, 2005-Ohio-1186. Infants ⇔ 222

Evidence of mother's past criminal charges for which she was acquitted was relevant to issue of whether mother's children had been neglected or dependent and was admissible in proceedings to determine if permanent custody of children should be awarded to county agency; agency alleged that mother was unable to care for her children because of her frequent arrests and resulting incarcerations, and fact that mother was in prison awaiting trial showed that mother was absent from the children for whom she was responsible for providing care and shelter. In re G.C. & M.C. (Ohio App. 8 Dist., Cuyahoga, 10-21-2004) No. 83994, 2004-Ohio-5607, 2004 WL 2367243, Unreported. Infants ⇔ 173.1

Evidence supported trial court's decision awarding permanent custody of mother's children to county agency, even though social worker testified that mother made a "total turn-around" and an "amazing change" in her parenting skills, and mother had not been convicted of criminal offenses with which she had been charged; other criminal charges against mother remained pending, mother had been incarcerated on such charges for more than a year, mother's repeated incarcerations prevented her from being present with her children and providing the care they needed, children required legally secure placement, and agency made diligent efforts in attempting to place children with mother's relatives. In re G.C. & M.C. (Ohio App. 8 Dist., Cuyahoga, 10-21-2004) No. 83994, 2004-Ohio-5607, 2004 WL 2367243, Unreported. Infants ⇔ 155

Factor, applicable when parent has placed child at substantial risk of harm two or more times due to alcohol or drug abuse and has rejected treatment two or more times or refused to participate in further treatment two or more times after a case plan, was inapplicable to mother challenging determination that grant of permanent custody of child to county agency was in best interests of child, although mother's case plan required her to be assessed for drug use, where there was no recommendation for treatment and no dispositional order requiring treatment. In re K. (Ohio App. 8 Dist., Cuyahoga, 09-02-2004) No. 83410, 2004-Ohio-4629, 2004 WL 1946141, Unreported. Infants ⇔ 155

Evidence supported juvenile court's finding that grant of permanent custody of mother's three children to county agency was in children's best interest; testimony showed that mother failed to maintain her home in clean and safe condition, which was reason for removal of children, mother was uncooperative with social workers, and mother failed to make appropriate efforts to clean and repair the home so that it would be fit for children. In re V.F. (Ohio App. 8 Dist., Cuyahoga, 08-26-2004) No. 83806, No. 83807, 2004-Ohio-4494, 2004 WL 1902560, Unreported. Infants ⇔ 156

Finding that mother was chemically dependent and that her dependency was so severe that it made her unable to provide adequate home for dependent children was not abuse of discretion in termination of parental rights proceeding, where mother, who denied drug use, repeatedly tested positive for drugs and was arrested for drug possession; expert testimony was not required to establish chemical dependency. In re Ross (Ohio App. 11 Dist., Geauga, 07-07-2004) No. 2003-G-2551, 2004-Ohio-3684, 2004 WL 1559742, Unreported. Infants ⇔ 155; Infants ⇔ 178

Trial court was required to make specific findings of fact with regard to all statutory factors to support finding that termination of biological father's parental rights was in child's best interest. In re Cravens (Ohio App. 3 Dist., Defiance, 05-10-2004) No. 4-03-48, 2004-Ohio-2356, 2004 WL 1049142, Unreported. Infants ⇔ 210

Evidence supported finding that termination of parents' parental rights and awarding Children Services Board (CSB) permanent custody of dependent and neglected child was in child's best interests; both parents had substance abuse problems that prevented them from caring for very young child without supervision despite having nearly two years to work on their case plans, mother seemed to try to achieve sobriety but she had been unable to do so even after losing parental rights to three older siblings of child, and father had refusal to even acknowledge that he had substance abuse problem. In re T.O. (Ohio App. 9 Dist., Summit, 03-31-2004) No. 21858, No. 21868, 2004-Ohio-1605, 2004 WL 742927, Unreported. Infants ⇔ 155

Granting permanent custody of dependent and neglected child to county children services board was in child's best interest; although father maintained regular visitation, some of father's urine tests were positive for cocaine, and father refused to acknowledge that he had substance abuse problem. In re T.O. (Ohio App. 9 Dist., Summit, 03-31-2004) No. 2185821868, 2004-Ohio-1605, 2004 WL 625816, Unreported. Infants ⇔ 155

Granting permanent custody of dependent and neglected child to county children services board was in child's best interest, where mother missed more than six months of visitation, failed to accomplish goals of case plan, had her parental rights to child's siblings involuntarily terminated, and continually relapsed into drug use. In re T.O. (Ohio App. 9 Dist., Summit, 03-31-2004) No. 2185821868, 2004-Ohio-1605, 2004 WL 625816, Unreported. Infants ⇔ 155; Infants ⇔ 157

Evidence supported trial court's finding that dependent child could not and should not in foreseeable future be placed with father, for purpose of termination of parental rights proceeding; father admittedly failed to complete any case plan goals or to attend parenting classes arranged for him. In re Strychalski (Ohio App. 7 Dist., Carroll, 03-26-2004) No. 03-CA-797, 2004-Ohio-1542, 2004 WL 612835, Unreported. Infants ⇔ 155

Clear and convincing evidence supported order granting permanent custody of child to county children services; mother's relatives had cared for child since he was two years old, there was no evidence of a maternal bond between mother and child, child had abandonment issues and feared being abandoned, mother had little contact with child for eight years, and children services was not required to develop a case plan to include mother since their efforts would have been futile. In re Leitwein (Ohio App. 4 Dist., Hocking, 03-12-2004) No. 03CA18, 2004-Ohio-1296, 2004 WL 540925, Unreported. Infants ⇔ 155; Infants ⇔ 157

Evidence was sufficient to establish, in dependent child proceeding that resulted in the termination of mother's parental rights, that mother did not comply with most of her case plan requirements; there was evidence that grandmother's home was unsafe for a mobile infant and that grandmother had provided inadequate supervision of mother's children in the past, mother's alleged reliance on her military brother for steady income or financial assistance was unsubstantiated, mother was diagnosed with bipolar disorder and a personality disorder but discounted the need for counseling, and mother did not address continuing issues regarding physical altercations between her and the child's father. In Re P. C. (Ohio App. 9 Dist., Summit, 03-17-2004) No. 21734, No. 21739, 2004-Ohio-1230, 2004 WL 509368, Unreported. Infants ⇔ 158

Evidence supported finding that termination of mother's parental rights and the grant of permanent custody to county children services board were in children's best interest; children had been placed together and agency was searching for a foster home that would adopt all three children, children's fathers had almost no contact with children, mother's relatives failed to show interest in assuming custody of children, and mother was unable to provide stable, secure environment due to her failure to complete case plans, her drug use, her inability to secure residence and employment, and her refusal to remedy situation that led to children's removal. In re Joiner (Ohio App. 11 Dist., Ashtabula, 03-12-2004) No. 2003-A-0110, 2004-Ohio-1158, 2004 WL 473260, Unreported, appeal not allowed 102 Ohio St.3d 1425, 807 N.E.2d 368, 2004-Ohio-2003. Infants ⇔ 155

Evidence supported trial court's finding that minor child could not be placed with either parent within a reasonable period of time, for purposes of determining whether parental rights could be terminated; father had failed to complete most of his case plan services, his current living situation consisted only of a sleeping room, mother's behavior during court proceedings was inappropriate and disruptive, mother had failed to alleviate conditions which led to placement of child with agency, that being her continued relationship with alleged sex offender, and parents had lifelong histories of significant psychological problems. In re Deserio (Ohio App. 5 Dist., Tuscarawas, 02-06-2004) No. 2003-AP-09 0073, No. 2003 AP 09 0078, 2004-Ohio-751, 2004 WL 309090, Unreported. Infants ⇐ 155; Infants ⇐ 156; Infants ⇐ 158

Evidence was sufficient to support finding that it was in children's best interests to grant permanent custody to County Children Services (CCS), although parents loved their children and vice versa; there was evidence that children's behavior improved in foster care, that children had been in temporary custody of CCS for 12 or more months of a consecutive 22-month period, that children showed signs of neglect after failed reunification attempt and that parents failed to take necessary actions to meet children's basic needs, and that parents lacked realistic plan for children's return. In re Myers Children (Ohio App. 4 Dist., Athens, 02-10-2004) No. 03CA23, 2004-Ohio-657, 2004 WL 257651, Unreported. Infants ⇐ 155; Infants ⇐ 156

Permanent custody of child properly was granted to County Children Services Board; mother was given nearly one year to find an adequate permanent home for child which she was unable to do, there was ongoing relationship between mother and convicted sex offender, and mother admitted she had not improved her home conditions as required by the case-plan. In re Malone (Ohio App. 3 Dist., Crawford, 02-09-2004) No. 3-03-25, 2004-Ohio-533, 2004 WL 231488, Unreported. Infants ⇐ 155

Evidence supported trial court's finding that grant of legal custody to paternal grandmother was in child's best interest; mother had not resolved her problems with instability, mother was not in a position to have custody of children, child had medical issues that required ongoing care, mother failed to attend all of child's medical appointments, mother had driven child in her car without a driver's license of insurance, and mother had engaged in altercations with members of grandmother's family with child nearby. In re N.P. (Ohio App. 9 Dist., Summit, 01-14-2004) No. 21707, 2004-Ohio-110, 2004 WL 57437, Unreported. Infants ⇐ 222

Children could not be placed with mother within a reasonable time given that mother had not addressed abuse that resulted in removal of children from home, and thus inability to place children with mother supported termination of mother's parental rights, although mother had complied with some of case plan's requirements; evidence corroborated mother's admission that mother had not and would not support her daughter regarding sexual abuse of daughter by stepfather, mother wanted her family to be together completely regardless of stepfather's sexual abuse of daughter and failure to seek treatment, and mother had not meaningfully addressed sexual abuse that mother experienced as child. In re Zorns (Ohio App. 10 Dist., Franklin, 10-23-2003) No. 02AP-1297, No. 02AP-1298, 2003-Ohio-5664, 2003 WL 22415613, Unreported, appeal not allowed 100 Ohio St.3d 1547, 800 N.E.2d 752, 2003-Ohio-6879. Infants ⇐ 156; Infants ⇐ 179

The trial court adequately considered child's interaction and relationship with his mother, in proceeding to terminate parental rights; trial court found that child and mother had good interaction during visits and that child was bonded to his parents, and the child's relationship with mother was only one factor that the trial court considered when determining whether it was in child's best interests to terminate mother's parental rights. In re Cornett (Ohio App. 12 Dist., Warren, 09-11-2003) No. CA2003-03-034, 2003-Ohio-4871, 2003 WL 22118857, Unreported. Infants ⇐ 210

Competent and credible evidence supported trial court award of permanent custody of child to county children services; child had been in the temporary custody of children services for at least 12 months of the 22 months before the hearing, child was not bonded to parents, child thrived in foster care but regressed when he had extended visitation with parents, and parents failed to continuously maintain a clean and safe home. In re Riley (Ohio App. 4 Dist., Washington, 07-25-2003) No. 03CA16, 2003-Ohio-4108, 2003 WL 21783368, Unreported. Infants ⇐ 155; Infants ⇐ 156

Evidence was sufficient to support finding that children could not have been placed with mother within a reasonable time, as would support awarding permanent custody of children to county; mother received extensive services continuously for approximately seven years, although she participated in case plan to best of her ability she was unable to remedy conditions leading to removal, she continued to demonstrate an inability to supervise, protect, or provide for her children, mother's depression and low intelligence quotient made internalizing parenting information provided by services difficult for her, continued contact with father was a continued concern, as he had been implicated as possible child abuser, mother was easily distracted and had difficulty interacting with children during visits, surrounded herself with persons who took advantage of her, and had no appropriate relatives or friends to help her with the children. In re Swisher (Ohio App. 5 Dist., Tuscarawas, 07-07-2003) No. 2003AP040028, 2003-Ohio-3747, 2003 WL 21652186, Unreported. Infants ⇐ 158

County made reasonable efforts to eliminate the need for continued removal of child from mother's care, thus supporting award of permanent custody of child to county; while case plan required mother, who was 16 years old at time of permanent placement, to comply with her probation rules, undergo substance abuse evaluation and treatment, attend school, seek and maintain employment, undergo a psychological assessment, and maintain contact with her child, mother repeatedly violated probation, was absent from school, was fired or quit two different jobs after one or two months, evaluation showed that she was a chemical abuser, bipolar, and suffering from oppositional defiant disorder, she failed to complete substance abuse program, her treatment team recommended she be placed in a group home with a goal of independent living, which would have required a minimum of six months of placement after her current detention, and while mother maintained contact with child, child had bonded with foster mother who wished to adopt her. McFarland v. Richland County Children Services Bd. (Ohio App. 5 Dist., Richland, 07-07-2003) No. 2003-CA-0020, 2003-Ohio-3746, 2003 WL 21652180, Unreported. Infants ⇐ 155

Evidence supported finding that the children could not be placed with mother within a reasonable time, in support of grant of permanent custody of the children to county department of children and family services; mother had not completed her GED, obtained appropriate housing, or obtained stable employment, as required under her caseplan. In re D.F. (Ohio App. 8 Dist., Cuyahoga, 06-19-2003) No. 81613, 2003-Ohio-3221, 2003 WL 21419537, Unreported. Infants ⇐ 155

Order terminating mother's parental rights to her three children was not against the manifest weight of the evidence; psychiatrist testified that mother was diagnosed with bipolar disorder, manic type severe, poly-substance abuse, and anti-social personalty traits, and that her prognosis was poor, counseling center casemanager testified that mother had been hospitalized six times in the past eight months, and that mother often failed to follow her doctor's recommendations, and no relatives of mother was qualified for placement of the children. In re A.C. (Ohio App. 9 Dist., Wayne, 05-28-2003) No. 02CA0053, No. 02CA0054, No. 02CA0055, 2003-Ohio-2714, 2003 WL 21223278, Unreported. Infants ⇐ 158

Awarding permanent custody of children to county children services board (CSB) was in children's best interest, and thus was warranted in dependency proceeding, where children's removal was third such incident based upon condition of home and personal hygiene of parents and children, in CSB's eight-year involvement with parents all reasonable efforts were made to help parents resolve primary problems, parents did not demonstrate their commitment to making recommended changes on a consistent and effective basis as set forth in case plan, and there was no indication that situation was likely to improve. In re Kuhn (Ohio App. 3 Dist., Crawford, 05-28-2003) No. 3-02-47, No. 3-02-48, No. 3-02-49, 2003-Ohio-2710, 2003 WL 21221328, Unreported. Infants ⇐ 155; Infants ⇐ 156

Substantial evidence supported termination of mother's parental rights over her minor child and placement of child in the permanent custody of the Children's Services Board; mother had history of substance abuse, child tested positive for cocaine at birth, mother refused to provide child with safe and appropriate care, failed to comply with the case plan requirements, and did not make herself available to contact for visitations with the child. In re J.L.T. (Ohio App. 9 Dist., Summit, 05-07-2003) No. 21359, 2003-Ohio-2346, 2003 WL 21040624, Unreported. Infants ⇐ 155; Infants ⇐ 156; Infants ⇐ 157

Clear and convincing evidence supported placement of mother's two children in the permanent custody of the Department of Children and Family Services; children were thriving in their respective placements, mother failed to comply with her case plan, she failed to consistently visit or communicate with the children, and she lacked employment, stable housing, or any means to provide adequate care and support for the children. In re D.B. (Ohio App. 8 Dist., Cuyahoga, 05-08-2003) No. 81652, No. 81654, 2003-Ohio-2304, 2003 WL 21029525, Unreported. Infants ⇐ 155; Infants ⇐ 157

Clear and convincing evidence established that awarding permanent custody of mother's four children to county was in their best interests; three oldest children were extremely bonded to each other, bond was very strong between children and the foster parent, whereas there was a minimal bond between mother and children, three oldest children expressed their desire to stay with foster parent who had cared for them for over a year and one half, youngest had never been in mother's care, no relatives were suitable caregivers, mother had limited coping skills, failed to supervise children, and apparently inflicted physical abuse upon at least two of her children. In re Pederson (Ohio App. 10 Dist., Franklin, 04-29-2003) No. 02AP-853, No. 02AP-856, No. 02AP-854, No. 02AP-855, 2003-Ohio-2138, 2003 WL 1962429, Unreported. Infants 155

Clear and convincing evidence established finding that mother's four children could not have been placed with either parent within a reasonable time or should not have been placed with either parent, as would support awarding permanent custody to county; three oldest children had been removed from mother's care in four of the five years preceding permanent custody proceedings, and had spent significant time living with the foster parent, county had provided numerous services to mother, but she continued leave children unsupervised, she was apparently unable to meet her own needs as well as those of others, had limited coping skills, and minimized the significance of supervision lapses and past physical abuse of her children. In re Pederson (Ohio App. 10 Dist., Franklin, 04-29-2003) No. 02AP-853, No. 02AP-856, No. 02AP-854, No. 02AP-855, 2003-Ohio-2138, 2003 WL 1962429, Unreported. Infants 155

Clear and convincing evidence supported finding that termination of mother's rights as to one and one-half-year-old daughter and awarding custody to county was in daughter's best interests; mother's last visit was eight months prior to permanency hearing, mother was convicted of complicity to gross sexual imposition and child endangering involving her 20-day-old niece, mother had not participated in sexual offender counseling as ordered by trial court, refused to acknowledge sexual offender allegations, referred to daughter during visits as "sexy girl," mother's parental rights to another child were terminated three years earlier, she was mildly mentally retarded and was unable to parent appropriately, consistently, or independently, daughter had special needs that presented challenges to caregivers, and she was very bonded with foster family who cared for her since she was three days old and who expressed interest in adopting her. In re Matter of Kilby (Ohio App. 12 Dist., Butler, 04-28-2003) No. CA2002-10-259, 2003-Ohio-2116, 2003 WL 1956100, Unreported. Infants 156; Infants 157; Infants 158

Evidence was sufficient to support finding that children could not have been placed with father within a reasonable period of time or should not have been placed with father, as would support awarding permanent custody of children to county; at time of permanent custody hearing, father had been incarcerated for three years and had not seen his children since that time, prior to current incarceration, father had been incarcerated for other criminal convictions, such incarceration prevented him from caring for children, and he was to remain in prison for approximately three more years. In re Nicole K. (Ohio App. 6 Dist., Lucas, 04-18-2003) No. L-02-1347, 2003-Ohio-1999, 2003 WL 1904403, Unreported. Infants 157

Clear and convincing evidence supported finding that awarding permanent custody of three children to county was in their best interests; children were initially removed from home after mother was arrested on charges of domestic violence and child endangering following her admission to severely beating her oldest child with a belt, county attempted to work with mother for over a year and a half but mother continued to abuse drugs, physically discipline children during visits, and engage in inappropriate relationships with men, the three children were extremely bonded to each other and had been placed together for almost one and one-half years in a "wonderful" foster home with a foster mother who apparently wished to adopt them, and youngest child had been in foster mother's care for 75% of his life. In re Ball/Butler Children (Ohio App. 5 Dist., Stark, 04-14-2003) No. 2003CA00015, 2003-Ohio-1899, 2003 WL 1874714, Unreported. Infants 155; Infants 156

Clear and convincing evidence supported trial court's decision to award permanent custody of child to county and terminate mother's parental rights as to child; mother, who suffered from psychological illnesses, failed to make sufficient progress towards any of her reunification goals, including securing suitable housing and employment, and obtaining medical counseling and medication, even though she had numerous, willing agencies and resources at her disposal. In re Simkins (Ohio App. 11 Dist., Trumbull, 04-14-2003) No. 2002-T-0173, 2003-Ohio-1884, 2003 WL 1871040, Unreported. Infants 158

Clear and convincing evidence supported finding that the child could not or should not be placed with mother or father within a reasonable time, as basis for award of permanent custody to county child protection agency, because the parent failed continuously and repeatedly to substantially remedy conditions causing child to be placed outside the child's home; child had been in agency's temporary custody for 12 or more months of a consecutive 22-month period, mother's apartment continued to be an unhealthy place to raise children, not simply because of lice, and mother's habit of falling asleep with burning cigarettes was still a concern at her new apartment. In re Nicholas Bruce Lee R. (Ohio App. 6 Dist., Huron, 03-13-2003) No. H-02-053, 2003-Ohio-1414, 2003 WL 1487341, Unreported. Infants 156

Trial court properly considered in permanent custody proceeding whether child's parents demonstrated a lack of commitment toward the child and had been unwilling to provide food, clothing, shelter, and other basic necessities for the child and, thus, could conclude that the child could not be placed with the parents within a reasonable period of time or should not be placed with them; record indicated that mother did not visit with the child on a consistent basis, when she did, she was detached from the child, letting him play with and talk to child's father, child's foster parents would not tell him when his parents were coming to visit because, on more than one occasion, his parents would schedule a time to meet with child and then not show up, neither parent kept child's inoculations up to date, and mother still lived in unsanitary and unsafe conditions, leaving dangerous objects lying around house and failing to remedy lice problem. In re Nicholas Bruce Lee R. (Ohio App. 6 Dist., Huron, 03-13-2003) No. H-02-053, 2003-Ohio-1414, 2003 WL 1487341, Unreported. Infants 156; Infants 157; Infants 159

Evidence was sufficient to support finding that termination of parents' rights as to their three children was in children's best interest; at time of termination proceedings parents were in process of obtaining a divorce, in year since permanent custody hearing neither party had completed counseling, mother had not found suitable housing, psychological evaluation indicated that neither parent had formed a bond with children, and, although parents were both capable of becoming good parents, they both tended to neglect children when emotionally stressed. In re Fricke (Ohio App. 3 Dist., Allen, 03-11-2003) No. 1-02-75, No. 1-02-76, No. 1-02-77, 2003-Ohio-1116, 2003 WL 952173, Unreported. Infants 155; Infants 156

Evidence was sufficient to support finding that paternal grandmother who sought custody of child would have permitted father, whose rights had been terminated, access to child in defiance of the State's advice, as would support determination that grant of permanent custody to State was in child's best interest; grandmother had accepted service of process for father, caseworker testified that she spoke to father on phone on morning of hearing at grandmother's address, indicating that father lived with grandmother, and at custody hearing grandmother did not deny that father would have had access to child. In re P.P. (Ohio App. 2 Dist., Montgomery, 03-07-2003) No. 19582, 2003-Ohio-1051, 2003 WL 863568, Unreported. Infants 222

Evidence was sufficient to support finding that child's need for legally secure placement could not have been achieved through placement with paternal grandmother, thus supporting finding that grant of permanent custody to State was in child's best interest; trial court was not required to award custody to a relative over the State, a home study by State caseworkers reported, though denied by grandmother, that grandmother did not know child's name or birth date, have sufficient room in her home for child, or have stable child care arranged, and grandmother was not prepared to care for child's special medical and developmental needs, whereas child's foster parents were prepared to adopt her, provided a very appropriate home, and were bonded with child, and child thrived in foster home. In re P.P. (Ohio App. 2 Dist., Montgomery, 03-07-2003) No. 19582, 2003-Ohio-1051, 2003 WL 863568, Unreported. Infants 222

Evidence was sufficient to support finding that child's custodial history supported determination that grant of permanent custody to State, rather than to paternal grandmother, was in child's best interest; child had been in temporary custody of State since shortly after birth and had been in the care of her foster parents since child's release from hospital following her birth. In re P.P. (Ohio App. 2 Dist., Montgomery, 03-07-2003) No. 19582, 2003-Ohio-1051, 2003 WL 863568, Unreported. Infants 222

Evidence was sufficient to support finding that trial court considered guardian ad litem's recommendation to temporarily place child with her paternal grandmother, thus supporting its finding that grant of permanent custody to State was in child's best interest; guardian ad litem made its position very clear at custody hearing, caseworker disagreed with guardian ad litem's statement that grandmother's home was appropriate for child, as home had very small bedrooms in which it would have been difficult to place a crib, guardian ad litem's report ignored caseworker's findings that grandmother didn't appear to be bonded with child, appreciate extent of child's medical needs, and did not plan to have consistent child care providers, which was concerning as child had special needs that needed to be addressed consistently with consistent persons. In re P.P. (Ohio App. 2 Dist., Montgomery, 03-07-2003) No. 19582, 2003-Ohio-1051, 2003 WL 863568, Unreported. Infants 208

Evidence was sufficient to support finding that children could not have been placed with mother within reasonable time or should not have been placed with mother, as would support granting permanent custody to county; children had been out of mother's custody for approximately 22 months, mother did not substantially comply with case plan, while children were in mother's care mother failed to consistently provide medicine, children and mother missed scheduled counseling sessions, mother provided unclean housing and insufficient food, children had better school attendance and less behavior problems when not in mother's care, and, although mother consistently exercised visitation, her parenting skills had not improved in two years. In re Alfrey (Ohio App. 2 Dist., Clark, 02-07-2003) No. 01CA0083, 2003-Ohio-608, 2003 WL 262587, Unreported. Infants ⇔ 155; Infants ⇔ 156; Infants ⇔ 159

Testimony of social worker, who was an expert in social work and diagnostic assessments, provided sufficient evidence that mother's illness prevented her from providing an adequate permanent home for child for at least one year, thus supporting trial court's decision to terminate mother's parental rights; expert testified that mother's personality disorder fell into the severe persistent mental illness category and that such illnesses generally persist for at least one year. In re Devin B. (Ohio App. 6 Dist., Lucas, 01-24-2003) No. L-02-1294, 2003-Ohio-307, 2003 WL 164858, Unreported. Infants ⇔ 181

Evidence supported the trial court's conclusion in dependency proceeding that minor child's mother failed to remedy the problems that caused the child to be placed outside the home, and that the child could not be placed with the mother within a reasonable time; mother's urine samples initially tested positive for marijuana, subsequently tested positive for cocaine, and she thereafter submitted only one sample until date of permanent custody trial, and mother missed 24 of her therapy treatment sessions, visited with her child sporadically, and was terminated during her second attempt to complete parenting classes after admitting that she used drugs daily. In re Alexander (Ohio App. 5 Dist., Stark, 01-13-2003) No. 2002CA00342, 2003-Ohio-136, 2003 WL 125070, Unreported. Infants ⇔ 155; Infants ⇔ 157

Evidence was sufficient to support finding that child could not have been placed with father within a reasonable time or should not have been placed with father, and that termination was in child's best interests; despite reasonable efforts by county, father failed to remedy conditions that caused child's removal from home, in that father was unwilling to provide food, clothing, shelter, and other basic necessities, demonstrated a lack of commitment toward child by failing to regularly support, visit, or communicate with him when able to do so, and father was unable to maintain steady employment, find independent housing, end his unstable relationship with child's mother for sake of his child, or achieve more than minimal parenting skills. In re Dylan R. (Ohio App. 6 Dist., Lucas, 01-10-2003) No. L-02-1267, 2003-Ohio-69, 2003 WL 99502, Unreported. Infants ⇔ 155; Infants ⇔ 156; Infants ⇔ 157

Evidence was sufficient to support finding that county made reasonable efforts to reunify mother with her three children prior to termination of her parental rights; county designed a case plan for parents to follow, made referrals for parents to engage in parenting class, assisted parents in engaging in development of living skills program, and while mother tried to comply reunification requirements, being intellectually challenged with an overall IQ of 55, mother required assistance of a co-parent, father was ordered to complete a substance abuse program, yet failed to do so, and failed every one of his urine screens, and while mother had also asked court to consider her brother as a co-parent, brother falsified his answers to a substance abuse evaluation by stating that there was no history of family alcohol abuse and he had never thought of suicide, and brother needed to address anger management and anxiety issues before being able to parent. In re Moore (Ohio App. 12 Dist., Butler, 01-06-2003) No. CA2002-03-065, No. CA2002-04-076, 2003-Ohio-9, 2003 WL 40746, Unreported. Infants ⇔ 155

Evidence was sufficient to support finding that grant of permanent custody to county was in three children's best interest; all three children were in same foster home, and bonded with foster family, children had been in foster care over 20 months, foster parents were willing to adopt children, while mother completed required parenting classes, she had an I.Q. of 55, had difficulty retaining skills, and needed ongoing support to raise children, while mother's brother filed for legal custody, he visited children only seven times between removal and filing for custody approximately 16 months later, and while father's interactions with children were good, and he completed parenting classes, he failed to complete a required substance abuse program, and failed every one of his urine screens. In re Moore (Ohio App. 12 Dist., Butler, 01-06-2003) No. CA2002-03-065, No. CA2002-04-076, 2003-Ohio-9, 2003 WL 40746, Unreported. Infants ⇔ 155; Infants ⇔ 179

Trial court's grant of permanent custody of dependent child to county department of jobs and family services (JFS) was not against manifest weight of the evidence; evidence indicated that biological father lived in another state at house owned by purported fiancee, father was on probation at time of hearing for battery and marijuana trafficking, father had history of problems with anger management, alcohol abuse, and drug use during time father was with biological mother, and father had not paid child support for at least two years. In re Willis (Ohio App. 5 Dist., Coshocton, 12-10-2002) No. 02 CA 15, 2002-Ohio-6795, 2002 WL 31761464, Unreported, appeal not allowed 98 Ohio St.3d 1463, 783 N.E.2d 521, 2003-Ohio-644. Infants ⇔ 178

Evidence supported finding that, prior to finding child dependent and granting permanent custody to county children services, child could not have been placed with his father within a reasonable time or that child should not have been placed with father; father failed to substantially remedy the conditions that led to the child's removal, father continued to have problems controlling his anger, father continued to engage in violent behavior, and father failed to obtain independent housing. In re Barnhart (Ohio App. 4 Dist., Athens, 10-30-2002) No. 02CA21, 2002-Ohio-6024, 2002 WL 31455952, Unreported. Infants ⇔ 155

A mother who shows no therapeutic improvement after attending six months of psychological counseling according to a case plan instituted after her daughter is sexually abused allegedly by the mother's husband, and who is unwilling to admit that her daughter was even abused at all despite contrary medical evidence and her daughter's own statements, is ill-equipped to protect her daughter from further possible abuse and the permanent termination of custody of her daughter is justified and supported by the manifest weight of the evidence. Matter of Misty B. (Ohio App. 6 Dist., Lucas, 08-18-1995) No. L-94-213, 1995 WL 490965, Unreported.

Clear and convincing evidence exists to show that children cannot be returned to their parents and permanent custody should be awarded to the county children services agency regardless of the possible ultimate placement of children by the agency when it is shown that (1) the mother and father have drug abuse problems and refuse to regularly attend treatment programs, (2) the father has been found guilty of sexually abusing his two-year-old daughter, (3) the children were left alone for a day and a half, and (4) the mother admits she is incapable of caring for the children. Matter of Catherine M. (Ohio App. 6 Dist., Lucas, 06-02-1995) No. L-94-110, 1995 WL 326354, Unreported.

Where natural mother of child in temporary foster care failed to remedy conditions concerning the appropriateness of home for child and supervised visitation between natural mother and child was unsuccessful, trial court properly granted permanent custody of child to public children services agency as several conditions delineated under RC 2151.414(E) existed. In re Schaupert, No. 92WD068, 1993 WL 306577 (6th Dist Ct App, Wood, 6–30–93).

Where defendant is sentenced to a minimum of eight years imprisonment and fails to produce evidence showing he will be released earlier than minimum sentence, trial court did not err in finding that defendant, due to his incarceration, will be unavailable to care for child at least 18 months after filing motion for permanent custody or dispositional hearing pursuant to RC 2151.414(E)(6) and awarding permanent custody to Children Services. Uehlein v Fuller, No. 92CA005431, 1993 WL 129333 (9th Dist Ct App, Lorain, 4–28–93).

Where mother, convicted of drug charges and incarcerated for violation of probation terms, showed little effort in meeting reunification goals of completing drug treatment and obtaining a job and apartment, trial court properly determined from consideration of factors in RC 2151.414(E) that placement of her five children in permanent custody of Children Services Board was in the children's best interests. Harris v Harris, No. 15866, 1993 WL 107844 (9th Dist Ct App, Summit, 4–14–93).

Invocation of statutory "12 of 22 months" rule, under which permanent custody may be granted to children's services agency if child has been in temporary custody of agency for 12 or more months within 22-month period, was not warranted in parental rights termination proceeding; it appeared that the reason for much of the time children were in agency's custody was agency's failure for period of several months to follow its own case plan to obtain psychological evaluation of mother and implement psychologist's recommendations. In re Alexis K. (Ohio App. 6 Dist., 03-24-2005) 160 Ohio App.3d 32, 825 N.E.2d 1148, 2005-Ohio-1380. Infants ⇔ 155

Fact that mother had been jailed, for violating terms of restitution on her bad-check criminal charges, for nearly three weeks during extended period of four to five months in which dispositional hearings were conducted in child neglect proceeding did not establish that mother was incarcerated at time of dispositional hearing and that she would be unable to care for children for at least 18 months after dispositional hearing, as element for terminating parent rights. In re Alexis K. (Ohio App. 6 Dist., 03-24-2005) 160 Ohio App.3d 32, 825 N.E.2d 1148, 2005-Ohio-1380. Infants ⇔ 157

Child born addicted to cocaine due to mother's drug use was per se abused, and thus, grant of permanent custody of child to state was in child's best interests, where child was physically and developmentally unhealthy since birth, child was constantly in need of medical attention and physical therapy, mother failed to comply with state's case plan on drug use and stable housing, and child did not know mother. In re Starkey (Ohio App. 7 Dist., 12-11-2002) 150 Ohio App.3d 612, 782 N.E.2d 665, 2002-Ohio-6892. Infants ⚖ 156

There was clear and convincing evidence that dependent children required legally secure placement, and thus, it was in children's best interests to be placed in permanent custody of state, even though guardian ad litem opined that children had bonded with mother and that mother should be given another chance to complete drug rehabilitation and procure stable housing, where mother was not committed to recovery, mother had failed to comply with case plan, mother had presumptively abandoned children, and mother's ability to provide needed stability to children was unrealistic. In re Starkey (Ohio App. 7 Dist., 12-11-2002) 150 Ohio App.3d 612, 782 N.E.2d 665, 2002-Ohio-6892. Infants ⚖ 155; Infants ⚖ 157

Evidence that mother and alleged father failed to remedy alleged sexual abuse of child by mother's boyfriend, which had caused child to be placed outside of mother's home, that mother and alleged father failed to regularly support, visit, or communicate with child when able to do so, and that mother and alleged father were currently incarcerated and therefore could not provide food, clothing, shelter, and other basic necessities for child or prevent child from suffering physical, emotional, or sexual abuse or physical, emotional, or mental neglect, supported decision to award permanent custody of dependent, neglected, and abused child to county children services board. In re T.C. (Ohio App. 3 Dist., 12-13-2000) 140 Ohio App.3d 409, 747 N.E.2d 881, 2000-Ohio-1769. Infants ⚖ 178

Sufficient evidence supported finding that mother failed, continuously and repeatedly for more than six months, to remedy conditions causing two children to be placed outside home, for purposes of child services agency's motion for permanent custody, even though mother claimed she had demonstrated ability to care for her youngest child and was working on reunification with a fourth child, where caseworker testified that mother did not have ability to care for more than one child at a time, mother made only minimal progress toward reunification with two removed children, and guardian ad litem testified that he believed mother would be overwhelmed if reunited with removed children. Lorain Cty. Children Serv. v. Keene (Ohio App. 9 Dist., 03-05-1997) 118 Ohio App.3d 535, 693 N.E.2d 833. Infants ⚖ 178

Trial court's finding that mother was unable to provide adequate home for children did not justify conclusion that children could not be placed with either parent within reasonable time or should not be placed with parents, for purpose of statute allowing for termination of parental rights, as inability to provide home was not specifically enumerated in statute, and inability was not equivalent to factor referring to unwillingness to provide home. In re William S. (Ohio, 03-04-1996) 75 Ohio St.3d 95, 661 N.E.2d 738, 1996-Ohio-182. Infants ⚖ 155

Court's simple statement that child could be adopted quite readily and that there was a great need for legally secure placement to provide stability in her life was insufficient to show that court considered statutory factors in determining that it was in best interest of the child for permanent custody to be placed in County Children Services Board. In re Brown (Ohio App. 3 Dist., 11-02-1994) 98 Ohio App.3d 337, 648 N.E.2d 576. Infants ⚖ 210

Trial court is required to make independent determination of relevant statutory criteria and all other relevant evidence independently for each child in multichild permanent custody proceeding; however, courts are not required to consider permanent custody decisions in a vacuum, i.e., how a parent mistreats another child in the household can be very relevant to permanent custody determination of child that is not mistreated in the same manner. In re Hiatt (Adams 1993) 86 Ohio App.3d 716, 621 N.E.2d 1222. Infants ⚖ 155; Infants ⚖ 156

Child need not be placed in risk of immediate and unavoidable harm before court can determine that such environment is unhealthy or unsafe so as to require placement of children in permanent custody with county agency. In re Hiatt (Adams 1993) 86 Ohio App.3d 716, 621 N.E.2d 1222. Infants ⚖ 155

Probability of child's adoption is just one statutory factor, out of all which are relevant, that trial court must consider before granting permanent custody of child to public children services agency. In re Shaeffer Children (Van Wert 1993) 85 Ohio App.3d 683, 621 N.E.2d 426, dismissed, jurisdictional motion overruled 67 Ohio St.3d 1451, 619 N.E.2d 419. Infants ⚖ 155

Under permanent custody statute, trial court could still properly determine that granting permanent custody to state agency is in child's best interest, even in absence of clear and convincing evidence of one of enumerated factors. In re Shaeffer Children (Van Wert 1993) 85 Ohio App.3d 683, 621 N.E.2d 426, dismissed, jurisdictional motion overruled 67 Ohio St.3d 1451, 619 N.E.2d 419. Infants ⚖ 155

Finding that granting permanent custody of father's two minor children to Department of Human Services (DHS) was in children's best interest and that children could not or should not be returned to father's custody was supported by evidence that father failed to remedy conditions causing children to be placed outside his home as he made no attempt to correct housing problems or fire safety violations until after hearing on permanent custody motion, and that he demonstrated lack of commitment toward children as he cancelled one scheduled visit with children and failed to attend another visit over seven months later. In re Shaeffer Children (Van Wert 1993) 85 Ohio App.3d 683, 621 N.E.2d 426, dismissed, jurisdictional motion overruled 67 Ohio St.3d 1451, 619 N.E.2d 419. Infants ⚖ 178

Evidence that father intended to teach child at home despite expert testimony that she needed to be taught in classroom because of behavior disorders, that child was ambivalent toward being reunited with father, that father had prison sentence and driving under influence (DUI) convictions, and that father arranged for child to see her mother after she relinquished custody, contrary to agency's instructions, supported determination that father was not suitable parent to take custody of child, and that it was therefore in child's best interest to terminate father's parental rights in looking toward child's adoption. In re Higby (Wayne 1992) 81 Ohio App.3d 466, 611 N.E.2d 403. Infants ⚖ 158

Evidence relating to natural mother's past parenting history and her inability to comply with prior reunification plans regarding her other children was relevant to juvenile court's determination of whether to commit one of her children to permanent custody of Department of Human Services. In re Brown (Hamilton 1989) 60 Ohio App.3d 136, 573 N.E.2d 1217. Infants ⚖ 173.1

RC 2151.414 sets out several factors to be considered in determining the existence of adequate parental care or lack thereof, including: (1) the extent to which the parents have conformed to court-ordered reunification plans; (2) the parents' existing mental and emotional status; and (3) any physical, emotional, or mental neglect of the child. In re Lay (Wayne 1987) 43 Ohio App.3d 78, 539 N.E.2d 664. Infants ⚖ 155; Infants ⚖ 156; Infants ⚖ 158

"Adequate parental care" does not require that both parents must be found capable of providing such care and although the possibility of compliance with the reunification plan by both parents is a consideration, the failure of one parent does not automatically mean the failure of both. In re Lay (Wayne 1987) 43 Ohio App.3d 78, 539 N.E.2d 664. Infants ⚖ 155

Where the sole parent's term of imprisonment is a lengthy one and where there is clear and convincing evidence that the child is without adequate parental care due to the imprisonment, it is proper for a court to consider the continuing imprisonment of the parent in determining whether or not the child will continue to be without adequate parental care and to terminate the imprisoned parent's rights under such circumstances. In re Hederson (Summit 1986) 30 Ohio App.3d 187, 507 N.E.2d 418, 30 O.B.R. 329.

Evidence supported finding that mother was an unfit parent, which trial court made when awarding child custody to half-brother; testimony indicated that mother grew marijuana inside of the home, child reported to the guardian ad litem that his parents were engaged in the sale of marijuana, there was testimony that child was once forced to sit on a garbage bag full of marijuana while riding in a car, and other testimony showed that mother was unable to provide a safe and stable home and that child had troubles at school. In re Rayl (Ohio App. 7 Dist., Belmont, 09-25-2002) No. 00-BA-55, 2002-Ohio-5176, 2002 WL 31160587, Unreported. Child Custody ⚖ 778

Evidence was sufficient to support finding that the grant of permanent custody to State, rather than with mother, was in the best interest of the child; child had no relationship with biological father, poor interrelationship and no bond with mother, a bond with prior custodians, but custodians refused to continue as such, and although child had a strong bond with biological brother, brother had no bond with mother and was reaching age of emancipation and would be able to continue a relationship with child, and child expressed that she did not wish to be placed with mother and that she wished to be adopted by a family. In re Gordon (Ohio App. 11 Dist., Trumbull, 09-20-2002) No. 2002-T-0073, 2002-Ohio-4959, 2002 WL 31107543, Unreported. Infants ⚖ 178

In termination of parental rights case, juvenile court acted within its discretion in refusing to conduct an in camera interview with the children in order to ascertain their wishes; guardian ad litem discussed the children's treatment with their clinical psychologist and she informed him that children needed stable, loving, and safe family surroundings, and guardian stated children echoed psychologist's sentiment when he interviewed them.

In re Funk (Ohio App. 11 Dist., Portage, 09-20-2002) No. 2002-P-0035, No. 2002-P-0036, 2002-Ohio-4958, 2002 WL 31107531, Unreported. Infants ⇐ 191

Clear and convincing evidence supported juvenile court's judgment terminating father's parental rights and awarding permanent custody to public agency; evidence showed that father suffered from a major depressive disorder that prevented him from providing his children with the safe, nurturing environment they required, and although his love for the children was unquestioned, he was either unable or unwilling to take the necessary steps to control his illness. In re Funk (Ohio App. 11 Dist., Portage, 09-20-2002) No. 2002-P-0035, No. 2002-P-0036, 2002-Ohio-4958, 2002 WL 31107531, Unreported. Infants ⇐ 181

Mother's efforts to comply with case plan in order to be reunited with her dependent children were insufficient, though mother contended she sought employment, given that mother was required to, but did not seek employment or assistance that would sufficiently provide for her housing needs; although mother sought employment, she did not hold one job for more than two weeks throughout the two years of the case plan, did admit that a two-week salary was insufficient to support her children, and there was no indication of when, if ever, mother was going to be able to support her children. In re Cather (Ohio App. 11 Dist., Portage, 08-30-2002) No. 2002-P-0014, No. 2002-P-0015, No. 2002-P-0016, 2002-Ohio-4519, 2002 WL 2022964, Unreported. Infants ⇐ 155

It was in the best interest of mother's minor children that the children be permanently placed in the custody of child protection agency, even though mother had completed her case plan; mother had worked at approximately ten jobs in the prior two years, mother had faced eviction twice and had her water turned off twice, mother had not followed through in obtaining services that could aid her, such as Social Security, consumer credit counseling, and case management, and mother's home had an ongoing problem with fleas, roaches and mice. In re Barker (Ohio App. 12 Dist., Butler, 07-29-2002) No. CA2001-12-293, 2002-Ohio-3871, 2002 WL 1758378, Unreported. Infants ⇐ 155

Substantial evidence supported termination of father's parental rights; psychiatrist testified that father was diagnosed with bipolar disorder, attention deficit hyperactivity disorder, antisocial personality disorder, and borderline intellectual functioning, and that he was not taking his medicine as prescribed; social service workers testified that neither father nor mother demonstrated an ability to care for the child, despite attending parenting classes. In re Hiltabidel (Ohio App. 9 Dist., Summit, 07-17-2002) No. 21009, 2002-Ohio-3627, 2002 WL 1596507, Unreported. Infants ⇐ 178

Child's best interests were served by juvenile court's terminating parental rights and awarding permanent custody to public services agency; child was in agency's temporary custody from day after her birth until the hearing, which was a period of over two years, parent was not the primary caregiver for child while both were in same foster home, and relationship between parent and child could be considered a child-child relationship rather than a mother-daughter relationship, in that parent would tease child by rejecting her after she pretended she wanted her to come and by offering her high calorie snack foods. In re Miqueal M. (Ohio App. 6 Dist., Lucas, 06-28-2002) No. L-02-1020, 2002-Ohio-3417, 2002 WL 1438664, Unreported. Infants ⇐ 155

Evidence, including testimony that mother had been living in motel with her children, that mother was employed as dancer/entertainer, that children had been in foster care for over three years, that mother had long history of drug and alcohol abuse and had spent great deal of time being rehabilitated and incarcerated for her multiple drunk driving convictions, that mother made virtually no progress on her case plan, visited children only 11 times out of possible 85, and failed to pay any child support, and that adoption by current foster parents was very likely, was sufficient to support termination of mother's parental rights. In re Stephens (Ohio App. 7 Dist., Columbiana, 06-05-2002) No. 2001 CO 56, 2002-Ohio-3057, 2002 WL 1376240, Unreported. Infants ⇐ 155

Best interests of child were served by granting agency's petition for permanent custody of child, given mother's failure to complete her case plan or determine child's paternity, her erratic history of drug use, her repeated incarceration, her lack of commitment toward child, evidenced by her failing to support, visit, or communicate with child when able to do so, her inability to maintain stable housing or employment, prior termination of her parental rights to child's older sibling, and her unwillingness to provide food, clothing, shelter, and other basic necessities for child, and given that agency had made reasonable efforts toward reunion and child had bonded with her foster mother. In re M.H. (Ohio App. 8 Dist., Cuyahoga, 06-13-2002) No. 80620, 2002-Ohio-2968, 2002 WL 1307426, Unreported. Infants ⇐ 222

Clear and convincing evidence supported determinations in dependency proceeding that two minor children could not and should not be placed with either parent within a reasonable time and that grant of permanent custody to county children's services agency was in children's best interest; despite numerous services offered by agency, parents did not fully complete those services, did not gain any insight into their problems from services that they did attend, and were inconsistent in their visits with children. In re Chianna C. (Ohio App. 6 Dist., Lucas, 06-07-2002) No. L-02-1019, 2002-Ohio-2800, 2002 WL 1303212, Unreported. Infants ⇐ 178

Evidence supported termination of mother's parental rights to her child; mother had long history of drug abuse and was unable to break her cycle of continual relapse, and thus child could not be placed with mother within a reasonable time, and termination was in child's best interests, given that mother had limited interaction with child because she was incarcerated, during visits with child at prison, mother's attention was not usually focused on child, child did not have visits with his siblings and thus was not integrated into family, and child had never lived with mother and barely knew her. In re Schafer (Ohio App. 9 Dist., Lorain, 06-05-2002) No. 02CA007991, 2002-Ohio-2661, 2002 WL 1263934, Unreported. Infants ⇐ 155

Evidence supported conclusion that termination of mother's parental rights to her six children was in children's best interests; children evinced behavior consistent with sexual abuse, father was convicted of gross sexual imposition (GSI) against child, despite father's conviction, mother denied father's culpability and harm suffered by children, mother testified unconvincingly that she would keep children away from father, mother failed to maintain mental health counseling, and even during temporary unsupervised time with children, children's clothes were soiled with urine due to lack of prompt attention and telephonic contact was had with their abusive father. In re Lansberry (Ohio App. 9 Dist., Summit, 06-05-2002) No. 20823, 2002-Ohio-2658, 2002 WL 1265539, Unreported. Infants ⇐ 178

Clear and convincing evidence supported finding that child could not be placed with father within a reasonable period of time, in support of termination of father's parental rights to child; father relinquished custody of child years ago because he was having marital difficulties and felt that he could not care for her any longer, he made no effort to be involved in the permanent custody proceedings, he failed to appear at the final hearing even though he was subpoenaed, he had accrued child support arrearages of $18,000.00, and he had failed to visit child. In re Borders (Ohio App. 12 Dist., Brown, 05-28-2002) No. CA2001-10-017, 2002-Ohio-2578, 2002 WL 1058119, Unreported. Infants ⇐ 178

Trial court judgment granting permanent custody of child to the county department of jobs and family service was in the child's best interests; granting permanent custody to county would not disrupt child's current placement, and testimony established that child was unable to cope with changes in her life, that contact with mother sometimes led to child acting out sexually and uncontrollably, which sometimes resulted in disruptions in child's foster placements, and that child had made considerable progress in her current placement. In re Borders (Ohio App. 12 Dist., Brown, 05-28-2002) No. CA2001-10-017, 2002-Ohio-2578, 2002 WL 1058119, Unreported. Infants ⇐ 226

The weight of the evidence supported the trial court's finding that it was in the child's best interest that the county department of jobs and family services be granted permanent custody of child; the court considered the statutory factors and found that mother exhibited a lack of interest in the proceedings, she failed to appear at the final hearing, her psychological and emotional makeup prevented her from providing a safe home environment, and she demonstrated a lack of commitment to adequately providing for child's needs and safety. In re Borders (Ohio App. 12 Dist., Brown, 05-28-2002) No. CA2001-10-017, 2002-Ohio-2578, 2002 WL 1058119, Unreported. Infants ⇐ 175.1

Evidence supported finding that child could not be placed with mother within a reasonable time, in termination of parental rights proceeding; mother was diagnosed with a narcissistic personality disorder, mother failed to attend many of her weekly mental health counseling sessions, caseworker testified that mother had difficulties with anger management, mother had past problems with illegal drug use, she had recently tested positive for marijuana on three occasions, and she failed to show up for regular drug screen tests. In re Pittman (Ohio App. 9 Dist., Summit, 05-08-2002) No. 20894, 2002-Ohio-2208, 2002 WL 987852, Unreported. Infants ⇐ 178

Mother's substantial compliance with her caseplan, in and of itself, did not warrant reversal of order granting permanent custody of child to the county children's services board; the primary focus in termination of parental rights proceedings was whether the parent remedied the conditions which originally caused the child's removal from the home. In re Pittman (Ohio App. 9 Dist., Summit, 05-08-2002) No. 20894, 2002-Ohio-2208, 2002 WL 987852, Unreported. Infants ⇐ 231

A parent's chronic substance abuse which prevents her from providing her child with an adequate permanent home in the present or within a year is adequate basis for terminating parental rights. In re Carroll (Ohio App. 9 Dist., Lorain, 10-10-2001) No. 01CA007857, 2001-Ohio-1423, 2001 WL 1192730, Unreported.

Where (1) a caseworker and psychologist state that a manic-depressive mother might be able to adequately parent her child if she would take medication and follow a program for six months, but the mother refuses to take the medication, (2) the mother drunkenly drove into a ditch with the child not in a safety-seat, and (3) the father's only contact with the child was one visit, the parent's mental and emotional problems make her "unable to provide an adequate permanent home for the child... in the foreseeable future" for purposes of RC 2151.414. In re Heyman, No. 96 APF02-194, 1996 WL 465238 (10th Dist Ct App, Franklin, 8-13-96).

6. Children's services agency duties

For purposes of determining whether children had been in agency custody for 12 of past consecutive 22 months, as required to support termination of mother's parental rights, periods of children's custody were required to be calculated as actual days in agency custody, and portions of months could not be counted as entire months. In re A.C. (Ohio App. 9 Dist., Summit, 06-30-2006) No. 23090, 2006-Ohio-3337, 2006 WL 1789853, Unreported. Infants ☞ 155

Evidence supported conclusion that children could not be placed with father within a reasonable time or should not be placed with him, as necessary to support termination of father's parental rights; father, who admitted causing incident which resulted in removal of children from his care, had convictions for child endangering and domestic violence, he did not benefit from his parenting class, he demonstrated inappropriate behavior when he was interacting with children, and he might have years of counseling ahead of him, given his psychological issues, including a diagnosis of immediate explosive disorder. In re E.T. (Ohio App. 9 Dist., Summit, 05-17-2006) No. 23017, 2006-Ohio-2413, 2006 WL 1329653, Unreported. Infants ☞ 158

Evidence supported conclusion that county children services board (CSB) provided reasonable case planning to father and made diligent and reasonable efforts toward reunification, as necessary to support termination of father's parental rights; father's initial case worker, who was temporarily assigned to father during a work stoppage, was inexperienced, but she was not unqualified, second case worker made numerous contacts with father to verify that services were provided as referred, she met with parents at court house, visitation center, and family team meetings, and she offered to meet with them at other times, but, according to case worker, father was not willing to do so. In re E.T. (Ohio App. 9 Dist., Summit, 05-17-2006) No. 23017, 2006-Ohio-2413, 2006 WL 1329653, Unreported. Infants ☞ 155

Allegations that parents whose children were removed from home by county social worker were not allowed to recover children after safety plan providing for children's placement with friends had been initiated, despite parents' best efforts to do so, that continued deprivation of children was involuntary, and that parents were effectively denied prompt hearing on children's placement supported claim against social worker for violating parents' procedural due process rights. Smith v. Williams-Ash (C.A.6 (Ohio), 12-06-2005) No. 04-4547, 173 Fed.Appx. 363, 2005 WL 3304101, Unreported. Infants ☞ 17

County social worker should have known that her alleged conduct in thwarting parents' attempts to have children returned to parents' home, after children were removed due to unsanitary conditions, and in effectively denying parents prompt hearing on children's placement had effect of violating parents' clearly established rights to procedural due process by involuntarily depriving parents of physical custody of children, and therefore qualified immunity did not apply to preclude social worker's liability under §§ 1983. Smith v. Williams-Ash (C.A.6 (Ohio), 12-06-2005) No. 04-4547, 173 Fed.Appx. 363, 2005 WL 3304101, Unreported. Civil Rights ☞ 1376(4)

County social worker's alleged conduct in thwarting parents' attempts to have children returned to parents' home, after children were removed due to unsanitary conditions, and in effectively denying parents prompt hearing on children's placement did not rise to the level of conscience-shocking behavior, and thus did not support substantive due process claim. Smith v. Williams-Ash (C.A.6 (Ohio), 12-06-2005) No. 04-4547, 173 Fed.Appx. 363, 2005 WL 3304101, Unreported. Infants ☞ 17

County department of children and family services made good-faith effort to implement reunification plan, in proceeding in which permanent custody of child was granted to department; department's motion for permanent custody only came after it had previously filed two extensions to maintain temporary custody in an effort to assist mother in her reunification efforts, and there was ample proof in the record to show that department social worker repeatedly made efforts to aid and help mother with her substance abuse issues, and thus, efforts satisfied good faith effort requirement imposed on department. In re T.W. (Ohio App. 8 Dist., Cuyahoga, 10-13-2005) No. 85845, 2005-Ohio-5446, 2005 WL 2600663, Unreported, appeal not allowed 108 Ohio St.3d 1418, 841 N.E.2d 321, 2006-Ohio-179, reconsideration denied 108 Ohio St.3d 1513, 844 N.E.2d 857, 2006-Ohio-1329. Infants ☞ 155

A lack of reasonable case planning effort of agency will be reversible error in a termination of parental rights proceeding only if the trial court's order of permanent custody is based solely upon statutory factor requiring the trial court to find that the child cannot or should not be returned to either parent because the parent failed to substantially remedy the conditions causing the child to be placed outside the home notwithstanding reasonable case planning and diligent efforts by the agency to assist the parents. In re S.T., V.T. & P.T. (Ohio App. 9 Dist., Summit, 09-14-2005) No. 22665, 2005-Ohio-4793, 2005 WL 2219613, Unreported. Infants ☞ 253

An agency is not precluded from moving for permanent custody before a child has been in the agency's temporary custody for at least 12 months; if a ground set forth in statute addressing circumstances under which courts may grant permanent custody, other than that permitting grant of permanent custody if child has been in temporary custody of agency for 12 or more months of consecutive 22 month period exists to support a grant of permanent custody, the agency may move for permanent custody on that other ground. In re Tucke (Ohio App. 5 Dist., Stark, 08-22-2005) No. 2005CA00077, 2005-Ohio-4409, 2005 WL 2045454, Unreported. Infants ☞ 193

Trial court's entry of order granting County Children Services Board's (MCCSB) motion to terminate mother's parental rights to her twin boys, despite MCCSB's failure to make reasonable efforts to reunite mother with children, was reversible error; although MCCSB developed case plan that included some limited supervised visitation provisions, this could hardly be called clear and convincing evidence that MCCSB made reasonable efforts at reunification. In re Bowers (Ohio App. 7 Dist., Mahoning, 08-18-2005) No. 04 MA 216, 2005-Ohio-4376, 2005 WL 2033100, Unreported. Infants ☞ 253

Child endangerment for which mother was convicted was not recognized under parental rights termination statute as an offense that allowed County Children Services Board (MCCSB) to bypass its responsibility to make reasonable efforts at reuniting children with parent before seeking termination. In re Bowers (Ohio App. 7 Dist., Mahoning, 08-18-2005) No. 04 MA 216, 2005-Ohio-4376, 2005 WL 2033100, Unreported. Infants ☞ 155

Evidence supported conclusion that county made reasonable, diligent efforts to effectuate goals of mother's case plan, in termination of parental rights proceeding; delay in performance of psychological evaluations for mother was due largely to mother's failure to attend appointments and her failure to cooperate with her caseworker in scheduling evaluation, and county diligently pursued goal of reunification by making services at health care provider available and by monitoring mother's use of those services and her progress, including scheduling appointments for her. In re Van Atta (Ohio App. 3 Dist., Hancock, 08-15-2005) No. 5-05-03, 2005-Ohio-4182, 2005 WL 1939418, Unreported. Infants ☞ 155

Clear and convincing evidence supported conclusion that children could not be placed with mother within a reasonable time and should not be placed with her, in termination of parental rights proceeding; county agency's case-planning with respect to mother was reasonable and its efforts to assist her were diligent, yet mother failed to complete case plan, mother failed to pay county child support for her children despite her ability to do so, and mother's repeated incarcerations prevented her from providing adequate care for her children. In re Amber L. (Ohio App. 6 Dist., Williams, 08-12-2005) No. 20230034, No. 20230035, No. 20230336, 2005-Ohio-4172, 2005 WL 1926515, Unreported. Infants ☞ 157

Sufficient evidence supported determination that county agency's case planning with respect to mother was reasonable and its efforts to assist her were diligent, in termination of parental rights proceeding; case plan sought to address mother's various mental health issues, long-term financial instability, criminal tendencies, and lack of parenting skills by providing her with means to obtain drug and alcohol assessments, parenting classes, anger management for her husband, psychological evaluation and treatment, individual therapy, promotion of financial stability, and participation in children's therapy programs, but, despite agency's efforts, mother failed to complete many of case plan's goals. In re Amber L. (Ohio App. 6 Dist., Williams, 08-12-2005) No. 20230034, No. 20230035, No. 20230336, 2005-Ohio-4172, 2005 WL 1926515, Unreported. Infants ☞ 155

County department of job and family services made reasonable efforts to develop and preserve parent-child relationship, in proceeding in which trial court granted permanent custody of child to county department of job and family services; in order to make it possible for mother to be reunified with child, department ordered mother to undergo psychological and substance abuse examination, and department facilitated visitation, provided information on services to mother, encouraged mother to work on case plan goals, and made efforts in locating relatives willing to care for child. In re Patfield (Ohio App. 11 Dist., Lake, 07-18-2005) No. 2005-L-007, 2005-Ohio-3769, 2005 WL 1714185, Unreported, appeal not allowed 106 Ohio St.3d 1548, 835 N.E.2d 728, 2005-Ohio-5343. Infants 155

Decision not to place child in permanent custody of County Children Services Board was not against manifest weight of evidence, despite finding that mother and father had parental rights involuntarily terminated with respect to sibling and had both been convicted of child endangerment; evidence did not show that father presented ongoing danger to child, and there was possibility that child could be placed with father within reasonable time if family counseling was conducted. In re Graves (Ohio App. 2 Dist., Montgomery, 03-25-2005) No. 20524, 2005-Ohio-1363, 2005 WL 678924, Unreported. Infants 156

Evidence supported trial court's finding that agency made reasonable efforts to prevent the removal of parents' child, thus supporting grant of permanent custody of child to county child protection agency; despite parents' lack of cooperation and failure to comply with court orders, agency continued to offer them encouragement and services, caseworker attempted to contact them and to set up drug screens and assessments, and agency was prevented from offering further services by parents' failure to submit to the screenings or to participate in the assessments. In re Ella C. (Ohio App. 6 Dist., Lucas, 01-04-2005) No. L-04-1207, 2005-Ohio-42, 2005 WL 30548, Unreported. Infants 155

In finding that dependent child could not or should not be placed with parents, trial court erred by relying on statutory factor that parents failed to remedy conditions that caused child's removal from their home, where children services board (CSB) failed to provide services to correct problems relating to parents' housing need, which was relied upon in removing child from home. In re B.E.M. (Ohio App. 9 Dist., Wayne, 09-22-2004) No. 04CA0028, 2004-Ohio-4959, 2004 WL 2244246, Unreported. Infants 231

Evidence in termination of parental rights proceeding supported finding that Geauga County Job and Family Services (GCJFS) used reasonable case planning and diligent efforts to assist parents to remedy problems that caused dependent children to be placed outside their home; case plan, which included counseling, chemical dependency assessments, and employment program, was designed to remedy parents' domestic violence, drug use, and unstable home. In re Ross (Ohio App. 11 Dist., Geauga, 07-07-2004) No. 2003-G-2551, 2004-Ohio-3684, 2004 WL 1559742, Unreported. Infants 155

Finding that it was in best interest of dependent children to grant permanent custody to County Children Services Board was not abuse of discretion, where children had been in Board's temporary custody for over three and one-half years, children needed secure placement, mother's witnesses had never met children or seen mother interact with children, and caseworker and guardian ad litem who had most contact with mother and children recommended that permanent custody be granted to Board. In re Bicanovsky (Ohio App. 7 Dist., Mahoning, 06-10-2004) No. 04-MA-5, 2004-Ohio-3034, 2004 WL 1321900, Unreported. Infants 222

County Children Services Board was required to file motion seeking permanent custody of dependent children, where children were in Board's custody for more that 12 months of consecutive 22-month period. In re Bicanovsky (Ohio App. 7 Dist., Mahoning, 06-10-2004) No. 04-MA-5, 2004-Ohio-3034, 2004 WL 1321900, Unreported. Infants 191

Trial court's determination that county made diligent efforts to return child to mother before seeking permanent custody of child was supported by evidence that county had provided mother with case plan that addressed her cocaine addiction and residence in county jail, and that it had provided her with more than normal opportunities for visitation. In re King (Ohio App. 11 Dist., Lake, 06-04-2004) No. 2004-L-013, 2004-Ohio-2919, 2004 WL 1238377, Unreported. Infants 155

Trial court was required to order the return of mother's child, while parental termination case was on appeal, where court denied Department of Job and Family Services' motion for permanent custody of child. In re Snow (Ohio App. 11 Dist., Portage, 03-29-2004) No. 2003-P-0118, 2004-Ohio-1532, 2004 WL 610201, Unreported. Infants 244.1

Children services agency lacked authority to file for permanent custody of children on basis that children had been in temporary custody of agency for 12 or more months of consecutive 22-month period, where, at time of filing, children had not been in agency's custody for full 12 months, even if children would have been in agency's custody for full 12 months at time of permanent custody hearing; parents were to be given full period of time to work toward reunification, agency could not benefit from delays between filing of motion and hearing on motion, and agency could not base motion on grounds that did not yet exist. In Re K.G. (Ohio App. 9 Dist., Wayne, 03-24-2004) No. 03CA0066, No. 03CA0067, No. 03CA0068, 2004-Ohio-1421, 2004 WL 573887, Unreported. Infants 200

Duty of county Child Protective Services Unit (CPSU) to make reasonable efforts to reunite mother with her children did not include duty to monitor or evaluate mother's efforts at reunification during period of mother's incarceration, absent contact by mother to make agency aware of her efforts; given significant involvement of CPSU both prior to children's removal, and thereafter, mother's lack of commitment to using resources offered by CPSU, her continuous criminal activity, and opportunity given to mother to inform caseworker about any programs in which she was involved while incarcerated, CPSU had no further obligation to provide services to mother while incarcerated. In re Vance (Ohio App. 3 Dist., Hancock, 12-22-2003) No. 5-03-16, No. 5-03-17, No. 5-03-18, 2003-Ohio-6991, 2003 WL 22994978, Unreported. Infants 155

In custody proceeding, trial court was not required to determine whether children could have been placed with either parent within a reasonable time, or should have been placed with either parent, where children were in custody of County Children Services for 12 or more months of a consecutive 22 month period. In re Damron (Ohio App. 10 Dist., Franklin, 10-30-2003) No. 03AP-419, 2003-Ohio-5810, 2003 WL 22455693, Unreported. Infants 210

Trial court's finding that there were reasonable efforts to reunify mother and child, when record reflected that county children services agency in fact made no efforts to reunite child with mother after removing child from home on ground that child could not be placed with either parent within a reasonable time due to parents' failure to remedy the conditions that originally caused child's removal, constituted harmless error, where several other statutory criteria justified grant of custody. In re Lewis (Ohio App. 4 Dist., Athens, 09-25-2003) No. 03CA12, 2003-Ohio-5262, 2003 WL 22267129, Unreported. Infants 253

County children services agency had duty to exercise reasonable efforts to reunify parent and child after child's removal from home when agency's efforts to obtain custody were based upon an allegation that child could not be placed with either parent within a reasonable time due to fact that parents had failed to remedy the conditions that originally caused child's removal. In re Lewis (Ohio App. 4 Dist., Athens, 09-25-2003) No. 03CA12, 2003-Ohio-5262, 2003 WL 22267129, Unreported. Infants 155

County children services agency did not have a duty to continue efforts to reunify mother with child after it filed complaint for permanent custody. In re Lewis (Ohio App. 4 Dist., Athens, 09-25-2003) No. 03CA12, 2003-Ohio-5262, 2003 WL 22267129, Unreported. Infants 155

Juvenile Court is not statutorily prohibited from granting permanent custody to Children's Services if a legally secure permanent placement could be achieved without granting permanent custody; statute provides that the court must determine whether child's needs require grant of permanent custody, regardless of possibility of an alternative placement. In re Bigham (Ohio App. 5 Dist., Fairfield, 06-30-2003) No. 03-CA-2, 2003-Ohio-3859, 2003 WL 21675676, Unreported. Infants 222

Trial court correctly determined, in permanent custody proceeding, that Department of Jobs and Family Services was required to prove the child could not be placed with either parent within a reasonable time, where child was not in temporary custody of Department for 12 of the last 24 months. In re Matuszczak (Ohio App. 5 Dist., Stark, 06-02-2003) No. 2003CA000100, 2003-Ohio-2892, 2003 WL 21290901, Unreported. Infants 155

County children services did not fail to make reasonable efforts to reunify family prior to filing for permanent custody of mother's children; county children services created and implemented two case plans and provided a myriad of services to mother, and while mother did take advantage of the services provided to her and clearly made significant efforts, mother failed to remedy the problems originally causing her children to be placed in temporary custody. In re Llewellyn (Ohio App. 5 Dist., Fairfield, 03-10-2003) No. 02CA10, No. 02CA11, No. 02CA12, 2003-Ohio-1102, 2003 WL 951401, Unreported. Infants 155

Mother failed to establish that the county job and family services agency failed to offer mother services designed to reunify her and the children; when the agency initially took custody, mother refused to cooperate with the agency in developing a caseplan, later mother fled out of state and her whereabouts were unknown or she was incarcerated, and, when mother was told how to arrange for visitation with the children, she failed to do so. In re Billingsley (Ohio App. 3 Dist., Putnam, 01-28-2003) No. 12-02-07,

No. 12-02-08, 2003-Ohio-344, 2003 WL 178661, Unreported. Infants ⚖ 155

County children services made reasonable efforts to treat mother's alleged personality disorder, thus supporting trial court's decision to terminate parental rights for mother's failure to remedy conditions that caused child to be placed outside her custody; counseling, group therapy and medication were made available to mother, but were not fully or properly utilized. In re Devin B. (Ohio App. 6 Dist., Lucas, 01-24-2003) No. L-02-1294, 2003-Ohio-307, 2003 WL 164858, Unreported. Infants ⚖ 158

Sufficient evidence supported finding that county children services board made reasonable attempt to reunify father and child; record indicated that board assisted father to meet goals of his case plan, and that board investigated possibility of placement with other relatives, but no evidence was presented to indicate that any relative wanted to, or could, assume custody of child. In re S.S. (Ohio App. 2 Dist., Montgomery, 01-24-2003) No. 19406, 2003-Ohio-319, 2003 WL 164598, Unreported. Infants ⚖ 178

A county children services agency failed to make a good faith effort to reunify a child with his father and failed to meet its burden of showing the child could not be placed with his father within a reasonable time where (1) although the father had no contact with his son for a number of years, he was unable to do so because the mother refused to allow him to see his son and moved so he would not know where the son lived; (2) the record is devoid of any proof that an award of permanent custody to the children services agency would facilitate adoption, especially since the child is aggressive and assaultive and has been relocated to many foster homes and hospitalized several times; (3) the children services agency never filed or attempted to implement a reunification plan for father and son, and had begun to implement its plan to obtain permanent custody and appeared reluctant to abandon or suspend that plan; (4) instead of facilitating any opportunity for the son to get to know his father, the children services agency may have hindered the father's attempts to contact or visit the child in the last six months; and (5) there is no evidence that the father could not provide a suitable home for the son upon completion of a case plan, and the father said he would do "whatever it takes" to reunify with his son. In re Forrest (Ohio App. 10 Dist., Franklin, 07-30-1996) No. 96APF02-211, 1996 WL 434180, Unreported.

Trial court properly determined per RC 2151.414(E) that it was in best interests of four children of woman twice incarcerated for drug trafficking to grant Children Services Board permanent custody of them, where woman made little progress toward remedying her drug addiction as called for in Board's reunification plan. Harris v Harris, No. 15902, 1993 WL 99996 (9th Dist Ct App, Summit, 4–7–93).

Before a public children-services agency or private child-placing agency can move for permanent custody of a child on the ground that the child has been in the temporary custody of the agency for at least 12 months of a consecutive 22–month period, the child must have been in the temporary custody of agency for at least 12 months of the 22–month period; in other words, the time that passes between the filing of a motion for permanent custody and the permanent-custody hearing does not count toward the 12–month period; abrogating In re Dyal, 2001 WL 925423. In re C.W. (Ohio, 12-08-2004) 104 Ohio St.3d 163, 818 N.E.2d 1176, 2004-Ohio-6411. Infants ⚖ 155

Former statutes concerning motions by children services agency for permanent custody of child, when read in pari materia, indicated legislature's intent that agency have current temporary custody when moving for permanent custody. In re Hayes (Ohio, 06-18-1997) 79 Ohio St.3d 46, 679 N.E.2d 680, reconsideration denied 79 Ohio St.3d 1492, 683 N.E.2d 793. Infants ⚖ 155

Termination of parental rights was warranted where children were removed from mother's home due to mother's dependency on crack cocaine which rendered her incapable of caring for children or providing them with decent home environment, 18 months later mother was still using crack cocaine and still needed counseling for chemical dependency, and on more than half a dozen occasions mother failed to avail herself of counseling services arranged for her. In re Shanequa H. (Ohio App. 6 Dist., 02-02-1996) 109 Ohio App.3d 142, 671 N.E.2d 1113. Infants ⚖ 155

Permanent custody statute authorizes granting of permanent custody to Department of Human Services (DHS) if trial court determined it to be in best interest of children and if trial court found that children could not be placed with their parents within reasonable time or should not be placed with their parents. In re Shaeffer Children (Van Wert 1993) 85 Ohio App.3d 683, 621 N.E.2d 426, dismissed, jurisdictional motion overruled 67 Ohio St.3d 1451, 619 N.E.2d 419. Infants ⚖ 155

Finding that grant of permanent custody to Department of Human Services (DHS) was in best interests of mother's two minor children was supported by evidence that children could not be returned to their mother within reasonable time due to her mental problems, that children were adoptable, even though they had special needs, and that placing children with adoptive parents would not pose problem. In re Shaeffer Children (Van Wert 1993) 85 Ohio App.3d 683, 621 N.E.2d 426, dismissed, jurisdictional motion overruled 67 Ohio St.3d 1451, 619 N.E.2d 419. Infants ⚖ 178; Infants ⚖ 181

A permanent custody award of a child to a county child services agency is supported by clear and convincing evidence that a reasonable possibility existed that the child would be adopted if the agency obtained permanent custody and that a permanent custody order would facilitate that adoption. In re McCrary (Madison 1991) 75 Ohio App.3d 601, 600 N.E.2d 347, dismissed, jurisdictional motion overruled 64 Ohio St.3d 1427, 594 N.E.2d 969. Infants ⚖ 178

A county children's services agency's temporary custody over a dependent child terminated under 1988 Am S 89, § 7, effective January 1, 1989, on January 1, 1990 where the child as of January 1, 1989, was in the temporary custody of the agency and not his mother, and the last recorded semiannual review was on September 11, 1989. In re McCrary (Madison 1991) 75 Ohio App.3d 601, 600 N.E.2d 347, dismissed, jurisdictional motion overruled 64 Ohio St.3d 1427, 594 N.E.2d 969.

Under termination of parental rights statute, public agency is not required to wait until a child has been in its custody for twenty-two months before filing a motion for permanent custody; statute only requires that the child be in agency's custody for twelve or more months of a consecutive twenty-two month period. In re T.B. (Ohio App. 9 Dist., Summit, 09-25-2002) No. 21124, 2002-Ohio-5036, 2002 WL 31114995, Unreported. Infants ⚖ 197

Public agency made reasonable efforts to reunify mother and child before trial court terminated parental rights and awarded agency permanent custody; agency attempted to locate mother at the beginning of the case, despite the fact that neither the child nor the child's father knew her address or telephone number and despite the fact that mother had been essentially uninvolved in the child's life for years, agency offered bus passes to fulfill mother's transportation needs, and mother failed to take advantage of opportunities provided by agency to establish or re-establish a relationship with her child. In re T.B. (Ohio App. 9 Dist., Summit, 09-25-2002) No. 21124, 2002-Ohio-5036, 2002 WL 31114995, Unreported. Infants ⚖ 155

Evidence supported award of permanent custody of three dependent or abused children to county department of jobs and family services; mother, during post-release control following her release in three months from her two-year prison sentence for child endangering, would not be permitted to have contact with one of the children, that child's psychologist opined the child needed the consistency of permanent placement, mother posed a safety risk to the children, mother did not complete "goodwill parenting" requirement of case plan or follow through on treatment recommendation, visitation had been limited while mother was in prison, and caseworker testified that the non-abused children could be safely placed with foster mother and that it was possible the abused child could be placed with the foster mother in the future. In re Campbell/Spicer Children (Ohio App. 5 Dist., Stark, 07-15-2002) No. 2002CA00056, 2002-Ohio-3696, 2002 WL 1585840, Unreported. Infants ⚖ 222

A children services agency must exercise diligence in attempting to reunify a family, and mere "reasonable efforts" are insufficient; the agency must diligently assist the parent to acquire the parenting skills necessary to regain custody of the child, and reunification of the family must be the only goal of the agency. In re Jeronic, No. 58619 and 58620+ (8th Dist Ct App, Cuyahoga, 6–27–91).

Where the trial court determines that it is in the best interest of a minor child to terminate parental rights permanently, the trial court may grant permanent custody to a county children services board without first granting temporary custody. In re Hollins, No. CA–703 (5th Dist Ct App, Guernsey, 3–29–83).

7. Hearings

Mother's lack of appropriate home for children and her own admitted prior history, including her previous inability to care for them, were sufficient to establish dependency on part of children at time of adjudicatory hearing. In re Elliott (Ohio App. 11 Dist., Ashtabula, 02-17-2006) No. 2005-A-0018, 2006-Ohio-738, 2006 WL 389595, Unreported. Infants ⚖ 156

Trial court abused its discretion, in child protection proceedings, in granting permanent custody of subject children to county Department of Children and Family Services (DCFS), where court signed proposed journal entry granting permanent custody to DCFS two days prior to conclusion of trial. In re S.J. (Ohio App. 8 Dist., Cuyahoga, 04-21-2005) No. 84410, 2005-Ohio-1854, 2005 WL 914692, Unreported. Infants ⚖ 221

Trial court did not abuse its discretion in proceeding to determine custody of abused, dependent, and neglected child by overruling father's objections to magistrate's decision awarding permanent custody to maternal grandmother, even though trial court's order stated "No formal hearing was held"; record of dispositional hearing before magistrate showed that magistrate did conduct evidentiary hearing, and statement in trial court's order most likely referred to trial court's denial of father's objections without a hearing, rather than to the proceedings before the magistrate. In re Dorie F. (Ohio App. 6 Dist., Lucas, 03-31-2005) No. L-04-1097, 2005-Ohio-1551, 2005 WL 736992, Unreported. Infants ⇐ 206

Evidence supported trial court's grant of permanent custody of parents' daughters to county child protection agency; mother and father had histories of failing to comply with case plans regarding other children, parents failed to comply with case plan regarding their daughters, mother failed to remedy drug problem, neither parent maintained employment or stable residence, parents failed to address their lack of education, parents failed to maintain clean living quarters, parents visitation was sporadic, and guardian ad litem recommended that grant of permanent custody to county child protection agency was in best interests of daughters. In re Grooms (Ohio App. 2 Dist., Clark, 12-03-2004) No. 2003 CA 50, 2004-Ohio-6782, 2004 WL 2903883, Unreported. Infants ⇐ 155; Infants ⇐ 156; Infants ⇐ 208

Evidence to support need to remove children from home was not necessary at dispositional hearing. In re R.H. (Ohio App. 8 Dist., Cuyahoga, 10-28-2004) No. 84051, 2004-Ohio-5734, 2004 WL 2425831, Unreported. Infants ⇐ 222

Juvenile court's denial of father's motion for a three-month continuance of his permanent custody hearing was not an abuse of discretion; father did not start to comply with his case plan until after the motion for permanent custody was filed, and he was also notified of the semi-annual review of the case plan and chose not to attend. In re Miller (Ohio App. 3 Dist., Auglaize, 06-14-2004) No. 2-04-02, 2004-Ohio-3023, 2004 WL 1302250, Unreported. Infants ⇐ 204

Juvenile court did not err by failing to inquire whether guardian ad litem's recommendation to grant Geauga County Job and Family Services (GCJFS) permanent child custody had changed after presentation of all evidence; statute requires guardian ad litem to submit written report to court prior to or at time of permanent custody hearing and guardian ad litem is not required to present testimony at hearing. In re Krems (Ohio App. 11 Dist., Geauga, 05-14-2004) No. 2003-G-2535, 2004-Ohio-2449, 2004 WL 1086974, Unreported. Infants ⇐ 208

Mother received adequate notice of final hearing in permanent custody case involving dependent children; mother was personally served with notice of the hearing, she failed to attend the hearing, her attorney informed her of the date of the final permanent custody hearing, and she failed to attend that hearing. In re Keith Lee P. (Ohio App. 6 Dist., Lucas, 04-16-2004) No. L-03-1266, 2004-Ohio-1976, 2004 WL 835989, Unreported. Infants ⇐ 198

Court failed to adequately discuss the children's wishes in termination of parental rights hearing when it stated that two children were not mature enough to express a meaningful opinion; guardian ad litem's report failed to mention children's wishes, guardian admitted he did not meet with those two children to discuss their wishes, and one child was eight years old and able to express opinion as to custody desire. In re Ridenour (Ohio App. 11 Dist., Lake, 04-16-2004) No. 2003-L-146, No. 2003-L-147, No. 2003-L-148, 2004-Ohio-1958, 2004 WL 834579, Unreported. Infants ⇐ 210

Guardian ad litem's failure to file report prior to termination of parental rights hearing was not prejudicial so as to require the reversal of the juvenile court's judgment awarding County Department of Job and Family Services permanent custody of children, where guardian testified at hearing as to his custody recommendation, recommendation at hearing was same as recommendation in report he subsequently filed, recommendation was consistent with evidence presented at hearing, and report did not contain any new facts, evidence, or opinions. In re Ridenour (Ohio App. 11 Dist., Lake, 04-16-2004) No. 2003-L-146, No. 2003-L-147, No. 2003-L-148, 2004-Ohio-1958, 2004 WL 834579, Unreported. Infants ⇐ 253

Trial court was required to hold dispositional hearing on motion, made by County Department of Children and Family Services and child's maternal aunt, to vacate permanent custody which had been previously granted to department, and to grant legal custody of child to her foster parents, and was required to provide notice of hearing to child's guardian ad litem; court was required to determine best interest of child, which could only be accomplished by considering all evidence concerning her custodial placement, including recommendation of guardian ad litem. In re G.R. (Ohio App. 8 Dist., Cuyahoga, 03-04-2004) No. 83146, 2004-Ohio-999, 2004 WL 397153, Unreported. Infants ⇐ 198; Infants ⇐ 203; Infants ⇐ 230.1

Trial court unlawfully terminated mother's parental rights without conducting a hearing to review child's best interests as required by statute. In re Robinson (Ohio App. 5 Dist., Stark, 01-20-2004) No. 2003CA00354, 2004-Ohio-376, 2004 WL 177720, Unreported. Infants ⇐ 203

Children services agency's case notes concerning alleged mental and physical abuse of dependent children by foster parents did not constitute newly discovered evidence entitling mother to new trial in termination of parental rights proceeding; new evidence did not impact trial court's determination that mother demonstrated an inability or unwillingness to protect children, and was not material to children's best interests in the future, in that agency sought to place children in a permanent adoptive home and foster parents did not wish to become permanent adoptive parents. In re West (Ohio App. 4 Dist., Athens, 11-19-2003) No. 03CA20, 2003-Ohio-6299, 2003 WL 22769711, Unreported. Infants ⇐ 211

Mother was not prejudiced by the trial court relying on the guardian ad litem's report in making its determination to grant permanent custody of child to county children services, even though the report was not filed at the time of the adjudicatory hearing; counsel for mother had a copy of the report at the hearing, the report was based on information provided by guardian ad litem for child, guardian ad litem for child was present at hearing and was subject to cross-examination, and report was filed immediately after the hearing. In re James (Ohio App. 10 Dist., Franklin, 09-30-2003) No. 03AP-373, 2003-Ohio-5208, 2003 WL 22232965, Unreported. Infants ⇐ 253

Trial court, in proceeding in which county children services agency sought permanent custody of child who had been previously adjudicated delinquent, was not required to prove, prior to granting permanent custody, that child could not be placed with mother within reasonable time, where child had been in agency's temporary custody for at least twelve months of a twenty-two month period. In re Beasley (Ohio App. 4 Dist., Scioto, 06-25-2003) No. 03CA2881, 2003-Ohio-3462, 2003 WL 21500016, Unreported. Infants ⇐ 155

Trial court's exercise of jurisdiction and decision to conduct permanent custody hearing for two dependent children was proper, even though grandmother of children had filed an appeal of trial court's denial of her motion to intervene prior to the permanent custody hearing; grandmother's notice of appeal did not constitute a final appealable order which would have divested the trial court of jurisdiction. In re The Cunningham Children (Ohio App. 5 Dist., Stark, 06-16-2003) No. 2003CA00042, No. 2003CA00090, 2003-Ohio-3176, 2003 WL 21398883, Unreported. Infants ⇐ 244.1

Late filing of guardian ad litem report in permanent custody proceedings, which report was filed after hearing but prior to magistrate's decision, did not prejudice mother, where mother was aware prior to hearing of guardian ad litem's recommendations contained in report, guardian ad litem testified during hearing and was subjected to cross-examination, and mother did not object during or after hearing to lack of a report. In re Honaker (Ohio App. 5 Dist., Richland, 05-07-2003) No. 03CA10, No. 03CA11, 2003-Ohio-2407, 2003 WL 21060699, Unreported. Infants ⇐ 253

Hearing on motion for permanent custody of dependent child was dispositional, rather than adjudicatory. In re Ashley E.D. (Ohio App. 6 Dist., Huron, 11-15-2002) No. H-02-025, 2002-Ohio-6238, 2002 WL 31529030, Unreported. Infants ⇐ 203

Trial court could lock door during hearing on termination of parental rights, where no one objected to the action of locking the doors, parents were present at the hearing, and there was no evidence that anyone was excluded from the hearing. In re Hayes (Ohio App. 5 Dist., Tuscarawas, 04-19-2002) No. 2001AP110099, No. 2001AP110098, 2002-Ohio-2446, 2002 WL 819216, Unreported. Infants ⇐ 203

The fact that RC 2151.414 does not contemplate or require more than one hearing to rule on a motion for permanent custody does not necessarily mean that a trial court is prohibited from holding more than one hearing; consequently, a trial court does not commit error when it bifurcates the hearing on the motion for permanent custody by sua sponte scheduling and holding an additional hearing to specifically address the adoptability of the minor child. In re Michael D. (Ohio App. 4 Dist., Jackson, 10-04-1995) No. 95CA760, 1995 WL 584516, Unreported.

Statutory prohibition against readjudication of neglect and dependency does not preclude the court from hearing, in connection with a proceeding for permanent custody, testimony that was presented or may have been relevant to the admission of neglect; rather, the prohibition is merely an attempt to emphasize that the outcome of the permanent custody hearing has no effect on the prior adjudication of neglect or the prior order of temporary custody, meaning that the parent cannot erase past findings of neglect by defeating the agency's motion for permanent custody. In re

Note 7

Nice (Ohio App. 7 Dist., 03-20-2001) 141 Ohio App.3d 445, 751 N.E.2d 552, 2001-Ohio-3214. Infants ⇐ 207

Trial court erred in failing to bifurcate hearing on alleged abuse and dependency from dispositional hearing; while court did hold separate dispositional hearing, order of adjudication, which was dispositional in nature, had already been signed and filed. In re Knotts (Ohio App. 3 Dist., 02-12-1996) 109 Ohio App.3d 267, 671 N.E.2d 1357. Infants ⇐ 203

Mother who was incarcerated did not have absolute right to attend permanent custody hearing regarding her two minor children, and was not entitled to writ of mandamus compelling continuance until after her release from incarceration. State ex rel. Vanderlaan v. Pollex (Ohio App. 6 Dist., 07-27-1994) 96 Ohio App.3d 235, 644 N.E.2d 1073. Convicts ⇐ 6; Infants ⇐ 204

Right of incarcerated parent to attend permanent custody hearing is within sound discretion of trial court. State ex rel. Vanderlaan v. Pollex (Ohio App. 6 Dist., 07-27-1994) 96 Ohio App.3d 235, 644 N.E.2d 1073. Infants ⇐ 203

Mother was provided with adequate notice of hearing to place her two minor children in permanent custody of Department of Human Services (DHS), despite her claim that DHS's motion for permanent custody failed to meet statutory notice requirements, in view of fact that statutory notice must be provided by court, not DHS, that notice given to mother by trial court contained all information required by statute, that mother waived any objection to inadequacies of notice when she elected to appear and participate with counsel, and that she did not raise issue of adequacy of notice at trial level. In re Shaeffer Children (Van Wert 1993) 85 Ohio App.3d 683, 621 N.E.2d 426, dismissed, jurisdictional motion overruled 67 Ohio St.3d 1451, 619 N.E.2d 419. Infants ⇐ 198

The requirement of RC 2151.414(A) that a court conduct a hearing to determine whether termination of parental rights is in the child's best interest does not mandate two hearings; upon a motion under RC 2151.413 to convert temporary custody to permanent custody, the court need hold only one hearing, which will be adjudicatory in its procedural nature. In re Hopkins (Hocking 1992) 78 Ohio App.3d 92, 603 N.E.2d 1138. Infants ⇐ 203

RC 2151.414 does not require a bifurcated hearing for the purpose of determining permanent custody. In re Jones (Cuyahoga 1985) 29 Ohio App.3d 176, 504 N.E.2d 719, 29 O.B.R. 206.

A bifurcated hearing is required in a proceeding for the permanent custody of a dependent or neglected child and the best interests of the child are to be considered during the dispositional phase of such proceeding. In re Lucas (Putnam 1985) 29 Ohio App.3d 165, 504 N.E.2d 472, 29 O.B.R. 194.

Statute governing hearings on motions for permanent custody by a county agency having been previously awarded temporary custody of children did not justify award of permanent custody to county, where there was no prayer for permanent custody in the complaints before the juvenile court, there were no citations on the parents or children specifying that permanent custody was being sought, and there was no prior award of temporary custody to a welfare department followed by a motion for an award of permanent custody. In re Snider (Defiance 1984) 14 Ohio App.3d 353, 471 N.E.2d 516, 14 O.B.R. 420. Infants ⇐ 197; Infants ⇐ 198; Infants ⇐ 222

A hearing on a complaint for permanent custody must be bifurcated according to Juv R 29 and Juv R 34 into separate adjudicatory and dispositional hearings, notwithstanding the contrary provisions of RC 2151.414, since Juv R 1(A) provides that all proceedings in a juvenile court are governed by the Rules of Juvenile Procedure. In re Vickers Children (Butler 1983) 14 Ohio App.3d 201, 470 N.E.2d 438, 14 O.B.R. 228.

8. Federal civil rights liability or 42 USC 1983

County was not liable in 1983 action for county social worker's acts of depriving mother of custody of her children without protecting her rights; mother did not claim that it was county's official policy to dispose of child custody issues without hearing each of the child's parents, and social worker and prosecutor involved in case were not final decisionmakers in county. Holloway v. Brush (C.A.6 (Ohio), 07-31-2000) 220 F.3d 767. Civil Rights ⇐ 1351(6)

Social workers are absolutely immune in 1983 suit only when they are acting in their capacity as legal advocates-initiating court actions or testifying under oath-not when they are performing administrative, investigative, or other functions. Holloway v. Brush (C.A.6 (Ohio), 07-31-2000) 220 F.3d 767. Civil Rights ⇐ 1373; Civil Rights ⇐ 1375; Civil Rights ⇐ 1376(1)

Counties and other local governments-while "persons" for the purposes of 1983 liability in the sense that they can be sued-do not enjoy the defenses of absolute and qualified immunity that are available to human defendants sued in their individual capacities. Holloway v. Brush (C.A.6 (Ohio), 07-31-2000) 220 F.3d 767. Civil Rights ⇐ 1376(4)

County social worker was not entitled to absolute immunity in 1983 action for failing to notify state court that children's mother had made contact and wished to assert her parental rights, telling mother that her parental rights had been severed when they had not yet been, and withholding information that would have enabled mother to raise her rights in court before her rights were severed; social worker was not acting in capacity of legal advocate in taking those actions. Holloway v. Brush (C.A.6 (Ohio), 07-31-2000) 220 F.3d 767. Civil Rights ⇐ 1376(4)

Doctrine of law of the case did not preclude Court of Appeals from ruling that social worker was not absolutely immune in 1983 action; issue of social worker's immunity from suit was never raised, much less decided, in any earlier action in which social worker had been involved. Holloway v. Brush (C.A.6 (Ohio), 07-31-2000) 220 F.3d 767. Courts ⇐ 99(1)

9. Grandparent visitation

Case plan statute requiring an abused, neglected, or dependent child to be placed in the legal custody of a suitable member of the child's extended family, as well as statute giving preference for placement with family members, did not apply to require placement of child with his maternal grandmother, where grandmother chose not to be considered for permanent custody of the child when approached for same by the county department of job and family services. In re Hoffman (Ohio App. 5 Dist., Stark, 03-03-2003) No. 2002CA0419, No. 2002CA0422, 2003-Ohio-1241, 2003 WL 1193770, Unreported. Infants ⇐ 222

Maternal grandparents of dependent children had standing to appeal juvenile court's order denying their motion to intervene in custody proceedings initiated by county children services agency; grandparents were not parties but they attempted to intervene, and their familial relationship to the children established requisite interest in the litigation and prejudice from the juvenile court's order. In re Fusik (Ohio App. 4 Dist., Athens, 08-19-2002) No. 02CA16, 2002-Ohio-4410, 2002 WL 1978880, Unreported. Infants ⇐ 242

RC 2151.414(D) is not a list of actions that the juvenile court must take in order to ensure the best interests of the child are met, but is a list of factors which the court must consider when determining whether the grant of permanent custody is in the best interests of the child, and therefore the court is not required to allow visitation of a child by a grandparent. In re Battaglia, No. CA2000–P–0084, 2001 WL 637399 (11th Dist Ct App, Portage, 6–8–01).

10. Best interests of child—Multiple siblings

It was in best interest of children previously adjudicated dependent to be placed in legal custody of children's maternal great-aunt, despite children's expressed desire to be with mother, where children were aged seven and four, respectively, and were exposed to domestic violence between father and mother while residing with mother, mother could not control children and did not make good parenting choices, mother's employment was persistently unstable, mother did not complete portions of case plan addressing drug and alcohol abuse, and children were thriving in care of great-aunt and her husband and also expressed desire to remain with her. In re D.P. (Ohio App. 10 Dist., Franklin, 09-27-2005) No. 05AP-117, No. 05AP-118, 2005-Ohio-5097, 2005 WL 2364946, Unreported, appeal allowed 108 Ohio St.3d 1472, 842 N.E.2d 1052, 2006-Ohio-665, affirmed 109 Ohio St.3d 207, 846 N.E.2d 853, 2006-Ohio-2185. Infants ⇐ 156

Termination of mother's parental rights was in children's best interests; children were bonded to their foster family and respite care family as equally as they were bonded with mother, and, both the foster parents and the respite care providers were interested in adopting children. In re Tucke (Ohio App. 5 Dist., Stark, 08-22-2005) No. 2005CA00077, 2005-Ohio-4409, 2005 WL 2045454, Unreported. Infants ⇐ 155

Finding that mother's parental rights to her six children should be terminated and permanent custody granted to county children services agency was not against the manifest weight of the evidence, where children had been in agency's custody for 12 out of 22 consecutive months, mother had failed to complete her case plan and was unable to provide for the children's basic needs, children were doing well in foster care, and mother had failed to engage in individual counseling relative to the children's disclosure of sexual abuse. In re J.L. (Ohio App. 8 Dist., Cuyahoga, 11-10-2004) No. 84368, 2004-Ohio-6024, 2004 WL 2578874, Unreported, appeal not allowed 104 Ohio St.3d 1463, 821 N.E.2d 578, 2005-Ohio-204. Infants ⇐ 155

Evidence supported juvenile court's finding that termination of parental rights was in children's best interest; mother had kept home in filthy and deplorable condition, mother had drug problem that contributed to her inability to care for the children, mother failed to participate in requested programs following completion of drug treatment program, mother did not complete all drug screens given to her, children interacted well with foster parents, foster parents were considering adopting children, and father had abandoned children. In re Abram (Ohio App. 10 Dist., Franklin, 09-21-2004) No. 04AP-220, No. 04AP-221, No. 04AP-224, 2004-Ohio-5435, 2004 WL 2283938, Unreported, appeal not allowed 104 Ohio St.3d 1441, 819 N.E.2d 1124, 2004-Ohio-7033. Infants ⇔ 155; Infants ⇔ 156; Infants ⇔ 157

There was clear and convincing evidence that it was in best interest of child that father's parental rights be terminated and permanent custody granted to county Department of Job and Family Services; evidence indicated that father had little parental attachment with child, child expressed that she did not want to live with father, and child had bond with half-sister and foster parent, with whom she lived. In re Gomer (Ohio App. 3 Dist., Wyandot, 04-05-2004) No. 16-03-19, No. 16-03-20, No. 16-03-21, 2004-Ohio-1723, 2004 WL 722978, Unreported, appeal not allowed 102 Ohio St.3d 1473, 809 N.E.2d 1159, 2004-Ohio-2830. Infants ⇔ 155

Trial court properly used date of completion of father's current prison sentence, rather than date of his eligibility for judicial release, to calculate date on which father would be released from prison, as factor in determination of children's best interests. In re Myers (Ohio App. 3 Dist., Seneca, 02-09-2004) No. 13-03-61, No. 13-03-65, No. 13-03-64, No. 13-03-63, No. 13-03-62, 2004-Ohio-539, 2004 WL 231796, Unreported. Infants ⇔ 157

Awarding permanent custody of children to county children services was in best interests of children, since mother had not demonstrated appropriate parenting skills when attending supervised visits, mother had caused emotional pain to daughter by telling daughter that mother believed that daughter lied about sexual abuse committed against daughter by stepfather, both children had lived in foster care for extended period of time, and children would have potentially faced same issues of abuse if children returned to mother's household. In re Zorns (Ohio App. 10 Dist., Franklin, 10-23-2003) No. 02AP-1297, No. 02AP-1298, 2003-Ohio-5664, 2003 WL 22415613, Unreported, appeal not allowed 100 Ohio St.3d 1547, 800 N.E.2d 752, 2003-Ohio-6879. Infants ⇔ 155; Infants ⇔ 156

There was sufficient evidence in record that it was in children's best interest that child services agency be granted permanent custody, to support permanency placement; record indicated children were doing well in their respective foster homes, that one foster family wished to adopt four of the six children, that domestic violence was often reported by children, that parents failed to address domestic violence issues, that children's guardian ad litem recommended permanent custody with agency, and that children were in need of legally secure placement, which parents had not provided. In re Sessoms (Ohio App. 12 Dist., Butler, 10-06-2003) No. CA2002-11-280, 2003-Ohio-5281, 2003 WL 22283495, Unreported. Infants ⇔ 155

Decision to terminate mother's parental rights and grant permanent custody of her two minor children to Children Services Board (CSB) was in children's best interest; mother and her two children were initially homeless and picked up on streets by police, children were not enrolled in school, mother repeatedly tested positive for cocaine and grandmother was also a cocaine user, children were doing well in foster care, mother failed to make any progress on her case plan, and she recently threatened suicide and was psychiatrically hospitalized for one week. In re L.A. (Ohio App. 9 Dist., Summit, 09-10-2003) No. 21531, 2003-Ohio-4790, 2003 WL 22093456, Unreported. Infants ⇔ 156; Infants ⇔ 158

Clear and convincing evidence supported finding that granting permanent custody of the children to county department of children and family services was in the best interest of the children; mother had a lengthy history with county, the children had previously been adjudicated neglected, the children were bonded with their foster family and one child had previously resided with the same family, third child was in need of constant medical care that mother could not provide, and guardian ad litem's written report stated that permanent custody would be in the children's best interests. In re D.F. (Ohio App. 8 Dist., Cuyahoga, 06-19-2003) No. 81613, 2003-Ohio-3221, 2003 WL 21419537, Unreported. Infants ⇔ 155

Continued long-term foster care, rather than award of permanent custody to county and subsequent adoption plan, was in best interests of four minor siblings; permanent custody would break up the siblings and likelihood of adoption was slim, foster parents were meeting the siblings' special needs and provided a stable home environment, and foster parents, although willing to continue foster care, were both in their sixties and financially could not accept the lesser adoption subsidy. In re Tanker (Ohio App. 8 Dist., 04-02-2001) 142 Ohio App.3d 159, 754 N.E.2d 813. Infants ⇔ 226

Clear and convincing evidence supported finding that it was in children's best interests to grant public children services agency's motion for permanent custody of mother's three children, and that award of custody was not against manifest weight of the evidence; mother had not maintained stable employment or housing for a period of two years, her children had been in foster care for more than 12 months of a consecutive 22 month period, mother admitted that one- bedroom apartment she shared with her mother would be an insufficient living situation for her and her children, children's foster mother testified that two of the children need ointments applied to their skin, and at least one of the children had asthma, which required special air purifiers, and there was no indication of when, if ever, mother was going to be able to support her children. In re Cather (Ohio App. 11 Dist., Portage, 08-30-2002) No. 2002-P-0014, No. 2002-P-0015, No. 2002-P-0016, 2002-Ohio-4519, 2002 WL 2022964, Unreported. Infants ⇔ 178

11. —— Permanent custody to county, best interests of child

Juvenile court's decision granting permanent custody of mother's 19-month-old child to county agency was in child's best interests; mother had somewhat abandoned child during visitation since the birth of her second child, child has bonded with his foster parents who were able to meet all of his special needs, child had been with his foster parents since he was nine days old, caseworker testified that child's need for a legally secure permanent placement could not be achieved without a grant of permanent custody to agency, and child's guardian ad litem recommended granting the agency permanent custody. In re C.E. (Ohio App. 12 Dist., Butler, 09-18-2006) No. CA2006-01-015, No. CA2006-02-024, 2006-Ohio-4827, 2006 WL 2663464, Unreported. Infants ⇔ 157

Clear and convincing evidence supported finding that father's children could not or should not be placed with him within a reasonable time, in support of termination of parental rights; father was incarcerated in a state penal institution since his conviction for murder, he was sentenced to 15 years to life, and he would be first eligible for parole more than 18 months after the filing of the motion for permanent custody and more than 18 months after the termination hearing. In re Lenix (Ohio App. 5 Dist., Ashland, 03-17-2006) No. 05-COA-039, 2006-Ohio-1294, 2006 WL 700953, Unreported. Infants ⇔ 157

Clear and convincing evidence supported finding that granting permanent custody of child to county children's service board, rather than to stepfather, child's prior legal custodian, was in child's best interest; the trial court found that stepfather had repeatedly placed child at risk, had recently lost custody of one of his own children, and had two others removed from his care and adjudicated neglected and dependent. In re Kenny B. (Ohio App. 6 Dist., Lucas, 03-03-2006) No. L-05-1227, 2006-Ohio-968, 2006 WL 513958, Unreported. Infants ⇔ 222

Clear and convincing evidence supported trial court's determination that awarding permanent custody of mother's three children to county agency was in the children's best interests; children were doing very well in their respective placements, and guardian ad litem recommended that permanent custody be granted. In re D.P. (Ohio App. 8 Dist., Cuyahoga, 03-02-2006) No. 86271, No. 86272, 2006-Ohio-937, 2006 WL 496058, Unreported. Infants ⇔ 208

Trial court did not abuse its discretion by finding that neglected child's need for a legally secure placement could not be accomplished without granting permanent custody to county children services; while record indicated that two potentially suitable relatives expressed some interest in adopting child, no relative expressed any such interest until child had been in the temporary custody of county children services for 16 months, and no party filed a motion requesting legal custody of child at any point during the 22 months child had been in the temporary custody of county children services of the commencement of the dispositional hearing. In re H.M. (Ohio App. 12 Dist., Clinton, 02-22-2006) No. CA2005-09-022, No. CA2005-09-023, 2006-Ohio-819, 2006 WL 443463, Unreported. Infants ⇔ 222

Evidence supported finding that granting permanent custody of neglected child to county children services was in child's best interests; evidence showed that, while mother and father completed portions of their case plan for reunification with child, neither had demonstrated an ability to refrain from illegal drug use throughout the time that the child had been in the temporary custody of county children services, which was the cause for removing the child from their custody. In re H.M. (Ohio App. 12 Dist., Clinton, 02-22-2006) No. CA2005-09-022, No. CA2005-09-023, 2006-Ohio-819, 2006 WL 443463, Unreported. Infants ⇔ 155

Termination of mother's parental rights and grant of permanent custody to county child protection agency, rather than placement in planned permanent living arrangement, was in best interests of disabled child; agency had been able to find adoptive homes for children with severe medical problems, agency worker testified that child's chances of adoption were "pretty high," child would not benefit from visitation with mother and would be unable to recognize her, and mother visited only sporadically and had exceeded a ninety day period without visitation. In re Wilson (Ohio App. 5 Dist., Stark, 11-14-2005) No. 2005CA00177, 2005-Ohio-6203, 2005 WL 3112867, Unreported. Infants ⇔ 157

Evidence at permanent custody hearing supported juvenile court's determination that it was in the best interest of father's minor child to be permanently placed in the custody of county agency; father had been incarcerated numerous times for domestic violence and DUI, he was diagnosed with cocaine dependence, alcohol and marijuana abuse, and antisocial personality disorder, along with several other disorders, he was incarcerated at the time of child's birth, and child had closely bonded with his foster parents. In re Aiken (Ohio App. 11 Dist., Lake, 11-15-2005) No. 2005-L-094, 2005-Ohio-6146, 2005 WL 3096548, Unreported. Infants ⇔ 158

Awarding county children services agency permanent custody of child, rather than placing child in the care of either of his parents or his maternal grandmother, was in the child's best interest, where child had well-established relationship with foster family, he did not inquire about his parents or comment upon their absence, grandmother had previously lost custody of her children to children services agency, grandmother stated that her fiancee probably had a criminal record, and grandmother failed her home inspection and made no effort to challenge or remedy the failure. In re Poke (Ohio App. 4 Dist., Lawrence, 09-23-2005) No. 05CA15, 2005-Ohio-5226, 2005 WL 2403893, Unreported. Infants ⇔ 222

Evidence supported finding it was in children's best interest to grant county children services board permanent custody of children; father had stipulated to sexually abusing oldest child, father admitted spanking all of the children with his hand, a belt, a paddle and a board, father admitted cursing in front of the children, and referring to them as "bitch," "dumb ass," and "stupid ass," father failed to comply with case plan requirement that he seek treatment for sexual offending, two of the children repeatedly expressed anger towards defendant for the abuse he imposed on them and consistently refused his efforts to visit with them, mother missed visitations with children and by the time of the permanent custody hearing had not had contact with any of the children for seven months, no bond existed between mother and any of the children, children had been doing well in foster care, and guardian ad litem stated the children needed a legally secure placement and such could not be accomplished without granting permanent custody. In re A.D. (Ohio App. 9 Dist., Summit, 09-30-2005) No. 22668, 2005-Ohio-5183, 2005 WL 2400960, Unreported. Infants ⇔ 157

Clear and convincing evidence established that mother posed an ongoing danger to her twin boys, thus supporting finding that children could not be placed with mother within reasonable period of time, and that placement of twin boys with County Children Services Board (MCCSB) was in the best interests of the children; mother committed crime of child endangerment, victims of crime were siblings of twin boys who were subject of parental rights termination hearing, and mother posed a danger to the boys by dropping one of them. In re Bowers (Ohio App. 7 Dist., Mahoning, 08-18-2005) No. 04 MA 216, 2005-Ohio-4376, 2005 WL 2033100, Unreported. Infants ⇔ 156

Grant of permanent custody of children to county child protection agency was in best interests of mothers' two children; although mother completed parenting course, mother failed to obtain satisfactory housing, mother had not had any contact with her children for seven months due to on-going legal problems, mother's previous visitation with children was inconsistent, there was little evidence of a continuing positive relationship between children and other relatives, children made progress with developmental and behavioral problems in foster care, mother had been convicted of child endangering and other offenses, foster parents were interested in adopting children, and children were in need of permanency. In re C.B. (Ohio App. 9 Dist., Summit, 08-24-2005) No. 22635, 2005-Ohio-4364, 2005 WL 2031752, Unreported. Infants ⇔ 156

Clear and convincing evidence supported conclusion that termination of mother's parental rights was in child's best interests; child's relationship with his mother was destructive, in that she was critical and demeaning of child and showed no affection for him, and mother allowed her boyfriend, who was verbally, emotionally, and physically abusive of child, to care for him. In re Van Atta (Ohio App. 3 Dist., Hancock, 08-15-2005) No. 5-05-03, 2005-Ohio-4182, 2005 WL 1939418, Unreported. Infants ⇔ 156

Clear and convincing evidence supported conclusion that termination of mother's parental rights was in children's best interest; children had not bonded with mother, but were readily able to bond with their foster mother, children stated that they did not want to visit mother, children had been in temporary custody of county for more than 12 months of consecutive 22 month period, children had emotional difficulties resulting from mother's relationship with boyfriend, who had been convicted of sexually abusing one of the children, and mother had abandoned children. In re Donell F. (Ohio App. 6 Dist., Lucas, 08-12-2005) No. L-04-1308, 2005-Ohio-4175, 2005 WL 1926512, Unreported. Infants ⇔ 157

Evidence was sufficient to support finding that award of permanent custody of children to agency was in children's best interest; three of four children had been in foster care for four years and one had been in foster case since birth, children had bonded with their respective foster parents and viewed them as parental figures, mother's relationship with children was more like that of a sibling than a parent, and children were in great need of secure, permanent placement due to abuse suffered by them, including sexual abuse of two of them, and mother's failure to secure stable residence. In re S.B. (Ohio App. 12 Dist., Butler, 07-25-2005) No. CA2004-12-305, No. CA2004-12-308, No. CA2004-12-306, No. CA2004-12-307, 2005-Ohio-3889, 2005 WL 1798271, Unreported. Infants ⇔ 155

Competent and credible evidence supported trial court's findings that children could not be placed with mother within reasonable time and that it was in children's best interest to grant permanent custody to county children services board; court found that mother had failed to substantially remedy conditions that caused children to be removed from her home, that mother's chemical dependency was so severe that it made her unable to provide adequate permanent home for children, that mother demonstrated lack of commitment toward children, that mother had abandoned children, and that mother had shown unwillingness to provide basic necessities for children. In re Culp (Ohio App. 3 Dist., Allen, 07-25-2005) No. 1-05-02, No. 1-05-03, No. 1-05-04, 2005-Ohio-3764, 2005 WL 1712883, Unreported. Infants ⇔ 180

Order terminating mother's parental rights and granting permanent custody of mother's children to Children Services Board was in best interests of children; county made reasonable efforts to prevent removal of children, mother failed to comply with case plan, mother's substance abuse was sufficiently severe to interfere with her ability to care for children, mother was incarcerated for crime committed against child, and there was no relative with whom children could be placed within reasonable time. In re Harris (Ohio App. 2 Dist., Montgomery, 07-15-2005) No. 20934, 2005-Ohio-3700, 2005 WL 1704920, Unreported. Infants ⇔ 156

Evidence was sufficient to support finding that child could not be placed with either mother or father, as basis for placing child into planned permanent living arrangement with county; father failed to comply with any part of case plan, father lived with mother but guardian ad litem never met him during any of eight visits, and mother had relapsed with respect to drug addiction at least five times during time child was in temporary custody. In re Wheeler (Ohio App. 5 Dist., Muskingum, 07-11-2005) No. CT 2005-0015, 2005-Ohio-3613, 2005 WL 1661981, Unreported. Infants ⇔ 222

Clear and convincing evidence supported trial court's determination that county department of children and family services should have permanent custody of child; child was in custody of department for more than 12 of past 22 months, and remained with same foster care provider for previous two years, record demonstrated that child could not and should not be placed with either parent within reasonable time, and parents had failed, for over six months, to remedy conditions that had caused child to be placed outside her home, had failed to implement changes needed for her return to home, and had shown inability to provide adequate permanent home for her. In re K.M. (Ohio App. 8 Dist., Cuyahoga, 07-14-2005) No. 85647, 2005-Ohio-3594, 2005 WL 1654569, Unreported, appeal not allowed 106 Ohio St.3d 1537, 835 N.E.2d 385, 2005-Ohio-5146. Infants ⇔ 155

County children services was not required to have custody of child for 12 out of previous 22 consecutive months before trial court could grant permanent custody to board. In re Woods (Ohio App. 5 Dist., Muskingum, 07-07-2005) No. CT2005-0011, 2005-Ohio-3561, 2005 WL 1645614, Unreported. Infants ⇔ 155

Evidence supported finding that it was in the best interest of child to grant permanent custody of child to county children services, rather than place child with maternal cousin who had permanent custody of child's sibling; cousin was the sole caregiver to two young children and an elderly man, psychologist opined that cousin would be intellectually pushing her limit and would be on overload with the additional of another child, caseworker testified that cousin sometimes had budgeting issues, and cousin had permitted parents of child to stay in her home and had permitted the children to be exposed to drug users. In re Woods (Ohio App. 5 Dist., Muskingum, 07-07-2005) No. CT2005-0008, 2005-Ohio-3563, 2005 WL 1645612, Unreported. Infants ⇔ 222

Trial court's finding that child could not be placed with parents in foreseeable future, and should not be placed with parents, and that best interests of child would be served by granting permanent custody to county department of job and family services was not against manifest weight of evidence; at time of permanent custody hearing, parents were incarcerated for physically restraining their child in manner which created risk of serious physical harm to child, and it was in child's best interest to be provided with safe and stable home environment, which could only be available through permanent custody. In re Stewart (Ohio App. 5 Dist., Coshocton, 07-12-2005) No. 05-CA-5, 2005-Ohio-3543, 2005 WL 1620451, Unreported. Infants ⇐ 156

Evidence supported trial court's finding that grant of permanent custody of father's children to county child protection agency was in best interests of children; father failed to take any responsibility for the situations which resulted in the removal of the children, father failed to comply with any aspect of case plan, father threatened agency and caseworkers, father was resistant to change and potentially dangerous to children, father had criminal record including conviction for child endangering, father had lost parental rights to other children, and father had child living with him despite court order prohibiting arrangement. In re Zink (Ohio App. 5 Dist., Licking, 07-05-2005) No. 2004CA0081, No. 2004CA00106, 2005-Ohio-3460, 2005 WL 1579312, Unreported. Infants ⇐ 155

Any error in requiring that mother have no contact with her husband, as part of her case plan, was harmless, in termination of parental rights proceeding; mother already had her parental rights to child's siblings terminated, and thus, trial court was required to enter a finding that child could not be placed with mother within a reasonable period of time. In re Spangler (Ohio App. 3 Dist., Hardin, 07-05-2005) No. 6-04-15, 2005-Ohio-3450, 2005 WL 1545777, Unreported. Infants ⇐ 253

Clear and convincing evidence supported trial court's determination that award of permanent custody of children to county children services was in children's best interest; children had been in custody of county child services for 12 or more months of consecutive 22-month period, parents had failed to substantially remedy conditions causing children to be placed outside home, parents had demonstrated lack of commitment toward children by failing to regularly support or visit them, parents were unwilling to provide basic necessities for children, and parents continued to use drugs after children had been removed from home. In re Briazanna G. (Ohio App. 6 Dist., Lucas, 06-24-2005) No. L-04-1366, 2005-Ohio-3206, 2005 WL 1492034, Unreported. Infants ⇐ 155

Grant of permanent custody of mother's two children to county child protection agency was in best interest of children; mother had neither income nor employment, mother often failed to take medication for her depression, mother attempted suicide while on case plan, mother was dependent on her boyfriend for housing, foster parents were willing to adopt children, children had been in the custody of agency for more than 18 months and had lived with their grandparents for the majority of their lives, and guardian ad litem recommended that grant of custody to agency would be in children's best interest. In re S.B. (Ohio App. 8 Dist., Cuyahoga, 06-23-2005) No. 85560, 2005-Ohio-3163, 2005 WL 1490128, Unreported. Infants ⇐ 208

Juvenile Court's decision to grant Children Services Board's (CSB) motion for permanent custody of child and deny maternal grandmother's motion for legal custody was in child's best interests; child was underweight and had several bruises and numerous fractured bones in various stages of healing when she was removed from her parents' home, both parents subsequently pled guilty to child endangering, mother's compliance with her case plan was very poor, while father's compliance was only slightly better, grandmother's relationship with child was not very strong, and grandmother reportedly admitted to guardian ad litem she wanted custody so that the child could see her mother. In re N.B. (Ohio App. 9 Dist., Summit, 06-22-2005) No. 22560, 2005-Ohio-3113, 2005 WL 1460302, Unreported. Infants ⇐ 156

Evidence supported finding that awarding permanent custody of infant child to county children services was in the best interest of child; child was not bonded to mother, guardian ad litem testified that child was doing well in foster care and neither parent seemed able to understand child's cues to address his needs, mother was unable to follow instructions to prepare child's bottle for feeding, child had been in foster care for three months at the time of the permanency hearing, and mother's parental rights had previously been terminated to two of her other children. In re West (Ohio App. 4 Dist., Athens, 06-10-2005) No. 05CA4, 2005-Ohio-2977, 2005 WL 1400029, Unreported. Infants ⇐ 155

Trial court's finding that granting permanent custody of father's five children to the county department of job and family services was in the best interest of children was not against the manifest weight of the evidence; father's children had psychological and behavioral problems, guardian ad litem and caseworker testified that none of the children sought visitation from father, and guardian ad litem testified that the children were receiving proper services for the first time in their lives. In re Bailey Children (Ohio App. 5 Dist., Stark, 06-13-2005) No. 2004 CA 00386, 2005-Ohio-2981, 2005 WL 1400026, Unreported. Infants ⇐ 178

Clear and convincing evidence supported finding that it was in child's best interest to grant permanent custody of child to county department of job and family services; child had been in the custody of department for 12 or more of the last consecutive 22 months, trial court found that father was too passive to intervene on behalf of child when mother was inappropriate, and child's behavior issues had dissipated since he was removed from the custody of parents and his speech had improved. In re Pappas (Ohio App. 5 Dist., Stark, 05-23-2005) No. 2005-CA-00060, 2005-Ohio-2592, 2005 WL 1242087, Unreported. Infants ⇐ 155

Grant of permanent custody of minor child to county social services agency was made in the consideration of the child's best interests and did not constitute an abuse of discretion; child, who suffered from speech and motor skills delays, was making excellent progress in foster care, bonded with foster family, was aware of the domestic violence issues involving father, and indicated she did not want to live with father unless her mother was present. In re Greathouse (Ohio App. 5 Dist., Fairfield, 05-18-2005) No. 04 CA 57, 2005-Ohio-2553, 2005 WL 1208850, Unreported. Infants ⇐ 155

Trial court's decision to grant permanent custody of minor child to County Children Services Board (CCSB) was supported by clear and convincing evidence that child could not be placed with either parent in reasonable period, that child should not be placed with either parent, and that granting permanent custody of child to CCSB was in child's best interest; although CCSB developed case plan for reuniting child and mother, mother failed to complete many of plan's objectives, and she made only limited progress in other objectives, mother refused to maintain employment, mother had substance abuse problems, mother's apartment was unfurnished and she refused to demonstrate she had food in apartment, she failed to complete counseling, failed to maintain contact with child, and failed to develop parenting skills, mother provided name of only one possible father, who was genetically excluded, and child had been in foster care for 23 months. In re Gresham (Ohio App. 2 Dist., Montgomery, 05-20-2005) No. 20916, 2005-Ohio-2512, 2005 WL 1207638, Unreported. Infants ⇐ 178

Trial court's finding that it was in daughter's best interest to grant Department of Job and Family Services' motion requesting permanent custody of daughter was not against the manifest of the evidence; mother failed to address her mental health issues, she failed to progress with her case plan goals, the interaction between mother and daughter was traumatic, and daughter was strongly bonded to her foster parents. In re Unger Children (Ohio App. 5 Dist., Coshocton, 05-12-2005) No. 04 CA 6, 2005-Ohio-2414, 2005 WL 1163915, Unreported. Infants ⇐ 158

Juvenile court lacked jurisdiction to grant permanent custody of mother and father's four minor children to the Guernsey County Children Services Board (CSB), where the court previously dismissed the action after having been notified by Gallia County Children Services of the physical custody of the children with said agency, and their intention to provide services. In re Chestnut (Ohio App. 5 Dist., Guernsey, 05-16-2005) No. 04-CA-28, No. 04-CA-30, No. 04-CA-42, 2005-Ohio-2412, 2005 WL 1162986, Unreported. Infants ⇐ 202

Best interests of father's biological child warranted granting permanent custody to Children Services Board (CSB), rather than a six-month extension of temporary custody; child had been in the custody of CSB for at least 12 of the prior 22 months, father had visited child consistently for only three months before the permanent custody hearing, his visitations had not progressed beyond two-hour weekly visits at the visitation center, he had made little progress on his case plan, and child was doing well in foster care. In re J.O. (Ohio App. 9 Dist., Summit, 05-18-2005) No. 22510, 2005-Ohio-2399, 2005 WL 1162976, Unreported. Infants ⇐ 230.1

Evidence supported conclusion that granting custody to county was in children's best interests, in permanent custody proceeding in which children had been removed from mother's custody; children were now cognitively at same or higher level than that of their parents, which would only make it more challenging for parents to supervise children, and parents used profanity when disciplining children and allowed them to go unsupervised for hours. In re McHugh Children (Ohio App. 5 Dist., Licking, 05-05-2005) No. 2004CA00091, 2005-Ohio-2345, 2005 WL 1125334, Unreported. Infants ⇐ 158

Evidence supported juvenile court's determination that it was in children's best interests to grant county agency's motion for permanent custody; case worker testified that mother often had a difficult time supervising the children during visitation and that her bond with one child was very strained, she further testified that one child had refused to attend visits for several months and became sullen and withdrawn after visiting mother, and guardian-ad-litem recommended the court grant the agency's

2151.414
Note 11

motion. In re Langford (Ohio App. 5 Dist., Stark, 05-09-2005) No. 2004CA00349, 2005-Ohio-2304, 2005 WL 1111220, Unreported. Infants ⇐ 208

In proceeding on county agency's motion for permanent custody, juvenile court was not required to make a finding that mother's two minor children could not or should not be placed with her, where court found that the children had been in the temporary custody of the agency for 12 of the past consecutive 22 months, and therefore, that it was in the best interest of the children to be in the permanent custody of the agency. In re Langford (Ohio App. 5 Dist., Stark, 05-09-2005) No. 2004CA00349, 2005-Ohio-2304, 2005 WL 1111220, Unreported. Infants ⇐ 210

Decision to grant county department of job and family services permanent custody of mother's three children was supported by competent evidence and was in the best interests of the children; mother was mildly mentally retarded, director of treatment and foster care program that cared for children stated that she saw no possibility of mother caring for all three children, mother's spouse had anger management issues, mother's home was unstable as she paid over 80% of her monthly income on the residence she shared with spouse and her other children, and mother's therapist admitted that mother could not parent the children without assistance. In re Hines (Ohio App. 5 Dist., Tuscarawas, 05-03-2005) No. 2004AP120072, 2005-Ohio-2266, 2005 WL 1077175, Unreported, appeal not allowed 106 Ohio St.3d 1488, 832 N.E.2d 739, 2005-Ohio-3978, reconsideration denied 106 Ohio St.3d 1537, 835 N.E.2d 385, 2005-Ohio-5146. Infants ⇐ 222

Mother could not raise for first time on appeal constitutional challenge to statute governing proceedings for permanent custody of child. In re Dailey (Ohio App. 10 Dist., Franklin, 05-05-2005) No. 04AP-1346, 2005-Ohio-2196, 2005 WL 1055783, Unreported, appeal not allowed 106 Ohio St.3d 1488, 832 N.E.2d 739, 2005-Ohio-3978. Infants ⇐ 243

Evidence supported trial court's finding that child could not be placed with either of her parents within a reasonable time, thus supporting grant of permanent custody of child to county child protection agency; father was incarcerated serving eleven-year prison term, mother did not contest placement of child with agency, mother was in prison and would not be able to care for child upon her release, no relatives were able to assume care and custody of child, and evidence suggested that child desired to be adopted by foster family. In re Noda (Ohio App. 11 Dist., Lake, 05-06-2005) No. 2004-L-212, 2005-Ohio-2213, 2005 WL 1048717, Unreported. Infants ⇐ 222

Sufficient evidence supported trial court's finding that permanent custody was in best interest of child, as would support court's decision to award permanent custody of child to county department of children and family services; child had been in custody of department since her birth and had never lived with mother, child's relationship with mother was "nonexistent," and grant of permanent custody was necessary for child to achieve a legally secure permanent placement. In re D.W. (Ohio App. 8 Dist., Cuyahoga, 04-21-2005) No. 84547, 2005-Ohio-1867, 2005 WL 926991, Unreported. Infants ⇐ 155

Children's best interests warranted termination of father's parental rights and placement in the permanent custody of Children Services Board (CSB); father had been sentenced to a three-year prison term on drug charges and, at the time of the permanent custody hearing, he had served less than one year of that term, and both children had been placed together in the same foster home and were doing well there. In re E.C. (Ohio App. 9 Dist., Summit, 04-06-2005) No. 22355, 2005-Ohio-1633, 2005 WL 767099, Unreported. Infants ⇐ 157

Children's best interests warranted termination of mother's parental rights and placement in the permanent custody of the Children Services Board (CSB); mother had been diagnosed with a personality disorder with paranoid traits and intermittent explosive disorder, her behavior was described by medical professionals and others as erratic, volatile, belligerent, and threatening, she discontinued her counseling sessions as well as her prescribed medication, and children were reportedly doing exceptionally well in foster care. In re I.K. (Ohio App. 9 Dist., Summit, 04-06-2005) No. 22424, 2005-Ohio-1634, 2005 WL 767093, Unreported. Infants ⇐ 158

Clear and convincing evidence supported finding that granting permanent custody of children to county children services was in children's best interest; children had been in and out of foster care for an extended period of time, and children were in need of legally secure permanent placement, as children's foster mother testified that the children were filthy and had injuries, such as open sores and infected cuts, and that the children were reluctant to visit with their mother and would often cry when dropped off for the visits. In re Ohler (Ohio App. 4 Dist., Hocking, 03-24-2005) No. 04CA8, 2005-Ohio-1583, 2005 WL 737580, Unreported. Infants ⇐ 156

Clear and convincing evidence supported finding that children could not, or should not, be reunited with either parent within a reasonable time, as required to grant permanent custody of children to county children services; mother suffered from impulsive anger and deficient parenting skills, and, while mother did complete some counseling, she again abused her stepdaughter, which led to county children services regaining temporary custody of all four children. In re Ohler (Ohio App. 4 Dist., Hocking, 03-24-2005) No. 04CA8, 2005-Ohio-1583, 2005 WL 737580, Unreported. Infants ⇐ 156

Clear and convincing evidence established that child had been in temporary custody of county children services agency for 12 or more months of a consecutive 22-month period, which, in turn, supported trial court's finding that child could not be placed or should not be placed with mother, in termination of parental rights proceeding. In re Bray (Ohio App. 10 Dist., Franklin, 03-31-2005) No. 04AP-842, 2005-Ohio-1540, 2005 WL 737401, Unreported. Infants ⇐ 179

Clear and convincing evidence supported conclusion that termination of mother's parental rights was in children's best interests; older child, who had fetal alcohol syndrome as result of mother's drinking during first few months of her pregnancy, had significant medical needs, but mother had not been taking child, who had also been diagnosed with a severe hearing impairment and cerebral palsy, for regular medical check-ups, mother was required to attend child's medical appointments as part of her case plan but had attended only half of the appointments, during unsupervised visit with children mother left them with an inappropriate caregiver and apparently went out drinking, and children had been in county's custody for most of their lives and were in need of legally secure placement. In re A.B. (Ohio App. 9 Dist., Summit, 03-23-2005) No. 22438, 2005-Ohio-1273, 2005 WL 662922, Unreported. Infants ⇐ 158

Trial court made requisite statutory findings on record to support order terminating father's parental rights; trial court adopted magistrate's decision recommending that permanent custody of children be awarded to County Children Services Board (CCSB), which found, among other things, that it was in the best interests of children to grant permanent custody to CCSB, after father had not visited with the dependent children since they were removed from his custody, that one child had already been placed with her maternal uncle, and that, eventually, siblings would be reunited in the same household. In re Bentley (Ohio App. 11 Dist., Ashtabula, 03-18-2005) No. 2004-A-0075, 2005-Ohio-1257, 2005 WL 639497, Unreported. Infants ⇐ 210

Evidence supported findings that children should not be placed with either parent within a reasonable period of time, and that an award of permanent custody to county child protection agency was in the children's best interests, thus supporting termination of mother's parental rights; mother failed to protect children from abuse, mother failed to seek necessary medical attention for child who was abused, and mother allowed children to be alone with father, despite father's volatile temper. In re Mark B. (Ohio App. 6 Dist., Lucas, 03-14-2005) No. L-04-1167, No. L-04-1168, 2005-Ohio-1220, 2005 WL 635022, Unreported. Infants ⇐ 159

Evidence supported trial court's findings that an award of permanent custody to county child protection agency was in child's best interest and that he could not be placed with his parents within a reasonable time or should not be placed with them in the foreseeable future, thus supporting termination of father's parental rights; child suffered from cerebral palsy, child failed to receive proper nutrition while in parents' care, parents missed appointments with nutritionist, parents failed to show interest in participating in the types of therapy child needed, father failed to visit child for over a year and a half, child was more attached to foster parents than to biological parents, child's health showed marked improvement since removal from parents' care, and child was in need of secure placement. In re B.L. (Ohio App. 10 Dist., Franklin, 03-17-2005) No. 04AP-1108, 2005-Ohio-1151, 2005 WL 615642, Unreported, stay denied 105 Ohio St.3d 1553, 828 N.E.2d 110, 2005-Ohio-2424, appeal not allowed 105 Ohio St.3d 1564, 828 N.E.2d 118, 2005-Ohio-2447, appeal not allowed 106 Ohio St.3d 1417, 830 N.E.2d 348, 2005-Ohio-3154, reconsideration denied 106 Ohio St.3d 1511, 833 N.E.2d 1251, 2005-Ohio-4605, certiorari denied 126 S.Ct. 443, 163 L.Ed.2d 337, rehearing denied, rehearing denied 126 S.Ct. 726, 163 L.Ed.2d 623. Infants ⇐ 159

Evidence in child protection proceedings was sufficient to support finding that grant of permanent custody of child to county Children Services Board was in child's best interest; mother did not timely participate in recommended counseling, did not prioritize obtaining prescription medication for her bipolar condition, and was living with man who had history of domestic violence, child was very comfortable in foster care, guardian ad litem recommended permanent custody with agency, child had been in temporary custody of agency for more than 12 months of consecutive 22-month period, mother had abandoned child, and mother's parental rights to another child had been terminated. In re S.P. (Ohio App. 12 Dist., Butler, 03-14-2005) No. CA2004-10-255, 2005-Ohio-1079, 2005 WL 578976, Unreported. Infants ⇐ 208

Credible evidence supported finding that granting permanent custody of children to the county department of children and family services was in the best interests of the children; children had been out of mother's custody for almost three years, mother continued to use drugs during the time the children were removed, mother had a long history of serious drug abuse, mother was involved in several criminal cases, mother's participation in in-patient drug counseling had been unsuccessful, mother suffered from mental illness, and mother had encouraged the children to misbehave and disrupt their foster home placements so no family would want them on a permanent basis. In re Ch.O. (Ohio App. 8 Dist., Cuyahoga, 03-10-2005) No. 84943, 2005-Ohio-1013, 2005 WL 563747, Unreported. Infants ⚖ 158

Evidence supported trial court's grant of permanent custody of father's child to county child protection agency; father failed to successfully complete significant elements of his case plan, despite opportunities to do so, father's failure to comply with specific directives of case plan indicated lack of commitment to child, child had never lived with father or mother and had bonded with foster family, child was in need of legally secure and permanent placement, and guardian ad litem supported grant of permanent custody to agency so that child could be adopted. In re M.B. (Ohio App. 10 Dist., Franklin, 03-08-2005) No. 04AP755, 2005-Ohio-986, 2005 WL 534904, Unreported. Infants ⚖ 208

Order granting Department of Children Services permanent custody of children was in their best interests; children had been removed from home twice and were in temporary custody of Department of Children Services in two counties for 12 or more months of consecutive 22 month period, children had bonded with relatives with whom they were placed, guardian ad litem recommended permanent custody with Department, mother had voluntarily relinquished custody, father of one child was unknown, and putative father was incarcerated and therefore unavailable to care for his child. In re Davis (Ohio App. 11 Dist., Ashtabula, 02-04-2005) No. 2004-A-0068, 2005-Ohio-411, 2005 WL 280507, Unreported. Infants ⚖ 208

Clear and convincing evidence supported the trial court determination that it was in the best interests of mother's two children to award permanent custody to the county children's services board; all four of mother's children had been diagnosed with failure to thrive syndrome, mother failed to bond with the children, the children had adjusted well to foster care, the children had been in the custody of the county children's services board for more than 12 of the last 22 consecutive months, mother was living with a known felon whose children had been removed from his custody by a children's services agency, mother missed visits with the children, and physicians who conducted psychological evaluations of mother both opined that mother was not presently able to parent the children. In re Hershberger & Smith (Ohio App. 3 Dist., Allen, 02-07-2005) No. 1-04-55, No. 1-04-61, 2005-Ohio-429, 2005 WL 280356, Unreported. Infants ⚖ 155

Juvenile court complied with Court of Appeals' instructions on remand of issuing a new judgment as to termination of mother's parental rights and children's permanent custody, taking into consideration children's wishes regarding their placement, where court, while acknowledging sincerity of children's wishes to remain with mother, found that those wishes did not outweigh the contrary evidence that returning them to mother's custody would not be in their best interest. In re Ridenour (Ohio App. 11 Dist., Lake, 01-28-2005) No. 2004-L-168, No. 2004-L-169, No. 2004-L-170, 2005-Ohio-349, 2005 WL 237332, Unreported. Infants ⚖ 254

Evidence that mother's level of mental retardation precluded her from learning necessary parenting skills, that mother suffered from seizure disorder, that mother was unable to parent child without constant supervision and help from other adults, and that despite extensive services mother had made no progress supported finding that child could not be placed with mother within reasonable amount of time, as grounds for terminating mother's parental rights. In re Sadie R. (Ohio App. 6 Dist., Lucas, 01-28-2005) No. L-04-1057, 2005-Ohio-325, 2005 WL 195489, Unreported. Infants ⚖ 158

Evidence supported finding that mother failed to remedy conditions that led to removal of children from home, as grounds for terminating mother's parental rights; children had been removed from home because of father's acts of domestic violence upon mother, yet mother enabled father to have access to herself and children despite condition of father's parole that he have no unsupervised contact, and mother seemed unwilling to protect herself and children from father. In re Delfino M. (Ohio App. 6 Dist., Lucas, 01-28-2005) No. L-04-1010, No. L-04-1009, 2005-Ohio-320, 2005 WL 195488, Unreported. Infants ⚖ 156

Evidence supported finding that father failed to remedy conditions that led to removal of children from home, as grounds for terminating father's parental rights; children had been removed from home due to father's repeated acts of domestic violence in their presence, father failed to avail himself of programs that were arranged for him, and he repeatedly violated conditions of parole that he have no unsupervised contact with children. In re Delfino M. (Ohio App. 6 Dist., Lucas, 01-28-2005) No. L-04-1010, No. L-04-1009, 2005-Ohio-320, 2005 WL 195488, Unreported. Infants ⚖ 156

Evidence did not support grant of permanent custody of children to county child protection agency; although mother had limited financial means and had a boyfriend with a criminal record, mother completed required anger management classes, expert testimony indicated that mother's low intelligence would not prohibit her from adequate parenting, mother had nearly saved enough money to get independent housing, evidence indicated that children responded well to mother's boyfriend, mother's displays of anger toward agency personnel were not unjustifiable, and there was no evidence that mother's completion of case plan failed to remedy the condition that caused the children to be removed from the home. In re Rashaun B. (Ohio App. 6 Dist., Lucas, 09-22-2004) No. L-03-1306, 2004-Ohio-7349, 2004 WL 3394820, Unreported. Infants ⚖ 181

County, which filed original complaint for permanent custody of mother's children, was not required to formulate reunification plan. In re Aaron F. (Ohio App. 6 Dist., Lucas, 12-30-2004) No. L-04-1156, 2004-Ohio-7152, 2004 WL 3017288, Unreported. Infants ⚖ 155

Evidence supported award of permanent custody of children to county; although children loved mother and desired to remain with her, she had violated no contact order, moved boyfriend into her trailer that had past domestic violence issues and sexual abuse allegation, and had violated her safety plan. In re Aaron F. (Ohio App. 6 Dist., Lucas, 12-30-2004) No. L-04-1156, 2004-Ohio-7152, 2004 WL 3017288, Unreported. Infants ⚖ 156

Evidence with respect to child's custodial history was sufficient to support trial court's finding that such factor weighed in favor of termination of parental rights and grant of permanent custody of child to agency; child was removed from her parents' care less than one month after she was born, had lived with same foster family since that time, and at time of hearing had been living with foster family for more than 12 consecutive months. In re Adams (Ohio App. 3 Dist., Seneca, 12-27-2004) No. 13-04-27, 2004-Ohio-7039, 2004 WL 2980493, Unreported. Infants ⚖ 155

Grant of permanent custody of child adjudicated neglected to agency, for placement with foster parents, was in child's best interests; child had almost no relationship with her extended family and severely limited relationship with her biological parents, biological parents had been unable to progress beyond supervised visitation since child was removed from their custody, child had continuously lived with her foster family for more than a year and a half, foster parents expressed interest in adopting child and demonstrated loving relationship with child, and child became upset when separated from her foster parents, but not when separated from her biological parents. In re Adams (Ohio App. 3 Dist., Seneca, 12-27-2004) No. 13-04-27, 2004-Ohio-7039, 2004 WL 2980493, Unreported. Infants ⚖ 155

Evidence in child protection proceedings was sufficient to support trial court's finding that subject child could not be placed with either of her parents within reasonable time, as required to support grant of permanent custody of child to agency; mother at first refused to attend, and then failed to complete, required substance abuse counseling, failed to actively participate in parenting classes, and demonstrated no skills learned in such classes, father failed to attend any counseling or parenting classes, neither parent found permanent housing or employment, and both parents were repeatedly incarcerated while child was in temporary custody of agency. In re Adams (Ohio App. 3 Dist., Seneca, 12-27-2004) No. 13-04-27, 2004-Ohio-7039, 2004 WL 2980493, Unreported. Infants ⚖ 155; Infants ⚖ 156; Infants ⚖ 157

Evidence supported findings that children could not be placed with either parent within a reasonable time and it was in children's best interest to be provided with a safe and stable home environment, which could only be available through grant of permanent custody to county agency; mother repeatedly failed to remedy problems which led to removal of children, mother had significant difficulty supervising one child who had physical, mental and emotional disabilities and struggled with aggressive and destructive behaviors, and caseworker testified that children were adoptable and current foster family showed a deep commitment to children and was interested in adoption. In re Shahan/Ramey Children (Ohio App. 5 Dist., Stark, 12-16-2004) No. 2004CA00300, 2004-Ohio-6973, 2004 WL 2940807, Unreported. Infants ⚖ 155

Some competent, credible evidence supported trial court's finding that granting permanent custody of dependent child to Athens County Children Services (ACCS) was in child's best interest; child had no relationship with father and inappropriate relationship with mother, child had been in temporary custody of ACCS for more than 12 of consecutive 22-month period, and child had caught up to appropriate grade level while living with foster family. In re Marano (Ohio App. 4 Dist., Athens, 12-09-2004) No. 04CA30, 2004-Ohio-6826, 2004 WL 2913586, Unreported. Infants ⇔ 155

Trial court was not required to consider children's paternal grandmother for placement before granting permanent custody of father's children to county child protection agency, where grandmother failed to file motion seeking legal custody. In re Grooms (Ohio App. 2 Dist., Clark, 12-03-2004) No. 2003 CA 50, 2004-Ohio-6782, 2004 WL 2903883, Unreported. Infants ⇔ 226

Sufficient, competent, and credible evidence supported trial court's finding that granting permanent child custody to department of job and family services was in children's best interest; children were living with foster parents who were willing to adopt them, children were adapting well to foster home, and case worker indicated that children needed consistency, which mother failed to provide. In re Hayes/Reichenbach Children (Ohio App. 5 Dist., Stark, 12-13-2004) No. 2004CA00278, 2004-Ohio-6751, 2004 WL 2896008, Unreported. Infants ⇔ 155

Conclusion that grant of permanent custody to county children services board was in child's best interest was supported by evidence that, while child was in board custody, mother chose to reside outside county to pursue her own interests and did not make much effort to maintain a family relationship with child, mother missed scheduled visits and never called to indicate she would be missing visits, even when mother had contact with child, it was not very meaningful, and, throughout 21 months that child lived away from mother, she made no attempt to communicate with him or foster parents via telephone or mail. In re J.J. (Ohio App. 9 Dist., Summit, 12-08-2004) No. 22236, 2004-Ohio-6538, 2004 WL 2808941, Unreported. Infants ⇔ 157

Evidence was sufficient to support trial court's conclusion that awarding permanent custody of child to county children services, rather than to maternal grandmother, was in child's best interest; grandmother failed to complete case plain, did not permit county children services to perform home study, continually argued with county children services' staff, and exposed breast to county children services' staff. In re A.U. (Ohio App. 2 Dist., Montgomery, 11-19-2004) No. 20583, No. 20585, 2004-Ohio-6219, 2004 WL 2659137, Unreported. Infants ⇔ 178

Evidence supported trial court's finding that granting Department of Job and Family Services (DJFS) permanent custody of mother's minor child served child's best interests; child expressed to her teachers and foster mother that she felt unloved at home, mother stated that she was afraid that child would kill her or one of her younger children, and mother was unable to consistently control child's behaviors. In re Lilley (Ohio App. 4 Dist., Lawrence, 11-09-2004) No. 04CA22, 2004-Ohio-6156, 2004 WL 2631490, Unreported. Infants ⇔ 155

Evidence in termination of parental rights proceeding supported trial court's finding that it was in the best interest of mother's two minor children to grant permanent custody to the Department of Job and Family Services; case worker testified the foster parents were willing to adopt both children, that the children were healthy and not suffering any physical, psychological, or developmental problems, and that she believed permanent custody was in the best interest of the children because mother had a long history of drug abuse and unstable housing. In re Robinson/ Brooks Children (Ohio App. 5 Dist., Stark, 11-15-2004) No. 2004-CA-00094, 2004-Ohio-6142, 2004 WL 2616425, Unreported. Infants ⇔ 155

Trial court made the requisite findings to award permanent custody of mother's four minor children to the Department of Children and Family Services (DCFS); children had been in the temporary custody of DCFS for more than three years, mother failed to benefit from repeated reunification efforts, she relapsed into cocaine use, and she failed to attend the permanent custody hearing. In re A.L. (Ohio App. 8 Dist., Cuyahoga, 11-18-2004) No. 83997, 2004-Ohio-6096, 2004 WL 2609783, Unreported. Infants ⇔ 155

Trial court did not abuse its discretion by failing to make specific findings as to factors for determining whether it was in children's best interest to terminate parental rights, where mother did not request findings of fact and conclusions of law and court indicated that statutory factors were considered. In re Sanders Children (Ohio App. 5 Dist., Tuscarawas, 10-29-2004) No. 2004 AP 08 0057, 2004-Ohio-5878, 2004 WL 2497028, Unreported. Infants ⇔ 155; Infants ⇔ 210

Awarding permanent custody of father's two minor children to children's services board (CSB) was in children's best interest, even if trial court incorrectly determined that the children could not be placed with father within a reasonable time; record reflected that the children had been in the temporary custody of the CSB for 12 or more months of a consecutive 22-month period. In re J.T. (Ohio App. 2 Dist., Greene, 10-15-2004) No. 2004-CA-10, 2004-Ohio-5797, 2004 WL 2444871, Unreported. Infants ⇔ 155

Trial court's determination that grant of permanent custody of child to county agency was in child's best interests was not against the manifest weight of the evidence; child had good relationship with foster parents and wanted to stay with them, mother did not have stable housing or employment, mother did not accept either her or child's need for ongoing psychological treatment and medication, mother failed to take medication to treat bipolar disease, and mother refused to continue or participate in counseling for her children. In re T.M., III (Ohio App. 8 Dist., Cuyahoga, 09-30-2004) No. 83933, 2004-Ohio-5222, 2004 WL 2340654, Unreported. Infants ⇔ 155; Infants ⇔ 158

Juvenile court was required to consider wishes of mother's nine-year-old child before determining that grant of permanent custody to county agency was in child's best interest; there was no evidence from guardian ad litem that child was not competent to express his wishes. In re T.M., III (Ohio App. 8 Dist., Cuyahoga, 09-30-2004) No. 83933, 2004-Ohio-5222, 2004 WL 2340654, Unreported. Infants ⇔ 207

Evidence supported finding that grant of permanent custody of father's child to county agency was in best interests of child; although father desired to care and provide for child, father was 30 years old and lived with parents, father never finished high school, father had criminal record and poor employment record, paternal grandmother who was to care for child when father was at work was already caring for three other young grandchildren, child had bonded with foster family, foster family wished to adopt child, child had special needs necessitating secure placement, father was absent during first year of child's life, and father did very little, if anything, to determine if he was child's father until he was notified of agency's desire to obtain permanent custody. In re A.C. (Ohio App. 12 Dist., Clermont, 10-18-2004) No. CA2004-05-041, 2004-Ohio-5531, 2004 WL 2340127, Unreported. Infants ⇔ 155; Infants ⇔ 157

Evidence supported juvenile court's determination that granting permanent custody of mother's five children to Cuyahoga County Department of Children and Family Services (CCDCFS) was in children's best interest; mother's interaction with her children was minimal, children loved their foster parents and referred to them as "mom" and "dad," and foster parents indicated their desire to adopt the children. In re C.C. (Ohio App. 8 Dist., Cuyahoga, 09-30-2004) No. 83793, 2004-Ohio-5213, 2004 WL 2340069, Unreported. Infants ⇔ 155

Since mother's children were in temporary custody of Cuyahoga County Department of Children and Family Services (CCDCFS) for 12 or more months of consecutive 22-month period, it was unnecessary for juvenile court, in determining whether to grant permanent custody of children to CCDCFS, to analyze whether children could be placed with mother within reasonable time or whether mother failed to remedy conditions causing children's removal. In re C.C. (Ohio App. 8 Dist., Cuyahoga, 09-30-2004) No. 83793, 2004-Ohio-5213, 2004 WL 2340069, Unreported. Infants ⇔ 155

Evidence supported juvenile court's finding that grant of permanent custody of children to county agency was in children's best interests; mother failed to interact with children appropriately during supervised visits, mother failed to appropriately supervise or discipline children, mother had continuing drug problem, placement with mother placed children at risk of exposure to illegal drugs and criminal activity, mother denied that she or her family had any problems, and children needed secure and stable placement. In re S.V. (Ohio App. 9 Dist., Summit, 10-13-2004) No. 22116, 2004-Ohio-5445, 2004 WL 2292825, Unreported. Infants ⇔ 155; Infants ⇔ 156

It was in children's best interests that permanent custody of children be granted to Children Services Board; children had bonded well with their current foster family, foster family was considering adopting children, children had been in temporary custody of Board for 29 consecutive months, ever since their initial removal from mother's home, mother had not completed requirements of her case plan as ordered by the court, mother had not achieved stability in her life, had not completed recommended counseling, and had refused to take medication prescribed for mood disorder, and legally secure placement could not be achieved without granting permanent custody to Board. In re D.L. (Ohio App. 12 Dist., Butler, 10-11-2004) No. CA2003-12-314, 2004-Ohio-5407, 2004 WL 2272061, Unreported. Infants ⇔ 155; Infants ⇔ 158

It was in children's best interests to grant permanent custody of children to Department of Job and Family Services; children could not be placed with either parent within reasonable amount of time, children had been in custody of Department for more than 12 months of a consecutive 22-month period, children had a good relationship with their foster parents, mother withheld medical treatment from child, and, although they were not married, father and mother resided together and any child placed in father's custody would necessarily be parented by mother as well, particularly considering father's role as breadwinner and mother's role as homemaker. In re A.C. (Ohio App. 12 Dist., Fayette, 10-11-2004) No. CA2004-

02-004, No. CA2004-02-005, 2004-Ohio-5408, 2004 WL 2271999, Unreported. Infants ⇐ 155; Infants ⇐ 159

Grant of permanent custody to Stark County Department of Jobs and Family Services was in the children's best interests; the children were special needs children and required continued counseling, each had been held back for a year in school, children's behavior had improved since their removal from mother's home, there was testimony that the children had a "not very strong bond" with mother, children were very well bonded with the foster parents, and children appeared to feel safe in the foster homes. In re Heldt/Woodson Children (Ohio App. 5 Dist., Stark, 09-27-2004) No. 2004CA00191, 2004-Ohio-5188, 2004 WL 2260574, Unreported. Infants ⇐ 155

The trial court order granting permanent custody of child to county department of job and family services, and denying paternal aunt custody, was in the best interests of child and was not an abuse of discretion; social services aide testified that father was difficult to work with and did not have an understanding of appropriate interaction with child, child was placed in a foster home with her biological brother, foster parents had adopted child's brother, child was bonded with foster parents, and caseworker had concerns about placing child with paternal aunt due to the presence of an adult stepson with a felony record in the home. In re Dixon (Ohio App. 5 Dist., Stark, 10-04-2004) No. 2004CA00134, 2004-Ohio-5361, 2004 WL 2260572, Unreported. Infants ⇐ 155; Infants ⇐ 222

Granting permanent custody of dependent child to children services board (CSB) was in child's best interest; although parents regularly visited child and expressed love for child, attempts to reunite child with family were unsuccessful, parents previously had their parental rights terminated as to some of child's siblings, and caseworkers recommended grant of custody to CSB. In re B.E.M. (Ohio App. 9 Dist., Wayne, 09-22-2004) No. 04CA0028, 2004-Ohio-4959, 2004 WL 2244246, Unreported. Infants ⇐ 155

Awarding permanent custody of children to children services board (CSB) was in children's best interest, where father's interaction with children did not progress beyond supervised visitation, father missed visitation, father did not interact with or stimulate children, children were doing well in foster care, and children needed stable environment. In re T.G. (Ohio App. 9 Dist., Wayne, 09-29-2004) No. 04CA0040, 2004-Ohio-5173, 2004 WL 2244123, Unreported. Infants ⇐ 155

Trial court's conclusion that it was in dependent children's best interest for permanent custody to be granted to department of job and family services was not against manifest weight of evidence; relatives could not take care of children, children had been placed in and removed from several foster homes, children had been in custody of department for more than 12 of last 22 months, and social worker, counselor, and guardian ad litem all agreed that it was in children's best interest to grant permanent custody to department. In re Sunderman/Daniels Children Minor Children (Ohio App. 5 Dist., Stark, 08-30-2004) No. 2004CA00093, 2004-Ohio-4608, 2004 WL 1941061, Unreported. Infants ⇐ 155

Granting permanent child custody to department of job and family services was in children's best interests; although father argued that he acted appropriately during visits and that children were bonded with his extended family, grandmother did not know where father lived when grandmother had temporary child custody, father did not immediately visit children when he returned to state, father previously engaged in criminal conduct, and father missed important hearings throughout case. In re Villanueva/Hampton Children Dependant Children (Ohio App. 5 Dist., Stark, 08-30-2004) No. 2004CA00126, 2004-Ohio-4610, 2004 WL 1933542, Unreported. Infants ⇐ 155

Clear and convincing evidence failed to support trial court's award of permanent child custody to children's services board, where trial court stated in performing analysis of best interest of children that mother abandoned child, no allegation was made and no evidence established that mother abandoned child, and, even if all other evidence supporting trial court's decision was believed, abandonment was such major factor that remand was required for new hearing. In re Hardy (Ohio App. 7 Dist., Mahoning, 08-23-2004) No. 04MA11, 2004-Ohio-4542, 2004 WL 1925973, Unreported. Infants ⇐ 180; Infants ⇐ 197; Infants ⇐ 254

Even if trial court's finding that dependent children could not be placed with either parent within reasonable amount of time was improper, trial court properly continued with inquiry as to best interest of children in proceeding in which children's services board sought permanent child custody, where court made alternative finding that children had been in board's custody for 12 or more months of consecutive 22 month period and grant of permanent custody could be supported by such alternative finding. In re Hardy (Ohio App. 7 Dist., Mahoning, 08-23-2004) No. 04MA11, 2004-Ohio-4542, 2004 WL 1925973, Unreported. Infants ⇐ 203

Finding that award of permanent custody of child, who suffered from chronic liver failure and who had been in temporary custody of Department of Children and Family Services (DCFS) for more than 12 months, to DCFS was in best interest of child was supported by manifest weight of the evidence; mother demonstrated a lack of commitment toward child by failing to regularly visit him, and failing to take advantage of services that would allow her to learn how to provide adequate care for child's medical needs. In re L.F. (Ohio App. 8 Dist., Cuyahoga, 08-26-2004) No. 83594, 2004-Ohio-4484, 2004 WL 1902519, Unreported. Infants ⇐ 157; Infants ⇐ 159

Evidence supported finding that granting permanent custody of child to county children services was in the best interests of child, in support of termination of parental rights; child looked to his foster parents for support, encouragement, and fulfillment of his basic needs, foster parents addressed child's medical needs and maintained child's occupational, physical, and speech therapy, and guardian ad litem recommended that permanent custody of child be granted to children services. In re M.L.J. (Ohio App. 10 Dist., Franklin, 08-19-2004) No. 04AP-152, 2004-Ohio-4358, 2004 WL 1853547, Unreported, appeal not allowed 103 Ohio St.3d 1528, 817 N.E.2d 410, 2004-Ohio-5852. Infants ⇐ 155; Infants ⇐ 208

Trial court finding that it was in the best interests of the children to grant permanent custody of the children to county jobs and family services, rather than place the children in a planned permanent living arrangement, was not an abuse of discretion; mother admitted that she was unable to take the children back into her home due to their behavior, foster parents had expressed an interest in adopting one or both of the children, and there was insufficient evidence to establish that the children had a significant positive relationship with mother. In re Hutzel (Ohio App. 5 Dist., Tuscarawas, 08-12-2004) No. 2004AP03-0028, 2004-Ohio-4337, 2004 WL 1846122, Unreported. Infants ⇐ 155; Infants ⇐ 199

Evidence supported finding that grant of permanent custody of child to county agency was in best interests of child; mother acted inappropriately when visiting child, child was bonded with foster family, guardian ad litem recommended granting permanent custody to county agency, child needed stable environment and mature caregiver, mother failed to obtain permanent job or housing, mother often switched residences or lived out of her car, child had been in temporary custody of children services agencies for 12 or more months of a consecutive 22–month period, and mother had no contact with child during eight months she was incarcerated. In re K.M. (Ohio App. 12 Dist., Butler, 08-09-2004) No. CA2004-02-052, 2004-Ohio-4152, 2004 WL 1765462, Unreported. Infants ⇐ 155; Infants ⇐ 157; Infants ⇐ 208

Evidence supported finding that granting permanent custody of mother's child to county children's services was in child's best interest, even though the trial court did not allow child to testify; child's caseworker stated that four-year-old child was not old enough to comprehend the situation, and guardian ad litem opined that child was too young and unable to express his wishes regarding the outcome of the proceedings. In re Wright (Ohio App. 10 Dist., Franklin, 08-03-2004) No. 04AP-435, 2004-Ohio-4045, 2004 WL 1729881, Unreported. Infants ⇐ 207

Evidence supported finding that granting permanent custody of children to county children services was in the best interests of the children; the children were bonded to their foster family, initial concerns regarding the development and behaviors of the children had alleviated while the children were in the care of foster family, mother's four older children were being cared for by relatives, parents had continued problems with drug and alcohol use and abuse, and parents had continued problems finding appropriate housing and stable employment. In re Brown (Ohio App. 10 Dist., Franklin, 08-03-2004) No. 04AP-169, No. 04-AP-181, No. 04AP-170, No. 04AP-180, 2004-Ohio-4044, 2004 WL 1729449, Unreported, appeal not allowed 103 Ohio St.3d 1495, 816 N.E.2d 1081, 2004-Ohio-5605. Infants ⇐ 155

To support grant of permanent custody of children to county agency, following determination that children had been in temporary custody of public children services agency for twelve or more months of a consecutive twenty-two month period, or that children had been abandoned, juvenile court was only required to make finding that grant of permanent custody was in best interests of children. In re Morgan (Ohio App. 3 Dist., Marion, 08-02-2004) No. 9-04-02, No. 9-04-03, 2004-Ohio-4018, 2004 WL 1717934, Unreported. Infants ⇐ 210

Evidence supported juvenile court's finding that grant of permanent custody to county agency was in best interest of mother's two children; mother's husband threatened children with a gun, children were afraid of mother's husband, mother was unwilling and unable to protect children from abusive husband, children had been in foster care for eighteen consecutive months prior to the permanent custody hearing, children had adapted to foster home and wished to be adopted, children were readily adoptable, and children needed stable future that mother could not provide. In re Morgan (Ohio App. 3 Dist., Marion, 08-02-2004) No. 9-04-02, No. 9-04-03, 2004-Ohio-4018, 2004 WL 1717934, Unreported. Infants ⇔ 156

Evidence supported finding termination of parental rights and grant of permanent custody of children to county children services was in best interests of children; children were fearful of father and distrustful of mother's ability to protect them, children's problems were worsened by contact with mother, children were closely bonded with foster parent, mother refused to believe children's allegations of father's abuse, mother waited nearly a full year after children's removal from their home before she separated from abusive father, children had been in temporary custody of county for total of 27 months, and children's need for stability and safety could be met by foster home. In re Brooks (Ohio App. 10 Dist., Franklin, 07-22-2004) No. 04AP-164, No. 04AP-201, No. 04AP-202, No. 04AP-165, 2004-Ohio-3887, 2004 WL 1631760, Unreported, appeal not allowed 103 Ohio St.3d 1495, 816 N.E.2d 1081, 2004-Ohio-5605. Infants ⇔ 155; Infants ⇔ 156

Trial court award of permanent custody of father's children to county department of children and family services was not an abuse of discretion; children had been in the temporary custody of the department for 35 months at the time of trial, father failed to complete programs required under his caseplan, father ignored son and his relationship with daughter had inappropriate aspects to it, foster parents were interested in providing a permanent home for the children, and mother stated the children were better off in foster care than with father. In re B.R. (Ohio App. 8 Dist., Cuyahoga, 07-22-2004) No. 83674, 2004-Ohio-3865, 2004 WL 1630507, Unreported. Infants ⇔ 155; Infants ⇔ 156

Finding that it was in dependent children's best interest to place them in permanent custody of Geauga County Job and Family Services (GCJFS) was not abuse of discretion; although mother loved children, mother continued to use drugs and was unable to maintain stable employment. In re Ross (Ohio App. 11 Dist., Geauga, 07-09-2004) No. 2003-G-2549, 2004-Ohio-3689, 2004 WL 1559781, Unreported, appeal not allowed 103 Ohio St.3d 1429, 814 N.E.2d 491, 2004-Ohio-4524. Infants ⇔ 155

Finding in termination of parental rights proceeding that it was not in dependent children's best interest to place them in grandmother's custody was not abuse of discretion, where grandmother had son who was incarcerated for murder and grandmother did not know about domestic violence involving children's parents. In re Ross (Ohio App. 11 Dist., Geauga, 07-09-2004) No. 2003-G-2549, 2004-Ohio-3689, 2004 WL 1559781, Unreported, appeal not allowed 103 Ohio St.3d 1429, 814 N.E.2d 491, 2004-Ohio-4524. Infants ⇔ 222

Evidence supported finding that it was in best interests of dependent children to be placed in the permanent custody of county department of job and family services; evidence indicated that children had little interaction with father, evidence indicated that children were attached and bonded to their foster family, guardian ad litem recommended that children be placed in the permanent custody of department, children had been in temporary custody of department for more than 12 months, and social worker testified that father had not contact with children for six months. In re Thompson (Ohio App. 11 Dist., Portage, 07-07-2004) No. 2004-P-0023, No. 2004-P-0024, 2004-Ohio-3686, 2004 WL 1559747, Unreported. Infants ⇔ 155; Infants ⇔ 208

Finding in termination of parental rights proceeding that it was not in dependent children's best interest to place them in grandmother's custody was not abuse of discretion, where grandmother had son who was incarcerated for murder and grandmother did not know about domestic violence involving children's parents. In re Ross (Ohio App. 11 Dist., Geauga, 07-07-2004) No. 2003-G-2551, 2004-Ohio-3684, 2004 WL 1559742, Unreported. Infants ⇔ 222

Finding that it was in dependent children's best interest to place them in permanent custody of Geauga County Job and Family Services (GCJFS) was not abuse of discretion; although mother loved children, mother continued to use drugs and was unable to maintain stable employment. In re Ross (Ohio App. 11 Dist., Geauga, 07-09-2004) No. 2003-G-2550, 2004-Ohio-3680, 2004 WL 1559729, Unreported, appeal not allowed 103 Ohio St.3d 1481, 816 N.E.2d 256, 2004-Ohio-5405. Infants ⇔ 155

Finding in termination of parental rights proceeding that it was not in dependent children's best interest to place them in grandmother's custody was not abuse of discretion, where grandmother had son who was incarcerated for murder and grandmother did not know about domestic violence involving children's parents. In re Ross (Ohio App. 11 Dist., Geauga, 07-09-2004) No. 2003-G-2550, 2004-Ohio-3680, 2004 WL 1559729, Unreported, appeal not allowed 103 Ohio St.3d 1481, 816 N.E.2d 256, 2004-Ohio-5405. Infants ⇔ 222

Granting permanent custody of dependent child to children services board was in child's best interest; although mother loved child, child had never been in mother's custody, child was in need of stable home, mother failed to demonstrate that she was able to care for child's basic needs, and permanent custody of child's sibling was previously granted to board. In re Baby Girl Elliott (Ohio App. 12 Dist., Butler, 07-06-2004) No. CA2003-10-256, 2004-Ohio-3539, 2004 WL 1485858, Unreported. Infants ⇔ 155

Clear and convincing evidence supported award of permanent custody of child to county department of jobs and family services (DJFS), in dependency case; mother was diagnosed with schizo-affective disorder, bipolar type, psychologist did not recommend giving child to mother absent mother's participation in treatment or therapy, caseworker testified that mother delayed complying with caseplan requirements for many months, and guardian ad litem's report recommended permanent custody due to the number of issues that still had to be addressed before child could be returned home to mother. In re Definbaugh (Ohio App. 5 Dist., Tuscarawas, 06-23-2004) No. 2004 AP 02 0010, 2004-Ohio-3367, 2004 WL 1445078, Unreported. Infants ⇔ 158; Infants ⇔ 208

Order granting permanent custody of mother's children to Children Services for purposes of adoption was in best interests of children; children had been in custody of Children Services for minimum 12 of 22 months, mother was incarcerated for indefinite period of time, mother had no contact with children, maternal grandmother who sought custody refused to acknowledge sexual abuse committed upon one of children while in her care, and other child had no relationship with grandmother, and children had bonded with foster parents. In re Brown (Ohio App. 10 Dist., Franklin, 06-24-2004) No. 03AP-969, 2004-Ohio-3314, 2004 WL 1405357, Unreported. Infants ⇔ 155; Infants ⇔ 157; Infants ⇔ 226

Trial court's determination that it was in dependent child's best interest to grant permanent custody to Franklin County Children Services (FCCS) was supported by clear and convincing evidence and was not against manifest weight of evidence; child had been in temporary custody of FCCS for 33 months, child needed legally secure placement that could not be achieved without grant of permanent custody, father admitted that he was not ready for child to be placed with him, mother continued to live with father who was untreated drug addict, and mother refused to take prescription medication to assist with her mental health. In re Andy-Jones (Ohio App. 10 Dist., Franklin, 06-24-2004) No. 03AP-1167, No. 03AP-1231, 2004-Ohio-3312, 2004 WL 1405319, Unreported, stay denied 103 Ohio St.3d 1425, 814 N.E.2d 489, 2004-Ohio-4524, appeal not allowed 103 Ohio St.3d 1429, 814 N.E.2d 491, 2004-Ohio-4524, appeal not allowed 103 Ohio St.3d 1465, 815 N.E.2d 680, 2004-Ohio-5056. Infants ⇔ 155; Infants ⇔ 158

Granting permanent custody of dependent children to department of jobs and family services was not against manifest weight of evidence; although mother claimed department failed to devise and implement case plan which was reasonably calculated to reunify children into home, case plan included goals of completing parenting skills and keeping family safe, and, regardless of mother's substantial compliance with case plan, mother was unable to successfully parent children and remedy problems which led to children's removal. In re Merryman/Wilson Children (Ohio App. 5 Dist., Stark, 06-14-2004) No. 2004 CA 00056, No. 2004 CA 00071, 2004-Ohio-3174, 2004 WL 1376278, Unreported. Infants ⇔ 155

Finding that it was in dependent child's best interest to grant permanent custody to department of jobs and family services was not against manifest weight of evidence; child was in department's temporary custody for 12 months within last 22 months and guardian ad litem and child therapist indicated that it was in child's best interest to grant permanent custody to department. In re Merryman/Wilson Children (Ohio App. 5 Dist., Stark, 06-14-2004) No. 2004 CA 00056, No. 2004 CA 00071, 2004-Ohio-3174, 2004 WL 1376278, Unreported. Infants ⇔ 155

Clear and convincing evidence supported finding that placing dependent children in permanent custody of department of job and family services was in children's best interest; mother failed to comply with case plans and was unable to find suitable housing, children needed secure placement, and children improved academically and socially while in foster care. In re Katrina T. (Ohio App. 6 Dist., Sandusky, 06-18-2004) No. S-03-024, 2004-Ohio-3164, 2004 WL 1368324, Unreported. Infants ⇔ 222

Failing to place dependent and neglected children with their aunt and uncle and, instead, granting permanent custody to department of job and family services was not error, where children had little prior contact with aunt and uncle, aunt and uncle had small home, family dog that was trained to attack could have been threat to children, and children associated uncle with grandfather, who sexually abused children. In re Katrina T. (Ohio App. 6 Dist., Sandusky, 06-18-2004) No. S-03-024, 2004-Ohio-3164, 2004 WL 1368324, Unreported. Infants ⇔ 222

Clear and convincing evidence supported finding that granting permanent custody of child to county department of children and family services was in child's best interest; mother and child showed little affection for each other, mother blamed child for the fact that he was in public custody, guardian ad litem testified that child expressed a desire to see mother but not to live with her, and child had made a positive adjustment to foster care and called his foster mother "mom" or "grandma" and his foster father "dad." In re R.N. (Ohio App. 8 Dist., Cuyahoga, 05-20-2004) No. 83121, 2004-Ohio-2560, 2004 WL 1118825, Unreported. Infants ⇔ 155

Juvenile court complied with statutory mandate that child's wishes be considered in permanent custody proceeding, where, in granting permanent child custody to Geauga County Job and Family Services (GCJFS), court indicated that child wished to live with mother, that child was eight years old, and that it was not uncommon for child of that age to desire to live with parent, regardless of circumstances. In re Krems (Ohio App. 11 Dist., Geauga, 05-14-2004) No. 2003-G-2535, 2004-Ohio-2449, 2004 WL 1086974, Unreported. Infants ⇔ 210

Evidence supported trial court's findings that county children services board made reasonable attempts at reunification and that granting board permanent custody of child was in child's best interests; evidence indicated that father was incarcerated, father intentionally avoided contact with board and child during proceeding, father had no contact with child since child was placed in board's custody, and father had not contributed to child's financial support for at least five years. In re K.S. (Ohio App. 12 Dist., Clinton, 05-03-2004) No. CA2003-12-029, 2004-Ohio-2208, 2004 WL 937319, Unreported. Infants ⇔ 155; Infants ⇔ 157

Children's best interests warranted termination of mother's parental rights and placement of children in permanent custody of Children Services Board (CSB); mother was unable to provide stable home for children due to long history of abusing alcohol and crack cocaine, children missed a lot of school during periods when mother was using drugs, and children were living in same foster home, had adjusted to living there, and seemed to be happy. In re J.O. (Ohio App. 9 Dist., Wayne, 04-28-2004) No. 03CA0076, 2004-Ohio-2121, 2004 WL 894571, Unreported. Infants ⇔ 155; Infants ⇔ 159

Evidence supported finding that grant of permanent custody to county agency was in best interests of child diagnosed with reactive attachment disorder; child had been in temporary custody of agency for twelve or more months out of a consecutive twenty-two month period, family counseling appropriate to child's unusual mental disorders had been arranged for family, parents were unable to provide the level of medical and personal attention and supervision that child required, and child's placement with a relative was no more likely to be successful than placement with his parents. In re C.W. (Ohio App. 2 Dist., Montgomery, 04-23-2004) No. 20140, 2004-Ohio-2040, 2004 WL 870126, Unreported. Infants ⇔ 155

Magistrate's conclusion that grant of permanent custody to county children's services board was in best interest of dependent children was supported by relevant statutory factors; magistrate indicated that guardian ad litem concluded that it was in children's best interest to grant board's motion for permanent custody, that child stated that she wanted to stay in foster home, that children had made significant developmental advances following removal from parents' home, and that children needed secure permanent placement. In re Paris (Ohio App. 11 Dist., Ashtabula, 04-16-2004) No. 2003-A-0133, No. 2003-A-0134, 2004-Ohio-1962, 2004 WL 833594, Unreported. Infants ⇔ 210

Evidence clearly and convincingly supported trial court's finding that granting permanent child custody to county children's services so as to effectuate adoption by maternal aunt was in child's best interest, where child was flourishing with aunt, aunt had son who was near child's age and who was like sibling to child, child had lived with aunt for nearly half his life, and guardian ad litem recommended such grant of custody. In re Samuel M. (Ohio App. 6 Dist., Lucas, 03-31-2004) No. L-03-1265, 2004-Ohio-1637, 2004 WL 628233, Unreported. Infants ⇔ 155

Trial court could grant permanent custody of dependent child to department of job and family services, even though child had not been in department's temporary custody for 12 or more months of consecutive 22-month period, where court found that dependent child's best interests would be served by granting permanent custody to department, that child could not and should not in foreseeable future be placed with father, and that mother abandoned child. In re Strychalski (Ohio App. 7 Dist., Carroll, 03-26-2004) No. 03-CA-797, 2004-Ohio-1542, 2004 WL 612835, Unreported. Infants ⇔ 155

Finding that dependent child's best interests would be served by granting permanent custody to department of job and family services was not abuse of trial court's discretion; although father exercised good portion of his visitation, he did not complete any of his case plan goals or agreed-upon parenting classes. In re Strychalski (Ohio App. 7 Dist., Carroll, 03-26-2004) No. 03-CA-797, 2004-Ohio-1542, 2004 WL 612835, Unreported. Infants ⇔ 155

Trial court was not required to rule out the option of legal custody to father, in dependent child proceeding, before awarding permanent custody of child to county child services board. In Re P. C. (Ohio App. 9 Dist., Summit, 03-17-2004) No. 21734, No. 21739, 2004-Ohio-1230, 2004 WL 509368, Unreported. Infants ⇔ 226

Evidence was sufficient to establish, in dependent child proceeding, that termination of mother's and father's parental rights was in best interest of child; though both parents regularly and appropriately participated in weekly visitation and loved the child, neither parent established regular employment or adequate housing, mother had not complied with requirement that she participate in anger management program, father only recently began participating in anger management program, mother did not participate in counseling for depression as required by case plan, father delayed required psychological assessment and it was not completed by time of permanent custody hearing, father had extensive criminal record, father was in arrears on child support payments, guardian ad litem indicated permanent custody was in best interest of the child, child had been in custody virtually her entire life, and mother had her parental rights terminated as to three other children. In Re P. C. (Ohio App. 9 Dist., Summit, 03-17-2004) No. 21734, No. 21739, 2004-Ohio-1230, 2004 WL 509368, Unreported. Infants ⇔ 158

Trial court finding that granting permanent custody of father's three children to the county department of job and family services in the best interests of the children was not against the manifest weight of the evidence; caseworker testified that father never visited with his children during the 18 months leading up to the best interests hearing, that he never provided care, custody, or control for the children in the time they were in custody, and that two of the children had serious medical conditions that required special attention and care. In re Foresha/Kinkel Children (Ohio App. 5 Dist., Stark, 02-09-2004) No. 2003CA00364, 2004-Ohio-578, 2004 WL 237987, Unreported. Infants ⇔ 155; Infants ⇔ 157

Evidence supported finding that it was in child's best interest to grant permanent custody of child to county children's services; expert testified that child was not bonded well to mother, evidence established that child's older brother, who lived with mother, was physically abusive to child, child formed a bond with her foster mother, child indicated that she did not want to return to mother, county children's services had custody of child on three prior occasions, expert testified that child had significant psychological problems that would require expert care, and mother had difficulty working with social service agencies. In re Nibert (Ohio App. 4 Dist., Gallia, 01-22-2004) No. 03CA19, 2004-Ohio-429, 2004 WL 193862, Unreported. Infants ⇔ 178

Trial court's finding that Children Services Board (CSB) made reasonable efforts to reunite child with her parents, a statutory finding required to support parental termination order, was against manifest weight of evidence; CSB conducted itself as if mother's losing her parental rights was a foregone conclusion, CSB never intended to make reasonable efforts to reunify mother with the child and only made limited efforts when ordered to do so by the trial court, when the parents fully complied with the CSB case plan, CSB refused parents' request for additional time with child, and CSB only set reunification as a goal for seven of the 23 months it had temporary custody of child. In re Elliott (Ohio App. 7 Dist., Jefferson, 01-26-2004) No. 03JE30, No. 03JE33, 2004-Ohio-388, 2004 WL 187413, Unreported. Infants ⇔ 155

Evidence supported trial court's decision that it was in best interests of children that children be placed in permanent custody of county department of family services; although grandmother desired custody of children, children were bonded to foster parents, foster parents wished to adopt children, and home study was thorough with well-reasoned conclusions justifying county's decision not to temporarily place the children with grandmother when they were first removed from parent's care. In re McCann (Ohio App. 12 Dist., Clermont, 01-26-2004) No. CA2003-02-017, 2004-Ohio-283, 2004 WL 111644, Unreported. Infants ⇔ 226

Evidence supported finding that granting permanent custody of child to county children's services was in child's best interests; three-year-old child had lived with her caretaker since she was 18 months old, she was bonded to her caretaker, and she thought of caretaker as her mother. In re Kierra D. (Ohio App. 6 Dist., Lucas, 01-22-2004) No. L-03-1164, 2004-Ohio-277, 2004 WL 102939, Unreported. Infants ⇔ 155

Evidence supported trial court's finding that grant of permanent custody of mother's child to Children Services Board was in child's best interest; child had been in temporary custody of Board for more than 12 of prior 22 months, mother failed to complete parenting classes, attend child's medical appointments or otherwise comply with requirements of case plan, child was medically fragile, child did not seem upset when mother failed to visit, mother had violated visitation guidelines, foster mother was a licensed emergency medical technician and was certified to care for medically fragile children, guardian encouraged termination of parental rights, and mother denied her own mental health issues. In re N.P. (Ohio App. 9

Dist., Summit, 01-14-2004) No. 21707, 2004-Ohio-110, 2004 WL 57437, Unreported. Infants ⇐ 222

Trial court acted within its discretion in not considering child's wish to be reunited with his grandmother when court placed child in the permanent custody of County Job & Family Services, where child suffered from numerous developmental delays, and child was of a young age. Swisher v. Tuscarawas County Job & Family Services (Ohio App. 5 Dist., Tuscarawas, 12-05-2003) No. 2003AP080060, No. 2003AP080066, 2003-Ohio-7317, 2003 WL 23269346, Unreported, appeal not allowed 101 Ohio St.3d 1453, 803 N.E.2d 401, 2004-Ohio-462. Infants ⇐ 226

Evidence supported trial court's placement of child in the permanent custody of County Job & Family Services, rather than placement with grandmother; grandmother could not alter her environment in a permanent manner to allow child to flourish, although grandmother made diligent efforts to follow all recommendations of her case plan, she was unable to apply that knowledge in a practical manner, and grandmother's history demonstrated her inability to protect minor children from inappropriate individuals. Swisher v. Tuscarawas County Job & Family Services (Ohio App. 5 Dist., Tuscarawas, 12-05-2003) No. 2003AP080060, No. 2003AP080066, 2003-Ohio-7317, 2003 WL 23269346, Unreported, appeal not allowed 101 Ohio St.3d 1453, 803 N.E.2d 401, 2004-Ohio-462. Infants ⇐ 222

There was clear and convincing evidence that mother failed continuously and repeatedly to substantially remedy the conditions causing her child to be placed outside her home, supporting grant of permanent custody of child to county Department of Children and Family Services (CCDCFS). In re R.C. (Ohio App. 8 Dist., Cuyahoga, 12-24-2003) No. 82453, 2003-Ohio-7062, 2003 WL 23009947, Unreported. Infants ⇐ 222

Order placing two children in permanent custody of Children Services Board was supported by findings children could not be placed with mother within reasonable time, that children had been in custody of Children Services Board for twelve or more months of consecutive 22-month period, that State made reasonable efforts to reunify mother with children, and that granting Children Services Board permanent custody was in best interest of children. In re Payne (Ohio App. 12 Dist., Clinton, 12-22-2003) No. CA2003-07-017, 2003-Ohio-7014, 2003 WL 22997800, Unreported. Infants ⇐ 222

Trial court sufficiently addressed child's wishes and best interest before terminating mother's parental rights, where court determined that child was too young to express her wishes concerning custody, and court considered child's best interests as expressed by the guardian ad litem. In re Salsgiver (Ohio App. 11 Dist., Geauga, 11-26-2003) No. 2003-G-2517, 2003-Ohio-6412, 2003 WL 22844229, Unreported. Infants ⇐ 210

Evidence in proceeding for termination of parental rights was sufficient to support conclusion that granting permanent custody of children to county children's services was in children's best interest and that children could not and should not be placed with either parent within reasonable time; mother and father suffered from mental illness and substance abuse problems, father had spent several periods of time incarcerated or in residential drug treatment facilities, he had physically abused one of their children and was not available to care for the children, and mother exhibited severe signs of instability. In re Dakota (Ohio App. 2 Dist., Greene, 10-24-2003) No. 02CA39, No. 02CA40, 2003-Ohio-5739, 2003 WL 22429293, Unreported. Infants ⇐ 156; Infants ⇐ 157; Infants ⇐ 158

Clear and convincing evidence supported trial court finding that granting county children services permanent custody of child was in child's best interests, in child dependency proceeding; caseworkers testified that child did not seem bonded to mother and that child was bonded with his foster mother, child's guardian ad litem recommended terminating parental rights, and child was in need of permanent placement and had been in foster care for three years. In re James (Ohio App. 10 Dist., Franklin, 09-30-2003) No. 03AP-373, 2003-Ohio-5208, 2003 WL 22232965, Unreported. Infants ⇐ 208

Granting permanent custody of two children to county department of job and family services was in best interest of children; children showed no signs of distress when they were separated from mother when visiting her in prison, placement with relatives could not be maintained permanently, and children were very happy with their current foster family. In re McDonald (Ohio App. 5 Dist., Delaware, 09-10-2003) No. 03 CA F 03 021, 2003-Ohio-4808, 2003 WL 22100693, Unreported. Infants ⇐ 155

Trial court's failure to place child in a planned permanent living arrangement, rather than terminating mother's parental rights and granting permanent custody of child to county children services board, did not constitute reversible error; child's foster father testified that child could be placed in residential care, that child's grades and attitude improved while child lived with foster family, and that child was able to function in a family-like setting and did not require institutional care. In re Bounds (Ohio App. 3 Dist., Allen, 09-08-2003) No. 1-03-11, 2003-Ohio-4733, 2003 WL 22071460, Unreported. Infants ⇐ 253

Evidence was sufficient to support finding that the best interests of dependent children would be served by granting permanent custody of children to county department job and family services; caseworker testified that mother did not seem to care if she visited children, caseworker testified that children bonded with their foster parents and they were capable of bonding with new foster parents, child indicated that she did not want to return to mother's custody, and children's therapist testified that current instability had a detrimental effect on children and that any harm caused by breaking the parental relationship would be outweighed by the benefits of stability occurring through permanent custody. In re Utt Children (Ohio App. 5 Dist., Stark, 08-27-2003) No. 2003CA00196, 2003-Ohio-4576, 2003 WL 22020802, Unreported. Infants ⇐ 178

Statute on factors to consider in determining child's best interests regarding permanent placement with children services agency requires the court to find the best option for the child once a determination has been made on uniting the child with family; the statute does not make the availability of a placement that would not require a termination of parental rights an all-controlling factor and does not even require the court to weigh that factor more heavily than other factors. In re Schaefer (Ohio, 10-25-2006) 2006-Ohio-5513, 2006 WL 3041370. Infants ⇐ 222

Trial court's ruling on best interests of child regarding permanent placement with children services agency was not required to determine by clear and convincing evidence that termination of mother's parental rights was not only a necessary option, but also the only option, or that no suitable relative was available for placement. In re Schaefer (Ohio, 10-25-2006) 2006-Ohio-5513, 2006 WL 3041370. Infants ⇐ 178

Child's need for a legally secure permanent placement and ability to achieve that type of placement without a grant of permanent custody to children services agency has no heightened importance over other statutory factors in determination of child's best interests in granting permanent custody to agency. In re Schaefer (Ohio, 10-25-2006) 2006-Ohio-5513, 2006 WL 3041370. Infants ⇐ 155

Grant of permanent custody of five-year-old child to county child protection agency was not supported by clear and convincing evidence, absent evidence of child's wishes regarding custody. In re Lopez (Ohio App. 3 Dist., 05-08-2006) 166 Ohio App.3d 688, 852 N.E.2d 1266, 2006-Ohio-2251. Infants ⇐ 178

Clear and convincing evidence supported findings that children were too young to express their wishes regarding custody, in proceeding in which county child protection agency sought permanent custody of children; two of the children were three years old, and the other was two years old, and all three children had language delays. In re Lopez (Ohio App. 3 Dist., 05-08-2006) 166 Ohio App.3d 688, 852 N.E.2d 1266, 2006-Ohio-2251. Infants ⇐ 207

Evidence supported finding that mother failed to substantially remedy the conditions that caused child to be placed outside of the home and that granting permanent custody to county department of children and family services was in child's best interest; mother made little effort to comply with her caseplan, she was in denial about child's serious mental health issues, she failed to visit child regularly, and there were no relatives available for placement. In re J.S. (Ohio App. 8 Dist., 05-06-2004) 157 Ohio App.3d 127, 809 N.E.2d 684, 2004-Ohio-2328. Infants ⇐ 155

Trial court finding that the county children services board made reasonable efforts to reunify child with father did not affect outcome of child dependency proceeding, even if the finding was in error; trial court terminated parental rights after finding that child had been in the temporary custody of children services board for more than 12 of the past 22 months, and the 12-month time requirement for termination did not require an inquiry into the reasonableness of reunification services and only required that the court address the best interest of the child. In re Stillman (Ohio App. 11 Dist., 11-19-2003) 155 Ohio App.3d 333, 801 N.E.2d 475, 2003-Ohio-6228, appeal not allowed 101 Ohio St.3d 1425, 802 N.E.2d 155, 2004-Ohio-123. Infants ⇐ 253

Genuine issue of material fact as to whether granting permanent custody of child to county children services board was in child's best interest precluded father's motion for summary judgment, filed in response to the county children services board motion for permanent custody of child. In re Stillman (Ohio App. 11 Dist., 11-19-2003) 155 Ohio App.3d 333, 801 N.E.2d 475, 2003-Ohio-6228, appeal not allowed 101 Ohio St.3d 1425, 802 N.E.2d 155, 2004-Ohio-123. Infants ⇐ 221

12. Review

Father's appeal of the trial court's denial of his objections to magistrate's decision, which found clear and convincing evidence that child was a neglected and dependent child, was not an issue that was capable of repetition, yet evaded review, which would allow the Court of Appeals to review a moot issue; the was no indication that father would ever be subject to a neglect or dependency action with regard to his surviving child, or that civil remedies to which he may be entitled would be impaired by the adjudication in the instant action. In re L.W. (Ohio App. 10 Dist., Franklin, 02-14-2006) No. 05AP-317, 2006-Ohio-644, 2006 WL 330089, Unreported, appeal not allowed 109 Ohio St.3d 1497, 848 N.E.2d 859, 2006-Ohio-2762. Infants ⚖ 247

Mother was not entitled to appellate review of claim that denial of continuance in proceedings to terminate parental rights violated constitutional right to parent children, where claim was not made subject of objection to magistrate's decision. In re Harris (Ohio App. 2 Dist., Montgomery, 07-15-2005) No. 20934, 2005-Ohio-3700, 2005 WL 1704920, Unreported. Infants ⚖ 243

County department of job and family services was not required to have children in its custody for at least 22 months before trial court could make finding pursuant statute allowing court to consider custodial history of child in determining what was in child's best interest, in proceeding in which permanent custody of children was granted to department; statute did not require that child be in the custody of department for 22 months, and only required that child be in department's custody for 12 out of previous 22 months. In re Speaks (Ohio App. 5 Dist., Licking, 06-20-2005) No. 2004 CA 0090, 2005-Ohio-3526, 2005 WL 1503572, Unreported, appeal not allowed 107 Ohio St.3d 1423, 837 N.E.2d 1208, 2005-Ohio-6124. Infants ⚖ 210

Court of Appeals would not review for plain error issue of whether trial court had erred in awarding permanent custody of child to county under statutory provision that allowed such an award when child has been in temporary custody of an agency for at least 12 months of a consecutive 22 month period, in dependency and neglect proceeding; mother had died during pendency of appeal, and, thus any return of child's custody to her was no longer relevant issue. In re Roberts (Ohio App. 5 Dist., Guernsey, 06-08-2005) No. 04 CA 29, 2005-Ohio-2843, 2005 WL 1364611, Unreported. Infants ⚖ 248.1

Mother waived on appeal issue of whether trial court had erred in awarding permanent custody of child to county under statutory provision that allowed such an award when child has been in temporary custody of an agency for at least 12 months of a consecutive 22 month period, in dependency and neglect proceeding, as mother failed to raise challenge on this basis at trial court level, even though county's counsel had indicated his reliance thereon during permanent custody hearing. In re Roberts (Ohio App. 5 Dist., Guernsey, 06-08-2005) No. 04 CA 29, 2005-Ohio-2843, 2005 WL 1364611, Unreported. Infants ⚖ 243

The Court of Appeals would not review trial court's decision overruling objections to magistrate's award of permanent custody to county and recommending termination of mother's and father's parental rights, where trial court's ruling was not submitted for review. In re Brown (Ohio App. 10 Dist., Franklin, 05-19-2005) No. 03AP-1205, No. 03AP-1206, 2005-Ohio-2425, 2005 WL 1177943, Unreported. Infants ⚖ 248.1

Mother waived for appellate review issue as to whether County Children Services Board (CCSB) violated Americans with Disabilities Act (ADA) by failing to provide mother reasonable accommodations for her personality disorder throughout parental rights termination proceedings, where mother failed to raise issue at trial. In re Ratliff (Ohio App. 10 Dist., Franklin, 03-24-2005) No. 04AP-803, 2005-Ohio-1301, 2005 WL 675798, Unreported, appeal not allowed 106 Ohio St.3d 1417, 830 N.E.2d 348, 2005-Ohio-3154. Infants ⚖ 243

Father's claims challenging trial court's finding at adjudicatory hearing that he had committed acts of domestic violence in presence of children and that he should have been provided with domestic violence counseling were not subject to review on appeal from disposition order terminating parental rights. In re Delfino M. (Ohio App. 6 Dist., Lucas, 01-28-2005) No. L-04-1010, No. L-04-1009, 2005-Ohio-320, 2005 WL 195488, Unreported. Infants ⚖ 248.1

Allowing counselor for dependent and neglected children to discuss diagnosis of children's psychological problems when counselor was not qualified as expert witness was not plain error in proceeding in which permanent custody was granted to department of job and family services, where, before eliciting such testimony from counselor, department established foundation for expert testimony by adducing information as to counselor's education, licensing, and years of work as counselor. In re Katrina T. (Ohio App. 6 Dist., Sandusky, 06-18-2004) No. S-03-024, 2004-Ohio-3164, 2004 WL 1368324, Unreported. Infants ⚖ 243

Whether trial court erred by allowing counselor for dependent and neglected children to discuss diagnosis of children's psychological problems when counselor was not qualified as expert witness could only be reviewed for plain error on appeal from grant of permanent custody to department of job and family services, where mother failed to object at trial to such testimony. In re Katrina T. (Ohio App. 6 Dist., Sandusky, 06-18-2004) No. S-03-024, 2004-Ohio-3164, 2004 WL 1368324, Unreported. Infants ⚖ 243

Remand of trial court order, which granted county children services permanent custody of mother's children, was required for court to issue findings addressing statutory factors to determine best interests of the children, where the court's order was deficient due to trial court's failure to conduct a best interests of the child determination on the record. In re Brooks (Ohio App. 10 Dist., Franklin, 10-07-2003) No. 03AP-282, No. 03AP-442, 2003-Ohio-5348, 2003 WL 22290239, Unreported. Infants ⚖ 210; Infants ⚖ 254

Evidence supported finding that dependent children had been in custody of county children services for twelve months in a 22-month consecutive period, as required to terminate mother's parental rights. In re Brooks (Ohio App. 10 Dist., Franklin, 10-07-2003) No. 03AP-282, No. 03AP-442, 2003-Ohio-5348, 2003 WL 22290239, Unreported. Infants ⚖ 178

An appellate court will not reverse a trial court's determination concerning parental rights and child custody unless the determination is not supported by sufficient evidence to meet the clear and convincing standard of proof; "clear and convincing evidence" is that level of proof which would cause the trier of fact to develop a firm belief or conviction as to the facts sought to be proven. Miller v. Greene Cty. Children's Serv. Bd. (Ohio App. 2 Dist., 08-05-2005) 162 Ohio App.3d 416, 833 N.E.2d 805, 2005-Ohio-4035. Infants ⚖ 252

The standard for appellate review in a permanent custody case is whether the trial court had clear and convincing evidence to make an award of permanent custody. In re Terrence (Ohio App. 6 Dist., 07-13-2005) 162 Ohio App.3d 229, 833 N.E.2d 306, 2005-Ohio-3600. Infants ⚖ 252

2151.415 Motions for dispositional orders; procedure

(A) Except for cases in which a motion for permanent custody described in division (D)(1) of section 2151.413 of the Revised Code is required to be made, a public children services agency or private child placing agency that has been given temporary custody of a child pursuant to section 2151.353 of the Revised Code, not later than thirty days prior to the earlier of the date for the termination of the custody order pursuant to division (F) of section 2151.353 of the Revised Code or the date set at the dispositional hearing for the hearing to be held pursuant to this section, shall file a motion with the court that issued the order of disposition requesting that any of the following orders of disposition of the child be issued by the court:

(1) An order that the child be returned home and the custody of the child's parents, guardian, or custodian without any restrictions;

(2) An order for protective supervision;

(3) An order that the child be placed in the legal custody of a relative or other interested individual;

(4) An order permanently terminating the parental rights of the child's parents;

(5) An order that the child be placed in a planned permanent living arrangement;

(6) In accordance with division (D) of this section, an order for the extension of temporary custody.

(B) Upon the filing of a motion pursuant to division (A) of this section, the court shall hold a dispositional hearing on the date set at the dispositional hearing held pursuant to section 2151.35 of the Revised Code, with notice to all parties to the action in accordance with the Juvenile Rules. After the dispositional hearing or at a date after the dispositional hearing that is not later than one year after the earlier of the date on which the complaint in the case was filed or the child was first placed into shelter care, the court, in accordance with the best interest of the child as supported by the evidence presented at the dispositional hearing, shall issue an order of disposition as set forth in division (A) of this section, except that all orders for permanent custody shall be made in accordance with sections 2151.413 and 2151.414 of the Revised Code. In issuing an order of disposition under this section, the court shall comply with section 2151.42 of the Revised Code.

(C)(1) If an agency pursuant to division (A) of this section requests the court to place a child into a planned permanent living arrangement, the agency shall present evidence to indicate why a planned permanent living arrangement is appropriate for the child, including, but not limited to, evidence that the agency has tried or considered all other possible dispositions for the child. A court shall not place a child in a planned permanent living arrangement, unless it finds, by clear and convincing evidence, that a planned permanent living arrangement is in the best interest of the child and that one of the following exists:

(a) The child, because of physical, mental, or psychological problems or needs, is unable to function in a family-like setting and must remain in residential or institutional care.

(b) The parents of the child have significant physical, mental, or psychological problems and are unable to care for the child because of those problems, adoption is not in the best interest of the child, as determined in accordance with division (D) of section 2151.414 of the Revised Code, and the child retains a significant and positive relationship with a parent or relative;

(c) The child is sixteen years of age or older, has been counseled on the permanent placement options available, is unwilling to accept or unable to adapt to a permanent placement, and is in an agency program preparing for independent living.

(2) If the court issues an order placing a child in a planned permanent living arrangement, both of the following apply:

(a) The court shall issue a finding of fact setting forth the reasons for its finding;

(b) The agency may make any appropriate placement for the child and shall develop a case plan for the child that is designed to assist the child in finding a permanent home outside of the home of the parents.

(D)(1) If an agency pursuant to division (A) of this section requests the court to grant an extension of temporary custody for a period of up to six months, the agency shall include in the motion an explanation of the progress on the case plan of the child and of its expectations of reunifying the child with the child's family, or placing the child in a permanent placement, within the extension period. The court shall schedule a hearing on the motion, give notice of its date, time, and location to all parties and the guardian ad litem of the child, and at the hearing consider the evidence presented by the parties and the guardian ad litem. The court may extend the temporary custody order of the child for a period of up to six months, if it determines at the hearing, by clear and convincing evidence, that the extension is in the best interest of the child, there has been significant progress on the case plan of the child, and there is reasonable cause to believe that the child will be reunified with one of the parents or otherwise permanently placed within the period of extension. In determining whether to extend the temporary custody of the child pursuant to this division, the court shall comply with section 2151.42 of the Revised Code. If the court extends the temporary custody of the child pursuant to this division, upon request it shall issue findings of fact.

(2) Prior to the end of the extension granted pursuant to division (D)(1) of this section, the agency that received the extension shall file a motion with the court requesting the issuance of one of the orders of disposition set forth in divisions (A)(1) to (5) of this section or requesting the court to extend the temporary custody order of the child for an additional period of up to six months. If the agency requests the issuance of an order of disposition under divisions (A)(1) to (5) of this section or does not file any motion prior to the expiration of the extension period, the court shall conduct a hearing in accordance with division (B) of this section and issue an appropriate order of disposition. In issuing an order of disposition, the court shall comply with section 2151.42 of the Revised Code.

If the agency requests an additional extension of up to six months of the temporary custody order of the child, the court shall schedule and conduct a hearing in the manner set forth in division (D)(1) of this section. The court may extend the temporary custody order of the child for an additional period of up to six months if it determines at the hearing, by clear and convincing evidence, that the additional extension is in the best interest of the child, there has been substantial additional progress since the original extension of temporary custody in the case plan of the child, there has been substantial additional progress since the original extension of temporary custody toward reunifying the child with one of the parents or otherwise permanently placing the child, and there is reasonable cause to believe that the child will be reunified with one of the parents or otherwise placed in a permanent setting before the expiration of the additional extension period. In determining whether to grant an additional extension, the court shall comply with section 2151.42 of the Revised Code. If the court extends the temporary custody of the child for an additional period pursuant to this division, upon request it shall issue findings of fact.

(3) Prior to the end of the extension of a temporary custody order granted pursuant to division (D)(2) of this section, the agency that received the extension shall file a motion with the court requesting the issuance of one of the orders of disposition set forth in divisions (A)(1) to (5) of this section. Upon the filing of the motion by the agency or, if the agency does not file the motion prior to the expiration of the extension period, upon its own motion, the court, prior to the expiration of the extension period, shall conduct a hearing in accordance with division (B) of this section and issue an appropriate order of disposition. In issuing an order of disposition, the court shall comply with section 2151.42 of the Revised Code.

(4) No court shall grant an agency more than two extensions of temporary custody pursuant to division (D) of this section.

(E) After the issuance of an order pursuant to division (B) of this section, the court shall retain jurisdiction over the child until the child attains the age of eighteen if the child is not mentally retarded, developmentally disabled, or physically impaired, the child attains the age of twenty-one if the child is mentally retarded, developmentally disabled, or physically impaired, or the child is adopted and a final decree of adoption is issued, unless the court's jurisdiction over the child is extended pursuant to division (E) of section 2151.353 of the Revised Code.

(F) The court, on its own motion or the motion of the agency or person with legal custody of the child, the child's guardian ad litem, or any other party to the action, may conduct a hearing with notice to all parties to determine whether any order issued pursuant to this section should be modified or terminated or whether any other dispositional order set forth in divisions (A)(1) to (5) of this section should be issued. After the hearing and consideration of all the evidence presented, the court, in accordance with the best interest of the child, may modify or terminate any order issued pursuant to this section or issue any dispositional order set forth in divisions (A)(1) to (5) of this section. In rendering a decision under this division, the court shall comply with section 2151.42 of the Revised Code.

(G) If the court places a child in a planned permanent living arrangement with a public children services agency or a private child placing agency pursuant to this section, the agency with which the child is placed in a planned permanent living arrangement shall not remove the child from the residential placement in which the child is originally placed pursuant to the case plan for the child or in which the child is placed with court approval pursuant to this division, unless the court and the guardian ad litem are given notice of the intended removal and the court issues an order approving the removal or unless the removal is necessary to protect the child from physical or emotional harm and the agency gives the court notice of the removal and of the reasons why the removal is necessary to protect the child from physical or emotional harm immediately after the removal of the child from the prior setting.

(H) If the hearing held under this section takes the place of an administrative review that otherwise would have been held under section 2151.416 of the Revised Code, the court at the hearing held under this section shall do all of the following in addition to any other requirements of this section:

(1) Determine the continued necessity for and the appropriateness of the child's placement;

(2) Determine the extent of compliance with the child's case plan;

(3) Determine the extent of progress that has been made toward alleviating or mitigating the causes necessitating the child's placement in foster care;

(4) Project a likely date by which the child may be returned to the child's home or placed for adoption or legal guardianship;

(5) Approve the permanency plan for the child consistent with section 2151.417 of the Revised Code.

(1999 H 176, eff. 10–29–99; 1998 H 484, eff. 3–18–99; 1996 H 274, eff. 8–8–96; 1988 S 89, eff. 1–1–89)

Historical and Statutory Notes

Amendment Note: 1999 H 176 substituted "a planned permanent living arrangement" for "long-term foster care" in the first paragraph in division (C)(2).

Amendment Note: 1998 H 484 inserted "Except for cases in which a motion for permanent custody described in division (D)(1) of section 2151.413 of the Revised Code is required to be made," in the first paragraph in division (A); substituted "a planned permanent living arrangement" for "long-term foster care" throughout divisions (A)(5), (C)(1), and (G); added the third sentence in division (B); added the fourth sentence in division (D)(1); added the third sentence in the first paragraph in division (D)(2); added the third sentence in the second paragraph in division (D)(2); added the third sentence in division (D)(3); added the third sentence in division (F); substituted "Approve the permanency plan for the child consistent with section 2151.417 of the Revised Code" for "Determine the future status of the child" in division (H)(5); and made changes to reflect gender neutral language and other nonsubstantive changes.

Amendment Note: 1996 H 274 substituted "retarded, developmentally disabled, or physically impaired" for "or physically handicapped" twice in division (E); and made changes to reflect gender neutral language.

Library References

Infants ⚖︎17, 197, 221, 222, 226, 230.
Westlaw Topic No. 211.
C.J.S. Adoption of Persons § 10.
C.J.S. Infants §§ 8 to 9, 55, 57, 69 to 85.
Baldwin's Ohio Legislative Service, 1988 Laws of Ohio, S 89—LSC Analysis, p 5–571

Research References

Encyclopedias

OH Jur. 3d Appellate Review § 90, Child Custody.
OH Jur. 3d Family Law § 1602, Prehearing Motions—Motion for Order of Disposition.
OH Jur. 3d Family Law § 1664, on Request for Permanent Custody—Factors to be Considered.
OH Jur. 3d Family Law § 1681, Conduct of Hearing; Advisement of Rights.
OH Jur. 3d Family Law § 1693, Permanent Custody.
OH Jur. 3d Family Law § 1701, Removal from Placement in Long-Term Foster Care.
OH Jur. 3d Family Law § 1703, Generally; Continuing Jurisdiction.
OH Jur. 3d Family Law § 1706, Modification or Vacation of Order.
OH Jur. 3d Family Law § 1711, Review Hearing.

Treatises and Practice Aids

Carlin, Baldwin's Ohio Practice, Merrick-Rippner Probate Law § 107:78, Disposition of Abused, Neglected, or Dependent Child—Temporary Custody.
Carlin, Baldwin's Ohio Practice, Merrick-Rippner Probate Law § 107:79, Disposition of Abused, Neglected, or Dependent Child—Legal Custody.
Carlin, Baldwin's Ohio Practice, Merrick-Rippner Probate Law § 107:80, Disposition of Abused, Neglected, or Dependent Child—Permanent Custody.
Carlin, Baldwin's Ohio Practice, Merrick-Rippner Probate Law § 107:82, Disposition of Abused, Neglected, or Dependent Child—Planned Permanent Living Arrangement.
Carlin, Baldwin's Ohio Practice, Merrick-Rippner Probate Law § 107:118, Modification of Dispositional Orders in Abuse, Neglect, and Dependency Proceedings.
Carlin, Baldwin's Ohio Practice, Merrick-Rippner Probate Law § 107:119, Custody Review Proceedings—Semiannual Administrative Review.
Carlin, Baldwin's Ohio Practice, Merrick-Rippner Probate Law § 107:120, Custody Review Hearing—Juvenile Court Dispositional Review.
Giannelli & Yeomans, Ohio Juvenile Law § 1:7, Juvenile Code.
Giannelli & Yeomans, Ohio Juvenile Law § 2:2, Age Jurisdiction.
Giannelli & Yeomans, Ohio Juvenile Law § 26:6, Goals & Priorities.
Giannelli & Yeomans, Ohio Juvenile Law § 30:6, Temporary Custody.
Giannelli & Yeomans, Ohio Juvenile Law § 31:2, Filing of Motion.
Giannelli & Yeomans, Ohio Juvenile Law § 31:4, Hearings on Permanent Custody Motions.
Giannelli & Yeomans, Ohio Juvenile Law § 31:9, Effect on Parental Rights.
Giannelli & Yeomans, Ohio Juvenile Law § 33:4, Abuse, Neglect, and Dependency Proceedings.
Giannelli & Yeomans, Ohio Juvenile Law § 16:14, Permanent & Temporary Custody Complaints; Planned Permanent Living Arrangements.
Giannelli & Yeomans, Ohio Juvenile Law § 23:13, Burden of Proof.
Giannelli & Yeomans, Ohio Juvenile Law § 25:14, Reasonable Efforts Determination; Abuse, Neglect & Dependency.
Giannelli & Yeomans, Ohio Juvenile Law § 30:10, Permanent Custody—Parental Placement Within Reasonable Time.
Giannelli & Yeomans, Ohio Juvenile Law § 30:13, Planned Permanent Living Arrangement.
Giannelli & Yeomans, Ohio Juvenile Law § 33:10, Child Custody Agency Commitment—Semiannual Administrative Review.
Giannelli & Yeomans, Ohio Juvenile Law § 33:11, Child Custody Agency Commitment—Juvenile Court Dispositional Review.

Notes of Decisions

Constitutional issues 1
Foster care 3
Temporary custody, extension 4
Termination of parental rights 5
Time limitation 2

---

1. Constitutional issues

Mother's procedural due process rights as guaranteed by US Const 14th amendment and O Const Art I § 16 were violated when juvenile court granted guardian ad litem's oral motion to award paternal grandmother legal custody of minor child without first requiring that, prior to the hearing, a written motion be filed by the paternal grandmother, as required by RC 2151.353(A)(3), or by the agency, as required by RC 2151.415(A)(3). In re Fleming, No. 63911, 1993 WL 277186 (8th Dist Ct App, Cuyahoga, 7–22–93).

Mother's due process rights were violated, in suit by county agency to obtain permanent custody of neglected child, when the trial court refused to allow mother to call relatives, who were considered for possible placement of child, to testify at hearing to modify child's disposition, though relatives did not file motion for custody; the parties had notice that relatives were possible custodians for child in advance of the hearing since the court had previously ordered the county job and family services to conduct a home study of relatives, the court had ordered visitation between child and relatives, and the hearing had been continued to provide child with an opportunity to spend more time with relatives, and the trial court permitted job and family services to present lengthy testimony concerning the appropriateness of relatives as a placement alternative at the hearing. In re Beatty (Ohio App. 5 Dist., 07-14-2006) 2006-Ohio-3698, 2006 WL 2022213. Infants ⇨ 230.1

A minor parent's due process rights are not violated by the application the six-month to two-year time frame for reunification of a parent and child on the ground that because minor parents often lack social and emotional maturity necessary to rear a child, the time frame is arbitrary since the six-month to two-year time frame is tightly drawn to attain only the state's interest in the future well being of the child, which dictates that the child not wait any longer than is necessary for parents to assume their rightful responsibilities. In re McCrary (Madison 1991) 75 Ohio App.3d 601, 600 N.E.2d 347, dismissed, jurisdictional motion overruled 64 Ohio St.3d 1427, 594 N.E.2d 969. Constitutional Law ⇨ 274(5); Infants ⇨ 132

2. Time limitation

Temporary custody of children in the care of a children's services agency is limited to a period of two years. In re D.J. (Ohio App. 2 Dist., Montgomery, 12-01-2006) No. 21666, 2006-Ohio-6304, 2006 WL 3462142, Unreported. Infants ⇨ 226

Five and a half month delay between the finding of delinquency and the disposition did not divest the court of jurisdiction; juvenile rule provided that after adjudication a court may continue a matter for disposition for not more than six months, and juvenile did not object to the continuances entered by the court. In re Homan (Ohio App. 5 Dist., Tuscarawas, 01-27-2003) No. 2002AP080067, 2003-Ohio-352, 2003 WL 183811, Unreported. Infants ⇨ 223.1

Juvenile court had the power to grant permanent custody to county, where it found by clear and convincing evidence that it was in child's best interest for county to take permanent custody, and child had been in the temporary custody of the county for well over 12 months in a consecutive 22-month period. In re Sullivan (Ohio App. 12 Dist., Butler, 01-21-2003) No. CA2002-03-061, 2003-Ohio-195, 2003 WL 138665, Unreported. Infants ⇨ 222

The time limitation in RC 2151.415(A) is directory, not mandatory, and, absent a showing of prejudice, failure to file a motion for extension of custody within the time constraints of RC 2151.415(A) is harmless error. In re Amy W. (Ohio App. 4 Dist., Jackson, 01-19-1995) No. 94CA737, 1995 WL 34789, Unreported.

With respect to statute providing that temporary custody order shall terminate one year after the earlier of the date on which the complaint in the case was filed or the child was first placed into shelter care, passing of sunset date does not divest juvenile courts of jurisdiction to enter dispositional orders. Holloway v. Clermont County Dept. of Human Services (Ohio, 10-22-1997) 80 Ohio St.3d 128, 684 N.E.2d 1217, 1997-Ohio-131. Infants ⇨ 222

Juvenile courts retain jurisdiction to issue dispositional order, even though statutory requirement that motion to continue original temporary custody order be filed within one year has not been fulfilled, provided that problems leading to original grant of temporary custody have not been resolved or sufficiently mitigated. In re Young Children (Ohio, 10-09-1996) 76 Ohio St.3d 632, 669 N.E.2d 1140, 1996-Ohio-45. Infants ⇨ 196; Infants ⇨ 197

New one-year limit for filing motion to continue original temporary custody order applies when new complaint is filed based on past facts discovered subsequent to original complaint or upon subsequent facts; new filing is not merely refiling of original complaint. In re Young Children (Ohio, 10-09-1996) 76 Ohio St.3d 632, 669 N.E.2d 1140, 1996-Ohio-45. Infants ⇨ 196; Infants ⇨ 197

Juvenile courts retained jurisdiction to decide untimely dispositional motions and, thus, juvenile courts were required to determine whether problems leading to original grant of temporary custody had been resolved or sufficiently mitigated when temporary custody order expired. In re Young Children (Ohio, 10-09-1996) 76 Ohio St.3d 632, 669 N.E.2d 1140, 1996-Ohio-45. Infants ⇨ 196; Infants ⇨ 197

Juvenile court retained jurisdiction to make dispositional order in best interests of child while problems that led to original grant of temporary custody had not been resolved or sufficiently mitigated, even though statutory requirement that motion to continue temporary custody order be filed within one year from date complaint was filed or child is first placed in temporary custody was violated. In re Young Children (Ohio, 10-09-1996) 76 Ohio St.3d 632, 669 N.E.2d 1140, 1996-Ohio-45. Infants ⇨ 196; Infants ⇨ 197

Statutory time periods for grant of temporary custody of child to public children's services agency and extension of temporary custody are mandatory, and failure to comply results in loss of authority by trial court to make any order as to custody of child until that authority has been reinvoked by filing of a new complaint. In re Omosun Children (Ohio App. 11 Dist., 10-16-1995) 106 Ohio App.3d 813, 667 N.E.2d 431. Infants ⇨ 193

If failure to render final dispositional order in dependency proceeding within required statutory two-year period can be attributed to existence of extenuating circumstances, it is not necessary for public children's services agency to give custody of child back to parents prior to filing of new complaint, i.e., agency's temporary custody of child can be continuous throughout entire period, and only instance in which child must be returned to parents is when failure of juvenile court and agency to comply with two-year limit cannot be explained by extenuating circumstances and purpose of filing new complaint is simply to circumvent statutory requirement. In re Omosun Children (Ohio App. 11 Dist., 10-16-1995) 106 Ohio App.3d 813, 667 N.E.2d 431. Infants ⇨ 222

Requirement that county children services board's motion to extend temporary custody be filed at least 30 days before temporary custody would expire was directory, rather than mandatory, and therefore failure to file within 30 days constituted no more than harmless error. Endsley v. Endsley (Wayne 1993) 89 Ohio App.3d 306, 624 N.E.2d 270. Infants ⇨ 230.1; Infants ⇨ 253

The county department of human services loses jurisdiction over neglected children, and cannot grant permanent custody to the department, where the "sunset" date lapsed before the ruling on the department's motion for permanent custody, which is improperly filed less than thirty days prior to the "sunset" date. In re Travis Children (Stark 1992) 80 Ohio App.3d 620, 609 N.E.2d 1356.

If a juvenile court commits to the temporary custody of a public children services agency a child who has been adjudicated to be unruly or delinquent pursuant to RC 2151.354(A)(1) or RC 2152.19(A)(1), respectively, the duration of the temporary custody order is subject to the time limitations set forth in RC 2151.353(F) and RC 2151.415. OAG 03-004.

A juvenile court retains jurisdiction over a child who has been adjudicated to be unruly or delinquent until the child attains twenty-one years of age, and may continue to make dispositional orders with respect to the child until that time, regardless of whether the court's order of temporary custody has expired under the time limitations set forth in RC 2151.353(F) and RC 2151.415. OAG 03-004.

3. Foster care

Evidence supported juvenile court's decision to grant foster parents' motion for legal custody of child who had been found dependent and removed from his biological parents' care, despite competing motion from child's paternal uncle and aunt; child was very young and had been in the foster parents' care since he was first placed in temporary custody, child had not established a relationship with uncle and aunt, and child had developed a strong bond with foster parents. In re Halstead (Ohio App. 7 Dist., Columbiana, 01-27-2005) No. 04 CO 37, 2005-Ohio-403, 2005 WL 289576, Unreported. Infants ⇨ 230.1

Phrase "is sixteen years of age or older," as used in foster care statute authorizing long-term placement to be based on child's opinion, refers to child who is at least sixteen when he or she expresses opinion, as opposed to when placement determination is made. In re Bacorn (Ohio App. 11 Dist., 12-23-1996) 116 Ohio App.3d 489, 688 N.E.2d 575. Infants ⇨ 154.1

Long-term foster care placement must be based on clear and convincing evidence that such disposition is in child's best interest and that statutory grounds for such placement exist. In re Bacorn (Ohio App. 11 Dist., 12-23-1996) 116 Ohio App.3d 489, 688 N.E.2d 575. Infants ⇨ 177

Trial court abused its discretion by relying solely on doctor's testimony to support determination that long-term foster care was in child's best interest, where doctor testified on two occasions that she had not seen child in two months and did not feel that she could make a knowledgeable recommendation as to whether child could be returned to her parents' home, or to any family-like setting. In re Bacorn (Ohio App. 11 Dist., 12-23-1996) 116 Ohio App.3d 489, 688 N.E.2d 575. Infants ⇨ 177

Trial court must issue findings of fact supporting determination that foster care is in child's best interests. In re Bacorn (Ohio App. 11 Dist., 12-23-1996) 116 Ohio App.3d 489, 688 N.E.2d 575. Infants ⇨ 210

Reviewing court could not sustain foster care placement supported by findings that were expressly based solely on stale expert testimony, even though there was other clear and convincing evidence in the record as a whole that supported placement. In re Bacorn (Ohio App. 11 Dist., 12-23-1996) 116 Ohio App.3d 489, 688 N.E.2d 575. Infants ⚖ 210; Infants ⚖ 253

A trial court does not err in failing to place a child in long-term foster care under RC 2151.353 pursuant to a county children services agency's RC 2151.413 motion for permanent custody where it grants such permanent custody to the agency; long–term foster care only becomes an alternative, by operation of RC 2151.415, where the motion for permanent custody is denied. In re McDaniel, No. 92–CA–359 (4th Dist Ct App, Adams, 2–11–93).

4. Temporary custody, extension

Trial court abused its discretion in denying mother's request for a six-month extension of county's temporary custody of children so that she could continue working on her case plan, in termination of parental rights proceeding, as mother had made significant progress on her case plan, and there was reasonable cause to believe that the children could be reunified with her within the period of extension. In re E.T. (Ohio App. 9 Dist., Summit, 05-17-2006) No. 23017, 2006-Ohio-2413, 2006 WL 1329653, Unreported. Infants ⚖ 230.1

Trial court did not abuse its discretion in denying father's request for a six-month extension of county's temporary custody of children so that he could continue working on his case plan, in termination of parental rights proceeding, as father did not make significant progress on his case plan, and there was no reason to believe that he would remedy his parenting problems within the next six months. In re E.T. (Ohio App. 9 Dist., Summit, 05-17-2006) No. 23017, 2006-Ohio-2413, 2006 WL 1329653, Unreported. Infants ⚖ 230.1

The trial court's denial of mother and father's motion for a six-month extension of temporary custody was an abuse of discretion, in child dependency proceeding, where the trial court erroneously determined that mother and father's children had been in the temporary custody of county children services board (CSB) for more than 12 of the previous 22 months, when actually the children had been in the custody of CSB for less than nine months when the motion for permanent custody was filed. In re E.T. (Ohio App. 9 Dist., Summit, 11-16-2005) No. 22720, 2005-Ohio-6087, 2005 WL 3050991, Unreported. Infants ⚖ 230.1

Passing of two-year statutory time period during which trial court could issue temporary custody orders and extensions of temporary custody orders with respect to dependent child did not divest juvenile court of jurisdiction to enter dispositional order granting permanent custody to county children services board; portion of delay arose from fact that appeal was taken from dependency adjudication and prior permanent custody award, and statute provides that juvenile court retains jurisdiction over dependent children to ensure their safety and proper treatment until they become adults. In re M.B. (Ohio App. 9 Dist., Summit, 10-27-2004) No. 22103, 2004-Ohio-5686, 2004 WL 2390987, Unreported. Infants ⚖ 196

A juvenile court does not lose jurisdiction to enter dispositional orders upon technical termination of temporary custody due to the expiration of the sunset date, especially where the problems that led to removal are unresolved. In re Hess (Ohio App. 7 Dist., Jefferson, 03-21-2003) No. 02 JE 37, 2003-Ohio-1429, 2003 WL 1465190, Unreported. Infants ⚖ 192

Juvenile court's "temporary custody" order, which continued proceedings on pending motion for permanent custody, was not an extension of temporary custody, and, thus, no new reunification case plan was required. In re Ware (Ohio App. 2 Dist., Montgomery, 10-16-2002) No. 19302, 2002-Ohio-6086, 2002 WL 31492584, Unreported. Infants ⚖ 231

Mother waived her contention that juvenile court lacked authority to extend, sua sponte, agency's temporary custody of four siblings, two of whom had been adjudicated neglected and two of whom had been adjudicated dependent, where extension was final appealable order and mother failed to appeal therefrom. In re Nice (Ohio App. 7 Dist., 03-20-2001) 141 Ohio App.3d 445, 751 N.E.2d 552, 2001-Ohio-3214. Infants ⚖ 242

Juvenile court was not required to schedule and notice separate hearing on extension of temporary custody of children following hearing on state's petition for permanent and legal custody, where agency had not requested extension of temporary custody, and where evidence at hearing on permanent and legal custody persuaded court that factors for extending temporary custody existed; mother was on notice, as result of prior hearing, that state wished to permanently terminate her parental rights with regard to two children and give legal custody of the other two children to a relative, and had opportunity to be heard on propriety of such dispositions. In re Nice (Ohio App. 7 Dist., 03-20-2001) 141 Ohio App.3d 445, 751 N.E.2d 552, 2001-Ohio-3214. Infants ⚖ 230.1

Where an agency requests an extension of temporary custody or the court wishes to extend temporary custody sua sponte where no other proceedings are occurring in the case, then the parent is entitled to notice and a hearing on the extension. In re Nice (Ohio App. 7 Dist., 03-20-2001) 141 Ohio App.3d 445, 751 N.E.2d 552, 2001-Ohio-3214. Infants ⚖ 230.1

Where public children services agency did not have requisite grant of temporary custody, instead of filing postdispositional motion for permanent custody, agency should have sought grant of temporary custody by asking court to modify its disposition terminating agency's grant of temporary custody or by filing a new complaint based on more recent allegations of abuse or on dependency theory. In re Miller (Ohio App. 2 Dist., 02-15-1995) 101 Ohio App.3d 199, 655 N.E.2d 252. Infants ⚖ 230.1

Parents were not prejudiced by failure of county children services board to include explanation of progress made under case plan and expectations for reunification in its motions to extend temporary custody, where parents were given notice of hearing and were afforded opportunity to appear, and court's decision to extend temporary custody was made in accordance with prescribed standard. Endsley v. Endsley (Wayne 1993) 89 Ohio App.3d 306, 624 N.E.2d 270. Infants ⚖ 253

Trial court's failure to hold hearing on county children services board's motion requesting a second six-month extension of its temporary custody of child before denying motion violated statute requiring court to do so, and required reversal of order granting permanent custody of child to board. In re collins (Ohio App. 9 Dist., Summit, 05-22-2002) No. CA20864, 2002-Ohio-2436, 2002 WL 1065681, Unreported. Infants ⚖ 203; Infants ⚖ 254

5. Termination of parental rights

County social worker's alleged conduct in thwarting parents' attempts to have children returned to parents' home, after children were removed due to unsanitary conditions, and in effectively denying parents prompt hearing on children's placement did not rise to the level of conscience-shocking behavior, and thus did not support substantive due process claim. Smith v. Williams-Ash (C.A.6 (Ohio), 12-06-2005) No. 04-4547, 173 Fed.Appx. 363, 2005 WL 3304101, Unreported. Infants ⚖ 17

County social worker should have known that her alleged conduct in thwarting parents' attempts to have children returned to parents' home, after children were removed due to unsanitary conditions, and in effectively denying parents prompt hearing on children's placement had effect of violating parents' clearly established rights to procedural due process by involuntarily depriving parents of physical custody of children, and therefore qualified immunity did not apply to preclude social worker's liability under §§ 1983. Smith v. Williams-Ash (C.A.6 (Ohio), 12-06-2005) No. 04-4547, 173 Fed.Appx. 363, 2005 WL 3304101, Unreported. Civil Rights ⚖ 1376(4)

Allegations that parents whose children were removed from home by county social worker were not allowed to recover children after safety plan providing for children's placement with friends had been initiated, despite parents' best efforts to do so, that continued deprivation of children was involuntary, and that parents were effectively denied prompt hearing on children's placement supported claim against social worker for violating parents' procedural due process rights. Smith v. Williams-Ash (C.A.6 (Ohio), 12-06-2005) No. 04-4547, 173 Fed.Appx. 363, 2005 WL 3304101, Unreported. Infants ⚖ 17

Awarding legal custody of abused child to paternal aunt and uncle was in child's best interests; child was five months old when removed from home after suffering fractures to both legs, child had lived outside home for 18 months at time of hearing, guardian ad litem and child's natural father recommended that aunt and uncle be awarded legal custody, child was in need of legally secured placement, child had bonded with aunt and uncle, and aunt and uncle were willing to provide child with stable and financially secure home environment. In re Starks (Ohio App. 2 Dist., Darke, 04-15-2005) No. 1646, 2005-Ohio-1912, 2005 WL 939851, Unreported. Infants ⚖ 222

Evidence supported determination that mother did not substantially comply with case plan for reunification, as grounds for granting legal custody of child adjudicated abused to paternal aunt and uncle, despite evidence that mother obtained and maintained suitable housing and complete parenting classes; mother did not obtain and maintain employment when medically able to do so, mother had not paid any court-ordered child support, mother attended court-ordered counseling on sporadic basis and had unresolved issues concerning impulse control and self-esteem, and mother failed to discontinue relationship with boyfriend who allegedly contributed to abuse of child that resulted in fractures to both legs, despite court order to do so. In re Starks (Ohio App. 2 Dist., Darke, 04-15-2005) No. 1646, 2005-Ohio-1912, 2005 WL 939851, Unreported. Infants ⚖ 155

Finding that abused child could not safely be returned to mother, as grounds for awarding legal custody to paternal aunt and uncle, was supported by evidence that results of mother's psychological exam revealed that mother was under great deal of stress and was at risk of engaging in physical and psychological abuse of children, and that mother continued to associate with boyfriend who was alleged to have played role in abuse which resulted in fractures to both of child's legs, despite court order that she discontinue contact with boyfriend. In re Starks (Ohio App. 2 Dist., Darke, 04-15-2005) No. 1646, 2005-Ohio-1912, 2005 WL 939851, Unreported. Infants ⚖ 158

Trial court order granting permanent custody of the children to county department of children and family services, rather than placing the children in a planned permanent living arrangement, was proper; there was no evidence that the children could not function in a family-like setting, there was no evidence that the children had a positive or significant relationship with father, and both children were under 16 years of age. In re B.R. (Ohio App. 8 Dist., Cuyahoga, 07-22-2004) No. 83674, 2004-Ohio-3865, 2004 WL 1630507, Unreported. Infants ⚖ 226

Trial court, in proceeding in which county children services agency sought permanent custody of delinquent child, did not abuse its discretion in finding that a planned permanent living arrangement (PPLA), rather than permanent custody, was in child's best interests. In re Beasley (Ohio App. 4 Dist., Scioto, 06-25-2003) No. 03CA2881, 2003-Ohio-3462, 2003 WL 21500016, Unreported. Infants ⚖ 222

Clear and convincing evidence supported finding that awarding children county services agency permanent custody of child, who had been previously adjudicated delinquent, was in child's best interests; evidence revealed that child had some history of committing sex offenses against other children, mother adamantly refused to allow the child to return to her home absent a "written guarantee" that he would not re-offend, and child had been in custody of county children services agency for over two years. In re Beasley (Ohio App. 4 Dist., Scioto, 06-25-2003) No. 03CA2881, 2003-Ohio-3462, 2003 WL 21500016, Unreported. Infants ⚖ 155

Evidence supported finding that granting permanent custody of mother's two children to the county job and family services agency would be in the best interest of the children; while children were in agency custody, warrants were issued for the arrest of their parents, both parents fled from the state, after both parents were arrested mother was sentenced to serve a four year and nine months sentence for attempted manufacturing of drugs, mother never provided any support for the children or assisted the agency in developing a caseplan, and while mother was out of state she made no attempts to contact her children. In re Billingsley (Ohio App. 3 Dist., Putnam, 01-28-2003) No. 12-02-07, No. 12-02-08, 2003-Ohio-344, 2003 WL 178661, Unreported. Infants ⚖ 157

Clear and convincing evidence supported determination that child could not be placed with father within reasonable time, for purposes of award of permanent custody to county children services board; record showed father failed to complete programs for substance abuse and domestic violence, and that he did not secure permanent housing, but continued to reside in the homes of various women. In re S.S. (Ohio App. 2 Dist., Montgomery, 01-24-2003) No. 19406, 2003-Ohio-319, 2003 WL 164598, Unreported. Infants ⚖ 178

Substantial evidence supported termination of mother's parental rights and award of permanent custody of children to county department of job and family services; mother admitted that she failed to complete parenting program or to undergo counseling, and mother was early into three-year prison sentence for child endangering. In re Mastache Children (Ohio App. 5 Dist., Stark, 01-21-2003) No. 2002CA00360, 2003-Ohio-260, 2003 WL 157330, Unreported. Infants ⚖ 156

Clear and convincing evidence supported termination of father's parental rights; children had been in custody of county department of children and family services for over three years, father failed to follow and complete his proposed case plan which ordered him to participate in substance abuse treatment and stay drug free, submit to random drug tests, complete parenting classes, and maintain stable employment, father demonstrated a lack of commitment toward children by failing to regularly support, visit, or communicate with them when able to do so, and he was unable to provide food, clothing, shelter, and other basic necessities for children. (Per O'Donnell, J., with two judges concurring in judgment only.) In re Harlston (Ohio App. 8 Dist., Cuyahoga, 01-23-2003) No. 80672, 2003-Ohio-282, 2003 WL 152939, Unreported, appeal not allowed 98 Ohio St.3d 1492, 785 N.E.2d 474, 2003-Ohio-1189. Infants ⚖ 155; Infants ⚖ 157

Trial court lacked authority to place children in a Planned Permanent Living Arrangement (PPLA) as an alternative to terminating father's parental rights; there was no evidence to suggest that father or county department of children and family services sought a PPLA, and there was no evidence presented to establish any of the other statutory requirements necessary for court to place children in a PPLA. (Per O'Donnell, J., with two judges concurring in judgment only). In re Harlston (Ohio App. 8 Dist., Cuyahoga, 01-23-2003) No. 80672, 2003-Ohio-282, 2003 WL 152939, Unreported, appeal not allowed 98 Ohio St.3d 1492, 785 N.E.2d 474, 2003-Ohio-1189. Infants ⚖ 226

The juvenile court has jurisdiction to hear a motion to terminate parental rights of a natural parent who is mentally retarded and functions at the level of a five- or six-year-old where the motion is made by the parties having legal custody of the child and the child remains in their custody without any change to the child's legal status. In re Bennett (Ohio App. 1 Dist., Hamilton, 11-15-1995) No. C-950035, 1995 WL 675968, Unreported.

Statute governing modification or termination of custody order regarding dependent child, not statute governing disposition of dependent child, applied to motion for permanent custody that was filed by county children services board (CSB); motion did not concern initial dispositional order following adjudication of dependency, but instead concerned modification of temporary-custody order after first six-month extension. In re A.S. (Ohio App. 9 Dist., 10-05-2005) 2005-Ohio-5309, 2005 WL 2446074. Infants ⚖ 230.1

Trial court had authority to consider dispositional option of planned permanent living arrangement (PPLA) when deciding whether to terminate mother's parental rights and grant permanent custody to county children services board (CSB), even though CSB never requested PPLA option; court, not CSB, had authority to make ultimate decision about disposition, statute governing initial disposition did not apply since court was considering modifying temporary-custody order after first six-month extension, and PPLA was one of dispositional alternatives available to court. In re A.S. (Ohio App. 9 Dist., 10-05-2005) 2005-Ohio-5309, 2005 WL 2446074. Infants ⚖ 230.1

Trial court's standard of review of a petition for legal custody not involving a termination of parental rights is not clear and convincing evidence, as it is in a permanent custody proceeding, but is merely preponderance of the evidence; legal custody where parental rights are not terminated is not as drastic a remedy as permanent custody. In re Nice (Ohio App. 7 Dist., 03-20-2001) 141 Ohio App.3d 445, 751 N.E.2d 552, 2001-Ohio-3214. Child Custody ⚖ 914

Clear and convincing evidence in child protection proceedings established that permanent custody of children previously adjudicated neglected was in children's best interests; mother and her husband failed to comply with their case plans, mother refused to acknowledge her husband's abuse of the children and his problem with anger control, injuries inflicted upon children by mother's husband had been severe, and children had been in agency's temporary custody for more than 12 months. In re Nice (Ohio App. 7 Dist., 03-20-2001) 141 Ohio App.3d 445, 751 N.E.2d 552, 2001-Ohio-3214. Infants ⚖ 178

Preponderance of the evidence supported juvenile court's award of legal custody of children adjudicated dependent to their paternal grandmother; guardian ad litem recommended that legal custody be given to grandmother, children's father had no objection to such arrangement, mother's husband had not completed recommended anger management counseling, children's twin siblings had been abused, mother refused to acknowledge that abuse had occurred, and evidence offered without objection established that children were in fear of their mother's husband due to inappropriate physical contact and that mother had characterized such contact as "just playing." In re Nice (Ohio App. 7 Dist., 03-20-2001) 141 Ohio App.3d 445, 751 N.E.2d 552, 2001-Ohio-3214. Infants ⚖ 179

Any error in juvenile court's finding, in proceedings on agency's second motion for permanent custody of children adjudicated neglected, that children could or should not be returned to either parent within reasonable time, was harmless, where clear and convincing evidence demonstrating that children had been in agency's temporary custody for more than 12 months was sufficient to support award of permanent custody to agency. In re Nice (Ohio App. 7 Dist., 03-20-2001) 141 Ohio App.3d 445, 751 N.E.2d 552, 2001-Ohio-3214. Infants ⚖ 253

Trial court's decision to terminate mother's parental rights and to grant legal custody of child to foster mother was supported by the evidence contained in the record and was in the best interest of the child; mother, who had limited parenting skills, told her doctors that she only took her psychotropic medication to get her child back and that, once reunified, she would discontinue her medication because she did not believe she suffered from any mental illness, and she abducted child from foster parents' home in violation of existing court orders and voluntarily absconded from court's jurisdiction to China. In re Zhang (Ohio App. 8 Dist., 06-10-1999) 135

Ohio App.3d 350, 734 N.E.2d 379, dismissed, appeal not allowed 87 Ohio St.3d 1417, 717 N.E.2d 1105, reconsideration stricken 87 Ohio St.3d 1437, 719 N.E.2d 2. Infants ⇌ 178; Infants ⇌ 226

In action to terminate parental rights, guardian ad litem's report was hearsay and could not be considered evidence, where report was not submitted under oath and guardian did not testify and was not subjected to direct or cross-examination. Matter of Duncan/Walker Children (Ohio App. 5 Dist., 03-18-1996) 109 Ohio App.3d 841, 673 N.E.2d 217. Infants ⇌ 174

2151.416 Administrative review of case plans

(A) Each agency that is required by section 2151.412 of the Revised Code to prepare a case plan for a child shall complete a semiannual administrative review of the case plan no later than six months after the earlier of the date on which the complaint in the case was filed or the child was first placed in shelter care. After the first administrative review, the agency shall complete semiannual administrative reviews no later than every six months. If the court issues an order pursuant to section 2151.414 or 2151.415 of the Revised Code, the agency shall complete an administrative review no later than six months after the court's order and continue to complete administrative reviews no later than every six months after the first review, except that the court hearing held pursuant to section 2151.417 of the Revised Code may take the place of any administrative review that would otherwise be held at the time of the court hearing. When conducting a review, the child's health and safety shall be the paramount concern.

(B) Each administrative review required by division (A) of this section shall be conducted by a review panel of at least three persons, including, but not limited to, both of the following:

(1) A caseworker with day-to-day responsibility for, or familiarity with, the management of the child's case plan;

(2) A person who is not responsible for the management of the child's case plan or for the delivery of services to the child or the parents, guardian, or custodian of the child.

(C) Each semiannual administrative review shall include, but not be limited to, a joint meeting by the review panel with the parents, guardian, or custodian of the child, the guardian ad litem of the child, and the child's foster care provider and shall include an opportunity for those persons to submit any written materials to be included in the case record of the child. If a parent, guardian, custodian, guardian ad litem, or foster care provider of the child cannot be located after reasonable efforts to do so or declines to participate in the administrative review after being contacted, the agency does not have to include them in the joint meeting.

(D) The agency shall prepare a written summary of the semiannual administrative review that shall include, but not be limited to, all of the following:

(1) A conclusion regarding the safety and appropriateness of the child's foster care placement;

(2) The extent of the compliance with the case plan of all parties;

(3) The extent of progress that has been made toward alleviating the circumstances that required the agency to assume temporary custody of the child;

(4) An estimated date by which the child may be returned to and safely maintained in the child's home or placed for adoption or legal custody;

(5) An updated case plan that includes any changes that the agency is proposing in the case plan;

(6) The recommendation of the agency as to which agency or person should be given custodial rights over the child for the six-month period after the administrative review;

(7) The names of all persons who participated in the administrative review.

(E) The agency shall file the summary with the court no later than seven days after the completion of the administrative review. If the agency proposes a change to the case plan as a result of the administrative review, the agency shall file the proposed change with the court at the time it files the summary. The agency shall give notice of the summary and proposed change in writing before the end of the next day after filing them to all parties and the child's guardian ad litem. All parties and the guardian ad litem shall have seven days after the date the notice is sent to object to and request a hearing on the proposed change.

(1) If the court receives a timely request for a hearing, the court shall schedule a hearing pursuant to section 2151.417 of the Revised Code to be held not later than thirty days after the court receives the request. The court shall give notice of the date, time, and location of the hearing to all parties and the guardian ad litem. The agency may implement the proposed change after the hearing, if the court approves it. The agency shall not implement the proposed change unless it is approved by the court.

(2) If the court does not receive a timely request for a hearing, the court may approve the proposed change without a hearing. If the court approves the proposed change without a hearing, it shall journalize the case plan with the change not later than fourteen days after the change is filed with the court. If the court does not approve the proposed change to the case plan, it shall schedule a review hearing to be held pursuant to section 2151.417 of the Revised Code no later than thirty days after the expiration of the fourteen-day time period and give notice of the date, time, and location of the hearing to all parties and the guardian ad litem of the child. If, despite the requirements of this division and division (D) of section 2151.417 of the Revised Code, the court neither approves and journalizes the proposed change nor conducts a hearing, the agency may implement the proposed change not earlier than fifteen days after it is submitted to the court.

(F) The director of job and family services may adopt rules pursuant to Chapter 119. of the Revised Code for procedures and standard forms for conducting administrative reviews pursuant to this section.

(G) The juvenile court that receives the written summary of the administrative review, upon determining, either from the written summary, case plan, or otherwise, that the custody or care arrangement is not in the best interest of the child, may terminate the custody of an agency and place the child in the custody of another institution or association certified by the department of job and family services under section 5103.03 of the Revised Code.

(2006 S 238, eff. 9–21–06; 2005 H 66, eff. 6–30–05; 1999 H 471, eff. 7–1–00; 1998 H 484, eff. 3–18–99; 1996 H 274, eff. 8–8–96; 1996 H 419, eff. 9–18–96; 1988 S 89, eff. 1–1–89)

Uncodified Law

1988 S 89, § 4: See Uncodified Law under 2151.414.

Historical and Statutory Notes

Ed. Note: 2151.416 is former 5103.151 amended and recodified by 1988 S 89, eff. 1–1–89; 1986 H 428; 1980 H 695; 1978 H 832; 1976 H 156.

Amendment Note: 2006 S 238 deleted division (H), which prior thereto read:

"(H) The department of job and family services shall report annually to the public and to the general assembly on the results of the review of case plans of each agency. The annual report shall include any information that is required by the department, including, but not limited to, all of the following:

"(1) A statistical analysis of the administrative reviews conducted pursuant to this section and section 2151.417 of the Revised Code;

"(2) The number of children in temporary or permanent custody for whom an administrative review was conducted, the number of children whose custody status changed during the period, the number of children whose residential placement changed during the period, and the number of residential placement changes for each child during the period;

"(3) An analysis of the utilization of public social services by agencies and parents or guardians, and the utilization of the adoption listing service of the department pursuant to section 5103.154 of the Revised Code."

Amendment Note: 2005 H 66 deleted "and on the results of the summaries submitted to the department under section 3107.10 of the Revised Code" in the first paragraph of division (H); deleted division (H)(4), which read: "(4) A compilation and analysis of data submitted to the department under section 3107.10 of the Revised Code"; and made other nonsubstantive changes.

Amendment Note: 1999 H 471 substituted "director of job and family services" for "department of human services" in division (F); and substituted "job and family" for "human" in divisions (G) and (H).

Amendment Note: 1998 H 484 added the fourth sentence in division (A); inserted "safety and" in division (D)(1); and inserted "and safely maintained in" in division (D)(4).

Amendment Note: 1996 H 274 rewrote division (E), which prior thereto read:

"(E)(1) If the agency, the parents, guardian, or custodian of the child, and the guardian ad litem and the attorney of the child agree to the need for changes in the case plan of the child and the terms of the changes, the revised case plan shall be signed by all parties and the guardian ad litem of the child and filed with the court together with the written summary of the administrative review no later than seven days after the completion of the administrative review. If the court does not object to the revised case plan, it shall journalize the case plan, within fourteen days after it is filed with the court. The agency may implement the proposed changes fourteen days after they are submitted to the court for approval, unless the court schedules a hearing under section 2151.417 of the Revised Code to consider the proposed changes. If the court does not approve of the revised case plan, it shall schedule a review hearing to be held pursuant to section 2151.417 of the Revised Code no later than thirty days after the filing of the case plan and written summary and give notice of the date, time, and location of the hearing to all parties and the guardian ad litem of the child.

"(2) If the agency, the parents, guardian, or custodian of the child, and the guardian ad litem and the attorney of the child do not agree to the need for changes to the case plan and to all of the proposed changes, the agency shall file its written summary of the administrative review with the court no later than seven days after the completion of the administrative review and request the court to conduct a review hearing pursuant to section 2151.417 of the Revised Code. The court shall schedule the hearing to be held no later than thirty days after the written summary was filed with the court and shall give notice of the date, time, and location of the hearing to all parties and the guardian ad litem of the child."

Amendment Note: 1996 H 419 substituted "the child's" for "his" in division (D)(4); substituted "institution or association certified by the department of human services under section 5103.03 of the Revised Code." for "public or private organization, society, association, agency, or individual certified pursuant to sections 5103.02 and 5103.03 of the Revised Code." in division (G); and substituted "5103.154" for "5103.152" in division (H)(3).

Ohio Administrative Code References

PCSA requirements for completing the case review, OAC 5101:2–38–09
Requirements for a semiannual administrative review, OAC 5101:2–38–10
Requirements of semiannual administrative review, OAC 5101:2–42–43

Library References

Infants ⊱17, 230.1.
Westlaw Topic No. 211.
C.J.S. Adoption of Persons § 10.
C.J.S. Infants §§ 8 to 9, 57, 69 to 85.

Baldwin's Ohio Legislative Service, 1996 H 274—LSC Analysis, p 5/L-697

Baldwin's Ohio Legislative Service, 1988 Laws of Ohio, S 89—LSC Analysis, p 5–571

Research References

Encyclopedias

OH Jur. 3d Family Law § 1429, Administrative Review.
OH Jur. 3d Family Law § 1602, Prehearing Motions—Motion for Order of Disposition.
OH Jur. 3d Family Law § 1633, Emergency Medical Care.
OH Jur. 3d Family Law § 1711, Review Hearing.

Treatises and Practice Aids

Carlin, Baldwin's Ohio Practice, Merrick-Rippner Probate Law § 98:16, Adoption—Types of Placement—Agency Adoptions—Administrative Review of Case Plans—Children Subject to Review.

Carlin, Baldwin's Ohio Practice, Merrick-Rippner Probate Law § 98:17, Adoption—Types of Placement—Agency Adoptions—Timing of Review.

Carlin, Baldwin's Ohio Practice, Merrick-Rippner Probate Law § 98:18, Adoption—Types of Placement—Agency Adoptions—Contents of Review.

Carlin, Baldwin's Ohio Practice, Merrick-Rippner Probate Law § 98:19, Adoption—Types of Placement—Agency Adoptions—Evaluation of Review.

Carlin, Baldwin's Ohio Practice, Merrick-Rippner Probate Law § 107:119, Custody Review Proceedings—Semiannual Administrative Review.

Giannelli & Yeomans, Ohio Juvenile Law § 1:7, Juvenile Code.

Giannelli & Yeomans, Ohio Juvenile Law § 33:10, Child Custody Agency Commitment—Semiannual Administrative Review.

Notes of Decisions

In general 1
Parties 2

1. In general

Trial court's denial of mother's motion to dismiss county agency's second motion for permanent custody of children did not deprive mother of opportunity to achieve goals of case plan, thus supporting termination of parental rights, even though county's second motion was filed before expiration of 4-month period allowed for reunification in order denying county's first motion for permanent custody; mother had two years to complete her case plans, plans were frequently modified in order to meet mother's need for psychological counseling and to reunify her with her children, and order denying agency's first motion for permanent custody was not a final, appealable order, but was subject to change and reconsideration at any time. In re Rachel K. & Glorietta K. (Ohio App. 6 Dist., Lucas, 09-30-2004) No. L-03-1061, 2004-Ohio-5239, 2004 WL 2334172, Unreported. Infants ⊱ 202

If a juvenile court, in making disposition of an unruly or delinquent child pursuant to RC 2151.354 or RC 2151.355, places the child into the temporary custody of the county department of human services in accordance with RC 2151.353 and the department provides services to that child, the county department of human services is required to develop and file with the court a case plan pursuant to RC 2151.412 and to hold semiannual reviews of the case plan pursuant to RC 2151.416. OAG 99–041.

2. Parties

Foster parents of a dependent child are proper parties to seek review of a dispositional judgment concerning placement of the foster child in their care. In re Moorehead (Montgomery 1991) 75 Ohio App.3d 711, 600 N.E.2d 778.

2151.417 Review by court issuing dispositional orders

(A) Any court that issues a dispositional order pursuant to section 2151.353, 2151.414, or 2151.415 of the Revised Code may review at any time the child's placement or custody arrangement, the case plan prepared for the child pursuant to section 2151.412 of the Revised Code, the actions of the public children services agency or private child placing agency in implementing that case plan, the child's permanency plan, if the child's permanency plan has been approved and any other aspects of the child's placement or custody arrangement. In conducting the review, the court shall determine the appropriateness of any agency actions, the safety and appropriateness of continuing the child's placement or custody arrangement, and whether any changes should be made with respect to the child's permanency plan or placement or custody arrangement or with respect to the actions of the agency under the child's placement or custody arrangement. Based upon the evidence presented at a hearing held after notice to all parties and the guardian ad litem of the child, the court may require the agency, the parents, guardian, or custodian of the child, and the physical custodians of the child to take any reasonable action that the court determines is necessary and in the best interest of the child or to discontinue any action that it determines is not in the best interest of the child.

(B) If a court issues a dispositional order pursuant to section 2151.353, 2151.414, or 2151.415 of the Revised Code, the court has continuing jurisdiction over the child as set forth in division (E)(1) of section 2151.353 of the Revised Code. The court may amend a dispositional order in accordance with division (E)(2) of section 2151.353 of the Revised Code at any time upon its own motion or upon the motion of any interested party. The court shall comply with section 2151.42 of the Revised Code in amending any dispositional order pursuant to this division.

(C) Any court that issues a dispositional order pursuant to section 2151.353, 2151.414, or 2151.415 of the Revised Code shall hold a review hearing one year after the earlier of the date on which the complaint in the case was filed or the child was first placed into shelter care to review the case plan prepared pursuant to section 2151.412 of the Revised Code and the child's placement or custody arrangement, to approve or review the permanency plan for the child, and to make changes to the case plan and placement or custody arrangement consistent with the permanency plan. The court shall schedule the review hearing at the time that it holds the dispositional hearing pursuant to section 2151.35 of the Revised Code.

The court shall hold a similar review hearing no later than every twelve months after the initial review hearing until the child is adopted, returned to the parents, or the court otherwise terminates the child's placement or custody arrangement, except that the dispositional hearing held pursuant to section 2151.415 of the Revised Code shall take the place of the first review hearing to be held under this section. The court shall schedule each subsequent review hearing at the conclusion of the review hearing immediately preceding the review hearing to be scheduled.

(D) If, within fourteen days after a written summary of an administrative review is filed with the court pursuant to section 2151.416 of the Revised Code, the court does not approve the proposed change to the case plan filed pursuant to division (E) of section 2151.416 of the Revised Code or a party or the guardian ad litem requests a review hearing pursuant to division (E) of that section, the court shall hold a review hearing in the same manner that it holds review hearings pursuant to division (C) of this section, except that if a review hearing is required by this division and if a hearing is to be held pursuant to division (C) of this section or section 2151.415 of the Revised Code, the hearing held pursuant to division (C) of this section or section 2151.415 of the Revised Code shall take the place of the review hearing required by this division.

(E) If a court determines pursuant to section 2151.419 of the Revised Code that a public children services agency or private child placing agency is not required to make reasonable efforts to prevent the removal of a child from the child's home, eliminate the continued removal of a child from the child's home, and return the child to the child's home, and the court does not return the child to the child's home pursuant to division (A)(3) of section 2151.419 of the Revised Code, the court shall hold a review hearing to approve the permanency plan for the child and, if appropriate, to make changes to the child's case plan and the child's placement or custody arrangement consistent with the permanency plan. The court may hold the hearing immediately following the determination under section 2151.419 of the Revised Code and shall hold it no later than thirty days after making that determination.

(F) The court shall give notice of the review hearings held pursuant to this section to every interested party, including, but not limited to, the appropriate agency employees who are responsible for the child's care and planning, the child's parents, any person who had guardianship or legal custody of the child prior to the custody order, the child's guardian ad litem, and the child. The court shall summon every interested party to appear at the review hearing and give them an opportunity to testify and to present other evidence with respect to the child's custody arrangement, including, but not limited to, the following: the case plan for the child the [sic] permanency plan, if one exists; the actions taken by the child's custodian; the need for a change in the child's custodian or caseworker; and the need for any specific action to be taken with respect to the child. The court shall require any interested party to testify or present other evidence when necessary to a proper determination of the issues presented at the review hearing.

(G) After the review hearing, the court shall take the following actions based upon the evidence presented:

(1) If an administrative review has been conducted, determine whether the conclusions of the review are supported by a preponderance of the evidence and approve or modify the case plan based upon that evidence;

(2) If the hearing was held under division (C) or (E) of this section, approve a permanency plan for the child that specifies whether and, if applicable, when the child will be safely returned home or placed for adoption, for legal custody, or in a planned permanent living arrangement. a permanency plan approved after a hearing under division (E) of this section shall not include any provision requiring the child to be returned to the child's home.

(3) If the child is in temporary custody, do all of the following:

(a) Determine whether the child can and should be returned home with or without an order for protective supervision;

(b) If the child can and should be returned home with or without an order for protective supervision, terminate the order for temporary custody;

(c) If the child cannot or should not be returned home with an order for protective supervision, determine whether the agency currently with custody of the child should retain custody or whether another public children services agency, private child placing agency, or an individual should be given custody of the child.

The court shall comply with section 2151.42 of the Revised Code in taking any action under this division.

(4) If the child is in permanent custody, determine what actions are required by the custodial agency and of any other organizations or persons in order to facilitate an adoption of the child and make any appropriate orders with respect to the custody arrangement or conditions of the child, including, but not limited to, a transfer of permanent custody to another public children services agency or private child placing agency;

(5) Journalize the terms of the updated case plan for the child.

(H) The court may appoint a referee or a citizens review board to conduct the review hearings that the court is required by this section to conduct, subject to the review and approval by the court of any determinations made by the referee or citizens review board. If the court appoints a citizens review board to conduct the review hearings, the board shall consist of one member representing the general public and four members who are trained or experienced in the care or placement of children and have training or experience in the fields of medicine, psychology, social work, education, or any related field. Of the initial appointments to the board, two shall be for a term of one year, two shall be for a term of two years, and one shall be for a term of three years, with all the terms ending one year after the date on which the appointment was made. Thereafter, all terms of the board members shall be for three years and shall end on the same day of the same month of the year as did the term that they succeed. Any member appointed to fill a vacancy occurring prior to the expiration of the term for which the member's predecessor was appointed shall hold office for the remainder of the term.

(I) A copy of the court's determination following any review hearing held pursuant to this section shall be sent to the custodial agency, the guardian ad litem of the child who is the subject of the review hearing, and, if that child is not the subject of a permanent commitment hearing, the parents of the child.

(J) If the hearing held under this section takes the place of an administrative review that otherwise would have been held under section 2151.416 of the Revised Code, the court at the hearing held under this section shall do all of the following in addition to any other requirements of this section:

(1) Determine the continued necessity for and the safety and appropriateness of the child's placement;

(2) Determine the extent of compliance with the child's case plan;

(3) Determine the extent of progress that has been made toward alleviating or mitigating the causes necessitating the child's placement in foster care;

(4) Project a likely date by which the child may be safely returned home or placed for adoption or legal custody.

(K)(1) Whenever the court is required to approve a permanency plan under this section or section 2151.415 of the Revised Code, the public children services agency or private child placing agency that filed the complaint in the case, has custody of the child, or will be given custody of the child shall develop a permanency plan for the child. The agency must file the plan with the court prior to the hearing under this section or section 2151.415 of the Revised Code.

(2) The permanency plan developed by the agency must specify whether and, if applicable, when the child will be safely returned home or placed for adoption or legal custody. If the agency determines that there is a compelling reason why returning the child home or placing the child for adoption or legal custody is not in the best interest of the child, the plan shall provide that the child will be placed in a planned permanent living arrangement. A permanency plan developed as a result of a determination made under division (A)(2) of section 2151.419 of the Revised Code may not include any provision requiring the child to be returned home.

(1998 H 484, eff. 3–18–99; 1996 H 274, eff. 8–8–96; 1988 S 89, eff. 1–1–89)

Uncodified Law

1988 S 89, § 4: See Uncodified Law under 2151.414.

Historical and Statutory Notes

Amendment Note: 1998 H 484 rewrote this section, which prior thereto read:

"(A) Any court that issues a dispositional order pursuant to section 2151.353, 2151.414, or 2151.415 of the Revised Code may review at any time the child's placement or custody arrangement, the case plan prepared for the child pursuant to section 2151.412 of the Revised Code, the actions of the public children services agency or private child placing agency in implementing that case plan, and any other aspects of the child's placement or custody arrangement. In conducting the review, the court shall determine the appropriateness of any agency actions, the appropriateness of continuing the child's placement or custody arrangement, and whether any changes should be made with respect to the child's placement or custody arrangement or with respect to the actions of the agency under the child's placement or custody arrangement. Based upon the evidence presented at a hearing held after notice to all parties and the guardian ad litem of the child, the court may require the agency, the parents, guardian, or custodian of the child, and the physical custodians of the child to take any reasonable action that the court determines is necessary and in the best interest of the child or to discontinue any action that it determines is not in the best interest of the child.

"(B) If a court issues a dispositional order pursuant to section 2151.353, 2151.414, or 2151.415 of the Revised Code, the court has continuing jurisdiction over the child as set forth in division (E)(1) of section 2151.353 of the Revised Code. The court may amend a dispositional order in accordance with division (E)(2) of section 2151.353 of the Revised Code at any time upon its own motion or upon the motion of any interested party.

"(C) Any court that issues a dispositional order pursuant to section 2151.353, 2151.414, or 2151.415 of the Revised Code shall hold a review hearing one year after the earlier of the date on which the complaint in the case was filed or the child was first placed into shelter care to review the case plan prepared pursuant to section 2151.412 of the Revised Code and to review the child's placement or custody arrangement. The court shall schedule the review hearing at the time that it holds the dispositional hearing pursuant to section 2151.35 of the Revised Code.

"The court shall hold a similar review hearing no later than every twelve months after the initial review hearing until the child is adopted, returned to the parents, or the court otherwise terminates the child's placement or custody arrangement, except that the dispositional hearing held pursuant to section 2151.415 of the Revised Code shall take the place of the first review hearing to be held under this section. The court shall schedule each subsequent review hearing at the conclusion of the review hearing immediately preceding the review hearing to be scheduled.

"(D) If, within fourteen days after a written summary of an administrative review is filed with the court pursuant to section 2151.416 of the Revised Code, the court does not approve the proposed change to the case plan filed pursuant to division (E) of section 2151.416 of the Revised Code or a party or the guardian ad litem requests a review hearing pursuant to division (E) of that section, the court shall hold a review hearing in the same manner that it holds review hearings pursuant to division (C) of this section, except that if a review hearing is required by this division and if a hearing is to be held pursuant to division (C) of this section or section 2151.415 of the Revised Code, the hearing held pursuant to division (C) of this section or section 2151.415 of the Revised Code shall take the place of the review hearing required by this division.

"(E) The court shall give notice of the review hearings held pursuant to this section to every interested party, including, but not limited to, the appropriate agency employees who are responsible for the child's care and planning, the child's parents, any person who had guardianship or legal custody of the child prior to the custody order, the child's guardian ad litem, and the child. The court shall summon every interested party to appear at the review hearing and give them an opportunity to testify and to present other evidence with respect to the child's custody arrangement, including, but not limited to, the case plan for the child, the actions taken by the child's custodian, the need for a change in the child's custodian or caseworker, or the need for any specific action to be taken with respect to the child. The court shall require any interested party to testify or present other evidence when necessary to a proper determination of the issues presented at the review hearing.

"(F) After the review hearing, the court shall take the following actions based upon the evidence presented:

"(1) Determine whether the conclusions of the administrative review are supported by a preponderance of the evidence and approve or modify the case plan based upon that evidence;

"(2) If the child is in temporary custody, do all of the following:

"(a) Determine whether the child can and should be returned home with or without an order for protective supervision;

"(b) If the child can and should be returned home with or without an order for protective supervision, terminate the order for temporary custody;

"(c) If the child cannot or should not be returned home with an order for protective supervision, determine whether the agency currently with custody of the child should retain custody or whether another public children services agency, private child placing agency, or an individual should be given custody of the child.

"(3) If the child is in permanent custody, determine what actions are required by the custodial agency and of any other organizations or persons in order to facilitate an adoption of the child and make any appropriate orders with respect to the custody arrangement or conditions of the child, including, but not limited to, a transfer of permanent custody to another public children services agency or private child placing agency;

"(4) Journalize the terms of the updated case plan for the child.

"(G) The court may appoint a referee or a citizens review board to conduct the review hearings that the court is required by this section to conduct, subject to the review and approval by the court of any determinations made by the referee or citizens review board. If the court appoints a citizens review board to conduct the review hearings, the board shall consist of one member representing the general public and four members who are trained or experienced in the care or placement of children and have training or experience in the fields of medicine, psychology, social work, education, or any related field. Of the initial appointments to the board, two shall be for a term of one year, two shall be for a term of two years, and one shall be for a term of three years, with all the terms ending one year after the date on which the appointment was made. Thereafter, all terms of the board members shall be for three years and shall end on the same day of the same month of the year as did the term that they succeed. Any member appointed to fill a vacancy occurring prior to the expiration of the term for which the member's predecessor was appointed shall hold office for the remainder of the term.

"(H) A copy of the court's determination following any review hearing held pursuant to this section shall be sent to the custodial agency, the guardian ad litem of the child who is the subject of the review hearing, and, if that child is not the subject of a permanent commitment hearing, the parents of the child.

"(I) If the hearing held under this section takes the place of an administrative review that otherwise would have been held under section 2151.416 of the Revised Code, the court at the hearing held under this section shall do all of the following in addition to any other requirements of this section:

"(1) Determine the continued necessity for and the appropriateness of the child's placement;

"(2) Determine the extent of compliance with the child's case plan;

"(3) Determine the extent of progress that has been made toward alleviating or mitigating the causes necessitating the child's placement in foster care;

"(4) Project a likely date by which the child may be returned home or placed for adoption or legal guardianship;

"(5) Determine the future status of the child."

Amendment Note: 1996 H 274 substituted "proposed change to the case plan filed pursuant to division (E) of section 2151.416 of the Revised Code or a party or the guardian ad litem requests a review hearing pursuant to division (E) of that section" for "revised case plan filed pursuant to division (E)(1) of section 2151.416 of the Revised Code or the agency requests a review hearing pursuant to division (E)(2) of section 2151.416 of the Revised Code" in division (D); and made changes to reflect gender neutral language.

Cross References

Public children services agencies, powers and duties, 5153.16

Library References

Infants ⇌17, 204, 230.1.
Westlaw Topic No. 211.
C.J.S. Adoption of Persons § 10.
C.J.S. Infants §§ 8 to 9, 50, 57, 62 to 67, 69 to 85.
Baldwin's Ohio Legislative Service, 1988 Laws of Ohio, S 89—LSC Analysis, p 5–571

Research References

Encyclopedias

OH Jur. 3d Family Law § 1428, Changes to Case Plan.
OH Jur. 3d Family Law § 1451, Powers and Duties as to Children in Need of Public Care or Protective Services.
OH Jur. 3d Family Law § 1602, Prehearing Motions—Motion for Order of Disposition.
OH Jur. 3d Family Law § 1654, Determination of Reasonable Efforts.
OH Jur. 3d Family Law § 1706, Modification or Vacation of Order.
OH Jur. 3d Family Law § 1711, Review Hearing.

Forms

Ohio Jurisprudence Pleading and Practice Forms § 96:43, Temporary and Permanent Custody.

Treatises and Practice Aids

Carlin, Baldwin's Ohio Practice, Merrick-Rippner Probate Law § 107:74, Reasonable Efforts Determination.
Carlin, Baldwin's Ohio Practice, Merrick-Rippner Probate Law § 107:118, Modification of Dispositional Orders in Abuse, Neglect, and Dependency Proceedings.
Carlin, Baldwin's Ohio Practice, Merrick-Rippner Probate Law § 107:119, Custody Review Proceedings—Semiannual Administrative Review.
Carlin, Baldwin's Ohio Practice, Merrick-Rippner Probate Law § 107:120, Custody Review Hearing—Juvenile Court Dispositional Review.
Carlin, Baldwin's Ohio Practice, Merrick-Rippner Probate Law § 107:174, Order Committing Child to Temporary Custody of Public or Private Agency or Foster Care—Form.
Carlin, Baldwin's Ohio Practice, Merrick-Rippner Probate Law § 107:175, Order Committing Child to Permanent Custody of Public or Private Agency—Form.
Carlin, Baldwin's Ohio Practice, Merrick-Rippner Probate Law § 107:176, Order Placing Child in Planned Permanent Living Arrangement—Form.
Giannelli & Yeomans, Ohio Juvenile Law § 1:7, Juvenile Code.
Giannelli & Yeomans, Ohio Juvenile Law § 26:5, Case Plan Amendments.
Giannelli & Yeomans, Ohio Juvenile Law § 30:6, Temporary Custody.
Giannelli & Yeomans, Ohio Juvenile Law § 31:2, Filing of Motion.
Giannelli & Yeomans, Ohio Juvenile Law § 33:4, Abuse, Neglect, and Dependency Proceedings.
Giannelli & Yeomans, Ohio Juvenile Law § 34:4, Final Order Requirement.
Giannelli & Yeomans, Ohio Juvenile Law § 16:14, Permanent & Temporary Custody Complaints; Planned Permanent Living Arrangements.
Giannelli & Yeomans, Ohio Juvenile Law § 25:14, Reasonable Efforts Determination; Abuse, Neglect & Dependency.
Giannelli & Yeomans, Ohio Juvenile Law § 33:10, Child Custody Agency Commitment—Semiannual Administrative Review.
Giannelli & Yeomans, Ohio Juvenile Law § 33:11, Child Custody Agency Commitment—Juvenile Court Dispositional Review.

Notes of Decisions

Continuance 6
Jurisdiction 3
Liability of government officials 8
Notice and hearing 7
Parties 5
Review at any time 4
Service of summons 1
Standing of foster family 2

---

1. Service of summons

The failure of a guardian ad litem to effectively secure the attendance of the subject of a placement review hearing, after attempting service on a county social services headquarters without a caseworker notation, does not require reversal of the court's judgment even though such service was not reasonably calculated to secure the ward's appearance where prejudice caused by the child's absence is not demonstrated and the guardian ad litem adequately protects the child's best interests by his presentation of evidence. Lovejoy v. Cuyahoga Cty. Dept. of Human Serv. (Cuyahoga 1991) 76 Ohio App.3d 514, 602 N.E.2d 405, dismissed, jurisdictional motion overruled 63 Ohio St.3d 1456, 590 N.E.2d 750.

2. Standing of foster family

Although a children services board does not appeal a dispositional judgment, this circumstance does not prevent it from arguing to preserve that part of the judgment denying a foster family's lack of standing to challenge the judgment at a review hearing. In re Moorehead (Montgomery 1991) 75 Ohio App.3d 711, 600 N.E.2d 778.

Foster parents of a dependent child are proper parties to seek review of a dispositional judgment concerning placement of the foster child in their care. In re Moorehead (Montgomery 1991) 75 Ohio App.3d 711, 600 N.E.2d 778.

3. Jurisdiction

Juvenile court had jurisdiction to order county department of children and family services to place child that was in permanent custody of department with child's present foster parents, upon guardian ad litem's motion for immediate hearing on department's proposed change of child's placement, but court lacked jurisdiction to order department to commence procedures to effect child's adoption by foster parents, since adoption matters were within exclusive jurisdiction of the probate court. In re A.W. (Ohio App. 8 Dist., Cuyahoga, 08-11-2005) No. 86078, 2005-Ohio-4127, 2005 WL 1910653, Unreported. Infants ⇐ 230.1

No new finding of dependency is required based upon circumstances of current placement of child before trial court may consider motion to modify or change dispositional order, as juvenile court retains jurisdiction following initial dispositional hearing until child reaches age of majority or is adopted, and may therefore hold additional hearings sua sponte or on motion of any party to reconsider original order. In re Hitchcock (Ohio App. 8 Dist., 11-21-1996) 120 Ohio App.3d 88, 696 N.E.2d 1090, stay granted 77 Ohio St.3d 1462, 672 N.E.2d 1119, stay denied 77 Ohio St.3d 1502, 673 N.E.2d 921, motion to vacate stay denied 77 Ohio St.3d 1521, 674 N.E.2d 373, appeal allowed 78 Ohio St.3d 1455, 677 N.E.2d 815, appeal dismissed as improvidently allowed 81 Ohio St.3d 1222, 689 N.E.2d 43, 1998-Ohio-653, stay denied 81 Ohio St.3d 1469, 690 N.E.2d 1288, stay denied 81 Ohio St.3d 1476, 691 N.E.2d 294. Infants ⇐ 230.1

Prospective adoptive parents were not entitled to writ of prohibition to prevent juvenile court judge from going forward with neglect proceeding while ordering that adoption proceedings be held in abeyance; judge's going forward in neglect proceeding was not unauthorized by law. State ex rel. Cuyahoga Cty. Dept. of Children & Family Serv. v. Ferreri (Ohio App. 8 Dist., 09-26-1994) 96 Ohio App.3d 660, 645 N.E.2d 837. Prohibition ⇐ 10(2)

In proceeding in which county children services board sought permanent custody of children as dependent, neglected and abused children, juvenile court had jurisdiction over children from dates of original adjudications of each child, and it would continue to have jurisdiction until each child reached age of 18. In re Doe Children (Ohio App. 6 Dist., 02-11-1994) 93 Ohio App.3d 134, 637 N.E.2d 977, cause dismissed 69 Ohio St.3d 1481, 634 N.E.2d 1027. Infants ⇐ 152; Infants ⇐ 196

4. Review at any time

Trial court did not abuse its discretion when it found that continued placement with foster family was in best interests of child born to minor mother; placement of child and her mother with foster family had been successful, and mother's parenting skills had been called into question, raising issue of child's safety. In re M. (Ohio App. 6 Dist., Wood, 07-16-2004) No. WD-03-092, 2004-Ohio-3798, 2004 WL 1595006, Unreported. Infants ⇐ 226

Following adjudication of child as dependent and neglected and award of temporary custody of child to aunt, which was later converted to one of legal custody, proper standard for trial court to apply in considering father's motion for legal custody was standard for amending dispositional order; consequently, trial court was required to consider whether it was in the best interest of child to return her to father. In re Osberry (Ohio App. 3 Dist., Allen, 10-14-2003) No. 1-03-26, 2003-Ohio-5462, 2003 WL 22336115, Unreported. Infants ⇐ 231

Trial court, which, upon mother's motion for permanent custody, adjudicated six-year-old child to be dependent, awarded legal custody to child's custodian of four years, and discontinued court-supervised visitation with mother, erred by failing to order an annual review hearing on such issues. In re Timberlake (Ohio App. 10 Dist., Franklin, 03-13-2003) No. 02AP-792, 2003-Ohio-1183, 2003 WL 1094078, Unreported. Infants ⇐ 203

Statute allowing the juvenile court to review at any time the placement or custody arrangement for an abused child did not apply to juvenile court's order placing unruly child in temporary custody of public children services agency, even if custody was awarded based on allegations of child abuse, where father was never charged with child abuse and child was not adjudicated as abused child. In re Kidd (Ohio App. 11 Dist., Lake, 12-27-2002) No. 2001-L-039, 2002-Ohio-7264, 2002 WL 31886759, Unreported. Infants ⇐ 192

While statute requires juvenile court to review dispositional order if any party files motion requesting modification or termination of order, statute and rule additionally allow juvenile court to review child's placement or custody arrangement at any time. In re Bowman (Ohio App. 9 Dist., 03-08-1995) 101 Ohio App.3d 599, 656 N.E.2d 355. Infants ⇐ 230.1

If a juvenile court, in making disposition of an unruly or delinquent child pursuant to RC 2151.354 or RC 2151.355, places the child into the temporary custody of the county department of human services in accordance with RC 2151.353, the juvenile court is required to hold periodic reviews pursuant to RC 2151.417 and Juv R 36(A). OAG 99–041.

5. Parties

Juvenile court order directing that child in permanent custody of county department of children and family services be placed with child's present foster parents, upon guardian ad litem's motion for immediate hearing on department's proposed change of child's placement, was not abuse of discretion; guardian ad litem advocated for child to remain with foster parents, the only parents child had ever known, and juvenile court properly evaluated the evidence and made sound, reasonable findings based on the record as to child's placement. In re A.W. (Ohio App. 8 Dist., Cuyahoga, 08-11-2005) No. 86078, 2005-Ohio-4127, 2005 WL 1910653, Unreported. Infants ⇐ 230.1

Adjudication of out-of-wedlock child as dependent and neglected implied parental unfitness, and thus trial court was not required to determine father's unsuitability as parent prior to awarding legal custody to child's aunt, even though mother allegedly misrepresented nonparentage to the father, who as a result had no contact with child prior to award, the basis for dependency was the mother's drug habit, and father's paternity was not confirmed until after the award. In re Osberry (Ohio App. 3 Dist., Allen, 10-14-2003) No. 1-03-26, 2003-Ohio-5462, 2003 WL 22336115, Unreported. Infants ⇐ 222

While statute regarding dispositional review hearings does not list a child's legal custodian at the time review hearing is ordered as an "interested party" entitled to notice of the review hearing, the list is not exhaustive. In re Bowman (Ohio App. 9 Dist., 03-08-1995) 101 Ohio App.3d 599, 656 N.E.2d 355. Infants ⇐ 230.1

6. Continuance

Where the juvenile court (1) has gone through the process of hearing pursuant to RC 2151.417, (2) has reviewed placement of the child with his mother, and (3) has satisfied itself as to such placement, it is not an abuse of discretion for the court to deny a motion for continuance brought by the child's former custodian. In re Mull, No. 13–96–38, 1997 WL 155412 (3d Dist Ct App, Seneca, 3–24–97).

7. Notice and hearing

Juvenile court was not required to schedule and notice separate hearing on extension of temporary custody of children following hearing on state's petition for permanent and legal custody, where agency had not requested extension of temporary custody, and where evidence at hearing on permanent and legal custody persuaded court that factors for extending temporary custody existed; mother was on notice, as result of prior hearing, that state wished to permanently terminate her parental rights with regard to two children and give legal custody of the other two children to a relative, and had opportunity to be heard on propriety of such dispositions. In re Nice (Ohio App. 7 Dist., 03-20-2001) 141 Ohio App.3d 445, 751 N.E.2d 552, 2001-Ohio-3214. Infants ⇐ 230.1

Where an agency requests an extension of temporary custody or the court wishes to extend temporary custody sua sponte where no other proceedings are occurring in the case, then the parent is entitled to notice and a hearing on the extension. In re Nice (Ohio App. 7 Dist., 03-20-2001) 141 Ohio App.3d 445, 751 N.E.2d 552, 2001-Ohio-3214. Infants ⇐ 230.1

8. Liability of government officials

Allegations that parents whose children were removed from home by county social worker were not allowed to recover children after safety plan providing for children's placement with friends had been initiated, despite parents' best efforts to do so, that continued deprivation of children was involuntary, and that parents were effectively denied prompt hearing on children's placement supported claim against social worker for violating parents' procedural due process rights. Smith v. Williams-Ash (C.A.6 (Ohio), 12-06-2005) No. 04-4547, 173 Fed.Appx. 363, 2005 WL 3304101, Unreported. Infants ⇐ 17

County social worker should have known that her alleged conduct in thwarting parents' attempts to have children returned to parents' home, after children were removed due to unsanitary conditions, and in effectively denying parents prompt hearing on children's placement had effect of violating parents' clearly established rights to procedural due process by involuntarily depriving parents of physical custody of children, and therefore qualified immunity did not apply to preclude social worker's liability under §§ 1983. Smith v. Williams-Ash (C.A.6 (Ohio), 12-06-2005) No. 04-

4547, 173 Fed.Appx. 363, 2005 WL 3304101, Unreported. Civil Rights ⊕ 1376(4)

County social worker's alleged conduct in thwarting parents' attempts to have children returned to parents' home, after children were removed due to unsanitary conditions, and in effectively denying parents prompt hearing on children's placement did not rise to the level of conscience-shocking behavior, and thus did not support substantive due process claim. Smith v. Williams-Ash (C.A.6 (Ohio), 12-06-2005) No. 04-4547, 173 Fed.Appx. 363, 2005 WL 3304101, Unreported. Infants ⊕ 17

2151.419 Hearings on efforts of agencies to prevent removal of children from homes

(A)(1) Except as provided in division (A)(2) of this section, at any hearing held pursuant to section 2151.28, division (E) of section 2151.31, or section 2151.314, 2151.33, or 2151.353 of the Revised Code at which the court removes a child from the child's home or continues the removal of a child from the child's home, the court shall determine whether the public children services agency or private child placing agency that filed the complaint in the case, removed the child from home, has custody of the child, or will be given custody of the child has made reasonable efforts to prevent the removal of the child from the child's home, to eliminate the continued removal of the child from the child's home, or to make it possible for the child to return safely home. The agency shall have the burden of proving that it has made those reasonable efforts. If the agency removed the child from home during an emergency in which the child could not safely remain at home and the agency did not have prior contact with the child, the court is not prohibited, solely because the agency did not make reasonable efforts during the emergency to prevent the removal of the child, from determining that the agency made those reasonable efforts. In determining whether reasonable efforts were made, the child's health and safety shall be paramount.

(2) If any of the following apply, the court shall make a determination that the agency is not required to make reasonable efforts to prevent the removal of the child from the child's home, eliminate the continued removal of the child from the child's home, and return the child to the child's home:

(a) The parent from whom the child was removed has been convicted of or pleaded guilty to one of the following:

(i) An offense under section 2903.01, 2903.02, or 2903.03 of the Revised Code or under an existing or former law of this state, any other state, or the United States that is substantially equivalent to an offense described in those sections and the victim of the offense was a sibling of the child or the victim was another child who lived in the parent's household at the time of the offense;

(ii) An offense under section 2903.11, 2903.12, or 2903.13 of the Revised Code or under an existing or former law of this state, any other state, or the United States that is substantially equivalent to an offense described in those sections and the victim of the offense is the child, a sibling of the child, or another child who lived in the parent's household at the time of the offense;

(iii) An offense under division (B)(2) of section 2919.22 of the Revised Code or under an existing or former law of this state, any other state, or the United States that is substantially equivalent to the offense described in that section and the child, a sibling of the child, or another child who lived in the parent's household at the time of the offense is the victim of the offense;

(iv) An offense under section 2907.02, 2907.03, 2907.04, 2907.05, or 2907.06 of the Revised Code or under an existing or former law of this state, any other state, or the United States that is substantially equivalent to an offense described in those sections and the victim of the offense is the child, a sibling of the child, or another child who lived in the parent's household at the time of the offense;

(v) A conspiracy or attempt to commit, or complicity in committing, an offense described in division (A)(2)(a)(i) or (iv) of this section.

(b) The parent from whom the child was removed has repeatedly withheld medical treatment or food from the child when the parent has the means to provide the treatment or food. If the parent has withheld medical treatment in order to treat the physical or mental illness or defect of the child by spiritual means through prayer alone, in accordance with the tenets of a recognized religious body, the court or agency shall comply with the requirements of division (A)(1) of this section.

(c) The parent from whom the child was removed has placed the child at substantial risk of harm two or more times due to alcohol or drug abuse and has rejected treatment two or more times or refused to participate in further treatment two or more times after a case plan issued pursuant to section 2151.412 of the Revised Code requiring treatment of the parent was journalized as part of a dispositional order issued with respect to the child or an order was issued by any other court requiring such treatment of the parent.

(d) The parent from whom the child was removed has abandoned the child.

(e) The parent from whom the child was removed has had parental rights involuntarily terminated pursuant to section 2151.353, 2151.414, or 2151.415 of the Revised Code with respect to a sibling of the child.

(3) At any hearing in which the court determines whether to return a child to the child's home, the court may issue an order that returns the child in situations in which the conditions described in divisions (A)(2)(a) to (e) of this section are present.

(B)(1) A court that is required to make a determination as described in division (A)(1) or (2) of this section shall issue written findings of fact setting forth the reasons supporting its determination. If the court makes a written determination under division (A)(1) of this section, it shall briefly describe in the findings of fact the relevant services provided by the agency to the family of the child and why those services did not prevent the removal of the child from the child's home or enable the child to return safely home.

(2) If a court issues an order that returns the child to the child's home in situations in which division (A)(2)(a), (b), (c), (d), or (e) of this section applies, the court shall issue written findings of fact setting forth the reasons supporting its determination.

(C) If the court makes a determination pursuant to division (A)(2) of this section, the court shall conduct a review hearing pursuant to section 2151.417 of the Revised Code to approve a permanency plan with respect to the child, unless the court issues an order returning the child home pursuant to division (A)(3) of this section. The hearing to approve the permanency plan may be held immediately following the court's determination pursuant to division (A)(2) of this section and shall be held no later than thirty days following that determination.

(1999 H 176, eff. 10–29–99; 1998 H 484, eff. 3–18–99; 1988 S 89, eff. 1–1–89)

Historical and Statutory Notes

Amendment Note: 1999 H 176 inserted ", division (E) of section 2151.31, or section 2151.314, 2151.33," and "removed the child from home," and added the third sentence in division (A)(1).

Amendment Note: 1998 H 484 rewrote this section, which prior thereto read:

"(A) At any hearing held pursuant to section 2151.28, division (E) of section 2151.31, or section 2151.314, 2151.33, or 2151.353 of the Revised Code at which the court removes a child from his home or continues the removal of a child from his home, the court shall determine whether the public children services agency or private child placing agency that filed the complaint in the case, removed the child from his home, has custody of the child, or will be given custody of the child has made reasonable efforts to prevent the removal of the child from his home, to eliminate the continued removal of the child from his home, or to make it possible for the child to return home. The agency shall have the burden of proving that it has made those reasonable efforts. If the agency removed the child from his home during an emergency in which the child could not safely remain at home and the agency did not have prior contact with the child, the court is not prohibited, solely because the agency did not make the reasonable efforts during the emergency to prevent the removal of the child, from determining that the agency made those reasonable efforts.

"(B) The court shall issue written finding of facts setting forth its determination under division (A) of this section. In its written finding of facts, the court shall briefly describe the relevant services provided by the agency to the family of the child and why those services did not prevent the removal of the child from his home or enable the child to return home."

Cross References

Cost charged to county of legal residence, determination of legal residence, transfer of child, 5153.20
Public children services agencies, powers and duties, 5153.16

Ohio Administrative Code References

Reasonable efforts, OAC 5101:2–39–05

Library References

Infants $\Longleftrightarrow$ 17, 155, 230.1.
Westlaw Topic No. 211.
C.J.S. Adoption of Persons § 10.
C.J.S. Infants §§ 8 to 9, 31, 33 to 50, 55, 57, 62, 69 to 85.
  Baldwin's Ohio Legislative Service, 1988 Laws of Ohio, S 89—LSC Analysis, p 5–571

Research References

Encyclopedias

OH Jur. 3d Family Law § 1451, Powers and Duties as to Children in Need of Public Care or Protective Services.
OH Jur. 3d Family Law § 1577, Detention Hearing; Notice—Conduct of Hearing.
OH Jur. 3d Family Law § 1596, Habeas Corpus.
OH Jur. 3d Family Law § 1634, Procedure.
OH Jur. 3d Family Law § 1654, Determination of Reasonable Efforts.
OH Jur. 3d Family Law § 1678, Generally—Placement of Child Until Dispositional Hearing.
OH Jur. 3d Family Law § 1711, Review Hearing.

Treatises and Practice Aids

Carlin, Baldwin's Ohio Practice, Merrick-Rippner Probate Law § 107:30, Detention Hearing.
Carlin, Baldwin's Ohio Practice, Merrick-Rippner Probate Law § 107:41, Prehearing Procedures in Juvenile Court—Temporary Orders Pending Hearing.
Carlin, Baldwin's Ohio Practice, Merrick-Rippner Probate Law § 107:74, Reasonable Efforts Determination.
Carlin, Baldwin's Ohio Practice, Merrick-Rippner Probate Law § 107:78, Disposition of Abused, Neglected, or Dependent Child—Temporary Custody.
Carlin, Baldwin's Ohio Practice, Merrick-Rippner Probate Law § 107:81, Disposition of Abused, Neglected, or Dependent Child—Permanent Custody—Best Interest Determination Factors.
Carlin, Baldwin's Ohio Practice, Merrick-Rippner Probate Law § 107:83, Motion for Permanent Custody of Abused, Neglected, or Dependent Child.
Giannelli & Yeomans, Ohio Juvenile Law § 1:7, Juvenile Code.
Giannelli & Yeomans, Ohio Juvenile Law § 19:6, Standard for Detention.
Giannelli & Yeomans, Ohio Juvenile Law § 20:2, Temporary Care Orders.
Giannelli & Yeomans, Ohio Juvenile Law § 20:4, Required Hearings.
Giannelli & Yeomans, Ohio Juvenile Law § 31:2, Filing of Motion.
Giannelli & Yeomans, Ohio Juvenile Law § 31:6, Findings.
Giannelli & Yeomans, Ohio Juvenile Law § 31:8, Implementation of Case Plan.
Giannelli & Yeomans, Ohio Juvenile Law § 34:4, Final Order Requirement.
Giannelli & Yeomans, Ohio Juvenile Law § 25:14, Reasonable Efforts Determination; Abuse, Neglect & Dependency.
Giannelli & Yeomans, Ohio Juvenile Law § 30:10, Permanent Custody—Parental Placement Within Reasonable Time.
Giannelli & Yeomans, Ohio Juvenile Law § 33:11, Child Custody Agency Commitment—Juvenile Court Dispositional Review.

Law Review and Journal Commentaries

State v. Parent Termination of Parental Rights: Contradictory Actions by the Ohio Legislature and the Ohio Supreme Court in 1996, Keith Wiens. 26 Cap U L Rev 673 (1997).

Notes of Decisions

Effective assistance of counsel 1
Reasonable efforts 2
"Siblings" 3

---

1. Effective assistance of counsel

Evidence supported finding that county jobs and family services made reasonable efforts to reunite mother with her children; mother was offered a case plan and supportive services to assist he in remedying the conditions that caused the children to be removed. In re Bierley (Ohio App. 5 Dist., Tuscarawas, 01-24-2005) No. 2004-AP-07-0049, 2005-Ohio-331, 2005 WL 217025, Unreported. Infants $\Longleftrightarrow$ 155

Statute requiring county agency to make reasonable efforts to prevent child's removal or to make it possible for child to return home with parent did not apply to agency's motion seeking permanent custody of child. In re T.T. (Ohio App. 12 Dist., Butler, 01-24-2005) No. CA2004-07-175, No. CA2004-08-198, 2005-Ohio-240, 2005 WL 123948, Unreported. Infants $\Longleftrightarrow$ 155

Parent's substantial compliance with case plan is not determinative as to whether agency has made reasonable efforts toward reunification, as required to support grant of permanent custody of child to county child protection agency. In re Smith (Ohio App. 3 Dist., Marion, 01-18-2005) No. 9-04-35, 2005-Ohio-149, 2005 WL 91639, Unreported. Infants $\Longleftrightarrow$ 155

Evidence supported finding that county child protection agency made reasonable efforts to reunify mother and child, thus supporting grant of permanent custody of child to county child protection agency; agency established and filed an individualized case plan, and case plan set forth reasonable requirements for compliance. In re Smith (Ohio App. 3 Dist., Marion, 01-18-2005) No. 9-04-35, 2005-Ohio-149, 2005 WL 91639, Unreported. Infants $\Longleftrightarrow$ 155

Evidence supported trial court's finding that agency made reasonable efforts to prevent the removal of parents' child, thus supporting grant of permanent custody of child to county child protection agency; despite parents' lack of cooperation and failure to comply with court orders, agency continued to offer them encouragement and services, caseworker attempted to contact them and to set up drug screens and assessments, and agency was prevented from offering further services by parents' failure to submit to the screenings or to participate in the assessments. In re Ella C. (Ohio App. 6 Dist., Lucas, 01-04-2005) No. L-04-1207, 2005-Ohio-42, 2005 WL 30548, Unreported. Infants $\Longleftrightarrow$ 155

County department of jobs and family services made reasonable efforts to eliminate continued removal of children from their home or make it possible for them to return home, as required for grant of permanent custody to agency; county had been working with the family for an extensive period of time with no significant improvement being shown by mother, mother failed to successfully complete any of court ordered services, failed to maintain safe and stable housing and failed to obtain and maintain employment, she failed to contribute to support of children, and her whereabouts were unknown during most of period that case was pending. In re Shahan/Ramey Children (Ohio App. 5 Dist., Stark, 12-16-2004) No. 2004CA00300, 2004-Ohio-6973, 2004 WL 2940807, Unreported. Infants $\Longleftrightarrow$ 155

Defense counsel did not render ineffective assistance at permanent custody hearing by failing to cross-examine guardian ad litem concerning child's statement in guardian ad litem's report that child wanted to return to mother's home if mother would not regress, where counsel never requested to cross-examine guardian ad litem, and statement in report was presented at hearing during direct examination of caseworker. In re Utt Children (Ohio App. 5 Dist., Stark, 08-27-2003) No. 2003CA00196, 2003-Ohio-4576, 2003 WL 22020802, Unreported. Infants $\Longleftrightarrow$ 205

2. Reasonable efforts

Evidence supported conclusion that county children services board (CSB) provided reasonable case planning to father and made diligent and reasonable efforts toward reunification, as necessary to support termination of father's parental rights; father's initial case worker, who was temporarily assigned to father during a work stoppage, was inexperienced, but she was not unqualified, second case worker made numerous contacts with father to verify that services were provided as referred, she met with parents at court house, visitation center, and family team meetings, and she offered to meet with them at other times, but, according to case worker, father was not willing to do so. In re E.T. (Ohio App. 9 Dist., Summit, 05-17-2006) No. 23017, 2006-Ohio-2413, 2006 WL 1329653, Unreported. Infants ⇌ 155

County children's services board made reasonable efforts to prevent removal of children from mother's home; mother was either living with friends in out-of-state, in transit to state, or living in a motel in state, agency tried to contact mother at telephone numbers provided by her attorney and herself, unsuccessfully, and agency, on its own initiative, tried unsuccessfully to obtain interstate compact home studies of the various purported residences mother had out-of-state, including that of her maternal grandmother. In re Elliott (Ohio App. 11 Dist., Ashtabula, 02-17-2006) No. 2005-A-0018, 2006-Ohio-738, 2006 WL 389595, Unreported. Infants ⇌ 155

County social worker's alleged conduct in thwarting parents' attempts to have children returned to parents' home, after children were removed due to unsanitary conditions, and in effectively denying parents prompt hearing on children's placement did not rise to the level of conscience-shocking behavior, and thus did not support substantive due process claim. Smith v. Williams-Ash (C.A.6 (Ohio), 12-06-2005) No. 04-4547, 173 Fed.Appx. 363, 2005 WL 3304101, Unreported. Infants ⇌ 17

County social worker should have known that her alleged conduct in thwarting parents' attempts to have children returned to parents' home, after children were removed due to unsanitary conditions, and in effectively denying parents prompt hearing on children's placement had effect of violating parents' clearly established rights to procedural due process by involuntarily depriving parents of physical custody of children, and therefore qualified immunity did not apply to preclude social worker's liability under §§ 1983. Smith v. Williams-Ash (C.A.6 (Ohio), 12-06-2005) No. 04-4547, 173 Fed.Appx. 363, 2005 WL 3304101, Unreported. Civil Rights ⇌ 1376(4)

Allegations that parents whose children were removed from home by county social worker were not allowed to recover children after safety plan providing for children's placement with friends had been initiated, despite parents' best efforts to do so, that continued deprivation of children was involuntary, and that parents were effectively denied prompt hearing on children's placement supported claim against social worker for violating parents' procedural due process rights. Smith v. Williams-Ash (C.A.6 (Ohio), 12-06-2005) No. 04-4547, 173 Fed.Appx. 363, 2005 WL 3304101, Unreported. Infants ⇌ 17

County children services board, after initially removing children from their home, made reasonable efforts to make it possible for the children to return safely home. In re A.D. (Ohio App. 9 Dist., Summit, 09-30-2005) No. 22668, 2005-Ohio-5183, 2005 WL 2400960, Unreported. Infants ⇌ 155

County children services board's failure to make requisite reasonable efforts to reunify mother and child before termination of mother's parental rights was harmless error, where board had a long and unsuccessful history of reunification attempts with respect to mother's other children, and mother had cognitive deficiencies that were not presently correctable and that affected mother's ability to parent appropriately. In re Meadows (Ohio App. 4 Dist., Scioto, 09-20-2005) No. 05CA3009, 2005-Ohio-5018, 2005 WL 2334681, Unreported. Infants ⇌ 253

County children services board failed to make reasonable reunification efforts before termination of parental rights of mother with whom board had a long and unsuccessful history of reunification attempts with respect to other children; board did not make any efforts with respect to child at issue. In re Meadows (Ohio App. 4 Dist., Scioto, 09-20-2005) No. 05CA3009, 2005-Ohio-5018, 2005 WL 2334681, Unreported. Infants ⇌ 155

Trial court's entry of order granting County Children Services Board's (MCCSB) motion to terminate mother's parental rights to her twin boys, despite MCCSB's failure to make reasonable efforts to reunite mother with children, was reversible error; although MCCSB developed case plan that included some limited supervised visitation provisions, this could hardly be called clear and convincing evidence that MCCSB made reasonable efforts at reunification. In re Bowers (Ohio App. 7 Dist., Mahoning, 08-18-2005) No. 04 MA 216, 2005-Ohio-4376, 2005 WL 2033100, Unreported. Infants ⇌ 253

Child endangerment for which mother was convicted was not recognized under parental rights termination statute as an offense that allowed County Children Services Board (MCCSB) to bypass its responsibility to make reasonable efforts at reuniting children with parent before seeking termination. In re Bowers (Ohio App. 7 Dist., Mahoning, 08-18-2005) No. 04 MA 216, 2005-Ohio-4376, 2005 WL 2033100, Unreported. Infants ⇌ 155

County department of job and family services made reasonable efforts to develop and preserve parent-child relationship, in proceeding in which trial court granted permanent custody of child to county department of job and family services; in order to make it possible for mother to be reunified with child, department ordered mother to undergo psychological and substance abuse examination, and department facilitated visitation, provided information on services to mother, encouraged mother to work on case plan goals, and made efforts in locating relatives willing to care for child. In re Patfield (Ohio App. 11 Dist., Lake, 07-18-2005) No. 2005-L-007, 2005-Ohio-3769, 2005 WL 1714185, Unreported. Infants ⇌ 155

Trial court was required to find that county children services had made reasonable efforts to prevent the removal of son, eliminate his continued removal, to make it possible for son to return safely home before entering dispositional order for mother's son, where mother did not stipulate to son's disposition, the record did not indicate what efforts children services had made to reunite son with mother, and case plan for son, which contained a goal of reunification with mother, was not approved until after the dispositional order was entered. In re Ohm (Ohio App. 4 Dist., Hocking, 07-01-2005) No. 05CA1, 2005-Ohio-3500, 2005 WL 1595245, Unreported. Infants ⇌ 210

Trial court failure to include a finding that county children services had made reasonable efforts to prevent the removal of mother's daughters, eliminate their continued removal, to make it possible for the children to return safely home was harmless error, where mother stipulated to the disposition of her daughters. In re Ohm (Ohio App. 4 Dist., Hocking, 07-01-2005) No. 05CA1, 2005-Ohio-3500, 2005 WL 1595245, Unreported. Infants ⇌ 253

County Children Services (ACCS) made reasonable efforts to reunify child with his parents, prior to petitioning for termination of father's parental rights; ACCS had a long and unsuccessful history of reunification attempts with mother and her other children, father was surrounded by relatives who abused drugs, although father denied any illegal drug use witnesses testified that they had observed him using illegal drugs, father had a history of violence against mother in front of the children, and a history of sexually abusing mother's children, all during ACCS's involvement with the family. In re Barnhart (Ohio App. 4 Dist., Athens, 05-26-2005) No. 05CA8, 2005-Ohio-2692, 2005 WL 1283675, Unreported. Infants ⇌ 155

County Children Services made reasonable attempts toward reunification with mother, as prerequisite to termination of mother's parental rights, despite unilateral suspension of visitation by county without seeking statutory amendment to case plan; county was authorized by court order to modify visitation as necessary, temporary suspension of visitation was necessary to allow mother time to recover from contagious illness, reinstatement of visitation was contingent on mother providing letter from physician that she was no longer contagious, county provided mother with medicine to treat illness, which mother refused to take, and county provided mother with substantial assistance, including financial support, referrals for drug and mental health counseling, and other assistance. In re Townsend (Ohio App. 4 Dist., Athens, 05-09-2005) No. 04CA46, 2005-Ohio-2473, 2005 WL 1190706, Unreported. Infants ⇌ 155

County Children Services' unilateral suspension of mother's telephone visitation with children in order to force compliance with mandatory drug screens without having followed statutory procedures for amending case plan did not warrant reversal of order terminating mother's parental rights, in view of trial court's findings that county made substantial efforts to prevent continued removal of children from mother's home, and that mother failed to comply with case plan. In re Townsend (Ohio App. 4 Dist., Athens, 05-09-2005) No. 04CA46, 2005-Ohio-2473, 2005 WL 1190706, Unreported. Infants ⇌ 253

County Job and Family Services made reasonable efforts to reunite father with children, as prerequisite for terminating parental rights, despite father's claim that he should have received counseling to help him understand emotional and mental health needs of children; father believed there were no problems with children when they were in his custody and he repeatedly refused further help. In re Hines (Ohio App. 5 Dist., Tuscarawas, 05-03-2005) No. 2004AP120071, 2005-Ohio-2267, 2005 WL 1075495, Unreported. Infants ⇌ 155

Father waived on appeal issue of whether trial court had erred in determining that county had made reasonable efforts to reunify family, in child dependency proceeding, as he failed to challenge this determination by filing objections as required by rule. In re Miller (Ohio App. 5 Dist., Licking, 02-24-2005) No. 04 CA 32, 2005-Ohio-856, 2005 WL 469260, Unreported. Infants ⚖ 243

County child services agency made reasonable efforts to reunify father with his children before seeking permanent custody, where it tailored a case plan specific to father, provided father with referrals for counseling, and provided him with financial assistance for housing. In re Cunningham (Ohio App. 4 Dist., Athens, 12-06-2004) No. 04CA39, 2004-Ohio-6568, 2004 WL 2809829, Unreported. Infants ⚖ 155

Evidence supported finding that county child protection agency made reasonable efforts to reunify minor child with mother, thus supporting grant of permanent custody of child to county child protection agency; agency provided case plan services to mother 55 hours a week, mother was provided with housing, and although mother's skills never improved, numerous attempts were made to teach mother how to care for her child. In re Keiondre S. (Ohio App. 6 Dist., Lucas, 11-24-2004) No. L-04-1025, 2004-Ohio-6316, 2004 WL 2690668, Unreported. Infants ⚖ 155

Department of Job and Family Services (DJFS) made reasonable efforts to reunify father's two minor children with him prior to seeking permanent custody of the children; DJFS developed a case plan that included the father, it attempted to locate him and to communicate with him, but father failed to communicate with the DJFS regarding the case plan. In re Keaton (Ohio App. 4 Dist., Ross, 11-19-2004) No. 04CA2785, No. 04CA2788, 2004-Ohio-6210, 2004 WL 2650249, Unreported. Infants ⚖ 155

Trial court's finding in permanent custody proceeding that reasonable efforts at reunification would be futile was not against the manifest weight of the evidence; mother, though having completed two prior case plans, was unable to provide a stable environment or the supervision necessary to protect the child's safety. In re Lilley (Ohio App. 4 Dist., Lawrence, 11-09-2004) No. 04CA22, 2004-Ohio-6156, 2004 WL 2631490, Unreported. Infants ⚖ 155

Statute requiring county agency to make reasonable efforts to prevent child's removal or to make it possible for child to return home with parent did not apply to agency's motion seeking permanent custody of child. In re A.C. (Ohio App. 12 Dist., Clermont, 10-18-2004) No. CA2004-05-041, 2004-Ohio-5531, 2004 WL 2340127, Unreported. Infants ⚖ 155

Mother challenging grant of permanent custody of children to county agency waived for appeal issue of whether trial court erred in finding that reasonable efforts were made to return children to mother's custody, where mother failed to raise claim in trial court. In re K. (Ohio App. 8 Dist., Cuyahoga, 09-02-2004) No. 83410, 2004-Ohio-4629, 2004 WL 1946141, Unreported. Infants ⚖ 243

Mother challenging grant of permanent custody of children to county agency failed to establish that agency failed to make reasonable efforts to return children to mother's custody; mother failed to cite authority supporting her claim that agency had duty to provide public housing, mother's admitted marijuana use disqualified mother from public housing, agency was not entity responsible for determining participation in public housing, and mother bore ultimate responsibility for insuring that she satisfied requirements for eligibility. In re K. (Ohio App. 8 Dist., Cuyahoga, 09-02-2004) No. 83410, 2004-Ohio-4629, 2004 WL 1946141, Unreported. Infants ⚖ 155; Infants ⚖ 241

Trial court was not required to find that the county department of job and family services used reasonable efforts to reunite family, in child dependency case; dependency case was not a permanent custody case. In re Narwrocki (Ohio App. 5 Dist., Stark, 08-09-2004) No. 2004-CA-00028, 2004-Ohio-4208, 2004 WL 1784525, Unreported. Infants ⚖ 210

Evidence supported finding that county agency made reasonable efforts to prevent child's removal from mother's home and that mother failed to take advantage of the services offered, thus supporting trial court's decision to grant permanent custody of child to county agency; mother was directed to complete a psychological evaluation and follow any recommendations, mother failed to complete and participate in counseling and training courses offered by county, mother had lived in at least nine places since child's removal and had been homeless on a couple occasions, and mother experienced financial difficulties due to her inability to hold a job. In re K.M. (Ohio App. 12 Dist., Butler, 08-09-2004) No. CA2004-02-052, 2004-Ohio-4152, 2004 WL 1765462, Unreported. Infants ⚖ 155

County children services' failure to consider placing father's children with paternal grandmother, and its alleged failure to require daughter to visit mother, did not contradict the finding that children services made reasonable efforts to prevent the continued removal of the children, in dependency case, where grandmother had no contact with child while father was in prison, she never filed a motion for custody of child, two of her own children were in jail and one was a prostitute, and she stated that child was better off in foster case, and daughter visited mother through the permanent custody hearing and expressed a desire to be adopted. In re Bailey (Ohio App. 4 Dist., Athens, 06-07-2004) No. 04CA11, 2004-Ohio-3628, 2004 WL 1531917, Unreported. Infants ⚖ 155

County children services made reasonable efforts to prevent the continued removal of children from father's custody, for the purpose of termination of parental rights proceeding; children services provided family-based services, housing relocation, transportation, financial aid, counseling, and visitation with parents. In re Bailey (Ohio App. 4 Dist., Athens, 06-07-2004) No. 04CA11, 2004-Ohio-3628, 2004 WL 1531917, Unreported. Infants ⚖ 155

Children services board, which was granted permanent custody of dependent child, made reasonable efforts to remedy problems that prevented child from being placed with mother; although mother argued that she completed relevant case plan services, mother was unable to use what she learned in real life situations, and case plan services mother did not complete, such as drug and alcohol assessment, were important. In re Baby Girl Elliott (Ohio App. 12 Dist., Butler, 07-06-2004) No. CA2003-10-256, 2004-Ohio-3539, 2004 WL 1485858, Unreported. Infants ⚖ 155

Evidence supported finding that the State made reasonable efforts to reunify father with his children, in termination of parental rights proceeding; children were placed in the custody of the State after protective supervision failed and parents were found in contempt due to their failure to comply with their case plan, failure to keep a clean and safe home, and failure to resolve a chronic head-lice problem, the State explored possible relative placement for the children, and in the year that the children were removed from father's custody he failed to attend anger management classes, complete court-ordered psychological counseling sessions, attend budget management sessions, or maintain a clean and safe home. In re H.E.R. (Ohio App. 2 Dist., Darke, 06-18-2004) No. 1631, 2004-Ohio-3138, 2004 WL 1366098, Unreported. Infants ⚖ 155

Evidence supported finding that county department of job and family services made reasonable efforts to prevent the removal of the children and eliminate the continued removal of the children, in dependency proceeding; department of job and family services developed a comprehensive caseplan to assist mother and step-father, the plan addressed issues including sex offender counseling, assistance with budgeting, parenting and life skills, and assistance to meet the special needs of the children. In re Caine (Ohio App. 5 Dist., Licking, 05-06-2004) No. 2003-CA-00118, 2004-Ohio-2270, 2004 WL 1047414, Unreported. Infants ⚖ 155

Evidence supported finding that county department of job and family services made reasonable efforts to eliminate the removal of mother's children and to make it possible for the children to return home, in support of granting permanent custody of children to county department of job and family services; mother was offered sexual abuse counseling, help with budgeting, parenting, and life skills, and assistance with meeting the special needs of the children. In re Caine (Ohio App. 5 Dist., Licking, 05-06-2004) No. 03-CA-115, 2004-Ohio-2326, 2004 WL 1045467, Unreported, appeal not allowed 102 Ohio St.3d 1534, 811 N.E.2d 1152, 2004-Ohio-3580. Infants ⚖ 155

County Children Services Board (CSB) was excepted from requirement to make reasonable efforts to reunite parents with their child before permanent custody could be awarded to agency; parents had previously had their parental rights terminated with respect to child's siblings. In re Richardson (Ohio App. 5 Dist., Guernsey, 04-27-2004) No. 04 CA 02, 2004-Ohio-2170, 2004 WL 911316, Unreported. Infants ⚖ 155

County Department of Job and Family Services: Children's Protective Services Unit (CPSU) made reasonable effort to reunite child and father, even though CPSU was not required to do so; father failed to complete mental health and substance abuse counseling despite CPSU's efforts to help father with payments for plan, and father failed to attend child's medical appointments. In re Jackson (Ohio App. 3 Dist., Hancock, 02-09-2004) No. 5-03-25, 2004-Ohio-542, 2004 WL 231513, Unreported. Infants ⚖ 155

Parents' prior involuntary termination of parental rights with regard to child's siblings exempted county Department of Job and Family Services: Children's Protective Services Unit (CPSU) from requirement that CPSU make reasonable efforts to reunite parents with child. In re Jackson (Ohio App. 3 Dist., Hancock, 02-09-2004) No. 5-03-25, 2004-Ohio-542, 2004 WL 231513, Unreported. Infants ⚖ 155

Trial court's finding that Children Services Board (CSB) made reasonable efforts to reunite child with her parents, a statutory finding required to support parental termination order, was against manifest weight of evidence; CSB conducted itself as if mother's losing her parental rights was a foregone conclusion, CSB never intended to make reasonable efforts to reunify mother with the child and only made limited efforts when ordered to do so by the trial court, when the parents fully complied with the CSB case plan, CSB refused parents' request for additional time with child, and CSB only set reunification as a goal for seven of the 23 months it had temporary custody of child. In re Elliott (Ohio App. 7 Dist., Jefferson, 01-26-2004) No. 03JE30, No. 03JE33, 2004-Ohio-388, 2004 WL 187413, Unreported. Infants 155

Trial court was under no obligation to make finding as to whether child could or could not be placed with either parent within reasonable amount of time, in support of its determination in parental termination proceeding, since child had been in temporary custody of Children Services Board for 12 or more months of consecutive 22-month period, a circumstance recognized by termination statute as relieving moving agency from its duty to make such showing. In re Elliott (Ohio App. 7 Dist., Jefferson, 01-26-2004) No. 03JE30, No. 03JE33, 2004-Ohio-388, 2004 WL 187413, Unreported. Infants 210

Failure to grant indigent mother's motion for appointment of psychological expert witness at State's expense, after granting Children Services Board's (CSB) motion that mother be evaluated by forensic psychologist, thereby making mother's mental health critical issue in parental termination proceeding, violated mother's due process rights; CSB expert's report and testimony regarding mother's mental health were central reasons why trial court granted CSB's motion for permanent custody, mother's mental health directly impacted trial court's conclusion that she was unfit to parent, and mother could not challenge testimony since trial court denied her request for similarly qualified expert. In re Elliott (Ohio App. 7 Dist., Jefferson, 01-26-2004) No. 03JE30, No. 03JE33, 2004-Ohio-388, 2004 WL 187413, Unreported. Constitutional Law 274(5); Infants 212

Paternal grandmother failed to show she was prejudiced by county agency's failure to file a case plan for father in child dependency proceedings, and thus grandmother did not have standing to challenge alleged error committed against father who did not contest or appeal permanent custody motion; agency made reasonable efforts to return children to their parents, but parents decided they did not want to or could not care for the children. In re McCann (Ohio App. 12 Dist., Clermont, 01-26-2004) No. CA2003-02-017, 2004-Ohio-283, 2004 WL 111644, Unreported. Infants 242

County children services agency made reasonable efforts to assist mother in satisfying case plan requirements regarding ability to be a mother for daughter who was in temporary custody of agency, thus supporting grant of permanent custody to agency, although agency did not provide any counseling referrals and failed to increase visitation with daughter, where agency was told mother had already enrolled in counseling, agency provided information and contacts for parenting classes, and agency discussed case plan with mother on several occasions. In re Nelson (Ohio App. 2 Dist., Montgomery, 01-23-2004) No. 19991, 2004-Ohio-268, 2004 WL 103021, Unreported. Infants 155

Sufficient evidence supported trial court finding that the family case plan was reasonable in its efforts to reunify parents with child, in child dependency proceeding; case plan addressed mother's cognitive issues by providing for a hands-on parent education plan, plan provided for visitation, mental health counseling for mother, and for parents to provide a safe and stable living environment and provide a stable income. In re Thomas (Ohio App. 3 Dist., Hancock, 11-03-2003) No. 5-03-08, 2003-Ohio-5885, 2003 WL 22474843, Unreported. Infants 155

Trial court's finding that there were reasonable efforts to reunify mother and child, when record reflected that county children services agency in fact made no efforts to reunite child with mother after removing child from home on ground that child could not be placed with either parent within a reasonable time due to parents' failure to remedy the conditions that originally caused child's removal, constituted harmless error, where several other statutory criteria justified grant of custody. In re Lewis (Ohio App. 4 Dist., Athens, 09-25-2003) No. 03CA12, 2003-Ohio-5262, 2003 WL 22267129, Unreported. Infants 253

County children services agency made reasonable efforts to prevent child's removal from her mother's home, where agency provided mother with substantial services both prior and subsequent to her first reunification with child, mental health counseling for child was provided, caseworker provided transportation to counseling, counseling referral was given to mother, case manager provided to mother parenting education, behavior modification, and nutritional and housekeeping assistance, and mother was given assistance in completing paperwork and obtaining medical evaluations. In re Lewis (Ohio App. 4 Dist., Athens, 09-25-2003) No. 03CA12, 2003-Ohio-5262, 2003 WL 22267129, Unreported. Infants 155

Trial court's findings of fact accompanying judgment granting permanent custody of mother's child to county agency minimally complied with statute requiring that such findings briefly describe services provided and why those services did not prevent removal of child from home, even though such findings were virtually identical to those made in similar judgment regarding child's brother, where trial court found that many efforts were made to assist mother, but she remained uncooperative, and it noted that mother had mental health issues that were not addressed despite county agency's efforts, and noted that mother had not visited child for over a month. In re Teasley (Ohio App. 10 Dist., Franklin, 09-25-2003) No. 03AP-196, No. 03AP-227, 2003-Ohio-5079, 2003 WL 22208789, Unreported. Infants 210

County department of job and family services made reasonable efforts to reunite children with mother, before department was granted permanent custody of children; case plan was prepared, but mother was serving 14-year prison sentence, possibility that Governor would grant her clemency, thereby reducing her sentence to as little as one year, was a long shot, and caseworker testified she was not aware of reunification services the department could provide mother in prison. In re McDonald (Ohio App. 5 Dist., Delaware, 09-10-2003) No. 03 CA F 03 021, 2003-Ohio-4808, 2003 WL 22100693, Unreported. Infants 155

Mother and father waived their appellate argument that the reasonable efforts bypass provision of child dependency statutes violated their rights under the Ohio and United States Constitutions and under the Americans with Disabilities Act, where mother and father failed to file any opposition to county job and family services motion that asked the court to find that the bypass provision applied, and they didn't file any opposition to the trial court order which found that the bypass provision applied. In re D.B. (Ohio App. 9 Dist., Medina, 08-27-2003) No. 03CA0015-M, No. 03CA0018-M, 2003-Ohio-4526, 2003 WL 22015445, Unreported. Infants 243

Evidence was sufficient to support finding that trial court made reasonable efforts to prevent the removal of 16-year-old child, who had been adjudicated dependent, from her parents' home prior to ordering removal; trial court found that home situation was deteriorating and, absent intervention, it would have continued to deteriorate, mother, who allegedly verbally and physically abused child, indicated that she believed she did not need counseling, guardian ad litem recommended removing child from home temporarily to facilitate counseling, and trial court indicated that temporary removal was a first step, and that after counseling had begun, situation was to be reevaluated to determine what further steps were in child's best interest. In re Day (Ohio App. 12 Dist., Clermont, 07-07-2003) No. CA2002-09-073, 2003-Ohio-3544, 2003 WL 21517343, Unreported. Infants 222

Trial court's finding, in permanent custody proceeding, that parents had failed to utilize resources of county children services agency to remedy conditions that caused children's removal from parents was mere surplusage, where statute required that, at any hearing where child is committed to permanent custody of agency, trial court must determine whether agency made reasonable efforts to return child to home, but statute did not require trial court to consider whether parents had utilized agency's resources to remedy conditions that caused removal. In re Myers (Ohio App. 4 Dist., Athens, 05-23-2003) No. 02CA50, 2003-Ohio-2776, 2003 WL 21246432, Unreported. Infants 210

Cuyahoga County Department of Children and Family Services (CCDCFS) made reasonable efforts to reunify mother and children, for purpose of proceeding in which CCDCFS was granted permanent custody of children, where CCDCFS referred mother to drug treatment and parenting programs and attempted to arrange visitation. In re C.N. (Ohio App. 8 Dist., Cuyahoga, 04-24-2003) No. 81813, 2003-Ohio-2048, 2003 WL 1924648, Unreported. Infants 155

Analysis of whether reasonable efforts were made to reunify mother and children was not required in determining whether to grant motion by Cuyahoga County Department of Children and Family Services (CCDCFS) to modify temporary custody of children to permanent custody. In re C.N. (Ohio App. 8 Dist., Cuyahoga, 04-24-2003) No. 81813, 2003-Ohio-2048, 2003 WL 1924648, Unreported. Infants 230.1

County seeking permanent custody of newborn made reasonable effort toward reunification of mother and father with their two-year-old daughter, even though they were not required to do so, as would support termination of their parental rights as to newborn in this separate case; although mother complained of a series of phone calls that were unreturned by county, county testified that at time mother made calls at issue, she resided in another state, significant periods of time existed wherein neither parent contacted the agency, father refused to provide his address and phone number to county, county returned nearly all phone calls and made repeated follow-up calls when a parent requested visitation or other assistance, and several caseworkers and counselors attempted to assist parents in satisfying case plan. In re Cook (Ohio App. 3 Dist., Seneca, 02-27-2003) No. 13-02-29, 2003-Ohio-868, 2003 WL 548484, Unreported. Infants ⊕ 155

Termination of mother's parental rights as to her six-year-old daughter, and both parents' rights as to their three-year-old son and two-year-old daughter in prior proceedings relieved the county from making reasonable reunification efforts between parents and their infant daughter in present termination case. In re Cook (Ohio App. 3 Dist., Seneca, 02-27-2003) No. 13-02-29, 2003-Ohio-868, 2003 WL 548484, Unreported. Infants ⊕ 155

County made a reasonable effort toward reunification of mother and father with their two-year-old daughter, as would support termination of parties' parental rights; although mother complained of a series of phone calls that were unreturned by county, county testified that at time mother made calls at issue, she resided in another state, significant periods of time existed wherein neither parent contacted the agency, father refused to provide his address and phone number to county, county returned nearly all phone calls, and made repeated follow-up calls when a parent requested visitation or other assistance, and several caseworkers and counselors attempted to assist parents in satisfying case plan. In re Cook (Ohio App. 3 Dist., Seneca, 02-27-2003) No. 13-02-27, 2003-Ohio-865, 2003 WL 547630, Unreported. Infants ⊕ 155

Termination of mother's parental rights as to her six-year-old daughter, and both parents' rights as to their three-year-old son in prior proceedings relieved the county from making reasonable reunification efforts with between parents and their two-year-old daughter in present termination case. In re Cook (Ohio App. 3 Dist., Seneca, 02-27-2003) No. 13-02-27, 2003-Ohio-865, 2003 WL 547630, Unreported. Infants ⊕ 155

Mother failed to establish that the county job and family services agency failed to offer mother services designed to reunify her and the children; when the agency initially took custody, mother refused to cooperate with the agency in developing a caseplan, later mother fled out of state and her whereabouts were unknown or she was incarcerated, and, when mother was told how to arrange for visitation with the children, she failed to do so. In re Billingsley (Ohio App. 3 Dist., Putnam, 01-28-2003) No. 12-02-07, No. 12-02-08, 2003-Ohio-344, 2003 WL 178661, Unreported. Infants ⊕ 155

County children services made reasonable efforts to treat mother's alleged personality disorder, thus supporting trial court's decision to terminate parental rights for mother's failure to remedy conditions that caused child to be placed outside her custody; counseling, group therapy and medication were made available to mother, but were not fully or properly utilized. In re Devin B. (Ohio App. 6 Dist., Lucas, 01-24-2003) No. L-02-1294, 2003-Ohio-307, 2003 WL 164858, Unreported. Infants ⊕ 158

County made reasonable efforts to make it possible to return child to father's care, as required to grant permanent custody of child to county. In re Dylan R. (Ohio App. 6 Dist., Lucas, 01-10-2003) No. L-02-1267, 2003-Ohio-69, 2003 WL 99502, Unreported. Infants ⊕ 155

County children services agency was not required to make reasonable efforts to reunify mother with minor child, for purposes of dependency proceeding, where permanent custody of child's siblings had been granted to agency prior to filing of dependency complaint. In re Llewellyn (Ohio App. 5 Dist., Fairfield, 12-18-2002) No. 2002CA51, 2002-Ohio-7188, 2002 WL 32005260, Unreported. Infants ⊕ 155

County failed to make a reasonable effort to reunify a mother and her daughter, and thus, reversal of trial court's judgment awarding permanent custody of daughter to county was required, even though county determined that mother failed to comply with her case plan, where mother, who had moved to a neighboring state while daughter was under temporary custody of county, requested that daughter be transferred to custody of neighboring state, no evidence suggested that neighboring state would not have accepted transfer, transfer would have been possible under the Interstate Compact on the Placement of Children, and county apparently ignored facts that mother had difficulty traveling back to state to be with her daughter and comply with her case plan, attainment of goals of case plan may have been enhanced by a transfer, and a transfer may have been a viable option. In re Secrest (Ohio App. 2 Dist., Montgomery, 12-20-2002) No. 19377, 2002-Ohio-7096, 2002 WL 31846268, Unreported. Infants ⊕ 155

Trial court, that entered order awarding permanent custody of child to Montgomery County Children Services (MCCS), substantially complied with statutory requirement that it make written findings regarding MCCS's attempt at reunification of parent and child, where trial court adopted findings of magistrate which included specific findings that MCCS had made reasonable efforts to return child to home via "case management; information/referral and substitute care," that these services did not enable child to return home, and that mother had failed to remedy conditions that caused child to be removed, because she failed to visit, support, or communicate with child, and had failed to provide medical treatment and food. In re Erin Secrest (Ohio App. 2 Dist., Montgomery, 12-20-2002) No. 19378, 2002-Ohio-7094, 2002 WL 31846262, Unreported. Infants ⊕ 210

County children's services board provided reasonable efforts to unify father with his children, prior to seeking termination of his parental rights; father's case plan was amended four times, each noting reunification as primary goal, counseling referrals were made to both parents, including referrals to treat father's alcohol problem, assigned caseworker and family aide frequented home to assist parents in acquiring necessary parenting skills, past referrals were made to parenting classes, and county was prevented from reunifying children with their parents due to their problems with maintaining a secure residence. In re Cook, Alleged Dependent Child (Ohio App. 3 Dist., Allen, 12-11-2002) No. 1-02-47, No. 1-02-48, No. 1-02-49, 2002-Ohio-6771, 2002 WL 31758704, Unreported. Infants ⊕ 155

Children Services Division (CSD) was not required to make reasonable efforts to reunify daughter with father, where record revealed that father's parental rights over son, daughter's sibling, had previously been involuntarily terminated, and that father had voluntarily surrendered parental rights to another daughter that same year. In re Daniels (Ohio App. 3 Dist., Shelby, 11-18-2002) No. 17-02-24, 2002-Ohio-6256, 2002 WL 31538808, Unreported. Infants ⊕ 155

Evidence supported finding that county jobs and family services made reasonable efforts to reunite the family, in termination of parental rights proceeding; when mother moved out of county her case was transferred to new county, new county arranged for mother to complete parenting classes, arranged for housing, paid for mother's electric bill, and arranged for mother's oldest child to be assessed, as required in mother's caseplan. In re Williamson (Ohio App. 5 Dist., Tuscarawas, 11-01-2002) No. 2002AP060050, 2002-Ohio-6069, 2002 WL 31492278, Unreported. Infants ⊕ 155

Evidence was sufficient to support finding that county agency, prior to filing petition for permanent custody and termination of parental rights, made reasonable efforts to implement a case plan that would have remedied situations which caused children to be removed from mother's home; record indicated that mother did not comply with case plan requirements that she address her mental and emotional problems, requirements were implemented in light of mother's history of auditory hallucinations that were telling her to harm her children, and mother failed to regularly take prescribed medications and missed scheduled appointments. In re Howard (Ohio App. 8 Dist., Cuyahoga, 10-24-2002) No. 78573, 2002-Ohio-5818, 2002 WL 31398668, Unreported. Infants ⊕ 155

Divesting a father of parental rights is error where (1) the children's services board fails to timely include the father in a case plan and does not provide him with a minimally adequate direction or opportunity regarding his rehabilitation as a parent, (2) the trial court fails to find that reunification would have been futile as required by RC 2151.419, and (3) the court improperly denies the father's motion for a continuance before the guardian ad litem submits a written report as mandated by RC 2151.414(C). In re Richard, Laqueeda, Shennell & Dominique (Ohio App. 2 Dist., Montgomery, 12-14-1994) No. 14140, No. 14200, 1994 WL 702071, Unreported.

Court of Appeals would not consider on appeal constitutionality, as applied to mother, of statute providing for permanent custody if in child's best interest and child has been in temporary custody of agency for 12 or more months of a consecutive 22-month period, where mother did not challenge constitutionality of statute at trial. In re Lopez (Ohio App. 3 Dist., 05-08-2006) 166 Ohio App.3d 688, 852 N.E.2d 1266, 2006-Ohio-2251. Infants ⊕ 243

County child protection agency used reasonable efforts to reunite father and child, as required by statute, for purposes of obtaining permanent custody; agency recognized that father spoke only Spanish and used reasonable efforts to obtain interpreters for him, although agency relied on woman with whom father was in a relationship as an interpreter for a period of a few months, father had Spanish speaking legal counsel throughout proceedings, and there was no evidence that father was unable to understand the various interpreters' translations. In re Lopez (Ohio App. 3 Dist., 05-08-2006) 166 Ohio App.3d 688, 852 N.E.2d 1266, 2006-Ohio-2251. Infants ⊕ 155

County was not diligent in efforts to unite child with either of natural parents where there were never any regularly scheduled visits, parents had simply been directed to make arrangements for weekly one-hour visits supervised by county employees in setting totally nonconducive to maintenance or development of close parent-child relationship, and parents and child received separate psychological evaluation as recommended by plan, but no counseling was ever suggested to assist parents in developing parenting skills or familial relationships. In re Brown (Ohio App. 3 Dist., 11-02-1994) 98 Ohio App.3d 337, 648 N.E.2d 576. Infants ⊕ 155

Juvenile court's repeated failures to comply with procedural and substantive requirements regarding emergency temporary custody orders were not of sufficient merit to require extraordinary remedy of habeas corpus, where complaint alleged that private child-placing agency had child voluntarily placed with it, where father allegedly testified that he was unable to care for child, and where complaint alleged that father was unfit because of alcoholism and substance abuse. Howard v. Catholic Social Serv. of Cuyahoga Cty., Inc. (Ohio, 08-31-1994) 70 Ohio St.3d 141, 637 N.E.2d 890, 1994-Ohio-219, reconsideration denied 70 Ohio St.3d 1457, 639 N.E.2d 796. Habeas Corpus ⇐ 532(2)

Risk of harm to children from their father, whose parental rights were terminated, was inherent in mother's continued custody and was not susceptible to any curative efforts by county agency; thus, neither reunification to revive actuality of risk nor empty efforts to avoid it was required for county agency to satisfy statutory requirement that it make "reasonable efforts" to eliminate continued removal of children from home, or to make it possible for children to return home. In re Pieper Children (Preble 1993) 85 Ohio App.3d 318, 619 N.E.2d 1059. Infants ⇐ 155

Public agency made reasonable efforts to return child to mother's home before trial court terminated parental rights and awarded permanent custody to agency; agency developed a case plan which outlined a specific plan of reunification, agency modified the visitation in order to accommodate mother's transportation difficulties, and agency provided mother with the opportunity to attend parenting classes and undergo psychological evaluations. In re Bair (Ohio App. 5 Dist., Richland, 09-10-2002) No. 02CA13, 2002-Ohio-5053, 2002 WL 31116692, Unreported. Infants ⇐ 155

"Case plans," intended to facilitate the reunification of families who have been temporarily separated, establish individualized concerns and goals, along with the steps that the parents and agency can take to achieve reunification. In re Sorg (Ohio App. 3 Dist., Hancock, 05-28-2002) No. 5-02-03, 2002-Ohio-2725, 2002 WL 1299762, Unreported. Infants ⇐ 222

Mother waived her appellate argument that the trial court erred when it determined that the county children's services board was not required to establish that reasonable efforts for reunification of mother and child had been made, in termination of parental rights proceeding, where mother failed to file any written objections to the trial court's decision to grant county's motion for a "reasonable efforts bypass," which excused county from making reasonable efforts to assist mother in reunification due to the prior involuntary termination of mother's parental rights to five of her other children. In re Pittman (Ohio App. 9 Dist., Summit, 05-08-2002) No. 20894, 2002-Ohio-2208, 2002 WL 987852, Unreported. Infants ⇐ 243

Granting an agency's motion for permanent custody is error absent a further finding in full conformity with RC 2151.419(B) that reasonable efforts at reunification were made or would have been futile. In re Lawson/Reid Children, No. 96-CA-0010, 1997 WL 189379 (2d Dist Ct App, Clark, 4-18-97).

3. "Siblings"

Evidence supported finding that county department of job and family services made reasonable efforts to reunite mother with her children, during dependency case; department had difficulty in locating mother since she lived in four different places in different counties in the year before the permanent custody hearing, the department sought mental health counseling for the children, and the department was responsible for initially reuniting mother with her children after she had abandoned them for six years. In re Hines (Ohio App. 5 Dist., Tuscarawas, 05-03-2005) No. 2004AP120072, 2005-Ohio-2266, 2005 WL 1077175, Unreported. Infants ⇐ 222

Father's son and father's daughter were siblings, despite fact that they had different mothers, for purposes of statute providing that children's services agency did not have to make reunification efforts when parent from whom child was removed had had parental rights involuntarily terminated with respect to child's sibling; children who had one or both parents in common were siblings under statute. In re Daniels (Ohio App. 3 Dist., Shelby, 11-18-2002) No. 17-02-24, 2002-Ohio-6256, 2002 WL 31538808, Unreported. Infants ⇐ 155

2151.42 Modification or termination of dispositional order

(A) At any hearing in which a court is asked to modify or terminate an order of disposition issued under section 2151.353, 2151.415, or 2151.417 of the Revised Code, the court, in determining whether to return the child to the child's parents, shall consider whether it is in the best interest of the child.

(B) An order of disposition issued under division (A)(3) of section 2151.353, division (A)(3) of section 2151.415, or section 2151.417 of the Revised Code granting legal custody of a child to a person is intended to be permanent in nature. A court shall not modify or terminate an order granting legal custody of a child unless it finds, based on facts that have arisen since the order was issued or that were unknown to the court at that time, that a change has occurred in the circumstances of the child or the person who was granted legal custody, and that modification or termination of the order is necessary to serve the best interest of the child.

(1999 H 176, eff. 10–29–99; 1998 H 484, eff. 3–18–99)

Historical and Statutory Notes

Ed. Note: Former 2151.42 repealed by 1972 H 511, eff. 1–1–74; 130 v H 83; 1953 H 1; GC 1639–46; see now 2919.21 and 2919.22 for provisions analogous to former 2151.42.

Pre–1953 H 1 Amendments: 121 v 557; 119 v 731; 117 v 520

Amendment Note: 1999 H 176 rewrote the section, which prior thereto read:

"(A) At any hearing in which a court is asked to modify or terminate an order of disposition issued under section 2151.353, 2151.415, or 2151.417 of the Revised Code, the court, in determining whether to return the child to the child's parents, shall consider whether it is in the best interest of the child. If the order of disposition that is the subject of a hearing under this section involves a previous award of legal custody under division (A)(3) of section 2151.353 of the Revised Code and is governed by division (E) of section 3109.04 of the Revised Code, the court shall comply with the requirements of division (E) of section 3109.04 of the Revised Code in its modification or termination of the order of disposition.

"(B) Additionally, an order of disposition issued under division (A)(3) of section 2151.353, division (A)(3) of section 2151.415, or section 2151.417 of the Revised Code granting legal custody of a child to a person is intended to be permanent in nature. A court shall not modify or terminate an order issued under either of those divisions or that section granting legal custody of a child to a person unless it finds, based on facts that have arisen since the order was issued or that were unknown to the court at that time, that a change has occurred in the circumstances of the child, the child's parents, or the person, and that modification or termination of the order is necessary to serve the best interest of the child."

Library References

Infants ⇐ 230.
Westlaw Topic No. 211.
C.J.S. Adoption of Persons § 10.
C.J.S. Infants §§ 57, 69 to 85.

Research References

Encyclopedias

OH Jur. 3d Family Law § 1602, Prehearing Motions—Motion for Order of Disposition.
OH Jur. 3d Family Law § 1662, on Request for Permanent Custody.
OH Jur. 3d Family Law § 1706, Modification or Vacation of Order.
OH Jur. 3d Family Law § 1711, Review Hearing.

Treatises and Practice Aids

Carlin, Baldwin's Ohio Practice, Merrick-Rippner Probate Law § 107:79, Disposition of Abused, Neglected, or Dependent Child—Legal Custody.
Giannelli & Yeomans, Ohio Juvenile Law § 30:6, Temporary Custody.
Giannelli & Yeomans, Ohio Juvenile Law § 31:2, Filing of Motion.
Giannelli & Yeomans, Ohio Juvenile Law § 33:4, Abuse, Neglect, and Dependency Proceedings.
Giannelli & Yeomans, Ohio Juvenile Law § 33:11, Child Custody Agency Commitment—Juvenile Court Dispositional Review.

Notes of Decisions

Evidence 1

1. Evidence

Sufficient evidence demonstrated a change of circumstances warranting finding that change of custody from mother to father was in best interest of children, where mother failed to cooperate with father's visitation or paternal grandmother's court-ordered right of first refusal for babysitting, son appeared to be overmedicated in an attempt to control behavior, and mother did not even inform father or grandmother of nature of medication, dosage, or other important factors bearing on proper child care. In re Dawkins (Ohio App. 10 Dist., Franklin, 08-26-2003) No. 02AP-1024, 2003-Ohio-4503, 2003 WL 22006829, Unreported. Child Custody ⇔ 558; Child Custody ⇔ 563; Child Custody ⇔ 569; Child Custody ⇔ 579

Trial court was permitted to consider, without additional, explanatory testimony, mother's positive marijuana test results in reaching its decision that returning her children to her custody was not in the children's best interests and to award legal custody to children's cousin and his wife. In re Beebe (Ohio App. 3 Dist., Allen, 04-15-2003) No. 1-02-84, 2003-Ohio-1888, 2003 WL 1873172, Unreported. Infants ⇔ 222; Infants ⇔ 231

2151.421 Persons required to report injury or neglect; procedures on receipt of report

(A)(1)(a) No person described in division (A)(1)(b) of this section who is acting in an official or professional capacity and knows, or has reasonable cause to suspect based on facts that would cause a reasonable person in a similar position to suspect, that a child under eighteen years of age or a mentally retarded, developmentally disabled, or physically impaired child under twenty-one years of age has suffered or faces a threat of suffering any physical or mental wound, injury, disability, or condition of a nature that reasonably indicates abuse or neglect of the child shall fail to immediately report that knowledge or reasonable cause to suspect to the entity or persons specified in this division. Except as provided in section 5120.173 of the Revised Code, the person making the report shall make it to the public children services agency or a municipal or county peace officer in the county in which the child resides or in which the abuse or neglect is occurring or has occurred. In the circumstances described in section 5120.173 of the Revised Code, the person making the report shall make it to the entity specified in that section.

(b) Division (A)(1)(a) of this section applies to any person who is an attorney; physician, including a hospital intern or resident; dentist; podiatrist; practitioner of a limited branch of medicine as specified in section 4731.15 of the Revised Code; registered nurse; licensed practical nurse; visiting nurse; other health care professional; licensed psychologist; licensed school psychologist; independent marriage and family therapist or marriage and family therapist; speech pathologist or audiologist; coroner; administrator or employee of a child day-care center; administrator or employee of a residential camp or child day camp; administrator or employee of a certified child care agency or other public or private children services agency; school teacher; school employee; school authority; person engaged in social work or the practice of professional counseling; agent of a county humane society; person, other than a cleric, rendering spiritual treatment through prayer in accordance with the tenets of a well-recognized religion; superintendent, board member, or employee of a county board of mental retardation; investigative agent contracted with by a county board of mental retardation; employee of the department of mental retardation and developmental disabilities; employee of a facility or home that provides respite care in accordance with section 5123.171 of the Revised Code; employee of a home health agency; employee of an entity that provides homemaker services; a person performing the duties of an assessor pursuant to Chapter 3107. or 5103. of the Revised Code; or third party employed by a public children services agency to assist in providing child or family related services.

(2) Except as provided in division (A)(3) of this section, an attorney or a physician is not required to make a report pursuant to division (A)(1) of this section concerning any communication the attorney or physician receives from a client or patient in an attorney-client or physician-patient relationship, if, in accordance with division (A) or (B) of section 2317.02 of the Revised Code, the attorney or physician could not testify with respect to that communication in a civil or criminal proceeding.

(3) The client or patient in an attorney-client or physician-patient relationship described in division (A)(2) of this section is deemed to have waived any testimonial privilege under division (A) or (B) of section 2317.02 of the Revised Code with respect to any communication the attorney or physician receives from the client or patient in that attorney-client or physician-patient relationship, and the attorney or physician shall make a report pursuant to division (A)(1) of this section with respect to that communication, if all of the following apply:

(a) The client or patient, at the time of the communication, is either a child under eighteen years of age or a mentally retarded, developmentally disabled, or physically impaired person under twenty-one years of age.

(b) The attorney or physician knows, or has reasonable cause to suspect based on facts that would cause a reasonable person in similar position to suspect, as a result of the communication or any observations made during that communication, that the client or patient has suffered or faces a threat of suffering any physical or mental wound, injury, disability, or condition of a nature that reasonably indicates abuse or neglect of the client or patient.

(c) The abuse or neglect does not arise out of the client's or patient's attempt to have an abortion without the notification of her parents, guardian, or custodian in accordance with section 2151.85 of the Revised Code.

(4)(a) No cleric and no person, other than a volunteer, designated by any church, religious society, or faith acting as a leader, official, or delegate on behalf of the church, religious society, or faith who is acting in an official or professional capacity, who knows, or has reasonable cause to believe based on facts that would cause a reasonable person in a similar position to believe, that a child under eighteen years of age or a mentally retarded, developmentally disabled, or physically impaired child under twenty-one years of age has suffered or faces a threat of suffering any physical or mental wound, injury, disability, or condition of a nature that reasonably indicates abuse or neglect of the child, and who knows, or has reasonable cause to believe based on facts that would cause a reasonable person in a similar position to believe, that another cleric or another person, other than a volunteer, designated by a church, religious society, or faith acting as a leader, official, or delegate on behalf of the church, religious society, or faith caused, or poses the threat of causing, the wound, injury, disability, or condition that reasonably indicates abuse or neglect shall fail to immediately report that knowledge or reasonable cause to believe to the entity or persons specified in this division. Except as provided in section 5120.173 of the Revised Code, the person making the report shall make it to the public children services agency or a municipal or county peace officer in the county in which the child resides or in which the abuse or neglect is occurring or has occurred. In the circumstances described in section 5120.173 of the Revised Code, the person making the report shall make it to the entity specified in that section.

(b) Except as provided in division (A)(4)(c) of this section, a cleric is not required to make a report pursuant to division (A)(4)(a) of this section concerning any communication the cleric receives from a penitent in a cleric-penitent relationship, if, in accordance with division (C) of section 2317.02 of the Revised Code, the cleric could not testify with respect to that communication in a civil or criminal proceeding.

(c) The penitent in a cleric-penitent relationship described in division (A)(4)(b) of this section is deemed to have waived any testimonial privilege under division (C) of section 2317.02 of the Revised Code with respect to any communication the cleric receives from the penitent in that cleric-penitent relationship, and the cleric shall make a report pursuant to division (A)(4)(a) of this section with respect to that communication, if all of the following apply:

(i) The penitent, at the time of the communication, is either a child under eighteen years of age or a mentally retarded, developmentally disabled, or physically impaired person under twenty-one years of age.

(ii) The cleric knows, or has reasonable cause to believe based on facts that would cause a reasonable person in a similar position to believe, as a result of the communication or any observations made during that communication, the penitent has suffered or faces a threat of suffering any physical or mental wound, injury, disability, or condition of a nature that reasonably indicates abuse or neglect of the penitent.

(iii) The abuse or neglect does not arise out of the penitent's attempt to have an abortion performed upon a child under eighteen years of age or upon a mentally retarded, developmentally disabled, or physically impaired person under twenty-one years of age without the notification of her parents, guardian, or custodian in accordance with section 2151.85 of the Revised Code.

(d) Divisions (A)(4)(a) and (c) of this section do not apply in a cleric-penitent relationship when the disclosure of any communication the cleric receives from the penitent is in violation of the sacred trust.

(e) As used in divisions (A)(1) and (4) of this section, "cleric" and "sacred trust" have the same meanings as in section 2317.02 of the Revised Code.

(B) Anyone who knows, or has reasonable cause to suspect based on facts that would cause a reasonable person in similar circumstances to suspect, that a child under eighteen years of age or a mentally retarded, developmentally disabled, or physically impaired person under twenty-one years of age has suffered or faces a threat of suffering any physical or mental wound, injury, disability, or other condition of a nature that reasonably indicates abuse or neglect of the child may report or cause reports to be made of that knowledge or reasonable cause to suspect to the entity or persons specified in this division. Except as provided in section 5120.173 of the Revised Code, a person making a report or causing a report to be made under this division shall make it or cause it to be made to the public children services agency or to a municipal or county peace officer. In the circumstances described in section 5120.173 of the Revised Code, a person making a report or causing a report to be made under this division shall make it or cause it to be made to the entity specified in that section.

(C) Any report made pursuant to division (A) or (B) of this section shall be made forthwith either by telephone or in person and shall be followed by a written report, if requested by the receiving agency or officer. The written report shall contain:

(1) The names and addresses of the child and the child's parents or the person or persons having custody of the child, if known;

(2) The child's age and the nature and extent of the child's injuries, abuse, or neglect that is known or reasonably suspected or believed, as applicable, to have occurred or of the threat of injury, abuse, or neglect that is known or reasonably suspected or believed, as applicable, to exist, including any evidence of previous injuries, abuse, or neglect;

(3) Any other information that might be helpful in establishing the cause of the injury, abuse, or neglect that is known or reasonably suspected or believed, as applicable, to have occurred or of the threat of injury, abuse, or neglect that is known or reasonably suspected or believed, as applicable, to exist.

Any person, who is required by division (A) of this section to report child abuse or child neglect that is known or reasonably suspected or believed to have occurred, may take or cause to be taken color photographs of areas of trauma visible on a child and, if medically indicated, cause to be performed radiological examinations of the child.

(D) As used in this division, "children's advocacy center" and "sexual abuse of a child" have the same meanings as in section 2151.425 of the Revised Code.

(1) When a municipal or county peace officer receives a report concerning the possible abuse or neglect of a child or the possible threat of abuse or neglect of a child, upon receipt of the report, the municipal or county peace officer who receives the report shall refer the report to the appropriate public children services agency.

(2) When a public children services agency receives a report pursuant to this division or division (A) or (B) of this section, upon receipt of the report, the public children services agency shall do both of the following:

(a) Comply with section 2151.422 of the Revised Code;

(b) If the county served by the agency is also served by a children's advocacy center and the report alleges sexual abuse of a child or another type of abuse of a child that is specified in the memorandum of understanding that creates the center as being within the center's jurisdiction, comply regarding the report with the protocol and procedures for referrals and investigations, with the coordinating activities, and with the authority or responsibility for performing or providing functions, activities, and services stipulated in the interagency agreement entered into under section 2151.428 of the Revised Code relative to that center.

(E) No township, municipal, or county peace officer shall remove a child about whom a report is made pursuant to this section from the child's parents, stepparents, or guardian or any other persons having custody of the child without consultation with the public children services agency, unless, in the judgment of the officer, and, if the report was made by physician, the physician, immediate removal is considered essential to protect the child from further abuse or neglect. The agency that must be consulted shall be the agency conducting the investigation of the report as determined pursuant to section 2151.422 of the Revised Code.

(F)(1) Except as provided in section 2151.422 of the Revised Code or in an interagency agreement entered into under section 2151.428 of the Revised Code that applies to the particular report, the public children services agency shall investigate, within twenty-four hours, each report of child abuse or child neglect that is known or reasonably suspected or believed to have occurred and of a threat of child abuse or child neglect that is known or reasonably suspected or believed to exist that is referred to it under this section to determine the circumstances surrounding the injuries, abuse, or neglect or the threat of injury, abuse, or neglect, the cause of the injuries, abuse, neglect, or threat, and the person or persons responsible. The investigation shall be made in cooperation with the law enforcement agency and in accordance with the memorandum of understanding prepared under division (J) of this section. A representative of the public children services agency shall, at the time of initial contact with the person subject to the investigation, inform the person of the specific complaints or allegations made against the person. The information shall be given in a manner that is consistent with division (H)(1) of this section and protects the rights of the person making the report under this section.

A failure to make the investigation in accordance with the memorandum is not grounds for, and shall not result in, the dismissal of any charges or complaint arising from the report or the suppression of any evidence obtained as a result of the report and does not give, and shall not be construed as giving, any rights or any grounds for appeal or post-conviction relief to any person. The public children services agency shall report each case the uniform statewide automated child welfare information system that the department of job and family services shall maintain in accordance with section 5101.13 of the Revised Code. The public children services agency shall submit a report of its investigation, in writing, to the law enforcement agency.

(2) The public children services agency shall make any recommendations to the county prosecuting attorney or city director of law that it considers necessary to protect any children that are brought to its attention.

(G)(1)(a) Except as provided in division (H)(3) of this section, anyone or any hospital, institution, school, health department, or agency participating in the making of reports under division (A) of this section, anyone or any hospital, institution, school, health department, or agency participating in good faith in the making of reports under division (B) of this section, and anyone participating in good faith in a judicial proceeding resulting from the reports, shall be immune from any civil or criminal liability for injury, death, or loss to person or property that otherwise might be incurred or imposed as a result of the making of the reports or the participation in the judicial proceeding.

(b) Notwithstanding section 4731.22 of the Revised Code, the physician-patient privilege shall not be a ground for excluding evidence regarding a child's injuries, abuse, or neglect, or the cause of the injuries, abuse, or neglect in any judicial proceeding resulting from a report submitted pursuant to this section.

(2) In any civil or criminal action or proceeding in which it is alleged and proved that participation in the making of a report under this section was not in good faith or participation in a judicial proceeding resulting from a report made under this section was not in good faith, the court shall award the prevailing party reasonable attorney's fees and costs and, if a civil action or proceeding is voluntarily dismissed, may award reasonable attorney's fees and costs to the party against whom the civil action or proceeding is brought.

(H)(1) Except as provided in divisions (H)(4) and (M) of this section, a report made under this section is confidential. The information provided in a report made pursuant to this section and the name of the person who made the report shall not be released for use, and shall not be used, as evidence in any civil action or proceeding brought against the person who made the report. In a criminal proceeding, the report is admissible in evidence in accordance with the Rules of Evidence and is subject to discovery in accordance with the Rules of Criminal Procedure.

(2) No person shall permit or encourage the unauthorized dissemination of the contents of any report made under this section.

(3) A person who knowingly makes or causes another person to make a false report under division (B) of this section that alleges that any person has committed an act or omission that resulted in a child being an abused child or a neglected child is guilty of a violation of section 2921.14 of the Revised Code.

(4) If a report is made pursuant to division (A) or (B) of this section and the child who is the subject of the report dies for any reason at any time after the report is made, but before the child attains eighteen years of age, the public children services agency or municipal or county peace officer to which the report was made or referred, on the request of the child fatality review board, shall submit a summary sheet of information providing a summary of the report to the review board of the county in which the deceased child resided at the time of death. On the request of the review board, the agency or peace officer may, at its discretion, make the report available to the review board. If the county served by the public children services agency is also served by a children's advocacy center and the report of alleged sexual abuse of a child or another type of abuse of a child is specified in the memorandum of understanding that creates the center as being within the center's jurisdiction, the agency or center shall perform the duties and functions specified in this division in accordance with the interagency agreement entered into under section 2151.428 of the Revised Code relative to that advocacy center.

(5) A public children services agency shall advise a person alleged to have inflicted abuse or neglect on a child who is the subject of a report made pursuant to this section, including a report alleging sexual abuse of a child or another type of abuse of a child referred to a children's advocacy center pursuant to an interagency agreement entered into under section 2151.428 of the Revised Code, in writing of the disposition of the investigation. The agency shall not provide to the person any information that identifies the person who made the report, statements of witnesses, or police or other investigative reports.

(I) Any report that is required by this section, other than a report that is made to the state highway patrol as described in section 5120.173 of the Revised Code, shall result in protective services and emergency supportive services being made available by the public children services agency on behalf of the children about whom the report is made, in an effort to prevent further neglect or abuse, to enhance their welfare, and, whenever possible, to preserve the family unit intact. The agency required to provide the services shall be the agency conducting the investigation of the report pursuant to section 2151.422 of the Revised Code.

(J)(1) Each public children services agency shall prepare a memorandum of understanding that is signed by all of the following:

(a) If there is only one juvenile judge in the county, the juvenile judge of the county or the juvenile judge's representative;

(b) If there is more than one juvenile judge in the county, a juvenile judge or the juvenile judges' representative selected by the juvenile judges or, if they are unable to do so for any reason, the juvenile judge who is senior in point of service or the senior juvenile judge's representative;

(c) The county peace officer;

(d) All chief municipal peace officers within the county;

(e) Other law enforcement officers handling child abuse and neglect cases in the county;

(f) The prosecuting attorney of the county;

(g) If the public children services agency is not the county department of job and family services, the county department of job and family services;

(h) The county humane society;

(i) If the public children services agency participated in the execution of a memorandum of understanding under section 2151.426 of the Revised Code establishing a children's advocacy center, each participating member of the children's advocacy center established by the memorandum.

(2) A memorandum of understanding shall set forth the normal operating procedure to be employed by all concerned officials in the execution of their respective responsibilities under this section and division (C) of section 2919.21, division (B)(1) of section 2919.22, division (B) of section 2919.23, and section 2919.24 of the Revised Code and shall have as two of its primary goals the elimination of all unnecessary interviews of children who are the subject of reports made pursuant to division (A) or (B) of this section and, when feasible, providing for only one interview of a child who is the subject of any report made pursuant to division (A) or (B) of this section. A failure to follow the procedure set forth in the memorandum by the concerned officials is not grounds for, and shall not result in, the dismissal of any charges or complaint arising from any reported case of abuse or neglect or the suppression of any evidence obtained as a result of any reported child abuse or child neglect and does not give, and shall not be construed as giving, any rights or any grounds for appeal or post-conviction relief to any person.

(3) A memorandum of understanding shall include all of the following:

(a) The roles and responsibilities for handling emergency and nonemergency cases of abuse and neglect;

(b) Standards and procedures to be used in handling and coordinating investigations of reported cases of child abuse and reported cases of child neglect, methods to be used in interviewing the child who is the subject of the report and who allegedly was abused or neglected, and standards and procedures addressing the categories of persons who may interview the child who is the subject of the report and who allegedly was abused or neglected.

(4) If a public children services agency participated in the execution of a memorandum of understanding under section 2151.426 of the Revised Code establishing a children's advocacy center, the agency shall incorporate the contents of that memorandum in the memorandum prepared pursuant to this section.

(K)(1) Except as provided in division (K)(4) of this section, a person who is required to make a report pursuant to division (A) of this section may make a reasonable number of requests of the public children services agency that receives or is referred the report, or of the children's advocacy center that is referred the report if the report is referred to a children's advocacy center pursuant to an interagency agreement entered into under section 2151.428 of the Revised Code, to be provided with the following information:

(a) Whether the agency or center has initiated an investigation of the report;

(b) Whether the agency or center is continuing to investigate the report;

(c) Whether the agency or center is otherwise involved with the child who is the subject of the report;

(d) The general status of the health and safety of the child who is the subject of the report;

(e) Whether the report has resulted in the filing of a complaint in juvenile court or of criminal charges in another court.

(2) A person may request the information specified in division (K)(1) of this section only if, at the time the report is made, the person's name, address, and telephone number are provided to the person who receives the report.

When a municipal or county peace officer or employee of a public children services agency receives a report pursuant to division (A) or (B) of this section the recipient of the report shall inform the person of the right to request the information described in division (K)(1) of this section. The recipient of the report shall include in the initial child abuse or child neglect report that the person making the report was so informed and, if provided at the time of the making of the report, shall include the person's name, address, and telephone number in the report.

Each request is subject to verification of the identity of the person making the report. If that person's identity is verified, the agency shall provide the person with the information described in division (K)(1) of this section a reasonable number of times, except that the agency shall not disclose any confidential information regarding the child who is the subject of the report other than the information described in those divisions.

(3) A request made pursuant to division (K)(1) of this section is not a substitute for any report required to be made pursuant to division (A) of this section.

(4) If an agency other than the agency that received or was referred the report is conducting the investigation of the report pursuant to section 2151.422 of the Revised Code, the agency conducting the investigation shall comply with the requirements of division (K) of this section.

(L) The director of job and family services shall adopt rules in accordance with Chapter 119. of the Revised Code to implement this section. The department of job and family services may enter into a plan of cooperation with any other governmental entity to aid in ensuring that children are protected from abuse and neglect. The department shall make recommendations to the attorney general that the department determines are necessary to protect children from child abuse and child neglect.

(M)(1) As used in this division:

(a) "Out-of-home care" includes a nonchartered nonpublic school if the alleged child abuse or child neglect, or alleged threat of child abuse or child neglect, described in a report received by a public children services agency allegedly occurred in or involved the nonchartered nonpublic school and the alleged perpetrator named in the report holds a certificate, permit, or license issued by the state board of education under section 3301.071 or Chapter 3319. of the Revised Code.

(b) "Administrator, director, or other chief administrative officer" means the superintendent of the school district if the out-of-home care entity subject to a report made pursuant to this section is a school operated by the district.

(2) No later than the end of the day following the day on which a public children services agency receives a report of alleged child abuse or child neglect, or a report of an alleged threat of child abuse or child neglect, that allegedly occurred in or involved an out-of-home care entity, the agency shall provide written notice of the allegations contained in and the person named as the alleged perpetrator in the report to the administrator, director, or other chief administrative officer of the out-of-home care entity that is the subject of the report unless the administrator, director, or other chief administrative officer is named as an alleged perpetrator in the report. If the administrator, director, or other chief administrative officer of an out-of-home care entity is named as an alleged perpetrator in a report of alleged child abuse or child neglect, or a report of an alleged threat of child abuse or child neglect, that allegedly occurred in or involved the out-of-home care entity, the agency shall provide the written notice to the owner or governing board of the out-of-home care entity that is the subject of the report. The agency shall not provide witness statements or police or other investigative reports.

(3) No later than three days after the day on which a public children services agency that conducted the investigation as determined pursuant to section 2151.422 of the Revised Code makes a disposition of an investigation involving a report of alleged child abuse or child neglect, or a report of an alleged threat of child abuse or child neglect, that allegedly occurred in or involved an out-of-home care entity, the agency shall send written notice of the disposition of the investigation to the administrator, director, or other chief administrative officer and the owner or governing board of the out-of-home care entity. The agency shall not provide witness statements or police or other investigative reports.

(2006 S 238, eff. 9–21–06; 2006 S 17, eff. 8–3–06; 2004 S 66, eff. 5–6–05; 2004 S 185, eff. 4–11–05; 2004 H 106, eff. 9–16–04; 2004 S 178, eff. 1–30–04; 2002 S 221, eff. 4–9–03; 2002 H 374, eff. 4–7–03; 2002 H 510, eff. 3–31–03; 2000 H 448, eff. 10–5–00; 1999 H 471, eff. 7–1–00; 1998 H 606, eff. 3–9–99; 1998 S 212, eff. 9–30–98; 1997 H 408, eff. 10–1–97; 1997 H 215, eff. 6–30–97; 1996 S 223, eff. 3–18–97; 1996 S 269, eff. 7–1–96; 1996 H 274, eff. 8–8–96; 1992 H 154, eff. 7–31–92; 1990 S 3, H 44; 1989 H 257; 1986 H 529, H 528; 1985 H 349; 1984 S 321; 1977 H 219; 1975 H 85; 1969 H 338, S 49; 131 v H 218; 130 v H 765)

Uncodified Law

2006 S 17 § 5: See Uncodified Law under RC 2151.03.

1999 H 121, § 3: See *Baldwin's Ohio Revised Code Annotated*, Uncodified Law under Ch 3314.

1990 S 3, § 6, eff. 4–11–91, reads: Each county shall amend its county plan of cooperation to comply with division (J) of section 2151.421 of the Revised Code, as amended by this act, when the plan is regularly scheduled to be revised. Prior to that time, the county does not have to amend its plan of cooperation; however, the appropriate officials of the county shall comply with division (J) of section 2151.421 of the Revised Code, as amended by this act, to the greatest extent possible.

Historical and Statutory Notes

Amendment Note: 2006 S 238 inserted "; employee of a facility or home that provides respite care in accordance with section 5123.171 of the Revised Code; employee of a home health agency; employee of an entity that provides homemaker services; a person performing the duties of an assessor pursuant to Chapter 3107. or 5103. of the Revised Code; or third party employed by a public children services agency to assist in providing child or family related services" in the last sentence of division (A)(1)(b); and made other nonsubstantive changes.

Amendment Note: 2006 S 17 rewrote this section. See *Baldwin's Ohio Legislative Service Annotated*, 2006, page 2/L-386, or the OH-LEGIS or OH-LEGIS-OLD database on WESTLAW for prior version of that section.

Amendment Note: 2004 S 66 redesignated division (D)(1); inserted the first sentence in division (D); substituted "do both of the following" for "comply" in division (D)(2); designated division (D)(2)(a); added division (D)2)(b) and inserted "Comply" in division (D)(2)(a); inserted "or in an interagency agreement entered into under section 2151.428 of the Revised Code that applies to the particular report" in division (F)(1); added the last sentence in division (H)(4); inserted ", including a report alleging sexual abuse of a child or another type of abuse of a child referred to a children's advocacy center pursuant to an interagency agreement entered into under section 2151.428 of the Revised Code," in division (H)(5); added division (j)(1)(i) and division (J)(4); inserted ", or of the children's advocacy center that is referred the report if the report is referred to a children's advocacy center pursuant to an interagency agreement entered into under section 2151.428 of the Revised Code," in division (K)(1); inserted "or center" in divisions (K)(1)(a)-(c); and made other nonsubstantive changes.

Amendment Note: 2004 S 185 added "A representative of the public children services agency shall, at the time of initial contract with the person subject to the investigation, inform the person of the specific complaints or allegations made against the person. The information shall be given in a manner that is consistent with division (H)(1) of this section and protects the rights of the person making the report under this section." in division (F)(1); and inserted "A" at the beginning of the next paragraph.

Amendment Note: 2004 H 106 deleted ", and (N)" in division (H)(1); added divisions (M)(1), (M)(1)(a) and (M)(1)(b); and designated division (M)(2) and redesignated former division (N) as new division (M)(3).

Amendment Note: 2004 S 178 inserted "; superintendent, board member, or employee of a county board of mental retardation; investigative agent contracted with by a county board of mental retardation; or employee of the department of mental retardation and developmental disabilities" at the end of division (A)(1)(b).

Amendment Note: 2002 S 221 added "agent of a county humane society;" to division (A)(1)(b); and added division (J)(1)(h).

Amendment Note: 2002 H 374 inserted "independent marriage and family therapist or marriage and family therapist;" preceding "speech pathologist" in division (A)(1)(b).

Amendment Note: 2002 H 510 inserted "to the entity or persons specified in this division. Except as provided in section 5120.173 of the Revised Code, the person making the report shall make it" and "In the circumstances described in section 5120.173 of the Revised Code, the person making the report shall make it to the entity specified in that section." in division (A)(1)(a); inserted "to the entity or persons specified in this division. Except as provided in section 5120.173 of the Revised Code, a person making a report or causing a report to be made under this division shall make it or cause it to be made" and "In the circumstances described in section 5120.173 of the Revised Code, a person making a report or causing a report to be made under this division shall make it or cause it to be made to the entity specified in that section." to division (B); substituted "When a municipal or county peace officer receives" with "Upon the receipt of" and inserted "upon receipt of the report," in division (D)(1); substituted "When a public children services agency receives" for "On receipt of" and inserted "upon receipt of the report," in division (D)(2); and inserted ", other than a report that is made to the state highway patrol as described in section 5120.173 of the Revised Code," in division (I).

Amendment Note: 2000 H 448 added new division (H)(4); redesignated former division (H)(4) as new division (H)(5); and inserted "in writing" in new division (H)(5).

Amendment Note: 1999 H 471 substituted "department of job and family services" for "state department of human services" in division (F)(1); substituted "job and family" for "human" twice in division (J)(1)(g); substituted "director of job and family services" for "department of human services" and inserted "of job and family services" in division (L); and made other nonsubstantive changes.

Amendment Note: 1998 H 606 deleted "or surgery" after "limited branch of medicine" and substituted "specified" for "defined" in division (A)(1)(b); designated divisions (G)(1)(a) and (G)(1)(b); and made other nonsubstantive changes.

Amendment Note: 1998 S 212 deleted "listed" following "No person described" in division (A)(1)(a); inserted "administrator or employee of a residential camp or child day camp;" in division (A)(1)(b); deleted "public" following "attorney of the county;" in division (J)(1)(f); deleted "agency" following "of human services" in division (J)(1)(g); and made other nonsubstantive changes.

Amendment Note: 1997 H 408 rewrote division (A)(1); changed references to county human services departments and county children services boards to references to public children services agencies throughout; and made corrective changes and other nonsubstantive changes. Prior to amendment, division (A)(1) read:

"(A)(1) No attorney, physician, including a hospital intern or resident, dentist, podiatrist, practitioner of a limited branch of medicine or surgery as defined in section 4731.15 of the Revised Code, registered nurse, licensed practical nurse, visiting nurse, other health care professional, licensed psychologist, licensed school psychologist, speech pathologist or audiologist, coroner, administrator or employee of a child day care center, administrator or employee of a certified child care agency or other public or private children services agency, school teacher, school employee, school authority, person engaged in social work or the practice of professional counseling, or person rendering spiritual treatment through prayer in accordance with the tenets of a well recognized religion, who is acting in an official or professional capacity and knows or suspects that a child under eighteen years of age or a mentally retarded, developmentally disabled, or physically impaired child under twenty-one years of age has suffered or faces a threat of suffering any physical or mental wound, injury, disability, or condition of a nature that reasonably indicates abuse or neglect of the child, shall fail to immediately report that knowledge or suspicion to the children services board, the county department of human services exercising the children services function, or a municipal or county peace officer in the county in which the child resides or in which the abuse or neglect is occurring or has occurred."

Amendment Note: 1997 H 215 rewrote this section; see *Baldwin's Ohio Legislative Service Annotated*, 1997, page 8/L–1492, or the OH–LEGIS or OH–LEGIS–OLD database on Westlaw, for text of previous version.

Amendment Note: 1996 S 223 substituted "person engaged in social work or the practice of professional counseling," for "social worker, licensed professional counselor," in division (A)(1); added the reference to township peace officers in division (E); rewrote division (K); and made changes to reflect gender neutral language and other nonsubstantive changes. Prior to amendment, division (K) read:

"(K)(1) When a municipal or county peace officer or an employee of a county department of human services or children services board receives a report pursuant to division (A) or (B) of this section, the person who receives the report, at the time he receives the report, shall inform the person making the report that, if the person making the report is required to make the report pursuant to division (A) of this section and if he provides his name, address, and telephone number at the time he makes the report, subject to verification of his identity, he may make a reasonable number of requests of the county department of human services or children services board that receives or is referred the report to provide him with the following information:

"(a) Whether the department or board has initiated an investigation of the report;

"(b) Whether the department or board is continuing to investigate the report;

"(c) Whether the department or board is otherwise involved with the child who is the subject of the report;

"(d) The general status of the health and safety of the child who is the subject of the report;

"(e) Whether the report has resulted in the filing of a complaint in juvenile court or of criminal charges in another court.

"(2) Any municipal or county peace officer or employee of a county department of human services or children services board who informs a person making a report pursuant to division (A) or (B) of this section of the person's right to request the information described in divisions (K)(1)(a) to (e) of this section shall include in the initial child abuse or child neglect report that the person making the report was so informed and, if provided at the time of the making of the report, shall include the person's name, address, and telephone number in the report.

"(3) Any person, who is required to make a report pursuant to division (A) of this section and who provides his name, address, and telephone number at the time he makes the report, may make a reasonable number of requests of the county department of human services or children services board that receives or is referred the report to provide him with the information described in divisions (K)(1)(a) to (e) of this section. Each request is subject to verification of the person's identity. A request made pursuant to division (K)(3) of this section is not a substitute for any report required to be made pursuant to division (A) of this section.

"(4) If the county department of human services or children services board receives or is referred a report pursuant to this section, if the person making the report is required to make the report pursuant to division (A) of this section, if that person provides his name, address, and telephone number at the time he makes the report, if that person requests the department or board to provide the information described in divisions (K)(1)(a) to (e) of this section, and if that person's identity is verified, the department or board shall provide the person with the information described in divisions (K)(1)(a) to (e) of this section a reasonable number of times, except that the department or board shall not disclose any confidential information regarding the child who is the subject of the report other than the information described in those divisions."

Amendment Note: 1996 S 269 changed a statutory reference from "division (B) of section 2919.21" to "division (C) of section 2919.21" in division (J); made changes to reflect gender neutral language; and made other nonsubstantive changes.

Amendment Note: 1996 H 274 substituted "mentally retarded, developmentally disabled, or physically impaired person" for "physically or mentally handicapped person" throughout; inserted "Except as provided in division (H)(4) of this section," in division (H)(1); added division (H)(4); added the second and third sentences in division (L); added divisions (M) and (N); and made changes to reflect gender neutral language.

Cross References

Penalty: 2151.99(A)
Abuse or neglect of minor inmate to be reported to state highway patrol, 5120.173
Anti-stalking protection orders, persons who may seek relief, 2903.214
Certification of Type B family day-care homes, inspections, 5104.11
Child abuse prevention, in-service training for school employees, 3319.073
Community schools, required terms of contracts, 3314.03
Contents of system, 5101.13
County children services boards, powers and duties, 5153.16
Disclosure of information relevant to evaluation of fitness of applicant for type A family day-care home or type B family day-care home, 5153.175
Evidence, privileged communications and acts, duty to report child abuse, 2317.02
Failure to report a felony or certain suspicious circumstances, 2921.22
Filing of power of attorney or affidavit with juvenile court, accompanying information, report to public children services agency, investigation, 3109.74
Memorandum of understanding to outline normal operating procedure, 5126.058
Mental retardation and developmental disabilities department, investigation of abuse or neglect by employees, 5123.51
Outpatient mental health services for minors, obligations of mental health professionals, 5122.04
Petition alleging domestic violence against minor children, 3113.31
Prevention of child abuse and child neglect, 3109.13 to 3109.18
Privileged communications and acts, 2317.02
Protection of children, 1717.14
Sealing of records, official records defined, 2953.51
Verification of power of attorney or affidavit, 3109.75

Ohio Administrative Code References

Access/confidentiality of child abuse and neglect information contained in the statewide automated child welfare database, OAC 5101:2-33-22
Access/confidentiality of information contained in the child abuse and neglect central registry, OAC 5101:2-34-38.1
Case records for children services, OAC 5101:2-33-23
Case records for children services, OAC 5101:2-39-02
Child abuse and neglect, interstate and intrastate referral procedures, protective service alerts, locating the child, OAC 5101:2-35-62 et seq.
Children services, definition of terms, OAC 5101:2-1-01
Children's protective services, OAC Ch 5101:2-34, Ch 5101:2-36
Child's education and health information, OAC 5101:2-38-08
Child's education and health information, OAC 5101:2-39-08.2
Confidentiality and dissemination of information relating to child abuse or neglect, OAC 5101:2-33-21, OAC 5101:2-34-38
Definition of terms for the implementation of the "Comprehensive Assessment and Planning Model - Interim Solution" and statewide automated child welfare database, OAC 5101:2-1-01.1
Documentation of comprehensive health care for children in custody, OAC 5101:2-42-66.2
Documentation of comprehensive health care for children in placement, OAC 5101:2-42-66.2
Emergency removal of a child from an out-of-home care setting, OAC 5101:2-39-03
Emergency removal of a child from an out-of-home care setting, OAC 5101:2-39-12.1
Expunction of identifying information from the central registry, OAC 5101:2-35-19
Family and children services information system (FACSIS) reporting requirements, OAC 5101:2-33-05
Intake and screening procedures for child abuse, neglect, dependency and family in need of services reports; and information and/or referral intakes, OAC 5101:2-36-01
Intrastate and interstate referral procedures for children's protective services, OAC 5101:2-35-62, OAC 5101:2-36-13
Joint planning and sharing of information among the PCSA and CDJFS, OAC 5101:2-33-28, OAC 5101:2-39-51
Justification to extend time frames for completion or waive completion of assessment/investigation activities, OAC 5101:2-36-11
Major unusual incidents, OAC 5123:2-17-02
PCSA case plan for children in custody or under protective supervision, OAC 5101:2-38-05
PCSA requirement for cross-referring reports of child abuse and/or neglect, OAC 5101:2-36-12
PCSA requirements for a deserted child assessment/investigation, OAC 5101:2-36-06
PCSA requirements for completing the family assessment, OAC 5101:2-37-03
PCSA requirements for completing the JFS 01510, "Family Decision Making Model: Safety Plan for Children", OAC 5101:2-34-37
PCSA requirements for completing the safety assessment, OAC 5101:2-37-01
PCSA requirements for conducting a specialized assessment/investigation, OAC 5101:2-36-04
PCSA requirements for conducting intra- familial (non-stranger) child abuse and neglect family assessments/investigations, OAC 5101:2-34-33
PCSA requirements for conducting out-of-home care and third party investigations, OAC 5101:2-34-34
PCSA requirements for conducting out-of-home perpetrator investigations and alleged child victim assessments, OAC 5101:2-34-36
PCSA requirements for conducting stranger danger investigations, OAC 5101:2-36-05
PCSA requirements for conducting third party assessment/investigations, OAC 5101:2-36-08
PCSA requirements for cross-referring reports of child abuse and neglect, OAC 5101:2-34-35
PCSA requirements for intra-familial child abuse and/or neglect assessment/investigations, OAC 5101:2-36-03
PCSA requirements for safety planning, OAC 5101:2-37-02
Procedures for intervening in cases involving alleged withholding of appropriate nutrition, hydration, medication, or medically indicated treatment from disabled infants with life-threatening conditions, OAC 5101:2-35-77
Procedures for intervening in cases involving alleged withholding of medically indicated treatment from disabled infants with life-threatening conditions, OAC 5101:2-36-07
Protective service alert, OAC 5101:2-36-14
Protective service alerts, OAC 5101:2-35-67
Removal of a child from his own home, OAC 5101:2-39-01, OAC 5101:2-39-12
Requirements for PCSA case plan for in-home supportive services without court order, OAC 5101:2-38-01
Screening child abuse and neglect reports, OAC 5101:2-34-06
Submittal of central registry reports on child abuse or neglect, OAC 5101:2-35-16

Supportive services for prevention of placement, reunification and life skills, OAC 5101:2–40–02

Supportive services, OAC 5101:2–39–07

The child abuse and neglect memorandum of understanding, OAC 5101:2–34–71

The county child abuse and neglect memorandum of understanding, OAC 5101:2–33–26

Library References

Infants ⊜13.5.

Westlaw Topic No. 211.

Baldwin's Ohio Legislative Service, 1996 H 274—LSC Analysis, p 5/L–697

Research References

Encyclopedias

2 Am. Jur. Proof of Facts 2d 365, Child Abuse--The Battered Child Syndrome.

6 Am. Jur. Proof of Facts 2d 345, Failure to Report Suspected Case of Child Abuse.

38 Am. Jur. Trials 1, Professional Liability for Failure to Report Child Abuse.

OH Jur. 3d Agency & Independent Contractors § 42, Effect of Death or Incompetence of Principal—Durable Power of Attorney; Nomination of Guardian of Principal or Minor Children.

OH Jur. 3d Criminal Law § 738, Tolling of Limitations Period—Child Abuse and Neglect Cases.

OH Jur. 3d Criminal Law § 1417, Other Similar Statutory Offenses.

OH Jur. 3d Defamation & Privacy § 75, Absolute Privilege.

OH Jur. 3d Evidence & Witnesses § 739, State Secrets and Communications to Public Officers.

OH Jur. 3d Evidence & Witnesses § 740, Communications Between Penitent and Spiritual Advisor.

OH Jur. 3d Evidence & Witnesses § 776, Generally; Express Waiver.

OH Jur. 3d Family Law § 1447, Record-Keeping Requirements.

OH Jur. 3d Family Law § 1451, Powers and Duties as to Children in Need of Public Care or Protective Services.

OH Jur. 3d Family Law § 1475, Investigation.

OH Jur. 3d Family Law § 1476, Confidentiality.

OH Jur. 3d Family Law § 1477, Immunity of Maker of Report.

OH Jur. 3d Family Law § 1478, Immunity of Maker of Report—Who May Claim Immunity.

OH Jur. 3d Family Law § 1479, Immunity of Maker of Report—Who May Not Claim Immunity.

OH Jur. 3d Family Law § 1736, Adult Acts Punishable in Juvenile Court—Failure to Report Child Abuse.

OH Jur. 3d Family Law § 1749, Sentence and Punishment.

OH Jur. 3d Family Law § 1062.1, Relinquishment of Child to Grandparent Through Power of Attorney.

OH Jur. 3d Family Law § 1062.2, Caretaker Authorization Affidavit.

OH Jur. 3d Government Tort Liability § 31, Defenses or Immunities of Subdivision and Employee.

OH Jur. 3d Government Tort Liability § 44, Statutory Liability.

OH Jur. 3d Government Tort Liability § 72, Liability With Respect to Particular Matters.

OH Jur. 3d Guardian & Ward § 86.1, Relinquishment to Grandparent Through Power of Attorney.

OH Jur. 3d Guardian & Ward § 86.2, Caretaker Authorization Affidavit.

Forms

Ohio Jurisprudence Pleading and Practice Forms § 119:19, Privilege—Absolute Privilege.

Ohio Jurisprudence Pleading and Practice Forms § 119:101, Absolute Privilege—Statements Made by Authorized Person to Appropriate Authority Regarding Suspected Child Abuse.

Treatises and Practice Aids

Klein, Darling, & Terez, Baldwin's Ohio Practice Civil Practice § 35:25, Other Means for Discovering Medical Reports.

Katz, Giannelli, Blair and Lipton, Baldwin's Ohio Practice, Criminal Law, § 84:7, Tolling.

Katz, Giannelli, Blair and Lipton, Baldwin's Ohio Practice, Criminal Law, § 110:9, False Report of Child Abuse.

Sowald & Morganstern, Baldwin's Ohio Practice Domestic Relations Law § 6:4, Communications Made in Mediation.

Sowald & Morganstern, Baldwin's Ohio Practice Domestic Relations Law § 37:8, Exceptions to Confidentiality—Reporting Statutes—Child Abuse.

Sowald & Morganstern, Baldwin's Ohio Practice Domestic Relations Law § 5:16, Civil Versus Criminal.

Sowald & Morganstern, Baldwin's Ohio Practice Domestic Relations Law § 34:21, Confidences—Exceptions.

Sowald & Morganstern, Baldwin's Ohio Practice Domestic Relations Law § 37:10, Exceptions to Confidentiality—Reporting Statutes—Felony.

Sowald & Morganstern, Baldwin's Ohio Practice Domestic Relations Law § 37:15, Privileged Communication—State Law Privileges—Psychologists and Physicians.

Sowald & Morganstern, Baldwin's Ohio Practice Domestic Relations Law § 37:32, Privileged Communication—Child Abuse Exception.

Giannelli and Snyder, Baldwin's Ohio Practice, Evidence, R 501, General Rule.

Giannelli and Snyder, Baldwin's Ohio Practice, Evidence, § 501.4, Ohio Statutory Privileges.

Giannelli and Snyder, Baldwin's Ohio Practice, Evidence, § 501.13, Attorney-Client Privilege: Waiver.

Giannelli and Snyder, Baldwin's Ohio Practice, Evidence, § 501.21, Physician-Patient Privilege: Exceptions.

Giannelli and Snyder, Baldwin's Ohio Practice, Evidence, § 501.22, Psychotherapist-Patient Privilege.

Giannelli and Snyder, Baldwin's Ohio Practice, Evidence, § 501.27, Clergy-Penitent Privilege.

Carlin, Baldwin's Ohio Practice, Merrick-Rippner Probate Law § 5:12, Evidentiary Matters—Privileged Communications—Protected Relationships—Counselors and Social Workers.

Carlin, Baldwin's Ohio Practice, Merrick-Rippner Probate Law § 108:1, Juvenile Court—Criminal Jurisdiction.

Carlin, Baldwin's Ohio Practice, Merrick-Rippner Probate Law § 108:9, Juvenile Court—Criminal Jurisdiction—Assignment of Case for Disposition.

Carlin, Baldwin's Ohio Practice, Merrick-Rippner Probate Law § 101:16, Outpatient Treatment of Minors—Disclosure.

Carlin, Baldwin's Ohio Practice, Merrick-Rippner Probate Law § 107:46, Adjudicatory Hearings—Child's Right to Guardian Ad Litem.

Carlin, Baldwin's Ohio Practice, Merrick-Rippner Probate Law § 107:52, Adjudicatory Hearings—Confidentiality of Juvenile Court Proceedings.

Carlin, Baldwin's Ohio Practice, Merrick-Rippner Probate Law § 107:54, Adjudicatory Hearings—Applicability of Physician-Patient Privilege.

Carlin, Baldwin's Ohio Practice, Merrick-Rippner Probate Law § 107:73, Alternatives for Disposition of Juvenile Cases.

Carlin, Baldwin's Ohio Practice, Merrick-Rippner Probate Law § 108:15, Juvenile Court—Visitation Right of Noncustodial Parent and Others.

Carlin, Baldwin's Ohio Practice, Merrick-Rippner Probate Law § 107:114, Juvenile Court Records—Confidentiality.

Adrine & Ruden, Ohio Domestic Violence Law § 8:6, Parents and Children.

Adrine & Ruden, Ohio Domestic Violence Law § 16:4, Confidentiality and Liability Concerns.

Giannelli & Yeomans, Ohio Juvenile Law § 9:7, Neglect—Subsistence, Education & Medical Care.

Giannelli & Yeomans, Ohio Juvenile Law § 14:1, Introduction.

Giannelli & Yeomans, Ohio Juvenile Law § 15:4, Mediation.

Giannelli & Yeomans, Ohio Juvenile Law § 20:2, Temporary Care Orders.

Giannelli & Yeomans, Ohio Juvenile Law § 21:2, Scope of Discovery; Rule 24.

Giannelli & Yeomans, Ohio Juvenile Law § 33:5, Other Proceedings.

Giannelli & Yeomans, Ohio Juvenile Law § 35:2, Confidentiality Requirement.

Giannelli & Yeomans, Ohio Juvenile Law § 35:3, Non-Juvenile Court Proceedings.

Giannelli & Yeomans, Ohio Juvenile Law § 9:11, Neglect—Out-Of-Home Care Neglect.

Giannelli & Yeomans, Ohio Juvenile Law § 14:16, Abuse, Neglect & Dependency Investigations.

Giannelli & Yeomans, Ohio Juvenile Law § 14:17, Child Abuse Reporting Statute.

Giannelli & Yeomans, Ohio Juvenile Law § 23:15, Evidence—Privileges.

Gotherman, Babbit and Lang, Baldwin's Ohio Practice, Local Government Law—Municipal, § 32:4, Imposition of Liability.

Gotherman, Babbit and Lang, Baldwin's Ohio Practice, Local Government Law—Municipal, § 6:17, Exception Where Confidentiality Required by Other Laws.

Hastings, Manoloff, Sheeran, & Stype, Ohio School Law § 24:9, Duty to Report Suspected Child Abuse or Neglect-In General.

Hastings, Manoloff, Sheeran, & Stype, Ohio School Law § 5:15, Rule-Making and Regulatory Power-Management of Schools.

Hastings, Manoloff, Sheeran, & Stype, Ohio School Law § 19:22, Sex Discrimination in Education-Sexual Harassment as Discrimination.

Hastings, Manoloff, Sheeran, & Stype, Ohio School Law § 24:10, Duty to Report Suspected Child Abuse or Neglect-Recognizing Child Abuse and Neglect.

Hastings, Manoloff, Sheeran, & Stype, Ohio School Law § 24:11, Duty to Report Suspected Child Abuse or Neglect-Definition of Child Abuse.

Hastings, Manoloff, Sheeran, & Stype, Ohio School Law § 24:13, Duty to Report Crimes-General Duty With Respect to Felonies.

Law Review and Journal Commentaries

Active Duty: Changes in reporting child abuse/neglect, Adam C. Miller. 41 Ohio Sch Boards Ass'n J 2 (February 1997).

Allegations of Child Sexual Abuse in Custody and Visitation Litigation: Recommendations for Improved Fact Finding and Child Protection, John E.B. Myers. 28 J Fam L 1 (1989–90).

Between A Rock And A Hard Place: Michigan Social Worker Liability For Child Abuse Investigations After *Achterhof v. Selvaggio*, Note. 22 U Tol L Rev 455 (Winter 1991).

Brodie v. Summit County Children Services Board: A Statutory Duty Exception to the Public Duty Rule for Children Service Agencies, Note. 18 Ohio N U L Rev 711 (1991).

Caseworker Liability for the Negligent Handling of Child Abuse Reports, Comment. 60 U Cin L Rev 191 (Summer 1991).

Child Abuse and Child Endangerment: Duties of School Officials and Employees Under R.C. 2151.421 and R.C. 2919.22, Mary A. Lentz. 2 Baldwin's Ohio Sch Serv 118 (November/December 1990).

Child Abuse Legislation and the Interdisciplinary Approach, Richard H. Hansen. 52 A B A J 734 (August 1966).

Child Protection Legal Process: Comparing The United States And Great Britain, Donald N. Duquette. 54 U Pitt L Rev 239 (Fall 1992).

Constitutional Law—Fourteenth Amendment—State Action—Substantive Due Process—The United States Supreme Court has held that the failure of a state operated child protection agency to provide adequate protection to a child from his parent's violence does not violate that child's rights under the substantive component of the Due Process Clause, Deshaney v Winnebago County Dept. of Social Servs., Note. 28 Duq L Rev 387 (Winter 1990).

Creating Therapist–Incest Offender Exception to Mandatory Child Abuse Reporting Statutes—When Psychiatrist Knows Best, Phyllis Coleman. 54 U Cin L Rev 1113 (1986).

Deal swiftly with sexual misconduct, Cheryl Thorpe Maimona. 40 Ohio Sch Boards Ass'n J 2 (February 1996).

Disclosure of Child Abuse or Neglect Records: Who Is the Watch Dog of Justice?, Mary A. Lentz. 3 Baldwin's Ohio Sch L J 33 (May/June 1991).

In re Barzak: Access to Children Services Board Files, David Hazelkorn. 19 Akron L Rev 237 (Fall 1985).

Interrogating Students at School, Richard J. Dickinson. 5 Baldwin's Ohio Sch L J 37 (July/August 1993).

"Let the Master Answer": Holding Schools Vicariously Liable When Employees Sexually Abuse Children, Richard Fossey and Todd A. Demitchell. 25 J L & Educ 575 (Fall 1996).

The Other Child Abuse—Munchausen Syndrome by Proxy, Mary A. Lentz. 8 Baldwin's Ohio Sch L J 41 (September/October 1996).

The Parent–Child Dilemma in the Courts, James W. Carpenter. 30 Ohio St L J 292 (Spring 1969).

Privileged Communications in Ohio and What's New on the Horizon: Ohio House Bill 52 Accountant–Client Privilege, Note. 31 Akron L Rev 505 (1998).

The Reporting of Child Abuse by Mandated Reporters and Ohio Law, Mary A. Lentz. 14 Baldwin's Ohio Sch L J 1 (March/April 2002).

School Personnel & Mandated Reporting of Child Maltreatment, Kevin S. Mahoney. 24 J L & Educ 227 (Spring 1995).

Statutory Privileges and Appellate Review—Polikoff Reaffirmed, William B. Baughman, Jr. 68 Clev B J 12 (October 1997).

Student Interrogation—Cooperating with outside agencies, Rachelle E. Bristol. 44 Ohio Sch Boards Ass'n J 2 (September 1999).

Tales of Sexual Panic in the Legal Academy: The Assault on Reverse Incest Suits, Edward Greer. (Ed. note: The author states the case against writers who would deny innocent fathers any legal recourse against incompetent or ideologically-motivated therapists who "retrieve memories" of nonexistent incidents of abuse.) 48 Case W Res L Rev 513 (Spring 1998).

Task force develops position paper: Issues surrounding child abuse and neglect, Elaine Buck. 28 Ohio Sch Boards Ass'n J 7 (November 1984).

Therapists' Liability to the Falsely Accused for Inducing Illusory Memories of Childhood Sexual Abuse—Current Remedies and a Proposed Statute, Joel Jay Finer. 11 J L & Health 45 (1996–97).

Tort Liability and Failure to report Sexual Abuse of a Minor, Mary A. Lentz. 16 Baldwin's Ohio Sch L J 13 (May/June 2004).

Understanding Faith: When Religious Parents Decline Conventional Medical Treatment for Their Children, Note. 45 Case W Res L Rev 891 (Spring 1995).

The Use of Juvenile Court Jurisdiction and Restraining Authority to Address the Problem of Maternal Drug Abuse in Ohio, Deborah A. Wainey. 18 Ohio N U L Rev 611 (1991).

Will The § 1983 Equal Protection Claim Solve The Equal Protection Problem Faced By Victims Of Domestic Violence? A Review Of *Balistreri, Watson, Hynson,* And *McKee*, Note. 29 J Fam L 635 (May 1991).

Notes of Decisions

Child day care center employees and administrators duty 11
Consequences of failure to report 6
Constitutional issues 1
Corpus delicti of crime 3
Immunity 5
Mother's duty 8
Political subdivision 12
Private organization's duty to report 9
Procedural issues 4
Professional counselors or social workers duty 13
Public children's services agency duty and authority 2
Public records disclosure 10
School teacher's duty 7

---

1. Constitutional issues

Child abuse reporting statute provided immunity for alleged violations of civil rights under the Ohio Constitution of subject of investigation, stemming from the report and investigation of child-abuse claim. Denver v. Casbeer (Ohio App. 1 Dist., Hamilton, 11-04-2005) No. C-050106, 2005-Ohio-5860, 2005 WL 2899631, Unreported, appeal not allowed 108 Ohio St.3d 1511, 844 N.E.2d 856, 2006-Ohio-1329. Civil Rights ⚖ 1737

Defendant was not in custody for purposes of *Miranda* when he was interviewed by Franklin County Children Services (FCCS) caseworker about sexual-abuse allegations; interview was conducted in standard room at FCCS offices, defendant was not secured in room in any way and was not instructed that he was not allowed to leave, nothing indicated that defendant was threatened or intimidated, defendant was aware that caseworker was not law enforcement officer, caseworker was not wearing badge, gun, or handcuffs, defendant was neither arrested nor threatened with arrest, no law enforcement officers were present at interview, and interview was not taped. State v. Thoman (Ohio App. 10 Dist., Franklin, 03-03-2005) No. 04AP-787, 2005-Ohio-898, 2005 WL 488390, Unreported. Criminal Law ⚖ 412.2(2)

Expense and inconvenience incurred by father in defending against child abuse allegations brought by state social services agency and agency employees, and humiliation and injury to father's reputation occasioned by such conduct, did not amount to taking of liberty or property interest required to support procedural due process claim under federal civil rights statute. Roe v. Franklin Cty. (Ohio App. 10 Dist., 03-12-1996) 109 Ohio

Note 1

App.3d 772, 673 N.E.2d 172, appeal not allowed 77 Ohio St.3d 1415, 670 N.E.2d 1003. Constitutional Law ⇔ 274(5); Infants ⇔ 17

The absolute immunity granted to persons reporting alleged child abuse to certain government agencies under RC 2151.421(G) does not deny equal protection or due process to persons falsely accused of child abuse or violate the due course of law provisions of O Const I §16; the statute is rationally related to the legitimate state interest of encouraging such reports, and those accused in such reports are not denied access to the courts to defend against false allegations. Cudlin v. Cudlin (Cuyahoga 1990) 64 Ohio App.3d 249, 580 N.E.2d 1170.

The fact that an individual charged with child mistreatment cannot discover records of a state protective service agency that investigated the matter, because the records are privileged information under state law, does not violate the defendant's Sixth Amendment rights to confront witnesses or to compel the attendance of witnesses whose existence could conceivably be discovered from the files; where the statute confers only a qualified privilege, however, due process requires that the trial judge review the records in camera for material information, at the defendant's request. (Ed. note: Pennsylvania statute construed in light of federal constitution.) Pennsylvania v. Ritchie (U.S.Pa. 1987) 107 S.Ct. 989, 480 U.S. 39, 94 L.Ed.2d 40.

Venue provisions of bypass procedure under Ohio parental notification of abortion statute permitted minor fearing disclosure of her activities to travel to any county in state to initiate bypass proceeding and to have abortion performed and thus did not violate minor's due process right to confidentiality. Akron Center for Reproductive Health v. Slaby (C.A.6 (Ohio) 1988) 854 F.2d 852, probable jurisdiction noted 109 S.Ct. 3239, 492 U.S. 916, 106 L.Ed.2d 586, reversed 110 S.Ct. 2972, 497 U.S. 502, 111 L.Ed.2d 405, on remand 911 F.2d 731, on remand 911 F.2d 733. Abortion And Birth Control ⇔ 1.30; Constitutional Law ⇔ 274(5)

State's statutory framework for investigating allegations of child abuse and neglect, including statute requiring county agency to investigate report of known or suspected abuse within 24 hours, did not supersede county social workers' obligations under Fourth Amendment so as to permit social workers' warrantless entry into private residence that was subject of anonymous report of unsafe conditions; report could have been investigated in accordance with Fourth Amendment, and social worker admitted that she fulfilled her statutory duty to commence investigation by making appointment with health inspector to visit home. Walsh v. Erie County Dept. of Job and Family Services (N.D.Ohio, 01-22-2003) 240 F.Supp.2d 731. Infants ⇔ 17

A father whose visitation rights are denied because of his former wife's false accusations of child abuse has no liberty interest in continued companionship and association with his child under the federal constitution that is cognizable in a civil rights suit under 42 USC 1983 or 1985. Norton v. Cobb (N.D.Ohio 1990) 744 F.Supp. 798.

A social service agency worker interviewing a person suspected of sexually molesting a child is not a law enforcement officer or agent where the social worker interviews the suspect after an interview with a deputy sheriff at the social service agency at the request of the suspect; thus, the social worker need not advise the "suspect" of his right to remain silent prior to recommencing the interview. State v Simpson, No. 1706 (4th Dist Ct App, Ross, 2–24–92).

2. Public children's services agency duty and authority

County children services board (CSB) was immune from liability, in action based on CSB's failure to investigate reports of child abuse, under the Political Subdivision Tort Liability Act (PSTLA); statute imposing duty of public children services agency to investigate a report of known or suspected child abuse within 24 hours did not expressly impose liability for failure to investigate reports of child abuse. Grimm v. Summit Cty. Children Servs. Bd. (Ohio App. 9 Dist., Summit, 05-17-2006) No. 22702, 2006-Ohio-2411, 2006 WL 1329689, Unreported. Infants ⇔ 17

Mother's communications to mental health counselor, which included statements that she had violently shaken child and had fantasies about causing her further harm, fell within exception to statutory privilege and were thus admissible in dependency proceeding, since they constituted indications of past child abuse and came within mandatory reporting law. In re Hauenstein (Ohio App. 3 Dist., Hancock, 06-07-2004) No. 5-03-38, No. 5-03-39, 2004-Ohio-2915, 2004 WL 1238288, Unreported. Witnesses ⇔ 214.5.

With the exception of initial child abuse reports made to peace officers, RC 2151.421 applies only to social service agency reports and does not prohibit the disclosure of criminal investigatory reports prepared by a law enforcement agency incident to the prosecution of a father for the murder of his infant when such documents are sought pursuant to RC 149.43 or in a public records mandamus action. State ex rel. Munici v. Kovacic (Ohio App. 8 Dist., Cuyahoga, 06-15-1994) No. 64818, 1994 WL 264265, Unreported.

Portions of city's police investigatory reports which referred to initial reports, to public children services agency, of suspected abuse of a child by police officers and of another child by two juveniles, were confidential, under the child-abuse reporting statute, and therefore were not subject to disclosure to newspaper publisher and reporter. State ex rel. Beacon Journal Publishing Co. v. Akron (Ohio, 12-15-2004) 104 Ohio St.3d 399, 819 N.E.2d 1087, 2004-Ohio-6557. Infants ⇔ 133

The authority and responsibility, under the child-abuse reporting statute, to conduct investigations of suspected abuse and to submit the necessary reports are vested solely in the children services agency, in cooperation with law enforcement agencies, and this responsibility may not be delegated to another agency, whether that agency is public or private. State ex rel. Beacon Journal Publishing Co. v. Akron (Ohio, 12-15-2004) 104 Ohio St.3d 399, 819 N.E.2d 1087, 2004-Ohio-6557. Infants ⇔ 17

Police investigatory reports are generally not confidential child-abuse investigatory reports under the child-abuse reporting statute, even if they are prepared by the police pursuant to a memorandum of understanding with a public children services agency. State ex rel. Beacon Journal Publishing Co. v. Akron (Ohio, 12-15-2004) 104 Ohio St.3d 399, 819 N.E.2d 1087, 2004-Ohio-6557. Infants ⇔ 133

Statute imposing duty on public children services agencies to investigate reports of known or suspected child abuse within twenty-four hours did not expressly impose liability on county children services board (CSB) and its employees for failure to investigate child abuse, and, thus, sovereign immunity precluded their liability in wrongful death action alleging that CSB knew or should have known about mother's previous acts of violence against her children, and that its negligent failure to investigate and remove child from mother's custody was proximate cause of child's death from injuries inflicted by mother; abrogating *Rich v Erie Cty. Dept. of Human Resources*, 106 Ohio App.3d 88, 665 N.E.2d 278, *Crago v. Lorain Cty. Commrs.*, 69 Ohio App.3d 24, 590 N.E.2d 15, and *Reed v. Perry Cty. Children's Serv.*, 1993 WL 274299. Marshall v. Montgomery Cty. Children Serv. Bd. (Ohio, 07-25-2001) 92 Ohio St.3d 348, 750 N.E.2d 549, 2001-Ohio-209. Infants ⇔ 17

In civil proceeding, records and reports compiled by departments of human services and children's services boards regarding allegations of child abuse are confidential and privileged. Johnson v. Johnson (Ohio App. 3 Dist., 03-05-1999) 134 Ohio App.3d 579, 731 N.E.2d 1144. Infants ⇔ 133

Compelling interest in protecting child's health and welfare overrode statutory confidentiality of records maintained by county Department of Human Services (DHS) concerning investigation into allegations of sexual abuse by former wife's boyfriend, on former wife's motion for change of custody of child; records were relevant to pending motion, good cause for request was established, and need for records outweighed statutory confidentiality considerations. Johnson v. Johnson (Ohio App. 3 Dist., 03-05-1999) 134 Ohio App.3d 579, 731 N.E.2d 1144. Infants ⇔ 133

Statutory protection against the use of reports of suspected child abuse in civil action against persons making the reports does not apply only to reports prepared by a children services agency, but extends to reports provided to such an agency from outside sources. Walters v. The Enrichment Ctr. of Wishing Well, Inc. (Ohio App. 8 Dist., 06-07-1999) 133 Ohio App.3d 66, 726 N.E.2d 1058, appeal not allowed 87 Ohio St.3d 1408, 716 N.E.2d 1170. Infants ⇔ 13

County agency could be held liable under state tort law for decision to return three-year-old child to mother's custody after removing child based on reports of abuse by mother's live-in companion, if action showed a failure to investigate reports of abuse or neglect or showed a reckless and wanton disregard for rights of child, who subsequently died from burns inflicted by mother's companion. Rich v. Erie Cty. Dept. of Human Resources (Ohio App. 6 Dist., 08-25-1995) 106 Ohio App.3d 88, 665 N.E.2d 278, dismissed, appeal not allowed 74 Ohio St.3d 1498, 659 N.E.2d 314. Infants ⇔ 17

County agency that returned three-year-old child to mother's custody after removing child based on reports of abuse by mother's live-in companion did not violate responsibility to investigate abuse reports or show a willful, reckless, or wanton disregard of child's rights, though department failed to file complaint, and though returning child was tragic mistake because child subsequently died from burns inflicted by mother's companion; department investigated abuse reports before removing child and sought to ameliorate problem by requiring parenting classes, and many of the procedural steps which department failed to follow, such as filing complaint, were clearly discretionary. Rich v. Erie Cty. Dept. of Human Resources (Ohio App. 6 Dist., 08-25-1995) 106 Ohio App.3d 88, 665

N.E.2d 278, dismissed, appeal not allowed 74 Ohio St.3d 1498, 659 N.E.2d 314. Infants ⇔ 17

When state voluntarily undertakes to protect neglected children from harm, it may also acquire a duty under state tort law to provide child with adequate protection and may be liable for doing so in a negligent fashion. Rich v. Erie Cty. Dept. of Human Resources (Ohio App. 6 Dist., 08-25-1995) 106 Ohio App.3d 88, 665 N.E.2d 278, dismissed, appeal not allowed 74 Ohio St.3d 1498, 659 N.E.2d 314. States ⇔ 112.2(1)

Duty imposed by statute requiring children services board to begin investigation of child abuse or neglect reports within 24 hours was owed to allegedly abused child, not to child's grandparents or any other person who files charge with board, and, thus, grandparents' claim that board violated statute did not set forth cause of action upon which relief could be granted to them under theory of negligence per se. Neuenschwander v. Wayne Cty. Children Serv. Bd. (Ohio App. 9 Dist., 02-02-1994) 92 Ohio App.3d 767, 637 N.E.2d 102, motion overruled 69 Ohio St.3d 1489, 635 N.E.2d 44. Infants ⇔ 17

Referee's release of confidential child abuse records of county department of human services, for review by court-appointed psychologist in determining custody action, represented usurpation of judicial decision-making power and was improper, where records were forwarded to psychologist before department was given opportunity to file objections and prior to judgment wherein trial court adopted referee's recommendations. Sharpe v. Sharpe (Lake 1993) 85 Ohio App.3d 638, 620 N.E.2d 916. Infants ⇔ 206

County department of human services' child abuse investigation report regarding foster child was report which was prohibited from being released by state law, except to extent that foster parents were required to be informed of allegation in and disposition of investigation, and thus, report was not subject to disclosure to foster parents under statute excepting from definition of "public record" records the release of which is prohibited by state or federal law. State ex rel. Renfro v. Cuyahoga County Dept. of Human Services (Ohio 1990) 54 Ohio St.3d 25, 560 N.E.2d 230, rehearing denied 55 Ohio St.3d 709, 563 N.E.2d 302. Records ⇔ 55

A children services board and its agents have a duty to investigate and report their findings as required by RC 2151.421 when a specific child is identified as abused or neglected, and the public duty doctrine may not be raised as a defense for agency failure to comply with such statutory requirements. Brodie v. Summit County Children Services Bd. (Ohio 1990) 51 Ohio St.3d 112, 554 N.E.2d 1301.

The presence in a young child of a sexually transmitted disease is a commonly accepted indicator of sexual abuse; consequently, a health facility's diagnosis of a chlamydia infection is the type of situation for which the general assembly has mandated reports to child welfare services, and the benefits to society from encouraging reporting and prosecution of child abuse by granting immunity outweigh any individual harm resulting from false reports. Criswell v. Brentwood Hosp. (Cuyahoga 1989) 49 Ohio App.3d 163, 551 N.E.2d 1315.

While some child abuse records may be confidential pursuant to child neglect reporting statute, such confidentiality is not absolute. Child Care Provider Certification Dept. v. Harris (Ohio App. 8 Dist., Cuyahoga, 07-25-2002) No. 80669, 2002-Ohio-3795, 2002 WL 1728540, Unreported, appeal not allowed 97 Ohio St.3d 1485, 780 N.E.2d 288, 2002-Ohio-6866. Infants ⇔ 133

County human services board and a children's services employee are not immune from an action for negligence by the parents of an allegedly abused child for failure to properly investigate and report an alleged instance of abuse under RC 2151.421 since they are not subject to general immunity granted to political subdivisions under RC 2744.02(A), nor are they immune under RC 2744.03(A)(6). Crago v. Lorain Cty. Commrs. (Lorain 1990) 69 Ohio App.3d 24, 590 N.E.2d 15, motion to certify overruled 57 Ohio St.3d 705, 566 N.E.2d 170.

Under RC 2151.421, a children's services board, its executive secretary, and a board of county commissioners are liable for failing to investigate allegations of child abuse where that failure is found to be a proximate cause of the children's death. Reed v Perry County Children's Servs, No. CA-429, 1993 WL 274299 (5th Dist Ct App, Perry, 6-29-93).

In investigating a report of child abuse pursuant to RC 2151.421, a public children services agency is required to consider the circumstances surrounding the injuries, abuse, or neglect or the threat of injury, abuse, or neglect; the cause of the injuries, abuse, neglect, or threat; and the person or persons responsible for the injuries, abuse, neglect, or threat. Thus, a public children services agency must consider whether, in accordance with RC 3319.41(G), a school teacher, principal, administrator, nonlicensed employee, or bus driver has used reasonable and necessary force and restraint to quell a disturbance threatening physical injury to others, to obtain possession of weapons or other dangerous objects upon the person or within the control of the pupil, for the purpose of self-defense, or for the protection of persons or property. OAG 02-019.

If, in investigating a report of child abuse pursuant to RC 2151.421, a public children services agency finds that action consisting of reasonable and necessary force and restraint was used by a school teacher, principal, administrator, nonlicensed employee, or bus driver in accordance with RC 3319.41(G) to quell a disturbance threatening physical injury to others, to obtain possession of weapons or other dangerous objects upon the person or within the control of the pupil, for the purpose of self-defense, or for the protection of persons or property, the public children services agency is precluded from finding that such action constituted child abuse for purposes of RC 2151.421. OAG 02-019.

When a public children services agency receives a report of the spanking of a student by a school administrator, the agency must assign the report a priority rating in accordance with OAC 5101:2-34-08; a report that is rated priority I, II, or III must be investigated as required by RC 2151.421, in accordance with the procedures prescribed in OAC 5101:2-34-32, 5101:2-34-33, and 5101:2-34-34, and a report that is rated priority IV may be resolved by termination pursuant to OAC 5101:2-34-08 if it is determined that the report alleges only action that is permitted under RC 3319.41 and 2919.22, for then the report does not constitute an allegation of abuse or neglect. OAG 92-082.

A public children services agency is required, pursuant to RC 2151.421(F)(1), to investigate as alleged child abuse a report received by it of an incident in which a sixteen-year-old female has been assaulted by her husband. OAG 92-073.

RC 2151.421 does not require that a public children services agency routinely share child abuse and neglect investigation materials with the air force office of special investigations, an agency of the federal government. OAG 92-046.

Each report and investigation of alleged child abuse or neglect made under RC 2151.421 is confidential and, pursuant to OAC 5101:2-34-38, the dissemination of such confidential information to an agency or organization is permitted only if the agency or organization has rules or policies governing the dissemination of confidential information that are consistent with those of OAC 5101:2-34-38. OAG 92-046.

A public children services agency may not share child abuse and neglect investigation materials with the air force office of special investigations unless the office has suitable rules or policies governing the dissemination of confidential information. OAG 92-046.

A public children services agency may disclose child abuse and neglect investigation materials to the air force office of special investigations when such disclosure is in compliance with RC 2151.421 and 5153.17, and OAC 5101:2-34-38 and is for purposes authorized by those provisions; the agency is not required to obtain assurance that the office will not use the materials for purposes other than criminal prosecution. OAG 92-046.

A public children services agency may, pursuant to OAC 5101:2-34-71, at 1991-92 OMR 280, include the air force office of special investigations as a voluntary subscriber to a county plan of cooperation prepared pursuant to RC 2151.421(J), if the office wishes to be a voluntary subscriber and if the agency determines that the participation of the office would be appropriate; if the office has suitable rules or policies governing the use and dissemination of confidential information, the office may receive investigatory materials as provided in the county plan of cooperation and in OAC 5101:2-34-38(D)(4). OAG 92-046.

Child abuse and neglect investigation records maintained by public children services agencies do not constitute "public records" within the meaning of RC 149.43 to which the right of public access attaches. Records of child abuse or neglect investigations under RC 2151.421(H)(1) and 5153.17 are "records the release of which is prohibited by state law" under RC 149.43(A)(1). OAG 91-003.

Public children services agencies are authorized to investigate reports of alleged child abuse or neglect or threats thereof at facilities operated by the mental health department pursuant to RC Ch 5122, by the mental retardation and developmental disabilities department pursuant to RC Ch 5123, by the youth services department pursuant to RC Ch 5139, at detention homes established pursuant to RC 2151.34, at the veterans' children's home operated pursuant to RC Ch 5909, and at public schools operating under standards set by the board of education pursuant to RC Ch 3301. OAG 89-108.

RC 2151.421 sets forth a comprehensive scheme for the reporting of allegations of child abuse and neglect and threats thereof and for the investigation of such reports by public children services agencies, which have authority to investigate all such reports within their counties of jurisdiction unless there is some provision of law restricting that authority with respect to particular persons or locations. OAG 89–108.

The powers of the highway patrol or special police officers designated by the highway patrol superintendent to investigate and to enforce laws on state properties and in state institutions do not restrict the authority of public children services agencies to investigate reports of alleged child abuse or neglect or threats thereof pertaining to such locations. OAG 89–108.

Public children services agencies are local agencies for purposes of RC Ch 1347, which governs the maintenance of personal information systems. OAG 89–084.

The provisions of RC 2151.421 impose the duties of investigation and disposition of reported cases of child abuse and neglect solely on children services boards and county welfare departments which have assumed the functions of a children services board, and, therefore, prohibit delegation of these duties to private entities. OAG 79–067.

3. Corpus delicti of crime

While the statute of limitations in a child sexual abuse case begins to run only when the corpus delicti of the crime is discovered and the general rule for discovery of corpus delecti in such a case is when the victim informs a responsible adult listed in RC 2151.421, a child abuse victim who has reached the age of majority is presumed to understand and acknowledge the act and the criminal nature of the act and, therefore, the statute of limitations begins to run after reaching the age of majority. State v. Wooldridge (Ohio App. 2 Dist., Montgomery, 10-08-1999) No. 17708, 1999 WL 812363, Unreported, appeal not allowed 88 Ohio St.3d 1416, 723 N.E.2d 121.

Community hospital did not have duty, under statute requiring it to report known or suspected child abuse, to report conduct of former employee, given that at time employment terminated, hospital had no reason to know or suspect any particular child was being abused or in danger of being abused by employee. Douglass v. Salem Community Hosp. (Ohio App. 7 Dist., 07-23-2003) 153 Ohio App.3d 350, 794 N.E.2d 107, 2003-Ohio-4006, appeal not allowed 100 Ohio St.3d 1530, 800 N.E.2d 47, 2003-Ohio-6458, reconsideration denied 101 Ohio St.3d 1471, 804 N.E.2d 43, 2004-Ohio-819. Infants ⚖ 13.5(1)

Corpus delicti of crime involving child abuse or neglect is discovered, and statute of limitations begins to run, when responsible adult, as listed in statute, has knowledge of both act and criminal nature of act. State v. Tillman (Ohio App. 9 Dist., 05-07-1997) 119 Ohio App.3d 449, 695 N.E.2d 792, motion for delayed appeal denied 90 Ohio St.3d 1471, 738 N.E.2d 382. Criminal Law ⚖ 148.1

Corpus delicti of crimes involving child abuse or neglect is discovered, for limitations purposes, when responsible adult has knowledge both of act and of criminal nature of act. State v. Weiss (Ohio App. 5 Dist., 08-08-1994) 96 Ohio App.3d 379, 645 N.E.2d 98, motion to certify denied 71 Ohio St.3d 1421, 642 N.E.2d 386. Criminal Law ⚖ 148.1

Corpus delicti of sexual abuse of five-year-old child was discovered when child's babysitter reported child's graphic account of abuse to county child services agency over seven years before defendant was indicted for sexual misconduct, and thus six-year statute of limitations had run. State v. Ritchie (Ohio App. 12 Dist., 07-11-1994) 95 Ohio App.3d 569, 642 N.E.2d 1168, dismissed, appeal not allowed 71 Ohio St.3d 1412, 641 N.E.2d 1111. Criminal Law ⚖ 154

That responsible adult has acquired knowledge of sexual abuse is not enough to commence limitation period; instead, period begins to run only if responsible adult required requisite knowledge while acting in his official or professional capacity. State v. Rosenberger (Ohio App. 9 Dist., 10-20-1993) 90 Ohio App.3d 735, 630 N.E.2d 435, motion overruled 68 Ohio St.3d 1473, 628 N.E.2d 1392. Criminal Law ⚖ 154

Sexual abuse was not discovered, and limitation period did not commence, until victim disclosed existence of sexual abuse during professional counseling. State v. Rosenberger (Ohio App. 9 Dist., 10-20-1993) 90 Ohio App.3d 735, 630 N.E.2d 435, motion overruled 68 Ohio St.3d 1473, 628 N.E.2d 1392. Criminal Law ⚖ 154

For purposes of RC 2901.13(F), the corpus delicti of crimes involving child abuse or neglect is discovered when a responsible adult, as listed in RC 2151.421, has knowledge of both the act and the criminal nature of the act. State v. Hensley (Ohio 1991) 59 Ohio St.3d 136, 571 N.E.2d 711. Criminal Law ⚖ 154

Evidence did not establish that corpus delicti of offenses of gross sexual imposition and rape of child under 13 years of age had been discovered by responsible adult acting in professional capacity with legal duty to report sexual abuse of child, and thus, limitations period did not begin to run for the offenses; defendant's girlfriend, who was not acting in her professional capacity, merely reported to law enforcement authorities that defendant took victim into bedroom, locked the door, and played loud music, victim denied allegations of sexual abuse when questioned by juvenile court judge, and other reports of sexual abuse were unsubstantiated. State v. Carpenter (Ohio App. 6 Dist., Erie, 05-10-2002) No. E-00-033, 2002-Ohio-2266, 2002 WL 1003520, Unreported, appeal reopened 2002-Ohio-4824, 2002 WL 31053828, appeal not allowed 96 Ohio St.3d 1513, 775 N.E.2d 855, 2002-Ohio-4950, appeal reopened 2004-Ohio-1036, 2004 WL 413288, appeal after new sentencing hearing 2006-Ohio-3048, 2006 WL 1661781, cause dismissed 110 Ohio St.3d 1450, 852 N.E.2d 197, 2006-Ohio-4085. Criminal Law ⚖ 150

For purposes of RC 2901.13(F), the corpus delicti of crimes involving child abuse or neglect is discovered when a person with an RC 2151.421 statutory duty to report child abuse learns of the abuse. State v Wright, No. 1870 (4th Dist Ct App, Scioto, 9–16–91).

The corpus delicti of a crime against a child is discovered when one who is required to report the crime discovers the crime and a prosecution for the crime is timely if commenced within the required limits following discovery. State v Sutter, No. 13749 (9th Dist Ct App, Summit, 11–15–89).

4. Procedural issues

Expert testimony was not required to establish breach of duty, proximate cause, or damages resulting from hospital's failure to timely report the suspected abuse of patient, a minor child; statute imposed a duty upon persons who provided medical and nonmedical services to report any knowledge or suspicion of abuse or neglect of a child, if hospital failed to report the suspected abuse of plaintiff it constituted negligence per se, and the issue of whether any hospital employee knew or suspected that patient was an abused or neglected child was a matter within the common knowledge and experience of law jurors. Grimm v. Summit Cty. Children Servs. Bd. (Ohio App. 9 Dist., Summit, 05-17-2006) No. 22702, 2006-Ohio-2411, 2006 WL 1329689, Unreported. Infants ⚖ 13.5(2)

Ordering department of children and family services prior to hearing in sexual predator classification proceeding to produce documents without reviewing documents in camera was abuse of trial court's discretion; information in records was sensitive in nature, disclosing records without in camera review would have potentially chilling effect on citizens' reports of abuse, and harm could be caused to those reporting abuse if records were disclosed. State v. Sahady (Ohio App. 8 Dist., Cuyahoga, 07-01-2004) No. 83247, 2004-Ohio-3481, 2004 WL 1472087, Unreported. Mental Health ⚖ 455

Records of department of children and family services are not absolutely privileged in sexual predator classification proceeding; although records are afforded confidentiality pursuant to statutes, this confidentiality is not absolute, but instead, access to records may be warranted if records are necessary and relevant to proceeding and good cause for disclosure is shown. State v. Sahady (Ohio App. 8 Dist., Cuyahoga, 07-01-2004) No. 83247, 2004-Ohio-3481, 2004 WL 1472087, Unreported. Witnesses ⚖ 216(1)

Father's allegation that school employee reported to children's services agency that child was bruised failed to state a cause of action against employee; employee had statutory duty to report any reasonable suspicion of child abuse, and father did not allege that employee's report was false, or was not based on reasonable suspicion. Tracy v. Tinnerman (Ohio App. 2 Dist., Miami, 12-12-2003) No. 2003-CA-21, 2003-Ohio-6675, 2003 WL 22927758, Unreported. Infants ⚖ 13.5(2)

A complaint is insufficient to support a claim that the county children services board fails to properly investigate sexual abuse and defames a party by putting his name on a list of sexual offenders where the complaint fails to state that the board did not follow the procedures set forth in the plan of cooperation and fails to claim that the board has the authority to remove the name from the central registry thus giving the party the relief requested. Dodson v. Shelby County Children Services Bd. (Ohio App. 3 Dist., Shelby, 04-23-1997) No. 17-96-20, 1997 WL 198919, Unreported.

A trial court's decision to deny defendant's motion for a protective order concerning a report of child abuse is an order entered in a special proceeding and is final and appealable. Walters, Jr. v. Enrichment Center of Wishing Well (Ohio App. 8 Dist., Cuyahoga, 03-28-1996) No. 69159, 1996 WL 139704, Unreported, motion to certify allowed 76 Ohio St.3d 1422, 667 N.E.2d 25, appeal not allowed 76 Ohio St.3d 1424, 667 N.E.2d 27, reversed 78 Ohio St.3d 118, 676 N.E.2d 890, 1997-Ohio-232.

When a child victim of sex offense tells a responsible person who is required by law to report the events to a peace officer or children's services agency, the statute of limitations begins to run as of that time, even if the child has not attained the age of majority. State v. Warren (Ohio App. 8 Dist., 08-10-2006) 2006-Ohio-4104, 2006 WL 2297294. Criminal Law ⇨ 148.1

Reports that document child abuse are not necessarily confidential child-abuse investigatory records under the child-abuse reporting statute. State ex rel. Beacon Journal Publishing Co. v. Akron (Ohio, 12-15-2004) 104 Ohio St.3d 399, 819 N.E.2d 1087, 2004-Ohio-6557. Infants ⇨ 133

The child-abuse reporting statute is not limited to cases of known or suspected abuse by parents, custodians, and guardians in family settings; it also applies to known or suspected abuse by other types of perpetrators, such as police officers or juvenile offenders. State ex rel. Beacon Journal Publishing Co. v. Akron (Ohio, 12-15-2004) 104 Ohio St.3d 399, 819 N.E.2d 1087, 2004-Ohio-6557. Infants ⇨ 13.5(1)

The General Assembly when imposing a duty to report abuse of a child did not intend to protect only the one specific minor student who was actually abused by a teacher. Yates v. Mansfield Bd. of Edn. (Ohio, 06-02-2004) 102 Ohio St.3d 205, 808 N.E.2d 861, 2004-Ohio-2491. Infants ⇨ 13.5(1)

The question of who is entitled to protection under the child abuse reporting statute in any given case depends on the circumstances and the relationships of the parties; in the typical case, the statute's mandatory reporting provisions will operate to protect only the specific child who is identified as abused because that child alone is in direct danger of further injury, but when the circumstances clearly indicate that there exists a danger of harm to another child from the same source and the reporter has an official or professional relationship with the other child, the statute does not withhold protection until such time as that child's personal security and bodily integrity are actually violated. Yates v. Mansfield Bd. of Edn. (Ohio, 06-02-2004) 102 Ohio St.3d 205, 808 N.E.2d 861, 2004-Ohio-2491. Infants ⇨ 13.5(1)

Use of word "reasonably," in statute requiring that certain persons report knowledge or suspicion of child abuse when there is a condition of a nature that reasonably indicates abuse or neglect of the child, clarifies that duty to report does not require absolute proof. Surdel v. MetroHealth Med. Ctr. (Ohio App. 8 Dist., 10-04-1999) 135 Ohio App.3d 141, 733 N.E.2d 281, dismissed, appeal not allowed 87 Ohio St.3d 1491, 722 N.E.2d 525. Infants ⇨ 13

Statute that protects information provided in a report of known or suspected child abuse to a children services agency from use as evidence in civil action against person making the report creates a testimonial privilege. Walters v. The Enrichment Ctr. of Wishing Well, Inc. (Ohio App. 8 Dist., 06-07-1999) 133 Ohio App.3d 66, 726 N.E.2d 1058, appeal not allowed 87 Ohio St.3d 1408, 716 N.E.2d 1170. Infants ⇨ 208

Day-care center that was sued by enrolled child's parents after its owner-director allegedly made bad-faith report to county agency of suspected child abuse was entitled, under child protection statute, to protective order preventing the depositions of employees concerning information contained in report. Walters v. The Enrichment Ctr. of Wishing Well, Inc. (Ohio App. 8 Dist., 06-07-1999) 133 Ohio App.3d 66, 726 N.E.2d 1058, appeal not allowed 87 Ohio St.3d 1408, 716 N.E.2d 1170. Infants ⇨ 208

Report of suspected child abuse, made by owner-director of day-care center to county department of social services, was protected from use in action against center and its owner-director by child's parents. Walters v. The Enrichment Ctr. of Wishing Well, Inc. (Ohio App. 8 Dist., 06-07-1999) 133 Ohio App.3d 66, 726 N.E.2d 1058, appeal not allowed 87 Ohio St.3d 1408, 716 N.E.2d 1170. Infants ⇨ 208

Parents are not included in definition of those "responsible adults" whose knowledge of act and criminal nature of act trigger limitation period on crime involving child abuse. State v. Tillman (Ohio App. 9 Dist., 05-07-1997) 119 Ohio App.3d 449, 695 N.E.2d 792, motion for delayed appeal denied 90 Ohio St.3d 1471, 738 N.E.2d 382. Criminal Law ⇨ 148.1

Requirement, for award of crime victim reparations, that criminally injurious conduct be reported to "law enforcement agency" or officer within 72 hours was satisfied by reporting incidents of sexual abuse to county children services board. In re Kramer (Ohio Ct.Cl., 06-28-1995) 86 Ohio Misc.2d 4, 684 N.E.2d 751. Criminal Law ⇨ 1220

Any privilege that attached to victim's communication with her psychologist was automatically waived, where victim was under 18 years of age, psychologist had reason to believe that victim had been sexually abused, and privileged communication did not arise from victim's attempt to get abortion. State v. Stewart (Ohio App. 9 Dist., 06-05-1996) 111 Ohio App.3d 525, 676 N.E.2d 912. Witnesses ⇨ 219(1)

In action brought by parents against day-care center for allegedly making bad faith report of child abuse, trial court's order denying center's motion for protective order as to certain documents allegedly pertaining to reports of child abuse was not a final appealable order. Walters v. Enrichment Center of Wishing Well, Inc. (Ohio, 04-02-1997) 78 Ohio St.3d 118, 676 N.E.2d 890, 1997-Ohio-232. Appeal And Error ⇨ 78(1)

Father's allegations that social services agency and agency employees published false statements regarding father having sexually abused his daughter when they filed complaint to that effect in juvenile court, that father suffered public humiliation when his name was placed on "central registry" and that false statements were published maliciously were sufficient to state defamation claim. Roe v. Franklin Cty. (Ohio App. 10 Dist., 03-12-1996) 109 Ohio App.3d 772, 673 N.E.2d 172, appeal not allowed 77 Ohio St.3d 1415, 670 N.E.2d 1003. Libel And Slander ⇨ 7(16)

Statute of limitations on charges of child abuse which allegedly occurred when victim's age ranged from eight to 12 years was tolled during child's minority, irrespective of victim's awareness of corpus delicti, and absent evidence that victim had told responsible adult of the abuse prior to attaining majority, tolling ceased no earlier than when victim turned 18. State v. Elsass (Ohio App. 10 Dist., 07-25-1995) 105 Ohio App.3d 277, 663 N.E.2d 1019. Criminal Law ⇨ 151.1

Under statute setting forth specific duty to report knowledge or suspicions of child abuse, plaintiffs bear burden of showing that they fall within class of individuals statute was designed to protect. Hite v. Brown (Ohio App. 8 Dist., 03-09-1995) 100 Ohio App.3d 606, 654 N.E.2d 452, appeal denied 73 Ohio St.3d 1414, 651 N.E.2d 1311. Infants ⇨ 13.5(1)

Statute of limitations begins to run on child-abuse prosecution once child-abuse victim attains age of 18 and understands criminal nature of act. State v. Weiss (Ohio App. 5 Dist., 08-08-1994) 96 Ohio App.3d 379, 645 N.E.2d 98, motion to certify denied 71 Ohio St.3d 1421, 642 N.E.2d 386. Criminal Law ⇨ 148.1

Statute of limitations began to run on child-abuse prosecution once child victim attained age of 18 and understood that what defendant had done was wrong, even though victim may not have been aware of exact nature of defendant's crime. State v. Weiss (Ohio App. 5 Dist., 08-08-1994) 96 Ohio App.3d 379, 645 N.E.2d 98, motion to certify denied 71 Ohio St.3d 1421, 642 N.E.2d 386. Criminal Law ⇨ 148.1

Child's age may toll statute of limitations on child abuse prosecution, even when child is not of tender years, if child is under 18 years of age and has sufficiently internalized defendant's abuse; whether such internalization is sufficient to toll statute of limitations in any given case is best left to trier of fact. State v. Weiss (Ohio App. 5 Dist., 08-08-1994) 96 Ohio App.3d 379, 645 N.E.2d 98, motion to certify denied 71 Ohio St.3d 1421, 642 N.E.2d 386. Criminal Law ⇨ 151.1

There is no presumption, for limitations purposes, that child-abuse victim understands and acknowledges defendant's act and criminal nature of act merely because victim attains age of majority. State v. Weiss (Ohio App. 5 Dist., 08-08-1994) 96 Ohio App.3d 379, 645 N.E.2d 98, motion to certify denied 71 Ohio St.3d 1421, 642 N.E.2d 386. Criminal Law ⇨ 151.1

Under six-year criminal statute of limitations, corpus delicti of crime involving sexual abuse of children is discovered when employee of children services agency or other "responsible adult," as that term is statutorily defined, has knowledge of both act itself and criminal nature of act. State v. Ritchie (Ohio App. 12 Dist., 07-11-1994) 95 Ohio App.3d 569, 642 N.E.2d 1168, dismissed, appeal not allowed 71 Ohio St.3d 1412, 641 N.E.2d 1111. Criminal Law ⇨ 154

In action arising from alleged sexual assault by clergyman on child, order that church produce communications from clergyman's mental health counselors for in camera inspection did not affect substantial right of church by forcing it to violate canon law and thus excessively entangling state in affairs of church, for purposes of determining whether order was final and appealable; canons at issue dealt with how church chose to handle files administratively, and statutory reporting requirement for cases of child abuse indicated legislative intent that church yield to state on such issues. Niemann v. Cooley (Ohio App. 1 Dist., 01-26-1994) 93 Ohio App.3d 81, 637 N.E.2d 943, dismissed, jurisdictional motion overruled 69 Ohio St.3d 1478, 634 N.E.2d 1025. Appeal And Error ⇨ 78(1)

Grandparents of allegedly abused child were not "affected by" statute imposing duty on children services board to investigate reports of child abuse or neglect, and, thus, grandparents did not have standing to seek declaratory judgment concerning such statute and the request for declaratory judgment could not present justiciable controversy; duty under statute was owed to allegedly abused child, not to any person who files a charge with board. Neuenschwander v. Wayne Cty. Children Serv. Bd. (Ohio App. 9 Dist., 02-02-1994) 92 Ohio App.3d 767, 637 N.E.2d 102, motion overruled 69 Ohio St.3d 1489, 635 N.E.2d 44. Declaratory Judgment ⇨ 300

Knowledge by victim's mother's neighbor, who was employed as paramedic, of victim's sexual abuse did not commence limitation period for prosecuting alleged abuser, where mother revealed her knowledge of abuse to neighbor as a personal friend, rather than in his professional capacity as paramedic. State v. Rosenberger (Ohio App. 9 Dist., 10-20-1993) 90 Ohio App.3d 735, 630 N.E.2d 435, motion overruled 68 Ohio St.3d 1473, 628 N.E.2d 1392. Criminal Law ⇐ 154

Judgment rejecting request of county department of human services that its confidential records remain sealed and not be reviewed by court-appointed psychologist in custody action was final appealable order. Sharpe v. Sharpe (Lake 1993) 85 Ohio App.3d 638, 620 N.E.2d 916. Infants ⇐ 242

Appeal taken by county department of human services, in challenging ruling that its confidential records be reviewed by court-appointed psychologist in determining custody action, was from actual order releasing confidential records for other than in camera review by court, rather than earlier judgment entry addressing department's motion to quash, for purposes of determining whether appeal was timely. Sharpe v. Sharpe (Lake 1993) 85 Ohio App.3d 638, 620 N.E.2d 916. Infants ⇐ 244.1

Ohio statute on judicial bypass for minor to obtain abortion without parental consent adequately ensures confidentiality without an exemption from requirements for reporting abuse; complete anonymity is not required, and the state is only required to take reasonable steps to prevent the public, not other governmental officials, from learning the minor's identity. Cincinnati Women's Services, Inc. v. Taft (S.D.Ohio, 09-08-2005) 2005 WL 2206219. Abortion And Birth Control ⇐ 124

Where a welfare department does not complete an investigation of alleged abuse by a noncustodial father within thirty days as required by RC 2151.421 but instead waits nearly one year to close the case because of the complaining mother's refusal to cooperate and the department's failure to take any of the steps available to it to secure cooperation, the father who was deprived of visitation for the entire period should have sought a writ of mandamus ordering the investigation to proceed and cannot sue the department in US district court under 42 USC 1983. Haag v. Cuyahoga County (N.D.Ohio 1985) 619 F.Supp. 262, affirmed 798 F.2d 1414.

County department of children and family services' allegations of child neglect, without further corroboration or explanation of the underlying facts by social worker and child care worker, who testified on behalf of county department of work & training that such findings had been made, did not constitute reliable, probative, and substantial evidence to support agency's revocation of provider's child care certification; department of work & training could have sought in camera inspection of the child abuse records or reports, and heard testimony from the case workers for department of children and family services who investigated the provider. Child Care Provider Certification Dept. v. Harris (Ohio App. 8 Dist., Cuyahoga, 07-25-2002) No. 80669, 2002-Ohio-3795, 2002 WL 1728540, Unreported, appeal not allowed 97 Ohio St.3d 1485, 780 N.E.2d 288, 2002-Ohio-6866. Asylums ⇐ 3

In camera inspection of child abuse records or reports was not only permitted, but was preferred, where child care provider sought judicial review of administrative decision revoking her child care certification, and evidence before trial court consisted of uncorroborated allegations of child neglect. Child Care Provider Certification Dept. v. Harris (Ohio App. 8 Dist., Cuyahoga, 07-25-2002) No. 80669, 2002-Ohio-3795, 2002 WL 1728540, Unreported, appeal not allowed 97 Ohio St.3d 1485, 780 N.E.2d 288, 2002-Ohio-6866. Infants ⇐ 133

A board of education may require by rule, adopted pursuant to RC 3313.20, that an investigator from a county children services board obtain parental consent or permit a school official to be present before allowing such investigator to interview a child on school property in the course of an investigation required to be conducted under RC 2151.421; the reasonableness of such rule is subject to judicial review. OAG 82-029.

The phrase "having reason to believe" as used in RC 2151.421 is equivalent to "known or suspected" as used in 45 CFR 1340.3-3(d). OAG 78-038.

The term "child neglect" as used in RC 2151.421 applies to children without proper parental care or guardianship as defined by RC 2151.05. OAG 78-038.

5. Immunity

Village and county social services department did not employ a policy encouraging its employees to fabricate child abuse investigations or to lie under oath, such that they could be held liable under §§ 1983 on claims of subject of allegedly fabricated investigation. Denver v. Casbeer (Ohio App. 1 Dist., Hamilton, 11-04-2005) No. C-050106, 2005-Ohio-5860, 2005 WL 2899631, Unreported, appeal not allowed 108 Ohio St.3d 1511, 844 N.E.2d 856, 2006-Ohio-1329. Civil Rights ⇐ 1351(6)

Social worker and police officer, whose testimony resulted in conviction of father of subject of child abuse investigation, were entitled to immunity from liability under §§ 1983 to subject of investigation. Denver v. Casbeer (Ohio App. 1 Dist., Hamilton, 11-04-2005) No. C-050106, 2005-Ohio-5860, 2005 WL 2899631, Unreported, appeal not allowed 108 Ohio St.3d 1511, 844 N.E.2d 856, 2006-Ohio-1329. Civil Rights ⇐ 1376(6)

A university hospital is immune from civil liability for reporting possible child abuse based upon X-rays of an eleven-month-old child which demonstrate a leg fracture and raise reasonable suspicion of a non-accidental injury. White v. University Hospitals of Cleveland (Ohio App. 8 Dist., Cuyahoga, 11-22-2000) No. 77694, 2000 WL 1739304, Unreported.

Purpose of statutory immunity for certain persons filing a report of suspected child abuse or neglect is that the societal benefits of preventing child abuse outweigh the individual harm that might arise from the filing of a false report. Liedtke v. Carrington (Ohio App. 8 Dist., 08-14-2001) 145 Ohio App.3d 396, 763 N.E.2d 213. Infants ⇐ 12(9)

Hospital, physician, and nurse who participated in making a report to a law enforcement agency of suspected child abuse fell within class of persons required by statute to report knowledge or suspicion of child abuse and, thus, were immune from liability to parents for alleged negligence and reckless conduct during course of investigation and in subsequent reporting of results of investigation to various agencies, regardless of whether reports were made in good faith or whether diagnosis of sexual abuse was a grave departure from applicable standard of care. Casbohm v. MetroHealth Med. Ctr. (Ohio App. 8 Dist., 09-25-2000) 140 Ohio App.3d 58, 746 N.E.2d 661. Infants ⇐ 17

Statutory immunity for making a mandatory report of suspected child abuse, or for making a permissive report of suspected abuse in good faith, is not limited to the initial reporter of suspected abuse, but also attaches to persons making subsequent reports after an investigation has begun. Surdel v. MetroHealth Med. Ctr. (Ohio App. 8 Dist., 10-04-1999) 135 Ohio App.3d 141, 733 N.E.2d 281, dismissed, appeal not allowed 87 Ohio St.3d 1491, 722 N.E.2d 525. Infants ⇐ 13

Persons who are required by statute to report suspected child abuse retain immunity from liability for such reports regardless of whether the report was made in good faith. Surdel v. MetroHealth Med. Ctr. (Ohio App. 8 Dist., 10-04-1999) 135 Ohio App.3d 141, 733 N.E.2d 281, dismissed, appeal not allowed 87 Ohio St.3d 1491, 722 N.E.2d 525. Infants ⇐ 13

Mental health counselors who counseled three minor sisters upon a referral from county authorities fell within class of persons required by statute to report knowledge or suspicion of child abuse, and were thus immune from liability to father for making reports resulting in criminal sex abuse charges against father, regardless of whether reports were made in good faith. Surdel v. MetroHealth Med. Ctr. (Ohio App. 8 Dist., 10-04-1999) 135 Ohio App.3d 141, 733 N.E.2d 281, dismissed, appeal not allowed 87 Ohio St.3d 1491, 722 N.E.2d 525. Infants ⇐ 17

Health care providers who performed diagnostic physical examinations of three minor sisters upon a referral from county authorities fell within class of persons required by statute to report knowledge or suspicion of child abuse, and therefore those providers were immune from liability to sisters' father for making reports resulting in criminal sex abuse charges against father, regardless of whether reports were made in good faith. Surdel v. MetroHealth Med. Ctr. (Ohio App. 8 Dist., 10-04-1999) 135 Ohio App.3d 141, 733 N.E.2d 281, dismissed, appeal not allowed 87 Ohio St.3d 1491, 722 N.E.2d 525. Infants ⇐ 17

Day-care center and its owner-director were immune from liability for any claims arising from owner-director's filing of report with county department of social services concerning suspected abuse of enrolled child by his father, regardless of whether report was filed in good faith. Walters v. The Enrichment Ctr. of Wishing Well, Inc. (Ohio App. 8 Dist., 06-07-1999) 133 Ohio App.3d 66, 726 N.E.2d 1058, appeal not allowed 87 Ohio St.3d 1408, 716 N.E.2d 1170. Infants ⇐ 208

Disclosures by a physician of otherwise confidential medical information made pursuant to statutory mandate are privileged, such as disclosure of occupational diseases or diseases which are infectious, contagious, or dangerous to public health, disclosure of medical conditions indicative of child abuse or neglect, and disclosure of injuries indicative of criminal conduct. Biddle v. Warren Gen. Hosp. (Ohio, 09-15-1999) 86 Ohio St.3d 395, 715 N.E.2d 518, 1999-Ohio-115. Health ⇐ 642

Immunity from civil or criminal liability is conferred by statute on any person reporting in good faith known or suspected abuse of child under 18 years of age to peace officer or children services board and on any person participating in judicial proceeding resulting from those reports. State v.

Thompson (Ohio App. 12 Dist., 10-17-1994) 97 Ohio App.3d 629, 647 N.E.2d 226. Infants ⇨ 13

Defendant who kept custody of child for three-day period without consent of child's mother was not entitled to defense of immunity based on good faith report of known or suspected child abuse where prosecution of defendant was not based on or result of defendant's reporting suspected abuse to police but was based on defendant's harboring of child without mother's permission and contrary to instructions of police officer. State v. Thompson (Ohio App. 12 Dist., 10-17-1994) 97 Ohio App.3d 629, 647 N.E.2d 226. Infants ⇨ 13

The immunity provided by the child abuse reporting statute, RC 2151.421(G), does not control a claim asserted in a state court under 42 USC 1983. Cudlin v. Cudlin (Cuyahoga 1990) 64 Ohio App.3d 249, 580 N.E.2d 1170.

Former RC 2151.421(G) confers immunity upon those who, as a result of a report of a known or suspected incident of child abuse and/or neglect, participate in a judicial proceeding. Gersper v. Ashtabula County Children Services Bd. (Ohio 1991) 59 Ohio St.3d 127, 570 N.E.2d 1120. Infants ⇨ 13

A child care center administrator enjoys a qualified privilege to report suspected child abuse; confronting and terminating a teacher for suspected child abuse do not constitute defamation absent a showing of actual malice. Lail v. Madisonville Child Care Project, Inc. (Hamilton 1989) 55 Ohio App.3d 37, 561 N.E.2d 1063.

Officers or agents of a children services bureau are immune from civil liability for the exercise of discretionary functions unless a plaintiff challenging the public officer's good faith can show that the official acted in willful, reckless, or wanton disregard of rights established under law. Brodie v. Summit County Children Services Bd. (Ohio 1990) 51 Ohio St.3d 112, 554 N.E.2d 1301. Infants ⇨ 17

Qualified immunity may not be asserted as a defense to an action alleging the failure of a public official to perform ministerial acts. Brodie v. Summit County Children Services Bd. (Ohio 1990) 51 Ohio St.3d 112, 554 N.E.2d 1301. Officers And Public Employees ⇨ 114

Division (G) of RC 2151.421 does not confer immunity upon those who fail to carry out the mandate of the statute. Brodie v. Summit County Children Services Bd. (Ohio 1990) 51 Ohio St.3d 112, 554 N.E.2d 1301.

The filing of false child abuse reports by an ex-spouse is immune from prosecution since the societal benefits of freely making reports outweigh the individual harm which arises from false reports. Hartley v. Hartley (Lucas 1988) 42 Ohio App.3d 160, 537 N.E.2d 706, motion to certify overruled 38 Ohio St.3d 717, 533 N.E.2d 787.

Under Ohio law, school district did not enjoy statutory immunity from liability for damages in student's state law claim for reckless indifference arising out of sexual relationship initiated by teacher, where student alleged that school district failed to observe statutory duties. Doe v. New Philadelphia Public Schools Bd. of Educ. (N.D.Ohio, 03-12-1998) 996 F.Supp. 741. Schools ⇨ 89.3

A federal court will enforce the doctrine of absolute judicial immunity and statutory immunity accorded participants in child abuse proceedings codified at RC 2151.421. Scarso v. Cuyahoga County Dept. of Human Services (N.D.Ohio 1989) 747 F.Supp. 381, affirmed in part and remanded 917 F.2d 1305.

City school district was not immune from claim of failure to report child abuse where RC 2744.02 provides exception to immunity when liability is expressly imposed by a section of the Revised Code, as is the case under RC 2151.421 which places a statutory duty to report upon teachers, school employees, and school authorities. Sprouse v Lucas Bd of Ed, No. L–98–1098, 1999 WL 128636 (6th Dist Ct App, Lucas, 3–12–99).

A police officer testifying before a grand jury in a sexual abuse proceeding is immunized from civil liability by RC 2151.421. Dunbar v Oregon, No. L–88–289 (6th Dist Ct App, Lucas, 5–5–89).

6. Consequences of failure to report

Jury award of $224,000 in damages to patient due to hospital's failure to report the known or suspected abuse of patient, a minor child, was not excessive and did not warrant a new trial; patient's stepfather was convicted of the rape that resulted in her pregnancy, and jury in present action awarded damages against stepfather in the amount of $4,110,000. Grimm v. Summit Cty. Children Servs. Bd. (Ohio App. 9 Dist., Summit, 05-17-2006) No. 22702, 2006-Ohio-2411, 2006 WL 1329689, Unreported. New Trial ⇨ 76(1)

Hospital was liable under the doctrine of respondeat superior for its employees' failure to report the known or suspected abuse or neglect of patient, a minor child; nurse who admitted patient noted on her chart that patient wanted stepfather to be named as the baby's father on the birth certificate and that patient verbalized a history of depression since being raped at age ten, second nurse observed patient being naked in the presence of stepfather, and hospital social worker's notes indicated that nurses had been concerned about stepfather's behavior. Grimm v. Summit Cty. Children Servs. Bd. (Ohio App. 9 Dist., Summit, 05-17-2006) No. 22702, 2006-Ohio-2411, 2006 WL 1329689, Unreported. Infants ⇨ 13.5(2)

An employee's liability for failure to report known or suspected abuse or neglect of child could be imputed to the employer under the doctrine of respondeat superior. Grimm v. Summit Cty. Children Servs. Bd. (Ohio App. 9 Dist., Summit, 05-17-2006) No. 22702, 2006-Ohio-2411, 2006 WL 1329689, Unreported. Labor And Employment ⇨ 3053

Evidence supported jury award of $224,000 in patient's personal injury case against hospital based on hospital's failure to report the known or suspected child abuse or neglect of patient; patient's stepfather, who was convicted by a jury of raping patient and was the father of her child, was present in the delivery room when patient gave birth, was seen in patient's hospital room when she was naked, and was present when patient was breastfeeding, and patient testified as to having nightmares as a result of being raped by her stepfather. Grimm v. Summit Cty. Children Servs. Bd. (Ohio App. 9 Dist., Summit, 05-17-2006) No. 22702, 2006-Ohio-2411, 2006 WL 1329689, Unreported. Damages ⇨ 192

Statute prohibiting the failure to report suspected child abuse contemplates individual-capacity suits against government officers. Doe v. Roman (Ohio App. 5 Dist., Tuscarawas, 12-04-2002) No. 2001-AP-05-0044, 2002-Ohio-6671, 2002 WL 31732468, Unreported, appeal not allowed 98 Ohio St.3d 1537, 786 N.E.2d 900, 2003-Ohio-1946. Infants ⇨ 13.5(2)

Statutory duty on part of local board of education to report high school teacher's sexual abuse of a female student to authorities was owed only to that student, and therefore board's failure to report that incident did not bring board within an exception to immunity in action by parents of another female student with whom same teacher subsequently engaged in sexual misconduct. Yates v. Mansfield Bd. of Edn. (Ohio App. 5 Dist., 11-20-2002) 150 Ohio App.3d 241, 780 N.E.2d 608, 2002-Ohio-6311, appeal allowed, reversed 99 Ohio St.3d 48, 788 N.E.2d 1062, 2003-Ohio-2461, reversed 102 Ohio St.3d 205, 808 N.E.2d 861, 2004-Ohio-2491. Schools ⇨ 89

Concern of the General Assembly in enacting the statute mandating the reporting of known or suspected child abuse was not the protection of political subdivisions or their employees from claims for damages, but the protection of children from abuse and neglect. Campbell v. Burton (Ohio, 07-25-2001) 92 Ohio St.3d 336, 750 N.E.2d 539, 2001-Ohio-206. Infants ⇨ 12(2)

Psychologist who fails to report knowledge or suspicion of child abuse has no duty to persons outside psychologist/patient relationship. Hite v. Brown (Ohio App. 8 Dist., 03-09-1995) 100 Ohio App.3d 606, 654 N.E.2d 452, appeal denied 73 Ohio St.3d 1414, 651 N.E.2d 1311. Infants ⇨ 13.5(2); Health ⇨ 751

Under statute setting forth specific duty to report knowledge or suspicions of child abuse, duty to report such knowledge or suspicion was owed to individual minor; thus, psychologist who allegedly failed to report his suspicions that minor had been molested owed no duty to others who allegedly were subsequently molested by same perpetrator. Hite v. Brown (Ohio App. 8 Dist., 03-09-1995) 100 Ohio App.3d 606, 654 N.E.2d 452, appeal denied 73 Ohio St.3d 1414, 651 N.E.2d 1311. Infants ⇨ 13.5(2); Health ⇨ 751

Defendant charged with contributing to unruliness of minor after he had custody of child against wishes of child's mother over three-day period did not make report in good faith of known or suspected abuse of child to authorities, and was not entitled to assert defense of statutory immunity from prosecution based on reporting, where defendant did not report abuse to authorities but took child from friend's home when child was not in danger of being abused and harbored child without mother's permission, returned child to mother following day, and after finally calling police did not follow police instructions, and defendant's wife admitted that she and defendant hid child from police. State v. Thompson (Ohio App. 12 Dist., 10-17-1994) 97 Ohio App.3d 629, 647 N.E.2d 226. Infants ⇨ 13

Genuine issues of material fact existed as to whether certain officials were employees of school board, and whether they reported high school teacher's sexual relationship with teacher, precluding summary judgment as to whether school board could be held vicariously liable under Ohio statute mandating reporting of injuries to or neglect of minors. Craig v. Lima

City Schools Bd of Educ. (N.D.Ohio, 08-31-2005) 384 F.Supp.2d 1136. Federal Civil Procedure ⇐ 2500

If school board employee failed to report high school teacher's sexual relationship with student, school board was potentially liable to student under Ohio statute mandating reporting of injuries to or neglect of minors. Craig v. Lima City Schools Bd of Educ. (N.D.Ohio, 08-31-2005) 384 F.Supp.2d 1136. Infants ⇐ 13.5(2)

Genuine issue of material fact existed as to whether counselor was employee or agent of school board, precluding summary judgment as to whether school board could be held vicariously liable under Ohio statute mandating reporting of injuries to or neglect of minors, for any failure by counselor to report teacher's sexual relationship with high school student. Craig v. Lima City Schools Bd of Educ. (N.D.Ohio, 08-31-2005) 384 F.Supp.2d 1136. Federal Civil Procedure ⇐ 2500

School board could not be held liable under Ohio statute mandating reporting of injuries to or neglect of minors, for any failure of high school teacher to report his own abuse of high school student. Craig v. Lima City Schools Bd of Educ. (N.D.Ohio, 08-31-2005) 384 F.Supp.2d 1136. Infants ⇐ 13.5(2)

A counseling case manager who is told by the manager of the apartment where one of her clients lives that the client is abusing her child, but who does not report the abuse because of an unsubstantiated belief that the police are acting on the matter, gives her employer just cause to fire her for violation of a work rule. In re Spero, UCBR B94–D1215–0000 (11–22–94).

7. School teacher's duty

Genuine issues of material fact as to whether high school principal engaged in outrageous conduct both by failing to conduct further investigation into alleged sexual misconduct by teacher and by failing to report matter to school social worker and whether student suffered severe emotional distress precluded summary judgment in favor of principal, in his individual capacity, in student's action for intentional infliction of emotional distress. Doe v. Roman (Ohio App. 5 Dist., Tuscarawas, 12-04-2002) No. 2001-AP-05-0044, 2002-Ohio-6671, 2002 WL 31732468, Unreported, appeal not allowed 98 Ohio St.3d 1537, 786 N.E.2d 900, 2003-Ohio-1946. Judgment ⇐ 181(27)

Genuine issue of material fact as to whether high school principal and school social worker should have reported alleged incidents of teacher's sexual misconduct before student's admissions precluded summary judgment in favor of principal and social worker, in their individual capacities, in student's action for failure to report suspected child abuse. Doe v. Roman (Ohio App. 5 Dist., Tuscarawas, 12-04-2002) No. 2001-AP-05-0044, 2002-Ohio-6671, 2002 WL 31732468, Unreported, appeal not allowed 98 Ohio St.3d 1537, 786 N.E.2d 900, 2003-Ohio-1946. Judgment ⇐ 181(27)

Statute providing immunity to employees of political subdivisions under certain circumstances did not apply in high school student's action against principal and school social worker for failure to report teacher's alleged sexual misconduct, since statute prohibiting the failure to report suspected abuse expressly imposed liability on school employees. Doe v. Roman (Ohio App. 5 Dist., Tuscarawas, 12-04-2002) No. 2001-AP-05-0044, 2002-Ohio-6671, 2002 WL 31732468, Unreported, appeal not allowed 98 Ohio St.3d 1537, 786 N.E.2d 900, 2003-Ohio-1946. Infants ⇐ 13.5(2)

Pursuant to former exception to sovereign immunity when liability is expressly imposed, a board of education may be held liable when its failure to report the sexual abuse of a minor student by a teacher in violation of the reporting statute proximately results in the sexual abuse of another minor student by the same teacher. Yates v. Mansfield Bd. of Edn. (Ohio, 06-02-2004) 102 Ohio St.3d 205, 808 N.E.2d 861, 2004-Ohio-2491. Schools ⇐ 89.3

The statutory duty to report abuse of a child does not run solely to the identified abused child in the situation where the reporter to whom that child's control and protection has been entrusted also has direct control over the alleged perpetrator, other potential victims, and the environment in which they are brought together; abrogating Curran v. Walsh Jesuit High School, 99 Ohio App.3d 696, 651 N.E.2d 1028. Yates v. Mansfield Bd. of Edn. (Ohio, 06-02-2004) 102 Ohio St.3d 205, 808 N.E.2d 861, 2004-Ohio-2491. Infants ⇐ 13.5(1)

City school superintendent and peer mediation coordinator for junior high school did not have sovereign immunity from action for damages by eighth grade student, alleging that coordinator violated statutory duty to report, to public children services agency or municipal or county peace officer, known or suspected abuse of the student. Campbell v. Burton (Ohio, 07-25-2001) 92 Ohio St.3d 336, 750 N.E.2d 539, 2001-Ohio-206. Schools ⇐ 63(3); Schools ⇐ 147

City board of education did not have sovereign immunity from action for damages by eighth grade student, alleging that peer mediation coordinator for junior high school violated statutory duty to report, to public children services agency or municipal or county peace officer, known or suspected abuse of the student. Campbell v. Burton (Ohio, 07-25-2001) 92 Ohio St.3d 336, 750 N.E.2d 539, 2001-Ohio-206. Schools ⇐ 89.3

Failure to perform duty imposed by statute requiring school teacher or authority having reason to believe that child has been abused or neglected to report information to proper authorities is actionable. Curran v. Walsh Jesuit High School (Ohio App. 9 Dist., 01-04-1995) 99 Ohio App.3d 696, 651 N.E.2d 1028, appeal not allowed 72 Ohio St.3d 1529, 649 N.E.2d 839. Action ⇐ 3; Infants ⇐ 13.5(1)

School was not liable to student who alleged that he had been sexually assaulted by teacher based on alleged violation of statute requiring school teacher or authority having reason to believe that child has been abused or neglected to report information to proper authorities where alleged breach of school's duty to report involved alleged abuse by teacher of student other than student who brought action. Curran v. Walsh Jesuit High School (Ohio App. 9 Dist., 01-04-1995) 99 Ohio App.3d 696, 651 N.E.2d 1028, appeal not allowed 72 Ohio St.3d 1529, 649 N.E.2d 839. Infants ⇐ 13.5(1)

Statute requiring school teacher or authority having reason to believe that child has been abused or neglected to report information to proper authorities imposes duty which is owed solely to minor child of whom reports have been received concerning abuse or neglect. Curran v. Walsh Jesuit High School (Ohio App. 9 Dist., 01-04-1995) 99 Ohio App.3d 696, 651 N.E.2d 1028, appeal not allowed 72 Ohio St.3d 1529, 649 N.E.2d 839. Infants ⇐ 13.5(1)

8. Mother's duty

Fact that child abuse reporting statute does not list parent or guardian as person required to report knowledge or suspicion of child abuse to appropriate governmental agency did not preclude finding that mother had special relationship with child, and that mother thus had duty to report father's alleged sexual abuse of daughter; statute is not exclusive listing of those persons who must report knowledge or suspicion of child abuse, and because mother had "special relationship" to daughter, statutory duty of care, protection and support created duty to stop alleged acts of abuse. Hite v. Brown (Ohio App. 8 Dist., 03-09-1995) 100 Ohio App.3d 606, 654 N.E.2d 452, appeal denied 73 Ohio St.3d 1414, 651 N.E.2d 1311. Infants ⇐ 13.5(1)

9. Private organization's duty to report

A big brother or big sister is not subject to the child abuse or neglect reporting requirements of RC 2151.421(A)(1), but a big brother or big sister who, during the course of his or her activities as a big brother or big sister, learns of or suspects child abuse or neglect, may, in accordance with RC 2151.421(B), report such knowledge or suspicion to one of the agencies or authorities described therein. OAG 97–031.

10. Public records disclosure

Trial court order quashing subpoena for child victim's county children's services records and granting protective orders for the records was not an abuse of discretion, during prosecution for rape and gross sexual imposition; trial court reviewed the records in camera and determined that the disclosure of the records would not have outweighed confidentiality considerations, and statute that allowed the admission of a report in a criminal proceeding referred to an incident report that was required to be made by a certain category of persons, was very limited in scope, and did not encompass the "records" that defendant sought to admit. State v. Dixon (Ohio App. 5 Dist., Richland, 07-26-2004) No. 03 CA 75, 2004-Ohio-3940, 2004 WL 1672194, Unreported, motion for delayed appeal denied 103 Ohio St.3d 1490, 816 N.E.2d 1078, 2004-Ohio-5605, appeal not allowed 105 Ohio St.3d 1438, 822 N.E.2d 810, 2005-Ohio-531, denial of post-conviction relief affirmed 2005-Ohio-2846, 2005 WL 1364615, appeal not allowed 106 Ohio St.3d 1556, 836 N.E.2d 581, 2005-Ohio-5531. Infants ⇐ 133; Witnesses ⇐ 16

Uniform incident report about rape crime was not protected from public disclosure by exemption for reports of child abuse, even though report allegedly set out a child abuse claim; uniform incident report did not request detailed information relating to a juvenile victim such as the name and address of the child's parents, the history of injury or abuse, or the potential threat of further abuse, and uniform incident reports were public records, even if they included information that would otherwise qualify under an exception to disclosure. State ex rel. Beacon Journal Pub. Co. v. Akron (Ohio App. 9 Dist., Summit, 07-24-2003) No. 21116, 2003 WL

21756380, Unreported, cause dismissed 100 Ohio St.3d 1405, 796 N.E.2d 534, 2003-Ohio-4948, affirmed in part, reversed in part 104 Ohio St.3d 399, 819 N.E.2d 1087, 2004-Ohio-6557. Infants ⇔ 133

None of the documents pertaining to internal police investigation involved a report of child abuse, made under child-abuse reporting statute, that was referred for investigation to the county Children Services Board, and thus documents were not exempt from disclosure, but rather were public records that had to be available for public inspection, even though documents might have contained some information that would have been included in an initial report of suspected child abuse, where documents were prepared for police investigatory purposes, not for an investigation of child abuse or neglect by a public children services agency. State ex rel. Beacon Journal Pub. Co. v. Akron (Ohio App. 9 Dist., Summit, 07-24-2003) No. 21116, 2003 WL 21756380, Unreported, cause dismissed 100 Ohio St.3d 1405, 796 N.E.2d 534, 2003-Ohio-4948, affirmed in part, reversed in part 104 Ohio St.3d 399, 819 N.E.2d 1087, 2004-Ohio-6557. Infants ⇔ 133

Confidentiality provision of child-abuse reporting statute, which encouraged reporting of suspected child abuse by assuring those making reports would remain confidential, only extended to investigations conducted by the public children services agency, and thus confidentially provision did not extend to criminal investigations or police internal investigations to preclude disclosure of documents relevant to investigations. State ex rel. Beacon Journal Pub. Co. v. Akron (Ohio App. 9 Dist., Summit, 07-24-2003) No. 21116, 2003 WL 21756380, Unreported, cause dismissed 100 Ohio St.3d 1405, 796 N.E.2d 534, 2003-Ohio-4948, affirmed in part, reversed in part 104 Ohio St.3d 399, 819 N.E.2d 1087, 2004-Ohio-6557. Infants ⇔ 133

Confidential county records containing any information as to whether adopted child had been victim of sexual abuse were not relevant to determination whether child committed sexual abuse upon plaintiffs' daughter, and thus, were not subject to disclosure in action for negligent supervision and related claims brought by plaintiffs against child's adoptive parents, church where adoptive father was pastor, and church trustees. Swartzentruber v. Orrville Grace Brethren Church (Ohio App. 9 Dist., 08-17-2005) 163 Ohio App.3d 96, 836 N.E.2d 619, 2005-Ohio-4264. Infants ⇔ 133

Recognizing that the confidentiality of records of child sexual abuse is not absolute, a trial court may conduct an in camera inspection of the reports and order disclosure upon finding that the reports are relevant to the pending action, that there is good cause for disclosure, and that disclosure outweighs the confidentiality considerations. Swartzentruber v. Orrville Grace Brethren Church (Ohio App. 9 Dist., 08-17-2005) 163 Ohio App.3d 96, 836 N.E.2d 619, 2005-Ohio-4264. Infants ⇔ 133

Confidential county records of child sexual abuse related to adopted child were statutorily privileged and not subject to disclosure until trial court first considered confidential nature of records by in camera review and determined that information in reports was relevant to claim. Swartzentruber v. Orrville Grace Brethren Church (Ohio App. 9 Dist., 08-17-2005) 163 Ohio App.3d 96, 836 N.E.2d 619, 2005-Ohio-4264. Infants ⇔ 133

Award of attorney fees to newspaper publisher and reporter was not warranted, under Public Records Act, though city had refused to disclose any portion of police department's uniform offense and incident report for rape of 14-year-old girl, and though information in the report which did not identify victim or her parents was not confidential under child-abuse reporting statute, where city had reasonably believed that disclosure of information might subject city and police chief to criminal liability for violating child-abuse reporting statute, and city had been genuinely concerned that disclosure might deter reporting of crimes concerning abused children. State ex rel. Beacon Journal Publishing Co. v. Akron (Ohio, 12-15-2004) 104 Ohio St.3d 399, 819 N.E.2d 1087, 2004-Ohio-6557. Records ⇔ 68

Information, in city police department's uniform offense and incident report for rape of 14-year-old girl, which would identify the victim and her parents, was confidential under child-abuse reporting statute, and therefore was not subject to disclosure to newspaper publisher and reporter, but information in the report concerning the rape, its general location, and the description of the perpetrators was not confidential and therefore was subject to disclosure. State ex rel. Beacon Journal Publishing Co. v. Akron (Ohio, 12-15-2004) 104 Ohio St.3d 399, 819 N.E.2d 1087, 2004-Ohio-6557. Infants ⇔ 133

Portions of city's police investigatory reports which referred to initial reports, to public children services agency, of suspected abuse of a child by police officers and of another child by two juveniles, were confidential, under the child-abuse reporting statute, and therefore were not subject to disclosure to newspaper publisher and reporter. State ex rel. Beacon Journal Publishing Co. v. Akron (Ohio, 12-15-2004) 104 Ohio St.3d 399, 819 N.E.2d 1087, 2004-Ohio-6557. Infants ⇔ 133

Statutory confidentiality of records and reports of alleged child abuse or neglect is not absolute. Johnson v. Johnson (Ohio App. 3 Dist., 03-05-1999) 134 Ohio App.3d 579, 731 N.E.2d 1144. Infants ⇔ 133

Reports prepared by county ombudsman office in investigating allegations of child abuse and neglect by staff members of juvenile detention center were not excepted from disclosure requirements of Public Records Act by statute providing for confidentiality of reports by persons required to report injury or neglect; such statute was directed to children services boards or departments of human services. State ex rel. Strothers v. Wertheim (Ohio, 10-22-1997) 80 Ohio St.3d 155, 684 N.E.2d 1239, 1997-Ohio-349, reconsideration denied 80 Ohio St.3d 1472, 687 N.E.2d 299, motion denied 81 Ohio St.3d 1469, 690 N.E.2d 1288. Records ⇔ 55

11. Child day care center employees and administrators duty

Administrators and employees of day-care centers have affirmative legal duty under child protection statute to report known or suspected child abuse. Walters v. The Enrichment Ctr. of Wishing Well, Inc. (Ohio App. 8 Dist., 06-07-1999) 133 Ohio App.3d 66, 726 N.E.2d 1058, appeal not allowed 87 Ohio St.3d 1408, 716 N.E.2d 1170. Infants ⇔ 13

12. Political subdivision

An employee of a political subdivision may be held liable for failure to perform a duty expressly imposed by the statute mandating the reporting of known or suspected child abuse. Campbell v. Burton (Ohio, 07-25-2001) 92 Ohio St.3d 336, 750 N.E.2d 539, 2001-Ohio-206. Municipal Corporations ⇔ 747(1)

Statute mandating the reporting of known or suspected child abuse, through its criminal penalty for failure to report, "expressly imposes liability," within meaning of Political Subdivision Tort Liability Act provisions creating exceptions from sovereign immunity of political subdivisions and their employees if the Revised Code expressly imposes liability. Campbell v. Burton (Ohio, 07-25-2001) 92 Ohio St.3d 336, 750 N.E.2d 539, 2001-Ohio-206. Municipal Corporations ⇔ 727

A political subdivision may be held liable for its employee's failure to perform a duty expressly imposed by the statute mandating the reporting of known or suspected child abuse. Campbell v. Burton (Ohio, 07-25-2001) 92 Ohio St.3d 336, 750 N.E.2d 539, 2001-Ohio-206. Municipal Corporations ⇔ 747(1)

13. Professional counselors or social workers duty

Allegations that parents whose children were removed from home by county social worker were not allowed to recover children after safety plan providing for children's placement with friends had been initiated, despite parents' best efforts to do so, that continued deprivation of children was involuntary, and that parents were effectively denied prompt hearing on children's placement supported claim against social worker for violating parents' procedural due process rights. Smith v. Williams-Ash (C.A.6 (Ohio), 12-06-2005) No. 04-4547, 173 Fed.Appx. 363, 2005 WL 3304101, Unreported. Infants ⇔ 17

County social worker should have known that her alleged conduct in thwarting parents' attempts to have children returned to parents' home, after children were removed due to unsanitary conditions, and in effectively denying parents prompt hearing on children's placement had effect of violating parents' clearly established rights to procedural due process by involuntarily depriving parents of physical custody of children, and therefore qualified immunity did not apply to preclude social worker's liability under §§ 1983. Smith v. Williams-Ash (C.A.6 (Ohio), 12-06-2005) No. 04-4547, 173 Fed.Appx. 363, 2005 WL 3304101, Unreported. Civil Rights ⇔ 1376(4)

County social worker's alleged conduct in thwarting parents' attempts to have children returned to parents' home, after children were removed due to unsanitary conditions, and in effectively denying parents prompt hearing on children's placement did not rise to the level of conscience-shocking behavior, and thus did not support substantive due process claim. Smith v. Williams-Ash (C.A.6 (Ohio), 12-06-2005) No. 04-4547, 173 Fed.Appx. 363, 2005 WL 3304101, Unreported. Infants ⇔ 17

Social worker represented a "responsible adult" and was thus obligated to report alleged instances of child abuse, even though social worker acted irresponsibly in not reporting abuse; record demonstrated that social worker had knowledge of the alleged abuse and its criminal nature. State v. Koerner (Ohio App. 2 Dist., Montgomery, 02-06-2004) No. 19830, 2004-Ohio-457, 2004 WL 225461, Unreported. Infants ⇔ 13.5(1)

2151.421
Note 13

High school psychologist, who had a statutory duty to report to county Department of Family and Children's Services her suspicion that high school student's father abused student, had statutory immunity from action by student's father in connection with report and subsequent investigation by the Department, although Department determined that father did not abuse student. Liedtke v. Carrington (Ohio App. 8 Dist., 08-14-2001) 145 Ohio App.3d 396, 763 N.E.2d 213. Infants ⇐ 13.5(2)

Information contained in report which high school psychologist filed with county Department of Family and Children's Services, which apparently indicated that high school student's father abused student and resulted in Department's investigation of father, was confidential and privileged, and thus father was not entitled to discovery of report in his action against psychologist stemming from the allegations of the report and the investigation, although Department determined that the allegations were unsubstantiated. Liedtke v. Carrington (Ohio App. 8 Dist., 08-14-2001) 145 Ohio App.3d 396, 763 N.E.2d 213. Witnesses ⇐ 216(1)

RC 2151.421(A) does not impose upon a professional counselor or social worker licensed under RC Ch 4757 the duty to report knowledge or suspicion of child abuse of an individual if, when the professional counselor or social worker learns of the child abuse, the individual no longer is a child under eighteen years of age or a mentally retarded, developmentally disabled, or physically impaired child under twenty-one years of age. However, if information provided to a professional counselor or social worker who is acting in an official or professional capacity gives that person reason to know or suspect that an individual who currently is a child is at risk of child abuse, RC 2151.421(A) requires that such knowledge or suspicion be reported. OAG 01–035.

2151.422 Investigations concerning children in domestic violence or homeless shelters; services; custody; confidentiality of information

(A) As used in this section, "homeless shelter" means a facility that provides accommodations to homeless individuals.

(B) On receipt of a notice pursuant to division (A), (B), or (D) of section 2151.421 of the Revised Code, the public children services agency shall determine whether the child subject to the report is living in a shelter for victims of domestic violence or a homeless shelter and whether the child was brought to that shelter pursuant to an agreement with a shelter in another county. If the child is living in a shelter and was brought there from another county, the agency shall immediately notify the public children services agency of the county from which the child was brought of the report and all the information contained in the report. On receipt of the notice pursuant to this division, the agency of the county from which the child was brought shall conduct the investigation of the report required pursuant to section 2151.421 of the Revised Code and shall perform all duties required of the agency under this chapter with respect to the child who is the subject of the report. If the child is not living in a shelter or the child was not brought to the shelter from another county, the agency that received the report pursuant to division (A), (B), or (D) of section 2151.421 of the Revised Code shall conduct the investigation required pursuant to section 2151.421 of the Revised Code and shall perform all duties required of the agency under this chapter with respect to the child who is the subject of the report. The agency of the county in which the shelter is located in which the child is living and the agency of the county from which the child was brought may ask the shelter to provide information concerning the child's residence address and county of residence to the agency.

(C) If a child is living in a shelter for victims of domestic violence or a homeless shelter and the child was brought to that shelter pursuant to an agreement with a shelter in another county, the public children services agency of the county from which the child was brought shall provide services to or take custody of the child if services or custody are needed or required under this chapter or section 5153.16 of the Revised Code.

(D) When a homeless shelter provides accommodations to a person, the shelter, on admitting the person to the shelter, shall determine, if possible, the person's last known residential address and county of residence. The information concerning the address and county of residence is confidential and may only be released to a public children services agency pursuant to this section.

(1997 H 215, eff. 6–30–97)

Historical and Statutory Notes

Ed. Note: Former 2151.422 repealed by 1978 H 565, eff. 11–1–78; 132 v S 316.

Cross References

Public children services agencies, powers and duties, 5153.16
Release of last known residential address of domestic violence shelter resident, 3113.40

Library References

Infants ⇐ 13.5, 17, 226.
Westlaw Topic No. 211.
C.J.S. Adoption of Persons § 10.
C.J.S. Infants §§ 8 to 9, 57, 70 to 77.

Research References

Encyclopedias
OH Jur. 3d Family Law § 1451, Powers and Duties as to Children in Need of Public Care or Protective Services.

Treatises and Practice Aids
Adrine & Ruden, Ohio Domestic Violence Law § 16:4, Confidentiality and Liability Concerns.

2151.423 Confidential information disclosure

A public children services agency shall disclose confidential information discovered during an investigation conducted pursuant to section 2151.421 or 2151.422 of the Revised Code to any federal, state, or local government entity that needs the information to carry out its responsibilities to protect children from abuse or neglect.

Information disclosed pursuant to this section is confidential and is not subject to disclosure pursuant to section 149.43 or 1347.08 of the Revised Code by the agency to whom the information was disclosed. The agency receiving the information shall maintain the confidentiality of information disclosed pursuant to this section.

(2006 S 238, eff. 9–21–06)

2151.424 Notice of dispositional hearings

(A) If a child has been placed in a certified foster home or is in the custody of a relative of the child, other than a parent of the child, a court, prior to conducting any hearing pursuant to division (E)(2) or (3) of section 2151.412 or section 2151.28, 2151.33, 2151.35, 2151.414, 2151.415, 2151.416, or 2151.417 of the Revised Code with respect to the child, shall notify the foster caregiver or relative of the date, time, and place of the hearing. At the hearing, the foster caregiver or relative may present evidence.

(B) If a public children services agency or private child placing agency has permanent custody of a child and a petition to adopt the child has been filed under Chapter 3107. of the Revised Code, the agency, prior to conducting a review under section 2151.416 of the Revised Code, or a court, prior to conducting a hearing under division (E)(2) or (3) of section 2151.412 or section 2151.416 or 2151.417 of the Revised Code, shall notify the prospective adoptive parent of the date, time, and place of the review or hearing. At the review or hearing, the prospective adoptive parent may present evidence.

(C) The notice and the opportunity to present evidence do not make the foster caregiver, relative, or prospective adoptive parent a party in the action or proceeding pursuant to which the review or hearing is conducted.

(2000 H 448, eff. 10–5–00; 1998 H 484, eff. 3–18–99)

Historical and Statutory Notes

Amendment Note: 2000 H 448 inserted "certified" in division (A).

Library References

Infants ⇌198, 226, 230.
Westlaw Topic No. 211.
C.J.S. Adoption of Persons § 10.
C.J.S. Infants §§ 57, 69 to 85.

Research References

Encyclopedias
OH Jur. 3d Family Law § 1603, Service of Motion; Notice of Hearing.

Treatises and Practice Aids
Carlin, Baldwin's Ohio Practice, Merrick-Rippner Probate Law § 107:56, Adjudicatory Hearings—Attendance of Parties at Hearing.
Carlin, Baldwin's Ohio Practice, Merrick-Rippner Probate Law § 107:72, Dispositional Hearings—Procedure.
Giannelli & Yeomans, Ohio Juvenile Law § 18:2, Issuance of Summons: Proper Parties.
Giannelli & Yeomans, Ohio Juvenile Law § 33:4, Abuse, Neglect, and Dependency Proceedings.

CHILDREN'S ADVOCACY CENTERS

2151.425 Definitions

As used in sections 2151.426 to 2151.428 of the Revised Code:

(A) "Children's advocacy center" means a center operated by participating entities within a county or two or more contiguous counties to perform functions and activities and provide services, in accordance with the interagency agreement entered into under section 2151.428 of the Revised Code, regarding reports received under section 2151.421 of the Revised Code of alleged sexual abuse of a child or another type of abuse of a child that is specified in the memorandum of understanding that creates the center as being within the center's jurisdiction and regarding the children who are the subjects of the report.

(B) "Sexual abuse of a child" means unlawful sexual conduct or sexual contact, as those terms are defined in section 2907.01 of the Revised Code, with a person under eighteen years of age or a mentally retarded, developmentally disabled, or physically impaired person under twenty-one years of age.

(2004 S 66, eff. 5–6–05)

Cross References

State plan for comprehensive child abuse and child neglect prevention, powers and duties of board, reports, list of funding sources, 3109.17

2151.426 Children's advocacy center; memorandum of understanding with other entities regarding child abuse

(A)(1) A children's advocacy center may be established to serve a single county by execution of a memorandum of understanding regarding the participation in the operation of the center by any of the following entities in the county to be served by the center:

(a) The public children services agency;

(b) Representatives of any county or municipal law enforcement agencies serving the county that investigate any of the types of abuse specified in the memorandum of understanding creating the center as being within the center's jurisdiction;

(c) The prosecuting attorney of the county or a village solicitor, city director of law, or similar chief legal officer of a municipal corporation in the county who prosecutes any of the types of abuse specified in the memorandum of understanding creating the center as being within the center's jurisdiction in the area to be served by the center;

(d) Any other entity considered appropriate by all of the other entities executing the memorandum.

(2) A children's advocacy center may be established to serve two or more contiguous counties if a memorandum of understanding regarding the participation in the operation of the center is executed by any of the entities described in division (A)(1) of this section in each county to be served by the center.

(3) Any memorandum of understanding executed under this section may include a provision that specifies types of abuse of a child, in addition to sexual abuse of a child, that are to be within the jurisdiction of the children's advocacy center created as a result of the execution of the memorandum. If a memorandum of understanding executed under this section does not include any provision of that nature, the children's advocacy center created as a result of the execution of the memorandum has jurisdiction only in relation to reports of alleged sexual abuse of a child.

(B) Each entity that participates in the execution of a memorandum of understanding under this section shall cooperate in all of the following:

(1) Developing a multidisciplinary team pursuant to section 2151.427 of the Revised Code to perform the functions and activities and provide the services specified in the interagency agreement entered into under section 2151.428 of the Revised Code, regarding reports received under section 2151.421 of the Revised Code of alleged sexual abuse of a child and reports of allegations of another type of abuse of a child that is specified in the memorandum of understanding that creates the center as being within the center's jurisdiction, and regarding the children who are the subjects of the reports;

(2) Participating in the operation of the center in compliance with standards for full membership established by the national children's alliance;

(3) Employing the center's staff.

(C) A center shall do both of the following:

(1) Operate in accordance with sections 2151.427 and 2151.428 of the Revised Code, the interagency agreement entered into under section 2151.428 of the Revised Code relative to the center, and the standards for full membership established by the national children's alliance;

(2) Register annually with the attorney general.

(2004 S 66, eff. 5–6–05)

Research References

Encyclopedias
OH Jur. 3d Family Law § 1475, Investigation.

2151.427 Multidisciplinary team; members; powers and duties

(A) The entities that participate in a memorandum of understanding executed under section 2151.426 of the Revised Code establishing a children's advocacy center shall assemble the center's multidisciplinary team.

(B)(1) The multidisciplinary team for a single county center shall consist of the following members who serve the county:

(a) Any county or municipal law enforcement officer;

(b) The executive director of the public children services agency or a designee of the executive director;

(c) The prosecuting attorney of the county or the prosecuting attorney's designee;

(d) A mental health professional;

(e) A medical health professional;

(f) A victim advocate;

(g) A center staff member;

(h) Any other person considered appropriate by all of the entities that executed the memorandum.

(2) If the center serves two or more contiguous counties, the multidisciplinary team shall consist of the members described in division (B)(1) of this section from the counties to be served by the center, with each county to be served by the center being represented on the multidisciplinary team by at least one member described in that division.

(C) The multidisciplinary team shall perform the functions and activities and provide the services specified in the interagency agreement entered into under section 2151.428 of the Revised Code, regarding reports received under section 2151.421 of the Revised Code of alleged sexual abuse of a child and reports of allegations of another type of abuse of a child that is specified in the memorandum of understanding that creates the center as being within the center's jurisdiction and regarding the children who are the subjects of the reports.

(2004 S 66, eff. 5–6–05)

Research References

Encyclopedias

OH Jur. 3d Family Law § 1475, Investigation.

2151.428 Interagency agreements relating to child abuse

(A) If a children's advocacy center is established under section 2151.426 of the Revised Code, in addition to the memorandum of understanding executed under that section, each public children services agency that participates in the execution of the memorandum of understanding, the children's advocacy center, and the children's advocacy center's multidisciplinary team assembled under section 2151.427 of the Revised Code shall enter into an interagency agreement that stipulates all of the following regarding reports received under section 2151.421 of the Revised Code of alleged sexual abuse of a child and reports of allegations of another type of abuse of a child that is specified in the memorandum of understanding that creates the center as being within the center's jurisdiction:

(1) The protocol and procedures for any and all referrals and investigations of the reports;

(2) Any and all coordinating activities between the parties that enter into the agreement;

(3) The authority or responsibility for performing any and all functions and activities, and providing any and all services, regarding the reports and the children who are the subjects of the reports.

(B) The parties that enter into an interagency agreement under division (A) of this section shall comply with the agreement in referring the reports, investigating the reports, coordinating the activities between the parties, and performing and providing the functions, activities, and services relative to the reports and the children who are the subjects of the reports.

(C) Nothing in this section, section 2151.421, or sections 2151.425 to 2151.427 of the Revised Code pertaining to the operation of a children's advocacy center shall relieve any public official or agency from any legal obligation or responsibility.

(2004 S 66, eff. 5–6–05)

Cross References

State plan for comprehensive child abuse and child neglect prevention, powers and duties of board, reports, list of funding sources, 3109.17

Research References

Encyclopedias

OH Jur. 3d Family Law § 1475, Investigation.

ADULT CASES

2151.43 Charges against adults; defendant bound over to grand jury

In cases against an adult under sections 2151.01 to 2151.54 of the Revised Code, any person may file an affidavit with the clerk of the juvenile court setting forth briefly, in plain and ordinary language, the charges against the accused who shall be tried thereon. When the child is a recipient of aid pursuant to Chapter 5107. or 5115. of the Revised Code, the county department of job and family services shall file charges against any person who fails to provide support to a child in violation of section 2919.21 of the Revised Code, unless the department files charges under section 3113.06 of the Revised Code, or unless charges of nonsupport are filed by a relative or guardian of the child, or unless action to enforce support is brought under Chapter 3115. of the Revised Code.

In such prosecution an indictment by the grand jury or information by the prosecuting attorney shall not be required. The clerk shall issue a warrant for the arrest of the accused, who, when arrested, shall be taken before the juvenile judge and tried according to such sections.

The affidavit may be amended at any time before or during the trial.

The judge may bind such adult over to the grand jury, where the act complained of constitutes a felony.

(1999 H 471, eff. 7–1–00; 1995 H 249, eff. 7–17–95; 1991 H 298, eff. 7–26–91; 1986 H 428; 1972 H 511; 1969 H 361; 132 v H 390; 127 v 847; 1953 H 1; GC 1639–39)

Historical and Statutory Notes

Pre–1953 H 1 Amendments: 119 v 731; 117 v 520, § 1

Amendment Note: 1999 H 471 substituted "job and family" for "human" in the first paragraph.

Amendment Note: 1995 H 249 removed a reference to Chapter 5113.

Cross References

Failure to pay maintenance cost, 3113.06

Library References

Child Support ⚖650, 652.
Criminal Law ⚖93.
Indictment and Information ⚖9.
Westlaw Topic Nos. 110, 210, 76E.
C.J.S. Criminal Law §§ 157 to 158.
C.J.S. Indictments and Informations § 13.
C.J.S. Parent and Child §§ 174, 208, 237, 359 to 365, 377.

Research References

Encyclopedias

OH Jur. 3d Family Law § 1739, Commencement of Proceedings.

OH Jur. 3d Family Law § 1740, Commencement of Proceedings—Charges in an Affidavit.

OH Jur. 3d Family Law § 1741, Commencement of Proceedings—Amendments to Affidavits.

Treatises and Practice Aids

Carlin, Baldwin's Ohio Practice, Merrick-Rippner Probate Law § 108:3, Juvenile Court—Criminal Jurisdiction—Proceedings for Nonsupport.

Carlin, Baldwin's Ohio Practice, Merrick-Rippner Probate Law § 108:4, Juvenile Court—Criminal Jurisdiction—Applicability of Rules of Criminal Procedure.

Carlin, Baldwin's Ohio Practice, Merrick-Rippner Probate Law § 108:5, Juvenile Court—Criminal Jurisdiction—Affidavit Charging Offense.

Carlin, Baldwin's Ohio Practice, Merrick-Rippner Probate Law § 108:6, Juvenile Court—Criminal Jurisdiction—Amended Affidavit.

Carlin, Baldwin's Ohio Practice, Merrick-Rippner Probate Law § 108:7, Juvenile Court—Criminal Jurisdiction—Issuance of Warrant.

Carlin, Baldwin's Ohio Practice, Merrick-Rippner Probate Law § 107:170, Summons on Adult Offender—Form.

Notes of Decisions

Bar to prosecution 2
Constitutional issues 1
Jurisdiction 4
Procedural issues 3

---

1. Constitutional issues

Procedure of filing complaint in juvenile court on charge of contributing to delinquency of minor and then binding prisoner over to Grand Jury upon concluding that felony over which juvenile court lacked jurisdiction had been committed did not violate federal right to be free from double jeopardy. Grear v. Maxwell (C.A.6 (Ohio) 1966) 8 Ohio Misc. 210, 355 F.2d 991, 35 O.O.2d 333, 37 O.O.2d 268, certiorari denied 86 S.Ct. 1580, 384 U.S. 957, 16 L.Ed.2d 552, rehearing denied 87 S.Ct. 27, 385 U.S. 893, 17 L.Ed.2d 127. Double Jeopardy ⇐ 33

2. Bar to prosecution

Compliance with common pleas court order fixing amount of support payments for minor child of divorced parents is a bar to prosecution for nonsupport in juvenile court. State v. Holl (Auglaize 1971) 25 Ohio App.2d 75, 266 N.E.2d 587, 54 O.O.2d 114.

3. Procedural issues

Where adult father filed motion to vacate previous orders and to dismiss proceedings of juvenile court as to custody of his child, and at hearing on such motion it was stipulated that the sole issue was court's jurisdiction to hear, decide and make order delivered therein on a stated date, there is no right of appeal to court of appeals on questions of law from court's order overruling such motion. In re Griffin (Montgomery 1943) 73 Ohio App. 110, 55 N.E.2d 133, 28 O.O. 177.

4. Jurisdiction

This section not only confers jurisdiction upon juvenile courts in certain cases, but goes further and prescribes that in such cases an information is not required, and that the court shall have jurisdiction to hear such matters on affidavit only, intention of the legislature being that the minor's correction might be quietly effected, the public not informed of his misconduct, and the child not be made the subject of public ridicule. Wilson v. Lasure (Perry 1930) 36 Ohio App. 107, 172 N.E. 694, 9 Ohio Law Abs. 295.

The court of common pleas and municipal courts have jurisdiction in offenses involving adults, concurrent with that of the juvenile court, arising under RC 2151.41 or RC 2151.42. 1958 OAG 2016.

Judge of the court of common pleas exercising jurisdiction as judge of juvenile court, does not have authority to lawfully sentence a female to the Ohio reformatory for women. 1931 OAG 2840.

2151.44 Complaint after hearing

If it appears at the hearing of a child that any person has abused or has aided, induced, caused, encouraged, or contributed to the dependency, neglect, or delinquency of a child or acted in a way tending to cause delinquency in such child, or that a person charged with the care, support, education, or maintenance of any child has failed to support or sufficiently contribute toward the support, education, and maintenance of such child, the juvenile judge may order a complaint filed against such person and proceed to hear and dispose of the case as provided in sections 2151.01 to 2151.54, inclusive, of the Revised Code.

On the request of the judge, the prosecuting attorney shall prosecute all adults charged with violating such sections.

(1953 H 1, eff. 10–1–53; GC 1639–40, 1639–42)

Historical and Statutory Notes

Pre–1953 H 1 Amendments: 117 v 520, § 1

Library References

Child Support ⇐650 to 669.
District and Prosecuting Attorneys ⇐8.
Infants ⇐13, 20.
Westlaw Topic Nos. 131, 211, 76E.
C.J.S. District and Prosecuting Attorneys §§ 20 to 21, 29.
C.J.S. Infants §§ 5, 92 to 100.
C.J.S. Parent and Child §§ 174, 208, 237, 359 to 377.

Research References

Encyclopedias

OH Jur. 3d Family Law § 1739, Commencement of Proceedings.

Treatises and Practice Aids

Carlin, Baldwin's Ohio Practice, Merrick-Rippner Probate Law § 108:8, Juvenile Court—Criminal Jurisdiction—Judicial Order to File Complaint.

Carlin, Baldwin's Ohio Practice, Merrick-Rippner Probate Law § 104:17, Juvenile Facilities—Creation of Detention Homes.

Carlin, Baldwin's Ohio Practice, Merrick-Rippner Probate Law § 106:10, Juvenile Court Jurisdiction—Neglected Child—Introduction.

Notes of Decisions

Juvenile court authority 1
Time of filing complaint 2

---

1. Juvenile court authority

When at a hearing upon a charge that a child is delinquent, neglected or dependent, it appears that a person has contributed to bring about the commission of any of these offenses, this section vests authority in a juvenile judge to order complaint filed against such person and proceed thereon. State v. Van Horn (Montgomery 1940) 32 Ohio Law Abs. 406.

2. Time of filing complaint

This section does not contemplate that no charge of contributing or tending to contribute to the delinquency of a minor may be filed until after hearing of a charge against the child. State v. Van Horn (Montgomery 1940) 32 Ohio Law Abs. 406.

2151.49 Suspension of sentence

In every case of conviction under sections 2151.01 to 2151.54 of the Revised Code, where imprisonment is imposed as part of the punishment, the juvenile judge may suspend sentence, before or during commitment, upon such condition as the juvenile judge imposes. In the case of conviction for nonsupport of a child who is receiving aid under Chapter 5107. or 5115. of the Revised Code, if the juvenile judge suspends sentence on condition that the person make payments for support, the payment shall be made to the county department of job and family services rather than to the child or custodian of the child.

The court, in accordance with sections 3119.29 to 3119.56 of the Revised Code, shall include in each support order made under this section the requirement that one or both of the parents provide for the health care needs of the child to the satisfaction of the court.

(2002 H 657, eff. 12–13–02; 2000 S 180, eff. 3–22–01; 1999 H 471, eff. 7–1–00; 1997 H 352, eff. 1–1–98; 1995 H 249, eff. 7–17–95; 1991 H 298, eff. 7–26–91; 1986 H 428; 132 v H 390; 1953 H 1; GC 1639–49)

Historical and Statutory Notes

Pre–1953 H 1 Amendments: 117 v 520, § 1

Amendment Note: 2002 H 657 substituted "3119.29" for "3119.30" and "3119.56" for "3119.58" in the last paragraph of the section.

Amendment Note: 2000 S 180 substituted "nonsupport" for "non support" in the first paragraph and "sections 3119.30 to 3119.58" for "section 3113.217" in the second paragraph.

Amendment Note: 1999 H 471 substituted "job and family" for "human" in the first paragraph.

Amendment Note: 1997 H 352 added the second paragraph; and made changes to reflect gender neutral language.

Amendment Note: 1995 H 249 removed a reference to Chapter 5113.

Cross References

Interfering with action to issue or modify support order, 2919.231
Modification of sentence, 2929.51
Presentence investigation, Crim R 32.2
Sentencing procedure, Crim R 32
Support of dependents, withholding personal earnings to pay support, bond, 3115.23

Library References

Child Support ⚖669.
Sentencing and Punishment ⚖1801, 1854, 1983.
Westlaw Topic Nos. 350H, 76E.
C.J.S. Criminal Law §§ 1549 to 1550, 1552 to 1556, 1560 to 1562.
C.J.S. Parent and Child §§ 375 to 376.

Research References

Encyclopedias

OH Jur. 3d Family Law § 1201, Minimum Child Support Order.
OH Jur. 3d Family Law § 1222, Interfering With Action to Issue or Modify Support Order.
OH Jur. 3d Family Law § 1241, Payment of Support by Obligor to Agency.
OH Jur. 3d Family Law § 1301, Hearing to Determine Withholding or Deduction Requirements.
OH Jur. 3d Family Law § 1308, Reissuance Upon Change in Obligor's Status.
OH Jur. 3d Family Law § 1750, Sentence and Punishment—Suspension of Sentence.

Treatises and Practice Aids

Katz, Giannelli, Blair and Lipton, Baldwin's Ohio Practice, Criminal Law, § 109:13, Interfering With Support Actions.
Carlin, Baldwin's Ohio Practice, Merrick-Rippner Probate Law § 108:1, Juvenile Court—Criminal Jurisdiction.
Carlin, Baldwin's Ohio Practice, Merrick-Rippner Probate Law § 108:12, Juvenile Court—Criminal Jurisdiction—Sentencing and Punishment of Convicted Adults.
Carlin, Baldwin's Ohio Practice, Merrick-Rippner Probate Law § 108:22, Juvenile Court—Parentage Act—Presumption of Paternity.
Carlin, Baldwin's Ohio Practice, Merrick-Rippner Probate Law § 108:48, Order on Hearing, Nonsupport of Illegitimate Child; Suspension of Sentence—Form.

Notes of Decisions

Enforcement of support payments 1
Procedural issues 2

1. Enforcement of support payments

Mandamus will not lie to recover money collected from non-custodial parents and retained by the county, since an action on an account is an adequate remedy. Creasy v. Waller (Ohio 1982) 1 Ohio St.3d 93, 438 N.E.2d 414, 1 O.B.R. 129.

Where the jurisdiction of the juvenile court has been invoked by the arrest of a father of minor children on a charge of nonsupport filed by the mother, and upon trial the father pleads guilty and is sentenced, which sentence is suspended and the defendant put on probation, the condition of the probation being that the defendant will pay a specified sum weekly for support, the minor children thereby become wards of the juvenile court and the subject of their support and the power to enforce the condition of probation is exclusively in that court until each child has reached the age of eighteen years, so that if the mother thereafter files a petition for divorce in the common pleas court and a divorce is granted to her, the common pleas court is without jurisdiction to deal with the custody and support of the minor children or to entertain an action filed by the mother against the father for alleged delinquencies in the weekly payments ordered as a condition of probation by the juvenile court, and the manner of enforcing such order of the juvenile court is to seek, by motion filed in the juvenile court, a revocation of the order of probation and to enforce against him the penalty of the judgment. Anderson v. Anderson (Cuyahoga 1965) 4 Ohio App.2d 90, 212 N.E.2d 643, 33 O.O.2d 145.

2. Procedural issues

Under this section, the juvenile court is authorized to "suspend sentence" either before or after commitment, which is construed to mean suspension of the execution, rather than postponement of imposition of sentence. Ex parte Keagy (Hamilton 1945) 76 Ohio App. 95, 63 N.E.2d 216, 43 Ohio Law Abs. 508, 31 O.O. 405.

The judge of a juvenile court is not authorized to suspend the execution of a sentence after a person has been imprisoned for violation of either former GC 1654 (RC 2151.41) or GC 1655 (RC 2151.42) and is not given authority to place such a person so imprisoned on parole or probation. 1934 OAG 2517.

2151.50 Forfeiture of bond

When, as a condition of suspension of sentence under section 2151.49 of the Revised Code, bond is required and given, upon the failure of a person giving such bond to comply with the conditions thereof, such bond may be forfeited, the suspension terminated by the juvenile judge, the original sentence executed as though it had not been suspended, and the term of any sentence imposed in such case shall commence from the date of imprisonment of such person after such forfeiture and termination of suspension. Any part of such sentence which may have been served shall be deducted from any such period of imprisonment. When such bond is forfeited the judge may issue execution thereon without further proceedings.

(1953 H 1, eff. 10–1–53; GC 1639–50)

Historical and Statutory Notes

Pre–1953 H 1 Amendments: 117 v 520, § 1

Library References

Child Support ⚖669.
Sentencing and Punishment ⚖2003, 2032, 2034.
Westlaw Topic Nos. 350H, 76E.
C.J.S. Criminal Law §§ 1560 to 1562, 1564 to 1568.
C.J.S. Parent and Child §§ 375 to 376.

Research References

Encyclopedias

OH Jur. 3d Family Law § 1750, Sentence and Punishment—Suspension of Sentence.

Treatises and Practice Aids

Carlin, Baldwin's Ohio Practice, Merrick-Rippner Probate Law § 108:4, Juvenile Court—Criminal Jurisdiction—Applicability of Rules of Criminal Procedure.

Carlin, Baldwin's Ohio Practice, Merrick-Rippner Probate Law § 108:12, Juvenile Court—Criminal Jurisdiction—Sentencing and Punishment of Convicted Adults.

Notes of Decisions

Aid to dependent children 1

1. Aid to dependent children

The provisions of this section are mandatory, and where an order for the payment of funds is made by the juvenile judge, it is the duty of the county to make payment in accordance therewith without regard to the fact that aid to the dependent children concerned is currently being extended under the aid to dependent children law. 1953 OAG 2426.

2151.52 Appeals on questions of law

The sections of the Revised Code and rules relating to appeals on questions of law from the court of common pleas shall apply to prosecutions of adults under this chapter, and from such prosecutions an appeal on a question of law may be taken to the court of appeals of the county under laws or rules governing appeals in other criminal cases to such court of appeals.

(1986 H 412, eff. 3–17–87; 129 v 290; 1953 H 1; GC 1639–51)

Historical and Statutory Notes

Pre–1953 H 1 Amendments: 117 v 520, § 1

Cross References

Applicability of rules of appellate procedure, scope, App R 1

Library References

Courts ⚖176.5.
Criminal Law ⚖1019, 1134(3).
Westlaw Topic Nos. 106, 110.
C.J.S. Criminal Law §§ 1703, 1705 to 1706.

Research References

Encyclopedias

OH Jur. 3d Family Law § 1753, Appeals from Prosecution of Adults.

Treatises and Practice Aids

Carlin, Baldwin's Ohio Practice, Merrick-Rippner Probate Law § 108:40, Juvenile Court—Appeal of Adult Cases.

Painter & Dennis, Ohio Appellate Practice § 1:23, Right to Appeal-Appeal from Lower to Higher Court.

Notes of Decisions

Good cause 1
Orders appealable 3
Orders not appealable 4
Procedural issues 2

1. Good cause

Where an appellant (from the juvenile court to the court of appeals) fails to make a showing of "good cause" preliminary to appealing, the appeal will be denied and the judgment of the lower court affirmed. State v. Parks (Franklin 1957) 105 Ohio App. 208, 152 N.E.2d 154, 6 O.O.2d 40.

Upon a motion for leave to appeal from a sentence imposed by the juvenile court, good cause is shown when a substantial question relating to the trial, conviction, and sentence of the defendant is raised incident to the appeal. State ex rel. Meng v. Todaro (Ottawa 1952) 92 Ohio App. 247, 109 N.E.2d 669, 49 O.O. 342.

2. Procedural issues

Bastardy proceeding is essentially a civil action and an appeal from a judgment therein is not controlled by this section. State ex rel. Pennington v. Barger (Butler 1943) 74 Ohio App. 58, 57 N.E.2d 815, 29 O.O. 243.

Where adult father filed motion to vacate previous orders and to dismiss proceedings of juvenile court, the one order, in part adjudicating that his child is a dependent child and the other awarding its exclusive custody to the mother, and at hearing on such motion it was stipulated that the sole issue was court's jurisdiction to hear, decide and make order delivered therein on a stated date, there is no right of appeal to Court of Appeals on questions of law from court's order overruling such motion. In re Griffin (Montgomery 1943) 73 Ohio App. 110, 55 N.E.2d 133, 28 O.O. 177. Infants ⚖ 242

3. Orders appealable

A juvenile court order finding children to be "neglected" and committing them to permanent custody of a child welfare board for ultimate adoption is a final appealable order. In re Masters (Ohio 1956) 165 Ohio St. 503, 137 N.E.2d 752, 60 O.O. 474.

The court of appeals has jurisdiction to review upon appeal on questions of law a final judgment of the division of domestic relations of the court of common pleas, entered in a proceeding brought to determine the status of a minor, alleged to be a "neglected child" as defined in GC 1639-3 (RC 2151.03). In re Hock (Hamilton 1947) 88 N.E.2d 597, 55 Ohio Law Abs. 73, appeal dismissed 149 Ohio St. 460, 78 N.E.2d 901, 37 O.O. 125.

4. Orders not appealable

Appellate court is given no jurisdiction to consider and determine proceedings on error which are on dependency charges affecting minors under age of eighteen years. Baker v. State (Franklin 1934) 17 Ohio Law Abs. 384. Courts ⚖ 240; Child Custody ⚖ 920

An order of a court, adjudging a minor to be a dependent child, is not appealable. In re Griffin (Montgomery 1943) 73 Ohio App. 110, 55 N.E.2d 133, 28 O.O. 177. Infants ⚖ 242

2151.53 Physical and mental examinations; records of examination; expenses

Any person coming within sections 2151.01 to 2151.54 of the Revised Code may be subjected to a physical examination by competent physicians, physician assistants, clinical nurse specialists, and certified nurse practitioners, and a mental examination by competent psychologists, psychiatrists, and clinical nurse specialists that practice the specialty of mental health or psychiatric mental health to be appointed by the juvenile court. Whenever any child is committed to any institution by virtue of such sections, a record of such examinations shall be sent with the commitment to such institution. The compensation of such physicians, physician assistants, clinical nurse specialists, certified nurse practitioners, psychologists, and psychiatrists and the expenses of such examinations shall be paid by the county treasurer upon specifically itemized vouchers, certified by the juvenile judge.

(2002 S 245, eff. 3–31–03; 1953 H 1, eff. 10–1–53; GC 1639–54)

Historical and Statutory Notes

Pre–1953 H 1 Amendments: 117 v 520, § 1

Amendment Note: 2002 S 245 rewrote this section, which prior thereto read:

"Any person coming within sections 2151.01 to 2151.54, inclusive, of the Revised Code, may be subjected to a physical and mental examination by competent physicians, psychologists, and psychiatrists to be appointed by the juvenile court. Whenever any child is committed to any institution by virtue of such sections, a record of such examinations shall be sent with the commitment to such institution. The compensation of such physicians, psychologists, and psychiatrists and the expenses of such examinations shall be paid by the county treasurer upon specifically itemized vouchers, certified by the juvenile judge."

Cross References

Social history, physical or mental examination, custody investigation, procedure, Juv R 32

Library References

Criminal Law ⚖ 627.5(1).
Infants ⚖ 208.
Westlaw Topic Nos. 110, 211.
C.J.S. Criminal Law §§ 322, 486 to 491, 493, 1210.
C.J.S. Infants §§ 50, 57 to 85.

Research References

Encyclopedias

OH Jur. 3d Family Law § 1723, Physicians, Psychologists, and Psychiatrists.
OH Jur. 3d Family Law § 1743, Adults in Custody of Juvenile Court.

Notes of Decisions

Disclosure of records 1

---

1. Disclosure of records

In prosecution for contributing to unruliness of a child, trial court did not err in refusing defense counsel access to victim's medical and psychiatric records and in conducting in camera inspection of those records without assistance of defense counsel. State v. Black (Hamilton 1993) 85 Ohio App.3d 771, 621 N.E.2d 484, dismissed, jurisdictional motion overruled 67 Ohio St.3d 1451, 619 N.E.2d 420. Criminal Law ⚖ 627.6(6); Criminal Law ⚖ 627.8(4)

FEES AND COSTS

2151.54 Fees and costs; waiver

The juvenile court shall tax and collect the same fees and costs as are allowed the clerk of the court of common pleas for similar services. No fees or costs shall be taxed in cases of delinquent, unruly, dependent, abused, or neglected children except as required by section 2743.70 or 2949.091 of the Revised Code or when specifically ordered by the court. The expense of transportation of children to places to which they have been committed, and the transportation of children to and from another state by police or other officers, acting upon order of the court, shall be paid from the county treasury upon specifically itemized vouchers certified to by the judge.

If a child is adjudicated to be a delinquent child or a juvenile traffic offender and the juvenile court specifically is required, by section 2743.70 or 2949.091 of the Revised Code or any other section of the Revised Code, to impose a specified sum of money as court costs in addition to any other court costs that the court is required or permitted by law to impose, the court shall not waive the payment of the specified additional court costs that the section of the Revised Code specifically requires the court to impose unless the court determines that the child is indigent and the court either waives the payment of all court costs or enters an order in its journal stating that no court costs are to be taxed in the case.

(1990 S 131, eff. 7–25–90; 1980 H 238; 1975 H 85; 1970 H 931; 1953 H 1; GC 1639–56)

Historical and Statutory Notes

Pre–1953 H 1 Amendments: 119 v 731; 117 v 520, § 1

Cross References

Common pleas court, fees and costs, Ch 2335

Library References

Costs ⚖ 284 to 317.
Infants ⚖ 212.
Westlaw Topic Nos. 102, 211.
C.J.S. Criminal Law §§ 1738 to 1751.
C.J.S. Infants §§ 57, 69 to 85.
Baldwin's Ohio Legislative Service, 1990 Laws of Ohio, S 131—LSC Analysis, p 5–623

Research References

Encyclopedias

OH Jur. 3d Family Law § 1518, Correctional Service—After-Care Services.
OH Jur. 3d Family Law § 1725, Transportation; Extradition.
OH Jur. 3d Family Law § 1752, Costs, Fees, and Expenses.

Treatises and Practice Aids

Carlin, Baldwin's Ohio Practice, Merrick-Rippner Probate Law § 108:10, Juvenile Court—Criminal Jurisdiction—Criminal Trial of Adults: Rules and Procedures.
Carlin, Baldwin's Ohio Practice, Merrick-Rippner Probate Law § 108:12, Juvenile Court—Criminal Jurisdiction—Sentencing and Punishment of Convicted Adults.
Carlin, Baldwin's Ohio Practice, Merrick-Rippner Probate Law § 107:111, Disposition of Unruly Children—Mandatory.
Carlin, Baldwin's Ohio Practice, Merrick-Rippner Probate Law § 107:129, Extradition of Delinquent Child.
Giannelli & Yeomans, Ohio Juvenile Law § 36:3, Extradition.

Notes of Decisions

In general 2
Automobiles for official use 4
Bail forfeiture 5
Cases of delinquent, unruly, dependent, abused, or neglected children 7
Constitutional issues 1
Sheriff's expenses 6
Transportation costs 3

---

1. Constitutional issues

1996 H 350, which amended more than 100 statutes and a variety of rules relating to tort and other civil actions, and which was an attempt to reenact provisions of law previously held unconstitutional by the Supreme Court of Ohio, is an act of usurpation of judicial power in violation of the doctrine of separation of powers; for that reason, and because of violation of the one-subject rule of the Ohio Constitution, 1996 H 350 is unconstitutional. State ex rel. Ohio Academy of Trial Lawyers v. Sheward (Ohio, 08-16-1999) 86 Ohio St.3d 451, 715 N.E.2d 1062, 1999-Ohio-123, reconsideration denied 87 Ohio St.3d 1409, 716 N.E.2d 1170.

Where court in juvenile proceeding had ordered imposition and suspension of fine contingent upon good behavior along with assessment of costs, and court had not imposed any form of detention as matter of punishment, order remanding child to the detention center for violation of order by failure to pay court costs, until costs were paid, constituted unconstitutional imprisonment for failure to pay debt. In re Rinehart (Ross 1983) 10 Ohio App.3d 318, 462 N.E.2d 448, 10 O.B.R. 523. Constitutional Law ⚖ 83(3); Infants ⚖ 223.1

2. In general

A county children services board is subject to the provisions of RC 2151.54 governing the taxation and collection of court costs by the juvenile court, and may be required to pay court costs that are taxed by the juvenile court in accordance with the provisions of that section. OAG 97–024, approved and followed by OAG 98–021.

When the Trumbull county children services board is a party to an action filed in the Trumbull county court of common pleas, domestic relations/juvenile division, the board is subject to the provisions of RC 2151.54 governing the taxation and collection of court costs. The Trumbull county children services board may be required to pay court costs that are taxed by the Trumbull county court of common pleas, domestic relations/juvenile division in accordance with the provisions of that section. OAG 97–024, approved and followed by OAG 98–021.

3. Transportation costs

Payment for transportation of child placed in home outside of state may be made from county treasury upon specifically itemized vouchers certified by judge of juvenile court. 1938 OAG 1918.

Where delinquent juveniles are sentenced to the boys industrial school or girls industrial home, the costs of the case and the expense of transporting said juveniles to the place to which they have been committed are payable by the county and not the state. 1921 OAG p 114.

4. Automobiles for official use

The expense of automobile owned by a probation officer, and used exclusively in carrying out the work of the juvenile court, may legally be paid from the county treasury under former GC 1682 (RC 2151.54); in the event that such automobile is used partially for the work of the court, and partially for the personal use of the owner, separations of such uses must be made. 1921 OAG p 1014.

There is no statutory authority for the purchase, with county funds, of an automobile for the use of a probation officer of a juvenile court. 1919 OAG p 1433.

Probation officer may use his own automobile in course of performance of his official duties and be reimbursed in the manner provided by former GC 1682 (RC 2151.54) for the expense of such use. 1919 OAG p 1433.

5. Bail forfeiture

Court costs and additional fees may not be deducted from the gross amount of fines and moneys to be distributed under RC 5503.04, except that when there is a forfeiture of bail, a court adjudging forfeiture may, pursuant to RC 2937.36, deduct accrued costs from the amount of bail prior to distribution of the bail proceeds under RC 5503.04. OAG 87–023.

6. Sheriff's expenses

Expenses incurred by a county sheriff in serving summonses, warrants, citations, subpoenas, writs, and other papers issued by a juvenile court in connection with cases filed therein shall, pursuant to RC 2151.19, be paid out of the monthly allowance made available therefor by a board of county commissioners under RC 325.07; such expenses shall not be taxed and collected by the juvenile court as fees or costs under RC 2151.54. OAG 89–086, clarified by OAG 98–021.

7. Cases of delinquent, unruly, dependent, abused, or neglected children

Court could not assess court costs against juvenile, in possession of marijuana delinquency proceedings, where delinquency proceedings against juvenile were dismissed. In re Graham (Ohio App. 7 Dist., Mahoning, 11-26-2002) No. 02CA67, 2002-Ohio-6615, 2002 WL 31718885, Unreported. Infants ⇔ 212

In juvenile court cases in which the Ohio rules of juvenile procedure apply, Ohio Juv R 17(B) grants a juvenile court the authority to tax as costs and collect from a party the fees of the county sheriff in serving subpoenas issued by the court and the fees of witnesses subpoenaed by the court. However, pursuant to RC 2151.54, such fees may not be taxed as costs and collected by a juvenile court in cases of delinquent, unruly, dependent, abused, or neglected children except when specifically ordered by the court. OAG 98–021.

Except in cases of delinquent, unruly, dependent, abused, or neglected children, RC 2151.54 grants a juvenile court the authority to tax and collect the same fees and costs as are allowed the clerk of the court of common pleas for similar services. No fees or costs shall be taxed by the juvenile court in cases of delinquent, unruly, dependent, abused, or neglected children except as required by RC 2743.70 or RC 2949.091 or when specifically ordered by the court. OAG 97–024, approved and followed by OAG 98–021.

Pursuant to RC 2151.54, no fees or costs shall be taxed by the Trumbull county court of common pleas, domestic relations/juvenile division in cases filed by the Trumbull county children services board in which a particular child is alleged to be delinquent, unruly, abused, neglected, or dependent, or in which the board seeks to obtain custody of such a child, except as required by RC 2743.70 or RC 2949.091 or when specifically ordered by the court. OAG 97–024, approved and followed by OAG 98–021.

2151.541 Additional fees for computer services

(A)(1) The juvenile judge may determine that, for the efficient operation of the juvenile court, additional funds are required to computerize the court, to make available computerized legal research services, or both. Upon making a determination that additional funds are required for either or both of those purposes, the judge shall do one of the following:

(a) If he is clerk of the court, charge one additional fee not to exceed three dollars on the filing of each cause of action or appeal under division (A), (Q), or (U) of section 2303.20 of the Revised Code;

(b) If the clerk of the court of common pleas serves as the clerk of the juvenile court pursuant to section 2151.12 of the Revised Code, authorize and direct the clerk to charge one additional fee not to exceed three dollars on the filing of each cause of action or appeal under division (A), (Q), or (U) of section 2303.20 of the Revised Code.

(2) All moneys collected under division (A)(1) of this section shall be paid to the county treasurer. The treasurer shall place the moneys from the fees in a separate fund to be disbursed, upon an order of the juvenile judge, in an amount no greater than the actual cost to the court of procuring and maintaining computerization of the court, computerized legal research services, or both.

(3) If the court determines that the funds in the fund described in division (A)(2) of this section are more than sufficient to satisfy the purpose for which the additional fee described in division (A)(1) of this section was imposed, the court may declare a surplus in the fund and expend those surplus funds for other appropriate technological expenses of the court.

(B)(1) If the juvenile judge is the clerk of the juvenile court, he may determine that, for the efficient operation of his court, additional funds are required to computerize the clerk's office and, upon that determination, may charge an additional fee, not to exceed ten dollars, on the filing of each cause of action or appeal, on the filing, docketing, and endorsing of each certificate of judgment, or on the docketing and indexing of each aid in execution or petition to vacate, revive, or modify a judgment under divisions (A), (P), (Q), (T), and (U) of section 2303.20 of the Revised Code. Subject to division (B)(2) of this section, all moneys collected under this division shall be paid to the county treasurer to be disbursed, upon an order of the juvenile judge and subject to appropriation by the board of county commissioners, in an amount no greater than the actual cost to the juvenile court of procuring and maintaining computer systems for the clerk's office.

(2) If the juvenile judge makes the determination described in division (B)(1) of this section, the board of county commissioners may issue one or more general obligation bonds for the purpose of procuring and maintaining the computer systems for the office of the clerk of the juvenile court. In addition to the purposes stated in division (B)(1) of this section for which the moneys collected under that division may be expended, the moneys additionally may be expended to pay debt charges on and financing costs related to any general obligation bonds issued pursuant to this division as they become due. General obligation bonds issued pursuant to this division are Chapter 133. securities.

(1992 S 246, eff. 3-24-93; 1992 H 405)

Cross References

Net indebtedness of county, securities not considered in calculation of, 133.07

Library References

Clerks of Courts ⚖28 to 29.
Infants ⚖212.
Westlaw Topic Nos. 211, 79.
C.J.S. Courts § 242.
C.J.S. Infants §§ 57, 69 to 85.

PLACEMENT OF CHILDREN IN FOSTER HOMES OUTSIDE COUNTIES OF RESIDENCE

2151.55 Persons entitled to oral communication of intended placement

When a private or governmental entity intends to place a child in a certified foster home in a county other than the county in which the child resided at the time of being removed from home, a representative of the placing entity shall orally communicate the intended placement to the foster caregiver with whom the child is to be placed and, if the child will attend the schools of the district in which the certified foster home is located, a representative of the school district's board of education.

(2000 H 332, eff. 1–1–01; 2000 H 448, eff. 10–5–00; 1999 H 283, eff. 9–29–99)

Historical and Statutory Notes

Ed. Note: The amendment of this section by 2000 H 332, eff. 1–1–01, and 2000 H 448, eff. 10–5–00, was identical. See *Baldwin's Ohio Legislative Service Annotated*, 2000, pages 6/L–2160 and 6/L–2233, or the OH–LEGIS or OH–LEGIS–OLD database on Westlaw, for original versions of these Acts.

Ed. Note: Former 2151.55 repealed by 1999 H 283, eff. 9–29–99; 1997 H 215, eff. 6–30–97.

Ed. Note: Prior 2151.55 repealed by 130 v H 299, eff. 10–7–63; 1953 H 1; GC 1639–59.

Pre–1953 H 1 Amendments: 117 v 520, § 1

Amendment Note: 2000 H 332 inserted "certified" twice throughout the section.

Amendment Note: 2000 H 448 inserted "certified" twice.

Library References

Infants ⚖17, 226.
Westlaw Topic No. 211.
C.J.S. Adoption of Persons § 10.
C.J.S. Infants §§ 8 to 9, 57, 70 to 77.

Research References

Treatises and Practice Aids

Carlin, Baldwin's Ohio Practice, Merrick-Rippner Probate Law § 105:1, Juvenile Court—Exclusive Original Jurisdiction.

Carlin, Baldwin's Ohio Practice, Merrick-Rippner Probate Law § 107:46, Adjudicatory Hearings—Child's Right to Guardian Ad Litem.

Giannelli & Yeomans, Ohio Juvenile Law § 13:2, Jurisdictional Requirements.

Giannelli & Yeomans, Ohio Juvenile Law § 13:5, Hearing.

Giannelli & Yeomans, Ohio Juvenile Law § 13:6, Case Law.

Giannelli & Yeomans, Ohio Juvenile Law App. D, Appendix D. Glossary.

Giannelli & Yeomans, Ohio Juvenile Law § 30:13, Planned Permanent Living Arrangement.

2151.551 Requirements of oral communication of intended placement

During the oral communication described in section 2151.55 of the Revised Code, the representative of the placing entity shall do the following:

(A) Discuss safety and well-being concerns regarding the child and, if the child attends school, the students, teachers, and personnel of the school;

(B) Provide the following information:

(1) A brief description of the reasons the child was removed from home;

(2) Services the child is receiving;

(3) The name of the contact person for the placing entity that is directly responsible for monitoring the child's placement;

(4) The telephone number of the placing entity and, if the child is in the temporary, permanent, or legal custody of a private or government entity other than the placing entity, the telephone number of the entity with custody;

(5) The previous school district attended by the child;

(6) The last known address of the child's parents.

(1999 H 283, eff. 9–29–99)

Library References

Infants ⚖17, 226.
Westlaw Topic No. 211.
C.J.S. Adoption of Persons § 10.
C.J.S. Infants §§ 8 to 9, 57, 70 to 77.

Research References

Treatises and Practice Aids

Hastings, Manoloff, Sheeran, & Stype, Ohio School Law § 23:2, Admission Requirements and Tuition Liability-Statutory Requirements in General.

2151.552 Time for provision of written information

No later than five days after a child described in section 2151.55 of the Revised Code is enrolled in school in the district described in that section, the placing entity shall provide in writing the information described in division (B) of section 2151.551 of the Revised Code to the school district and the child's foster caregiver.

(1999 H 283, eff. 9–29–99)

Library References

Infants ⚖17, 226.
Westlaw Topic No. 211.
C.J.S. Adoption of Persons § 10.
C.J.S. Infants §§ 8 to 9, 57, 70 to 77.

Research References

Treatises and Practice Aids

Hastings, Manoloff, Sheeran, & Stype, Ohio School Law § 23:2, Admission Requirements and Tuition Liability-Statutory Requirements in General.

2151.553 School district procedures for receiving information

Each school district board of education shall implement a procedure for receiving the information described in section 2151.552 of the Revised Code.

(1999 H 283, eff. 9–29–99)

Library References

Schools ⇌20, 45.
Westlaw Topic No. 345.
C.J.S. Schools and School Districts §§ 7, 74, 76, 195.

Research References

Treatises and Practice Aids

Hastings, Manoloff, Sheeran, & Stype, Ohio School Law § 23:2, Admission Requirements and Tuition Liability-Statutory Requirements in General.

2151.554 Provision of written information to juvenile court

When a private or governmental entity places a child who has been adjudicated to be an unruly or delinquent child in a certified foster home in a county other than the county in which the child resided at the time of being removed from home, the placing entity shall provide the following information in writing to the juvenile court of the county in which the certified foster home is located:

(A) The information listed in divisions (B)(2) to (4) of section 2151.551 of the Revised Code;

(B) A brief description of the facts supporting the adjudication that the child is unruly or delinquent;

(C) The name and address of the foster caregiver;

(D) Safety and well-being concerns with respect to the child and community.

(2000 H 332, eff. 1–1–01; 2000 H 448, eff. 10–5–00; 1999 H 283, eff. 9–29–99)

Historical and Statutory Notes

Ed. Note: The amendment of this section by 2000 H 332, eff. 1–1–01, and 2000 H 448, eff. 10–5–00, was identical. See *Baldwin's Ohio Legislative Service Annotated*, 2000, pages 6/L–2160 and 6/L–2233, or the OH–LEGIS or OH–LEGIS–OLD database on Westlaw, for original versions of these Acts.

Amendment Note: 2000 H 332 inserted "certified" twice in the introductory paragraph.

Amendment Note: 2000 H 448 inserted "certified" twice in the introductory paragraph.

Library References

Infants ⇌17, 133, 226.
Westlaw Topic No. 211.
C.J.S. Adoption of Persons § 10.
C.J.S. Infants §§ 8 to 9, 57, 69 to 85.

INTERSTATE COMPACT ON JUVENILES

2151.56 Interstate compact on juveniles

The governor is hereby authorized to execute a compact on behalf of this state with any other state or states legally joining therein in the form substantially as follows:

THE INTERSTATE COMPACT ON JUVENILES

The contracting states solemnly agree:

Article I —Findings and Purposes

That juveniles who are not under proper supervision and control, or who have absconded, escaped or run away, are likely to endanger their own health, morals and welfare, and the health, morals and welfare of others. The cooperation of the states party to this compact is therefore necessary to provide for the welfare and protection of juveniles and of the public with respect to (1) cooperative supervision of delinquent juveniles on probation or parole; (2) the return, from one state to another, of delinquent juveniles who have escaped or absconded; (3) the return, from one state to another, of nondelinquent juveniles who have run away from home; and (4) additional measures for the protection of juveniles and of the public, which any two or more of the party states may find desirable to undertake cooperatively. In carrying out the provisions of this compact the party states shall be guided by the noncriminal, reformative and protective policies which guide their laws concerning delinquent, neglected or dependent juveniles generally. It shall be the policy of the states party to this compact to cooperate and observe their respective responsibilities for the prompt return and acceptance of juveniles and delinquent juveniles who become subject to the provisions of this compact. The provisions of this compact shall be reasonably and liberally construed to accomplish the foregoing purposes.

Article II —Existing Rights and Remedies

That all remedies and procedures provided by this compact shall be in addition to and not in substitution for other rights, remedies and procedures, and shall not be in derogation of parental rights and responsibilities.

Article III —Definitions

That, for the purposes of this compact, "delinquent juvenile" means any juvenile who has been adjudged delinquent and who, at the time the provisions of this compact are invoked, is still subject to the jurisdiction of the court that has made such adjudication or to the jurisdiction or supervision of an agency or institution pursuant to an order of such court; "probation or parole" means any kind of conditional release of juveniles authorized under the laws of the states party hereto; "court" means any court having jurisdiction over delinquent, neglected or dependent children; "state" means any state, territory or possessions of the United States, the District of Columbia, and the Commonwealth of Puerto Rico; and "residence" or any variant thereof means a place at which a home or regular place of abode is maintained.

Article IV —Return of Runaways

(a) That the parent, guardian, person or agency entitled to legal custody of a juvenile who has not been adjudged delinquent but who has run away without the consent of such parent, guardian, person or agency may petition the appropriate court in the demanding state for the issuance of a requisition for his return. The petition shall state the name and age of the juvenile, the name of the petitioner and the basis of entitlement to the juvenile's custody, the circumstances of his running away, his location if known at the time application is made, and such other facts as may tend to show that the juvenile who has run away is endangering his own welfare or the welfare of others and is not an emancipated minor. The petition shall be verified by affidavit, shall be executed in duplicate, and shall be accompanied by two certified copies of the document or documents on which the petitioner's entitlement to the juvenile's custody is based, such as birth records, letters of guardianship, or custody decrees. Such further affidavits and other documents as may be deemed proper may be submitted with such petition. The judge of the court to which this application is made may hold a hearing thereon to determine whether for the purposes of this compact the petitioner is entitled to the legal custody of the juvenile, whether or not it appears that the juvenile has in fact run away without consent, whether or not he is an emancipated minor, and whether or not it is in the best interest of the juvenile to compel his return to the state. If the judge determines, either with or without a hearing, that the juvenile should be returned, he shall present to the appropriate court or to the executive authority of the state where the juvenile is alleged to be located a written requisition for the return of such juvenile. Such requisition shall set forth the name and age of the juvenile, the determination of the court that the juvenile has run away without the consent of a parent, guardian, person or agency entitled to his legal custody, and that it is in the best interest and for the protection of such juvenile that he be returned. In the event that a proceeding for the adjudication of the juvenile as a delinquent, neglected or dependent juvenile is pending in the court at the time when such juvenile runs away, the court may issue a requisition for the return of such juvenile upon its own motion, regardless of the consent of the parent, guardian, person or agency entitled to legal custody, reciting therein the nature and circumstances of the pending proceeding. The requisition shall in every case be executed in duplicate and shall be signed by the judge. One copy of the requisition shall be filed with the compact administrator of the demanding state, there to remain on file subject to the provisions of law governing records of such court. Upon the receipt of a requisition demanding the return of a juvenile who has run away, the court or the executive authority to whom the requisition is addressed shall issue an order to any peace officer or other appropriate person directing him to take into custody and detain such juvenile. Such detention order must substantially recite the facts necessary to the validity of its issuance hereunder. No juvenile detained upon such order shall be delivered over to the officer whom the court demanding him shall have appointed to receive him, unless he shall first be taken forthwith before a judge of a court in the state, who shall inform him of the demand made for his return, and who may appoint counsel or guardian ad litem for him. If the judge of such court shall find that the requisition is in order, he shall deliver such juvenile over to the officer whom the court demanding him shall have appointed to receive him. The judge, however, may fix a reasonable time to be allowed for the purpose of testing the legality of the proceeding.

Upon reasonable information that a person is a juvenile who has run away from another state party to this compact without the consent of a parent, guardian, person or agency entitled to his legal custody, such juvenile may be taken into custody without a requisition and brought forthwith before a judge of the appropriate court who may appoint counsel or guardian ad litem for such juvenile and who shall determine after a hearing whether sufficient cause exists to hold the person, subject to the order of the court, for his own protection and welfare, for such a time not exceeding ninety days as will enable his return to another state party to this compact pursuant to a requisition for his return from a court of that state. If, at the time when a state seeks the return of a juvenile who has run away, there is pending in the state wherein he is found any criminal charge, or any proceeding to have him adjudicated a delinquent juvenile for an act committed in such state, or if he is suspected of having committed within such state a criminal offense or an act of juvenile delinquency, he shall not be returned without the consent of such state until discharged from prosecution or other form of proceeding, imprisonment, detention or supervision for such offense or juvenile delinquency. The duly accredited officers of any state party to this compact, upon the establishment of their authority and the identity of the juvenile being returned, shall be permitted to transport such juvenile through any and all states party to this compact, without interference. Upon his return to the state from which he ran away, the juvenile shall be subject to such further proceedings as may be appropriate under the laws of that state.

(b) That the state to which a juvenile is returned under this Article shall be responsible for payment of the transportation costs of such return.

(c) That "juvenile" as used in this Article means any person who is a minor under the law of the state of residence of the parent, guardian, person or agency entitled to the legal custody of such minor.

Article V —Return of Escapees and Absconders

(a) That the appropriate person or authority from whose probation or parole supervision a delinquent juvenile has absconded or from whose institutional custody he has escaped shall present to the appropriate court or to the executive authority of the state where the delinquent juvenile is alleged to be located a written requisition for the return of such delinquent juvenile. Such requisition shall state the name and age of the delinquent juvenile, the particulars of his adjudication as a delinquent juvenile, the circumstances of the breach of the terms of his probation or parole or of his escape from an institution or agency vested with his legal custody or supervision, and the location of such delinquent juvenile, if known, at the time the requisition is made. The requisition shall be verified by affidavit, shall be executed in duplicate, and shall be accompanied by two certified copies of the judgment, formal adjudication, or order of commitment which subjects such delinquent juvenile to probation or parole or to the legal custody of the institution or agency concerned. Such further affidavits and other documents as may be deemed proper may be submitted with such requisition. One copy of the requisition shall be filed with the compact administrator of the demanding state, there to remain on file subject to the provisions of law governing records of the appropriate court. Upon the receipt of a requisition demanding the return of a delinquent juvenile who has absconded or escaped, the court or the executive authority to whom the requisition is addressed shall issue an order to any peace officer or other appropriate person directing him to take into custody and detain such delinquent juvenile. Such detention order must substantially recite the facts necessary to the validity of its issuance hereunder. No delinquent juvenile detained upon such order shall be delivered over to the officer whom the appropriate person or authority demanding him shall have appointed to receive him, unless he shall first be taken forthwith before a judge of an appropriate court in the state, who shall inform him of the demand made for his return and who may appoint counsel or guardian ad litem for him. If the judge of such court shall find that the requisition is in order, he shall deliver such delinquent juvenile over to the officer whom the appropriate person or authority demanding him shall have appointed to receive him. The judge, however, may fix a reasonable time to be allowed for the purpose of testing the legality of the proceeding.

Upon reasonable information that a person is a delinquent juvenile who has absconded while on probation or parole, or escaped from an institution or agency vested with his legal custody or supervision in any state party to this compact, such person may be taken into custody in any other state party to this compact without a requisition. But in such event, he must be taken forthwith before a judge of the appropriate court, who may appoint counsel or guardian ad litem for such person and who shall determine, after a hearing, whether sufficient cause exists to hold the person subject to the order of the court for such a time, not exceeding ninety days, as will enable his detention under a detention order issued on a requisition pursuant to this Article. If, at the time when a state seeks the return of a delinquent juvenile who has either absconded while on probation or parole or escaped from an institution or agency vested with his legal custody or supervision, there is pending in the state wherein he is detained any criminal charge or any proceeding to have him adjudicated a delinquent juvenile for an act committed in such state, or if he is suspected of having committed within such state a criminal offense or an act of juvenile delinquency, he shall not be returned without the consent of such state until discharged from prosecution or other form of proceeding, imprisonment, detention or supervision for such offense or juvenile delinquency. The duly accredited officers of any state party to this compact, upon the establishment of their authority and the identity of the delinquent juvenile being returned, shall be permitted to transport such delinquent juvenile through any and all states party to this compact, without interference. Upon his return to the state from which he escaped or absconded, the delinquent juvenile shall be subject to such further proceedings as may be appropriate under the laws of that state.

(b) That the state to which a delinquent juvenile is returned under this Article shall be responsible for the payment of the transportation costs of such return.

Article VI —Voluntary Return Procedure

That any delinquent juvenile who has absconded while on probation or parole, or escaped from an institution or agency vested with his legal custody or supervision in any state party to this compact, and any juvenile who has run away from any state party to this compact, who is taken into custody without a requisition in another state party to this compact under the provisions of Article IV (a) or of Article V (a), may consent to his immediate return to the state from which he absconded, escaped or ran away. Such consent shall be given by the juvenile or delinquent juvenile and his counsel or guardian ad litem if any, by executing or subscribing a writing, in the presence of a judge of the appropriate court, which states that the juvenile or delinquent juvenile and his counsel or guardian ad litem, if any, consent to his return to the demanding state. Before such consent shall be executed or subscribed, however, the judge, in the presence of counsel or guardian ad litem, if any, shall inform the juvenile or delinquent juvenile of his rights under this compact. When the consent has been duly executed, it shall be forwarded to and filed with the compact administrator of the state in which the court is located and the judge shall direct the officer having the juvenile or delinquent juvenile in custody to deliver him to the duly accredited officer or officers of the state demanding his return, and shall cause to be delivered to such officer or officers a copy of the consent. The court may, however, upon the request of the state to which the juvenile or delinquent juvenile is being returned, order him to return unaccompanied to such state and shall provide him with a copy of such court order; in such event a copy of the consent shall be forwarded to the compact administrator of the state to which said juvenile or delinquent juvenile is ordered to return.

Article VII —Cooperative Supervision of Probationers and Parolees

(a) That the duly constituted judicial and administrative authorities of a state party to this compact (herein called "sending state") may permit any delinquent juvenile within such state, placed on probation or parole, to reside in any other state party to this compact (herein called "receiving state") while on probation or parole, and the receiving state shall accept such delinquent juvenile, if the parent, guardian or person entitled to the legal custody of such delinquent juvenile is residing or undertakes to reside within the receiving state. Before granting such permission, opportunity shall be given to the receiving state to make such investigations as it deems necessary. The authorities of the sending state shall send to the authorities of the receiving state copies of pertinent court orders, social case studies and all other available information which may be of value to and assist the receiving state in supervising a probationer or parolee under this compact. A receiving state, in its discretion, may agree to accept supervision of a probationer or parolee in cases where the parent, guardian or person entitled to the legal custody of the delinquent juvenile is not a resident of the receiving state, and if so accepted the sending state may transfer supervision accordingly.

(b) That each receiving state will assume the duties of visitation and of supervision over any such delinquent juvenile and in the exercise of those duties will be governed by the same standards of visitation and supervision that prevail for its own delinquent juveniles released on probation or parole.

(c) That, after consultation between the appropriate authorities of the sending state and of the receiving state as to the desirability and necessity of returning such a delinquent juvenile, the duly accredited officers of a sending state may enter a receiving state and there apprehend and retake any such delinquent juvenile on probation or parole. For that purpose, no formalities will be required, other than establishing the authority of the officer and the identity of the delinquent juvenile to be retaken and returned. The decision of the sending state to retake a delinquent juvenile on probation or parole shall be conclusive upon and not reviewable within the receiving state, but if, at the time the sending state seeks to retake a delinquent juvenile on probation or parole, there is pending against him within the receiving state any criminal charge or any proceeding to have him adjudicated a delinquent juvenile for any act committed in such state, or if he is suspected of having committed within such state a criminal offense or an act of juvenile delinquency, he shall not be returned without the consent of the receiving state until discharged from prosecution or other form of proceeding, imprisonment, detention or supervision for such offense or juvenile delinquency. The duly accredited officers of the sending state shall be permitted to transport delinquent juveniles being so returned through any and all states party to this compact, without interference.

(d) That the sending state shall be responsible under this Article for paying the costs of transporting any delinquent juvenile to the receiving state or of returning any delinquent juvenile to the sending state.

Article VIII —Responsibility for Costs

(a) That the provisions of Articles IV(b), V(b) and VII(d) of this compact shall not be construed to alter or affect any internal relationship among the departments, agencies and officers of and in the government of a party state, or between a party state and its subdivisions, as to the payment of costs, or responsibilities therefor.

(b) That nothing in this compact shall be construed to prevent any party state or subdivision thereof from asserting any right against any person, agency or other entity in regard to costs for which such party state or subdivision thereof may be responsible pursuant to Articles IV(b), V(b) or VII(d) of this compact.

Article IX —Detention Practices

That, to every extent possible, it shall be the policy of states party to this compact that no juvenile or delinquent juvenile shall be placed or detained in any prison, jail or lockup nor be detained or transported in association with criminal, vicious or dissolute persons.

Article X —Supplementary Agreements

That the duly constituted administrative authorities of a state party to this compact may enter into supplementary agreements with any other state or states party hereto for the cooperative care, treatment and rehabilitation of delinquent juveniles whenever they shall find that such agreements will improve the facilities or programs available for such care, treatment and rehabilitation. Such care, treatment and rehabilitation may be provided in an institution located within any state entering into such supplementary agreement. Such supplementary agreements shall (1) provide the rates to be paid for the care, treatment and custody of such delinquent juveniles, taking into consideration the character of facilities, services and subsistence furnished; (2) provide that the delinquent juvenile shall be given a court hearing prior to his being sent to another state for care, treatment and custody; (3) provide that the state receiving such a delinquent juvenile in one of its institutions shall act solely as agent for the state sending such delinquent juvenile; (4) provide that the sending state shall at all times retain jurisdiction over delinquent juveniles sent to an institution in another state; (5) provide for reasonable inspection of such institutions by the sending state; (6) provide that the consent of the parent, guardian, person or agency entitled to the legal custody of said delinquent juvenile shall be secured prior to his being sent to another state; and (7) make provision for such other matters and details as shall be necessary to protect the rights and equities of such delinquent juveniles and of the cooperating states.

Article XI —Acceptance of Federal and Other Aid

That any state party to this compact may accept any and all donations, gifts and grants of money, equipment and services from the federal or any local government, or any agency thereof and from any person, firm or corporation, for any of the purposes and functions of this compact, and may receive and utilize the same subject to the terms, conditions and regulations governing such donations, gifts and grants.

Article XII —Compact Administrators

That the governor of each state party to this compact shall designate an officer who, acting jointly with like officers of other party states, shall promulgate rules and regulations to carry out more effectively the terms and provisions of this compact.

Article XIII —Execution of Compact

That this compact shall become operative immediately upon its execution by any state as between it and any other state or states so executing. When executed it shall have the full force and effect of law within such state, the form of execution to be in accordance with the laws of the executing state.

Article XIV —Renunciation

That this compact shall continue in force and remain binding upon each executing state until renounced by it. Renunciation of this compact shall be by the same authority which executed it, by sending six months' notice in writing of its intention to withdraw from the compact to the other states party hereto. The duties and obligations of a renouncing state under Article VII hereof shall continue as to parolees and probationers residing therein at the time of withdrawal until retaken or finally discharged. Supplementary agreements entered into under Article X hereof shall be subject to renunciation as provided by such supplementary agreements, and shall not be subject to the six months' renunciation notice of the present Article.

Article XV —Severability

That the provisions of this compact shall be severable and if any phrase, clause, sentence or provision of this compact is declared to be contrary to the constitution of any participating state or of the United States or the applicability thereof to any government, agency, person or circumstance is held invalid, the validity of the remainder of this compact and the applicability thereof to any government, agency, person or circumstance shall not be affected thereby. If this compact shall be held contrary to the constitution of any state participating therein, the compact shall remain in full force and effect as to the remaining states and in full force and effect as to the state affected as to all severable matters.

(1988 H 790, eff. 3-16-89; 127 v 530)

Comparative Laws

Ala.—Code 1975, § 44-2-10.
Alaska—AS 47.15.010 to 47.15.080.
Ariz.—A.R.S. § 8-361 to 8-367.
Ark.—A.C.A. § 9-29-101 to 9-29-108.
Cal.—West's Ann.Cal.Welf. & Inst.Code, § 1300.
Colo.—West's C.R.S.A. § 24-60-701 to 24-60-708.
Conn.—C.G.S.A. § 46b-151.
D.C.—D.C. Official Code, 2001 Ed. § 24-1101 to 24-1106.
Del.—31 Del.C. § 5203, 5221 to 5228.
Fla.—West's F.S.A. § 985.501 to 985.507.
Ga.—O.C.G.A. § 39-3-1 to 39-3-7.
Hawaii—HRS § 582-1 to 582-8.
Idaho—I.C. § 16-1901 to 16-1910.
Ill.—45 ILCS 10/0.01 to 10/7.
Ind.—West's A.I.C. 31-37-23-1 to 31-37-23-10.
Iowa—I.C.A. § 232.171, 232.172.
Kan.—K.S.A. 38-1001 to 38-1006.
Ky.—Baldwin's KRS 615.010, 615.020.
La.—LSA-C.C. arts. 1623 to 1657.
Mass.—M.G.L.A. c. 119 App., § 1-1 to 1-7.
Md.—Code 1957, art. 83C, § 3-102 to 3-109.
Me.—34-A M.R.S.A. § 9001 to 9016.
Mich.—M.C.L.A. § 3.701 to 3.706.
Minn.—M.S.A. § 260.51 to 260.57.
Miss.—Code 1972, § 43-25-1 to 43-25-17.
Mo.—V.A.M.S. § 210.570 to 210.600.
Mont.—MCA 41-6-101 to 41-6-106.
N.C.—G.S. § 7B-2800 to 7B-2827.
N.D.—NDCC 27-22-01 to 27-22-06.
Neb.—R.R.S.1943, § 43-1001 to 43-1009.
Nev.—N.R.S. 62I.010 to 62I.070.
N.H.—RSA 169-A:1 to 169-A:9.
N.J.—N.J.S.A. 9:23-1 to 9:23-4.
N.M.—NMSA 1978, § 32A-10-9.
N.Y.—McKinney's Unconsol. Laws, § 1801 to 1806.
Okl.—10 Okl.St.Ann. § 531 to 537.
Ore.—ORS 417.010 to 417.080.
Pa.—62 P.S. § 731 et seq.
R.I.—Gen.Laws 1956, § 14-6-1 to 14-6-11.
S.C.—Code 1976, § 20-7-8075.
S.D.—SDCL 26-12-1 to 26-12-13.
Tenn.—T.C.A. § 37-4-101 to 37-4-106.
Tex.—V.T.C.A., Family Code § 60.001 to 60.009.
Utah—U.C.A.1953, 55-12-1 to 55-12-6.
Va.—Va. Code Ann. § 16.1-323 to 16.1-330.
Vt.—33 V.S.A. § 5701 to 5703.
Wash.—West's RCWA 13.24.010 to 13.24.900.
Wis.—W.S.A. 938.991.
W.Va.—Code, 49-8-1 to 49-8-7.
Wyo.—Wyo.Stat.Ann., § 14-6-101.

Cross References

Jurisdiction of juvenile court under interstate compact, 2151.23
Procedure not otherwise specified, Juv R 45

Library References

Infants ⟸17, 151, 192, 277.
States ⟸6.
Westlaw Topic Nos. 211, 360.
C.J.S. Infants §§ 8 to 9, 31, 33, 41, 53 to 55, 62, 198, 206 to 213, 276.
C.J.S. States §§ 29, 142.

Research References

Encyclopedias
OH Jur. 3d Family Law § 1524, Administrator.
OH Jur. 3d Family Law § 1688, Unruly Child.

Forms
Ohio Jurisprudence Pleading and Practice Forms § 2:8, Courts of Common Pleas—Juvenile Division.
Ohio Jurisprudence Pleading and Practice Forms § 6:83, Residence.

Treatises and Practice Aids
Carlin, Baldwin's Ohio Practice, Merrick-Rippner Probate Law § 105:1, Juvenile Court—Exclusive Original Jurisdiction.
Carlin, Baldwin's Ohio Practice, Merrick-Rippner Probate Law § 107:128, Interstate Compacts.
Carlin, Baldwin's Ohio Practice, Merrick-Rippner Probate Law § 107:129, Extradition of Delinquent Child.
Giannelli & Yeomans, Ohio Juvenile Law § 17:4, Transfer of Venue.
Giannelli & Yeomans, Ohio Juvenile Law § 19:2, Place of Detention.
Giannelli & Yeomans, Ohio Juvenile Law § 29:3, Unruly—Delinquency Dispositions.

Giannelli & Yeomans, Ohio Juvenile Law § 36:2, Interstate Compact on Juveniles.

Notes of Decisions

Juvenile delinquents 2
Transportation costs 1

1. Transportation costs

When a runaway or delinquent juvenile is returned to Ohio from another state party to the interstate compact on juveniles, under RC 2151.56, Art IV(b) or Art V(b), the state of Ohio is responsible for payment of the return transportation costs, and the person or entity with legal custody of such juvenile is the party within the state which is responsible for the transportation costs of his return, unless the juvenile court, in its disposition of a delinquent juvenile under RC 2151.355(A), transferred the responsibility for the physical care and custody of the delinquent juvenile to another person or entity, which is then responsible for the payment of such costs. OAG 89–107.

2. Juvenile delinquents

For purposes of RC 2151.56, a person over the age of twenty-one may qualify as a "delinquent juvenile," provided that the person has been adjudged delinquent by the sending state and, at the time the provisions of RC 2151.56 are invoked, is subject to the jurisdiction of the court in the sending state that made the adjudication or the jurisdiction or supervision of an agency or institution pursuant to an order of such court. OAG 88–050.

RC 2151.39 is not applicable to the acceptance of a juvenile delinquent by the Ohio compact administrator pursuant to RC 2151.56 to RC 2151.61. 1959 OAG 758.

2151.57 Compact administrator; powers and duties

Pursuant to section 2151.56 of the Revised Code, the governor is hereby authorized and empowered, with the advice and consent of the senate, to designate an officer who shall be the compact administrator and who, acting jointly with like officers of other party states, shall promulgate rules and regulations to carry out more effectively the terms of the compact. Such compact administrator shall serve subject to the pleasure of the governor. The compact administrator is hereby authorized, empowered and directed to cooperate with all departments, agencies and officers of and in the government of this state and its subdivisions in facilitating the proper administration of the compact or of any supplementary agreement or agreements entered into by this state thereunder.

(127 v 530, eff. 9–17–57)

Library References

Infants ⇐17.
States ⇐6.
Westlaw Topic Nos. 211, 360.
C.J.S. Infants §§ 8 to 9.
C.J.S. States §§ 29, 142.

Research References

Encyclopedias
OH Jur. 3d Family Law § 1524, Administrator.

Treatises and Practice Aids
Carlin, Baldwin's Ohio Practice, Merrick-Rippner Probate Law § 107:128, Interstate Compacts.

2151.58 Supplementary agreements

The compact administrator is hereby authorized and empowered to enter into supplementary agreements with appropriate officials of other states pursuant to the compact. In the event that such supplementary agreement shall require or contemplate the use of any institution or facility of this state or require or contemplate the provision of any service by this state, said supplementary agreement shall have no force or effect until approved by the head of the department or agency under whose jurisdiction the institution or facility is operated or whose department or agency will be charged with the rendering of such service.

(127 v 530, eff. 9–17–57)

Library References

Infants ⇐17.
States ⇐6.
Westlaw Topic Nos. 211, 360.
C.J.S. Infants §§ 8 to 9.
C.J.S. States §§ 29, 142.

Research References

Encyclopedias
OH Jur. 3d Family Law § 1524, Administrator.

2151.59 Discharge of financial obligations

The compact administrator, subject to the approval of the director of budget and management, may make or arrange for any payments necessary to discharge any financial obligations imposed upon this state by the compact or by any supplementary agreement entered into thereunder.

(1985 H 201, eff. 7–1–85; 127 v 530)

Library References

Infants ⇐17.
States ⇐6.
Westlaw Topic Nos. 211, 360.
C.J.S. Infants §§ 8 to 9.
C.J.S. States §§ 29, 142.

Research References

Encyclopedias
OH Jur. 3d Family Law § 1524, Administrator.

Treatises and Practice Aids
Carlin, Baldwin's Ohio Practice, Merrick-Rippner Probate Law § 107:128, Interstate Compacts.

2151.60 Enforcement by agencies of state and subdivisions

The courts, departments, agencies and officers of this state and its subdivisions shall enforce this compact and shall do all things appropriate to the effectuation of its purposes and intent which may be within their respective jurisdictions.

(127 v 530, eff. 9–17–57)

Library References

Infants ⇐17, 151, 192, 277.
States ⇐6.
Westlaw Topic Nos. 211, 360.
C.J.S. Infants §§ 8 to 9, 31, 33, 41, 53 to 55, 62, 198, 206 to 213, 276.
C.J.S. States §§ 29, 142.

Research References

Encyclopedias
OH Jur. 3d Family Law § 1525, Enforcement of Compact.

Notes of Decisions

Juvenile delinquent 1

1. Juvenile delinquent

RC 2151.39 is not applicable to the acceptance of a juvenile delinquent by the Ohio compact administrator pursuant to RC 2151.56 to RC 2151.61. 1959 OAG 758.

2151.61 Additional article

In addition to any procedure provided in Articles IV and VI of the compact for the return of any runaway juvenile, the particular states, the juvenile or his parents, the courts, or other legal custodian involved may agree upon and adopt any other plan or procedure legally authorized under the laws of this state and the other respective party states for the return of any such runaway juvenile.

Article XVI — Additional Article

The governor is hereby authorized and directed to execute, with any other state or states legally joining in the same, an amendment to the interstate compact on juveniles in substantially the following form:

"(a) That this Article shall provide additional remedies, and shall be binding only as among and between those party states which specifically execute the same.

(b) For the purposes of Article XVI(c), "child", as used herein, means any minor within the jurisdictional age limits of any court in the home state.

(c) When any child is brought before a court of a state of which such child is not a resident, and such state is willing to permit such child's return to the home state of such child, such home state, upon being so advised by the state in which such proceeding is pending, shall immediately institute proceedings to determine the residence and jurisdictional facts as to such child in such home state, and upon finding that such child is in fact a resident of said state and subject to the jurisdiction of the court thereof, shall within five days authorize the return of such child to the home state, and to the parent or custodial agency legally authorized to accept such custody in such home state, and at the expense of such home state, to be paid from such funds as such home state may procure, designate, or provide, prompt action being of the essence.

(d) All provisions and procedures of Articles V and VI of the interstate compact on juveniles shall be construed to apply to any juvenile charged with being a delinquent juvenile for the violation of any criminal law. Any juvenile charged with being a delinquent juvenile for violating any criminal law shall be returned to the requesting state upon a requisition to the state where the juvenile may be found. A petition in the case shall be filed in a court of competent jurisdiction in the requesting state where the violation of criminal law is alleged to have been committed. The petition may be filed regardless of whether the juvenile has left the state before or after the filing of the petition. The requisition described in Article V of the compact shall be forwarded by the judge of the county in which the petition has been filed."

(1992 H 154, eff. 7–31–92; 127 v 530)

Cross References

Judges of the division of domestic relations, 2301.03

Library References

Infants ⚖151, 192.
States ⚖6.
Westlaw Topic Nos. 211, 360.
C.J.S. Infants §§ 31, 33, 41, 53 to 55, 62.
C.J.S. States §§ 29, 142.

Research References

Encyclopedias

OH Jur. 3d Family Law § 1581, Alleged Delinquent or Unruly Child or Juvenile Traffic Offender.
OH Jur. 3d Family Law § 1583, Alleged Neglected, Abused, or Dependent Child.
OH Jur. 3d Family Law § 1688, Unruly Child.

Treatises and Practice Aids

Carlin, Baldwin's Ohio Practice, Merrick-Rippner Probate Law § 107:128, Interstate Compacts.
Giannelli & Yeomans, Ohio Juvenile Law § 19:2, Place of Detention.
Giannelli & Yeomans, Ohio Juvenile Law § 29:3, Unruly—Delinquency Dispositions.
Giannelli & Yeomans, Ohio Juvenile Law § 36:3, Extradition.

FOSTER CARE

FACILITIES FOR TRAINING, TREATMENT, AND REHABILITATION OF JUVENILES

2151.65 Facilities for treatment of juveniles; joint boards; admission

Upon the advice and recommendation of the juvenile judge, the board of county commissioners may provide by purchase, lease, construction, or otherwise a school, forestry camp, or other facility or facilities where delinquent children, as defined in section 2152.02 of the Revised Code, dependent children, abused children, unruly children, as defined in section 2151.022 of the Revised Code, or neglected children or juvenile traffic offenders may be held for training, treatment, and rehabilitation. Upon the joint advice and recommendation of the juvenile judges of two or more adjoining or neighboring counties, the boards of county commissioners of such counties may form themselves into a joint board and proceed to organize a district for the establishment and support of a school, forestry camp, or other facility or facilities for the use of the juvenile courts of such counties, where delinquent, dependent, abused, unruly, or neglected children, or juvenile traffic offenders may be held for treatment, training, and rehabilitation, by using a site or buildings already established in one such county, or by providing for the purchase of a site and the erection of the necessary buildings thereon. Such county or district school, forestry camp, or other facility or facilities shall be maintained as provided in Chapters 2151. and 2152. of the Revised Code. Children who are adjudged to be delinquent, dependent, neglected, abused, unruly, or juvenile traffic offenders may be committed to and held in any such school, forestry camp, or other facility or facilities for training, treatment, and rehabilitation.

The juvenile court shall determine:

(A) The children to be admitted to any school, forestry camp, or other facility maintained under this section;

(B) The period such children shall be trained, treated, and rehabilitated at such facility;

(C) The removal and transfer of children from such facility.

(2000 S 179, § 3, eff. 1–1–02; 1980 S 168, eff. 10–2–80; 1975 H 85; 130 v H 879)

Historical and Statutory Notes

Amendment Note: 2000 S 179, § 3, eff. 1–1–02, substituted "2152.02" for "2151.02" and "Chapters 2151. and 2152." for "sections 2151.01 to 2151.80" in the first paragraph; and made other nonsubstantive changes.

Cross References

Acquisition, construction, or renovation of facilities, 307.021
Additional disposition orders for delinquent children; 2152.19
Adoption of rules for payment of assistance, 5139.29
Issuance of self-supporting securities to finance permanent improvements of juvenile detention facility districts, 133.152
Resolution relative to tax levy in excess of ten-mill limitation, 5705.19
Standards of construction prerequisite to financial assistance of facilities for rehabilitation of delinquent juveniles, 5139.27
Tax levy law, detention home district is "subdivision," 5705.01
Transfer of child committed to facility, 5139.30
Uniform bond law, fiscal officer, subdivision and taxing authority defined, definitions, 133.01
Withdrawal of county from district, continuity of district tax levy, 2151.78

Library References

Infants ⚖226, 271.
Westlaw Topic No. 211.
C.J.S. Adoption of Persons § 10.
C.J.S. Infants §§ 57, 70 to 77, 271.

Research References

Encyclopedias

OH Jur. 3d Family Law § 1718, Cost of Education.
OH Jur. 3d Taxation § 62, Generally, Local Purposes.

Treatises and Practice Aids

Carlin, Baldwin's Ohio Practice, Merrick-Rippner Probate Law § 104:18, Juvenile Facilities—Creation of Schools, Forestry Camps, and Other Facilities.
Carlin, Baldwin's Ohio Practice, Merrick-Rippner Probate Law § 107:73, Alternatives for Disposition of Juvenile Cases.
Carlin, Baldwin's Ohio Practice, Merrick-Rippner Probate Law § 107:84, Disposition of Delinquent Children—Prior to January 1, 2002.
Carlin, Baldwin's Ohio Practice, Merrick-Rippner Probate Law § 107:90, Disposition Orders for Delinquent Children, Effective January 1, 2002.
Giannelli & Yeomans, Ohio Juvenile Law § 27:6, County or Private Facility Commitment.
Giannelli & Yeomans, Ohio Juvenile Law § 30:2, General Principles for Abuse, Neglect and Dependency Dispositions.
Giannelli & Yeomans, Ohio Juvenile Law § 30:3, Costs of Dispositions.
Hastings, Manoloff, Sheeran, & Stype, Ohio School Law § 23:2, Admission Requirements and Tuition Liability-Statutory Requirements in General.

Notes of Decisions

Employees 3
Legal counsel 1
Liability 4
Operating costs 2

---

1. Legal counsel

Where a joint board of county commissioners is created for the purpose of constructing and maintaining a multicounty detention and treatment facility for the training and treatment of juveniles, the joint board of county commissioners may employ legal counsel. OAG 83–064.

Where a joint board of county commissioners is created for the purpose of constructing and maintaining a multicounty detention and treatment facility for the training and treatment of juveniles, the county prosecuting attorneys of the participating counties have no duty to provide legal counsel for the joint board of county commissioners. OAG 83–064.

2. Operating costs

RC 2151.3412 and RC 2151.77 require that the costs of operating and maintaining district juvenile detention and rehabilitation facilities be apportioned among the counties participating in the district on the basis of the counties' actual use of such facilities where no levy has been approved pursuant to RC 5705.19(A). Neither a joint board of county commissioners formed pursuant to RC 2151.34 and RC 2151.65 nor a district board of trustees appointed pursuant to RC 2151.343 and RC 2151.68 has the authority to direct or permit the apportionment of such costs in any other manner. OAG 84–052.

3. Employees

District court's determination that genuine issues of material fact, concerning whether employee's position at juvenile detention facility was "classified" position such that he was entitled to due process hearing before being removed from position, precluded summary judgment for juvenile judge, who removed employee from position, on qualified immunity grounds, was not "final decision" over which Court of Appeals had jurisdiction. Davis v. Rawson (C.A.6 (Ohio), 05-15-2002) No. 00-4405, 35 Fed.Appx. 185, 2002 WL 1001020, Unreported. Federal Courts ⚖ 595

4. Liability

Juvenile corrections officer failed to establish that juvenile correctional facility committed workplace intentional tort that resulted in corrections officer being assaulted by juvenile; corrections officer's supervisor followed internal policies and had discretion in determining how to de-escalate resistant youth. Nichols v. Indian River Juvenile Correctional Facility (Ohio Ct.Cl., 05-09-2005) No. 2004-06852, 2005-Ohio-2541, 2005 WL 1208946, Unreported. Infants ⚖ 280

Juvenile corrections officer failed to establish that juvenile correctional facility was liable for intentional infliction of emotional distress following assault of corrections officer by juvenile; even if juvenile continued to taunt corrections officer, Court of Claims would not interfere with juvenile correctional facility's decision with classification and placement of inmates, and corrections officer did not suffer from severe emotional distress as result of actions of juvenile correctional facility. Nichols v. Indian River Juvenile Correctional Facility (Ohio Ct.Cl., 05-09-2005) No. 2004-06852, 2005-Ohio-2541, 2005 WL 1208946, Unreported. Infants ⚖ 280

County juvenile training facility, constructed pursuant to state statutory scheme but primarily county-funded, was not an arm of the state and thus not entitled to sovereign immunity in former resident's §§1983 action, even though under statutory scheme county acted as "state agenc[y]" in constructing facility and even though county juvenile court, a branch of state government, controlled admissions, appointed supervisor and set his salary, and had discretion over facility's budget; county rather than state would pay damages judgment against facility, and county rather than state or juvenile court made decision whether to create facility to begin with. S.J. v. Hamilton County, Ohio (C.A.6 (Ohio), 06-22-2004) 374 F.3d 416. Federal Courts ⚖ 270

2151.651 Application for financial assistance for acquisition or construction of facilities

The board of county commissioners of a county which, either separately or as part of a district, is planning to establish a school, forestry camp, or other facility under section 2151.65 of the Revised Code, to be used exclusively for the rehabilitation of children between the ages of twelve to eighteen years, other than psychotic or mentally retarded children, who are designated delinquent children, as defined in section 2152.02 of the Revised Code, or unruly children, as defined in section 2151.022 of the Revised Code, by order of a juvenile court, may make application to the department of youth services, created under section 5139.01 of the Revised Code, for financial assistance in defraying the county's share of the cost of acquisition or construction of such school, camp, or other facility, as provided in section 5139.27 of the Revised Code. Such application shall be made on forms prescribed and furnished by the department.

(2000 S 179, § 3, eff. 1–1–02; 1981 H 440, eff. 11–23–81; 1980 S 168; 131 v H 943)

Historical and Statutory Notes

Amendment Note: 2000 S 179, § 3, eff. 1–1–02, substituted "2152.02" for "2151.01"; deleted "division (B) of" before "section 5139.01"; and made other nonsubstantive changes.

Cross References

Inspection of youth rehabilitation facilities, 5139.31

Standards of construction prerequisite to financial assistance of facilities for rehabilitation of delinquent juveniles, 5139.27

Library References

Infants ⇐271.
States ⇐123.
Westlaw Topic Nos. 211, 360.
C.J.S. Infants § 271.
C.J.S. States § 226.

Research References

Encyclopedias

OH Jur. 3d Penal & Correctional Institutions § 56, Finances.

Treatises and Practice Aids

Carlin, Baldwin's Ohio Practice, Merrick-Rippner Probate Law § 104:18, Juvenile Facilities—Creation of Schools, Forestry Camps, and Other Facilities.

2151.653 Program of education; teachers

The board of county commissioners of a county or the board of trustees of a district maintaining a school, forestry camp, or other facility established under section 2151.65 of the Revised Code, shall provide a program of education for the youths admitted to such school, forestry camp, or other facility. Either of such boards and the board of education of any school district may enter into an agreement whereby such board of education provides teachers for such school, forestry camp, or other facility, or permits youths admitted to such school, forestry camp, or other facility to attend a school or schools within such school district, or both. Either of such boards may enter into an agreement with the appropriate authority of any university, college, or vocational institution to assist in providing a program of education for the youths admitted to such school, forestry camp, or other facility.

(131 v H 943, eff. 8–10–65)

Library References

Infants ⇐226, 275.
Westlaw Topic No. 211.
C.J.S. Adoption of Persons § 10.
C.J.S. Infants §§ 57, 70 to 77, 198, 206 to 213, 274.

2151.654 Agreements for admission of children from counties not maintaining facilities

The board of county commissioners of a county or the board of trustees of a district maintaining a school, forestry camp, or other facility established under section 2151.65 of the Revised Code, may enter into an agreement with the board of county commissioners of a county which does not maintain such a school, forestry camp, or other facility, to admit to such school, forestry camp, or other facility a child from the county not maintaining such a school, forestry camp, or other facility.

(131 v H 943, eff. 8–10–65)

Library References

Counties ⇐107.
Infants ⇐271.
Westlaw Topic Nos. 104, 211.
C.J.S. Counties § 147.
C.J.S. Infants § 271.

2151.655 County taxing authority may submit securities issue to electors for support of schools, detention homes, forestry camps, or other facilities; permissible agreements to pay costs of permanent improvements of districts

(A) The taxing authority of a county may issue general obligation securities of the county under Chapter 133. of the Revised Code to pay such county's share, either separately or as a part of a district, of the cost of acquiring schools, detention facilities, forestry camps, or other facilities, or any combination thereof, under section 2152.41 or 2151.65 of the Revised Code, or of acquiring sites for and constructing, enlarging, or otherwise improving such schools, detention facilities, forestry camps, other facilities, or combinations thereof.

(B) The joint board of county commissioners, as the taxing authority of a detention facility district, or a district organized under section 2151. 65 of the Revised Code, or of a combined district organized under sections 2152.41 and 2151.65 of the Revised Code, may submit to the electors of the district the question of issuing general obligation bonds of the district to pay the cost of acquiring, constructing, enlarging, or otherwise improving sites, buildings, and facilities for any purposes for which the district was organized. The election on such question shall be submitted and held under section 133.18 of the Revised Code.

(C)(1) To pay the cost of permanent improvements of the district, the board of trustees of a detention facility district, of a district organized under section 2151.65 of the Revised Code, or of a combined district organized under sections 2152.41 and 2151.65 of the Revised Code may enter into an agreement with the several boards of county commissioners constituting the joint board of county commissioners. The agreement shall provide for each such board of county commissioners to pay the district a share of such costs for a stated term from the proceeds of a tax levied by the board under division (F) or (R) of section 5705.19 of the Revised Code or from funds of the county otherwise lawfully available to pay the county's share of the costs of the district's permanent improvements. County shares shall be allocated on the basis prescribed in the agreement, which may include an allocation in proportion to the taxable value of each county or in proportion to the number of children from each county who are maintained in district facilities.

More than one agreement may be entered into under this division with respect to a district, and more than one agreement may exist at the same time with respect to a district. An agreement entered into under this division may be amended if the amendment is mutually agreed to by the board of trustees of the district and the several boards of county commissioners constituting the joint board of county commissioners.

If a board of county commissioners withdraws from the district before the end of the term of the agreement, the board shall be required to make payments as required in the agreement until all debt charges or loan repayments for which such payments are pledged are paid in full, unless the board of trustees agrees otherwise.

(2) In any such district where the board of trustees has entered into an agreement under division (C)(1) of this section, the joint board of county commissioners, as the taxing authority of a district, may issue self-supporting securities of the district under section 133.152 of the Revised Code for the purpose of paying the cost of permanent improvements of the district. If such securities are issued, the term of an agreement shall be for no fewer years than the maximum maturity of securities secured by a pledge of payments made under the agreement.

(3) In any such district where the board of trustees has entered into an agreement under division (C)(1) of this section, the joint board of county commissioners, as the taxing authority of a district, may obtain loans from a financial institution to be repaid

from amounts to be paid to the district under the agreement by the boards of county commissioners constituting the joint board of county commissioners.

(2006 S 125, eff. 7–20–06; 2000 S 179, § 3, eff. 1–1–02; 1989 H 230, eff. 10–30–89)

Historical and Statutory Notes

Ed. Note: 2151.655 is former 133.151, amended and recodified by 1989 H 230, eff. 10–30–89; 1972 H 258; 1970 H 1135; 131 v H 943.

Amendment Note: 2006 S 125 inserted "joint board of county commissioners, as the" in the first sentence of division (B); and added division (C).

Amendment Note: 2000 S 179, § 3, eff. 1–1–02, substituted "facilities" for "homes" twice and "2152.41" for "2151.34" in division (A); and substituted "facility" for "home" and "2152.41" for "2151.34" in division (B).

Cross References

Issuance of self-supporting securities to finance permanent improvements of juvenile detention facility districts, 133.152
Uniform bond law, definitions, 133.01

Library References

Counties ⚖149, 172 to 181.
Infants ⚖271.
Westlaw Topic Nos. 104, 211.
C.J.S. Counties §§ 185, 187, 218 to 221.
C.J.S. Infants § 271.
    Baldwin's Ohio Legislative Service, 1989 Laws of Ohio, H 230—LSC Analysis, p 5–925

2151.66 Annual tax assessments

The joint boards of county commissioners of district schools, forestry camps, or other facility or facilities created under section 2151.65 of the Revised Code, shall make annual assessments of taxes sufficient to support and defray all necessary expenses of such school, forestry camp, or other facility or facilities.

(130 v H 879, eff. 10–14–63)

Library References

Counties ⚖193.
Westlaw Topic No. 104.
C.J.S. Counties §§ 227, 233.

Research References

Encyclopedias
OH Jur. 3d Penal & Correctional Institutions § 56, Finances.

2151.67 Receipt and use of gifts, grants, devises, bequests and public moneys

The board of county commissioners of a county or the board of trustees of a district maintaining a school, forestry camp, or other facility established or to be established under section 2151.65 of the Revised Code may receive gifts, grants, devises, and bequests, either absolutely or in trust, and may receive any public moneys made available to it. Each of such boards shall use such gifts, grants, devises, bequests, and public moneys in whatever manner it determines is most likely to carry out the purposes for which such school, forestry camp, or other facility was or is to be established.

(132 v H 1, eff. 2–21–67; 131 v H 943)

Historical and Statutory Notes

Ed. Note: Former 2151.67 repealed by 131 v H 943, eff. 8–10–65; 130 v H 879.

Library References

Counties ⚖47, 154.5.
Westlaw Topic No. 104.
C.J.S. Counties §§ 70 to 73.

Research References

Encyclopedias
OH Jur. 3d Penal & Correctional Institutions § 56, Finances.

2151.68 Board of trustees

Immediately upon the organization of the joint board of county commissioners as provided by section 2151.65 of the Revised Code, or so soon thereafter as practicable, such joint board of county commissioners shall appoint a board of not less than five trustees, which shall hold office and perform its duties until the first annual meeting after the choice of an established site and buildings, or after the selection and purchase of a building site, at which time such joint board of county commissioners shall appoint a board of not less than five trustees, one of whom shall hold office for a term of one year, one for the term of two years, one for the term of three years, half of the remaining number for the term of four years, and the remainder for the term of five years. Annually thereafter, the joint board of county commissioners shall appoint one or more trustees, each of whom shall hold office for the term of five years, to succeed any trustee whose term of office expires. A trustee may be appointed to succeed himself upon such board of trustees, and all appointments to such board of trustees shall be made from persons who are recommended and approved by the juvenile court judge or judges of the county of which such person is a resident. The annual meeting of the board of trustees shall be held on the first Tuesday in May in each year.

(130 v H 879, eff. 10–14–63)

Ohio Administrative Code References

County department of job and family services responsibilities for certification, OAC 5101:2–14–61

Library References

Infants ⚖273.
Westlaw Topic No. 211.
C.J.S. Infants § 272.

Research References

Encyclopedias
OH Jur. 3d Penal & Correctional Institutions § 54, District Boards of Trustees.

Notes of Decisions

Operating costs 1

1. **Operating costs**

RC 2151.3412 and RC 2151.77 require that the costs of operating and maintaining district juvenile detention and rehabilitation facilities be apportioned among the counties participating in the district on the basis of the counties' actual use of such facilities where no levy has been approved pursuant to RC 5705.19(A). Neither a joint board of county commissioners formed pursuant to RC 2151.34 and RC 2151.65 nor a district board of trustees appointed pursuant RC 2151.343 and RC 2151.68 has the authority to direct or permit the apportionment of such costs in any other manner. OAG 84–052.

2151.69 Board meetings; compensation

A majority of the trustees appointed under section 2151.68 of the Revised Code constitutes a quorum. Board meetings shall be held at least quarterly. The presiding juvenile court judge of each of the counties of the district organized pursuant to section 2151.65 of the Revised Code shall attend such meetings, or shall designate a member of his staff to do so. The members of the board shall receive no compensation for their services, except their actual traveling expenses, which, when properly certified, shall be allowed and paid by the treasurer.

(130 v H 879, eff. 10–14–63)

Library References

Infants ⇐273.
Westlaw Topic No. 211.
C.J.S. Infants § 272.

Research References

Encyclopedias

OH Jur. 3d Penal & Correctional Institutions § 54, District Boards of Trustees.

2151.70 Appointment of superintendent; bond; compensation; duties

The judge, in a county maintaining a school, forestry camp, or other facility or facilities created under section 2151.65 of the Revised Code, shall appoint the superintendent of any such facility. In the case of a district facility created under such section, the board of trustees shall appoint the superintendent. A superintendent, before entering upon his duties, shall give bond with sufficient surety to the judge or to the board, as the case may be, in such amount as may be fixed by the judge or the board, such bond being conditioned upon the full and faithful accounting of the funds and properties coming into his hands.

Compensation of the superintendent and other necessary employees of a school, forestry camp, or other facility or facilities shall be fixed by the judge in the case of a county facility, or by the board of trustees in the case of a district facility. Such compensation and other expenses of maintaining the facility shall be paid in the manner prescribed in section 2151.13 of the Revised Code in the case of a county facility, or in accordance with rules and regulations provided for in section 2151.77 of the Revised Code in the case of a district facility.

The superintendent of a facility shall appoint all employees of such facility. All such employees, except the superintendent, shall be in the classified civil service.

The superintendent of a school, forestry camp, or other facility shall have entire executive charge of such facility, under supervision of the judge, in the case of a county facility, or under supervision of the board of trustees, in the case of a district facility. The superintendent shall control, manage, and operate the facility, and shall have custody of its property, files, and records.

(130 v H 879, eff. 10–14–63)

Cross References

Classified civil service defined, 124.01
Official bond, 3.30 to 3.34

Library References

Infants ⇐273.
Westlaw Topic No. 211.
C.J.S. Infants § 272.

Research References

Encyclopedias

OH Jur. 3d Penal & Correctional Institutions § 55, Officers and Employees.

2151.71 Operation of facilities

District schools, forestry camps, or other facilities created under section 2151.65 of the Revised Code shall be established, operated, maintained, and managed in the same manner, so far as applicable, as county schools, forestry camps, or other facilities.

(130 v H 879, eff. 10–14–63)

Library References

Infants ⇐275.
Westlaw Topic No. 211.
C.J.S. Infants §§ 198, 206 to 213, 274.

2151.72 Selection of site for district facility

When the board of trustees appointed under section 2151.68 of the Revised Code does not choose an established institution in one of the counties of the district, it may select a suitable site for the erection of a district school, forestry camp, or other facility or facilities created under section 2151.65 of the Revised Code.

(130 v H 879, eff. 10–14–63)

Library References

Infants ⇐271, 273.
Westlaw Topic No. 211.
C.J.S. Infants §§ 271 to 272.

Research References

Encyclopedias

OH Jur. 3d Penal & Correctional Institutions § 54, District Boards of Trustees.

2151.73 Apportionment of trustees; executive committee

Each county in the district, organized under section 2151.65 of the Revised Code, shall be entitled to one trustee, and in districts composed of but two counties, each county shall be entitled to not less than two trustees. In districts composed of more than four counties, the number of trustees shall be sufficiently increased so that there shall always be an uneven number of trustees constituting such board. The county in which a district school, forestry camp, or other facility created under section 2151.65 of the Revised Code is located shall have not less than two trustees, who, in the interim period between the regular meetings of the board of trustees, shall act as an executive committee in the discharge of all business pertaining to the school, forestry camp, or other facility.

(130 v H 879, eff. 10–14–63)

Library References

Infants ⇐273.
Westlaw Topic No. 211.
C.J.S. Infants § 272.

Research References

Encyclopedias

OH Jur. 3d Penal & Correctional Institutions § 54, District Boards of Trustees.

2151.74 Removal of trustee

The joint board of county commissioners organized under section 2151.65 of the Revised Code may remove any trustee appointed under section 2151.68 of the Revised Code, but no such removal shall be made on account of the religious or political convictions of such trustee. The trustee appointed to fill any vacancy shall hold his office for the unexpired term of his predecessor.

(130 v H 879, eff. 10–14–63)

Library References

Infants ☞273.
Westlaw Topic No. 211.
C.J.S. Infants § 272.

Research References

Encyclopedias

OH Jur. 3d Penal & Correctional Institutions § 54, District Boards of Trustees.

2151.75 Interim duties of trustees; trustees fund; reports

In the interim, between the selection and purchase of a site, and the erection and occupancy of a district school, forestry camp, or other facility or facilities created under section 2151.65 of the Revised Code, the joint board of county commissioners provided by section 2151.65 of the Revised Code may delegate to a board of trustees appointed under section 2151.68 of the Revised Code, such powers and duties as, in its judgment, will be of general interest or aid to the institution. Such joint board of county commissioners may appropriate a trustees' fund, to be expended by the board of trustees in payment of such contracts, purchases, or other expenses necessary to the wants or requirements of the school, forestry camp, or other facility or facilities which are not otherwise provided for. The board of trustees shall make a complete settlement with the joint board of county commissioners once each six months, or quarterly if required, and shall make a full report of the condition of the school, forestry camp, or other facility or facilities and inmates, to the board of county commissioners, and to the juvenile court of each of the counties.

(130 v H 879, eff. 10–14–63)

Library References

Infants ☞273.
Westlaw Topic No. 211.
C.J.S. Infants § 272.

Research References

Encyclopedias

OH Jur. 3d Penal & Correctional Institutions § 54, District Boards of Trustees.

2151.76 Authority for choice, construction, and furnishing of district facility

The choice of an established site and buildings, or the purchase of a site, stock, implements, and general farm equipment, should there be a farm, the erection of buildings, and the completion and furnishing of the district school, forestry camp, or other facility or facilities for occupancy, shall be in the hands of the joint board of county commissioners organized under section 2151.65 of the Revised Code. Such joint board of county commissioners may delegate all or a portion of these duties to the board of trustees provided for under section 2151.68 of the Revised Code, under such restrictions and regulations as the joint board of county commissioners imposes.

(130 v H 879, eff. 10–14–63)

Library References

Counties ☞47, 103 to 105(1).
Infants ☞271.
Westlaw Topic Nos. 104, 211.
C.J.S. Counties §§ 70 to 73, 143 to 147.
C.J.S. Infants § 271.

Research References

Encyclopedias

OH Jur. 3d Penal & Correctional Institutions § 54, District Boards of Trustees.

2151.77 Capital and current expenses of district

When an established site and buildings are used for a district school, forestry camp, or other facility or facilities created under section 2151.65 of the Revised Code the joint board of county commissioners organized under section 2151.65 of the Revised Code shall cause the value of such site and buildings to be properly appraised. This appraisal value, or in case of the purchase of a site, the purchase price and the cost of all betterments and additions thereto, shall be paid by the counties comprising the district, in proportion to the taxable property of each county, as shown by its tax duplicate. The current expenses of maintaining the school, forestry camp, or other facility or facilities and the cost of ordinary repairs thereto shall be paid by each such county in accordance with one of the following methods as approved by the joint board of county commissioners:

(A) In proportion to the number of children from such county who are maintained in the school, forestry camp, or other facility or facilities during the year;

(B) By a levy submitted by the joint board of county commissioners under division (A) of section 5705.19 of the Revised Code and approved by the electors of the district;

(C) In proportion to the taxable property of each county, as shown by its tax duplicate;

(D) In any combination of the methods for payment described in division (A), (B), or (C) of this section.

The board of trustees shall, with the approval of the joint board of county commissioners, adopt rules for the management of funds used for the current expenses of maintaining the school, forestry camp, or other facility or facilities.

(1988 H 365, eff. 6–14–88; 1972 H 258; 130 v H 879)

Library References

Counties ☞137.
Infants ☞271.
Westlaw Topic Nos. 104, 211.
C.J.S. Counties § 175.
C.J.S. Infants § 271.

Research References

Encyclopedias

OH Jur. 3d Penal & Correctional Institutions § 56, Finances.

Notes of Decisions

Operating costs   1

---

1. Operating costs

RC 2151.3412 and RC 2151.77 require that the costs of operating and maintaining district juvenile detention and rehabilitation facilities be apportioned among the counties participating in the district on the basis of the counties' actual use of such facilities where no levy has been approved pursuant to RC 5705.19(A). Neither a joint board of county commissioners formed pursuant to RC 2151.34 and RC 2151.65 nor a district board of trustees appointed pursuant to RC 2151.343 and RC 2151.68 has the authority to direct or permit the apportionment of such costs in any other manner. OAG 84–052.

2151.78 Withdrawal of county from district; continuity of district tax levy

The board of county commissioners of any county within a school, forestry camp, or other facility or facilities district may, upon the recommendation of the juvenile court of such county, withdraw from such district and dispose of its interest in such school, forestry camp, or other facility or facilities selling or leasing its right, title, and interest in the site, buildings, furniture, and equipment to any counties in the district, at such price and upon such terms as are agreed upon among the boards of county commissioners of the counties concerned. Section 307.10 of the Revised Code does not apply to this section. The net proceeds of any such sale or lease shall be paid into the treasury of the withdrawing county.

Any county withdrawing from such district or from a combined district organized under sections 2152.41 and 2151.65 of the Revised Code shall continue to have levied against its tax duplicate any tax levied by the district during the period in which the county was a member of the district for current operating expenses, permanent improvements, or the retirement of bonded indebtedness. Such levy shall continue to be a levy against such duplicate of the county until such time that it expires or is renewed.

Members of the board of trustees of a district school, forestry camp, or other facility or facilities who are residents of a county withdrawing from such district are deemed to have resigned their positions upon the completion of the withdrawal procedure provided by this section. Vacancies then created shall be filled according to sections 2151.68 and 2151.74 of the Revised Code.

(2000 S 179, § 3, eff. 1–1–02; 1972 H 258, eff. 1–27–72; 130 v H 879)

Historical and Statutory Notes

Amendment Note: 2000 S 179, § 3, eff. 1–1–02, substituted "2152.41" for "2151.34" in the second paragraph; and made other nonsubstantive changes.

Library References

Infants ⟐271.
Westlaw Topic No. 211.
C.J.S. Infants § 271.

2151.79 Designation of fiscal officer of district; duties of county auditors

The county auditor of the county having the greatest population, or, with the unanimous concurrence of the county auditors of the counties composing a facilities district, the auditor of the county wherein the facility is located, shall be the fiscal officer of a district organized under section 2151.65 of the Revised Code or a combined district organized under sections 2152.41 and 2151.65 of the Revised Code. The county auditors of the several counties composing a school, forestry camp, or other facility or facilities district, shall meet at the district school, forestry camp, or other facility or facilities not less than once in each six months, to review accounts and to transact such other duties in connection with the institution as pertain to the business of their office.

(2000 S 179, § 3, eff. 1–1–02; 1974 H 1033, eff. 10–2–74; 1972 H 258; 130 v H 879)

Historical and Statutory Notes

Amendment Note: 2000 S 179, § 3, eff. 1–1–02, substituted "2152.41" for "2151.34".

Library References

Counties ⟐91.
Westlaw Topic No. 104.
C.J.S. Counties § 128.

Research References

Encyclopedias
OH Jur. 3d Penal & Correctional Institutions § 56, Finances.

2151.80 Expenses of members of boards of county commissioners

Each member of the board of county commissioners who meets by appointment to consider the organization of a district school, forestry camp, or other facility or facilities shall, upon presentation of properly certified accounts, be paid his necessary expenses upon a warrant drawn by the county auditor of his county.

(130 v H 879, eff. 10–14–63)

Library References

Counties ⟐46.
Westlaw Topic No. 104.
C.J.S. Counties § 68.

MISCELLANEOUS PROVISIONS

2151.85 Minor female's complaint for abortion; hearing; appeal

(A) A woman who is pregnant, unmarried, under eighteen years of age, and unemancipated and who wishes to have an abortion without the notification of her parents, guardian, or custodian may file a complaint in the juvenile court of the county in which she has a residence or legal settlement, in the juvenile court of any county that borders to any extent the county in which she has a residence or legal settlement, or in the juvenile court of the county in which the hospital, clinic, or other facility in which the abortion would be performed or induced is located, requesting the issuance of an order authorizing her to consent to the performance or inducement of an abortion without the notification of her parents, guardian, or custodian.

The complaint shall be made under oath and shall include all of the following:

(1) A statement that the complainant is pregnant;

(2) A statement that the complainant is unmarried, under eighteen years of age, and unemancipated;

(3) A statement that the complainant wishes to have an abortion without the notification of her parents, guardian, or custodian;

(4) An allegation of either or both of the following:

(a) That the complainant is sufficiently mature and well enough informed to intelligently decide whether to have an abortion without the notification of her parents, guardian, or custodian;

(b) That one or both of her parents, her guardian, or her custodian was engaged in a pattern of physical, sexual, or emotional abuse against her, or that the notification of her parents, guardian, or custodian otherwise is not in her best interest.

(5) A statement as to whether the complainant has retained an attorney and, if she has retained an attorney, the name, address, and telephone number of her attorney.

(B)(1) The court shall fix a time for a hearing on any complaint filed pursuant to division (A) of this section and shall keep a record of all testimony and other oral proceedings in the action. The court shall hear and determine the action and shall not refer any portion of it to a referee. The hearing shall be held at the earliest possible time, but not later than the fifth business day after the day that the complaint is filed. The court shall enter judgment on the complaint immediately after the hearing is concluded. If the hearing required by this division is not held by the fifth business day after the complaint is filed, the failure to hold the hearing shall be considered to be a constructive order of the court authorizing the complainant to consent to the performance or inducement of an abortion without the notification of her parent, guardian, or custodian, and the complainant and any other person may rely on the constructive order to the same extent as if the court actually had issued an order under this section authorizing the complainant to consent to the performance or inducement of an abortion without such notification.

(2) The court shall appoint a guardian ad litem to protect the interests of the complainant at the hearing that is held pursuant to this section. If the complainant has not retained an attorney, the court shall appoint an attorney to represent her. If the guardian ad litem is an attorney admitted to the practice of law in this state, the court also may appoint him to serve as the complainant's attorney.

(C)(1) If the complainant makes only the allegation set forth in division (A)(4)(a) of this section and if the court finds, by clear and convincing evidence, that the complainant is sufficiently mature and well enough informed to decide intelligently whether to have an abortion, the court shall issue an order authorizing the complainant to consent to the performance or inducement of an abortion without the notification of her parents, guardian, or custodian. If the court does not make the finding specified in this division, it shall dismiss the complaint.

(2) If the complainant makes only the allegation set forth in division (A)(4)(b) of this section and if the court finds, by clear and convincing evidence, that there is evidence of a pattern of physical, sexual, or emotional abuse of the complainant by one or both of her parents, her guardian, or her custodian, or that the notification of the parents, guardian, or custodian of the complainant otherwise is not in the best interest of the complainant, the court shall issue an order authorizing the complainant to consent to the performance or inducement of an abortion without the notification of her parents, guardian, or custodian. If the court does not make the finding specified in this division, it shall dismiss the complaint.

(3) If the complainant makes both of the allegations set forth in divisions (A)(4)(a) and (b) of this section, the court shall proceed as follows:

(a) The court first shall determine whether it can make the finding specified in division (C)(1) of this section and, if so, shall issue an order pursuant to that division. If the court issues such an order, it shall not proceed pursuant to division (C)(3)(b) of this section. If the court does not make the finding specified in division (C)(1) of this section, it shall proceed pursuant to division (C)(3)(b) of this section.

(b) If the court pursuant to division (C)(3)(a) of this section does not make the finding specified in division (C)(1) of this section, it shall proceed to determine whether it can make the finding specified in division (C)(2) of this section and, if so, shall issue an order pursuant to that division. If the court does not make the finding specified in division (C)(2) of this section, it shall dismiss the complaint.

(D) The court shall not notify the parents, guardian, or custodian of the complainant that she is pregnant or that she wants to have an abortion.

(E) If the court dismisses the complaint, it immediately shall notify the complainant that she has a right to appeal under section 2505.073 of the Revised Code.

(F) Each hearing under this section shall be conducted in a manner that will preserve the anonymity of the complainant. The complaint and all other papers and records that pertain to an action commenced under this section shall be kept confidential and are not public records under section 149.43 of the Revised Code.

(G) The clerk of the supreme court shall prescribe complaint and notice of appeal forms that shall be used by a complainant filing a complaint under this section and by an appellant filing an appeal under section 2505.073 of the Revised Code. The clerk of each juvenile court shall furnish blank copies of the forms, without charge, to any person who requests them.

(H) No filing fee shall be required of, and no court costs shall be assessed against, a complainant filing a complaint under this section or an appellant filing an appeal under section 2505.073 of the Revised Code.

(I) As used in this section, "unemancipated" means that a woman who is unmarried and under eighteen years of age has not entered the armed services of the United States, has not become employed and self-subsisting, or has not otherwise become independent from the care and control of her parent, guardian, or custodian.

(1985 H 319, eff. 3-24-86)

Cross References

Appeal from dismissal of minor female's complaint for abortion, 2505.073
Attempt to have abortion without parental notice not creating patient-physician relationship, 2151.421

Library References

Abortion and Birth Control ⚖0.5.
Westlaw Topic No. 4.

Research References

ALR Library
77 ALR 5th 1, Validity, Construction, and Application of Statutes Requiring Parental Notification of or Consent to Minor's Abortion.

Encyclopedias
OH Jur. 3d Family Law § 1481, Permission for Abortion Without Notice to Parents.
OH Jur. 3d Family Law § 1482, Permission for Abortion Without Notice to Parents—Requirements for Granting Permission.

Forms
Ohio Forms Legal and Business § 28:44, Form Drafting Principles—Consent to Medical Treatment.
Ohio Jurisprudence Pleading and Practice Forms § 48:7, Public Records.
Ohio Jurisprudence Pleading and Practice Forms § 84:70, Juvenile Court—Notice of Appeal.

Treatises and Practice Aids
Katz, Giannelli, Blair and Lipton, Baldwin's Ohio Practice, Criminal Law, § 109:3, Abortion.
Carlin, Baldwin's Ohio Practice, Merrick-Rippner Probate Law § 107:2, Types of Complaints.
Carlin, Baldwin's Ohio Practice, Merrick-Rippner Probate Law § 107:7, Jurisdiction and Venue for Juvenile Proceedings.
Carlin, Baldwin's Ohio Practice, Merrick-Rippner Probate Law § 106:21, Juvenile Court Jurisdiction—Consent for Abortion—Minor Female's Complaint for Abortion.
Carlin, Baldwin's Ohio Practice, Merrick-Rippner Probate Law § 106:22, Juvenile Court Jurisdiction—Consent for Abortion—Quantum of Proof in Abortion Consent Hearings.
Carlin, Baldwin's Ohio Practice, Merrick-Rippner Probate Law § 106:32, Complaint for an Order Authorizing Consent to an Abortion Without Notification—Form.
Carlin, Baldwin's Ohio Practice, Merrick-Rippner Probate Law § 106:33, Journal Order—Form.
Carlin, Baldwin's Ohio Practice, Merrick-Rippner Probate Law § 107:10, Contents and Issuance of Summons.

Carlin, Baldwin's Ohio Practice, Merrick-Rippner Probate Law § 107:43, Scheduling Juvenile Court Hearing.

Carlin, Baldwin's Ohio Practice, Merrick-Rippner Probate Law § 107:45, Adjudicatory Hearings—Parties' Right to Counsel.

Carlin, Baldwin's Ohio Practice, Merrick-Rippner Probate Law § 107:46, Adjudicatory Hearings—Child's Right to Guardian Ad Litem.

Carlin, Baldwin's Ohio Practice, Merrick-Rippner Probate Law § 107:49, Adjudicatory Hearings—Conduct of Hearing by Magistrate.

Carlin, Baldwin's Ohio Practice, Merrick-Rippner Probate Law § 107:52, Adjudicatory Hearings—Confidentiality of Juvenile Court Proceedings.

Carlin, Baldwin's Ohio Practice, Merrick-Rippner Probate Law § 107:59, Adjudicatory Hearings—Proof Beyond a Reasonable Doubt.

Carlin, Baldwin's Ohio Practice, Merrick-Rippner Probate Law § 107:60, Adjudicatory Hearings—Right to Transcript of Proceedings.

Carlin, Baldwin's Ohio Practice, Merrick-Rippner Probate Law § 107:62, Adjudicatory Hearings—Procedure for Hearing on Minor Female's Complaint for Abortion.

Carlin, Baldwin's Ohio Practice, Merrick-Rippner Probate Law § 107:72, Dispositional Hearings—Procedure.

Carlin, Baldwin's Ohio Practice, Merrick-Rippner Probate Law § 107:114, Juvenile Court Records—Confidentiality.

Carlin, Baldwin's Ohio Practice, Merrick-Rippner Probate Law § 107:124, Appeals—Juvenile Court Judgments—Abortion Authorization Cases.

Carlin, Baldwin's Ohio Practice, Merrick-Rippner Probate Law § 107:187, Order Authorizing Performance of Abortion Without Parental Notification—Form.

Carlin, Baldwin's Ohio Practice, Merrick-Rippner Probate Law § 107:188, Notice of Appeal from Order Dismissing Complaint Seeking Abortion Without Parental Notification—Form.

Painter & Dennis, Ohio Appellate Practice § 3:26, Accelerated Calendar Cases-In General.

Hennenberg & Reinhart, Ohio Criminal Defense Motions F 2.43, Motion for Sanctions for Violations of R.C. Chapter 149 (Public Records Act)-Discovery Demands and Motions.

Hennenberg & Reinhart, Ohio Criminal Defense Motions F 2.45, Motion to Inspect Public Records-Discovery Demands and Motions.

Giannelli & Yeomans, Ohio Juvenile Law § 1:8, Rules of Juvenile Procedure.

Giannelli & Yeomans, Ohio Juvenile Law § 12:2, Jurisdictional Requirements.

Giannelli & Yeomans, Ohio Juvenile Law § 12:3, Complaint.

Giannelli & Yeomans, Ohio Juvenile Law § 12:4, Attorney & Guardian Ad Litem.

Giannelli & Yeomans, Ohio Juvenile Law § 12:5, Venue.

Giannelli & Yeomans, Ohio Juvenile Law § 12:6, Summons.

Giannelli & Yeomans, Ohio Juvenile Law § 12:7, Scheduling the Hearing.

Giannelli & Yeomans, Ohio Juvenile Law § 12:8, Hearing.

Giannelli & Yeomans, Ohio Juvenile Law § 12:9, Case Law.

Giannelli & Yeomans, Ohio Juvenile Law § 23:3, Right to Counsel.

Giannelli & Yeomans, Ohio Juvenile Law § 35:2, Confidentiality Requirement.

Giannelli & Yeomans, Ohio Juvenile Law App. D, Appendix D. Glossary.

Giannelli & Yeomans, Ohio Juvenile Law § 12:10, Appeals.

Hastings, Manoloff, Sheeran, & Stype, Ohio School Law § 44:2, Definition of Public Records.

Law Review and Journal Commentaries

Abortion counseling and the schools, Van D. Keating. 34 Ohio Sch Boards Ass'n J 2 (August 1990).

House Bill 899: Counseling for Minors Seeking Abortions Without Parental Notification, Bernadette A. Champa. 2 Health L J Ohio 99 (January/February 1991).

A Look at "Parental Notification of Abortion" in Ohio (Better Known as "Parental Bypass"), Hon. William K. Weaver. 14 Lake Legal Views 1 (July 1991).

Ohio Abortion Notification Law Ruled Constitutional, William A. Kurtz. 1 Prob L J Ohio 14 (September/October 1990).

Ohio Parental Notification Law For A Minor's Abortion: *Akron II*, Sue Ganske Graziano and Robert Holmes. 15 Ohio N U L Rev 543 (1988).

Parental Notification and a Minor's Right to an Abortion After *Hodgson & Akron II*, Sue Ganske Graziano. 18 Ohio N U L Rev 581 (1991).

Update on Ohio Abortion Notification Law, William A. Kurtz. 1 Prob L J Ohio 36 (November/December 1990).

When Is a Pregnant Minor Mature? When Is an Abortion in Her Best Interest? The Ohio Supreme Court Applies Ohio's Abortion Parental Notification Law, Note. 60 U Cin L Rev 907 (Winter 1992).

Notes of Decisions

Constitutional issues 1
Evidence of maturity 3
Pattern of abuse 5
Procedural issues 4
Public records 2

---

1. Constitutional issues

As RC 2151.85 has been declared unconstitutional, RC 2919.12(B)(1) is unconstitutional, as there is no judicial bypass of parental consent. In re Doe (Ohio Com.Pl. 1990) 57 Ohio Misc.2d 20, 565 N.E.2d 891.

The notice provisions of RC 2151.85(D) violate the rulemaking authority of the Supreme Court, in O Const Art IV §5(B), as Juv R 15(A) requires that parents of a juvenile be notified of any proceedings involving the child; therefore, RC 2151.85 is unconstitutional. Further CP Sup R 76(H), promulgated in furtherance of RC 2151.85, conflicts with Juv R 15(A), and in such situations, the juvenile rule controls. In re Doe (Ohio Com.Pl. 1990) 57 Ohio Misc.2d 20, 565 N.E.2d 891.

Intent of institutional abortion providers and physician to violate Ohio's judicial bypass system for minor seeking abortion was not determinative of standing of providers and physician to bring action challenging constitutionality of system. Cleveland Surgi–Center, Inc. v. Jones (C.A.6 (Ohio) 1993) 2 F.3d 686, certiorari denied 114 S.Ct. 696, 510 U.S. 1046, 126 L.Ed.2d 663. Constitutional Law ⇔ 42.1(1)

Institutional abortion providers and physician lacked standing to bring action challenging constitutionality of Ohio's judicial bypass system for minor seeking abortion; real complaint was that certain state court judges were making wrong decisions under constitutional statute and there was no constitutional or statutory authority that permitted federal court to review decisions of state courts. Cleveland Surgi–Center, Inc. v. Jones (C.A.6 (Ohio) 1993) 2 F.3d 686, certiorari denied 114 S.Ct. 696, 510 U.S. 1046, 126 L.Ed.2d 663. Courts ⇔ 509

Although it is conceded the law may recognize the right of parents to notice before abortionists sell their services to immature and dependent minor children, so long as a secret means is afforded to determine a minor child's claim an abortion is in her best interest or that she is mature, emancipated, and thus entitled to seek an abortion, a statute serving these ends will be struck down where it (1) imposes a duty on the abortionist to notify the parents; (2) allows a court considering a minor's maturity or best interest to consider both these factors if both are pleaded but not if only one is pleaded; (3) calls for the minor to give her real name and an address where the court can reach her during the secret proceedings on her maturity and best interest; and (4) could take twenty-two days for the secret ''bypass'' proceedings to determine whether an abortion without notice to parents will be permitted. Akron Center for Reproductive Health v. Slaby (C.A.6 (Ohio) 1988) 854 F.2d 852, probable jurisdiction noted 109 S.Ct. 3239, 492 U.S. 916, 106 L.Ed.2d 586, reversed 110 S.Ct. 2972, 497 U.S. 502, 111 L.Ed.2d 405, on remand 911 F.2d 731, on remand 911 F.2d 733.

Under RC 2151.85 a minor's parents need not even be notified of an abortion if "clear and convincing evidence" shows the minor is "mature" or it is in her "best interests" the parents remain uninformed; because this burden of proof is greater than a preponderance of the evidence standard, however, it could result in "erroneous determinations" allowing parents to be told, and is therefore unconstitutional. Akron Center for Reproductive Health v. Rosen (N.D.Ohio 1986) 633 F.Supp. 1123, amended 110 F.R.D. 576, appeal dismissed 805 F.2d 1033, appeal dismissed 805 F.2d 1036, affirmed 854 F.2d 852, probable jurisdiction noted 109 S.Ct. 3239, 492 U.S. 916, 106 L.Ed.2d 586, reversed 110 S.Ct. 2972, 497 U.S. 502, 111 L.Ed.2d 405, on remand 911 F.2d 731, on remand 911 F.2d 733.

A minor can obtain an abortion without notification of her parent if she is "mature" or it is in her "best interest"; under RC 2151.85 the judge is to consider only the ground the minor asserts in her complaint, or both if she asserts both; RC 2151.85 is held unconstitutional, however, because it does not require the judge to consider both grounds where the minor asserts only one. Akron Center for Reproductive Health v. Rosen (N.D.Ohio 1986) 633 F.Supp. 1123, amended 110 F.R.D. 576, appeal dismissed 805 F.2d 1033, appeal dismissed 805 F.2d 1036, affirmed 854 F.2d 852, probable jurisdiction noted 109 S.Ct. 3239, 492 U.S. 916, 106 L.Ed.2d 586, reversed 110 S.Ct. 2972, 497 U.S. 502, 111 L.Ed.2d 405, on remand 911 F.2d 731, on remand 911 F.2d 733.

The "constructive order" allowing an abortion under RC 2151.85 if the juvenile court does not act is insufficient notice to the abortionist that he may proceed, and is constitutionally inadequate. Akron Center for Reproductive Health v. Rosen (N.D.Ohio 1986) 633 F.Supp. 1123, amended 110 F.R.D. 576, appeal dismissed 805 F.2d 1033, appeal dismissed 805 F.2d 1036, affirmed 854 F.2d 852, probable jurisdiction noted 109 S.Ct. 3239, 492 U.S. 916, 106 L.Ed.2d 586, reversed 110 S.Ct. 2972, 497 U.S. 502, 111 L.Ed.2d 405, on remand 911 F.2d 731, on remand 911 F.2d 733.

2. Public records

The public is entitled to secure from the records pertaining to each case filed under RC 2505.073 (1) the docket number, (2) the name of the judge, and (3) the decision, including, if appropriate, a properly redacted opinion. State ex rel. The Cincinnati Post v. Second Dist. Court of Appeals (Ohio 1992) 65 Ohio St.3d 378, 604 N.E.2d 153.

3. Evidence of maturity

Clear and convincing evidence existed that 17-year-old minor was sufficiently mature and well informed to have abortion without parental notification; evidence indicated that minor sought to avoid potential and probable conflict with parents, minor had 3.2 grade point average in high school, minor had participated in extracurricular school activities, minor had been accepted by a college, minor had received counseling about options other termination of pregnancy, and minor considered and understood risks and benefits of abortion and foster care and options to abortion. In re Doe (Ohio App. 1 Dist., Hamilton, 04-01-2005) No. C-050133, 2005-Ohio-1559, 2005 WL 736666, Unreported. Abortion And Birth Control ⇔ 0.5

Juvenile demonstrated that she was sufficiently mature to have abortion without parental notification; juvenile had maintained fairly good grades in school, had made plans for her future education, had obtained at least a partial scholarship to support her future educational plans, admitted that she was not in a position to assume responsibility for child, and had obtained medical counseling to prevent future pregnancies and was aware of medical consequences of her choice to have abortion, and juvenile would be 18 in a month and able to have an abortion without notifying her parents. In re Petition of Doe (Ohio App. 10 Dist., Franklin, 12-05-2003) No. 03AP-1185, 2003-Ohio-6509, 2003 WL 22871690, Unreported. Abortion And Birth Control ⇔ 0.5

Clear and convincing evidence of minor female's maturity and intelligence entitled her to order authorizing her to consent to abortion without notification of her parents, even though minor had not consulted with a physician or clinic where abortion would be performed, and minor had not spoken with a person who had had an abortion; minor conducted Internet research regarding procedure and its risks, minor had considered and rejected adoption as an alternative, minor consulted with social services agency over the Internet, and minor who lived in a small community could not be expected to find a person who had had an abortion to discuss the experience. In re Doe (Ohio App. 2 Dist., Clark, 09-16-2002) No. 02CA0067, 2002-Ohio-6081, 2002 WL 31492302, Unreported. Abortion And Birth Control ⇔ 0.5; Infants ⇔ 11

Evidence was sufficient to find that juvenile was not sufficiently mature and well enough informed to intelligently decide whether to have an abortion without notification of her parent; although juvenile was an honor student and had plans to attend college, she testified that she called the abortion clinic when she learned that she was pregnant, that she would begin using birth control, despite having indicated that she would not continue to be sexually active, and acknowledged that she was not asserting that the trial court erred in finding that she failed to demonstrate that notification of her parent of her desire to have an abortion was not in her best interest. In re Jane Doe 01-01 (Ohio App. 8 Dist., 01-17-2001) 141 Ohio App.3d 20, 749 N.E.2d 807. Abortion And Birth Control ⇔ 0.5

Finding that 17 year old female was not sufficiently mature and well enough informed to intelligently decide whether to terminate her pregnancy without notifying her parents was an abuse of discretion; she was a high school senior, an A and B student who had held part-time employment, and she testified that neither she nor her boyfriend was financially capable of supporting a child, that she had regularly used birth control devices, that she was aware of her options, and that she feared the information could destroy her already tenuous relationship with her parents. In re Complaint of Jane Doe (Ohio App. 4 Dist., 10-08-1999) 134 Ohio App.3d 569, 731 N.E.2d 751. Abortion And Birth Control ⇔ 0.5

Failure to grant juvenile petition to terminate her pregnancy without parental notification was abuse of discretion on record; juvenile clearly demonstrated both that she was sufficiently mature and well enough informed to intelligently decide whether to have abortion and that notification of her parents was not in her best interest. In re Complaint of Jane Doe (Franklin 1992) 83 Ohio App.3d 904, 615 N.E.2d 1142. Abortion And Birth Control ⇔ 0.5

A juvenile who properly establishes that she is nearly eighteen years of age, has done well in high school, is employed and saving the earnings for college, which she will be starting within six months, proves by clear and convincing evidence that she is "sufficiently mature" to terminate a pregnancy without the need for parental notification; without other evidence in the record to establish the contrary in such circumstances, the trial court abuses its discretion by finding insufficient maturity. In re Complaint of Jane Doe (Franklin 1993) 83 Ohio App.3d 98, 613 N.E.2d 1112.

Seventeen-year-old girl was sufficiently mature and well enough informed to decide intelligently to have an abortion without notification of her parent; the girl stated that she would have the abortion anyway when she turned 18–years-old, but the procedure was much safer if she had it sooner, girl had graduated from high school, girl had an excellent academic record and earned a full scholarship to college, and girl had considered adoption and foster care alternatives. In re Doe (Ohio App. 1 Dist., Hamilton, 07-10-2002) No. C-020443, 2002-Ohio-3926, 2002 WL 1769389, Unreported. Abortion And Birth Control ⇔ 0.5

A trial court's refusal to allow a minor to terminate a pregnancy without parental notification pursuant to RC 2151.85(A) constitutes an abuse of discretion where the record establishes the minor is a seventeen-year-old senior in high school, taking college preparatory classes, and maintaining a 3.6 grade point average, the minor is employed part time and will start college in the fall, the minor has informed her boyfriend of the pregnancy and her boyfriend supports her decision to have an abortion, and the minor and her boyfriend are not financially or emotionally prepared to take care of a child. In re Doe, No. 93AP–529, 1993 WL 172353 (10th Dist Ct App, Franklin, 4–21–93).

4. Procedural issues

Absent an abuse of discretion by the juvenile court, the dismissal of a complaint brought by an unemancipated pregnant minor seeking authorization to have an abortion shall not be disturbed. In re Jane Doe 01-01 (Ohio App. 8 Dist., 01-17-2001) 141 Ohio App.3d 20, 749 N.E.2d 807. Abortion And Birth Control ⇔ 0.5

While the correctness of a juvenile court's dismissal of a complaint requesting an order authorizing consent to an abortion without parental notification must be scrutinized on a case-by-case basis, a reviewing court must evaluate the trial court's determination under an abuse of discretion standard. In re Jane Doe 01-01 (Ohio App. 8 Dist., 01-17-2001) 141 Ohio App.3d 20, 749 N.E.2d 807. Abortion And Birth Control ⇔ 0.5

Failure of Juvenile Division of Common Pleas Court to hold hearing on minor's request for order authorizing her to terminate her pregnancy without parental notification constituted a constructive order authorizing minor to consent to performance or inducement of abortion without parental notice, which could be relied on by minor, and any other person, to same extent as if court had actually issued an order permitting parental notification bypass procedure. In re Jane Doe (Ohio App. 4 Dist., 12-17-1999) 135 Ohio App.3d 719, 735 N.E.2d 504. Abortion And Birth Control ⇔ 0.5

When reviewing trial court judgments concerning parental notification as to a minor female's termination of pregnancy, appellate courts must determine whether the trial court abused its discretion in finding that the appellant did not prove either of the statutory grounds by clear and convincing evidence. In re Complaint of Jane Doe (Ohio App. 4 Dist., 10-08-1999) 134 Ohio App.3d 569, 731 N.E.2d 751. Abortion And Birth Control ⇔ 0.5

In a proceeding in which a juvenile is requesting authorization to terminate her pregnancy without parental notification, the role of the trial and appellate courts is to focus upon the factors prescribed by the General Assembly, not to question the wisdom of a legislative enactment. In re Complaint of Jane Doe (Ohio App. 4 Dist., 10-08-1999) 134 Ohio App.3d 569, 731 N.E.2d 751. Abortion And Birth Control ⇔ 0.5

Absent an abuse of discretion by the juvenile court, the dismissal of a complaint brought by an unemancipated pregnant minor seeking authorization to have an abortion pursuant to RC 2151.85 shall not be disturbed.

In re Jane Doe 1 (Ohio 1991) 57 Ohio St.3d 135, 566 N.E.2d 1181. Abortion And Birth Control ⇔ 0.5

Judicial bypass procedure of Ohio statute requiring parental notification of abortion complies with Fourteenth Amendment, even though minor must sign complaint form to initiate bypass procedure unless she has counsel and must supply name of one parent in four different places, even though State employees might unlawfully disclose minor's identity, and even if procedure may take 22 days in rare case; statute permits minor to show sufficient maturity, requires court to authorize abortion if it is in minor's best interest or if minor has shown pattern of abuse, prohibits court from notifying parents, guardian, or custodian, requires court of appeals to preserve minor's anonymity and confidentiality on appeal, and contains sufficient requirements for expedition of procedure. Ohio v. Akron Center for Reproductive Health (U.S.Ohio 1990) 110 S.Ct. 2972, 497 U.S. 502, 111 L.Ed.2d 405, on remand 911 F.2d 731, on remand 911 F.2d 733. Abortion And Birth Control ⇔ 1.30; Constitutional Law ⇔ 274(5)

The state need not provide counsel to a minor appealing from a juvenile court decision on parental notice, nor need it provide for an appeal to the supreme court. Akron Center for Reproductive Health v. Rosen (N.D.Ohio 1986) 633 F.Supp. 1123, amended 110 F.R.D. 576, appeal dismissed 805 F.2d 1033, appeal dismissed 805 F.2d 1036, affirmed 854 F.2d 852, probable jurisdiction noted 109 S.Ct. 3239, 492 U.S. 916, 106 L.Ed.2d 586, reversed 110 S.Ct. 2972, 497 U.S. 502, 111 L.Ed.2d 405, on remand 911 F.2d 731, on remand 911 F.2d 733.

5. Pattern of abuse

Trial court should have considered history of parental physical abuse and threats of further physical abuse in determining whether minor should be allowed to terminate her pregnancy without parental notification, even though court found that statutory criteria for abortion without parental consent on basis of minor's maturity were not satisfied, where another statutory provision contained other criteria for abortion without parental consent based on parental abuse. In re Complaint of Jane Doe (Ohio App. 10 Dist., 08-16-1994) 96 Ohio App.3d 435, 645 N.E.2d 134. Abortion And Birth Control ⇔ 0.5

Minor, who was only a matter of days from her 18th birthday, was entitled to terminate her pregnancy without parental notification, where minor graphically described horrible home life which more than justified her desire to conceal her pregnancy from her parents. In re Complaint of Jane Doe (Ohio App. 10 Dist., 08-16-1994) 96 Ohio App.3d 435, 645 N.E.2d 134. Abortion And Birth Control ⇔ 0.5

2151.86 Criminal records check; disqualification from employment

(A)(1) The appointing or hiring officer of any entity that appoints or employs any person responsible for a child's care in out-of-home care shall request the superintendent of BCII to conduct a criminal records check with respect to any person who is under final consideration for appointment or employment as a person responsible for a child's care in out-of-home care, except that section 3319.39 of the Revised Code shall apply instead of this section if the out-of-home care entity is a public school, educational service center, or chartered nonpublic school.

(2) The administrative director of an agency, or attorney, who arranges an adoption for a prospective adoptive parent shall request the superintendent of BCII to conduct a criminal records check with respect to that prospective adoptive parent and all persons eighteen years of age or older who reside with the prospective adoptive parent.

(3) Before a recommending agency submits a recommendation to the department of job and family services on whether the department should issue a certificate to a foster home under section 5103.03 of the Revised Code, the administrative director of the agency shall request that the superintendent of BCII conduct a criminal records check with respect to the prospective foster caregiver and all other persons eighteen years of age or older who reside with the foster caregiver.

(B) If a person subject to a criminal records check does not present proof that the person has been a resident of this state for the five-year period immediately prior to the date upon which the criminal records check is requested or does not provide evidence that within that five-year period the superintendent of BCII has requested information about the person from the federal bureau of investigation in a criminal records check, the appointing or hiring officer, administrative director, or attorney shall request that the superintendent of BCII obtain information from the federal bureau of investigation as a part of the criminal records check. If the person subject to the criminal records check presents proof that the person has been a resident of this state for that five-year period, the officer, director, or attorney may request that the superintendent of BCII include information from the federal bureau of investigation in the criminal records check.

An appointing or hiring officer, administrative director, or attorney required by division (A) of this section to request a criminal records check shall provide to each person subject to a criminal records check a copy of the form prescribed pursuant to division (C)(1) of section 109.572 of the Revised Code and a standard impression sheet to obtain fingerprint impressions prescribed pursuant to division (C)(2) of section 109.572 of the Revised Code, obtain the completed form and impression sheet from the person, and forward the completed form and impression sheet to the superintendent of BCII at the time the criminal records check is requested.

Any person subject to a criminal records check who receives pursuant to this division a copy of the form prescribed pursuant to division (C)(1) of section 109.572 of the Revised Code and a copy of an impression sheet prescribed pursuant to division (C)(2) of that section and who is requested to complete the form and provide a set of fingerprint impressions shall complete the form or provide all the information necessary to complete the form and shall provide the impression sheet with the impressions of the person's fingerprints. If a person subject to a criminal records check, upon request, fails to provide the information necessary to complete the form or fails to provide impressions of the person's fingerprints, the appointing or hiring officer shall not appoint or employ the person as a person responsible for a child's care in out-of-home care, a probate court may not issue a final decree of adoption or an interlocutory order of adoption making the person an adoptive parent, and the department of job and family services shall not issue a certificate authorizing the prospective foster caregiver to operate a foster home.

(C)(1) No appointing or hiring officer shall appoint or employ a person as a person responsible for a child's care in out-of-home care, the department of job and family services shall not issue a certificate under section 5103.03 of the Revised Code authorizing a prospective foster caregiver to operate a foster home, and no probate court shall issue a final decree of adoption or an interlocutory order of adoption making a person an adoptive parent if the person or, in the case of a prospective foster caregiver or prospective adoptive parent, any person eighteen years of age or older who resides with the prospective foster caregiver or prospective adoptive parent previously has been convicted of or pleaded guilty to any of the following, unless the person meets rehabilitation standards established in rules adopted under division (F) of this section:

(a) A violation of section 2903.01, 2903.02, 2903.03, 2903.04, 2903.11, 2903.12, 2903.13, 2903.16, 2903.21, 2903.34, 2905.01, 2905.02, 2905.05, 2907. 02, 2907.03, 2907.04, 2907.05, 2907.06, 2907.07, 2907.08, 2907.09, 2907.21, 2907.22, 2907.23, 2907.25, 2907.31, 2907.32, 2907.321, 2907.322, 2907.323, 2909.02, 2909.03, 2911.01, 2911.02, 2911.11, 2911.12, 2919.12, 2919.22, 2919.24, 2919.25, 2923. 12, 2923.13, 2923.161, 2925.02, 2925.03, 2925.04, 2925.05, 2925.06, or 3716.11 of the Revised Code, a violation of section 2905.04 of the Revised Code as it existed prior to July 1, 1996, a violation of section 2919.23 of the Revised Code that would have been a violation of section 2905.04 of the Revised Code as it existed prior to July 1, 1996, had the violation been committed prior to that date, a violation of section 2925.11 of the Revised Code that is not a minor drug possession offense, or felonious sexual penetration in violation of former section 2907.12 of the Revised Code;

(b) A violation of an existing or former law of this state, any other state, or the United States that is substantially equivalent to any of the offenses described in division (C)(1)(a) of this section.

(2) The appointing or hiring officer may appoint or employ a person as a person responsible for a child's care in out-of-home care conditionally until the criminal records check required by this section is completed and the officer receives the results of the criminal records check. If the results of the criminal records check indicate that, pursuant to division (C)(1) of this section, the person subject to the criminal records check does not qualify for appointment or employment, the officer shall release the person from appointment or employment.

(D) The appointing or hiring officer, administrative director, or attorney shall pay to the bureau of criminal identification and investigation the fee prescribed pursuant to division (C)(3) of section 109.572 of the Revised Code for each criminal records check conducted in accordance with that section upon a request pursuant to division (A) of this section. The officer, director, or attorney may charge the person subject to the criminal records check a fee for the costs the officer, director, or attorney incurs in obtaining the criminal records check. A fee charged under this division shall not exceed the amount of fees the officer, director, or attorney pays for the criminal records check. If a fee is charged under this division, the officer, director, or attorney shall notify the person who is the applicant at the time of the person's initial application for appointment or employment, an adoption to be arranged, or a certificate to operate a foster home of the amount of the fee and that, unless the fee is paid, the person who is the applicant will not be considered for appointment or employment or as an adoptive parent or foster caregiver.

(E) The report of any criminal records check conducted by the bureau of criminal identification and investigation in accordance with section 109.572 of the Revised Code and pursuant to a request made under division (A) of this section is not a public record for the purposes of section 149.43 of the Revised Code and shall not be made available to any person other than the person who is the subject of the criminal records check or the person's representative; the appointing or hiring officer, administrative director, or attorney requesting the criminal records check or the officer's, director's, or attorney's representative; the department of job and family services or a county department of job and family services; and any court, hearing officer, or other necessary individual involved in a case dealing with the denial of employment, a final decree of adoption or interlocutory order of adoption, or a foster home certificate.

(F) The director of job and family services shall adopt rules in accordance with Chapter 119. of the Revised Code to implement this section. The rules shall include rehabilitation standards a person who has been convicted of or pleaded guilty to an offense listed in division (C)(1) of this section must meet for an appointing or hiring officer to appoint or employ the person as a person responsible for a child's care in out-of-home care, a probate court to issue a final decree of adoption or interlocutory order of adoption making the person an adoptive parent, or the department to issue a certificate authorizing the prospective foster caregiver to operate a foster home.

(G) An appointing or hiring officer, administrative director, or attorney required by division (A) of this section to request a criminal records check shall inform each person who is the applicant, at the time of the person's initial application for appointment or employment, an adoption to be arranged, or a foster home certificate, that the person subject to the criminal records check is required to provide a set of impressions of the person's fingerprints and that a criminal records check is required to be conducted and satisfactorily completed in accordance with section 109.572 of the Revised Code.

(H) The department of job and family services may waive the requirement that a criminal records check based on fingerprints be conducted for an adult resident of a prospective adoptive or foster home or the home of a foster caregiver if the recommending agency documents to the department's satisfaction that the adult resident is physically unable to comply with the fingerprinting requirement and poses no danger to foster children or adoptive children who may be placed in the home. In such cases, the recommending or approving agency shall request that the bureau of criminal identification and investigation conduct a criminal records check using the person's name and social security number.

(I) As used in this section:

(1) "Children's hospital" means any of the following:

(a) A hospital registered under section 3701.07 of the Revised Code that provides general pediatric medical and surgical care, and in which at least seventy-five per cent of annual inpatient discharges for the preceding two calendar years were individuals less than eighteen years of age;

(b) A distinct portion of a hospital registered under section 3701.07 of the Revised Code that provides general pediatric medical and surgical care, has a total of at least one hundred fifty registered pediatric special care and pediatric acute care beds, and in which at least seventy-five per cent of annual inpatient discharges for the preceding two calendar years were individuals less than eighteen years of age;

(c) A distinct portion of a hospital, if the hospital is registered under section 3701.07 of the Revised Code as a children's hospital and the children's hospital meets all the requirements of division (I)(3)(a) of this section.

(2) "Criminal records check" has the same meaning as in section 109.572 of the Revised Code.

(3) "Minor drug possession offense" has the same meaning as in section 2925.01 of the Revised Code.

(4) "Person responsible for a child's care in out-of-home care" has the same meaning as in section 2151.011 of the Revised Code, except that it does not include a prospective employee of the department of youth services or a person responsible for a child's care in a hospital or medical clinic other than a children's hospital.

(5) "Person subject to a criminal records check" means the following:

(a) A person who is under final consideration for appointment or employment as a person responsible for a child's care in out-of-home care;

(b) A prospective adoptive parent;

(c) A prospective foster caregiver;

(d) A person eighteen years old or older who resides with a prospective foster caregiver or a prospective adoptive parent.

(6) "Recommending agency" means a public children services agency, private child placing agency, or private noncustodial agency to which the department of job and family services has delegated a duty to inspect and approve foster homes.

(7) "Superintendent of BCII" means the superintendent of the bureau of criminal identification and investigation.

(2004 H 106, eff. 9–16–04; 2004 H 117, eff. 9–3–04; 2000 H 448, eff. 10–5–00; 1999 H 471, eff. 7–1–00; 1998 H 446, eff. 8–5–98; 1996 S 269, eff. 7–1–96; 1996 H 445, eff. 9–3–96; 1995 S 2, eff. 7–1–96; 1993 S 38, eff. 10–29–93)

Uncodified Law

1993 S 38, § 3, eff. 10–29–93, reads: Sections 3301.54, 5104.09, and 5126.28 of the Revised Code, as amended by this act, and sections 109.572, 2151.86, 3301.32, 3301.541, 3319.39, 3701.881, 5104.012, 5104.013, and 5153.111 of the Revised Code, as enacted by this act, apply only to persons who apply for employment for a position on or after the effective date of this act.

Historical and Statutory Notes

Ed. Note: The legal review and technical services staff of the Legislative Service Commission has issued an opinion regarding the treatment of multiple amendments [2004 H 106, eff. 9–16–04 and 2004 H 117, eff. 9–3–04] under R.C. 1.52. The opinions are neither legally authoritative nor binding, but are provided as a general indication that the amendments of the several acts [2004 H 106, eff. 9–16–04 and 2004 H 117, eff. 9–3–04] may be included pursuant to the R.C. 1.52(B) rule of construction which requires all the amendments to be given effect if they can reasonably be put into simultaneous operation. See *Baldwin's Ohio Legislative Service Annotated*, 2004, pages 5/L–1034 and 5/L–733, or the OH-LEGIS or OH-LEGIS-OLD database on Westlaw, for original versions of these Acts.

Amendment Note: 2004 H 106, eff. 9–16–04, inserted ", except that section 3319.39 of the Revised Code shall apply instead of this section if the out-of-home care entity is a public school, educational service center, or chartered nonpublic school" in division (A)(1).

Amendment Note: 2004 H 117 inserted "and all persons eighteen years of age or older who reside with the prospective adoptive parent" in division (A)(2); inserted ", the department of job and family services shall not issue a certificate under section 5103.03 of the Revised Code authorizing a prospective foster caregiver to operate a foster home," and "or, in the case of a prospective foster caregiver or prospective adoptive parent, any person eighteen years of age or older who resides with the prospective foster caregiver or prospective adoptive parent" in division (C)(1); inserted "2909.02, 2909.03" in division (C)(1)(a); deleted division (C)(2) through (C)(2)(b); deleted the paragraph designation in division (C)(3); deleted "or (2)" in division (F); added division (H); designated division (I); substituted "(I)" for "(H)" in newly division (I)(c); and inserted "or a prospective adoptive parent" in division (I)(5)(d). Prior to amendment, deleted division (C)(2) through (C)(2)(b) read:

"(2) The department of job and family services shall not issue a certificate under section 5103.03 of the Revised Code authorizing a prospective foster caregiver to operate a foster home if the department has been notified that the foster caregiver or any person eighteen years of age or older who resides with the foster caregiver has been convicted of or pleaded guilty to a violation of one of the following offenses, unless the foster caregiver or other person meets rehabilitation standards established in rules adopted under division (F) of this section:

"(a) Any offense listed in division (C)(1)(a) of this section or section 2909.02 or 2909.03 of the Revised Code;

"(b) An existing or former law of this state, any other state, or the United States that is substantially equivalent to any offense listed in division (C)(1)(a) of this section or section 2909.02 or 2909.03 of the Revised Code."

Amendment Note: 2000 H 448 rewrote this section, which prior thereto read:

"(A)(1) The appointing or hiring officer of any entity that employs any person responsible for a child's care in out-of-home care shall request the superintendent of the bureau of criminal identification and investigation to conduct a criminal records check with respect to any applicant who has applied to the entity for employment as a person responsible for a child's care in out-of-home care. The administrative director of any entity that designates a person as a prospective adoptive parent or as a prospective foster parent shall request the superintendent to conduct a criminal records check with respect to that person. If the applicant, prospective adoptive parent, or prospective foster parent does not present proof that the applicant or prospective adoptive or foster parent has been a resident of this state for the five-year period immediately prior to the date upon which the criminal records check is requested or does not provide evidence that within that five-year period the superintendent has requested information about the applicant or prospective adoptive or foster parent from the federal bureau of investigation in a criminal records check, the appointing or hiring officer or administrative director shall request that the superintendent obtain information from the federal bureau of investigation as a part of the criminal records check. If the applicant, prospective adoptive parent, or prospective foster parent presents proof that the applicant or prospective adoptive or foster parent has been a resident of this state for that five-year period, the appointing or hiring officer or administrator may request that the superintendent include information from the federal bureau of investigation in the criminal records check.

"(2) Any person required by division (A)(1) of this section to request a criminal records check shall provide to each applicant, prospective adoptive parent, or prospective foster parent a copy of the form prescribed pursuant to division (C)(1) of section 109.572 of the Revised Code and a standard impression sheet to obtain fingerprint impressions prescribed pursuant to division (C)(2) of section 109.572 of the Revised Code, obtain the completed form and impression sheet from each applicant, prospective adoptive parent, or prospective foster parent, and forward the completed form and impression sheet to the superintendent of the bureau of criminal identification and investigation at the time the person requests a criminal records check pursuant to division (A)(1) of this section.

"(3) Any applicant, prospective adoptive parent, or prospective foster parent who receives pursuant to division (A)(2) of this section a copy of the form prescribed pursuant to division (C)(1) of section 109.572 of the Revised Code and a copy of an impression sheet prescribed pursuant to division (C)(2) of that section and who is requested to complete the form and provide a set of fingerprint impressions shall complete the form or provide all the information necessary to complete the form and shall provide the impression sheet with the impressions of the applicant's or prospective adoptive or foster parent's fingerprints. If an applicant, prospective adoptive parent, or prospective foster parent, upon request, fails to provide the information necessary to complete the form or fails to provide impressions of the applicant's or prospective adoptive or foster parent's fingerprints, the entity shall not employ that applicant for any position for which a criminal records check is required by division (A)(1) of this section and shall not consider the prospective adoptive parent or prospective foster parent as an adoptive parent or foster parent.

"(B)(1) No entity shall employ a person as a person responsible for a child's care in out-of-home care or permit a person to become an adoptive parent or foster parent if the person previously has been convicted of or pleaded guilty to any of the following, unless the person meets rehabilitation standards established in rules adopted under division (E) of this section:

"(a) A violation of section 2903.01, 2903.02, 2903.03, 2903.04, 2903.11, 2903.12, 2903.13, 2903.16, 2903.21, 2903.34, 2905.01, 2905.02, 2905.05, 2907.02, 2907.03, 2907.04, 2907.05, 2907.06, 2907.07, 2907.08, 2907.09, 2907.21, 2907.22, 2907.23, 2907.25, 2907.31, 2907.32, 2907.321, 2907.322, 2907.323, 2911.01, 2911.02, 2911.11, 2911.12, 2919.12, 2919.22, 2919.24, 2919.25, 2923.12, 2923.13, 2923.161, 2925.02, 2925.03, 2925.04, 2925.05, 2925.06, or 3716.11 of the Revised Code, a violation of section 2905.04 of the Revised Code as it existed prior to July 1, 1996, a violation of section 2919.23 of the Revised Code that would have been a violation of section 2905.04 of the Revised Code as it existed prior to July 1, 1996, had the violation been committed prior to that date, a violation of section 2925.11 of the Revised Code that is not a minor drug possession offense, or felonious sexual penetration in violation of former section 2907.12 of the Revised Code;

"(b) A violation of an existing or former law of this state, any other state, or the United States that is substantially equivalent to any of the offenses described in division (B)(1)(a) of this section.

"(2) An out-of-home care entity may employ an applicant conditionally until the criminal records check required by this section is completed and the entity receives the results of the criminal records check. If the results of the criminal records check indicate that, pursuant to division (B)(1) of this section, the applicant does not qualify for employment, the entity shall release the applicant from employment.

"(C)(1) The out-of-home care entity shall pay to the bureau of criminal identification and investigation the fee prescribed pursuant to division (C)(3) of section 109.572 of the Revised Code for each criminal records check conducted in accordance with that section upon a request pursuant to division (A)(1) of this section.

"(2) An out-of-home care entity may charge an applicant, prospective adoptive parent, or prospective foster parent a fee for the costs it incurs in obtaining a criminal records check under this section. A fee charged under this division shall not exceed the amount of fees the entity pays under division (C)(1) of this section. If a fee is charged under this division, the entity shall notify the applicant, prospective adoptive parent, or prospective foster parent at the time of the person's initial application for employment or for becoming an adoptive parent or foster parent of the amount of the fee and that, unless the fee is paid, the entity will not consider the person for employment or as an adoptive parent or foster parent.

"(D) The report of any criminal records check conducted by the bureau of criminal identification and investigation in accordance with section 109.572 of the Revised Code and pursuant to a request made under division (A)(1) of this section is not a public record for the purposes of section 149.43 of the Revised Code and shall not be made available to any person other than the applicant, prospective adoptive parent, or prospective foster parent who is the subject of the criminal records check or the applicant's or prospective adoptive or foster parent's representative; the entity requesting the criminal records check or its representative; the department of job and family services or a county department of job and family services; and any court, hearing officer, or other necessary individual involved in a case dealing with the denial of employment to the applicant or the denial of consideration as an adoptive parent or foster parent.

"(E) The director of job and family services shall adopt rules pursuant to Chapter 119. of the Revised Code to implement this section. The rules shall include rehabilitation standards a person who has been convicted of or pleaded guilty to an offense listed in division (B)(1) of this section must meet for an entity to employ the person as a person responsible for a child's care in out-of-home care or permit the person to become an adoptive parent or foster parent.

"(F) Any person required by division (A)(1) of this section to request a criminal records check shall inform each person, at the time of the person's initial application for employment with an entity as a person responsible for a child's care in out-of-home care or the person's initial application for becoming an adoptive parent or foster parent, that the person is required to provide a set of impressions of the person's fingerprints and that a criminal records check is required to be conducted and satisfactorily completed in accordance with section 109.572 of the Revised Code if the person comes under final consideration for appointment or employment as a precondition to employment for that position or if the person is to be given final consideration as an adoptive parent or foster parent.

"(G) As used in this section:

"(1) 'Applicant' means a person who is under final consideration for appointment or employment as a person responsible for a child's care in out-of-home care.

"(2) 'Person responsible for a child's care in out-of-home care' has the same meaning as in section 2151.011 of the Revised Code, except that it does not include a prospective employee of the department of youth services or a person responsible for a child's care in a hospital or medical clinic other than a children's hospital.

"(3) 'Children's hospital' means any of the following:

"(a) A hospital registered under section 3701.07 of the Revised Code that provides general pediatric medical and surgical care, and in which at least seventy-five per cent of annual inpatient discharges for the preceding two calendar years were individuals less than eighteen years of age;

"(b) A distinct portion of a hospital registered under section 3701.07 of the Revised Code that provides general pediatric medical and surgical care, has a total of at least one hundred fifty registered pediatric special care and pediatric acute care beds, and in which at least seventy-five per cent of annual inpatient discharges for the preceding two calendar years were individuals less than eighteen years of age;

"(c) A distinct portion of a hospital, if the hospital is registered under section 3701.07 of the Revised Code as a children's hospital and the children's hospital meets all the requirements of division (G)(3)(a) of this section.

"(4) 'Criminal records check' has the same meaning as in section 109.572 of the Revised Code.

"(5) 'Minor drug possession offense' has the same meaning as in section 2925.01 of the Revised Code."

Amendment Note: 1999 H 471 substituted "department of job and family services or a county department of job and family services" for "state department of human services or a county department of human services" in division (D); and substituted "director of job and family services" for "department of human services" in division (E).

Amendment Note: 1998 H 446 rewrote the first paragraph in division (B)(1) and division (E), which prior thereto read:

"(B)(1) Except as provided in rules adopted by the department of human services in accordance with division (E) of this section, no entity shall employ a person as a person responsible for a child's care in out-of-home care or permit a person to become an adoptive parent or foster parent if the person previously has been convicted of or pleaded guilty to any of the following:"

"(E) The department of human services shall adopt rules pursuant to Chapter 119. of the Revised Code to implement this section, including rules specifying circumstances under which an out-of-home care entity may hire a person who has been convicted of an offense listed in division (B)(1) of this section but who meets standards in regard to rehabilitation set by the department."

Amendment Note: 1996 S 269 deleted a statutory reference to section "2905.04," following "2905.02," and inserted "a violation of section 2905.04 of the Revised Code as it existed prior to July 1, 1996, a violation of section 2919.23 of the Revised Code that would have been a violation of section 2905.04 of the Revised Code as it existed prior to July 1, 1996, had the violation been committed prior to that date," in division (B)(1)(a).

Amendment Note: 1996 H 445 substituted "the entity shall not employ that applicant for any position for which a criminal records check is required by division (A)(1) of this section and shall not consider the prospective adoptive parent or prospective foster parent as an adoptive parent or foster parent" for "that applicant or prospective adoptive or foster parent shall not be employed for any position for which a criminal records check is required by division (A)(1) of this section or be considered as a prospective adoptive parent or prospective foster parent" in division (A)(3); removed a reference to section 2907.12 from, and inserted "or felonious sexual penetration in violation of former section 2907.12 of the Revised Code" in, division (B)(1)(a); and made other nonsubstantive changes.

Amendment Note: 1995 S 2 inserted "2925.04, 2925.05, 2925.06," and "or a violation of section 2925.11 of the Revised Code that is not a minor drug possession offense" in division (B)(1)(a); added division (G)(5); and made changes to reflect gender neutral language and other nonsubstantive changes.

Cross References

Adoption, issuance of final decree or interlocutory order, 3107.14
Application for adoption by foster caregiver seeking to adopt foster child, 3107.012
Crisis care facilities, 5103.13
Requests for criminal records checks by criminal identification and investigation bureau, 109.57

Ohio Administrative Code References

Application for professional certification, OAC 5101:2–14–02
Definitions, criminal records check, OAC 5101:2–14–01
General requirements for initial application for child placement, OAC 5101:2–7–02
Limited certification, OAC 5101:2–14–55 et seq.
Offenses which disqualify persons from being a certified child care provider, an emergency caregiver or substitute caregiver, OAC 5101:2–14–11
Personnel and prohibited convictions for employment, OAC 5101:2–5–09
Personnel, OAC 5139–35–05, 5139–37–05
Personnel and prohibited convictions for employment, OAC 5101:2–5–09
Restrictions concerning provision of adoption services, OAC 5101:2–48–10

Library References

Criminal Law ⚖1226(2).
Infants ⚖17, 17.5, 226.
Westlaw Topic Nos. 110, 211.
C.J.S. Adoption of Persons § 10.
C.J.S. Criminal Law § 1734.
C.J.S. Infants §§ 8 to 9, 57, 70 to 77.

Research References

Encyclopedias

OH Jur. 3d Criminal Law § 673, Filing Identification Information.
OH Jur. 3d Criminal Law § 678, Entities Responsible for Care of Children.
OH Jur. 3d Family Law § 928, Investigation.
OH Jur. 3d Family Law § 1413, Care of Dependent, Neglected, or Delinquent Children.
OH Jur. 3d Family Law § 1417, Criteria for Private Placement.
OH Jur. 3d Family Law § 1467, Criminal Records Check for Employees.
OH Jur. 3d Schools, Universities, & Colleges § 107, Failure of Board to Fill Vacancy or to Perform Other Duties; Criminal Records Check.

Treatises and Practice Aids

Carlin, Baldwin's Ohio Practice, Merrick-Rippner Probate Law § 98:12, Adoption—Suitability of Adoptive Parents—Regulation of Persons With Criminal Record.
Carlin, Baldwin's Ohio Practice, Merrick-Rippner Probate Law § 107:76, Disposition of Abused, Neglected, or Dependent Child—Types of Orders Court May Make.
Adrine & Ruden, Ohio Domestic Violence Law § 7:12, Collateral Effects of a Guilty Plea or of Being Found Guilty—Employment.

Law Review and Journal Commentaries

The Liberty Interests of Foster Parents and the Future of Foster Care, Comment. 63 U Cin L Rev 403 (1994).

2151.861 Random sampling of registered child day camps; effect of noncompliance relating to criminal records check

(A) The department of job and family services may periodically conduct a random sampling of registered child day camps to determine compliance with section 2151.86 of the Revised Code.

(B)(1) No child day camp shall fail to comply with section 2151.86 of the Revised Code in regards to a person it appoints or employs.

(2) If the department determines that a child day camp has violated division (B)(1) of this section, the department shall do both of the following:

(a) Consider imposing a civil penalty on the child day camp in an amount that shall not exceed ten per cent of the camp's gross revenues for the full month immediately preceding the month in which the violation occurred. If the camp was not operating for the entire calendar month preceding the month in which the violation occurred, the penalty shall be five hundred dollars.

(b) Order the child day camp to initiate a criminal records check of the person who is the subject of the violation within a specified period of time.

(3) If, within the specified period of time, the child day camp fails to comply with an order to initiate a criminal records check of the person who is the subject of the violation or to release the person from the appointment or employment, the department shall do both of the following:

(a) Impose a civil penalty in an amount not less than the amount previously imposed and that shall not exceed twice the amount permitted by division (B)(2)(a) of this section;

(b) Order the child day camp to initiate a criminal records check of the person who is the subject of the violation within a specified period of time.

(C) If the department determines that a child day camp has violated division (B)(1) of this section, the department may post a notice at a prominent place at the camp that states that the camp has failed to conduct criminal records checks of its appointees or employees as required by section 2151.86 of the Revised Code. Once the camp demonstrates to the department that the camp is in compliance with that section, the department shall permit the camp to remove the notice.

(D) The department shall include on the department's web site a list of child day camps that the department has determined from a random sample to be not in compliance with the criminal records check requirements of section 2151.86 of the Revised Code. The department shall remove a camp's name from the list when the camp demonstrates to the department that the camp is in compliance with that section.

(E) For the purposes of divisions (C) and (D) of this section, a child day camp will be considered to be in compliance with section 2151.86 of the Revised Code by doing any of the following:

(1) Requesting that the bureau of criminal identification and investigation conduct a criminal records check regarding the person who is the subject of the violation of division (B)(1) of this section and, if the person does not qualify for the appointment or employment, releasing the person from the appointment or employment;

(2) Releasing the person who is the subject of the violation from the appointment or employment.

(F) The attorney general shall commence and prosecute to judgment a civil action in a court of competent jurisdiction to collect any civil penalty imposed under this section that remains unpaid.

(G) A child day camp may appeal any action the department takes under divisions (B) to (D) of this section to the court of common pleas of the county in which the camp is located.

(2004 H 11, eff. 5–18–05)

Library References

Infants ⟸13.
Westlaw Topic No. 211.
C.J.S. Infants §§ 5, 92 to 93.

Research References

Encyclopedias
OH Jur. 3d Family Law § 1408, Statutory Protection of Minors.
OH Jur. 3d Family Law § 1487, "Delinquent Child".
OH Jur. 3d Family Law § 1489, "Unruly Child".

Forms
Ohio Jurisprudence Pleading and Practice Forms § 2:8, Courts of Common Pleas—Juvenile Division.

Treatises and Practice Aids
Katz, Giannelli, Blair and Lipton, Baldwin's Ohio Practice, Criminal Law, § 113:3, Illegal Cigarettes.
Carlin, Baldwin's Ohio Practice, Merrick-Rippner Probate Law § 105:1, Juvenile Court—Exclusive Original Jurisdiction.
Carlin, Baldwin's Ohio Practice, Merrick-Rippner Probate Law § 106:1, Juvenile Court Jurisdiction—Delinquent Child—Definition: Evidence of Delinquency.
Carlin, Baldwin's Ohio Practice, Merrick-Rippner Probate Law § 106:8, Juvenile Court Jurisdiction—Unruly Child—Definition: Evidence of Unruliness.
Carlin, Baldwin's Ohio Practice, Merrick-Rippner Probate Law § 106:25, Tobacco Use by Child.
Giannelli & Yeomans, Ohio Juvenile Law § 8:2, Unruly Child Defined.
Giannelli & Yeomans, Ohio Juvenile Law § 8:6, Unruly—Status Offenses.

PENALTIES

2151.99 Penalties

(A)(1) Except as otherwise provided in division (A)(2) of this section, whoever violates division (D)(2) or (3) of section 2151.313 or division, (A)(4), (H)(2)[1] of section 2151.421 of the Revised Code is guilty of a misdemeanor of the fourth degree.

(2) Whoever violates division (A)(4) of section 2151.421 of the Revised Code knowing that a child has been abused or neglected and knowing that the person who committed the abuse or neglect was a cleric or another person, other than a volunteer, designated by a church, religious society, or faith acting as a leader, official, or delegate on behalf of the church, religious society, or faith, is guilty of a misdemeanor of the first degree if the person who violates division (A)(4) of this section and the person who committed the abuse or neglect belong to the same church, religious society, or faith.

(B) Whoever violates division (D)(1) of section 2151.313 of the Revised Code is guilty of a minor misdemeanor.

(C) Whoever violates division (A)(1) of section 2151.421 of the Revised Code shall be punished as follows:

(1) Except as otherwise provided in division (C)(2) of this section, the offender is guilty of a misdemeanor of the fourth degree.

(2) The offender is guilty of a misdemeanor of the first degree if the child who is the subject of the required report that the offender fails to make suffers or faces the threat of suffering the physical or mental wound, injury, disability, or condition that

would be the basis of the required report when the child is under the direct care or supervision of the offender who is then acting in the offender's official or professional capacity or when the child is under the direct care or supervision of another person over whom the offender while acting in the offender's official or professional capacity has supervisory control.

(2006 S 137, eff. 3–30–07; 2006 S 17, eff. 8–3–06; 2000 S 179, § 3, eff. 1–1–02; 1998 H 173, eff. 7–29–98; 1989 H 257, eff. 8–3–89; 1986 H 529; 1985 H 349; 1984 H 258; 1972 H 511; 1969 H 320; 130 v H 765; 1953 H 1)

¹ Language appears as the result of the harmonization of 2006 S 137 and 2006 S 17.

Uncodified Law

2006 S 17 § 5: See Uncodified Law under RC 2151.03.

Historical and Statutory Notes

Ed. Note: Comparison of these amendments [2006 S 137, eff. 3–30–07 and 2006 S 17, eff. 8–3–06] in pursuance of section 1.52 of the Revised Code discloses that they are not irreconcilable so that they are required by that section to be harmonized to give effect to each amendment. In recognition of this rule of construction, changes made by 2006 S 137, eff. 3–30–07, and 2006 S 17, eff. 8–3–06, have been incorporated in the above amendment. See *Baldwin's Ohio Legislative Service Annotated*, 2006, pages 7/L–2769 and 2/L–1137, or the OH–LEGIS or OH–LEGIS–OLD database on Westlaw, for original versions of these Acts.

Amendment Note: 2006 S 17 rewrote division (A), which prior thereto read:

"(A) Whoever violates division (D)(2) or (3) of section 2151.313 or division (A)(1) or (H)(2) of section 2151.421 of the Revised Code is guilty of a misdemeanor of the fourth degree."

Amendment Note: 2000 S 179, § 3, eff. 1–1–02, deleted former division (C), which read:

"(C) Whoever violates division (C) of section 2151.62 of the Revised Code is guilty of a minor misdemeanor."

Amendment Note: 1998 H 173 added division (C).

Cross References

Imposing sentence for misdemeanor, 2929.22
Judges of the court of domestic relations, juvenile court responsibility, 2301.03
Penalties for misdemeanor, 2929.21

Library References

Infants ⚖13, 13.5(2), 17.
Municipal Corporations ⚖190.
Westlaw Topic Nos. 211, 268.
C.J.S. Infants §§ 5, 8 to 9, 92 to 93.
C.J.S. Municipal Corporations §§ 450 to 453, 474 to 476, 503, 505, 508.

Research References

Encyclopedias

OH Jur. 3d Family Law § 1476, Confidentiality.
OH Jur. 3d Family Law § 1572, Fingerprints and Photographs of Children.
OH Jur. 3d Family Law § 1736, Adult Acts Punishable in Juvenile Court—Failure to Report Child Abuse.
OH Jur. 3d Family Law § 1737, Adult Acts Punishable in Juvenile Court—Failure to Follow Procedures for Fingerprinting and Photographing Children Involved in Crimes.
OH Jur. 3d Family Law § 1749, Sentence and Punishment.
OH Jur. 3d Government Tort Liability § 31, Defenses or Immunities of Subdivision and Employee.
OH Jur. 3d Government Tort Liability § 44, Statutory Liability.

Treatises and Practice Aids

Carlin, Baldwin's Ohio Practice, Merrick-Rippner Probate Law § 108:1, Juvenile Court—Criminal Jurisdiction.
Carlin, Baldwin's Ohio Practice, Merrick-Rippner Probate Law § 108:9, Juvenile Court—Criminal Jurisdiction—Assignment of Case for Disposition.
Carlin, Baldwin's Ohio Practice, Merrick-Rippner Probate Law § 107:24, Use and Release of Juvenile Records.
Carlin, Baldwin's Ohio Practice, Merrick-Rippner Probate Law § 107:114, Juvenile Court Records—Confidentiality.
Giannelli & Yeomans, Ohio Juvenile Law § 14:15, Fingerprints & Photographs.
Hastings, Manoloff, Sheeran, & Stype, Ohio School Law § 24:9, Duty to Report Suspected Child Abuse or Neglect-In General.

Law Review and Journal Commentaries

Deal swiftly with sexual misconduct, Cheryl Thorpe Maimona. 40 Ohio Sch Boards Ass'n J 2 (February 1996).

Notes of Decisions

Ability to pay 3
Constitutional issues 1
Liability imposed 4
Probation conditions 2

---

1. Constitutional issues

RC 2151.99 is constitutional. State v. Ducey (Franklin 1970) 25 Ohio App.2d 50, 266 N.E.2d 233, 54 O.O.2d 80.

2. Probation conditions

Where the jurisdiction of the juvenile court has been invoked by the arrest of a father of minor children upon a charge of nonsupport filed by the mother, and upon trial the father pleads guilty and is sentenced, which sentence is suspended and the defendant put on probation, the condition of the probation being that the defendant will pay a specified sum weekly for support, the minor children thereby become wards of the juvenile court and the subject of their support and the power to enforce the condition of probation is exclusively in that court until each child has reached the age of eighteen years, so that if the mother thereafter files a petition for divorce in the common pleas court and a divorce is granted to her, the common pleas court is without jurisdiction to deal with the custody and support of the minor children or to entertain an action filed by the mother against the father for alleged delinquencies in the weekly payments ordered as a condition of probation by the juvenile court, and the manner of enforcing such order of the juvenile court is to seek, by motion filed in the juvenile court, a revocation of the order of probation and to enforce against him the penalty of the judgment. Anderson v. Anderson (Cuyahoga 1965) 4 Ohio App.2d 90, 212 N.E.2d 643, 33 O.O.2d 145.

3. Ability to pay

Only that class of persons capable of paying support money, but failing to do so, may be prosecuted under RC 2151.42 and RC 2151.99. State v. Ducey (Franklin 1970) 25 Ohio App.2d 50, 266 N.E.2d 233, 54 O.O.2d 80.

Judge of juvenile court may not commit child who has been found to be delinquent child, or juvenile traffic offender, to county jail upon failure, refusal, or inability of such child to pay fine and court costs. OAG 70–143.

4. Liability imposed

Statute mandating the reporting of known or suspected child abuse, through its criminal penalty for failure to report, "expressly imposes liability," within meaning of Political Subdivision Tort Liability Act provisions creating exceptions from sovereign immunity of political subdivisions and their employees if the Revised Code expressly imposes liability. Campbell v. Burton (Ohio, 07-25-2001) 92 Ohio St.3d 336, 750 N.E.2d 539, 2001-Ohio-206. Municipal Corporations ⚖ 727

CHAPTER 2152

JUVENILE COURTS—CRIMINAL PROVISIONS

GENERAL PROVISIONS

Section	
2152.01	Purposes; applicability of law
2152.02	Definitions
2152.021	Complaint; indictment
2152.03	Transfer of cases to juvenile court
2152.04	Social histories of delinquent children

DISPOSITIONAL ORDERS

2152.10	Mandatory transfer; discretionary transfer
2152.11	More restrictive dispositions for commission of enhanced acts
2152.12	Transfer of cases from juvenile court
2152.13	Serious youthful offender dispositional sentence
2152.14	Invoking adult portion of sentence
2152.16	Commitment of delinquent children to custody of youth services department
2152.17	Felony specifications
2152.18	Place and duration of institutionalization; records; notice to schools and victims
2152.19	Additional disposition orders for delinquent children
2152.191	Application of certain sections of Revised Code to child adjudicated a delinquent child for committing sexually oriented offense
2152.192	Court or child welfare agency to notify institution or association of adjudication of child as delinquent for committing sexually oriented offense
2152.20	Fines; costs; restitution; forfeitures
2152.20	Fines; costs; restitution; forfeitures (later effective date)
2152.201	Recovery of costs where offense constitutes act of terrorism
2152.202	Recovery of costs from juvenile drug abuse offenders
2152.21	Disposition of juvenile traffic offender
2152.22	Relinquishment of juvenile court control; judicial release

PLACE OF DETENTION

2152.26	Delinquent child or juvenile traffic offender to be held only in specified places

DETENTION FACILITIES

2152.41	Juvenile detention facility
2152.42	Superintendents of facilities
2152.43	Assistance in operation of facilities from department of youth services; tax assessment
2152.44	District detention facility trustees

ORDERS RESTRAINING PARENTS

2152.61	Orders restraining parents, guardians, or custodians

JURY TRIALS

2152.67	Jury trial; procedure

MISCELLANEOUS PROVISIONS

2152.71	Records and reports; statistical summaries
2152.72	Information provided to foster caregivers or prospective adoptive parents regarding delinquent children; psychological examination
2152.73	Court participation in delinquency prevention activities
2152.74	DNA specimen collected from juvenile adjudged delinquent

SEX OFFENSES

2152.81	Deposition of child sex offense victim

JUVENILE OFFENDER REGISTRANTS

2152.811	Child adjudicated a child delinquent for committing a sexually oriented offense
2152.82	Juvenile offender registrant
2152.821	Testimony of mentally retarded or developmentally disabled victim
2152.83	Order classifying child as juvenile offender registrant; hearing to review effectiveness of disposition and treatment
2152.84	Hearings; orders
2152.85	Petitioning of judge by juvenile offender registrant
2152.851	Effect of redesignation of offense on existing order

PENALTIES

2152.99	Penalties

GENERAL PROVISIONS

Uncodified Law

2000 S 179, § 10, eff. 4–9–01, reads:

The General Assembly hereby states its intention to do the following in the remainder of the 123rd General Assembly and in the 124th General Assembly:

(A) Address the issue of competency in juvenile proceedings and its various aspects;

(B) Review and continue to support the RECLAIM Ohio program and the alternative schools program;

(C) Review and address the anticipated costs of implementing this act.

Cross References

Corrupt activity, engaging in pattern of, penalties not limited, 2923.32, 2923.34

2152.01 Purposes; applicability of law

(A) The overriding purposes for dispositions under this chapter are to provide for the care, protection, and mental and physical development of children subject to this chapter, protect the public interest and safety, hold the offender accountable for the offender's actions, restore the victim, and rehabilitate the offender. These purposes shall be achieved by a system of graduated sanctions and services.

(B) Dispositions under this chapter shall be reasonably calculated to achieve the overriding purposes set forth in this section, commensurate with and not demeaning to the seriousness of the delinquent child's or the juvenile traffic offender's conduct and its impact on the victim, and consistent with dispositions for similar acts committed by similar delinquent children and juvenile traffic offenders. The court shall not base the disposition on the race, ethnic background, gender, or religion of the delinquent child or juvenile traffic offender.

(C) To the extent they do not conflict with this chapter, the provisions of Chapter 2151. of the Revised Code apply to the proceedings under this chapter.

(2000 S 179, § 3, eff. 1–1–02)

Cross References

Judges of the divisions of domestic relations, 2301.03

Library References

Infants ⚖68.2, 132.
Westlaw Topic No. 211.
C.J.S. Infants §§ 32, 41, 198 to 207.

Research References

Encyclopedias

OH Jur. 3d Family Law § 1527, Attitude as to Juvenile Offenses.

OH Jur. 3d Family Law § 1531, Construction of Statutes.

Treatises and Practice Aids

Katz, Giannelli, Blair and Lipton, Baldwin's Ohio Practice, Criminal Law, § 128:2, Transfer to Criminal Courts.

Carlin, Baldwin's Ohio Practice, Merrick-Rippner Probate Law § 104:3, Juvenile Court—Purpose and Function.

Carlin, Baldwin's Ohio Practice, Merrick-Rippner Probate Law § 105:8, Juvenile Court—Age Jurisdiction.

Carlin, Baldwin's Ohio Practice, Merrick-Rippner Probate Law § 105:9, Juvenile Court—Waiver of Jurisdiction.

Carlin, Baldwin's Ohio Practice, Merrick-Rippner Probate Law § 106:4, Juvenile Court Jurisdiction—Delinquent Child—Non-Criminal Nature of Delinquency Proceedings.

Carlin, Baldwin's Ohio Practice, Merrick-Rippner Probate Law § 107:73, Alternatives for Disposition of Juvenile Cases.

Carlin, Baldwin's Ohio Practice, Merrick-Rippner Probate Law § 107:84, Disposition of Delinquent Children—Prior to January 1, 2002.

Carlin, Baldwin's Ohio Practice, Merrick-Rippner Probate Law § 107:85, Disposition of Delinquent Children—Mandatory Dispositions—Prior to January 1, 2002.

Carlin, Baldwin's Ohio Practice, Merrick-Rippner Probate Law § 107:86, Disposition of Delinquent Children—Previous Convictions—Prior to January 1, 2002.

Carlin, Baldwin's Ohio Practice, Merrick-Rippner Probate Law § 107:87, Disposition of Delinquent Children—Further Disposition of Delinquent Children—Prior to January 1, 2002.

Carlin, Baldwin's Ohio Practice, Merrick-Rippner Probate Law § 107:89, Custody of Department of Youth Services.

Carlin, Baldwin's Ohio Practice, Merrick-Rippner Probate Law § 107:102, Serious Youthful Offenders, Effective January 1, 2002.

Giannelli & Yeomans, Ohio Juvenile Law § 1:7, Juvenile Code.

Giannelli & Yeomans, Ohio Juvenile Law § 4:1, Introduction.

Giannelli & Yeomans, Ohio Juvenile Law § 5:8, Discretionary Syo Dispositions.

Giannelli & Yeomans, Ohio Juvenile Law § 22:8, Discretionary Transfer.

Giannelli & Yeomans, Ohio Juvenile Law § 27:3, Department of Youth Services Commitment.

Notes of Decisions

Constitutional issues 1
Polygraph test 2

1. Constitutional issues

Rational basis existed for treating juvenile and adult offenders differently with respect to the imposition of consecutive terms of commitment, and thus statute permitting juvenile to be sentenced to consecutive terms without requiring juvenile court to make findings similar to those required prior to imposition of consecutive sentences on adult offenders did not deprive juvenile of equal protection; objectives of juvenile justice system differed from those of adult criminal justice system, in that focus was on protection, development, and rehabilitation of juveniles. In re R.L. (Ohio App. 8 Dist., Cuyahoga, 01-06-2005) No. 84543, No. 84545, No. 84546, 2005-Ohio-26, 2005 WL 23343, Unreported. Infants ⇐ 132

Statute allowing a trial court to sentence a juvenile, who committed two or more acts that would be felonies if committed by an adult, to consecutive sentences without first making specific findings did not violate equal protection; the purpose of juvenile court was to provide for the care, protection, and development of children, protecting the public, and rehabilitating child, the purpose of felony sentencing was protect the public and to punish the offender, and juveniles could apply for judicial release at any time during their commitment. In re Slater (Ohio App. 9 Dist., Wayne, 09-22-2004) No. 04CA0004, No. 04CA0005, 2004-Ohio-4961, 2004 WL 2244249, Unreported, appeal not allowed 105 Ohio St.3d 1439, 822 N.E.2d 811, 2005-Ohio-531. Constitutional Law ⇐ 242.1(4); Infants ⇐ 132

Condition of probation for juvenile following adjudications that he had committed rape and gross sexual imposition, that he submit to and pass polygraph tests as may be directed by his probation officer or therapists, did not eliminate juvenile's rights against self-incrimination, and thus juvenile could assert them before giving answers that might incriminate himself. In re D.S. (Ohio, 11-29-2006) 111 Ohio St.3d 361, 856 N.E.2d 921, 2006-Ohio-5851. Infants ⇐ 225

2. Polygraph test

Condition of probation for juvenile following adjudications that he had committed rape and gross sexual imposition, that he submit to and pass polygraph tests as may be directed by his probation officer or therapists, was not reasonable, as no witness specifically asked for a polygraph to be used with juvenile, and there was no evidence that it would serve as a therapeutic tool for him. In re D.S. (Ohio, 11-29-2006) 111 Ohio St.3d 361, 856 N.E.2d 921, 2006-Ohio-5851. Infants ⇐ 225

Before a polygraph can be considered to be a reasonable probationary condition for a juvenile, there must be a showing that a polygraph is needed for therapeutic reasons in a particular case, that is, for the treatment and monitoring of the juvenile's behavior. In re D.S. (Ohio, 11-29-2006) 111 Ohio St.3d 361, 856 N.E.2d 921, 2006-Ohio-5851. Infants ⇐ 225

2152.02 Definitions

As used in this chapter:

(A) "Act charged" means the act that is identified in a complaint, indictment, or information alleging that a child is a delinquent child.

(B) "Admitted to a department of youth services facility" includes admission to a facility operated, or contracted for, by the department and admission to a comparable facility outside this state by another state or the United States.

(C)(1) "Child" means a person who is under eighteen years of age, except as otherwise provided in divisions (C)(2) to (6) of this section.

(2) Subject to division (C)(3) of this section, any person who violates a federal or state law or a municipal ordinance prior to attaining eighteen years of age shall be deemed a "child" irrespective of that person's age at the time the complaint with respect to that violation is filed or the hearing on the complaint is held.

(3) Any person who, while under eighteen years of age, commits an act that would be a felony if committed by an adult and who is not taken into custody or apprehended for that act until after the person attains twenty-one years of age is not a child in relation to that act.

(4) Any person whose case is transferred for criminal prosecution pursuant to section 2152.12 of the Revised Code shall be deemed after the transfer not to be a child in the transferred case.

(5) Any person whose case is transferred for criminal prosecution pursuant to section 2152.12 of the Revised Code and who subsequently is convicted of or pleads guilty to a felony in that case, and any person who is adjudicated a delinquent child for the commission of an act, who has a serious youthful offender dispositional sentence imposed for the act pursuant to section 2152.13 of the Revised Code, and whose adult portion of the dispositional sentence is invoked pursuant to section 2152.14 of the Revised Code, shall be deemed after the transfer or invocation not to be a child in any case in which a complaint is filed against the person.

(6) The juvenile court has jurisdiction over a person who is adjudicated a delinquent child or juvenile traffic offender prior to attaining eighteen years of age until the person attains twenty-one years of age, and, for purposes of that jurisdiction related to that adjudication, except as otherwise provided in this division, a person who is so adjudicated a delinquent child or juvenile traffic offender shall be deemed a "child" until the person attains twenty-one years of age. If a person is so adjudicated a delinquent child or juvenile traffic offender and the court makes a disposition of the person under this chapter, at any time after the

person attains eighteen years of age, the places at which the person may be held under that disposition are not limited to places authorized under this chapter solely for confinement of children, and the person may be confined under that disposition, in accordance with division (F)(2) of section 2152.26 of the Revised Code, in places other than those authorized under this chapter solely for confinement of children.

(D) "Chronic truant" means any child of compulsory school age who is absent without legitimate excuse for absence from the public school the child is supposed to attend for seven or more consecutive school days, ten or more school days in one school month, or fifteen or more school days in a school year.

(E) "Community corrections facility," "public safety beds," "release authority," and "supervised release" have the same meanings as in section 5139.01 of the Revised Code.

(F) "Delinquent child" includes any of the following:

(1) Any child, except a juvenile traffic offender, who violates any law of this state or the United States, or any ordinance of a political subdivision of the state, that would be an offense if committed by an adult;

(2) Any child who violates any lawful order of the court made under this chapter or under Chapter 2151. of the Revised Code other than an order issued under section 2151.87 of the Revised Code;

(3) Any child who violates division (C) of section 2907.39 or division (A) of section 2923.211 or division (C)(1) or (D) of section 2925.55 of the Revised Code;

(4) Any child who is a habitual truant and who previously has been adjudicated an unruly child for being a habitual truant;

(5) Any child who is a chronic truant.

(G) "Discretionary serious youthful offender" means a person who is eligible for a discretionary SYO and who is not transferred to adult court under a mandatory or discretionary transfer.

(H) "Discretionary SYO" means a case in which the juvenile court, in the juvenile court's discretion, may impose a serious youthful offender disposition under section 2152.13 of the Revised Code.

(I) "Discretionary transfer" means that the juvenile court has discretion to transfer a case for criminal prosecution under division (B) of section 2152.12 of the Revised Code.

(J) "Drug abuse offense," "felony drug abuse offense," and "minor drug possession offense" have the same meanings as in section 2925.01 of the Revised Code.

(K) "Electronic monitoring" and "electronic monitoring device" have the same meanings as in section 2929.01 of the Revised Code.

(L) "Economic loss" means any economic detriment suffered by a victim of a delinquent act or juvenile traffic offense as a direct and proximate result of the delinquent act or juvenile traffic offense and includes any loss of income due to lost time at work because of any injury caused to the victim and any property loss, medical cost, or funeral expense incurred as a result of the delinquent act or juvenile traffic offense. "Economic loss" does not include non-economic loss or any punitive or exemplary damages.

(M) "Firearm" has the same meaning as in section 2923.11 of the Revised Code.

(N) "Juvenile traffic offender" means any child who violates any traffic law, traffic ordinance, or traffic regulation of this state, the United States, or any political subdivision of this state, other than a resolution, ordinance, or regulation of a political subdivision of this state the violation of which is required to be handled by a parking violations bureau or a joint parking violations bureau pursuant to Chapter 4521. of the Revised Code.

(O) A "legitimate excuse for absence from the public school the child is supposed to attend" has the same meaning as in section 2151.011 of the Revised Code.

(P) "Mandatory serious youthful offender" means a person who is eligible for a mandatory SYO and who is not transferred to adult court under a mandatory or discretionary transfer.

(Q) "Mandatory SYO" means a case in which the juvenile court is required to impose a mandatory serious youthful offender disposition under section 2152.13 of the Revised Code.

(R) "Mandatory transfer" means that a case is required to be transferred for criminal prosecution under division (A) of section 2152.12 of the Revised Code.

(S) "Mental illness" has the same meaning as in section 5122.01 of the Revised Code.

(T) "Mentally retarded person" has the same meaning as in section 5123.01 of the Revised Code.

(U) "Monitored time" and "repeat violent offender" have the same meanings as in section 2929.01 of the Revised Code.

(V) "Of compulsory school age" has the same meaning as in section 3321.01 of the Revised Code.

(W) "Public record" has the same meaning as in section 149.43 of the Revised Code.

(X) "Serious youthful offender" means a person who is eligible for a mandatory SYO or discretionary SYO but who is not transferred to adult court under a mandatory or discretionary transfer.

(Y) "Sexually oriented offense," "habitual sex offender," "juvenile offender registrant," "sexual predator," "presumptive registration-exempt sexually oriented offense," "registration-exempt sexually oriented offense," "child-victim oriented offense," "habitual child-victim offender," and "child-victim predator" have the same meanings as in section 2950.01 of the Revised Code.

(Z) "Traditional juvenile" means a case that is not transferred to adult court under a mandatory or discretionary transfer, that is eligible for a disposition under sections 2152.16, 2152.17, 2152.19, and 2152.20 of the Revised Code, and that is not eligible for a disposition under section 2152.13 of the Revised Code.

(AA) "Transfer" means the transfer for criminal prosecution of a case involving the alleged commission by a child of an act that would be an offense if committed by an adult from the juvenile court to the appropriate court that has jurisdiction of the offense.

(BB) "Category one offense" means any of the following:

(1) A violation of section 2903.01 or 2903.02 of the Revised Code;

(2) A violation of section 2923.02 of the Revised Code involving an attempt to commit aggravated murder or murder.

(CC) "Category two offense" means any of the following:

(1) A violation of section 2903.03, 2905.01, 2907.02, 2909.02, 2911.01, or 2911.11 of the Revised Code;

(2) A violation of section 2903.04 of the Revised Code that is a felony of the first degree;

(3) A violation of section 2907.12 of the Revised Code as it existed prior to September 3, 1996.

(DD) "Non–economic loss" means nonpecuniary harm suffered by a victim of a delinquent act or juvenile traffic offense as a result of or related to the delinquent act or juvenile traffic offense, including, but not limited to, pain and suffering; loss of society, consortium, companionship, care, assistance, attention, protection, advice, guidance, counsel, instruction, training, or education; mental anguish; and any other intangible loss.

(2006 H 23, eff. 8–17–06; 2006 S 53, eff. 5–17–06; 2004 H 52, eff. 6–1–04; 2003 S 5, § 3, eff. 1–1–04; 2003 S 5, § 1, eff. 7–31–03; 2002 H 490, eff. 1–1–04; 2002 H 400, eff. 4–3–03; 2001 S 3, eff. 1–1–02; 2000 S 179, § 3, eff. 1–1–02)

Uncodified Law

2001 S 3, § 4, eff. 10–26–01, reads, in part:

Section 2152.02 of the Revised Code, as presented in this act, includes matter that was amended into former section 2151.02 of the Revised Code by S.B. 218 of the 123rd General Assembly. Paragraphs of former section 2151.02 of the Revised Code were transferred to section 2152.02 of the Revised Code by S.B. 179 of the 123rd General Assembly as part of its general revision of the juvenile sentencing laws. The General Assembly, applying the principle stated in division (B) of section 1.52 of the Revised Code that amendments are to be harmonized if reasonably capable of simultaneous operation, finds that the version of section 2152.02 of the Revised Code presented in this act is the resulting version of the section in effect prior to the date of the section as presented in this act.

Historical and Statutory Notes

Ed. Note: The legal review and technical services staff of the Legislative Service Commission has issued an opinion regarding the treatment of multiple amendments. The opinion is neither legally authoritative nor binding, but is provided as a general indication that the amendments of the several acts [2006 H 23, eff. 8–17–06 and 2006 S 53, eff. 5–17–06] may be harmonized pursuant to the rule of construction contained in R.C. 1.52(B) requiring all amendments be given effect if they can reasonably be put into simultaneous operation. See *Baldwin's Ohio Legislative Service Annotated*, 2006, pages 3/L–1243 and 1/L–220, or the OH-LEGIS or OH-LEGIS-OLD database on Westlaw, for original versions of these Acts.

Ed. Note: RC 2152.02 contains, in part, provisions analogous to former RC 2151.02 and 2151.021, repealed by 2000 S 179, eff. 1–1–02.

Amendment Note: 2006 H 23 inserted "division (C) of section 2907.39 or" in division (F)(3).

Amendment Note: 2006 S 53 inserted "or division (C)(1) or (D) of section 2925.55" in division (F)(3).

Amendment Note: 2004 H 52 inserted "or juvenile traffic offense" throughout division (L); inserted "direct and proximate" in the first sentence of division (L); added the last sentence of division (L); and added new division (DD).

Amendment Note: 2003 S 5, § 1 and 3, rewrote division (Y), which prior thereto read:

"(Y) 'Sexually oriented offense,' 'habitual sex offender,' 'juvenile sex offender registrant,' and 'sexual predator' have the same meanings as in section 2950.01 of the Revised Code."

Amendment Note: 2002 H 490 rewrote division (K), which prior thereto read:

"(K) 'Electronic monitoring device,' 'certified electronic monitoring device,' 'electronically monitored house arrest,' 'electronic monitoring system,' and 'certified electronic monitoring system' have the same meanings as in section 2929.23 of the Revised Code."

Amendment Note: 2002 H 400 rewrote division (C)(6), which prior thereto read:

"(6) The juvenile court has jurisdiction over a person who is adjudicated a delinquent child or juvenile traffic offender prior to attaining eighteen years of age until the person attains twenty-one years of age, and, for purposes of that jurisdiction related to that adjudication, a person who is so adjudicated a delinquent child or juvenile traffic offender shall be deemed a 'child' until the person attains twenty-one years of age."

Amendment Note: 2001 S 3 rewrote division (Y) which prior thereto read:

"(Y) 'Sexually oriented offense' has the same meaning as in section 2950.01 of the Revised Code."

Library References

Infants ⚖68.2, 132.
Westlaw Topic No. 211.
C.J.S. Infants §§ 32, 41, 198 to 207.

Research References

Encyclopedias

OH Jur. 3d Family Law § 1485, "Child".
OH Jur. 3d Family Law § 1487, "Delinquent Child".
OH Jur. 3d Family Law § 1488, "Juvenile Traffic Offender".
OH Jur. 3d Family Law § 1500, Relating to Persons.
OH Jur. 3d Family Law § 1581, Alleged Delinquent or Unruly Child or Juvenile Traffic Offender.
OH Jur. 3d Family Law § 1487.5, Sexually Oriented and Child-Victim Offenders.
OH Jur. 3d Family Law § 1488.5, "Truant".
OH Jur. 3d Family Law § 1698.6, Sexually Oriented and Child-Victim Offenses; Registration.

Treatises and Practice Aids

Katz, Giannelli, Blair and Lipton, Baldwin's Ohio Practice, Criminal Law, § 109:14, Contributing to Unruliness or Delinquency.

Carlin, Baldwin's Ohio Practice, Merrick-Rippner Probate Law § 105:8, Juvenile Court—Age Jurisdiction.

Carlin, Baldwin's Ohio Practice, Merrick-Rippner Probate Law § 106:1, Juvenile Court Jurisdiction—Delinquent Child—Definition: Evidence of Delinquency.

Carlin, Baldwin's Ohio Practice, Merrick-Rippner Probate Law § 106:7, Juvenile Court Jurisdiction—Juvenile Traffic Offender—Quantum of Proof in Juvenile Traffic Offender Hearings.

Carlin, Baldwin's Ohio Practice, Merrick-Rippner Probate Law § 12:13, Wrongful Death—Damages—Stacking of Uninsured/Underinsured Motorist Coverage.

Carlin, Baldwin's Ohio Practice, Merrick-Rippner Probate Law § 107:27, Detention Separate from Adult Detainees.

Carlin, Baldwin's Ohio Practice, Merrick-Rippner Probate Law § 107:65, Mandatory Transfer, Effective January 1, 2002.

Carlin, Baldwin's Ohio Practice, Merrick-Rippner Probate Law § 107:73, Alternatives for Disposition of Juvenile Cases.

Carlin, Baldwin's Ohio Practice, Merrick-Rippner Probate Law § 107:105, Commitment of Delinquent Children to the Custody of Department of Youth Services, Effective January 1, 2002.

Carlin, Baldwin's Ohio Practice, Merrick-Rippner Probate Law § 107:136, Complaint, Delinquent Child—Form.

Painter, Ohio Driving Under the Influence § 12:45, Juvenile and "Underage" Offenders—Generally.

Giannelli & Yeomans, Ohio Juvenile Law § 1:7, Juvenile Code.

Giannelli & Yeomans, Ohio Juvenile Law § 2:3, Child Subject to Adult Prosecution.

Giannelli & Yeomans, Ohio Juvenile Law § 2:7, Detention of "Children" Over the Age of 18 Years.

Giannelli & Yeomans, Ohio Juvenile Law § 4:2, Delinquent Child Defined.

Giannelli & Yeomans, Ohio Juvenile Law § 4:5, Truancy.

Giannelli & Yeomans, Ohio Juvenile Law § 4:6, Court Order Violations.

Giannelli & Yeomans, Ohio Juvenile Law § 5:5, Syo Enhancements.

Giannelli & Yeomans, Ohio Juvenile Law § 7:2, Traffic Offenders.

Giannelli & Yeomans, Ohio Juvenile Law § 8:4, Unruly—Truancy.

Giannelli & Yeomans, Ohio Juvenile Law § 8:6, Unruly—Status Offenses.

Giannelli & Yeomans, Ohio Juvenile Law § 16:8, Delinquency Complaints.

Giannelli & Yeomans, Ohio Juvenile Law § 22:1, Introduction.

Giannelli & Yeomans, Ohio Juvenile Law § 22:4, Improper Transfer; Lack of Jurisdiction.

Giannelli & Yeomans, Ohio Juvenile Law § 22:7, Mandatory Transfer.

Giannelli & Yeomans, Ohio Juvenile Law § 27:7, Community Control Sanctions.

Giannelli & Yeomans, Ohio Juvenile Law § 28:6, Commitment to Juvenile Facility.

Giannelli & Yeomans, Ohio Juvenile Law § 29:3, Unruly—Delinquency Dispositions.

Giannelli & Yeomans, Ohio Juvenile Law App. D, Appendix D. Glossary.

Giannelli & Yeomans, Ohio Juvenile Law § 22:22, Transfer of Jurisdiction.

Giannelli & Yeomans, Ohio Juvenile Law § 27:10, House Arrest & Electronic Monitoring.

Giannelli & Yeomans, Ohio Juvenile Law § 27:13, Restitution.

Hastings, Manoloff, Sheeran, & Stype, Ohio School Law § 20:19, Enforcement Procedures-Investigation.

Hastings, Manoloff, Sheeran, & Stype, Ohio School Law § 24:27, Contributing to the Delinquency or Unruliness of a Minor.

Notes of Decisions

Constitutional issues   1
Evidence of delinquency   3
Juvenile traffic offender, evidence   2

---

1. Constitutional issues

The constitutional guaranty of due process of law was violated by the commitment of a 15-year-old boy as a juvenile delinquent where no notice was given to the parents that the boy was being taken into custody, no copy of the petition was served on them, the petition did not allege the basis for the charge of delinquency, the complainant did not attend the hearing, no one was sworn, no transcript or recording was made, no memorandum or record of the substance of the proceeding was prepared, a referral report filed by probation officers with the court was not disclosed to the parents or the boy, and the court did not advise the parents or the boy that they had a right to counsel, that the boy did not have to testify or make a statement, or that incriminating statements made by the boy might result in his commitment as a delinquent. Application of Gault (U.S.Ariz. 1967) 87 S.Ct. 1428, 387 U.S. 1, 18 L.Ed.2d 527, 40 O.O.2d 378.

2. Juvenile traffic offender, evidence

Evidence was sufficient in adjudicatory traffic offender proceeding to support finding that juvenile failed to stop for red traffic signal in violation of municipal ordinance; although juvenile argued state failed to demonstrate that traffic signal was placed in accordance with municipal ordinance, police officer testified regarding existence of traffic signal, photographs of traffic signal were introduced, such evidence created permissive inference that traffic signal was placed in accordance with municipal ordinance, and juvenile did not present any evidence to contrary. In re S.C. (Ohio App. 2 Dist., Miami, 10-15-2004) No. 2004-CA-14, 2004-Ohio-5800, 2004 WL 2445334, Unreported, appeal not allowed 105 Ohio St.3d 1453, 823 N.E.2d 457, 2005-Ohio-763. Automobiles ⇐ 355(1)

Trial court's finding in adjudicatory traffic offender proceeding that juvenile failed to stop for red traffic signal in violation of municipal ordinance was not against manifest weight of evidence; although witness testified that traffic signal was yellow when juvenile drove into intersection, witness testified that she and juvenile were good friends, and police officer testified that traffic signal was red when juvenile drove into intersection. In re S.C. (Ohio App. 2 Dist., Miami, 10-15-2004) No. 2004-CA-14, 2004-Ohio-5800, 2004 WL 2445334, Unreported, appeal not allowed 105 Ohio St.3d 1453, 823 N.E.2d 457, 2005-Ohio-763. Automobiles ⇐ 355(1)

When child violates criminal statute, he or she should be charged with being delinquent child, not juvenile traffic offender, but when child violates traffic law, he or she should be charged as being juvenile traffic offender, not delinquent child. In re Elliott (Fayette 1993) 87 Ohio App.3d 816, 623 N.E.2d 217. Infants ⇐ 197

Juvenile could not be found to be juvenile traffic offender when complaint alleged only that she was delinquent child by reason of having committed aggravated vehicular assault; state had failed to prove that juvenile violated any criminal statute, and trial court's finding that she had nonetheless committed reckless operation of motor vehicle resulted in amendment of complaint, after adjudicatory hearing, charging juvenile with something entirely different than that with which she was originally charged, thus violating her due process rights. In re Elliott (Fayette 1993) 87 Ohio App.3d 816, 623 N.E.2d 217. Constitutional Law ⇐ 255(4); Infants ⇐ 197

When child violates criminal statute, he or she should be charged with being delinquent child, not juvenile traffic offender, but when child violates traffic law, he or she should be charged as being juvenile traffic offender, not delinquent child. In re Elliott (Fayette 1993) 87 Ohio App.3d 816, 623 N.E.2d 217. Infants ⇐ 197

Juvenile proceedings involving juvenile traffic offenders are not criminal proceedings and do not try the alleged juvenile offender for any crime, either misdemeanor or felony; thus, RC 2945.71 to 2945.73 does not apply to juvenile traffic offense proceedings. In re Washburn (Wyandot 1990) 70 Ohio App.3d 178, 590 N.E.2d 855.

Picture of stop sign that was admitted into evidence in a proceeding to adjudicate driver as juvenile traffic offender raised a permissive inference that the sign was in compliance with the uniform traffic control device manual, even though the officer could not testify as to the date the sign was placed or the exact shape of the sign. In re McDonald (Ohio App. 5 Dist., Licking, 05-17-2002) No. 02-CA-21, 2002-Ohio-2548, 2002 WL 1050323, Unreported. Automobiles ⇐ 353; Criminal Law ⇐ 446

A trial court's finding a juvenile to be a juvenile traffic offender must be reversed where the complaint filed in the juvenile court alleges the juvenile was a delinquent child by reason of having committed aggravated vehicular assault because a juvenile traffic offender pursuant to RC 2151.021 is a completely separate concept from that of a delinquent child pursuant to RC 2151.02. In re Elliot, No. CA92-07-012, 1993 WL 265493 (12th Dist Ct App, Fayette, 7-19-93).

3. Evidence of delinquency

The trial court's adjudication of juvenile as a delinquent child was supported by sufficient evidence and was not against the manifest weight of the evidence; juvenile was adjudicated delinquent by reason of grand theft and violation of probation, victim and his girlfriend testified that they worked the third shift, that when they returned to victim's residence after work they discovered they had been robbed and guns, ammunition, jewelry, and electronic equipment was missing, and that when they left for work the victim's two daughters were the only people in the residence, juvenile's cousin testified that he went with juvenile to the victim's residence, that the victim's daughter let them in, that they took the victim's guns and hid them, and that he returned to the victim's residence later that night with juvenile and another male and obtained some electrical equipment from the victim's daughters, and police officer testified that one of the juveniles involved told police where they could find the stolen items and that all stolen items were recovered. In re R.T. (Ohio App. 9 Dist., Lorain, 03-22-2006) No. 05CA008728, No. 05CA008742, 2006-Ohio-1311, 2006 WL 709057, Unreported. Infants ⇐ 176

Evidence that juvenile inflicted physical harm upon victim was sufficient to support his adjudication as delinquent based upon commission of aggravated burglary; not long after juvenile pushed victim out of his way and into her van in order to flee, victim was seen to have red mark on her cheek. In re C.W. (Ohio App. 12 Dist., Butler, 08-01-2005) No. CA2004-12-312, 2005-Ohio-3905, 2005 WL 1799317, Unreported. Infants ⇐ 153

Evidence that juvenile entered into victim's garage with purpose to commit criminal offense was sufficient to support his adjudication as delinquent based upon commission of aggravated burglary; at time victim confronted juvenile, juvenile was holding 12-pack of beer belonging to victim under his arm and was looking around at shelves in garage, juvenile refused to put beer down upon being asked to do so, and juvenile dropped beer and ran after victim told him that police were going to be called. In re C.W. (Ohio App. 12 Dist., Butler, 08-01-2005) No. CA2004-12-312, 2005-Ohio-3905, 2005 WL 1799317, Unreported. Infants ⇐ 176

Circumstantial evidence that juvenile entered into victim's garage by stealth was sufficient to support his adjudication as delinquent based upon commission of aggravated burglary; juvenile was not invited into victim's garage and entered without permission, victim saw juvenile and his companion walking between houses and noted his quick disappearance, and, when victim arrived at her garage, juvenile was already inside and his companion was standing outside facing street, permitting reasonable inference that companion was acting as lookout. In re C.W. (Ohio App. 12 Dist., Butler, 08-01-2005) No. CA2004-12-312, 2005-Ohio-3905, 2005 WL 1799317, Unreported. Infants ⇐ 176

Juvenile's delinquency adjudication based on chronic truancy was against the manifest weight of the evidence, where juvenile's absence was due to his father's refusal to allow him to attend school. In re Whittekind (Ohio App. 4 Dist., Washington, 12-17-2004) No. 04CA22, 2004-Ohio-7282, 2004 WL 3090246, Unreported. Infants ⇐ 153

Juvenile's adjudication as a delinquent child as a result of committing gross sexual imposition was not against the manifest weight of the evidence; witnesses testified that juvenile admitted putting five-year old victim's penis in his mouth, officer testified that juvenile admitted inappropriately touching and kissing victim, victim's mother testified that victim's behavior changed following the incident, and there was no innocent explanation for juvenile's placement of his mouth on the victim's mouth, chest, and penis. In re Higginbotham (Ohio App. 4 Dist., Lawrence, 10-27-2004) No. 04CA26, 2004-Ohio-6004, 2004 WL 2569446, Unreported. Infants ⇐ 176

Adjudication of delinquency, based on the offense of cruelty to animals, was not against the manifest weight of the evidence; cousin of juvenile testified that juvenile suggested that they place kittens in glass jars and then smash the jars in train tracks, and that juvenile got the jars and they placed the kittens inside and smashed the jars on the train tracks, and friend of juvenile testified that juvenile brought him to the train tracks, told him that he placed kittens in jars and smashed the jars against the train tracks, and that he saw three dead kittens. In re Definbaugh (Ohio App. 5 Dist., Tuscarawas, 11-13-2003) No. 2003AP03-0021, 2003-Ohio-6138, 2003 WL 22717957, Unreported. Infants ⇐ 176

There was sufficient evidence identifying juvenile as robber to support delinquency finding; juvenile admitted being in area, he was identified as robber by victim, who knew juvenile because they lived in same neighborhood, victim's wife saw juvenile by side of truck in which victim was robbed, both victim and his wife described what robber was wearing, and when juvenile was arrested, his clothing matched their description. In re Good (Ohio App. 12 Dist., 02-24-1997) 118 Ohio App.3d 371, 692 N.E.2d 1072, dismissed, appeal not allowed 79 Ohio St.3d 1418, 680 N.E.2d 156. Infants ⇐ 176

Juvenile failed to show how outcome of trial was affected by allegedly improper admission of testimony that handgun was found approximately one block from robbery location, to which juvenile did not object at trial; evidence relied upon by trial judge in his finding of delinquency was victim's testimony that juvenile used small shiny pistol. In re Good (Ohio App. 12 Dist., 02-24-1997) 118 Ohio App.3d 371, 692 N.E.2d 1072, dismissed, appeal not allowed 79 Ohio St.3d 1418, 680 N.E.2d 156. Infants ⇐ 253

Evidence was insufficient to establish that negligence of juvenile who was driving van was cause of death of individual who had been riding on running board of van and who died shortly after either jumping from or falling from van as van left parking lot, as would support conviction of delinquency on basis of grounds of vehicular homicide; no admissible evidence provided basis for finding that negligence of driver caused death, and it could just as easily be surmised that individual's own negligence, or that of emergency medical personal who negligently inserted intubation tube, caused death. State v. Fouty (Ohio App. 2 Dist., 03-29-1996) 110 Ohio App.3d 130, 673 N.E.2d 681. Infants ⇐ 176

Although a complaining witness may refer to one or more particular statutes as being violated by a child, a juvenile court may find a violation of another statute and determine that the accused is a delinquent child. In re Burgess (Preble 1984) 13 Ohio App.3d 374, 469 N.E.2d 967, 13 O.B.R. 456. Infants ⇐ 210

Prohibition will not lie to dismiss indictment for aggravated murder against defendant previously found to be delinquent child for identical offense. DuBose v. Court of Common Pleas of Trumbull County (Ohio 1980) 64 Ohio St.2d 169, 413 N.E.2d 1205, 18 O.O.3d 385.

The violation of RC 2903.07, vehicular homicide, when committed by a juvenile is an act of delinquency, not a juvenile traffic offense. In re Fox (Ohio Com.Pl. 1979) 60 Ohio Misc. 31, 395 N.E.2d 918, 14 O.O.3d 80.

It is abuse of discretion for juvenile court to recognize juvenile to common pleas court in absence of finding that such juvenile was delinquent and where evidence fails to disclose that such juvenile would not be proper subject for rehabilitation under provisions of juvenile code or that such recognizance was necessary as protection to public. In re Mack (Hamilton 1970) 22 Ohio App.2d 201, 260 N.E.2d 619, 51 O.O.2d 400. Infants ⇐ 68.7(2)

Juvenile court must, as condition of order for juvenile to appear before common pleas court, find such juvenile to be delinquent under RC 2151.01 to RC 2151.54. In re Mack (Hamilton 1970) 22 Ohio App.2d 201, 260 N.E.2d 619, 51 O.O.2d 400.

Where a seventeen-year-old boy sells a non-prescription drug containing substances defined as poisonous but not hallucinogenic to his schoolmates, it is a violation of RC 3719.32 and sufficient to support a finding of delinquency, though it is not a felony allowing commitment to the reformatory. In re Baker (Ohio 1969) 20 Ohio St.2d 142, 254 N.E.2d 363, 49 O.O.2d 473.

Any adjudication of delinquency must be supported by clear and convincing evidence. In re Agler (Ohio 1969) 19 Ohio St.2d 70, 249 N.E.2d 808, 48 O.O.2d 85. Infants ⇐ 176

Delinquency proceedings in juvenile court do not require indictment or trial by jury. In re Agler (Ohio 1969) 19 Ohio St.2d 70, 249 N.E.2d 808, 48 O.O.2d 85. Infants ⇐ 197; Jury ⇐ 19.5

Proof of possession, use, or control by a juvenile of a hallucinogen is sufficient evidence upon which a juvenile court can find such juvenile a delinquent under RC Ch 2151. In re Baker (Hocking 1969) 18 Ohio App.2d 276, 248 N.E.2d 620, 47 O.O.2d 411.

Under existing Ohio law, proceedings in juvenile court are civil in nature and not criminal, and a juvenile court judge acts within his authority when, in a hearing to determine the delinquency status of a child under RC 2151.02, he denies a request for a jury trial and decides the case on the preponderance of the evidence. In re Benn (Cuyahoga 1969) 18 Ohio App.2d 97, 247 N.E.2d 335, 47 O.O.2d 170. Infants ⇐ 209

Where a demurrer is sustained to a complaint (delinquency) filed in a juvenile court, and no citation is issued or custody order made pursuant to a subsequently amended complaint, an order, made concurrently with the sustaining of the demurrer, that the child involved "remain in the custody" of certain officials, is a nullity; and the retention of custody of such child thereunder is illegal. In re Quickle (Allen 1961) 114 Ohio App. 78, 180 N.E.2d 275, 18 O.O.2d 370.

Proceedings in a juvenile court are civil in nature, the customary rules of evidence governing civil actions must be followed, and hearsay evidence is not admissible; and a mere preponderance of the evidence is sufficient to warrant a determination that a minor is a delinquent, even though such determination involves a finding that a criminal statute has been violated by such minor. (See also In re Gault, 387 US 1, 87 SCt 1428, 18 LEd(2d) 527 (1967).) State v. Shardell (Cuyahoga 1958) 107 Ohio App. 338, 153 N.E.2d 510, 79 Ohio Law Abs. 534, 8 O.O.2d 262.

Where the parents of a female person under sixteen years of age actively participate in enabling such person to enter into a marriage relationship, such participation constitutes acts tending to cause the child to become a "delinquent child" and the parents "act in a way tending to cause delinquency in such child." State v. Gans (Ohio 1958) 168 Ohio St. 174, 151 N.E.2d 709, 68 A.L.R.2d 736, 5 O.O.2d 472, certiorari denied 79 S.Ct. 722, 359 U.S. 945, 3 L.Ed.2d 678. Infants ⇐ 13

Where it is charged that a defendant did "act in a way tending to cause delinquency" in a child, it is not necessary, for a conviction, to establish actual delinquency, but only that the acts of the defendant were within themselves of such a nature that they would tend to cause delinquency in such child. State v. Gans (Ohio 1958) 168 Ohio St. 174, 151 N.E.2d 709, 68 A.L.R.2d 736, 5 O.O.2d 472, certiorari denied 79 S.Ct. 722, 359 U.S. 945, 3 L.Ed.2d 678. Infants ⇐ 20

Ordinarily, a minor child does not commit any act of delinquency so long as he or she acts under and in accordance with instructions of duly constituted law enforcement officers who are acting within the course of their duties as such. State v. Miclau (Ohio 1957) 167 Ohio St. 38, 146 N.E.2d 293, 4 O.O.2d 6. Infants ⇐ 153

Conviction for contributing to delinquency of minor by owner of restaurant for serving liquor to fifteen year old girl accompanied by police officers reversed upon ground evidence was inadmissible because means of procuring it was illegal and against public policy, and upon ground that the defendant, acting upon orders of police officers, did not commit any delinquency. State v. Miclau (Cuyahoga 1957) 104 Ohio App. 347, 140 N.E.2d 596, 5 O.O.2d 36, affirmed 167 Ohio St. 38, 146 N.E.2d 293, 4 O.O.2d 6.

An affidavit charging a person with contributing toward the delinquency of a minor child which neither charges that such child is a delinquent nor sets forth facts showing such child to be a delinquent and which does not set forth facts showing any conduct on the part of the accused which would tend to cause the delinquency of such child, does not charge an offense, and in a prosecution under such affidavit, it is error for the court to convict and sentence the accused, suspend execution of the sentence, and, thereafter, to revoke such suspension and order the sentence executed. State v. Holbrook (Logan 1954) 95 Ohio App. 526, 121 N.E.2d 81, 54 O.O. 135. Indictment And Information ⇐ 110(48)

A conviction for the offense of contributing to the delinquency of a minor will not be disturbed on appeal, where competent evidence was introduced at the trial showing that the defendant, a married man, twenty-nine years of age and with a family, persistently associated with a sixteen year old girl in such a way as to disrupt her life and morals. State ex rel. Meng v. Todaro (Ohio 1954) 161 Ohio St. 348, 119 N.E.2d 281, 53 O.O. 252.

A finding or adjudication in a separate proceeding that a minor is delinquent is not a condition precedent to the maintenance of a prosecution for contributing to the delinquency of the minor, where the affidavit filed against the one charged with contributing to the delinquency and the evidence on his trial shows that the minor is delinquent. State ex rel. Meng v. Todaro (Ohio 1954) 161 Ohio St. 348, 119 N.E.2d 281, 53 O.O. 252.

An affidavit charging a person with contributing to the delinquency of a minor child, "in that he did act as a receiver of stolen property from the said minor," which neither charges that such child is a delinquent nor sets forth facts showing such child to be a delinquent and which does not set forth facts showing that the accused in any way contributed to the delinquency of such child, does not charge an offense. State v. Kiessling

(Defiance 1952) 93 Ohio App. 524, 114 N.E.2d 154, 51 O.O. 225. Infants ⇨ 20

Where affidavit for contributing to delinquency of minor alleged that the minor by "improperly" associating with defendant, a married man, "until late hours at night" so deported herself "as to injure or endanger" her "morals or health," it contains facts sufficient to show the minor a delinquent child under this section. State v. Mahoney (Carroll 1948) 87 N.E.2d 496, 54 Ohio Law Abs. 218, appeal dismissed 150 Ohio St. 392, 82 N.E.2d 544, 38 O.O. 239. Infants ⇨ 20

There can be no valid conviction on an affidavit which does not charge an offense against the laws of the state, and a plea of guilty will not cure such defect in affidavit. State v. Zaras (Hancock 1947) 81 Ohio App. 152, 78 N.E.2d 74, 36 O.O. 460. Indictment And Information ⇨ 202(5)

An affidavit drawn pursuant to GC 1639–45 (RC 2151.41) charging an accused with contributing to delinquency of a minor but which does not set forth facts showing such minor to be a delinquent within purview of this section, does not charge an offense against the laws of Ohio. State v. Zaras (Hancock 1947) 81 Ohio App. 152, 78 N.E.2d 74, 36 O.O. 460. Infants ⇨ 20

"Delinquent" and "dependent" children as defined by act (98 v 314) are sufficiently distinguished by the act to avoid such confusion in management and control after they become wards of the court as will invalidate the act for indefiniteness. Travis v. State (Ohio Cir. 1909) 21 Ohio C.D. 492, 12 Ohio C.C.(N.S.) 374, affirmed 82 Ohio St. 439, 92 N.E. 1125, 8 Ohio Law Rep. 91. Infants ⇨ 132; Statutes ⇨ 47

In a prosecution under former GC 1644 (RC 2151.02) of a minor for immoral conduct and delinquency, character evidence is inadmissible and former immoral conduct cannot be shown; the purpose of the section is reformatory and not retaliatory. State v. Hawkins (Ohio Juv. 1910) 56 W.L.B. 166.

Selling or handling of intoxicating liquors by minor under eighteen years of age is act of delinquency under this section. State v. Butler (Ohio Juv. 1943) 11 Ohio Supp. 18, 38 Ohio Law Abs. 211, 25 O.O. 567.

Evidence was sufficient to support delinquency adjudication of juvenile based on juvenile's commission of retaliation and aggravated menacing offenses. In re Rumph (Ohio App. 9 Dist., Summit, 09-04-2002) No. 20886, 2002-Ohio-4525, 2002 WL 2009212, Unreported. Infants ⇨ 176

In accordance with RC 5119.64 et seq., juvenile runaways who are apprehended by law enforcement officials may not be placed in juvenile detention facilities even though suitable shelter is unavailable; however, if such a youth is determined to be a delinquent child as defined in RC 2151.02, an unruly child as defined in RC 2151.022, or a juvenile traffic offender as defined in RC 2151.021, he may be processed through the juvenile justice system and placed in a juvenile detention facility. OAG 77–063.

An adjudication and disposition of delinquency conforms to the general policies of RC Ch 2151 where the doctor retained to assess a child testifies that the eight-year-old had a general awareness that dousing straw with lighter fluid and igniting it next to a building would likely lead to a serious fire, from which the trial court may properly conclude that the child knew that his conduct would probably cause serious property damage. In re Archie, No. 95–CA–33, 1995 WL 723044 (2d Dist Ct App, Greene, 12–6–95).

A thirteen-year-old juvenile may be found delinquent by reason of committing rape where the prosecution does not present evidence of his ability to emit semen; this is not a requirement of RC 2907.02 and there is no longer a rebuttable presumption that a male under the age of fourteen is incapable of rape. In re Wilson, No. 10909 (2d Dist Ct App, Montgomery, 12–1–88).

A sixteen-year-old delinquent child who purposely causes the death of her father in violation of RC 2903.02 and 2151.02 is not amenable to rehabilitation within the juvenile system despite the lack of a physical examination where testimony and evidence coupled with the nature and severity of the act suggest a callous indifference for human life that could pose a threat to the community even beyond the juvenile's twenty-first birthday. State v Berenyi, No. 11–97–01, 1997 WL 576357 (3d Dist Ct App, Paulding, 9–18–97).

In accordance with RC 5119.64 et seq., juvenile runaways who are apprehended by law enforcement officials may not be placed in juvenile detention facilities even though suitable shelter is unavailable; however, if such a youth is determined to be a delinquent child as defined in RC 2151.02, an unruly child as defined in RC 2151.022, or a juvenile traffic offender as defined in RC 2151.021, he may be processed through the juvenile justice system and placed in a juvenile detention facility. OAG 77–063.

2152.021 Complaint; indictment

(A)(1) Subject to division (A)(2) of this section, any person having knowledge of a child who appears to be a juvenile traffic offender or to be a delinquent child may file a sworn complaint with respect to that child in the juvenile court of the county in which the child has a residence or legal settlement or in which the traffic offense or delinquent act allegedly occurred. The sworn complaint may be upon information and belief, and, in addition to the allegation that the child is a delinquent child or a juvenile traffic offender, the complaint shall allege the particular facts upon which the allegation that the child is a delinquent child or a juvenile traffic offender is based.

If a child appears to be a delinquent child who is eligible for a serious youthful offender dispositional sentence under section 2152.11 of the Revised Code and if the prosecuting attorney desires to seek a serious youthful offender dispositional sentence under section 2152.13 of the Revised Code in regard to the child, the prosecuting attorney of the county in which the alleged delinquency occurs may initiate a case in the juvenile court of the county by presenting the case to a grand jury for indictment, by charging the child in a bill of information as a serious youthful offender pursuant to section 2152.13 of the Revised Code, by requesting a serious youthful offender dispositional sentence in the original complaint alleging that the child is a delinquent child, or by filing with the juvenile court a written notice of intent to seek a serious youthful offender dispositional sentence.

(2) Any person having knowledge of a child who appears to be a delinquent child for being an habitual or chronic truant may file a sworn complaint with respect to that child and the parent, guardian, or other person having care of the child in the juvenile court of the county in which the child has a residence or legal settlement or in which the child is supposed to attend public school. The sworn complaint may be upon information and belief and shall contain the following allegations:

(a) That the child is a delinquent child for being a chronic truant or an habitual truant who previously has been adjudicated an unruly child for being a habitual truant and, in addition, the particular facts upon which that allegation is based;

(b) That the parent, guardian, or other person having care of the child has failed to cause the child's attendance at school in violation of section 3321.38 of the Revised Code and, in addition, the particular facts upon which that allegation is based.

(B) Any person with standing under applicable law may file a complaint for the determination of any other matter over which the juvenile court is given jurisdiction by section 2151.23 of the Revised Code. The complaint shall be filed in the county in which the child who is the subject of the complaint is found or was last known to be found.

(C) Within ten days after the filing of a complaint or the issuance of an indictment, the court shall give written notice of the filing of the complaint or the issuance of an indictment and of the substance of the complaint or indictment to the superintendent of a city, local, exempted village, or joint vocational school district if the complaint or indictment alleges that a child committed an act that would be a criminal offense if committed by an adult, that the child was sixteen years of age or older at the time of the commission of the alleged act, and that the alleged act is any of the following:

(1) A violation of section 2923.122 of the Revised Code that relates to property owned or controlled by, or to an activity held under the auspices of, the board of education of that school district;

(2) A violation of section 2923.12 of the Revised Code, of a substantially similar municipal ordinance, or of section 2925.03 of the Revised Code that was committed on property owned or controlled by, or at an activity held under the auspices of, the board of education of that school district;

(3) A violation of section 2925.11 of the Revised Code that was committed on property owned or controlled by, or at an activity held under the auspices of, the board of education of that school district, other than a violation of that section that would be a minor drug possession offense if committed by an adult;

(4) A violation of section 2903.01, 2903.02, 2903.03, 2903.04, 2903.11, 2903.12, 2907.02, or 2907.05 of the Revised Code, or a violation of former section 2907.12 of the Revised Code, that was committed on property owned or controlled by, or at an activity held under the auspices of, the board of education of that school district, if the victim at the time of the commission of the alleged act was an employee of the board of education of that school district;

(5) Complicity in any violation described in division (C)(1), (2), (3), or (4) of this section that was alleged to have been committed in the manner described in division (C)(1), (2), (3), or (4) of this section, regardless of whether the act of complicity was committed on property owned or controlled by, or at an activity held under the auspices of, the board of education of that school district.

(D) A public children services agency, acting pursuant to a complaint or an action on a complaint filed under this section, is not subject to the requirements of section 3127.23 of the Revised Code.

(E) For purposes of the record to be maintained by the clerk under division (B) of section 2152.71 of the Revised Code, when a complaint is filed that alleges that a child is a delinquent child, the court shall determine if the victim of the alleged delinquent act was sixty-five years of age or older or permanently and totally disabled at the time of the alleged commission of the act.

(2004 S 185, eff. 4–11–05; 2000 S 179, § 3, eff. 1–1–02)

Historical and Statutory Notes

Amendment Note: 2004 S 185 substituted "3127.23" for "3109.27" in division (D).

Library References

Automobiles ⇌351.1.
Infants ⇌197.
Westlaw Topic Nos. 211, 48A.
C.J.S. Infants § 55.
C.J.S. Motor Vehicles §§ 1344, 1365 to 1371, 1397 to 1400, 1442 to 1443, 1473, 1486 to 1487, 1496, 1508, 1518, 1526, 1532, 1543 to 1547, 1550.

Research References

Encyclopedias
OH Jur. 3d Family Law § 1576, Detention Hearing; Notice.
OH Jur. 3d Family Law § 1590, Who May File Complaint.

Treatises and Practice Aids
Carlin, Baldwin's Ohio Practice, Merrick-Rippner Probate Law § 104:5, Juvenile Courts—Constitutional Issues—Right to Notice, Counsel, and Trial.
Carlin, Baldwin's Ohio Practice, Merrick-Rippner Probate Law § 107:2, Types of Complaints.
Carlin, Baldwin's Ohio Practice, Merrick-Rippner Probate Law § 107:3, Contents of Juvenile Complaint—Facts Establishing Jurisdiction.
Carlin, Baldwin's Ohio Practice, Merrick-Rippner Probate Law § 107:7, Jurisdiction and Venue for Juvenile Proceedings.
Carlin, Baldwin's Ohio Practice, Merrick-Rippner Probate Law § 107:8, Notice to School Officials.
Carlin, Baldwin's Ohio Practice, Merrick-Rippner Probate Law § 107:84, Disposition of Delinquent Children—Prior to January 1, 2002.
Carlin, Baldwin's Ohio Practice, Merrick-Rippner Probate Law § 107:136, Complaint, Delinquent Child—Form.
Giannelli & Yeomans, Ohio Juvenile Law § 14:3, Custody, Arrests & Stops.
Giannelli & Yeomans, Ohio Juvenile Law § 15:2, Intake.
Giannelli & Yeomans, Ohio Juvenile Law § 16:1, Introduction.
Giannelli & Yeomans, Ohio Juvenile Law § 16:7, Content of Complaint; Designating Type of Case.
Giannelli & Yeomans, Ohio Juvenile Law § 16:8, Delinquency Complaints.
Giannelli & Yeomans, Ohio Juvenile Law § 16:9, Traffic Offender Complaints.
Giannelli & Yeomans, Ohio Juvenile Law § 17:2, Proper Venue.
Giannelli & Yeomans, Ohio Juvenile Law § 32:3, Responsibilities to Victims and Others.

Notes of Decisions

Constitutional issues 1

1. Constitutional issues

Ohio's serious youthful offender sentencing scheme does not violate principles of due process; scheme does not unconstitutionally "target" very young offenders or unconstitutionally treat juveniles as adults, and while the scheme does, under certain circumstances, subject juveniles to adult punishment, the statute was crafted to take into account juvenile-adult distinctions. In re J.B. (Ohio App. 12 Dist., Butler, 12-30-2005) No. CA2004-09-226, 2005-Ohio-7029, 2005 WL 3610482, Unreported. Infants ⇌ 69(2)

Ohio's serious youthful offender sentencing scheme does not violate the Eighth Amendment's prohibition against cruel and unusual punishment; scheme does not provide for penalties against juveniles so greatly disproportionate to the offenses committed that those penalties shock the sense of justice in the community, scheme prohibits the imposition of the most severe adult punishment, and the scheme reserves adult punishment only for serious juvenile offenders not capable of being rehabilitated within the juvenile system. In re J.B. (Ohio App. 12 Dist., Butler, 12-30-2005) No. CA2004-09-226, 2005-Ohio-7029, 2005 WL 3610482, Unreported. Sentencing And Punishment ⇌ 1607

2152.03 Transfer of cases to juvenile court

When a child is arrested under any charge, complaint, affidavit, or indictment for a felony or a misdemeanor, proceedings regarding the child initially shall be in the juvenile court in accordance with this chapter. If the child is taken before a judge of a county court, a mayor, a judge of a municipal court, or a judge of a court of common pleas other than a juvenile court, the judge of the county court, mayor, judge of the municipal court, or judge of the court of common pleas shall transfer the case to the juvenile court, and, upon the transfer, the proceedings shall be in accordance with this chapter. Upon the transfer, all further proceedings under the charge, complaint, information, or indictment shall be discontinued in the court of the judge of the county court, mayor, municipal judge, or judge of the court of common pleas other than a juvenile court subject to section 2152.12 of the Revised Code. The case relating to the child then shall be within the exclusive jurisdiction of the juvenile court, subject to section 2152.12 of the Revised Code.

(2000 S 179, § 3, eff. 1–1–02)

Historical and Statutory Notes

Ed. Note: 2152.03 is former 2151.25, amended and recodified by 2000 S 179, § 3, eff. 1-1-02; 1995 H 1, eff. 1-1-96; 1975 H 205, eff. 1-1-76; 1969 H 320; 129 v 582; 1953 H 1; GC 1639-29.

Amendment Note: 2000 S 179, § 3, eff. 1–1–02, substituted "2152.12" for "2151.26" twice; and made other nonsubstantive changes.

Amendment Note: 1995 H 1 inserted "subject to section 2151.26 of the Revised Code" throughout, and made other nonsubstantive changes.

Cross References

Certification to juvenile court, 3109.06
Minor under sixteen not to be confined with adult prisoner, 341.11
Right to counsel, 2151.352

Library References

Infants ⟸68.6.
Westlaw Topic No. 211.
C.J.S. Infants §§ 41, 198 to 207.

Research References

Treatises and Practice Aids

Carlin, Baldwin's Ohio Practice, Merrick-Rippner Probate Law § 105:9, Juvenile Court—Waiver of Jurisdiction.

Carlin, Baldwin's Ohio Practice, Merrick-Rippner Probate Law § 107:14, Police Investigation of Juveniles—Custodial Interrogation.

Giannelli & Yeomans, Ohio Juvenile Law § 2:4, Mistaken or Concealed Age.

Giannelli & Yeomans, Ohio Juvenile Law § 3:3, Concurrent Jurisdiction.

Giannelli & Yeomans, Ohio Juvenile Law § 22:4, Improper Transfer; Lack of Jurisdiction.

Notes of Decisions

Ed. Note: This section contains annotations from former RC 2151.25.

Age of defendant 2
Charge 4
Confessions 6
Constitutional issues 1
Extradition 5
Failure to object to jurisdiction 3
Procedural issues 7

---

1. Constitutional issues

A voluntary confession to the perpetration of murder, obtained from a seventeen-year-old high school senior, which confession was made before indictment on said charge and while the accused was under arrest for a misdemeanor, is admissible in evidence (1) where the accused was first advised that "he would not be compelled to give a statement... if he wanted to give a statement it would be by his own free will and that statement would be used for or against him in court"; (2) where the accused was further advised that "he could secure the services of an attorney;" and (3) where there is no showing that the confession was obtained by inquisitorial processes, without the procedural safeguards of due process, and by such compulsion that the confession is irreconcilable with the possession of mental freedom. State v. Stewart (Summit 1963) 120 Ohio App. 199, 201 N.E.2d 793, 29 O.O.2d 4, affirmed 176 Ohio St. 156, 198 N.E.2d 439, 27 O.O.2d 42, certiorari denied 85 S.Ct. 443, 379 U.S. 947, 13 L.Ed.2d 544.

2. Age of defendant

Whether a boy convicted of a felony was under eighteen and should have been taken before the juvenile court under former GC 1659 (RC 2151.25) cannot be tried on habeas corpus, the jurisdiction of the convicting court not having been challenged until after trial. Ex parte Pharr (Ohio App. 1 Dist. 1919) 10 Ohio App. 395, 31 Ohio C.A. 465.

Upon the trial and conviction of a minor under eighteen in the common pleas court, the remedy is by proceeding in error. Ex parte Pharr (Ohio App. 1 Dist. 1919) 10 Ohio App. 395, 31 Ohio C.A. 465.

Common pleas court had subject matter jurisdiction over murder prosecution where, although defendant claimed that he was not more than 18 years old on date of offense, defendant was unsure of his actual birth date, documentary evidence from county children's services contained two conflicting birth dates almost four years apart, and bone marrow test indicated that defendant was approximately 20 years of age on date of offense. State v. Neguse (Franklin 1991) 71 Ohio App.3d 596, 594 N.E.2d 1116. Infants ⟸68.5.

Defendant charged with misdemeanor who, although only seventeen, misrepresented her age as twenty, could not after conviction assert a right to be tried in juvenile court. State v. Peterson (Ohio Mun. 1966) 9 Ohio Misc. 154, 223 N.E.2d 838, 38 O.O.2d 220, 38 O.O.2d 245.

One over eighteen years old when tried for rape committed when under such age held not entitled to have trial transferred to juvenile court. Scopillitti v. State (Cuyahoga 1932) 41 Ohio App. 221, 180 N.E. 740, 11 Ohio Law Abs. 461, 36 Ohio Law Rep. 187. Criminal Law ⟸101(3); Infants ⟸68.6.

Superintendent of Ohio state reformatory has no right to refuse to receive person committed to that institution by court having general jurisdiction to try felonies even though he has reason to believe that person committed was under eighteen and had not had benefit of proceedings under GC 1639–29 (RC 2151.25) and GC 1639–32 (RC 2151.26). 1944 OAG 6813.

Under authority of this act, juvenile court has exclusive jurisdiction of all persons under eighteen charged with arson or other burnings as contained in GC 12433 (RC 2907.02) and 12436 (RC 2907.07). 1939 OAG 726.

There is no statutory authority permitting a justice of peace or mayor to bind over a minor under eighteen to the court of common pleas to await action of grand jury; such magistrate has no jurisdiction to dispose of a case against a minor under eighteen other than to transfer the case to the juvenile judge. 1921 OAG p 114.

3. Failure to object to jurisdiction

Defendant who was 22 years old at time of trial waived personal jurisdiction of juvenile court when he did not disclose during trial that he was 17 years old at time he was alleged to have committed offense, and did not raise issue until after he was found guilty and sentenced. State v. Tillman (Lorain 1990) 66 Ohio App.3d 464, 585 N.E.2d 550, appeal after new trial 119 Ohio App.3d 449, 695 N.E.2d 792. Infants ⟸68.7(1)

A juvenile who submits without challenge to the jurisdiction of a municipal court cannot thereafter secure release in a habeas corpus action on the ground that the judgment and sentence of the municipal court is void for want of jurisdiction. Hemphill v. Johnson (Montgomery 1972) 31 Ohio App.2d 241, 287 N.E.2d 828, 60 O.O.2d 404. Habeas Corpus ⟸535

A minor charged with a felony, who does not object to the jurisdiction of the court of common pleas on the ground of his minority by raising that question before such court, loses his right to object after sentence by that court. Mellott v. Alvis (Franklin 1959) 109 Ohio App. 486, 162 N.E.2d 623, 81 Ohio Law Abs. 532, 12 O.O.2d 23. Infants ⟸68.8

Where a seventeen year old defendant charged with operating a motor vehicle without the owner's consent did not object to the jurisdiction of the common pleas court on the ground of his minority by raising that question in such court, he has lost his right to object after sentence by that court. Mellott v. Alvis (Franklin 1959) 109 Ohio App. 486, 162 N.E.2d 623, 81 Ohio Law Abs. 532, 12 O.O.2d 23. Infants ⟸68.8

The juvenile and general divisions of a court of common pleas possess concurrent jurisdiction over a juvenile accused of a crime, and the juvenile division has not been divested of personal jurisdiction over one whose disposition is returned to it after the accused initially waived his right to be judged in that tribunal. State ex rel. Leis v. Black (Hamilton 1975) 45 Ohio App.2d 191, 341 N.E.2d 853, 74 O.O.2d 270.

4. Charge

2151.25 does not apply until the juvenile involved is actually charged with a crime. State v. Carder (Ohio 1966) 9 Ohio St.2d 1, 222 N.E.2d 620, 38 O.O.2d 1.

When warrant has been issued by a juvenile court and minor has been arrested thereunder, upon a complaint charging him or her with being a delinquent child, the juvenile court has exclusive jurisdiction over such minor. State ex rel. Heth v. Moloney (Ohio 1933) 126 Ohio St. 526, 186 N.E. 362.

5. Extradition

A minor under eighteen who escapes from either boys industrial school or girls industrial school and flees to another state may not be returned to this state under provisions of Uniform Extradition Act. 1946 OAG 1378.

A person, who may be a child under eighteen years of age, charged with a crime in this state and who fled to another state may be returned to this state under Uniform Extradition Act; upon the return of such person, if he was a child at the time the crime was committed, he should be taken before the juvenile judge or, if taken before any other court, such other court shall transfer case to the juvenile judge as provided in this section. 1945 OAG 395.

6. Confessions

A voluntary confession to the perpetration of murder obtained from a sixteen and three-fourths year old high school junior, which confession was made before indictment and while the accused was detained for investigation, is admissible in evidence (1) where the accused had been allowed to consult with an attorney prior to being questioned, (2) where the accused first was advised that he did not have to talk, (3) where the accused, when told that his parents and another attorney were there and waiting to see him, stated that he did not want to see them, and (4) where there is no showing that the confession was obtained by inquisitorial processes. State v. Carder (Fairfield 1965) 3 Ohio App.2d 381, 210 N.E.2d 714, 32 O.O.2d 524, affirmed 9 Ohio St.2d 1, 222 N.E.2d 620, 38 O.O.2d 1.

Accused detained for eighteen days during which time he saw no one except his interrogators and who was regularly questioned and was the victim of physical and psychological coercion did not confess voluntarily, and admission of confession in 1955 was erroneous. Jordan v. Cardwell (N.D.Ohio 1971) 334 F.Supp. 193.

7. Procedural issues

Court of common pleas lacked subject matter jurisdiction to convict 17-year-old defendant of grand theft and, thus, judgment of conviction against him was void ab initio; since defendant was child under statute and was never bound over by juvenile court, juvenile court retained exclusive jurisdiction over defendant's case. State v. Wilson (Ohio, 08-09-1995) 73 Ohio St.3d 40, 652 N.E.2d 196, 1995-Ohio-217. Infants ⚖ 68.5

Absent proper bindover procedure pursuant to statute, juvenile court has exclusive subject matter jurisdiction over any case concerning child who is alleged to be delinquent. State v. Wilson (Ohio, 08-09-1995) 73 Ohio St.3d 40, 652 N.E.2d 196, 1995-Ohio-217. Infants ⚖ 68.5

RC 5141.16 was repealed by subsequently enacted provisions of RC 2151.25 and RC 2151.26. State v. Worden (Ohio 1955) 162 Ohio St. 593, 124 N.E.2d 817, 55 O.O. 483.

The juvenile court does not have exclusive jurisdiction of the prosecution of a minor until the case is transferred to it. Harris v. Alvis (Franklin 1950) 104 N.E.2d 182, 61 Ohio Law Abs. 311.

The statute relating to the arrest of minors, has application only to arrests in criminal cases. Durst v. Griffith (Hocking 1932) 43 Ohio App. 44, 182 N.E. 519, 12 Ohio Law Abs. 522, 37 Ohio Law Rep. 183.

When a justice of the peace under former GC 1659 (RC 2151.25) transferred the case of a minor to the juvenile judge, fees and costs of the justice of the peace and his constable, originally made, followed the case for allowance and payments under former GC 1682 (RC 2151.54). 1935 OAG 4109.

2152.04 Social histories of delinquent children

A child who is alleged to be, or who is adjudicated, a delinquent child may be confined in a place of juvenile detention provided under section 2152.41 of the Revised Code for a period not to exceed ninety days, during which time a social history may be prepared to include court record, family history, personal history, school and attendance records, and any other pertinent studies and material that will be of assistance to the juvenile court in its disposition of the charges against that alleged or adjudicated delinquent child.

(2000 S 179, § 3, eff. 1–1–02)

Library References

Infants ⚖192, 201, 223.
Westlaw Topic No. 211.
C.J.S. Infants §§ 41, 53 to 55, 57, 69 to 85.

Research References

Encyclopedias

OH Jur. 3d Family Law § 1570, Apprehension.

Treatises and Practice Aids

Carlin, Baldwin's Ohio Practice, Merrick-Rippner Probate Law § 107:28, Children Subject to Detention.

Giannelli & Yeomans, Ohio Juvenile Law § 19:1, Introduction.

Giannelli & Yeomans, Ohio Juvenile Law § 19:6, Standard for Detention.

DISPOSITIONAL ORDERS

2152.10 Mandatory transfer; discretionary transfer

(A) A child who is alleged to be a delinquent child is eligible for mandatory transfer and shall be transferred as provided in section 2152.12 of the Revised Code in any of the following circumstances:

(1) The child is charged with a category one offense and either of the following apply:

(a) The child was sixteen years of age or older at the time of the act charged.

(b) The child was fourteen or fifteen years of age at the time of the act charged and previously was adjudicated a delinquent child for committing an act that is a category one or category two offense and was committed to the legal custody of the department of youth services upon the basis of that adjudication.

(2) The child is charged with a category two offense, other than a violation of section 2905.01 of the Revised Code, the child was sixteen years of age or older at the time of the commission of the act charged, and either or both of the following apply:

(a) The child previously was adjudicated a delinquent child for committing an act that is a category one or a category two offense and was committed to the legal custody of the department of youth services on the basis of that adjudication.

(b) The child is alleged to have had a firearm on or about the child's person or under the child's control while committing the act charged and to have displayed the firearm, brandished the firearm, indicated possession of the firearm, or used the firearm to facilitate the commission of the act charged.

(3) Division (A)(2) of section 2152.12 of the Revised Code applies.

(B) Unless the child is subject to mandatory transfer, if a child is fourteen years of age or older at the time of the act charged and if the child is charged with an act that would be a felony if committed by an adult, the child is eligible for discretionary transfer to the appropriate court for criminal prosecution. In determining whether to transfer the child for criminal prosecution, the juvenile court shall follow the procedures in section 2152.12 of the Revised Code. If the court does not transfer the child and if the court adjudicates the child to be a delinquent child for the act charged, the court shall issue an order of disposition in accordance with section 2152.11 of the Revised Code.

(2002 H 393, eff. 7–5–02; 2000 S 179, § 3, eff. 1–1–02)

Historical and Statutory Notes

Amendment Note: 2002 H 393 inserted "brandished the firearm," in division (A)(2)(b).

Library References

Infants ⚖68.5, 68.7.
Westlaw Topic No. 211.
C.J.S. Infants §§ 41, 198 to 207.

Research References

Treatises and Practice Aids

Katz, Giannelli, Blair and Lipton, Baldwin's Ohio Practice, Criminal Law, § 128:2, Transfer to Criminal Courts.

Carlin, Baldwin's Ohio Practice, Merrick-Rippner Probate Law § 107:64, Mandatory Transfer.

Carlin, Baldwin's Ohio Practice, Merrick-Rippner Probate Law § 107:65, Mandatory Transfer, Effective January 1, 2002.

Carlin, Baldwin's Ohio Practice, Merrick-Rippner Probate Law § 107:66, Discretionary Transfer.

Carlin, Baldwin's Ohio Practice, Merrick-Rippner Probate Law § 107:69, Court's Discretion to Transfer or Retain Jurisdiction.

Carlin, Baldwin's Ohio Practice, Merrick-Rippner Probate Law § 107:189, Order Transferring Action for Criminal Prosecution in Common Pleas Court, Effective January 1, 2002—Form.

Giannelli & Yeomans, Ohio Juvenile Law § 4:4, Ohio Penal Law.

Giannelli & Yeomans, Ohio Juvenile Law § 4:6, Court Order Violations.

Giannelli & Yeomans, Ohio Juvenile Law § 22:1, Introduction.

Giannelli & Yeomans, Ohio Juvenile Law § 22:5, Transfer Age Requirement.

Giannelli & Yeomans, Ohio Juvenile Law § 22:7, Mandatory Transfer.

Giannelli & Yeomans, Ohio Juvenile Law § 22:8, Discretionary Transfer.

Giannelli & Yeomans, Ohio Juvenile Law § 22:9, Amenability Hearing Procedures.

Notes of Decisions

Age of juvenile at time of criminal act 2
Firearm 1

---

1. Firearm

Juvenile court lacked subject matter jurisdiction to accept admission from 16 year old defendant who was charged with aggravated robbery with a firearm specification. In re Graham (Ohio App. 7 Dist., 05-17-2002) 147 Ohio App.3d 452, 770 N.E.2d 1123, 2002-Ohio-2407. Infants ⚖ 196

Remand was required for juvenile court to determine if it had jurisdiction over 16 year old defendant who was charged with aggravated robbery with a firearm specification. In re Graham (Ohio App. 7 Dist., 05-17-2002) 147 Ohio App.3d 452, 770 N.E.2d 1123, 2002-Ohio-2407. Infants ⚖ 254

If a juvenile offender meets defined criteria, the juvenile court may, or in specific cases shall, transfer the case to the general division of the common pleas court; in specified situations, transfer to the general division is mandatory, one such mandatory transfer situation is where the juvenile is alleged to have used a firearm in commission of certain crimes. In re Graham (Ohio App. 7 Dist., 05-17-2002) 147 Ohio App.3d 452, 770 N.E.2d 1123, 2002-Ohio-2407. Infants ⚖ 68.7(1)

2. Age of juvenile at time of criminal act

Juvenile court should have considered discretionary bindover factors in ruling on State's motion to bind over juveniles to common pleas court, where juveniles were age 14 or over at time of criminal acts, they were charged with engaging in pattern of criminal gang activity, a second-degree felony, and juvenile court had determined that there was probable cause to believe that juveniles had committed offense. In re Stanley (Ohio App. 7 Dist., 03-14-2006) 165 Ohio App.3d 726, 848 N.E.2d 540, 2006-Ohio-1279. Infants ⚖ 68.7(2)

2152.11 More restrictive dispositions for commission of enhanced acts

(A) A child who is adjudicated a delinquent child for committing an act that would be a felony if committed by an adult is eligible for a particular type of disposition under this section if the child was not transferred under section 2152.12 of the Revised Code. If the complaint, indictment, or information charging the act includes one or more of the following factors, the act is considered to be enhanced, and the child is eligible for a more restrictive disposition under this section:

(1) The act charged against the child would be an offense of violence if committed by an adult.

(2) During the commission of the act charged, the child used a firearm, displayed a firearm, brandished a firearm, or indicated that the child possessed a firearm and actually possessed a firearm.

(3) The child previously was admitted to a department of youth services facility for the commission of an act that would have been aggravated murder, murder, a felony of the first or second degree if committed by an adult, or an act that would have been a felony of the third degree and an offense of violence if committed by an adult.

(B) If a child is adjudicated a delinquent child for committing an act that would be aggravated murder or murder if committed by an adult, the child is eligible for whichever of the following is appropriate:

(1) Mandatory SYO, if the act allegedly was committed when the child was fourteen or fifteen years of age;

(2) Discretionary SYO, if the act was committed when the child was ten, eleven, twelve, or thirteen years of age;

(3) Traditional juvenile, if divisions (B)(1) and (2) of this section do not apply.

(C) If a child is adjudicated a delinquent child for committing an act that would be attempted aggravated murder or attempted murder if committed by an adult, the child is eligible for whichever of the following is appropriate:

(1) Mandatory SYO, if the act allegedly was committed when the child was fourteen or fifteen years of age;

(2) Discretionary SYO, if the act was committed when the child was ten, eleven, twelve, or thirteen years of age;

(3) Traditional juvenile, if divisions (C)(1) and (2) of this section do not apply.

(D) If a child is adjudicated a delinquent child for committing an act that would be a felony of the first degree if committed by an adult, the child is eligible for whichever of the following is appropriate:

(1) Mandatory SYO, if the act allegedly was committed when the child was sixteen or seventeen years of age, and the act is enhanced by the factors described in division (A)(1) and either division (A)(2) or (3) of this section;

(2) Discretionary SYO, if any of the following applies:

(a) The act was committed when the child was sixteen or seventeen years of age, and division (D)(1) of this section does not apply.

(b) The act was committed when the child was fourteen or fifteen years of age.

(c) The act was committed when the child was twelve or thirteen years of age, and the act is enhanced by any factor described in division (A)(1), (2), or (3) of this section.

(d) The act was committed when the child was ten or eleven years of age, and the act is enhanced by the factors described in division (A)(1) and either division (A)(2) or (3) of this section.

(3) Traditional juvenile, if divisions (D)(1) and (2) of this section do not apply.

(E) If a child is adjudicated a delinquent child for committing an act that would be a felony of the second degree if committed by an adult, the child is eligible for whichever of the following is appropriate:

(1) Discretionary SYO, if the act was committed when the child was fourteen, fifteen, sixteen, or seventeen years of age;

(2) Discretionary SYO, if the act was committed when the child was twelve or thirteen years of age, and the act is enhanced by any factor described in division (A)(1), (2), or (3) of this section;

(3) Traditional juvenile, if divisions (E)(1) and (2) of this section do not apply.

(F) If a child is adjudicated a delinquent child for committing an act that would be a felony of the third degree if committed by an adult, the child is eligible for whichever of the following is appropriate:

(1) Discretionary SYO, if the act was committed when the child was sixteen or seventeen years of age;

(2) Discretionary SYO, if the act was committed when the child was fourteen or fifteen years of age, and the act is enhanced by any factor described in division (A)(1), (2), or (3) of this section;

(3) Traditional juvenile, if divisions (F)(1) and (2) of this section do not apply.

(G) If a child is adjudicated a delinquent child for committing an act that would be a felony of the fourth or fifth degree if committed by an adult, the child is eligible for whichever of the following dispositions is appropriate:

(1) Discretionary SYO, if the act was committed when the child was sixteen or seventeen years of age, and the act is enhanced by any factor described in division (A)(1), (2), or (3) of this section;

(2) Traditional juvenile, if division (G)(1) of this section does not apply.

(H) The following table describes the dispositions that a juvenile court may impose on a delinquent child:

OFFENSE CATEGORY (Enhancement factors)	AGE 16 & 17	AGE 14 & 15	AGE 12 & 13	AGE 10 & 11
Murder/aggravated Murder	N/A	MSYO, TJ	DSYO, TJ	DSYO, TJ
Attempted Murder/Attempted Aggravated Murder	N/A	MSYO, TJ	DSYO, TJ	DSYO, TJ
F1 (enhanced by offense of violence factor and either disposition firearm factor or previous DYS admission factor)	MSYO, TJ	DSYO, TJ	DSYO, TJ	DSYO, TJ
F1 (enhanced by any single or other combination of enhancement factors)	DSYO, TJ	DSYO, TJ	DSYO, TJ	TJ
F1 (not enhanced)	DSYO, TJ	DSYO, TJ	TJ	TJ
F2 (enhanced by any enhancement factor)	DSYO, TJ	DSYO, TJ	DSYO, TJ	TJ
F2 (not enhanced)	DSYO, TJ	DSYO, TJ	TJ	TJ
F3 (enhanced by any enhancement factor)	DSYO, TJ	DSYO, TJ	TJ	TJ
F3 (not enhanced)	DSYO, TJ	TJ	TJ	TJ
F4 (enhanced by any enhancement factor)	DSYO, TJ	TJ	TJ	TJ
F4 (not enhanced)	TJ	TJ	TJ	TJ
F5 (enhanced by any enhancement factor)	DSYO, TJ	TJ	TJ	TJ
F5 (not enhanced)	TJ	TJ	TJ	TJ

(I) The table in division (H) of this section is for illustrative purposes only. If the table conflicts with any provision of divisions (A) to (G) of this section, divisions (A) to (G) of this section shall control.

(J) Key for table in division (H) of this section:

(1) "Any enhancement factor" applies when the criteria described in division (A)(1), (2), or (3) of this section apply.

(2) The "disposition firearm factor" applies when the criteria described in division (A)(2) of this section apply.

(3) "DSYO" refers to discretionary serious youthful offender disposition.

(4) "F1" refers to an act that would be a felony of the first degree if committed by an adult.

(5) "F2" refers to an act that would be a felony of the second degree if committed by an adult.

(6) "F3" refers to an act that would be a felony of the third degree if committed by an adult.

(7) "F4" refers to an act that would be a felony of the fourth degree if committed by an adult.

(8) "F5" refers to an act that would be a felony of the fifth degree if committed by an adult.

(9) "MSYO" refers to mandatory serious youthful offender disposition.

(10) The "offense of violence factor" applies when the criteria described in division (A)(1) of this section apply.

(11) The "previous DYS admission factor" applies when the criteria described in division (A)(3) of this section apply.

(12) "TJ" refers to traditional juvenile.

(2000 S 179, § 3, eff. 1–1–02)

Library References

Infants ⚖69(3), 223.
Westlaw Topic No. 211.
C.J.S. Infants §§ 57, 69 to 85, 198, 207 to 209.

Research References

Encyclopedias
OH Jur. 3d Family Law § 1500, Relating to Persons.
OH Jur. 3d Family Law § 1503, Relating to Procedure.
OH Jur. 3d Family Law § 1590, Who May File Complaint.

Treatises and Practice Aids
Carlin, Baldwin's Ohio Practice, Merrick-Rippner Probate Law § 107:102, Serious Youthful Offenders, Effective January 1, 2002.
Carlin, Baldwin's Ohio Practice, Merrick-Rippner Probate Law § 107:103, Enhanced Dispositions as a Serious Youthful Offender, Effective January 1, 2002.
Giannelli & Yeomans, Ohio Juvenile Law § 5:5, Syo Enhancements.
Giannelli & Yeomans, Ohio Juvenile Law § 5:7, Mandatory Syo Dispositions.
Giannelli & Yeomans, Ohio Juvenile Law § 5:8, Discretionary Syo Dispositions.

Notes of Decisions

Constitutional issues 1

1. Constitutional issues

Ohio's serious youthful offender sentencing scheme does not violate the Eighth Amendment's prohibition against cruel and unusual punishment; scheme does not provide for penalties against juveniles so greatly disproportionate to the offenses committed that those penalties shock the sense of justice in the community, scheme prohibits the imposition of the most severe adult punishment, and the scheme reserves adult punishment only for serious juvenile offenders not capable of being rehabilitated within the juvenile system. In re J.B. (Ohio App. 12 Dist., Butler, 12-30-2005) No. CA2004-09-226, 2005-Ohio-7029, 2005 WL 3610482, Unreported. Sentencing And Punishment ⚖ 1607

Ohio's serious youthful offender sentencing scheme does not violate principles of due process; scheme does not unconstitutionally "target" very young offenders or unconstitutionally treat juveniles as adults, and while the scheme does, under certain circumstances, subject juveniles to adult punishment, the statute was crafted to take into account juvenile-adult distinctions. In re J.B. (Ohio App. 12 Dist., Butler, 12-30-2005) No. CA2004-09-226, 2005-Ohio-7029, 2005 WL 3610482, Unreported. Infants ⚖ 69(2)

2152.12 Transfer of cases from juvenile court

(A)(1)(a) After a complaint has been filed alleging that a child is a delinquent child for committing an act that would be aggravated murder, murder, attempted aggravated murder, or attempted murder if committed by an adult, the juvenile court at a hearing shall transfer the case if the child was sixteen or seventeen years of age at the time of the act charged and there is probable cause to believe that the child committed the act charged. The juvenile court also shall transfer the case at a hearing if the child was fourteen or fifteen years of age at the time of the act charged, if section 2152.10 of the Revised Code provides that the child is eligible for mandatory transfer, and if there is probable cause to believe that the child committed the act charged.

(b) After a complaint has been filed alleging that a child is a delinquent child by reason of committing a category two offense, the juvenile court at a hearing shall transfer the case if section 2152.10 of the Revised Code requires the mandatory transfer of the case and there is probable cause to believe that the child committed the act charged.

(2) The juvenile court also shall transfer a case in the circumstances described in division (C)(5) of section 2152.02 of the Revised Code or if either of the following applies:

(a) A complaint is filed against a child who is eligible for a discretionary transfer under section 2152.10 of the Revised Code and who previously was convicted of or pleaded guilty to a felony in a case that was transferred to a criminal court.

(b) A complaint is filed against a child who is domiciled in another state alleging that the child is a delinquent child for committing an act that would be a felony if committed by an adult, and, if the act charged had been committed in that other state, the child would be subject to criminal prosecution as an adult under the law of that other state without the need for a transfer of jurisdiction from a juvenile, family, or similar noncriminal court to a criminal court.

(B) Except as provided in division (A) of this section, after a complaint has been filed alleging that a child is a delinquent child for committing an act that would be a felony if committed by an adult, the juvenile court at a hearing may transfer the case if the court finds all of the following:

(1) The child was fourteen years of age or older at the time of the act charged.

(2) There is probable cause to believe that the child committed the act charged.

(3) The child is not amenable to care or rehabilitation within the juvenile system, and the safety of the community may require that the child be subject to adult sanctions. In making its decision under this division, the court shall consider whether the applicable factors under division (D) of this section indicating that the case should be transferred outweigh the applicable factors under division (E) of this section indicating that the case should not be transferred. The record shall indicate the specific factors that were applicable and that the court weighed.

(C) Before considering a transfer under division (B) of this section, the juvenile court shall order an investigation, including a mental examination of the child by a public or private agency or a person qualified to make the examination. The child may waive the examination required by this division if the court finds that the waiver is competently and intelligently made. Refusal to submit to a mental examination by the child constitutes a waiver of the examination.

(D) In considering whether to transfer a child under division (B) of this section, the juvenile court shall consider the following relevant factors, and any other relevant factors, in favor of a transfer under that division:

(1) The victim of the act charged suffered physical or psychological harm, or serious economic harm, as a result of the alleged act.

(2) The physical or psychological harm suffered by the victim due to the alleged act of the child was exacerbated because of the physical or psychological vulnerability or the age of the victim.

(3) The child's relationship with the victim facilitated the act charged.

(4) The child allegedly committed the act charged for hire or as a part of a gang or other organized criminal activity.

(5) The child had a firearm on or about the child's person or under the child's control at the time of the act charged, the act charged is not a violation of section 2923.12 of the Revised Code, and the child, during the commission of the act charged, allegedly used or displayed the firearm, brandished the firearm, or indicated that the child possessed a firearm.

(6) At the time of the act charged, the child was awaiting adjudication or disposition as a delinquent child, was under a community control sanction, or was on parole for a prior delinquent child adjudication or conviction.

(7) The results of any previous juvenile sanctions and programs indicate that rehabilitation of the child will not occur in the juvenile system.

(8) The child is emotionally, physically, or psychologically mature enough for the transfer.

(9) There is not sufficient time to rehabilitate the child within the juvenile system.

(E) In considering whether to transfer a child under division (B) of this section, the juvenile court shall consider the following relevant factors, and any other relevant factors, against a transfer under that division:

(1) The victim induced or facilitated the act charged.

(2) The child acted under provocation in allegedly committing the act charged.

(3) The child was not the principal actor in the act charged, or, at the time of the act charged, the child was under the negative influence or coercion of another person.

(4) The child did not cause physical harm to any person or property, or have reasonable cause to believe that harm of that nature would occur, in allegedly committing the act charged.

(5) The child previously has not been adjudicated a delinquent child.

(6) The child is not emotionally, physically, or psychologically mature enough for the transfer.

(7) The child has a mental illness or is a mentally retarded person.

(8) There is sufficient time to rehabilitate the child within the juvenile system and the level of security available in the juvenile system provides a reasonable assurance of public safety.

(F) If one or more complaints are filed alleging that a child is a delinquent child for committing two or more acts that would be offenses if committed by an adult, if a motion is made alleging that division (A) of this section applies and requires that the case or cases involving one or more of the acts charged be transferred for, and if a motion also is made requesting that the case or cases involving one or more of the acts charged be transferred pursuant to division (B) of this section, the juvenile court, in deciding the motions, shall proceed in the following manner:

(1) Initially, the court shall decide the motion alleging that division (A) of this section applies and requires that the case or cases involving one or more of the acts charged be transferred.

(2) If the court determines that division (A) of this section applies and requires that the case or cases involving one or more of the acts charged be transferred, the court shall transfer the case or cases in accordance with the that division. After the transfer pursuant to division (A) of this section, the court shall decide, in accordance with division (B) of this section, whether to grant the motion requesting that the case or cases involving one or more of the acts charged be transferred pursuant to that division. Notwithstanding division (B) of this section, prior to transferring a case pursuant to division (A) of this section, the court is not required to consider any factor specified in division

(D) or (E) of this section or to conduct an investigation under division (C) of this section.

(3) If the court determines that division (A) of this section does not require that the case or cases involving one or more of the acts charged be transferred, the court shall decide in accordance with division (B) of this section whether to grant the motion requesting that the case or cases involving one or more of the acts charged be transferred pursuant to that division.

(G) The court shall give notice in writing of the time, place, and purpose of any hearing held pursuant to division (A) or (B) of this section to the child's parents, guardian, or other custodian and to the child's counsel at least three days prior to the hearing.

(H) No person, either before or after reaching eighteen years of age, shall be prosecuted as an adult for an offense committed prior to becoming eighteen years of age, unless the person has been transferred as provided in division (A) or (B) of this section or unless division (J) of this section applies. Any prosecution that is had in a criminal court on the mistaken belief that the person who is the subject of the case was eighteen years of age or older at the time of the commission of the offense shall be deemed a nullity, and the person shall not be considered to have been in jeopardy on the offense.

(I) Upon the transfer of a case under division (A) or (B) of this section, the juvenile court shall state the reasons for the transfer on the record, and shall order the child to enter into a recognizance with good and sufficient surety for the child's appearance before the appropriate court for any disposition that the court is authorized to make for a similar act committed by an adult. The transfer abates the jurisdiction of the juvenile court with respect to the delinquent acts alleged in the complaint, and, upon the transfer, all further proceedings pertaining to the act charged shall be discontinued in the juvenile court, and the case then shall be within the jurisdiction of the court to which it is transferred as described in division (H) of section 2151.23 of the Revised Code.

(J) If a person under eighteen years of age allegedly commits an act that would be a felony if committed by an adult and if the person is not taken into custody or apprehended for that act until after the person attains twenty-one years of age, the juvenile court does not have jurisdiction to hear or determine any portion of the case charging the person with committing that act. In those circumstances, divisions (A) and (B) of this section do not apply regarding the act, and the case charging the person with committing the act shall be a criminal prosecution commenced and heard in the appropriate court having jurisdiction of the offense as if the person had been eighteen years of age or older when the person committed the act. All proceedings pertaining to the act shall be within the jurisdiction of the court having jurisdiction of the offense, and that court has all the authority and duties in the case as it has in other criminal cases in that court.

(2000 S 179, § 3, eff. 1–1–02)

Uncodified Law

1995 H 1, § 3: See Uncodified Law under 2151.011.

1991 H 27, § 3, eff. 10–10–91, reads: The provisions of section 2151.26 of the Revised Code, as amended by this act, apply only to offenses that are committed on or after the effective date of this act.

Historical and Statutory Notes

Ed. Note: 2152.12 is former 2151.26, amended and recodified by 2000 S 179, § 3, eff. 1–1–02; 1996 H 124, eff. 3–31–97; 1996 S 269, eff. 7–1–96; 1995 S 2, eff. 7–1–96; 1995 H 1, eff. 1–1–96; 1991 H 27, eff. 10–10–91; 1986 H 499; 1983 S 210; 1981 H 440; 1978 H 119; 1971 S 325; 1969 H 320.

Amendment Note: 2000 S 179, § 3, eff. 1–1–02, rewrote this section. See *Baldwin's Ohio Legislative Service Annotated*, 2000, page 11/L–3649, or the OH–LEGIS or OH–LEGIS–OLD database on Westlaw, for prior version of this section.

Amendment Note: 1996 H 124 deleted a reference to former section 2907.12 from division (A)(2)(a); added division (A)(2)(c); inserted "and subject to division (C)(4) of this section" in the first paragraph in division (C)(1); inserted "Subject to division (C)(4) of this section," in the first paragraph in division (C)(2); added division (C)(4); inserted "or unless division (G) of this section applies" in division (E); added division (G); and made other nonsubstantive changes.

Amendment Note: 1996 S 269 substituted "a felony" for "an aggravated felony" in division (A)(2)(b); added division (a)(4); inserted "or the act charged" in the introductory paragraph of division (B); deleted "be alleged in the complaint" preceding "When determining" in division (C)(2); and made other nonsubstantive changes.

Amendment Note: 1995 S 2 deleted a reference to section 2901.01 from division (B)(1); deleted "would constitute an aggravated felony of the first or second degree or" from and inserted ", or third" in division (G); and made changes to reflect gender neutral language and other nonsubstantive changes.

Amendment Note: 1995 H 1 rewrote this section, which previously read:

"(A)(1) Except as provided in division (A)(2) of this section, after a complaint has been filed alleging that a child is a delinquent child for committing an act that would constitute a felony if committed by an adult, the court at a hearing may transfer the case for criminal prosecution to the appropriate court having jurisdiction of the offense, after making the following determinations:

"(a) The child was fifteen years of age or older at the time of the conduct charged;

"(b) There is probable cause to believe that the child committed the act alleged;

"(c) After an investigation, including a mental and physical examination of the child made by a public or private agency or a person qualified to make the examination, and after consideration of all relevant information and factors, including any fact required to be considered by division (B)(2) of this section, that there are reasonable grounds to believe that:

"(i) He is not amenable to care or rehabilitation or further care or rehabilitation in any facility designed for the care, supervision, and rehabilitation of delinquent children;

"(ii) The safety of the community may require that he be placed under legal restraint, including, if necessary, for the period extending beyond his majority.

"(2) After a complaint has been filed alleging that a child is a delinquent child for committing an act that would constitute aggravated murder or murder if committed by an adult, the court at a hearing shall transfer the case for criminal prosecution to the appropriate court having jurisdiction of the offense, if the court determines at the hearing that both of the following apply:

"(a) There is probable cause to believe that the child committed the alleged act.

"(b) The child previously has been adjudicated a delinquent child for the commission of an act that would constitute aggravated murder or murder if committed by an adult.

"(B)(1) The court, when determining whether to transfer a case pursuant to division (A)(1) of this section, shall determine if the victim of the delinquent act was sixty-five years of age or older or permanently and totally disabled at the time of the commission of the act and whether the act alleged, if actually committed, would be an offense of violence, as defined in section 2901.01 of the Revised Code, if committed by an adult. Regardless of whether or not the child knew the age of the victim, if the court determines that the victim was sixty-five years of age or older or permanently and totally disabled, that fact shall be considered by the court in favor of transfer, but shall not control the decision of the court. Additionally, if the court determines that the act alleged, if actually committed, would be an offense of violence, as defined in section 2901.01 of the Revised Code, if committed by an adult, that fact shall be considered by the court in favor of transfer, but shall not control the decision of the court.

"(2)(a) As used in division (B)(2)(b) of this section, "foreign jurisdiction" means any state other than this state, any foreign country or nation, or any province, territory, or other political subdivision of any foreign country or nation.

"(b) The court, when determining whether to transfer a case pursuant to division (A)(1) of this section, shall determine whether the child is domiciled in this state or in a foreign jurisdiction and, if the child is domiciled in a foreign jurisdiction, whether the law of that foreign jurisdiction would subject him to criminal prosecution as an adult for the alleged act without the need for any transfer of jurisdiction from a juvenile, family, or similar noncriminal court to a criminal court if that act had been committed in that foreign jurisdiction. If the court determines that the child is domiciled in a foreign jurisdiction and that, if the alleged act had been committed in that foreign jurisdiction, the law of that foreign jurisdiction would subject him to criminal prosecution as an adult for that act without the need for any transfer of jurisdiction from a juvenile, family, or similar noncriminal court to a criminal court, the court shall consider that fact, along with all other relevant information and factors, in determining whether there are reasonable grounds to believe that the child is not amenable to care or rehabilitation or further care or rehabilitation, as described in division (A)(1)(c)(i) of this section, and whether there are reasonable grounds to believe that the safety of the community may require that the child be placed under legal restraint, as described in division (A)(1)(c)(ii) of this section.

"(C) The child may waive the examination required by division (A)(1)(c) of this section, if the court finds the waiver competently and intelligently made. Refusal to submit to a mental and physical examination by the child constitutes waiver of the examination.

"(D) Notice in writing of the time, place, and purpose of any hearing held pursuant to division (A) of this section shall be given to the child's parents, guardian, or other custodian and his counsel at least three days prior to the hearing.

"(E) No child, either before or after reaching eighteen years of age, shall be prosecuted as an adult for an offense committed prior to becoming eighteen, unless the child has been transferred as provided in this section. Any prosecution that is had in a criminal court on the mistaken belief that the child was eighteen years of age or older at the time of the commission of the offense shall be deemed a nullity, and the child shall not be considered to have been in jeopardy on the offense.

"(F) Upon such transfer, the juvenile court shall state the reasons for the transfer and order the child to enter into a recognizance with good and sufficient surety for his appearance before the appropriate court for any disposition that the court is authorized to make for a like act committed by an adult. The transfer abates the jurisdiction of the juvenile court with respect to the delinquent acts alleged in the complaint.

"(G) Any child whose case is transferred for criminal prosecution pursuant to this section and who subsequently is convicted in that case thereafter shall be prosecuted as an adult in the appropriate court for any future act that he is alleged to have committed that if committed by an adult would constitute the offense of murder or aggravated murder, or would constitute an aggravated felony of the first or second degree or a felony of the first or second degree."

Cross References

Imprisoned minors deemed emancipated for purpose of consent to medical treatment, 5120.172
Relinquishment of jurisdiction, procedure, Juv R 30
Sex offenders, definitions, 2950.01
Social history, physical and mental examinations, custody investigation, Juv R 32
Youth services department, category one offense and category two offense defined, 5139.01

Library References

Infants ⚖68.7.
Westlaw Topic No. 211.
C.J.S. Infants §§ 41, 198 to 207.

Research References

Encyclopedias

OH Jur. 3d Criminal Law § 2013, Transfers from Juvenile Court for Criminal Prosecution; Relinquishment of Jurisdiction.
OH Jur. 3d Family Law § 1515, Powers.
OH Jur. 3d Family Law § 1562, Notice and Hearing.
OH Jur. 3d Family Law § 1563, Determination by Court.
OH Jur. 3d Family Law § 1564, Waiver of Mental or Physical Examination.
OH Jur. 3d Family Law § 1565, Order of Transfer; Resumption of Jurisdiction by Juvenile Court.
OH Jur. 3d Family Law § 1571, Apprehension—Release on Bail.
OH Jur. 3d Family Law § 1626, Right Under Juvenile Court Law and Rules.
OH Jur. 3d Family Law § 1698.5, Serious Youthful Offender.

Treatises and Practice Aids

Katz, Giannelli, Blair and Lipton, Baldwin's Ohio Practice, Criminal Law, § 128:2, Transfer to Criminal Courts.
Carlin, Baldwin's Ohio Practice, Merrick-Rippner Probate Law § 105:7, Juvenile Court—Attachment of Jurisdiction.
Carlin, Baldwin's Ohio Practice, Merrick-Rippner Probate Law § 105:8, Juvenile Court—Age Jurisdiction.
Carlin, Baldwin's Ohio Practice, Merrick-Rippner Probate Law § 107:63, Transfer of Jurisdiction to Criminal Court—Introduction.
Carlin, Baldwin's Ohio Practice, Merrick-Rippner Probate Law § 107:64, Mandatory Transfer.
Carlin, Baldwin's Ohio Practice, Merrick-Rippner Probate Law § 107:65, Mandatory Transfer, Effective January 1, 2002.
Carlin, Baldwin's Ohio Practice, Merrick-Rippner Probate Law § 107:66, Discretionary Transfer.
Carlin, Baldwin's Ohio Practice, Merrick-Rippner Probate Law § 107:67, Procedural Due Process Requirements in Transfer Proceedings.
Carlin, Baldwin's Ohio Practice, Merrick-Rippner Probate Law § 107:69, Court's Discretion to Transfer or Retain Jurisdiction.
Carlin, Baldwin's Ohio Practice, Merrick-Rippner Probate Law § 107:90, Disposition Orders for Delinquent Children, Effective January 1, 2002.
Carlin, Baldwin's Ohio Practice, Merrick-Rippner Probate Law § 107:102, Serious Youthful Offenders, Effective January 1, 2002.
Carlin, Baldwin's Ohio Practice, Merrick-Rippner Probate Law § 107:189, Order Transferring Action for Criminal Prosecution in Common Pleas Court, Effective January 1, 2002—Form.
Giannelli & Yeomans, Ohio Juvenile Law § 1:7, Juvenile Code.
Giannelli & Yeomans, Ohio Juvenile Law § 2:3, Child Subject to Adult Prosecution.
Giannelli & Yeomans, Ohio Juvenile Law § 2:4, Mistaken or Concealed Age.
Giannelli & Yeomans, Ohio Juvenile Law § 3:3, Concurrent Jurisdiction.
Giannelli & Yeomans, Ohio Juvenile Law § 4:4, Ohio Penal Law.
Giannelli & Yeomans, Ohio Juvenile Law § 21:6, Social History Report.
Giannelli & Yeomans, Ohio Juvenile Law § 22:1, Introduction.
Giannelli & Yeomans, Ohio Juvenile Law § 22:4, Improper Transfer; Lack of Jurisdiction.
Giannelli & Yeomans, Ohio Juvenile Law § 22:5, Transfer Age Requirement.
Giannelli & Yeomans, Ohio Juvenile Law § 22:6, Probable Cause Requirement.
Giannelli & Yeomans, Ohio Juvenile Law § 22:7, Mandatory Transfer.
Giannelli & Yeomans, Ohio Juvenile Law § 22:8, Discretionary Transfer.
Giannelli & Yeomans, Ohio Juvenile Law § 22:9, Amenability Hearing Procedures.
Giannelli & Yeomans, Ohio Juvenile Law § 32:3, Responsibilities to Victims and Others.
Giannelli & Yeomans, Ohio Juvenile Law App. D, Appendix D. Glossary.
Giannelli & Yeomans, Ohio Juvenile Law § 22:10, Mental Examination.
Giannelli & Yeomans, Ohio Juvenile Law § 22:12, Notice.
Giannelli & Yeomans, Ohio Juvenile Law § 22:17, Statement of Reasons.
Giannelli & Yeomans, Ohio Juvenile Law § 22:22, Transfer of Jurisdiction.

Law Review and Journal Commentaries

Children, the Death Penalty and the Eighth Amendment: An Analysis of Stanford v. Kentucky. 35 Vill L Rev 641 (1990).

Death penalty for minors: Who should decide?, Comment. 20 S Ill U L J 621 (Spring 1996).

The Effect of the Double Jeopardy Clause on Juvenile Proceedings, James G. Carr. 6 U Tol L Rev 1 (Fall 1974).

Is the Trend to Expand Juvenile Transfer Statutes Just an Easy Answer to a Complex Problem?, Comment. 26 U Tol L Rev 979 (Summer 1995).

Judge's Column, Hon. William W. Weaver. (Ed. note: Judge Weaver of the Lake County Juvenile Court highlights the effects of 1995 H 1 on juvenile law and procedure and provides flow charts to explain the new procedures.) 19 Lake Legal Views 1 (January 1996).

Ohio Gets Tough on Juvenile Crime: An Analysis of Ohio's 1996 Amendments Concerning the Bindover of Violent Juvenile Offenders to the Adult System and Related Legislation, Susan R. Bell. 66 U Cin L Rev 207 (Fall 1997).

Rights of passage: Analysis of waiver of juvenile court jurisdiction. 64 Fordham L Rev 2425 (1995).

Sentencing Juvenile Murderers: Punish the Last Offender or Save the Next Victim?, Victor L. Streib. 26 U Tol L Rev 765 (Summer 1995).

Serious and habitual juvenile offender statutes: Reconciling punishment and rehabilitation within the juvenile justice system. 48 Vand L Rev 479 (1995).

Symposium: They Grow Up So Fast: When Juveniles Commit Adult Crimes, Hon. W. Don Reader, et al. 29 Akron L Rev 473 (Spring 1996).

Notes of Decisions

Ed. Note: This section contains annotations from former RC 2151.26.

Constitutional issues 1
Criteria for transfer 3
Disqualification of judge 8
Evidence 4
Grand jury indictment and bindover to adult facility 7
Mental exam 5
Procedural issues 2
Public access 9
Waiver of jurisdiction 6

---

1. Constitutional issues

Grand jury was free to indict defendant on kidnapping charges, even though juvenile court did not specifically transfer those charges when it bound the case over to the general division of the court of common pleas; juvenile court clearly transferred the entire case to the general division, charges that were issued by the grand jury were based on the same delinquent acts under review in the juvenile court, and the kidnapping charges did not involve any additional circumstances beyond those that were under review in the juvenile court. State v. Barnette (Ohio App. 7 Dist., Mahoning, 12-28-2004) No. 02 CA 65, 2004-Ohio-7211, 2004 WL 3090228, Unreported, opinion corrected on denial of reconsideration 2005-Ohio-477, 2005 WL 293804, appeal allowed 105 Ohio St.3d 1559, 828 N.E.2d 115, 2005-Ohio-2447, reversed in part 109 Ohio St.3d 313, 847 N.E.2d 1174, 2006-Ohio-2109. Infants ⚖ 68.7(5)

Supreme Court's decision in *State v Hanning*, that statute requiring juvenile bindover for use of firearm was inapplicable unless juvenile personally possessed firearm, applied retroactively to habeas petition filed by juvenile whose conviction became final before decision was rendered; decision did not involve new constitutional rule, but instead merely determined what juvenile bindover statute had meant since its enactment. Johnson v. Timmerman-Cooper (Ohio, 11-28-2001) 93 Ohio St.3d 614, 757 N.E.2d 1153, 2001-Ohio-1803. Courts ⚖ 100(1)

Teague v Lane and *Pinch v. Maxwell,* which govern retroactivity of new constitutional rules of criminal procedure, did not apply to determination of whether of *State v. Hanning*, which provided that statute requiring juvenile bindover for use of firearm is inapplicable unless juvenile personally possessed firearm, applied to habeas petition filed by juvenile whose conviction became final before *Hanning* was decided; *Hanning* did not involve new constitutional rule, but instead merely determined what juvenile bindover statute had meant since its enactment. Agee v. Russell (Ohio, 08-15-2001) 92 Ohio St.3d 540, 751 N.E.2d 1043, 2001-Ohio-1279. Courts ⚖ 100(1)

Teague v Lane, which governs retroactivity of new constitutional rules of criminal procedure, is inapplicable to cases in which court determines meaning of statute enacted by legislature. Agee v. Russell (Ohio, 08-15-2001) 92 Ohio St.3d 540, 751 N.E.2d 1043, 2001-Ohio-1279. Courts ⚖ 100(1)

Statute providing for transfer of certain juveniles to General Division for criminal prosecution as an adult did not violate juvenile's due process or equal protection rights, nor did it conflict with juvenile procedure rule governing relinquishment of jurisdiction for purposes of criminal prosecution. State v. Agee (Ohio App. 2 Dist., 05-21-1999) 133 Ohio App.3d 441, 728 N.E.2d 442, dismissed, appeal not allowed 86 Ohio St.3d 1489, 716 N.E.2d 721, denial of habeas corpus affirmed 92 Ohio St.3d 540, 751 N.E.2d 1043, 2001-Ohio-1279. Constitutional Law ⚖ 242.1(4); Constitutional Law ⚖ 255(4); Infants ⚖ 68.7(2)

At probable cause hearing on delinquency adjudication petition, juvenile has right to attorney, to cross-examination, to present evidence, to remain silent, to inspect any exhibits prior to their introduction, and to receive proper notice and service prior to hearing. In re Hunter (Ohio Com.Pl., 07-12-1999) 99 Ohio Misc.2d 107, 716 N.E.2d 802. Infants ⚖ 205; Infants ⚖ 207

While juvenile's probable cause hearing must measure up to essentials of due process and fair treatment, hearing need not conform with all requirements of criminal trial, adjudicatory hearing, or administrative hearing, and juvenile need not be afforded all rights that he or she may have for trial. In re Hunter (Ohio Com.Pl., 07-12-1999) 99 Ohio Misc.2d 107, 716 N.E.2d 802. Constitutional Law ⚖ 255(4); Infants ⚖ 203

Bindover proceeding is not "adjudicative," as the juvenile's guilt or innocence is not at issue; accordingly, fundamental fairness and due process do not obligate the juvenile court to rule on or to suppress evidence allegedly obtained in violation of *Miranda*. State v. Whisenant (Ohio App. 11 Dist., 03-30-1998) 127 Ohio App.3d 75, 711 N.E.2d 1016, dismissed, appeal not allowed 83 Ohio St.3d 1416, 698 N.E.2d 1005. Constitutional Law ⚖ 255(4); Infants ⚖ 68.7(3)

"Mandatory bindover" or waiver of jurisdiction proceeding in a juvenile matter must measure up to the essentials of due process and fair treatment. In re A.M. (Ohio Com.Pl., 05-28-1998) 92 Ohio Misc.2d 4, 699 N.E.2d 574, affirmed 139 Ohio App.3d 303, 743 N.E.2d 937, appeal not allowed 91 Ohio St.3d 1431, 741 N.E.2d 895. Constitutional Law ⚖ 255(4)

Jeopardy does not attach to a probable cause hearing in a "mandatory bindover" or waiver of juvenile jurisdiction proceeding in a juvenile matter, and therefore subsequent trial as an adult does not place the juvenile in double jeopardy. In re A.M. (Ohio Com.Pl., 05-28-1998) 92 Ohio Misc.2d 4, 699 N.E.2d 574, affirmed 139 Ohio App.3d 303, 743 N.E.2d 937, appeal not allowed 91 Ohio St.3d 1431, 741 N.E.2d 895. Double Jeopardy ⚖ 33

Juvenile court may, in its discretion, admit juvenile to bail in action wherein request for waiver of jurisdiction has been made seeking transfer of matter for prosecution as adult. In re K.G. (Ohio Com.Pl., 10-23-1997) 89 Ohio Misc.2d 16, 693 N.E.2d 1186. Infants ⚖ 68.3

Juvenile has due process rights, and a right to fair treatment in bindover process from juvenile court to criminal court. State v. Payne (Ohio App. 3 Dist., 03-13-1997) 118 Ohio App.3d 699, 693 N.E.2d 1159. Constitutional Law ⚖ 255(4)

Under Ohio procedure for binding juveniles over for prosecution as adults, jeopardy attaches, for double jeopardy purposes, when juvenile is adjudged delinquent, but not to preliminary or probable cause hearing. State v. Payne (Ohio App. 3 Dist., 03-13-1997) 118 Ohio App.3d 699, 693 N.E.2d 1159. Double Jeopardy ⚖ 62

Jeopardy did not attach, for double jeopardy purposes, during preliminary hearing held in juvenile court before juvenile was bound over for prosecution as adult, and thus, criminal prosecution did not violate double jeopardy clause, even though juvenile court judge stated at preliminary hearing that State had met its burden of proving probable cause and had, in addition, demonstrated juvenile's guilt beyond a reasonable doubt; judge's statements were merely extraneous, and juvenile was not adjudged delinquent, subjected to any sanctions, or otherwise punished during hearing. State v. Payne (Ohio App. 3 Dist., 03-13-1997) 118 Ohio App.3d 699, 693 N.E.2d 1159. Double Jeopardy ⚖ 62

Juvenile who was transferred to criminal court for prosecution as adult on assault charges received fair and impartial hearing, as required by due process clause, on his amenability for rehabilitation as juvenile, even though juvenile court judge had made statement during preliminary hearing that juvenile had, beyond a reasonable doubt, committed offense in question. State v. Payne (Ohio App. 3 Dist., 03-13-1997) 118 Ohio App.3d 699, 693 N.E.2d 1159. Constitutional Law ⚖ 255(4); Infants ⚖ 68.7(3)

Child's right to be represented by counsel at hearing to determine whether juvenile court shall relinquish its jurisdiction for purposes of criminal prosecution may not be waived. Gaskins v. Shiplevy (Ohio, 12-06-1995) 74 Ohio St.3d 149, 656 N.E.2d 1282, 1995-Ohio-262. Infants ⚖ 68.4

Public has First Amendment right of access to delinquency proceeding which corresponds to public's interest in criminal matters. In re N.H. (Ohio Com.Pl., 06-09-1992) 63 Ohio Misc.2d 285, 626 N.E.2d 697. Constitutional Law ⚖ 90.1(3); Infants ⚖ 203

Public's interest in access to juvenile delinquency proceedings is accentuated when alleged delinquent is subject to pending motion to transfer for prosecution as adult. In re N.H. (Ohio Com.Pl., 06-09-1992) 63 Ohio Misc.2d 285, 626 N.E.2d 697. Infants ⚖ 68.7(3)

Note 1

Alleged falsity of news broadcast in suggesting that juvenile had prior record for rape and kidnapping did not require closing probable cause and amenability hearings in juvenile delinquency case, even though the broadcast would likely endanger fairness of trial as adult; state's agents and judge knew difference between facts of prior case and scenario presented in broadcast, and there was no reason to believe that any more harm would result from permitting public access to further proceedings. In re N.H. (Ohio Com.Pl., 06-09-1992) 63 Ohio Misc.2d 285, 626 N.E.2d 697. Infants ⇐ 203

In case involving juvenile delinquency, rather than neglect, abuse, or dependency, greater weight can be given to public's interest in observing the proceedings, because the matter involved is much closer to adult criminal proceedings. In re N.H. (Ohio Com.Pl., 06-09-1992) 63 Ohio Misc.2d 285, 626 N.E.2d 697. Infants ⇐ 203

A minor criminal defendant, by entering a plea of guilty, does not waive his objections to constitutional deficiencies in the hearing wherein the juvenile court relinquished jurisdiction to the court of common pleas. State v. Riggins (Cuyahoga 1980) 68 Ohio App.2d 1, 426 N.E.2d 504, 22 O.O.3d 1. Criminal Law ⇐ 273.4(1)

Transfer of case by juvenile court to common pleas court, pursuant to RC 2151.26 permitting child to be tried as adult, does not violate any constitutional rights of such child. State v. Anderson (Franklin 1971) 28 Ohio App.2d 234, 277 N.E.2d 64, 57 O.O.2d 345, affirmed in part, reversed in part 30 Ohio St.2d 66, 282 N.E.2d 568, 59 O.O.2d 85.

The prosecution of a juvenile as an adult after an adjudicatory hearing in juvenile court violates the Double Jeopardy Clause of US Const Am 5, since the object of the hearing is to determine whether the juvenile had committed acts that violated a criminal law and whose potential consequences included both the stigma inherent in that determination and the deprivation of liberty for many years. Breed v. Jones (U.S.Cal. 1975) 95 S.Ct. 1779, 421 U.S. 519, 44 L.Ed.2d 346, on remand 519 F.2d 1314. Double Jeopardy ⇐ 33

Defendant's pro se objections to magistrate's report, which restated his position that juvenile court proceeding held preliminarily to binding him over for trial as adult was actually delinquency adjudication so that state's subsequent prosecution of him as adult offender for same crimes violated his double jeopardy rights, should have been broadly construed as objection on ground that his case fell within exception to correctness presumption afforded state court factual findings in habeas corpus action when factual determination was not fairly supported by record, and thus, district court should have made inquiry as to whether exception was applicable. Sellers v. Morris (C.A.6 (Ohio) 1988) 840 F.2d 352. United States Magistrates ⇐ 21

A juvenile court hearing under RC 2151.26 to determine if a juvenile should be transferred to common pleas court for trial as an adult is not adjudicatory in nature or purpose and double jeopardy does not attach to such a hearing when the hearing is preliminary in nature and the juvenile court makes determinations, unrelated to an alleged offense, that affect the juvenile's transfer to common pleas court. (See also Johnson v Perini, 644 F(2d) 573 (6th Cir Ohio 1981).) Keener v. Taylor (C.A.6 (Ohio) 1981) 640 F.2d 839, 22 O.O.3d 248.

Dispute as to whether the court followed the proper procedure under RC 2151.26 does not rise to a constitutional level requiring federal habeas corpus relief. Keener v. Taylor (C.A.6 (Ohio) 1981) 640 F.2d 839, 22 O.O.3d 248.

Procedure for determining whether a juvenile defendant should be tried as a juvenile or an adult is not an adjudicatory proceeding to which double jeopardy attaches. Keener v. Taylor (C.A.6 (Ohio) 1981) 640 F.2d 839, 22 O.O.3d 248.

Where the Ohio statute required a full investigation of the facts underlying a charge of delinquency and a finding of delinquency that the accused had committed acts in violation of Ohio law, jeopardy attached at a hearing at which accused was bound over for trial as an adult. Sims v. Engle (C.A.6 (Ohio) 1980) 619 F.2d 598, certiorari denied 101 S.Ct. 1403, 450 U.S. 936, 67 L.Ed.2d 372.

In a bindover proceeding a juvenile is denied effective assistance of counsel where his attorney fails to present any evidence in opposition to the prosecutor's bindover request and the record contains very little information concerning (1) the juvenile's prior offenses, (2) disposition of those offenses, (3) extent of the probation services offered, and (4) previous attempts to rehabilitate the juvenile. State v Lett, No. 95–CA–2094, 1996 WL 511732 (4th Dist Ct App, Ross, 9–11–96).

Statutes are presumed constitutional and the burden is on a defendant to demonstrate the contrary; therefore, where a defendant alleges, without analysis, that RC 2151.26 and Juv R 30(E) are unconstitutionally void for vagueness, because they fail to provide a workable standard to insure equal treatment among juvenile defendants, that burden is not met. State v Brown, No. 52757 (8th Dist Ct App, Cuyahoga, 10–8–87).

State, in seeking juvenile's transfer to adult court on basis of gun specification, must demonstrate probable cause to believe that juvenile possessed and displayed, brandished, indicated possession of, or used firearm in commission of offense; permitting transfer on basis of mere allegation of gun specification violates due process, and application of probable cause standard of proof to firearm portion of allegation in mandatory waiver of jurisdiction matter is consistent with legislatively imposed burden of probable cause contained in waiver of jurisdiction statute. In re B.S. (Ohio Com.Pl. 1998) 103 Ohio Misc.2d 34, 725 N.E.2d 362.

2. Procedural issues

Doctrine of res judicata precluded appellate review on direct appeal of claim that bindover from juvenile court on charges of aggravated burglary and aggravated robbery was invalid based on alleged lack of evidence to prove firearm specifications, where claim was raised and rejected on pretrial petition for writ of habeas corpus, in view of evidence that juvenile and accomplice both threatened to shoot victims, that both victims were struck in head with firearm, and that both juvenile and accomplice personally controlled and used firearm to facilitate offenses. State v. Goins (Ohio App. 7 Dist., Mahoning, 03-21-2005) No. 02 CA 68, 2005-Ohio-1439, 2005 WL 704865, Unreported, appeal allowed 106 Ohio St.3d 1503, 833 N.E.2d 1246, 2005-Ohio-4605, reversed in part 109 Ohio St.3d 313, 847 N.E.2d 1174, 2006-Ohio-2109. Habeas Corpus ⇐ 894.1

Bind-over order lacking requisite findings, due to juvenile court's incorrect treatment of offenses with which juvenile was charged as mandatory bind-over offenses, was ineffective to relinquish exclusive jurisdiction of juvenile court over action originally commenced as delinquency proceeding. State v. Washington (Ohio App. 2 Dist., Montgomery, 01-07-2005) No. 20226, 2005-Ohio-58, 2005 WL 38760, Unreported. Infants ⇐ 68.7(3)

Juvenile court should have considered discretionary bindover factors in ruling on State's motion to bind over juveniles to common pleas court, where juveniles were age 14 or over at time of criminal acts, they were charged with engaging in pattern of criminal gang activity, a second-degree felony, and juvenile court had determined that there was probable cause to believe that juveniles had committed offense. In re Stanley (Ohio App. 7 Dist., 03-14-2006) 165 Ohio App.3d 726, 848 N.E.2d 540, 2006-Ohio-1279. Infants ⇐ 68.7(2)

Petitioner had adequate remedy at law by appeal to raise his claims that his convictions and sentence were void because his bindover from juvenile court was defective, and, as such, he was not entitled to habeas relief; juvenile court's bindover entry indicated that proper procedures were followed, probable cause finding regarding kidnapping charge was based in part on evidence presented to juvenile court and not solely on waiver of probable cause hearing that petitioner alleged was invalid, and petitioner had already unsuccessfully raised his claim concerning improper bindover based upon lack of a physical examination in his direct appeal. Smith v. Bradshaw (Ohio, 04-26-2006) 109 Ohio St.3d 50, 845 N.E.2d 516, 2006-Ohio-1829. Habeas Corpus ⇐ 291

Juvenile court lacked subject matter jurisdiction to accept admission from 16 year old defendant who was charged with aggravated robbery with a firearm specification. In re Graham (Ohio App. 7 Dist., 05-17-2002) 147 Ohio App.3d 452, 770 N.E.2d 1123, 2002-Ohio-2407. Infants ⇐ 196

Juvenile courts have exclusive initial subject matter jurisdiction over any case involving a child alleged to be delinquent for having committed an act that would constitute a felony if committed by an adult. In re Graham (Ohio App. 7 Dist., 05-17-2002) 147 Ohio App.3d 452, 770 N.E.2d 1123, 2002-Ohio-2407. Infants ⇐ 196

Remand was required for juvenile court to determine if it had jurisdiction over 16 year old defendant who was charged with aggravated robbery with a firearm specification. In re Graham (Ohio App. 7 Dist., 05-17-2002) 147 Ohio App.3d 452, 770 N.E.2d 1123, 2002-Ohio-2407. Infants ⇐ 254

Writ of habeas corpus was an appropriate remedy, even if alternative remedies were available and juvenile was possibly subject to a discretionary bindover in the future, where sentencing court patently and unambiguously lacked jurisdiction to convict and sentence juvenile of the charged offenses when she had not been lawfully transferred to that court. Johnson v. Timmerman-Cooper (Ohio, 11-28-2001) 93 Ohio St.3d 614, 757 N.E.2d 1153, 2001-Ohio-1803. Habeas Corpus ⇐ 280; Habeas Corpus ⇐ 535

Preliminary hearing in delinquency adjudication proceeding to determine probable cause was not adjudicatory hearing for purposes of filing of discovery motions; juvenile's guilt or innocence was not at issue, and bindover to adult court was still possibility. In re Hunter (Ohio Com.Pl., 07-12-1999) 99 Ohio Misc.2d 107, 716 N.E.2d 802. Infants ⚖ 201

General rule that court may deny or limit discovery in delinquency adjudication proceeding upon showing that granting discovery may impede criminal prosecution of minor as adult or of an adult charged with offense arising from same transaction, while applicable when there is adjudicatory hearing pending on juvenile and that juvenile has co-delinquent who has pending bindover hearing and/or adult co-defendant who has trial pending, is not applicable to preliminary probable cause hearings. In re Hunter (Ohio Com.Pl., 07-12-1999) 99 Ohio Misc.2d 107, 716 N.E.2d 802. Infants ⚖ 201

Rule requiring the state to respond to discovery requests in juvenile matters applies to "mandatory bindover" or waiver of jurisdiction proceedings wherein the court determines whether probable cause exists to transfer the matter for prosecution of the juvenile as an adult. In re A.M. (Ohio Com.Pl., 05-28-1998) 92 Ohio Misc.2d 4, 699 N.E.2d 574, affirmed 139 Ohio App.3d 303, 743 N.E.2d 937, appeal not allowed 91 Ohio St.3d 1431, 741 N.E.2d 895. Infants ⚖ 68.7(3)

Probable cause hearing in a "mandatory bindover" or waiver of jurisdiction proceeding is both an "adjudicatory hearing" and a "hearing" as those terms are used in the rules governing juvenile matters. In re A.M. (Ohio Com.Pl., 05-28-1998) 92 Ohio Misc.2d 4, 699 N.E.2d 574, affirmed 139 Ohio App.3d 303, 743 N.E.2d 937, appeal not allowed 91 Ohio St.3d 1431, 741 N.E.2d 895. Infants ⚖ 68.7(3)

Appeal from order denying mandatory bindover became ripe following amenability hearing where trial court bound over juvenile and order became final and appealable. In re Langston (Ohio App. 5 Dist., 03-03-1997) 119 Ohio App.3d 1, 694 N.E.2d 468. Infants ⚖ 68.8

Juvenile courts have exclusive initial subject-matter jurisdiction over any case involving person alleged to be delinquent for having committed, when younger than 18 years of age, act which would constitute felony if committed by adult. State v. Golphin (Ohio, 04-29-1998) 81 Ohio St.3d 543, 692 N.E.2d 608, 1998-Ohio-336. Infants ⚖ 68.5

Legislative elimination of requirement that allegedly delinquent child be given physical examination before juvenile court relinquishes jurisdiction could not be applied retroactively. State v. Golphin (Ohio, 04-29-1998) 81 Ohio St.3d 543, 692 N.E.2d 608, 1998-Ohio-336. Infants ⚖ 68.2

Under former versions of statute and rule governing bind-over procedures, juvenile court failed to properly relinquish jurisdiction over allegedly delinquent child where no physical examination was performed; thus, prosecution of child in common pleas court was void ab initio. State v. Golphin (Ohio, 04-29-1998) 81 Ohio St.3d 543, 692 N.E.2d 608, 1998-Ohio-336. Infants ⚖ 68.7(1)

Habeas corpus did not lie in defendant's challenge to constitutionality of statutory grant of jurisdiction to general division to try juvenile as adult after transfer of case from juvenile court by mandatory statutory bindover procedure; defendant had adequate remedy at law in form of appeal following any conviction, defendant was not attacking statutes pursuant to which he was charged with crimes, and challenge did not allege noncompliance with bindover procedure and was brought prior to any conviction. In re Writ of Habeas Corpus for Baker (Ohio App. 10 Dist., 12-05-1996) 116 Ohio App.3d 580, 688 N.E.2d 1068, cause dismissed 78 Ohio St.3d 1443, 677 N.E.2d 354. Habeas Corpus ⚖ 232; Habeas Corpus ⚖ 289; Habeas Corpus ⚖ 535

Juvenile court enjoys wide latitude in determining whether to relinquish jurisdiction of juvenile, and its ultimate decision will not be reversed absent abuse of discretion. State v. Lopez (Ohio App. 9 Dist., 07-17-1996) 112 Ohio App.3d 659, 679 N.E.2d 1155. Infants ⚖ 68.7(2); Infants ⚖ 68.8

Juvenile court is not bound by expert opinions in determining whether juvenile is amenable to rehabilitation and should thus not be bound over as an adult. State v. Lopez (Ohio App. 9 Dist., 07-17-1996) 112 Ohio App.3d 659, 679 N.E.2d 1155. Infants ⚖ 68.7(3)

Until juvenile court either begins to hear evidence in an adjudicatory hearing, or divests itself of jurisdiction by transferring child for prosecution as an adult, determination of child's amenability to care and rehabilitation in juvenile justice system is subject to reconsideration upon motion filed by party. In re K.W. (Ohio Com.Pl., 10-02-1995) 73 Ohio Misc.2d 20, 657 N.E.2d 611. Infants ⚖ 68.7(4)

Original determination, that child was amenable to care and rehabilitation in juvenile justice system, would be set aside prior to adjudicatory hearing and jurisdiction would be transferred to Common Pleas Court; child failed to appear for adjudicatory hearing and after turning age 18 was arrested as an adult for carrying concealed weapon, escaped from juvenile detention center one week after being placed there, and was rearrested for receiving stolen property and carrying concealed weapon. In re K.W. (Ohio Com.Pl., 10-02-1995) 73 Ohio Misc.2d 20, 657 N.E.2d 611. Infants ⚖ 68.7(4)

Court of common pleas lacked subject matter jurisdiction to convict 17-year-old defendant of grand theft and, thus, judgment of conviction against him was void ab initio; since defendant was child under statute and was never bound over by juvenile court, juvenile court retained exclusive jurisdiction over defendant's case. State v. Wilson (Ohio, 08-09-1995) 73 Ohio St.3d 40, 652 N.E.2d 196, 1995-Ohio-217. Infants ⚖ 68.5

Absent proper bindover procedure pursuant to statute, juvenile court has exclusive subject matter jurisdiction over any case concerning child who is alleged to be delinquent. State v. Wilson (Ohio, 08-09-1995) 73 Ohio St.3d 40, 652 N.E.2d 196, 1995-Ohio-217. Infants ⚖ 68.5

In cases involving challenges to certification of juveniles to adult courts, counsel is required to include specific language in the text of the praecipe to the clerk of courts requesting all pertinent documents from both the juvenile division and the general division of the court of common pleas to establish that the case is a final appealable order. State v. Houston (Lucas 1990) 70 Ohio App.3d 152, 590 N.E.2d 839. Infants ⚖ 68.8

Notice of a juvenile court hearing to bind over a minor for trial as an adult must be given his mother by either mail or publication where personal service failed because her whereabouts were unknown; absent such notice, a minor's rape and grand theft convictions will be reversed even where the adult sister he lived with was present at both the hearing and the trial. State v. Taylor (Auglaize 1985) 26 Ohio App.3d 69, 498 N.E.2d 211, 26 O.B.R. 243.

Once a juvenile is bound over in any county in Ohio pursuant to RC 2151.26 and Juv R 30, that juvenile is bound over for all felonies committed in other counties of this state, as well as for future felonies he may commit. State v. Adams (Ohio 1982) 69 Ohio St.2d 120, 431 N.E.2d 326, 23 O.O.3d 164. Infants ⚖ 68.7(4)

Informal proceedings conducted in a juvenile court in 1962 for the purpose of determining whether or not to bind over a juvenile defendant to be tried as an adult do not constitute an "adjudicatory hearing" as described in Breed v Jones, 421 US 519, 95 SCt 1779, 44 LEd(2d) 346 (1975). State v. Sims (Cuyahoga 1977) 55 Ohio App.2d 285, 380 N.E.2d 1350, 9 O.O.3d 417. Double Jeopardy ⚖ 33

An order by a juvenile court pursuant to RC 2151.26 transferring a child to the court of common pleas for criminal prosecution is not a final appealable order. In re Becker (Ohio 1974) 39 Ohio St.2d 84, 314 N.E.2d 158, 68 O.O.2d 50. Infants ⚖ 68.8

A hearing under RC 2151.26 is a preliminary stage of the juvenile judicial process and contemplates that the court should have considerable latitude within which to determine whether it should retain jurisdiction. State v. Carmichael (Ohio 1973) 35 Ohio St.2d 1, 298 N.E.2d 568, 64 O.O.2d 1, certiorari denied 94 S.Ct. 922, 414 U.S. 1161, 39 L.Ed.2d 113.

RC 2151.26 does not require specific language to be used by a juvenile court in journalizing its finding that a child is delinquent and it can do so without ever using the word "delinquent," as long as a reading of its entry reasonably apprises the reader that such a finding was made. State v. Carter (Ohio 1971) 27 Ohio St.2d 135, 272 N.E.2d 119, 56 O.O.2d 75.

A finding of delinquency by the juvenile court unaccompanied by any disposition thereof is not a final appealable order. (See also In re Whittington, 13 App(2d) 11, 233 NE(2d) 333 (1967); vacated by 391 US 341, 88 SCt 1507, 20 LEd(2d) 625 (1968).) In re Whittington (Fairfield 1969) 17 Ohio App.2d 164, 245 N.E.2d 364, 46 O.O.2d 237. Infants ⚖ 242

An order made under RC 2151.26 recognizing a juvenile to appear before the common pleas court is a final appealable order. (See also In re Whittington, 13 App(2d) 11, 233 NE(2d) 333 (1967); vacated by 391 US 341, 88 SCt 1507, 20 LEd(2d) 625 (1968).) In re Whittington (Fairfield 1969) 17 Ohio App.2d 164, 245 N.E.2d 364, 46 O.O.2d 237. Infants ⚖ 242

The order of a juvenile court pursuant to RC 2151.26 for a child charged with a felony to appear before the common pleas court is a final order under RC 2505.02. State v. Yoss (Carroll 1967) 10 Ohio App.2d 47, 225 N.E.2d 275, 39 O.O.2d 81.

RC 5141.16 was repealed by subsequently enacted provisions of RC 2151.25 and RC 2151.26. State v. Worden (Ohio 1955) 162 Ohio St. 593, 124 N.E.2d 817, 55 O.O. 483.

Where the judge of the juvenile court, after a hearing and examinations as required by GC 1639–32, binds over a minor under eighteen years of age accused of murder in the first degree to the court of common pleas for such disposition as the latter court is authorized to make for a like act committed by an adult, and such minor, after indictment by a grand jury and a plea of not guilty upon arraignment, appears before the judge of the common pleas court presiding at the time in the trial of criminal cases in open court with counsel of his own choosing, elects to be tried by the court without a jury by signing in open court a waiver (pursuant to GC 13442-4, and who later appears with his counsel before a three-judge court, makes application to such judges for permission to withdraw his former plea of not guilty and to enter a plea of guilty, and such judges are satisfied that the defendant has an intelligent understanding of the effect of his plea of guilty and waiver of trial by jury, no error may be predicated on the refusal of a trial by jury after such court has determined the degree of crime and pronounced sentence accordingly. State v. Frohner (Ohio 1948) 150 Ohio St. 53, 80 N.E.2d 868, 37 O.O. 406.

An adjudication of a fourteen-year-old boy as delinquent was vacated and the case remanded to allow Ohio courts to consider the impact of the Gault decision. (See also In re Whittington, 17 App(2d) 164, 245 NE(2d) 364 (1969), reversed sub nom State ex rel Whittington v Barr, 19 OS(2d) 21, 249 NE(2d) 773 (1969), for disposition of case on remand.) In re Whittington (U.S.Ohio 1968) 88 S.Ct. 1507, 391 U.S. 341, 20 L.Ed.2d 625, 45 O.O.2d 31, on remand 17 Ohio App.2d 164, 245 N.E.2d 364, 46 O.O.2d 237.

Under Ohio law, an adult adjudication may follow juvenile proceedings for the same offense, so long as the prior juvenile proceedings are limited to determining the juvenile's amenability to transfer for adult adjudication and do not decide the juvenile's guilt. Robertson v. Morgan (C.A.6 (Ohio), 09-14-2000) 227 F.3d 589, rehearing denied. Infants ⇨ 68.7(2); Infants ⇨ 68.7(3)

Doctrine of res judicata barred inmate from filing third petition for writ of habeas corpus, in which he claimed that his conviction and sentence were void due to fact he was never given physical examination before juvenile court bound him over for trial as an adult, where inmate could have raised such claim in his two prior habeas corpus actions. State ex rel. Childs v. Lazaroff (Ohio 2001) 90 Ohio St.3d 519, 739 N.E.2d 802, 2001 –Ohio- 9.

Habeas petition in which petitioner who alleged that conviction for which he was incarcerated occurred when he was 17 years old and that no bindover from juvenile court to adult court occurred stated potentially good cause of action in habeas corpus, even though petitioner may have possessed adequate remedy at law. State ex rel. Harris v. Anderson (Ohio 1996) 76 Ohio St.3d 193, 667 N.E.2d 1, 1996 –Ohio- 412.

Habeas corpus petition which alleges that court lacked jurisdiction over petitioner due to improper bindover from juvenile court states potentially good cause of action in habeas corpus. State ex rel. Harris v. Anderson (Ohio 1996) 76 Ohio St.3d 193, 667 N.E.2d 1, 1996 –Ohio- 412.

Contention by petitioner, who sought habeas corpus relief on basis that no proper bindover from juvenile court had occurred prior to his conviction, that he was 17 years old at time of commission of offenses was sufficient to meet particularity requirement to withstand dismissal, as petitioner was not required to provide supporting documentation of his age in petition in order to satisfy particularity requirement. State ex rel. Harris v. Anderson (Ohio 1996) 76 Ohio St.3d 193, 667 N.E.2d 1, 1996 –Ohio- 412.

Prohibition will not lie to test validity of order transferring jurisdiction of juvenile to adult division on ground order fails to state the reasons therefor; alleged error should be raised on appeal. State ex rel. Torres v. Simmons (Ohio 1981) 68 Ohio St.2d 118, 428 N.E.2d 862, 22 O.O.3d 340.

If a juvenile is accused of committing a felony, the ninety-day period established by RC 2945.71(C)(2) and (D) for commencing trial does not begin to run until the juvenile court relinquishes jurisdiction and transfers the accused to the "adult" court. State ex rel. Williams v. Court of Common Pleas of Lucas County (Ohio 1975) 42 Ohio St.2d 433, 329 N.E.2d 680, 71 O.O.2d 410.

Under former GC 1639 (RC 2151.23), GC 1647 (RC 2151.27) and GC 1681 (RC 2151.26), transfer by court of common pleas of felony case against minor to court of domestic relations merely gives latter court information and authority to act thereon. State ex rel. Brown v. Hoffman (Hamilton 1926) 23 Ohio App. 348, 155 N.E. 499, 5 Ohio Law Abs. 6.

While juvenile was bound over on charges related to one incident, he was not bound over for additional offenses and, therefore, his prosecution as an adult in the general division on those additional offenses was void ab initio because, although the offenses might have been effectively transferred, prior to 1996, with the charges upon which the juvenile was formally bound over, Am Sub HB §1 changed the law and demanded that a valid, formal bindover occur for each charge. State v Fryerson, No. 71683, 2000 WL 146567 (8th Dist Ct App, Cuyahoga, 2–10–00).

Where a defendant is a juvenile at the time he commits theft but is an adult at the time he receives the stolen property, the judgment of conviction for theft is vacated where no complaint for delinquency was ever brought against the defendant in juvenile court, there was no bindover from juvenile court to common pleas court, and the defendant was indicted, charged, and tried as an adult in common pleas court without subject matter jurisdiction for an offense committed while a juvenile. State v Wilson, No. C–930429, 1994 WL 176901 (1st Dist Ct App, Hamilton, 5–11–94), affirmed by 73 Ohio St.3d 40 (1995).

Where a case is pending against a juvenile in a foreign county, such case must be transferred to the juvenile's home county, if, at any time prior to dispositional order, proceedings against the juvenile are pending in his home county. Furthermore, such mandatory transfer may not be avoided by the foreign county through the use of a bindover proceeding. State v Payne, No. 81–CA–22 (4th Dist Ct App, Pickaway, 7–28–82).

Former GC 1681 (RC 2151.26), is discretionary and not mandatory; division of domestic relations may try the juvenile for delinquency or bind him over to the court of common pleas for indictment, etc. State v Wessel, 28 LR 104 (CP, Hamilton 1927).

3. Criteria for transfer

Record supported juvenile court's conclusions that 17-year-old defendant charged with delinquency for aggravated robbery was not amenable to rehabilitation and that adult sanctions were necessary for community safety, as required for juvenile court to relinquish jurisdiction and transfer defendant to general division for prosecution as adult, even though defendant argued in part that there was evidence from psychological evaluation that he was both emotionally and psychologically immature; juvenile court expressly based its decision on defendant's prior conduct, failure of juvenile-justice system to rehabilitate him, and gravity of alleged crime. State v. Terrell (Ohio App. 6 Dist., Lucas, 09-16-2005) No. L-04-1131, 2005-Ohio-4871, 2005 WL 2249586, Unreported. Infants ⇨ 68.7(3)

No bind-over proceeding or hearing was required in juvenile court before matter against juvenile defendant could proceed in court of common pleas, in prosecution for carrying a concealed weapon and possession of crack cocaine; defendant had previously been convicted of a felony in court of common pleas, and thus no longer satisfied definition of "child" over which juvenile court had exclusive original jurisdiction, and juvenile court had no discretion regarding whether defendant who had previously been convicted of a felony in court of common pleas would be tried as and adult, but was required to transfer case to court of common pleas. State v. Washington (Ohio App. 2 Dist., Montgomery, 09-30-2004) No. 200218, 2004-Ohio-5283, 2004 WL 2245103, Unreported. Infants ⇨ 68.7(3)

Juvenile court acted within its discretion in binding over juvenile defendant to the general division to be tried as an adult on charges of rape, burglary and kidnapping; although one expert believed defendant could be rehabilitated before age 21, another expert testified that defendant was unlikely to avail himself of intervention strategies available through juvenile court system, defendant demonstrated conduct disorder, defendant's prognosis for future criminal activity was moderate to high, and defendant had refused to participate in treatment programs in the past. State v. Tooill (Ohio App. 5 Dist., Fairfield, 08-27-2004) No. 03-CA-36, 2004-Ohio-4533, 2004 WL 1921096, Unreported. Infants ⇨ 68.7(2)

For purposes of binding juvenile over to court of common pleas, juvenile court acted within its discretion when it concluded that defendant, who was 15 years old at the time of alleged murder and had not previously been convicted of a felony or adjudicated a delinquent child, was not amenable to care or rehabilitation in a juvenile facility, even though expert witnesses for both the prosecution and defense testified that it was possible or probable that defendant suffered from Attention Deficit Hyperactivity Disorder (ADHD) and that any treatment for ADHD would be better found in the juvenile system; neither expert witness explained how ADHD led to defendant's alleged conduct in the case, defendant demonstrated some reticence toward rehabilitation, expert witness testified that it would take longer than normal for defendant to be rehabilitated, and defendant was alleged to have committed murder, a serious offense normally requiring longer periods of rehabilitation. State v. Lallathin (Ohio App. 7 Dist., Noble, 06-26-2003) No. 299, 2003-Ohio-3478, 2003 WL 21500290, Unreported, appeal not allowed 100 Ohio St.3d 1433, 797 N.E.2d 513, 2003-Ohio-5396, denial of post-conviction relief affirmed 2004-Ohio-7066, 2004 WL 2980379, appeal not allowed 105 Ohio St.3d 1519, 826 N.E.2d 316, 2005-Ohio-1880. Infants ⇨ 68.7(3)

Trial court did not abuse its discretion in relinquishing its jurisdiction of juvenile's case and transferring juvenile for prosecution as adult; several witnesses testified that juvenile was threat to community and himself and that juvenile had engaged in violent behavior which had escalated, and none of the witnesses was able to state that juvenile would be amenable to rehabilitation in juvenile justice system or that there would be no need for legal restraint beyond age of 21. State v. Shreves (Ohio App. 6 Dist.,

Lucas, 06-06-2003) No. L-02-1075, 2003-Ohio-2911, 2003 WL 21299925, Unreported. Infants ⇐ 68.7(3)

Evidence in record in bindover proceedings with respect to juvenile charged with murder was sufficient to support juvenile court's conclusion that juvenile was emotionally, physically and psychologically mature enough to be transferred to adult justice system, where assistant administrator at juvenile's school testified that juvenile was neither more nor less mature than other boys in his age group, examining psychologists concluded that juvenile was of average intelligence and had adequate intellectual abilities, and competency report indicated that juvenile would be capable of assisting in his defense and that he was competent at time of act with which he was charged. State v. West (Ohio App. 4 Dist., 06-30-2006) 2006-Ohio-3518, 2006 WL 1868310. Infants ⇐ 68.7(3)

Evidence in record in bindover proceedings with respect to juvenile charged with murder was sufficient to support juvenile court's conclusion that insufficient time existed to rehabilitate juvenile within juvenile justice system, despite juvenile's comparatively young age, 14, at time of murder, where murder was especially brutal, vicious, and unprovoked, and one court-appointed psychologist testified that juvenile did not exhibit motivation to participate in counseling, was very avoidant, and was likely to actively resist therapeutic treatment, which treatment would be entirely voluntary in absence of diagnosis. State v. West (Ohio App. 4 Dist., 06-30-2006) 2006-Ohio-3518, 2006 WL 1868310. Infants ⇐ 68.7(3)

Testimony in bindover proceedings of court-appointed psychologists and juvenile facility psychologist was sufficient to support finding of juvenile court that court-appointed psychologists did not make specific diagnosis and that juvenile would thus not receive treatment or medication in juvenile facility; court-appointed psychologists testified that they did not make specific diagnosis of juvenile's psychological condition, and juvenile facility psychologist testified that juvenile would not receive course of medication or treatment in absence of diagnosis and that juvenile's participation in specific treatment programs described by all testifying experts as potentially beneficial to him would be voluntary. State v. West (Ohio App. 4 Dist., 06-30-2006) 2006-Ohio-3518, 2006 WL 1868310. Infants ⇐ 68.7(3)

Juvenile court did not abuse its discretion, in proceedings for transfer of jurisdiction to general division of the court of common pleas, in determining that juvenile charged with murder was not amenable to care or rehabilitation within juvenile system and that safety of community might require that juvenile be subject to adult sanctions, where juvenile court found that murder was brutal, vicious, and unprovoked, that juvenile had callous indifference and utter disregard for human life, and that juvenile had adequate mental capacity, had no disability from any mental illness, and was emotionally, physically, and psychologically mature enough to be transferred as adult. State v. West (Ohio App. 4 Dist., 06-30-2006) 2006-Ohio-3518, 2006 WL 1868310. Infants ⇐ 68.7(2)

Juvenile court was not bound by opinions of court-appointed psychologists, in bindover proceedings with respect to juvenile charged with murder, to effect that juvenile was amenable to treatment and rehabilitation within juvenile system. State v. West (Ohio App. 4 Dist., 06-30-2006) 167 Ohio App.3d 598, 856 N.E.2d 285, 2006-Ohio-3518. Infants ⇐ 68.7(3)

Evidence in record in bindover proceedings with respect to juvenile charged with murder was sufficient to support juvenile court's conclusion that juvenile was emotionally, physically and psychologically mature enough to be transferred to adult justice system, where assistant administrator at juvenile's school testified that juvenile was neither more nor less mature than other boys in his age group, examining psychologists concluded that juvenile was of average intelligence and had adequate intellectual abilities, and competency report indicated that juvenile would be capable of assisting in his defense and that he was competent at time of act with which he was charged. State v. West (Ohio App. 4 Dist., 06-30-2006) 167 Ohio App.3d 598, 856 N.E.2d 285, 2006-Ohio-3518. Infants ⇐ 68.7(3)

Evidence in record in bindover proceedings with respect to juvenile charged with murder was sufficient to support juvenile court's conclusion that insufficient time existed to rehabilitate juvenile within juvenile justice system, despite juvenile's comparatively young age, 14, at time of murder, where murder was especially brutal, vicious, and unprovoked, and one court-appointed psychologist testified that juvenile did not exhibit motivation to participate in counseling, was very avoidant, and was likely to actively resist therapeutic treatment, which treatment would be entirely voluntary in absence of diagnosis. State v. West (Ohio App. 4 Dist., 06-30-2006) 167 Ohio App.3d 598, 856 N.E.2d 285, 2006-Ohio-3518. Infants ⇐ 68.7(3)

Juvenile court did not abuse its discretion, in proceedings for transfer of jurisdiction to general division of the court of common pleas, in determining that juvenile charged with murder was not amenable to care or rehabilitation within juvenile system and that safety of community might require that juvenile be subject to adult sanctions, where juvenile court found that murder was brutal, vicious, and unprovoked, that juvenile had callous indifference and utter disregard for human life, and that juvenile had adequate mental capacity, had no disability from any mental illness, and was emotionally, physically, and psychologically mature enough to be transferred as adult. State v. West (Ohio App. 4 Dist., 06-30-2006) 167 Ohio App.3d 598, 856 N.E.2d 285, 2006-Ohio-3518. Infants ⇐ 68.7(2)

Court of Common Pleas had subject matter jurisdiction to hear defendant's case, following his bind-over from juvenile division, as juvenile division, in its bind-over entry, specifically stated that it found probable cause and that defendant was 17 years of age at time of conduct charged, and juvenile division went on to explain factors it considered in making its determination that defendant was not amenable to care or rehabilitation in the juvenile system, in compliance with provisions of statute and rule governing transfer of cases from juvenile court. State v. Mock (Ohio Com.Pl., 09-26-2005) 136 Ohio Misc.2d 21, 846 N.E.2d 108, 2005-Ohio-7142. Infants ⇐ 68.7(4)

Juvenile charged with aggravated murder by aggravated robbery and other felonies was not amenable to care and rehabilitation within juvenile system, and thus transfer of case to general division of court of common pleas was appropriate; victim was beaten to death and her car was stolen, her affectionate relationship with juvenile facilitated act, juvenile was on parole with Department of Youth Services at time of murder, juvenile had extensive criminal history and had failed all rehabilitative programs, 4-1/2 years would not be sufficient time to rehabilitate child, and, had murder occurred one month later, transfer to adult court would have been mandatory upon showing of probable cause. In re Lynch (Ohio Com.Pl., 05-12-2003) 123 Ohio Misc.2d 81, 789 N.E.2d 1206, 2003-Ohio-2690. Infants ⇐ 68.7(2)

If a juvenile offender meets defined criteria, the juvenile court may, or in specific cases shall, transfer the case to the general division of the common pleas court; in specified situations, transfer to the general division is mandatory, one such mandatory transfer situation is where the juvenile is alleged to have used a firearm in commission of certain crimes. In re Graham (Ohio App. 7 Dist., 05-17-2002) 147 Ohio App.3d 452, 770 N.E.2d 1123, 2002-Ohio-2407. Infants ⇐ 68.7(1)

Mandatory transfer removes discretion from judges in the transfer decision in certain situations, such as where the juvenile is alleged to have used a gun in commission of certain crimes. State v. Hanning (Ohio, 06-07-2000) 89 Ohio St.3d 86, 728 N.E.2d 1059, 2000-Ohio-436. Infants ⇐ 68.7(2)

Complicity statute did not allow juvenile to be bound over to adult court on basis of allegation that his adult accomplice possessed a handgun during commission of aggravated robbery. State v. Hanning (Ohio, 06-07-2000) 89 Ohio St.3d 86, 728 N.E.2d 1059, 2000-Ohio-436. Infants ⇐ 68.7(3)

Juvenile who allegedly aided and abetted another in the commission of aggravated robbery of gas station, but who did not hold the gun during the robbery, was subject to mandatory bindover provision and, thus, was properly bound over to the General Division for criminal prosecution as an adult; complicity to aggravated robbery was category two offense for purposes of mandatory bindover provision. State v. Agee (Ohio App. 2 Dist., 05-21-1999) 133 Ohio App.3d 441, 728 N.E.2d 442, dismissed, appeal not allowed 86 Ohio St.3d 1489, 716 N.E.2d 721, denial of habeas corpus affirmed 92 Ohio St.3d 540, 751 N.E.2d 1043, 2001-Ohio-1279. Infants ⇐ 68.7(3)

To bind juvenile over as an adult, it is not necessary that court resolve each of pertinent rule's factors against juvenile. State v. Lopez (Ohio App. 9 Dist., 07-17-1996) 112 Ohio App.3d 659, 679 N.E.2d 1155. Infants ⇐ 68.7(2)

In determining whether juvenile could be bound over as an adult on charges of burglary and assault, juvenile court could consider testimony of arresting officer as to violent nature of crime. State v. Lopez (Ohio App. 9 Dist., 07-17-1996) 112 Ohio App.3d 659, 679 N.E.2d 1155. Infants ⇐ 68.7(3)

In deciding whether to relinquish its jurisdiction and permit state to prosecute child as adult, juvenile court enjoys wide latitude of discretion. State v. Hopfer (Ohio App. 2 Dist., 07-12-1996) 112 Ohio App.3d 521, 679 N.E.2d 321, dismissed, appeal not allowed 77 Ohio St.3d 1488, 673 N.E.2d 146, reconsideration denied 77 Ohio St.3d 1550, 674 N.E.2d 1187. Infants ⇐ 68.7(2)

In reviewing juvenile court's decision to permit state to prosecute child as adult, test is not whether appellate court would have reached same result upon evidence before juvenile court; test is whether juvenile court abused discretion confided in it. State v. Hopfer (Ohio App. 2 Dist., 07-12-1996) 112 Ohio App.3d 521, 679 N.E.2d 321, dismissed, appeal not allowed 77 Ohio St.3d 1488, 673 N.E.2d 146, reconsideration denied 77 Ohio St.3d 1550, 674 N.E.2d 1187. Infants ⇔ 68.8

In deciding whether juvenile court abused its discretion in permitting state to prosecute child as adult, appellate court had to determine whether juvenile court's decision was "unreasonable" (that is, without any reasonable basis), arbitrary, or unconscionable. State v. Hopfer (Ohio App. 2 Dist., 07-12-1996) 112 Ohio App.3d 521, 679 N.E.2d 321, dismissed, appeal not allowed 77 Ohio St.3d 1488, 673 N.E.2d 146, reconsideration denied 77 Ohio St.3d 1550, 674 N.E.2d 1187. Infants ⇔ 68.8

Any evidence that reasonably supports juvenile court's decision to relinquish jurisdiction over child and permit state to prosecute child as adult will suffice to sustain that court's judgment. State v. Hopfer (Ohio App. 2 Dist., 07-12-1996) 112 Ohio App.3d 521, 679 N.E.2d 321, dismissed, appeal not allowed 77 Ohio St.3d 1488, 673 N.E.2d 146, reconsideration denied 77 Ohio St.3d 1550, 674 N.E.2d 1187. Infants ⇔ 68.8

Juvenile court need not find that any of the statutory circumstances for determining child's amenability to care or rehabilitation within juvenile penal system specifically weighs against child before it relinquishes jurisdiction over child and permits state to prosecute child as adult, as long as totality of evidence supports finding that child is not amenable to treatment. State v. Hopfer (Ohio App. 2 Dist., 07-12-1996) 112 Ohio App.3d 521, 679 N.E.2d 321, dismissed, appeal not allowed 77 Ohio St.3d 1488, 673 N.E.2d 146, reconsideration denied 77 Ohio St.3d 1550, 674 N.E.2d 1187. Infants ⇔ 68.7(3)

Juvenile court did not abuse its discretion in relinquishing jurisdiction over 17-year-old child and permitting state to prosecute her as adult for murdering her newborn baby and grossly abusing its corpse, notwithstanding child's excellent academic record, lack of criminal history, clean disciplinary record, and previously stable family, where psychologist provided sufficient expert testimony about child's lack of remorse and skewed, self-focused value system to support conclusion that she would not be amenable to rehabilitation or treatment within juvenile penal system, child's age at time of hearing was only three months short of 18, and nature and severity of child's alleged act suggested callous indifference for human life which could pose threat to community even after she turned 21. State v. Hopfer (Ohio App. 2 Dist., 07-12-1996) 112 Ohio App.3d 521, 679 N.E.2d 321, dismissed, appeal not allowed 77 Ohio St.3d 1488, 673 N.E.2d 146, reconsideration denied 77 Ohio St.3d 1550, 674 N.E.2d 1187. Infants ⇔ 68.7(3)

In assessing probability of rehabilitating child within juvenile justice system, juvenile court enjoys wide latitude to entertain or relinquish jurisdiction, and ultimate decision lies within its sound discretion. In re Williams (Ohio App. 10 Dist., 05-14-1996) 111 Ohio App.3d 120, 675 N.E.2d 1254, dismissed, appeal not allowed 77 Ohio St.3d 1470, 673 N.E.2d 136. Infants ⇔ 68.7(2)

Juvenile who was almost 18 years old when he allegedly murdered 14-year-old girl after considering candidates for murder for approximately two months was not amenable to rehabilitation, and safety of community required that juvenile be placed under legal restrictions beyond age of majority despite fact that juvenile had no prior record, achieved above average grades in school, and worked steadily since junior high and, thus, jurisdiction of juvenile could be transferred for prosecution as adult. In re Snitzky (Ohio Com.Pl., 08-01-1995) 73 Ohio Misc.2d 52, 657 N.E.2d 1379. Infants ⇔ 68.7(2)

After complaint has been filed alleging that child is delinquent by reason of having committed act that would constitute felony if committed by adult, court at a hearing may transfer case for criminal prosecution to the appropriate court having jurisdiction of the offense, after making the following determinations: after investigation, including mental and physical examination of child made by public or private agency, there are reasonable grounds to believe that he is not amenable to care or rehabilitation in facility designed for care of delinquent children and safety of the community may require that he be placed under legal restraint. Gaskins v. Shiplevy (Ohio, 12-06-1995) 74 Ohio St.3d 149, 656 N.E.2d 1282, 1995-Ohio-262. Infants ⇔ 68.7(2); Infants ⇔ 68.7(4)

A juvenile court has no jurisdiction to rule on a delinquency complaint alleging rape where the complaint is filed after the alleged delinquent has reached the age of twenty-one, even though the fact that the alleged offense was committed before the juvenile's fifteenth birthday precludes the relinquishment of jurisdiction to an adult court. In re C. (Ohio Com.Pl. 1991) 61 Ohio Misc.2d 610, 580 N.E.2d 1182.

In making assessment of probability of rehabilitating child within juvenile justice system, juvenile court enjoys wide latitude to entertain or relinquish jurisdiction, and ultimate decision lies within its sound discretion. State v. Watson (Ohio 1989) 47 Ohio St.3d 93, 547 N.E.2d 1181. Infants ⇔ 68.7(2)

A minor does not have the right to be tried as an adult and there is no provision for bind-over upon motion of a minor. State v. Smith (Cuyahoga 1985) 29 Ohio App.3d 194, 504 N.E.2d 1121, 29 O.B.R. 237.

The court of common pleas has no authority to review the factual findings of the juvenile court on the issue of amenability to rehabilitation, such issue must be presented after trial on appeal to the court of appeals. State v. Whiteside (Allen 1982) 6 Ohio App.3d 30, 452 N.E.2d 332, 6 O.B.R. 140.

The duty imposed upon the juvenile court, before ordering a relinquishment of jurisdiction, is, after investigation, to find that there are reasonable grounds to believe that the child is one who will not be readily brought to yield, submit, and respond to care, supervision, and rehabilitation in any facility designed for such care of delinquent children and that the safety of the community may require legal restraint beyond the child's majority. State v. Whiteside (Allen 1982) 6 Ohio App.3d 30, 452 N.E.2d 332, 6 O.B.R. 140. Infants ⇔ 68.7(2)

What constitutes "reasonable grounds" for relinquishing jurisdiction under RC 2151.26(A)(3) is within the sound discretion of the court, after an "investigation" is made. State v. Carmichael (Ohio 1973) 35 Ohio St.2d 1, 298 N.E.2d 568, 64 O.O.2d 1, certiorari denied 94 S.Ct. 922, 414 U.S. 1161, 39 L.Ed.2d 113. Infants ⇔ 68.7(2)

It is abuse of discretion for juvenile court to recognize juvenile to common pleas court in absence of finding that such juvenile was delinquent and where evidence fails to disclose that such juvenile would not be proper subject for rehabilitation under provisions of juvenile code or that such recognizance was necessary as protection to public. In re Mack (Hamilton 1970) 22 Ohio App.2d 201, 260 N.E.2d 619, 51 O.O.2d 400. Infants ⇔ 68.7(2)

Juvenile court must, as condition of order for juvenile to appear before common pleas court, find such juvenile to be delinquent under RC 2151.01 to RC 2151.54. In re Mack (Hamilton 1970) 22 Ohio App.2d 201, 260 N.E.2d 619, 51 O.O.2d 400.

Pursuant to RC 2151.26 as it existed immediately prior to November 19, 1969, where a juvenile was charged with being a delinquent child, and where the juvenile court sought to bind that child over to the court of common pleas, the child must first have been found to be a delinquent child; and, if so found, the juvenile court must also have found that the child could not be rehabilitated within the exercise of the exclusive jurisdiction of the juvenile court. In re Jackson (Ohio 1970) 21 Ohio St.2d 215, 257 N.E.2d 74, 50 O.O.2d 447. Infants ⇔ 68.7(3)

Pursuant to RC 2151.26 as it existed immediately prior to November 19, 1969, where the evidence before a juvenile court was sufficient to support a finding that there was probable cause to believe a delinquent child had committed an act which could be a felony if committed by an adult, that court could properly bind the child over to the court of common pleas. In re Jackson (Ohio 1970) 21 Ohio St.2d 215, 257 N.E.2d 74, 50 O.O.2d 447. Infants ⇔ 68.7(3)

It is an abuse of discretion for the juvenile court under RC 2151.26 to recognize a fourteen year old youth to appear before the common pleas court when the evidence is insufficient to support a finding that he is other than a fit subject for rehabilitation under the provisions of the juvenile code, and insufficient to support a finding that recognizing him to common pleas court is necessary as a protection to the public. (See also In re Whittington, 13 App(2d) 11, 233 NE(2d) 333 (1967); vacated by 391 US 341, 88 SCt 1507, 20 LEd(2d) 625 (1968).) In re Whittington (Fairfield 1969) 17 Ohio App.2d 164, 245 N.E.2d 364, 46 O.O.2d 237. Infants ⇔ 68.7(2)

There was sufficient evidence for Ohio state court to order juvenile to be tried as an adult; juvenile did poorly in school while on probation, juvenile was almost 18 when attack occurred, and state judge determined that safety of community might require juvenile's confinement beyond age 21. Robertson v. Morgan (C.A.6 (Ohio), 09-14-2000) 227 F.3d 589, rehearing denied. Infants ⇔ 68.7(3)

Department of Youth Services had been unsuccessful in rehabilitating juvenile defendant on his previous commitments, juvenile defendant had a poor school record that consisted of him being disciplined for tardiness and school disruption, and evidence indicated juvenile defendant had been a habitual behavioral problem in the community. State v. Gibson (Ohio App. 5 Dist., Licking, 05-01-2002) No. 01CA00081, 2002-Ohio-2513, 2002 WL 925252, Unreported.

Refusal by court of domestic relations to hear case of infant charged with felony, transferred to it by court of common pleas, is equivalent to exercise of discretion, under former GC 1681 (RC 2151.26), of transferring case to court of common pleas, which was required to dispose of case as though originally transferred to it by domestic relations court. State ex rel.

Brown v. Hoffman (Hamilton 1926) 23 Ohio App. 348, 155 N.E. 499, 5 Ohio Law Abs. 6.

Juvenile court errs in binding over a seventeen-year-old defendant for adult criminal prosecution upon a finding that defendant's actions in aiding and abetting the co-defendant who actually possessed the firearm during the commission of an aggravated robbery were sufficient to invoke the mandatory bindover provision of RC 2151.26(B)(4)(b). State v Hanning, No. 98AP–380, 1999 WL 64221 (10th Dist Ct App, Franklin, 2–9–99), affirmed 89 Ohio St.3d 86 (2000).

A sixteen-year-old delinquent child who purposely causes the death of her father in violation of RC 2903.02 and 2151.02 is not amenable to rehabilitation within the juvenile system despite the lack of a physical examination where testimony and evidence coupled with the nature and severity of the act suggest a callous indifference for human life that could pose a threat to the community even beyond the juvenile's twenty-first birthday. State v Berenyi, No. 11–97–01, 1997 WL 576357 (3d Dist Ct App, Paulding, 9–18–97).

The juvenile court was well within its discretion in determining that there were reasonable grounds to believe that a seventeen-year-old charged with aggravated murder was not amenable to rehabilitation in a juvenile treatment facility and in transferring jurisdiction to the general division after a full evidentiary hearing and careful examination of all the statutory factors showed that (1) the defendant was adjudicated delinquent in 1990 and 1991 for acts which if committed by an adult would be violent felonies, (2) rehabilitation after these offenses was not successful, (3) school officials were unsuccessful at disciplining him and his family was not cooperative in rectifying his disrespectful behavior, and (4) the murder victim was seventy-seven years old and was shot three times in the head at point-blank range while he was lying on the floor. State v Metz, No. 96CA03, 1997 WL 305220 (4th Dist Ct App, Washington, 6–4–97).

The decision to relinquish juvenile court jurisdiction rests with the juvenile court; expert testimony as to the amenability of a defendant to rehabilitation in juvenile facilities is not binding on the court. State v Dickens, No. 12967 (9th Dist Ct App, Summit, 9–23–87).

Under this section, when a child alleged to be delinquent is said to have committed an act which would be a felony if committed by an adult, the juvenile judge cannot order such child to enter into a recognizance for his appearance before the court of common pleas until after a full investigation and mental and physical examination has been made. 1945 OAG 395.

Case of a boy between sixteen and twenty-one who has committed an act which, if committed by an adult, would be a felony may be transferred, under this section, to common pleas court. 1938 OAG 3439.

4. Evidence

Juvenile court did not abuse its discretion by ordering that juvenile defendant be bound over for adult prosecution for murder and robbery offenses; evidence at the amenability hearing established that defendant was manipulative and exploited the trust of those who cared for him, evidence indicated that even in the restricted setting of his foster home the criminal nature of juvenile's behavior was escalating, and psychological evaluation of court-appointed psychologist concluded that any behavioral improvements displayed by juvenile were superficial. State. v. Moorer (Ohio App. 11 Dist., Geauga, 10-24-2003) No. 2001-G-2353, No. 2001-G-2354, 2003-Ohio-5698, 2003 WL 22427822, Unreported, appeal not allowed 101 Ohio St.3d 1489, 805 N.E.2d 539, 2004-Ohio-1293. Infants ⚖ 68.7(2)

Juvenile court considered relevant factors before allowing juvenile to be bound over for adult prosecution for murder and robbery offenses; stipulation existed that victims sustained physical harm to their persons during the robbery and that juvenile used a firearm to commit the robbery, record further demonstrated that both victims were over the age of five and under the age of sixty-five at the time of the robbery, evidence established that neither victim was disabled and that juvenile had never been committed to rehabilitation prior to the offense, and juvenile court appropriately considered the seriousness of the offense, as evidence was presented that revealed juvenile's actions were premeditated and occurred in a deliberate manner. State v. Moorer (Ohio App. 11 Dist., Geauga, 10-24-2003) No. 2001-G-2353, No. 2001-G-2354, 2003-Ohio-5698, 2003 WL 22427822, Unreported, appeal not allowed 101 Ohio St.3d 1489, 805 N.E.2d 539, 2004-Ohio-1293. Infants ⚖ 68.7(2)

Evidence was sufficient to support juvenile court's finding that probable cause existed that 17-year-old defendant committed murder, requiring bindover to the trial court, and that he committed aggravated arson, allowing for discretionary bindover; a fire was located at back of victim's house and a car port was located in back of house, allowing for inference that car may have been parked there, and defendant's mother testified that defendant told her that on night of incident he went to house, threw oil into vehicle owned by an apparent relative of victim, lit a match and then returned home. State v. Kitchen (Ohio App. 5 Dist., Ashland, 09-22-2003) No. 02CA056, 2003-Ohio-5017, 2003 WL 22174602, Unreported, appeal not allowed 101 Ohio St.3d 1423, 802 N.E.2d 154, 2004-Ohio-123. Infants ⚖ 68.7(3)

Record in bindover proceedings with respect to juvenile charged with murder contained some basis for juvenile court's findings that reports of court-appointed psychologists did not adequately address risk of harm presented upon juvenile's eventual release from juvenile system, where one expert testified at hearing that she believed that juvenile's risk of harm would decrease "to a significant level" while he was in treatment, and other expert's report indicated expectation that juvenile would have continuing conduct problems in adulthood. State. v. West (Ohio App. 4 Dist., 06-30-2006) 167 Ohio App.3d 598, 856 N.E.2d 285, 2006-Ohio-3518. Infants ⚖ 68.7(3)

Testimony in bindover proceedings of court-appointed psychologists and juvenile facility psychologist was sufficient to support finding of juvenile court that court-appointed psychologists did not make specific diagnosis and that juvenile would thus not receive treatment or medication in juvenile facility; court-appointed psychologists testified that they did not make specific diagnosis of juvenile's psychological condition, and juvenile facility psychologist testified that juvenile would not receive course of medication or treatment in absence of diagnosis and that juvenile's participation in specific treatment programs described by all testifying experts as potentially beneficial to him would be voluntary. State. v. West (Ohio App. 4 Dist., 06-30-2006) 167 Ohio App.3d 598, 856 N.E.2d 285, 2006-Ohio-3518. Infants ⚖ 68.7(3)

Juvenile's allegations that she was erroneously bound over for trial as an adult, under the mandatory bindover statute, even though she did not personally possess firearm, raised a viable habeas corpus claim. Johnson v. Timmerman-Cooper (Ohio, 11-28-2001) 93 Ohio St.3d 614, 757 N.E.2d 1153, 2001-Ohio-1803. Habeas Corpus ⚖ 535

State produced sufficient evidence to satisfy statutory criteria for binding juvenile over to General Division for criminal prosecution as an adult for aggravated murder; juvenile was 17 years old at time of offense, juvenile had gun in his possession the day before murder of gas station clerk, juvenile test-fired gun twice the day of murder, juvenile had stated to friend that he had been thinking of "pulling a 187," juvenile and accomplice tried to recruit others to participate in robbery of gas station, juvenile and accomplice carried out their plan, and juvenile hid gun under rock and planned to retrieve it when things "cooled off." State. v. Agee (Ohio App. 2 Dist., 05-21-1999) 133 Ohio App.3d 441, 728 N.E.2d 442, dismissed, appeal not allowed 86 Ohio St.3d 1489, 716 N.E.2d 721, denial of habeas corpus affirmed 92 Ohio St.3d 540, 751 N.E.2d 1043, 2001-Ohio-1279. Infants ⚖ 68.7(3)

Evidence in a juvenile murder suspect's bindover proceeding, including the gruesome facts of the murder, supported the conclusion that the suspect was not amenable to rehabilitation in the juvenile court, even though prior attempts at such rehabilitation had been limited to probation. State. v. Whisenant (Ohio App. 11 Dist., 03-30-1998) 127 Ohio App.3d 75, 711 N.E.2d 1016, dismissed, appeal not allowed 83 Ohio St.3d 1416, 698 N.E.2d 1005. Infants ⚖ 68.7(3)

Evidence supported juvenile court's determination that 16-year-old juvenile charged with delinquency would not be amenable to rehabilitation; victim died from blow to back of head allegedly administered by juvenile with baseball bat. State. v. Campbell (Hamilton 1991) 74 Ohio App.3d 352, 598 N.E.2d 1244, dismissed, jurisdictional motion overruled 62 Ohio St.3d 1431, 578 N.E.2d 823. Infants ⚖ 68.7(3)

Defendant's conviction for murder was supported by testimony that defendant shot victim because victim called defendant's gun a toy, and that, prior to shooting, there had been no argument or other provocation between victim and defendant. State. v. Neguse (Franklin 1991) 71 Ohio App.3d 596, 594 N.E.2d 1116. Homicide ⚖ 1134

Where the record before a juvenile court contains sufficient credible evidence pertaining to each factor listed in Juv R 30(E), the court's determination to transfer the case for trial of the juvenile as an adult will be upheld, absent an abuse of discretion, even without any written statement of the court on those factors. State v. Douglas (Ohio 1985) 20 Ohio St.3d 34, 485 N.E.2d 711, 20 O.B.R. 282.

Where a seventeen-year-old boy sells a non-prescription drug containing substances defined as poisonous but not hallucinogenic to his schoolmates, it is a violation of RC 3719.32 and sufficient to support a finding of delinquency, though it is not a felony allowing commitment to the reformatory. In re Baker (Ohio 1969) 20 Ohio St.2d 142, 254 N.E.2d 363, 49 O.O.2d 473.

Note 4

Proof of possession, use, or control by a juvenile of a hallucinogen is sufficient evidence upon which a juvenile court can find such juvenile a delinquent under RC Ch 2151. In re Baker (Hocking 1969) 18 Ohio App.2d 276, 248 N.E.2d 620, 47 O.O.2d 411.

A proceeding against a juvenile charged with being a delinquent is civil in nature and not criminal, and a preponderance of the evidence is sufficient to warrant a determination that such juvenile is a delinquent, notwithstanding that acts are charged which, if committed by an adult and proved beyond a reasonable doubt, would constitute a felony. (See also In re Whittington, 17 App(2d) 164, 245 NE(2d) 364 (1969), reversed sub nom State ex rel Whittington v Barr, 19 OS(2d) 21, 249 NE(2d) 773 (1969).) In re Whittington (Fairfield 1967) 13 Ohio App.2d 11, 233 N.E.2d 333, 42 O.O.2d 39, vacated 88 S.Ct. 1507, 391 U.S. 341, 20 L.Ed.2d 625, 45 O.O.2d 31, on remand 17 Ohio App.2d 164, 245 N.E.2d 364, 46 O.O.2d 237. Infants ⇐ 176; Infants ⇐ 194.1

Under RC 2151.26 a child who is charged with committing a felony is entitled to a hearing at which he may present evidence as to his mental condition. State v. Yoss (Carroll 1967) 10 Ohio App.2d 47, 225 N.E.2d 275, 39 O.O.2d 81.

Evidence that a juvenile was sixteen years and seven months old at the time of the murder and in seemingly satisfactory mental and physical health, his past adjudications as a delinquent, the juvenile's admission to selling drugs and using both drugs and alcohol, his association with friends with whom he had engaged in criminal behavior, and his expulsion from high school for setting fire to a trash can, supports a trial court decision to bind the juvenile over to be tried as an adult pursuant to Juv R 30(E) and RC 2151.26. State v Ruple, No. 15726, 1993 WL 290201 (9th Dist Ct App, Summit, 8–4–93).

Evidence at probable cause hearing that juvenile entered home not his own through unlocked door, that no confrontation occurred within home, that juvenile fled residence while carrying video game, that juvenile carried handgun tucked into rear waistband of his pants, and that handgun was only seen from rear as juvenile fled, while sufficient to establish probable cause to believe that juvenile committed aggravated burglary, was insufficient to establish probable cause to believe that juvenile somehow employed firearm in course thereof, as required to trigger juvenile's mandatory bindover to adult court. In re B.S. (Ohio Com.Pl. 1998) 103 Ohio Misc.2d 34, 725 N.E.2d 362.

5. Mental exam

For purposes of binding juvenile over to court of common pleas, juvenile court acted within its discretion when it found that the safety of the community might require that defendant, who was 15 years old at the time of alleged murder and had not previously been convicted of a felony or adjudicated a delinquent child, be placed in legal restraint, even after reaching the age of majority; expert witnesses for both prosecution and defense testified that the results of defendant's mental examination showed that he had an increased risk for future violence, defendant scored very high in a test suggesting aggressive, antisocial behavior and scored in a "moderate to high risk" category on another test, demonstrating a risk of violence 13 times more than the general public, and defendant was using drugs and alcohol, increasing his risk of violence. State v. Lallathin (Ohio App. 7 Dist., Noble, 06-26-2003) No. 299, 2003-Ohio-3478, 2003 WL 21500290, Unreported, appeal not allowed 100 Ohio St.3d 1433, 797 N.E.2d 513, 2003-Ohio-5396, denial of post-conviction relief affirmed 2004-Ohio-7066, 2004 WL 2980379, appeal not allowed 105 Ohio St.3d 1519, 826 N.E.2d 316, 2005-Ohio-1880. Infants ⇐ 68.7(3)

For purposes of binding juvenile over to court of common pleas, juvenile court acted within its discretion when it concluded that defendant, who was 15 years old at the time of alleged murder and had not previously been convicted of a felony or adjudicated a delinquent child, was not amenable to care or rehabilitation in a juvenile facility, even though expert witnesses for both the prosecution and defense testified that it was possible or probable that defendant suffered from Attention Deficit Hyperactivity Disorder (ADHD) and that any treatment for ADHD would be better found in the juvenile system; neither expert witness explained how ADHD led to defendant's alleged conduct in the case, defendant demonstrated some reticence toward rehabilitation, expert witness testified that it would take longer than normal for defendant to be rehabilitated, and defendant was alleged to have committed murder, a serious offense normally requiring longer periods of rehabilitation. State v. Lallathin (Ohio App. 7 Dist., Noble, 06-26-2003) No. 299, 2003-Ohio-3478, 2003 WL 21500290, Unreported, appeal not allowed 100 Ohio St.3d 1433, 797 N.E.2d 513, 2003-Ohio-5396, denial of post-conviction relief affirmed 2004-Ohio-7066, 2004 WL 2980379, appeal not allowed 105 Ohio St.3d 1519, 826 N.E.2d 316, 2005-Ohio-1880. Infants ⇐ 68.7(3)

Where a juvenile court has made full investigation, including mental and physical examination, of minor charged with a felony and has ordered such minor into a recognizance for his appearance before court of common pleas for such disposition as court of common pleas is authorized to make for a like act committed by an adult and it is not suggested or otherwise brought to attention of court of common pleas that accused is not then sane, trial court is not required to proceed further to examine into question of sanity of such defendant. State v. Frohner (Ohio 1948) 150 Ohio St. 53, 80 N.E.2d 868, 37 O.O. 406. Criminal Law ⇐ 625(1)

A writ of procedendo will issue where a juvenile court finds a minor in contempt for refusal to submit to a mental examination and suspends proceedings pending compliance with the order for a mental examination, a knowing, voluntary refusal to submit to the examination constitutes a waiver of the right to a mental examination, RC 2151.26(C). State ex rel. Doe v. Tracy (Warren 1988) 51 Ohio App.3d 198, 555 N.E.2d 674, cause dismissed 39 Ohio St.3d 713, 534 N.E.2d 95.

Juvenile was not entitled to appointment of private psychiatric examiner of the court's choosing other than the court's psychologist, at the State's expense, in proceeding to determine whether juvenile court jurisdiction should be waived and whether juvenile should be prosecuted as adult in the Common Pleas Court; proceeding was not phase in which juvenile's life or liberty was expressly at stake, and any incriminating matter which might be obtained during the mental examination with the court psychologist could not be used for anything other than the waiver determination itself. State ex rel. A Juvenile v. Hoose (Lake 1988) 43 Ohio App.3d 109, 539 N.E.2d 704, cause dismissed 39 Ohio St.3d 713, 534 N.E.2d 94.

Commitment of a fifteen year old to a state institution pursuant to RC 2151.26 for purpose of examination is not an act for which a writ of prohibition will issue. State ex rel. Harris v. Common Pleas Court, Division of Probate and Juvenile (Ross 1970) 25 Ohio App.2d 78, 266 N.E.2d 589, 54 O.O.2d 115.

6. Waiver of jurisdiction

Exclusive subject matter jurisdiction of juvenile court cannot be waived; abrogating Tillman, 585 N.E.2d 550, 66 Ohio App.3d 464. State v. Wilson (Ohio, 08-09-1995) 73 Ohio St.3d 40, 652 N.E.2d 196, 1995-Ohio-217. Infants ⇐ 68.5

The entry of a plea and failure by a criminal defendant to inform the court prior to the entry of sentence that he was a juvenile at the time the charged offenses are alleged to have been committed waives the issue of the personal jurisdiction of the general division of a common pleas court. State v. Tillman (Lorain 1990) 66 Ohio App.3d 464, 585 N.E.2d 550, appeal after new trial 119 Ohio App.3d 449, 695 N.E.2d 792.

Indigent juvenile offender is entitled to a record in hearing conducted for purpose of determining whether juvenile court may waive jurisdiction and bind offender over to court of common pleas for criminal prosecution. State v. Ross (Greene 1970) 23 Ohio App.2d 215, 262 N.E.2d 427, 52 O.O.2d 311. Infants ⇐ 68.7(3)

Where a juvenile court, in the jurisdiction in which an offender resides, waives jurisdiction so that the offender will be tried by a common pleas court, such defendant is entitled to a trial in the county where the offense occurred. In re Davis (Ohio Juv. 1961) 179 N.E.2d 198, 87 Ohio Law Abs. 222, 22 O.O.2d 108.

A minor, charged with a felony, who does not object to the jurisdiction of the court of common pleas on the ground of his minority by raising that question before such court, loses his right to object after sentence by that court. Mellott v. Alvis (Franklin 1959) 109 Ohio App. 486, 162 N.E.2d 623, 81 Ohio Law Abs. 532, 12 O.O.2d 23. Infants ⇐ 68.8

Where a seventeen year old defendant charged with operating a motor vehicle without the owner's consent did not object to the jurisdiction of the common pleas court on the ground of his minority by raising that question in such court, he has lost his right to object after sentence by that court. Mellott v. Alvis (Franklin 1959) 109 Ohio App. 486, 162 N.E.2d 623, 81 Ohio Law Abs. 532, 12 O.O.2d 23. Infants ⇐ 68.8

Juvenile Court made the findings required in order to relinquish jurisdiction over juvenile, who was charged with attempted murder of his elderly neighbor, to Common Pleas Court; Juvenile Court found that juvenile was not amenable to care or rehabilitation in any facility designed for the care, supervision and rehabilitation of delinquent children and that the safety of the community might require that juvenile be placed under legal restraint for a period extending beyond his majority, and doctor stated that juvenile, who was 15 when crime was committed, could not comply with the typical role obligations for a child at his age. State v. Tomlin (Ohio App. 8 Dist., Cuyahoga, 09-19-2002) No. 79750, 2002-Ohio-4889, 2002 WL 31087431, Unreported. Infants ⇐ 68.7(4)

Absent proper bindover procedure pursuant to statute, jurisdiction of juvenile court is exclusive and cannot be waived. State ex rel. Harris v. Anderson (Ohio 1996) 76 Ohio St.3d 193, 667 N.E.2d 1, 1996 –Ohio- 412.

The juvenile and general divisions of a court of common pleas possess concurrent jurisdiction over a juvenile accused of a crime, and the juvenile division has not been divested of personal jurisdiction over one whose disposition is returned to it after the accused initially waived his right to be judged in that tribunal. State ex rel. Leis v. Black (Hamilton 1975) 45 Ohio App.2d 191, 341 N.E.2d 853, 74 O.O.2d 270.

Firearm specification as set forth in statute governing mandatory waivers of juvenile court jurisdiction is an essential portion of "the act charged" for purposes of probable cause hearing in mandatory bindover proceeding. In re B.S. (Ohio Com.Pl. 1998) 103 Ohio Misc.2d 34, 725 N.E.2d 362.

7. Grand jury indictment and bindover to adult facility

Juvenile court division did not have jurisdiction over defendant's case, where defendant was bound over and indicted in the general division after his eighteenth birthday. State v. Sherrills (Ohio App. 8 Dist., Cuyahoga, 05-19-2005) No. 85655, No. 85656, 2005-Ohio-2467, 2005 WL 1190729, Unreported. Infants ⇐ 68.7(3)

Trial court did not lack jurisdiction over kidnapping charges that were not explicitly included in bindover order from juvenile court with charges of attempted aggravated murder, aggravated robbery, and other crimes; grand jury had statutory authority to issue indictments for kidnapping that derived from offenses charged in juvenile proceeding. State v. Goins (Ohio App. 7 Dist., Mahoning, 03-21-2005) No. 02 CA 68, 2005-Ohio-1439, 2005 WL 704865, Unreported, appeal allowed 106 Ohio St.3d 1503, 833 N.E.2d 1246, 2005-Ohio-4605, reversed in part 109 Ohio St.3d 313, 847 N.E.2d 1174, 2006-Ohio-2109. Infants ⇐ 68.7(1)

Inmate's allegation that common pleas court did not have jurisdiction to enter a conviction or sentence, based upon juvenile court's purported failure to administer a physical examination prior to his amenability hearing and bindover, raised a sufficient claim of jurisdictional error to sustain his writ of habeas corpus action. Snitzky v. Wilson (Ohio App. 11 Dist., Trumbull, 12-23-2004) No. 2003-T-0095, 2004-Ohio-7229, 2004 WL 3090238, Unreported. Habeas Corpus ⇐ 670(10)

Common pleas court possessed jurisdiction over claimant who had been convicted of charges that were subject to mandatory bindover from juvenile court, even though it lacked jurisdiction to sentence claimant on charges that were not subject to mandatory bindover and thus were not properly bound over to common pleas court, and thus claimant could not maintain false imprisonment charge against Department of Rehabilitation and Correction for confinement following conviction on charges; department did not initiate proceedings leading to confinement, but was under statutory duty to maintain custody of plaintiff pursuant to court's sentencing entry that did not appear to be invalid on its face, and there was no evidence that department had knowledge that the judgment of sentence by common pleas court was improper. Fryerson v. Ohio Dept. of Rehab. & Corr. (Ohio Ct.Cl., 10-09-2002) 120 Ohio Misc.2d 50, 778 N.E.2d 153, 2002-Ohio-5757, affirmed 2003-Ohio-2730, 2003 WL 21234932, appeal not allowed 100 Ohio St.3d 1412, 796 N.E.2d 538, 2003-Ohio-4948. False Imprisonment ⇐ 12

Where the court of common pleas had some jurisdiction over claimant at time of order of bindover from juvenile court, the court's entry of sentence does not give rise to an action against Department of Rehabilitation and Correction for false imprisonment, where the charges relating to the offense, although erroneous, appeared valid on the face of the order of commitment. Fryerson v. Ohio Dept. of Rehab. & Corr. (Ohio Ct.Cl., 10-09-2002) 120 Ohio Misc.2d 50, 778 N.E.2d 153, 2002-Ohio-5757, affirmed 2003-Ohio-2730, 2003 WL 21234932, appeal not allowed 100 Ohio St.3d 1412, 796 N.E.2d 538, 2003-Ohio-4948. False Imprisonment ⇐ 12

Domicile at time of offense, rather than at time of bindover hearing, governed determination of whether minor was "domiciled in another state" within meaning of bindover statute, so that he could be tried as adult for offense committed within state. State v. Simpson (Ohio App. 5 Dist., 06-17-2002) 148 Ohio App.3d 221, 772 N.E.2d 707, 2002-Ohio-3077. Infants ⇐ 68.7(2)

Minor's domicile was in South Carolina at the time he committed an aggravated robbery in Ohio, and thus he was subject to Ohio's bindover statute that allowed him to be tried as an adult, though minor was staying with relative in Ohio; minor had been in Ohio less than a month when he committed the offense, and soon thereafter returned to South Carolina to live with his mother. State v. Simpson (Ohio App. 5 Dist., 06-17-2002) 148 Ohio App.3d 221, 772 N.E.2d 707, 2002-Ohio-3077. Infants ⇐ 68.7(3)

State v Hanning, which provided that statute requiring juvenile bindover for use of firearm in commission of certain crimes is inapplicable unless juvenile personally possessed firearm, applies retrospectively. Agee v. Russell (Ohio, 08-15-2001) 92 Ohio St.3d 540, 751 N.E.2d 1043, 2001-Ohio-1279. Courts ⇐ 100(1); Infants ⇐ 68.7(1)

Common pleas court's general division did not patently and unambiguously lack jurisdiction to try, convict, and sentence juvenile for, inter alia, aggravated murder with accompanying firearm specifications, and thus, because juvenile had adequate remedy by appeal to raise his claim that mandatory bindover was improper, habeas corpus relief was unavailable; record did not show that juvenile court judge relied on complicity statute to transfer juvenile based on accomplice's use of firearm, and juvenile was subject to mandatory bindover on grounds that act charged was category one offense, that he was sixteen years of age or older at time of act charged, and that there was probable cause to believe that he committed act charged. Agee v. Russell (Ohio, 08-15-2001) 92 Ohio St.3d 540, 751 N.E.2d 1043, 2001-Ohio-1279. Habeas Corpus ⇐ 289; Infants ⇐ 68.7(2)

State v Hanning, which provided that statute requiring juvenile bindover for use of firearm in commission of certain crimes is inapplicable unless juvenile personally possessed firearm, is limited to cases in which mandatory bindover is based on firearm specification; it does not apply to cases in which mandatory bindover is based on other grounds, such as probable cause to believe that juvenile committed category one offense when he was sixteen years of age or older. Agee v. Russell (Ohio, 08-15-2001) 92 Ohio St.3d 540, 751 N.E.2d 1043, 2001-Ohio-1279. Infants ⇐ 68.7(2)

Statute requiring mandatory bindover to adult criminal court after a probable cause finding did not conflict with juvenile rule relating to bindover, as by its very language, juvenile rule was a discretionary provision and only affected discretionary bindovers, not those mandated by criminal statute. In re Langston (Ohio App. 5 Dist., 03-03-1997) 119 Ohio App.3d 1, 694 N.E.2d 468. Infants ⇐ 68.2

Where a grandmother states to a juvenile court that she has legal custody of a minor in a "bind-over" proceeding, the notice requirements of RC 2151.26 have been satisfied when the grandmother has been given proper notice. State v. Parks (Montgomery 1988) 51 Ohio App.3d 194, 555 N.E.2d 671.

RC 2151.355(A)(9) does not authorize the juvenile court to exercise unlimited discretion in sentencing a delinquent child, and there is no authority for it to commit a delinquent juvenile to a jail for adult offenders, absent a finding that housing in an appropriate juvenile facility is unavailable, or that the public safety and protection so require. State v. Grady (Cuyahoga 1981) 3 Ohio App.3d 174, 444 N.E.2d 51, 3 O.B.R. 199.

When a minor is transferred from the juvenile court to the court of common pleas on a charge which would constitute a felony if committed by an adult, the grand jury is empowered to return any indictment under the facts submitted to it and is not confined to returning indictments only on charges originally filed in the juvenile court. State v. Adams (Ohio 1982) 69 Ohio St.2d 120, 431 N.E.2d 326, 23 O.O.3d 164.

When felony charge against a minor transferred from the juvenile court to the court of common pleas under former GC 1681 (RC 2151.26), the grand jury is empowered to return any indictment proper under the facts submitted to it. State v. Klingenberger (Ohio 1925) 113 Ohio St. 418, 149 N.E. 395, 3 Ohio Law Abs. 675, 23 Ohio Law Rep. 588.

Former GC 1681 (RC 2151.26), that a delinquent child charged with a felony may be recognized to the common pleas for trial, is not in conflict with former GC 1652 (RC 2151.35) for sending him to the state reformatory; it is permissive and not mandatory. Leonard v. Licker (Ohio App. 1914) 26 Ohio C.D. 427, 23 Ohio C.C.(N.S.) 442, 3 Ohio App. 377.

If the charge of a particular offense would invoke the mandatory bindover provisions of RC 2151.26, then the charge of complicity in that offense, pursuant to RC 2923.03, would also invoke those mandatory bindover provisions. OAG 97–014.

In appropriate circumstances, a juvenile offender whose case has been transferred to the court of common pleas for prosecution as an adult pursuant to RC 2151.26 may, upon conviction, be ordered or committed to a community-based correctional facility established pursuant to RC 2301.51 to 2301.58. OAG 97–013.

Superintendent of Ohio state reformatory has no right to refuse to receive person committed to that institution by court having general jurisdiction to try felonies even though he has reason to believe that person committed was under eighteen years of age at time of his arraignment and conviction and had not had benefit of proceedings under GC 1639–29 (RC 2151.25) and GC 1639–32 (RC 2151.26). 1944 OAG 6813.

2152.12
Note 8

8. Disqualification of judge

Former rulings of a juvenile court judge demonstrating that the motion to transfer a youth for prosecution as an adult was granted in more than one-half of the cases in which the motion was considered are contrary to a claim that former rulings demonstrate a predisposition to deny such motions and therefore the rulings do not provide grounds for disqualification. In re Disqualification of Ruben (Ohio, 09-14-1995) No. 95-AP-109, No. 9536, 77 Ohio St.3d 1232, 674 N.E.2d 348, Unreported.

9. Public access

Closure of delinquency proceedings for 17–year–old charged with aggravated murder, aggravated attempted murder, and aggravated robbery was abuse of discretion; public interest in proceedings outweighed bare assertion by juvenile's attorney that permitting access would not be in juvenile's best interest, in view of juvenile's near-adult age at time of alleged offenses, minimal likelihood that probable cause hearing would disclose confidential information, gravity of offenses, and fact that juvenile would be subject to mandatory bindover to adult court if probable cause was found. State ex rel. Plain Dealer Publishing Co. v. Geauga Cty. Court of Common Pleas, Juv. Div. (Ohio 2000) 90 Ohio St.3d 79, 734 N.E.2d 1214, 2000 –Ohio- 35.

2152.13 Serious youthful offender dispositional sentence

(A) A juvenile court may impose a serious youthful offender dispositional sentence on a child only if the prosecuting attorney of the county in which the delinquent act allegedly occurred initiates the process against the child in accordance with this division, and the child is an alleged delinquent child who is eligible for the dispositional sentence. The prosecuting attorney may initiate the process in any of the following ways:

(1) Obtaining an indictment of the child as a serious youthful offender;

(2) The child waives the right to indictment, charging the child in a bill of information as a serious youthful offender;

(3) Until an indictment or information is obtained, requesting a serious youthful offender dispositional sentence in the original complaint alleging that the child is a delinquent child;

(4) Until an indictment or information is obtained, if the original complaint does not request a serious youthful offender dispositional sentence, filing with the juvenile court a written notice of intent to seek a serious youthful offender dispositional sentence within twenty days after the later of the following, unless the time is extended by the juvenile court for good cause shown:

(a) The date of the child's first juvenile court hearing regarding the complaint;

(b) The date the juvenile court determines not to transfer the case under section 2152.12 of the Revised Code.

After a written notice is filed under division (A)(4) of this section, the juvenile court shall serve a copy of the notice on the child and advise the child of the prosecuting attorney's intent to seek a serious youthful offender dispositional sentence in the case.

(B) If an alleged delinquent child is not indicted or charged by information as described in division (A)(1) or (2) of this section and if a notice or complaint as described in division (A)(3) or (4) of this section indicates that the prosecuting attorney intends to pursue a serious youthful offender dispositional sentence in the case, the juvenile court shall hold a preliminary hearing to determine if there is probable cause that the child committed the act charged and is by age eligible for, or required to receive, a serious youthful offender dispositional sentence.

(C) (1) A child for whom a serious youthful offender dispositional sentence is sought has the right to a grand jury determination of probable cause that the child committed the act charged and that the child is eligible by age for a serious youthful offender dispositional sentence. The grand jury may be impaneled by the court of common pleas or the juvenile court.

Once a child is indicted, or charged by information or the juvenile court determines that the child is eligible for a serious youthful offender dispositional sentence, the child is entitled to an open and speedy trial by jury in juvenile court and to be provided with a transcript of the proceedings. The time within which the trial is to be held under Title XXIX of the Revised Code commences on whichever of the following dates is applicable:

(a) If the child is indicted or charged by information, on the date of the filing of the indictment or information.

(b) If the child is charged by an original complaint that requests a serious youthful offender dispositional sentence, on the date of the filing of the complaint.

(c) If the child is not charged by an original complaint that requests a serious youthful offender dispositional sentence, on the date that the prosecuting attorney files the written notice of intent to seek a serious youthful offender dispositional sentence.

(2) If the child is detained awaiting adjudication, upon indictment or being charged by information, the child has the same right to bail as an adult charged with the offense the alleged delinquent act would be if committed by an adult. Except as provided in division (D) of section 2152.14 of the Revised Code, all provisions of Title XXIX of the Revised Code and the Criminal Rules shall apply in the case and to the child. The juvenile court shall afford the child all rights afforded a person who is prosecuted for committing a crime including the right to counsel and the right to raise the issue of competency. The child may not waive the right to counsel.

(D) (1) If a child is adjudicated a delinquent child for committing an act under circumstances that require the juvenile court to impose upon the child a serious youthful offender dispositional sentence under section 2152.11 of the Revised Code, all of the following apply:

(a) The juvenile court shall impose upon the child a sentence available for the violation, as if the child were an adult, under Chapter 2929. of the Revised Code, except that the juvenile court shall not impose on the child a sentence of death or life imprisonment without parole.

(b) The juvenile court also shall impose upon the child one or more traditional juvenile dispositions under sections 2152.16, 2152.19, and 2152.20, and, if applicable, section 2152.17 of the Revised Code.

(c) The juvenile court shall stay the adult portion of the serious youthful offender dispositional sentence pending the successful completion of the traditional juvenile dispositions imposed.

(2)(a) If a child is adjudicated a delinquent child for committing an act under circumstances that allow, but do not require, the juvenile court to impose on the child a serious youthful offender dispositional sentence under section 2152.11 of the Revised Code, all of the following apply:

(i) If the juvenile court on the record makes a finding that, given the nature and circumstances of the violation and the history of the child, the length of time, level of security, and types of programming and resources available in the juvenile system alone are not adequate to provide the juvenile court with a reasonable expectation that the purposes set forth in section 2152.01 of the Revised Code will be met, the juvenile court may impose upon the child a sentence available for the violation, as if the child were an adult, under Chapter 2929. of the Revised Code, except that the juvenile court shall not impose on the child a sentence of death or life imprisonment without parole.

(ii) If a sentence is imposed under division (D) (2)(a)(i) of this section, the juvenile court also shall impose upon the child one or more traditional juvenile dispositions under sections 2152.16,

2152.19, and 2152.20 and, if applicable, section 2152.17 of the Revised Code.

(iii) The juvenile court shall stay the adult portion of the serious youthful offender dispositional sentence pending the successful completion of the traditional juvenile dispositions imposed.

(b) If the juvenile court does not find that a sentence should be imposed under division (D) (2)(a)(i) of this section, the juvenile court may impose one or more traditional juvenile dispositions under sections 2152.16, 2152.19, 2152.20, and, if applicable, section 2152.17 of the Revised Code.

(3) A child upon whom a serious youthful offender dispositional sentence is imposed under division (D) (1) or (2) of this section has a right to appeal under division (A)(1), (3), (4), (5), or (6) of section 2953.08 of the Revised Code the adult portion of the serious youthful offender dispositional sentence when any of those divisions apply. The child may appeal the adult portion, and the court shall consider the appeal as if the adult portion were not stayed.

(2002 H 393, eff. 7–5–02; 2000 S 179, § 3, eff. 1–1–02)

Uncodified Law

2000 S 179, § 8, eff. 4–9–01, reads:

The General Assembly hereby encourages the Supreme Court to take appropriate action to collect data from each juvenile court in this state on both the number of alleged delinquent children for whom a serious youthful offender dispositional sentence is sought pursuant to section 2152.13 of the Revised Code and the number of jury trials held in the juvenile courts annually as a result of serious youthful offender dispositional sentences being sought for alleged delinquent children, and to prepare and submit to the General Assembly a report containing the data so collected.

Historical and Statutory Notes

Amendment Note: 2002 H 393 rewrote this section which prior thereto read:

"(A) A juvenile court may impose a serious youthful offender dispositional sentence on a child only if the prosecuting attorney of the county in which the delinquent act allegedly occurred initiates the process against the child in accordance with this division or division (B) of this section, and the child is an alleged delinquent child who is eligible for the dispositional sentence. The prosecuting attorney may initiate the process in any of the following ways:

"(1) The child is indicted as a serious youthful offender or is charged in a bill of information as a serious youthful offender.

"(2) The original complaint alleging that the child is a delinquent child requests a serious youthful offender dispositional sentence.

"(B) Unless the original complaint includes a notice of intent to seek that type of sentence, the prosecuting attorney shall file with the juvenile court a written notice of intent to seek a serious youthful offender dispositional sentence within twenty days after the later of the following, unless the time is extended by the juvenile court for good cause shown:

"(1) The date of the child's first juvenile court hearing regarding the complaint;

"(2) The date the juvenile court determines not to transfer the case under section 2152.12 of the Revised Code.

"After a written notice is filed under this division, the juvenile court shall serve a copy of the notice on the child and advise the child of the prosecuting attorney's intent to seek a serious youthful offender dispositional sentence in the case.

"(C) If an alleged delinquent child is not indicted or charged by information as described in division (A) of this section and if a notice or complaint as described in division (A)(3) or (B) of this section indicates that the prosecuting attorney intends to pursue a serious youthful offender dispositional sentence in the case, the juvenile court shall hold a preliminary hearing to determine if there is probable cause that the child committed the act charged and is by age eligible for, or required to receive, a serious youthful offender dispositional sentence.

"(D)(1) A child for whom a serious youthful offender dispositional sentence is sought has the right to a grand jury determination of probable cause that the child committed the act charged and that the child is eligible by age for a serious youthful offender dispositional sentence. The grand jury may be impaneled by the court of common pleas or the juvenile court.

"Once a child is indicted, or charged by information or the juvenile court determines that the child is eligible for a serious youthful offender dispositional sentence, the child is entitled to an open and speedy trial by jury in juvenile court and to be provided with a transcript of the proceedings. The time within which the trial is to be held under Title XXIX of the Revised Code commences on whichever of the following dates is applicable:

"(a) If the child is indicted or charged by information, on the date of the filing of the indictment or information.

"(b) If the child is charged by an original complaint that requests a serious youthful offender dispositional sentence, on the date of the filing of the complaint.

"(c) If the child is not charged by an original complaint that requests a serious youthful offender dispositional sentence, on the date that the prosecuting attorney files the written notice of intent to seek a serious youthful offender dispositional sentence.

"(2) If the child is detained awaiting adjudication, upon indictment or being charged by information, the child has the same right to bail as an adult charged with the offense the alleged delinquent act would be if committed by an adult. Except as provided in division (D) of section 2152.14 of the Revised Code, all provisions of Title XXIX of the Revised Code and the Criminal Rules shall apply in the case and to the child. The juvenile court shall afford the child all rights afforded a person who is prosecuted for committing a crime including the right to counsel and the right to raise the issue of competency. The child may not waive the right to counsel.

"(E)(1) If a child is adjudicated a delinquent child for committing an act under circumstances that require the juvenile court to impose upon the child a serious youthful offender dispositional sentence under section 2152.11 of the Revised Code, all of the following apply:

"(a) The juvenile court shall impose upon the child a sentence available for the violation, as if the child were an adult, under Chapter 2929. of the Revised Code, except that the juvenile court shall not impose on the child a sentence of death or life imprisonment without parole.

"(b) The juvenile court also shall impose upon the child one or more traditional juvenile dispositions under sections 2152.16 and 2152.19 of the Revised Code.

"(c) The juvenile court shall stay the adult portion of the serious youthful offender dispositional sentence pending the successful completion of the traditional juvenile dispositions imposed.

"(2)(a) If a child is adjudicated a delinquent child for committing an act under circumstances that allow, but do not require, the juvenile court to impose on the child a serious youthful offender dispositional sentence under section 2152.11 of the Revised Code, all of the following apply:

"(i) If the juvenile court on the record makes a finding that, given the nature and circumstances of the violation and the history of the child, the length of time, level of security, and types of programming and resources available in the juvenile system alone are not adequate to provide the juvenile court with a reasonable expectation that the purposes set forth in section 2152.01 of the Revised Code will be met, the juvenile court may impose upon the child a sentence available for the violation, as if the child were an adult, under Chapter 2929. of the Revised Code, except that the juvenile court shall not impose on the child a sentence of death or life imprisonment without parole.

"(ii) If a sentence is imposed under division (E)(2)(a)(i) of this section, the juvenile court also shall impose upon the child one or more traditional juvenile dispositions under sections 2152.16, 2152.19, and 2152.20 and, if applicable, section 2152.17 of the Revised Code.

"(iii) The juvenile court shall stay the adult portion of the serious youthful offender dispositional sentence pending the successful completion of the traditional juvenile dispositions imposed.

"(b) If the juvenile court does not find that a sentence should be imposed under division (E)(2)(a)(i) of this section, the juvenile court may impose one or more traditional juvenile dispositions under sections 2152.16, 2152.19, and, if applicable, section 2152.17 of the Revised Code.

"(3) A child upon whom a serious youthful offender dispositional sentence is imposed under division (E)(1) or (2) of this section has a right to appeal under division (A)(1), (3), (4), (5), or (6) of section 2953.08 of the Revised Code the adult portion of the serious youthful offender dispositional sentence when any of those divisions apply. The child may appeal the adult portion, and the court shall consider the appeal as if the adult portion were not stayed."

Library References

Infants ⟸69(3).
Westlaw Topic No. 211.
C.J.S. Infants §§ 198, 207 to 209.

Research References

Encyclopedias

OH Jur. 3d Family Law § 1500, Relating to Persons.
OH Jur. 3d Family Law § 1503, Relating to Procedure.
OH Jur. 3d Family Law § 1515, Powers.
OH Jur. 3d Family Law § 1536, Terms, Sessions, and Places of Court.
OH Jur. 3d Family Law § 1570, Apprehension.
OH Jur. 3d Family Law § 1576, Detention Hearing; Notice.
OH Jur. 3d Family Law § 1587, Transfer to County of Residence.
OH Jur. 3d Family Law § 1590, Who May File Complaint.
OH Jur. 3d Family Law § 1656, Right to Jury Trial.
OH Jur. 3d Family Law § 1698.5, Serious Youthful Offender.

Treatises and Practice Aids

Katz, Giannelli, Blair and Lipton, Baldwin's Ohio Practice, Criminal Law, § 62:7, Juvenile Cases.

Carlin, Baldwin's Ohio Practice, Merrick-Rippner Probate Law § 107:52, Adjudicatory Hearings—Confidentiality of Juvenile Court Proceedings.

Carlin, Baldwin's Ohio Practice, Merrick-Rippner Probate Law § 107:65, Mandatory Transfer, Effective January 1, 2002.

Carlin, Baldwin's Ohio Practice, Merrick-Rippner Probate Law § 107:89, Custody of Department of Youth Services.

Carlin, Baldwin's Ohio Practice, Merrick-Rippner Probate Law § 107:102, Serious Youthful Offenders, Effective January 1, 2002.

Carlin, Baldwin's Ohio Practice, Merrick-Rippner Probate Law § 107:104, Requests to Invoke Adult Portion of Serious Youthful Offender Disposition, Effective January 1, 2002.

Carlin, Baldwin's Ohio Practice, Merrick-Rippner Probate Law § 107:168, Bond in Delinquency Complaint—Form.

Giannelli & Yeomans, Ohio Juvenile Law § 5:3, Syo Charging; Preliminary Hearing.

Giannelli & Yeomans, Ohio Juvenile Law § 5:6, Syo Adjudicatory Hearing.

Giannelli & Yeomans, Ohio Juvenile Law § 5:7, Mandatory Syo Dispositions.

Giannelli & Yeomans, Ohio Juvenile Law § 5:8, Discretionary Syo Dispositions.

Giannelli & Yeomans, Ohio Juvenile Law § 5:9, Procedural Rights.

Giannelli & Yeomans, Ohio Juvenile Law § 14:3, Custody, Arrests & Stops.

Giannelli & Yeomans, Ohio Juvenile Law § 19:1, Introduction.

Giannelli & Yeomans, Ohio Juvenile Law § 19:6, Standard for Detention.

Giannelli & Yeomans, Ohio Juvenile Law § 19:9, Bail.

Giannelli & Yeomans, Ohio Juvenile Law § 23:4, Waiver of Right to Counsel.

Giannelli & Yeomans, Ohio Juvenile Law § 23:7, Mental Competency.

Giannelli & Yeomans, Ohio Juvenile Law § 5:13, Syo Appeals.

Giannelli & Yeomans, Ohio Juvenile Law App. D, Appendix D. Glossary.

Giannelli & Yeomans, Ohio Juvenile Law § 19:12, Closure of Hearing.

Giannelli & Yeomans, Ohio Juvenile Law § 23:10, Jury Trials.

Giannelli & Yeomans, Ohio Juvenile Law § 23:11, Public Trials; Gag Orders.

Giannelli & Yeomans, Ohio Juvenile Law § 23:29, Speedy Trial.

Giannelli & Yeomans, Ohio Juvenile Law § 23:30, Right to a Transcript.

Notes of Decisions

Constitutional issues 1

1. Constitutional issues

Ohio's serious youthful offender sentencing scheme does not violate principles of due process; scheme does not unconstitutionally "target" very young offenders or unconstitutionally treat juveniles as adults, and while the scheme does, under certain circumstances, subject juveniles to adult punishment, the statute was crafted to take into account juvenile-adult distinctions. In re J.B. (Ohio App. 12 Dist., Butler, 12-30-2005) No. CA2004-09-226, 2005-Ohio-7029, 2005 WL 3610482, Unreported. Infants ⟸ 69(2)

Ohio's serious youthful offender sentencing scheme does not violate the Eighth Amendment's prohibition against cruel and unusual punishment; scheme does not provide for penalties against juveniles so greatly disproportionate to the offenses committed that those penalties shock the sense of justice in the community, scheme prohibits the imposition of the most severe adult punishment, and the scheme reserves adult punishment only for serious juvenile offenders not capable of being rehabilitated within the juvenile system. In re J.B. (Ohio App. 12 Dist., Butler, 12-30-2005) No. CA2004-09-226, 2005-Ohio-7029, 2005 WL 3610482, Unreported. Sentencing And Punishment ⟸ 1607

2152.14 Invoking adult portion of sentence

(A)(1) The director of youth services may request the prosecuting attorney of the county in which is located the juvenile court that imposed a serious youthful offender dispositional sentence upon a person to file a motion with that juvenile court to invoke the adult portion of the dispositional sentence if all of the following apply to the person:

(a) The person is at least fourteen years of age.

(b) The person is in the institutional custody, or an escapee from the custody, of the department of youth services.

(c) The person is serving the juvenile portion of the serious youthful offender dispositional sentence.

(2) The motion shall state that there is reasonable cause to believe that either of the following misconduct has occurred and shall state that at least one incident of misconduct of that nature occurred after the person reached fourteen years of age:

(a) The person committed an act that is a violation of the rules of the institution and that could be charged as any felony or as a first degree misdemeanor offense of violence if committed by an adult.

(b) The person has engaged in conduct that creates a substantial risk to the safety or security of the institution, the community, or the victim.

(B) If a person is at least fourteen years of age, is serving the juvenile portion of a serious youthful offender dispositional sentence, and is on parole or aftercare from a department of youth services facility, or on community control, the director of youth services, the juvenile court that imposed the serious youthful offender dispositional sentence on the person, or the probation department supervising the person may request the prosecuting attorney of the county in which is located the juvenile court to file a motion with the juvenile court to invoke the adult portion of the dispositional sentence. The prosecuting attorney may file a motion to invoke the adult portion of the dispositional sentence even if no request is made. The motion shall state that there is reasonable cause to believe that either of the following occurred and shall state that at least one incident of misconduct of that nature occurred after the person reached fourteen years of age:

(1) The person committed an act that is a violation of the conditions of supervision and that could be charged as any felony or as a first degree misdemeanor offense of violence if committed by an adult.

(2) The person has engaged in conduct that creates a substantial risk to the safety or security of the community or of the victim.

(C) If the prosecuting attorney declines a request to file a motion that was made by the department of youth services or the supervising probation department under division (A) or (B) of this section or fails to act on a request made under either division by the department within a reasonable time, the department of youth services or the supervising probation department may file a motion of the type described in division (A) or (B) of this section with the juvenile court to invoke the adult portion of the serious youthful offender dispositional sentence. If the prosecuting attorney declines a request to file a motion that was made by the juvenile court under division (B) of this section or fails to act on a request from the court under that division within a reasonable time, the juvenile court may hold the hearing described in division (D) of this section on its own motion.

(D) Upon the filing of a motion described in division (A), (B), or (C) of this section, the juvenile court may hold a hearing to determine whether to invoke the adult portion of a person's serious juvenile offender dispositional sentence. The juvenile court shall not invoke the adult portion of the dispositional sentence without a hearing. At the hearing the person who is the subject of the serious youthful offender disposition has the right to be present, to receive notice of the grounds upon which the adult sentence portion is sought to be invoked, to be represented by counsel including counsel appointed under Juvenile Rule 4(A), to be advised on the procedures and protections set forth in the Juvenile Rules, and to present evidence on the person's own behalf, including evidence that the person has a mental illness or is a mentally retarded person. The person may not waive the right to counsel. The hearing shall be open to the public. If the person presents evidence that the person has a mental illness or is a mentally retarded person, the juvenile court shall consider that evidence in determining whether to invoke the adult portion of the serious youthful offender dispositional sentence.

(E)(1) The juvenile court may invoke the adult portion of a person's serious youthful offender dispositional sentence if the juvenile court finds all of the following on the record by clear and convincing evidence:

(a) The person is serving the juvenile portion of a serious youthful offender dispositional sentence.

(b) The person is at least fourteen years of age and has been admitted to a department of youth services facility, or criminal charges are pending against the person.

(c) The person engaged in the conduct or acts charged under division (A), (B), or (C) of this section, and the person's conduct demonstrates that the person is unlikely to be rehabilitated during the remaining period of juvenile jurisdiction.

(2) The court may modify the adult sentence the court invokes to consist of any lesser prison term that could be imposed for the offense and, in addition to the prison term or in lieu of the prison term if the prison term was not mandatory, any community control sanction that the offender was eligible to receive at sentencing.

(F) If a juvenile court issues an order invoking the adult portion of a serious youthful offender dispositional sentence under division (E) of this section, the juvenile portion of the dispositional sentence shall terminate, and the department of youth services shall transfer the person to the department of rehabilitation and correction or place the person under another sanction imposed as part of the sentence. The juvenile court shall state in its order the total number of days that the person has been held in detention or in a facility operated by, or under contract with, the department of youth services under the juvenile portion of the dispositional sentence. The time the person must serve on a prison term imposed under the adult portion of the dispositional sentence shall be reduced by the total number of days specified in the order plus any additional days the person is held in a juvenile facility or in detention after the order is issued and before the person is transferred to the custody of the department of rehabilitation and correction. In no case shall the total prison term as calculated under this division exceed the maximum prison term available for an adult who is convicted of violating the same sections of the Revised Code.

Any community control imposed as part of the adult sentence or as a condition of a judicial release from prison shall be under the supervision of the entity that provides adult probation services in the county. Any post-release control imposed after the offender otherwise is released from prison shall be supervised by the adult parole authority.

(2002 H 393, eff. 7–5–02; 2000 S 179, § 3, eff. 1–1–02)

Historical and Statutory Notes

Amendment Note: 2002 H 393 inserted "and shall state that at least one incident of misconduct of that nature occurred after the person reached fourteen years of age:" at the end of division (B); and rewrote division (E) which prior thereto read:

"(E) The juvenile court may invoke the adult portion of a person's serious youthful offender dispositional sentence if the juvenile court finds all of the following on the record by clear and convincing evidence:

"(1) The person is serving the juvenile portion of a serious youthful offender dispositional sentence.

"(2) The person is at least fourteen years of age and has been admitted to a department of youth services facility, or criminal charges are pending against the person.

"(3) The person engaged in the conduct or acts charged under division (A), (B), or (C) of this section, and the person's conduct demonstrates that the person is unlikely to be rehabilitated during the remaining period of juvenile jurisdiction."

Library References

Infants ⚖69(3), 69(7), 225.
Westlaw Topic No. 211.
C.J.S. Infants §§ 57, 69 to 85, 198, 207 to 209.

Research References

Encyclopedias
OH Jur. 3d Family Law § 1515, Powers.
OH Jur. 3d Family Law § 1706, Modification or Vacation of Order.
OH Jur. 3d Family Law § 1698.5, Serious Youthful Offender.

Treatises and Practice Aids
Carlin, Baldwin's Ohio Practice, Merrick-Rippner Probate Law § 107:65, Mandatory Transfer, Effective January 1, 2002.
Carlin, Baldwin's Ohio Practice, Merrick-Rippner Probate Law § 107:102, Serious Youthful Offenders, Effective January 1, 2002.
Carlin, Baldwin's Ohio Practice, Merrick-Rippner Probate Law § 107:104, Requests to Invoke Adult Portion of Serious Youthful Offender Disposition, Effective January 1, 2002.
Giannelli & Yeomans, Ohio Juvenile Law § 5:9, Procedural Rights.
Giannelli & Yeomans, Ohio Juvenile Law § 5:10, Invoking Adult Sentences.
Giannelli & Yeomans, Ohio Juvenile Law § 5:11, Invoking Adult Sentence Hearing.
Giannelli & Yeomans, Ohio Juvenile Law § 5:12, Subsequent Procedures.
Giannelli & Yeomans, Ohio Juvenile Law App. D, Appendix D. Glossary.

Notes of Decisions

Constitutional issues 1

---

1. Constitutional issues

Ohio's serious youthful offender sentencing scheme does not violate the Eighth Amendment's prohibition against cruel and unusual punishment; scheme does not provide for penalties against juveniles so greatly disproportionate to the offenses committed that those penalties shock the sense of justice in the community, scheme prohibits the imposition of the most severe adult punishment, and the scheme reserves adult punishment only for serious juvenile offenders not capable of being rehabilitated within the juvenile system. In re J.B. (Ohio App. 12 Dist., Butler, 12-30-2005) No. CA2004-09-226, 2005-Ohio-7029, 2005 WL 3610482, Unreported. Sentencing And Punishment ☞ 1607

Ohio's serious youthful offender sentencing scheme does not violate principles of due process; scheme does not unconstitutionally "target" very young offenders or unconstitutionally treat juveniles as adults, and while the scheme does, under certain circumstances, subject juveniles to adult punishment, the statute was crafted to take into account juvenile-adult distinctions. In re J.B. (Ohio App. 12 Dist., Butler, 12-30-2005) No. CA2004-09-226, 2005-Ohio-7029, 2005 WL 3610482, Unreported. Infants ☞ 69(2)

2152.16 Commitment of delinquent children to custody of youth services department

(A)(1) If a child is adjudicated a delinquent child for committing an act that would be a felony if committed by an adult, the juvenile court may commit the child to the legal custody of the department of youth services for secure confinement as follows:

(a) For an act that would be aggravated murder or murder if committed by an adult, until the offender attains twenty-one years of age;

(b) For a violation of section 2923.02 of the Revised Code that involves an attempt to commit an act that would be aggravated murder or murder if committed by an adult, a minimum period of six to seven years as prescribed by the court and a maximum period not to exceed the child's attainment of twenty-one years of age;

(c) For a violation of section 2903.03, 2905.01, 2909.02, or 2911.01 or division (A) of section 2903.04 of the Revised Code or for a violation of any provision of section 2907.02 of the Revised Code other than division (A)(1)(b) of that section when the sexual conduct or insertion involved was consensual and when the victim of the violation of division (A)(1)(b) of that section was older than the delinquent child, was the same age as the delinquent child, or was less than three years younger than the delinquent child, for an indefinite term consisting of a minimum period of one to three years, as prescribed by the court, and a maximum period not to exceed the child's attainment of twenty-one years of age;

(d) If the child is adjudicated a delinquent child for committing an act that is not described in division (A)(1)(b) or (c) of this section and that would be a felony of the first or second degree if committed by an adult, for an indefinite term consisting of a minimum period of one year and a maximum period not to exceed the child's attainment of twenty-one years of age;

(e) For committing an act that would be a felony of the third, fourth, or fifth degree if committed by an adult or for a violation of division (A) of section 2923.211 of the Revised Code, for an indefinite term consisting of a minimum period of six months and a maximum period not to exceed the child's attainment of twenty-one years of age.

(2) In each case in which a court makes a disposition under this section, the court retains control over the commitment for the minimum period specified by the court in divisions (A)(1)(a) to (e) of this section. During the minimum period, the department of youth services shall not move the child to a nonsecure setting without the permission of the court that imposed the disposition.

(B) (1) Subject to division (B)(2) of this section, if a delinquent child is committed to the department of youth services under this section, the department may release the child at any time after the minimum period specified by the court in division (A)(1) of this section ends.

(2) A commitment under this section is subject to a supervised release or to a discharge of the child from the custody of the department for medical reasons pursuant to section 5139.54 of the Revised Code, but, during the minimum period specified by the court in division (A)(1) of this section, the department shall obtain court approval of a supervised release or discharge under that section.

(C) If a child is adjudicated a delinquent child, at the dispositional hearing and prior to making any disposition pursuant to this section, the court shall determine whether the delinquent child previously has been adjudicated a delinquent child for a violation of a law or ordinance. If the delinquent child previously has been adjudicated a delinquent child for a violation of a law or ordinance, the court, for purposes of entering an order of disposition of the delinquent child under this section, shall consider the previous delinquent child adjudication as a conviction of a violation of the law or ordinance in determining the degree of the offense the current act would be had it been committed by an adult. This division also shall apply in relation to the imposition of any financial sanction under section 2152.19 of the Revised Code.

(2002 H 393, eff. 7–5–02; 2000 S 179, § 3, eff. 1–1–02)

Historical and Statutory Notes

Amendment Note: 2002 H 393 inserted "minimum" before and deleted "of court control" after "period" in division (A)(2); and rewrote division (B) which prior thereto read:

"(B) If a delinquent child is committed to the department of youth services under this section, the department may release the child at any time after the period of court control imposed under division (A)(1) of this section ends."

Cross References

Order of commitment to department of youth services, 5139.05

Library References

Infants ☞223.1, 277 to 278, 281.
Westlaw Topic No. 211.
C.J.S. Infants §§ 57, 69 to 85, 198, 206 to 213, 276 to 277, 280.

Research References

Encyclopedias
OH Jur. 3d Family Law § 1515, Powers.
OH Jur. 3d Family Law § 1698.5, Serious Youthful Offender.

Treatises and Practice Aids
Carlin, Baldwin's Ohio Practice, Merrick-Rippner Probate Law § 107:89, Custody of Department of Youth Services.
Carlin, Baldwin's Ohio Practice, Merrick-Rippner Probate Law § 107:102, Serious Youthful Offenders, Effective January 1, 2002.
Carlin, Baldwin's Ohio Practice, Merrick-Rippner Probate Law § 107:105, Commitment of Delinquent Children to the Custody of Department of Youth Services, Effective January 1, 2002.
Giannelli & Yeomans, Ohio Juvenile Law § 1:7, Juvenile Code.
Giannelli & Yeomans, Ohio Juvenile Law § 4:4, Ohio Penal Law.
Giannelli & Yeomans, Ohio Juvenile Law § 4:6, Court Order Violations.
Giannelli & Yeomans, Ohio Juvenile Law § 5:7, Mandatory Syo Dispositions.
Giannelli & Yeomans, Ohio Juvenile Law § 5:8, Discretionary Syo Dispositions.
Giannelli & Yeomans, Ohio Juvenile Law § 16:8, Delinquency Complaints.
Giannelli & Yeomans, Ohio Juvenile Law § 27:1, Introduction.
Giannelli & Yeomans, Ohio Juvenile Law § 27:3, Department of Youth Services Commitment.
Giannelli & Yeomans, Ohio Juvenile Law § 27:4, Dys Release.
Giannelli & Yeomans, Ohio Juvenile Law § 33:9, Department of Youth Services.

Notes of Decisions

"Act that would be a felony" if by adult 3
Commitment to government custody 1

Sexual conduct 2

1. Commitment to government custody

Juvenile court did not abuse its discretion, in delinquency proceedings, in imposing indefinite commitment to Department of Youth Services (DYS), despite juvenile's lack of prior record and assertion of remorse, where juvenile was adjudicated delinquent for committing gross sexual imposition as fourth-degree felony and misdemeanor disorderly conduct, juvenile denied any inappropriate behavior in connection with offense of gross sexual imposition, juvenile was described by staff member of pre-release office as being manipulative, and juvenile's statements concerning remorse were not made until disposition. In re Wisdom (Ohio App. 5 Dist., Stark, 02-28-2005) No. 2004CA00187, 2005-Ohio-930, 2005 WL 503407, Unreported. Infants ⇐ 223.1

Trial court order of disposition, which committed juvenile to Youth Services for a minimum of six months, up to his 21st birthday, was not an abuse of discretion; juvenile was adjudicated delinquent for breaking and entering, the owners of the business juvenile broke into were related to juvenile, and juvenile had previously been adjudicated unruly and provided an opportunity to change his behavior pattern. In re Homan (Ohio App. 5 Dist., Tuscarawas, 01-27-2003) No. 2002AP080067, 2003-Ohio-352, 2003 WL 183811, Unreported. Infants ⇐ 223.1

2. Sexual conduct

Minor who engaged in non-forcible sexual contact with a five-year-old girl was delinquent, even though girl consented to the conduct, where minor was nine or ten at the time of the offense, minor was presumably of greater physical and intellectual development, and evidence indicated that minor used manipulative threats to obtain compliance from other victim. In re N.K. (Ohio App. 8 Dist., Cuyahoga, 12-24-2003) No. 82332, 2003-Ohio-7059, 2003 WL 23009113, Unreported. Infants ⇐ 153

3. "Act that would be a felony" if by adult

Juvenile's act of ethnic intimidation with criminal damaging as a predicate offense would have been a misdemeanor of the first degree if committed by an adult and, therefore, portion of juvenile's sentence committing him to Department of Youth Services (DYS) was void. In re J.W. (Ohio App. 12 Dist., Butler, 12-30-2004) No. CA2004-02-036, No. CA2004-03-061, 2004-Ohio-7139, 2004 WL 3015755, Unreported. Infants ⇐ 223.1

2152.17 Felony specifications

(A) Subject to division (D) of this section, if a child is adjudicated a delinquent child for committing an act, other than a violation of section 2923.12 of the Revised Code, that would be a felony if committed by an adult and if the court determines that, if the child was an adult, the child would be guilty of a specification of the type set forth in section 2941.141, 2941. 144, 2941.145, 2941.146, 2941.1412, 2941.1414, or 2941.1415 of the Revised Code, in addition to any commitment or other disposition the court imposes for the underlying delinquent act, all of the following apply:

(1) If the court determines that the child would be guilty of a specification of the type set forth in section 2941.141 of the Revised Code, the court may commit the child to the department of youth services for the specification for a definite period of up to one year.

(2) If the court determines that the child would be guilty of a specification of the type set forth in section 2941.145 of the Revised Code or if the delinquent act is a violation of division (A)(1) or (2) of section 2903.06 of the Revised Code and the court determines that the child would be guilty of a specification of the type set forth in section 2941.1415 of the Revised Code, the court shall commit the child to the department of youth services for the specification for a definite period of not less than one and not more than three years, and the court also shall commit the child to the department for the underlying delinquent act under sections 2152.11 to 2152.16 of the Revised Code.

(3) If the court determines that the child would be guilty of a specification of the type set forth in section 2941.144, 2941.146, or 2941.1412 of the Revised Code or if the delinquent act is a violation of division (A)(1) or (2) of section 2903.06 of the Revised Code and the court determines that the child would be guilty of a specification of the type set forth in section 2941.1414 of the Revised Code, the court shall commit the child to the department of youth services for the specification for a definite period of not less than one and not more than five years, and the court also shall commit the child to the department for the underlying delinquent act under sections 2152.11 to 2152.16 of the Revised Code.

(B) Division (A) of this section also applies to a child who is an accomplice to the same extent the firearm specifications would apply to an adult accomplice in a criminal proceeding.

(C) If a child is adjudicated a delinquent child for committing an act that would be aggravated murder, murder, or a first, second, or third degree felony offense of violence if committed by an adult and if the court determines that, if the child was an adult, the child would be guilty of a specification of the type set forth in section 2941.142 of the Revised Code in relation to the act for which the child was adjudicated a delinquent child, the court shall commit the child for the specification to the legal custody of the department of youth services for institutionalization in a secure facility for a definite period of not less than one and not more than three years, subject to division (D)(2) of this section, and the court also shall commit the child to the department for the underlying delinquent act.

(D)(1) If the child is adjudicated a delinquent child for committing an act that would be an offense of violence that is a felony if committed by an adult and is committed to the legal custody of the department of youth services pursuant to division (A)(1) of section 2152.16 of the Revised Code and if the court determines that the child, if the child was an adult, would be guilty of a specification of the type set forth in section 2941.1411 of the Revised Code in relation to the act for which the child was adjudicated a delinquent child, the court may commit the child to the custody of the department of youth services for institutionalization in a secure facility for up to two years, subject to division (D)(2) of this section.

(2) A court that imposes a period of commitment under division (A) of this section is not precluded from imposing an additional period of commitment under division (C) or (D)(1) of this section, a court that imposes a period of commitment under division (C) of this section is not precluded from imposing an additional period of commitment under division (A) or (D)(1) of this section, and a court that imposes a period of commitment under division (D)(1) of this section is not precluded from imposing an additional period of commitment under division (A) or (C) of this section.

(E) The court shall not commit a child to the legal custody of the department of youth services for a specification pursuant to this section for a period that exceeds five years for any one delinquent act. Any commitment imposed pursuant to division (A), (B), (C), or (D)(1) of this section shall be in addition to, and shall be served consecutively with and prior to, a period of commitment ordered under this chapter for the underlying delinquent act, and each commitment imposed pursuant to division (A), (B), (C), or (D)(1) of this section shall be in addition to, and shall be served consecutively with, any other period of commitment imposed under those divisions. If a commitment is imposed under division (A) or (B) of this section and a commitment also is imposed under division (C) of this section, the period imposed under division (A) or (B) of this section shall be served prior to the period imposed under division (C) of this section.

In each case in which a court makes a disposition under this section, the court retains control over the commitment for the entire period of the commitment.

The total of all the periods of commitment imposed for any specification under this section and for the underlying offense shall not exceed the child's attainment of twenty-one years of age.

(F) If a child is adjudicated a delinquent child for committing two or more acts that would be felonies if committed by an adult and if the court entering the delinquent child adjudication orders the commitment of the child for two or more of those acts to the legal custody of the department of youth services for institutionalization in a secure facility pursuant to section 2152.13 or 2152.16 of the Revised Code, the court may order that all of the periods of commitment imposed under those sections for those acts be served consecutively in the legal custody of the department of youth services, provided that those periods of commitment shall be in addition to and commence immediately following the expiration of a period of commitment that the court imposes pursuant to division (A), (B), (C), or (D)(1) of this section. A court shall not commit a delinquent child to the legal custody of the department of youth services under this division for a period that exceeds the child's attainment of twenty-one years of age.

(2006 H 95, eff. 8-3-06; 2004 H 52, eff. 6-1-04; 2002 H 130, § 3, eff. 1-1-02 [1]; 2002 H 393, eff. 7-5-02; 2000 S 179, § 3, eff. 1-1-02)

[1] O Const Art II, § 1c and 1d, and RC 1.471, state that codified sections of law are subject to the referendum unless providing for tax levies, state appropriations, or are emergency in nature. Since this Act is apparently not an exception, and 1-1-02 is within the ninety-day period, the effective date should probably be 4-7-03.

Uncodified Law

2002 H 130, § 5, eff. 4-7-03, reads, in part:

(B) Section 2152.17 of the Revised Code, as presented in this act, includes matter that was amended into former section 2151.355 of the Revised Code by Am. Sub. S.B. 222 of the 123rd General Assembly. Paragraphs of former section 2151.355 of the Revised Code containing Am. Sub. S.B. 222 amendments were transferred to section 2152.17 of the Revised Code by Am. Sub. S.B. 179 of the 123rd General Assembly as part of its general revision of the juvenile sentencing laws. The General Assembly, applying the principle stated in division (B) of section 1.52 of the Revised Code that amendments are to be harmonized if reasonably capable of simultaneous operation, finds that the version of section 2152.17 of the Revised Code presented in this act is the resulting version of the section in effect prior to the effective date of the section as presented in this act.

Historical and Statutory Notes

Amendment Note: 2006 H 95 deleted division (G), which read:

"(G) If a child is adjudicated a delinquent child for committing an act that if committed by an adult would be aggravated murder, murder, rape, felonious sexual penetration in violation of former section 2907.12 of the Revised Code, involuntary manslaughter, a felony of the first or second degree resulting in the death of or physical harm to a person, complicity in or an attempt to commit any of those offenses, or an offense under an existing or former law of this state that is or was substantially equivalent to any of those offenses and if the court in its order of disposition for that act commits the child to the custody of the department of youth services, the adjudication shall be considered a conviction for purposes of a future determination pursuant to Chapter 2929. of the Revised Code as to whether the child, as an adult, is a repeat violent offender."

Amendment Note: 2004 H 52 inserted "2941.1413, or 2941.1414 in division (A); inserted "or if the delinquent act is a violation of division (A)(1) or (2) of section 2903.06 of the Revised Code and the court determines that the child would be guilty of a specification of the type set forth in section 2941.1414 of the Revised Code" in division (A)(2); inserted "or if the delinquent act is a violation of division (A)(1) or (2) of section 2903.06 of the Revised Code and the court determines that the child would be guilty of specification of the type set forth in section 2941.1413 of the Revised Code"; and made other nonsubstantive changes.

Amendment Note: 2002 H 130 inserted ", or 2941.1412" in divisions (A) and (A)(3); inserted "(2)" after "subject to division (D)" in division (C); rewrote the first two paragraphs of division (D); redesignated the last two paragraphs of former division (D) as new division (E) and inserted "or (D)(1)" twice; redesignated former division (E) as new division (F) and inserted "or (D)(1)"; redesignated former division (F) as new division (G); and made other nonsubstantive changes. Prior to amendment the first two paragraphs of division (D) read:

"(D) If the child is adjudicated a delinquent child for committing an act that would be an offense of violence that is a felony if committed by an adult and is committed to the legal custody of the department of youth services pursuant to division (A)(4), (5), or (6) of this section and if the court determines that the child, if the child was an adult, would be guilty of a specification of the type set forth in section 2941.1411 of the Revised Code in relation to the act for which the child was adjudicated a delinquent child, the court may commit the child to the custody of the department of youth services for institutionalization in a secure facility for two years, subject to division (A)(7)(d) of this section.

"(d) A court that imposes a period of commitment under division (A)(7)(a) of this section is not precluded from imposing an additional period of commitment under division (A)(7)(b) or (c) of this section, a court that imposes a period of commitment under division (A)(7)(b) of this section is not precluded from imposing an additional period of commitment under division (A)(7)(a) or (c) of this section, and a court that imposes a period of commitment under division (A)(7)(c) of this section is not precluded from imposing an additional period of commitment under division (A)(7)(a) or (b) of this section."

Amendment Note: 2002 H 393 added "(2)" to division (C); and rewrote divisions (D) through (F), which prior thereto read:

"(D) If the child is adjudicated a delinquent child for committing an act that would be an offense of violence that is a felony if committed by an adult and is committed to the legal custody of the department of youth services pursuant to division (A)(4), (5), or (6) of this section and if the court determines that the child, if the child was an adult, would be guilty of a specification of the type set forth in section 2941.1411 of the Revised Code in relation to the act for which the child was adjudicated a delinquent child, the court may commit the child to the custody of the department of youth services for institutionalization in a secure facility for two years, subject to division (A)(7)(d) of this section.

"(d) A court that imposes a period of commitment under division (A)(7)(a) of this section is not precluded from imposing an additional period of commitment under division (A)(7)(b) or (c) of this section, a court that imposes a period of commitment under division (A)(7)(b) of this section is not precluded from imposing an additional period of commitment under division (A)(7)(a) or (c) of this section, and a court that imposes a period of commitment under division (A)(7)(c) of this section is not precluded from imposing an additional period of commitment under division (A)(7)(a) or (b) of this section.

"The court shall not commit a child to the legal custody of the department of youth services for a specification pursuant to this section for a period that exceeds five years for any one delinquent act. Any commitment imposed pursuant to division (A), (B), or (C) of this section shall be in addition to, and shall be served consecutively with and prior to, a period of commitment ordered under this chapter for the underlying delinquent act, and each commitment imposed pursuant to division (A), (B), or (C) of this section shall be in addition to, and shall be served consecutively with, any other period of commitment imposed under those divisions. If a commitment is imposed under division (A) or (B) of this section and a commitment also is imposed under division (C) of this section, the period imposed under division (A) or (B) of this section shall be served prior to the period imposed under division (C) of this section.

"The total of all the periods of commitment imposed for any specification under this section and for the underlying offense shall not exceed the child's attainment of twenty-one years of age.

"(E) If a child is adjudicated a delinquent child for committing two or more acts that would be felonies if committed by an adult and if the court entering the delinquent child adjudication orders the commitment of the child for two or more of those acts to the legal custody of the department of youth services for institutionalization in a secure facility pursuant to section 2152.13 or 2152.16 of the Revised Code, the court may order that all of the periods of commitment imposed under those sections for those acts be served consecutively in the legal custody of the department of youth services, provided that those periods of commitment shall be in addition to and commence immediately following the expiration of a period of commitment that the court imposes pursuant to division (A), (B), or (C) of this section. A court shall not commit a delinquent child to the legal custody of the department of youth services under this division for a period that exceeds the child's attainment of twenty-one years of age.

"(F) If a child is adjudicated a delinquent child for committing an act that if committed by an adult would be aggravated murder, murder, rape, felonious sexual penetration in violation of former section 2907.12 of the Revised Code, involuntary manslaughter, a felony of the first or second degree resulting in the death of or physical harm to a person, complicity in or an attempt to commit any of those offenses, or an offense under an existing or former law of this state that is or was substantially equivalent to any of those offenses and if the court in its order of disposition for that act commits the child to the custody of the department of youth services, the adjudication shall be considered a conviction for purposes of a future determination pursuant to Chapter 2929. of the Revised Code as to whether the child, as an adult, is a repeat violent offender."

Cross References

Specifications concerning drug or alcohol related vehicular homicide of peace officer in construction zone and prior convictions, 2941.1415

Library References

Infants ⇔223.1.
Sentencing and Punishment ⇔1291.
Westlaw Topic Nos. 211, 350H.
C.J.S. Criminal Law §§ 1643, 1645 to 1646, 1650.
C.J.S. Infants §§ 57, 69 to 85.

Research References

Encyclopedias

OH Jur. 3d Criminal Law § 570, Different Penalties for Identical Conduct.
OH Jur. 3d Criminal Law § 3283, Three-Year Term.
OH Jur. 3d Criminal Law § 3284, One-Year Term.
OH Jur. 3d Criminal Law § 3290, Use of Firearm from Moving Vehicle.
OH Jur. 3d Criminal Law § 3291, Automatic or Silencer-Equipped Firearm.
OH Jur. 3d Criminal Law § 3292, Participation in Criminal Gang Activity.
OH Jur. 3d Family Law § 1515, Powers.
OH Jur. 3d Family Law § 1689, Juvenile Traffic Offender.
OH Jur. 3d Family Law § 1696, Commitment to Youth Commission.
OH Jur. 3d Family Law § 1698.5, Serious Youthful Offender.

Treatises and Practice Aids

Carlin, Baldwin's Ohio Practice, Merrick-Rippner Probate Law § 106:4, Juvenile Court Jurisdiction—Delinquent Child—Non-Criminal Nature of Delinquency Proceedings.
Carlin, Baldwin's Ohio Practice, Merrick-Rippner Probate Law § 107:73, Alternatives for Disposition of Juvenile Cases.
Carlin, Baldwin's Ohio Practice, Merrick-Rippner Probate Law § 107:89, Custody of Department of Youth Services.
Carlin, Baldwin's Ohio Practice, Merrick-Rippner Probate Law § 107:92, Enhanced Dispositions Due to Felony Specifications, Effective January 1, 2002.
Carlin, Baldwin's Ohio Practice, Merrick-Rippner Probate Law § 107:102, Serious Youthful Offenders, Effective January 1, 2002.
Giannelli & Yeomans, Ohio Juvenile Law § 4:4, Ohio Penal Law.
Giannelli & Yeomans, Ohio Juvenile Law § 5:8, Discretionary Syo Dispositions.
Giannelli & Yeomans, Ohio Juvenile Law § 27:3, Department of Youth Services Commitment.
Giannelli & Yeomans, Ohio Juvenile Law § 27:18, "Catch-All" Provision.

Notes of Decisions

Constitutional issues   1

---

1. Constitutional issues

Juvenile waived his state and federal equal protection challenge to statute authorizing juvenile court to impose consecutive commitments upon delinquent juveniles without making findings equivalent to those required for imposition of consecutive sentences upon adult offenders, by failing to object to his consecutive commitments or otherwise raise issue before the juvenile court. In re S.C. (Ohio App. 2 Dist., Montgomery, 02-25-2005) No. CIV.A. 20562, No. CIV.A. 20564, No. CIV.A. 20565, No. CIV.A. 20563, 2005-Ohio-810, 2005 WL 435215, Unreported. Infants ⇔ 243

Juvenile's trial counsel did not provide ineffective assistance in delinquency proceeding by failing to challenge the imposition of consecutive terms of commitment in the three cases against juvenile; imposition of consecutive terms was proper. In re R.L. (Ohio App. 8 Dist., Cuyahoga, 01-06-2005) No. 84543, No. 84545, No. 84546, 2005-Ohio-26, 2005 WL 23323, Unreported. Infants ⇔ 205

Statute allowing a trial court to sentence a juvenile, who committed two or more acts that would be felonies if committed by an adult, to consecutive sentences without first making specific findings did not violate equal protection; the purpose of juvenile court was to provide for the care, protection, and development of children, protecting the public, and rehabilitating child, the purpose of felony sentencing was protect the public and to punish the offender, and juveniles could apply for judicial release at any time during their commitment. In re Slater (Ohio App. 9 Dist., Wayne, 09-22-2004) No. 04CA0004, No. 04CA0005, 2004-Ohio-4961, 2004 WL 2244249, Unreported, appeal not allowed 105 Ohio St.3d 1439, 822 N.E.2d 811, 2005-Ohio-531. Constitutional Law ⇔ 242.1(4); Infants ⇔ 132

Juveniles were not "suspect class," and thus, issue whether statute allowing trial court in delinquency proceedings to impose consecutive dispositions for multiple offenses violated equal protection by not requiring statutory findings with supporting reasons as required to impose consecutive sentences for adults was not subject to strict scrutiny review; rather, issue was subject to rational basis review to determine whether differential treatment was related to legitimate state interest. In re Chappell (Ohio App. 7 Dist., 11-29-2005) 164 Ohio App.3d 628, 843 N.E.2d 823, 2005-Ohio-6451. Constitutional Law ⇔ 242.1(4)

Juvenile adjudicated delinquent for committing assault was not similarly situated to adult defendant, and thus, statute allowing for imposition of consecutive terms of commitment for multiple offenses did not violate equal protection by not requiring trial court to make statutory findings with supporting reasons, as required for imposition of consecutive sentences; although one of purposes of juvenile delinquency proceedings was to punish offender and to deter crime, focus of juvenile commitment remained on development and rehabilitation of juvenile. In re Chappell (Ohio App. 7 Dist., 11-29-2005) 164 Ohio App.3d 628, 843 N.E.2d 823, 2005-Ohio-6451. Infants ⇔ 132

2152.18 Place and duration of institutionalization; records; notice to schools and victims

(A) When a juvenile court commits a delinquent child to the custody of the department of youth services pursuant to this chapter, the court shall not designate the specific institution in which the department is to place the child but instead shall specify that the child is to be institutionalized in a secure facility.

(B) When a juvenile court commits a delinquent child to the custody of the department of youth services pursuant to this chapter, the court shall state in the order of commitment the total number of days that the child has been held in detention in connection with the delinquent child complaint upon which the order of commitment is based. The department shall reduce the minimum period of institutionalization that was ordered by both the total number of days that the child has been so held in detention as stated by the court in the order of commitment and the total number of any additional days that the child has been held in detention subsequent to the order of commitment but prior to the transfer of physical custody of the child to the department.

(C)(1) When a juvenile court commits a delinquent child to the custody of the department of youth services pursuant to this chapter, the court shall provide the department with the child's medical records, a copy of the report of any mental examination of the child ordered by the court, the Revised Code section or sections the child violated and the degree of each violation, the warrant to convey the child to the department, a copy of the court's journal entry ordering the commitment of the child to the legal custody of the department, a copy of the arrest record pertaining to the act for which the child was adjudicated a delinquent child, a copy of any victim impact statement pertaining to the act, and any other information concerning the child that the department reasonably requests. The court also shall complete the form for the standard predisposition investigation report that the department furnishes pursuant to section 5139.04 of the Revised Code and provide the department with the completed form.

The department may refuse to accept physical custody of a delinquent child who is committed to the legal custody of the department until the court provides to the department the documents specified in this division. No officer or employee of the department who refuses to accept physical custody of a delinquent child who is committed to the legal custody of the department shall be subject to prosecution or contempt of court for the refusal if the court fails to provide the documents specified in this division at the time the court transfers the physical custody of the child to the department.

(2) Within twenty working days after the department of youth services receives physical custody of a delinquent child from a juvenile court, the court shall provide the department with a certified copy of the child's birth certificate and the child's social security number or, if the court made all reasonable efforts to obtain the information but was unsuccessful, with documentation of the efforts it made to obtain the information.

(3) If an officer is preparing pursuant to section 2947.06 or 2951.03 of the Revised Code or Criminal Rule 32.2 a presentence investigation report pertaining to a person, the department shall make available to the officer, for use in preparing the report, any records or reports it possesses regarding that person that it received from a juvenile court pursuant to division (C)(1) of this section or that pertain to the treatment of that person after the person was committed to the custody of the department as a delinquent child.

(D)(1) Within ten days after an adjudication that a child is a delinquent child, the court shall give written notice of the adjudication to the superintendent of a city, local, exempted village, or joint vocational school district, and to the principal of the school the child attends, if the basis of the adjudication was the commission of an act that would be a criminal offense if committed by an adult, if the act was committed by the delinquent child when the child was fourteen years of age or older, and if the act is any of the following:

(a) An act that would be a felony or an offense of violence if committed by an adult, an act in the commission of which the child used or brandished a firearm, or an act that is a violation of section 2907.06, 2907.07, 2907.08, 2907.09, 2907.24, or 2907.241 of the Revised Code and that would be a misdemeanor if committed by an adult;

(b) A violation of section 2923.12 of the Revised Code or of a substantially similar municipal ordinance that would be a misdemeanor if committed by an adult and that was committed on property owned or controlled by, or at an activity held under the auspices of, the board of education of that school district;

(c) A violation of division (A) of section 2925.03 or 2925.11 of the Revised Code that would be a misdemeanor if committed by an adult, that was committed on property owned or controlled by, or at an activity held under the auspices of, the board of education of that school district, and that is not a minor drug possession offense;

(d) An act that would be a criminal offense if committed by an adult and that results in serious physical harm to persons or serious physical harm to property while the child is at school, on any other property owned or controlled by the board, or at an interscholastic competition, an extracurricular event, or any other school program or activity;

(e) Complicity in any violation described in division (D)(1)(a), (b), (c), or (d) of this section that was alleged to have been committed in the manner described in division (D)(1)(a), (b), (c), or (d) of this section, regardless of whether the act of complicity was committed on property owned or controlled by, or at an activity held under the auspices of, the board of education of that school district.

(2) The notice given pursuant to division (D)(1) of this section shall include the name of the child who was adjudicated to be a delinquent child, the child's age at the time the child committed the act that was the basis of the adjudication, and identification of the violation of the law or ordinance that was the basis of the adjudication.

(3) Within fourteen days after committing a delinquent child to the custody of the department of youth services, the court shall give notice to the school attended by the child of the child's commitment by sending to that school a copy of the court's journal entry ordering the commitment. As soon as possible after receipt of the notice described in this division, the school shall provide the department with the child's school transcript. However, the department shall not refuse to accept a child committed to it, and a child committed to it shall not be held in a county or district detention facility, because of a school's failure to provide the school transcript that it is required to provide under this division.

(4) Within fourteen days after discharging or releasing a child from an institution under its control, the department of youth services shall provide the court and the superintendent of the school district in which the child is entitled to attend school under section 3313.64 or 3313.65 of the Revised Code with the following:

(a) An updated copy of the child's school transcript;

(b) A report outlining the child's behavior in school while in the custody of the department;

(c) The child's current individualized education program, as defined in section 3323.01 of the Revised Code, if such a program has been developed for the child;

(d) A summary of the institutional record of the child's behavior.

The department also shall provide the court with a copy of any portion of the child's institutional record that the court specifically requests, within five working days of the request.

(E) At any hearing at which a child is adjudicated a delinquent child or as soon as possible after the hearing, the court shall notify all victims of the delinquent act who may be entitled to a recovery under any of the following sections of the right of the victims to recover, pursuant to section 3109.09 of the Revised Code, compensatory damages from the child's parents; of the right of the victims to recover, pursuant to section 3109.10 of the Revised Code, compensatory damages from the child's parents for willful and malicious assaults committed by the child; and of the right of the victims to recover an award of reparations pursuant to sections 2743.51 to 2743.72 of the Revised Code.

(2004 H 106, eff. 9–16–04; 2002 H 393, eff. 7–5–02; 2002 H 247, eff. 5–30–02; 2000 S 179, § 3, eff. 1–1–02)

Uncodified Law

2002 H 393, § 5, eff. 7–5–02, reads, in part:

(B) Section 2152.18 of the Revised Code, as presented in this act, includes matter that was amended into former section 2151.355 of the Revised Code by Am. Sub. S.B. 181 of the 123rd General Assembly. Paragraphs of former section 2151.355 of the Revised Code containing S.B. 181 amendments were transferred to section 2152.18 of the Revised Code by S.B. 179 of the 123rd General Assembly as part of its general revision of the juvenile sentencing laws. The General Assembly, applying the principle stated in division (B) of section 1.52 of the Revised Code that amendments are to be harmonized if reasonably capable of simultaneous operation, finds that the version of section 2152.18 of the Revised Code presented in this act is the resulting version of the section in effect prior to the effective date of the section as presented in this act.

2002 H 247, § 3, eff. 5–30–02, reads:

Section 2152.18 of the Revised Code, as presented in this act, includes matter that was amended into former section 2151.355 of the Revised Code by Am. Sub. S.B. 181 of the 123rd General Assembly. Paragraphs of former section 2151.355 of the Revised Code containing S.B. 181 amendments were transferred to section 2152.18 of the Revised Code by S.B. 179 of the 123rd General Assembly as part of its general revision of the juvenile sentencing laws. The General Assembly, applying the principle stated in division (B) of section 1.52 of the Revised Code that amendments are to be harmonized if reasonably capable of simultaneous operation, finds that the version of section 2152.18 of the Revised Code presented in this act is the resulting version of the section in effect prior to the effective date of the section as presented in this act.

Historical and Statutory Notes

Ed. Note: 2152.18, 2152.19 and 2152.20 contain provisions analogous to former 2151.355, repealed by 2000 S 179, § 4, eff. 1–1–02.

Amendment Note: 2004 H 106 Rewrote division (D)(4). Prior to amendment, division (D)(4) read, "Within fourteen days after releasing a child from an institution under its control, the department of youth services shall provide the court and the school with an updated copy of the child's school transcript and a summary of the institutional record of the child. The department also shall provide the court with a copy of any portion of the child's institutional record that the court specifically requests, within five working days of the request."

Amendment Note: 2002 H 393 deleted "2907.04" before "2907.06" in division (D)(1)(a); and substituted "(D)" for "(K)" in division (D)(2).

Amendment Note: 2002 H 247 added new division (C)(3); deleted "2907.04" before "2907.06" in division (D)(1)(a); and substituted "(D)" for "(K)" after "pursuant to division" in division (D)(2).

Cross References

Order of commitment to department of youth services; release; records; parental rights, 5139.05
Presentence investigation reports, mandatory consideration of certain information, 2951.03
Pupil to provide certain information; request for records from prior school; notice to police of failure to produce records; notification of power of attorney or caretaker authorization affidavit; notification of shelter care for victims of domestic violence, 3313.672
Victim impact statement, presentence investigation report, 2930.13

Library References

Infants ⚖ 133, 274, 278.
Westlaw Topic No. 211.
C.J.S. Infants §§ 57, 69 to 85, 198, 206 to 213, 273, 277.

Research References

Encyclopedias

OH Jur. 3d Family Law § 1517, Correctional Service—Children Committed to Commission.
OH Jur. 3d Family Law § 1715, Expenses of Committed Children; Liability of Parent or Guardian.
OH Jur. 3d Penal & Correctional Institutions § 78, Records and Reports.
OH Jur. 3d Schools, Universities, & Colleges § 276, Restrictions on Admission to Public Schools.

Treatises and Practice Aids

Carlin, Baldwin's Ohio Practice, Merrick-Rippner Probate Law § 107:84, Disposition of Delinquent Children—Prior to January 1, 2002.
Carlin, Baldwin's Ohio Practice, Merrick-Rippner Probate Law § 107:105, Commitment of Delinquent Children to the Custody of Department of Youth Services, Effective January 1, 2002.
Giannelli & Yeomans, Ohio Juvenile Law § 27:3, Department of Youth Services Commitment.
Giannelli & Yeomans, Ohio Juvenile Law § 32:3, Responsibilities to Victims and Others.
Giannelli & Yeomans, Ohio Juvenile Law § 33:8, Contempt.
Giannelli & Yeomans, Ohio Juvenile Law § 25:13, Judgment & Records.
Giannelli & Yeomans, Ohio Juvenile Law § 27:18, "Catch-All" Provision.
Hastings, Manoloff, Sheeran, & Stype, Ohio School Law § 20:3, Compulsory School Attendance-In General.
Hastings, Manoloff, Sheeran, & Stype, Ohio School Law § 23:2, Admission Requirements and Tuition Liability-Statutory Requirements in General.
Hastings, Manoloff, Sheeran, & Stype, Ohio School Law § 24:16, Notice to Board of Certain Crimes Committed by Employees, Students or Others-Notice to Board of Student Crimes.

Notes of Decisions

Ed. Note: This section contains annotations from former RC 2151.355.)

Credit for days in detention 2
Final appealable order 1

---

1. Final appealable order

The imposition of a penalty pursuant to RC 2151.355(A)(6) is a dispositional order and as such is a final appealable order. In re Sekulich (Ohio 1981) 65 Ohio St.2d 13, 417 N.E.2d 1014, 19 O.O.3d 192.

A finding of delinquency by the juvenile court accompanied only by a commitment to the temporary custody of the Ohio youth commission for the purpose of diagnostic study and report as provided by RC 5139.05(B) is not a final order subject to appeal, and such commitment constitutes merely a procedural incident. In re Bolden (Allen 1973) 37 Ohio App.2d 7, 306 N.E.2d 166, 66 O.O.2d 26. Infants ⚖ 242

2. Credit for days in detention

Juvenile was entitled to credit for time served at juvenile residential center pending disposition of motions to impose his suspended sentence after probation violation. In re Marlin (Ohio App. 3 Dist., Paulding, 03-28-2005) No. 11-04-15, 2005-Ohio-1429, 2005 WL 696871, Unreported. Infants ⚖ 225

2152.19 Additional disposition orders for delinquent children

(A) If a child is adjudicated a delinquent child, the court may make any of the following orders of disposition, in addition to any other disposition authorized or required by this chapter:

(1) Any order that is authorized by section 2151.353 of the Revised Code for the care and protection of an abused, neglected, or dependent child;

(2) Commit the child to the temporary custody of any school, camp, institution, or other facility operated for the care of delinquent children by the county, by a district organized under section 2152.41 or 2151.65 of the Revised Code, or by a private agency or organization, within or without the state, that is authorized and qualified to provide the care, treatment, or placement required, including, but not limited to, a school, camp, or facility operated under section 2151.65 of the Revised Code;

(3) Place the child in a detention facility or district detention facility operated under section 2152.41 of the Revised Code, for up to ninety days;

(4) Place the child on community control under any sanctions, services, and conditions that the court prescribes. As a condition of community control in every case and in addition to any other condition that it imposes upon the child, the court shall require the child to abide by the law during the period of community control. As referred to in this division, community control includes, but is not limited to, the following sanctions and conditions:

(a) A period of basic probation supervision in which the child is required to maintain contact with a person appointed to supervise the child in accordance with sanctions imposed by the court;

(b) A period of intensive probation supervision in which the child is required to maintain frequent contact with a person appointed by the court to supervise the child while the child is seeking or maintaining employment and participating in training, education, and treatment programs as the order of disposition;

(c) A period of day reporting in which the child is required each day to report to and leave a center or another approved reporting location at specified times in order to participate in work, education or training, treatment, and other approved programs at the center or outside the center;

(d) A period of community service of up to five hundred hours for an act that would be a felony or a misdemeanor of the first degree if committed by an adult, up to two hundred hours for an act that would be a misdemeanor of the second, third, or fourth degree if committed by an adult, or up to thirty hours for an act that would be a minor misdemeanor if committed by an adult;

(e) A requirement that the child obtain a high school diploma, a certificate of high school equivalence, vocational training, or employment;

(f) A period of drug and alcohol use monitoring;

(g) A requirement of alcohol or drug assessment or counseling, or a period in an alcohol or drug treatment program with a level of security for the child as determined necessary by the court;

(h) A period in which the court orders the child to observe a curfew that may involve daytime or evening hours;

(i) A requirement that the child serve monitored time;

(j) A period of house arrest without electronic monitoring or continuous alcohol monitoring;

(k) A period of electronic monitoring or continuous alcohol monitoring without house arrest, or house arrest with electronic monitoring or continuous alcohol monitoring or both electronic monitoring and continuous alcohol monitoring, that does not exceed the maximum sentence of imprisonment that could be imposed upon an adult who commits the same act.

A period of house arrest with electronic monitoring or continuous alcohol monitoring or both electronic monitoring and continuous alcohol monitoring, imposed under this division shall not extend beyond the child's twenty-first birthday. If a court imposes a period of house arrest with electronic monitoring or continuous alcohol monitoring or both electronic monitoring and continuous alcohol monitoring, upon a child under this division, it shall require the child: to remain in the child's home or other specified premises for the entire period of house arrest with electronic monitoring or continuous alcohol monitoring or both except when the court permits the child to leave those premises to go to school or to other specified premises. Regarding electronic monitoring, the court also shall require the child to be monitored by a central system that can determine the child's location at designated times; to report periodically to a person designated by the court; and to enter into a written contract with the court agreeing to comply with all requirements imposed by the court, agreeing to pay any fee imposed by the court for the costs of the house arrest with electronic monitoring, and agreeing to waive the right to receive credit for any time served on house arrest with electronic monitoring toward the period of any other dispositional order imposed upon the child if the child violates any of the requirements of the dispositional order of house arrest with electronic monitoring. The court also may impose other reasonable requirements upon the child.

Unless ordered by the court, a child shall not receive credit for any time served on house arrest with electronic monitoring or continuous alcohol monitoring or both toward any other dispositional order imposed upon the child for the act for which was imposed the dispositional order of house arrest with electronic monitoring or continuous alcohol monitoring. As used in this division and division (A)(4)(*l*) of this section, "continuous alcohol monitoring" has the same meaning as in section 2929.01 of the Revised Code.

(*l*) A suspension of the driver's license, probationary driver's license, or temporary instruction permit issued to the child for a period of time prescribed by the court, or a suspension of the registration of all motor vehicles registered in the name of the child for a period of time prescribed by the court. A child whose license or permit is so suspended is ineligible for issuance of a license or permit during the period of suspension. At the end of the period of suspension, the child shall not be reissued a license or permit until the child has paid any applicable reinstatement fee and complied with all requirements governing license reinstatement.

(5) Commit the child to the custody of the court;

(6) Require the child to not be absent without legitimate excuse from the public school the child is supposed to attend for five or more consecutive days, seven or more school days in one school month, or twelve or more school days in a school year;

(7)(a) If a child is adjudicated a delinquent child for being a chronic truant or a habitual truant who previously has been adjudicated an unruly child for being a habitual truant, do either or both of the following:

(i) Require the child to participate in a truancy prevention mediation program;

(ii) Make any order of disposition as authorized by this section, except that the court shall not commit the child to a facility described in division (A)(2) or (3) of this section unless the court determines that the child violated a lawful court order made pursuant to division (C)(1)(e) of section 2151.354 of the Revised Code or division (A)(6) of this section.

(b) If a child is adjudicated a delinquent child for being a chronic truant or a habitual truant who previously has been adjudicated an unruly child for being a habitual truant and the court determines that the parent, guardian, or other person having care of the child has failed to cause the child's attendance at school in violation of section 3321.38 of the Revised Code, do either or both of the following:

(i) Require the parent, guardian, or other person having care of the child to participate in a truancy prevention mediation program;

(ii) Require the parent, guardian, or other person having care of the child to participate in any community service program, preferably a community service program that requires the involvement of the parent, guardian, or other person having care of the child in the school attended by the child.

(8) Make any further disposition that the court finds proper, except that the child shall not be placed in any of the following:

(a) A state correctional institution, a county, multicounty, or municipal jail or workhouse, or another place in which an adult convicted of a crime, under arrest, or charged with a crime is held;

(b) A community corrections facility, if the child would be covered by the definition of public safety beds for purposes of sections 5139.41 to 5139.43 of the Revised Code if the court exercised its authority to commit the child to the legal custody of the department of youth services for institutionalization or institutionalization in a secure facility pursuant to this chapter.

(B) If a child is adjudicated a delinquent child, in addition to any order of disposition made under division (A) of this section, the court, in the following situations and for the specified periods of time, shall suspend the child's temporary instruction permit, restricted license, probationary driver's license, or nonresident operating privilege, or suspend the child's ability to obtain such a permit:

(1) If the child is adjudicated a delinquent child for violating section 2923.122 of the Revised Code, impose a class four suspension of the child's license, permit, or privilege from the range specified in division (A)(4) of section 4510.02 of the Revised Code or deny the child the issuance of a license or permit in accordance with division (F)(1) of section 2923.122 of the Revised Code.

(2) If the child is adjudicated a delinquent child for committing an act that if committed by an adult would be a drug abuse offense or for violating division (B) of section 2917.11 of the Revised Code, suspend the child's license, permit, or privilege for a period of time prescribed by the court. The court, in its discretion, may terminate the suspension if the child attends and satisfactorily completes a drug abuse or alcohol abuse education, intervention, or treatment program specified by the court. Dur-

ing the time the child is attending a program described in this division, the court shall retain the child's temporary instruction permit, probationary driver's license, or driver's license, and the court shall return the permit or license if it terminates the suspension as described in this division.

(C) The court may establish a victim-offender mediation program in which victims and their offenders meet to discuss the offense and suggest possible restitution. If the court obtains the assent of the victim of the delinquent act committed by the child, the court may require the child to participate in the program.

(D)(1) If a child is adjudicated a delinquent child for committing an act that would be a felony if committed by an adult and if the child caused, attempted to cause, threatened to cause, or created a risk of physical harm to the victim of the act, the court, prior to issuing an order of disposition under this section, shall order the preparation of a victim impact statement by the probation department of the county in which the victim of the act resides, by the court's own probation department, or by a victim assistance program that is operated by the state, a county, a municipal corporation, or another governmental entity. The court shall consider the victim impact statement in determining the order of disposition to issue for the child.

(2) Each victim impact statement shall identify the victim of the act for which the child was adjudicated a delinquent child, itemize any economic loss suffered by the victim as a result of the act, identify any physical injury suffered by the victim as a result of the act and the seriousness and permanence of the injury, identify any change in the victim's personal welfare or familial relationships as a result of the act and any psychological impact experienced by the victim or the victim's family as a result of the act, and contain any other information related to the impact of the act upon the victim that the court requires.

(3) A victim impact statement shall be kept confidential and is not a public record. However, the court may furnish copies of the statement to the department of youth services if the delinquent child is committed to the department or to both the adjudicated delinquent child or the adjudicated delinquent child's counsel and the prosecuting attorney. The copy of a victim impact statement furnished by the court to the department pursuant to this section shall be kept confidential and is not a public record. If an officer is preparing pursuant to section 2947.06 or 2951.03 of the Revised Code or Criminal Rule 32.2 a presentence investigation report pertaining to a person, the court shall make available to the officer, for use in preparing the report, a copy of any victim impact statement regarding that person. The copies of a victim impact statement that are made available to the adjudicated delinquent child or the adjudicated delinquent child's counsel and the prosecuting attorney pursuant to this division shall be returned to the court by the person to whom they were made available immediately following the imposition of an order of disposition for the child under this chapter.

The copy of a victim impact statement that is made available pursuant to this division to an officer preparing a criminal presentence investigation report shall be returned to the court by the officer immediately following its use in preparing the report.

(4) The department of youth services shall work with local probation departments and victim assistance programs to develop a standard victim impact statement.

(E) If a child is adjudicated a delinquent child for being a chronic truant or a habitual truant who previously has been adjudicated an unruly child for being a habitual truant and the court determines that the parent, guardian, or other person having care of the child has failed to cause the child's attendance at school in violation of section 3321.38 of the Revised Code, in addition to any order of disposition it makes under this section, the court shall warn the parent, guardian, or other person having care of the child that any subsequent adjudication of the child as an unruly or delinquent child for being a habitual or chronic truant may result in a criminal charge against the parent, guardian, or other person having care of the child for a violation of division (C) of section 2919.21 or section 2919.24 of the Revised Code.

(F)(1) During the period of a delinquent child's community control granted under this section, authorized probation officers who are engaged within the scope of their supervisory duties or responsibilities may search, with or without a warrant, the person of the delinquent child, the place of residence of the delinquent child, and a motor vehicle, another item of tangible or intangible personal property, or other real property in which the delinquent child has a right, title, or interest or for which the delinquent child has the express or implied permission of a person with a right, title, or interest to use, occupy, or possess if the probation officers have reasonable grounds to believe that the delinquent child is not abiding by the law or otherwise is not complying with the conditions of the delinquent child's community control. The court that places a delinquent child on community control under this section shall provide the delinquent child with a written notice that informs the delinquent child that authorized probation officers who are engaged within the scope of their supervisory duties or responsibilities may conduct those types of searches during the period of community control if they have reasonable grounds to believe that the delinquent child is not abiding by the law or otherwise is not complying with the conditions of the delinquent child's community control. The court also shall provide the written notice described in division (E)(2) of this section to each parent, guardian, or custodian of the delinquent child who is described in that division.

(2) The court that places a child on community control under this section shall provide the child's parent, guardian, or other custodian with a written notice that informs them that authorized probation officers may conduct searches pursuant to division (E)(1) of this section. The notice shall specifically state that a permissible search might extend to a motor vehicle, another item of tangible or intangible personal property, or a place of residence or other real property in which a notified parent, guardian, or custodian has a right, title, or interest and that the parent, guardian, or custodian expressly or impliedly permits the child to use, occupy, or possess.

(G) If a juvenile court commits a delinquent child to the custody of any person, organization, or entity pursuant to this section and if the delinquent act for which the child is so committed is a sexually oriented offense that is not a registration-exempt sexually oriented offense or is a child-victim oriented offense, the court in the order of disposition shall do one of the following:

(1) Require that the child be provided treatment as described in division (A)(2) of section 5139.13 of the Revised Code;

(2) Inform the person, organization, or entity that it is the preferred course of action in this state that the child be provided treatment as described in division (A)(2) of section 5139.13 of the Revised Code and encourage the person, organization, or entity to provide that treatment.

(2004 H 163, eff. 9–23–04; 2003 S 5, § 3, eff. 1–1–04; 2003 S 5, § 1, eff. 7–31–03; 2003 H 95, § 3.13, eff. 1–1–04; 2003 H 95, § 1, eff. 9–26–03; 2002 H 490, eff. 1–1–04; 2002 H 400, § 4, eff. 1–1–04; 2002 H 400, § 1, eff. 4–3–03; 2002 S 123, eff. 1–1–04; 2002 H 393, eff. 7–5–02; 2002 H 247, eff. 5–30–02; 2001 S 3, eff. 1–1–02; 2000 S 179, § 3, eff. 1–1–02)

Uncodified Law

2001 S 3, § 5, eff. 10–26–01, reads:

Section 2152.19 of the Revised Code, as presented in this act, includes matter that was amended into former section 2151.355 of the Revised Code by Am. Sub. S.B. 181 of the 123rd General Assembly. Paragraphs of former section 2151.355 of the Revised Code containing S.B. 181 amendments were transferred to section 2152.19 of the Revised Code by Am. Sub. S.B. 179 of the 123rd General Assembly as part of its general revision of the juvenile sentencing laws. The General Assembly, applying the principle stated in division (B) of section 1.52 of the Revised Code that amendments are to be harmonized if reasonably capable of simultaneous operation, finds that the version of section 2152.19 of the Revised Code presented in this act is the resulting version of the section in effect prior to the effective date of the section as presented in this act.

Historical and Statutory Notes

Ed. Note: 2152.18, 2152.19 and 2152.20 contain provisions analogous to former 2151.355, repealed by 2000 S 179, § 4, eff. 1–1–02.

Amendment Note: 2004 H 163 inserted "or continuous alcohol monitoring", "or both electronic monitoring and continuous alcohol monitoring," and "or continuous alcohol monitoring or both" throughout subdivisions (A)(4)(j) and (k); inserted ". Regarding electronic monitoring, the court also shall require the child" preceding "to be monitored by a central system" in the second paragraph of subdivision (A)(4)(k); inserted the last sentence of subdivision (A)(4)(k); and made other nonsubstantive changes.

Amendment Note: 2003 S 5 inserted "that is not a registration-exempt sexually oriented offense or is a child-victim oriented offense" in division (G).

Amendment Note: 2003 H 95, § 1 and 3, substituted "5139.43" for "5139.45" in Division (A)(8)(b).

Amendment Note: 2002 H 490 substituted "with electronic monitoring" for "electronically monitored" throughout the section; and deleted "to wear, otherwise have attached to the child's person, or otherwise be subject to monitoring by a certified electronic monitoring device or to participate in the operation of and monitoring by a certified electronic monitoring system;" after "the child:" in the first paragraph of division (A)(3)(k).

Amendment Note: 2002 H 400, § 1, added ", including, but not limited to, a school, camp, or facility operated under section 2151.65 of the Revised Code;" to division (A)(2); added new (A)(3); renumbered existing divisions (A)(3) through (A)(7) as (A)(4) through (A)(8); added "or (3)" to division (A)(7)(a)(ii); and changed "(5)" to "(6)" in division (A)(7)(a)(ii).

Amendment Note: 2002 S 123 inserted "for a period of time prescribed by the court" twice in division (A)(3)(*l*); and rewrote division (B), which prior thereto read:

"(B) If a child is adjudicated a delinquent child, in addition to any order of disposition made under division (A) of this section, the court, in the following situations, shall suspend the child's temporary instruction permit, restricted license, probationary driver's license, or nonresident operating privilege, or suspend the child's ability to obtain such a permit:

"(1) The child is adjudicated a delinquent child for violating section 2923.122 of the Revised Code, with the suspension and denial being in accordance with division (E)(1)(a), (c), (d), or (e) of section 2923.122 of the Revised Code.

"(2) The child is adjudicated a delinquent child for committing an act that if committed by an adult would be a drug abuse offense or for violating division (B) of section 2917.11 of the Revised Code, with the suspension continuing until the child attends and satisfactorily completes a drug abuse or alcohol abuse education, intervention, or treatment program specified by the court. During the time the child is attending the program, the court shall retain any temporary instruction permit, probationary driver's license, or driver's license issued to the child, and the court shall return the permit or license when the child satisfactorily completes the program."

Amendment Note: 2002 H 393 rewrote division (G) which prior thereto read:

"(G) If a juvenile court commits a delinquent child to the custody of any person, organization, or entity pursuant to this section and if the delinquent act for which the child is so committed is a sexually oriented offense, the court in the order of disposition shall inform the person, organization, or entity that it is the preferred course of action in this state that the child be provided treatment as described in division (A)(2) of section 5139.13 of the Revised Code and shall encourage the person, organization, or entity to provide that treatment."

Amendment Note: 2002 H 247 made nonsubstantive changes and rewrote division (D)(3), which prior thereto read:

"(3) A victim impact statement shall be kept confidential and is not a public record. However, the court may furnish copies of the statement to the department of youth services if the delinquent child is committed to the department or to both the adjudicated delinquent child and the adjudicated delinquent child's counsel and the prosecuting attorney. The copy of a victim impact statement furnished by the court to the department pursuant to this section shall be kept confidential and is not a public record. The copies of a victim impact statement that are made available to the adjudicated delinquent child or the adjudicated delinquent child's counsel and the prosecuting attorney pursuant to this division shall be returned to the court by the person to whom they were made available immediately following the imposition of an order of disposition for the child under this chapter."

Amendment Note: 2001 S 3 added new division (G).

Cross References

Agreement to reimburse juvenile court for foster care maintenance costs and associated administrative and training costs, 2151.152

Presentence investigation reports, mandatory consideration of certain information, 2951.03

Library References

Infants ⟂223.
Westlaw Topic No. 211.
C.J.S. Infants §§ 57, 69 to 85.

Research References

Encyclopedias

OH Jur. 3d Family Law § 1548, Juvenile Traffic Offenders—Orders of Disposition.

OH Jur. 3d Family Law § 1688, Unruly Child.

OH Jur. 3d Family Law § 1689, Juvenile Traffic Offender.

OH Jur. 3d Family Law § 1698.6, Sexually Oriented and Child-Victim Offenses; Registration.

Treatises and Practice Aids

Carlin, Baldwin's Ohio Practice, Merrick-Rippner Probate Law § 104:19, Juvenile Facilities—Participation With Service Providers.

Carlin, Baldwin's Ohio Practice, Merrick-Rippner Probate Law § 107:61, Adjudicatory Hearings—Notice to Victims of Crime of Right to Recover Damages and Victim-Impact Statements.

Carlin, Baldwin's Ohio Practice, Merrick-Rippner Probate Law § 107:89, Custody of Department of Youth Services.

Carlin, Baldwin's Ohio Practice, Merrick-Rippner Probate Law § 107:90, Disposition Orders for Delinquent Children, Effective January 1, 2002.

Carlin, Baldwin's Ohio Practice, Merrick-Rippner Probate Law § 107:101, Mandatory Suspension of Driver's License, Effective January 1, 2002.

Carlin, Baldwin's Ohio Practice, Merrick-Rippner Probate Law § 107:102, Serious Youthful Offenders, Effective January 1, 2002.

Carlin, Baldwin's Ohio Practice, Merrick-Rippner Probate Law § 107:105, Commitment of Delinquent Children to the Custody of Department of Youth Services, Effective January 1, 2002.

Carlin, Baldwin's Ohio Practice, Merrick-Rippner Probate Law § 107:108, Disposition of Juvenile Traffic Offender—Commitment to Detention Home or Institution.

Carlin, Baldwin's Ohio Practice, Merrick-Rippner Probate Law § 107:112, Disposition of Unruly Children—Permissive.

Carlin, Baldwin's Ohio Practice, Merrick-Rippner Probate Law § 107:113, Juvenile Court's Authority Over Parents.

Carlin, Baldwin's Ohio Practice, Merrick-Rippner Probate Law § 107:180, Rules of Probation—Form.

Painter, Ohio Driving Under the Influence § 12:29, Statutory Penalties—Both Tiers—House Arrest With Electronic Monitoring (Haem).

Painter, Ohio Driving Under the Influence § 12:45, Juvenile and "Underage" Offenders—Generally.

Giannelli & Yeomans, Ohio Juvenile Law § 4:6, Court Order Violations.

Giannelli & Yeomans, Ohio Juvenile Law § 5:7, Mandatory Syo Dispositions.

Giannelli & Yeomans, Ohio Juvenile Law § 5:8, Discretionary Syo Dispositions.

Giannelli & Yeomans, Ohio Juvenile Law § 14:7, Probation Searches.

Giannelli & Yeomans, Ohio Juvenile Law § 15:4, Mediation.

Giannelli & Yeomans, Ohio Juvenile Law § 16:8, Delinquency Complaints.

Giannelli & Yeomans, Ohio Juvenile Law § 19:6, Standard for Detention.

Giannelli & Yeomans, Ohio Juvenile Law § 21:7, Court Records.

Giannelli & Yeomans, Ohio Juvenile Law § 21:8, Victim Impact Statement.

Giannelli & Yeomans, Ohio Juvenile Law § 27:2, Dispositional Alternatives.

Giannelli & Yeomans, Ohio Juvenile Law § 27:5, Child Protective Services.

Giannelli & Yeomans, Ohio Juvenile Law § 27:6, County or Private Facility Commitment.

Giannelli & Yeomans, Ohio Juvenile Law § 27:7, Community Control Sanctions.

Giannelli & Yeomans, Ohio Juvenile Law § 27:8, Probation.

Giannelli & Yeomans, Ohio Juvenile Law § 27:9, Drug & Alcohol Dispositions.

Giannelli & Yeomans, Ohio Juvenile Law § 28:6, Commitment to Juvenile Facility.

Giannelli & Yeomans, Ohio Juvenile Law § 29:2, Unruly—Dispositional Alternatives.

Giannelli & Yeomans, Ohio Juvenile Law § 29:3, Unruly—Delinquency Dispositions.

Giannelli & Yeomans, Ohio Juvenile Law § 32:2, Jurisdiction Over Parents and Others.

Giannelli & Yeomans, Ohio Juvenile Law § 32:3, Responsibilities to Victims and Others.

Giannelli & Yeomans, Ohio Juvenile Law § 35:2, Confidentiality Requirement.

Giannelli & Yeomans, Ohio Juvenile Law § 25:11, Victim Participation.

Giannelli & Yeomans, Ohio Juvenile Law § 27:10, House Arrest & Electronic Monitoring.

Giannelli & Yeomans, Ohio Juvenile Law § 27:11, Driving Privileges.

Giannelli & Yeomans, Ohio Juvenile Law § 27:14, Forfeiture.

Giannelli & Yeomans, Ohio Juvenile Law § 27:16, Truancy Dispositions.

Giannelli & Yeomans, Ohio Juvenile Law § 27:17, Court Custody.

Giannelli & Yeomans, Ohio Juvenile Law § 27:18, "Catch-All" Provision.

Giannelli & Yeomans, Ohio Juvenile Law § 27:19, Plural Dispositions.

Giannelli & Yeomans, Ohio Juvenile Law § 27:20, Victim-Mediation.

Hastings, Manoloff, Sheeran, & Stype, Ohio School Law § 20:20, Enforcement Procedures-Consequences.

Notes of Decisions

Ed. Note: This section contains annotations from former RC 2151.35 and RC 2151.355.

Adult facilities   8
Commitment to government custody, detention home   3
Constitutional issues   1
Drug offenses   7
Education   4
Evidence   2
Procedural issues   5
Traffic offenses   6

---

1. Constitutional issues

Juvenile did not have legitimate expectation that his sentence of probation was complete at time the court prosecuted probation violations and extended his probation, and thus, juvenile failed to establish double jeopardy violation, where juvenile's probation was conditioned upon his compliance with terms and conditions of probation, including completion of sexual offender counseling, and such condition was not completed. In re Walker (Ohio App. 10 Dist., Franklin, 04-29-2003) No. 02AP-421, 2003-Ohio-2137, 2003 WL 1962419, Unreported, appeal not allowed 99 Ohio St.3d 1542, 795 N.E.2d 681, 2003-Ohio-4671. Double Jeopardy ⇔ 33

Juvenile failed to establish due process violation as to notice of when his probation expired, where juvenile signed terms and conditions of probation, indicating his awareness, as provided in terms and conditions, that probation continued until sexual offender counseling was completed. In re Walker (Ohio App. 10 Dist., Franklin, 04-29-2003) No. 02AP-421, 2003-Ohio-2137, 2003 WL 1962419, Unreported, appeal not allowed 99 Ohio St.3d 1542, 795 N.E.2d 681, 2003-Ohio-4671. Constitutional Law ⇔ 255(4); Infants ⇔ 225

Pressure placed on juvenile defendant to make self-incriminating statements to social worker during alcohol and drug assessment in connection with probation violation, or risk perceived undesired consequence of negative recommendation from social worker with respect to sentencing, did not rise to level of compulsion forbidden by Fifth Amendment; defendant's choice was not between self-incrimination and incarceration, and to some extent, defendant and his counsel requested alcohol and drug assessment. State v. Johnson (Ohio App. 10 Dist., 08-16-2005) 2005-Ohio-4243, 2005 WL 1953065. Infants ⇔ 68.7(3)

Juvenile court must give the minor notice as to why a previously suspended commitment is ordered reinstituted, if the court imposes a previously suspended commitment as a further disposition. In re Royal (Ohio App. 7 Dist., 03-01-1999) 132 Ohio App.3d 496, 725 N.E.2d 685. Infants ⇔ 198

Juvenile's challenge to manifest weight of evidence supporting his adjudication as delinquent by reason of acts constituting felony drug abuse, although rendered moot by appellate finding that reversal was required for erroneous admission of untrustworthy hearsay, would nevertheless be addressed on appeal, as issue affected juvenile's constitutional protection against double jeopardy. In re Carter (Ohio App. 4 Dist., 11-06-1997) 123 Ohio App.3d 532, 704 N.E.2d 625. Double Jeopardy ⇔ 33; Infants ⇔ 247

Three conditions of probation imposed upon a juvenile who pushed his brother through a plate glass window during an argument that he is not to go to a specified place of business, not to associate with a specified individual, and not to dress as a female infringe upon a juvenile's constitutional rights and have no relation to a charge of domestic violence. In re Miller (Lucas 1992) 82 Ohio App.3d 81, 611 N.E.2d 451.

Imposing consecutive terms of commitment for distinct and unrelated offenses occurring at different times is within the juvenile court's authority to order, and the argument that these consecutive terms serve only to punish rather than rehabilitate is without merit. In re Samkas (Cuyahoga 1992) 80 Ohio App.3d 240, 608 N.E.2d 1172, dismissed, jurisdictional motion overruled 65 Ohio St.3d 1431, 600 N.E.2d 676.

RC 2151.35(E) which authorizes the juvenile court to commit a male child over sixteen years of age who has committed an act which if committed by an adult would be a felony to the Ohio state reformatory (the same institution to which adults convicted of a felony are committed) without providing to such juvenile equal rights of due process of law, is an unconstitutional denial of rights secured by US Const Am 14. State v. Fisher (Tuscarawas 1969) 17 Ohio App.2d 183, 245 N.E.2d 358, 46 O.O.2d 247. Constitutional Law ⇔ 255(4); Infants ⇔ 132; Statutes ⇔ 64(6)

A curfew ordinance that restricts minor children at nighttime can be constitutionally valid; however, a curfew ordinance must not exceed the bounds of reasonableness. City of Eastlake v. Ruggiero (Lake 1966) 7 Ohio App.2d 212, 220 N.E.2d 126, 36 O.O.2d 345. Municipal Corporations ⇔ 625

Due process does not require that counsel be permitted at the staffings of indefinite committees at Lima state hospital. Davis v. Balson (N.D.Ohio 1978) 461 F.Supp. 842, 11 O.O.3d 360.

Trial court's imposition of juvenile's suspended commitment to Department of Youth Services (DYS) did not violate juvenile's Fourteenth Amendment equal protection rights on grounds that a court could not revoke an adult's probation after adult's term of probation had expired, where court did not revoke juvenile's probation, rather it merely exercised its continuing jurisdiction over him by imposing a suspended commitment after the end of his probation period. In re Braun (Ohio App. 4 Dist., Washington, 06-07-2002) No. 01CA42, 2002-Ohio-3021, 2002 WL 1376182, Unreported. Constitutional Law ⇔ 242.1(4); Infants ⇔ 225

Imposition of juvenile's suspended commitment to the Department of Youth Services (DYS) after his discharge from probation did not violate juvenile's right to notice or his Fourteenth Amendment right to due process, where court had conditioned suspension on both probation and upon separate order requiring good behavior until age of 21, and court imposed commitment not based upon a probation violation, but upon juvenile's poor behavior. In re Braun (Ohio App. 4 Dist., Washington, 06-07-2002) No. 01CA42, 2002-Ohio-3021, 2002 WL 1376182, Unreported. Constitutional Law ⇔ 255(4); Infants ⇔ 69(1)

Trial court did not violate juvenile's constitutional protection from double jeopardy by imposing both a suspended commitment to the Department of Youth Services (DYS) conditioned upon good behavior in one paragraph of its dispositional order, and a period of probation in a separate paragraph of order, where juvenile statute provided court with numerous dispositional options, including probation, commitment to the DYS, and any other disposition that court deemed proper, and did not list these options in the alternative. In re Braun (Ohio App. 4 Dist., Washington, 06-07-2002) No. 01CA42, 2002-Ohio-3021, 2002 WL 1376182, Unreported. Infants ⇔ 69(1)

Note 1

A juvenile court errs when it revokes a juvenile's probation status without affording the right to counsel at the dispositional hearing and by failing to provide the opportunity to secure counsel for the probation revocation hearing where (1) the juvenile pleads true at the adjudication hearing and is not informed of right to counsel, (2) there is no inquiry into the desire for counsel, and (3) there is no indication of a waiver of right to counsel. In re Sproule, Nos. 00CA007575 and 00CA007580, 2001 WL 39594 (9th Dist Ct App, Lorain, 1–17–01).

Any construction of RC 2151.354 that would allow commitment of an "unruly" child to the legal custody of the Ohio youth commission would be a violation of due process of law, and therefore an improper construction. OAG 72–071.

2. Evidence

Evidence was insufficient to support juvenile's adjudication as delinquent by reason of commission of disorderly conduct; even if juvenile's rude comment and profane gesture, the middle finger, to two individuals constituted fighting words, the record lacked evidence that her comment and gesture inflicted injury or provoked either individuals to an immediate retaliatory breach of the peace, with one victim testifying that juvenile's actions did not incite any feelings of retaliation at all. In re Fechuch (Ohio App. 5 Dist., Tuscarawas, 08-16-2005) No. 2005 AP 02 0012, 2005-Ohio-4342, 2005 WL 2002268, Unreported. Infants ⚖ 176

Trial court acted within its discretion in committing juvenile to Department of Youth Services after he was adjudicated delinquent for burglary and aggravated arson, even though juvenile argued that his prior record suggested that alternative services were available; juvenile was adjudicated delinquent for two felony offenses, and trial court found that juvenile was menace to community and that community needed to be protected. State v. O'Brien (Ohio App. 5 Dist., Stark, 07-18-2005) No. 2004CA00370, 2005-Ohio-3765, 2005 WL 1713549, Unreported. Infants ⚖ 223.1

Evidence presented at juvenile's probation revocation hearing was sufficient to support finding that juvenile violated the terms of his probation; counsel for juvenile admitted the violation. In re A.B. (Ohio App. 9 Dist., Wayne, 09-08-2004) No. 04CA0017, No. 04CA0018, 2004-Ohio-4724, 2004 WL 1969355, Unreported. Infants ⚖ 225

Weight of evidence supported finding of delinquency for aggravated robbery, despite fact that one victim could not identify juvenile and the other victim had to be brought close to juvenile in order to identify him at the scene, since she was not wearing corrective eyewear on the night in question; juvenile was apprehended shortly after crime occurred, and only a couple of blocks away from scene, victim's identification of juvenile's clothing was accurate, and victim was certain about her description and identification of juvenile. In re J.K. (Ohio App. 8 Dist., Cuyahoga, 04-08-2004) No. 82824, 2004-Ohio-1792, 2004 WL 744828, Unreported. Infants ⚖ 176

There was insufficient evidence to support adjudication of delinquency for burglary and theft; state failed to present any evidence linking juvenile to crime, state failed to present testimony of either of two arresting officers or any details surrounding juvenile's arrest, victim did not identify juvenile as perpetrator, no witness positively identified juvenile at crime scene, and no testimony was offered about whether stolen items were in his possession. In re C.L. (Ohio App. 8 Dist., Cuyahoga, 03-04-2004) No. 82609, 2004-Ohio-987, 2004 WL 396344, Unreported. Infants ⚖ 176

Witnesses' pretrial identifications of juvenile as shooter were sufficiently reliable to allow admission of witnesses' identifications in juvenile's delinquency adjudication for felonious assault; first witness knew juvenile prior to shooting and the two had been together for several hours proceeding the shooting, and second witness had the opportunity to see juvenile both before and during the shooting, and he was quite certain of his identification. In re Tims (Ohio App. 2 Dist., Montgomery, 02-13-2004) No. 20047, 2004-Ohio-674, 2004 WL 260317, Unreported. Infants ⚖ 173.1

Sufficient evidence existed to identify juvenile as the shooter to support his adjudication of delinquency for felonious assault; two witnesses identified juvenile as the shooter, victim identified juvenile as the individual who shot him, and victim testified he knew juvenile from their neighborhood and had seen him just hours before the shooting. In re Tims (Ohio App. 2 Dist., Montgomery, 02-13-2004) No. 20047, 2004-Ohio-674, 2004 WL 260317, Unreported. Infants ⚖ 176

Decision to place child in temporary custody of juvenile probation department was supported by evidence which revealed history of escalating conflict in the home, alcohol abuse, sexual abuse, and significant physical and psychological issues, and testimony of representative from juvenile's school that juvenile's environment was having a negative impact upon her. In re Hutzel (Ohio App. 5 Dist., Tuscarawas, 04-29-2003) No. 2002AP110087, 2003-Ohio-2288, 2003 WL 21025820, Unreported. Infants ⚖ 223.1

Finding that juvenile was delinquent by reason of gross sexual imposition was not against the manifest weight of the evidence; witness testified that juvenile and victim went into his clubhouse and juvenile placed a piece of wood over the door, that he observed the activity in the clubhouse through a peep hole, that he saw juvenile pull up the victim's shirt, kiss her on her chest and cheeks, pull her pants down, place her on top of him, and move himself up and down, and mother of victim testified that when she asked victim was happened she said "he sexed me." In re Hoyle (Ohio App. 5 Dist., Stark, 12-23-2002) No. 2002CA00266, 2002-Ohio-7212, 2002 WL 31874994, Unreported. Infants ⚖ 176

Trial court's erroneous admission, in delinquency adjudication proceeding, of hearsay statement of juvenile's adult codefendant, was prejudicial to juvenile and required reversal of adjudication, where evidence remaining after exclusion of hearsay statement was not overwhelming evidence of juvenile's guilt and reasonable probability existed that exclusion of statement from adjudication proceeding would have affected result. In re Carter (Ohio App. 4 Dist., 11-06-1997) 123 Ohio App.3d 532, 704 N.E.2d 625. Infants ⚖ 174; Infants ⚖ 253

Any adjudication of delinquency must be supported by clear and convincing evidence. In re Agler (Ohio 1969) 19 Ohio St.2d 70, 249 N.E.2d 808, 48 O.O.2d 85. Infants ⚖ 176

It is an abuse of discretion for the juvenile court under RC 2151.26 to recognize a fourteen-year-old youth to appear before the common pleas court when the evidence is insufficient to support a finding that he is other than a fit subject for rehabilitation under the provisions of the juvenile code, and insufficient to support a finding that recognizing him to common pleas court is necessary as a protection to the public. (See also In re Whittington, 13 App(2d) 11, 233 NE(2d) 333 (1967); vacated by 391 US 341, 88 SCt 1507, 20 LEd(2d) 625 (1968).) In re Whittington (Fairfield 1969) 17 Ohio App.2d 164, 245 N.E.2d 364, 46 O.O.2d 237. Infants ⚖ 68.7(2)

A proceeding against a juvenile charged with being a delinquent is civil in nature and not criminal, and a preponderance of the evidence is sufficient to warrant a determination that such juvenile is a delinquent, notwithstanding that acts are charged which, if committed by an adult and proved beyond a reasonable doubt, would constitute a felony. (See also In re Whittington, 13 App(2d) 11, 233 NE(2d) 333 (1967); vacated by 391 US 341, 88 SCt 1507, 20 LEd(2d) 625 (1968).) In re Agler (Defiance 1968) 15 Ohio App.2d 240, 240 N.E.2d 874, 44 O.O.2d 482, reversed 19 Ohio St.2d 70, 249 N.E.2d 808, 48 O.O.2d 85. Infants ⚖ 176; Infants ⚖ 194.1

The word "allow" as used in an ordinance prohibiting a parent or guardian of any child to allow such child to do something means either "permit" or "neglect to restrain or prevent"; it requires actual or constructive knowledge on the part of the parent or guardian. City of Eastlake v. Ruggiero (Lake 1966) 7 Ohio App.2d 212, 220 N.E.2d 126, 36 O.O.2d 345. Municipal Corporations ⚖ 622

In a petty theft of a box of donuts committed by a trio of juveniles, a defense of abandoned property fails based on one party's testimony that she did not know what was in the box and "it is reasonable that a person seeing an abandoned box in front of the store, which if it contained property for resale by the store, would be a health department violation would think the property was abandoned;" in addition, the court's finding of delinquent by reason of petty theft is supported by testimony of two police officers who are watching the store because of previous reports that donuts ordered by the store were being stolen shortly after delivery and (1) the officers see the trio of juveniles watching a delivery truck as it places donuts on the steps of a dairy store at 2 in the morning, (2) the trio walks to the alley behind the dairy, (3) one of the them walks up the wheelchair ramp to the back door and picks up one of the boxes as the other two stay at the corner of the store, (4) the juvenile walks down the ramp to where the two are waiting, and (5) all three begin looking through the box to see what kind of donuts there are. In re Fahrni, No. 1998CA00072, 1999 WL 4501 (5th Dist Ct App, Stark, 12–14–98).

A one-year commitment to the Department of Youth Services is appropriate in the case of a juvenile who is seventeen years of age at the time of the dispositional hearing and is involved in the robbery of a bank and the use of a gun. In re Williams, No. 15152, 1995 WL 628014 (2d Dist Ct App, Montgomery, 10–25–95).

Where several witnesses identified juvenile defendant as the young man who stabbed an elementary school teacher in her classroom, there was substantial evidence upon which trier of fact could conclude that all elements of felonious assault in violation of RC 2903.11 had been proven beyond a reasonable doubt, and trial court properly adjudicated defendant a delinquent. State v Harthorne, No. L–92–169, 1993 WL 306630 (6th Dist Ct App, Lucas, 6–30–93).

3. Commitment to government custody, detention home

Under governing statute, juvenile who was placed on probation following delinquency adjudication could not be held in county jail pending trial on alleged parole violation, even though he was 18 years of age at time of arrest for parole violation, but should have been placed in a juvenile facility. In re Raypole (Ohio App. 12 Dist., Fayette, 03-10-2003) No. CA2002-01-001, No. CA2002-01-002, 2003-Ohio-1066, 2003 WL 928976, Unreported. Infants 225

Order committing juvenile adjudicated delinquent to county juvenile center following probation violation was not abuse of discretion; juvenile had committed act which, if committed by adult, amounted to third degree felony, juvenile violated probation on numerous occasions, and juvenile's overall conduct, including assault on mother and refusal to follow instructions, indicated he had not made necessary adjustments in attitude or conduct. In re Goudy (Ohio App. 4 Dist., Washington, 01-21-2003) No. 02CA49, 2003-Ohio-547, 2003 WL 251956, Unreported. Infants 225

Trial court order of disposition, which committed juvenile to Youth Services for a minimum of six months, up to his 21st birthday, was not an abuse of discretion; juvenile was adjudicated delinquent for breaking and entering, the owners of the business juvenile broke into were related to juvenile, and juvenile had previously been adjudicated unruly and provided an opportunity to change his behavior pattern. In re Homan (Ohio App. 5 Dist., Tuscarawas, 01-27-2003) No. 2002AP080067, 2003-Ohio-352, 2003 WL 183811, Unreported. Infants 223.1

Juvenile, who attempted to challenge his confinement at a juvenile detention center with a pending order to transfer him to the Division of Youth Services, was not entitled to a writ of mandamus to compel his release from the juvenile detention facility; juvenile had adequate remedies at law through an appeal and a motion for contempt to raise the issue of whether juvenile court judge, on remand, had violated a Court of Appeals mandate. State ex rel. Borden v. Hendon (Ohio, 07-24-2002) 96 Ohio St.3d 64, 771 N.E.2d 247, 2002-Ohio-3525. Mandamus 3(3); Mandamus 4(4)

Where *Anders* brief and court's independent review of record indicated that trial court proceedings contained no error prejudicial to juvenile's rights in connection with revocation of his probation and commitment to Department of Youth Services (DYS) and juvenile defendant had been allowed sufficient opportunity to respond to *Anders* brief, affirmance of trial court's judgment revoking probation was appropriate. In re Unrue (Ohio App. 4 Dist., 08-23-1996) 113 Ohio App.3d 844, 682 N.E.2d 686. Infants 253

When determining appropriate length of commitment, juvenile court must look not only at delinquent act, but also at overall conduct and behavior of juvenile, juvenile's history, remorse shown by juvenile, and other societal factors. In re Caldwell (Ohio, 07-31-1996) 76 Ohio St.3d 156, 666 N.E.2d 1367, 1996-Ohio-410. Infants 223.1

Juvenile court is authorized to impose consecutive terms of commitment upon delinquent minor for separate delinquent acts, whether or not acts arise from same set of operative facts. In re Caldwell (Ohio, 07-31-1996) 76 Ohio St.3d 156, 666 N.E.2d 1367, 1996-Ohio-410. Infants 223.1

Juvenile court properly ordered consecutive term of commitment for each of three separate delinquent acts by juvenile, receiving stolen goods and two counts of aggravated vehicular assault, in light of serious nature of actions, of juvenile's obvious lack of remorse, of his disregard for school, and of his prior probation for auto theft. In re Caldwell (Ohio, 07-31-1996) 76 Ohio St.3d 156, 666 N.E.2d 1367, 1996-Ohio-410. Infants 223.1

Trial court was authorized to order placement of delinquent minor, who was in temporary custody of county children services board, into residential treatment facility. In re Lawson (Ohio App. 10 Dist., 11-08-1994) 98 Ohio App.3d 456, 648 N.E.2d 889. Infants 223.1

A juvenile delinquent defendant who has already been committed to the youth services department's custody for a minimum of twelve months for robbery and grand theft may be sentenced to a consecutive six-month term for safecracking. In re Samkas (Cuyahoga 1992) 80 Ohio App.3d 240, 608 N.E.2d 1172, dismissed, jurisdictional motion overruled 65 Ohio St.3d 1431, 600 N.E.2d 676.

A final order of disposition of a child found to be delinquent, as prescribed by RC 2151.355, may not include, as punishment or otherwise, confinement or detention in a juvenile detention home. In re Bolden (Allen 1973) 37 Ohio App.2d 7, 306 N.E.2d 166, 66 O.O.2d 26. Infants 223.1

Commitment of juvenile to the Department of Youth Services for a minimum of five years and a maximum of juvenile's attainment of age 21 was an abuse of discretion, and thus remand for a new disposition hearing was required; juvenile was adjudicated delinquent for committing one count of complicity to felonious assault, and the statute governing juvenile dispositional orderers provided that if a juvenile committed an act which would be a second degree felony if committed by an adult, as complicity to felonious assault would, the juvenile should be committed to the Department of Youth Services for a minimum period of one year. In re Richardson (Ohio App. 7 Dist., Mahoning, 06-27-2002) No. 01 CA 78, 2002-Ohio-3461, 2002 WL 1483880, Unreported, reconsideration denied 2002-Ohio-6709, 2002 WL 31743108. Infants 69(1); Infants 254

Trial court retained subject matter jurisdiction to lift the suspension of juvenile's commitment to Department of Youth Services (DYS) after the end of his probation period, where trial court conditioned suspension of commitment on both probation and a separate order requiring juvenile to be of good behavior until age of 21. In re Braun (Ohio App. 4 Dist., Washington, 06-07-2002) No. 01CA42, 2002-Ohio-3021, 2002 WL 1376182, Unreported. Infants 196

Commitment of a fifteen year old to a state institution pursuant to RC 2151.26 for purpose of examination is not an act for which a writ of prohibition will issue. State ex rel. Harris v. Common Pleas Court, Division of Probate and Juvenile (Ross 1970) 25 Ohio App.2d 78, 266 N.E.2d 589, 54 O.O.2d 115.

Probable cause to arrest is not required where officers approach a group of juveniles and ask them to identify themselves and the juveniles scatter and run which provides the officers with reasonable articulable suspicion to inquire further; repeated profanity can be sufficiently provocative to sustain a conviction under RC 2917.11 of a juvenile who is belligerent, profane and violent and convictions for disorderly conduct, resisting arrest and assault on a peace officer in addition to the juvenile's prior conviction for resisting arrest involving a physical altercation with law enforcement officers justifies sentencing to the custody of the Ohio youth commission until the juvenile's twenty-first birthday. In re Hefner, No. 848, 1998 WL 346846 (5th Dist Ct App, Morrow, 5–29–98).

Consecutive commitment orders may be issued by a juvenile court only pursuant to RC 2921.34 on a juvenile found delinquent of escape, and the juvenile court is without jurisdiction to impose consecutive commitments in delinquency cases arising from the same set of operative facts; once a child is adjudicated delinquent and turned over to the custody of the department of youth services, the juvenile court is without jurisdiction to instruct the department how the commitment shall be served. In re Caldwell, Nos. 94APF07–996 and 94APF07–997, 1995 WL 3832 (10th Dist Ct App, Franklin, 1–9–95).

Juvenile court has discretionary authority to issue consecutive commitment orders pursuant to RC 2151.355(A)(11). In re Bremmer, No. 62088 (8th Dist Ct App, Cuyahoga, 4–1–93).

As the unauthorized absence from a residential treatment center or group home by a juvenile committed to such premises by a juvenile court constitutes escape, an adjudication of delinquency premised on such an act is not a status offense; therefore, a child may be placed in a juvenile detention facility. In re Wells, No. CA–8287, CA–8347, and CA–8307 (5th Dist Ct App, Stark, 3–18–91).

A juvenile court in a post-dispositional setting may sentence a child found to be delinquent to a detention home, provided the home is in compliance with the statutory requisites concerning the care, treatment, and training of delinquent children. In re Hale, No. WD–85–74 (6th Dist Ct App, Wood, 4–25–86).

A juvenile court has no authority pursuant to RC 2151.38(B) or 2151.38(C) to release a child committed to the youth services department under RC 2151.355(A)(4) to 2151.355(A)(6) for institutional care after expiration of the applicable minimum period of institutionalization. The effect of RC 2151.38(A), therefore, is that the juvenile court's jurisdiction to release a child terminates when the child has completed the minimum period of institutionalization. OAG 93–079.

If a request for early release is made pursuant to one of the procedures specified in RC 2151.38(B) prior to expiration of the minimum period of institutionalization imposed under RC 2151.355(A)(4) to 2151.355(A)(6), and the hearing is rescheduled or continued beyond the expiration of the minimum period of institutionalization, the juvenile court does not acquire or retain jurisdiction to grant an early release after that date. The court's jurisdiction over releases after the minimum period of confinement is limited to that set out in RC 2151.38(C). OAG 93–079.

A minor youth who has been committed to the youth services department pursuant to RC 2151.355 and 5139.05 and who wishes to get married must first obtain consent, as required by RC 3101.01 and Juv R 42, from one or both parents, from one of the alternative authorities named in RC 3101.01, or from the juvenile court as provided in Juv R 42(A). The youth services department has no authority to either consent or withhold consent to the marriage of a minor committed to its custody. OAG 89–046.

For purposes of a home furlough for a child committed to the legal custody of the youth services department for institutionalization under RC 2151.355(A)(4) or (5), said department may not allow the child to leave prior to the expiration of the minimum statutory commitment period without approval of the committing court pursuant to RC 2151.38(B); approval of the court is not required after expiration of that period and the department may allow the child to leave in accordance with RC 2151.38(C) and 5139.06. OAG 88–062.

For purposes of a home furlough for a child committed to the legal custody of the youth services department for institutionalization under RC 2151.355(A)(6), the department may not allow the child to leave before his attainment of the age of twenty-one years without approval of the committing court pursuant to RC 2151.38(B). OAG 88–062.

The Ohio youth commission may pursuant to RC 5139.281 adopt a rule requiring the separation of an adjudicated delinquent where extraordinary circumstances make such separation necessary for the care, treatment or training of such youth, or where necessary to insure the safety of that youth, or any other youth in the detention home. OAG 77–006.

1976 H 1196, eff. 8–9–76, does not operate to prohibit the commingling of pre-adjudicated and post-adjudicated youth confined in a district detention home. OAG 77–006.

Both the existing juvenile code and the juvenile rules require a hearing before a temporary commitment to the Ohio youth commission can be made permanent, which hearing requires the presence of the youth involved. OAG 72–071.

The placement or detention of delinquent, dependent, neglected children, or juvenile traffic offenders, is upon final disposition of the juvenile court and does not include placement in a detention home provided under RC 2151.34. 1963 OAG 553; overruled to the extent that it is inconsistent with OAG 80–101.

4. Education

A juvenile court is prohibited from placing a child under the legal custody of the youth services department in a specific school since the department, and not the court, has the right to determine where and with whom a juvenile should be placed; thus, a trial court's order requiring the youth services department to place a juvenile parole violator at a specific private, out-of-state school is erroneous. In re Sanders (Cuyahoga 1991) 72 Ohio App.3d 655, 595 N.E.2d 974, motion overruled 61 Ohio St.3d 1422, 574 N.E.2d 1093.

When a juvenile court commits a delinquent child to an out-of-state private residential facility pursuant to RC 2151.355, the cost of educating the child is paid with funds from the state subsidy provided in RC 2151.357; if such subsidy is insufficient, any remaining educational expense is to be paid by the court as provided in RC 2151.36. OAG 89–006.

5. Procedural issues

Magistrate lacked authority to suspend juvenile's right to obtain driver's license until his twenty-first birthday, upon juvenile's adjudication as delinquent, where juvenile was not sentenced to community control sanctions or adjudicated delinquent on basis of any statutorily enumerated offense. In re Spears (Ohio App. 5 Dist., Licking, 04-17-2006) No. 2005-CA-93, 2006-Ohio-1920, 2006 WL 1011201, Unreported. Infants 223.1

Trial court had statutory authority to sentence juvenile to state Department of Youth Services (DYS) following juvenile's admission to offenses of participation in a criminal gang and drug trafficking, because juvenile committed acts that would have been felonies of second and fourth degree if committed by adult. In re Harris (Ohio App. 10 Dist., Franklin, 05-15-2003) No. 02AP-1188, 2003-Ohio-2485, 2003 WL 21101271, Unreported. Infants 223.1

Extending juvenile's probation past specified date so that juvenile could complete sexual offender counseling was proper, even though state did not assert probation violation in motion to extend probation, where terms and conditions of probation required juvenile to serve probation until specified date or until conditions were completed, one condition was completion of sexual offender counseling, and probation officers, therapist, and juvenile's mother urged court to extend probation. In re Walker (Ohio App. 10 Dist., Franklin, 04-29-2003) No. 02AP-421, 2003-Ohio-2137, 2003 WL 1962419, Unreported, appeal not allowed 99 Ohio St.3d 1542, 795 N.E.2d 681, 2003-Ohio-4671. Infants 225

Juvenile's probation period did not expire on specified date, but continued until all conditions of his probation were completed, including completion of sexual offender counseling, where terms and conditions of probation required juvenile to serve probation until specified date or until conditions were completed and one condition was completion of sexual offender counseling. In re Walker (Ohio App. 10 Dist., Franklin, 04-29-2003) No. 02AP-421, 2003-Ohio-2137, 2003 WL 1962419, Unreported, appeal not allowed 99 Ohio St.3d 1542, 795 N.E.2d 681, 2003-Ohio-4671. Infants 225

Juvenile waived all but plain error in trial court's alleged failure to establish jurisdiction over him in delinquency proceeding, where juvenile did not raise that objection below. In re Ball (Ohio App. 3 Dist., Allen, 01-30-2003) No. 1-02-72, 2003-Ohio-395, 2003 WL 193519, Unreported. Infants 243

Trial court established proper jurisdiction in juvenile delinquency proceeding by eliciting testimony by subject of proceeding, at preliminary hearing, that he was 16 years old and by making a finding in judgment entry of commitment that subject of proceeding was born on a particular date and was therefore a juvenile. In re Ball (Ohio App. 3 Dist., Allen, 01-30-2003) No. 1-02-72, 2003-Ohio-395, 2003 WL 193519, Unreported. Infants 196

State had right to appeal from juvenile court's probable cause findings in mandatory-bindover hearing in delinquency adjudication proceedings. In re S.J. (Ohio, 07-13-2005) 106 Ohio St.3d 11, 829 N.E.2d 1207, 2005-Ohio-3215, on remand 2005-Ohio-6353, 2005 WL 3215227. Infants 68.8

State's filing of notice of appeal from juvenile court's probable-cause rulings in mandatory-bindover hearing divested juvenile court of any jurisdiction to proceed with delinquency adjudication during pendency of appeal. In re S.J. (Ohio, 07-13-2005) 106 Ohio St.3d 11, 829 N.E.2d 1207, 2005-Ohio-3215, on remand 2005-Ohio-6353, 2005 WL 3215227. Infants 68.8

Juvenile court lacks jurisdiction to proceed with an adjudication of a child as delinquent after a notice of appeal has been filed from an order of that court, as the adjudication of a child during the pendency of an appeal interferes with and is inconsistent with the jurisdiction of the appellate court. In re S.J. (Ohio, 07-13-2005) 106 Ohio St.3d 11, 829 N.E.2d 1207, 2005-Ohio-3215, on remand 2005-Ohio-6353, 2005 WL 3215227. Infants 244.1

Juvenile court, in imposing order of disposition on delinquent juvenile under statute allowing court to make further dispositional order if court found it be proper, is not restricted to imposing disposition prescribed under another statute within Juvenile Code. In re Jacobs (Ohio App. 3 Dist., 06-04-2002) 148 Ohio App.3d 173, 772 N.E.2d 671, 2002-Ohio-2844. Infants 223.1

Amended charge of acts constituting second-degree felonious assault by means of deadly weapon if committed by adult was not lesser included offense of original charge of third-degree attempted felonious assault, for purposes of amending the complaint after adjudicatory hearing in juvenile delinquency proceeding; second–degree felony adjudication carried longer minimum term of confinement for juvenile than third-degree felony adjudication, attempted felonious assault could be committed without felonious assault by means of deadly weapon also being committed, and attempted felonious assault did not contain deadly weapon element. In re Reed (Ohio App. 8 Dist., 01-17-2002) 147 Ohio App.3d 182, 769 N.E.2d 412, 2002-Ohio-43. Infants 197

Court has wide latitude in order of disposition that it may make with respect to child ultimately adjudicated delinquent; because purpose of maintaining juvenile court is different from that of criminal justice system for adults, juvenile court is given discretion to make any disposition that court finds proper. In re Bracewell (Ohio App. 1 Dist., 04-17-1998) 126 Ohio App.3d 133, 709 N.E.2d 938, dismissed, appeal not allowed 82 Ohio St.3d 1481, 696 N.E.2d 1087. Infants 223.1

Forfeiture proceedings are applicable to juveniles, and juvenile courts have jurisdiction to hear and decide forfeiture matters, in light of statute providing that forfeiture division should be liberally construed to give effect to legislative intent enacting division that forfeiture and contraband provisions apply to property possessed, or possessed and owned, by persons under 18 years of age in the same manner as those provisions apply to property possessed, or possessed and owned, by adults. In re Harman (Ohio Com.Pl., 03-11-1994) 63 Ohio Misc.2d 529, 635 N.E.2d 96. Forfeitures 1; Forfeitures 5

A prior adjudication of delinquency predicated on a theft offense constitutes a previous conviction of a theft offense for the purpose of determining disposition pursuant to RC 2151.355(A). In re Russell (Ohio 1984) 12 Ohio St.3d 304, 466 N.E.2d 553, 12 O.B.R. 377. Infants 223.1

The trial court exceeded its authority by attempting both to impose a fine and transfer the matter to another jurisdiction. In re Sekulich (Ohio

1981) 65 Ohio St.2d 13, 417 N.E.2d 1014, 19 O.O.3d 192. Infants 221; Infants 224

Where a court, having acquired jurisdiction over a child by virtue of a divorce action between the child's parents, certifies the matter of the child's custody to a juvenile court, the consent of the juvenile court having been first obtained, the juvenile court has exclusive jurisdiction over the child's custody by virtue of RC 3109.06 and RC 2151.23(D) and a finding of unfitness of the parents or that there is no suitable relative to have custody is not a necessary prerequisite to such certification, and while such certification shall be deemed to be the complaint in the juvenile court, it does not constitute a complaint in the juvenile court that such child is dependent or neglected and those dispositions provided for under RC 2151.353, RC 2151.354, and RC 2151.355 are not applicable to the disposition of such a child, disposition thereof being subject to and controlled by RC 3109.04. In re Height (Van Wert 1975) 47 Ohio App.2d 203, 353 N.E.2d 887, 1 O.O.3d 279.

The authority of the juvenile court under RC 2151.355(I) is limited to dispositions provided by other statutes. In re Cox (Mahoning 1973) 36 Ohio App.2d 65, 301 N.E.2d 907, 65 O.O.2d 51.

Where a child, as defined in RC 2151.011(B)(1), who has been adjudicated a delinquent beyond a reasonable doubt leaves the jurisdiction of the juvenile court so that such court cannot dispose of his case, the juvenile court has authority under RC 2151.355(I) to treat such person as an adult and to impose upon such person the penalty prescribed in the statute he violated and which constituted the basis for the adjudication of delinquency. In re Cox (Mahoning 1973) 36 Ohio App.2d 65, 301 N.E.2d 907, 65 O.O.2d 51. Infants 223.1

Juvenile had notice that good behavior requirement of his suspended commitment to Department of Youth Services (DYS) continued through age 21, even though probation period had ended; trial court conditioned suspension on both probation and a clear order, separate and apart from probation order, requiring juvenile to engage in good behavior through age of 21. In re Braun (Ohio App. 4 Dist., Washington, 06-07-2002) No. 01CA42, 2002-Ohio-3021, 2002 WL 1376182, Unreported. Infants 69(1)

A trial court errs in not giving a juvenile credit for time served after she pleads true to a charge of violating a prior order where the violation of a prior court order stems from a condition of probation and is not a separate criminal offense bringing with it a separate sentence and the only criminal charge against the juvenile is the original charge of arson. In re Dillard, Nos. 2001CA00093 and 2001CA00121, 2001 WL 1548758 (5th Dist Ct App, Stark, 12-3-01).

The juvenile court is without jurisdiction to order three consecutive commitments to the department of youth services as a result of three delinquent acts arising from the same operative facts. In re Caldwell, Nos. 94APF07-996+, 1995 WL 46199 (10th Dist Ct App, Franklin, 1-31-95), reversed by 76 Ohio St.3d 156 (1996).

Ordering a juvenile who has twice been adjudicated delinquent to serve a second indefinite term of commitment consecutive to a prior commitment order arising from distinct and unrelated offenses during a different time frame is within the discretion of a juvenile court pursuant to RC 2151.355. In re Hill, Nos. 14-93-7+, 1993 WL 291068 (3d Dist Ct App, Union, 7-7-93).

Pursuant to RC 2152.74(B)(3), a juvenile court must order the collection of a DNA specimen from a juvenile placed on some form of probation supervision pursuant to RC 2152.19(A)(4) on or after May 18, 2005. OAG 05-037.

If a juvenile court commits to the temporary custody of a public children services agency a child who has been adjudicated to be unruly or delinquent pursuant to RC 2151.354(A)(1) or RC 2152.19(A)(1), respectively, the duration of the temporary custody order is subject to the time limitations set forth in RC 2151.353(F) and RC 2151.415. OAG 03-004.

A juvenile court retains jurisdiction over a child who has been adjudicated to be unruly or delinquent until the child attains twenty-one years of age, and may continue to make dispositional orders with respect to the child until that time, regardless of whether the court's order of temporary custody has expired under the time limitations set forth in RC 2151.353(F) and RC 2151.415. OAG 03-004.

If a juvenile court, in making disposition of an unruly or delinquent child pursuant to RC 2151.354 or RC 2151.355, places the child into the temporary custody of the county department of human services in accordance with RC 2151.353 and the department provides services to that child, the county department of human services is required to develop and file with the court a case plan pursuant to RC 2151.412 and to hold semiannual reviews of the case plan pursuant to RC 2151.416. OAG 99-041.

If a juvenile court, in making disposition of an unruly or delinquent child pursuant to RC 2151.354 or RC 2151.355, places the child into the temporary custody of the county department of human services in accordance with RC 2151.353, the juvenile court is required to hold periodic reviews pursuant to RC 2151.417 and Juv R 36(A). OAG 99-041.

If a juvenile court schedules an early release hearing pursuant to RC 2151.38(B) after expiration of the applicable minimum period of institutionalization imposed under RC 2151.355(A)(4) to 2151.355(A)(6) and orders the youth services department to deliver the child for the hearing and to present a treatment plan for post-institutional care as described in RC 2151.38(B)(2)(c), the youth services department should raise the issue of lack of jurisdiction by motion in that proceeding. OAG 93-079.

When a runaway or delinquent juvenile is returned to Ohio from another state party to the interstate compact on juveniles, under RC 2151.56, Art IV(b) or Art V(b), the state of Ohio is responsible for payment of the return transportation costs, and the person or entity with legal custody of such juvenile is the party within the state which is responsible for the transportation costs of his return, unless the juvenile court, in its disposition of a delinquent juvenile under RC 2151.355(A), transferred the responsibility for the physical care and custody of the delinquent juvenile to another person or entity, which is then responsible for the payment of such costs. OAG 89-107.

6. Traffic offenses

A juvenile court's permanent revocation of a juvenile's driver's license is not authorized by statute following a determination of delinquency resulting from a vehicular homicide. In re Finlaw (Greene 1990) 69 Ohio App.3d 474, 590 N.E.2d 1340.

A juvenile court lacks jurisdiction under RC 2151.355 to revoke a juvenile delinquent's driver's license for life; however, RC 2151.355(A)(4) grants the authority to impose institutionalization to age twenty-one and, therefore, probation with conditions, such as the revocation of the juvenile's driver's license to age twenty-one, in lieu of institutionalization, would be proper. In re Weber (Cuyahoga 1989) 61 Ohio App.3d 636, 573 N.E.2d 730.

The driving privileges of a juvenile adjudicated delinquent due to an admission of aggravated vehicular homicide while under the influence of alcohol may not be permanently revoked, as an adjudication of delinquency is not a conviction as required by RC 4507.16(D). In re Finlaw, No. 89-CA-0078 (2d Dist Ct App, Greene, 9-20-90).

7. Drug offenses

A juvenile court does not have the jurisdiction to reimpose a suspended commitment to a Department of Youth Services facility after a juvenile has been released from probation. In re Cross (Ohio, 09-11-2002) 96 Ohio St.3d 328, 774 N.E.2d 258, 2002-Ohio-4183. Infants 225

Evidence that juvenile passenger in car stopped by police used alias upon being questioned, which was sole admissible evidence of guilt presented in delinquency adjudication proceeding, was insufficient to convince reasonable trier of fact, beyond reasonable doubt, that juvenile knowingly exercised dominion and control over cocaine found in purse of adult passenger, as required to support juvenile's adjudication as delinquent by reason of acts which would, if committed by adult, constituted felony drug abuse; only evidence that juvenile exerted actual control over purse at any time was improperly admitted hearsay. In re Carter (Ohio App. 4 Dist., 11-06-1997) 123 Ohio App.3d 532, 704 N.E.2d 625. Infants 176

Where a juvenile is adjudicated delinquent for drug trafficking, the car used in the offense is not subject to forfeiture under RC 2933.41 because a juvenile is incapable of committing a felony. In re Forfeiture of 1979 Mazda (Wayne 1989) 48 Ohio App.3d 51, 547 N.E.2d 1238.

Where a juvenile is adjudged delinquent for possession of marijuana and drug paraphernalia and his father admits to using and intending to continue using marijuana, the court may order the father to undergo urinalysis as a condition of the juvenile sentence. In re Dague, No. 87-CA-12 (5th Dist Ct App, Delaware, 10-22-87).

8. Adult facilities

Juvenile court's error in placing juvenile in county jail pending trial for alleged violation of parole was not prejudicial and thus did not warrant reversal. In re Raypole (Ohio App. 12 Dist., Fayette, 03-10-2003) No. CA2002-01-001, No. CA2002-01-002, 2003-Ohio-1066, 2003 WL 928976, Unreported. Infants 253

Juvenile who was 17 years of age at time he committed vehicular manslaughter forming basis of his adjudication, but was to turn 18 years old 38 days into his 90–day confinement was statutory "child" for purposes of disposition or sentencing, and court was limited to dispositional alternatives available in sentencing juveniles. In re Hennessey (Ohio App. 3 Dist., 09-13-2001) 146 Ohio App.3d 743, 768 N.E.2d 663, 2001-Ohio-2267, appeal not allowed 94 Ohio St.3d 1431, 761 N.E.2d 47. Infants ⚖ 223.1

After a child is adjudicated delinquent, a trial court may choose from the statutory dispositions when sentencing, which include imposing a period of confinement, but is expressly precluded from placing the child in any state correctional institution, county, multicounty, or municipal jail or workhouse, or other place in which an adult convicted of a crime, under arrest, or charged with a crime is held. In re Hennessey (Ohio App. 3 Dist., 09-13-2001) 146 Ohio App.3d 743, 768 N.E.2d 663, 2001-Ohio-2267, appeal not allowed 94 Ohio St.3d 1431, 761 N.E.2d 47. Infants ⚖ 223.1

Delinquent children may not be housed in any adult facility. In re Hennessey (Ohio App. 3 Dist., 09-13-2001) 146 Ohio App.3d 743, 768 N.E.2d 663, 2001-Ohio-2267, appeal not allowed 94 Ohio St.3d 1431, 761 N.E.2d 47. Infants ⚖ 223.1

Juvenile court's wide latitude to make "any further disposition that the court finds proper" with respect to a delinquent child, or to order a commitment to "any other suitable place designated by the court," does not include placement in an adult county jail; the plain language of the applicable statutes prohibits the court from ordering a delinquent child to serve any time in the county jail even though he is chronologically an adult. In re Hennessey (Ohio App. 3 Dist., 09-13-2001) 146 Ohio App.3d 743, 768 N.E.2d 663, 2001-Ohio-2267, appeal not allowed 94 Ohio St.3d 1431, 761 N.E.2d 47. Infants ⚖ 223.1

Juvenile court was without authority to commit juvenile to adult facility as part of his disposition, where juvenile was 17 years of age at time he committed vehicular manslaughter forming basis of his adjudication, but was to turn 18 years old 38 days into his 90–day confinement. In re Hennessey (Ohio App. 3 Dist., 09-13-2001) 146 Ohio App.3d 743, 768 N.E.2d 663, 2001-Ohio-2267, appeal not allowed 94 Ohio St.3d 1431, 761 N.E.2d 47. Infants ⚖ 223.1

A juvenile court has no jurisdiction to rule on a delinquency complaint alleging rape where the complaint is filed after the alleged delinquent has reached the age of twenty-one, even though the fact that the alleged offense was committed before the juvenile's fifteenth birthday precludes the relinquishment of jurisdiction to an adult court. In re C. (Ohio Com.Pl. 1991) 61 Ohio Misc.2d 610, 580 N.E.2d 1182.

RC 2151.355(A)(9) does not authorize the juvenile court to exercise unlimited discretion in sentencing a delinquent child, and there is no authority for it to commit a delinquent juvenile to a jail for adult offenders, absent a finding that housing in an appropriate juvenile facility is unavailable, or that the public safety and protection so require. State v. Grady (Cuyahoga 1981) 3 Ohio App.3d 174, 444 N.E.2d 51, 3 O.B.R. 199.

Juveniles adjudicated as delinquent for commission of act which if committed by adult would be felony may be committed by court to custody of department of mental hygiene and correction for purpose of training and rehabilitation only, in which case custody of such juveniles must be completely separate and apart from and free of any contact with adult convicts, but if such custody of such juveniles is, in fact, not for training and rehabilitation or is a commingling with adult convicts, such defalcation is administrative matter and should not invalidate nor affect an otherwise valid commitment or power to commit. In re Tsesmilles (Columbiana 1970) 24 Ohio App.2d 153, 265 N.E.2d 308, 53 O.O.2d 363.

The commitment of a juvenile to the Ohio state reformatory by a juvenile court under the provisions of former 2151.35(E) is prejudicially erroneous where the evidence fails to establish that the acts committed by the juvenile were such that they would constitute a felony if committed by an adult. In re Baker (Ohio 1969) 20 Ohio St.2d 142, 254 N.E.2d 363, 49 O.O.2d 473.

A juvenile court is without authority to order a delinquent child to serve a term of incarceration in an adult correctional facility or to place him on adult probation even though he is chronologically an adult when "sentenced" and was sixteen when the incidents giving rise to the complaint took place. In re Campbell, No. 96-L-133, 1997 WL 401546 (11th Dist Ct App, Lake, 6-27-97).

Judge of juvenile court may not commit child who has been found to be delinquent child, or juvenile traffic offender, to county jail upon failure, refusal, or inability of such child to pay fine and court costs. OAG 70–143.

2152.191 Application of certain sections of Revised Code to child adjudicated a delinquent child for committing sexually oriented offense

If a child is adjudicated a delinquent child for committing a sexually oriented offense that is not a registration-exempt sexually oriented offense or for committing a child-victim oriented offense, if the child is fourteen years of age or older at the time of committing the offense, and if the child committed the offense on or after January 1, 2002, both of the following apply:

(A) Sections 2152.82 to 2152.85 and Chapter 2950. of the Revised Code apply to the child and the adjudication.

(B) In addition to any order of disposition it makes of the child under this chapter, the court may make any determination, adjudication, or order authorized under sections 2152.82 to 2152.85 and Chapter 2950. of the Revised Code and shall make any determination, adjudication, or order required under those sections and that chapter.

(2003 S 5, eff. 7–31–03; 2001 S 3, eff. 1–1–02)

Historical and Statutory Notes

Amendment Note: 2003 S 5 inserted "that is not a registration-exempt sexually oriented offense or for committing a child-victim oriented offense" and substituted "January 1, 2002, both" for "the effective date of this section, all" in the first paragraph.

Library References

Infants ⚖ 227(2).
Westlaw Topic No. 211.
C.J.S. Infants §§ 41, 53 to 54, 57, 69 to 85.

Research References

Encyclopedias

OH Jur. 3d Family Law § 1698.6, Sexually Oriented and Child-Victim Offenses; Registration.

Treatises and Practice Aids

Katz, Giannelli, Blair and Lipton, Baldwin's Ohio Practice, Criminal Law, § 121:4, Sexual Offender Classification Hearing.

Giannelli & Yeomans, Ohio Juvenile Law § 6:1, Introduction.

2152.192 Court or child welfare agency to notify institution or association of adjudication of child as delinquent for committing sexually oriented offense

If a court or child welfare agency places a delinquent child in an institution or association, as defined in section 5103.02 of the Revised Code, that is certified by the department of job and family services pursuant to section 5103.03 of the Revised Code and if that child has been adjudicated delinquent for committing an act that is a sexually oriented offense in either a prior delinquency adjudication or in the most recent delinquency adjudication, the court or child welfare agency shall notify the operator of the institution or association and the sheriff of the county in which the institution or association is located that the child has been adjudicated delinquent for committing an act that is a sexually oriented offense.

(2006 H 95, eff. 8–3–06)

2152.20 Fines; costs; restitution; forfeitures

Note: See also following version of this section, eff. 7-1-07.

(A) If a child is adjudicated a delinquent child or a juvenile traffic offender, the court may order any of the following dispositions, in addition to any other disposition authorized or required by this chapter:

(1) Impose a fine in accordance with the following schedule:

(a) For an act that would be a minor misdemeanor or an unclassified misdemeanor if committed by an adult, a fine not to exceed fifty dollars;

(b) For an act that would be a misdemeanor of the fourth degree if committed by an adult, a fine not to exceed one hundred dollars;

(c) For an act that would be a misdemeanor of the third degree if committed by an adult, a fine not to exceed one hundred fifty dollars;

(d) For an act that would be a misdemeanor of the second degree if committed by an adult, a fine not to exceed two hundred dollars;

(e) For an act that would be a misdemeanor of the first degree if committed by an adult, a fine not to exceed two hundred fifty dollars;

(f) For an act that would be a felony of the fifth degree or an unclassified felony if committed by an adult, a fine not to exceed three hundred dollars;

(g) For an act that would be a felony of the fourth degree if committed by an adult, a fine not to exceed four hundred dollars;

(h) For an act that would be a felony of the third degree if committed by an adult, a fine not to exceed seven hundred fifty dollars;

(i) For an act that would be a felony of the second degree if committed by an adult, a fine not to exceed one thousand dollars;

(j) For an act that would be a felony of the first degree if committed by an adult, a fine not to exceed one thousand five hundred dollars;

(k) For an act that would be aggravated murder or murder if committed by an adult, a fine not to exceed two thousand dollars.

(2) Require the child to pay costs;

(3) Unless the child's delinquent act or juvenile traffic offense would be a minor misdemeanor if committed by an adult or could be disposed of by the juvenile traffic violations bureau serving the court under Traffic Rule 13.1 if the court has established a juvenile traffic violations bureau, require the child to make restitution to the victim of the child's delinquent act or juvenile traffic offense or, if the victim is deceased, to a survivor of the victim in an amount based upon the victim's economic loss caused by or related to the delinquent act or juvenile traffic offense. The court may not require a child to make restitution pursuant to this division if the child's delinquent act or juvenile traffic offense would be a minor misdemeanor if committed by an adult or could be disposed of by the juvenile traffic violations bureau serving the court under Traffic Rule 13.1 if the court has established a juvenile traffic violations bureau. If the court requires restitution under this division, the restitution shall be made directly to the victim in open court or to the probation department that serves the jurisdiction or the clerk of courts on behalf of the victim.

If the court requires restitution under this division, the restitution may be in the form of a cash reimbursement paid in a lump sum or in installments, the performance of repair work to restore any damaged property to its original condition, the performance of a reasonable amount of labor for the victim or survivor of the victim, the performance of community service work, any other form of restitution devised by the court, or any combination of the previously described forms of restitution.

If the court requires restitution under this division, the court may base the restitution order on an amount recommended by the victim or survivor of the victim, the delinquent child, the juvenile traffic offender, a presentence investigation report, estimates or receipts indicating the cost of repairing or replacing property, and any other information, provided that the amount the court orders as restitution shall not exceed the amount of the economic loss suffered by the victim as a direct and proximate result of the delinquent act or juvenile traffic offense. If the court decides to order restitution under this division and the amount of the restitution is disputed by the victim or survivor or by the delinquent child or juvenile traffic offender, the court shall hold a hearing on the restitution. If the court requires restitution under this division, the court shall determine, or order the determination of, the amount of restitution to be paid by the delinquent child or juvenile traffic offender. All restitution payments shall be credited against any recovery of economic loss in a civil action brought by or on behalf of the victim against the delinquent child or juvenile traffic offender or the delinquent child's or juvenile traffic offender's parent, guardian, or other custodian.

If the court requires restitution under this division, the court may order that the delinquent child or juvenile traffic offender pay a surcharge, in an amount not exceeding five per cent of the amount of restitution otherwise ordered under this division, to the entity responsible for collecting and processing the restitution payments.

The victim or the survivor of the victim may request that the prosecuting authority file a motion, or the delinquent child or juvenile traffic offender may file a motion, for modification of the payment terms of any restitution ordered under this division. If the court grants the motion, it may modify the payment terms as it determines appropriate.

(4) Require the child to reimburse any or all of the costs incurred for services or sanctions provided or imposed, including, but not limited to, the following:

(a) All or part of the costs of implementing any community control imposed as a disposition under section 2152.19 of the Revised Code, including a supervision fee;

(b) All or part of the costs of confinement in a residential facility described in section 2152.19 of the Revised Code or in a department of youth services institution, including, but not limited to, a per diem fee for room and board, the costs of medical and dental treatment provided, and the costs of repairing property the delinquent child damaged while so confined. The amount of reimbursement ordered for a child under this division shall not exceed the total amount of reimbursement the child is able to pay as determined at a hearing and shall not exceed the actual cost of the confinement. The court may collect any reimbursement ordered under this division. If the court does not order reimbursement under this division, confinement costs may be assessed pursuant to a repayment policy adopted under section 2929.37 of the Revised Code and division (D) of section 307.93, division (A) of section 341.19, division (C) of section 341.23 or 753.16, division (C) of section 2301.56, or division (B) of section 341.14, 753.02, 753.04, or 2947.19 of the Revised Code.

(B)(1) If a child is adjudicated a delinquent child for violating section 2923.32 of the Revised Code, the court shall enter an order of criminal forfeiture against the child in accordance with divisions (B)(3), (4), (5), and (6) and (C) to (F) of section 2923.32 of the Revised Code.

(2) Sections 2925.41 to 2925.45 of the Revised Code apply to children who are adjudicated or could be adjudicated by a juvenile court to be delinquent children for an act that, if committed by an adult, would be a felony drug abuse offense. Subject to division (B) of section 2925.42 and division (E) of section 2925.43 of the Revised Code, a delinquent child of that nature loses any right to the possession of, and forfeits to the state any right, title, and interest that the delinquent child may have in, property as defined in section 2925.41 of the Revised Code and further described in section 2925.42 or 2925.43 of the Revised Code.

(3) Sections 2923.44 to 2923.47 of the Revised Code apply to children who are adjudicated or could be adjudicated by a juvenile court to be delinquent children for an act in violation of section 2923.42 of the Revised Code. Subject to division (B) of section 2923.44 and division (E) of section 2923. 45 of the Revised Code, a delinquent child of that nature loses any right to the possession of, and forfeits to the state any right, title, and interest that the delinquent child may have in, property as defined in section 2923.41 of the Revised Code and further described in section 2923.44 or 2923. 45 of the Revised Code.

(C) The court may hold a hearing if necessary to determine whether a child is able to pay a sanction under this section.

(D) If a child who is adjudicated a delinquent child is indigent, the court shall consider imposing a term of community service under division (A) of section 2152.19 of the Revised Code in lieu of imposing a financial sanction under this section. If a child who is adjudicated a delinquent child is not indigent, the court may impose a term of community service under that division in lieu of, or in addition to, imposing a financial sanction under this section. The court may order community service for an act that if committed by an adult would be a minor misdemeanor.

If a child fails to pay a financial sanction imposed under this section, the court may impose a term of community service in lieu of the sanction.

(E) The clerk of the court, or another person authorized by law or by the court to collect a financial sanction imposed under this section, may do any of the following:

(1) Enter into contracts with one or more public agencies or private vendors for the collection of the amounts due under the financial sanction, which amounts may include interest from the date of imposition of the financial sanction;

(2) Permit payment of all, or any portion of, the financial sanction in installments, by credit or debit card, by another type of electronic transfer, or by any other reasonable method, within any period of time, and on any terms that the court considers just, except that the maximum time permitted for payment shall not exceed five years. The clerk may pay any fee associated with processing an electronic transfer out of public money and may charge the fee to the delinquent child.

(3) To defray administrative costs, charge a reasonable fee to a child who elects a payment plan rather than a lump sum payment of a financial sanction.

(2006 H 162, eff. 10-12-06; 2004 H 52, eff. 6-1-04; 2002 H 490, eff. 1-1-04; 2002 H 170, eff. 9-6-02; 2000 S 179, § 3, eff. 1-1-02)

Note: See also following version of this section, eff. 7-1-07.

2152.20 Fines; costs; restitution; forfeitures (later effective date)

Note: See also preceding version of this section in effect until 7-1-07.

(A) If a child is adjudicated a delinquent child or a juvenile traffic offender, the court may order any of the following dispositions, in addition to any other disposition authorized or required by this chapter:

(1) Impose a fine in accordance with the following schedule:

(a) For an act that would be a minor misdemeanor or an unclassified misdemeanor if committed by an adult, a fine not to exceed fifty dollars;

(b) For an act that would be a misdemeanor of the fourth degree if committed by an adult, a fine not to exceed one hundred dollars;

(c) For an act that would be a misdemeanor of the third degree if committed by an adult, a fine not to exceed one hundred fifty dollars;

(d) For an act that would be a misdemeanor of the second degree if committed by an adult, a fine not to exceed two hundred dollars;

(e) For an act that would be a misdemeanor of the first degree if committed by an adult, a fine not to exceed two hundred fifty dollars;

(f) For an act that would be a felony of the fifth degree or an unclassified felony if committed by an adult, a fine not to exceed three hundred dollars;

(g) For an act that would be a felony of the fourth degree if committed by an adult, a fine not to exceed four hundred dollars;

(h) For an act that would be a felony of the third degree if committed by an adult, a fine not to exceed seven hundred fifty dollars;

(i) For an act that would be a felony of the second degree if committed by an adult, a fine not to exceed one thousand dollars;

(j) For an act that would be a felony of the first degree if committed by an adult, a fine not to exceed one thousand five hundred dollars;

(k) For an act that would be aggravated murder or murder if committed by an adult, a fine not to exceed two thousand dollars.

(2) Require the child to pay costs;

(3) Unless the child's delinquent act or juvenile traffic offense would be a minor misdemeanor if committed by an adult or could be disposed of by the juvenile traffic violations bureau serving the court under Traffic Rule 13.1 if the court has established a juvenile traffic violations bureau, require the child to make restitution to the victim of the child's delinquent act or juvenile traffic offense or, if the victim is deceased, to a survivor of the victim in an amount based upon the victim's economic loss caused by or related to the delinquent act or juvenile traffic offense. The court may not require a child to make restitution pursuant to this division if the child's delinquent act or juvenile traffic offense would be a minor misdemeanor if committed by an adult or could be disposed of by the juvenile traffic violations bureau serving the court under Traffic Rule 13.1 if the court has established a juvenile traffic violations bureau. If the court requires restitution under this division, the restitution shall be made directly to the victim in open court or to the probation department that serves the jurisdiction or the clerk of courts on behalf of the victim.

If the court requires restitution under this division, the restitution may be in the form of a cash reimbursement paid in a lump sum or in installments, the performance of repair work to restore any damaged property to its original condition, the performance of a reasonable amount of labor for the victim or survivor of the victim, the performance of community service work, any other form of restitution devised by the court, or any combination of the previously described forms of restitution.

If the court requires restitution under this division, the court may base the restitution order on an amount recommended by the victim or survivor of the victim, the delinquent child, the juvenile traffic offender, a presentence investigation report, estimates or receipts indicating the cost of repairing or replacing property, and any other information, provided that the amount the court orders as restitution shall not exceed the amount of the economic loss suffered by the victim as a direct and proximate result of the delinquent act or juvenile traffic offense. If the court decides to order restitution under this division and the amount of the restitution is disputed by the victim or survivor or by the delinquent child or juvenile traffic offender, the court shall hold a hearing on the restitution. If the court requires restitution under this division, the court shall determine, or order the determination of, the amount of restitution to be paid by the delinquent child or juvenile traffic offender. All restitution payments shall be credited against any recovery of economic loss in a civil action brought by or on behalf of the victim against the delinquent child or juvenile traffic offender or the delinquent child's or juvenile traffic offender's parent, guardian, or other custodian.

If the court requires restitution under this division, the court may order that the delinquent child or juvenile traffic offender pay a surcharge, in an amount not exceeding five per cent of the amount of restitution otherwise ordered under this division, to the entity responsible for collecting and processing the restitution payments.

The victim or the survivor of the victim may request that the prosecuting authority file a motion, or the delinquent child or juvenile traffic offender may file a motion, for modification of the payment terms of any restitution ordered under this division. If the court grants the motion, it may modify the payment terms as it determines appropriate.

(4) Require the child to reimburse any or all of the costs incurred for services or sanctions provided or imposed, including, but not limited to, the following:

(a) All or part of the costs of implementing any community control imposed as a disposition under section 2152.19 of the Revised Code, including a supervision fee;

(b) All or part of the costs of confinement in a residential facility described in section 2152.19 of the Revised Code or in a department of youth services institution, including, but not limited to, a per diem fee for room and board, the costs of medical and dental treatment provided, and the costs of repairing property the delinquent child damaged while so confined. The amount of reimbursement ordered for a child under this division shall not exceed the total amount of reimbursement the child is able to pay as determined at a hearing and shall not exceed the actual cost of the confinement. The court may collect any reimbursement ordered under this division. If the court does not order reimbursement under this division, confinement costs may be assessed pursuant to a repayment policy adopted under section 2929.37 of the Revised Code and division (D) of section 307.93, division (A) of section 341.19, division (C) of section 341.23 or 753.16, division (C) of section 2301.56, or division (B) of section 341.14, 753.02, 753.04, or 2947.19 of the Revised Code.

(B) Chapter 2981. of the Revised Code applies to a child who is adjudicated a delinquent child for violating section 2923.32 or 2923.42 of the Revised Code or for committing an act that, if committed by an adult, would be a felony drug abuse offense.

(3) Sections 2923.44 to 2923.47 of the Revised Code apply to children who are adjudicated or could be adjudicated by a juvenile court to be delinquent children for an act in violation of section 2923.42 of the Revised Code. Subject to division (B) of section 2923.44 and division (E) of section 2923.45 of the Revised Code, a delinquent child of that nature loses any right to the possession of, and forfeits to the state any right, title, and interest that the delinquent child may have in, property as defined in section 2923.41 of the Revised Code and further described in section 2923.44 or 2923.45 of the Revised Code.

(C) The court may hold a hearing if necessary to determine whether a child is able to pay a sanction under this section.

(D) If a child who is adjudicated a delinquent child is indigent, the court shall consider imposing a term of community service under division (A) of section 2152.19 of the Revised Code in lieu of imposing a financial sanction under this section. If a child who is adjudicated a delinquent child is not indigent, the court may impose a term of community service under that division in lieu of, or in addition to, imposing a financial sanction under this section. The court may order community service for an act that if committed by an adult would be a minor misdemeanor.

If a child fails to pay a financial sanction imposed under this section, the court may impose a term of community service in lieu of the sanction.

(E) The clerk of the court, or another person authorized by law or by the court to collect a financial sanction imposed under this section, may do any of the following:

(1) Enter into contracts with one or more public agencies or private vendors for the collection of the amounts due under the financial sanction, which amounts may include interest from the date of imposition of the financial sanction;

(2) Permit payment of all, or any portion of, the financial sanction in installments, by credit or debit card, by another type of electronic transfer, or by any other reasonable method, within any period of time, and on any terms that the court considers just, except that the maximum time permitted for payment shall not exceed five years. The clerk may pay any fee associated with processing an electronic transfer out of public money and may charge the fee to the delinquent child.

(3) To defray administrative costs, charge a reasonable fee to a child who elects a payment plan rather than a lump sum payment of a financial sanction.

(2006 H 241, eff. 7–1–07; 2006 H 162, eff. 10–12–06; 2004 H 52, eff. 6–1–04; 2002 H 490, eff. 1–1–04; 2002 H 170, eff. 9–6–02; 2000 S 179, § 3, eff. 1–1–02)

Note: See also preceding version of this section in effect until 7-1-07.

Historical and Statutory Notes

Ed. Note: 2152.18, 2152.19 and 2152.20 contain provisions analogous to former 2151.355, repealed by 2000 S 179, § 4, eff. 1–1–02.

Amendment Note: 2006 H 162 inserted "division (C) of section 2301.56," after "753.16," and deleted "2301.56" after "753.04," in the last sentence of division (A)(4)(b).

Amendment Note: 2004 H 52 rewrote division (A)(3), which prior thereto read:

"(3) Require the child to make restitution to the victim of the child's delinquent act or, if the victim is deceased, to a survivor of the victim in an amount based upon the victim's economic loss caused by or related to the delinquent act. Restitution required under this division shall be made directly to the victim in open court or to the probation department that serves the jurisdiction or the clerk of courts on behalf of the victim. The restitution may include reimbursement to third parties, other than the delinquent child's insurer, for amounts paid to the victim or to any survivor of the victim for economic loss resulting from the delinquent act. If reimbursement to a third party is required, the reimbursement shall be made to any governmental agency to repay any amounts the agency paid to the victim or any survivor of the victim before any reimbursement is made to any other person.

"Restitution required under this division may be in the form of a cash reimbursement paid in a lump sum or in installments, the performance of repair work to restore any damaged property to its original condition, the performance of a reasonable amount of labor for the victim or survivor of the victim, the performance of community service work, any other form of restitution devised by the court, or any combination of the previously described forms of restitution.

"The court may base the restitution order under this division on an amount recommended by the victim or survivor of the victim, the delinquent child, a presentence investigation report, estimates or receipts indicating the cost of repairing or replacing property, and any other information. If the amount of the restitution is disputed by the victim or survivor or by the delinquent child, the court shall hold a hearing on the restitution. The court shall determine, or order the determination of, the amount of restitution to be paid by the delinquent child. All restitution payments shall be credited against any recovery of economic loss in a civil action brought by or on behalf of the victim against the delinquent child or the delinquent child's parent, guardian, or other custodian.

"The court may order that the delinquent child pay a surcharge, in an amount not exceeding five per cent of the amount of restitution otherwise ordered under this division, to the entity responsible for collecting and processing the restitution payments.

"The victim or the survivor of the victim may request that the prosecuting authority file a motion, or the delinquent child may file a motion, for modification of the payment terms of any restitution ordered under this division. If the court grants the motion, it may modify the payment terms as it determines appropriate."

Amendment Note: 2002 H 490 rewrote the fifth paragraph of division (A)((3), which prior thereto read:

"The victim or the survivor of the victim may request that the prosecuting authority file a motion, or the delinquent child may file a motion, for modification of the payment terms of any restitution ordered under this division, based on a substantial change in the delinquent child's ability to pay."

Amendment Note: 2002 H 170 rewrote the last sentence of division (A)(4)(b), which prior thereto read:

"If the court does not order reimbursement under this division, confinement costs may be assessed pursuant to a repayment policy adopted under division (E) of section 307.93, division (A) of section 341.06, division (C) of section 341.23, or division (C) of section 753.02, 753.04, 2301.56, or 2947.19 of the Revised Code."

Cross References

Victim impact statement, presentence investigation report, 2930.13

Library References

Automobiles ⟐359.
Costs ⟐304.
Infants ⟐69(1), 212, 224.
Westlaw Topic Nos. 102, 211, 48A.
C.J.S. Infants §§ 57, 69 to 85, 198, 206 to 209.
C.J.S. Motor Vehicles §§ 1336, 1352, 1380, 1414 to 1419, 1442, 1451 to 1452, 1484, 1486 to 1487, 1503, 1510, 1523, 1526, 1539, 1543 to 1544, 1546 to 1547, 1550.

Research References

Encyclopedias

OH Jur. 3d Family Law § 1547, Juvenile Traffic Offenders.
OH Jur. 3d Family Law § 1548, Juvenile Traffic Offenders—Orders of Disposition.
OH Jur. 3d Family Law § 1689, Juvenile Traffic Offender.
OH Jur. 3d Family Law § 1706, Modification or Vacation of Order.

Treatises and Practice Aids

Carlin, Baldwin's Ohio Practice, Merrick-Rippner Probate Law § 107:91, Disposition of Delinquent Children—Financial Sanctions, Effective January 1, 2002.
Carlin, Baldwin's Ohio Practice, Merrick-Rippner Probate Law § 107:102, Serious Youthful Offenders, Effective January 1, 2002.
Carlin, Baldwin's Ohio Practice, Merrick-Rippner Probate Law § 107:107, Disposition of Juvenile Traffic Offender—Permissive.
Carlin, Baldwin's Ohio Practice, Merrick-Rippner Probate Law § 107:130, Forfeiture Proceedings.
Painter, Ohio Driving Under the Influence § 12:46, Juvenile and "Underage" Offenders—Juvenile Offender.
Giannelli & Yeomans, Ohio Juvenile Law § 5:8, Discretionary Syo Dispositions.
Giannelli & Yeomans, Ohio Juvenile Law § 27:1, Introduction.
Giannelli & Yeomans, Ohio Juvenile Law § 27:8, Probation.
Giannelli & Yeomans, Ohio Juvenile Law § 28:3, Financial Sanctions.
Giannelli & Yeomans, Ohio Juvenile Law § 28:5, Restitution.
Giannelli & Yeomans, Ohio Juvenile Law § 32:3, Responsibilities to Victims and Others.
Giannelli & Yeomans, Ohio Juvenile Law § 27:12, Fines.
Giannelli & Yeomans, Ohio Juvenile Law § 27:13, Restitution.
Giannelli & Yeomans, Ohio Juvenile Law § 27:14, Forfeiture.
Giannelli & Yeomans, Ohio Juvenile Law § 27:15, Costs & Reimbursements.

Law Review and Journal Commentaries

In Favor of 'Trina's Law': A Proposal to Allow Crime Victims in Ohio to Use the Criminal Convictions of the Perpetrators as Collateral Estoppel in Subsequent Civil Cases. The Center for Law and Justice at the University of Cincinnati College of Law, 32 Cap U L Rev 351 (Winter 2003).

Notes of Decisions

Ed. Note: This section contains annotations from former RC 2151.355.

Appeals, restitution 1
Attorney fee reimbursement 6
Constitutional issues 7
Exclusions, restitution 2
Medical bills, restitution 3
Procedural issues 4
Restitution 1-3
    Appeals 1
    Exclusions 2
    Medical bills 3
Valuation of loss 5

1. Restitution—Appeals

Juvenile court restitution order requiring juvenile, who was adjudicated delinquent after admission to complaint alleging vehicular homicide, to pay for victim's funeral expenses was within court's discretion under statute allowing court to make further dispositional order if court found it be proper, although statute concerning dispositional orders specifically provided for restitution only in case of theft. In re Jacobs (Ohio App. 3 Dist., 06-04-2002) 148 Ohio App.3d 173, 772 N.E.2d 671, 2002-Ohio-2844. Infants ⟐ 224

Even if juvenile court, in imposing order of disposition on delinquent juvenile under statute allowing court to make further dispositional order if court found it be proper, was required to impose disposition prescribed by another statute, court satisfied that requirement in ordering juvenile, who admitted to complaint alleging vehicular homicide, to pay victim's funeral expenses, since disposition fell within statute requiring juvenile traffic offenders to make restitution for damages caused by juvenile. In re Jacobs (Ohio App. 3 Dist., 06-04-2002) 148 Ohio App.3d 173, 772 N.E.2d 671, 2002-Ohio-2844. Infants ⟐ 224

Juvenile court properly ordered delinquent juvenile, who admitted to complaint alleging vehicular homicide, to pay victim's funeral expenses as restitution as part of disposition, although juvenile contended that his compliance with statute requiring carrying of automobile insurance discharged his obligation for funeral expenses; juvenile court ordered reimbursement in order to rehabilitate juvenile and make juvenile accept personal responsibility for loss to victim's family. In re Jacobs (Ohio App. 3 Dist., 06-04-2002) 148 Ohio App.3d 173, 772 N.E.2d 671, 2002-Ohio-2844. Infants ⟐ 224

An order of the juvenile court which overrules the child's objections to the referee's report but defers the issue of restitution for a later time without specifying the amount of restitution or the method of payment is not a final appealable order pursuant to RC 2505.02. In re Holmes (Hamilton 1980) 70 Ohio App.2d 75, 434 N.E.2d 747, 24 O.O.3d 93. Infants ⟐ 242

2. —— Exclusions, restitution

Public policy embodied by Ohio Juvenile Code was not violated by interpreting criminal acts exclusion in homeowners' policy to bar liability coverage for wrongful death action against insureds' minor son arising out of incident in which decedent fell into river and drowned after son struck him because son had been adjudicated delinquent based on committing offense of involuntary manslaughter. Allstate Ins. Co. v. Cutcher (N.D.Ohio, 01-29-1996) 920 F.Supp. 796, affirmed 114 F.3d 1186. Insurance ⟐ 2278(4)

Under Ohio law, criminal acts exclusion in homeowners' policy barred liability coverage for wrongful death action against insureds' minor son arising out of incident in which decedent fell into river and drowned after son struck him, where son had been adjudicated delinquent based on committing offense of involuntary manslaughter, notwithstanding that adjudication of delinquency is not criminal conviction. Allstate Ins. Co. v. Cutcher (N.D.Ohio, 01-29-1996) 920 F.Supp. 796, affirmed 114 F.3d 1186. Insurance ⟐ 2278(4)

An award made to a victim of crime is exempt under RC 2743.66(D) from a restitution order issued pursuant to RC 2151.355. In re Wood, No. 9–84–44 (3d Dist Ct App, Marion, 4–14–86).

RC Ch 4109, governing the employment of minors, is applicable to all arrangements under which minors are employed to provide other persons with services, including cadet firefighting programs and juvenile court restitution orders, whether or not compensation is paid for such services, except to the extent such arrangements come within the exceptions set forth in RC 4109.06. OAG 87–104.

3. —— Medical bills, restitution

Although RC 2151.355 specifically provides only for restitution for property damage and theft, a juvenile court may order a delinquent to make restitution in the amount of the medical expenses incurred by an assault victim, as the language of RC 2155.355(A)(10) is broad enough to encompass such an order. In re Lambert (Lawrence 1989) 63 Ohio App.3d 121, 577 N.E.2d 1184.

Statutory authority "to make any disposition that the court finds proper" authorizes a juvenile court to order restitution of medical bills to the victim by a juvenile offender. In re Branham (Ohio App. 2 Dist., Clark, 03-29-2002) No. 2001-CA-56, 2002-Ohio-1797, 2002 WL 471830, Unreported. Infants 224

4. Procedural issues

Remand was required, on appeal from imposition of court costs and restitution in delinquency adjudication proceedings, to permit juvenile court to consider imposition of community service in lieu of financial sanctions, where juvenile was not advised that he could be ordered to pay court costs and restitution and record did not reflect that magistrate or juvenile court considered community service in lieu of sanctions as required by statute. In re Spears (Ohio App. 5 Dist., Licking, 04-17-2006) No. 2005-CA-93, 2006-Ohio-1920, 2006 WL 1011201, Unreported. Infants 254

Juvenile court was not statutorily required to impose community control sanctions, rather than financial sanctions, upon indigent juvenile; rather, juvenile court was required to consider community service in lieu of financial sanctions. In re Spears (Ohio App. 5 Dist., Licking, 04-17-2006) No. 2005-CA-93, 2006-Ohio-1920, 2006 WL 1011201, Unreported. Infants 225

Juvenile was not statutorily entitled to indigency hearing prior to imposition of financial sanctions following adjudication of delinquency. In re Spears (Ohio App. 5 Dist., Licking, 04-17-2006) No. 2005-CA-93, 2006-Ohio-1920, 2006 WL 1011201, Unreported. Infants 203

Order that indigent juvenile reimburse court for costs of sex offender evaluation and court costs as part of disposition for assault on school official and attempted gross sexual imposition did not violate statute requiring trial court to consider imposing term of community service. In re C.P. (Ohio App. 9 Dist., Lorain, 04-20-2005) No. 04CA008534, No. 04CA008535, 2005-Ohio-1819, 2005 WL 901209, Unreported. Infants 212

Hearing to determine juvenile's ability to pay financial sanctions as part of disposition for assault on school official and attempted gross sexual imposition was discretionary with court, not mandatory. In re C.P. (Ohio App. 9 Dist., Lorain, 04-20-2005) No. 04CA008534, No. 04CA008535, 2005-Ohio-1819, 2005 WL 901209, Unreported. Infants 203

Juvenile court did not err in failing to consider imposing a term of community service in lieu of court costs in delinquency proceeding, given juvenile's failure to apprise the court of his indigent status at the dispositional hearing. (Per Harsha, J., with one judge concurring in judgment only). In re Carter (Ohio App. 4 Dist., Jackson, 12-30-2004) No. 04CA15, No. 04CA16, 2004-Ohio-7285, 2004 WL 3090250, Unreported. Infants 212

Decision whether to conduct a hearing to determine if a juvenile adjudicated a delinquent child is able to pay court costs is within the juvenile court's discretion. (Per Harsha, J., with one judge concurring in judgment only). In re Carter (Ohio App. 4 Dist., Jackson, 12-30-2004) No. 04CA15, No. 04CA16, 2004-Ohio-7285, 2004 WL 3090250, Unreported. Infants 212

Any error in trial court's failure to consider community service in lieu of financial sanctions following juvenile's adjudication as delinquent was harmless, where court decided to hold hearing on financial sanctions prior to juvenile's release from custody. In re McClanahan (Ohio App. 5 Dist., Tuscarawas, 08-02-2004) No. 2004AP010004, 2004-Ohio-4113, 2004 WL 1758408, Unreported, appeal not allowed 104 Ohio St.3d 1426, 819 N.E.2d 709, 2004-Ohio-6585. Infants 253

Following adjudication proceeding, failing to hold hearing to determine whether juvenile delinquent was able to pay financial sanctions imposed upon him, including fines, court costs, and costs of confinement, was not abuse of discretion, where use of word "may" in statute providing that court may hold hearing to determine whether juvenile was able to pay sanction indicated that court was not required to hold hearing, juvenile did not request hearing on his ability to pay financial sanctions, and juvenile was not incarcerated for non-payment of fine. In re McClanahan (Ohio App. 5 Dist., Tuscarawas, 08-02-2004) No. 2004AP010004, 2004-Ohio-4113, 2004 WL 1758408, Unreported, appeal not allowed 104 Ohio St.3d 1426, 819 N.E.2d 709, 2004-Ohio-6585. Infants 203

Trial court did not violate mandates of juvenile disposition statute by not giving juvenile community service in lieu of the $1,450.00 fine; statute stated that court "shall consider" community service, and by reviewing motion to vacate fines and costs and subsequently denying same, court "considered" issue and rejected it. In re Hopkins (Ohio App. 5 Dist., Stark, 09-22-2003) No. 2003CA00007, 2003-Ohio-5081, 2003 WL 22209852, Unreported. Infants 223.1

Court could not assess court costs against juvenile, in possession of marijuana delinquency proceedings, where delinquency proceedings against juvenile were dismissed. In re Graham (Ohio App. 7 Dist., Mahoning, 11-26-2002) No. 02CA67, 2002-Ohio-6615, 2002 WL 31718885, Unreported. Infants 212

5. Valuation of loss

No absolute requirement existed that victim demonstrate the amount of her loss through documentary evidence, in order to collect restitution from juvenile who had been adjudicated as delinquent; amount of loss could be established through victim's testimony. In re Hatfield (Ohio App. 4 Dist., Lawrence, 10-03-2003) No. 03CA14, 2003-Ohio-5404, 2003 WL 22318010, Unreported. Infants 224

Evidence established victim's loss was $74,800, as basis for collecting restitution from juvenile after juvenile was adjudicated delinquent based on his admission to committing acts constituting burglary, theft, and safecracking; victim testified that before the burglary, she had counted $100,000 in cash in safe, that after the burglary only $8,000 remained, that sheriff recovered $17,000, that she had to pay $1,000 deductible to insurance company, and that she received $200 from insurer. In re Hatfield (Ohio App. 4 Dist., Lawrence, 10-03-2003) No. 03CA14, 2003-Ohio-5404, 2003 WL 22318010, Unreported. Criminal Law 224

6. Attorney fee reimbursement

Juvenile court erred by not making a determination on the record that juvenile, as an indigent defendant, had the ability to pay the court-appointed counsel fees imposed upon him as a sanction; there was no indication that juvenile court considered imposing a term of community service in lieu of requiring juvenile to pay his court-appointed attorney fees, and court failed to make an affirmative determination that juvenile had, or reasonably could be expected to have, the means to pay all or some part of the cost of the legal services rendered to him. In re J.W. (Ohio App. 12 Dist., Butler, 12-30-2004) No. CA2004-02-036, No. CA2004-03-061, 2004-Ohio-7139, 2004 WL 3015755, Unreported. Infants 212

7. Constitutional issues

Defense counsel provided ineffective assistance of counsel during delinquency proceeding by failing to object to juvenile court's imposition of court costs; counsel was aware that the juvenile court had appointed him to represent juvenile because juvenile was indigent, and, since counsel did not apprise the court of juvenile's indigent status, the court did not engage in the proper analysis before imposing court costs. In re Carter (Ohio App. 4 Dist., Jackson, 12-30-2004) No. 04CA15, No. 04CA16, 2004-Ohio-7285, 2004 WL 3090250, Unreported. Infants 205

2152.201 Recovery of costs where offense constitutes act of terrorism

(A) In addition to any other dispositions authorized or required by this chapter, the juvenile court making disposition of a child adjudicated a delinquent child for committing a violation of section 2909.22, 2909.23, or 2909.24 of the Revised Code or a violation of section 2921.32 of the Revised Code when the offense or act committed by the person aided or to be aided as described in that section is an act of terrorism may order the child to pay to the state, municipal, or county law enforcement agencies that handled the investigation and prosecution all of the costs that the state, municipal corporation, or county reasonably incurred in the investigation and prosecution of the violation. The court shall hold a hearing to determine the amount of costs to be imposed under this section. The court may hold the hearing as part of the dispositional hearing for the child.

(B) If a child is adjudicated a delinquent child for committing a violation of section 2909.23 or 2909.24 of the Revised Code and if any political subdivision incurred any response costs as a result of, or in making any response to, the threat of the specified offense involved in the violation of section 2909.23 of the Revised Code or the actual specified offense involved in the violation of section 2909.24 of the Revised Code, in addition to any other dispositions authorized or required by this chapter, the juvenile court making disposition of the child for the violation may order the child to reimburse the involved political subdivision for the response costs it so incurred.

(C) As used in this section, "response costs" and "act of terrorism" have the same meanings as in section 2909.21 of the Revised Code.

(2002 S 184, eff. 5–15–02)

Library References

Infants ⚖︎212.
Westlaw Topic No. 211.
C.J.S. Infants §§ 57, 69 to 85.

Law Review and Journal Commentaries

Ohio Responds to the Threat of Terrorism, Eric Skidmore. 17 Ohio Law 6 (January/February 2003).

2152.202 Recovery of costs from juvenile drug abuse offenders

(A) In addition to the dispositions authorized or required under section 2152.20 of the Revised Code and to any costs otherwise authorized or required under any provision of law, the juvenile court making disposition of a child adjudicated a delinquent child for committing an act that would be a drug abuse offense if committed by an adult may order the child to pay to the state, municipal, or county law enforcement agencies that handled the investigation and prosecution all of the costs that the state, municipal corporation, or county reasonably incurred in having tests performed under section 2925.51 of the Revised Code or in any other manner on any substance that was the basis of, or involved in, the delinquent act to determine whether the substance contained any amount of a controlled substance if the results of the tests indicate that the substance tested contained any controlled substance. No court shall order a delinquent child under this section to pay the costs of tests performed on a substance if the results of the tests do not indicate that the substance tested contained any controlled substance.

The court shall hold a hearing to determine the amount of costs to be imposed under this section. The court may hold the hearing as part of the dispositional hearing for the child.

(B) As used in this section, "controlled substance" has the same meaning as in section 3719.01 of the Revised Code.

(2006 H 163, eff. 10–12–06)

2152.21 Disposition of juvenile traffic offender

(A) Unless division (C) of this section applies, if a child is adjudicated a juvenile traffic offender, the court may make any of the following orders of disposition:

(1) Impose costs and one or more financial sanctions in accordance with section 2152.20 of the Revised Code;

(2) Suspend the child's driver's license, probationary driver's license, or temporary instruction permit for a definite period not exceeding two years or suspend the registration of all motor vehicles registered in the name of the child for a definite period not exceeding two years. A child whose license or permit is so suspended is ineligible for issuance of a license or permit during the period of suspension. At the end of the period of suspension, the child shall not be reissued a license or permit until the child has paid any applicable reinstatement fee and complied with all requirements governing license reinstatement.

(3) Place the child on community control;

(4) If the child is adjudicated a juvenile traffic offender for an act other than an act that would be a minor misdemeanor if committed by an adult and other than an act that could be disposed of by the juvenile traffic violations bureau serving the court under Traffic Rule 13.1 if the court has established a juvenile traffic violations bureau, require the child to make restitution pursuant to division (A)(3) of section 2152.20 of the Revised Code;

(5)(a) If the child is adjudicated a juvenile traffic offender for committing a violation of division (A) of section 4511.19 of the Revised Code or of a municipal ordinance that is substantially equivalent to that division, commit the child, for not longer than five days, to either of the following:

(i) The temporary custody of a detention facility or district detention facility established under section 2152.41 of the Revised Code;

(ii) The temporary custody of any school, camp, institution, or other facility for children operated in whole or in part for the care of juvenile traffic offenders of that nature by the county, by a district organized under section 2151.65 or 2152.41 of the Revised Code, or by a private agency or organization within the state that is authorized and qualified to provide the care, treatment, or placement required.

(b) If an order of disposition committing a child to the temporary custody of a home, school, camp, institution, or other facility of that nature is made under division (A)(5)(a) of this section, the length of the commitment shall not be reduced or diminished as a credit for any time that the child was held in a place of detention or shelter care, or otherwise was detained, prior to entry of the order of disposition.

(6) If, after making a disposition under divisions (A)(1) to (5) of this section, the court finds upon further hearing that the child has failed to comply with the orders of the court and the child's operation of a motor vehicle constitutes the child a danger to the child and to others, the court may make any disposition authorized by divisions (A)(1), (4), (5), and (8) of section 2152.19 of the Revised Code, except that the child may not be committed to or placed in a secure correctional facility unless authorized by division (A)(5) of this section, and commitment to or placement in a detention facility may not exceed twenty-four hours.

(B) If a child is adjudicated a juvenile traffic offender for violating division (A) or (B) of section 4511.19 of the Revised Code, in addition to any order of disposition made under division (A) of this section, the court shall impose a class six suspension of the temporary instruction permit, probationary driver's license, or driver's license issued to the child from the range specified in division (A)(6) of section 4510.02 of the Revised Code. The court, in its discretion, may terminate the suspension if the child attends and satisfactorily completes a drug abuse or alcohol abuse education, intervention, or treatment program specified by the court. During the time the child is attending a program as described in this division, the court shall retain the child's temporary instruction permit, probationary driver's license, or driver's license issued, and the court shall return the permit or license if it terminates the suspension as described in this division.

(C) If a child is adjudicated a juvenile traffic offender for violating division (B)(1) of section 4513.263 of the Revised Code, the court shall impose the appropriate fine set forth in division (G) of that section. If a child is adjudicated a juvenile traffic offender for violating division (B)(3) of section 4513.263 of the Revised Code and if the child is sixteen years of age or older, the court shall impose the fine set forth in division (G)(2) of that section. If a child is adjudicated a juvenile traffic offender for violating division (B)(3) of section 4513.263 of the Revised Code and if the child is under sixteen years of age, the court shall not impose a fine but may place the child on probation or community control.

(D) A juvenile traffic offender is subject to sections 4509.01 to 4509.78 of the Revised Code.

(2004 H 52, eff. 6–1–04; 2002 H 400, § 4, eff. 1–1–04; 2002 H 400, § 1, eff. 4–3–03; 2002 S 123, eff. 1–1–04; 2000 S 179, § 3, eff. 1–1–02)

Historical and Statutory Notes

Ed. Note: 2152.21 is former 2151.356, amended and recodified by 2000 S 179, § 3, eff. 1–1–02; 2000 S 181, eff. 9–4–00; 1998 H 2, eff. 1–1–99; 1997 S 35, eff. 1–1–99; 1996 H 265, eff. 3–3–97; 1995 H 1, eff. 1–1–96; 1992 S 98, eff. 11–12–92; 1992 H 154, H 118; 1990 S 131; 1989 H 381, H 330, H 329; 1988 H 643; 1986 H 428, S 54; 1977 H 222, H 1; 1970 H 931; 1969 H 320.

Amendment Note: 2004 H 52 rewrote division (A)(4) and substituted "or 2152.41" for "2152.41 or" in division (A)(5)(a)(ii). Prior to amendment, division (A)(4) read:

"(4) Require the child to make restitution for all damages caused by the child's traffic violation;"

Amendment Note: 2002 H 400, § 1, rewrote "divisions (A)(1), (3), (4), and (7) of section 2152.19" as "divisions (A)(1), (4), (5), and (8) of section 2152.19" in division (A)(6).

Amendment Note: 2002 S 123 inserted "for a definite period not exceeding two years" in division (A)(2); made other nonsubstantive changes to the section; and rewrote division (B), which prior thereto read:

"(B) If a child is adjudicated a juvenile traffic offender for violating division (A) or (B) of section 4511.19 of the Revised Code, in addition to any order of disposition made under division (A) of this section, the court shall suspend the temporary instruction permit, probationary driver's license, or driver's license issued to the child for a definite period of at least three months but not more than two years or, at the discretion of the court, until the child attends and satisfactorily completes a drug abuse or alcohol abuse education, intervention, or treatment program specified by the court. During the time the child is attending the program, the court shall retain any temporary instruction permit, probationary driver's license, or driver's license issued to the child and shall return the permit or license when the child satisfactorily completes the program."

Amendment Note: 2000 S 179, § 3, eff. 1–1–02, rewrote this section, which prior thereto read:

"(A) Unless division (C) of this section applies, if a child is adjudicated a juvenile traffic offender, the court may make any of the following orders of disposition:

"(1) Impose a fine and costs in accordance with the schedule set forth in section 2151.3512 of the Revised Code;

"(2) Suspend the child's driver's license, probationary driver's license, or temporary instruction permit or the registration of all motor vehicles registered in the name of the child for the period that the court prescribes. A child whose license or permit is so suspended is ineligible for issuance of a license or permit during the period of suspension. At the end of the period of suspension, the child shall not be reissued a license or permit until the child has paid any applicable reinstatement fee and complied with all requirements governing license reinstatement.

"(3) Revoke the child's driver's license, probationary driver's license, or temporary instruction permit or the registration of all motor vehicles registered in the name of the child. A child whose license or permit is so revoked is ineligible for issuance of a license or permit during the period of revocation. At the end of the period of revocation, the child shall not be reissued a license or permit until the child has paid any applicable reinstatement fee and complied with all requirements governing license reinstatement.

"(4) Place the child on probation;

"(5) Require the child to make restitution for all damages caused by the child's traffic violation or any part of the damages;

"(6) If the child is adjudicated a juvenile traffic offender for committing a violation of division (A) of section 4511.19 of the Revised Code or of a municipal ordinance that is substantially comparable to that division, commit the child, for not longer than five days, to the temporary custody of a detention home or district detention home established under section 2151.34 of the Revised Code, or to the temporary custody of any school, camp, institution, or other facility for children operated in whole or in part for the care of juvenile traffic offenders of that nature by the county, by a district organized under section 2151.34 or 2151.65 of the Revised Code, or by a private agency or organization within the state that is authorized and qualified to provide the care, treatment, or placement required. If an order of disposition committing a child to the temporary custody of a home, school, camp, institution, or other facility of that nature is made under division (A)(6) of this section, the length of the commitment shall not be reduced or diminished as a credit for any time that the child was held in a place of detention or shelter care, or otherwise was detained, prior to entry of the order of disposition.

"(7) If, after making a disposition under divisions (A)(1) to (6) of this section, the court finds upon further hearing that the child has failed to comply with the orders of the court and the child's operation of a motor vehicle constitutes the child a danger to the child and to others, the court may make any disposition authorized by divisions (A)(1), (A)(2), (A)(10) to (11), and (A)(22) of section 2151.355 of the Revised Code, except that the child may not be committed to or placed in a secure correctional facility unless authorized by division (A)(6) of this section, and commitment to or placement in a detention home may not exceed twenty-four hours.

"(B) If a child is adjudicated a juvenile traffic offender for violating division (A) of section 4511.19 of the Revised Code, the court shall suspend or revoke the temporary instruction permit, probationary driver's license, or driver's license issued to the child for a period of time prescribed by the court or, at the discretion of the court, until the child attends and satisfactorily completes a drug abuse or alcohol abuse education, intervention, or treatment program specified by the court. During the time the child is attending the program, the court shall retain any temporary instruction permit, probationary driver's license, or driver's license issued to the child and shall return the permit or license when the child satisfactorily completes the program. If a child is adjudicated a juvenile traffic offender for violating division (B) of section 4511.19 of the Revised Code, the court shall suspend the temporary instruction permit, probationary driver's license, or driver's license issued to the child for a period of not less than sixty days nor more than two years.

"(C) If a child is adjudicated a juvenile traffic offender for violating division (B)(1) or (2) of section 4513.263 of the Revised Code, the court shall impose the appropriate fine set forth in section 4513.99 of the Revised Code. If a child is adjudicated a juvenile traffic offender for violating division (B)(3) of section 4513.263 of the Revised Code and if the child is sixteen years of age or older, the court shall impose the fine set forth in division (G) of section 4513.99 of the Revised Code. If a child is adjudicated a juvenile traffic offender for violating division (B)(3) of section 4513.263 of the Revised Code and if the child is under sixteen years of age, the court shall not impose a fine but may place the child on probation.

"(D) A juvenile traffic offender is subject to sections 4509.01 to 4509.78 of the Revised Code."

Amendment Note: 2000 S 181 substituted "(A)(10) to (11), and (A)(22)" for "(A)(7) to (A)(10), and (A)(21)" in division (A)(7).

Amendment Note: 1998 H 2 substituted "(A)(2), (A)(7) to (A)(10), and (A)(21)" for "(2), and (A)(7) to (11)" in division (A)(7).

Amendment Note: 1997 S 35 inserted "driver's license" and "or temporary instruction permit", substituted "driver's" for "operator's", and added the second and third sentences, in division (A)(2); inserted "driver's license" and "or temporary instruction permit", and added the second and third sentences, in division (A)(3); rewrote division (B); and made other nonsubstantive changes. Prior to amendment, division (B) read:

"(B) If a child is adjudicated a juvenile traffic offender for violating division (A) of section 4511.19 of the Revised Code, the court shall suspend or revoke the temporary instruction permit or probationary driver's license issued to the child until the child attains eighteen years of age or attends, at the discretion of the court, and satisfactorily completes a drug abuse or alcohol abuse education, intervention, or treatment program specified by the court. During the time the child is attending the program, the court shall retain any temporary instruction permit or probationary license issued to the child and shall return the permit or license when the child satisfactorily completes the program. If a child is adjudicated a juvenile traffic offender for violating division (B) of section 4511.19 of the Revised Code, the court shall suspend the temporary instruction permit or probationary driver's license issued to the child for the shorter period of sixty days or until the child attains eighteen years of age."

Amendment Note: 1996 H 265 substituted "the child's" for "his" in division (A)(5); and substituted "(A)(1), (2), and (A)(7) to (11)" for "(A)(1) to (3) and (A)(6) to (10)" and inserted ", except that the child may not be committed to or placed in a secure correctional facility unless authorized by division (A)(6) of this section, and commitment to or placement in a detention home may not exceed twenty-four hours" in division (A)(7).

Amendment Note: 1995 H 1 substituted "adjudicated" for "found to be" throughout; substituted "and costs in accordance with the schedule set forth in section 2151.3512 of the Revised Code" for "not to exceed fifty dollars and costs" in division (A)(1); substituted "violating" for "having committed any act that if committed by an adult would be a drug abuse offense, as defined in section 2925.01 of the Revised Code, a violation of division (B) of section 2917.11 of the Revised Code, or a violation of" in division (B); substituted "violating" for "having committed an act that if committed by an adult would be a violation of" throughout division (C); and made changes to reflect gender neutral language and other nonsubstantive changes.

Cross References

Adjudicatory hearing, procedure, Juv R 29
Dispositional hearing, procedure, Juv R 34

Library References

Automobiles ⚖=359.
Infants ⚖=69(1).
Westlaw Topic Nos. 211, 48A.
C.J.S. Infants §§ 198, 206 to 209.
C.J.S. Motor Vehicles §§ 1336, 1352, 1380, 1414 to 1419, 1442, 1451 to 1452, 1484, 1486 to 1487, 1503, 1510, 1523, 1526, 1539, 1543 to 1544, 1546 to 1547, 1550.
Baldwin's Ohio Legislative Service, 1990 Laws of Ohio, S 131—LSC Analysis, p 5–623

Research References

Encyclopedias

OH Jur. 3d Family Law § 1547, Juvenile Traffic Offenders.
OH Jur. 3d Family Law § 1548, Juvenile Traffic Offenders—Orders of Disposition.
OH Jur. 3d Family Law § 1689, Juvenile Traffic Offender.

Treatises and Practice Aids

Carlin, Baldwin's Ohio Practice, Merrick-Rippner Probate Law § 107:106, Disposition of Juvenile Traffic Offender—Mandatory.
Carlin, Baldwin's Ohio Practice, Merrick-Rippner Probate Law § 107:107, Disposition of Juvenile Traffic Offender—Permissive.
Carlin, Baldwin's Ohio Practice, Merrick-Rippner Probate Law § 107:108, Disposition of Juvenile Traffic Offender—Commitment to Detention Home or Institution.
Carlin, Baldwin's Ohio Practice, Merrick-Rippner Probate Law § 107:109, Disposition of Juvenile Traffic Offender—Violations of Seat Belt Law.
Painter, Ohio Driving Under the Influence § 12:45, Juvenile and "Underage" Offenders—Generally.
Painter, Ohio Driving Under the Influence § 12:46, Juvenile and "Underage" Offenders—Juvenile Offender.
Giannelli & Yeomans, Ohio Juvenile Law § 19:2, Place of Detention.
Giannelli & Yeomans, Ohio Juvenile Law § 28:2, Suspension or Revocation.
Giannelli & Yeomans, Ohio Juvenile Law § 28:3, Financial Sanctions.
Giannelli & Yeomans, Ohio Juvenile Law § 28:4, Community Control and Probation.
Giannelli & Yeomans, Ohio Juvenile Law § 28:5, Restitution.
Giannelli & Yeomans, Ohio Juvenile Law § 28:6, Commitment to Juvenile Facility.
Giannelli & Yeomans, Ohio Juvenile Law § 28:7, Seat Belt Law Violations.
Giannelli & Yeomans, Ohio Juvenile Law § 28:10, Imposition of Adult Penalties.

Law Review and Journal Commentaries

Preventing Violence in Ohio's Schools, Comment. 33 Akron L Rev 311 (2000).

Notes of Decisions

Ed. Note: This section contains annotations from former RC 2151.35 and 2151.356.

Admissibility of evidence in other actions 2
Court authority 4
Fines and costs 1
Restitution 3

---

1. Fines and costs

Juvenile's appeal from his adjudication as a juvenile traffic offender was moot following his voluntary payment of fine, given that juvenile failed to make any claim of collateral disability or loss of civil rights; although points were assessed to his driving record and he could be subject to higher insurance premiums, juvenile's ability to drive was not impaired by the adjudication. In re S.J.K. (Ohio App. 9 Dist., Summit, 02-15-2006) No. 22721, 2006-Ohio-653, 2006 WL 335624, Unreported, motion to certify allowed 109 Ohio St.3d 1493, 848 N.E.2d 856, 2006-Ohio-2762, appeal allowed 109 Ohio St.3d 1494, 848 N.E.2d 857, 2006-Ohio-2762. Infants ⚖= 247

Under RC 4513.35, where the arrest for a traffic offense is by one other than a state highway patrolman, with prosecution and money fine paid, fifty per cent of such fine is to be paid to the county law library association, for the free use of such facilities by judges and other public officials, through the county treasurer, municipal court, or juvenile court, pursuant to RC 3375.53; where the arrest is made by a township officer for a traffic offense, fifty per cent of the fine is to be paid into the township general fund and the other fifty per cent arising from such arrests is to be paid to the county law library association. State ex rel. Akron Law Library Ass'n v. Weil (Summit 1968) 16 Ohio App.2d 151, 242 N.E.2d 664, 45 O.O.2d 433.

Fines imposed upon juvenile traffic offenders pursuant to RC 2151.356(A) must be paid to the general fund of the county treasury pursuant to RC 2949.11 rather than to the county law library association pursuant to RC 3375.52 or RC 3375.53. OAG 82–062; overruled to the extent that it is inconsistent with OAG 87–023.

Judge of juvenile court may not commit child who has been found to be delinquent child, or juvenile traffic offender, to county jail upon failure, refusal, or inability of such child to pay fine and court costs. OAG 70–143.

2. Admissibility of evidence in other actions

RC 2151.358 does not prohibit the use of records pertaining to traffic violations, kept pursuant to RC 4507.40, in a driver's license revocation hearing conducted after the accused has attained majority. Gebell v. Dollison (Clermont 1978) 57 Ohio App.2d 198, 386 N.E.2d 845, 9 O.O.3d 23, 11 O.O.3d 187. Infants ⚖= 133

The judgment of a juvenile court finding juvenile to be a traffic offender was admissible in action by an insurance company to invalidate liability policy issued upon answer by juvenile's father that no one in his household had been convicted of a traffic offense where there was other testimony sufficient to support the court's findings of fact. Allstate Ins. Co. v. Cook (C.A.6 (Ohio) 1963) 324 F.2d 752, 26 O.O.2d 192.

3. Restitution

Even if juvenile court, in imposing order of disposition on delinquent juvenile under statute allowing court to make further dispositional order if court found it be proper, was required to impose disposition prescribed by another statute, court satisfied that requirement in ordering juvenile, who admitted to complaint alleging vehicular homicide, to pay victim's funeral expenses, since disposition fell within statute requiring juvenile traffic offenders to make restitution for damages caused by juvenile. In re Jacobs (Ohio App. 3 Dist., 06-04-2002) 148 Ohio App.3d 173, 772 N.E.2d 671, 2002-Ohio-2844. Infants ⚖= 224

Juvenile court could suspend juvenile offender's driver's license only until offender's eighteenth birthday, regardless of status of restitution order, absent finding that offender had failed to comply with orders of court and that his operation of motor vehicle constituted danger to himself and others. State v. Minix (Ohio App. 4 Dist., 02-24-1995) 101 Ohio App.3d 380, 655 N.E.2d 789. Automobiles ⇐ 144.2(8)

While juvenile court may generally order restitution from offending juvenile driver, court is not statutorily permitted to use restitution order to suspend juvenile's driver's license beyond that time proscribed by statute, i.e., juvenile's eighteenth birthday, absent application of statute that requires finding that juvenile has failed to comply with orders of court and that his operation of motor vehicle constitutes danger to himself and others. State v. Minix (Ohio App. 4 Dist., 02-24-1995) 101 Ohio App.3d 380, 655 N.E.2d 789. Automobiles ⇐ 144.2(8)

RC Ch 4109, governing the employment of minors, is applicable to all arrangements under which minors are employed to provide other persons with services, including cadet firefighting programs and juvenile court restitution orders, whether or not compensation is paid for such services, except to the extent such arrangements come within the exceptions set forth in RC 4109.06. OAG 87–104.

4. Court authority

Public policy to ensure accountability and compel respect for court orders did not warrant judicial exception to the legislatively imposed limits on juvenile court jurisdiction to the age of twenty-one years. In re R.K. (Ohio App. 8 Dist., Cuyahoga, 12-16-2004) No. 84948, 2004-Ohio-6918, 2004 WL 2931013, Unreported, appeal not allowed 105 Ohio St.3d 1561, 828 N.E.2d 117, 2005-Ohio-2447. Infants ⇐ 196

Juvenile court did not have authority to impose indefinite driving suspensions beyond juvenile traffic offender's twenty-first birthday. In re R.K. (Ohio App. 8 Dist., Cuyahoga, 12-16-2004) No. 84948, 2004-Ohio-6918, 2004 WL 2931013, Unreported, appeal not allowed 105 Ohio St.3d 1561, 828 N.E.2d 117, 2005-Ohio-2447. Infants ⇐ 223.1

Trial court lacked authority pursuant to statute to suspend driver's license of juvenile convicted of operating motor vehicle after consuming alcohol while under age of 21, where juvenile had already turned 18 by time of sentencing; governing statutes require suspension for shorter period of 60 days or until child attained 18 years of age. In re Eric W. (Ohio App. 6 Dist., 08-09-1996) 113 Ohio App.3d 367, 680 N.E.2d 1275. Automobiles ⇐ 144.1(1.11); Automobiles ⇐ 144.2(8)

The authority granted a juvenile court in RC 2151.35 to make certain specified dispositions and commitments of children in matters before it can be exercised by such court only if the child before it is found to be a juvenile traffic offender or is delinquent, neglected or dependent. In re Darst (Franklin 1963) 117 Ohio App. 374, 192 N.E.2d 287, 24 O.O.2d 144.

If juvenile violated probation previously imposed for a juvenile traffic offense, court could not sentence him to 90 days in a detention home, and thus, by imposing such a sentence on juvenile the court erased 90 days of potential credit for time served which would shorten his commitment to Ohio Department of Youth Services (ODYS) on other offenses, requiring remand for new probation revocation proceedings. In re Lett (Ohio App. 7 Dist., Mahoning, 09-18-2002) No. 01 CA 222, 2002-Ohio-5023, 2002 WL 31115583, Unreported. Infants ⇐ 225

A probationary license does not necessarily terminate automatically upon reaching the age of eighteen; a juvenile court has the authority to suspend or revoke a juvenile traffic offender's probationary license beyond the offender's eighteenth birthday. State v Elliott, No. CA99–04–048, 2000 WL 127097 (12th Dist Ct App, Warren, 1–24–00).

The driver's license of a juvenile who violates RC 4511.19(B) cannot be suspended by the common pleas court, juvenile division, past the juvenile's eighteenth birthday. In re Eric W, No. E–95–074, 1996 WL 446845 (6th Dist Ct App, Erie, 8–9–96).

2152.22 Relinquishment of juvenile court control; judicial release

(A) When a child is committed to the legal custody of the department of youth services under this chapter, the juvenile court relinquishes control with respect to the child so committed, except as provided in divisions (B), (C), and (G) of this section or in sections 2152.82 to 2152.85 of the Revised Code. Subject to divisions (B) and (C) of this section, sections 2151.353 and 2151.412 to 2151.421 of the Revised Code, sections 2152.82 to 2152.85 of the Revised Code, and any other provision of law that specifies a different duration for a dispositional order, all other dispositional orders made by the court under this chapter shall be temporary and shall continue for a period that is designated by the court in its order, until terminated or modified by the court or until the child attains twenty-one years of age.

The department shall not release the child from a department facility and as a result shall not discharge the child or order the child's release on supervised release prior to the expiration of the minimum period specified by the court in division (A)(1) of section 2152.16 of the Revised Code and any term of commitment imposed under section 2152.17 of the Revised Code or prior to the child's attainment of twenty-one years of age, except upon the order of a court pursuant to division (B) or (C) of this section or in accordance with section 5139.54 of the Revised Code.

(B)(1) The court that commits a delinquent child to the department may grant judicial release of the child to court supervision under this division during the first half of the prescribed minimum term for which the child was committed to the department or, if the child was committed to the department until the child attains twenty-one years of age, during the first half of the prescribed period of commitment that begins on the first day of commitment and ends on the child's twenty-first birthday, provided any commitment imposed under division (A), (B), (C), or (D) of section 2152.17 of the Revised Code has ended.

(2) If the department of youth services desires to release a child during a period specified in division (B)(1) of this section, it shall request the court that committed the child to grant a judicial release of the child to court supervision. During whichever of those periods is applicable, the child or the parents of the child also may request that court to grant a judicial release of the child to court supervision. Upon receipt of a request for a judicial release to court supervision from the department, the child, or the child's parent, or upon its own motion, the court that committed the child shall do one of the following: approve the release by journal entry; schedule within thirty days after the request is received a time for a hearing on whether the child is to be released; or reject the request by journal entry without conducting a hearing.

If the court rejects an initial request for a release under this division by the child or the child's parent, the child or the child's parent may make one additional request for a judicial release to court supervision within the applicable period. The additional request may be made no earlier than thirty days after the filing of the prior request for a judicial release to court supervision. Upon the filing of a second request for a judicial release to court supervision, the court shall either approve or disapprove the release by journal entry or schedule within thirty days after the request is received a time for a hearing on whether the child is to be released.

(3) If a court schedules a hearing under division (B)(2) of this section, it may order the department to deliver the child to the court on the date set for the hearing and may order the department to present to the court a report on the child's progress in the institution to which the child was committed and recommendations for conditions of supervision of the child by the court after release. The court may conduct the hearing without the child being present. The court shall determine at the hearing whether the child should be granted a judicial release to court supervision.

If the court approves the release, it shall order its staff to prepare a written treatment and rehabilitation plan for the child that may include any conditions of the child's release that were recommended by the department and approved by the court. The committing court shall send the juvenile court of the county in which the child is placed a copy of the recommended plan. The court of the county in which the child is placed may adopt the recommended conditions set by the committing court as an order of the court and may add any additional consistent conditions it considers appropriate. If a child is granted a judicial release to court supervision, the release discharges the child from the custody of the department of youth services.

(C)(1) The court that commits a delinquent child to the department may grant judicial release of the child to department of youth services supervision under this division during the second half of the prescribed minimum term for which the child was committed to the department or, if the child was committed to the department until the child attains twenty-one years of age, during the second half of the prescribed period of commitment that begins on the first day of commitment and ends on the child's twenty-first birthday, provided any commitment imposed under division (A), (B), (C), or (D) of section 2152.17 of the Revised Code has ended.

(2) If the department of youth services desires to release a child during a period specified in division (C)(1) of this section, it shall request the court that committed the child to grant a judicial release to department of youth services supervision. During whichever of those periods is applicable, the child or the child's parent also may request the court that committed the child to grant a judicial release to department of youth services supervision. Upon receipt of a request for judicial release to department of youth services supervision, the child, or the child's parent, or upon its own motion at any time during that period, the court shall do one of the following: approve the release by journal entry; schedule a time within thirty days after receipt of the request for a hearing on whether the child is to be released; or reject the request by journal entry without conducting a hearing.

If the court rejects an initial request for release under this division by the child or the child's parent, the child or the child's parent may make one or more subsequent requests for a release within the applicable period, but may make no more than one request during each period of ninety days that the child is in a secure department facility after the filing of a prior request for early release. Upon the filing of a request for release under this division subsequent to an initial request, the court shall either approve or disapprove the release by journal entry or schedule a time within thirty days after receipt of the request for a hearing on whether the child is to be released.

(3) If a court schedules a hearing under division (C)(2) of this section, it may order the department to deliver the child to the court on the date set for the hearing and shall order the department to present to the court at that time a treatment plan for the child's post-institutional care. The court may conduct the hearing without the child being present. The court shall determine at the hearing whether the child should be granted a judicial release to department of youth services supervision.

If the court approves the judicial release to department of youth services supervision, the department shall prepare a written treatment and rehabilitation plan for the child pursuant to division (E) of this section that shall include the conditions of the child's release. It shall send the committing court and the juvenile court of the county in which the child is placed a copy of the plan. The court of the county in which the child is placed may adopt the conditions set by the department as an order of the court and may add any additional consistent conditions it considers appropriate, provided that the court may not add any condition that decreases the level or degree of supervision specified by the department in its plan, that substantially increases the financial burden of supervision that will be experienced by the department, or that alters the placement specified by the department in its plan. If the court of the county in which the child is placed adds to the department's plan any additional conditions, it shall enter those additional conditions in its journal and shall send to the department a copy of the journal entry of the additional conditions.

If the court approves the judicial release to department of youth services supervision, the actual date on which the department shall release the child is contingent upon the department finding a suitable placement for the child. If the child is to be returned to the child's home, the department shall return the child on the date that the court schedules for the child's release or shall bear the expense of any additional time that the child remains in a department facility. If the child is unable to return to the child's home, the department shall exercise reasonable diligence in finding a suitable placement for the child, and the child shall remain in a department facility while the department finds the suitable placement.

(D) If a child is released under division (B) or (C) of this section and the court of the county in which the child is placed has reason to believe that the child's deportment is not in accordance with the conditions of the child's judicial release, the court of the county in which the child is placed shall schedule a time for a hearing to determine whether the child violated any of the post-release conditions, and, if the child was released under division (C) of this section, divisions (A) to (E) of section 5139.52 of the Revised Code apply regarding the child.

If that court determines at the hearing that the child violated any of the post-release conditions, the court, if it determines that the violation was a serious violation, may order the child to be returned to the department for institutionalization, consistent with the original order of commitment of the child, or in any case may make any other disposition of the child authorized by law that the court considers proper. If the court of the county in which the child is placed orders the child to be returned to a department of youth services institution, the time during which the child was held in a secure department facility prior to the child's judicial release shall be considered as time served in fulfilling the prescribed period of institutionalization that is applicable to the child under the child's original order of commitment. If the court orders the child returned to a department institution, the child shall remain in institutional care for a minimum of three months or until the child successfully completes a revocation program of a duration of not less than thirty days operated either by the department or by an entity with which the department has contracted to provide a revocation program.

(E) The department of youth services, prior to the release of a child pursuant to division (C) of this section, shall do all of the following:

(1) After reviewing the child's rehabilitative progress history and medical and educational records, prepare a written treatment and rehabilitation plan for the child that includes conditions of the release;

(2) Completely discuss the conditions of the plan prepared pursuant to division (E)(1) of this section and the possible penalties for violation of the plan with the child and the child's parents, guardian, or legal custodian;

(3) Have the plan prepared pursuant to division (E)(1) of this section signed by the child, the child's parents, legal guardian, or custodian, and any authority or person that is to supervise, control, and provide supportive assistance to the child at the time of the child's release pursuant to division (C) of this section;

(4) Prior to the child's release, file a copy of the treatment plan prepared pursuant to division (E)(1) of this section with the committing court and the juvenile court of the county in which the child is to be placed.

(F) The department of youth services shall file a written progress report with the committing court regarding each child released pursuant to division (C) of this section at least once every thirty days unless specifically directed otherwise by the court. The report shall indicate the treatment and rehabilitative progress of the child and the child's family, if applicable, and shall include any suggestions for altering the program, custody, living arrangements, or treatment. The department shall retain legal custody of a child so released until it discharges the child or until the custody is terminated as otherwise provided by law.

(G) When a child is committed to the legal custody of the department of youth services, the court retains jurisdiction to perform the functions specified in section 5139.51 of the Revised Code with respect to the granting of supervised release by the release authority and to perform the functions specified in section 5139.52 of the Revised Code with respect to violations of the conditions of supervised release granted by the release authority and to the revocation of supervised release granted by the release authority.

(2002 H 393, eff. 7–5–02; 2001 S 3, eff. 1–1–02; 2000 S 179, § 3, eff. 1–1–02)

Historical and Statutory Notes

Amendment Note: 2002 H 393 rewrote divisions (A), (B), and (C)(1) which prior thereto read:

"(A) When a child is committed to the legal custody of the department of youth services under this chapter, the juvenile court relinquishes control with respect to the child so committed, except as provided in divisions (B), (C), and (G) of this section or in sections 2152.82 to 2152.85 of the Revised Code. Subject to divisions (B) and (C) of this section, sections 2151.353 and 2151.412 to 2151.421 of the Revised Code, sections 2152.82 to 2152.85 of the Revised Code, and any other provision of law that specifies a different duration for a dispositional order, all other dispositional orders made by the court under this chapter shall be temporary and shall continue for a period that is designated by the court in its order, until terminated or modified by the court or until the child attains twenty-one years of age.

"The department shall not release the child from a department facility and as a result shall not discharge the child or order the child's release on supervised release prior to the expiration of the period of court control over the child or prior to the child's attainment of twenty-one years of age, except upon the order of a court pursuant to division (B) or (C) of this section or in accordance with section 5139.54 of the Revised Code.

"(B)(1) The court that commits a delinquent child to the department may grant judicial release of the child to court supervision under this division, during any of the following periods that are applicable, provided any commitment imposed under division (A), (B), or (C) of section 2152.17 of the Revised Code has ended:

"(a) If the child was given a disposition under section 2152.16 of the Revised Code for committing an act that would be a felony of the third, fourth, or fifth degree if committed by an adult, at any time during the first ninety days of the period of court control over the child;

"(b) If the child was given a disposition under section 2152.13 or 2152.16 of the Revised Code, or both of those sections, for committing an act that would be a felony of the first or second degree if committed by an adult, at any time during the first one hundred eighty days of the period of court control over the child;

"(c) If the child was committed to the department until the child attains twenty-one years of age for an act that would be aggravated murder or murder if committed by an adult, at any time during the first half of the prescribed period of that commitment of the child.

"(2) If the department of youth services desires to release a child during a period specified in division (B)(1) of this section, it shall request the court that committed the child to grant a judicial release of the child to court supervision. During whichever of those periods is applicable, the child or the parents of the child also may request that court to grant a judicial release of the child to court supervision. Upon receipt of a request for a judicial release to court supervision from the department, the child, or the child's parent, or upon its own motion, the court that committed the child shall do one of the following: approve the release by journal entry; schedule within thirty days after the request is received a time for a hearing on whether the child is to be released; or reject the request by journal entry without conducting a hearing.

"If the court rejects an initial request for a release under this division by the child or the child's parent, the child or the child's parent may make one additional request for a judicial release to court supervision within the applicable period. The additional request may be made no earlier than thirty days after the filing of the prior request for a judicial release to court supervision. Upon the filing of a second request for a judicial release to court supervision, the court shall either approve or disapprove the release by journal entry or schedule within thirty days after the request is received a time for a hearing on whether the child is to be released.

"(3) If a court schedules a hearing under division (B)(2) of this section, it may order the department to deliver the child to the court on the date set for the hearing and may order the department to present to the court a report on the child's progress in the institution to which the child was committed and recommendations for conditions of supervision of the child by the court after release. The court may conduct the hearing without the child being present. The court shall determine at the hearing whether the child should be granted a judicial release to court supervision.

"If the court approves the release, it shall order its staff to prepare a written treatment and rehabilitation plan for the child that may include any conditions of the child's release that were recommended by the department and approved by the court. The committing court shall send the juvenile court of the county in which the child is placed a copy of the recommended plan. The court of the county in which the child is placed may adopt the recommended conditions set by the committing court as an order of the court and may add any additional consistent conditions it considers appropriate. If a child is granted a judicial release to court supervision, the release discharges the child from the custody of the department of youth services.

"(C)(1) The court that commits a delinquent child to the department may grant judicial release of the child to department of youth services supervision under this division, during any of the following periods that are applicable, provided any commitment imposed under division (A), (B), or (C) of section 2152.17 of the Revised Code has ended:

"(a) If the child was given a disposition under section 2152.16 of the Revised Code for an act that would be a felony of the third, fourth, or fifth degree if committed by an adult, at any time during the period of court control over the child, provided that at least ninety days of that period have elapsed;

"(b) If the child was given a disposition under section 2152.13 or 2152.16 of the Revised Code, or both of those sections, for an act that would be a felony of the first or second degree if committed by an adult, at any time during the period of court control over the child, provided that at least one hundred eighty days of that period have elapsed;

"(c) If the child was committed to the department for an act that would be aggravated murder or murder if committed by an adult until the child attains twenty-one years of age, at any time during the second half of the prescribed period of that commitment of the child."

Amendment Note: 2001 S 3 inserted "or in sections 2152.82 to 2152.85 of the Revised Code" and "sections 2152.82 to 2152.85 of the Revised Code" in the first paragraph of division (A)

Library References

Infants ⇌225, 273, 281.
Westlaw Topic No. 211.
C.J.S. Infants §§ 57, 69 to 85, 198, 206 to 213, 272, 280.

Research References

Encyclopedias

OH Jur. 3d Family Law § 1705, Effect on Court's Jurisdiction of Child's Commitment to Public Agency—Commitment to Youth Commission.

Treatises and Practice Aids

Carlin, Baldwin's Ohio Practice, Merrick-Rippner Probate Law § 107:89, Custody of Department of Youth Services.

Carlin, Baldwin's Ohio Practice, Merrick-Rippner Probate Law § 107:92, Enhanced Dispositions Due to Felony Specifications, Effective January 1, 2002.

Carlin, Baldwin's Ohio Practice, Merrick-Rippner Probate Law § 107:121, Custody Review Hearing—Revocation of Probation or Parole.

Carlin, Baldwin's Ohio Practice, Merrick-Rippner Probate Law § 107:146, Complaint for Violation of Parole—Form.

Carlin, Baldwin's Ohio Practice, Merrick-Rippner Probate Law § 107:184, Terms and Conditions of Child's Release from Department of Youth Services—Form.

Carlin, Baldwin's Ohio Practice, Merrick-Rippner Probate Law § 107:185, Order Committing Child to Department of Youth Services Upon Parole Revocation—Form.

Giannelli & Yeomans, Ohio Juvenile Law § 27:4, Dys Release.

Giannelli & Yeomans, Ohio Juvenile Law § 33:9, Department of Youth Services.

PLACE OF DETENTION

2152.26 Delinquent child or juvenile traffic offender to be held only in specified places

(A) Except as provided in divisions (B) and (F) of this section, a child alleged to be or adjudicated a delinquent child or a juvenile traffic offender may be held only in the following places:

(1) A certified foster home or a home approved by the court;

(2) A facility operated by a certified child welfare agency;

(3) Any other suitable place designated by the court.

(B) In addition to the places listed in division (A) of this section, a child alleged to be or adjudicated a delinquent child may be held in a detention facility for delinquent children that is under the direction or supervision of the court or other public authority or of a private agency and approved by the court and a child adjudicated a delinquent child may be held in accordance with division (F)(2) of this section in a facility of a type specified in that division. Division (B) of this section does not apply to a child alleged to be or adjudicated a delinquent child for chronic truancy, unless the child violated a lawful court order made pursuant to division (A)(6) of section 2152.19 of the Revised Code. Division (B) of this section also does not apply to a child alleged to be or adjudicated a delinquent child for being an habitual truant who previously has been adjudicated an unruly child for being an habitual truant, unless the child violated a lawful court order made pursuant to division (C)(1)(e) of section 2151.354 of the Revised Code.

(C)(1) Except as provided under division (C)(1) of section 2151.311 of the Revised Code or division (A)(5) of section 2152.21 of the Revised Code, a child alleged to be or adjudicated a juvenile traffic offender may not be held in any of the following facilities:

(a) A state correctional institution, county, multicounty, or municipal jail or workhouse, or other place in which an adult convicted of crime, under arrest, or charged with a crime is held.

(b) A secure correctional facility.

(2) Except as provided under this section, sections 2151.56 to 2151.61, and divisions (A)(5) and (6) of section 2152.21 of the Revised Code, a child alleged to be or adjudicated a juvenile traffic offender may not be held for more than twenty-four hours in a detention facility.

(D) Except as provided in division (F) of this section or in division (C) of section 2151.311, in division (C)(2) of section 5139.06 and section 5120.162, or in division (B) of section 5120.16 of the Revised Code, a child who is alleged to be or is adjudicated a delinquent child may not be held in a state correctional institution, county, multicounty, or municipal jail or workhouse, or other place where an adult convicted of crime, under arrest, or charged with crime is held.

(E) Unless the detention is pursuant to division (F) of this section or division (C) of section 2151.311, division (C)(2) of section 5139.06 and section 5120.162, or division (B) of section 5120.16 of the Revised Code, the official in charge of the institution, jail, workhouse, or other facility shall inform the court immediately when a child, who is or appears to be under the age of eighteen years, is received at the facility, and shall deliver the child to the court upon request or transfer the child to a detention facility designated by the court.

(F)(1) If a case is transferred to another court for criminal prosecution pursuant to section 2152.12 of the Revised Code, the child may be transferred for detention pending the criminal prosecution in a jail or other facility in accordance with the law governing the detention of persons charged with crime. Any child so held shall be confined in a manner that keeps the child beyond the range of touch of all adult detainees. The child shall be supervised at all times during the detention.

(2) If a person is adjudicated a delinquent child or juvenile traffic offender and the court makes a disposition of the person under this chapter, at any time after the person attains eighteen years of age, the person may be held under that disposition in places other than those specified in division (A) of this section, including, but not limited to, a county, multicounty, or municipal jail or workhouse, or other place where an adult convicted of crime, under arrest, or charged with crime is held.

(3)(a) A person alleged to be a delinquent child may be held in places other than those specified in division (A) of this section, including, but not limited to, a county, multicounty, or municipal jail, if the delinquent act that the child allegedly committed would be a felony if committed by an adult, and if either of the following applies:

(i) The person attains eighteen years of age before the person is arrested or apprehended for that act.

(ii) The person is arrested or apprehended for that act before the person attains eighteen years of age, but the person attains eighteen years of age before the court orders a disposition in the case.

(b) If, pursuant to division (F)(3)(a) of this section, a person is held in a place other than a place specified in division (A) of this section, the person has the same rights to bail as an adult charged with the same offense who is confined in a jail pending trial.

(2002 H 400, eff. 4–3–03; 2000 S 179, § 3, eff. 1–1–02)

Historical and Statutory Notes

Ed. Note: 2152.26 is former 2151.312, amended and recodified by 2000 S 179, § 3, eff. 1–1–02; 2000 H 332, eff. 1–1–01; 2000 H 448, eff. 10–5–00; 2000 S 181, eff. 9–4–00; 1997 H 1, eff. 7–1–98; 1996 H 124, eff. 3–31–97; 1996 H 265, eff. 3–3–97; 1994 H 571, eff. 10–6–94; 1993 H 152, eff. 7–1–93; 1992 S 331; 1989 H 166; 1981 H 440; 1975 H 85; 1969 H 320.

Amendment Note: 2002 H 400 added "and a child adjudicated a delinquent child may be held in accordance with division (F)(2) of this section in a facility of a type specified in that division" to the first sentence of division (B); changed "(A)(5)" to "(A)(6)" in the second sentence of division (B); changed "division (A)(5)" to "divisions (A)(5) and (6)" in division (C)(2); and rewrote division (F), which prior thereto read:

"(F) If a case is transferred to another court for criminal prosecution pursuant to section 2152.12 of the Revised Code, the child may be transferred for detention pending the criminal prosecution in a jail or other facility in accordance with the law governing the detention of persons charged with crime. Any child so held shall be confined in a manner that keeps the child beyond the range of touch of all adult detainees. The child shall be supervised at all times during the detention."

Amendment Note: 2000 S 179, § 3, eff. 1–1–02, rewrote this section, which prior thereto read:

"(A) Except as provided in divisions (B) and (F) of this section, a child alleged to be or adjudicated a delinquent child, an unruly child, or a juvenile traffic offender may be held only in the following places:

"(1) A certified foster home or a home approved by the court;

"(2) A facility operated by a certified child welfare agency;

"(3) Any other suitable place designated by the court.

"(B) In addition to the places listed in division (A) of this section, a child alleged to be or adjudicated a delinquent child may be held in a detention home or center for delinquent children that is under the direction or supervision of the court or other public authority or of a private agency and approved by the court. Division (B) of this section does not apply to a child alleged to be or adjudicated a delinquent child for chronic truancy, unless the child violated a lawful court order made pursuant to division (A)(23) of section 2151.355 of the Revised Code. Division (B) of this section also does not apply to a child alleged to be or adjudicated a delinquent child for being an habitual truant who previously has been adjudicated an unruly child for being an habitual truant, unless the child violated a lawful court order made pursuant to division (C)(1)(e) of section 2151.354 of the Revised Code.

"(C)(1) Except as provided under division (C)(1) of section 2151.311 of the Revised Code or division (A)(6) of section 2151.356 of the Revised Code, a child alleged to be or adjudicated a neglected child, an abused child, a dependent child, an unruly child, or a juvenile traffic offender may not be held in any of the following facilities:

"(a) A state correctional institution, county, multicounty, or municipal jail or workhouse, or other place in which an adult convicted of crime, under arrest, or charged with a crime is held.

"(b) A secure correctional facility.

"(2) Except as provided under sections 2151.56 to 2151.61 and division (A)(6) of section 2151.356 of the Revised Code and division (C)(3) of this section, a child alleged to be or adjudicated an unruly child or a juvenile traffic offender may not be held for more than twenty-four hours in a detention home. A child alleged to be or adjudicated a neglected child, an abused child, or a dependent child shall not be held in a detention home.

"(3) A child who is alleged to be or who is adjudicated an unruly child and who is taken into custody on a Saturday, Sunday, or legal holiday, as listed in section 1.14 of the Revised Code, may be held in a detention home until the next succeeding day that is not a Saturday, Sunday, or legal holiday.

"(D) Except as provided in division (F) of this section or in division (C) of section 2151.311, in division (C)(2) of section 5139.06 and section 5120.162, or in division (B) of section 5120.16 of the Revised Code, a child who is alleged to be or is adjudicated a delinquent child may not be held in a state correctional institution, county, multicounty, or municipal jail or workhouse, or other place where an adult convicted of crime, under arrest, or charged with crime is held.

"(E) Unless the detention is pursuant to division (F) of this section or division (C) of section 2151.311, division (C)(2) of section 5139.06 and section 5120.162, or division (B) of section 5120.16 of the Revised Code, the official in charge of the institution, jail, workhouse, or other facility shall inform the court immediately when a child, who is or appears to be under the age of eighteen years, is received at the facility, and shall deliver the child to the court upon request or transfer the child to a detention facility designated by the court.

"(F) If a case is transferred to another court for criminal prosecution pursuant to section 2151.26 of the Revised Code, the child may be transferred for detention pending the criminal prosecution in a jail or other facility in accordance with the law governing the detention of persons charged with crime. Any child so held shall be confined in a manner that keeps the child beyond the range of touch of all adult detainees. The child shall be supervised at all times during the detention."

Amendment Note: 2000 H 332 deleted "family" before "foster home" in division (A)(1).

Amendment Note: 2000 H 448 deleted "family" after "certified" in division (A)(1).

Amendment Note: 2000 S 181 added the second and third sentences in division (B).

Amendment Note: 1997 H 1 substituted "(F)" for "(C)" and "(C)(2)" for "(C)(3)" in divisions (D) and (E).

Amendment Note: 1996 H 124 added the references to sections 2151.312(C) and 5120.16(B) throughout division (B); substituted "a manner that keeps the child beyond the range of touch of" for "a room totally separate by both sight and sound from" in division (C); and made changes to reflect gender neutral language and other nonsubstantive changes.

Amendment Note: 1996 H 265 rewrote this section, which prior thereto read:

"(A) A child alleged to be a delinquent child, an unruly child, or a juvenile traffic offender may be held only in the following places:

"(1) A certified family foster home or a home approved by the court;

"(2) A facility operated by a certified child welfare agency;

"(3) A detention home or center for delinquent children which is under the direction or supervision of the court or other public authority or of a private agency and approved by the court;

"(4) Any other suitable place designated by the court.

"(B) Except as provided in division (C) of section 2151.311 or in division (C)(3) of section 5139.06 and section 5120.162 of the Revised Code, a child shall not be held in a state correctional institution, county, multicounty, or municipal jail or workhouse, or other place where an adult convicted of crime, under arrest, or charged with crime is held. Unless the detention is pursuant to division (C) of section 2151.311 or pursuant to division (C)(3) of section 5139.06 and section 5120.162 of the Revised Code, the official in charge of the institution, jail, workhouse, or other facility shall inform the court immediately when a child, who is or appears to be under the age of eighteen years, is received at the facility, and shall deliver him to the court upon request or transfer him to a detention facility designated by the court.

"(C) If a case is transferred to another court for criminal prosecution pursuant to section 2151.26 of the Revised Code, the child may be transferred for detention pending the criminal prosecution in a jail or other facility in accordance with the law governing the detention of persons charged with crime. Any child so held shall be confined in a room totally separate by both sight and sound from all adult detainees. The child shall be supervised at all times during the detention.

"(D) A child who is alleged to be a neglected, abused, or dependent child shall not be held in a state correctional institution, county, multicounty, or municipal jail, or other place where any adult convicted of crime, under arrest, or charged with crime is held. The alleged neglected, abused, or dependent child shall not be held in a detention home or a center for children who are alleged to be delinquent children."

Amendment Note: 1994 H 571 substituted "correctional" for "penal or reformatory" in divisions (B) and (D).

Amendment Note: 1993 H 152 inserted "family" in division (A)(1).

Cross References

Detention and shelter care, Juv R 7

Library References

Infants ⟲68.3, 192.
Westlaw Topic No. 211.
C.J.S. Infants §§ 41, 53 to 55, 198 to 207.

Research References

Encyclopedias

OH Jur. 3d Family Law § 1581, Alleged Delinquent or Unruly Child or Juvenile Traffic Offender.

OH Jur. 3d Family Law § 1582, Alleged Delinquent or Unruly Child or Juvenile Traffic Offender—Transfer of Child Upon Transfer of Case for Criminal Prosecution.

OH Jur. 3d Family Law § 1583, Alleged Neglected, Abused, or Dependent Child.

Treatises and Practice Aids

Carlin, Baldwin's Ohio Practice, Merrick-Rippner Probate Law § 107:27, Detention Separate from Adult Detainees.

Carlin, Baldwin's Ohio Practice, Merrick-Rippner Probate Law § 107:28, Children Subject to Detention.

Carlin, Baldwin's Ohio Practice, Merrick-Rippner Probate Law § 107:31, Bail.

Carlin, Baldwin's Ohio Practice, Merrick-Rippner Probate Law § 107:73, Alternatives for Disposition of Juvenile Cases.

Carlin, Baldwin's Ohio Practice, Merrick-Rippner Probate Law § 107:90, Disposition Orders for Delinquent Children, Effective January 1, 2002.

Painter, Ohio Driving Under the Influence § 12:45, Juvenile and "Underage" Offenders—Generally.

Giannelli & Yeomans, Ohio Juvenile Law § 2:7, Detention of "Children" Over the Age of 18 Years.

Giannelli & Yeomans, Ohio Juvenile Law § 19:1, Introduction.

Giannelli & Yeomans, Ohio Juvenile Law § 19:2, Place of Detention.

Giannelli & Yeomans, Ohio Juvenile Law § 19:9, Bail.

Giannelli & Yeomans, Ohio Juvenile Law § 27:18, "Catch-All" Provision.

Giannelli & Yeomans, Ohio Juvenile Law § 28:10, Imposition of Adult Penalties.

Law Review and Journal Commentaries

Deprived of "Fatal Liberty": The Rhetoric of Child Saving and the Reality of Juvenile Incarceration, J. Herbie DiFonzo. 26 U Tol L Rev 855 (Summer 1995).

Notes of Decisions

Ed. Note: This section contains annotations from former RC 2151.312.

Adult detention facility 5
Counsel 2
Delinquent child placement 6
Jail 1

Juvenile detention facility 4
State institution 3

---

1. Jail

Juvenile court's error in placing juvenile in county jail pending trial for alleged violation of parole was not prejudicial and thus did not warrant reversal. In re Raypole (Ohio App. 12 Dist., Fayette, 03-10-2003) No. CA2002-01-001, No. CA2002-01-002, 2003-Ohio-1066, 2003 WL 928976, Unreported. Infants 253

RC 2151.355(A)(9) does not authorize the juvenile court to exercise unlimited discretion in sentencing a delinquent child, and there is no authority for it to commit a delinquent juvenile to a jail for adult offenders, absent a finding that housing in an appropriate juvenile facility is unavailable, or that the public safety and protection so require. State v. Grady (Cuyahoga 1981) 3 Ohio App.3d 174, 444 N.E.2d 51, 3 O.B.R. 199.

A juvenile court judge who, illegally and unconstitutionally but nevertheless "judicially," sends juveniles to a county jail in violation of RC 2151.312(A)(4) is absolutely immune from damages in a 42 USC 1983 action, as are the sheriff, warden, and other corrections officers who carried out the orders. Doe v. McFaul (N.D.Ohio 1984) 599 F.Supp. 1421.

A county and its commissioners are not subject to liability for failing to overrule, countermand, challenge, or otherwise interfere with a juvenile court judge's illegal and unconstitutional, yet seemingly valid order to incarcerate juveniles in the county jail in violation of RC 2151.312(A)(4). Doe v. McFaul (N.D.Ohio 1984) 599 F.Supp. 1421.

Where a judge remands juveniles who are not being bound over for prosecution as adults to a county jail which lacks the capacity to counsel or even safeguard juveniles, and where the judge acts not because of a lack of proper facilities under RC 2151.312(A)(4) but because of theories propounded in a "television movie," the incarceration of the juveniles violates their statutory rights and also constitutes cruel and unusual punishment. Doe v. McFaul (N.D.Ohio 1984) 599 F.Supp. 1421.

2. Counsel

Juvenile rule and statute guarantee right to counsel for all indigent parties in juvenile proceedings. Holley v. Higgins (Franklin 1993) 86 Ohio App.3d 240, 620 N.E.2d 251. Infants 205

Indigent parties to juvenile court proceedings have a right to counsel under RC 2151.312 and Juv R 4(A). Lowry v. Lowry (Ross 1988) 48 Ohio App.3d 184, 549 N.E.2d 176.

3. State institution

Commitment of a fifteen year old to a state institution pursuant to RC 2151.26 for purpose of examination is not an act for which a writ of prohibition will issue. State ex rel. Harris v. Common Pleas Court, Division of Probate and Juvenile (Ross 1970) 25 Ohio App.2d 78, 266 N.E.2d 589, 54 O.O.2d 115.

4. Juvenile detention facility

Under governing statute, juvenile who was placed on probation following delinquency adjudication could not be held in county jail pending trial on alleged parole violation, even though he was 18 years of age at time of arrest for parole violation, but should have been placed in a juvenile facility. In re Raypole (Ohio App. 12 Dist., Fayette, 03-10-2003) No. CA2002-01-001, No. CA2002-01-002, 2003-Ohio-1066, 2003 WL 928976, Unreported. Infants 225

Order committing juvenile adjudicated delinquent to county juvenile center following probation violation was not abuse of discretion; juvenile had committed act which, if committed by adult, amounted to third degree felony, juvenile violated probation on numerous occasions, and juvenile's overall conduct, including assault on mother and refusal to follow instructions, indicated he had not made necessary adjustments in attitude or conduct. In re Goudy (Ohio App. 4 Dist., Washington, 01-21-2003) No. 02CA49, 2003-Ohio-547, 2003 WL 251956, Unreported. Infants 225

Juvenile who was 17 years of age at time he committed vehicular manslaughter forming basis of his adjudication, but was to turn 18 years old 38 days into his 90–day confinement was statutory "child" for purposes of disposition or sentencing, and court was limited to dispositional alternatives available in sentencing juveniles. In re Hennessey (Ohio App. 3 Dist., 09-13-2001) 146 Ohio App.3d 743, 768 N.E.2d 663, 2001-Ohio-2267, appeal not allowed 94 Ohio St.3d 1431, 761 N.E.2d 47. Infants 223.1

In accordance with RC 5119.64 et seq., juvenile runaways who are apprehended by law enforcement officials may not be placed in juvenile detention facilities even though suitable shelter is unavailable; however, if such a youth is determined to be a delinquent child as defined in RC 2151.02, an unruly child as defined in RC 2151.022, or a juvenile traffic offender as defined in RC 2151.021, he may be processed through the juvenile justice system and placed in a juvenile detention facility. OAG 77–063.

5. Adult detention facility

After a child is adjudicated delinquent, a trial court may choose from the statutory dispositions when sentencing, which include imposing a period of confinement, but is expressly precluded from placing the child in any state correctional institution, county, multicounty, or municipal jail or workhouse, or other place in which an adult convicted of a crime, under arrest, or charged with a crime is held. In re Hennessey (Ohio App. 3 Dist., 09-13-2001) 146 Ohio App.3d 743, 768 N.E.2d 663, 2001-Ohio-2267, appeal not allowed 94 Ohio St.3d 1431, 761 N.E.2d 47. Infants 223.1

Delinquent children may not be housed in any adult facility. In re Hennessey (Ohio App. 3 Dist., 09-13-2001) 146 Ohio App.3d 743, 768 N.E.2d 663, 2001-Ohio-2267, appeal not allowed 94 Ohio St.3d 1431, 761 N.E.2d 47. Infants 223.1

Juvenile court's wide latitude to make "any further disposition that the court finds proper" with respect to a delinquent child, or to order a commitment to "any other suitable place designated by the court," does not include placement in an adult county jail; the plain language of the applicable statutes prohibits the court from ordering a delinquent child to serve any time in the county jail even though he is chronologically an adult. In re Hennessey (Ohio App. 3 Dist., 09-13-2001) 146 Ohio App.3d 743, 768 N.E.2d 663, 2001-Ohio-2267, appeal not allowed 94 Ohio St.3d 1431, 761 N.E.2d 47. Infants 223.1

Juvenile court was without authority to commit juvenile to adult facility as part of his disposition, where juvenile was 17 years of age at time he committed vehicular manslaughter forming basis of his adjudication, but was to turn 18 years old 38 days into his 90–day confinement. In re Hennessey (Ohio App. 3 Dist., 09-13-2001) 146 Ohio App.3d 743, 768 N.E.2d 663, 2001-Ohio-2267, appeal not allowed 94 Ohio St.3d 1431, 761 N.E.2d 47. Infants 223.1

If the county adult detention facility is designed with a space which is enclosed on all sides, that is distinct, set apart and disconnected so that no child over the age of fifteen placed in that space will come in contact or communication with any adult convicted of or arrested for a crime, and the public interest and safety require the detention of such child when a delinquent detention facility is not available, the use of such adult facility is authorized. OAG 70–015.

6. Delinquent child placement

A child who is alleged to be delinquent because of a domestic violence offense may be placed in any setting authorized by RC 2151.312(A). OAG 96–061.

DETENTION FACILITIES

2152.41 Juvenile detention facility

(A) Upon the recommendation of the judge, the board of county commissioners shall provide, by purchase, lease, construction, or otherwise, a detention facility that shall be within a convenient distance of the juvenile court. The facility shall not be used for the confinement of adults charged with criminal offenses. The facility may be used to detain alleged delinquent children until final disposition for evaluation pursuant to section 2152.04 of the Revised Code, to confine children who are adjudicated delinquent children and placed in the facility pursuant to division (A)(3) of section 2152.19 of the Revised Code, and to confine children who are adjudicated juvenile traffic offenders and committed to the facility under division (A)(5) or (6) of section 2152.21 of the Revised Code.

(B) Upon the joint recommendation of the juvenile judges of two or more neighboring counties, the boards of county commissioners of the counties shall form themselves into a joint board and proceed to organize a district for the establishment and support of a detention facility for the use of the juvenile courts of those counties, in which alleged delinquent children may be detained as provided in division (A) of this section, by using a site or buildings already established in one of the counties or by providing for the purchase of a site and the erection of the necessary buildings on the site.

A child who is adjudicated to be a juvenile traffic offender for having committed a violation of division (A) of section 4511.19 of the Revised Code or of a municipal ordinance that is substantially comparable to that division may be confined in a detention facility or district detention facility pursuant to division (A)(5) of section 2152.21 of the Revised Code, provided the child is kept separate and apart from alleged delinquent children.

Except as otherwise provided by law, district detention facilities shall be established, operated, maintained, and managed in the same manner so far as applicable as county detention facilities.

Members of the board of county commissioners who meet by appointment to consider the organization of a district detention home, upon presentation of properly certified accounts, shall be paid their necessary expenses upon a warrant drawn by the county auditor of their county.

The county auditor of the county having the greatest population or, with the unanimous concurrence of the county auditors of the counties composing a district, the auditor of the county in which the detention facility is located shall be the fiscal officer of a detention facility district. The county auditors of the several counties composing a detention facility district shall meet at the district detention facility, not less than once in six months, to review accounts and to transact any other duties in connection with the institution that pertain to the business of their office.

(C) In any county in which there is no detention facility or that is not served by a district detention facility, the juvenile court may enter into a contract, subject to the approval of the board of county commissioners, with another juvenile court, another county's detention facility, or a joint county detention facility. Alternately, the board of county commissioners shall provide funds for the boarding of children, who would be eligible for detention under division (A) of this section, temporarily in private homes or in certified foster homes approved by the court for a period not exceeding sixty days or until final disposition of their cases, whichever comes first. The court also may arrange with any public children services agency or private child placing agency to receive, or private noncustodial agency for temporary care of, children within the jurisdiction of the court.

If the court arranges for the board of children temporarily detained in certified foster homes or through any private child placing agency, the county shall pay a reasonable sum to be fixed by the court for the board of those children. In order to have certified foster homes available for service, an agreed monthly subsidy may be paid and a fixed rate per day for care of children actually residing in the certified foster home.

(D) The board of county commissioners of any county within a detention facility district, upon the recommendation of the juvenile court of that county, may withdraw from the district and sell or lease its right, title, and interest in the site, buildings, furniture, and equipment of the facility to any counties in the district, at any price and upon any such terms that are agreed upon among the boards of county commissioners of the counties concerned. Section 307.10 of the Revised Code does not apply to this division. The net proceeds of any sale or lease under this division shall be paid into the treasury of the withdrawing county.

The members of the board of trustees of a district detention facility who are residents of a county withdrawing from the district are deemed to have resigned their positions upon the completion of the withdrawal procedure provided by this division. The vacancies then created shall be filled as provided in this section.

(E) The children to be admitted for care in a county or district detention facility established under this section, the period during which they shall be cared for in the facility, and the removal and transfer of children from the facility shall be determined by the juvenile court that ordered the child's detention.

(2002 H 400, eff. 4–3–03; 2000 S 179, § 3, eff. 1–1–02)

Historical and Statutory Notes

Ed. Note: 2152.41 is former 2151.34, amended and recodified by 2000 S 179, § 3, eff. 1–1–02; 2000 H 332, eff. 1–1–01; 2000 H 448, eff. 10–5–00; 1996 H 265, eff. 3–3–97; 1993 H 152, eff. 7–1–93; 1990 H 837, S 131; 1989 H 166; 1988 S 89; 1986 H 428; 1981 H 440; 1976 H 1196; 1975 H 85; 1970 H 931; 1969 H 320, S 49; 128 v 1211; 1953 H 1; GC 1639–22.

Pre–1953 H 1 Amendments: 121 v 557; 117 v 520

Amendment Note: 2002 H 400 rewrote division (A), which prior thereto read:

"(A) Upon the recommendation of the judge, the board of county commissioners shall provide, by purchase, lease, construction, or otherwise, a detention facility that shall be within a convenient distance of the juvenile court. The facility shall not be used for the confinement of adults charged with criminal offenses. The facility may be used to detain alleged delinquent children until final disposition for evaluation pursuant to section 2152.04 of the Revised Code and for children adjudicated juvenile traffic offenders under division (A)(5) or (6) of section 2152.21 of the Revised Code."

Amendment Note: 2000 S 179, § 3, eff. 1–1–02, rewrote this section, which prior thereto read:

"A child who is alleged to be or adjudicated a delinquent child may be confined in a place of juvenile detention for a period not to exceed ninety days, during which time a social history may be prepared to include court record, family history, personal history, school and attendance records, and any other pertinent studies and material that will be of assistance to the juvenile court in its disposition of the charges against that juvenile offender.

"Upon the advice and recommendation of the judge, the board of county commissioners shall provide, by purchase, lease, construction, or otherwise, a place to be known as a detention home that shall be within a convenient distance of the juvenile court and shall not be used for the confinement of adults charged with criminal offenses and in which delinquent children may be detained until final disposition. Upon the joint advice and recommendation of the juvenile judges of two or more adjoining or neighboring counties, the boards of county commissioners of the counties shall form themselves into a joint board and proceed to organize a district for the establishment and support of a detention home for the use of the juvenile courts of those counties, in which delinquent children may be detained until final disposition, by using a site or buildings already established in one of the counties or by providing for the purchase of a site and the erection of the necessary buildings on the site.

"A child who is adjudicated to be a juvenile traffic offender for having committed a violation of division (A) of section 4511.19 of the Revised Code or of a municipal ordinance that is substantially comparable to that division may be confined in a detention home or district detention home pursuant to division (A)(6) of section 2151.356 of the Revised Code, provided the child is kept separate and apart from alleged delinquent children.

"The county or district detention home shall be maintained as provided in sections 2151.01 to 2151.54 of the Revised Code. In any county in which there is no detention home or that is not served by a district detention home, the board of county commissioners shall provide funds for the boarding of such children temporarily in private homes. Children who are alleged to be or have been adjudicated delinquent children may be detained after a complaint is filed in the detention home until final disposition of their cases or in certified foster homes or in any other home approved by the court, if any are available, for a period not exceeding sixty days or until final disposition of their cases, whichever comes first. The court also may arrange with any public children services agency or private child placing agency to receive, or private noncustodial agency for temporary care of, the children within the jurisdiction of the court. A district detention home approved for such purpose by the department of youth services under section 5139.281 of the Revised Code may receive children committed to its temporary custody under section 2151.355 of the Revised Code and provide the care, treatment, and training required.

"If a detention home is established as an agency of the court or a district detention home is established by the courts of several counties as provided in this section, it shall be furnished and carried on, as far as possible, as a family home in charge of a superintendent or matron in a nonpunitive neutral atmosphere. The judge, or the directing board of a district detention home, may appoint a superintendent, a matron, and other necessary employees for the home and fix their salaries. During the school year, when possible, a comparable educational program with competent and trained staff shall be provided for those children of school age. A sufficient number of trained recreational personnel shall be included among the staff to assure wholesome and profitable leisure-time activities. Medical and mental health services shall be made available to ensure the courts all possible treatment facilities shall be given to those children placed under their care. In the case of a county detention home, the salaries shall be paid in the same manner as is provided by section 2151.13 of the Revised Code for other employees of the court, and the necessary expenses incurred in maintaining the detention home shall be paid by the county. In the case of a district detention home, the salaries and the necessary expenses incurred in maintaining the district detention home shall be paid as provided in sections 2151.341 to 2151.3415 of the Revised Code.

"If the court arranges for the board of children temporarily detained in certified foster homes or arranges for the board of those children through any private child placing agency, a reasonable sum to be fixed by the court for the board of those children shall be paid by the county. In order to have certified foster homes available for service, an agreed monthly subsidy may be paid and a fixed rate per day for care of children actually residing in the certified foster home."

Amendment Note: 2000 H 332 deleted "family" before "foster home in the fourth paragraph; substituted "certified" for "family" throughout the last paragraph; and made other nonsubstantive changes.

Amendment Note: 2000 H 448 deleted "family" after "certified" in the third sentence in the third paragraph; substituted "certified" for "family" three times in the last paragraph; and made other nonsubstantive changes.

Amendment Note: 1996 H 265 inserted "or adjudicated" in the first sentence in the first paragraph; removed references to unruly, dependent, neglected, and abused children and juvenile traffic offenders throughout this section; and rewrote the fourth paragraph, which prior thereto read:

"The county or district detention home shall be maintained as provided in sections 2151.01 to 2151.54 of the Revised Code. In any county in which there is no detention home or that is not served by a district detention home, the board of county commissioners shall provide funds for the boarding of such children temporarily in private homes. Children who are alleged to be or have been adjudicated delinquent, unruly, dependent, neglected, or abused children or juvenile traffic offenders, after a complaint is filed, may be detained in the detention home or in certified family foster homes until final disposition of their case. The court may arrange for the boarding of such children in certified family foster homes or in uncertified family foster homes for a period not exceeding sixty days, subject to the supervision of the court, or may arrange with any children services agency, or private child placing agency to receive, or private noncustodial agency for temporary care children within the jurisdiction of the court. A district detention home approve for such purpose by the department of youth services under section 5139.281 of the Revised Code may receive children committed to its temporary custody under section 2151.355 of the Revised Code and provide the care, treatment, and training required."

Amendment Note: 1993 H 152 changed "foster home" to "family foster home" throughout; and deleted "may enter into a contract with a public children services agency," before "private child placing agency" in the final paragraph.

Cross References

Actions against political subdivisions, negligence or omission in performing governmental or proprietary functions, Ch 2744
Adoption of rules for payment of assistance, 5139.29
Conditions of financial assistance for construction or acquisition of detention home, 5139.271
County taxing authority may submit securities issue to electors for support of schools, detention homes, forestry camps, or other facilities; permissible agreements to pay costs of permanent improvements of districts, 2151.655
Detention and shelter care, Juv R 7
Division of social administration, examination of institutions, 5103.03
Issuance of self-supporting securities to finance permanent improvements of juvenile detention facility districts, 133.152
Resolution relative to tax levy in excess of ten-mill limitation, 5705.19
Tax levy law, detention home districts, 5705.01
Uniform bond law, fiscal officer, subdivision and taxing authority defined, definitions, 133.01
Withdrawal of county from district, continuity of district tax levy, 2151.78

Library References

Infants ⇌192.
Westlaw Topic No. 211.
C.J.S. Infants §§ 41, 53 to 55.
Baldwin's Ohio Legislative Service, 1988 Laws of Ohio, S 89—LSC Analysis, p 5–571; 1990 Laws of Ohio, S 131—LSC Analysis, p 5–623

Research References

Encyclopedias
OH Jur. 3d Family Law § 1504, Generally; County Detention Homes.
OH Jur. 3d Family Law § 1505, Operation, Maintenance, and Management of Detention Homes.
OH Jur. 3d Family Law § 1506, Operation, Maintenance, and Management of Detention Homes—Superintendent and Other Employees.
OH Jur. 3d Family Law § 1507, Boarding Children in Private Homes.
OH Jur. 3d Family Law § 1540, Court Personnel.
OH Jur. 3d Family Law § 1581, Alleged Delinquent or Unruly Child or Juvenile Traffic Offender.
OH Jur. 3d Family Law § 1718, Cost of Education.

Treatises and Practice Aids
Carlin, Baldwin's Ohio Practice, Merrick-Rippner Probate Law § 104:13, Juvenile Court—Appropriations.
Carlin, Baldwin's Ohio Practice, Merrick-Rippner Probate Law § 104:17, Juvenile Facilities—Creation of Detention Homes.
Carlin, Baldwin's Ohio Practice, Merrick-Rippner Probate Law § 107:88, Adult Sentence for Juvenile.
Carlin, Baldwin's Ohio Practice, Merrick-Rippner Probate Law § 107:90, Disposition Orders for Delinquent Children, Effective January 1, 2002.
Carlin, Baldwin's Ohio Practice, Merrick-Rippner Probate Law § 107:108, Disposition of Juvenile Traffic Offender—Commitment to Detention Home or Institution.
Painter, Ohio Driving Under the Influence § 12:46, Juvenile and "Underage" Offenders—Juvenile Offender.
Giannelli & Yeomans, Ohio Juvenile Law § 27:6, County or Private Facility Commitment.
Giannelli & Yeomans, Ohio Juvenile Law § 28:6, Commitment to Juvenile Facility.
Hastings, Manoloff, Sheeran, & Stype, Ohio School Law § 23:2, Admission Requirements and Tuition Liability-Statutory Requirements in General.

Law Review and Journal Commentaries

Constitutional Law—Institutionalized Juveniles Have a Right to Rehabilitative Treatment, Note. 4 Cap U L Rev 85 (1975).

Deprived of "Fatal Liberty": The Rhetoric of Child Saving and the Reality of Juvenile Incarceration, J. Herbie DiFonzo. 26 U Tol L Rev 855 (Summer 1995).

Rethinking The Relationship Between Juvenile Courts And Treatment Agencies—An Administrative Law Approach, Leslie J. Harris. 28 J Fam L 217 (1990).

Notes of Decisions

Ed. Note: This section contains annotations from former RC 2151.34.

Constitutional issues 1
Education 3
Employees 4-6
    Establishment; costs, detention home 5
    Placement of juveniles, detention home 6
Establishment; costs, detention home, employees 5
Investigation of abuse at home 8
Jail or other adult facility 2
Place 7
Placement of juveniles, detention home, employees 6

---

1. Constitutional issues

County juvenile training facility, constructed pursuant to state statutory scheme but primarily county-funded, was not an arm of the state and thus not entitled to sovereign immunity in former resident's §§1983 action, even though under statutory scheme county acted as "state agenc[y]" in constructing facility and even though county juvenile court, a branch of state government, controlled admissions, appointed supervisor and set his salary, and had discretion over facility's budget; county rather than state would pay damages judgment against facility, and county rather than state or juvenile court made decision whether to create facility to begin with. S.J. v. Hamilton County, Ohio (C.A.6 (Ohio), 06-22-2004) 374 F.3d 416. Federal Courts ⇐ 270

Even though a juvenile detention center detainee was able to commit suicide by tying his t-shirt to the wire mesh in his door and hanging himself, the center's lack of more modern and efficient facilities does not deprive the detainee of his constitutional rights where the facilities, including the cell doors, were at all relevant times in accordance with state standards. Picciuto v. Lucas Cty. Bd. of Commrs. (Lucas 1990) 69 Ohio App.3d 789, 591 N.E.2d 1287, motion to certify overruled 58 Ohio St.3d 715, 570 N.E.2d 281.

A juvenile detention center's policy of not allowing new detainees off their floor for twenty-four hours does not violate the due process rights of a detainee who commits suicide where the detainee showed no signs he was contemplating suicide, and the policy prevents the spreading of illness pending a medical examination on the new detainee and prevents unnecessary disruption in the facility by hot-tempered detainees. Picciuto v. Lucas Cty. Bd. of Commrs. (Lucas 1990) 69 Ohio App.3d 789, 591 N.E.2d 1287, motion to certify overruled 58 Ohio St.3d 715, 570 N.E.2d 281.

County commissioners are not empowered by GC 1639–22 (RC 2151.34) to acquire a detention home upon a request by the judge of the court exercising the power and jurisdiction conferred by former Ohio Code, Title IV, Ch 8. 1949 OAG 1231.

2. Jail or other adult facility

Where a county has no separate juvenile detention home as provided in RC 2151.34 and the only facility for the detention of juveniles, as ordered and authorized by the juvenile judge, is a juvenile ward which is separated and secluded from the adult sections but is located in the county jail, and where, pursuant to verbal directions by the chief probation officer of the juvenile court, an eight-year-old boy, in the company of his father who was arrested by deputy sheriffs at 1:30 a.m., is placed by the deputy sheriffs, together with his father, in the juvenile ward in the county jail until the mother of the boy could come to take the boy home, and where the boy and his father are in the juvenile ward in the county jail for approximately one and one-half hours when the mother arrived and took the boy home, the sheriff of the county is not liable in damages in an action for false imprisonment brought by the mother on behalf of the boy, for the detention of the boy placed in the juvenile ward by his deputy sheriffs under the specific directions of the chief probation officer of the juvenile court. Garland v. Dustman (Portage 1969) 19 Ohio App.2d 292, 251 N.E.2d 153, 48 O.O.2d 408.

A county jail is a prison within the meaning of GC 1639–22 (RC 2151.34). Ex parte Karnes (Williams 1953) 121 N.E.2d 156, 67 Ohio Law Abs. 449.

Judge of juvenile court may not commit child who has been found to be delinquent child, or juvenile traffic offender, to county jail upon failure, refusal, or inability of such child to pay fine and court costs. OAG 70–143.

If the county adult detention facility is designed with a space which is enclosed on all sides, that is distinct, set apart and disconnected so that no child over the age of fifteen placed in that space will come in contact or communication with any adult convicted of or arrested for a crime, and the public interest and safety require the detention of such child when a delinquent detention facility is not available, the use of such adult facility is authorized. OAG 70–015.

A juvenile detention home is a place not used for the confinement of adult persons, and such a home should be separate and apart from buildings in which adult persons are confined; accordingly, such a juvenile detention home may not properly be established in a county jail, even though one complete floor of the jail would be used for such purpose, and the intention would be to keep the one floor separate and apart from the rest of the jail. 1962 OAG 2814.

Juvenile under fourteen may not, pending final disposition of his case, be confined in a cell in the upper part of the county jail even though such cell is separate and apart from the county jail proper. 1918 OAG p 1592.

3. Education

RC 2151.357 does not require the school district of residence of a child placed in a detention home by a juvenile court to pay the cost of nonacademic summer activities provided for the child by the detention home. OAG 85–028.

Pursuant to RC 2151.357, when a child is placed in a detention home established under RC 2151.34, the child's school district as determined by the court is responsible for paying the cost of the education of the child. OAG 80–101.

When it is not possible for the governing authorities of a juvenile detention home to provide "a comparable educational program," an educational program shall be provided by the school district in which the home is located and the expense thereof shall be assumed by the county. 1963 OAG 261; overruled to the extent that it is inconsistent with OAG 80–101.

Board of education may forbid attendance of inmates of home at public schools of district. 1921 OAG p 942.

4. Employees

Full-time juvenile court employees working part time at a juvenile detention center may be terminated from their part-time employment by the administrative judge of a juvenile court notwithstanding oral promises of continued employment that may have been made by the superintendent of the juvenile detention facility, as the terms of employment at juvenile detention facilities are governed by statute, not the doctrine of employment at will. Abbott v. Stepanik (Cuyahoga 1990) 64 Ohio App.3d 719, 582 N.E.2d 1082, dismissed, jurisdictional motion overruled 50 Ohio St.3d 717, 553 N.E.2d 1364.

Juvenile detention facility employees are not classified civil service employees, and are not entitled to protection under RC 124.34 against termination for other than just cause. Abbott v. Stepanik (Cuyahoga 1990) 64 Ohio App.3d 719, 582 N.E.2d 1082, dismissed, jurisdictional motion overruled 50 Ohio St.3d 717, 553 N.E.2d 1364. Infants ⇐ 273; Officers And Public Employees ⇐ 69.4

County commissioners are under no statutory duty to provide safe cells at a county-run detention center for juveniles and cannot be held liable in a negligence action brought by parents of a child who committed suicide in the detention center where the center employees are under the direct authority of the juvenile court and the commissioners have no control over how the money they appropriate for the center is spent. Picciuto v. Lucas Cty. Bd. of Commrs. (Lucas 1990) 69 Ohio App.3d 789, 591 N.E.2d 1287, motion to certify overruled 58 Ohio St.3d 715, 570 N.E.2d 281.

Employees of a juvenile detention center that is advised by juvenile court judges but has its own budget from the county and is administered by a board of trustees are not "officers of the court" but, instead, employees of the trustees. In re Five County Joint Juvenile Detention Center, SERB 85–050 (9–27–85).

5. —— Establishment; costs, detention home

Mandamus will not issue to compel county commissioners to provide juvenile detention facility if funds are not available therefor. State ex rel. Johns v. Board of County Commrs. of Richland County (Ohio 1972) 29 Ohio St.2d 6, 278 N.E.2d 19, 58 O.O.2d 65.

A writ of mandamus will issue to compel county commissioner to make provision for a detention home. State ex rel. Ray v. South (Ohio 1964) 176 Ohio St. 241, 198 N.E.2d 919, 27 O.O.2d 133.

Until the juvenile judge or juvenile judges advise and recommend the establishment of a county or a district detention home pursuant to RC 2151.34, there is no legal authority to levy a tax for that purpose nor for a tax levy in the alternative. OAG 66–173.

There is no statutory authority to submit a proposed district levy to the voters of such district for the purpose of building a district detention home pursuant to RC 2151.34 et seq. either before or after the formation of a district board of trustees. OAG 66–173.

If a district detention home is established pursuant to RC 2151.34, the board of county commissioners of each participating county shall provide for its proportionate share of the costs of establishing, maintaining, and supporting the detention home. OAG 66–173.

In case a juvenile detention home is established, it is under the supervision of the juvenile judge who also has the sole authority to appoint necessary employees for such home, and the county, through the board of county commissioners, has a duty to provide sufficient funds for the operation of the home. 1961 OAG 2034.

Where a juvenile judge of a county advised and recommended that a detention home be provided at a certain location and the board has taken no action in this regard for two years, the advice and recommendation for the establishment of a detention home are still in effect, and the board, while not being required to follow the specific recommendation as to location, has a mandatory duty to provide a detention home within a convenient distance of the juvenile court. 1961 OAG 2034.

A judge of the court exercising the powers and jurisdiction conferred by former Ohio Code, Title IV, Ch 8, is limited to advising and recommending the need of a detention home and the extent of the facilities required to fulfill that need; such advice and recommendation is a prerequisite to the exercise of the mandatory duty imposed upon the county commissioners to provide a detention home by this section. 1949 OAG 1231.

Where zoning ordinance establishes an area called a dwelling-house district and provides that "in a dwelling or apartment occupied as a private residence one or more rooms may be rented or table-board furnished," the temporary placing by juvenile court of four or fewer children for care in a private home in a single residence in said district is not a violation of such zoning ordinance. 1944 OAG 7011.

Detention quarters may be legally and properly maintained at county home, in charge of a superintendent or matron appointed by judge of juvenile court, to be paid on salary or per diem basis. 1938 OAG 2804.

It is mandatory that the board of county commissioners provide a juvenile detention home within a convenient distance of the juvenile court under this section. 1938 OAG 2804.

If the judge of the juvenile court advises and recommends the establishment of a detention home, it is mandatory upon the county commissioners to purchase or lease a detention home within a convenient distance of the court, not used for the confinement of adult persons charged with criminal offenses and which can be furnished and carried on as far as possible, as a family home, and the court is authorized to commit a delinquent child to such detention home. 1938 OAG 2803.

The superintendent of the detention home cannot be allowed a fixed amount per meal for the sustenance of the children in the home; allowances may be made only for the actual sums expended. 1930 OAG 1489.

Under former GC 1670 (RC 2151.34), upon the advice and recommendation of the juvenile judge, the commissioners should purchase or lease a detention home; in counties having a population less than forty thousand the commissioners are authorized to provide the necessary persons to care for said home and for the children therein. 1917 OAG p 1518.

6. —— Placement of juveniles, detention home

Sentencing option of detention in a juvenile detention facility is available to juvenile courts as a post-dispositional remedy. In re Hennessey (Ohio App. 3 Dist., 09-13-2001) 146 Ohio App.3d 743, 768 N.E.2d 663, 2001-Ohio-2267, appeal not allowed 94 Ohio St.3d 1431, 761 N.E.2d 47. Infants ⚖ 223.1

Juvenile's appeal from that portion of dispositional order sentencing him to detention in juvenile detention facility was required to be dismissed, where juvenile had already served his sentence and had been released, rendering it impossible for Court of Appeals to grant any effective relief. In re Hennessey (Ohio App. 3 Dist., 09-13-2001) 146 Ohio App.3d 743, 768 N.E.2d 663, 2001-Ohio-2267, appeal not allowed 94 Ohio St.3d 1431, 761 N.E.2d 47. Infants ⚖ 242

A final order of disposition of a child found to be delinquent, as prescribed by RC 2151.355, may not include, as punishment or otherwise, confinement or detention in a juvenile detention home. In re Bolden (Allen 1973) 37 Ohio App.2d 7, 306 N.E.2d 166, 66 O.O.2d 26. Infants ⚖ 223.1

Commitment of a fifteen year old to a state institution pursuant to RC 2151.26 for purpose of examination is not an act for which a writ of prohibition will issue. State ex rel. Harris v. Common Pleas Court, Division of Probate and Juvenile (Ross 1970) 25 Ohio App.2d 78, 266 N.E.2d 589, 54 O.O.2d 115.

A juvenile court in a post-dispositional setting may sentence a child found to be delinquent to a detention home, provided the home is in compliance with the statutory requisites concerning the care, treatment, and training of delinquent children. In re Hale, No. WD-85-74 (6th Dist Ct App, Wood, 4-25-86).

1976 H 1196, eff. 8-9-76, does not operate to prohibit the commingling of pre-adjudicated and post-adjudicated youth confined in a district detention home. OAG 77-006.

A detention home provided by authority of RC 2151.34 is for the detention of "delinquent, dependent, neglected children, or juvenile traffic offenders… until final disposition." 1963 OAG 553; overruled to the extent that it is inconsistent with OAG 80-101.

The placement or detention of delinquent, dependent, neglected children, or juvenile traffic offenders, is upon final disposition of the juvenile court and does not include placement in a detention home provided under RC 2151.34. 1963 OAG 553; overruled to the extent that it is inconsistent with OAG 80-101.

7. Place

Judge of juvenile court has power to place a child under its jurisdiction in custody of relative or other fit person in home outside state. 1938 OAG 1918.

8. Investigation of abuse at home

Public children services agencies are authorized to investigate reports of alleged child abuse or neglect or threats thereof at facilities operated by the mental health department pursuant to RC Ch 5122, by the mental retardation and developmental disabilities department pursuant to RC Ch 5123, by the youth services department pursuant to RC Ch 5139, at detention homes established pursuant to RC 2151.34, at the veterans' children's home operated pursuant to RC Ch 5909, and at public schools operating under standards set by the board of education pursuant to RC Ch 3301. OAG 89-108.

2152.42 Superintendents of facilities

(A) Any detention facility established under section 2152.41 of the Revised Code shall be under the direction of a superintendent. The superintendent shall be appointed by, and under the direction of, the judge or judges or, for a district facility, the board of trustees of the facility. The superintendent serves at the pleasure of the juvenile court or, in a district detention facility, at the pleasure of the board of trustees.

Before commencing work as superintendent, the person appointed shall obtain a bond, with sufficient surety, conditioned upon the full and faithful accounting of the funds and properties under the superintendent's control.

The superintendent, under the supervision and subject to the rules and regulations of the board, shall control, manage, operate, and have general charge of the facility and shall have the custody of its property, files, and records.

(B) For a county facility, the superintendent shall appoint all employees of the facility, who shall be in the unclassified civil service. The salaries shall be paid as provided by section 2151.13 of the Revised Code for other employees of the court, and the necessary expenses incurred in maintaining the facility shall be paid by the county.

For a district facility, the superintendent shall appoint other employees of the facility and fix their compensation, subject to approval of the board of trustees. Employees of a district facility, except for the superintendent, shall be in the classified civil service.

(C) During the school year, when possible, a comparable educational program with competent and trained staff shall be provided for children of school age who are in the facility. A sufficient number of trained recreational personnel shall be included among the staff. Medical and mental health services shall be made available.

(2000 S 179, § 3, eff. 1-1-02)

Library References

Infants ⚖192.
Westlaw Topic No. 211.
C.J.S. Infants §§ 41, 53 to 55.

Research References

Encyclopedias

OH Jur. 3d Family Law § 1540, Court Personnel.

Treatises and Practice Aids

Carlin, Baldwin's Ohio Practice, Merrick-Rippner Probate Law § 104:17, Juvenile Facilities—Creation of Detention Homes.

Giannelli & Yeomans, Ohio Juvenile Law § 19:11, Detention Facilities.

2152.43 Assistance in operation of facilities from department of youth services; tax assessment

(A) A board of county commissioners that provides a detention facility and the board of trustees of a district detention facility may apply to the department of youth services under section 5139.281 of the Revised Code for assistance in defraying the cost of operating and maintaining the facility. The application shall be made on forms prescribed and furnished by the department.

The board of county commissioners of each county that participates in a district detention facility may apply to the department of youth services for assistance in defraying the county's share of the cost of acquisition or construction of the facility, as provided in section 5139.271 of the Revised Code. Application shall be made in accordance with rules adopted by the department. No county shall be reimbursed for expenses incurred in the acquisition or construction of a district detention facility that serves a district having a population of less than one hundred thousand.

(B)(1) The joint boards of county commissioners of district detention facilities shall defray all necessary expenses of the facility not paid from funds made available under section 5139.281 of the Revised Code, through annual assessments of taxes, through gifts, or through other means.

If any county withdraws from a district under division (D) of section 2152.41 of the Revised Code, it shall continue to have levied against its tax duplicate any tax levied by the district during the period in which the county was a member of the district for current operating expenses, permanent improvements, or the retirement of bonded indebtedness. The levy shall continue to be a levy against the tax duplicate of the county until the time that it expires or is renewed.

(2) The current expenses of maintaining the facility not paid from funds made available under section 5139.281 of the Revised Code or division (C) of this section, and the cost of ordinary repairs to the facility, shall be paid by each county in accordance with one of the following methods as approved by the joint board of county commissioners:

(a) In proportion to the number of children from that county who are maintained in the facility during the year;

(b) By a levy submitted by the joint board of county commissioners under division (A) of section 5705.19 of the Revised Code and approved by the electors of the district;

(c) In proportion to the taxable property of each county, as shown by its tax duplicate;

(d) In any other method agreed upon by unanimous vote of the joint board of county commissioners.

(C) When any person donates or bequeaths any real or personal property to a county or district detention facility, the juvenile court or the trustees of the facility may accept and use the gift, consistent with the best interest of the institution and the conditions of the gift.

(2005 H 66, eff. 9-29-05; 2000 S 179, § 3, eff. 1-1-02)

Historical and Statutory Notes

Ed. Note: 2152.43 is former 2151.341, amended and recodified by 2000 S 179, § 3, eff. 1-1-02; 1981 H 440, eff. 11-23-81; 1977 S 221; 1976 H 1196; 128 v 1211.

Amendment Note: 2005 H 66 rewrote division (B)(2)(d), which prior thereto read:

"(d) In any combination of the methods for payment described in division (B)(2)(a), (b), or (c) of this section."

Amendment Note: 2000 S 179, § 3, eff. 1-1-02, rewrote this section, which prior thereto read:

"A board of county commissioners that provides a detention home and the board of trustees of a district detention home may make application to the department of youth services under section 5139.281 of the Revised Code for financial assistance in defraying the cost of operating and maintaining the home. Such application shall be made on forms prescribed and furnished by the department. The joint boards of county commissioners of district detention homes shall make annual assessments of taxes sufficient to support and defray all necessary expenses of such home not paid from funds made available under section 5139.281 of the Revised Code."

Cross References

Inspection of facilities by youth commission, 5139.31

Library References

Counties ⇐193.
States ⇐123.
Westlaw Topic Nos. 104, 360.
C.J.S. Counties §§ 227, 233.
C.J.S. States § 226.

Research References

Encyclopedias

OH Jur. 3d Family Law § 1510, Costs of Acquisition and Operation.

Treatises and Practice Aids

Carlin, Baldwin's Ohio Practice, Merrick-Rippner Probate Law § 104:17, Juvenile Facilities—Creation of Detention Homes.

2152.44 District detention facility trustees

(A) As soon as practical after the organization of the joint board of county commissioners as provided by section 2152.41 of the Revised Code, the joint board shall appoint a board of not less than five trustees. The board shall hold office until the first annual meeting after the choice of an established site and buildings, or after the selection and purchase of a building site. At that time, the joint board of county commissioners shall appoint a board of not less than five trustees, one of whom shall hold office for a term of one year, one for a term of two years, one for a term of three years, half of the remaining number for a term of four years, and the remainder for a term of five years. Annually thereafter, the joint board of county commissioners shall appoint one or more trustees, each of whom shall hold office for a term of five years, to succeed the trustee or trustees whose term of office expires. A trustee may be appointed to successive terms. Any person appointed as a trustee shall be recommended and approved by the juvenile court judge or judges of the county of which the person resides.

At least one trustee shall reside in each county in the district. In districts composed of two counties, each county shall be entitled to not less than two trustees. In districts composed of more than four counties, the number of trustees shall be sufficiently increased, provided that there shall always be an uneven number of trustees on the board. The county in which a district detention facility is located shall have not less than two trustees, who, in the interim period between the regular meetings of the trustees, shall act as an executive committee in the discharge of all business pertaining to the facility.

The joint board of county commissioners may remove any trustee for good cause. The trustee appointed to fill any vacancy shall hold the office for the unexpired term of the predecessor trustee.

(B) The annual meeting of the board of trustees shall be held on the first Tuesday in May in each year.

A majority of the board constitutes a quorum. Other board meetings shall be held at least quarterly. The juvenile court judge of each county of the district, or the judge's designee, shall attend the meetings. The members of the board shall receive no compensation for their services, except their actual and necessary expenses. The treasurer shall pay the member's traveling expenses when properly certified.

(C) When the board of trustees does not choose an established institution in one of the counties of the district, it may select a suitable site for the erection of a district detention facility. The site must be easily accessible, conducive to health, economy in purchasing or in building, and the general interest of the facility and its residents, and be as near as practicable to the geographical center of the district.

In the interim between the selection and purchase of a site, and the erection and occupancy of the district detention facility, the joint board of county commissioners provided under section 2152.41 of the Revised Code may delegate to the board of trustees any powers and duties that, in its judgment, will be of general interest or aid to the institution. The joint board of county commissioners may appropriate a trustees' fund, to be expended by the trustees for contracts, purchases, or other necessary expenses of the facility. The trustees shall make a complete settlement with the joint board of county commissioners once each six months, or quarterly if required, and shall make to the board of county commissioners and to the juvenile court of each of the counties a full report of the condition of the facility and residents.

(D) The choice of an established site and buildings, or the purchase of a site, stock, implements, and general farm equipment, should there be a farm, the erection of buildings, and the completion and furnishing of the district detention facility for occupancy, shall be in the hands of the joint board of county commissioners organized under section 2152.41 of the Revised Code. The joint board of county commissioners may delegate all or a portion of these duties to the board of trustees, under any restrictions that the joint board of county commissioners imposes.

When an established site and buildings are used for a district detention facility, the joint board of county commissioners shall cause the value of that site and those buildings to be properly appraised. This appraisal value, or in case of the purchase of a site, the purchase price and the cost of all improvements thereto, shall be paid by the counties comprising the district, in proportion to the taxable property of each county, as shown by its tax duplicate.

(E) Once a district is established, the trustees shall operate, maintain, and manage the facility as provided in sections 2152.41 to 2152.43 of the Revised Code and, on and after the effective date of this amendment and notwithstanding any provision of the Revised Code to the contrary, may adopt bylaws regarding the daily operation, maintenance, and management of the facility. No bylaw adopted pursuant to this division may supersede any provision of the Revised Code.

(2006 H 530, eff. 6–30–06; 2000 S 179, § 3, eff. 1–1–02)

Historical and Statutory Notes

Ed. Note: 2152.44 is former 2151.343, amended and recodified by 2000 S 179, § 3, eff. 1–1–02; 128 v 1211, eff. 11-2-59.

Amendment Note: 2006 H 530 substituted "2152.41" for "2151.41" in the first sentence of the second paragraph of division (C); and rewrote division (E). Prior to amendment, division (E) read:

"(E) Once a district is established, the trustees shall operate, maintain, and manage the facility as provided in sections 2152.41 to 2152.43 of the Revised Code."

Amendment Note: 2000 S 179, § 3, eff. 1–1–02, rewrote this section, which prior thereto read:

"Immediately upon the organization of the joint board of county commissioners as provided by section 2151.34 of the Revised Code, or so soon thereafter as practicable, such joint board of county commissioners shall appoint a board of not less than five trustees, which shall hold office for and perform its duties until the first annual meeting after the choice of an established site and buildings, or after the selection and purchase of a building site, at which time such joint board of county commissioners shall appoint a board of not less than five trustees, one of whom shall hold office for a term of one year, one for the term of two years, one for the term of three years, half of the remaining number for the term of four years, and the remainder for the term of five years. Annually thereafter, the joint board of county commissioners shall appoint one or more trustees, each of whom shall hold office for the term of five years, to succeed the trustee or trustees whose term of office shall expire. A trustee may be appointed to succeed himself upon such board of trustees, and all appointments to such board of trustees shall be made from persons who are recommended and approved by the juvenile court judge or judges of the county of which such person is resident. The annual meeting of the board of trustees shall be held on the first Tuesday in May in each year."

Library References

Infants ⚖=192.
Westlaw Topic No. 211.
C.J.S. Infants §§ 41, 53 to 55.

Notes of Decisions

Ed. Note: This section contains annotations from former RC 2151.343.

Board members 2
Costs 1

1. Costs

RC 2151.3412 and RC 2151.77 require that the costs of operating and maintaining district juvenile detention and rehabilitation facilities be apportioned among the counties participating in the district on the basis of the counties' actual use of such facilities where no levy has been approved pursuant to RC 5705.19(A). Neither a joint board of county commissioners formed pursuant to RC 2151.34 and RC 2151.65 nor a district board of trustees appointed pursuant to RC 2151.343 and RC 2151.68 has the authority to direct or permit the apportionment of such costs in any other manner. OAG 84–052.

2. Board members

There is nothing to preclude a juvenile court judge from being appointed a member of a board of trustees of a district detention home, if it is physically possible for one person to discharge the duties of both positions. OAG 66–112.

ORDERS RESTRAINING PARENTS

2152.61 Orders restraining parents, guardians, or custodians

(A) In any proceeding in which a child has been adjudicated a delinquent child or a juvenile traffic offender, on the application of a party or the court's own motion, the court may make an order restraining or otherwise controlling the conduct of any parent, guardian, or other custodian in the relationship of the individual to the child if the court finds that an order of that type necessary to do either of the following:

(1) Control any conduct or relationship that will be detrimental or harmful to the child;

(2) Control any conduct or relationship that will tend to defeat the execution of the order of disposition made or to be made.

(B) Due notice of the application or motion and the grounds for the application or motion under division (A) of this section, and an opportunity to be heard, shall be given to the person against whom the order under that division is directed. The order may include a requirement that the child's parent, guardian, or other custodian enter into a recognizance with sufficient surety, conditioned upon the faithful discharge of any conditions or control required by the court.

(C) A person's failure to comply with any order made by the court under this section is contempt of court under Chapter 2705. of the Revised Code.

(2000 S 179, § 3, eff. 1–1–02)

Library References

Infants ⬥69(1), 221.
Westlaw Topic No. 211.
C.J.S. Infants §§ 57, 69 to 85, 198, 206 to 209.

Research References

Treatises and Practice Aids

Carlin, Baldwin's Ohio Practice, Merrick-Rippner Probate Law § 107:113, Juvenile Court's Authority Over Parents.

Carlin, Baldwin's Ohio Practice, Merrick-Rippner Probate Law § 107:127, Contempt of Court in Juvenile Proceedings.

Giannelli & Yeomans, Ohio Juvenile Law § 32:2, Jurisdiction Over Parents and Others.

Giannelli & Yeomans, Ohio Juvenile Law § 28:11, Parental Orders.

Notes of Decisions

Notice and hearing 1

---

1. Notice and hearing

Trial court, in restricting contact between mother and juvenile after dismissing drug paraphernalia possession charges against juvenile based on finding that juvenile's mother had left paraphernalia with juvenile, was not required to comply with statute governing notice and hearing requirements "[i]n any proceeding in which a child has been adjudicated a delinquent child" for orders restraining parents, guardians, or custodians in relationship with juvenile, since, the charges having been dismissed, juvenile was not adjudicated a delinquent child. In re Boucher (Ohio App. 2 Dist., Champaign, 10-24-2003) No. 2003 CA 20, 2003-Ohio-5719, 2003 WL 22427769, Unreported. Infants ⬥ 198; Infants ⬥ 203

JURY TRIALS

2152.67   Jury trial; procedure

Any adult who is arrested or charged under any provision in this chapter and who is charged with a crime may demand a trial by jury, or the juvenile judge upon the judge's own motion may call a jury. A demand for a jury trial shall be made in writing in not less than three days before the date set for trial, or within three days after counsel has been retained, whichever is later. Sections 2945.17 and 2945.23 to 2945.36 of the Revised Code, relating to the drawing and impaneling of jurors in criminal cases in the court of common pleas, other than in capital cases, shall apply to a jury trial under this section. The compensation of jurors and costs of the clerk and sheriff shall be taxed and paid in the same manner as in criminal cases in the court of common pleas.

(2000 S 179, § 3, eff. 1–1–02)

Historical and Statutory Notes

Ed. Note: 2152.67 is former 2151.47, recodified by 2000 S 179, § 3, eff. 1–1–02; 2000 S 181, eff. 9–4–00; 1969 H 1, eff. 3–18–69; 132 v S 55; 1953 H 1; GC 1639–44.

Amendment Note: 2000 S 181 rewrote this section, which prior thereto read:

"Any adult arrested under section 2151.01 to 2151.54, inclusive, of the Revised Code, may demand a trial by jury, or the juvenile judge upon his own motion may call a jury. A demand for a jury trial must be made in writing in not less than three days before the date set for trial, or within three days after counsel has been retained, whichever is later. Sections 2945.17 and 2945.22 to 2945.36, inclusive, of the Revised Code, relating to the drawing and impaneling of jurors in criminal cases in the court of common pleas, other than in capital cases, shall apply to such jury trial. The compensation of jurors and costs of the clerk and sheriff shall be taxed and paid as in criminal cases in the court of common pleas."

Cross References

Jury trial, Crim R 23

Library References

Jury ⬥19.5, 22(2).
Westlaw Topic No. 230.
C.J.S. Juries §§ 7, 122, 140 to 141.

Research References

Encyclopedias

OH Jur. 3d Family Law § 1744, Trial by Jury.
OH Jur. 3d Family Law § 1752, Costs, Fees, and Expenses.
OH Jur. 3d Jury § 233, Compensation of Trial Jurors.

Notes of Decisions

Ed. Note: This section contains annotations from former RC 2151.47.

Referees 2
Waiver of jury trial 1

---

1. Waiver of jury trial

A defendant in a misdemeanor case may waive trial by jury orally. State v. Edwards (Montgomery 1952) 117 N.E.2d 444, 66 Ohio Law Abs. 479.

By former GC 1651 (RC 2151.35, RC 2151.47), a defendant in the juvenile court charged with contributing to juvenile delinquency, might waive a jury orally as in other misdemeanor cases. Walton v. State (Ohio App. 1914) 27 Ohio C.D. 12, 19 Ohio C.C.(N.S.) 452, 3 Ohio App. 97.

This section gives defendant right to demand a jury trial, and provides that if he does not, the judge, upon his own motion, may call a jury; but that does not give trial judge right to call a jury where defendant, in compliance with GC 13442–4 (RC 2945.05), expressly waives a trial by jury and elects to be tried by the court; when that is done, GC 13442–5 (RC 2945.06) makes it the mandatory duty of the trial judge to try the case without a jury. (See also Baker v State, 19 Abs 126 (App, Summit 1935).) Baker v State, 15 Abs 505 (App, Summit 1933).

2. Referees

A juvenile judge has no authority to commit the trial of a criminal charge against an adult to a referee, and any proceedings so committed are null and void. State v. Eddington (Marion 1976) 52 Ohio App.2d 312, 369 N.E.2d 1054, 6 O.O.3d 317. Criminal Law ⬥ 254.1

MISCELLANEOUS PROVISIONS

2152.71   Records and reports; statistical summaries

(A)(1) The juvenile court shall maintain records of all official cases brought before it, including, but not limited to, an appearance docket, a journal, and, in cases pertaining to an alleged delinquent child, arrest and custody records, complaints, journal entries, and hearing summaries. The court shall maintain a separate docket for traffic cases and shall record all traffic cases on the separate docket instead of on the general appearance docket. The parents, guardian, or other custodian of any child affected, if they are living, or the nearest of kin of the child, if the parents are deceased, may inspect these records, either in person or by counsel, during the hours in which the court is open. Division (A)(1) of this section does not require the release or authorize the inspection of arrest or incident reports, law enforcement investigatory reports or records, or witness statements.

(2) The juvenile court shall send to the superintendent of the bureau of criminal identification and investigation, pursuant to section 109.57 of the Revised Code, a weekly report containing a summary of each case that has come before it and that involves

the disposition of a child who is a delinquent child for committing an act that would be a felony or an offense of violence if committed by an adult.

(B) The clerk of the court shall maintain a statistical record that includes all of the following:

(1) The number of complaints that are filed with, or indictments or information made to, the court that allege that a child is a delinquent child, in relation to which the court determines under division (D) of section 2151.27 of the Revised Code that the victim of the alleged delinquent act was sixty-five years of age or older or permanently and totally disabled at the time of the alleged commission of the act;

(2) The number of complaints, indictments, or information described in division (B)(1) of this section that result in the child being adjudicated a delinquent child;

(3) The number of complaints, indictments, or information described in division (B)(2) of this section in which the act upon which the delinquent child adjudication is based caused property damage or would be a theft offense, as defined in division (K) of section 2913.01 of the Revised Code, if committed by an adult;

(4) The number of complaints, indictments, or information described in division (B)(3) of this section that result in the delinquent child being required as an order of disposition made under division (A) of section 2152.20 of the Revised Code to make restitution for all or part of the property damage caused by the child's delinquent act or for all or part of the value of the property that was the subject of the delinquent act that would be a theft offense if committed by an adult;

(5) The number of complaints, indictments, or information described in division (B)(2) of this section in which the act upon which the delinquent child adjudication is based would have been an offense of violence if committed by an adult;

(6) The number of complaints, indictments, or information described in division (B)(5) of this section that result in the delinquent child being committed as an order of disposition made under section 2152.16, divisions (A) and (B) of section 2152.17, or division (A)(2) of section 2152.19 of the Revised Code to any facility for delinquent children operated by the county, a district, or a private agency or organization or to the department of youth services;

(7) The number of complaints, indictments, or information described in division (B)(1) of this section that result in the case being transferred for criminal prosecution to an appropriate court having jurisdiction of the offense under section 2152.12 of the Revised Code.

(C) The clerk of the court shall compile an annual summary covering the preceding calendar year showing all of the information for that year contained in the statistical record maintained under division (B) of this section. The statistical record and the annual summary shall be public records open for inspection. Neither the statistical record nor the annual summary shall include the identity of any party to a case.

(D) Not later than June of each year, the court shall prepare an annual report covering the preceding calendar year showing the number and kinds of cases that have come before it, the disposition of the cases, and any other data pertaining to the work of the court that the juvenile judge directs. The court shall file copies of the report with the board of county commissioners. With the approval of the board, the court may print or cause to be printed copies of the report for distribution to persons and agencies interested in the court or community program for dependent, neglected, abused, or delinquent children and juvenile traffic offenders. The court shall include the number of copies ordered printed and the estimated cost of each printed copy on each copy of the report printed for distribution.

(E) If an officer is preparing pursuant to section 2947.06 or 2951.03 of the Revised Code or Criminal Rule 32.2 a presentence investigation report pertaining to a person, the court shall make available to the officer, for use in preparing the report, any records it possesses regarding any adjudications of that person as a delinquent child or regarding the dispositions made relative to those adjudications. The records to be made available pursuant to this division include, but are not limited to, any social history or report of a mental or physical examination regarding the person that was prepared pursuant to Juvenile Rule 32.

(2002 H 393, eff. 7–5–02; 2002 H 247, eff. 5–30–02; 2000 S 179, § 3, eff. 1–1–02)

Historical and Statutory Notes

Ed. Note: A special endorsement by the Legislative Service Commission states, "Comparison of these amendments [2002 H 393, eff. 7–5–02 and 2002 H 247, eff. 5–30–02] in pursuance of section 1.52 of the Revised Code discloses that they are not irreconcilable so that they are required by that section to be harmonized to give effect to each amendment." In recognition of this rule of construction, changes made by 2002 H 393, eff. 7–5–02, and 2002 H 247, eff. 5–30–02, have been incorporated in the above amendment. See *Baldwin's Ohio Legislative Service Annotated*, 2002 pages 3/L–553 and 2/L–121, or the OH–LEGIS or OH–LEGIS–OLD database on Westlaw, for original versions of these Acts.

Ed. Note: 2152.71 is former 2151.18, amended and recodified by 2000 S 179, § 3, eff. 1–1–02; 2000 S 181, eff. 9–4–00; 1999 H 3, eff. 11–22–99; 1998 H 2, eff. 1–1–99; 1996 H 124, eff. 3–31–97; 1995 H 1, eff. 1–1–96; 1993 H 152, eff. 7–1–93; 1990 S 268; 1984 S 5; 1981 H 440; 1979 H 394; 1975 H 85; 127 v 547; 1953 H 1; GC 1639–13.

Amendment Note: 2002 H 393 inserted the last two sentences in division (A)(1); and substituted "2152.19" for "2159.19" in division (B)(6).

Amendment Note: 2002 H 247 substituted "2152.19" for "2159.19" in division (B)(6); and added new division (E).

Amendment Note: 2000 S 179, § 3, eff. 1–1–02, rewrote division (A)(1); added references to indictments and informations throughout the section; substituted "section 2152.16, divisions (A) and (B) of section 2152.17, or division (A)(2) of section 2152.19" for "division (A)(3), (4), (5), (6), or (7) of section 2151.355" in division (B)(6); and substituted "2152.12" for '2151.26" in division (B)(8). Prior to amendment, division (A)(1) read:

"(A)(1) The juvenile court shall maintain records of all official cases brought before it, including, but not limited to, an appearance docket, a journal, a cashbook, records of the type required by division (A)(2) of section 2151.35 of the Revised Code, and, in cases pertaining to an alleged delinquent child, arrest and custody records, complaints, journal entries, and hearing summaries. The court shall maintain a separate docket for traffic cases and shall record all traffic cases on the separate docket instead of on the general appearance docket. The parents of any child affected, if they are living, or the nearest of kin of the child, if the parents are deceased, may inspect these records, either in person or by counsel during the hours in which the court is open."

Amendment Note: 2000 S 181 inserted ", but not limited to," and ", records of the type required by division (A)(2) of section 2151.35 of the Revised Code, and, in cases pertaining to an alleged delinquent child, arrest and custody records, complaints, journal entries, and hearing summaries" in division (A)(1); substituted "(A)(9)" for "(A)(8)(b)" in division (B)(4); and made other nonsubstantive changes.

Amendment Note: 1999 H 3 substituted "the disposition of a child who" for "an adjudication of a child" in division (A)(2).

Amendment Note: 1998 H 2 rewrote division (A)(2); and made other changes to reflect gender neutral language. Prior to amendment, division (A)(2) read:

"(2) The juvenile court shall send to the superintendent of the bureau of criminal identification and investigation, pursuant to section 109.57 of the Revised Code, a weekly report containing a summary of each case that has come before it and that involves an adjudication that a child is a delinquent child for committing a designated delinquent act or juvenile offense, as defined in section 109.57 of the Revised Code."

Amendment Note: 1996 H 124 substituted "a designated delinquent act or juvenile offense, as defined in section 109.57" for "an act that is a category one offense or a category two offense, as defined in section 2151.26" in division (A)(2).

Amendment Note: 1995 H 1 designated division (A)(1); added division (A)(2); rewrote division (B)(7); and made other nonsubstantive changes. Prior to amendment, division (B)(7) read:

"(7) The number of complaints described in division (B)(1) of this section that result in the case being transferred for criminal prosecution to an appropriate court having jurisdiction of the offense, under division (A) of section 2151.26 of the Revised Code, or that involve an act of a child that is required to be prosecuted in an appropriate court having jurisdiction of the offense, under division (G) of that section."

Amendment Note: 1993 H 152 substituted "cases" for "offenses" in division (A); designated division (C); inserted "statistical" before "record" in division (C); deleted former division (C); and deleted "or that the department of youth services requests" following "juvenile judge directs" and "department and with the" prior to "board of county commissioners" in division (D). Prior to amendment, division (C) read:

"(C) The juvenile court shall submit quarterly to the department of youth services, on forms provided by the department, the number of juveniles who were adjudicated delinquent children during the immediately preceding month for the commission of an act that would be a felony if committed by an adult, the number of those delinquent children who were committed to the department, and any other data regarding all official cases of the court that the department reasonably requests. The department shall publish this data on a statewide basis in statistical form at least annually. The department shall not publish the identity of any party to a case."

Cross References

Judges of the court of domestic relations, juvenile court responsibility, 2301.03
Presentence investigation reports, mandatory consideration of certain information, 2951.03

Library References

Courts ⚖113.
Infants ⚖133.
Westlaw Topic Nos. 106, 211.
C.J.S. Courts §§ 179, 181.
C.J.S. Infants §§ 57, 69 to 85.

Research References

Encyclopedias

OH Jur. 3d Courts & Judges § 205, Records of Court Judgments and Proceedings, and Miscellaneous Records Prescribed by Statute.
OH Jur. 3d Courts & Judges § 207, Dockets.
OH Jur. 3d Family Law § 1539, Powers and Duties—Records and Reports.

Treatises and Practice Aids

Carlin, Baldwin's Ohio Practice, Merrick-Rippner Probate Law § 106:1, Juvenile Court Jurisdiction—Delinquent Child—Definition: Evidence of Delinquency.
Carlin, Baldwin's Ohio Practice, Merrick-Rippner Probate Law § 107:1, Intake.
Carlin, Baldwin's Ohio Practice, Merrick-Rippner Probate Law § 107:86, Disposition of Delinquent Children—Previous Convictions—Prior to January 1, 2002.
Carlin, Baldwin's Ohio Practice, Merrick-Rippner Probate Law § 107:114, Juvenile Court Records—Confidentiality.
Carlin, Baldwin's Ohio Practice, Merrick-Rippner Probate Law § 107:115, Juvenile Court Records—Statistical.
Giannelli & Yeomans, Ohio Juvenile Law § 35:2, Confidentiality Requirement.

Law Review and Journal Commentaries

Preventing Violence in Ohio's Schools, Comment. 33 Akron L Rev 311 (2000).
Rights of passage: Analysis of waiver of juvenile court jurisdiction. 64 Fordham L Rev 2425 (1995).
Symposium: They Grow Up So Fast: When Juveniles Commit Adult Crimes, Hon. W. Don Reader, et al. 29 Akron L Rev 473 (Spring 1996).

Notes of Decisions

Ed. Note: This section contains annotations from former RC 2151.18.

Orders 2
Records 1

---

1. Records

The judge of the juvenile court of Hamilton county is not the clerk of his own court, when exercising the powers and jurisdictions conferred in RC 2151.01 to RC 2151.54, and mandamus will not lie to require him to exhibit to the attorneys representing a minor charged with a crime "all books, records, papers, [and] dockets… in all cases and proceedings involving" such minor. State ex rel. Hibbard v. Hoffman (Hamilton 1955) 101 Ohio App. 547, 137 N.E.2d 606, 1 O.O.2d 454.

In cases arising under this act, the entries and minutes made in the appearance docket and journal of the juvenile court are the only "record" required by law to be kept. 1921 OAG p 114.

2. Orders

Legitimation order filed in probate court with consent of mother did not bar subsequent parentage action wherein mother sought child support arrearages; application of doctrine of res judicata would violate state's strong public policy favoring protection of children and their support, health, maintenance and welfare, and would also violate equal protection. Lewis v. Chapin (Ohio App. 8 Dist., 03-21-1994) 93 Ohio App.3d 695, 639 N.E.2d 848   Children Out-of-wedlock ⚖ 33; Constitutional Law ⚖ 225.1

A court may not, by a nunc pro tunc order entered after term, enter an order which was not made or directed to be made during term.   Reynolds v Reynolds, 12 App 63, 31 CC(NS) 129 (1919).

2152.72 Information provided to foster caregivers or prospective adoptive parents regarding delinquent children; psychological examination

(A) This section applies only to a child who is or previously has been adjudicated a delinquent child for an act to which any of the following applies:

(1) The act is a violation of section 2903.01, 2903.02, 2903.03, 2903.04, 2903.11, 2903.12, 2903.13, 2907.02, 2907.03, or 2907.05 of the Revised Code.

(2) The act is a violation of section 2923.01 of the Revised Code and involved an attempt to commit aggravated murder or murder.

(3) The act would be a felony if committed by an adult, and the court determined that the child, if an adult, would be guilty of a specification found in section 2941.141, 2941.144, or 2941.145 of the Revised Code or in another section of the Revised Code that relates to the possession or use of a firearm during the commission of the act for which the child was adjudicated a delinquent child.

(4) The act would be an offense of violence that is a felony if committed by an adult, and the court determined that the child, if an adult, would be guilty of a specification found in section 2941.1411 of the Revised Code or in another section of the Revised Code that relates to the wearing or carrying of body armor during the commission of the act for which the child was adjudicated a delinquent child.

(B)(1) Except as provided in division (E) of this section, a public children services agency, private child placing agency, private noncustodial agency, or court, the department of youth services, or another private or government entity shall not place a child in a certified foster home or for adoption until it provides the foster caregivers or prospective adoptive parents with all of the following:

(a) A written report describing the child's social history;

(b) A written report describing all the acts committed by the child the entity knows of that resulted in the child being adjudicated a delinquent child and the disposition made by the court, unless the records pertaining to the acts have been sealed pursuant to section 2151.356 of the Revised Code;

(c) A written report describing any other violent act committed by the child of which the entity is aware;

(d) The substantial and material conclusions and recommendations of any psychiatric or psychological examination conducted on the child or, if no psychological or psychiatric examination of the child is available, the substantial and material conclusions and recommendations of an examination to detect mental and emotional disorders conducted in compliance with the requirements of Chapter 4757. of the Revised Code by an independent social worker, social worker, professional clinical counselor, or professional counselor licensed under that chapter. The entity shall not provide any part of a psychological, psychiatric, or mental and emotional disorder examination to the foster caregivers or prospective adoptive parents other than the substantial and material conclusions.

(2) Notwithstanding sections 2151.356 to 2151.358 of the Revised Code, if records of an adjudication that a child is a delinquent child have been sealed pursuant to those sections and an entity knows the records have been sealed, the entity shall provide the foster caregivers or prospective adoptive parents a written statement that the records of a prior adjudication have been sealed.

(C)(1) The entity that places the child in a certified foster home or for adoption shall conduct a psychological examination of the child unless either of the following applies:

(a) An entity is not required to conduct the examination if an examination was conducted no more than one year prior to the child's placement, and division (C)(1)(b) of this section does not apply.

(b) An entity is not required to conduct the examination if a foster caregiver seeks to adopt the foster caregiver's foster child, and an examination was conducted no more than two years prior to the date the foster caregiver seeks to adopt the child.

(2) No later than sixty days after placing the child, the entity shall provide the foster caregiver or prospective adoptive parents a written report detailing the substantial and material conclusions and recommendations of the examination conducted pursuant to this division.

(D)(1) Except as provided in divisions (D)(2) and (3) of this section, the expenses of conducting the examinations and preparing the reports and assessment required by division (B) or (C) of this section shall be paid by the entity that places the child in the certified foster home or for adoption.

(2) When a juvenile court grants temporary or permanent custody of a child pursuant to any section of the Revised Code, including section 2151.33, 2151.353, 2151.354, or 2152.19 of the Revised Code, to a public children services agency or private child placing agency, the court shall provide the agency the information described in division (B) of this section, pay the expenses of preparing that information, and, if a new examination is required to be conducted, pay the expenses of conducting the examination described in division (C) of this section. On receipt of the information described in division (B) of this section, the agency shall provide to the court written acknowledgment that the agency received the information. The court shall keep the acknowledgment and provide a copy to the agency. On the motion of the agency, the court may terminate the order granting temporary or permanent custody of the child to that agency, if the court does not provide the information described in division (B) of this section.

(3) If one of the following entities is placing a child in a certified foster home or for adoption with the assistance of or by contracting with a public children services agency, private child placing agency, or a private noncustodial agency, the entity shall provide the agency with the information described in division (B) of this section, pay the expenses of preparing that information, and, if a new examination is required to be conducted, pay the expenses of conducting the examination described in division (C) of this section:

(a) The department of youth services if the placement is pursuant to any section of the Revised Code including section 2152.22, 5139.06, 5139.07, 5139.38, or 5139.39 of the Revised Code;

(b) A juvenile court with temporary or permanent custody of a child pursuant to section 2151.354 or 2152.19 of the Revised Code;

(c) A public children services agency or private child placing agency with temporary or permanent custody of the child.

The agency receiving the information described in division (B) of this section shall provide the entity described in division (D)(3)(a) to (c) of this section that sent the information written acknowledgment that the agency received the information and provided it to the foster caregivers or prospective adoptive parents. The entity shall keep the acknowledgment and provide a copy to the agency. An entity that places a child in a certified foster home or for adoption with the assistance of or by contracting with an agency remains responsible to provide the information described in division (B) of this section to the foster caregivers or prospective adoptive parents unless the entity receives written acknowledgment that the agency provided the information.

(E) If a child is placed in a certified foster home as a result of an emergency removal of the child from home pursuant to division (D) of section 2151.31 of the Revised Code, an emergency change in the child's case plan pursuant to division (E)(3) of section 2151.412 of the Revised Code, or an emergency placement by the department of youth services pursuant to this chapter or Chapter 5139. of the Revised Code, the entity that places the child in the certified foster home shall provide the information described in division (B) of this section no later than ninety-six hours after the child is placed in the certified foster home.

(F) On receipt of the information described in divisions (B) and (C) of this section, the foster caregiver or prospective adoptive parents shall provide to the entity that places the child in the foster caregiver's or prospective adoptive parents' home a written acknowledgment that the foster caregiver or prospective adoptive parents received the information. The entity shall keep the acknowledgment and provide a copy to the foster caregiver or prospective adoptive parents.

(G) No person employed by an entity subject to this section and made responsible by that entity for the child's placement in a certified foster home or for adoption shall fail to provide the foster caregivers or prospective adoptive parents with the information required by divisions (B) and (C) of this section.

(H) It is not a violation of any duty of confidentiality provided for in the Revised Code or a code of professional responsibility for a person or government entity to provide the substantial and material conclusions and recommendations of a psychiatric or psychological examination, or an examination to detect mental and emotional disorders, in accordance with division (B)(1)(d) or (C) of this section.

(I) As used in this section:

(1) "Body armor" has the same meaning as in section 2941.1411 of the Revised Code.

(2) "Firearm" has the same meaning as in section 2923.11 of the Revised Code.

(2006 H 137, eff. 10–9–06; 2001 S 27, eff. 3–15–02; 2000 S 179, § 3, eff. 1–1–02)

Uncodified Law

2001 S 27, § 7, eff. 3–15–02, reads:

The amendment of section 2151.62 of the Revised Code is not intended to supersede its amendment and renumbering by Am. Sub. S.B. 179 of the 123rd General Assembly. Paragraphs of section 2151.62 of the Revised Code that are amended by this act were moved to section 2152.72 of the Revised Code by Am. Sub. S.B. 179, effective January 1, 2002, as part of its revision of the juvenile sentencing laws. Therefore, section 2152.72 of the Revised Code is amended by this act to continue, on and after January 1, 2002, the amendments this act is making to section 2151.62 of the Revised Code; section 2151.62 of the Revised Code as amended by this act is superseded on January 1, 2002, by the section as it results from its amendment and renumbering by Am. Sub. S.B. 179; and section 2152.72 of the Revised Code as amended by this act takes effect on January 1, 2002 [1].

[1] O Const Art II, § 1c and 1d, and RC 1.471 state that codified sections of law are subject to the referendum unless providing for tax levies, state appropriations, or are emergency in nature. Since this Act is apparently not an exception, and January 1, 2002, is within the ninety-day period, the Secretary of State has assigned an effective date of March 15, 2002.

Historical and Statutory Notes

Ed. Note: 2152.72 is former 2151.62, amended and recodified by 2000 S 179, § 3, eff. 1–1–02; 2000 S 222, eff. 3–22–01; 2000 H 332, eff. 1–1–01; 2000 H 448, eff. 10–5–00; 1998 H 173, eff. 7–29–98.

Amendment Note: 2006 H 137 substituted "2151.358" with "2151.356" in subdivision (B)(1)(b) and substituted "section" with "sections 2151.356 to" and "that section" with "those sections" in division (B)(2).

Amendment Note: 2001 S 27 inserted "or for adoption" and "or prospective adoptive parents" throughout the section; rewrote division (C); and made other nonsubstantive changes throughout the section. Prior to amendment, division (C) read:

"(C) The entity that places the child in a certified foster home shall conduct a psychological examination of the child, except that the entity is not required to conduct the examination if such an examination was conducted no more than one year prior to the child's placement. No later than sixty days after placing the child, the entity shall provide the foster caregiver a written report detailing the substantial and material conclusions and recommendations of the examination conducted pursuant to this division."

Amendment Note: 2000 S 179, § 3, eff. 1–1–02, substituted "2152.19" for "2151.355" in divisions (D)(2) and (D)(3)(b); substituted "2152,22" for "2151.38" in division (D)(3)(a); and made other nonsubstantive changes.

Amendment Note: 2000 S 222 deleted ", as defined in section 2923.11 of the Revised Code," after "firearm" in division (A)(3); and added divisions (A)(4) and (I).

Amendment Note: 2000 H 332 inserted "certified" throughout the section.

Amendment Note: 2000 H 448 inserted "certified" before "foster home" throughout the section.

Cross References

Content of preplacement training program, 5103.039

Ohio Administrative Code References

Adoptive placement procedures, OAC 5101:2–48–16
Pre-adoptive staffing, matching and placement procedures, OAC 5101:2–48–16

Library References

Adoption ⟝5.
Infants ⟝17, 226.
Westlaw Topic Nos. 17, 211.
C.J.S. Adoption of Persons §§ 10, 18 to 24.
C.J.S. Infants §§ 8 to 9, 57, 70 to 77.

Research References

Treatises and Practice Aids

Carlin, Baldwin's Ohio Practice, Merrick-Rippner Probate Law § 107:84, Disposition of Delinquent Children—Prior to January 1, 2002.

Giannelli & Yeomans, Ohio Juvenile Law § 32:3, Responsibilities to Victims and Others.

2152.73 Court participation in delinquency prevention activities

A juvenile court may participate with other public or private agencies of the county served by the court in programs that have as their objective the prevention and control of juvenile delinquency. The juvenile judge may assign employees of the court, as part of their regular duties, to work with organizations concerned with combatting conditions known to contribute to delinquency, providing adult sponsors for children who have been found to be delinquent children, and developing wholesome youth programs.

The juvenile judge may accept and administer on behalf of the court gifts, grants, bequests, and devises made to the court for the purpose of preventing delinquency.

(2000 S 179, § 3, eff. 1–1–02)

Historical and Statutory Notes

Ed. Note: 2152.73 is former 2151.11, amended and recodified by 2000 S 179, § 3, eff. 1–1–02; 131 v H 449, eff. 11–11–65.

Amendment Note: 2000 S 179, § 3, eff. 1–1–02, made nonsubstantive changes.

Cross References

Intake, Juv R 9

Library References

Courts ⟝55, 174.1.
Westlaw Topic No. 106.
C.J.S. Courts §§ 107 to 109.

Research References

Encyclopedias

OH Jur. 3d Family Law § 1537, Powers and Duties.

Treatises and Practice Aids

Carlin, Baldwin's Ohio Practice, Merrick-Rippner Probate Law § 104:19, Juvenile Facilities—Participation With Service Providers.

2152.74 DNA specimen collected from juvenile adjudged delinquent

(A) As used in this section, "DNA analysis" and "DNA specimen" have the same meanings as in section 109.573 of the Revised Code.

(B)(1) A child who is adjudicated a delinquent child for committing an act listed in division (D) of this section and who is committed to the custody of the department of youth services, placed in a detention facility or district detention facility pursuant to division (A)(3) of section 2152.19 of the Revised Code, or placed in a school, camp, institution, or other facility for delinquent children described in division (A)(2) of section 2152.19 of the Revised Code shall submit to a DNA specimen collection procedure administered by the director of youth services if committed to the department or by the chief administrative officer of the detention facility, district detention facility, school, camp, institution, or other facility for delinquent children to which the child was committed or in which the child was placed. If the court commits the child to the department of youth services, the director of youth services shall cause the DNA specimen to be collected from the child during the intake process at an institution operated by or under the control of the department. If the court commits the child to or places the child in a detention facility, district detention facility, school, camp, institution, or other facility for delinquent children, the chief administrative officer of the detention facility, district detention facility, school, camp, institution, or facility to which the child is committed or in which the child is placed shall cause the DNA specimen to be collected from the child during the intake process for the detention facility, district detention facility, school, camp, institution, or facility. The DNA specimen shall be collected from the child in accordance with division (C) of this section.

(2) If a child is adjudicated a delinquent child for committing an act listed in division (D) of this section, is committed to or placed in the department of youth services, a detention facility or district detention facility, or a school, camp, institution, or other facility for delinquent children, and does not submit to a DNA specimen collection procedure pursuant to division (B)(1) of this section, prior to the child's release from the custody of the department of youth services, from the custody of the detention facility or district detention facility, or from the custody of the school, camp, institution, or facility, the child shall submit to, and the director of youth services or the chief administrator of the detention facility, district detention facility, school, camp, institution, or facility to which the child is committed or in which the child was placed shall administer, a DNA specimen collection procedure at the institution operated by or under the control of the department of youth services or at the detention facility, district detention facility, school, camp, institution, or facility to which the child is committed or in which the child was placed. The DNA specimen shall be collected in accordance with division (C) of this section.

(3) If a child is adjudicated a delinquent child for committing an act listed in division (D) of this section, is not committed to or placed in the department of youth services, a detention facility or district detention facility, or a school, camp, institution, or other facility for delinquent children described in division (A)(2) or (3) of section 2152.19 of the Revised Code, and does not provide a DNA specimen pursuant to division (B)(1) or (2) of this section, the juvenile court shall order the child to report to the county probation department immediately after disposition to submit to a DNA specimen collection procedure administered by the chief administrative officer of the county probation department. The DNA specimen shall be collected from the child in accordance with division (C) of this section.

(C) If the DNA specimen is collected by withdrawing blood from the child or a similarly invasive procedure, a physician, registered nurse, licensed practical nurse, duly licensed clinical laboratory technician, or other qualified medical practitioner shall collect in a medically approved manner the DNA specimen required to be collected pursuant to division (B) of this section. If the DNA specimen is collected by swabbing for buccal cells or a similarly noninvasive procedure, this section does not require that the DNA specimen be collected by a qualified medical practitioner of that nature. No later than fifteen days after the date of the collection of the DNA specimen, the director of youth services or the chief administrative officer of the detention facility, district detention facility, school, camp, institution, or other facility for delinquent children to which the child is committed or in which the child was placed shall cause the DNA specimen to be forwarded to the bureau of criminal identification and investigation in accordance with procedures established by the superintendent of the bureau under division (H) of section 109.573 of the Revised Code. The bureau shall provide the specimen vials, mailing tubes, labels, postage, and instruction needed for the collection and forwarding of the DNA specimen to the bureau.

(D) The director of youth services and the chief administrative officer of a detention facility, district detention facility, school, camp, institution, or other facility for delinquent children shall cause a DNA specimen to be collected in accordance with divisions (B) and (C) of this section from each child in its custody who is adjudicated a delinquent child for committing any of the following acts:

(1) An act that would be a felony if committed by an adult;

(2) A violation of any law that would be a misdemeanor if committed by an adult and that arose out of the same facts and circumstances and same act as did a charge against the child of a violation of section 2903.01, 2903.02, 2905.01, 2907.02, 2907.03, 2907.05, or 2911.11 of the Revised Code that previously was dismissed or amended or as did a charge against the child of a violation of section 2907.12 of the Revised Code as it existed prior to September 3, 1996, that previously was dismissed or amended;

(3) A violation of section 2919.23 of the Revised Code that would be a misdemeanor if committed by an adult and that would have been a violation of section 2905.04 of the Revised Code as it existed prior to July 1, 1996, had the violation been committed prior to that date;

(4) A violation of section 2923.03 of the Revised Code involving complicity in committing a violation of section 2907.04 of the Revised Code that would be a misdemeanor if committed by an adult.

(2005 H 66, eff. 6–30–05; 2004 H 525, eff. 5–18–05; 2002 H 400, eff. 4–3–03; 2002 H 427, eff. 8–29–02; 2000 S 179, § 3, eff. 1–1–02)

Historical and Statutory Notes

Ed. Note: The legal review and technical services staff of the Legislative Service Commission has issued an opinion regarding the treatment of multiple amendments [2005 H 66, eff. 6–30–05 and 2004 H 525, eff. 5–18–05] under R.C. 1.52 stating, "The amendment by HB 66 is ineffective. The amendment by HB 525 resulted in repealing the language HB 66 attempted to amend. The cross-reference did not exist and therefore could not be amended.' The opinions are neither legally authoritative nor binding, but are provided as a general indication that the amendments of the several acts [2005 H 66, eff. 6–30–05 and 2004 H 525, eff. 5–18–05] may be included pursuant to the R.C. 1.52(B) rule of construction which requires all the amendments to be given effect if they can reasonably be put into simultaneous operation. See *Baldwin's Ohio Legislative Service Annotated*, 2005, page 5/L–856 and 2004, page 11/L–2631, or the OH-LEGIS or OH-LEGIS-OLD database on Westlaw, for original versions of these Acts.

Ed. Note: 2152.74 is former 2151.315, amended and recodified by 2000 S 179, § 3, eff. 1–1–02; 2000 H 442, eff. 10–17–00; 1998 H 526, eff. 9–1–98; 1996 H 124, eff. 3–31–97; 1996 S 269, eff. 7–1–96; 1995 H 5, eff. 8–30–95.

Amendment Note: 2005 H 66 substituted "5502.61" for "181.51" in the first paragraph of division (E).

Amendment Note: 2004 H 525 rewrote this section, which prior thereto read:

"(A) As used in this section, 'DNA analysis' and 'DNA specimen' have the same meanings as in section 109.573 of the Revised Code.

"(B)(1) A child who is adjudicated a delinquent child for committing an act listed in division (D) of this section and who is committed to the custody of the department of youth services, placed in a detention facility or district detention facility pursuant to division (A)(3) of section 2152.19 of the Revised Code, or placed in a school, camp, institution, or other facility for delinquent children described in division (A)(2) of section 2152.19 of the Revised Code shall submit to a DNA specimen collection procedure administered by the director of youth services if committed to the department or by the chief administrative officer of the detention facility, district detention facility, school, camp, institution, or other facility for delinquent children to which the child was committed or in which the child was placed. If the court commits the child to the department of youth services, the director of youth services shall cause the DNA specimen to be collected from the child during the intake process at an institution operated by or under the control of the department. If the court commits the child to or places the child in a detention facility, district detention facility, school, camp, institution, or other facility for delinquent children, the chief administrative officer of the detention facility, district detention facility, school, camp, institution, or facility to which the child is committed or in which the child is placed shall cause the DNA specimen to be collected from the child during the intake process for the detention facility, district detention facility, school, camp, institution, or facility. In accordance with division (C) of this section, the director or the chief administrative officer shall cause the DNA specimen to be forwarded to the bureau of criminal identification and investigation no later than fifteen days after the date of the collection of the DNA specimen. The DNA specimen shall be collected from the child in accordance with division (C) of this section.

"(2) If a child is adjudicated a delinquent child for committing an act listed in division (D) of this section, is committed to or placed in the department of youth services, a detention facility or district detention facility, or a school, camp, institution, or other facility for delinquent children, and does not submit to a DNA specimen collection procedure pursuant to division (B)(1) of this section, prior to the child's release from the custody of the department of youth services, from the custody of the detention facility or district detention facility, or from the custody of the school, camp, institution, or facility, the child shall submit to, and the director of youth services or the chief administrator of the detention facility, district detention facility, school, camp, institution, or facility to which the child is committed or in which the child was placed shall administer, a DNA specimen collection procedure at the institution operated by or under the control of the department of youth services or at the detention facility, district detention facility, school, camp, institution, or facility to which the child is committed or in which the child was placed. In accordance with division (C) of this section, the director or the chief administrative officer shall cause the DNA specimen to be forwarded to the bureau of criminal identification and investigation no later than fifteen days after the date of the collection of the DNA specimen. The DNA specimen shall be collected in accordance with division (C) of this section.

"(C) If the DNA specimen is collected by withdrawing blood from the child or a similarly invasive procedure, a physician, registered nurse, licensed practical nurse, duly licensed clinical laboratory technician, or other qualified medical practitioner shall collect in a medically approved manner the DNA specimen required to be collected pursuant to division (B) of this section. If the DNA specimen is collected by swabbing for buccal cells or a similarly noninvasive procedure, this section does not require that the DNA specimen be collected by a qualified medical practitioner of that nature. No later than fifteen days after the date of the collection of the DNA specimen, the director of youth services or the chief administrative officer of the detention facility, district detention facility, school, camp, institution, or other facility for delinquent children to which the child is committed or in which the child was placed shall cause the DNA specimen to be forwarded to the bureau of criminal identification and investigation in accordance with procedures established by the superintendent of the bureau under division (H) of section 109.573 of the Revised Code. The bureau shall provide the specimen vials, mailing tubes, labels, postage, and instruction needed for the collection and forwarding of the DNA specimen to the bureau.

"(D) The director of youth services and the chief administrative officer of a detention facility, district detention facility, school, camp, institution, or other facility for delinquent children shall cause a DNA specimen to be collected in accordance with divisions (B) and (C) of this section from each child in its custody who is adjudicated a delinquent child for committing any of the following acts:

"(1) A violation of section 2903.01, 2903.02, 2903.11, 2905.01, 2907.02, 2907.03, 2907.05, 2911.01, 2911.02, 2911.11, or 2911.12 of the Revised Code;

"(2) A violation of section 2907.12 of the Revised Code as it existed prior to September 3, 1996;

"(3) An attempt to commit a violation of section 2903.01, 2903.02, 2907.02, 2907.03, or 2907.05 of the Revised Code or to commit a violation of section 2907.12 of the Revised Code as it existed prior to September 3, 1996;

"(4) A violation of any law that arose out of the same facts and circumstances and same act as did a charge against the child of a violation of section 2903.01, 2903.02, 2905.01, 2907.02, 2907.03, 2907.05, or 2911.11 of the Revised Code that previously was dismissed or amended or as did a charge against the child of a violation of section 2907.12 of the Revised Code as it existed prior to September 3, 1996, that previously was dismissed or amended;

"(5) A violation of section 2905.02 or 2919.23 of the Revised Code that would have been a violation of section 2905.04 of the Revised Code as it existed prior to July 1, 1996, had the violation been committed prior to that date;

"(6) A felony violation of any law that arose out of the same facts and circumstances and same act as did a charge against the child of a violation of section 2903.11, 2911.01, 2911.02, or 2911.12 of the Revised Code that previously was dismissed or amended;

"(7) A violation of section 2923.01 of the Revised Code involving a conspiracy to commit a violation of section 2903.01, 2903.02, 2905.01, 2911.01, 2911.02, 2911.11, or 2911.12 of the Revised Code;

"(8) A violation of section 2923.03 of the Revised Code involving complicity in committing a violation of section 2903.01, 2903.02, 2903.11, 2905.01, 2907.02, 2907.03, 2907.04, 2907.05, 2911.01, 2911.02, 2911.11, or 2911.12 of the Revised Code or a violation of section 2907.12 of the Revised Code as it existed prior to September 3, 1996.

"(E) The director of youth services and the chief administrative officer of a detention facility, district detention facility, school, camp, institution, or other facility for delinquent children is not required to comply with this section in relation to the following acts until the superintendent of the bureau of criminal identification and investigation gives agencies in the juvenile justice system, as defined in section 181.51 of the Revised Code, in the state official notification that the state DNA laboratory is prepared to accept DNA specimens of that nature:

"(1) A violation of section 2903.11, 2911.01, 2911.02, or 2911.12 of the Revised Code;

"(2) An attempt to commit a violation of section 2903.01 or 2903.02 of the Revised Code;

"(3) A felony violation of any law that arose out of the same facts and circumstances and same act as did a charge against the child of a violation of section 2903.11, 2911.01, 2911.02, or 2911.12 of the Revised Code that previously was dismissed or amended;

"(4) A violation of section 2923.01 of the Revised Code involving a conspiracy to commit a violation of section 2903.01, 2903.02, 2905.01, 2911.01, 2911.02, 2911.11, or 2911.12 of the Revised Code;

"(5) A violation of section 2923.03 of the Revised Code involving complicity in committing a violation of section 2903.01, 2903.02, 2903.11, 2905.01, 2907.02, 2907.03, 2907.04, 2907.05, 2911.01, 2911.02, 2911.11, or 2911.12 of the Revised Code or a violation of section 2907.12 of the Revised Code as it existed prior to September 3, 1996."

Amendment Note: 2002 H 400 added "detention facility, district detention facility," in divisions (C), (D) and (E); added "or in which the child was placed" to the third sentence of division (C); and rewrote division (B), which prior thereto read:

"(B)(1) A child who is adjudicated a delinquent child for committing an act listed in division (D) of this section and who is committed to the custody of the department of youth services or to a school, camp, institution, or other facility for delinquent children described in division (A)(2) of section 2152.19 of the Revised Code shall submit to a DNA specimen collection procedure administered by the director of youth services if committed to the department or by the chief administrative officer of the school, camp, institution, or other facility for delinquent children to which the child was committed. If the court commits the child to the department of youth services, the director of youth services shall cause the DNA specimen to be collected from the child during the intake process at an institution operated by or under the control of the department. If the court commits the child to a school, camp, institution, or other facility for delinquent children, the chief administrative officer of the school, camp, institution, or facility to which the child is committed shall cause the DNA specimen to be collected from the child during the intake process for the school, camp, institution, or facility. In accordance with division (C) of this section, the director or the chief administrative officer shall cause the DNA specimen to be forwarded to the bureau of criminal identification and investigation no later than fifteen days after the date of the collection of the DNA specimen. The DNA specimen shall be collected from the child in accordance with division (C) of this section.

"(2) If a child is adjudicated a delinquent child for committing an act listed in division (D) of this section, is committed to the department of youth services or to a school, camp, institution, or other facility for delinquent children, and does not submit to a DNA specimen collection procedure pursuant to division (B)(1) of this section, prior to the child's release from the custody of the department of youth services or from the custody of the school, camp, institution, or facility, the child shall submit to, and the director of youth services or the chief administrator of the school, camp, institution, or facility to which the child is committed shall administer, a DNA specimen collection procedure at the institution operated by or under the control of the department of youth services or at the school, camp, institution, or facility to which the child is committed. In accordance with division (C) of this section, the director or the chief administrative officer shall cause the DNA specimen to be forwarded to the bureau of criminal identification and investigation no later than fifteen days after the date of the collection of the DNA specimen. The DNA specimen shall be collected in accordance with division (C) of this section.".

Amendment Note: 2002 H 427 rewrote divisions (C), (D) and (E), which prior thereto read:

"(C) A physician, registered nurse, licensed practical nurse, duly licensed clinical laboratory technician, or other qualified medical practitioner shall collect in a medically approved manner the DNA specimen required to be collected pursuant to division (B) of this section. No later than fifteen days after the date of the collection of the DNA specimen, the director of youth services or the chief administrative officer of the school, camp, institution, or other facility for delinquent children to which the child is committed shall cause the DNA specimen to be forwarded to the bureau of criminal identification and investigation in accordance with procedures established by the superintendent of the bureau under division (H) of section 109.573 of the Revised Code. The bureau shall provide the specimen vials, mailing tubes, labels, postage, and instruction needed for the collection and forwarding of the DNA specimen to the bureau.

"(D) The director of youth services and the chief administrative officer of a school, camp, institution, or other facility for delinquent children shall cause a DNA specimen to be collected in accordance with divisions (B) and (C) of this section from each child in its custody who is adjudicated a delinquent child for committing any of the following acts:

"(1) A violation of section 2903.01, 2903.02, 2905.01, 2907.02, 2907.03, 2907.05, or 2911.11 of the Revised Code;

"(2) A violation of section 2907.12 of the Revised Code as it existed prior to September 3, 1996;

"(3) An attempt to commit a violation of section 2907.02, 2907.03, or 2907.05 of the Revised Code or to commit a violation of section 2907.12 of the Revised Code as it existed prior to September 3, 1996;

"(4) A violation of any law that arose out of the same facts and circumstances and same act as did a charge against the child of a violation of section 2903.01, 2903.02, 2905.01, 2907.02, 2907.03, 2907.05, or 2911.11 of the Revised Code that previously was dismissed or amended or as did a charge against the child of a violation of section 2907.12 of the Revised Code as it existed prior to September 3, 1996, that previously was dismissed or amended;

"(5) A violation of section 2905.02 or 2919.23 of the Revised Code that would have been a violation of section 2905.04 of the Revised Code as it existed prior to July 1, 1996, had the violation been committed prior to that date.

"(E) The director of youth services and the chief administrative officer of a school, camp, institution, or other facility for delinquent children is not required to comply with this section until the superintendent of the bureau of criminal identification and investigation gives agencies in the juvenile justice system, as defined in section 181.51 of the Revised Code, in the state official notification that the state DNA laboratory is prepared to accept DNA specimens."

Amendment Note: 2000 S 179, § 3, eff. 1–1–02, substituted "division (2) of section 2152.19" for "division (3) of section 2151.355" in division (B)(1).

Amendment Note: 2000 H 442 deleted "2907.04," after "2907.03" in divisions (D)(1), (D)(3), and (D)(4).

Amendment Note: 1998 H 526 added references to sections 2903.01, 2903.02, 2905.01, and 2911.11 and inserted "or amended" twice in division (D)(4).

Amendment Note: 1996 H 124 rewrote division (D), which prior thereto read:

"(D) The director of youth services and the chief administrative officer of a school, camp, institution, or other facility for delinquent children shall cause a DNA specimen to be collected in accordance with divisions (B) and (C) of this section from each child in its custody who is adjudicated a delinquent child for committing any of the following acts:

"(1) A violation of section 2903.01, 2903.02, 2905.01, 2907.02, 2907.03, 2907.04, 2907.05, 2907.12, or 2911.11 of the Revised Code;

"(2) An attempt to commit a violation of section 2907.02, 2907.03, 2907.04, 2907.05, or 2907.12 of the Revised Code;

"(3) A violation of any law that arose out of the same facts and circumstances and same act as did a charge against the child of a violation of section 2907.02, 2907.03, 2907.04, 2907.05, or 2907.12 of the Revised Code that previously was dismissed;

"(4) A violation of section 2905.02 or 2919.23 of the Revised Code that would have been a violation of section 2905.04 of the Revised Code as it existed prior to July 1, 1996, had the violation been committed prior to that date.

Amendment Note: 1996 S 269 deleted "that if committed by an adult would be an offense" following "an act" in divisions (B)(1) and (B)(2); substituted "is adjudicated" for "was adjudicated", "is committed" for "was committed", and "does not submit" for "did not submit" in division (B)(2); substituted "any of the following acts" for "an act that if committed by an adult would be one of the following offenses" in the introductory paragraph of division (D); added division (D)(4); and made other nonsubstantive changes.

Cross References

Effect of sealed records, retention, limited disclosure, 2151.357
Reparations fund, DNA specimens, administration and analysis costs, 2743.191

Library References

Infants ⚖=275.
Westlaw Topic No. 211.
C.J.S. Infants §§ 198, 206 to 213, 274.
Baldwin's Ohio Legislative Service, 1995 H 5—LSC Analysis, p 5/L–336

Research References

Treatises and Practice Aids

Carlin, Baldwin's Ohio Practice, Merrick-Rippner Probate Law § 106:5, Juvenile Court Jurisdiction—Delinquent Child—Dna Testing of Certain Delinquent Children.

Carlin, Baldwin's Ohio Practice, Merrick-Rippner Probate Law § 107:91, Disposition of Delinquent Children—Financial Sanctions, Effective January 1, 2002.

Giannelli & Yeomans, Ohio Juvenile Law § 14:8, Dna Databases.

Notes of Decisions

Ed. Note: This section contains annotations from former RC 2151.315.

Admissions 2
Constitutional issues 1

---

1. Constitutional issues

Required collection of blood sample for DNA identification purposes from juveniles who are adjudicated delinquent on certain charges does not constitute an unreasonable search and seizure under the Fourth Amendment; reasonable doubt standard for proof of delinquency imposes substantially greater burden than the probable cause standard required for a search warrant, and the minimal intrusion of taking a blood sample is outweighed by state's legitimate interest in recording the identity of a person who is lawfully incarcerated, committed to a secure care facility, or on probation. In re Nicholson (Ohio App. 8 Dist., 02-16-1999) 132 Ohio App.3d 303, 724 N.E.2d 1217, dismissed, appeal not allowed 86 Ohio St.3d 1403, 711 N.E.2d 231. Infants ⚖ 201; Searches And Seizures ⚖ 78

Pursuant to RC 2152.74(B)(3), a juvenile court must order the collection of a DNA specimen from a juvenile placed on some form of probation supervision pursuant to RC 2152.19(A)(4) on or after May 18, 2005. OAG 05–037.

If a juvenile released from one of the Department of Youth Services' institutions before May 18, 2005, and currently on supervised release pursuant to RC 5139.51(B) has not previously submitted to a DNA specimen collection procedure pursuant to RC 2152.74(B)(1), RC 2152.74(B)(2) authorizes the collection of a DNA specimen from the juvenile. OAG 05–037.

RC 2152.74(B)(3) authorizes the collection of a DNA specimen from a juvenile who was not committed to, or placed in, the custody of the Department of Youth Services or an entity described in RC 2152.19(A)(2) or RC 2152.19(A)(3) and who has not previously submitted to a DNA specimen collection procedure pursuant to RC 2152.74(B)(1) or RC 2152.74(B)(2) when the juvenile is currently required to comply with the terms of a dispositional order issued by a juvenile court under RC Chapter 2152 before May 18, 2005. OAG 05–037.

2. Admissions

Requirement that juvenile who admitted delinquency on charge of gross sexual imposition provide a DNA sample was not a "consequence" of the admission of which trial court was obligated to inform him prior to accepting the admission; requirement was remedial and did not have a direct and immediate effect upon the range of juvenile's punishment. In re Nicholson (Ohio App. 8 Dist., 02-16-1999) 132 Ohio App.3d 303, 724 N.E.2d 1217, dismissed, appeal not allowed 86 Ohio St.3d 1403, 711 N.E.2d 231. Infants ⚖ 199

Whether State Department of Youth Services could properly require that juvenile provide blood sample for DNA identification, after failing to inform him of that requirement when he admitted his delinquency on charge of gross sexual imposition, was waived in proceeding to enjoin department from taking blood sample, where juvenile failed to seek a withdrawal of his admission. In re Nicholson (Ohio App. 8 Dist., 02-16-1999) 132 Ohio App.3d 303, 724 N.E.2d 1217, dismissed, appeal not allowed 86 Ohio St.3d 1403, 711 N.E.2d 231. Infants ⇔ 243

SEX OFFENSES

2152.81 Deposition of child sex offense victim

(A)(1) As used in this section, "victim" includes any of the following persons:

(a) A person who was a victim of a violation identified in division (A)(2) of this section or an act that would be an offense of violence if committed by an adult;

(b) A person against whom was directed any conduct that constitutes, or that is an element of, a violation identified in division (A)(2) of this section or an act that would be an offense of violence if committed by an adult.

(2) In any proceeding in juvenile court involving a complaint, indictment, or information in which a child is charged with a violation of section 2905.03, 2905.05, 2907.02, 2907.03, 2907.05, 2907.06, 2907.07, 2907.09, 2907.21, 2907.23, 2907.24, 2907.31, 2907.32, 2907.321, 2907.322, 2907.323, or 2919.22 of the Revised Code or an act that would be an offense of violence if committed by an adult and in which an alleged victim of the violation or act was a child who was less than thirteen years of age when the complaint or information was filed or the indictment was returned, the juvenile judge, upon motion of an attorney for the prosecution, shall order that the testimony of the child victim be taken by deposition. The prosecution also may request that the deposition be videotaped in accordance with division (A)(3) of this section. The judge shall notify the child victim whose deposition is to be taken, the prosecution, and the attorney for the child who is charged with the violation or act of the date, time, and place for taking the deposition. The notice shall identify the child victim who is to be examined and shall indicate whether a request that the deposition be videotaped has been made. The child who is charged with the violation or act shall have the right to attend the deposition and the right to be represented by counsel. Depositions shall be taken in the manner provided in civil cases, except that the judge in the proceeding shall preside at the taking of the deposition and shall rule at that time on any objections of the prosecution or the attorney for the child charged with the violation or act. The prosecution and the attorney for the child charged with the violation or act shall have the right, as at an adjudication hearing, to full examination and cross-examination of the child victim whose deposition is to be taken. If a deposition taken under this division is intended to be offered as evidence in the proceeding, it shall be filed in the juvenile court in which the action is pending and is admissible in the manner described in division (B) of this section. If a deposition of a child victim taken under this division is admitted as evidence at the proceeding under division (B) of this section, the child victim shall not be required to testify in person at the proceeding. However, at any time before the conclusion of the proceeding, the attorney for the child charged with the violation or act may file a motion with the judge requesting that another deposition of the child victim be taken because new evidence material to the defense of the child charged has been discovered that the attorney for the child charged could not with reasonable diligence have discovered prior to the taking of the admitted deposition. Any motion requesting another deposition shall be accompanied by supporting affidavits. Upon the filing of the motion and affidavits, the court may order that additional testimony of the child victim relative to the new evidence be taken by another deposition. If the court orders the taking of another deposition under this provision, the deposition shall be taken in accordance with this division; if the admitted deposition was a videotaped deposition taken in accordance with division (A)(3) of this section, the new deposition also shall be videotaped in accordance with that division, and, in other cases, the new deposition may be videotaped in accordance with that division.

(3) If the prosecution requests that a deposition to be taken under division (A)(2) of this section be videotaped, the juvenile judge shall order that the deposition be videotaped in accordance with this division. If a juvenile judge issues an order to video tape the deposition, the judge shall exclude from the room in which the deposition is to be taken every person except the child victim giving the testimony, the judge, one or more interpreters if needed, the attorneys for the prosecution and the child who is charged with the violation or act, any person needed to operate the equipment to be used, one person chosen by the child victim giving the deposition, and any person whose presence the judge determines would contribute to the welfare and well-being of the child victim giving the deposition. The person chosen by the child victim shall not be a witness in the proceeding and, both before and during the deposition, shall not discuss the testimony of the child victim with any other witness in the proceeding. To the extent feasible, any person operating the recording equipment shall be restricted to a room adjacent to the room in which the deposition is being taken, or to a location in the room in which the deposition is being taken that is behind a screen or mirror so that the person operating the recording equipment can see and hear, but cannot be seen or heard by, the child victim giving the deposition during the deposition. The child who is charged with the violation or act shall be permitted to observe and hear the testimony of the child victim giving the deposition on a monitor, shall be provided with an electronic means of immediate communication with the attorney of the child who is charged with the violation or act during the testimony, and shall be restricted to a location from which the child who is charged with the violation or act cannot be seen or heard by the child victim giving the deposition, except on a monitor provided for that purpose. The child victim giving the deposition shall be provided with a monitor on which the child victim can observe, while giving testimony, the child who is charged with the violation or act. The judge, at the judge's discretion, may preside at the deposition by electronic means from outside the room in which the deposition is to be taken; if the judge presides by electronic means, the judge shall be provided with monitors on which the judge can see each person in the room in which the deposition is to be taken and with an electronic means of communication with each person in that room, and each person in the room shall be provided with a monitor on which that person can see the judge and with an electronic means of communication with the judge. A deposition that is videotaped under this division shall be taken and filed in the manner described in division (A)(2) of this section and is admissible in the manner described in this division and division (B) of this section, and, if a deposition that is videotaped under this division is admitted as evidence at the proceeding, the child victim shall not be required to testify in person at the proceeding. No deposition videotaped under this division shall be admitted as evidence at any proceeding unless division (B) of this section is satisfied relative to the deposition and all of the following apply relative to the recording:

(a) The recording is both aural and visual and is recorded on film or videotape, or by other electronic means.

(b) The recording is authenticated under the Rules of Evidence and the Rules of Criminal Procedure as a fair and accurate representation of what occurred, and the recording is not altered other than at the direction and under the supervision of the judge in the proceeding.

(c) Each voice on the recording that is material to the testimony on the recording or the making of the recording, as determined by the judge, is identified.

(d) Both the prosecution and the child who is charged with the violation or act are afforded an opportunity to view the recording before it is shown in the proceeding.

(B)(1) At any proceeding in relation to which a deposition was taken under division (A) of this section, the deposition or a part of it is admissible in evidence upon motion of the prosecution if the testimony in the deposition or the part to be admitted is not excluded by the hearsay rule and if the deposition or the part to be admitted otherwise is admissible under the Rules of Evidence. For purposes of this division, testimony is not excluded by the hearsay rule if the testimony is not hearsay under Evidence Rule 801; if the testimony is within an exception to the hearsay rule set forth in Evidence Rule 803; if the child victim who gave the testimony is unavailable as a witness, as defined in Evidence Rule 804, and the testimony is admissible under that rule; or if both of the following apply:

(a) The child who is charged with the violation or act had an opportunity and similar motive at the time of the taking of the deposition to develop the testimony by direct, cross, or redirect examination.

(b) The judge determines that there is reasonable cause to believe that, if the child victim who gave the testimony in the deposition were to testify in person at the proceeding, the child victim would experience serious emotional trauma as a result of the child victim's participation at the proceeding.

(2) Objections to receiving in evidence a deposition or a part of it under division (B) of this section shall be made as provided in civil actions.

(3) The provisions of divisions (A) and (B) of this section are in addition to any other provisions of the Revised Code, the Rules of Juvenile Procedure, the Rules of Criminal Procedure, or the Rules of Evidence that pertain to the taking or admission of depositions in a juvenile court proceeding and do not limit the admissibility under any of those other provisions of any deposition taken under division (A) of this section or otherwise taken.

(C) In any proceeding in juvenile court involving a complaint, indictment, or information in which a child is charged with a violation listed in division (A)(2) of this section or an act that would be an offense of violence if committed by an adult and in which an alleged victim of the violation or offense was a child who was less than thirteen years of age when the complaint or information was filed or indictment was returned, the prosecution may file a motion with the juvenile judge requesting the judge to order the testimony of the child victim to be taken in a room other than the room in which the proceeding is being conducted and be televised, by closed circuit equipment, into the room in which the proceeding is being conducted to be viewed by the child who is charged with the violation or act and any other persons who are not permitted in the room in which the testimony is to be taken but who would have been present during the testimony of the child victim had it been given in the room in which the proceeding is being conducted. Except for good cause shown, the prosecution shall file a motion under this division at least seven days before the date of the proceeding. The juvenile judge may issue the order upon the motion of the prosecution filed under this division, if the judge determines that the child victim is unavailable to testify in the room in which the proceeding is being conducted in the physical presence of the child charged with the violation or act, due to one or more of the reasons set forth in division (E) of this section. If a juvenile judge issues an order of that nature, the judge shall exclude from the room in which the testimony is to be taken every person except a person described in division (A)(3) of this section. The judge, at the judge's discretion, may preside during the giving of the testimony by electronic means from outside the room in which it is being given, subject to the limitations set forth in division (A)(3) of this section. To the extent feasible, any person operating the televising equipment shall be hidden from the sight and hearing of the child victim giving the testimony, in a manner similar to that described in division (A)(3) of this section. The child who is charged with the violation or act shall be permitted to observe and hear the testimony of the child victim giving the testimony on a monitor, shall be provided with an electronic means of immediate communication with the attorney of the child who is charged with the violation or act during the testimony, and shall be restricted to a location from which the child who is charged with the violation or act cannot be seen or heard by the child victim giving the testimony, except on a monitor provided for that purpose. The child victim giving the testimony shall be provided with a monitor on which the child victim can observe, while giving testimony, the child who is charged with the violation or act.

(D) In any proceeding in juvenile court involving a complaint, indictment, or information in which a child is charged with a violation listed in division (A)(2) of this section or an act that would be an offense of violence if committed by an adult and in which an alleged victim of the violation or offense was a child who was less than thirteen years of age when the complaint or information was filed or the indictment was returned, the prosecution may file a motion with the juvenile judge requesting the judge to order the testimony of the child victim to be taken outside of the room in which the proceeding is being conducted and be recorded for showing in the room in which the proceeding is being conducted before the judge, the child who is charged with the violation or act, and any other persons who would have been present during the testimony of the child victim had it been given in the room in which the proceeding is being conducted. Except for good cause shown, the prosecution shall file a motion under this division at least seven days before the date of the proceeding. The juvenile judge may issue the order upon the motion of the prosecution filed under this division, if the judge determines that the child victim is unavailable to testify in the room in which the proceeding is being conducted in the physical presence of the child charged with the violation or act, due to one or more of the reasons set forth in division (E) of this section. If a juvenile judge issues an order of that nature, the judge shall exclude from the room in which the testimony is to be taken every person except a person described in division (A)(3) of this section. To the extent feasible, any person operating the recording equipment shall be hidden from the sight and hearing of the child victim giving the testimony, in a manner similar to that described in division (A)(3) of this section. The child who is charged with the violation or act shall be permitted to observe and hear the testimony of the child victim giving the testimony on a monitor, shall be provided with an electronic means of immediate communication with the attorney of the child who is charged with the violation or act during the testimony, and shall be restricted to a location from which the child who is charged with the violation or act cannot be seen or heard by the child victim giving the testimony, except on a monitor provided for that purpose. The child victim giving the testimony shall be provided with a monitor on which the child victim can observe, while giving testimony, the child who is charged with the violation or act. No order for the taking of testimony by recording shall be issued under this division unless the provisions set forth in divisions (A)(3)(a), (b), (c), and (d) of this section apply to the recording of the testimony.

(E) For purposes of divisions (C) and (D) of this section, a juvenile judge may order the testimony of a child victim to be taken outside of the room in which a proceeding is being conducted if the judge determines that the child victim is unavailable to testify in the room in the physical presence of the child charged with the violation or act due to one or more of the following circumstances:

(1) The persistent refusal of the child victim to testify despite judicial requests to do so;

(2) The inability of the child victim to communicate about the alleged violation or offense because of extreme fear, failure of memory, or another similar reason;

(3) The substantial likelihood that the child victim will suffer serious emotional trauma from so testifying.

(F)(1) If a juvenile judge issues an order pursuant to division (C) or (D) of this section that requires the testimony of a child victim in a juvenile court proceeding to be taken outside of the room in which the proceeding is being conducted, the order shall specifically identify the child victim to whose testimony it applies, the order applies only during the testimony of the specified child victim, and the child victim giving the testimony shall not be required to testify at the proceeding other than in accordance with the order. The authority of a judge to close the taking of a deposition under division (A)(3) of this section or a proceeding under division (C) or (D) of this section is in addition to the authority of a judge to close a hearing pursuant to section 2151.35 of the Revised Code.

(2) A juvenile judge who makes any determination regarding the admissibility of a deposition under divisions (A) and (B) of this section, the videotaping of a deposition under division (A)(3) of this section, or the taking of testimony outside of the room in which a proceeding is being conducted under division (C) or (D) of this section, shall enter the determination and findings on the record in the proceeding.

(2000 S 179, § 3, eff. 1–1–02)

Historical and Statutory Notes

Ed. Note: 2152.81 is former 2151.3511, amended and recodified by 2000 S 179, § 3, eff. 1–1–02; 2000 H 442, eff. 10–17–00; 1997 S 53, eff. 10–14–97; 1996 H 445, eff. 9–3–96; 1986 H 108, eff. 10–14–86.

Amendment Note: 2000 S 179, § 3, eff. 1–1–02, added references to indictments and informations throughout the section.

Amendment Note: 2000 H 442 deleted "2907.04," after "2907.03" in division (A)(2).

Amendment Note: 1997 S 53 added division (A)(1); redesignated former division (A)(2) as division (A)(3); designated division (A)(2); inserted references to Revised Code sections 2905.03, 2905.05, 2907.07, 2907.09, 2907.23 and 2907.24 in division (A)(2); substituted references to division (A)(2) with references to division (A)(3) throughout; substituted "less than thirteen" for "under eleven" in divisions (A)(2), (C) and (D); inserted "or an act that would be an offense of violence if committed by an adult" in divisions (A)(2), (C) and (D); and made changes to reflect gender neutral language and other nonsubstantive changes.

Amendment Note: 1996 H 445 removed a reference to section 2907.12 from the first sentence in division (A)(1); and made changes to reflect gender neutral language and other nonsubstantive changes.

Cross References

Bureau of criminal identification and investigation, recording and televising equipment for child sex offense victims, 109.54

Library References

Infants ⇐174, 201, 207.
Westlaw Topic No. 211.
C.J.S. Infants §§ 41 to 54, 58 to 67.

Research References

Encyclopedias

OH Jur. 3d Criminal Law § 466, Proceedings or Stages of Trial to Which Right Applies.
OH Jur. 3d Evidence & Witnesses § 253, Statements of Children With Respect to Sexual or Physical Abuse as Hearsay.
OH Jur. 3d Family Law § 1641, Depositions.

Treatises and Practice Aids

Giannelli and Snyder, Baldwin's Ohio Practice, Evidence, R 801, Definitions.
Giannelli and Snyder, Baldwin's Ohio Practice, Evidence, R 803, Hearsay Exceptions; Availability of Declarant Immaterial.
Giannelli and Snyder, Baldwin's Ohio Practice, Evidence, R 804, Hearsay Exceptions; Declarant Unavailable.
1 Giannelli and Snyder, Baldwin's Ohio Practice, Evidence, Index, Index.
Carlin, Baldwin's Ohio Practice, Merrick-Rippner Probate Law § 107:35, Depositions in Juvenile Proceedings.
Carlin, Baldwin's Ohio Practice, Merrick-Rippner Probate Law § 107:37, Testimony of Child Sex Offense Victims.
Carlin, Baldwin's Ohio Practice, Merrick-Rippner Probate Law § 107:38, Videotaped Depositions.
Carlin, Baldwin's Ohio Practice, Merrick-Rippner Probate Law § 107:39, Testimony on Closed Circuit Television or Recording.
Giannelli & Yeomans, Ohio Juvenile Law § 23:17, Evidence—Separation of Witnesses.

Law Review and Journal Commentaries

A Model Statute to Provide Foreign–Language Interpreters in the Ohio Courts, Alice J. Baker. 30 U Tol L Rev 593 (Summer 1999).

Navigating Between Scylla and Charybdis: Ohio's Efforts to Protect Children Without Eviscerating the Rights of Criminal Defendants–Evidentiary Considerations and the Rebirth of Confrontation Clause Analysis in Child Abuse Cases, Myrna S. Raeder. 25 U Tol L Rev 43 (1994).

Notes of Decisions

Ed. Note: This section contains annotations from former RC 2151.3511.

Age of victim 1
Televised testimony 2

---

1. Age of victim

RC 2151.3511 applies only when the accused is a child and the victim is a child under the age of eleven years. In re Burchfield (Athens 1988) 51 Ohio App.3d 148, 555 N.E.2d 325.

2. Televised testimony

Sufficient evidence supported trial court's decision to allow children who witnessed sexual abuse of other children to testify via closed circuit television from outside courtroom in juvenile delinquency proceeding, pursuant to statute allowing such testimony by child victims of sexual abuse, where physician testified that children who observe sexual abuse of another child can have problems discussing those observations in front of perpetrator, and child witnesses testified that they were afraid of juvenile and had been threatened by juvenile and another perpetrator. In re Howard (Ohio App. 12 Dist., 03-31-1997) 119 Ohio App.3d 33, 694 N.E.2d 488, dismissed, appeal not allowed 79 Ohio St.3d 1482, 683 N.E.2d 787. Infants ⇐ 207

Trial court's erroneous failure to enter factual findings in support of its determination that child victims of sexual abuse and children who witnessed abuse could testify via closed circuit television outside courtroom was harmless and did not violate juvenile's constitutional right to confront accusers in delinquency proceeding based on charges of rape and felonious sexual penetration; record contained sufficient evidence to support court's determination, and child witnesses testified under oath, were subject to full cross-examination, were able to be observed by judge and juvenile as they testified, and were able to observe juvenile as they testified. In re Howard (Ohio App. 12 Dist., 03-31-1997) 119 Ohio App.3d 33, 694 N.E.2d 488, dismissed, appeal not allowed 79 Ohio St.3d 1482, 683 N.E.2d 787. Infants ⇐ 253

Special procedure designed to allow child sexual abuse victim to testify at trial through closed circuit television is permissible if state proves necessity of such procedure; necessity determination must be made on case-by-case basis after court has heard evidence on issue, and court must find not only that child victim would suffer trauma due to presence of accused, but that emotional stress from which child would suffer would be significant. In re Howard (Ohio App. 12 Dist., 03-31-1997) 119 Ohio App.3d 33, 694 N.E.2d 488, dismissed, appeal not allowed 79 Ohio St.3d 1482, 683 N.E.2d 787. Witnesses ⇐ 228

JUVENILE OFFENDER REGISTRANTS

2152.811 Child adjudicated a child delinquent for committing a sexually oriented offense

If a court adjudicates a child a delinquent child for committing a presumptive registration-exempt sexually oriented offense, the court may determine pursuant to section 2950.021 of the Revised Code, prior to making an order of disposition for the child, that the child potentially should be subjected to classification as a juvenile offender registrant under sections 2152.82, 2152.83, 2152.84, or 2152.85 of the Revised Code and to registration under section 2950.04 of the Revised Code and all other duties and responsibilities generally imposed under Chapter 2950. of the Revised Code upon persons who are adjudicated delinquent children for committing a sexually oriented offense other than a presumptive registration-exempt sexually oriented offense. If the court so determines, divisions (B)(1) and (3) of section 2950.021 of the Revised Code apply, and the court shall proceed as described in those divisions.

(2003 S 5, eff. 7–31–03)

Library References

Infants ⚖227(2).
Westlaw Topic No. 211.
C.J.S. Infants §§ 41, 53 to 54, 57, 69 to 85.

Research References

Encyclopedias
OH Jur. 3d Family Law § 1698.6, Sexually Oriented and Child-Victim Offenses; Registration.

2152.82 Juvenile offender registrant

(A) The court that adjudicates a child a delinquent child shall issue as part of the dispositional order an order that classifies the child a juvenile offender registrant and specifies that the child has a duty to comply with sections 2950.04, 2950.041, 2950.05, and 2950.06 of the Revised Code if all of the following apply:

(1) The act for which the child is adjudicated a delinquent child is a sexually oriented offense that is not a registration-exempt sexually oriented offense or is a child-victim oriented offense that the child committed on or after January 1, 2002.

(2) The child was fourteen, fifteen, sixteen, or seventeen years of age at the time of committing the offense.

(3) The court has determined that the child previously was convicted of, pleaded guilty to, or was adjudicated a delinquent child for committing any sexually oriented offense or child-victim oriented offense, regardless of when the prior offense was committed and regardless of the child's age at the time of committing the offense.

(B) An order required under division (A) of this section shall be issued at the time the judge makes the orders of disposition for the delinquent child. Prior to issuing the order required by division (A) of this section, the judge shall conduct the hearing and make the determinations required by division (B) of section 2950.09 of the Revised Code regarding a sexually oriented offense that is not a registration-exempt sexually oriented offense or division (B) of section 2950.091 of the Revised Code regarding a child-victim oriented offense to determine if the child is to be classified a sexual predator or a child-victim predator, shall make the determinations required by division (E) of section 2950.09 of the Revised Code regarding a sexually oriented offense that is not a registration-exempt sexually oriented offense or division (E) of section 2950.091 of the Revised Code regarding a child-victim oriented offense to determine if the child is to be classified a habitual sex offender or a habitual child-victim offender, and shall otherwise comply with those divisions. When a judge issues an order under division (A) of this section, all of the following apply:

(1) The judge shall include in the order any determination that the delinquent child is, or is not, a sexual predator or child-victim predator or is, or is not, a habitual sex offender or habitual child-victim offender that the judge makes pursuant to division (B) or (E) of section 2950.09 or 2950.091 of the Revised Code and any related information required or authorized under the division under which the determination is made, including, but not limited to, any requirement imposed by the court subjecting a child who is a habitual sex offender or habitual child-victim offender to community notification provisions as described in division (E) of section 2950.09 or 2950.091 of the Revised Code.

(2) The judge shall include in the order a statement that, upon completion of the disposition of the delinquent child that was made for the sexually oriented offense or child-victim oriented offense upon which the order is based, a hearing will be conducted, and the order and any determinations included in the order are subject to modification or termination pursuant to sections 2152.84 and 2152.85 of the Revised Code.

(3) The judge shall provide to the delinquent child and to the delinquent child's parent, guardian, or custodian the notice required under divisions (A) and (B) of section 2950.03 of the Revised Code and shall provide as part of that notice a copy of the order.

(4) The judge shall include the order in the delinquent child's dispositional order and shall specify in the dispositional order that the order issued under division (A) of this section was made pursuant to this section.

(C) An order issued under division (A) of this section and any determinations included in the order shall remain in effect for the period of time specified in section 2950.07 of the Revised Code, subject to a modification or termination of the order under section 2152.84 or 2152.85 of the Revised Code, and section 2152.851 of the Revised Code applies regarding the order and the determinations. If an order is issued under division (A) of this section, the child's attainment of eighteen or twenty-one years of age does not affect or terminate the order, and the order remains in effect for the period of time described in this division.

(D) A court that adjudicates a child a delinquent child for a sexually oriented offense that is a registration-exempt sexually oriented offense shall not issue based on that adjudication an order under this section that classifies the child a juvenile offender registrant and specifies that the child has a duty to comply with sections 2950.04, 2950.041, 2950.05, and 2950.06 of the Revised Code.

(2003 S 5, eff. 7–31–03; 2002 H 393, eff. 7–5–02; 2001 S 3, eff. 1–1–02)

Historical and Statutory Notes

Amendment Note: 2003 S 5 substituted "comply with sections" for "register under section" and inserted ", 2950.041, 2950.05, and 2950.06" before "of the Revised Code" in the first paragraph; inserted "that is not a registration-exempt sexually oriented offense or is a child-victim oriented offense" to division (1); inserted "or child-victim oriented offense" to division (3); inserted "regarding a sexually oriented offense that is not a registration-exempt sexually oriented offense or division (B) of section 2950.091 of the Revised Code regarding a child-victim oriented offense" before "to determine if the child" and inserted "or a child-victim predator" before "shall make the determinations", deleted "that" after "by division (E) of", inserted "2950.09 of the Revised Code regarding a sexually oriented offense that is not a registration-exempt sexually oriented offense or division (E) of section 2950.091 of the Revised Code regarding a child-victim oriented offense" before "to determine if the child is to be classified as a habitual sex offender", inserted "or a habitual child-victim offender" before ", and shall otherwise comply", inserted ", or is not," before "sexual predator", inserted "or child-victim predator" before "or is", inserted ",or is not," before "a habitual sex offender", inserted "or habitual child-victim offender" before "that the judge makes", inserted "or 2950.091" before "of the Revised Code", inserted "or habitual child-victim offender" before "to community notification", deleted "that" after "division (E) of", and inserted "2950.09.09 or 2950.091 of the Revised Code" to division (B)(1); inserted "or child-victim oriented offense" before "upon which the order is based" in division (B)(2); deleted "a copy of the order" before "to the delinquent", deleted ", as part of" before "the notice", substituted "required" for "provided" before "under divisions (A) and (B)" and inserted "and shall provide as part of that notice a copy of the order" to division (B)(3); inserted ", and section 2152.851 of the Revised Code applies regarding the order and the determinations" to the end of the first sentence in division (C); and added new division (D).

Amendment Note: 2002 H 393 rewrote divisions (A) and (B) which prior thereto read:

"(A) If a child is adjudicated a delinquent child for committing on or after the effective date of this section a sexually oriented offense, the juvenile court judge who adjudicates the child a delinquent child shall issue an order that classifies the child a juvenile sex offender registrant and specifies that the child has a duty to register under section 2950.04 of the Revised Code if the delinquent child was fourteen, fifteen, sixteen, or seventeen years of age at the time of committing the offense, and the delinquent child previously was adjudicated a delinquent child for committing any sexually oriented offense, regardless of when the prior offense was committed and regardless of the delinquent child's age at the time of committing the offense.

"(B) An order required under division (A) of this section shall be issued at the time the judge makes the orders of disposition for the delinquent child. Prior to issuing the order, the judge shall conduct the hearing and make the determinations required by, and otherwise comply with, divisions (B) and (E) of section 2950.09 of the Revised Code. When a judge issues an order under division (A) of this section, all of the following apply:"

Cross References

Adjudication of offender as sexual predator or as habitual sex offender; exclusion of registration-exempt sexually oriented offense, 2950.09.
Child-victim oriented offenses; duty of registration of offender or delinquent child, 2950.041.
Determination of offender as child-victim predator; hearing, 2950.091.
Determination of requirement to register as sex offender with sheriff, 2950.021.
Manner of registering as sex offenders, 2950.04.
Notice of duty to register as sex offender and related requirements, 2950.03.
Sex offenders, definitions, 2950.01.

Library References

Infants ⚖227(2).
Westlaw Topic No. 211.
C.J.S. Infants §§ 41, 53 to 54, 57, 69 to 85.

Research References

Encyclopedias

OH Jur. 3d Criminal Law § 3241, Sexual Predator Hearing; Notice—Inclusion of Finding in Sentence.
OH Jur. 3d Criminal Law § 3447, Generally; Constitutionality.
OH Jur. 3d Criminal Law § 3453, Duties of Institution Officials.
OH Jur. 3d Criminal Law § 3454, Duties of Courts.
OH Jur. 3d Family Law § 1697, Notification of Victims.
OH Jur. 3d Family Law § 1698.6, Sexually Oriented and Child-Victim Offenses; Registration.

Treatises and Practice Aids

1 Giannelli and Snyder, Baldwin's Ohio Practice, Evidence, Index, Index.
Carlin, Baldwin's Ohio Practice, Merrick-Rippner Probate Law § 105:1, Juvenile Court—Exclusive Original Jurisdiction.
Carlin, Baldwin's Ohio Practice, Merrick-Rippner Probate Law § 107:89, Custody of Department of Youth Services.
Carlin, Baldwin's Ohio Practice, Merrick-Rippner Probate Law § 107:93, Classification of Juvenile Sex Offender Registrant, Effective January 1, 2002...
Carlin, Baldwin's Ohio Practice, Merrick-Rippner Probate Law § 107:94, Classification of Juvenile Sex Offender Registrant, Effective January 1, 2002 (If Charged With a Sexually Oriented Offense on or After January 1, 2002 and is 16-17 Years Old at the Time of...
Carlin, Baldwin's Ohio Practice, Merrick-Rippner Probate Law § 107:95, Classification of Juvenile Sex Offender Registrant, Effective January 1, 2002 (If Charged With a Sexually Oriented Offense on or After January 1, 2002 and is 14-15 Years Old at the Time of...
Carlin, Baldwin's Ohio Practice, Merrick-Rippner Probate Law § 107:96, Classification of Juvenile Sex Offender Registrant, Effective January 1, 2002—Hearing After Completion of the Dispositions Ordered Under RC 2152.82 and RC 2152.83—Continuation or Modification...
Carlin, Baldwin's Ohio Practice, Merrick-Rippner Probate Law § 107:97, Classification of Juvenile Sex Offender Registrant, Effective January 1, 2002—Subsequent Petition for Reclassification or Declassification of Orders Issued Pursuant to RC 2152.82, RC 2152.83 and...
Carlin, Baldwin's Ohio Practice, Merrick-Rippner Probate Law § 107:100, Frequency and Duration of Registration Based on the Classification of a Juvenile Sex Offender Registrant.
Giannelli & Yeomans, Ohio Juvenile Law § 6:1, Introduction.
Giannelli & Yeomans, Ohio Juvenile Law § 6:5, "Sexual Predator" Defined.
Giannelli & Yeomans, Ohio Juvenile Law § 6:9, Juvenile Offender Registrant—Repeat Offender Classification.
Giannelli & Yeomans, Ohio Juvenile Law § 6:10, Juvenile Offender Registrant—Mandatory Classification.
Giannelli & Yeomans, Ohio Juvenile Law § 6:11, Juvenile Offender Registrant—Discretionary Classification.

2152.821 Testimony of mentally retarded or developmentally disabled victim

(A) As used in this section:

(1) "Mentally retarded person" and "developmentally disabled person" have the same meanings as in section 5123.01 of the Revised Code.

(2) "Mentally retarded or developmentally disabled victim" includes any of the following persons:

(a) A mentally retarded person or developmentally disabled person who was a victim of a violation identified in division (B)(1) of this section or an act that would be an offense of violence if committed by an adult;

(b) A mentally retarded person or developmentally disabled person against whom was directed any conduct that constitutes, or that is an element of, a violation identified in division (B)(1) of this section or an act that would be an offense of violence if committed by an adult.

(B)(1) In any proceeding in juvenile court involving a complaint, indictment, or information in which a child is charged with a violation of section 2903.16, 2903.34, 2903.341, 2907.02, 2907.03, 2907.05, 2907.21, 2907. 23, 2907.24, 2907.32, 2907.321, 2907.322, or 2907.323 of the Revised Code or an act that would be an offense of violence if committed by an adult and in which an alleged victim of the violation or act was a mentally retarded person or developmentally disabled person, the juvenile judge, upon motion of the prosecution, shall order that the testimony of the mentally retarded or developmentally disabled victim be taken by deposition. The prosecution also may request that the deposition be videotaped in accordance with division (B)(2) of this section. The judge shall notify the mentally retarded or developmentally disabled victim whose deposition is to be taken, the prosecution, and the attorney for the child who is charged with the violation or act of the date, time, and place for taking the deposition. The notice shall identify the mentally retarded or developmentally disabled victim who is to be examined and shall indicate whether a request that the deposition be videotaped has been made. The child who is charged with the violation or act shall have the right to attend the deposition and the right to be represented by counsel. Depositions shall be taken in the manner provided in civil cases, except that the judge in the proceeding shall preside at the taking of the deposition and shall rule at that time on any objections of the prosecution or the attorney for the child charged with the violation or act. The prosecution and the attorney for the child charged with the violation or act shall have the right, as at an adjudication hearing, to full examination and cross-examination of the mentally retarded or developmentally disabled victim whose deposition is to be taken.

If a deposition taken under this division is intended to be offered as evidence in the proceeding, it shall be filed in the juvenile court in which the action is pending and is admissible in the manner described in division (C) of this section. If a deposition of a mentally retarded or developmentally disabled victim taken under this division is admitted as evidence at the proceeding under division (C) of this section, the mentally retarded or developmentally disabled victim shall not be required to testify in person at the proceeding.

At any time before the conclusion of the proceeding, the attorney for the child charged with the violation or act may file a motion with the judge requesting that another deposition of the mentally retarded or developmentally disabled victim be taken because new evidence material to the defense of the child charged has been discovered that the attorney for the child charged could not with reasonable diligence have discovered prior to the taking of the admitted deposition. Any motion requesting another deposition shall be accompanied by supporting affidavits. Upon the filing of the motion and affidavits, the court may order that additional testimony of the mentally retarded or developmentally disabled victim relative to the new evidence be taken by another deposition. If the court orders the taking of another deposition under this provision, the deposition shall be taken in accordance with this division. If the admitted deposition was a videotaped deposition taken in accordance with division (B)(2) of this section, the new deposition also shall be videotaped in accordance with that division. In other cases, the new deposition may be videotaped in accordance with that division.

(2) If the prosecution requests that a deposition to be taken under division (B)(1) of this section be videotaped, the juvenile judge shall order that the deposition be videotaped in accordance with this division. If a juvenile judge issues an order to video tape the deposition, the judge shall exclude from the room in which the deposition is to be taken every person except the mentally retarded or developmentally disabled victim giving the testimony, the judge, one or more interpreters if needed, the attorneys for the prosecution and the child who is charged with the violation or act, any person needed to operate the equipment to be used, one person chosen by the mentally retarded or developmentally disabled victim giving the deposition, and any person whose presence the judge determines would contribute to the welfare and well-being of the mentally retarded or developmentally disabled victim giving the deposition. The person chosen by the mentally retarded or developmentally disabled victim shall not be a witness in the proceeding and, both before and during the deposition, shall not discuss the testimony of the victim with any other witness in the proceeding. To the extent feasible, any person operating the recording equipment shall be restricted to a room adjacent to the room in which the deposition is being taken, or to a location in the room in which the deposition is being taken that is behind a screen or mirror so that the person operating the recording equipment can see and hear, but cannot be seen or heard by, the mentally retarded or developmentally disabled victim giving the deposition during the deposition.

The child who is charged with the violation or act shall be permitted to observe and hear the testimony of the mentally retarded or developmentally disabled victim giving the deposition on a monitor, shall be provided with an electronic means of immediate communication with the attorney of the child who is charged with the violation or act during the testimony, and shall be restricted to a location from which the child who is charged with the violation or act cannot be seen or heard by the mentally retarded or developmentally disabled victim giving the deposition, except on a monitor provided for that purpose. The mentally retarded or developmentally disabled victim giving the deposition shall be provided with a monitor on which the mentally retarded or developmentally disabled victim can observe, while giving testimony, the child who is charged with the violation or act. The judge, at the judge's discretion, may preside at the deposition by electronic means from outside the room in which the deposition is to be taken; if the judge presides by electronic means, the judge shall be provided with monitors on which the judge can see each person in the room in which the deposition is to be taken and with an electronic means of communication with each person in that room, and each person in the room shall be provided with a monitor on which that person can see the judge and with an electronic means of communication with the judge. A deposition that is videotaped under this division shall be taken and filed in the manner described in division (B)(1) of this section and is admissible in the manner described in this division and division (C) of this section. If a deposition that is videotaped under this division is admitted as evidence at the proceeding, the mentally retarded or developmentally disabled victim shall not be required to testify in person at the proceeding. No deposition videotaped under this division shall be admitted as evidence at any proceeding unless division (C) of this section is satisfied relative to the deposition and all of the following apply relative to the recording:

(a) The recording is both aural and visual and is recorded on film or videotape, or by other electronic means.

(b) The recording is authenticated under the Rules of Evidence and the Rules of Criminal Procedure as a fair and accurate representation of what occurred, and the recording is not altered other than at the direction and under the supervision of the judge in the proceeding.

(c) Each voice on the recording that is material to the testimony on the recording or the making of the recording, as determined by the judge, is identified.

(d) Both the prosecution and the child who is charged with the violation or act are afforded an opportunity to view the recording before it is shown in the proceeding.

(C)(1) At any proceeding in relation to which a deposition was taken under division (B) of this section, the deposition or a part of it is admissible in evidence upon motion of the prosecution if the testimony in the deposition or the part to be admitted is not excluded by the hearsay rule and if the deposition or the part to be admitted otherwise is admissible under the Rules of Evidence. For purposes of this division, testimony is not excluded by the hearsay rule if the testimony is not hearsay under Evidence Rule 801; the testimony is within an exception to the hearsay rule set forth in Evidence Rule 803; the mentally retarded or developmentally disabled victim who gave the testimony is unavailable as a witness, as defined in Evidence Rule 804, and the testimony is admissible under that rule; or both of the following apply:

(a) The child who is charged with the violation or act had an opportunity and similar motive at the time of the taking of the deposition to develop the testimony by direct, cross, or redirect examination.

(b) The judge determines that there is reasonable cause to believe that, if the mentally retarded or developmentally disabled victim who gave the testimony in the deposition were to testify in person at the proceeding, the mentally retarded or developmentally disabled victim would experience serious emotional trauma as a result of the mentally retarded or developmentally disabled victim's participation at the proceeding.

(2) Objections to receiving in evidence a deposition or a part of it under division (C) of this section shall be made as provided in civil actions.

(3) The provisions of divisions (B) and (C) of this section are in addition to any other provisions of the Revised Code, the Rules of Juvenile Procedure, the Rules of Criminal Procedure, or the Rules of Evidence that pertain to the taking or admission of depositions in a juvenile court proceeding and do not limit the admissibility under any of those other provisions of any deposition taken under division (B) of this section or otherwise taken.

(D) In any proceeding in juvenile court involving a complaint, indictment, or information in which a child is charged with a violation listed in division (B)(1) of this section or an act that would be an offense of violence if committed by an adult and in which an alleged victim of the violation or offense was a mentally retarded or developmentally disabled person, the prosecution may file a motion with the juvenile judge requesting the judge to order the testimony of the mentally retarded or developmentally disabled victim to be taken in a room other than the room in which the proceeding is being conducted and be televised, by closed circuit equipment, into the room in which the proceeding is being conducted to be viewed by the child who is charged with the violation or act and any other persons who are not permitted in the room in which the testimony is to be taken but who would have been present during the testimony of the mentally retarded or developmentally disabled victim had it been given in the room in which the proceeding is being conducted. Except for good cause shown, the prosecution shall file a motion under this division at least seven days before the date of the proceeding. The juvenile judge may issue the order upon the motion of the prosecution filed under this division, if the judge determines that the mentally retarded or developmentally disabled victim is unavailable to testify in the room in which the proceeding is being conducted in the physical presence of the child charged with the violation or act for one or more of the reasons set forth in division (F) of this section. If a juvenile judge issues an order of that nature, the judge shall exclude from the room in which the testimony is to be taken every person except a person described in division (B)(2) of this section. The judge, at the judge's discretion, may preside during the giving of the testimony by electronic means from outside the room in which it is being given, subject to the limitations set forth in division (B)(2) of this section. To the extent feasible, any person operating the televising equipment shall be hidden from the sight and hearing of the mentally retarded or developmentally disabled victim giving the testimony, in a manner similar to that described in division (B)(2) of this section. The child who is charged with the violation or act shall be permitted to observe and hear the testimony of the mentally retarded or developmentally disabled victim giving the testimony on a monitor, shall be provided with an electronic means of immediate communication with the attorney of the child who is charged with the violation or act during the testimony, and shall be restricted to a location from which the child who is charged with the violation or act cannot be seen or heard by the mentally retarded or developmentally disabled victim giving the testimony, except on a monitor provided for that purpose. The mentally retarded or developmentally disabled victim giving the testimony shall be provided with a monitor on which the mentally retarded or developmentally disabled victim can observe, while giving testimony, the child who is charged with the violation or act.

(E) In any proceeding in juvenile court involving a complaint, indictment, or information in which a child is charged with a violation listed in division (B)(1) of this section or an act that would be an offense of violence if committed by an adult and in which an alleged victim of the violation or offense was a mentally retarded or developmentally disabled person, the prosecution may file a motion with the juvenile judge requesting the judge to order the testimony of the mentally retarded or developmentally disabled victim to be taken outside of the room in which the proceeding is being conducted and be recorded for showing in the room in which the proceeding is being conducted before the judge, the child who is charged with the violation or act, and any other persons who would have been present during the testimony of the mentally retarded or developmentally disabled victim had it been given in the room in which the proceeding is being conducted. Except for good cause shown, the prosecution shall file a motion under this division at least seven days before the date of the proceeding. The juvenile judge may issue the order upon the motion of the prosecution filed under this division, if the judge determines that the mentally retarded or developmentally disabled victim is unavailable to testify in the room in which the proceeding is being conducted in the physical presence of the child charged with the violation or act, due to one or more of the reasons set forth in division (F) of this section. If a juvenile judge issues an order of that nature, the judge shall exclude from the room in which the testimony is to be taken every person except a person described in division (B)(2) of this section. To the extent feasible, any person operating the recording equipment shall be hidden from the sight and hearing of the mentally retarded or developmentally disabled victim giving the testimony, in a manner similar to that described in division (B)(2) of this section. The child who is charged with the violation or act shall be permitted to observe and hear the testimony of the mentally retarded or developmentally disabled victim giving the testimony on a monitor, shall be provided with an electronic means of immediate communication with the attorney of the child who is charged with the violation or act during the testimony, and shall be restricted to a location from which the child who is charged with the violation or act cannot be seen or heard by the mentally retarded or developmentally disabled victim giving the testimony, except on a monitor provided for that purpose. The mentally retarded or developmentally disabled victim giving the testimony shall be provided with a monitor on which the mentally retarded or developmentally disabled victim can observe, while giving testimony, the child who is charged with the violation or act. No order for the taking of testimony by recording shall be issued under this division unless the provisions set forth in divisions (B)(2)(a), (b), (c), and (d) of this section apply to the recording of the testimony.

(F) For purposes of divisions (D) and (E) of this section, a juvenile judge may order the testimony of a mentally retarded or developmentally disabled victim to be taken outside of the room in which a proceeding is being conducted if the judge determines that the mentally retarded or developmentally disabled victim is unavailable to testify in the room in the physical presence of the child charged with the violation or act due to one or more of the following circumstances:

(1) The persistent refusal of the mentally retarded or developmentally disabled victim to testify despite judicial requests to do so;

(2) The inability of the mentally retarded or developmentally disabled victim to communicate about the alleged violation or offense because of extreme fear, failure of memory, or another similar reason;

(3) The substantial likelihood that the mentally retarded or developmentally disabled victim will suffer serious emotional trauma from so testifying.

(G)(1) If a juvenile judge issues an order pursuant to division (D) or (E) of this section that requires the testimony of a mentally retarded or developmentally disabled victim in a juvenile court proceeding to be taken outside of the room in which the proceeding is being conducted, the order shall specifically identify the mentally retarded or developmentally disabled victim to whose testimony it applies, the order applies only during the testimony of the specified mentally retarded or developmentally disabled victim, and the mentally retarded or developmentally disabled victim giving the testimony shall not be required to testify at the proceeding other than in accordance with the order. The authority of a judge to close the taking of a deposition under division (B)(2) of this section or a proceeding under division (D) or (E) of this section is in addition to the authority of a judge to close a hearing pursuant to section 2151.35 of the Revised Code.

(2) A juvenile judge who makes any determination regarding the admissibility of a deposition under divisions (B) and (C) of this section, the videotaping of a deposition under division (B)(2) of this section, or the taking of testimony outside of the room in which a proceeding is being conducted under division (D) or (E) of this section shall enter the determination and findings on the record in the proceeding.

(2004 S 178, eff. 1–30–04)

Library References

Infants ⚖201, 207.
Westlaw Topic No. 211.
C.J.S. Infants §§ 41 to 54, 62 to 67.

Research References

Encyclopedias

OH Jur. 3d Family Law § 1641, Depositions.
OH Jur. 3d Family Law § 1672, Testimony of Child.

Treatises and Practice Aids

1 Giannelli and Snyder, Baldwin's Ohio Practice, Evidence, Index, Index.

Carlin, Baldwin's Ohio Practice, Merrick-Rippner Probate Law § 107:37, Testimony of Child Sex Offense Victims.

Carlin, Baldwin's Ohio Practice, Merrick-Rippner Probate Law § 107:38, Videotaped Depositions.

Carlin, Baldwin's Ohio Practice, Merrick-Rippner Probate Law § 107:39, Testimony on Closed Circuit Television or Recording.

2152.83 Order classifying child as juvenile offender registrant; hearing to review effectiveness of disposition and treatment

(A)(1) The court that adjudicates a child a delinquent child shall issue as part of the dispositional order or, if the court commits the child for the delinquent act to the custody of a secure facility, shall issue at the time of the child's release from the secure facility, an order that classifies the child a juvenile offender registrant and specifies that the child has a duty to comply with sections 2950.04, 2950.041, 2950.05, and 2950.06 of the Revised Code if all of the following apply:

(a) The act for which the child is or was adjudicated a delinquent child is a sexually oriented offense that is not a registration-exempt sexually oriented offense or is a child-victim oriented offense that the child committed on or after January 1, 2002.

(b) The child was sixteen or seventeen years of age at the time of committing the offense.

(c) The court was not required to classify the child a juvenile offender registrant under section 2152.82 of the Revised Code.

(2) Prior to issuing the order required by division (A)(2) of this section, the judge shall conduct the hearing and make the determinations required by division (B) of section 2950.09 of the Revised Code regarding a sexually oriented offense that is not a registration-exempt sexually oriented offense or division (B) of section 2950.091 of the Revised Code regarding a child-victim oriented offense to determine if the child is to be classified a sexual predator or a child-victim predator, shall make the determinations required by division (E) of section 2950.09 of the Revised Code regarding a sexually oriented offense that is not a registration-exempt sexually oriented offense or division (E) of section 2950.091 of the Revised Code regarding a child-victim oriented offense to determine if the child is to be classified a habitual sex offender or a habitual child-victim offender, and shall otherwise comply with those divisions. When a judge issues an order under division (A)(1) of this section, the judge shall include in the order all of the determinations and information identified in division (B)(1) of section 2152.82 of the Revised Code that are relevant.

(B)(1) The court that adjudicates a child a delinquent child, on the judge's own motion, may conduct at the time of disposition of the child or, if the court commits the child for the delinquent act to the custody of a secure facility, may conduct at the time of the child's release from the secure facility, a hearing for the purposes described in division (B)(2) of this section if all of the following apply:

(a) The act for which the child is adjudicated a delinquent child is a sexually oriented offense that is not a registration-exempt sexually oriented offense or is a child-victim oriented offense that the child committed on or after January 1, 2002.

(b) The child was fourteen or fifteen years of age at the time of committing the offense.

(c) The court was not required to classify the child a juvenile offender registrant under section 2152.82 of the Revised Code.

(2) A judge shall conduct a hearing under division (B)(1) of this section to review the effectiveness of the disposition made of the child and of any treatment provided for the child placed in a secure setting and to determine whether the child should be classified a juvenile offender registrant. The judge may conduct the hearing on the judge's own initiative or based upon a recommendation of an officer or employee of the department of youth services, a probation officer, an employee of the court, or a prosecutor or law enforcement officer. If the judge conducts the hearing, upon completion of the hearing, the judge, in the judge's discretion and after consideration of the factors listed in division (E) of this section, shall do either of the following:

(a) Decline to issue an order that classifies the child a juvenile offender registrant and specifies that the child has a duty to comply with sections 2950.04, 2950.041, 2950.05, and 2950.06 of the Revised Code;

(b) Issue an order that classifies the child a juvenile offender registrant and specifies that the child has a duty to comply with sections 2950.04, 2950.041, 2950.05, and 2950.06 of the Revised Code and, if the judge conducts a hearing as described in division (C) of this section to determine whether the child is a sexual predator or child-victim predator or a habitual sex offender or habitual child-victim offender, include in the order a statement that the judge has determined that the child is, or is not, a sexual predator, child-victim predator, habitual sex offender, or habitual child-victim offender, whichever is applicable.

(C) A judge may issue an order under division (B) of this section that contains a determination that a delinquent child is a sexual predator or child-victim predator only if the judge, in accordance with the procedures specified in division (B) of section 2950.09 of the Revised Code regarding sexual predators or division (B) of section 2950.091 of the Revised Code regarding child-victim predators, determines at the hearing by clear and convincing evidence that the child is a sexual predator or a child-victim predator. A judge may issue an order under division (B) of this section that contains a determination that a delinquent child is a habitual sex offender or a habitual child-victim offender only if the judge at the hearing determines as described in division (E) of section 2950.09 of the Revised Code regarding habitual sex offenders or division (E) of section 2950.091 of the Revised Code regarding habitual child-victim offenders that the child is a habitual sex offender or a habitual child-victim offender. If the judge issues an order under division (B) of this section that contains a determination that a delinquent child is a habitual sex offender or a habitual child-victim offender, the judge may impose a requirement subjecting the child to community notification provisions as described in division (E) of section 2950.09 or 2950.091 of the Revised Code, whichever is applicable. If the court conducts a hearing as described in this division to determine whether the child is a sexual predator or child-victim predator or a habitual sex offender or habitual child-victim offender, the judge shall comply with division (B) or (E) of section 2950.09 or 2950.091 of the Revised Code, whichever is applicable, in all regards.

(D) If a judge issues an order under division (A) or (B) of this section, the judge shall provide to the delinquent child and to the delinquent child's parent, guardian, or custodian a copy of the order and a notice containing the information described in divisions (A) and (B) of section 2950.03 of the Revised Code. The judge shall provide the notice at the time of the issuance of the order and shall comply with divisions (B) and (C) of that section regarding that notice and the provision of it.

The judge also shall include in the order a statement that, upon completion of the disposition of the delinquent child that was made for the sexually oriented offense or child-victim oriented offense upon which the order is based, a hearing will be conducted and the order is subject to modification or termination pursuant to section 2152.84 of the Revised Code.

(E) In making a decision under division (B) of this section as to whether a delinquent child should be classified a juvenile offender registrant and, if so, whether the child also is a sexual predator or child-victim predator or a habitual sex offender or habitual child-victim offender, a judge shall consider all relevant factors, including, but not limited to, all of the following:

(1) The nature of the sexually oriented offense that is not a registration-exempt sexually oriented offense or the child-victim oriented offense committed by the child;

(2) Whether the child has shown any genuine remorse or compunction for the offense;

(3) The public interest and safety;

(4) The factors set forth in division (B)(3) of section 2950.09 or 2950.091 of the Revised Code, whichever is applicable;

(5) The factors set forth in divisions (B) and (C) of section 2929.12 of the Revised Code as those factors apply regarding the delinquent child, the offense, and the victim;

(6) The results of any treatment provided to the child and of any follow-up professional assessment of the child.

(F) An order issued under division (A) or (B) of this section and any determinations included in the order shall remain in effect for the period of time specified in section 2950.07 of the Revised Code, subject to a modification or termination of the order under section 2152.84 of the Revised Code, and section 2152.851 of the Revised Code applies regarding the order and the determinations. The child's attainment of eighteen or twenty-one years of age does not affect or terminate the order, and the order remains in effect for the period of time described in this division.

(G) A court that adjudicates a child a delinquent child for a sexually oriented offense that is a registration-exempt sexually oriented offense shall not issue based on that adjudication an order under this section that classifies the child a juvenile offender registrant and specifies that the child has a duty to comply with sections 2950.04, 2950.041, 2950.05, and 2950.06 of the Revised Code.

(H) As used in the section, "secure facility" has the same meaning as in section 2950.01 of the Revised Code.

(2003 S 5, eff. 7–31–03; 2002 H 393, eff. 7–5–02; 2001 S 3, eff. 1–1–02)

Historical and Statutory Notes

Amendment Note: 2003 S 5 rewrote the section, which prior thereto read:

"(A)(1) The court that adjudicates a child a delinquent child shall issue as part of the dispositional order or, if the court commits the child for the delinquent act to the custody of a secure facility, shall issue at the time of the child's release from the secure facility, an order that classifies the child a juvenile sex offender registrant and specifies that the child has a duty to register under section 2950.04 of the Revised Code if all of the following apply:

"(a) The act for which the child is or was adjudicated a delinquent child is a sexually oriented offense that the child committed on or after January 1, 2002.

"(b) The child was sixteen or seventeen years of age at the time of committing the offense.

"(c) The court was not required to classify the child a juvenile sex offender registrant under section 2152.82 of the Revised Code.

"(2) Prior to issuing the order required by division (A)(2) of this section, the judge shall conduct the hearing and make the determinations required by division (B) of section 2950.09 of the Revised Code to determine if the child is to be classified as a sexual predator, shall make the determinations required by division (E) of that section to determine if the child is to be classified as a habitual sex offender, and shall otherwise comply with those divisions. When a judge issues an order under division (A)(1) of this section, the judge shall include in the order all of the determinations and information identified in division (B)(1) of section 2152.82 of the Revised Code that are relevant.

"(B)(1) The court that adjudicates a child a delinquent child, on the judge's own motion, may conduct at the time of disposition of the child or, if the court commits the child for the delinquent act to the custody of a secure facility, may conduct at the time of the child's release from the secure facility, a hearing for the purposes described in division (B)(2) of this section if all of the following apply:

"(a) The act for which the child is adjudicated a delinquent child is a sexually oriented offense that the child committed on or after January 1, 2002.

"(b) The child was fourteen or fifteen years of age at the time of committing the offense.

"(c) The court was not required to classify the child a juvenile sex offender registrant under section 2152.82 of the Revised Code.

"(2) A judge shall conduct a hearing under division (B)(1) of this section to review the effectiveness of the disposition made of the child and of any treatment provided for the child placed in a secure setting and to determine whether the child should be classified a juvenile sex offender registrant. The judge may conduct the hearing on the judge's own initiative or based upon a recommendation of an officer or employee of the department of youth services, a probation officer, an employee of the court, or a prosecutor or law enforcement officer. If the judge conducts the hearing, upon completion of the hearing, the judge, in the judge's discretion and after consideration of the factors listed in division (E) of this section, shall do either of the following:

"(a) Decline to issue an order that classifies the child a juvenile sex offender registrant and specifies that the child has a duty to register under section 2950.04 of the Revised Code;

"(b) Issue an order that classifies the child a juvenile sex offender registrant and specifies that the child has a duty to register under section 2950.04 of the Revised Code and, if the judge determines as described in division (C) of this section that the child is a sexual predator or a habitual sex offender, include in the order a statement that the judge has determined that the child is a sexual predator or a habitual sex offender, whichever is applicable.

"(C) A judge may issue an order under division (B) of this section that contains a determination that a delinquent child is a sexual predator only if the judge, in accordance with the procedures specified in division (B) of section 2950.09 of the Revised Code, determines at the hearing by clear and convincing evidence that the child is a sexual predator. A judge may issue an order under division (B) of this section that contains a determination that a delinquent child is a habitual sex offender only if the judge at the hearing determines as described in division (E) of section 2950.09 of the Revised Code that the child is a habitual sex offender. If the judge issues an order under division (B) of this section that contains a determination that a delinquent child is a habitual sex offender, the judge may impose a requirement subjecting the child to community notification provisions as described in division (E) of section 2950.09 of the Revised Code.

"(D) If a judge issues an order under division (A) or (B) of this section, the judge shall provide to the delinquent child and to the delinquent child's parent, guardian, or custodian a copy of the order and a notice containing the information described in divisions (A) and (B) of section 2950.03 of the Revised Code. The judge shall provide the notice at the time of the issuance of the order, shall provide the notice as described in division (B)(1)(c) of that section, and shall comply with divisions (B)(1), (B)(2), and (C) of that section regarding that notice.

"The judge also shall include in the order a statement that, upon completion of the disposition of the delinquent child that was made for the sexually oriented offense upon which the order is based, a hearing will be conducted and the order is subject to modification or termination pursuant to section 2152.84 of the Revised Code.

"(E) In making a decision under division (B) of this section as to whether a delinquent child should be classified a juvenile sex offender registrant and, if so, whether the child also is a sexual predator or a habitual sex offender, a judge shall consider all relevant factors, including, but not limited to, all of the following:

"(1) The nature of the sexually oriented offense committed by the child;

"(2) Whether the child has shown any genuine remorse or compunction for the offense;

"(3) The public interest and safety;

"(4) The factors set forth in division (B)(3) of section 2950.09 of the Revised Code;

"(5) The factors set forth in divisions (B) and (C) of section 2929.12 of the Revised Code as those factors apply regarding the delinquent child, the offense, and the victim;

"(6) The results of any treatment provided to the child and of any follow-up professional assessment of the child.

"(F) An order issued under division (A) or (B) of this section shall remain in effect for the period of time specified in section 2950.07 of the Revised Code, subject to a modification or termination of the order under section 2152.84 of the Revised Code. The child's attainment of eighteen or twenty-one years of age does not affect or terminate the order, and the order remains in effect for the period of time described in this division.

"(G) As used in the section, 'secure facility' has the same meaning as in section 2950.01 of the Revised Code."

Amendment Note: 2002 H 393 rewrote divisions (A), (B), and (C) which prior thereto read:

"(A) If a child is adjudicated a delinquent child for committing on or after the effective date of this section a sexually oriented offense, if the child was sixteen or seventeen years of age at the time of committing the offense, and if the juvenile court judge was not required to classify the child a juvenile sex offender registrant under section 2152.82 of the Revised Code, upon the child's discharge or release from a secure facility or at the time of disposition if the judge does not commit the child to the custody of a secure facility, the juvenile court judge who adjudicated the child a delinquent child, or that judge's successor in office, shall issue an order that classifies the child a juvenile sex offender registrant and specifies that the child has a duty to register under section 2950.04 of the Revised Code. Prior to issuing the order, the judge shall conduct the hearing and make the determinations required by, and otherwise comply with, divisions (B) and (E) of section 2950.09 of the Revised Code. When a judge issues an order under division (A) of this section, the judge shall include in the order any determination that the delinquent child is a sexual predator or is a habitual sex offender that the judge makes pursuant to division (B) or (E) of section 2950.09 of the Revised Code and any related information required or authorized under the division under which the determination is made, including, but not limited to, any requirement imposed by the court subjecting a child who is a habitual sex offender to community notification provisions as described in division (E) of that section.

"(B) If a child is adjudicated a delinquent child for committing on or after the effective date of this section a sexually oriented offense, if the delinquent child was fourteen or fifteen years of age at the time of committing the offense, and if the juvenile court judge was not required to classify the child a juvenile sex offender registrant under section 2152.82 of the Revised Code, upon the child's discharge or release from a secure facility or at the time of disposition if the judge does not commit the child to the custody of a secure facility, the juvenile court judge who adjudicated the child a delinquent child, or that judge's successor in office, may, on the judge's own motion, conduct a hearing to review the effectiveness of the disposition and of any treatment provided for a child placed in a secure setting and to determine whether the child should be classified a juvenile sex offender registrant. The judge may conduct the hearing on the judge's own initiative or based upon a recommendation of an officer or employee of the department of youth services, a probation officer, an employee of the court, or a prosecutor or law enforcement officer. If the judge conducts the hearing, upon completion of the hearing, the judge, in the judge's discretion and after consideration of the factors listed in division (E) of this section, shall do either of the following:

"(1) Decline to issue an order that classifies the child a juvenile sex offender registrant and specifies that the child has a duty to register under section 2950.04 of the Revised Code;

"(2) Issue an order that classifies the child a juvenile sex offender registrant and specifies that the child has a duty to register under section 2950.04 of the Revised Code and, if the judge determines as described in division (C) of this section that the child is a sexual predator or a habitual sex offender, include in the order a statement that the judge has determined that the child is a sexual predator or a habitual sex offender, whichever is applicable.

"(C) A judge may issue an order under division (B) of this section that contains a determination that a delinquent child is a sexual predator only if the judge, in accordance with the procedures specified in division (B) of section 2950.09 of the Revised Code, determines at the hearing by clear and convincing evidence that the child is a sexual predator. A judge may issue an order under division (B) of this section that contains a determination that a delinquent child is a habitual sex offender only if the judge determines at the hearing as described in division (E) of section 2950.09 of the Revised Code that the child is a habitual sex offender. If the judge issues an order under division (B) of this section that contains a determination that a delinquent child is a habitual sex offender, the judge may impose a requirement subjecting the child to community notification provisions as described in division (E) of section 2950.09 of the Revised Code."

Cross References

Adjudication of offender as sexual predator or as habitual sex offender; exclusion of registration-exempt sexually oriented offense, 2950.09.
Child-victim oriented offenses; duty of registration of offender or delinquent child, 2950.041.
Community notification of sex offender registration, 2950.11
Determination of offender as child-victim predator; hearing, 2950.091.
Determination of requirement to register as sex offender with sheriff, 2950.021.
Manner of registering as sex offenders, 2950.04.
Notice of duty to register as sex offender and related requirements, 2950.03.
Sex offenders, definitions, 2950.01.

Library References

Infants ⚖227(2).
Westlaw Topic No. 211.
C.J.S. Infants §§ 41, 53 to 54, 57, 69 to 85.

Research References

Encyclopedias

OH Jur. 3d Criminal Law § 3447, Generally; Constitutionality.
OH Jur. 3d Criminal Law § 3453, Duties of Institution Officials.
OH Jur. 3d Criminal Law § 3454, Duties of Courts.
OH Jur. 3d Family Law § 1626, Right Under Juvenile Court Law and Rules.
OH Jur. 3d Family Law § 1487.5, Sexually Oriented and Child-Victim Offenders.
OH Jur. 3d Family Law § 1628.1, Ineffective Assistance of Counsel.
OH Jur. 3d Family Law § 1698.6, Sexually Oriented and Child-Victim Offenses; Registration.

Treatises and Practice Aids

1 Giannelli and Snyder, Baldwin's Ohio Practice, Evidence, Index, Index.
Carlin, Baldwin's Ohio Practice, Merrick-Rippner Probate Law § 107:93, Classification of Juvenile Sex Offender Registrant, Effective January 1, 2002...
Carlin, Baldwin's Ohio Practice, Merrick-Rippner Probate Law § 107:94, Classification of Juvenile Sex Offender Registrant, Effective January 1, 2002 (If Charged With a Sexually Oriented Offense on or After January 1, 2002 and is 16-17 Years Old at the Time of...
Carlin, Baldwin's Ohio Practice, Merrick-Rippner Probate Law § 107:95, Classification of Juvenile Sex Offender Registrant, Effective January 1, 2002 (If Charged With a Sexually Oriented Offense on or After January 1, 2002 and is 14-15 Years Old at the Time of...
Carlin, Baldwin's Ohio Practice, Merrick-Rippner Probate Law § 107:96, Classification of Juvenile Sex Offender Registrant, Effective January 1, 2002—Hearing After Completion of the Dispositions Ordered Under RC 2152.82 and RC 2152.83—Continuation or Modification...
Carlin, Baldwin's Ohio Practice, Merrick-Rippner Probate Law § 107:97, Classification of Juvenile Sex Offender Registrant, Effective January 1, 2002—Subsequent Petition for Reclassification or Declassification of Orders Issued Pursuant to RC 2152.82, RC 2152.83 and...
Carlin, Baldwin's Ohio Practice, Merrick-Rippner Probate Law § 107:100, Frequency and Duration of Registration Based on the Classification of a Juvenile Sex Offender Registrant.
Giannelli & Yeomans, Ohio Juvenile Law § 6:10, Juvenile Offender Registrant—Mandatory Classification.
Giannelli & Yeomans, Ohio Juvenile Law § 6:11, Juvenile Offender Registrant—Discretionary Classification.
Giannelli & Yeomans, Ohio Juvenile Law § 6:12, Dispositional Completion Hearing.
Giannelli & Yeomans, Ohio Juvenile Law § 6:13, Petitions for Reclassification or Declassification.

Notes of Decisions

Sexually oriented offense 1

---

1. Sexually oriented offense

Adjudication as juvenile sex offender registrant following delinquency adjudication for gross sexual imposition was supported by findings that juvenile was 14 years old and victim was nine, offense involved juvenile placing hand inside victim's pants in vaginal region, prior assault charge had been amended from charge of gross sexual imposition, juvenile did not successfully complete court-ordered sex offender therapy, that juvenile reoffended after 23 sessions of treatment, and that juvenile appeared to view victims not as people, but as objects. In re J.F.F. (Ohio App. 2 Dist., Miami, 04-15-2005) No. 2004 CA 34, 2005-Ohio-1906, 2005 WL 937852, Unreported. Infants ⇔ 227(2)

Adjudication as juvenile sex offender registrant following delinquency adjudication for gross sexual imposition did not require prior adjudication for qualifying sexually oriented offense. In re J.F.F. (Ohio App. 2 Dist., Miami, 04-15-2005) No. 2004 CA 34, 2005-Ohio-1906, 2005 WL 937852, Unreported. Infants ⇔ 227(2)

A trial court has discretion following its adjudication of a juvenile as delinquent to classify the juvenile as a sex predator prior to the juvenile's treatment in a secure facility. In re Callahan (Ohio App. 5 Dist., Ashland, 02-24-2005) No. 04COA064, 2005-Ohio-735, 2005 WL 449832, Unreported. Infants ⇔ 227(2)

The trial court's classification of juvenile as a juvenile sex offender registrant was proper; trial court adjudicated juvenile delinquent after it found that juvenile committed sexual battery, and statute provided that a 16- or 17-year-old juvenile who committed a sexually-oriented offense could be classified as a juvenile sex offender registrant. In re Thomas (Ohio App. 8 Dist., Cuyahoga, 12-02-2004) No. 83579, No. 83580, 2004-Ohio-6415, 2004 WL 2756224, Unreported. Infants ⇔ 227(2)

2152.84 Hearings; orders

(A)(1) When a juvenile court judge issues an order under section 2152.82 or division (A) or (B) of section 2152.83 of the Revised Code that classifies a delinquent child a juvenile offender registrant and specifies that the child has a duty to comply with sections 2950.04, 2950.041, 2950.05, and 2950.06 of the Revised Code, upon completion of the disposition of that child made for the sexually oriented offense that is not a registration-exempt sexually oriented offense or the child-victim oriented offense on which the juvenile offender registrant order was based, the judge or the judge's successor in office shall conduct a hearing to review the effectiveness of the disposition and of any treatment provided for the child, to determine the risks that the child might reoffend, and to determine whether the prior classification of the child as a juvenile offender registrant and, if applicable, as a sexual predator or child-victim predator or as a habitual sex offender or habitual child-victim offender should be continued, modified, or terminated as provided under division (A)(2) of this section.

(2) Upon completion of a hearing under division (A)(1) of this section, the judge, in the judge's discretion and after consideration of the factors listed in division (E) of section 2152.83 of the Revised Code, shall do one of the following, as applicable:

(a) Enter an order that continues the classification of the delinquent child made in the prior order issued under section 2152.82 or division (A) or (B) of section 2152.83 of the Revised Code, and any sexual predator, child-victim predator, habitual sex offender, or habitual child-victim offender determination included in the order;

(b) If the prior order was issued under section 2152.82 or division (A) of section 2152.83 of the Revised Code and includes a determination by the judge that the delinquent child is a sexual predator or child-victim predator, enter, as applicable, an order that contains a determination that the child no longer is a sexual predator, the reason or reasons for that determination, and either a determination that the child is a habitual sex offender or a determination that the child remains a juvenile offender registrant but is not a sexual predator or habitual sex offender, or an order that contains a determination that the child no longer is a child-victim predator, the reason or reasons for that determination, and either a determination that the child is a habitual child-victim offender or a determination that the child remains a juvenile offender registrant but is not a child-victim predator or habitual child-victim offender;

(c) If the prior order was issued under section 2152.82 or division (A) of section 2152.83 of the Revised Code and does not include a sexual predator or child-victim predator determination as described in division (A)(2)(b) of this section but includes a determination by the judge that the delinquent child is a habitual sex offender or a habitual child-victim offender, enter, as applicable, an order that contains a determination that the child no longer is a habitual sex offender and a determination that the child remains a juvenile sex offender registrant but is not a habitual offender, or an order that contains a determination that the child no longer is a habitual child-victim offender and a determination that the child remains a juvenile offender registrant but is not a habitual child-victim offender;

(d) If the prior order was issued under division (B) of section 2152.83 of the Revised Code and includes a determination by the judge that the delinquent child is a sexual predator or child-victim predator, enter, as applicable, an order that contains a determination that the child no longer is a sexual predator, the reason or reasons for that determination, and either a determination that the child is a habitual sex offender, a determination that the child remains a juvenile offender registrant but is not a sexual predator or habitual sex offender, or a determination that the child no longer is a juvenile offender registrant and no longer has a duty to comply with sections 2950.04, 2950.05, and 2950.06 of the Revised Code, or an order that contains a determination that the child no longer is a child-victim predator, the reason or reasons for that determination, and either a determination that the child is a habitual child-victim offender, a determination that the child remains a juvenile offender registrant but is not a child-victim predator or habitual child-victim offender, or a determination that the child no longer is a juvenile offender registrant and no longer has a duty to comply with sections 2950.041, 2950.05, and 2950.06 of the Revised Code;

(e) If the prior order was issued under division (B) of section 2152.83 of the Revised Code and does not include a sexual predator or child-victim predator determination as described in division (A)(2)(d) of this section but includes a determination by the judge that the delinquent child is a habitual sex offender or habitual child-victim offender, enter, as applicable, an order that contains a determination that the child no longer is a habitual sex offender and either a determination that the child remains a juvenile offender registrant but is not a sexual predator or habitual sex offender or a determination that the child no longer is a juvenile offender registrant and no longer has a duty to comply with sections 2950.04, 2950.05, and 2950.06 of the Revised Code, or an order that contains a determination that the child no longer is a habitual child-victim offender and either a determination that the child remains a juvenile offender registrant but is not a child-victim predator or habitual child-victim offender or a determination that the child no longer is a juvenile offender registrant and no longer has a duty to comply with sections 2950.041, 2950.05, and 2950.06 of the Revised Code;

(f) If the prior order was issued under division (B) of section 2152.83 of the Revised Code and does not include a sexual predator or child-victim predator determination or a habitual sex offender or habitual child-victim offender determination as described in divisions (A)(2)(d) and (e) of this section, enter, as applicable, an order that contains a determination that the delinquent child no longer is a juvenile offender registrant and no longer has a duty to comply with sections 2950.04, 2950.05, and 2950.06 of the Revised Code, or an order that contains a determination that the delinquent child no longer is a juvenile offender registrant and no longer has a duty to comply with sections 2950.041, 2950.05, and 2950.06 of the Revised Code.

(B) If a judge issues an order under division (A)(2)(a) of this section that continues the prior classification of the delinquent child as a juvenile offender registrant and any sexual predator or habitual sex offender determination included in the order, or that continues the prior classification of the delinquent child as a juvenile offender registrant and any child-victim predator or habitual child-victim offender determination included in the order, the prior classification and the prior determination, if applicable, shall remain in effect.

A judge may issue an order under division (A)(2) of this section that contains a determination that a child no longer is a sexual predator or no longer is a child-victim predator only if the judge, in accordance with the procedures specified in division (D)(1) of section 2950.09 of the Revised Code regarding a sexual predator, determines at the hearing by clear and convincing evidence that the delinquent child is unlikely to commit a sexually oriented offense in the future, or the judge, in accordance with the procedures specified in division (D)(1) of section 2950.091 of the Revised Code regarding a child-victim predator, determines at the hearing by clear and convincing evidence that the delinquent child is unlikely to commit a child-victim oriented offense in the future. If the judge issues an order of that type, the judge shall provide the notifications described in division (D)(1) of section 2950.09 or 2950.091 of the Revised Code, whichever is applicable, and the recipient of the notification shall comply with the provisions of that division.

If a judge issues an order under division (A)(2) of this section that otherwise reclassifies the delinquent child, the judge shall provide a copy of the order to the bureau of criminal identification and investigation, and the bureau, upon receipt of the copy of the order, promptly shall notify the sheriff with whom the child most recently registered under section 2950.04 or 2950.041 of the Revised Code of the reclassification.

(C) If a judge issues an order under any provision of division (A)(2) of this section, the judge shall provide to the delinquent child and to the delinquent child's parent, guardian, or custodian a copy of the order and a notice containing the information described in divisions (A) and (B) of section 2950.03 of the Revised Code. The judge shall provide the notice at the time of the issuance of the order and shall comply with divisions (B) and (C) of that section regarding that notice and the provision of it.

(D) In making a decision under division (A) of this section, a judge shall consider all relevant factors, including, but not limited to, the factors listed in division (E) of section 2152.83 of the Revised Code.

(E) An order issued under division (A)(2) of this section and any determinations included in the order shall remain in effect for the period of time specified in section 2950.07 of the Revised Code, subject to a modification or termination of the order under section 2152.85 of the Revised Code, and section 2152.851 of the Revised Code applies regarding the order and the determinations. If an order is issued under division (A)(2) of this section, the child's attainment of eighteen or twenty-one years of age does not affect or terminate the order, and the order remains in effect for the period of time described in this division.

(2003 S 5, eff. 7–31–03; 2002 H 393, eff. 7–5–02; 2001 S 3, eff. 1–1–02)

Historical and Statutory Notes

Amendment Note: 2003 S 5 rewrote the section, which prior thereto read:

"(A)(1) When a juvenile court judge issues an order under section 2152.82 or division (A) or (B) of section 2152.83 of the Revised Code that classifies a delinquent child a juvenile sex offender registrant and specifies that the child has a duty to register under section 2950.04 of the Revised Code, upon completion of the disposition of that child made for the sexually oriented offense on which the juvenile sex offender registrant order was based, the judge or the judge's successor in office shall conduct a hearing to review the effectiveness of the disposition and of any treatment provided for the child, to determine the risks that the child might re-offend, and to determine whether the prior classification of the child as a juvenile sex offender registrant and, if applicable, as a sexual predator or habitual sex offender should be continued, modified, or terminated as provided under division (A)(2) of this section.

"(2) Upon completion of a hearing under division (A)(1) of this section, the judge, in the judge's discretion and after consideration of the factors listed in division (E) of section 2152.83 of the Revised Code, shall do one of the following, as applicable:

"(a) Enter an order that continues the classification of the delinquent child made in the prior order issued under section 2152.82 or division (A) or (B) of section 2152.83 of the Revised Code, and any sexual predator or habitual sex offender determination included in the order;

"(b) If the prior order was issued under section 2152.82 or division (A) of section 2152.83 of the Revised Code and includes a determination by the judge that the delinquent child is a sexual predator, enter an order that contains a determination that the delinquent child no longer is a sexual predator and that also contains either a determination that the delinquent child is a habitual sex offender or a determination that the delinquent child remains a juvenile sex offender registrant but is not a sexual predator or habitual sex offender;

"(c) If the prior order was issued under section 2152.82 or division (A) of section 2152.83 of the Revised Code and does not include a sexual predator determination as described in division (A)(2)(b) of this section but includes a determination by the judge that the delinquent child is a habitual sex offender, enter an order that contains a determination that the delinquent child no longer is a habitual sex offender and that also contains a determination that the delinquent child remains a juvenile sex offender registrant but is not a habitual sex offender;

"(d) If the prior order was issued under division (B) of section 2152.83 of the Revised Code and includes a determination by the judge that the delinquent child is a sexual predator, enter an order that contains a determination that the delinquent child no longer is a sexual predator and that also contains a determination that the delinquent child is a habitual sex offender, a determination that the delinquent child remains a juvenile sex offender registrant but is not a sexual predator or habitual sex offender, or a determination that specifies that the delinquent child no longer is a juvenile sex offender registrant and no longer has a duty to register under section 2950.04 of the Revised Code;

"(e) If the prior order was issued under division (B) of section 2152.83 of the Revised Code and does not include a sexual predator determination as described in division (A)(2)(d) of this section but includes a determination by the judge that the delinquent child is a habitual sex offender, enter an order that contains a determination that the child no longer is a habitual sex offender and that also contains either a determination that the child remains a juvenile sex offender registrant but is not a sexual predator or habitual sex offender or a determination that specifies that the child no longer is a juvenile sex offender registrant and no longer has a duty to register under section 2950.04 of the Revised Code;

"(f) If the prior order was issued under division (B) of section 2152.83 of the Revised Code and does not include a sexual predator determination or a habitual sex offender determination as described in divisions (A)(2)(d) and (e) of this section, enter an order that contains a determination that the delinquent child no longer is a juvenile sex offender registrant and no longer has a duty to register under section 2950.04 of the Revised Code.

"(B) If a judge issues an order under division (A)(2)(a) of this section that continues the prior classification of the delinquent child as a juvenile sex offender registrant and any sexual predator or habitual sex offender determination included in the order, the prior classification and the prior determination, if applicable, shall remain in effect.

"A judge may issue an order under division (A)(2) of this section that contains a determination that a child no longer is a sexual predator only if the judge, in accordance with the procedures specified in division (D)(1) of section 2950.09 of the Revised Code, determines at the hearing by clear and convincing evidence that the delinquent child is unlikely to commit a sexually oriented offense in the future. If the judge issues an order of that type, the judge shall provide the notifications described in division (D)(1) of section 2950.09 of the Revised Code, and the recipient of the notification shall comply with the provisions of that division.

"If a judge issues an order under division (A)(2) of this section that otherwise reclassifies the delinquent child, the judge shall provide a copy of the order to the bureau of criminal identification and investigation, and the bureau, upon receipt of the copy of the order, promptly shall notify the sheriff with whom the child most recently registered under section 2950.04 of the Revised Code of the reclassification.

"(C) If a judge issues an order under any provision of division (A)(2) of this section, the judge shall provide to the delinquent child and to the delinquent child's parent, guardian, or custodian a copy of the order and a notice containing the information described in divisions (A) and (B) of section 2950.03 of the Revised Code. The judge shall provide the notice at the time of the issuance of the order, shall provide the notice as described in division (B)(1)(c) of that section, and shall comply with divisions (B)(1), (B)(2), and (C) of that section regarding that notice.

"(D) In making a decision under division (A) of this section, a judge shall consider all relevant factors, including, but not limited to, the factors listed in division (E) of section 2152.83 of the Revised Code.

"(E) An order issued under division (A)(2) of this section and any determinations included in the order shall remain in effect for the period of time specified in section 2950.07 of the Revised Code, subject to a modification or termination of the order under section 2152.85 of the Revised Code. If an order is issued under division (A)(2) of this section, the child's attainment of eighteen or twenty-one years of age does not affect or terminate the order, and the order remains in effect for the period of time described in this division."

Amendment Note: 2002 H 393 rewrote this section which prior thereto read:

"(A)(1) When a juvenile court judge issues an order under section 2152.82 or division (A) or (B) of section 2152.83 of the Revised Code that classifies a delinquent child a juvenile sex offender registrant and specifies that the child has a duty to register under section 2950.04 of the Revised Code, upon completion of the disposition of that delinquent child that the judge made for the sexually oriented offense on which the juvenile sex offender registrant order was based, the judge or the judge's successor in office shall conduct a hearing to do all of the following:

"(a) Review the effectiveness of the disposition and of any treatment provided for the child;

"(b) If the order also contains a determination that the delinquent child is a sexual predator or habitual sex offender that the court made pursuant to division (B) or (E) of section 2950.09 of the Revised Code, determine whether the classification of the child as a sexual predator, habitual sex offender, or juvenile sex offender registrant should be continued or modified or, regarding an order issued under division (B) of section 2152.83 of the Revised Code, terminated;

"(c) If the order was issued under division (B) of section 2152.83 of the Revised Code and does not contain a sexual predator determination that the court makes as described in division (A)(1)(b) of this section, determine whether the classification of the child as a juvenile sex offender registrant should be continued, modified, or terminated.

"(2) Upon completion of a hearing under division (A)(1) of this section, the judge, in the judge's discretion and after consideration of the factors listed in division (E) of this section, shall do one of the following, as applicable:

"(a) Enter an order that continues the classification of the delinquent child made in the order issued under section 2152.82 or division (A) or (B) of section 2152.83 of the Revised Code, and any sexual predator or habitual sex offender determination included in the order;

"(b) If the order was issued under section 2152.82 or division (A) of section 2152.83 of the Revised Code and includes a determination by the judge that the delinquent child is a sexual predator, enter an order that contains a determination that the delinquent child no longer is a sexual predator and that also contains either a determination that the delinquent child is a habitual sex offender or a determination that the delinquent child remains a juvenile sex offender registrant but is not a sexual predator or habitual sex offender;

"(c) If the order was issued under section 2152.82 or division (A) of section 2152.83 of the Revised Code and does not include a sexual predator determination as described in division (A)(2)(b) of this section but includes a determination by the judge that the delinquent child is a habitual sex offender, enter an order that contains a determination that the delinquent child no longer is a habitual sex offender and that also contains a determination that the delinquent child remains a juvenile sex offender registrant but is not a habitual sex offender;

"(d) If the order was issued under division (B) of section 2152.83 of the Revised Code and includes a determination by the judge that the delinquent child is a sexual predator, enter an order that contains a determination that the delinquent child no longer is a sexual predator and that also contains a determination that the delinquent child is a habitual sex offender, a determination that the delinquent child remains a juvenile sex offender registrant but is not a sexual predator or habitual sex offender, or a determination that specifies that the delinquent child no longer is a juvenile sex offender registrant and no longer has a duty to register under section 2950.04 of the Revised Code;

"(e) If the order was issued under division (B) of section 2152.83 of the Revised Code and does not include a sexual predator determination as described in division (A)(2)(d) of this section but includes a determination by the judge that the delinquent child is a habitual sex offender, enter an order that contains a determination that the child no longer is a habitual sex offender and that also contains either a determination that the child remains a juvenile sex offender registrant but is not a sexual predator or habitual sex offender or a determination that specifies that the child no longer is a juvenile sex offender registrant and no longer has a duty to register under section 2950.04 of the Revised Code;

"(f) If the order was issued under division (B) of section 2152.83 of the Revised Code and the order does not include a sexual predator determination or a habitual sex offender determination as described in divisions (A)(2)(d) and (e) of this section, enter an order that contains a determination that the delinquent child no longer is a juvenile sex offender registrant and no longer has a duty to register under section 2950.04 of the Revised Code.

"(B) If a judge issues an order under division (A)(2)(a) of this section that continues the prior classification of the delinquent child as a juvenile sex offender registrant and any sexual predator or habitual sex offender determination included in the order, the prior classification and the prior determination, if applicable, shall remain in effect.

"A judge may issue an order under division (A)(2) of this section that contains a determination that a child no longer is a sexual predator only if the judge, in accordance with the procedures specified in division (D)(1) of section 2950.09 of the Revised Code, determines at the hearing by clear and convincing evidence that the delinquent child is unlikely to commit a sexually oriented offense in the future. If the judge issues an order of that type, the judge shall provide the notifications described in division (D)(1) of section 2950.09 of the Revised Code, and the recipient of the notification shall comply with the provisions of that division.

"(C) If a judge issues an order under any provision of division (A)(2) of this section, the judge shall provide to the delinquent child and to the delinquent child's parent, guardian, or custodian a copy of the order and a notice containing the information described in divisions (A) and (B) of section 2950.03 of the Revised Code. The judge shall provide the notice at the time of the issuance of the order, shall provide the notice as described in division (B)(1)(c) of that section, and shall comply with divisions (B)(1), (B)(2), and (C) of that section regarding that notice.

"(D) In making a decision under division (A) of this section, a judge shall consider all relevant factors, including, but not limited to, the factors listed in division (E) of section 2152.83 of the Revised Code.

"(E) An order issued under division (A)(2) of this section and any determinations included in the order shall remain in effect for the period of time specified in section 2950.07 of the Revised Code, subject to a modification or termination of the order under section 2152.85 of the Revised Code. If an order is issued under division (A)(2) of this section, the child's attainment of eighteen or twenty-one years of age does not affect or terminate the order, and the order remains in effect for the period of time described in this division."

Cross References

Adjudication of offender as sexual predator or as habitual sex offender; exclusion of registration-exempt sexually oriented offense, 2950.09.
Child-victim oriented offenses; duty of registration of offender or delinquent child, 2950.041.
Community notification of sex offender registration, 2950.11
Determination of offender as child-victim predator; hearing, 2950.091.
Determination of requirement to register as sex offender with sheriff, 2950.021.
Manner of registering as sex offenders, 2950.04.
Notice of duty to register as sex offender and related requirements, 2950.03.
Sex offenders, definitions, 2950.01.
Verification of current address of residence, school, or place of employment, 2950.06.

Ohio Administrative Code References

Completion and transmittal of forms and information, OAC 109:5-2-02
Completion and transmittal of forms, OAC 109:5-2-02

Library References

Infants ⇐227(2), 230.1.
Westlaw Topic No. 211.
C.J.S. Adoption of Persons § 10.
C.J.S. Infants §§ 41, 53 to 54, 57, 69 to 85.

Research References

Encyclopedias

OH Jur. 3d Criminal Law § 3447, Generally; Constitutionality.

OH Jur. 3d Family Law § 1487.5, Sexually Oriented and Child-Victim Offenders.

OH Jur. 3d Family Law § 1698.6, Sexually Oriented and Child-Victim Offenses; Registration.

Treatises and Practice Aids

1 Giannelli and Snyder, Baldwin's Ohio Practice, Evidence, Index, Index.

Carlin, Baldwin's Ohio Practice, Merrick-Rippner Probate Law § 107:93, Classification of Juvenile Sex Offender Registrant, Effective January 1, 2002...

Carlin, Baldwin's Ohio Practice, Merrick-Rippner Probate Law § 107:94, Classification of Juvenile Sex Offender Registrant, Effective January 1, 2002 (If Charged With a Sexually Oriented Offense on or After January 1, 2002 and is 16-17 Years Old at the Time of...

Carlin, Baldwin's Ohio Practice, Merrick-Rippner Probate Law § 107:95, Classification of Juvenile Sex Offender Registrant, Effective January 1, 2002 (If Charged With a Sexually Oriented Offense on or After January 1, 2002 and is 14-15 Years Old at the Time of...

Carlin, Baldwin's Ohio Practice, Merrick-Rippner Probate Law § 107:96, Classification of Juvenile Sex Offender Registrant, Effective January 1, 2002—Hearing After Completion of the Dispositions Ordered Under RC 2152.82 and RC 2152.83—Continuation or Modification...

Carlin, Baldwin's Ohio Practice, Merrick-Rippner Probate Law § 107:97, Classification of Juvenile Sex Offender Registrant, Effective January 1, 2002—Subsequent Petition for Reclassification or Declassification of Orders Issued Pursuant to RC 2152.82, RC 2152.83 and...

Carlin, Baldwin's Ohio Practice, Merrick-Rippner Probate Law § 107:100, Frequency and Duration of Registration Based on the Classification of a Juvenile Sex Offender Registrant.

Giannelli & Yeomans, Ohio Juvenile Law § 6:9, Juvenile Offender Registrant—Repeat Offender Classification.

Giannelli & Yeomans, Ohio Juvenile Law § 6:10, Juvenile Offender Registrant—Mandatory Classification.

Giannelli & Yeomans, Ohio Juvenile Law § 6:11, Juvenile Offender Registrant—Discretionary Classification.

Giannelli & Yeomans, Ohio Juvenile Law § 6:12, Dispositional Completion Hearing.

Giannelli & Yeomans, Ohio Juvenile Law § 6:13, Petitions for Reclassification or Declassification.

Notes of Decisions

Classification as predator, timing 1

1. Classification as predator, timing

A trial court has discretion following its adjudication of a juvenile as delinquent to classify the juvenile as a sex predator prior to the juvenile's treatment in a secure facility. In re Callahan (Ohio App. 5 Dist., Ashland, 02-24-2005) No. 04COA064, 2005-Ohio-735, 2005 WL 449832, Unreported. Infants ⇨ 227(2)

2152.85 Petitioning of judge by juvenile offender registrant

(A) Upon the expiration of the applicable period of time specified in division (B)(1) or (2) of this section, a delinquent child who has been classified pursuant to this section or section 2152.82 or 2152.83 of the Revised Code a juvenile offender registrant may petition the judge who made the classification, or that judge's successor in office, to do one of the following:

(1) If the order containing the juvenile offender registrant classification also includes a determination by the juvenile court judge that the delinquent child is a sexual predator or child-victim predator in the manner described in section 2152.82 or 2152.83 of the Revised Code and that determination remains in effect, to enter, as applicable, an order that contains a determination that the child no longer is a sexual predator, the reason or reasons for that determination, and either a determination that the child is a habitual sex offender or a determination that the child remains a juvenile offender registrant but is not a sexual predator or habitual sex offender, or an order that contains a determination that the child no longer is a child-victim predator, the reason or reasons for that determination, and either a determination that the child is a habitual child-victim offender or a determination that the child remains a juvenile offender registrant but is not a child-victim predator or habitual child-victim offender;

(2) If the order containing the juvenile offender registrant classification under section 2152.82 or 2152.83 of the Revised Code or under division (C)(2) of this section pursuant to a petition filed under division (A) of this section does not include a sexual predator or child-victim predator determination as described in division (A)(1) of this section but includes a determination by the juvenile court judge that the delinquent child is a habitual sex offender or a habitual child-victim offender in the manner described in section 2152.82 or 2152.83 of the Revised Code, or in this section, and that determination remains in effect, to enter, as applicable, an order that contains a determination that the child no longer is a habitual sex offender and either a determination that the child remains a juvenile offender registrant or a determination that the child no longer is a juvenile offender registrant and no longer has a duty to comply with sections 2950.04, 2950.05, and 2950.06 of the Revised Code, or an order that contains a determination that the child no longer is a habitual child-victim offender and either a determination that the child remains a juvenile offender registrant or a determination that the child no longer is a juvenile offender registrant and no longer has a duty to comply with sections 2950.041, 2950.05, and 2950.06 of the Revised Code;

(3) If the order containing the juvenile offender registrant classification under section 2152.82 or 2152.83 of the Revised Code or under division (C)(2) of this section pursuant to a petition filed under division (A) of this section does not include a sexual predator or child-victim predator determination or a habitual sex offender or habitual child-victim offender determination as described in division (A)(1) or (2) of this section, to enter, as applicable, an order that contains a determination that the child no longer is a juvenile offender registrant and no longer has a duty to comply with sections 2950.04, 2950.05, and 2950.06 of the Revised Code, or an order that contains a determination that the child no longer is a juvenile offender registrant and no longer has a duty to comply with sections 2950.041, 2950.05, and 2950.06 of the Revised Code.

(B) A delinquent child who has been adjudicated a delinquent child for committing on or after January 1, 2002, a sexually oriented offense that is not a registration-exempt sexually oriented offense and who has been classified a juvenile offender registrant relative to that offense or who has been adjudicated a delinquent child for committing on or after that date a child-victim oriented offense and who has been classified a juvenile offender registrant relative to that offense may file a petition under division (A) of this section requesting reclassification or declassification as described in that division after the expiration of one of the following periods of time:

(1) The delinquent child initially may file a petition not earlier than three years after the entry of the juvenile court judge's order after the mandatory hearing conducted under section 2152.84 of the Revised Code.

(2) After the delinquent child's initial filing of a petition under division (B)(1) of this section, the child may file a second petition not earlier than three years after the judge has entered an order deciding the petition under division (B)(1) of this section.

(3) After the delinquent child's filing of a petition under division (B)(2) of this section, thereafter, the delinquent child may file a petition under this division upon the expiration of five years after the judge has entered an order deciding the petition under division (B)(2) of this section or the most recent petition the delinquent child has filed under this division.

(C) Upon the filing of a petition under divisions (A) and (B) of this section, the judge may review the prior classification or determination in question and, upon consideration of all relevant factors and information, including, but not limited to the factors listed in division (E) of section 2152.83 of the Revised Code, the judge, in the judge's discretion, shall do one of the following:

(1) Enter an order denying the petition;

(2) Issue an order that reclassifies or declassifies the delinquent child, in the requested manner specified in division (A)(1), (2), or (3) of this section.

(D) If a judge issues an order under division (C) of this section that denies a petition, the prior classification of the delinquent child as a juvenile offender registrant, and the prior determination that the child is a sexual predator, child-victim predator, habitual sex offender, or habitual child-victim offender, if applicable, shall remain in effect.

A judge may issue an order under division (C) of this section that contains a determination that a child no longer is a sexual predator or no longer is a child-victim predator only if the judge conducts a hearing and, in accordance with the procedures specified in division (D)(1) of section 2950.09 of the Revised Code regarding a sexual predator, determines at the hearing by clear and convincing evidence that the delinquent child is unlikely to commit a sexually oriented offense in the future, or, in accordance with the procedures specified in division (D)(1) of section 2950.091 of the Revised Code regarding a child-victim predator, determines at the hearing by clear and convincing evidence that the delinquent child is unlikely to commit a child-victim oriented offense in the future. If the judge issues an order of that type, the judge shall provide the notifications described in division (D)(1) of section 2950.09 or 2950.091 of the Revised Code, whichever is applicable, and the recipient of the notification shall comply with the provisions of that division.

A judge may issue an order under division (C) of this section that contains a determination that a delinquent child is a habitual sex offender or a habitual child-victim offender only if the judge conducts a hearing and determines at the hearing as described in division (E) of section 2950.09 of the Revised Code regarding habitual sex offenders or division (E) of section 2950.091 of the Revised Code regarding habitual child-victim offenders that the child is a habitual sex offender or a habitual child-victim offender. If the judge issues an order that contains a determination that a delinquent child is a habitual sex offender or a habitual child-victim offender, the judge may impose a requirement subjecting the child to community notification provisions as described in that division.

(E) If a judge issues an order under division (C) of this section, the judge shall provide to the delinquent child and to the delinquent child's parent, guardian, or custodian a copy of the order and a notice containing the information described in divisions (A) and (B) of section 2950.03 of the Revised Code. The judge shall provide the notice at the time of the issuance of the order and shall comply with divisions (B) and (C) of that section regarding that notice and the provision of it.

(F) An order issued under division (C) of this section shall remain in effect for the period of time specified in section 2950.07 of the Revised Code, subject to a further modification or a termination of the order under this section, and section 2152.851 of the Revised Code applies regarding the order and the determinations. If an order is issued under division (C) of this section, the child's attainment of eighteen or twenty-one years of age does not affect or terminate the order, and the order remains in effect for the period of time described in this division.

(2003 S 5, eff. 7–31–03; 2001 S 3, eff. 1–1–02)

Historical and Statutory Notes

Amendment Note: 2003 S 5 rewrote the section, which prior thereto read:

"(A) Upon the expiration of the applicable period of time specified in division (B)(1) or (2) of this section, a delinquent child who has been classified pursuant to this section or section 2152.82 or 2152.83 of the Revised Code a juvenile sex offender registrant may petition the judge who made the classification, or that judge's successor in office, to do one of the following:

"(1) If the order containing the juvenile sex offender registrant classification also includes a determination by the juvenile court judge that the delinquent child is a sexual predator relative to the sexually oriented offense in the manner described in section 2152.82 or 2152.83 of the Revised Code and that determination remains in effect, to enter an order that contains a determination that the child no longer is a sexual predator and that also contains either a determination that the child is a habitual sex offender or a determination that the child remains a juvenile sex offender registrant but is not a sexual predator or habitual sex offender;

"(2) If the order containing the juvenile sex offender registrant classification under section 2152.82 or 2152.83 of the Revised Code or under division (C)(2) of this section pursuant to a petition filed under division (A) of this section does not include a sexual predator determination as described in division (A)(1) of this section but includes a determination by the juvenile court judge that the delinquent child is a habitual sex offender relative to the sexually oriented offense in the manner described in section 2152.82 or 2152.83 of the Revised Code, or in this section, and that determination remains in effect, to enter an order that contains a determination that the child no longer is a habitual sex offender and that also contains either a determination that the child remains a juvenile sex offender registrant or a determination that the child no longer is a juvenile sex offender registrant and no longer has a duty to register under section 2950.04 of the Revised Code;

"(3) If the order containing the juvenile sex offender registrant classification under section 2152.82 or 2152.83 of the Revised Code or under division (C)(2) of this section pursuant to a petition filed under division (A) of this section does not include a sexual predator or habitual sex offender determination as described in division (A)(1) or (2) of this section, to enter an order that contains a determination that the child no longer is a juvenile sex offender registrant and no longer has a duty to register under section 2950.04 of the Revised Code.

"(B) A delinquent child who has been adjudicated a delinquent child for committing on or after the effective date of this section a sexually oriented offense and who has been classified a juvenile sex offender registrant relative to that sexually oriented offense may file a petition under division (A) of this section requesting reclassification or declassification as described in that division after the expiration of one of the following periods of time:

"(1) The delinquent child initially may file a petition not earlier than three years after the entry of the juvenile court judge's order after the mandatory hearing conducted under section 2152.84 of the Revised Code.

"(2) After the delinquent child's initial filing of a petition under division (B)(1) of this section, the child may file a second petition not earlier than three years after the judge has entered an order deciding the petition under division (B)(1) of this section.

"(3) After the delinquent child's filing of a petition under division (B)(2) of this section, thereafter, the delinquent child may file a petition under this division upon the expiration of five years after the judge has entered an order deciding the petition under division (B)(2) of this section or the most recent petition the delinquent child has filed under this division.

"(C) Upon the filing of a petition under divisions (A) and (B) of this section, the judge may review the prior classification or determination in question and, upon consideration of all relevant factors and information, including, but not limited to the factors listed in division (E) of section 2152.83 of the Revised Code, the judge, in the judge's discretion, shall do one of the following:

"(1) Enter an order denying the petition;

"(2) Issue an order that reclassifies or declassifies the delinquent child, in the requested manner specified in division (A)(1), (2), or (3) of this section.

"(D) If a judge issues an order under division (C) of this section that denies a petition, the prior classification of the delinquent child as a juvenile sex offender registrant, and the prior determination that the child is a sexual predator or habitual sex offender, if applicable, shall remain in effect.

"A judge may issue an order under division (C) of this section that contains a determination that a child no longer is a sexual predator only if the judge conducts a hearing and, in accordance with the procedures specified in division (D)(1) of section 2950.09 of the Revised Code, determines at the hearing by clear and convincing evidence that the delinquent child is unlikely to commit a sexually oriented offense in the future. If the judge issues an order of that type, the judge shall provide the notifications described in division (D)(1) of section 2950.09 of the Revised Code, and the recipient of the notification shall comply with the provisions of that division.

"A judge may issue an order under division (C) of this section that contains a determination that a delinquent child is a habitual sex offender only if the judge conducts a hearing and determines at the hearing as described in division (E) of section 2950.09 of the Revised Code that the child is a habitual sex offender. If the judge issues an order that contains a determination that a delinquent child is a habitual sex offender , the judge may impose a requirement subjecting the child to community notification provisions as described in that division.

"(E) If a judge issues an order under division (C) of this section, the judge shall provide to the delinquent child and to the delinquent child's parent, guardian, or custodian a copy of the order and a notice containing the information described in divisions (A) and (B) of section 2950.03 of the Revised Code. The judge shall provide the notice at the time of the issuance of the order, shall provide the notice as described in division (B)(1)(c) of section 2950.03 of the Revised Code, and shall comply with divisions (B)(1), (B)(2), and (C) of that section regarding that notice.

"(F) An order issued under division (C) of this section shall remain in effect for the period of time specified in section 2950.07 of the Revised Code, subject to a further modification or a termination of the order under this section. If an order is issued under division (C) of this section, the child's attainment of eighteen or twenty-one years of age does not affect or terminate the order, and the order remains in effect for the period of time described in this division."

Cross References

Adjudication of offender as sexual predator or as habitual sex offender; exclusion of registration-exempt sexually oriented offense, 2950.09.
Child-victim oriented offenses; duty of registration of offender or delinquent child, 2950.041.
Community notification of sex offender registration, 2950.11.
Determination of offender as child-victim predator; hearing, 2950.091.
Determination of requirement to register as sex offender with sheriff, 2950.021.
Manner of registering as sex offenders, 2950.04.
Notice of duty to register as sex offender and related requirements, 2950.03.
Sex offenders, definitions, 2950.01.
Verification of current address of residence, school, or place of employment, 2950.06.

Ohio Administrative Code References

Completion and transmittal of forms and information, OAC 109:5–2–02
Completion and transmittal of forms, OAC 109:5–2–02

Library References

Infants ⇌227(2), 230.1.
Westlaw Topic No. 211.
C.J.S. Adoption of Persons § 10.
C.J.S. Infants §§ 41, 53 to 54, 57, 69 to 85.

Research References

Encyclopedias

OH Jur. 3d Criminal Law § 3447, Generally; Constitutionality.
OH Jur. 3d Family Law § 1487.5, Sexually Oriented and Child-Victim Offenders.
OH Jur. 3d Family Law § 1698.6, Sexually Oriented and Child-Victim Offenses; Registration.

Treatises and Practice Aids

1 Giannelli and Snyder, Baldwin's Ohio Practice, Evidence, Index, Index.
Carlin, Baldwin's Ohio Practice, Merrick-Rippner Probate Law § 105:1, Juvenile Court—Exclusive Original Jurisdiction.
Carlin, Baldwin's Ohio Practice, Merrick-Rippner Probate Law § 107:89, Custody of Department of Youth Services.
Carlin, Baldwin's Ohio Practice, Merrick-Rippner Probate Law § 107:93, Classification of Juvenile Sex Offender Registrant, Effective January 1, 2002...
Carlin, Baldwin's Ohio Practice, Merrick-Rippner Probate Law § 107:94, Classification of Juvenile Sex Offender Registrant, Effective January 1, 2002 (If Charged With a Sexually Oriented Offense on or After January 1, 2002 and is 16-17 Years Old at the Time of...
Carlin, Baldwin's Ohio Practice, Merrick-Rippner Probate Law § 107:95, Classification of Juvenile Sex Offender Registrant, Effective January 1, 2002 (If Charged With a Sexually Oriented Offense on or After January 1, 2002 and is 14-15 Years Old at the Time of...
Carlin, Baldwin's Ohio Practice, Merrick-Rippner Probate Law § 107:96, Classification of Juvenile Sex Offender Registrant, Effective January 1, 2002—Hearing After Completion of the Dispositions Ordered Under RC 2152.82 and RC 2152.83—Continuation or Modification...
Carlin, Baldwin's Ohio Practice, Merrick-Rippner Probate Law § 107:97, Classification of Juvenile Sex Offender Registrant, Effective January 1, 2002—Subsequent Petition for Reclassification or Declassification of Orders Issued Pursuant to RC 2152.82, RC 2152.83 and...
Carlin, Baldwin's Ohio Practice, Merrick-Rippner Probate Law § 107:100, Frequency and Duration of Registration Based on the Classification of a Juvenile Sex Offender Registrant.
Giannelli & Yeomans, Ohio Juvenile Law § 6:1, Introduction.
Giannelli & Yeomans, Ohio Juvenile Law § 6:5, "Sexual Predator" Defined.
Giannelli & Yeomans, Ohio Juvenile Law § 6:9, Juvenile Offender Registrant—Repeat Offender Classification.
Giannelli & Yeomans, Ohio Juvenile Law § 6:10, Juvenile Offender Registrant—Mandatory Classification.
Giannelli & Yeomans, Ohio Juvenile Law § 6:13, Petitions for Reclassification or Declassification.

2152.851 Effect of redesignation of offense on existing order

(A) If, prior to the effective date of this section, a judge issues an order under section 2152.82, 2152.83, 2152.84, or 2152.85 of the Revised Code that classifies a delinquent child a juvenile offender registrant and if, on and after the effective date of this section, the sexually oriented offense upon which the order was based no longer is considered a sexually oriented offense but instead is a child-victim oriented offense, notwithstanding the redesignation of the offense, the order shall remain in effect for the period described in the section under which it was issued, the order shall be considered for all purposes to be an order that classifies the child a juvenile offender registrant, division (A)(2)(b) of section 2950.041 of the Revised Code applies regarding the child, and the duty to register imposed pursuant to that division shall be considered, for purposes of section 2950.07 of the Revised Code and for all other purposes, to be a continuation of the duty imposed upon the child prior to the effective date of this section under the order issued under section 2152.82, 2152.83, 2152.84, or 2152.85 and Chapter 2950. of the Revised Code.

(B) If an order of the type described in division (A) of this section included a classification or determination that the delinquent child was a sexual predator or habitual sex offender, notwithstanding the redesignation of the offense upon which the determination was based, all of the following apply:

(1) Divisions (A)(1) and (2) or (E)(1) and (2) of section 2950.091 of the Revised Code apply regarding the child and the judge's order made prior to the effective date of this section shall be considered for all purposes to be an order that classifies the child as described in those divisions;

(2) The child's classification or determination under divisions (A)(1) and (2) or (E)(1) and (2) of section 2950.091 of the Revised Code shall be considered, for purposes of section 2950.07 of the Revised Code and for all other purposes, to be a continuation of classification or determination made prior to the effective date of this section;

(3) The child's duties under Chapter 2950. of the Revised Code relative to that classification or determination shall be considered for all purposes to be a continuation of the duties related to that classification or determination as they existed prior to the effective date of this section.

(2003 S 5, eff. 7–31–03)

Library References

Infants ⚖227(2), 230.1.
Westlaw Topic No. 211.
C.J.S. Adoption of Persons § 10.
C.J.S. Infants §§ 41, 53 to 54, 57, 69 to 85.

Research References

Encyclopedias

OH Jur. 3d Family Law § 1487.5, Sexually Oriented and Child-Victim Offenders.

OH Jur. 3d Family Law § 1698.6, Sexually Oriented and Child-Victim Offenses; Registration.

PENALTIES

2152.99 Penalties

Whoever violates division (G) of section 2152.72 of the Revised Code is guilty of a minor misdemeanor.

(2000 S 179, § 3, eff. 1–1–02)

Library References

Infants ⚖17.
Westlaw Topic No. 211.
C.J.S. Infants §§ 8 to 9.

CHAPTER 2153

CUYAHOGA COUNTY JUVENILE COURT

Section
2153.01 Juvenile court of Cuyahoga county established

JUDGES
2153.02 Judges; qualifications
2153.03 Nomination and election of judges; term of office; administrative judge
2153.05 Substitute judge; vacancies
2153.06 Removal from office

COURT ADMINISTRATION AND OFFICIALS
2153.07 Accommodations for court
2153.08 Administrative judge shall be clerk of court; may appoint deputies and clerks; bonds
2153.081 Additional fees for computer services
2153.09 Compensation of employees
2153.10 Bond of clerk; amount
2153.11 Bailiffs; compensation

GENERAL PROVISIONS
2153.12 Calendar of court; term
2153.13 Contempt proceedings
2153.14 Seal of court; form
2153.15 May vacate and modify judgments
2153.16 Jurisdiction and powers
2153.17 Laws now in force to apply

Cross References

Common pleas courts; probate and other divisions; jurisdiction, O Const Art IV §4
Judicial power vested in courts, O Const Art IV §1

2153.01 Juvenile court of Cuyahoga county established

There is hereby established within the court of common pleas of Cuyahoga county a juvenile division, which shall be styled "the court of common pleas, juvenile court division," referred to in sections 2153.02 to 2153.17 of the Revised Code, as "the juvenile court."

(1972 H 574, eff. 6–29–72)

Historical and Statutory Notes

Ed. Note: Former 2153.01 repealed by 1972 H 574, eff. 6–29–72; 1953 H 1; GC 1683–12.

Pre–1953 H 1 Amendments: 114 v 45, § 1; 108 v Pt 1, 380; 107 v 732

Library References

Courts ⚖50.
Westlaw Topic No. 106.
C.J.S. Courts § 106.

Research References

Encyclopedias

OH Jur. 3d Courts & Judges § 18, Courts of Common Pleas—Juvenile Division and Juvenile Courts.
OH Jur. 3d Courts & Judges § 70, Judges in Cuyahoga County; Administrative Judge.

Forms

Ohio Jurisprudence Pleading and Practice Forms § 2:25, Powers and Duties Via Particular Courts—Juvenile Division.
Ohio Jurisprudence Pleading and Practice Forms § 5:40, Divisions of the Common Pleas Courts—Generally.

Notes of Decisions

Pamphlets 1

1. **Pamphlets**

Authority of juvenile court to expend public funds to publish and distribute pamphlets discussed. 1944 OAG 6877.

JUDGES

2153.02 Judges; qualifications

The juvenile court shall consist of six judges, each of whom, at the time of his election or appointment, shall be a qualified elector and resident of Cuyahoga county and shall have been admitted to practice as an attorney at law in this state for a period of at least six years immediately preceding his appointment or commencement of his term. They shall be elected and designated as judges of the court of common pleas, juvenile court division, and shall exercise the same powers and jurisdiction and receive the same compensation as other judges of the court of common pleas.

(1984 H 113, eff. 1–8–85; 1976 H 468; 1972 H 574; 127 v 482; 1953 H 1; GC 1683–13)

Historical and Statutory Notes

Pre–1953 H 1 Amendments: 121 v 290; 114 v 45; 108 v Pt 1, 380; 107 v 732

Cross References

Compensation of judges, 141.04 to 141.07
Filling vacancy in judgeship, O Const Art IV §13

Library References

Judges ⚖3 to 5.
Westlaw Topic No. 227.
C.J.S. Judges §§ 12 to 19.

Research References

Encyclopedias

OH Jur. 3d Courts & Judges § 30, Time of Election; Additional Judges.
OH Jur. 3d Courts & Judges § 35, Generally; Admission to Practice as Attorney.
OH Jur. 3d Courts & Judges § 36, Qualifications as Elector; Residency.
OH Jur. 3d Courts & Judges § 70, Judges in Cuyahoga County; Administrative Judge.
OH Jur. 3d Courts & Judges § 105, Juvenile Division.

Forms

Ohio Jurisprudence Pleading and Practice Forms § 2:20, Qualifications and Selection in General.

2153.03 Nomination and election of judges; term of office; administrative judge

Each of the judges of the juvenile court division shall be elected for six years at the general election immediately preceding the year in which the term, as provided in this section, commences, and the judge's successor shall be elected at the general election immediately preceding the expiration of such term.

Each judge shall be elected by the electors of Cuyahoga county in the same manner as is provided for the election of judges of the court of common pleas. The terms of office of the judges of the juvenile court shall begin as follows: January 1, 1959, January 2, 1959, January 1, 1963, January 2, 1963, January 3, 1977, and January 3, 1987. Each of the judges of the juvenile court shall have the same judicial duties.

In addition to the judge's regular judicial duties, one of the judges shall be the administrator of the juvenile court's subdivisions and departments.

The administrative judge shall be elected in the manner provided by rule 3 of the rules adopted by the supreme court of Ohio for the superintendence of the common pleas court. During any absence from the court by the administrative judge, the administrative judge may designate one of the other judges to serve in the administrative judge's place and stead as the clerk of the court and as the administrator of the court's subdivisions and departments.

(1995 H 99, eff. 8-22-95; 1984 H 113, eff. 1-8-85; 1976 H 468; 1972 H 574; 127 v 482; 1953 H 1; GC 1683-14)

Historical and Statutory Notes

Pre–1953 H 1 Amendments: 121 v 290; 114 v 45; 108 Pt 1, 380; 107 v 732

Amendment Note: 1995 H 99 substituted "immediately" for "next" twice in the first paragraph; and made other changes to reflect gender neutral language.

Cross References

Election of judges of common pleas court, 2301.01
Election, term, and compensation of judges; assignment of retired judges, O Const Art IV §6
Time for holding elections for state and local officers; terms of office, O Const Art XVII §1

Library References

Courts ⚖70.
Judges ⚖3, 7.
Westlaw Topic Nos. 106, 227.
C.J.S. Courts § 123.
C.J.S. Judges §§ 12 to 13, 21 to 24, 27 to 29.

Research References

Encyclopedias

OH Jur. 3d Courts & Judges § 29, Generally; Elective Nature of Office.
OH Jur. 3d Courts & Judges § 32, Term of Office.
OH Jur. 3d Courts & Judges § 33, Commencement of Term.
OH Jur. 3d Courts & Judges § 70, Judges in Cuyahoga County; Administrative Judge.

Forms

Ohio Jurisprudence Pleading and Practice Forms § 2:20, Qualifications and Selection in General.

Notes of Decisions

Employees 1

---

1. Employees

Full-time juvenile court employees working part time at a juvenile detention center may be terminated from their part-time employment by the administrative judge of a juvenile court notwithstanding oral promises of continued employment that may have been made by the superintendent of the juvenile detention facility, as the terms of employment at juvenile detention facilities are governed by statute, not the doctrine of employment at will. Abbott v. Stepanik (Cuyahoga 1990) 64 Ohio App.3d 719, 582 N.E.2d 1082, dismissed, jurisdictional motion overruled 50 Ohio St.3d 717, 553 N.E.2d 1364.

An administrative judge of the juvenile division of a court of common pleas is not authorized to enter into an employment agreement with employees of the court. Malone v. Court of Common Pleas of Cuyahoga County (Ohio 1976) 45 Ohio St.2d 245, 344 N.E.2d 126, 74 O.O.2d 413. Courts ⚖ 55

2153.05 Substitute judge; vacancies

In case of the temporary absence or disability of a juvenile judge, or when the volume of cases pending in the juvenile court necessitates the assistance of an additional judge, and upon the request of a juvenile judge, the presiding judge of the court of common pleas of Cuyahoga county shall designate a judge of the court of common pleas of Cuyahoga county to act as juvenile judge during the absence or disability. If no judge of the court of common pleas is available for that purpose, the chief justice of the supreme court shall designate a juvenile judge, a probate judge, or a judge of the court of common pleas from another county to act as judge. Such judge shall receive the compensation for his services and expenses that is provided by section 141.07 of the Revised Code for judges of the courts of common pleas designated by the chief justice to hold court outside their respective counties.

Vacancies occurring in the office of the juvenile judge of Cuyahoga county shall be filled in the manner prescribed for the filling of vacancies in the office of the judges of the courts of common pleas.

(1995 H 151, eff. 12-4-95; 1953 H 1, eff. 10-1-53; GC 1683-16)

Historical and Statutory Notes

Pre–1953 H 1 Amendments: 121 v 290; 114 v 46; 108 v Pt 1, 380; 107 v 732

Amendment Note: 1995 H 151 deleted "chief justice or, in his absence, the" before "presiding judge" in the first sentence of the first paragraph; and made other nonsubstantive changes.

Library References

Judges ⇨13, 16.
Westlaw Topic No. 227.
C.J.S. Judges §§ 161 to 162, 164 to 167, 169.

Research References

Encyclopedias

OH Jur. 3d Courts & Judges § 71, Assignment of Judges.
OH Jur. 3d Courts & Judges § 104, Courts of Common Pleas and Divisions.
OH Jur. 3d Courts & Judges § 105, Juvenile Division.

2153.06 Removal from office

A juvenile judge is subject to the same disabilities and may be removed from office for the same causes and in the same manner as a judge of the court of common pleas.

(1953 H 1, eff. 10–1–53; GC 1683–17)

Historical and Statutory Notes

Pre–1953 H 1 Amendments: 114 v 46, § 6; 108 v Pt 1, 380; 107 v 732

Cross References

Removal of judge, 3.08, 2701.11, 2701.12; O Const Art II §38, O Const Art IV §17

Library References

Judges ⇨11.
Westlaw Topic No. 227.
C.J.S. Judges §§ 29, 35 to 36, 40 to 52.

Research References

Encyclopedias

OH Jur. 3d Courts & Judges § 148, Grounds for Forfeiture of Office.

COURT ADMINISTRATION AND OFFICIALS

2153.07 Accommodations for court

The board of county commissioners of Cuyahoga county shall provide suitable accommodations, facilities, and equipment for the juvenile court, its officers, and employees. The expense of maintaining and operating the court shall be paid out of the treasury of Cuyahoga county.

(1953 H 1, eff. 10–1–53; GC 1683–18)

Historical and Statutory Notes

Pre–1953 H 1 Amendments: 114 v 46, § 7; 108 v Pt 1, 380; 107 v 732

Library References

Courts ⇨72 to 74.
Westlaw Topic No. 106.
C.J.S. Courts §§ 7, 121.

Research References

Encyclopedias

OH Jur. 3d Family Law § 1536, Terms, Sessions, and Places of Court.

2153.08 Administrative judge shall be clerk of court; may appoint deputies and clerks; bonds

The administrative juvenile judge shall have the care and custody of the files, papers, books, records, and moneys pertaining to the juvenile court, and shall be the clerk of said court, with all the powers and duties of a clerk of the court of common pleas in connection with the business of said juvenile court. He may appoint and employ such deputies, clerks, stenographers, and other assistants and attaches as are reasonably necessary in connection with the work of said court, and shall file with the county auditor certificates of such appointments. Any such appointee may be dismissed by the administrative judge. Each appointee shall qualify by taking the oath of office required of the clerk of the court of common pleas under sections 3.22 and 3.23 of the Revised Code. When so qualified, each deputy clerk may perform the duties of the clerk and shall have the same powers as a deputy clerk of the court of common pleas in matters of which the court of common pleas now has concurrent jurisdiction by virtue of section 2151.07 of the Revised Code. The administrative judge may require any of his appointees to give bond in the sum of not less than one thousand dollars, conditioned for the honest and faithful performance of his duties. The approval of the sureties, the terms, the filing, and the beneficiaries of such bonds shall be the same as in the case of the bond of the clerk under section 2153.10 of the Revised Code. The clerk shall not be personally liable for the default, misfeasance, or nonfeasance of any appointee from whom a bond has been required, approved, and filed as provided in this section.

(1972 H 574, eff. 6–29–72; 1953 H 1; GC 1683–20)

Historical and Statutory Notes

Pre–1953 H 1 Amendments: 114 v 47, § 9

Library References

Clerks of Courts ⇨4.
Courts ⇨55, 57.
Judges ⇨33.
Westlaw Topic Nos. 106, 227, 79.
C.J.S. Courts §§ 107 to 109, 239.
C.J.S. Judges § 54.
C.J.S. Stenographers §§ 2 to 21.

Research References

Encyclopedias

OH Jur. 3d Courts & Judges § 70, Judges in Cuyahoga County; Administrative Judge.
OH Jur. 3d Courts & Judges § 112, Insurance; Liability for Acts of Subordinates.
OH Jur. 3d Courts & Judges § 185, Appointment or Election, in General—County Courts; Other Courts.
OH Jur. 3d Courts & Judges § 188, Official Bonds.
OH Jur. 3d Courts & Judges § 189, Oath of Office.
OH Jur. 3d Courts & Judges § 205, Records of Court Judgments and Proceedings, and Miscellaneous Records Prescribed by Statute.
OH Jur. 3d Courts & Judges § 211, Custody of Papers.
OH Jur. 3d Courts & Judges § 216, Powers and Duties of Deputies and Assistants.
OH Jur. 3d Courts & Judges § 217, Civil Action, Generally; Defenses.
OH Jur. 3d Family Law § 1540, Court Personnel.

Treatises and Practice Aids

Carlin, Baldwin's Ohio Practice, Merrick-Rippner Probate Law § 104:14, Juvenile Court—Clerk.
Giannelli & Yeomans, Ohio Juvenile Law § 15:2, Intake.

Notes of Decisions

Assistants and employees 2

Employment agreement 1

1. Employment agreement

An administrative judge of the juvenile division of a court of common pleas is not authorized to enter into an employment agreement with employees of the court. Malone v. Court of Common Pleas of Cuyahoga County (Ohio 1976) 45 Ohio St.2d 245, 344 N.E.2d 126, 74 O.O.2d 413. Courts ⇔ 55

2. Assistants and employees

County juvenile center employees appointed by the juvenile court under RC 2151.13 and 2153.08 serve at the pleasure of the court, are not "public employees" for purposes of RC 4117.01(C) and have no right to hold a representation election; the fact they are appointed as deputy clerks to administer oaths does not make them employees of the clerk. Service Employees International Union, Local 47 v SERB, 1996 SERB 4–39 (CP, Franklin, 7–10–95).

2153.081 Additional fees for computer services

(A)(1) The juvenile judges may determine that, for the efficient operation of their court, additional funds are required to computerize the court, to make available computerized legal research services, or both. Upon making a determination that additional funds are required for either or both of those purposes, the judges shall authorize and direct the clerk or a deputy clerk of the court to charge one additional fee not to exceed three dollars on the filing of each cause of action or appeal under division (A), (Q), or (U) of section 2303.20 of the Revised Code.

(2) All moneys collected under division (A)(1) of this section shall be paid to the county treasurer. The treasurer shall place the moneys from the fees in a separate fund to be disbursed, upon an order of the juvenile judges, in an amount no greater than the actual cost to the court of procuring and maintaining computer systems for the clerk's office, computerized legal research services, or both.

(3) If the court determines that the funds in the fund described in division (A)(2) of this section are more than sufficient to satisfy the purpose for which the additional fee described in division (A)(1) of this section was imposed, the court may declare a surplus in the fund and expend those surplus funds for other appropriate technological expenses of the court.

(B)(1) The juvenile judges may determine that, for the efficient operation of their court, additional funds are required to computerize the office of the clerk of the juvenile court and, upon that determination, may authorize and direct the clerk or a deputy clerk of the court to charge an additional fee, not to exceed ten dollars, on the filing of each cause of action or appeal, on the filing, docketing, and endorsing of each certificate of judgment, or on the docketing and indexing of each aid in execution or petition to vacate, revive, or modify a judgment under divisions (A), (P), (Q), (T), and (U) of section 2303.20 of the Revised Code. Subject to division (B)(2) of this section, all moneys collected under this division shall be paid to the county treasurer to be disbursed, upon an order of the juvenile judges and subject to appropriation by the board of county commissioners, in an amount no greater than the actual cost to the juvenile court of procuring and maintaining computer systems for the clerk's office.

(2) If the juvenile judges make the determination described in division (B)(1) of this section, the board of county commissioners may issue one or more general obligation bonds for the purpose of procuring and maintaining the computer systems for the office of the clerk of the juvenile court. In addition to the purposes stated in division (B)(1) of this section for which the moneys collected under that division may be expended, the moneys additionally may be expended to pay debt charges on and financing costs related to any general obligation bonds issued pursuant to this division as they become due. General obligation bonds issued pursuant to this division are Chapter 133. securities.

(1992 S 246, eff. 3–24–93; 1992 H 405)

Cross References

Net indebtedness of county, securities not considered in calculation of, 133.07

Library References

Clerks of Courts ⇔ 28 to 29.
Westlaw Topic No. 79.
C.J.S. Courts § 242.

Research References

Encyclopedias

OH Jur. 3d Courts & Judges § 70, Judges in Cuyahoga County; Administrative Judge.

2153.09 Compensation of employees

The compensation of the employees of the juvenile court shall be fixed by the administrative juvenile judge, which compensation shall not exceed in the aggregate the amount fixed by the board of county commissioners for such purpose. Such compensation so fixed shall be paid from the county treasury in semimonthly installments on the warrant of the county auditor.

(1972 H 574, eff. 6–29–72; 1953 H 1; GC 1683–21)

Historical and Statutory Notes

Pre–1953 H 1 Amendments: 114 v 47, § 10

Library References

Courts ⇔ 55.
Westlaw Topic No. 106.
C.J.S. Courts §§ 107 to 109.

Research References

Treatises and Practice Aids

Carlin, Baldwin's Ohio Practice, Merrick-Rippner Probate Law § 104:16, Juvenile Court—Employees.

Giannelli & Yeomans, Ohio Juvenile Law § 15:2, Intake.

Notes of Decisions

Employment agreement 1

1. Employment agreement

An administrative judge of the juvenile division of a court of common pleas is not authorized to enter into an employment agreement with employees of the court. Malone v. Court of Common Pleas of Cuyahoga County (Ohio 1976) 45 Ohio St.2d 245, 344 N.E.2d 126, 74 O.O.2d 413. Courts ⇔ 55

2153.10 Bond of clerk; amount

Before entering upon the duties of his office, the administrative juvenile judge, as judge and clerk of the juvenile court, and each judge shall execute and file with the county treasurer of Cuyahoga county a bond in the sum of not less than five thousand dollars, to be determined by the board of county commissioners of Cuyahoga county, with sufficient surety, to be approved by said board, conditioned for the faithful performance of such duties as clerk. Said bond shall be given for the benefit of Cuyahoga county, the state, and any person who may suffer loss by reason of a default in any of the conditions of said bond.

(1972 H 574, eff. 6–29–72; 1953 H 1; GC 1683–22)

Historical and Statutory Notes

Pre–1953 H 1 Amendments: 114 v 47, § 11

Cross References

Official bond, 3.30 to 3.34

Library References

Judges ⚖5, 37.
Westlaw Topic No. 227.
C.J.S. Judges §§ 15 to 19, 93 to 94.

Research References

Encyclopedias
OH Jur. 3d Courts & Judges § 38, Official Bond.
OH Jur. 3d Courts & Judges § 188, Official Bonds.

2153.11 Bailiffs; compensation

The administrative juvenile judge may appoint one or more bailiffs to preserve order and perform such other duties as such judge requires, as provided for constables in section 2701.07 of the Revised Code. The compensation of any such appointee shall be fixed and paid on the same basis as provided by section 2701.08 of the Revised Code for the compensation of constables in the court of common pleas of Cuyahoga county.

(1972 H 574, eff. 6–29–72; 1953 H 1; GC 1683–23)

Historical and Statutory Notes

Pre–1953 H 1 Amendments: 114 v 48, § 12

Library References

Courts ⚖58.
Westlaw Topic No. 106.
C.J.S. Courts § 108.

Research References

Encyclopedias
OH Jur. 3d Family Law § 1540, Court Personnel.

GENERAL PROVISIONS

2153.12 Calendar of court; term

The calendar of the juvenile court shall be divided into four terms of three months each commencing on the first day of January, April, July, and October of each year. All actions and other business of the court pending at the expiration of any term of court shall be continued to the following term of court without any special or general entry or order to that effect. The juvenile judges may adjourn the court from day to day or to any other day in the same term whenever, in their opinion, the business of the court permits.

(1953 H 1, eff. 10–1–53; GC 1683–24)

Historical and Statutory Notes

Pre–1953 H 1 Amendments: 114 v 48, § 13

Library References

Courts ⚖63, 65, 68.
Westlaw Topic No. 106.
C.J.S. Courts §§ 111 to 114, 116, 120.

Research References

Encyclopedias
OH Jur. 3d Family Law § 1536, Terms, Sessions, and Places of Court.

Treatises and Practice Aids
Carlin, Baldwin's Ohio Practice, Merrick-Rippner Probate Law § 104:12, Juvenile Court—Term.

2153.13 Contempt proceedings

The juvenile court has the same jurisdiction in contempt of court proceedings provided for the court of common pleas and for other courts of record.

(1953 H 1, eff. 10–1–53; GC 1683–25)

Historical and Statutory Notes

Pre–1953 H 1 Amendments: 114 v 48, § 14

Cross References

Contempt of court, Ch 2705

Library References

Contempt ⚖30.
Courts ⚖175.
Infants ⚖221.
Westlaw Topic Nos. 106, 211, 93.
C.J.S. Contempt §§ 45, 48, 55 to 56.
C.J.S. Infants §§ 57, 69 to 85.

Research References

Encyclopedias
OH Jur. 3d Family Law § 1545, Contempt.

2153.14 Seal of court; form

The juvenile court shall have a seal which shall consist of the coat of arms of the state within a circle one and one-fourth inches in diameter and shall be surrounded by the words, "the juvenile court of Cuyahoga county, Ohio." Such seal shall have no other words or device engraved thereon. Such seal shall be affixed to the processes of the court, which shall be attested and be in the general form and served as provided for process of the court of common pleas.

(132 v H 164, eff. 12–15–67; 1953 H 1; GC 1683–26)

Historical and Statutory Notes

Pre–1953 H 1 Amendments: 114 v 48, § 15

Cross References

Service of process, Civ R 4 to 6

Research References

Encyclopedias
OH Jur. 3d Family Law § 1537, Powers and Duties.

2153.15 May vacate and modify judgments

The juvenile court has the same power to vacate and modify its own judgments or orders during or after term as the probate court has under section 2101.33 of the Revised Code, and may adopt, publish, and revise rules and regulations for practice in said court not inconsistent with sections 2153.01 to 2153.17, inclusive, of the Revised Code.

(1953 H 1, eff. 10–1–53; GC 1683–27)

Historical and Statutory Notes

Pre–1953 H 1 Amendments: 114 v 48, § 15

Library References

Courts ⚖47.
Westlaw Topic No. 106.
C.J.S. Courts § 2.

Research References

Encyclopedias

OH Jur. 3d Family Law § 1538, Powers and Duties—Rules as to Practice and Procedure.
OH Jur. 3d Family Law § 1706, Modification or Vacation of Order.

Forms

Ohio Jurisprudence Pleading and Practice Forms § 2:8, Courts of Common Pleas—Juvenile Division.

Treatises and Practice Aids

Carlin, Baldwin's Ohio Practice, Merrick-Rippner Probate Law § 107:117, Proceedings After Judgment—Continuing Jurisdiction of Juvenile Court.

Giannelli & Yeomans, Ohio Juvenile Law § 33:2, Motions.

2153.16 Jurisdiction and powers

The juvenile court shall exercise the jurisdiction and powers conferred upon the court by Chapters 2151. and 2152. and other sections of the Revised Code, unless the jurisdiction and powers are inconsistent with sections 2153.01 to 2153.17 of the Revised Code or are plainly inapplicable.

(2000 S 179, § 3, eff. 1–1–02; 1972 H 574, eff. 6–29–72; 127 v 847; 1953 H 1; GC 1683–28)

Historical and Statutory Notes

Pre–1953 H 1 Amendments: 114 v 49, § 17

Amendment Note: 2000 S 179, § 3, eff. 1–1–02, added the reference to Chapter 2152; and made other nonsubstantive changes.

Library References

Courts ⚖176.
Infants ⚖230.1.
Westlaw Topic Nos. 106, 211.
C.J.S. Adoption of Persons § 10.
C.J.S. Infants §§ 57, 69 to 85.

Research References

Encyclopedias

OH Jur. 3d Courts & Judges § 70, Judges in Cuyahoga County; Administrative Judge.

Notes of Decisions

Information distribution 1

1. Information distribution

Authority of juvenile court to expend public funds to publish and distribute pamphlets discussed. 1944 OAG 6877.

2153.17 Laws now in force to apply

The sections of the Revised Code regulating the manner and grounds of appeal from any judgment, order, or decree rendered by the court of common pleas in the exercise of juvenile jurisdiction shall apply to the juvenile court.

(1953 H 1, eff. 10–1–53; GC 1683–29)

Historical and Statutory Notes

Pre–1953 H 1 Amendments: 114 v 49, § 18

Cross References

Appeals from juvenile court, 2151.52

Research References

Encyclopedias

OH Jur. 3d Courts & Judges § 70, Judges in Cuyahoga County; Administrative Judge.

Treatises and Practice Aids

Giannelli & Yeomans, Ohio Juvenile Law § 34:2, Types of Cases.

Notes of Decisions

Notice of appeal 2
Procedural issues 3
Right to counsel 1

1. Right to counsel

Habeas corpus will not lie based upon an allegation of denial of counsel to a juvenile adjudicated delinquent inasmuch as a right of appeal to the Court of Appeals exists in such case. In re Piazza (Ohio 1966) 7 Ohio St.2d 102, 218 N.E.2d 459, 36 O.O.2d 84.

2. Notice of appeal

A Court of Appeals may allow amendment of timely filed notice of appeal and certification so that there is full compliance with applicable rule, and thus state would be permitted to amend its original certification to comply with formalized procedure established by Juvenile Rule, which required certification that appeal from granting of motion to suppress statements made to investigators was not taken for purpose of delay and that granting of motion had rendered proof available to state so weak that any reasonable possibility of proving complaint's allegations had been destroyed. In re Hester (Franklin 1981) 1 Ohio App.3d 24, 437 N.E.2d 1218, 1 O.B.R. 85. Infants ⚖ 244.1.

3. Procedural issues

An order of a juvenile division transferring child to court of common pleas, general division, is not a final appealable order, and therefore, a contention that the transfer was erroneous is properly raised on appeal from juvenile's conviction. State v. Whiteside (Allen 1982) 6 Ohio App.3d 30, 452 N.E.2d 332, 6 O.B.R. 140. Infants ⚖ 68.8.

OHIO REVISED CODE
TITLES 23 TO 57
(Selected Provisions)

Complete to February 28, 2007

CHAPTER		CHAPTER	
2301	Organization	4505	Certificate of Motor Vehicle Title Law
2305	Jurisdiction; Limitation of Actions	4507	Driver's License Law
2717	Change of Name	4511	Traffic Laws—Operation of Motor Vehicles
2901	General Provisions	5101	Job and Family Services Department—General Provisions
2945	Trial	5103	Placement of Children
3103	Husband and Wife	5122	Hospitalization of Mentally Ill
3105	Divorce, Legal Separation, Annulment, Dissolution of Marriage	5123	Department of Mental Retardation and Developmental Disabilities
3107	Adoption	5126	County Boards of Mental Retardation and Developmental Disabilities
3109	Children	5302	Statutory Forms of Land Conveyance
3111	Parentage	5305	Dower
3705	Vital Statistics	5731	Estate Tax
3923	Sickness and Accident Insurance	5747	Income Tax

CHAPTER 2301

ORGANIZATION

JUDGES

Section
2301.03 Judges of the divisions of domestic relations

TERMS OF COURT

2301.05 Term for any division set at one year; part terms for jury service

JUDGES

2301.03 Judges of the divisions of domestic relations

(A) In Franklin county, the judges of the court of common pleas whose terms begin on January 1, 1953, January 2, 1953, January 5, 1969, January 5, 1977, and January 2, 1997, and successors, shall have the same qualifications, exercise the same powers and jurisdiction, and receive the same compensation as other judges of the court of common pleas of Franklin county and shall be elected and designated as judges of the court of common pleas, division of domestic relations. They shall have all the powers relating to juvenile courts, and all cases under Chapters 2151. and 2152. of the Revised Code, all parentage proceedings under Chapter 3111. of the Revised Code over which the juvenile court has jurisdiction, and all divorce, dissolution of marriage, legal separation, and annulment cases shall be assigned to them. In addition to the judge's regular duties, the judge who is senior in point of service shall serve on the children services board and the county advisory board and shall be the administrator of the domestic relations division and its subdivisions and departments.

(B) In Hamilton county:

(1) The judge of the court of common pleas, whose term begins on January 1, 1957, and successors, and the judge of the court of common pleas, whose term begins on February 14, 1967, and successors, shall be the juvenile judges as provided in Chapters 2151. and 2152. of the Revised Code, with the powers and jurisdiction conferred by those chapters.

(2) The judges of the court of common pleas whose terms begin on January 5, 1957, January 16, 1981, and July 1, 1991, and successors, shall be elected and designated as judges of the court of common pleas, division of domestic relations, and shall have assigned to them all divorce, dissolution of marriage, legal separation, and annulment cases coming before the court. On or after the first day of July and before the first day of August of 1991 and each year thereafter, a majority of the judges of the division of domestic relations shall elect one of the judges of the division as administrative judge of that division. If a majority of the judges of the division of domestic relations are unable for any reason to elect an administrative judge for the division before the first day of August, a majority of the judges of the Hamilton county court of common pleas, as soon as possible after that date, shall elect one of the judges of the division of domestic relations as administrative judge of that division. The term of the administrative judge shall begin on the earlier of the first day of August of the year in which the administrative judge is elected or the date on which the administrative judge is elected by a majority of the judges of the Hamilton county court of common pleas and shall terminate on the date on which the administrative judge's successor is elected in the following year.

In addition to the judge's regular duties, the administrative judge of the division of domestic relations shall be the administrator of the domestic relations division and its subdivisions and departments and shall have charge of the employment, assignment, and supervision of the personnel of the division engaged in handling, servicing, or investigating divorce, dissolution of marriage, legal separation, and annulment cases, including any referees considered necessary by the judges in the discharge of their various duties.

The administrative judge of the division of domestic relations also shall designate the title, compensation, expense allowances, hours, leaves of absence, and vacations of the personnel of the division, and shall fix the duties of its personnel. The duties of the personnel, in addition to those provided for in other sections of the Revised Code, shall include the handling, servicing, and investigation of divorce, dissolution of marriage, legal separation, and annulment cases and counseling and conciliation services that may be made available to persons requesting them, whether or not the persons are parties to an action pending in the division.

The board of county commissioners shall appropriate the sum of money each year as will meet all the administrative expenses of the division of domestic relations, including reasonable expenses of the domestic relations judges and the division counselors and other employees designated to conduct the handling, servicing, and investigation of divorce, dissolution of marriage, legal separation, and annulment cases, conciliation and counseling, and all matters relating to those cases and counseling, and the expenses involved in the attendance of division personnel at domestic relations and welfare conferences designated by the division, and the further sum each year as will provide for the adequate operation of the division of domestic relations.

The compensation and expenses of all employees and the salary and expenses of the judges shall be paid by the county treasurer from the money appropriated for the operation of the division, upon the warrant of the county auditor, certified to by the administrative judge of the division of domestic relations.

The summonses, warrants, citations, subpoenas, and other writs of the division may issue to a bailiff, constable, or staff investigator of the division or to the sheriff of any county or any marshal, constable, or police officer, and the provisions of law relating to the subpoenaing of witnesses in other cases shall apply insofar as they are applicable. When a summons, warrant, citation, subpoena, or other writ is issued to an officer, other than a bailiff, constable, or staff investigator of the division, the expense of serving it shall be assessed as a part of the costs in the case involved.

(3) The judge of the court of common pleas of Hamilton county whose term begins on January 3, 1997, and the successor to that judge whose term begins on January 3, 2003, shall each be elected and designated for one term only as the drug court judge of the court of common pleas of Hamilton county. The successors to the judge whose term begins on January 3, 2003, shall be elected and designated as judges of the general division of the court of common pleas of Hamilton county and shall not have the authority granted by division (B)(3) of this section. The drug court judge may accept or reject any case referred to the drug court judge under division (B)(3) of this section. After the drug court judge accepts a referred case, the drug court judge has full authority over the case, including the authority to conduct arraignment, accept pleas, enter findings and dispositions, conduct trials, order treatment, and if treatment is not successfully completed pronounce and enter sentence.

A judge of the general division of the court of common pleas of Hamilton county and a judge of the Hamilton county municipal court may refer to the drug court judge any case, and any companion cases, the judge determines meet the criteria described under divisions (B)(3)(a) and (b) of this section. If the drug court judge accepts referral of a referred case, the case, and any companion cases, shall be transferred to the drug court judge. A judge may refer a case meeting the criteria described in divisions (B)(3)(a) and (b) of this section that involves a violation of a condition of a community control sanction to the drug court judge, and, if the drug court judge accepts the referral, the referring judge and the drug court judge have concurrent jurisdiction over the case.

A judge of the general division of the court of common pleas of Hamilton county and a judge of the Hamilton county municipal court may refer a case to the drug court judge under division (B)(3) of this section if the judge determines that both of the following apply:

(a) One of the following applies:

(i) The case involves a drug abuse offense, as defined in section 2925.01 of the Revised Code, that is a felony of the third or fourth degree if the offense is committed prior to July 1, 1996, a felony of the third, fourth, or fifth degree if the offense is committed on or after July 1, 1996, or a misdemeanor.

(ii) The case involves a theft offense, as defined in section 2913.01 of the Revised Code, that is a felony of the third or fourth degree if the offense is committed prior to July 1, 1996, a felony of the third, fourth, or fifth degree if the offense is committed on or after July 1, 1996, or a misdemeanor, and the defendant is drug or alcohol dependent or in danger of becoming drug or alcohol dependent and would benefit from treatment.

(b) All of the following apply:

(i) The case involves an offense for which a community control sanction may be imposed or is a case in which a mandatory prison term or a mandatory jail term is not required to be imposed.

(ii) The defendant has no history of violent behavior.

(iii) The defendant has no history of mental illness.

(iv) The defendant's current or past behavior, or both, is drug or alcohol driven.

(v) The defendant demonstrates a sincere willingness to participate in a fifteen-month treatment process.

(vi) The defendant has no acute health condition.

(vii) If the defendant is incarcerated, the county prosecutor approves of the referral.

(4) If the administrative judge of the court of common pleas of Hamilton county determines that the volume of cases pending before the drug court judge does not constitute a sufficient caseload for the drug court judge, the administrative judge, in accordance with the Rules of Superintendence for Courts of Common Pleas, shall assign individual cases to the drug court judge from the general docket of the court. If the assignments so occur, the administrative judge shall cease the assignments when the administrative judge determines that the volume of cases pending before the drug court judge constitutes a sufficient caseload for the drug court judge.

(5) As used in division (B) of this section, "community control sanction," "mandatory prison term," and "mandatory jail term" have the same meanings as in section 2929.01 of the Revised Code.

(C)(1) In Lorain county:

(a) The judges of the court of common pleas whose terms begin on January 3, 1959, January 4, 1989, January 2, 1999, and February 9, 2009, and successors, shall have the same qualifications, exercise the same powers and jurisdiction, and receive the same compensation as the other judges of the court of common pleas of Lorain county and shall be elected and designated as the judges of the court of common pleas, division of domestic relations. They shall have all of the powers relating to juvenile courts, and all cases under Chapters 2151. and 2152. of the Revised Code, all parentage proceedings over which the juvenile court has jurisdiction, and all divorce, dissolution of marriage, legal separation, and annulment cases shall be assigned to them, except cases that for some special reason are assigned to some other judge of the court of common pleas.

(b) On and after January 1, 2006, the judges of the court of common pleas, division of domestic relations, in addition to the powers and jurisdiction set forth in division (C)(1)(a) of this section, shall have jurisdiction over matters that are within the jurisdiction of the probate court under Chapter 2101. and other provisions of the Revised Code. From January 1, 2006, through February 8, 2009, the judges of the court of common pleas, division of domestic relations, shall exercise probate jurisdiction concurrently with the probate judge.

(c) The judge of the court of common pleas, division of domestic relations, whose term begins on February 9, 2009, is the successor to the probate judge who was elected in 2002 for a term that began on February 9, 2003.

(2)(a) From January 1, 2006, through February 8, 2009, with respect to Lorain county, all references in law to the probate court shall be construed as references to both the probate court and the court of common pleas, division of domestic relations, and all references in law to the probate judge shall be construed as references to both the probate judge and the judges of the court of common pleas, division of domestic relations. On and after February 9, 2009, with respect to Lorain county, all references in law to the probate court shall be construed as references to the court of common pleas, division of domestic relations, and all references to the probate judge shall be construed as references to the judges of the court of common pleas, division of domestic relations.

(b) On and after February 9, 2009, with respect to Lorain county, all references in law to the clerk of the probate court shall be construed as references to the judge who is serving pursuant to Rule 4 of the Rules of Superintendence for the Courts of Ohio as the administrative judge of the court of common pleas, division of domestic relations.

(D) In Lucas county:

(1) The judges of the court of common pleas whose terms begin on January 1, 1955, and January 3, 1965, and successors, shall have the same qualifications, exercise the same powers and jurisdiction, and receive the same compensation as other judges of the court of common pleas of Lucas county and shall be elected and designated as judges of the court of common pleas, division of domestic relations. All divorce, dissolution of marriage, legal separation, and annulment cases shall be assigned to them.

The judge of the division of domestic relations, senior in point of service, shall be considered as the presiding judge of the court of common pleas, division of domestic relations, and shall be charged exclusively with the assignment and division of the work of the division and the employment and supervision of all other personnel of the domestic relations division.

(2) The judges of the court of common pleas whose terms begin on January 5, 1977, and January 2, 1991, and successors shall have the same qualifications, exercise the same powers and jurisdiction, and receive the same compensation as other judges of the court of common pleas of Lucas county, shall be elected and designated as judges of the court of common pleas, juvenile division, and shall be the juvenile judges as provided in Chapters 2151. and 2152. of the Revised Code with the powers and jurisdictions conferred by those chapters. In addition to the judge's regular duties, the judge of the court of common pleas, juvenile division, senior in point of service, shall be the administrator of the juvenile division and its subdivisions and departments and shall have charge of the employment, assignment, and supervision of the personnel of the division engaged in handling, servicing, or investigating juvenile cases, including any referees considered necessary by the judges of the division in the discharge of their various duties.

The judge of the court of common pleas, juvenile division, senior in point of service, also shall designate the title, compensation, expense allowance, hours, leaves of absence, and vacation of the personnel of the division and shall fix the duties of the personnel of the division. The duties of the personnel, in addition to other statutory duties include the handling, servicing, and investigation of juvenile cases and counseling and conciliation services that may be made available to persons requesting them, whether or not the persons are parties to an action pending in the division.

(3) If one of the judges of the court of common pleas, division of domestic relations, or one of the judges of the juvenile division is sick, absent, or unable to perform that judge's judicial duties or the volume of cases pending in that judge's division necessitates it, the duties shall be performed by the judges of the other of those divisions.

(E) In Mahoning county:

(1) The judge of the court of common pleas whose term began on January 1, 1955, and successors, shall have the same qualifications, exercise the same powers and jurisdiction, and receive the same compensation as other judges of the court of common pleas of Mahoning county, shall be elected and designated as judge of the court of common pleas, division of domestic relations, and shall be assigned all the divorce, dissolution of marriage, legal separation, and annulment cases coming before the court. In addition to the judge's regular duties, the judge of the court of common pleas, division of domestic relations, shall be the administrator of the domestic relations division and its subdivisions and departments and shall have charge of the employment, assignment, and supervision of the personnel of the division engaged in handling, servicing, or investigating divorce, dissolution of marriage, legal separation, and annulment cases, including any referees considered necessary in the discharge of the various duties of the judge's office.

The judge also shall designate the title, compensation, expense allowances, hours, leaves of absence, and vacations of the personnel of the division and shall fix the duties of the personnel of the division. The duties of the personnel, in addition to other statutory duties, include the handling, servicing, and investigation of divorce, dissolution of marriage, legal separation, and annulment cases and counseling and conciliation services that may be made available to persons requesting them, whether or not the persons are parties to an action pending in the division.

(2) The judge of the court of common pleas whose term began on January 2, 1969, and successors, shall have the same qualifications, exercise the same powers and jurisdiction, and receive the same compensation as other judges of the court of common pleas of Mahoning county, shall be elected and designated as judge of the court of common pleas, juvenile division, and shall be the juvenile judge as provided in Chapters 2151. and 2152. of the Revised Code, with the powers and jurisdictions conferred by those chapters. In addition to the judge's regular duties, the judge of the court of common pleas, juvenile division, shall be the administrator of the juvenile division and its subdivisions and departments and shall have charge of the employment, assignment, and supervision of the personnel of the division engaged in handling, servicing, or investigating juvenile cases, including any referees considered necessary by the judge in the discharge of the judge's various duties.

The judge also shall designate the title, compensation, expense allowances, hours, leaves of absence, and vacation of the personnel of the division and shall fix the duties of the personnel of the division. The duties of the personnel, in addition to other statutory duties, include the handling, servicing, and investigation of juvenile cases and counseling and conciliation services that may be made available to persons requesting them, whether or not the persons are parties to an action pending in the division.

(3) If a judge of the court of common pleas, division of domestic relations or juvenile division, is sick, absent, or unable to perform that judge's judicial duties, or the volume of cases pending in that judge's division necessitates it, that judge's duties shall be performed by another judge of the court of common pleas.

(F) In Montgomery county:

(1) The judges of the court of common pleas whose terms begin on January 2, 1953, and January 4, 1977, and successors,

shall have the same qualifications, exercise the same powers and jurisdiction, and receive the same compensation as other judges of the court of common pleas of Montgomery county and shall be elected and designated as judges of the court of common pleas, division of domestic relations. These judges shall have assigned to them all divorce, dissolution of marriage, legal separation, and annulment cases.

The judge of the division of domestic relations, senior in point of service, shall be charged exclusively with the assignment and division of the work of the division and shall have charge of the employment and supervision of the personnel of the division engaged in handling, servicing, or investigating divorce, dissolution of marriage, legal separation, and annulment cases, including any necessary referees, except those employees who may be appointed by the judge, junior in point of service, under this section and sections 2301.12, 2301.18, and 2301.19 of the Revised Code. The judge of the division of domestic relations, senior in point of service, also shall designate the title, compensation, expense allowances, hours, leaves of absence, and vacation of the personnel of the division and shall fix their duties.

(2) The judges of the court of common pleas whose terms begin on January 1, 1953, and January 1, 1993, and successors, shall have the same qualifications, exercise the same powers and jurisdiction, and receive the same compensation as other judges of the court of common pleas of Montgomery county, shall be elected and designated as judges of the court of common pleas, juvenile division, and shall be, and have the powers and jurisdiction of, the juvenile judge as provided in Chapters 2151. and 2152. of the Revised Code.

In addition to the judge's regular duties, the judge of the court of common pleas, juvenile division, senior in point of service, shall be the administrator of the juvenile division and its subdivisions and departments and shall have charge of the employment, assignment, and supervision of the personnel of the juvenile division, including any necessary referees, who are engaged in handling, servicing, or investigating juvenile cases. The judge, senior in point of service, also shall designate the title, compensation, expense allowances, hours, leaves of absence, and vacation of the personnel of the division and shall fix their duties. The duties of the personnel, in addition to other statutory duties, shall include the handling, servicing, and investigation of juvenile cases and of any counseling and conciliation services that are available upon request to persons, whether or not they are parties to an action pending in the division.

If one of the judges of the court of common pleas, division of domestic relations, or one of the judges of the court of common pleas, juvenile division, is sick, absent, or unable to perform that judge's duties or the volume of cases pending in that judge's division necessitates it, the duties of that judge may be performed by the judge or judges of the other of those divisions.

(G) In Richland county:

(1) The judge of the court of common pleas whose term begins on January 1, 1957, and successors, shall have the same qualifications, exercise the same powers and jurisdiction, and receive the same compensation as the other judges of the court of common pleas of Richland county and shall be elected and designated as judge of the court of common pleas, division of domestic relations. That judge shall be assigned and hear all divorce, dissolution of marriage, legal separation, and annulment cases, all domestic violence cases arising under section 3113.31 of the Revised Code, and all post-decree proceedings arising from any case pertaining to any of those matters. The division of domestic relations has concurrent jurisdiction with the juvenile division of the court of common pleas of Richland county to determine the care, custody, or control of any child not a ward of another court of this state, and to hear and determine a request for an order for the support of any child if the request is not ancillary to an action for divorce, dissolution of marriage, annulment, or legal separation, a criminal or civil action involving an allegation of domestic violence, or an action for support brought under Chapter 3115. of the Revised Code. Except in cases that are subject to the exclusive original jurisdiction of the juvenile court, the judge of the division of domestic relations shall be assigned and hear all cases pertaining to paternity or parentage, the care, custody, or control of children, parenting time or visitation, child support, or the allocation of parental rights and responsibilities for the care of children, all proceedings arising under Chapter 3111. of the Revised Code, all proceedings arising under the uniform interstate family support act contained in Chapter 3115. of the Revised Code, and all post-decree proceedings arising from any case pertaining to any of those matters.

In addition to the judge's regular duties, the judge of the court of common pleas, division of domestic relations, shall be the administrator of the domestic relations division and its subdivisions and departments. The judge shall have charge of the employment, assignment, and supervision of the personnel of the domestic relations division, including any magistrates the judge considers necessary for the discharge of the judge's duties. The judge shall also designate the title, compensation, expense allowances, hours, leaves of absence, vacation, and other employment-related matters of the personnel of the division and shall fix their duties.

(2) The judge of the court of common pleas whose term begins on January 3, 2005, and successors, shall have the same qualifications, exercise the same powers and jurisdiction, and receive the same compensation as other judges of the court of common pleas of Richland county, shall be elected and designated as judge of the court of common pleas, juvenile division, and shall be, and have the powers and jurisdiction of, the juvenile judge as provided in Chapters 2151. and 2152. of the Revised Code. Except in cases that are subject to the exclusive original jurisdiction of the juvenile court, the judge of the juvenile division shall not have jurisdiction or the power to hear, and shall not be assigned, any case pertaining to paternity or parentage, the care, custody, or control of children, parenting time or visitation, child support, or the allocation of parental rights and responsibilities for the care of children or any post-decree proceeding arising from any case pertaining to any of those matters. The judge of the juvenile division shall not have jurisdiction or the power to hear, and shall not be assigned, any proceeding under the uniform interstate family support act contained in Chapter 3115. of the Revised Code.

In addition to the judge's regular duties, the judge of the juvenile division shall be the administrator of the juvenile division and its subdivisions and departments. The judge shall have charge of the employment, assignment, and supervision of the personnel of the juvenile division who are engaged in handling, servicing, or investigating juvenile cases, including any magistrates whom the judge considers necessary for the discharge of the judge's various duties.

The judge of the juvenile division also shall designate the title, compensation, expense allowances, hours, leaves of absence, and vacation of the personnel of the division and shall fix their duties. The duties of the personnel, in addition to other statutory duties, include the handling, servicing, and investigation of juvenile cases and providing any counseling, conciliation, and mediation services that the court makes available to persons, whether or not the persons are parties to an action pending in the court, who request the services.

(H) In Stark county, the judges of the court of common pleas whose terms begin on January 1, 1953, January 2, 1959, and January 1, 1993, and successors, shall have the same qualifications, exercise the same powers and jurisdiction, and receive the same compensation as other judges of the court of common pleas of Stark county and shall be elected and designated as judges of the court of common pleas, division of domestic relations. They shall have all the powers relating to juvenile courts, and all cases under Chapters 2151. and 2152. of the Revised Code, all parentage proceedings over which the juvenile court has jurisdiction, and all divorce, dissolution of marriage, legal separation, and annulment cases, except cases that are assigned to some other judge of the court of common pleas for some special reason, shall be assigned to the judges.

The judge of the division of domestic relations, second most senior in point of service, shall have charge of the employment and supervision of the personnel of the division engaged in handling, servicing, or investigating divorce, dissolution of marriage, legal separation, and annulment cases, and necessary referees required for the judge's respective court.

The judge of the division of domestic relations, senior in point of service, shall be charged exclusively with the administration of sections 2151.13, 2151.16, 2151.17, and 2152.71 of the Revised Code and with the assignment and division of the work of the division and the employment and supervision of all other personnel of the division, including, but not limited to, that judge's necessary referees, but excepting those employees who may be appointed by the judge second most senior in point of service. The senior judge further shall serve in every other position in which the statutes permit or require a juvenile judge to serve.

(I) In Summit county:

(1) The judges of the court of common pleas whose terms begin on January 4, 1967, and January 6, 1993, and successors, shall have the same qualifications, exercise the same powers and jurisdiction, and receive the same compensation as other judges of the court of common pleas of Summit county and shall be elected and designated as judges of the court of common pleas, division of domestic relations. The judges of the division of domestic relations shall have assigned to them and hear all divorce, dissolution of marriage, legal separation, and annulment cases that come before the court. Except in cases that are subject to the exclusive original jurisdiction of the juvenile court, the judges of the division of domestic relations shall have assigned to them and hear all cases pertaining to paternity, custody, visitation, child support, or the allocation of parental rights and responsibilities for the care of children and all post-decree proceedings arising from any case pertaining to any of those matters. The judges of the division of domestic relations shall have assigned to them and hear all proceedings under the uniform interstate family support act contained in Chapter 3115. of the Revised Code.

The judge of the division of domestic relations, senior in point of service, shall be the administrator of the domestic relations division and its subdivisions and departments and shall have charge of the employment, assignment, and supervision of the personnel of the division, including any necessary referees, who are engaged in handling, servicing, or investigating divorce, dissolution of marriage, legal separation, and annulment cases. That judge also shall designate the title, compensation, expense allowances, hours, leaves of absence, and vacations of the personnel of the division and shall fix their duties. The duties of the personnel, in addition to other statutory duties, shall include the handling, servicing, and investigation of divorce, dissolution of marriage, legal separation, and annulment cases and of any counseling and conciliation services that are available upon request to all persons, whether or not they are parties to an action pending in the division.

(2) The judge of the court of common pleas whose term begins on January 1, 1955, and successors, shall have the same qualifications, exercise the same powers and jurisdiction, and receive the same compensation as other judges of the court of common pleas of Summit county, shall be elected and designated as judge of the court of common pleas, juvenile division, and shall be, and have the powers and jurisdiction of, the juvenile judge as provided in Chapters 2151. and 2152. of the Revised Code. Except in cases that are subject to the exclusive original jurisdiction of the juvenile court, the judge of the juvenile division shall not have jurisdiction or the power to hear, and shall not be assigned, any case pertaining to paternity, custody, visitation, child support, or the allocation of parental rights and responsibilities for the care of children or any post-decree proceeding arising from any case pertaining to any of those matters. The judge of the juvenile division shall not have jurisdiction or the power to hear, and shall not be assigned, any proceeding under the uniform interstate family support act contained in Chapter 3115. of the Revised Code.

The juvenile judge shall be the administrator of the juvenile division and its subdivisions and departments and shall have charge of the employment, assignment, and supervision of the personnel of the juvenile division, including any necessary referees, who are engaged in handling, servicing, or investigating juvenile cases. The judge also shall designate the title, compensation, expense allowances, hours, leaves of absence, and vacation of the personnel of the division and shall fix their duties. The duties of the personnel, in addition to other statutory duties, shall include the handling, servicing, and investigation of juvenile cases and of any counseling and conciliation services that are available upon request to persons, whether or not they are parties to an action pending in the division.

(J) In Trumbull county, the judges of the court of common pleas whose terms begin on January 1, 1953, and January 2, 1977, and successors, shall have the same qualifications, exercise the same powers and jurisdiction, and receive the same compensation as other judges of the court of common pleas of Trumbull county and shall be elected and designated as judges of the court of common pleas, division of domestic relations. They shall have all the powers relating to juvenile courts, and all cases under Chapters 2151. and 2152. of the Revised Code, all parentage proceedings over which the juvenile court has jurisdiction, and all divorce, dissolution of marriage, legal separation, and annulment cases shall be assigned to them, except cases that for some special reason are assigned to some other judge of the court of common pleas.

(K) In Butler county:

(1) The judges of the court of common pleas whose terms begin on January 1, 1957, and January 4, 1993, and successors, shall have the same qualifications, exercise the same powers and jurisdiction, and receive the same compensation as other judges of the court of common pleas of Butler county and shall be elected and designated as judges of the court of common pleas, division of domestic relations. The judges of the division of domestic relations shall have assigned to them all divorce, dissolution of marriage, legal separation, and annulment cases coming before the court, except in cases that for some special reason are assigned to some other judge of the court of common pleas. The judge senior in point of service shall be charged with the assignment and division of the work of the division and with the employment and supervision of all other personnel of the domestic relations division.

The judge senior in point of service also shall designate the title, compensation, expense allowances, hours, leaves of absence, and vacations of the personnel of the division and shall fix their duties. The duties of the personnel, in addition to other statutory duties, shall include the handling, servicing, and investigation of divorce, dissolution of marriage, legal separation, and annulment cases and providing any counseling and conciliation services that the division makes available to persons, whether or not the persons are parties to an action pending in the division, who request the services.

(2) The judges of the court of common pleas whose terms begin on January 3, 1987, and January 2, 2003, and successors, shall have the same qualifications, exercise the same powers and jurisdiction, and receive the same compensation as other judges of the court of common pleas of Butler county, shall be elected and designated as judges of the court of common pleas, juvenile division, and shall be the juvenile judges as provided in Chapters 2151. and 2152. of the Revised Code, with the powers and jurisdictions conferred by those chapters. The judge of the court

of common pleas, juvenile division, who is senior in point of service, shall be the administrator of the juvenile division and its subdivisions and departments. The judge, senior in point of service, shall have charge of the employment, assignment, and supervision of the personnel of the juvenile division who are engaged in handling, servicing, or investigating juvenile cases, including any referees whom the judge considers necessary for the discharge of the judge's various duties.

The judge, senior in point of service, also shall designate the title, compensation, expense allowances, hours, leaves of absence, and vacation of the personnel of the division and shall fix their duties. The duties of the personnel, in addition to other statutory duties, include the handling, servicing, and investigation of juvenile cases and providing any counseling and conciliation services that the division makes available to persons, whether or not the persons are parties to an action pending in the division, who request the services.

(3) If a judge of the court of common pleas, division of domestic relations or juvenile division, is sick, absent, or unable to perform that judge's judicial duties or the volume of cases pending in the judge's division necessitates it, the duties of that judge shall be performed by the other judges of the domestic relations and juvenile divisions.

(L)(1) In Cuyahoga county, the judges of the court of common pleas whose terms begin on January 8, 1961, January 9, 1961, January 18, 1975, January 19, 1975, and January 13, 1987, and successors, shall have the same qualifications, exercise the same powers and jurisdiction, and receive the same compensation as other judges of the court of common pleas of Cuyahoga county and shall be elected and designated as judges of the court of common pleas, division of domestic relations. They shall have all the powers relating to all divorce, dissolution of marriage, legal separation, and annulment cases, except in cases that are assigned to some other judge of the court of common pleas for some special reason.

(2) The administrative judge is administrator of the domestic relations division and its subdivisions and departments and has the following powers concerning division personnel:

(a) Full charge of the employment, assignment, and supervision;

(b) Sole determination of compensation, duties, expenses, allowances, hours, leaves, and vacations.

(3) "Division personnel" include persons employed or referees engaged in hearing, servicing, investigating, counseling, or conciliating divorce, dissolution of marriage, legal separation and annulment matters.

(M) In Lake county:

(1) The judge of the court of common pleas whose term begins on January 2, 1961, and successors, shall have the same qualifications, exercise the same powers and jurisdiction, and receive the same compensation as the other judges of the court of common pleas of Lake county and shall be elected and designated as judge of the court of common pleas, division of domestic relations. The judge shall be assigned all the divorce, dissolution of marriage, legal separation, and annulment cases coming before the court, except in cases that for some special reason are assigned to some other judge of the court of common pleas. The judge shall be charged with the assignment and division of the work of the division and with the employment and supervision of all other personnel of the domestic relations division.

The judge also shall designate the title, compensation, expense allowances, hours, leaves of absence, and vacations of the personnel of the division and shall fix their duties. The duties of the personnel, in addition to other statutory duties, shall include the handling, servicing, and investigation of divorce, dissolution of marriage, legal separation, and annulment cases and providing any counseling and conciliation services that the division makes available to persons, whether or not the persons are parties to an action pending in the division, who request the services.

(2) The judge of the court of common pleas whose term begins on January 4, 1979, and successors, shall have the same qualifications, exercise the same powers and jurisdiction, and receive the same compensation as other judges of the court of common pleas of Lake county, shall be elected and designated as judge of the court of common pleas, juvenile division, and shall be the juvenile judge as provided in Chapters 2151. and 2152. of the Revised Code, with the powers and jurisdictions conferred by those chapters. The judge of the court of common pleas, juvenile division, shall be the administrator of the juvenile division and its subdivisions and departments. The judge shall have charge of the employment, assignment, and supervision of the personnel of the juvenile division who are engaged in handling, servicing, or investigating juvenile cases, including any referees whom the judge considers necessary for the discharge of the judge's various duties.

The judge also shall designate the title, compensation, expense allowances, hours, leaves of absence, and vacation of the personnel of the division and shall fix their duties. The duties of the personnel, in addition to other statutory duties, include the handling, servicing, and investigation of juvenile cases and providing any counseling and conciliation services that the division makes available to persons, whether or not the persons are parties to an action pending in the division, who request the services.

(3) If a judge of the court of common pleas, division of domestic relations or juvenile division, is sick, absent, or unable to perform that judge's judicial duties or the volume of cases pending in the judge's division necessitates it, the duties of that judge shall be performed by the other judges of the domestic relations and juvenile divisions.

(N) In Erie county:

(1) The judge of the court of common pleas whose term begins on January 2, 1971, and the successors to that judge whose terms begin before January 2, 2007, shall have the same qualifications, exercise the same powers and jurisdiction, and receive the same compensation as the other judge of the court of common pleas of Erie county and shall be elected and designated as judge of the court of common pleas, division of domestic relations. The judge shall have all the powers relating to juvenile courts, and shall be assigned all cases under Chapters 2151. and 2152. of the Revised Code, parentage proceedings over which the juvenile court has jurisdiction, and divorce, dissolution of marriage, legal separation, and annulment cases, except cases that for some special reason are assigned to some other judge.

On or after January 2, 2007, the judge of the court of common pleas who is elected in 2006 shall be the successor to the judge of the domestic relations division whose term expires on January 1, 2007, shall be designated as judge of the court of common pleas, juvenile division, and shall be the juvenile judge as provided in Chapters 2151. and 2152. of the Revised Code with the powers and jurisdictions conferred by those chapters.

(2) The judge of the court of common pleas, general division, whose term begins on January 1, 2005, and successors, the judge of the court of common pleas, general division whose term begins on January 2, 2005, and successors, and the judge of the court of common pleas, general division, whose term begins February 9, 2009, and successors, shall have assigned to them, in addition to all matters that are within the jurisdiction of the general division of the court of common pleas, all divorce, dissolution of marriage, legal separation, and annulment cases coming before the court, and all matters that are within the jurisdiction of the probate court under Chapter 2101., and other provisions, of the Revised Code.

(O) In Greene county:

(1) The judge of the court of common pleas whose term begins on January 1, 1961, and successors, shall have the same qualifications, exercise the same powers and jurisdiction, and receive the same compensation as the other judges of the court of common pleas of Greene county and shall be elected and designated as the judge of the court of common pleas, division of domestic relations. The judge shall be assigned all divorce, dissolution of marriage, legal separation, annulment, uniform reciprocal support enforcement, and domestic violence cases and all other cases related to domestic relations, except cases that for some special reason are assigned to some other judge of the court of common pleas.

The judge shall be charged with the assignment and division of the work of the division and with the employment and supervision of all other personnel of the division. The judge also shall designate the title, compensation, hours, leaves of absence, and vacations of the personnel of the division and shall fix their duties. The duties of the personnel of the division, in addition to other statutory duties, shall include the handling, servicing, and investigation of divorce, dissolution of marriage, legal separation, and annulment cases and the provision of counseling and conciliation services that the division considers necessary and makes available to persons who request the services, whether or not the persons are parties in an action pending in the division. The compensation for the personnel shall be paid from the overall court budget and shall be included in the appropriations for the existing judges of the general division of the court of common pleas.

(2) The judge of the court of common pleas whose term begins on January 1, 1995, and successors, shall have the same qualifications, exercise the same powers and jurisdiction, and receive the same compensation as the other judges of the court of common pleas of Greene county, shall be elected and designated as judge of the court of common pleas, juvenile division, and, on or after January 1, 1995, shall be the juvenile judge as provided in Chapters 2151. and 2152. of the Revised Code with the powers and jurisdiction conferred by those chapters. The judge of the court of common pleas, juvenile division, shall be the administrator of the juvenile division and its subdivisions and departments. The judge shall have charge of the employment, assignment, and supervision of the personnel of the juvenile division who are engaged in handling, servicing, or investigating juvenile cases, including any referees whom the judge considers necessary for the discharge of the judge's various duties.

The judge also shall designate the title, compensation, expense allowances, hours, leaves of absence, and vacation of the personnel of the division and shall fix their duties. The duties of the personnel, in addition to other statutory duties, include the handling, servicing, and investigation of juvenile cases and providing any counseling and conciliation services that the court makes available to persons, whether or not the persons are parties to an action pending in the court, who request the services.

(3) If one of the judges of the court of common pleas, general division, is sick, absent, or unable to perform that judge's judicial duties or the volume of cases pending in the general division necessitates it, the duties of that judge of the general division shall be performed by the judge of the division of domestic relations and the judge of the juvenile division.

(P) In Portage county, the judge of the court of common pleas, whose term begins January 2, 1987, and successors, shall have the same qualifications, exercise the same powers and jurisdiction, and receive the same compensation as the other judges of the court of common pleas of Portage county and shall be elected and designated as judge of the court of common pleas, division of domestic relations. The judge shall be assigned all divorce, dissolution of marriage, legal separation, and annulment cases coming before the court, except in cases that for some special reason are assigned to some other judge of the court of common pleas. The judge shall be charged with the assignment and division of the work of the division and with the employment and supervision of all other personnel of the domestic relations division.

The judge also shall designate the title, compensation, expense allowances, hours, leaves of absence, and vacations of the personnel of the division and shall fix their duties. The duties of the personnel, in addition to other statutory duties, shall include the handling, servicing, and investigation of divorce, dissolution of marriage, legal separation, and annulment cases and providing any counseling and conciliation services that the division makes available to persons, whether or not the persons are parties to an action pending in the division, who request the services.

(Q) In Clermont county, the judge of the court of common pleas, whose term begins January 2, 1987, and successors, shall have the same qualifications, exercise the same powers and jurisdiction, and receive the same compensation as the other judges of the court of common pleas of Clermont county and shall be elected and designated as judge of the court of common pleas, division of domestic relations. The judge shall be assigned all divorce, dissolution of marriage, legal separation, and annulment cases coming before the court, except in cases that for some special reason are assigned to some other judge of the court of common pleas. The judge shall be charged with the assignment and division of the work of the division and with the employment and supervision of all other personnel of the domestic relations division.

The judge also shall designate the title, compensation, expense allowances, hours, leaves of absence, and vacations of the personnel of the division and shall fix their duties. The duties of the personnel, in addition to other statutory duties, shall include the handling, servicing, and investigation of divorce, dissolution of marriage, legal separation, and annulment cases and providing any counseling and conciliation services that the division makes available to persons, whether or not the persons are parties to an action pending in the division, who request the services.

(R) In Warren county, the judge of the court of common pleas, whose term begins January 1, 1987, and successors, shall have the same qualifications, exercise the same powers and jurisdiction, and receive the same compensation as the other judges of the court of common pleas of Warren county and shall be elected and designated as judge of the court of common pleas, division of domestic relations. The judge shall be assigned all divorce, dissolution of marriage, legal separation, and annulment cases coming before the court, except in cases that for some special reason are assigned to some other judge of the court of common pleas. The judge shall be charged with the assignment and division of the work of the division and with the employment and supervision of all other personnel of the domestic relations division.

The judge also shall designate the title, compensation, expense allowances, hours, leaves of absence, and vacations of the personnel of the division and shall fix their duties. The duties of the personnel, in addition to other statutory duties, shall include the handling, servicing, and investigation of divorce, dissolution of marriage, legal separation, and annulment cases and providing any counseling and conciliation services that the division makes available to persons, whether or not the persons are parties to an action pending in the division, who request the services.

(S) In Licking county, the judges of the court of common pleas, whose terms begin on January 1, 1991, and January 1, 2005, and successors, shall have the same qualifications, exercise the same powers and jurisdiction, and receive the same compensation as the other judges of the court of common pleas of Licking county and shall be elected and designated as judges of the court of common pleas, division of domestic relations. The judges shall be assigned all divorce, dissolution of marriage, legal separation, and annulment cases, all cases arising under Chapter 3111. of the Revised Code, all proceedings involving child support, the allocation of parental rights and responsibilities for the care of children and the designation for the children of a place of residence and legal custodian, parenting time, and visitation, and all post-decree proceedings and matters arising from those cases and proceedings, except in cases that for some special reason are assigned to another judge of the court of common pleas. The administrative judge of the division of domestic relations shall be charged with the assignment and division of the work of the division and with the employment and supervision of the personnel of the division.

The administrative judge of the division of domestic relations shall designate the title, compensation, expense allowances, hours, leaves of absence, and vacations of the personnel of the division and shall fix the duties of the personnel of the division. The duties of the personnel of the division, in addition to other statutory duties, shall include the handling, servicing, and investigation of divorce, dissolution of marriage, legal separation, and annulment cases, cases arising under Chapter 3111. of the Revised Code, and proceedings involving child support, the allocation of parental rights and responsibilities for the care of children and the designation for the children of a place of residence and legal custodian, parenting time, and visitation and providing any counseling and conciliation services that the division makes available to persons, whether or not the persons are parties to an action pending in the division, who request the services.

(T) In Allen county, the judge of the court of common pleas, whose term begins January 1, 1993, and successors, shall have the same qualifications, exercise the same powers and jurisdiction, and receive the same compensation as the other judges of the court of common pleas of Allen county and shall be elected and designated as judge of the court of common pleas, division of domestic relations. The judge shall be assigned all divorce, dissolution of marriage, legal separation, and annulment cases, all cases arising under Chapter 3111. of the Revised Code, all proceedings involving child support, the allocation of parental rights and responsibilities for the care of children and the designation for the children of a place of residence and legal custodian, parenting time, and visitation, and all post-decree proceedings and matters arising from those cases and proceedings, except in cases that for some special reason are assigned to another judge of the court of common pleas. The judge shall be charged with the assignment and division of the work of the division and with the employment and supervision of the personnel of the division.

The judge shall designate the title, compensation, expense allowances, hours, leaves of absence, and vacations of the personnel of the division and shall fix the duties of the personnel of the division. The duties of the personnel of the division, in addition to other statutory duties, shall include the handling, servicing, and investigation of divorce, dissolution of marriage, legal separation, and annulment cases, cases arising under Chapter 3111. of the Revised Code, and proceedings involving child support, the allocation of parental rights and responsibilities for the care of children and the designation for the children of a place of residence and legal custodian, parenting time, and visitation, and providing any counseling and conciliation services that the division makes available to persons, whether or not the persons are parties to an action pending in the division, who request the services.

(U) In Medina county, the judge of the court of common pleas whose term begins January 1, 1995, and successors, shall have the same qualifications, exercise the same powers and jurisdiction, and receive the same compensation as other judges of the court of common pleas of Medina county and shall be elected and designated as judge of the court of common pleas, division of domestic relations. The judge shall be assigned all divorce, dissolution of marriage, legal separation, and annulment cases, all cases arising under Chapter 3111. of the Revised Code, all proceedings involving child support, the allocation of parental rights and responsibilities for the care of children and the designation for the children of a place of residence and legal custodian, parenting time, and visitation, and all post-decree proceedings and matters arising from those cases and proceedings, except in cases that for some special reason are assigned to another judge of the court of common pleas. The judge shall be charged with the assignment and division of the work of the division and with the employment and supervision of the personnel of the division.

The judge shall designate the title, compensation, expense allowances, hours, leaves of absence, and vacations of the personnel of the division and shall fix the duties of the personnel of the division. The duties of the personnel, in addition to other statutory duties, include the handling, servicing, and investigation of divorce, dissolution of marriage, legal separation, and annulment cases, cases arising under Chapter 3111. of the Revised Code, and proceedings involving child support, the allocation of parental rights and responsibilities for the care of children and the designation for the children of a place of residence and legal custodian, parenting time, and visitation, and providing counseling and conciliation services that the division makes available to persons, whether or not the persons are parties to an action pending in the division, who request the services.

(V) In Fairfield county, the judge of the court of common pleas whose term begins January 2, 1995, and successors, shall have the same qualifications, exercise the same powers and jurisdiction, and receive the same compensation as the other judges of the court of common pleas of Fairfield county and shall be elected and designated as judge of the court of common pleas, division of domestic relations. The judge shall be assigned all divorce, dissolution of marriage, legal separation, and annulment cases, all cases arising under Chapter 3111. of the Revised Code, all proceedings involving child support, the allocation of parental rights and responsibilities for the care of children and the designation for the children of a place of residence and legal custodian, parenting time, and visitation, and all post-decree proceedings and matters arising from those cases and proceedings, except in cases that for some special reason are assigned to another judge of the court of common pleas. The judge also has concurrent jurisdiction with the probate-juvenile division of the court of common pleas of Fairfield county with respect to and may hear cases to determine the custody of a child, as defined in section 2151.011 of the Revised Code, who is not the ward of another court of this state, cases that are commenced by a parent, guardian, or custodian of a child, as defined in section 2151.011 of the Revised Code, to obtain an order requiring a parent of the child to pay child support for that child when the request for that order is not ancillary to an action for divorce, dissolution of marriage, annulment, or legal separation, a criminal or civil action involving an allegation of domestic violence, an action for support under Chapter 3115. of the Revised Code, or an action that is within the exclusive original jurisdiction of the probate-juvenile division of the court of common pleas of Fairfield county and that involves an allegation that the child is an abused, neglected, or dependent child, and post-decree proceedings and matters arising from those types of cases.

The judge of the domestic relations division shall be charged with the assignment and division of the work of the division and with the employment and supervision of the personnel of the division.

The judge shall designate the title, compensation, expense allowances, hours, leaves of absence, and vacations of the personnel of the division and shall fix the duties of the personnel of the division. The duties of the personnel of the division, in addition to other statutory duties, shall include the handling, servicing, and investigation of divorce, dissolution of marriage, legal separation, and annulment cases, cases arising under Chapter 3111. of the Revised Code, and proceedings involving child support, the allocation of parental rights and responsibilities for the care of children and the designation for the children of a place of residence and legal custodian, parenting time, and visitation, and providing any counseling and conciliation services that the division makes available to persons, regardless of whether the persons are parties to an action pending in the division, who request the services. When the judge hears a case to determine the custody of a child, as defined in section 2151.011 of the Revised Code, who is not the ward of another court of this state or a case that is commenced by a parent, guardian, or custodian of a child, as defined in section 2151.011 of the Revised Code, to obtain an order requiring a parent of the child to pay child support for that child when the request for that order is not ancillary to an action for divorce, dissolution of marriage, annulment, or legal separation, a criminal or civil action involving an allegation of domestic violence, an action for support under Chapter 3115. of the Revised Code, or an action that is within the exclusive original jurisdiction of the probate-juvenile division of the court of common pleas of Fairfield county and that involves an allegation that the child is an abused, neglected, or dependent child, the duties of the personnel of the domestic relations division also include the handling, servicing, and investigation of those types of cases.

(W)(1) In Clark county, the judge of the court of common pleas whose term begins on January 2, 1995, and successors, shall have the same qualifications, exercise the same powers and jurisdiction, and receive the same compensation as other judges of the court of common pleas of Clark county and shall be elected and designated as judge of the court of common pleas, domestic relations division. The judge shall have all the powers relating to juvenile courts, and all cases under Chapters 2151. and 2152. of the Revised Code and all parentage proceedings under Chapter 3111. of the Revised Code over which the juvenile court has jurisdiction shall be assigned to the judge of the division of domestic relations. All divorce, dissolution of marriage, legal separation, annulment, uniform reciprocal support enforcement, and other cases related to domestic relations shall be assigned to the domestic relations division, and the presiding judge of the court of common pleas shall assign the cases to the judge of the domestic relations division and the judges of the general division.

(2) In addition to the judge's regular duties, the judge of the division of domestic relations shall serve on the children services board and the county advisory board.

(3) If the judge of the court of common pleas of Clark county, division of domestic relations, is sick, absent, or unable to perform that judge's judicial duties or if the presiding judge of the court of common pleas of Clark county determines that the volume of cases pending in the division of domestic relations necessitates it, the duties of the judge of the division of domestic relations shall be performed by the judges of the general division or probate division of the court of common pleas of Clark county, as assigned for that purpose by the presiding judge of that court, and the judges so assigned shall act in conjunction with the judge of the division of domestic relations of that court.

(X) In Scioto county, the judge of the court of common pleas whose term begins January 2, 1995, and successors, shall have the same qualifications, exercise the same powers and jurisdiction, and receive the same compensation as other judges of the court of common pleas of Scioto county and shall be elected and designated as judge of the court of common pleas, division of domestic relations. The judge shall be assigned all divorce, dissolution of marriage, legal separation, and annulment cases, all cases arising under Chapter 3111. of the Revised Code, all proceedings involving child support, the allocation of parental rights and responsibilities for the care of children and the designation for the children of a place of residence and legal custodian, parenting time, visitation, and all post-decree proceedings and matters arising from those cases and proceedings, except in cases that for some special reason are assigned to another judge of the court of common pleas. The judge shall be charged with the assignment and division of the work of the division and with the employment and supervision of the personnel of the division.

The judge shall designate the title, compensation, expense allowances, hours, leaves of absence, and vacations of the personnel of the division and shall fix the duties of the personnel of the division. The duties of the personnel, in addition to other statutory duties, include the handling, servicing, and investigation of divorce, dissolution of marriage, legal separation, and annulment cases, cases arising under Chapter 3111. of the Revised Code, and proceedings involving child support, the allocation of parental rights and responsibilities for the care of children and the designation for the children of a place of residence and legal custodian, parenting time, and visitation, and providing counseling and conciliation services that the division makes available to persons, whether or not the persons are parties to an action pending in the division, who request the services.

(Y) In Auglaize county, the judge of the probate and juvenile divisions of the Auglaize county court of common pleas also shall be the administrative judge of the domestic relations division of the court and shall be assigned all divorce, dissolution of marriage, legal separation, and annulment cases coming before the court. The judge shall have all powers as administrator of the domestic relations division and shall have charge of the personnel engaged in handling, servicing, or investigating divorce, dissolution of marriage, legal separation, and annulment cases, including any referees considered necessary for the discharge of the judge's various duties.

(Z)(1) In Marion county, the judge of the court of common pleas whose term begins on February 9, 1999, and the successors to that judge, shall have the same qualifications, exercise the same powers and jurisdiction, and receive the same compensation as the other judges of the court of common pleas of Marion county and shall be elected and designated as judge of the court of common pleas, domestic relations-juvenile-probate division. Except as otherwise specified in this division, that judge, and the successors to that judge, shall have all the powers relating to juvenile courts, and all cases under Chapters 2151. and 2152. of the Revised Code, all cases arising under Chapter 3111. of the Revised Code, all divorce, dissolution of marriage, legal separation, and annulment cases, all proceedings involving child support, the allocation of parental rights and responsibilities for the care of children and the designation for the children of a place of residence and legal custodian, parenting time, and visitation, and all post-decree proceedings and matters arising from those cases and proceedings shall be assigned to that judge and the successors to that judge. Except as provided in division (Z)(2) of this section and notwithstanding any other provision of any section of the Revised Code, on and after February 9, 2003, the judge of the court of common pleas of Marion county whose term begins on February 9, 1999, and the successors to that judge, shall have all the powers relating to the probate division of the court of common pleas of Marion county in addition to the powers previously specified in this division, and shall exercise concurrent jurisdiction with the judge of the probate division of that court over all matters that are within the jurisdiction of the probate division of that court under Chapter 2101., and other provisions, of the Revised Code in addition to the jurisdiction of the domestic relations-juvenile-probate division of that court otherwise specified in division (Z)(1) of this section.

(2) The judge of the domestic relations-juvenile-probate division of the court of common pleas of Marion county or the judge of the probate division of the court of common pleas of Marion county, whichever of those judges is senior in total length of service on the court of common pleas of Marion county, regardless of the division or divisions of service, shall serve as the clerk of the probate division of the court of common pleas of Marion county.

(3) On and after February 9, 2003, all references in law to "the probate court," "the probate judge," "the juvenile court," or "the judge of the juvenile court" shall be construed, with respect to Marion county, as being references to both "the probate division" and "the domestic relations-juvenile-probate division" and as being references to both "the judge of the probate division" and "the judge of the domestic relations- juvenile-probate division." On and after February 9, 2003, all references in law to "the clerk of the probate court" shall be construed, with respect to Marion county, as being references to the judge who is serving pursuant

to division (Z)(2) of this section as the clerk of the probate division of the court of common pleas of Marion county.

(AA) In Muskingum county, the judge of the court of common pleas whose term begins on January 2, 2003, and successors, shall have the same qualifications, exercise the same powers and jurisdiction, and receive the same compensation as the other judges of the court of common pleas of Muskingum county and shall be elected and designated as the judge of the court of common pleas, division of domestic relations. The judge shall be assigned all divorce, dissolution of marriage, legal separation, and annulment cases, all cases arising under Chapter 3111. of the Revised Code, all proceedings involving child support, the allocation of parental rights and responsibilities for the care of children and the designation for the children of a place of residence and legal custodian, parenting time, and visitation, and all post-decree proceedings and matters arising from those cases and proceedings, except in cases that for some special reason are assigned to another judge of the court of common pleas. The judge shall be charged with the assignment and division of the work of the division and with the employment and supervision of the personnel of the division.

The judge shall designate the title, compensation, expense allowances, hours, leaves of absence, and vacations of the personnel of the division and shall fix the duties of the personnel of the division. The duties of the personnel of the division, in addition to other statutory duties, shall include the handling, servicing, and investigation of divorce, dissolution of marriage, legal separation, and annulment cases, cases arising under Chapter 3111. of the Revised Code, and proceedings involving child support, the allocation of parental rights and responsibilities for the care of children and the designation for the children of a place of residence and legal custodian, parenting time, and visitation and providing any counseling and conciliation services that the division makes available to persons, whether or not the persons are parties to an action pending in the division, who request the services.

(BB) In Henry county, the judge of the court of common pleas whose term begins on January 1, 2005, and successors, shall have the same qualifications, exercise the same powers and jurisdiction, and receive the same compensation as the other judge of the court of common pleas of Henry county and shall be elected and designated as the judge of the court of common pleas, division of domestic relations. The judge shall have all of the powers relating to juvenile courts, and all cases under Chapter 2151. or 2152. of the Revised Code, all parentage proceedings arising under Chapter 3111. of the Revised Code over which the juvenile court has jurisdiction, all divorce, dissolution of marriage, legal separation, and annulment cases, all proceedings involving child support, the allocation of parental rights and responsibilities for the care of children and the designation for the children of a place of residence and legal custodian, parenting time, and visitation, and all post-decree proceedings and matters arising from those cases and proceedings shall be assigned to that judge, except in cases that for some special reason are assigned to the other judge of the court of common pleas.

(CC)(1) In Logan county, the judge of the court of common pleas whose term begins January 2, 2005, and the successors to that judge, shall have the same qualifications, exercise the same powers and jurisdiction, and receive the same compensation as the other judges of the court of common pleas of Logan county and shall be elected and designated as judge of the court of common pleas, domestic relations-juvenile-probate division. Except as otherwise specified in this division, that judge, and the successors to that judge, shall have all the powers relating to juvenile courts, and all cases under Chapters 2151. and 2152. of the Revised Code, all cases arising under Chapter 3111. of the Revised Code, all divorce, dissolution of marriage, legal separation, and annulment cases, all proceedings involving child support, the allocation of parental rights and responsibilities for the care of children and designation for the children of a place of residence and legal custodian, parenting time, and visitation, and all post-decree proceedings and matters arising from those cases and proceedings shall be assigned to that judge and the successors to that judge. Notwithstanding any other provision of any section of the Revised Code, on and after January 2, 2005, the judge of the court of common pleas of Logan county whose term begins on January 2, 2005, and the successors to that judge, shall have all the powers relating to the probate division of the court of common pleas of Logan county in addition to the powers previously specified in this division and shall exercise concurrent jurisdiction with the judge of the probate division of that court over all matters that are within the jurisdiction of the probate division of that court under Chapter 2101., and other provisions, of the Revised Code in addition to the jurisdiction of the domestic relations-juvenile-probate division of that court otherwise specified in division (CC)(1) of this section.

(2) The judge of the domestic relations-juvenile-probate division of the court of common pleas of Logan county or the probate judge of the court of common pleas of Logan county who is elected as the administrative judge of the probate division of the court of common pleas of Logan county pursuant to Rule 4 of the Rules of Superintendence shall be the clerk of the probate division and juvenile division of the court of common pleas of Logan county. The clerk of the court of common pleas who is elected pursuant to section 2303.01 of the Revised Code shall keep all of the journals, records, books, papers, and files pertaining to the domestic relations cases.

(3) On and after January 2, 2005, all references in law to "the probate court," "the probate judge," "the juvenile court," or "the judge of the juvenile court" shall be construed, with respect to Logan county, as being references to both "the probate division" and the "domestic relations-juvenile-probate division" and as being references to both "the judge of the probate division" and the "judge of the domestic relations-juvenile-probate division." On and after January 2, 2005, all references in law to "the clerk of the probate court" shall be construed, with respect to Logan county, as being references to the judge who is serving pursuant to division (CC)(2) of this section as the clerk of the probate division of the court of common pleas of Logan county.

(DD) If a judge of the court of common pleas, division of domestic relations, or juvenile judge, of any of the counties mentioned in this section is sick, absent, or unable to perform that judge's judicial duties or the volume of cases pending in the judge's division necessitates it, the duties of that judge shall be performed by another judge of the court of common pleas of that county, assigned for that purpose by the presiding judge of the court of common pleas of that county to act in place of or in conjunction with that judge, as the case may require.

(2005 S 128, eff. 12–20–05; 2004 H 38, eff. 6–17–04; 2003 H 86, § 3, eff. 1–1–04; 2003 H 86, § 1, eff. 11–13–03; 2003 H 95, § 3.13, eff. 1–1–04; 2003 H 95, § 1, eff. 9–26–03; 2003 H 26, eff. 8–8–03; 2002 H 490, eff. 1–1–04; 2002 H 530, eff. 12–18–02; 2002 H 8, eff. 8–5–02; 2002 H 393, eff. 7–5–02; 2001 H 11, § 3, eff. 1–1–02; 2001 H 11, § 1, eff. 10–31–01; 2000 S 179, § 3, eff. 1–1–02; 2000 S 180, eff. 3–22–01; 2000 H 583, eff. 6–14–00; 1998 H 444, eff. 1–15–98; 1997 H 408, eff. 10–1–97; 1996 H 377, eff. 10–17–96; 1996 S 269, eff. 7–1–96; 1995 H 151, eff. 12–4–95; 1994 H 21, eff. 2–4–94; 1992 S 273, eff. 3–6–92; 1990 H 211, H 514, H 837, H 648, H 390; 1987 S 171; 1986 H 815; 1984 H 113, H 82; 1982 H 245; 1980 H 961; 1978 H 246; 1976 H 468; 1975 S 145, H 1; 1974 H 233, H 818; 1973 S 201; 1969 S 49, H 7; 132 v H 880; 131 v H 165; 130 v H 151, H 467; 128 v 147; 127 v 475; 126 v 778; 125 v 896; 1953 H 1; Source—GC 1532, 1532–1, 1532–2)

Uncodified Law

2002 H 530, § 7, eff. 12–18–02, reads:

The amendment by this act to division (B)(3) of section 2301.33 [sic.] of the Revised Code is identical to the amendment of that division of that section by Sub. H.B. 8 of the 124th General Assembly. The United States

District Court of the Southern District of Ohio, in *Bookfriends, Inc. v. Taft*, 232 F. Supp.2d 932 (2002), issued a preliminary injunction enjoining to an uncertain extent the operation of Sub. H.B. 8. By thus re-enacting the amendment of Sub. H.B. 8 to division (B)(3) of section 2301.33 [sic.] of the Revised Code, the General Assembly intends to confirm that the amendment is nevertheless effective as part of the law.

Historical and Statutory Notes

Ed. Note: Guidelines for Assignment of Judges were announced by the Chief Justice of the Ohio Supreme Court on 5-24-88, and revised 2-25-94 and 3-25-94, but not adopted as rules pursuant to O Const Art IV § 5. For the full text, see 37 OS(3d) xxxix, 61 OBar A-2 (6-13-88) and 69 OS(3d) XCIX, 67 OBar xiii (4-18-94).

Amendment Note: 2005 S 128 rewrote division (C), which prior thereto read:

"(C) In Lorain county, the judges of the court of common pleas whose terms begin on January 3, 1959, January 4, 1989, and January 2, 1999, and successors, shall have the same qualifications, exercise the same powers and jurisdiction, and receive the same compensation as the other judges of the court of common pleas of Lorain county and shall be elected and designated as the judges of the court of common pleas, division of domestic relations. They shall have all of the powers relating to juvenile courts, and all cases under Chapters 2151. and 2152. of the Revised Code, all parentage proceedings over which the juvenile court has jurisdiction, and all divorce, dissolution of marriage, legal separation, and annulment cases shall be assigned to them, except cases that for some special reason are assigned to some other judge of the court of common pleas."

Amendment Note: 2004 H 38 deleted "to that judge" and "that come before the court" in the second sentence of division (G)(1); added "all domestic violence cases arising under section 3113.31 of the Revised Code, and all post-decree proceedings arising from any case pertaining to any of those matters." and the next sentence immediately following in division (G)(1); inserted "or parentage, the care", "or control of children, parenting time or" and ", all proceedings arising under uniform interstate family support act contained in Chapter 3115. of the Revised Code," in division (G)(1); deleted the last sentence in division (G)(1), which read "The judge of the division of domestic relations shall have assigned to that judge and hear all proceedings under the uniform interstate family support act contained in Chapter 3115. of the Revised Code."; and added the last paragraph in division (G)(1).

In division (G)(2), inserted "or parentage, the care" and "or control of children, parenting time or" in the second to the last sentence; and inserted "In addition to the judge's regular duties, the" in the second paragraph of division (G)(2). In division (S), inserted "and January 1, 2005,"; inserted "administrative" and "of the division of domestic relations" in the last sentence of the first paragraph of division (S) and the first sentence of the second paragraph of division (S). Division (AA) was rewritten and prior thereto read:

"(AA) In Muskingum county, the judge of the court of common pleas whose term begins on January 2, 2003, and successors, shall have the same qualifications, exercise the same powers and jurisdiction, and receive the same compensation as the other judges of the court of common pleas of Muskingum county and shall be elected and designated as the judge of the court of common pleas, division of domestic relations. The judge shall be assigned and hear all divorce, dissolution of marriage, legal separation, and annulment cases and all proceedings under the uniform interstate family support act contained in Chapter 3115. of the Revised Code. Except in cases that are subject to the exclusive original jurisdiction of the juvenile court, the judge shall be assigned and hear all cases pertaining to paternity, visitation, child support, the allocation of parental rights and responsibilities for the care of children, and the designation for the children of a place of residence and legal custodian, and all post-decree proceedings arising from any case pertaining to any of those matters."

Amendment Note: 2003 H 86, § 1 and 3, designated division (N)(1) and inserted "to that judge whose terms begin before January 2, 2007" therein; added the second paragraph in division (N)(1) and added division (N)(2); redesignated former division (CC) as division (DD) and added new division (CC); and made other nonsubstantive changes.

Amendment Note: 2003 H 95, § 1 and 3.13, rewrote Division (G), which prior thereto read:

"(G) In Richland county, the judge of the court of common pleas whose term begins on January 1, 1957, and successors, shall have the same qualifications, exercise the same powers and jurisdiction, and receive the same compensation as the other judges of the court of common pleas of Richland county and shall be elected and designated as judge of the court of common pleas, division of domestic relations. That judge shall have all of the powers relating to juvenile courts, and all cases under Chapters 2151. and 2152. of the Revised Code, all parentage proceedings over which the juvenile court has jurisdiction, and all divorce, dissolution of marriage, legal separation, and annulment cases shall be assigned to that judge, except in cases that for some special reason are assigned to some other judge of the court of common pleas."

Amendment Note: 2003 H 26 added new division (BB); and redesignated former division (BB) as new division (CC).

Amendment Note: 2002 H 490 substituted "condition of a community control sanction" for "term of probation" in the second paragraph of division (B)(3); inserted new division (B)(5); and rewrote division (B)(3)(b)(i), which prior thereto read: "(i) the case involves a probationable offense or a case in which a mandatory prison term is not required to be imposed."

Amendment Note: 2002 H 530 rewrote the first sentence of division (B)(3), which prior thereto read:

"(3) The judge of the court of common pleas of Hamilton county whose term begins on January 3, 1997, shall be elected and designated for one term only as the drug court judge of the court of common pleas of Hamilton county, and the successors to that judge shall be elected and designated as judges of the general division of the court of common pleas of Hamilton county and shall not have the authority granted by division (B)(3) of this section."

Amendment Note: 2002 H 8 rewrote the first sentence of division (B)(3) which prior thereto read:

"(3) The judge of the court of common pleas of Hamilton county whose term begins on January 3, 1997, shall be elected and designated for one term only as the drug court judge of the court of common pleas of Hamilton county, and the successors to that judge shall be elected and designated as judges of the general division of the court of common pleas of Hamilton county and shall not have the authority granted by division (B)(3) of this section."

Amendment Note: 2002 H 393 rewrote division (AA) which prior thereto read:

"(AA) In Muskingum county, the judge of the court of common pleas whose term begins on January 2, 2003, and successors, shall have the same qualifications, exercise the same powers and jurisdiction, and receive the same compensation as the other judges of the court of common pleas of Muskingum county and shall be elected and designated as the judge of the court of common pleas, division of domestic relations. The judge shall have all of the powers relating to juvenile courts and shall be assigned all cases under Chapter 2151. or 2152. of the Revised Code, all parentage proceedings over which the juvenile court has jurisdiction, all divorce, dissolution of marriage, legal separation, and annulment cases, all cases arising under Chapter 3111. of the Revised Code, all proceedings involving child support, the allocation of parental rights and responsibilities for the care of children, the designation for the children of a place of residence and legal custodian, and all post-decree proceedings and matters arising from those cases and proceedings, except cases that for some special reason are assigned to some other judge of the court of common pleas."

Amendment Note: 2001 H 11, § 1 and 3 substituted "county" for "County" in division (B)(3); substituted "judges" for "judge" three times and "terms begin" for "term begins" once and inserted "and January 2, 2003", "who is senior in point of service" and ", senior in point of service," twice in division (K)(2); added new division (AA); and redesignated former division (AA) as new division (BB).

Amendment Note: 2000 S 179, § 3, eff. 1-1-02, added references to Chapter 2152 throughout the section; substituted "2152.71" for "2151.18" in the third paragraph in division (H); and made other nonsubstantive changes.

Amendment Note: 2000 S 180 added "parenting time," throughout the section.

Amendment Note: 2000 H 583 added the third and fourth sentences in the first paragraphs in divisions (I)(1) and (I)(2); and made other nonsubstantive changes.

Amendment Note: 1998 H 444, in division (C), inserted "and January 2, 1999,"; added new division (Z); redesignated former division (Z) as new division (AA); and made other nonsubstantive changes.

Amendment Note: 1997 H 408 deleted "as administrator of the bureau of aid to dependent children and shall serve" before "in every other position" in the third paragraph in division (H); and made other nonsubstantive changes.

Amendment Note: 1996 H 377 rewrote division (V); made changes to reflect gender neutral language; and made other nonsubstantive changes. Prior thereto division (V) read:

"(V) In Fairfield county, the judge of the court of common pleas whose term begins January 2, 1995, and successors, shall have the same qualifications, exercise the same powers and jurisdiction, and receive the same compensation as the other judges of the court of common pleas of Fairfield county and shall be elected and designated as judge of the court of common pleas, division of domestic relations. The judge shall have assigned to him all the divorce, dissolution of marriage, legal separation, and annulment cases, all cases arising under Chapter 3111. of the Revised Code, all proceedings involving child support, the allocation of parental rights and responsibilities for the care of children and the designation for the children of a place of residence and legal custodian, and visitation, and all post-decree proceedings and matters arising from those cases and proceedings, except in cases that for some special reason are assigned to another judge of the court of common pleas. The judge shall be charged with the assignment and division of the work of the division and with the employment and supervision of the personnel of the division.

"The judge shall designate the title, compensation, expense allowances, hours, leaves of absence, and vacations of the personnel of the division and shall fix the duties of the personnel of the division. The duties of the personnel of the division, in addition to other statutory duties, shall include the handling, servicing, and investigation of divorce, dissolution of marriage, legal separation, and annulment cases, cases arising under Chapter 3111. of the Revised Code, and proceedings involving child support, the allocation of parental rights and responsibilities for the care of children and the designation for the children of a place of residence and legal custodian, and visitation, and providing any counseling and conciliation services that the division makes available to persons, regardless of whether the persons are parties to an action pending in the division, who request the services."

Amendment Note: 1996 S 269 inserted "and January 2, 1997" in division (A); made changes to reflect gender neutral language; and made other nonsubstantive changes.

Amendment Note: 1995 H 151 added divisions (B)(3) and (B)(4); designated division (W)(1); deleted "chief justice or" before "presiding judge" in division (Z); and made other nonsubstantive changes.

Amendment Note: 1994 H 21 inserted "of marriage" after "dissolution" throughout; changed references to domestic relations courts to references to domestic relations divisions throughout; substituted "referees" for "references" in divisions (D)(2), (E)(1), and (E)(2); deleted ", on and after January 3, 1987," before "shall be the juvenile judge" in the first paragraph of division (K)(2); deleted ", on and after January 1, 1985," after "In Greene county" at the beginning of division (O); added division (O)(2); redesignated former division (O)(2) as division (O)(3); added "and the judge of the juvenile division" at the end of division (O)(3); substituted "the allocation of parental rights and responsibilities for the care of children and the designation for the children of a place of residence and legal custodian" for "child custody" throughout divisions (S) and (T); added divisions (U) through (Y); and redesignated former division (U) as division (Z).

Library References

Judges ⚖3 to 5, 24.
Westlaw Topic No. 227.
C.J.S. Judges §§12 to 20, 35, 53 to 56, 59 to 65.

TERMS OF COURT

2301.05 Term for any division set at one year; part terms for jury service

The term of any division of a court of common pleas is one calendar year, which may, by written order of the judges of the division, be divided into parts for purposes of Chapter 2313. of the Revised Code.

(1976 H 390, eff. 8–6–76)

Historical and Statutory Notes

Ed. Note: Former 2301.05 repealed by 1976 H 390, eff. 8–6–76; 1953 H 1; GC 1533.

Pre–1953 H 1 Amendments: 106 v 462; RS 457

Library References

Courts ⚖63, 65.
Westlaw Topic No. 106.
C.J.S. Courts §§ 111 to 114, 120.

CHAPTER 2305

JURISDICTION; LIMITATION OF ACTIONS

LIMITATIONS—REAL ESTATE

Section
2305.04 Recovery of real estate

LIMITATIONS—TORTS

2305.09 Four years; certain torts
2305.10 Product liability, bodily injury or injury to personal property; when certain causes of action arise

LIMITATIONS—MISCELLANEOUS

2305.11 Time limitations for bringing certain actions
2305.12 On official bond
2305.121 Limitation of actions pertaining to revocable trust made irrevocable by death of grantor—Repealed

SAVING PROVISIONS

2305.16 Disabilities; tolling of statute of limitations

MISCELLANEOUS PROVISIONS

2305.19 Saving in case of reversal
2305.21 Survival of actions

Comparative Laws

Ind.—West's A.I.C. Title 34 Article 11.
Ky.—Baldwin's KRS 413.010 et seq.
Mich.—M.C.L.A. § 600.5801 et seq.
N.Y.—McKinney's CPLR § 201 et seq.

LIMITATIONS—REAL ESTATE

2305.04 Recovery of real estate

An action to recover the title to or possession of real property shall be brought within twenty-one years after the cause of action accrued, but if a person entitled to bring the action is, at the time the cause of action accrues, within the age of minority or of unsound mind, the person, after the expiration of twenty-one years from the time the cause of action accrues, may bring the action within ten years after the disability is removed.

(1990 S 125, eff. 1–13–91; 1953 H 1; GC 11219)

Uncodified Law

1990 S 125, § 4, eff. 7–13–90, reads: Sections 2305.04, 2305.11, 2305.16, and 2743.16 of the Revised Code, as amended by this act, shall apply only to causes of action that accrue on or after the date specified in Section 3 of this act, which is six months after the effective date of this act.

Historical and Statutory Notes

Pre–1953 H 1 Amendments: RS 4977, 4978

Library References

Limitation of Actions ⚖19, 72.
Westlaw Topic No. 241.
C.J.S. Limitations of Actions §§ 40, 112 to 114.

LIMITATIONS—TORTS

2305.09 Four years; certain torts

An action for any of the following causes shall be brought within four years after the cause thereof accrued:

(A) For trespassing upon real property;

(B) For the recovery of personal property, or for taking or detaining it;

(C) For relief on the ground of fraud;

(D) For an injury to the rights of the plaintiff not arising on contract nor enumerated in sections 1304.35, 2305.10 to 2305.12, and 2305.14 of the Revised Code;

(E) For relief on the grounds of a physical or regulatory taking of real property.

If the action is for trespassing under ground or injury to mines, or for the wrongful taking of personal property, the causes thereof shall not accrue until the wrongdoer is discovered; nor, if it is for fraud, until the fraud is discovered.

(2004 H 161, eff. 5–31–04; 1994 S 147, eff. 8–19–94; 129 v 13, eff. 7–1–62; 1953 H 1; GC 11224)

Uncodified Law

2004 S 80, § 3(B): See *Baldwin's Ohio Revised Code Annotated*, Uncodified Law under RC 2305.131.

2004 S 80, § 3, eff. 4–7–05, reads, in part:

(C) In enacting division (D)(2) of section 2125.02 and division (C) of section 2305.10 of the Revised Code in this act, it is the intent of the General Assembly to do all of the following:

(1) To declare that the ten-year statute of repose prescribed by division (D)(2) of section 2125.02 and division (C) of section 2305.10 of the Revised Code, as enacted by this act, are specific provisions intended to promote a greater interest than the interest underlying the general four-year statute of limitations prescribed by section 2305.09 of the Revised Code, the general two-year statutes of limitations prescribed by sections 2125.02 and 2305.10 of the Revised Code, and other general statutes of limitations prescribed by the Revised Code;

(2) To declare that, subject to the two-year exceptions prescribed in division (D)(2)(d) of section 2125.02 and in division (C)(4) of section 2305.10 of the Revised Code, the ten-year statutes of repose shall serve as a limitation upon the commencement of a civil action in accordance with an otherwise applicable statute of limitations prescribed by the Revised Code;

(3) To recognize that subsequent to the delivery of a product, the manufacturer or supplier lacks control over the product, over the uses made of the product, and over the conditions under which the product is used;

(4) To recognize that under the circumstances described in division (C)(3) of this section, it is more appropriate for the party or parties who have had control over the product during the intervening time period to be responsible for any harm caused by the product;

(5) To recognize that, more than ten years after a product has been delivered, it is very difficult for a manufacturer or supplier to locate reliable evidence and witnesses regarding the design, production, or marketing of the product, thus severely disadvantaging manufacturers or suppliers in their efforts to defend actions based on a product liability claim;

(6) To recognize the inappropriateness of applying current legal and technological standards to products manufactured many years prior to the commencement of an action based on a product liability claim;

(7) To recognize that a statute of repose for product liability claims would enhance the competitiveness of Ohio manufacturers by reducing their exposure to disruptive and protracted liability with respect to products long out of their control, by increasing finality in commercial transactions, and by allowing manufacturers to conduct their affairs with increased certainty;

(8) To declare that division (D)(2) of section 2125.02 and division (C) of section 2305.10 of the Revised Code, as enacted by this act, strike a rational balance between the rights of prospective claimants and the rights of product manufacturers and suppliers and to declare that the ten-year statutes of repose prescribed in those sections are rational periods of repose intended to preclude the problems of stale litigation but not to affect civil actions against those in actual control and possession of a product at the time that the product causes an injury to real or personal property, bodily injury, or wrongful death;

Historical and Statutory Notes

Pre–1953 H 1 Amendments: 112 v 237; RS 4982

Amendment Note: 2004 H 161 added new division (E) and made other nonsubstantive changes.

Amendment Note: 1994 S 147 substituted "1304.35" for "1304.29" in division (D).

Library References

Limitation of Actions ⚖20, 32(1), 37(1), 95(7), 100(1).
Westlaw Topic No. 241.
C.J.S. Limitations of Actions §§ 34, 47, 68, 71, 176, 192.

2305.10 Product liability, bodily injury or injury to personal property; when certain causes of action arise

(A) Except as provided in division (C) or (E) of this section, an action based on a product liability claim and an action for bodily injury or injuring personal property shall be brought within two years after the cause of action accrues. Except as provided in divisions (B)(1), (2), (3), (4), and (5) of this section, a cause of action accrues under this division when the injury or loss to person or property occurs.

(B)(1) For purposes of division (A) of this section, a cause of action for bodily injury that is not described in division (B)(2), (3), (4), or (5) of this section and that is caused by exposure to hazardous or toxic chemicals, ethical drugs, or ethical medical devices accrues upon the date on which the plaintiff is informed by competent medical authority that the plaintiff has an injury that is related to the exposure, or upon the date on which by the exercise of reasonable diligence the plaintiff should have known that the plaintiff has an injury that is related to the exposure, whichever date occurs first.

(2) For purposes of division (A) of this section, a cause of action for bodily injury caused by exposure to chromium in any of its chemical forms accrues upon the date on which the plaintiff is informed by competent medical authority that the plaintiff has an injury that is related to the exposure, or upon the date on which by the exercise of reasonable diligence the plaintiff should have known that the plaintiff has an injury that is related to the exposure, whichever date occurs first.

(3) For purposes of division (A) of this section, a cause of action for bodily injury incurred by a veteran through exposure to chemical defoliants or herbicides or other causative agents, including agent orange, accrues upon the date on which the plaintiff is informed by competent medical authority that the plaintiff has an injury that is related to the exposure, or upon the date on which by the exercise of reasonable diligence the plaintiff should have known that the plaintiff has an injury that is related to the exposure, whichever date occurs first.

(4) For purposes of division (A) of this section, a cause of action for bodily injury caused by exposure to diethylstilbestrol or other nonsteroidal synthetic estrogens, including exposure before birth, accrues upon the date on which the plaintiff is informed by competent medical authority that the plaintiff has an injury that is related to the exposure, or upon the date on which by the

exercise of reasonable diligence the plaintiff should have known that the plaintiff has an injury that is related to the exposure, whichever date occurs first.

(5) For purposes of division (A) of this section, a cause of action for bodily injury caused by exposure to asbestos accrues upon the date on which the plaintiff is informed by competent medical authority that the plaintiff has an injury that is related to the exposure, or upon the date on which by the exercise of reasonable diligence the plaintiff should have known that the plaintiff has an injury that is related to the exposure, whichever date occurs first.

(C)(1) Except as otherwise provided in divisions (C)(2), (3), (4), (5), (6), and (7) of this section or in section 2305.19 of the Revised Code, no cause of action based on a product liability claim shall accrue against the manufacturer or supplier of a product later than ten years from the date that the product was delivered to its first purchaser or first lessee who was not engaged in a business in which the product was used as a component in the production, construction, creation, assembly, or rebuilding of another product.

(2) Division (C)(1) of this section does not apply if the manufacturer or supplier of a product engaged in fraud in regard to information about the product and the fraud contributed to the harm that is alleged in a product liability claim involving that product.

(3) Division (C)(1) of this section does not bar an action based on a product liability claim against a manufacturer or supplier of a product who made an express, written warranty as to the safety of the product that was for a period longer than ten years and that, at the time of the accrual of the cause of action, has not expired in accordance with the terms of that warranty.

(4) If the cause of action relative to a product liability claim accrues during the ten-year period described in division (C)(1) of this section but less than two years prior to the expiration of that period, an action based on the product liability claim may be commenced within two years after the cause of action accrues.

(5) If a cause of action relative to a product liability claim accrues during the ten-year period described in division (C)(1) of this section and the claimant cannot commence an action during that period due to a disability described in section 2305.16 of the Revised Code, an action based on the product liability claim may be commenced within two years after the disability is removed.

(6) Division (C)(1) of this section does not bar an action for bodily injury caused by exposure to asbestos if the cause of action that is the basis of the action accrues upon the date on which the plaintiff is informed by competent medical authority that the plaintiff has an injury that is related to the exposure, or upon the date on which by the exercise of reasonable diligence the plaintiff should have known that the plaintiff has an injury that is related to the exposure, whichever date occurs first.

(7)(a) Division (C)(1) of this section does not bar an action based on a product liability claim against a manufacturer or supplier of a product if all of the following apply:

(i) The action is for bodily injury.

(ii) The product involved is a substance or device described in division (B)(1), (2), (3), or (4) of this section.

(iii) The bodily injury results from exposure to the product during the ten-year period described in division (C)(1) of this section.

(b) If division (C)(7)(a) of this section applies regarding an action, the cause of action accrues upon the date on which the claimant is informed by competent medical authority that the bodily injury was related to the exposure to the product, or upon the date on which by the exercise of reasonable diligence the claimant should have known that the bodily injury was related to the exposure to the product, whichever date occurs first. The action based on the product liability claim shall be commenced within two years after the cause of action accrues and shall not be commenced more than two years after the cause of action accrues.

(D) This section does not create a new cause of action or substantive legal right against any person involving a product liability claim.

(E) An action brought by a victim of childhood sexual abuse asserting any claim resulting from childhood sexual abuse, as defined in section 2305.111 of the Revised Code, shall be brought as provided in division (C) of that section.

(F) As used in this section:

(1) "Agent orange," "causative agent," and "veteran" have the same meanings as in section 5903.21 of the Revised Code.

(2) "Ethical drug," "ethical medical device," "manufacturer," "product," "product liability claim," and "supplier" have the same meanings as in section 2307.71 of the Revised Code.

(3) "Harm" means injury, death, or loss to person or property.

(G) This section shall be considered to be purely remedial in operation and shall be applied in a remedial manner in any civil action commenced on or after April 7, 2005, in which this section is relevant, regardless of when the cause of action accrued and notwithstanding any other section of the Revised Code or prior rule of law of this state, but shall not be construed to apply to any civil action pending prior to April 7, 2005.

(2006 S 17, eff. 8–3–06; 2004 S 80, eff. 4–7–05; 2001 S 108, § 2.01, eff. 7–6–01; 2001 S 108, § 2.02, eff. 7–6–01; 1996 H 350, eff. 1–27–97 [1]; 1984 H 72, eff. 5–31–84; 1982 S 406; 1980 H 716; 1953 H 1; GC 11224–1)

[1] See *Baldwin's Ohio Revised Code Annotated*, Notes of Decisions, *State ex rel. Ohio Academy of Trial Lawyers v. Sheward* (Ohio 1999), 86 Ohio St.3d 451, 715 N.E.2d 1062.

Uncodified Law

2006 S 17, § 5, eff. 8–3–06, reads:

If any provision of a section of the Revised Code as amended or enacted by this act or the application of the provision to any person or circumstance is held invalid, the invalidity does not affect other provisions or applications of the section or related sections that can be given effect without the invalid provision or application, and to this end the provisions are severable.

2004 S 80, § 3(B): See *Baldwin's Ohio Revised Code Annotated*, Uncodified Law under RC 2305.131.

2004 S 80, § 3(C): See Uncodified Law under RC 2305.09.

2001 S 108, § 1: See *Baldwin's Ohio Revised Code Annotated*, Uncodified Law under 2305.251.

2001 S 108, § 3, eff. 7–6–01, reads, in part:

(A) In Section 2.01 of this act:

(3) Sections 109.36, 2117.06, 2125.01, 2125.02, 2125.04, 2305.10, 2305.16, 2305.27, 2305.38, 2307.31, 2307.32, 2307.75, 2307.80, 2315.01, 2315.19, 2501.02, 2744.06, 3722.08, 4112.14, 4113.52, 4171.10, and 4399.18 of the Revised Code are revived and amended, supersede the versions of the same sections that are repealed by Section 2.02 of this act, and include amendments that gender neutralize the language of the sections (as contemplated by section 1.31 of the Revised Code) and that correct apparent error.

Historical and Statutory Notes

Ed. Note: The amendment of this section by 1996 H 350, eff. 1–27–97, was repealed by 2001 S 108, § 2.02, eff. 7–6–01. See *Baldwin's Ohio Legislative Service Annotated*, 1996, page 10/L–3385, and 2001, page 6/L–1441, or the OH–LEGIS or OH–LEGIS–OLD database on Westlaw, for original versions of these Acts.

Pre–1953 H 1 Amendments: 112 v 238

Amendment Note: 2006 S 17 inserted "or (E)" in the first sentence of division (A); added new language as division (E); redesignated former division (E) and (F) as (F) and (G), respectively; and substituted "April 7,

2005" for "the effective date of this amendment" twice in newly designated division (G).

Amendment Note: 2004 S 80 rewrote this section, which prior thereto read:

"An action for bodily injury or injuring personal property shall be brought within two years after the cause thereof arose.

"For purposes of this section, a cause of action for bodily injury caused by exposure to asbestos or to chromium in any of its chemical forms arises upon the date on which the plaintiff is informed by competent medical authority that the plaintiff has been injured by such exposure, or upon the date on which, by the exercise of reasonable diligence, the plaintiff should have become aware that the plaintiff had been injured by the exposure, whichever date occurs first.

"For purposes of this section, a cause of action for bodily injury incurred by a veteran through exposure to chemical defoliants or herbicides or other causative agents, including agent orange, arises upon the date on which the plaintiff is informed by competent medical authority that the plaintiff has been injured by such exposure.

"As used in this section, "agent orange," "causative agent," and "veteran" have the same meanings as in section 5903.21 of the Revised Code.

"For purposes of this section, a cause of action for bodily injury which may be caused by exposure to diethylstilbestrol or other nonsteroidal synthetic estrogens, including exposure before birth, upon the date on which the plaintiff learns from a licensed physician that the plaintiff has an injury which may be related to such exposure, or upon the date on which by the exercise of reasonable diligence the plaintiff should have become aware that the plaintiff has an injury which may be related to such exposure, whichever date occurs first."

Amendment Note: 1996 H 350 rewrote this section, which prior thereto read:

"An action for bodily injury or injuring personal property shall be brought within two years after the cause thereof arose.

"For purposes of this section, a cause of action for bodily injury caused by exposure to asbestos or to chromium in any of its chemical forms arises upon the date on which the plaintiff is informed by competent medical authority that he has been injured by such exposure, or upon the date on which, by the exercise of reasonable diligence, he should have become aware that he had been injured by the exposure, whichever date occurs first.

"For purposes of this section, a cause of action for bodily injury incurred by a veteran through exposure to chemical defoliants or herbicides or other causative agents, including agent orange, arises upon the date on which the plaintiff is informed by competent medical authority that he has been injured by such exposure.

"As used in this section, "agent orange," "causative agent," and "veteran" have the same meanings as in section 5903.21 of the Revised Code.

"For purposes of this section, a cause of action for bodily injury which may be caused by exposure to diethylstilbestrol or other nonsteroidal synthetic estrogens, including exposure before birth, arises upon the date on which the plaintiff learns from a licensed physician that he has an injury which may be related to such exposure, or upon the date on which by the exercise of reasonable diligence he should have become aware that he has an injury which may be related to such exposure, whichever date occurs first."

Library References

Limitation of Actions ⟜31, 32(1), 55(3) to 55(5), 95(4.1, 7).
Westlaw Topic No. 241.
C.J.S. Limitations of Actions §§ 68 to 71, 159, 166 to 167, 170 to 176, 180, 183.
C.J.S. Physicians, Surgeons, and other Health to Care Providers § 108.
Baldwin's Ohio Legislative Service, 1996 H 350—LSC Analysis, p 10/L-3476

LIMITATIONS—MISCELLANEOUS

2305.11 Time limitations for bringing certain actions

(A) An action for libel, slander, malicious prosecution, or false imprisonment, an action for malpractice other than an action upon a medical, dental, optometric, or chiropractic claim, or an action upon a statute for a penalty or forfeiture shall be commenced within one year after the cause of action accrued, provided that an action by an employee for the payment of unpaid minimum wages, unpaid overtime compensation, or liquidated damages by reason of the nonpayment of minimum wages or overtime compensation shall be commenced within two years after the cause of action accrued.

(B) A civil action for unlawful abortion pursuant to section 2919.12 of the Revised Code, a civil action authorized by division (H) of section 2317.56 of the Revised Code, a civil action pursuant to division (B)(1) or (2) of section 2307.51 of the Revised Code for performing a dilation and extraction procedure or attempting to perform a dilation and extraction procedure in violation of section 2919.15 of the Revised Code, and a civil action pursuant to division (B)(1) or (2) of section 2307.52 of the Revised Code for terminating or attempting to terminate a human pregnancy after viability in violation of division (A) or (B) of section 2919.17 of the Revised Code shall be commenced within one year after the performance or inducement of the abortion, within one year after the attempt to perform or induce the abortion in violation of division (A) or (B) of section 2919.17 of the Revised Code, within one year after the performance of the dilation and extraction procedure, or, in the case of a civil action pursuant to division (B)(2) of section 2307.51 of the Revised Code, within one year after the attempt to perform the dilation and extraction procedure.

(C) As used in this section, "medical claim," "dental claim," "optometric claim," and "chiropractic claim" have the same meanings as in section 2305.113 of the Revised Code.

(2002 S 281, eff. 4–11–03; 2002 H 412, eff. 11–7–02; 2001 S 108, § 2.01, eff. 7–6–01; 2001 S 108, § 2.02, eff. 7–6–01; 1996 H 350, eff. 1–27–97 [1]*; 1995 H 135, eff. 11–15–95; 1992 S 124, eff. 4–16–93; 1991 H 108; 1990 S 125, S 80; 1987 S 327; 1985 H 319; 1984 S 183; 1981 H 243; 1976 H 1426; 1975 H 682; 1974 H 989; 1953 H 1; GC 11225)*

[1] See *Baldwin's Ohio Revised Code Annotated*, Notes of Decisions, *State ex rel. Ohio Academy of Trial Lawyers v. Sheward* (Ohio 1999), 86 Ohio St.3d 451, 715 N.E.2d 1062.

Uncodified Law

2002 S 281, § 6 through 8, eff. 4–11–03, read:

Section 6. (A) Sections 1751.67, 2117.06, 2305.11, 2305.15, 2305.234, 2317.02, 2317.54, 2323.56, 2711.21, 2711.22, 2711.23, 2711.24, 2743.02, 2743.43, 2919.16, 3923.63, 3923.64, 3929.71, and 5111.018 of the Revised Code, as amended by this act, and sections 2303.23, 2305.113, 2323.41, 2323.42, 2323.43, and 2323.55 of the Revised Code, as enacted by this act, apply to civil actions upon a medical claim, dental claim, optometric claim, or chiropractic claim in which the act or omission that constitutes the alleged basis of the claim occurs on or after the effective date of this act.

(B) As used in this section, "medical claim," "dental claim," "optometric claim," and "chiropractic claim" have the same meanings as in section 2305.113 of the Revised Code.

Section 7. If any item of law that constitutes the whole or part of a section of law contained in this act, or if any application of any item of law that constitutes the whole or part of a section of law contained in this act, is held invalid, the invalidity does not affect other items of law or applications of items of law that can be given effect without the invalid item of law or application. To this end, the items of law of which the sections contained in this act are composed, and their applications, are independent and severable.

Section 8. If any item of law that constitutes the whole or part of a section of law contained in this act, or if any application of any item of law contained in this act, is held to be preempted by federal law, the preemption of the item of law or its application does not affect other items of law or applications of items of law that can be given affect. The items of law of which the sections of this act are composed, and their applications, are independent and severable.

2002 H 412, § 3, eff. 11–7–02, reads:

Nothing in this act applies to proceedings or appeals involving workers' compensation claims under Chapter 4121. or 4123. of the Revised Code.

2002 H 412, § 4, eff. 11–7–02, reads:

If any provision of section 2305.11, 2315.21, 3721.02, or 3721.17 of the Revised Code, as amended by this act, any provision of section 5111.411 of the Revised Code, as enacted by this act, or the application of any provision of those sections to any person or circumstance is held invalid, the invalidity does not affect other provisions or applications of the particular section or related sections that can be given effect without the invalid provision or application, and to this end the provisions of the particular section are severable.

2001 S 108, § 1: See *Baldwin's Ohio Revised Code Annotated*, Uncodified Law under 2305.251.

2001 S 108, § 3: See *Baldwin's Ohio Revised Code Annotated*, Uncodified Law under 2305.01.

1995 H 135, § 3, eff. 11–15–95, reads: The General Assembly declares that its intent in enacting sections 2307.51 and 2919.15 and in amending section 2305.11 of the Revised Code in this act is to prevent the unnecessary use of a specific procedure used in performing an abortion. This intent is based on a state interest in preventing unnecessary cruelty to the human fetus.

1990 S 125, § 4, eff. 7–13–90, reads: Sections 2305.04, 2305.11, 2305.16, and 2743.16 of the Revised Code, as amended by this act, shall apply only to causes of action that accrue on or after the date specified in Section 3 of this act, which is six months after the effective date of this act.

Historical and Statutory Notes

Ed. Note: The amendment of this section by 1996 H 350, eff. 1–27–97, was repealed by 2001 S 108, § 2.02, eff. 7–6–01. See *Baldwin's Ohio Legislative Service Annotated*, 1996, page 10/L–3388, and 2001, page 6/L–1441, or the OH–LEGIS or OH–LEGIS–OLD database on Westlaw, for original versions of these Acts.

Pre–1953 H 1 Amendments: 122 v H 319; 120 v 646; RS 4983

Amendment Note: 2002 S 281 rewrote divisions (B) through (D) which prior thereto read:

"(B)(1) Subject to division (B)(2) of this section, an action upon a medical, dental, optometric, or chiropractic claim shall be commenced within one year after the cause of action accrued, except that, if prior to the expiration of that one-year period, a claimant who allegedly possesses a medical, dental, optometric, or chiropractic claim gives to the person who is the subject of that claim written notice that the claimant is considering bringing an action upon that claim, that action may be commenced against the person notified at any time within one hundred eighty days after the notice is so given.

"(2) Except as to persons within the age of minority or of unsound mind, as provided by section 2305.16 of the Revised Code:

"(a) In no event shall any action upon a medical, dental, optometric, or chiropractic claim be commenced more than four years after the occurrence of the act or omission constituting the alleged basis of the medical, dental, optometric, or chiropractic claim.

"(b) If an action upon a medical, dental, optometric, or chiropractic claim is not commenced within four years after the occurrence of the act or omission constituting the alleged basis of the medical, dental, optometric, or chiropractic claim, then, notwithstanding the time when the action is determined to accrue under division (B)(1) of this section, any action upon that claim is barred.

"(C) A civil action for unlawful abortion pursuant to section 2919.12 of the Revised Code, a civil action authorized by division (H) of section 2317.56 of the Revised Code, a civil action pursuant to division (B)(1) or (2) of section 2307.51 of the Revised Code for performing a dilation and extraction procedure or attempting to perform a dilation and extraction procedure in violation of section 2919.15 of the Revised Code, and a civil action pursuant to division (B)(1) or (2) of section 2307.52 of the Revised Code for terminating or attempting to terminate a human pregnancy after viability in violation of division (A) or (B) of section 2919.17 of the Revised Code shall be commenced within one year after the performance or inducement of the abortion, within one year after the attempt to perform or induce the abortion in violation of division (A) or (B) of section 2919.17 of the Revised Code, within one year after the performance of the dilation and extraction procedure, or, in the case of a civil action pursuant to division (B)(2) of section 2307.51 of the Revised Code, within one year after the attempt to perform the dilation and extraction procedure.

"(D) As used in this section:

"(1) "Hospital" includes any person, corporation, association, board, or authority that is responsible for the operation of any hospital licensed or registered in the state, including, but not limited to, those that are owned or operated by the state, political subdivisions, any person, any corporation, or any combination thereof. "Hospital" also includes any person, corporation, association, board, entity, or authority that is responsible for the operation of any clinic that employs a full-time staff of physicians practicing in more than one recognized medical specialty and rendering advice, diagnosis, care, and treatment to individuals. 'Hospital" does not include any hospital operated by the government of the United States or any of its branches.

"(2) "Physician" means a person who is licensed to practice medicine and surgery or osteopathic medicine and surgery by the state medical board or a person who otherwise is authorized to practice medicine and surgery or osteopathic medicine and surgery in this state.

"(3) "Medical claim" means any claim that is asserted in any civil action against a physician, podiatrist, hospital, home, or residential facility, against any employee or agent of a physician, podiatrist, hospital, home, or residential facility, or against a registered nurse or physical therapist, and that arises out of the medical diagnosis, care, or treatment of any person. "Medical claim" includes the following:

"(a) Derivative claims for relief that arise from the medical diagnosis, care, or treatment of a person;

"(b) Claims that arise out of the medical diagnosis, care, or treatment of any person and to which either of the following apply:

"(i) The claim results from acts or omissions in providing medical care.

"(ii) The claim results from the hiring, training, supervision, retention, or termination of caregivers providing medical diagnosis, care, or treatment.

"(c) Claims that arise out of the medical diagnosis, care, or treatment of any person and that are brought under section 3721.17 of the Revised Code.

"(4) "Podiatrist" means any person who is licensed to practice podiatric medicine and surgery by the state medical board.

"(5) "Dentist" means any person who is licensed to practice dentistry by the state dental board.

"(6) "Dental claim" means any claim that is asserted in any civil action against a dentist, or against any employee or agent of a dentist, and that arises out of a dental operation or the dental diagnosis, care, or treatment of any person. "Dental claim" includes derivative claims for relief that arise from a dental operation or the dental diagnosis, care, or treatment of a person.

"(7) "Derivative claims for relief" include, but are not limited to, claims of a parent, guardian, custodian, or spouse of an individual who was the subject of any medical diagnosis, care, or treatment, dental diagnosis, care, or treatment, dental operation, optometric diagnosis, care, or treatment, or chiropractic diagnosis, care, or treatment, that arise from that diagnosis, care, treatment, or operation, and that seek the recovery of damages for any of the following:

"(a) Loss of society, consortium, companionship, care, assistance, attention, protection, advice, guidance, counsel, instruction, training, or education, or any other intangible loss that was sustained by the parent, guardian, custodian, or spouse;

"(b) Expenditures of the parent, guardian, custodian, or spouse for medical, dental, optometric, or chiropractic care or treatment, for rehabilitation services, or for other care, treatment, services, products, or accommodations provided to the individual who was the subject of the medical diagnosis, care, or treatment, the dental diagnosis, care, or treatment, the dental operation, the optometric diagnosis, care, or treatment, or the chiropractic diagnosis, care, or treatment.

"(8) "Registered nurse" means any person who is licensed to practice nursing as a registered nurse by the state board of nursing.

"(9) "Chiropractic claim" means any claim that is asserted in any civil action against a chiropractor, or against any employee or agent of a chiropractor, and that arises out of the chiropractic diagnosis, care, or treatment of any person. "Chiropractic claim" includes derivative claims for relief that arise from the chiropractic diagnosis, care, or treatment of a person.

"(10) "Chiropractor" means any person who is licensed to practice chiropractic by the chiropractic examining board.

"(11) "Optometric claim" means any claim that is asserted in any civil action against an optometrist, or against any employee or agent of an optometrist, and that arises out of the optometric diagnosis, care, or treatment of any person. "Optometric claim" includes derivative claims for relief that arise from the optometric diagnosis, care, or treatment of a person.

"(12) "Optometrist" means any person licensed to practice optometry by the state board of optometry.

"(13) "Physical therapist" means any person who is licensed to practice physical therapy under Chapter 4755. of the Revised Code.

"(14) "Home" has the same meaning as in section 3721.10 of the Revised Code.

"(15) "Residential facility" means a facility licensed under section 5123.19 of the Revised Code."

Amendment Note: 2002 H 412 rewrote division (D)(3), added divisions (D)(14) and (D)(15); and made other nonsubstantive changes. Prior to amendment division (D)(3) read:

"(3) 'Medical claim' means any claim that is asserted in any civil action against a physician, podiatrist, or hospital, against any employee or agent of a physician, podiatrist, or hospital, or against a registered nurse or physical therapist, and that arises out of the medical diagnosis, care, or treatment of any person. 'Medical claim' includes derivative claims for relief that arise from the medical diagnosis, care, or treatment of a person."

Amendment Note: 1996 H 350 rewrote divisions (A) and (B); and inserted ", midwife," and "and a claim that is asserted in a civil action against a hospital and that is based on negligent credentialing" in division (D)(3). Prior to amendment, divisions (A) and (B) read:

"(A) An action for libel, slander, malicious prosecution, or false imprisonment, an action for malpractice other than an action upon a medical, dental, optometric, or chiropractic claim, or an action upon a statute for a penalty or forfeiture shall be commenced within one year after the cause of action accrued, provided that an action by an employee for the payment of unpaid minimum wages, unpaid overtime compensation, or liquidated damages by reason of the nonpayment of minimum wages or overtime compensation shall be commenced within two years after the cause of action accrued.

"(B)(1) Subject to division (B)(2) of this section, an action upon a medical, dental, optometric, or chiropractic claim shall be commenced within one year after the cause of action accrued, except that, if prior to the expiration of that one-year period, a claimant who allegedly possesses a medical, dental, optometric, or chiropractic claim gives to the person who is the subject of that claim written notice that the claimant is considering bringing an action upon that claim, that action may be commenced against the person notified at any time within one hundred eighty days after the notice is so given.

"(2) Except as to persons within the age of minority or of unsound mind, as provided by section 2305.16 of the Revised Code:

"(a) In no event shall any action upon a medical, dental, optometric, or chiropractic claim be commenced more than four years after the occurrence of the act or omission constituting the alleged basis of the medical, dental, optometric, or chiropractic claim.

"(b) If an action upon a medical, dental, optometric, or chiropractic claim is not commenced within four years after the occurrence of the act or omission constituting the alleged basis of the medical, dental, optometric, or chiropractic claim, then, notwithstanding the time when the action is determined to accrue under division (B)(1) of this section, any action upon that claim is barred."

Amendment Note: 1995 H 135 inserted "cause of" in division (B)(1); rewrote division (C); and substituted "a" for "any" and inserted "or a person who otherwise is authorized to practice medicine and surgery or osteopathic medicine and surgery in this state" in division (D)(2). Prior to amendment, division (C) read:

"(C) A civil action for unlawful abortion pursuant to section 2919.12 of the Revised Code or a civil action authorized by division (H) of section 2317.56 of the Revised Code shall be commenced within one year after the abortion."

Library References

False Imprisonment ⚖18.
Health ⚖811.
Libel and Slander ⚖76.
Limitation of Actions ⚖55(3), 72(1), 74(1).
Malicious Prosecution ⚖44.
Westlaw Topic Nos. 168, 198H, 237, 241, 249.

C.J.S. Libel and Slander.
C.J.S. Injurious Falsehood § 122.
C.J.S. Limitations of Actions §§ 112 to 113, 116 to 117, 159, 166, 171 to 175.
C.J.S. Malicious Prosecution or Wrongful Litigation § 64.
C.J.S. Physicians, Surgeons, and other Health to Care Providers § 108.
Baldwin's Ohio Legislative Service, 1996 H 350—LSC Analysis, p 10/L-3476

2305.12   On official bond

An action on the official bond, or undertaking of an officer, assignee, trustee, executor, administrator, or guardian, or on a bond or undertaking given in pursuance of statute, shall be brought within ten years after the cause thereof accrued.

(1953 H 1, eff. 10–1–53; GC 11226)

Historical and Statutory Notes

Pre–1953 H 1 Amendments: RS 4976, 4984

Library References

Appeal and Error ⚖1243.
Assignments ⚖128.
Executors and Administrators ⚖537(5).
Guardian and Ward ⚖182(3).
Limitation of Actions ⚖22(8).
Mental Health ⚖192.
Officers and Public Employees ⚖139.
Trusts ⚖387.
Westlaw Topic Nos. 30, 38, 162, 196, 241, 257A, 283, 390.
C.J.S. Appeal and Error § 1082.
C.J.S. Assignments § 116.
C.J.S. Limitations of Actions § 58.
C.J.S. Officers and Public Employees § 376.
C.J.S. Trover and Conversion §§ 770 to 777.

2305.121   Limitation of actions pertaining to revocable trust made irrevocable by death of grantor—Repealed

(2006 H 416, eff. 1–1–07; 2002 H 345, eff. 7–23–02)

Historical and Statutory Notes

Ed. Note: Former RC 2305.121 amended and recodified as RC 5806.04 by 2006 H 416, eff. 1–1–07.

SAVING PROVISIONS

2305.16   Disabilities; tolling of statute of limitations

Unless otherwise provided in sections 1302.98, 1304.35, and 2305.04 to 2305.14 of the Revised Code, if a person entitled to bring any action mentioned in those sections, unless for penalty or forfeiture, is, at the time the cause of action accrues, within the age of minority or of unsound mind, the person may bring it within the respective times limited by those sections, after the disability is removed. When the interests of two or more parties are joint and inseparable, the disability of one shall inure to the benefit of all.

After the cause of action accrues, if the person entitled to bring the action becomes of unsound mind and is adjudicated as such by a court of competent jurisdiction or is confined in an institution or hospital under a diagnosed condition or disease which renders the person of unsound mind, the time during which the person is of unsound mind and so adjudicated or so confined shall not be computed as any part of the period within which the action must be brought.

(2001 S 108, § 2.01, eff. 7–6–01; 2001 S 108, § 2.02, eff. 7–6–01; 1996 H 350, eff. 1–27–97 [1]; 1994 S 147, eff. 8–19–94; 1990 S 125, eff. 1–13–91; 131 v H 439; 129 v 13; 127 v 619; 1953 H 1; GC 11229)

[1] See *Baldwin's Ohio Revised Code Annotated*, Notes of Decisions, *State ex rel. Ohio Academy of Trial Lawyers v. Sheward* (Ohio 1999), 86 Ohio St.3d 451, 715 N.E.2d 1062.

Uncodified Law

2001 S 108, § 1: See *Baldwin's Ohio Revised Code Annotated*, Uncodified Law under 2305.251.

2001 S 108, § 3: See *Baldwin's Ohio Revised Code Annotated*, Uncodified Law under 2305.10.

1990 S 125, § 4, eff. 7–13–90, reads: Sections 2305.04, 2305.11, 2305.16, and 2743.16 of the Revised Code, as amended by this act, shall apply only to causes of action that accrue on or after the date specified in Section 3 of this act, which is six months after the effective date of this act.

Historical and Statutory Notes

Ed. Note: The amendment of this section by 1996 H 350, eff. 1–27–97, was repealed by 2001 S 108, § 2.02, eff. 7–6–01. See *Baldwin's Ohio Legislative Service Annotated*, 1996, page 10/L–3393, and 2001, page 6/L–1441, or the OH–LEGIS or OH–LEGIS–OLD database on Westlaw, for original versions of these Acts.

Pre–1953 H 1 Amendments: RS 4986

Amendment Note: 1996 H 350 added the reference to section 2744.04 in the first paragraph; and made changes to reflect gender neutral language and other nonsubstantive changes.

Amendment Note: 1994 S 147 substituted "1304.35" for "1304.29" in the first paragraph.

Library References

Limitation of Actions ⚖72, 74, 94.
Westlaw Topic No. 241.
C.J.S. Limitations of Actions §§ 100, 112 to 114, 116.

MISCELLANEOUS PROVISIONS

2305.19 Saving in case of reversal

(A) In any action that is commenced or attempted to be commenced, if in due time a judgment for the plaintiff is reversed or if the plaintiff fails otherwise than upon the merits, the plaintiff or, if the plaintiff dies and the cause of action survives, the plaintiff's representative may commence a new action within one year after the date of the reversal of the judgment or the plaintiff's failure otherwise than upon the merits or within the period of the original applicable statute of limitations, whichever occurs later. This division applies to any claim asserted in any pleading by a defendant.

(B) If the defendant in an action described in division (A) of this section is a foreign or domestic corporation, and whether its charter prescribes the manner or place of service of process on the defendant, and if it passes into the hands of a receiver before the expiration of the one year period or the period of the original applicable statute of limitations, whichever is applicable, as described in that division, then service to be made within one year following the original service or attempt to begin the action may be made upon that receiver or the receiver's cashier, treasurer, secretary, clerk, or managing agent, or if none of these officers can be found, by a copy left at the office or the usual place of business of any of those agents or officers of the receiver with the person having charge of the office or place of business. If that corporation is a railroad company, summons may be served on any regular ticket or freight agent of the receiver, and if there is no regular ticket or freight agent of the receiver, then upon any conductor of the receiver, in any county in the state in which the railroad is located. The summons shall be returned as if served on that defendant corporation.

(2004 H 161, eff. 5–31–04; 1953 H 1, eff. 10–1–53; GC 11233)

Historical and Statutory Notes

Pre–1953 H 1 Amendments: RS 4991

Amendment Note: 2004 H 161 rewrote the section which prior thereto read:

"In an action commenced, or attempted to be commenced, if in due time a judgment for the plaintiff is reversed, or if the plaintiff fails otherwise than upon the merits, and the time limited for the commencement of such action at the date of reversal or failure has expired, the plaintiff, or, if he dies and the cause of action survives, his representatives may commence a new action within one year after such date. This provision applies to any claim asserted in any pleading by a defendant. If the defendant is a corporation, foreign or domestic, and whether its charter prescribes the manner and place, or either, of service of process thereon, and it passes into the hands of a receiver before the expiration of such year, then service to be made within the year following such original service or attempt to begin the action may be made upon such receiver or his cashier, treasurer, secretary, clerk, or managing agent, or if none of these officers can be found, by a copy left at the office or the usual place of business of such agents or officers of the receiver with the person having charge thereof. If such corporation is a railroad company, summons may be served on any regular ticket or freight agent of the receiver, and if there is no such agent, then upon any conductor of the receiver, in any county in the state in which the railroad is located. The summons shall be returned as if served on such defendant."

Library References

Limitation of Actions ⚖130(12).
Westlaw Topic No. 241.
C.J.S. Limitations of Actions §§ 241, 250.

2305.21 Survival of actions

In addition to the causes of action which survive at common law, causes of action for mesne profits, or injuries to the person or property, or for deceit or fraud, also shall survive; and such actions may be brought notwithstanding the death of the person entitled or liable thereto.

(1953 H 1, eff. 10–1–53; GC 11235)

Historical and Statutory Notes

Ed. Note: Survival of actions and revivor of actions are terms frequently confused. This section provides that particular causes of action survive the death of the party injured. See 2311.21, which provides that no pending action shall abate by the death of either party.

Pre–1953 H 1 Amendments: RS 4975

Comparative Laws

Mich.—M.C.L.A. § 600.2921.
N.Y.—McKinney's EPTL 11–3.2.

Library References

Abatement and Revival ⚖51.
Westlaw Topic No. 2.

CHAPTER 2717

CHANGE OF NAME

Section
2717.01　Proceedings to change name of person

Comparative Laws

Cal.—West's Ann.Cal.C.C.P. § 1275 et seq.
Ind.—West's A.I.C. 34-28-2-1.
Mich.—M.C.L.A. § 711.1.

2717.01　Proceedings to change name of person

(A) A person desiring a change of name may file an application in the probate court of the county in which the person resides. The application shall set forth that the applicant has been a bona fide resident of that county for at least one year prior to the filing of the application, the cause for which the change of name is sought, and the requested new name.

Notice of the application shall be given once by publication in a newspaper of general circulation in the county at least thirty days before the hearing on the application. The notice shall set forth the court in which the application was filed, the case number, and the date and time of the hearing.

Upon proof that proper notice was given and that the facts set forth in the application show reasonable and proper cause for changing the name of the applicant, the court may order the change of name.

(B) An application for change of name may be made on behalf of a minor by either of the minor's parents, a legal guardian, or a guardian ad litem. When application is made on behalf of a minor, in addition to the notice and proof required pursuant to division (A) of this section, the consent of both living, legal parents of the minor shall be filed, or notice of the hearing shall be given to the parent or parents not consenting by certified mail, return receipt requested. If there is no known father of the minor, the notice shall be given to the person who the mother of the minor alleges to be the father. If no father is so alleged, or if either parent or the address of either parent is unknown, notice pursuant to division (A) of this section shall be sufficient as to the father or parent.

Any additional notice required by this division may be waived in writing by any person entitled to the notice.

(1986 S 248, eff. 12-17-86; 1975 S 145; 1973 S 1; 130 v S 83; 1953 H 1; GC 12209)

Historical and Statutory Notes

Pre–1953 H 1 Amendments:　RS 5853

Library References

Children Out-of-Wedlock ⚖1.
Names ⚖20.
Westlaw Topic Nos. 269, 76H.
C.J.S. Children Out-of-Wedlock §§ 2 to 11.
C.J.S. Names §§ 7, 21 to 28.

CHAPTER 2901

GENERAL PROVISIONS

GENERAL PROVISIONS

Section
2901.01　Definitions
2901.01　Definitions (later effective date)
2901.05　Presumption of innocence; proof of offense; of affirmative defense; as to each; reasonable doubt
2901.07　DNA testing of certain prisoners

GENERAL PROVISIONS

2901.01　Definitions

Note: See also following version of this section, eff. 7-1-07.

(A) As used in the Revised Code:

(1) "Force" means any violence, compulsion, or constraint physically exerted by any means upon or against a person or thing.

(2) "Deadly force" means any force that carries a substantial risk that it will proximately result in the death of any person.

(3) "Physical harm to persons" means any injury, illness, or other physiological impairment, regardless of its gravity or duration.

(4) "Physical harm to property" means any tangible or intangible damage to property that, in any degree, results in loss to its value or interferes with its use or enjoyment. "Physical harm to property" does not include wear and tear occasioned by normal use.

(5) "Serious physical harm to persons" means any of the following:

(a) Any mental illness or condition of such gravity as would normally require hospitalization or prolonged psychiatric treatment;

(b) Any physical harm that carries a substantial risk of death;

(c) Any physical harm that involves some permanent incapacity, whether partial or total, or that involves some temporary, substantial incapacity;

(d) Any physical harm that involves some permanent disfigurement or that involves some temporary, serious disfigurement;

(e) Any physical harm that involves acute pain of such duration as to result in substantial suffering or that involves any degree of prolonged or intractable pain.

(6) "Serious physical harm to property" means any physical harm to property that does either of the following:

(a) Results in substantial loss to the value of the property or requires a substantial amount of time, effort, or money to repair or replace;

(b) Temporarily prevents the use or enjoyment of the property or substantially interferes with its use or enjoyment for an extended period of time.

(7) "Risk" means a significant possibility, as contrasted with a remote possibility, that a certain result may occur or that certain circumstances may exist.

(8) "Substantial risk" means a strong possibility, as contrasted with a remote or significant possibility, that a certain result may occur or that certain circumstances may exist.

(9) "Offense of violence" means any of the following:

(a) A violation of section 2903.01, 2903.02, 2903.03, 2903.04, 2903.11, 2903.12, 2903.13, 2903.15, 2903.21, 2903.211, 2903.22, 2905.01, 2905.02, 2905.11, 2907.02, 2907.03, 2907.05, 2909.02, 2909.03, 2909.24, 2911.01, 2911.02, 2911.11, 2917.01, 2917.02, 2917.03, 2917.31, 2919.25, 2921.03, 2921.04, 2921.34, or 2923.161, of division (A)(1), (2), or (3) of section 2911.12, or of division (B)(1), (2), (3), or (4) of section 2919.22 of the Revised Code or felonious sexual penetration in violation of former section 2907.12 of the Revised Code;

(b) A violation of an existing or former municipal ordinance or law of this or any other state or the United States, substantially equivalent to any section, division, or offense listed in division (A)(9)(a) of this section;

(c) An offense, other than a traffic offense, under an existing or former municipal ordinance or law of this or any other state or the United States, committed purposely or knowingly, and involving physical harm to persons or a risk of serious physical harm to persons;

(d) A conspiracy or attempt to commit, or complicity in committing, any offense under division (A)(9)(a), (b), or (c) of this section.

(10)(a) "Property" means any property, real or personal, tangible or intangible, and any interest or license in that property. "Property" includes, but is not limited to, cable television service, other telecommunications service, telecommunications devices, information service, computers, data, computer software, financial instruments associated with computers, other documents associated with computers, or copies of the documents, whether in machine or human readable form, trade secrets, trademarks, copyrights, patents, and property protected by a trademark, copyright, or patent. "Financial instruments associated with computers" include, but are not limited to, checks, drafts, warrants, money orders, notes of indebtedness, certificates of deposit, letters of credit, bills of credit or debit cards, financial transaction authorization mechanisms, marketable securities, or any computer system representations of any of them.

(b) As used in division (A)(10) of this section, "trade secret" has the same meaning as in section 1333.61 of the Revised Code, and "telecommunications service" and "information service" have the same meanings as in section 2913.01 of the Revised Code.

(c) As used in divisions (A)(10) and (13) of this section, "cable television service," "computer," "computer software," "computer system," "computer network," "data," and "telecommunications device" have the same meanings as in section 2913.01 of the Revised Code.

(11) "Law enforcement officer" means any of the following:

(a) A sheriff, deputy sheriff, constable, police officer of a township or joint township police district, marshal, deputy marshal, municipal police officer, member of a police force employed by a metropolitan housing authority under division (D) of section 3735.31 of the Revised Code, or state highway patrol trooper;

(b) An officer, agent, or employee of the state or any of its agencies, instrumentalities, or political subdivisions, upon whom, by statute, a duty to conserve the peace or to enforce all or certain laws is imposed and the authority to arrest violators is conferred, within the limits of that statutory duty and authority;

(c) A mayor, in the mayor's capacity as chief conservator of the peace within the mayor's municipal corporation;

(d) A member of an auxiliary police force organized by county, township, or municipal law enforcement authorities, within the scope of the member's appointment or commission;

(e) A person lawfully called pursuant to section 311.07 of the Revised Code to aid a sheriff in keeping the peace, for the purposes and during the time when the person is called;

(f) A person appointed by a mayor pursuant to section 737.01 of the Revised Code as a special patrolling officer during riot or emergency, for the purposes and during the time when the person is appointed;

(g) A member of the organized militia of this state or the armed forces of the United States, lawfully called to duty to aid civil authorities in keeping the peace or protect against domestic violence;

(h) A prosecuting attorney, assistant prosecuting attorney, secret service officer, or municipal prosecutor;

(i) A veterans' home police officer appointed under section 5907.02 of the Revised Code;

(j) A member of a police force employed by a regional transit authority under division (Y) of section 306.35 of the Revised Code;

(k) A special police officer employed by a port authority under section 4582.04 or 4582.28 of the Revised Code;

(*l*) The house sergeant at arms if the house sergeant at arms has arrest authority pursuant to division (E)(1) of section 101.311 of the Revised Code and an assistant house sergeant at arms;

(m) A special police officer employed by a municipal corporation at a municipal airport, or other municipal air navigation facility, that has scheduled operations, as defined in section 119.3 of Title 14 of the Code of Federal Regulations, 14 C.F.R. 119.3, as amended, and that is required to be under a security program and is governed by aviation security rules of the transportation security administration of the United States department of transportation as provided in Parts 1542. and 1544. of Title 49 of the Code of Federal Regulations, as amended.

(12) "Privilege" means an immunity, license, or right conferred by law, bestowed by express or implied grant, arising out of status, position, office, or relationship, or growing out of necessity.

(13) "Contraband" means any property described in the following categories:

(a) Property that in and of itself is unlawful for a person to acquire or possess;

(b) Property that is not in and of itself unlawful for a person to acquire or possess, but that has been determined by a court of this state, in accordance with law, to be contraband because of its use in an unlawful activity or manner, of its nature, or of the circumstances of the person who acquires or possesses it, including, but not limited to, goods and personal property described in division (D) of section 2913.34 of the Revised Code;

(c) Property that is specifically stated to be contraband by a section of the Revised Code or by an ordinance, regulation, or resolution;

(d) Property that is forfeitable pursuant to a section of the Revised Code, or an ordinance, regulation, or resolution, including, but not limited to, forfeitable firearms, dangerous ordnance, obscene materials, and goods and personal property described in division (D) of section 2913.34 of the Revised Code;

(e) Any controlled substance, as defined in section 3719.01 of the Revised Code, or any device, paraphernalia, money as defined in section 1301.01 of the Revised Code, or other means of exchange that has been, is being, or is intended to be used in an attempt or conspiracy to violate, or in a violation of, Chapter 2925. or 3719. of the Revised Code;

(f) Any gambling device, paraphernalia, money as defined in section 1301.01 of the Revised Code, or other means of exchange that has been, is being, or is intended to be used in an attempt or conspiracy to violate, or in the violation of, Chapter 2915. of the Revised Code;

(g) Any equipment, machine, device, apparatus, vehicle, vessel, container, liquid, or substance that has been, is being, or is intended to be used in an attempt or conspiracy to violate, or in the violation of, any law of this state relating to alcohol or tobacco;

(h) Any personal property that has been, is being, or is intended to be used in an attempt or conspiracy to commit, or in the commission of, any offense or in the transportation of the fruits of any offense;

(i) Any property that is acquired through the sale or other transfer of contraband or through the proceeds of contraband, other than by a court or a law enforcement agency acting within the scope of its duties;

(j) Any computer, computer system, computer network, computer software, or other telecommunications device that is used in a conspiracy to commit, an attempt to commit, or the commission of any offense, if the owner of the computer, computer system, computer network, computer software, or other telecommunications device is convicted of or pleads guilty to the offense in which it is used;

(k) Any property that is material support or resources and that has been, is being, or is intended to be used in an attempt or conspiracy to violate, or in the violation of, section 2909.22, 2909.23, or 2909.24 of the Revised Code or of section 2921.32 of the Revised Code when the offense or act committed by the person aided or to be aided as described in that section is an act of terrorism. As used in division (A)(13)(k) of this section, "material support or resources" and "act of terrorism" have the same meanings as in section 2909.21 of the Revised Code.

(14) A person is "not guilty by reason of insanity" relative to a charge of an offense only if the person proves, in the manner specified in section 2901.05 of the Revised Code, that at the time of the commission of the offense, the person did not know, as a result of a severe mental disease or defect, the wrongfulness of the person's acts.

(B)(1)(a) Subject to division (B)(2) of this section, as used in any section contained in Title XXIX of the Revised Code that sets forth a criminal offense, "person" includes all of the following:

(i) An individual, corporation, business trust, estate, trust, partnership, and association;

(ii) An unborn human who is viable.

(b) As used in any section contained in Title XXIX of the Revised Code that does not set forth a criminal offense, "person" includes an individual, corporation, business trust, estate, trust, partnership, and association.

(c) As used in division (B)(1)(a) of this section:

(i) "Unborn human" means an individual organism of the species Homo sapiens from fertilization until live birth.

(ii) "Viable" means the stage of development of a human fetus at which there is a realistic possibility of maintaining and nourishing of a life outside the womb with or without temporary artificial life-sustaining support.

(2) Notwithstanding division (B)(1)(a) of this section, in no case shall the portion of the definition of the term "person" that is set forth in division (B)(1)(a)(ii) of this section be applied or construed in any section contained in Title XXIX of the Revised Code that sets forth a criminal offense in any of the following manners:

(a) Except as otherwise provided in division (B)(2)(a) of this section, in a manner so that the offense prohibits or is construed as prohibiting any pregnant woman or her physician from performing an abortion with the consent of the pregnant woman, with the consent of the pregnant woman implied by law in a medical emergency, or with the approval of one otherwise authorized by law to consent to medical treatment on behalf of the pregnant woman. An abortion that violates the conditions described in the immediately preceding sentence may be punished as a violation of section 2903.01, 2903.02, 2903.03, 2903.04, 2903.05, 2903.06, 2903.08, 2903.11, 2903.12, 2903.13, 2903.14, 2903.21, or 2903.22 of the Revised Code, as applicable. An abortion that does not violate the conditions described in the second immediately preceding sentence, but that does violate section 2919.12, division (B) of section 2919.13, or section 2919.151, 2919.17, or 2919.18 of the Revised Code, may be punished as a violation of section 2919.12, division (B) of section 2919.13, or section 2919.151, 2919.17, or 2919.18 of the Revised Code, as applicable. Consent is sufficient under this division if it is of the type otherwise adequate to permit medical treatment to the pregnant woman, even if it does not comply with section 2919.12 of the Revised Code.

(b) In a manner so that the offense is applied or is construed as applying to a woman based on an act or omission of the woman that occurs while she is or was pregnant and that results in any of the following:

(i) Her delivery of a stillborn baby;

(ii) Her causing, in any other manner, the death in utero of a viable, unborn human that she is carrying;

(iii) Her causing the death of her child who is born alive but who dies from one or more injuries that are sustained while the child is a viable, unborn human;

(iv) Her causing her child who is born alive to sustain one or more injuries while the child is a viable, unborn human;

(v) Her causing, threatening to cause, or attempting to cause, in any other manner, an injury, illness, or other physiological impairment, regardless of its duration or gravity, or a mental illness or condition, regardless of its duration or gravity, to a viable, unborn human that she is carrying.

(C) As used in Title XXIX of the Revised Code:

(1) "School safety zone" consists of a school, school building, school premises, school activity, and school bus.

(2) "School," "school building," and "school premises" have the same meanings as in section 2925.01 of the Revised Code.

(3) "School activity" means any activity held under the auspices of a board of education of a city, local, exempted village, joint vocational, or cooperative education school district; a governing authority of a community school established under Chapter 3314. of the Revised Code; a governing board of an educational service center; or the governing body of a nonpublic school for which the state board of education prescribes minimum standards under section 3301.07 of the Revised Code.

(4) "School bus" has the same meaning as in section 4511.01 of the Revised Code.

(2002 H 675, eff. 3–14–03; 2002 H 364, eff 4–8–03; 2002 H 545, eff. 3–19–03; 2002 S 184, eff. 5–15–02; 2000 S 317, eff. 3–22–01; 2000 S 351, eff. 8–18–00; 2000 S 137, eff. 5–17–00; 1999 S 107, eff. 3–23–00; 1999 H 162, eff. 8–25–99; 1999 S 1, eff. 8–6–99; 1998 H 565, eff. 3–30–99; 1996 S 277, eff. 3–31–97; 1996 S 269, eff. 7–1–96; 1996 S 239, eff. 9–6–96; 1996 H 445, eff. 9–3–96; 1995 S 2, eff. 7–1–96; 1991 S 144, eff. 8–8–91; 1991 H 77; 1990 S 24; 1988 H 708, § 1)

Note: See also following version of this section, eff. 7-1-07.

2901.01 Definitions (later effective date)

Note: See also preceding version of this section in effect until 7-1-07.

(A) As used in the Revised Code:

(1) "Force" means any violence, compulsion, or constraint physically exerted by any means upon or against a person or thing.

(2) "Deadly force" means any force that carries a substantial risk that it will proximately result in the death of any person.

(3) "Physical harm to persons" means any injury, illness, or other physiological impairment, regardless of its gravity or duration.

(4) "Physical harm to property" means any tangible or intangible damage to property that, in any degree, results in loss to its value or interferes with its use or enjoyment. "Physical harm to property" does not include wear and tear occasioned by normal use.

(5) "Serious physical harm to persons" means any of the following:

(a) Any mental illness or condition of such gravity as would normally require hospitalization or prolonged psychiatric treatment;

(b) Any physical harm that carries a substantial risk of death;

(c) Any physical harm that involves some permanent incapacity, whether partial or total, or that involves some temporary, substantial incapacity;

(d) Any physical harm that involves some permanent disfigurement or that involves some temporary, serious disfigurement;

(e) Any physical harm that involves acute pain of such duration as to result in substantial suffering or that involves any degree of prolonged or intractable pain.

(6) "Serious physical harm to property" means any physical harm to property that does either of the following:

(a) Results in substantial loss to the value of the property or requires a substantial amount of time, effort, or money to repair or replace;

(b) Temporarily prevents the use or enjoyment of the property or substantially interferes with its use or enjoyment for an extended period of time.

(7) "Risk" means a significant possibility, as contrasted with a remote possibility, that a certain result may occur or that certain circumstances may exist.

(8) "Substantial risk" means a strong possibility, as contrasted with a remote or significant possibility, that a certain result may occur or that certain circumstances may exist.

(9) "Offense of violence" means any of the following:

(a) A violation of section 2903.01, 2903.02, 2903.03, 2903.04, 2903.11, 2903.12, 2903.13, 2903.15, 2903.21, 2903.211, 2903.22, 2905.01, 2905.02, 2905.11, 2907.02, 2907.03, 2907.05, 2909.02, 2909.03, 2909.24, 2911.01, 2911.02, 2911.11, 2917.01, 2917.02, 2917.03, 2917.31, 2919.25, 2921.03, 2921.04, 2921.34, or 2923.161, of division (A)(1), (2), or (3) of section 2911.12, or of division (B)(1), (2), (3), or (4) of section 2919.22 of the Revised Code or felonious sexual penetration in violation of former section 2907.12 of the Revised Code;

(b) A violation of an existing or former municipal ordinance or law of this or any other state or the United States, substantially equivalent to any section, division, or offense listed in division (A)(9)(a) of this section;

(c) An offense, other than a traffic offense, under an existing or former municipal ordinance or law of this or any other state or the United States, committed purposely or knowingly, and involving physical harm to persons or a risk of serious physical harm to persons;

(d) A conspiracy or attempt to commit, or complicity in committing, any offense under division (A)(9)(a), (b), or (c) of this section.

(10)(a) "Property" means any property, real or personal, tangible or intangible, and any interest or license in that property. "Property" includes, but is not limited to, cable television service, other telecommunications service, telecommunications devices, information service, computers, data, computer software, financial instruments associated with computers, other documents associated with computers, or copies of the documents, whether in machine or human readable form, trade secrets, trademarks, copyrights, patents, and property protected by a trademark, copyright, or patent. "Financial instruments associated with computers" include, but are not limited to, checks, drafts, warrants, money orders, notes of indebtedness, certificates of deposit, letters of credit, bills of credit or debit cards, financial transaction authorization mechanisms, marketable securities, or any computer system representations of any of them.

(b) As used in division (A)(10) of this section, "trade secret" has the same meaning as in section 1333.61 of the Revised Code, and "telecommunications service" and "information service" have the same meanings as in section 2913.01 of the Revised Code.

(c) As used in divisions (A)(10) and (13) of this section, "cable television service," "computer," "computer software," "computer system," "computer network," "data," and "telecommunications device" have the same meanings as in section 2913.01 of the Revised Code.

(11) "Law enforcement officer" means any of the following:

(a) A sheriff, deputy sheriff, constable, police officer of a township or joint township police district, marshal, deputy marshal, municipal police officer, member of a police force employed by a metropolitan housing authority under division (D) of section 3735.31 of the Revised Code, or state highway patrol trooper;

(b) An officer, agent, or employee of the state or any of its agencies, instrumentalities, or political subdivisions, upon whom, by statute, a duty to conserve the peace or to enforce all or certain laws is imposed and the authority to arrest violators is conferred, within the limits of that statutory duty and authority;

(c) A mayor, in the mayor's capacity as chief conservator of the peace within the mayor's municipal corporation;

(d) A member of an auxiliary police force organized by county, township, or municipal law enforcement authorities, within the scope of the member's appointment or commission;

(e) A person lawfully called pursuant to section 311.07 of the Revised Code to aid a sheriff in keeping the peace, for the purposes and during the time when the person is called;

(f) A person appointed by a mayor pursuant to section 737.01 of the Revised Code as a special patrolling officer during riot or emergency, for the purposes and during the time when the person is appointed;

(g) A member of the organized militia of this state or the armed forces of the United States, lawfully called to duty to aid civil authorities in keeping the peace or protect against domestic violence;

(h) A prosecuting attorney, assistant prosecuting attorney, secret service officer, or municipal prosecutor;

(i) A veterans' home police officer appointed under section 5907.02 of the Revised Code;

(j) A member of a police force employed by a regional transit authority under division (Y) of section 306.35 of the Revised Code;

(k) A special police officer employed by a port authority under section 4582.04 or 4582.28 of the Revised Code;

(*l*) The house of representatives sergeant at arms if the house of representatives sergeant at arms has arrest authority pursuant to division (E)(1) of section 101.311 of the Revised Code and an assistant house of representatives sergeant at arms;

(m) A special police officer employed by a municipal corporation at a municipal airport, or other municipal air navigation facility, that has scheduled operations, as defined in section 119.3 of Title 14 of the Code of Federal Regulations, 14 C.F.R. 119.3, as amended, and that is required to be under a security program and is governed by aviation security rules of the transportation security administration of the United States department of transportation as provided in Parts 1542. and 1544. of Title 49 of the Code of Federal Regulations, as amended.

(12) "Privilege" means an immunity, license, or right conferred by law, bestowed by express or implied grant, arising out of status, position, office, or relationship, or growing out of necessity.

(13) "Contraband" means any property that is illegal for a person to acquire or possess under a statute, ordinance, or rule, or that a trier of fact lawfully determines to be illegal to possess by reason of the property's involvement in an offense. "Contraband" includes, but is not limited to, all of the following:

(a) Any controlled substance, as defined in section 3719.01 of the Revised Code, or any device or paraphernalia;

(b) Any unlawful gambling device or paraphernalia;

(c) Any dangerous ordnance or obscene material.

(14) A person is "not guilty by reason of insanity" relative to a charge of an offense only if the person proves, in the manner specified in section 2901.05 of the Revised Code, that at the time of the commission of the offense, the person did not know, as a result of a severe mental disease or defect, the wrongfulness of the person's acts.

(B)(1)(a) Subject to division (B)(2) of this section, as used in any section contained in Title XXIX of the Revised Code that sets forth a criminal offense, "person" includes all of the following:

(i) An individual, corporation, business trust, estate, trust, partnership, and association;

(ii) An unborn human who is viable.

(b) As used in any section contained in Title XXIX of the Revised Code that does not set forth a criminal offense, "person" includes an individual, corporation, business trust, estate, trust, partnership, and association.

(c) As used in division (B)(1)(a) of this section:

(i) "Unborn human" means an individual organism of the species Homo sapiens from fertilization until live birth.

(ii) "Viable" means the stage of development of a human fetus at which there is a realistic possibility of maintaining and nourishing of a life outside the womb with or without temporary artificial life-sustaining support.

(2) Notwithstanding division (B)(1)(a) of this section, in no case shall the portion of the definition of the term "person" that is set forth in division (B)(1)(a)(ii) of this section be applied or construed in any section contained in Title XXIX of the Revised Code that sets forth a criminal offense in any of the following manners:

(a) Except as otherwise provided in division (B)(2)(a) of this section, in a manner so that the offense prohibits or is construed as prohibiting any pregnant woman or her physician from performing an abortion with the consent of the pregnant woman, with the consent of the pregnant woman implied by law in a medical emergency, or with the approval of one otherwise authorized by law to consent to medical treatment on behalf of the pregnant woman. An abortion that violates the conditions described in the immediately preceding sentence may be punished as a violation of section 2903.01, 2903.02, 2903.03, 2903.04, 2903.05, 2903.06, 2903.08, 2903.11, 2903.12, 2903.13, 2903.14, 2903.21, or 2903.22 of the Revised Code, as applicable. An abortion that does not violate the conditions described in the second immediately preceding sentence, but that does violate section 2919.12, division (B) of section 2919.13, or section 2919.151, 2919.17, or 2919.18 of the Revised Code, may be punished as a violation of section 2919.12, division (B) of section 2919.13, or section 2919.151, 2919.17, or 2919.18 of the Revised Code, as applicable. Consent is sufficient under this division if it is of the type otherwise adequate to permit medical treatment to the pregnant woman, even if it does not comply with section 2919.12 of the Revised Code.

(b) In a manner so that the offense is applied or is construed as applying to a woman based on an act or omission of the woman that occurs while she is or was pregnant and that results in any of the following:

(i) Her delivery of a stillborn baby;

(ii) Her causing, in any other manner, the death in utero of a viable, unborn human that she is carrying;

(iii) Her causing the death of her child who is born alive but who dies from one or more injuries that are sustained while the child is a viable, unborn human;

(iv) Her causing her child who is born alive to sustain one or more injuries while the child is a viable, unborn human;

(v) Her causing, threatening to cause, or attempting to cause, in any other manner, an injury, illness, or other physiological impairment, regardless of its duration or gravity, or a mental illness or condition, regardless of its duration or gravity, to a viable, unborn human that she is carrying.

(C) As used in Title XXIX of the Revised Code:

(1) "School safety zone" consists of a school, school building, school premises, school activity, and school bus.

(2) "School," "school building," and "school premises" have the same meanings as in section 2925.01 of the Revised Code.

(3) "School activity" means any activity held under the auspices of a board of education of a city, local, exempted village, joint vocational, or cooperative education school district; a governing authority of a community school established under Chapter 3314. of the Revised Code; a governing board of an educational service center; or the governing body of a nonpublic school for which the state board of education prescribes minimum standards under section 3301.07 of the Revised Code.

(4) "School bus" has the same meaning as in section 4511.01 of the Revised Code.

(2006 H 241, eff. 7-1-07; 2002 H 675, eff. 3-14-03; 2002 H 364, eff. 4-8-03; 2002 H 545, eff. 3-19-03; 2002 S 184, eff. 5-15-02; 2000 S 317, eff. 3-22-01; 2000 H 351, eff. 8-18-00; 2000 S 137, eff. 5-17-00; 1999 S 107, eff. 3-23-00; 1999 H 162, eff. 8-25-99; 1999 S 1, eff. 8-6-99; 1998 H 565, eff. 3-30-99; 1996 S 277, eff. 3-31-97; 1996 S 269, eff. 7-1-96; 1996 S 239, eff. 9-6-96; 1996 H 445, eff. 9-3-96; 1995 S 2, eff. 7-1-96; 1991 S 144, eff. 8-8-91; 1991 H 77; 1990 S 24; 1988 H 708, § 1)

Note: See also preceding version of this section in effect until 7-1-07.

Uncodified Law

1996 S 269, § 3, eff. 7-1-96, amended 1995 S 2, § 5, to read:

Sec. 5. The provisions of the Revised Code in existence prior to July 1, 1996, shall apply to a person upon whom a court imposed a term of imprisonment prior to that date and, notwithstanding division (B) of section 1.58 of the Revised Code, to a person upon whom a court, on or after that date and in accordance with the law in existence prior to that date, imposes a term of imprisonment for an offense that was committed prior to that date.

The provisions of the Revised Code in existence on and after July 1, 1996, apply to a person who commits an offense on or after that date.

Historical and Statutory Notes

Ed. Note: In the version eff. 7–1–07, comparison of these amendments [2006 H 241, eff. 7–1–07 and 2002 H 364, eff. 4–8–03] in pursuance of section 1.52 of the Revised Code discloses that they are not substantively irreconcilable so that they are required by that section to be harmonized to give effect to each amendment. In recognition of this rule of construction, changes made by 2006 H 241, eff. 7–1–07, and 2002 H 364, eff. 4–8–03, have been incorporated in the above amendment. See *Baldwin's Ohio Legislative Service Annotated*, 2006, page 7/L–__, and 2002, page 12/L–3050, or the OH–LEGIS or OH–LEGIS–OLD database on Westlaw, for original versions of these Acts.

Ed. Note: In the version eff. 3–14–03, a special endorsement by the Legislative Service Commission states, "Comparison of these amendments [2002 H 675, eff. 3–14–03, 2002 H 364, eff. 4–8–03, and 2002 H 545, eff. 3–19–03] in pursuance of section 1.52 of the Revised Code discloses that they are not irreconcilable so that they are required by that section to be harmonized to give effect to each amendment." In recognition of this rule of construction, changes made by 2002 H 675, eff. 3–14–03, 2002 H 364, eff. 4–8–03, and 2002 H 545, eff. 3–19–03, have been incorporated in the above amendment. See *Baldwin's Ohio Legislative Service Annotated*, 2002, pages 12/L–2105, 12/L–3050 and 12/L–2320, or the OH–LEGIS or OH–LEGIS–OLD database on Westlaw, for original versions of these Acts.

Ed. Note: Former 2901.01 repealed by 1988 H 708, § 2, eff. 4–19–88; 1988 H 708, § 18; 1987 H 231, § 1, 6, H 261, § 1, 3; 1986 H 428, § 1, 13, S 69, § 1, 3, H 49, § 1, 3; 1984 H 129, § 1, 3, H 632, S 183; 1982 H 269, § 4, S 199, H 437; 1972 H 511.

Ed. Note: Prior 2901.01 repealed by 1972 H 511, eff. 1–1–74; 1953 H 1; GC 12399, 12400; see now 2903.01 for provisions analogous to prior 2901.01.

Pre–1953 H 1 Amendments: 120 v 413; 118 v 288, § 25; RS 6808

Amendment Note: 2002 H 675 made nonsubstantive changes to the section.

Amendment Note: 2002 H 364 inserted "; a governing authority of a community school established under Chapter 3314. of the Revised Code" in division (C)(3); inserted "nonpublic" before "school" in division (C)(3); and made other nonsubstantive changes.

Amendment Note: 2002 H 545 added new division (A)(11)(m).

Amendment Note: 2002 S 184 added new division (A)(13)(k); and made other nonsubstantive changes.

Amendment Note: 2000 S 317 added division (A)(11)(*l*); and made other nonsubstantive changes.

Amendment Note: 2000 H 351 inserted "or" after "2919.13," twice and substituted "2919.151" for "2919.15" twice in division (B)(2)(a).

Amendment Note: 2000 S 137 added division (A)(11)(k); and made other nonsubstantive changes.

Amendment Note: 1999 S 107 deleted "2903.07," after "2903.06," in division (B)(2)(a).

Amendment Note: 1999 H 162 inserted "2913.15" and "or of division (B)(1), (2), (3), or (4) of section 2919.22" in division (A)(9)(a); and made other nonsubstantive changes.

Amendment Note: 1999 S 1 added division (C).

Amendment Note: 1998 H 565 rewrote division (A)(10); inserted ", or other telecommunications device" twice in division (A)(13)(j); and made other nonsubstantive changes. Prior to amendment, division (A)(10) read:

"(10)(a) 'Property' means any property, real or personal, tangible or intangible, and any interest or license in that property. 'Property' includes, but is not limited to, cable television service, computer data, computer software, financial instruments associated with computers, and other documents associated with computers, or copies of the documents, whether in machine or human readable form. 'Financial instruments associated with computers' include, but are not limited to, checks, drafts, warrants, money orders, notes of indebtedness, certificates of deposit, letters of credit, bills of credit or debit cards, financial transaction authorization mechanisms, marketable securities, or any computer system representations of any of them.

"(b) As used in this division and division (A)(13) of this section, 'cable television service,' 'computer,' 'computer software,' 'computer system,' 'computer network,' and 'data' have the same meaning as in section 2913.01 of the Revised Code."

Amendment Note: 1996 S 277 substituted "(A)(13)" for "(M)" in division (A)(10)(b); inserted ", including, but not limited to, goods and personal property described in division (D) of section 2913.34 of the Revised Code" in division (A)(13)(b); inserted ", and goods and personal property described in division (D) of section 2913.34 of the Revised Code" in division (A)(13)(d); and made other nonsubstantive changes.

Amendment Note: 1996 S 269 deleted a statutory reference to section "2911.12," following "2911.11" and inserted "or of division (A)(1), (2), or (3) of section 2911.12" in division (I)(1); inserted "or division" in division (I)(2); made other changes to reflect gender neutral language; and made other nonsubstantive changes.

Amendment Note: 1996 S 239 designated division (A); redesignated former divisions (A) through (N) as divisions (A)(1) through (A)(14); redesignated former divisions (E)(1) through (E)(5) as divisions (A)(5)(a) through (A)(5)(e); redesignated former divisions (F)(1) and (F)(2) as divisions (A)(6)(a) and (A)(6)(b); redesignated former divisions (I)(1) through (I)(4) as divisions (A)(9)(a) through (A)(9)(d); redesignated former divisions (J)(1) and (J)(2) as divisions (A)(10)(a) and (A)(10)(b); redesignated former divisions (K)(1) through (K)(10) as divisions (A)(11)(a) through (A)(11)(j); redesignated former divisions (M)(1) through (M)(10) as divisions (A)(13)(a) through (A)(13)(j); substituted "(A)(9)(a)" for "(I)(1)" in division (A)(9)(b); substituted "(A)(9)(a), (b), or (c)" for "(I)(1), (2), or (3)" in division (A)(9)(d); added division (B); and made changes to reflect gender neutral language.

Amendment Note: 1996 H 445 deleted "2907.12," and added "or felonious sexual penetration in violation of former section 2907.12 of the Revised Code" in division (I)(1); added "or offense" following "to any section" in division (I)(2); and substituted "patrolling" for "patrolman or" in division (K)(6).

Amendment Note: 1995 S 2 added references to sections 2903.211, 2907.05, 2921.04, and 2923.161 in and removed references to sections 2909.04, 2909.05, 2921.35, 2923.12, and 2923.13 from division (I)(1); added division (K)(10); and made changes to reflect gender neutral language and other nonsubstantive changes.

Library References

Criminal Law ⇔5.
Westlaw Topic No. 110.
C.J.S. Criminal Law §§ 19, 21.

2901.05 Presumption of innocence; proof of offense; of affirmative defense; as to each; reasonable doubt

(A) Every person accused of an offense is presumed innocent until proven guilty beyond a reasonable doubt, and the burden of proof for all elements of the offense is upon the prosecution. The burden of going forward with the evidence of an affirmative defense, and the burden of proof, by a preponderance of the evidence, for an affirmative defense, is upon the accused.

(B) As part of its charge to the jury in a criminal case, the court shall read the definitions of "reasonable doubt" and "proof beyond a reasonable doubt," contained in division (D) of this section.

(C) As used in this section, an "affirmative defense" is either of the following:

(1) A defense expressly designated as affirmative;

(2) A defense involving an excuse or justification peculiarly within the knowledge of the accused, on which he can fairly be required to adduce supporting evidence.

(D) "Reasonable doubt" is present when the jurors, after they have carefully considered and compared all the evidence, cannot say they are firmly convinced of the truth of the charge. It is a doubt based on reason and common sense. Reasonable doubt is not mere possible doubt, because everything relating to human affairs or depending on moral evidence is open to some possible or imaginary doubt. "Proof beyond a reasonable doubt" is proof of such character that an ordinary person would be willing to rely and act upon it in the most important of his own affairs.

(1978 H 1168, eff. 11–1–78; 1972 H 511)

Historical and Statutory Notes

Ed. Note: 2901.05 contains provisions analogous to former 2945.04, repealed by 1973 H 716, eff. 1–1–74.

Ed. Note: Former 2901.05 repealed by 1972 H 511, eff. 1–1–74; 1953 H 1; GC 12403; see now 2903.02 for provisions analogous to former 2901.05.

Pre–1953 H 1 Amendments: 124 v H 53; RS 6810

Library References

Criminal Law ⚖308, 328, 330, 561, 789.
Westlaw Topic No. 110.
C.J.S. Criminal Law §§ 682 to 683, 686, 688 to 689, 696, 1108, 1342.

2901.07 DNA testing of certain prisoners

(A) As used in this section:

(1) "DNA analysis" and "DNA specimen" have the same meanings as in section 109.573 of the Revised Code.

(2) "Jail" and "community-based correctional facility" have the same meanings as in section 2929.01 of the Revised Code.

(3) "Post–release control" has the same meaning as in section 2967.01 of the Revised Code.

(B)(1) Regardless of when the conviction occurred or the guilty plea was entered, a person who has been convicted of, is convicted of, has pleaded guilty to, or pleads guilty to a felony offense and who is sentenced to a prison term or to a community residential sanction in a jail or community-based correctional facility for that offense pursuant to section 2929.16 of the Revised Code, and a person who has been convicted of, is convicted of, has pleaded guilty to, or pleads guilty to a misdemeanor offense listed in division (D) of this section and who is sentenced to a term of imprisonment for that offense shall submit to a DNA specimen collection procedure administered by the director of rehabilitation and correction or the chief administrative officer of the jail or other detention facility in which the person is serving the term of imprisonment. If the person serves the prison term in a state correctional institution, the director of rehabilitation and correction shall cause the DNA specimen to be collected from the person during the intake process at the reception facility designated by the director. If the person serves the community residential sanction or term of imprisonment in a jail, a community-based correctional facility, or another county, multicounty, municipal, municipal-county, or multicounty-municipal detention facility, the chief administrative officer of the jail, community-based correctional facility, or detention facility shall cause the DNA specimen to be collected from the person during the intake process at the jail, community-based correctional facility, or detention facility. The DNA specimen shall be collected in accordance with division (C) of this section.

(2) Regardless of when the conviction occurred or the guilty plea was entered, if a person has been convicted of, is convicted of, has pleaded guilty to, or pleads guilty to a felony offense or a misdemeanor offense listed in division (D) of this section, is serving a prison term, community residential sanction, or term of imprisonment for that offense, and does not provide a DNA specimen pursuant to division (B)(1) of this section, prior to the person's release from the prison term, community residential sanction, or imprisonment, the person shall submit to, and the director of rehabilitation and correction or the chief administrative officer of the jail, community-based correctional facility, or detention facility in which the person is serving the prison term, community residential sanction, or term of imprisonment shall administer, a DNA specimen collection procedure at the state correctional institution, jail, community-based correctional facility, or detention facility in which the person is serving the prison term, community residential sanction, or term of imprisonment. The DNA specimen shall be collected in accordance with division (C) of this section.

(3)(a) Regardless of when the conviction occurred or the guilty plea was entered, if a person has been convicted of, is convicted of, has pleaded guilty to, or pleads guilty to a felony offense or a misdemeanor offense listed in division (D) of this section and the person is on probation, released on parole, under transitional control, on community control, on post-release control, or under any other type of supervised release under the supervision of a probation department or the adult parole authority for that offense, the person shall submit to a DNA specimen collection procedure administered by the chief administrative officer of the probation department or the adult parole authority. The DNA specimen shall be collected in accordance with division (C) of this section. If the person refuses to submit to a DNA specimen collection procedure as provided in this division, the person may be subject to the provisions of section 2967.15 of the Revised Code.

(b) If a person to whom division (B)(3)(a) of this section applies is sent to jail or is returned to a jail, community-based correctional facility, or state correctional institution for a violation of the terms and conditions of the probation, parole, transitional control, other release, or post-release control, if the person was or will be serving a term of imprisonment, prison term, or community residential sanction for committing a felony offense or for committing a misdemeanor offense listed in division (D) of this section, and if the person did not provide a DNA specimen pursuant to division (B)(1), (2) or (3)(a) of this section, the person shall submit to, and the director of rehabilitation and correction or the chief administrative officer of the jail or community-based correctional facility shall administer, a DNA specimen collection procedure at the jail, community-based correctional facility, or state correctional institution in which the person is serving the term of imprisonment, prison term, or community residential sanction. The DNA specimen shall be collected from the person in accordance with division (C) of this section.

(4) Regardless of when the conviction occurred or the guilty plea was entered, if a person has been convicted of, is convicted of, has pleaded guilty to, or pleads guilty to a felony offense or a misdemeanor offense listed in division (D) of this section, the person is not sentenced to a prison term, a community residential sanction in a jail or community-based correctional facility, a term of imprisonment, or any type of supervised release under the supervision of a probation department or the adult parole authority, and the person does not provide a DNA specimen pursuant to division (B)(1), (2), (3)(a), or (3)(b) of this section, the sentencing court shall order the person to report to the county probation department immediately after sentencing to submit to a DNA specimen collection procedure administered by the chief administrative officer of the county probation office. If the person is incarcerated at the time of sentencing, the person shall submit to a DNA specimen collection procedure administered by the director of rehabilitation and correction or the chief administrative officer of the jail or other detention facility in which the person is incarcerated. The DNA specimen shall be collected in accordance with division (C) of this section.

(C) If the DNA specimen is collected by withdrawing blood from the person or a similarly invasive procedure, a physician, registered nurse, licensed practical nurse, duly licensed clinical laboratory technician, or other qualified medical practitioner shall collect in a medically approved manner the DNA specimen required to be collected pursuant to division (B) of this section. If the DNA specimen is collected by swabbing for buccal cells or a similarly noninvasive procedure, this section does not require that the DNA specimen be collected by a qualified medical practitioner of that nature. No later than fifteen days after the date of the collection of the DNA specimen, the director of rehabilitation and correction or the chief administrative officer of the jail, community-based correctional facility, or other county, multicounty, municipal, municipal-county, or multicounty-municipal detention facility, in which the person is serving the prison term, community residential sanction, or term of imprisonment shall cause the DNA specimen to be forwarded to the bureau of criminal identification and investigation in accordance with procedures established by the superintendent of the bureau under division (H) of section 109.573 of the Revised Code. The bureau shall provide the specimen vials, mailing tubes, labels, postage, and instructions needed for the collection and forwarding of the DNA specimen to the bureau.

(D) The director of rehabilitation and correction, the chief administrative officer of the jail, community-based correctional facility, or other county, multicounty, municipal, municipal-county, or multicounty-municipal detention facility, or the chief administrative officer of a county probation department or the adult parole authority shall cause a DNA specimen to be collected in accordance with divisions (B) and (C) of this section from a person in its custody or under its supervision who has been convicted of, is convicted of, has pleaded guilty to, or pleads guilty to any felony offense or any of the following misdemeanor offenses:

(1) A misdemeanor violation, an attempt to commit a misdemeanor violation, or complicity in committing a misdemeanor violation of section 2907.04 of the Revised Code;

(2) A misdemeanor violation of any law that arose out of the same facts and circumstances and same act as did a charge against the person of a violation of section 2903.01, 2903.02, 2905.01, 2907.02, 2907.03, 2907.04, 2907.05, or 2911.11 of the Revised Code that previously was dismissed or amended or as did a charge against the person of a violation of section 2907.12 of the Revised Code as it existed prior to September 3, 1996, that previously was dismissed or amended;

(3) A misdemeanor violation of section 2919.23 of the Revised Code that would have been a violation of section 2905.04 of the Revised Code as it existed prior to July 1, 1996, had it been committed prior to that date;

(4) A sexually oriented offense or a child-victim oriented offense, both as defined in section 2950.01 of the Revised Code, that is a misdemeanor, if, in relation to that offense, the offender has been adjudicated a sexual predator, child-victim predator, habitual sex offender, or habitual child-victim offender, all as defined in section 2950.01 of the Revised Code.

(E) The director of rehabilitation and correction may prescribe rules in accordance with Chapter 119. of the Revised Code to collect a DNA specimen, as provided in this section, from an offender whose supervision is transferred from another state to this state in accordance with the interstate compact for adult offender supervision described in section 5149.21 of the Revised Code.

(2006 S 262, eff. 7–11–06; 2005 H 66, eff. 6–30–05 (see Historical and Statutory Notes); 2004 H 525, eff. 5–18–05; 2003 S 5, eff. 7–31–03; 2002 H 427, eff. 8–29–02; 1998 H 526, eff. 9–1–98; 1997 S 111, eff. 3–17–98; 1996 H 124, eff. 3–31–97; 1996 H 180, eff. 1–1–97; 1996 S 269, eff. 7–1–96; 1995 H 5, eff. 8–30–95)

Uncodified Law

2006 S 262, § 3, eff. 7–11–06, reads:

(A) The General Assembly hereby declares that its purpose in amending section 2901.07 of the Revised Code in Sections 1 and 2 of this act is to reaffirm that it is the General Assembly's intent that, under that section as it existed prior to the effective date of this act, a person who is in any of the categories of offenders described in division (B)(1), (2), (3), or (4) of that section in relation to a conviction of or plea of guilty to a felony offense or a misdemeanor offense listed in division (D) of that section is subject to the DNA specimen collection provisions of divisions (B) and (C) of that section regardless of when the conviction of or plea of guilty to the felony offense or the misdemeanor offense occurs or is entered.

(B) The General Assembly declares that it believes that the amendments to section 2901.07 of the Revised Code made in Sections 1 and 2 of this act are not substantive in nature and merely clarify that divisions (B)(1), (2), and (3) and (C) of that section operate as described in division (A) of this Section, and that the amendments to section 2901.07 of the Revised Code made in Sections 1 and 2 of this act thus are remedial in nature. The General Assembly declares that it intends that the clarifying, remedial amendments to section 2901.07 of the Revised Code made in Sections 1 and 2 of this act apply to all convicted offenders described in division (A) of this Section, regardless of when they were convicted of or pleaded guilty to the felony or the specified misdemeanor or are convicted of or plead guilty to the felony or the specified misdemeanor.

(C) In compliance with the Ohio Supreme Court decision in *Van Fossen v. Babcock & Wilcox Co.* (1988), 36 Ohio St.3d 100, and with section 1.48 of the Revised Code, the General Assembly expressly states its intent that the amendments to section 2901.07 of the Revised Code made in Sections 1 and 2 of this act shall apply retrospectively.

Historical and Statutory Notes

Ed. Note: The legal review and technical services staff of the Legislative Service Commission has issued an opinion regarding the treatment of multiple amendments [2005 H 66, eff. 6–30–05 and 2004 H 525, eff. 5–18–05] under R.C. 1.52 stating, "H 525 prevails. The amendment by HB 66 is ineffective. The amendment by HB 525 in effect repealed the section HB 66 attempted to amend. Since the amendment by HB 525 was in effect the section HB 66 tried to amend did not exist." The opinions are neither legally authoritative nor binding. See *Baldwin's Ohio Legislative Service Annotated*, 2005, page 5/L–873, and 2004, page 11/L–2635, or the OH-LEGIS or OH-LEGIS-OLD database on Westlaw, for original versions of these Acts.

Ed. Note: Former 2901.07 repealed by 1972 H 511, eff. 1–1–74, 1953 H 1; GC 12401–1; see now 2903.04 for provisions analogous to former 2901.07.

Pre–1953 H 1 Amendments: 124 v H 444

Amendment Note: 2006 S 262 inserted "Regardless of when the conviction occurred or the guilty plea was entered," at the beginning of divisions (B)(1), (2), (3)(a), and (4); inserted "has been convicted of," preceding "is convicted of" and inserted ", has pleaded guilty to," following 'is convicted of" in divisions (B)(1), (2), (3)(a), (4), and (D); inserted "for that offense" preceding "pursuant to section" in division (B)(1); and inserted "for that offense" preceding "shall submit to a DNA" in divisions (B)(1) and (B)(3)(a); inserted "to whom division (B)(3)(a) of this section applies" in division (B)(3)(b); and made other nonsubstantive changes.

Amendment Note: 2005 H 66 substituted "5502.61" for "181.51" in the first paragraph of division (E).

Amendment Note: 2004 H 525 rewrote divisions (B) through (E), which prior thereto read:

"(B)(1) A person who is convicted of or pleads guilty to a felony offense listed in division (D) of this section and who is sentenced to a prison term or to a community residential sanction in a jail or community-based correctional facility pursuant to section 2929.16 of the Revised Code, and a person who is convicted of or pleads guilty to a misdemeanor offense listed in division (D) of this section and who is sentenced to a term of imprisonment shall submit to a DNA specimen collection procedure administered by the director of rehabilitation and correction or the chief administrative officer of the jail or other detention facility in which the person is serving the term of imprisonment. If the person serves the prison term in a state correctional institution, the director of rehabilitation and correction shall cause the DNA specimen to be collected from the person during the intake process at the reception facility designated by the director. If the person serves the community residential sanction or term of imprisonment in a jail, a community-based correctional facility, or another county, multicounty, municipal, municipal-county, or multicounty-municipal detention facility, the chief administrative officer of the jail, community-based correctional facility, or detention facility shall cause the DNA specimen to be collected from the person during the intake process at the jail, community-based correctional facility, or detention facility. In accordance with division (C) of this section, the director or the chief administrative officer shall cause the DNA specimen to be forwarded to the bureau of criminal identification and investigation no later than fifteen days after the date of the collection of the DNA specimen. The DNA specimen shall be collected in accordance with division (C) of this section.

"(2) If a person is convicted of or pleads guilty to an offense listed in division (D) of this section, is serving a prison term, community residential sanction, or term of imprisonment for that offense, and does not provide a DNA specimen pursuant to division (B)(1) of this section, prior to the person's release from the prison term, community residential sanction, or imprisonment, the person shall submit to, and the director of rehabilitation and correction or the chief administrative officer of the jail, community-based correctional facility, or detention facility in which the person is serving the prison term, community residential sanction, or term of imprisonment shall administer, a DNA specimen collection procedure at the state correctional institution, jail, community-based correctional facility, or detention facility in which the person is serving the prison term, community residential sanction, or term of imprisonment. In accordance with division (C) of this section, the director or the chief administrative officer shall cause the DNA specimen to be forwarded to the bureau of criminal identification and investigation no later than fifteen days after the date of the collection of the DNA specimen. The DNA specimen shall be collected in accordance with division (C) of this section.

"(3) If a person sentenced to a term of imprisonment or serving a prison term or community residential sanction for committing an offense listed in division (D) of this section is on probation, is released on parole, under transitional control, or on another type of release, or is on post-release control, if the person is under the supervision of a probation department or the adult parole authority, if the person is sent to jail or is returned to a jail, community-based correctional facility, or state correctional institution for a violation of the terms and conditions of the probation, parole, transitional control, other release, or post-release control, if the person was or will be serving a term of imprisonment, prison term, or community residential sanction for committing an offense listed in division (D) of this section, and if the person did not provide a DNA specimen pursuant to division (B)(1) or (2) of this section, the person shall submit to, and the director of rehabilitation and correction or the chief administrative officer of the jail or community-based correctional facility shall administer, a DNA specimen collection procedure at the jail, community-based correctional facility, or state correctional institution in which the person is serving the term of imprisonment, prison term, or community residential sanction. In accordance with division (C) of this section, the director or the chief administrative officer shall cause the DNA specimen to be forwarded to the bureau of criminal identification and investigation no later than fifteen days after the date of the collection of the DNA specimen. The DNA specimen shall be collected from the person in accordance with division (C) of this section.

"(C) If the DNA specimen is collected by withdrawing blood from the person or a similarly invasive procedure, a physician, registered nurse, licensed practical nurse, duly licensed clinical laboratory technician, or other qualified medical practitioner shall collect in a medically approved manner the DNA specimen required to be collected pursuant to division (B) of this section. If the DNA specimen is collected by swabbing for buccal cells or a similarly noninvasive procedure, this section does not require that the DNA specimen be collected by a qualified medical practitioner of that nature. No later than fifteen days after the date of the collection of the DNA specimen, the director of rehabilitation and correction or the chief administrative officer of the jail, community-based correctional facility, or any county, multicounty, municipal, municipal-county, or multicounty-municipal detention facility, in which the person is serving the prison term, community residential sanction, or term of imprisonment shall cause the DNA specimen to be forwarded to the bureau of criminal identification and investigation in accordance with procedures established by the superintendent of the bureau under division (H) of section 109.573 of the Revised Code. The bureau shall provide the specimen vials, mailing tubes, labels, postage, and instructions needed for the collection and forwarding of the DNA specimen to the bureau.

"(D) The director of rehabilitation and correction and the chief administrative officer of the jail, community-based correctional facility, or other county, multicounty, municipal, municipal-county, or multicounty-municipal detention facility shall cause a DNA specimen to be collected in accordance with divisions (B) and (C) of this section from a person in its custody who is convicted of or pleads guilty to any of the following offenses:

"(1) A violation of section 2903.01, 2903.02, 2903.11, 2905.01, 2907.02, 2907.03, 2907.04, 2907.05, 2911.01, 2911.02, 2911.11, or 2911.12 of the Revised Code;

"(2) A violation of section 2907.12 of the Revised Code as it existed prior to September 3, 1996;

"(3) An attempt to commit a violation of section 2903.01, 2903.02, 2907.02, 2907.03, 2907.04, or 2907.05 of the Revised Code or to commit a violation of section 2907.12 of the Revised Code as it existed prior to September 3, 1996;

"(4) A violation of any law that arose out of the same facts and circumstances and same act as did a charge against the person of a violation of section 2903.01, 2903.02, 2905.01, 2907.02, 2907.03, 2907.04, 2907.05, or 2911.11 of the Revised Code that previously was dismissed or amended or as did a charge against the person of a violation of section 2907.12 of the Revised Code as it existed prior to September 3, 1996, that previously was dismissed or amended;

"(5) A violation of section 2905.02 or 2919.23 of the Revised Code that would have been a violation of section 2905.04 of the Revised Code as it existed prior to July 1, 1996, had it been committed prior to that date;

"(6) A sexually oriented offense or a child-victim oriented offense, both as defined in section 2950.01 of the Revised Code, if, in relation to that offense, the offender has been adjudicated a sexual predator or a child-victim predator, both as defined in section 2950.01 of the Revised Code;

"(7) A felony violation of any law that arose out of the same facts and circumstances and same act as did a charge against the person of a violation of section 2903.11, 2911.01, 2911.02, or 2911.12 of the Revised Code that previously was dismissed or amended;

"(8) A conspiracy to commit a violation of section 2903.01, 2903.02, 2905.01, 2911.01, 2911.02, 2911.11, or 2911.12 of the Revised Code;

"(9) Complicity in committing a violation of section 2903.01, 2903.02, 2903.11, 2905.01, 2907.02, 2907.03, 2907.04, 2907.05, 2911.01, 2911.02, 2911. 11, or 2911.12 of the Revised Code or a violation of section 2907.12 of the Revised Code as it existed prior to September 3, 1996.

"(E) The director of rehabilitation and correction or a chief administrative officer of a jail, community-based correctional facility, or other detention facility described in division (B) of this section in relation to the following offenses is not required to comply with this section until the superintendent of the bureau of criminal identification and investigation gives agencies in the criminal justice system, as defined in section 181.51 of the Revised Code, in the state official notification that the state DNA laboratory is prepared to accept DNA specimens of that nature:

"(1) A violation of section 2903.11, 2911.01, 2911.02, or 2911.12 of the Revised Code;

"(2) An attempt to commit a violation of section 2903.01 or 2903.02 of the Revised Code;

"(3) A felony violation of any law that arose out of the same facts and circumstances and same act as did a charge against the person of a violation of section 2903.11, 2911.01, 2911.02, or 2911.12 of the Revised Code that previously was dismissed or amended;

"(4) A conspiracy to commit a violation of section 2903.01, 2903.02, 2905.01, 2911.01, 2911.02, 2911.11, or 2911.12 of the Revised Code;

"(5) Complicity in committing a violation of section 2903.01, 2903.02, 2903.11, 2905.01, 2907.02, 2907.03, 2907.04, 2907.05, 2911.01, 2911.02, 2911. 11, or 2911.12 of the Revised Code or a violation of section 2907.12 of the Revised Code as it existed prior to September 3, 1996."

Amendment Note: 2003 S 5 rewrote division (D)(6), which prior thereto read:

"(6) A sexually oriented offense, as defined in section 2950.01 of the Revised Code, if, in relation to that offense, the offender has been adjudicated as being a sexual predator, as defined in section 2950. 01 of the Revised Code;"

Amendment Note: 2002 H 427 rewrote divisions (B)(3), (C), (D) and (E), which prior thereto read:

"(3) If a person serving a prison term or community residential sanction for a felony is released on parole, under transitional control, or on another type of release or is on post-release control, if the person is under the supervision of the adult parole authority, if the person is returned to a jail, community-based correctional facility, or state correctional institution for a violation of the terms and conditions of the parole, transitional control, other release, or post-release control, if the person was or will be serving a prison term or community residential sanction for committing an offense listed in division (D) of this section, and if the person did not provide a DNA specimen pursuant to division (B)(1) or (2) of this section, the person shall submit to, and the director of rehabilitation and correction or the chief administrative officer of the jail or community-based correctional facility shall administer, a DNA specimen collection procedure at the jail, community-based correctional facility, or state correctional institution in which the person is serving the prison term or community residential sanction. In accordance with division (C) of this section, the director or the chief administrative officer shall cause the DNA specimen to be forwarded to the bureau of criminal identification and investigation no later than fifteen days after the date of the collection of the DNA specimen. The DNA specimen shall be collected from the person in accordance with division (C) of this section.

"(C) A physician, registered nurse, licensed practical nurse, duly licensed clinical laboratory technician, or other qualified medical practitioner shall collect in a medically approved manner the DNA specimen required to be collected pursuant to division (B) of this section. No later than fifteen days after the date of the collection of the DNA specimen, the director of rehabilitation and correction or the chief administrative officer of the jail, community-based correctional facility, or other county, multi-county, municipal, municipal-county, or multicounty-municipal detention facility, in which the person is serving the prison term, community residential sanction, or term of imprisonment shall cause the DNA specimen to be forwarded to the bureau of criminal identification and investigation in accordance with procedures established by the superintendent of the bureau under division (H) of section 109.573 of the Revised Code. The bureau shall provide the specimen vials, mailing tubes, labels, postage, and instructions needed for the collection and forwarding of the DNA specimen to the bureau.

"(D) The director of rehabilitation and correction and the chief administrative officer of the jail, community-based correctional facility, or other county, multicounty, municipal, municipal-county, or multicounty-municipal detention facility shall cause a DNA specimen to be collected in accordance with divisions (B) and (C) of this section from a person in its custody who is convicted of or pleads guilty to any of the following offenses:

"(1) A violation of section 2903.01, 2903.02, 2905.01, 2907.02, 2907.03, 2907.04, 2907.05, or 2911.11 of the Revised Code;

"(2) A violation of section 2907.12 of the Revised Code as it existed prior to September 3, 1996;

"(3) An attempt to commit a violation of section 2907.02, 2907.03, 2907.04, or 2907.05 of the Revised Code or to commit a violation of section 2907.12 of the Revised Code as it existed prior to September 3, 1996;

"(4) A violation of any law that arose out of the same facts and circumstances and same act as did a charge against the person of a violation of section 2903.01, 2903.02, 2905.01, 2907.02, 2907.03, 2907.04, 2907.05, or 2911.11 of the Revised Code that previously was dismissed or amended or as did a charge against the person of a violation of section 2907.12 of the Revised Code as it existed prior to September 3, 1996, that previously was dismissed or amended;

"(5) A violation of section 2905.02 or 2919.23 of the Revised Code that would have been a violation of section 2905.04 of the Revised Code as it existed prior to July 1, 1996, had it been committed prior to that date;

"(6) A sexually oriented offense, as defined in section 2950.01 of the Revised Code, if, in relation to that offense, the offender has been adjudicated as being a sexual predator, as defined in section 2950.01 of the Revised Code.

"(E) The director of rehabilitation and correction or a chief administrative officer of a jail, community-based correctional facility, or other detention facility described in division (B) of this section is not required to comply with this section until the superintendent of the bureau of criminal identification and investigation gives agencies in the criminal justice system, as defined in section 181.51 of the Revised Code, in the state official notification that the state DNA laboratory is prepared to accept DNA specimens."

Amendment Note: 1998 H 526 added references to sections 2903.01, 2903.02, 2905.01, and 2911.11 and inserted "or amended" twice in division (D)(4).

Amendment Note: 1997 S 111 substituted "2967.01" for "2967.28" in division (A)(3); substituted "under transitional control" and "transitional control" for "furlough" in division (B)(3); and made other nonsubstantive changes.

Amendment Note: 1996 S 269 rewrote the section, which prior thereto read:

"(A) As used in this section, "DNA analysis" and "DNA specimen" have the same meanings as in section 109.573 of the Revised Code.

"(B)(1) A person who is convicted of or pleads guilty to committing an offense listed in division (D) of this section and who is sentenced to a term of imprisonment shall submit to a DNA specimen collection procedure administered by the director of rehabilitation and correction or the chief administrative officer of the detention facility, jail, or workhouse in which the person is serving the term of imprisonment. If the person serves the term of imprisonment in a state correctional institution, the director of rehabilitation and correction shall cause the DNA specimen to be collected from the person during the intake process at the reception facility designated by the director. If the person serves the term of imprisonment in a county, multicounty, municipal, municipal-county, or multicounty-municipal detention facility or a jail or workhouse, the chief administrative officer of the detention facility, jail, or workhouse shall cause the DNA specimen to be collected from the person during the intake process at the detention facility, jail, or workhouse. In accordance with division (C) of this section, the director of rehabilitation and correction or the chief administrative officer of the detention facility, jail, or workhouse in which the person is serving the term of imprisonment shall cause the DNA specimen to be forwarded to the bureau of criminal identification and investigation no later than fifteen days after the date of the collection of the DNA specimen. The DNA specimen shall be collected in accordance with division (C) of this section.

"(2) If a person is convicted of or pleads guilty to committing an offense listed in division (D) of this section, is serving a term of imprisonment for that offense, and did not provide a DNA specimen pursuant to division (B)(1) of this section, prior to the person's release from imprisonment, the person shall submit to, and director of rehabilitation and correction or the chief administrative officer of the detention facility, jail, or workhouse in which the person is serving the term of imprisonment shall administer, a DNA specimen collection procedure at the state correctional institution, detention facility, jail, or workhouse in which the person is serving the term of imprisonment. In accordance with division (C) of this section, the director of rehabilitation and correction or the chief administrative officer of the detention facility, jail, or workhouse in which the person is serving the term of imprisonment shall cause the DNA specimen to be forwarded to the bureau of criminal identification and investigation no later than fifteen days after the date of the collection of the DNA specimen. The DNA specimen shall be collected in accordance with division (C) of this section.

"(3) If an inmate is released on parole, furlough, or other release, is under the supervision of the adult parole authority, is returned to a state correctional institution for a violation of a condition of his parole, furlough, or other release, was or will be serving a term of imprisonment for committing an offense listed in division (D) of this section, and did not provide a DNA specimen pursuant to division (B)(1) or (2) of this section, the inmate shall submit to, and the director of rehabilitation and correction shall administer, a DNA specimen collection procedure at the state correctional institution in which the person is serving the term of imprisonment. In accordance with division (C) of this section, the director of rehabilitation and correction shall cause the DNA specimen to be forwarded to the bureau of criminal identification and investigation no later than fifteen days after the date of the collection of the DNA specimen. The DNA specimen shall be collected from the inmate in accordance with division (C) of this section.

"(C) A physician, registered nurse, licensed practical nurse, duly licensed clinical laboratory technician, or other qualified medical practitioner shall collect in a medically approved manner the DNA specimen required to be collected pursuant to division (B) of this section. No later than fifteen days after the date of the collection of the DNA specimen, the director of rehabilitation and correction or the chief administrative officer of the county, multicounty, municipal, municipal-county, or multicounty-municipal detention facility, jail, or workhouse in which the person is serving the term of imprisonment shall cause the DNA specimen to be forwarded to the bureau of criminal identification and investigation in accordance with procedures established by the superintendent of the bureau under division (H) of section 109.573 of the Revised Code. The bureau shall provide the specimen vials, mailing tubes, labels, postage, and instructions needed for the collection and forwarding of the DNA specimen to the bureau.

"(D) The director of rehabilitation and correction and the chief administrative officer of the county, multicounty, municipal, municipal-county, or multicounty-municipal detention facility or jail or workhouse shall cause a DNA specimen to be collected in accordance with divisions (B) and (C) of this section from a person in its custody who is convicted of or pleads guilty to one of the following offenses:

"(1) A violation of section 2903.01, 2903.02, 2905.01, 2905.04, 2907.02, 2907.03, 2907.04, 2907.05, 2907.12, or 2911.11 of the Revised Code;

"(2) An attempt to commit a violation of section 2907.02, 2907.03, 2907.04, 2907.05, or 2907.12 of the Revised Code;

"(3) A violation that arose out of the same facts and circumstances and same act as did a charge against the person of a violation of section 2907.02, 2907.03, 2907.04, 2907.05, or 2907.12 of the Revised Code that was previously dismissed.

"(E) The director of rehabilitation and correction or a chief administrative officer of a detention facility, jail, or workhouse described in division (B) of this section is not required to comply with this section until the superintendent of the bureau of criminal identification and investigation gives agencies in the criminal justice system, as defined in section 181.51 of the Revised Code, in the state official notification that the state DNA laboratory is prepared to accept DNA specimens."

Amendment Note: 1996 H 124 rewrote division (D), which prior thereto read:

"(D) The director of rehabilitation and correction and the chief administrative officer of the jail, community-based correctional facility, or other county, multicounty, municipal, municipal-county, or multicounty-municipal detention facility shall cause a DNA specimen to be collected in accordance with divisions (B) and (C) of this section from a person in its custody who is convicted of or pleads guilty to any of the following offenses:

"(1) A violation of section 2903.01, 2903.02, 2905.01, 2907.02, 2907.03, 2907.04, 2907.05, 2907.12, or 2911.11 of the Revised Code;

"(2) An attempt to commit a violation of section 2907.02, 2907.03, 2907.04, 2907.05, or 2907.12 of the Revised Code;

"(3) A violation of any law that arose out of the same facts and circumstances and same act as did a charge against the person of a violation of section 2907.02, 2907.03, 2907.04, 2907.05, or 2907.12 of the Revised Code that previously was dismissed;

"(4) A violation of section 2905.02 or 2919.23 of the Revised Code that would have been a violation of section 2905.04 of the Revised Code as it existed prior to July 1, 1996, had it been committed prior to that date;

"(5) A sexually oriented offense, as defined in section 2950.01 of the Revised Code, if, in relation to that offense, the offender has been adjudicated as being a sexual predator, as defined in section 2950.01 of the Revised Code."

Amendment Note: 1996 H 180 made amendments identical to 1996 S 269 and added division (D)(5).

Library References

Searches and Seizures ⚖78.
Westlaw Topic No. 349.
C.J.S. Searches and Seizures §§ 31, 103 to 106.
Baldwin's Ohio Legislative Service, 1995 H 5—LSC Analysis, p 5/L–336

CHAPTER 2945

TRIAL

INSANITY

Section	
2945.37	Competence to stand trial; raising of issue; procedures; municipal courts
2945.371	Evaluations of mental condition
2945.38	Effect of findings; treatment or continuing evaluation and treatment of incompetent; medication; disposition of defendant; report; additional hearings; discharge
2945.39	Civil commitment; expiration of time for treatment; jurisdiction; hearing; reports
2945.391	Applicability of not guilty by reason of insanity plea; impairment of reason not defense
2945.392	Battered woman syndrome
2945.40	Verdict of not guilty by reason of insanity; effects; procedures; hearings; rights; commitment
2945.401	Nonsecured status or termination of commitment; reports on competence; jurisdiction; hearing
2945.402	Conditional release

INSANITY

2945.37 Competence to stand trial; raising of issue; procedures; municipal courts

(A) As used in sections 2945.37 to 2945.402 of the Revised Code:

(1) "Prosecutor" means a prosecuting attorney or a city director of law, village solicitor, or similar chief legal officer of a municipal corporation who has authority to prosecute a criminal case that is before the court or the criminal case in which a defendant in a criminal case has been found incompetent to stand trial or not guilty by reason of insanity.

(2) "Examiner" means either of the following:

(a) A psychiatrist or a licensed clinical psychologist who satisfies the criteria of division (I)(1) of section 5122.01 of the Revised Code or is employed by a certified forensic center designated by the department of mental health to conduct examinations or evaluations.

(b) For purposes of a separate mental retardation evaluation that is ordered by a court pursuant to division (H) of section 2945.371 of the Revised Code, a psychologist designated by the director of mental retardation and developmental disabilities pursuant to that section to conduct that separate mental retardation evaluation.

(3) "Nonsecured status" means any unsupervised, off-grounds movement or trial visit from a hospital or institution, or any conditional release, that is granted to a person who is found incompetent to stand trial and is committed pursuant to section 2945.39 of the Revised Code or to a person who is found not guilty by reason of insanity and is committed pursuant to section 2945.40 of the Revised Code.

(4) "Unsupervised, off-grounds movement" includes only off-grounds privileges that are unsupervised and that have an expectation of return to the hospital or institution on a daily basis.

(5) "Trial visit" means a patient privilege of a longer stated duration of unsupervised community contact with an expectation of return to the hospital or institution at designated times.

(6) "Conditional release" means a commitment status under which the trial court at any time may revoke a person's conditional release and order the rehospitalization or reinstitutionalization of the person as described in division (A) of section 2945.402 of the Revised Code and pursuant to which a person who is found incompetent to stand trial or a person who is found not guilty by reason of insanity lives and receives treatment in the community for a period of time that does not exceed the maximum prison term or term of imprisonment that the person could have received for the offense in question had the person been convicted of the offense instead of being found incompetent to stand trial on the charge of the offense or being found not guilty by reason of insanity relative to the offense.

(7) "Licensed clinical psychologist," "mentally ill person subject to hospitalization by court order," and "psychiatrist" have the same meanings as in section 5122.01 of the Revised Code.

(8) "Mentally retarded person subject to institutionalization by court order" has the same meaning as in section 5123.01 of the Revised Code.

(B) In a criminal action in a court of common pleas, a county court, or a municipal court, the court, prosecutor, or defense may raise the issue of the defendant's competence to stand trial. If the issue is raised before the trial has commenced, the court shall hold a hearing on the issue as provided in this section. If the issue is raised after the trial has commenced, the court shall hold a hearing on the issue only for good cause shown or on the court's own motion.

(C) The court shall conduct the hearing required or authorized under division (B) of this section within thirty days after the issue is raised, unless the defendant has been referred for evaluation in which case the court shall conduct the hearing within ten days after the filing of the report of the evaluation or, in the case of a defendant who is ordered by the court pursuant to division (H) of section 2945.371 of the Revised Code to undergo a separate mental retardation evaluation conducted by a psychologist designated by the director of mental retardation and developmental disabilities, within ten days after the filing of the report of the separate mental retardation evaluation under that division. A hearing may be continued for good cause.

(D) The defendant shall be represented by counsel at the hearing conducted under division (C) of this section. If the defendant is unable to obtain counsel, the court shall appoint counsel under Chapter 120. of the Revised Code or under the authority recognized in division (C) of section 120.06, division (E) of section 120.16, division (E) of section 120.26, or section 2941.51 of the Revised Code before proceeding with the hearing.

(E) The prosecutor and defense counsel may submit evidence on the issue of the defendant's competence to stand trial. A written report of the evaluation of the defendant may be admitted into evidence at the hearing by stipulation, but, if either the prosecution or defense objects to its admission, the report may be admitted under sections 2317.36 to 2317.38 of the Revised Code or any other applicable statute or rule.

(F) The court shall not find a defendant incompetent to stand trial solely because the defendant is receiving or has received treatment as a voluntary or involuntary mentally ill patient under Chapter 5122. or a voluntary or involuntary mentally retarded resident under Chapter 5123. of the Revised Code or because the defendant is receiving or has received psychotropic drugs or other medication, even if the defendant might become incompetent to stand trial without the drugs or medication.

(G) A defendant is presumed to be competent to stand trial. If, after a hearing, the court finds by a preponderance of the evidence that, because of the defendant's present mental condition, the defendant is incapable of understanding the nature and objective of the proceedings against the defendant or of assisting in the defendant's defense, the court shall find the defendant incompetent to stand trial and shall enter an order authorized by section 2945.38 of the Revised Code.

(H) Municipal courts shall follow the procedures set forth in sections 2945.37 to 2945.402 of the Revised Code. Except as provided in section 2945.371 of the Revised Code, a municipal court shall not order an evaluation of the defendant's competence to stand trial or the defendant's mental condition at the time of the commission of the offense to be conducted at any hospital operated by the department of mental health. Those evaluations shall be performed through community resources including, but not limited to, certified forensic centers, court probation departments, and community mental health agencies. All expenses of the evaluations shall be borne by the legislative authority of the municipal court, as defined in section 1901.03 of the Revised Code, and shall be taxed as costs in the case. If a defendant is found incompetent to stand trial or not guilty by reason of insanity, a municipal court may commit the defendant as provided in sections 2945.38 to 2945.402 of the Revised Code [1]

(1996 S 285, eff. 7–1–97; 1988 S 156, eff. 7–1–89; 1981 H 694; 1980 S 297; 1978 H 565)

[1] So in original.

Historical and Statutory Notes

Ed. Note: 2945.37 contains provisions analogous to former 2947.25, repealed by 1972 H 511, eff. 1–1–74.

Ed. Note: Former 2945.37 repealed by 1978 H 565, eff. 11–1–78; 1976 S 368; 1953 H 1; GC 13441–1.

Pre–1953 H 1 Amendments: 113 v 177, Ch 19, § 1

Amendment Note: 1996 S 285 rewrote this section, which previously read:

"(A) In a criminal action in a court of common pleas or municipal court, the court, prosecutor, or defense may raise the issue of the defendant's competence to stand trial. If the issue is raised before trial, the court shall hold a hearing on the issue as provided in this section. If the issue is raised after trial has begun, the court shall hold a hearing on the issue only for good cause shown.

"A defendant is presumed competent to stand trial, unless it is proved by a preponderance of the evidence in a hearing under this section that because of his present mental condition he is incapable of understanding the nature and objective of the proceedings against him or of presently assisting in his defense.

"The court shall not find a defendant incompetent to stand trial solely because he is receiving or has received treatment as a voluntary or involuntary mentally ill patient or mentally retarded resident under Chapter 5122. or 5123. of the Revised Code or because he is receiving or has received psychotropic drugs or other medication under medical supervision, even though without the drugs or medication the defendant might become incompetent to stand trial.

"The court shall conduct the hearing within thirty days after the issue is raised, unless the defendant has been referred for examination under section 2945.371 of the Revised Code, in which case the court shall conduct the hearing within ten days after the filing of the report required by that section. A hearing may be continued for good cause shown.

"The defendant shall be represented by counsel at the hearing. If the defendant is unable to obtain counsel, the court shall appoint counsel under Chapter 120. of the Revised Code before proceeding with the hearing.

"The prosecutor and defense counsel may submit evidence on the issue of the defendant's competence to stand trial. A written report made under section 2945.371 of the Revised Code may be admitted into evidence at the hearing by stipulation of the prosecution and defense counsel, but if either objects to its admission, the report may be admitted under sections 2317.36 to 2317.38 of the Revised Code or other applicable statute or rule. A report made under section 2945.37 of the Revised Code is inadmissible into evidence in the criminal action against the defendant, but in such an action the prosecutor or defense counsel may call as witnesses any persons who examined the defendant or prepared a report pursuant to a referral under section 2945.371 of the Revised Code.

"Upon the evidence submitted, the court shall determine the defendant's competence to stand trial and shall make an order under section 2945.38 of the Revised Code.

"(B) As used in sections 2945.37 to 2945.40 of the Revised Code, 'prosecutor' means the prosecuting attorney, village solicitor, city director of law, or similar officer who has the authority to prosecute a criminal case that is before the court or a criminal case in which the person was found incompetent to stand trial or found not guilty by reason of insanity.

"(C) Municipal courts shall follow the procedures set forth in sections 2945.37 to 2945.40 of the Revised Code, except as provided in this division. Notwithstanding sections 2945.371 and 2945.39 of the Revised Code, a municipal court shall not order an evaluation of the defendant's competence to stand trial or the defendant's mental condition at the time of the commission of the offense to be conducted at any hospital operated by the department of mental health. Such evaluations shall be performed through community resources including, but not limited to, certified forensic centers, court probation departments, and community mental health agencies, and all expenses of such evaluations shall be borne by the court and taxed as costs in the case. If a defendant is found incompetent to stand trial or not guilty by reason of insanity, a municipal court may commit him as provided in section 2945.38 or 2945.40 of the Revised Code, whichever is applicable, except that the court shall make no commitment to the Oakwood forensic center."

Library References

Criminal Law ⇐623.
Mental Health ⇐432, 434.
Westlaw Topic Nos. 110, 257A.
C.J.S. Criminal Law §§ 549 to 557.

Baldwin's Ohio Legislative Service, 1988 Laws of Ohio, S 156—LSC Analysis, p 5–284

2945.371 Evaluations of mental condition

(A) If the issue of a defendant's competence to stand trial is raised or if a defendant enters a plea of not guilty by reason of insanity, the court may order one or more evaluations of the defendant's present mental condition or, in the case of a plea of not guilty by reason of insanity, of the defendant's mental condition at the time of the offense charged. An examiner shall conduct the evaluation.

(B) If the court orders more than one evaluation under division (A) of this section, the prosecutor and the defendant may recommend to the court an examiner whom each prefers to perform one of the evaluations. If a defendant enters a plea of not guilty by reason of insanity and if the court does not designate an examiner recommended by the defendant, the court shall inform the defendant that the defendant may have independent expert evaluation and that, if the defendant is unable to obtain independent expert evaluation, it will be obtained for the defendant at public expense if the defendant is indigent.

(C) If the court orders an evaluation under division (A) of this section, the defendant shall be available at the times and places established by the examiners who are to conduct the evaluation. The court may order a defendant who has been released on bail or recognizance to submit to an evaluation under this section. If a defendant who has been released on bail or recognizance refuses to submit to a complete evaluation, the court may amend the conditions of bail or recognizance and order the sheriff to take the defendant into custody and deliver the defendant to a center, program, or facility operated or certified by the department of mental health or the department of mental retardation and developmental disabilities where the defendant may be held for evaluation for a reasonable period of time not to exceed twenty days.

(D) A defendant who has not been released on bail or recognizance may be evaluated at the defendant's place of detention. Upon the request of the examiner, the court may order the sheriff to transport the defendant to a program or facility operated by the department of mental health or the department of mental retardation and developmental disabilities, where the defendant may be held for evaluation for a reasonable period of time not to exceed twenty days, and to return the defendant to the place of detention after the evaluation. A municipal court may make an order under this division only upon the request of a certified forensic center examiner.

(E) If a court orders the evaluation to determine a defendant's mental condition at the time of the offense charged, the court shall inform the examiner of the offense with which the defendant is charged.

(F) In conducting an evaluation of a defendant's mental condition at the time of the offense charged, the examiner shall consider all relevant evidence. If the offense charged involves the use of force against another person, the relevant evidence to be considered includes, but is not limited to, any evidence that the defendant suffered, at the time of the commission of the offense, from the "battered woman syndrome."

(G) The examiner shall file a written report with the court within thirty days after entry of a court order for evaluation, and the court shall provide copies of the report to the prosecutor and defense counsel. The report shall include all of the following:

(1) The examiner's findings;

(2) The facts in reasonable detail on which the findings are based;

(3) If the evaluation was ordered to determine the defendant's competence to stand trial, all of the following findings or recommendations that are applicable:

(a) Whether the defendant is capable of understanding the nature and objective of the proceedings against the defendant or of assisting in the defendant's defense;

(b) If the examiner's opinion is that the defendant is incapable of understanding the nature and objective of the proceedings against the defendant or of assisting in the defendant's defense, whether the defendant presently is mentally ill or mentally retarded and, if the examiner's opinion is that the defendant presently is mentally retarded, whether the defendant appears to be a mentally retarded person subject to institutionalization by court order;

(c) If the examiner's opinion is that the defendant is incapable of understanding the nature and objective of the proceedings against the defendant or of assisting in the defendant's defense, the examiner's opinion as to the likelihood of the defendant becoming capable of understanding the nature and objective of the proceedings against the defendant and of assisting in the defendant's defense within one year if the defendant is provided with a course of treatment;

(d) If the examiner's opinion is that the defendant is incapable of understanding the nature and objective of the proceedings against the defendant or of assisting in the defendant's defense and that the defendant presently is mentally ill or mentally retarded, the examiner's recommendation as to the least restrictive treatment alternative, consistent with the defendant's treatment needs for restoration to competency and with the safety of the community.

(4) If the evaluation was ordered to determine the defendant's mental condition at the time of the offense charged, the examiner's findings as to whether the defendant, at the time of the offense charged, did not know, as a result of a severe mental disease or defect, the wrongfulness of the defendant's acts charged.

(H) If the examiner's report filed under division (G) of this section indicates that in the examiner's opinion the defendant is incapable of understanding the nature and objective of the proceedings against the defendant or of assisting in the defendant's defense and that in the examiner's opinion the defendant appears to be a mentally retarded person subject to institutionalization by court order, the court shall order the defendant to undergo a separate mental retardation evaluation conducted by a psychologist designated by the director of mental retardation and developmental disabilities. Divisions (C) to (F) of this section apply in relation to a separate mental retardation evaluation conducted under this division. The psychologist appointed under this division to conduct the separate mental retardation evaluation shall file a written report with the court within thirty days after the entry of the court order requiring the separate mental retardation evaluation, and the court shall provide copies of the report to the prosecutor and defense counsel. The report shall include all of the information described in divisions (G)(1) to (4) of this section. If the court orders a separate mental retardation evaluation of a defendant under this division, the court shall not conduct a hearing under divisions (B) to (H) of section 2945.37 of the Revised Code regarding that defendant until a report of the separate mental retardation evaluation conducted under this division has been filed. Upon the filing of that report, the court shall conduct the hearing within the period of time specified in division (C) of section 2945.37 of the Revised Code.

(I) An examiner appointed under divisions (A) and (B) of this section or under division (H) of this section to evaluate a defendant to determine the defendant's competence to stand trial also may be appointed to evaluate a defendant who has entered a plea of not guilty by reason of insanity, but an examiner of that nature shall prepare separate reports on the issue of competence to stand trial and the defense of not guilty by reason of insanity.

(J) No statement that a defendant makes in an evaluation or hearing under divisions (A) to (H) of this section relating to the defendant's competence to stand trial or to the defendant's mental condition at the time of the offense charged shall be used against the defendant on the issue of guilt in any criminal action or proceeding, but, in a criminal action or proceeding, the prosecutor or defense counsel may call as a witness any person who evaluated the defendant or prepared a report pursuant to a referral under this section. Neither the appointment nor the testimony of an examiner appointed under this section precludes the prosecutor or defense counsel from calling other witnesses or presenting other evidence on competency or insanity issues.

(K) Persons appointed as examiners under divisions (A) and (B) of this section or under division (H) of this section shall be paid a reasonable amount for their services and expenses, as certified by the court. The certified amount shall be paid by the county in the case of county courts and courts of common pleas and by the legislative authority, as defined in section 1901.03 of the Revised Code, in the case of municipal courts.

(2001 S 122, eff. 2–20–02; 1996 S 285, eff. 7–1–97; 1980 H 965, eff. 4–9–81; 1980 H 900, S 297; 1978 H 565)

Historical and Statutory Notes

Amendment Note: 2001 S 122 added new division G(3)(c) and redesignated former division G(3)(c) as new division G(3)(d).

Amendment Note: 1996 S 285 rewrote this section, which previously read:

"(A) If the issue of a defendant's competence to stand trial is raised under section 2945.37 of the Revised Code, the court may order one or more, but not more than three evaluations of the defendant's mental condition. The court shall do either of the following:

"(1) Order that each evaluation be conducted through examination of the defendant by a forensic center designated by the department of mental health to conduct such examinations and make such evaluations in the area in which the court is located or by any other program or facility that is designated by the department of mental health or the department of mental retardation and developmental disabilities to conduct such examinations and make such evaluations provided the center, program, or facility is operated by the appropriate department or is certified by such department as being in compliance with the standards established under division (J) of section 5119.01 or division (C) of section 5123.04 of the Revised Code;

"(2) Designate a center, program, or facility other than one designated by the department to conduct the examination.

"In any case, the court may designate examiners other than the personnel of the center, program, facility, or department to make the examination. If more than one examination is ordered, the prosecutor and the defendant may recommend to the court an examiner whom each prefers to perform one of the examinations.

"(B) If an evaluation is ordered, the defendant shall be available at the times and places established by the center, program, facility, or examiners. The court may order a defendant who has been released on bail or recognizance to submit to an examination under this section. If a defendant who has been released on bail or recognizance refuses to submit to a complete examination, the court may amend the conditions of bail or recognizance and order the sheriff to take the defendant into custody and deliver him to a center, program, or facility operated or certified by the department where he may be held for examination for a reasonable period of time not to exceed twenty days.

"(C) A defendant who has not been released on bail or recognizance may be examined at his place of detention. The court at the request of the examiner may order the sheriff to transport the defendant to a program or facility operated by the department of mental health or the department of mental retardation and developmental disabilities, where he may be held for examination for a reasonable period of time not to exceed twenty days, and to return the defendant to the place of detention after the examination. Such an order may be made by a municipal court only upon the request of a certified forensic center examiner.

"(D) The examiner shall file a written report with the court within thirty days after entry of an order for examination. The court shall provide copies of the report to the prosecutor and defense counsel. The report shall contain the findings of the examiner, the facts in reasonable detail on which the findings are based, and the opinion of the examiner as to the defendant's competence to stand trial. If the examiner reports that in his opinion the defendant is incompetent to stand trial, he shall also state his opinion on the likelihood of the defendant's becoming competent to stand trial within one year and if, in his opinion, the defendant is mentally ill or mentally retarded.

"(E) An examiner appointed under this section may also be appointed under section 2945.39 of the Revised Code to examine a defendant who has entered a plea of not guilty by reason of insanity, but such an examiner shall prepare separate reports on the issue of competence to stand trial and the defense of not guilty by reason of insanity.

"(F) As used in this chapter, 'examiner' means a psychiatrist or licensed clinical psychologist, as defined in section 5122.01 of the Revised Code; provided that a licensed clinical psychologist shall meet the criteria of division (I)(1) of section 5122.01 of the Revised Code or be employed by a certified forensic center designated by the department of mental health to conduct examinations."

Library References

Criminal Law ⬌623.
Mental Health ⬌434.
Westlaw Topic Nos. 110, 257A.
C.J.S. Criminal Law §§ 549 to 557.

2945.38 Effect of findings; treatment or continuing evaluation and treatment of incompetent; medication; disposition of defendant; report; additional hearings; discharge

(A) If the issue of a defendant's competence to stand trial is raised and if the court, upon conducting the hearing provided for in section 2945.37 of the Revised Code, finds that the defendant is competent to stand trial, the defendant shall be proceeded against as provided by law. If the court finds the defendant competent to stand trial and the defendant is receiving psychotropic drugs or other medication, the court may authorize the continued administration of the drugs or medication or other appropriate treatment in order to maintain the defendant's competence to stand trial, unless the defendant's attending physician advises the court against continuation of the drugs, other medication, or treatment.

(B)(1)(a) If, after taking into consideration all relevant reports, information, and other evidence, the court finds that the defendant is incompetent to stand trial and that there is a substantial probability that the defendant will become competent to stand trial within one year if the defendant is provided with a course of treatment, the court shall order the defendant to undergo treatment. If the defendant has been charged with a felony offense and if, after taking into consideration all relevant reports, information, and other evidence, the court finds that the defendant is incompetent to stand trial, but the court is unable at that time to determine whether there is a substantial probability that the defendant will become competent to stand trial within one year if the defendant is provided with a course of treatment, the court shall order continuing evaluation and treatment of the defendant for a period not to exceed four months to determine whether there is a substantial probability that the defendant will become competent to stand trial within one year if the defendant is provided with a course of treatment.

(b) The court order for the defendant to undergo treatment or continuing evaluation and treatment under division (B)(1)(a) of this section shall specify that the treatment or continuing evaluation and treatment shall occur at a facility operated by the department of mental health or the department of mental retardation and developmental disabilities, at a facility certified by either of those departments as being qualified to treat mental illness or mental retardation, at a public or private community mental health or mental retardation facility, or by a psychiatrist or another mental health or mental retardation professional. The order may restrict the defendant's freedom of movement as the court considers necessary. The prosecutor in the defendant's case shall send to the chief clinical officer of the hospital or facility, the managing officer of the institution, the director of the program, or the person to which the defendant is committed copies of relevant police reports and other background information that pertains to the defendant and is available to the prosecutor unless the prosecutor determines that the release of any of the information in the police reports or any of the other background information to unauthorized persons would interfere with the effective prosecution of any person or would create a substantial risk of harm to any person.

In determining placement alternatives, the court shall consider the extent to which the person is a danger to the person and to others, the need for security, and the type of crime involved and shall order the least restrictive alternative available that is consistent with public safety and treatment goals. In weighing these factors, the court shall give preference to protecting public safety.

(c) If the defendant is found incompetent to stand trial, if the chief clinical officer of the hospital or facility, the managing officer of the institution, the director of the program, or the person to which the defendant is committed for treatment or continuing evaluation and treatment under division (B)(1)(b) of this section determines that medication is necessary to restore the defendant's competency to stand trial, and if the defendant lacks the capacity to give informed consent or refuses medication, the chief clinical officer, managing officer, director, or person to which the defendant is committed for treatment or continuing evaluation and treatment may petition the court for authorization for the involuntary administration of medication. The court shall hold a hearing on the petition within five days of the filing of the petition if the petition was filed in a municipal court or a county court regarding an incompetent defendant charged with a misdemeanor or within ten days of the filing of the petition if the petition was filed in a court of common pleas regarding an incompetent defendant charged with a felony offense. Following the hearing, the court may authorize the involuntary administration of medication or may dismiss the petition.

(2) If the court finds that the defendant is incompetent to stand trial and that, even if the defendant is provided with a course of treatment, there is not a substantial probability that the defendant will become competent to stand trial within one year, the court shall order the discharge of the defendant, unless upon motion of the prosecutor or on its own motion, the court either seeks to retain jurisdiction over the defendant pursuant to section 2945.39 of the Revised Code or files an affidavit in the probate court for the civil commitment of the defendant pursuant to Chapter 5122. or 5123. of the Revised Code alleging that the defendant is a mentally ill person subject to hospitalization by court order or a mentally retarded person subject to institutionalization by court order. If an affidavit is filed in the probate court, the trial court shall send to the probate court copies of all written reports of the defendant's mental condition that were prepared pursuant to section 2945.371 of the Revised Code.

The trial court may issue the temporary order of detention that a probate court may issue under section 5122.11 or 5123.71 of the Revised Code, to remain in effect until the probable cause or initial hearing in the probate court. Further proceedings in the probate court are civil proceedings governed by Chapter 5122. or 5123. of the Revised Code.

(C) No defendant shall be required to undergo treatment, including any continuing evaluation and treatment, under division (B)(1) of this section for longer than whichever of the following periods is applicable:

(1) One year, if the most serious offense with which the defendant is charged is one of the following offenses:

(a) Aggravated murder, murder, or an offense of violence for which a sentence of death or life imprisonment may be imposed;

(b) An offense of violence that is a felony of the first or second degree;

(c) A conspiracy to commit, an attempt to commit, or complicity in the commission of an offense described in division (C)(1)(a) or (b) of this section if the conspiracy, attempt, or complicity is a felony of the first or second degree.

(2) Six months, if the most serious offense with which the defendant is charged is a felony other than a felony described in division (C)(1) of this section;

(3) Sixty days, if the most serious offense with which the defendant is charged is a misdemeanor of the first or second degree;

(4) Thirty days, if the most serious offense with which the defendant is charged is a misdemeanor of the third or fourth degree, a minor misdemeanor, or an unclassified misdemeanor.

(D) Any defendant who is committed pursuant to this section shall not voluntarily admit the defendant or be voluntarily admitted to a hospital or institution pursuant to section 5122.02, 5122.15, 5123.69, or 5123.76 of the Revised Code.

(E) Except as otherwise provided in this division, a defendant who is charged with an offense and is committed to a hospital or other institution by the court under this section shall not be granted unsupervised on-grounds movement, supervised off-grounds movement, or nonsecured status. The court may grant a defendant supervised off-grounds movement to obtain medical treatment or specialized habilitation treatment services if the person who supervises the treatment or the continuing evaluation and treatment of the defendant ordered under division (B)(1)(a) of this section informs the court that the treatment or continuing evaluation and treatment cannot be provided at the hospital or the institution to which the defendant is committed. The chief clinical officer of the hospital or the managing officer of the institution to which the defendant is committed or a designee of either of those persons may grant a defendant movement to a medical facility for an emergency medical situation with appropriate supervision to ensure the safety of the defendant, staff, and community during that emergency medical situation. The chief clinical officer of the hospital or the managing officer of the institution shall notify the court within twenty-four hours of the defendant's movement to the medical facility for an emergency medical situation under this division.

(F) The person who supervises the treatment or continuing evaluation and treatment of a defendant ordered to undergo treatment or continuing evaluation and treatment under division (B)(1)(a) of this section shall file a written report with the court at the following times:

(1) Whenever the person believes the defendant is capable of understanding the nature and objective of the proceedings against the defendant and of assisting in the defendant's defense;

(2) For a felony offense, fourteen days before expiration of the maximum time for treatment as specified in division (C) of this section and fourteen days before the expiration of the maximum time for continuing evaluation and treatment as specified in division (B)(1)(a) of this section, and, for a misdemeanor offense, ten days before the expiration of the maximum time for treatment, as specified in division (C) of this section;

(3) At a minimum, after each six months of treatment;

(4) Whenever the person who supervises the treatment or continuing evaluation and treatment of a defendant ordered under division (B)(1)(a) of this section believes that there is not a substantial probability that the defendant will become capable of understanding the nature and objective of the proceedings against the defendant or of assisting in the defendant's defense even if the defendant is provided with a course of treatment.

(G) A report under division (F) of this section shall contain the examiner's findings, the facts in reasonable detail on which the findings are based, and the examiner's opinion as to the defendant's capability of understanding the nature and objective of the proceedings against the defendant and of assisting in the defendant's defense. If, in the examiner's opinion, the defendant remains incapable of understanding the nature and objective of the proceedings against the defendant and of assisting in the defendant's defense and there is a substantial probability that the defendant will become capable of understanding the nature and objective of the proceedings against the defendant and of assisting in the defendant's defense if the defendant is provided with a course of treatment, if in the examiner's opinion the defendant remains mentally ill or mentally retarded, and if the maximum time for treatment as specified in division (C) of this section has not expired, the report also shall contain the examiner's recommendation as to the least restrictive treatment alternative that is consistent with the defendant's treatment needs for restoration to competency and with the safety of the community. The court shall provide copies of the report to the prosecutor and defense counsel.

(H) If a defendant is committed pursuant to division (B)(1) of this section, within ten days after the treating physician of the defendant or the examiner of the defendant who is employed or retained by the treating facility advises that there is not a substantial probability that the defendant will become capable of understanding the nature and objective of the proceedings against the defendant or of assisting in the defendant's defense even if the defendant is provided with a course of treatment, within ten days after the expiration of the maximum time for treatment as specified in division (C) of this section, within ten days after the expiration of the maximum time for continuing evaluation and treatment as specified in division (B)(1)(a) of this section, within thirty days after a defendant's request for a hearing that is made after six months of treatment, or within thirty days after being advised by the treating physician or examiner that the defendant is competent to stand trial, whichever is the earliest, the court shall conduct another hearing to determine if the defendant is competent to stand trial and shall do whichever of the following is applicable:

(1) If the court finds that the defendant is competent to stand trial, the defendant shall be proceeded against as provided by law.

(2) If the court finds that the defendant is incompetent to stand trial, but that there is a substantial probability that the defendant will become competent to stand trial if the defendant is provided with a course of treatment, and the maximum time for treatment as specified in division (C) of this section has not expired, the court, after consideration of the examiner's recommendation, shall order that treatment be continued, may change the facility or program at which the treatment is to be continued, and shall specify whether the treatment is to be continued at the same or a different facility or program.

(3) If the court finds that the defendant is incompetent to stand trial, if the defendant is charged with an offense listed in division (C)(1) of this section, and if the court finds that there is not a substantial probability that the defendant will become competent to stand trial even if the defendant is provided with a course of treatment, or if the maximum time for treatment relative to that offense as specified in division (C) of this section has expired, further proceedings shall be as provided in sections 2945.39, 2945.401, and 2945.402 of the Revised Code.

(4) If the court finds that the defendant is incompetent to stand trial, if the most serious offense with which the defendant is charged is a misdemeanor or a felony other than a felony listed in division (C)(1) of this section, and if the court finds that there is not a substantial probability that the defendant will become competent to stand trial even if the defendant is provided with a course of treatment, or if the maximum time for treatment relative to that offense as specified in division (C) of this section has expired, the court shall dismiss the indictment, information, or complaint against the defendant. A dismissal under this division is not a bar to further prosecution based on the same conduct. The court shall discharge the defendant unless the court or prosecutor files an affidavit in probate court for civil commitment pursuant to Chapter 5122. or 5123. of the Revised Code. If an affidavit for civil commitment is filed, the court may detain the defendant for ten days pending civil commitment. All of the following provisions apply to persons charged with a misdemeanor or a felony other than a felony listed in division (C)(1) of this section who are committed by the probate court subsequent to the court's or prosecutor's filing of an affidavit for civil commitment under authority of this division:

(a) The chief clinical officer of the hospital or facility, the managing officer of the institution, the director of the program, or the person to which the defendant is committed or admitted shall do all of the following:

(i) Notify the prosecutor, in writing, of the discharge of the defendant, send the notice at least ten days prior to the discharge unless the discharge is by the probate court, and state in the notice the date on which the defendant will be discharged;

(ii) Notify the prosecutor, in writing, when the defendant is absent without leave or is granted unsupervised, off-grounds movement, and send this notice promptly after the discovery of the absence without leave or prior to the granting of the unsupervised, off-grounds movement, whichever is applicable;

(iii) Notify the prosecutor, in writing, of the change of the defendant's commitment or admission to voluntary status, send the notice promptly upon learning of the change to voluntary status, and state in the notice the date on which the defendant was committed or admitted on a voluntary status.

(b) Upon receiving notice that the defendant will be granted unsupervised, off-grounds movement, the prosecutor either shall re-indict the defendant or promptly notify the court that the prosecutor does not intend to prosecute the charges against the defendant.

(I) If a defendant is convicted of a crime and sentenced to a jail or workhouse, the defendant's sentence shall be reduced by the total number of days the defendant is confined for evaluation to determine the defendant's competence to stand trial or treatment under this section and sections 2945.37 and 2945.371 of the Revised Code or by the total number of days the defendant is confined for evaluation to determine the defendant's mental condition at the time of the offense charged.

(2001 S 122, eff. 2–20–02; 1996 S 285, eff. 7–1–97; 1996 S 269, eff. 7–1–96; 1988 S 156, eff. 7–1–89; 1980 H 965, H 900, S 297; 1978 H 565; 1975 S 185; 1953 H 1; GC 13441–2)

Uncodified Law

2001 S 122, § 3, eff. 2–20–02, reads:

This act presents section 2945.38 of the Revised Code as it existed prior to its amendment by Am. Sub. S.B. 285 of the 121st General Assembly. The revived version of that section supersedes the version of that section repealed by Section 2 of this act and omits and repeals all changes made to that section by Am. Sub. S.B. 285 of the 121st General Assembly. The omission and repeal of those changes is not intended to have any substantive effect and is intended to present in this act the version of section 2945.38 of the Revised Code that is currently effective. The repeal of section 2945.38 of the Revised Code by Section 2 of this act is to give effect to the holding of the Ohio Supreme Court in State v. Sullivan (2001), 90 Ohio St.3d 502, that section 2945.38 of the Revised Code, as amended by Am. Sub. S.B. 285 of the 121st General Assembly, is unconstitutional.

Historical and Statutory Notes

Pre–1953 H 1 Amendments: 113 v 177, Ch 19, § 2

Amendment Note: 2001 S 122 rewrote the section, which prior thereto read:

"(A) If the issue of a defendant's competence to stand trial is raised and if the court, upon conducting the hearing provided for in section 2945.37 of the Revised Code, finds that the defendant is competent to stand trial, the defendant shall be proceeded against as provided by law. If the court finds the defendant competent to stand trial and the defendant is receiving psychotropic drugs or other medication, the court may authorize the continued administration of the drugs or medication or other appropriate treatment in order to maintain the defendant's competence to stand trial, unless the defendant's attending physician advises the court against continuation of the drugs, other medication, or treatment.

"(B) After taking into consideration all relevant reports, information, and other evidence, the court shall order a defendant who is found incompetent to stand trial to undergo treatment at a facility operated by the department of mental health or the department of mental retardation and developmental disabilities, treatment at a facility certified by either of those departments as being qualified to treat mental illness or mental retardation, treatment at a public or private community mental health or mental retardation facility, private treatment by a psychiatrist or another mental health or mental retardation professional. The order may restrict the defendant's freedom of movement as the court considers necessary.

The prosecutor in the defendant's case shall send to the chief clinical officer of the hospital or facility, the managing officer of the institution, the director of the program, or the person to which the defendant is committed copies of relevant police reports and other background information that pertains to the defendant and is available to the prosecutor unless the prosecutor determines that the release of any of the information in the police reports or any of the other background information to unauthorized persons would interfere with the effective prosecution of any person or would create a substantial risk of harm to any person.

"In determining placement alternatives, the court shall consider the extent to which the person is a danger to the person and to others, the need for security, and the type of crime involved and shall order the least restrictive alternative available that is consistent with public safety and treatment goals. In weighing these factors, the court shall give preference to protecting public safety.

"If the defendant is found incompetent to stand trial, if the chief clinical officer of the hospital or facility, the managing officer of the institution, the director of the program, or the person to which the defendant is committed determines that medication is necessary to restore the defendant's competency to stand trial, and if the defendant lacks the capacity to give informed consent or refuses medication, the chief clinical officer, managing officer, director, or person to which the defendant is committed may petition for, and the court may authorize, the involuntary administration of medication.

"(C) No defendant shall be required to undergo treatment under this section for longer than whichever of the following periods is applicable:

"(1) One year, if the most serious offense with which the defendant is charged is one of the following offenses:

"(a) Aggravated murder, murder, or an offense of violence for which a sentence of death or life imprisonment may be imposed;

"(b) An offense of violence that is a felony of the first or second degree;

"(c) A conspiracy to commit, an attempt to commit, or complicity in the commission of an offense described in division (C)(1)(a) or (b) of this section if the conspiracy, attempt, or complicity is a felony of the first or second degree.

"(2) Six months, if the most serious offense with which the defendant is charged is a felony other than a felony described in division (C)(1) of this section;

"(3) Sixty days, if the most serious offense with which the defendant is charged is a misdemeanor.

"(D) Any defendant who is committed pursuant to this section shall not voluntarily admit the defendant or be voluntarily admitted to a hospital or institution pursuant to section 5122.02, 5122.15, 5123.69, or 5123.76 of the Revised Code.

"(E) A defendant charged with an offense and committed to a hospital or other institution by the court under this section shall not be granted unsupervised on-grounds movement, supervised off-grounds movement, or nonsecured status.

"(F) The person who supervises the treatment of a defendant ordered to undergo treatment under division (B) of this section shall file a written report with the court at the following times:

"(1) Whenever the person believes the defendant is capable of understanding the nature and objective of the proceedings against the defendant and of assisting in the defendant's defense;

"(2) For a felony offense, fourteen days before expiration of the maximum time for treatment as specified in division (C) of this section, and, for a misdemeanor offense, ten days before the expiration of the maximum time for treatment as specified in division (C) of this section;

"(3) At a minimum, after each six months of treatment.

"(G) A report under division (F) of this section shall contain the examiner's findings, the facts in reasonable detail on which the findings are based, and the examiner's opinion as to the defendant's capability of understanding the nature and objective of the proceedings against the defendant and of assisting in the defendant's defense. If, in the examiner's opinion, the defendant remains incapable of understanding the nature and objective of the proceedings against the defendant or of assisting in the defendant's defense and also remains mentally ill or mentally retarded, and if the maximum time for treatment as specified in division (C) of this section has not expired, the report also shall contain the examiner's recommendation as to the least restrictive treatment alternative that is consistent with the defendant's treatment needs for restoration to competency and with the safety of the community. The court shall provide copies of the report to the prosecutor and defense counsel.

"(H) Within ten days after the expiration of the maximum time for treatment as specified in division (C) of this section, within thirty days after a defendant's request for a hearing that is made after six months of treatment, or within thirty days after being advised by the treating physician that the defendant is competent to stand trial, whichever is earlier, the court shall conduct another hearing to determine if the defendant is competent to stand trial and shall do whichever of the following is applicable:

"(1) If the court finds that the defendant is competent to stand trial, the defendant shall be proceeded against as provided by law.

"(2) If the court finds that the defendant is incompetent to stand trial and the maximum time for treatment as specified in division (C) of this section has not expired, the court, after consideration of the examiner's recommendation, shall order that treatment be continued until the expiration of the maximum time for treatment, may change the facility or program at which the treatment is to be continued, and shall specify whether the treatment is to be continued at the same or a different facility or program.

"(3) If the court finds that the defendant is incompetent to stand trial, if the defendant is charged with an offense listed in division (C)(1) of this section, and if the maximum time for treatment relative to that offense as specified in that division has expired, further proceedings shall be as provided in sections 2945.39, 2945.401, and 2945.402 of the Revised Code.

"(4) If the court finds that the defendant is incompetent to stand trial, if the most serious offense with which the defendant is charged is a misdemeanor or a felony other than a felony listed in division (C)(1) of this section, and if the maximum time for treatment relative to that offense as specified in division (C) of this section has expired, the court shall dismiss the indictment, information, or complaint against the defendant. A dismissal under this division is not a bar to further prosecution based on the same conduct. The court shall discharge the defendant unless the court or prosecutor files an affidavit in probate court for civil commitment pursuant to Chapter 5122. or 5123. of the Revised Code. If an affidavit for civil commitment is filed, the court may detain the defendant for ten days pending civil commitment. All of the following provisions apply to persons charged with a misdemeanor or a felony other than a felony listed in division (C)(1) of this section who are committed by the probate court subsequent to the court's or prosecutor's filing of an affidavit for civil commitment under authority of this division:

"(a) The chief clinical officer of the hospital or facility, the managing officer of the institution, the director of the program, or the person to which the defendant is committed or admitted shall do all of the following:

"(i) Notify the prosecutor, in writing, of the discharge of the defendant, send the notice at least ten days prior to the discharge unless the discharge is by the probate court, and state in the notice the date on which the defendant will be discharged;

"(ii) Notify the prosecutor, in writing, when the defendant is absent without leave or is granted unsupervised, off-grounds movement, and send this notice promptly after the discovery of the absence without leave or prior to the granting of the unsupervised, off-grounds movement, whichever is applicable;

"(iii) Notify the prosecutor, in writing, of the change of the defendant's commitment or admission to voluntary status, send the notice promptly upon learning of the change to voluntary status, and state in the notice the date on which the defendant was committed or admitted on a voluntary status.

"(b) Upon receiving notice that the defendant will be granted unsupervised, off-grounds movement, the prosecutor either shall re-indict the defendant or promptly notify the court that the prosecutor does not intend to prosecute the charges against the defendant.

"(I) If a defendant is convicted of a crime and sentenced to a jail or workhouse, the defendant's sentence shall be reduced by the total number of days the defendant is confined for evaluation to determine the defendant's competence to stand trial or treatment under this section and sections 2945.37 and 2945.371 of the Revised Code or by the total number of days the defendant is confined for evaluation to determine the defendant's mental condition at the time of the offense charged."

Amendment Note: 1996 S 269 substituted "prison term" for "minimum sentence" and "term of imprisonment" for "maximum sentence" in the second paragraph of division (D); substituted "prison term or term of imprisonment" for "sentence" in division (H)(2); made changes to reflect gender neutral language; and made other nonsubstantive changes.

Amendment Note: 1996 S 285 rewrote this section. See Baldwin's Ohio Legislative Service, 1996, p 12/L–3524, or the OH–LEGIS or OH–LEGIS–OLD database on WESTLAW, for prior version of this section.

Library References

Criminal Law ⚖623.
Mental Health ⚖432 to 436.
Westlaw Topic Nos. 110, 257A.
C.J.S. Criminal Law §§ 549 to 557.
C.J.S. Mental Health §§ 235 to 241, 248.

Baldwin's Ohio Legislative Service, 1988 Laws of Ohio, S 156—LSC Analysis, p 5–284

2945.39 Civil commitment; expiration of time for treatment; jurisdiction; hearing; reports

(A) If a defendant who is charged with an offense described in division (C)(1) of section 2945.38 of the Revised Code is found incompetent to stand trial, after the expiration of the maximum time for treatment as specified in division (C) of that section or after the court finds that there is not a substantial probability that the defendant will become competent to stand trial even if the defendant is provided with a course of treatment, one of the following applies:

(1) The court or the prosecutor may file an affidavit in probate court for civil commitment of the defendant in the manner provided in Chapter 5122. or 5123. of the Revised Code. If the court or prosecutor files an affidavit for civil commitment, the court may detain the defendant for ten days pending civil commitment. If the probate court commits the defendant subsequent to the court's or prosecutor's filing of an affidavit for civil commitment, the chief clinical officer of the hospital or facility, the managing officer of the institution, the director of the program, or the person to which the defendant is committed or admitted shall send to the prosecutor the notices described in divisions (H)(4)(a)(i) to (iii) of section 2945.38 of the Revised Code within the periods of time and under the circumstances specified in those divisions.

(2) On the motion of the prosecutor or on its own motion, the court may retain jurisdiction over the defendant if, at a hearing, the court finds both of the following by clear and convincing evidence:

(a) The defendant committed the offense with which the defendant is charged.

(b) The defendant is a mentally ill person subject to hospitalization by court order or a mentally retarded person subject to institutionalization by court order.

(B) In making its determination under division (A)(2) of this section as to whether to retain jurisdiction over the defendant, the court may consider all relevant evidence, including, but not limited to, any relevant psychiatric, psychological, or medical testimony or reports, the acts constituting the offense charged, and any history of the defendant that is relevant to the defendant's ability to conform to the law.

(C) If the court conducts a hearing as described in division (A)(2) of this section and if the court does not make both findings described in divisions (A)(2)(a) and (b) of this section by clear and convincing evidence, the court shall dismiss the indictment, information, or complaint against the defendant. Upon the dismissal, the court shall discharge the defendant unless the court or prosecutor files an affidavit in probate court for civil commitment of the defendant pursuant to Chapter 5122. or 5123. of the Revised Code. If the court or prosecutor files an affidavit for civil commitment, the court may order that the defendant be detained for up to ten days pending the civil commitment. If the probate court commits the defendant subsequent to the court's or prosecutor's filing of an affidavit for civil commitment, the chief clinical officer of the hospital or facility, the managing officer of the institution, the director of the program, or the person to which the defendant is committed or admitted shall send to the prosecutor the notices described in divisions (H)(4)(a)(i) to (iii) of section 2945.38 of the Revised Code within the periods of time and under the circumstances specified in those divisions. A dismissal of charges under this division is not a bar to further criminal proceedings based on the same conduct.

(D)(1) If the court conducts a hearing as described in division (A)(2) of this section and if the court makes the findings described in divisions (A)(2)(a) and (b) of this section by clear and convincing evidence, the court shall commit the defendant to a hospital operated by the department of mental health, a facility operated by the department of mental retardation and developmental disabilities, or another medical or psychiatric facility, as appropriate. In determining the place and nature of the commitment, the court shall order the least restrictive commitment alternative available that is consistent with public safety and the welfare of the defendant. In weighing these factors, the court shall give preference to protecting public safety.

(2) If a court makes a commitment of a defendant under division (D)(1) of this section, the prosecutor shall send to the place of commitment all reports of the defendant's current mental condition and, except as otherwise provided in this division, any other relevant information, including, but not limited to, a transcript of the hearing held pursuant to division (A)(2) of this section, copies of relevant police reports, and copies of any prior arrest and conviction records that pertain to the defendant and that the prosecutor possesses. The prosecutor shall send the reports of the defendant's current mental condition in every case of commitment, and, unless the prosecutor determines that the release of any of the other relevant information to unauthorized persons would interfere with the effective prosecution of any person or would create a substantial risk of harm to any person, the prosecutor also shall send the other relevant information. Upon admission of a defendant committed under division (D)(1) of this section, the place of commitment shall send to the board of alcohol, drug addiction, and mental health services or the community mental health board serving the county in which the charges against the defendant were filed a copy of all reports of the defendant's current mental condition and a copy of the other relevant information provided by the prosecutor under this division, including, if provided, a transcript of the hearing held pursuant to division (A)(2) of this section, the relevant police reports, and the prior arrest and conviction records that pertain to the defendant and that the prosecutor possesses.

(3) If a court makes a commitment under division (D)(1) of this section, all further proceedings shall be in accordance with sections 2945.401 and 2945.402 of the Revised Code.

(2001 S 122, eff. 2–20–02; 1996 S 285, eff. 7–1–97)

Historical and Statutory Notes

Ed. Note: Former 2945.39 repealed by 1996 S 285, eff. 7–1–97; 1990 H 484, eff. 11–5–90; 1981 H 1; 1980 H 965, H 736, S 297, H 900; 1978 H 565.

Ed. Note: Prior 2945.39 repealed by 1978 H 565, eff. 11–1–78; 1972 H 511; 132 v S 523; 1953 H 1; GC 13441–3.

Pre–1953 H 1 Amendments: 113 v 177, Ch 19, § 3

Amendment Note: 2001 S 122 inserted "or after the court finds that there is not a substantial probability that the defendant will become competent to stand trial even if the defendant is provided with a course of treatment" in division (A); and made other nonsubstantive changes.

Library References

Mental Health ⚖434, 436.
Westlaw Topic No. 257A.
C.J.S. Criminal Law §§ 549 to 554.
C.J.S. Mental Health §§ 238 to 240.

2945.391 Applicability of not guilty by reason of insanity plea; impairment of reason not defense

For purposes of sections 2945.371, 2945.40, 2945.401, and 2945.402 and Chapters 5122. and 5123. of the Revised Code, a person is "not guilty by reason of insanity" relative to a charge of an offense only as described in division (A)(14) of section 2901.01 of the Revised Code. Proof that a person's reason, at the time of the commission of an offense, was so impaired that the person did not have the ability to refrain from doing the person's act or acts, does not constitute a defense.

(1996 S 285, eff. 7–1–97; 1996 S 239, eff. 9–6–96; 1990 S 24, eff. 7–24–90)

Historical and Statutory Notes

Amendment Note: 1996 S 239 substituted "(A)(14)" for "(N)"; and made changes to reflect gender neutral language.

Amendment Note: 1996 S 285 substituted "sections 2945.371, 2945.401, and 2945.402" for "section 2945.40" in the first sentence.

2945.392 Battered woman syndrome

(A) The declarations set forth in division (A) of section 2901.06 of the Revised Code apply in relation to this section.

(B) If a defendant is charged with an offense involving the use of force against another and the defendant enters a plea to the charge of not guilty by reason of insanity, the defendant may introduce expert testimony of the "battered woman syndrome" and expert testimony that the defendant suffered from that syndrome as evidence to establish the requisite impairment of the defendant's reason, at the time of the commission of the offense, that is necessary for a finding that the defendant is not guilty by reason of insanity. The introduction of any expert testimony under this division shall be in accordance with the Ohio Rules of Evidence.

(1996 S 285, eff. 7–1–97; 1990 H 484, eff. 11–5–90)

Historical and Statutory Notes

Amendment Note: 1996 S 285 substituted "defendant" for "person" in division (B).

Library References

Criminal Law ⇌474.4(3).
Westlaw Topic No. 110.
C.J.S. Criminal Law § 1067.

2945.40 Verdict of not guilty by reason of insanity; effects; procedures; hearings; rights; commitment

(A) If a person is found not guilty by reason of insanity, the verdict shall state that finding, and the trial court shall conduct a full hearing to determine whether the person is a mentally ill person subject to hospitalization by court order or a mentally retarded person subject to institutionalization by court order. Prior to the hearing, if the trial judge believes that there is probable cause that the person found not guilty by reason of insanity is a mentally ill person subject to hospitalization by court order or mentally retarded person subject to institutionalization by court order, the trial judge may issue a temporary order of detention for that person to remain in effect for ten court days or until the hearing, whichever occurs first.

Any person detained pursuant to a temporary order of detention issued under this division shall be held in a suitable facility, taking into consideration the place and type of confinement prior to and during trial.

(B) The court shall hold the hearing under division (A) of this section to determine whether the person found not guilty by reason of insanity is a mentally ill person subject to hospitalization by court order or a mentally retarded person subject to institutionalization by court order within ten court days after the finding of not guilty by reason of insanity. Failure to conduct the hearing within the ten-day period shall cause the immediate discharge of the respondent, unless the judge grants a continuance for not longer than ten court days for good cause shown or for any period of time upon motion of the respondent.

(C) If a person is found not guilty by reason of insanity, the person has the right to attend all hearings conducted pursuant to sections 2945.37 to 2945.402 of the Revised Code. At any hearing conducted pursuant to one of those sections, the court shall inform the person that the person has all of the following rights:

(1) The right to be represented by counsel and to have that counsel provided at public expense if the person is indigent, with the counsel to be appointed by the court under Chapter 120. of the Revised Code or under the authority recognized in division (C) of section 120.06, division (E) of section 120.16, division (E) of section 120.26, or section 2941.51 of the Revised Code;

(2) The right to have independent expert evaluation and to have that independent expert evaluation provided at public expense if the person is indigent;

(3) The right to subpoena witnesses and documents, to present evidence on the person's behalf, and to cross-examine witnesses against the person;

(4) The right to testify in the person's own behalf and to not be compelled to testify;

(5) The right to have copies of any relevant medical or mental health document in the custody of the state or of any place of commitment other than a document for which the court finds that the release to the person of information contained in the document would create a substantial risk of harm to any person.

(D) The hearing under division (A) of this section shall be open to the public, and the court shall conduct the hearing in accordance with the Rules of Civil Procedure. The court shall make and maintain a full transcript and record of the hearing proceedings. The court may consider all relevant evidence, including, but not limited to, any relevant psychiatric, psychological, or medical testimony or reports, the acts constituting the offense in relation to which the person was found not guilty by reason of insanity, and any history of the person that is relevant to the person's ability to conform to the law.

(E) Upon completion of the hearing under division (A) of this section, if the court finds there is not clear and convincing evidence that the person is a mentally ill person subject to hospitalization by court order or a mentally retarded person subject to institutionalization by court order, the court shall discharge the person, unless a detainer has been placed upon the person by the department of rehabilitation and correction, in which case the person shall be returned to that department.

(F) If, at the hearing under division (A) of this section, the court finds by clear and convincing evidence that the person is a mentally ill person subject to hospitalization by court order or a mentally retarded person subject to institutionalization by court order, it shall commit the person to a hospital operated by the department of mental health, a facility operated by the department of mental retardation and developmental disabilities, or another medical or psychiatric facility, as appropriate, and further proceedings shall be in accordance with sections 2945.401 and 2945.402 of the Revised Code. In determining the place and nature of the commitment, the court shall order the least restrictive commitment alternative available that is consistent with public safety and the welfare of the person. In weighing these factors, the court shall give preference to protecting public safety.

(G) If a court makes a commitment of a person under division (F) of this section, the prosecutor shall send to the place of commitment all reports of the person's current mental condition, and, except as otherwise provided in this division, any other relevant information, including, but not limited to, a transcript of the hearing held pursuant to division (A) of this section, copies of relevant police reports, and copies of any prior arrest and conviction records that pertain to the person and that the prosecutor possesses. The prosecutor shall send the reports of the person's current mental condition in every case of commitment, and, unless the prosecutor determines that the release of any of the other relevant information to unauthorized persons would interfere with the effective prosecution of any person or would create a substantial risk of harm to any person, the prosecutor also shall send the other relevant information. Upon admission of a person committed under division (F) of this section, the place of commitment shall send to the board of alcohol, drug addiction, and mental health services or the community mental health board serving the county in which the charges against the person were filed a copy of all reports of the person's current mental condition and a copy of the other relevant information provided by the prosecutor under this division, including, if provided, a transcript of the hearing held pursuant to division (A) of this section, the relevant police reports, and the prior arrest and conviction records that pertain to the person and that the prosecutor possesses.

(H) A person who is committed pursuant to this section shall not voluntarily admit the person or be voluntarily admitted to a hospital or institution pursuant to sections 5122.02, 5122.15, 5123.69, or 5123.76 of the Revised Code.

(1996 S 285, eff. 7–1–97; 1996 H 567, eff. 10–29–96; 1994 H 571, eff. 10–6–94; 1990 S 24, eff. 7–24–90; 1988 S 156; 1981 H 1; 1980 H 965, S 297; 1978 H 565)

Historical and Statutory Notes

Ed. Note: 2945.40 contains provisions analogous to former 2947.26 to 2947.28, repealed by 1972 H 511, eff. 1–1–74.

Ed. Note: Former 2945.40 repealed by 1978 H 565, eff. 11–1–78; 1953 H 1; GC 13441–4.

Pre–1953 H 1 Amendments: 113 v 178, Ch 19, § 4

Amendment Note: 1996 S 285 rewrote this section. See Baldwin's Ohio Legislative Service, 1996, p 12/L–3532, or the OH–LEGIS or OH–LEGIS–OLD database on WESTLAW, for prior version of this section.

Amendment Note: 1996 H 567 deleted "the attorney general" preceding "and the prosecutor" in the first sentence, and "and attorney general" following "the prosecutor" in the second sentence, of division (D)(4); deleted "to the attorney general and" preceding "to the prosecutor" in division (E); deleted "the attorney general" preceding "and the prosecutor" throughout in the first paragraph of division (F); deleted "and the attorney general" following "give the prosecutor" in the second paragraph of division (F); deleted the final sentence in division (G); and made other changes to reflect gender neutral language. Prior thereto the final sentence in division (G) read:

"An attorney designated by the attorney general shall represent the hospital, facility, program, or institution to which the person was committed, if the person has been committed."

Amendment Note: 1994 H 571 substituted "correctional" for "penal" in division (D)(6).

Library References

Criminal Law ⚖47.
Mental Health ⚖439.
Westlaw Topic Nos. 110, 257A.
C.J.S. Criminal Law §§ 99 to 108.
C.J.S. Mental Health §§ 241 to 246.

Baldwin's Ohio Legislative Service, 1988 Laws of Ohio, S 156—LSC Analysis, p 5–284

2945.401 Nonsecured status or termination of commitment; reports on competence; jurisdiction; hearing

(A) A defendant found incompetent to stand trial and committed pursuant to section 2945.39 of the Revised Code or a person found not guilty by reason of insanity and committed pursuant to section 2945.40 of the Revised Code shall remain subject to the jurisdiction of the trial court pursuant to that commitment, and to the provisions of this section, until the final termination of the commitment as described in division (J)(1) of this section. If the jurisdiction is terminated under this division because of the final termination of the commitment resulting from the expiration of the maximum prison term or term of imprisonment described in division (J)(1)(b) of this section, the court or prosecutor may file an affidavit for the civil commitment of the defendant or person pursuant to Chapter 5122. or 5123. of the Revised Code.

(B) A hearing conducted under any provision of sections 2945.37 to 2945.402 of the Revised Code shall not be conducted in accordance with Chapters 5122. and 5123. of the Revised Code. Any person who is committed pursuant to section 2945.39 or 2945.40 of the Revised Code shall not voluntarily admit the person or be voluntarily admitted to a hospital or institution pursuant to section 5122.02, 5122.15, 5123.69, or 5123.76 of the Revised Code. All other provisions of Chapters 5122. and 5123. of the Revised Code regarding hospitalization or institutionalization shall apply to the extent they are not in conflict with this chapter. A commitment under section 2945.39 or 2945.40 of the Revised Code shall not be terminated and the conditions of the commitment shall not be changed except as otherwise provided in division (D)(2) of this section with respect to a mentally retarded person subject to institutionalization by court order or except by order of the trial court.

(C) The hospital, facility, or program to which a defendant or person has been committed under section 2945.39 or 2945.40 of the Revised Code shall report in writing to the trial court, at the times specified in this division, as to whether the defendant or person remains a mentally ill person subject to hospitalization by court order or a mentally retarded person subject to institutionalization by court order and, in the case of a defendant committed under section 2945.39 of the Revised Code, as to whether the defendant remains incompetent to stand trial. The hospital, facility, or program shall make the reports after the initial six months of treatment and every two years after the initial report is made. The trial court shall provide copies of the reports to the prosecutor and to the counsel for the defendant or person. Within thirty days after its receipt pursuant to this division of a report from a hospital, facility, or program, the trial court shall hold a hearing on the continued commitment of the defendant or person or on any changes in the conditions of the commitment of the defendant or person. The defendant or person may request a change in the conditions of confinement, and the trial court shall conduct a hearing on that request if six months or more have elapsed since the most recent hearing was conducted under this section.

(D)(1) Except as otherwise provided in division (D)(2) of this section, when a defendant or person has been committed under section 2945.39 or 2945.40 of the Revised Code, at any time after evaluating the risks to public safety and the welfare of the defendant or person, the chief clinical officer of the hospital, facility, or program to which the defendant or person is committed may recommend a termination of the defendant's or person's commitment or a change in the conditions of the defendant's or person's commitment.

Except as otherwise provided in division (D)(2) of this section, if the chief clinical officer recommends on-grounds unsupervised movement, off-grounds supervised movement, or nonsecured status for the defendant or person or termination of the defendant's or person's commitment, the following provisions apply:

(a) If the chief clinical officer recommends on-grounds unsupervised movement or off-grounds supervised movement, the chief clinical officer shall file with the trial court an application for approval of the movement and shall send a copy of the application to the prosecutor. Within fifteen days after receiving the application, the prosecutor may request a hearing on the application and, if a hearing is requested, shall so inform the chief clinical officer. If the prosecutor does not request a hearing within the fifteen-day period, the trial court shall approve the application by entering its order approving the requested movement or, within five days after the expiration of the fifteen-day period, shall set a date for a hearing on the application. If the prosecutor requests a hearing on the application within the fifteen-day period, the trial court shall hold a hearing on the application within thirty days after the hearing is requested. If the trial court, within five days after the expiration of the fifteen-day period, sets a date for a hearing on the application, the trial court shall hold the hearing within thirty days after setting the hearing date. At least fifteen days before any hearing is held under this division, the trial court shall give the prosecutor written notice of the date, time, and place of the hearing. At the conclusion of each hearing conducted under this division, the trial court either shall approve or disapprove the application and shall enter its order accordingly.

(b) If the chief clinical officer recommends termination of the defendant's or person's commitment at any time or if the chief clinical officer recommends the first of any nonsecured status for the defendant or person, the chief clinical officer shall send written notice of this recommendation to the trial court and to the local forensic center. The local forensic center shall evaluate the committed defendant or person and, within thirty days after its receipt of the written notice, shall submit to the trial court and the chief clinical officer a written report of the evaluation. The trial court shall provide a copy of the chief clinical officer's written notice and of the local forensic center's written report to the prosecutor and to the counsel for the defendant or person. Upon the local forensic center's submission of the report to the trial court and the chief clinical officer, all of the following apply:

(i) If the forensic center disagrees with the recommendation of the chief clinical officer, it shall inform the chief clinical officer and the trial court of its decision and the reasons for the decision. The chief clinical officer, after consideration of the forensic center's decision, shall either withdraw, proceed with, or modify and proceed with the recommendation. If the chief clinical officer proceeds with, or modifies and proceeds with, the recommendation, the chief clinical officer shall proceed in accordance with division (D)(1)(b)(iii) of this section.

(ii) If the forensic center agrees with the recommendation of the chief clinical officer, it shall inform the chief clinical officer and the trial court of its decision and the reasons for the decision, and the chief clinical officer shall proceed in accordance with division (D)(1)(b)(iii) of this section.

(iii) If the forensic center disagrees with the recommendation of the chief clinical officer and the chief clinical officer proceeds with, or modifies and proceeds with, the recommendation or if the forensic center agrees with the recommendation of the chief clinical officer, the chief clinical officer shall work with the board of alcohol, drug addiction, and mental health services or community mental health board serving the area, as appropriate, to develop a plan to implement the recommendation. If the defendant or person is on medication, the plan shall include, but shall not be limited to, a system to monitor the defendant's or person's compliance with the prescribed medication treatment plan. The system shall include a schedule that clearly states when the defendant or person shall report for a medication compliance check. The medication compliance checks shall be based upon the effective duration of the prescribed medication, taking into account the route by which it is taken, and shall be scheduled at intervals sufficiently close together to detect a potential increase in mental illness symptoms that the medication is intended to prevent.

The chief clinical officer, after consultation with the board of alcohol, drug addiction, and mental health services or the community mental health board serving the area, shall send the recommendation and plan developed under division (D)(1)(b)(iii) of this section, in writing, to the trial court, the prosecutor and the counsel for the committed defendant or person. The trial court shall conduct a hearing on the recommendation and plan developed under division (D)(1)(b)(iii) of this section. Divisions (D)(1)(c) and (d) and (E) to (J) of this section apply regarding the hearing.

(c) If the chief clinical officer's recommendation is for nonsecured status or termination of commitment, the prosecutor may obtain an independent expert evaluation of the defendant's or person's mental condition, and the trial court may continue the hearing on the recommendation for a period of not more than thirty days to permit time for the evaluation.

The prosecutor may introduce the evaluation report or present other evidence at the hearing in accordance with the Rules of Evidence.

(d) The trial court shall schedule the hearing on a chief clinical officer's recommendation for nonsecured status or termination of commitment and shall give reasonable notice to the prosecutor and the counsel for the defendant or person. Unless continued for independent evaluation at the prosecutor's request or for other good cause, the hearing shall be held within thirty days after the trial court's receipt of the recommendation and plan.

(2)(a) Division (D)(1) of this section does not apply to on-grounds unsupervised movement of a defendant or person who has been committed under section 2945.39 or 2945.40 of the Revised Code, who is a mentally retarded person subject to institutionalization by court order, and who is being provided residential habilitation, care, and treatment in a facility operated by the department of mental retardation and developmental disabilities.

(b) If, pursuant to section 2945.39 of the Revised Code, the trial court commits a defendant who is found incompetent to stand trial and who is a mentally retarded person subject to institutionalization by court order, if the defendant is being provided residential habilitation, care, and treatment in a facility operated by the department of mental retardation and developmental disabilities, if an individual who is conducting a survey for the department of health to determine the facility's compliance with the certification requirements of the medicaid program under Chapter 5111. of the Revised Code and Title XIX of the "Social Security Act," 49 Stat. 620 (1935), 42 U.S.C.A. 301, as amended, cites the defendant's receipt of the residential habilitation, care, and treatment in the facility as being inappropriate under the certification requirements, if the defendant's receipt of the residential habilitation, care, and treatment in the facility potentially jeopardizes the facility's continued receipt of federal medicaid moneys, and if as a result of the citation the chief clinical officer of the facility determines that the conditions of the defendant's commitment should be changed, the department of mental retardation and developmental disabilities may cause the defendant to be removed from the particular facility and, after evaluating the risks to public safety and the welfare of the defendant and after determining whether another type of placement is consistent with the certification requirements, may place the defendant in another facility that the department selects as an appropriate facility for the defendant's continued receipt of residential habilitation, care, and treatment and that is a no less secure setting than the facility in which the defendant had been placed at the time of the citation. Within three days after the defendant's removal and alternative placement under the circumstances described in division (D)(2)(b) of this section, the department of mental retardation and developmental disabilities shall notify the trial court and the prosecutor in writing of the removal and alternative placement.

The trial court shall set a date for a hearing on the removal and alternative placement, and the hearing shall be held within twenty-one days after the trial court's receipt of the notice from the department of mental retardation and developmental disabilities. At least ten-days before the hearing is held, the trial court shall give the prosecutor, the department of mental retardation and developmental disabilities, and the counsel for the defendant written notice of the date, time, and place of the hearing. At the hearing, the trial court shall consider the citation issued by the individual who conducted the survey for the department of health to be prima-facie evidence of the fact that the defendant's commitment to the particular facility was inappropriate under the certification requirements of the medicaid program under chapter 5111. of the Revised Code and Title XIX of the "Social Security Act," 49 Stat. 620 (1935), 42 U.S.C.A. 301, as amended, and potentially jeopardizes the particular facility's continued receipt of federal medicaid moneys. At the conclusion of the hearing, the trial court may approve or disapprove the defendant's removal and alternative placement. If the trial court approves the defendant's removal and alternative placement, the department of mental retardation and developmental disabilities may continue the defendant's alternative placement. If the trial court disapproves the defendant's removal and alternative placement, it shall enter an order modifying the defendant's removal and alternative placement, but that order shall not require the department of mental retardation and developmental disabilities to replace the defendant for purposes of continued residential habilitation, care, and treatment in the facility associated with the citation issued by the individual who conducted the survey for the department of health.

(E) In making a determination under this section regarding nonsecured status or termination of commitment, the trial court shall consider all relevant factors, including, but not limited to, all of the following:

(1) Whether, in the trial court's view, the defendant or person currently represents a substantial risk of physical harm to the defendant or person or others;

(2) Psychiatric and medical testimony as to the current mental and physical condition of the defendant or person;

(3) Whether the defendant or person has insight into the dependant's or person's condition so that the defendant or person will continue treatment as prescribed or seek professional assistance as needed;

(4) The grounds upon which the state relies for the proposed commitment;

(5) Any past history that is relevant to establish the defendant's or person's degree of conformity to the laws, rules, regulations, and values of society;

(6) If there is evidence that the defendant's or person's mental illness is in a state of remission, the medically suggested cause and degree of the remission and the probability that the defendant or person will continue treatment to maintain the remissive state of the defendant's or person's illness should the defendant's or person's commitment conditions be altered.

(F) At any hearing held pursuant to division (C) or (D)(1) or (2) of this section, the defendant or the person shall have all the rights of a defendant or person at a commitment hearing as described in section 2945.40 of the Revised Code.

(G) In a hearing held pursuant to division (C) or (D)(1) of this section, the prosecutor has the burden of proof as follows:

(1) For a recommendation of termination of commitment, to show by clear and convincing evidence that the defendant or person remains a mentally ill person subject to hospitalization by court order or a mentally retarded person subject to institutionalization by court order;

(2) For a recommendation for a change in the conditions of the commitment to a less restrictive status, to show by clear and convincing evidence that the proposed change represents a threat to public safety or a threat to the safety of any person.

(H) In a hearing held pursuant to division (C) or (D)(1) or (2) of this section, the prosecutor shall represent the state or the public interest.

(I) At the conclusion of a hearing conducted under division (D)(1) of this section regarding a recommendation from the chief clinical officer of a hospital, program, or facility, the trial court may approve, disapprove, or modify the recommendation and shall enter an order accordingly.

(J)(1) A defendant or person who has been committed pursuant to section 2945.39 or 2945.40 of the Revised Code continues to be under the jurisdiction of the trial court until the final termination of the commitment. For purposes of division (J) of this section, the final termination of a commitment occurs upon the earlier of one of the following:

(a) The defendant or person no longer is a mentally ill person subject to hospitalization by court order or a mentally retarded person subject to institutionalization by court order, as determined by the trial court;

(b) The expiration of the maximum prison term or term of imprisonment that the defendant or person could have received if the defendant or person had been convicted of the most serious offense with which the defendant or person is charged or in relation to which the defendant or person was found not guilty by reason of insanity;

(c) The trial court enters an order terminating the commitment under the circumstances described in division (J)(2)(a)(ii) of this section.

(2)(a) If a defendant is found incompetent to stand trial and committed pursuant to section 2945.39 of the Revised Code, if neither of the circumstances described in divisions (J)(1)(a) and (b) of this section applies to that defendant, and if a report filed with the trial court pursuant to division (C) of this section indicates that the defendant presently is competent to stand trial or if, at any other time during the period of the defendant's commitment, the prosecutor, the counsel for the defendant, or the chief clinical officer of the hospital, facility, or program to which the defendant is committed files an application with the trial court alleging that the defendant presently is competent to stand trial and requesting a hearing on the competency issue or the trial court otherwise has reasonable cause to believe that the defendant presently is competent to stand trial and determines on its own motion to hold a hearing on the competency issue, the trial court shall schedule a hearing on the competency of the defendant to stand trial, shall give the prosecutor, the counsel for the defendant, and the chief clinical officer notice of the date, time, and place of the hearing at least fifteen days before the hearing, and shall conduct the hearing within thirty days of the filing of the application or of its own motion. If, at the conclusion of the hearing, the trial court determines that the defendant presently is capable of understanding the nature and objective of the proceedings against the defendant and of assisting in the defendant's defense, the trial court shall order that the defendant is competent to stand trial and shall be proceeded against as provided by law with respect to the applicable offenses described in division (C)(1) of section 2945.38 of the Revised Code and shall enter whichever of the following additional orders is appropriate:

(i) If the trial court determines that the defendant remains a mentally ill person subject to hospitalization by court order or a mentally retarded person subject to institutionalization by court order, the trial court shall order that the defendant's commitment to the hospital, facility, or program be continued during the pendency of the trial on the applicable offenses described in division (C)(1) of section 2945.38 of the Revised Code.

(ii) If the trial court determines that the defendant no longer is a mentally ill person subject to hospitalization by court order or a mentally retarded person subject to institutionalization by court order, the trial court shall order that the defendant's commitment to the hospital, facility, or program shall not be continued during the pendency of the trial on the applicable offenses described in division (C)(1) of section 2945.38 of the Revised Code. This order shall be a final termination of the commitment for purposes of division (J)(1)(c) of this section.

(b) If, at the conclusion of the hearing described in division (J)(2)(a) of this section, the trial court determines that the defendant remains incapable of understanding the nature and objective of the proceedings against the defendant or of assisting in the defendant's defense, the trial court shall order that the defendant continues to be incompetent to stand trial, that the defendant's commitment to the hospital, facility, or program shall be continued, and that the defendant remains subject to the jurisdiction of the trial court pursuant to that commitment, and to the provisions of this section, until the final termination of the commitment as described in division (J)(1) of this section.

(1996 S 285, eff. 7–1–97)

Library References

Mental Health ⚖439.
Westlaw Topic No. 257A.
C.J.S. Mental Health §§ 241 to 246.

2945.402 Conditional release

(A) In approving a conditional release, the trial court may set any conditions on the release with respect to the treatment, evaluation, counseling, or control of the defendant or person that the court considers necessary to protect the public safety and the welfare of the defendant or person. The trial court may revoke a defendant's or person's conditional release and order rehospitalization or reinstitutionalization at any time the conditions of the release have not been satisfied, provided that the revocation shall be in accordance with this section.

(B) A conditional release is a commitment. The hearings on continued commitment as described in section 2945.401 of the Revised Code apply to a defendant or person on conditional release.

(C) A person, agency, or facility that is assigned to monitor a defendant or person on conditional release immediately shall notify the trial court on learning that the defendant or person being monitored has violated the terms of the conditional release. Upon learning of any violation of the terms of the conditional release, the trial court may issue a temporary order of detention or, if necessary, an arrest warrant for the defendant or person. Within ten court days after the defendant's or person's detention or arrest, the trial court shall conduct a hearing to determine whether the conditional release should be modified or terminated. At the hearing, the defendant or person shall have the same rights as are described in division (C) of section 2945.40 of the Revised Code. The trial court may order a continuance of the ten-court-day period for no longer than ten days for good cause shown or for any period on motion of the defendant or person. If the trial court fails to conduct the hearing within the ten-court-day period and does not order a continuance in accordance with this division, the defendant or person shall be restored to the prior conditional release status.

(D) The trial court shall give all parties reasonable notice of a hearing conducted under this section. At the hearing, the prosecutor shall present the case demonstrating that the defendant or person violated the terms of the conditional release. If the court finds by a preponderance of the evidence that the defendant or person violated the terms of the conditional release, the court may continue, modify, or terminate the conditional release and shall enter its order accordingly.

(1996 S 285, eff. 7–1–97)

Library References

Mental Health ⚖439.
Westlaw Topic No. 257A.
C.J.S. Mental Health §§ 241 to 246.

CHAPTER 3103

HUSBAND AND WIFE

Section
3103.03   Duty of married person to support self, spouse, and children; duration of duty to support; third person's recovery of support; funeral expenses of spouse
3103.031 Parental duty of support
3103.05   Contracts
3103.06   Contracts affecting marriage

3103.03 Duty of married person to support self, spouse, and children; duration of duty to support; third person's recovery of support; funeral expenses of spouse

(A) Each married person must support the person's self and spouse out of the person's property or by the person's labor. If a married person is unable to do so, the spouse of the married person must assist in the support so far as the spouse is able. The biological or adoptive parent of a minor child must support the parent's minor children out of the parent's property or by the parent's labor.

(B) Notwithstanding section 3109.01 of the Revised Code and to the extent provided in section 3319.86 of the Revised Code, the parental duty of support to children shall continue beyond the age of majority as long as the child continuously attends on a full-time basis any recognized and accredited high school. That duty of support shall continue during seasonal vacation periods.

(C) If a married person neglects to support the person's spouse in accordance with this section, any other person, in good faith, may supply the spouse with necessaries for the support of the spouse and recover the reasonable value of the necessaries supplied from the married person who neglected to support the spouse unless the spouse abandons that person without cause.

(D) If a parent neglects to support the parent's minor child in accordance with this section and if the minor child in question is unemancipated, any other person, in good faith, may supply the minor child with necessaries for the support of the minor child and recover the reasonable value of the necessaries supplied from the parent who neglected to support the minor child.

(E) If a decedent during the decedent's lifetime has purchased an irrevocable preneed funeral contract pursuant to section 1109.75 of the Revised Code, then the duty of support owed to a spouse pursuant to this section does not include an obligation to pay for the funeral expenses of the deceased spouse. This division does not preclude a surviving spouse from assuming by contract the obligation to pay for the funeral expenses of the deceased spouse.

(2000 S 180, eff. 3–22–01; 1997 H 352, eff. 1–1–98; 1996 H 538, eff. 1–1–97; 1992 S 10, eff. 7–15–92; 1990 S 3, H 346; 1973 S 1; 1953 H 1; GC 8002–3; Source—GC 7997)

Uncodified Law

1990 H 346, § 3, eff. 5–31–90, reads, in part:

(A) Sections 1 and 2 of this act shall apply only to the estates of decedents who die on or after the effective date of this act.

Historical and Statutory Notes

Pre–1953 H 1 Amendments: 124 v S 65

Amendment Note: 2000 S 180 rewrote division (B) which prior thereto read:

"(B) Notwithstanding section 3109.01 of the Revised Code, the parental duty of support to children, including the duty of a parent to pay support pursuant to a child support order, shall continue beyond the age of majority as long as the child continuously attends on a full-time basis any recognized and accredited high school or a court-issued child support order provides that the duty of support continues beyond the age of majority. Except in cases in which a child support order requires the duty of support to continue for any period after the child reaches age nineteen, the order shall not remain in effect after the child reaches age nineteen. That duty of support shall continue during seasonal vacation periods."

Amendment Note: 1997 H 352 inserted or a court-issued child support order provides that the duty of support continues beyond the age of majority" and added the second sentence in division (B); and made changes to reflect gender neutral language.

Amendment Note: 1996 H 538 substituted "1109.75" for "1107.33" in division (E).

Comparative Laws

Fla.—West's F.S.A. § 61.13.
Ill.—ILCS 750 16/1 et seq.
La.—LSA-R.S. 14:74; LSA-C.C. art. 123.
N.Y.—McKinney's Family Court Act § 411 et seq.

Library References

Child Support ⚖22, 33.
Children Out-of-Wedlock ⚖21.
Husband and Wife ⚖4, 19.
Westlaw Topic Nos. 205, 76E, 76H.
C.J.S. Children Out-of-Wedlock §§ 40 to 42, 122.
C.J.S. Husband and Wife §§ 48 to 55.
C.J.S. Parent and Child §§ 156 to 158, 162 to 167, 172, 193.

Baldwin's Ohio Legislative Service, 1990 Laws of Ohio, H 346—LSC Analysis, p 5–87

3103.031 Parental duty of support

A biological parent of a child, a man determined to be the natural father of a child under sections 3111.01 to 3111.18 or 3111.20 to 3111.85 of the Revised Code, a parent who adopts a minor child pursuant to Chapter 3107. of the Revised Code, or a parent whose signed acknowledgment of paternity has become final pursuant to section 2151.232, 3111.25, or 3111.821 of the Revised Code assumes the parental duty of support for that child. Notwithstanding section 3109.01 of the Revised Code and to the extent provided in section 3119.86 of the Revised Code, the parental duty of support to the child shall continue beyond the age of majority as long as the child continuously attends on a full-time basis any recognized and accredited high school. That duty of support shall continue during seasonal vacation periods.

(2000 S 180, eff. 3–22–01; 1997 H 352, eff. 1–1–98; 1992 S 10, eff. 7–15–92)

Uncodified Law

1992 S 10, § 5, eff. 7–15–92, reads, in part: Section 3103.031 of the Revised Code, as enacted by this act, shall apply only to a father who signs a child's birth certificate on or after the effective date of this act.

Historical and Statutory Notes

Amendment Note: 2000 S 180 rewrote this section which prior thereto read:

"A biological parent of a child, a man determined to be the natural father of a child under sections 3111.01 to 3111.19 or 3111.20 to 3111.29 of the Revised Code, a parent who adopts a minor child pursuant to Chapter 3107. of the Revised Code, or a parent whose signed acknowledgment of paternity has become final pursuant to section 2151.232, 3111.211, or 5101.314 of the Revised Code assumes the parental duty of support for that child. Notwithstanding section 3109.01 of the Revised Code, the parental duty of support to the child shall continue beyond the age of majority as long as the child continuously attends on a full-time basis any recognized and accredited high school or a court-issued child support order provides that the duty of support continues beyond the age of majority. Except in cases in which a child support order requires the duty of support to continue for any period after the child reaches age nineteen, the order shall not remain in effect after the child reaches age nineteen. That duty of support shall continue during seasonal vacation periods."

Amendment Note: 1997 H 352 rewrote this section, which prior thereto read:

"A biological parent of a child, a man determined to be the natural father of a child under sections 3111.01 to 3111.19 or 3111.20 to 3111.29 of the Revised Code, a parent who adopts a minor child pursuant to Chapter 3107. of the Revised Code, a parent who acknowledges parentage on the child's birth certificate as provided in section 3705.09 of the Revised Code, or a parent whose signed acknowledgment of paternity is entered upon the probate court's journal under section 2105.18 of the Revised Code assumes the parental duty of support for that child. Notwithstanding section 3109.01 of the Revised Code, the parental duty of support to the child shall continue beyond the age of majority as long as the child continuously attends on a full-time basis any recognized and accredited high school. That duty of support shall continue during seasonal vacation periods."

Library References

Child Support ⚖33.
Children Out-of-Wedlock ⚖21.
Westlaw Topic Nos. 76E, 76H.
C.J.S. Children Out-of-Wedlock §§ 40 to 42, 122.
C.J.S. Parent and Child § 162.

3103.05 Contracts

A husband or wife may enter into any engagement or transaction with the other, or with any other person, which either might if unmarried; subject, in transactions between themselves, to the general rules which control the actions of persons occupying confidential relations with each other.

(1953 H 1, eff. 10–1–53; GC 8002–5; Source—GC 7999)

Historical and Statutory Notes

Pre–1953 H 1 Amendments: 124 v S 65

Comparative Laws

Ga.—O.C.G.A. § 19-3-10.
Ill.—ILCS 750 65/6.
Iowa—I.C.A. § 597.18.
Ky.—Baldwin's KRS 404.020.
Mass.—M.G.L.A. c. 209, § 2.
Minn.—M.S.A. § 519.03.
N.C.—G.S. § 52-2.
Neb.—R.R.S.1943, § 42–202.

N.J.—N.J.S.A. 37:2-16 et seq.
N.M.—NMSA 1978, § 40-2-2.

Library References

Husband and Wife ⚖17, 36 to 51, 79.
Westlaw Topic No. 205.
C.J.S. Husband and Wife §§ 44 to 46, 87 to 94, 97 to 101, 108.

3103.06 Contracts affecting marriage

A husband and wife cannot, by any contract with each other, alter their legal relations, except that they may agree to an immediate separation and make provisions for the support of either of them and their children during the separation.

(1953 H 1, eff. 10–1–53; GC 8002–6; Source—GC 8000)

Historical and Statutory Notes

Pre–1953 H 1 Amendments: 124 v S 65

Library References

Child Support ⚖43.
Divorce ⚖11.5.
Husband and Wife ⚖29, 30, 278.
Westlaw Topic Nos. 134, 205, 76E.
C.J.S. Husband and Wife §§ 60 to 73, 86, 220 to 224, 235 to 236.
C.J.S. Parent and Child §§ 156, 167, 176 to 179, 182, 209, 224.

CHAPTER 3105

DIVORCE, LEGAL SEPARATION, ANNULMENT, DISSOLUTION OF MARRIAGE

DIVORCE; GENERAL PROVISIONS

Section
3105.01 Grounds for divorce
3105.06 Notice by publication authorized in certain cases
3105.10 Power to dissolve marriage; enforcement of separation agreement providing for child support; condonation and recrimination defenses eliminated; effect on dower
3105.12 Evidence of marriage; common law marriage prohibited

LEGAL SEPARATION; DIVISION OF PROPERTY; SPOUSAL SUPPORT

3105.17 Grounds for legal separation

CHILD CUSTODY AND SUPPORT

3105.21 Custody and support of children; support orders

ANNULMENT

3105.31 Grounds for annulment

DIVORCE; GENERAL PROVISIONS

3105.01 Grounds for divorce

The court of common pleas may grant divorces for the following causes:

(A) Either party had a husband or wife living at the time of the marriage from which the divorce is sought;

(B) Willful absence of the adverse party for one year;

(C) Adultery;

(D) Extreme cruelty;

(E) Fraudulent contract;

(F) Any gross neglect of duty;

(G) Habitual drunkenness;

(H) Imprisonment of the adverse party in a state or federal correctional institution at the time of filing the complaint;

(I) Procurement of a divorce outside this state, by a husband or wife, by virtue of which the party who procured it is released from the obligations of the marriage, while those obligations remain binding upon the other party;

(J) On the application of either party, when husband and wife have, without interruption for one year, lived separate and apart without cohabitation;

(K) Incompatibility, unless denied by either party.

A plea of res judicata or of recrimination with respect to any provision of this section does not bar either party from obtaining a divorce on this ground.

(1994 H 571, eff. 10–6–94; 1990 H 514, eff. 1–1–91; 1989 H 129; 1982 H 477; 1974 H 233, S 348; 1953 H 1; GC 8003–1; Source—GC 11979)

Historical and Statutory Notes

Pre–1953 H 1 Amendments: 124 v S 65

Amendment Note: 1994 H 571 substituted "correctional" for "penal" in division (H).

Comparative Laws

Ariz.—A.R.S. § 25-312.
Ark.—A.C.A. § 9-12-301.
Conn.—C.G.S.A. § 46b-40.
Fla.—West's F.S.A. § 61.052.
Ga.—O.C.G.A. § 19-5-3 et seq.
Idaho—I.C. § 32-603 et seq.
Ind.—West's A.I.C. 31–15–2–3.
La.—LSA-C.C. art. 103.
Mass.—M.G.L.A. c. 208, § 1 et seq.
Me.—19-A M.R.S.A. § 902.
Mich.—M.C.L.A. § 552.6.
Minn.—M.S.A. § 518.06.
Mo.—V.A.M.S. § 452.305.
Neb.—R.R.S.1943, § 42-349, 42-361.
N.J.—N.J.S.A. 2A:34-2.
N.M.—NMSA 1978, § 40-4-1 et seq.
N.Y.—McKinney's Domestic Relations Law § 170.
Okl.—43 Okl.St.Ann. § 101.
Tex.—V.T.C.A. Family Code § 6.001 et seq.
W.Va.—Code, 48-5-201 et seq.

Library References

Divorce ⚖12 to 38.
Westlaw Topic No. 134.
C.J.S. Divorce §§ 13 to 70, 74.

3105.06 Notice by publication authorized in certain cases

If the residence of a defendant in an action for divorce, annulment, or legal separation is unknown, or if the defendant is not a resident of this state or is a resident of this state but absent from the state, notice of the pendency of the action shall be given by publication as provided by the Rules of Civil Procedure.

(1990 H 514, eff. 1–1–91; 1979 H 248; 1971 H 602; 1970 H 1201; 130 v H 467; 1953 H 1; GC 8003–7; Source—GC 11984)

Historical and Statutory Notes

Pre–1953 H 1 Amendments: 124 v S 65

Library References

Divorce ⚖︎79.
Westlaw Topic No. 134.
C.J.S. Divorce § 120.

3105.10 Power to dissolve marriage; enforcement of separation agreement providing for child support; condonation and recrimination defenses eliminated; effect on dower

(A) The court of common pleas shall hear any of the causes for divorce or annulment charged in the complaint and may, upon proof to the satisfaction of the court, pronounce the marriage contract dissolved and both of the parties released from their obligations.

(B)(1) A separation agreement providing for the support of children eighteen years of age or older is enforceable by the court of common pleas.

(2) A separation agreement that was voluntarily entered into by the parties may be enforceable by the court of common pleas upon the motion of either party to the agreement, if the court determines that it would be in the interests of justice and equity to require enforcement of the separation agreement.

(3) If a court of common pleas has a division of domestic relations, all cases brought for enforcement of a separation agreement under division (B)(1) or (2) of this section shall be assigned to the judges of that division.

(C) A plea of condonation or recrimination is not a bar to a divorce.

(D) Upon the granting of a divorce, on a complaint or counterclaim, by force of the judgment, each party shall be barred of all right of dower in real estate situated within this state of which the other was seized at any time during coverture.

(E) Upon the granting of a judgment for legal separation, when by the force of the judgment real estate is granted to one party, the other party is barred of all right of dower in the real estate and the court may provide that each party shall be barred of all rights of dower in the real estate acquired by either party at any time subsequent to the judgment.

"Dower" as used in this section has the meaning set forth in section 2103.02 of the Revised Code.

(1990 H 514, eff. 1–1–91; 1975 H 370; 1974 H 233; 130 v H 467; 1953 H 1; GC 8003–11; Source—GC 11986)

Historical and Statutory Notes

Pre–1953 H 1 Amendments: 124 v S 65

Library References

Child Support ⚖︎43.
Courts ⚖︎50.
Divorce ⚖︎57, 99, 321.5.
Dower and Curtesy ⚖︎52.
Husband and Wife ⚖︎278.
Marriage ⚖︎60(0.5).
Westlaw Topic Nos. 106, 134, 136, 205, 253, 76E.
C.J.S. Courts § 106.
C.J.S. Divorce §§ 96, 150.
C.J.S. Dower and Curtesy §§ 51, 159.
C.J.S. Husband and Wife §§ 220 to 224, 235 to 236.
C.J.S. Marriage §§ 63, 67.
C.J.S. Parent and Child §§ 156, 167, 176 to 179, 182, 209, 224.

3105.12 Evidence of marriage; common law marriage prohibited

(A) Except as provided in division (B) of this section, proof of cohabitation and reputation of the marriage of a man and woman is competent evidence to prove their marriage, and, in the discretion of the court, that proof may be sufficient to establish their marriage for a particular purpose.

(B)(1) On and after October 10, 1991, except as provided in divisions (B)(2) and (3) of this section, common law marriages are prohibited in this state, and the marriage of a man and woman may occur in this state only if the marriage is solemnized by a person described in section 3101.08 of the Revised Code and only if the marriage otherwise is in compliance with Chapter 3101. of the Revised Code.

(2) Common law marriages that occurred in this state prior to October 10, 1991, and that have not been terminated by death, divorce, dissolution of marriage, or annulment remain valid on and after October 10, 1991.

(3) Common law marriages that satisfy all of the following remain valid on and after October 10, 1991:

(a) They came into existence prior to October 10, 1991, or come into existence on or after that date, in another state or nation that recognizes the validity of common law marriages in accordance with all relevant aspects of the law of that state or nation.

(b) They have not been terminated by death, divorce, dissolution of marriage, annulment, or other judicial determination in this or another state or in another nation.

(c) They are not otherwise deemed invalid under section 3101.01 of the Revised Code.

(4) On and after October 10, 1991, all references in the Revised Code to common law marriages or common law marital relationships, including the references in sections 2919.25, 3113.31, and 3113.33 of the Revised Code, shall be construed to mean only common law marriages as described in divisions (B)(2) and (3) of this section.

(2004 H 272, eff. 5–7–04; 1991 H 32, eff. 10–10–91; 1953 H 1; GC 8003–13; Source—GC 11989)

Historical and Statutory Notes

Pre–1953 H 1 Amendments: 124 v S 65

Amendment Note: 2004 H 272 substituted "October 10, 1991" for "the effective date of this amendment" throughout the section; and added new division (B)(3)(c).

Comparative Laws

Fla.—West's F.S.A. § 741.211.
Idaho—I.C. § 32-201.
Ill.—ILCS 750 5/214.
Ky.—Baldwin's KRS 402.020.
N.J.—N.J.S.A. 37:1-10.

Library References

Marriage ⚖︎13, 50(5).
Westlaw Topic No. 253.
C.J.S. Marriage §§ 10, 19, 56.

LEGAL SEPARATION; DIVISION OF PROPERTY; SPOUSAL SUPPORT

3105.17 Grounds for legal separation

(A) Either party to the marriage may file a complaint for divorce or for legal separation, and when filed the other may file a counterclaim for divorce or for legal separation. The court of common pleas may grant divorces for the causes set forth in section 3105.01 of the Revised Code. The court of common pleas may grant legal separation on a complaint or counterclaim, regardless of whether the parties are living separately at the time the complaint or counterclaim is filed, for the following causes:

(1) Either party had a husband or wife living at the time of the marriage from which legal separation is sought;

(2) Willful absence of the adverse party for one year;

(3) Adultery;

(4) Extreme cruelty;

(5) Fraudulent contract;

(6) Any gross neglect of duty;

(7) Habitual drunkenness;

(8) Imprisonment of the adverse party in a state or federal correctional institution at the time of filing the complaint;

(9) On the application of either party, when husband and wife have, without interruption for one year, lived separate and apart without cohabitation;

(10) Incompatibility, unless denied by either party.

(B) The filing of a complaint or counterclaim for legal separation or the granting of a decree of legal separation under this section does not bar either party from filing a complaint or counterclaim for a divorce or annulment or obtaining a divorce or annulment.

(1994 H 571, eff. 10–6–94; 1990 H 514, eff. 1–1–91; 1974 H 233; 1953 H 1; GC 8003–18; Source—GC 11997)

Historical and Statutory Notes

Pre–1953 H 1 Amendments: 124 v S 65

Amendment Note: 1994 H 571 substituted "correctional" for "penal" in division (A)(8).

Library References

Divorce ⚖12 to 38, 171.
Westlaw Topic No. 134.
C.J.S. Divorce §§ 13 to 70, 74, 262 to 263, 265 to 266.

CHILD CUSTODY AND SUPPORT

3105.21 Custody and support of children; support orders

(A) Upon satisfactory proof of the causes in the complaint for divorce, annulment, or legal separation, the court of common pleas shall make an order for the disposition, care, and maintenance of the children of the marriage, as is in their best interests, and in accordance with section 3109.04 of the Revised Code.

(B) Upon the failure of proof of the causes in the complaint, the court may make the order for the disposition, care, and maintenance of any dependent child of the marriage as is in the child's best interest, and in accordance with section 3109.04 of the Revised Code.

(C) Any court of common pleas that makes or modifies an order for child support under this section shall comply with Chapters 3119., 3121., 3123., and 3125. of the Revised Code. If any person required to pay child support under an order made under this section on or after April 15, 1985, or modified on or after December 1, 1986, is found in contempt of court for failure to make support payments under the order, the court that makes the finding, in addition to any other penalty or remedy imposed, shall assess all court costs arising out of the contempt proceeding against the person and require the person to pay any reasonable attorney's fees of any adverse party, as determined by the court, that arose in relation to the act of contempt.

(2000 S 180, eff. 3–22–01; 1997 H 352, eff. 1–1–98; 1993 H 173, eff. 12–31–93; 1992 S 10; 1990 H 514, H 591; 1988 H 708; 1987 H 231; 1986 H 509; 1984 H 614; 1974 H 233)

Historical and Statutory Notes

Ed. Note: Former RC 3105.21(D) related to the duration of support orders beyond the child's eighteenth birthday. See now RC 3119.86 for provisions analogous to former RC 3105.21(D).

Ed. Note: Former 3105.21 repealed by 1970 H 1201, eff. 7–1–71; 130 v H 467; 1953 H 1; GC 8003–22; Source—GC 11998.

Pre–1953 H 1 Amendments: 124 v S 65

Amendment Note: 2000 S 180 rewrote division (C) and deleted division (D). Prior to amendment and deletion divisions (C) and (D) read:

"(C) Each order for child support made or modified under this section shall include as part of the order a general provision, as described in division (A)(1) of section 3113.21 of the Revised Code, requiring the withholding or deduction of income or assets of the obligor under the order as described in division (D) of section 3113.21 of the Revised Code, or another type of appropriate requirement as described in division (D)(3), (D)(4), or (H) of that section, to ensure that withholding or deduction from the income or assets of the obligor is available from the commencement of the support order for collection of the support and of any arrearages that occur; a statement requiring all parties to the order to notify the child support enforcement agency in writing of their current mailing address, current residence address, current residence telephone number, current driver's license number, and any changes to that information; and a notice that the requirement to notify the agency of all changes to that information continues until further notice from the court. Any court of common pleas that makes or modifies an order for child support under this section shall comply with sections 3113.21 to 3113.219 of the Revised Code. If any person required to pay child support under an order made under this section on or after April 15, 1985, or modified on or after December 1, 1986, is found in contempt of court for failure to make support payments under the order, the court that makes the finding, in addition to any other penalty or remedy imposed, shall assess all court costs arising out of the contempt proceeding against the person and require the person to pay any reasonable attorney's fees of any adverse party, as determined by the court, that arose in relation to the act of contempt.

"(D) Notwithstanding section 3109.01 of the Revised Code, if a court issues a child support order under this section, the order shall remain in effect beyond the child's eighteenth birthday as long as the child continuously attends on a full-time basis any recognized and accredited high school or the order provides that the duty of support of the child continues beyond the child's eighteenth birthday. Except in cases in which the order provides that the duty of support continues for any period after the child reaches age nineteen, the order shall not remain in effect after the child reaches age nineteen. Any parent ordered to pay support under a child support order issued under this section shall continue to pay support under the order, including during seasonal vacation periods, until the order terminates."

Amendment Note: 1997 H 352 deleted "on or after December 31, 1993," before "shall include", substituted "income" for "wages" twice and "(D)(3), (D)(4)" for "(D)(6), (D)(7)", inserted "current residence telephone number, current driver's license number,", and deleted "on or after April 12, 1990," before "shall comply", in division (C); inserted "or the order provides that the duty of support of the child continues beyond the child's eighteenth birthday" and added the second sentence in division (D); and made other nonsubstantive changes.

Amendment Note: 1993 H 173 rewrote division (C) before the first semicolon, which previously read:

"(C) Each order for child support made or modified under this section on or after December 1, 1986, shall be accompanied by one or more orders described in division (D) or (H) of section 3113.21 of the Revised Code, whichever is appropriate under the requirements of that section".

Library References

Child Custody ⇔9.
Child Support ⇔11, 496.
Westlaw Topic Nos. 76D, 76E.
C.J.S. Parent and Child §§ 55, 58 to 59, 203 to 205.

Baldwin's Ohio Legislative Service, 1990 Laws of Ohio, H 591—LSC Analysis, p 5–576

ANNULMENT

3105.31 Grounds for annulment

A marriage may be annulled for any of the following causes existing at the time of the marriage:

(A) That the party in whose behalf it is sought to have the marriage annulled was under the age at which persons may be joined in marriage as established by section 3101.01 of the Revised Code, unless after attaining such age such party cohabited with the other as husband or wife;

(B) That the former husband or wife of either party was living and the marriage with such former husband or wife was then and still is in force;

(C) That either party has been adjudicated to be mentally incompetent, unless such party after being restored to competency cohabited with the other as husband or wife;

(D) That the consent of either party was obtained by fraud, unless such party afterwards, with full knowledge of the facts constituting the fraud, cohabited with the other as husband or wife;

(E) That the consent to the marriage of either party was obtained by force, unless such party afterwards cohabited with the other as husband or wife;

(F) That the marriage between the parties was never consummated although otherwise valid.

(130 v H 467, eff. 9–24–63)

Comparative Laws

Ark.—A.C.A. § 9-12-201.
Conn.—C.G.S.A. § 46b-40.
Ga.—O.C.G.A. § 19-4-1 et seq.
Idaho—I.C. § 32-501 et seq.
Ill.—ILCS 750 5/301 et seq.
Ky.—Baldwin's KRS 403.120.
Mass.—M.G.L.A. c. 207, § 15.
Mich.—M.C.L.A. § 552.1.
Neb.—R.R.S.1943, § 42–374.
N.M.—NMSA 1978, § 40–1–9.
Wis.—W.S.A. 767.03.

Library References

Marriage ⇔58.
Westlaw Topic No. 253.
C.J.S. Marriage §§ 15 to 16, 18, 36 to 42, 63, 65.

CHAPTER 3107

ADOPTION

GENERAL PROVISIONS

Section	
3107.01	Definitions
3107.011	Representation by agency or attorney; false statements
3107.012	Application for adoption by foster caregiver seeking to adopt foster child
3107.013	Information about adoption
3107.014	Home study assessor; qualifications, registry
3107.015	Training programs for assessors
3107.016	Schedule of training
3107.02	Persons who may be adopted
3107.03	Persons who may adopt
3107.031	Home study
3107.032	Multiple children assessment
3107.033	Rules for conducting home study
3107.034	Abuse and neglect determination summary report
3107.04	Venue; caption of petition for adoption
3107.05	Petition; documents to be filed with clerk
3107.051	Submission of petition for adoption
3107.055	Accounting; disbursements

CONSENTS AND PUTATIVE FATHER REGISTRY

3107.06	Consents required
3107.061	Adoption of child without putative father's consent
3107.062	Putative father registry
3107.063	Request to search registry
3107.064	Required search of registry prior to adoption; exceptions
3107.065	Rules, registration form, and informational campaign for registry
3107.07	Consents not required
3107.071	Parental consent required despite voluntary permanent custody surrender agreement; exceptions
3107.08	Execution of consent

Section	
3107.081	Conditions for court acceptance of parental consent
3107.082	Assessor's meeting with parent prior to parent's consent to adoption
3107.083	Form authorizing release of information
3107.084	Withdrawal of consent

HISTORY OF BIOLOGICAL PARENTS

3107.09	Social and medical histories of biological parents
3107.091	Biological parent may add medical and social history to records concerning adopted person

ACCOUNTING TO COURT

3107.10	Out of county adoption; notice and information sharing
3107.101	Prospective home visits

COURT PROCEEDINGS

3107.11	Hearing and notice
3107.12	Prefinalization assessment and report
3107.13	Residence in adoptive home
3107.14	Court's discretion; final decree or interlocutory order
3107.141	Order to redo or supplement report or history; appointment of different assessor
3107.15	Effects of final decree
3107.16	Appeals; finality of decree
3107.161	Contested adoption; factors considered; best interest of child

RECORDS

3107.17	Confidentiality; records; access to histories of biological parents; rights of parties concerning proposed correction or expansion; procedures
3107.18	Recognition of decrees of other jurisdictions and countries
3107.19	Information forwarded to human services department

Section

ACCESS TO ADOPTION RECORDS BY ADOPTEES

3107.38 Adoptee's written request or petition to see adoption file
3107.39 Definitions
3107.40 Release of identifying information; consent of biological parents or siblings; procedures; withdrawal of release
3107.41 Rights of an adult who believes he is an adopted person; birth record; procedures
3107.42 Records declared not public
3107.43 Revealing information without statutory authority; penalty
3107.44 Rights of adult who believes he is adopted; release of information to petitioner; immunity from liability

ACCESS TO ADOPTION RECORDS BY BIRTH PARENTS AND SIBLINGS

3107.45 Definitions
3107.46 Denial or authorization of release form; rescinding of form
3107.47 Adoptee or adoptee's parents requesting copy of adoption file
3107.48 Adoptee's request that health department assist birth parents or siblings in finding adoptee's name by adoption
3107.49 Birth parent or sibling's request for assistance in finding adoptee's name by adoption
3107.50 Denial of release form; authorization of release form
3107.51 Form for adoptee's requesting assistance for birth parents or siblings finding adoptee's name by adoption
3107.52 Records not public
3107.53 No liability for release of information

OPEN ADOPTIONS

3107.60 Definitions
3107.61 Profiles of prospective adoptive parents shown to birth parent
3107.62 Nonbinding open adoption option
3107.63 Birth parent requesting open adoption of child voluntarily placed for adoption
3107.65 Prohibitions in open adoptions
3107.66 Written request for information on adoption
3107.67 Agency or attorney providing probate court with adoption records upon permanently ceasing to arrange adoptions
3107.68 Birth parent providing information and photographs

PENALTIES

3107.99 Penalties

Comparative Laws

Uniform Adoption Act

Table of Jurisdictions Wherein Act Has Been Adopted.

For text of Uniform Act, and variation notes and annotation materials for adopting jurisdictions, see Uniform Laws Annotated, Master Edition, Volume 9, Pt. IA.

Jurisdiction	Statutory Citation
Alaska	AS 25.23.005 to 25.23.240.
Arkansas	A.C.A. § 9–9–201 to 9–9–224.
North Dakota	NDCC 14–15–01 to 14–15–23.

Comparative Laws

Ariz.—A.R.S. § 8-101 et seq.
Ark.—A.C.A. § 9-9-201 et seq.
Fla.—West's F.S.A. § 63.012 et seq.
Ga.—O.C.G.A. § 19-8-1 et seq.
Idaho—I.C. § 16-1501 et seq.
Ill.—ILCS 750 50/1 et seq.
Ind.—West's A.I.C. 31–19–2–1 et seq.
Iowa—I.C.A. § 600.1 et seq.
Ky.—Baldwin's KRS 199.470 et seq.
Mass.—M.G.L.A. c. 210, § 1 et seq.
Me.—18-A M.R.S.A. § 9–101 et seq.
Mich.—M.C.L.A. § 710.21 et seq.
Minn.—M.S.A. § 259.21 et seq.
Mo.—V.A.M.S. § 453.010 et seq.
N.C.—G.S. § 48-1-100 et seq.
Neb.—R.R.S.1943, § 43–101 et seq.
N.J.—N.J.S.A. 9:3-37 et seq.
N.Y.—McKinney's Domestic Relations Law § 109 et seq.
Tenn.—T.C.A. § 36-1-101 et seq.
Tex.—V.T.C.A. Family Code § 162.001 et seq.
Wis.—W.S.A. 48.81 et seq.
W.Va.—Code, 48–22–101 et seq.

GENERAL PROVISIONS

3107.01 Definitions

As used in sections 3107.01 to 3107.19 of the Revised Code:

(A) "Agency" means any public or private organization certified, licensed, or otherwise specially empowered by law or rule to place minors for adoption.

(B) "Attorney" means a person who has been admitted to the bar by order of the Ohio supreme court.

(C) "Child" means a son or daughter, whether by birth or by adoption.

(D) "Court" means the probate courts of this state, and when the context requires, means the court of any other state empowered to grant petitions for adoption.

(E) "Foster caregiver" has the same meaning as in section 5103.02 of the Revised Code.

(F) "Identifying information" means any of the following with regard to a person: first name, last name, maiden name, alias, social security number, address, telephone number, place of employment, number used to identify the person for the purpose of the statewide education management information system established pursuant to section 3301.0714 of the Revised Code, and any other number federal or state law requires or permits to be used to identify the person.

(G) "Minor" means a person under the age of eighteen years.

(H) "Putative father" means a man, including one under age eighteen, who may be a child's father and to whom all of the following apply:

(1) He is not married to the child's mother at the time of the child's conception or birth;

(2) He has not adopted the child;

(3) He has not been determined, prior to the date a petition to adopt the child is filed, to have a parent and child relationship with the child by a court proceeding pursuant to sections 3111.01 to 3111.18 of the Revised Code, a court proceeding in another state, an administrative agency proceeding pursuant to sections 3111.38 to 3111.54 of the Revised Code, or an administrative agency proceeding in another state;

(4) He has not acknowledged paternity of the child pursuant to sections 3111.21 to 3111.35 of the Revised Code.

(2000 S 180, eff. 3–22–01; 2000 H 448, eff. 10–5–00; 1997 H 352, eff. 1–1–98; 1997 H 408, eff. 10–1–97; 1996 H 274, eff. 9–18–96; 1996 H 419, eff. 9–18–96; 1976 H 156, eff. 1–1–77)

Uncodified Law

1996 H 419, § 5: See Uncodified Law under 3107.06.

Historical and Statutory Notes

Ed. Note: Former 3107.01 repealed by 1976 H 156, eff. 1–1–77; 1973 S 1; 1953 H 1; GC 8004–1; Source—GC 10512–9.

Pre–1953 H 1 Amendments: 124 v S 65

Amendment Note: 2000 S 180 substituted "3111.18" for "3111.19", "3111.38" for "3111.20" and "3111.54" for "3111.29" in division (B)(3); and substituted "3111.25" for "3111.211" and "3111.821" for "5101.314" in division (B)(4).

Amendment Note: 2000 H 448 added new division (E) and redesignated former divisions (E) through (G) as new divisions (F) through (H).

Amendment Note: 1997 H 352 substituted "5101.314" for "2105.18" in division (G)(4).

Amendment Note: 1997 H 408 deleted former division (G); and redesignated former division (H) as new division (G). Prior to deletion, former division (G) read:

"(G) 'Private child placing agency,' 'private noncustodial agency,' and 'public children services agency' have the same meanings as in section 2151.011 of the Revised Code."

Amendment Note: 1996 H 274 added division (H)(4).

Amendment Note: 1996 H 419 rewrote this section, which previously read:

"As used in sections 3107.01 to 3107.19 of the Revised Code, unless the context otherwise requires:

"(A) 'Child' means a son or daughter, whether by birth or by adoption;

"(B) 'Court' means the probate courts of this state, and when the context requires, means the court of any other state empowered to grant petitions for adoption;

"(C) 'Minor' means a person under the age of eighteen years;

"(D) 'Agency' means any public or private organization certified, licensed, or otherwise specially empowered by law or rule to place minors for adoption."

Library References

Adoption ⟲1 to 25.
Westlaw Topic No. 17.
C.J.S. Adoption of Persons §§ 1 to 9, 15 to 164.
C.J.S. Conflict of Laws § 57.
Baldwin's Ohio Legislative Service, 1996 H 419—LSC Analysis, 3/L–336

3107.011 Representation by agency or attorney; false statements

(A) A person seeking to adopt a minor shall utilize an agency or attorney to arrange the adoption. Only an agency or attorney may arrange an adoption. An attorney may not represent with regard to the adoption both the person seeking to adopt and the parent placing a child for adoption.

Any person may informally aid or promote an adoption by making a person seeking to adopt a minor aware of a minor who will be or is available for adoption.

(B) A person seeking to adopt a minor who knowingly makes a false statement that is included in an application submitted to an agency or attorney to obtain services of that agency or attorney in arranging an adoption is guilty of the offense of falsification under section 2921.13 of the Revised Code.

(2006 S 238, eff. 9–21–06; 1996 H 419, eff. 9–18–96)

Historical and Statutory Notes

Amendment Note: 2006 S 238 designated division (A) and added division (B).

Library References

Adoption ⟲4, 6.
Infants ⟲17.
Westlaw Topic Nos. 17, 211.
C.J.S. Adoption of Persons §§ 10 to 21, 27 to 45, 140.
C.J.S. Infants §§ 6, 8 to 9.
Baldwin's Ohio Legislative Service, 1996 H 419—LSC Analysis, 3/L–336

3107.012 Application for adoption by foster caregiver seeking to adopt foster child

(A) A foster caregiver may use the application prescribed under division (B) of this section to obtain the services of an agency to arrange an adoption for the foster caregiver if the foster caregiver seeks to adopt the foster caregiver's foster child who has resided in the foster caregiver's home for at least twelve months prior to the date the foster caregiver submits the application to the agency.

(B) The department of job and family services shall prescribe an application for a foster caregiver to use under division (A) of this section. The application shall not require that the foster caregiver provide any information the foster caregiver already provided the department, or undergo an inspection the foster caregiver already underwent, to obtain a foster home certificate under section 5103.03 of the Revised Code.

(C) An agency that receives an application prescribed under division (B) of this section from a foster caregiver authorized to use the application shall not require, as a condition of the agency accepting or approving the application, that the foster caregiver undergo a criminal records check under section 2151.86 of the Revised Code as a prospective adoptive parent. The agency shall inform the foster caregiver, in accordance with division (G) of section 2151.86 of the Revised Code, that the foster caregiver must undergo the criminal records check before a court may issue a final decree of adoption or interlocutory order of adoption under section 3107.14 of the Revised Code.

(2000 H 448, eff. 10–5–00)

Historical and Statutory Notes

Ed. Note: Former 3107.012 amended and recodified as 3107.014 by 2000 H 448, eff. 10–5–00; 1998 H 446, eff. 8–5–98; 1996 H 419, eff. 9–18–96.

Library References

Adoption ⟲11.
Infants ⟲17, 226.
Westlaw Topic Nos. 17, 211.
C.J.S. Adoption of Persons §§ 10 to 14, 41, 80 to 83.
C.J.S. Infants §§ 6, 8 to 9, 43, 73 to 92.

3107.013 Information about adoption

An agency arranging an adoption pursuant to an application submitted to the agency under section 3107.012 of the Revised Code for a foster caregiver seeking to adopt the foster caregiver's foster child shall provide the foster caregiver information about adoption, including information about state adoption law, adoption assistance available pursuant to section 5153.163 of the Revised Code and Title IV–E of the "Social Security Act," 94 Stat. 501, 42 U.S.C.A. 670 (1980), as amended, the types of behavior that the prospective adoptive parents may anticipate from children who have experienced abuse and neglect, suggested interventions and the assistance available if the child exhibits those types of behavior after adoption, and other adoption issues the department of job and family services identifies. The agency shall provide the information to the foster caregiver in accordance with rules the department of job and family services shall adopt in accordance with Chapter 119. of the Revised Code.

(2001 S 27, eff. 3–15–02; 2000 H 448, eff. 10–5–00)

Historical and Statutory Notes

Ed. Note: Former 3107.013 amended and recodified as 3107.015 by 2000 H 448, eff. 10–5–00; 1999 H 471, eff. 7–1–00; 1996 H 419, eff. 6–20–96.

Amendment Note: 2001 S 27 rewrote this section which prior thereto read:

"An agency arranging an adoption pursuant to an application submitted to the agency under section 3107.012 of the Revised Code for a foster caregiver seeking to adopt the foster caregiver's foster child shall offer to provide the foster caregiver information about adoption, including information about state adoption law, adoption assistance available pursuant to section 5153.163 of the Revised Code and Title IV–E of the "Social Security Act," 94 Stat. 501, 42 U.S.C.A. 670 (1980), as amended, and other adoption issues the department of job and family services identifies. If the foster caregiver informs the agency that the foster caregiver wants the information, the agency shall provide the information to the foster caregiver in accordance with rules the department of job and family services shall adopt in accordance with Chapter 119. of the Revised Code."

Library References

Infants ⚖17, 226.
Westlaw Topic No. 211.
C.J.S. Adoption of Persons §§ 10 to 14, 41.
C.J.S. Infants §§ 6, 8 to 9, 43, 73 to 92.

3107.014 Home study assessor; qualifications, registry

(A) Except as provided in division (B) of this section, only an individual who meets all of the following requirements may perform the duties of an assessor under sections 3107.031, 3107.032, 3107.082, 3107.09, 3107.101, 3107.12, 5103.0324, and 5103.152 of the Revised Code:

(1) The individual must be in the employ of, appointed by, or under contract with a court, public children services agency, private child placing agency, or private noncustodial agency;

(2) The individual must be one of the following:

(a) A professional counselor, social worker, or marriage and family therapist licensed under Chapter 4757. of the Revised Code;

(b) A psychologist licensed under Chapter 4732. of the Revised Code;

(c) A student working to earn a four-year, post-secondary degree, or higher, in a social or behavior science, or both, who conducts assessor's duties under the supervision of a professional counselor, social worker, or marriage and family therapist licensed under Chapter 4757. of the Revised Code or a psychologist licensed under Chapter 4732. of the Revised Code. Beginning July 1, 2009, a student is eligible under this division only if the supervising professional counselor, social worker, marriage and family therapist, or psychologist has completed training in accordance with rules adopted under section 3107.015 of the Revised Code.

(d) A civil service employee engaging in social work without a license under Chapter 4757. of the Revised Code, as permitted by division (A)(5) of section 4757.41 of the Revised Code;

(e) A former employee of a public children services agency who, while so employed, conducted the duties of an assessor.

(3) The individual must complete training in accordance with rules adopted under section 3107.015 of the Revised Code.

(B) An individual in the employ of, appointed by, or under contract with a court prior to September 18, 1996, to conduct adoption investigations of prospective adoptive parents may perform the duties of an assessor under sections 3107.031, 3107.032, 3107.082, 3107.09, 3107.101, 3107.12, 5103.0324, and 5103.152 of the Revised Code if the individual complies with division (A)(3) of this section regardless of whether the individual meets the requirement of division (A)(2) of this section.

(C) A court, public children services agency, private child placing agency, or private noncustodial agency may employ, appoint, or contract with an assessor in the county in which a petition for adoption is filed and in any other county or location outside this state where information needed to complete or supplement the assessor's duties may be obtained. More than one assessor may be utilized for an adoption.

(D) Not later than January 1, 2008, the department of job and family services shall develop and maintain an assessor registry. The registry shall list all individuals who are employed, appointed by, or under contract with a court, public children services agency, private child placing agency, or private noncustodial agency and meet the requirements of an assessor as described in this section. A public children services agency, private child placing agency, private noncustodial agency, court, or any other person may contact the department to determine if an individual is listed in the assessor registry. An individual listed in the assessor registry shall immediately inform the department when that individual is no longer employed, appointed by, or under contract with a court, public children services agency, private child placing agency, or private noncustodial agency to perform the duties of an assessor as described in this section. The director of job and family services shall adopt rules in accordance with Chapter 119. of the Revised Code necessary for the implementation, contents, and maintenance of the registry, and any sanctions related to the provision of information, or the failure to provide information, that is needed for the proper operation of the assessor registry.

(2006 S 238, eff. 9–21–06; 2000 H 448, eff. 10–5–00)

Historical and Statutory Notes

Ed. Note: 3107.014 is former 3107.012, amended and recodified by 2000 H 448, eff. 10–5–00; 1998 H 446, eff. 8–5–98; 1996 H 419, eff. 9–18–96.

Amendment Note: 2006 S 238 rewrote this section. See *Baldwin's Ohio Legislative Service Annotated*, 2006, page 3/L–1574, or the OH–LEGIS or OH–LEGIS–OLD database on WESTLAW, for prior version of this section.

Amendment Note: 2000 H 448 inserted "5103.0324" in divisions (A) and (B); added new division (A)(2)(e); and substituted "3107.015" for "3107.013" in division (A)(3).

Amendment Note: 1998 H 446 substituted "in the employ of, appointed by," for "employed by" and inserted "court," in division (A)(1); substituted "division (A)(5) of section 4757.41" for "division (E) of section 4757.16" in division (A)(2)(d); rewrote division (B); and added division (C). Prior to amendment, division (B) read:

"(B) An individual employed by a court prior to the effective date of this section to conduct home studies of prospective adoptive parents may conduct home studies under section 3107.031 of the Revised Code if the individual complies with division (A)(3) of this section."

Library References

Infants ⚖17.
Westlaw Topic No. 211.
C.J.S. Adoption of Persons §§ 10 to 14, 41.
C.J.S. Infants §§ 6, 8 to 9.
Baldwin's Ohio Legislative Service, 1996 H 419—LSC Analysis, 3/L–336

3107.015 Training programs for assessors

The director of job and family services shall adopt rules in accordance with Chapter 119. of the Revised Code governing the training an individual must complete for the purpose of division (A)(3) of section 3107.014 of the Revised Code. The training shall include courses on adoption placement practice, federal and state adoption assistance programs, and post adoption support services.

(2006 S 238, eff. 9–21–06; 2000 H 448, eff. 10–5–00)

Historical and Statutory Notes

Ed. Note: 3107.015 is former 3107.013, amended and recodified by 2000 H 448, eff. 10–5–00; 1999 H 471, eff. 7–1–00; 1996 H 419, eff. 6–20–96.

Amendment Note: 2006 S 238 substituted "The" for "Not later than ninety days after June 20, 1996, the" and substituted "training" for "education programs" in the first sentence; and substituted "training" for "education programs" in the second sentence.

Amendment Note: 2000 H 448 substituted "June 20, 1996" for "the effective date of this section" and "3107.014" for "3107.012".

Amendment Note: 1999 H 471 substituted "director of job and family services" for "department of human services".

Library References

Infants ⇌17.
Westlaw Topic No. 211.
C.J.S. Adoption of Persons §§ 10 to 14, 41.
C.J.S. Infants §§ 6, 8 to 9.
Baldwin's Ohio Legislative Service, 1996 H 419—LSC Analysis, 3/L–336

3107.016 Schedule of training

The department of job and family services shall develop a schedule of training that meets the requirements established in rules adopted pursuant to section 3107.015 of the Revised Code. The schedule shall include enough training to provide all agencies equal access to the training. The department shall distribute the schedule to all agencies.

(2006 S 238, eff. 9–21–06; 2000 H 448, eff. 10–5–00)

Historical and Statutory Notes

Amendment Note: 2006 S 238 rewrote this section, which prior thereto read:

"The department of job and family services shall develop a schedule of education programs that meet the requirements established in rules adopted pursuant to section 3107.015 of the Revised Code. The schedule shall include enough programs to provide all agencies equal access to the programs. The department shall distribute the schedule to all agencies."

Library References

Infants ⇌17.
Westlaw Topic No. 211.
C.J.S. Adoption of Persons §§ 10 to 14, 41.
C.J.S. Infants §§ 6, 8 to 9.

3107.02 Persons who may be adopted

(A) Any minor may be adopted.

(B) An adult may be adopted under any of the following conditions:

(1) If the adult is totally and permanently disabled;

(2) If the adult is determined to be a mentally retarded person as defined in section 5123.01 of the Revised Code;

(3) If the adult had established a child-foster caregiver or child-stepparent relationship with the petitioners as a minor, and the adult consents to the adoption;

(4) If the adult was, at the time of the adult's eighteenth birthday, in the permanent custody of a public children services agency or a private child placing agency, and the adult consents to the adoption.

(C) When proceedings to adopt a minor are initiated by the filing of a petition, and the eighteenth birthday of the minor occurs prior to the decision of the court, the court shall require the person who is to be adopted to submit a written statement of consent or objection to the adoption. If an objection is submitted, the petition shall be dismissed, and if a consent is submitted, the court shall proceed with the case, and may issue an interlocutory order or final decree of adoption.

(D) Any physical examination of the individual to be adopted as part of or in contemplation of a petition to adopt may be conducted by any health professional authorized by the Revised Code to perform physical examinations, including a physician assistant, a clinical nurse specialist, a certified nurse practitioner, or a certified nurse-midwife. Any written documentation of the physical examination shall be completed by the healthcare professional who conducted the examination.

(E) An adult who consents to an adoption pursuant to division (B)(4) of this section shall provide the court with the name and contact information of the public children services agency or private child placing agency that had permanent custody of that adult. The petitioner shall request verification from the agency as to whether the adult was or was not in the permanent custody of that agency at the time of the adult's eighteenth birthday and provide the verification to the court.

(2006 S 238, eff. 9–21–06; 2002 S 245, eff. 3–31–03; 2000 H 448, eff. 10–5–00; 1984 H 71, eff. 9–20–84; 1981 H 1; 1976 H 156)

Historical and Statutory Notes

Ed. Note: Former 3107.02 repealed by 1976 H 156, eff. 1–1–77; 1953 H 1; GC 8004–2; Source—GC 10512–10; see now 3107.03 for provisions analogous to former 3107.02.

Pre–1953 H 1 Amendments: 124 v S 65

Amendment Note: 2006 S 238 added division (B)(4) and (E); and made other nonsubstantive changes.

Amendment Note: 2002 S 245 added division (D).

Amendment Note: 2000 H 448 substituted "caregiver" for "parent" in division (B)(3); and made changes to reflect gender neutral language.

Library References

Adoption ⇌5, 9.1, 13.
Westlaw Topic No. 17.
C.J.S. Adoption of Persons §§ 22 to 27, 46 to 47, 77, 93 to 102.

3107.03 Persons who may adopt

The following persons may adopt:

(A) A husband and wife together, at least one of whom is an adult;

(B) An unmarried adult;

(C) The unmarried minor parent of the person to be adopted;

(D) A married adult without the other spouse joining as a petitioner if any of the following apply:

(1) The other spouse is a parent of the person to be adopted and supports the adoption;

(2) The petitioner and the other spouse are separated under section 3103.06 or 3105.17 of the Revised Code;

(3) The failure of the other spouse to join in the petition or to support the adoption is found by the court to be by reason of prolonged unexplained absence, unavailability, incapacity, or circumstances that make it impossible or unreasonably difficult to obtain either the support or refusal of the other spouse.

(1996 H 419, eff. 9–18–96; 1976 H 156, eff. 1–1–77)

Historical and Statutory Notes

Ed. Note: 3107.03 is analogous to former 3107.02, repealed by 1976 H 156, eff. 1–1–77.

Ed. Note: Former 3107.03 repealed by 1976 H 156, eff. 1–1–77; 1969 S 49; 1953 H 1; GC 8004–3; Source—GC 10512–11; see now 3107.05 for provisions analogous to former 3107.03.

Pre–1953 H 1 Amendments: 124 v S 65

Amendment Note: 1996 H 419 substituted "supports," "support," and "support" for "consents to," "consent to," and "consent," respectively, in divisions (D)(1) and (3).

Library References

Adoption ⟾4.
Westlaw Topic No. 17.
C.J.S. Adoption of Persons §§ 15 to 21, 27.
Baldwin's Ohio Legislative Service, 1996 H 419—LSC Analysis, 3/L–336

3107.031 Home study

Except as otherwise provided in this section, an assessor shall conduct a home study for the purpose of ascertaining whether a person seeking to adopt a minor is suitable to adopt. A written report of the home study shall be filed with the court at least ten days before the petition for adoption is heard.

A person seeking to adopt a minor who knowingly makes a false statement that is included in the written report of a home study conducted pursuant to this section is guilty of the offense of falsification under section 2921.13 of the Revised Code, and such a home study shall not be filed with the court. If such a home study is filed with the court, the court may strike the home study from the court's records.

The report shall contain the opinion of the assessor as to whether the person who is the subject of the report is suitable to adopt a minor, any multiple children assessment required under section 3107.032 of the Revised Code, and other information and documents specified in rules adopted by the director of job and family services under section 3107.033 of the Revised Code. The assessor shall not consider the person's age when determining whether the person is suitable to adopt if the person is old enough to adopt as provided by section 3107.03 of the Revised Code.

An assessor may request departments or agencies within or outside this state to assist in the home study as may be appropriate and to make a written report to be included with and attached to the report to the court. The assessor shall make similar home studies and reports on behalf of other assessors designated by the courts of this state or another place.

Upon order of the court, the costs of the home study and other proceedings shall be paid by the person seeking to adopt, and, if the home study is conducted by a public agency or public employee, the part of the cost representing any services and expenses shall be taxed as costs and paid into the state treasury or county treasury, as the court may direct.

On request, the assessor shall provide the person seeking to adopt a copy of the report of the home study. The assessor shall delete from that copy any provisions concerning the opinion of other persons, excluding the assessor, of the person's suitability to adopt a minor.

This section does not apply to a foster caregiver seeking to adopt the foster caregiver's foster child if the foster child has resided in the foster caregiver's home for at least twelve months prior to the date the foster caregiver submits an application prescribed under division (B) of section 3107.012 of the Revised Code to the agency arranging the adoption.

(2006 S 238, eff. 9–21–06; 2000 H 448, eff. 10–5–00; 1999 H 471, eff. 7–1–00; 1996 H 274, eff. 9–18–96; 1996 H 419, eff. 9–18–96)

Historical and Statutory Notes

Ed. Note: 3107.031 is former 3107.12, amended and recodified by 1996 H 419, eff. 9–18–96; 1984 H 84, eff. 3–19–85; 1978 S 340; 1976 H 156.

Amendment Note: 2006 S 238 added the second paragraph; inserted ", any multiple children assessment required under section 3107.032 of the Revised Code," and substituted "3107.033" for "3107.032" in the first sentence of the third paragraph.

Amendment Note: 2000 H 448 substituted "Except as otherwise provided in this section, an" for "an"; and added the last paragraph.

Amendment Note: 1999 H 471 substituted "director of job and family services" for "department of human services" in the second paragraph.

Amendment Note: 1996 H 274 deleted "Except when a stepparent adopts a stepchild," from the beginning of the first paragraph.

Amendment Note: 1996 H 419 rewrote this section, which formerly read:

"(A) An investigation shall be made by the department of human services, an agency, or other person appointed by the court into the conditions and antecedents of a minor sought to be adopted and of the petitioner, for the purpose of ascertaining whether the adoptive home is a suitable home for the minor and whether the proposed adoption is in the best interest of the minor. If the minor is in the custody of the department or an agency, the department or agency shall perform the investigation.

"(B) A written report of the investigation as described in division (C) of this section shall be filed with the court at least ten days before the petition for adoption is heard.

"(C) The report of the investigation shall contain, in addition to any other information that the court requires regarding the petitioner or the minor sought to be adopted, the following information:

"(1) The physical and mental health, emotional stability, and personal integrity of the petitioner and the ability of the petitioner to provide for the needs of the minor;

"(2) The physical, mental, and developmental condition of the minor;

"(3) The minor's family background, including names and identifying data regarding the biological or other legal parents, and, except when the adoption is by a stepparent or grandparent, the social and medical histories described in division (D) of this section, to the extent that they can be prepared;

"(4) The reasons for the minor's placement with persons other than his biological or other legal parents, their attitude toward the proposed adoption, and the circumstances under which the minor came to be placed in the home of the petitioner;

"(5) The attitude of the minor toward the proposed adoption in any case in which the minor's age makes this feasible;

"(6) The recommendation of the investigator as to the granting or denial of the petition for adoption.

"(D)(1) The department of human services shall prescribe, and shall supply for purposes of an investigation pursuant to division (A) of this section, forms for the taking of the social and medical histories of the biological parents of minors sought to be adopted.

"(2) Except when an adoption is by a stepparent or grandparent, the department, an agency, and any other person appointed by a court to make an investigation pursuant to division (A) of this section, to the extent possible, shall record the social and medical histories of the biological parents of the minor sought to be adopted, using the forms prescribed pursuant to division (D)(1) of this section. The investigator shall not include on the forms the names of the biological parents or other ancestors of the minor, or any identifying data that would allow a person, except the court or the investigator, to determine the identity of the biological parents or other ancestors.

"(3) The social history of the biological parents of a minor sought to be adopted shall describe and identify the ethnic, racial, religious, marital, physical characteristics, educational, cultural, talent and hobby, and work experience background of the biological parents of the minor. The medical history of the biological parents of a minor sought to be adopted shall identify major diseases, malformations, allergies, ear or eye defects, major conditions, and major health problems of the biological parents that are or may be congenital or familial. These histories may include other social and medical information relative to the biological parents, and shall include social and medical information relative to the minor's other ancestors.

"The social and medical histories may be obtained through interviews with the biological parents or other persons, and from any available records if a parent or any legal guardian of a parent consents to the release of information contained in a record. If the investigator considers it necessary, it may request that a parent undergo a medical examination. In obtaining social and medical histories of a biological parent, an investigator shall inform the biological parent, or a person other than a biological parent who provides information pursuant to this section, of the purpose and use of the histories and of his right to correct or expand the histories at any time.

"(4) A biological parent, or a person other than a biological parent who provided information in the preparation of the social and medical histories of the biological parents of a minor, may cause, in accordance with this division, the histories to be corrected or expanded to include different or additional types of information. A biological parent or such a person may cause the histories to be corrected or expanded at any time prior or subsequent to the adoption of the minor, including, but not limited to, at any time after the minor becomes an adult. A biological parent may cause the histories to be corrected or expanded even if he did not provide any information to the investigator at the time the histories were prepared.

"To cause the histories to be corrected or expanded, a biological parent or such a person shall provide the information that he wishes to have included, or shall specify the information that he wishes to have corrected, to one of the following, whichever is appropriate under the circumstances:

"(a) subject to division (D)(4)(b) of this section, if the biological parent or person knows the investigator that prepared the histories, to the investigator;

"(b) if the biological parent or person does not know the investigator that prepared the histories, if he ascertains that the investigator has ceased to exist, or if an investigator other than the department of human services refuses to assist him, to the clerk of the court involved in the adoption or, if that court is not known, to the department of health.

"If an investigator receives information from a biological parent or such a person pursuant to division (D)(4)(a) of this section and is willing to assist the biological parent or person, it shall determine whether the information is of a type that divisions (D)(2) and (3) of this section permit to be included in the histories and, to the best of its ability, whether the information is accurate. If it determines the information is of a permissible type and accurate, the investigator shall cause the histories to be corrected or expanded to reflect the information. If, at the time the information is received, the histories have been filed with the court as required by division (D)(6) of this section, the clerk of the court shall cooperate with the investigator in the correcting or expanding of the histories.

"If the department of health or a clerk receives information from a biological parent or such a person pursuant to division (D)(4)(b) of this section, it shall determine whether the information is of a type that divisions (D)(2) and (3) of this section permit to be included in the histories and, to the best of its ability, whether the information is accurate. If a clerk determines the information is of a permissible type and accurate, he shall cause the histories to be corrected or expanded to reflect the information. If the department of health so determines, the clerk of the court involved shall cooperate with the department in the correcting or expanding of the histories.

"(5) An investigator shall comply, to the extent possible, with division (D)(3) of this section, but neither the failure of the investigator to obtain all or any part of the information mentioned in that division nor the refusal of a biological parent to supply information shall invalidate, delay, or otherwise affect the adoption.

"(6) An investigator shall file, as part of the report required by division (B) of this section, the social and medical histories of the biological parents prepared, to the extent possible, pursuant to divisions (D)(2) and (3) of this section. The court promptly shall provide a copy of the social and medical histories filed with it to the petitioner. No interlocutory order or final decree of adoption shall be entered by a court, in a case involving the adoption of a minor, if either the histories of his biological parents have not been so filed or the copy of the histories has not been so provided.

"(E) The department of human services, an agency, or a person, when required to make an investigation pursuant to division (A) of this section, may request departments or agencies within or outside this state to make or assist in the investigation as may be appropriate and to make a written report which shall be included with and attached to the report to the court. The department, an agency, or a person appointed to make an investigation pursuant to division (A) of this section shall make similar investigations and reports on behalf of departments, agencies, or persons designated by the courts of this state or another place.

"(F) Upon order of the court, the costs of the investigation and other proceedings shall be paid by the petitioner, and, if the investigation is conducted by a public agency or public employee, the part of the cost representing any services and expenses shall be taxed as costs and paid into the state treasury or county treasury, as the court may direct."

Library References

Adoption ⚖ 9.1, 13.
Westlaw Topic No. 17.
C.J.S. Adoption of Persons §§ 46 to 47, 77, 93 to 102.
Baldwin's Ohio Legislative Service, 1996 H 419—LSC Analysis, 3/L–336

3107.032 Multiple children assessment

(A) Except as provided in division (C) of this section, each time a person seeking to adopt a minor or foster child will have at least five children residing in the prospective adoptive home after the minor or foster child to be adopted is placed in the home, an assessor, on behalf of an agency or attorney arranging an adoption pursuant to sections 3107.011 or 3107.012 of the Revised Code, shall complete a multiple children assessment during the home study. The multiple children assessment shall evaluate the ability of the person seeking to adopt in meeting the needs of the minor or foster child to be adopted and continuing to meet the needs of the children residing in the home. The assessor shall include the multiple children assessment in the written report of the home study filed pursuant to section 3107.031 of the Revised Code.

(B) The director of job and family services shall adopt rules in accordance with Chapter 119. of the Revised Code necessary for an assessor to complete a multiple children assessment.

(C) This section does not apply to an adoption by a stepparent whose spouse is a biological or adoptive parent of the minor to be adopted.

(2006 S 238, eff. 9–21–06)

Historical and Statutory Notes

Ed. Note: Former RC 3107.032 amended and recodified as RC 3107.033 by 2006 S 238, eff. 9–21–06; 1999 H 471, eff. 7–1–00; 1996 H 419, eff. 6–20–96.

3107.033 Rules for conducting home study

Not later than January 1, 2008, the director of job and family services shall adopt rules in accordance with Chapter 119. of the Revised Code specifying both of the following:

(A) The manner in which a home study is to be conducted and the information and documents to be included in a home study report, which shall include, pursuant to section 3107.034 of the Revised Code, a summary report of a search of the uniform statewide automated child welfare information system established in section 5101.13 of the Revised Code;

(B) A procedure under which a person whose application for adoption has been denied as a result of a search of the uniform statewide automated child welfare information system established in section 5101.13 of the Revised Code as part of the home study may appeal the denial to the agency that employed the assessor who filed the report.

(2006 S 238, eff. 9–21–06)

Historical and Statutory Notes

Ed. Note: RC 3107.033 is former RC 3107.032, amended and recodified by 2006 S 238, eff. 9–21–06; 1999 H 471, eff. 7–1–00; 1996 H 419, eff. 6–20–96.

Amendment Note: 2006 S 238 rewrote this section, which prior thereto read:

"Not later than ninety days after June 20, 1996, the director of job and family services shall adopt rules in accordance with Chapter 119. of the Revised Code specifying the manner in which a home study is to be conducted and the information and documents to be included in a home study report."

Amendment Note: 1999 H 471 substituted "June 20, 1996" for "the effective date of this section" and "director of job and family services" for "department of human services".

Library References

Adoption ⚖9.1, 13.
Infants ⚖17.
Westlaw Topic Nos. 17, 211.
C.J.S. Adoption of Persons §§ 10 to 14, 41, 46 to 47, 77, 93 to 102.
C.J.S. Infants §§ 6, 8 to 9.

Baldwin's Ohio Legislative Service, 1996 H 419—LSC Analysis, 3/L-336

3107.034 Abuse and neglect determination summary report

(A) The summary report of a search of the uniform statewide automated child welfare information system established in section 5101.13 of the Revised Code that is required under section 3107.033 of the Revised Code shall contain, if applicable, a chronological list of abuse and neglect determinations or allegations of which the person seeking to adopt is subject and in regards to which a public children services agency has done one of the following:

(1) Determined that abuse or neglect occurred;

(2) Initiated an investigation, and the investigation is ongoing;

(3) Initiated an investigation and the agency was unable to determine whether abuse or neglect occurred.

(B) The summary report required under section 3107.033 of the Revised Code shall not contain any of the following:

(1) An abuse and neglect determination of which the person seeking to adopt is subject and in regards to which a public children services agency determined that abuse or neglect did not occur;

(2) Information or reports the dissemination of which is prohibited by, or interferes with eligibility under, the "Child Abuse Prevention and Treatment Act," 88 Stat. 4 (1974), 42 U.S.C. 5101 et seq., as amended;

(3) The name of the person who or entity that made, or participated in the making of, the report of abuse or neglect.

(C)(1) An application for adoption may be denied based on a summary report containing the information described under division (A)(1) of this section, when considered within the totality of the circumstances. An application that is denied may be appealed using the procedure adopted pursuant to division (B) of section 3107.033 of the Revised Code.

(2) An application for adoption shall not be denied solely based on a summary report containing the information described under division (A)(2) or (3) of this section.

(2006 S 238, eff. 9-21-06)

3107.04 Venue; caption of petition for adoption

(A) A petition for adoption shall be filed in the court in the county in which the person to be adopted was born, or in which, at the time of filing the petition, the petitioner or the person to be adopted or parent of the person to be adopted resides, or in which the petitioner is stationed in military service, or in which the agency having the permanent custody of the person to be adopted is located.

(B) If the court finds in the interest of justice that the case should be heard in another forum, the court may stay the proceedings or dismiss the petition in whole or in part on any conditions that are just, or certify the case to another court.

(C) The caption of a petition for adoption shall be styled, "In the matter of adoption of _____". The person to be adopted shall be designated in the caption under the name by which he is to be known if the petition is granted.

(1976 H 156, eff. 1-1-77)

Historical and Statutory Notes

Ed. Note: Former 3107.04 repealed by 1976 H 156, eff. 1-1-77; 1975 S 145; 1953 H 1; GC 8004-4; Source—GC 10512-12; see now 3107.11 for provisions analogous to former 3107.04.

Pre-1953 H 1 Amendments: 124 v S 65

Library References

Adoption ⚖10, 11.
Westlaw Topic No. 17.
C.J.S. Adoption of Persons §§ 78 to 83.

3107.05 Petition; documents to be filed with clerk

(A) A petition for adoption shall be prepared and filed according to the procedure for commencing an action under the Rules of Civil Procedure. It shall include the following information:

(1) The date and place of birth of the person to be adopted, if known;

(2) The name of the person to be adopted, if known;

(3) The name to be used for the person to be adopted;

(4) The date of placement of a minor and the name of the person placing the minor;

(5) The full name, age, place, and duration of residence of the petitioner;

(6) The marital status of the petitioner, including the date and place of marriage, if married;

(7) The relationship to the petitioner of the person to be adopted;

(8) That the petitioner has facilities and resources suitable to provide for the nurture and care of the person to be adopted, and that it is the desire of the petitioner to establish the relationship of parent and child with the person to be adopted;

(9) A description and estimate of value of all property of the person to be adopted;

(10) The name and address, if known, of any person whose consent to the adoption is required, but who has not consented, and facts that explain the lack of the consent normally required to the adoption.

(B) A certified copy of the birth certificate of the person to be adopted, if available, and ordinary copies of the required consents, and relinquishments of consents, if any, shall be filed with the clerk.

(1976 H 156, eff. 1-1-77)

Historical and Statutory Notes

Ed. Note: 3107.05 is analogous to former 3107.03, repealed by 1976 H 156, eff. 1-1-77.

Ed. Note: Former 3107.05 repealed by 1976 H 156, eff. 1-1-77; 1969 S 49; 1953 H 1; GC 8004-5; Source—GC 10512-13; see now 3107.12 for provisions analogous to former 3107.05.

Pre-1953 H 1 Amendments: 124 v S 65

Library References

Adoption ⬅︎11.
Westlaw Topic No. 17.
C.J.S. Adoption of Persons §§ 80 to 83.

3107.051 Submission of petition for adoption

(A) Except as provided in division (B) of this section, a person seeking to adopt a minor, or the agency or attorney arranging the adoption, shall submit a petition for the minor's adoption no later than ninety days after the date the minor is placed in the person's home. Failure to file a petition within the time provided by this division does not affect a court's jurisdiction to hear the petition and is not grounds for denying the petition.

(B) This section does not apply if any of the following apply:

(1) The person seeking to adopt the minor is the minor's stepparent;

(2) The minor was not originally placed in the person's home with the purpose of the person adopting the minor;

(3) The minor is a "child with special needs," as defined by the director of job and family services in accordance with section 5153.163 of the Revised Code.

(1999 H 471, eff. 7–1–00; 1996 H 419, eff. 9–18–96)

Historical and Statutory Notes

Amendment Note: 1999 H 471 substituted "director of job and family services" for "department of human services" in division (B)(3).

Library References

Adoption ⬅︎9.1.
Westlaw Topic No. 17.
C.J.S. Adoption of Persons §§ 46, 77.
Baldwin's Ohio Legislative Service, 1996 H 419—LSC Analysis, 3/L–336

3107.055 Accounting; disbursements

(A) Notwithstanding section 3107.01 of the Revised Code, as used in this section, "agency" does not include a public children services agency.

(B) An agency or attorney, whichever arranges a minor's adoption, shall file with the court a preliminary estimate accounting not later than the time the adoption petition for the minor is filed with the court. The agency or attorney, whichever arranges the adoption, also shall file a final accounting with the court before a final decree of adoption is issued or an interlocutory order of adoption is finalized for the minor. The agency or attorney shall complete and file accountings in a manner acceptable to the court.

An accounting shall specify all disbursements of anything of value the petitioner, a person on the petitioner's behalf, and the agency or attorney made and has agreed to make in connection with the minor's permanent surrender under division (B) of section 5103.15 of the Revised Code, placement under section 5103.16 of the Revised Code, and adoption under this chapter. The agency or attorney shall include in an accounting an itemization of each expense listed in division (C) of this section. The itemization of the expenses specified in divisions (C)(3) and (4) of this section shall show the amount the agency or attorney charged or is going to charge for the services and the actual cost to the agency or attorney of providing the services. An accounting shall indicate whether any expenses listed in division (C) of this section do not apply to the adoption proceeding for which the accounting is filed.

The agency or attorney shall include with a preliminary estimate accounting and a final accounting a written statement signed by the petitioner that the petitioner has reviewed the accounting and attests to its accuracy.

(C) No petitioner, person acting on a petitioner's behalf, or agency or attorney shall make or agree to make any disbursements in connection with the minor's permanent surrender, placement, or adoption other than for the following:

(1) Physician expenses incurred on behalf of the birth mother or minor in connection with prenatal care, delivery, and confinement prior to or following the minor's birth;

(2) Hospital or other medical facility expenses incurred on behalf of the birth mother or minor in connection with the minor's birth;

(3) Expenses charged by the attorney arranging the adoption for providing legal services in connection with the placement and adoption, including expenses incurred by the attorney pursuant to sections 3107.031, 3107.032, 3107.081, 3107.082, 3107.09, 3107.101, and 3107.12 of the Revised Code;

(4) Expenses charged by the agency arranging the adoption for providing services in connection with the permanent surrender and adoption, including the agency's application fee and the expenses incurred by the agency pursuant to sections 3107.031, 3107.032, 3107.09, 3107.101, 3107.12, 5103.151, and 5103.152 of the Revised Code;

(5) Temporary costs of routine maintenance and medical care for a minor required under section 5103.16 of the Revised Code if the person seeking to adopt the minor refuses to accept placement of the minor;

(6) Guardian ad litem fees incurred on behalf of the minor in any court proceedings;

(7) Foster care expenses incurred in connection with any temporary care and maintenance of the minor;

(8) Court expenses incurred in connection with the minor's permanent surrender, placement, and adoption.

(D) If a court determines from an accounting that an amount that is going to be disbursed for an expense listed in division (C) of this section is unreasonable, the court may order a reduction in the amount to be disbursed. If a court determines from an accounting that an unreasonable amount was disbursed for an expense listed in division (C) of this section, the court may order the person who received the disbursement to refund to the person who made the disbursement an amount the court orders.

If a court determines from an accounting that a disbursement for an expense not permitted by division (C) of this section is going to be made, the court may issue an injunction prohibiting the disbursement. If a court determines from an accounting that a disbursement for an expense not permitted by division (C) of this section was made, the court may order the person who received the disbursement to return it to the person who made the disbursement.

If a court determines that a final accounting does not completely report all the disbursements that are going to be made or have been made in connection with the minor's permanent surrender, placement, and adoption, the court shall order the agency or attorney to file with the court an accounting that completely reports all such disbursements.

The agency or attorney shall file the final accounting with the court not later than ten days prior to the date scheduled for the final hearing on the adoption. The court may not issue a final decree of adoption or finalize an interlocutory order of adoption of a minor until at least ten days after the agency or attorney files the final accounting.

(E) This section does not apply to an adoption by a stepparent whose spouse is a biological or adoptive parent of the minor.

(2006 S 238, eff. 9–21–06)

Historical and Statutory Notes

Ed. Note: RC 3107.055 is former RC 3107.10, amended and recodified by 2006 S 238, eff. 9–21–06; 2005 H 66, eff. 6–30–05; 1999 H 471, eff. 7–1–00; 1996 H 274, eff. 9–18–96; 1996 H 419, eff. 9–18–96; 1986 H 428, eff. 12–23–86; 1978 H 832; 1976 H 156.

Amendment Note: 2006 S 238 inserted "3107.032," and "3107.101," in divisions (C)(3) and (C)(4).

Amendment Note: 2005 H 66 deleted division (E) and redesignated former division (F) as new division (E). Prior to amendment, former division (E) read:

"(E) At the conclusion of each adoption proceeding, the court shall prepare a summary of the proceeding, and on or before the tenth day of each month, send copies of the summaries for all proceedings concluded during the preceding calendar month to the department of job and family services. The summary shall contain:

"(1) A notation of the nature and approximate value or amount of anything paid in connection with the proceeding, compiled from the final accounting required by division (B) of this section and indicating the category of division (C) of this section to which any payment relates;

"(2) If the court has not issued a decree because of the requirements of division (D) of this section, a notation of that fact and a statement of the reason for refusing to issue the decree, related to the financial data summarized under division (E)(1) of this section;

"(3) If the adoption was arranged by an attorney, a notation of that fact.

"The summary shall contain no information identifying by name any party to the proceeding or any other person, but may contain additional narrative material that the court considers useful to an analysis of the summary."

Amendment Note: 1999 H 471 substituted "job and family" for "human" in the introductory paragraph in division (E).

Amendment Note: 1996 H 274 substituted "may" for "shall" in the fourth paragraph in division (D).

Amendment Note: 1996 H 419 rewrote this section, which prior thereto read:

"(A) The petitioner in any proceeding for the adoption of a minor shall file, before the petition is heard, a full accounting in a manner acceptable to the court of all disbursements of anything of value made or agreed to be made by or on behalf of the petitioner in connection with the placement or adoption of the minor. The accounting shall show any payments made or to be made by or on behalf of the petitioner in connection with the placement or adoption.

"(B) A petitioner shall not make or agree to make any disbursements in connection with the placement or adoption of a minor other than for the following:

"(1) Physician expenses incurred in connection with prenatal care and confinement or in connection with the birth of the minor to be adopted;

"(2) Hospital expenses incurred in connection with the birth of the minor to be adopted;

"(3) Attorneys' fees incurred in providing legal services in connection with the placement of the minor to be adopted or in connection with legal services provided to initiate and pursue the adoption proceedings;

"(4) Agency expenses incurred for providing services in connection with the adoption or in connection with placement services provided by an agency under section 5103.16 of the Revised Code;

"(5) Temporary costs of routine maintenance and medical care for a minor required under section 5103.16 of the Revised Code if the person seeking to adopt the minor refuses to accept placement of the minor.

"(C) The court shall review and approve, prior to the entry of any decree of adoption, all expenses made or agreed to be made by a petitioner in connection with the adoption of a minor. The court shall not issue a decree of adoption if after a hearing it determines that any of the expenses incurred by the petitioner were unreasonable or were for services other than those permitted under division (B) of this section or if after a hearing it determines that the petitioner has failed to report all of the expenses incurred in connection with the placement or adoption of the minor.

"(D) At the conclusion of each adoption proceeding, the court shall prepare a summary of the proceeding, and on or before the tenth day of each month, send copies of the summaries for all proceedings concluded during the preceding calendar month to the department of human services. The summary shall contain:

"(1) A notation of the nature and approximate value or amount of anything paid in connection with the proceeding, compiled from the accounting required by division (A) of this section and indicating the category of division (B) of this section to which any payment relates;

"(2) If the court has not issued a decree because of the requirements of division (C) of this section, a notation of that fact and a statement of the reason for refusing to issue the decree, related to the financial data summarized under division (D)(1) of this section;

"(3) If placement in the petitioners' home was privately arranged under section 5103.16 of the Revised Code, a notation of that fact.

"The summary shall contain no information identifying by name any party to the proceeding or any other person, but may contain additional narrative material that the court considers useful to an analysis of the summary.

"(E) This section does not apply to an adoption by a stepparent whose spouse is a biological or adoptive parent of the minor."

Library References

Adoption ⚖6, 7.5, 13.
Westlaw Topic No. 17.
C.J.S. Adoption of Persons §§ 28 to 47, 56, 70 to 73, 93 to 102, 140.

Baldwin's Ohio Legislative Service, 1996 H 419—LSC Analysis, 3/L–336

CONSENTS AND PUTATIVE FATHER REGISTRY

3107.06 Consents required

Unless consent is not required under section 3107.07 of the Revised Code, a petition to adopt a minor may be granted only if written consent to the adoption has been executed by all of the following:

(A) The mother of the minor;

(B) The father of the minor, if any of the following apply:

(1) The minor was conceived or born while the father was married to the mother;

(2) The minor is his child by adoption;

(3) Prior to the date the petition was filed, it was determined by a court proceeding pursuant to sections 3111.01 to 3111.18 of the Revised Code, a court proceeding in another state, an administrative proceeding pursuant to sections 3111.38 to 3111.54 of the Revised Code, or an administrative proceeding in another state that he has a parent and child relationship with the minor;

(4) He acknowledged paternity of the child and that acknowledgment has become final pursuant to section 2151.232, 3111.25, or 3111.821 of the Revised Code.

(C) The putative father of the minor;

(D) Any person or agency having permanent custody of the minor or authorized by court order to consent;

(E) The juvenile court that has jurisdiction to determine custody of the minor, if the legal guardian or custodian of the minor is not authorized by law or court order to consent to the adoption;

(F) The minor, if more than twelve years of age, unless the court, finding that it is in the best interest of the minor, determines that the minor's consent is not required.

(2000 S 180, eff. 3–22–01; 1997 H 352, eff. 1–1–98; 1996 H 274, eff. 9–18–96; 1996 H 419, eff. 9–18–96; 1988 H 790, eff. 3–16–89; 1986 H 476; 1982 H 245; 1976 H 156)

Uncodified Law

1996 H 419, § 5, eff. 6–20–96, reads: The amendment made by this act to sections 3107.06 and 3107.07 of the Revised Code concerning a putative father, as defined in section 3107.01 of the Revised Code, consenting to his child's adoption apply only if the child is born on or after January 1, 1997.

Whether a putative father's consent to the adoption of his child born prior to January 1, 1997, is required shall be determined in accordance with sections 3107.06 and 3107.07 of the Revised Code as those sections exist immediately prior to their amendment by this act.

Historical and Statutory Notes

Ed. Note: Former 3107.06 repealed by 1976 H 156, eff. 1–1–77; 1975 S 145; 1969 S 49; 130 v S 155; 129 v 498; 126 v 392; 1953 H 1; GC 8004–6; Source—GC 10512–14; see now 3107.07 and 3107.09 for provisions analogous to former 3107.06.

Pre–1953 H 1 Amendments: 124 v S 65

Amendment Note: 1997 H 352 rewrote division (B)(4), which prior thereto read:

"(4) He acknowledged paternity of the child pursuant to section 2105.18 of the Revised Code."

Amendment Note: 1996 H 274 added division (B)(4).

Amendment Note: 1996 H 419 rewrote division (B); added new division (C); redesignated former divisions (C) through (E) as divisions (D) through (F), respectively; and deleted former section (F). Prior to amendment and deletion, divisions (B) and (F) read:

"(B) The father of the minor, if the minor was conceived or born while the father was married to the mother, if the minor is his child by adoption, or if the minor has been established to be his child by a court proceeding;

"(F) Subject to division (B) of section 3107.07 of the Revised Code, the putative father, if he:

"(1) Is alleged to be the father of the minor in proceedings brought under sections 3111.01 to 3111.19 of the Revised Code at any time before the placement of the minor in the home of the petitioner;

"(2) Has acknowledged the child in a writing sworn to before a notary public at any time before the placement of the minor in the home of the petitioner;

"(3) Has signed the birth certificate of the child as an informant as provided in section 3705.09 of the Revised Code;

"(4) Has filed an objection to the adoption with the agency having custody of the minor or the department of human services at any time before the placement of the minor in the home of the petitioner, or with the probate court or the department of human services within thirty days of the filing of a petition to adopt the minor or its placement in the home of the petitioner, whichever occurs first."

Comparative Laws

Ariz.—A.R.S. § 8-106 et seq.
Ark.—A.C.A. § 9-9-206 et seq.
Fla.—West's F.S.A. § 63.062 et seq.
Idaho—I.C. § 16-1503, 16-1504.
Ill.—ILCS 750 50/8 et seq.
Ind.—West's A.I.C. 31–19–9–1 et seq.
Iowa—I.C.A. § 600.7.
Ky.—Baldwin's KRS 199.500.
Mass.—M.G.L.A. c. 210, § 2 et seq.
Me.—18-A M.R.S.A. § 9–302.
Mich.—M.C.L.A. § 710.43 et seq.
Minn.—M.S.A. § 259.24.
Mo.—V.A.M.S. § 453.040, 453.050.
N.C.—G.S. § 48-3-601 et seq.
N.Y.—McKinney's Domestic Relations Law § 111.
Okl.—10 Okl.St.Ann. § 7503–2.1.
Tenn.—T.C.A. § 36-1-108 et seq.
Tex.—V.T.C.A. Family Code § 162.010, 162.011.

Library References

Adoption ⇐7.1 to 7.2(3).
Westlaw Topic No. 17.
C.J.S. Adoption of Persons §§ 49 to 57, 59 to 61.
Baldwin's Ohio Legislative Service, 1996 H 419—LSC Analysis, 3/L–336

3107.061 Adoption of child without putative father's consent

A man who has sexual intercourse with a woman is on notice that if a child is born as a result and the man is the putative father, the child may be adopted without his consent pursuant to division (B) of section 3107.07 of the Revised Code.

(1996 H 419, eff. 6–20–96)

Library References

Adoption ⇐7.2(3), 7.3.
Westlaw Topic No. 17.
C.J.S. Adoption of Persons §§ 56 to 58, 62.
Baldwin's Ohio Legislative Service, 1996 H 419—LSC Analysis, 3/L–336

3107.062 Putative father registry

The department of job and family services shall establish a putative father registry. To register, a putative father must complete a registration form prescribed under section 3107.065 of the Revised Code and submit it to the department. The registration form shall include the putative father's name; the address or telephone number at which he wishes to receive, pursuant to section 3107.11 of the Revised Code, notice of a petition to adopt the minor he claims as his child; and the name of the mother of the minor.

A putative father may register before or not later than thirty days after the birth of the child. No fee shall be charged for registration.

On receipt of a completed registration form, the department shall indicate on the form the date of receipt and file it in the putative father registry. The department shall maintain registration forms in a manner that enables it to access a registration form using either the name of the putative father or of the mother.

(1999 H 471, eff. 7–1–00; 1996 H 274, eff. 9–18–96; 1996 H 419, eff. 9–18–96)

Historical and Statutory Notes

Amendment Note: 1999 H 471 substituted "job and family" for "human" in the first paragraph.

Amendment Note: 1996 H 274 substituted "not later than thirty days" for ", to the extent provided by division (B)(1) of section 3107.07 of the Revised Code," in the second paragraph.

Library References

Adoption ⇐7.2(3).
Westlaw Topic No. 17.
C.J.S. Adoption of Persons § 56.
Baldwin's Ohio Legislative Service, 1996 H 419—LSC Analysis, 3/L–336

3107.063 Request to search registry

A mother or an agency or attorney arranging a minor's adoption may request at any time that the department of job and family services search the putative father registry to determine whether a man is registered as the minor's putative father. The request shall include the mother's name. On receipt of the request, the department shall search the registry. If the department determines that a man is registered as the minor's putative father, it shall provide the mother, agency, or attorney a certified copy of the man's registration form. If the department determines that no man is registered as the minor's putative father, it shall provide the mother, agency, or attorney a certified written statement to that effect. The department shall specify in the statement the date the search request was submitted. No fee shall be charged for searching the registry.

Division (B) of section 3107.17 of the Revised Code does not apply to this section.

(1999 H 471, eff. 7–1–00; 1996 H 274, eff. 9–18–96; 1996 H 419, eff. 9–18–96)

Historical and Statutory Notes

Amendment Note: 1999 H 471 substituted "job and family" for "human" in the first paragraph.

Amendment Note: 1996 H 274 deleted "Not sooner than thirty one days after the birth of a minor," from the beginning of, and inserted "at any time" in, the first sentence in the first paragraph; and made other nonsubstantive changes.

Library References

Adoption ⚖7.2(3).
Westlaw Topic No. 17.
C.J.S. Adoption of Persons § 56.
Baldwin's Ohio Legislative Service, 1996 H 419—LSC Analysis, 3/L–336

3107.064 Required search of registry prior to adoption; exceptions

(A) Except as provided in division (B) of this section, a court shall not issue a final decree of adoption or finalize an interlocutory order of adoption unless the mother placing the minor for adoption or the agency or attorney arranging the adoption files with the court a certified document provided by the department of job and family services under section 3107.063 of the Revised Code. The court shall not accept the document unless the date the department places on the document pursuant to that section is thirty-one or more days after the date of the minor's birth.

(B) The document described in division (A) of this section is not required if any of the following apply:

(1) The mother was married at the time the minor was conceived or born;

(2) The parent placing the minor for adoption previously adopted the minor;

(3) Prior to the date a petition to adopt the minor is filed, a man has been determined to have a parent and child relationship with the minor by a court proceeding pursuant to sections 3111.01 to 3111.18 of the Revised Code, a court proceeding in another state, an administrative agency proceeding pursuant to sections 3111.38 to 3111.54 of the Revised Code, or an administrative agency proceeding in another state;

(4) The minor's father acknowledged paternity of the minor and that acknowledgment has become final pursuant to section 2151.232, 3111.25, or 3111.821 of the Revised Code;

(5) A public children services agency has permanent custody of the minor pursuant to Chapter 2151. or division (B) of section 5103.15 of the Revised Code after both parents lost or surrendered parental rights, privileges, and responsibilities over the minor.

(2000 S 180, eff. 3–22–01; 1999 H 471, eff. 7–1–00; 1997 H 352, eff. 1–1–98; 1996 H 274, eff. 9–18–96; 1996 H 419, eff. 9–18–96)

Historical and Statutory Notes

Amendment Note: 2000 S 180 substituted "3111.18" for "3111.19", "3111.38" for "3111.20" and "3111.54" for "3111.29" in division (B)(3); and substituted "3111.25" for "3111.211" and "3111.821" for "5101.314" in division (B)(4).

Amendment Note: 1999 H 471 substituted "job and family" for "human" in division (A).

Amendment Note: 1997 H 352 rewrote division (B)(4), which prior thereto read:

"(4) The minor's father acknowledged paternity of the minor pursuant to section 2105.18 of the Revised Code."

Amendment Note: 1996 H 274 added the second sentence in division (A); added division (B)(4); and redesignated former division (B)(4) as division (B)(5).

Library References

Adoption ⚖7.2(3), 13.
Westlaw Topic No. 17.
C.J.S. Adoption of Persons §§ 46 to 47, 56, 93 to 102.
Baldwin's Ohio Legislative Service, 1996 H 419—LSC Analysis, 3/L–336

3107.065 Rules, registration form, and informational campaign for registry

Not later than ninety days after the effective date of this section, the director of job and family services shall do both of the following:

(A) Adopt rules in accordance with Chapter 119. of the Revised Code governing the putative father registry. The rules shall establish the registration form to be used by a putative father under section 3107.062 of the Revised Code.

(B) Establish a campaign to promote awareness of the putative father registry. The campaign shall include informational materials about the registry.

(1999 H 471, eff. 7–1–00; 1996 H 419, eff. 6–20–96)

Historical and Statutory Notes

Amendment Note: 1999 H 471 substituted "director of job and family services" for "department of human services" in the introductory paragraph.

Library References

Adoption ⚖7.2(3).
Infants ⚖17.
Westlaw Topic Nos. 17, 211.
C.J.S. Adoption of Persons §§ 10 to 14, 41, 56.
C.J.S. Infants §§ 6, 8 to 9.
Baldwin's Ohio Legislative Service, 1996 H 419—LSC Analysis, 3/L–336

3107.07 Consents not required

Consent to adoption is not required of any of the following:

(A) A parent of a minor, when it is alleged in the adoption petition and the court finds after proper service of notice and hearing, that the parent has failed without justifiable cause to communicate with the minor or to provide for the maintenance and support of the minor as required by law or judicial decree for a period of at least one year immediately preceding either the filing of the adoption petition or the placement of the minor in the home of the petitioner.

(B) The putative father of a minor if either of the following applies:

(1) The putative father fails to register as the minor's putative father with the putative father registry established under section 3107.062 of the Revised Code not later than thirty days after the minor's birth;

(2) The court finds, after proper service of notice and hearing, that any of the following are the case:

(a) The putative father is not the father of the minor;

(b) The putative father has willfully abandoned or failed to care for and support the minor;

(c) The putative father has willfully abandoned the mother of the minor during her pregnancy and up to the time of her surrender of the minor, or the minor's placement in the home of the petitioner, whichever occurs first.

(C) Except as provided in section 3107.071 of the Revised Code, a parent who has entered into a voluntary permanent custody surrender agreement under division (B) of section 5103.15 of the Revised Code;

(D) A parent whose parental rights have been terminated by order of a juvenile court under Chapter 2151. of the Revised Code;

(E) A parent who is married to the petitioner and supports the adoption;

(F) The father, or putative father, of a minor if the minor is conceived as the result of the commission of rape by the father or putative father and the father or putative father is convicted of or pleads guilty to the commission of that offense. As used in this division, "rape" means a violation of section 2907.02 of the Revised Code or a similar law of another state.

(G) A legal guardian or guardian ad litem of a parent judicially declared incompetent in a separate court proceeding who has failed to respond in writing to a request for consent, for a period of thirty days, or who, after examination of the written reasons for withholding consent, is found by the court to be withholding consent unreasonably;

(H) Any legal guardian or lawful custodian of the person to be adopted, other than a parent, who has failed to respond in writing to a request for consent, for a period of thirty days, or who, after examination of the written reasons for withholding consent, is found by the court to be withholding consent unreasonably;

(I) The spouse of the person to be adopted, if the failure of the spouse to consent to the adoption is found by the court to be by reason of prolonged unexplained absence, unavailability, incapacity, or circumstances that make it impossible or unreasonably difficult to obtain the consent or refusal of the spouse;

(J) Any parent, legal guardian, or other lawful custodian in a foreign country, if the person to be adopted has been released for adoption pursuant to the laws of the country in which the person resides and the release of such person is in a form that satisfies the requirements of the immigration and naturalization service of the United States department of justice for purposes of immigration to the United States pursuant to section 101(b)(1)(F) of the "Immigration and Nationality Act," 75 Stat. 650 (1961), 8 U.S.C. 1101(b)(1)(F), as amended or reenacted.

(K) Except as provided in divisions (G) and (H) of this section, a juvenile court, agency, or person given notice of the petition pursuant to division (A)(1) of section 3107.11 of the Revised Code that fails to file an objection to the petition within fourteen days after proof is filed pursuant to division (B) of that section that the notice was given;

(L) Any guardian, custodian, or other party who has temporary custody of the child.

(1999 H 176, eff. 10–29–99; 1998 H 484, eff. 3–18–99; 1996 H 274, eff. 9–18–96; 1996 H 419, eff. 9–18–96; 1986 H 428, eff. 12–23–86; 1980 S 205; 1977 H 1; 1976 H 156)

Uncodified Law

1996 H 419, § 5: See Uncodified Law under 3107.06.

Historical and Statutory Notes

Ed. Note: 3107.07 contains provisions analogous to former 3107.06, repealed by 1976 H 156, eff. 1–1–77.

Ed. Note: Former 3107.07 repealed by 1976 H 156, eff. 1–1–77; 1953 H 1; GC 8004–7; Source—GC 10512–17.

Pre–1953 H 1 Amendments: 124 v S 65

Amendment Note: 1999 H 176 substituted "(A)(1)" for "(A)(2)" in division (K).

Amendment Note: 1998 H 484 added division (L).

Amendment Note: 1996 H 274 deleted ", or for reasons beyond his control, other than lack of knowledge of the minor's birth, is not able to register within that time period and fails to register not later than ten days after it becomes possible to register" from the end of division (B)(1).

Amendment Note: 1996 H 419 rewrote divisions (B) and (C); added divisions (E), (F), and (K); redesignated former divisions (E) through (H) as (G) through (J), respectively; and made changes to reflect gender neutral language throughout. Prior to amendment, divisions (B) and (C) read:

"(B) The putative father of a minor if the putative father fails to file an objection with the court, the department of human services, or the agency having custody of the minor as provided in division (F)(4) of section 3107.06 of the Revised Code, or files an objection with the court, department, or agency and the court finds, after proper service of notice and hearing, that he is not the father of the minor, or that he has willfully abandoned or failed to care for and support the minor, or abandoned the mother of the minor during her pregnancy and up to the time of her surrender of the minor, or its placement in the home of the petitioner, whichever occurs first;

"(C) A parent who has relinquished his right to consent under section 5103.15 of the Revised Code;"

Library References

Adoption ⇔7.3 to 7.4(6).
Westlaw Topic No. 17.
C.J.S. Adoption of Persons §§ 56 to 58, 62 to 68.

Baldwin's Ohio Legislative Service, 1996 H 419—LSC Analysis, 3/L–336

3107.071 Parental consent required despite voluntary permanent custody surrender agreement; exceptions

If a parent enters into a voluntary permanent custody surrender agreement under division (B)(2) of section 5103.15 of the Revised Code on or after the effective date of this section, the parent's consent to the adoption of the child who is the subject of the agreement is required unless all of the following requirements are met:

(A) In the case of a parent whose child, if adopted, will be an adopted person as defined in section 3107.45 of the Revised Code:

(1) The parent does all of the following:

(a) Signs the component of the form prescribed under division (A)(1)(a) of section 3107.083 of the Revised Code;

(b) Checks either the "yes" or "no" space provided on the component of the form prescribed under division (A)(1)(b) of section 3107.083 of the Revised Code and signs that component;

(c) If the parent is the mother, completes and signs the component of the form prescribed under division (A)(1)(c) of section 3107.083 of the Revised Code.

(2) The agency provides the parent the opportunity to sign, if the parent chooses to do so, the components of the form prescribed under divisions (A)(1)(d), (e), and (f) of section 3107.083 of the Revised Code;

(3) The agency files with the juvenile and probate courts the form prescribed under division (A)(1) of section 3107.083 of the Revised Code signed by the parent, provides a copy of the form signed by the parent to the parent, and keeps a copy of the form signed by the parent in the agency's records.

The court shall keep a copy of the form signed by the parent in the court records.

(B) In the case of a parent whose child, if adopted, will be an adopted person as defined in section 3107.39 of the Revised Code:

(1) The parent does both of the following:

(a) Signs the component of the form prescribed under division (B)(1)(a) of section 3107.083 of the Revised Code;

(b) If the parent is the mother, completes and signs the component of the form prescribed under division (B)(1)(b) of section 3107.083 of the Revised Code.

(2) The agency provides the parent the opportunity to sign, if the parent chooses to do so, the components of the form prescribed under divisions (B)(1)(c), (d), and (e) of section 3107.083 of the Revised Code at the time the parent enters into the agreement with the agency;

(3) The agency files the form signed by the parent with the juvenile and probate courts, provides a copy of the form signed by the parent to the parent, and keeps a copy of the form signed by the parent in the agency's records.

The court shall keep a copy of the form signed by the parent in the court records.

(1999 H 471, eff. 7–1–00; 1996 H 419, eff. 9–18–96)

Historical and Statutory Notes

Amendment Note: 1999 H 471 deleted "by the department of human services" after "prescribed" in divisions (A)(1)(a) and (B)(1)(a); and made other nonsubstantive changes.

Library References

Adoption ⚖═7.3.
Westlaw Topic No. 17.
C.J.S. Adoption of Persons §§ 56 to 58, 62.
Baldwin's Ohio Legislative Service, 1996 H 419—LSC Analysis, 3/L–336

3107.08 Execution of consent

(A) The required consent to adoption may be executed at any time after seventy-two hours after the birth of a minor, and shall be executed in the following manner:

(1) If by the person to be adopted, in the presence of the court;

(2) If by a parent of the person to be adopted, in accordance with section 3107.081 of the Revised Code;

(3) If by an agency, by the executive head or other authorized representative, in the presence of a person authorized to take acknowledgments;

(4) If by any other person, in the presence of the court or in the presence of a person authorized to take acknowledgments;

(5) If by a juvenile court, by appropriate order.

(B) A consent which does not name or otherwise identify the prospective adoptive parent is valid if it contains a statement by the person giving consent that it was voluntarily executed irrespective of disclosure of the name or other identification of the prospective adoptive parent.

(1996 H 419, eff. 9–18–96; 1976 H 156, eff. 1–1–77)

Historical and Statutory Notes

Ed. Note: Former 3107.08 repealed by 1976 H 156, eff. 1–1–77; 1975 S 145; 1953 H 1; GC 8004–8; Source—GC 10512–16.

Pre–1953 H 1 Amendments: 124 v S 65

Amendment Note: 1996 H 419 added division (A)(2); redesignated former divisions (A)(2) through (4) as (A)(3) through (5), respectively; substituted "acknowledgments" for "acknowledgements" in divisions (A)(3) and (4); deleted "except a minor" following "If by any other person" in division (A)(4); added "juvenile" in division (A)(5); deleted former division (A)(5), which read: "(5) If by a minor parent, pursuant to section 5103.16 of the Revised Code"; substituted "adoptive" for "adopting" twice in division (B); and made a nonsubstantive change.

Library References

Adoption ⚖═7.5.
Westlaw Topic No. 17.
C.J.S. Adoption of Persons §§ 56, 70 to 73.
Baldwin's Ohio Legislative Service, 1996 H 419—LSC Analysis, 3/L–336

3107.081 Conditions for court acceptance of parental consent

(A) Except as provided in divisions (B), (E), and (F) of this section, a parent of a minor, who will be, if adopted, an adopted person as defined in section 3107.45 of the Revised Code, shall do all of the following as a condition of a court accepting the parent's consent to the minor's adoption:

(1) Appear personally before the court;

(2) Sign the component of the form prescribed under division (A)(1)(a) of section 3107.083 of the Revised Code;

(3) Check either the "yes" or "no" space provided on the component of the form prescribed under division (A)(1)(b) of section 3107.083 of the Revised Code and sign that component;

(4) If the parent is the mother, complete and sign the component of the form prescribed under division (A)(1)(c) of section 3107.083 of the Revised Code.

At the time the parent signs the components of the form prescribed under divisions (A)(1)(a), (b), and (c) of section 3107.083 of the Revised Code, the parent may sign, if the parent chooses to do so, the components of the form prescribed under divisions (A)(1)(d), (e), and (f) of that section. After the parent signs the components required to be signed and any discretionary components the parent chooses to sign, the parent, or the attorney arranging the adoption, shall file the form and parent's consent with the court. The court or attorney shall give the parent a copy of the form and consent. The court and attorney shall keep a copy of the form and consent in the court and attorney's records of the adoption.

The court shall question the parent to determine that the parent understands the adoption process, the ramifications of consenting to the adoption, each component of the form prescribed under division (A)(1) of section 3107.083 of the Revised Code, and that the minor and adoptive parent may receive identifying information about the parent in accordance with section 3107.47 of the Revised Code unless the parent checks the "no" space provided on the component of the form prescribed under division (A)(1)(b) of section 3107.083 of the Revised Code or has a denial of release form filed with the department of health under section 3107.46 of the Revised Code. The court also shall question the parent to determine that the parent's consent to the adoption and any decisions the parent makes in filling out the form prescribed under division (A)(1) of section 3107.083 of the Revised Code are made voluntarily.

(B) The parents of a minor, who is less than six months of age and will be, if adopted, an adopted person as defined in section 3107.45 of the Revised Code, may consent to the minor's adoption without personally appearing before a court if both parents do all of the following:

(1) Execute a notarized statement of consent to the minor's adoption before the attorney arranging the adoption;

(2) Sign the component of the form prescribed under division (A)(1)(a) of section 3107.083 of the Revised Code;

(3) Check either the "yes" or "no" space provided on the component of the form prescribed under division (A)(1)(b) of section 3107.083 of the Revised Code and sign that component.

At the time the parents sign the components of the form prescribed under divisions (A)(1)(a) and (b) of section 3107.083 of the Revised Code, the mother shall complete and sign the component of the form prescribed under division (A)(1)(c) of that section and the attorney arranging the adoption shall provide the parents the opportunity to sign, if they choose to do so, the components of the form prescribed under divisions (A)(1)(d), (e), and (f) of that section. At the time the petition to adopt the minor is submitted to the court, the attorney shall file the parents' consents and forms with the court. The attorney shall give the parents a copy of the consents and forms. At the time the attorney files the consents and forms with the court, the attorney also shall file with the court all other documents the director of job and family services requires by rules adopted under division (D) of section 3107.083 of the Revised Code to be filed with the court. The court and attorney shall keep a copy of the consents, forms, and documents in the court and attorney's records of the adoption.

(C) Except as provided in divisions (D), (E), and (F) of this section, a parent of a minor, who will be, if adopted, an adopted person as defined in section 3107.39 of the Revised Code, shall do all of the following as a condition of a court accepting the parent's consent to the minor's adoption:

(1) Appear personally before the court;

(2) Sign the component of the form prescribed under division (B)(1)(a) of section 3107.083 of the Revised Code;

(3) If the parent is the mother, complete and sign the component of the form prescribed under division (B)(1)(b) of section 3107.083 of the Revised Code.

At the time the parent signs the components prescribed under divisions (B)(1)(a) and (b) of section 3107.083 of the Revised Code, the parent may sign, if the parent chooses to do so, the components of the form prescribed under divisions (B)(1)(c), (d), and (e) of that section. After the parent signs the components required to be signed and any discretionary components the parent chooses to sign, the parent, or the attorney arranging the adoption, shall file the form and parent's consent with the court. The court or attorney shall give the parent a copy of the form and consent. The court and attorney shall keep a copy of the form and consent in the court and attorney's records of the adoption.

The court shall question the parent to determine that the parent understands the adoption process, the ramifications of consenting to the adoption, and each component of the form prescribed under division (B)(1) of section 3107.083 of the Revised Code. The court also shall question the parent to determine that the parent's consent to the adoption and any decisions the parent makes in filling out the form are made voluntarily.

(D) The parent of a minor who is less than six months of age and will be, if adopted, an adopted person as defined in section 3107.39 of the Revised Code may consent to the minor's adoption without personally appearing before a court if the parent does all of the following:

(1) Executes a notarized statement of consent to the minor's adoption before the attorney arranging the adoption;

(2) Signs the component of the form prescribed under division (B)(1)(a) of section 3107.083 of the Revised Code;

(3) If the parent is the mother, completes and signs the component of the form prescribed under division (B)(1)(b) of section 3107.083 of the Revised Code.

At the time the parent signs the components of the form prescribed under divisions (B)(1)(a) and (b) of section 3107.083 of the Revised Code, the attorney arranging the adoption shall provide the parent the opportunity to sign, if the parent chooses to do so, the components of the form prescribed under divisions (B)(1)(c), (d), and (e) of that section. At the time the petition to adopt the minor is submitted to the court, the attorney shall file the parent's consent and form with the court. The attorney shall give the parent a copy of the consent and form. At the time the attorney files the consent and form with the court, the attorney also shall file with the court all other documents the director of job and family services requires by rules adopted under division (D) of section 3107.083 of the Revised Code to be filed with the court. The court and attorney shall keep a copy of the consent, form, and documents in the court and attorney's records of the adoption.

(E) If a minor is to be adopted by a stepparent, the parent who is not married to the stepparent may consent to the minor's adoption without appearing personally before a court if the parent executes consent in the presence of a person authorized to take acknowledgments. The attorney arranging the adoption shall file the consent with the court and give the parent a copy of the consent. The court and attorney shall keep a copy of the consent in the court and attorney's records of the adoption.

(F) If a parent of a minor to be adopted resides in another state, the parent may consent to the minor's adoption without appearing personally before a court if the parent executes consent in the presence of a person authorized to take acknowledgments. The attorney arranging the adoption shall file the consent with the court and give the parent a copy of the consent. The court and attorney shall keep a copy of the consent in the court and attorney's records of the adoption.

(1999 H 471, eff. 7–1–00; 1996 H 274, eff. 9–18–96; 1996 H 419, eff. 9–18–96)

Historical and Statutory Notes

Amendment Note: 1999 H 471 deleted "by the department of human services" after "prescribed" in divisions (A)(2), (B)(2), (C)(2), and (D)(2); substituted "director of job and family services" for "department of human services" in the final paragraphs in divisions (B) and (D); and made other nonsubstantive changes.

Amendment Note: 1996 H 274 substituted "At the time the petition to adopt the minor is submitted to the court" for "Not later than two business days after the parents execute consent and sign the components of the form required to be signed and any discretionary components the parents choose to sign" in the final paragraph in division (B); and for "Not later than two business days after the parents execute consent and signs the components of the form required to be signed and any discretionary components the parent chooses to sign" in the final paragraph in division (D).

Library References

Adoption ⚖7.5, 13.
Westlaw Topic No. 17.
C.J.S. Adoption of Persons §§ 46 to 47, 56, 70 to 73, 93 to 102.
Baldwin's Ohio Legislative Service, 1996 H 419—LSC Analysis, 3/L–336

3107.082 Assessor's meeting with parent prior to parent's consent to adoption

Not less than seventy-two hours prior to the date a parent executes consent to the adoption of the parent's child under section 3107.081 of the Revised Code, an assessor shall meet in person with the parent and do both of the following unless the child is to be adopted by a stepparent or the parent resides in another state:

(A) Provide the parent with a copy of the written materials about adoption prepared under division (C) of section 3107.083 of the Revised Code, discuss with the parent the adoption process and ramifications of a parent consenting to a child's adoption, and provide the parent the opportunity to review the materials and to ask questions about the materials, discussion, and related matters;

(B) Unless the child, if adopted, will be an adopted person as defined in section 3107.39 of the Revised Code, inform the parent that the child and the adoptive parent may receive, in accordance with section 3107.47 of the Revised Code, identifying information about the parent that is contained in the child's adoption file maintained by the department of health unless the parent checks the "no" space provided on the component of the form prescribed under division (A)(1)(b) of section 3107.083 of the Revised Code or signs and has filed with the department a denial of release form prescribed under section 3107.50 of the Revised Code.

(1999 H 471, eff. 7–1–00; 1996 H 419, eff. 9–18–96)

Historical and Statutory Notes

Amendment Note: 1999 H 471 deleted "by the department of human services" after "prepared" in division (A).

Library References

Adoption ⚖️7.5.
Westlaw Topic No. 17.
C.J.S. Adoption of Persons §§ 56, 70 to 73.
Baldwin's Ohio Legislative Service, 1996 H 419—LSC Analysis, 3/L–336

3107.083 Form authorizing release of information

Not later than ninety days after June 20, 1996, the director of job and family services shall do all of the following:

(A)(1) For a parent of a child who, if adopted, will be an adopted person as defined in section 3107.45 of the Revised Code, prescribe a form that has the following six components:

(a) A component the parent signs under section 3107.071, 3107.081, or 5103.151 of the Revised Code to indicate the requirements of section 3107.082 or 5103.152 of the Revised Code have been met. The component shall be as follows:

"Statement Concerning Ohio Law
and Adoption Materials

By signing this component of this form, I acknowledge that it has been explained to me, and I understand, that, if I check the space on the next component of this form that indicates that I authorize the release, the adoption file maintained by the Ohio Department of Health, which contains identifying information about me at the time of my child's birth, will be released, on request, to the adoptive parent when the adoptee is at least age eighteen but younger than age twenty-one and to the adoptee when he or she is age twenty-one or older. It has also been explained to me, and I understand, that I may prohibit the release of identifying information about me contained in the adoption file by checking the space on the next component of this form that indicates that I do not authorize the release of the identifying information. It has additionally been explained to me, and I understand, that I may change my mind regarding the decision I make on the next component of this form at any time and as many times as I desire by signing, dating, and having filed with the Ohio Department of Health a denial of release form or authorization of release form prescribed and provided by the Department of Health and providing the Department two items of identification.

By signing this component of this form, I also acknowledge that I have been provided a copy of written materials about adoption prepared by the Ohio Department of Job and Family Services, the adoption process and ramifications of consenting to adoption or entering into a voluntary permanent custody surrender agreement have been discussed with me, and I have been provided the opportunity to review the materials and ask questions about the materials and discussion.

Signature of biological parent: _____
Signature of witness: _____
Date: ...."

(b) A component the parent signs under section 3107.071, 3107.081, or 5103.151 of the Revised Code regarding the parent's decision whether to allow identifying information about the parent contained in an adoption file maintained by the department of health to be released to the parent's child and adoptive parent pursuant to section 3107.47 of the Revised Code. The component shall be as follows:

"Statement Regarding Release
of Identifying Information

The purpose of this component of this form is to allow a biological parent to decide whether to allow the Ohio Department of Health to provide an adoptee and adoptive parent identifying information about the adoptee's biological parent contained in an adoption file maintained by the Department. Please check one of the following spaces:

___YES, I authorize the Ohio Department of Health to release identifying information about me, on request, to the adoptive parent when the adoptee is at least age eighteen but younger than age twenty-one and to the adoptee when he or she is age twenty-one or older.

___NO, I do not authorize the release of identifying information about me to the adoptive parent or adoptee.

Signature of biological parent: _____
Signature of witness: _____
Date: ...."

(c) A component the parent, if the mother of the child, completes and signs under section 3107.071, 3107.081, or 5103.151 of the Revised Code to indicate, to the extent of the mother's knowledge, all of the following:

(i) Whether the mother, during her pregnancy, was a recipient of the medical assistance program established under Chapter 5111. of the Revised Code or other public health insurance program and, if so, the dates her eligibility began and ended;

(ii) Whether the mother, during her pregnancy, was covered by private health insurance and, if so, the dates the coverage began and ended, the name of the insurance provider, the type of coverage, and the identification number of the coverage;

(iii) The name and location of the hospital, freestanding birth center, or other place where the mother gave birth and, if different, received medical care immediately after giving birth;

(iv) The expenses of the obstetrical and neonatal care;

(v) Whether the mother has been informed that the adoptive parent or the agency or attorney arranging the adoption are to pay expenses involved in the adoption, including expenses the mother has paid and expects to receive or has received reimbursement, and, if so, what expenses are to be or have been paid and an estimate of the expenses;

(vi) Any other information related to expenses the department determines appropriate to be included in this component.

(d) A component the parent may sign to authorize the agency or attorney arranging the adoption to provide to the child or adoptive parent materials, other than photographs of the parent, that the parent requests be given to the child or adoptive parent pursuant to section 3107.68 of the Revised Code.

(e) A component the parent may sign to authorize the agency or attorney arranging the adoption to provide to the child or adoptive parent photographs of the parent pursuant to section 3107.68 of the Revised Code.

(f) A component the parent may sign to authorize the agency or attorney arranging the adoption to provide to the child or adoptive parent the first name of the parent pursuant to section 3107.68 of the Revised Code.

(2) State at the bottom of the form that the parent is to receive a copy of the form the parent signed.

(3) Provide copies of the form prescribed under this division to probate and juvenile courts, public children services agencies, private child placing agencies, private noncustodial agencies, attorneys, and persons authorized to take acknowledgments.

(B)(1) For a parent of a child who, if adopted, will become an adopted person as defined in section 3107.39 of the Revised Code, prescribe a form that has the following five components:

(a) A component the parent signs under section 3107.071, 3107.081, or 5103.151 of the Revised Code to attest that the requirement of division (A) of section 3107.082 or division (A) of section 5103.152 of the Revised Code has been met;

(b) A component the parent, if the mother of the child, completes and signs under section 3107.071, 3107.081, or 5103.151 of the Revised Code to indicate, to the extent of the mother's knowledge, all of the following:

(i) Whether the mother, during her pregnancy, was a recipient of the medical assistance program established under Chapter 5111. of the Revised Code or other public health insurance program and, if so, the dates her eligibility began and ended;

(ii) Whether the mother, during her pregnancy, was covered by private health insurance and, if so, the dates the coverage began and ended, the name of the insurance provider, the type of coverage, and the identification number of the coverage;

(iii) The name and location of the hospital, freestanding birth center, or other place where the mother gave birth and, if different, received medical care immediately after giving birth;

(iv) The expenses of the obstetrical and neonatal care;

(v) Whether the mother has been informed that the adoptive parent or the agency or attorney arranging the adoption are to pay expenses involved in the adoption, including expenses the mother has paid and expects to receive or has received reimbursement for, and, if so, what expenses are to be or have been paid and an estimate of the expenses;

(vi) Any other information related to expenses the department determines appropriate to be included in the component.

(c) A component the parent may sign to authorize the agency or attorney arranging the adoption to provide to the child or adoptive parent materials, other than photographs of the parent, that the parent requests be given to the child or adoptive parent pursuant to section 3107.68 of the Revised Code.

(d) A component the parent may sign to authorize the agency or attorney arranging the adoption to provide to the child or adoptive parent photographs of the parent pursuant to section 3107.68 of the Revised Code.

(e) A component the parent may sign to authorize the agency or attorney arranging the adoption to provide to the child or adoptive parent the first name of the parent pursuant to section 3107.68 of the Revised Code.

(2) State at the bottom of the form that the parent is to receive a copy of the form the parent signed.

(3) Provide copies of the form prescribed under this division to probate and juvenile courts, public children services agencies, private child placing agencies, private noncustodial agencies, and attorneys.

(C) Prepare the written materials about adoption that are required to be given to parents under division (A) of section 3107.082 and division (A) of section 5103.152 of the Revised Code. The materials shall provide information about the adoption process, including ramifications of a parent consenting to a child's adoption or entering into a voluntary permanent custody surrender agreement. The materials also shall include referral information for professional counseling and adoption support organizations. The director shall provide the materials to assessors.

(D) Adopt rules in accordance with Chapter 119. of the Revised Code specifying the documents that must be filed with a probate court under divisions (B) and (D) of section 3107.081 of the Revised Code and a juvenile court under divisions (C) and (E) of section 5103.151 of the Revised Code.

(1999 H 471, eff. 7–1–00; 1996 H 419, eff. 6–20–96)

Historical and Statutory Notes

Amendment Note: 1999 H 471 substituted "June 20, 1996" for "the effective date of this section" and "director of job and family services" for "department of human services" in the introductory paragraph; substituted "Job and Family" for "Human" in the form in division (A)(1); and substituted "director" for "department" in division (C).

Library References

Adoption ⟸7.5.
Health ⟸397.
Westlaw Topic Nos. 17, 198H.
C.J.S. Adoption of Persons §§ 56, 70 to 73.
C.J.S. Health and Environment §§ 24, 74.
   Baldwin's Ohio Legislative Service, 1996 H 419—LSC Analysis, 3/L–336

3107.084 Withdrawal of consent

(A) A consent to adoption is irrevocable and cannot be withdrawn after the entry of an interlocutory order or after the entry of a final decree of adoption when no interlocutory order has been entered. The consent of a minor is not voidable by reason of the minor's age.

(B) A consent to adoption may be withdrawn prior to the entry of an interlocutory order or prior to the entry of a final decree of adoption when no interlocutory order has been entered if the court finds after hearing that the withdrawal is in the best interest of the person to be adopted and the court by order authorizes the withdrawal of consent. Notice of the hearing shall be given to the petitioner, the person seeking the withdrawal of consent, and the agency placing the minor for adoption.

(1996 H 419, eff. 9–18–96)

Historical and Statutory Notes

Ed. Note: 3107.084 is former 3107.09, amended and recodified by 1996 H 419, eff. 9–18–96; 1976 H 156, eff. 1–1–77.

Amendment Note: 1996 H 419 amended this section by substituting "the minor's age" for "his minority" at the end of division (A).

Library References

Adoption ⟸7.6.
Westlaw Topic No. 17.
C.J.S. Adoption of Persons §§ 56, 74 to 76.
   Baldwin's Ohio Legislative Service, 1996 H 419—LSC Analysis, 3/L–336

HISTORY OF BIOLOGICAL PARENTS

3107.09 Social and medical histories of biological parents

(A) The department of job and family services shall prescribe and supply forms for the taking of social and medical histories of the biological parents of a minor available for adoption.

(B) An assessor shall record the social and medical histories of the biological parents of a minor available for adoption, unless the minor is to be adopted by the minor's stepparent or grandparent. The assessor shall use the forms prescribed pursuant to division (A) of this section. The assessor shall not include on the forms identifying information about the biological parents or other ancestors of the minor.

(C) A social history shall describe and identify the age; ethnic, racial, religious, marital, and physical characteristics; and educational, cultural, talent and hobby, and work experience background of the biological parents of the minor. A medical history shall identify major diseases, malformations, allergies, ear or eye defects, major conditions, and major health problems of the biological parents that are or may be congenital or familial. These histories may include other social and medical information relative to the biological parents and shall include social and medical information relative to the minor's other ancestors.

The social and medical histories may be obtained through interviews with the biological parents or other persons and from any available records if a biological parent or any legal guardian of a biological parent consents to the release of information contained in a record. An assessor who considers it necessary may request that a biological parent undergo a medical examination. In obtaining social and medical histories of a biological parent, an assessor shall inform the biological parent, or a person other than a biological parent who provides information pursuant to this section, of the purpose and use of the histories and of the biological parent's or other person's right to correct or expand the histories at any time.

(D) A biological parent, or another person who provided information in the preparation of the social and medical histories of the biological parents of a minor, may cause the histories to be corrected or expanded to include different or additional types of information. The biological parent or other person may cause the histories to be corrected or expanded at any time prior or subsequent to the adoption of the minor, including any time after the minor becomes an adult. A biological parent may cause the histories to be corrected or expanded even if the biological parent did not provide any information to the assessor at the time the histories were prepared.

To cause the histories to be corrected or expanded, a biological parent or other person who provided information shall provide the information to be included or specify the information to be corrected to whichever of the following is appropriate under the circumstances:

(1) Subject to division (D)(2) of this section, if the biological parent or other person knows the assessor who prepared the histories, to the assessor;

(2) If the biological parent or person does not know the assessor or finds that the assessor has ceased to perform assessments, to the court involved in the adoption or, if that court is not known, to the department of health.

An assessor who receives information from a biological parent or other person pursuant to division (D)(1) of this section shall determine whether the information is of a type that divisions (B) and (C) of this section permit to be included in the histories. If the assessor determines the information is of a permissible type, the assessor shall cause the histories to be corrected or expanded to reflect the information. If, at the time the information is received, the histories have been filed with the court as required by division (E) of this section, the court shall cooperate with the assessor in correcting or expanding the histories.

If the department of health or a court receives information from a biological parent or other person pursuant to division (D)(2) of this section, it shall determine whether the information is of a type that divisions (B) and (C) of this section permit to be included in the histories. If a court determines the information is of a permissible type, the court shall cause the histories to be corrected or expanded to reflect the information. If the department of health so determines, the court involved shall cooperate with the department in the correcting or expanding of the histories.

An assessor or the department of health shall notify a biological parent or other person in writing if the assessor or department determines that information the biological parent or other person provided or specified for inclusion in a history is not of a type that may be included in a history. On receipt of the notice, the biological parent or other person may petition the court involved in the adoption to make a finding as to whether the information is of a type that may be included in a history. On receipt of the petition, the court shall issue its finding without holding a hearing. If the court finds that the information is of a type that may be included in a history, it shall cause the history to be corrected or expanded to reflect the information.

(E) An assessor shall file the social and medical histories of the biological parents prepared pursuant to divisions (B) and (C) of this section with the court with which a petition to adopt the biological parents' child is filed. The court promptly shall provide a copy of the social and medical histories filed with it to the petitioner. In a case involving the adoption of a minor by any person other than the minor's stepparent or grandparent, a court may refuse to issue an interlocutory order or final decree of adoption if the histories of the biological parents have not been so filed, unless the assessor certifies to the court that information needed to prepare the histories is unavailable for reasons beyond the assessor's control.

(1999 H 471, eff. 7–1–00; 1996 H 419, eff. 9–18–96)

Historical and Statutory Notes

Ed. Note: Former 3107.09 amended and recodified as 3107.084 by 1996 H 419, eff. 9–18–96; 1976 H 156, eff. 1–1–77.

Ed. Note: Prior 3107.09 repealed by 1976 H 156, eff. 1–1–77; 1969 S 49; 1953 H 1; GC 8004–9; Source—GC 10512–18; see now 3107.14 for provisions analogous to former 3107.09.

Pre–1953 H 1 Amendments: 124 v S 65

Amendment Note: 1999 H 471 substituted "job and family" for "human" in division (A).

Library References

Adoption ⚖13.
Health ⚖396.
Westlaw Topic Nos. 17, 198H.
C.J.S. Adoption of Persons §§ 46 to 47, 93 to 102.
C.J.S. Health and Environment § 24.
Baldwin's Ohio Legislative Service, 1996 H 419—LSC Analysis, 3/L–336

3107.091 Biological parent may add medical and social history to records concerning adopted person

(A) As used in this section, "biological parent" means a biological parent whose offspring, as a minor, was adopted and with respect to whom a medical and social history was not prepared prior or subsequent to the adoption.

(B) A biological parent may request the department of job and family services to provide the biological parent with a copy of the social and medical history forms prescribed by the department pursuant to section 3107.09 of the Revised Code. The department, upon receipt of such a request, shall provide the forms to the biological parent, if the biological parent indicates that the forms are being requested so that the adoption records of the biological parent's offspring will include a social and medical history of the biological parent.

In completing the forms, the biological parent may include information described in division (C) of section 3107.09 of the Revised Code, but shall not include identifying information. When the biological parent has completed the forms to the extent the biological parent wishes to provide information, the biological parent shall return them to the department. The department shall review the completed forms, and shall determine whether the information included by the biological parent is of a type permissible under divisions (B) and (C) of section 3107.09 of the Revised Code and, to the best of its ability, whether the information is accurate. If it determines that the forms contain accurate, permissible information, the department, after excluding from the forms any information the department deems impermissible, shall file them with the court that entered the interlocutory order or final decree of adoption in the adoption case. If the department needs assistance in determining that court, the department of health, upon request, shall assist it.

The department of job and family services shall notify the biological parent in writing if it excludes from the biological parent's social and medical history forms information deemed impermissible. On receipt of the notice, the biological parent may petition the court with which the forms were filed to make a finding as to whether the information is permissible. On receipt of the petition, the court shall issue its finding without holding a hearing. If the court finds the information is permissible, it shall cause the information to be included on the forms.

Upon receiving social and medical history forms pursuant to this section, a court shall cause them to be filed in the records pertaining to the adoption case.

Social and medical history forms completed by a biological parent pursuant to this section may be corrected or expanded by the biological parent in accordance with division (D) of section 3107.09 of the Revised Code.

Access to the histories shall be granted in accordance with division (D) of section 3107.17 of the Revised Code.

(1999 H 471, eff. 7–1–00; 1996 H 419, eff. 9–18–96)

Historical and Statutory Notes

Ed. Note: 3107.091 is former 3107.121, amended and recodified by 1996 H 419, eff. 9–18–96; 1984 H 84, eff. 3–19–85.

Amendment Note: 1999 H 471 substituted "job and family" for "human" in the first and third paragraphs in division (B).

Amendment Note: 1996 H 419 amended this section (former 3107.121) by substituting "the biological parent" and "the biological parent's" for "he," "him," and "his" throughout the section; substituting "3107.09" for "3107.12" throughout the section; substituting "information" for "data as described in division (D)(2) of that section" in the first sentence of the second paragraph of division (B); substituting "information the department deems impermissible" for "impermissible information" and "divisions (B) and (C) of section 3107.09" for "divisions (D)(2) and (3) of section 3107.12" in the second paragraph of division (B); adding the third paragraph of division (B); deleting "the clerk of" preceding "a court shall cause them to be filed" in the fourth paragraph of division (B); and substituting "division (D) of section 3107.09" for "division (D)(4) of section 3107.12" in the fifth paragraph of division (B).

Library References

Adoption ⇌13.
Health ⇌396.
Westlaw Topic Nos. 17, 198H.
C.J.S. Adoption of Persons §§ 46 to 47, 93 to 102.
C.J.S. Health and Environment § 24.
Baldwin's Ohio Legislative Service, 1996 H 419—LSC Analysis, 3/L–336

ACCOUNTING TO COURT

3107.10 Out of county adoption; notice and information sharing

(A)(1) A public children services agency arranging an adoption in a county other than the county where that public children services agency is located, private child placing agency, or private noncustodial agency, or an attorney arranging an adoption, shall notify the public children services agency in the county in which the prospective adoptive parent resides within ten days after initiation of a home study required under section 3107.031 of the Revised Code.

(2) After a public children services agency has received notification pursuant to division (A)(1) of this section, both the public children services agency arranging an adoption in a county other than the county where that public children services agency is located, private child placing agency, private noncustodial agency, or attorney arranging an adoption, and the public children services agency shall share relevant information regarding the prospective adoptive parent as soon as possible after initiation of the home study.

(B) A public children services agency arranging an adoption in a county other than the county where that public children services agency is located, private child placing agency, or private noncustodial agency, or an attorney arranging an adoption, shall notify the public children services agency in the county in which the prospective adoptive parent resides of an impending adoptive placement not later than ten days prior to that placement. Notification shall include a description of the special needs and the age of the prospective adoptive child and the name of the prospective adoptive parent and number of children that will be residing in the prospective adoptive home when the prospective adoptive child is placed in the prospective adoptive home.

(C) An agency or attorney sharing relevant information pursuant to this section is immune from liability in a civil action to recover damages for injury, death, or loss to person or property allegedly caused by any act or omission in connection with sharing relevant information unless the acts or omissions are with malicious purpose, in bad faith, or in a wanton or reckless manner.

(D) The director of job and family services shall adopt rules in accordance with Chapter 119. of the Revised Code necessary for the implementation and execution of this section, including, but not limited to, a definition of "relevant information" for the purposes of division (A) of this section.

(E) This section does not apply to an adoption by a stepparent whose spouse is a biological or adoptive parent of the minor to be adopted.

(2006 S 238, eff. 9–21–06)

Historical and Statutory Notes

Ed. Note: Former RC 3107.10 amended and recodified as RC 3107.055 by 2006 S 238, eff. 9–21–06; 2005 H 66, eff. 6–30–05; 1999 H 471, eff. 7–1–00; 1996 H 274, eff. 9–18–96; 1996 H 419, eff. 9–18–96; 1986 H 428, eff. 12–23–86; 1978 H 832; 1976 H 156.

Ed. Note: Prior 3107.10 repealed by 1976 H 156, eff. 1–1–77; 1953 H 1; GC 8004–10; Source—GC 10512–19; see now 3107.14 for provisions analogous to former 3107.10.

Pre–1953 H 1 Amendments: 124 v S 65

3107.101 Prospective home visits

(A) Not later than seven days after a minor to be adopted is placed in a prospective adoptive home pursuant to section 5103.16 of the Revised Code, the assessor providing placement or post placement services in the prospective adoptive home shall conduct a prospective adoptive home visit in that home, every thirty days, until the court issues a final decree of adoption. During the prospective adoptive home visits, the assessor shall evaluate the progression of the placement in the prospective adoptive home. The assessor shall include the evaluation in the prefinalization assessment required under section 3107.12 of the Revised Code.

(B) During the prospective home visit required under division (A) of this section, the assessor shall make face-to-face contact with the prospective adoptive parent and the minor to be adopted. The assessor shall make contact, as prescribed by rule under division (C) of this section, with all other children or adults residing in the prospective adoptive home.

(C) The director of job and family services shall adopt rules in accordance with Chapter 119. of the Revised Code necessary for the implementation and execution of this section.

(D) This section does not apply to an adoption by a stepparent whose spouse is a biological or adoptive parent of the minor to be adopted.

(2006 S 238, eff. 9-21-06)

COURT PROCEEDINGS

3107.11 Hearing and notice

(A) After the filing of a petition to adopt an adult or a minor, the court shall fix a time and place for hearing the petition. The hearing may take place at any time more than thirty days after the date on which the minor is placed in the home of the petitioner. At least twenty days before the date of hearing, notice of the filing of the petition and of the time and place of hearing shall be given by the court to all of the following:

(1) Any juvenile court, agency, or person whose consent to the adoption is required by this chapter but who has not consented;

(2) A person whose consent is not required as provided by division (A), (G), (H), or (I) of section 3107.07 of the Revised Code and has not consented;

(3) Any guardian, custodian, or other party who has temporary custody or permanent custody of the child.

Notice shall not be given to a person whose consent is not required as provided by division (B), (C), (D), (E), (F), or (J) of section 3107.07, or section 3107.071, of the Revised Code. Second notice shall not be given to a juvenile court, agency, or person whose consent is not required as provided by division (K) of section 3107.07 of the Revised Code because the court, agency, or person failed to file an objection to the petition within fourteen days after proof was filed pursuant to division (B) of this section that a first notice was given to the court, agency, or person pursuant to division (A)(1) of this section.

(B) All notices required under this section shall be given as specified in the Rules of Civil Procedure. Proof of the giving of notice shall be filed with the court before the petition is heard.

(1999 H 176, eff. 10-29-99; 1998 H 484, eff. 3-18-99; 1996 H 419, eff. 9-18-96; 1986 H 428, eff. 12-23-86; 1978 H 832; 1976 H 156)

Historical and Statutory Notes

Ed. Note: 3107.11 is analogous to former 3107.04, repealed by 1976 H 156, eff. 1-1-77.

Ed. Note: Former 3107.11 repealed by 1976 H 156, eff. 1-1-77; 130 v H 202; 1953 H 1; GC 8004-11; Source—GC 10512-20; see now 3107.14 and 3107.19 for provisions analogous to former 3107.11.

Pre-1953 H 1 Amendments: 124 v S 65

Amendment Note: 1999 H 176 deleted former division (A)(1); redesignated former divisions (A)(2) through (A)(4) as new divisions (A)(1) through (A)(3); deleted "The notice to the department of human services shall be accompanied by a copy of the petition." from the beginning of the final paragraph in division (A); and substituted "(A)(1)" for "(A)(2)" in the final paragraph in division (A). Prior to deletion, former division (A)(1) read:

"(1) The department of human services."

Amendment Note: 1998 H 484 added division (A)(4).

Amendment Note: 1996 H 419 added "juvenile" to division (A)(2); substituted "consent is not required as provided by division (A), (G), (H), or (I) of section 3107.07 of the Revised Code and has not consented." for "consent is dispensed with upon any ground mentioned in divisions (A), (E), (F), and (G) of section 3107.07 of the Revised Code, but who has not consented." in division (A)(3); and added the second and third sentences of the second paragraph of division (A)(3).

Library References

Adoption ⚖ 12, 13.
Westlaw Topic No. 17.
C.J.S. Adoption of Persons §§ 46 to 47, 84 to 102.
Baldwin's Ohio Legislative Service, 1996 H 419—LSC Analysis, 3/L-336

3107.12 Prefinalization assessment and report

(A) Except as provided in division (B) of this section, an assessor shall conduct a prefinalization assessment of a minor and petitioner before a court issues a final decree of adoption or finalizes an interlocutory order of adoption for the minor. On completion of the assessment, the assessor shall prepare a written report of the assessment and provide a copy of the report to the court before which the adoption petition is pending.

The report of a prefinalization assessment shall include all of the following:

(1) The adjustment of the minor and the petitioner to the adoptive placement;

(2) The present and anticipated needs of the minor and the petitioner, as determined by a review of the minor's medical and social history, for adoption-related services, including assistance under Title IV–E of the "Social Security Act," 94 Stat. 501 (1980), 42 U.S.C.A. 670, as amended, or section 5153.163 of the Revised Code and counseling, case management services, crisis services, diagnostic services, and therapeutic counseling.

(3) The physical, mental, and developmental condition of the minor;

(4) If known, the minor's biological family background, including identifying information about the biological or other legal parents;

(5) The reasons for the minor's placement with the petitioner, the petitioner's attitude toward the proposed adoption, and the circumstances under which the minor was placed in the home of the petitioner;

(6) The attitude of the minor toward the proposed adoption, if the minor's age makes this feasible;

(7) If the minor is an Indian child, as defined in 25 U.S.C.A. 1903(4), how the placement complies with the "Indian Child Welfare Act of 1978," 92 Stat. 3069, 25 U.S.C.A. 1901, as amended;

(8) If known, the minor's psychological background, including prior abuse of the child and behavioral problems of the child;

(9) If applicable, the documents or forms required under sections 3107.032, 3107.10, and 3107.101 of the Revised Code.

The assessor shall file the prefinalization report with the court not later than twenty days prior to the date scheduled for the final hearing on the adoption unless the court determines there is good cause for filing the report at a later date.

The assessor shall provide a copy of the written report of the assessment to the petitioner with the identifying information about the biological or other legal parents redacted.

(B) This section does not apply if the petitioner is the minor's stepparent, unless a court, after determining a prefinalization assessment is in the best interest of the minor, orders that an assessor conduct a prefinalization assessment.

(C) The director of job and family services shall adopt rules in accordance with Chapter 119. of the Revised Code defining "counseling," "case management services," "crisis services," "diagnostic services," and "therapeutic counseling" for the purpose of this section.

(2006 S 238, eff. 9-21-06; 2001 S 27, eff. 3-15-02; 2000 H 448, eff. 10-5-00; 1999 H 471, eff. 7-1-00; 1998 H 446, eff. 8-5-98; 1996 H 274, eff. 9-18-96; 1996 H 419, eff. 9-18-96)

Historical and Statutory Notes

Ed. Note: Former 3107.12 amended and recodified as 3107.031 by 1996 H 419, eff. 9–18–96; 1984 H 84, eff. 3–19–85; 1978 S 340; 1976 H 156.

Ed. Note: Prior 3107.12 repealed by 1976 H 156, eff. 1–1–77; 1953 H 1; GC 8004–12; Source—GC 10512–21; see now 3107.14 for provisions analogous to former 3107.12.

Pre–1953 H 1 Amendments: 124 v S 65

Amendment Note: 2006 S 238 added division (A)(9) and made other nonsubstantive changes.

Amendment Note: 2001 S 27 added new division (A)(8); added the last sentence of division (A); and rewrote division (B) which prior thereto read:

"(B) This section does not apply if the petitioner is the minor's stepparent, unless a court, after determining a prefinalization assessment is in the best interest of the minor, orders that an assessor conduct a prefinalization assessment. This section also does not apply if the petitioner is the minor's foster caregiver and the minor has resided in the petitioner's home as the foster caregiver's foster child for at least twelve months prior to the date the petitioner submits an application prescribed under division (B) of section 3107.012 of the Revised Code to the agency arranging the adoption."

Amendment Note: 2000 H 448 added the last sentence in division (B).

Amendment Note: 1999 H 471 substituted "director of job and family services" for "department of human services" in division (C).

Amendment Note: 1998 H 446 designated new division (A) and inserted "Except as provided in division (B) of this section," in the first paragraph therein; redesignated former divisions (A) through (G) as new divisions (A)(1) through (A)(7); added new division (B); designated new division (C); and made other nonsubstantive changes.

Amendment Note: 1996 H 274 deleted "Except in the case of a stepparent adopting a stepchild," from the beginning of the first paragraph.

Library References

Adoption ⚖=13.
Westlaw Topic No. 17.
C.J.S. Adoption of Persons §§ 46 to 47, 93 to 102.
Baldwin's Ohio Legislative Service, 1996 H 419—LSC Analysis, 3/L–336

3107.13 Residence in adoptive home

(A) A final decree of adoption shall not be issued and an interlocutory order of adoption does not become final, until the person to be adopted has lived in the adoptive home for at least six months after placement by an agency, or for at least six months after the department of job and family services or the court has been informed of the placement of the person with the petitioner, and the department or court has had an opportunity to observe or investigate the adoptive home, or in the case of adoption by a stepparent, until at least six months after the filing of the petition, or until the child has lived in the home for at least six months.

(B) In the case of a foster caregiver adopting a foster child or person adopting a child to whom the person is related, the court shall apply the amount of time the child lived in the foster caregiver's or relative's home prior to the date the foster caregiver or relative files the petition to adopt the child toward the six-month waiting period established by division (A) of this section.

(2000 H 448, eff. 10–5–00; 1999 H 471, eff. 7–1–00; 1996 H 419, eff. 9–18–96; 1986 H 428, eff. 12–23–86; 1980 S 205; 1976 H 156)

Historical and Statutory Notes

Ed. Note: Former 3107.13 repealed by 1976 H 156, eff. 1–1–77; 1971 S 267; 132 v S 326; 129 v 1566; 1953 H 1; GC 8004–13; Source—GC 10512–23; see now 3107.15 for provisions analogous to former 3107.13.

Pre–1953 H 1 Amendments: 124 v S 65

Amendment Note: 2000 H 448 substituted "caregiver" for "parent" throughout the section.

Amendment Note: 1999 H 471 substituted "job and family" for "human" in division (A).

Amendment Note: 1996 H 419 designated division (A) and added division (B).

Library References

Adoption ⚖=14.
Westlaw Topic No. 17.
C.J.S. Adoption of Persons §§ 103 to 108, 130 to 135, 140.
Baldwin's Ohio Legislative Service, 1996 H 419—LSC Analysis, 3/L–336

3107.14 Court's discretion; final decree or interlocutory order

(A) The petitioner and the person sought to be adopted shall appear at the hearing on the petition, unless the presence of either is excused by the court for good cause shown.

(B) The court may continue the hearing from time to time to permit further observation, investigation, or consideration of any facts or circumstances affecting the granting of the petition, and may examine the petitioners separate and apart from each other.

(C) If, at the conclusion of the hearing, the court finds that the required consents have been obtained or excused and that the adoption is in the best interest of the person sought to be adopted as supported by the evidence, it may issue, subject to division (C)(1) of section 2151.86, section 3107.064, and division (E) of section 3107.09 of the Revised Code, and any other limitations specified in this chapter, a final decree of adoption or an interlocutory order of adoption, which by its own terms automatically becomes a final decree of adoption on a date specified in the order, which, except as provided in division (B) of section 3107.13 of the Revised Code, shall not be less than six months or more than one year from the date of issuance of the order, unless sooner vacated by the court for good cause shown. In determining whether the adoption is in the best interest of the person sought to be adopted, the court shall not consider the age of the petitioner if the petitioner is old enough to adopt as provided by section 3107.03 of the Revised Code.

In an interlocutory order of adoption, the court shall provide for observation, investigation, and a further report on the adoptive home during the interlocutory period.

(D) If the requirements for a decree under division (C) of this section have not been satisfied or the court vacates an interlocutory order of adoption, or if the court finds that a person sought to be adopted was placed in the home of the petitioner in violation of law, the court shall dismiss the petition and may determine the agency or person to have temporary or permanent custody of the person, which may include the agency or person that had custody prior to the filing of the petition or the petitioner, if the court finds it is in the best interest of the person as supported by the evidence, or if the person is a minor, the court may certify the case to the juvenile court of the county where the minor is then residing for appropriate action and disposition.

(E) The issuance of a final decree or interlocutory order of adoption for an adult adoption under division (A)(4) of section 3107.02 of the Revised Code shall not disqualify that adult for services under section 2151.82 or 2151.83 of the Revised Code.

(2006 S 238, eff. 9–21–06; 2000 H 448, eff. 10–5–00; 1998 H 446, eff. 8–5–98; 1996 H 419, eff. 9–18–96; 1984 H 84, eff. 3–19–85; 1976 H 156)

Historical and Statutory Notes

Ed. Note: 3107.14 contains provisions analogous to former 3107.08 to 3107.12, repealed by 1976 H 156, eff. 1–1–77.

Ed. Note: Former 3107.14 repealed by 1976 H 156, eff. 1–1–77; 130 v H 202; 1953 H 1; GC 8004–14; Source—GC 10512–22; see now 3107.17 for provisions analogous to former 3107.14.

Pre–1953 H 1 Amendments: 124 v S 65

Amendment Note: 2006 S 238 designated division (D) and added division (E).

Amendment Note: 2000 H 448 substituted "(C)" for "(B)" after "subject to division" in division (C).

Amendment Note: 1998 H 446 inserted "division (B)(1) of section 2151.86," in the first paragraph in division (C); and made other nonsubstantive changes.

Amendment Note: 1996 H 419 substituted "as supported by the evidence, it may issue, subject to section 3107.064, division (E) of section 3107.09 of the Revised Code," for "it may issue, subject to division (D)(6) of section 3107.12 of the Revised Code" in division (C); added "except as provided in division (B) of section 3107.13 of the Revised Code," preceding "shall not be less than six months or more than one year" in division (C); added the second sentence in the first paragraph of division (C); added "as supported by the evidence," preceding "or if the person is a minor" in division (D); and made other nonsubstantive changes.

Library References

Adoption ⚖13, 14, 16.
Westlaw Topic No. 17.
C.J.S. Adoption of Persons §§ 46 to 47, 93 to 108, 119 to 135, 140.
Baldwin's Ohio Legislative Service, 1996 H 419—LSC Analysis, 3/L–336

3107.141 Order to redo or supplement report or history; appointment of different assessor

After an assessor files a home study report under section 3107.031, a social and medical history under section 3107.09, or a prefinalization assessment report under section 3107.12 of the Revised Code, or the department of job and family services files a social and medical history under section 3107.091 of the Revised Code, a court may do either or both of the following if the court determines the report or history does not comply with the requirements governing the report or history or, in the case of a home study or prefinalization assessment report, does not enable the court to determine whether an adoption is in the best interest of the minor to be adopted:

(A) Order the assessor or department to redo or supplement the report or history in a manner the court directs;

(B) Appoint a different assessor to redo or supplement the report or history in a manner the court directs.

(1999 H 471, eff. 7–1–00; 1998 H 446, eff. 8–5–98)

Historical and Statutory Notes

Amendment Note: 1999 H 471 substituted "job and family" for "human" in the introductory paragraph.

Library References

Adoption ⚖13.
Westlaw Topic No. 17.
C.J.S. Adoption of Persons §§ 46 to 47, 93 to 102.

3107.15 Effects of final decree

(A) A final decree of adoption and an interlocutory order of adoption that has become final as issued by a court of this state, or a decree issued by a jurisdiction outside this state as recognized pursuant to section 3107.18 of the Revised Code, shall have the following effects as to all matters within the jurisdiction or before a court of this state, whether issued before or after May 30, 1996:

(1) Except with respect to a spouse of the petitioner and relatives of the spouse, to relieve the biological or other legal parents of the adopted person of all parental rights and responsibilities, and to terminate all legal relationships between the adopted person and the adopted person's relatives, including the adopted person's biological or other legal parents, so that the adopted person thereafter is a stranger to the adopted person's former relatives for all purposes including inheritance and the interpretation or construction of documents, statutes, and instruments, whether executed before or after the adoption is decreed, which do not expressly include the person by name or by some designation not based on a parent and child or blood relationship;

(2) To create the relationship of parent and child between petitioner and the adopted person, as if the adopted person were a legitimate blood descendant of the petitioner, for all purposes including inheritance and applicability of statutes, documents, and instruments, whether executed before or after the adoption is decreed, and whether executed or created before or after May 30, 1996, which do not expressly exclude an adopted person from their operation or effect;

(3) Notwithstanding division (A)(2) of this section, a person who is eighteen years of age or older at the time the person is adopted, and the adopted person's lineal descendants, are not included as recipients of gifts, devises, bequests, or other transfers of property, including transfers in trust made to a class of persons including, but not limited to, children, grandchildren, heirs, issue, lineal descendants, and next of kin, for purposes of inheritance and applicability of statutes, documents, and instruments, whether executed or created before or after May 30, 1996, unless the document or instrument expressly includes the adopted person by name or expressly states that it includes a person who is eighteen years of age or older at the time the person is adopted.

(B) Notwithstanding division (A) of this section, if a parent of a child dies without the relationship of parent and child having been previously terminated and a spouse of the living parent thereafter adopts the child, the child's rights from or through the deceased parent for all purposes, including inheritance and applicability or construction of documents, statutes, and instruments, are not restricted or curtailed by the adoption.

(C) Notwithstanding division (A) of this section, if the relationship of parent and child has not been terminated between a parent and that parent's child and a spouse of the other parent of the child adopts the child, a grandparent's or relative's right to companionship or visitation pursuant to section 3109.11 of the Revised Code is not restricted or curtailed by the adoption.

(D) An interlocutory order of adoption, while it is in force, has the same legal effect as a final decree of adoption. If an interlocutory order of adoption is vacated, it shall be as though void from its issuance, and the rights, liabilities, and status of all affected persons that have not become vested are governed accordingly.

(2002 H 509, eff. 3–14–03; 2000 S 180, eff. 3–22–01; 1996 S 129, eff. 5–30–96; 1976 H 156, eff. 1–1–77)

Uncodified Law

2002 H 509, § 3, eff. 3–14–03, reads:

No liability shall arise against any one of the following that, prior to the effective date of this section, authorized or was otherwise responsible for a distribution or other payment or a transfer of property that is inconsistent with division (A)(3) of section 3107.15 of the Revised Code, as amended by this act:

(1) A fiduciary under a trust instrument, will, or other document;

(2) A bank, savings and loan association, credit union, or society for savings, in connection with written contracts described in sections 2131.10 and 2131.11 of the Revised Code;

(3) A registering entity, as defined in division (H) of section 1709.01 of the Revised Code, for a transfer-on-death made pursuant to Chapter 1709. of the Revised Code.

Historical and Statutory Notes

Ed. Note: 3107.15 contains provisions analogous to former 3107.13, repealed by 1976 H 156, eff. 1–1–77.

Amendment Note: 2002 H 509 added division (A)(3).

Amendment Note: 2000 S 180 substituted "May 30, 1996" for "the effective date of this amendment" in divisions (A) and (A)(2); added new division (C); and redesignated former division (C) as new division (D).

Amendment Note: 1996 S 129 inserted "or a decree issued by a jurisdiction outside this state as recognized pursuant to section 3107.18 of the Revised Code" and "whether issued before or after the effective date of this amendment" in division (A); inserted "and whether executed or created before or after the effective date of this amendment" in division (A)(2); and made changes to reflect gender neutral language and other nonsubstantive changes throughout.

Library References

Adoption ⚖14, 20 to 24.
Westlaw Topic No. 17.
C.J.S. Adoption of Persons §§ 103 to 108, 130 to 135, 137 to 138, 140 to 145, 152 to 154, 156 to 164.

3107.16 Appeals; finality of decree

(A) Appeals from the probate court are subject to the Rules of Appellate Procedure and, to the extent not in conflict with those rules, Chapter 2505. of the Revised Code. Unless there is good cause for delay, appeals shall be heard on an expedited basis.

(B) Subject to the disposition of an appeal, upon the expiration of one year after an adoption decree is issued, the decree cannot be questioned by any person, including the petitioner, in any manner or upon any ground, including fraud, misrepresentation, failure to give any required notice, or lack of jurisdiction of the parties or of the subject matter, unless, in the case of the adoption of a minor, the petitioner has not taken custody of the minor, or, in the case of the adoption of a minor by a stepparent, the adoption would not have been granted but for fraud perpetrated by the petitioner or the petitioner's spouse, or, in the case of the adoption of an adult, the adult had no knowledge of the decree within the one-year period.

(1996 H 419, eff. 9–18–96; 1986 H 412, eff. 3–17–87; 1976 H 156)

Historical and Statutory Notes

Amendment Note: 1996 H 419 added the second sentence to division (A).

Library References

Adoption ⚖14 to 16.
Westlaw Topic No. 17.
C.J.S. Adoption of Persons §§ 103 to 135, 140.
Baldwin's Ohio Legislative Service, 1996 H 419—LSC Analysis, 3/L–336

3107.161 Contested adoption; factors considered; best interest of child

(A) As used in this section, "the least detrimental available alternative" means the alternative that would have the least long-term negative impact on the child.

(B) When a court makes a determination in a contested adoption concerning the best interest of a child, the court shall consider all relevant factors including, but not limited to, all of the following:

(1) The least detrimental available alternative for safeguarding the child's growth and development;

(2) The age and health of the child at the time the best interest determination is made and, if applicable, at the time the child was removed from the home;

(3) The wishes of the child in any case in which the child's age and maturity makes this feasible;

(4) The duration of the separation of the child from a parent;

(5) Whether the child will be able to enter into a more stable and permanent family relationship, taking into account the conditions of the child's current placement, the likelihood of future placements, and the results of prior placements;

(6) The likelihood of safe reunification with a parent within a reasonable period of time;

(7) The importance of providing permanency, stability, and continuity of relationships for the child;

(8) The child's interaction and interrelationship with the child's parents, siblings, and any other person who may significantly affect the child's best interest;

(9) The child's adjustment to the child's current home, school, and community;

(10) The mental and physical health of all persons involved in the situation;

(11) Whether any person involved in the situation has been convicted of, pleaded guilty to, or accused of any criminal offense involving any act that resulted in a child being abused or neglected; whether the person, in a case in which a child has been adjudicated to be an abused or neglected child, has been determined to be the perpetrator of the abusive or neglectful act that is the basis of the adjudication; whether the person has been convicted of, pleaded guilty to, or accused of a violation of section 2919.25 of the Revised Code involving a victim who at the time of the commission of the offense was a member of the person's family or household; and whether the person has been convicted of, pleaded guilty to, or accused of any offense involving a victim who at the time of the commission of the offense was a member of the person's family or household and caused physical harm to the victim in the commission of the offense.

(C) A person who contests an adoption has the burden of providing the court material evidence needed to determine what is in the best interest of the child and must establish that the child's current placement is not the least detrimental available alternative.

(1996 S 292, eff. 11–6–96; 1996 H 419, eff. 9–18–96)

Uncodified Law

1996 S 292, § 4, eff. 11–6–96, reads: The repeal by this act of division (C) of section 3107.161 of the Revised Code shall not be construed to change the public policy of this state regarding the status of a child in a contested adoption and whether the child may be represented by independent counsel as the public policy existed immediately prior to the enactment of Am. Sub. H.B. 419 of the 121st General Assembly.

Historical and Statutory Notes

Amendment Note: 1996 S 292 added division (A); redesignated former division (A) as division (B); added division (B)(1); redesignated former divisions (A)(1) through (A)(10) as divisions (B)(2) through (B)(11); redesignated former division (B) as division (C); and deleted former division (C), which previously read:

"(C) A child in a contested adoption has full party status and may be represented by independent counsel."

Library References

Adoption ⚖4.
Westlaw Topic No. 17.
C.J.S. Adoption of Persons §§ 15 to 21, 27.
Baldwin's Ohio Legislative Service, 1996 H 419—LSC Analysis, 3/L–336

RECORDS

3107.17 Confidentiality; records; access to histories of biological parents; rights of parties concerning proposed correction or expansion; procedures

(A) All hearings held under sections 3107.01 to 3107.19 of the Revised Code shall be held in closed court without the admittance of any person other than essential officers of the court, the parties, the witnesses of the parties, counsel, persons who have not previously consented to an adoption but who are required to consent, and representatives of the agencies present to perform their official duties.

(B)(1) Except as provided in divisions (B)(2) and (D) of this section and sections 3107.39 to 3107.44 and 3107.60 to 3107.68 of the Revised Code, no person or governmental entity shall knowingly reveal any information contained in a paper, book, or record pertaining to an adoption that is part of the permanent record of a court or maintained by the department of job and family services, an agency, or attorney without the consent of a court.

(2) An agency or attorney may examine the agency's or attorney's own papers, books, and records pertaining to an adoption without a court's consent for official administrative purposes. The department of job and family services may examine its own papers, books, and records pertaining to an adoption, or such papers, books, and records of an agency, without a court's consent for official administrative, certification, and eligibility determination purposes.

(C) The petition, the interlocutory order, the final decree of adoption, and other adoption proceedings shall be recorded in a book kept for such purposes and shall be separately indexed. The book shall be a part of the records of the court, and all consents, affidavits, and other papers shall be properly filed.

(D) All forms that pertain to the social or medical histories of the biological parents of an adopted person and that were completed pursuant to section 3107.09 or 3107.091 of the Revised Code shall be filed only in the permanent record kept by the court. During the minority of the adopted person, only the adoptive parents of the person may inspect the forms. When an adopted person reaches majority, only the adopted person may inspect the forms. Under the circumstances described in this division, an adopted person or the adoptive parents are entitled to inspect the forms upon requesting the clerk of the court to produce them.

(E)(1) The department of job and family services shall prescribe a form that permits any person who is authorized by division (D) of this section to inspect forms that pertain to the social or medical histories of the biological parents and that were completed pursuant to section 3107.09 or 3107.091 of the Revised Code to request notice if any correction or expansion of either such history, made pursuant to division (D) of section 3107.09 of the Revised Code, is made a part of the permanent record kept by the court. The form shall be designed to facilitate the provision of the information and statements described in division (E)(3) of this section. The department shall provide copies of the form to each court. A court shall provide a copy of the request form to each adoptive parent when a final decree of adoption is entered and shall explain to each adoptive parent at that time that an adoptive parent who completes and files the form will be notified of any correction or expansion of either the social or medical history of the biological parents of the adopted person made during the minority of the adopted person that is made a part of the permanent record kept by the court, and that, during the adopted person's minority, the adopted person may inspect the forms that pertain to those histories. Upon request, the court also shall provide a copy of the request form to any adoptive parent during the minority of the adopted person and to an adopted person who has reached the age of majority.

(2) Any person who is authorized to inspect forms pursuant to division (D) of this section who wishes to be notified of corrections or expansions pursuant to division (D) of section 3107.09 of the Revised Code that are made a part of the permanent record kept by the court shall file with the court, on a copy of the form prescribed by the department of job and family services pursuant to division (E)(1) of this section, a request for such notification that contains the information and statements required by division (E)(3) of this section. A request may be filed at any time if the person who files the request is authorized at that time to inspect forms that pertain to the social or medical histories.

(3) A request for notification as described in division (E)(2) of this section shall contain all of the following information:

(a) The adopted person's name and mailing address at that time;

(b) The name of each adoptive parent, and if the adoptive person is a minor at the time of the filing of the request, the mailing address of each adoptive parent at that time;

(c) The adopted person's date of birth;

(d) The date of entry of the final decree of adoption;

(e) A statement requesting the court to notify the person who files the request, at the address provided in the request, if any correction or expansion of either the social or medical history of the biological parents is made a part of the permanent record kept by the court;

(f) A statement that the person who files the request is authorized, at the time of the filing, to inspect the forms that pertain to the social and medical histories of the biological parents;

(g) The signature of the person who files the request.

(4) Upon the filing of a request for notification in accordance with division (E)(2) of this section, the clerk of the court in which it is filed immediately shall insert the request in the permanent record of the case. A person who has filed the request and who wishes to update it with respect to a new mailing address may inform the court in writing of the new address. Upon its receipt, the court promptly shall insert the new address into the permanent record by attaching it to the request. Thereafter, any notification described in this division shall be sent to the new address.

(5) Whenever a social or medical history of a biological parent is corrected or expanded and the correction or expansion is made a part of the permanent record kept by the court, the court shall ascertain whether a request for notification has been filed in accordance with division (E)(2) of this section. If such a request has been filed, the court shall determine whether, at that time, the person who filed the request is authorized, under division (D) of this section, to inspect the forms that pertain to the social or medical history of the biological parents. If the court determines that the person who filed the request is so authorized, it immediately shall notify the person that the social or medical history has record kept by the court, and that the forms that pertain to the records may be inspected in accordance with division (D) of this section.

(2006 S 238, eff. 9–21–06; 1999 H 471, eff. 7–1–00; 1996 H 419, eff. 9–18–96; 1984 H 84, eff. 3–19–85; 1978 H 832, S 340; 1976 H 156)

Historical and Statutory Notes

Ed. Note: 3107.17 contains provisions analogous to former 3107.14, repealed by 1976 H 156, eff. 1–1–77.

Amendment Note: 2006 S 238 deleted "a placement under section 5103.16 of the Revised Code or to" after "pertaining to" in division (B)(1);

and substituted "an" for "a placement or" after "pertaining to" twice in division (B)(2).

Amendment Note: 1999 H 471 substituted "job and family" for "human" in divisions (B)(1), (B)(2), (E)(1), and (E)(2).

Amendment Note: 1996 H 419 rewrote division (B); deleted "probate" preceding "court" in divisions (C) and (E)(1); substituted "section 3107.09 or 3107.091 of the Revised Code" for "division (D) of section 3107.12 or section 3107.121 of the Revised Code" in division (D); substituted "section 3107.09 or 3107.091 of the Revised Code to request notice if any correction or expansion of either such history, made pursuant to division (D) of section 3107.09 of the Revised Code" for "division (D) of section 3107.12 or section 3107.121 of the Revised Code to request that he be notified if any correction or expansion of either such history, made pursuant to division (D)(4) of section 3107.12 of the Revised Code" in division (E)(1); substituted "division (D) of section 3107.09 of the Revised Code" for "division (D)(4) of section 3107.12 of the Revised Code" in division (E)(2); and made changes to reflect gender neutral language throughout the section. Prior to amendment, former division (B) read:

"(B) All papers, books, and records pertaining to a placement under section 5103.16 of the Revised Code or an adoption, whether part of the permanent record of the court or of a file in the department of human services or in an agency, are, except as provided in division (D) of this section, subject to inspection only upon consent of the court."

Comparative Laws

Idaho—I.C. § 16-1511.
Ill.—ILCS 750 50/18.
Ind.—West's A.I.C. 31-19-19-1 et seq.
Iowa—I.C.A. § 600.24.
Ky.—Baldwin's KRS 199.570.
Mass.—M.G.L.A. c. 210, § 5c.
Me.—18-A M.R.S.A. § 9-310.
Mo.—V.A.M.S. § 453.120.
N.C.—G.S. § 48-9-101 et seq.
N.J.—N.J.S.A. 9:3-51.
Wis.—W.S.A. 48.93.

Library References

Adoption ⚖13.
Health ⚖396.
Infants ⚖17.
Records ⚖32.
Westlaw Topic Nos. 17, 198H, 211, 326.
C.J.S. Adoption of Persons §§ 10 to 14, 41, 46 to 47, 93 to 102.
C.J.S. Health and Environment § 24.
C.J.S. Infants §§ 6, 8 to 9.
C.J.S. Records §§ 65, 67 to 75.

Baldwin's Ohio Legislative Service, 1996 H 419—LSC Analysis, 3/L-336

3107.18 Recognition of decrees of other jurisdictions and countries

(A) Except when giving effect to such a decree would violate the public policy of this state, a court decree terminating the relationship of parent and child, or establishing the relationship by adoption, issued pursuant to due process of law by a court of any jurisdiction outside this state, whether within or outside the United States, shall be recognized in this state, and the rights and obligations of the parties as to all matters within the jurisdiction of this state, including, without limitation, those matters specified in section 3107.15 of the Revised Code, shall be determined as though the decree were issued by a court of this state. A decree or certificate of adoption that is issued under the laws of a foreign country and that is verified and approved by the immigration and naturalization service of the United States shall be recognized in this state. Nothing in this section prohibits a court from issuing a final decree of adoption or interlocutory order of adoption pursuant to section 3107.14 of the Revised Code for a person the petitioner has adopted pursuant to a decree or certificate of adoption recognized in this state that was issued outside the United States.

(B) If a child born in a foreign country is placed with adoptive parents or an adoptive parent in this state for the purpose of adoption and if the adoption previously has been finalized in the country of the child's birth, the adoptive parent or parents may bring a petition in the probate court in their county of residence requesting that the court issue a final decree of adoption or an interlocutory order of adoption pursuant to section 3107.14 of the Revised Code. In a proceeding on the petition, proof of finalization of the adoption outside the United States is prima-facie evidence of the consent of the parties who are required to give consent even if the foreign decree or certificate of adoption was issued with respect to only one of two adoptive parents who seek to adopt the child in this state.

(C) At the request of a person who has adopted a person pursuant to a decree or certificate of adoption recognized in this state that was issued outside the United States, the court of the county in which the person making the request resides shall order the department of health to issue a foreign birth record for the adopted person under division (A)(4) of section 3705.12 of the Revised Code. The court may specify a change of name for the child and, if a physician has recommended a revision of the birth date, a revised birth date. The court shall send to the department with its order a copy of the foreign adoption decree or certificate of adoption and, if the foreign decree or certificate of adoption is not in English, a translation certified as to its accuracy by the translator and provided by the person who requested the order.

(2000 S 173, eff. 10–10–00; 1996 H 274, eff. 9–18–96; 1996 H 419, eff. 9–18–96; 1996 H 266, eff. 5–15–96; 1976 H 156, eff. 1–1–77)

Historical and Statutory Notes

Amendment Note: 2000 S 173 substituted "3107.14" for "3701.14"; and made other nonsubstantive changes.

Amendment Note: 1996 H 274 deleted "of common pleas" before "of the county" in division (C).

Amendment Note: 1996 H 419 designated division (A); added the second and third sentences to division (A); and added divisions (B) and (C).

Amendment Note: 1996 H 266 designated division (A) and added the second and third sentences therein; and added divisions (B) and (C).

Library References

Adoption ⚖25.
Westlaw Topic No. 17.
C.J.S. Adoption of Persons §§ 139, 155.
C.J.S. Conflict of Laws § 57.

Baldwin's Ohio Legislative Service, 1996 H 419—LSC Analysis, 3/L-336

3107.19 Information forwarded to human services department

If the adopted person was born in this state or outside the United States, the court shall forward all of the following to the department of health within thirty days after an adoption decree becomes final:

(A) A copy of the adopted person's certificate of adoption;

(B) The form prescribed under division (A)(1) of section 3107.083 of the Revised Code, if a parent filled out and signed the form pursuant to section 3107.071, 3107.081, or 5103.151 of the Revised Code;

(C) A statement of whether the adopted person is an adopted person as defined in section 3107.39 or 3107.45 of the Revised Code.

If the adopted person was born in another state of the United States, the court shall forward a copy of the adopted person's certificate of adoption to that state's vital statistics office within thirty days after an adoption decree becomes final.

(1999 H 176, eff. 10–29–99; 1996 H 419, eff. 9–18–96; 1986 H 428, eff. 12–23–86; 1976 H 156)

Historical and Statutory Notes

Ed. Note: 3107.19 is analogous to provisions of former 3107.11, repealed by 1976 H 156, eff. 1–1–77.

Amendment Note: 1999 H 176 deleted "Within thirty days after an adoption decree becomes final, the court shall forward a copy of the decree to the department of human services of this state for statistical purposes." from the beginning of the introductory paragraph; and substituted "within thirty days after an adoption decree becomes final" for "at the time of forwarding the adoption decree to the department of human services" in the introductory and final paragraphs.

Amendment Note: 1996 H 419 rewrote this section, which prior thereto read:

"Within thirty days after an adoption decree becomes final, the clerk of the court shall prepare an application for a birth record of the adopted person and forward the application to the appropriate vital statistics office of the place, if known, where the adopted person was born, and forward a copy of the decree to the department of human services of this state for statistical purposes."

Comparative Laws

Ark.—A.C.A. § 9-9-219.
Mich.—M.C.L.A. § 710.67.

Library References

Records ⚖32.
Westlaw Topic No. 326.
C.J.S. Records §§ 65, 67 to 75.
Baldwin's Ohio Legislative Service, 1996 H 419—LSC Analysis, 3/L–336

ACCESS TO ADOPTION RECORDS BY ADOPTEES

3107.38 Adoptee's written request or petition to see adoption file

(A) As used in this section:

(1) "Adoption file" means the file maintained by the department of health under section 3705.12 of the Revised Code.

(2) "Items of identification" include a motor vehicle driver's or commercial driver's license, an identification card issued under sections 4507.50 to 4507.52 of the Revised Code, a marriage application, a social security card, a credit card, a military identification card, or an employee identification card.

(B) An adopted person whose birth occurred in this state and whose adoption was decreed prior to January 1, 1964, may do either or both of the following:

(1) Submit a written request to the department of health for the department to provide the adopted person with a copy of the contents of the adopted person's adoption file. The request shall provide the adopted person's address, notarized signature, and be accompanied by two items of identification of the adopted person. If the adopted person submits such a request, the fee required by section 3705.241 of the Revised Code is paid, and the department has an adoption file for the adopted person, the department shall mail to the adopted person, at the address provided in the request, a copy of the contents of the adopted person's adoption file.

(2) File a petition pursuant to section 3107.41 of the Revised Code for the release of information regarding the adopted person's name by birth and the identity of the adopted person's biological parent and biological sibling.

(1996 H 419, eff. 9–18–96)

Library References

Records ⚖32.
Westlaw Topic No. 326.
C.J.S. Records §§ 65, 67 to 75.
Baldwin's Ohio Legislative Service, 1996 H 419—LSC Analysis, 3/L–336

3107.39 Definitions

As used in sections 3107.39 to 3107.44 of the Revised Code:

(A) "Adopted person" means a person who, as a minor, was adopted and who, prior to September 18, 1996, became available or potentially available for adoption. For the purpose of this division, a person was available or potentially available for adoption prior to September 18, 1996, if, prior to that date, either of the following occurred:

(1) At least one of the person's biological parents executed consent to person's adoption;

(2) A probate court entered a finding that the consent of at least one of the person's biological parents to the person's adoption was not needed as determined pursuant to section 3107.07 of the Revised Code.

(B) "Adopted sibling" means an adopted person who has a biological sibling.

(C) "Agency" means any public or private organization that is certified by the department of job and family services to place minors for adoption.

(D) "Biological parent" means a parent, by birth, of an adopted person.

(E) "Biological sibling" means a sibling, by birth, of an adopted person.

(F) "Effective release" means a release that is filed by a biological parent or biological sibling of an adopted person, and with respect to which a withdrawal of release has not been filed by that biological parent or biological sibling.

(G) "File of releases" means the file that is established by the department of health pursuant to division (C) of section 3107.40 of the Revised Code.

(H) "Final decree of adoption" includes an interlocutory order of adoption that has become final.

(I) "Identifying information" has the same meaning as in section 3107.01 of the Revised Code.

(J) "Offspring" means a child, by birth, of a person.

(K) "Petition for release of information" means the petition filed in a probate court in accordance with section 3107.41 of the Revised Code.

(L) "Release" means the form that is filed, pursuant to division (B) of section 3107.40 of the Revised Code, by a biological parent or biological sibling with the department of health and that contains the information, statement, and matter required by division (B)(3) of that section.

(M) "Withdrawal of release" means the form that is filed, pursuant to division (D) of section 3107.40 of the Revised Code, by a biological parent or biological sibling with the department of health and that contains the information, statement, and matter required by division (D)(3) of that section.

(1999 H 471, eff. 7–1–00; 1996 H 419, eff. 9–18–96; 1988 H 790, eff. 3–16–89; 1984 H 84)

Historical and Statutory Notes

Amendment Note: 1999 H 471 substituted "September 18, 1996" for "the effective date of this amendment" twice in the introductory paragraph in division (A); and substituted "job and family" for "human" in division (C).

Amendment Note: 1996 H 419 rewrote this section, which prior thereto read:

"As used in sections 3107.39 to 3107.44 of the Revised Code:

"(A) 'Adopted person' means a person who, as a minor, was adopted pursuant to a final decree of adoption entered by a court.

"(B) 'Agency' means any public or private organization that is certified by the department of human services to place minors for adoption.

"(C) 'Biological parent' means a parent, by birth, of an adopted person and, for purposes of section 3107.40 of the Revised Code, includes a parent, by birth, of a minor who has been placed for adoption.

"(D) 'Biological sibling' means a sibling, by birth, of an adopted person and, for purposes of section 3107.40 of the Revised Code, includes a sibling, by birth, of a minor who has been placed for adoption.

"(E) 'Effective release' means a release that is filed by a biological parent or biological sibling of an adopted person, and with respect to which a withdrawal of release has not been filed by that biological parent or biological sibling.

"(F) 'File of releases' means the file that is established by the department of health pursuant to division (C) of section 3107.40 of the Revised Code.

"(G) 'Final decree of adoption' includes an interlocutory order of adoption that has become final.

"(H) 'Identifying information' means information that is described in either of the following categories:

"(1) Information that is likely to assist an adopted person in identifying his name by birth or one or both of his biological parents and that is described in any of the following categories:

"(a) The information is contained in the copy of the adopted person's original birth record that is obtained by an agency pursuant to an order of a probate judge to the department of health to provide the agency with a copy of the person's original birth record.

"(b) If the probate court in which the petition for release of identifying information is filed is the court that entered the final decree of adoption in the adoption proceedings pertaining to the adopted person, the information is contained in the adoption records of that court. Such information includes, but is not limited to, the addresses of the adopted person's biological parents at the time of the entry of the decree.

"(c) The information is contained in a release filed by a biological parent of the adopted person and is obtained by an agency pursuant to division (B)(2) of section 3107.41 of the Revised Code.

"(d) The information is contained in a probate court's or agency's records and relates to any deceased biological parent of the adopted person.

"(2) If the adopted person's original birth record contains the name of only one of his biological parents, a statement that informs the adopted person of this fact.

"'Identifying information' does not include information that pertains to a biological sibling of the adopted person.

"(I) 'Offspring' means a child, by birth, of a person.

"(J) 'Adopted sibling' means a sibling, by birth, of a person who has been adopted or in relation to whom an adoption petition has been filed.

"(K) 'Petition for release of information' means the petition filed in a probate court in accordance with section 3107.41 of the Revised Code.

"(L) 'Release' means the form that is filed, pursuant to division (B) of section 3107.40 of the Revised Code, by a biological parent or biological sibling with the department of health and that contains the information, statement, and matter required by division (B)(3) of that section.

"(M) 'Withdrawal of release' means the form that is filed, pursuant to division (D) of section 3107.40 of the Revised Code, by a biological parent or biological sibling with the department of health and that contains the information, statement, and matter required by division (D)(3) of that section."

Library References

Records ⚖=32.
Westlaw Topic No. 326.
C.J.S. Records §§ 65, 67 to 75.

Baldwin's Ohio Legislative Service, 1996 H 419—LSC Analysis, 3/L–336

3107.40 Release of identifying information; consent of biological parents or siblings; procedures; withdrawal of release

(A) The department of health shall prescribe a form that permits any biological parent to authorize the release of identifying information, in accordance with section 3107.41 of the Revised Code, to the biological parent's offspring and a form that permits any biological sibling to authorize the release of specified information, in accordance with section 3107.41 of the Revised Code, to the biological sibling's adopted sibling. The forms shall be designed in a manner that permits the biological parent or biological sibling, whichever is applicable, to supply the information, statement, and matter required by division (B)(3) of this section. The department shall prepare written instructions that explain to biological parents and biological siblings the manner in which the applicable form is to be completed; the information, statement, and matter required by division (B)(3) of this section; and the manner in which the completed form is to be filed by a biological parent or biological sibling with the department.

The department shall provide copies of the forms and the instructions to agencies located in, and to the probate courts of, this state. Upon request of any biological parent or biological sibling, the department shall provide the parent or sibling with a copy of the applicable form and the instructions. If an agency or a probate court has copies of the applicable form and the instructions available, the agency or probate court shall provide, upon request, a copy of the applicable form and the instructions to any biological parent or biological sibling.

(B)(1) Any biological parent or biological sibling who wishes to obtain a copy of the applicable form prescribed and the instructions prepared by the department pursuant to division (A) of this section, may obtain them from the department or from an agency located in, or a probate court of, this state, if the agency or probate court has copies of the form and instructions available.

(2) Any biological parent who wishes to authorize the release of identifying information, in accordance with section 3107.41 of the Revised Code, to the biological parent's offspring, and any biological sibling who wishes to authorize the release of specified information, in accordance with section 3107.41 of the Revised Code, to the biological sibling's adopted sibling shall file with the department, on a copy of the applicable form prescribed by it pursuant to division (A) of this section, a release that contains the information, statement, and matter required by division (B)(3) of this section. A release may be filed with the department at any time.

(3) A release shall contain at least the following:

(a) For a biological parent:

(i) The complete name of the biological parent who is filing the release, at the time of its filing with the department and at the time the adoption petition for the biological parent's offspring was filed, if the biological parent knows when the petition was filed;

(ii) The complete name and date of birth, as set forth in the original birth record, of the offspring of the biological parent to whom the biological parent authorizes the release of identifying information in accordance with section 3107.41 of the Revised Code;

(iii) A statement authorizing the release of identifying information, in accordance with section 3107.41 of the Revised Code, to that offspring;

(iv) The written signature of the biological parent, the biological parent's residential mailing address, and the date upon which the release is filed with the department.

(b) For a biological sibling:

(i) The complete name of the biological sibling who is filing the release, at the time of its filing with the department and at the time the adoption petition for the biological sibling's adopted sibling was filed, if the biological sibling knows when the petition was filed;

(ii) The complete name and date of birth, as set forth in the original birth record, of the adopted sibling to whom the biological sibling authorizes the release of the specified information in accordance with section 3107.41 of the Revised Code;

(iii) A statement authorizing the release of the information specified in the release, in accordance with section 3107.41 of the Revised Code, to that adopted sibling;

(iv) The signature of the biological sibling, the biological sibling's residential mailing address, and the date upon which the release is filed with the department.

(4)(a) A release of a biological parent also may contain information that is not required by division (B)(3)(a) of this section and that the biological parent wishes to reveal, in accordance with section 3107.41 of the Revised Code, to the biological parent's offspring. This information shall not include information pertaining to the other biological parent of the offspring or information pertaining to a biological sibling of the offspring.

(b) A release of a biological sibling also may contain information that is not required by division (B)(3)(b) of this section and that the biological sibling wishes to reveal, in accordance with section 3107.41 of the Revised Code, to the biological sibling's adopted sibling. This information shall not include information pertaining to either biological parent of the adopted person or information pertaining to any biological sibling of the adopted person other than the sibling filing the release.

(C) The department shall establish and maintain a file of releases that shall be organized in the manner described in this section and be used in accordance with section 3107.41 of the Revised Code. If any biological parent or biological sibling files with the department a release that has been completed in accordance with the applicable provisions of division (B) of this section, the department shall accept it and place it in the file of releases in accordance with this division.

The department shall place each release accepted pursuant to this division in the file of releases in alphabetical order, according to the surname of the offspring or adopted sibling to whom it pertains, as set forth in the release. The department shall maintain an index to the file of releases that shall list each offspring and each adopted sibling in alphabetical order, according to the surname set forth in the release. The department also shall maintain a separate, alphabetical index to the file of releases that shall list each biological parent and each biological sibling who files a release according to the biological parent's or biological sibling's name at the time of the filing of the release or, if the release indicates that the biological parent or biological sibling had a different name at the time of the filing of an adoption petition, according to the biological parent's or biological sibling's name at that time; and that shall cross-reference each biological parent and each biological sibling listing to the listing of the biological parent's offspring or biological sibling's adopted sibling, whichever is applicable, that is contained in the other index to the file of releases.

(D)(1) The department of health shall prescribe a form that permits any biological parent or biological sibling who has filed a release with the department pursuant to division (B) of this section to withdraw the release. The form shall be designed in a manner that permits the biological parent or biological sibling to supply the information, statement, and matter required by division (D)(3) of this section. Upon request of any biological parent or biological sibling who has filed a release with the department pursuant to division (B) of this section, the department shall provide a copy of the form to the biological parent or biological sibling.

(2) At any time after filing a release with the department, a biological parent or biological sibling may withdraw the release by filing with the department, on a form prescribed by it pursuant to division (D)(1) of this section, a withdrawal of release that contains the information, statement, and matter required by division (D)(3) of this section.

(3) A withdrawal of release shall contain all the following:

(a) The information that the biological parent set forth in the release in accordance with divisions (B)(3)(a)(i) and (ii) of this section, or that the biological sibling set forth in the release in accordance with divisions (B)(3)(b)(i) and (ii) of this section, whichever is applicable;

(b) A statement withdrawing the authorization of the biological parent to release identifying information, in accordance with section 3107.41 of the Revised Code, to the biological parent's offspring, or withdrawing the authorization of the biological sibling to release specified information, in accordance with section 3107.41 of the Revised Code, to the biological sibling's adopted sibling, whichever is applicable;

(c) The written signature of the biological parent or biological sibling, the biological parent's or biological sibling's residential mailing address, and the date upon which the withdrawal of release is filed with the department.

(4) If any biological parent or biological sibling who previously filed a release with the department, files with the department a withdrawal of release that has been completed in accordance with division (D)(3) of this section, the department shall accept the withdrawal of release and place it in the file of releases together with and attached to the release previously filed by the biological parent or biological sibling. Upon request of the biological parent or biological sibling, the department shall provide the biological parent or biological sibling with a copy of the withdrawal of release.

Upon the withdrawal of a release, the department shall note in the index to the file of releases that lists each biological parent and biological sibling who files a release, the fact that the biological parent or biological sibling has filed the withdrawal of release. This notation shall be placed in the index next to the biological parent's or biological sibling's name and the cross-reference to the listing of the biological parent's offspring or the biological sibling's adopted sibling in the other index to the file of releases.

(1996 H 419, eff. 9–18–96; 1988 H 790, eff. 3–16–89; 1984 H 84)

Historical and Statutory Notes

Amendment Note: 1996 H 419 deleted divisions (A)(1) and (2) and redesignated division (A)(3) as division (A); rewrote divisions (B)(3)(a)(i) and (B)(3)(b)(i); and made changes to reflect gender neutral language. Prior to amendment, divisions (A)(1) and (2), (B)(3)(a)(i) and (B)(3)(b)(i), respectively, read:

"(A)(1) The department of human services shall prescribe the procedure to be used by agencies for informing the biological parents of their right to file a form that permits them to authorize the release of identifying information to their offspring, in accordance with section 3107.41 of the Revised Code. The procedure shall include instructions for advising the biological parents of their right to authorize the release of identifying information at the time of the transfer of permanent custody, in accordance with section 5103.15 or Chapter 2151. of the Revised Code, or when a consent to adoption is filed, whichever occurs first.

"(2) A probate court that is acting upon an application filed pursuant to section 5103.16 of the Revised Code shall prescribe the procedure for notification of the biological parents of their right to file a form that permits them to authorize the release of identifying information to their offspring, in accordance with section 3107.41 of the Revised Code."

"(i) The complete name of the biological parent who is filing the release, at the time of its filing with the department; and, if prior to the filing of the release, an adoption petition has been filed or a final decree of adoption entered relative to the offspring described in division (B)(3)(a)(ii) of this section, and the biological parent is aware of the adoption proceedings, the complete name of that biological parent at the time of the filing of the adoption petition [.]"

"(i) The complete name of the biological sibling who is filing the release, at the time of its filing with the department and, if prior to the filing of the release, an adoption petition has been filed or a final decree of adoption entered regarding the adopted sibling described in division (B)(3)(b)(ii) of this section and the biological sibling is aware of the adoption proceedings, the complete name of that biological sibling at the time of the filing of the adoption petition [.]"

Library References

Health ⚖︎397.
Records ⚖︎32.
Westlaw Topic Nos. 198H, 326.
C.J.S. Health and Environment §§ 24, 74.
C.J.S. Records §§ 65, 67 to 75.

Baldwin's Ohio Legislative Service, 1996 H 419—LSC Analysis, 3/L–336

3107.41 Rights of an adult who believes he is an adopted person; birth record; procedures

(A)(1) Any person who is twenty-one years of age or older and who believes he is an adopted person may file a petition for the release of information regarding his name by birth, and the identity of his biological parents and biological siblings, as follows:

(a) If the person is a resident of this state, the petition shall be filed in the probate court of the county in which he resides or in the probate court that entered the final decree of adoption in the adoption proceedings pertaining to him;

(b) If the person is not a resident of this state, the petition shall be filed in the probate court that entered the final decree of adoption in the adoption proceedings pertaining to him, or, if the person does not know which probate court entered that decree, in the probate court of any county.

(2) The petition shall be accompanied by the fee that the probate court has fixed pursuant to division (E) of section 2101.16 of the Revised Code.

(B)(1) Upon the filing of a petition for the release of such information and the payment of the fee fixed by the probate court, the probate judge to whom the petition is assigned shall do each of the following:

(a) Appoint the agency that was involved in the adoption proceeding to perform the tasks described in divisions (B)(2), (C), and (D) of this section, or if no agency was involved in the proceeding, it is not possible to determine the agency involved, or the court determines that it is not feasible for the agency involved in the proceeding to perform those tasks, appoint any agency to perform those tasks;

(b) Issue an order to the department of health that requires it to provide the agency appointed pursuant to division (B)(1)(a) of this section with a copy of the original birth record of the petitioner or with the identity of the court involved in the petitioner's adoption if the department does not possess the original birth record of the petitioner;

(c) Give a certified copy of the order issued pursuant to division (B)(1)(b) of this section to the appointed agency;

(d) Require the appointed agency to perform the tasks described in division (B)(2) of this section within the time that the judge shall prescribe, which time shall be no later than ninety days from the date of appointment or as extended by the judge for good cause shown.

(2)(a) An agency appointed pursuant to division (B)(1) of this section shall present, by mail or in another reasonable manner, the certified copy of the order issued pursuant to division (B)(1) of this section to the department of health. Upon receipt of the order, the department shall provide the agency with a copy of the original birth record of the petitioner, if any. If the department possesses no original birth record of the petitioner, it shall inform the agency, in writing, of this fact and shall provide the agency with the identity of the court that was involved in the petitioner's adoption, and the agency, upon receipt of this information, shall present, by mail or in another reasonable manner, a copy of the order issued pursuant to division (B)(1) of this section and a copy of the information provided by the department to that court and shall request the court to provide the agency with a copy of the original birth record of the petitioner. Upon receipt of the copy of the order and the copy of the information provided by the department, the court shall provide the agency with a copy of the original birth record of the petitioner, if any. If the court possesses no copy of the original birth record of the petitioner, it shall inform the agency of this fact, and, if the court determines that the petitioner was born outside of this state, the department also shall inform the agency of the petitioner's state of birth and shall provide the agency with any pertinent information contained in its file that normally is noted on a birth record in this state.

(b) If the agency receives a copy of the petitioner's original birth record, it shall inspect the record. If the agency determines, upon the inspection, that the petitioner is not an adopted person, it shall report this determination to the probate court in writing. If it determines, upon the inspection, that the petitioner is an adopted person, it shall contact the department of health and request the department to determine whether the file of releases contains a release or releases filed by one or both of the petitioner's biological parents and authorizing the release of identifying information to him, to determine whether the file of releases contains a release or releases filed by any biological sibling of the petitioner and authorizing the release of specified information to him, to determine whether a withdrawal of release also has been filed with respect to any such release, and to provide the agency with a copy of each release with respect to which a withdrawal of release has not been filed. If the agency determines, upon the inspection, that the petitioner is an adopted person, the agency also shall review its records to determine whether they indicate that one or both of the petitioner's biological parents as indicated on the petitioner's original birth record are deceased.

Upon receipt of an agency's request as described in this division, the department of health shall search the file of releases to determine whether it contains a release or releases filed by one or both of the petitioner's biological parents and authorizing the release of identifying information to him, to determine whether it contains a release or releases filed by any biological sibling of the petitioner and authorizing the release of specified information to him, and to determine whether a withdrawal of release also has been filed with respect to any such release. The department promptly shall inform the agency, in writing, of its findings and provide the agency with a copy of each such release with respect to which a withdrawal of release has not been filed.

(c) If the department of health informs an agency either that the file of releases does not contain a release or releases filed by one or both of the petitioner's biological parents that authorize the release of identifying information to him and does not contain a release or releases filed by any biological sibling of the petitioner that authorize the release of specified information to him or that it contains at least one such release but a withdrawal of release has been filed that negates each such release, the agency shall report its determination that the petitioner is an adopted person and the findings of the department to the probate court, in writing, and shall attach to the report the copy of the petitioner's original birth record. If the department informs the agency that the file of releases contains a release or releases filed by one or both of the petitioner's biological parents that authorize the release of identifying information to him for which no withdrawal has been filed or contains a release or releases filed by any biological sibling of the petitioner for which no withdrawal has been filed, and provides the agency with a copy of each such release, the agency shall report its determination that the petitioner is an adopted person and the findings of the department to the probate court, in writing, and shall attach to the report the copy of the petitioner's original birth record and the copy of each release provided by the department. In either case, if the agency after its review of records, has determined that one or both of the petitioner's biological parents as indicated on the petitioner's original birth record are deceased, the agency also shall report that fact to the probate court, in writing, and shall identify the deceased parent or parents.

If the department informs the agency that it possesses no original birth record of the petitioner, the agency shall report that fact and the identity of the court that was involved in the petitioner's adoption, as provided by the department, to the probate court, in writing; if the court that was involved in the adoption informs the agency that it possesses no copy of the original birth record of the petitioner, the agency also shall report that fact to the probate court, in writing; and if the court that was involved in the adoption informs the agency that the petitioner was born outside of this state, the agency also shall report that fact and the identity of the other state to the probate court, in writing.

(d) An agency shall perform all tasks required of it by division (B)(2) of this section within the time prescribed by the probate judge pursuant to division (B)(1)(d) of this section.

(C) Upon receipt of an agency's report submitted pursuant to division (B)(2) of this section, the probate judge shall review the records of the court to determine whether they indicate that one or both of the petitioner's biological parents as indicated on the petitioner's original birth record are deceased, and shall do whichever of the following is appropriate:

(1) If the agency determined that the petitioner is not an adopted person, or if no original birth record was possessed by the department of health and no copy of such record was possessed by the court that was involved in the petitioner's adoption, the judge shall enter an order dismissing the petition, which order shall state the reason for the dismissal.

(2) If the agency determined that the petitioner is an adopted person, if the department of health informed the agency either that the file of releases does not contain a release or releases filed by one or both of the petitioner's biological parents that authorize the release of identifying information to him and does not contain a release or releases filed by any biological sibling that authorizes the release of specified information to him or that the file of releases contains at least one such release but a withdrawal of release has been filed that negates each such release, if the agency did not inform the court that it had determined that one or both of the petitioner's biological parents as indicated on the petitioner's original birth record were deceased, and if the court did not determine that one or both of the petitioner's biological parents as indicated on that record were deceased, the judge shall order that the petition remain pending until withdrawn by the petitioner and order the department of health to note its pendency in the file of releases according to the surname of the petitioner as set forth in his original birth record; shall inform the petitioner that he is an adopted person and, if known, of the county in which the adoption proceedings occurred; shall inform the petitioner that information regarding his name by birth and the identity of his biological parents and biological siblings may not be released at that time because the file of releases at that time does not contain an effective release that authorizes the release of any such information to him; and shall inform the petitioner that, upon the subsequent filing of a release by or the death of either of his biological parents, or the subsequent filing of a release by any of his biological siblings, the petition will be acted upon within thirty days of the filing in accordance with division (E) of this section.

(3) If the agency determined that the petitioner is an adopted person and either the agency informed the court that it had determined that one or both of the petitioner's biological parents as indicated on the petitioner's original birth record were deceased or the court determined that one or both of the petitioner's biological parents as indicated on that record were deceased, the judge shall proceed as follows:

(a) The judge shall inform the petitioner that he is an adopted person and, if known, of the county in which the adoption proceedings occurred;

(b) The judge shall inform the petitioner that one or both of his biological parents, whichever is applicable, is deceased, provided that the information provided under this requirement shall not identify either biological parent of the petitioner;

(c) If two biological parents were indicated on the petitioner's original birth record, if only one of those biological parents is deceased, and if an effective release of the surviving biological parent that authorizes the release of identifying information to the petitioner was provided the agency by the department of health, the judge shall comply with division (C)(4) of this section in relation to the surviving biological parent, and the judge may enter an order granting the petition in relation to the deceased biological parent and requiring the agency and the department of health to release identifying information in relation to the deceased biological parent, subject to the limitations of division (D)(2) of this section and within the time prescribed by the judge;

(d) If two biological parents were indicated on the petitioner's original birth record, if only one of those biological parents is deceased, and if either no effective release of the surviving biological parent that authorizes the release of identifying information to the petitioner is contained in the file of releases or such an effective release is contained in the file but the judge does not enter an order of a type described in division (C)(3)(c) of this section, the judge shall inform the petitioner that one of his biological parents is deceased, shall order that the petition remain pending until withdrawn by the petitioner and order the department of health to note its pendency in the file of releases according to the surname of the petitioner as set forth in his original birth record, and shall inform the petitioner that upon the subsequent filing of a release by or the death of the surviving biological parent, the petition will be acted on in accordance with division (E) of this section;

(e) If two biological parents were indicated on the petitioner's original birth record and both of them are deceased or if only one biological parent was indicated on that record and is deceased, the judge may enter an order granting the petition in relation to each such deceased biological parent and requiring the agency and the department of health to release identifying information in relation to each such deceased biological parent to the petitioner, subject to the limitations of division (D)(2) of this section and within the time prescribed by the judge; if the judge does not enter such an order the petition shall be dismissed;

(f) The judge shall comply with division (C)(4)(d) of this section in relation to any biological sibling of the petitioner who has filed a release that authorizes the release of information to the petitioner and that has not been withdrawn.

(4) If the agency determined that the petitioner is an adopted person and the department of health provided the agency with a copy of each release that authorizes the release of identifying information or specified information to him, the judge shall do each of the following that applies:

(a) Enter an order granting the petition in relation to each biological parent who has filed a release that has not been withdrawn;

(b) Inform the petitioner that he is an adopted person and, if known, of the county in which the adoption proceedings occurred;

(c) In relation to a biological parent:

(i) Require the agency to release identifying information to the petitioner, subject to the limitations of division (D)(2) of this section and within the time prescribed by the judge;

(ii) If an effective release of only one of the petitioner's biological parents that authorizes the release of information to him is contained in the file of releases and either the agency has informed the court that it has determined that the other biological parent is deceased or the court has determined that the other biological parent is deceased, comply with division (C)(3) of this section in relation to the deceased biological parent;

(iii) If an effective release of only one of the petitioner's biological parents that authorizes the release of identifying information to him is contained in the file of releases, if the agency has not informed the court that it has determined that the other biological parent is deceased, and if the court has not determined that the other biological parent is deceased, order that the petition remain pending as to the other biological parent until withdrawn by the petitioner and order the department of health to note its pendency in the file of releases according to the surname of the petitioner as set forth in his original birth record, and inform the petitioner that, upon the subsequent filing of a release by or the death of that biological parent or the filing of a release by any biological sibling, the petition will be acted upon within thirty days of the filing in accordance with division (E) of this section.

(d) In relation to a biological sibling:

(i) If the agency or the court has determined that each biological parent indicated on the petitioner's original birth record is deceased or has filed a release authorizing the release of identifying information to the petitioner that has not been withdrawn, enter an order granting the petition in relation to the biological sibling, require the agency to release the information specified in the biological sibling's release to the petitioner, subject to the limitations of division (D)(2) of this section and within the time prescribed by the judge;

(ii) Order that the petition remain pending until withdrawn by the petitioner and order the department of health to note its pendency in the file of releases according to the surname of the petitioner as set forth in his original birth record, and inform the petitioner that, upon the subsequent filing of a release by any biological sibling or biological parent whose effective release is not contained in the file, the petition will be acted upon within thirty days in accordance with division (E) of this section.

(D)(1) Each agency that is required by an order of a probate judge entered under division (C)(3) or (4) of this section to release information to a petitioner shall do both of the following:

(a) Gather all the information that is subject to the order that it is permitted to release;

(b) Subject to the limitations of division (D)(2) of this section and within the time prescribed by the judge, release to the petitioner the information that is subject to the order that it is permitted to release.

(2)(a) Except as otherwise provided in this division, if a biological parent of a petitioner is deceased or an effective release of a biological parent of a petitioner is contained in the file of releases, and an agency is required by an order of a probate judge entered under division (C)(3) or (4) of this section to release identifying information pertaining to that biological parent to the petitioner, the agency shall not release to the petitioner any identifying information pertaining to a surviving biological parent who filed a withdrawal of release, a surviving biological parent who did not file a release, or a deceased biological parent other than in the circumstances described in division (C)(3) of this section, or any information pertaining to a biological sibling of the petitioner. The agency shall release identifying information pertaining to any biological parent of the petitioner who the probate court's or agency's records indicates is deceased in accordance with an order to do so issued under division (C)(3) of this section, and if a biological sibling has filed an effective release, shall release the information specified in the release, in accordance with any order issued under division (C)(4) of this section requiring the release.

(b) Except as otherwise provided in this division, if an effective release of a biological sibling of a petitioner is in the file of releases and an agency is required by an order of a probate judge entered under division (C)(4) of this section to release information specified in the release of that biological sibling to the petitioner, the agency shall not release to the petitioner any information pertaining to a biological sibling of the petitioner who filed a withdrawal of release or who did not file a release, or any identifying information pertaining to a biological parent of the petitioner. The agency shall release identifying information pertaining to any biological parent of the petitioner who the probate court's or agency's records indicate is deceased in accordance with an order to do so issued under division (C)(3) of this section, and shall release identifying information pertaining to any biological parent who has filed an effective release, in accordance with any order issued by a probate judge under division (C)(4) of this section requiring the release of identifying information.

(E) The petition of a petitioner to whom no information is released in relation to a biological parent in accordance with an order entered pursuant to division (C)(2) of this section, or in accordance with division (C)(3) or (4) of this section, shall remain pending until withdrawn by the petitioner. The petition of a petitioner to whom identifying information is released concerning only one biological parent in accordance with an order entered pursuant to division (C)(3) or (4) of this section shall remain pending as to the other biological parent and as to biological siblings until withdrawn by the petitioner. At the same time as it enters the order under division (C)(2), (3), or (4) of this section, the probate court in which the petition is pending shall order the department of health promptly to provide both the agency appointed pursuant to division (B)(1) of this section and the court with a copy of each release that subsequently is filed by one or both of the petitioner's biological parents, or by the petitioner's other biological parent, whichever is applicable, or by a biological sibling of the petitioner, and that authorizes the release of identifying information to the petitioner, and promptly to notify the agency and the court of the death of a surviving biological parent as indicated on the petitioner's original birth record for whom no identifying information had been released relative to the petition for release, of which the department gains knowledge. Upon receipt of a copy of any such release or of notice of the death of any such biological parent, the probate judge, within thirty days of the date on which the release was filed with the department or the date on which the department gained knowledge of the death, shall do each thing listed in divisions (C)(3)(a) to (f) or (4)(a) to (d) of this section that applies.

Any petitioner who has filed a petition with the probate court that is to remain pending under this division and who wishes to update it with respect to a new mailing address may inform the department in writing, through the court, of the new address. The court shall promptly file the writing with the department and provide the department with the petitioner's name as set forth in his original birth record. The department shall attach the writing to the notation of pendency of the petition contained in the file of releases. Any petitioner who has filed a petition with the probate court that is to remain pending under this division may file a written withdrawal of the petition with the court at any time. Upon the filing of such a withdrawal, the court shall enter an order dismissing the petition, and shall notify both the agency appointed pursuant to division (B)(1) of this section and the department of health of the withdrawal, and upon receipt of such a notice, the department does not have to provide copies of any subsequently filed releases to the agency or the court, as otherwise would be required by this division.

(F) An agency that performs any task described in this division relative to or in connection with a petition for the release of identifying information filed under this section may be reimbursed a reasonable portion of the fee charged for the filing of that petition, in accordance with division (D) of section 2101.16

of the Revised Code, for any services it renders in performing any such task.

(1989 S 46, eff. 1–1–90; 1988 H 790; 1984 H 84)

Library References

Health ⇌397.
Records ⇌32 to 34, 58.
Westlaw Topic Nos. 198H, 326.
C.J.S. Health and Environment §§ 24, 74.
C.J.S. Records §§ 63 to 65, 67 to 75, 86, 99 to 100, 104 to 105, 107.

3107.42 Records declared not public

(A) The following records are not public records subject to inspection or copying under section 149.43 of the Revised Code:

(1) The file of releases;

(2) The indices to the file of releases;

(3) Releases and withdrawals of releases in the file of releases, and information contained in them;

(4) Probate court and agency records pertaining to proceedings under sections 3107.39 to 3107.44 of the Revised Code.

(B) No adopted person who is the subject of personal information contained in a record listed in division (A) of this section may inspect or copy all or part of any such record.

(1984 H 84, eff. 3–19–85)

Library References

Records ⇌32.
Westlaw Topic No. 326.
C.J.S. Records §§ 65, 67 to 75.

3107.43 Revealing information without statutory authority; penalty

(A) No employee or officer of the department of health shall knowingly reveal whether any release or withdrawal of release is included in the file of releases, knowingly provide a copy of any release or withdrawal of release in the files of releases, or knowingly reveal any information contained in any release or withdrawal of release in the file of releases, to any person unless authorized to do so by sections 3107.39 to 3107.44 of the Revised Code.

(B)(1) No agency, officer of an agency, or employee of an agency shall knowingly reveal any information regarding the name by birth of an adopted person or the identity of an adopted person's biological parents or biological siblings to a person who filed a petition for the release of such information unless a probate judge has entered an order under division (C)(3) or (4) of section 3107.41 of the Revised Code requiring the agency, officer, or employee to release such information to the petitioner.

(2) No agency required to release information regarding the name by birth of an adopted person or the identity of an adopted person's biological parents or biological siblings to a petitioner by an order entered by a probate judge under division (C)(3) or (4) of section 3107.41 of the Revised Code, officer of such an agency, or employee of such an agency shall knowingly reveal any information in violation of division (D)(2) of section 3107.41 of the Revised Code.

(C) Whoever violates this section is guilty of a minor misdemeanor.

(1984 H 84, eff. 3–19–85)

Library References

Health ⇌984.
Records ⇌31.
Westlaw Topic Nos. 198H, 326.
C.J.S. Criminal Law § 449.
C.J.S. Health and Environment § 89.
C.J.S. Records §§ 74 to 92.

3107.44 Rights of adult who believes he is adopted; release of information to petitioner; immunity from liability

No agency, officer of an agency, or employee of an agency that releases any information to a petitioner pursuant to an order entered by a probate judge under division (C)(3) or (4) of section 3107.41 of the Revised Code is liable in damages in a civil action to any person for injury, death, or loss allegedly arising from the release of the information to the petitioner, or is criminally liable for the release of the information to the petitioner, if the agency, officer, or employee makes a good faith effort to comply with division (D) of section 3107.41 of the Revised Code in its release of that information.

(1984 H 84, eff. 3–19–85)

Library References

Health ⇌367.
Infants ⇌17.
Westlaw Topic Nos. 198H, 211.
C.J.S. Adoption of Persons §§ 10 to 14, 41.
C.J.S. Health and Environment §§ 9, 16 to 26, 44 to 45.
C.J.S. Infants §§ 6, 8 to 9.

ACCESS TO ADOPTION RECORDS BY BIRTH PARENTS AND SIBLINGS

3107.45 Definitions

As used in sections 3107.45 to 3107.53 of the Revised Code:

(A) "Adopted person" means a person who, as a minor, was adopted but is not an "adopted person" as defined in section 3107.39 of the Revised Code.

(B) "Adoption file" means the file maintained by the department of health under section 3705.12 of the Revised Code.

(C) "Adoptive parent" means a person who adopted an adopted person.

(D) "Authorization of release form" means the form prescribed under division (A)(2) of section 3107.50 of the Revised Code.

(E) "Birth parent" means the biological parent of an adopted person.

(F) "Birth sibling" means a biological sibling of an adopted person.

(G) "Denial of release form" means either of the following:

(1) The component of the form prescribed under division (A)(1)(b) of section 3107.083 if the birth parent checked the "no" space provided on that component.

(2) The form prescribed under division (A)(1) of section 3107.50 of the Revised Code.

(H) "Effective denial of release form" means a denial of release form that has not been rescinded by an authorization of release form pursuant to division (B) of section 3107.46 of the Revised Code.

(I) "Final decree of adoption" includes an interlocutory order of adoption that has become final.

(J) "Identifying information" has the same meaning as in section 3107.01 of the Revised Code.

(K) "Items of identification" include a motor vehicle driver's or commercial driver's license, an identification card issued under sections 4507.50 to 4507.52 of the Revised Code, a marriage application, a social security card, a credit card, a military identification card, or an employee identification card.

(1996 H 419, eff. 9–18–96)

Library References

Records ⬅32.
Westlaw Topic No. 326.
C.J.S. Records §§ 65, 67 to 75.

Baldwin's Ohio Legislative Service, 1996 H 419—LSC Analysis, 3/L–336

3107.46 Denial or authorization of release form; rescinding of form

(A) A birth parent who did not check, pursuant to section 3107.071, 3107.081, or 5103.151 of the Revised Code, the "no" space provided on the component of the form prescribed pursuant to division (A)(1)(b) of section 3107.083 of the Revised Code may sign, date, and have filed with the department of health a denial of release form prescribed under section 3107.50 of the Revised Code. A birth parent who signs an authorization of release form under division (B) of this section may rescind that form by signing, dating, and having filed with the department of health a denial of release form prescribed under section 3107.50 of the Revised Code. If, at the time of submitting the denial of release form, the birth parent provides the department two items of identification, the department shall file the form in the adoption file of the adopted person indicated on the form.

(B) If an adoption file contains a birth parent's denial of release form, the birth parent may rescind that form by signing, dating, and having filed with the department of health an authorization of release form. If, at the time of submitting the authorization of release form, the birth parent provides the department two items of identification, the department shall file the form in the adoption file of the adopted person indicated on the form.

(C) After a birth parent submits a denial of release form or an authorization of release form under this section, the department of health shall provide the birth parent a copy of the form.

(D) A birth parent may rescind an authorization of release form pursuant to division (A) of this section and rescind a denial of release form pursuant to division (B) of this section as many times as the birth parent wishes.

(1996 H 419, eff. 9–18–96)

Library References

Records ⬅32, 35.
Westlaw Topic No. 326.
C.J.S. Records §§ 65, 67 to 75, 86, 92.

Baldwin's Ohio Legislative Service, 1996 H 419—LSC Analysis, 3/L–336

3107.47 Adoptee or adoptee's parents requesting copy of adoption file

(A) An adopted person age twenty-one or older, or an adoptive parent of an adopted person at least age eighteen but under age twenty-one, may submit a request to the department of health for a copy of the contents of the adopted person's adoption file. If the adopted person includes with the request the adopted person's notarized signature and copies of two items of identification, or the adoptive parent includes with the request the adoptive parent's notarized signature and copies of two items of identification, the department shall do the following:

(1) If there is not an effective denial of release form for either birth parent in the adopted person's adoption file and the fee required by section 3705.241 of the Revised Code is paid, provide the adopted person or adoptive parent a copy of the contents of the adopted person's adoption file;

(2) If there is an effective denial of release form for each birth parent in the adopted person's adoption file, refuse to provide the adopted person or adoptive parent a copy of the contents of the adopted person's adoption file;

(3) If there is an effective denial of release form for only one of the birth parents in the adopted person's adoption file and the fee required by section 3705.241 of the Revised Code is paid, provide the adopted person or adoptive parent a copy of the contents of the adopted person's adoption file with all identifying information about the birth parent for whom there is an effective denial of release form deleted.

(B) If an adopted person or adoptive parent is denied a copy of the contents of the adopted person's adoption file or receives a copy of the contents with identifying information about one of the birth parents deleted, the department of health shall inform the adopted person or adoptive parent that it will notify the adopted person or adoptive parent if the department subsequently receives an authorization of release form from one or both birth parents and the adopted person or adoptive parent submits to the department a request to be notified. An adopted person or adoptive parent who submits a request to be notified shall provide the department the adopted person's or adoptive parent's address and notify the department of any change of address. An adopted person or adoptive parent who subsequently decides not to be notified may submit a statement with the department for the department not to notify the adopted person or adoptive parent.

The department shall notify the adopted person or adoptive parent if the department receives an authorization of release form from one or both birth parents and the adopted person or adoptive parent submitted a request to be notified and has not subsequently submitted a statement not to be notified. If the adopted person or adoptive parent contacts the department after being notified and indicates a desire to receive the information the department may provide, the department shall provide the adopted person or adoptive parent information in accordance with division (A) of this section.

(1996 H 419, eff. 9–18–96)

Library References

Records ⬅32, 33.
Westlaw Topic No. 326.
C.J.S. Records §§ 63, 65, 67 to 75.

Baldwin's Ohio Legislative Service, 1996 H 419—LSC Analysis, 3/L–336

3107.48 Adoptee's request that health department assist birth parents or siblings in finding adoptee's name by adoption

(A) An adopted person age twenty-one or older may submit a request with the department of health for the department to assist the adopted person's birth parent or birth sibling in finding the adopted person's name by adoption pursuant to section 3107.49 of the Revised Code. The adopted person shall submit the request on a form prescribed by the department under section 3107.51 of the Revised Code. If the adopted person provides all the information required by section 3107.51 of the Revised Code on the form, the department shall file it in the adopted person's adoption file and assist the birth parent or birth sibling in finding the adopted person's name by adoption unless the adopted person rescinds the request pursuant to division (B) of this section.

(B) An adopted person who has requested under division (A) of this section that the department of health assist the adopted person's birth parent or birth sibling in finding the adopted person's name by adoption pursuant to section 3107.49 of the Revised Code may rescind the request and prohibit the department from assisting the birth parent or birth sibling in finding the adopted person's name by adoption pursuant to section 3107.49 of the Revised Code. The department shall remove the request from the adopted person's adoption file and destroy the request to rescind the request if the adopted person does both of the following:

(1) Makes a written request to the department;

(2) Provides to the department the adopted person's residence address, notarized signature, and two items of identification of the adopted person.

(C) An adopted person may submit requests under division (A) of this section and rescind requests under division (B) of this section as many times as the adopted person wishes.

(1996 H 419, eff. 9–18–96)

Library References

Records ⚖︎33, 34.
Westlaw Topic No. 326.
C.J.S. Records §§ 63 to 64, 71, 74 to 75, 86.

Baldwin's Ohio Legislative Service, 1996 H 419—LSC Analysis, 3/L–336

3107.49 Birth parent or sibling's request for assistance in finding adoptee's name by adoption

(A) A birth parent, or birth sibling age twenty-one or older, may submit a request to the department of health for assistance in finding an adopted person's name by adoption. The department shall examine the adopted person's adoption file to determine the adopted person's name by adoption and provide the birth parent or birth sibling with the adopted person's name by adoption if all of the following are the case:

(1) The adopted person's adoption file contains a request submitted by the adopted person under division (A) of section 3107.48 of the Revised Code that the department assist the birth parent or birth sibling in finding the adopted person's name by adoption;

(2) The adopted person was the child of the birth parent or sibling of the birth sibling before the adoption;

(3) In the case of a request by a birth parent, the court that issued the adopted person's final decree of adoption sends the department, in accordance with division (B) of this section, a notice stating that the birth parent's parental rights concerning the adopted person were not involuntarily terminated pursuant to Chapter 2151. of the Revised Code;

(4) The request is in writing and includes the birth parent's or birth sibling's residence address and notarized signature, one or more items of identification of the birth parent or birth sibling, and the adopted person's name and date of birth as it appears on the original birth record;

(5) The department has an adoption file for the adopted person and is able to determine the adopted person's name by adoption from the file's contents.

(B) If a birth parent requests assistance from the department of health in finding an adopted person's name by adoption, the department shall request the court that issued the adopted person's final decree of adoption to determine whether the birth parent's parental rights concerning the adopted person were involuntarily terminated pursuant to Chapter 2151. of the Revised Code. The department shall provide to the court any information the department has and the court needs to make the determination. On request from the department, the court shall make the determination. After making the determination, the court shall send a notice to the department stating whether the birth parent's parental rights were so involuntarily terminated.

(C) If a birth parent or birth sibling does not know all the information about the adopted person that the department needs to be able to find the adopted person's adoption file, the department shall, if it is known which court issued the adopted person's final decree of adoption, ask the court to find the information about the adopted person from its records. The department shall provide to the court any information the department receives from the birth parent or birth sibling that the court needs to find the information. On the department's request, the court shall provide to the department any information the court has that will aid the department in finding the adopted person's adoption file.

(D) If a birth parent or birth sibling is denied assistance in finding an adopted person's name by adoption because the adopted person's adoption file does not contain a request submitted by the adopted person under division (A) of section 3107.48 of the Revised Code, the department shall inform the birth parent or birth sibling that it will notify the birth parent or birth sibling if the adopted person subsequently submits a request under division (A) of section 3107.48 of the Revised Code and the birth parent or birth sibling submits to the department a request to be notified. A birth parent or birth sibling who submits a request to be notified shall provide the department the birth parent's or birth sibling's address and shall notify the department of any change of address. A birth parent or birth sibling who subsequently decides not to be notified may submit a statement with the department for the department not to notify the birth parent or birth sibling. The department shall notify the birth parent or birth sibling if the adopted person submits a request under division (A) of section 3107.48 of the Revised Code and the birth parent or birth sibling has submitted a request to be notified and not subsequently submitted a statement not to be notified.

(1996 H 419, eff. 9–18–96)

Library References

Records ⚖︎33, 34.
Westlaw Topic No. 326.
C.J.S. Records §§ 63 to 64, 71, 74 to 75, 86.

Baldwin's Ohio Legislative Service, 1996 H 419—LSC Analysis, 3/L–336

3107.50 Denial of release form; authorization of release form

(A) Not later than ninety days after the effective date of this section, the department of health shall prescribe the following forms:

(1) A denial of release form to be used by a birth parent under division (A) of section 3107.46 of the Revised Code. The form shall explain that the birth parent may rescind the denial of release at any time by signing, dating, and having filed with the department of health an authorization of release form pursuant to division (B) of section 3107.46 of the Revised Code.

(2) An authorization of release form to be used by a birth parent under division (B) of section 3107.46 of the Revised Code. The form shall state that the birth parent may rescind the authorization of release at any time by signing, dating, and having filed with the department of health a denial of release form pursuant to division (A) of that section.

(B) On request of a birth parent, the department shall provide a copy of a denial of release form or authorization of release form to the birth parent.

(1996 H 419, eff. 6–20–96)

Library References

Records ⚖=35.
Westlaw Topic No. 326.
C.J.S. Records §§ 71, 86, 92.
Baldwin's Ohio Legislative Service, 1996 H 419—LSC Analysis, 3/L–336

3107.51 Form for adoptee's requesting assistance for birth parents or siblings finding adoptee's name by adoption

(A) Not later than ninety days after the effective date of this section, the department of health shall prescribe a form with which an adopted person may make a request under division (A) of section 3107.48 of the Revised Code. The form shall require all of the following information:

(1) The residence address of the adopted person;

(2) The adopted person's name and date of birth as it appears on the adopted person's new birth record;

(3) The notarized signature of the adopted person;

(4) Any other information considered necessary by the department.

(B) The form shall include instructions that explain how it is to be completed and filed with the department. The department shall include on the form information that advises the adopted person that the adopted person may, in accordance with division (B) of section 3107.48 of the Revised Code, rescind the request at any time, and shall include instructions on how to do so.

(C) On request of an adopted person, the department shall provide the adopted person with a copy of the form.

(1996 H 419, eff. 6–20–96)

Library References

Records ⚖=34.
Westlaw Topic No. 326.
C.J.S. Records §§ 63 to 64, 71, 74 to 75, 86.
Baldwin's Ohio Legislative Service, 1996 H 419—LSC Analysis, 3/L–336

3107.52 Records not public

(A) The department of health's records pertaining to proceedings under sections 3107.45 to 3107.53 of the Revised Code are not public records subject to inspection or copying under section 149.43 of the Revised Code.

(B) No person who is the subject of personal information contained in a record listed in division (A) of this section may inspect or copy all or part of any such record except pursuant to section 3107.47 of the Revised Code.

(1996 H 419, eff. 9–18–96)

Library References

Health ⚖=396 to 397.
Records ⚖=32, 33.
Westlaw Topic Nos. 198H, 326.
C.J.S. Health and Environment §§ 24, 74.
C.J.S. Records §§ 63, 65, 67 to 75.
Baldwin's Ohio Legislative Service, 1996 H 419—LSC Analysis, 3/L–336

3107.53 No liability for release of information

No officer or employee of the department of health who releases any information contained in an adopted person's adoption file or provides a copy of the contents of an adopted person's adoption file to a person who requests the copy pursuant to section 3107.47 or 3107.49 of the Revised Code is liable in damages in a civil action to any person for injury, death, or loss allegedly arising from the release to the person or is criminally liable for the release if the officer or employee releases the information or copy in accordance with section 3107.47 or 3107.49 of the Revised Code.

(1996 H 419, eff. 9–18–96)

Library References

Health ⚖=367.
Westlaw Topic No. 198H.
C.J.S. Health and Environment §§ 9, 16 to 26, 44 to 45.
Baldwin's Ohio Legislative Service, 1996 H 419—LSC Analysis, 3/L–336

OPEN ADOPTIONS

3107.60 Definitions

As used in sections 3107.60 to 3107.68 of the Revised Code:

(A) "Agency," "attorney," and "identifying information" have the same meanings as in section 3107.01 of the Revised Code.

(B) "Nonidentifying information" means any information that is not identifying information, including all of the following:

(1) A birth parent's age at the time the birth parent's child is adopted;

(2) The medical and genetic history of the birth parents;

(3) The age, sex, and medical and genetic history of an adopted person's birth sibling and extended family members;

(4) A person's heritage and ethnic background, educational level, general physical appearance, religion, occupation, and cause of death;

(5) Any information that may be included in a social and medical history as specified in divisions (B) and (C) of section 3107.09 of the Revised Code.

(1996 H 419, eff. 9–18–96)

Library References

Adoption ⚖=6.
Westlaw Topic No. 17.
C.J.S. Adoption of Persons §§ 28 to 45, 140.
Baldwin's Ohio Legislative Service, 1996 H 419—LSC Analysis, 3/L–336

3107.61 Profiles of prospective adoptive parents shown to birth parent

At the request of a birth parent who voluntarily chooses to have a child placed for adoption, the agency or attorney arranging the child's placement and adoption may provide the birth parent profiles of prospective adoptive parents who an assessor has recommended pursuant to a home study under section 3107.031 of the Revised Code be approved to adopt a child. At the request of the birth parent, the agency or attorney may include identifying information about a prospective adoptive parent in the profile if the prospective adoptive parent agrees to the inclusion of the identifying information. If a birth parent chooses a prospective adoptive parent from a profile, the agency or attorney shall give that prospective adoptive parent priority when determining with whom the agency or attorney will place the child.

(1996 H 419, eff. 9–18–96)

Library References

Adoption ⚖=6.
Westlaw Topic No. 17.
C.J.S. Adoption of Persons §§ 28 to 45, 140.

3107.62 Nonbinding open adoption option

An agency or attorney arranging a child's adoptive placement shall inform the child's birth parent and prospective adoptive parent that the birth parent and prospective adoptive parent may enter into a nonbinding open adoption in accordance with section 3107.63 of the Revised Code.

(1996 H 274, eff. 9–18–96; 1996 H 419, eff. 9–18–96)

Historical and Statutory Notes

Amendment Note: 1996 H 274 deleted "or 3107.64" after "3107.63".

Library References

Adoption ⚖6.
Westlaw Topic No. 17.
C.J.S. Adoption of Persons §§ 28 to 45, 140.

Baldwin's Ohio Legislative Service, 1996 H 419—LSC Analysis, 3/L–336

3107.63 Birth parent requesting open adoption of child voluntarily placed for adoption

(A) A birth parent who voluntarily chooses to have the birth parent's child placed for adoption may request that the agency or attorney arranging the child's adoptive placement provide for the birth parent and prospective adoptive parent to enter into an open adoption with terms acceptable to the birth parent and prospective adoptive parent. Except as provided in division (B) of this section, the agency or attorney shall provide for the open adoption if the birth parent and prospective adoptive parent agree to the terms of the open adoption.

(B) An agency or attorney arranging a child's adoptive placement may refuse to provide for the birth parent and prospective adoptive parent to enter into an open adoption. If the agency or attorney refuses, the agency or attorney shall offer to refer the birth parent to another agency or attorney the agency or attorney knows will provide for the open adoption.

(1996 H 419, eff. 9–18–96)

Library References

Adoption ⚖6.
Westlaw Topic No. 17.
C.J.S. Adoption of Persons §§ 28 to 45, 140.

Baldwin's Ohio Legislative Service, 1996 H 419—LSC Analysis, 3/L–336

3107.65 Prohibitions in open adoptions

(A) No open adoption shall do any of the following:

(1) Provide for the birth parent to share with the prospective adoptive parent parental control and authority over the child placed for adoption or in any manner limit the adoptive parent's full parental control and authority over the adopted child;

(2) Deny the adoptive parent or child access to forms pertaining to the social or medical histories of the birth parent if the adoptive parent or child is entitled to them under section 3107.17 of the Revised Code;

(3) Deny the adoptive parent or child access to a copy of the contents of the child's adoption file if the adoptive parent or child is entitled to them under section 3107.47 of the Revised Code;

(4) Deny the adoptive parent, child, birth parent, birth sibling, or other relative access to nonidentifying information that is accessible pursuant to section 3107.66 of the Revised Code or to materials, photographs, or information that is accessible pursuant to section 3107.68 of the Revised Code;

(5) Provide for the open adoption to be binding or enforceable.

(B) A probate court may not refuse to approve a proposed placement pursuant to division (D)(1) of section 5103.16 of the Revised Code or to issue a final decree of adoption or interlocutory order of adoption under section 3107.14 of the Revised Code on the grounds that the birth parent and prospective adoptive parent have entered into an open adoption unless the court issues a finding that the terms of the open adoption violate division (A) of this section or are not in the best interest of the child. A probate court may not issue a final decree of adoption or interlocutory order of adoption that nullifies or alters the terms of an open adoption unless the court issues a finding that the terms violate division (A) of this section or are not in the best interest of the child.

(C) Subject to divisions (A) and (B) of this section, an open adoption may provide for the exchange of any information, including identifying information, and have any other terms. All terms of an open adoption are voluntary and any person who has entered into an open adoption may withdraw from the open adoption at any time. An open adoption is not enforceable. At the request of a person who has withdrawn from an open adoption, the court with jurisdiction over the adoption shall issue an order barring any other person who was a party to the open adoption from taking any action pursuant to the open adoption.

(1996 H 274, eff. 9–18–96; 1996 H 419, eff. 9–18–96)

Historical and Statutory Notes

Amendment Note: 1996 H 274 deleted "or relative" after "birth parent" in division (A)(1); and deleted ", or relative of the child to be adopted and prospective adoptive parent," after "adoptive parent" in division (B).

Library References

Adoption ⚖6, 13.
Health ⚖396.
Records ⚖32.
Westlaw Topic Nos. 17, 198H, 326.
C.J.S. Adoption of Persons §§ 28 to 47, 93 to 102, 140.
C.J.S. Health and Environment § 24.
C.J.S. Records §§ 65, 67 to 75.

Baldwin's Ohio Legislative Service, 1996 H 419—LSC Analysis, 3/L–336

3107.66 Written request for information on adoption

(A) As used in this section:

(1) "Adopted person" includes both an "adopted person" as defined in section 3107.39 of the Revised Code and an "adopted person" as defined in section 3107.45 of the Revised Code.

(2) "Adoptive parent" means a person who adopted an adopted person.

(3) "Birth parent" means the biological parent of an adopted person.

(4) "Birth sibling" means a biological sibling of an adopted person.

(B) An adopted person age eighteen or older, an adoptive parent of an adopted person under age eighteen, or an adoptive family member of a deceased adopted person may submit a written request to the agency or attorney who arranged the adopted person's adoption, or the probate court that finalized the adopted person's adoption, for the agency, attorney, or court to provide the adopted person, adoptive parent, or adoptive family member information about the adopted person's birth parent or birth sibling contained in the agency's, attorney's, or court's adoption records that is nonidentifying information. Except as provided in division (C) of this section, the agency, attorney, or court shall provide the adopted person, adoptive parent, or adoptive family member the information sought within a reasonable amount of time. The agency, attorney, or court may charge a reasonable fee for providing the information.

A birth parent of an adopted person, a birth sibling age eighteen or older, or a birth family member of a deceased birth parent may submit a written request to the agency or attorney who arranged the adopted person's adoption, or the probate court that finalized the adoption, for the agency, attorney, or court to provide the birth parent, birth sibling, or birth family member information about the adopted person or adoptive parent contained in the agency's, attorney's, or court's adoption records that is nonidentifying information. Except as provided in division (C) of this section, the agency, attorney, or court shall provide the birth parent, birth sibling, or birth family member the information sought within a reasonable amount of time. The agency, attorney, or court may charge a reasonable fee for providing the information.

(C) An agency or attorney that has permanently ceased to arrange adoptions is not subject to division (B) of this section. If the adoption records of such an agency or attorney are held by a probate court, person, or other governmental entity pursuant to section 3107.67 of the Revised Code, the adopted person, adoptive parent, adoptive family member, birth parent, birth sibling, or birth family member may submit the written request that otherwise would be submitted to the agency or attorney under division (B) of this section to the court, person, or other governmental entity that holds the records. On receipt of the request, the court, person, or other governmental entity shall provide the information that the agency or attorney would have been required to provide within a reasonable amount of time. The court, person, or other governmental entity may charge a reasonable fee for providing the information.

(D) Prior to providing nonidentifying information pursuant to division (B) or (C) of this section, the person or governmental entity providing the information shall review the record to ensure that all identifying information about any person contained in the record is deleted.

(2006 S 238, eff. 9–21–06; 1996 H 419, eff. 9–18–96)

Historical and Statutory Notes

Amendment Note: 2006 S 238 rewrote division (A), which prior thereto read:

"(A) As used in this section, 'adopted person,' 'adoptive parent,' 'birth parent,' and 'birth sibling' have the same meanings as in section 3107.45 of the Revised Code."

Library References

Adoption ⚖=6.
Infants ⚖=17.
Records ⚖=33.
Westlaw Topic Nos. 17, 211, 326.
C.J.S. Adoption of Persons §§ 10 to 14, 28 to 45, 140.
C.J.S. Infants §§ 6, 8 to 9.
C.J.S. Records §§ 63, 74 to 75.

Baldwin's Ohio Legislative Service, 1996 H 419—LSC Analysis, 3/L–336

3107.67 Agency or attorney providing probate court with adoption records upon permanently ceasing to arrange adoptions

(A) For the purpose of division (C) of section 3107.66 of the Revised Code, an agency or attorney that arranged an adoption shall provide the probate court that finalized the adoption with the agency's or attorney's records of the adoption when the agency or attorney permanently ceases to arrange adoptions.

If an agency permanently ceases to arrange adoptions because the person operating the agency has died or become incapacitated or the attorney ceases to arrange adoptions because the attorney has died or become incapacitated, the person responsible for disposing of the agency's or attorney's records shall provide the court with the adoption records. If no one is responsible for disposing of the records, the person responsible for administering the estate or managing the resources of the attorney or the person who operated the agency shall provide the court with the adoption records.

If the attorney who permanently ceases to arrange adoptions is in practice with another attorney, the attorney may provide the adoption records to the other attorney rather than the court if the other attorney agrees to act in the place of the first attorney for the purpose of section 3107.66 of the Revised Code. The person responsible for the practice of the first attorney shall provide the adoption records to the probate court that finalized the adoption when the practice no longer includes an attorney who agrees to act in the first attorney's place for the purpose of section 3107.66 of the Revised Code.

(B) A probate court that receives adoption records under division (A) of this section may transfer the records to a person or governmental entity that voluntarily accepts the records. If the court finds a person or governmental entity that accepts the adoption records, the court shall maintain a directory for the purpose of informing a person seeking the records where the records are held.

(1996 H 419, eff. 9–18–96)

Library References

Adoption ⚖=6.
Infants ⚖=17.
Records ⚖=13.
Westlaw Topic Nos. 17, 211, 326.
C.J.S. Adoption of Persons §§ 10 to 14, 28 to 45, 140.
C.J.S. Infants §§ 6, 8 to 9.
C.J.S. Records § 32.

Baldwin's Ohio Legislative Service, 1996 H 419—LSC Analysis, 3/L–336

3107.68 Birth parent providing information and photographs

A birth parent who signs the component of the form prescribed pursuant to division (A)(1)(d), or (B)(1)(c), of section 3107.083 of the Revised Code shall provide the materials the birth parent requests be given to the birth parent's child or adoptive parent to the agency or attorney arranging the adoption. At the request of the birth parent's child or adoptive parent, the agency or attorney shall provide the materials to the child or adoptive parent.

A birth parent who signs the component of the form prescribed pursuant to division (A)(1)(e), or (B)(1)(d), of section 3107.083 of the Revised Code shall provide the photographs of the birth parent that the birth parent requests be given to the birth parent's child or adoptive parent to the agency or attorney arranging the adoption. At the request of the birth parent's child or adoptive parent, the agency or attorney shall provide the photographs to the child or adoptive parent.

If a birth parent has signed the component of the form prescribed pursuant to division (A)(1)(f), or (B)(1)(e), of section 3107.083 of the Revised Code authorizing the agency or attorney that arranged the adoption of the birth parent's child to provide the child or adoptive parent the first name of the birth parent, the agency or attorney may provide the birth parent's first name to the child or adoptive parent at the request of the child or adoptive parent.

An agency or attorney arranging a child's adoption shall provide the adoptive parent the child's social security number.

(1996 H 419, eff. 9–18–96)

Library References

Adoption ⚖=6.

Infants ⟲17.
Westlaw Topic Nos. 17, 211.
C.J.S. Adoption of Persons §§ 10 to 14, 28 to 45, 140.
C.J.S. Infants §§ 6, 8 to 9.
Baldwin's Ohio Legislative Service, 1996 H 419—LSC Analysis, 3/L–336

Library References

Health ⟲984.
Records ⟲31.
Westlaw Topic Nos. 198H, 326.
C.J.S. Criminal Law § 449.
C.J.S. Health and Environment § 89.
C.J.S. Records §§ 74 to 92.

Baldwin's Ohio Legislative Service, 1996 H 419—LSC Analysis, 3/L–336

PENALTIES

3107.99 Penalties

Whoever violates division (B)(1) of section 3107.17 of the Revised Code is guilty of a misdemeanor of the third degree.

(1996 H 419, eff. 9–18–96)

CHAPTER 3109

CHILDREN

GENERAL PROVISIONS

Section
3109.01 Age of majority

PARENTAL RIGHTS AND RESPONSIBILITIES

3109.04 Court awarding parental rights and responsibilities; shared parenting; modifications; best interests of child; child's wishes
3109.042 Designation of residential parent and legal custodian
3109.043 Temporary order regarding allocation of parental rights and responsibilities while action pending
3109.05 Support orders; medical needs
3109.051 Parenting time rights
3109.06 Certification to juvenile court

LIABILITY OF PARENTS

3109.09 Damages recoverable against parent of minor who willfully damages property or commits theft offense; community service
3109.10 Liability of parents for assaults by their children

VISITATION RIGHTS OF RELATIVES

3109.11 Visitation rights of grandparents and other relatives when parent deceased
3109.12 Visitation rights of grandparents and other relatives when child's mother unmarried

PREVENTION OF CHILD ABUSE AND CHILD NEGLECT

3109.19 Duty of parents to support children of unemancipated minor children

UNIFORM CHILD CUSTODY JURISDICTION LAW

3109.21 to 3109.37 Uniform Child Custody Jurisdiction Law—Repealed

PARENT CONVICTED OF KILLING OTHER PARENT

3109.41 Definitions
3109.42 Unavailability of custody for parent convicted of killing other parent
3109.43 Unavailability of visitation rights for parent convicted of killing other parent
3109.44 Notice of conviction
3109.45 Termination of visitation order upon receipt of notice of conviction
3109.46 Termination of custody order upon receipt of notice of conviction; deemed new complaint for custody
3109.47 Custody or visitation order when in best interest of child
3109.48 Court order and consent of custodian required for visitation

Section

GRANDPARENT POWER OF ATTORNEY OR CARETAKER AUTHORIZATION AFFIDAVIT

3109.51 Definitions
3109.52 Power of attorney to grandparents for care, physical custody and control of child
3109.53 Form and content of power of attorney
3109.54 Signature and notarization
3109.55 Notice to nonresidential parent and legal custodian; exceptions; method of delivery; contents of notice
3109.56 Conditions determining execution of power of attorney by one or both parents
3109.57 Conditions required for creation of power of attorney
3109.58 Certain pending actions prohibiting creation of power of attorney
3109.59 Termination; filing of revocation of initial power of attorney or subsequent power of attorney
3109.60 Notice required upon termination of grandparent's power of attorney
3109.61 Immunity from liability for good faith reliance on power of attorney
3109.62 Effect of military power of attorney
3109.65 Authority of grandparent to execute caretaker authorization affidavit
3109.66 Form and content of caretaker authorization affidavit
3109.67 Execution of affidavit
3109.68 Affidavit not permitted when certain proceedings are pending
3109.69 Effect of executed affidavit
3109.70 Termination of affidavit
3109.71 Notice required upon termination of affidavit
3109.72 Negation, reversal, or disapproval of action taken pursuant to affidavit
3109.73 Immunity from liability for good faith reliance on affidavit
3109.74 Filing of power of attorney or affidavit with juvenile court; accompanying information; report to public children services agency; investigation
3109.75 Verification of power of attorney or affidavit
3109.76 Requirements regarding subsequent powers of attorney or affidavits
3109.77 Hearing; notice; de novo review
3109.78 Creation of power of attorney or affidavit for participation in academic or interscholastic programs prohibited
3109.79 Effect of power of attorney or affidavit on administrative or court child support order
3109.80 Only one power of attorney or affidavit in effect per child

GENERAL PROVISIONS

3109.01 Age of majority

All persons of the age of eighteen years or more, who are under no legal disability, are capable of contracting and are of full age for all purposes.

(1973 S 1, eff. 1-1-74; 1953 H 1; GC 8005-1; Source—GC 8023)

Historical and Statutory Notes

Pre-1953 H 1 Amendments: 124 v S 65

Library References

Infants ⇌1, 46.
Westlaw Topic No. 211.
C.J.S. Infants §§ 1 to 3, 209 to 213, 253, 268, 275.

PARENTAL RIGHTS AND RESPONSIBILITIES

3109.04 Court awarding parental rights and responsibilities; shared parenting; modifications; best interests of child; child's wishes

(A) In any divorce, legal separation, or annulment proceeding and in any proceeding pertaining to the allocation of parental rights and responsibilities for the care of a child, upon hearing the testimony of either or both parents and considering any mediation report filed pursuant to section 3109.052 of the Revised Code and in accordance with sections 3127.01 to 3127.53 of the Revised Code, the court shall allocate the parental rights and responsibilities for the care of the minor children of the marriage. Subject to division (D)(2) of this section, the court may allocate the parental rights and responsibilities for the care of the children in either of the following ways:

(1) If neither parent files a pleading or motion in accordance with division (G) of this section, if at least one parent files a pleading or motion under that division but no parent who filed a pleading or motion under that division also files a plan for shared parenting, or if at least one parent files both a pleading or motion and a shared parenting plan under that division but no plan for shared parenting is in the best interest of the children, the court, in a manner consistent with the best interest of the children, shall allocate the parental rights and responsibilities for the care of the children primarily to one of the parents, designate that parent as the residential parent and the legal custodian of the child, and divide between the parents the other rights and responsibilities for the care of the children, including, but not limited to, the responsibility to provide support for the children and the right of the parent who is not the residential parent to have continuing contact with the children.

(2) If at least one parent files a pleading or motion in accordance with division (G) of this section and a plan for shared parenting pursuant to that division and if a plan for shared parenting is in the best interest of the children and is approved by the court in accordance with division (D)(1) of this section, the court may allocate the parental rights and responsibilities for the care of the children to both parents and issue a shared parenting order requiring the parents to share all or some of the aspects of the physical and legal care of the children in accordance with the approved plan for shared parenting. If the court issues a shared parenting order under this division and it is necessary for the purpose of receiving public assistance, the court shall designate which one of the parents' residences is to serve as the child's home. The child support obligations of the parents under a shared parenting order issued under this division shall be determined in accordance with Chapters 3119., 3121., 3123., and 3125. of the Revised Code.

(B)(1) When making the allocation of the parental rights and responsibilities for the care of the children under this section in an original proceeding or in any proceeding for modification of a prior order of the court making the allocation, the court shall take into account that which would be in the best interest of the children. In determining the child's best interest for purposes of making its allocation of the parental rights and responsibilities for the care of the child and for purposes of resolving any issues related to the making of that allocation, the court, in its discretion, may and, upon the request of either party, shall interview in chambers any or all of the involved children regarding their wishes and concerns with respect to the allocation.

(2) If the court interviews any child pursuant to division (B)(1) of this section, all of the following apply:

(a) The court, in its discretion, may and, upon the motion of either parent, shall appoint a guardian ad litem for the child.

(b) The court first shall determine the reasoning ability of the child. If the court determines that the child does not have sufficient reasoning ability to express the child's wishes and concern with respect to the allocation of parental rights and responsibilities for the care of the child, it shall not determine the child's wishes and concerns with respect to the allocation. If the court determines that the child has sufficient reasoning ability to express the child's wishes or concerns with respect to the allocation, it then shall determine whether, because of special circumstances, it would not be in the best interest of the child to determine the child's wishes and concerns with respect to the allocation. If the court determines that, because of special circumstances, it would not be in the best interest of the child to determine the child's wishes and concerns with respect to the allocation, it shall not determine the child's wishes and concerns with respect to the allocation and shall enter its written findings of fact and opinion in the journal. If the court determines that it would be in the best interests of the child to determine the child's wishes and concerns with respect to the allocation, it shall proceed to make that determination.

(c) The interview shall be conducted in chambers, and no person other than the child, the child's attorney, the judge, any necessary court personnel, and, in the judge's discretion, the attorney of each parent shall be permitted to be present in the chambers during the interview.

(3) No person shall obtain or attempt to obtain from a child a written or recorded statement or affidavit setting forth the child's wishes and concerns regarding the allocation of parental rights and responsibilities concerning the child. No court, in determining the child's best interest for purposes of making its allocation of the parental rights and responsibilities for the care of the child or for purposes of resolving any issues related to the making of that allocation, shall accept or consider a written or recorded statement or affidavit that purports to set forth the child's wishes and concerns regarding those matters.

(C) Prior to trial, the court may cause an investigation to be made as to the character, family relations, past conduct, earning ability, and financial worth of each parent and may order the parents and their minor children to submit to medical, psychological, and psychiatric examinations. The report of the investigation and examinations shall be made available to either parent or the parent's counsel of record not less than five days before trial, upon written request. The report shall be signed by the investigator, and the investigator shall be subject to cross-examination by either parent concerning the contents of the report. The court may tax as costs all or any part of the expenses for each investigation.

If the court determines that either parent previously has been convicted of or pleaded guilty to any criminal offense involving any act that resulted in a child being a neglected child, that either parent previously has been determined to be the perpetrator of the neglectful act that is the basis of an adjudication that a child is a neglected child, or that there is reason to believe that either parent has acted in a manner resulting in a child being a neglected child, the court shall consider that fact against naming that parent the residential parent and against granting a shared parenting decree. When the court allocates parental rights and responsibilities for the care of children or determines whether to grant shared parenting in any proceeding, it shall consider whether either parent or any member of the household of either parent has been convicted of or pleaded guilty to a violation of section 2919.25 of the Revised Code or a sexually oriented offense involving a victim who at the time of the commission of the offense was a member of the family or household that is the subject of the proceeding, has been convicted of or pleaded guilty to any sexually oriented offense or other offense involving a victim who at the time of the commission of the offense was a member of the family or household that is the subject of the proceeding and caused physical harm to the victim in the commission of the offense, or has been determined to be the perpetrator of the abusive act that is the basis of an adjudication that a child is an abused child. If the court determines that either parent has been convicted of or pleaded guilty to a violation of section 2919.25 of the Revised Code or a sexually oriented offense involving a victim who at the time of the commission of the offense was a member of the family or household that is the subject of the proceeding, has been convicted of or pleaded guilty to any sexually oriented offense or other offense involving a victim who at the time of the commission of the offense was a member of the family or household that is the subject of the proceeding and caused physical harm to the victim in the commission of the offense, or has been determined to be the perpetrator of the abusive act that is the basis of an adjudication that a child is an abused child, it may designate that parent as the residential parent and may issue a shared parenting decree or order only if it determines that it is in the best interest of the child to name that parent the residential parent or to issue a shared parenting decree or order and it makes specific written findings of fact to support its determination.

(D)(1)(a) Upon the filing of a pleading or motion by either parent or both parents, in accordance with division (G) of this section, requesting shared parenting and the filing of a shared parenting plan in accordance with that division, the court shall comply with division (D)(1)(a)(i), (ii), or (iii) of this section, whichever is applicable:

(i) If both parents jointly make the request in their pleadings or jointly file the motion and also jointly file the plan, the court shall review the parents' plan to determine if it is in the best interest of the children. If the court determines that the plan is in the best interest of the children, the court shall approve it. If the court determines that the plan or any part of the plan is not in the best interest of the children, the court shall require the parents to make appropriate changes to the plan to meet the court's objections to it. If changes to the plan are made to meet the court's objections, and if the new plan is in the best interest of the children, the court shall approve the plan. If changes to the plan are not made to meet the court's objections, or if the parents attempt to make changes to the plan to meet the court's objections, but the court determines that the new plan or any part of the new plan still is not in the best interest of the children, the court may reject the portion of the parents' pleadings or deny their motion requesting shared parenting of the children and proceed as if the request in the pleadings or the motion had not been made. The court shall not approve a plan under this division unless it determines that the plan is in the best interest of the children.

(ii) If each parent makes a request in the parent's pleadings or files a motion and each also files a separate plan, the court shall review each plan filed to determine if either is in the best interest of the children. If the court determines that one of the filed plans is in the best interest of the children, the court may approve the plan. If the court determines that neither filed plan is in the best interest of the children, the court may order each parent to submit appropriate changes to the parent's plan or both of the filed plans to meet the court's objections, or may select one of the filed plans and order each parent to submit appropriate changes to the selected plan to meet the court's objections. If changes to the plan or plans are submitted to meet the court's objections, and if any of the filed plans with the changes is in the best interest of the children, the court may approve the plan with the changes. If changes to the plan or plans are not submitted to meet the court's objections, or if the parents submit changes to the plan or plans to meet the court's objections but the court determines that none of the filed plans with the submitted changes is in the best interest of the children, the court may reject the portion of the parents' pleadings or deny their motions requesting shared parenting of the children and proceed as if the requests in the pleadings or the motions had not been made. If the court approves a plan under this division, either as originally filed or with submitted changes, or if the court rejects the portion of the parents' pleadings or denies their motions requesting shared parenting under this division and proceeds as if the requests in the pleadings or the motions had not been made, the court shall enter in the record of the case findings of fact and conclusions of law as to the reasons for the approval or the rejection or denial. Division (D)(1)(b) of this section applies in relation to the approval or disapproval of a plan under this division.

(iii) If each parent makes a request in the parent's pleadings or files a motion but only one parent files a plan, or if only one parent makes a request in the parent's pleadings or files a motion and also files a plan, the court in the best interest of the children may order the other parent to file a plan for shared parenting in accordance with division (G) of this section. The court shall review each plan filed to determine if any plan is in the best interest of the children. If the court determines that one of the filed plans is in the best interest of the children, the court may approve the plan. If the court determines that no filed plan is in the best interest of the children, the court may order each parent to submit appropriate changes to the parent's plan or both of the filed plans to meet the court's objections or may select one filed plan and order each parent to submit appropriate changes to the selected plan to meet the court's objections. If changes to the plan or plans are submitted to meet the court's objections, and if any of the filed plans with the changes is in the best interest of the children, the court may approve the plan with the changes. If changes to the plan or plans are not submitted to meet the court's objections, or if the parents submit changes to the plan or plans to meet the court's objections but the court determines that none of the filed plans with the submitted changes is in the best interest of the children, the court may reject the portion of the parents' pleadings or deny the parents' motion or reject the portion of the parents' pleadings or deny their motions requesting shared parenting of the children and proceed as if the request or requests or the motion or motions had not been made. If the court approves a plan under this division, either as originally filed or with submitted changes, or if the court rejects the portion of the pleadings or denies the motion or motions requesting shared parenting under this division and proceeds as if the request or requests or the motion or motions had not been made, the court shall enter in the record of the case findings of fact and conclusions of law as to the reasons for the approval or the rejection or denial. Division (D)(1)(b) of this section applies in relation to the approval or disapproval of a plan under this division.

(b) The approval of a plan under division (D)(1)(a)(ii) or (iii) of this section is discretionary with the court. The court shall not approve more than one plan under either division and shall not approve a plan under either division unless it determines that the plan is in the best interest of the children. If the court, under either division, does not determine that any filed plan or any filed plan with submitted changes is in the best interest of the children, the court shall not approve any plan.

(c) Whenever possible, the court shall require that a shared parenting plan approved under division (D)(1)(a)(i), (ii), or (iii) of this section ensure the opportunity for both parents to have frequent and continuing contact with the child, unless frequent and continuing contact with any parent would not be in the best interest of the child.

(d) If a court approves a shared parenting plan under division (D)(1)(a)(i), (ii), or (iii) of this section, the approved plan shall be incorporated into a final shared parenting decree granting the parents the shared parenting of the children. Any final shared parenting decree shall be issued at the same time as and shall be appended to the final decree of dissolution, divorce, annulment, or legal separation arising out of the action out of which the question of the allocation of parental rights and responsibilities for the care of the children arose.

No provisional shared parenting decree shall be issued in relation to any shared parenting plan approved under division (D)(1)(a)(i), (ii), or (iii) of this section. A final shared parenting decree issued under this division has immediate effect as a final decree on the date of its issuance, subject to modification or termination as authorized by this section.

(2) If the court finds, with respect to any child under eighteen years of age, that it is in the best interest of the child for neither parent to be designated the residential parent and legal custodian of the child, it may commit the child to a relative of the child or certify a copy of its findings, together with as much of the record and the further information, in narrative form or otherwise, that it considers necessary or as the juvenile court requests, to the juvenile court for further proceedings, and, upon the certification, the juvenile court has exclusive jurisdiction.

(E)(1)(a) The court shall not modify a prior decree allocating parental rights and responsibilities for the care of children unless it finds, based on facts that have arisen since the prior decree or that were unknown to the court at the time of the prior decree, that a change has occurred in the circumstances of the child, the child's residential parent, or either of the parents subject to a shared parenting decree, and that the modification is necessary to serve the best interest of the child. In applying these standards, the court shall retain the residential parent designated by the prior decree or the prior shared parenting decree, unless a modification is in the best interest of the child and one of the following applies:

(i) The residential parent agrees to a change in the residential parent or both parents under a shared parenting decree agree to a change in the designation of residential parent.

(ii) The child, with the consent of the residential parent or of both parents under a shared parenting decree, has been integrated into the family of the person seeking to become the residential parent.

(iii) The harm likely to be caused by a change of environment is outweighed by the advantages of the change of environment to the child.

(b) One or both of the parents under a prior decree allocating parental rights and responsibilities for the care of children that is not a shared parenting decree may file a motion requesting that the prior decree be modified to give both parents shared rights and responsibilities for the care of the children. The motion shall include both a request for modification of the prior decree and a request for a shared parenting order that complies with division (G) of this section. Upon the filing of the motion, if the court determines that a modification of the prior decree is authorized under division (E)(1)(a) of this section, the court may modify the prior decree to grant a shared parenting order, provided that the court shall not modify the prior decree to grant a shared parenting order unless the court complies with divisions (A) and (D)(1) of this section and, in accordance with those divisions, approves the submitted shared parenting plan and determines that shared parenting would be in the best interest of the children.

(2) In addition to a modification authorized under division (E)(1) of this section:

(a) Both parents under a shared parenting decree jointly may modify the terms of the plan for shared parenting approved by the court and incorporated by it into the shared parenting decree. Modifications under this division may be made at any time. The modifications to the plan shall be filed jointly by both parents with the court, and the court shall include them in the plan, unless they are not in the best interest of the children. If the modifications are not in the best interests of the children, the court, in its discretion, may reject the modifications or make modifications to the proposed modifications or the plan that are in the best interest of the children. Modifications jointly submitted by both parents under a shared parenting decree shall be effective, either as originally filed or as modified by the court, upon their inclusion by the court in the plan. Modifications to the plan made by the court shall be effective upon their inclusion by the court in the plan.

(b) The court may modify the terms of the plan for shared parenting approved by the court and incorporated by it into the shared parenting decree upon its own motion at any time if the court determines that the modifications are in the best interest of the children or upon the request of one or both of the parents under the decree. Modifications under this division may be made at any time. The court shall not make any modification to the plan under this division, unless the modification is in the best interest of the children.

(c) The court may terminate a prior final shared parenting decree that includes a shared parenting plan approved under division (D)(1)(a)(i) of this section upon the request of one or both of the parents or whenever it determines that shared parenting is not in the best interest of the children. The court may terminate a prior final shared parenting decree that includes a shared parenting plan approved under division (D)(1)(a)(ii) or (iii) of this section if it determines, upon its own motion or upon the request of one or both parents, that shared parenting is not in the best interest of the children. If modification of the terms of the plan for shared parenting approved by the court and incorporated by it into the final shared parenting decree is attempted under division (E)(2)(a) of this section and the court rejects the modifications, it may terminate the final shared parenting decree if it determines that shared parenting is not in the best interest of the children.

(d) Upon the termination of a prior final shared parenting decree under division (E)(2)(c) of this section, the court shall proceed and issue a modified decree for the allocation of parental rights and responsibilities for the care of the children under the standards applicable under divisions (A), (B), and (C) of this section as if no decree for shared parenting had been granted and as if no request for shared parenting ever had been made.

(F)(1) In determining the best interest of a child pursuant to this section, whether on an original decree allocating parental rights and responsibilities for the care of children or a modification of a decree allocating those rights and responsibilities, the court shall consider all relevant factors, including, but not limited to:

(a) The wishes of the child's parents regarding the child's care;

(b) If the court has interviewed the child in chambers pursuant to division (B) of this section regarding the child's wishes and concerns as to the allocation of parental rights and responsibilities concerning the child, the wishes and concerns of the child, as expressed to the court;

(c) The child's interaction and interrelationship with the child's parents, siblings, and any other person who may significantly affect the child's best interest;

(d) The child's adjustment to the child's home, school, and community;

(e) The mental and physical health of all persons involved in the situation;

(f) The parent more likely to honor and facilitate court-approved parenting time rights or visitation and companionship rights;

(g) Whether either parent has failed to make all child support payments, including all arrearages, that are required of that parent pursuant to a child support order under which that parent is an obligor;

(h) Whether either parent or any member of the household of either parent previously has been convicted of or pleaded guilty to any criminal offense involving any act that resulted in a child being an abused child or a neglected child; whether either parent, in a case in which a child has been adjudicated an abused child or a neglected child, previously has been determined to be the perpetrator of the abusive or neglectful act that is the basis of an adjudication; whether either parent or any member of the household of either parent previously has been convicted of or pleaded guilty to a violation of section 2919.25 of the Revised Code or a sexually oriented offense involving a victim who at the time of the commission of the offense was a member of the family or household that is the subject of the current proceeding; whether either parent or any member of the household of either parent previously has been convicted of or pleaded guilty to any offense involving a victim who at the time of the commission of the offense was a member of the family or household that is the subject of the current proceeding and caused physical harm to the victim in the commission of the offense; and whether there is reason to believe that either parent has acted in a manner resulting in a child being an abused child or a neglected child;

(i) Whether the residential parent or one of the parents subject to a shared parenting decree has continuously and willfully denied the other parent's right to parenting time in accordance with an order of the court;

(j) Whether either parent has established a residence, or is planning to establish a residence, outside this state.

(2) In determining whether shared parenting is in the best interest of the children, the court shall consider all relevant factors, including, but not limited to, the factors enumerated in division (F)(1) of this section, the factors enumerated in section 3119.23 of the Revised Code, and all of the following factors:

(a) The ability of the parents to cooperate and make decisions jointly, with respect to the children;

(b) The ability of each parent to encourage the sharing of love, affection, and contact between the child and the other parent;

(c) Any history of, or potential for, child abuse, spouse abuse, other domestic violence, or parental kidnapping by either parent;

(d) The geographic proximity of the parents to each other, as the proximity relates to the practical considerations of shared parenting;

(e) The recommendation of the guardian ad litem of the child, if the child has a guardian ad litem.

(3) When allocating parental rights and responsibilities for the care of children, the court shall not give preference to a parent because of that parent's financial status or condition.

(G) Either parent or both parents of any children may file a pleading or motion with the court requesting the court to grant both parents shared parental rights and responsibilities for the care of the children in a proceeding held pursuant to division (A) of this section. If a pleading or motion requesting shared parenting is filed, the parent or parents filing the pleading or motion also shall file with the court a plan for the exercise of shared parenting by both parents. If each parent files a pleading or motion requesting shared parenting but only one parent files a plan or if only one parent files a pleading or motion requesting shared parenting and also files a plan, the other parent as ordered by the court shall file with the court a plan for the exercise of shared parenting by both parents. The plan for shared parenting shall be filed with the petition for dissolution of marriage, if the question of parental rights and responsibilities for the care of the children arises out of an action for dissolution of marriage, or, in other cases, at a time at least thirty days prior to the hearing on the issue of the parental rights and responsibilities for the care of the children. A plan for shared parenting shall include provisions covering all factors that are relevant to the care of the children, including, but not limited to, provisions covering factors such as physical living arrangements, child support obligations, provision for the children's medical and dental care, school placement, and the parent with which the children will be physically located during legal holidays, school holidays, and other days of special importance.

(H) If an appeal is taken from a decision of a court that grants or modifies a decree allocating parental rights and responsibilities for the care of children, the court of appeals shall give the case calendar priority and handle it expeditiously.

(I) As used in this section:

(1) "Abused child" has the same meaning as in section 2151.031 of the Revised Code, and "neglected child" has the same meaning as in section 2151.03 of the Revised Code.

(2) "Sexually oriented offense" has the same meaning as in section 2950.01 of the Revised Code.

(J) As used in the Revised Code, "shared parenting" means that the parents share, in the manner set forth in the plan for shared parenting that is approved by the court under division (D)(1) and described in division (K)(6) of this section, all or some of the aspects of physical and legal care of their children.

(K) For purposes of the Revised Code:

(1) A parent who is granted the care, custody, and control of a child under an order that was issued pursuant to this section prior to April 11, 1991, and that does not provide for shared parenting has "custody of the child" and "care, custody, and control of the child" under the order, and is the "residential parent," the "residential parent and legal custodian," or the "custodial parent" of the child under the order.

(2) A parent who primarily is allocated the parental rights and responsibilities for the care of a child and who is designated as the residential parent and legal custodian of the child under an order that is issued pursuant to this section on or after April 11, 1991, and that does not provide for shared parenting has "custody of the child" and "care, custody, and control of the child" under the order, and is the "residential parent," the "residential parent and legal custodian," or the "custodial parent" of the child under the order.

(3) A parent who is not granted custody of a child under an order that was issued pursuant to this section prior to April 11, 1991, and that does not provide for shared parenting is the "parent who is not the residential parent," the "parent who is not the residential parent and legal custodian," or the "noncustodial parent" of the child under the order.

(4) A parent who is not primarily allocated the parental rights and responsibilities for the care of a child and who is not designated as the residential parent and legal custodian of the child under an order that is issued pursuant to this section on or after April 11, 1991, and that does not provide for shared parenting is the "parent who is not the residential parent," the "parent who is not the residential parent and legal custodian," or the "noncustodial parent" of the child under the order.

(5) Unless the context clearly requires otherwise, if an order is issued by a court pursuant to this section and the order provides for shared parenting of a child, both parents have "custody of the child" or "care, custody, and control of the child" under the order, to the extent and in the manner specified in the order.

(6) Unless the context clearly requires otherwise and except as otherwise provided in the order, if an order is issued by a court pursuant to this section and the order provides for shared parenting of a child, each parent, regardless of where the child is

physically located or with whom the child is residing at a particular point in time, as specified in the order, is the "residential parent," the "residential parent and legal custodian," or the "custodial parent" of the child.

(7) Unless the context clearly requires otherwise and except as otherwise provided in the order, a designation in the order of a parent as the residential parent for the purpose of determining the school the child attends, as the custodial parent for purposes of claiming the child as a dependent pursuant to section 152(e) of the "Internal Revenue Code of 1986," 100 Stat. 2085, 26 U.S.C.A. 1, as amended, or as the residential parent for purposes of receiving public assistance pursuant to division (A)(2) of this section, does not affect the designation pursuant to division (K)(6) of this section of each parent as the "residential parent," the "residential parent and legal custodian," or the "custodial parent" of the child.

(L) The court shall require each parent of a child to file an affidavit attesting as to whether the parent, and the members of the parent's household, have been convicted of or pleaded guilty to any of the offenses identified in divisions (C) and (F)(1)(h) of this section.

(2006 S 260, eff. 1–2–07; 2004 S 185, eff. 4–11–05; 2000 S 180, eff. 3–22–01; 1994 H 415, eff. 11–9–94; 1993 S 115, eff. 10–12–93; 1990 S 3, H 514, H 591; 1983 H 93; 1981 S 39, H 71; 1977 S 135; 1975 H 370, H 1; 1974 H 740, H 233; 131 v H 745; 1953 H 1; GC 8005–4; Source—GC 8033)

Historical and Statutory Notes

Pre–1953 H 1 Amendments: 124 v S 65

Amendment Note: 2004 S 185 substituted "3127.01 to 3127.53" for "3109.21 to 3109.36" in division (A).

Amendment Note: 2000 S 180 substituted "Chapters 3119., 3121., 3123., and 3125.," for "section 3113.215" in division (A)(2); inserted "court-approved parenting time rights or" and deleted "approved by the court" after "companionship rights" in division (F)(1)(f); substituted "parent's" for "parent his or her" and "parenting time" for "visitation" in division (F)(1)(i); deleted "division (B)(3) of" after "enumerated" and substituted '3119.23" for "3113.215" in division (F)(2); and made changes to reflect gender neutral language.

Amendment Note: 1994 H 415 rewrote division (E)(2); substituted "the parent with which the children will be physically located during legal holidays, school holidays, and other days of special importance" for "visitation" in division (G); inserted "and described in division (K)(6)" in division (J); substituted "each" for "the" and inserted ", regardless of where the child is physically located or" in division (K)(6); and rewrote division (K)(7). Prior to amendment, divisions (E)(2) and (K)(7) read:

"(2) In addition to a modification authorized under division (E)(1) of this section:

"(a) Both parents under a shared parenting decree jointly may modify the terms of the plan for shared parenting approved by the court and incorporated by it into the shared parenting decree. Modifications under this division may be made in relation to a final decree at any time and may be made in relation to a provisional decree issued prior to April 11, 1991, at any time prior to sixty days after the date of issuance of the provisional decree. The modifications to the plan shall be filed jointly by both parents with the court, and the court shall include them in the plan, unless they are not in the best interest of the children, in which case the court may reject the modifications. Modifications jointly submitted by both parents under a shared parenting decree shall be effective upon their inclusion by the court in the plan. A modification to a provisional plan issued prior to April 11, 1991, that is made under this division does not affect or extend the ninety-day period during which the provisional plan may be terminated upon motion of either parent or the court itself.

"(b) The court may modify the terms of the plan for shared parenting approved by the court and incorporated by it into the shared parenting decree upon the request of one or both of the parents under the decree. Modifications under this division may be made in relation to a final decree at any time and may be made in relation to a provisional decree issued prior to April 11, 1991, at any time prior to sixty days after the date of issuance of the provisional decree. The court shall not make any modifications to the plan under this division, unless the modification is in the best interest of the children and, if the plan was approved under division (D)(1)(a)(i) of this section, unless both parents agree to the modification. A modification to a provisional plan issued prior to April 11, 1991, that is made under this division does not affect or extend the ninety-day period during which the provisional plan may be terminated upon motion of either parent or the court itself, as described in divisions (E)(2)(c), (d), and (e) of this section.

"(c) The court shall terminate a provisional shared parenting decree issued prior to April 11, 1991, if either parent or the court itself makes a motion to terminate the provisional decree at any time prior to the expiration of ninety days after the date of its issuance. The court itself may make a motion to terminate a provisional decree only if it has reason to believe that the plan incorporated into the provisional decree is not in the best interest of the children and that it cannot be modified so as to be in the best interest of the children or if it has reason to believe that shared parenting itself is not in the best interest of the children. If the court has reason to believe that the plan incorporated into the provisional decree is not in the best interest of the children but that it can be modified so as to be in the best interest of the children, the plan may be modified in accordance with division (E)(2)(a) or (b) of this section regardless of whether the sixty-day period that normally applies in relation to modification of provisional decrees under those divisions has expired. If a provisional decree is terminated under this division, the court shall proceed in accordance with division (E)(2)(e) of this section. If neither parent nor the court itself makes a motion to terminate a provisional decree prior to the expiration of the ninety-day period, the provisional decree immediately and without need for further action shall become final on the ninetieth day after the date of its issuance, subject to modification or termination authorized by this section. Division (E)(2)(c) of this section does not apply in relation to a final shared parenting decree.

"(d) The court may terminate a prior final shared parenting decree that includes a shared parenting plan approved under division (D)(1)(a)(i) of this section upon the request of one or both of the parents or whenever it determines that shared parenting is not in the best interest of the children. The court may terminate a prior final shared parenting decree that includes a shared parenting plan approved under division (D)(1)(a)(ii) or (iii) of this section if it determines, upon its own motion or upon the request of one or both parents, that shared parenting is not in the best interest of the children. If modification of the terms of the plan for shared parenting approved by the court and incorporated by it into the final shared parenting decree is attempted under division (E)(2)(a) of this section and the court rejects the modifications, it may terminate the final shared parenting decree if it determines that shared parenting is not in the best interest of the children.

"(e) Upon the termination of a provisional shared parenting decree issued prior to April 11, 1991, or a prior final shared parenting decree under division (E)(2)(c) or (d) of this section, the court shall proceed and issue a modified decree for the allocation of parental rights and responsibilities for the care of the children under the standards applicable under divisions (A), (B), and (C) of this section as if no decree for shared parenting had been granted and as if no request for shared parenting ever had been made."

"(7) Unless the context clearly requires otherwise and except as otherwise provided in the order, if an order is issued by a court pursuant to this section and the order provides for shared parenting of a child, the parent with whom the child is not to reside at a particular point in time, as specified in the order, is the 'parent who is not the residential parent,' the 'parent who is not the residential parent and legal custodian,' or the 'noncustodial parent' of the child at that point in time."

Amendment Note: 1993 S 115 substituted "April 11, 1991" for "the effective date of this amendment" in division (E); changed a reference to section 3109.05(A) to a reference to section 3113.215(B)(3) in the first paragraph of division (F)(2); and substituted "April 11, 1991" for "the effective date of this amendment" in division (K).

Library References

Child Custody ⇔1 to 662.

Westlaw Topic No. 76D.

C.J.S. Adoption of Persons §§ 140 to 141, 143.

C.J.S. Parent and Child §§ 55 to 155, 157, 203.

Baldwin's Ohio Legislative Service, 1990 Laws of Ohio, H 591—LSC Analysis, p 5–576

3109.042 Designation of residential parent and legal custodian

An unmarried female who gives birth to a child is the sole residential parent and legal custodian of the child until a court of competent jurisdiction issues an order designating another person as the residential parent and legal custodian. A court designating the residential parent and legal custodian of a child described in this section shall treat the mother and father as standing upon an equality when making the designation.

(1997 H 352, eff. 1-1-98)

Library References

Children Out-of-Wedlock ⚖20 to 20.3.
Westlaw Topic No. 76H.
C.J.S. Children Out-of-Wedlock §§ 11 to 12, 34 to 38.

3109.043 Temporary order regarding allocation of parental rights and responsibilities while action pending

In any proceeding pertaining to the allocation of parental rights and responsibilities for the care of a child, when requested in the complaint, answer, or counterclaim, or by motion served with the pleading, upon satisfactory proof by affidavit duly filed with the clerk of the court, the court, without oral hearing and for good cause shown, may make a temporary order regarding the allocation of parental rights and responsibilities for the care of the child while the action is pending.

If a parent and child relationship has not already been established pursuant to section 3111.02 of the Revised Code, the court may take into consideration when determining whether to award parenting time, visitation rights, or temporary custody to a putative father that the putative father is named on the birth record of the child, the child has the putative father's surname, or a clear pattern of a parent and child relationship between the child and the putative father exists.

(2006 H 136, eff. 5-17-06)

3109.05 Support orders; medical needs

(A)(1) In a divorce, dissolution of marriage, legal separation, or child support proceeding, the court may order either or both parents to support or help support their children, without regard to marital misconduct. In determining the amount reasonable or necessary for child support, including the medical needs of the child, the court shall comply with Chapter 3119. of the Revised Code.

(2) The court, in accordance with Chapter 3119. of the Revised Code, shall include in each support order made under this section the requirement that one or both of the parents provide for the health care needs of the child to the satisfaction of the court, and the court shall include in the support order a requirement that all support payments be made through the office of child support in the department of job and family services.

(3) The court shall comply with Chapters 3119., 3121., 3123., and 3125. of the Revised Code when it makes or modifies an order for child support under this section.

(B) The juvenile court has exclusive jurisdiction to enter the orders in any case certified to it from another court.

(C) If any person required to pay child support under an order made under division (A) of this section on or after April 15, 1985, or modified on or after December 1, 1986, is found in contempt of court for failure to make support payments under the order, the court that makes the finding, in addition to any other penalty or remedy imposed, shall assess all court costs arising out of the contempt proceeding against the person and require the person to pay any reasonable attorney's fees of any adverse party, as determined by the court, that arose in relation to the act of contempt and, on or after July 1, 1992, shall assess interest on any unpaid amount of child support pursuant to section 3123.17 of the Revised Code.

(D) The court shall not authorize or permit the escrowing, impoundment, or withholding of any child support payment ordered under this section or any other section of the Revised Code because of a denial of or interference with a right of parenting time granted to a parent in an order issued under this section or section 3109.051 or 3109.12 of the Revised Code or companionship or visitation granted in an order issued under this section, section 3109.051, 3109.11, 3109.12, or any other section of the Revised Code, or as a method of enforcing the specific provisions of any such order dealing with parenting time or visitation.

(2000 S 180, eff. 3-22-01; 1999 H 471, eff. 7-1-00; 1997 H 352, eff. 1-1-98; 1993 H 173, eff. 12-31-93; 1993 S 115; 1992 S 10; 1990 S 3, H 514, H 591, H 15; 1988 H 708; 1987 H 231; 1986 H 509; 1984 H 614; 1981 H 694, H 71; 1974 H 233; 1971 H 163, H 544; 1953 H 1; GC 8005-5; Source—GC 8034)

Historical and Statutory Notes

Ed. Note: Former RC 3109.05(E) related to the duration of support orders. See now RC 3119.86 for provisions analogous to former RC 3109.05(E).

Pre-1953 H 1 Amendments: 124 v S 65

Amendment Note: 2000 S 180 substituted "Chapter 3119" for "sections 3113.21 to 3113.219" in division (A)(1) and (A)(2); rewrote division (A)(3); substituted "3123.17" for "3113.219"; rewrote division (D); and deleted division (E). Prior to amendment or deletion divisions (A)(3), (D), and (E) read:

"(3) Each order for child support made or modified under this section shall include as part of the order a general provision, as described in division (A)(1) of section 3113.21 of the Revised Code, requiring the withholding or deduction of income or assets of the obligor under the order as described in division (D) or (H) of section 3113.21 of the Revised Code, or another type of appropriate requirement as described in division (D)(3), (D)(4), or (H) of that section, to ensure that withholding or deduction from the income or assets of the obligor is available from the commencement of the support order for collection of the support and of any arrearages that occur; a statement requiring both parents to notify the child support enforcement agency in writing of their current mailing address; current residence address, current residence telephone number, current driver's license number, and any changes to that information, and a notice that the requirement to notify the agency of all changes to that information continues until further notice from the court. The court shall comply with sections 3113.21 to 3113.219 of the Revised Code when it makes or modifies an order for child support under this section.

"(D) The court shall not authorize or permit the escrowing, impoundment, or withholding of any child support payment ordered under this section or any other section of the Revised Code because of a denial of or interference with a right of companionship or visitation granted in an order issued under this section, section 3109.051, 3109.11, 3109.12, or any other section of the Revised Code, or as a method of enforcing the specific provisions of any such order dealing with visitation.

"(E) Notwithstanding section 3109.01 of the Revised Code, if a court issues a child support order under this section, the order shall remain in effect beyond the child's eighteenth birthday as long as the child continuously attends on a full-time basis any recognized and accredited high school or the order provides that the duty of support of the child continues beyond the child's eighteenth birthday. Except in cases in which the order provides that the duty of support continues for any period after the child reaches age nineteen, the order shall not remain in effect after the child reaches age nineteen. Any parent ordered to pay support under a child support order issued under this section shall continue to pay support under the order, including during seasonal vacation periods, until the order terminates."

Amendment Note: 1999 H 471 substituted "job and family" for "human" in division (A)(2).

Amendment Note: 1997 H 352 substituted "division of child support in the department of human services" for "child support enforcement agency" in division (A)(2); deleted "on or after December 31, 1993," before "shall include", substituted "income" for "wages" twice and "(D)(3), (D)(4)" for "(D)(6), (D)(7)", and inserted "current residence telephone number, current driver's license number,", in division (A)(3); inserted "or the order provides that the duty of support of the child continues beyond the child's eighteenth birthday" and added the second sentence in division (E); and made other nonsubstantive changes.

Amendment Note: 1993 H 173 rewrote division (A)(3) before the first semi-colon, which previously read:

"(3) Each order for child support made or modified under this section on or after December 1, 1986, shall be accompanied by one or more orders described in division (D) or (H) of section 3113.21 of the Revised Code, whichever is appropriate under the requirements of that section".

Amendment Note: 1993 S 115 rewrote division (A)(1), which previously read:

"(A)(1) In a divorce, dissolution of marriage, legal separation, or child support proceeding, the court may order either or both parents to support or help support their children, without regard to marital misconduct. In determining the amount reasonable or necessary for child support, including the medical needs of the child, the court shall comply with sections 3113.21 to 3113.219 of the Revised Code and shall consider all relevant factors, including, but not limited to, all of the following:

"(a) The financial resources and the earning ability of the child;

"(b) The relative financial resources, other assets and resources, and needs of the residential parent and of the parent who is not the residential parent, when a decree for shared parenting is not issued;

"(c) The standard of living and circumstances of each parent and the standard of living the child would have enjoyed had the marriage continued;

"(d) The physical and emotional condition and needs of the child;

"(e) The financial resources, other assets and resources, and needs of both parents, when a decree for shared parenting is issued;

"(f) The need and capacity of the child for an education, and the educational opportunities that would have been available to him had the circumstances requiring a court order for his support not arisen;

"(g) The earning ability of each parent;

"(h) The age of the child;

"(i) The responsibility of each parent for the support of others;

"(j) The value of services contributed by the residential parent."

Comparative Laws

Ariz.—A.R.S. § 25-320.
Ark.—A.C.A. § 9-12-312.
Conn.—C.G.S.A. § 46b-84.
Ga.—O.C.G.A. § 19-6-17.
Ill.—ILCS 750 5/505.
Ind.—West's A.I.C. 31-16-6-1 et seq.
Ky.—Baldwin's KRS 403.210.
La.—LSA-C.C. art. 227.
Mass.—M.G.L.A. c. 208, § 28.
Mich.—M.C.L.A. § 552.151 et seq.
Mo.—V.A.M.S. § 452.340.
Neb.—R.R.S.1943, § 42-364 et seq.
N.J.—N.J.S.A. 2A:34-23.
N.M.—NMSA 1978, § 40-4-7.
Wash.—West's RCWA 26.09.100.
Wis.—W.S.A. 767.25.
W.Va.—Code, 48-12-101 et seq.

Library References

Child Custody ⚖️874.
Child Support ⚖️11, 109 to 114, 397, 425, 496.
Westlaw Topic Nos. 76D, 76E.
C.J.S. Parent and Child §§ 166, 171, 180, 200 to 201, 203 to 205.

Baldwin's Ohio Legislative Service, 1990 Laws of Ohio, H 591—LSC Analysis, p 5-576

3109.051 Parenting time rights

(A) If a divorce, dissolution, legal separation, or annulment proceeding involves a child and if the court has not issued a shared parenting decree, the court shall consider any mediation report filed pursuant to section 3109. 052 of the Revised Code and, in accordance with division (C) of this section, shall make a just and reasonable order or decree permitting each parent who is not the residential parent to have parenting time with the child at the time and under the conditions that the court directs, unless the court determines that it would not be in the best interest of the child to permit that parent to have parenting time with the child and includes in the journal its findings of fact and conclusions of law. Whenever possible, the order or decree permitting the parenting time shall ensure the opportunity for both parents to have frequent and continuing contact with the child, unless frequent and continuing contact by either parent with the child would not be in the best interest of the child. The court shall include in its final decree a specific schedule of parenting time for that parent. Except as provided in division (E)(6) of section 3113.31 of the Revised Code, if the court, pursuant to this section, grants parenting time to a parent or companionship or visitation rights to any other person with respect to any child, it shall not require the public children services agency to provide supervision of or other services related to that parent's exercise of parenting time or that person's exercise of companionship or visitation rights with respect to the child. This section does not limit the power of a juvenile court pursuant to Chapter 2151. of the Revised Code to issue orders with respect to children who are alleged to be abused, neglected, or dependent children or to make dispositions of children who are adjudicated abused, neglected, or dependent children or of a common pleas court to issue orders pursuant to section 3113.31 of the Revised Code.

(B)(1) In a divorce, dissolution of marriage, legal separation, annulment, or child support proceeding that involves a child, the court may grant reasonable companionship or visitation rights to any grandparent, any person related to the child by consanguinity or affinity, or any other person other than a parent, if all of the following apply:

(a) The grandparent, relative, or other person files a motion with the court seeking companionship or visitation rights.

(b) The court determines that the grandparent, relative, or other person has an interest in the welfare of the child.

(c) The court determines that the granting of the companionship or visitation rights is in the best interest of the child.

(2) A motion may be filed under division (B)(1) of this section during the pendency of the divorce, dissolution of marriage, legal separation, annulment, or child support proceeding or, if a motion was not filed at that time or was filed at that time and the circumstances in the case have changed, at any time after a decree or final order is issued in the case.

(C) When determining whether to grant parenting time rights to a parent pursuant to this section or section 3109.12 of the Revised Code or to grant companionship or visitation rights to a grandparent, relative, or other person pursuant to this section or section 3109.11 or 3109.12 of the Revised Code, when establishing a specific parenting time or visitation schedule, and when determining other parenting time matters under this section or section 3109.12 of the Revised Code or visitation matters under this section or section 3109.11 or 3109.12 of the Revised Code, the court shall consider any mediation report that is filed pursuant to section 3109.052 of the Revised Code and shall consider all other relevant factors, including, but not limited to, all of the factors listed in division (D) of this section. In considering the factors listed in division (D) of this section for purposes of determining whether to grant parenting time or visitation rights, establishing a specific parenting time or visitation schedule, determining other parenting time matters under this section or section 3109.12 of the Revised Code or visitation matters under this section or under section 3109.11 or 3109.12 of the Revised Code, and resolving any issues related to the making of any determination with respect to parenting time or visitation rights or the establishment of any specific parenting time or visitation schedule, the court, in its discretion, may interview in chambers any or all involved children regarding their wishes and concerns. If the court interviews any child concerning the child's wishes and concerns regarding those parenting time or visitation matters, the interview shall be conducted in chambers, and no person other than the child, the child's attorney, the judge, any necessary court personnel, and, in the judge's discretion, the attorney of each parent shall be permitted to be present in the chambers during the interview. No person shall obtain or attempt to obtain from a child a written or recorded statement or affidavit setting forth the wishes and concerns of the child regarding those parenting time or visitation matters. A court, in considering the factors listed in division (D) of this section for purposes of determining whether to grant any parenting time or visitation rights, establishing a parenting time or visitation schedule, determining other parenting time matters under this section or section 3109.12 of the Revised Code or visitation matters under this section or under section 3109.11 or 3109.12 of the Revised Code, or resolving any issues related to the making of any determination with respect to parenting time or visitation rights or the establishment of any specific parenting time or visitation schedule, shall not accept or consider a written or recorded statement or affidavit that purports to set forth the child's wishes or concerns regarding those parenting time or visitation matters.

(D) In determining whether to grant parenting time to a parent pursuant to this section or section 3109.12 of the Revised Code or companionship or visitation rights to a grandparent, relative, or other person pursuant to this section or section 3109.11 or 3109.12 of the Revised Code, in establishing a specific parenting time or visitation schedule, and in determining other parenting time matters under this section or section 3109.12 of the Revised Code or visitation matters under this section or section 3109.11 or 3109.12 of the Revised Code, the court shall consider all of the following factors:

(1) The prior interaction and interrelationships of the child with the child's parents, siblings, and other persons related by consanguinity or affinity, and with the person who requested companionship or visitation if that person is not a parent, sibling, or relative of the child;

(2) The geographical location of the residence of each parent and the distance between those residences, and if the person is not a parent, the geographical location of that person's residence and the distance between that person's residence and the child's residence;

(3) The child's and parents' available time, including, but not limited to, each parent's employment schedule, the child's school schedule, and the child's and the parents' holiday and vacation schedule;

(4) The age of the child;

(5) The child's adjustment to home, school, and community;

(6) If the court has interviewed the child in chambers, pursuant to division (C) of this section, regarding the wishes and concerns of the child as to parenting time by the parent who is not the residential parent or companionship or visitation by the grandparent, relative, or other person who requested companionship or visitation, as to a specific parenting time or visitation schedule, or as to other parenting time or visitation matters, the wishes and concerns of the child, as expressed to the court;

(7) The health and safety of the child;

(8) The amount of time that will be available for the child to spend with siblings;

(9) The mental and physical health of all parties;

(10) Each parent's willingness to reschedule missed parenting time and to facilitate the other parent's parenting time rights, and with respect to a person who requested companionship or visitation, the willingness of that person to reschedule missed visitation;

(11) In relation to parenting time, whether either parent previously has been convicted of or pleaded guilty to any criminal offense involving any act that resulted in a child being an abused child or a neglected child; whether either parent, in a case in which a child has been adjudicated an abused child or a neglected child, previously has been determined to be the perpetrator of the abusive or neglectful act that is the basis of the adjudication; and whether there is reason to believe that either parent has acted in a manner resulting in a child being an abused child or a neglected child;

(12) In relation to requested companionship or visitation by a person other than a parent, whether the person previously has been convicted of or pleaded guilty to any criminal offense involving any act that resulted in a child being an abused child or a neglected child; whether the person, in a case in which a child has been adjudicated an abused child or a neglected child, previously has been determined to be the perpetrator of the abusive or neglectful act that is the basis of the adjudication; whether either parent previously has been convicted of or pleaded guilty to a violation of section 2919.25 of the Revised Code involving a victim who at the time of the commission of the offense was a member of the family or household that is the subject of the current proceeding; whether either parent previously has been convicted of an offense involving a victim who at the time of the commission of the offense was a member of the family or household that is the subject of the current proceeding and caused physical harm to the victim in the commission of the offense; and whether there is reason to believe that the person has acted in a manner resulting in a child being an abused child or a neglected child;

(13) Whether the residential parent or one of the parents subject to a shared parenting decree has continuously and willfully denied the other parent's right to parenting time in accordance with an order of the court;

(14) Whether either parent has established a residence or is planning to establish a residence outside this state;

(15) In relation to requested companionship or visitation by a person other than a parent, the wishes and concerns of the child's parents, as expressed by them to the court;

(16) Any other factor in the best interest of the child.

(E) The remarriage of a residential parent of a child does not affect the authority of a court under this section to grant parenting time rights with respect to the child to the parent who is not the residential parent or to grant reasonable companionship or visitation rights with respect to the child to any grandparent, any person related by consanguinity or affinity, or any other person.

(F)(1) If the court, pursuant to division (A) of this section, denies parenting time to a parent who is not the residential parent or denies a motion for reasonable companionship or visitation rights filed under division (B) of this section and the parent or movant files a written request for findings of fact and conclusions of law, the court shall state in writing its findings of fact and conclusions of law in accordance with Civil Rule 52.

(2) On or before July 1, 1991, each court of common pleas, by rule, shall adopt standard parenting time guidelines. A court shall have discretion to deviate from its standard parenting time guidelines based upon factors set forth in division (D) of this section.

(G)(1) If the residential parent intends to move to a residence other than the residence specified in the parenting time order or decree of the court, the parent shall file a notice of intent to relocate with the court that issued the order or decree. Except as provided in divisions (G)(2), (3), and (4) of this section, the court shall send a copy of the notice to the parent who is not the residential parent. Upon receipt of the notice, the court, on its own motion or the motion of the parent who is not the residential parent, may schedule a hearing with notice to both parents to determine whether it is in the best interest of the child to revise the parenting time schedule for the child.

(2) When a court grants parenting time rights to a parent who is not the residential parent, the court shall determine whether that parent has been convicted of or pleaded guilty to a violation of section 2919.25 of the Revised Code involving a victim who at the time of the commission of the offense was a member of the family or household that is the subject of the proceeding, has been convicted of or pleaded guilty to any other offense involving a victim who at the time of the commission of the offense was a member of the family or household that is the subject of the proceeding and caused physical harm to the victim in the commission of the offense, or has been determined to be the perpetrator of the abusive act that is the basis of an adjudication that a child is an abused child. If the court determines that that parent has not been so convicted and has not been determined to be the perpetrator of an abusive act that is the basis of a child abuse adjudication, the court shall issue an order stating that a copy of any notice of relocation that is filed with the court pursuant to division (G)(1) of this section will be sent to the parent who is given the parenting time rights in accordance with division (G)(1) of this section.

If the court determines that the parent who is granted the parenting time rights has been convicted of or pleaded guilty to a violation of section 2919.25 of the Revised Code involving a victim who at the time of the commission of the offense was a member of the family or household that is the subject of the proceeding, has been convicted of or pleaded guilty to any other offense involving a victim who at the time of the commission of the offense was a member of the family or household that is the subject of the proceeding and caused physical harm to the victim in the commission of the offense, or has been determined to be the perpetrator of the abusive act that is the basis of an adjudication that a child is an abused child, it shall issue an order stating that that parent will not be given a copy of any notice of relocation that is filed with the court pursuant to division (G)(1) of this section unless the court determines that it is in the best interest of the children to give that parent a copy of the notice of relocation, issues an order stating that that parent will be given a copy of any notice of relocation filed pursuant to division (G)(1) of this section, and issues specific written findings of fact in support of its determination.

(3) If a court, prior to April 11, 1991, issued an order granting parenting time rights to a parent who is not the residential parent and did not require the residential parent in that order to give the parent who is granted the parenting time rights notice of any change of address and if the residential parent files a notice of relocation pursuant to division (G)(1) of this section, the court shall determine if the parent who is granted the parenting time rights has been convicted of or pleaded guilty to a violation of section 2919.25 of the Revised Code involving a victim who at the time of the commission of the offense was a member of the family or household that is the subject of the proceeding, has been convicted of or pleaded guilty to any other offense involving a victim who at the time of the commission of the offense was a member of the family or household that is the subject of the proceeding and caused physical harm to the victim in the commission of the offense, or has been determined to be the perpetrator of the abusive act that is the basis of an adjudication that a child is an abused child. If the court determines that the parent who is granted the parenting time rights has not been so convicted and has not been determined to be the perpetrator of an abusive act that is the basis of a child abuse adjudication, the court shall issue an order stating that a copy of any notice of relocation that is filed with the court pursuant to division (G)(1) of this section will be sent to the parent who is granted parenting time rights in accordance with division (G)(1) of this section.

If the court determines that the parent who is granted the parenting time rights has been convicted of or pleaded guilty to a violation of section 2919.25 of the Revised Code involving a victim who at the time of the commission of the offense was a member of the family or household that is the subject of the proceeding, has been convicted of or pleaded guilty to any other offense involving a victim who at the time of the commission of the offense was a member of the family or household that is the subject of the proceeding and caused physical harm to the victim in the commission of the offense, or has been determined to be the perpetrator of the abusive act that is the basis of an adjudication that a child is an abused child, it shall issue an order stating that that parent will not be given a copy of any notice of relocation that is filed with the court pursuant to division (G)(1) of this section unless the court determines that it is in the best interest of the children to give that parent a copy of the notice of relocation, issues an order stating that that parent will be given a copy of any notice of relocation filed pursuant to division (G)(1) of this section, and issues specific written findings of fact in support of its determination.

(4) If a parent who is granted parenting time rights pursuant to this section or any other section of the Revised Code is authorized by an order issued pursuant to this section or any other court order to receive a copy of any notice of relocation that is filed pursuant to division (G)(1) of this section or pursuant to court order, if the residential parent intends to move to a residence other than the residence address specified in the parenting time order, and if the residential parent does not want the parent who is granted the parenting time rights to receive a copy of the relocation notice because the parent with parenting time rights has been convicted of or pleaded guilty to a violation of section 2919.25 of the Revised Code involving a victim who at the time of the commission of the offense was a member of the family or household that is the subject of the proceeding, has been convicted of or pleaded guilty to any other offense involving a victim who at the time of the commission of the offense was a member of the family or household that is the subject of the proceeding and caused physical harm to the victim in the commission of the offense, or has been determined to be the perpetrator of the abusive act that is the basis of an adjudication that a child is an abused child, the residential parent may file a motion with the court requesting that the parent who is granted the parenting time rights not receive a copy of any notice of relocation. Upon the filing of the motion, the court shall schedule a hearing on the motion and give both parents notice of the date, time, and location of the hearing. If the court determines that the parent who is granted the parenting time rights has been so convicted or has been determined to be the perpetrator of an abusive act that is the basis of a child abuse adjudication, the court shall issue an order stating that the parent who is granted the parenting time rights will not be given a copy of any notice of relocation that is filed with the court pursuant to division (G)(1) of this section or that the residential parent is no longer required to give that parent a copy of any notice of relocation unless the court determines that it is in the best interest of the children to give that parent a copy of the notice of relocation, issues an order stating that that parent will be given a copy of any notice of relocation filed pursuant to division (G)(1) of this section, and issues specific written findings of fact in support of its determination. If it does not so find, it shall dismiss the motion.

(H)(1) Subject to section 3125.16 and division (F) of section 3319.321 of the Revised Code, a parent of a child who is not the residential parent of the child is entitled to access, under the same terms and conditions under which access is provided to the residential parent, to any record that is related to the child and to which the residential parent of the child legally is provided access, unless the court determines that it would not be in the best interest of the child for the parent who is not the residential parent to have access to the records under those same terms and conditions. If the court determines that the parent of a child who is not the residential parent should not have access to records related to the child under the same terms and conditions as provided for the residential parent, the court shall specify the terms and conditions under which the parent who is not the residential parent is to have access to those records, shall enter its written findings of facts and opinion in the journal, and shall issue an order containing the terms and conditions to both the residential parent and the parent of the child who is not the residential parent. The court shall include in every order issued pursuant to this division notice that any keeper of a record who knowingly fails to comply with the order or division (H) of this section is in contempt of court.

(2) Subject to section 3125.16 and division (F) of section 3319.321 of the Revised Code, subsequent to the issuance of an order under division (H)(1) of this section, the keeper of any record that is related to a particular child and to which the residential parent legally is provided access shall permit the parent of the child who is not the residential parent to have access to the record under the same terms and conditions under which access is provided to the residential parent, unless the residential parent has presented the keeper of the record with a copy of an order issued under division (H)(1) of this section that limits the terms and conditions under which the parent who is not the residential parent is to have access to records pertaining to the child and the order pertains to the record in question. If the residential parent presents the keeper of the record with a copy of that type of order, the keeper of the record shall permit the parent who is not the residential parent to have access to the record only in accordance with the most recent order that has been issued pursuant to division (H)(1) of this section and presented to the keeper by the residential parent or the parent who is not the residential parent. Any keeper of any record who knowingly fails to comply with division (H) of this section or with any order issued pursuant to division (H)(1) of this section is in contempt of court.

(3) The prosecuting attorney of any county may file a complaint with the court of common pleas of that county requesting the court to issue a protective order preventing the disclosure pursuant to division (H)(1) or (2) of this section of any confidential law enforcement investigatory record. The court shall schedule a hearing on the motion and give notice of the date, time, and location of the hearing to all parties.

(I) A court that issues a parenting time order or decree pursuant to this section or section 3109.12 of the Revised Code shall determine whether the parent granted the right of parenting time is to be permitted access, in accordance with section 5104.011 of the Revised Code, to any child day-care center that is, or that in the future may be, attended by the children with whom the right of parenting time is granted. Unless the court determines that the parent who is not the residential parent should not have access to the center to the same extent that the residential parent is granted access to the center, the parent who is not the residential parent and who is granted parenting time rights is entitled to access to the center to the same extent that the residential parent is granted access to the center. If the court determines that the parent who is not the residential parent should not have access to the center to the same extent that the residential parent is granted such access under division (C) of section 5104.011 of the Revised Code, the court shall specify the terms and conditions under which the parent who is not the residential parent is to have access to the center, provided that the access shall not be greater than the access that is provided to the residential parent under division (C) of section 5104.011 of the Revised Code, the court shall enter its written findings of fact and opinions in the journal, and the court shall include the terms and conditions of access in the parenting time order or decree.

(J)(1) Subject to division (F) of section 3319.321 of the Revised Code, when a court issues an order or decree allocating parental rights and responsibilities for the care of a child, the parent of the child who is not the residential parent of the child is entitled to access, under the same terms and conditions under which access is provided to the residential parent, to any student activity that is related to the child and to which the residential parent of the child legally is provided access, unless the court determines that it would not be in the best interest of the child to grant the parent who is not the residential parent access to the student activities under those same terms and conditions. If the court determines that the parent of the child who is not the residential parent should not have access to any student activity that is related to the child under the same terms and conditions as provided for the residential parent, the court shall specify the terms and conditions under which the parent who is not the residential parent is to have access to those student activities, shall enter its written findings of facts and opinion in the journal, and shall issue an order containing the terms and conditions to both the residential parent and the parent of the child who is not the residential parent. The court shall include in every order issued pursuant to this division notice that any school official or employee who knowingly fails to comply with the order or division (J) of this section is in contempt of court.

(2) Subject to division (F) of section 3319.321 of the Revised Code, subsequent to the issuance of an order under division (J)(1) of this section, all school officials and employees shall permit the parent of the child who is not the residential parent to have access to any student activity under the same terms and conditions under which access is provided to the residential parent of the child, unless the residential parent has presented the school official or employee, the board of education of the school, or the governing body of the chartered nonpublic school with a copy of an order issued under division (J)(1) of this section that limits the terms and conditions under which the parent who is not the residential parent is to have access to student activities related to the child and the order pertains to the student activity in question. If the residential parent presents the school official or employee, the board of education of the school, or the governing body of the chartered nonpublic school with a copy of that type of order, the school official or employee shall permit the parent who is not the residential parent to have access to the student activity only in accordance with the most recent order that has been issued pursuant to division (J)(1) of this section and presented to the school official or employee, the board of education of the school, or the governing body of the chartered nonpublic school by the residential parent or the parent who is not the residential parent. Any school official or employee who knowingly fails to comply with division (J) of this section or with any order issued pursuant to division (J)(1) of this section is in contempt of court.

(K) If any person is found in contempt of court for failing to comply with or interfering with any order or decree granting parenting time rights issued pursuant to this section or section 3109.12 of the Revised Code or companionship or visitation rights issued pursuant to this section, section 3109.11 or 3109.12 of the Revised Code, or any other provision of the Revised Code, the court that makes the finding, in addition to any other penalty or remedy imposed, shall assess all court costs arising out of the contempt proceeding against the person and require the person to pay any reasonable attorney's fees of any adverse party, as determined by the court, that arose in relation to the act of contempt, and may award reasonable compensatory parenting time or visitation to the person whose right of parenting time or visitation was affected by the failure or interference if such compensatory parenting time or visitation is in the best interest of the child. Any compensatory parenting time or visitation awarded under this division shall be included in an order issued by the court and, to the extent possible, shall be governed by the same terms and conditions as was the parenting time or visitation that was affected by the failure or interference.

(L) Any parent who requests reasonable parenting time rights with respect to a child under this section or section 3109.12 of the Revised Code or any person who requests reasonable companionship or visitation rights with respect to a child under this section, section 3109.11 or 3109.12 of the Revised Code, or any other provision of the Revised Code may file a motion with the court requesting that it waive all or any part of the costs that may accrue in the proceedings. If the court determines that the movant is indigent and that the waiver is in the best interest of the child, the court, in its discretion, may waive payment of all or any part of the costs of those proceedings.

(M) The juvenile court has exclusive jurisdiction to enter the orders in any case certified to it from another court.

(N) As used in this section:

(1) "Abused child" has the same meaning as in section 2151.031 of the Revised Code, and "neglected child" has the same meaning as in section 2151.03 of the Revised Code.

(2) "Record" means any record, document, file, or other material that contains information directly related to a child, including, but not limited to, any of the following:

(a) Records maintained by public and nonpublic schools;

(b) Records maintained by facilities that provide child care, as defined in section 5104.01 of the Revised Code, publicly funded child care, as defined in section 5104.01 of the Revised Code, or pre-school services operated by or under the supervision of a school district board of education or a nonpublic school;

(c) Records maintained by hospitals, other facilities, or persons providing medical or surgical care or treatment for the child;

(d) Records maintained by agencies, departments, instrumentalities, or other entities of the state or any political subdivision of the state, other than a child support enforcement agency. Access to records maintained by a child support enforcement agency is governed by section 3125.16 of the Revised Code.

(3) "Confidential law enforcement investigatory record" has the same meaning as in section 149.43 of the Revised Code.

(2004 H 11, eff. 5–18–05; 2000 S 180, eff. 3–22–01; 1997 H 408, eff. 10–1–97; 1996 H 274, eff. 8–8–96; 1991 H 155, eff. 7–22–91; 1990 S 3, H 15)

Historical and Statutory Notes

Amendment Note: 2004 H 11 substituted "care" for "day care" in division (N)(2)(b).

Amendment Note: 2000 S 180 rewrote this section which prior thereto read:

"(A) If a divorce, dissolution, legal separation, or annulment proceeding involves a child and if the court has not issued a shared parenting decree, the court shall consider any mediation report filed pursuant to section 3109.052 of the Revised Code and, in accordance with division (C) of this section, shall make a just and reasonable order or decree permitting each parent who is not the residential parent to visit the child at the time and under the conditions that the court directs, unless the court determines that it would not be in the best interest of the child to permit that parent to visit the child and includes in the journal its findings of fact and conclusions of law. Whenever possible, the order or decree permitting the visitation shall ensure the opportunity for both parents to have frequent and continuing contact with the child, unless frequent and continuing contact by either parent with the child would not be in the best interest of the child. The court shall include in its final decree a specific schedule of visitation for that parent. Except as provided in division (E)(6) of section 3113.31 of the Revised Code, if the court, pursuant to this section, grants any person companionship or visitation rights with respect to any child, it shall not require the public children services agency to provide supervision of or other services related to that person's exercise of companionship or visitation rights with respect to the child. This section does not limit the power of a juvenile court pursuant to Chapter 2151. of the Revised Code to issue orders with respect to children who are alleged to be abused, neglected, or dependent children or to make dispositions of children who are adjudicated abused, neglected, or dependent children or of a common pleas court to issue orders pursuant to section 3113.31 of the Revised Code.

"(B)(1) In a divorce, dissolution of marriage, legal separation, annulment, or child support proceeding that involves a child, the court may grant reasonable companionship or visitation rights to any grandparent, any person related to the child by consanguinity or affinity, or any other person other than a parent, if all of the following apply:

"(a) The grandparent, relative, or other person files a motion with the court seeking companionship or visitation rights.

"(b) The court determines that the grandparent, relative, or other person has an interest in the welfare of the child.

"(c) The court determines that the granting of the companionship or visitation rights is in the best interest of the child.

"(2) A motion may be filed under division (B)(1) of this section during the pendency of the divorce, dissolution of marriage, legal separation, annulment, or child support proceeding or, if a motion was not filed at that time or was filed at that time and the circumstances in the case have changed, at any time after a decree or final order is issued in the case.

"(C) When determining whether to grant companionship or visitation rights to a parent, grandparent, relative, or other person pursuant to this section or section 3109.11 or 3109.12 of the Revised Code, when establishing a specific visitation schedule, and when determining other visitation matters under this section or section 3109.11 or 3109.12 of the Revised Code, the court shall consider any mediation report that is filed pursuant to section 3109.052 of the Revised Code and shall consider all other relevant factors, including, but not limited to, all of the factors listed in division (D) of this section. In considering the factors listed in division (D) of this section for purposes of determining whether to grant visitation rights, establishing a specific visitation schedule, determining other visitation matters under this section or under section 3109.11 or 3109.12 of the Revised Code, and resolving any issues related to the making of any determination with respect to visitation rights or the establishment of any specific visitation schedule, the court, in its discretion, may interview in chambers any or all involved children regarding their wishes and concerns. If the court interviews any child concerning the child's wishes and concerns regarding those visitation matters, the interview shall be conducted in chambers, and no person other than the child, the child's attorney, the judge, any necessary court personnel, and, in the judge's discretion, the attorney of each parent shall be permitted to be present in the chambers during the interview. No person shall obtain or attempt to obtain from a child a written or recorded statement or affidavit setting forth the wishes and concerns of the child regarding those visitation matters. A court, in considering the factors listed in division (D) of this section for purposes of determining whether to grant any visitation rights, establishing a visitation schedule, determining other visitation matters under this section or under section 3109.11 or 3109.12 of the Revised Code, or resolving any issues related to the making of any determination with respect to visitation rights or the establishment of any specific visitation schedule, shall not accept or consider a written or recorded statement or affidavit that purports to set forth the child's wishes or concerns regarding those visitation matters.

"(D) In determining whether to grant companionship or visitation rights to a parent, grandparent, relative, or other person pursuant to this section or section 3109.11 or 3109.12 of the Revised Code, in establishing a specific visitation schedule, and in determining other visitation matters under this section or section 3109.11 or 3109.12 of the Revised Code, the court shall consider all of the following factors:

"(1) The prior interaction and interrelationships of the child with the child's parents, siblings, and other persons related by consanguinity or affinity, and with the person who requested companionship or visitation if that person is not a parent, sibling, or relative of the child;

"(2) The geographical location of the residence of each parent and the distance between those residences, and if the person who requested companionship or visitation is not a parent, the geographical location of that person's residence and the distance between that person's residence and the child's residence;

"(3) The child's and parents' available time, including, but not limited to, each parent's employment schedule, the child's school schedule, and the child's and the parents' holiday and vacation schedule;

"(4) The age of the child;

"(5) The child's adjustment to home, school, and community;

"(6) If the court has interviewed the child in chambers, pursuant to division (C) of this section, regarding the wishes and concerns of the child as to visitation by the parent who is not the residential parent or companionship or visitation by the grandparent, relative, or other person who requested the companionship or visitation, as to a specific visitation schedule, or as to other visitation matters, the wishes and concerns of the child, as expressed to the court;

"(7) The health and safety of the child;

"(8) The amount of time that will be available for the child to spend with siblings;

"(9) The mental and physical health of all parties;

"(10) Each parent's willingness to reschedule missed visitation and to facilitate the other parent's visitation rights, and if the person who requested companionship or visitation is not a parent, the willingness of that person to reschedule missed visitation;

"(11) In relation to visitation by a parent, whether either parent previously has been convicted of or pleaded guilty to any criminal offense involving any act that resulted in a child being an abused child or a neglected child; whether either parent, in a case in which a child has been adjudicated an abused child or a neglected child, previously has been determined to be the perpetrator of the abusive or neglectful act that is the basis of the adjudication; and whether there is reason to believe that either parent has acted in a manner resulting in a child being an abused child or a neglected child;

"(12) In relation to requested companionship or visitation by a person other than a parent, whether the person previously has been convicted of or pleaded guilty to any criminal offense involving any act that resulted in a child being an abused child or a neglected child; whether the person, in a case in which a child has been adjudicated an abused child or a neglected child, previously has been determined to be the perpetrator of the abusive or neglectful act that is the basis of the adjudication; whether either parent previously has been convicted of or pleaded guilty to a violation of section 2919.25 of the Revised Code involving a victim who at the time of the commission of the offense was a member of the family or household that is the subject of the current proceeding; whether either parent previously has been convicted of an offense involving a victim who at the time of the commission of the offense was a member of the family or household that is the subject of the current proceeding and caused physical harm to the victim in the commission of the offense; and whether there is reason to believe that the person has acted in a manner resulting in a child being an abused child or a neglected child;

"(13) Whether the residential parent or one of the parents subject to a shared parenting decree has continuously and willfully denied the other parent's right to visitation in accordance with an order of the court;

"(14) Whether either parent has established a residence or is planning to establish a residence outside this state;

"(15) Any other factor in the best interest of the child.

"(E) The remarriage of a residential parent of a child does not affect the authority of a court under this section to grant visitation rights with respect to the child to the parent who is not the residential parent or to grant reasonable companionship or visitation rights with respect to the child to any grandparent, any person related by consanguinity or affinity, or any other person.

"(F)(1) If the court, pursuant to division (A) of this section, denies visitation to a parent who is not the residential parent or denies a motion for reasonable companionship or visitation rights filed under division (B) of this section and the parent or movant files a written request for findings of fact and conclusions of law, the court shall state in writing its findings of fact and conclusions of law in accordance with Civil Rule 52.

"(2) On or before July 1, 1991, each court of common pleas, by rule, shall adopt standard visitation guidelines. A court shall have discretion to deviate from its standard visitation guidelines based upon factors set forth in division (D) of this section.

"(G)(1) If the residential parent intends to move to a residence other than the residence specified in the visitation order or decree of the court, the parent shall file a notice of intent to relocate with the court that issued the order or decree. Except as provided in divisions (G)(2), (3), and (4) of this section, the court shall send a copy of the notice to the parent who is not the residential parent. Upon receipt of the notice, the court, on its own motion or the motion of the parent who is not the residential parent, may schedule a hearing with notice to both parents to determine whether it is in the best interest of the child to revise the visitation schedule for the child.

"(2) When a court grants visitation or companionship rights to a parent who is not the residential parent, the court shall determine whether that parent has been convicted of or pleaded guilty to a violation of section 2919.25 of the Revised Code involving a victim who at the time of the commission of the offense was a member of the family or household that is the subject of the proceeding, has been convicted of or pleaded guilty to any other offense involving a victim who at the time of the commission of the offense was a member of the family or household that is the subject of the proceeding and caused physical harm to the victim in the commission of the offense, or has been determined to be the perpetrator of the abusive act that is the basis of an adjudication that a child is an abused child. If the court determines that that parent has not been so convicted and has not been determined to be the perpetrator of an abusive act that is the basis of a child abuse adjudication, the court shall issue an order stating that a copy of any notice of relocation that is filed with the court pursuant to division (G)(1) of this section will be sent to the parent who is given the visitation or companionship rights in accordance with division (G)(1) of this section.

"If the court determines that the parent who is granted the visitation or companionship rights has been convicted of or pleaded guilty to a violation of section 2919.25 of the Revised Code involving a victim who at the time of the commission of the offense was a member of the family or household that is the subject of the proceeding, has been convicted of or pleaded guilty to any other offense involving a victim who at the time of the commission of the offense was a member of the family or household that is the subject of the proceeding and caused physical harm to the victim in the commission of the offense, or has been determined to be the perpetrator of the abusive act that is the basis of an adjudication that a child is an abused child, it shall issue an order stating that that parent will not be given a copy of any notice of relocation that is filed with the court pursuant to division (G)(1) of this section unless the court determines that it is in the best interest of the children to give that parent a copy of the notice of relocation, issues an order stating that that parent will be given a copy of any notice of relocation filed pursuant to division (G)(1) of this section, and issues specific written findings of fact in support of its determination.

"(3) If a court, prior to April 11, 1991, issued an order granting visitation or companionship rights to a parent who is not the residential parent and did not require the residential parent in that order to give the parent who is granted the visitation or companionship rights notice of any change of address and if the residential parent files a notice of relocation pursuant to division (G)(1) of this section, the court shall determine if the parent who is granted the visitation or companionship rights has been convicted of or pleaded guilty to a violation of section 2919.25 of the Revised Code involving a victim who at the time of the commission of the offense was a member of the family or household that is the subject of the proceeding, has been convicted of or pleaded guilty to any other offense involving a victim who at the time of the commission of the offense was a member of the family or household that is the subject of the proceeding and caused physical harm to the victim in the commission of the offense, or has been determined to be the perpetrator of the abusive act that is the basis of an adjudication that a child is an abused child. If the court determines that the parent who is granted the visitation or companionship rights has not been so convicted and has not been determined to be the perpetrator of an abusive act that is the basis of a child abuse adjudication, the court shall issue an order stating that a copy of any notice of relocation that is filed with the court pursuant to division (G)(1) of this section will be sent to the parent who is granted visitation or companionship rights in accordance with division (G)(1) of this section.

"If the court determines that the parent who is granted the visitation or companionship rights has been convicted of or pleaded guilty to a violation of section 2919.25 of the Revised Code involving a victim who at the time of the commission of the offense was a member of the family or household that is the subject of the proceeding, has been convicted of or pleaded guilty to any other offense involving a victim who at the time of the commission of the offense was a member of the family or household that is the subject of the proceeding and caused physical harm to the victim in the commission of the offense, or has been determined to be the perpetrator of the abusive act that is the basis of an adjudication that a child is an abused child, it shall issue an order stating that that parent will not be given a copy of any notice of relocation that is filed with the court pursuant to division (G)(1) of this section unless the court determines that it is in the best interest of the children to give that parent a copy of the notice of relocation, issues an order stating that that parent will be given a copy of any notice of relocation filed pursuant to division (G)(1) of this section, and issues specific written findings of fact in support of its determination.

"(4) If a parent who is granted visitation or companionship rights pursuant to this section or any other section of the Revised Code is authorized by an order issued pursuant to this section or any other court order to receive a copy of any notice of relocation that is filed pursuant to division (G)(1) of this section or pursuant to court order, if the residential parent intends to move to a residence other than the residence address specified in the visitation or companionship order, and if the residential parent does not want the parent who is granted the visitation or companionship rights to receive a copy of the relocation notice because the parent with visitation or companionship rights has been convicted of or pleaded guilty to a violation of section 2919.25 of the Revised Code involving a victim who at the time of the commission of the offense was a member of the family or household that is the subject of the proceeding, has been convicted of or pleaded guilty to any other offense involving a victim who at the time of the commission of the offense was a member of the family or household that is the subject of the proceeding and caused physical harm to the victim in the commission of the offense, or has been determined to be the perpetrator of the abusive act that is the basis of an adjudication that a child is an abused child, the residential parent may file a motion with the court requesting that the parent who is granted the visitation or companionship rights not receive a copy of any notice of relocation. Upon the filing of the motion, the court shall schedule a hearing on the motion and give both parents notice of the date, time, and location of the hearing. If the court determines that the parent who is granted the visitation or companionship rights has been so convicted or has been determined to be the perpetrator of an abusive act that is the basis of a child abuse adjudication, the court shall issue an order stating that the parent who is granted the visitation or companionship rights will not be given a copy of any notice of relocation that is filed with the court pursuant to division (G)(1) of this section or that the residential parent is no longer required to give that parent a copy of any notice of relocation unless the court determines that it is in the best interest of the children to give that parent a copy of the notice of relocation, issues an order stating that that parent will be given a copy of any notice of relocation filed pursuant to division (G)(1) of this section, and issues specific written findings of fact in support of its determination. If it does not so find, it shall dismiss the motion.

"(H)(1) Subject to division (F)(2) of section 2301.35 and division (F) of section 3319.321 of the Revised Code, a parent of a child who is not the residential parent of the child is entitled to access, under the same terms and conditions under which access is provided to the residential parent, to any record that is related to the child and to which the residential parent of the child legally is provided access, unless the court determines that it would not be in the best interest of the child for the parent who is not the residential parent to have access to the records under those same terms and conditions. If the court determines that the parent of a child who is not the residential parent should not have access to records related to the child under the same terms and conditions as provided for the residential parent, the court shall specify the terms and conditions under which the parent who is not the residential parent is to have access to those records, shall enter its written findings of facts and opinion in the journal, and shall issue an order containing the terms and conditions to both the residential parent and the parent of the child who is not the residential parent. The court shall include in every order issued pursuant to this division notice that any keeper of a record who knowingly fails to comply with the order or division (H) of this section is in contempt of court.

"(2) Subject to division (F)(2) of section 2301.35 and division (F) of section 3319.321 of the Revised Code, subsequent to the issuance of an order under division (H)(1) of this section, the keeper of any record that is related to a particular child and to which the residential parent legally is provided access shall permit the parent of the child who is not the residential parent to have access to the record under the same terms and conditions under which access is provided to the residential parent, unless the residential parent has presented the keeper of the record with a copy of an order issued under division (H)(1) of this section that limits the terms and conditions under which the parent who is not the residential parent is to have access to records pertaining to the child and the order pertains to the record in question. If the residential parent presents the keeper of the record with a copy of that type of order, the keeper of the record shall permit the parent who is not the residential parent to have access to the record only in accordance with the most recent order that has been issued pursuant to division (H)(1) of this section and presented to the keeper by the residential parent or the parent who is not the residential parent. Any keeper of any record who knowingly fails to comply with division (H) of this section or with any order issued pursuant to division (H)(1) of this section is in contempt of court.

"(3) The prosecuting attorney of any county may file a complaint with the court of common pleas of that county requesting the court to issue a protective order preventing the disclosure pursuant to division (H)(1) or (2) of this section of any confidential law enforcement investigatory record. The court shall schedule a hearing on the motion and give notice of the date, time, and location of the hearing to all parties.

"(I) A court that issues a visitation order or decree pursuant to this section, section 3109.11 or 3109.12 of the Revised Code, or any other provision of the Revised Code shall determine whether the parent granted the right of visitation is to be permitted access, in accordance with section 5104.011 of the Revised Code, to any child day-care center that is, or that in the future may be, attended by the children with whom the right of visitation is granted. Unless the court determines that the parent who is not the residential parent should not have access to the center to the same extent that the residential parent is granted access to the center, the parent who is not the residential parent and who is granted visitation or companionship rights is entitled to access to the center to the same extent that the residential parent is granted access to the center. If the court determines that the parent who is not the residential parent should not have access to the center to the same extent that the residential parent is granted such access under division (C) of section 5104.011 of the Revised Code, the court shall specify the terms and conditions under which the parent who is not the residential parent is to have access to the center, provided that the access shall not be greater than the access that is provided to the residential parent under division (C) of section 5104.011 of the Revised Code, the court shall enter its written findings of fact and opinions in the journal, and the court shall include the terms and conditions of access in the visitation order or decree.

"(J)(1) Subject to division (F) of section 3319.321 of the Revised Code, when a court issues an order or decree allocating parental rights and responsibilities for the care of a child, the parent of the child who is not the residential parent of the child is entitled to access, under the same terms and conditions under which access is provided to the residential parent, to any student activity that is related to the child and to which the residential parent of the child legally is provided access, unless the court determines that it would not be in the best interest of the child to grant the parent who is not the residential parent access to the student activities under those same terms and conditions. If the court determines that the parent of the child who is not the residential parent should not have access to any student activity that is related to the child under the same terms and conditions as provided for the residential parent, the court shall specify the terms and conditions under which the parent who is not the residential parent is to have access to those student activities, shall enter its written findings of facts and opinion in the journal, and shall issue an order containing the terms and conditions to both the residential parent and the parent of the child who is not the residential parent. The court shall include in every order issued pursuant to this division notice that any school official or employee who knowingly fails to comply with the order or division (J) of this section is in contempt of court.

"(2) Subject to division (F) of section 3319.321 of the Revised Code, subsequent to the issuance of an order under division (J)(1) of this section, all school officials and employees shall permit the parent of the child who is not the residential parent to have access to any student activity under the same terms and conditions under which access is provided to the residential parent of the child, unless the residential parent has presented the school official or employee, the board of education of the school, or the governing body of the chartered nonpublic school with a copy of an order issued under division (J)(1) of this section that limits the terms and conditions under which the parent who is not the residential parent is to have access to student activities related to the child and the order pertains to the student activity in question. If the residential parent presents the school official or employee, the board of education of the school, or the governing body of the chartered nonpublic school with a copy of that type of order, the school official or employee shall permit the parent who is not the residential parent to have access to the student activity only in accordance with the most recent order that has been issued pursuant to division (J)(1) of this section and presented to the school official or employee, the board of education of the school, or the governing body of the chartered nonpublic school by the residential parent or the parent who is not the residential parent. Any school official or employee who knowingly fails to comply with division (J) of this section or with any order issued pursuant to division (J)(1) of this section is in contempt of court.

"(K) If any person is found in contempt of court for failing to comply with or interfering with any order or decree granting companionship or visitation rights that is issued pursuant to this section, section 3109.11 or 3109.12 of the Revised Code, or any other provision of the Revised Code, the court that makes the finding, in addition to any other penalty or remedy imposed, shall assess all court costs arising out of the contempt proceeding against the person and require the person to pay any reasonable attorney's fees of any adverse party, as determined by the court, that arose in relation to the act of contempt, and may award reasonable compensatory visitation to the person whose right of visitation was affected by the failure or interference if such compensatory visitation is in the best interest of the child. Any compensatory visitation awarded under this division shall be included in an order issued by the court and, to the extent possible, shall be governed by the same terms and conditions as was the visitation that was affected by the failure or interference.

"(L) Any person who requests reasonable companionship or visitation rights with respect to a child under this section, section 3109.11 or 3109.12 of the Revised Code, or any other provision of the Revised Code may file a motion with the court requesting that it waive all or any part of the costs that may accrue in the proceedings under this section, section 3109.11, or section 3109.12 of the Revised Code. If the court determines that the movant is indigent and that the waiver is in the best interest of the child, the court, in its discretion, may waive payment of all or any part of the costs of those proceedings.

"(M) The juvenile court has exclusive jurisdiction to enter the orders in any case certified to it from another court.

"(N) As used in this section:

"(1) "Abused child" has the same meaning as in section 2151.031 of the Revised Code, and "neglected child" has the same meaning as in section 2151.03 of the Revised Code.

"(2) "Record" means any record, document, file, or other material that contains information directly related to a child, including, but not limited to, any of the following:

"(a) Records maintained by public and nonpublic schools;

"(b) Records maintained by facilities that provide child day-care, as defined in section 5104.01 of the Revised Code, publicly funded child day-care, as defined in section 5104.01 of the Revised Code, or pre-school services operated by or under the supervision of a school district board of education or a nonpublic school;

"(c) Records maintained by hospitals, other facilities, or persons providing medical or surgical care or treatment for the child;

"(d) Records maintained by agencies, departments, instrumentalities, or other entities of the state or any political subdivision of the state, other than a child support enforcement agency. Access to records maintained by a child support enforcement agency is governed by division (F)(2) of section 2301.35 of the Revised Code.

"(3) "Confidential law enforcement investigatory record" has the same meaning as in section 149.43 of the Revised Code."

Amendment Note: 1997 H 408 substituted "division (F)(2) of section 2301.35" for "division (G)(2) of section 2301.35" in divisions (H)(1), (H)(2), and (N)(2)(d); and made changes to reflect gender neutral language.

Amendment Note: 1996 H 274 added the fourth and fifth sentences in division (A); substituted "legal separation" for "alimony" in division (B)(2); and made changes to reflect gender neutral language.

Library References

Child Custody ⇐175 to 231, 270 to 329.
Westlaw Topic No. 76D.
C.J.S. Adoption of Persons §§ 140 to 141, 143.

3109.06 Certification to juvenile court

Any court, other than a juvenile court, that has jurisdiction in any case respecting the allocation of parental rights and responsibilities for the care of a child under eighteen years of age and the designation of the child's place of residence and legal custodian or in any case respecting the support of a child under eighteen years of age, may, on its own motion or on motion of any interested party, with the consent of the juvenile court, certify the record in the case or so much of the record and such further information, in narrative form or otherwise, as the court deems necessary or the juvenile court requests, to the juvenile court for further proceedings; upon the certification, the juvenile court shall have exclusive jurisdiction.

In cases in which the court of common pleas finds the parents unsuitable to have the parental rights and responsibilities for the care of the child or children and unsuitable to provide the place of residence and to be the legal custodian of the child or children, consent of the juvenile court shall not be required to such certification. This section applies to actions pending on August 28, 1951.

In any case in which a court of common pleas, or other court having jurisdiction, has issued an order that allocates parental rights and responsibilities for the care of minor children and designates their place of residence and legal custodian of minor children, has made an order for support of minor children, or has done both, the jurisdiction of the court shall not abate upon the death of the person awarded custody but shall continue for all purposes during the minority of the children. The court, upon its own motion or the motion of either parent or of any interested person acting on behalf of the children, may proceed to make further disposition of the case in the best interests of the children and subject to sections 3109.42 to 3109.48 of the Revised Code. If the children are under eighteen years of age, it may certify them, pursuant to this section, to the juvenile court of any county for further proceedings. After certification to a juvenile court, the jurisdiction of the court of common pleas, or other court, shall cease, except as to any payments of spousal support due for the spouse and support payments due and unpaid for the children at the time of the certification.

Any disposition made pursuant to this section, whether by a juvenile court after a case is certified to it, or by any court upon the death of a person awarded custody of a child, shall be made in accordance with sections 3109.04 and 3109.42 to 3109.48 of the Revised Code. If an appeal is taken from a decision made pursuant to this section that allocates parental rights and responsibilities for the care of a minor child and designates the child's place of residence and legal custodian, the court of appeals shall give the case calendar priority and handle it expeditiously.

(1999 H 191, eff. 10–20–99; 1990 S 3, eff. 4–11–91; 1990 H 514; 1983 H 93; 1953 H 1; GC 8005–6; Source—GC 8034–1)

Historical and Statutory Notes

Pre–1953 H 1 Amendments: 124 v S 65

Amendment Note: 1999 H 191 inserted "and subject to sections 3109.42 to 3109.48 of the Revised Code" in the third paragraph; inserted "and 3109.42 to 3109.48" in the fourth paragraph; and made other nonsubstantive changes.

Library References

Courts ⇐483 to 488(4).
Westlaw Topic No. 106.
C.J.S. Courts §§ 193 to 202.

LIABILITY OF PARENTS

3109.09 Damages recoverable against parent of minor who willfully damages property or commits theft offense; community service

(A) As used in this section, "parent" means one of the following:

(1) Both parents unless division (A)(2) or (3) of this section applies;

(2) The parent designated the residential parent and legal custodian pursuant to an order issued under section 3109.04 of the Revised Code that is not a shared parenting order;

(3) The custodial parent of a child born out of wedlock with respect to whom no custody order has been issued.

(B) Any owner of property, including any board of education of a city, local, exempted village, or joint vocational school district, may maintain a civil action to recover compensatory damages not exceeding ten thousand dollars and court costs from the parent of a minor if the minor willfully damages property belonging to the owner or commits acts cognizable as a "theft offense," as defined in section 2913.01 of the Revised Code, involving the property of the owner. The action may be joined with an action under Chapter 2737. of the Revised Code against the minor, or the minor and the minor's parent, to recover the property regardless of value, but any additional damages recovered from the parent pursuant to this section shall be limited to compensatory damages not exceeding ten thousand dollars, as authorized by this section. A finding of willful destruction of property or of committing acts cognizable as a theft offense is not dependent upon a prior finding that the child is a delinquent child or upon the child's conviction of any criminal offense.

(C)(1) If a court renders a judgment in favor of a board of education of a city, local, exempted village, or joint vocational school district in an action brought pursuant to division (B) of this section, if the board of education agrees to the parent's performance of community service in lieu of full payment of the judgment, and if the parent who is responsible for the payment of the judgment agrees to voluntarily participate in the performance of community service in lieu of full payment of the judgment, the court may order the parent to perform community service in lieu of providing full payment of the judgment.

(2) If a court, pursuant to division (C)(1) of this section, orders a parent to perform community service in lieu of providing full payment of a judgment, the court shall specify in its order the amount of the judgment, if any, to be paid by the parent, the type and number of hours of community service to be performed by the parent, and any other conditions necessary to carry out the order.

(D) This section shall not apply to a parent of a minor if the minor was married at the time of the commission of the acts or violations that would otherwise give rise to a civil action commenced under this section.

(E) Any action brought pursuant to this section shall be commenced and heard as in other civil actions.

(F) The monetary limitation upon compensatory damages set forth in this section does not apply to a civil action brought pursuant to section 2307.70 of the Revised Code.

(1996 H 601, eff. 10–29–96; 1992 H 154, eff. 7–31–92; 1990 S 3; 1988 H 708; 1986 H 158, S 316; 1978 H 456; 1969 S 10; 132 v H 257; 131 v H 159)

Historical and Statutory Notes

Amendment Note: 1996 H 601 added divisions (A) and (A)(1) to (A)(3); redesignated former divisions (A) to (E) as divisions (B) to (F) respectively; substituted "ten thousand dollars" for "six thousand dollars" throughout and "parent of a minor" for "parents who have the parental rights and responsibilities for the care of a minor, and are the residential parents and legal custodians of a minor" in division (B); substituted "This section shall not apply to a parent" for "For purposes of this section, the parents of a minor do not have parental rights and responsibilities for the care of the minor and are not the residential parents and legal custodians of the minor" and "would otherwise give" for "gave" in division (D); changed references from "parents" to "parent" throughout; made changes to reflect gender neutral language; and made other nonsubstantive changes.

Comparative Laws

Ill.—ILCS 740 115/1 et seq.
Ind.—West's A.I.C. 34-31-4-1, 34-31-4-2.
Ky.—Baldwin's KRS 405.025.
Mich.—M.C.L.A. § 600.2913.

Library References

Parent and Child ⇐13.5(2).
Westlaw Topic No. 285.
C.J.S. Parent and Child §§ 191, 310.

3109.10 Liability of parents for assaults by their children

As used in this section, "parent" has the same meaning as in section 3109.09 of the Revised Code.

Any person is entitled to maintain an action to recover compensatory damages in a civil action, in an amount not to exceed ten thousand dollars and costs of suit in a court of competent jurisdiction, from the parent of a child under the age of eighteen if the child willfully and maliciously assaults the person by a means or force likely to produce great bodily harm. A finding of willful and malicious assault by a means or force likely to produce great bodily harm is not dependent upon a prior finding that the child is a delinquent child.

Any action brought pursuant to this section shall be commenced and heard as in other civil actions for damages.

The monetary limitation upon compensatory damages set forth in this section does not apply to a civil action brought pursuant to section 2307.70 of the Revised Code.

(1996 H 601, eff. 10–29–96; 1995 H 18, eff. 11–24–95; 1990 S 3, eff. 4–11–91; 1986 S 316; 1969 S 11)

Historical and Statutory Notes

Amendment Note: 1996 H 601 inserted the first paragraph; substituted "ten thousand dollars" for "six thousand dollars", deleted "parents who have the parental rights and responsibilities for the care of a child under the age of eighteen, and from any" following "jurisdiction, from the" and "who is the residential parent and legal custodian" preceding "of a child" in the second paragraph; and made other nonsubstantive changes.

Amendment Note: 1995 H 18 substituted "six" for "two", "parent" for "parents", and "custodian" for "custodians"; added "from any parent", "is", and "under the age of eighteen"; and made nonsubstantive changes.

Library References

Parent and Child ⇐13.5(2).
Westlaw Topic No. 285.
C.J.S. Parent and Child §§ 191, 310.

VISITATION RIGHTS OF RELATIVES

3109.11 Visitation rights of grandparents and other relatives when parent deceased

If either the father or mother of an unmarried minor child is deceased, the court of common pleas of the county in which the minor child resides may grant the parents and other relatives of the deceased father or mother reasonable companionship or visitation rights with respect to the minor child during the child's minority if the parent or other relative files a complaint requesting reasonable companionship or visitation rights and if the court determines that the granting of the companionship or visitation rights is in the best interest of the minor child. In determining whether to grant any person reasonable companionship or visitation rights with respect to any child, the court shall consider all relevant factors, including, but not limited to, the factors set forth in division (D) of section 3109.051 of the Revised Code. Divisions (C), (K), and (L) of section 3109.051 of the Revised Code apply to the determination of reasonable companionship or visitation rights under this section and to any order granting any such rights that is issued under this section.

The remarriage of the surviving parent of the child or the adoption of the child by the spouse of the surviving parent of the child does not affect the authority of the court under this section to grant reasonable companionship or visitation rights with respect to the child to a parent or other relative of the child's deceased father or mother.

If the court denies a request for reasonable companionship or visitation rights made pursuant to this section and the complainant files a written request for findings of fact and conclusions of law, the court shall state in writing its findings of fact and conclusions of law in accordance with Civil Rule 52.

Except as provided in division (E)(6) of section 3113.31 of the Revised Code, if the court, pursuant to this section, grants any person companionship or visitation rights with respect to any child, it shall not require the public children services agency to provide supervision of or other services related to that person's exercise of companionship or visitation rights with respect to the child. This section does not limit the power of a juvenile court pursuant to Chapter 2151. of the Revised Code to issue orders with respect to children who are alleged to be abused, neglected, or dependent children or to make dispositions of children who are adjudicated abused, neglected, or dependent children or of a common pleas court to issue orders pursuant to section 3113.31 of the Revised Code.

(2000 S 180, eff. 3–22–01; 1996 H 274, eff. 8–8–96; 1990 S 3, eff. 4–11–91; 1990 H 15; 1971 H 163)

Historical and Statutory Notes

Amendment Note: 2000 S 180 inserted "or the adoption of the child by the spouse of the surviving parent of the child" in the second paragraph.

Amendment Note: 1996 H 274 added the fourth paragraph; and made changes to reflect gender neutral language.

Library References

Child Custody ⊂⊃270 to 274, 289.
Westlaw Topic No. 76D.

3109.12 Visitation rights of grandparents and other relatives when child's mother unmarried

(A) If a child is born to an unmarried woman, the parents of the woman and any relative of the woman may file a complaint requesting the court of common pleas of the county in which the child resides to grant them reasonable companionship or visitation rights with the child. If a child is born to an unmarried woman and if the father of the child has acknowledged the child and that acknowledgment has become final pursuant to section 2151.232, 3111.25, or 3111.821 of the Revised Code or has been determined in an action under Chapter 3111. of the Revised Code to be the father of the child, the father may file a complaint requesting that the court of appropriate jurisdiction of the county in which the child resides grant him reasonable parenting time rights with the child and the parents of the father and any relative of the father may file a complaint requesting that the court grant them reasonable companionship or visitation rights with the child.

(B) The court may grant the parenting time rights or companionship or visitation rights requested under division (A) of this section, if it determines that the granting of the parenting time rights or companionship or visitation rights is in the best interest of the child. In determining whether to grant reasonable parenting time rights or reasonable companionship or visitation rights with respect to any child, the court shall consider all relevant factors, including, but not limited to, the factors set forth in division (D) of section 3109.051 of the Revised Code. Divisions (C), (K), and (L) of section 3109.051 of the Revised Code apply to the determination of reasonable parenting time rights or reasonable companionship or visitation rights under this section and to any order granting any such rights that is issued under this section.

The marriage or remarriage of the mother or father of a child does not affect the authority of the court under this section to grant the natural father reasonable parenting time rights or the parents or relatives of the natural father or the parents or relatives of the mother of the child reasonable companionship or visitation rights with respect to the child.

If the court denies a request for reasonable parenting time rights or reasonable companionship or visitation rights made pursuant to division (A) of this section and the complainant files a written request for findings of fact and conclusions of law, the court shall state in writing its findings of fact and conclusions of law in accordance with Civil Rule 52.

Except as provided in division (E)(6) of section 3113.31 of the Revised Code, if the court, pursuant to this section, grants parenting time rights or companionship or visitation rights with respect to any child, it shall not require the public children services agency to provide supervision of or other services related to that parent's exercise of parenting time rights with the child or that person's exercise of companionship or visitation rights with the child. This section does not limit the power of a juvenile court pursuant to Chapter 2151. of the Revised Code to issue orders with respect to children who are alleged to be abused, neglected, or dependent children or to make dispositions of children who are adjudicated abused, neglected, or dependent children or of a common pleas court to issue orders pursuant to section 3113.31 of the Revised Code.

(2000 S 180, eff. 3–22–01; 1997 H 352, eff. 1–1–98; 1996 H 274, eff. 8–8–96; 1990 S 3, eff. 4–11–91; 1990 H 15)

Historical and Statutory Notes

Amendment Note: 2000 S 180 rewrote this section which prior thereto read:

"(A) If a child is born to an unmarried woman, the parents of the woman and any relative of the woman may file a complaint requesting the court of common pleas of the county in which the child resides to grant them reasonable companionship or visitation rights with the child. If a child is born to an unmarried woman and if the father of the child has acknowledged the child and that acknowledgment has become final pursuant to section 2151.232, 3111.211, or 5101.314 of the Revised Code or has been determined in an action under Chapter 3111. of the Revised Code to be the father of the child, the father, the parents of the father, and any relative of the father may file a complaint requesting the court of common pleas of the county in which the child resides to grant them reasonable companionship or visitation rights with respect to the child.

"(B) The court may grant the companionship or visitation rights requested under division (A) of this section, if it determines that the granting of the companionship or visitation rights is in the best interest of the child. In determining whether to grant any person reasonable companionship or visitation rights with respect to any child, the court shall consider all relevant factors, including, but not limited to, the factors set forth in division (D) of section 3109.051 of the Revised Code. Divisions (C), (K), and (L) of section 3109.051 of the Revised Code apply to the determination of reasonable companionship or visitation rights under this section and to any order granting any such rights that is issued under this section.

"The marriage or remarriage of the mother or father of a child does not affect the authority of the court under this section to grant the natural father, the parents or relatives of the natural father, or the parents or relatives of the mother of the child reasonable companionship or visitation rights with respect to the child.

"If the court denies a request for reasonable companionship or visitation rights made pursuant to division (A) of this section and the complainant files a written request for findings of fact and conclusions of law, the court shall state in writing its findings of fact and conclusions of law in accordance with Civil Rule 52.

"Except as provided in division (E)(6) of section 3113.31 of the Revised Code, if the court, pursuant to this section, grants any person companionship or visitation rights with respect to any child, it shall not require the public children services agency to provide supervision of or other services related to that person's exercise of companionship or visitation rights with respect to the child. This section does not limit the power of a juvenile court pursuant to Chapter 2151. of the Revised Code to issue orders with respect to children who are alleged to be abused, neglected, or dependent children or to make dispositions of children who are adjudicated abused, neglected, or dependent children or of a common pleas court to issue orders pursuant to section 3113.31 of the Revised Code.

Amendment Note: 1997 H 352 inserted "and that acknowledgment has become final" and substituted "2151.232, 3111.211, or 5101.314" for "2105.18" in division (A).

Amendment Note: 1996 H 274 added the fourth paragraph in division (B).

Library References

Children Out-of-Wedlock ⊂⊃20.9.
Westlaw Topic No. 76H.

PREVENTION OF CHILD ABUSE AND CHILD NEGLECT

3109.19 Duty of parents to support children of unemancipated minor children

(A) As used in this section, "minor" has the same meaning as in section 3107.01 of the Revised Code.

(B)(1) If a child is born to parents who are unmarried and unemancipated minors, a parent of one of the minors is providing support for the minors' child, and the minors have not signed an acknowledgment of paternity or a parent and child relationship has not been established between the child and the male minor, the parent who is providing support for the child may request a determination of the existence or nonexistence of a parent and child relationship between the child and the male minor pursuant to Chapter 3111. of the Revised Code.

(2) If a child is born to parents who are unmarried and unemancipated minors, a parent of one of the minors is providing support for the child, and the minors have signed an acknowledgment of paternity that has become final pursuant to section 2151.232, 3111.25, or 3111.821 of the Revised Code or a parent and child relationship has been established between the child and the male minor pursuant to Chapter 3111. of the Revised Code, the parent who is providing support for the child may file a complaint requesting that the court issue an order or may request the child support enforcement agency of the county in which the child resides to issue an administrative order requiring all of the minors' parents to pay support for the child.

(C)(1) On receipt of a complaint filed under division (B)(2) of this section, the court shall schedule a hearing to determine, in accordance with Chapters 3119., 3121., 3123., and 3125. of the Revised Code, the amount of child support the minors' parents are required to pay, the method of paying the support, and the method of providing for the child's health care needs. On receipt of a request under division (B)(2) of this section, the agency shall schedule a hearing to determine, in accordance with Chapters 3119., 3121., 3123., and 3125. of the Revised Code, the amount of child support the minors' parents are required to pay, the method of paying the support, and the method of providing for the child's health care needs. At the conclusion of the hearing, the court or agency shall issue an order requiring the payment of support of the child and provision for the child's health care needs. The court or agency shall calculate the child support amount using the income of the minors' parents instead of the income of the minors. If any of the minors' parents are divorced, the court or agency shall calculate the child support as if they were married, and issue a child support order requiring the parents to pay a portion of any support imposed as a separate obligation. If a child support order issued pursuant to section 2151.23, 2151.231, 2151.232, 3111.13, or 3111.81 of the Revised Code requires one of the minors to pay support for the child, the amount the minor is required to pay shall be deducted from any amount that minor's parents are required to pay pursuant to an order issued under this section. The hearing shall be held not later than sixty days after the day the complaint is filed or the request is made nor earlier than thirty days after the court or agency gives the minors' parents notice of the action.

(2) An order issued by an agency for the payment of child support shall include a notice stating all of the following: that the parents of the minors may object to the order by filing a complaint pursuant to division (B)(2) of this section with the court requesting that the court issue an order requiring the minors' parents to pay support for the child and provide for the child's health care needs; that the complaint may be filed no later than thirty days after the date of the issuance of the agency's order; and that, if none of the parents of the minors file a complaint pursuant to division (B)(2) of this section, the agency's order is final and enforceable by a court and may be modified and enforced only in accordance with Chapters 3119., 3121., 3123., and 3125. of the Revised Code.

(D) An order issued by a court or agency under this section shall remain in effect, except as modified pursuant to Chapters 3119., 3121., 3123., and 3125. of the Revised Code until the occurrence of any of the following:

(1) The minor who resides with the parents required to pay support under this section reaches the age of eighteen years, dies, marries, enlists in the armed services, is deported, gains legal or physical custody of the child, or is otherwise emancipated.

(2) The child who is the subject of the order dies, is adopted, is deported, or is transferred to the legal or physical custody of the minor who lives with the parents required to pay support under this section.

(3) The minor's parents to whom support is being paid pursuant to this section is no longer providing any support for the child.

(E) The minor's parents to whom support is being paid under a child support order issued by a court or agency pursuant to this section shall notify, and the minor's parents who are paying support may notify the child support enforcement agency of the occurrence of any event described in division (D) of this section. A willful failure to notify the agency as required by this division is contempt of court with respect to a court child support order. Upon receiving notification pursuant to this division, the agency shall comply with sections 3119.90 to 3119.94 of the Revised Code.

(2000 S 180, eff. 3-22-01; 1997 H 352, eff. 1-1-98; 1995 H 167, eff. 11-15-95)

Historical and Statutory Notes

Amendment Note: 2000 S 180 substituted "3111.25" for "3111.211" and "3111.821" for "5101.314" in division (B)(2); substituted "Chapters 3119., 3121., 3123., and 3125." for "sections 3113.21 to 3113.219" in the first sentence of division (C)(1); substituted "Chapters 3119., 3121., 3123., and 3125." for "sections 3111.23 to 3111.28 and 3113.215" in the second sentence of division (C)(1); deleted "3111.20, 3111.22" and "3111.13" and substituted "3111.81" for "3122." in the sixth sentence of division (C)(1); substituted "Chapters 3119., 3121., 3123., and 3125." for "sections 3111.23 to 3111.28 and sections 3113.21 to 3113.219" in division (C)(2); and rewrote divisions (D) and (E). Prior to amendment divisions (D) and (E) read:

"(D) An order issued by a court or agency under this section shall remain in effect, except as modified pursuant to sections 3113.21 to 3113.219 of the Revised Code with respect to a court-issued child support order or pursuant to sections 3111.23 to 3111.28 and 3113.215 of the Revised Code with respect to an administrative child support order, until the occurrence of any of the following:

"(1) The minor who resides with the parents required to pay support under this section reaches the age of eighteen years, dies, marries, enlists in the armed services, is deported, gains legal or physical custody of the child, or is otherwise emancipated.

"(2) The child who is the subject of the order dies, is adopted, is deported, or is transferred to the legal or physical custody of the minor who lives with the parents required to pay support under this section.

"(3) The minor's parents to whom support is being paid pursuant to this section is no longer providing any support for the child.

"(E)(1) The minor's parents to whom support is being paid under a child support order issued by a court pursuant to this section shall notify, and the minor's parents who are paying support may notify the child support enforcement agency of the occurrence of any event described in division (D) of this section. A willful failure to notify the agency as required by this division is contempt of court. Upon receiving notification pursuant to this division, the agency shall comply with division (G)(4) of section 3113.21 of the Revised Code.

"(2) The minor's parents to whom support is being paid under a child support order issued by the agency pursuant to this section shall notify, and the minor's parents who are paying support may notify the child support enforcement agency of the occurrence of any event described in division (D) of this section. Upon receiving notification pursuant to this division, the agency shall comply with division (E)(4) of section 3111.23 of the Revised Code."

Amendment Note: 1997 H 352 inserted "that has become final" and substituted "2151.232, 3111.211, or 5101.314" for "2105.18" in division (A)(2); inserted "and the method of providing for the child's health care needs" twice and "2151.231, 2151.232,", and substituted "3111.211" for "3111.21", in division (C)(1); inserted "and provide for the child's health care needs" in division (C)(2); and made other nonsubstantive changes.

Library References

Children Out-of-Wedlock ⚖=21(1), 34 to 35.
Westlaw Topic No. 76H.
C.J.S. Children Out-of-Wedlock §§ 40 to 42, 46, 49, 85 to 90, 122.

UNIFORM CHILD CUSTODY JURISDICTION LAW

Comparative Laws
Uniform Child Custody Jurisdiction Act
Table of Jurisdictions Wherein Act Has Been Adopted.

For text of Uniform Act, and variation notes and annotation materials for adopting jurisdictions, see Uniform Laws Annotated, Master Edition, Volume 9, Pt. I.

Jurisdiction	Statutory Citation
Indiana	West's A.I.C. 31–17–3–1 to 31–17–3–25.
Kentucky	KRS 403.400 to 403.350.
Louisiana	LSA–R.S. 13:1700 to 13:1724.
Maryland	Code, Family Law, § 9.5–101 to 9.5–111.
Massachusetts	M.G.L.A. c. 209B, § 1 to 14.
Mississippi	Code 1972, § 93–27–101 to 93–27–112.
Missouri	V.A.M.S. § 452.440 to 452.550.
New Hampshire	RSA 458–A:1 to 458–A:25.
New Jersey	N.J.S.A. 2A:34–53 et seq.
Pennsylvania	23 Pa.C.S.A. § 5402 et seq.
South Carolina	Code 1976, § 20–7–782 to 20–7–830.
South Dakota	SDCL 26–5b–101 to 26–5b–112.
Vermont	15 V.S.A. § 1031 to 1051.
Virgin Islands	16 V.I.C. § 115 to 139.
Wisconsin	W.S.A. 822.01 to 822.25.
Wyoming	Wyo.Stat.Ann., § 20–5–201 to 20–5–212.

3109.21 to 3109.37 Uniform Child Custody Jurisdiction Law—Repealed

(2004 S 185, eff. 4–11–05; 2000 S 180, eff. 3–22–01; 1996 H 274, eff. 8–8–96; 1990 S 3, eff. 4–11–91; 1977 S 135)

Historical and Statutory Notes

Ed Note: Former RC 3109.27 amended and recodified as RC 3127.23 by 2004 S 185, eff. 4–11–05.

Ed Note: Former RC 3109.29 amended and recodified as RC 3127.24 by 2004 S 185, eff. 4–11–05.

Ed Note: Former RC 3109.37 amended and recodified as RC 3127.06 by 2004 S 185, eff. 4–11–05.

PARENT CONVICTED OF KILLING OTHER PARENT

3109.41 Definitions

As used in sections 3109.41 to 3109.48 of the Revised Code:

(A) A person is "convicted of killing" if the person has been convicted of or pleaded guilty to a violation of section 2903.01, 2903.02, or 2903.03 of the Revised Code.

(B) "Custody order" means an order designating a person as the residential parent and legal custodian of a child under section 3109.04 of the Revised Code or any order determining custody of a child under section 2151.23, 2151.33, 2151.353, 2151.354, 2151.415, 2151.417, 2152.16, 2152.17, 2152.19, 2152.21, or 3113.31 of the Revised Code.

(C) "Visitation order" means an order issued under division (B)(1)(c) of section 2151.33 or under section 2151.412, 3109.051, 3109.12, or 3113.31 of the Revised Code.

(2000 S 179, § 3, eff. 1–1–02; 1999 H 191, eff. 10–20–99)

Historical and Statutory Notes

Amendment Note: 2000 S 179, § 3, eff. 1–1–02, deleted "2151.355, 2151.356," before "2151.415," and inserted "2152.16, 2152.17, 2152.19, 2152.21," in division (B).

Library References

Child Custody ⚖=61.
Westlaw Topic No. 76D.
C.J.S. Parent and Child § 79.

3109.42 Unavailability of custody for parent convicted of killing other parent

Except as provided in section 3109.47 of the Revised Code, if a parent is convicted of killing the other parent of a child, no court shall issue a custody order designating the parent as the residential parent and legal custodian of the child or granting custody of the child to the parent.

(1999 H 191, eff. 10–20–99)

Library References

Child Custody ⚖=61.
Westlaw Topic No. 76D.
C.J.S. Parent and Child § 79.

3109.43 Unavailability of visitation rights for parent convicted of killing other parent

Except as provided in section 3109.47 of the Revised Code, if a parent is convicted of killing the other parent of a child, no court shall issue a visitation order granting the parent visitation rights with the child.

(1999 H 191, eff. 10–20–99)

Library References

Child Custody ⚖=200.
Westlaw Topic No. 76D.

3109.44 Notice of conviction

Upon receipt of notice that a visitation order is pending or has been issued granting a parent visitation rights with a child or a custody order is pending or has been issued designating a parent as the residential parent and legal custodian of a child or granting custody of a child to a parent prior to that parent being convicted of killing the other parent of the child, the court in which the parent is convicted of killing the other parent shall immediately notify the court that issued the visitation or custody order of the conviction.

(1999 H 191, eff. 10–20–99)

Library References

Child Custody ⚖=61, 200.
Criminal Law ⚖=1226(2).
Westlaw Topic Nos. 110, 76D.
C.J.S. Criminal Law § 1734.
C.J.S. Parent and Child § 79.

3109.45 Termination of visitation order upon receipt of notice of conviction

On receipt of notice under section 3109.44 of the Revised Code, a court that issued a visitation order described in that section shall terminate the order.

(1999 H 191, eff. 10–20–99)

Library References

Child Custody ⚖577.
Westlaw Topic No. 76D.
C.J.S. Parent and Child § 143.

3109.46 Termination of custody order upon receipt of notice of conviction; deemed new complaint for custody

If the court to which notice is sent under section 3109.44 of the Revised Code is a juvenile court that issued a custody order described in that section, the court shall retain jurisdiction over the order. If the court to which notice is sent is not a juvenile court but the court issued a custody order described in that section, the court shall transfer jurisdiction over the custody order to the juvenile court of the county in which the child has a residence or legal settlement.

On receipt of the notice in cases in which the custody order was issued by a juvenile court or after jurisdiction is transferred, the juvenile court with jurisdiction shall terminate the custody order.

The termination order shall be treated as a complaint filed under section 2151.27 of the Revised Code alleging the child subject of the custody order to be a dependent child. If a juvenile court issued the terminated custody order under a prior juvenile proceeding under Chapter 2151. of the Revised Code in which the child was adjudicated an abused, neglected, dependent, unruly, or delinquent child or a juvenile traffic offender, the court shall treat the termination order as a new complaint.

(1999 H 191, eff. 10–20–99)

Library References

Child Custody ⚖559.
Westlaw Topic No. 76D.
C.J.S. Parent and Child § 143.

3109.47 Custody or visitation order when in best interest of child

(A) A court may do one of the following with respect to a parent convicted of killing the other parent of a child if the court determines, by clear and convincing evidence, that it is in the best interest of the child and the child consents:

(1) Issue a custody order designating the parent as the residential parent and legal custodian of the child or granting custody of the child to that parent;

(2) Issue a visitation order granting that parent visitation rights with the child.

(B) When considering the ability of a child to consent and the validity of a child's consent under this section, the court shall consider the wishes of the child, as expressed directly by the child or through the child's guardian ad litem, with due regard for the maturity of the child.

(1999 H 191, eff. 10–20–99)

Library References

Child Custody ⚖61, 78, 200, 204.
Westlaw Topic No. 76D.
C.J.S. Parent and Child §§ 70 to 71, 79.

3109.48 Court order and consent of custodian required for visitation

No person, with the child of the parent present, shall visit the parent who has been convicted of killing the child's other parent unless a court has issued an order granting the parent visitation rights with the child and the child's custodian or legal guardian consents to the visit.

(1999 H 191, eff. 10–20–99)

Library References

Child Custody ⚖200.
Westlaw Topic No. 76D.

GRANDPARENT POWER OF ATTORNEY OR CARETAKER AUTHORIZATION AFFIDAVIT

3109.51 Definitions

As used in sections 3109.52 to 3109.80 of the Revised Code:

(A) "Child" means a person under eighteen years of age.

(B) "Custodian" means an individual with legal custody of a child.

(C) "Guardian" means an individual granted authority by a probate court pursuant to Chapter 2111. of the Revised Code to exercise parental rights over a child to the extent provided in the court's order and subject to the residual parental rights, privileges, and responsibilities of the child's parents.

(D) "Legal custody" and "residual parental rights, privileges, and responsibilities" have the same meanings as in section 2151.011 of the Revised Code.

(2004 H 130, eff. 7–20–04)

Library References

Powers ⚖7.
Westlaw Topic No. 307.
C.J.S. Powers § 3.

3109.52 Power of attorney to grandparents for care, physical custody and control of child

The parent, guardian, or custodian of a child may create a power of attorney that grants to a grandparent of the child with whom the child is residing any of the parent's, guardian's, or custodian's rights and responsibilities regarding the care, physical custody, and control of the child, including the ability to enroll the child in school, to obtain from the school district educational and behavioral information about the child, to consent to all school-related matters regarding the child, and to consent to medical, psychological, or dental treatment for the child. The power of attorney may not grant authority to consent to the marriage or adoption of the child. The power of attorney does not affect the rights of the parent, guardian, or custodian of the child in any future proceeding concerning custody of the child or the allocation of parental rights and responsibilities for the care of the child and does not grant legal custody to the attorney in fact.

(2004 H 130, eff. 7-20-04)

Library References

Powers ⇌5 to 7, 17.
Westlaw Topic No. 307.
C.J.S. Powers §§ 2 to 4, 14 to 18.

3109.53 Form and content of power of attorney

To create a power of attorney under section 3109.52 of the Revised Code, a parent, guardian, or custodian shall use a form that is identical in form and content to the following:

POWER OF ATTORNEY

I, the undersigned, residing at..........., in the county of ...., state of.........., hereby appoint the child's grandparent, ..., residing at.........., in the county of.........., in the state of Ohio, with whom the child of whom I am the parent, guardian, or custodian is residing, my attorney in fact to exercise any and all of my rights and responsibilities regarding the care, physical custody, and control of the child,.........., born.........., having social security number (optional).........., except my authority to consent to marriage or adoption of the child.........., and to perform all acts necessary in the execution of the rights and responsibilities hereby granted, as fully as I might do if personally present. The rights I am transferring under this power of attorney include the ability to enroll the child in school, to obtain from the school district educational and behavioral information about the child, to consent to all school-related matters regarding the child, and to consent to medical, psychological, or dental treatment for the child. This transfer does not affect my rights in any future proceedings concerning the custody of the child or the allocation of the parental rights and responsibilities for the care of the child and does not give the attorney in fact legal custody of the child. This transfer does not terminate my right to have regular contact with the child.

I hereby certify that I am transferring the rights and responsibilities designated in this power of attorney because one of the following circumstances exists:

(1) I am: (a) Seriously ill, incarcerated or about to be incarcerated, (b) Temporarily unable to provide financial support or parental guidance to the child, (c) Temporarily unable to provide adequate care and supervision of the child because of my physical or mental condition, (d) Homeless or without a residence because the current residence is destroyed or otherwise uninhabitable, or (e) In or about to enter a residential treatment program for substance abuse;

(2) I am a parent of the child, the child's other parent is deceased, and I have authority to execute the power of attorney; or

(3) I have a well-founded belief that the power of attorney is in the child's best interest.

I hereby certify that I am not transferring my rights and responsibilities regarding the child for the purpose of enrolling the child in a school or school district so that the child may participate in the academic or interscholastic athletic programs provided by that school or district.

I understand that this document does not authorize a child support enforcement agency to redirect child support payments to the grandparent designated as attorney in fact. I further understand that to have an existing child support order modified or a new child support order issued administrative or judicial proceedings must be initiated.

If there is a court order naming me the residential parent and legal custodian of the child who is the subject of this power of attorney and I am the sole parent signing this document, I hereby certify that one of the following is the case:

(1) I have made reasonable efforts to locate and provide notice of the creation of this power of attorney to the other parent and have been unable to locate that parent;

(2) The other parent is prohibited from receiving a notice of relocation; or

(3) The parental rights of the other parent have been terminated by order of a juvenile court.

This POWER OF ATTORNEY is valid until the occurrence of whichever of the following events occurs first: (1) one year elapses following the date this POWER OF ATTORNEY is notarized; (2) I revoke this POWER OF ATTORNEY in writing; (3) the child ceases to reside with the grandparent designated as attorney in fact; (4) this POWER OF ATTORNEY is terminated by court order; (5) the death of the child who is the subject of the power of attorney; or (6) the death of the grandparent designated as the attorney in fact.

WARNING: DO NOT EXECUTE THIS POWER OF ATTORNEY IF ANY STATEMENT MADE IN THIS INSTRUMENT IS UNTRUE. FALSIFICATION IS A CRIME UNDER SECTION 2921.13 OF THE REVISED CODE, PUNISHABLE BY THE SANCTIONS UNDER CHAPTER 2929. OF THE REVISED CODE, INCLUDING A TERM OF IMPRISONMENT OF UP TO 6 MONTHS, A FINE OF UP TO $1,000, OR BOTH.

Witness my hand this...... day of............,......

....
Parent/Custodian/Guardian's signature

....
Parent's signature

....
Grandparent designated as attorney in fact

State of Ohio   )
) ss:
County of ....   )

Subscribed, sworn to, and acknowledged before me this...... day of ....,.............

....
Notary Public

Notices:

1. A power of attorney may be executed only if one of the following circumstances exists: (1) The parent, guardian, or custodian of the child is: (a) Seriously ill, incarcerated or about to be incarcerated; (b) Temporarily unable to provide financial support or parental guidance to the child; (c) Temporarily unable to provide adequate care and supervision of the child because of the parent's, guardian's, or custodian's physical or mental condition; (d) Homeless or without a residence because the current residence is destroyed or otherwise uninhabitable; or (e) In or about to enter a residential treatment program for substance abuse; (2) One of the child's parents is deceased and the other parent, with authority to do so, seeks to execute a power of attorney; or (3) The parent, guardian, or custodian has a well-founded belief that the power of attorney is in the child's best interest.

2. The signatures of the parent, guardian, or custodian of the child and the grandparent designated as the attorney in fact must be notarized by an Ohio notary public.

3. A parent, guardian, or custodian who creates a power of attorney must notify the parent of the child who is not the residential parent and legal custodian of the child unless one of the following circumstances applies: (a) the parent is

prohibited from receiving a notice of relocation in accordance with section 3109.051 of the Revised Code of the creation of the power of attorney; (b) the parent's parental rights have been terminated by order of a juvenile court pursuant to Chapter 2151. of the Revised Code; (c) the parent cannot be located with reasonable efforts; (d) both parents are executing the power of attorney. The notice must be sent by certified mail not later than five days after the power of attorney is created and must state the name and address of the person designated as the attorney in fact.

4. A parent, guardian, or custodian who creates a power of attorney must file it with the juvenile court of the county in which the attorney in fact resides, or any other court that has jurisdiction over the child under a previously filed motion or proceeding. The power of attorney must be filed not later than five days after the date it is created and be accompanied by a receipt showing that the notice of creation of the power of attorney was sent to the parent who is not the residential parent and legal custodian by certified mail.

5. A parent, guardian, or custodian who creates a second or subsequent power of attorney regarding a child who is the subject of a prior power of attorney must file the power of attorney with the juvenile court of the county in which the attorney in fact resides or any other court that has jurisdiction over the child under a previously filed motion or proceeding. On filing, the court will schedule a hearing to determine whether the power of attorney is in the child's best interest.

6. This power of attorney does not affect the rights of the child's parents, guardian, or custodian regarding any future proceedings concerning the custody of the child or the allocation of the parental rights and responsibilities for the care of the child and does not give the attorney in fact legal custody of the child.

7. A person or entity that relies on this power of attorney, in good faith, has no obligation to make any further inquiry or investigation.

8. This power of attorney terminates on the occurrence of whichever of the following occurs first: (1) one year elapses following the date the power of attorney is notarized; (2) the power of attorney is revoked in writing by the person who created it; (3) the child ceases to live with the grandparent who is the attorney in fact; (4) the power of attorney is terminated by court order; (5) the death of the child who is the subject of the power of attorney; or (6) the death of the grandparent designated as the attorney in fact.

(If this power of attorney terminates other than by the death of the attorney in fact, the grandparent who served as the attorney in fact shall notify, in writing, all of the following:

(a) Any schools, health care providers, or health insurance coverage provider with which the child has been involved through the grandparent;

(b) Any other person or entity that has an ongoing relationship with the child or grandparent such that the other person or entity would reasonably rely on the power of attorney unless notified of the termination;

(c) The court in which the power of attorney was filed after its creation; and

(d) The parent who is not the residential parent and legal custodian of the child who is required to be given notice of its creation. The grandparent shall make the notifications not later than one week after the date the power of attorney terminates.

9. If this power of attorney is terminated by written revocation of the person who created it, or the revocation is regarding a second or subsequent power of attorney, a copy of the revocation must be filed with the court with which that power of attorney was filed.

Additional information:

To the grandparent designated as attorney in fact:

1. If the child stops living with you, you are required to notify, in writing, any school, health care provider, or health care insurance provider to which you have given this power of attorney. You are also required to notify, in writing, any other person or entity that has an ongoing relationship with you or the child such that the person or entity would reasonably rely on the power of attorney unless notified. The notification must be made not later than one week after the child stops living with you.

2. You must include with the power of attorney the following information:

(a) The child's present address, the addresses of the places where the child has lived within the last five years, and the name and present address of each person with whom the child has lived during that period;

(b) Whether you have participated as a party, a witness, or in any other capacity in any other litigation, in this state or any other state, that concerned the allocation, between the parents of the same child, of parental rights and responsibilities for the care of the child and the designation of the residential parent and legal custodian of the child or that otherwise concerned the custody of the same child;

(c) Whether you have information of any parenting proceeding concerning the child pending in a court of this or any other state;

(d) Whether you know of any person who has physical custody of the child or claims to be a parent of the child who is designated the residential parent and legal custodian of the child or to have parenting time rights with respect to the child or to be a person other than a parent of the child who has custody or visitation rights with respect to the child;

(e) Whether you previously have been convicted of or pleaded guilty to any criminal offense involving any act that resulted in a child being an abused child or a neglected child or previously have been determined, in a case in which a child has been adjudicated an abused child or a neglected child, to be the perpetrator of the abusive or neglectful act that was the basis of the adjudication.

To school officials:

1. Except as provided in section 3313.649 of the Revised Code, this power of attorney, properly completed and notarized, authorizes the child in question to attend school in the district in which the grandparent designated as attorney in fact resides and that grandparent is authorized to provide consent in all school-related matters and to obtain from the school district educational and behavioral information about the child. This power of attorney does not preclude the parent, guardian, or custodian of the child from having access to all school records pertinent to the child.

2. The school district may require additional reasonable evidence that the grandparent lives in the school district.

3. A school district or school official that reasonably and in good faith relies on this power of attorney has no obligation to make any further inquiry or investigation.

To health care providers:

1. A person or entity that acts in good faith reliance on a power of attorney to provide medical, psychological, or dental treatment, without actual knowledge of facts contrary to those stated in the power of attorney, is not subject to criminal liability or to civil liability to any person or entity, and is not subject to professional disciplinary action, solely for such reliance if the power of attorney is completed and the signatures of the parent, guardian, or custodian of the child and the grandparent designated as attorney in fact are notarized.

2. The decision of a grandparent designated as attorney in fact, based on a power of attorney, shall be honored by a health care facility or practitioner, school district, or school official.

(2004 H 130, eff. 7–20–04)

Library References

Powers ⇐8.
Westlaw Topic No. 307.
C.J.S. Powers § 7.

3109.54 Signature and notarization

A power of attorney created pursuant to section 3109.52 of the Revised Code must be signed by the parent, guardian, or custodian granting it and by the grandparent designated as the attorney in fact. For the power of attorney to be effective, the signatures must be notarized. The child's social security number need not appear on the power of attorney for the power of attorney to be effective.

(2004 H 130, eff. 7–20–04)

Library References

Powers ⇐8.
Westlaw Topic No. 307.
C.J.S. Powers § 7.

3109.55 Notice to nonresidential parent and legal custodian; exceptions; method of delivery; contents of notice

(A) A person who creates a power of attorney under section 3109.52 of the Revised Code shall send notice of the creation to the parent of the child who is not the residential parent and legal custodian of the child unless one of the following is the case:

(1) The parent is prohibited from receiving a notice of relocation in accordance with section 3109.051 of the Revised Code.

(2) The parent's parental rights have been terminated by order of a juvenile court pursuant to Chapter 2151. of the Revised Code.

(3) The parent cannot be located with reasonable efforts.

(4) The power of attorney is being created by both parents.

(B) The notice shall be sent by certified mail not later than five days after the power of attorney is created. The notice shall state the name and address of the person designated as the attorney in fact.

(2004 H 130, eff. 7–20–04)

Library References

Powers ⇐10.
Westlaw Topic No. 307.
C.J.S. Powers § 9.

3109.56 Conditions determining execution of power of attorney by one or both parents

When a parent seeks to create a power of attorney pursuant to section 3109.52 of the Revised Code, all of the following apply:

(A) The power of attorney shall be executed by both parents if any of the following apply:

(1) The parents are married to each other and are living as husband and wife.

(2) The child is the subject of a shared parenting order issued pursuant to section 3109.04 of the Revised Code.

(3) The child is the subject of a custody order issued pursuant to section 3109.04 of the Revised Code unless one of the following is the case:

(a) The parent who is not the residential parent and legal custodian is prohibited from receiving a notice of relocation in accordance with section 3109.051 of the Revised Code.

(b) The parental rights of the parent who is not the residential parent and legal custodian have been terminated by order of a juvenile court pursuant to Chapter 2151. of the Revised Code.

(c) The parent who is not the residential parent and legal custodian cannot be located with reasonable efforts.

(B) In all other cases, the power of attorney may be executed only by one of the following persons:

(1) The parent who is the residential parent and legal custodian of the child, as determined by court order or as provided in section 3109.042 of the Revised Code;

(2) The parent with whom the child is residing the majority of the school year in cases in which no court has issued an order designating a parent as the residential parent and legal custodian of the child or section 3109.042 of the Revised Code is not applicable.

(2004 H 130, eff. 7–20–04)

Library References

Powers ⇐6, 10.
Westlaw Topic No. 307.
C.J.S. Powers §§ 2, 9.

3109.57 Conditions required for creation of power of attorney

(A) Except as provided in division (B) of this section and subject to sections 3109.56 and 3109.58 of the Revised Code, a parent, guardian, or custodian may create a power of attorney under section 3109.52 of the Revised Code only under the following circumstances:

(1) The parent, guardian, or custodian of the child is any of the following:

(a) Seriously ill, incarcerated, or about to be incarcerated;

(b) Temporarily unable to provide financial support or parental guidance to the child;

(c) Temporarily unable to provide adequate care and supervision of the child because of the parent's, guardian's, or custodian's physical or mental condition;

(d) Homeless or without a residence because the current residence is destroyed or otherwise uninhabitable;

(e) In or about to enter a residential treatment program for substance abuse.

(2) The parent, guardian, or custodian of the child has a well-founded belief that the power of attorney is in the child's best interest.

(B) In addition to the circumstances described in division (A) of this section and subject to sections 3109.56 and 3109.58 of the Revised Code, a parent may execute a power of attorney if the other parent of the child is deceased.

(2004 H 130, eff. 7–20–04)

Library References

Powers ⇐5, 10.
Westlaw Topic No. 307.
C.J.S. Powers §§ 2, 9.

3109.58 Certain pending actions prohibiting creation of power of attorney

(A) As used in this section, "temporary custody," "permanent custody," and "planned permanent living arrangement" have the same meanings as in section 2151.011 of the Revised Code.

(B) A power of attorney created pursuant to section 3109.52 of the Revised Code may not be executed with respect to a child while any of the following proceedings are pending regarding the child:

(1) A proceeding for the appointment of a guardian for, or the adoption of, the child;

(2) A juvenile proceeding in which one of the following applies:

(a) The temporary, permanent, or legal custody of the child or the placement of the child in a planned permanent living arrangement has been requested.

(b) The child is the subject of an ex parte emergency custody order issued under division (D) of section 2151.31 of the Revised Code, and no hearing has yet been held regarding the child under division (A) of section 2151.314 of the Revised Code.

(c) The child is the subject of a temporary custody order issued under section 2151.33 of the Revised Code.

(3) A proceeding for divorce, dissolution, legal separation, annulment, or allocation of parental rights and responsibilities regarding the child.

(2004 H 130, eff. 7–20–04)

Library References

Powers ⚖10, 31.
Westlaw Topic No. 307.
C.J.S. Powers §§ 9, 25.

3109.59 Termination; filing of revocation of initial power of attorney or subsequent power of attorney

(A) A power of attorney created under section 3109.52 of the Revised Code terminates on the occurrence of whichever of the following events occurs first:

(1) One year elapses following the date the power of attorney is notarized.

(2) The power of attorney is revoked in writing by the person who created it.

(3) The child ceases to reside with the grandparent designated the attorney in fact.

(4) The power of attorney is terminated by court order.

(5) The death of the child who is the subject of the power of attorney.

(6) The death of the grandparent designated as the attorney in fact.

(B) Not later than five days after a power of attorney is terminated pursuant to division (A)(2) of this section, a copy of the revocation of an initial power of attorney or a second or subsequent power of attorney must be filed with the court with which the power of attorney is filed pursuant to section 3109.76 of the Revised Code.

(2004 H 130, eff. 7–20–04)

Library References

Powers ⚖13 to 15.
Westlaw Topic No. 307.
C.J.S. Powers §§ 10 to 11.

3109.60 Notice required upon termination of grandparent's power of attorney

When a power of attorney created pursuant to section 3109.52 of the Revised Code terminates pursuant to division (A)(1), (A)(2), (A)(3), (A)(4), or (A)(5) of section 3109.59 of the Revised Code, the grandparent designated as the attorney in fact shall notify, in writing, all of the following:

(A) The school district in which the child attends school;

(B) The child's health care providers;

(C) The child's health insurance coverage provider;

(D) The court in which the power of attorney was filed under section 3109.74 of the Revised Code;

(E) The parent who is not the residential parent and legal custodian and who is required to be given notice under section 3109.55 of the Revised Code;

(F) Any other person or entity that has an ongoing relationship with the child or grandparent such that the person or entity would reasonably rely on the power of attorney unless notified of the termination.

The grandparent shall make the notifications not later than one week after the date the power of attorney terminates.

(2004 H 130, eff. 7–20–04)

Library References

Powers ⚖13 to 15.
Westlaw Topic No. 307.
C.J.S. Powers §§ 10 to 11.

3109.61 Immunity from liability for good faith reliance on power of attorney

A person who, in good faith, relies on or takes action in reliance on a power of attorney created under section 3109.52 of the Revised Code is immune from any criminal or civil liability for injury, death, or loss to persons or property that might otherwise be incurred or imposed solely as a result of the person's reliance or action. The person is not subject to any disciplinary action from an entity that licenses or certifies the person.

Any medical, psychological, or dental treatment provided to a child in reliance on a power of attorney created under section 3109.52 of the Revised Code shall be considered to have been provided in good faith if the person providing the treatment had no actual knowledge of opposition by the parent, guardian, or custodian.

This section does not provide immunity from civil or criminal liability to any person for actions that are wanton, reckless, or inconsistent with the ordinary standard of care required to be exercised by anyone acting in the same capacity as the person.

(2004 H 130, eff. 7–20–04)

Library References

Criminal Law ⚖31, 37.20.
Negligence ⚖500.
Torts ⚖121.
Westlaw Topic Nos. 110, 272, 379.
C.J.S. Criminal Law §§ 14, 46 to 49, 56, 88, 93 to 94.
C.J.S. Negligence §§ 226, 654.

3109.62 Effect of military power of attorney

A military power of attorney executed pursuant to section 574(a) of the "National Defense Authorization Act for Fiscal Year 1994," 107 Stat. 1674 (1993), 10 U.S.C. 1044b, that grants a person's rights and responsibilities regarding the care, custody, and control of the person's child, including the ability to enroll the child in school, to obtain from the school district educational and behavioral information about the child, to consent to all school-related matters regarding the child, and to consent to medical, psychological, or dental treatment for the child shall be considered a power of attorney created pursuant to sections 3109.51 to 3109.61 of the Revised Code, as long as the military power of attorney, according to its terms, remains in effect.

(2004 H 130, eff. 7–20–04)

Library References

Armed Services ⇐20.7.
Westlaw Topic No. 34.
C.J.S. Armed Services §§ 1, 67, 71.

3109.65 Authority of grandparent to execute caretaker authorization affidavit

(A) Except as provided in division (B) of this section, if a child is living with a grandparent who has made reasonable attempts to locate and contact both of the child's parents, or the child's guardian or custodian, but has been unable to do so, the grandparent may obtain authority to exercise care, physical custody, and control of the child including authority to enroll the child in school, to discuss with the school district the child's educational progress, to consent to all school-related matters regarding the child, and to consent to medical, psychological, or dental treatment for the child by executing a caretaker authorization affidavit in accordance with section 3109.67 of the Revised Code.

(B) The grandparent may execute a caretaker authorization affidavit without attempting to locate the following parent:

(1) If paternity has not been established with regard to the child, the child's father.

(2) If the child is the subject of a custody order, the following parent:

(a) A parent who is prohibited from receiving a notice of relocation in accordance with section 3109.051 of the Revised Code;

(b) A parent whose parental rights have been terminated by order of a juvenile court pursuant to Chapter 2151. of the Revised Code.

(2004 H 130, eff. 7–20–04)

Library References

Parent and Child ⇐15.
Westlaw Topic No. 285.
C.J.S. Parent and Child §§ 345 to 350, 357 to 358.

3109.66 Form and content of caretaker authorization affidavit

The caretaker authorization affidavit that a grandparent described in section 3109.65 of the Revised Code may execute shall be identical in form and content to the following:

CARETAKER AUTHORIZATION AFFIDAVIT

Use of this affidavit is authorized by sections 3109.65 to 3109.73 of the Ohio Revised Code.

Completion of items 1–7 and the signing and notarization of this affidavit is sufficient to authorize the grandparent signing to exercise care, physical custody, and control of the child who is its subject, including authority to enroll the child in school, to discuss with the school district the child's educational progress, to consent to all school-related matters regarding the child, and to consent to medical, psychological, or dental treatment for the child.

The child named below lives in my home, I am 18 years of age or older, and I am the child's grandparent.

1. Name of child:
2. Child's date and year of birth:
3. Child's social security number (optional):
4. My name:
5. My home address:
6. My date and year of birth:
7. My Ohio driver's license number or identification card number:
8. Despite having made reasonable attempts, I am either:
   (a) Unable to locate or contact the child's parents, or the child's guardian or custodian; or
   (b) I am unable to locate or contact one of the child's parents and I am not required to contact the other parent because paternity has not been established; or
   (c) I am unable to locate or contact one of the child's parents and I am not required to contact the other parent because there is a custody order regarding the child and one of the following is the case:
   (i) The parent has been prohibited from receiving notice of a relocation; or
   (ii) The parental rights of the parent have been terminated.
9. I hereby certify that this affidavit is not being executed for the purpose of enrolling the child in a school or school district so that the child may participate in the academic or interscholastic athletic programs provided by that school or district.

I understand that this document does not authorize a child support enforcement agency to redirect child support payments. I further understand that to have an existing child support order modified or a new child support order issued administrative or judicial proceedings must be initiated.

WARNING: DO NOT SIGN THIS FORM IF ANY OF THE ABOVE STATEMENTS ARE INCORRECT. FALSIFICATION IS A CRIME UNDER SECTION 2921.13 OF THE REVISED CODE, PUNISHABLE BY THE SANCTIONS UNDER CHAPTER 2929. OF THE REVISED CODE, INCLUDING A TERM OF IMPRISONMENT OF UP TO 6 MONTHS, A FINE OF UP TO $1,000, OR BOTH.

I declare that the foregoing is true and correct:

Signed: .... Date: ....
Grandparent

State of Ohio   )
) ss:
County of ....   )

Subscribed, sworn to, and acknowledged before me this...... day of ....,............

....
Notary Public

Notices:
1. The grandparent's signature must be notarized by an Ohio notary public.
2. The grandparent who executed this affidavit must file it with the juvenile court of the county in which the grandparent resides or any other court that has jurisdiction over the child under a previously filed motion or proceeding not later than five days after the date it is executed.

3. A grandparent who executes a second or subsequent caretaker authorization affidavit regarding a child who is the subject of a prior caretaker authorization affidavit must file the affidavit with the juvenile court of the county in which the grandparent resides or any other court that has jurisdiction over the child under a previously filed motion or proceeding. On filing, the court will schedule a hearing to determine whether the caretaker authorization affidavit is in the child's best interest.
4. This affidavit does not affect the rights of the child's parents, guardian, or custodian regarding the care, physical custody, and control of the child, and does not give the grandparent legal custody of the child.
5. A person or entity that relies on this affidavit, in good faith, has no obligation to make any further inquiry or investigation.
6. This affidavit terminates on the occurrence of whichever of the following occurs first: (1) one year elapses following the date the affidavit is notarized; (2) the child ceases to live with the grandparent who signs this form; (3) the parent, guardian, or custodian of the child acts to negate, reverse, or otherwise disapprove an action or decision of the grandparent who signed this affidavit; or (4) the affidavit is terminated by court order; (5) the death of the child who is the subject of the affidavit; or (6) the death of the grandparent who executed the affidavit.

A parent, guardian, or custodian may negate, reverse, or disapprove a grandparent's action or decision only by delivering written notice of negation, reversal, or disapproval to the grandparent and the person acting on the grandparent's action or decision in reliance on this affidavit.

If this affidavit terminates other than by the death of the grandparent, the grandparent who signed this affidavit shall notify, in writing, all of the following:

a) Any schools, health care providers, or health insurance coverage provider with which the child has been involved through the grandparent;

(b) Any other person or entity that has an ongoing relationship with the child or grandparent such that the person or entity would reasonably rely on the affidavit unless notified of the termination;

(c) The court in which the affidavit was filed after its creation.

The grandparent shall make the notifications not later than one week after the date the affidavit terminates.

7. The decision of a grandparent to consent to or to refuse medical treatment or school enrollment for a child is superseded by a contrary decision of a parent, custodian, or guardian of the child, unless the decision of the parent, guardian, or custodian would jeopardize the life, health, or safety of the child.

Additional information:

To caretakers:

1. If the child stops living with you, you are required to notify, in writing, any school, health care provider, or health care insurance provider to which you have given this affidavit. You are also required to notify, in writing, any other person or entity that has an ongoing relationship with you or the child such that the person or entity would reasonably rely on the affidavit unless notified. The notifications must be made not later than one week after the child stops living with you.
2. If you do not have the information requested in item 7 (Ohio driver's license or identification card), provide another form of identification such as your social security number or medicaid number.
3. You must include with the caretaker authorization affidavit the following information:

(a) The child's present address, the addresses of the places where the child has lived within the last five years, and the name and present address of each person with whom the child has lived during that period;

(b) Whether you have participated as a party, a witness, or in any other capacity in any other litigation, in this state or any other state, that concerned the allocation, between the parents of the same child, of parental rights and responsibilities for the care of the child and the designation of the residential parent and legal custodian of the child or that otherwise concerned the custody of the same child;

(c) Whether you have information of any parenting proceeding concerning the child pending in a court of this or any other state;

(d) Whether you know of any person who has physical custody of the child or claims to be a parent of the child who is designated the residential parent and legal custodian of the child or to have parenting time rights with respect to the child or to be a person other than a parent of the child who has custody or visitation rights with respect to the child;

(e) Whether you previously have been convicted of or pleaded guilty to any criminal offense involving any act that resulted in a child being an abused child or a neglected child or previously have been determined, in a case in which a child has been adjudicated an abused child or a neglected child, to be the perpetrator of the abusive or neglectful act that was the basis of the adjudication.

To school officials:

1. This affidavit, properly completed and notarized, authorizes the child in question to attend school in the district in which the grandparent who signed this affidavit resides and the grandparent is authorized to provide consent in all school-related matters and to discuss with the school district the child's educational progress. This affidavit does not preclude the parent, guardian, or custodian of the child from having access to all school records pertinent to the child.
2. The school district may require additional reasonable evidence that the grandparent lives at the address provided in item 5.
3. A school district or school official that reasonably and in good faith relies on this affidavit has no obligation to make any further inquiry or investigation.
4. The act of a parent, guardian, or custodian of the child to negate, reverse, or otherwise disapprove an action or decision of the grandparent who signed this affidavit constitutes termination of this affidavit. A parent, guardian, or custodian may negate, reverse, or disapprove a grandparent's action or decision only by delivering written notice of negation, reversal, or disapproval to the grandparent and the person acting on the grandparent's action or decision in reliance on this affidavit.

To health care providers:

1. A person or entity that acts in good faith reliance on a CARETAKER AUTHORIZATION AFFIDAVIT to provide medical, psychological, or dental treatment, without actual knowledge of facts contrary to those stated in the affidavit, is not subject to criminal liability or to civil liability to any person or entity, and is not subject to professional disciplinary action, solely for such reliance if the applicable portions of the form are completed and the grandparent's signature is notarized.
2. The decision of a grandparent, based on a CARETAKER AUTHORIZATION AFFIDAVIT, shall be honored by a health care facility or practitioner, school district, or school official unless the health care facility or practitioner or educational facility or official has actual knowledge that a parent, guardian, or custodian of a child has made a contravening decision to consent to or to refuse medical treatment for the child.
3. The act of a parent, guardian, or custodian of the child to negate, reverse, or otherwise disapprove an action or decision of the grandparent who signed this affidavit constitutes termination of this affidavit. A parent, guardian, or custodian may negate, reverse, or disapprove a grandparent's action or decision only by delivering written notice of negation, rever-

sal, or disapproval to the grandparent and the person acting on the grandparent's action or decision in reliance on this affidavit.

(2004 H 130, eff. 7-20-04)

Library References

Parent and Child ⚖=15.
Westlaw Topic No. 285.
C.J.S. Parent and Child §§ 345 to 350, 357 to 358.

3109.67 Execution of affidavit

A caretaker authorization affidavit described in section 3109.66 of the Revised Code is executed when the affidavit is completed, signed by a grandparent described in section 3109.65 of the Revised Code, and notarized.

(2004 H 130, eff. 7-20-04)

Library References

Parent and Child ⚖=15.
Westlaw Topic No. 285.
C.J.S. Parent and Child §§ 345 to 350, 357 to 358.

3109.68 Affidavit not permitted when certain proceedings are pending

(A) As used in this section, "temporary custody," "permanent custody," and "planned permanent living arrangement" have the same meanings as in section 2151.011 of the Revised Code.

(B) A caretaker authorization affidavit may not be executed with respect to a child while any of the following proceedings are pending regarding the child:

(1) A proceeding for the appointment of a guardian for, or the adoption of, the child;

(2) A juvenile proceeding in which one of the following applies:

(a) The temporary, permanent, or legal custody of the child or the placement of the child in a planned permanent living arrangement has been requested.

(b) The child is the subject of an ex parte emergency custody order issued under division (D) of section 2151.31 of the Revised Code, and no hearing has yet been held regarding the child under division (A) of section 2151.314 of the Revised Code.

(c) The child is the subject of a temporary custody order issued under section 2151.33 of the Revised Code.

(3) A proceeding for divorce, dissolution, legal separation, annulment, or allocation of parental rights and responsibilities regarding the child.

(2004 H 130, eff. 7-20-04)

Library References

Parent and Child ⚖=15.
Westlaw Topic No. 285.
C.J.S. Parent and Child §§ 345 to 350, 357 to 358.

3109.69 Effect of executed affidavit

Once a caretaker authorization affidavit has been executed under section 3109.67 of the Revised Code, the grandparent may exercise care, physical custody, and control of the child, including enrolling the child in school, discussing with the school district the child's educational progress, consenting to all school-related matters regarding the child, and consenting to medical, psychological, or dental treatment for the child. The affidavit does not affect the rights and responsibilities of the parent, guardian, or custodian regarding the child, does not grant legal custody to the grandparent, and does not grant authority to the grandparent to consent to the marriage or adoption of the child.

(2004 H 130, eff. 7-20-04)

Library References

Parent and Child ⚖=15.
Westlaw Topic No. 285.
C.J.S. Parent and Child §§ 345 to 350, 357 to 358.

3109.70 Termination of affidavit

An executed caretaker authorization affidavit shall terminate on the occurrence of whichever of the following comes first:

(A) One year elapses following the date the affidavit is notarized.

(B) The child ceases to reside with the grandparent.

(C) The parent, guardian, or custodian of the child who is the subject of the affidavit acts, in accordance with section 3109.72 of the Revised Code, to negate, reverse, or otherwise disapprove an action or decision of the grandparent who signed the affidavit with respect to the child.

(D) The affidavit is terminated by court order.

(E) The death of the child who is the subject of the affidavit.

(F) The death of the grandparent who executed the affidavit.

(2004 H 130, eff. 7-20-04)

Library References

Parent and Child ⚖=15.
Westlaw Topic No. 285.
C.J.S. Parent and Child §§ 345 to 350, 357 to 358.

3109.71 Notice required upon termination of affidavit

When a caretaker authorization affidavit terminates pursuant to division (A), (B), (C), (D), or (E) of section 3109.70 of the Revised Code, the grandparent shall notify, in writing, the school district in which the child attends school, the child's health care providers, the child's health insurance coverage provider, the court in which the affidavit was filed under section 3109.74 of the Revised Code, and any other person or entity that has an ongoing relationship with the child or grandparent such that the person or entity would reasonably rely on the affidavit unless notified of the termination. The grandparent shall make the notifications not later than one week after the date the affidavit terminates.

(2004 H 130, eff. 7-20-04)

Library References

Parent and Child ⚖=15.
Westlaw Topic No. 285.
C.J.S. Parent and Child §§ 345 to 350, 357 to 358.

3109.72 Negation, reversal, or disapproval of action taken pursuant to affidavit

The parent, guardian, or custodian of a child may negate, reverse, or otherwise disapprove any action taken or decision made pursuant to a caretaker authorization affidavit unless negation, reversal, or disapproval would jeopardize the life, health, or safety of the child. A parent, guardian, or custodian may negate, reverse, or disapprove a caretaker's action or decision only by delivering written notice of negation, reversal, or disapproval to the caretaker and the person responding to the caretaker's action or decision in reliance on the affidavit. The act to negate, reverse, or disapprove the action or decision, regardless of whether it is effective, terminates the affidavit.

(2004 H 130, eff. 7–20–04)

Library References

Parent and Child ⇌15.
Westlaw Topic No. 285.
C.J.S. Parent and Child §§ 345 to 350, 357 to 358.

3109.73 Immunity from liability for good faith reliance on affidavit

A person who, in good faith, relies on or takes action in reliance on a caretaker authorization affidavit is immune from any criminal or civil liability for injury, death, or loss to persons or property that might otherwise be incurred or imposed solely as a result of the reliance or action. The person is not subject to any disciplinary action from an entity that licenses or certifies the person. Any medical, psychological, or dental treatment provided to a child in reliance on an affidavit with respect to the child shall be considered to have been provided in good faith if the person providing the treatment had no actual knowledge of opposition by the parent, guardian, or custodian.

This section does not provide immunity from civil or criminal liability to any person for actions that are wanton, reckless, or inconsistent with the ordinary standard of care required to be exercised by anyone acting in the same capacity as the person.

(2004 H 130, eff. 7–20–04)

Library References

Criminal Law ⇌31, 37.20.
Negligence ⇌500.
Torts ⇌121.
Westlaw Topic Nos. 110, 272, 379.
C.J.S. Criminal Law §§ 14, 46 to 49, 56, 88, 93 to 94.
C.J.S. Negligence §§ 226, 654.

3109.74 Filing of power of attorney or affidavit with juvenile court; accompanying information; report to public children services agency; investigation

(A) A person who creates a power of attorney under section 3109.52 of the Revised Code or executes a caretaker authorization affidavit under section 3109.67 of the Revised Code shall file the power of attorney or affidavit with the juvenile court of the county in which the grandparent designated as attorney in fact or grandparent who executed the affidavit resides or any other court that has jurisdiction over the child under a previously filed motion or proceeding. The power of attorney or affidavit shall be filed not later than five days after the date it is created or executed and may be sent to the court by certified mail.

(B) A power of attorney filed under this section shall be accompanied by a receipt showing that the notice of creation of the power of attorney was sent to the parent who is not the residential parent and legal custodian by certified mail under section 3109.55 of the Revised Code.

(C)(1) The grandparent designated as attorney in fact or the grandparent who executed the affidavit shall include with the power of attorney or the caretaker authorization affidavit the information described in section 3109.27 of the Revised Code.

(2) If the grandparent provides information that the grandparent previously has been convicted of or pleaded guilty to any criminal offense involving any act that resulted in a child being an abused child or a neglected child or previously has been determined, in a case in which a child has been adjudicated an abused child or a neglected child, to be the perpetrator of the abusive or neglectful act that was the basis of the adjudication, the court may report that information to the public children services agency pursuant to section 2151.421 of the Revised Code. Upon the receipt of that information, the public children services agency shall initiate an investigation pursuant to section 2151.421 of the Revised Code.

(3) If the court has reason to believe that a power of attorney or caretaker authorization affidavit is not in the best interest of the child, the court may report that information to the public children services agency pursuant to section 2151.421 of the Revised Code. Upon receipt of that information, the public children services agency shall initiate an investigation pursuant to section 2151.421 of the Revised Code. The public children services agency shall submit a report of its investigation to the court not later than thirty days after the court reports the information to the public children services agency or not later than forty-five days after the court reports the information to the public children services agency when information that is needed to determine the case disposition cannot be compiled within thirty days and the reasons are documented in the case record.

(D) The court shall waive any filing fee imposed for the filing of the power of attorney or caretaker authorization affidavit.

(2004 H 130, eff. 7–20–04)

Library References

Parent and Child ⇌15.
Powers ⇌10.
Westlaw Topic Nos. 285, 307.
C.J.S. Parent and Child §§ 345 to 350, 357 to 358.
C.J.S. Powers § 9.

3109.75 Verification of power of attorney or affidavit

On the request of the person in charge of admissions of a school or a person described under division (A)(1)(b) of section 2151.421 of the Revised Code, the court in which the power of attorney or caretaker authorization affidavit was filed shall verify whether a power of attorney or caretaker authorization affidavit has been filed under section 3109.74 of the Revised Code with respect to a child.

(2004 H 130, eff. 7–20–04)

Library References

Parent and Child ⇌15.
Powers ⇌10.
Westlaw Topic Nos. 285, 307.
C.J.S. Parent and Child §§ 345 to 350, 357 to 358.
C.J.S. Powers § 9.

3109.76 Requirements regarding subsequent powers of attorney or affidavits

If a second or subsequent power of attorney is created under section 3109.52 of the Revised Code regarding a child who is the subject of a prior power of attorney or a second or subsequent caretaker authorization affidavit is executed under section 3109.67 of the Revised Code regarding a child who is the subject of a prior affidavit, the person who creates the power of attorney or executes the affidavit must file it with the juvenile court of the county in which the grandparent designated as attorney in fact or the grandparent who executed the affidavit resides or with any other court that has jurisdiction over the child under a previously filed motion or proceeding.

(2004 H 130, eff. 7–20–04)

Library References

Parent and Child ⇐15.
Powers ⇐10.
Westlaw Topic Nos. 285, 307.
C.J.S. Parent and Child §§ 345 to 350, 357 to 358.
C.J.S. Powers § 9.

3109.77 Hearing; notice; de novo review

(A) On the filing of a power of attorney or caretaker authorization affidavit under section 3109.76 of the Revised Code, the court in which the power of attorney or caretaker authorization affidavit was filed shall schedule a hearing to determine whether the power of attorney or affidavit is in the child's best interest. The court shall provide notice of the date, time, and location of the hearing to the parties and to the parent who is not the residential parent and legal custodian unless one of the following circumstances applies:

(1) In accordance with section 3109.051 of the Revised Code, that parent is not to be given a notice of relocation.

(2) The parent's parental rights have been terminated by order of a juvenile court pursuant to Chapter 2151. of the Revised Code.

(3) The parent cannot be located with reasonable efforts.

(4) The power of attorney was created by both parents.

(B) The hearing shall be held not later than ten days after the date the power of attorney or affidavit was filed with the court. At the hearing, the parties and the parent who is not the residential parent and legal custodian may present evidence and be represented by counsel.

(C) At the conclusion of the hearing, the court may take any of the following actions that the court determines is in the child's best interest:

(1) Approve the power of attorney or affidavit. If approved, the power of attorney or affidavit shall remain in effect unless otherwise terminated under section 3109.59 of the Revised Code with respect to a power of attorney or section 3109.70 of the Revised Code with respect to an affidavit.

(2) Issue an order terminating the power of attorney or affidavit and ordering the child returned to the child's parent, guardian, or custodian. If the parent, guardian, or custodian of the child cannot be located, the court shall treat the filing of the power of attorney or affidavit with the court as a complaint under section 2151.27 of the Revised Code that the child is a dependent child.

(3) Treat the filing of the power of attorney or affidavit as a petition for legal custody and award legal custody of the child to the grandparent designated as the attorney in fact under the power of attorney or to the grandparent who executed the affidavit.

(D) The court shall conduct a de novo review of any order issued under division (C) of this section if all of the following apply regarding the parent who is not the residential parent and legal custodian:

(1) The parent did not appear at the hearing from which the order was issued.

(2) The parent was not represented by counsel at the hearing.

(3) The parent filed a motion with the court not later than fourteen days after receiving notice of the hearing pursuant to division (A) of this section.

(2004 H 130, eff. 7–20–04)

Library References

Parent and Child ⇐15.
Powers ⇐10.
Westlaw Topic Nos. 285, 307.
C.J.S. Parent and Child §§ 345 to 350, 357 to 358.
C.J.S. Powers § 9.

3109.78 Creation of power of attorney or affidavit for participation in academic or interscholastic programs prohibited

(A) No person shall create a power of attorney under section 3109.52 of the Revised Code or execute a caretaker authorization affidavit under section 3109.67 of the Revised Code for the purpose of enrolling the child in a school or school district so that the child may participate in the academic or interscholastic athletic programs provided by the school or school district.

(B) A person who violates division (A) of this section is in violation of section 2921.13 of the Revised Code and is guilty of falsification, a misdemeanor of the first degree.

(C) A power of attorney created, or an affidavit executed, in violation of this section is void as of the date of its creation or execution.

(2004 H 130, eff. 7–20–04)

Library References

Parent and Child ⇐15.
Powers ⇐5.
Westlaw Topic Nos. 285, 307.
C.J.S. Parent and Child §§ 345 to 350, 357 to 358.
C.J.S. Powers § 2.

3109.79 Effect of power of attorney or affidavit on administrative or court child support order

As used in this section, "administrative child support order" and "court child support order" have the same meanings as in section 3119.01 of the Revised Code.

A power of attorney created under section 3109.52 of the Revised Code or a caretaker authorization affidavit executed under section 3109.67 of the Revised Code shall not affect the enforcement of an administrative child support order or court child support order, unless a child support enforcement agency, with respect to an administrative child support order, or a court, with respect to either order, issues an order providing otherwise.

(2004 H 130, eff. 7–20–04)

Library References

Child Support ⇐440, 465.
Westlaw Topic No. 76E.
C.J.S. Parent and Child §§ 175, 236, 239 to 240.

3109.80 Only one power of attorney or affidavit in effect per child

Only one power of attorney created under section 3109.52 of the Revised Code or one caretaker authorization executed under section 3109.67 of the Revised Code may be in effect for a child at one time.

(2004 H 130, eff. 7–20–04)

Library References

Parent and Child ⇐15.

Powers ⚖︎10.
Westlaw Topic Nos. 285, 307.

C.J.S. Parent and Child §§ 345 to 350, 357 to 358.
C.J.S. Powers § 9.

CHAPTER 3111

PARENTAGE

PRELIMINARY PROVISIONS

Section	
3111.01	Definition
3111.02	Parent and child relationship; how established; reciprocity
3111.03	Presumptions as to father and child relationship

PRACTICE AND PROCEDURE

Section	
3111.04	Action to determine father and child relationship
3111.05	Limitation of action
3111.06	Jurisdiction
3111.07	Necessary parties; intervenors
3111.08	Civil nature of action to establish father and child relationship; judgment; default judgment
3111.09	Genetic tests and DNA records
3111.10	Admissible evidence
3111.11	Pretrial procedures
3111.111	Temporary support order pending action objecting to parentage determination
3111.12	Testimony; admissibility of genetic test results or DNA records
3111.13	Effects of judgment; support orders; contempt; prohibitions on certain arrearages
3111.14	Fees for experts; court costs
3111.15	Enforcement of support order
3111.16	Continuing jurisdiction
3111.17	Action to determine mother and child relationship
3111.18	New birth record
3111.19	Interference with parentage action

ACKNOWLEDGMENT OF PATERNITY

Section	
3111.20	Birth record
3111.21	Signing and notarizing of acknowledgment
3111.22	Signed and notarized acknowledgment of paternity to be sent to office of child support
3111.23	Acknowledgment of paternity
3111.24	Examination of acknowledgment; return of incorrect acknowledgment; entry of acknowledgment information into birth registry
3111.25	Final and enforceable acknowledgment
3111.26	Effect of final and enforceable acknowledgment
3111.27	Rescission of acknowledgment
3111.28	Rescission of acknowledgment for fraud, duress, or material mistake of fact
3111.29	Complaint for child support
3111.30	Department of health to receive notice of acknowledgment; preparation of new birth certificate consistent with acknowledgment
3111.31	Acknowledgment of paternity affidavit
3111.32	Pamphlets
3111.33	Availability of pamphlets and acknowledgment of paternity affidavits
3111.34	Rules specifying additional evidence for new birth certificate
3111.35	Rules

ADMINISTRATIVE DETERMINATION OF EXISTENCE OR NONEXISTENCE OF PARENT AND CHILD RELATIONSHIP

Section	
3111.38	Existence or nonexistence of parent and child relationship
3111.381	Requirements to bring action; jurisdiction
3111.39	Multiple requests for determination of existence or nonexistence of parent and child relationship

Section	
3111.40	Contents of request for administrative determination of existence or nonexistence of parent and child relationship
3111.41	Administrative office to consider request; order; genetic tests
3111.42	Notice to accompany order for genetic testing; contents
3111.421	Rules of civil procedure to apply
3111.43	Notice of request to determine existence or nonexistence of parent and child relationship
3111.44	Conference; genetic testing
3111.45	Qualified examiner to conduct genetic testing; report of test results
3111.46	Duties of administrative officer upon receipt of test results
3111.47	Failure to submit to genetic testing
3111.48	Notice of right to bring actions
3111.49	Objection to administrative order; finality of order
3111.50	Inconclusive administrative orders; action to establish parent and child relationship
3111.51	Contents of administrative orders; exceptions
3111.52	Change of child's surname
3111.53	Administrative officers
3111.54	Finding of contempt
3111.58	Preparation of new birth record pursuant to determination of parent and child relationship
3111.61	Collection of samples and genetic testing
3111.611	Rules governing establishment of on-site genetic testing programs

BIRTH REGISTRY AND PUTATIVE FATHER REGISTRY

Section	
3111.64	Birth registry
3111.65	Maintenance and accessibility of birth registry
3111.66	Filing of orders
3111.67	Rules for birth registry
3111.69	Examining putative father registry

MISCELLANEOUS PROVISIONS

Section	
3111.71	Contracts with local hospitals for staff to meet with certain unmarried women
3111.72	Requirements of contract
3111.73	Reports
3111.74	Requirements when presumed father is not man who signed or is attempting to sign acknowledgment

PARENTAL SUPPORT

Section	
3111.77	Duty of parental support
3111.78	Actions permitted to require man to pay support and provide for health care needs
3111.80	Administrative hearings
3111.81	Administrative order for payment of support and provision for child's health care
3111.82	Party may raise existence or nonexistence of relationship
3111.821	Determination of existence of parent and child relationship
3111.83	Registration of order
3111.831	Development of system and procedure for safekeeping and retrieval of orders
3111.832	Fee not to be charged
3111.84	Action for payment of support and provision for child's health care

Section

3111.85 Effect of support orders issued under former R.C. 3111.21 prior to January 1, 1998

NON–SPOUSAL ARTIFICIAL INSEMINATION

3111.88 Definitions
3111.89 Sections applicable to non-spousal artificial insemination
3111.90 Supervision by physician
3111.91 Fresh semen; frozen semen; medical history of donor; laboratory studies
3111.92 Consents to non-spousal insemination of married woman
3111.93 Recipient information and statements; date of insemination to be recorded
3111.94 Physician's files; confidential information; donor information; action for file inspection
3111.95 Husband rather than donor regarded as natural father of child
3111.96 Effect of physician's failure to comply with statutes

EMBRYO DONATION

3111.97 Birth mother regarded as natural mother; effect of husband's consent

PENALTIES

3111.99 Penalties

Comparative Laws
Uniform Parentage Act
Table of Jurisdictions Wherein Act Has Been Adopted.

For text of Uniform Act, and variation notes and annotation materials for adopting jurisdictions, see Uniform Laws Annotated, Master Edition, Volume 9B.

Jurisdiction	Statutory Citation
Alabama	Code 1975, § 26–17–1 to 26–17–22.
California	West's Ann.Cal.Fam. Code, § 7600 to 7730.
Colorado	West's C.R.S.A. § 19–4–101 to 19–4–130.
Hawaii	HRS § 584–1 to 584–26.
Illinois	S.H.A. 750 ILCS 45/1 to 45/27.
Kansas	K.S.A. 38–1110 to 38–1138.
Minnesota	M.S.A. § 257.51 to 257.75.
Missouri	V.A.M.S. § 210.817 to 210.853.
Montana	MCA 40–6–101 to 40–6–135.
Nevada	N.R.S. 126.011 to 126.371.
New Jersey	N.J.S.A. 9:17–38 to 9:17–59.
New Mexico	NMSA 1978 § 40–11–1 to 40–11–23.
North Dakota	NDCC 14–20–01 to 14–20–66.
Rhode Island	Gen. Laws 1956, § 15–8–1 to 15–8–28.

PRELIMINARY PROVISIONS

3111.01 Definition

(A) As used in sections 3111.01 to 3111.85 of the Revised Code, "parent and child relationship" means the legal relationship that exists between a child and the child's natural or adoptive parents and upon which those sections and any other provision of the Revised Code confer or impose rights, privileges, duties, and obligations. The "parent and child relationship" includes the mother and child relationship and the father and child relationship.

(B) The parent and child relationship extends equally to all children and all parents, regardless of the marital status of the parents.

(2000 S 180, eff. 3–22–01; 1992 S 10, eff. 7–15–92; 1986 H 476; 1982 H 245)

Uncodified Law

1992 S 10, § 5, eff. 7–15–92, reads, in part: Sections 3111.01 to 3111.19 of the Revised Code, as enacted or amended by this act, shall apply only to an action brought under sections 3111.01 to 3111.19 of the Revised Code on or after the effective date of this act.

1982 H 245, § 3: See Uncodified Law under 3111.04.

Historical and Statutory Notes

Ed. Note: Former 3111.01 repealed by 1982 H 245, eff. 6–29–82; 1975 S 145; 127 v 1039; 1953 H 1; GC 8006–1; Source—GC 12110.

Pre–1953 H 1 Amendments: 124 v S 65

Amendment Note: 2000 S 180 substituted "3111.85" for "3111.01" in division (A).

Library References

Children Out-of-Wedlock ⚖1.
Parent and Child ⚖1.
Westlaw Topic Nos. 285, 76H.
C.J.S. Children Out-of-Wedlock §§ 2 to 11.
C.J.S. Parent and Child §§ 1 to 12, 201.

3111.02 Parent and child relationship; how established; reciprocity

(A) The parent and child relationship between a child and the child's natural mother may be established by proof of her having given birth to the child or pursuant to sections 3111.01 to 3111.18 or 3111.20 to 3111.85 of the Revised Code. The parent and child relationship between a child and the natural father of the child may be established by an acknowledgment of paternity as provided in sections 3111.20 to 3111.35 of the Revised Code, and pursuant to sections 3111.01 to 3111.18 or 3111.38 to 3111.54 of the Revised Code. The parent and child relationship between a child and the adoptive parent of the child may be established by proof of adoption or pursuant to Chapter 3107. of the Revised Code.

(B) A court that is determining a parent and child relationship pursuant to this chapter shall give full faith and credit to a parentage determination made under the laws of this state or another state, regardless of whether the parentage determination was made pursuant to a voluntary acknowledgement of paternity, an administrative procedure, or a court proceeding.

(2000 S 180, eff. 3–22–01; 1997 H 352, eff. 1–1–98; 1994 S 355, eff. 12–9–94; 1992 S 10, eff. 7–15–92; 1986 H 476; 1982 H 245)

Uncodified Law

1994 S 355, § 5: See Uncodified Law under 3111.08.
1992 S 10, § 5: See Uncodified Law under 3111.01.
1982 H 245, § 3: See Uncodified Law under 3111.04.

Historical and Statutory Notes

Ed. Note: Former 3111.02 repealed by 1982 H 245, eff. 6–29–82; 127 v 1039; 1953 H 1; GC 8006–2; Source—GC 12125; see now 3111.04 for provisions analogous to former 3111.02.

Pre–1953 H 1 Amendments: 124 v S 65

Amendment Note: 2000 S 180 rewrote division (A) which prior thereto read:

"(A) The parent and child relationship between a child and the child's natural mother may be established by proof of her having given birth to the child or pursuant to sections 3111.01 to 3111.19 or 3111.20 to 3111.29 of the Revised Code. The parent and child relationship between a child and the natural father of the child may be established by an acknowledgment of paternity as provided in section 5101.314 of the Revised Code, and pursuant to sections 3111.01 to 3111.19 or 3111.20 to 3111.29 of the Revised Code. The parent and child relationship between a child and the adoptive parent of the child may be established by proof of adoption or pursuant to Chapter 3107. of the Revised Code."

Amendment Note: 1997 H 352 substituted "an acknowledgment of paternity" for "a probate court entering an acknowledgment upon its journal" and "5101.314" for "2105.18" in division (A).

Amendment Note: 1994 S 355 designated division (A) and added division (B).

Library References

Adoption ⇌17 to 18.
Children Out-of-Wedlock ⇌1, 12, 30 to 75.
Judgment ⇌815.
Westlaw Topic Nos. 17, 228, 76H.
C.J.S. Adoption of Persons §§ 6, 136, 146 to 150.
C.J.S. Children Out-of-Wedlock §§ 2 to 11, 23, 25, 41, 46 to 52, 66, 70 to 141.
C.J.S. Judgments §§ 965 to 979.

3111.03 Presumptions as to father and child relationship

(A) A man is presumed to be the natural father of a child under any of the following circumstances:

(1) The man and the child's mother are or have been married to each other, and the child is born during the marriage or is born within three hundred days after the marriage is terminated by death, annulment, divorce, or dissolution or after the man and the child's mother separate pursuant to a separation agreement.

(2) The man and the child's mother attempted, before the child's birth, to marry each other by a marriage that was solemnized in apparent compliance with the law of the state in which the marriage took place, the marriage is or could be declared invalid, and either of the following applies:

(a) The marriage can only be declared invalid by a court and the child is born during the marriage or within three hundred days after the termination of the marriage by death, annulment, divorce, or dissolution;

(b) The attempted marriage is invalid without a court order and the child is born within three hundred days after the termination of cohabitation.

(3) An acknowledgment of paternity has been filed pursuant to section 3111.23 or former section 5101.314 of the Revised Code and has not become final under former section 3111.211 or 5101.314 or section 2151.232, 3111.25, or 3111.821 of the Revised Code.

(B) A presumption that arises under this section can only be rebutted by clear and convincing evidence that includes the results of genetic testing, except that a presumption that is conclusive as provided in division (A) of section 3111.95 or division (B) of section 3111.97 of the Revised Code cannot be rebutted. An acknowledgment of paternity that becomes final under section 2151.232, 3111.25, or 3111.821 of the Revised Code is not a presumption and shall be considered a final and enforceable determination of paternity unless the acknowledgment is rescinded under section 3111.28 or 3119.962 of the Revised Code. If two or more conflicting presumptions arise under this section, the court shall determine, based upon logic and policy considerations, which presumption controls.

(C)(1) Except as provided in division (C)(2) of this section, a presumption of paternity that arose pursuant to this section prior to March 22, 2001, shall remain valid on and after that date unless rebutted pursuant to division (B) of this section. This division does not apply to a determination described in division (B)(3) of this section as division (B)(3) of this section existed prior to March 22, 2001.

(2) A presumption of paternity that arose prior to March 22, 2001, based on an acknowledgment of paternity that became final under former section 3111.211 or 5101.314 or section 2151.232 of the Revised Code is not a presumption and shall be considered a final and enforceable determination of paternity unless the acknowledgment is rescinded under section 3111.28 or 3119.962 of the Revised Code.

(2006 H 102, eff. 6–15–06; 2000 S 180, eff. 3–22–01; 1999 H 471, eff. 7–1–00; 1997 H 352, eff. 1–1–98; 1992 S 10, eff. 7–15–92; 1990 S 3; 1988 H 790; 1986 H 476; 1982 H 245)

Uncodified Law

1992 S 10, § 5: See Uncodified Law under 3111.01.

1982 H 245, § 3: See Uncodified Law under 3111.04.

Historical and Statutory Notes

Ed. Note: 3111.03 contains provisions analogous to former 3105.13 and 3105.33, repealed by 1982 H 245, eff. 6–29–82.

Ed. Note: Former 3111.03 repealed by 1982 H 245, eff. 6–29–82; 1953 H 1; GC 8006–3; Source—GC 12134; see now 3111.04 for provisions analogous to former 3111.03.

Pre–1953 H 1 Amendments: 124 v S 65

Amendment Note: 2006 H 102 inserted "or division (B) of section 3111.97" in division (B); and substituted "March 22, 2001," for "the effective date of this amendment" in division (C).

Amendment Note: 2000 S 180 rewrote this section which prior thereto read:

"(A) A man is presumed to be the natural father of a child under any of the following circumstances:

"(1) The man and the child's mother are or have been married to each other, and the child is born during the marriage or is born within three hundred days after the marriage is terminated by death, annulment, divorce, or dissolution or after the man and the child's mother separate pursuant to a separation agreement.

"(2) The man and the child's mother attempted, before the child's birth, to marry each other by a marriage that was solemnized in apparent compliance with the law of the state in which the marriage took place, the marriage is or could be declared invalid, and either of the following applies:

"(a) The marriage can only be declared invalid by a court and the child is born during the marriage or within three hundred days after the termination of the marriage by death, annulment, divorce, or dissolution;

"(b) The attempted marriage is invalid without a court order and the child is born within three hundred days after the termination of cohabitation.

"(3) The man and the child's mother, after the child's birth, married or attempted to marry each other by a marriage solemnized in apparent compliance with the law of the state in which the marriage took place, and either of the following occurs:

"(a) The man has acknowledged his paternity of the child in a writing sworn to before a notary public;

"(b) The man is required to support the child by a written voluntary promise or by a court order.

"(4) An acknowledgment of paternity filed with the division of child support in the department of job and family services becomes final pursuant to section 2151.232, 3111.211, or 5101.314 of the Revised Code.

"(5) A court or administrative body, pursuant to section 3111.09, 3111.22, or 3115.52 of the Revised Code or otherwise, has ordered that genetic tests be conducted on the natural mother and alleged natural father voluntarily agreed to genetic testing pursuant to former section 3111.21 of the Revised Code to determine the father and child relationship and the results of the genetic tests indicate a probability of ninety-nine per cent or greater that the man is the biological father of the child.

"(B)(1) A presumption arises under division (A)(3) of this section regardless of the validity or invalidity of the marriage of the parents. A presumption that arises under this section can only be rebutted by clear and convincing evidence that includes the results of genetic testing, except that a presumption that arises under division (A)(1) or (2) of this section is conclusive as provided in division (A) of section 3111.37 of the Revised Code and cannot be rebutted. If two or more conflicting presumptions arise under this section, the court shall determine, based upon logic and policy considerations, which presumption controls. If a determination described in division (B)(3) of this section conflicts with a presumption that arises under this section the determination is controlling.

"(2) Notwithstanding division (B)(1) of this section, a presumption that arises under division (A)(4) of this section may only be rebutted as provided in division (B)(2) of section 5101.314 of the Revised Code.

"(3) Notwithstanding division (A)(5) of this section, a final and enforceable determination finding the existence of a father and child relationship pursuant to former section 3111.21 or section 3111.22 of the Revised Code that is based on the results of genetic tests ordered pursuant to either of those sections, is not a presumption.

"(C) A presumption of paternity that arose pursuant to this section prior to January 1, 1998, shall remain valid on and after that date unless rebutted pursuant to division (B) of this section. This division does not apply to a determination described in division (B)(3) of this section."

Amendment Note: 1999 H 471 substituted "job and family" for "human" in division (A)(4); and substituted "January 1, 1998" for "the effective date of this amendment" in division (C).

Amendment Note: 1997 H 352 deleted former division (A)(3)(b); redesignated former division (A)(3)(c) as new division (A)(3)(b); deleted former division (A)(4); redesignated former divisions (A)(5) and (A)(6) as new divisions (A)(4) and (A)(5) and rewrote those divisions; designated division (B)(1) and added the fourth sentence therein; added divisions (B)(2), (B)(3), and (C); and made other nonsubstantive changes. Prior to amendment, former divisions (A)(3)(b) and (A)(4) through (A)(6) read:

"(b) The man, with his consent, is named as the child's father on the child's birth certificate;"

"(4) The man, with his consent, signs the child's birth certificate as an informant as provided in section 3705.09 of the Revised Code."

"(5) A court enters upon its journal an acknowledgment of paternity pursuant to section 2105.18 of the Revised Code.

"(6) A court or administrative body, pursuant to section 3111.09 or 3115.24 of the Revised Code or otherwise, has ordered that genetic tests be conducted or the natural mother and alleged natural father voluntarily agreed to genetic testing pursuant to section 3111.21 or 3111.22 of the Revised Code to determine the father and child relationship and the results of the genetic tests indicate a probability of ninety-five per cent or greater that the man is the biological father of the child."

Library References

Children Out-of-Wedlock ⇌3, 43.
Westlaw Topic No. 76H.
C.J.S. Children Out-of-Wedlock §§ 13 to 17, 51, 99 to 100.

PRACTICE AND PROCEDURE

3111.04 Action to determine father and child relationship

(A) An action to determine the existence or nonexistence of the father and child relationship may be brought by the child or the child's personal representative, the child's mother or her personal representative, a man alleged or alleging himself to be the child's father, the child support enforcement agency of the county in which the child resides if the child's mother, father, or alleged father is a recipient of public assistance or of services under Title IV–D of the "Social Security Act," 88 Stat. 2351 (1975), 42 U.S.C.A. 651, as amended, or the alleged father's personal representative.

(B) An agreement does not bar an action under this section.

(C) If an action under this section is brought before the birth of the child and if the action is contested, all proceedings, except service of process and the taking of depositions to perpetuate testimony, may be stayed until after the birth.

(D) A recipient of public assistance or of services under Title IV–D of the "Social Security Act," 88 Stat. 2351 (1975), 42 U.S.C.A. 651, as amended, shall cooperate with the child support enforcement agency of the county in which a child resides to obtain an administrative determination pursuant to sections 3111.38 to 3111.54 of the Revised Code, or, if necessary, a court determination pursuant to sections 3111.01 to 3111.18 of the Revised Code, of the existence or nonexistence of a parent and child relationship between the father and the child. If the recipient fails to cooperate, the agency may commence an action to determine the existence or nonexistence of a parent and child relationship between the father and the child pursuant to sections 3111.01 to 3111.18 of the Revised Code.

(E) As used in this section, "public assistance" means medical assistance under Chapter 5111. of the Revised Code, assistance under Chapter 5107. of the Revised Code, disability financial assistance under Chapter 5115. of the Revised Code, or disability medical assistance under Chapter 5115. of the Revised Code.

(2006 H 136, eff. 5–17–06; 2003 H 95, eff. 6–26–03; 2000 S 180, eff. 3–22–01; 1997 H 352, eff. 1–1–98; 1992 S 10, eff. 7–15–92; 1982 H 245)

Uncodified Law

1992 S 10, § 5: See Uncodified Law under 3111.01.

1982 H 245, § 3, eff. 6–29–82, reads: An action may be commenced pursuant to sections 3111.01 to 3111.19 of the Revised Code, as enacted by Section 1 of this act, to establish the father and child relationship, or the mother and child relationship, irrespective of whether a child is born prior to, or on or after, the effective date of this act.

Historical and Statutory Notes

Ed. Note: Former 3111.04 repealed by 1982 H 245, eff. 6–29–82; 127 v 1039; 125 v 184; 1953 H 1; GC 8006–4; Source—GC 12111. 3111.04 contains provisions analogous to former 3111.02 and 3111.03, repealed by 1982 H 245, eff. 6–29–82.

Pre–1953 H 1 Amendments: 124 v S 65

Amendment Note: 2006 H 136 inserted ", father, or alleged father" in division (A).

Amendment Note: 2003 H 95 substituted "disability financial assistance" for "or disability assistance", and inserted ", or disability medical assistance under Chapter 5115. of the Revised Code", in Subdivision (E).

Amendment Note: 2000 S 180 substituted "sections 3111.38 to 3111.54" for "section 3111.22" and "3111.18" for "3111.19" twice in division (D).

Amendment Note: 1997 H 352 rewrote this section, which prior thereto read:

"(A) An action to determine the existence or nonexistence of the father and child relationship may be brought by the child or the child's personal representative, the child's mother or her personal representative, a man alleged or alleging himself to be the child's father, the child support enforcement agency of the county in which the child resides if the child's mother is a recipient of public assistance as defined in section 2301.351 of the Revised Code or of services under Title IV–D of the "Social Security Act," 88 Stat. 2351 (1975), 42 U.S.C.A. 651, as amended, or the alleged father's personal representative.

"(B) An agreement does not bar an action under this section.

"(C) If an action under this section is brought before the birth of the child and if the action is contested, all proceedings, except service of process and the taking of depositions to perpetuate testimony, may be stayed until after the birth.

"(D) A recipient of public assistance as defined in section 2301.351 of the Revised Code or of services under Title IV–D of the "Social Security Act," 88 Stat. 2351 (1975), 42 U.S.C.A. 651, as amended, shall request the child support enforcement agency of the county in which a child resides to make an administrative determination of the existence or nonexistence of a parent and child relationship between the father and the child pursuant to section 3111.22 of the Revised Code before the recipient commences an action to determine the existence or nonexistence of that parent and child relationship."

Library References

Children Out-of-Wedlock ⟐30, 33 to 34.
Social Security and Public Welfare ⟐4.16.
Westlaw Topic Nos. 356A, 76H.
C.J.S. Children Out-of-Wedlock §§ 46, 49, 70, 77 to 80, 85 to 90.
C.J.S. Social Security and Public Welfare §§ 28 to 33, 52 to 53.

3111.05 Limitation of action

An action to determine the existence or nonexistence of the father and child relationship may not be brought later than five years after the child reaches the age of eighteen. Neither section 3111.04 of the Revised Code nor this section extends the time within which a right of inheritance or a right to a succession may be asserted beyond the time provided by Chapter 2105., 2107., 2113., 2117., or 2123. of the Revised Code.

(1982 H 245, eff. 6–29–82)

Uncodified Law

1992 S 10, § 5: See Uncodified Law under 3111.01.

1982 H 245, § 3: See Uncodified Law under 3111.04.

Historical and Statutory Notes

Ed. Note: Former 3111.05 repealed by 1982 H 245, eff. 6–29–82; 127 v 1039; 125 v 184; 1953 H 1; GC 8006–5; Source—GC 12112.

Pre–1953 H 1 Amendments: 124 v S 65

Library References

Children Out-of-Wedlock ⟐38.
Westlaw Topic No. 76H.
C.J.S. Children Out-of-Wedlock §§ 48, 66, 81 to 82.

3111.06 Jurisdiction

(A) Except as otherwise provided in division (B) or (C) of section 3111.381 of the Revised Code, an action authorized under sections 3111.01 to 3111.18 of the Revised Code may be brought in the juvenile court or other court with jurisdiction under section 2101.022 or 2301.03 of the Revised Code of the county in which the child, the child's mother, or the alleged father resides or is found or, if the alleged father is deceased, of the county in which proceedings for the probate of the alleged father's estate have been or can be commenced, or of the county in which the child is being provided support by the county department of job and family services of that county. An action pursuant to sections 3111.01 to 3111.18 of the Revised Code to object to an administrative order issued pursuant to former section 3111.21 or 3111.22 or sections 3111.38 to 3111.54 of the Revised Code determining the existence or nonexistence of a parent and child relationship that has not become final and enforceable, may be brought only in the juvenile court or other court with jurisdiction of the county in which the child support enforcement agency that issued the order is located. If an action for divorce, dissolution, or legal separation has been filed in a court of common pleas, that court of common pleas has original jurisdiction to determine if the parent and child relationship exists between one or both of the parties and any child alleged or presumed to be the child of one or both of the parties.

(B) A person who has sexual intercourse in this state submits to the jurisdiction of the courts of this state as to an action brought under sections 3111.01 to 3111.18 of the Revised Code with respect to a child who may have been conceived by that act of intercourse. In addition to any other method provided by the Rules of Civil Procedure, personal jurisdiction may be acquired by personal service of summons outside this state or by certified mail with proof of actual receipt.

(2006 H 136, eff. 5–17–06; 2000 S 180, eff. 3–22–01; 1999 H 471, eff. 7–1–00; 1997 H 352, eff. 1–1–98; 1990 H 514, eff. 1–1–91; 1986 H 476; 1982 H 245)

Uncodified Law

1992 S 10, § 5: See Uncodified Law under 3111.01.

1982 H 245, § 3: See Uncodified Law under 3111.04.

Historical and Statutory Notes

Ed. Note: Former 3111.06 repealed by 1982 H 245, eff. 6–29–82; 127 v 1039; 125 v 184; 1953 H 1; GC 8006–6; Source—GC 12113. 3111.06 contains provisions analogous to former 3111.08, repealed by 1982 H 245, eff. 6–29–82.

Pre–1953 H 1 Amendments: 124 v S 65

Amendment Note: 2006 H 136 substituted "Except as otherwise provided in division (B) or (C) of section 3111.381 of the Revised Code, an" for "An" in the first sentence of division (A).

Amendment Note: 2000 S 180 rewrote division (A) and substituted "3111.18" for "3111.19" in division (B). Prior to amendment division (A) read:

"(A) The juvenile court has original jurisdiction of any action authorized under sections 3111.01 to 3111.19 of the Revised Code. An action may be brought under those sections in the juvenile court of the county in which the child, the child's mother, or the alleged father resides or is found or, if the alleged father is deceased, of the county in which proceedings for the probate of the alleged father's estate have been or can be commenced, or of the county in which the child is being provided support by the county department of job and family services of that county. An action pursuant to sections 3111.01 to 3111.19 of the Revised Code to object to an administrative order issued pursuant to former section 3111.21 or section 3111.22 of the Revised Code determining the existence or nonexistence of a parent and child relationship that has not become final and enforceable, may be brought only in the juvenile court of the county in which the child support enforcement agency that issued the order is located. If an action for divorce, dissolution, or legal separation has been filed in a court of common pleas, that court of common pleas has original jurisdiction to determine if the parent and child relationship exists between one or both of the parties and any child alleged or presumed to be the child of one or both of the parties."

Amendment Note: 1999 H 471 substituted "county department of job and family services" for "department of human services" in division (A).

Amendment Note: 1997 H 352 added the third sentence in division (A); and made changes to reflect gender neutral language.

Library References

Children Out-of-Wedlock ⟐36.
Westlaw Topic No. 76H.
C.J.S. Children Out-of-Wedlock §§ 47, 83.

3111.07 Necessary parties; intervenors

(A) The natural mother, each man presumed to be the father under section 3111.03 of the Revised Code, and each man alleged to be the natural father shall be made parties to the action brought pursuant to sections 3111.01 to 3111.18 of the Revised Code or, if not subject to the jurisdiction of the court, shall be given notice of the action pursuant to the Rules of Civil Procedure and shall be given an opportunity to be heard. The child support enforcement agency of the county in which the action is brought also shall be given notice of the action pursuant to the Rules of Civil Procedure and shall be given an opportunity to be heard. The court may align the parties. The child shall be made a party to the action unless a party shows good cause for not doing so. Separate counsel shall be appointed for the child if the court finds that the child's interests conflict with those of the mother.

If the person bringing the action knows that a particular man is not or, based upon the facts and circumstances present, could not be the natural father of the child, the person bringing the action shall not allege in the action that the man is the natural father of the child and shall not make the man a party to the action.

(B) If an action is brought pursuant to sections 3111.01 to 3111.18 of the Revised Code and the child to whom the action pertains is or was being provided support by the department of job and family services, a county department of job and family services, or another public agency, the department, county department, or agency may intervene for purposes of collecting or recovering the support.

(2006 H 136, eff. 5–17–06; 2000 S 180, eff. 3–22–01; 1999 H 471, eff. 7–1–00; 1997 H 352, eff. 1–1–98; 1992 S 10, eff. 7–15–92; 1990 H 591; 1986 H 428, H 476; 1982 H 245)

Uncodified Law

1992 S 10, § 5: See Uncodified Law under 3111.01.

1982 H 245, § 3: See Uncodified Law under 3111.04.

Historical and Statutory Notes

Ed. Note: Former 3111.07 repealed by 1982 H 245, eff. 6–29–82; 127 v 1039; 125 v 184; 1953 H 1; GC 8006–7; Source—GC 12114; see now 3111.19 for provisions analogous to former 3111.07.

Pre–1953 H 1 Amendments: 124 v S 65

Amendment Note: 2006 H 136 rewrote the first paragraph of division (A) which prior thereto read:

"(A) The natural mother, each man presumed to be the father under section 3111.03 of the Revised Code, each man alleged to be the natural father, and, if the party who initiates the action is a recipient of public assistance as defined in section 3111.04 of the Revised Code or if the responsibility for the collection of support for the child who is the subject of the action has been assumed by the child support enforcement agency under Title IV–D of the "Social Security Act," 88 Stat. 2351 (1975), 42 U.S.C.A. 651, as amended, the child support enforcement agency of the county in which the child resides shall be made parties to the action brought pursuant to sections 3111.01 to 3111.18 of the Revised Code or, if not subject to the jurisdiction of the court, shall be given notice of the action pursuant to the Rules of Civil Procedure and shall be given an opportunity to be heard. The court may align the parties. The child shall be made a party to the action unless a party shows good cause for not doing so. Separate counsel shall be appointed for the child if the court finds that the child's interests conflict with those of the mother."

Amendment Note: 2000 S 180 substituted "3111.18" for "3111.19" in divisions (A) and (B).

Amendment Note: 1999 H 471 substituted "job and family" for "human" twice in division (B).

Amendment Note: 1997 H 352 substituted "3111.04" for "2301.351" in the first paragraph in division (A).

Library References

Children Out-of-Wedlock ⚖30, 34.
Westlaw Topic No. 76H.
C.J.S. Children Out-of-Wedlock §§ 46, 49, 70, 85 to 90.
Baldwin's Ohio Legislative Service, 1990 Laws of Ohio, H 591—LSC Analysis, p 5–576

3111.08 Civil nature of action to establish father and child relationship; judgment; default judgment

(A) An action brought pursuant to sections 3111.01 to 3111.18 of the Revised Code to declare the existence or nonexistence of the father and child relationship is a civil action and shall be governed by the Rules of Civil Procedure unless a different procedure is specifically provided by those sections.

(B) If an action is brought against a person to declare the existence or nonexistence of the father and child relationship between that person and a child and the person in his answer admits the existence or nonexistence of the father and child relationship as alleged in the action, the court shall enter judgment in accordance with section 3111.13 of the Revised Code. If the person against whom the action is brought fails to plead or otherwise defend against the action, the opposing party may make an oral or written motion for default judgment pursuant to the Rules of Civil Procedure. The court shall render a judgment by default against the person after hearing satisfactory evidence of the truth of the statements in the complaint.

(2000 S 180, eff. 3–22–01; 1994 S 355, eff. 12–9–94; 1992 S 10, eff. 7–15–92; 1990 H 591; 1986 H 476; 1982 H 245)

Uncodified Law

1994 S 355, § 5, eff. 12–9–94, reads: The provisions of this act that apply to actions brought under Chapter 3111. of the Revised Code to determine paternity apply only to actions initiated on or after the effective date of this act.

1992 S 10, § 5: See Uncodified Law under 3111.01.

1982 H 245, § 3: See Uncodified Law under 3111.04.

Historical and Statutory Notes

Ed. Note: Former 3111.08 repealed by 1982 H 245, eff. 6–29–82; 1976 H 390; 127 v 1039; 1953 H 1; GC 8006–8; Source—GC 12115; see now 3111.06 for provisions analogous to former 3111.08.

Pre–1953 H 1 Amendments: 124 v S 65

Amendment Note: 2000 S 180 substituted "3111.18" for "3111.19" in division (A).

Amendment Note: 1994 S 355 rewrote division (B), which previously read:

"(B) If an action is brought against a person to declare the existence or nonexistence of the father and child relationship between that person and a child and the person in his answer admits the existence or nonexistence of the father and child relationship as alleged in the action, the court shall enter judgment in accordance with section 3111.13 of the Revised Code. If the person against whom the action is brought does not admit the existence or nonexistence of the father and child relationship, the court, upon its own motion, may order, and, upon the motion of any party to the action, shall order genetic tests to be taken in accordance with section 3111.09 of the Revised Code. If genetic tests are ordered upon the motion of a party or the court, the court shall order that the child's mother, the child, the alleged father, and any other defendant submit to the genetic tests in accordance with section 3111.09 of the Revised Code. A willful failure to submit to genetic tests as ordered by the court is contempt of court. If the person against whom the action is brought does not appear personally or by counsel at a pretrial hearing scheduled under section 3111.11 of the Revised Code, the opposing party may file a written motion for default judgment against the person. The motion, along with a notice of the date and time when it is to be heard, shall be served upon the person in the same manner as is provided for service of a complaint under the Rules of Civil Procedure. The court may render a judgment by default against the person after hearing satisfactory evidence of the truth of the statements in the complaint."

Library References

Children Out-of-Wedlock ⚖30, 63.
Westlaw Topic No. 76H.
C.J.S. Children Out-of-Wedlock §§ 46, 70, 90, 120 to 126.
Baldwin's Ohio Legislative Service, 1990 Laws of Ohio, H 591—LSC Analysis, p 5–576

3111.09 Genetic tests and DNA records

(A)(1) In any action instituted under sections 3111.01 to 3111.18 of the Revised Code, the court, upon its own motion, may order and, upon the motion of any party to the action, shall order the child's mother, the child, the alleged father, and any other person who is a defendant in the action to submit to genetic tests. Instead of or in addition to genetic testing ordered pursuant to this section, the court may use the following information to determine the existence of a parent and child relationship between the child and the child's mother, the alleged father, or another defendant:

(a) A DNA record of the child's mother, the child, the alleged father, or any other defendant that is stored in the DNA database pursuant to section 109.573 of the Revised Code;

(b) Results of genetic tests conducted on the child, the child's mother, the alleged father, or any other defendant pursuant to former section 3111.21 or 3111.22 or sections 3111.38 to 3111.54 of the Revised Code.

If the court intends to use the information described in division (A)(1)(a) of this section, it shall order the superintendent of the bureau of criminal identification and investigation to disclose the information to the court. If the court intends to use the genetic test results described in division (A)(1)(b) of this section, it shall order the agency that ordered the tests to provide the report of the genetic test results to the court.

(2) If the child support enforcement agency is not made a party to the action, the clerk of the court shall schedule the genetic testing no later than thirty days after the court issues its order. If the agency is made a party to the action, the agency shall schedule the genetic testing in accordance with the rules adopted by the director of job and family services pursuant to section 3111.611 of the Revised Code. If the alleged father of a child brings an action under sections 3111.01 to 3111.18 of the Revised Code and if the mother of the child willfully fails to submit to genetic testing or if the mother is the custodian of the child and willfully fails to submit the child to genetic testing, the court, on the motion of the alleged father, shall issue an order determining the existence of a parent and child relationship between the father and the child without genetic testing. If the mother or other guardian or custodian of the child brings an action under sections 3111.01 to 3111.18 of the Revised Code and if the alleged father of the child willfully fails to submit himself to genetic testing or, if the alleged father is the custodian of the child and willfully fails to submit the child to genetic testing, the court shall issue an order determining the existence of a parent and child relationship between the father and the child without genetic testing. If a party shows good cause for failing to submit to genetic testing or for failing to submit the child to genetic testing, the court shall not consider the failure to be willful.

(3) Except as provided in division (A)(4) of this section, any fees charged for the tests shall be paid by the party that requests them, unless the custodian of the child is represented by the child support enforcement agency in its role as the agency providing enforcement of child support orders under Title IV–D of the "Social Security Act," 88 Stat. 2351 (1975), 42 U.S.C. 651, as amended, the custodian is a participant in Ohio works first under Chapter 5107. of the Revised Code for the benefit of the child, or the defendant in the action is found to be indigent, in which case the child support enforcement agency shall pay the costs of genetic testing. The child support enforcement agency, within guidelines contained in that federal law, shall use funds received pursuant to Title IV–D of the "Social Security Act," 88 Stat. 2351 (1975), 42 U.S.C. 651, as amended, to pay the fees charged for the tests.

Except as provided in division (A)(4) of this section, if there is a dispute as to who shall pay the fees charged for genetic testing, the child support enforcement agency shall pay the fees, but neither the court nor the agency shall delay genetic testing due to a dispute as to who shall pay the genetic testing fees. The child support enforcement agency or the person who paid the fees charged for the genetic testing may seek reimbursement for the genetic testing fees from the person against whom the court assesses the costs of the action. Any funds used in accordance with this division by the child support enforcement agency shall be in addition to any other funds that the agency is entitled to receive as a result of any contractual provision for specific funding allocations for the agency between the county, the state, and the federal government.

(4) If, pursuant to former section 3111.21 or 3111.22 or sections 3111.38 to 3111.54 of the Revised Code, the agency has previously conducted genetic tests on the child, child's mother, alleged father, or any other defendant and the current action pursuant to section 3111.01 to 3111.18 of the Revised Code has been brought to object to the result of those previous tests, the agency shall not be required to pay the fees for conducting genetic tests pursuant to this section on the same persons.

(B)(1) The genetic tests shall be made by qualified examiners who are authorized by the court or the department of job and family services. An examiner conducting a genetic test, upon the completion of the test, shall send a complete report of the test results to the clerk of the court that ordered the test or, if the agency is a party to the action, to the child support enforcement agency of the county in which the court that ordered the test is located.

(2) If a court orders the superintendent of the bureau of criminal identification and investigation to disclose information regarding a DNA record stored in the DNA database pursuant to section 109.573 of the Revised Code, the superintendent shall send the information to the clerk of the court that issued the order or, if the agency is a party to the action, to the child support enforcement agency of the county in which the court that issued the order is located.

(3) If a court orders the child support enforcement agency to provide the report of the genetic test results obtained pursuant to former section 3111.21 or 3111.22 or sections 3111.38 to 3111.54 of the Revised Code, the agency shall send the information to the person or government entity designated by the court that issued the order.

(4) The clerk, agency, or person or government entity under division (B)(3) of this section that receives a report or information pursuant to division (B)(1), (2), or (3) of this section shall mail a copy of the report or information to the attorney of record for each party or, if a party is not represented by an attorney, to the party. The clerk, agency, or person or government entity under division (B)(3) of this section that receives a copy of the report or information shall include with the report or information sent to an attorney of record of a party or a party a notice that the party may object to the admission into evidence of the report or information by filing a written objection as described in division (D) of section 3111.12 of the Revised Code with the court that ordered the tests or ordered the disclosure of the information no later than fourteen days after the report or information was mailed to the attorney of record or to the party. The examiners may be called as witnesses to testify as to their findings. Any party may demand that other qualified examiners perform independent genetic tests under order of the court. The number and qualifications of the independent examiners shall be determined by the court.

(C) Nothing in this section prevents any party to the action from producing other expert evidence on the issue covered by this section, but, if other expert witnesses are called by a party to the action, the fees of these expert witnesses shall be paid by the party calling the witnesses and only ordinary witness fees for these expert witnesses shall be taxed as costs in the action.

(D) If the court finds that the conclusions of all the examiners are that the alleged father is not the father of the child, the court shall enter judgment that the alleged father is not the father of the child. If the examiners disagree in their findings or conclusions, the court shall determine the father of the child based upon all the evidence.

(E) As used in sections 3111.01 to 3111.85 of the Revised Code:

(1) "Genetic tests" and "genetic testing" mean either of the following:

(a) Tissue or blood tests, including tests that identify the presence or absence of common blood group antigens, the red blood cell antigens, human lymphocyte antigens, serum enzymes, serum proteins, or genetic markers;

(b) Deoxyribonucleic acid typing of blood or buccal cell samples.

"Genetic test" and "genetic testing" may include the typing and comparison of deoxyribonucleic acid derived from the blood of one individual and buccal cells of another.

(2) "DNA record" and "DNA database" have the same meanings as in section 109.573 of the Revised Code.

(2000 S 180, eff. 3–22–01; 1999 H 471, eff. 7–1–00; 1997 H 352, eff. 1–1–98; 1997 H 408, eff. 10–1–97; 1996 H 357, eff. 9–19–96; 1995 H 5, eff. 8–30–95; 1994 S 355, eff. 12–9–94; 1992 S 10, eff. 7–15–92; 1990 H 591; 1988 H 708; 1987 H 231; 1986 H 476; 1982 H 245)

Uncodified Law

1994 S 355, § 5: See Uncodified Law under 3111.08.

1992 S 10, § 5: See Uncodified Law under 3111.01.

1982 H 245, § 3: See Uncodified Law under 3111.04.

Historical and Statutory Notes

Ed. Note: RC 3111.09 contains provisions analogous to former RC 3111.16, repealed by 1982 H 245, eff. 6–29–82.

Ed. Note: Former RC 3111.09 repealed by 1982 H 245, eff. 6–29–82; 1953 H 1; GC 8006–9; Source—GC 12116.

Pre–1953 H 1 Amendments: 124 v S 65

Amendment Note: 2000 S 180 substituted "3111.18" for "3111.19" once in division (A)(1), twice in division (A)(2), and once in division (A)(4); inserted "or sections 3111.38 to 3111.54" in division (A)(1)(b), (A)(4), and (B)(3); substituted "3111.611" for "2301.35" in division (A)(2); substituted "3111.85" for "3111.29" in division (E); and made other nonsubstantive changes.

Amendment Note: 1999 H 471 substituted "director of job and family services" for "department of human services" in division (A)(2); and substituted "job and family" for "human" in division (B)(1).

Amendment Note: 1997 H 352 split division (A) into paragraphs; designated division (A)(1) and rewrote that division; designated division (A)(2) and inserted "on the motion of the alleged father" therein; designated division (A)(3) and inserted "Except as provided in division (A)(4) of this section," at the beginning thereof; added division (A)(4) and new division (B)(3); redesignated former division (B)(3) as new division (B)(4) and inserted "or person or government entity under division (B) of this section" twice and ", (2), or (3)" therein; deleted "or jury" before "shall determine" in division (D); and made other nonsubstantive changes.

Amendment Note: 1997 H 408 split the paragraphs in division (A); and substituted "participant in Ohio works first" for "recipient of aid to dependent children" in the second paragraph in division (A).

Amendment Note: 1996 H 357 substituted "either of the following:" for "a series of serological" in division (E)(1); designated and rewrote division (E)(1)(a); and added division (E)(1)(b) and the final paragraph in division (E)(1). Prior to amendment, the provisions now contained in division (E)(1)(a) read "tests, that are either immunological or biochemical or both immunological and biochemical in nature, and that are specifically selected because of their known genetic transmittance. 'Genetic tests' and 'genetic testing' include, but are not limited to, tests for the presence or absence of the common blood group antigens, the red blood cell antigens, human lymphocyte antigens, serum enzymes, and serum proteins and for the comparison of the deoxyribonucleic acid."

Amendment Note: 1995 H 5 added the third sentence in division (A); designated division (B)(1); added division (B)(2); designated division (B)(3); added all references to DNA record information and deleted "(1)" after "(D)" in the second sentence in division (B)(3); designated division (E)(1); added division (E)(2); and made other nonsubstantive changes.

Amendment Note: 1994 S 355 added the second through the fourth sentence in division (B).

Library References

Children Out-of-Wedlock ⚖45, 58.
Westlaw Topic No. 76H.
C.J.S. Children Out-of-Wedlock §§ 51, 75, 99, 110.
 Baldwin's Ohio Legislative Service, 1995 H 5—LSC Analysis, p 5/L–336
 Baldwin's Ohio Legislative Service, 1990 Laws of Ohio, H 591—LSC Analysis, p 5–576

3111.10 Admissible evidence

In an action brought under sections 3111.01 to 3111.18 of the Revised Code, evidence relating to paternity may include:

(A) Evidence of sexual intercourse between the mother and alleged father at any possible time of conception;

(B) An expert's opinion concerning the statistical probability of the alleged father's paternity, which opinion is based upon the duration of the mother's pregnancy;

(C) Genetic test results, weighted in accordance with evidence, if available, of the statistical probability of the alleged father's paternity;

(D) Medical evidence relating to the alleged father's paternity of the child based on tests performed by experts. If a man has been identified as a possible father of the child, the court may, and upon the request of a party shall, require the child, the mother, and the man to submit to appropriate tests. Any fees charged for the tests shall be paid by the party that requests them unless the court orders the fees taxed as costs in the action.

(E) All other evidence relevant to the issue of paternity of the child.

(2000 S 180, eff. 3–22–01; 1986 H 476, eff. 9–24–86; 1982 H 245)

Uncodified Law

1992 S 10, § 5: See Uncodified Law under 3111.01.

1982 H 245, § 3: See Uncodified Law under 3111.04.

Historical and Statutory Notes

Ed. Note: Former 3111.10 repealed by 1982 H 245, eff. 6–29–82; 127 v 1039; 1953 H 1; GC 8006–10; Source—GC 12117.

Pre–1953 H 1 Amendments: 124 v S 65

Amendment Note: 2000 S 180 substituted '3111.18" for "3111.19" in the first sentence of the section.

Library References

Children Out-of-Wedlock ⚖44 to 51.
Westlaw Topic No. 76H.
C.J.S. Children Out-of-Wedlock §§ 51, 75, 99, 101.

3111.11 Pretrial procedures

If the person against whom an action is brought pursuant to sections 3111.01 to 3111.18 of the Revised Code does not admit in his answer the existence or nonexistence of the father and child relationship, the court shall hold a pretrial hearing, in accordance with the Civil Rules, at a time set by the court. At the pretrial hearing, the court shall notify each party to the action that the party may file a motion requesting the court to order the child's mother, the alleged father, and any other person who is a defendant in the action to submit to genetic tests and, if applicable, to the appropriate tests referred to in section 3111.10 of the Revised Code. When the court determines that all pretrial matters have been completed, the action shall be set for trial.

(2000 S 180, eff. 3–22–01; 1986 H 476, eff. 9–24–86; 1982 H 245)

Uncodified Law

1992 S 10, § 5: See Uncodified Law under 3111.01.

1982 H 245, § 3: See Uncodified Law under 3111.04.

Historical and Statutory Notes

Ed. Note: Former 3111.11 repealed by 1982 H 245, eff. 6–29–82; 1953 H 1; GC 8006–11; Source—GC 12118.

Pre–1953 H 1 Amendments: 124 v S 65

Amendment Note: 2000 S 180 substituted "3111.18" for "3111.19" in the first sentence of the section.

Library References

Children Out-of-Wedlock ⚖︎39, 58.
Westlaw Topic No. 76H.
C.J.S. Children Out-of-Wedlock §§ 50, 72 to 75, 90 to 94, 110.

3111.111 Temporary support order pending action objecting to parentage determination

If an action is brought pursuant to sections 3111.01 to 3111.18 of the Revised Code to object to a determination made pursuant to former section 3111.21 or 3111.22 or sections 3111.38 to 3111.54 of the Revised Code that the alleged father is the natural father of a child, the court, on its own motion or on the motion of either party, shall issue a temporary order for the support of the child pursuant to Chapters 3119., 3121., 3123., and 3125. of the Revised Code requiring the alleged father to pay support to the natural mother or the guardian or legal custodian of the child. The order shall remain in effect until the court issues a judgment in the action pursuant to section 3111.13 of the Revised Code that determines the existence or nonexistence of a father and child relationship. If the court, in its judgment, determines that the alleged father is not the natural father of the child, the court shall order the person to whom the temporary support was paid under the order to repay the alleged father all amounts paid for support under the temporary order.

(2000 S 180, eff. 3–22–01; 1997 H 352, eff. 1–1–98)

Historical and Statutory Notes

Amendment Note: 2000 S 180 substituted "3111.18" for "3111.19"; inserted "or sections 3111.38 to 3111.54"; substituted "Chapters 3119., 3121., 3123., and 3125." for "section 3113.21 to 3113.219"; and made other nonsubstantive changes.

Library References

Children Out-of-Wedlock ⚖︎67.
Westlaw Topic No. 76H.
C.J.S. Children Out-of-Wedlock §§ 122 to 126.

3111.12 Testimony; admissibility of genetic test results or DNA records

(A) In an action under sections 3111.01 to 3111.18 of the Revised Code, the mother of the child and the alleged father are competent to testify and may be compelled to testify by subpoena. If a witness refuses to testify upon the ground that the testimony or evidence of the witness might tend to incriminate the witness and the court compels the witness to testify, the court may grant the witness immunity from having the testimony of the witness used against the witness in subsequent criminal proceedings.

(B) Testimony of a physician concerning the medical circumstances of the mother's pregnancy and the condition and characteristics of the child upon birth is not privileged.

(C) Testimony relating to sexual access to the mother by a man at a time other than the probable time of conception of the child is inadmissible in evidence, unless offered by the mother.

(D) If, pursuant to section 3111.09 of the Revised Code, a court orders genetic tests to be conducted, orders disclosure of information regarding a DNA record stored in the DNA database pursuant to section 109.573 of the Revised Code, or intends to use a report of genetic test results obtained from tests conducted pursuant to former section 3111.21 or 3111.22 or sections 3111.38 to 3111.54 of the Revised Code, a party may object to the admission into evidence of any of the genetic test results or of the DNA record information by filing a written objection with the court that ordered the tests or disclosure or intends to use a report of genetic test results. The party shall file the written objection with the court no later than fourteen days after the report of the test results or the DNA record information is mailed to the attorney of record of a party or to a party. The party making the objection shall send a copy of the objection to all parties.

If a party files a written objection, the report of the test results or the DNA record information shall be admissible into evidence as provided by the Rules of Evidence. If a written objection is not filed, the report of the test results or the DNA record information shall be admissible into evidence without the need for foundation testimony or other proof of authenticity or accuracy.

(E) If a party intends to introduce into evidence invoices or other documents showing amounts expended to cover pregnancy and confinement and genetic testing, the party shall notify all other parties in writing of that intent and include copies of the invoices and documents. A party may object to the admission into evidence of the invoices or documents by filing a written objection with the court that is hearing the action no later than fourteen days after the notice and the copies of the invoices and documents are mailed to the attorney of record of each party or to each party.

If a party files a written objection, the invoices and other documents shall be admissible into evidence as provided by the Rules of Evidence. If a written objection is not filed, the invoices or other documents are admissible into evidence without the need for foundation testimony or other evidence of authenticity or accuracy.

(F) A juvenile court or other court with jurisdiction under section 2101.022 or 2301.03 of the Revised Code shall give priority to actions under sections 3111.01 to 3111.18 of the Revised Code and shall issue an order determining the existence or nonexistence of a parent and child relationship no later than one hundred twenty days after the date on which the action was brought in the juvenile court or other court with jurisdiction.

(2000 S 180, eff. 3–22–01; 1997 H 352, eff. 1–1–98; 1995 H 5, eff. 8–30–95; 1994 S 355, eff. 12–9–94; 1992 S 10, eff. 7–15–92; 1986 H 476; 1982 H 245)

Uncodified Law

1994 S 355, § 5: See Uncodified Law under 3111.08.

1992 S 10, § 5: See Uncodified Law under 3111.01.

1982 H 245, § 3: See Uncodified Law under 3111.04.

Historical and Statutory Notes

Ed. Note: RC 3111.12 contains provisions analogous to former RC 3111.15, repealed by 1982 H 245, eff. 6–29–82.

Ed. Note: Former RC 3111.12 repealed by 1982 H 245, eff. 6–29–82; 1953 H 1; GC 8006–12; Source—GC 12119.

Pre–1953 H 1 Amendments: 124 v S 65

Amendment Note: 2000 S 180 substituted "3111.18" for "3111.19" in division (A); inserted "or sections 3111.38 to 3111.54" in division (D);

rewrote division (F); and made other nonsubstantive changes. Prior to amendment division (F) read:

"(F) A juvenile court shall give priority to actions under sections 3111.01 to 3111.19 of the Revised Code and shall issue an order determining the existence or nonexistence of a parent and child relationship no later than one hundred twenty days after the date on which the action was brought in the juvenile court."

Amendment Note: 1997 H 352 rewrote divisions (D) and (E), which prior thereto read:

"(D) If, pursuant to section 3111.09 of the Revised Code, a court orders genetic tests to be conducted or orders disclosure of information regarding a DNA record stored in the DNA database pursuant to section 109.573 of the Revised Code, a party may object to the admission into evidence of the report of the test results or of the DNA record information by filing a written objection with the court that ordered the tests or disclosure. The party shall file the written objection with the court no later than fourteen days after the report of the test results or the DNA record information is mailed to the attorney of record of a party or to a party. The party making the objection shall send a copy of the objection to all parties.

"If a party files a written objection, the report of the test results or the DNA record information shall be admissible into evidence as provided by the Rules of Evidence. If a written objection is not filed, the report of the test results or the DNA record information shall be admissible into evidence without the need for foundation testimony or other proof of authenticity or accuracy.

"(E) Any party to an action brought pursuant to sections 3111.01 to 3111.19 of the Revised Code may demand a jury trial by filing the demand within three days after the action is set for trial. If a jury demand is not filed within the three-day period, the trial shall be by the court.

"If the action is tried to a jury, the verdict of the jury is limited only to the parentage of the child, and all other matters involved in the action shall be determined by the court following the rendering of the verdict."

Amendment Note: 1995 H 5 added all references to DNA record information in division (D); and made changes to reflect gender neutral language.

Amendment Note: 1994 S 355 added division (D); and redesignated former divisions (D) and (E) as divisions (E) and (F).

Library References

Children Out-of-Wedlock ⚖45 to 46, 50, 58, 65.
Criminal Law ⚖42.
Witnesses ⚖7, 83, 211(2).
Westlaw Topic Nos. 110, 410, 76H.
C.J.S. Children Out-of-Wedlock §§ 51, 75, 99, 101, 110, 120.
C.J.S. Criminal Law §§ 78 to 86.
C.J.S. Witnesses §§ 2, 20 to 31, 204, 341 to 346, 348 to 355.

3111.13 Effects of judgment; support orders; contempt; prohibitions on certain arrearages

(A) The judgment or order of the court determining the existence or nonexistence of the parent and child relationship is determinative for all purposes.

(B) If the judgment or order of the court is at variance with the child's birth record, the court may order that a new birth record be issued under section 3111.18 of the Revised Code.

(C) Except as otherwise provided in this section, the judgment or order may contain, at the request of a party and if not prohibited under federal law, any other provision directed against the appropriate party to the proceeding, concerning the duty of support, the payment of all or any part of the reasonable expenses of the mother's pregnancy and confinement, the furnishing of bond or other security for the payment of the judgment, or any other matter in the best interest of the child. After entry of the judgment or order, the father may petition that he be designated the residential parent and legal custodian of the child or for parenting time rights in a proceeding separate from any action to establish paternity. Additionally, if the mother is unmarried, the father may file a complaint requesting the granting of reasonable parenting time rights, and the parents of the father, any relative of the father, the parents of the mother, and any relative of the mother may file a complaint requesting the granting of reasonable companionship or visitation rights, with the child pursuant to section 3109.12 of the Revised Code.

The judgment or order shall contain any provision required by section 3111.14 of the Revised Code.

(D) Support judgments or orders ordinarily shall be for periodic payments that may vary in amount. In the best interest of the child, the purchase of an annuity may be ordered in lieu of periodic payments of support if the purchase agreement provides that any remaining principal will be transferred to the ownership and control of the child on the child's attainment of the age of majority.

(E) In determining the amount to be paid by a parent for support of the child and the period during which the duty of support is owed, a court enforcing the obligation of support shall comply with Chapters 3119., 3121., 3123., and 3125. of the Revised Code.

(F)(1) Any court that makes or modifies an order for child support under this section shall comply with Chapters 3119., 3121., 3123., and 3125. of the Revised Code. If any person required to pay child support under an order made under this section on or after April 15, 1985, or modified on or after December 1, 1986, is found in contempt of court for failure to make support payments under the order, the court that makes the finding, in addition to any other penalty or remedy imposed, shall assess all court costs arising out of the contempt proceeding against the person and require the person to pay any reasonable attorney's fees of any adverse party, as determined by the court, that arose in relation to the act of contempt.

(2) When a court determines whether to require a parent to pay an amount for that parent's failure to support a child prior to the date the court issues an order requiring that parent to pay an amount for the current support of that child, it shall consider all relevant factors, including, but not limited to, any monetary contribution either parent of the child made to the support of the child prior to the court issuing the order requiring the parent to pay an amount for the current support of the child.

(3)(a) A court shall not require a parent to pay an amount for that parent's failure to support a child prior to the date the court issues an order requiring that parent to pay an amount for the current support of that child or to pay all or any part of the reasonable expenses of the mother's pregnancy and confinement, if both of the following apply:

(i) At the time of the initial filing of an action to determine the existence of the parent and child relationship with respect to that parent, the child was over three years of age.

(ii) Prior to the initial filing of an action to determine the existence of the parent and child relationship with respect to that parent, the alleged father had no knowledge and had no reason to have knowledge of his alleged paternity of the child.

(b) For purposes of division (F)(4)(a)(ii) of this section, the mother of the child may establish that the alleged father had or should have had knowledge of the paternity of the child by showing, by a preponderance of the evidence, that she performed a reasonable and documented effort to contact and notify the alleged father of his paternity of the child.

(c) A party is entitled to obtain modification of an existing order for arrearages under this division regardless of whether the judgment, court order, or administrative support order from which relief is sought was issued prior to, on, or after October 27, 2000.

(G) As used in this section, "birth record" has the same meaning as in section 3705.01 of the Revised Code.

(H) Unless the court has reason to believe that a person named in the order is a potential victim of domestic violence, any order issued pursuant to this section finding the existence of a parent and child relationship shall contain the full names, addresses, and social security numbers of the mother and father of the child and the full name and address of the child.

(2000 S 180, eff. 3-22-01; 2000 H 242, eff. 10-27-00; 1997 H 352, eff. 1-1-98; 1993 H 173, eff. 12-31-93; 1993 S 115; 1992 S 10; 1990 S 3, H 591, H 15; 1988 H 790, H 708; 1987 H 231; 1986 H 509; 1984 H 614; 1982 H 245)

Uncodified Law

2000 H 242, § 3, eff. 10-27-00, reads:

The General Assembly hereby declares that it is a person's or male minor's substantive right to obtain relief from a final judgment, court order, or administrative determination or order that determines that the person or male minor is the father of a child or that requires the person or male minor to pay child support for a child. The person or male minor may obtain relief from a final judgment, court order, or administrative determination or order only if relief is granted based on genetic evidence that the person or male minor is not the father of the child who is the subject of the judgment, order, or determination.

1992 S 10, § 5: See Uncodified Law under 3111.01.

1982 H 245, § 3: See Uncodified Law under 3111.04.

Historical and Statutory Notes

Ed. Note: RC 3111.13 contains provisions analogous to former RC 3111.17, repealed by 1982 H 245, eff. 6-29-82.

Ed. Note: Former RC 3111.13 repealed by 1982 H 245, eff. 6-29-82; 1953 H 1; GC 8006-13; Source—GC 12120; see now RC 3119.86 for provisions analogous to former RC 3111.13(F)(2), which related to the duration of support orders.

Pre-1953 H 1 Amendments: 124 v S 65

Amendment Note: 2000 S 180 rewrote this section which prior thereto read:

"(A) The judgment or order of the court determining the existence or nonexistence of the parent and child relationship is determinative for all purposes.

"(B) If the judgment or order of the court is at variance with the child's birth record, the court may order that a new birth record be issued under section 3111.18 of the Revised Code.

"(C) Except as otherwise provided in this section, the judgment or order may contain any other provision directed against the appropriate party to the proceeding, concerning the duty of support, the furnishing of bond or other security for the payment of the judgment, or any other matter in the best interest of the child. The judgment or order shall direct the father to pay all or any part of the reasonable expenses of the mother's pregnancy and confinement. After entry of the judgment or order, the father may petition that he be designated the residential parent and legal custodian of the child or for visitation rights in a proceeding separate from any action to establish paternity. Additionally, if the mother is unmarried, the father, the parents of the father, any relative of the father, the parents of the mother, and any relative of the mother may file a complaint pursuant to section 3109.12 of the Revised Code requesting the granting under that section of reasonable companionship or visitation rights with respect to the child.

"The judgment or order shall contain any provision required by section 3111.14 of the Revised Code.

"(D) Support judgments or orders ordinarily shall be for periodic payments that may vary in amount. In the best interest of the child, a lump-sum payment or the purchase of an annuity may be ordered in lieu of periodic payments of support.

"(E) In determining the amount to be paid by a parent for support of the child and the period during which the duty of support is owed, a court enforcing the obligation of support shall comply with sections 3113.21 to 3113.219 of the Revised Code.

"(F)(1) Each order for child support made or modified under this section shall include as part of the order a general provision, as described in division (A)(1) of section 3113.21 of the Revised Code, requiring the withholding or deduction of income or assets of the obligor under the order as described in division (D) or (H) of section 3113.21 of the Revised Code, or another type of appropriate requirement as described in division (D)(3), (D)(4), or (H) of that section, to ensure that withholding or deduction from the income or assets of the obligor is available from the commencement of the support order for collection of the support and of any arrearages that occur; a statement requiring all parties to the order to notify the child support enforcement agency in writing of their current mailing address, current residence address, current residence telephone number, current driver's license number, and any changes to that information; and a notice that the requirement to notify the agency of all changes to that information continues until further notice from the court. Any court that makes or modifies an order for child support under this section shall comply with sections 3113.21 to 3113.219 of the Revised Code. If any person required to pay child support under an order made under this section on or after April 15, 1985, or modified on or after December 1, 1986, is found in contempt of court for failure to make support payments under the order, the court that makes the finding, in addition to any other penalty or remedy imposed, shall assess all court costs arising out of the contempt proceeding against the person and require the person to pay any reasonable attorney's fees of any adverse party, as determined by the court, that arose in relation to the act of contempt.

"(2) Notwithstanding section 3109.01 of the Revised Code, if a court issues a child support order under this section, the order shall remain in effect beyond the child's eighteenth birthday as long as the child continuously attends on a full-time basis any recognized and accredited high school or the order provides that the duty of support of the child continues beyond the child's eighteenth birthday. Except in cases in which the order provides that the duty of support continues for any period after the child reaches nineteen years of age, the order shall not remain in effect after the child reaches age nineteen. Any parent ordered to pay support under a child support order issued under this section shall continue to pay support under the order, including during seasonal vacation periods, until the order terminates.

"(3) When a court determines whether to require a parent to pay an amount for that parent's failure to support a child prior to the date the court issues an order requiring that parent to pay an amount for the current support of that child, it shall consider all relevant factors, including, but not limited to, any monetary contribution either parent of the child made to the support of the child prior to the court issuing the order requiring the parent to pay an amount for the current support of the child.

"(4)(a) A court shall not require a parent to pay an amount for that parent's failure to support a child prior to the date the court issues an order requiring that parent to pay an amount for the current support of that child or to pay all or any part of the reasonable expenses of the mother's pregnancy and confinement, if both of the following apply:

"(i) At the time of the initial filing of an action to determine the existence of the parent and child relationship with respect to that parent, the child was over three years of age.

"(ii) Prior to the initial filing of an action to determine the existence of the parent and child relationship with respect to that parent, the alleged father had no knowledge and had no reason to have knowledge of his alleged paternity of the child.

"(b) For purposes of division (F)(4)(a)(ii) of this section, the mother of the child may establish that the alleged father had or should have had knowledge of the paternity of the child by showing, by a preponderance of the evidence, that she performed a reasonable and documented effort to contact and notify the alleged father of his paternity of the child.

"(c) A party is entitled to obtain modification of an existing order for arrearages under this division regardless of whether the judgment, court order, or administrative support order from which relief is sought was issued prior to, on, or after the effective date of this amendment.

"(G) As used in this section, "birth record" has the same meaning as in section 3705.01 of the Revised Code.

"(H) Unless the court has reason to believe that a person named in the order is a potential victim of domestic violence, any order issued pursuant to this section finding the existence of a parent and child relationship shall contain the full names, addresses, and social security numbers of the mother and father of the child and the full name and address of the child."

Amendment Note: 2000 H 242 substituted "Except as otherwise provided in this section, the" for "the" in division (C); and added new division (F)(4).

Amendment Note: 1997 H 352 deleted "division (B) of" before "section 3111.14" in the second paragraph in division (C); deleted "on or after December 31, 1993," before "shall include," substituted "income" for "wages" twice and "(D)(3), (D)(4)" for "(D)(6), (D)(7)", inserted "current residence telephone number, current driver's license number,", and deleted "on or after April 12, 1990," before "shall comply", in division (F)(1); inserted "or the order provides that the duty of support of the child continues beyond the child's eighteenth birthday" and added the second sentence in division (F)(2); added division (H); and made other nonsubstantive changes.

Amendment Note: 1993 H 173 rewrote division (F)(1) before the first semi-colon, which previously read:

"(F)(1) Each order for child support made or modified under this section on or after December 1, 1986, shall be accompanied by one or more orders described in division (D) or (H) of section 3113.21 of the Revised Code, whichever is appropriate under the requirements of that section".

Amendment Note: 1993 S 115 rewrote division (E), which previously read:

"(E) In determining the amount to be paid by a parent for support of the child and the period during which the duty of support is owed, a court enforcing the obligation of support shall comply with sections 3113.21 to 3113.219 of the Revised Code, and shall consider all relevant factors, including, but not limited to, all of the following:

"(1) The physical and emotional condition and needs of the child;

"(2) The standard of living and circumstances of each parent and the standard of living the child would have enjoyed had the parents been married;

"(3) The relative financial resources, other assets and resources, and needs of each parent;

"(4) The earning ability of each parent;

"(5) The need and capacity of the child for education, and the educational opportunities that would have been available to him had the parents been married;

"(6) The age of the child;

"(7) The financial resources and the earning ability of the child;

"(8) The responsibility of each parent for the support of others;

"(9) The value of services contributed by the parent who is the residential parent and legal custodian."

Library References

Children Out-of-Wedlock ⇌68, 69.
Westlaw Topic No. 76H.
C.J.S. Children Out-of-Wedlock §§ 126 to 128.
   Baldwin's Ohio Legislative Service, 1990 Laws of Ohio, H 591—LSC Analysis, p 5–576

3111.14 Fees for experts; court costs

The court may order reasonable fees for experts and other costs of the action and pretrial proceedings, including genetic tests, to be paid by the parties in proportions and at times determined by the court. The court may order the proportion of any party to be paid by the court, and, before or after payment by any party or the county, may order all or part of the fees and costs to be taxed as costs in the action.

(1992 S 10, eff. 7–15–92; 1990 H 591; 1982 H 245)

Uncodified Law

1992 S 10, § 5: See Uncodified Law under 3111.01.
1982 H 245, § 3: See Uncodified Law under 3111.04.

Historical and Statutory Notes

Ed. Note: RC 3111.14 contains provisions analogous to former RC 3111.17, repealed by 1982 H 245, eff. 6–29–82.

Ed. Note: Former RC 3111.14 repealed by 1982 H 245, eff. 6–29–82; 1953 H 1; GC 8006–14; Source—GC 12121.

Pre–1953 H 1 Amendments: 124 v S 65

Library References

Children Out-of-Wedlock ⇌75.
Westlaw Topic No. 76H.
C.J.S. Children Out-of-Wedlock §§ 52, 75, 140 to 141.
   Baldwin's Ohio Legislative Service, 1990 Laws of Ohio, H 591—LSC Analysis, p 5–576

3111.15 Enforcement of support order

(A) If the existence of the father and child relationship is declared or if paternity or a duty of support has been adjudicated under sections 3111.01 to 3111.18 of the Revised Code or under prior law, the obligation of the father may be enforced in the same or other proceedings by the mother, the child, or the public authority that has furnished or may furnish the reasonable expenses of pregnancy, confinement, education, support, or funeral, or by any other person, including a private agency, to the extent that any of them may furnish, has furnished, or is furnishing these expenses.

(B) The court may order support payments to be made to the mother, the clerk of the court, or a person or agency designated to administer them for the benefit of the child under the supervision of the court.

(C) Willful failure to obey the judgment or order of the court is a civil contempt of the court.

(2000 S 180, eff. 3–22–01; 1986 H 476, eff. 9–24–86; 1982 H 245)

Uncodified Law

1992 S 10, § 5: See Uncodified Law under 3111.01.
1982 H 245, § 3: See Uncodified Law under 3111.04.

Historical and Statutory Notes

Ed. Note: Former 3111.15 repealed by 1982 H 245, eff. 6–29–82; 125 v 184; 1953 H 1; GC 8006–15; Source—GC 12122; see now 3111.12 for provisions analogous to former 3111.15. 3111.15 contains provisions analogous to former 3111.17, repealed by 1982 S 245, eff. 6–29–82.

Pre–1953 H 1 Amendments: 124 v S 65

Amendment Note: 2000 S 180 substituted "3111.18" for "3111.19" in division (A).

Library References

Children Out-of-Wedlock ⇌69.
Westlaw Topic No. 76H.
C.J.S. Children Out-of-Wedlock § 128.

3111.16 Continuing jurisdiction

The court has continuing jurisdiction to modify or revoke a judgment or order issued under sections 3111.01 to 3111.18 of the Revised Code to provide for future education and support and a judgment or order issued with respect to matters listed in divisions (C) and (D) of section 3111.13 and division (B) of section 3111.15 of the Revised Code, except that a court entering a judgment or order for the purchase of an annuity under division (D) of section 3111.13 of the Revised Code may specify that the judgment or order may not be modified or revoked.

(2000 S 180, eff. 3–22–01; 1986 H 476, eff. 9–24–86; 1982 H 245)

Uncodified Law

1992 S 10, § 5: See Uncodified Law under 3111.01.
1982 H 245, § 3: See Uncodified Law under 3111.04.

Historical and Statutory Notes

Ed. Note: Former 3111.16 repealed by 1982 H 245, eff. 6–29–82; 1975 S 145; 1953 H 1; GC 8006–16; Source—GC 12122–1; see now 3111.09 for provisions analogous to former 3111.16.

Pre–1953 H 1 Amendments: 124 v S 65

Amendment Note: 2000 S 180 substituted "3111.18" for "3111.19"; and deleted "the payment of a lump sum or" before "the purchase of an annuity".

Library References

Children Out-of-Wedlock ⚖64.
Westlaw Topic No. 76H.
C.J.S. Children Out-of-Wedlock §§ 120 to 121.

3111.17 Action to determine mother and child relationship

Any interested party may bring an action to determine the existence or nonexistence of a mother and child relationship. Insofar as practicable, the provisions of sections 3111.01 to 3111.18 of the Revised Code that are applicable to the father and child relationship shall apply to an action brought under this section.

(2000 S 180, eff. 3–22–01; 1986 H 476, eff. 9–24–86; 1982 H 245)

Uncodified Law

1992 S 10, § 5: See Uncodified Law under 3111.01.

1982 H 245, § 3: See Uncodified Law under 3111.04.

Historical and Statutory Notes

Ed. Note: Former 3111.17 repealed by 1982 H 245, eff. 6–29–82; 1975 S 145; 1970 S 460; 125 v 184; 1953 H 1; GC 8006–17; Source—GC 12123; see now 3111.13 to 3111.15 for provisions analogous to former 3111.17, and 3111.03, 3111.04, and 3111.15 for annotations from former 3111.17.

Pre–1953 H 1 Amendments: 124 v S 65

Amendment Note: 2000 S 180 substituted "3111.18" for "3111.19".

Library References

Children Out-of-Wedlock ⚖1, 30 to 75.
Westlaw Topic No. 76H.
C.J.S. Children Out-of-Wedlock §§ 2 to 11, 41, 46 to 52, 66, 70 to 141.

3111.18 New birth record

As used in this section, "birth record" has the meaning given in section 3705.01 of the Revised Code.

Upon the order of a court of this state or upon the request of a court of another state, the department of health shall prepare a new birth record consistent with the findings of the court and shall substitute the new record for the original birth record.

(1988 H 790, eff. 3–16–89; 1982 H 245)

Uncodified Law

1992 S 10, § 5: See Uncodified Law under 3111.01.

1982 H 245, § 3: See Uncodified Law under 3111.04.

Historical and Statutory Notes

Ed. Note: Former 3111.18 repealed by 1982 H 245, eff. 6–29–82; 1953 H 1; GC 8006–18; Source—GC 12124.

Pre–1953 H 1 Amendments: 124 v S 65

Library References

Health ⚖397.
Westlaw Topic No. 198H.
C.J.S. Health and Environment §§ 24, 74.

3111.19 Interference with parentage action

No person, by using physical harassment or threats of violence against another person, shall interfere with the other person's initiation or continuance of, or attempt to prevent the other person from initiating or continuing, an action under sections 3111.01 to 3111.18 of the Revised Code.

(2000 S 180, eff. 3–22–01)

Uncodified Law

1992 S 10, § 5: See Uncodified Law under 3111.01.

1982 H 245, § 3: See Uncodified Law under 3111.04.

Historical and Statutory Notes

Ed. Note: 3111.19 is former 3111.29, amended and recodified by 2000 S 180, eff. 3–22–01; 1992 S 10, eff. 7–15–92.

Ed. Note: Former 3111.19 repealed by 2000 S 180, eff. 3–22–01; 1993 S 115, eff. 10–12–93; 1982 H 245.

Ed. Note: Prior 3111.19 repealed by 1982 H 245, eff. 6–29–82; 127 v 1039; 1953 H 1; GC 8006–19; Source—GC 12128.

Pre–1953 H 1 Amendments: 124 v S 65

Amendment Note: 2000 S 180 substituted "3111.18" for "3111.19"; and made changes to reflect gender neutral language.

Library References

Obstructing Justice ⚖6.
Westlaw Topic No. 282.
C.J.S. Obstructing Justice or Governmental Administration §§ 3 to 8, 37 to 38.

ACKNOWLEDGMENT OF PATERNITY

3111.20 Birth record

As used in sections 3111.21 to 3111.85 of the Revised Code, "birth record" has the same meaning as in section 3705.01 of the Revised Code.

(2000 S 180, eff. 3–22–01)

Uncodified Law

2001 S 99, § 4, eff. 10–31–01, reads:

Section 3121.01 of the Revised Code, as presented in this act, includes matter that was amended into former sections 3111.20 and 3113.21 of the Revised Code by Sub. H.B. 535 of the 123rd General Assembly. Paragraphs of former sections 3111.20 and 3113.21 of the Revised Code containing H.B. 535 amendments were transferred to section 3121.01 of the Revised Code by Am. Sub. S.B. 180 of the 123rd General Assembly as part of its general revision of the child support laws. Inclusion of the H.B. 535 amendments in section 3121.01 of the Revised Code is in recognition of the principle stated in division (B) of section 1.52 of the Revised Code that amendments are to be harmonized if capable of simultaneous operation. The version of section 3121.01 of the Revised Code presented in this act therefore is the resulting version in effect prior to the effective date of the section in this act.

Historical and Statutory Notes

Ed. Note: RC 3111.20 contains provisions analogous to former RC 5101.314(F), repealed by 2000 S 180, eff. 3–22–01.

Ed. Note: Former 3111.20 repealed by 2000 S 180, eff. 3–22–01; 2000 H 535, eff. 4–1–01; 2000 H 509, eff. 9–21–00; 1999 H 471, eff. 7–1–00; 1999 H 222, eff. 11–2–99; 1997 H 352, eff. 1–1–98; 1997 H 408, eff. 10–1–97; 1996 H 710, § 7, eff. 6–11–96; 1995 H 167, eff. 6–11–96; 1992 S 10, eff. 7–15–92.

Ed. Note: Former RC 3111.20(A) contained definitions related to the parental obligation of support. See now RC 3119.01; 3121.01; 3123.01; 3125.01 for provisions analogous to former RC 3111.20(A).

Ed. Note: Former RC 3111.20(B) related to the duty of support of a presumed father. See now RC 3111.77 for provisions analogous to former RC 3111.20(B).

Ed. Note: Former RC 3111.20(C) and (D) related to administrative support actions. See now RC 3111.78; 3111.80; 3111.81; 3111.82; 3111.821 for provisions analogous to former RC 3111.20(C).

Ed. Note: Prior 3111.20 repealed by 1982 H 245, eff. 6–29–82; 1975 S 145; 127 v 1039; 1953 H 1; GC 8006–20; Source—GC 12129.

Ed. Note: The effective date of the amendment of this section by 1995 H 167 was changed from 11–15–96 to 6–11–96 by 1996 H 710, § 7, eff. 6–11–96.

Pre–1953 H 1 Amendments: 124 v S 65

Library References

Health ⬤397.
Westlaw Topic No. 198H.
C.J.S. Health and Environment §§ 24, 74.

3111.21 Signing and notarizing of acknowledgment

If the natural mother and alleged father of a child sign an acknowledgment of paternity affidavit prepared pursuant to section 3111.31 of the Revised Code with respect to that child at a child support enforcement agency, the agency shall provide a notary public to notarize the acknowledgment.

(2000 S 180, eff. 3–22–01)

Historical and Statutory Notes

Ed. Note: Former 3111.21 repealed by 2000 S 180, eff. 3–22–01; 1999 H 471, eff. 7–1–00; 1997 H 352, eff. 1–1–98.

Ed. Note: Former RC 3111.21 contained provisions specifying CSEA actions upon receipt of a notarized acknowledgement of paternity. See now RC 3111.22 for provisions analogous to those deleted from current RC 3111.21, as amended by 2000 S 180, eff. 3–22–01.

Ed. Note: Prior 3111.21 repealed by 1997 H 352, eff. 1–1–98; 1996 H 710, § 7, eff. 6–11–96; 1995 H 167, eff. 6–11–96; 1992 S 10, eff. 7–15–92.

Ed. Note: Prior 3111.21 repealed by 1982 H 245, eff. 6–29–82; 1953 H 1; GC 8006–21; Source—GC 12130.

Ed. Note: The effective date of the amendment of this section by 1995 H 167 was changed from 11–15–96 to 6–11–96 by 1996 H 710, § 7, eff. 6–11–96.

Pre–1953 H 1 Amendments: 124 v S 65

Library References

Children Out-of-Wedlock ⬤21(2).
Westlaw Topic No. 76H.
C.J.S. Children Out-of-Wedlock §§ 40 to 42, 122.

3111.22 Signed and notarized acknowledgment of paternity to be sent to office of child support

A child support enforcement agency shall send a signed and notarized acknowledgment of paternity to the office of child support in the department of job and family services pursuant to section 3111.23 of the Revised Code. The agency shall send the acknowledgment no later than ten days after it has been signed and notarized. If the agency knows a man is presumed under section 3111.03 of the Revised Code to be the father of the child and the presumed father is not the man who signed an acknowledgment with respect to the child, the agency shall not notarize or send the acknowledgment with respect to the child pursuant to this section.

(2000 S 180, eff. 3–22–01)

Historical and Statutory Notes

Ed. Note: RC 3111.22 contains provisions analogous to those deleted from current RC 3111.21, as amended by 2000 S 180, eff. 3–22–01.

Ed. Note: Former 3111.22 repealed by 2000 S 180, eff. 3–22–01; 1999 H 471, eff. 7–1–00; 1997 H 352, eff. 1–1–98; 1996 H 710, § 7, eff. 6–11–96; 1995 H 167, eff. 6–11–96; 1992 S 10, eff. 7–15–92.

Ed. Note: Former RC 3111.22(A) related to availability of de novo court actions to determine paternity. See now RC 3111.381 for provisions analogous to former RC 3111.22(A).

Ed. Note: Former RC 3111.22(B) related to requests for administrative paternity determinations. See now RC 3111.38; 3111.39; 3111.40 for provisions analogous to former RC 3111.22(B).

Ed. Note: Former RC 3111.22(C) related to notice, order and testing procedures for paternity testing in administrative proceedings. See now RC 3111.41; 3111.42; 3111.421; 3111.44; 3111.45; 3111.46; 3111.48 for provisions analogous to former RC 3111.22(C).

Ed. Note: Former RC 3111.22(D) related to appeal of conclusive paternity determination. See now RC 3111.49 for provisions analogous to former RC 3111.22(D).

Ed. Note: Former RC 3111.22(E) related to administrative support orders based on administrative paternity determinations. See now RC 3111.80; 3111.81 for provisions analogous to former RC 3111.22(E).

Ed. Note: Former RC 3111.22(F) related to paternity determinations deemed inconclusive due to failure to submit to testing. See now RC 3111.47; 3111.50 for provisions analogous to former RC 3111.22(F).

Ed. Note: Former RC 3111.22(G) related to the contents of administrative paternity orders, including name changes. See now RC 3111.51; 3111.52 for provisions analogous to former RC 3111.22(G).

Ed. Note: Former RC 3111.22(H) related to the effect of prior administrative paternity determinations. See now RC 3111.85 for provisions analogous to former RC 3111.22(H).

Ed. Note: Prior 3111.22 repealed by 1982 H 245, eff. 6–29–82; 1953 H 1; GC 8006–22; Source—GC 12131.

Ed. Note: The effective date of the amendment of this section by 1995 H 167 was changed from 11–15–96 to 6–11–96 by 1996 H 710, § 7, eff. 6–11–96.

Pre–1953 H 1 Amendments: 124 v S 65

Library References

Children Out-of-Wedlock ⬤21(2).
Westlaw Topic No. 76H.
C.J.S. Children Out-of-Wedlock §§ 40 to 42, 122.

3111.23 Acknowledgment of paternity

The natural mother, the man acknowledging he is the natural father, or the other custodian or guardian of a child, a child support enforcement agency pursuant to section 3111.22 of the Revised Code, a local registrar of vital statistics pursuant to section 3705.091 of the Revised Code, or a hospital staff person pursuant to section 3727.17 of the Revised Code, in person or by mail, may file an acknowledgment of paternity with the office of child support in the department of job and family services, acknowledging that the child is the child of the man who signed the acknowledgment. The acknowledgment of paternity shall be made on the affidavit prepared pursuant to section 3111.31 of the Revised Code, shall be signed by the natural mother and the man acknowledging that he is the natural father, and each signature shall be notarized. The mother and man may sign and have the signature notarized outside of each other's presence. An acknowledgment shall be sent to the office no later than ten days after it has been signed and notarized. If a person knows a man is presumed under section 3111.03 of the Revised Code to be the father of the child described in this section and that the presumed father is not the man who signed an acknowledgment with respect to the child, the person shall not notarize or file the acknowledgment pursuant to this section.

(2000 S 180, eff. 3–22–01)

Historical and Statutory Notes

Ed. Note: RC 3111.23 contains provisions analogous to former RC 5101.314(A)(1), repealed by 2000 S 180, eff. 3–22–01.

Ed. Note: Former 3111.23 repealed by 2000 S 180, eff. 3–22–01; 1999 H 471, eff. 7–1–00; 1998 S 170, eff. 3–30–99; 1997 H 352, eff. 1–1–98;

1997 H 408, eff. 10–1–97; 1996 S 292, eff. 11–6–96; 1996 H 710, § 7, eff. 6–11–96; 1995 H 167, eff. 6–11–96; 1993 H 173, eff. 12–31–93; 1992 S 10.

Ed. Note: Former RC 3111.23(A) contained various provisions relating to the issuance of withholding/deduction orders. See now RC 3121.02; 3121.0311; 3121.032; 3121.035; 3121.27; 3121.33; 3121.34 for provisions analogous to former RC 3111.23(A).

Ed. Note: Former RC 3111.23(B) related to the required contents of withholding/deduction notices. See now RC 3121.03; 3121.036; 3121.037 for provisions analogous to former 3111.23(B).

Ed. Note: Former RC 3111.23(C) related to the number of notices or orders required. See now RC 3121.033 for provisions analogous to former RC 3111.23(C).

Ed. Note: Former RC 3111.23(D) related to priority among multiple withholding/deduction notices. See now RC 3121.034 for provisions analogous to former RC 3111.23(D).

Ed. Note: Former RC 3111.23(E) related to service and notice requirements, including termination. See now RC 3121.23; 3121.24; 3121.29; 3119.87; 3119.88; 3119.89; 3119.90; 3119.93; 3119.94 for provisions analogous to former RC 3111.23(E).

Ed. Note: Former RC 3111.23(F) related to disposition of lump sum payments. See now RC 3121.12 for provisions analogous to former RC 3111.23(F).

Ed. Note: Former RC 3111.23(G) related to specific contents of withholding/deduction orders. See now RC 3121.30; 3121.039; 3121.038 for provisions analogous to former RC 3111.23(G).

Ed. Note: Former RC 3111.23(H) related to termination by payment of arrearages. See now 3123.13 for provisions analogous to former RC 3111.23(H).

Ed. Note: Former RC 3111.23(I) related to payment of arrearages to ODHS. See now RC 3123.19 for provisions analogous to former RC 3111.23(I).

Ed. Note: Prior 3111.23 repealed by 1982 H 245, eff. 6–29–82; 1953 H 1; GC 8006–23; Source—GC 12132.

Ed. Note: The effective date of the amendment of this section by 1995 H 167 was changed from 11–15–96 to 6–11–96 by 1996 H 710, § 7, eff. 6–11–96.

Pre–1953 H 1 Amendments: 124 v S 65

Library References

Children Out-of-Wedlock ⚖21(2).
Westlaw Topic No. 76H.
C.J.S. Children Out-of-Wedlock §§ 40 to 42, 122.

3111.24 Examination of acknowledgment; return of incorrect acknowledgment; entry of acknowledgment information into birth registry

(A) On the filing of an acknowledgment, the office of child support shall examine the acknowledgment to determine whether it is completed correctly. The office shall make the examination no later than five days after the acknowledgment is filed. If the acknowledgment is completed correctly, the office shall comply with division (B) of this section. If the acknowledgment is not completed correctly, the office shall return it to the person or entity that filed it. The person or entity shall have ten days from the date the office sends the acknowledgment back to correct it and return it to the office. The office shall send, along with the acknowledgment, a notice stating what needs to be corrected and the amount of time the person or entity has to make the corrections and return the acknowledgment to the office.

If the person or entity returns the acknowledgment in a timely manner, the office shall examine the acknowledgment again to determine whether it has been correctly completed. If the acknowledgment has been correctly completed, the office shall comply with division (B) of this section. If the acknowledgment has not been correctly completed the second time or if the acknowledgment is not returned to the office in a timely manner, the acknowledgment is invalid and the office shall return it to the person or entity and shall not enter it into the birth registry. If the office returns an acknowledgment the second time, it shall send a notice to the person or entity stating the errors in the acknowledgment and that the acknowledgment is invalid.

(B) If the office determines an acknowledgment is correctly completed, the office shall enter the information on the acknowledgment into the birth registry pursuant to sections 3111.64 and 3111.65 of the Revised Code. After entering the information in the registry, the office shall send the acknowledgment to the department of health for storage pursuant to section 3705.091 of the Revised Code. The office may request that the department of health send back to the office any acknowledgment that is being stored by the department of health pursuant to that section.

(2000 S 180, eff. 3–22–01)

Historical and Statutory Notes

Ed. Note: RC 3111.24 contains provisions analogous to former RC 5101.314(A)(2), repealed by 2000 S 180, eff. 3–22–01.

Ed. Note: Former 3111.24 repealed by 2000 S 180, eff. 3–22–01; 1999 H 471, eff. 7–1–00; 1997 H 352, eff. 1–1–98; 1993 H 173, eff. 12–31–93; 1992 S 10.

Ed. Note: Former RC 3111.24 related to collection and disbursement procedures pursuant to withholding/deduction orders. See now RC 3121.18; 3121.19; 3121.20; 3121.21; 3121.50 for provisions analogous to former RC 3111.24.

Ed. Note: Prior 3111.24 repealed by 1982 H 245, eff. 6–29–82; 1953 H 1; GC 8006–24; Source—GC 12133.

Pre–1953 H 1 Amendments: 124 v S 65

Library References

Children Out-of-Wedlock ⚖21(2).
Health ⚖397.
Westlaw Topic Nos. 198H, 76H.
C.J.S. Children Out-of-Wedlock §§ 40 to 42, 122.
C.J.S. Health and Environment §§ 24, 74.

3111.25 Final and enforceable acknowledgment

An acknowledgment of paternity is final and enforceable without ratification by a court when the acknowledgment has been filed with the office of child support, the information on the acknowledgment has been entered in the birth registry, and the acknowledgment has not been rescinded and is not subject to possible recission [sic] pursuant to section 3111.27 of the Revised Code.

(2000 S 180, eff. 3–22–01)

Historical and Statutory Notes

Ed. Note: RC 3111.25 contains provisions analogous to former RC 5101.314(A)(3)(a) and (b), repealed by 2000 S 180, eff. 3–22–01.

Ed. Note: Former 3111.25 repealed by 2000 S 180, eff. 3–22–01; 1999 H 471, eff. 7–1–00; 1997 H 352, eff. 1–1–98; 1993 H 173, eff. 12–31–93; 1992 S 10.

Ed. Note: Former RC 3111.25 related to restrictions on employers of obligors. See now RC 3121.38; 3121.39 for provisions analogous to former RC 3111.25.

Library References

Children Out-of-Wedlock ⚖21(2).
Westlaw Topic No. 76H.
C.J.S. Children Out-of-Wedlock §§ 40 to 42, 122.

3111.26 Effect of final and enforceable acknowledgment

After an acknowledgment of paternity becomes final and enforceable, the child is the child of the man who signed the acknowledgment of paternity, as though born to him in lawful wedlock. If the mother is unmarried, the man who signed the acknowledgment of paternity may file a complaint requesting the granting of reasonable parenting time with the child under section 3109.12 of the Revised Code and the parents of the man who signed the acknowledgment of paternity, any relative of the man who signed the acknowledgment of paternity, the parents of the mother, and any relative of the mother may file a complaint pursuant to that section requesting the granting of reasonable companionship or visitation rights with the child. Once the acknowledgment becomes final the man who signed the acknowledgment of paternity assumes the parental duty of support.

(2000 S 180, eff. 3–22–01)

Historical and Statutory Notes

Ed. Note: RC 3111.26 contains provisions analogous to portions of former RC 5101.314(A)(4)(a), repealed by 2000 S 180, eff. 3–22–01.

Ed. Note: Former 3111.26 repealed by 2000 S 180, eff. 3–22–01; 1997 H 352, eff. 1–1–98; 1992 S 10, eff. 7–15–92.

Ed. Note: Former RC 3111.26 related to contingency if unable to obtain service. See now RC 3111.43 for provisions analogous to former RC 3111.26.

Library References

Children Out-of-Wedlock ⇌20.2, 21(2).
Westlaw Topic No. 76H.
C.J.S. Children Out-of-Wedlock §§ 40 to 42, 122.

3111.27 Rescission of acknowledgment

(A) Except as provided in section 2151.232 or 3111.821 of the Revised Code, for an acknowledgment of paternity filed with the office of child support to be rescinded both of the following must occur:

(1) Not later than sixty days after the date of the latest signature on the acknowledgment, one of the persons who signed it must do both of the following:

(a) Request a determination under section 3111.38 of the Revised Code of whether there is a parent and child relationship between the man who signed the acknowledgment and the child who is the subject of it;

(b) Give the office written notice of having complied with division (A)(1)(a) of this section and include in the notice the name of the child support enforcement agency conducting genetic tests to determine whether there is a parent and child relationship;

(2) An order must be issued under section 3111.46 of the Revised Code determining whether there is a parent and child relationship between the man and the child.

(B) Not later than the end of the business day following the business day on which the office receives a notice under division (A)(1)(b) of this section, it shall contact the agency indicated in the notice to verify that the person sending it has complied with division (A)(1) of this section. If the office verifies compliance, and the notice was sent within the time limit required by this section, the office shall note in its records the date the notice was received and that the acknowledgment to which the notice pertains is subject to recission [*sic*]. The office shall direct the agency to notify the office of the agency's issuance of an order described in division (A)(2) of this section. On receipt from an agency of notice that an order described in division (A)(2) of this section has been issued, the acknowledgment to which the order pertains shall be rescinded as of the date.

If the office is unable to verify compliance with division (A)(1) of this section, it shall note in its records the date the notice under division (A)(1)(b) of this section was received and that compliance with division (A)(1) of this section was not verified.

(2000 S 180, eff. 3–22–01)

Historical and Statutory Notes

Ed. Note: RC 3111.27 contains provisions analogous to former RC 5101.314(B)(1)(a) and (b), repealed by 2000 S 180, eff. 3–22–01.

Ed. Note: Former 3111.27 repealed by 2000 S 180, eff. 3–22–01; 1999 H 471, eff. 7–1–00; 1997 H 352, eff. 1–1–98; 1996 H 710, § 7, eff. 6–11–96; 1995 H 167, eff. 6–11–96; 1992 S 10, eff. 7–15–92.

Ed. Note: Former RC 3111.27 related to administrative review of support orders. See now RC 3119.60; 3119.61; 3119.72; 3119.73; 3119.76 for provisions analogous to former RC 3111.27.

Ed. Note: The effective date of the amendment of this section by 1995 H 167 was changed from 11–15–96 to 6–11–96 by 1996 H 710, § 7, eff. 6–11–96.

Library References

Children Out-of-Wedlock ⇌21(2).
Westlaw Topic No. 76H.
C.J.S. Children Out-of-Wedlock §§ 40 to 42, 122.

3111.28 Rescission of acknowledgment for fraud, duress, or material mistake of fact

After an acknowledgment becomes final pursuant to section 2151.232, 3111.25, or 3111.821 of the Revised Code, a man presumed to be the father of the child pursuant to section 3111.03 of the Revised Code who did not sign the acknowledgment, either person who signed the acknowledgment, or a guardian or legal custodian of the child may bring an action to rescind the acknowledgment on the basis of fraud, duress, or material mistake of fact. The court shall treat the action as an action to determine the existence or nonexistence of a parent and child relationship pursuant to sections 3111.01 to 3111.18 of the Revised Code. An action pursuant to this section shall be brought no later than one year after the acknowledgment becomes final. The action may be brought in one of the following courts in the county in which the child, the guardian or custodian of the child, or either person who signed the acknowledgment resides: the juvenile court or the domestic relations division of the court of common pleas that has jurisdiction pursuant to section 2101.022 or 2301.03 of the Revised Code to hear and determine cases arising under Chapter 3111. of the Revised Code.

(2000 S 180, eff. 3–22–01)

Historical and Statutory Notes

Ed. Note: RC 3111.28 contains provisions analogous to former RC 5101.314(B)(2), repealed by 2000 S 180, eff. 3–22–01.

Ed. Note: Former 3111.28 repealed by 2000 S 180, eff. 3–22–01; 1997 H 352, eff. 1–1–98; 1996 H 710, § 7, eff. 6–11–96; 1995 H 167, eff. 6–11–96; 1993 H 173, eff. 12–31–93; 1992 S 10.

Ed. Note: Former RC 3111.28 related to failure by payor or obligor to cooperate in administrative review. See now RC 3119.72 for provisions analogous to former RC 3111.28.

Ed. Note: The effective date of the amendment of this section by 1995 H 167 was changed from 11–15–96 to 6–11–96 by 1996 H 710, § 7, eff. 6–11–96.

Library References

Children Out-of-Wedlock ⇌21(2).
Westlaw Topic No. 76H.

3111.29 Complaint for child support

Once an acknowledgment of paternity becomes final under section 3111.25 of the Revised Code, the mother or other custodian or guardian of the child may file a complaint pursuant to section 2151.231 of the Revised Code in the juvenile court or other court with jurisdiction under section 2101.022 or 2301.03 of the Revised Code of the county in which the child or the guardian or legal custodian of the child resides requesting that the court order the father to pay an amount for the support of the child, may contact the child support enforcement agency for assistance in obtaining the order, or may request that an administrative officer of a child support enforcement agency issue an administrative order for the payment of child support pursuant to section 3111.81 of the Revised Code.

(2000 S 180, eff. 3–22–01)

Historical and Statutory Notes

Ed. Note: RC 3111.29 contains provisions analogous to former RC 5101.314(A)(4)(b), repealed by 2000 S 180, eff. 3–22–01.

Ed. Note: Former 3111.29 amended and recodified as 3111.19 by 2000 S 180, eff. 3–22–01; 1992 S 10, eff. 7–15–92.

Library References

Children Out-of-Wedlock ⇌21(2), 30, 32.
Westlaw Topic No. 76H.
C.J.S. Children Out-of-Wedlock §§ 40 to 42, 46, 70, 90, 122.

3111.30 Department of health to receive notice of acknowledgment; preparation of new birth certificate consistent with acknowledgment

Once an acknowledgment of paternity becomes final, the office of child support shall notify the department of health of the acknowledgment. If the original birth record is inconsistent with the acknowledgment, on receipt of the notice, the department of health shall, in accordance with section 3705.09 of the Revised Code, prepare a new birth record consistent with the acknowledgment and substitute the new record for the original birth record.

(2000 S 180, eff. 3–22–01)

Historical and Statutory Notes

Ed. Note: RC 3111.30 contains provisions analogous to former RC 5101.314(A)(4)(c), repealed by 2000 S 180, eff. 3–22–01.

Ed. Note: Former 3111.30 amended and recodified as 3111.88 by 2000 S 180, eff. 3–22–01; 1986 H 476, eff. 9–24–86.

Library References

Health ⇌397.
Westlaw Topic No. 198H.
C.J.S. Health and Environment §§ 24, 74.

3111.31 Acknowledgment of paternity affidavit

The department of job and family services shall prepare an acknowledgment of paternity affidavit that includes in boldface type at the top of the affidavit the rights and responsibilities of and the due process safeguards afforded to a person who acknowledges that he is the natural father of a child, including that if an alleged father acknowledges a parent and child relationship he assumes the parental duty of support, that both signators waive any right to bring an action pursuant to sections 3111.01 to 3111.18 of the Revised Code or make a request pursuant to section 3111.38 of the Revised Code, other than for purposes of rescinding the acknowledgment pursuant to section 3111.27 of the Revised Code in order to ensure expediency in resolving the question of the existence of a parent and child relationship, that either parent may rescind the acknowledgment pursuant to section 3111.27 of the Revised Code, that an action may be brought pursuant to section 3111.28 of the Revised Code, or a motion may be filed pursuant to section 3119.961 of the Revised Code, to rescind the acknowledgment, and that the natural father has the right to petition a court pursuant to section 3109.12 of the Revised Code for an order granting him reasonable parenting time with respect to the child and to petition the court for custody of the child pursuant to section 2151.23 of the Revised Code. The affidavit shall include all of the following:

(A) Basic instructions for completing the form, including instructions that both the natural father and the mother of the child are required to sign the statement, that they may sign the statement without being in each other's presence, and that the signatures must be notarized;

(B) Blank spaces to enter the full name, social security number, date of birth and address of each parent;

(C) Blank spaces to enter the full name, date of birth, and the residence of the child;

(D) A blank space to enter the name of the hospital or department of health code number assigned to the hospital, for use in situations in which the hospital fills out the form pursuant to section 3727.17 of the Revised Code;

(E) An affirmation by the mother that the information she supplied is true to the best of her knowledge and belief and that she is the natural mother of the child named on the form and assumes the parental duty of support of the child;

(F) An affirmation by the father that the information he supplied is true to the best of his knowledge and belief, that he has received information regarding his legal rights and responsibilities, that he consents to the jurisdiction of the courts of this state, and that he is the natural father of the child named on the form and assumes the parental duty of support of the child;

(G) Signature lines for the mother of the child and the natural father;

(H) Signature lines for the notary public;

(I) An instruction to include or attach any other evidence necessary to complete the new birth record that is required by the department by rule.

(2000 S 180, eff. 3–22–01)

Historical and Statutory Notes

Ed. Note: RC 3111.31 contains provisions analogous to former RC 5101.324(D)(1), repealed by 2000 S 180, eff. 3–22–01.

Ed. Note: Former 3111.31 amended and recodified as 3111.89 by 2000 S 180, eff. 3–22–01; 1986 H 476, eff. 9–24–86.

Library References

Children Out-of-Wedlock ⇌21(2).
Infants ⇌17.
Westlaw Topic Nos. 211, 76H.
C.J.S. Adoption of Persons §§ 10 to 14, 41.
C.J.S. Children Out-of-Wedlock §§ 40 to 42, 122.
C.J.S. Infants §§ 6, 8 to 9.

3111.32 Pamphlets

The department of job and family services shall prepare pamphlets that discuss the benefit of establishing a parent and child relationship, the proper procedure for establishing a parent and child relationship between a father and his child, and a toll-free telephone number that interested persons may call for more information regarding the procedures for establishing a parent and child relationship.

(2000 S 180, eff. 3–22–01)

Historical and Statutory Notes

Ed. Note: RC 3111.32 contains provisions analogous to portions of former RC 5101.324(C), repealed by 2000 S 180, eff. 3–22–01.

Ed. Note: Former 3111.32 recodified as 3111.90 by 2000 S 180, eff. 3–22–01; 1986 H 476, eff. 9–24–86.

Library References

Infants ⚖17.
Westlaw Topic No. 211.
C.J.S. Adoption of Persons §§ 10 to 14, 41.
C.J.S. Infants §§ 6, 8 to 9.

3111.33 Availability of pamphlets and acknowledgment of paternity affidavits

The department of job and family services shall make available the pamphlets and the acknowledgment of paternity affidavits and statements to the department of health, to each hospital it has a contract with pursuant to section 3727.17 of the Revised Code, and to any individual who requests a pamphlet. The department of job and family services shall make available the affidavit acknowledging paternity to each county child support enforcement agency, the department of health, and any other person or agency that requests copies.

(2000 S 180, eff. 3–22–01)

Historical and Statutory Notes

Ed. Note: RC 3111.33 contains provisions analogous to portions of former RC 5101.324(C) and (D)(3), repealed by 2000 S 180, eff. 3–22–01.

Ed. Note: Former 3111.33 recodified as 3111.91 by 2000 S 180, eff. 3–22–01; 1986 H 476, eff. 9–24–86.

Library References

Infants ⚖17.
Westlaw Topic No. 211.
C.J.S. Adoption of Persons §§ 10 to 14, 41.
C.J.S. Infants §§ 6, 8 to 9.

3111.34 Rules specifying additional evidence for new birth certificate

The director of job and family services, in consultation with the department of health, shall adopt rules specifying additional evidence necessary to complete a new birth record that is required to be included with an acknowledgment of paternity affidavit.

(2000 S 180, eff. 3–22–01)

Historical and Statutory Notes

Ed. Note: RC 3111.34 contains provisions analogous to former RC 5101.324(D)(2), repealed by 2000 S 180, eff. 3–22–01.

Ed. Note: Former 3111.34 amended and recodified as 3111.92 by 2000 S 180, eff. 3–22–01; 1986 H 476, eff. 9–24–86.

Library References

Health ⚖397.
Westlaw Topic No. 198H.
C.J.S. Health and Environment §§ 24, 74.

3111.35 Rules

The director of job and family services shall adopt rules pursuant to Chapter 119. of the Revised Code to implement sections 3111.20 to 3111.34 of the Revised Code that are consistent with Title IV–D of the "Social Security Act," 88 Stat. 2351, 42 U.S.C. 651 et seq., as amended.

(2000 S 180, eff. 3–22–01)

Historical and Statutory Notes

Ed. Note: RC 3111.35 contains provisions analogous to former RC 5101.314(E), repealed by 2000 S 180, eff. 3–22–01.

Ed. Note: Former 3111.35 amended and recodified as 3111.93 by 2000 S 180, eff. 3–22–01; 1986 H 476, eff. 9–24–86.

Library References

Infants ⚖17.
Social Security and Public Welfare ⚖194 to 194.1.
Westlaw Topic Nos. 211, 356A.
C.J.S. Adoption of Persons §§ 10 to 14, 41.
C.J.S. Infants §§ 6, 8 to 9.
C.J.S. Social Security and Public Welfare §§ 206, 209 to 213, 215, 227, 229.

ADMINISTRATIVE DETERMINATION OF EXISTENCE OR NONEXISTENCE OF PARENT AND CHILD RELATIONSHIP

3111.38 Existence or nonexistence of parent and child relationship

At the request of a person described in division (A) of section 3111.04 of the Revised Code the child support enforcement agency of the county in which a child resides or in which the guardian or legal custodian of the child resides shall determine the existence or nonexistence of a parent and child relationship between an alleged father and the child.

(2000 S 180, eff. 3–22–01)

Historical and Statutory Notes

Ed. Note: RC 3111.38 contains provisions analogous to portions of former RC 3111.22(B), repealed by 2000 S 180, eff. 3–22–01.

Ed. Note: Former 3111.38 amended and recodified as 3111.96 by 2000 S 180, eff. 3–22–01; 1986 H 476, eff. 9–24–86.

Library References

Children Out-of-Wedlock ⚖30.
Westlaw Topic No. 76H.
C.J.S. Children Out-of-Wedlock §§ 46, 70, 90.

3111.381 Requirements to bring action; jurisdiction

(A) Except as provided in divisions (B), (C), (D), and (E) of this section, no person may bring an action under sections 3111.01 to 3111.18 of the Revised Code unless the person has requested an administrative determination under section 3111.38 of the Revised Code of the existence or nonexistence of a parent and child relationship.

(B) An action to determine the existence or nonexistence of a parent and child relationship may be brought by the child's mother in the appropriate division of the court of common pleas in the county in which the child resides, without requesting an administrative determination, if the child's mother brings the action in order to request an order to determine the allocation of parental rights and responsibilities, the payment of all or any part of the reasonable expenses of the mother's pregnancy and confinement, or support of the child. The clerk of the court shall forward a copy of the complaint to the child support enforcement agency of the county in which the complaint is filed.

(C) An action to determine the existence or nonexistence of a parent and child relationship may be brought by the putative father of the child in the appropriate division of the court of common pleas in the county in which the child resides, without requesting an administrative determination, if the putative father brings the action in order to request an order to determine the allocation of parental rights and responsibilities. The clerk of the court shall forward a copy of the complaint to the child support enforcement agency of the county in which the complaint is filed.

(D) If services are requested by the court, under divisions (B) and (C) of this section, of the child support enforcement agency to determine the existence or nonexistence of a parent and child relationship, a Title IV–D application must be completed and delivered to the child support enforcement agency.

(E) If the alleged father of a child is deceased and proceedings for the probate of the estate of the alleged father have been or can be commenced, the court with jurisdiction over the probate proceedings shall retain jurisdiction to determine the existence or nonexistence of a parent and child relationship between the alleged father and any child without an administrative determination being requested from a child support enforcement agency.

If an action for divorce, dissolution of marriage, or legal separation, or an action under section 2151.231 or 2151.232 of the Revised Code requesting an order requiring the payment of child support and provision for the health care of a child, has been filed in a court of common pleas and a question as to the existence or nonexistence of a parent and child relationship arises, the court in which the original action was filed shall retain jurisdiction to determine the existence or nonexistence of the parent and child relationship without an administrative determination being requested from a child support enforcement agency.

If a juvenile court or other court with jurisdiction under section 2101.022 or 2301.03 of the Revised Code issues a support order under section 2151.231 or 2151.232 of the Revised Code relying on a presumption under section 3111.03 of the Revised Code, the juvenile court or other court with jurisdiction that issued the support order shall retain jurisdiction if a question as to the existence of a parent and child relationship arises.

(2006 H 136, eff. 5–17–06; 2000 S 180, eff. 3–22–01)

Historical and Statutory Notes

Ed. Note: RC 3111.381 contains provisions analogous to former RC 3111.22(A), repealed by 2000 S 180, eff. 3–22–01.

Amendment Note: 2006 H 136 inserted references to divisions (C), (D), and (E) in division (A); added new divisions (B), (C), and (D); redesignated former division (B) as (E); and made other nonsubstantive changes.

Library References

Children Out-of-Wedlock ⚖33, 36.
Westlaw Topic No. 76H.
C.J.S. Children Out-of-Wedlock §§ 46 to 47, 77 to 80, 83, 90.

3111.39 Multiple requests for determination of existence or nonexistence of parent and child relationship

If more than one child support enforcement agency receives a request to determine the existence or nonexistence of a parent and child relationship concerning the same child and each agency is an appropriate agency for the filing of the request as provided in section 3111.38 of the Revised Code, the agency that receives the request first shall act on the request. If an agency that receives a request is not the appropriate agency for the filing of the request, the agency shall forward the request to the agency of the county in which the child or the guardian or legal custodian of the child resides, and the latter agency shall proceed with the request.

(2000 S 180, eff. 3–22–01)

Historical and Statutory Notes

Ed. Note: RC 3111.39 contains provisions analogous to portions of former RC 3111.22(B), repealed by 2000 S 180, eff. 3–22–01.

Library References

Children Out-of-Wedlock ⚖30.
Westlaw Topic No. 76H.
C.J.S. Children Out-of-Wedlock §§ 46, 70, 90.

3111.40 Contents of request for administrative determination of existence or nonexistence of parent and child relationship

A request for an administrative determination of the existence or nonexistence of a parent and child relationship shall contain all of the following:

(A) The name, birthdate, and current address of the alleged father of the child;

(B) The name, social security number, and current address of the mother of the child;

(C) The name and last known address of the alleged father of the child;

(D) The name and birthdate of the child.

(2000 S 180, eff. 3–22–01)

Historical and Statutory Notes

Ed. Note: RC 3111.40 contains provisions analogous to former RC 3111.22(B)(1) to (4), repealed by 2000 S 180, eff. 3–22–01.

Library References

Children Out-of-Wedlock ⚖30.
Westlaw Topic No. 76H.
C.J.S. Children Out-of-Wedlock §§ 46, 70, 90.

3111.41 Administrative office to consider request; order; genetic tests

On receiving a request for a determination of the existence or nonexistence of a parent and child relationship, a child support enforcement agency shall assign an administrative officer to consider the request. The officer shall issue an order requiring the child, mother, and alleged father to submit to genetic testing. The order shall specify the date of the genetic tests for the mother, alleged father, and child, which shall be no later than forty-five days after the date of assignment of the administrative officer. The tests shall be conducted in accordance with the rules adopted by the director of job and family services under section 3111.611 of the Revised Code.

(2000 S 180, eff. 3–22–01)

Historical and Statutory Notes

Ed. Note: RC 3111.41 contains provisions analogous to portions of former RC 3111.22(C)(1), repealed by 2000 S 180, eff. 3–22–01.

Library References

Children Out-of-Wedlock ⚖30.
Westlaw Topic No. 76H.

C.J.S. Children Out-of-Wedlock §§ 46, 70, 90.

3111.42 Notice to accompany order for genetic testing; contents

A child support enforcement agency shall attach a notice to each order for genetic testing and send both to the mother and the alleged father. The notice shall state all of the following:

(A) That the agency has been asked to determine the existence of a parent and child relationship between a child and the alleged named father;

(B) The name and birthdate of the child of which the man is alleged to be the natural father;

(C) The name of the mother and the alleged natural father;

(D) The rights and responsibilities of a parent;

(E) That the child, the mother, and the alleged father must submit to genetic testing at the date, time, and place determined by the agency in the order issued pursuant to section 3111.41 of the Revised Code;

(F) The administrative procedure for determining the existence of a parent and child relationship;

(G) That if the alleged father or natural mother willfully fails to submit to genetic testing, or the alleged father, natural mother, or the custodian of the child willfully fails to submit the child to genetic testing, the agency will issue an order that it is inconclusive whether the alleged father is the child's natural father;

(H) That if the alleged father or natural mother willfully fails to submit to genetic testing, or the alleged father, natural mother, or custodian of the child willfully fails to submit the child to genetic testing, they may be found in contempt of court.

(2000 S 180, eff. 3–22–01)

Historical and Statutory Notes

Ed. Note: RC 3111.42 contains provisions analogous to portions of former RC 3111.22(C)(1), repealed by 2000 S 180, eff. 3–22–01.

Library References

Children Out-of-Wedlock ⇐30.
Westlaw Topic No. 76H.
C.J.S. Children Out-of-Wedlock §§ 46, 70, 90.

3111.421 Rules of civil procedure to apply

The notice and order described in section 3111.42 of the Revised Code shall be sent in accordance with the provisions of the Rules of Civil Procedure that govern service of process, except to the extent that the provisions of the Civil Rules by their nature are clearly inapplicable and except that references in the provisions of the Civil Rules to the court or to the clerk of the court shall be construed as being references to the child support enforcement agency or the administrative officer.

(2000 S 180, eff. 3–22–01)

Historical and Statutory Notes

Ed. Note: RC 3111.421 contains provisions analogous to portions of former RC 3111.22(C)(1), repealed by 2000 S 180, eff. 3–22–01.

Library References

Children Out-of-Wedlock ⇐30.
Westlaw Topic No. 76H.
C.J.S. Children Out-of-Wedlock §§ 46, 70, 90.

3111.43 Notice of request to determine existence or nonexistence of parent and child relationship

If a child support enforcement agency is asked to determine the existence or nonexistence of a parent and child relationship, the administrative officer shall provide notice of the request pursuant to the Rules of Civil Procedure to the natural mother of the child who is the subject of the request, each man presumed under section 3111.03 of the Revised Code to be the father of the child, and each man alleged to be the natural father. If the agency is unable to obtain service of process on the presumed father, alleged father, or natural mother within the time prescribed by section 3111.41 of the Revised Code, the agency shall proceed with genetic testing of all of those persons who are present on the date scheduled for the testing.

(2000 S 180, eff. 3–22–01)

Historical and Statutory Notes

Ed. Note: RC 3111.43 contains provisions analogous to former RC 3111.26, repealed by 2000 S 180, eff. 3–22–01.

Library References

Children Out-of-Wedlock ⇐30.
Westlaw Topic No. 76H.
C.J.S. Children Out-of-Wedlock §§ 46, 70, 90.

3111.44 Conference; genetic testing

After issuing a genetic testing order, the administrative officer may schedule a conference with the mother and the alleged father to provide information. If a conference is scheduled and no other man is presumed to be the father of the child under section 3111.03 of the Revised Code, the administrative officer shall provide the mother and alleged father the opportunity to sign an acknowledgment of paternity affidavit prepared pursuant to section 3111.31 of the Revised Code. If they sign an acknowledgment of paternity, the administrative officer shall cancel the genetic testing order the officer had issued. Regardless of whether a conference is held, if the mother and alleged father do not sign an acknowledgment of paternity affidavit or if an affidavit cannot be notarized or filed because another man is presumed under section 3111.03 of the Revised Code to be the father of the child, the child, the mother, and the alleged father shall submit to genetic testing in accordance with the order issued by the administrative officer.

(2000 S 180, eff. 3–22–01)

Historical and Statutory Notes

Ed. Note: RC 3111.44 contains provisions analogous to portions of former RC 3111.22(C)(1), repealed by 2000 S 180, eff. 3–22–01.

Library References

Children Out-of-Wedlock ⇐30.
Westlaw Topic No. 76H.
C.J.S. Children Out-of-Wedlock §§ 46, 70, 90.

3111.45 Qualified examiner to conduct genetic testing; report of test results

The genetic testing required under an administrative genetic testing order shall be conducted by a qualified examiner authorized by the department of job and family services. On completion of the genetic tests, the examiner shall send a complete report of the test results to the agency.

(2000 S 180, eff. 3–22–01)

Historical and Statutory Notes

Ed. Note: RC 3111.45 contains provisions analogous to portions of former RC 3111.22(C)(2), repealed by 2000 S 180, eff. 3–22–01.

Library References

Children Out-of-Wedlock ⇌30.
Westlaw Topic No. 76H.
C.J.S. Children Out-of-Wedlock §§ 46, 70, 90.

3111.46 Duties of administrative officer upon receipt of test results

On receipt of the genetic test results, the administrative officer shall do one of the following:

(A) If the results of the genetic testing show a ninety-nine per cent or greater probability that the alleged father is the natural father of the child, the administrative officer of the agency shall issue an administrative order that the alleged father is the father of the child who is the subject of the proceeding.

(B) If the results of genetic testing show less than a ninety-nine per cent probability that the alleged father is the natural father of the child, the administrative officer shall issue an administrative order that the alleged father is not the father of the child who is the subject of the proceeding.

An order issued pursuant to this section shall be sent to parties in accordance with the Civil Rule governing service and filing of pleadings and other papers subsequent to the original complaint.

(2000 S 180, eff. 3–22–01)

Historical and Statutory Notes

Ed. Note: RC 3111.46 contains provisions analogous to former RC 3111.22(C)(2)(a) to (c), repealed by 2000 S 180, eff. 3–22–01.

Library References

Children Out-of-Wedlock ⇌30.
Westlaw Topic No. 76H.
C.J.S. Children Out-of-Wedlock §§ 46, 70, 90.

3111.47 Failure to submit to genetic testing

If the alleged natural father or the natural mother willfully fails to submit to genetic testing or if either parent or any other person who is the custodian of the child willfully fails to submit the child to genetic testing, the agency shall enter an administrative order stating that it is inconclusive as to whether the alleged natural father is the natural father of the child.

(2000 S 180, eff. 3–22–01)

Historical and Statutory Notes

Ed. Note: RC 3111.47 contains provisions analogous to portions of former RC 3111.22(F), repealed by 2000 S 180, eff. 3–22–01.

Library References

Children Out-of-Wedlock ⇌30.
Westlaw Topic No. 76H.
C.J.S. Children Out-of-Wedlock §§ 46, 70, 90.

3111.48 Notice of right to bring actions

An administrative officer shall include in an order issued under section 3111.46 of the Revised Code a notice that contains the information described in section 3111.49 of the Revised Code informing the mother, father, and the guardian or legal custodian of the child of the right to bring an action under sections 3111.01 to 3111.18 of the Revised Code and of the effect of failure to timely bring the action.

An agency shall include in an administrative order issued under section 3111.47 of the Revised Code a notice that contains the information described in section 3111.50 of the Revised Code informing the parties of their right to bring an action under sections 3111.01 to 3111.18 of the Revised Code.

(2000 S 180, eff. 3–22–01)

Historical and Statutory Notes

Ed. Note: RC 3111.48 contains provisions analogous to portions of former RC 3111.22(C)(2), repealed by 2000 S 180, eff. 3–22–01.

Library References

Children Out-of-Wedlock ⇌30.
Westlaw Topic No. 76H.
C.J.S. Children Out-of-Wedlock §§ 46, 70, 90.

3111.49 Objection to administrative order; finality of order

The mother, alleged father, and guardian or legal custodian of a child may object to an administrative order determining the existence or nonexistence of a parent and child relationship by bringing, within thirty days after the date the administrative officer issues the order, an action under sections 3111.01 to 3111.18 of the Revised Code in the juvenile court or other court with jurisdiction under section 2101.022 or 2301.03 of the Revised Code in the county in which the child support enforcement agency that employs the administrative officer who issued the order is located. If the action is not brought within the thirty-day period, the administrative order is final and enforceable by a court and may not be challenged in an action or proceeding under Chapter 3111. of the Revised Code.

(2000 S 180, eff. 3–22–01)

Historical and Statutory Notes

Ed. Note: RC 3111.49 contains provisions analogous to former RC 3111.22(D), repealed by 2000 S 180, eff. 3–22–01.

Library References

Children Out-of-Wedlock ⇌30.
Westlaw Topic No. 76H.
C.J.S. Children Out-of-Wedlock §§ 46, 70, 90.

3111.50 Inconclusive administrative orders; action to establish parent and child relationship

If a child support enforcement agency issues an administrative order stating that it is inconclusive as to whether the alleged natural father is the natural father of the child, any of the parties may bring an action under sections 3111.01 to 3111.18 of the Revised Code to establish a parent and child relationship.

(2000 S 180, eff. 3–22–01)

Historical and Statutory Notes

Ed. Note: RC 3111.50 contains provisions analogous to portions of former RC 3111.22(F), repealed by 2000 S 180, eff. 3–22–01.

Library References

Children Out-of-Wedlock ⇌34.
Westlaw Topic No. 76H.
C.J.S. Children Out-of-Wedlock §§ 49, 85 to 90.

3111.51 Contents of administrative orders; exceptions

Unless the child support enforcement agency has reason to believe that a person named in the order is a potential victim of domestic violence, any administrative order finding the existence of a parent and child relationship shall contain the full names, addresses, and social security numbers of the mother and father of the child who is the subject of the order and the full name and address of the child.

(2000 S 180, eff. 3–22–01)

Historical and Statutory Notes

Ed. Note: RC 3111.51 contains provisions analogous to portions of former RC 3111.22(G), repealed by 2000 S 180, eff. 3–22–01.

Library References

Children Out-of-Wedlock ⇔30.
Westlaw Topic No. 76H.
C.J.S. Children Out-of-Wedlock §§ 46, 70, 90.

3111.52 Change of child's surname

The child support enforcement agency, as part of an administrative order determining the existence of a parent and child relationship, may order the surname of the child subject to the determination to be changed and order the change to be made on the child's birth record consistent with the order if both the parties agree to the change.

(2000 S 180, eff. 3–22–01)

Historical and Statutory Notes

Ed. Note: RC 3111.52 contains provisions analogous to portions of former RC 3111.22(G), repealed by 2000 S 180, eff. 3–22–01.

Library References

Children Out-of-Wedlock ⇔1, 30.
Health ⇔397.
Westlaw Topic Nos. 198H, 76H.
C.J.S. Children Out-of-Wedlock §§ 2 to 11, 46, 70, 90.
C.J.S. Health and Environment §§ 24, 74.

3111.53 Administrative officers

(A) A child support enforcement agency, in accordance with the rules adopted by the director of job and family services pursuant to division (B) of this section, shall employ an administrative officer, contract with another entity to provide an administrative officer, or contract with an individual to serve as an administrative officer to issue administrative orders determining the existence or nonexistence of a parent and child relationship, requiring the payment of child support, or both.

(B) The director of job and family services shall adopt rules in accordance with Chapter 119. of the Revised Code regulating administrative officers who issue administrative orders described in division (A) of this section, including the following:

(1) The qualifications of the administrative officer;

(2) Any other procedures, requirements, or standards necessary for the employment of the administrative officer.

(2000 S 180, eff. 3–22–01)

Historical and Statutory Notes

Ed. Note: 3111.53 is former 2301.358, amended and recodified by 2000 S 180, eff. 3–22–01; 1999 H 471, eff. 7–1–00; 1997 H 352, eff. 1–1–98; 1996 H 710, § 7, eff. 6–11–96; 1995 H 167, eff. 6–11–96; 1992 S 10, eff. 7–15–92.

Ed. Note: The effective date of the amendment of this section by 1995 H 167 was changed from 11–15–96 to 6–11–96 by 1996 H 710, § 7, eff. 6–11–96.

Amendment Note: 2000 S 180 rewrote this section which prior thereto read:

"(A) A child support enforcement agency, in accordance with the rules adopted by the director of job and family services pursuant to division (B) of this section, shall employ an administrative officer, contract with another entity to provide an administrative officer, or contract with an individual to serve as an administrative officer to issue, in accordance with sections 3111.22 to 3111.29 and 3113.215 of the Revised Code, administrative orders determining the existence or nonexistence of a parent and child relationship and requiring the payment of child support, or in accordance with sections 3111.20, 3111.23 to 3111.29, and 3113.215 of the Revised Code, administrative orders requiring the payment of child support.

"(B) The director of job and family services shall adopt rules in accordance with Chapter 119. of the Revised Code regulating administrative officers who issue administrative orders described in division (A) of this section, including, but not limited to:

"(1) The qualifications of the administrative officer;

"(2) Any other procedures, requirements, or standards necessary for the employment of the administrative officer."

Amendment Note: 1999 H 471 substituted "director of job and family services" for "department of human services" in division (A) and in the introductory paragraph in division (B).

Amendment Note: 1997 H 352 substituted "3111.22" for "3111.21".

Amendment Note: 1995 H 167 inserted ", or in accordance with sections 3111.20, 3111.23 to 3111.29, and 3113.215 of the Revised Code, administrative orders requiring the payment of child support" in division (A); deleted ", in accordance with sections 3111.21 to 3111.29 and 3113.215 of the Revised Code" before "administrative orders" in division (B); and substituted "described in division (A) of this section" for "determining the existence or nonexistence of a parent and child relationship and requiring the payment of child support" in division (B).

Library References

Infants ⇔17.
Westlaw Topic No. 211.
C.J.S. Adoption of Persons §§ 10 to 14, 41.
C.J.S. Infants §§ 6, 8 to 9.

3111.54 Finding of contempt

If an alleged father or natural mother willfully fails to submit to genetic testing, or if the alleged father, natural mother, or any other person who is the custodian of the child willfully fails to submit the child to genetic testing, as required by an order for genetic testing issued under section 3111.41 of the Revised Code, the child support enforcement agency that issued the order may request that the juvenile court or other court with jurisdiction under section 2101.022 or 2301.03 of the Revised Code of the county in which the agency is located find the alleged father, natural mother, or other person in contempt pursuant to section 2705.02 of the Revised Code.

(2000 S 180, eff. 3–22–01)

Historical and Statutory Notes

Ed. Note: RC 3111.54 contains provisions analogous to former RC 3111.242(B), repealed by 2000 S 180, eff. 3–22–01.

Library References

Administrative Law and Procedure ⇔937.
Children Out-of-Wedlock ⇔30.

Infants ⇐17.
Westlaw Topic Nos. 15A, 211, 76H.
C.J.S. Adoption of Persons §§ 10 to 14, 41.
C.J.S. Children Out-of-Wedlock §§ 46, 70, 90.
C.J.S. Infants §§ 6, 8 to 9.
C.J.S. Public Administrative Law and Procedure § 501.

3111.58 Preparation of new birth record pursuant to determination of parent and child relationship

If an administrative order determining the existence or nonexistence of a parent and child relationship includes a finding that the child's father is a man other than the man named in the child's birth record as the father or is otherwise at variance with the child's birth record, the agency that made the determination shall notify the department of health of the determination as soon as any period for objection to the determination provided for in former section 3111.21 or 3111.22 or section 3111.49 of the Revised Code has elapsed.

On receipt of notice under this section or notice from an agency of another state with authority to make paternity determinations that has made a determination of the existence or nonexistence of a parent and child relationship, the department of health shall prepare a new birth record consistent with the agency's determination and substitute the new record for the original birth record.

(2000 S 180, eff. 3–22–01)

Historical and Statutory Notes

Ed. Note: 3111.58 is former 3111.221, amended and recodified by 2000 S 180, eff. 3–22–01; 1997 H 352, eff. 1–1–98.

Amendment Note: 2000 S 180 deleted the first paragraph of the section; inserted "3111.22 or" in the new first paragraph; and substituted "3111.49" for "3111.22" in the new first paragraph. Prior to deletion the former first paragraph read:

"As used in this section, 'birth record' has the same meaning as in section 3705.01 of the Revised Code."

Library References

Health ⇐397.
Westlaw Topic No. 198H.
C.J.S. Health and Environment §§ 24, 74.

3111.61 Collection of samples and genetic testing

If a child support enforcement agency is made a party to an action brought to establish a parent and child relationship under sections 3111.01 to 3111.18 of the Revised Code and the court orders the parties to the action to submit to genetic testing or the agency orders the parties to submit to genetic testing under section 3111.41 of the Revised Code, the agency shall provide for collection of samples and performance of genetic testing in accordance with generally accepted medical techniques. If a court ordered the genetic testing, the agency shall inform the court of the procedures for collecting the samples and performing the genetic tests, in accordance with the rules governing on-site genetic testing adopted by the director of job and family services pursuant to section 3111.611 of the Revised Code.

(2000 S 180, eff. 3–22–01)

Historical and Statutory Notes

Ed. Note: 3111.61 is former 2301.356, amended and recodified by 2000 S 180, eff. 3–22–01; 1999 H 471, eff. 7–1–00; 1997 H 352, eff. 1–1–98; 1996 H 357, eff. 9–19–96; 1992 S 10, eff. 7–15–92.

Amendment Note: 2000 S 180 substituted "3111.18" for "3111.19", "section 3111.41" for "sections 3111.22 to 3111.29", and "3111.611" for "2305.35".

Amendment Note: 1999 H 471 substituted "director of job and family services" for "department of human services".

Amendment Note: 1997 H 352 substituted "the agency orders the parties to submit to" for "if the natural mother and alleged natural father voluntarily agree to be bound by" and "3111.22" for "3111.21"; and made other nonsubstantive changes.

Amendment Note: 1996 H 357 substituted "provide for collection of samples and performance of genetic testing in accordance with generally accepted medical techniques. If" for "make available a medically trained phlebotomist to withdraw the necessary blood samples and an authorized examiner to perform the genetic tests. The agency shall provide the phlebotomist, the examiner, and a location to withdraw the blood samples, and, if"; inserted "the agency" and substituted "collecting the samples" for "withdrawing the blood samples" in the final sentence; and made other nonsubstantive changes.

Library References

Children Out-of-Wedlock ⇐58.
Westlaw Topic No. 76H.
C.J.S. Children Out-of-Wedlock §§ 75, 110.

3111.611 Rules governing establishment of on-site genetic testing programs

The director of job and family services shall adopt in accordance with Chapter 119. of the Revised Code rules governing the establishment by child support enforcement agencies of on-site genetic testing programs to be used in actions under sections 3111.01 to 3111.18 of the Revised Code and in administrative procedures under sections 3111.38 to 3111.54 of the Revised Code. The rules shall include provisions relating to the environment in which a blood or buccal cell sample may be drawn, the medical personnel who may draw a sample, the trained personnel who may perform the genetic comparison, the types of genetic testing that may be performed on a sample, and the procedure for notifying the court of the location at which the sample will be drawn, who will draw the sample, and who will perform the genetic testing on the sample, and any other procedures or standards the director determines are necessary for the implementation of on-site genetic testing.

(2000 S 180, eff. 3–22–01)

Historical and Statutory Notes

Ed. Note: RC 3111.611 contains provisions analogous to former RC 2301.35(D)(2), repealed by 2000 S 180, eff. 3–22–01.

Library References

Children Out-of-Wedlock ⇐58.
Infants ⇐17.
Westlaw Topic Nos. 211, 76H.
C.J.S. Adoption of Persons §§ 10 to 14, 41.
C.J.S. Children Out-of-Wedlock §§ 75, 110.
C.J.S. Infants §§ 6, 8 to 9.

BIRTH REGISTRY AND PUTATIVE FATHER REGISTRY

3111.64 Birth registry

The office of child support in the department of job and family services shall establish and maintain a birth registry that shall contain all of the following information contained in orders determining the existence of a parent and child relationship and acknowledgments of paternity required to be filed with the office:

(A) The names of the parents of the child subject to the order or acknowledgment;

(B) The name of the child;

(C) The resident address of each parent and each parent's social security number.

(2000 S 180, eff. 3–22–01)

Historical and Statutory Notes

Ed. Note: RC 3111.64 contains provisions analogous to former RC 5101.314(D)(1), repealed by 2000 S 180, eff. 3–22–01.

Library References

Health ⚖397.
Infants ⚖17.
Westlaw Topic Nos. 198H, 211.
C.J.S. Adoption of Persons §§ 10 to 14, 41.
C.J.S. Health and Environment §§ 24, 74.
C.J.S. Infants §§ 6, 8 to 9.

3111.65 Maintenance and accessibility of birth registry

The birth registry shall be maintained as part of and be accessible through the automated system created pursuant to section 3125.07 of the Revised Code. The office of child support shall make comparisons of the information in the registry with the information maintained by the department of job and family services pursuant to sections 3107.062 and 3121.894 of the Revised Code. The office shall make the comparisons in the manner and in the time intervals required by the rules adopted pursuant to section 3111.67 of the Revised Code.

(2000 S 180, eff. 3–22–01)

Historical and Statutory Notes

Ed. Note: RC 3111.65 contains provisions analogous to former RC 5101.314(D)(2), repealed by 2000 S 180, eff. 3–22–01.

Library References

Health ⚖397.
Infants ⚖17.
Westlaw Topic Nos. 198H, 211.
C.J.S. Adoption of Persons §§ 10 to 14, 41.
C.J.S. Health and Environment §§ 24, 74.
C.J.S. Infants §§ 6, 8 to 9.

3111.66 Filing of orders

A court or child support enforcement agency, whichever is applicable, shall file the following with the office of child support:

(A) An order issued pursuant to section 3111.13 of the Revised Code on or after January 1, 1998;

(B) An order issued pursuant to section 3111.22 of the Revised Code on or after January 1, 1998, that has become final and enforceable;

(C) An order issued pursuant to section 3111.46 of the Revised Code on or after the effective date of this section.

On the filing of an order pursuant to this section, the office shall enter the information on the order in the birth registry.

(2000 S 180, eff. 3–22–01)

Historical and Statutory Notes

Ed. Note: RC 3111.66 contains provisions analogous to former RC 5101.314(C), repealed by 2000 S 180, eff. 3–22–01.

Library References

Children Out-of-Wedlock ⚖63.
Records ⚖3.
Westlaw Topic Nos. 326, 76H.
C.J.S. Children Out-of-Wedlock §§ 120 to 126.
C.J.S. Records § 4.

3111.67 Rules for birth registry

The director of job and family services shall adopt rules pursuant to Chapter 119. of the Revised Code to implement the requirements of sections 3111.64 to 3111.66 of the Revised Code that are consistent with Title IV–D of the "Social Security Act," 88 Stat. 2351, 42 U.S.C. 651 et seq., as amended.

(2000 S 180, eff. 3–22–01)

Historical and Statutory Notes

Ed. Note: RC 3111.67 contains provisions analogous to former RC 5101.314(E), repealed by 2000 S 180, eff. 3–22–01.

Library References

Health ⚖397.
Infants ⚖17.
Social Security and Public Welfare ⚖194 to 194.1.
Westlaw Topic Nos. 198H, 211, 356A.
C.J.S. Adoption of Persons §§ 10 to 14, 41.
C.J.S. Health and Environment §§ 24, 74.
C.J.S. Infants §§ 6, 8 to 9.
C.J.S. Social Security and Public Welfare §§ 206, 209 to 213, 215, 227, 229.

3111.69 Examining putative father registry

The office of child support in the department of job and family services and a child support enforcement agency may examine the putative father registry established under section 3107.062 of the Revised Code to locate an absent parent for the purpose of the office or agency carrying out its duties under the child and spousal support enforcement programs established under Chapter 3125. of the Revised Code. Neither the office nor an agency shall use the information it receives from the registry for any purpose other than child and spousal support enforcement.

(2000 S 180, eff. 3–22–01)

Historical and Statutory Notes

Ed. Note: 3111.69 is former 5101.313, amended and recodified by 2000 S 180, eff. 3–22–01; 1999 H 471, eff. 7–1–00; 1996 H 419, eff. 9–18–96.

Amendment Note: 2000 S 180 substituted "office" for "division" three times and "Chapter 3125" for "section 5101.31".

Library References

Children Out-of-Wedlock ⚖30.
Infants ⚖17.
Westlaw Topic Nos. 211, 76H.
C.J.S. Adoption of Persons §§ 10 to 14, 41.
C.J.S. Children Out-of-Wedlock §§ 46, 70, 90.
C.J.S. Infants §§ 6, 8 to 9.
Baldwin's Ohio Legislative Service, 1996 H 419—LSC Analysis, 3/L–336

MISCELLANEOUS PROVISIONS

3111.71 Contracts with local hospitals for staff to meet with certain unmarried women

The department of job and family services shall enter into a contract with local hospitals for the provision of staff by the hospitals to meet with unmarried women who give birth in or en route to the particular hospital. On or before April 1, 1998, each hospital shall enter into a contract with the department of job and family services pursuant to this section regarding the duties imposed by this section and section 3727.17 of the Revised Code concerning paternity establishment. A hospital that fails to enter into a contract shall not receive the fee from the department for correctly signed and notarized affidavits submitted by the hospital.

(2000 S 180, eff. 3–22–01)

Historical and Statutory Notes

Ed. Note: RC 3111.71 contains provisions analogous to portions of former 2301.357(B), repealed by 2000 S 180, eff. 3–22–01.

Library References

Health ⚖=256.
Infants ⚖=17.
Westlaw Topic Nos. 198H, 211.
C.J.S. Adoption of Persons §§ 10 to 14, 41.
C.J.S. Infants §§ 6, 8 to 9.

3111.72 Requirements of contract

The contract between the department of job and family services and a local hospital shall require all of the following:

(A) That the hospital provide a staff person to meet with each unmarried mother who gave birth in or en route to the hospital within twenty-four hours of the birth or before the mother is released from the hospital;

(B) That the staff person attempt to meet with the father of the unmarried mother's child if possible;

(C) That the staff person explain to the unmarried mother and the father, if he is present, the benefit to the child of establishing a parent and child relationship between the father and the child and the various proper procedures for establishing a parent and child relationship;

(D) That the staff person present to the unmarried mother and, if possible, the father, the pamphlet or statement regarding the rights and responsibilities of a natural parent that is prepared and provided by the department of job and family services pursuant to section 3111.32 of the Revised Code;

(E) That the staff person provide the mother and, if possible, the father, all forms and statements necessary to voluntarily establish a parent and child relationship, including, but not limited to, the acknowledgment of paternity affidavit prepared by the department of job and family services pursuant to section 3111.31 of the Revised Code;

(F) That the staff person, at the request of both the mother and father, help the mother and father complete any form or statement necessary to establish a parent and child relationship;

(G) That the hospital provide a notary public to notarize an acknowledgment of paternity affidavit signed by the mother and father;

(H) That the staff person present to an unmarried mother who is not participating in the Ohio works first program established under Chapter 5107. or receiving medical assistance under Chapter 5111. of the Revised Code an application for Title IV–D services;

(I) That the staff person forward any completed acknowledgment of paternity, no later than ten days after it is completed, to the office of child support in the department of job and family services;

(J) That the department of job and family services pay the hospital twenty dollars for every correctly signed and notarized acknowledgment of paternity affidavit from the hospital.

(2000 S 180, eff. 3–22–01)

Historical and Statutory Notes

Ed. Note: RC 3111.72 contains provisions analogous to portions of former 2301.357(B), repealed by 2000 S 180, eff. 3–22–01.

Library References

Health ⚖=256.
Infants ⚖=17.
Westlaw Topic Nos. 198H, 211.
C.J.S. Adoption of Persons §§ 10 to 14, 41.
C.J.S. Infants §§ 6, 8 to 9.

3111.73 Reports

Not later than July 1, 1998, and the first day of each July thereafter, the department of job and family services shall complete a report on the hospitals that have not entered into contracts described in this section. The department shall submit the report to the chairperson and ranking minority member of the committees of the house of representatives and senate with primary responsibility for issues concerning paternity establishment.

(2000 S 180, eff. 3–22–01)

Historical and Statutory Notes

Ed. Note: RC 3111.73 contains provisions analogous to former 2301.357(C), repealed by 2000 S 180, eff. 3–22–01.

Library References

Health ⚖=256.
Infants ⚖=17.
Westlaw Topic Nos. 198H, 211.
C.J.S. Adoption of Persons §§ 10 to 14, 41.
C.J.S. Infants §§ 6, 8 to 9.

3111.74 Requirements when presumed father is not man who signed or is attempting to sign acknowledgment

If the hospital knows or determines that a man is presumed under section 3111.03 of the Revised Code to be the father of a child and that the presumed father is not the man who signed or is attempting to sign an acknowledgment with respect to the child, the hospital shall take no further action with regard to the acknowledgment and shall not send the acknowledgment to the office of child support.

(2000 S 180, eff. 3–22–01)

Historical and Statutory Notes

Ed. Note: RC 3111.74 contains provisions analogous to former 2301.357(D), repealed by 2000 S 180, eff. 3–22–01.

Library References

Children Out-of-Wedlock ⚖=21(2).
Health ⚖=256.
Westlaw Topic Nos. 198H, 76H.
C.J.S. Children Out-of-Wedlock §§ 40 to 42, 122.

PARENTAL SUPPORT

3111.77 Duty of parental support

A man who is presumed to be the natural father of a child pursuant to section 3111.03 of the Revised Code assumes the parental duty of support with respect to the child as provided in section 3103.031 of the Revised Code.

(2000 S 180, eff. 3–22–01)

Historical and Statutory Notes

Ed. Note: RC 3111.77 contains provisions analogous to former RC 3111.20(B), repealed by 2000 S 180, eff. 3–22–01.

Library References

Children Out-of-Wedlock ⬄21(2).
Westlaw Topic No. 76H.
C.J.S. Children Out-of-Wedlock §§ 40 to 42, 122.

3111.78 Actions permitted to require man to pay support and provide for health care needs

A parent, guardian, or legal custodian of a child, the person with whom the child resides, or the child support enforcement agency of the county in which the child, parent, guardian, or legal custodian of the child resides may do the following to require a man to pay support and provide for the health care needs of the child if the man is presumed to be the natural father of the child under section 3111.03 of the Revised Code:

(A) If the presumption is not based on an acknowledgment of paternity, file a complaint pursuant to section 2151.231 of the Revised Code in the juvenile court or other court with jurisdiction under section 2101.022 or 2301.03 of the Revised Code of the county in which the child, parent, guardian, or legal custodian resides;

(B) Ask an administrative officer of a child support enforcement agency to issue an administrative order pursuant to section 3111.81 of the Revised Code;

(C) Contact a child support enforcement agency for assistance in obtaining an order for support and the provision of health care for the child.

(2000 S 180, eff. 3–22–01)

Historical and Statutory Notes

Ed. Note: RC 3111.78 contains provisions analogous to portions of former RC 3111.20(C), repealed by 2000 S 180, eff. 3–22–01.

Library References

Children Out-of-Wedlock ⬄30, 34.
Westlaw Topic No. 76H.
C.J.S. Children Out-of-Wedlock §§ 46, 49, 70, 85 to 90.

3111.80 Administrative hearings

If a request for issuance of an administrative support order is made under section 3111.29 or 3111.78 of the Revised Code or an administrative officer issues an administrative order determining the existence of a parent and child relationship under section 3111.46 of the Revised Code, the administrative officer shall schedule an administrative hearing to determine, in accordance with Chapters 3119. and 3121. of the Revised Code, the amount of child support any parent is required to pay, the method of payment of child support, and the method of providing for the child's health care.

The administrative officer shall send the mother and the father of the child notice of the date, time, place, and purpose of the administrative hearing. With respect to an administrative hearing scheduled pursuant to an administrative order determining, pursuant to section 3111.46 of the Revised Code, the existence of a parent and child relationship, the officer shall attach the notice of the administrative hearing to the order and send it in accordance with that section. The Rules of Civil Procedure shall apply regarding the sending of the notice, except to the extent the civil rules, by their nature, are clearly inapplicable and except that references in the civil rules to the court or the clerk of the court shall be construed as being references to the child support enforcement agency or the administrative officer.

The hearing shall be held no later than sixty days after the request is made under section 3111.29 or 3111.78 of the Revised Code or an administrative officer issues an administrative order determining the existence of a parent and child relationship under section 3111.46 of the Revised Code. The hearing shall not be held earlier than thirty days after the officer gives the mother and father notice of the hearing.

(2000 S 180, eff. 3–22–01)

Historical and Statutory Notes

Ed. Note: RC 3111.80 contains provisions analogous to former RC 3111.22(E)(1), and provisions analogous to portions of former RC 3111.20(D), both repealed by 2000 S 180, eff. 3–22–01.

Library References

Children Out-of-Wedlock ⬄30.
Westlaw Topic No. 76H.
C.J.S. Children Out-of-Wedlock §§ 46, 70, 90.

3111.81 Administrative order for payment of support and provision for child's health care

After the hearing under section 3111.80 of the Revised Code is completed, the administrative officer may issue an administrative order for the payment of support and provision for the child's health care. The order shall do all of the following:

(A) Require periodic payments of support that may vary in amount, except that, if it is in the best interest of the child, the administrative officer may order the purchase of an annuity in lieu of periodic payments of support if the purchase agreement provides that any remaining principal will be transferred to the ownership and control of the child on the child's attainment of the age of majority;

(B) Require the parents to provide for the health care needs of the child in accordance with sections 3119.29 to 3119.56 of the Revised Code;

(C) Include a notice that contains the information described in section 3111.84 of the Revised Code informing the mother and the father of the right to object to the order by bringing an action for the payment of support and provision of the child's health care under section 2151.231 of the Revised Code and the effect of a failure to timely bring the action.

(2002 H 657, eff. 12–13–02; 2000 S 180, eff. 3–22–01)

Historical and Statutory Notes

Ed. Note: RC 3111.81 contains provisions analogous to former RC 3111.20(D)(1) and (2), and provisions analogous to former RC 3111.22(E)(1)(a) to (c), repealed by 2000 S 180, eff. 3–22–01.

Amendment Note: 2002 H 657 substituted "3119.29" for "3119.30" and "3119.56" for "3119.58" in division (B); and made other nonsubstantive changes.

Library References

Children Out-of-Wedlock ⇐30.
Westlaw Topic No. 76H.
C.J.S. Children Out-of-Wedlock §§ 46, 70, 90.

3111.82 Party may raise existence or nonexistence of relationship

A party to a request made under section 3111.78 of the Revised Code for an administrative support order may raise the issue of the existence or nonexistence of a parent and child relationship.

(2000 S 180, eff. 3–22–01)

Historical and Statutory Notes

Ed. Note: RC 3111.82 contains provisions analogous to portions of former RC 3111.20(C) and former RC 3111.211(A), both repealed by 2000 S 180, eff. 3–22–01.

Library References

Children Out-of-Wedlock ⇐30.
Westlaw Topic No. 76H.
C.J.S. Children Out-of-Wedlock §§ 46, 70, 90.

3111.821 Determination of existence of parent and child relationship

If a request is made pursuant to section 3111.78 of the Revised Code for an administrative support order and the issue of the existence or nonexistence of a parent and child relationship is raised, the administrative officer shall treat the request as a request made pursuant to section 3111.38 of the Revised Code and determine the issue in accordance with that section. If the request made under section 3111.78 of the Revised Code is made based on an acknowledgment of paternity that has not become final, the administrative officer shall promptly notify the office of child support in the department of job and family services when the officer issues an order determining the existence or nonexistence of a parent and child relationship with respect to the child who is the subject of the acknowledgment of paternity. On receipt of the notice by the office, the acknowledgment of paternity shall be considered rescinded.

If the parties do not raise the issue of the existence or nonexistence of a parent and child relationship pursuant to the request made under section 3111.78 of the Revised Code and an administrative order is issued pursuant to section 3111.81 of the Revised Code prior to the date the acknowledgment of paternity becomes final, the acknowledgment shall be considered final as of the date of the issuance of the order. An administrative order issued pursuant to section 3111.81 of the Revised Code shall not affect an acknowledgment that becomes final prior to the issuance of the order.

(2000 S 180, eff. 3–22–01)

Historical and Statutory Notes

Ed. Note: RC 3111.821 contains provisions analogous to portions of former RC 3111.20(C) and former RC 3111.211(A), both repealed by 2000 S 180, eff. 3–22–01.

Library References

Children Out-of-Wedlock ⇐30.
Westlaw Topic No. 76H.
C.J.S. Children Out-of-Wedlock §§ 46, 70, 90.

3111.83 Registration of order

An administrative officer who issues an administrative support order for the payment of support and provision for a child's health care shall register the order or cause the order to be registered in the system established under section 3111.831 of the Revised Code or with the clerk of the court of appropriate jurisdiction of the county served by the administrative officer's child support enforcement agency.

(2000 S 180, eff. 3–22–01)

Library References

Children Out-of-Wedlock ⇐30.
Westlaw Topic No. 76H.
C.J.S. Children Out-of-Wedlock §§ 46, 70, 90.

3111.831 Development of system and procedure for safekeeping and retrieval of orders

Each child support enforcement agency may develop a system and procedure for the organized safekeeping and retrieval of administrative support orders for the payment of support and provision for the child's health care.

(2000 S 180, eff. 3–22–01)

Library References

Infants ⇐17.
Westlaw Topic No. 211.
C.J.S. Adoption of Persons §§ 10 to 14, 41.
C.J.S. Infants §§ 6, 8 to 9.

3111.832 Fee not to be charged

If an administrative support order is registered with the clerk of a court of appropriate jurisdiction, the clerk shall not charge a fee for the registration and shall assign the order a case number.

(2000 S 180, eff. 3–22–01)

Library References

Clerks of Courts ⇐18, 67.
Westlaw Topic No. 79.
C.J.S. Courts §§ 242 to 243, 249, 251, 254.

3111.84 Action for payment of support and provision for child's health care

The mother or father of a child who is the subject of an administrative support order may object to the order by bringing an action for the payment of support and provision for the child's health care under section 2151.231 of the Revised Code in the juvenile court or other court with jurisdiction under section 2101.022 or 2301.03 of the Revised Code of the county in which the child support enforcement agency that employs the administrative officer is located. The action shall be brought not later than thirty days after the date of the issuance of the administrative support order. If neither the mother nor the father brings an action for the payment of support and provision for the child's health care within that thirty-day period, the administrative support order is final and enforceable by a court and may be modified only as provided in Chapters 3119., 3121., and 3123. of the Revised Code.

(2000 S 180, eff. 3–22–01)

Library References

Children Out-of-Wedlock ⬅30, 34, 38.
Westlaw Topic No. 76H.
C.J.S. Children Out-of-Wedlock §§ 46, 48 to 49, 66, 70, 81 to 82, 85 to 90.

3111.85 Effect of support orders issued under former R.C. 3111.21 prior to January 1, 1998

An administrative support order issued pursuant to former section 3111.21 of the Revised Code prior to January 1, 1998, that is in effect on the effective date of this section shall remain in effect on and after the effective date of this section and shall be considered an administrative support order issued pursuant to section 3111.81 of the Revised Code for all purposes.

(2000 S 180, eff. 3–22–01)

Historical and Statutory Notes

Ed. Note: RC 3111.85 contains provisions analogous to former RC 3111.22(H), repealed by 2000 S 180, eff. 3-22-01.

Library References

Children Out-of-Wedlock ⬅31.
Westlaw Topic No. 76H.
C.J.S. Children Out-of-Wedlock §§ 41, 46, 70 to 71.

NON–SPOUSAL ARTIFICIAL INSEMINATION

3111.88 Definitions

As used in sections 3111.88 to 3111.96 of the Revised Code:

(A) "Artificial insemination" means the introduction of semen into the vagina, cervical canal, or uterus through instruments or other artificial means.

(B) "Donor" means a man who supplies semen for a non-spousal artificial insemination.

(C) "Non–spousal artificial insemination" means an artificial insemination of a woman with the semen of a man who is not her husband.

(D) "Physician" means a person who is licensed pursuant to Chapter 4731. of the Revised Code to practice medicine or surgery or osteopathic medicine or surgery in this state.

(E) "Recipient" means a woman who has been artificially inseminated with the semen of a donor.

(2000 S 180, eff. 3–22–01)

Historical and Statutory Notes

Ed. Note: 3111.88 is former 3111.30, amended and recodified by 2000 S 180, eff. 3–22–01; 1986 H 476, eff. 9-24-86.

Amendment Note: 2000 S 180 substituted "3111.88" for "3111.30" and "3111.96" for "3111.38" in the first sentence of the section.

Library References

Children Out-of-Wedlock ⬅1.
Westlaw Topic No. 76H.
C.J.S. Children Out-of-Wedlock §§ 2 to 11.

3111.89 Sections applicable to non-spousal artificial insemination

Sections 3111.88 to 3111.96 of the Revised Code deal with non-spousal artificial insemination for the purpose of impregnating a woman so that she can bear a child that she intends to raise as her child. These sections do not deal with the artificial insemination of a wife with the semen of her husband or with surrogate motherhood.

(2000 S 180, eff. 3–22–01)

Historical and Statutory Notes

Ed. Note: 3111.89 is former 3111.31, amended and recodified by 2000 S 180, eff. 3–22–01; 1986 H 476, eff. 9-24-86.

Amendment Note: 2000 S 180 substituted "3111.88" for "3111.30" and "3111.96" for "3111.38" in the first sentence of the section.

Library References

Children Out-of-Wedlock ⬅1.
Westlaw Topic No. 76H.
C.J.S. Children Out-of-Wedlock §§ 2 to 11.

3111.90 Supervision by physician

A non-spousal artificial insemination shall be performed by a physician or a person who is under the supervision and control of a physician. Supervision requires the availability of a physician for consultation and direction, but does not necessarily require the personal presence of the physician who is providing the supervision.

(2000 S 180, eff. 3–22–01)

Historical and Statutory Notes

Ed. Note: 3111.90 is former 3111.32, recodified by 2000 S 180, eff. 3-22-01; 1986 H 476, eff. 9-24-86.

Library References

Health ⬅192.
Westlaw Topic No. 198H.

3111.91 Fresh semen; frozen semen; medical history of donor; laboratory studies

(A) In a non-spousal artificial insemination, fresh or frozen semen may be used, provided that the requirements of division (B) of this section are satisfied.

(B)(1) A physician, physician assistant, clinical nurse specialist, certified nurse practitioner, certified nurse-midwife, or person under the supervision and control of a physician may use fresh semen for purposes of a non-spousal artificial insemination, only if within one year prior to the supplying of the semen, all of the following occurred:

(a) A complete medical history of the donor, including, but not limited to, any available genetic history of the donor, was obtained by a physician, a physician assistant, a clinical nurse specialist, or a certified nurse practitioner.

(b) The donor had a physical examination by a physician, a physician assistant, a clinical nurse specialist, or a certified nurse practitioner.

(c) The donor was tested for blood type and RH factor.

(2) A physician, physician assistant, clinical nurse specialist, certified nurse practitioner, certified nurse-midwife, or person under the supervision and control of a physician may use frozen semen for purposes of a non-spousal artificial insemination only if all the following apply:

(a) The requirements set forth in division (B)(1) of this section are satisfied;

(b) In conjunction with the supplying of the semen, the semen or blood of the donor was the subject of laboratory studies that the physician involved in the non-spousal artificial insemination considers appropriate. The laboratory studies may include, but are not limited to, venereal disease research laboratories, karotyping, GC culture, cytomegalo, hepatitis, kem-zyme, Tay–Sachs, sickle-cell, ureaplasma, HLTV–III, and chlamydia.

(c) The physician involved in the non-spousal artificial insemination determines that the results of the laboratory studies are acceptable results.

(3) Any written documentation of a physical examination conducted pursuant to division (B)(1)(b) of this section shall be completed by the individual who conducted the examination.

(2002 S 245, eff. 3–31–03; 2000 S 180, eff. 3–22–01)

Historical and Statutory Notes

Ed. Note: 3111.91 is former 3111.33, recodified by 2000 S 180, eff. 3–22–01; 1986 H 476, eff. 9–24–86.

Amendment Note: 2002 S 245 added ", physician assistant, clinical nurse specialist, certified nurse practitioner, certified nurse-midwife," to division (B)(2); added division (B)(3); and rewrote division (B)(1), which prior thereto read:

"(B)(1) A physician or person under the supervision and control of a physician may use fresh semen for purposes of a non-spousal artificial insemination, only if within one year prior to the supplying of the semen, a complete medical history of the donor, including, but not limited to, any available genetic history of the donor, was obtained by a physician, the donor had a physical examination by a physician, and the donor was tested for blood type and RH factor."

Library References

Health ⚖=192.
Westlaw Topic No. 198H.

3111.92 Consents to non-spousal insemination of married woman

The non-spousal artificial insemination of a married woman may occur only if both she and her husband sign a written consent to the artificial insemination as described in section 3111.93 of the Revised Code.

(2000 S 180, eff. 3–22–01)

Historical and Statutory Notes

Ed. Note: 3111.92 is former 3111.34, amended and recodified by 2000 S 180, eff. 3–22–01; 1986 H 476, eff. 9–24–86.

Amendment Note: 2000 S 180 substituted "3111.93" for "3111.35".

Library References

Health ⚖=905.
Westlaw Topic No. 198H.

3111.93 Recipient information and statements; date of insemination to be recorded

(A) Prior to a non-spousal artificial insemination, the physician associated with it shall do the following:

(1) Obtain the written consent of the recipient on a form that the physician shall provide. The written consent shall contain all of the following:

(a) The name and address of the recipient and, if married, her husband;

(b) The name of the physician;

(c) The proposed location of the performance of the artificial insemination;

(d) A statement that the recipient and, if married, her husband consent to the artificial insemination;

(e) If desired, a statement that the recipient and, if married, her husband consent to more than one artificial insemination if necessary;

(f) A statement that the donor shall not be advised by the physician or another person performing the artificial insemination as to the identity of the recipient or, if married, her husband and that the recipient and, if married, her husband shall not be advised by the physician or another person performing the artificial insemination as to the identity of the donor;

(g) A statement that the physician is to obtain necessary semen from a donor and, subject to any agreed upon provision as described in division (A)(1)(n) of this section, that the recipient and, if married, her husband shall rely upon the judgment and discretion of the physician in this regard;

(h) A statement that the recipient and, if married, her husband understand that the physician cannot be responsible for the physical or mental characteristics of any child resulting from the artificial insemination;

(i) A statement that there is no guarantee that the recipient will become pregnant as a result of the artificial insemination;

(j) A statement that the artificial insemination shall occur in compliance with sections 3111.88 to 3111.96 of the Revised Code;

(k) A brief summary of the paternity consequences of the artificial insemination as set forth in section 3111.95 of the Revised Code;

(*l*) The signature of the recipient and, if married, her husband;

(m) If agreed to, a statement that the artificial insemination will be performed by a person who is under the supervision and control of the physician;

(n) Any other provision that the physician, the recipient, and, if married, her husband agree to include.

(2) Upon request, provide the recipient and, if married, her husband with the following information to the extent the physician has knowledge of it:

(a) The medical history of the donor, including, but not limited to, any available genetic history of the donor and persons related to him by consanguinity, the blood type of the donor, and whether he has an RH factor;

(b) The race, eye and hair color, age, height, and weight of the donor;

(c) The educational attainment and talents of the donor;

(d) The religious background of the donor;

(e) Any other information that the donor has indicated may be disclosed.

(B) After each non-spousal artificial insemination of a woman, the physician associated with it shall note the date of the artificial insemination in the physician's records pertaining to the woman and the artificial insemination, and retain this information as provided in section 3111.94 of the Revised Code.

(2000 S 180, eff. 3–22–01)

Historical and Statutory Notes

Ed. Note: 3111.93 is former 3111.35, amended and recodified by 2000 S 180, eff. 3–22–01; 1986 H 476, eff. 9–24–86.

Amendment Note: 2000 S 180 substituted "3111.88" for "3111.30" and "3111.96" for "3111.38" in division (A)(1)(j); substituted "3111.95" for "3111.37" in division (A)(1)(k); substituted "3111.94" for "3111.36" in division (B); and made changes to reflect gender neutral language.

Library References

Health ⚖=905 to 906.
Westlaw Topic No. 198H.

3111.94 Physician's files; confidential information; donor information; action for file inspection

(A) The physician who is associated with a non-spousal artificial insemination shall place the written consent obtained pursuant to division (A)(1) of section 3111.93 of the Revised Code, information provided to the recipient and, if married, her husband pursuant to division (A)(2) of that section, other information concerning the donor that the physician possesses, and other matters concerning the artificial insemination in a file that shall bear the name of the recipient. This file shall be retained by the physician in the physician's office separate from any regular medical chart of the recipient, and shall be confidential, except as provided in divisions (B) and (C) of this section. This file is not a public record under section 149.43 of the Revised Code.

(B) The written consent form and information provided to the recipient and, if married, her husband pursuant to division (A)(2) of section 3111.93 of the Revised Code shall be open to inspection only until the child born as the result of the non-spousal artificial insemination is twenty-one years of age, and only to the recipient or, if married, her husband upon request to the physician.

(C) Information pertaining to the donor that was not provided to the recipient and, if married, her husband pursuant to division (A)(2) of section 3111.93 of the Revised Code and that the physician possesses shall be kept in the file pertaining to the non-spousal artificial insemination for at least five years from the date of the artificial insemination. At the expiration of this period, the physician may destroy such information or retain it in the file.

The physician shall not make this information available for inspection by any person during the five-year period or, if the physician retains the information after the expiration of that period, at any other time, unless the following apply:

(1) A child is born as a result of the artificial insemination, an action is filed by the recipient, her husband if she is married, or a guardian of the child in the domestic relations division or, if there is no domestic relations division, the general division of the court of common pleas of the county in which the office of the physician is located, the child is not twenty-one years of age or older, and the court pursuant to division (C)(2) of this section issues an order authorizing the inspection of specified types of information by the recipient, husband, or guardian;

(2) Prior to issuing an order authorizing an inspection of information, the court shall determine, by clear and convincing evidence, that the information that the recipient, husband, or guardian wishes to inspect is necessary for or helpful in the medical treatment of the child born as a result of the artificial insemination, and shall determine which types of information in the file are germane to the medical treatment and are to be made available for inspection by the recipient, husband, or guardian in that regard. An order only shall authorize the inspection of information germane to the medical treatment of the child.

(2000 S 180, eff. 3–22–01)

Historical and Statutory Notes

Ed. Note: 3111.94 is former 3111.36, amended and recodified by 2000 S 180, eff. 3–22–01; 1986 H 476, eff. 9–24–86.

Amendment Note: 2000 S 180 substituted "3111.93" for "3111.35" in divisions (A), (B), and (C); and made changes to reflect gender neutral language.

Library References

Health ⇔196.
Westlaw Topic No. 198H.

3111.95 Husband rather than donor regarded as natural father of child

(A) If a married woman is the subject of a non-spousal artificial insemination and if her husband consented to the artificial insemination, the husband shall be treated in law and regarded as the natural father of a child conceived as a result of the artificial insemination, and a child so conceived shall be treated in law and regarded as the natural child of the husband. A presumption that arises under division (A)(1) or (2) of section 3111.03 of the Revised Code is conclusive with respect to this father and child relationship, and no action or proceeding under sections 3111.01 to 3111.18 or sections 3111.38 to 3111.54 of the Revised Code shall affect the relationship.

(B) If a woman is the subject of a non-spousal artificial insemination, the donor shall not be treated in law or regarded as the natural father of a child conceived as a result of the artificial insemination, and a child so conceived shall not be treated in law or regarded as the natural child of the donor. No action or proceeding under sections 3111.01 to 3111.18 or sections 3111.38 to 3111.54 of the Revised Code shall affect these consequences.

(2000 S 180, eff. 3–22–01)

Historical and Statutory Notes

Ed. Note: 3111.95 is former 3111.37, amended and recodified by 2000 S 180, eff. 3–22–01; 2000 H 242, eff. 10–27–00; 1997 H 352, eff. 1–1–98; 1986 H 476, eff. 9–24–86.

Amendment Note: 2000 S 180 substituted "3111.18" for "3111.19" and "sections 3111.38 to 3111.54" for "section 3111.22 or 3113.2111" in division (A); and substituted "3111.18" for "3111.19" and "sections 3111.38 to 3111.54" for "section 3111.22".

Amendment Note: 2000 H 242 inserted "or 3113.2111".

Amendment Note: 1997 H 352 inserted "or proceeding" and "or section 3111.22" in divisions (A) and (B).

Library References

Children Out-of-Wedlock ⇔3, 10, 35.
Westlaw Topic No. 76H.
C.J.S. Children Out-of-Wedlock §§ 13 to 17, 23, 46, 49, 90.

3111.96 Effect of physician's failure to comply with statutes

The failure of a physician or person under the supervision and control of a physician to comply with the applicable requirements of sections 3111.88 to 3111.95 of the Revised Code shall not affect the legal status, rights, or obligations of a child conceived as a result of a non-spousal artificial insemination, a recipient, a husband who consented to the non-spousal artificial insemination of his wife, or the donor. If a recipient who is married and her husband make a good faith effort to execute a written consent that is in compliance with section 3111.93 of the Revised Code relative to a non-spousal artificial insemination, the failure of the written consent to so comply shall not affect the paternity consequences set forth in division (A) of section 3111.95 of the Revised Code.

(2000 S 180, eff. 3–22–01)

Historical and Statutory Notes

Ed. Note: 3111.96 is former 3111.38, amended and recodified by 2000 S 180, eff. 3–22–01; 1986 H 476, eff. 9–24–86.

Amendment Note: 2000 S 180 substituted "3111.88" for "3111.30", "3111.95" for "3111.37" twice, and "3111.93" for "3111.35".

Library References

Children Out-of-Wedlock ⇔3, 10, 35.

Health ⚖︎905 to 906.

Westlaw Topic Nos. 198H, 76H.

C.J.S. Children Out-of-Wedlock §§ 13 to 17, 23, 46, 49, 90.

EMBRYO DONATION

3111.97 Birth mother regarded as natural mother; effect of husband's consent

(A) A woman who gives birth to a child born as a result of embryo donation shall be treated in law and regarded as the natural mother of the child, and the child shall be treated in law and regarded as the natural child of the woman. No action or proceeding under this chapter shall affect the relationship.

(B) If a married woman gives birth to a child born as a result of embryo donation to which her husband consented, the husband shall be treated in law and regarded as the natural father of the child, and the child shall be treated in law and regarded as the natural child of the husband. A presumption that arises under division (A)(1) or (2) of section 3111.03 of the Revised Code is conclusive with respect to this father and child relationship, and no action or proceeding under this chapter shall affect the relationship.

(C) If a married woman gives birth to a child born as a result of embryo donation to which her husband has not consented, a presumption that arises under division (A)(1) or (2) of section 3111.03 of the Revised Code that the husband is the father of the child may be rebutted by clear and convincing evidence that includes the lack of consent to the embryo donation.

(D) As used in this division, "donor" means an individual who produced genetic material used to create an embryo, consents to the implantation of the embryo in a woman who is not the individual or the individual's wife, and at the time of the embryo donation does not intend to raise the resulting child as the individual's own.

If an individual who produced genetic material used to create an embryo dies, the other person who produced genetic material used to create the embryo may consent to donate the embryo. In such a case, the deceased person shall be deemed a donor for the purposes of this section.

A donor shall not be treated in law or regarded as a parent of a child born as a result of embryo donation. A donor shall have no parental responsibilities and shall have no right, obligation, or interest with respect to a child resulting from the donation.

(E) This section deals with embryo donation for the purpose of impregnating a woman so that she can bear a child that she intends to raise as her child.

(2006 H 102, eff. 6-15-06)

PENALTIES

3111.99 Penalties

Whoever violates section 3111.19 of the Revised Code is guilty of interfering with the establishment of paternity, a misdemeanor of the first degree.

(2000 S 180, eff. 3-22-01; 1999 H 471, eff. 7-1-00; 1997 H 352, eff. 1-1-98; 1996 H 710, § 7, eff. 6-11-96; 1995 H 167, eff. 6-11-96; 1995 S 2, eff. 7-1-96; 1992 S 10, eff. 7-15-92)

Uncodified Law

1996 H 710, § 15, eff. 6-11-96, reads, in part:

(A) The amendments to sections 2151.231, 2301.34, 2301.35, 2301.351, 2301.358, 2705.02, 3111.20, 3111.21, 3111.22, 3111.23, 3111.241, 3111.242, 3111.27, 3111.28, 3111.99, 3113.21, 3113.214, 3113.215, 3113.99, 4723.07, and 4723.09 of the Revised Code by Sub. H.B. 167 of the 121st General Assembly take effect, and their existing interim versions are correspondingly repealed, on the date this act takes effect and not on November 15, 1996 [.]

Historical and Statutory Notes

Ed. Note: Former RC 3111.99 related to penalties for non-compliance with support orders. See now RC 3121.99; 3121.59 for provisions analogous to former RC 3111.99.

Ed. Note: The effective date of the amendment of this section by 1995 H 167 was changed from 11-15-96 to 6-11-96 by 1996 H 710, § 7, eff. 6-11-96.

Amendment Note: 2000 S 180 rewrote this section which prior thereto read:

"(A) For purposes of this section, "administrative support order" and "obligor" have the same meaning as in section 3111.20 of the Revised Code.

"(B) Whoever violates section 3111.29 of the Revised Code is guilty of interfering with the establishment of paternity, a misdemeanor of the first degree.

"(C) An obligor who violates division (B)(1)(c) of section 3111.23 of the Revised Code shall be fined not more than fifty dollars for a first offense, not more than one hundred dollars for a second offense, and not more than five hundred dollars for each subsequent offense.

"(D) An obligor who violates division (E)(2) of section 3111.23 of the Revised Code shall be fined not more than fifty dollars for a first offense, not more than one hundred dollars for a second offense, and not more than five hundred dollars for each subsequent offense.

"(E) A fine imposed pursuant to division (C) or (D) of this section shall be paid to the division of child support in the department of job and family services or, pursuant to division (H)(4) of section 2301.35 of the Revised Code, the child support enforcement agency. The amount of the fine that does not exceed the amount of arrearage the obligor owes under the administrative support order shall be disbursed in accordance with the support order. The amount of the fine that exceeds the amount of the arrearage under the support order shall be called program income and shall be collected in accordance with section 5101.325 of the Revised Code."

Amendment Note: 1999 H 471 substituted "job and family" for "human" in division (E).

Amendment Note: 1997 H 352 substituted "division of child support in the department of human services or, pursuant to division (H) of section 2301.35 of the Revised Code, the child support enforcement agency" for "child support enforcement agency administering the obligor's child support order" and "called program income and shall be collected in accordance with section 5101.325 of the Revised Code" for "used by the agency for the administration of its program for child support enforcement" in division (E).

Amendment Note: 1995 S 2 deleted the former second sentence, which read:

"If the offender previously has been convicted of or pleaded guilty to a violation of section 3111.29 or 2919.231 of the Revised Code, interfering with the establishment of paternity is a felony of the fourth degree."

Amendment Note: 1995 H 167 added division (A); designated division (B); and added divisions (C), (D), and (E).

Library References

Obstructing Justice ⚖︎6, 21.

Westlaw Topic No. 282.

C.J.S. Obstructing Justice or Governmental Administration §§ 3 to 8, 37 to 38, 47.

CHAPTER 3705

VITAL STATISTICS

STATEWIDE REGISTRATION SYSTEM; ADMINISTRATIVE PROVISIONS

Section
3705.071 Duties of local registrar of vital statistics upon death of person under eighteen years of age

BIRTH CERTIFICATES

3705.09 Filing of birth certificates; birth certificate of legitimatized child
3705.091 Signing, notarizing, and sending of acknowledgment of paternity; affidavits
3705.15 Registration of unrecorded birth; correction of birth record; costs

STATEWIDE REGISTRATION SYSTEM; ADMINISTRATIVE PROVISIONS

3705.071 Duties of local registrar of vital statistics upon death of person under eighteen years of age

On receipt of a death certificate of a person who was under eighteen years of age at death, the local registrar of vital statistics shall determine the county in which the person resided at the time of death. If the county of residence was other than the county in which the person died, the registrar, after registering the certificate and no later than four weeks after receiving it, shall make a copy of the certificate and send it to the local registrar of vital statistics of the county in which the person resided at the time of death.

(2000 H 448, eff. 10-5-00)

Library References

Health ☞398.
Westlaw Topic No. 198H.
C.J.S. Health and Environment §§ 24, 74.

BIRTH CERTIFICATES

3705.09 Filing of birth certificates; birth certificate of legitimatized child

(A) A birth certificate for each live birth in this state shall be filed in the registration district in which it occurs within ten days after such birth and shall be registered if it has been completed and filed in accordance with this section.

(B) When a birth occurs in or en route to an institution, the person in charge of the institution or a designated representative shall obtain the personal data, prepare the certificate, secure the signatures required, and file the certificate within ten days with the local registrar of vital statistics. The physician in attendance shall provide the medical information required by the certificate and certify to the facts of birth within seventy-two hours after the birth.

(C) When a birth occurs outside an institution, the birth certificate shall be prepared and filed by one of the following in the indicated order of priority:

(1) The physician in attendance at or immediately after the birth;

(2) Any other person in attendance at or immediately after the birth;

(3) The father;

(4) The mother;

(5) The person in charge of the premises where the birth occurred.

(D) Either of the parents of the child or other informant shall attest to the accuracy of the personal data entered on the birth certificate in time to permit the filing of the certificate within the ten days prescribed in this section.

(E) When a birth occurs in a moving conveyance within the United States and the child is first removed from the conveyance in this state, the birth shall be registered in this state and the place where it is first removed shall be considered the place of birth. When a birth occurs on a moving conveyance while in international waters or air space or in a foreign country or its air space and the child is first removed from the conveyance in this state, the birth shall be registered in this state but the record shall show the actual place of birth insofar as can be determined.

(F)(1) If the mother of a child was married at the time of either conception or birth or between conception and birth, the child shall be registered in the surname designated by the mother, and the name of the husband shall be entered on the certificate as the father of the child. The presumption of paternity shall be in accordance with section 3111.03 of the Revised Code.

(2) If the mother was not married at the time of conception or birth or between conception and birth, the child shall be registered by the surname designated by the mother. The name of the father of such child shall also be inserted on the birth certificate if both the mother and the father sign an acknowledgement of paternity affidavit before the birth record has been sent to the local registrar. If the father is not named on the birth certificate pursuant to division (F)(1) or (2) of this section, no other information about the father shall be entered on the record.

(G) When a man is presumed, found, or declared to be the father of a child, according to section 2105.26, sections 3111.01 to 3111.18, former section 3111.21, or sections 3111.38 to 3111.54 of the Revised Code, or the father has acknowledged the child as his child in an acknowledgment of paternity, and the acknowledgment has become final pursuant to section 2151.232, 3111.25, or 3111.821 of the Revised Code, and documentary evidence of such fact is submitted to the department of health in such form as the director may require, a new birth record shall be issued by the department which shall have the same overall appearance as the record which would have been issued under this section if a marriage had occurred before the birth of such child. Where handwriting is required to effect such appearance, the department shall supply it. Upon the issuance of such new birth record, the original birth record shall cease to be a public record. Except as provided in division (C) of section 3705.091 of the Revised Code, the original record and any documentary evidence supporting the new registration of birth shall be placed in an envelope which shall be sealed by the department and shall not be open to inspection or copy unless so ordered by a court of competent jurisdiction.

The department shall then promptly forward a copy of the new birth record to the local registrar of vital statistics of the district in which the birth occurred, and such local registrar shall file a copy of such new birth record along with and in the same manner as the other copies of birth records in such local registrar's possession. All copies of the original birth record in the possession of the local registrar or the probate court, as well as any and all index references to it, shall be destroyed. Such new birth record, as well as any certified or exact copy of it, when properly authenticated by a duly authorized person shall be prima-facie evidence in all courts and places of the facts stated in it.

(H) When a woman who is a legal resident of this state has given birth to a child in a foreign country that does not have a system of registration of vital statistics, a birth record may be filed in the office of vital statistics on evidence satisfactory to the director of health.

(I) Every birth certificate filed under this section on or after July 1, 1990, shall be accompanied by all social security numbers that have been issued to the parents of the child, unless the division of child support in the department of job and family services, acting in accordance with regulations prescribed under the "Family Support Act of 1988," 102 Stat. 2353, 42 U.S.C.A. 405, as amended, finds good cause for not requiring that the numbers be furnished with the certificate. The parents' social security numbers shall not be recorded on the certificate. The local registrar of vital statistics shall transmit the social security numbers to the state office of vital statistics in accordance with section 3705.07 of the Revised Code. No social security number obtained under this division shall be used for any purpose other than child support enforcement.

(2001 H 85, eff. 10–31–01; 2000 S 180, eff. 3–22–01; 1999 H 471, eff. 7–1–00; 1997 H 352, eff. 1–1–98; 1990 H 591, eff. 4–12–90; 1989 H 112, § 4; 1988 H 790)

Historical and Statutory Notes

Ed. Note: 3705.09 is former 3705.15, amended and recodified by 1989 H 112, § 4, and 1988 H 790, eff. 3–16–89; 1986 H 476; 1982 H 245; 130 v H 202; 126 v 1005; 1953 H 1; GC 1261–52a.

Ed. Note: 3705.09 contains provisions analogous to former 3705.14, repealed by 1989 H 112, § 4, and 1988 H 790, eff. 3–16–89.

Ed. Note: Former 3705.09 repealed by 1989 H 112, § 4, and 1988 H 790, eff. 3–16–89; 129 v 240; 1953 H 1; GC 1261–47a.

Pre–1953 H 1 Amendments: 124 v H 42

Library References

Health ⚖397.
Westlaw Topic No. 198H.
C.J.S. Health and Environment §§ 24, 74.

Baldwin's Ohio Legislative Service, 1990 Laws of Ohio, H 591—LSC Analysis, p 5–576

3705.091 Signing, notarizing, and sending of acknowledgment of paternity; affidavits

(A) If the natural mother and alleged father of a child sign an acknowledgment of paternity affidavit prepared pursuant to section 3111.31 of the Revised Code with respect to that child at the office of the local registrar, the local registrar shall provide a notary public to notarize the acknowledgment. The local registrar shall send a signed and notarized acknowledgment of paternity to the office of child support in the department of job and family services pursuant to section 3111.22 of the Revised Code. The local registrar shall send the acknowledgment no later than ten days after it has been signed and notarized. If the local registrar knows a man is presumed under section 3111.03 of the Revised Code to be the father of the child and that the presumed father is not the man who signed or is attempting to sign an acknowledgment with respect to the child, the local registrar shall not notarize or send the acknowledgment pursuant to this section.

(B) The local registrar of vital statistics shall provide an acknowledgment of paternity affidavit described in division (A) of this section to any person that requests it.

(C) The department of health shall store all acknowledgments of paternity affidavits it receives pursuant to section 3111.24 of the Revised Code. The department of health shall send to the office any acknowledgment the department is storing that the office requests. The department of health shall adopt rules pursuant to Chapter 119. of the Revised Code to govern the method of storage of the acknowledgments and to implement this section.

(D) The department of health and the department of job and family services shall enter into an agreement regarding expenses incurred by the department of health in comparing acknowledgment of paternity affidavits to birth records and storage of acknowledgment of paternity affidavits.

(2000 S 180, eff. 3–22–01; 1999 H 471, eff. 7–1–00; 1997 H 352, eff. 1–1–98)

Library References

Health ⚖397.
Westlaw Topic No. 198H.
C.J.S. Health and Environment §§ 24, 74.

3705.15 Registration of unrecorded birth; correction of birth record; costs

Whoever claims to have been born in this state, and whose registration of birth is not recorded, or has been lost or destroyed, or has not been properly and accurately recorded, may file an application for registration of birth or correction of the birth record in the probate court of the county of the person's birth or residence or the county in which the person's mother resided at the time of the person's birth. If the person is a minor the application shall be signed by either parent or the person's guardian.

(A) An application to correct a birth record shall set forth all of the available facts required on a birth record and the reasons for making the application, and shall be verified by the applicant. Upon the filing of the application the court may fix a date for a hearing, which shall not be less than seven days after the filing date. The court may require one publication of notice of the hearing in a newspaper of general circulation in the county at least seven days prior to the date of the hearing. The application shall be supported by the affidavit of the physician in attendance. If an affidavit is not available the application shall be supported by the affidavits of at least two persons having knowledge of the facts stated in the application, by documentary evidence, or by other evidence the court deems sufficient.

The probate judge, if satisfied that the facts are as stated, shall make an order correcting the birth record, except that in the case of an application to correct the date of birth, the judge shall make the order only if any date shown as the date the attending physician signed the birth record or the date the local registrar filed the record is consistent with the corrected date of birth. If supported by sufficient evidence, the judge may include in an order correcting the date of birth an order correcting the date the attending physician signed the birth record or the date the local registrar filed the record.

(B) An application of a person whose registration of birth is not recorded, or has been lost or destroyed, must comply with division (A) of this section. Upon the filing of the application the court may fix a date for a hearing, which shall not be less than seven days after the filing date. The court may require one publication of notice of the hearing in a newspaper of general circulation in the county at least seven days prior to the date of the hearing. The probate judge, or a special master commissioner, shall personally examine the applicant in open court and shall take sworn testimony on the application which shall include the testimony of at least two credible witnesses, or clear and convincing documentary evidence. The probate court may conduct any necessary investigation, and shall permit the applicant and all witnesses presented to be cross-examined by any interested person, or by the prosecuting attorney of the county. When a witness or the applicant is unable to appear in open court, the court may authorize the taking of the witness's or applicant's deposition. The court may cause a complete record to be taken of the hearing, shall file it with the other papers in the case, and may order the transcript of the testimony to be filed and made a matter of record in the court. Upon being satisfied that notice of the hearing on the application has been given by publication, if required, and that the claim of the applicant is true, the court shall make a finding upon all the facts required on a birth record, and shall order the registration of the birth of the applicant. The court shall forthwith transmit to the director of health a certified summary of its finding and order, on a form prescribed by the director, who shall file it in the records of the central division of vital statistics.

(C) The director may forward a copy of the summary for the registration of a birth in the director's office to the appropriate local registrar of vital statistics.

A certified copy of the birth record corrected or registered by court order as provided in this section shall have the same legal effect for all purposes as an original birth record.

The application, affidavits, findings, and orders of the court, together with a transcript of the testimony if ordered by the court, for the correction of a birth record or for the registration of a birth, shall be recorded in a book kept for that purpose and shall be properly indexed. The book shall become a part of the records of the probate court.

(D)(1) Except as provided in division (D)(2) of this section, whenever a correction is ordered in a birth record under division (A) of this section, the court ordering the correction shall forthwith forward to the department of health a certified copy of the order containing such information as will enable the department to prepare a new birth record. Thereupon, the department shall record a new birth record using the correct information supplied by the court and the new birth record shall have the same overall appearance as the original record which would have been issued under this chapter. Where handwriting is required to effect that appearance, the department shall supply it. Upon the preparation and filing of the new birth record, the original birth record and index references shall cease to be a public record. The original record and all other information pertaining to it shall be placed in an envelope which shall be sealed by the department, and its contents shall not be open to inspection or copy unless so ordered by the probate court of the county that ordered the correction.

The department shall promptly forward a copy of the new birth record to the local registrar of vital statistics of the district in which the birth occurred and the local registrar shall file a copy of the new birth record along with and in the same manner as the other copies of birth records in the local registrar's possession. All copies of the original birth record, as well as any and all other papers, documents, and index references pertaining to it, in the possession of the local registrar shall be destroyed. The probate court shall retain permanently in the file of its proceedings such information as will enable the court to identify both the original birth record and the new birth record.

The new birth record, as well as any certified copies of it when properly authenticated by a duly authorized person, shall be prima-facie evidence in all courts and places of the facts therein stated.

(2) If the correction ordered in the birth record under division (A) of this section involves a change in the date of birth of the applicant and the department of health determines that the corrected date of birth is inconsistent with the date shown as the date the attending physician signed the birth record or the date the local registrar filed the record, the department shall request that the court reconsider the order and, if appropriate, make a new order in which the dates are consistent. If the court does not make a new order within a reasonable time, instead of issuing a new birth record, the department shall file and record the court's order in the same manner as other birth records and make a cross-reference on the original and on the corrected record.

(E) The probate court shall assess costs of registering a birth or correcting a birth record under this section against the person who makes application for the registration or correction.

(1996 H 355, eff. 4–2–96; 1990 H 210, eff. 6–28–90; 1988 H 790)

Historical and Statutory Notes

Ed. Note: 3705.15 is former 3705.20, amended and recodified by 1988 H 790, eff. 3–16–89; 132 v H 534; 1953 H 1; GC 1261–57.

Ed. Note: Former 3705.15 amended and recodified as 3705.09 by 1989 H 112, § 4, and 1988 H 790, eff. 3–16–89; 1986 H 476; 1982 H 245; 130 v H 202; 126 v 1005; 1953 H 1; GC 1261–52a.

Pre–1953 H 1 Amendments: 120 v 447

Library References

Health ☞397.
Westlaw Topic No. 198H.
C.J.S. Health and Environment §§ 24, 74.

CHAPTER 3923

SICKNESS AND ACCIDENT INSURANCE

Section
3923.061 Interest on insurance proceeds

3923.061 Interest on insurance proceeds

(A) On and after January 1, 2003, any insurance company authorized to do business in this state shall pay interest, in accordance with division (B) of this section and subject to division (C) of this section, on any proceeds that become due pursuant to the terms of a policy of sickness and accident insurance due to the death of the insured by sickness or accident.

(B) The interest payable pursuant to division (A) of this section shall be computed from the date of the death of the insured to the date of the payment of the proceeds and shall be at whichever of the following rates is greater:

(1) The annual short-term applicable federal rate for purposes of section 1274(d) of the Internal Revenue Code, as defined in section 5747.01 of the Revised Code, in effect for the month in which the insured died;

(2) The current rate of interest on proceeds left on deposit with the company under an interest settlement option contained in the policy of sickness and accident insurance.

(C) Division (A) or (B) of this section does not require the payment of interest unless the insured was a resident of this state on the date of the insured's death and unless the beneficiary under the policy of sickness and accident insurance elects in writing to receive, or a written election has been made for the beneficiary to receive, the proceeds of the policy by means of a lump sum payment.

(2002 H 345, eff. 7–23–02)

Library References

Insurance ☞3396.
Westlaw Topic No. 217.

C.J.S. Insurance § 1631.

CHAPTER 4505

CERTIFICATE OF MOTOR VEHICLE TITLE LAW

OBTAINING A CERTIFICATE OF TITLE; SURRENDER AND CANCELLATION

Section
4505.06 Application for certificate of title; conditions; fees; sales taxes; valuation; odometer reading; methods of payment; return in case of casual sale; manufactured or mobile homes
4505.10 Certificate of title when ownership changed by operation of law

Uncodified Law

1999 H 163, § 17, eff. 3-31-99, reads:

There is hereby created the Task Force on Motor Vehicle Titling, consisting of the Director of Public Safety, the Registrar of Motor Vehicles, two members of the Senate, both of whom shall be appointed by the President of the Senate but only one of whom shall be of the same political party as the President, two members of the House of Representatives, both of whom shall be appointed by the Speaker of the House of Representatives but only one of whom shall be of the same political party as the Speaker, a representative of the Office of the Attorney General designated by the Attorney General, a representative of the Department of Taxation designated by the Tax Commissioner, three members of the Ohio Clerks of Court Association, one of whom shall be appointed by the Governor and two of whom shall be selected by the Association as its representatives, the president of the Ohio Automobile Dealers Association or the president's representative, the president of the Ohio Auto Auction Association or the president's representative, one person who represents a company that is a member of the Ohio Telecommunications Industry Association and is appointed by the Governor, one person who represents a company that is engaged in the business of providing financing for the purchase or leasing of motor vehicles and is appointed by the Governor, and two members of the public at large who are appointed by the Governor.

The President, Speaker, and Governor shall make their appointments, and the Tax Commissioner and Attorney General shall each designate a representative, within two weeks after the effective date of this section, and the President and Speaker shall select jointly a chairperson of the Task Force from among the four legislative members.

The Task Force shall evaluate the current state of technology to determine whether the creation of an efficient, integrated, and accurate system of delivering information regarding ownership and other interests and related data and information relating to motor vehicles, including the area of motor vehicle titling, is feasible, and if so, a general estimate of the costs involved in creating such a system. The Task Force shall evaluate any recent advancements in the electronic transfer of information that would make creation of such a system possible. The Task Force shall make any recommendations regarding actions that would need to be taken to create such a system.

The Task Force shall submit its report, including its evaluations and recommendations, to the Governor and the General Assembly not later than one hundred eighty days after the effective date of this section, and then the Task Force shall cease to exist.

This section is not subject to the referendum. Therefore, under Ohio Constitution, Article II, Section 1d and section 1.471 of the Revised Code, this section goes into immediate effect when this act becomes law.

OBTAINING A CERTIFICATE OF TITLE; SURRENDER AND CANCELLATION

4505.06 Application for certificate of title; conditions; fees; sales taxes; valuation; odometer reading; methods of payment; return in case of casual sale; manufactured or mobile homes

(A)(1) Application for a certificate of title shall be made in a form prescribed by the registrar of motor vehicles and shall be sworn to before a notary public or other officer empowered to administer oaths. The application shall be filed with the clerk of any court of common pleas. An application for a certificate of title may be filed electronically by any electronic means approved by the registrar in any county with the clerk of the court of common pleas of that county. Any payments required by this chapter shall be considered as accompanying any electronically transmitted application when payment actually is received by the clerk. Payment of any fee or taxes may be made by electronic transfer of funds.

(2) The application for a certificate of title shall be accompanied by the fee prescribed in section 4505.09 of the Revised Code. The fee shall be retained by the clerk who issues the certificate of title and shall be distributed in accordance with that section. If a clerk of a court of common pleas, other than the clerk of the court of common pleas of an applicant's county of residence, issues a certificate of title to the applicant, the clerk shall transmit data related to the transaction to the automated title processing system.

(3) If a certificate of title previously has been issued for a motor vehicle in this state, the application for a certificate of title also shall be accompanied by that certificate of title duly assigned, unless otherwise provided in this chapter. If a certificate of title previously has not been issued for the motor vehicle in this state, the application, unless otherwise provided in this chapter, shall be accompanied by a manufacturer's or importer's certificate or by a certificate of title of another state from which the motor vehicle was brought into this state. If the application refers to a motor vehicle last previously registered in another state, the application also shall be accompanied by the physical inspection certificate required by section 4505.061 of the Revised Code. If the application is made by two persons regarding a motor vehicle in which they wish to establish joint ownership with right of survivorship, they may do so as provided in section 2131.12 of the Revised Code. If the applicant requests a designation of the motor vehicle in beneficiary form so that upon the death of the owner of the motor vehicle, ownership of the motor vehicle will pass to a designated transfer-on-death beneficiary or beneficiaries, the applicant may do so as provided in section 2131.13 of the Revised Code. A person who establishes ownership of a motor vehicle that is transferable on death in accordance with section 2131.13 of the Revised Code may terminate that type of ownership or change the designation of the transfer-on-death beneficiary or beneficiaries by applying for a certificate of title pursuant to this section. The clerk shall retain the evidence of title presented by the applicant and on which the certificate of title is issued, except that, if an application for a certificate of title is filed electronically by an electronic motor vehicle dealer on behalf of the purchaser of a motor vehicle, the clerk shall retain the completed electronic record to which the dealer converted the certificate of title application and other required documents. The registrar, after consultation with the attorney general, shall adopt rules that govern the location at which, and the manner in which, are stored the actual application and all other documents relating to the sale of a motor vehicle when an electronic motor vehicle dealer files the application for a certificate of title electronically on behalf of the purchaser.

The clerk shall use reasonable diligence in ascertaining whether or not the facts in the application for a certificate of title are true by checking the application and documents accompanying it or the electronic record to which a dealer converted the application and accompanying documents with the records of motor vehicles in the clerk's office. If the clerk is satisfied that the applicant is the owner of the motor vehicle and that the application is in the proper form, the clerk, within five business days after the application is filed and except as provided in section 4505.021 of the Revised Code, shall issue a physical certificate of title over the clerk's signature and sealed with the clerk's seal, unless the applicant specifically requests the clerk not to issue a physical certificate of title and instead to issue an electronic certificate of title. For purposes of the transfer of a certificate of title, if the clerk is satisfied that the secured party has duly discharged a lien notation but has not canceled the lien notation with a clerk, the clerk may cancel the lien notation on the automated title processing system and notify the clerk of the county of origin.

(4) In the case of the sale of a motor vehicle to a general buyer or user by a dealer, by a motor vehicle leasing dealer selling the motor vehicle to the lessee or, in a case in which the leasing dealer subleased the motor vehicle, the sublessee, at the end of the lease agreement or sublease agreement, or by a manufactured home broker, the certificate of title shall be obtained in the name of the buyer by the dealer, leasing dealer, or manufactured home broker, as the case may be, upon application signed by the buyer. The certificate of title shall be issued, or the process of entering the certificate of title application information into the automated title processing system if a physical certificate of title is not to be issued shall be completed, within five business days after the application for title is filed with the clerk. If the buyer of the motor vehicle previously leased the motor vehicle and is buying the motor vehicle at the end of the lease pursuant to that lease, the certificate of title shall be obtained in the name of the buyer by the motor vehicle leasing dealer who previously leased the motor vehicle to the buyer or by the motor vehicle leasing dealer who subleased the motor vehicle to the buyer under a sublease agreement.

In all other cases, except as provided in section 4505.032 and division (D)(2) of section 4505.11 of the Revised Code, such certificates shall be obtained by the buyer.

(5)(a)(i) If the certificate of title is being obtained in the name of the buyer by a motor vehicle dealer or motor vehicle leasing dealer and there is a security interest to be noted on the certificate of title, the dealer or leasing dealer shall submit the application for the certificate of title and payment of the applicable tax to a clerk within seven business days after the later of the delivery of the motor vehicle to the buyer or the date the dealer or leasing dealer obtains the manufacturer's or importer's certificate, or certificate of title issued in the name of the dealer or leasing dealer, for the motor vehicle. Submission of the application for the certificate of title and payment of the applicable tax within the required seven business days may be indicated by postmark or receipt by a clerk within that period.

(ii) Upon receipt of the certificate of title with the security interest noted on its face, the dealer or leasing dealer shall forward the certificate of title to the secured party at the location noted in the financing documents or otherwise specified by the secured party.

(iii) A motor vehicle dealer or motor vehicle leasing dealer is liable to a secured party for a late fee of ten dollars per day for each certificate of title application and payment of the applicable tax that is submitted to a clerk more than seven business days but less than twenty-one days after the later of the delivery of the motor vehicle to the buyer or the date the dealer or leasing dealer obtains the manufacturer's or importer's certificate, or certificate of title issued in the name of the dealer or leasing dealer, for the motor vehicle and, from then on, twenty-five dollars per day until the application and applicable tax are submitted to a clerk.

(b) In all cases of transfer of a motor vehicle, the application for certificate of title shall be filed within thirty days after the assignment or delivery of the motor vehicle. If an application for a certificate of title is not filed within the period specified in division (A)(5)(b) of this section, the clerk shall collect a fee of five dollars for the issuance of the certificate, except that no such fee shall be required from a motor vehicle salvage dealer, as defined in division (A) of section 4738.01 of the Revised Code, who immediately surrenders the certificate of title for cancellation. The fee shall be in addition to all other fees established by this chapter, and shall be retained by the clerk. The registrar shall provide, on the certificate of title form prescribed by section 4505.07 of the Revised Code, language necessary to give evidence of the date on which the assignment or delivery of the motor vehicle was made.

(6) As used in division (A) of this section, "lease agreement," "lessee," and "sublease agreement" have the same meanings as in section 4505.04 of the Revised Code.

(B)(1) The clerk, except as provided in this section, shall refuse to accept for filing any application for a certificate of title and shall refuse to issue a certificate of title unless the dealer or manufactured home broker or the applicant, in cases in which the certificate shall be obtained by the buyer, submits with the application payment of the tax levied by or pursuant to Chapters 5739. and 5741. of the Revised Code based on the purchaser's county of residence. Upon payment of the tax in accordance with division (E) of this section, the clerk shall issue a receipt prescribed by the registrar and agreed upon by the tax commissioner showing payment of the tax or a receipt issued by the commissioner showing the payment of the tax. When submitting payment of the tax to the clerk, a dealer shall retain any discount to which the dealer is entitled under section 5739.12 of the Revised Code.

(2) For receiving and disbursing such taxes paid to the clerk by a resident of the clerk's county, the clerk may retain a poundage fee of one and one one-hundredth per cent, and the clerk shall pay the poundage fee into the certificate of title administration fund created by section 325.33 of the Revised Code. The clerk shall not retain a poundage fee from payments of taxes by persons who do not reside in the clerk's county.

A clerk, however, may retain from the taxes paid to the clerk an amount equal to the poundage fees associated with certificates of title issued by other clerks of courts of common pleas to applicants who reside in the first clerk's county. The registrar, in consultation with the tax commissioner and the clerks of the courts of common pleas, shall develop a report from the automated title processing system that informs each clerk of the amount of the poundage fees that the clerk is permitted to retain from those taxes because of certificates of title issued by the clerks of other counties to applicants who reside in the first clerk's county.

(3) In the case of casual sales of motor vehicles, as defined in section 4517.01 of the Revised Code, the price for the purpose of determining the tax shall be the purchase price on the assigned certificate of title executed by the seller and filed with the clerk by the buyer on a form to be prescribed by the registrar, which shall be prima-facie evidence of the amount for the determination of the tax.

(4) Each county clerk shall forward to the treasurer of state all sales and use tax collections resulting from sales of motor vehicles, off-highway motorcycles, and all-purpose vehicles during a calendar week on or before the Friday following the close of that week. If, on any Friday, the offices of the clerk of courts or the state are not open for business, the tax shall be forwarded to the treasurer of state on or before the next day on which the offices are open. Every remittance of tax under division (B)(4) of this section shall be accompanied by a remittance report in such form as the tax commissioner prescribes. Upon receipt of a tax remittance and remittance report, the treasurer of state shall date stamp the report and forward it to the tax commissioner. If the tax due for any week is not remitted by a clerk of courts as required under division (B)(4) of this section, the commissioner may require the clerk to forfeit the poundage fees for the sales made during that week. The treasurer of state may require the

clerks of courts to transmit tax collections and remittance reports electronically.

(C)(1) If the transferor indicates on the certificate of title that the odometer reflects mileage in excess of the designed mechanical limit of the odometer, the clerk shall enter the phrase "exceeds mechanical limits" following the mileage designation. If the transferor indicates on the certificate of title that the odometer reading is not the actual mileage, the clerk shall enter the phrase "nonactual: warning—odometer discrepancy" following the mileage designation. The clerk shall use reasonable care in transferring the information supplied by the transferor, but is not liable for any errors or omissions of the clerk or those of the clerk's deputies in the performance of the clerk's duties created by this chapter.

The registrar shall prescribe an affidavit in which the transferor shall swear to the true selling price and, except as provided in this division, the true odometer reading of the motor vehicle. The registrar may prescribe an affidavit in which the seller and buyer provide information pertaining to the odometer reading of the motor vehicle in addition to that required by this section, as such information may be required by the United States secretary of transportation by rule prescribed under authority of subchapter IV of the "Motor Vehicle Information and Cost Savings Act," 86 Stat. 961 (1972), 15 U.S.C. 1981.

(2) Division (C)(1) of this section does not require the giving of information concerning the odometer and odometer reading of a motor vehicle when ownership of a motor vehicle is being transferred as a result of a bequest, under the laws of intestate succession, to a survivor pursuant to section 2106.18, 2131.12, or 4505.10 of the Revised Code, to a transfer-on-death beneficiary or beneficiaries pursuant to section 2131.13 of the Revised Code, in connection with the creation of a security interest or for a vehicle with a gross vehicle weight rating of more than sixteen thousand pounds.

(D) When the transfer to the applicant was made in some other state or in interstate commerce, the clerk, except as provided in this section, shall refuse to issue any certificate of title unless the tax imposed by or pursuant to Chapter 5741. of the Revised Code based on the purchaser's county of residence has been paid as evidenced by a receipt issued by the tax commissioner, or unless the applicant submits with the application payment of the tax. Upon payment of the tax in accordance with division (E) of this section, the clerk shall issue a receipt prescribed by the registrar and agreed upon by the tax commissioner, showing payment of the tax.

For receiving and disbursing such taxes paid to the clerk by a resident of the clerk's county, the clerk may retain a poundage fee of one and one one-hundredth per cent. The clerk shall not retain a poundage fee from payments of taxes by persons who do not reside in the clerk's county.

A clerk, however, may retain from the taxes paid to the clerk an amount equal to the poundage fees associated with certificates of title issued by other clerks of courts of common pleas to applicants who reside in the first clerk's county. The registrar, in consultation with the tax commissioner and the clerks of the courts of common pleas, shall develop a report from the automated title processing system that informs each clerk of the amount of the poundage fees that the clerk is permitted to retain from those taxes because of certificates of title issued by the clerks of other counties to applicants who reside in the first clerk's county.

When the vendor is not regularly engaged in the business of selling motor vehicles, the vendor shall not be required to purchase a vendor's license or make reports concerning those sales.

(E) The clerk shall accept any payment of a tax in cash, or by cashier's check, certified check, draft, money order, or teller check issued by any insured financial institution payable to the clerk and submitted with an application for a certificate of title under division (B) or (D) of this section. The clerk also may accept payment of the tax by corporate, business, or personal check, credit card, electronic transfer or wire transfer, debit card, or any other accepted form of payment made payable to the clerk. The clerk may require bonds, guarantees, or letters of credit to ensure the collection of corporate, business, or personal checks. Any service fee charged by a third party to a clerk for the use of any form of payment may be paid by the clerk from the certificate of title administration fund created in section 325.33 of the Revised Code, or may be assessed by the clerk upon the applicant as an additional fee. Upon collection, the additional fees shall be paid by the clerk into that certificate of title administration fund.

The clerk shall make a good faith effort to collect any payment of taxes due but not made because the payment was returned or dishonored, but the clerk is not personally liable for the payment of uncollected taxes or uncollected fees. The clerk shall notify the tax commissioner of any such payment of taxes that is due but not made and shall furnish the information to the commissioner that the commissioner requires. The clerk shall deduct the amount of taxes due but not paid from the clerk's periodic remittance of tax payments, in accordance with procedures agreed upon by the tax commissioner. The commissioner may collect taxes due by assessment in the manner provided in section 5739.13 of the Revised Code.

Any person who presents payment that is returned or dishonored for any reason is liable to the clerk for payment of a penalty over and above the amount of the taxes due. The clerk shall determine the amount of the penalty, and the penalty shall be no greater than that amount necessary to compensate the clerk for banking charges, legal fees, or other expenses incurred by the clerk in collecting the returned or dishonored payment. The remedies and procedures provided in this section are in addition to any other available civil or criminal remedies. Subsequently collected penalties, poundage fees, and title fees, less any title fee due the state, from returned or dishonored payments collected by the clerk shall be paid into the certificate of title administration fund. Subsequently collected taxes, less poundage fees, shall be sent by the clerk to the treasurer of state at the next scheduled periodic remittance of tax payments, with information as the commissioner may require. The clerk may abate all or any part of any penalty assessed under this division.

(F) In the following cases, the clerk shall accept for filing an application and shall issue a certificate of title without requiring payment or evidence of payment of the tax:

(1) When the purchaser is this state or any of its political subdivisions, a church, or an organization whose purchases are exempted by section 5739.02 of the Revised Code;

(2) When the transaction in this state is not a retail sale as defined by section 5739.01 of the Revised Code;

(3) When the purchase is outside this state or in interstate commerce and the purpose of the purchaser is not to use, store, or consume within the meaning of section 5741.01 of the Revised Code;

(4) When the purchaser is the federal government;

(5) When the motor vehicle was purchased outside this state for use outside this state;

(6) When the motor vehicle is purchased by a nonresident of this state for immediate removal from this state, and will be permanently titled and registered in another state, as provided by division (B)(23) of section 5739.02 of the Revised Code, and upon presentation of a copy of the affidavit provided by that section, and a copy of the exemption certificate provided by section 5739.03 of the Revised Code.

(G) An application, as prescribed by the registrar and agreed to by the tax commissioner, shall be filled out and sworn to by the buyer of a motor vehicle in a casual sale. The application shall contain the following notice in bold lettering: "WARNING TO TRANSFEROR AND TRANSFEREE (SELLER AND BUY-

ER): You are required by law to state the true selling price. A false statement is in violation of section 2921.13 of the Revised Code and is punishable by six months' imprisonment or a fine of up to one thousand dollars, or both. All transfers are audited by the department of taxation. The seller and buyer must provide any information requested by the department of taxation. The buyer may be assessed any additional tax found to be due."

(H) For sales of manufactured homes or mobile homes occurring on or after January 1, 2000, the clerk shall accept for filing, pursuant to Chapter 5739. of the Revised Code, an application for a certificate of title for a manufactured home or mobile home without requiring payment of any tax pursuant to section 5739.02, 5741.021, 5741.022, or 5741.023 of the Revised Code, or a receipt issued by the tax commissioner showing payment of the tax. For sales of manufactured homes or mobile homes occurring on or after January 1, 2000, the applicant shall pay to the clerk an additional fee of five dollars for each certificate of title issued by the clerk for a manufactured or mobile home pursuant to division (H) of section 4505.11 of the Revised Code and for each certificate of title issued upon transfer of ownership of the home. The clerk shall credit the fee to the county certificate of title administration fund, and the fee shall be used to pay the expenses of archiving those certificates pursuant to division (A) of section 4505.08 and division (H)(3) of section 4505.11 of the Revised Code. The tax commissioner shall administer any tax on a manufactured or mobile home pursuant to Chapters 5739. and 5741. of the Revised Code.

(I) Every clerk shall have the capability to transact by electronic means all procedures and transactions relating to the issuance of motor vehicle certificates of title that are described in the Revised Code as being accomplished by electronic means.

(2005 H 66, eff. 6–30–05; 2005 H 68, eff. 6–29–05; 2004 H 230, eff. 9–16–04; 2003 S 37, eff. 10–21–03; 2003 H 95, eff. 6–26–03; 2002 H 345, eff. 7–23–02; 2001 S 59, eff. 10–31–01; 2000 H 672, eff. 4–9–01; 1999 H 163, § 21, eff. 7–1–99; 1999 H 163, § 1, eff. 3–31–99; 1998 H 611, eff. 7–1–99; 1998 S 142, eff. 3–30–99; 1998 S 213, eff. 7–29–98; 1997 H 39, eff. 9–16–97; 1996 S 182, eff. 12–3–96; 1996 H 353, eff. 9–17–96; 1995 S 134, eff. 8–25–95; 1995 H 117, eff. 9–29–95; 1994 H 687, eff. 10–12–94; 1994 H 458, eff. 7–20–94; 1990 H 346, eff. 5–31–90; 1989 H 381; 1987 H 419, S 10; 1986 H 382; 1983 S 115; 1981 H 671, H 275; 1977 S 78; 1976 H 741, H 612; 1973 H 31; 1971 S 222, H 651; 1970 H 855; 132 v H 919; 131 v H 150; 128 v 421; 1953 H 1; GC 6290–5)

Uncodified Law

2001 S 59, § 6: See *Baldwin's Ohio Revised Code Annotated*, Uncodified Law under RC 4505.021.

Historical and Statutory Notes

Pre–1953 H 1 Amendments: 124 v S 111; 117 v 726, 373; 114 v 824, § 2; 114 v 173

4505.10 Certificate of title when ownership changed by operation of law

(A) In the event of the transfer of ownership of a motor vehicle by operation of law, as upon inheritance, devise, bequest, order in bankruptcy, insolvency, replevin, or execution sale, a motor vehicle is sold to satisfy storage or repair charges, or repossession is had upon default in performance of the terms of a security agreement as provided in Chapter 1309. of the Revised Code and the secured party has notified the debtor as required by division (B) of section 1309.611 of the Revised Code, a clerk of a court of common pleas, upon the surrender of the prior certificate of title or the manufacturer's or importer's certificate, or, when that is not possible, upon presentation of satisfactory proof to the clerk of ownership and rights of possession to the motor vehicle, and upon payment of the fee prescribed in section 4505.09 of the Revised Code and presentation of an application for certificate of title, may issue to the applicant a certificate of title to the motor vehicle. Only an affidavit by the person or agent of the person to whom possession of the motor vehicle has passed, setting forth the facts entitling the person to the possession and ownership, together with a copy of the journal entry, court order, or instrument upon which the claim of possession and ownership is founded, is satisfactory proof of ownership and right of possession. If the applicant cannot produce that proof of ownership, the applicant may apply directly to the registrar of motor vehicles and submit the evidence the applicant has, and the registrar, if the registrar finds the evidence sufficient, then may authorize a clerk to issue a certificate of title. If the registrar finds the evidence insufficient, the applicant may petition the court of common pleas for a court order ordering the clerk to issue a certificate of title. The court shall grant or deny the petition based on the sufficiency of the evidence presented to the court. If, from the records in the office of the clerk involved, there appears to be any lien on the motor vehicle, the certificate of title shall contain a statement of the lien unless the application is accompanied by proper evidence of its extinction.

(B) A clerk shall transfer a decedent's interest in one or two automobiles to the surviving spouse of the decedent, as provided in section 2106.18 of the Revised Code, upon receipt of the title or titles. An affidavit executed by the surviving spouse shall be submitted to the clerk with the title or titles. The affidavit shall give the date of death of the decedent, shall state that each automobile for which the decedent's interest is to be so transferred is not disposed of by testamentary disposition, and shall provide an approximate value for each automobile selected to be transferred by the surviving spouse. The affidavit shall also contain a description for each automobile for which the decedent's interest is to be so transferred. The transfer does not affect any liens upon any automobile for which the decedent's interest is so transferred.

(C) Upon the death of one of the persons who have established joint ownership with right of survivorship under section 2131.12 of the Revised Code in a motor vehicle, and upon presentation to a clerk of the title and the certificate of death of the decedent, the clerk shall transfer title to the motor vehicle to the survivor. The transfer does not affect any liens upon any motor vehicle so transferred.

(D) Upon the death of the owner of a motor vehicle designated in beneficiary form under section 2131.13 of the Revised Code, upon application for a certificate of title by the transfer-on-death beneficiary or beneficiaries designated pursuant to that section, and upon presentation to the clerk of the certificate of title and the certificate of death of the decedent, the clerk shall transfer the motor vehicle and issue a certificate of title to the transfer-on-death beneficiary or beneficiaries. The transfer does not affect any liens upon the motor vehicle so transferred.

(2004 H 230, eff. 9–16–04; 2002 H 345, eff. 7–23–02; 2001 S 59, eff. 10–31–01; 2001 S 74, eff. 7–1–01; 2001 H 73, eff. 6–29–01; 1996 H 353, eff. 9–17–96; 1995 H 156, eff. 3–11–96; 1994 H 458, eff. 7–20–94; 1990 H 346, eff. 5–31–90; 1984 S 260; 1976 S 466; 1975 S 145; 129 v 13; 1953 H 1; GC 6290–10)

Uncodified Law

2001 S 59, § 6: See *Baldwin's Ohio Revised Code Annotated*, Uncodified Law under 4505.021.

Historical and Statutory Notes

Pre–1953 H 1 Amendments: 117 v 373; 114 v 824, § 2; 114 v 173

CHAPTER 4507

DRIVER'S LICENSE LAW

GENERAL PROVISIONS

Section
4507.02 License required as driver or commercial driver on public or private property; surrender of out-of-state license; impounding license plates; restricted license plates
4507.06 Form and contents of application for license; registration of voters
4507.07 Licenses of minors; signature by an adult; identification required; notice of liability; not imputed where proof of financial responsibility exists; exceptions to examination requirement
4507.071 Probationary licenses; restrictions
4507.08 Restrictions against issuance of license; probationary license, or temporary instruction permit; reinstatement of suspended license

Uncodified Law

1997 S 35, § 7, eff. 1-30-98, reads: The Department of Public Safety shall maintain records and statistics indicating the driving history of persons who are issued probationary driver's licenses on and after the effective date of this act, including crash records, traffic violation convictions, and driver's license suspensions and revocations. The Department shall compile the records and statistics in an appropriate format and, not later than two years after the effective date of this section, shall submit to the presiding officers of the General Assembly a report analyzing the information and comparing the relative records of juvenile drivers before and after the effective date of this act.

GENERAL PROVISIONS

4507.02 License required as driver or commercial driver on public or private property; surrender of out-of-state license; impounding license plates; restricted license plates

(A)(1) No person shall permit the operation of a motor vehicle upon any public or private property used by the public for purposes of vehicular travel or parking knowing the operator does not have a valid driver's license issued to the operator by the registrar of motor vehicles under this chapter or a valid commercial driver's license issued under Chapter 4506. of the Revised Code. Whoever violates this division is guilty of a misdemeanor of the first degree.

(2) No person shall receive a driver's license, or a motorcycle operator's endorsement of a driver's or commercial driver's license, unless and until the person surrenders to the registrar all valid licenses issued to the person by another jurisdiction recognized by this state. The registrar shall report the surrender of a license to the issuing authority, together with information that a license is now issued in this state. The registrar shall destroy any such license that is not returned to the issuing authority. No person shall be permitted to have more than one valid license at any time.

(B)(1) If a person is convicted of a violation of section 4510.11, 4510.14, 4510.16 when division (B)(3) of that section applies, or 4510.21 of the Revised Code or if division (F) of section 4507.164 of the Revised Code applies, the trial judge of any court, in addition to or independent of any other penalties provided by law or ordinance, shall impound the identification license plates of any motor vehicle registered in the name of the person. If a person is convicted of a violation of section 4510.16 of the Revised Code and division (B)(2) of that section applies, the trial judge of any court, in addition to or independent of any other penalties provided by law or ordinance, may impound the identification license plates of any motor vehicle registered in the name of the person. The court shall send the impounded license plates to the registrar, who may retain the license plates until the driver's or commercial driver's license of the owner has been reinstated or destroy them pursuant to section 4503.232 of the Revised Code.

If the license plates of a person convicted of a violation of any provision of those sections have been impounded in accordance with the provisions of this division, the court shall notify the registrar of that action. The notice shall contain the name and address of the driver, the serial number of the driver's driver's or commercial driver's license, the serial numbers of the license plates of the motor vehicle, and the length of time for which the license plates have been impounded. The registrar shall record the data in the notice as part of the driver's permanent record.

(2) Any motor vehicle owner who has had the license plates of a motor vehicle impounded pursuant to division (B)(1) of this section may apply to the registrar, or to a deputy registrar, for restricted license plates that shall conform to the requirements of section 4503.231 of the Revised Code. The registrar or deputy registrar forthwith shall notify the court of the application and, upon approval of the court, shall issue restricted license plates to the applicant. Until the driver's or commercial driver's license of the owner is reinstated, any new license plates issued to the owner also shall conform to the requirements of section 4503.231 of the Revised Code.

The registrar or deputy registrar shall charge the owner of a vehicle the fees provided in section 4503.19 of the Revised Code for restricted license plates that are issued in accordance with this division, except upon renewal as specified in section 4503.10 of the Revised Code, when the regular fee as provided in section 4503.04 of the Revised Code shall be charged. The registrar or deputy registrar shall charge the owner of a vehicle the fees provided in section 4503.19 of the Revised Code whenever restricted license plates are exchanged, by reason of the reinstatement of the driver's or commercial driver's license of the owner, for those ordinarily issued.

(3) If an owner wishes to sell a motor vehicle during the time the restricted license plates provided under division (B)(2) of this section are in use, the owner may apply to the court that impounded the license plates of the motor vehicle for permission to transfer title to the motor vehicle. If the court is satisfied that the sale will be made in good faith and not for the purpose of circumventing the provisions of this section, it may certify its consent to the owner and to the registrar of motor vehicles who shall enter notice of the transfer of the title of the motor vehicle in the vehicle registration record.

If, during the time the restricted license plates provided under division (B)(2) of this section are in use, the title to a motor vehicle is transferred by the foreclosure of a chattel mortgage, a sale upon execution, the cancellation of a conditional sales contract, or by order of a court, the court shall notify the registrar of the action and the registrar shall enter notice of the transfer of the title to the motor vehicle in the vehicle registration record.

(C) This section is not intended to change or modify any provision of Chapter 4503. of the Revised Code with respect to the taxation of motor vehicles or the time within which the taxes on motor vehicles shall be paid.

(2006 H 461, eff. 4-4-07; 2005 H 68, eff. 6-29-05; 2004 H 163, eff. 9-23-04; 2002 S 123, eff. 1-1-04; 1999 H 163, eff. 6-30-99; 1997 S 60, eff. 10-21-97; 1994 S 20, eff. 4-20-95; 1994 H 687, eff. 10-12-94; 1993 S 62, § 1, eff. 9-1-93; 1993 S 62, § 4; 1992 S 275; 1990 S 131; 1989 H 381; 1987 H 419; 1986 S 262, S 356)

Uncodified Law

1999 H 86, § 3, eff. 6–29–99, amended 1999 H 163, § 16, to read:

A task force to study the Bureau of Motor Vehicles' existing method of random selection to verify financial responsibility is hereby established. The task force shall study the method and make recommendations on changes to the General Assembly on or before August 1, 1999. The task force shall consist of twelve members, including the Director of Public Safety, or the Director's designee and the Superintendent of Insurance. The Speaker of the House of Representatives shall appoint five members of the House of Representatives to the task force, no more than three of whom shall be from the same political party as the Speaker. The President of the Senate shall appoint five members of the Senate to the task force, no more than three of whom shall be from the same political party as the President. The Speaker and President shall make their appointments within two weeks after the effective date of this section, and shall jointly select the chairperson of the task force. The Director of Public Safety, or the Director's designee, and the legislative members of the task force shall be voting members. The Superintendent of Insurance shall be a nonvoting member. After making its recommendations to the General Assembly, the task force shall cease to exist.

This section is not subject to the referendum. Therefore, under Ohio Constitution, Article II, Section 1d and section 1.471 of the Revised Code, this section goes into immediate effect when Am. Sub. H.B. No. 163 of the 123rd General Assembly becomes law.

1999 H 163, § 14, eff. 6–30–99, amended 1994 S 20, § 3, as amended by 1997 H 215, § 179, to read:

(A) Not later than January 1, 1998, the Registrar of Motor Vehicles shall adopt rules in accordance with Chapter 119. of the Revised Code to establish a pilot program requiring that persons randomly selected within the pilot program according to a method developed by the Registrar be required to verify the existence of proof of financial responsibility. Not later than January 1, 2000, the Registrar shall adopt rules in accordance with Chapter 119. of the Revised Code to establish a permanent program requiring that persons randomly selected on a statewide basis be required to verify the existence of proof of financial responsibility. In adopting the rules, the Registrar may consider relevant findings and recommendations of the Task Force on the Enforcement of the Financial Responsibility Laws of Ohio.

(B) The rules of the registrar for the pilot project shall do all of the following:

(1) Establish a three-step process for written notification to the owner of a vehicle randomly selected to submit proof of financial responsibility, with the last notification, when necessary for an owner who fails to respond to the previous notices, to be sent by certified mail, return receipt requested. If the second notice is returned as not deliverable, the registrar shall make reasonable efforts to determine if the owner's address has changed before sending the third notice.

(2) Allow an order of the Registrar imposing the civil penalties required under division (A)(2) of section 4509.101 of the Revised Code to be issued upon the failure of a vehicle owner to provide proof of financial responsibility in response to the initial notice, but to be implemented in regard to owners who fail to respond only after the owner has failed to respond to the third notice sent by certified mail or the certified mail is returned as refused or not deliverable.

(3) Require the Registrar, when recording the necessary information for an order imposing the civil penalties required under division (A)(2) of section 4509.101 of the Revised Code, to distinctly indicate the type of suspension and impoundment when the suspension of the person's license and the impoundment of the person's certificate of registration and license plates results from a failure to respond to the random verification.

(4) Establish procedures for a person to provide proof of financial responsibility at the office of a deputy registrar if the operating privileges or registration rights of the person are suspended because of a failure to respond to a financial responsibility random verification request.

(C) If the suspension of a person's license and the impoundment of the person's certificate of registration and license plates results from a failure to respond to a random verification, the registrar distinctly shall indicate the type of suspension and impoundment when putting the information of such an order into the law enforcement automated data system and recording the information as part of the person's permanent record.

Historical and Statutory Notes

Ed. Note: RC 4507.02 and RC 4507.99 related to driving under suspension other than under the Financial Responsibility Law, or in violation of a license restriction. See now RC 4510.11 for provisions analogous to former RC 4507.02 and RC 4507.99.

Ed. Note: RC 4507.02(E) and RC 4511.192 related to affirmative defenses. See now RC 4510.04 for provisions analogous to former RC 4507.02(E) and RC 4511.192.

Ed. Note: RC 4507.02(C) and RC 4507.99(A) related to the failure to reinstate a license. See now RC 4510.21 for provisions analogous to former RC 4507.02(C) and RC 4507.99(A).

Ed. Note: RC 4507.02(B)(1) and RC 4507.99(C) related to driving under financial responsibility suspension. See now RC 4510.16 and RC 4510.161 for provisions analogous to former RC 4507.02(B)(1) and RC 4507.99(C).

Ed. Note: RC 4507.02(D)(2), RC 4507.99(B), RC 4511.192(A) and (B), and RC 4511.99(B) related to the offense of driving under OMVI suspension or revocation. See now RC 4510.14 for provisions analogous to former RC 4507.02(D)(2), RC 4507.99(B), RC 4511.192(A) and (B), and RC 4511.99(B).

Ed. Note: RC 4507.02 is former RC 4507.38, amended and recodified by 1986 S 356, eff. 9–24–86; 1982 S 432; 132 v S 451, H 518; 131 v H 274; 130 v H 393; 1953 H 1; GC 6296–29.

Ed. Note: 4507.02 contains provisions analogous to former 4507.39, repealed by 1986 S 356, eff. 9–24–86.

Ed. Note: Former 4507.02 repealed by 1986 S 356, eff. 9–24–86; 1969 H 636; 132 v H 380; 131 v H 215; 1953 H 1; GC 6296–4.

Ed. Note: The effective date of the amendment of this section by 1992 S 275 was changed from 7–1–93 to 9–1–93 by 1993 S 62, § 4, eff. 6–30–93.

Pre–1953 H 1 Amendments: 116 v Pt 2, 33, § 4

Library References

Automobiles ⚖41, 137, 326.

Westlaw Topic No. 48A.

C.J.S. Motor Vehicles §§ 106 et seq., 148 et seq., 638, 639, 651.

Baldwin's Ohio Legislative Service, 1990 Laws of Ohio, S 131—LSC Analysis, p 5–623

4507.06 Form and contents of application for license; registration of voters

(A)(1) Every application for a driver's license or motorcycle operator's license or endorsement, or duplicate of any such license or endorsement, shall be made upon the approved form furnished by the registrar of motor vehicles and shall be signed by the applicant.

Every application shall state the following:

(a) The applicant's name, date of birth, social security number if such has been assigned, sex, general description, including height, weight, color of hair, and eyes, residence address, including county of residence, duration of residence in this state, and country of citizenship;

(b) Whether the applicant previously has been licensed as an operator, chauffeur, driver, commercial driver, or motorcycle operator and, if so, when, by what state, and whether such license is suspended or canceled at the present time and, if so, the date of and reason for the suspension or cancellation;

(c) Whether the applicant is now or ever has been afflicted with epilepsy, or whether the applicant now is suffering from any physical or mental disability or disease and, if so, the nature and extent of the disability or disease, giving the names and addresses of physicians then or previously in attendance upon the applicant;

(d) Whether an applicant for a duplicate driver's license, or duplicate license containing a motorcycle operator endorsement has pending a citation for violation of any motor vehicle law or ordinance, a description of any such citation pending, and the date of the citation;

(e) Whether the applicant wishes to certify willingness to make an anatomical gift under section 2108.04 of the Revised Code, which shall be given no consideration in the issuance of a license or endorsement;

(f) Whether the applicant has executed a valid durable power of attorney for health care pursuant to sections 1337.11 to 1337.17 of the Revised Code or has executed a declaration governing the use or continuation, or the withholding or withdrawal, of life-sustaining treatment pursuant to sections 2133.01 to 2133.15 of the Revised Code and, if the applicant has executed either type of instrument, whether the applicant wishes the applicant's license to indicate that the applicant has executed the instrument.

(2) Every applicant for a driver's license shall be photographed in color at the time the application for the license is made. The application shall state any additional information that the registrar requires.

(B) The registrar or a deputy registrar, in accordance with section 3503.11 of the Revised Code, shall register as an elector any person who applies for a driver's license or motorcycle operator's license or endorsement under division (A) of this section, or for a renewal or duplicate of the license or endorsement, if the applicant is eligible and wishes to be registered as an elector. The decision of an applicant whether to register as an elector shall be given no consideration in the decision of whether to issue the applicant a license or endorsement, or a renewal or duplicate.

(C) The registrar or a deputy registrar, in accordance with section 3503.11 of the Revised Code, shall offer the opportunity of completing a notice of change of residence or change of name to any applicant for a driver's license or endorsement under division (A) of this section, or for a renewal or duplicate of the license or endorsement, if the applicant is a registered elector who has changed the applicant's residence or name and has not filed such a notice.

(2002 S 123, eff. 1–1–04; 1998 H 354, eff. 7–9–98; 1996 H 353, eff. 9–17–96; 1994 S 300, eff. 1–1–95; 1992 H 427, eff. 10–8–92; 1990 H 21; 1989 H 381; 1986 H 428)

Historical and Statutory Notes

Ed. Note: Former 4507.06 repealed by 1986 H 428, eff. 12–23–86; 1984 H 183; 1977 S 125; 1975 H 650; 1974 S 313; 132 v H 1007, S 452, S 43, H 193, H 380, S 259; 126 v 253; 1953 H 1; GC 6296–9.

Pre–1953 H 1 Amendments: 123 v 246; 120 v 289, § 1; 116 v Pt 2, 33, § 9

Library References

Automobiles ⊂⊃139.
Westlaw Topic No. 48A.
C.J.S. Motor Vehicles § 156.

4507.07 Licenses of minors; signature by an adult; identification required; notice of liability; not imputed where proof of financial responsibility exists; exceptions to examination requirement

(A) The registrar of motor vehicles shall not grant the application of any minor under eighteen years of age for a probationary license, a restricted license, or a temporary instruction permit, unless the application is signed by one of the minor's parents, the minor's guardian, another person having custody of the applicant, or, if there is no parent or guardian, a responsible person who is willing to assume the obligation imposed under this section.

At the time a minor under eighteen years of age submits an application for a license or permit at a driver's license examining station, the adult who signs the application shall present identification establishing that the adult is the individual whose signature appears on the application. The registrar shall prescribe, by rule, the types of identification that are suitable for the purposes of this paragraph. If the adult who signs the application does not provide identification as required by this paragraph, the application shall not be accepted.

When a minor under eighteen years of age applies for a probationary license, a restricted license, or a temporary instruction permit, the registrar shall give the adult who signs the application notice of the potential liability that may be imputed to the adult pursuant to division (B) of this section and notice of how the adult may prevent any liability from being imputed to the adult pursuant to that division.

(B) Any negligence, or willful or wanton misconduct, that is committed by a minor under eighteen years of age when driving a motor vehicle upon a highway shall be imputed to the person who has signed the application of the minor for a probationary license, restricted license, or temporary instruction permit, which person shall be jointly and severally liable with the minor for any damages caused by the negligence or the willful or wanton misconduct. This joint and several liability is not subject to section 2307.22 or 2315.36 of the Revised Code with respect to a tort claim that otherwise is subject to that section.

There shall be no imputed liability imposed under this division if a minor under eighteen years of age has proof of financial responsibility with respect to the operation of a motor vehicle owned by the minor or, if the minor is not the owner of a motor vehicle, with respect to the minor's operation of any motor vehicle, in the form and in the amounts required under Chapter 4509. of the Revised Code.

(C) Any person who has signed the application of a minor under eighteen years of age for a license or permit subsequently may surrender to the registrar the license or temporary instruction permit of the minor and request that the license or permit be canceled. The registrar then shall cancel the license or temporary instruction permit, and the person who signed the application of the minor shall be relieved from the liability imposed by division (B) of this section.

(D) Any minor under eighteen years of age whose probationary license, restricted license, or temporary instruction permit is surrendered to the registrar by the person who signed the application for the license or permit and whose license or temporary instruction permit subsequently is canceled by the registrar may obtain a new license or temporary instruction permit without having to undergo the examinations otherwise required by sections 4507.10 and 4507.12 of the Revised Code and without having to tender the fee for that license or temporary instruction permit, if the minor is able to produce another parent, guardian, other person having custody of the minor, or other adult, and that adult is willing to assume the liability imposed under division (B) of this section. That adult shall comply with the procedures contained in division (A) of this section.

(2004 S 80, eff. 4–7–05; 2002 S 120, eff. 4–9–03; 2001 S 108, § 2.01, eff. 7–6–01; 1997 S 35, eff. 1–1–99; 1996 H 350, eff. 1–27–97 [1]; 1989 H 71, eff. 9–22–89; 1987 H 1; 1979 H 522; 132 v S 95; 130 v H 772; 127 v 839; 1953 H 1; GC 6296–10)

[1] See *Baldwin's Ohio Revised Code Annotated*, Notes of Decisions, *State ex rel. Ohio Academy of Trial Lawyers v. Sheward* (Ohio 1999), 86 Ohio St.3d 451, 715 N.E.2d 1062.

Uncodified Law

2002 S 120, § 3, eff. 4–9–03, reads:

Sections 1775.14, 2307.011, 2307.22, 2307.23, 2307.24, 2307.25, 2307.26, 2307.27, 2307.28, 2307.29, 2315.32, 2315.33, 2315.34, 2315.35, 2315.36, 2315.41, 2315.42, 2315.43, 2315.44, 2315.45, 2315.46, 4171.10, 4507.07, and 5703.54 of the Revised Code, as amended or enacted, by this act, apply only to causes of action that accrue on or after the effective date of this act. Any cause of action that accrues prior to the effective date of this act is governed by the law in effect when the cause of action accrued.

2001 S 108, § 1, eff. 7–6–01, reads:

It is the intent of this act (1) to repeal the Tort Reform Act, Am. Sub. H.B. 350 of the 121st General Assembly, 146 Ohio Laws 3867, in conformity with the Supreme Court of Ohio's decision in *State, ex rel. Ohio Academy of Trial Lawyers, v. Sheward* (1999), 86 Ohio St.3d 451; (2) to clarify the status of the law; and (3) to revive the law as it existed prior to the Tort Reform Act.

2001 S 108, § 3, eff. 7–6–01, reads, in part:

(A) In Section 2.01 of this act:

(1) Sections 1701.95, 1707.01, 2305.25, 2305.251, 2305.37, 2307.60, 2307.61, 2743.18, 2743.19, 2744.01, 2744.02, 2744.03, 2744.05, 3123.17, 4112.02, 4507.07, 4513.263, 4582.27, and 5111.81 of the Revised Code, which have been amended by acts subsequent to their amendment by Am. Sub. H.B. 350 of the 121st General Assembly, are amended to remove matter inserted by, or to revive matter removed by, Am. Sub. H.B. 350. Amendments made by Am. Sub. H.B. 350 or the subsequent acts that are independent of the purposes of Am. Sub. H.B. 350 are retained.

Historical and Statutory Notes

Pre–1953 H 1 Amendments: 120 v 289, § 1; 119 v 701, § 1; 116 v Pt 2, 33, § 10

Library References

Automobiles ⬌139, 195(1), 195(3).
Westlaw Topic No. 48A.
C.J.S. Motor Vehicles §§ 156, 431 to 434.

4507.071 Probationary licenses; restrictions

(A) No driver's license shall be issued to any person under eighteen years of age, except that a probationary license may be issued to a person who is at least sixteen years of age and has held a temporary instruction permit for a period of at least six months.

(B)(1)(a) No holder of a probationary driver's license who has not attained the age of seventeen years shall operate a motor vehicle upon a highway or any public or private property used by the public for purposes of vehicular travel or parking between the hours of midnight and six a.m. unless the holder is accompanied by the holder's parent or guardian.

(b) No holder of a probationary driver's license who has attained the age of seventeen years but has not attained the age of eighteen years shall operate a motor vehicle upon a highway or any public or private property used by the public for purposes of vehicular travel or parking between the hours of one a.m. and five a.m. unless the holder is accompanied by the holder's parent or guardian.

(2)(a) Subject to division (D)(1)(a) of this section, division (B)(1)(a) of this section does not apply to the holder of a probationary driver's license who is traveling to or from work between the hours of midnight and six a.m. and has in the holder's immediate possession written documentation from the holder's employer.

(b) Division (B)(1)(b) of this section does not apply to the holder of a probationary driver's license who is traveling to or from work between the hours of one a.m. and five a.m. and has in the holder's immediate possession written documentation from the holder's employer.

(3) An employer is not liable in damages in a civil action for any injury, death, or loss to person or property that allegedly arises from, or is related to, the fact that the employer provided an employee who is the holder of a probationary driver's license with the written documentation described in division (B)(2) of this section.

The registrar of motor vehicles shall make available at no cost a form to serve as the written documentation described in division (B)(2) of this section, and employers and holders of probationary driver's licenses may utilize that form or may choose to utilize any other written documentation to meet the requirements of that division.

(4) No holder of a probationary driver's license who is less than seventeen years of age shall operate a motor vehicle upon a highway or any public or private property used by the public for purposes of vehicular travel or parking with more than one person who is not a family member occupying the vehicle unless the probationary license holder is accompanied by the probationary license holder's parent, guardian, or custodian.

(C) It is an affirmative defense to a violation of division (B)(1)(a) or (b) of this section if, at the time of the violation, the holder of the probationary driver's license was traveling to or from an official function sponsored by the school the holder attends, or an emergency existed that required the holder to operate a motor vehicle in violation of division (B)(1)(a) or (b) of this section, or the holder was an emancipated minor.

(D)(1)(a) If a person is issued a probationary driver's license prior to attaining the age of seventeen years and the person pleads guilty to, is convicted of, or is adjudicated in juvenile court of having committed a moving violation during the six-month period commencing on the date on which the person is issued the probationary driver's license, the holder must be accompanied by the holder's parent or guardian whenever the holder is operating a motor vehicle upon a highway or any public or private property used by the public for purposes of vehicular parking during whichever of the following time periods applies:

(i) If, on the date the holder of the probationary driver's license pleads guilty to, is convicted of, or is adjudicated in juvenile court of having committed the moving violation, the holder has not attained the age of sixteen years six months, during the six-month period commencing on that date;

(ii) If, on the date the holder pleads guilty to, is convicted of, or is adjudicated in juvenile court of having committed the moving violation, the holder has attained the age of sixteen years six months but not seventeen years, until the person attains the age of seventeen years.

(b) If the holder of a probationary driver's license commits a moving violation during the six-month period after the person is issued the probationary driver's license and before the person attains the age of seventeen years and on the date the person pleads guilty to, is convicted of, or is adjudicated in juvenile court of having committed the moving violation the person has attained the age of seventeen years, or if the person commits the moving violation during the six-month period after the person is issued the probationary driver's license and after the person attains the age of seventeen years, the holder is not subject to the restriction described in divisions (D)(1)(a)(i) and (ii) of this section unless the court or juvenile court imposes such a restriction upon the holder.

(2) No person shall violate division (D)(1)(a) of this section.

(E) No holder of a probationary license shall operate a motor vehicle upon a highway or any public or private property used by the public for purposes of vehicular travel or parking unless the total number of occupants of the vehicle does not exceed the total number of occupant restraining devices originally installed in the motor vehicle by its manufacturer, and each occupant of the vehicle is wearing all of the available elements of a properly adjusted occupant restraining device.

(F) A restricted license may be issued to a person who is fourteen or fifteen years of age upon proof of hardship satisfactory to the registrar of motor vehicles.

(G) Notwithstanding any other provision of law to the contrary, no law enforcement officer shall cause the operator of a motor vehicle being operated on any street or highway to stop the motor vehicle for the sole purpose of determining whether each occupant of the motor vehicle is wearing all of the available elements of a properly adjusted occupant restraining device as required by division (E) of this section, or for the sole purpose of issuing a ticket, citation, or summons if the requirement in that division has been or is being violated, or for causing the arrest of or commencing a prosecution of a person for a violation of that requirement.

(H) Notwithstanding any other provision of law to the contrary, no law enforcement officer shall cause the operator of a motor vehicle being operated on any street or highway to stop the motor vehicle for the sole purpose of determining whether a violation of division (B)(1)(a) or (b) of this section has been or is being committed or for the sole purpose of issuing a ticket, citation, or summons for such a violation or for causing the arrest of or commencing a prosecution of a person for such violation.

(I) As used in this section:

(1) "Occupant restraining device" has the same meaning as in section 4513.263 of the Revised Code.

(2) "Family member" of a probationary license holder includes any of the following:

(a) A spouse;

(b) A child or stepchild;

(c) A parent, stepparent, grandparent, or parent-in-law;

(d) An aunt or uncle;

(e) A sibling, whether of the whole or half blood or by adoption, a brother-in-law, or a sister-in-law;

(f) A son or daughter of the probationary license holder's stepparent if the stepparent has not adopted the probationary license holder;

(g) An eligible adult, as defined in section 4507.05 of the Revised Code.

(3) "Moving violation" means any violation of any statute or ordinance that regulates the operation of vehicles, streetcars, or trackless trolleys on the highways or streets. "Moving violation" does not include a violation of section 4513.263 of the Revised Code or a substantially equivalent municipal ordinance, or a violation of any statute or ordinance regulating pedestrians or the parking of vehicles, vehicle size or load limitations, vehicle fitness requirements, or vehicle registration.

(J) Whoever violates division (B)(1) or (4), (D)(2), or (E) of this section is guilty of a minor misdemeanor.

(2006 H 343, eff. 4-6-07; 2002 S 123, eff. 1-1-04; 1997 S 35, eff. 1-1-99)

4507.08 Restrictions against issuance of license; probationary license, or temporary instruction permit; reinstatement of suspended license

(A) No probationary license shall be issued to any person under the age of eighteen who has been adjudicated an unruly or delinquent child or a juvenile traffic offender for having committed any act that if committed by an adult would be a drug abuse offense, as defined in section 2925.01 of the Revised Code, a violation of division (B) of section 2917.11, or a violation of division (A) of section 4511.19 of the Revised Code, unless the person has been required by the court to attend a drug abuse or alcohol abuse education, intervention, or treatment program specified by the court and has satisfactorily completed the program.

(B) No temporary instruction permit or driver's license shall be issued to any person whose license has been suspended, during the period for which the license was suspended, nor to any person whose license has been canceled, under Chapter 4510. or any other provision of the Revised Code.

(C) No temporary instruction permit or driver's license shall be issued to any person whose commercial driver's license is suspended under Chapter 4510. or any other provision of the Revised Code during the period of the suspension.

No temporary instruction permit or driver's license shall be issued to any person when issuance is prohibited by division (A) of section 4507.091 of the Revised Code.

(D) No temporary instruction permit or driver's license shall be issued to, or retained by, any of the following persons:

(1) Any person who is an alcoholic, or is addicted to the use of controlled substances to the extent that the use constitutes an impairment to the person's ability to operate a motor vehicle with the required degree of safety;

(2) Any person who is under the age of eighteen and has been adjudicated an unruly or delinquent child or a juvenile traffic offender for having committed any act that if committed by an adult would be a drug abuse offense, as defined in section 2925.01 of the Revised Code, a violation of division (B) of section 2917.11, or a violation of division (A) of section 4511.19 of the Revised Code, unless the person has been required by the court to attend a drug abuse or alcohol abuse education, intervention, or treatment program specified by the court and has satisfactorily completed the program;

(3) Any person who, in the opinion of the registrar, is afflicted with or suffering from a physical or mental disability or disease that prevents the person from exercising reasonable and ordinary control over a motor vehicle while operating the vehicle upon the highways, except that a restricted license effective for six months may be issued to any person otherwise qualified who is or has been subject to any condition resulting in episodic impairment of consciousness or loss of muscular control and whose condition, in the opinion of the registrar, is dormant or is sufficiently under medical control that the person is capable of exercising reasonable and ordinary control over a motor vehicle. A restricted license effective for six months shall be issued to any person who otherwise is qualified and who is subject to any condition that causes episodic impairment of consciousness or a loss of muscular control if the person presents a statement from a licensed physician that the person's condition is under effective medical control and the period of time for which the control has been continuously maintained, unless, thereafter, a medical examination is ordered and, pursuant thereto, cause for denial is found.

A person to whom a six-month restricted license has been issued shall give notice of the person's medical condition to the registrar on forms provided by the registrar and signed by the licensee's physician. The notice shall be sent to the registrar six months after the issuance of the license. Subsequent restricted licenses issued to the same individual shall be effective for six months.

(4) Any person who is unable to understand highway warnings or traffic signs or directions given in the English language;

(5) Any person making an application whose driver's license or driving privileges are under cancellation, revocation, or suspension in the jurisdiction where issued or any other jurisdiction, until the expiration of one year after the license was canceled or revoked or until the period of suspension ends. Any person whose application is denied under this division may file a petition in the municipal court or county court in whose jurisdiction the person resides agreeing to pay the cost of the proceedings and alleging that the conduct involved in the offense that resulted in suspension, cancellation, or revocation in the foreign jurisdiction would not have resulted in a suspension, cancellation, or revocation had the offense occurred in this state. If the petition is granted, the petitioner shall notify the registrar by a certified copy of the court's findings and a license shall not be denied under this division.

(6) Any person who is under a class one or two suspension imposed for a violation of section 2903.01, 2903.02, 2903.04, 2903.06, 2903.08, 2903.11, 2921.331, or 2923.02 of the Revised Code or whose driver's or commercial driver's license or permit was permanently revoked prior to January 1, 2004, for a substantially equivalent violation pursuant to section 4507.16 of the Revised Code;

(7) Any person who is not a resident or temporary resident of this state.

(E) No person whose driver's license or permit has been suspended under Chapter 4510. of the Revised Code or any other provision of the Revised Code shall have driving privileges reinstated if the registrar determines that a warrant has been issued in this state or any other state for the person's arrest and that warrant is an active warrant.

(2006 H 461, eff. 4–4–07; 2005 S 9, eff. 4–14–06; 2002 S 123, eff. 1–1–04; 2000 S 180, eff. 3–22–01; 1997 S 35, eff. 1–1–99; 1997 H 141, eff. 3–3–98; 1997 S 60, eff. 10–21–97; 1995 H 167, eff. 5–15–97; 1994 S 82, eff. 5–4–94; 1993 S 62, § 1, eff. 9–1–93; 1993 S 62, § 4; 1992 S 275; 1989 H 381, H 330, H 329; 1988 H 643; 1986 S 262; 1980 H 965; 1979 H 328; 1977 H 71; 1975 H 300; 1974 S 313; 1973 S 1; 131 v H 183, H 274; 130 v H 758, H 772; 129 v 1448, 582; 128 v 539; 127 v 789, 839; 1953 H 1; GC 6296–7)

CHAPTER 4511

TRAFFIC LAWS—OPERATION OF MOTOR VEHICLES

TRAFFIC CONTROL DEVICES AND SIGNS

Section
4511.12 Obeying traffic control devices
4511.13 Signal lights
4511.15 Flashing traffic signals

OPERATION OF MOTOR VEHICLE WHILE INTOXICATED

4511.19 Driving while under the influence of alcohol or drugs; tests; presumptions; penalties; immunity for those withdrawing blood
4511.191 Chemical tests for determining alcoholic content of blood; effect of refusal to submit to test; seizure of license; indigent drivers alcohol treatment funds; procedures

TRANSPORTATION OF SCHOOL CHILDREN

4511.75 Stopping for school bus; signals on bus

TRAFFIC CONTROL DEVICES AND SIGNS

4511.12 Obeying traffic control devices

(A) No pedestrian, driver of a vehicle, or operator of a streetcar or trackless trolley shall disobey the instructions of any traffic control device placed in accordance with this chapter, unless at the time otherwise directed by a police officer.

No provision of this chapter for which signs are required shall be enforced against an alleged violator if at the time and place of the alleged violation an official sign is not in proper position and sufficiently legible to be seen by an ordinarily observant person. Whenever a particular section of this chapter does not state that signs are required, that section shall be effective even though no signs are erected or in place.

(B) Except as otherwise provided in this division, whoever violates this section is guilty of a minor misdemeanor. If, within one year of the offense, the offender previously has been convicted of or pleaded guilty to one predicate motor vehicle or traffic offense, whoever violates this section is guilty of a misdemeanor of the fourth degree. If, within one year of the offense, the offender previously has been convicted of two or more predicate motor vehicle or traffic offenses, whoever violates this section is guilty of a misdemeanor of the third degree.

(2002 S 123, eff. 1–1–04; 1989 H 258, eff. 11–2–89; 1953 H 1; GC 6307–12)

Historical and Statutory Notes

Pre–1953 H 1 Amendments: 124 v S 227; 119 v 766, § 12

Historical and Statutory Notes

Ed. Note: The effective date of the amendment of this section by 1992 S 275 was changed from 7–1–93 to 9–1–93 by 1993 S 62, § 4, eff. 6–30–93.

Pre–1953 H 1 Amendments: 123 v 246; 120 v 289, § 1; 119 v 701, § 1; 116 v Pt 2, 33, § 7

Library References

Automobiles ⚖138.
Westlaw Topic No. 48A.
C.J.S. Motor Vehicles §§ 154, 155.

Amendment Note: 2002 S 123 designated the existing section as new division (A); and added new division (B).

Library References

Automobiles ⚖335.
Westlaw Topic No. 48A.
C.J.S. Motor Vehicles § 606 et seq.

4511.13 Signal lights

Whenever traffic is controlled by traffic control signals exhibiting different colored lights, or colored lighted arrows, successively one at a time or in combination, only the colors green, red, and yellow shall be used, except for special pedestrian signals carrying words or symbols, and said lights shall indicate and apply to drivers of vehicles, streetcars, and trackless trolleys and to pedestrians as follows:

(A) Green indication:

(1) Vehicular traffic, streetcars, and trackless trolleys, facing a circular green signal may proceed straight through or turn right or left unless a sign at such place prohibits either such turn. But vehicular traffic, streetcars, and trackless trolleys, including vehicles, streetcars, and trackless trolleys turning right or left, shall yield the right-of-way to other vehicles, streetcars, trackless trolleys, and pedestrians lawfully within the intersection or an adjacent crosswalk at the time such signal is exhibited.

(2) Vehicular traffic, streetcars, and trackless trolleys facing a green arrow signal, shown alone or in combination with another indication, may cautiously enter the intersection only to make the movement indicated by such arrow, or such other movement as is permitted by other indications shown at the same time. Such vehicular traffic, streetcars, and trackless trolleys shall yield the right-of-way to pedestrians lawfully within an adjacent crosswalk and to other traffic lawfully using the intersection.

(3) Unless otherwise directed by a pedestrian-control signal, as provided in section 4511.14 of the Revised Code, pedestrians facing any green signal, except when the sole green signal is a turn arrow, may proceed across the roadway within any marked or unmarked crosswalk.

(B) Steady yellow indication:

(1) Vehicular traffic, streetcars, and trackless trolleys facing a steady circular yellow or yellow arrow signal are thereby warned that the related green movement is being terminated or that a red indication will be exhibited immediately thereafter when vehicular traffic, streetcars and trackless trolleys shall not enter the intersection.

(2) Pedestrians facing a steady circular yellow or yellow arrow signal, unless otherwise directed by a pedestrian-control signal as provided in section 4511.14 of the Revised Code, are thereby advised that there is insufficient time to cross the roadway before a red indication is shown and no pedestrian shall then start to cross the roadway.

(C) Steady red indication:

(1) Vehicular traffic, streetcars, and trackless trolleys facing a steady red signal alone shall stop at a clearly marked stop line, but if none, before entering the crosswalk on the near side of the intersection, or if none, then before entering the intersection and shall remain standing until an indication to proceed is shown except as provided in divisions (C)(2) and (3) of this section.

(2) Unless a sign is in place prohibiting a right turn as provided in division (C)(5) of this section, vehicular traffic, streetcars, and trackless trolleys facing a steady red signal may cautiously enter the intersection to make a right turn after stopping as required by division (C)(1) of this section. Such vehicular traffic, streetcars, and trackless trolleys shall yield the right-of-way to pedestrians lawfully within an adjacent crosswalk and to other traffic lawfully using the intersection.

(3) Unless a sign is in place prohibiting a left turn as provided in division (C)(5) of this section, vehicular traffic, streetcars, and trackless trolleys facing a steady red signal on a one-way street that intersects another one-way street on which traffic moves to the left may cautiously enter the intersection to make a left turn into the one-way street after stopping as required by division (C)(1) of this section, and yielding the right-of-way to pedestrians lawfully within an adjacent crosswalk and to other traffic lawfully using the intersection.

(4) Unless otherwise directed by a pedestrian-control signal as provided in section 4511.14 of the Revised Code, pedestrians facing a steady red signal alone shall not enter the roadway.

(5) Local authorities may by ordinance, or the director of transportation on state highways may, prohibit a right or a left turn against a steady red signal at any intersection, which shall be effective when signs giving notice thereof are posted at the intersection.

(D) In the event an official traffic-control signal is erected and maintained at a place other than an intersection, the provisions of this section shall be applicable except as to those provisions which by their nature can have no application. Any stop required shall be made at a sign or marking on the pavement indicating where the stop shall be made, but in the absence of any such sign or marking the stop shall be made at the signal.

(1984 H 703, eff. 3-28-85; 1977 H 171; 1974 H 99, S 263; 130 v S 71; 1953 H 1; GC 6307-13)

Historical and Statutory Notes

Pre-1953 H 1 Amendments: 124 v S 227; 119 v 766, § 13

Library References

Automobiles ⚖=5(2), 329.
Westlaw Topic No. 48A.
C.J.S. Motor Vehicles §§ 26, 653.

4511.15 Flashing traffic signals

Whenever an illuminated flashing red or yellow traffic signal is used in a traffic signal or with a traffic sign it shall require obedience as follows:

(A) Flashing red stop signal: Operators of vehicles, trackless trolleys, and streetcars shall stop at a clearly marked stop line, but if none, before entering the crosswalk on the near side of the intersection, or if none, then at the point nearest the intersecting roadway where the driver has a view of approaching traffic on the intersecting roadway before entering it, and the right to proceed shall be subject to the rules applicable after making a stop at a stop sign.

(B) Flashing yellow caution signal: Operators of vehicles, trackless trolleys, and streetcars may proceed through the intersection or past such signal only with caution.

This section shall not apply at railroad grade crossings. Conduct of drivers of vehicles, trackless trolleys, and streetcars approaching railroad grade crossings shall be governed by sections 4511.61 and 4511.62 of the Revised Code.

(1974 H 995, eff. 1-1-75; 1953 H 1; GC 6307-15)

Historical and Statutory Notes

Pre-1953 H 1 Amendments: 119 v 766, § 15

Library References

Automobiles ⚖=5(2), 329.
Westlaw Topic No. 48A.
C.J.S. Motor Vehicles §§ 26, 653.

OPERATION OF MOTOR VEHICLE WHILE INTOXICATED

4511.19 Driving while under the influence of alcohol or drugs; tests; presumptions; penalties; immunity for those withdrawing blood

(A)(1) No person shall operate any vehicle, streetcar, or trackless trolley within this state, if, at the time of the operation, any of the following apply:

(a) The person is under the influence of alcohol, a drug of abuse, or a combination of them.

(b) The person has a concentration of eight-hundredths of one per cent or more but less than seventeen-hundredths of one per cent by weight per unit volume of alcohol in the person's whole blood.

(c) The person has a concentration of ninety-six-thousandths of one per cent or more but less than two hundred four-thousandths of one per cent by weight per unit volume of alcohol in the person's blood serum or plasma.

(d) The person has a concentration of eight-hundredths of one gram or more but less than seventeen-hundredths of one gram by weight of alcohol per two hundred ten liters of the person's breath.

(e) The person has a concentration of eleven-hundredths of one gram or more but less than two hundred thirty-eight-thousandths of one gram by weight of alcohol per one hundred milliliters of the person's urine.

(f) The person has a concentration of seventeen-hundredths of one per cent or more by weight per unit volume of alcohol in the person's whole blood.

(g) The person has a concentration of two hundred four-thousandths of one per cent or more by weight per unit volume of alcohol in the person's blood serum or plasma.

(h) The person has a concentration of seventeen-hundredths of one gram or more by weight of alcohol per two hundred ten liters of the person's breath.

(i) The person has a concentration of two hundred thirty-eight-thousandths of one gram or more by weight of alcohol per one hundred milliliters of the person's urine.

(j) Except as provided in division (K) of this section, the person has a concentration of any of the following controlled substances or metabolites of a controlled substance in the person's whole blood, blood serum or plasma, or urine that equals or exceeds any of the following:

(i) The person has a concentration of amphetamine in the person's urine of at least five hundred nanograms of amphetamine per milliliter of the person's urine or has a concentration of amphetamine in the person's whole blood or blood serum or plasma of at least one hundred nanograms of amphetamine per milliliter of the person's whole blood or blood serum or plasma.

(ii) The person has a concentration of cocaine in the person's urine of at least one hundred fifty nanograms of cocaine per milliliter of the person's urine or has a concentration of cocaine in the person's whole blood or blood serum or plasma of at least fifty nanograms of cocaine per milliliter of the person's whole blood or blood serum or plasma.

(iii) The person has a concentration of cocaine metabolite in the person's urine of at least one hundred fifty nanograms of cocaine metabolite per milliliter of the person's urine or has a concentration of cocaine metabolite in the person's whole blood or blood serum or plasma of at least fifty nanograms of cocaine metabolite per milliliter of the person's whole blood or blood serum or plasma.

(iv) The person has a concentration of heroin in the person's urine of at least two thousand nanograms of heroin per milliliter of the person's urine or has a concentration of heroin in the person's whole blood or blood serum or plasma of at least fifty nanograms of heroin per milliliter of the person's whole blood or blood serum or plasma.

(v) The person has a concentration of heroin metabolite (6–monoacetyl morphine) in the person's urine of at least ten nanograms of heroin metabolite (6–monoacetyl morphine) per milliliter of the person's urine or has a concentration of heroin metabolite (6–monoacetyl morphine) in the person's whole blood or blood serum or plasma of at least ten nanograms of heroin metabolite (6–monoacetyl morphine) per milliliter of the person's whole blood or blood serum or plasma.

(vi) The person has a concentration of L.S.D. in the person's urine of at least twenty-five nanograms of L.S.D. per milliliter of the person's urine or a concentration of L.S.D. in the person's whole blood or blood serum or plasma of at least ten nanograms of L.S.D. per milliliter of the person's whole blood or blood serum or plasma.

(vii) The person has a concentration of marihuana in the person's urine of at least ten nanograms of marihuana per milliliter of the person's urine or has a concentration of marihuana in the person's whole blood or blood serum or plasma of at least two nanograms of marihuana per milliliter of the person's whole blood or blood serum or plasma.

(viii) Either of the following applies:

(I) The person is under the influence of alcohol, a drug of abuse, or a combination of them, and, as measured by gas chromatography mass spectrometry, the person has a concentration of marihuana metabolite in the person's urine of at least fifteen nanograms of marihuana metabolite per milliliter of the person's urine or has a concentration of marihuana metabolite in the person's whole blood or blood serum or plasma of at least five nanograms of marihuana metabolite per milliliter of the person's whole blood or blood serum or plasma.

(II) As measured by gas chromatography mass spectrometry, the person has a concentration of marihuana metabolite in the person's urine of at least thirty-five nanograms of marihuana metabolite per milliliter of the person's urine or has a concentration of marihuana metabolite in the person's whole blood or blood serum or plasma of at least fifty nanograms of marihuana metabolite per milliliter of the person's whole blood or blood serum or plasma.

(ix) The person has a concentration of methamphetamine in the person's urine of at least five hundred nanograms of methamphetamine per milliliter of the person's urine or has a concentration of methamphetamine in the person's whole blood or blood serum or plasma of at least one hundred nanograms of methamphetamine per milliliter of the person's whole blood or blood serum or plasma.

(x) The person has a concentration of phencyclidine in the person's urine of at least twenty-five nanograms of phencyclidine per milliliter of the person's urine or has a concentration of phencyclidine in the person's whole blood or blood serum or plasma of at least ten nanograms of phencyclidine per milliliter of the person's whole blood or blood serum or plasma.

(2) No person who, within twenty years of the conduct described in division (A)(2)(a) of this section, previously has been convicted of or pleaded guilty to a violation of this division, division (A)(1) or (B) of this section, or a municipal OVI offense shall do both of the following:

(a) Operate any vehicle, streetcar, or trackless trolley within this state while under the influence of alcohol, a drug of abuse, or a combination of them;

(b) Subsequent to being arrested for operating the vehicle, streetcar, or trackless trolley as described in division (A)(2)(a) of this section, being asked by a law enforcement officer to submit to a chemical test or tests under section 4511.191 of the Revised Code, and being advised by the officer in accordance with section 4511.192 of the Revised Code of the consequences of the person's refusal or submission to the test or tests, refuse to submit to the test or tests.

(B) No person under twenty-one years of age shall operate any vehicle, streetcar, or trackless trolley within this state, if, at the time of the operation, any of the following apply:

(1) The person has a concentration of at least two-hundredths of one per cent but less than eight-hundredths of one per cent by weight per unit volume of alcohol in the person's whole blood.

(2) The person has a concentration of at least three-hundredths of one per cent but less than ninety-six-thousandths of one per cent by weight per unit volume of alcohol in the person's blood serum or plasma.

(3) The person has a concentration of at least two-hundredths of one gram but less than eight-hundredths of one gram by weight of alcohol per two hundred ten liters of the person's breath.

(4) The person has a concentration of at least twenty-eight one-thousandths of one gram but less than eleven-hundredths of one gram by weight of alcohol per one hundred milliliters of the person's urine.

(C) In any proceeding arising out of one incident, a person may be charged with a violation of division (A)(1)(a) or (A)(2) and a violation of division (B)(1), (2), or (3) of this section, but the person may not be convicted of more than one violation of these divisions.

(D)(1)(a) In any criminal prosecution or juvenile court proceeding for a violation of division (A)(1)(a) of this section or for an equivalent offense, the result of any test of any blood or urine withdrawn and analyzed at any health care provider, as defined in section 2317.02 of the Revised Code, may be admitted with expert testimony to be considered with any other relevant and competent evidence in determining the guilt or innocence of the defendant.

(b) In any criminal prosecution or juvenile court proceeding for a violation of division (A) or (B) of this section or for an equivalent offense, the court may admit evidence on the concentration of alcohol, drugs of abuse, controlled substances, metabolites of a controlled substance, or a combination of them in the defendant's whole blood, blood serum or plasma, breath, urine, or other bodily substance at the time of the alleged violation as shown by chemical analysis of the substance withdrawn within three hours of the time of the alleged violation. The three-hour time limit specified in this division regarding the admission of evidence does not extend or affect the two-hour time limit specified in division (A) of section 4511.192 of the Revised Code as the maximum period of time during which a person may consent to a chemical test or tests as described in that section. The court may admit evidence on the concentration of alcohol, drugs of abuse, or a combination of them as described in this division when a person submits to a blood, breath, urine, or other bodily substance test at the request of a law enforcement officer under section 4511.191 of the Revised Code or a blood or urine sample is obtained pursuant to a search warrant. Only a physician, a registered nurse, or a qualified technician, chemist, or phlebotomist shall withdraw a blood sample for the purpose of determining the alcohol, drug, controlled substance, metabolite of a controlled substance, or combination content of the whole blood, blood serum, or blood plasma. This limitation does not apply to the taking of breath or urine specimens. A person authorized to withdraw blood under this division may refuse to withdraw blood under this division, if in that person's opinion, the physical welfare of the person would be endangered by the withdrawing of blood.

The bodily substance withdrawn under division (D)(1)(b) of this section shall be analyzed in accordance with methods approved by the director of health by an individual possessing a valid permit issued by the director pursuant to section 3701.143 of the Revised Code.

(2) In a criminal prosecution or juvenile court proceeding for a violation of division (A) of this section or for an equivalent offense, if there was at the time the bodily substance was withdrawn a concentration of less than the applicable concentration of alcohol specified in divisions (A)(1)(b), (c), (d), and (e) of this section or less than the applicable concentration of a listed controlled substance or a listed metabolite of a controlled substance specified for a violation of division (A)(1)(j) of this section, that fact may be considered with other competent evidence in determining the guilt or innocence of the defendant. This division does not limit or affect a criminal prosecution or juvenile court proceeding for a violation of division (B) of this section or for an equivalent offense that is substantially equivalent to that division.

(3) Upon the request of the person who was tested, the results of the chemical test shall be made available to the person or the person's attorney, immediately upon the completion of the chemical test analysis.

If the chemical test was obtained pursuant to division (D)(1)(b) of this section, the person tested may have a physician, a registered nurse, or a qualified technician, chemist, or phlebotomist of the person's own choosing administer a chemical test or tests, at the person's expense, in addition to any administered at the request of a law enforcement officer. The form to be read to the person to be tested, as required under section 4511.192 of the Revised Code, shall state that the person may have an independent test performed at the person's expense. The failure or inability to obtain an additional chemical test by a person shall not preclude the admission of evidence relating to the chemical test or tests taken at the request of a law enforcement officer.

(4)(a) As used in divisions (D)(4)(b) and (c) of this section, "national highway traffic safety administration" means the national highway traffic safety administration established as an administration of the United States department of transportation under 96 Stat. 2415 (1983), 49 U.S.C.A. 105.

(b) In any criminal prosecution or juvenile court proceeding for a violation of division (A) or (B) of this section, of a municipal ordinance relating to operating a vehicle while under the influence of alcohol, a drug of abuse, or alcohol and a drug of abuse, or of a municipal ordinance relating to operating a vehicle with a prohibited concentration of alcohol, a controlled substance, or a metabolite of a controlled substance in the blood, breath, or urine, if a law enforcement officer has administered a field sobriety test to the operator of the vehicle involved in the violation and if it is shown by clear and convincing evidence that the officer administered the test in substantial compliance with the testing standards for any reliable, credible, and generally accepted field sobriety tests that were in effect at the time the tests were administered, including, but not limited to, any testing standards then in effect that were set by the national highway traffic safety administration, all of the following apply:

(i) The officer may testify concerning the results of the field sobriety test so administered.

(ii) The prosecution may introduce the results of the field sobriety test so administered as evidence in any proceedings in the criminal prosecution or juvenile court proceeding.

(iii) If testimony is presented or evidence is introduced under division (D)(4)(b)(i) or (ii) of this section and if the testimony or evidence is admissible under the Rules of Evidence, the court shall admit the testimony or evidence and the trier of fact shall give it whatever weight the trier of fact considers to be appropriate.

(c) Division (D)(4)(b) of this section does not limit or preclude a court, in its determination of whether the arrest of a person was supported by probable cause or its determination of any other matter in a criminal prosecution or juvenile court proceeding of a type described in that division, from considering evidence or testimony that is not otherwise disallowed by division (D)(4)(b) of this section.

(E)(1) Subject to division (E)(3) of this section, in any criminal prosecution or juvenile court proceeding for a violation of division (A)(1)(b), (c), (d), (e), (f), (g), (h), (i), or (j) or (B)(1), (2), (3), or (4) of this section or for an equivalent offense that is substantially equivalent to any of those divisions, a laboratory report from any laboratory personnel issued a permit by the department of health authorizing an analysis as described in this division that contains an analysis of the whole blood, blood serum or plasma, breath, urine, or other bodily substance tested and that contains all of the information specified in this division shall be admitted as prima-facie evidence of the information and statements that the report contains. The laboratory report shall contain all of the following:

(a) The signature, under oath, of any person who performed the analysis;

(b) Any findings as to the identity and quantity of alcohol, a drug of abuse, a controlled substance, a metabolite of a controlled substance, or a combination of them that was found;

(c) A copy of a notarized statement by the laboratory director or a designee of the director that contains the name of each certified analyst or test performer involved with the report, the analyst's or test performer's employment relationship with the laboratory that issued the report, and a notation that performing an analysis of the type involved is part of the analyst's or test performer's regular duties;

(d) An outline of the analyst's or test performer's education, training, and experience in performing the type of analysis involved and a certification that the laboratory satisfies appropriate quality control standards in general and, in this particular analysis, under rules of the department of health.

(2) Notwithstanding any other provision of law regarding the admission of evidence, a report of the type described in division (E)(1) of this section is not admissible against the defendant to whom it pertains in any proceeding, other than a preliminary hearing or a grand jury proceeding, unless the prosecutor has served a copy of the report on the defendant's attorney or, if the defendant has no attorney, on the defendant.

(3) A report of the type described in division (E)(1) of this section shall not be prima-facie evidence of the contents, identity, or amount of any substance if, within seven days after the defendant to whom the report pertains or the defendant's attor-

ney receives a copy of the report, the defendant or the defendant's attorney demands the testimony of the person who signed the report. The judge in the case may extend the seven-day time limit in the interest of justice.

(F) Except as otherwise provided in this division, any physician, registered nurse, or qualified technician, chemist, or phlebotomist who withdraws blood from a person pursuant to this section, and any hospital, first-aid station, or clinic at which blood is withdrawn from a person pursuant to this section, is immune from criminal liability and civil liability based upon a claim of assault and battery or any other claim that is not a claim of malpractice, for any act performed in withdrawing blood from the person. The immunity provided in this division is not available to a person who withdraws blood if the person engages in willful or wanton misconduct.

(G)(1) Whoever violates any provision of divisions (A)(1)(a) to (i) or (A)(2) of this section is guilty of operating a vehicle under the influence of alcohol, a drug of abuse, or a combination of them. Whoever violates division (A)(1)(j) of this section is guilty of operating a vehicle while under the influence of a listed controlled substance or a listed metabolite of a controlled substance. The court shall sentence the offender for either offense under Chapter 2929. of the Revised Code, except as otherwise authorized or required by divisions (G)(1)(a) to (e) of this section:

(a) Except as otherwise provided in division (G)(1)(b), (c), (d), or (e) of this section, the offender is guilty of a misdemeanor of the first degree, and the court shall sentence the offender to all of the following:

(i) If the sentence is being imposed for a violation of division (A)(1)(a), (b), (c), (d), (e), or (j) of this section, a mandatory jail term of three consecutive days. As used in this division, three consecutive days means seventy-two consecutive hours. The court may sentence an offender to both an intervention program and a jail term. The court may impose an jail term in addition to the three-day mandatory jail term or intervention program. However, in no case shall the cumulative jail term imposed for the offense exceed six months.

The court may suspend the execution of the three-day jail term under this division if the court, in lieu of that suspended term, places the offender under a community control sanction pursuant to section 2929.25 of the Revised Code and requires the offender to attend, for three consecutive days, a drivers' intervention program certified under section 3793.10 of the Revised Code. The court also may suspend the execution of any part of the three-day jail term under this division if it places the offender under a community control sanction pursuant to section 2929.25 of the Revised Code for part of the three days, requires the offender to attend for the suspended part of the term a drivers' intervention program so certified, and sentences the offender to a jail term equal to the remainder of the three consecutive days that the offender does not spend attending the program. The court may require the offender, as a condition of community control and in addition to the required attendance at a drivers' intervention program, to attend and satisfactorily complete any treatment or education programs that comply with the minimum standards adopted pursuant to Chapter 3793. of the Revised Code by the director of alcohol and drug addiction services that the operators of the drivers' intervention program determine that the offender should attend and to report periodically to the court on the offender's progress in the programs. The court also may impose on the offender any other conditions of community control that it considers necessary.

(ii) If the sentence is being imposed for a violation of division (A)(1)(f), (g), (h), or (i) or division (A)(2) of this section, except as otherwise provided in this division, a mandatory jail term of at least three consecutive days and a requirement that the offender attend, for three consecutive days, a drivers' intervention program that is certified pursuant to section 3793.10 of the Revised Code. As used in this division, three consecutive days means seventy-two consecutive hours. If the court determines that the offender is not conducive to treatment in a drivers' intervention program, if the offender refuses to attend a drivers' intervention program, or if the jail at which the offender is to serve the jail term imposed can provide a driver's intervention program, the court shall sentence the offender to a mandatory jail term of at least six consecutive days.

The court may require the offender, under a community control sanction imposed under section 2929.25 of the Revised Code, to attend and satisfactorily complete any treatment or education programs that comply with the minimum standards adopted pursuant to Chapter 3793. of the Revised Code by the director of alcohol and drug addiction services, in addition to the required attendance at drivers' intervention program, that the operators of the drivers' intervention program determine that the offender should attend and to report periodically to the court on the offender's progress in the programs. The court also may impose any other conditions of community control on the offender that it considers necessary.

(iii) In all cases, a fine of not less than two hundred fifty and not more than one thousand dollars;

(iv) In all cases, a class five license suspension of the offender's driver's or commercial driver's license or permit or nonresident operating privilege from the range specified in division (A)(5) of section 4510.02 of the Revised Code. The court may grant limited driving privileges relative to the suspension under sections 4510.021 and 4510.13 of the Revised Code.

(b) Except as otherwise provided in division (G)(1)(e) of this section, an offender who, within six years of the offense, previously has been convicted of or pleaded guilty to one violation of division (A) or (B) of this section or one other equivalent offense is guilty of a misdemeanor of the first degree. The court shall sentence the offender to all of the following:

(i) If the sentence is being imposed for a violation of division (A)(1)(a), (b), (c), (d), (e), or (j) of this section, a mandatory jail term of ten consecutive days. The court shall impose the ten-day mandatory jail term under this division unless, subject to division (G)(3) of this section, it instead imposes a sentence under that division consisting of both a jail term and a term of house arrest with electronic monitoring, with continuous alcohol monitoring, or with both electronic monitoring and continuous alcohol monitoring. The court may impose a jail term in addition to the ten-day mandatory jail term. The cumulative jail term imposed for the offense shall not exceed six months.

In addition to the jail term or the term of house arrest with electronic monitoring or continuous alcohol monitoring or both types of monitoring and jail term, the court may require the offender to attend a drivers' intervention program that is certified pursuant to section 3793.10 of the Revised Code. If the operator of the program determines that the offender is alcohol dependent, the program shall notify the court, and, subject to division (I) of this section, the court shall order the offender to obtain treatment through an alcohol and drug addiction program authorized by section 3793.02 of the Revised Code.

(ii) If the sentence is being imposed for a violation of division (A)(1)(f), (g), (h), or (i) or division (A)(2) of this section, except as otherwise provided in this division, a mandatory jail term of twenty consecutive days. The court shall impose the twenty-day mandatory jail term under this division unless, subject to division (G)(3) of this section, it instead imposes a sentence under that division consisting of both a jail term and a term of house arrest with electronic monitoring, with continuous alcohol monitoring, or with both electronic monitoring and continuous alcohol monitoring. The court may impose a jail term in addition to the twenty-day mandatory jail term. The cumulative jail term imposed for the offense shall not exceed six months.

In addition to the jail term or the term of house arrest with electronic monitoring or continuous alcohol monitoring or both types of monitoring and jail term, the court may require the offender to attend a driver's intervention program that is certified pursuant to section 3793.10 of the Revised Code. If the operator of the program determines that the offender is alcohol dependent, the program shall notify the court, and, subject to division (I) of this section, the court shall order the offender to obtain treatment through an alcohol and drug addiction program authorized by section 3793.02 of the Revised Code.

(iii) In all cases, notwithstanding the fines set forth in Chapter 2929. of the Revised Code, a fine of not less than three hundred fifty and not more than one thousand five hundred dollars;

(iv) In all cases, a class four license suspension of the offender's driver's license, commercial driver's license, temporary instruction permit, probationary license, or nonresident operating privilege from the range specified in division (A)(4) of section 4510.02 of the Revised Code. The court may grant limited driving privileges relative to the suspension under sections 4510.021 and 4510.13 of the Revised Code.

(v) In all cases, if the vehicle is registered in the offender's name, immobilization of the vehicle involved in the offense for ninety days in accordance with section 4503.233 of the Revised Code and impoundment of the license plates of that vehicle for ninety days.

(c) Except as otherwise provided in division (G)(1)(e) of this section, an offender who, within six years of the offense, previously has been convicted of or pleaded guilty to two violations of division (A) or (B) of this section or other equivalent offenses is guilty of a misdemeanor. The court shall sentence the offender to all of the following:

(i) If the sentence is being imposed for a violation of division (A)(1)(a), (b), (c), (d), (e), or (j) of this section, a mandatory jail term of thirty consecutive days. The court shall impose the thirty-day mandatory jail term under this division unless, subject to division (G)(3) of this section, it instead imposes a sentence under that division consisting of both a jail term and a term of house arrest with electronic monitoring, with continuous alcohol monitoring, or with both electronic monitoring and continuous alcohol monitoring. The court may impose a jail term in addition to the thirty-day mandatory jail term. Notwithstanding the jail terms set forth in sections 2929.21 to 2929.28 of the Revised Code, the additional jail term shall not exceed one year, and the cumulative jail term imposed for the offense shall not exceed one year.

(ii) If the sentence is being imposed for a violation of division (A)(1)(f), (g), (h), or (i) or division (A)(2) of this section, a mandatory jail term of sixty consecutive days. The court shall impose the sixty-day mandatory jail term under this division unless, subject to division (G)(3) of this section, it instead imposes a sentence under that division consisting of both a jail term and a term of house arrest with electronic monitoring, with continuous alcohol monitoring, or with both electronic monitoring and continuous alcohol monitoring. The court may impose a jail term in addition to the sixty-day mandatory jail term. Notwithstanding the jail terms set forth in sections 2929.21 to 2929.28 of the Revised Code, the additional jail term shall not exceed one year, and the cumulative jail term imposed for the offense shall not exceed one year.

(iii) In all cases, notwithstanding the fines set forth in Chapter 2929. of the Revised Code, a fine of not less than five hundred fifty and not more than two thousand five hundred dollars;

(iv) In all cases, a class three license suspension of the offender's driver's license, commercial driver's license, temporary instruction permit, probationary license, or nonresident operating privilege from the range specified in division (A)(3) of section 4510.02 of the Revised Code. The court may grant limited driving privileges relative to the suspension under sections 4510.021 and 4510.13 of the Revised Code.

(v) In all cases, if the vehicle is registered in the offender's name, criminal forfeiture of the vehicle involved in the offense in accordance with section 4503.234 of the Revised Code. Division (G)(6) of this section applies regarding any vehicle that is subject to an order of criminal forfeiture under this division.

(vi) In all cases, participation in an alcohol and drug addiction program authorized by section 3793.02 of the Revised Code, subject to division (I) of this section.

(d) Except as otherwise provided in division (G)(1)(e) of this section, an offender who, within six years of the offense, previously has been convicted of or pleaded guilty to three or four violations of division (A) or (B) of this section or other equivalent offenses or an offender who, within twenty years of the offense, previously has been convicted of or pleaded guilty to five or more violations of that nature is guilty of a felony of the fourth degree. The court shall sentence the offender to all of the following:

(i) If the sentence is being imposed for a violation of division (A)(1)(a), (b), (c), (d), (e), or (j) of this section, a mandatory prison term of one, two, three, four, or five years as required by and in accordance with division (G)(2) of section 2929.13 of the Revised Code if the offender also is convicted of or also pleads guilty to a specification of the type described in section 2941.1413 of the Revised Code or, in the discretion of the court, either a mandatory term of local incarceration of sixty consecutive days in accordance with division (G)(1) of section 2929.13 of the Revised Code or a mandatory prison term of sixty consecutive days in accordance with division (G)(2) of that section if the offender is not convicted of and does not plead guilty to a specification of that type. If the court imposes a mandatory term of local incarceration, it may impose a jail term in addition to the sixty-day mandatory term, the cumulative total of the mandatory term and the jail term for the offense shall not exceed one year, and, except as provided in division (A)(1) of section 2929.13 of the Revised Code, no prison term is authorized for the offense. If the court imposes a mandatory prison term, notwithstanding division (A)(4) of section 2929.14 of the Revised Code, it also may sentence the offender to a definite prison term that shall be not less than six months and not more than thirty months and the prison terms shall be imposed as described in division (G)(2) of section 2929.13 of the Revised Code. If the court imposes a mandatory prison term or mandatory prison term and additional prison term, in addition to the term or terms so imposed, the court also may sentence the offender to a community control sanction for the offense, but the offender shall serve all of the prison terms so imposed prior to serving the community control sanction.

(ii) If the sentence is being imposed for a violation of division (A)(1)(f), (g), (h), or (i) or division (A)(2) of this section, a mandatory prison term of one, two, three, four, or five years as required by and in accordance with division (G)(2) of section 2929.13 of the Revised Code if the offender also is convicted of or also pleads guilty to a specification of the type described in section 2941.1413 of the Revised Code or, in the discretion of the court, either a mandatory term of local incarceration of one hundred twenty consecutive days in accordance with division (G)(1) of section 2929.13 of the Revised Code or a mandatory prison term of one hundred twenty consecutive days in accordance with division (G)(2) of that section if the offender is not convicted of and does not plead guilty to a specification of that type. If the court imposes a mandatory term of local incarceration, it may impose a jail term in addition to the one hundred twenty-day mandatory term, the cumulative total of the mandatory term and the jail term for the offense shall not exceed one year, and, except as provided in division (A)(1) of section 2929.13 of the Revised Code, no prison term is authorized for the offense. If the court imposes a mandatory prison term, notwithstanding division (A)(4) of section 2929.14 of the Revised Code, it also may sentence the offender to a definite prison term that shall be not less than six months and not more than thirty months and the prison terms shall be imposed as described in division (G)(2) of section 2929.13 of the Revised Code. If the court imposes a mandatory prison term or mandatory prison term and additional prison term, in addition to the term or terms so imposed, the court also may sentence the offender to a community control sanction for the offense, but the offender shall serve all of the prison terms so imposed prior to serving the community control sanction.

(iii) In all cases, notwithstanding section 2929.18 of the Revised Code, a fine of not less than eight hundred nor more than ten thousand dollars;

(iv) In all cases, a class two license suspension of the offender's driver's license, commercial driver's license, temporary instruction permit, probationary license, or nonresident operating privilege from the range specified in division (A)(2) of section 4510.02 of the Revised Code. The court may grant limited driving privileges relative to the suspension under sections 4510.021 and 4510.13 of the Revised Code.

(v) In all cases, if the vehicle is registered in the offender's name, criminal forfeiture of the vehicle involved in the offense in accordance with section 4503.234 of the Revised Code. Division (G)(6) of this section applies regarding any vehicle that is subject to an order of criminal forfeiture under this division.

(vi) In all cases, participation in an alcohol and drug addiction program authorized by section 3793.02 of the Revised Code, subject to division (I) of this section.

(vii) In all cases, if the court sentences the offender to a mandatory term of local incarceration, in addition to the mandatory term, the court, pursuant to section 2929.17 of the Revised Code, may impose a term of house arrest with electronic monitoring. The term shall not commence until after the offender has served the mandatory term of local incarceration.

(e) An offender who previously has been convicted of or pleaded guilty to a violation of division (A) of this section that was a felony, regardless of when the violation and the conviction or guilty plea occurred, is guilty of a felony of the third degree. The court shall sentence the offender to all of the following:

(i) If the offender is being sentenced for a violation of division (A)(1)(a), (b), (c), (d), (e), or (j) of this section, a mandatory prison term of one, two, three, four, or five years as required by and in accordance with division (G)(2) of section 2929.13 of the Revised Code if the offender also is convicted of or also pleads guilty to a specification of the type described in section 2941.1413 of the Revised Code or a mandatory prison term of sixty consecutive days in accordance with division (G)(2) of section 2929.13 of the Revised Code if the offender is not convicted of and does not plead guilty to a specification of that type. The court may impose a prison term in addition to the mandatory prison term. The cumulative total of a sixty-day mandatory prison term and the additional prison term for the offense shall not exceed five years. In addition to the mandatory prison term or mandatory prison term and additional prison term the court imposes, the court also may sentence the offender to a community control sanction for the offense, but the offender shall serve all of the prison terms so imposed prior to serving the community control sanction.

(ii) If the sentence is being imposed for a violation of division (A)(1)(f), (g), (h), or (i) or division (A)(2) of this section, a mandatory prison term of one, two, three, four, or five years as required by and in accordance with division (G)(2) of section 2929.13 of the Revised Code if the offender also is convicted of or also pleads guilty to a specification of the type described in section 2941.1413 of the Revised Code or a mandatory prison term of one hundred twenty consecutive days in accordance with division (G)(2) of section 2929.13 of the Revised Code if the offender is not convicted of and does not plead guilty to a specification of that type. The court may impose a prison term in addition to the mandatory prison term. The cumulative total of a one hundred twenty-day mandatory prison term and the additional prison term for the offense shall not exceed five years. In addition to the mandatory prison term or mandatory prison term and additional prison term the court imposes, the court also may sentence the offender to a community control sanction for the offense, but the offender shall serve all of the prison terms so imposed prior to serving the community control sanction.

(iii) In all cases, notwithstanding section 2929.18 of the Revised Code, a fine of not less than eight hundred nor more than ten thousand dollars;

(iv) In all cases, a class two license suspension of the offender's driver's license, commercial driver's license, temporary instruction permit, probationary license, or nonresident operating privilege from the range specified in division (A)(2) of section 4510.02 of the Revised Code. The court may grant limited driving privileges relative to the suspension under sections 4510.021 and 4510.13 of the Revised Code.

(v) In all cases, if the vehicle is registered in the offender's name, criminal forfeiture of the vehicle involved in the offense in accordance with section 4503.234 of the Revised Code. Division (G)(6) of this section applies regarding any vehicle that is subject to an order of criminal forfeiture under this division.

(vi) In all cases, participation in an alcohol and drug addiction program authorized by section 3793.02 of the Revised Code, subject to division (I) of this section.

(2) An offender who is convicted of or pleads guilty to a violation of division (A) of this section and who subsequently seeks reinstatement of the driver's or occupational driver's license or permit or nonresident operating privilege suspended under this section as a result of the conviction or guilty plea shall pay a reinstatement fee as provided in division (F)(2) of section 4511.191 of the Revised Code.

(3) If an offender is sentenced to a jail term under division (G)(1)(b)(i) or (ii) or (G)(1)(c)(i) or (ii) of this section and if, within sixty days of sentencing of the offender, the court issues a written finding on the record that, due to the unavailability of space at the jail where the offender is required to serve the term, the offender will not be able to begin serving that term within the sixty-day period following the date of sentencing, the court may impose an alternative sentence under this division that includes a term of house arrest with electronic monitoring, with continuous alcohol monitoring, or with both electronic monitoring and continuous alcohol monitoring.

As an alternative to a mandatory jail term of ten consecutive days required by division (G)(1)(b)(i) of this section, the court, under this division, may sentence the offender to five consecutive days in jail and not less than eighteen consecutive days of house arrest with electronic monitoring, with continuous alcohol monitoring, or with both electronic monitoring and continuous alcohol monitoring. The cumulative total of the five consecutive days in jail and the period of house arrest with electronic monitoring, continuous alcohol monitoring, or both types of monitoring shall not exceed six months. The five consecutive days in jail do not have to be served prior to or consecutively to the period of house arrest.

As an alternative to the mandatory jail term of twenty consecutive days required by division (G)(1)(b)(ii) of this section, the court, under this division, may sentence the offender to ten consecutive days in jail and not less than thirty-six consecutive days of house arrest with electronic monitoring, with continuous alcohol monitoring, or with both electronic monitoring and continuous alcohol monitoring. The cumulative total of the ten consecutive days in jail and the period of house arrest with electronic monitoring, continuous alcohol monitoring, or both types of monitoring shall not exceed six months. The ten consecutive days in jail do not have to be served prior to or consecutively to the period of house arrest.

As an alternative to a mandatory jail term of thirty consecutive days required by division (G)(1)(c)(i) of this section, the court, under this division, may sentence the offender to fifteen consecutive days in jail and not less than fifty-five consecutive days of house arrest with electronic monitoring, with continuous alcohol monitoring, or with both electronic monitoring and continuous alcohol monitoring. The cumulative total of the fifteen consecutive days in jail and the period of house arrest with electronic monitoring, continuous alcohol monitoring, or both types of monitoring shall not exceed one year. The fifteen consecutive days in jail do not have to be served prior to or consecutively to the period of house arrest.

As an alternative to the mandatory jail term of sixty consecutive days required by division (G)(1)(c)(ii) of this section, the court, under this division, may sentence the offender to thirty consecutive days in jail and not less than one hundred ten consecutive days of house arrest with electronic monitoring, with continuous alcohol monitoring, or with both electronic monitoring and continuous alcohol monitoring. The cumulative total of the thirty consecutive days in jail and the period of house arrest with electronic monitoring, continuous alcohol monitoring, or both types of monitoring shall not exceed one year. The thirty consecutive days in jail do not have to be served prior to or consecutively to the period of house arrest.

(4) If an offender's driver's or occupational driver's license or permit or nonresident operating privilege is suspended under division (G) of this section and if section 4510.13 of the Revised Code permits the court to grant limited driving privileges, the court may grant the limited driving privileges in accordance with that section. If division (A)(7) of that section requires that the court impose as a condition of the privileges that the offender must display on the vehicle that is driven subject to the privileges restricted license plates that are issued under section 4503.231 of the Revised Code, except as provided in division (B) of that section, the court shall impose that condition as one of the conditions of the limited driving privileges granted to the offender, except as provided in division (B) of section 4503.231 of the Revised Code.

(5) Fines imposed under this section for a violation of division (A) of this section shall be distributed as follows:

(a) Twenty-five dollars of the fine imposed under division (G)(1)(a)(iii), thirty-five dollars of the fine imposed under division (G)(1)(b)(iii), one hundred twenty-three dollars of the fine imposed under division (G)(1)(c)(iii), and two hundred ten dollars of the fine imposed under division (G)(1)(d)(iii) or (e)(iii) of this section shall be paid to an enforcement and education fund established by the legislative authority of the law enforcement agency in this state that primarily was responsible for the arrest of the offender, as determined by the court that imposes the fine. The agency shall use this share to pay only those costs it incurs in enforcing this section or a municipal OVI ordinance and in informing the public of the laws governing the operation of a vehicle while under the influence of alcohol, the dangers of the operation of a vehicle under the influence of alcohol, and other information relating to the operation of a vehicle under the influence of alcohol and the consumption of alcoholic beverages.

(b) Fifty dollars of the fine imposed under division (G)(1)(a)(iii) of this section shall be paid to the political subdivision that pays the cost of housing the offender during the offender's term of incarceration. If the offender is being sentenced for a violation of division (A)(1)(a), (b), (c), (d), (e), or (j) of this section and was confined as a result of the offense prior to being sentenced for the offense but is not sentenced to a term of incarceration, the fifty dollars shall be paid to the political subdivision that paid the cost of housing the offender during that period of confinement. The political subdivision shall use the share under this division to pay or reimburse incarceration or treatment costs it incurs in housing or providing drug and alcohol treatment to persons who violate this section or a municipal OVI ordinance, costs of any immobilizing or disabling device used on the offender's vehicle, and costs of electronic house arrest equipment needed for persons who violate this section.

(c) Twenty-five dollars of the fine imposed under division (G)(1)(a)(iii) and fifty dollars of the fine imposed under division (G)(1)(b)(iii) of this section shall be deposited into the county or municipal indigent drivers' alcohol treatment fund under the control of that court, as created by the county or municipal corporation under division (N) of section 4511.191 of the Revised Code.

(d) One hundred fifteen dollars of the fine imposed under division (G)(1)(b)(iii), two hundred seventy-seven dollars of the fine imposed under division (G)(1)(c)(iii), and four hundred forty dollars of the fine imposed under division (G)(1)(d)(iii) or (e)(iii) of this section shall be paid to the political subdivision that pays the cost of housing the offender during the offender's term of incarceration. The political subdivision shall use this share to pay or reimburse incarceration or treatment costs it incurs in housing or providing drug and alcohol treatment to persons who violate this section or a municipal OVI ordinance, costs for any immobilizing or disabling device used on the offender's vehicle, and costs of electronic house arrest equipment needed for persons who violate this section.

(e) The balance of the fine imposed under division (G)(1)(a)(iii), (b)(iii), (c)(iii), (d)(iii), or (e)(iii) of this section shall be disbursed as otherwise provided by law.

(6) If title to a motor vehicle that is subject to an order of criminal forfeiture under division (G)(1)(c), (d), or (e) of this section is assigned or transferred and division (B)(2) or (3) of section 4503.234 of the Revised Code applies, in addition to or independent of any other penalty established by law, the court may fine the offender the value of the vehicle as determined by publications of the national auto dealers association. The proceeds of any fine so imposed shall be distributed in accordance with division (C)(2) of that section.

(7) As used in division (G) of this section, "electronic monitoring," "mandatory prison term," and "mandatory term of local incarceration" have the same meanings as in section 2929.01 of the Revised Code.

(H) Whoever violates division (B) of this section is guilty of operating a vehicle after underage alcohol consumption and shall be punished as follows:

(1) Except as otherwise provided in division (H)(2) of this section, the offender is guilty of a misdemeanor of the fourth degree. In addition to any other sanction imposed for the offense, the court shall impose a class six suspension of the offender's driver's license, commercial driver's license, temporary instruction permit, probationary license, or nonresident operating privilege from the range specified in division (A)(6) of section 4510.02 of the Revised Code.

(2) If, within one year of the offense, the offender previously has been convicted of or pleaded guilty to one or more violations of division (A) or (B) of this section or other equivalent offenses, the offender is guilty of a misdemeanor of the third degree. In addition to any other sanction imposed for the offense, the court shall impose a class four suspension of the offender's driver's license, commercial driver's license, temporary instruction permit, probationary license, or nonresident operating privilege from the range specified in division (A)(4) of section 4510.02 of the Revised Code.

(3) If the offender also is convicted of or also pleads guilty to a specification of the type described in section 2941.1416 of the Revised Code and if the court imposes a jail term for the violation of division (B) of this section, the court shall impose upon the offender an additional definite jail term pursuant to division (E) of section 2929.24 of the Revised Code.

(I)(1) No court shall sentence an offender to an alcohol treatment program under this section unless the treatment program complies with the minimum standards for alcohol treatment programs adopted under Chapter 3793. of the Revised Code by the director of alcohol and drug addiction services.

(2) An offender who stays in a drivers' intervention program or in an alcohol treatment program under an order issued under this section shall pay the cost of the stay in the program. However, if the court determines that an offender who stays in an alcohol treatment program under an order issued under this section is unable to pay the cost of the stay in the program, the court may order that the cost be paid from the court's indigent drivers' alcohol treatment fund.

(J) If a person whose driver's or commercial driver's license or permit or nonresident operating privilege is suspended under this section files an appeal regarding any aspect of the person's trial or sentence, the appeal itself does not stay the operation of the suspension.

(K) Division (A)(1)(j) of this section does not apply to a person who operates a vehicle, streetcar, or trackless trolley while the person has a concentration of a listed controlled substance or a listed metabolite of a controlled substance in the person's whole blood, blood serum or plasma, or urine that equals or exceeds the amount specified in that division, if both of the following apply:

(1) The person obtained the controlled substance pursuant to a prescription issued by a licensed health professional authorized to prescribe drugs.

(2) The person injected, ingested, or inhaled the controlled substance in accordance with the health professional's directions.

(L) The prohibited concentrations of a controlled substance or a metabolite of a controlled substance listed in division (A)(1)(j) of this section also apply in a prosecution of a violation of division (D) of section 2923.16 of the Revised Code in the same manner as if the offender is being prosecuted for a prohibited concentration of alcohol.

(M) All terms defined in section 4510.01 of the Revised Code apply to this section. If the meaning of a term defined in section 4510.01 of the Revised Code conflicts with the meaning of the same term as defined in section 4501.01 or 4511.01 of the Revised Code, the term as defined in section 4510.01 of the Revised Code applies to this section.

(N)(1) The Ohio Traffic Rules in effect on January 1, 2004, as adopted by the supreme court under authority of section 2937.46 of the Revised Code, do not apply to felony violations of this section. Subject to division (N)(2) of this section, the Rules of Criminal Procedure apply to felony violations of this section.

(2) If, on or after January 1, 2004, the supreme court modifies the Ohio Traffic Rules to provide procedures to govern felony violations of this section, the modified rules shall apply to felony violations of this section.

(2006 H 461, eff. 4-4-07; 2006 S 8, eff. 8-17-06; 2004 H 163, eff. 9-23-04; 2003 H 87, § 4, eff. 1-1-04; 2003 H 87, § 1, eff. 6-30-03; 2002 S 163, § 3, eff. 1-1-04; 2002 S 163, § 1, eff 4-9-03; 2002 H 490, eff. 1-1-04; 2002 S 123, eff. 1-1-04; 1999 S 22, eff. 5-17-00; 1994 S 82, eff. 5-4-94; 1990 H 837, eff. 7-25-90; 1990 S 131; 1986 S 262; 1982 S 432; 1974 H 995; 1971 S 14; 1970 H 874; 132 v H 380; 130 v S 41; 125 v 461; 1953 H 1; GC 6307-19)

Historical and Statutory Notes

Ed. Note: RC 4511.19 contains provisions analogous to former RC 4507.16(B) and 4511.99(A), repealed by 2002 S 123, eff. 1-1-04.

Ed. Note: RC 4511.19 contains provisions analogous to former RC 4507.16(E) and 4511.99(N), repealed by 2002 S 123, eff. 1-1-04.

Pre-1953 H 1 Amendments: 119 v 766, § 19

Amendment Note: 2006 S 8 added division (A)(1)(j); inserted "controlled substances, metabolites of a controlled substance," in the first sentence of the first paragraph of division (D)(1) and substituted "three" for "two" before "hours" in that same sentence; added the second sentence in the first paragraph of division (D)(1); inserted "controlled substance, metabolite of a controlled substance," and substituted "combination" for "alcohol and drug" in the first sentence of the second paragraph of division (D)(1); inserted "or less than the applicable concentration of a listed controlled substance or a listed metabolite of a controlled substance specified for a violation of division (A)(1)(j) of this section" in the first sentence of division (D)(2); inserted ", a controlled substance, or a metabolite of a controlled substance" in division (D)(4)(b) and (E)(1)(b); rewrote the first paragraph of division (E)(1); added the second sentence and inserted "for either offense" in the third sentence of the first paragraph of division (G)(1); inserted ", or (j)" in the first sentence of division (G)(1)(a)(i), (G)(1)(b)(i), (G)(1)(c)(i), (G)(1)(d)(i), (G)(1)(d)(i) and the second sentence of division (G)(5)(b); rewrote divisions (K) through (L); and made other nonsubstantive changes. Prior to amendment, the first paragraph of division (E)(1) and divisions (K) through (L) read, respectively:

"(E)(1) Subject to division (E)(3) of this section, in any criminal prosecution or juvenile court proceeding for a violation of division (A)(1)(b), (c), (d), (e), (f), (g), (h), or (i) or (B)(1), (2), (3), or (4) of this section or for an equivalent offense that is substantially equivalent to any of those divisions, a laboratory report from any forensic laboratory certified by the department of health that contains an analysis of the whole blood, blood serum or plasma, breath, urine, or other bodily substance tested and that contains all of the information specified in this division shall be admitted as prima-facie evidence of the information and statements that the report contains. The laboratory report shall contain all of the following:

"(K) All terms defined in section 4510.01 of the Revised Code apply to this section. If the meaning of a term defined in section 4510.01 of the Revised Code conflicts with the meaning of the same term as defined in section 4501.01 or 4511.01 of the Revised Code, the term as defined in section 4510.01 of the Revised Code applies to this section.

"(L)(1) The Ohio Traffic Rules in effect on January 1, 2004, as adopted by the supreme court under authority of section 2937.46 of the Revised Code, do not apply to felony violations of this section. Subject to division (L)(2) of this section, the Rules of Criminal Procedure apply to felony violations of this section.

"(2) If, on or after January 1, 2004, the supreme court modifies the Ohio Traffic Rules to provide procedures to govern felony violations of this section, the modified rules shall apply to felony violations of this section."

Amendment Note: 2004 H 163 redesignated former divisions (A), (A)(1), (A)(2), (A)(3), (A)(4), (A)(5), (A)(6), (A)(7), (A)(8), and (A)(9) as divisions (A)(1), (A)(1)(a), (A)(1)(b), (A)(1)(c), (A)(1)(d), (A)(1)(e), (A)(1)(f), (A)(1)(g), (A)(1)(h), and (A)(1)(i), respectively; added new division (A)(2); inserted "(a) or (A)(2)" in division (C); substituted "(1)(b), (c), (d), and (e)" for "(2), (3), (4), and (5)" in division (D)(2); substituted "(1)(b), (c), (d), (e), (f), (g), (h), or (i)" for "(2), (3), (4), (5), (6), (7), (8), or (9)" in division (E)(1); inserted "(a)" and substituted "(i) or (A)(2)" for "(9)" in division (G)(1); substituted "(a), (b), (c), (d), or (e)" for ", (2), (3), (4), or (5)" in division (G)(1)(a)(i); substituted "(1)(f), (g), (h), or (i) or division (A)(2)" for "(6), (7), (8), or (9)" in division (G)(1)(a)(ii); substituted "(a), (b), (c), (d), or (e)" for ", (2), (3), (4), or (5)" in division (G)(1)(b)(i); inserted ", with continuous alcohol monitoring, or with both electronic monitoring and continuous alcohol monitoring" in divisions (G)(1)(b)(i), (ii), (G)(1)(c)(i), (ii), and (G)(3); substituted "four" for "more" and inserted "or an offender who, within twenty years of the offense, previously has been convicted of or pleaded guilty to five or more violations of that nature" in the first paragraph of division (G)(1)(d); inserted "or continuous alcohol monitoring or both types of monitoring" in divisions (G)(1)(b)(i) and (ii); inserted ", continuous alcohol monitoring, or both types of monitoring" in division (G)(3); substituted "(1)(f), (g), (h), or (i) or division (A)(2)" for "(6), (7), (8), or (9)" in divisions (G)(1)(b)(ii) and (G)(1)(c)(ii); substituted "(a), (b), (c), (d), or (e)" for ", (2), (3), (4), or (5)" in division (G)(1)(c)(i); substituted "in accordance with that section. If division (A)(7) of that section requires that" for "only if", "impose" for "imposes", and "a condition" for "one of the conditions" in division (G)(4); inserted ", the court shall impose that condition as one of the conditions of the limited driving privileges granted to the offender, except as provided in division (B) of section 4503.231 of the Revised Code" at the end of division (G)(4); substituted "(a), (b), (c), (d), or (e)" for ", (2), (3), (4), or (5)" in division (G)(5)(b); added division (H)(3); rewrote divisions (G)(1)(d)(i), (G)(1)(d)(ii), (G)(1)(e)(i), and (G)(1)(e)(ii). Prior to amendment, divisions (G)(1)(d)(i), (G)(1)(d)(ii), (G)(1)(e)(i), and (G)(1)(e)(ii) read:

"(i) If the sentence is being imposed for a violation of division (A)(1), (2), (3), (4), or (5) of this section, in the discretion of the court, either a mandatory term of local incarceration of sixty consecutive days in accordance with division (G)(1) of section 2929.13 of the Revised Code or a mandatory prison term of sixty consecutive days in accordance with division (G)(2) of that section. If the court imposes a mandatory term of local incarceration, it may impose a jail term in addition to the sixty-day mandatory term, the cumulative total of the mandatory term and the jail term for the offense shall not exceed one year, and no prison term is authorized for the offense. If the court imposes a mandatory prison term, notwithstanding division (A)(4) of section 2929.14 of the Revised Code, it also may sentence the offender to a definite prison term that shall be not less than six months and not more than thirty months, the prison terms shall be imposed as described in division (G)(2) of section 2929.13 of the Revised Code, and no term of local incarceration, community residential sanction, or nonresidential sanction is authorized for the offense.

"(ii) If the sentence is being imposed for a violation of division (A)(6), (7), (8), or (9) of this section, in the discretion of the court, either a mandatory term of local incarceration of one hundred twenty consecutive days in accordance with division (G)(1) of section 2929.13 of the Revised Code or a mandatory prison term of one hundred twenty consecutive days in accordance with division (G)(2) of that section. If the court imposes a mandatory term of local incarceration, it may impose a jail term in addition to the one hundred twenty-day mandatory term, the cumulative total of the mandatory term and the jail term for the offense shall not exceed one year, and no prison term is authorized for the offense. If the court imposes a mandatory prison term, notwithstanding division (A)(4) of section 2929.14 of the Revised Code, it also may sentence the offender to a definite prison term that shall be not less than six months and not more than thirty months, the prison terms shall be imposed as described in division (G)(2) of section 2929.13 of the Revised Code, and no term of local incarceration, community residential sanction, or nonresidential sanction is authorized for the offense."

"(i) If the offender is being sentenced for a violation of division (A)(1), (2), (3), (4), or (5) of this section, a mandatory prison term of sixty consecutive days in accordance with division (G)(2) of section 2929.13 of the Revised Code. The court may impose a prison term in addition to the sixty-day mandatory prison term. The cumulative total of the mandatory prison term and the additional prison term for the offense shall not exceed five years. No term of local incarceration, community residential sanction, or nonresidential sanction is authorized for the offense.

"(ii) If the sentence is being imposed for a violation of division (A)(6), (7), (8), or (9) of this section, a mandatory prison term of one hundred twenty consecutive days in accordance with division (G)(2) of section 2929.13 of the Revised Code. The court may impose a prison term in addition to the one hundred twenty-day mandatory prison term. The cumulative total of the mandatory prison term and the additional prison term for the offense shall not exceed five years. No term of local incarceration, community residential sanction, or nonresidential sanction is authorized for the offense."

Amendment Note: 2002 H 490 rewrote division (G); and substituted "January 1, 2004" for "the effective date of this amendment" in division (L). Prior to amendment division (G) read:

"(G)(1) Whoever violates any provision of divisions (A)(1) to (9) of this section is guilty of operating a vehicle under the influence of alcohol, a drug of abuse, or a combination of them. The court shall sentence the offender under Chapter 2929. of the Revised Code, except as otherwise authorized or required by divisions (G)(1)(a) to (e) of this section:

"(a) Except as otherwise provided in division (G)(1)(b), (c), (d), or (e) of this section, the offender is guilty of a misdemeanor of the first degree, and the court shall sentence the offender to all of the following:

"(i) If the sentence is being imposed for a violation of division (A)(1), (2), (3), (4), or (5) of this section, a mandatory jail term of three consecutive days. As used in this division, three consecutive days means seventy-two consecutive hours. The court may sentence an offender to both an intervention program and a jail term. The court may impose a jail term in addition to the three-day mandatory jail term or intervention program. However, in no case shall the cumulative jail term imposed for the offense exceed six months.

"The court may suspend the execution of the three-day jail term under this division if the court, in lieu of that suspended term, places the offender on probation and requires the offender to attend, for three consecutive days, a drivers' intervention program certified under section 3793.10 of the Revised Code. The court also may suspend the execution of any part of the three-day jail term under this division if it places the offender on probation for part of the three days, requires the offender to attend for the suspended part of the term a drivers' intervention program so certified, and sentences the offender to a jail term equal to the remainder of the three consecutive days that the offender does not spend attending the program. The court may require the offender, as a condition of probation and in addition to the required attendance at a drivers' intervention program, to attend and satisfactorily complete any treatment or education programs that comply with the minimum standards adopted pursuant to Chapter 3793. of the Revised Code by the director of alcohol and drug addiction services that the operators of the drivers' intervention program determine that the offender should attend and to report periodically to the court on the offender's progress in the programs. The court also may impose on the offender any other conditions of probation that it considers necessary.

"(ii) If the sentence is being imposed for a violation of division (A)(6), (7), (8), or (9) of this section, except as otherwise provided in this division, a mandatory jail term of at least three consecutive days and a requirement that the offender attend, for three consecutive days, a drivers' intervention program that is certified pursuant to section 3793.10 of the Revised Code. As used in this division, three consecutive days means seventy-two consecutive hours. If the court determines that the offender is not conducive to treatment in a drivers' intervention program, if the offender refuses to attend a drivers' intervention program, or if the jail at which the offender is to serve the jail term imposed can provide a driver's intervention program, the court shall sentence the offender to a mandatory jail term of at least six consecutive days.

"The court may require the offender, as a condition of probation, to attend and satisfactorily complete any treatment or education programs that comply with the minimum standards adopted pursuant to Chapter 3793. of the Revised Code by the director of alcohol and drug addiction services, in addition to the required attendance at drivers' intervention program, that the operators of the drivers' intervention program determine that the offender should attend and to report periodically to the court on the offender's progress in the programs. The court also may impose any other conditions of probation on the offender that it considers necessary.

"(iii) In all cases, a fine of not less than two hundred fifty and not more than one thousand dollars;

"(iv) In all cases, a class five license suspension of the offender's driver's or commercial driver's license or permit or nonresident operating privilege from the range specified in division (A)(5) of section 4510.02 of the Revised Code. The court may grant limited driving privileges relative to the suspension under sections 4510.021 and 4510.13 of the Revised Code.

"(b) Except as otherwise provided in division (G)(1)(e) of this section, an offender who, within six years of the offense, previously has been convicted of or pleaded guilty to one violation of division (A) or (B) of this section or one other equivalent offense is guilty of a misdemeanor of the first degree. The court shall sentence the offender to all of the following:

"(i) If the sentence is being imposed for a violation of division (A)(1), (2), (3), (4), or (5) of this section, a mandatory jail term of ten consecutive days. The court shall impose the ten-day mandatory jail term under this division unless, subject to division (G)(3) of this section, it instead imposes a sentence under that division consisting of both a jail term and a term of electronically monitored house arrest. The court may impose a jail term in addition to the ten-day mandatory jail term. The cumulative jail term imposed for the offense shall not exceed six months.

"In addition to the jail term or the term of electronically monitored house arrest and jail term, the court may require the offender to attend a drivers' intervention program that is certified pursuant to section 3793.10 of the Revised Code. If the operator of the program determines that the offender is alcohol dependent, the program shall notify the court, and, subject to division (I) of this section, the court shall order the offender to obtain treatment through an alcohol and drug addiction program authorized by section 3793.02 of the Revised Code.

"(ii) If the sentence is being imposed for a violation of division (A)(6), (7), (8), or (9) of this section, except as otherwise provided in this division, a mandatory jail term of twenty consecutive days. The court shall impose the twenty-day mandatory jail term under this division unless, subject to division (G)(3) of this section, it instead imposes a sentence under that division consisting of both a jail term and a term of electronically monitored house arrest. The court may impose a jail term in addition to the twenty-day mandatory jail term. The cumulative jail term imposed for the offense shall not exceed six months.

"In addition to the jail term or the term of electronically monitored house arrest and jail term, the court may require the offender to attend a driver's intervention program that is certified pursuant to section 3793.10 of the Revised Code. If the operator of the program determines that the offender is alcohol dependent, the program shall notify the court, and, subject to division (I) of this section, the court shall order the offender to obtain treatment through an alcohol and drug addiction program authorized by section 3793.02 of the Revised Code.

"(iii) In all cases, notwithstanding the fines set forth in Chapter 2929. of the Revised Code, a fine of not less than three hundred fifty and not more than one thousand five hundred dollars;

"(iv) In all cases, a class four license suspension of the offender's driver's license, commercial driver's license, temporary instruction permit, probationary license, or nonresident operating privilege from the range specified in division (A)(4) of section 4510.02 of the Revised Code. The court may grant limited driving privileges relative to the suspension under sections 4510.021 and 4510.13 of the Revised Code.

"(v) In all cases, if the vehicle is registered in the offender's name, immobilization of the vehicle involved in the offense for ninety days in accordance with section 4503.233 of the Revised Code and impoundment of the license plates of that vehicle for ninety days.

"(c) Except as otherwise provided in division (G)(1)(e) of this section, an offender who, within six years of the offense, previously has been convicted of or pleaded guilty to two violations of division (A) or (B) of this section or other equivalent offenses is guilty of a misdemeanor. The court shall sentence the offender to all of the following:

"(i) If the sentence is being imposed for a violation of division (A)(1), (2), (3), (4), or (5) of this section, a mandatory jail term of thirty consecutive days. The court shall impose the thirty-day mandatory jail term under this division unless, subject to division (G)(3) of this section, it instead imposes a sentence under that division consisting of both a jail term and a term of electronically monitored house arrest. The court may impose a jail term in addition to the thirty-day mandatory jail term. Notwithstanding the terms of imprisonment set forth in Chapter 2929. of the Revised Code, the additional jail term shall not exceed one year, and the cumulative jail term imposed for the offense shall not exceed one year.

"(ii) If the sentence is being imposed for a violation of division (A)(6), (7), (8), or (9) of this section, a mandatory jail term of sixty consecutive days. The court shall impose the sixty-day mandatory jail term under this division unless, subject to division (G)(3) of this section, it instead imposes a sentence under that division consisting of both a jail term and a term of electronically monitored house arrest. The court may impose a jail term in addition to the sixty-day mandatory jail term. Notwithstanding the terms of imprisonment set forth in Chapter 2929. of the Revised Code, the additional jail term shall not exceed one year, and the cumulative jail term imposed for the offense shall not exceed one year.

"(iii) In all cases, notwithstanding the fines set forth in Chapter 2929. of the Revised Code, a fine of not less than five hundred fifty and not more than two thousand five hundred dollars;

"(iv) In all cases, a class three license suspension of the offender's driver's license, commercial driver's license, temporary instruction permit, probationary license, or nonresident operating privilege from the range specified in division (A)(3) of section 4510.02 of the Revised Code. The court may grant limited driving privileges relative to the suspension under sections 4510.021 and 4510.13 of the Revised Code.

"(v) In all cases, if the vehicle is registered in the offender's name, criminal forfeiture of the vehicle involved in the offense in accordance with section 4503.234 of the Revised Code. Division (G)(6) of this section applies regarding any vehicle that is subject to an order of criminal forfeiture under this division.

"(vi) In all cases, participation in an alcohol and drug addiction program authorized by section 3793.02 of the Revised Code, subject to division (I) of this section.

"(d) Except as otherwise provided in division (G)(1)(e) of this section, an offender who, within six years of the offense, previously has been convicted of or pleaded guilty to three or more violations of division (A) or (B) of this section or other equivalent offenses is guilty of a felony of the fourth degree. The court shall sentence the offender to all of the following:

"(i) If the sentence is being imposed for a violation of division (A)(1), (2), (3), (4), or (5) of this section, in the discretion of the court, either a mandatory term of local incarceration of sixty consecutive days in accordance with division (G)(1) of section 2929.13 of the Revised Code or a mandatory prison term of sixty consecutive days of imprisonment in accordance with division (G)(2) of that section. If the court imposes a mandatory term of local incarceration, it may impose a jail term in addition to the sixty-day mandatory term, the cumulative total of the mandatory term and the jail term for the offense shall not exceed one year, and no prison term is authorized for the offense. If the court imposes a mandatory prison term, notwithstanding division (A)(4) of section 2929.14 of the Revised Code, it also may sentence the offender to a definite prison term that shall be not less than six months and not more than thirty months, the prison terms shall be imposed as described in division (G)(2) of section 2929.13 of the Revised Code, and no term of local incarceration, community residential sanction, or nonresidential sanction is authorized for the offense.

"(ii) If the sentence is being imposed for a violation of division (A)(6), (7), (8), or (9) of this section, in the discretion of the court, either a mandatory term of local incarceration of one hundred twenty consecutive days in accordance with division (G)(1) of section 2929.13 of the Revised Code or a mandatory prison term of one hundred twenty consecutive days in accordance with division (G)(2) of that section. If the court imposes a mandatory term of local incarceration, it may impose a jail term in addition to the one hundred twenty-day mandatory term, the cumulative total of the mandatory term and the jail term for the offense shall not exceed one year, and no prison term is authorized for the offense. If the court imposes a mandatory prison term, notwithstanding division (A)(4) of section 2929.14 of the Revised Code, it also may sentence the offender to a definite prison term that shall be not less than six months and not more than thirty months, the prison terms shall be imposed as described in division (G)(2) of section 2929.13 of the Revised Code, and no term of local incarceration, community residential sanction, or nonresidential sanction is authorized for the offense.

"(iii) In all cases, notwithstanding section 2929.18 of the Revised Code, a fine of not less than eight hundred nor more than ten thousand dollars;

"(iv) In all cases, a class two license suspension of the offender's driver's license, commercial driver's license, temporary instruction permit, probationary license, or nonresident operating privilege from the range specified in division (A)(2) of section 4510.02 of the Revised Code. The court may grant limited driving privileges relative to the suspension under sections 4510.021 and 4510.13 of the Revised Code.

"(v) In all cases, if the vehicle is registered in the offender's name, criminal forfeiture of the vehicle involved in the offense in accordance with section 4503.234 of the Revised Code. Division (G)(6) of this section applies regarding any vehicle that is subject to an order of criminal forfeiture under this division.

"(vi) In all cases, participation in an alcohol and drug addiction program authorized by section 3793.02 of the Revised Code, subject to division (I) of this section.

"(vii) In all cases, if the court sentences the offender to a mandatory term of local incarceration, in addition to the mandatory term, the court, pursuant to section 2929.17 of the Revised Code, may impose a term of electronically monitored house arrest. The term shall not commence until after the offender has served the mandatory term of local incarceration.

"(e) An offender who previously has been convicted of or pleaded guilty to a violation of division (A) of this section that was a felony, regardless of when the violation and the conviction or guilty plea occurred, is guilty of a felony of the third degree. The court shall sentence the offender to all of the following:

"(i) If the offender is being sentenced for a violation of division (A)(1), (2), (3), (4), or (5) of this section, a mandatory prison term of sixty consecutive days in accordance with division (G)(2) of section 2929.13 of the Revised Code. The court may impose a prison term in addition to the sixty-day mandatory prison term. The cumulative total of the mandatory prison term and the additional prison term for the offense shall not exceed five years. No term of local incarceration, community residential sanction, or nonresidential sanction is authorized for the offense.

"(ii) If the sentence is being imposed for a violation of division (A)(6), (7), (8), or (9) of this section, a mandatory prison term of one hundred twenty consecutive days in accordance with division (G)(2) of section 2929.13 of the Revised Code. The court may impose a prison term in addition to the one hundred twenty-day mandatory prison term. The cumulative total of the mandatory prison term and the additional prison term for the offense shall not exceed five years. No term of local incarceration, community residential sanction, or nonresidential sanction is authorized for the offense.

"(iii) In all cases, notwithstanding section 2929.18 of the Revised Code, a fine of not less than eight hundred nor more than ten thousand dollars;

"(iv) In all cases, a class two license suspension of the offender's driver's license, commercial driver's license, temporary instruction permit, probationary license, or nonresident operating privilege from the range specified in division (A)(2) of section 4510.02 of the Revised Code. The court may grant limited driving privileges relative to the suspension under sections 4510.021 and 4510.13 of the Revised Code.

"(v) In all cases, if the vehicle is registered in the offender's name, criminal forfeiture of the vehicle involved in the offense in accordance with section 4503.234 of the Revised Code. Division (G)(6) of this section applies regarding any vehicle that is subject to an order of criminal forfeiture under this division.

"(vi) In all cases, participation in an alcohol and drug addiction program authorized by section 3793.02 of the Revised Code, subject to division (I) of this section.

"(2) An offender who is convicted of or pleads guilty to a violation of division (A) of this section and who subsequently seeks reinstatement of the driver's or occupational driver's license or permit or nonresident operating privilege suspended under this section as a result of the conviction or guilty plea shall pay a reinstatement fee as provided in division (F)(2) of section 4511.191 of the Revised Code.

"(3) If an offender is sentenced to a jail term under division (G)(1)(b)(i) or (ii) or (G)(1)(c)(i) or (ii) of this section and if, within sixty days of sentencing of the offender, the court issues a written finding on the record that, due to the unavailability of space at the jail where the offender is required to serve the term, the offender will not be able to begin serving that term within the sixty-day period following the date of sentencing, the court may impose an alternative sentence under this division that includes a term of electronically monitored house arrest, as defined in section 2929.23 of the Revised Code.

"As an alternative to a mandatory jail term of ten consecutive days required by division (G)(1)(b)(i) of this section, the court, under this division, may sentence the offender to five consecutive days in jail and not less than eighteen consecutive days of electronically monitored house arrest. The cumulative total of the five consecutive days in jail and the period of electronically monitored house arrest shall not exceed six months. The five consecutive days in jail do not have to be served prior to or consecutively to the period of house arrest.

"As an alternative to the mandatory jail term of twenty consecutive days required by division (G)(1)(b)(ii) of this section, the court, under this division, may sentence the offender to ten consecutive days in jail and not less than thirty-six consecutive days of electronically monitored house arrest. The cumulative total of the ten consecutive days in jail and the period of electronically monitored house arrest shall not exceed six months. The ten consecutive days in jail do not have to be served prior to or consecutively to the period of house arrest.

"As an alternative to a mandatory jail term of thirty consecutive days required by division (G)(1)(c)(i) of this section, the court, under this division, may sentence the offender to fifteen consecutive days in jail and not less than fifty-five consecutive days of electronically monitored house arrest. The cumulative total of the fifteen consecutive days in jail and the period of electronically monitored house arrest shall not exceed one year. The fifteen consecutive days in jail do not have to be served prior to or consecutively to the period of house arrest.

"As an alternative to the mandatory jail term of sixty consecutive days required by division (G)(1)(c)(ii) of this section, the court, under this division, may sentence the offender to thirty consecutive days in jail and not less than one hundred ten consecutive days of electronically monitored house arrest. The cumulative total of the thirty consecutive days in jail and the period of electronically monitored house arrest shall not exceed one year. The thirty consecutive days in jail do not have to be served prior to or consecutively to the period of house arrest.

"(4) If an offender's driver's or occupational driver's license or permit or nonresident operating privilege is suspended under division (G) of this section and if section 4510.13 of the Revised Code permits the court to grant limited driving privileges, the court may grant the limited driving privileges only if the court imposes as one of the conditions of the privileges that the offender must display on the vehicle that is driven subject to the privileges restricted license plates that are issued under section 4503.231 of the Revised Code, except as provided in division (B) of that section.

"(5) Fines imposed under this section for a violation of division (A) of this section shall be distributed as follows:

"(a) Twenty-five dollars of the fine imposed under division (G)(1)(a)(iii), thirty-five dollars of the fine imposed under division (G)(1)(b)(iii), one hundred twenty-three dollars of the fine imposed under division (G)(1)(c)(iii), and two hundred ten dollars of the fine imposed under division (G)(1)(d)(iii) or (e)(iii) of this section shall be paid to an enforcement and education fund established by the legislative authority of the law enforcement agency in this state that primarily was responsible for the arrest of the offender, as determined by the court that imposes the fine. The agency shall use this share to pay only those costs it incurs in enforcing this section or a municipal OVI ordinance and in informing the public of the laws governing the operation of a vehicle while under the influence of alcohol, the dangers of the operation of a vehicle under the influence of alcohol, and other information relating to the operation of a vehicle under the influence of alcohol and the consumption of alcoholic beverages.

"(b) Fifty dollars of the fine imposed under division (G)(1)(a)(iii) of this section shall be paid to the political subdivision that pays the cost of housing the offender during the offender's term of incarceration. If the offender is being sentenced for a violation of division (A)(1), (2), (3), (4), or (5) of this section and was confined as a result of the offense prior to being sentenced for the offense but is not sentenced to a term of incarceration, the fifty dollars shall be paid to the political subdivision that paid the cost of housing the offender during that period of confinement. The political subdivision shall use the share under this division to pay or reimburse incarceration or treatment costs it incurs in housing or providing drug and alcohol treatment to persons who violate this section or a municipal OVI ordinance, costs of any immobilizing or disabling device used on the offender's vehicle, and costs of electronic house arrest equipment needed for persons who violate this section.

"(c) Twenty-five dollars of the fine imposed under division (G)(1)(a)(iii) and fifty dollars of the fine imposed under division (G)(1)(b)(iii) of this section shall be deposited into the county or municipal indigent drivers' alcohol treatment fund under the control of that court, as created by the county or municipal corporation under division (N) of section 4511.191 of the Revised Code.

"(d) One hundred fifteen dollars of the fine imposed under division (G)(1)(b)(iii), two hundred seventy-seven dollars of the fine imposed under division (G)(1)(c)(iii), and four hundred forty dollars of the fine imposed under division (G)(1)(d)(iii) or (e)(iii) of this section shall be paid to the political subdivision that pays the cost of housing the offender during the offender's term of incarceration. The political subdivision shall use this share to pay or reimburse incarceration or treatment costs it incurs in housing or providing drug and alcohol treatment to persons who violate this section or a municipal OVI ordinance, costs for any immobilizing or disabling device used on the offender's vehicle, and costs of electronic house arrest equipment needed for persons who violate this section.

"(e) The balance of the fine imposed under division (G)(1)(a)(iii), (b)(iii), (c)(iii), (d)(iii), or (e)(iii) of this section shall be disbursed as otherwise provided by law.

"(6) If title to a motor vehicle that is subject to an order of criminal forfeiture under division (G)(1)(c), (d), or (e) of this section is assigned or transferred and division (B)(2) or (3) of section 4503.234 of the Revised Code applies, in addition to or independent of any other penalty established by law, the court may fine the offender the value of the vehicle as determined by publications of the national auto dealers association. The proceeds of any fine so imposed shall be distributed in accordance with division (C)(2) of that section."

Amendment Note: 2003 H 87, § 1 substituted "eight-hundredths" for "ten-hundredths" and "eleven-hundredths" for "fourteen-hundredths" throughout the section; and made other nonsubstantive changes.

Amendment Note: 2003 H 87, § 4 substituted "eight-hundredths" for "ten-hundredths", "eleven-hundredths" for "fourteen-hundredths", and "ninety-six-thousandths" for "twelve-hundredths" throughout the section.

Amendment Note: 2002 S 163, § 1, added "division (A) or (B) of" to division (D)(1); added new division (D)(4); and redesignated former division (D)(4) as (D)(5).

Amendment Note: 2002 S 163, § 3, added "division (A) or (B) of" to division (D)(1); added division (D)(4); and substituted "January 1, 2004" for "the effective date of this amendment" in divisions (L)(1) and (2).

Amendment Note: 2002 S 123 rewrote the section, which prior thereto read:

"(A) No person shall operate any vehicle, streetcar, or trackless trolley within this state, if any of the following apply:

"(1) The person is under the influence of alcohol, a drug of abuse, or alcohol and a drug of abuse;

"(2) The person has a concentration of ten-hundredths of one per cent or more but less than seventeen-hundredths of one per cent by weight of alcohol in the person's blood;

"(3) The person has a concentration of ten-hundredths of one gram or more but less than seventeen-hundredths of one gram by weight of alcohol per two hundred ten liters of the person's breath;

"(4) The person has a concentration of fourteen-hundredths of one gram or more but less than two hundred thirty-eight-thousandths of one gram by weight of alcohol per one hundred milliliters of the person's urine;

"(5) The person has a concentration of seventeen-hundredths of one per cent or more by weight of alcohol in the person's blood;

"(6) The person has a concentration of seventeen-hundredths of one gram or more by weight of alcohol per two hundred ten liters of the person's breath;

"(7) The person has a concentration of two hundred thirty-eight-thousandths of one gram or more by weight of alcohol per one hundred milliliters of the person's urine.

"(B) No person under twenty-one years of age shall operate any vehicle, streetcar, or trackless trolley within this state, if any of the following apply:

"(1) The person has a concentration of at least two-hundredths of one per cent but less than ten-hundredths of one per cent by weight of alcohol in the person's blood;

"(2) The person has a concentration of at least two-hundredths of one gram but less than ten-hundredths of one gram by weight of alcohol per two hundred ten liters of the person's breath;

"(3) The person has a concentration of at least twenty-eight one-thousandths of one gram but less than fourteen-hundredths of one gram by weight of alcohol per one hundred milliliters of the person's urine.

"(C) In any proceeding arising out of one incident, a person may be charged with a violation of division (A)(1) and a violation of division (B)(1), (2), or (3) of this section, but the person may not be convicted of more than one violation of these divisions.

"(D)(1) In any criminal prosecution or juvenile court proceeding for a violation of this section, of a municipal ordinance relating to operating a vehicle while under the influence of alcohol, a drug of abuse, or alcohol and a drug of abuse, or of a municipal ordinance relating to operating a vehicle with a prohibited concentration of alcohol in the blood, breath, or urine, the court may admit evidence on the concentration of alcohol, drugs of abuse, or alcohol and drugs of abuse in the defendant's blood, breath, urine, or other bodily substance at the time of the alleged violation as shown by chemical analysis of the defendant's blood, urine, breath, or other bodily substance withdrawn within two hours of the time of the alleged violation.

"When a person submits to a blood test at the request of a police officer under section 4511.191 of the Revised Code, only a physician, a registered nurse, or a qualified technician or chemist shall withdraw blood for the purpose of determining its alcohol, drug, or alcohol and drug content. This limitation does not apply to the taking of breath or urine specimens. A physician, a registered nurse, or a qualified technician or chemist may refuse to withdraw blood for the purpose of determining the alcohol, drug, or alcohol and drug content of the blood, if in the opinion of the physician, nurse, technician, or chemist the physical welfare of the person would be endangered by the withdrawing of blood.

"Such bodily substance shall be analyzed in accordance with methods approved by the director of health by an individual possessing a valid permit issued by the director of health pursuant to section 3701.143 of the Revised Code.

"(2) In a criminal prosecution or juvenile court proceeding for a violation of division (A) of this section, of a municipal ordinance relating to operating a vehicle while under the influence of alcohol, a drug of abuse, or alcohol and a drug of abuse, or of a municipal ordinance substantially equivalent to division (A) of this section relating to operating a vehicle with a prohibited concentration of alcohol in the blood, breath, or urine, if there was at the time the bodily substance was withdrawn a concentration of less than ten-hundredths of one per cent by weight of alcohol in the defendant's blood, less than ten-hundredths of one gram by weight of alcohol per two hundred ten liters of the defendant's breath, or less than fourteen-hundredths of one gram by weight of alcohol per one hundred milliliters of the defendant's urine, such fact may be considered with other competent evidence in determining the guilt or innocence of the defendant. This division does not limit or affect a criminal prosecution or juvenile court proceeding for a violation of division (B) of this section or of a municipal ordinance substantially equivalent to division (B) of this section relating to operating a vehicle with a prohibited concentration of alcohol in the blood, breath, or urine.

"(3) Upon the request of the person who was tested, the results of the chemical test shall be made available to the person or the person's attorney or agent immediately upon the completion of the chemical test analysis.

"The person tested may have a physician, a registered nurse, or a qualified technician or chemist of the person's own choosing administer a chemical test or tests in addition to any administered at the request of a police officer, and shall be so advised. The failure or inability to obtain an additional chemical test by a person shall not preclude the admission of evidence relating to the chemical test or tests taken at the request of a police officer.

"(4) Any physician, registered nurse, or qualified technician or chemist who withdraws blood from a person pursuant to this section, and any hospital, first-aid station, or clinic at which blood is withdrawn from a person pursuant to this section, is immune from criminal liability, and from civil liability that is based upon a claim of assault and battery or based upon any other claim that is not in the nature of a claim of malpractice, for any act performed in withdrawing blood from the person."

Amendment Note: 1999 S 22 inserted "but less than seventeen-hundredths of one per cent" in division (A)(2); inserted "but less than seventeen-hundredths of one gram" in division (A)(3); inserted "but less than two hundred thirty-eight-thousandths of one gram" in division (A)(4); added divisions (A)(5) through (A)(7); and made changes to reflect gender neutral language.

Amendment Note: 1994 S 82 substituted "twenty-one" for "eighteen" in the first paragraph of division (B); designated divisions (D)(1) through (4); inserted "or juvenile court proceeding" in division (D)(1); and rewrote division (D)(2), which previously read:

"If there was at the time the bodily substance was withdrawn a concentration of less than ten-hundredths of one per cent by weight of alcohol in the defendant's blood, less than ten-hundredths of one gram by weight of alcohol per two hundred ten liters of his breath, or less than fourteen-hundredths of one gram by weight of alcohol per one hundred milliliters of his urine, such fact may be considered with other competent evidence in determining the guilt or innocence of the defendant."

Library References

Automobiles ⚘332, 411 to 426.
Westlaw Topic No. 48A.
C.J.S. Motor Vehicles §§ 625 to 637.

Baldwin's Ohio Legislative Service, 1990 Laws of Ohio, S 131—LSC Analysis, p 5–623

4511.191 Chemical tests for determining alcoholic content of blood; effect of refusal to submit to test; seizure of license; indigent drivers alcohol treatment funds; procedures

(A)(1) "Physical control" has the same meaning as in section 4511.194 of the Revised Code.

(2) Any person who operates a vehicle, streetcar, or trackless trolley upon a highway or any public or private property used by the public for vehicular travel or parking within this state or who is in physical control of a vehicle, streetcar, or trackless trolley shall be deemed to have given consent to a chemical test or tests of the person's whole blood, blood serum or plasma, breath, or urine to determine the alcohol, drug of abuse, controlled substance, metabolite of a controlled substance, or combination content of the person's whole blood, blood serum or plasma, breath, or urine if arrested for a violation of division (A) or (B) of section 4511.19 of the Revised Code, section 4511.194 of the Revised Code or a substantially equivalent municipal ordinance, or a municipal OVI ordinance.

(3) The chemical test or tests under division (A)(2) of this section shall be administered at the request of a law enforcement officer having reasonable grounds to believe the person was operating or in physical control of a vehicle, streetcar, or trackless trolley in violation of a division, section, or ordinance identified in division (A)(2) of this section. The law enforcement agency by which the officer is employed shall designate which of the tests shall be administered.

(4) Any person who is dead or unconscious, or who otherwise is in a condition rendering the person incapable of refusal, shall be deemed to have consented as provided in division (A)(2) of this section, and the test or tests may be administered, subject to sections 313.12 to 313.16 of the Revised Code.

(B)(1) Upon receipt of the sworn report of a law enforcement officer who arrested a person for a violation of division (A) or (B) of section 4511.19 of the Revised Code, section 4511.194 of the Revised Code or a substantially equivalent municipal ordinance, or a municipal OVI ordinance that was completed and sent to the registrar and a court pursuant to section 4511.192 of the Revised Code in regard to a person who refused to take the designated chemical test, the registrar shall enter into the registrar's records the fact that the person's driver's or commercial driver's license or permit or nonresident operating privilege was suspended by the arresting officer under this division and that section and the period of the suspension, as determined under this section. The suspension shall be subject to appeal as provided in section 4511.197 of the Revised Code. The suspension shall be for whichever of the following periods applies:

(a) Except when division (B)(1)(b), (c), or (d) of this section applies and specifies a different class or length of suspension, the suspension shall be a class C suspension for the period of time specified in division (B)(3) of section 4510.02 of the Revised Code.

(b) If the arrested person, within six years of the date on which the person refused the request to consent to the chemical test, had refused one previous request to consent to a chemical test, the suspension shall be a class B suspension imposed for the period of time specified in division (B)(2) of section 4510.02 of the Revised Code.

(c) If the arrested person, within six years of the date on which the person refused the request to consent to the chemical test, had refused two previous requests to consent to a chemical test, the suspension shall be a class A suspension imposed for the period of time specified in division (B)(1) of section 4510.02 of the Revised Code.

(d) If the arrested person, within six years of the date on which the person refused the request to consent to the chemical test, had refused three or more previous requests to consent to a chemical test, the suspension shall be for five years.

(2) The registrar shall terminate a suspension of the driver's or commercial driver's license or permit of a resident or of the operating privilege of a nonresident, or a denial of a driver's or commercial driver's license or permit, imposed pursuant to division (B)(1) of this section upon receipt of notice that the person has entered a plea of guilty to, or that the person has been convicted after entering a plea of no contest to, operating a vehicle in violation of section 4511.19 of the Revised Code or in violation of a municipal OVI ordinance, if the offense for which the conviction is had or the plea is entered arose from the same incident that led to the suspension or denial.

The registrar shall credit against any judicial suspension of a person's driver's or commercial driver's license or permit or nonresident operating privilege imposed pursuant to section 4511.19 of the Revised Code, or pursuant to section 4510.07 of the Revised Code for a violation of a municipal OVI ordinance, any time during which the person serves a related suspension imposed pursuant to division (B)(1) of this section.

(C)(1) Upon receipt of the sworn report of the law enforcement officer who arrested a person for a violation of division (A) or (B) of section 4511.19 of the Revised Code or a municipal OVI ordinance that was completed and sent to the registrar and a court pursuant to section 4511.192 of the Revised Code in regard to a person whose test results indicate that the person's whole blood, blood serum or plasma, breath, or urine contained at least the concentration of alcohol specified in division (A)(1)(b), (c), (d), or (e) of section 4511.19 of the Revised Code or at least the concentration of a listed controlled substance or a listed metabolite of a controlled substance specified in division (A)(1)(j) of section 4511.19 of the Revised Code, the registrar shall enter into the registrar's records the fact that the person's driver's or commercial driver's license or permit or nonresident operating privilege was suspended by the arresting officer under this division and section 4511.192 of the Revised Code and the period of the suspension, as determined under divisions (F)(1) to (4) of this section. The suspension shall be subject to appeal as provided in section 4511.197 of the Revised Code. The suspension described in this division does not apply to, and shall not be imposed upon, a person arrested for a violation of section 4511.194 of the Revised Code or a substantially equivalent municipal ordinance who submits to a designated chemical test. The suspension shall be for whichever of the following periods applies:

(a) Except when division (C)(1)(b), (c), or (d) of this section applies and specifies a different period, the suspension shall be a class E suspension imposed for the period of time specified in division (B)(5) of section 4510.02 of the Revised Code.

(b) The suspension shall be a class C suspension for the period of time specified in division (B)(3) of section 4510.02 of the Revised Code if the person has been convicted of or pleaded guilty to, within six years of the date the test was conducted, one violation of division (A) or (B) of section 4511.19 of the Revised Code or one other equivalent offense.

(c) If, within six years of the date the test was conducted, the person has been convicted of or pleaded guilty to two violations of a statute or ordinance described in division (C)(1)(b) of this section, the suspension shall be a class B suspension imposed for the period of time specified in division (B)(2) of section 4510.02 of the Revised Code.

(d) If, within six years of the date the test was conducted, the person has been convicted of or pleaded guilty to more than two violations of a statute or ordinance described in division (C)(1)(b) of this section, the suspension shall be a class A suspension imposed for the period of time specified in division (B)(1) of section 4510.02 of the Revised Code.

(2) The registrar shall terminate a suspension of the driver's or commercial driver's license or permit of a resident or of the operating privilege of a nonresident, or a denial of a driver's or commercial driver's license or permit, imposed pursuant to division (C)(1) of this section upon receipt of notice that the person has entered a plea of guilty to, or that the person has been convicted after entering a plea of no contest to, operating a vehicle in violation of section 4511.19 of the Revised Code or in violation of a municipal OVI ordinance, if the offense for which the conviction is had or the plea is entered arose from the same incident that led to the suspension or denial.

The registrar shall credit against any judicial suspension of a person's driver's or commercial driver's license or permit or nonresident operating privilege imposed pursuant to section 4511.19 of the Revised Code, or pursuant to section 4510.07 of the Revised Code for a violation of a municipal OVI ordinance, any time during which the person serves a related suspension imposed pursuant to division (C)(1) of this section.

(D)(1) A suspension of a person's driver's or commercial driver's license or permit or nonresident operating privilege under this section for the time described in division (B) or (C) of this section is effective immediately from the time at which the arresting officer serves the notice of suspension upon the arrested person. Any subsequent finding that the person is not guilty of the charge that resulted in the person being requested to take the chemical test or tests under division (A) of this section does not affect the suspension.

(2) If a person is arrested for operating a vehicle, streetcar, or trackless trolley in violation of division (A) or (B) of section 4511.19 of the Revised Code or a municipal OVI ordinance, or for being in physical control of a vehicle, streetcar, or trackless trolley in violation of section 4511.194 of the Revised Code or a substantially equivalent municipal ordinance, regardless of whether the person's driver's or commercial driver's license or permit or nonresident operating privilege is or is not suspended under division (B) or (C) of this section or Chapter 4510. of the Revised Code, the person's initial appearance on the charge resulting from the arrest shall be held within five days of the person's arrest or the issuance of the citation to the person, subject to any continuance granted by the court pursuant to section 4511.197 of the Revised Code regarding the issues specified in that division.

(E) When it finally has been determined under the procedures of this section and sections 4511.192 to 4511.197 of the Revised Code that a nonresident's privilege to operate a vehicle within this state has been suspended, the registrar shall give information in writing of the action taken to the motor vehicle administrator of the state of the person's residence and of any state in which the person has a license.

(F) At the end of a suspension period under this section, under section 4511.194, section 4511.196, or division (G) of section 4511.19 of the Revised Code, or under section 4510.07 of the Revised Code for a violation of a municipal OVI ordinance and upon the request of the person whose driver's or commercial driver's license or permit was suspended and who is not otherwise subject to suspension, cancellation, or disqualification, the registrar shall return the driver's or commercial driver's license or permit to the person upon the occurrence of all of the conditions specified in divisions (F)(1) and (2) of this section:

(1) A showing that the person has proof of financial responsibility, a policy of liability insurance in effect that meets the minimum standards set forth in section 4509.51 of the Revised Code, or proof, to the satisfaction of the registrar, that the person is able to respond in damages in an amount at least equal to the minimum amounts specified in section 4509.51 of the Revised Code.

(2) Subject to the limitation contained in division (F)(3) of this section, payment by the person to the bureau of motor vehicles of a license reinstatement fee of four hundred twenty-five dollars, which fee shall be deposited in the state treasury and credited as follows:

(a) One hundred twelve dollars and fifty cents shall be credited to the statewide treatment and prevention fund created by section 4301.30 of the Revised Code. The fund shall be used to pay the costs of driver treatment and intervention programs operated pursuant to sections 3793.02 and 3793.10 of the Revised Code. The director of alcohol and drug addiction services shall determine the share of the fund that is to be allocated to alcohol and drug addiction programs authorized by section 3793.02 of the Revised Code, and the share of the fund that is to be allocated to drivers' intervention programs authorized by section 3793.10 of the Revised Code.

(b) Seventy-five dollars shall be credited to the reparations fund created by section 2743.191 of the Revised Code.

(c) Thirty-seven dollars and fifty cents shall be credited to the indigent drivers alcohol treatment fund, which is hereby established. Except as otherwise provided in division (F)(2)(c) of this section, moneys in the fund shall be distributed by the department of alcohol and drug addiction services to the county indigent drivers alcohol treatment funds, the county juvenile indigent drivers alcohol treatment funds, and the municipal indigent drivers alcohol treatment funds that are required to be established by counties and municipal corporations pursuant to this section, and shall be used only to pay the cost of an alcohol and drug addiction treatment program attended by an offender or juvenile traffic offender who is ordered to attend an alcohol and drug addiction treatment program by a county, juvenile, or municipal court judge and who is determined by the county, juvenile, or municipal court judge not to have the means to pay for the person's attendance at the program or to pay the costs specified in division (H)(4) of this section in accordance with that division. In addition, a county, juvenile, or municipal court judge may use moneys in the county indigent drivers alcohol treatment fund, county juvenile indigent drivers alcohol treatment fund, or municipal indigent drivers alcohol treatment fund to pay for the cost of the continued use of an electronic continuous alcohol monitoring device as described in divisions (H)(3) and (4) of this section. Moneys in the fund that are not distributed to a county indigent drivers alcohol treatment fund, a county juvenile indigent drivers alcohol treatment fund, or a municipal indigent drivers alcohol treatment fund under division (H) of this section because the director of alcohol and drug addiction services does not have the information necessary to identify the county or municipal corporation where the offender or juvenile offender was arrested may be transferred by the director of budget and management to the statewide treatment and prevention fund created by section 4301.30 of the Revised Code, upon certification of the amount by the director of alcohol and drug addiction services.

(d) Seventy-five dollars shall be credited to the Ohio rehabilitation services commission established by section 3304.12 of the Revised Code, to the services for rehabilitation fund, which is hereby established. The fund shall be used to match available federal matching funds where appropriate, and for any other purpose or program of the commission to rehabilitate people with disabilities to help them become employed and independent.

(e) Seventy-five dollars shall be deposited into the state treasury and credited to the drug abuse resistance education programs fund, which is hereby established, to be used by the attorney general for the purposes specified in division (F)(4) of this section.

(f) Thirty dollars shall be credited to the state bureau of motor vehicles fund created by section 4501.25 of the Revised Code.

(g) Twenty dollars shall be credited to the trauma and emergency medical services grants fund created by section 4513.263 of the Revised Code.

(3) If a person's driver's or commercial driver's license or permit is suspended under this section, under section 4511.196 or division (G) of section 4511.19 of the Revised Code, under section 4510.07 of the Revised Code for a violation of a municipal OVI ordinance or under any combination of the suspensions described in division (F)(3) of this section, and if the suspensions arise from a single incident or a single set of facts and circumstances, the person is liable for payment of, and shall be required to pay to the bureau, only one reinstatement fee of four hundred twenty-five dollars. The reinstatement fee shall be distributed by the bureau in accordance with division (F)(2) of this section.

(4) The attorney general shall use amounts in the drug abuse resistance education programs fund to award grants to law enforcement agencies to establish and implement drug abuse resistance education programs in public schools. Grants awarded to a law enforcement agency under this section shall be used by the agency to pay for not more than fifty per cent of the amount of the salaries of law enforcement officers who conduct drug abuse resistance education programs in public schools. The attorney general shall not use more than six per cent of the amounts the attorney general's office receives under division (F)(2)(e) of this section to pay the costs it incurs in administering the grant program established by division (F)(2)(e) of this section and in providing training and materials relating to drug abuse resistance education programs.

The attorney general shall report to the governor and the general assembly each fiscal year on the progress made in establishing and implementing drug abuse resistance education programs. These reports shall include an evaluation of the effectiveness of these programs.

(G) Suspension of a commercial driver's license under division (B) or (C) of this section shall be concurrent with any period of disqualification under section 3123.611 or 4506.16 of the Revised Code or any period of suspension under section 3123.58 of the Revised Code. No person who is disqualified for life from holding a commercial driver's license under section 4506.16 of the Revised Code shall be issued a driver's license under Chapter 4507. of the Revised Code during the period for which the commercial driver's license was suspended under division (B) or (C) of this section. No person whose commercial driver's license is suspended under division (B) or (C) of this section shall be issued a driver's license under Chapter 4507. of the Revised Code during the period of the suspension.

(H)(1) Each county shall establish an indigent drivers alcohol treatment fund, each county shall establish a juvenile indigent drivers alcohol treatment fund, and each municipal corporation in which there is a municipal court shall establish an indigent drivers alcohol treatment fund. All revenue that the general assembly appropriates to the indigent drivers alcohol treatment fund for transfer to a county indigent drivers alcohol treatment fund, a county juvenile indigent drivers alcohol treatment fund, or a municipal indigent drivers alcohol treatment fund, all portions of fees that are paid under division (F) of this section and that are credited under that division to the indigent drivers alcohol treatment fund in the state treasury for a county indigent drivers alcohol treatment fund, a county juvenile indigent drivers alcohol treatment fund, or a municipal indigent drivers alcohol treatment fund, and all portions of fines that are specified for deposit into a county or municipal indigent drivers alcohol treatment fund by section 4511.193 of the Revised Code shall be deposited into that county indigent drivers alcohol treatment fund, county juvenile indigent drivers alcohol treatment fund, or municipal indigent drivers alcohol treatment fund in accordance with division (H)(2) of this section. Additionally, all portions of fines that are paid for a violation of section 4511.19 of the Revised Code or of any prohibition contained in Chapter 4510. of the Revised Code, and that are required under section 4511.19 or any provision of Chapter 4510. of the Revised Code to be deposited into a county indigent drivers alcohol treatment fund or municipal indigent drivers alcohol treatment fund shall be deposited into the appropriate fund in accordance with the applicable division.

(2) That portion of the license reinstatement fee that is paid under division (F) of this section and that is credited under that division to the indigent drivers alcohol treatment fund shall be deposited into a county indigent drivers alcohol treatment fund, a county juvenile indigent drivers alcohol treatment fund, or a municipal indigent drivers alcohol treatment fund as follows:

(a) If the suspension in question was imposed under this section, that portion of the fee shall be deposited as follows:

(i) If the fee is paid by a person who was charged in a county court with the violation that resulted in the suspension, the portion shall be deposited into the county indigent drivers alcohol treatment fund under the control of that court;

(ii) If the fee is paid by a person who was charged in a juvenile court with the violation that resulted in the suspension, the portion shall be deposited into the county juvenile indigent drivers alcohol treatment fund established in the county served by the court;

(iii) If the fee is paid by a person who was charged in a municipal court with the violation that resulted in the suspension, the portion shall be deposited into the municipal indigent drivers alcohol treatment fund under the control of that court.

(b) If the suspension in question was imposed under section 4511.19 of the Revised Code or under section 4510.07 of the Revised Code for a violation of a municipal OVI ordinance, that portion of the fee shall be deposited as follows:

(i) If the fee is paid by a person whose license or permit was suspended by a county court, the portion shall be deposited into the county indigent drivers alcohol treatment fund under the control of that court;

(ii) If the fee is paid by a person whose license or permit was suspended by a municipal court, the portion shall be deposited into the municipal indigent drivers alcohol treatment fund under the control of that court.

(3) Expenditures from a county indigent drivers alcohol treatment fund, a county juvenile indigent drivers alcohol treatment fund, or a municipal indigent drivers alcohol treatment fund shall be made only upon the order of a county, juvenile, or municipal court judge and only for payment of the cost of the attendance at an alcohol and drug addiction treatment program of a person who is convicted of, or found to be a juvenile traffic offender by reason of, a violation of division (A) of section 4511.19 of the Revised Code or a substantially similar municipal ordinance, who is ordered by the court to attend the alcohol and drug addiction treatment program, and who is determined by the court to be unable to pay the cost of attendance at the treatment program or for payment of the costs specified in division (H)(4) of this section in accordance with that division. The alcohol and drug addiction services board or the board of alcohol, drug addiction, and mental health services established pursuant to section 340.02 or 340.021 of the Revised Code and serving the alcohol, drug addiction, and mental health service district in which the court is located shall administer the indigent drivers alcohol treatment program of the court. When a court orders an offender or juvenile traffic offender to attend an alcohol and drug addiction treatment program, the board shall determine which program is suitable to meet the needs of the offender or juvenile traffic offender, and when a suitable program is located and space is available at the program, the offender or juvenile traffic offender shall attend the program designated by the board. A reasonable amount not to exceed five per cent of the amounts credited to and deposited into the county indigent drivers alcohol treatment fund, the county juvenile indigent drivers alcohol treatment fund, or the municipal indigent drivers alcohol treatment fund serving every court whose program is administered by that board shall be paid to the board to cover the costs it incurs in administering those indigent drivers alcohol treatment programs.

In addition, a county, juvenile, or municipal court judge may use moneys in the county indigent drivers alcohol treatment fund, county juvenile indigent drivers alcohol treatment fund, or municipal indigent drivers alcohol treatment fund to pay for the continued use of an electronic continuous alcohol monitoring device by an offender or juvenile traffic offender, in conjunction with a treatment program approved by the department of alcohol and drug addiction services, when such use is determined clinically necessary by the treatment program and when the court determines that the offender or juvenile traffic offender is unable to pay all or part of the daily monitoring of the device.

(4) If a county, juvenile, or municipal court determines, in consultation with the alcohol and drug addiction services board or the board of alcohol, drug addiction, and mental health services established pursuant to section 340.02 or 340.021 of the Revised Code and serving the alcohol, drug addiction, and mental health district in which the court is located, that the funds in the county indigent drivers alcohol treatment fund, the county juvenile indigent drivers alcohol treatment fund, or the municipal indigent drivers alcohol treatment fund under the control of the court are more than sufficient to satisfy the purpose for which the fund was established, as specified in divisions (H)(1) to (3) of this section, the court may declare a surplus in the fund. If the court declares a surplus in the fund, the court may expend the amount of the surplus in the fund for:

(a) Alcohol and drug abuse assessment and treatment of persons who are charged in the court with committing a criminal offense or with being a delinquent child or juvenile traffic offender and in relation to whom both of the following apply:

(i) The court determines that substance abuse was a contributing factor leading to the criminal or delinquent activity or the juvenile traffic offense with which the person is charged.

(ii) The court determines that the person is unable to pay the cost of the alcohol and drug abuse assessment and treatment for which the surplus money will be used.

(b) All or part of the cost of purchasing electronic continuous alcohol monitoring devices to be used in conjunction with division (H)(3) of this section.

(2006 S 8, eff. 8–17–06; 2005 H 66, eff. 9–29–05; 2004 H 163, eff. 9–23–04; 2003 H 87, eff. 6–30–03; 2002 S 123, eff. 1–1–04; 2000 S 180, eff. 3–22–01; 2000 H 138, eff. 11–3–00; 1999 S 22, eff. 5–17–00; 1999 S 107, eff. 3–23–00; 1999 H 283, eff. 6–30–99; 1998 S 80, eff. 9–16–98; 1997 S 60, eff. 10–21–97; 1997 S 85, eff. 5–15–97; 1997 H 210, eff. 6–30–97; 1996 S 166, § 6, eff. 5–15–97; 1996 S 166, § 1, eff. 10–17–96; 1996 H 353, § 4, eff. 5–15–97; 1996 H 353, § 1, eff. 9–17–96; 1995 H 167, eff. 5–15–97; 1995 S 2, eff. 7–1–96; 1995 H 117, eff. 6–30–95; 1994 H 687, eff. 10–12–94; 1994 H 236, eff. 9–29–94; 1994 S 82, eff. 5–4–94; 1993 H 152, eff. 7–1–93; 1993 S 62, § 1, 4; 1992 S 275; 1990 H 837, S 131; 1989 H 317, H 381, H 329; 1988 H 643, S 308; 1987 H 303; 1986 S 262; 1985 H 201; 1982 S 432; 1978 H 469; 1977 H 219; 1976 H 451; 1975 H 1; 1971 H 792; 1969 H 1; 132 v S 512, H 380)

Uncodified Law

2003 H 87, § 7, eff. 6–30–03, reads:

The amendment of section 4511.191 of the Revised Code by this act does not supersede the earlier amendment with delayed effective date of that section by Am. Sub. S.B. 123 of the 124th General Assembly.

Historical and Statutory Notes

Ed. Note: The effective date of the amendment of this section by 1992 S 275 was changed from 7–1–93 to 9–1–93 by 1993 S 62, § 4, eff. 6–30–93.

Amendment Note: 2006 S 8 inserted "of abuse, controlled substance, metabolite of a controlled substance" and "combination" and deleted "alcohol and drug" in division (A)(2); and inserted "or at least the concentration of a listed controlled substance or a listed metabolite of a controlled substance specified in division (A)(1)(j) of section 4511.19 of the Revised Code" in the first sentence of division (C)(1).

Amendment Note: 2005 H 66 substituted "to" for "through" in division (E); added the third sentence in division (F)(2)(c); substituted "(F)(4)" for "(L)(4)" in division (F)(2)(e); substituted "(F)" for "(L)" in the second sentence of division (H)(1); added the second paragraph in division (H)(3); designated new division (H)(4)(a); redesignated former division (H)(4)(a) and (H)(4)(b) as (H)(4)(i) and (H)(4)(ii); added division (H)(4)(b); moved "alcohol" from the end of division (H)(4) to the beginning of division (H)(4)(a); and made other nonsubstantive changes.

Amendment Note: 2004 H 163 inserted "or a substantially equivalent municipal ordinance" in divisions (A)(2), (B)(1), (C)(1), and (D)(2); inserted "that the person" preceding "has been convicted" and substituted "after entering a plea of no contest to" for "of" in the first paragraph of divisions (B)(2) and (C)(2); and substituted "(1)(b), (c), (d), or (e)" for "(2), (3), (4), or (5)" in division (C)(1).

Amendment Note: 2003 H 87 substituted "eight-hundredths" for "ten-hundredths" and "eleven-hundredths" for "fourteen-hundredths" throughout the section; deleted ", 2903.07," after "or section 2903.06" and inserted "or former section 2903.07" and "former" after "is substantially similar to" in division (I)(4); and substituted "(4)" for "(2)(e)" twice in the first paragraph of division (L)(4).

Amendment Note: 2002 S 123 rewrote the section, which prior thereto read:

"(A) Any person who operates a vehicle upon a highway or any public or private property used by the public for vehicular travel or parking within this state shall be deemed to have given consent to a chemical test or tests of the person's blood, breath, or urine for the purpose of determining the alcohol, drug, or alcohol and drug content of the person's blood, breath, or urine if arrested for operating a vehicle while under the influence of alcohol, a drug of abuse, or alcohol and a drug of abuse or for operating a vehicle with a prohibited concentration of alcohol in the blood, breath, or urine. The chemical test or tests shall be administered at the request of a police officer having reasonable grounds to believe the person to have been operating a vehicle upon a highway or any public or private property used by the public for vehicular travel or parking in this state while under the influence of alcohol, a drug of abuse, or alcohol and a drug of abuse or with a prohibited concentration of alcohol in the blood, breath, or urine. The law enforcement agency by which the officer is employed shall designate which of the tests shall be administered.

"(B) Any person who is dead or unconscious, or who is otherwise in a condition rendering the person incapable of refusal, shall be deemed not to have withdrawn consent as provided by division (A) of this section and the test or tests may be administered, subject to sections 313.12 to 313.16 of the Revised Code.

"(C)(1) Any person under arrest for operating a vehicle while under the influence of alcohol, a drug of abuse, or alcohol and a drug of abuse or for operating a vehicle with a prohibited concentration of alcohol in the blood, breath, or urine shall be advised at a police station, or at a hospital, first-aid station, or clinic to which the person has been taken for first-aid or medical treatment, of both of the following:

"(a) The consequences, as specified in division (E) of this section, of the person's refusal to submit upon request to a chemical test designated by the law enforcement agency as provided in division (A) of this section;

"(b) The consequences, as specified in division (F) of this section, of the person's submission to the designated chemical test if the person is found to have a prohibited concentration of alcohol in the blood, breath, or urine.

"(2)(a) The advice given pursuant to division (C)(1) of this section shall be in a written form containing the information described in division (C)(2)(b) of this section and shall be read to the person. The form shall contain a statement that the form was shown to the person under arrest and read to the person in the presence of the arresting officer and either another police officer, a civilian police employee, or an employee of a hospital, first-aid station, or clinic, if any, to which the person has been taken for first-aid or medical treatment. The witnesses shall certify to this fact by signing the form.

"(b) The form required by division (C)(2)(a) of this section shall read as follows:

"'You now are under arrest for operating a vehicle while under the influence of alcohol, a drug of abuse, or both alcohol and a drug of abuse and will be requested by a police officer to submit to a chemical test to determine the concentration of alcohol, drugs of abuse, or alcohol and drugs of abuse in your blood, breath, or urine.

"If you refuse to submit to the requested test or if you submit to the requested test and are found to have a prohibited concentration of alcohol in your blood, breath, or urine, your driver's or commercial driver's license or permit or nonresident operating privilege immediately will be suspended for the period of time specified by law by the officer, on behalf of the registrar of motor vehicles. You may appeal this suspension at your initial appearance before the court that hears the charges against you resulting from the arrest, and your initial appearance will be conducted no later than five days after the arrest. This suspension is independent of the penalties for the offense, and you may be subject to other penalties upon conviction.'

"(D)(1) If a person under arrest as described in division (C)(1) of this section is not asked by a police officer to submit to a chemical test designated as provided in division (A) of this section, the arresting officer shall seize the Ohio or out-of-state driver's or commercial driver's license or permit of the person and immediately forward the seized license or permit to the court in which the arrested person is to appear on the charge for which the person was arrested. If the arrested person does not have the person's driver's or commercial driver's license or permit on the person's self or in the person's vehicle, the arresting officer shall order the arrested person to surrender it to the law enforcement agency that employs the officer within twenty-four hours after the arrest, and, upon the surrender, the officer's employing agency immediately shall forward the license or permit to the court in which the arrested person is to appear on the charge for which the person was arrested. Upon receipt of the license or permit, the court shall retain it pending the initial appearance of the arrested person and any action taken under section 4511.196 of the Revised Code.

"If a person under arrest as described in division (C)(1) of this section is asked by a police officer to submit to a chemical test designated as provided in division (A) of this section and is advised of the consequences of the person's refusal or submission as provided in division (C) of this section and if the person either refuses to submit to the designated chemical test or the person submits to the designated chemical test and the test results indicate that the person's blood contained a concentration of ten-hundredths of one per cent or more by weight of alcohol, the person's breath contained a concentration of ten-hundredths of one gram or more by weight of alcohol per two hundred ten liters of the person's breath, or the person's urine contained a concentration of fourteen-hundredths of one gram or more by weight of alcohol per one hundred milliliters of the person's urine at the time of the alleged offense, the arresting officer shall do all of the following:

"(a) On behalf of the registrar, serve a notice of suspension upon the person that advises the person that, independent of any penalties or sanctions imposed upon the person pursuant to any other section of the Revised Code or any other municipal ordinance, the person's driver's or commercial driver's license or permit or nonresident operating privilege is suspended, that the suspension takes effect immediately, that the suspension will last at least until the person's initial appearance on the charge that will be held within five days after the date of the person's arrest or the issuance of a citation to the person, and that the person may appeal the suspension at the initial appearance; seize the Ohio or out-of-state driver's or commercial driver's license or permit of the person; and immediately forward the seized license or permit to the registrar. If the arrested person does not have the person's driver's or commercial driver's license or permit on the person's self or in the person's vehicle, the arresting officer shall order the person to surrender it to the law enforcement agency that employs the officer within twenty-four hours after the service of the notice of suspension, and, upon the surrender, the officer's employing agency immediately shall forward the license or permit to the registrar.

"(b) Verify the current residence of the person and, if it differs from that on the person's driver's or commercial driver's license or permit, notify the registrar of the change;

"(c) In addition to forwarding the arrested person's driver's or commercial driver's license or permit to the registrar, send to the registrar, within forty-eight hours after the arrest of the person, a sworn report that includes all of the following statements:

"(i) That the officer had reasonable grounds to believe that, at the time of the arrest, the arrested person was operating a vehicle upon a highway or public or private property used by the public for vehicular travel or parking within this state while under the influence of alcohol, a drug of abuse, or alcohol and a drug of abuse or with a prohibited concentration of alcohol in the blood, breath, or urine;

"(ii) That the person was arrested and charged with operating a vehicle while under the influence of alcohol, a drug of abuse, or alcohol and a drug of abuse or with operating a vehicle with a prohibited concentration of alcohol in the blood, breath, or urine;

"(iii) That the officer asked the person to take the designated chemical test, advised the person of the consequences of submitting to the chemical test or refusing to take the chemical test, and gave the person the form described in division (C)(2) of this section;

"(iv) That the person refused to submit to the chemical test or that the person submitted to the chemical test and the test results indicate that the person's blood contained a concentration of ten-hundredths of one per cent or more by weight of alcohol, the person's breath contained a concentration of ten-hundredths of one gram or more by weight of alcohol per two hundred ten liters of the person's breath, or the person's urine contained a concentration of fourteen-hundredths of one gram or more by weight of alcohol per one hundred milliliters of the person's urine at the time of the alleged offense;

"(v) That the officer served a notice of suspension upon the person as described in division (D)(1)(a) of this section.

"(2) The sworn report of an arresting officer completed under division (D)(1)(c) of this section shall be given by the officer to the arrested person at the time of the arrest or sent to the person by regular first class mail by the registrar as soon thereafter as possible, but no later than fourteen days after receipt of the report. An arresting officer may give an unsworn report to the arrested person at the time of the arrest provided the report is complete when given to the arrested person and subsequently is sworn to by the arresting officer. As soon as possible, but no later than forty-eight hours after the arrest of the person, the arresting officer shall send a copy of the sworn report to the court in which the arrested person is to appear on the charge for which the person was arrested.

"(3) The sworn report of an arresting officer completed and sent to the registrar and the court under divisions (D)(1)(c) and (D)(2) of this section is prima-facie proof of the information and statements that it contains and shall be admitted and considered as prima-facie proof of the information and statements that it contains in any appeal under division (H) of this section relative to any suspension of a person's driver's or commercial driver's license or permit or nonresident operating privilege that results from the arrest covered by the report.

"(E)(1) Upon receipt of the sworn report of an arresting officer completed and sent to the registrar and a court pursuant to divisions (D)(1)(c) and (D)(2) of this section in regard to a person who refused to take the designated chemical test, the registrar shall enter into the registrar's records the fact that the person's driver's or commercial driver's license or permit or nonresident operating privilege was suspended by the arresting officer under division (D)(1)(a) of this section and the period of the suspension, as determined under divisions (E)(1)(a) to (d) of this section. The suspension shall be subject to appeal as provided in this section and shall be for whichever of the following periods applies:

"(a) If the arrested person, within five years of the date on which the person refused the request to consent to the chemical test, had not refused a previous request to consent to a chemical test of the person's blood, breath, or urine to determine its alcohol content, the period of suspension shall be one year. If the person is a resident without a license or permit to operate a vehicle within this state, the registrar shall deny to the person the issuance of a driver's or commercial driver's license or permit for a period of one year after the date of the alleged violation.

"(b) If the arrested person, within five years of the date on which the person refused the request to consent to the chemical test, had refused one previous request to consent to a chemical test of the person's blood, breath, or urine to determine its alcohol content, the period of suspension or denial shall be two years.

"(c) If the arrested person, within five years of the date on which the person refused the request to consent to the chemical test, had refused two previous requests to consent to a chemical test of the person's blood, breath, or urine to determine its alcohol content, the period of suspension or denial shall be three years.

"(d) If the arrested person, within five years of the date on which the person refused the request to consent to the chemical test, had refused three or more previous requests to consent to a chemical test of the person's blood, breath, or urine to determine its alcohol content, the period of suspension or denial shall be five years.

"(2) The suspension or denial imposed under division (E)(1) of this section shall continue for the entire one-year, two-year, three-year, or five-year period, subject to appeal as provided in this section and subject to termination as provided in division (K) of this section.

"(F) Upon receipt of the sworn report of an arresting officer completed and sent to the registrar and a court pursuant to divisions (D)(1)(c) and (D)(2) of this section in regard to a person whose test results indicate that the person's blood contained a concentration of ten-hundredths of one per cent or more by weight of alcohol, the person's breath contained a concentration of ten-hundredths of one gram or more by weight of alcohol per two hundred ten liters of the person's breath, or the person's urine contained a concentration of fourteen-hundredths of one gram or more by weight of alcohol per one hundred milliliters of the person's urine at the time of the alleged offense, the registrar shall enter into the registrar's records the fact that the person's driver's or commercial driver's license or permit or nonresident operating privilege was suspended by the arresting officer under division (D)(1)(a) of this section and the period of the suspension, as determined under divisions (F)(1) to (4) of this section. The suspension shall be subject to appeal as provided in this section and shall be for whichever of the following periods that applies:

"(1) Except when division (F)(2), (3), or (4) of this section applies and specifies a different period of suspension or denial, the period of the suspension or denial shall be ninety days.

"(2) The period of suspension or denial shall be one year if the person has been convicted, within six years of the date the test was conducted, of a violation of one of the following:

"(a) Division (A) or (B) of section 4511.19 of the Revised Code;

"(b) A municipal ordinance relating to operating a vehicle while under the influence of alcohol, a drug of abuse, or alcohol and a drug of abuse;

"(c) A municipal ordinance relating to operating a vehicle with a prohibited concentration of alcohol in the blood, breath, or urine;

"(d) Section 2903.04 of the Revised Code in a case in which the offender was subject to the sanctions described in division (D) of that section;

"(e) Division (A)(1) of section 2903.06 or division (A)(1) of section 2903.08 of the Revised Code or a municipal ordinance that is substantially similar to either of those divisions;

"(f) Division (A)(2), (3), or (4) of section 2903.06, division (A)(2) of section 2903.08, or former section 2903.07 of the Revised Code, or a municipal ordinance that is substantially similar to any of those divisions or that former section, in a case in which the jury or judge found that at the time of the commission of the offense the offender was under the influence of alcohol, a drug of abuse, or alcohol and a drug of abuse;

"(g) A statute of the United States or of any other state or a municipal ordinance of a municipal corporation located in any other state that is substantially similar to division (A) or (B) of section 4511.19 of the Revised Code.

"(3) If the person has been convicted, within six years of the date the test was conducted, of two violations of a statute or ordinance described in division (F)(2) of this section, the period of the suspension or denial shall be two years.

"(4) If the person has been convicted, within six years of the date the test was conducted, of more than two violations of a statute or ordinance described in division (F)(2) of this section, the period of the suspension or denial shall be three years.

"(G)(1) A suspension of a person's driver's or commercial driver's license or permit or nonresident operating privilege under division (D)(1)(a) of this section for the period of time described in division (E) or (F) of this section is effective immediately from the time at which the arresting officer serves the notice of suspension upon the arrested person. Any subsequent finding that the person is not guilty of the charge that resulted in the person being requested to take, or in the person taking, the chemical test or tests under division (A) of this section affects the suspension only as described in division (H)(2) of this section.

"(2) If a person is arrested for operating a vehicle while under the influence of alcohol, a drug of abuse, or alcohol and a drug of abuse or for operating a vehicle with a prohibited concentration of alcohol in the blood, breath, or urine and regardless of whether the person's driver's or commercial driver's license or permit or nonresident operating privilege is or is not suspended under division (E) or (F) of this section, the person's initial appearance on the charge resulting from the arrest shall be held within five days of the person's arrest or the issuance of the citation to the person, subject to any continuance granted by the court pursuant to division (H)(1) of this section regarding the issues specified in that division.

"(H)(1) If a person is arrested for operating a vehicle while under the influence of alcohol, a drug of abuse, or alcohol and a drug of abuse or for operating a vehicle with a prohibited concentration of alcohol in the blood, breath, or urine and if the person's driver's or commercial driver's license or permit or nonresident operating privilege is suspended under division (E) or (F) of this section, the person may appeal the suspension at the person's initial appearance on the charge resulting from the arrest in the court in which the person will appear on that charge. If the person appeals the suspension at the person's initial appearance, the appeal does not stay the operation of the suspension. Subject to division (H)(2) of this section, no court has jurisdiction to grant a stay of a suspension imposed under division (E) or (F) of this section, and any order issued by any court that purports to grant a stay of any suspension imposed under either of those divisions shall not be given administrative effect.

"If the person appeals the suspension at the person's initial appearance, either the person or the registrar may request a continuance of the appeal. Either the person or the registrar shall make the request for a continuance of the appeal at the same time as the making of the appeal. If either the person or the registrar requests a continuance of the appeal, the court may grant the continuance. The court also may continue the appeal on its own motion. The granting of a continuance applies only to the conduct of the appeal of the suspension and does not extend the time within which the initial appearance must be conducted, and the court shall proceed with all other aspects of the initial appearance in accordance with its normal procedures. Neither the request for nor the granting of a continuance stays the operation of the suspension that is the subject of the appeal.

"If the person appeals the suspension at the person's initial appearance, the scope of the appeal is limited to determining whether one or more of the following conditions have not been met:

"(a) Whether the law enforcement officer had reasonable ground to believe the arrested person was operating a vehicle upon a highway or public or private property used by the public for vehicular travel or parking within this state while under the influence of alcohol, a drug of abuse, or alcohol and a drug of abuse or with a prohibited concentration of alcohol in the blood, breath, or urine and whether the arrested person was in fact placed under arrest;

"(b) Whether the law enforcement officer requested the arrested person to submit to the chemical test designated pursuant to division (A) of this section;

"(c) Whether the arresting officer informed the arrested person of the consequences of refusing to be tested or of submitting to the test;

"(d) Whichever of the following is applicable:

"(i) Whether the arrested person refused to submit to the chemical test requested by the officer;

"(ii) Whether the chemical test results indicate that the arrested person's blood contained a concentration of ten-hundredths of one per cent or more by weight of alcohol, the person's breath contained a concentration of ten-hundredths of one gram or more by weight of alcohol per two hundred ten liters of the person's breath, or the person's urine contained a concentration of fourteen-hundredths of one gram or more by weight of alcohol per one hundred milliliters of the person's urine at the time of the alleged offense.

"(2) If the person appeals the suspension at the initial appearance, the judge or referee of the court or the mayor of the mayor's court shall determine whether one or more of the conditions specified in divisions (H)(1)(a) to (d) of this section have not been met. The person who appeals the suspension has the burden of proving, by a preponderance of the evidence, that one or more of the specified conditions has not been met. If during the appeal at the initial appearance the judge or referee of the court or the mayor of the mayor's court determines that all of those conditions have been met, the judge, referee, or mayor shall uphold the suspension, shall continue the suspension, and shall notify the registrar of the decision on a form approved by the registrar. Except as otherwise provided in division (H)(2) of this section, if the suspension is upheld or if the person does not appeal the suspension at the person's initial appearance under division (H)(1) of this section, the suspension shall continue until the complaint alleging the violation for which the person was arrested and in relation to which the suspension was imposed is adjudicated on the merits by the judge or referee of the trial court or by the mayor of the mayor's court. If the suspension was imposed under division (E) of this section and it is continued under this division, any subsequent finding that the person is not guilty of the charge that resulted in the person being requested to take the chemical test or tests under division (A) of this section does not terminate or otherwise affect the suspension. If the suspension was imposed under division (F) of this section and it is continued under this division, the suspension shall terminate if, for any reason, the person subsequently is found not guilty of the charge that resulted in the person taking the chemical test or tests under division (A) of this section.

"If, during the appeal at the initial appearance, the judge or referee of the trial court or the mayor of the mayor's court determines that one or more of the conditions specified in divisions (H)(1)(a) to (d) of this section have not been met, the judge, referee, or mayor shall terminate the suspension, subject to the imposition of a new suspension under division (B) of section 4511.196 of the Revised Code; shall notify the registrar of the decision on a form approved by the registrar; and, except as provided in division (B) of section 4511.196 of the Revised Code, shall order the registrar to return the driver's or commercial driver's license or permit to the person or to take such measures as may be necessary, if the license or permit was destroyed under section 4507.55 of the Revised Code, to permit the person to obtain a replacement driver's or commercial driver's license or permit from the registrar or a deputy registrar in accordance with that section. The court also shall issue to the person a court order, valid for not more than ten days from the date of issuance, granting the person operating privileges for that period of time.

"If the person appeals the suspension at the initial appearance, the registrar shall be represented by the prosecuting attorney of the county in which the arrest occurred if the initial appearance is conducted in a juvenile court or county court, except that if the arrest occurred within a city or village within the jurisdiction of the county court in which the appeal is conducted, the city director of law or village solicitor of that city or village shall represent the registrar. If the appeal is conducted in a municipal court, the registrar shall be represented as provided in section 1901.34 of the Revised Code. If the appeal is conducted in a mayor's court, the registrar shall be represented by the city director of law, village solicitor, or other chief legal officer of the municipal corporation that operates that mayor's court.

"(I)(1)(a) A person is not entitled to request, and a court shall not grant to the person, occupational driving privileges under division (I)(1) of this section if a person's driver's or commercial driver's license or permit or nonresident operating privilege has been suspended pursuant to division (E) of this section, and the person, within the preceding seven years, has refused three previous requests to consent to a chemical test of the person's blood, breath, or urine to determine its alcohol content or has been convicted of or pleaded guilty to three or more violations of one or more of the following:

"(i) Division (A) or (B) of section 4511.19 of the Revised Code;

"(ii) A municipal ordinance relating to operating a vehicle while under the influence of alcohol, a drug of abuse, or alcohol and a drug of abuse;

"(iii) A municipal ordinance relating to operating a vehicle with a prohibited concentration of alcohol in the blood, breath, or urine;

"(iv) Section 2903.04 of the Revised Code in a case in which the person was subject to the sanctions described in division (D) of that section;

"(v) Division (A)(1) of section 2903.06 or division (A)(1) of section 2903.08 of the Revised Code or a municipal ordinance that is substantially similar to either of those divisions;

"(vi) Division (A)(2), (3), or (4) of section 2903.06, division (A)(2) of section 2903.08, or former section 2903.07 of the Revised Code, or a municipal ordinance that is substantially similar to any of those divisions or that former section, in a case in which the jury or judge found that the person was under the influence of alcohol, a drug of abuse, or alcohol and a drug of abuse;

"(vii) A statute of the United States or of any other state or a municipal ordinance of a municipal corporation located in any other state that is substantially similar to division (A) or (B) of section 4511.19 of the Revised Code.

"(b) Any other person who is not described in division (I)(1)(a) of this section and whose driver's or commercial driver's license or nonresident operating privilege has been suspended pursuant to division (E) of this section may file a petition requesting occupational driving privileges in the common pleas court, municipal court, county court, mayor's court, or, if the person is a minor, juvenile court with jurisdiction over the related criminal or delinquency case. The petition may be filed at any time subsequent to the date on which the notice of suspension is served upon the arrested person. The person shall pay the costs of the proceeding, notify the registrar of the filing of the petition, and send the registrar a copy of the petition.

"In the proceedings, the registrar shall be represented by the prosecuting attorney of the county in which the arrest occurred if the petition is filed in the juvenile court, county court, or common pleas court, except that, if the arrest occurred within a city or village within the jurisdiction of the county court in which the petition is filed, the city director of law or village solicitor of that city or village shall represent the registrar. If the petition is filed in the municipal court, the registrar shall be represented as provided in section 1901.34 of the Revised Code. If the petition is filed in a mayor's court, the registrar shall be represented by the city director of law, village solicitor, or other chief legal officer of the municipal corporation that operates the mayor's court.

"The court, if it finds reasonable cause to believe that suspension would seriously affect the person's ability to continue in the person's employment, may grant the person occupational driving privileges during the period of suspension imposed pursuant to division (E) of this section, subject to the limitations contained in this division and division (I)(2) of this section. The court may grant the occupational driving privileges, subject to the limitations contained in this division and division (I)(2) of this section, regardless of whether the person appeals the suspension at the person's initial appearance under division (H)(1) of this section or appeals the decision of the court made pursuant to the appeal conducted at the initial appearance, and, if the person has appealed the suspension or decision, regardless of whether the matter at issue has been heard or decided by the court. The court shall not grant occupational driving privileges for employment as a driver of commercial motor vehicles to any person who is disqualified from operating a commercial motor vehicle under section 3123.611 or 4506.16 of the Revised Code or whose commercial driver's license or commercial driver's temporary instruction permit has been suspended under section 3123.58 of the Revised Code.

"(2)(a) In granting occupational driving privileges under division (I)(1) of this section, the court may impose any condition it considers reasonable and necessary to limit the use of a vehicle by the person. The court shall deliver to the person a permit card, in a form to be prescribed by the court, setting forth the time, place, and other conditions limiting the defendant's use of a vehicle. The grant of occupational driving privileges shall be conditioned upon the person's having the permit in the person's possession at all times during which the person is operating a vehicle.

"A person granted occupational driving privileges who operates a vehicle for other than occupational purposes, in violation of any condition imposed by the court, or without having the permit in the person's possession, is guilty of a violation of section 4507.02 of the Revised Code.

"(b) The court may not grant a person occupational driving privileges under division (I)(1) of this section when prohibited by a limitation contained in that division or during any of the following periods of time:

"(i) The first thirty days of suspension imposed upon a person who, within five years of the date on which the person refused the request to consent to a chemical test of the person's blood, breath, or urine to determine its alcohol content and for which refusal the suspension was imposed, had not refused a previous request to consent to a chemical test of the person's blood, breath, or urine to determine its alcohol content;

"(ii) The first ninety days of suspension imposed upon a person who, within five years of the date on which the person refused the request to consent to a chemical test of the person's blood, breath, or urine to determine its alcohol content and for which refusal the suspension was imposed, had refused one previous request to consent to a chemical test of the person's blood, breath, or urine to determine its alcohol content;

"(iii) The first year of suspension imposed upon a person who, within five years of the date on which the person refused the request to consent to a chemical test of the person's blood, breath, or urine to determine its alcohol content and for which refusal the suspension was imposed, had refused two previous requests to consent to a chemical test of the person's blood, breath, or urine to determine its alcohol content;

"(iv) The first three years of suspension imposed upon a person who, within five years of the date on which the person refused the request to consent to a chemical test of the person's blood, breath, or urine to determine its alcohol content and for which refusal the suspension was imposed, had refused three or more previous requests to consent to a chemical test of the person's blood, breath, or urine to determine its alcohol content.

"(3) The court shall give information in writing of any action taken under this section to the registrar.

"(4) If a person's driver's or commercial driver's license or permit or nonresident operating privilege has been suspended pursuant to division (F) of this section, and the person, within the preceding seven years, has been convicted of or pleaded guilty to three or more violations of division (A) or (B) of section 4511.19 of the Revised Code, a municipal ordinance relating to operating a vehicle while under the influence of alcohol, a drug of abuse, or alcohol and a drug of abuse, a municipal ordinance relating to operating a vehicle with a prohibited concentration of alcohol in the blood, breath, or urine, section 2903.04 of the Revised Code in a case in which the person was subject to the sanctions described in division (D) of that section, or section 2903.06, 2903.07, or 2903.08 of the Revised Code or a municipal ordinance that is substantially similar to section 2903.07 of the Revised Code in a case in which the jury or judge found that the person was under the influence of alcohol, a drug of abuse, or alcohol and a drug of abuse, or a statute of the United States or of any other state or a municipal ordinance of a municipal corporation located in any other state that is substantially similar to division (A) or (B) of section 4511.19 of the Revised Code, the person is not entitled to request, and the court shall not grant to the person, occupational driving privileges under this division. Any other person whose driver's or commercial driver's license or nonresident operating privilege has been suspended pursuant to division (F) of this section may file in the court specified in division (I)(1)(b) of this section a petition requesting occupational driving privileges in accordance with section 4507.16 of the Revised Code. The petition may be filed at any time subsequent to the date on which the arresting officer serves the notice of suspension upon the arrested person. Upon the making of the request, occupational driving privileges may be granted in accordance with section 4507.16 of the Revised Code. The court may grant the occupational driving privileges, subject to the limitations contained in section 4507.16 of the Revised Code, regardless of whether the person appeals the suspension at the person's initial appearance under division (H)(1) of this section or appeals the decision of the court made pursuant to the appeal conducted at the initial appearance, and, if the person has appealed the suspension or decision, regardless of whether the matter at issue has been heard or decided by the court.

"(J) When it finally has been determined under the procedures of this section that a nonresident's privilege to operate a vehicle within this state has been suspended, the registrar shall give information in writing of the action taken to the motor vehicle administrator of the state of the person's residence and of any state in which the person has a license.

"(K) A suspension of the driver's or commercial driver's license or permit of a resident, a suspension of the operating privilege of a nonresident, or a denial of a driver's or commercial driver's license or permit pursuant to division (E) or (F) of this section shall be terminated by the registrar upon receipt of notice of the person's entering a plea of guilty to, or of the person's conviction of, operating a vehicle while under the influence of alcohol, a drug of abuse, or alcohol and a drug of abuse or with a prohibited concentration of alcohol in the blood, breath, or urine, if the offense for which the plea is entered or that resulted in the conviction arose from the same incident that led to the suspension or denial.

"The registrar shall credit against any judicial suspension of a person's driver's or commercial driver's license or permit or nonresident operating privilege imposed pursuant to division (B) or (E) of section 4507.16 of the Revised Code any time during which the person serves a related suspension imposed pursuant to division (E) or (F) of this section.

"(L) At the end of a suspension period under this section, section 4511.196, or division (B) of section 4507.16 of the Revised Code and upon the request of the person whose driver's or commercial driver's license or permit was suspended and who is not otherwise subject to suspension, revocation, or disqualification, the registrar shall return the driver's or commercial driver's license or permit to the person upon the person's compliance with all of the conditions specified in divisions (L)(1) and (2) of this section:

"(1) A showing by the person that the person has proof of financial responsibility, a policy of liability insurance in effect that meets the minimum standards set forth in section 4509.51 of the Revised Code, or proof, to the satisfaction of the registrar, that the person is able to respond in damages in an amount at least equal to the minimum amounts specified in section 4509.51 of the Revised Code.

"(2) Subject to the limitation contained in division (L)(3) of this section, payment by the person of a license reinstatement fee of four hundred twenty-five dollars to the bureau of motor vehicles, which fee shall be deposited in the state treasury and credited as follows:

"(a) One hundred twelve dollars and fifty cents shall be credited to the statewide treatment and prevention fund created by section 4301.30 of the Revised Code. The fund shall be used to pay the costs of driver treatment and intervention programs operated pursuant to sections 3793.02 and 3793.10 of the Revised Code. The director of alcohol and drug addiction services shall determine the share of the fund that is to be allocated to alcohol and drug addiction programs authorized by section 3793.02 of the Revised Code, and the share of the fund that is to be allocated to drivers' intervention programs authorized by section 3793.10 of the Revised Code.

"(b) Seventy-five dollars shall be credited to the reparations fund created by section 2743.191 of the Revised Code.

"(c) Thirty-seven dollars and fifty cents shall be credited to the indigent drivers alcohol treatment fund, which is hereby established. Except as otherwise provided in division (L)(2)(c) of this section, moneys in the fund shall be distributed by the department of alcohol and drug addiction services to the county indigent drivers alcohol treatment funds, the county juvenile indigent drivers alcohol treatment funds, and the municipal indigent drivers alcohol treatment funds that are required to be established by counties and municipal corporations pursuant to division (N) of this section, and shall be used only to pay the cost of an alcohol and drug addiction treatment program attended by an offender or juvenile traffic offender who is ordered to attend an alcohol and drug addiction treatment program by a county, juvenile, or municipal court judge and who is determined by the county, juvenile, or municipal court judge not to have the means to pay for attendance at the program or to pay the costs specified in division (N)(4) of this section in accordance with that division. Moneys in the fund that are not distributed to a county indigent drivers alcohol treatment fund, a county juvenile indigent drivers alcohol treatment fund, or a municipal indigent drivers alcohol treatment fund under division (N) of this section because the director of alcohol and drug addiction services does not have the information necessary to identify the county or municipal corporation where the offender or juvenile offender was arrested may be transferred by the director of budget and management to the statewide treatment and prevention fund created by section 4301.30 of the Revised Code, upon certification of the amount by the director of alcohol and drug addiction services.

"(d) Seventy-five dollars shall be credited to the Ohio rehabilitation services commission established by section 3304.12 of the Revised Code, to the services for rehabilitation fund, which is hereby established. The fund shall be used to match available federal matching funds where appropriate, and for any other purpose or program of the commission to rehabilitate people with disabilities to help them become employed and independent.

"(e) Seventy-five dollars shall be deposited into the state treasury and credited to the drug abuse resistance education programs fund, which is hereby established, to be used by the attorney general for the purposes specified in division (L)(4) of this section.

"(f) Thirty dollars shall be credited to the state bureau of motor vehicles fund created by section 4501.25 of the Revised Code.

"(g) Twenty dollars shall be credited to the trauma and emergency medical services grants fund created by section 4513.263 of the Revised Code.

"(3) If a person's driver's or commercial driver's license or permit is suspended under division (E) or (F) of this section, section 4511.196, or division (B) of section 4507.16 of the Revised Code, or any combination of the suspensions described in division (L)(3) of this section, and if the suspensions arise from a single incident or a single set of facts and circumstances, the person is liable for payment of, and shall be required to pay to the bureau, only one reinstatement fee of four hundred five dollars. The reinstatement fee shall be distributed by the bureau in accordance with division (L)(2) of this section.

"(4) The attorney general shall use amounts in the drug abuse resistance education programs fund to award grants to law enforcement agencies to establish and implement drug abuse resistance education programs in public schools. Grants awarded to a law enforcement agency under division (L)(2)(e) of this section shall be used by the agency to pay for not more than fifty per cent of the amount of the salaries of law enforcement officers who conduct drug abuse resistance education programs in public schools. The attorney general shall not use more than six per cent of the amounts the attorney general's office receives under division (L)(2)(e) of this section to pay the costs it incurs in administering the grant program established by division (L)(2)(e) of this section and in providing training and materials relating to drug abuse resistance education programs.

"The attorney general shall report to the governor and the general assembly each fiscal year on the progress made in establishing and implementing drug abuse resistance education programs. These reports shall include an evaluation of the effectiveness of these programs.

"(M) Suspension of a commercial driver's license under division (E) or (F) of this section shall be concurrent with any period of disqualification under section 3123.611 or 4506.16 of the Revised Code or any period of suspension under section 3123.58 of the Revised Code. No person who is disqualified for life from holding a commercial driver's license under section 4506.16 of the Revised Code shall be issued a driver's license under Chapter 4507. of the Revised Code during the period for which the commercial driver's license was suspended under division (E) or (F) of this section, and no person whose commercial driver's license is suspended under division (E) or (F) of this section shall be issued a driver's license under that chapter during the period of the suspension.

"(N)(1) Each county shall establish an indigent drivers alcohol treatment fund, each county shall establish a juvenile indigent drivers alcohol treatment fund, and each municipal corporation in which there is a municipal court shall establish an indigent drivers alcohol treatment fund. All revenue that the general assembly appropriates to the indigent drivers alcohol treatment fund for transfer to a county indigent drivers alcohol treatment fund, a county juvenile indigent drivers alcohol treatment fund, or a municipal indigent drivers alcohol treatment fund, all portions of fees that are paid under division (L) of this section and that are credited under that division to the indigent drivers alcohol treatment fund in the state treasury for a county indigent drivers alcohol treatment fund, a county juvenile indigent drivers alcohol treatment fund, or a municipal indigent drivers alcohol treatment fund, and all portions of fines that are specified for deposit into a county or municipal indigent drivers alcohol treatment fund by section 4511.193 of the Revised Code shall be deposited into that county indigent drivers alcohol treatment fund, county juvenile indigent drivers alcohol treatment fund, or municipal indigent drivers alcohol treatment fund in accordance with division (N)(2) of this section. Additionally, all portions of fines that are paid for a violation of section 4511.19 of the Revised Code or division (B)(2) of section 4507.02 of the Revised Code, and that are required under division (A)(1), (2), (5), or (6) of section 4511.99 or division (B)(5) of section 4507.99 of the Revised Code to be deposited into a county indigent drivers alcohol treatment fund or municipal indigent drivers alcohol treatment fund shall be deposited into the appropriate fund in accordance with the applicable division.

"(2) That portion of the license reinstatement fee that is paid under division (L) of this section and that is credited under that division to the indigent drivers alcohol treatment fund shall be deposited into a county indigent drivers alcohol treatment fund, a county juvenile indigent drivers alcohol treatment fund, or a municipal indigent drivers alcohol treatment fund as follows:

"(a) If the suspension in question was imposed under this section, that portion of the fee shall be deposited as follows:

"(i) If the fee is paid by a person who was charged in a county court with the violation that resulted in the suspension, the portion shall be deposited into the county indigent drivers alcohol treatment fund under the control of that court;

"(ii) If the fee is paid by a person who was charged in a juvenile court with the violation that resulted in the suspension, the portion shall be deposited into the county juvenile indigent drivers alcohol treatment fund established in the county served by the court;

"(iii) If the fee is paid by a person who was charged in a municipal court with the violation that resulted in the suspension, the portion shall be deposited into the municipal indigent drivers alcohol treatment fund under the control of that court.

"(b) If the suspension in question was imposed under division (B) of section 4507.16 of the Revised Code, that portion of the fee shall be deposited as follows:

"(i) If the fee is paid by a person whose license or permit was suspended by a county court, the portion shall be deposited into the county indigent drivers alcohol treatment fund under the control of that court;

"(ii) If the fee is paid by a person whose license or permit was suspended by a municipal court, the portion shall be deposited into the municipal indigent drivers alcohol treatment fund under the control of that court.

"(3) Expenditures from a county indigent drivers alcohol treatment fund, a county juvenile indigent drivers alcohol treatment fund, or a municipal indigent drivers alcohol treatment fund shall be made only upon the order of a county, juvenile, or municipal court judge and only for payment of the cost of the attendance at an alcohol and drug addiction treatment program of a person who is convicted of, or found to be a juvenile traffic offender by reason of, a violation of division (A) of section 4511.19 of the Revised Code or a substantially similar municipal ordinance, who is ordered by the court to attend the alcohol and drug addiction treatment program, and who is determined by the court to be unable to pay the cost of attendance at the treatment program or for payment of the costs specified in division (N)(4) of this section in accordance with that division. The alcohol and drug addiction services board or the board of alcohol, drug addiction, and mental health services established pursuant to section 340.02 or 340.021 of the Revised Code and serving the alcohol, drug addiction, and mental health service district in which the court is located shall administer the indigent drivers alcohol treatment program of the court. When a court orders an offender or juvenile traffic offender to attend an alcohol and drug addiction treatment program, the board shall determine which program is suitable to meet the needs of the offender or juvenile traffic offender, and when a suitable program is located and space is available at the program, the offender or juvenile traffic offender shall attend the program designated by the board. A reasonable amount not to exceed five per cent of the amounts credited to and deposited into the county indigent drivers alcohol treatment fund, the county juvenile indigent drivers alcohol treatment fund, or the municipal indigent drivers alcohol treatment fund serving every court whose program is administered by that board shall be paid to the board to cover the costs it incurs in administering those indigent drivers alcohol treatment programs.

"(4) If a county, juvenile, or municipal court determines, in consultation with the alcohol and drug addiction services board or the board of alcohol, drug addiction, and mental health services established pursuant to section 340.02 or 340.021 of the Revised Code and serving the alcohol, drug addiction, and mental health district in which the court is located, that the funds in the county indigent drivers alcohol treatment fund, the county juvenile indigent drivers alcohol treatment fund, or the municipal indigent drivers alcohol treatment fund under the control of the court are more than sufficient to satisfy the purpose for which the fund was established, as specified in divisions (N)(1) to (3) of this section, the court may declare a surplus in the fund. If the court declares a surplus in the fund, the court may expend the amount of the surplus in the fund for alcohol and drug abuse assessment and treatment of persons who are charged in the court with committing a criminal offense or with being a delinquent child or juvenile traffic offender and in relation to whom both of the following apply:

"(a) The court determines that substance abuse was a contributing factor leading to the criminal or delinquent activity or the juvenile traffic offense with which the person is charged.

"(b) The court determines that the person is unable to pay the cost of the alcohol and drug abuse assessment and treatment for which the surplus money will be used."

Amendment Note: 2000 S 180 substituted "3123.611" for "2301.374" and inserted "or whose commercial driver's license or commercial driver's temporary instruction permit has been suspended under section 3123.58 of the Revised Code" in the third paragraph of division (I)(1)(b); and substituted "3123.611" for "2301.374" and inserted "or any period of suspension under section 3123.58 of the Revised Code" in division (M).

Amendment Note: 2000 H 138 inserted "twenty" after "four hundred" in division (L)(2); added new division (L)(2)(g); and made other nonsubstantive changes.

Amendment Note: 1999 S 22 inserted ", (5), or (6)" in division (N)(1); and made other nonsubstantive changes.

Amendment Note: 1999 S 107 rewrote divisions (F)(2) and (I)(1); and substituted "(I)(1)(b)" for "(I)(1)" in division (I)(4). Prior to amendment, divisions (F)(2) and (I)(1) read:

"(2) If the person has been convicted, within six years of the date the test was conducted, of one violation of division (A) or (B) of section 4511.19 of the Revised Code, a municipal ordinance relating to operating a vehicle while under the influence of alcohol, a drug of abuse, or alcohol and a drug of abuse, a municipal ordinance relating to operating a vehicle with a prohibited concentration of alcohol in the blood, breath, or urine, section 2903.04 of the Revised Code in a case in which the offender was subject to the sanctions described in division (D) of that section, or section 2903.06, 2903.07, or 2903.08 of the Revised Code or a municipal ordinance that is substantially similar to section 2903.07 of the Revised Code in a case in which the jury or judge found that at the time of the commission of the offense the offender was under the influence of alcohol, a drug of abuse, or alcohol and a drug of abuse, or a statute of the United States or of any other state or a municipal ordinance of a municipal corporation located in any other state that is substantially similar to division (A) or (B) of section 4511.19 of the Revised Code, the period of the suspension or denial shall be one year."

"(I)(1) If a person's driver's or commercial driver's license or permit or nonresident operating privilege has been suspended pursuant to division (E) of this section, and the person, within the preceding seven years, has refused three previous requests to consent to a chemical test of the person's blood, breath, or urine to determine its alcohol content or has been convicted of or pleaded guilty to three or more violations of division (A) or (B) of section 4511.19 of the Revised Code, a municipal ordinance relating to operating a vehicle while under the influence of alcohol, a drug of abuse, or alcohol and a drug of abuse, a municipal ordinance relating to operating a vehicle with a prohibited concentration of alcohol in the blood, breath, or urine, section 2903.04 of the Revised Code in a case in which the person was subject to the sanctions described in division (D) of that section, or section 2903.06, 2903.07, or 2903.08 of the Revised Code or a municipal ordinance that is substantially similar to section 2903.07 of the Revised Code in a case in which the jury or judge found that the person was under the influence of alcohol, a drug of abuse, or alcohol and a drug of abuse, or a statute of the United States or of any other state or a municipal ordinance of a municipal corporation located in any other state that is substantially similar to division (A) or (B) of section 4511.19 of the Revised Code, the person is not entitled to request, and the court shall not grant to the person, occupational driving privileges under this division. Any other person whose driver's or commercial driver's license or nonresident operating privilege has been suspended pursuant to division (E) of this section may file a petition requesting occupational driving privileges in the common pleas court, municipal court, county court, mayor's court, or, if the person is a minor, juvenile court with jurisdiction over the related criminal or delinquency case. The petition may be filed at any time subsequent to the date on which the notice of suspension is served upon the arrested person. The person shall pay the costs of the proceeding, notify the registrar of the filing of the petition, and send the registrar a copy of the petition.

"In the proceedings, the registrar shall be represented by the prosecuting attorney of the county in which the arrest occurred if the petition is filed in the juvenile court, county court, or common pleas court, except that, if the arrest occurred within a city or village within the jurisdiction of the county court in which the petition is filed, the city director of law or village solicitor of that city or village shall represent the registrar. If the petition is filed in the municipal court, the registrar shall be represented as provided in section 1901.34 of the Revised Code. If the petition is filed in a mayor's court, the registrar shall be represented by the city director of law, village solicitor, or other chief legal officer of the municipal corporation that operates the mayor's court.

"The court, if it finds reasonable cause to believe that suspension would seriously affect the person's ability to continue in the person's employment, may grant the person occupational driving privileges during the period of suspension imposed pursuant to division (E) of this section, subject to the limitations contained in this division and division (I)(2) of this section. The court may grant the occupational driving privileges, subject to the limitations contained in this division and division (I)(2) of this section, regardless of whether the person appeals the suspension at the person's initial appearance under division (H)(1) of this section or appeals the decision of the court made pursuant to the appeal conducted at the initial appearance, and, if the person has appealed the suspension or decision, regardless of whether the matter at issue has been heard or decided by the court. The court shall not grant occupational driving privileges to any person who, within seven years of the filing of the petition, has refused three previous requests to consent to a chemical test of the person's blood, breath, or urine to determine its alcohol content or has been convicted of or pleaded guilty to three or more violations of division (A) or (B) of section 4511.19 of the Revised Code, a municipal ordinance relating to operating a vehicle while under the influence of alcohol, a drug of abuse, or alcohol and a drug of abuse, a municipal ordinance relating to operating a vehicle with a prohibited concentration of alcohol in the blood, breath, or urine, section 2903.04 of the Revised Code in a case in which the person was subject to the sanctions described in division (D) of that section, or section 2903.06, 2903.07, or 2903.08 of the Revised Code or a municipal ordinance that is substantially similar to section 2903.07 of the Revised Code in a case in which the jury or judge found that the person was under the influence of alcohol, a drug of abuse, or alcohol and a drug of abuse, or a statute of the United States or of any other state or a municipal ordinance of a municipal corporation located in any other state that is substantially similar to division (A) or (B) of section 4511.19 of the Revised Code, and shall not grant occupational driving privileges for employment as a driver of commercial motor vehicles to any person who is disqualified from operating a commercial motor vehicle under section 2301.374 or 4506.16 of the Revised Code."

Amendment Note: 1999 H 283 substituted "statewide treatment and prevention fund created by section 4301.30 of the Revised Code" for "drivers' treatment and intervention fund, which is hereby established" in division (L)(2)(a); and substituted "statewide treatment and prevention fund created by section 4301.30 of the Revised Code" for "drivers' treatment and intervention fund, created in division (L)(2)(a) of this section" in division (L)(2)(c).

Amendment Note: 1998 S 80 deleted "for refusal to submit to a chemical test to determine the alcohol, drug, or alcohol and drug content of the person's blood, breath, or urine" following "driver's license or permit", inserted "or (F)", deleted "after entering a plea of no contest under Criminal Rule 11 to" following "of the person's conviction", and inserted "or that resulted in the conviction", in the first paragraph in division (K); substituted "person's compliance with" for "occurrence of" and "conditions specified in divisions (L)(1) and (2) of this section" for "following" in the first paragraph in division (L); inserted "subject to the limitation contained in division (L)(3) of this section," in the first paragraph in division (L)(2); changed the license reinstatement fee referenced in the first paragraph in division (L)(2) from $280 to $405; changed the contribution to the driver's treatment and intervention fund referenced in division (L)(2)(a) from $75 to $112.50; changed the contribution to the reparations fund referenced in division (L)(2)(b) from $50 to $75; changed the contribution to the indigent drivers alcohol treatment fund referenced in division (L(2)(c) from $25 to $37.50; inserted "or to pay the costs specified in division (N)(4) of this section in accordance with that division" in division (L)(2)(c); changed the contribution to the Ohio rehabilitation services commission referenced in division (L)(2)(d) from $50 to $75; changed the contribution to the drug abuse resistance education programs fund referenced in division (L)(2)(e) from $50 to $75; substituted "(L)(4)" for "(L)(2)(e)" in division (L)(2)(e); added division (L)(3); designated division (L)(4); inserted "or for payment of the costs specified in division (N)(4) of this section in accordance with that division" and "alcohol and drug addiction services board or the" and added a reference to section 340.021 in division (N)(3); added division (N)(4); and made changes to reflect gender neutral language and other nonsubstantive changes.

Amendment Note: 1997 S 60 inserted "the United States or of" following "a statute of" at one location in division (F)(2), at two locations in division (I)(1), and at one location in division (I)(4); deleted "place at which the arrest occurred" and "arresting officer serves him" in the first paragraph of division (I)(1); inserted "common please court", "mayor's court" and "related criminal or delinquency case" in the first paragraph of division (I)(1); inserted "or common please court," in the second paragraph of division (I)(1); and added "If the petition is filed in a mayor's court, the registrar shall be represented by the city director of law, village solicitor, or other chief legal officer of the municipal corporation that operates the mayor's court." in the second paragraph of division (I)(1).

Amendment Note: 1997 S 85 substituted "six" for "ten" in divisions (F)(2) through (F)(4); and made a corrective change in division (L)(2)(a).

Amendment Note: 1997 H 210 substituted "eighty" for "fifty" in the first paragraph in division (L)(2); and added division (L)(2)(f).

Amendment Note: 1996 S 166, § 1, eff. 10–17–96, substituted "six years" for "five years" in divisions (F)(2) to (F)(4); added division (O); and made changes to reflect gender neutral language.

Amendment Note: 1996 S 166, § 6, eff. 5–15–97, substituted "ten years" for "five years" in divisions (F)(2) to (F)(4); and made changes to reflect gender neutral language.

Amendment Note: 1996 H 353, § 1, eff. 9–17–96, inserted "or a statute of any other state or a municipal ordinance of a municipal corporation located in any other state that is substantially similar to division (A) or (B) of section 4511.19 of the Revised Code," in division (F)(2), in the first and final paragraphs of division (I)(1), and in division (I)(4); inserted "on a form approved by the registrar" in the first and second paragraphs of division (H)(2); substituted "established" for "created in the state treasury" in division (L)(1)(c); added the second paragraph in division (N)(3); made changes to reflect gender neutral language; and made other nonsubstantive changes.

Amendment Note: 1996 H 353, § 4, eff. 5–15–97, harmonized the versions of this section as amended by 1995 H 167, § 1, eff. 5–15–97, and 1996 H 353, § 1, eff. 7–1–96; and deleted a former second paragraph of division (N)(3), which prior thereto read:

"This is an interim section effective until May 15, 1997."

Amendment Note: 1995 S 2 added division (F)(1); redesignated former division (F)(1) as division (F)(2) and substituted "one year" for "ninety days" therein; deleted former division (F)(2); and made other changes to reflect gender neutral language. Prior to amendment, former division (F)(2) read:

"(2) If the person has been convicted, within five years of the date the test was conducted, of one violation of a statute or ordinance described in division (F)(1) of this section, the period of the suspension or denial shall be one year."

Amendment Note: 1995 H 117 rewrote division (L)(2)(c), which previously read:

"(c) Twenty-five dollars shall be credited to the indigent drivers alcohol treatment fund, which is hereby created in the state treasury. Except as otherwise provided in division (L)(2)(c) of this section, moneys in the fund shall be distributed by the department of alcohol and drug addiction services to the county indigent drivers alcohol treatment funds, the county juvenile indigent drivers alcohol treatment funds, and the municipal indigent drivers treatment funds that are required to be established by counties and municipal corporations pursuant to division (N) of this section, and shall be used only to pay the cost of an alcohol and drug addiction treatment program attended by an offender or juvenile traffic offender who is ordered to attend an alcohol and drug addiction treatment program by a county, juvenile, or municipal court judge and who is determined by the county, juvenile, or municipal court judge not to have the means to pay for his attendance at the program. The department shall retain those moneys in the fund that are not distributed to a county indigent drivers alcohol treatment fund, a county juvenile indigent drivers alcohol treatment fund, or a municipal indigent drivers alcohol treatment fund under division (N) of this section. The department may use the amounts so retained for administrative purposes or distribute them to treatment programs."

Amendment Note: 1995 H 167 added references to section 2301.374 in the third paragraph in division (I)(1) and in division (M); and made other changes to reflect gender neutral language.

Amendment Note: 1994 S 82 inserted "division (A) or (B) of" in division (F)(1); added the references to county juvenile indigent drivers alcohol treatment funds in division (L)(2)(c); and rewrote division (N), which previously read:

"(N) Each county shall establish an indigent drivers alcohol treatment fund, and each municipal corporation in which there is a municipal court shall establish an indigent drivers alcohol treatment fund. All revenue that the general assembly appropriates to the indigent drivers alcohol treatment fund for a county or municipal corporation, all portions of fees that are paid under division (L) of this section and that are credited under that division to the indigent drivers alcohol treatment fund in the state treasury for a county or municipal indigent drivers alcohol treatment fund, and all portions of fines that are specified for deposit into a county or municipal indigent drivers alcohol treatment fund by division (A) of section 4511.99 or by section 4511.193 of the Revised Code shall be deposited into that county's or municipal corporation's indigent drivers alcohol treatment fund. That portion of the fee paid under division (L) of this section by a person whose driver's or commercial driver's license or permit was suspended by a county court or by a juvenile court and which is credited to the indigent drivers alcohol treatment fund shall be deposited in that county's indigent drivers alcohol treatment fund, and that portion of the fee paid under division (L) of this section by a person whose driver's or commercial driver's license or permit was suspended by a municipal court and which is credited to the indigent drivers alcohol treatment fund shall be deposited in that municipal corporation's indigent drivers alcohol treatment fund. Expenditures from a county or municipal indigent drivers alcohol treatment fund shall be made only upon order of a county, juvenile, or municipal court judge and only for payment of the cost of the attendance at an alcohol and drug addiction treatment program of a person who is convicted of, or found to be a juvenile traffic offender by reason of, a violation of section 4511.19 of the Revised Code or a substantially similar municipal ordinance, who is ordered by the court to attend the alcohol and drug addiction treatment program, and who is determined by the court to be unable to pay the cost of his attendance at the treatment program. The board of alcohol, drug addiction, and mental health services established pursuant to section 340.02 of the Revised Code serving the alcohol, drug addiction, and mental health service district in which the court is located shall administer the indigent drivers alcohol treatment program of the court. When a court orders an offender to attend an alcohol and drug addiction treatment program, the board shall determine which program is suitable to meet the needs of the offender, and when a suitable program is located and space is available at the program, the offender shall attend the program designated by the board. A reasonable amount not to exceed five per cent of the amounts credited to and deposited into the county or municipal indigent drivers alcohol treatment fund of every court whose program is administered by that board shall be paid to the board to cover the costs it incurs in administering the indigent drivers alcohol treatment programs of the courts located in its district.".

Amendment Note: 1994 H 236 rewrote division (I)(1); inserted "when prohibited by a limitation contained in that division or" in the first paragraph of division (I)(2)(b); and rewrote division (I)(4). Prior to amendment, divisions (I)(1) and (I)(4) read, respectively:

"(I)(1) A person whose driver's or commercial driver's license or permit or nonresident operating privilege has been suspended pursuant to division (E) of this section may file a petition requesting occupational driving privileges in the municipal court, county court, or, if the person is a minor, juvenile court with jurisdiction over the place at which the arrest occurred. The petition may be filed at any time subsequent to the date on which the arresting officer serves the notice of suspension upon the arrested person. The person shall pay the costs of the proceeding, notify the registrar of the filing of the petition, and send the registrar a copy of the petition.

"In the proceedings, the registrar shall be represented by the prosecuting attorney of the county in which the arrest occurred if the petition is filed in the juvenile court or county court, except that, if the arrest occurred within a city or village within the jurisdiction of the county court in which the petition is filed, the city director of law or village solicitor of that city or village shall represent the registrar. If the petition is filed in the municipal court, the registrar shall be represented as provided in section 1901.34 of the Revised Code.

"The court, if it finds reasonable cause to believe that suspension would seriously affect the person's ability to continue in his employment, may grant the person occupational driving privileges during the period of suspension imposed pursuant to division (E) of this section, subject to the limitations contained in this division and division (I)(2) of this section. The court may grant the occupational driving privileges, subject to the limitations contained in this division and division (I)(2) of this section, regardless of whether the person appeals the suspension at his initial appearance under division (H)(1) of this section or appeals the decision of the court made pursuant to the appeal conducted at the initial appearance, and, if the person has appealed the suspension or decision, regardless of whether the matter at issue has been heard or decided by the court. The court shall not grant occupational driving privileges for employment as a driver of commercial motor vehicles to any person who is disqualified from operating a commercial motor vehicle under section 4506.16 of the Revised Code.

"(4) A person whose driver's or commercial driver's license or permit or nonresident operating privilege has been suspended pursuant to division (F) of this section may file in the court specified in division (I)(1) of this section a petition requesting occupational driving privileges in accordance with section 4507.16 of the Revised Code. The petition may be filed at any time subsequent to the date on which the arresting officer serves the notice of suspension upon the arrested person. Upon the making of the request, occupational driving privileges may be granted in accordance with section 4507.16 of the Revised Code. The court may grant the occupational driving privileges, subject to the limitations contained in section 4507.16 of the Revised Code, regardless of whether the person appeals the suspension at his initial appearance under division (H)(1) of this section or appeals the decision of the court made pursuant to the appeal conducted at the initial appearance, and, if the person has appealed the suspension or decision, regardless of whether the matter at issue has been heard or decided by the court."

Amendment Note: 1994 H 687 added the second sentence in division (D)(2); and inserted ", if the license or permit was destroyed under section 4507.55 of the Revised Code," and "in accordance with that section" in the second paragraph of division (H)(2).

Amendment Note: 1993 S 62 rewrote this section; see *Baldwin's Ohio Legislative Service*, 1993 Laws of Ohio, S 62, p 5–208.

Amendment Note: 1993 H 152 substituted "two hundred fifty" for "two hundred twenty-five" in the first paragraph of division (L)(2); substituted "Fifty" for "Twenty-five" in division (L)(2)(b); and inserted "which is hereby created," in the first paragraph of division (L)(2)(e).

Library References

Automobiles ⚖144.1(1.20), 411 to 426.
Westlaw Topic No. 48A.
C.J.S. Motor Vehicles §§ 164.16, 631 to 637.
  Baldwin's Ohio Legislative Service, 1990 Laws of Ohio, S 131—LSC Analysis, p 5–623
  Baldwin's Ohio Legislative Service, 1993 Laws of Ohio, S 62—LSC Analysis, p 5–220

TRANSPORTATION OF SCHOOL CHILDREN

4511.75 Stopping for school bus; signals on bus

(A) The driver of a vehicle, streetcar, or trackless trolley upon meeting or overtaking from either direction any school bus stopped for the purpose of receiving or discharging any school child, person attending programs offered by community boards of mental health and county boards of mental retardation and developmental disabilities, or child attending a program offered by a head start agency, shall stop at least ten feet from the front or rear of the school bus and shall not proceed until such school bus resumes motion, or until signaled by the school bus driver to proceed.

It is no defense to a charge under this division that the school bus involved failed to display or be equipped with an automatically extended stop warning sign as required by division (B) of this section.

(B) Every school bus shall be equipped with amber and red visual signals meeting the requirements of section 4511.771 of the Revised Code, and an automatically extended stop warning sign of a type approved by the state board of education, which shall be actuated by the driver of the bus whenever but only whenever the bus is stopped or stopping on the roadway for the purpose of receiving or discharging school children, persons attending programs offered by community boards of mental health and county boards of mental retardation and developmental disabilities, or children attending programs offered by head start agencies. A school bus driver shall not actuate the visual signals or the stop warning sign in designated school bus loading areas where the bus is entirely off the roadway or at school buildings when children or persons attending programs offered by community boards of mental health and county boards of mental retardation and developmental disabilities are loading or unloading at curbside or at buildings when children attending programs offered by head start agencies are loading or unloading at curbside. The visual signals and stop warning sign shall be synchronized or otherwise operated as required by rule of the board.

(C) Where a highway has been divided into four or more traffic lanes, a driver of a vehicle, streetcar, or trackless trolley need not stop for a school bus approaching from the opposite direction which has stopped for the purpose of receiving or discharging any school child, persons attending programs offered by community boards of mental health and county boards of mental retardation and developmental disabilities, or children attending programs offered by head start agencies. The driver of any vehicle, streetcar, or trackless trolley overtaking the school bus shall comply with division (A) of this section.

(D) School buses operating on divided highways or on highways with four or more traffic lanes shall receive and discharge all school children, persons attending programs offered by community boards of mental health and county boards of mental retardation and developmental disabilities, and children attending programs offered by head start agencies on their residence side of the highway.

(E) No school bus driver shall start the driver's bus until after any child, person attending programs offered by community boards of mental health and county boards of mental retardation and developmental disabilities, or child attending a program offered by a head start agency who may have alighted therefrom has reached a place of safety on the child's or person's residence side of the road.

(F)(1) Whoever violates division (A) of this section may be fined an amount not to exceed five hundred dollars. A person who is issued a citation for a violation of division (A) of this section is not permitted to enter a written plea of guilty and waive the person's right to contest the citation in a trial but instead must appear in person in the proper court to answer the charge.

(2) In addition to and independent of any other penalty provided by law, the court or mayor may impose upon an offender who violates this section a class seven suspension of the offender's driver's license, commercial driver's license, temporary instruction permit, probationary license, or nonresident operating privilege from the range specified in division (A)(7) of section 4510.02 of the Revised Code. When a license is suspended under this section, the court or mayor shall cause the offender to deliver the license to the court, and the court or clerk of the court immediately shall forward the license to the registrar of motor vehicles, together with notice of the court's action.

(G) As used in this section:

(1) "Head start agency" has the same meaning as in section 3301.32 of the Revised Code.

(2) "School bus," as used in relation to children who attend a program offered by a head start agency, means a bus that is owned and operated by a head start agency, is equipped with an automatically extended stop warning sign of a type approved by

the state board of education, is painted the color and displays the markings described in section 4511.77 of the Revised Code, and is equipped with amber and red visual signals meeting the requirements of section 4511.771 of the Revised Code, irrespective of whether or not the bus has fifteen or more children aboard at any time. "School bus" does not include a van owned and operated by a head start agency, irrespective of its color, lights, or markings.

(2005 H 66, eff. 6–30–05; 2003 H 95, § 3.13, eff. 7–1–04; 2002 S 123, eff. 1–1–04; 1998 H 618, eff. 3–22–99; 1984 H 478, eff. 3–28–85; 1980 S 160; 1978 S 389; 1975 H 369; 1974 H 995; 125 v 167; 1953 H 1; GC 6307–73)

Uncodified Law

2003 H 95, § 193, eff. 6–26–03, reads:

The amendment by this act of the version of section 4511.75 of the Revised Code that is scheduled to take effect January 1, 2004, and the items of law of which that amendment is composed, are not subject to the referendum under Ohio Constitution, Article II, Section 1d and section 1.471 of the Revised Code and go into effect on July 1, 2004.

Historical and Statutory Notes

Pre–1953 H 1 Amendments: 123 v 614; 119 v 766, § 73

Amendment Note: 2005 H 66 substituted "3301.32" for "3301.31" in division (G)(1).

Amendment Note: 2003 H 95 deleted "division (A)(1) of" following "has the same meaning as in" in division (G)(1).

Amendment Note: 2002 S 123 redesignated existing division (F) as new division (G) and added new division (F).

Amendment Note: 1998 H 618 added references to children attending programs offered by head start agencies throughout the section; added division (F); and made changes to reflect gender neutral language and other nonsubstantive changes.

Library References

Automobiles ☞333.
Schools ☞159 1/2(1), 159 1/2(6).
Westlaw Topic Nos. 48A, 345.
C.J.S. Civil Rights § 134.
C.J.S. Motor Vehicles §§ 684, 714.
C.J.S. Schools and School Districts §§ 475, 481.

CHAPTER 5101

JOB AND FAMILY SERVICES DEPARTMENT—GENERAL PROVISIONS

PROTECTIVE SERVICES FOR ADULTS

Section
5101.60 Definitions
5101.61 Duty to report suspected abuse of adult
5101.62 County department of job and family services to investigate
5101.63 Court may restrain interference
5101.64 Protective services
5101.65 Department may petition court
5101.66 Procedures
5101.67 Hearing; order; placement; renewal or modification
5101.68 Interference by another; procedures
5101.69 Emergency provision for protective services
5101.70 Determination of ability to pay
5101.71 County to implement; training

Uncodified Law

1999 H 470, § 12, eff. 3–14–00, reads:

On July 1, 2000:

(A) The Bureau of Employment Services shall cease to exist. Employees of the Bureau of Employment Services are hereby transferred to the Department of Job and Family Services or the Department of Commerce, as appropriate. The vehicles and equipment assigned to the employees are transferred to the Department of Job and Family Services or the Department of Commerce, as appropriate.

(B) The assets, liabilities, other equipment not provided for, and records, irrespective of form or medium, of the Bureau of Employment Services are transferred to the Department of Job and Family Services or the Department of Commerce, as appropriate. The Department of Job and Family Services and the Department of Commerce are successors to, assume the obligations of, and otherwise constitute the continuation of, the Bureau of Employment Services.

(C) Business commenced but not completed by the Administrator or the Bureau of Employment Services on July 1, 2000, shall be completed by the Director or Department of Job and Family Services or the Director or Department of Commerce, as appropriate, in the same manner, and with the same effect, as if completed by the Administrator or Bureau of Employment Services. No validation, cure, right, privilege, remedy, obligation, or liability is lost or impaired by reason of the transfer required by this section but shall be administered by the Director or Department of Job and Family Services or the Director or Department of Commerce, as appropriate.

(D) The rules, orders, and determinations pertaining to the Bureau of Employment Services continue in effect as rules, orders, and determinations of the Department of Job and Family Services or the Department of Commerce, as appropriate, until modified or rescinded by those Departments.

(E) No judicial or administrative action or proceeding pending on July 1, 2000, is affected by the transfer of functions from the Administrator or Bureau of Employment Services to the Director or Department of Job and Family Services or the Director or Department of Commerce, and shall be prosecuted or defended in the name of the Director or Department of Job and Family Services or the Director or Department of Commerce, as appropriate. On application to the court or other tribunal, the Director or Department of Job and Family Services or the Director or Department of Commerce, whichever is appropriate, shall be substituted as a party in such actions and proceedings.

(F) When the Administrator or Bureau of Employment Services is referred to in any statute, rule, contract, grant, or other document, the reference is hereby deemed to refer to the Director or Department of Job and Family Services or the Director or Department of Commerce, as appropriate.

1999 H 470, § 16, eff. 3–14–00, reads:

Effective July 1, 2000, except as provided in Section 15 of this act, the functions the Bureau of Employment Services performs under a grant agreement with the United States Department of Labor are assigned to the Department of Job and Family Services.

1999 H 470, § 17, eff. 3–14–00, reads:

On and after July 1, 2000, if necessary to ensure the integrity of the numbering of the Administrative Code, the Director of the Legislative Service Commission shall renumber the rules of the Bureau of Employment Services and the Department of Human Services to reflect their transfer to the Department of Job and Family Services and the Department of Commerce.

1999 H 470, § 18, eff. 3–14–00, reads:

On and after July 1, 2000, in addition to the positions described in division (A)(26) of section 124.11 of the Revised Code, the Director of Job and Family Services may appoint up to five additional positions to the unclassified service that the Director determines to be involved in policy development and implementation. These additional positions shall expire no later than June 30, 2002.

1999 H 470, § 19, eff. 3–14–00, reads:

During the period beginning July 1, 2000, and ending June 30, 2002, the Director of Job and Family Services has the authority to establish, change, and abolish positions for the Department of Job and Family Services, and to assign, reassign, classify, reclassify, transfer, reduce, promote, or demote all employees of the Department of Job and Family Services who are not subject to Chapter 4117. of the Revised Code.

This authority includes assigning or reassigning an exempt employee, as defined in section 124.152 of the Revised Code, to a bargaining unit classification if the Director determines that the bargaining unit classification is the proper classification for that employee. The Director's actions shall be consistent with the requirements of 5 C.F.R. 900.603 for those employees subject to such requirements. If an employee in the E–1 pay range is to be assigned, reassigned, classified, reclassified, transferred, reduced, or demoted to a position in a lower classification during the period specified in this section, the Director, or in the case of a transfer outside the Department, the Director of Administrative Services, shall assign the employee to the appropriate classification and place the employee in Step X. The employee shall not receive any increase in compensation until the maximum rate of pay for that classification exceeds the employee's compensation.

Actions taken by the Director of Job and Family Services or the Director of Administrative Services pursuant to this section are not subject to appeal to the State Personnel Board of Review.

1999 H 470, § 21, eff. 3–14–00, reads:

The Director of Human Services and the Administrator of the Bureau of Employment Services may jointly or separately enter into one or more contracts with private or government entities for staff training and development to facilitate the transfer of the staff and duties of the Bureau of Employment Services to the Department of Job and Family Services. Division (B) of section 127.16 of the Revised Code does not apply to contracts entered into under this section.

1999 H 470, § 22, eff. 3–14–00, reads:

The Director of Human Services and the Administrator of the Bureau of Employment Services, the boards of county commissioners, and the chief elected official of municipal corporations may enter into negotiations to amend an existing partnership agreement or to enter into a new partnership agreement consistent with this act. Any such amended or new partnership agreement shall be drafted in the name of the Department of Job and Family Services. The amended or new partnership agreement may be executed before July 1, 2000, if the amendment or agreement does not become effective sooner than July 1, 2000.

1997 H 215, § 148, eff. 6–30–97, reads:

From October 1, 1997, to July 1, 1998, the Director of Human Services has full authority to establish, change, and abolish positions for, and to assign, reassign, classify, reclassify, transfer, reduce, promote, or demote, all employees of the Department of Human Services who are not subject to Chapter 4117. of the Revised Code. If an employee is to be assigned, reassigned, classified, reclassified, transferred, reduced, or demoted during this period to a position in a classification assigned to a pay range lower than the pay range to which the employee's classification on the effective date of this section is assigned, the Director or, in the case of a transfer outside the Department, the Director of Administrative Services shall assign the employee to the appropriate classification and place the employee in Step X. The employee shall not receive any increase in compensation until the maximum rate of pay for that classification exceeds the employee's compensation. The Director of Human Services shall report to the Speaker and Minority Leader of the House of Representatives and the President and Minority Leader of the Senate on any actions taken by the Director under this section regarding employees of the Department. The Director shall make the report on an annual basis in 1997 and 1998.

1997 H 408, § 4, eff. 10–1–97, reads:

A rule adopted by the Department of Human Services under Chapter 5101. or 5107. of the Revised Code or pursuant to Executive Order 96–73V prior to the effective date of this act remains valid and enforceable until repealed by the Department notwithstanding the abolition of the Aid to Dependent Children Program and the Job Opportunities and Basic Skills Training Program and creation of the Ohio Works First Program and the Prevention, Retention, and Contingency Program.

No later than July 1, 1998, the Department shall, to the extent allowable under rule making authority, conduct a review and repeal all rules that, as a result of enactment of this act, are no longer applicable to the administration of the Department's programs.

1995 H 167, § 5, eff. 10–25–95, reads:

The Department of Human Services shall establish an employment assistance program. Under the program, the Department shall provide a wage subsidy to an employer who enters into a written contract with a county department of human services under which the employer agrees to do all of the following:

(A) Employ either of the following:

(1) A recipient of Disability Assistance Medical Assistance eligible for such assistance pursuant to division (B)(2)(f) of section 5115.01 of the Revised Code;

(2) A former recipient of General Assistance who received General Assistance under former Chapter 5113. of the Revised Code for at least one month during the period July 1, 1994 to June 30, 1995;

(B) Pay the Disability Assistance Medical Assistance recipient or former General Assistance recipient at least minimum wage;

(C) Employ the Disability Assistance Medical Assistance recipient or former General Assistance recipient in a position that is reasonably expected to be either permanent or to lead to permanent employment with the employer;

(D) Provide the Disability Assistance Medical Assistance recipient or former General Assistance recipient not less than twenty hours a week of employment.

If the employer signs the contract, the Department shall pay the employer three hundred dollars not later than the first day of the Disability Assistance Medical Assistance recipient's or former General Assistance recipient's employment. If the employer complies with the contract, the Department also shall pay the employer two hundred dollars not later than ninety days after the three hundred dollar payment is made.

The Department shall prescribe the contract to be used for the employment assistance program. The Department shall provide county departments of human services as many copies of the contract as the county departments need.

The Department may adopt rules in accordance with section 111.15 of the Revised Code to implement the employment assistance program.

A county department shall not enter into any new contract under this section after June 30, 1997.

PROTECTIVE SERVICES FOR ADULTS

5101.60 Definitions

As used in sections 5101.60 to 5101.71 of the Revised Code:

(A) "Abuse" means the infliction upon an adult by self or others of injury, unreasonable confinement, intimidation, or cruel punishment with resulting physical harm, pain, or mental anguish.

(B) "Adult" means any person sixty years of age or older within this state who is handicapped by the infirmities of aging or who has a physical or mental impairment which prevents the person from providing for the person's own care or protection, and who resides in an independent living arrangement. An "independent living arrangement" is a domicile of a person's own choosing, including, but not limited to, a private home, apartment, trailer, or rooming house. Except as otherwise provided in this division, "independent living arrangement" includes a community alternative home licensed pursuant to section 3724.03 of the Revised Code but does not include other institutions or facilities licensed by the state, or facilities in which a person resides as a result of voluntary, civil, or criminal commitment. "Independent living arrangement" does include adult care facilities licensed pursuant to Chapter 3722. of the Revised Code.

(C) "Caretaker" means the person assuming the responsibility for the care of an adult on a voluntary basis, by contract, through receipt of payment for care, as a result of a family relationship, or by order of a court of competent jurisdiction.

(D) "Court" means the probate court in the county where an adult resides.

(E) "Emergency" means that the adult is living in conditions which present a substantial risk of immediate and irreparable physical harm or death to self or any other person.

(F) "Emergency services" means protective services furnished to an adult in an emergency.

(G) "Exploitation" means the unlawful or improper act of a caretaker using an adult or an adult's resources for monetary or personal benefit, profit, or gain.

(H) "In need of protective services" means an adult known or suspected to be suffering from abuse, neglect, or exploitation to an extent that either life is endangered or physical harm, mental anguish, or mental illness results or is likely to result.

(I) "Incapacitated person" means a person who is impaired for any reason to the extent that the person lacks sufficient understanding or capacity to make and carry out reasonable decisions concerning the person's self or resources, with or without the assistance of a caretaker. Refusal to consent to the provision of services shall not be the sole determinative that the person is incapacitated. "Reasonable decisions" are decisions made in daily living which facilitate the provision of food, shelter, clothing, and health care necessary for life support.

(J) "Mental illness" means a substantial disorder of thought, mood, perception, orientation, or memory that grossly impairs judgment, behavior, capacity to recognize reality, or ability to meet the ordinary demands of life.

(K) "Neglect" means the failure of an adult to provide for self the goods or services necessary to avoid physical harm, mental anguish, or mental illness or the failure of a caretaker to provide such goods or services.

(L) "Peace officer" means a peace officer as defined in section 2935.01 of the Revised Code.

(M) "Physical harm" means bodily pain, injury, impairment, or disease suffered by an adult.

(N) "Protective services" means services provided by the county department of job and family services or its designated agency to an adult who has been determined by evaluation to require such services for the prevention, correction, or discontinuance of an act of as well as conditions resulting from abuse, neglect, or exploitation. Protective services may include, but are not limited to, case work services, medical care, mental health services, legal services, fiscal management, home health care, homemaker services, housing-related services, guardianship services, and placement services as well as the provision of such commodities as food, clothing, and shelter.

(O) "Working day" means Monday, Tuesday, Wednesday, Thursday, and Friday, except when such day is a holiday as defined in section 1.14 of the Revised Code.

(1999 H 471, eff. 7–1–00; 1989 H 253, eff. 11–15–90; 1989 S 2; 1986 H 428; 1981 H 694)

Library References

Mental Health ⇌101, 102.
Statutes ⇌179.
Westlaw Topic Nos. 257A, 361.
C.J.S. Insane Persons § 108 to 110, 128, 143.
C.J.S. Statutes § 306, 309.

5101.61 Duty to report suspected abuse of adult

(A) As used in this section:

(1) "Senior service provider" means any person who provides care or services to a person who is an adult as defined in division (B) of section 5101.60 of the Revised Code.

(2) "Ambulatory health facility" means a nonprofit, public or proprietary freestanding organization or a unit of such an agency or organization that:

(a) Provides preventive, diagnostic, therapeutic, rehabilitative, or palliative items or services furnished to an outpatient or ambulatory patient, by or under the direction of a physician or dentist in a facility which is not a part of a hospital, but which is organized and operated to provide medical care to outpatients;

(b) Has health and medical care policies which are developed with the advice of, and with the provision of review of such policies, an advisory committee of professional personnel, including one or more physicians, one or more dentists, if dental care is provided, and one or more registered nurses;

(c) Has a medical director, a dental director, if dental care is provided, and a nursing director responsible for the execution of such policies, and has physicians, dentists, nursing, and ancillary staff appropriate to the scope of services provided;

(d) Requires that the health care and medical care of every patient be under the supervision of a physician, provides for medical care in a case of emergency, has in effect a written agreement with one or more hospitals and other centers or clinics, and has an established patient referral system to other resources, and a utilization review plan and program;

(e) Maintains clinical records on all patients;

(f) Provides nursing services and other therapeutic services in accordance with programs and policies, with such services supervised by a registered professional nurse, and has a registered professional nurse on duty at all times of clinical operations;

(g) Provides approved methods and procedures for the dispensing and administration of drugs and biologicals;

(h) Has established an accounting and record keeping system to determine reasonable and allowable costs;

(i) "Ambulatory health facilities" also includes an alcoholism treatment facility approved by the joint commission on accreditation of healthcare organizations as an alcoholism treatment facility or certified by the department of alcohol and drug addiction services, and such facility shall comply with other provisions of this division not inconsistent with such accreditation or certification.

(3) "Community mental health facility" means a facility which provides community mental health services and is included in the comprehensive mental health plan for the alcohol, drug addiction, and mental health service district in which it is located.

(4) "Community mental health service" means services, other than inpatient services, provided by a community mental health facility.

(5) "Home health agency" means an institution or a distinct part of an institution operated in this state which:

(a) Is primarily engaged in providing home health services;

(b) Has home health policies which are established by a group of professional personnel, including one or more duly licensed doctors of medicine or osteopathy and one or more registered professional nurses, to govern the home health services it provides and which includes a requirement that every patient must be under the care of a duly licensed doctor of medicine or osteopathy;

(c) Is under the supervision of a duly licensed doctor of medicine or doctor of osteopathy or a registered professional nurse who is responsible for the execution of such home health policies;

(d) Maintains comprehensive records on all patients;

(e) Is operated by the state, a political subdivision, or an agency of either, or is operated not for profit in this state and is licensed or registered, if required, pursuant to law by the appropriate department of the state, county, or municipality in which it furnishes services; or is operated for profit in this state, meets all the requirements specified in divisions (A)(5)(a) to (d) of this section, and is certified under Title XVIII of the "Social Security Act," 49 Stat. 620 (1935), 42 U.S.C. 301, as amended.

(6) "Home health service" means the following items and services, provided, except as provided in division (A)(6)(g) of this section, on a visiting basis in a place of residence used as the patient's home:

(a) Nursing care provided by or under the supervision of a registered professional nurse;

(b) Physical, occupational, or speech therapy ordered by the patient's attending physician;

(c) Medical social services performed by or under the supervision of a qualified medical or psychiatric social worker and under the direction of the patient's attending physician;

(d) Personal health care of the patient performed by aides in accordance with the orders of a doctor of medicine or osteopathy and under the supervision of a registered professional nurse;

(e) Medical supplies and the use of medical appliances;

(f) Medical services of interns and residents-in-training under an approved teaching program of a nonprofit hospital and under the direction and supervision of the patient's attending physician;

(g) Any of the foregoing items and services which:

(i) Are provided on an outpatient basis under arrangements made by the home health agency at a hospital or skilled nursing facility;

(ii) Involve the use of equipment of such a nature that the items and services cannot readily be made available to the patient in the patient's place of residence, or which are furnished at the hospital or skilled nursing facility while the patient [sic.] there to receive any item or service involving the use of such equipment.

Any attorney, physician, osteopath, podiatrist, chiropractor, dentist, psychologist, any employee of a hospital as defined in section 3701.01 of the Revised Code, any nurse licensed under Chapter 4723. of the Revised Code, any employee of an ambulatory health facility, any employee of a home health agency, any employee of an adult care facility as defined in section 3722.01 of the Revised Code, any employee of a community alternative home as defined in section 3724.01 of the Revised Code, any employee of a nursing home, residential care facility, or home for the aging, as defined in section 3721.01 of the Revised Code, any senior service provider, any peace officer, coroner, clergyman, any employee of a community mental health facility, and any person engaged in social work or counseling having reasonable cause to believe that an adult is being abused, neglected, or exploited, or is in a condition which is the result of abuse, neglect, or exploitation shall immediately report such belief to the county department of job and family services. This section does not apply to employees of any hospital or public hospital as defined in section 5122.01 of the Revised Code.

(B) Any person having reasonable cause to believe that an adult has suffered abuse, neglect, or exploitation may report, or cause reports to be made of such belief to the department.

(C) The reports made under this section shall be made orally or in writing except that oral reports shall be followed by a written report if a written report is requested by the department. Written reports shall include:

(1) The name, address, and approximate age of the adult who is the subject of the report;

(2) The name and address of the individual responsible for the adult's care, if any individual is, and if the individual is known;

(3) The nature and extent of the alleged abuse, neglect, or exploitation of the adult;

(4) The basis of the reporter's belief that the adult has been abused, neglected, or exploited.

(D) Any person with reasonable cause to believe that an adult is suffering abuse, neglect, or exploitation who makes a report pursuant to this section or who testifies in any administrative or judicial proceeding arising from such a report, or any employee of the state or any of its subdivisions who is discharging responsibilities under section 5101.62 of the Revised Code shall be immune from civil or criminal liability on account of such investigation, report, or testimony, except liability for perjury, unless the person has acted in bad faith or with malicious purpose.

(E) No employer or any other person with the authority to do so shall discharge, demote, transfer, prepare a negative work performance evaluation, or reduce benefits, pay, or work privileges, or take any other action detrimental to an employee or in any way retaliate against an employee as a result of the employee's having filed a report under this section.

(F) Neither the written or oral report provided for in this section nor the investigatory report provided for in section 5101.62 of the Revised Code shall be considered a public record as defined in section 149.43 of the Revised Code. Information contained in the report shall upon request be made available to the adult who is the subject of the report, to agencies authorized by the department to receive information contained in the report, and to legal counsel for the adult.

(1999 H 471, eff. 7–1–00; 1995 H 117, eff. 9–29–95; 1989 H 317, eff. 10–10–89; 1989 H 253, S 2; 1987 S 124; 1985 H 66; 1981 H 694)

Library References

Asylums ⇐3.
Mental Health ⇐101, 102.
Statutes ⇐179.
Westlaw Topic Nos. 43, 257A, 361.
C.J.S. Asylums and Institutional Care Facilities § 5 to 8.
C.J.S. Insane Persons § 108 to 110, 128, 143.
C.J.S. Statutes § 306, 309.

5101.62 County department of job and family services to investigate

The county department of job and family services shall be responsible for the investigation of all reports provided for in section 5101.61 and all cases referred to it under section 5126.31 of the Revised Code and for evaluating the need for and, to the extent of available funds, providing or arranging for the provision of protective services. The department may designate another agency to perform the department's duties under this section.

Investigation of the report provided for in section 5101.61 or a case referred to the department under section 5126.31 of the Revised Code shall be initiated within twenty-four hours after the department receives the report or case if any emergency exists; otherwise investigation shall be initiated within three working days.

Investigation of the need for protective services shall include a face-to-face visit with the adult who is the subject of the report, preferably in the adult's residence, and consultation with the person who made the report, if feasible, and agencies or persons who have information about the adult's alleged abuse, neglect, or exploitation.

The department shall give written notice of the intent of the investigation and an explanation of the notice in language reasonably understandable to the adult who is the subject of the investigation, at the time of the initial interview with that person.

Upon completion of the investigation, the department shall determine from its findings whether or not the adult who is the subject of the report is in need of protective services. No adult shall be determined to be abused, neglected, or in need of protective services for the sole reason that, in lieu of medical treatment, the adult relies on or is being furnished spiritual treatment through prayer alone in accordance with the tenets and practices of a church or religious denomination of which the adult is a member or adherent. The department shall write a report which confirms or denies the need for protective services and states why it reached this conclusion.

(1999 H 471, eff. 7–1–00; 1988 H 403, eff. 3–16–89; 1986 H 428; 1981 H 694)

Library References

Mental Health ⊙=101, 102.
Westlaw Topic No. 257A.
C.J.S. Insane Persons § 108 to 110, 128, 143.

5101.63 Court may restrain interference

If, during the course of an investigation conducted under section 5101.62 of the Revised Code, any person, including the adult who is the subject of the investigation, denies or obstructs access to the residence of the adult, the county department of job and family services may file a petition in court for a temporary restraining order to prevent the interference or obstruction. The court shall issue a temporary restraining order to prevent the interference or obstruction if it finds there is reasonable cause to believe that the adult is being or has been abused, neglected, or exploited and access to the person's residence has been denied or obstructed. Such a finding is prima-facie evidence that immediate and irreparable injury, loss, or damage will result, so that notice is not required. After obtaining an order restraining the obstruction of or interference with the access of the protective services representative, the representative may be accompanied to the residence by a peace officer.

(1999 H 471, eff. 7–1–00; 1988 H 403, eff. 3–16–89; 1986 H 428; 1981 H 694)

Library References

Mental Health ⊙=101, 102.
Westlaw Topic No. 257A.
C.J.S. Insane Persons § 108 to 110, 128, 143.

5101.64 Protective services

Any person who requests or consents to receive protective services shall receive such services only after an investigation and determination of a need for protective services, which investigation shall be performed in the same manner as the investigation of a report pursuant to sections 5101.62 and 5101.63 of the Revised Code. If the person withdraws consent, the protective services shall be terminated.

(1981 H 694, eff. 11–15–81)

Library References

Mental Health ⊙=101, 102, 104.1.
Westlaw Topic No. 257A.
C.J.S. Insane Persons § 108 to 111, 128, 143.

5101.65 Department may petition court

If the county department of job and family services determines that an adult is in need of protective services and is an incapacitated person, the department may petition the court for an order authorizing the provision of protective services. The petition shall state the specific facts alleging the abuse, neglect, or exploitation and shall include a proposed protective service plan. Any plan for protective services shall be specified in the petition.

(1999 H 471, eff. 7–1–00; 1986 H 428, eff. 12–23–86; 1981 H 694)

Library References

Mental Health ⊙=103, 126.
Westlaw Topic No. 257A.
C.J.S. Insane Persons § 133.

5101.66 Procedures

Notice of a petition for the provision of court-ordered protective services as provided for in section 5101.65 of the Revised Code shall be personally served upon the adult who is the subject of the petition at least five working days prior to the date set for the hearing as provided in section 5101.67 of the Revised Code. Notice shall be given orally and in writing in language reasonably understandable to the adult. The notice shall include the names of all petitioners, the basis of the belief that protective services are needed, the rights of the adult in the court proceedings, and the consequences of a court order for protective services. The adult shall be informed of his right to counsel and his right to appointed counsel if he is indigent and if appointed counsel is requested. Written notice by certified mail shall also be given to the adult's guardian, legal counsel, caretaker, and spouse, if any, or if he has none of these, to his adult children or next of kin, if any, or to any other person as the court may require. The adult who is the subject of the petition may not waive notice as provided in this section.

(1981 H 694, eff. 11–15–81)

Library References

Mental Health ⊙=127.1 to 130.
Westlaw Topic No. 257A.
C.J.S. Insane Persons § 134 to 137.

5101.67 Hearing; order; placement; renewal or modification

(A) The court shall hold a hearing on the petition as provided in section 5101.65 of the Revised Code within fourteen days after its filing. The adult who is the subject of the petition shall have the right to be present at the hearing, present evidence, and examine and cross-examine witnesses. The adult shall be represented by counsel unless the right to counsel is knowingly waived. If the adult is indigent, the court shall appoint counsel to represent the adult. If the court determines that the adult lacks the capacity to waive the right to counsel, the court shall appoint counsel to represent the adult's interests.

(B) If the court finds, on the basis of clear and convincing evidence, that the adult has been abused, neglected, or exploited, is in need of protective services, and is incapacitated, and no person authorized by law or by court order is available to give consent, it shall issue an order requiring the provision of protective services only if they are available locally.

(C) If the court orders placement under this section it shall give consideration to the choice of residence of the adult. The court may order placement in settings which have been approved by the department of job and family services as meeting at least minimum community standards for safety, security, and the requirements of daily living. The court shall not order an institutional placement unless it has made a specific finding entered in the record that no less restrictive alternative can be found to meet the needs of the individual. No individual may be committed to a hospital or public hospital as defined in section 5122.01 of the Revised Code pursuant to this section.

(D) The placement of an adult pursuant to court order as provided in this section shall not be changed unless the court authorized the transfer of placement after finding compelling reasons to justify the transfer. Unless the court finds that an emergency exists, the court shall notify the adult of a transfer at least thirty days prior to the actual transfer.

(E) A court order provided for in this section shall remain in effect for no longer than six months. Thereafter, the county department of job and family services shall review the adult's need for continued services and, if the department determines that there is a continued need, it shall apply for a renewal of the order for additional periods of no longer than one year each. The adult who is the subject of the court-ordered services may petition for modification of the order at any time.

(1999 H 471, eff. 7–1–00; 1986 H 428, eff. 12–23–86; 1981 H 694)

Library References

Mental Health ⟲137.1 to 147.
Westlaw Topic No. 257A.

5101.68 Interference by another; procedures

(A) If an adult has consented to the provision of protective services but any other person refuses to allow such provision, the county department of human services may petition the court for a temporary restraining order to restrain the person from interfering with the provision of protective services for the adult.

(B) The petition shall state specific facts sufficient to demonstrate the need for protective services, the consent of the adult, and the refusal of some other person to allow the provision of these services.

(C) Notice of the petition shall be given in language reasonably understandable to the person alleged to be interfering with the provision of services;

(D) The court shall hold a hearing on the petition within fourteen days after its filing. If the court finds that the protective services are necessary, that the adult has consented to the provisions of such services, and that the person who is the subject of the petition has prevented such provision, the court shall issue a temporary restraining order to restrain the person from interfering with the provision of protective services to the adult.

(1986 H 428, eff. 12–23–86; 1981 H 694)

Library References

Injunction ⟲94.
Mental Health ⟲103, 134, 160.1.
Westlaw Topic Nos. 212, 257A.
C.J.S. Injunctions § 140 to 141, 146 to 148.
C.J.S. Insane Persons § 142.

5101.69 Emergency provision for protective services

(A) Upon petition by the county department of human services, the court may issue an order authorizing the provision of protective services on an emergency basis to an adult. The petition for any emergency order shall include:

(1) The name, age, and address of the adult in need of protective services;

(2) The nature of the emergency;

(3) The proposed protective services;

(4) The petitioner's reasonable belief, together with facts supportive thereof, as to the existence of the circumstances described in divisions (D)(1) to (3) of this section;

(5) Facts showing the petitioner's attempts to obtain the adult's consent to the protective services.

(B) Notice of the filing and contents of the petition provided for in division (a) of this section, the rights of the person in the hearing provided for in division (C) of this section, and the possible consequences of a court order, shall be given to the adult. Notice shall also be given to the spouse of the adult or, if he has none, to his adult children or next of kin, and his guardian, if any, if his whereabouts are known. The notice shall be given in language reasonably understandable to its recipients at least twenty-four hours prior to the hearing provided for in this section. The court may waive the twenty-four hour notice requirement upon a showing that:

(1) Immediate and irreparable physical harm to the adult or others will result from the twenty-four hour delay; and

(2) Reasonable attempts have been made to notify the adult, his spouse, or, if he has none, his adult children or next of kin, if any, and his guardian, if any, if his whereabouts are known.

Notice of the court's determination shall be given to all persons receiving notice of the filing of the petition provided for in this division.

(C) Upon receipt of a petition for an order for emergency services, the court shall hold a hearing no sooner than twenty-four and no later than seventy-two hours after the notice provided for in division (B) of this section has been given, unless the court has waived the notice. The adult who is the subject of the petition shall have the right to be present at the hearing, present, evidence, and examine and cross-examine witnesses.

(D) The court shall issue an order authorizing the provision of protective services on an emergency basis if it finds, on the basis of clear and convincing evidence, that:

(1) The adult is an incapacitated person;

(2) An emergency exists;

(3) No person authorized by law or court order to give consent for the adult is available or willing to consent to emergency services.

(E) In issuing an emergency order, the court shall adhere to the following limitations:

(1) The court shall order only such protective services as are necessary and available locally to remove the conditions creating the emergency, and the court shall specifically designate those protective services the adult shall receive;

(2) The court shall not order any change of residence under this section unless the court specifically finds that a change of residence is necessary;

(3) The court may order emergency services only for fourteen days. The department may petition the court for a renewal of the order for a fourteen-day period upon a showing that continuation of the order is necessary to remove the emergency.

(4) In its order the court shall authorize the director of the department or his designee to give consent for the person for the approved emergency services until the expiration of the order;

(5) The court shall not order a person to a hospital or public hospital as defined in section 5122.01 of the Revised Code.

(F) If the department determines that the adult continues to need protective services after the order provided for in division (D) of this section has expired, the department may petition the court for an order to continue protective services, pursuant to section 5101.65 of the Revised Code. After the filing of the petition, the department may continue to provide protective services pending a hearing by the court.

(1986 H 428, eff. 12–23–86; 1981 H 694)

Library References

Mental Health ⟲179.
Physicians and Surgeons ⟲44.
Westlaw Topic Nos. 257A, 299.
C.J.S. Hospitals § 7.
C.J.S. Insane Persons § 158 to 159.
C.J.S. Right to Die § 4 to 6, 8.

5101.70 Determination of ability to pay

(A) If it appears that an adult in need of protective services has the financial means sufficient to pay for such services, the county department of job and family services shall make an evaluation regarding such means. If the evaluation establishes that the adult has such financial means, the department shall initiate procedures for reimbursement pursuant to rules promulgated by the department. If the evaluation establishes that the adult does not have such financial means, the services shall be provided in accordance with the policies and procedures established by the department of job and family services for the provision of welfare assistance. An adult shall not be required to pay for court-ordered protective services unless the court determines upon a showing by the department that the adult is financially able to pay and the court orders the adult to pay.

(B) Whenever the department has petitioned the court to authorize the provision of protective services and the adult who is the subject of the petition is indigent, the court shall appoint legal counsel.

(1999 H 471, eff. 7–1–00; 1986 H 428, eff. 12–23–86; 1981 H 694)

Library References

Mental Health ⇌133.
Westlaw Topic No. 257A.
C.J.S. Insane Persons § 139 to 140.

5101.71 County to implement; training

(A) The county departments of job and family services shall implement sections 5101.60 to 5101.71 of the Revised Code. The department of job and family services may provide a program of ongoing, comprehensive, formal training to county departments and other agencies authorized to implement sections 5101.60 to 5101.71 of the Revised Code. Training shall not be limited to the procedures for implementing section 5101.62 of the Revised Code.

(B) The director of job and family services may adopt rules in accordance with section 111.15 of the Revised Code governing the county departments' implementation of sections 5101.60 to 5101.71 of the Revised Code. The rules adopted pursuant to this division may include a requirement that the county departments provide on forms prescribed by the rules a plan of proposed expenditures, and a report of actual expenditures, of funds necessary to implement sections 5101.60 to 5101.71 of the Revised Code.

(1999 H 471, eff. 7–1–00; 1991 H 298, eff. 7–26–91; 1989 H 111; 1986 H 428; 1981 H 694)

Library References

Mental Health ⇌5.
Westlaw Topic No. 257A.

CHAPTER 5103

PLACEMENT OF CHILDREN

FOSTER CAREGIVERS AND FOSTER HOME CERTIFICATES

Section
5103.03 Powers and duties of department in certification of institutions for children

CARE AND PLACEMENT OF CHILDREN

5103.15 Placing of child in public or private institution; agreements to be in writing; social and medical histories required
5103.151 Conditions for juvenile court approving parent's agreement for child's adoption
5103.152 Assessor's meeting with birth parent prior to parent's consenting to adoption
5103.16 Placing of children; assumption of responsibility for expenses
5103.162 Immunity from liability
5103.17 Advertising; enforcement

INTERSTATE COMPACT ON THE PLACEMENT OF CHILDREN

5103.20 Interstate compact for the placement of children
5103.21 Interstate compact for the placement of children; rulemaking
5103.22 Definition
5103.23 Appropriate authority in receiving state—Repealed
5103.24 Agreements authorized; approval—Repealed
5103.25 Reciprocal recognition of inspections—Repealed
5103.26 Court placing child in another state—Repealed
5103.27 Authority of governor—Repealed
5103.28 Construction of chapter regarding termination of parental rights—Repealed

Library References

Infants ⇌226 to 229, 271.
Westlaw Topic No. 211.
C.J.S. Infants §§ 42, 53, 54, 57, 69 to 85.
C.J.S. Reformatories §§ 1 to 5.

FOSTER CAREGIVERS AND FOSTER HOME CERTIFICATES

5103.03 Powers and duties of department in certification of institutions for children

(A) The director of job and family services shall adopt rules as necessary for the adequate and competent management of institutions or associations.

(B)(1) Except for facilities under the control of the department of youth services, places of detention for children established and maintained pursuant to sections 2152.41 to 2152.44 of the Revised Code, and child day-care centers subject to Chapter 5104. of the Revised Code, the department of job and family services every two years shall pass upon the fitness of every institution and association that receives, or desires to receive and care for children, or places children in private homes.

(2) When the department of job and family services is satisfied as to the care given such children, and that the requirements of the statutes and rules covering the management of such institutions and associations are being complied with, it shall issue to the institution or association a certificate to that effect. A certificate is valid for two years, unless sooner revoked by the department. When determining whether an institution or association meets a particular requirement for certification, the department may consider the institution or association to have met the requirement if the institution or association shows to the department's satisfaction that it has met a comparable requirement to be accredited by a nationally recognized accreditation organization.

(3) The department may issue a temporary certificate valid for less than one year authorizing an institution or association to operate until minimum requirements have been met.

(4) An institution or association that knowingly makes a false statement that is included as a part of certification under this section is guilty of the offense of falsification under section

2921.13 of the Revised Code and the department shall not certify that institution or association.

(C) The department may revoke a certificate if it finds that the institution or association is in violation of law or rule. No juvenile court shall commit a child to an association or institution that is required to be certified under this section if its certificate has been revoked or, if after revocation, the date of reissue is less than fifteen months prior to the proposed commitment.

(D) Every two years, on a date specified by the department, each institution or association desiring certification or recertification shall submit to the department a report showing its condition, management, competency to care adequately for the children who have been or may be committed to it or to whom it provides care or services, the system of visitation it employs for children placed in private homes, and other information the department requires.

(E) The department shall, not less than once each year, send a list of certified institutions and associations to each juvenile court and certified association or institution.

(F) No person shall receive children or receive or solicit money on behalf of such an institution or association not so certified or whose certificate has been revoked.

(G) The director may delegate by rule any duties imposed on it by this section to inspect and approve family foster homes and specialized foster homes to public children services agencies, private child placing agencies, or private noncustodial agencies.

(H) If the director of job and family services determines that an institution or association that cares for children is operating without a certificate, the director may petition the court of common pleas in the county in which the institution or association is located for an order enjoining its operation. The court shall grant injunctive relief upon a showing that the institution or association is operating without a certificate.

(I) If both of the following are the case, the director of job and family services may petition the court of common pleas of any county in which an institution or association that holds a certificate under this section operates for an order, and the court may issue an order, preventing the institution or association from receiving additional children into its care or an order removing children from its care:

(1) The department has evidence that the life, health, or safety of one or more children in the care of the institution or association is at imminent risk.

(2) The department has issued a proposed adjudication order pursuant to Chapter 119. of the Revised Code to deny renewal of or revoke the certificate of the institution or association.

(2006 S 238, eff. 9–21–06; 2004 H 117, eff. 9–3–04; 2002 H 424, eff. 3–14–03; 2000 S 179, § 3, eff. 1–1–02; 2000 H 332, eff. 1–1–01; 1999 H 471, eff. 7–1–00; 1996 H 419, eff. 9–18–96; 1993 H 152, eff. 7–1–93; 1986 H 428; 1981 H 440; 1969 S 105; 130 v H 299; 128 v 1126; 1953 H 1; GC 1352–1)

Uncodified Law

2000 H 332, § 3: See *Baldwin's Ohio Revised Code Annotated*, Uncodified Law under RC 5103.031.

Historical and Statutory Notes

Pre–1953 H 1 Amendments: 103 v 866

Library References

Administrative Law and Procedure ⚖381.
Infants ⚖17, 272, 273.
States ⚖67, 73.
Westlaw Topic Nos. 15A, 211, 360.
C.J.S. Infants § 8 to 9, 271 to 272.
C.J.S. Public Administrative Law And Procedure § 87, 91.

C.J.S. States § 120 to 121, 130 to 138, 140.

CARE AND PLACEMENT OF CHILDREN

5103.15 Placing of child in public or private institution; agreements to be in writing; social and medical histories required

(A)(1) The parents, guardian, or other persons having the custody of a child may enter into an agreement with any public children services agency or private child placing agency, whereby the child is placed without the approval of the juvenile court in the temporary custody of the agency for a period of time of up to thirty days, except that an agreement for temporary custody can be for a period of time of up to sixty days without court approval if the agreement is executed solely for the purpose of obtaining the adoption of a child who is less than six months of age on the date of the execution of the agreement.

(2) Except as provided in division (A)(3) of this section for agreements entered into to obtain the adoption of a child under the age of six months, any public children services agency or private child placing agency that obtains, without court approval, temporary custody of a child pursuant to an agreement executed in accordance with this division may request the juvenile court of the county in which the child has a residence or legal settlement for an original thirty-day extension of the temporary custody agreement. Upon the filing of a request for the extension of the temporary custody agreement, the juvenile court shall determine whether the extension is in the best interest of the child and may extend the temporary custody agreement for a period of thirty days beyond the initial thirty-day period for which court approval is not required by this division. The agency requesting the original extension shall file a case plan, prepared pursuant to section 2151.412 of the Revised Code, with the court at the same time that it files its request for an extension.

At the expiration of the original thirty-day extension period, the agency may request the juvenile court to grant an additional thirty-day extension of the temporary custody agreement. Upon the filing of the request for the additional extension, the juvenile court may extend the temporary custody agreement for a period of thirty days beyond the original thirty-day extension period if it determines that the additional extension is in the best interest of the child. The agency shall file an updated version of the child's case plan at the same time that it files its request for an additional extension.

At the expiration of an additional thirty-day extension period and at the expiration of the original thirty-day extension period if the agency does not request an additional thirty-day extension, the agency shall either return the child to the child's parents, guardian, or other person having custody of the child or file a complaint with the court pursuant to section 2151.27 of the Revised Code requesting temporary or permanent custody of the child. The complaint shall be accompanied by a case plan prepared in accordance with section 2151.412 of the Revised Code.

(3) Any public children services agency or private child placing agency that obtains, without court approval and solely for the purpose of obtaining the adoption of the child, temporary custody of a child who is under the age of six months pursuant to an agreement executed in accordance with this division may request the juvenile court in the county in which the child has a residence or legal settlement to grant a thirty day extension of the temporary custody agreement. Upon the filing of the request, the court shall determine whether the extension is in the best interest of the child and may extend the temporary custody agreement for a period of thirty days beyond the sixty day period for which the court approval is not required by this division. The agency requesting the extension shall file a case plan, prepared pursuant to section 2151.412 of the Revised Code, with the court at the same time that it files its request for an extension.

At the expiration of the thirty day extension, the agency shall either return the child to the parents, guardian, or other person having custody of the child or file a complaint with the court pursuant to section 2151.27 of the Revised Code requesting temporary or permanent custody of the child. The complaint shall be accompanied by a case plan prepared in accordance with section 2151.412 of the Revised Code.

(B)(1) Subject to, except as provided in division (B)(2) of this section, juvenile court approval, the parents, guardian, or other persons having custody of a child may enter into an agreement with a public children services agency or private child placing agency surrendering the child into the permanent custody of the agency. An agency that enters into such an agreement may take and care for the child or place the child in a family home.

A private child placing agency or public children services agency that seeks permanent custody of a child pursuant to division (B)(1) of this section shall file a request with the juvenile court of the county in which the child has a residence or legal settlement for approval of the agency's permanent surrender agreement with the parents, guardian, or other persons having custody of the child. Not later than fourteen business days after the request is filed, the juvenile court shall determine whether the permanent surrender agreement is in the best interest of the child. The court may approve the permanent surrender agreement if it determines that the agreement is in the best interest of the child and, in the case of an agreement between a parent and an agency, the requirements of section 5103.151 of the Revised Code are met. The agency requesting the approval of the permanent surrender agreement shall file a case plan, prepared pursuant to section 2151.412 of the Revised Code, with the court at the same time that it files its request for the approval of the permanent surrender agreement.

(2) The parents of a child less than six months of age may enter into an agreement with a private child placing agency surrendering the child into the permanent custody of the agency without juvenile court approval if the agreement is executed solely for the purpose of obtaining the adoption of the child. The agency shall, not later than two business days after entering into the agreement, notify the juvenile court. The agency also shall notify the court not later than two business days after the agency places the child for adoption. The court shall journalize the notices it receives under division (B)(2) of this section.

(C) The agreements provided for in this section shall be in writing, on forms prescribed and furnished by the department, and may contain any proper and legal stipulations for proper care of the child, and may authorize the public children services agency or private child placing agency when such agreements are for permanent care and custody to appear in any proceeding for the legal adoption of the child, and consent to the child's adoption, as provided in section 3107.06 of the Revised Code. If an agreement for permanent care and custody of a child is executed, social and medical histories shall be completed in relation to the child in accordance with section 3107.09 of the Revised Code. The adoption order of the probate court judge made upon the consent shall be binding upon the child and the child's parents, guardian, or other person, as if those persons were personally in court and consented to the order, whether made party to the proceeding or not.

(D) An agreement entered into under this section by a parent under age eighteen is as valid as an agreement entered into by a parent age eighteen or older.

(1996 H 419, eff. 9–18–96; 1988 S 89, eff. 1–1–89; 1984 H 84; 1976 H 156; 1953 H 1; GC 1352–12)

Historical and Statutory Notes

Pre–1953 H 1 Amendments: 110 v 265

Library References

Adoption ⬄6.
Infants ⬄222.
Westlaw Topic Nos. 17, 211.
C.J.S. Adoption of Persons § 25 to 40.
C.J.S. Infants § 57, 69 to 85.

Baldwin's Ohio Legislative Service, 1988 Laws of Ohio, S 89—LSC Analysis, p 5–571

5103.151 Conditions for juvenile court approving parent's agreement for child's adoption

(A) As used in this section and in section 5103.152 of the Revised Code, "identifying information" has the same meaning as in section 3107.01 of the Revised Code.

(B) Except as provided in division (C) of this section, a parent of a minor who will be, if adopted, an adopted person as defined in section 3107.45 of the Revised Code shall do all of the following as a condition of a juvenile court approving the parent's agreement with a public children services agency or private child placing agency under division (B)(1) of section 5103.15 of the Revised Code:

(1) Appear personally before the court;

(2) Sign the component of the form prescribed under division (A)(1)(a) of section 3107.083 of the Revised Code;

(3) Check either the "yes" or "no" space provided on the component of the form prescribed under division (A)(1)(b) of section 3107.083 of the Revised Code and sign that component;

(4) If the parent is the mother, complete and sign the component of the form prescribed under division (A)(1)(c) of section 3107.083 of the Revised Code.

At the time the parent signs the components of the form prescribed under divisions (A)(1)(a), (b), and (c) of section 3107.083 of the Revised Code, the parent may sign, if the parent chooses to do so, the components of the form prescribed under divisions (A)(1)(d), (e), and (f) of that section. After the parent signs the components required to be signed and any discretionary components the parent chooses to sign, the parent or agency shall file the form and agreement with the court. The court or agency shall give the parent a copy of the form and agreement. The court and agency shall keep a copy of the form and agreement in the court and agency's records. The agency shall file a copy of the form and agreement with the probate court with which a petition to adopt the child who is the subject of the agreement is filed.

The juvenile court shall question the parent to determine that the parent understands the adoption process, the ramifications of entering into a voluntary permanent custody surrender agreement, each component of the form prescribed under division (A)(1) of section 3107.083 of the Revised Code, and that the child and adoptive parent may receive identifying information about the parent in accordance with section 3107.47 of the Revised Code unless the parent checks the "no" space provided on the component of the form prescribed under division (A)(1)(b) of section 3107.083 of the Revised Code or has a denial of release form filed with the department of health under section 3107.46 of the Revised Code. The court also shall question the parent to determine that the parent enters into the permanent custody surrender agreement voluntarily and any decisions the parent makes in filling out the form prescribed under division (A)(1) of section 3107.083 of the Revised Code are made voluntarily.

(C) A juvenile court may approve an agreement entered into under division (B)(1) of section 5103.15 of the Revised Code between a public children services agency or private child placing agency and the parents of a child who is less than six months of age and will be, if adopted, an adopted person as defined in section 3107.45 of the Revised Code without the parents personally appearing before the court if both parents do all of the following:

(1) Enter into the agreement with the agency;

(2) Sign the component of the form prescribed under division (A)(1)(a) of section 3107.083 of the Revised Code;

(3) Check either the "yes" or "no" space provided on the component of the form prescribed under division (A)(1)(b) of section 3107.083 of the Revised Code and sign that component.

At the time the parents sign the components of the form prescribed under divisions (A)(1)(a) and (b) of section 3107.083 of the Revised Code, the mother shall complete and sign the component of the form prescribed under division (A)(1)(c) of that section and the agency shall provide the parents the opportunity to sign, if they choose to do so, the components of the form prescribed under divisions (A)(1)(d), (e), and (f) of that section. Not later than two business days after the parents enter into the agreements and sign the components of the form required to be signed and any discretionary components the parents choose to sign, the agency shall file the agreements and forms with the court. The agency shall give the parents a copy of the agreements and forms. At the time the agency files the agreements and forms with the court, the agency also shall file with the court all other documents the director of job and family services requires by rules adopted under division (D) of section 3107.083 of the Revised Code to be filed with the court. The court and agency shall keep a copy of the agreements, forms, and documents in the court and attorney's records. The agency shall file a copy of the agreements, forms, and documents with the probate court with which a petition to adopt the child who is the subject of the agreement is filed.

(D) Except as provided in division (E) of this section, a parent of a minor, who will be, if adopted, an adopted person as defined in section 3107.39 of the Revised Code, shall do all of the following as a condition of a juvenile court approving the parent's agreement with a public children services agency or private child placing agency under division (B)(1) of section 5103.15 of the Revised Code:

(1) Appear personally before the court;

(2) Sign the component of the form prescribed under division (B)(1)(a) of section 3107.081 of the Revised Code;

(3) If the parent is the mother, complete and sign the component of the form prescribed under division (B)(1)(b) of section 3107.083 of the Revised Code.

At the time the parent signs the components prescribed under division (B)(1)(a) and (b) of section 3107.081 of the Revised Code, the parent may sign, if the parent chooses to do so, the components of the form prescribed under divisions (B)(1)(c), (d), and (e) of that section. After the parent signs the components required to be signed and any discretionary components the parent chooses to sign, the parent or agency shall file the form and agreement with the court. The court or agency shall give the parent a copy of the form and agreement. The court and agency shall keep a copy of the form and agreement in the court and agency's records. The agency shall file a copy of the form and agreement with the probate court with which a petition to adopt the child who is the subject of the agreement is filed.

The juvenile court shall question the parent to determine that the parent understands the adoption process, the ramifications of entering into a voluntary permanent custody surrender agreement, and each component of the form prescribed under division (B)(1) of section 3107.083 of the Revised Code. The court also shall question the parent to determine that the parent enters into the permanent custody surrender agreement voluntarily and any decisions the parent makes in filling out the form are made voluntarily.

(E) A juvenile court may approve an agreement entered into under division (B)(1) of section 5103.15 of the Revised Code between a public children services agency or private child placing agency and the parent of a child who is less than six months of age and will be, if adopted, an adopted person as defined in section 3107.39 of the Revised Code without the parent personally appearing before the court if the parent does both of the following:

(1) Signs the component of the form prescribed under division (B)(1)(a) of section 3107.083 of the Revised Code;

(2) If the parent is the mother, completes and signs the component of the form prescribed under division (B)(1)(b) of section 3107.083 of the Revised Code.

At the time the parent signs that component, the agency shall provide the parent the opportunity to sign, if the parent chooses to do so, the components of the form prescribed under divisions (B)(1)(c), (d), and (e) of section 3107.083 of the Revised Code. Not later than two business days after the parent enters into the agreement and signs the components of the form required to be signed and any discretionary components the parent chooses to sign, the agency shall file the agreement and form with the court. The agency shall give the parent a copy of the agreement and form. At the time the agency files the agreement and form with the court, the agency also shall file with the court all other documents the director of job and family services requires by rules adopted under division (D) of section 3107.083 of the Revised Code to be filed with the court. The court and agency shall keep a copy of the agreement, form, and documents in the court and agency's records. The agency shall file a copy of the agreement, form, and documents with the probate court with which a petition to adopt the child who is the subject of the agreement is filed.

(1999 H 471, eff. 7–1–00; 1996 H 419, eff. 9–18–96)

Historical and Statutory Notes

Ed. Note: Former 5103.151 amended and recodified as 2151.416 by 1988 S 89, eff. 1–1–89; 1986 H 428; 1980 H 695; 1978 H 832; 1976 H 156.

Library References

Adoption ⟸13, 14.
Infants ⟸203, 210, 222.
Westlaw Topic Nos. 17, 211.
C.J.S. Adoption of Persons § 49 to 50, 88 to 102, 124 to 128.
C.J.S. Infants § 51 to 52, 57, 62 to 85.
Baldwin's Ohio Legislative Service, 1996 H 419—LSC Analysis, 3/L–336

5103.152 Assessor's meeting with birth parent prior to parent's consenting to adoption

Not less than seventy-two hours before a public children services agency or private child placing agency enters into an agreement with a parent under division (B) of section 5103.15 of the Revised Code, an assessor shall meet in person with the parent and do both of the following:

(A) Provide the parent with a copy of the written materials about adoption prepared by the department of job and family services under division (C) of section 3107.083 of the Revised Code, discuss with the parent the adoption process and ramifications of a parent entering into a voluntary permanent custody surrender agreement, and provide the parent the opportunity to review the materials and ask questions about the materials, discussion, and related matters.

(B) Unless the child who is the subject of the agreement, if adopted, will be an adopted person as defined in section 3107.39 of the Revised Code, inform the parent that the parent's child and the adoptive parent may receive, in accordance with section

3107.47 of the Revised Code, identifying information about the parent that is contained in the child's adoption file maintained by the department of health unless the parent checks the "no" space provided on the component of the form prescribed under division (A)(1)(b) of section 3107.083 of the Revised Code or signs and has filed with the department a denial of release form prescribed under section 3107.50 of the Revised Code.

(1999 H 471, eff. 7-1-00; 1996 H 419, eff. 9-18-96)

Historical and Statutory Notes

Ed. Note: Former 5103.152 amended and recodified as 5103.154 by 1996 H 419, eff. 9-18-96; 1994 S 226, eff. 1-1-95; 1991 H 298, eff. 7-26-91; 1986 H 428; 1980 H 378; 1976 H 156.

Library References

Adoption ⚖17.1.
Infants ⚖222.
Westlaw Topic Nos. 17, 211.
C.J.S. Adoption of Persons § 133, 140.
C.J.S. Infants § 57, 69 to 85.

Baldwin's Ohio Legislative Service, 1996 H 419—LSC Analysis, 3/L-336

5103.16 Placing of children; assumption of responsibility for expenses

(A) Pursuant to section 5103.18 of the Revised Code and except as otherwise provided in this section, no child shall be placed or accepted for placement under any written or oral agreement or understanding that transfers or surrenders the legal rights, powers, or duties of the legal parent, parents, or guardian of the child into the temporary or permanent custody of any association or institution that is not certified by the department of job and family services under section 5103.03 of the Revised Code, without the written consent of the office in the department that oversees the interstate compact on placement of children established under section 5103.20 of the Revised Code, or by a commitment of a juvenile court, or by a commitment of a probate court as provided in this section. A child may be placed temporarily without written consent or court commitment with persons related by blood or marriage or in a legally licensed boarding home.

(B)(1) Associations and institutions certified under section 5103.03 of the Revised Code for the purpose of placing children in free foster homes or for legal adoption shall keep a record of the temporary and permanent surrenders of children. This record shall be available for separate statistics, which shall include a copy of an official birth record and all information concerning the social, mental, and medical history of the children that will aid in an intelligent disposition of the children in case that becomes necessary because the parents or guardians fail or are unable to reassume custody.

(2) No child placed on a temporary surrender with an association or institution shall be placed permanently in a foster home or for legal adoption. All surrendered children who are placed permanently in foster homes or for adoption shall have been permanently surrendered, and a copy of the permanent surrender shall be a part of the separate record kept by the association or institution.

(C) Any agreement or understanding to transfer or surrender the legal rights, powers, or duties of the legal parent or parents and place a child with a person seeking to adopt the child under this section shall be construed to contain a promise by the person seeking to adopt the child to pay the expenses listed in divisions (C)(1), (2), and (4) of section 3107.055 of the Revised Code and, if the person seeking to adopt the child refuses to accept placement of the child, to pay the temporary costs of routine maintenance and medical care for the child in a hospital, foster home, or other appropriate place for up to thirty days or until other custody is established for the child, as provided by law, whichever is less.

(D) No child shall be placed or received for adoption or with intent to adopt unless placement is made by a public children services agency, an institution or association that is certified by the department of job and family services under section 5103.03 of the Revised Code to place children for adoption, or custodians in another state or foreign country, or unless all of the following criteria are met:

(1) Prior to the placement and receiving of the child, the parent or parents of the child personally have applied to, and appeared before, the probate court of the county in which the parent or parents reside, or in which the person seeking to adopt the child resides, for approval of the proposed placement specified in the application and have signed and filed with the court a written statement showing that the parent or parents are aware of their right to contest the decree of adoption subject to the limitations of section 3107.16 of the Revised Code;

(2) The court ordered an independent home study of the proposed placement to be conducted as provided in section 3107.031 of the Revised Code, and after completion of the home study, the court determined that the proposed placement is in the best interest of the child;

(3) The court has approved of record the proposed placement.

In determining whether a custodian has authority to place children for adoption under the laws of a foreign country, the probate court shall determine whether the child has been released for adoption pursuant to the laws of the country in which the child resides, and if the release is in a form that satisfies the requirements of the immigration and naturalization service of the United States department of justice for purposes of immigration to this country pursuant to section 101(b)(1)(F) of the "Immigration and Nationality Act," 75 Stat. 650 (1961), 8 U.S.C. 1101 (b)(1)(F), as amended or reenacted.

If the parent or parents of the child are deceased or have abandoned the child, as determined under division (A) of section 3107.07 of the Revised Code, the application for approval of the proposed adoptive placement may be brought by the relative seeking to adopt the child, or by the department, board, or organization not otherwise having legal authority to place the orphaned or abandoned child for adoption, but having legal custody of the orphaned or abandoned child, in the probate court of the county in which the child is a resident, or in which the department, board, or organization is located, or where the person or persons with whom the child is to be placed reside. Unless the parent, parents, or guardian of the person of the child personally have appeared before the court and applied for approval of the placement, notice of the hearing on the application shall be served on the parent, parents, or guardian.

The consent to placement, surrender, or adoption executed by a minor parent before a judge of the probate court or an authorized deputy or referee of the court, whether executed within or outside the confines of the court, is as valid as though executed by an adult. A consent given as above before an employee of a children services agency that is licensed as provided by law, is equally effective, if the consent also is accompanied by an affidavit executed by the witnessing employee or employees to the effect that the legal rights of the parents have been fully explained to the parents, prior to the execution of any consent, and that the action was done after the birth of the child.

If the court approves a placement, the prospective adoptive parent with whom the child is placed has care, custody, and control of the child pending further order of the court.

(E) This section does not apply to an adoption by a stepparent, a grandparent, or a guardian.

(2006 S 238, eff. 9-21-06; 1999 H 471, eff. 7-1-00; 1999 H 59, eff. 10-29-99; 1996 H 274, eff. 9-18-96; 1996 H 419, eff. 9-18-96; 1988 H 790, eff. 3-16-89; 1988 H 708; 1986 H 428, S 248, § 1, 3; 1978 H 832; 1976 H 156; 1975 S 145; 1969 S 49; 132 v H 1; 131 v H 287; 129 v 1776; 1953 H 1; GC 1352-13)

Uncodified Law

1986 S 248, § 5, eff. 12-17-86, reads:

Division (D)(2) of section 5103.16 of the Revised Code, as enacted by this act, does not mean and shall not be construed to mean either of the following:

(A) That, prior to the effective date of this act, the placement and receipt for adoption or with intent to adopt of foreign children was not permissible by residents of this state under section 5103.16 of the Revised Code;

(B) That any placement for adoption or with intent to adopt that occurred at any time on or after January 1, 1983, and prior to the effective date of this act, that involved a child or children who were residents of a foreign country and a person or persons who were residing in this state, and that, consistent with section 5103.16 of the Revised Code as it existed immediately prior to the effective date of this act, was made by custodians in a foreign country, was not authorized under the law of this state.

Historical and Statutory Notes

Pre-1953 H 1 Amendments: 110 v 265

Library References

Infants ⇔222, 226.
Westlaw Topic No. 211.
C.J.S. Adoption of Persons § 10 to 12.
C.J.S. Infants § 57, 69 to 85.

5103.162 Immunity from liability

(A) Except as provided in division (B) of this section, a foster caregiver shall be immune from liability in a civil action to recover damages for injury, death, or loss to person or property allegedly caused by an act or omission in connection with a power, duty, responsibility, or authorization under this chapter or under rules adopted under authority of this chapter.

(B) The immunity described in division (A) of this section does not apply to a foster caregiver if, in relation to the act or omission in question, any of the following applies:

(1) The act or omission was manifestly outside the scope of the foster caregiver's power, duty, responsibility, or authorization.

(2) The act or omission was with malicious purpose, in bad faith, or in a wanton or reckless manner.

(3) Liability for the act or omission is expressly imposed by a section of the Revised Code.

(2006 S 238, eff. 9-21-06)

5103.17 Advertising; enforcement

Subject to section 5103.16 of the Revised Code, no person or government entity, other than a private child placing agency or private noncustodial agency certified by the department of job and family services under section 5103.03 of the Revised Code or a public children services agency, shall advertise that the person or government entity will adopt children or place them in foster homes, hold out inducements to parents to part with their offspring, or in any manner knowingly become a party to the separation of a child from the child's parents or guardians, except through a juvenile court or probate court commitment.

If the department of job and family services has reasonable cause to believe a violation of this section has been committed, the department shall notify the attorney general or the county prosecutor, city attorney, village solicitor, or other chief legal officer of the political subdivision in which the violation has allegedly occurred. On receipt of the notification, the attorney general, county prosecutor, city attorney, village solicitor, or other chief legal officer shall take action to enforce this section through injunctive relief or criminal charge.

(1999 H 471, eff. 7-1-00; 1996 H 419, eff. 9-18-96; 1986 S 248, eff. 12-17-86; 129 v 1776; 1953 H 1; GC 1352-14, 12789-1)

Historical and Statutory Notes

Pre-1953 H 1 Amendments: 110 v 265

Library References

Adoption ⇔3.
Infants ⇔222, 226.
Westlaw Topic Nos. 17, 211.
C.J.S. Adoption of Persons § 6 to 12.
C.J.S. Infants § 57, 69 to 85.

INTERSTATE COMPACT ON THE PLACEMENT OF CHILDREN

5103.20 Interstate compact for the placement of children

The interstate compact for the placement of children is hereby enacted into law and entered into with all other jurisdictions legally joining therein in form substantially as follows:

ARTICLE I.

PURPOSE

The purpose of this compact is to:

(A) Provide a process through which children subject to this compact are placed in safe and suitable homes in a timely manner.

(B) Facilitate ongoing supervision of a placement, the delivery of services, and communication between the states.

(C) Provide operating procedures that will ensure that children are placed in safe and suitable homes in a timely manner.

(D) Provide for the promulgation and enforcement of administrative rules implementing the provisions of this compact and regulating the covered activities of the member states.

(E) Provide for uniform data collection and information sharing between member states under this compact.

(F) Promote coordination between this compact, the Interstate Compacts for Juveniles, the Interstate Compact on Adoption and Medical Assistance and other compacts affecting the placement of and which provide services to children otherwise subject to this compact.

(G) Provide for a state's continuing legal jurisdiction and responsibility for placement and care of a child that it would have had if the placement were intrastate.

(H) Provide for the promulgation of guidelines, in collaboration with Indian tribes, for interstate cases involving Indian children as is or may be permitted by federal law.

ARTICLE II.

DEFINITIONS

As used in this compact:

(A) "Approved placement" means the receiving state has determined after an assessment that the placement is both safe and suitable for the child and is in compliance with the applicable laws of the receiving state governing the placement of children therein.

(B) "Assessment" means an evaluation of a prospective placement to determine whether the placement meets the individualized needs of the child, including but not limited to the child's safety and stability, health and well-being, and mental, emotional, and physical development.

(C) "Child" means an individual who has not attained the age of eighteen (18).

(D) "Default" means the failure of a member state to perform the obligations or responsibilities imposed upon it by this compact, the bylaws or rules of the Interstate Commission.

(E) "Indian tribe" means any Indian tribe, band, nation, or other organized group or community of Indians recognized as eligible for services provided to Indians by the Secretary of the Interior because of their status as Indians, including any Alaskan native village as defined in section 3 (c) of the Alaska Native Claims Settlement Act at 43 USC section 1602(c).

(F) "Interstate Commission for the Placement of Children" means the commission that is created under Article VIII of this compact and which is generally referred to as the Interstate Commission.

(G) "Jurisdiction" means the power and authority of a court to hear and decide matters.

(H) "Member state" means a state that has enacted this compact.

(I) "Non–custodial parent" means a person who, at the time of the commencement of court proceedings in the sending state, does not have sole legal custody of the child or has joint legal custody of a child, and who is not the subject of allegations or findings of child abuse or neglect.

(J) "Non–member state" means a state which has not enacted this compact.

(K) "Notice of residential placement" means information regarding a placement into a residential facility provided to the receiving state including, but not limited to the name, date, and place of birth of the child, the identity and address of the parent or legal guardian, evidence of authority to make the placement, and the name and address of the facility in which the child will be placed. Notice of residential placement shall also include information regarding a discharge and any unauthorized absence from the facility.

(L) "Placement" means the act by a public or private child placing agency intended to arrange for the care or custody of a child in another state.

(M) "Private child placing agency" means any private corporation, agency, foundation, institution, or charitable organization, or any private person or attorney that facilitates, causes, or is involved in the placement of a child from one state to another and that is not an instrumentality of the state or acting under color of state law.

(N) "Provisional placement" means that the receiving state has determined that the proposed placement is safe and suitable, and, to the extent allowable, the receiving state has temporarily waived its standards or requirements otherwise applicable to prospective foster or adoptive parents so as to not delay the placement. Completion of the receiving state requirements regarding training for prospective foster or adoptive parents shall not delay an otherwise safe and suitable placement.

(O) "Public child placing agency" means any government child welfare agency or child protection agency or a private entity under contract with such an agency, regardless of whether they act on behalf of a state, county, municipality, or other governmental unit and which facilitates, causes, or is involved in the placement of a child from one state to another.

(P) "Receiving state" means the state to which a child is sent, brought, or caused to be sent or brought.

(Q) "Relative" means someone who is related to the child as a parent, step-parent, sibling by half or whole blood or by adoption, grandparent, aunt, uncle, or first cousin or a non-relative with such significant ties to the child that they may be regarded as relatives as determined by the court in the sending state.

(R) "Residential Facility" means a facility providing a level of care that is sufficient to substitute for parental responsibility or foster care, and is beyond what is needed for assessment or treatment of an acute condition. For purposes of the compact, residential facilities do not include institutions primarily educational in character, hospitals, or other medical facilities.

(S) "Rule" means a written directive, mandate, standard, or principle issued by the Interstate Commission promulgated pursuant to Article XI of this compact that is of general applicability and that implements, interprets or prescribes a policy or provision of the compact. "Rule" has the force and effect of statutory law in a member state, and includes the amendment, repeal, or suspension of an existing rule.

(T) "Sending state" means the state from which the placement of a child is initiated.

(U) "Service member's permanent duty station" means the military installation where an active duty Armed Services member is currently assigned and is physically located under competent orders that do not specify the duty as temporary.

(V) "Service member's state of local residence" means the state in which the active duty Armed Services member is considered a resident for tax and voting purposes.

(W) "State" means a state of the United States, the District of Columbia, the Commonwealth of Puerto Rico, the U.S. Virgin Islands, Guam, American Samoa, the Northern Marianas Islands and any other territory of the United States.

(X) "State court" means a judicial body of a state that is vested by law with responsibility for adjudicating cases involving abuse, neglect, deprivation, delinquency or status offenses of individuals who have not attained the age of eighteen (18).

(Y) "Supervision" means monitoring provided by the receiving state once a child has been placed in a receiving state pursuant to this compact.

ARTICLE III.

APPLICABILITY

(A) Except as otherwise provided in Article III, Section B, this compact shall apply to:

(1) The interstate placement of a child subject to ongoing court jurisdiction in the sending state, due to allegations or findings that the child has been abused, neglected, or deprived as defined by the laws of the sending state, provided, however, that the placement of such a child into a residential facility shall only require notice of residential placement to the receiving state prior to placement.

(2) The interstate placement of a child adjudicated delinquent or unmanageable based on the laws of the sending state and subject to ongoing court jurisdiction of the sending state if:

(a) The child is being placed in a residential facility in another member state and is not covered under another compact; or

(b) The child is being placed in another member state and the determination of safety and suitability of the placement and services required is not provided through another compact.

(3) The interstate placement of any child by a public child placing agency or private child placing agency as defined in this compact as a preliminary step to a possible adoption.

(B) The provisions of this compact shall not apply to:

(1) The interstate placement of a child with a non-relative in a receiving state by a parent with the legal authority to make such a placement provided, however, that the placement is not intended to effectuate an adoption.

(2) The interstate placement of a child by one relative with the lawful authority to make such a placement directly with a relative in a receiving state.

(3) The placement of a child, not subject to Article III, Section A, into a residential facility by his parent.

(4) The placement of a child with a non-custodial parent provided that:

(a) The non-custodial parent proves to the satisfaction of a court in the sending state a substantial relationship with the child; and

(b) The court in the sending state makes a written finding that placement with the non-custodial parent is in the best interests of the child; and

(c) The court in the sending state dismisses its jurisdiction over the child's case.

(5) A child entering the United States from a foreign country for the purpose of adoption or leaving the United States to go to a foreign country for the purpose of adoption in that country.

(6) Cases in which a U.S. citizen child living overseas with his family, at least one of whom is in the U.S. Armed Services, and who is stationed overseas, is removed and placed in a state.

(7) The sending of a child by a public child placing agency or a private child placing agency for a visit as defined by the rules of the Interstate Commission.

(C) For purposes of determining the applicability of this compact to the placement of a child with a family in the Armed Services, the public child placing agency or private child placing agency may choose the state of the service member's permanent duty station or the service member's declared legal residence.

(D) Nothing in this compact shall be construed to prohibit the concurrent application of the provisions of this compact with other applicable interstate compacts including the Interstate Compact for Juveniles and the Interstate Compact on Adoption and Medical Assistance. The Interstate Commission may in cooperation with other interstate compact commissions having responsibility for the interstate movement, placement or transfer of children, promulgate like rules to ensure the coordination of services, timely placement of children, and the reduction of unnecessary or duplicative administrative or procedural requirements.

ARTICLE IV.

JURISDICTION

(A) The sending state shall retain jurisdiction over a child with respect to all matters of custody and disposition of the child which it would have had if the child had remained in the sending state. Such jurisdiction shall also include the power to order the return of the child to the sending state.

(B) When an issue of child protection or custody is brought before a court in the receiving state, such court shall confer with the court of the sending state to determine the most appropriate forum for adjudication.

(C) In accordance with its own laws, the court in the sending state shall have authority to terminate its jurisdiction if:

(1) The child is reunified with the parent in the receiving state who is the subject of allegations or findings of abuse or neglect, only with the concurrence of the public child placing agency in the receiving state; or

(2) The child is adopted; or

(3) The child reaches the age of majority under the laws of the sending state; or

(4) The child achieves legal independence pursuant to the laws of the sending state; or

(5) A guardianship is created by a court in the receiving state with the concurrence of the court in the sending state; or

(6) An Indian tribe has petitioned for and received jurisdiction from the court in the sending state; or

(7) The public child placing agency of the sending state requests termination and has obtained the concurrence of the public child placing agency in the receiving the state.

(D) When a sending state court terminates its jurisdiction, the receiving state child placing agency shall be notified.

(E) Nothing in this article shall defeat a claim of jurisdiction by a receiving state court sufficient to deal with an act of truancy, delinquency, crime or behavior involving a child as defined by the laws of the receiving state committed by the child in the receiving state which would be a violation of its laws.

(F) Nothing in this article shall limit the receiving state's ability to take emergency jurisdiction for the protection of the child.

ARTICLE V.

ASSESSMENTS

(A) Prior to sending, bringing, or causing a child to be sent or brought into a receiving state, the public child placing agency shall provide a written request for assessment to the receiving state.

(B) Prior to the sending, bringing, or causing a child to be sent or brought into a receiving state, the private child placing agency shall:

(1) Provide evidence that the applicable laws of the sending state have been complied with; and

(2) Certification that the consent or relinquishment is in compliance with applicable law of the birth parent's state of residence or, where permitted, the laws of the state of where the finalization of the adoption will occur; and

(3) Request through the public child placing agency in the sending state an assessment to be conducted in the receiving state; and

(4) Upon completion of the assessment, obtain the approval of the public child placing agency in the receiving state.

(C) The procedures for making and the request for an assessment shall contain all information and be in such form as provided for in the rules of the Interstate Commission.

(D) Upon receipt of a request from the public child welfare agency of the sending state, the receiving state shall initiate an assessment of the proposed placement to determine its safety and suitability. If the proposed placement is a placement with a relative, the public child placing agency of the sending state may request a determination of whether the placement qualifies as a provisional placement.

(E) The public child placing agency in the receiving state may request from the public child placing agency or the private child placing agency in the sending state, and shall be entitled to receive supporting or additional information necessary to complete the assessment.

(F) The public child placing agency in the receiving state shall complete or arrange for the completion of the assessment within the timeframes established by the rules of the Interstate Commission.

(G) The Interstate Commission may develop uniform standards for the assessment of the safety and suitability of interstate placements.

ARTICLE VI.

PLACEMENT AUTHORITY

(A) Except as provided in Article VI, Section C, no child subject to this compact shall be placed into a receiving state until approval for such placement is obtained.

(B) If the public child placing agency in the receiving state does not approve the proposed placement then the child shall not be placed. The receiving state shall provide written documentation of any such determination in accordance with the rules promulgated by the Interstate Commission. Such determination is not subject to judicial review in the sending state.

(C) If the proposed placement is not approved, any interested party shall have standing to seek an administrative review of the receiving state's determination.

(1) The administrative review and any further judicial review associated with the determination shall be conducted in the receiving state pursuant to its applicable administrative procedures.

(2) If a determination not to approve the placement of the child in the receiving state is overturned upon review, the placement shall be deemed approved, provided however that all administrative or judicial remedies have been exhausted or the time for such remedies has passed.

ARTICLE VII.

STATE RESPONSIBILITY

(A) For the interstate placement of a child made by a public child placing agency or state court:

(1) The public child placing agency in the sending state shall have financial responsibility for:

(a) The ongoing support and maintenance for the child during the period of the placement, unless otherwise provided for in the receiving state; and

(b) As determined by the public child placing agency in the sending state, services for the child beyond the public services for which the child is eligible in the receiving state.

(2) The receiving state shall only have financial responsibility for:

(a) Any assessment conducted by the receiving state; and

(b) Supervision conducted by the receiving state at the level necessary to support the placement as agreed upon by the public child placing agencies of the receiving and sending state.

(3) Nothing in this provision shall prohibit public child placing agencies in the sending state from entering into agreements with licensed agencies or persons in the receiving state to conduct assessments and provide supervision.

(B) For the placement of a child by a private child placing agency preliminary to a possible adoption, the private child placing agency shall be:

(1) Legally responsible for the child during the period of placement as provided for in the law of the sending state until the finalization of the adoption.

(2) Financially responsible for the child absent a contractual agreement to the contrary.

(C) A private child placing agency shall be responsible for any assessment conducted in the receiving state and any supervision conducted by the receiving state at the level required by the laws of the receiving state or the rules of the Interstate Commission.

(D) The public child placing agency in the receiving state shall provide timely assessments, as provided for in the rules of the Interstate Commission.

(E) The public child placing agency in the receiving state shall provide, or arrange for the provision of, supervision and services for the child, including timely reports, during the period of the placement.

(F) Nothing in this compact shall be construed as to limit the authority of the public child placing agency in the receiving state from contracting with a licensed agency or person in the receiving state for an assessment or the provision of supervision or services for the child or otherwise authorizing the provision of supervision or services by a licensed agency during the period of placement.

(G) Each member state shall provide for coordination among its branches of government concerning the state's participation in, and compliance with, the compact and Interstate Commission activities, through the creation of an advisory council or use of an existing body or board.

(H) Each member state shall establish a central state compact office, which shall be responsible for state compliance with the compact and the rules of the Interstate Commission.

(I) The public child placing agency in the sending state shall oversee compliance with the provisions of the Indian Child Welfare Act (25 USC 1901 et seq.) for placements subject to the provisions of this compact, prior to placement.

(J) With the consent of the Interstate Commission, states may enter into limited agreements that facilitate the timely assessment and provision of services and supervisions of placements under this compact.

ARTICLE VIII.

INTERSTATE COMMISSION FOR THE PLACEMENT OF CHILDREN

The member states hereby establish, by way of this compact, a commission known as the "Interstate Commission for the Placement of Children." The activities of the Interstate Commission are the formation of public policy and are a discretionary state function. The Interstate Commission shall:

(A) Be joint commission of the member states and shall have the responsibilities, powers and duties set forth herein, and such additional powers as may be conferred upon it by subsequent concurrent action of the respective legislatures of the member states.

(B) Consist of one commissioner from each member state who shall be appointed by the executive head of the state human services administration with ultimate responsibility for the child welfare program. The appointed commissioner shall have the legal authority to vote on policy related matters governed by this compact binding the state.

(1) Each member state represented at a meeting of the Interstate Commission is entitled to one vote.

(2) A majority of the member states shall constitute a quorum for the transaction of business, unless a larger quorum is required by the bylaws of the Interstate Commission.

(3) A representative shall not delegate a vote to another member state.

(4) A representative may delegate voting authority to another person from their state for a specified meeting.

(C) In addition to the commissioners of each member state, the Interstate Commission shall include persons who are members of interested organizations as defined in the bylaws or rules of the Interstate Commission. Such members shall be ex officio and shall not be entitled to vote on any matter before the Interstate Commission.

(D) Establish an executive committee which shall have the authority to administer the day-to-day operations and administration of the Interstate Commission. It shall not have the power to engage in rulemaking.

ARTICLE IX.

POWERS AND DUTIES OF THE INTERSTATE COMMISSION

The Interstate Commission shall have the following powers:

(A) To promulgate rules and take all necessary actions to effect the goals, purposes, and obligations as enumerated in this compact.

(B) To provide for dispute resolution among member states.

(C) To issue, upon request of a member state, advisory opinions concerning the meaning or interpretation of the interstate compact, its bylaws, rules, or actions.

(D) To enforce compliance with this compact or the bylaws or rules of the Interstate Commission pursuant to Article XII.

(E) Collect standardized data concerning the interstate placement of children subject to this compact as directed through its rules which shall specify the data to be collected, the means of collection, and data exchange and reporting requirements.

(F) To establish and maintain offices as may be necessary for the transacting of its business.

(G) To purchase and maintain insurance and bonds.

(H) To hire or contract for services of personnel or consultants as necessary to carry out its functions under the compact and establish personnel qualification policies, and rates of compensation.

(I) To establish and appoint committees and officers including, but not limited to, an executive committee as required by Article X.

(J) To accept any and all donations and grants of money, equipment, supplies, materials, and services, and to receive, utilize, and dispose thereof.

(K) To lease, purchase, accept contributions or donations of, or otherwise to own, hold, improve or use any property, real, personal, or mixed.

(L) To sell, convey, mortgage, pledge, lease, exchange, abandon, or otherwise dispose of any property, real, personal, or mixed.

(M) To establish a budget and make expenditures.

(N) To adopt a seal and bylaws governing the management and operation of the Interstate Commission.

(O) To report annually to the legislatures, governors, the judiciary, and state advisory councils of the member states concerning the activities of the Interstate Commission during the preceding year. Such reports shall also include any recommendations that may have been adopted by the Interstate Commission.

(P) To coordinate and provide education, training, and public awareness regarding the interstate movement of children for officials involved in such activity.

(Q) To maintain books and records in accordance with the bylaws of the Interstate Commission.

(R) To perform such functions as may be necessary or appropriate to achieve the purposes of this compact.

ARTICLE X.

ORGANIZATION AND OPERATION OF THE INTERSTATE COMMISSION

(A) Bylaws:

(1) Within 12 months after the first Interstate Commission meeting, the Interstate Commission shall adopt bylaws to govern its conduct as may be necessary or appropriate to carry out the purposes of the compact.

(2) The Interstate Commission's bylaws and rules shall establish conditions and procedures under which the Interstate Commission shall make its information and official records available to the public for inspection or copying. The Interstate Commission may exempt from disclosure information or official records to the extent they would adversely affect personal privacy rights or proprietary interests.

(B) Meetings:

(1) The Interstate Commission shall meet at least once each calendar year. The chairperson may call additional meetings and, upon the request of a simple majority of the member states shall call additional meetings.

(2) Public notice shall be given by the Interstate Commission of all meetings and all meetings shall be open to the public, except as set forth in the rules or as otherwise provided in the compact. The Interstate Commission and its committees may close a meeting, or portion thereof, where it determines by two-thirds vote that an open meeting would be likely to:

(a) Relate solely to the Interstate Commission's internal personnel practices and procedures; or

(b) Disclose matters specifically exempted from disclosure by federal law; or

(c) Disclose financial or commercial information which is privileged, proprietary, or confidential in nature; or

(d) Involve accusing a person of a crime, or formally censuring a person; or

(e) Disclose information of a personal nature where disclosure would constitute a clearly unwarranted invasion of personal privacy or physically endanger one or more persons; or

(f) Disclose investigative records compiled for law enforcement purposes; or

(g) Specifically relate to the Interstate Commission's participation in a civil action or other legal proceeding.

(3) For a meeting, or portion of a meeting, closed pursuant to this provision, the Interstate Commission's legal counsel or designee shall certify that the meeting may be closed and shall reference each relevant exemption provision. The Interstate Commission shall keep minutes which shall fully and clearly describe all matters discussed in a meeting and shall provide a full and accurate summary of actions taken, and the reasons therefore, including a description of the views expressed and the record of a roll call vote. All documents considered in connection with an action shall be identified in such minutes. All minutes and documents of a closed meeting shall remain under

seal, subject to release by a majority vote of the Interstate Commission or by court order.

(4) The bylaws may provide for meetings of the Interstate Commission to be conducted by telecommunication or other electronic communication.

(C) Officers and Staff:

(1) The Interstate Commission may, through its executive committee, appoint or retain a staff director for such period, upon such terms and conditions and for such compensation as the Interstate Commission may deem appropriate. The staff director shall serve as secretary to the Interstate Commission, but shall not have a vote. The staff director may hire and supervise such other staff as may be authorized by the Interstate Commission.

(2) The Interstate Commission shall elect, from among its members, a chairperson and a vice chairperson of the executive committee and other necessary officers, each of whom shall have such authority and duties as may be specified in the bylaws.

(D) Qualified Immunity, Defense and Indemnification:

(1) The Interstate Commission's staff director and its employees shall be immune from suit and liability, either personally or in their official capacity, for a claim for damage to or loss of property or personal injury or other civil liability caused by or arising out of or relating to an actual or alleged act, error, or omission that occurred, or that such person had a reasonable basis for believing occurred within the scope of Commission employment, duties, or responsibilities; provided, that such person shall not be protected from suit or liability for damage, loss, injury, or liability caused by a criminal act or the intentional or willful and wanton misconduct of such person.

(a) The liability of the Interstate Commission's staff director and employees or Interstate Commission representatives, acting within the scope of such person's employment or duties for acts, errors, or omissions occurring within such person's state may not exceed the limits of liability set forth under the Constitution and laws of that state for state officials, employees, and agents. The Interstate Commission is considered to be an instrumentality of the states for the purposes of any such action. Nothing in this subsection shall be construed to protect such person from suit or liability for damage, loss, injury, or liability caused by a criminal act or the intentional or willful and wanton misconduct of such person.

(b) The Interstate Commission shall defend the staff director and its employees and, subject to the approval of the Attorney General or other appropriate legal counsel of the member state shall defend the commissioner of a member state in a civil action seeking to impose liability arising out of an actual or alleged act, error or omission that occurred within the scope of Interstate Commission employment, duties or responsibilities, or that the defendant had a reasonable basis for believing occurred within the scope of Interstate Commission employment, duties, or responsibilities, provided that the actual or alleged act, error, or omission did not result from intentional or willful and wanton misconduct on the part of such person.

(c) To the extent not covered by the state involved, member state, or the Interstate Commission, the representatives or employees of the Interstate Commission shall be held harmless in the amount of a settlement or judgment, including attorney's fees and costs, obtained against such persons arising out of an actual or alleged act, error, or omission that occurred within the scope of Interstate Commission employment, duties, or responsibilities, or that such persons had a reasonable basis for believing occurred within the scope of the Interstate Commission employment, duties, or responsibilities, provided that the actual or alleged act, error, or omission did not result from intentional or willful and wanton misconduct on the part of such persons.

ARTICLE XI.

RULEMAKING FUNCTIONS OF THE INTERSTATE COMMISSION

(A) The Interstate Commission shall promulgate and publish rules in order to effectively and efficiently achieve the purposes of the compact.

(B) Rulemaking shall occur pursuant to the criteria set forth in this article and the bylaws and rules adopted pursuant thereto. Such rulemaking shall substantially conform to the principles of the "Model State Administrative Procedures Act," 1981 Act, Uniform Laws Annotated, Vol. 15, p.1 (2000), or such other administrative procedure acts as the Interstate Commission deems appropriate consistent with due process requirements under the United States Constitution as now or hereafter interpreted by the U.S. Supreme Court. All rules and amendments shall become binding as of the date specified, as published with the final version of the rule as approved by the Interstate Commission.

(C) When promulgating a rule, the Interstate Commission shall, at a minimum:

(1) Publish the proposed rule's entire text stating the reason(s) for that proposed rule; and

(2) Allow and invite any and all persons to submit written data, facts, opinions and arguments, which information shall be added to the record, and be made publicly available; and

(3) Promulgate a final rule and its effective date, if appropriate, based on input from state or local officials, or interested parties.

(D) Rules promulgated by the Interstate Commission shall have the force and effect of statutory law and shall supersede any state law, rule or regulation to the extent of any conflict.

(E) Not later than 60 days after a rule is promulgated, an interested person may file a petition in the U.S. District Court for the District of Columbia or in the Federal District Court where the Interstate Commission's principal office is located for judicial review of such rule. If the court finds that the Interstate Commission's action is not supported by substantial evidence in the rulemaking record, the court shall hold the rule unlawful and set it aside.

(F) If a majority of the legislatures of the member states rejects a rule, those states may by enactment of a statute or resolution in the same manner used to adopt the compact cause that such rule shall have no further force and effect in any member state.

(G) The existing rules governing the operation of the Interstate Company on the Placement of Children superseded by this act shall be null and void no less than 12, but no more than 24 months after the first meeting of the Interstate Commission created hereunder, as determined by the members during the first meeting.

(H) Within the first 12 months of operation, the Interstate Commission shall promulgate rules addressing the following:

(1) Transition rules;

(2) Forms and procedures;

(3) Time lines;

(4) Data collection and reporting;

(5) Rulemaking;

(6) Visitation;

(7) Progress reports/supervision;

(8) Sharing of information/confidentiality;

(9) Financing of the Interstate Commission;

(10) Mediation, arbitration and dispute resolution;

(11) Education, training and technical assistance;

(12) Enforcement;

(13) Coordination with other interstate compacts.

(I) Upon determination by a majority of the members of the Interstate Commission that an emergency exists:

(1) The Interstate Commission may promulgate an emergency rule only if it is required to:

(a) Protect the children covered by this compact from an imminent threat to their health, safety and well-being; or

(b) Prevent loss of federal or state funds; or

(c) Meet a deadline for the promulgation of an administrative rule required by federal law.

(2) An emergency rule shall become effective immediately upon adoption, provided that the usual rulemaking procedures provided hereunder shall be retroactively applied to said rule as soon as reasonably possible, but no later than 90 days after the effective date of the emergency rule.

(3) An emergency rule shall be promulgated as provided for in the rules of the Interstate Commission.

ARTICLE XII.

OVERSIGHT, DISPUTE RESOLUTION, ENFORCEMENT

(A) Oversight:

(1) The Interstate Commission shall oversee the administration and operations of the compact.

(2) The executive, legislative and judicial branches of state government in each member state shall enforce this compact and the rules of the Interstate Commission and shall take all actions necessary and appropriate to effectuate the compact's purposes and intent. The compact and its rules shall supercede state law, rules or regulations to the extent of any conflict therewith.

(3) All courts shall take judicial notice of the compact and the rules in any judicial or administrative proceeding in a member state pertaining to the subject matter of this compact.

(4) The Interstate Commission shall be entitled to receive service of process in any action in which the validity of a compact provision or rule is the issue for which a judicial determination has been sought and shall have standing to intervene in any proceedings. Failure to provide service of process to the Interstate Commission shall render any judgment, order or other determination, however so captioned or classified, void as to the Interstate Commission, this compact, its bylaws or rules of the Interstate Commission.

(B) Dispute Resolution:

(1) The Interstate Commission shall attempt, upon the request of a member state, to resolve disputes which are subject to the compact and which may arise among member states and between member and non-member states.

(2) The Interstate Commission shall promulgate a rule providing for both mediation and binding dispute resolution for disputes among compacting states. The costs of such mediation or dispute resolution shall be the responsibility of the parties to the dispute.

(C) Enforcement:

(1) If the Interstate Commission determines that a member state has defaulted in the performance of its obligations or responsibilities under this compact, its bylaws or rules, the Interstate Commission may:

(a) Provide remedial training and specific technical assistance; or

(b) Provide written notice to the defaulting state and other member states, of the nature of the default and the means of curing the default. The Interstate Commission shall specify the conditions by which the defaulting state must cure its default; or

(c) By majority vote of the members, initiate against a defaulting member state legal action in the United States District Court for the District of Columbia or, at the discretion of the Interstate Commission, in the federal district where the Interstate Commission has its principal offices, to enforce compliance with the provisions of the compact, its bylaws or rules. The relief sought may include both injunctive relief and damages. In the event judicial enforcement is necessary the prevailing party shall be awarded all costs of such litigation including reasonable attorney's fees; or

(d) Avail itself of any other remedies available under state law or the regulation of official or professional conduct.

ARTICLE XIII.

FINANCING OF THE COMMISSION

(A) The Interstate Commission shall pay, or provide for the payment of the reasonable expenses of its establishment, organization and ongoing activities.

(B) The Interstate Commission may levy on and collect an annual assessment from each member state to cover the cost of the operations and activities of the Interstate Commission and its staff which must be in a total amount sufficient to cover the Interstate Commission's annual budget as approved by its members each year. The aggregate annual assessment amount shall be allocated based upon a formula to be determined by the Interstate Commission which shall promulgate a rule binding upon all member states.

(C) The Interstate Commission shall not incur obligations of any kind prior to securing the funds adequate to meet the same; nor shall the Interstate Commission pledge the credit of any of the member states, except by and with the authority of the member state.

(D) The Interstate Commission shall keep accurate accounts of all receipts and disbursements. The receipts and disbursements of the Interstate Commission shall be subject to the audit and accounting procedures established under its bylaws. However, all receipts and disbursements of funds handled by the Interstate Commission shall be audited yearly by a certified or licensed public accountant and the report of the audit shall be included in and become part of the annual report of the Interstate Commission.

ARTICLE XIV.

MEMBER STATES, EFFECTIVE DATE AND AMENDMENT

(A) Any state is eligible to become a member state.

(B) The compact shall become effective and binding upon legislative enactment of the compact into law by no less than 35 states. The effective date shall be the later of July 1, 2007 or upon enactment of the compact into law by the 35th state. Thereafter it shall become effective and binding as to any other member state upon enactment of the compact into law by that state. The governors of non-member states or their designees shall be invited to participate in the activities of the Interstate Commission on a non-voting basis prior to adoption of the compact by all states.

(C) The Interstate Commission may propose amendments to the compact for enactment by the member states. No amendment shall become effective and binding on the member states unless and until it is enacted into law by unanimous consent of the member states.

ARTICLE XV.

WITHDRAWAL AND DISSOLUTION

(A) Withdrawal:

(1) Once effective, the compact shall continue in force and remain binding upon each and every member state; provided that a member state may withdraw from the compact specifically repealing the statute which enacted the compact into law.

(2) Withdrawal from this compact shall be by the enactment of a statute repealing the same. The effective date of withdrawal shall be the effective date of the repeal of the statute.

(3) The withdrawing state shall immediately notify the president of the Interstate Commission in writing upon the introduction of legislation repealing this compact in the withdrawing state. The Interstate Commission shall then notify the other member states of the withdrawing state's intent to withdraw.

(4) The withdrawing state is responsible for all assessments, obligations and liabilities incurred through the effective date of withdrawal.

(5) Reinstatement following withdrawal of a member state shall occur upon the withdrawing stated reenacting the compact or upon such later date as determined by the members of the Interstate Commission.

(B) Dissolution of Compact:

(1) This compact shall dissolve effective upon the date of the withdrawal or default of the member state which reduces the membership in the compact to one member state.

(2) Upon the dissolution of this compact, the compact becomes null and void and shall be of no further force or effect, and the business and affairs of the Interstate Commission shall be concluded and surplus funds shall be distributed in accordance with the bylaws.

ARTICLE XVI.

SEVERABILITY AND CONSTRUCTION

(A) The provisions of this compact shall be severable, and if any phrase, clause, sentence or provision is deemed unenforceable, the remaining provisions of the compact shall be enforceable.

(B) The provisions of this compact shall be liberally construed to effectuate its purposes.

(C) Nothing in this compact shall be construed to prohibit the concurrent applicability of other interstate compacts to which the states are members.

ARTICLE XVII.

BINDING EFFECT OF COMPACT AND OTHER LAWS

(A) Other Laws:

(1) Nothing herein prevents the enforcement of any other law of a member state that is not inconsistent with this compact.

(2) All member states' laws conflicting with this compact or its rules are superseded to the extent of the conflict.

(B) Binding Effect of the Compact:

(1) All lawful actions of the Interstate Commission, including all rules and bylaws promulgated by the Interstate Commission, are binding upon the member states.

(2) All agreements between the Interstate Commission and the member states are binding in accordance with their terms.

(3) In the event any provision of the compact exceeds the constitutional limits imposed on the legislature of any member state, such provision shall be ineffective to the extent of the conflict with the constitutional provision in question in that member state.

ARTICLE XVIII.

INDIAN TRIBES

Notwithstanding any other provision in this compact, the Interstate Commission may promulgate guidelines to permit Indian tribes to utilize the compact to achieve any or all of the purposes of the compact as specified in Article I. The Interstate Commission shall make reasonable efforts to consult with Indian tribes in promulgating guidelines to reflect the diverse circumstances of the various Indian tribes.

(2006 S 238, eff. 9–21–06)

Historical and Statutory Notes

Ed. Note: Former RC 5103.20 repealed by 2006 S 238, eff. 9–21–06; 1975 H 247, eff. 1–1–76.

Comparative Laws

Ala.—Code 1975, § 44–2–20 to 44–2–26.
Alaska—AS 47.70.010 to 47.70.080.
Ariz.—A.R.S. § 8-548 to 8-548.07.
Ark.—A.C.A. § 9-29-201 to 9-29-208.
Cal.—West's Ann.Cal.Fam.Code, § 7900 to 7912.
Colo.—West's C.R.S.A. § 24–60–1801 to 24–60–1803.
Conn.—C.G.S.A. § 17a-125 to 17a-182.
D.C.—D.C. Official Code, 2001 Ed. § 4–1421.
Del.—31 Del.C. § 381 to 389.
Fla.—West's F.S.A. § 409.401 to 409.405.
Ga.—O.C.G.A. § 39-4-1 to 39–4–10.
Hawaii—HRS § 350E–1 to 350E–9.
Idaho—I.C. § 16-2101 to 16–2107.
Ill.—45 ILCS 15/0.01 to 15/9.
Ind.—West's A.I.C. 12–17–8–1 to 12–17–8–8.
Iowa—I.C.A. § 232.158 to 232.168.
Kan.—K.S.A. 38-1201 to 38–1206.
Ky.—Baldwin's KRS 615.030 to 615.050, 615.990.
La.—LSA-C.C. arts. 1608 to 1622.
Mass.—M.G.L.A. c. 119 App., § 2–1 to 2–8.
Md.—Code, Family Law, § 5–601 to 5–611.
Me.—22 M.R.S.A. § 4191 to 4247.
Mich.—M.C.L.A. § 3.711 to 3.717.
Minn.—M.S.A. § 260.851 to 260.91.
Miss.—Code 1972, § 43–18–1 to 43–18–17.
Mo.—V.A.M.S. § 210.620 to 210.640.
Mont.—MCA 41–4–101 to 41–4–109.
N.C.—G.S. § 7B-3800 to 7B–3806.
N.D.—NDCC 14–13–01 to 14–13–08.
Neb.—R.R.S.1943, 43–1101, 43–1102.
Nev.—N.R.S. 127.320 to 127.350.
N.H.—RSA 170-A:1 to 170–A:7.
N.J.—N.J.S.A. 9:23-5 to 9:23–18.
N.M.—NMSA 1978, § 32A–11–1 to 32A–11–7.
N.Y.—McKinney's Social Services Law § 374a.
Okl.—10 Okl.St.Ann. § 571 to 576.
Ore.—ORS 417.200 to 417.260.
Pa.—62 P.S. § 761 to 765.
R.I.—Gen.Laws 1956, § 40–15–1 to 40–15–10.
S.C.—Code 1976, § 20–7–1980 to 20–7–2070.
S.D.—SDCL 26–13–1 to 26–13–9.
Tenn.—T.C.A. § 37-4-201 to 37–4–207.
Tex.—V.T.C.A., Family Code, § 162.101 to 162.107.
Utah—U.C.A.1953, 62A-4a-701 to 62A-4a-709.
Va.—Va. Code Ann. § 63.2–1000 to 63.2–1105.

V.I.—34 V.I.C. § 121 to 127.
Vt.—32 V.S.A. § 5901 to 5927.
Wash.—West's RCWA 26.34.010 to 26.34.080.
Wis.—W.S.A. 48.988, 48.989.
W.Va.—Code 49–2A–1, 49–2A–2.
Wyo.—Wyo.Stat.Ann., § 14–5–101 to 14–5–108.

Library References

Infants ⚖222, 229.
States ⚖6.
Westlaw Topic Nos. 211, 360.
C.J.S. Infants § 57, 69 to 85.
C.J.S. States § 31 to 32, 143.

5103.21 Interstate compact for the placement of children; rulemaking

The department of job and family services may adopt rules necessary for the implementation of section 5103.20 of the Revised Code.

(2006 S 238, eff. 9–21–06)

Historical and Statutory Notes

Ed. Note: Former RC 5103.21 repealed by 2006 S 238, eff. 9–21–06; 1975 H 247, eff. 1–1–76.

Library References

Infants ⚖228, 229.
States ⚖6.
Westlaw Topic Nos. 211, 360.
C.J.S. Infants § 42, 53 to 54, 57, 69 to 85.
C.J.S. States § 31 to 32, 143.

5103.22 Definition

As used in division (B) of Article VIII of section 5103.20 of the Revised Code, "state human services administration" means the department of job and family services.

(2006 S 238, eff. 9–21–06)

Historical and Statutory Notes

Ed. Note: Former RC 5103.22 repealed by 2006 S 238, eff. 9–21–06; 1999 H 471, eff. 7–1–00; 1986 H 428, eff. 12–23–86; 1975 H 247, eff. 1–1–76.

Library References

Infants ⚖222, 229.
States ⚖6.
Westlaw Topic Nos. 211, 360.
C.J.S. Infants § 57, 69 to 85.
C.J.S. States § 31 to 32, 143.

5103.23 Appropriate authority in receiving state—Repealed

(2006 S 238, eff. 9–21–06; 1999 H 471, eff. 7–1–00; 1986 H 428, eff. 12–23–86; 1975 H 247)

5103.24 Agreements authorized; approval—Repealed

(2006 S 238, eff. 9–21–06; 1985 H 201, eff. 7–1–85; 1975 H 247)

5103.25 Reciprocal recognition of inspections—Repealed

(2006 S 238, eff. 9–21–06; 1975 H 247, eff. 1–1–76)

5103.26 Court placing child in another state—Repealed

(2006 S 238, eff. 9–21–06; 1975 H 247, eff. 1–1–76)

5103.27 Authority of governor—Repealed

(2006 S 238, eff. 9–21–06; 1975 H 247, eff. 1–1–76)

5103.28 Construction of chapter regarding termination of parental rights—Repealed

(2006 S 238, eff. 9–21–06; 1975 H 247, eff. 1–1–76)

CHAPTER 5122

HOSPITALIZATION OF MENTALLY ILL

DEFINITIONS

Section
5122.01 Definitions

APPLICABILITY OF PROVISIONS

5122.011 Applicability of provisions; conflicts

VOLUNTARY HOSPITALIZATION; OUTPATIENT MENTAL HEALTH SERVICES

5122.02 Admission of voluntary adult patients; voluntary admission of minors and incompetent adults; admission of persons found not guilty by reason of insanity
5122.03 Right to release of voluntary patients
5122.04 Outpatient mental health services for minors

INVOLUNTARY HOSPITALIZATION; EMERGENCY HOSPITALIZATION

5122.05 Admission of involuntary patients
5122.09 Person released without probable cause hearing; record expunged
5122.10 Emergency hospitalization; examination; disposition

Section

JUDICIAL HOSPITALIZATION

5122.11 Judicial hospitalization; affidavit; temporary detention order
5122.12 Notice of hearing
5122.13 Investigation by court
5122.14 Pre–hearing medical examination
5122.141 Hearing to determine if person is mentally ill subject to hospitalization; continuance; discharge; interim order; waiver of hearing
5122.15 Full hearing; ninety–day order; disposition of respondent
5122.16 Hospitalization to federal facility
5122.17 Temporary detention
5122.18 Notice of hospitalization
5122.19 Medical examination after admission

TRANSFER; DISCHARGE; TRIAL VISITS

5122.20 Transfer of involuntary patients; notice
5122.21 Discharge by chief clinical officer

HOSPITALIZATION OF MENTALLY ILL

Section
5122.22 Trial visits
5122.23 Vital statistics of public hospital reported to department
5122.231 Alcohol, drug addiction, and mental health services
5122.25 Rehearings
5122.26 Patient absent without leave

RIGHTS OF PATIENTS

5122.27 Standards of care
5122.271 Consent of patient or his guardian required for certain treatment; other conditions of treatment; procedure in medical emergency
5122.28 Limits on mandatory labor by patients
5122.29 Rights as patients
5122.30 Right to writ of habeas corpus
5122.301 Rights of patients and former patients not affected
5122.31 Disclosure of information
5122.311 Notification of identity of mentally ill person subject to hospitalization by court order or person becoming involuntary patient; compilation and maintenance of notices

GENERAL PROVISIONS

5122.32 Confidentiality of quality assurance records
5122.33 Additional powers of department
5122.34 Liability

PRACTICE AND PROCEDURE

5122.35 Jurisdiction of probate court
5122.36 Expenses; transcript
5122.38 Competency adjudication for present and former patients; notice of hearing; journal entry
5122.39 Guardianship; priorities and prohibitions
5122.41 Transfer of court papers; patient's estate; special guardian
5122.42 Rules of construction
5122.43 Paying costs and expenses of proceedings
5122.44 Definitions
5122.45 Creation of compilations
5122.46 Department of mental health access to records for purposes of creating compilations
5122.47 Copies of compilations deposited with historical society and state library

PENALTIES

5122.99 Penalties

Library References

Mental Health ⚖1.
Westlaw Topic No. 257A.
C.J.S. Insane Persons § 3.

DEFINITIONS

5122.01 Definitions

As used in this chapter and Chapter 5119. of the Revised Code:

(A) "Mental illness" means a substantial disorder of thought, mood, perception, orientation, or memory that grossly impairs judgment, behavior, capacity to recognize reality, or ability to meet the ordinary demands of life.

(B) "Mentally ill person subject to hospitalization by court order" means a mentally ill person who, because of the person's illness:

(1) Represents a substantial risk of physical harm to self as manifested by evidence of threats of, or attempts at, suicide or serious self-inflicted bodily harm;

(2) Represents a substantial risk of physical harm to others as manifested by evidence of recent homicidal or other violent behavior, evidence of recent threats that place another in reasonable fear of violent behavior and serious physical harm, or other evidence of present dangerousness;

(3) Represents a substantial and immediate risk of serious physical impairment or injury to self as manifested by evidence that the person is unable to provide for and is not providing for the person's basic physical needs because of the person's mental illness and that appropriate provision for those needs cannot be made immediately available in the community; or

(4) Would benefit from treatment in a hospital for the person's mental illness and is in need of such treatment as manifested by evidence of behavior that creates a grave and imminent risk to substantial rights of others or the person.

(C)(1) "Patient" means, subject to division (C)(2) of this section, a person who is admitted either voluntarily or involuntarily to a hospital or other place under section 2945.39, 2945.40, 2945.401, or 2945.402 of the Revised Code subsequent to a finding of not guilty by reason of insanity or incompetence to stand trial or under this chapter, who is under observation or receiving treatment in such place.

(2) "Patient" does not include a person admitted to a hospital or other place under section 2945.39, 2945.40, 2945.401, or 2945.402 of the Revised Code to the extent that the reference in this chapter to patient, or the context in which the reference occurs, is in conflict with any provision of sections 2945.37 to 2945.402 of the Revised Code.

(D) "Licensed physician" means a person licensed under the laws of this state to practice medicine or a medical officer of the government of the United States while in this state in the performance of the person's official duties.

(E) "Psychiatrist" means a licensed physician who has satisfactorily completed a residency training program in psychiatry, as approved by the residency review committee of the American medical association, the committee on post-graduate education of the American osteopathic association, or the American osteopathic board of neurology and psychiatry, or who on July 1, 1989, has been recognized as a psychiatrist by the Ohio state medical association or the Ohio osteopathic association on the basis of formal training and five or more years of medical practice limited to psychiatry.

(F) "Hospital" means a hospital or inpatient unit licensed by the department of mental health under section 5119.20 of the Revised Code, and any institution, hospital, or other place established, controlled, or supervised by the department under Chapter 5119. of the Revised Code.

(G) "Public hospital" means a facility that is tax-supported and under the jurisdiction of the department of mental health.

(H) "Community mental health agency" means any agency, program, or facility with which a board of alcohol, drug addiction, and mental health services contracts to provide the mental health services listed in section 340.09 of the Revised Code.

(I) "Licensed clinical psychologist" means a person who holds a current valid psychologist license issued under section 4732.12 or 4732.15 of the Revised Code, and in addition, meets either of the following criteria:

(1) Meets the educational requirements set forth in division (B) of section 4732.10 of the Revised Code and has a minimum of two years' full-time professional experience, or the equivalent as determined by rule of the state board of psychology, at least one year of which shall be post-doctoral, in clinical psychological work in a public or private hospital or clinic or in private practice, diagnosing and treating problems of mental illness or mental retardation under the supervision of a psychologist who is licensed or who holds a diploma issued by the American board of professional psychology, or whose qualifications are substantially similar to those required for licensure by the state board of

psychology when the supervision has occurred prior to enactment of laws governing the practice of psychology;

(2) Meets the educational requirements set forth in division (B) of section 4732.15 of the Revised Code and has a minimum of four years' full-time professional experience, or the equivalent as determined by rule of the state board of psychology, in clinical psychological work in a public or private hospital or clinic or in private practice, diagnosing and treating problems of mental illness or mental retardation under supervision, as set forth in division (I)(1) of this section.

(J) "Health officer" means any public health physician; public health nurse; or other person authorized by or designated by a city health district; a general health district; or a board of alcohol, drug addiction, and mental health services to perform the duties of a health officer under this chapter.

(K) "Chief clinical officer" means the medical director of a hospital, or a community mental health agency, or a board of alcohol, drug addiction, and mental health services, or, if there is no medical director, the licensed physician responsible for the treatment a hospital or community mental health agency provides. The chief clinical officer may delegate to the attending physician responsible for a patient's care the duties imposed on the chief clinical officer by this chapter. Within a community mental health agency, the chief clinical officer shall be designated by the governing body of the agency and shall be a licensed physician or licensed clinical psychologist who supervises diagnostic and treatment services. A licensed physician or licensed clinical psychologist designated by the chief clinical officer may perform the duties and accept the responsibilities of the chief clinical officer in the chief clinical officer's absence.

(L) "Working day" or "court day" means Monday, Tuesday, Wednesday, Thursday, and Friday, except when such day is a holiday.

(M) "Indigent" means unable without deprivation of satisfaction of basic needs to provide for the payment of an attorney and other necessary expenses of legal representation, including expert testimony.

(N) "Respondent" means the person whose detention, commitment, hospitalization, continued hospitalization or commitment, or discharge is being sought in any proceeding under this chapter.

(O) "Legal rights service" means the service established under section 5123.60 of the Revised Code.

(P) "Independent expert evaluation" means an evaluation conducted by a licensed clinical psychologist, psychiatrist, or licensed physician who has been selected by the respondent or the respondent's counsel and who consents to conducting the evaluation.

(Q) "Court" means the probate division of the court of common pleas.

(R) "Expunge" means:

(1) The removal and destruction of court files and records, originals and copies, and the deletion of all index references;

(2) The reporting to the person of the nature and extent of any information about the person transmitted to any other person by the court;

(3) Otherwise insuring that any examination of court files and records in question shall show no record whatever with respect to the person;

(4) That all rights and privileges are restored, and that the person, the court, and any other person may properly reply that no such record exists, as to any matter expunged.

(S) "Residence" means a person's physical presence in a county with intent to remain there, except that:

(1) If a person is receiving a mental health service at a facility that includes nighttime sleeping accommodations, residence means that county in which the person maintained the person's primary place of residence at the time the person entered the facility;

(2) If a person is committed pursuant to section 2945.38, 2945.39, 2945.40, 2945.401, or 2945.402 of the Revised Code, residence means the county where the criminal charges were filed.

When the residence of a person is disputed, the matter of residence shall be referred to the department of mental health for investigation and determination. Residence shall not be a basis for a board's denying services to any person present in the board's service district, and the board shall provide services for a person whose residence is in dispute while residence is being determined and for a person in an emergency situation.

(T) "Admission" to a hospital or other place means that a patient is accepted for and stays at least one night at the hospital or other place.

(U) "Prosecutor" means the prosecuting attorney, village solicitor, city director of law, or similar chief legal officer who prosecuted a criminal case in which a person was found not guilty by reason of insanity, who would have had the authority to prosecute a criminal case against a person if the person had not been found incompetent to stand trial, or who prosecuted a case in which a person was found guilty.

(V) "Treatment plan" means a written statement of reasonable objectives and goals for an individual established by the treatment team, with specific criteria to evaluate progress towards achieving those objectives. The active participation of the patient in establishing the objectives and goals shall be documented. The treatment plan shall be based on patient needs and include services to be provided to the patient while the patient is hospitalized and after the patient is discharged. The treatment plan shall address services to be provided upon discharge, including but not limited to housing, financial, and vocational services.

(W) "Community control sanction" has the same meaning as in section 2929.01 of the Revised Code.

(X) "Post–release control sanction" has the same meaning as in section 2967.01 of the Revised Code.

(2002 H 490, eff. 1–1–04; 1996 S 285, eff. 7–1–97; 1989 H 317, eff. 10–10–89; 1988 S 156; 1980 H 965, H 900, S 297; 1977 H 725, H 1; 1976 H 244; 1972 H 494; 1970 H 874; 130 v H 758; 129 v 1448)

Historical and Statutory Notes

Ed. Note: 5122.01 contains provisions analogous to former 2947.24, repealed by 1972 H 511, eff. 1–1–74.

Library References

Mental Health ⚖31, 32.

Statutes ⚖179.

Westlaw Topic Nos. 257A, 361.

C.J.S. Insane Persons § 45 to 47, 49 to 50, 53 to 54, 60 to 64, 66.

C.J.S. Statutes § 306, 309.

Baldwin's Ohio Legislative Service, 1988 Laws of Ohio, S 156—LSC Analysis, p 5–284

APPLICABILITY OF PROVISIONS

5122.011 Applicability of provisions; conflicts

The provisions of this chapter regarding hospitalization apply to a person who is found incompetent to stand trial or not guilty by reason of insanity and is committed pursuant to section 2945.39, 2945.40, 2945.401, or 2945.402 of the Revised Code to the extent that the provisions are not in conflict with any provision of sections 2945.37 to 2945.402 of the Revised Code. If a provision of this chapter is in conflict with a provision in sections

2945.37 to 2945.402 of the Revised Code regarding a person who has been so committed, the provision in sections 2945.37 to 2945.402 of the Revised Code shall control regarding that person.

(1996 S 285, eff. 7–1–97)

Library References

Mental Health ⚖32.
Westlaw Topic No. 257A.
C.J.S. Insane Persons § 45 to 46, 49 to 50, 54, 60 to 64, 66.

VOLUNTARY HOSPITALIZATION; OUTPATIENT MENTAL HEALTH SERVICES

5122.02 Admission of voluntary adult patients; voluntary admission of minors and incompetent adults; admission of persons found not guilty by reason of insanity

(A) Except as provided in division (D) of this section, any person who is eighteen years of age or older and who is, appears to be, or believes self to be mentally ill may make written application for voluntary admission to the chief medical officer of a hospital.

(B) Except as provided in division (D) of this section, the application also may be made on behalf of a minor by a parent, a guardian of the person, or the person with custody of the minor, and on behalf of an adult incompetent person by the guardian or the person with custody of the incompetent person.

Any person whose admission is applied for under division (A) or (B) of this section may be admitted for observation, diagnosis, care, or treatment, in any hospital unless the chief clinical officer finds that hospitalization is inappropriate, and except that, in the case of a public hospital, no person shall be admitted without the authorization of the board of the person's county of residence.

(C) If a minor or person adjudicated incompetent due to mental illness whose voluntary admission is applied for under division (B) of this section is admitted, the court shall determine, upon petition by the legal rights service, private or otherwise appointed counsel, a relative, or one acting as next friend, whether the admission or continued hospitalization is in the best interest of the minor or incompetent.

The chief clinical officer shall discharge any voluntary patient who has recovered or whose hospitalization the officer determines to be no longer advisable and may discharge any voluntary patient who refuses to accept treatment consistent with the written treatment plan required by section 5122.27 of the Revised Code.

(D) A person who is found incompetent to stand trial or not guilty by reason of insanity and who is committed pursuant to section 2945.39, 2945.40, 2945.401, or 2945.402 of the Revised Code shall not voluntarily admit himself or herself or be voluntarily admitted to a hospital pursuant to this section until after the final termination of the commitment, as described in division (J) of section 2945.401 of the Revised Code.

(1996 S 285, eff. 7–1–97; 1988 S 156, eff. 7–1–89; 1980 H 965, S 297; 1977 H 725; 1976 H 244; 1972 H 494; 1970 H 874; 129 v 1448)

Historical and Statutory Notes

Ed. Note: 5122.02 is analogous to former 5125.32, repealed by 129 v 1448, eff. 10–25–61.

Library References

Mental Health ⚖31, 37.1, 432, 439.1.
Westlaw Topic No. 257A.
C.J.S. Criminal Law § 549 to 554.

C.J.S. Insane Persons § 45, 47, 53, 241 to 245.
Baldwin's Ohio Legislative Service, 1988 Laws of Ohio, S 156—LSC Analysis, p 5–284

5122.03 Right to release of voluntary patients

A patient admitted under section 5122.02 of the Revised Code who requests release in writing, or whose release is requested in writing by the patient's counsel, legal guardian, parent, spouse, or adult next of kin shall be released forthwith, except that when:

(A) The patient was admitted on the patient's own application and the request for release is made by a person other than the patient, release may be conditional upon the agreement of the patient; or

(B) The chief clinical officer of the hospital, within three court days from the receipt of the request for release, files or causes to be filed with the court of the county where the patient is hospitalized or of the county where the patient is a resident, an affidavit under section 5122.11 of the Revised Code. Release may be postponed until the hearing held under section 5122.141 of the Revised Code. A telephone communication within three court days from the receipt of the request for release from the chief clinical officer to the court, indicating that the required affidavit has been mailed, is sufficient compliance with the time limit for filing such affidavit.

Unless the patient is released within three days from the receipt of the request by the chief clinical officer, the request shall serve as a request for an initial hearing under section 5122.141 of the Revised Code. If the court finds that the patient is a mentally ill person subject to hospitalization by court order, all provisions of this chapter with respect to involuntary hospitalization apply to such person.

Judicial proceedings for hospitalization shall not be commenced with respect to a voluntary patient except pursuant to this section.

Sections 5121.30 to 5121.56 of the Revised Code apply to persons received in a hospital operated by the department of mental health on a voluntary application.

The chief clinical officer of the hospital shall provide reasonable means and arrangements for informing patients of their rights to release as provided in this section and for assisting them in making and presenting requests for release or for a hearing under section 5122.141 of the Revised Code.

Before a patient is released from a public hospital, the chief clinical officer shall, when possible, notify the board of the patient's county of residence of the patient's pending release after the chief clinical officer has informed the patient that the board will be so notified.

(2005 H 66, eff. 1–1–06; 1988 S 156, eff. 7–1–89; 1980 H 900; 1977 H 725; 1976 H 244; 130 v H 758; 129 v 1448)

Historical and Statutory Notes

Ed. Note: 5122.03 is analogous to former 5125.33, repealed by 129 v 1448, eff. 10–25–61.

Library References

Mental Health ⚖31, 59.1.
Westlaw Topic No. 257A.
C.J.S. Insane Persons § 45, 47, 53, 83.
Baldwin's Ohio Legislative Service, 1988 Laws of Ohio, S 156—LSC Analysis, p 5–284

5122.04 Outpatient mental health services for minors

(A) Upon the request of a minor fourteen years of age or older, a mental health professional may provide outpatient mental health services, excluding the use of medication, without the consent or knowledge of the minor's parent or guardian. Except as otherwise provided in this section, the minor's parent or guardian shall not be informed of the services without the minor's consent unless the mental health professional treating the minor determines that there is a compelling need for disclosure based on a substantial probability of harm to the minor or to other persons, and if the minor is notified of the mental health professional's intent to inform the minor's parent, or guardian.

(B) Services provided to a minor pursuant to this section shall be limited to not more than six sessions or thirty days of services whichever occurs sooner. After the sixth session or thirty days of services the mental health professional shall terminate the services or, with the consent of the minor, notify the parent, or guardian, to obtain consent to provide further outpatient services.

(C) The minor's parent or guardian shall not be liable for the costs of services which are received by a minor under division (A).

(D) Nothing in this section relieves a mental health professional from the obligations of section 2151.421 of the Revised Code.

(E) As used in this section, "Mental health professional" has the same meaning as in section 340.02 of the Revised Code.

(1988 S 156, eff. 7–1–89)

Historical and Statutory Notes

Ed. Note: Former 5122.04 amended and recodified as 5119.06 by 1980 H 900, eff. 7–1–80; 1976 H 244; 1972 H 494; 1970 H 970; 1969 H 688; 129 v 1448.

Library References

Mental Health ⇐21, 31.
Westlaw Topic No. 257A.
C.J.S. Insane Persons § 17 to 20, 45, 47, 53.
  Baldwin's Ohio Legislative Service, 1988 Laws of Ohio, S 156—LSC Analysis, p 5–284

INVOLUNTARY HOSPITALIZATION; EMERGENCY HOSPITALIZATION

5122.05 Admission of involuntary patients

(A) The chief clinical officer of a hospital may, and the chief clinical officer of a public hospital in all cases of psychiatric medical emergencies, shall receive for observation, diagnosis, care, and treatment any person whose admission is applied for under any of the following procedures:

(1) Emergency procedure, as provided in section 5122.10 of the Revised Code;

(2) Judicial procedure as provided in sections 2945.38, 2945.39, 2945.40, 2945.401, 2945.402, and 5122.11 to 5122.15 of the Revised Code.

Upon application for such admission, the chief clinical officer of a hospital immediately shall notify the board of the patient's county of residence. To assist the hospital in determining whether the patient is subject to involuntary hospitalization and whether alternative services are available, the board or an agency the board designates promptly shall assess the patient unless the board or agency already has performed such assessment, or unless the commitment is pursuant to section 2945.38, 2945.39, 2945.40, 2945.401, or 2945.402 of the Revised Code.

(B) No person who is being treated by spiritual means through prayer alone, in accordance with a recognized religious method of healing, may be involuntarily committed unless the court has determined that the person represents a substantial risk of impairment or injury to self or others;

(C) Any person who is involuntarily detained in a hospital or otherwise is in custody under this chapter, immediately upon being taken into custody, shall be informed and provided with a written statement that the person may do any of the following:

(1) Immediately make a reasonable number of telephone calls or use other reasonable means to contact an attorney, a licensed physician, or a licensed clinical psychologist, to contact any other person or persons to secure representation by counsel, or to obtain medical or psychological assistance, and be provided assistance in making calls if the assistance is needed and requested;

(2) Retain counsel and have independent expert evaluation of the person's mental condition and, if the person is unable to obtain an attorney or independent expert evaluation, be represented by court-appointed counsel or have independent expert evaluation of the person's mental condition, or both, at public expense if the person is indigent;

(3) Have a hearing to determine whether or not the person is a mentally ill person subject to hospitalization by court order.

(1996 S 285, eff. 7–1–97; 1996 S 310, eff. 6–20–96; 1988 S 156, eff. 7–1–89; 1980 S 297; 1977 H 725; 1976 H 244; 129 v 1448)

Library References

Mental Health ⇐31, 37.1 to 42.
Westlaw Topic No. 257A.
C.J.S. Insane Persons § 45, 47 to 49, 53 to 56, 58 to 70.
  Baldwin's Ohio Legislative Service, 1988 Laws of Ohio, S 156—LSC Analysis, p 5–284

5122.09 Person released without probable cause hearing; record expunged

If a person taken into custody under section 5122.10 or 5122.11 of the Revised Code is released from custody before having an initial hearing, a court that has made a file or record relating to the person during this period shall expunge it.

(1988 S 156, eff. 7–1–89; 1977 H 725)

Historical and Statutory Notes

Ed. Note: Former 5122.09 repealed by 1976 H 244, eff. 8–26–76; 1972 H 494; 129 v 1448.

Library References

Mental Health ⇐40.
Westlaw Topic No. 257A.
C.J.S. Insane Persons § 48.
  Baldwin's Ohio Legislative Service, 1988 Laws of Ohio, S 156—LSC Analysis, p 5–284

5122.10 Emergency hospitalization; examination; disposition

Any psychiatrist, licensed clinical psychologist, licensed physician, health officer, parole officer, police officer, or sheriff may take a person into custody, or the chief of the adult parole authority or a parole or probation officer with the approval of the chief of the authority may take a parolee, an offender under a community control sanction or a post-release control sanction, or an offender under transitional control into custody and may immediately transport the parolee, offender on community control or post-release control, or offender under transitional control to a hospital or, notwithstanding section 5119.20 of the Revised Code, to a general hospital not licensed by the department of mental health where the parolee, offender on community control or post-release control, or offender under transitional control may be held for the period prescribed in this section, if the psychiatrist, licensed clinical psychologist, licensed physician, health officer, parole officer, police officer, or sheriff has reason to believe that the person is a mentally ill person subject to hospitalization by court order under division (B) of section 5122.01 of the Revised Code, and represents a substantial risk of physical harm to self or others if allowed to remain at liberty pending examination.

A written statement shall be given to such hospital by the transporting psychiatrist, licensed clinical psychologist, licensed physician, health officer, parole officer, police officer, chief of the adult parole authority, parole or probation officer, or sheriff stating the circumstances under which such person was taken into custody and the reasons for the psychiatrist's, licensed clinical psychologist's, licensed physician's, health officer's, parole officer's, police officer's, chief of the adult parole authority's, parole or probation officer's, or sheriff's belief. This statement shall be made available to the respondent or the respondent's attorney upon request of either.

Every reasonable and appropriate effort shall be made to take persons into custody in the least conspicuous manner possible. A person taking the respondent into custody pursuant to this section shall explain to the respondent: the name, professional designation, and agency affiliation of the person taking the respondent into custody; that the custody-taking is not a criminal arrest; and that the person is being taken for examination by mental health professionals at a specified mental health facility identified by name.

If a person taken into custody under this section is transported to a general hospital, the general hospital may admit the person, or provide care and treatment for the person, or both, notwithstanding section 5119.20 of the Revised Code, but by the end of twenty-four hours after arrival at the general hospital, the person shall be transferred to a hospital as defined in section 5122.01 of the Revised Code.

A person transported or transferred to a hospital or community mental health agency under this section shall be examined by the staff of the hospital or agency within twenty-four hours after arrival at the hospital or agency. If to conduct the examination requires that the person remain overnight, the hospital or agency shall admit the person in an unclassified status until making a disposition under this section. After the examination, if the chief clinical officer of the hospital or agency believes that the person is not a mentally ill person subject to hospitalization by court order, the chief clinical officer shall release or discharge the person immediately unless a court has issued a temporary order of detention applicable to the person under section 5122.11 of the Revised Code. After the examination, if the chief clinical officer believes that the person is a mentally ill person subject to hospitalization by court order, the chief clinical officer may detain the person for not more than three court days following the day of the examination and during such period admit the person as a voluntary patient under section 5122.02 of the Revised Code or file an affidavit under section 5122.11 of the Revised Code. If neither action is taken and a court has not otherwise issued a temporary order of detention applicable to the person under section 5122.11 of the Revised Code, the chief clinical officer shall discharge the person at the end of the three-day period unless the person has been sentenced to the department of rehabilitation and correction and has not been released from the person's sentence, in which case the person shall be returned to that department.

(2002 H 490, eff. 1-1-04; 1997 S 111, eff. 3-17-98; 1988 S 156, eff. 7-1-89; 1981 H 1; 1980 H 965, S 52, S 297, H 900; 1977 H 725; 1976 H 244; 1972 H 494; 130 v H 758; 129 v 1448)

Library References

Mental Health ⇐31, 36, 37.1, 43.
Westlaw Topic No. 257A.
C.J.S. Insane Persons § 45, 47, 49 to 53, 59, 63, 70.
   Baldwin's Ohio Legislative Service, 1988 Laws of Ohio, S 156—LSC Analysis, p 5–284

JUDICIAL HOSPITALIZATION

5122.11 Judicial hospitalization; affidavit; temporary detention order

Proceedings for the hospitalization of a person pursuant to sections 5122.11 to 5122.15 of the Revised Code shall be commenced by the filing of an affidavit in the manner and form prescribed by the department of mental health, by any person or persons with the court, either on reliable information or actual knowledge, whichever is determined to be proper by the court. This section does not apply to the hospitalization of a person pursuant to section 2945.39, 2945.40, 2945.401, or 2945.402 of the Revised Code.

The affidavit shall contain an allegation setting forth the specific category or categories under division (B) of section 5122.01 of the Revised Code upon which the jurisdiction of the court is based and a statement of alleged facts sufficient to indicate probable cause to believe that the person is a mentally ill person subject to hospitalization by court order. The affidavit may be accompanied, or the court may require that the affidavit be accompanied, by a certificate of a psychiatrist, or a certificate signed by a licensed clinical psychologist and a certificate signed by a licensed physician stating that the person who issued the certificate has examined the person and is of the opinion that the person is a mentally ill person subject to hospitalization by court order, or shall be accompanied by a written statement by the applicant, under oath, that the person has refused to submit to an examination by a psychiatrist, or by a licensed clinical psychologist and licensed physician.

Upon receipt of the affidavit, if a judge of the court or a referee who is an attorney at law appointed by the court has probable cause to believe that the person named in the affidavit is a mentally ill person subject to hospitalization by court order, the judge or referee may issue a temporary order of detention ordering any health or police officer or sheriff to take into custody and transport the person to a hospital or other place designated in section 5122.17 of the Revised Code, or may set the matter for further hearing.

The person may be observed and treated until the hearing provided for in section 5122.141 of the Revised Code. If no such hearing is held, the person may be observed and treated until the hearing provided for in section 5122.15 of the Revised Code.

(1996 S 285, eff. 7-1-97; 1988 S 156, eff. 7-1-89; 1980 H 965, H 900, S 297; 1976 H 244; 1972 H 494; 130 v H 758; 129 v 1448)

Historical and Statutory Notes

Ed. Note: 5122.11 is analogous to prior 5123.18, former 5125.34, and 5125.35, repealed by 129 v 1448, eff. 10–25–61.

Library References

Mental Health ⇐37.1 to 40.
Westlaw Topic No. 257A.
C.J.S. Insane Persons § 48, 53, 56, 58.
   Baldwin's Ohio Legislative Service, 1988 Laws of Ohio, S 156—LSC Analysis, p 5–284

5122.12 Notice of hearing

After receipt of the affidavit required by section 5122.11 of the Revised Code, the court shall cause written notice by mail or otherwise of any hearing as the court directs to be given to the following persons:

(A) The respondent;

(B) The respondent's legal guardian, if any, the respondent's spouse, if any, and the respondent's parents, if respondent is a minor, if these persons' addresses are known to the court or can be obtained through exercise of reasonable diligence;

(C) The person who filed the affidavit;

(D) Any one person designated by the respondent; but if the respondent does not make a selection, the notice shall be sent to the adult next of kin other than the person who filed the affidavit if that person's address is known to the court or can be obtained through exercise of reasonable diligence;

(E) The respondent's counsel;

(F) The director, chief clinical officer, or the respective designee of the hospital, board, agency, or facility to which the person has been committed;

(G) The board of alcohol, drug addiction, and mental health services serving the respondent's county of residence or an agency the board designates.

Any person entitled to notice under this section, with the exception of the respondent, may waive the notice.

A copy of the affidavit and temporary order of detention shall be served with the notice to the parties and to respondent's counsel, if counsel has been appointed or retained.

(1996 S 285, eff. 7–1–97; 1989 H 317, eff. 10–10–89; 1988 S 156; 1980 S 297; 1976 H 244; 129 v 1448)

Historical and Statutory Notes

Ed. Note: 5122.12 is analogous to former 5123.21 and 5125.35, repealed by 129 v 1448, eff. 10-25-61.

Library References

Mental Health ⟶39.
Westlaw Topic No. 257A.
C.J.S. Insane Persons § 56.
Baldwin's Ohio Legislative Service, 1988 Laws of Ohio, S 156—LSC Analysis, p 5–284

5122.13 Investigation by court

Upon receipt of the affidavit required by section 5122.11 of the Revised Code, the court shall refer the affidavit to the board of alcohol, drug addiction, and mental health services or an agency the board designates to assist the court in determining whether the respondent is subject to hospitalization and whether alternative services are available, unless the agency or board has already performed such screening. The board or agency shall review the allegations of the affidavit and other information relating to whether or not the person named in the affidavit or statement is a mentally ill person subject to hospitalization by court order, and the availability of appropriate treatment alternatives.

The person who conducts the investigation shall promptly make a report to the court, in writing, in open court or in chambers, as directed by the court and a full record of the report shall be made by the court. The report is not admissible as evidence for the purpose of establishing whether or not the respondent is a mentally ill person subject to hospitalization by court order, but shall be considered by the court in its determination of an appropriate placement for any person after that person is found to be a mentally ill person subject to hospitalization.

The court, prior to the hearing under section 5122.141 of the Revised Code, shall release a copy of the investigative report to the respondent's counsel.

Nothing in this section precludes a judge or referee from issuing a temporary order of detention pursuant to section 5122.11 of the Revised Code.

(1989 H 317, eff. 10–10–89; 1988 S 156; 1977 H 725; 1976 H 244; 129 v 1448)

Library References

Mental Health ⟶41 to 43.
Westlaw Topic No. 257A.
C.J.S. Insane Persons § 49, 54 to 55, 59 to 70.
Baldwin's Ohio Legislative Service, 1988 Laws of Ohio, S 156—LSC Analysis, p 5–284

5122.14 Pre–hearing medical examination

Immediately after acceptance of an affidavit required under section 5122.11 of the Revised Code, the court may appoint a psychiatrist, or a licensed clinical psychologist and a licensed physician to examine the respondent, and at the first hearing held pursuant to section 5122.141 of the Revised Code, such psychiatrist, or licensed clinical psychologist and licensed physician, shall report to the court his findings as to the mental condition of respondent, and his need for custody, care, or treatment in a mental hospital. The court may accept as evidence the written report of a psychiatrist, or the written report of a licensed clinical psychologist and a licensed physician, designated by the board of alcohol, drug addiction, and mental health services as the report and findings referred to in this section.

The examination, if possible, shall be held at a hospital or other medical facility, at the home of the respondent, or at any other suitable place least likely to have a harmful effect on the respondent's health.

The court shall prior to a hearing under section 5122.141 or 5122.15 of the Revised Code release a copy of the report to the respondent's counsel.

(1989 H 317, eff. 10–10–89; 1988 S 156; 1976 H 244; 130 v H 758; 129 v 1448)

Historical and Statutory Notes

Ed. Note: 5122.14 is analogous to former 5123.23 and 5125.32, repealed by 129 v 1448, eff. 10-25-61.

Library References

Mental Health ⟶37.1, 43.
Westlaw Topic No. 257A.
C.J.S. Insane Persons § 53, 59, 63, 70.
Baldwin's Ohio Legislative Service, 1988 Laws of Ohio, S 156—LSC Analysis, p 5–284

5122.141 Hearing to determine if person is mentally ill subject to hospitalization; continuance; discharge; interim order; waiver of hearing

(A) A respondent who is involuntarily placed in a hospital or other place as designated in section 5122.10 or 5122.17 of the Revised Code, or with respect to whom proceedings have been instituted under section 5122.11 of the Revised Code, shall be afforded a hearing to determine whether or not the respondent is a mentally ill person subject to hospitalization by court order. The hearing shall be conducted pursuant to section 5122.15 of the Revised Code.

(B) The hearing shall be conducted within five court days from the day on which the respondent is detained or an affidavit is filed, whichever occurs first, in a physical setting not likely to have a harmful effect on the respondent, and may be conducted in a hospital in or out of the county. On the motion of the respondent, his counsel, the chief clinical officer, or on its own motion, and for good cause shown, the court may order a continuance of the hearing. The continuance may be for no more than ten days from the day on which the respondent is detained or on which an affidavit is filed, whichever occurs first. Failure to conduct the hearing within this time shall effect an immediate discharge of the respondent. If the proceedings are not reinstituted within thirty days, all records of the proceedings shall be expunged.

(C) If the court does not find that the respondent is a mentally ill person subject to hospitalization by court order, it shall order his immediate discharge, and shall expunge all record of the proceedings during this period.

(D) If the court finds that the respondent is a mentally ill person subject to hospitalization by court order, the court may issue an interim order of detention ordering any health or police officer or sheriff to take into custody and transport such person to a hospital or other place designated in section 5122.17 of the Revised Code, where the respondent may be observed and treated.

(E) A respondent or his counsel, after obtaining the consent of the respondent, may waive the hearing provided for in this section. In such case, unless the person has been discharged, a mandatory full hearing shall be held by the thirtieth day after the original involuntary detention of the respondent. Failure to conduct the mandatory full hearing within this time limit shall result in the immediate discharge of the respondent.

(F) Where possible, the initial hearing shall be held before the respondent is taken into custody.

(1988 S 156, eff. 7–1–89; 1980 S 297; 1977 H 725; 1976 H 244)

Historical and Statutory Notes

Ed. Note: 5122.141 contains provisions analogous to former 2947.25, repealed by 1972 H 511, eff. 1–1–74.

Library References

Mental Health ⇒40, 41, 44.
Westlaw Topic No. 257A.
C.J.S. Insane Persons § 48 to 49, 54, 59 to 64, 66 to 73.
Baldwin's Ohio Legislative Service, 1988 Laws of Ohio, S 156—LSC Analysis, p 5–284

5122.15 Full hearing; ninety–day order; disposition of respondent

(A) Full hearings shall be conducted in a manner consistent with this chapter and with due process of law. The hearings shall be conducted by a judge of the probate court or a referee designated by a judge of the probate court and may be conducted in or out of the county in which the respondent is held. Any referee designated under this division shall be an attorney.

(1) With the consent of the respondent, the following shall be made available to counsel for the respondent:

(a) All relevant documents, information, and evidence in the custody or control of the state or prosecutor;

(b) All relevant documents, information, and evidence in the custody or control of the hospital in which the respondent currently is held, or in which the respondent has been held pursuant to this chapter;

(c) All relevant documents, information, and evidence in the custody or control of any hospital, facility, or person not included in division (A)(1)(a) or (b) of this section.

(2) The respondent has the right to attend the hearing and to be represented by counsel of the respondent's choice. The right to attend the hearing may be waived only by the respondent or counsel for the respondent after consultation with the respondent.

(3) If the respondent is not represented by counsel, is absent from the hearing, and has not validly waived the right to counsel, the court shall appoint counsel immediately to represent the respondent at the hearing, reserving the right to tax costs of appointed counsel to the respondent, unless it is shown that the respondent is indigent. If the court appoints counsel, or if the court determines that the evidence relevant to the respondent's absence does not justify the absence, the court shall continue the case.

(4) The respondent shall be informed that the respondent may retain counsel and have independent expert evaluation. If the respondent is unable to obtain an attorney, the respondent shall be represented by court-appointed counsel. If the respondent is indigent, court-appointed counsel and independent expert evaluation shall be provided as an expense under section 5122.43 of the Revised Code.

(5) The hearing shall be closed to the public, unless counsel for the respondent, with the permission of the respondent, requests that the hearing be open to the public.

(6) If the hearing is closed to the public, the court, for good cause shown, may admit persons who have a legitimate interest in the proceedings. If the respondent, the respondent's counsel, the designee of the director or of the chief clinical officer objects to the admission of any person, the court shall hear the objection and any opposing argument and shall rule upon the admission of the person to the hearing.

(7) The affiant under section 5122.11 of the Revised Code shall be subject to subpoena by either party.

(8) The court shall examine the sufficiency of all documents filed and shall inform the respondent, if present, and the respondent's counsel of the nature and content of the documents and the reason for which the respondent is being detained, or for which the respondent's placement is being sought.

(9) The court shall receive only reliable, competent, and material evidence.

(10) Unless proceedings are initiated pursuant to section 5120.17 or 5139.08 of the Revised Code or proceedings are initiated regarding a resident of the service district of a board of alcohol, drug addiction, and mental health services that elects under division (B)(3)(b) of section 5119.62 of the Revised Code not to accept the amount allocated to it under division (B)(1) of that section, an attorney that the board designates shall present the case demonstrating that the respondent is a mentally ill person subject to hospitalization by court order. The attorney shall offer evidence of the diagnosis, prognosis, record of treatment, if any, and less restrictive treatment plans, if any. In proceedings pursuant to section 5120.17 or 5139.08 of the Revised Code and in proceedings in which the respondent is a resident of a service district of a board that elects under division (B)(3)(b) of section 5119.62 of the Revised Code not to accept the amount allocated to it under division (B)(1) of that section, the attorney general shall designate an attorney who shall present the case demonstrating that the respondent is a mentally ill person subject to hospitalization by court order. The attorney shall offer evidence of the diagnosis, prognosis, record of treatment, if any, and less restrictive treatment plans, if any.

(11) The respondent or the respondent's counsel has the right to subpoena witnesses and documents and to examine and cross-examine witnesses.

(12) The respondent has the right, but shall not be compelled, to testify, and shall be so advised by the court.

(13) On motion of the respondent or the respondent's counsel for good cause shown, or on the court's own motion, the court may order a continuance of the hearing.

(14) If the respondent is represented by counsel and the respondent's counsel requests a transcript and record, or if the respondent is not represented by counsel, the court shall make and maintain a full transcript and record of the proceeding. If the respondent is indigent and the transcript and record is made, a copy shall be provided to the respondent upon request and be treated as an expense under section 5122.43 of the Revised Code.

(15) To the extent not inconsistent with this chapter, the Rules of Civil Procedure are applicable.

(B) Unless, upon completion of the hearing the court finds by clear and convincing evidence that the respondent is a mentally ill person subject to hospitalization by court order, it shall order the respondent's discharge immediately.

(C) If, upon completion of the hearing, the court finds by clear and convincing evidence that the respondent is a mentally ill person subject to hospitalization by court order, the court shall order the respondent for a period not to exceed ninety days to any of the following:

(1) A hospital operated by the department of mental health if the respondent is committed pursuant to section 5139.08 of the Revised Code;

(2) A nonpublic hospital;

(3) The veterans' administration or other agency of the United States government;

(4) A board of alcohol, drug addiction, and mental health services or agency the board designates;

(5) Receive private psychiatric or psychological care and treatment;

(6) Any other suitable facility or person consistent with the diagnosis, prognosis, and treatment needs of the respondent.

(D) Any order made pursuant to division (C)(2), (3), (5), or (6) of this section shall be conditioned upon the receipt by the court of consent by the hospital, facility, agency, or person to accept the respondent.

(E) In determining the place to which, or the person with whom, the respondent is to be committed, the court shall consider the diagnosis, prognosis, preferences of the respondent and the projected treatment plan for the respondent and shall order the implementation of the least restrictive alternative available and consistent with treatment goals. If the court determines that the least restrictive alternative available that is consistent with treatment goals is inpatient hospitalization, the court's order shall so state.

(F) During such ninety-day period the hospital; facility; board of alcohol, drug addiction, and mental health services; agency the board designates; or person shall examine and treat the individual. If, at any time prior to the expiration of the ninety-day period, it is determined by the hospital, facility, board, agency, or person that the respondent's treatment needs could be equally well met in an available and appropriate less restrictive environment, both of the following apply:

(1) The respondent shall be released from the care of the hospital, agency, facility, or person immediately and shall be referred to the court together with a report of the findings and recommendations of the hospital, agency, facility, or person; and

(2) The hospital, agency, facility, or person shall notify the respondent's counsel or the attorney designated by a board of alcohol, drug addiction, and mental health services or, if the respondent was committed to a board or an agency designated by the board, it shall place the respondent in the least restrictive environment available consistent with treatment goals and notify the court and the respondent's counsel of the placement.

The court shall dismiss the case or order placement in the least restrictive environment.

(G)(1) Except as provided in divisions (G)(2) and (3) of this section, any person who has been committed under this section, or for whom proceedings for hospitalization have been commenced pursuant to section 5122.11 of the Revised Code, may apply at any time for voluntary admission to the hospital, facility, agency that the board designates, or person to which the person was committed. Upon admission as a voluntary patient the chief clinical officer of the hospital, agency, or other facility, or the person immediately shall notify the court, the patient's counsel, and the attorney designated by the board, if the attorney has entered the proceedings, in writing of that fact, and, upon receipt of the notice, the court shall dismiss the case.

(2) A person who is found incompetent to stand trial or not guilty by reason of insanity and who is committed pursuant to section 2945.39, 2945.40, 2945.401, or 2945.402 of the Revised Code shall not voluntarily commit the person pursuant to this section until after the final termination of the commitment, as described in division (J) of section 2945.401 of the Revised Code.

(H) If, at the end of the first ninety-day period or any subsequent period of continued commitment, there has been no disposition of the case, either by discharge or voluntary admission, the hospital, facility, board, agency, or person shall discharge the patient immediately, unless at least ten days before the expiration of the period the attorney the board designates or the prosecutor files with the court an application for continued commitment. The application of the attorney or the prosecutor shall include a written report containing the diagnosis, prognosis, past treatment, a list of alternative treatment settings and plans, and identification of the treatment setting that is the least restrictive consistent with treatment needs. The attorney the board designates or the prosecutor shall file the written report at least three days prior to the full hearing. A copy of the application and written report shall be provided to the respondent's counsel immediately.

The court shall hold a full hearing on applications for continued commitment at the expiration of the first ninety-day period and at least every two years after the expiration of the first ninety-day period.

Hearings following any application for continued commitment are mandatory and may not be waived.

Upon request of a person who is involuntarily committed under this section, or the person's counsel, that is made more than one hundred eighty days after the person's last full hearing, mandatory or requested, the court shall hold a full hearing on the person's continued commitment. Upon the application of a person involuntarily committed under this section, supported by an affidavit of a psychiatrist or licensed clinical psychologist, alleging that the person no longer is a mentally ill person subject to hospitalization by court order, the court for good cause shown may hold a full hearing on the person's continued commitment prior to the expiration of one hundred eighty days after the person's last full hearing. Section 5122.12 of the Revised Code applies to all hearings on continued commitment.

If the court, after a hearing for continued commitment finds by clear and convincing evidence that the respondent is a mentally ill person subject to hospitalization by court order, the court may order continued commitment at places specified in division (C) of this section.

(I) Unless the admission is pursuant to section 5120.17 or 5139.08 of the Revised Code, the chief clinical officer of the hospital or agency admitting a respondent pursuant to a judicial proceeding, within ten working days of the admission, shall make a report of the admission to the board of alcohol, drug addiction, and mental health services serving the respondent's county of residence.

(J) A referee appointed by the court may make all orders that a judge may make under this section and sections 5122.11 and 5122.141 of the Revised Code, except an order of contempt of court. The orders of a referee take effect immediately. Within fourteen days of the making of an order by a referee, a party may file written objections to the order with the court. The filed objections shall be considered a motion, shall be specific, and shall state their grounds with particularity. Within ten days of the filing of the objections, a judge of the court shall hold a hearing on the objections and may hear and consider any testimony or other evidence relating to the respondent's mental condition. At the conclusion of the hearing, the judge may ratify, rescind, or modify the referee's order.

(K) An order of the court under division (C), (H), or (J) of this section is a final order.

(L) Before a board, or an agency the board designates, may place an unconsenting respondent in an inpatient setting from a less restrictive placement, the board or agency shall do all of the following:

(1) Determine that the respondent is in immediate need of treatment in an inpatient setting because the respondent represents a substantial risk of physical harm to the respondent or others if allowed to remain in a less restrictive setting;

(2) On the day of placement in the inpatient setting or on the next court day, file with the court a motion for transfer to an inpatient setting or communicate to the court by telephone that the required motion has been mailed;

(3) Ensure that every reasonable and appropriate effort is made to take the respondent to the inpatient setting in the least conspicuous manner possible;

(4) Immediately notify the board's designated attorney and the respondent's attorney.

At the respondent's request, the court shall hold a hearing on the motion and make a determination pursuant to division (E) of this section within five days of the placement.

(M) Before a board, or an agency the board designates, may move a respondent from one residential placement to another, the board or agency shall consult with the respondent about the placement. If the respondent objects to the placement, the proposed placement and the need for it shall be reviewed by a qualified mental health professional who otherwise is not involved in the treatment of the respondent.

(1996 S 285, eff. 7–1–97; 1996 H 567, eff. 10–29–96; 1996 S 310, eff. 6–20–96; 1989 H 317, eff. 10–10–89; 1988 S 156; 1980 H 965, S 297, H 900; 1977 H 725; 1976 H 244; 1972 H 494; 130 v H 758; 129 v 1448)

Historical and Statutory Notes

Ed. Note: 5122.15 contains provisions analogous to former 2947.26 to 2947.28, repealed by 1972 H 511, eff. 1–1–74.

Library References

Mental Health ⚖41, 42, 51.1.
Westlaw Topic No. 257A.
C.J.S. Insane Persons §§ 49, 54 to 55, 59 to 70, 86 to 92.
　Baldwin's Ohio Legislative Service, 1988 Laws of Ohio, S 156—LSC Analysis, p 5–284

5122.16　Hospitalization to federal facility

If a person, ordered to be hospitalized pursuant to section 5122.15 of the Revised Code, is eligible for hospital care or treatment by the veterans' administration or other agency of the United States government, such hospitalization may be ordered to those facilities provided by section 5905.02 of the Revised Code.

(1976 H 244, eff. 8–26–76; 129 v 1448)

Library References

Mental Health ⚖31, 35, 56.
Westlaw Topic No. 257A.
C.J.S. Insane Persons §§ 45, 47, 53, 70, 100.

5122.17　Temporary detention

Pending his removal to a hospital, a person taken into custody or ordered to be hospitalized pursuant to this chapter may be detained for not more than forty-eight hours in a licensed rest or nursing home, a licensed or unlicensed hospital, a community mental health agency, or a county home, but he shall not be detained in a nonmedical facility used for detention of persons charged with or convicted of penal offenses unless the court finds that a less restrictive alternative cannot be made available.

(1988 S 156, eff. 7–1–89; 1976 H 244; 129 v 1448)

Library References

Mental Health ⚖40.
Westlaw Topic No. 257A.
C.J.S. Insane Persons § 48.
　Baldwin's Ohio Legislative Service, 1988 Laws of Ohio, S 156—LSC Analysis, p 5–284

5122.18　Notice of hospitalization

Whenever a person has been involuntarily detained at or admitted to a hospital, community mental health agency, or other facility at the request of anyone other than the person's legal guardian, spouse, or next of kin under this chapter, the chief clinical officer of the hospital, agency, or other facility in which the person is temporarily detained under section 5122.17 of the Revised Code shall immediately notify the person's legal guardian, spouse or next of kin, and counsel, if these persons can be ascertained through exercise of reasonable diligence. If a person voluntarily remains at or is admitted to a hospital, agency, or other facility, such notification shall not be given without his consent. The chief clinical officer of the hospital, agency, or other facility shall inform a person voluntarily remaining at or admitted to a hospital, agency, or other facility that he may authorize such notification.

(1988 S 156, eff. 7–1–89; 1977 H 725; 1976 H 244; 129 v 1448)

Library References

Mental Health ⚖39, 40.
Westlaw Topic No. 257A.
C.J.S. Insane Persons §§ 48, 56.
　Baldwin's Ohio Legislative Service, 1988 Laws of Ohio, S 156—LSC Analysis, p 5–284

5122.19　Medical examination after admission

Every person transported to a hospital or community mental health agency pursuant to sections 5122.11 to 5122.16 of the Revised Code, shall be examined by the staff of the hospital or agency as soon as practicable after his arrival at the hospital or agency. Such an examination shall be held within twenty-four hours after the time of arrival, and if the chief clinical officer fails after such an examination to certify that in his opinion the person is a mentally ill person subject to hospitalization by court order, the person shall be immediately released.

(1988 S 156, eff. 7–1–89; 1977 H 725; 1976 H 244; 1972 H 494; 130 v H 758; 129 v 1448)

Library References

Mental Health ⚖31, 51.1.
Westlaw Topic No. 257A.
C.J.S. Insane Persons §§ 45, 47, 53, 86 to 92.
　Baldwin's Ohio Legislative Service, 1988 Laws of Ohio, S 156—LSC Analysis, p 5–284

TRANSFER; DISCHARGE; TRIAL VISITS

5122.20　Transfer of involuntary patients; notice

The director of mental health or the director's designee may transfer, or authorize the transfer of, an involuntary patient, or a consenting voluntary patient hospitalized pursuant to section

5122.02 or sections 5122.11 to 5122.15 of the Revised Code, from one public hospital to another, or to a hospital, community mental health agency, or other facility offering treatment or other services for mental illness, if the medical director of the department of mental health determines that it would be consistent with the medical needs of the patient to do so. If such a transfer is made to a private facility, the transfer shall be conditioned upon the consent of the facility.

Before an involuntary patient may be transferred to a more restrictive setting, the chief clinical officer shall file a motion with the court requesting the court to amend its order of placement issued under section 5122.15 of the Revised Code. At the patient's request, the court shall hold a hearing on the motion at which the patient has the same rights as at a full hearing under section 5122.15 of the Revised Code. The hearing shall be held within ten days after the date on which the respondent was transferred to the more restrictive setting or on which the motion was filed, whichever is earlier. On the motion of the respondent, the respondent's counsel, or the chief clinical officer, or on its own motion, and for good cause shown, the court may order a continuance of the hearing for up to ten days.

Whenever an involuntary patient is transferred, written notice of the transfer shall be given to the patient's legal guardian, parents, spouse, and counsel, or, if none is known, to the patient's nearest known relative or friend. If the patient is a minor, the department, before making such a transfer, shall make a minute of the order for the transfer and the reason for it upon its record and shall send a certified copy at least seven days prior to the transfer to the person shown by its record to have had the care or custody of the minor immediately prior to the minor's commitment. Whenever a consenting voluntary patient is transferred, the notification shall be given only at the patient's request. The chief clinical officer shall advise a voluntary patient who is being transferred that the patient may decide if the notification shall be given. In all such transfers, due consideration shall be given to the wishes of the patient, and the relationship of the patient to the patient's family, legal guardian, or friends, so as to maintain the relationship and encourage visits beneficial to the patient.

When a voluntary patient whose medical or psychological needs are found by the chief clinical officer to warrant a transfer refuses to be transferred to an alternate facility, the chief clinical officer may file an affidavit for a hearing under section 5122.11 of the Revised Code.

(1996 S 285, eff. 7–1–97; 1988 S 156, eff. 7–1–89; 1980 H 965, H 900, S 297; 1978 H 565; 1977 H 725; 1976 H 244; 1972 H 494; 129 v 1448)

Historical and Statutory Notes

Ed. Note: 5122.20 is analogous to former 5123.47, repealed by 129 v 1448, eff. 10–25–61.

Library References

Mental Health ⚖56.
Westlaw Topic No. 257A.
C.J.S. Insane Persons § 100.
 Baldwin's Ohio Legislative Service, 1988 Laws of Ohio, S 156—LSC Analysis, p 5–284

5122.21 Discharge by chief clinical officer

(A) The chief clinical officer shall as frequently as practicable, and at least once every thirty days, examine or cause to be examined every patient, and, whenever the chief clinical officer determines that the conditions justifying involuntary hospitalization or commitment no longer obtain, shall, except as provided in division (C) of this section, discharge the patient not under indictment or conviction for crime and immediately make a report of the discharge to the department of mental health. The chief clinical officer may discharge a patient who is under an indictment, a sentence of imprisonment, a community control sanction, or a post-release control sanction or on parole ten days after written notice of intent to discharge the patient has been given by personal service or certified mail, return receipt requested, to the court having criminal jurisdiction over the patient. Except when the patient was found not guilty by reason of insanity and the defendant's commitment is pursuant to section 2945.40 of the Revised Code, the chief clinical officer has final authority to discharge a patient who is under an indictment, a sentence of imprisonment, a community control sanction, or a post-release control sanction or on parole.

(B) After a finding pursuant to section 5122.15 of the Revised Code that a person is a mentally ill person subject to hospitalization by court order, the chief clinical officer of the hospital or agency to which the person is ordered or to which the person is transferred under section 5122.20 of the Revised Code, may, except as provided in division (C) of this section, grant a discharge without the consent or authorization of any court.

Upon discharge, the chief clinical officer shall notify the court that caused the judicial hospitalization of the discharge from the hospital.

(2002 H 490, eff. 1–1–04; 1996 S 285, eff. 7–1–97; 1988 S 156, eff. 7–1–89; 1980 H 965, S 297, H 900; 1977 H 725; 1976 H 244; 1972 H 494; 1969 H 1; 132 v H 15; 130 v H 758; 129 v 1448)

Historical and Statutory Notes

Ed. Note: 5122.21 is analogous to former 5123.50, repealed by 129 v 1448, eff. 10–25–61.

Library References

Mental Health ⚖59.1, 60.
Westlaw Topic No. 257A.
C.J.S. Insane Persons § 83 to 84.
 Baldwin's Ohio Legislative Service, 1988 Laws of Ohio, S 156—LSC Analysis, p 5–284

5122.22 Trial visits

When the chief clinical officer of a hospital considers it in the best interest of a patient, the officer may permit the patient to leave the hospital on a trial visit. The trial visit shall be for the period of time the chief clinical officer determines, but shall not exceed ninety days, unless extended for subsequent periods not to exceed ninety days after evaluation of the patient's condition.

The chief clinical officer, upon releasing a patient on trial visit, may impose requirements and conditions in relation to the patient while the patient is absent from the hospital that are consistent with the treatment plan.

The chief clinical officer of the hospital from which the patient is released on trial visit may at any time revoke the trial visit if there is reason to believe that it is in the best interests of the patient to be returned to the hospital.

If the revocation of the trial visit is not voluntarily complied with, the chief clinical officer, within five days, shall authorize any health or police officer or sheriff to take the patient into custody and transport the patient to the hospital.

At the completion of the trial visit, the chief clinical officer shall take whatever measures are necessary to enable the patient to return to the hospital.

If an involuntarily committed patient has successfully completed one year of continuous trial visit, the chief clinical officer shall discharge the patient subject to any applicable notice requirements of section 5122.21 of the Revised Code.

(1996 S 285, eff. 7–1–97; 1988 S 156, eff. 7–1–89; 1980 S 297; 1976 H 244; 129 v 1448)

Historical and Statutory Notes

Ed. Note: 5122.22 is analogous to former 5123.49, repealed by 129 v 1448, eff. 10–25–61.

Library References

Mental Health ⇐58.
Westlaw Topic No. 257A.
C.J.S. Insane Persons § 101.
  Baldwin's Ohio Legislative Service, 1988 Laws of Ohio, S 156—LSC Analysis, p 5–284

5122.23 Vital statistics of public hospital reported to department

The chief clinical officer of a public hospital shall immediately report to the department of mental health and the board of alcohol, drug addiction, and mental health services serving the patient's county of residence the removal, death, escape, discharge, or trial visit of any patient hospitalized under section 5122.15 of the Revised Code, or the return of such an escaped or visiting patient to the department, the probate judge of the county from which such patient was hospitalized, and the probate judge of the county of residence of such patient. In case of death, the chief clinical officer also shall notify one or more of the nearest relatives of the deceased patient, if known to him, by letter, telegram, or telephone. If the place of residence of such relative is unknown to the chief clinical officer, immediately upon receiving notification the probate judge shall in the speediest manner possible notify such relatives, if known to him.

The chief clinical officer of a public hospital, upon the request of the probate judge of the county from which a patient was hospitalized or the probate judge of the county of residence of such a patient, shall make a report to the judge of the condition of any patient under the care, treatment, custody, or control of the chief clinical officer.

(1989 H 317, eff. 10–10–89; 1988 S 156; 1980 H 900)

Historical and Statutory Notes

Ed. Note: Former 5122.23 repealed by 1976 H 244, eff. 8–26–76; 1972 H 494; 130 v H 758; 129 v 1448.

Library References

Mental Health ⇐31, 51.1.
Westlaw Topic No. 257A.
C.J.S. Insane Persons § 45, 47, 53, 86 to 92.
  Baldwin's Ohio Legislative Service, 1988 Laws of Ohio, S 156—LSC Analysis, p 5–284

5122.231 Alcohol, drug addiction, and mental health services

Any person who has been hospitalized or committed under this chapter may, at any time, apply to the board of alcohol, drug addiction, and mental health services serving his county of residence for services listed in section 340.09 of the Revised Code.

(1989 H 317, eff. 10–10–89; 1988 S 156; 1980 H 900; 1972 H 494; 130 v H 6)

Library References

Mental Health ⇐51.1.
Westlaw Topic No. 257A.
C.J.S. Insane Persons § 86 to 92.
  Baldwin's Ohio Legislative Service, 1988 Laws of Ohio, S 156—LSC Analysis, p 5–284

5122.25 Rehearings

Upon the request of a hospital, person, board, agency, or facility who has custody of a patient hospitalized pursuant to section 5122.15 of the Revised Code, or on the order of the court, such patient may be called for a rehearing at such place within the county of his residence or the county where such patient is hospitalized as the court designates. The hearing shall be conducted pursuant to section 5122.15 of the Revised Code.

(1988 S 156, eff. 7–1–89; 1980 H 900; 1976 H 244; 129 v 1448)

Historical and Statutory Notes

Ed. Note: 5122.25 is analogous to former 5123.24, repealed by 129 v 1448, eff. 10–25–61.

Library References

Mental Health ⇐33, 37.1, 41.
Westlaw Topic No. 257A.
C.J.S. Insane Persons §§ 49, 53 to 54, 57, 59 to 64, 66 to 70.
  Baldwin's Ohio Legislative Service, 1988 Laws of Ohio, S 156—LSC Analysis, p 5–284

5122.26 Patient absent without leave

(A) If a patient is absent without leave, on a verbal or written order issued within five days of the time of the unauthorized absence by the department of mental health, the chief clinical officer of the hospital from which the patient is absent without leave, or the court of either the county from which the patient was committed or in which the patient is found, any health or police officer or sheriff may take the patient into custody and transport the patient to the hospital in which the patient was hospitalized or to a place that is designated in the order. The officer immediately shall report such fact to the agency that issued the order.

The chief clinical officer of a hospital may discharge a patient who is under an indictment, a sentence of imprisonment, a community control sanction, or a post-release control sanction or on parole and who has been absent without leave for more than thirty days but shall give written notice of the discharge to the court with criminal jurisdiction over the patient. The chief clinical officer of a hospital may discharge any other patient who has been absent without leave for more than fourteen days.

The chief clinical officer shall take all proper measures for the apprehension of an escaped patient. The expense of the return of an escaped patient shall be borne by the hospital where the patient is hospitalized.

(B)(1) Subject to division (B)(2) of this section, no patient hospitalized under Chapter 5122. of the Revised Code whose absence without leave was caused or contributed to by the patient's mental illness shall be subject to a charge of escape.

(2) Division (B)(1) of this section does not apply to any person who was hospitalized, institutionalized, or confined in a facility under an order made pursuant to or under authority of section 2945.37, 2945.371, 2945.38, 2945.39, 2945.40, 2945.401, or 2945.402 of the Revised Code and who escapes from the facility, from confinement in a vehicle for transportation to or from the facility, or from supervision by an employee of the facility that is incidental to hospitalization, institutionalization, or confinement in the facility and that occurs outside the facility, in violation of section 2921.34 of the Revised Code.

(2002 H 490, eff. 1–1–04; 1996 S 285, eff. 7–1–97; 1993 H 42, eff. 2–9–94; 1988 S 156; 1980 H 900; 1977 H 725; 1976 H 244; 1972 H 494; 129 v 1448)

Historical and Statutory Notes

Ed. Note: 5122.26 is analogous to former 5123.54, repealed by 129 v 1448, eff. 10–25–61.

Library References

Mental Health ⬬31.
Westlaw Topic No. 257A.
C.J.S. Insane Persons § 45, 47, 53.
Baldwin's Ohio Legislative Service, 1988 Laws of Ohio, S 156—LSC Analysis, p 5–284

RIGHTS OF PATIENTS

5122.27 Standards of care

The chief clinical officer of the hospital or his designee shall assure that all patients hospitalized or committed pursuant to this chapter shall:

(A) Receive, within twenty days of their admission sufficient professional care to assure that an evaluation of current status, differential diagnosis, probable prognosis, and description of the current treatment plan is stated on the official chart;

(B) Have a written treatment plan consistent with the evaluation, diagnosis, prognosis, and goals which shall be provided, upon request of the patient or patient's counsel, to the patient's counsel and to any private physician or licensed clinical psychologist designated by the patient or his counsel or to the legal rights service;

(C) Receive treatment consistent with the treatment plan. The department of mental health shall set standards for treatment provided to such patients, consistent wherever possible with standards set by the joint commission on accreditation of healthcare organizations.

(D) Receive periodic reevaluations of the treatment plan by the professional staff at intervals not to exceed ninety days;

(E) Be provided with adequate medical treatment for physical disease or injury;

(F) Receive humane care and treatment, including without limitation, the following:

(1) The least restrictive environment consistent with the treatment plan;

(2) The necessary facilities and personnel required by the treatment plan;

(3) A humane psychological and physical environment;

(4) The right to obtain current information concerning his treatment program and expectations in terms that he can reasonably understand;

(5) Participation in programs designed to afford him substantial opportunity to acquire skills to facilitate his return to the community or to terminate an involuntary commitment;

(6) The right to be free from unnecessary or excessive medication;

(7) Freedom from restraints or isolation unless it is stated in a written order by the chief clinical officer or his designee, or the patient's individual physician or psychologist in a private or general hospital.

(G) Be notified of their rights under the law within twenty-four hours of admission, according to rules established by the legal rights service.

If the chief clinical officer of the hospital is unable to provide the treatment required by divisions (C), (E), and (F) of this section for any patient hospitalized pursuant to Chapter 5122. of the Revised Code, he shall immediately notify the patient, the court, the legal rights service, the director of mental health, and the patient's counsel and legal guardian, if known. If within ten days after receipt of such notification by the director, he is unable to effect a transfer of the patient, pursuant to section 5122.20 of the Revised Code, to a hospital, community mental health agency, or other medical facility where treatment is available, or has not received an order of the court to the contrary, the involuntary commitment of any patient hospitalized pursuant to Chapter 5122. of the Revised Code and defined as a mentally ill person subject to hospitalization by court order under division (B)(4) of section 5122.01 of the Revised Code shall automatically be terminated.

(1988 S 156, eff. 7–1–89; 1980 H 900; 1976 H 244; 129 v 1448)

Library References

Mental Health ⬬51.1, 51.5, 51.15.
Westlaw Topic No. 257A.
C.J.S. Insane Persons § 86 to 96, 98.
Baldwin's Ohio Legislative Service, 1988 Laws of Ohio, S 156—LSC Analysis, p 5–284

5122.271 Consent of patient or his guardian required for certain treatment; other conditions of treatment; procedure in medical emergency

(A) Except as provided in divisions (C), (D), and (E) of this section, the chief clinical officer or, in a nonpublic hospital, the attending physician responsible for a patient's care shall provide all information, including expected physical and medical consequences, necessary to enable any patient of a hospital for the mentally ill to give a fully informed, intelligent, and knowing consent, the opportunity to consult with independent specialists and counsel, and the right to refuse consent for any of the following:

(1) Surgery;

(2) Convulsive therapy;

(3) Major aversive interventions;

(4) Sterilizations;

(5) Any unusually hazardous treatment procedures;

(6) Psycho–surgery.

(B) No patient shall be subjected to any of the procedures listed in divisions (A)(4) to (6) of this section until both the patient's informed, intelligent, and knowing consent and the approval of the court have been obtained, except that court approval is not required for a legally competent and voluntary patient in a nonpublic hospital.

(C) If, after providing the information required under division (A) of this section to the patient, the chief clinical officer or attending physician concludes that a patient is physically or mentally unable to receive the information required for surgery under division (A)(1) of this section, or has been adjudicated incompetent, the information may be provided to the patient's natural or court-appointed guardian, who may give an informed, intelligent, and knowing written consent.

If a patient is physically or mentally unable to receive the information required for surgery under division (A)(1) of this section and has no guardian, the information, the recommendation of the chief clinical officer, and the concurring judgment of a licensed physician who is not a full-time employee of the state may be provided to the court in the county in which the hospital is located, which may approve the surgery. Before approving the surgery, the court shall notify the legal rights service created by section 5123.60 of the Revised Code, and shall notify the patient of the rights to consult with counsel, to have counsel appointed by the court if the patient is indigent, and to contest the recommendation of the chief clinical officer.

(D) If, in a medical emergency, and after providing the information required under division (A) of this section to the patient, it is the judgment of one licensed physician that delay in obtaining surgery would create a grave danger to the health of the patient, it may be administered without the consent of the patient or the patient's guardian if the necessary information is provided to the patient's spouse or next of kin to enable that person to give informed, intelligent, and knowing written consent. If no spouse or next of kin can reasonably be contacted, or if the spouse or next of kin is contacted, but refuses to consent, the surgery may be performed upon the written authorization of the chief clinical officer or, in a nonpublic hospital, upon the written authorization of the attending physician responsible for the patient's care, and after the approval of the court has been obtained. However, if delay in obtaining court approval would create a grave danger to the life of the patient, the chief clinical officer or, in a nonpublic hospital, the attending physician responsible for the patient's care may authorize surgery, in writing, without court approval. If the surgery is authorized without court approval, the chief clinical officer or the attending physician who made the authorization and the physician who performed the surgery shall each execute an affidavit describing the circumstances constituting the emergency and warranting the surgery and the circumstances warranting their not obtaining prior court approval. The affidavit shall be filed with the court with which the request for prior approval would have been filed within five court days after the surgery, and a copy of the affidavit shall be placed in the patient's file and be given to the guardian, spouse, or next of kin of the patient, to the hospital at which the surgery was performed, and to the legal rights service created by section 5123.60 of the Revised Code.

(E) Major aversive interventions shall not be used unless a patient continues to engage in behavior destructive to self or others after other forms of therapy have been attempted. Major aversive interventions may be applied if approved by the director of mental health. The director of the legal rights service created by section 5123.60 of the Revised Code shall be notified of any proposed major aversive intervention prior to review by the director of mental health. Major aversive interventions shall not be applied to a voluntary patient without the informed, intelligent, and knowing written consent of the patient or the patient's guardian.

(F) Unless there is substantial risk of physical harm to self or others, or other than under division (D) of this section, this chapter does not authorize any form of compulsory medical, psychological, or psychiatric treatment of any patient who is being treated by spiritual means through prayer alone in accordance with a recognized religious method of healing without specific court authorization.

(G) For purposes of this section, "convulsive therapy" does not include defibrillation.

(1996 H 670, eff. 12–2–96; 1991 H 128, eff. 7–1–91; 1990 H 764; 1988 S 156; 1980 S 209, H 900; 1978 S 415; 1977 H 725; 1976 H 244)

Library References

Mental Health ⇐51.15, 57.
Westlaw Topic No. 257A.
C.J.S. Insane Persons § 8 to 13, 93 to 96, 98.
    Baldwin's Ohio Legislative Service, 1988 Laws of Ohio, S 156—LSC Analysis, p 5–284

5122.28 Limits on mandatory labor by patients

No patient of a hospital for the mentally ill shall be compelled to perform labor which involves the operation, support, or maintenance of the hospital or for which the hospital is under contract with an outside organization. Privileges or release from the hospital shall not be conditional upon the performance of such labor. Patients who volunteer to perform such labor shall be compensated at a rate derived from the value of work performed, having reference to the prevailing wage rate for comparable work or wage rates established under section 4111.06 of the Revised Code.

A patient may be required to perform therapeutic tasks which do not involve the operation, support, or maintenance of the hospital if those tasks are an integrated part of the patient's treatment plan and supervised by a person qualified to oversee the therapeutic aspects of the activity.

A patient may be required to perform tasks of a personal housekeeping nature.

(1976 H 244, eff. 8–26–76; 129 v 1448)

Library References

Mental Health ⇐31, 51.5.
Westlaw Topic No. 257A.
C.J.S. Insane Persons § 45, 47, 53, 86 to 90, 92.

5122.29 Rights as patients

All patients hospitalized or committed pursuant to this chapter have the following rights:

(A) The right to a written list of all rights enumerated in this chapter, to that person, his legal guardian, and his counsel. If the person is unable to read, the list shall be read and explained to him.

(B) The right at all times to be treated with consideration and respect for his privacy and dignity, including without limitation, the following:

(1) At the time a person is taken into custody for diagnosis, detention, or treatment under Chapter 5122. of the Revised Code, the person taking him into custody shall take reasonable precautions to preserve and safeguard the personal property in the possession of or on the premises occupied by that person;

(2) A person who is committed, voluntarily or involuntarily, shall be given reasonable protection from assault or battery by any other person.

(C) The right to communicate freely with and be visited at reasonable times by his private counsel or personnel of the legal rights service and, unless prior court restriction has been obtained, to communicate freely with and be visited at reasonable times by his personal physician or psychologist.

(D) The right to communicate freely with others, unless specifically restricted in the patient's treatment plan for clear treatment reasons, including without limitation the following:

(1) To receive visitors at reasonable times;

(2) To have reasonable access to telephones to make and receive confidential calls, including a reasonable number of free calls if unable to pay for them and assistance in calling if requested and needed.

(E) The right to have ready access to letter writing materials, including a reasonable number of stamps without cost if unable to pay for them, and to mail and receive unopened correspondence and assistance in writing if requested and needed.

(F) The right to the following personal privileges consistent with health and safety:

(1) To wear his own clothes and maintain his own personal effects;

(2) To be provided an adequate allowance for or allotment of neat, clean, and seasonable clothing if unable to provide his own;

(3) To maintain his personal appearance according to his own personal taste, including head and body hair;

(4) To keep and use personal possessions, including toilet articles;

(5) To have access to individual storage space for his private use;

(6) To keep and spend a reasonable sum of his own money for expenses and small purchases;

(7) To receive and possess reading materials without censorship, except when the materials create a clear and present danger to the safety of persons in the facility.

(G) The right to reasonable privacy, including both periods of privacy and places of privacy.

(H) The right to free exercise of religious worship within the facility, including a right to services and sacred texts that are within the reasonable capacity of the facility to supply, provided that no patient shall be coerced into engaging in any religious activities.

(I) The right to social interaction with members of either sex, subject to adequate supervision, unless such social interaction is specifically withheld under a patient's written treatment plan for clear treatment reasons.

As used in this section, "clear treatment reasons" means that permitting the patient to communicate freely with others will present a substantial risk of physical harm to the patient or others or will substantially preclude effective treatment of the patient. If a right provided under this section is restricted or withheld for clear treatment reasons, the patient's written treatment plan shall specify the treatment designed to eliminate the restriction or withholding of the right at the earliest possible time.

(1988 S 156, eff. 7-1-89; 1980 H 900; 1977 H 725; 1976 H 244; 1972 H 494; 129 v 1448)

Library References

Mental Health ⚖31, 51.1.
Westlaw Topic No. 257A.
C.J.S. Insane Persons § 45, 47, 53, 86 to 92.
Baldwin's Ohio Legislative Service, 1988 Laws of Ohio, S 156—LSC Analysis, p 5-284

5122.30 Right to writ of habeas corpus

Any person detained pursuant to this chapter or section 2945.39, 2945.40, 2945.401, or 2945.402 of the Revised Code shall be entitled to the writ of habeas corpus upon proper petition by self or by a friend to any court generally empowered to issue the writ of habeas corpus in the county in which the person is detained.

No person may bring a petition for a writ of habeas corpus that alleges that a person involuntarily detained pursuant to this chapter no longer is a mentally ill person subject to hospitalization by court order unless the person shows that the release procedures of division (H) of section 5122.15 of the Revised Code are inadequate or unavailable.

(1996 S 285, eff. 7-1-97; 1980 H 965, eff. 4-9-81; 1976 H 244; 129 v 1448)

Library References

Habeas Corpus ⚖233.
Westlaw Topic No. 197.
C.J.S. Habeas Corpus § 132 to 135.

5122.301 Rights of patients and former patients not affected

No person shall be deprived of any public or private employment solely because of having been admitted to a hospital or otherwise receiving services, voluntarily or involuntarily, for a mental illness or other mental disability.

Any person admitted to a hospital or otherwise taken into custody, voluntarily or involuntarily, under this chapter retains all civil rights not specifically denied in the Revised Code or removed by an adjudication of incompetence following a judicial proceeding other than a proceeding under sections 5122.11 to 5122.15 of the Revised Code.

As used in this section, "civil rights" includes, without limitation, the rights to contract, hold a professional, occupational, or motor vehicle driver's or commercial driver's license, marry or obtain a divorce, annulment, or dissolution of marriage, make a will, vote, and sue and be sued.

(1989 H 381, eff. 7-1-89; 1988 S 156; 1977 H 725; 1976 H 244)

Library References

Mental Health ⚖31.
Westlaw Topic No. 257A.
C.J.S. Insane Persons § 45, 47, 53.
Baldwin's Ohio Legislative Service, 1988 Laws of Ohio, S 156—LSC Analysis, p 5-284

5122.31 Disclosure of information

(A) All certificates, applications, records, and reports made for the purpose of this chapter and sections 2945.38, 2945.39, 2945.40, 2945.401, and 2945.402 of the Revised Code, other than court journal entries or court docket entries, and directly or indirectly identifying a patient or former patient or person whose hospitalization has been sought under this chapter, shall be kept confidential and shall not be disclosed by any person except:

(1) If the person identified, or the person's legal guardian, if any, or if the person is a minor, the person's parent or legal guardian, consents, and if the disclosure is in the best interests of the person, as may be determined by the court for judicial records and by the chief clinical officer for medical records;

(2) When disclosure is provided for in this chapter or section 5123.60 of the Revised Code;

(3) That hospitals, boards of alcohol, drug addiction, and mental health services, and community mental health agencies may release necessary medical information to insurers and other third-party payers, including government entities responsible for processing and authorizing payment, to obtain payment for goods and services furnished to the patient;

(4) Pursuant to a court order signed by a judge;

(5) That a patient shall be granted access to the patient's own psychiatric and medical records, unless access specifically is restricted in a patient's treatment plan for clear treatment reasons;

(6) That hospitals and other institutions and facilities within the department of mental health may exchange psychiatric records and other pertinent information with other hospitals, institutions, and facilities of the department, and with community mental health agencies and boards of alcohol, drug addiction, and mental health services with which the department has a current agreement for patient care or services. Records and information that may be released pursuant to this division shall be limited to medication history, physical health status and history, financial status, summary of course of treatment in the hospital, summary of treatment needs, and a discharge summary, if any.

(7) That a patient's family member who is involved in the provision, planning, and monitoring of services to the patient may receive medication information, a summary of the patient's diagnosis and prognosis, and a list of the services and personnel available to assist the patient and the patient's family, if the patient's treating physician determines that the disclosure would be in the best interests of the patient. No such disclosure shall

be made unless the patient is notified first and receives the information and does not object to the disclosure.

(8) That community mental health agencies may exchange psychiatric records and certain other information with the board of alcohol, drug addiction, and mental health services and other agencies in order to provide services to a person involuntarily committed to a board. Release of records under this division shall be limited to medication history, physical health status and history, financial status, summary of course of treatment, summary of treatment needs, and discharge summary, if any.

(9) That information may be disclosed to the executor or the administrator of an estate of a deceased patient when the information is necessary to administer the estate;

(10) That records in the possession of the Ohio historical society may be released to the closest living relative of a deceased patient upon request of that relative;

(11) That information may be disclosed to staff members of the appropriate board or to staff members designated by the director of mental health for the purpose of evaluating the quality, effectiveness, and efficiency of services and determining if the services meet minimum standards. Information obtained during such evaluations shall not be retained with the name of any patient.

(12) That records pertaining to the patient's diagnosis, course of treatment, treatment needs, and prognosis shall be disclosed and released to the appropriate prosecuting attorney if the patient was committed pursuant to section 2945.38, 2945.39, 2945.40, 2945.401, or 2945.402 of the Revised Code, or to the attorney designated by the board for proceedings pursuant to involuntary commitment under this chapter.

(13) That the department of mental health may exchange psychiatric hospitalization records, other mental health treatment records, and other pertinent information with the department of rehabilitation and correction to ensure continuity of care for inmates who are receiving mental health services in an institution of the department of rehabilitation and correction. The department shall not disclose those records unless the inmate is notified, receives the information, and does not object to the disclosure. The release of records under this division is limited to records regarding an inmate's medication history, physical health status and history, summary of course of treatment, summary of treatment needs, and a discharge summary, if any.

(14) That a community mental health agency that ceases to operate may transfer to either a community mental health agency that assumes its caseload or to the board of alcohol, drug addiction, and mental health services of the service district in which the patient resided at the time services were most recently provided any treatment records that have not been transferred elsewhere at the patient's request.

(B) Before records are disclosed pursuant to divisions (A) (3), (6), and (8) of this section, the custodian of the records shall attempt to obtain the patient's consent for the disclosure. No person shall reveal the contents of a medical record of a patient except as authorized by law.

(C) The managing officer of a hospital who releases necessary medical information under division (A)(3) of this section to allow an insurance carrier or other third party payor to comply with section 5121.43 of the Revised Code shall neither be subject to criminal nor civil liability.

(2005 H 66, eff. 1–1–06; 2001 H 94, eff. 9–5–01; 1996 S 285, eff. 7–1–97; 1996 S 310, eff. 6–20–96; 1989 H 317, eff. 10–10–89; 1988 S 156; 1980 H 900; 1977 H 725; 1976 H 244; 129 v 1448)

Library References

Mental Health ⟲21.
Westlaw Topic No. 257A.
C.J.S. Insane Persons § 17 to 20.

Baldwin's Ohio Legislative Service, 1988 Laws of Ohio, S 156—LSC Analysis, p 5–284

5122.311 Notification of identity of mentally ill person subject to hospitalization by court order or person becoming involuntary patient; compilation and maintenance of notices

(A) Notwithstanding any provision of the Revised Code to the contrary, if, on or after the effective date of this section, an individual is found by a court to be a mentally ill person subject to hospitalization by court order or becomes an involuntary patient other than one who is a patient only for purposes of observation, the probate judge who made the adjudication or the chief clinical officer of the hospital, agency, or facility in which the person is an involuntary patient shall notify the bureau of criminal identification and investigation, on the form described in division (C) of this section, of the identity of the individual. The notification shall be transmitted by the judge or the chief clinical officer not later than seven days after the adjudication or commitment.

(B) The bureau of criminal identification and investigation shall compile and maintain the notices it receives under division (A) of this section and shall use them for the purpose of conducting incompetency records checks pursuant to section 311.41 of the Revised Code. The notices and the information they contain are confidential, except as provided in this division, and are not public records.

(C) The attorney general, by rule adopted under Chapter 119. of the Revised Code, shall prescribe and make available to all probate judges and all chief clinical officers a form to be used by them for the purpose of making the notifications required by division (A) of this section.

(2004 H 12, eff. 4–8–04)

GENERAL PROVISIONS

5122.32 Confidentiality of quality assurance records

(A) As used in this section:

(1) "Quality assurance committee" means a committee that is appointed in the central office of the department of mental health by the director of mental health, a committee of a hospital or community setting program, a committee established pursuant to section 5119.47 of the Revised Code of the department of mental health appointed by the managing officer of the hospital or program, or a duly authorized subcommittee of a committee of that nature and that is designated to carry out quality assurance program activities.

(2) "Quality assurance program" means a comprehensive program within the department of mental health to systematically review and improve the quality of medical and mental health services within the department and its hospitals and community setting programs, the safety and security of persons receiving medical and mental health services within the department and its hospitals and community setting programs, and the efficiency and effectiveness of the utilization of staff and resources in the delivery of medical and mental health services within the department and its hospitals and community setting programs. "Quality assurance program" includes the central office quality assurance committees, morbidity and mortality review committees, quality assurance programs of community setting programs, quality assurance committees of hospitals operated by the department of mental health, and the office of licensure and certification of the department.

(3) "Quality assurance program activities" include collecting or compiling information and reports required by a quality assur-

ance committee, receiving, reviewing, or implementing the recommendations made by a quality assurance committee, and credentialing, privileging, infection control, tissue review, peer review, utilization review including access to patient care records, patient care assessment records, and medical and mental health records, medical and mental health resource management, mortality and morbidity review, and identification and prevention of medical or mental health incidents and risks, whether performed by a quality assurance committee or by persons who are directed by a quality assurance committee.

(4) "Quality assurance records" means the proceedings, discussion, records, findings, recommendations, evaluations, opinions, minutes, reports, and other documents or actions that emanate from quality assurance committees, quality assurance programs, or quality assurance program activities. "Quality assurance records" does not include aggregate statistical information that does not disclose the identity of persons receiving or providing medical or mental health services in department of mental health institutions.

(B)(1) Except as provided in division (E) of this section, quality assurance records are confidential and are not public records under section 149.43 of the Revised Code, and shall be used only in the course of the proper functions of a quality assurance program.

(2) Except as provided in division (E) of this section, no person who possesses or has access to quality assurance records and who knows that the records are quality assurance records shall willfully disclose the contents of the records to any person or entity.

(C)(1) Except as provided in division (E) of this section, no quality assurance record shall be subject to discovery in, and is not admissible in evidence, in any judicial or administrative proceeding.

(2) Except as provided in division (E) of this section, no member of a quality assurance committee or a person who is performing a function that is part of a quality assurance program shall be permitted or required to testify in a judicial or administrative proceeding with respect to quality assurance records or with respect to any finding, recommendation, evaluation, opinion, or other action taken by the committee, member, or person.

(3) Information, documents, or records otherwise available from original sources are not to be construed as being unavailable for discovery or admission in evidence in a judicial or administrative proceeding merely because they were presented to a quality assurance committee. No person testifying before a quality assurance committee or person who is a member of a quality assurance committee shall be prevented from testifying as to matters within the person's knowledge, but the witness cannot be asked about the witness' testimony before the quality assurance committee or about an opinion formed by the person as a result of the quality assurance committee proceedings.

(D)(1) A person who, without malice and in the reasonable belief that the information is warranted by the facts known to the person, provides information to a person engaged in quality assurance program activities is not liable for damages in a civil action for injury, death, or loss to person or property to any person as a result of providing the information.

(2) A member of a quality assurance committee, a person engaged in quality assurance program activities, and an employee of the department of mental health shall not be liable in damages in a civil action for injury, death, or loss to person or property to any person for any acts, omissions, decisions, or other conduct within the scope of the functions of the quality assurance program.

(3) Nothing in this section shall relieve any institution or individual from liability arising from the treatment of a patient.

(E) Quality assurance records may be disclosed, and testimony may be provided concerning quality assurance records, only to the following persons or entities:

(1) Persons who are employed or retained by the department of mental health and who have authority to evaluate or implement the recommendations of a state-operated hospital, community setting program, or central office quality assurance committee;

(2) Public or private agencies or organizations if needed to perform a licensing or accreditation function related to department of mental health hospitals or community setting programs, or to perform monitoring of a hospital or program of that nature as required by law.

(F) A disclosure of quality assurance records pursuant to division (E) of this section does not otherwise waive the confidential and privileged status of the disclosed quality assurance records.

(G) Nothing in this section shall limit the access of the legal rights service to records or personnel as set forth in sections 5123.60 to 5123.604 of the Revised Code. Nothing in this section shall limit the admissibility of documentary or testimonial evidence in an action brought by the legal rights service in its own name or on behalf of a client.

(1997 S 111, eff. 3–17–98)

Historical and Statutory Notes

Ed. Note: Former 5122.32 repealed by 1976 H 244, eff. 8–26–76; 129 v 1448.

Library References

Mental Health ☞21.
Westlaw Topic No. 257A.
C.J.S. Insane Persons § 17 to 20.

5122.33 Additional powers of department

The department of mental health may prescribe the form of applications, reports, records, and medical certificates provided for under this chapter, and the information required to be contained therein; require reports from the chief clinical officer of any public hospital relating to the admission, examination, diagnosis, release, or discharge of any patient; visit each such hospital regularly to review the admission procedures of all new patients admitted between visits; investigate by personal visit complaints made by any patient or by any person on behalf of a patient; and adopt such rules as are reasonably necessary to effectuate the provisions of this chapter.

(1988 S 156, eff. 7–1–89; 1980 H 900; 1976 H 244; 1972 H 494; 129 v 1448)

Library References

Mental Health ☞20.
Westlaw Topic No. 257A.
C.J.S. Insane Persons § 14 to 16.
    Baldwin's Ohio Legislative Service, 1988 Laws of Ohio, S 156—LSC Analysis, p 5–284

5122.34 Liability

(A) Persons, including, but not limited to, boards of alcohol, drug addiction, and mental health services and community mental health agencies, acting in good faith, either upon actual knowledge or information thought by them to be reliable, who procedurally or physically assist in the hospitalization or discharge, determination of appropriate placement, or in judicial proceedings of a person under this chapter, do not come within any criminal provisions, and are free from any liability to the person hospitalized or to any other person.

(B) Regardless of whether any affirmative action has been taken under this chapter with respect to a mental health client or patient and except as otherwise provided in section 2305.51 of the Revised Code, no person shall be liable for any harm that results to any other person as a result of failing to disclose any confidential information about the mental health client or patient, or failing to otherwise attempt to protect such other person from harm by such client or patient.

(C) This section applies to expert witnesses who testify at hearings under this chapter.

(D) The immunity from liability conferred by this section is in addition to and not in limitation of any immunity conferred by any other section of the Revised Code or by judicial precedent.

(1999 H 71, eff. 9–15–99; 1989 H 317, eff. 10–10–89; 1988 S 156; 1977 H 725; 1976 H 244; 130 v H 758; 129 v 1448)

Uncodified Law

1999 H 71, § 3, eff. 9–15–99, reads:

In amending section 5122.34 and in enacting section 2305.51 of the Revised Code, it is the intent of the General Assembly to respectfully disagree with and supersede the statutory construction holdings of the Ohio Supreme Court relative to section 5122.34 of the Revised Code as set forth in *Estates of Morgan v. Fairfield Family Counseling Ctr.* (1997), 77 Ohio St. 3d 284, under heading G of section I at 304–305, and, thereby, to supersede the second, third, and fourth syllabus paragraph holdings of the Court in that case.

Library References

Mental Health ⟶51.20.
Westlaw Topic No. 257A.
C.J.S. Insane Persons § 93 to 99.
  Baldwin's Ohio Legislative Service, 1988 Laws of Ohio, S 156—LSC Analysis, p 5–284

PRACTICE AND PROCEDURE

5122.35 Jurisdiction of probate court

(A) In a case in which the jurisdiction of a court has not been specifically given or the procedure provided for, the court in the county in which a person alleged to be mentally ill is found shall have full, complete, and general jurisdiction to make disposition of such person in accordance with the procedure prescribed by Chapter 5122. of the Revised Code.

(B) When an affidavit is filed in the court as provided in section 5122.11 of the Revised Code, and the person alleged to be mentally ill is detained in a hospital located in another county, the court of the county in which such hospital is located shall, upon the request of the court receiving the affidavit, hold a hearing and make disposition of such person in accordance with Chapter 5122. of the Revised Code.

(1980 H 900, eff. 7–1–80; 1976 H 244; 1969 H 688; 129 v 1448)

Library References

Mental Health ⟶33.
Westlaw Topic No. 257A.
C.J.S. Insane Persons § 57.

5122.36 Expenses; transcript

If the legal residence of a person suffering from mental illness is in another county of the state, the necessary expense of his return shall be a proper charge against the county of residence. If an adjudication and order of hospitalization by the county of temporary residence is required, the regular probate court fees and expenses incident to the order of hospitalization, under this chapter, and any other expense incurred in his behalf, shall be charged to and paid by the county of his legal residence upon the approval and certificate of the probate judge thereof. A certified transcript of all proceedings had in the ordering court shall be sent to the probate court of the county of the residence of such person. The court shall enter and record such transcript. The certified transcript shall be prima-facie evidence of the residence of such person. When the residence of the person cannot be established as represented by the ordering court, the matter of residence shall be referred to the department of mental health for investigation and determination.

(1980 H 900, eff. 7–1–80)

Historical and Statutory Notes

Ed. Note: 5122.36 is former 5123.29 amended and recodified by 1980 H 900, eff. 7–1–80; 1977 H 1; 1972 H 494; 129 v 1448; 125 v 823; 1953 H 1; GC 1890–33.

Ed. Note: Former 5122.36 repealed by 1976 H 244, eff. 8–26–76; 130 v H 758; 129 v 1448.

Library References

Mental Health ⟶46, 56, 79.
Westlaw Topic No. 257A.
C.J.S. Insane Persons § 80 to 81, 100, 204, 207.

5122.38 Competency adjudication for present and former patients; notice of hearing; journal entry

Each individual now or formerly hospitalized pursuant to this chapter or former Chapter 5123. of the Revised Code, is entitled to an adjudication of competency or incompetency or termination of guardianship upon written request by any such individual, his guardian, or the chief clinical officer to the probate court. The court, on its own motion, may initiate such a hearing.

Upon filing of such application, or on the court's own motion, notice of the purpose, time, and place of the hearing shall be given to the person upon whose affidavit such adjudication was made, to the guardian of the applicant, and to his spouse at his residence, if such address is known.

Upon hearing, if it is proven that such applicant is competent, the court shall so find and enter the finding on its journal. The adjudicating court shall send a transcript of the adjudication to the county of the patient's residence.

(1988 S 156, eff. 7–1–89; 130 v H 758, H 1; 129 v 1448)

Library References

Mental Health ⟶6, 37.1, 59.1 to 61.
Westlaw Topic No. 257A.
C.J.S. Insane Persons § 4, 21, 23 to 36, 42 to 44, 53, 83 to 85.
  Baldwin's Ohio Legislative Service, 1988 Laws of Ohio, S 156—LSC Analysis, p 5–284

5122.39 Guardianship; priorities and prohibitions

(A) Mentally ill minors shall remain under the natural guardianship of their parents, notwithstanding hospitalization pursuant to this chapter, unless parental rights have been terminated pursuant to a court finding that the minor is neglected or dependent. Where a mentally ill minor is found to be dependent or neglected, the public children's services agency in the county of residence has final guardianship authority and responsibility.

(B) In no case shall the guardianship of a mentally ill person be assigned to the chief medical officer or any staff member of a hospital, board, or agency from which the person is receiving mental health services.

(1997 H 408, eff. 10–1–97; 1988 S 156, eff. 7–1–89; 1986 H 428; 1976 H 244)

Library References

Mental Health ⚖=31, 101, 102.

Westlaw Topic No. 257A.

C.J.S. Insane Persons § 45, 47, 53, 108 to 110, 128, 143.

Baldwin's Ohio Legislative Service, 1988 Laws of Ohio, S 156—LSC Analysis, p 5–284

5122.41 Transfer of court papers; patient's estate; special guardian

The court, upon making an order hospitalizing a person under this chapter, shall immediately transmit to the chief clinical officer of the hospital, copies, under his official seal, of court papers in the case, including the certificate of the medical witnesses and of his findings in the case.

Upon hospitalization, the chief clinical officer of the hospital to which the patient is admitted shall take possession of all money and other valuables that may be upon the person of the patient, and shall within ten days file a list thereof with the probate judge of the county of which the patient is a resident. If the amount of money is fifty dollars or less it shall be retained and expended by the chief clinical officer of the hospital for the benefit of the patient. Unless a guardian of the estate of the patient has already been appointed, the probate judge may, upon his own motion and without notice, appoint a special guardian of the estate of the patient. Any special guardian, before being appointed, shall file a bond approved by the probate judge in the same amount as is required by section 2109.04 of the Revised Code. A special guardian as provided for in this section, and while acting as such, shall be governed by all laws applicable to guardians of the estates of either minors or incompetents. The special guardian shall be allowed such compensation for his services as the court thinks reasonable, provided he forthwith performs all the duties incumbent upon him.

(1988 S 156, eff. 7–1–89; 1980 H 900; 1977 H 725; 1976 H 244)

Library References

Mental Health ⚖=31, 44, 211.

Westlaw Topic No. 257A.

C.J.S. Insane Persons § 45, 47, 53, 66, 71 to 73, 165.

Baldwin's Ohio Legislative Service, 1988 Laws of Ohio, S 156—LSC Analysis, p 5–284

5122.42 Rules of construction

Nothing in this chapter limits any rights, privileges, or immunities under the constitution, and laws of the United States or this state.

(1977 H 725, eff. 3–16–78; 1976 H 244)

Library References

Mental Health ⚖=2.

Westlaw Topic No. 257A.

C.J.S. Insane Persons § 22.

5122.43 Paying costs and expenses of proceedings

(A) Costs, fees, and expenses of all proceedings held under this chapter shall be paid as follows:

(1) To police and health officers, other than sheriffs or their deputies, the same fees allowed to constables, to be paid upon the approval of the probate judge;

(2) To sheriffs or their deputies, the same fees allowed for similar services in the court of common pleas;

(3) To physicians or licensed clinical psychologists acting as expert witnesses and to other expert witnesses designated by the court, an amount determined by the court;

(4) To other witnesses, the same fees and mileage as for attendance at the court of common pleas, to be paid upon the approval of the probate judge;

(5) To a person, other than the sheriff or the sheriff's deputies, for taking a mentally ill person to a hospital or removing a mentally ill person from a hospital, the actual necessary expenses incurred, specifically itemized, and approved by the probate judge;

(6) To assistants who convey mentally ill persons to the hospital when authorized by the probate judge, a fee set by the probate court, provided the assistants are not drawing a salary from the state or any political subdivision of the state, and their actual necessary expenses incurred, provided that the expenses are specifically itemized and approved by the probate judge;

(7) To an attorney appointed by the probate division for an indigent who allegedly is a mentally ill person pursuant to any section of this chapter, the fees that are determined by the probate division. When those indigent persons are before the court, all filing and recording fees shall be waived.

(8) To a referee who is appointed to conduct proceedings under this chapter that involve a respondent whose domicile is or, before the respondent's hospitalization, was not the county in which the proceedings are held, compensation as fixed by the probate division, but not more than the compensation paid for similar proceedings for respondents whose domicile is in the county in which the proceedings are held;

(9) To a court reporter appointed to make a transcript of proceedings under this chapter, the compensation and fees allowed in other cases under section 2101.08 of the Revised Code.

(B) A county shall pay for the costs, fees, and expenses described in division (A) of this section with money appropriated pursuant to section 2101.11 of the Revised Code. A county may seek reimbursement from the department of mental health by submitting a request and certification by the county auditor of the costs, fees, and expenses to the department within two months of the date the costs, fees, and expenses are incurred by the county.

Each fiscal year, based on past allocations, historical utilization, and other factors the department considers appropriate, the department shall allocate for each county an amount for reimbursements under this section. The total of all the allocations shall equal the amount appropriated for the fiscal year to the department specifically for the purposes of this section.

On receipt, the department shall review each request for reimbursement and prepare a voucher for the amount of the costs, fees, and expenses incurred by the county, provided that the total amount of money paid to all counties in each fiscal year shall not exceed the total amount of moneys specifically appropriated to the department for these purposes.

The department's total reimbursement to each county shall be the lesser of the full amount requested or the amount allocated for the county under this division. In addition, the department shall distribute any surplus remaining from the money appropriated for the fiscal year to the department for the purposes of this section as follows to counties whose full requests exceed their allocations:

(1) If the surplus is sufficient to reimburse such counties the full amount of their requests, each such county shall receive the full amount of its request;

(2) If the surplus is insufficient, each such county shall receive a percentage of the surplus determined by dividing the difference between the county's full request and its allocation by the difference between the total of the full requests of all such counties and the total of the amounts allocated for all such counties.

The department may adopt rules in accordance with Chapter 119. of the Revised Code to implement the payment of costs, fees, and expenses under this section.

(1997 H 215, eff. 9-29-97; 1992 H 427, eff. 10-8-92; 1985 H 238; 1983 H 291; 1981 H 694; 1980 H 900)

Library References

Mental Health ⚖46.
Westlaw Topic No. 257A.
C.J.S. Insane Persons § 80 to 81.

5122.44 Definitions

As used in sections 5122.44 to 5122.47 of the Revised Code:

(A) "Compilation" means a written list of the following information, as the department of mental health is able to reasonably ascertain, for every patient who was buried, entombed, or inurned prior to the effective date of this section in a cemetery located on the grounds of or adjacent to the grounds of a public hospital:

(1) Name;

(2) Date of birth;

(3) Date of death or burial;

(4) Specific physical location of the burial, entombment, or inurnment, including the plot or grave site number if available.

(B) "Patient" means an individual who died while admitted to a public hospital that was under the control of the department of mental health.

(C) "Record" has the same meaning as in section 149.011 of the Revised Code.

(D) "State agency" means every organized body, office, or agency established by the laws of the state for the exercise of any function of state government.

(2004 H 398, eff. 3-31-05)

5122.45 Creation of compilations

The department of mental health shall create a separate compilation for each cemetery located on the grounds of or adjacent to the grounds of a public hospital that is under the control of the department on the effective date of this section. The compilation shall be created within a reasonable time not exceeding three years after the effective date of this section. The department shall use its best efforts to create the most complete compilations possible using records in the department's possession and records obtained in accordance with section 5122.46 of the Revised Code.

(2004 H 398, eff. 3-31-05)

5122.46 Department of mental health access to records for purposes of creating compilations

The Ohio historical society and each state agency shall, at the request of the department of mental health, provide the department access to records and information in the possession of the historical society or state agency for purposes of creating compilations.

(2004 H 398, eff. 3-31-05)

5122.47 Copies of compilations deposited with historical society and state library

The department of mental health shall deposit a copy of each compilation with the Ohio historical society and the state library as soon as a compilation is completed. The department shall not disclose any record or information used to create a compilation except as provided in sections 149.43 and 5122.31 of the Revised Code.

(2004 H 398, eff. 3-31-05)

PENALTIES

5122.99 Penalties

A person who violates division (B)(2) of section 5122.32 of the Revised Code shall be fined not more than two thousand five hundred dollars on a first offense and not more than twenty thousand dollars on a subsequent offense.

(1997 S 111, eff. 3-17-98)

Historical and Statutory Notes

Ed. Note: Former 5122.99 amended and recodified as 3793.99 by 1989 H 317, eff. 10-10-89; 1975 H 300; 1972 H 521.

Library References

Penalties ⚖2, 3.
Westlaw Topic No. 295.
C.J.S. Penalties § 4 to 5.

CHAPTER 5123

DEPARTMENT OF MENTAL RETARDATION AND DEVELOPMENTAL DISABILITIES

DEFINITIONS; GENERAL PROVISIONS

Section	
5123.01	Definitions
5123.011	Director to adopt rules establishing definitions (first version)
5123.011	Applicability of provisions; conflicts (second version)
5123.012	Eligibility determinations

POWERS AND DUTIES

Section	
5123.02	Department of mental retardation and developmental disabilities; powers and duties
5123.021	Determination of need for specialized services for mentally retarded persons seeking admission to nursing facility
5123.03	Duties and authority of department
5123.031	Miscellaneous powers and duties

Section	
5123.032	Closure of developmental centers; notice; independent study; report; closure commission
5123.04	Duties of director
5123.042	Residential services
5123.043	Administrative resolution of complaints
5123.044	Determination of compliance; department to provide assistance
5123.045	Certification of home and community-based services providers
5123.046	Approval or disapproval of components of plan
5123.047	Payment of nonfederal share of medicaid expenditures
5123.049	Rulemaking governing authorization and payment of home and community-based services and Medicaid case management services
5123.0410	Individual who moves to new county to receive comparable services
5123.0411	Mandamus action
5123.0412	Fees
5123.0413	Rules governing payment of extraordinary costs

DIVISIONS AND BUREAUS

5123.05	Audits
5123.051	Payment agreements; purchase of service fund
5123.06	Establishment of divisions
5123.07	Bureau of research; powers and duties

PERSONNEL; GENERAL PROVISIONS

5123.08	Reassignments; rights to reinstatement
5123.081	Criminal records check; form and standard impression sheet; violations preventing employment; fee; confidentiality of reports; conditional employment
5123.082	Rules for certification or registration of employees
5123.083	Certificate holders in default on child support orders
5123.09	Managing officers of institutions
5123.091	Authority to change purpose of institution

CITIZEN'S ADVISORY COUNCILS

5123.092	Citizen's advisory councils
5123.093	Duties of councils; resident or staff abuse

MISCELLANEOUS POWERS AND DUTIES OF DEPARTMENT AND DIRECTOR

5123.10	Bonds
5123.11	Agreements with colleges of medicine and universities with psychology schools; residency training and clinical clerkships; residency training costs paid by department
5123.12	Agreements with college
5123.122	Rate of support for minor children
5123.13	Special police
5123.14	Powers to investigate
5123.15	Appointment of competent agency or person; contents of credentials

CARE OUTSIDE HOSPITAL; RESIDENTIAL FACILITIES

5123.17	Care outside hospital
5123.171	Respite care services
5123.172	Information to be furnished by providers
5123.18	Contracts for residential services
5123.181	Double billings to be eliminated; agreements for services
5123.182	Supported living
5123.19	Licensing of residential facilities
5123.191	Receiver for residential facility
5123.192	Nursing homes with intermediate care for the mentally retarded beds
5123.194	Waiver of support collection requirements for individuals moving into independent living arrangements
5123.20	Prohibitions
5123.21	Transfer between institutions
5123.211	Residential services for former residents of closed institutions

Section	

REAL ESTATE

5123.22	Appropriation of real property
5123.221	Cultivation of lands
5123.23	Oil and gas leases
5123.24	Petition to conduct business within prohibited distance of institution

FISCAL PROVISIONS

5123.25	Purchasing; competitive bidding; exceptions
5123.26	Fiscal procedures
5123.27	Grants, devises, gifts, or bequests; accounting; annual report
5123.28	Care of residents' money and property; disposition on death
5123.29	Designated funds
5123.30	Accounting standards

RECORDS AND REPORTS

5123.31	Records concerning residents
5123.33	Annual report of department

PURPOSE OF CHAPTER

5123.34	Statement of purposes

STATE AND FEDERAL ASSISTANCE

5123.35	Developmental disabilities council
5123.351	Duties concerning eligibility for state reimbursement of expenses
5123.352	Community mental retardation and developmental disabilities trust fund
5123.36	Agreements to assist with construction of local facilities
5123.37	Application to sell facility to acquire replacement facility
5123.371	Payment of proceeds after sale
5123.372	Deadline for notification of readiness to acquire replacement facility
5123.373	Agreement for director to pay percentage of cost of replacement facility
5123.374	Rescission of approval to sell facility
5123.375	MR/DD community capital replacement facilities fund

PATIENTS' CLOTHING

5123.39	Clothing
5123.40	Services fund for individuals with mental retardation and developmental disabilities

REGISTRY OF ABUSIVE OR NEGLECTFUL EMPLOYEES

5123.50	Definitions
5123.51	Review of reports of abuse or neglect; investigations; hearings; inclusion of employee in registry; notice
5123.52	Registry of abusive or neglectful employees
5123.53	Removal of individuals from registry
5123.54	Rules
5123.541	Prohibition on sexual conduct with mentally retarded or developmentally disabled individual; inclusion in registry; reporting of violations
5123.542	Entities required to give notice of conduct causing possible inclusion in registry

GUARDIANSHIP, TRUSTEESHIP, OR CONSERVATORSHIP APPOINTMENTS

5123.55	Definitions
5123.56	Establishment of protective service system; duty and authority of division of mental retardation; charge prohibited
5123.57	Evaluation and annual review
5123.58	Agencies that may be guardian
5123.59	Bond of trustee

Section

LEGAL RIGHTS SERVICE; OMBUDSMAN SECTION; ABUSE OF MENTALLY RETARDED ADULT

5123.60 Legal rights service; legal rights service commission; administrator's duties
5123.601 Legal rights service ombudsman section
5123.602 Access to providers' premises; communication with mentally retarded and developmentally disabled persons
5123.603 Duties of ombudsman section
5123.604 Retaliation for disclosures to ombudsperson section prohibited; notice of investigations
5123.61 Duty of certain persons to report believed abuse of mentally retarded or developmentally disabled adult; registry office; immunity
5123.611 Report of findings following review of report of abuse, neglect, or major unusual incident
5123.612 Rules regarding reporting of incidents
5123.613 Reports
5123.614 Reports; independent review or investigation
5123.62 Rights of persons with mental retardation or developmental disability
5123.63 Rights list to be furnished to providers; posting and distribution of list
5123.64 Familiarity and compliance with rights list; remedies for violations

INSTITUTIONALIZATION OF MENTALLY RETARDED PERSONS

5123.67 Purposes of chapter
5123.69 Voluntary admission; discharge
5123.70 Request of voluntarily admitted resident for release
5123.701 Person may apply for his admission for short-term care
5123.71 Involuntary institutionalization; procedure; rights of person detained
5123.711 Assessment of an individual's needs; request for assessment

PRACTICE AND PROCEDURE

5123.72 Designee of director to present case for state
5123.73 Notice of hearing
5123.74 Procedures prior to emergency institutionalization; probable cause hearing
5123.75 Probable cause hearing; procedure
5123.76 Conduct of hearing; respondent's rights; disposition; post–admission rights
5123.77 Temporary detention

MISCELLANEOUS PROVISIONS

5123.79 Administrative discharge; review of need for institutionalization
5123.80 Trial visits
5123.801 Trial visit or discharge visit expenses; clothing
5123.81 Procedure on absence without leave
5123.811 Report of removal; death
5123.82 Application of discharged person for additional care; outpatient care
5123.83 Civil and employment rights
5123.84 Freedom to communicate
5123.85 Plans for care required
5123.851 Personal effects of discharged resident
5123.86 Knowledge essential to informed consent to procedures; exceptions; procedure in medical emergency
5123.87 Limits on labor required of residents
5123.88 Petition for writ of habeas corpus
5123.89 Confidentiality of records; exceptions
5123.90 Duty of attorney general
5123.91 Immunity from liability
5123.92 Venue
5123.93 Guardianships
5123.95 Transmittal of records; patient's clothing to be provided; patient's estate; special guardian
5123.96 Costs, fees, and expenses of proceedings

Section

5123.97 Preservation of case record
5123.99 Penalties

Uncodified Law

1993 H 152, § 68.01, eff. 7–1–93, reads, in part:

Community Residential

Notwithstanding Chapters 5123. and 5126. of the Revised Code, the Department of Mental Retardation and Developmental Disabilities may develop community programs that enable persons with mental retardation and developmental disabilities to live in the community. Notwithstanding Chapter 5121. and section 5123.122 of the Revised Code, the department may waive the support collection requirements of those statutes for persons in community programs developed by the department under this section. The department shall adopt rules or may use existing rules for the implementation of these programs.

Library References

Asylums ⟲3 to 6.
Mental Health ⟲20.
Westlaw Topic Nos. 43, 257A.
C.J.S. Asylums and Institutional Care Facilities §§ 3 to 13.
C.J.S. Insane Persons § 3.

DEFINITIONS; GENERAL PROVISIONS

5123.01 Definitions

As used in this chapter:

(A) "Chief medical officer" means the licensed physician appointed by the managing officer of an institution for the mentally retarded with the approval of the director of mental retardation and developmental disabilities to provide medical treatment for residents of the institution.

(B) "Chief program director" means a person with special training and experience in the diagnosis and management of the mentally retarded, certified according to division (C) of this section in at least one of the designated fields, and appointed by the managing officer of an institution for the mentally retarded with the approval of the director to provide habilitation and care for residents of the institution.

(C) "Comprehensive evaluation" means a study, including a sequence of observations and examinations, of a person leading to conclusions and recommendations formulated jointly, with dissenting opinions if any, by a group of persons with special training and experience in the diagnosis and management of persons with mental retardation or a developmental disability, which group shall include individuals who are professionally qualified in the fields of medicine, psychology, and social work, together with such other specialists as the individual case may require.

(D) "Education" means the process of formal training and instruction to facilitate the intellectual and emotional development of residents.

(E) "Habilitation" means the process by which the staff of the institution assists the resident in acquiring and maintaining those life skills that enable the resident to cope more effectively with the demands of the resident's own person and of the resident's environment and in raising the level of the resident's physical, mental, social, and vocational efficiency. Habilitation includes but is not limited to programs of formal, structured education and training.

(F) "Health officer" means any public health physician, public health nurse, or other person authorized or designated by a city or general health district.

(G) "Home and community-based services" means medicaid-funded home and community-based services specified in division (B) (1) of section 5111.87 of the Revised Code provided under the medicaid waiver components the department of mental retardation and developmental disabilities administers pursuant to section 5111.871 of the Revised Code.

(H) "Indigent person" means a person who is unable, without substantial financial hardship, to provide for the payment of an attorney and for other necessary expenses of legal representation, including expert testimony.

(I) "Institution" means a public or private facility, or a part of a public or private facility, that is licensed by the appropriate state department and is equipped to provide residential habilitation, care, and treatment for the mentally retarded.

(J) "Licensed physician" means a person who holds a valid certificate issued under Chapter 4731. of the Revised Code authorizing the person to practice medicine and surgery or osteopathic medicine and surgery, or a medical officer of the government of the United States while in the performance of the officer's official duties.

(K) "Managing officer" means a person who is appointed by the director of mental retardation and developmental disabilities to be in executive control of an institution for the mentally retarded under the jurisdiction of the department.

(L) "Medicaid" has the same meaning as in section 5111.01 of the Revised Code.

(M) "Medicaid case management services" means case management services provided to an individual with mental retardation or other developmental disability that the state medicaid plan requires.

(N) "Mentally retarded person" means a person having significantly subaverage general intellectual functioning existing concurrently with deficiencies in adaptive behavior, manifested during the developmental period.

(O) "Mentally retarded person subject to institutionalization by court order" means a person eighteen years of age or older who is at least moderately mentally retarded and in relation to whom, because of the person's retardation, either of the following conditions exist:

(1) The person represents a very substantial risk of physical impairment or injury to self as manifested by evidence that the person is unable to provide for and is not providing for the person's most basic physical needs and that provision for those needs is not available in the community;

(2) The person needs and is susceptible to significant habilitation in an institution.

(P) "A person who is at least moderately mentally retarded" means a person who is found, following a comprehensive evaluation, to be impaired in adaptive behavior to a moderate degree and to be functioning at the moderate level of intellectual functioning in accordance with standard measurements as recorded in the most current revision of the manual of terminology and classification in mental retardation published by the American association on mental retardation.

(Q) As used in this division, "substantial functional limitation," "developmental delay," and "established risk" have the meanings established pursuant to section 5123.011 of the Revised Code.

"Developmental disability" means a severe, chronic disability that is characterized by all of the following:

(1) It is attributable to a mental or physical impairment or a combination of mental and physical impairments, other than a mental or physical impairment solely caused by mental illness as defined in division (A) of section 5122.01 of the Revised Code.

(2) It is manifested before age twenty-two.

(3) It is likely to continue indefinitely.

(4) It results in one of the following:

(a) In the case of a person under three years of age, at least one developmental delay or an established risk;

(b) In the case of a person at least three years of age but under six years of age, at least two developmental delays or an established risk;

(c) In the case of a person six years of age or older, a substantial functional limitation in at least three of the following areas of major life activity, as appropriate for the person's age: self–care, receptive and expressive language, learning, mobility, self-direction, capacity for independent living, and, if the person is at least sixteen years of age, capacity for economic self-sufficiency.

(5) It causes the person to need a combination and sequence of special, interdisciplinary, or other type of care, treatment, or provision of services for an extended period of time that is individually planned and coordinated for the person.

(R) "Developmentally disabled person" means a person with a developmental disability.

(S) "State institution" means an institution that is tax-supported and under the jurisdiction of the department.

(T) "Residence" and "legal residence" have the same meaning as "legal settlement," which is acquired by residing in Ohio for a period of one year without receiving general assistance prior to July 17, 1995, under former Chapter 5113. of the Revised Code, financial assistance under Chapter 5115. of the Revised Code, or assistance from a private agency that maintains records of assistance given. A person having a legal settlement in the state shall be considered as having legal settlement in the assistance area in which the person resides. No adult person coming into this state and having a spouse or minor children residing in another state shall obtain a legal settlement in this state as long as the spouse or minor children are receiving public assistance, care, or support at the expense of the other state or its subdivisions. For the purpose of determining the legal settlement of a person who is living in a public or private institution or in a home subject to licensing by the department of job and family services, the department of mental health, or the department of mental retardation and developmental disabilities, the residence of the person shall be considered as though the person were residing in the county in which the person was living prior to the person's entrance into the institution or home. Settlement once acquired shall continue until a person has been continuously absent from Ohio for a period of one year or has acquired a legal residence in another state. A woman who marries a man with legal settlement in any county immediately acquires the settlement of her husband. The legal settlement of a minor is that of the parents, surviving parent, sole parent, parent who is designated the residential parent and legal custodian by a court, other adult having permanent custody awarded by a court, or guardian of the person of the minor, provided that:

(1) A minor female who marries shall be considered to have the legal settlement of her husband and, in the case of death of her husband or divorce, she shall not thereby lose her legal settlement obtained by the marriage.

(2) A minor male who marries, establishes a home, and who has resided in this state for one year without receiving general assistance prior to July 17, 1995, under former Chapter 5113. of the Revised Code, financial assistance under Chapter 5115. of the Revised Code, or assistance from a private agency that maintains records of assistance given shall be considered to have obtained a legal settlement in this state.

(3) The legal settlement of a child under eighteen years of age who is in the care or custody of a public or private child caring agency shall not change if the legal settlement of the parent changes until after the child has been in the home of the parent for a period of one year.

No person, adult or minor, may establish a legal settlement in this state for the purpose of gaining admission to any state institution.

(U)(1) "Resident" means, subject to division (R) (2) of this section, a person who is admitted either voluntarily or involuntarily to an institution or other facility pursuant to section 2945.39, 2945.40, 2945.401, or 2945.402 of the Revised Code subsequent to a finding of not guilty by reason of insanity or incompetence to stand trial or under this chapter who is under observation or receiving habilitation and care in an institution.

(2) "Resident" does not include a person admitted to an institution or other facility under section 2945.39, 2945.40, 2945.401, or 2945.402 of the Revised Code to the extent that the reference in this chapter to resident, or the context in which the reference occurs, is in conflict with any provision of sections 2945.37 to 2945.402 of the Revised Code.

(V) "Respondent" means the person whose detention, commitment, or continued commitment is being sought in any proceeding under this chapter.

(W) "Working day" and "court day" mean Monday, Tuesday, Wednesday, Thursday, and Friday, except when such day is a legal holiday.

(X) "Prosecutor" means the prosecuting attorney, village solicitor, city director of law, or similar chief legal officer who prosecuted a criminal case in which a person was found not guilty by reason of insanity, who would have had the authority to prosecute a criminal case against a person if the person had not been found incompetent to stand trial, or who prosecuted a case in which a person was found guilty.

(Y) "Court" means the probate division of the court of common pleas.

(2005 H 66, eff. 7–1–05; 2003 H 95, eff. 6–26–03; 2001 H 94, eff. 6–6–01; 2000 H 538, eff. 9–22–00; 1999 H 471, eff. 7–1–00; 1996 S 285, eff. 7–1–97; 1995 H 249, eff. 7–17–95; 1994 H 694, eff. 11–11–94; 1993 S 21, eff. 10–29–93; 1991 H 298; 1990 S 3, H 569; 1987 H 231; 1981 H 1; 1980 H 965, H 900)

Historical and Statutory Notes

Ed. Note: 5123.01 is former 5123.68 amended and recodified by 1980 H 900, eff. 7–1–80; 1980 S 297; 1974 S 336.

Ed. Note: Former 5123.01 repealed by 129 v 1448, eff. 10–25–61; 1953 H 1; GC 1890–19.

Pre–1953 H 1 Amendments: 121 v 423; 119 v 616; 117 v 550

Library References

Mental Health ⚖2, 20.
Statutes ⚖179.
Westlaw Topic Nos. 257A, 361.
C.J.S. Insane Persons § 14 to 16, 22.
C.J.S. Statutes § 306, 309.

5123.011 Director to adopt rules establishing definitions (first version)

Note: See also following version of this section, and Publisher's Note.

The director of mental retardation and developmental disabilities shall adopt rules in accordance with Chapter 119. of the Revised Code that establish definitions of "substantial functional limitation," "developmental delay," "established risk," "biological risk," and "environmental risk."

(1992 S 156, eff. 1–10–92; 1990 H 569)

Note: See also following version of this section, and Publisher's Note.

5123.011 Applicability of provisions; conflicts (second version)

Note: See also preceding version of this section, and Publisher's Note.

The provisions of this chapter regarding institutionalization apply to a person who is found incompetent to stand trial or not guilty by reason of insanity and is committed pursuant to section 2945.39, 2945.40, 2945.401, or 2945.402 of the Revised Code to the extent that the provisions are not in conflict with any provision of sections 2945.37 to 2945.402 of the Revised Code. If a provision of this chapter is in conflict with a provision in sections 2945.37 to 2945.402 of the Revised Code regarding a person who has been so committed, the provision in sections 2945.37 to 2945.402 of the Revised Code shall control regarding that person.

(1996 S 285, eff. 7–1–97)

Note: See also preceding version of this section, and Publisher's Note.

Historical and Statutory Notes

Publisher's Note: 5123.011 was enacted by 1996 S 285, eff. 7–1–97. However, a separate statute, as enacted by 1990 H 569, eff. 11–11–90, and amended by 1992 S 156, eff. 1–10–92, also exists at that number. See *Baldwin's Ohio Legislative Service*, 1992, page 5–1, and 1996, page 12/L–3563, or the OH–LEGIS or OH–LEGIS–OLD database on WESTLAW, for original versions of these Acts.

Library References

Mental Health ⚖2, 20.
Westlaw Topic No. 257A.
C.J.S. Insane Persons § 14 to 16, 22.

5123.012 Eligibility determinations

(A) As used in this section:

(1) "Biological risk" and "environmental risk" have the meanings established pursuant to section 5123.011 of the Revised Code.

(2) "Handicapped preschool child" has the same meaning as in section 3323.01 of the Revised Code.

(B) Except as provided in division (C) of this section, the department of mental retardation and developmental disabilities shall make eligibility determinations in accordance with the definition of "developmental disability" in section 5123.01 of the Revised Code. The department may adopt rules in accordance with Chapter 119. of the Revised Code establishing eligibility for programs and services for either of the following:

(1) Individuals under age six who have a biological risk or environmental risk of a developmental delay;

(2) Any handicapped preschool child eligible for services under section 3323.02 of the Revised Code whose handicap is not attributable solely to mental illness as defined in section 5122.01 of the Revised Code.

(C)(1) The department shall make determinations of eligibility for protective services in accordance with sections 5123.55 to 5123.59 of the Revised Code.

(2) Determinations of whether a mentally retarded person is subject to institutionalization by court order shall be made in accordance with sections 5123.71 to 5123.76 of the Revised Code and shall be based on the definition of "mentally retarded person subject to institutionalization by court order" in section 5123.01 of the Revised Code.

(3) All persons who were eligible for services and enrolled in programs offered by the department of mental retardation and developmental disabilities pursuant to this chapter on July 1,

1991, shall continue to be eligible for those services and to be enrolled in those programs as long as they are in need of services.

(1994 H 694, eff. 11–11–94; 1992 S 156, eff. 1–10–92; 1990 H 569)

Library References

Mental Health ⇔3.1, 20, 31.
Westlaw Topic No. 257A.
C.J.S. Insane Persons § 2, 6, 14 to 16, 45, 47, 53.

POWERS AND DUTIES

5123.02 Department of mental retardation and developmental disabilities; powers and duties

The department of mental retardation and developmental disabilities shall do the following:

(A) Promote comprehensive statewide programs and services for persons with mental retardation or a developmental disability and their families wherever they reside in the state. These programs shall include public education, prevention, diagnosis, treatment, training, and care.

(B) Provide administrative leadership for statewide services which include residential facilities, evaluation centers, and community classes which are wholly or in part financed by the department of mental retardation and developmental disabilities as provided by section 5123.26 of the Revised Code;

(C) Develop and maintain, to the extent feasible, data on all services and programs for persons with mental retardation or a developmental disability, that are provided by governmental and private agencies;

(D) Make periodic determinations of the number of persons with mental retardation or a developmental disability requiring services in the state;

(E) Provide leadership to local authorities in planning and developing community-wide services for persons with mental retardation or a developmental disability and their families;

(F) Promote programs of professional training and research in cooperation with other state departments, agencies, and institutions of higher learning.

(2000 H 538, eff. 9–22–00; 1996 H 629, eff. 3–13–97; 1990 H 569, eff. 7–1–91; 1980 H 965, H 900)

Uncodified Law

2005 H 66, § 209.09.12, eff. 6–30–05, reads:

Developmental centers of the Department of Mental Retardation and Developmental Disabilities may provide services to persons with mental retardation or developmental disabilities living in the community or to providers of services to these persons. The department may develop a method for recovery of all costs associated with the provisions of these services.

2005 H 66, § 209.09.16, eff. 6–30–05, reads:

The Department of Mental Retardation and Developmental Disabilities shall transfer the administrative duties related to the operation of the Ohio Family and Children First Cabinet Council to the Department of Mental Health. As part of the transfer, all of the following shall occur on July 1, 2005, or as soon as possible thereafter as the Departments of Mental Retardation and Developmental Disabilities and Mental Health are able to make the transfers:

(A) Individuals employed by the Department of Mental Retardation and Developmental Disabilities on June 30, 2005, to perform administrative functions for the Ohio Family and Children First Cabinet Council shall be transferred to the Department of Mental Health.

(B) The assets, liabilities, equipment, and records, irrespective of form or medium, related to the administrative duties of the Ohio Family and Children First Cabinet Council shall transfer or be transferred to the Department of Mental Health;

(C) The Department of Mental Health shall assume the obligations of the Ohio Family and Children First Cabinet Council's administrative duties.

2005 H 66, § 209.09.21, eff. 6–30–05, reads:

(1) "Family support services," "home and community-based services," "service and support administration," and "supported living" have the same meaning as in section 5126.01 of the Revised Code.

(2) "Intermediate care facility for the mentally retarded" has the same meaning as in section 5111.20 of the Revised Code.

(B) If one or more new beds obtain certification as an intermediate-care-facility-for-the-mentally-retarded bed on or after the effective date of this section, the Director of Mental Retardation and Developmental Disabilities shall transfer funds to the Department of Job and Family Services to pay the nonfederal share of the cost under the Medicaid Program for those beds. The Director shall use only the following funds for the transfer:

(1) If the beds are located in a county served by a county board of mental retardation and developmental disabilities that does not initiate or support the beds' certification, funds appropriated to the Department of Mental Retardation and Developmental Disabilities for home and community-based services and supported living for which the Director is authorized to make allocations to county boards;

(2) If the beds are located in a county served by a county board that initiates or supports the beds' certification, funds appropriated to the Department for family support services, service and support administration, and other services for which the Director is authorized to make allocations to counties.

(C) The funds that the Director transfers under division (B)(2) of this section shall be funds that the Director has allocated to the county board serving the county in which the beds are located unless the amount of the allocation is insufficient to pay the entire nonfederal share of the cost under the Medicaid Program for those beds. If the allocation is insufficient, the Director shall use as much of such funds allocated to other counties as is needed to make up the difference.

2001 H 94, § 63.39, eff. 6–6–01, reads, in part:

The Department of Mental Retardation and Developmental Disabilities shall arrange for a study to be completed no later than January 1, 2003, of the implications of the "Health Insurance Portability and Accountability Act of 1996," Pub. L. No. 104–191, 110 Stat. 1955, 42 U.S.C.A. 300gg–42, as amended, on payment systems for Medicaid-funded services to individuals with mental retardation or other developmental disability, including the Multi–Agency Community Services Information System and similar payment systems. The study shall include consideration of the feasibility of a payment system under which a county board of mental retardation and developmental disabilities pays claims directly to persons and government entities under contract with the county board to provide Medicaid-funded services to individuals with mental retardation or other developmental disability.

2001 H 94, § 63.39: See *Baldwin's Ohio Revised Code Annotated*, Uncodified Law under 5111.871.

2001 H 94, § 75.03, eff. 6–6–01, reads:

Developmental centers of the Department of Mental Retardation and Developmental Disabilities may provide services to persons with mental retardation or developmental disabilities living in the community or to providers of services to these persons. The department may develop a methodology for recovery of all costs associated with the provisions of these services.

2001 H 94, § 75.04, eff. 6–6–01, reads:

As used in this section, "service and support administration" has the same meaning as in section 5126.01 of the Revised Code, as amended by this act.

Wherever case management services are referred to in any law, contract, or other document, the reference shall be deemed to refer to service and support administration. No action or proceeding pending on the effective date of this section is affected by the renaming of case management services as service and support administration.

The Department of Mental Retardation and Developmental Disabilities shall adopt, amend, and rescind rules as necessary to reflect the renaming of case management services as service and support administration. All boards of mental retardation and developmental disabilities and the entities with which they contract for services shall rename the titles of their employees who provide service and support administration. All boards and contracting entities shall make corresponding changes to all employment contracts.

2001 H 94, § 75.06, eff. 6–6–01, reads:

(A) There is hereby created the Executive Branch Committee on Medicaid Redesign and Expansion of MRDD Services. The committee shall consist of all of the following individuals:

(1) One representative of the Governor appointed by the Governor;

(2) Two representatives of the Department of Mental Retardation and Developmental Disabilities appointed by the Director of Mental Retardation and Developmental Disabilities;

(3) Two representatives of the Department of Job and Family Services appointed by the Director of Job and Family Services;

(4) One representative of the Office of Budget and Management appointed by the Director of Budget and Management;

(5) One representative of The Arc of Ohio appointed by the organization's board of trustees;

(6) One representative of the Ohio Association of County Boards of Mental Retardation and Developmental Disabilities appointed by the association's board of trustees;

(7) One representative of the Ohio Superintendents of County Boards of Mental Retardation and Developmental Disabilities appointed by the organization's board of trustees;

(8) One representative of the Ohio Provider Resource Association appointed by the association's board of trustees;

(9) One representative of the Ohio Health Care Association appointed by the association's board of trustees;

(10) One representative of individuals with mental retardation or other developmental disability appointed by the Director of Mental Retardation and Developmental Disabilities.

(B) The Governor shall appoint the chairperson of the committee. Members of the committee shall serve without compensation or reimbursement, except to the extent that serving on the committee is considered a part of their regular employment duties.

(C) The committee shall meet at times determined by the chairperson to do all of the following:

(1) Review the effect that the provisions of this act regarding Medicaid funding for services to individuals with mental retardation or other developmental disability have on the funding and provision of services to such individuals;

(2) Identify issues related to, and barriers to, the effective implementation of those provisions of this act with the goal of meeting the needs of individuals with mental retardation or other developmental disability;

(3) Establish effective means for resolving the issues and barriers, including advocating changes to state law, rules, or both.

(D) The committee shall finish a preliminary report on its actions no later than one year after the effective date of this section and a final report on its actions no later than three years after the effective date of this section. The committee shall submit the reports to the Governor and Directors of Mental Retardation and Developmental Disabilities and Job and Family Services. The committee shall cease to exist on submission of the final report unless the Governor issues an executive order providing for the committee to continue.

2001 H 405, § 4 and 5, eff. 12–13–01, read:

Section 4. As used in this section, "Residential Facility Waiver transition" means the transition, due to the upcoming termination of the Residential Facility Waiver, of individuals who receive services under the Residential Facility Waiver to other home and community-based services as defined in section 5126.01 of the Revised Code.

Consistent with the Medicaid redesign plan that the Department of Job and Family Services submitted to the Centers for Medicaid and Medicare Services to comply with an audit conducted by the centers, the Department of Mental Retardation and Developmental Disabilities shall develop a plan to implement the Residential Facilities Waiver transition. The plan shall identify how the needs of the individuals to be transferred are to be met, including ways that the Residential Facility Waiver's service capacity can be reconfigured on a statewide, regional, or county specific basis. The plan shall also specify the date, which shall not be later than September 1, 2002, that the moratorium established under Section 5 of this act is to terminate. The Department of Mental Retardation and Developmental Disabilities shall complete the plan in time for the Executive Branch Committee on Medicaid Redesign and Expansion MRDD Services, created by Am. Sub. H.B. 94 of the 124th General Assembly, to review the plan and submit recommended changes to the Department by May 31, 2002. The Committee shall finish its review and submit suggested changes to the Department of Mental Retardation and Developmental Disabilities not later than that date. Not later than sixty days after the Committee submits suggested changes to the Department, the Department and the Department of Job and Family Services shall establish protocols for county boards of mental retardation and developmental disabilities and private and government entities under contract with a county board to provide services under the Residential Facility Waiver to follow in implementing the plan.

The Department of Mental Retardation and Developmental Disabilities shall identify costs associated with the plan developed under this section and sources of funding available to pay the costs.

Not later than February 8, 2002, each county board of mental retardation and developmental disabilities that has a contract with one or more private or government entities to provide services under the Residential Facility Waiver shall jointly develop a plan with the providers for the implementation of the Residential Facility Waiver transition as concerns individuals who reside in a residential facility with a license capacity of five or fewer beds. The boards and providers shall develop the plan in accordance with a protocol the Departments of Job and Family Services and Mental Retardation and Developmental Disabilities shall jointly establish.

Section 5. (A) Notwithstanding Chapter 5111. of the Revised Code, until the date specified in the plan that the Department of Mental Retardation and Developmental Disabilities develops under Section 4 of this act and except as provided in division (B) of this section, the number of intermediate care facility for the mentally retarded beds eligible for Medicaid payment shall not be higher than the number of such beds eligible for such payment on the effective date of this section.

(B) The Department of Job and Family Services may issue one or more waivers of division (A) of this section in the event that an emergency, as determined by the Department, exists. In determining whether to issue a waiver, the Department of Job and Family Services shall consider the recommendation of the Department of Mental Retardation and Developmental Disabilities.

2000 S 346, § 13, eff. 12–8–00, reads:

(A) There is hereby created the Ticket To Work Program Evaluation Committee, which shall consist of the following members:

(1) Three members of the Senate appointed by the President of the Senate, no more than two of whom shall belong to the same political party as the President;

(2) Three members of the House of Representatives appointed by the Speaker of the House of Representatives, no more than two of whom shall belong to the same political party as the Speaker;

(3) The Director of Job and Family Services or the designee of the Director;

(4) The Administrator of the Rehabilitation Services Commission or the designee of the Administrator;

(5) The Director of Mental Retardation and Developmental Disabilities or the designee of the Director;

(6) The Director of Mental Health or the designee of the Director;

(7) The Director of Budget and Management or the designee of the Director.

The Committee shall select from its members a Chairperson and Vice-Chairperson.

(B) The Committee shall do all of the following:

(1) Determine the costs associated with establishing in Ohio a ticket to work and self-sufficiency program under the "Ticket To Work and Work Incentives Improvement Act of 1999," 113 Stat. 1860, 42 U.S.C.A. 1320b-19, as well as sources of funds that may be available for the program;

(2) Determine the number of people likely to enroll in such a program;

(3) Determine the barriers and impediments to establishing such a program;

(4) Address any other issues the Committee considers pertinent.

(C) Not later than March 31, 2001, the Committee shall complete its work and submit a report on the matters specified in division (B) of this section to the President and Minority Leader of the Senate and the Speaker and Minority Leader of the House of Representatives. The Legislative Service Commission shall serve as staff to the Committee. On submission of the report, the Committee shall cease to exist.

Historical and Statutory Notes

Ed. Note: 5123.02 is former 5119.061 amended and recodified by 1980 H 900, eff. 7–1–80; 1972 H 494; 1970 H 970; 1969 H 1; 132 v H 178.

Ed. Note: Former 5123.02 repealed by 129 v 1448, eff. 10–25–61; 125 v 823; 1953 H 1; GC 154–60c.

Pre–1953 H 1 Amendments: 121 v 423; 119 v 109

Library References

Mental Health ⚖20.
Westlaw Topic No. 257A.
C.J.S. Insane Persons § 14 to 16.

5123.021 Determination of need for specialized services for mentally retarded persons seeking admission to nursing facility

(A) As used in this section, "mentally retarded individual" and "specialized services" have the same meanings as in section 5111.202 of the Revised Code.

(B)(1) Except as provided in division (B)(2) of this section and rules adopted under division (E)(3) of this section, for purposes of section 5111.202 of the Revised Code, the department of mental retardation and developmental disabilities shall determine in accordance with section 1919(e)(7) of the "Social Security Act," 49 Stat. 620 (1935), 42 U.S.C.A. 301, as amended, and regulations adopted under section 1919(f)(8)(A) of that act whether, because of the individual's physical and mental condition, a mentally retarded individual seeking admission to a nursing facility requires the level of services provided by a nursing facility and, if the individual requires that level of services, whether the individual requires specialized services for mental retardation.

(2) A determination under this division is not required for any of the following:

(a) An individual seeking readmission to a nursing facility after having been transferred from a nursing facility to a hospital for care;

(b) An individual who meets all of the following conditions:

(i) The individual is admitted to the nursing facility directly from a hospital after receiving inpatient care at the hospital;

(ii) The individual requires nursing facility services for the condition for which the individual received care in the hospital;

(iii) The individual's attending physician has certified, before admission to the nursing facility, that the individual is likely to require less than thirty days of nursing facility services.

(c) An individual transferred from one nursing facility to another nursing facility, with or without an intervening hospital stay.

(C) Except as provided in rules adopted under division (F)(3) of this section, the department of mental retardation and developmental disabilities shall review and determine, for each resident of a nursing facility who is mentally retarded, whether the resident, because of the resident's physical and mental condition, requires the level of services provided by a nursing facility and whether the resident requires specialized services for mental retardation. The review and determination shall be conducted in accordance with section 1919(e)(7) of the "Social Security Act" and the regulations adopted under section 1919(f)(8)(A) of the act. The review and determination shall be completed promptly after a nursing facility has notified the department that there has been a significant change in the resident's mental or physical condition.

(D)(1) In the case of a nursing facility resident who has continuously resided in a nursing facility for at least thirty months before the date of a review and determination under division (C) of this section, if the resident is determined not to require the level of services provided by a nursing facility, but is determined to require specialized services for mental retardation, the department, in consultation with the resident's family or legal representative and care givers, shall do all of the following:

(a) Inform the resident of the institutional and noninstitutional alternatives covered under the state plan for medical assistance;

(b) Offer the resident the choice of remaining in the nursing facility or receiving covered services in an alternative institutional or noninstitutional setting;

(c) Clarify the effect on eligibility for services under the state plan for medical assistance if the resident chooses to leave the facility, including its effect on readmission to the facility;

(d) Provide for or arrange for the provision of specialized services for the resident's mental retardation in the setting chosen by the resident.

(2) In the case of a nursing facility resident who has continuously resided in a nursing facility for less than thirty months before the date of the review and determination under division (C) of this section, if the resident is determined not to require the level of services provided by a nursing facility, but is determined to require specialized services for mental retardation, or if the resident is determined to require neither the level of services provided by a nursing facility nor specialized services for mental retardation, the department shall act in accordance with its alternative disposition plan approved by the United States department of health and human services under section 1919(e)(7)(E) of the "Social Security Act."

(3) In the case of an individual who is determined under division (B) or (C) of this section to require both the level of services provided by a nursing facility and specialized services for mental retardation, the department of mental retardation and developmental disabilities shall provide or arrange for the provision of the specialized services needed by the individual or resident while residing in a nursing facility.

(E) The department of mental retardation and developmental disabilities shall adopt rules in accordance with Chapter 119. of the Revised Code that do all of the following:

(1) Establish criteria to be used in making the determinations required by divisions (B) and (C) of this section. The criteria shall not exceed the criteria established by regulations adopted by the United States department of health and human services under section 1919(f)(8)(A) of the "Social Security Act."

(2) Specify information to be provided by the individual or nursing facility resident being assessed;

(3) Specify any circumstances, in addition to circumstances listed in division (B) of this section, under which determinations under divisions (B) and (C) of this section are not required to be made.

(1996 H 629, eff. 3–13–97; 1992 S 124, eff. 4–16–93)

Library References

Mental Health ⚖3.1, 14.1, 20.
Westlaw Topic No. 257A.
C.J.S. Insane Persons § 2, 6, 14 to 16, 37.

5123.03 Duties and authority of department

(A) The department of mental retardation and developmental disabilities shall do all of the following:

(1) Maintain, operate, manage, and govern all state institutions for the care, treatment, and training of the mentally retarded;

(2) Designate all such institutions by appropriate names;

(3) Provide and designate facilities for the custody, care, and special treatment of persons of the following classes:

(a) Dangerous persons in state institutions for the mentally retarded who represent a serious threat to the safety of the other patients of the institution;

(b) Persons charged with crimes who are found incompetent to stand trial or not guilty by reason of insanity and who are also mentally retarded persons subject to institutionalization by court order.

(4) Have control of all institutions maintained in part by the state for the care, treatment, and training of the mentally retarded;

(5) Administer the laws relative to persons in such institutions in an efficient, economical, and humane manner;

(6) Ascertain by actual examinations and inquiry whether institutionalizations are made according to law.

(B) The department may do any of the following:

(1) Subject to section 5139.08 of the Revised Code, receive from the department of youth services for observation, diagnosis, care, habilitation, or placement any children in the custody of the department of youth services;

(2) Receive for observation any minor from a public institution other than an institution under the jurisdiction of the department of mental retardation and developmental disabilities, from a private charitable institution, or from a person having legal custody of such a minor, upon such terms as are proper;

(3) Receive from the department of mental health any patient in the custody of the department who is transferred to the department of mental retardation and developmental disabilities upon such terms and conditions as may be agreed upon by the two departments.

(C) In addition to the powers and duties expressly conferred by this section, the department may take any other action necessary for the full and efficient executive, administrative, and fiscal supervision of the state institutions described in this section.

(1996 S 310, eff. 6–20–96; 1993 S 21, eff. 10–29–93; 1983 H 291; 1981 H 440; 1980 H 965, H 900)

Uncodified Law

2001 H 405, § 4 and 5: See Uncodified Law under 5123.02.

Historical and Statutory Notes

Ed. Note: Former 5123.03 repealed by 1980 H 900, eff. 7–1–80; 1976 H 244; 1972 H 494; 1970 H 970; 129 v 1448; 125 v 823; 1953 H 1; GC 1890–7.

Pre–1953 H 1 Amendments: 121 v 423; 119 v 616; 117 v 550

Library References

Asylums ⇔2.
Mental Health ⇔20.
Westlaw Topic Nos. 43, 257A.
C.J.S. Asylums and Institutional Care Facilities § 2 to 4.
C.J.S. Insane Persons § 14 to 16.

5123.031 Miscellaneous powers and duties

The director of mental retardation and developmental disabilities may require the performance of duties by the officers of the institutions under the jurisdiction of the department of mental retardation and developmental disabilities so as fully to meet the requirements, intents, and purposes of this chapter. In case of an apparent conflict between the powers conferred upon any managing officer and those conferred by this chapter upon the department, the presumption shall be conclusive in favor of the department.

The director shall adopt rules for the nonpartisan management of the institutions under the jurisdiction of the department. An officer or employee of the department or any officer or employee of any institution under its control who, by solicitation or otherwise, exerts his influence directly or indirectly to induce any other officer or employee of the department or any of its institutions to adopt his political views or to favor any particular person, issue, or candidate for office shall be removed from his office or position, by the department in case of an officer or employee, and by the governor in case of the director.

The managing officer of any institution under the jurisdiction of the department shall submit reports to the director relating to the admission, examination, comprehensive evaluation, diagnosis, release, or discharge of any resident.

The director, or a person designated by him, shall visit each institution regularly to review the admission procedures of all new residents and to investigate complaints made by any resident or by any person on behalf of a resident.

The director shall prescribe the forms of affidavits, applications, comprehensive evaluations, orders of institutionalization and release, and all other forms that are required in the institutionalization, admission, and release of all persons with respect to institutions under the jurisdiction of the department, and of reports and records provided for under this chapter.

(1994 H 694, eff. 11–11–94)

Historical and Statutory Notes

Ed. Note: Former 5123.031 amended and recodified as 5119.41 by 1980 H 900, eff. 7–1–80; 1979 H 204; 1977 S 221; 1976 H 1215.

Library References

Asylums ⇔3.
Mental Health ⇔20.
Westlaw Topic Nos. 43, 257A.
C.J.S. Asylums and Institutional Care Facilities § 5 to 8.
C.J.S. Insane Persons § 14 to 16.

5123.032 Closure of developmental centers; notice; independent study; report; closure commission

(A) As used in this section, "developmental center" means any institution or facility of the department of mental retardation and developmental disabilities that, on or after the effective date of this section, is named, designated, or referred to as a developmental center.

(B) Notwithstanding any other provision of law, on and after the effective date of this section, any closure of a developmental center shall be subject to, and in accordance with, this section. Notwithstanding any other provision of law, if the governor announced on or after January 1, 2003, and prior to the effective date of this section the intended closure of a developmental center and if the closure identified in the announcement has not occurred prior to the effective date of this section, the closure identified in the announcement shall be subject to the criteria set forth in this section as if the announcement had been made on or after the effective date of this section, except for the time at which the notice to the general assembly must be provided as identified in division (C) of this section.

(C) Notwithstanding any other provision of law, on and after the effective date of this section, at least ten days prior to making any official, public announcement that the governor intends to close one or more developmental centers, the governor shall notify the general assembly in writing that the governor intends to close one or more developmental centers. Notwithstanding any other provision of law, if the governor announced on or after January 1, 2003, and prior to the effective date of this section the intended closure of a developmental center and if the closure identified in the announcement has not occurred prior to the effective date of this section, not later than ten days after the effective date of this section, the governor shall notify the general assembly in writing of the prior announcement and that the governor intends to close the center identified in the prior announcement, and the notification to the general assembly shall constitute, for purposes of this section, the governor's official, public announcement that the governor intends to close that center.

The notice required by this division shall identify by name each developmental center that the governor intends to close or, if the governor has not determined any specific developmental center to close, shall state the governor's general intent to close one or more developmental centers. When the governor notifies the general assembly as required by this division, the legislative service commission promptly shall conduct an independent study of the developmental centers of the department of mental retardation and developmental disabilities and of the department's operation of the centers, and the study shall address relevant criteria and factors, including, but not limited to, all of the following:

(1) The manner in which the closure of developmental centers in general would affect the safety, health, well-being, and lifestyle of the centers' residents and their family members and would affect public safety and, if the governor's notice identifies by name one or more developmental centers that the governor intends to close, the manner in which the closure of each center so identified would affect the safety, health, well-being, and lifestyle of the center's residents and their family members and would affect public safety;

(2) The availability of alternate facilities;

(3) The cost effectiveness of the facilities identified for closure;

(4) A comparison of the cost of residing at a facility identified for closure and the cost of new living arrangements;

(5) The geographic factors associated with each facility and its proximity to other similar facilities;

(6) The impact of collective bargaining on facility operations;

(7) The utilization and maximization of resources;

(8) Continuity of the staff and ability to serve the facility population;

(9) Continuing costs following closure of a facility;

(10) The impact of the closure on the local economy;

(11) Alternatives and opportunities for consolidation with other facilities;

(12) How the closing of a facility identified for closure relates to the department's plans for the future of developmental centers in this state;

(13) The effect of the closure of developmental centers in general upon the state's fiscal resources and fiscal status and, if the governor's notice identifies by name one or more developmental centers that the governor intends to close, the effect of the closure of each center so identified upon the state's fiscal resources and fiscal status.

(D) The legislative service commission shall complete the study required by division (C) of this section, and prepare a report that contains its findings, not later than sixty days after the governor makes the official, public announcement that the governor intends to close one or more developmental centers as described in division (C) of this section. The commission shall provide a copy of the report to each member of the general assembly who requests a copy of the report.

Not later than the date on which the legislative service commission is required to complete the report under this division, the mental retardation and developmental disabilities developmental center closure commission is hereby created as described in division (E) of this section. The officials with the duties to appoint members of the closure commission, as described in division (E) of this section, shall appoint the specified members of the closure commission, and, as soon as possible after the appointments, the closure commission shall meet for the purposes described in that division. Upon completion of the report and the creation of the closure commission under this division, the legislative service commission promptly shall provide a copy of the report to the closure commission and shall present the report as described in division (E) of this section.

(E)(1) A mental retardation and developmental disabilities developmental center closure commission shall be created at the time and in the manner specified in division (D) of this section. The closure commission consists of six members. One member shall be the director of the department of mental retardation and developmental disabilities. One member shall be the director of the department of health. One member shall be a private executive with expertise in facility utilization, in economics, or in both facility utilization and economics, jointly appointed by the speaker of the house of representatives and the president of the senate. The member appointed for expertise in facility utilization, economics, or both may not be a member of the general assembly and may not have a developmental center identified for closure by the governor in the county in which the member resides. One member shall be a member of the board of the Ohio civil service employees' association, jointly appointed by the speaker of the house of representatives and the president of the senate. One member shall be either a family member of a resident of a developmental center or a representative of a mental retardation and developmental disabilities advocacy group, jointly appointed by the speaker of the house of representatives and the president of the senate. The member appointed who is a family member of a developmental center resident or a representative of an advocacy group may not be a member of the general assembly. One member shall be a member of the law enforcement community, appointed by the governor. The officials with the duties to appoint members of the closure commission shall make the appointments, and the closure commission shall meet, within the time periods specified in division (D) of this section. The members of the closure commission shall serve without compensation. At the closure commission's first meeting, the members shall organize and appoint a chairperson and vice-chairperson.

The closure commission shall meet as often as is necessary for the purpose of making the recommendations to the governor that are described in this division. The closure commission's meetings shall be open to the public, and the closure commission shall accept public testimony. The legislative service commission shall appear before the closure commission and present the report the legislative service commission prepared under division (D) of this section. The closure commission shall meet for the purpose of making recommendations to the governor, which recommendations may include all of the following:

(a) Whether any developmental center should be closed;

(b) If the recommendation described in division (E)(1)(a) of this section is that one or more developmental centers should be closed, which center or centers should be closed;

(c) If the governor's notice described in division (C) of this section identifies by name one or more developmental centers that the governor intends to close, whether the center or centers so identified should be closed.

(2) The mental retardation and developmental disabilities developmental center closure commission, not later than sixty days after it receives the report of the legislative service commission under division (D) of this section, shall prepare a report containing its recommendations to the governor. The closure commission shall send a copy of the report to the governor and to each member of the general assembly who requests a copy of the report. Upon receipt of the closure commission's report, the

governor shall review and consider the commission's recommendation. The governor shall do one of the following:

(a) Follow the recommendation of the commission;

(b) Close no developmental center;

(c) Take other action that the governor determines is necessary for the purpose of expenditure reductions or budget cuts and state the reasons for the action.

The governor's decision is final. Upon the governor's making of the decision, the closure commission shall cease to exist. Another closure commission shall be created under this section each time the governor subsequently makes an official, public announcement that the governor intends to close one or more developmental centers.

(2004 S 178, eff. 1–30–04)

5123.04 Duties of director

(A) The director of mental retardation and developmental disabilities is the executive head of the department of mental retardation and developmental disabilities. All duties conferred on the department and its institutions by law or by order of the director shall be performed under such rules as the director prescribes, and shall be under the director's control. The director shall establish bylaws for the government of all institutions under the jurisdiction of the department. Except as otherwise is provided as to appointments by chiefs of divisions, the director shall appoint such employees as are necessary for the efficient conduct of the department, and shall prescribe their titles and duties. If the director is not a licensed physician, decisions relating to medical diagnosis and treatment shall be the responsibility of a licensed physician appointed by the director.

(B) The director shall adopt rules for the proper execution of the powers and duties of the department.

(C) The director shall adopt rules establishing standards that mental retardation programs and facilities shall follow when performing evaluations of the mental condition of defendants ordered by the court under section 2919.271 or 2945.371 of the Revised Code, and for the treatment of defendants who have been found incompetent to stand trial under section 2945.38 of the Revised Code, and certify the compliance of such programs and facilities with the standards.

(D) On behalf of the department, the director has the authority to, and responsibility for, entering into contracts and other agreements.

(E) The director shall adopt rules in accordance with Chapter 119. of the Revised Code that do all of the following:

(1) Specify the supplemental services that may be provided through a trust authorized by section 5815.28 of the Revised Code;

(2) Establish standards for the maintenance and distribution to a beneficiary of assets of a trust authorized by section 5815.28 of the Revised Code.

(F) The director shall provide monitoring of county boards of mental retardation and developmental disabilities.

(2006 H 416, eff. 1–1–07; 1996 S 285, eff. 7–1–97; 1996 H 670, eff. 12–2–96; 1995 S 2, eff. 7–1–96; 1994 H 694, eff. 11–11–94; 1993 S 21, eff. 10–29–93; 1992 S 124, H 536; 1986 S 322; 1985 H 475; 1983 H 291; 1980 H 965, H 900)

Uncodified Law

1993 H 152, § 68.01: See Uncodified Law under 5123.18.

1992 S 124, § 8, eff. 4–16–93, reads: In enacting sections 1339.51 and 5111.15 and in amending sections 2101.24, 5119.01, 5121.04, 5121.10, 5123.04, 5123.18, and 5123.28 of the Revised Code, the General Assembly hereby declares its intent to supersede the effect of the holding of the Ohio Supreme Court in the December 31, 1968, decision in *Bureau of Support v. Kreitzer* (1968), 16 Ohio St. 2d 147.

Historical and Statutory Notes

Ed. Note: Former 5123.04 repealed by 1980 H 900, eff. 7–1–80; 1972 H 494; 126 v 1157; 1953 H 1; GC 1890–8.

Pre–1953 H 1 Amendments: 117 v 550, § 8

Library References

Asylums ⚖3.
Mental Health ⚖20.
Westlaw Topic Nos. 43, 257A.
C.J.S. Asylums and Institutional Care Facilities § 5 to 8.
C.J.S. Insane Persons § 14 to 16.

Baldwin's Ohio Legislative Service Annotated, 2006 H 416 LSC Analysis, p 3/L-1709

5123.042 Residential services

(A) The director of mental retardation and developmental disabilities shall adopt rules in accordance with Chapter 119. of the Revised Code establishing the following:

(1) Uniform standards under which:

(a) A person or agency shall submit plans to the county board of mental retardation and developmental disabilities for the development of residential services for individuals with mental retardation or a developmental disability within the county;

(b) The county board must review the plans and recommend providers for the services.

(2) The eligibility criteria for selecting persons and agencies to provide residential services, which shall take into consideration the recommendations of the county board.

(B) The county board, in accordance with its comprehensive service plan, shall review all proposals for the development of residential services that are submitted to it and shall, if the proposals are acceptable to the county board, recommend providers for the development of residential services within the county. The department shall approve proposals for the development of residential services within counties based upon the availability of funds and in accordance with rules adopted under division (A)(2) of this section.

No county board shall recommend providers for the development of residential services if the county board is an applicant to provide services. In cases of possible conflict of interest, the director shall appoint a committee that shall, in accordance with the approved county comprehensive service plan, review and recommend to the director providers for the services.

If a county board fails to establish an approved comprehensive service plan, the director may establish residential services development goals for the county board based on documented need as determined by the department. If a county board fails to develop or implement such a plan in accordance with the rules adopted under this section, the department may, without the involvement of the county board, review and select providers for the development of residential services in the county.

(2000 H 538, eff. 9–22–00; 1994 H 694, eff. 11–11–94)

Library References

Mental Health ⚖20.
Westlaw Topic No. 257A.
C.J.S. Insane Persons § 14 to 16.

5123.043 Administrative resolution of complaints

(A) The director of mental retardation and developmental disabilities shall adopt rules establishing procedures for administrative resolution of complaints filed under division (B) of this section and section 5126.06 of the Revised Code. The rules shall be adopted in accordance with Chapter 119. of the Revised Code.

(B) Except as provided in division (C) of this section, any person or county board of mental retardation and developmental disabilities that has a complaint involving any of the programs, services, policies, or administrative practices of the department of mental retardation and developmental disabilities or any of the entities under contract with the department, may file a complaint with the department. Prior to commencing a civil action regarding the complaint, a person or county board shall attempt to have the complaint resolved through the administrative resolution process established in the rules adopted under this section. After exhausting the administrative resolution process, the person or county board may commence a civil action if the complaint is not settled to the person's or county board's satisfaction.

(C) An employee of the department may not file under this section a complaint related to the terms and conditions of employment for the employee.

(D) This section does not apply to a conflict between a county board of mental retardation and developmental disabilities and a person or government entity that provides or seeks to provide services to an individual with mental retardation or other developmental disability. Section 5126.036 of the Revised Code applies to such a conflict.

(2001 H 405, eff. 12–13–01; 2001 H 94, eff. 6–6–01; 1996 H 629, eff. 3–13–97; 1994 H 694, eff. 11–11–94)

Library References

Mental Health ⇐20.
Westlaw Topic No. 257A.
C.J.S. Insane Persons § 14 to 16.

5123.044 Determination of compliance; department to provide assistance

The department of mental retardation and developmental disabilities shall determine whether county boards of mental retardation and developmental disabilities are in compliance with section 5126.046 of the Revised Code. The department shall provide assistance to an individual with mental retardation or other developmental disability who requests assistance with the individual's right under section 5126.046 of the Revised Code to choose a provider of habilitation, vocational, community employment, residential, or supported living services if the department is notified of a county board's alleged violation of the individual's right to choose such a provider.

(2001 H 94, eff. 6–6–01)

5123.045 Certification of home and community-based services providers

No person or government entity shall receive payment for providing home and community-based services unless the person or government entity is one of the following:

(A) Certified under section 5123.16 of the Revised Code;

(B) Licensed as a residential facility under section 5123.19 of the Revised Code.

(2005 H 66, eff. 7–1–05; 2001 H 94, eff. 6–6–01)

Uncodified Law

2005 H 66, § 209.09.27, eff. 6–30–05, reads:

(A) A person or government entity described in division (A) of section 5123.045 of the Revised Code shall not receive payment for home and community-based services unless both of the following are the case:

(1) The individuals who receive the services reside with not more than three other individuals with mental retardation or an other developmental disability unless the individuals are related by blood or marriage.

(2) Except as provided in division (B) of this section, the person or government entity does not provide to the individuals who receive the services a residence and home and community-based services.

(B) A person described in division (A) of section 5123.045 of the Revised Code may receive payment for home and community-based services and provide a residence to the individuals who receive the services if one of the following is the case:

(1) The person lives in the residence and provides the services to not more than three individuals who reside in the residence at any one time.

(2) The person is an association of family members related to two or more of the individuals who reside in the residence and provides the services to not more than four individuals who reside in the residence at any one time.

5123.046 Approval or disapproval of components of plan

The department of mental retardation and developmental disabilities shall review each component of the three-calendar year plan it receives from a county board of mental retardation and developmental disabilities under section 5126.054 of the Revised Code and, in consultation with the department of job and family services and office of budget and management, approve each component that includes all the information and conditions specified in that section. The fourth component of the plan shall be approved or disapproved not later than forty-five days after the fourth component is submitted to the department under division (B)(3) of section 5126.054 of the Revised Code. If the department approves all four components of the plan, the plan is approved. Otherwise, the plan is disapproved. If the plan is disapproved, the department shall take action against the county board under division (B) of section 5126.056 of the Revised Code.

In approving plans under this section, the department shall ensure that the aggregate of all plans provide for the increased enrollment into home and community-based services during each state fiscal year of at least five hundred individuals who did not receive residential services, supported living, or home and community-based services the prior state fiscal year if the department has enough additional enrollment available for this purpose.

The department shall establish protocols that the department shall use to determine whether a county board is complying with the programmatic and financial accountability mechanisms and achieving outcomes specified in its approved plan. If the department determines that a county board is not in compliance with the mechanisms or achieving the outcomes specified in its approved plan, the department may take action under division (F) of section 5126.055 of the Revised Code.

(2005 H 66, eff. 7–1–05; 2001 H 405, eff. 12–13–01; 2001 H 94, eff. 6–6–01)

5123.047 Payment of nonfederal share of medicaid expenditures

(A) The department of mental retardation and developmental disabilities shall pay the nonfederal share of medicaid expenditures for medicaid case management services if the services are provided to an individual with mental retardation or other developmental disability who a county board of mental retardation and developmental disabilities has determined under section 5126.041 of the Revised Code is not eligible for county board services.

(B) The department shall pay the nonfederal share of medicaid expenditures for home and community-based services if any of the following apply:

(1) The services are provided to an individual with mental retardation or other developmental disability who a county board has determined under section 5126.041 of the Revised Code is not eligible for county board services;

(2) The services are provided to an individual with mental retardation or other developmental disability given priority for the services pursuant to division (D)(3) of section 5126.042 of the Revised Code. The department shall pay the nonfederal share of medicaid expenditures for home and community-based services provided to such an individual for as long as the individual continues to be eligible for and receive the services, regardless of whether the services are provided after June 30, 2003.

(3) An agreement entered into under section 5123.048 of the Revised Code requires that the department pay the nonfederal share of medicaid expenditures for the services.

(2005 H 66, eff. 7–1–05; 2001 H 94, eff. 6–6–01)

5123.049 Rulemaking governing authorization and payment of home and community-based services and Medicaid case management services

The director of mental retardation and developmental disabilities shall adopt rules in accordance with Chapter 119. of the Revised Code governing the authorization and payment of home and community-based services and medicaid case management services. The rules shall provide for private providers of the services to receive one hundred per cent of the medicaid allowable payment amount and for government providers of the services to receive the federal share of the medicaid allowable payment, less the amount withheld as a fee under section 5123.0412 of the Revised Code and any amount that may be required by rules adopted under section 5123.0413 of the Revised Code to be deposited into the state MR/DD risk fund. The rules shall establish the process by which county boards of mental retardation and developmental disabilities shall certify and provide the nonfederal share of medicaid expenditures that the county board is required by division (A) of section 5126.057 of the Revised Code to pay. The process shall require a county board to certify that the county board has funding available at one time for two months costs for those expenditures. The process may permit a county board to certify that the county board has funding available at one time for more than two months costs for those expenditures.

(2005 H 66, eff. 7–1–05; 2001 H 405, eff. 12–13–01; 2001 H 94, eff. 6–6–01)

5123.0410 Individual who moves to new county to receive comparable services

An individual with mental retardation or other developmental disability who moves from one county in this state to another county in this state shall receive home and community-based services in the new county that are comparable in scope to the home and community-based services the individual receives in the prior county at the time the individual moves. If the county board serving the county to which the individual moves determines under section 5126.041 of the Revised Code that the individual is eligible for county board services, the county board shall ensure that the individual receives the comparable services. If the county board determines that the individual is not eligible for county board services, the department of mental retardation and developmental disabilities shall ensure that the individual receives the comparable services.

If the home and community-based services that the individual receives at the time the individual moves include supported living or residential services, the department shall reduce the amount the department allocates to the county board serving the county the individual left for those supported living or residential services by an amount that equals the payment the department authorizes or projects, or both, for those supported living or residential services from the last day the individual resides in the county to the last day of the state fiscal year in which the individual moves. The department shall increase the amount the department allocates to the county board serving the county the individual moves to by the same amount. The department shall make the reduction and increase effective the day the department determines the individual has residence in the new county. The department shall determine the amount that is to be reduced and increased in accordance with the department's rules for authorizing payments for home and community-based services established adopted under section 5123.049 of the Revised Code. The department shall annualize the reduction and increase for the subsequent state fiscal year as necessary.

(2001 H 94, eff. 6–6–01)

5123.0411 Mandamus action

The department of mental retardation and developmental disabilities may bring a mandamus action against a county board of mental retardation and developmental disabilities that fails to pay the nonfederal share of medicaid expenditures that the county board is required by division (A) of section 5126.057 of the Revised Code to pay. The department may bring the mandamus action in the court of common pleas of the county served by the county board or in the Franklin county court of common pleas.

(2001 H 405, eff. 12–13–01; 2001 H 94, eff. 6–6–01)

5123.0412 Fees

(A) The department of mental retardation and developmental disabilities shall charge each county board of mental retardation and developmental disabilities an annual fee equal to one and one-half per cent of the total value of all medicaid paid claims for medicaid case management services and home and community-based services provided during the year to an individual eligible for services from the county board. No county board shall pass the cost of a fee charged to the county board under this section on to another provider of these services.

(B) The fees collected under this section shall be deposited into the ODMR/DD administration and oversight fund and the ODJFS administration and oversight fund, both of which are hereby created in the state treasury. The portion of the fees to be deposited into the ODMR/DD administration and oversight fund and the portion of the fees to be deposited into the ODJFS administration and oversight fund shall be the portion specified in an interagency agreement entered into under division (C) of this section. The department of mental retardation and developmental disabilities shall use the money in the ODMR/DD administration and oversight fund and the department of job and family services shall use the money in the ODJFS administration and oversight fund for both of the following purposes:

(1) The administrative and oversight costs of medicaid case management services and home and community-based services. The administrative and oversight costs shall include costs for staff, systems, and other resources the departments need and dedicate solely to the following duties associated with the services:

(a) Eligibility determinations;

(b) Training;

(c) Fiscal management;

(d) Claims processing;

(e) Quality assurance oversight;

(f) Other duties the departments identify.

(2) Providing technical support to county boards' local administrative authority under section 5126.055 of the Revised Code for the services.

(C) The departments of mental retardation and developmental disabilities and job and family services shall enter into an interagency agreement to do both of the following:

(1) Specify which portion of the fees collected under this section is to be deposited into the ODMR/DD administration and oversight fund and which portion is to be deposited into the ODJFS administration and oversight fund;

(2) Provide for the departments to coordinate the staff whose costs are paid for with money in the ODMR/DD administration and oversight fund and the ODJFS administration and oversight fund.

(D) The departments shall submit an annual report to the director of budget and management certifying how the departments spent the money in the ODMR/DD administration and oversight fund and the ODJFS administration and oversight fund for the purposes specified in division (B) of this section.

(2005 H 66, eff. 7-1-05; 2001 H 94, eff. 6-6-01)

5123.0413 Rules governing payment of extraordinary costs

(A) The department of mental retardation and developmental disabilities, in consultation with the department of job and family services, office of budget and management, and county boards of mental retardation and developmental disabilities, shall adopt rules in accordance with Chapter 119. of the Revised Code no later than January 1, 2002, establishing a method of paying for extraordinary costs, including extraordinary costs for services to individuals with mental retardation or other developmental disability, and ensure the availability of adequate funds in the event a county property tax levy for services for individuals with mental retardation or other developmental disability fails. The rules may provide for using and managing either or both of the following:

(1) A state MR/DD risk fund, which is hereby created in the state treasury;

(2) A state insurance against MR/DD risk fund, which is hereby created in the state treasury.

(B) Beginning January 1, 2002, the department of job and family services may not request approval from the United States secretary of health and human services to increase the number of slots for home and community-based services until the rules required by division (A) of this section are in effect.

(2006 H 530, eff. 6-30-06; 2001 H 94, eff. 6-6-01)

DIVISIONS AND BUREAUS

5123.05 Audits

The department of mental retardation and developmental disabilities may conduct audits of the services and programs that either receive funds through the department or are subject to regulation by the department. Audits shall be conducted in accordance with procedures prescribed by the department. Records created or received by the department in connection with an audit are not public records under section 149.43 of the Revised Code until a report of the audit is released by the department.

(2000 H 538, eff. 9-22-00)

Historical and Statutory Notes

Ed. Note: Former 5123.05 amended and recodified as 5123.06 by 2000 H 538, eff. 9-22-00; 1997 H 215, eff. 9-29-97; 1990 H 569, eff. 7-1-91; 1986 S 322; 1980 H 900.

Ed. Note: Prior 5123.05 amended and recodified as 5119.17 by 1980 H 900, eff. 7-1-80; 1972 H 494; 131 v H 457; 126 v 1157; 1953 H 1; GC 1890-9.

Pre-1953 H 1 Amendments: 121 v 423; 119 v 616; 117 v 550

Library References

Mental Health ⚖20.
Westlaw Topic No. 257A.
C.J.S. Insane Persons § 14 to 16.

5123.051 Payment agreements; purchase of service fund

(A) If the department of mental retardation and developmental disabilities determines pursuant to an audit conducted under section 5123.05 of the Revised Code or a reconciliation conducted under section 5123.18 or 5123.199 of the Revised Code that money is owed the state by a provider of a service or program, the department may enter into a payment agreement with the provider. The agreement shall include the following:

(1) A schedule of installment payments whereby the money owed the state is to be paid in full within a period not to exceed one year;

(2) A provision that the provider may pay the entire balance owed at any time during the term of the agreement;

(3) A provision that if any installment is not paid in full within forty-five days after it is due, the entire balance owed is immediately due and payable;

(4) Any other terms and conditions that are agreed to by the department and the provider.

(B) The department may include a provision in a payment agreement that requires the provider to pay interest on the money owed the state. The department, in its discretion, shall determine whether to require the payment of interest and, if it so requires, the rate of interest. Neither the obligation to pay interest nor the rate of interest is subject to negotiation between the department and the provider.

(C) If the provider fails to pay any installment in full within forty-five days after its due date, the department shall certify the entire balance owed to the attorney general for collection under section 131.02 of the Revised Code. The department may withhold funds from payments made to a provider under section 5123.18 or 5123.199 of the Revised Code to satisfy a judgment secured by the attorney general.

(D) The purchase of service fund is hereby created. Money credited to the fund shall be used solely for purposes of section 5123.05 of the Revised Code.

(2003 H 95, eff. 9-26-03; 2000 H 538, eff. 9-22-00)

Historical and Statutory Notes

Ed. Note: 5123.051 is former 5123.183, amended and recodified by 2000 H 538, eff. 9-22-00; 1994 H 435, eff. 11-9-94; 1992 S 331, eff. 11-13-92.

Library References

Mental Health ⚖20.
Westlaw Topic No. 257A.
C.J.S. Insane Persons § 14 to 16.

5123.06 Establishment of divisions

The director of mental retardation and developmental disabilities may establish divisions in the department of mental retardation and developmental disabilities and prescribe their powers and duties.

Each division shall consist of a deputy director and the officers and employees, including those in institutions, necessary for the performance of the functions assigned to it. The director shall supervise the work of each division and be responsible for the determination of general policies in the exercise of powers vested in the department and powers assigned to each division. The deputy director of each division shall be responsible to the director for the organization, direction, and supervision of the work of the division and the exercise of the powers and the performance of the duties of the department assigned to the division, and, with the approval of the director, may establish bureaus or other administrative units in the division.

Appointment to the position of deputy director of a division may be made from persons holding positions in the classified service in the department.

The deputy director of each division shall be a person who has had special training and experience in the type of work with the performance of which the division is charged.

Each deputy director of a division, under the director, shall have entire executive charge of the division to which the deputy director is appointed. Subject to sections 124.01 to 124.64 of the Revised Code, and civil service rules, the deputy director of a division shall, with the approval of the director, select and appoint the necessary employees in the deputy director's division and may remove those employees for cause.

(2000 H 538, eff. 9–22–00)

Historical and Statutory Notes

Ed. Note: 5123.06 is former 5123.05, admended and recodified by 2000 H 538, eff. 9-22-00; 1997 H 215, eff. 9-29-97; 1990 H 569, eff. 7-1-91; 1986 S 322; 1980 H 900.

Ed. Note: Former 5123.06 repealed by 1997 H 215, eff. 9-29-97; 1980 H 900, eff. 7-1-80.

Ed. Note: Prior 5123.06 amended and recodified as 5123.27 by 1980 H 900, eff. 7-1-80; 1976 H 1215; 1972 H 494; 1970 H 970; 125 v 823; 1953 H 1; GC 1890-10.

Pre–1953 H 1 Amendments: 121 v 423; 119 v 616; 117 v 550

Library References

Mental Health ⇐20.
States ⇐50.
Westlaw Topic Nos. 257A, 360.
C.J.S. Insane Persons § 14 to 16.
C.J.S. States § 61, 85, 123.

5123.07 Bureau of research; powers and duties

There may be created in the department of mental retardation and developmental disabilities a bureau of research. The bureau shall:

(A) Plan, direct, and coordinate all research programs conducted by the department;

(B) Provide continuing evaluation of research programs;

(C) Direct and coordinate scientific investigations and studies as undertaken under this section.

The department shall institute and encourage scientific investigation by the staffs of the various institutions under its control and supervision, and publish bulletins and reports of the scientific and clinical work done in such institutions. Scientific investigation in the department shall be undertaken and continued only with the approval of the director of mental retardation and developmental disabilities.

(1986 S 322, eff. 4–4–86; 1980 H 900)

Historical and Statutory Notes

Ed. Note: 5123.07 is former 5129.011 amended and recodified by 1980 H 900, eff. 7-1-80; 1972 H 494.

Ed. Note: Former 5123.07 repealed by 126 v 1157, eff. 10-1-55; 125 v 823; 1953 H 1; GC 1890-11.

Pre–1953 H 1 Amendments: 119 v 616, § 1; 117 v 550, § 11

Library References

Mental Health ⇐20.
States ⇐45.
Westlaw Topic Nos. 257A, 360.
C.J.S. Insane Persons § 14 to 16.
C.J.S. States § 79 to 80, 82, 136.

PERSONNEL; GENERAL PROVISIONS

5123.08 Reassignments; rights to reinstatement

An appointing officer may appoint a person who holds a certified position in the classified service within the department of mental retardation and developmental disabilities to a position in the unclassified service within the department. A person appointed pursuant to this section to a position in the unclassified service shall retain the right to resume the position and status held by the person in the classified service immediately prior to the person's appointment to the position in the unclassified service, regardless of the number of positions the person held in the unclassified service. An employee's right to resume a position in the classified service may only be exercised when an appointing authority demotes the employee to a pay range lower than the employee's current pay range or revokes the employee's appointment to the unclassified service. An employee forfeits the right to resume a position in the classified service when the employee is removed from the position in the unclassified service due to incompetence, inefficiency, dishonesty, drunkenness, immoral conduct, insubordination, discourteous treatment of the public, neglect of duty, violation of this chapter or Chapter 124. of the Revised Code, the rules of the director of mental retardation and developmental disabilities or the director of administrative services, any other failure of good behavior, any other acts of misfeasance, malfeasance, or nonfeasance in office, or conviction of a felony. An employee also forfeits the right to resume a position in the classified service upon transfer to a different agency.

Reinstatement to a position in the classified service shall be to a position substantially equal to that position in the classified service held previously, as certified by the director of administrative services. If the position the person previously held in the classified service has been placed in the unclassified service or is otherwise unavailable, the person shall be appointed to a position in the classified service within the department that the director of administrative services certifies is comparable in compensation to the position the person previously held in the classified service. Service in the position in the unclassified service shall be counted as service in the position in the classified service held by the person immediately prior to the person's appointment to the position in the unclassified service. When a person is reinstated to a position in the classified service as provided in this section, the person is entitled to all rights, status, and benefits accruing to the position in the classified service during the time of the person's service in the position in the unclassified service.

(2006 H 699, eff. 3–29–07; 1980 H 1017, eff. 1–15–81; 1980 H 900)

Historical and Statutory Notes

Ed. Note: Former 5123.08 repealed by 1980 H 900, eff. 7–1–80; 1972 H 494; 129 v 1448; 1953 H 1; GC 1890–12.

Pre–1953 H 1 Amendments: 117 v 550, § 12

Library References

Mental Health ⚖20.
Officers and Public Employees ⚖11.7.
States ⚖53.
Westlaw Topic Nos. 257A, 283, 360.
C.J.S. Insane Persons § 14 to 16.
C.J.S. Officers and Public Employees § 92 to 98.
C.J.S. States § 81 to 83, 86, 93 to 98, 101, 136.

5123.081 Criminal records check; form and standard impression sheet; violations preventing employment; fee; confidentiality of reports; conditional employment

(A) As used in this section:

(1) "Applicant" means a person who is under final consideration for appointment to or employment with the department of mental retardation and developmental disabilities, including, but not limited to, a person who is being transferred to the department and an employee who is being recalled or reemployed after a layoff.

(2) "Criminal records check" has the same meaning as in section 109.572 of the Revised Code.

(3) "Minor drug possession offense" has the same meaning as in section 2925.01 of the Revised Code.

(B) The director of mental retardation and developmental disabilities shall request the superintendent of the bureau of criminal identification and investigation to conduct a criminal records check with respect to each applicant, except that the director is not required to request a criminal records check for an employee of the department who is being considered for a different position or is returning after a leave of absence or seasonal break in employment, as long as the director has no reason to believe that the employee has committed any of the offenses listed or described in division (E) of this section.

If the applicant does not present proof that the applicant has been a resident of this state for the five-year period immediately prior to the date upon which the criminal records check is requested, the director shall request that the superintendent of the bureau obtain information from the federal bureau of investigation as a part of the criminal records check for the applicant. If the applicant presents proof that the applicant has been a resident of this state for that five-year period, the director may request that the superintendent of the bureau include information from the federal bureau of investigation in the criminal records check. For purposes of this division, an applicant may provide proof of residency in this state by presenting, with a notarized statement asserting that the applicant has been a resident of this state for that five-year period, a valid driver's license, notification of registration as an elector, a copy of an officially filed federal or state tax form identifying the applicant's permanent residence, or any other document the director considers acceptable.

(C) The director shall provide to each applicant a copy of the form prescribed pursuant to division (C)(1) of section 109.572 of the Revised Code, provide to each applicant a standard impression sheet to obtain fingerprint impressions prescribed pursuant to division (C)(2) of section 109.572 of the Revised Code, obtain the completed form and impression sheet from each applicant, and forward the completed form and impression sheet to the superintendent of the bureau of criminal identification and investigation at the time the criminal records check is requested.

Any applicant who receives pursuant to this division a copy of the form prescribed pursuant to division (C)(1) of section 109.572 of the Revised Code and a copy of an impression sheet prescribed pursuant to division (C)(2) of that section and who is requested to complete the form and provide a set of fingerprint impressions shall complete the form or provide all the information necessary to complete the form and shall provide the material with the impressions of the applicant's fingerprints. If an applicant, upon request, fails to provide the information necessary to complete the form or fails to provide impressions of the applicant's fingerprints, the director shall not employ the applicant.

(D) The director may request any other state or federal agency to supply the director with a written report regarding the criminal record of each applicant. With regard to an applicant who becomes a department employee, if the employee holds an occupational or professional license or other credentials, the director may request that the state or federal agency that regulates the employee's occupation or profession supply the director with a written report of any information pertaining to the employee's criminal record that the agency obtains in the course of conducting an investigation or in the process of renewing the employee's license or other credentials.

(E) Except as provided in division (K)(2) of this section and in rules adopted by the director in accordance with division (M) of this section, the director shall not employ a person to fill a position with the department who has been convicted of or pleaded guilty to any of the following:

(1) A violation of section 2903.01, 2903.02, 2903.03, 2903.04, 2903.11, 2903.12, 2903.13, 2903.16, 2903.21, 2903.34, 2903.341, 2905.01, 2905.02, 2905.05, 2907.02, 2907.03, 2907.04, 2907.05, 2907.06, 2907.07, 2907.08, 2907. 09, 2907.21, 2907.22, 2907.23, 2907.25, 2907.31, 2907.32, 2907.321, 2907.322, 2907.323, 2911.01, 2911.02, 2911.11, 2911.12, 2919.12, 2919.22, 2919.24, 2919.25, 2923.12, 2923.13, 2923.161, 2925.02, 2925.03, 2925.04, 2925.05, 2925.06, or 3716.11 of the Revised Code, a violation of section 2905.04 of the Revised Code as it existed prior to July 1, 1996, a violation of section 2919.23 of the Revised Code that would have been a violation of section 2905.04 of the Revised Code as it existed prior to July 1, 1996, had the violation occurred prior to that date, a violation of section 2925.11 of the Revised Code that is not a minor drug possession offense, or felonious sexual penetration in violation of former section 2907.12 of the Revised Code;

(2) A felony contained in the Revised Code that is not listed in this division, if the felony bears a direct and substantial relationship to the duties and responsibilities of the position being filled;

(3) Any offense contained in the Revised Code constituting a misdemeanor of the first degree on the first offense and a felony on a subsequent offense, if the offense bears a direct and substantial relationship to the position being filled and the nature of the services being provided by the department;

(4) A violation of an existing or former municipal ordinance or law of this state, any other state, or the United States, if the offense is substantially equivalent to any of the offenses listed or described in division (E)(1), (2), or (3) of this section.

(F) Prior to employing an applicant, the director shall require the applicant to submit a statement with the applicant's signature attesting that the applicant has not been convicted of or pleaded guilty to any of the offenses listed or described in division (E) of this section. The director also shall require the applicant to sign an agreement under which the applicant agrees to notify the director within fourteen calendar days if, while employed with the department, the applicant is ever formally charged with, convicted of, or pleads guilty to any of the offenses listed or described in division (E) of this section. The agreement shall inform the applicant that failure to report formal charges, a conviction, or a guilty plea may result in being dismissed from employment.

(G) The director shall pay to the bureau of criminal identification and investigation the fee prescribed pursuant to division (C)(3) of section 109.572 of the Revised Code for each criminal records check requested and conducted pursuant to this section.

(H)(1) Any report obtained pursuant to this section is not a public record for purposes of section 149.43 of the Revised Code and shall not be made available to any person, other than the applicant who is the subject of the records check or criminal records check or the applicant's representative, the department or its representative, a county board of mental retardation and developmental disabilities, and any court, hearing officer, or other necessary individual involved in a case dealing with the denial of employment to the applicant or the denial, suspension, or revocation of a certificate or evidence of registration under section 5123.082 of the Revised Code.

(2) An individual for whom the director has obtained reports under this section may submit a written request to the director to have copies of the reports sent to any state agency, entity of local government, or private entity. The individual shall specify in the request the agencies or entities to which the copies are to be sent. On receiving the request, the director shall send copies of the reports to the agencies or entities specified.

The director may request that a state agency, entity of local government, or private entity send copies to the director of any report regarding a records check or criminal records check that the agency or entity possesses, if the director obtains the written consent of the individual who is the subject of the report.

(I) The director shall request the registrar of motor vehicles to supply the director with a certified abstract regarding the record of convictions for violations of motor vehicle laws of each applicant who will be required by the applicant's employment to transport individuals with mental retardation or a developmental disability or to operate the department's vehicles for any other purpose. For each abstract provided under this section, the director shall pay the amount specified in section 4509.05 of the Revised Code.

(J) The director shall provide each applicant with a copy of any report or abstract obtained about the applicant under this section.

(K)(1) The director shall inform each person, at the time of the person's initial application for employment, that the person is required to provide a set of impressions of the person's fingerprints and that a criminal records check is required to be conducted and satisfactorily completed in accordance with section 109.572 of the Revised Code if the person comes under final consideration for employment as a precondition to employment in a position.

(2) The director may employ an applicant pending receipt of reports requested under this section. The director shall terminate employment of any such applicant if it is determined from the reports that the applicant failed to inform the director that the applicant had been convicted of or pleaded guilty to any of the offenses listed or described in division (E) of this section.

(L) The director may charge an applicant a fee for costs the director incurs in obtaining reports, abstracts, or fingerprint impressions under this section. A fee charged under this division shall not exceed the amount of the fees the director pays under divisions (G) and (I) of this section. If a fee is charged under this division, the director shall notify the applicant of the amount of the fee at the time of the applicant's initial application for employment and that, unless the fee is paid, the director will not consider the applicant for employment.

(M) The director shall adopt rules in accordance with Chapter 119. of the Revised Code to implement this section, including rules specifying circumstances under which the director may employ a person who has been convicted of or pleaded guilty to an offense listed or described in division (E) of this section but who meets standards in regard to rehabilitation set by the director.

(2004 S 178, eff. 1–30–04; 2000 H 538, eff. 9–22–00)

Historical and Statutory Notes

Ed. Note: Former 5123.081 repealed by 2000 H 538, eff. 9–22–00; 1984 H 235, eff. 6–7–84.

Library References

Criminal Law ⚖1226(2).
Mental Health ⚖20.
Westlaw Topic Nos. 110, 257A.
C.J.S. Criminal Law § 1734 to 1736.
C.J.S. Insane Persons § 14 to 16.

5123.082 Rules for certification or registration of employees

(A) The director of mental retardation and developmental disabilities shall adopt rules in accordance with Chapter 119. of the Revised Code:

(1) Designating positions of employment for which the director determines that certification or evidence of registration is required as a condition of employment in the department of mental retardation and developmental disabilities, entities that contract with the department or county boards of mental retardation and developmental disabilities to operate programs or provide services to persons with mental retardation and developmental disabilities, or other positions of employment in programs that serve those persons. The rules shall designate the position of investigative agent, as defined in section 5126.20 of the Revised Code, as a position for which certification is required.

(2) Establishing levels of certification or registration for each position for which certification or registration is required;

(3) Establishing for each level of each position the requirements that must be met to obtain certification or registration, including standards regarding education, specialized training, and experience. The standards shall take into account the nature and needs of persons with mental retardation or a developmental disability and the specialized techniques needed to serve them. The requirements for an investigative agent shall be the same as the certification requirements for an investigative agent under section 5126.25 of the Revised Code.

(4) Establishing renewal schedules and renewal requirements for certification and registration, including standards regarding education, specialized training, and experience. The renewal requirements for an investigative agent shall be the same as the renewal requirements for an investigative agent under section 5126.25 of the Revised Code.

(5) Establishing procedures for denial, suspension, and revocation of a certificate or evidence of registration, including appeal procedures;

(6) Establishing other requirements needed to carry out this section.

(B) The director shall issue, renew, deny, suspend, or revoke a certificate or evidence of registration in accordance with rules adopted under this section. The director shall deny, suspend, or revoke a certificate or evidence of registration if the director finds, pursuant to an adjudication conducted in accordance with Chapter 119. of the Revised Code, that an applicant for or holder of a certificate or evidence of registration is guilty of intemperate, immoral, or other conduct unbecoming to the applicant's or holder's position, or is guilty of incompetence or negligence within the scope of the applicant's or holder's duties. The director shall deny or revoke a certificate or evidence of registration after the director finds, pursuant to an adjudication conducted in accordance with Chapter 119. of the Revised Code, that the applicant for or holder of the certificate or evidence of registration has been convicted of or pleaded guilty to any of the offenses listed or described in division (E) of section 5126.28 of the Revised Code, unless the individual meets standards for rehabilitation that the director establishes in the rules adopted under that section. Evidence supporting such allegations must be presented to the director in writing, and the director shall provide prompt notice of the allegations to the person who is the subject of the allegations. A denial, suspension, or revocation may be appealed in accordance with the procedures established in rules adopted under this section.

(C) A person holding a valid certificate or evidence of registration under this section on the effective date of any rules adopted under this section that increase the certification or registration standards shall have the period that the rules prescribe, but not less than one year after the effective date of the rules, to meet the new standards.

(D) No person shall be employed in a position for which certification or registration is required under rules adopted under this section, unless the person holds a valid certificate or evidence of registration for the position.

(2001 H 94, eff. 6–6–01; 2000 H 538, eff. 9–22–00; 1996 H 629, eff. 3–13–97; 1992 H 387, eff. 5–4–92; 1986 S 322)

Library References

Asylums ⇌3.
Mental Health ⇌20.
Westlaw Topic Nos. 43, 257A.
C.J.S. Asylums and Institutional Care Facilities § 5 to 8.
C.J.S. Insane Persons § 14 to 16.

5123.083 Certificate holders in default on child support orders

On receipt of a notice pursuant to section 3123.43 of the Revised Code, the director of mental retardation and developmental disabilities shall comply with sections 3123.41 to 3123.50 of the Revised Code and any applicable rules adopted under section 3123.63 of the Revised Code with respect to a certificate or evidence of registration issued pursuant to this chapter.

(2000 S 180, eff. 3–22–01; 1996 H 629, eff. 3–13–97; 1995 H 167, eff. 11–15–96)

Library References

Asylums ⇌3.
Mental Health ⇌20.
Westlaw Topic Nos. 43, 257A.
C.J.S. Asylums and Institutional Care Facilities § 5 to 8.
C.J.S. Insane Persons § 14 to 16.

5123.09 Managing officers of institutions

Subject to the rules of the department of mental retardation and developmental disabilities, each institution under the jurisdiction of the department shall be under the control of a managing officer to be known as a superintendent or by other appropriate title. The managing officer shall be appointed by the director of mental retardation and developmental disabilities and shall be in the unclassified service and serve at the pleasure of the director. Each managing officer shall be of good moral character and have skill, ability, and experience in the managing officer's profession. Appointment to the position of managing officer of an institution may be made from persons holding positions in the classified service in the department.

The managing officer, under the director, shall have entire executive charge of the institution for which the managing officer is appointed, except as provided in section 5119.16 of the Revised Code. Subject to civil service rules and rules adopted by the department, the managing officer shall appoint the necessary employees, and the managing officer or the director may remove those employees for cause. A report of all appointments, resignations, and discharges shall be filed with the appropriate division at the close of each month.

After conference with the managing officer of each institution, the director shall determine the number of employees to be appointed to the various institutions and clinics.

(2000 H 538, eff. 9–22–00; 1984 S 112, eff. 1–10–85; 1980 H 900)

Historical and Statutory Notes

Ed. Note: Former 5123.09 amended and recodified as 5119.45 by 1980 H 900, eff. 7–1–80; 1972 H 494; 1970 H 970; 125 v 823; 1953 H 1; GC 1890–13.

Pre–1953 H 1 Amendments: 117 v 550, § 13

Library References

Asylums ⇌4.
Mental Health ⇌20.
Westlaw Topic Nos. 43, 257A.
C.J.S. Asylums and Institutional Care Facilities § 9 to 10.
C.J.S. Insane Persons § 14 to 16.

5123.091 Authority to change purpose of institution

The director of mental retardation and developmental disabilities may, by rule and with the approval of the governor, change the purpose for which any institution under the control of the department is being used. The director may designate a new or another use for the institution, provided the change of use and new designation has for its objective improvement in the classification, segregation, care, education, cure, or rehabilitation of the persons admitted.

(1980 H 965, eff. 4–9–81)

Library References

Asylums ⇌3.
Mental Health ⇌20.
Westlaw Topic Nos. 43, 257A.
C.J.S. Asylums and Institutional Care Facilities § 5 to 8.
C.J.S. Insane Persons § 14 to 16.

CITIZEN'S ADVISORY COUNCILS

5123.092 Citizen's advisory councils

(A) There is hereby established at each institution and branch institution under the control of the department of mental retardation and developmental disabilities a citizen's advisory council consisting of thirteen members. At least seven of the members shall be persons who are not providers of mental retardation services. Each council shall include parents or other relatives of residents of institutions under the control of the department, community leaders, professional persons in relevant fields, and persons who have an interest in or knowledge of mental retardation. The managing officer of the institution shall be a nonvoting member of the council.

(B) The director of mental retardation and developmental disabilities shall be the appointing authority for the voting members of each citizen's advisory council. Each time the term of a voting member expires, the remaining members of the council shall recommend to the director one or more persons to serve on the council. The director may accept a nominee of the council or reject the nominee or nominees. If the director rejects the nominee or nominees, the remaining members of the advisory council shall further recommend to the director one or more other persons to serve on the advisory council. This procedure shall continue until a member is appointed to the advisory council.

Each advisory council shall elect from its appointed members a chairperson, vice-chairperson, and a secretary to serve for terms of one year. Advisory council officers shall not serve for more than two consecutive terms in the same office. A majority of the advisory council members constitutes a quorum.

(C) Terms of office shall be for three years, each term ending on the same day of the same month of the year as did the term which it succeeds. No member shall serve more than two consecutive terms, except that any former member may be appointed if one year or longer has elapsed since the member served two consecutive terms. Each member shall hold office from the date of appointment until the end of the term for which the member was appointed. Any vacancy shall be filled in the same manner in which the original appointment was made, and the appointee to a vacancy in an unexpired term shall serve the balance of the term of the original appointee. Any member shall continue in office subsequent to the expiration date of the member's term until the member's successor takes office, or until a period of sixty days has elapsed, whichever occurs first.

(D) Members shall be expected to attend all meetings of the advisory council. Unexcused absence from two successive regularly scheduled meetings shall be considered prima-facie evidence of intent not to continue as a member. The chairperson of the board shall, after a member has been absent for two successive regularly scheduled meetings, direct a letter to the member asking if the member wishes to remain in membership. If an affirmative reply is received, the member shall be retained as a member except that, if, after having expressed a desire to remain a member, the member then misses a third successive regularly scheduled meeting without being excused, the chairperson shall terminate the member's membership.

(E) A citizen's advisory council shall meet six times annually, or more frequently if three council members request the chairperson to call a meeting. The council shall keep minutes of each meeting and shall submit them to the managing officer of the institution with which the council is associated, the department of mental retardation and developmental disabilities, and the legal rights service.

(F) Members of citizen's advisory councils shall receive no compensation for their services, except that they shall be reimbursed for their actual and necessary expenses incurred in the performance of their official duties by the institution with which they are associated from funds allocated to it, provided that reimbursement for those expenses shall not exceed limits imposed upon the department of mental retardation and developmental disabilities by administrative rules regulating travel within this state.

(G) The councils shall have reasonable access to all patient treatment and living areas and records of the institution, except those records of a strictly personal or confidential nature. The councils shall have access to a patient's personal records with the consent of the patient or the patient's legal guardian or, if the patient is a minor, with the consent of the parent or legal guardian of the patient.

(H) As used in this section, "branch institution" means a facility that is located apart from an institution and is under the control of the managing officer of the institution.

(2000 H 538, eff. 9–22–00; 1996 H 670, eff. 12–2–96; 1993 S 21, eff. 10–29–93; 1986 H 428; 1983 H 291; 1982 S 550; 1981 H 694)

Uncodified Law

1996 H 670, § 27, as subsequently amended: See *Baldwin's Ohio Revised Code Annotated*, Uncodified Law under RC 101.83.

Library References

Asylums ⚖3.
Mental Health ⚖20.
Westlaw Topic Nos. 43, 257A.
C.J.S. Asylums and Institutional Care Facilities § 5 to 8.
C.J.S. Insane Persons § 14 to 16.

5123.093 Duties of councils; resident or staff abuse

The citizen's advisory councils established under section 5123.092 of the Revised Code shall:

(A) Transmit verbal or written information from any person or organization associated with the institution or within the community, that an advisory council considers important, to the joint council on mental retardation and developmental disabilities created by section 101.37 of the Revised Code and the director of mental retardation and developmental disabilities;

(B) Review the records of all applicants to any unclassified position at the institution, except for resident physician positions filled under section 5123.11 of the Revised Code;

(C) Review and evaluate institutional employee training and continuing education programs;

(D) On or before the thirty-first day of January of each year, submit a written report to the joint council on mental retardation and developmental disabilities and the director of mental retardation and developmental disabilities regarding matters affecting the institution including, but not limited to, allegations of dehumanizing practices and violations of individual or legal rights;

(E) Review institutional budgets, programs, services, and planning;

(F) Develop and maintain relationships within the community with community mental retardation and developmental disabilities organizations;

(G) Participate in the formulation of the institution's objectives, administrative procedures, program philosophy, and long range goals;

(H) Bring any matter that an advisory council considers important to the attention of the joint council on mental retardation and developmental disabilities and the director of mental retardation and developmental disabilities;

(I) Recommend to the director of mental retardation and developmental disabilities persons for appointment to citizen's advisory councils;

(J) Adopt any rules or procedures necessary to carry out this section.

The chairperson of the advisory council or the chairperson's designee shall be notified within twenty-four hours of any alleged incident of abuse to a resident or staff member by anyone. Incidents of resident or staff abuse shall include, but not be limited to, sudden deaths, accidents, suicides, attempted suicides, injury caused by other persons, alleged criminal acts, errors in prescribing or administering medication, theft from clients, fires, epidemic disease, administering unprescribed drugs, unauthorized use of restraint, withholding of information concerning alleged abuse, neglect, or any deprivation of rights as defined in Chapter 5122. or 5123. of the Revised Code.

(1996 H 670, eff. 12–2–96; 1982 S 550, eff. 11–26–82; 1981 H 694)

Library References

Asylums ⇌3.
Mental Health ⇌20.
Westlaw Topic Nos. 43, 257A.
C.J.S. Asylums and Institutional Care Facilities § 5 to 8.
C.J.S. Insane Persons § 14 to 16.

MISCELLANEOUS POWERS AND DUTIES OF DEPARTMENT AND DIRECTOR

5123.10 Bonds

The department of mental retardation and developmental disabilities shall require any of its employees and each officer and employee of every institution under its control who may be charged with custody or control of any money or property belonging to the state or who is required to give bond to give a surety company bond, properly conditioned, in a sum to be fixed by the department which, when approved by the department, shall be filed in the office of the secretary of state. The cost of such bonds, when approved by the department, shall be paid from funds available for the department. The bonds required or authorized by this section may, in the discretion of the director of mental retardation and developmental disabilities, be individual, schedule, or blanket bonds.

(1980 H 900, eff. 7–1–80)

Historical and Statutory Notes

Ed. Note: Former 5123.10 repealed by 129 v 1448, eff. 10–25–61; 1953 H 1; GC 1890–14.

Pre–1953 H 1 Amendments: 119 v 616, § 1; 117 v 550, § 14

Library References

Asylums ⇌3.
Mental Health ⇌20.
Westlaw Topic Nos. 43, 257A.
C.J.S. Asylums and Institutional Care Facilities § 5 to 8.
C.J.S. Insane Persons § 14 to 16.

5123.11 Agreements with colleges of medicine and universities with psychology schools; residency training and clinical clerkships; residency training costs paid by department

(A) The director of mental retardation and developmental disabilities may enter into an agreement with the boards of trustees or boards of directors of two or more universities in which there is a college of medicine or college of osteopathic medicine, or of two or more colleges of medicine or colleges of osteopathic medicine, or any combination of those universities and colleges, to establish, manage, and conduct residency medical training programs. The agreement may also provide for clinical clerkships for medical students. The director shall also enter into an agreement with the boards of trustees or boards of directors of one or more universities in which there is a school of professional psychology to establish, manage, and conduct residency psychological training programs.

(B) The department shall pay all costs incurred by a university or college that relate directly to the training of resident physicians or psychologists in programs developed under this section. The director of mental retardation and developmental disabilities shall ensure that any procedures and limitations imposed for the purpose of reimbursing universities or colleges, or for direct payment of residents' salaries, are incorporated into agreements between the department and the universities or colleges. Any agreement shall provide that residency training for a physician shall not exceed four calendar years.

(2000 H 538, eff. 9–22–00; 1996 H 670, eff. 12–2–96; 1980 H 900, eff. 7–1–80)

Historical and Statutory Notes

Ed. Note: Former 5123.11 repealed by 1980 H 900, eff. 7–1–80; 1972 H 494; 1969 H 688; 125 v 823; 1953 H 1; GC 1890–15. See now 5120.17 for provisions analogous to former 5125.11.

Pre–1953 H 1 Amendments: 121 v 423; 119 v 616; 117 v 550

Library References

Mental Health ⇌20.
Westlaw Topic No. 257A.
C.J.S. Insane Persons § 14 to 16.

5123.12 Agreements with college

The director of mental retardation and developmental disabilities may enter into an agreement with boards of trustees or boards of directors of one or more universities, colleges, or schools to establish, manage, and conduct residency training programs for students enrolled in courses of studies for occupations or professions which may be determined by the director to be needed by the department to provide adequate care and treatment for the residents of any institution administered by the director.

(1980 H 900, eff. 7–1–80)

Historical and Statutory Notes

Ed. Note: Former 5123.12 amended and recodified as 5123.17 by 1980 H 900, eff. 7–1–80; 1972 H 494; 1970 H 970; 1969 H 688; 129 v 1448; 125 v 823; 1953 H 1; GC 1890–15a.

Pre–1953 H 1 Amendments: 121 v 423

Library References

Mental Health ⇌20.
Westlaw Topic No. 257A.
C.J.S. Insane Persons § 14 to 16.

5123.122 Rate of support for minor children

Notwithstanding section 5121.04 of the Revised Code and except as provided in section 5123.194 of the Revised Code, the liable relative of a mentally retarded or developmentally disabled person who is a minor receiving residential services pursuant to a contract entered into with the department of mental retardation and developmental disabilities under section 5123.18 of the Revised Code shall be charged for the minor's support the percentage of a base support rate determined in accordance with division (B)(2) of section 5121.04 of the Revised Code.

(1997 H 215, eff. 6–30–97; 1994 H 435, eff. 11–9–94; 1990 H 569, eff. 7–1–91; 1980 H 900; 1977 H 862; 1974 H 1320)

Uncodified Law

1994 H 435, § 3: See Uncodified Law under 5123.18.

1993 H 152, § 68.01, eff. 7–1–93, reads, in part:

Community Residential

Notwithstanding Chapters 5123. and 5126. of the Revised Code, the Department of Mental Retardation and Developmental Disabilities may develop community programs that enable persons with mental retardation and developmental disabilities to live in the community. Notwithstanding Chapter 5121. and section 5123.122 of the Revised Code, the department may waive the support collection requirements of those statutes for persons in community programs developed by the department under this section. The department shall adopt rules or may use existing rules for the implementation of these programs.

Library References

Mental Health ⇐75.
Westlaw Topic No. 257A.
C.J.S. Insane Persons § 203, 205, 207.

5123.13 Special police

(A) As used in this section, "felony" has the same meaning as in section 109.511 of the Revised Code.

(B)(1) Subject to division (C) of this section, upon the recommendation of the director of mental retardation and developmental disabilities, the managing officer of an institution under the jurisdiction of the department of mental retardation and developmental disabilities may designate one or more employees to be special police officers of the department. The special police officers shall take an oath of office, wear the badge of office, and give bond for the proper and faithful discharge of their duties in an amount that the director requires.

(2) In accordance with section 109.77 of the Revised Code, the special police officers shall be required to complete successfully a peace officer basic training program approved by the Ohio peace officer training commission and to be certified by the commission. The cost of the training shall be paid by the department of mental retardation and developmental disabilities.

(3) Special police officers, on the premises of institutions under the jurisdiction of the department of mental retardation and developmental disabilities and subject to the rules of the department, shall protect the property of the institutions and the persons and property of patients in the institutions, suppress riots, disturbances, and breaches of the peace, and enforce the laws of the state and the rules of the department for the preservation of good order. They may arrest any person without a warrant and detain the person until a warrant can be obtained under the circumstances described in division (F) of section 2935.03 of the Revised Code.

(C)(1) The managing officer of an institution under the jurisdiction of the department of mental retardation and developmental disabilities shall not designate an employee as a special police officer of the department pursuant to division (B)(1) of this section on a permanent basis, on a temporary basis, for a probationary term, or on other than a permanent basis if the employee previously has been convicted of or has pleaded guilty to a felony.

(2)(a) The managing officer of an institution under the jurisdiction of the department of mental retardation and developmental disabilities shall terminate the employment as a special police officer of the department of an employee designated as a special police officer under division (B)(1) of this section if that employee does either of the following:

(i) Pleads guilty to a felony;

(ii) Pleads guilty to a misdemeanor pursuant to a negotiated plea agreement as provided in division (D) of section 2929.43 of the Revised Code in which the employee agrees to surrender the certificate awarded to that employee under section 109.77 of the Revised Code.

(b) The managing officer shall suspend from employment as a special police officer of the department an employee designated as a special police officer under division (B)(1) of this section if that employee is convicted, after trial, of a felony. If the special police officer files an appeal from that conviction and the conviction is upheld by the highest court to which the appeal is taken or if the special police officer does not file a timely appeal, the managing officer shall terminate the employment of that special police officer. If the special police officer files an appeal that results in that special police officer's acquittal of the felony or conviction of a misdemeanor, or in the dismissal of the felony charge against that special police officer, the managing officer shall reinstate that special police officer. A special police officer of the department who is reinstated under division (C)(2)(b) of this section shall not receive any back pay unless that special police officer's conviction of the felony was reversed on appeal, or the felony charge was dismissed, because the court found insufficient evidence to convict the special police officer of the felony.

(3) Division (C) of this section does not apply regarding an offense that was committed prior to January 1, 1997.

(4) The suspension from employment, or the termination of the employment, of a special police officer under division (C)(2) of this section shall be in accordance with Chapter 119. of the Revised Code.

(2002 H 490, eff. 1–1–04; 1996 H 670, eff. 12–2–96; 1996 H 566, eff. 10–16–96; 1993 H 42, eff. 2–9–94; 1992 S 49; 1981 H 694; 1980 H 900)

Historical and Statutory Notes

Ed. Note: Former 5123.13 amended and recodified as 5119.25 by 1980 H 900, eff. 7–1–80; 1972 H 494; 1969 H 1; 132 v H 357; 129 v 1448; 125 v 823; 1953 H 1; GC 1890–16.

Pre–1953 H 1 Amendments: 121 v 423; 119 v 616; 117 v 550

Library References

Asylums ⇐4.
Mental Health ⇐20.
Westlaw Topic Nos. 43, 257A.
C.J.S. Asylums and Institutional Care Facilities § 9 to 10.
C.J.S. Insane Persons § 14 to 16.

5123.14 Powers to investigate

The department of mental retardation and developmental disabilities may make such investigations as are necessary in the performance of its duties and to that end the director of mental retardation and developmental disabilities shall have the same power as a judge of a county court to administer oaths and to enforce the attendance and testimony of witnesses and the production of books or papers.

The department shall keep a record of such investigations stating the time, place, charges or subject, witnesses summoned and examined, and its conclusions.

In matters involving the conduct of an officer, a stenographic report of the evidence shall be taken and a copy of such report, with all documents introduced, kept on file at the office of the department.

The fees of witnesses for attendance and travel shall be the same as in the court of common pleas, but no officer or employee of the institution under investigation is entitled to such fees.

Any judge of the probate court or of the court of common pleas, upon application of the department, may compel the attendance of witnesses, the production of books or papers, and the giving of testimony before the department, by a judgment for contempt or otherwise, in the same manner as in cases before said courts.

(1980 H 900, eff. 7–1–80)

Historical and Statutory Notes

Ed. Note: Former 5123.14 repealed by 1980 H 900, eff. 7–1–80; 1972 H 494; 130 v H 1; 129 v 1448; 1953 H 1; GC 1890–17.

Pre–1953 H 1 Amendments: 119 v 616, § 1; 117 v 550, § 17

Library References

Mental Health ⇔20.
Westlaw Topic No. 257A.
C.J.S. Insane Persons § 14 to 16.

5123.15 Appointment of competent agency or person; contents of credentials

The department of mental retardation and developmental disabilities may appoint and commission any competent agency or person, to serve without compensation, as a special agent, investigator, or representative to perform a designated duty for and in behalf of the department. Specific credentials shall be given by the department to each person so designated, and each credential shall state the:

(A) Name;

(B) Agency with which such person is connected;

(C) Purpose of appointment;

(D) Date of expiration of appointment;

(E) Such information as the department considers proper.

(1980 H 900, eff. 7–1–80)

Historical and Statutory Notes

Ed. Note: 5123.15 is former 5119.38 amended and recodified by 1980 H 900, eff. 7–1–80; 1972 H 494; 125 v 823; Source—GC 1359.

Ed. Note: Former 5123.15 repealed by 1980 H 900, eff. 7–1–80; 1972 H 494; 1970 H 970; 129 v 1448; 1953 H 1; GC 1890–18.

Pre–1953 H 1 Amendments: 119 v 616, § 1; 117 v 550, § 18

Library References

Mental Health ⇔20.
Westlaw Topic No. 257A.
C.J.S. Insane Persons § 14 to 16.

CARE OUTSIDE HOSPITAL; RESIDENTIAL FACILITIES

5123.17 Care outside hospital

The department of mental retardation and developmental disabilities may provide for the custody, supervision, control, treatment, and training of persons with mental retardation or a developmental disability elsewhere than within the enclosure of an institution under its jurisdiction, if the department so determines with respect to any individual or group of individuals. In all such cases, the department shall ensure adequate and proper supervision for the protection of those persons and of the public.

(2000 H 538, eff. 9–22–00; 1990 H 569, eff. 7–1–91; 1980 H 900)

Historical and Statutory Notes

Ed. Note: 5123.17 is former 5123.12 amended and recodified by 1980 H 900, eff. 7–1–80; 1972 H 494; 1970 H 970; 1969 H 688; 129 v 1448; 125 v 823; 1953 H 1; GC 1890–15a.

Ed. Note: Former 5123.17 amended and recodified as 5119.21 by 1980 H 900, eff. 7–1–80; 1978 H 870; 1972 H 494; 1953 H 1; GC 1890–21.

Pre–1953 H 1 Amendments: 119 v 616; 117 v 550, § 21

Library References

Mental Health ⇔31, 51.1.
Westlaw Topic No. 257A.
C.J.S. Insane Persons § 45, 47, 53, 86 to 92.

5123.171 Respite care services

As used in this section, "respite care" means appropriate, short-term, temporary care provided to a mentally retarded or developmentally disabled person to sustain the family structure or to meet planned or emergency needs of the family.

The department of mental retardation and developmental disabilities shall provide respite care services to persons with mental retardation or a developmental disability for the purpose of promoting self-sufficiency and normalization, preventing or reducing inappropriate institutional care, and furthering the unity of the family by enabling the family to meet the special needs of a mentally retarded or developmentally disabled person.

In order to be eligible for respite care services under this section, the mentally retarded or developmentally disabled person must be in need of habilitation services as defined in section 5126.01 of the Revised Code.

Respite care may be provided in a facility licensed under section 5123.19 of the Revised Code or certified as an intermediate care facility for the mentally retarded under Title XIX of the "Social Security Act," 49 Stat. 620 (1935), 42 U.S.C. 301, as amended, or certified as a respite care home under section 5126.05 of the Revised Code.

The department shall develop a system for locating vacant beds that are available for respite care and for making information on vacant beds available to users of respite care services. Facilities certified as intermediate care facilities for the mentally retarded and facilities holding contracts with the department for the provision of residential services under section 5123.18 of the Revised Code shall report vacant beds to the department but shall not be required to accept respite care clients.

The director of mental retardation and developmental disabilities shall adopt, and may amend or rescind, rules in accordance with Chapter 119. of the Revised Code for both of the following:

(A) Certification by county boards of mental retardation and developmental disabilities of respite care homes;

(B) Provision of respite care services authorized by this section. Rules adopted under this division shall establish all of the following:

(1) A formula for distributing funds appropriated for respite care services;

(2) Standards for supervision, training and quality control in the provision of respite care services;

(3) Eligibility criteria for emergency respite care services.

(1993 S 21, eff. 10–29–93; 1990 H 569; 1989 H 257; 1983 H 291)

Uncodified Law

1993 H 152, § 68.01, eff. 7–1–93, reads, in part:

Family Resource Services

Notwithstanding sections 5123.171, 5123.19, 5123.20, and 5126.11 of the Revised Code, the Department of Mental Retardation and Developmental Disabilities may implement programs funded by appropriation item 322–451, Family Resource Services, to provide assistance to persons with mental retardation or developmental disabilities and their families who are living in the community. The department shall establish rules to implement these programs.

Library References

Mental Health ⇔20, 51.1.
Westlaw Topic No. 257A.
C.J.S. Insane Persons § 14 to 16, 86 to 92.

5123.172 Information to be furnished by providers

(A) As used in this section:

(1) "Provider" means any person or government agency that owns, operates, manages, or is employed or under contract to operate a residential facility licensed under section 5123.19 of the Revised Code.

(2) "Related to a provider" means that a person or government agency is affiliated with a provider, has control over the provider or is controlled by the provider, or is a member of the provider's family.

(3) "Member of the provider's family" means the provider's spouse, natural or adoptive parent, stepparent, natural or adoptive child, stepchild, sibling, stepsister, stepbrother, half-brother, half-sister, daughter-in-law, son-in-law, brother-in-law, sister-in-law, grandparent, or grandchild.

(B) Prior to entering into a contract with the department of mental retardation and developmental disabilities under section 5123.18 of the Revised Code and as required thereafter, every provider holding or negotiating a contract with the department shall report upon the request of the department, in the form and on the schedule established in rules adopted by the department in accordance with Chapter 119. of the Revised Code, the following information:

(1) The name and address of every person holding a financial interest of five per cent or more in the management or operation of the residential facility;

(2) The names and addresses of members of the board of trustees or directors of the residential facility or of the management contractor;

(3) Every contract or business transaction between the provider and any person or government agency related to the provider if such contract or transaction would affect rates of payment under section 5123.18 of the Revised Code.

(C) The department shall make reports filed under division (B) of this section available to the appropriate county board of mental retardation and developmental disabilities and any other appropriate public agencies.

(D) Any provider who fails to comply with reporting requirements of this section shall be subject to a civil penalty not to exceed one thousand dollars for each violation and to possible license revocation.

(1994 H 435, eff. 11–9–94; 1986 S 322, eff. 4–4–86)

Library References

Asylums ⇐3.
Westlaw Topic No. 43.
C.J.S. Asylums and Institutional Care Facilities § 5 to 8.

5123.18 Contracts for residential services

(A) As used in this section:

(1) "Contractor" means a person or government agency that enters into a contract with the department of mental retardation and developmental disabilities under this section.

(2) "Government agency" means a state agency as defined in section 117.01 of the Revised Code or a similar agency of a political subdivision of the state.

(3) "Residential services" means the services necessary for an individual with mental retardation or a developmental disability to live in the community, including room and board, clothing, transportation, personal care, habilitation, supervision, and any other services the department considers necessary for the individual to live in the community.

(B)(1) The department of mental retardation and developmental disabilities may enter into a contract with a person or government agency to provide residential services to individuals with mental retardation or developmental disabilities in need of residential services. Contracts for residential services shall be of the following types:

(a) Companion home contracts—contracts under which the contractor is an individual, the individual is the primary caregiver, and the individual owns or leases and resides in the home in which the services are provided.

(b) Agency–operated companion home contracts—contracts under which the contractor subcontracts, for purposes of coordinating the provision of residential services, with one or more individuals who are primary caregivers and own or lease and reside in the homes in which the services are provided.

(c) Community home contracts—contracts for residential services under which the contractor owns or operates a home that is used solely to provide residential services.

(d) Combined agency-operated companion home and community home contracts.

(2) A companion home contract shall cover not more than one home. An agency-operated companion home contract or a community home contract may cover more than one home.

(C) Contracts shall be in writing and shall provide for payment to be made to the contractor at the times agreed to by the department and the contractor. Each contract shall specify the period during which it is valid, the amount to be paid for residential services, and the number of individuals for whom payment will be made. Contracts may be renewed.

(D) To be eligible to enter into a contract with the department under this section, the person or government agency and the home in which the residential services are provided must meet all applicable standards for licensing or certification by the appropriate government agency. In addition, if the residential facility is operated as a nonprofit entity, the members of the board of trustees or board of directors of the facility must not have a financial interest in or receive financial benefit from the facility, other than reimbursement for actual expenses incurred in attending board meetings.

(E)(1) The department shall determine the payment amount assigned to an initial contract. To the extent that the department determines sufficient funds are available, the payment amount assigned to an initial contract shall be equal to the average amount assigned to contracts for other homes that are of the same type and size and serve individuals with similar needs, except that if an initial contract is the result of a change of contractor or ownership, the payment amount assigned to the contract shall be the lesser of the amount assigned to the previous contract or the contract's total adjusted predicted funding need calculated under division (I) of this section.

(2) A renewed contract shall be assigned a payment amount in accordance with division (K) of this section.

(3) When a contractor relocates a home to another site at which residential services are provided to the same individuals, the payment amount assigned to the contract for the new home shall be the payment amount assigned to the contract at the previous location.

(F)(1) Annually, a contractor shall complete an assessment of each individual to whom the contractor provides residential services to predict the individual's need for routine direct services staff. The department shall establish by rule adopted in accordance with Chapter 119. of the Revised Code the assessment instrument to be used by contractors to make assessments. Assessments shall be submitted to the department not later than the thirty-first day of January of each year.

A contractor shall submit a revised assessment for an individual if there is a substantial, long-term change in the nature of the individual's needs. A contractor shall submit revised assessments for all individuals receiving residential services if there is a change in the composition of the home's residents.

(2) Annually, a contractor shall submit a cost report to the department specifying the costs incurred in providing residential services during the immediately preceding calendar year. Only costs actually incurred by a contractor shall be reported on a cost report. Cost reports shall be prepared according to a uniform chart of accounts approved by the department and shall be submitted on forms prescribed by the department.

(3) The department shall not renew the contract held by a contractor who fails to submit the assessments or cost reports required under this division.

(4) The department shall adopt rules as necessary regarding the submission of assessments and cost reports under this division. The rules shall be adopted in accordance with Chapter 119. of the Revised Code.

(G) Prior to renewing a contract entered into under this section, the department shall compute the contract's total predicted funding need and total adjusted predicted funding need. The department shall also compute the contract's unmet funding need if the payment amount assigned to the contract is less than the total adjusted predicted funding need. The results of these calculations shall be used to determine the payment amount assigned to the renewed contract.

(H)(1) A contract's total predicted funding need is an amount equal to the sum of the predicted funding needs for the following cost categories:

(a) Routine direct services staff;

(b) Dietary, program supplies, and specialized staff;

(c) Facility and general services;

(d) Administration.

(2) Based on the assessments submitted by the contractor, the department shall compute the contract's predicted funding need for the routine direct services staff cost category by multiplying the number of direct services staff predicted to be necessary for the home by the sum of the following:

(a) Entry level wages paid during the immediately preceding cost reporting period to comparable staff employed by the county board of mental retardation and developmental disabilities of the county in which the home is located;

(b) Fringe benefits and payroll taxes as determined by the department using state civil service statistics from the same period as the cost reporting period.

(3) The department shall establish by rule adopted in accordance with Chapter 119. of the Revised Code the method to be used to compute the predicted funding need for the dietary, program supplies, and specialized staff cost category; the facility and general services cost category; and the administration cost category. The rules shall not establish a maximum amount that may be attributed to the dietary, program supplies, and specialized staff cost category. The rules shall establish a process for determining the combined maximum amount that may be attributed to the facility and general services cost category and the administration cost category.

(I)(1) A contract's total adjusted predicted funding need is the contract's total predicted funding need with adjustments made for the following:

(a) Inflation, as provided under division (I)(2) of this section;

(b) The predicted cost of complying with new requirements established under federal or state law that were not taken into consideration when the total predicted funding need was computed;

(c) Changes in needs based on revised assessments submitted by the contractor.

(2) In adjusting the total predicted funding need for inflation, the department shall use either the consumer price index compound annual inflation rate calculated by the United States department of labor for all items or another index or measurement of inflation designated in rules that the department shall adopt in accordance with Chapter 119. of the Revised Code.

When a contract is being renewed for the first time, and the contract is to begin on the first day of July, the inflation adjustment applied to the contract's total predicted funding need shall be the estimated rate of inflation for the calendar year in which the contract is renewed. If the consumer price index is being used, the department shall base its estimate on the rate of inflation calculated for the three-month period ending the thirty-first day of March of that calendar year. If another index or measurement is being used, the department shall base its estimate on the most recent calculations of the rate of inflation available under the index or measurement. Each year thereafter, the inflation adjustment shall be estimated in the same manner, except that if the estimated rate of inflation for a year is different from the actual rate of inflation for that year, the difference shall be added to or subtracted from the rate of inflation estimated for the next succeeding year.

If a contract begins at any time other than July first, the inflation adjustment applied to the contract's total predicted funding need shall be determined by a method comparable to that used for contracts beginning July first. The department shall adopt rules in accordance with Chapter 119. of the Revised Code establishing the method to be used.

(J) A contract's unmet funding need is the difference between the payment amount assigned to the contract and the total adjusted predicted funding need, if the payment amount assigned is less than the total adjusted predicted funding need.

(K) The payment amount to be assigned to a contract being renewed shall be determined by comparing the total adjusted predicted funding need with the payment amount assigned to the current contract.

(1) If the payment amount assigned to the current contract equals or exceeds the total adjusted predicted funding need, the payment amount assigned to the renewed contract shall be the same as that assigned to the current contract, unless a reduction is made pursuant to division (L) of this section.

(2) If the payment amount assigned to the current contract is less than the total adjusted predicted funding need, the payment amount assigned to the renewed contract shall be increased if the department determines that funds are available for such increases. The amount of a contract's increase shall be the same percentage of the available funds that the contract's unmet funding need is of the total of the unmet funding need for all contracts.

(L) When renewing a contract provided for in division (B) of this section other than a companion home contract, the department may reduce the payment amount assigned to a renewed contract if the sum of the contractor's allowable reported costs and the maximum efficiency incentive is less than ninety-one and one-half per cent of the amount received pursuant to this section during the immediately preceding contract year.

The department shall adopt rules in accordance with Chapter 119. of the Revised Code establishing a formula to be used in computing the maximum efficiency incentive, which shall be at least four per cent of the weighted average payment amount to be made to all contractors during the contract year. The maximum efficiency incentive shall be computed annually.

(M) The department may increase the payment amount assigned to a contract based on the contract's unmet funding need at times other than when the contract is renewed. The department may develop policies for determining priorities in making such increases.

(N)(1) In addition to the contracts provided for in division (B) of this section, the department may enter into the following contracts:

(a) A contract to pay the cost of beginning operation of a new home that is to be funded under a companion home contract, agency-operated companion home contract, community home contract, or combined agency-operated companion home and community home contract.

(b) A contract to pay the cost associated with increasing the number of individuals served by a home funded under a companion home contract, agency-operated companion home contract, community home contract, or combined agency-operated companion home and community home contract.

(2) The department shall adopt rules as necessary regarding contracts entered into under this division. The rules shall be adopted in accordance with Chapter 119. of the Revised Code.

(O) Except for companion home contracts, the department shall conduct a reconciliation of the amount earned under a contract and the actual costs incurred by the contractor. An amount is considered to have been earned for delivering a service at the time the service is delivered. The department shall adopt rules in accordance with Chapter 119. of the Revised Code establishing procedures for conducting reconciliations.

A reconciliation shall be based on the annual cost report submitted by the contractor. If a reconciliation reveals that a contractor owes money to the state, the amount owed shall be collected in accordance with section 5123.051 of the Revised Code.

When conducting reconciliations, the department shall review all reported costs that may be affected by transactions required to be reported under division (B)(3) of section 5123.172 of the Revised Code. If the department determines that such transactions have increased the cost reported by a contractor, the department may disallow or adjust the cost allowable for payment. The department shall adopt rules in accordance with Chapter 119. of the Revised Code establishing standards for disallowances or adjustments.

(P) The department may audit the contracts it enters into under this section. Audits may be conducted by the department or an entity with which the department contracts to perform the audits. The department shall adopt rules in accordance with Chapter 119. of the Revised Code establishing procedures for conducting audits.

An audit may include the examination of a contractor's financial books and records, the costs incurred by a contractor in providing residential services, and any other relevant information specified by the department. An audit shall not be commenced more than four years after the expiration of the contract to be audited, except in cases where the department has reasonable cause to believe that a contractor has committed fraud.

If an audit reveals that a contractor owes money to the state, the amount owed, subject to an adjudication hearing under this division, shall be collected in accordance with section 5123.051 of the Revised Code. If an audit reveals that a reconciliation conducted under this section resulted in the contractor erroneously paying money to the state, the department shall refund the money to the contractor, or, in lieu of making a refund, the department may offset the erroneous payment against any money determined as a result of the audit to be owed by the contractor to the state. The department is not required to pay interest on any money refunded under this division.

In conducting audits or making determinations of amounts owed by a contractor and amounts to be refunded or offset, the department shall not be bound by the results of reconciliations conducted under this section, except with regard to cases involving claims that have been certified pursuant to section 5123.051 of the Revised Code to the attorney general for collection for which a full and final settlement has been reached or a final judgment has been made from which all rights of appeal have expired or been exhausted.

Not later than ninety days after an audit's completion, the department shall provide the contractor a copy of a report of the audit. The report shall state the findings of the audit, including the amount of any money the contractor is determined to owe the state.

(Q) The department shall adopt rules specifying the amount that will be allowed under a reconciliation or audit for the cost incurred by a contractor for compensation of owners, administrators, and other personnel. The rules shall be adopted in accordance with Chapter 119. of the Revised Code.

(R) Each contractor shall, for at least seven years, maintain fiscal records related to payments received pursuant to this section.

(S) The department may enter into shared funding agreements with other government agencies to fund contracts entered into under this section. The amount of each agency's share of the cost shall be determined through negotiations with the department. The department's share shall not exceed the amount it would have paid without entering into the shared funding agreement, nor shall it be reduced by any amounts contributed by the other parties to the agreement.

(T) Except as provided in section 5123.194 of the Revised Code, an individual who receives residential services pursuant to divisions (A) through (U) of this section and the individual's liable relatives or guardians shall pay support charges in accordance with Chapter 5121. of the Revised Code.

(U) The department may make reimbursements or payments for any of the following pursuant to rules adopted under this division:

(1) Unanticipated, nonrecurring costs associated with the health or habilitation of a person who resides in a home funded under a contract provided for in division (B) of this section;

(2) The cost of staff development training for contractors if the director of mental retardation and developmental disabilities has given prior approval for the training;

(3) Fixed costs that the department, pursuant to the rules, determines relate to the continued operation of a home funded under a contract provided for in division (B) of this section when a short term vacancy occurs and the contractor has diligently attempted to fill the vacancy.

The department shall adopt rules in accordance with Chapter 119. of the Revised Code establishing standards for use in determining which costs it may make payment or reimbursements for under this division.

(V) In addition to the rules required or authorized to be adopted under this section, the department may adopt any other rules necessary to implement divisions (A) through (U) of this section. The rules shall be adopted in accordance with Chapter 119. of the Revised Code.

(W) The department may delegate to county boards of mental retardation and developmental disabilities its authority under this section to negotiate and enter into contracts or subcontracts for residential services. In the event that it elects to delegate its authority, the department shall adopt rules in accordance with Chapter 119. of the Revised Code for the boards' administration of the contracts or subcontracts. In administering the contracts or subcontracts, the boards shall be subject to all applicable provisions of Chapter 5126. of the Revised Code and shall not be subject to the provisions of divisions (A) to (V) of this section.

Subject to the department's rules, a board may require the following to contribute to the cost of the residential services an individual receives pursuant to this division: the individual or the individual's estate, the individual's spouse, the individual's guardian, and, if the individual is under age eighteen, either or both of the individual's parents. Chapter 5121. of the Revised Code shall not apply to individuals or entities that are subject to making contributions under this division. In calculating contributions to be made under this division, a board, subject to the department's rules, may allow an amount to be kept for meeting the personal needs of the individual who receives residential services.

(2000 H 538, eff. 9–22–00; 1997 H 215, eff. 6–30–97; 1994 H 435, eff. 11–9–94)

Uncodified Law

1994 H 435, § 3, eff. 11–9–94, reads: The purpose of this act, except for the amendment of division (J) of section 5123.191 of the Revised Code, is to establish a funding system for the Purchase of Service Program operated by the Department of Mental Retardation and Developmental Disabilities that is based on the needs of the individuals with mental retardation or developmental disabilities who receive the residential and other community services offered through the program.

1993 H 152, § 68.01, eff. 7–1–93 reads, in part:

Shared Funding Agreement

Notwithstanding division (J) of section 5123.18 of the Revised Code, as an alternative to the contracting procedures of divisions (A), (C), (E), and (N) of that section, the Director of the Department of Mental Retardation and Developmental Disabilities may enter into shared funding agreements with other state agencies, local public agencies, political subdivisions, or providers for the provision of residential services meeting applicable government standards at a rate negotiated with the other agencies. The department's share shall not exceed the purchase of service ceiling rate.

The department's share shall not be reduced by supplemental funds included in the shared funding agreement. Subject to the availability of the department's funds, the department may renegotiate rates at any time.

State agencies, local public agencies, political subdivisions or providers shall have the right to appeal a negotiated or proposed shared funding rate to the director based on the provisions of this section, substandard care, or inaccurate cost reports. The appeal process shall be established pursuant to rules in accordance with Chapter 119. of the Revised Code.

Purchase of Service

Notwithstanding sections 5123.04, 5123.18, 5123.19, and 5123.20 of the Revised Code, the Department of Mental Retardation and Developmental Disabilities may develop a funding system to provide residential services and support to eligible individuals under appropriation item 322–450, Purchase of Service. Notwithstanding Chapter 5121. and section 513.122 of the Revised Code, the department may waive support collection requirements for individuals preparing to move into supported or independent living arrangements.

The department shall adopt rules to implement this section.

1992 S 124, § 8, eff. 4–16–93, reads: In enacting sections 1339.51 and 5111.15 and in amending sections 2101.24, 5119.01, 5121.04, 5121.10, 5123,04, 5123.18, and 5123.28 of the Revised Code, the General Assembly hereby declares its intent to supersede the effect of the holding of the Ohio Supreme Court in the December 31, 1968, decision in *Bureau of Support v. Kreitzer* (1968), 16 Ohio St. 2d 147.

Historical and Statutory Notes

Ed. Note: Former 5123.18 repealed by 1994 H 435, eff. 11–9–94; 1992 S 124, eff. 4–16–93; 1990 H 569; 1989 H 257; 1986 S 322; 1985 H 238, H 201; 1982 S 550, H 902; 1981 H 694; 1980 S 160, H 900.

Ed. Note: Former 5123.18 was former 5123.121, amended and recodified by 1980 H 900, eff. 7–1–80; 1979 H 204; 1977 H 1; 1973 H 761.

Ed. Note: Prior 5123.18 amended and recodified as 5123.19 by 1980 H 900, eff. 7–1–80; 1977 S 71.

Ed. Note: Prior 5123.18 repealed by 1977 S 71, eff. 10–31–77; 1972 H 494; 1970 S 367.

Prior 5123.18 repealed by 129 v 1448, eff. 10–25–61; 1953 H 1; GC 1890–23; see now 5122.11 for provisions analogous to prior 5123.18.

Pre–1953 H 1 Amendments: 121 v 423; 119 v 616; 117 v 550

Library References

Asylums ⇔1, 3.
Mental Health ⇔20, 51.
Westlaw Topic Nos. 43, 257A.
C.J.S. Asylums and Institutional Care Facilities § 2 to 3, 5 to 8.
C.J.S. Insane Persons § 14 to 16, 86 to 92.

5123.181 Double billings to be eliminated; agreements for services

The director of mental retardation and developmental disabilities and the director of job and family services shall, in concert with each other, eliminate all double billings and double payments for services on behalf of persons with mental retardation or another developmental disability in intermediate care facilities. The department of mental retardation and developmental disabilities may enter into contracts with providers of services for the purpose of making payments to the providers for services rendered to eligible clients who are persons with mental retardation or a developmental disability over and above the services authorized and paid under Chapter 5111. of the Revised Code. Payments authorized under this section and section 5123.18 of the Revised Code shall not be subject to audit findings pursuant to Chapter 5111. of the Revised Code, unless an audit determines that payment was made to the provider for services that were not rendered in accordance with the provisions of the provider agreement entered into with the department of job and family services or the department of mental retardation and developmental disabilities pursuant to this section.

(2000 H 538, eff. 9–22–00; 1999 H 471, eff. 7–1–00; 1990 H 569, eff. 7–1–91; 1986 H 428; 1980 S 160.)

Library References

Mental Health ⇔20.
Westlaw Topic No. 257A.
C.J.S. Insane Persons § 14 to 16.

5123.182 Supported living

This section in effect until July 1, 1995.

(A) As used in this section:

(1) "Residential services" and "supported living" have the same meanings as in section 5126.01 of the Revised Code.

(2) "Provider" has the same meaning as in section 5126.40 of the Revised Code.

(B) The department of mental retardation and developmental disabilities shall adopt rules under Chapter 119. of the Revised Code governing provision of supported living by the department.

(C) On receipt of a resolution adopted by a county board of mental retardation and developmental disabilities under section 5126.40 of the Revised Code stating that the board has elected to plan, develop, and contract for supported living, the department shall cease to enter into new contracts with providers of supported living in that county without the approval of the county board, but the department may renew contracts in effect on the date of its receipt of the resolution. If a county board does not pass such a resolution, the department shall, in accordance with the rules adopted under this section, provide supported living for residents of the county who are mentally retarded or developmentally disabled individuals.

(D) The department shall ensure that services are furnished in a manner that provides for the individual's health, safety, and welfare.

The department shall plan and request additional appropriations for the provision of residential services for all mentally retarded or developmentally disabled persons eligible for residential services who are on waiting lists for the services.

On the closing for any reason of a residential facility as defined in section 5123.19 of the Revised Code, the department may develop and contract for any necessary residential services for mentally retarded or developmentally disabled persons who are leaving the facility. If state or federal funding is available, with the consent of a county board of mental retardation and developmental disabilities, the department may delegate to the board the responsibility for developing and contracting for supported living in accordance with sections 5126.40 to 5126.47 of the Revised Code for county residents who are leaving the facility.

The department shall maintain records of all individuals receiving residential services arranged with money from the department or licensed or certified by the department. Annually each county board shall report information specified by the department about persons receiving services.

(1994 H 694, eff. 11–11–94; 1990 H 569, eff. 7–1–91; 1990 H 697; 1989 H 257)

Uncodified Law

1994 H 435, § 3: See Uncodified Law under 5123.18.

Historical and Statutory Notes

Ed. Note: Former 5123.182, as enacted by 1989 H 111, eff. 7–1–89, was repealed by 1990 H 359, eff. 3–13–90.

Library References

Asylums ⚖=1, 3.
Mental Health ⚖=20.
Westlaw Topic Nos. 43, 257A.
C.J.S. Asylums and Institutional Care Facilities § 2 to 3, 5 to 8.
C.J.S. Insane Persons § 14 to 16.

5123.19 Licensing of residential facilities

(A) As used in this section and in sections 5123.191, 5123.194, 5123.196, 5123.198, and 5123.20 of the Revised Code:

(1)(a) "Residential facility" means a home or facility in which a mentally retarded or developmentally disabled person resides, except the home of a relative or legal guardian in which a mentally retarded or developmentally disabled person resides, a respite care home certified under section 5126.05 of the Revised Code, a county home or district home operated pursuant to Chapter 5155. of the Revised Code, or a dwelling in which the only mentally retarded or developmentally disabled residents are in an independent living arrangement or are being provided supported living.

(b) "Intermediate care facility for the mentally retarded" means a residential facility that is considered an intermediate care facility for the mentally retarded for the purposes of Chapter 5111. of the Revised Code.

(2) "Political subdivision" means a municipal corporation, county, or township.

(3) "Independent living arrangement" means an arrangement in which a mentally retarded or developmentally disabled person resides in an individualized setting chosen by the person or the person's guardian, which is not dedicated principally to the provision of residential services for mentally retarded or developmentally disabled persons, and for which no financial support is received for rendering such service from any governmental agency by a provider of residential services.

(4) "Supported living" has the same meaning as in section 5126.01 of the Revised Code.

(5) "Licensee" means the person or government agency that has applied for a license to operate a residential facility and to which the license was issued under this section.

(B) Every person or government agency desiring to operate a residential facility shall apply for licensure of the facility to the director of mental retardation and developmental disabilities unless the residential facility is subject to section 3721.02, 3722.04, 5103.03, or 5119.20 of the Revised Code. Notwithstanding Chapter 3721. of the Revised Code, a nursing home that is certified as an intermediate care facility for the mentally retarded under Title XIX of the "Social Security Act," 79 Stat. 286 (1965), 42 U.S.C.A. 1396, as amended, shall apply for licensure of the portion of the home that is certified as an intermediate care facility for the mentally retarded.

(C) Subject to section 5123.196 of the Revised Code, the director of mental retardation and developmental disabilities shall license the operation of residential facilities. An initial license shall be issued for a period that does not exceed one year, unless the director denies the license under division (D) of this section. A license shall be renewed for a period that does not exceed three years, unless the director refuses to renew the license under division (D) of this section. The director, when issuing or renewing a license, shall specify the period for which the license is being issued or renewed. A license remains valid for the length of the licensing period specified by the director, unless the license is terminated, revoked, or voluntarily surrendered.

(D) If it is determined that an applicant or licensee is not in compliance with a provision of this chapter that applies to residential facilities or the rules adopted under such a provision, the director may deny issuance of a license, refuse to renew a license, terminate a license, revoke a license, issue an order for the suspension of admissions to a facility, issue an order for the placement of a monitor at a facility, issue an order for the immediate removal of residents, or take any other action the director considers necessary consistent with the director's authority under this chapter regarding residential facilities. In the director's selection and administration of the sanction to be imposed, all of the following apply:

(1) The director may deny, refuse to renew, or revoke a license, if the director determines that the applicant or licensee has demonstrated a pattern of serious noncompliance or that a violation creates a substantial risk to the health and safety of residents of a residential facility.

(2) The director may terminate a license if more than twelve consecutive months have elapsed since the residential facility was last occupied by a resident or a notice required by division (J) of this section is not given.

(3) The director may issue an order for the suspension of admissions to a facility for any violation that may result in sanctions under division (D)(1) of this section and for any other violation specified in rules adopted under division (G)(2) of this section. If the suspension of admissions is imposed for a violation that may result in sanctions under division (D)(1) of this section, the director may impose the suspension before providing an opportunity for an adjudication under Chapter 119. of the Revised Code. The director shall lift an order for the suspension of admissions when the director determines that the violation that formed the basis for the order has been corrected.

(4) The director may order the placement of a monitor at a residential facility for any violation specified in rules adopted under division (G)(2) of this section. The director shall lift the order when the director determines that the violation that formed the basis for the order has been corrected.

(5) If the director determines that two or more residential facilities owned or operated by the same person or government entity are not being operated in compliance with a provision of this chapter that applies to residential facilities or the rules adopted under such a provision, and the director's findings are based on the same or a substantially similar action, practice,

circumstance, or incident that creates a substantial risk to the health and safety of the residents, the director shall conduct a survey as soon as practicable at each residential facility owned or operated by that person or government entity. The director may take any action authorized by this section with respect to any facility found to be operating in violation of a provision of this chapter that applies to residential facilities or the rules adopted under such a provision.

(6) When the director initiates license revocation proceedings, no opportunity for submitting a plan of correction shall be given. The director shall notify the licensee by letter of the initiation of the proceedings. The letter shall list the deficiencies of the residential facility and inform the licensee that no plan of correction will be accepted. The director shall also notify each affected resident, the resident's guardian if the resident is an adult for whom a guardian has been appointed, the resident's parent or guardian if the resident is a minor, and the county board of mental retardation and developmental disabilities.

(7) Pursuant to rules which shall be adopted in accordance with Chapter 119. of the Revised Code, the director may order the immediate removal of residents from a residential facility whenever conditions at the facility present an immediate danger of physical or psychological harm to the residents.

(8) In determining whether a residential facility is being operated in compliance with a provision of this chapter that applies to residential facilities or the rules adopted under such a provision, or whether conditions at a residential facility present an immediate danger of physical or psychological harm to the residents, the director may rely on information obtained by a county board of mental retardation and developmental disabilities or other governmental agencies.

(9) In proceedings initiated to deny, refuse to renew, or revoke licenses, the director may deny, refuse to renew, or revoke a license regardless of whether some or all of the deficiencies that prompted the proceedings have been corrected at the time of the hearing.

(E) The director shall establish a program under which public notification may be made when the director has initiated license revocation proceedings or has issued an order for the suspension of admissions, placement of a monitor, or removal of residents. The director shall adopt rules in accordance with Chapter 119. of the Revised Code to implement this division. The rules shall establish the procedures by which the public notification will be made and specify the circumstances for which the notification must be made. The rules shall require that public notification be made if the director has taken action against the facility in the eighteen-month period immediately preceding the director's latest action against the facility and the latest action is being taken for the same or a substantially similar violation of a provision of this chapter that applies to residential facilities or the rules adopted under such a provision. The rules shall specify a method for removing or amending the public notification if the director's action is found to have been unjustified or the violation at the residential facility has been corrected.

(F)(1) Except as provided in division (F)(2) of this section, appeals from proceedings initiated to impose a sanction under division (D) of this section shall be conducted in accordance with Chapter 119. of the Revised Code.

(2) Appeals from proceedings initiated to order the suspension of admissions to a facility shall be conducted in accordance with Chapter 119. of the Revised Code, unless the order was issued before providing an opportunity for an adjudication, in which case all of the following apply:

(a) The licensee may request a hearing not later than ten days after receiving the notice specified in section 119.07 of the Revised Code.

(b) If a timely request for a hearing is made, the hearing shall commence not later than thirty days after the department receives the request.

(c) After commencing, the hearing shall continue uninterrupted, except for Saturdays, Sundays, and legal holidays, unless other interruptions are agreed to by the licensee and the director.

(d) If the hearing is conducted by a hearing examiner, the hearing examiner shall file a report and recommendations not later than ten days after the close of the hearing.

(e) Not later than five days after the hearing examiner files the report and recommendations, the licensee may file objections to the report and recommendations.

(f) Not later than fifteen days after the hearing examiner files the report and recommendations, the director shall issue an order approving, modifying, or disapproving the report and recommendations.

(g) Notwithstanding the pendency of the hearing, the director shall lift the order for the suspension of admissions when the director determines that the violation that formed the basis for the order has been corrected.

(G) In accordance with Chapter 119. of the Revised Code, the director shall adopt and may amend and rescind rules for licensing and regulating the operation of residential facilities, including intermediate care facilities for the mentally retarded. The rules for intermediate care facilities for the mentally retarded may differ from those for other residential facilities. The rules shall establish and specify the following:

(1) Procedures and criteria for issuing and renewing licenses, including procedures and criteria for determining the length of the licensing period that the director must specify for each license when it is issued or renewed;

(2) Procedures and criteria for denying, refusing to renew, terminating, and revoking licenses and for ordering the suspension of admissions to a facility, placement of a monitor at a facility, and the immediate removal of residents from a facility;

(3) Fees for issuing and renewing licenses;

(4) Procedures for surveying residential facilities;

(5) Requirements for the training of residential facility personnel;

(6) Classifications for the various types of residential facilities;

(7) Certification procedures for licensees and management contractors that the director determines are necessary to ensure that they have the skills and qualifications to properly operate or manage residential facilities;

(8) The maximum number of persons who may be served in a particular type of residential facility;

(9) Uniform procedures for admission of persons to and transfers and discharges of persons from residential facilities;

(10) Other standards for the operation of residential facilities and the services provided at residential facilities;

(11) Procedures for waiving any provision of any rule adopted under this section.

(H) Before issuing a license, the director of the department or the director's designee shall conduct a survey of the residential facility for which application is made. The director or the director's designee shall conduct a survey of each licensed residential facility at least once during the period the license is valid and may conduct additional inspections as needed. A survey includes but is not limited to an on-site examination and evaluation of the residential facility, its personnel, and the services provided there.

In conducting surveys, the director or the director's designee shall be given access to the residential facility; all records, accounts, and any other documents related to the operation of the facility; the licensee; the residents of the facility; and all persons acting on behalf of, under the control of, or in connection with the licensee. The licensee and all persons on behalf of, under the control of, or in connection with the licensee shall cooperate with the director or the director's designee in conducting the survey.

Following each survey, unless the director initiates a license revocation proceeding, the director or the director's designee shall provide the licensee with a report listing any deficiencies, specifying a timetable within which the licensee shall submit a plan of correction describing how the deficiencies will be corrected, and, when appropriate, specifying a timetable within which the licensee must correct the deficiencies. After a plan of correction is submitted, the director or the director's designee shall approve or disapprove the plan. A copy of the report and any approved plan of correction shall be provided to any person who requests it.

The director shall initiate disciplinary action against any department employee who notifies or causes the notification to any unauthorized person of an unannounced survey of a residential facility by an authorized representative of the department.

(I) In addition to any other information which may be required of applicants for a license pursuant to this section, the director shall require each applicant to provide a copy of an approved plan for a proposed residential facility pursuant to section 5123.042 of the Revised Code. This division does not apply to renewal of a license.

(J) A licensee shall notify the owner of the building in which the licensee's residential facility is located of any significant change in the identity of the licensee or management contractor before the effective date of the change if the licensee is not the owner of the building.

Pursuant to rules which shall be adopted in accordance with Chapter 119. of the Revised Code, the director may require notification to the department of any significant change in the ownership of a residential facility or in the identity of the licensee or management contractor. If the director determines that a significant change of ownership is proposed, the director shall consider the proposed change to be an application for development by a new operator pursuant to section 5123.042 of the Revised Code and shall advise the applicant within sixty days of the notification that the current license shall continue in effect or a new license will be required pursuant to this section. If the director requires a new license, the director shall permit the facility to continue to operate under the current license until the new license is issued, unless the current license is revoked, refused to be renewed, or terminated in accordance with Chapter 119. of the Revised Code.

(K) A county board of mental retardation and developmental disabilities, the legal rights service, and any interested person may file complaints alleging violations of statute or department rule relating to residential facilities with the department. All complaints shall be in writing and shall state the facts constituting the basis of the allegation. The department shall not reveal the source of any complaint unless the complainant agrees in writing to waive the right to confidentiality or until so ordered by a court of competent jurisdiction.

The department shall adopt rules in accordance with Chapter 119. of the Revised Code establishing procedures for the receipt, referral, investigation, and disposition of complaints filed with the department under this division.

(L) The department shall establish procedures for the notification of interested parties of the transfer or interim care of residents from residential facilities that are closing or are losing their license.

(M) Before issuing a license under this section to a residential facility that will accommodate at any time more than one mentally retarded or developmentally disabled individual, the director shall, by first class mail, notify the following:

(1) If the facility will be located in a municipal corporation, the clerk of the legislative authority of the municipal corporation;

(2) If the facility will be located in unincorporated territory, the clerk of the appropriate board of county commissioners and the fiscal officer of the appropriate board of township trustees.

The director shall not issue the license for ten days after mailing the notice, excluding Saturdays, Sundays, and legal holidays, in order to give the notified local officials time in which to comment on the proposed issuance.

Any legislative authority of a municipal corporation, board of county commissioners, or board of township trustees that receives notice under this division of the proposed issuance of a license for a residential facility may comment on it in writing to the director within ten days after the director mailed the notice, excluding Saturdays, Sundays, and legal holidays. If the director receives written comments from any notified officials within the specified time, the director shall make written findings concerning the comments and the director's decision on the issuance of the license. If the director does not receive written comments from any notified local officials within the specified time, the director shall continue the process for issuance of the license.

(N) Any person may operate a licensed residential facility that provides room and board, personal care, habilitation services, and supervision in a family setting for at least six but not more than eight persons with mental retardation or a developmental disability as a permitted use in any residential district or zone, including any single-family residential district or zone, of any political subdivision. These residential facilities may be required to comply with area, height, yard, and architectural compatibility requirements that are uniformly imposed upon all single-family residences within the district or zone.

(O) Any person may operate a licensed residential facility that provides room and board, personal care, habilitation services, and supervision in a family setting for at least nine but not more than sixteen persons with mental retardation or a developmental disability as a permitted use in any multiple-family residential district or zone of any political subdivision, except that a political subdivision that has enacted a zoning ordinance or resolution establishing planned unit development districts may exclude these residential facilities from those districts, and a political subdivision that has enacted a zoning ordinance or resolution may regulate these residential facilities in multiple-family residential districts or zones as a conditionally permitted use or special exception, in either case, under reasonable and specific standards and conditions set out in the zoning ordinance or resolution to:

(1) Require the architectural design and site layout of the residential facility and the location, nature, and height of any walls, screens, and fences to be compatible with adjoining land uses and the residential character of the neighborhood;

(2) Require compliance with yard, parking, and sign regulation;

(3) Limit excessive concentration of these residential facilities.

(P) This section does not prohibit a political subdivision from applying to residential facilities nondiscriminatory regulations requiring compliance with health, fire, and safety regulations and building standards and regulations.

(Q) Divisions (N) and (O) of this section are not applicable to municipal corporations that had in effect on June 15, 1977, an ordinance specifically permitting in residential zones licensed residential facilities by means of permitted uses, conditional uses, or special exception, so long as such ordinance remains in effect without any substantive modification.

(R)(1) The director may issue an interim license to operate a residential facility to an applicant for a license under this section if either of the following is the case:

(a) The director determines that an emergency exists requiring immediate placement of persons in a residential facility, that insufficient licensed beds are available, and that the residential facility is likely to receive a permanent license under this section within thirty days after issuance of the interim license.

(b) The director determines that the issuance of an interim license is necessary to meet a temporary need for a residential facility.

(2) To be eligible to receive an interim license, an applicant must meet the same criteria that must be met to receive a permanent license under this section, except for any differing procedures and time frames that may apply to issuance of a permanent license.

(3) An interim license shall be valid for thirty days and may be renewed by the director for a period not to exceed one hundred fifty days.

(4) The director shall adopt rules in accordance with Chapter 119. of the Revised Code as the director considers necessary to administer the issuance of interim licenses.

(S) Notwithstanding rules adopted pursuant to this section establishing the maximum number of persons who may be served in a particular type of residential facility, a residential facility shall be permitted to serve the same number of persons being served by the facility on the effective date of the rules or the number of persons for which the facility is authorized pursuant to a current application for a certificate of need with a letter of support from the department of mental retardation and developmental disabilities and which is in the review process prior to April 4, 1986.

(T) The director or the director's designee may enter at any time, for purposes of investigation, any home, facility, or other structure that has been reported to the director or that the director has reasonable cause to believe is being operated as a residential facility without a license issued under this section.

The director may petition the court of common pleas of the county in which an unlicensed residential facility is located for an order enjoining the person or governmental agency operating the facility from continuing to operate without a license. The court may grant the injunction on a showing that the person or governmental agency named in the petition is operating a residential facility without a license. The court may grant the injunction, regardless of whether the residential facility meets the requirements for receiving a license under this section.

(2005 S 107, eff. 12–20–05; 2003 H 95, eff. 6–26–03; 2002 S 191, eff. 3–31–03; 2000 H 538, eff. 9–22–00; 1997 H 215, eff. 6–30–97; 1995 H 117, eff. 9–29–95; 1994 H 694, eff. 11–11–94; 1993 S 21, eff. 10–29–93; 1993 H 152; 1992 S 331; 1991 S 233, § 1, 4; 1990 H 569, § 1, 4; 1989 H 253, H 332, § 1, 3, H 257; 1988 S 155; 1987 H 499; 1986 S 322; 1985 H 238; 1983 H 159; 1980 H 900)

Uncodified Law

1997 H 215, § 150, eff. 6–30–97, reads:

Moratorium for New MR/DD Residential Facility Beds

(A) During the period beginning July 1, 1997, and ending June 30, 1999, the Department of Mental Retardation and Developmental Disabilities shall not issue development approval for, nor license under section 5123.19 of the Revised Code, new residential facility beds for persons with mental retardation or developmental disabilities, except that the department may approve the development or licensure, or both, of such new beds in an emergency. The department shall adopt rules in accordance with Chapter 119. of the Revised Code specifying what constitutes an emergency for the purposes of this section.

(B) For the purposes of division (A) of this section, the following shall not be considered new beds:

(1) Beds relocated from one facility to another, if the facility from which the beds are relocated reduces the number of its beds by the same number of beds that are relocated to the other facility;

(2) Beds to replace others that the Director of Health determines no longer comply with the standards of the Medical Assistance Program established under Chapter 5111. of the Revised Code and Title XIX of the "Social Security Act," 49 Stat. 620 (1935), 42 U.S.C.A. 301, as amended.

1995 H 117, § 7, eff. 6–30–95, amended 1994 H 715, § 31, to read:

(A) During the period beginning July 22, 1994, and ending June 30, 1997, the Department of Mental Retardation and Developmental Disabilities shall not issue development approval for, nor license under section 5123.19 of the Revised Code, new residential facility beds for persons with mental retardation or developmental disabilities, except that the Department may approve the development or licensure, or both, of such new beds in an emergency. The Department shall adopt rules in accordance with Chapter 119. of the Revised Code specifying what constitutes an emergency for the purposes of this section.

(B) For the purposes of division (A) of this section, the following shall not be considered new beds:

(1) Beds relocated from one facility to another, if the facility from which the beds are relocated reduces the number of its beds by the same number of beds that are relocated to the other facility;

(2) Beds to replace others that the Director of Health determines no longer comply with the standards of the Medical Assistance Program established under Chapter 5111. of the Revised Code and Title XIX of the "Social Security Act," 49 Stat. 620 (1935), 42 U.S.C.A. 301, as amended.

(C) This section does not prohibit the Department from licensing beds for which the Department issued development approval prior to July 22, 1994.

1995 H 117, § 157, eff. 6–30–95, reads: Any rest home license that is valid on the effective date of this section shall be considered a residential care facility license. This section shall take effect on the ninety-first day after this act is filed with the Secretary of State.

1993 H 152, § 68.01: See Uncodified Law under 5123.171.

1993 H 152, § 68.01: See Uncodified Law under 5123.18.

1989 H 24, § 3, eff. 6–30–89, amended 1987 H 499, § 13, to read:

Notwithstanding section 5123.19 of the Revised Code as amended by Am. Sub. H.B. 499 of the 117th General Assembly any nursing home that on the effective date of that act contained beds that the Department of Health had certified prior to the effective date of that act as intermediate care facility for the mentally retarded beds under Title XIX of the "Social Security Act," 49 Stat. 620 (1935), 42 U.S.C. 301, as amended, or any nursing home that on the effective date of Am. Sub. H.B. 499 of the 117th General Assembly had an application pending before the Department to convert intermediate care facility beds to intermediate care facility for the mentally retarded beds, shall not be required to apply for licensure under section 5123.19 of the Revised Code, but shall be subject to the requirements for licensure as a nursing home and to any other requirements of Chapter 3721. of the Revised Code and any rules adopted under that chapter, and shall be subject to sections 3702.51 to 3702.60 and 3702.99 of the Revised Code and any rules adopted under those sections, unless:

(A) The nursing home's certification or provider agreement as an intermediate care facility for the mentally retarded is subject to a final order of nonrenewal or termination with respect to which all appeal rights have been exhausted and the facility intends to apply for recertification; or

(B) The nursing home intends to increase its number of beds certified as intermediate care facility for the mentally retarded beds. In such a case, the nursing home shall be required to apply for licensure of the additional beds under section 5123.19 of the Revised Code."

Historical and Statutory Notes

Ed. Note: 5123.19 is former 5123.18 amended and recodified by 1980 H 900, eff. 7–1–80; 1977 S 71.

Ed. Note: Former 5123.19 amended and recodified as 5123.20 by 1980 H 900, eff. 7–1–80; 1977 S 71; 1970 S 367; 125 v 119; 1953 H 1; GC 1890–24.

Ed. Note: The amendment of this section by 1989 H 332, § 3—as subsequently amended, eff. 11–15–91—was repealed by 1991 S 233, § 4, eff. 11–15–91. See *Baldwin's Ohio Legislative Service*, 1989 Laws of Ohio, page 5–753, 1990 Laws of Ohio, page 5–848, and 1991 Laws of Ohio, pages 5–852 and 5–854.

Pre–1953 H 1 Amendments: 121 v 423; 119 v 616; 117 v 550

Library References

Asylums ⇔3, 6.

Mental Health ⇌20.
Westlaw Topic Nos. 43, 257A.
C.J.S. Asylums and Institutional Care Facilities § 5 to 8, 13.
C.J.S. Insane Persons § 14 to 16.

5123.191 Receiver for residential facility

(A) The court of common pleas or a judge thereof in the judge's county, or the probate court, may appoint a receiver to take possession of and operate a residential facility licensed by the department of mental retardation and developmental disabilities, in causes pending in such courts respectively, when conditions existing at the facility present a substantial risk of physical or mental harm to residents and no other remedies at law are adequate to protect the health, safety, and welfare of the residents. Conditions at the facility that may present such risk of harm include, but are not limited to, instances when any of the following occur:

(1) The residential facility is in violation of state or federal law or regulations.

(2) The facility has had its license revoked or procedures for revocation have been initiated, or the facility is closing or intends to cease operations.

(3) Arrangements for relocating residents need to be made.

(4) Insolvency of the operator, licensee, or landowner threatens the operation of the facility.

(5) The facility or operator has demonstrated a pattern and practice of repeated violations of state or federal laws or regulations.

(B) A court in which a petition is filed pursuant to this section shall notify the person holding the license for the facility and the department of mental retardation and developmental disabilities of the filing. The court shall order the department to notify the legal rights service, facility owner, facility operator, county board of mental retardation and developmental disabilities, facility residents, and residents' parents and guardians of the filing of the petition.

The court shall provide a hearing on the petition within five court days of the time it was filed, except that the court may appoint a receiver prior to that time if it determines that the circumstances necessitate such action. Following a hearing on the petition, and upon a determination that the appointment of a receiver is warranted, the court shall appoint a receiver and notify the department of mental retardation and developmental disabilities and appropriate persons of this action.

(C) A residential facility for which a receiver has been named is deemed to be in compliance with section 5123.19 and Chapter 3721. of the Revised Code for the duration of the receivership.

(D) When the operating revenue of a residential facility in receivership is insufficient to meet its operating expenses, including the cost of bringing the facility into compliance with state or federal laws or regulations, the court may order the state to provide necessary funding, except as provided in division (K) of this section. The state shall provide such funding, subject to the approval of the controlling board. The court may also order the appropriate authorities to expedite all inspections necessary for the issuance of licenses or the certification of a facility, and order a facility to be closed if it determines that reasonable efforts cannot bring the facility into substantial compliance with the law.

(E) In establishing a receivership, the court shall set forth the powers and duties of the receiver. The court may generally authorize the receiver to do all that is prudent and necessary to safely and efficiently operate the residential facility within the requirements of state and federal law, but shall require the receiver to obtain court approval prior to making any single expenditure of more than five thousand dollars to correct deficiencies in the structure or furnishings of a facility. The court shall closely review the conduct of the receiver it has appointed and shall require regular and detailed reports. The receivership shall be reviewed at least every sixty days.

(F) A receivership established pursuant to this section shall be terminated, following notification of the appropriate parties and a hearing, if the court determines either of the following:

(1) The residential facility has been closed and the former residents have been relocated to an appropriate facility.

(2) Circumstances no longer exist at the facility that present a substantial risk of physical or mental harm to residents, and there is no deficiency in the facility that is likely to create a future risk of harm.

Notwithstanding division (F)(2) of this section, the court shall not terminate a receivership for a residential facility that has previously operated under another receivership unless the responsibility for the operation of the facility is transferred to an operator approved by the court and the department of mental retardation and developmental disabilities.

(G) The department of mental retardation and developmental disabilities may, upon its own initiative or at the request of an owner, operator, or resident of a residential facility, or at the request of a resident's guardian or relative, a county board of mental retardation and developmental disabilities, or the legal rights service, petition the court to appoint a receiver to take possession of and operate a residential facility. When the department has been requested to file a petition by any of the parties listed above, it shall, within forty-eight hours of such request, either file such a petition or notify the requesting party of its decision not to file. If the department refuses to file, the requesting party may file a petition with the court requesting the appointment of a receiver to take possession of and operate a residential facility.

Petitions filed pursuant to this division shall include the following:

(1) A description of the specific conditions existing at the facility which present a substantial risk of physical or mental harm to residents;

(2) A statement of the absence of other adequate remedies at law;

(3) The number of individuals residing at the facility;

(4) A statement that the facts have been brought to the attention of the owner or licensee and that conditions have not been remedied within a reasonable period of time or that the conditions, though remedied periodically, habitually exist at the facility as a pattern or practice;

(5) The name and address of the person holding the license for the facility and the address of the department of mental retardation and developmental disabilities.

The court may award to an operator appropriate costs and expenses, including reasonable attorney's fees, if it determines that a petitioner has initiated a proceeding in bad faith or merely for the purpose of harassing or embarrassing the operator.

(H) Except for the department of mental retardation and developmental disabilities or a county board of mental retardation and developmental disabilities, no party or person interested in an action shall be appointed a receiver pursuant to this section.

To assist the court in identifying persons qualified to be named as receivers, the director of mental retardation and developmental disabilities or the director's designee shall maintain a list of the names of such persons. The director shall, in accordance with Chapter 119. of the Revised Code, establish standards for evaluating persons desiring to be included on such a list.

(I) Before a receiver enters upon the duties of that person, the receiver must be sworn to perform the duties of receiver faithfully, and, with surety approved by the court, judge, or clerk, execute a bond to such person, and in such sum as the court or judge directs, to the effect that such receiver will faithfully discharge the duties of receiver in the action, and obey the orders of the court therein.

(J) Under the control of the appointing court, a receiver may bring and defend actions in the receiver's own name as receiver and take and keep possession of property.

The court shall authorize the receiver to do the following:

(1) Collect payment for all goods and services provided to the residents or others during the period of the receivership at the same rate as was charged by the licensee at the time the petition for receivership was filed, unless a different rate is set by the court;

(2) Honor all leases, mortgages, and secured transactions governing all buildings, goods, and fixtures of which the receiver has taken possession and continues to use, subject to the following conditions:

(a) In the case of a rental agreement, only to the extent of payments that are for the use of the property during the period of the receivership;

(b) In the case of a purchase agreement only to the extent of payments that come due during the period of the receivership;

(c) If the court determines that the cost of the lease, mortgage, or secured transaction was increased by a transaction required to be reported under division (B)(3) of section 5123.172 of the Revised Code, only to the extent determined by the court to be the fair market value for use of the property during the period of the receivership.

(3) If transfer of residents is necessary, provide for the orderly transfer of residents by doing the following:

(a) Cooperating with all appropriate state and local agencies in carrying out the transfer of residents to alternative community placements;

(b) Providing for the transportation of residents' belongings and records;

(c) Helping to locate alternative placements and develop discharge plans;

(d) Preparing residents for the trauma of discharge;

(e) Permitting residents or guardians to participate in transfer or discharge planning except when an emergency exists and immediate transfer is necessary.

(4) Make periodic reports on the status of the residential program to the appropriate state agency, county board of mental retardation and developmental disabilities, parents, guardians, and residents;

(5) Compromise demands or claims;

(6) Generally do such acts respecting the residential facility as the court authorizes.

(K) Neither the receiver nor the department of mental retardation and developmental disabilities is liable for debts incurred by the owner or operator of a residential facility for which a receiver has been appointed.

(L) The department of mental retardation and developmental disabilities may contract for the operation of a residential facility in receivership. The department shall establish the conditions of a contract. A condition may be the same as, similar to, or different from a condition established by section 5123.18 of the Revised Code and the rules adopted under that section for a contract entered into under that section. Notwithstanding any other provision of law, contracts that are necessary to carry out the powers and duties of the receiver need not be competitively bid.

(M) The department of mental retardation and developmental disabilities, the department of job and family services, and the department of health shall provide technical assistance to any receiver appointed pursuant to this section.

(1999 H 471, eff. 7–1–00; 1994 H 435, eff. 11–9–94; 1993 S 21, eff. 10–29–93; 1986 S 322)

Uncodified Law

1994 H 435, § 3: See Uncodified Law under 5123.18.

Library References

Asylums ⚖3, 6.
Westlaw Topic No. 43.
C.J.S. Asylums and Institutional Care Facilities § 5 to 8, 13.

5123.192 Nursing homes with intermediate care for the mentally retarded beds

Notwithstanding section 5123.19 of the Revised Code, any nursing home that on June 30, 1987, contained beds that the department of health had certified prior to June 30, 1987, as intermediate care facility for the mentally retarded beds under Title XIX of the "Social Security Act," 49 Stat. 620 (1935), 42 U.S.C. 301, as amended, or any nursing home that on June 30, 1987, had an application pending before the department to convert intermediate care facility beds to intermediate care facility for the mentally retarded beds, shall not be required to apply for licensure under section 5123.19 of the Revised Code, shall be subject to the requirements for licensure as a nursing home and all other requirements of Chapter 3721. of the Revised Code and any rules adopted under that chapter, and shall be subject to sections 3702.51 to 3702.62 of the Revised Code and any rules adopted under those sections, unless either of the following applies:

(A) The nursing home's certification or provider agreement as an intermediate care facility for the mentally retarded is subject to a final order of nonrenewal or termination with respect to which all appeal rights have been exhausted and the facility intends to apply for recertification;

(B) The nursing home intends to increase its number of beds certified as intermediate care facility for the mentally retarded beds. In such a case, the nursing home shall be required to apply for licensure of the additional beds under section 5123.19 of the Revised Code.

(1995 S 50, eff. 4–20–95)

Historical and Statutory Notes

Ed. Note: 5123.192 is former 1987 H 499, § 13, amended and codified by 1995 S 50, eff. 4–20–95; 1989 H 24, § 3, eff. 6–30–89; 1987 H 499, § 13, eff. 6–30–87.

Ed. Note: Former 5123.192 amended and recodified as 5126.431 by 1994 H 694, eff. 11–11–94; 1989 H 257, eff. 8–3–89.

Library References

Asylums ⚖3.
Westlaw Topic No. 43.
C.J.S. Asylums and Institutional Care Facilities § 5 to 8.

5123.194 Waiver of support collection requirements for individuals moving into independent living arrangements

In the case of an individual who resides in a residential facility and is preparing to move into an independent living arrangement and the individual's liable relative, the department of mental retardation and developmental disabilities may waive the support collection requirements of sections 5121.04, 5123.122, and

5123.18 of the Revised Code for the purpose of allowing income or resources to be used to acquire items necessary for independent living. The department shall adopt rules in accordance with section 111.15 of the Revised Code to implement this section, including rules that establish the method the department shall use to determine when an individual is preparing to move into an independent living arrangement.

(1997 H 215, eff. 6–30–97)

Library References

Mental Health ⇐72, 73.
Westlaw Topic No. 257A.
C.J.S. Insane Persons § 203 to 207.

5123.20 Prohibitions

As used in this section, "supported living" has the same meaning as in section 5126.01 of the Revised Code.

No person or government agency shall operate a residential facility or receive a mentally retarded or developmentally disabled person as a resident of a residential facility unless the facility is licensed under section 5123.19 of the Revised Code, and no person or government agency shall operate a respite care home or receive a mentally retarded or developmentally disabled person in a respite care home unless the home is certified under section 5126.05 of the Revised Code.

No person or government agency shall provide supported living unless that person or government agency is certified under section 5126.431 of the Revised Code.

(1994 H 694, eff. 11–11–94; 1993 S 21, eff. 10–29–93; 1990 H 569; 1989 H 257; 1980 H 900)

Uncodified Law

1993 H 152, § 68.01: See Uncodified Law under 5123.171.

1993 H 152, § 68.01: See Uncodified Law under 5123.18.

Historical and Statutory Notes

Ed. Note: 5123.20 is former 5123.19 amended and recodified by 1980 H 900, eff. 7–1–80; 1977 S 71; 1970 S 367; Source—GC 1890–24.

Ed. Note: Former 5123.20 amended and recodified as 5119.22 by 1980 H 900, eff. 7–1–80; 1978 H 870; prior 5123.20 repealed by 129 v 1448, eff. 10–25–61; 1953 H 1

Library References

Asylums ⇐3.
Westlaw Topic No. 43.
C.J.S. Asylums and Institutional Care Facilities § 5 to 8.

5123.21 Transfer between institutions

The director of mental retardation and developmental disabilities or the director's designee may transfer or authorize the transfer of an involuntary resident or a consenting voluntary resident from one public institution to another or to an institution other than a public institution or other facility, if the director determines that it would be consistent with the habilitation needs of the resident to do so.

Before an involuntary resident may be transferred to a more restrictive setting, the managing officer of the institution shall file a motion with the court requesting the court to amend its order of placement issued under section 5123.76 of the Revised Code. At the resident's request, the court shall hold a hearing on the motion at which the resident has the same rights as at a full hearing under section 5123.76 of the Revised Code.

Whenever a resident is transferred, the director shall give written notice of the transfer to the resident's legal guardian, parents, spouse, and counsel, or, if none is known, to the resident's nearest known relative or friend. If the resident is a minor, the department before making such a transfer shall make a minute of the order for the transfer and the reason for it upon its record and shall send a certified copy at least seven days prior to the transfer to the person shown by its record to have had the care or custody of the minor immediately prior to the minor's commitment. Whenever a consenting voluntary resident is transferred, the notification shall be given only at the resident's request. The managing officer shall advise a voluntary resident who is being transferred that the patient may decide if such a notification shall be given. In all such transfers, due consideration shall be given to the relationship of the resident to the resident's family, legal guardian, or friends, so as to maintain relationships and encourage visits beneficial to the resident.

(2000 H 538, eff. 9–22–00; 1996 S 285, eff. 7–1–97; 1980 H 965, eff. 4–9–81; 1980 H 900)

Historical and Statutory Notes

Ed. Note: 5123.21 is former 5123.78 amended and recodified by 1980 H 900, eff. 7–1–80; 1980 S 297; 1978 H 565; 1974 S 336.

Ed. Note: Former 5123.21 repealed by 129 v 1448, eff. 10–25–61; 126 v 313; 1953 H 1; GC 1890–25; see now 5122.12 for provisions analogous to former 5123.21.

Pre–1953 H 1 Amendments: 121 v 423; 119 v 616; 117 v 550

Library References

Asylums ⇐5.
Westlaw Topic Nos. 43, 357A.
C.J.S. Asylums and Institutional Care Facilities § 11 to 12.
C.J.S. Sodomy § 2 to 6.

5123.211 Residential services for former residents of closed institutions

(A) As used in this section, "residential services" and "supported living" have the same meanings as in section 5126.01 of the Revised Code.

(B) The department of mental retardation and developmental disabilities shall provide or arrange provision of residential services for each person who, on or after July 1, 1989, ceases to be a resident of a state institution because of closure of the institution or a reduction in the institution's population by forty per cent or more within a period of one year. The services shall be provided in the county in which the person chooses to reside and shall consist of one of the following as determined appropriate by the department in consultation with the county board of mental retardation and developmental disabilities of the county in which the services are to be provided:

(1) Residential services provided pursuant to section 5123.18 of the Revised Code;

(2) Supported living provided pursuant to section 5123.182 of the Revised Code;

(3) Residential services for which reimbursement is made under the medical assistance program established under section 5111.01 of the Revised Code;

(4) Residential services provided in a manner or setting approved by the director of mental retardation and developmental disabilities.

(C) Not less than six months prior to closing a state institution or reducing a state institution's population by forty per cent or more within a period of one year, the department shall identify those counties in which individuals leaving the institution have chosen to reside and notify the county boards of mental retardation and developmental disabilities in those counties of the need to develop the services specified in division (B) of this section. The notice shall specify the number of individuals requiring services who plan to reside in the county and indicate the amount of funds the department will use to provide or arrange services for those individuals.

(D) In each county in which one or more persons receive residential services pursuant to division (B) of this section, the department shall provide or arrange provision of residential services, or shall distribute moneys to the county board of mental retardation and developmental disabilities to provide or arrange provision of residential services, for an equal number of persons with mental retardation or developmental disabilities in that county who the county board has determined need residential services but are not receiving them.

(1991 H 298, eff. 7–26–91; 1990 H 359)

Library References

Mental Health ⇐20, 51.1.
Westlaw Topic No. 257A.
C.J.S. Insane Persons § 14 to 16, 86 to 92.

REAL ESTATE

5123.22 Appropriation of real property

When it is necessary for an institution under the jurisdiction of the department of mental retardation and developmental disabilities to acquire any real estate, right-of-way, or easement in real estate in order to accomplish the purposes for which it was organized or is being conducted, and the department is unable to agree with the owner of such property upon the price to be paid therefor, such property may be appropriated in the manner provided for the appropriation of property for other state purposes.

Any instrument by which real property is acquired pursuant to this section shall identify the agency of the state that has the use and benefit of the real property as specified in section 5301.012 of the Revised Code.

(1999 H 19, eff. 10–26–99; 1980 H 900, eff. 7–1–80)

Historical and Statutory Notes

Ed. Note: Former 5123.22 repealed by 129 v 1448, eff. 10–25–61; 1953 H 1; GC 1890–26.

Pre–1953 H 1 Amendments: 119 v 616; 117 v 550, § 26

Library References

Mental Health ⇐20.
States ⇐85.
Westlaw Topic Nos. 257A, 360.
C.J.S. Insane Persons § 14 to 16.
C.J.S. States § 145.

5123.221 Cultivation of lands

The department of mental retardation and developmental disabilities shall determine and direct what lands belonging to institutions under its control shall be cultivated.

The department of agriculture, the department of health, and the Ohio state university shall cooperate with the department of mental retardation and developmental disabilities, and the managing officer of each institution mentioned in section 5123.03 of the Revised Code, in making such cooperative tests as are necessary to determine the quality, strength, and purity of supplies, the value and use of farm lands, or the conditions and needs of mechanical equipment.

The department may direct the purchase of any materials, supplies, or other articles for any institution subject to its jurisdiction from any other such institution at the reasonable market value, such value to be fixed by the department, and payments therefor shall be made as between institutions in the manner provided for payment for supplies.

(1985 H 201, eff. 7–1–85; 1980 H 900)

Library References

Mental Health ⇐20.
States ⇐87.
Westlaw Topic Nos. 257A, 360.
C.J.S. Insane Persons § 14 to 16.
C.J.S. States § 146.

5123.23 Oil and gas leases

The director of mental retardation and developmental disabilities may lease, for oil and gas, any real estate owned by the state and placed under the supervision of the department of mental retardation and developmental disabilities, to any person, upon such terms and for such number of years, not more than forty, as will be for the best interest of the state. No such lease shall be agreed upon or entered into before the proposal to lease the property has been advertised once each week for four weeks in a newspaper of general circulation in the county in which the property is located. The lease shall be made with the person offering the best terms to the state.

The director, in such lease, may grant to the lessee the right to use so much of the surface of the land as may be reasonably necessary to carry on the work of prospecting for, extracting, piping, storing, and removing all oil or gas, and for depositing waste material and maintaining such buildings and constructions as are reasonably necessary for exploring or prospecting for such oil and gas.

All leases made under this section shall be prepared by the attorney general and approved by the governor. All money received from any such leases shall be paid into the state treasury to the credit of the general revenue fund.

(1986 S 312, eff. 9–24–86; 1983 H 291; 1980 H 900)

Historical and Statutory Notes

Ed. Note: Former 5123.23 repealed by 129 v 1448, eff. 10–25–61; 128 v 522; 126 v 313; 125 v 823, 119; 1953 H 1; GC 1890–27.

Pre–1953 H 1 Amendments: 121 v 423; 119 v 616; 117 v 550

Library References

Mental Health ⇐20.
States ⇐87.
Westlaw Topic Nos. 257A, 360.
C.J.S. Insane Persons § 14 to 16.
C.J.S. States § 146.

5123.24 Petition to conduct business within prohibited distance of institution

A person, firm, or corporation may file a petition in the court of common pleas of the county in which an institution under the jurisdiction of the department of mental retardation and developmental disabilities is located, in which petition the desire to erect or carry on at a less distance than that prescribed in section 3767.19 of the Revised Code shall be set forth, the business prohibited, the precise point of its establishment, and the reasons and circumstances, in its opinion, why the erection or carrying on thereof would not annoy or endanger the health, convenience, or recovery of the residents of such institution. The petitioner shall give notice in a newspaper of general circulation in the county of the pendency and prayer of the petition for at least six consecutive weeks before the day set for hearing the petition and serve a written notice upon the superintendent of the institution at least thirty days before the day set for hearing the petition.

If, upon the hearing of the petition, it appears that the notice has been given as required and the court is of the opinion that no good reason exists why such establishment may not be erected or such business carried on and that by the erection or carrying on thereof at the point named, the institution will sustain no detriment, the court may issue an order granting the prayer of the petitioner. Thereafter the petitioner may locate such establishment or carry on such business at the point named in the petition.

(1980 H 900, eff. 7–1–80)

Historical and Statutory Notes

Ed. Note: Former 5123.24 repealed by 129 v 1448, eff. 10–25–61; 125 v 119; 1953 H 1; GC 1890–28; see now 5122.14 for provisions analogous to former 5123.24.

Pre–1953 H 1 Amendments: 119 v 616, § 1; 117 v 550, § 28

Library References

Mental Health ⇌20.
Westlaw Topic No. 257A.
C.J.S. Insane Persons § 14 to 16.

FISCAL PROVISIONS

5123.25 Purchasing; competitive bidding; exceptions

The department of administrative services shall purchase all supplies needed for the proper support and maintenance of the institutions under the control of the department of mental retardation and developmental disabilities in accordance with the competitive selection procedures of Chapter 125. of the Revised Code and such rules as the department of administrative services adopts. All bids shall be publicly opened on the day and hour and at the place specified in the advertisement.

Preference shall be given to bidders in localities wherein the institution is located, if the price is fair and reasonable and not greater than the usual price.

The department of administrative services may require such security as it considers proper to accompany the bids and shall fix the security to be given by the contractor.

The department of administrative services may reject any or all bids and secure new bids, if for any reason it is considered for the best interest of the state to do so, and it may authorize the managing officer of any institution to purchase perishable goods and supplies for use in cases of emergency, in which cases the managing officer shall certify such fact in writing and the department of administrative services shall record the reasons for the purchases.

(1993 H 152, eff. 7–1–93; 1987 H 88; 1980 H 900)

Historical and Statutory Notes

Ed. Note: Former 5123.25 repealed by 129 v 1448, eff. 10–25–61; 1953 H 1; GC 1890–29.

Pre–1953 H 1 Amendments: 119 v 616, § 1; 117 v 550, § 29

Library References

Mental Health ⇌20.
States ⇌98.
Westlaw Topic Nos. 257A, 360.
C.J.S. Insane Persons § 14 to 16.
C.J.S. States § 160 to 167.

5123.26 Fiscal procedures

The treasurer of state shall have charge of all funds under the jurisdiction of the department of mental retardation and developmental disabilities and shall pay out the same only in accordance with Chapter 5123. of the Revised Code.

The department shall cause to be furnished a contract of indemnity to cover all moneys and funds received by it or by its managing officers, employees, or agents while such moneys or funds are in the possession of such managing officers, employees, or agents. Such funds are designated as follows:

(A) Funds which are due and payable to the treasurer of state as provided by Chapter 131. of the Revised Code;

(B) Those funds which are held in trust by the managing officers, employees, or agents of the institution as local funds or accounts under the jurisdiction of the department.

Such contract of indemnity shall be made payable to the state and the premium for such contract of indemnity may be paid from any of the funds received for the use of the department under this chapter or Chapter 5121. of the Revised Code.

Funds collected from various sources, such as the sale of goods, farm products, and all miscellaneous articles, shall be transmitted on or before Monday of each week to the treasurer of state and a detailed statement of such collections shall be made to the division of business administration by each managing officer.

(1980 H 900, eff. 7–1–80)

Historical and Statutory Notes

Ed. Note: Former 5123.26 repealed by 129 v 1448, eff. 10–25–61; 1953 H 1; GC 1890–30.

Pre–1953 H 1 Amendments: 117 v 550, § 30

Library References

States ⇌121.
Westlaw Topic No. 360.
C.J.S. States § 203, 223.

5123.27 Grants, devises, gifts, or bequests; accounting; annual report

The director of mental retardation and developmental disabilities may accept, hold, and administer in trust on behalf of the state, if it is for the public interest, any grant, devise, gift, or bequest of money or property made to the state for the use or benefit of any institution under the jurisdiction of the department of mental retardation and developmental disabilities or for the use and benefit of persons with mental retardation or a developmental disability under the control of the department. If the trust so provides, the money or property may be used for any work which the department is authorized to undertake.

The department shall keep such gift, grant, devise, or bequest as a distinct property or fund and, if it is in money, shall invest it in the manner provided by law. The department may deposit in a proper trust company or savings bank any money left in trust during a specified life or lives and shall adopt rules governing the deposit, transfer, withdrawal, or investment of the money and the income from it.

The department shall, in the manner prescribed by the director of budget and management pursuant to section 126.21 of the Revised Code, account for all money or property received or expended under this section. The records, together with a statement certified by the depository showing the money deposited there to the credit of the trust, shall be open to public inspection. The director of budget and management may require the department to file a report with the director on any particular portion, or the whole, of any trust property received or expended by it.

The department shall, upon the expiration of any trust according to its terms, dispose of the money or property held under the trust in the manner provided in the instrument creating the trust. If the instrument creating the trust failed to make any terms of disposition, or if no trust was in evidence, the decedent resident's money, saving or commercial deposits, dividends or distributions, bonds, or any other interest-bearing debt certificate or stamp issued by the United States government shall escheat to the state. All such unclaimed intangible personal property of a former resident shall be retained by the managing officer in such institution for the period of one year, during which time every possible effort shall be made to find the former resident or the former resident's legal representative.

If after a period of one year from the time the resident has left the institution or has died, the managing officer has been unable to locate the person or the person's legal representative, then, upon proper notice of that fact, the director shall at that time formulate in writing a method of disposition on the minutes of the department authorizing the managing officer to convert such intangible personal property to cash to be paid into the state treasury to the credit of the general revenue fund.

The department shall include in its annual report a statement of all such money and property and the terms and conditions relating to them.

(2000 H 538, eff. 9–22–00; 1990 H 569, eff. 7–1–91; 1985 H 201; 1984 H 250; 1980 H 900)

Historical and Statutory Notes

Ed. Note: 5123.27 is former 5123.06 amended and recodified by 1980 H 900, eff. 7–1–80; 1976 H 1215; 1972 H 494; 1970 H 970; 125 v 823; 1953 H 1; GC 1890–10.

Ed. Note: Former 5123.27 repealed by 1974 S 336, eff. 7–1–75; 1972 H 494; 129 v 1448; 125 v 823; 1953 H 1; GC 1890–31.

Pre–1953 H 1 Amendments: 119 v 616, § 1; 117 v 550, § 31

Library References

Mental Health ⇔20, 101, 102, 211, 212.
Westlaw Topic No. 257A.
C.J.S. Insane Persons § 14 to 16, 108 to 110, 128, 143, 165.

5123.28 Care of residents' money and property; disposition on death

(A) Except as otherwise provided in this division, money or property deposited with managing officers of institutions under the jurisdiction of the department of mental retardation and developmental disabilities by any resident under the department's control or by relatives, guardians, conservators, and others for the special benefit of such resident, as well as all other funds and all other income paid to the resident, to the resident's estate, or on the resident's behalf, or paid to the managing officer or to the institution as representative payee or otherwise paid on the resident's behalf, shall remain in the hands of such managing officers in appropriate accounts for use accordingly. Each such managing officer shall keep itemized book accounts of the receipt and disposition of such money and property, which book shall be open at all times to the inspection of the department. The director of mental retardation and developmental disabilities shall adopt rules governing the deposit, transfer, withdrawal, or investment of such funds and the income of the funds, as well as rules under which such funds and income shall be paid by managing officers, institutions, or district managers for the support of such residents pursuant to Chapter 5121. of the Revised Code, or for their other needs.

This division does not require, and shall not be construed as requiring, the deposit of the principal or income of a trust created pursuant to section 5815.28 of the Revised Code with managing officers of institutions under the jurisdiction of the department.

(B) Whenever any resident confined in a state institution under the jurisdiction of the department dies, escapes, or is discharged from the institution, any personal funds of the resident remain in the hands of the managing officer of the institution, and no demand is made upon the managing officer by the owner of the funds or the owner's legally appointed representative, the managing officer shall hold the funds in the personal deposit fund for a period of at least one year during which time the managing officer shall make every effort possible to locate the owner or the owner's legally appointed representative. If, at the end of this period, no demand has been made for the funds, the managing officer shall dispose of the funds as follows:

(1) All money in a personal deposit fund in excess of ten dollars due for the support of a resident, shall be paid in accordance with Chapter 5121. of the Revised Code.

(2) All money in a personal deposit fund in excess of ten dollars not due for the support of a resident, shall be placed to the credit of the institution's local account designated as the "industrial and entertainment" fund.

(3) The first ten dollars to the credit of a resident shall be placed to the credit of the institution's local account designated as the "industrial and entertainment" fund.

(C) Whenever any resident in any state institution subject to the jurisdiction of the department dies, escapes, or is discharged from the institution, any personal effects of the resident remain in the hands of the managing officer of the institution, and no demand is made upon the managing officer by the owner of the personal effects or the owner's legally appointed representative, the managing officer shall hold and dispose of the personal effects in the following manner. All the miscellaneous personal effects shall be held for a period of at least one year, during which time the managing officer shall make every effort possible to locate the owner or the owner's legal representative. If, at the end of this period, no demand has been made by the owner of the property or the owner's legal representative, the managing officer shall file with the county recorder of the county of commitment of such owner, all deeds, wills, contract mortgages, or assignments. The balance of the personal effects shall be sold at public auction after being duly advertised, and the funds turned over to the treasurer of state for credit to the general revenue fund. If any of the property is not of a type to be filed with the county recorder and is not salable at public auction, the managing officer of the institution shall destroy that property.

(2006 H 416, eff. 1–1–07; 1993 S 21, eff. 10–29–93; 1992 S 124; 1980 H 965, H 900)

Uncodified Law

1992 S 124, § 8, eff. 4–16–93, reads: In enacting sections 1339.51 and 5111.15 and in amending sections 2101.24, 5119.01, 5121.04, 5121.10, 5123,04, 5123.18, and 5123.28 of the Revised Code, the General Assembly hereby declares its intent to supersede the effect of the holding of the Ohio Supreme Court in the December 31, 1968, decision in *Bureau of Support v. Kreitzer* (1968), 16 Ohio St. 2d 147.

Historical and Statutory Notes

Ed. Note: Former 5123.28 repealed by 1974 S 336, eff. 7–1–75; 1972 H 494; 125 v 823; 1953 H 1; GC 1890–32.

Pre–1953 H 1 Amendments: 119 v 616, § 1; 117 v 550, § 32

Library References

Mental Health ⇔211, 212, 218.
Westlaw Topic No. 257A.
C.J.S. Insane Persons § 165, 182.

Baldwin's Ohio Legislative Service Annotated, 2006 H 416 LSC Analysis, p 3/L-1709

5123.29 Designated funds

Each managing officer of an institution under the jurisdiction of the department of mental retardation and developmental disabilities, with the approval of the director of mental retardation and developmental disabilities, may establish funds in the institutions under the jurisdiction of the department, designated as follows:

(A) Industrial and entertainment fund for the entertainment and welfare of the residents of the institution.

(B) Commissary fund for the benefit of residents of the institution. Commissary revenue in excess of operating costs and reserve shall be considered profits. All profits from the commissary fund operations shall be paid into the industrial and entertainment fund, and used only for the entertainment and welfare of residents.

The director shall establish rules for the operation of the industrial and entertainment and commissary funds.

(1980 H 900, eff. 7–1–80)

Historical and Statutory Notes

Ed. Note: Former 5123.29 amended and recodified as 5122.36 by 1980 H 900, eff. 7–1–80; 1977 H 1; 1972 H 494; 129 v 1448; 125 v 823; 1953 H 1; GC 1890-33.

Pre–1953 H 1 Amendments: 119 v 616, § 1; 117 v 550, § 33

Library References

Asylums ⚖=6.
Mental Health ⚖=20.
Westlaw Topic Nos. 43, 257A.
C.J.S. Asylums and Institutional Care Facilities § 13.
C.J.S. Insane Persons § 14 to 16.

5123.30 Accounting standards

The department of mental retardation and developmental disabilities shall keep in its office a proper and complete set of books and accounts with each institution, which shall clearly show the nature and amount of every expenditure authorized and made at such institution, and which shall contain an account of all appropriations made by the general assembly and of all other funds, together with the disposition of such funds.

The department shall prescribe the form of vouchers, records, and methods of keeping accounts at each of the institutions, which shall be as nearly uniform as possible. The department may examine the records of any institution at any time.

The department may authorize any of its bookkeepers, accountants, or employees to examine the records, accounts, and vouchers or take an inventory of the property of any institution, or do whatever is necessary, and pay the actual and reasonable expenses incurred in such service when an itemized account is filed and approved.

(1980 H 900, eff. 7–1–80)

Historical and Statutory Notes

Ed. Note: Former 5123.30 repealed by 129 v 1448, eff. 10–25–61; 126 v 313; 1953 H 1; GC 1890-34.

Pre–1953 H 1 Amendments: 119 v 616, § 1; 117 v 550, § 34

Library References

Asylums ⚖=6.
Mental Health ⚖=20.
Westlaw Topic Nos. 43, 257A.
C.J.S. Asylums and Institutional Care Facilities § 13.
C.J.S. Insane Persons § 14 to 16.

RECORDS AND REPORTS

5123.31 Records concerning residents

The department of mental retardation and developmental disabilities shall keep in its office, accessible only to its employees, except by the consent of the department or the order of the judge of a court of record, a record showing the name, residence, sex, age, nativity, occupation, condition, and date of entrance or commitment of every resident in the institutions governed by it, the date, cause, and terms of discharge and the condition of such person at the time of leaving, and also a record of all transfers from one institution to another, and, if such person dies while in the care or custody of the department, the date and cause of death. These and such other facts as the department requires shall be furnished by the managing officer of each institution within ten days after the commitment, entrance, death, or discharge of a resident.

In case of an accident or injury or peculiar death of a resident the managing officer shall make a special report to the department within twenty-four hours thereafter, giving the circumstances as fully as possible.

(1980 H 900, eff. 7–1–80)

Historical and Statutory Notes

Ed. Note: Former 5123.31 repealed by 1976 H 244, eff. 8–26–76; 1972 H 494; 1970 H 970; 129 v 1448; 128 v 333; 1953 H 1; GC 1890-35.

Pre–1953 H 1 Amendments: 119 v 616, § 1; 117 v 550, § 35

Library References

Mental Health ⚖=21.
Westlaw Topic No. 257A.
C.J.S. Insane Persons § 17 to 20.

5123.33 Annual report of department

In its annual report, the department of mental retardation and developmental disabilities shall include a list of the officers and agents employed, and complete financial statement of the various institutions under its control. The report shall describe the condition of each institution, and shall state, as to each institution, whether:

(A) The moneys appropriated have been economically and judiciously expended;

(B) The objects of the institutions have been accomplished;

(C) The laws in relation to such institutions have been fully complied with;

(D) All parts of the state are equally benefited by the institutions.

Such annual report shall be accompanied by the reports of the managing officers, such other information as the department considers proper, and the department's recommendations for the more effective accomplishment of the general purpose of this chapter.

(1980 H 900, eff. 7–1–80)

Historical and Statutory Notes

Ed. Note: Former 5123.33 repealed by 1980 H 900, eff. 7–1–80; 1976 H 244; 129 v 1448; 1953 H 1; GC 1890-37.

Pre–1953 H 1 Amendments: 121 v 423; 119 v 616; 117 v 550

Library References

Mental Health ⟶20.
Westlaw Topic No. 257A.
C.J.S. Insane Persons § 14 to 16.

PURPOSE OF CHAPTER

5123.34 Statement of purposes

This chapter attempts to do all of the following:

(A) Provide humane and scientific treatment and care and the highest attainable degree of individual development for persons with mental retardation or a developmental disability;

(B) Promote the study of the causes of mental retardation and developmental disabilities, with a view to ultimate prevention;

(C) Secure by uniform and systematic management the highest attainable degree of economy in the administration of the institutions under the control of the department of mental retardation and developmental disabilities.

Sections 5123.02 to 5123.04, 5123.042, 5123.043, 5123. 10, 5123.21, 5123.221, 5123.25, and 5123.31 of the Revised Code shall be liberally construed to attain these purposes.

(2005 H 66, eff. 7–1–05; 2000 H 538, eff. 9–22–00; 1997 H 215, eff. 6–30–97; 1994 H 694, eff. 11–11–94; 1990 H 569, eff. 7–1–91; 1980 H 900)

Historical and Statutory Notes

Ed. Note: Former 5123.34 repealed by 129 v 1448, eff. 10–25–61; 1953 H 1; GC 1890–38.

Pre–1953 H 1 Amendments: 117 v 550, § 38

Library References

Mental Health ⟶31, 51.1.
Statutes ⟶184, 235.
Westlaw Topic Nos. 257A, 361.
C.J.S. Insane Persons § 45, 47, 53, 86 to 92.
C.J.S. Statutes § 306, 316, 376.

STATE AND FEDERAL ASSISTANCE

5123.35 Developmental disabilities council

(A) There is hereby created the Ohio developmental disabilities council, which shall serve as an advocate for all persons with developmental disabilities. The council shall act in accordance with the "Developmental Disabilities Assistance and Bill of Rights Act," 98 Stat. 2662 (1984), 42 U.S.C. 6001, as amended. The governor shall appoint the members of the council in accordance with 42 U.S.C. 6024.

(B) The Ohio developmental disabilities council shall develop the state plan required by federal law as a condition of receiving federal assistance under 42 U.S.C. 6021 to 6030. The department of mental retardation and developmental disabilities, as the state agency selected by the governor for purposes of receiving the federal assistance, shall receive, account for, and disburse funds based on the state plan and shall provide assurances and other administrative support services required as a condition of receiving the federal assistance.

(C) The federal funds may be disbursed through grants to or contracts with persons and government agencies for the provision of necessary or useful goods and services for developmentally disabled persons. The Ohio developmental disabilities council may award the grants or enter into the contracts.

(D) The Ohio developmental disabilities council may award grants to or enter into contracts with a member of the council or an entity that the member represents if all of the following apply:

(1) The member serves on the council as a representative of one of the principal state agencies concerned with services for persons with developmental disabilities as specified in 42 U.S.C. 6024(b)(3), a representative of a university affiliated program as defined in 42 U.S.C. 6001(18), or a representative of the legal rights service created under section 5123.60 of the Revised Code.

(2) The council determines that the member or the entity the member represents is capable of providing the goods or services specified under the terms of the grant or contract.

(3) The member has not taken part in any discussion or vote of the council related to awarding the grant or entering into the contract, including service as a member of a review panel established by the council to award grants or enter into contracts or to make recommendations with regard to awarding grants or entering into contracts.

(E) A member of the Ohio developmental disabilities council is not in violation of Chapter 102. or section 2921.42 of the Revised Code with regard to receiving a grant or entering into a contract under this section if the requirements of division (D) of this section have been met.

(2005 S 124, eff. 6–27–05; 2004 H 516, eff. 12–30–04; 1993 S 21, eff. 10–29–93)

Uncodified Law

2005 S 124, § 6, eff. 6–27–05, reads:

It is the intent of the General Assembly in amending sections 101.23, 101.83, 101.84, 101.85, 101.86, 122.011, 122.40, 123.151, 149.56, 307.674, 340.02, 1501.04, 1502.04, 1502.05, 1502.11, 1502.12, 1506.30, 1506.34, 1506.35, 1517.02, 1517.23, 1518.01, 1518.03, 1551.35, 3358.10, 3375. 61, 3375.62, 3383.01, 3383.02, 3383.03, 3383.04, 3383.05, 3383.06, 3383.07, 3383.08, 3383.09, 3746.09, 3746.35, 3747.02, 3748.01, 3748.02, 3748.04, 3748. 05, 3748.16, 3929.482, 3929.85, 3931.01, 3955.05, 3960.06, 4117.01, 4121.442, 4167.09, 4167.25, 4167.27, 4731.143, 4741.03, 4755.481, 4981.03, 5123.35, and 5123.352 of the Revised Code in this act to confirm the amendments to those sections and the resulting versions of those sections that took effect on December 30, 2004, in accordance with Section 10 of Am. Sub. H.B. 516 of the 125th General Assembly. It also is the intent of the General Assembly, in part, in amending Section 4 of Am. Sub. H.B. 516 of the 125th General Assembly in this act to confirm the text of that uncodified section of law as it took effect on December 30, 2004, in accordance with Section 10 of Am. Sub. H.B. 516 of the 125th General Assembly. This act does not affect, and shall not be construed as affecting, the other amendments, enactments, or repeals of codified or uncodified law made by Am. Sub. H.B. 516 of the 125th General Assembly which took effect on December 30, 2004, in accordance with Section 10 of that legislation, all of which it is the intent of the General Assembly to confirm in this act, including, but not limited to, the following amendments, enactments, or repeals pertaining to the implementation of the report of the Sunset Review Committee and related purposes set forth in Am. Sub. H.B. 516's title: the amendments to sections 122.133, 164.07, 1517.05, 2505.02, 3746.04, 3929.682, and 4582.12 of the Revised Code, the repeals of sections 122.09, 125.24, 149.32, 149.321, 149.322, 1502.10, 1506.37, 1517.03, 1517.04, 3354.161, 3355.121, 3357.161, 3375.47, 3746.08, 3747.04, 3747.05, 3747.06, 3747.061, 3747.07, 3747.08, 3747.09, 3747.10, 3747.11, 3747.12, 3747.13, 3747.14, 3747.15, 3747. 16, 3747.17, 3747.18, 3747.19, 3747.20, 3747.21, 3747.22, 3748.09, 3929.71, 3929.72, 3929.721, 3929.73, 3929.75, 3929.76, 3929.77, 3929.78, 3929.79, 3929.80, 3929.81, 3929.82, 3929.83, 3929.84, 4121.443, 4167.26, 5101.93, 5119.81, 5119.82, and 5123.353 of the Revised Code, the enactments of uncodified law in its Sections 3, 6, 9, 10, 11, and 12, and the repeals of Section 6 of Am. Sub. S.B. 163 of the 124th General Assembly, Section 6 of Sub. S.B. 27 of the 124th General Assembly, Section 10 of Sub. H.B. 548 of the 123rd General Assembly, Section 3 of Am. H.B. 280 of the 121st General Assembly, Section 27 of Sub. H.B. 670 of the 121st General Assembly, Section 3 of Am. S.B. 208 of the 120th General Assembly, and Section 3 of Sub. H.B. 508 of the 119th General Assembly. The General Assembly, thus, further declares this section and the related provisions of Sections 1 and 3 of this act to be remedial legislation solely intended to confirm the operation on and after December 30, 2004, of the amendments, enactments, and repeals of codified and uncodified law made by Am. Sub. H.B. 516 of the 125th General Assembly.

Historical and Statutory Notes

Ed. Note: Former 5123.35 repealed by 1993 S 21, eff. 10–29–93; 1990 H 569; 1980 H 900.

Ed. Note: Prior 5123.35 repealed by 129 v 1448, eff. 10–25–61; 1953 H 1; GC 1890–39.

Pre–1953 H 1 Amendments: 121 v 423; 119 v 616; 117 v 550

Library References

Mental Health ⚖20.
States ⚖45, 46.
Westlaw Topic Nos. 257A, 360.
C.J.S. Insane Persons § 14 to 16.
C.J.S. States § 61, 79 to 80, 82, 84, 102, 136.

5123.351 Duties concerning eligibility for state reimbursement of expenses

The director of mental retardation and developmental disabilities, with respect to the eligibility for state reimbursement of expenses incurred by facilities and programs established and operated under Chapter 5126. of the Revised Code for persons with mental retardation or a developmental disability, shall do all of the following:

(A) Make rules that may be necessary to carry out the purposes of Chapter 5126. and sections 5123.35, 5123.351, and 5123.36 of the Revised Code;

(B) Define minimum standards for qualifications of personnel, professional services, and in-service training and educational leave programs;

(C) Review and evaluate community programs and make recommendations for needed improvements to county boards of mental retardation and developmental disabilities and to program directors;

(D) Withhold state reimbursement, in whole or in part, from any county or combination of counties for failure to comply with Chapter 5126. or section 5123.35 or 5123.351 of the Revised Code or rules of the department of mental retardation and developmental disabilities;

(E) Withhold state funds from an agency, corporation, or association denying or rendering service on the basis of race, color, sex, religion, ancestry, national origin, disability as defined in section 4112.01 of the Revised Code, or inability to pay;

(F) Provide consultative staff service to communities to assist in ascertaining needs and in planning and establishing programs.

(2000 H 538, eff. 9–22–00; 1999 H 264, eff. 3–17–00; 1993 S 21, eff. 10–29–93; 1990 H 569; 1980 H 965)

Library References

Mental Health ⚖20.
Westlaw Topic No. 257A.
C.J.S. Insane Persons § 14 to 16.

5123.352 Community mental retardation and developmental disabilities trust fund

There is hereby created in the state treasury the community mental retardation and developmental disabilities trust fund. The director of mental retardation and developmental disabilities, not later than sixty days after the end of each fiscal year, shall certify to the director of budget and management the amount of all the unexpended, unencumbered balances of general revenue fund appropriations made to the department of mental retardation and developmental disabilities for the fiscal year, excluding appropriations for rental payments to the Ohio public facilities commission, and the amount of any other funds held by the department in excess of amounts necessary to meet the department's operating costs and obligations pursuant to this chapter and Chapter 5126. of the Revised Code. On receipt of the certification, the director of budget and management shall transfer cash to the trust fund in an amount up to, but not exceeding, the total of the amounts certified by the director of mental retardation and developmental disabilities, except in cases in which the transfer will involve more than twenty million dollars. In such cases, the director of budget and management shall notify the controlling board and must receive the board's approval of the transfer prior to making the transfer.

All moneys in the trust fund shall be distributed in accordance with section 5126.19 of the Revised Code.

(2005 S 124, eff. 6–27–05; 2004 H 516, eff. 12–30–04; 2004 S 189, eff. 6–29–04; 1993 S 21, eff. 10–29–93)

Uncodified Law

2005 S 124, § 6: See Uncodified Law under RC 5123.35.

Library References

States ⚖127.
Westlaw Topic No. 360.
C.J.S. States § 228.

5123.36 Agreements to assist with construction of local facilities

(A) To the extent funds are available and on application by a county board of mental retardation and developmental disabilities or private nonprofit agency incorporated to provide mental retardation or developmental disability services, the director of mental retardation and developmental disabilities may enter into an agreement with the county board or agency to assist the county board or agency with a mental retardation or developmental disability construction project. Except as provided by division (B) of this section, the director may provide up to ninety per cent of the total project cost where circumstances warrant. The director may, where circumstances warrant, use existing facilities or other in-kind match for the local share of the communities' share of the cost.

(B) Upon the recommendation of the director, for projects of the highest priority of the department of mental retardation and developmental disabilities, the controlling board may authorize the director to provide more than ninety per cent of the total cost of a project under this section.

(C) A county board is eligible for funds under this section for a project bid on or after January 1, 1992, under either section 153.07 or 307.86 of the Revised Code, as long as all other applicable requirements were followed.

(D) The director may not assist a project under this section unless the controlling board or director of budget and management also approves the project pursuant to section 126.14 of the Revised Code.

(2006 H 530, eff. 3–30–06; 1994 H 694, eff. 11–11–94; 1993 S 21, eff. 10–29–93; 1990 H 569; 1980 S 160, H 900)

Historical and Statutory Notes

Ed. Note: Former 5123.36 repealed by 129 v 1448, eff. 10–25–61; 1953 H 1; GC 1890–40.

Pre–1953 H 1 Amendments: 119 v 616, § 1; 117 v 550, § 40

Library References

Mental Health ⚖20.
States ⚖86.
Westlaw Topic Nos. 257A, 360.

C.J.S. Insane Persons § 14 to 16.
C.J.S. States § 147.

5123.37 Application to sell facility to acquire replacement facility

A county board of mental retardation and developmental disabilities or private, nonprofit agency that receives state funds pursuant to an agreement with the director of mental retardation and developmental disabilities under section 5123.36 of the Revised Code to acquire a facility may apply to the director for approval to sell the facility before the terms of the agreement expire for the purpose of acquiring a replacement facility to be used to provide mental retardation or developmental disability services to individuals the county board or agency serves. The application shall be made on a form the director shall prescribe. The county board or agency shall include in the application the specific purpose for which the replacement facility is to be used. The director may refuse to approve the application if the director determines that any of the following apply:

(A) The application is incomplete or indicates that the county board or agency is unable to purchase a replacement facility.

(B) The replacement facility would not be used to continue to provide mental retardation or developmental disability services that the director determines are appropriate for the individuals the county board or agency serves.

(C) The county board or agency has failed to comply with a provision of Chapter 5123. or 5126. of the Revised Code or a rule adopted by the director.

(D) Approving the application would be inconsistent with the plans and priorities of the department of mental retardation and developmental disabilities.

(2006 H 530, eff. 3–30–06)

Historical and Statutory Notes

Ed. Note: Former RC 5123.37 repealed by 1974 S 336, eff. 7–1–75; 129 v 1448; 127 v 835; 125 v 119; 1953 H 1; GC 1890–41, 1890–42.

5123.371 Payment of proceeds after sale

If the director of mental retardation and developmental disabilities approves an application submitted under section 5123.37 of the Revised Code, the county board of mental retardation and developmental disabilities or private, nonprofit agency that submitted the application shall, after selling the facility for which the county board or agency received approval to sell, pay to the director the portion of the proceeds that equals the amount that the director determines the county board or agency owes the department of mental retardation and developmental disabilities, including the department's security interest in the facility, for the state funds used to acquire the facility.

(2006 H 530, eff. 3–30–06)

5123.372 Deadline for notification of readiness to acquire replacement facility

If the director of mental retardation and developmental disabilities approves an application submitted under section 5123.37 of the Revised Code, the director shall establish a deadline by which the county board of mental retardation and developmental disabilities or private, nonprofit agency that submitted the application must notify the director that the county board or agency is ready to acquire a replacement facility to be used for the purpose stated in the application. The director may extend the deadline as many times as the director determines necessary.

(2006 H 530, eff. 3–30–06)

5123.373 Agreement for director to pay percentage of cost of replacement facility

If, on or before the deadline or, if any, the last extended deadline established under section 5123.372 of the Revised Code for a county board of mental retardation and developmental disabilities or private, nonprofit agency, the county board or agency notifies the director of mental retardation and developmental disabilities that the county board or agency is ready to acquire the replacement facility, the director shall enter into an agreement with the county board or agency that provides for the director to pay to the county board or agency a percentage of the cost of acquiring the replacement facility. The agreement shall specify the amount that the director shall pay. The amount may be the amount of the security interest that the department of mental retardation and developmental disabilities had in the previous facility or a different amount. The agreement may provide for the department to hold a security interest in the replacement facility.

(2006 H 530, eff. 3–30–06)

5123.374 Rescission of approval to sell facility

(A) The director of mental retardation and developmental disabilities may rescind approval of an application submitted under section 5123.37 of the Revised Code if either of the following occurs:

(1) The county board of mental retardation and developmental disabilities or private, nonprofit agency that submitted the application fails, on or before the deadline or, if any, the last extended deadline established under section 5123.372 of the Revised Code for the county board or agency, to notify the director that the county board or agency is ready to acquire the replacement facility.

(2) The county board or agency at any time notifies the director that the county board or agency no longer intends to acquire a replacement facility.

(B) If the director rescinds approval of an application, the director shall use any funds the county board or agency paid to the director under section 5123.371 of the Revised Code to assist mental retardation or developmental disabilities construction projects under section 5123.36 of the Revised Code.

(2006 H 530, eff. 3–30–06)

5123.375 MR/DD community capital replacement facilities fund

The MR/DD community capital replacement facilities fund is hereby created in the state treasury. The director of mental retardation and developmental disabilities shall credit all amounts paid to the director under section 5123.371 of the Revised Code to the fund. The director shall use the money in the fund as follows:

(A) To make payments to county boards of mental retardation and developmental disabilities and private, nonprofit agencies pursuant to agreements entered into under section 5123.373 of the Revised Code;

(B) To provide, pursuant to section 5123.374 of the Revised Code, assistance for mental retardation or developmental disabilities construction projects under section 5123.36 of the Revised Code.

(2006 H 530, eff. 3–30–06)

PATIENTS' CLOTHING

5123.39 Clothing

If not otherwise furnished, the probate judge shall see that each patient hospitalized under section 5123.76 of the Revised Code is properly attired for transportation, and, in addition, the institution shall be furnished a complete change of clothing for such patient, which shall be paid for on the certificate of the probate judge and the order of the county auditor from the county treasury. Such clothing shall be new or as good as new.

(1988 S 156, eff. 7-1-88; 1978 H 565; 129 v 1448; 1953 H 1; GC 1890-44)

Historical and Statutory Notes

Pre-1953 H 1 Amendments: 121 v 423; 119 v 616; 117 v 550

Library References

Mental Health ⚖31.
Westlaw Topic No. 257A.
C.J.S. Insane Persons § 45, 47, 53.
Baldwin's Ohio Legislative Service, 1988 Laws of Ohio, S 156—LSC Analysis, p 5-284

5123.40 Services fund for individuals with mental retardation and developmental disabilities

There is hereby created in the state treasury the services fund for individuals with mental retardation and developmental disabilities. On the death of the beneficiary of a trust created pursuant to section 5815.28 of the Revised Code, the portion of the remaining assets of the trust specified in the trust instrument shall be deposited to the credit of the fund.

Money credited to the fund shall be used for individuals with mental retardation and developmental disabilities. In accordance with Chapter 119. of the Revised Code, the department of mental retardation and developmental disabilities may adopt any rules necessary to implement this section.

(2006 H 416, eff. 1-1-07; 1992 S 124, eff. 4-16-93)

Historical and Statutory Notes

Ed. Note: Former 5123.40 amended and recodified as 5121.12 by 1980 H 900, eff. 7-1-80; 1969 H 688; 1953 H 1; GC 1890-46.

Pre-1953 H 1 Amendments: 121 v 423; 120 v 309; 119 v 616; 117 v 550

Library References

States ⚖127.
Westlaw Topic No. 360.
C.J.S. States § 228.
Baldwin's Ohio Legislative Service Annotated, 2006 H 416 LSC Analysis, p 3/L-1709

REGISTRY OF ABUSIVE OR NEGLECTFUL EMPLOYEES

5123.50 Definitions

As used in this section and sections 5123.51, 5123.52, and 5123.541 of the Revised Code:

(A) "Abuse" means all of the following:

(1) The use of physical force that can reasonably be expected to result in physical harm or serious physical harm;

(2) Sexual abuse;

(3) Verbal abuse.

(B) "Misappropriation" means depriving, defrauding, or otherwise obtaining the real or personal property of an individual by any means prohibited by the Revised Code, including violations of Chapter 2911. or 2913. of the Revised Code.

(C) "MR/DD employee" means all of the following:

(1) An employee of the department of mental retardation and developmental disabilities;

(2) An employee of a county board of mental retardation and developmental disabilities;

(3) An employee in a position that includes providing specialized services to an individual with mental retardation or another developmental disability.

(D) "Neglect" means, when there is a duty to do so, failing to provide an individual with any treatment, care, goods, or services that are necessary to maintain the health and safety of the individual.

(E) "Physical harm" and "serious physical harm" have the same meanings as in section 2901.01 of the Revised Code.

(F) "Sexual abuse" means unlawful sexual conduct or sexual contact.

(G) "Specialized services" means any program or service designed and operated to serve primarily individuals with mental retardation or a developmental disability, including a program or service provided by an entity licensed or certified by the department of mental retardation and developmental disabilities. A program or service available to the general public is not a specialized service.

(H) "Verbal abuse" means purposely using words to threaten, coerce, intimidate, harass, or humiliate an individual.

(I) "Sexual conduct," "sexual contact," and "spouse" have the same meanings as in section 2907.01 of the Revised Code.

(2004 S 178, eff. 1-30-04; 2002 S 191, eff. 12-31-03; 2000 S 171, eff. 11-22-00)

Historical and Statutory Notes

Ed. Note: Former 5123.50 repealed by 129 v 1448, eff. 10-25-61; 128 v 522; 126 v 313; 125 v 823, 119; 1953 H 1; GC 1890-63; see now 5122.21 for provisions analogous to former 5123.50.

Pre-1953 H 1 Amendments: 121 v 423; 119 v 616; 117 v 550

Library References

Asylums ⚖3, 4.
Statutes ⚖179.
Westlaw Topic Nos. 43, 361.
C.J.S. Asylums and Institutional Care Facilities § 5 to 10.
C.J.S. Statutes § 306, 309.

5123.51 Review of reports of abuse or neglect; investigations; hearings; inclusion of employee in registry; notice

(A) In addition to any other action required by sections 5123.61 and 5126. 31 of the Revised Code, the department of mental retardation and developmental disabilities shall review each report the department receives of abuse or neglect of an individual with mental retardation or a developmental disability or misappropriation of an individual's property that includes an allegation that an MR/DD employee committed or was responsible for the abuse, neglect, or misappropriation. The department shall review a report it receives from a public children services agency only after the agency completes its investigation pursuant to section 2151.421 of the Revised Code. On receipt of a notice under section 2930.061 or 5123.541 of the Revised Code, the department shall review the notice.

(B) The department shall do both of the following:

(1) Investigate the allegation or adopt the findings of an investigation or review of the allegation conducted by another person or government entity and determine whether there is a reasonable basis for the allegation;

(2) If the department determines that there is a reasonable basis for the allegation, conduct an adjudication pursuant to Chapter 119. of the Revised Code.

(C)(1) The department shall appoint an independent hearing officer to conduct any hearing conducted pursuant to division (B)(2) of this section, except that, if the hearing is regarding an employee of the department who is represented by a union, the department and a representative of the union shall jointly select the hearing officer.

(2)(a) Except as provided in division (C)(2)(b) of this section, no hearing shall be conducted under division (B)(2) of this section until any criminal proceeding or collective bargaining arbitration concerning the same allegation has concluded.

(b) The department may conduct a hearing pursuant to division (B)(2) of this section before a criminal proceeding concerning the same allegation is concluded if both of the following are the case:

(i) The department notifies the prosecutor responsible for the criminal proceeding that the department proposes to conduct a hearing.

(ii) The prosecutor consents to the hearing.

(3) In conducting a hearing pursuant to division (B)(2) of this section, the hearing officer shall do all of the following:

(a) Determine whether there is clear and convincing evidence that the MR/DD employee has done any of the following:

(i) Misappropriated property of one or more individuals with mental retardation or a developmental disability that has a value, either separately or taken together, of one hundred dollars or more;

(ii) Misappropriated property of an individual with mental retardation or a developmental disability that is designed to be used as a check, draft, negotiable instrument, credit card, charge card, or device for initiating an electronic fund transfer at a point of sale terminal, automated teller machine, or cash dispensing machine;

(iii) Knowingly abused such an individual;

(iv) Recklessly abused or neglected such an individual, with resulting physical harm;

(v) Negligently abused or neglected such an individual, with resulting serious physical harm;

(vi) Recklessly neglected such an individual, creating a substantial risk of serious physical harm;

(vii) Engaged in sexual conduct or had sexual contact with an individual with mental retardation or another developmental disability who was not the MR/DD employee's spouse and for whom the MR/DD employee was employed or under a contract to provide care;

(viii) Unreasonably failed to make a report pursuant to division (C) of section 5123.61 of the Revised Code when the employee knew or should have known that the failure would result in a substantial risk of harm to an individual with mental retardation or a developmental disability.

(b) Give weight to the decision in any collective bargaining arbitration regarding the same allegation;

(c) Give weight to any relevant facts presented at the hearing.

(D)(1) Unless the director of mental retardation and developmental disabilities determines that there are extenuating circumstances and except as provided in division (E) of this section, if the director, after considering all of the factors listed in division (C)(3) of this section, finds that there is clear and convincing evidence that an MR/DD employee has done one or more of the things described in division (C)(3)(a) of this section the director shall include the name of the employee in the registry established under section 5123.52 of the Revised Code.

(2) Extenuating circumstances the director must consider include the use of physical force by an MR/DD employee that was necessary as self-defense.

(3) If the director includes an MR/DD employee in the registry established under section 5123.52 of the Revised Code, the director shall notify the employee, the person or government entity that employs or contracts with the employee, the individual with mental retardation or a developmental disability who was the subject of the report and that individual's legal guardian, if any, the attorney general, and the prosecuting attorney or other law enforcement agency. If the MR/DD employee holds a license, certificate, registration, or other authorization to engage in a profession issued pursuant to Title XLVII of the Revised Code, the director shall notify the appropriate agency, board, department, or other entity responsible for regulating the employee's professional practice.

(4) If an individual whose name appears on the registry is involved in a court proceeding or arbitration arising from the same facts as the allegation resulting in the individual's placement on the registry, the disposition of the proceeding or arbitration shall be noted in the registry next to the individual's name.

(E) In the case of an allegation concerning an employee of the department, after the hearing conducted pursuant to division (B)(2) of this section, the director of health or that director's designee shall review the decision of the hearing officer to determine whether the standard described in division (C)(3) of this section has been met. If the director or designee determines that the standard has been met and that no extenuating circumstances exist, the director or designee shall notify the director of mental retardation and developmental disabilities that the MR/DD employee is to be included in the registry established under section 5123.52 of the Revised Code. If the director of mental retardation and developmental disabilities receives such notification, the director shall include the MR/DD employee in the registry and shall provide the notification described in division (D)(3) of this section.

(F) If the department is required by Chapter 119. of the Revised Code to give notice of an opportunity for a hearing and the MR/DD employee subject to the notice does not timely request a hearing in accordance with section 119.07 of the Revised Code, the department is not required to hold a hearing.

(G) Files and records of investigations conducted pursuant to this section are not public records as defined in section 149.43 of the Revised Code, but, on request, the department shall provide copies of those files and records to the attorney general, a prosecuting attorney, or a law enforcement agency.

(2004 S 178, eff. 1–30–04; 2000 S 171, eff. 11–22–00)

Historical and Statutory Notes

Ed. Note: Former 5123.51 repealed by 129 v 1448, eff. 10–25–61; 126 v 313; 1953 H 1; GC 1890–63a.

Pre–1953 H 1 Amendments: 121 v 321

Library References

Asylums ⟐3, 4.

Westlaw Topic No. 43.

C.J.S. Asylums and Institutional Care Facilities § 5 to 10.

5123.52 Registry of abusive or neglectful employees

(A) The department of mental retardation and developmental disabilities shall establish a registry of MR/DD employees consisting of the names of MR/DD employees included in the registry pursuant to section 5123.51 of the Revised Code.

(B) Before a person or government entity hires, contracts with, or employs an individual as an MR/DD employee, the person or government entity shall inquire whether the individual is included in the registry.

(C) When it receives an inquiry regarding whether an individual is included in the registry, the department shall inform the person making the inquiry whether the individual is included in the registry.

(D)(1) Except as otherwise provided in a collective bargaining agreement entered into under Chapter 4117. of the Revised Code that is in effect on the effective date of this section, no person or government entity shall hire, contract with, or employ as an MR/DD employee an individual who is included in the registry. Notwithstanding sections 4117.08 and 4117.10 of the Revised Code, no agreement entered into under Chapter 4117. of the Revised Code after the effective date of this section may contain any provision that in any way limits the effect or operation of this section.

(2) Neither the department nor any county board of mental retardation and developmental disabilities may enter into a new contract or renew a contract with a person or government entity that fails to comply with division (D)(1) of this section until the department or board is satisfied that the person or government entity will comply.

(3) A person or government entity that fails to hire or retain as an MR/DD employee a person because the person is included in the registry shall not be liable in damages in a civil action brought by the employee or applicant for employment. Termination of employment pursuant to division (D)(1) of this section constitutes a discharge for just cause for the purposes of section 4141.29 of the Revised Code.

(E) Information contained in the registry is a public record for the purposes of section 149.43 of the Revised Code and is subject to inspection and copying under section 1347.08 of the Revised Code.

(2000 S 171, eff. 11–22–00)

Historical and Statutory Notes

Ed. Note: Former 5123.52 repealed by 129 v 1448, eff. 10–25–61; 125 v 823; 1953 H 1; GC 1890–63b.

Pre–1953 H 1 Amendments: 121 v 423

Library References

Asylums ⚖3, 4.
Westlaw Topic No. 43.
C.J.S. Asylums and Institutional Care Facilities § 5 to 10.

5123.53 Removal of individuals from registry

An individual who is included in the registry may petition the director of mental retardation and developmental disabilities for removal from the registry. If the director determines that good cause exists, the director shall remove the individual from the registry and may properly reply to an inquiry that the individual is not included in the registry. Good cause includes meeting rehabilitation standards established in rules adopted under section 5123.54 of the Revised Code.

(2000 S 171, eff. 11–22–00)

Historical and Statutory Notes

Ed. Note: Former 5123.53 amended and recodified as 5123.801 by 1980 H 900, eff. 7–1–80; 1972 H 494; 1970 H 970; 129 v 1448; 1953 H 1; GC 1890–64.

Pre–1953 H 1 Amendments: 117 v 550, § 64

Library References

Asylums ⚖3, 4.
Westlaw Topic No. 43.
C.J.S. Asylums and Institutional Care Facilities § 5 to 10.

5123.54 Rules

The director of mental retardation and developmental disabilities shall adopt rules under Chapter 119. of the Revised Code to implement sections 5123.51, 5123.52, and 5123.53 of the Revised Code. The rules shall establish rehabilitation standards for the purposes of section 5123.53 of the Revised Code and specify circumstances, other than meeting the standards, that constitute good cause for the purposes of that section.

(2000 S 171, eff. 11–22–00)

Historical and Statutory Notes

Ed. Note: Former 5123.54 repealed by 129 v 1448, eff. 10–25–61; 126 v 313; 125 v 823, 119; 1953 H 1; GC 1890–65; see now 5122.26 for provisions analogous to former 5123.54.

Pre–1953 H 1 Amendments: 119 v 616, § 1; 117 v 550, § 65

Library References

Asylums ⚖3, 4.
Westlaw Topic No. 43.
C.J.S. Asylums and Institutional Care Facilities § 5 to 10.

5123.541 Prohibition on sexual conduct with mentally retarded or developmentally disabled individual; inclusion in registry; reporting of violations

(A) No MR/DD employee shall engage in any sexual conduct or have any sexual contact with an individual with mental retardation or another developmental disability for whom the MR/DD employee is employed or under a contract to provide care unless the individual is the MR/DD employee's spouse.

(B) Any MR/DD employee who violates division (A) of this section shall be eligible to be included in the registry regarding misappropriation, abuse, neglect, or other specified misconduct by MR/DD employees established under section 5123.52 of the Revised Code, in addition to any other sanction or penalty authorized or required by law.

(C)(1) Any person listed in division (C)(2) of section 5123.61 of the Revised Code who has reason to believe that an MR/DD employee has violated division (A) of this section shall immediately report that belief to the department of mental retardation and developmental disabilities.

(2) Any person who has reason to believe that an MR/DD employee has violated division (A) of this section may report that belief to the department of mental retardation and developmental disabilities.

(2004 S 178, eff. 1–30–04)

5123.542 Entities required to give notice of conduct causing possible inclusion in registry

(A) Each of the following shall annually provide a written notice to each of its MR/DD employees explaining the conduct for which an MR/DD employee may be included in the registry established under section 5123.52 of the Revised Code:

(1) The department of mental retardation and developmental disabilities;

(2) Each county board of mental retardation and developmental disabilities;

(3) Each contracting entity, as defined in section 5126.281 of the Revised Code;

(4) Each owner, operator, or administrator of a residential facility, as defined in section 5123.19 of the Revised Code;

(5) Each owner, operator, or administrator of a program certified by the department to provide supported living.

(B) The notice described in division (A) of this section shall be in a form and provided in a manner prescribed by the department of mental retardation and developmental disabilities. The form shall be the same for all persons and entities required to provide notice under division (A) of this section.

(C) The fact that an MR/DD employee does not receive the notice required by this section does not exempt the employee from inclusion in the registry established under section 5123.52 of the Revised Code.

(2004 S 178, eff. 1-30-04)

GUARDIANSHIP, TRUSTEESHIP, OR CONSERVATORSHIP APPOINTMENTS

5123.55 Definitions

As used in sections 5123.55 to 5123.59 of the Revised Code:

(A) "Guardian" means a guardian of the person, limited guardian, interim guardian, or emergency guardian pursuant to appointment by the probate court under Chapter 2111. of the Revised Code.

(B) "Trustee" means a trustee appointed by and accountable to the probate court, in lieu of a guardian and without a judicial determination of incompetency, with respect to an estate of ten thousand dollars or less.

(C) "Protector" means an agency under contract with the department of mental retardation and developmental disabilities acting with or without court appointment to provide guidance, service, and encouragement in the development of maximum self-reliance to a person with mental retardation or a developmental disability, independent of any determination of incompetency.

(D) "Protective service" means performance of the duties of a guardian, trustee, or conservator, or acting as a protector, with respect to a person with mental retardation or a developmental disability.

(E) "Conservator" means a conservator of the person pursuant to an appointment by a probate court under Chapter 2111. of the Revised Code.

(2000 H 538, eff. 9-22-00; 1990 H 569, eff. 7-1-91; 1989 S 46; 1981 H 694; 1980 H 900)

Historical and Statutory Notes

Ed. Note: 5123.55 is former 5119.85 amended and recodified by 1980 H 900, eff. 7-1-80; 1978 S 415; 1971 H 290.

Ed. Note: Former 5123.55 repealed by 1980 H 900, eff. 7-1-80; 1970 H 970; 129 v 1448; 126 v 313; 125 v 823, 119; 1953 H 1; GC 1890-66.

Pre-1953 H 1 Amendments: 119 v 616, § 1; 117 v 550, § 66

Library References

Mental Health ⚖101, 102.
Statutes ⚖179.
Westlaw Topic Nos. 257A, 361.
C.J.S. Insane Persons § 108 to 110, 128, 143.
C.J.S. Statutes § 306, 309.

5123.56 Establishment of protective service system; duty and authority of division of mental retardation; charge prohibited

The department of mental retardation and developmental disabilities shall develop a statewide system of protective service in accordance with rules and standards established by the department. With respect to this program, the department may enter into a contract with any responsible public or private agency for provision of protective service by the agency, and the contract may permit the agency to charge the person receiving services fees for services provided.

No costs or fees shall be charged by a probate court for the filing of a petition for guardianship, trusteeship, protectorship, or conservatorship under sections 5123.55 to 5123.59 of the Revised Code, or for any service performed by a probate court, or by any state agency in the course of petitioning for protective services, or for any protective services provided under those sections.

An agency that provides protective services pursuant to a contract with another agency or a court may charge the agency or court fees for the services provided.

(1990 H 697, eff. 7-17-90; 1989 S 46; 1980 H 900)

Historical and Statutory Notes

Ed. Note: 5123.56 is former 5119.86 amended and recodified by 1980 H 900, eff. 7-1-80; 1976 S 295; 1971 H 290.

Ed. Note: Former 5123.56 amended and recodified as 5123.811 by 1980 H 900, eff. 7-1-80; 1972 H 494; 1970 H 970; 129 v 1448; 125 v 823; 1953 H 1; GC 1890-67.

Pre-1953 H 1 Amendments: 119 v 616, § 1; 117 v 550, § 67

Library References

Mental Health ⚖20, 101 to 103.
Westlaw Topic No. 257A.
C.J.S. Insane Persons § 14 to 16, 108 to 110, 128, 143.

5123.57 Evaluation and annual review

No guardianship or trusteeship appointment shall be made under sections 5123.55 to 5123.59 of the Revised Code and no person shall be accepted for service by a protector under those sections unless a comprehensive evaluation has been made in a clinic or other facility approved by the department of mental retardation and developmental disabilities. The evaluation shall include a medical, psychological, social, and educational evaluation, and a copy of the evaluation shall be filed with the department.

Any agency that is appointed as a guardian, trustee, or conservator under sections 5123.55 to 5123.59 of the Revised Code or accepted as a protector under those sections shall provide for a review at least once each year in writing of the physical, mental, and social condition of each mentally retarded or developmentally disabled person for whom it is acting as guardian, trustee, or protector. An agency providing protective services under contract with the department shall file these reports with the department of mental retardation and developmental disabilities. Any record of the department or agency pertaining to a mentally retarded or developmentally disabled person shall not be a public record under section 149.43 of the Revised Code. Information contained in those records shall not be disclosed publicly in such a manner as to identify individuals, but may be made available to persons approved by the director of mental retardation and developmental disabilities or the court.

(1990 H 569, eff. 7–1–91; 1989 S 46; 1980 H 900)

Historical and Statutory Notes

Ed. Note: 5123.57 is former 5119.87 amended and recodified by 1980 H 900, eff. 7–1–80; 1971 H 290.

Ed. Note: Former 5123.57 repealed by 129 v 1448, eff. 10–25–61; 126 v 313; 125 v 823, 119; 1953 H 1; GC 1890–68.

Pre–1953 H 1 Amendments: 121 v 423; 119 v 616; 117 v 550

5123.58 Agencies that may be guardian

An agency providing protective services under contract with the department of mental retardation and developmental disabilities may be nominated under any of the following conditions as guardian, trustee, protector, conservator, or as trustee and protector of a mentally retarded or developmentally disabled person:

(A) The person who needs or believes he needs protective service may make application in writing.

(B) Any interested person may make application in writing on behalf of a mentally retarded or developmentally disabled person.

(C) A parent may name the department or agency as guardian or successor guardian in a will.

(D) A parent may name the department or agency as guardian, trustee, or protector, to assume such duties during the parent's lifetime.

If the results of the comprehensive evaluation required under section 5123.57 of the Revised Code indicate that the person named in the nomination is in need of protective services, the agency or service either shall reject or accept the nomination as guardian, trustee, or conservator, subject to appointment by the probate court, or reject or accept the nomination as protector, or trustee and protector.

At the time the nomination is accepted or when an appointment is made by the court, the mentally retarded or developmentally disabled person and any person who made application for service on his behalf under this section shall be informed by the agency, service, or court of the procedure for terminating the appointment or service. The agency or service shall cease to provide protective service as a protector pursuant to nomination under division (A), (B), or (D) of this section when a written request for termination is received by the agency from or on behalf of the mentally retarded or developmentally disabled person. If the agency or service believes the person to be in need of protective service, the agency or service may file an application for guardianship, trusteeship, or protectorship with the probate court. Termination of any court appointment as guardian, trustee, or protector shall be by order of the probate court.

(1990 H 569, eff. 7–1–91; 1989 S 46; 1986 S 322; 1980 H 900)

Historical and Statutory Notes

Ed. Note: 5123.58 is former 5119.88 amended and recodified by 1980 H 900, eff. 7–1–80; 1978 S 415; 1971 H 290.

Ed. Note: Former 5123.58 repealed by 129 v 1448, eff. 10–25–61; 125 v 823; 1953 H 1; GC 1890–107.

Pre–1953 H 1 Amendments: 119 v 616, § 1; 117 v 802; 117 v 550, § 107

Library References

Mental Health ⟲103, 116.1, 117, 126.
Westlaw Topic No. 257A.
C.J.S. Insane Persons § 123 to 125, 129, 133.

5123.59 Bond of trustee

Before entering upon the duties of trustee, an agency under contract with the department of mental retardation and developmental disabilities may require any of its employees having custody or control of funds or property to give bond to the probate court with sufficient surety, conditioned upon the full and faithful accounting of all trust funds which he holds. The amount of the bond shall be determined by the court and may be modified by the court.

(1989 S 46, eff. 1–1–90; 1980 H 900)

Historical and Statutory Notes

Ed. Note: 5123.59 is former 5119.89 amended and recodified by 1980 H 900, eff. 7–1–80; 1971 H 290.

Ed. Note: Former 5123.59 repealed by 129 v 1448, eff. 10–25–61; 1953 H 1; GC 1890–108.

Pre–1953 H 1 Amendments: 121 v 423; 119 v 616; 117 v 550

Library References

Mental Health ⟲116.1.
Westlaw Topic No. 257A.
C.J.S. Insane Persons § 123 to 125, 129.

LEGAL RIGHTS SERVICE; OMBUDSMAN SECTION; ABUSE OF MENTALLY RETARDED ADULT

5123.60 Legal rights service; legal rights service commission; administrator's duties

(A) A legal rights service is hereby created and established to protect and advocate the rights of mentally ill persons, mentally retarded persons, developmentally disabled persons, and other disabled persons who may be represented by the service pursuant to division (L) of this section; to receive and act upon complaints concerning institutional and hospital practices and conditions of institutions for mentally retarded or developmentally disabled persons and hospitals for the mentally ill; and to assure that all persons detained, hospitalized, discharged, or institutionalized, and all persons whose detention, hospitalization, discharge, or institutionalization is sought or has been sought under this chapter or Chapter 5122. of the Revised Code are fully informed of their rights and adequately represented by counsel in proceedings under this chapter or Chapter 5122. of the Revised Code and in any proceedings to secure the rights of those persons. Notwithstanding the definitions of "mentally retarded person" and "developmentally disabled person" in section 5123.01 of the Revised Code, the legal rights service shall determine who is a mentally retarded or developmentally disabled person for purposes of this section and sections 5123.601 to 5123.604 of the Revised Code.

(B) In regard to those persons detained, hospitalized, or institutionalized under Chapter 5122. of the Revised Code, the legal rights service shall undertake formal representation only of those persons who are involuntarily detained, hospitalized, or institutionalized pursuant to sections 5122.10 to 5122.15 of the Revised Code, and those voluntarily detained, hospitalized, or institutionalized who are minors, who have been adjudicated incompetent, who have been detained, hospitalized, or institutionalized in a public hospital, or who have requested representation by the legal rights service. If a person referred to in division (A) of this section voluntarily requests in writing that the legal rights service terminate participation in the person's case, such involvement shall cease.

(C) Any person voluntarily hospitalized or institutionalized in a public hospital under division (A) of section 5122.02 of the Revised Code, after being fully informed of the person's rights under division (A) of this section, may, by written request, waive assistance by the legal rights service if the waiver is knowingly and intelligently made, without duress or coercion.

The waiver may be rescinded at any time by the voluntary patient or resident, or by the voluntary patient's or resident's legal guardian.

(D)(1) The legal rights service commission is hereby created for the purposes of appointing an administrator of the legal rights service, advising the administrator, assisting the administrator in developing a budget, advising the administrator in establishing and annually reviewing a strategic plan, creating a procedure for filing and determination of grievances against the legal rights service, and establishing general policy guidelines, including guidelines for the commencement of litigation, for the legal rights service. The commission may adopt rules to carry these purposes into effect and may receive and act upon appeals of personnel decisions by the administrator.

(2) The commission shall consist of seven members. One member, who shall serve as chairperson, shall be appointed by the chief justice of the supreme court, three members shall be appointed by the speaker of the house of representatives, and three members shall be appointed by the president of the senate. At least two members shall have experience in the field of developmental disabilities, and at least two members shall have experience in the field of mental health. No member shall be a provider or related to a provider of services to mentally retarded, developmentally disabled, or mentally ill persons.

(3) Terms of office of the members of the commission shall be for three years, each term ending on the same day of the month of the year as did the term which it succeeds. Each member shall serve subsequent to the expiration of the member's term until a successor is appointed and qualifies, or until sixty days has elapsed, whichever occurs first. No member shall serve more than two consecutive terms.

All vacancies in the membership of the commission shall be filled in the manner prescribed for regular appointments to the commission and shall be limited to the unexpired terms.

(4) The commission shall meet at least four times each year. Members shall be reimbursed for their necessary and actual expenses incurred in the performance of their official duties.

(5) The administrator of the legal rights service shall serve at the pleasure of the commission.

The administrator shall be a person who has had special training and experience in the type of work with which the legal rights service is charged. If the administrator is not an attorney, the administrator shall seek legal counsel when appropriate. The salary of the administrator shall be established in accordance with section 124.14 of the Revised Code.

(E) The legal rights service shall be completely independent of the department of mental health and the department of mental retardation and developmental disabilities and, notwithstanding section 109.02 of the Revised Code, shall also be independent of the office of the attorney general. The administrator of the legal rights service, staff, and attorneys designated by the administrator to represent persons detained, hospitalized, or institutionalized under this chapter or Chapter 5122. of the Revised Code shall have ready access to the following:

(1) During normal business hours and at other reasonable times, all records relating to expenditures of state and federal funds or to the commitment, care, treatment, and habilitation of all persons represented by the legal rights service, including those who may be represented pursuant to division (L) of this section, or persons detained, hospitalized, institutionalized, or receiving services under this chapter or Chapter 340., 5119., 5122., or 5126. of the Revised Code that are records maintained by the following entities providing services for those persons: departments; institutions; hospitals; community residential facilities; boards of alcohol, drug addiction, and mental health services; county boards of mental retardation and developmental disabilities; contract agencies of those boards; and any other entity providing services to persons who may be represented by the service pursuant to division (L) of this section;

(2) Any records maintained in computerized data banks of the departments or boards or, in the case of persons who may be represented by the service pursuant to division (L) of this section, any other entity that provides services to those persons;

(3) During their normal working hours, personnel of the departments, facilities, boards, agencies, institutions, hospitals, and other service-providing entities;

(4) At any time, all persons detained, hospitalized, or institutionalized; persons receiving services under this chapter or Chapter 340., 5119., 5122., or 5126. of the Revised Code; and persons who may be represented by the service pursuant to division (L) of this section.

(F) The administrator of the legal rights service shall do the following:

(1) Administer and organize the work of the legal rights service and establish administrative or geographic divisions as the administrator considers necessary, proper, and expedient;

(2) Adopt and promulgate rules that are not in conflict with rules adopted by the commission and prescribe duties for the efficient conduct of the business and general administration of the legal rights service;

(3) Appoint and discharge employees, and hire experts, consultants, advisors, or other professionally qualified persons as the administrator considers necessary to carry out the duties of the legal rights service;

(4) Apply for and accept grants of funds, and accept charitable gifts and bequests;

(5) Prepare and submit a budget to the general assembly for the operation of the legal rights service. At least thirty days prior to submitting the budget to the general assembly, the administrator shall provide a copy of the budget to the commission for review and comment. When submitting the budget to the general assembly, the administrator shall include a copy of any written comments returned by the commission to the administrator.

(6) Enter into contracts and make expenditures necessary for the efficient operation of the legal rights service;

(7) Annually prepare a report of activities and submit copies of the report to the governor, the chief justice of the supreme court, the president of the senate, the speaker of the house of representatives, the director of mental health, and the director of mental retardation and developmental disabilities, and make the report available to the public;

(8) Upon request of the commission or of the chairperson of the commission, report to the commission on specific litigation issues or activities.

(G)(1) The legal rights service may act directly or contract with other organizations or individuals for the provision of the services envisioned under this section.

(2) Whenever possible, the administrator shall attempt to facilitate the resolution of complaints through administrative channels. Subject to division (G)(3) of this section, if attempts at administrative resolution prove unsatisfactory, the administrator may pursue any legal, administrative, and other appropriate remedies or approaches that may be necessary to accomplish the purposes of this section.

(3) The administrator may not pursue a class action lawsuit under division (G)(2) of this section when attempts at administrative resolution of a complaint prove unsatisfactory under that division unless both of the following have first occurred:

(a) At least four members of the commission, by their affirmative vote, have consented to the pursuit of the class action lawsuit;

(b) At least five members of the commission are present at the meeting of the commission at which that consent is obtained.

(4) Subject to division (G)(5) of this section, relationships between personnel and the agents of the legal rights service and its clients shall be fiduciary relationships, and all communications shall be confidential, as if between attorney and client.

(5) Any person who has been represented by the legal rights service or who has applied for and been denied representation and who files a grievance with the service concerning the representation or application may appeal the decision of the service on the grievance to the commission. The person may appeal notwithstanding any objections of the person's legal guardian. The commission may examine any records relevant to the appeal and shall maintain the confidentiality of any records that are required to be kept confidential.

(H) The legal rights service, on the order of the administrator, with the approval by an affirmative vote of at least four members of the commission, may compel by subpoena the appearance and sworn testimony of any person the administrator reasonably believes may be able to provide information or to produce any documents, books, records, papers, or other information necessary to carry out its duties.

(I) The legal rights service may conduct public hearings.

(J) The legal rights service may request from any governmental agency any cooperation, assistance, services, or data that will enable it to perform its duties.

(K) In any malpractice action filed against the administrator of the legal rights service, a member of the staff of the legal rights service, or an attorney designated by the administrator to perform legal services under division (E) of this section, the state shall, when the administrator, member, or attorney has acted in good faith and in the scope of employment, indemnify the administrator, member, or attorney for any judgment awarded or amount negotiated in settlement, and for any court costs or legal fees incurred in defense of the claim.

This division does not limit or waive, and shall not be construed to limit or waive, any defense that is available to the legal rights service, its administrator or employees, persons under a personal services contract with it, or persons designated under division (E) of this section, including, but not limited to, any defense available under section 9.86 of the Revised Code.

(L) In addition to providing services to mentally ill, mentally retarded, or developmentally disabled persons, when a grant authorizing the provision of services to other individuals is accepted pursuant to division (F)(4) of this section, the legal rights service and its ombudsperson section may provide advocacy or ombudsperson services to those other individuals and exercise any other authority granted by this section or sections 5123.601 to 5123.604 of the Revised Code on behalf of those individuals. Determinations of whether an individual is eligible for services under this division shall be made by the legal rights service.

(2003 H 95, eff. 9–26–03; 2001 H 94, eff. 9–5–01; 1999 H 283, eff. 9–29–99; 1994 H 694, eff. 11–11–94; 1993 H 152, eff. 7–1–93; 1992 S 156; 1990 H 569; 1989 H 317; 1988 S 156; 1986 S 322; 1983 H 291; 1980 H 900)

Uncodified Law

1996 H 670, § 27, as subsequently amended: See *Baldwin's Ohio Revised Code Annotated*, Uncodified Law under RC 101.83.

Historical and Statutory Notes

Ed. Note: 5123.60 is former 5123.94 amended and recodified by 1980 H 900, eff. 7–1–80; 1979 H 1; 1978 S 415; 1977 S 115; 1976 H 244; 1975 H 155; 1974 S 336.

Ed. Note: Former 5123.60 repealed by 129 v 1448, eff. 10–25–61; 128 v 333; 125 v 823; 1953 H 1; GC 1890–109.

Pre–1953 H 1 Amendments: 119 v 616, § 1; 117 v 550, § 109

Library References

Mental Health ⇐20, 31.
States ⇐45, 68, 73.
Westlaw Topic Nos. 257A, 360.
C.J.S. Insane Persons § 14 to 16, 45, 47, 53.
C.J.S. States § 79 to 80, 82, 120, 130 to 136, 139 to 140.
Baldwin's Ohio Legislative Service, 1988 Laws of Ohio, S 156—LSC Analysis, p 5–284

5123.601 Legal rights service ombudsman section

(A) As used in sections 5123.601 to 5123.604 of the Revised Code, "provider" means any person or governmental agency that furnishes one or more services to one or more mentally retarded, developmentally disabled, or mentally ill persons.

(B) There is hereby created within the legal rights service the ombudsman section. The administrator of the legal rights service shall adopt rules in accordance with Chapter 119. of the Revised Code establishing procedures for receiving complaints and conducting investigations for the purposes of resolving and mediating complaints from mentally retarded, developmentally disabled, or mentally ill persons, their relatives, their guardians, and interested citizens, public officials, and governmental agencies or any deficiencies which come to its attention concerning any activity, practice, policy, or procedure it determines is adversely affecting or may adversely affect the health, safety, welfare, and civil or human rights of any mentally retarded, developmentally disabled, or mentally ill persons. After initial investigation, the section may decline to accept any complaint it determines is frivolous, vexatious, or not made in good faith. The section shall attempt to resolve the complaint at the lowest appropriate administrative level, unless otherwise provided by law. The procedures shall require the section to:

(1) Acknowledge the receipt of a complaint by sending written notice to the complainant no more than seven days after it receives the complaint;

(2) When appropriate, provide written notice to the department of mental retardation and developmental disabilities or the department of mental health and any other appropriate agency within seven days after receiving the complaint;

(3) Immediately refer a complaint made under this section to the department of mental retardation and developmental disabilities and to any other appropriate governmental agency, whenever the complaint involves an immediate and substantial threat to the health or safety of a mentally retarded or developmentally disabled person, or to the department of mental health and to any other appropriate governmental agency, whenever the complaint involves an immediate and substantial threat to the health or safety of a mentally ill person. The department or an agency designated by the department shall report its findings and actions no later than forty-eight hours following its receipt of the complaint.

(4) Within seven days after identifying a deficiency in the treatment of a mentally retarded, developmentally disabled, or mentally ill person that pertains to misconduct, breach of duty, or noncompliance with state or federal laws, local ordinances, or rules or regulations adopted under those laws or ordinances that are administered by a governmental agency, refer the matter in writing to the appropriate state agency. The state agency shall

report on its actions and findings within seven days of receiving the matter.

(5) Advise the complainant and any mentally retarded, developmentally disabled, or mentally ill person mentioned in the complaint, no more than thirty days after it receives the complaint, of any action it has taken and of any opinions and recommendations it has with respect to the complaint.

(6) Attempt to resolve the complaint by using informal techniques of mediation, conciliation, and persuasion. If the complaint cannot be resolved by the use of these informal techniques or if the act, practice, policy, or procedure that is the subject of the complaint adversely affects the health, safety, welfare, or civil or human rights of a mentally retarded, developmentally disabled, or mentally ill person, the section may recommend to the appropriate authorities or the administrator of the legal rights service that appropriate actions be taken.

(7) Report its opinions or recommendations to the parties involved after attempting to resolve a complaint through informal techniques of mediation, conciliation, or persuasion. The section may request any party affected by the opinions or recommendations to notify the section, within a time period specified by the section, of any action the party has taken on the section's recommendations.

(C) The section may make public any of its opinions or recommendations concerning a complaint, the responses of persons and governmental agencies to its opinions or recommendations, and any act, practice, policy, or procedure that adversely affects or may adversely affect the health, safety, welfare, or civil or human rights of a mentally retarded, developmentally disabled, or mentally ill person.

(D) The section shall at all times maintain confidentiality under sections 5123.601 to 5123.604 of the Revised Code concerning the identities of mentally retarded, developmentally disabled, or mentally ill persons, complainants, witnesses, and other involved parties who provide it with information unless the person, in writing, authorizes the release of the information.

Nothing in this section shall prohibit the legal rights service from taking appropriate action when the administrator determines it is necessary.

(E) Whenever information is disclosed indicating the commission of a crime or a violation of standards of professional conduct, the legal rights service shall, within seven days of receiving the complaint or identifying the information during its investigation, refer the matter to the attorney general, county prosecutor, other law enforcement official, or regulatory board, as appropriate, to investigate the crime or violation. The section may disclose any information permitted by law that is necessary to resolve the matter referred. The section shall monitor and maintain records on every matter it refers under this division.

(1988 S 156, eff. 7–1–88; 1986 S 322)

Library References

Mental Health ⌾20, 31.
Westlaw Topic No. 257A.
C.J.S. Insane Persons § 14 to 16, 45, 47, 53.
   Baldwin's Ohio Legislative Service, 1988 Laws of Ohio, S 156—LSC Analysis, p 5–284

5123.602 Access to providers' premises; communication with mentally retarded and developmentally disabled persons

The ombudsman section of the legal rights service may, in order to carry out its duties under this chapter, make necessary inquiries and obtain information it considers necessary. For those purposes the section shall have ready access to the premises and records of all providers of services to mentally retarded, developmentally disabled, or mentally ill persons and shall have the right to communicate in a private and confidential setting with any mentally retarded, developmentally disabled, or mentally ill persons, with their parents, guardians, or advocates, and with employees of any provider.

(1988 S 156, eff. 7–1–88; 1986 S 322)

Library References

Mental Health ⌾20.
Westlaw Topic No. 257A.
C.J.S. Insane Persons § 14 to 16.
   Baldwin's Ohio Legislative Service, 1988 Laws of Ohio, S 156—LSC Analysis, p 5–284

5123.603 Duties of ombudsman section

The ombudsman section of the legal rights service shall:

(A) Publicize its existence, functions, and activities, and the procedures for filing a complaint under section 5123.601 of the Revised Code, and send this information in written form to each provider with instructions that the information is to be posted in a conspicuous place accessible to residents, visitors, and employees;

(B) Maintain the confidentiality of all its records and files;

(C) Not be required to testify in any court with respect to any matters it is required to maintain as confidential;

(D) Collect, compile, and analyze data relating to complaints, investigations, or other actions or conditions, for the purpose of helping prepare the annual report required by division (F)(7) of section 5123.60 of the Revised Code and identifying and resolving significant systemic problems affecting mentally retarded, developmentally disabled, or mentally ill persons;

(E) Recommend or propose to other governmental agencies changes in policies and rules that affect mentally retarded, developmentally disabled, or mentally ill persons;

(F) Establish, maintain, and publicize a toll-free number for receiving complaints.

(1988 S 156, eff. 7–1–88; 1986 S 322)

Library References

Mental Health ⌾20.
Westlaw Topic No. 257A.
C.J.S. Insane Persons § 14 to 16.
   Baldwin's Ohio Legislative Service, 1988 Laws of Ohio, S 156—LSC Analysis, p 5–284

5123.604 Retaliation for disclosures to ombudsperson section prohibited; notice of investigations

(A) No one shall take a discriminatory, disciplinary, or retaliatory action against any officer or employee of a provider, any mentally retarded, developmentally disabled, or mentally ill person, the parents or guardian of a mentally retarded, developmentally disabled, or mentally ill person, or any volunteer or advocate for a mentally retarded, developmentally disabled, or mentally ill person, for any communication these persons make or information they disclose in good faith to the ombudsperson section of the legal rights service.

(B) No person shall knowingly interfere with lawful actions of the ombudsperson section, refuse entry to its representatives, fail to comply with its lawful demands, or offer any compensation, gratuity, or promise thereof in an effort to influence the outcome of any matter being considered by the section.

(C) The department of mental retardation and developmental disabilities shall immediately notify the ombudsperson section of all investigations of major unusual incidents or life-threatening situations, as defined in rules adopted by the department, involving mentally retarded and developmentally disabled persons, and shall furnish copies of all relevant reports within forty-eight hours after receipt. The department of mental health shall notify the ombudsperson section of all major unusual incidents or life-threatening situations, as defined in rules adopted by the department, involving mentally ill persons within forty-eight hours after receipt of the report of the incident or situation. The departments of health and job and family services shall notify the department of mental retardation and developmental disabilities of all allegations and investigations of abuse, neglect, or life-threatening situations involving mentally retarded or developmentally disabled persons. Any other state agency with information concerning abuse, neglect, or life-threatening situations involving mentally retarded or developmentally disabled persons shall report that information immediately to the department of mental retardation and developmental disabilities.

Nothing in this section or section 5123.60, 5123.601, or 5123.602 of the Revised Code shall preclude any department or board, its contract agencies, a community residential facility, or other governmental entity from carrying out its responsibility as prescribed by law.

(1999 H 471, eff. 7–1–00; 1988 S 156, eff. 7–1–88; 1986 S 322)

Library References

Asylums ☞4.
Mental Health ☞20, 31.
Westlaw Topic Nos. 43, 257A.
C.J.S. Asylums and Institutional Care Facilities § 9 to 10.
C.J.S. Insane Persons § 14 to 16, 45, 47, 53.
 Baldwin's Ohio Legislative Service, 1988 Laws of Ohio, S 156—LSC Analysis, p 5–284

5123.61 Duty of certain persons to report believed abuse of mentally retarded or developmentally disabled adult; registry office; immunity

(A) As used in this section:

(1) "Law enforcement agency" means the state highway patrol, the police department of a municipal corporation, or a county sheriff.

(2) "Abuse" has the same meaning as in section 5123.50 of the Revised Code, except that it includes a misappropriation, as defined in that section.

(3) "Neglect" has the same meaning as in section 5123.50 of the Revised Code.

(B) The department of mental retardation and developmental disabilities shall establish a registry office for the purpose of maintaining reports of abuse, neglect, and other major unusual incidents made to the department under this section and reports received from county boards of mental retardation and developmental disabilities under section 5126.31 of the Revised Code. The department shall establish committees to review reports of abuse, neglect, and other major unusual incidents.

(C)(1) Any person listed in division (C)(2) of this section, having reason to believe that a person with mental retardation or a developmental disability has suffered or faces a substantial risk of suffering any wound, injury, disability, or condition of such a nature as to reasonably indicate abuse or neglect of that person, shall immediately report or cause reports to be made of such information to the entity specified in this division. Except as provided in section 5120.173 of the Revised Code or as otherwise provided in this division, the person making the report shall make it to a law enforcement agency or to the county board of mental retardation and developmental disabilities. If the report concerns a resident of a facility operated by the department of mental retardation and developmental disabilities the report shall be made either to a law enforcement agency or to the department. If the report concerns any act or omission of an employee of a county board of mental retardation and developmental disabilities, the report immediately shall be made to the department and to the county board.

(2) All of the following persons are required to make a report under division (C)(1) of this section:

(a) Any physician, including a hospital intern or resident, any dentist, podiatrist, chiropractor, practitioner of a limited branch of medicine as specified in section 4731.15 of the Revised Code, hospital administrator or employee of a hospital, nurse licensed under Chapter 4723. of the Revised Code, employee of an ambulatory health facility as defined in section 5101.61 of the Revised Code, employee of a home health agency, employee of an adult care facility licensed under Chapter 3722. of the Revised Code, or employee of a community mental health facility;

(b) Any school teacher or school authority, social worker, psychologist, attorney, peace officer, coroner, or residents' rights advocate as defined in section 3721.10 of the Revised Code;

(c) A superintendent, board member, or employee of a county board of mental retardation and developmental disabilities; an administrator, board member, or employee of a residential facility licensed under section 5123.19 of the Revised Code; an administrator, board member, or employee of any other public or private provider of services to a person with mental retardation or a developmental disability, or any MR/DD employee, as defined in section 5123.50 of the Revised Code;

(d) A member of a citizen's advisory council established at an institution or branch institution of the department of mental retardation and developmental disabilities under section 5123.092 of the Revised Code;

(e) A clergyman who is employed in a position that includes providing specialized services to an individual with mental retardation or another developmental disability, while acting in an official or professional capacity in that position, or a person who is employed in a position that includes providing specialized services to an individual with mental retardation or another developmental disability and who, while acting in an official or professional capacity, renders spiritual treatment through prayer in accordance with the tenets of an organized religion.

(3)(a) The reporting requirements of this division do not apply to members of the legal rights service commission or to employees of the legal rights service.

(b) An attorney or physician is not required to make a report pursuant to division (C)(1) of this section concerning any communication the attorney or physician receives from a client or patient in an attorney-client or physician-patient relationship, if, in accordance with division (A) or (B) of section 2317.02 of the Revised Code, the attorney or physician could not testify with respect to that communication in a civil or criminal proceeding, except that the client or patient is deemed to have waived any testimonial privilege under division (A) or (B) of section 2317.02 of the Revised Code with respect to that communication and the attorney or physician shall make a report pursuant to division (C)(1) of this section, if both of the following apply:

(i) The client or patient, at the time of the communication, is a person with mental retardation or a developmental disability.

(ii) The attorney or physician knows or suspects, as a result of the communication or any observations made during that communication, that the client or patient has suffered or faces a substantial risk of suffering any wound, injury, disability, or condition of a nature that reasonably indicates abuse or neglect of the client or patient.

(4) Any person who fails to make a report required under division (C) of this section and who is an MR/DD employee, as

defined in section 5123.50 of the Revised Code, shall be eligible to be included in the registry regarding misappropriation, abuse, neglect, or other specified misconduct by MR/DD employees established under section 5123.52 of the Revised Code.

(D) The reports required under division (C) of this section shall be made forthwith by telephone or in person and shall be followed by a written report. The reports shall contain the following:

(1) The names and addresses of the person with mental retardation or a developmental disability and the person's custodian, if known;

(2) The age of the person with mental retardation or a developmental disability;

(3) Any other information that would assist in the investigation of the report.

(E) When a physician performing services as a member of the staff of a hospital or similar institution has reason to believe that a person with mental retardation or a developmental disability has suffered injury, abuse, or physical neglect, the physician shall notify the person in charge of the institution or that person's designated delegate, who shall make the necessary reports.

(F) Any person having reasonable cause to believe that a person with mental retardation or a developmental disability has suffered or faces a substantial risk of suffering abuse or neglect may report or cause a report to be made of that belief to the entity specified in this division. Except as provided in section 5120.173 of the Revised Code or as otherwise provided in this division, the person making the report shall make it to a law enforcement agency or the county board of mental retardation and developmental disabilities. If the person is a resident of a facility operated by the department of mental retardation and developmental disabilities, the report shall be made to a law enforcement agency or to the department. If the report concerns any act or omission of an employee of a county board of mental retardation and developmental disabilities, the report immediately shall be made to the department and to the county board.

(G)(1) Upon the receipt of a report concerning the possible abuse or neglect of a person with mental retardation or a developmental disability, the law enforcement agency shall inform the county board of mental retardation and developmental disabilities or, if the person is a resident of a facility operated by the department of mental retardation and developmental disabilities, the director of the department or the director's designee.

(2) On receipt of a report under this section that includes an allegation of action or inaction that may constitute a crime under federal law or the law of this state, the department of mental retardation and developmental disabilities shall notify the law enforcement agency.

(3) When a county board of mental retardation and developmental disabilities receives a report under this section that includes an allegation of action or inaction that may constitute a crime under federal law or the law of this state, the superintendent of the board or an individual the superintendent designates under division (H) of this section shall notify the law enforcement agency. The superintendent or individual shall notify the department of mental retardation and developmental disabilities when it receives any report under this section.

(4) When a county board of mental retardation and developmental disabilities receives a report under this section and believes that the degree of risk to the person is such that the report is an emergency, the superintendent of the board or an employee of the board the superintendent designates shall attempt a face-to-face contact with the person with mental retardation or a developmental disability who allegedly is the victim within one hour of the board's receipt of the report.

(H) The superintendent of the board may designate an individual to be responsible for notifying the law enforcement agency and the department when the county board receives a report under this section.

(I) An adult with mental retardation or a developmental disability about whom a report is made may be removed from the adult's place of residence only by law enforcement officers who consider that the adult's immediate removal is essential to protect the adult from further injury or abuse or in accordance with the order of a court made pursuant to section 5126.33 of the Revised Code.

(J) A law enforcement agency shall investigate each report of abuse or neglect it receives under this section. In addition, the department, in cooperation with law enforcement officials, shall investigate each report regarding a resident of a facility operated by the department to determine the circumstances surrounding the injury, the cause of the injury, and the person responsible. The investigation shall be in accordance with the memorandum of understanding prepared under section 5126.058 of the Revised Code. The department shall determine, with the registry office which shall be maintained by the department, whether prior reports have been made concerning an adult with mental retardation or a developmental disability or other principals in the case. If the department finds that the report involves action or inaction that may constitute a crime under federal law or the law of this state, it shall submit a report of its investigation, in writing, to the law enforcement agency. If the person with mental retardation or a developmental disability is an adult, with the consent of the adult, the department shall provide such protective services as are necessary to protect the adult. The law enforcement agency shall make a written report of its findings to the department.

If the person is an adult and is not a resident of a facility operated by the department, the county board of mental retardation and developmental disabilities shall review the report of abuse or neglect in accordance with sections 5126.30 to 5126.33 of the Revised Code and the law enforcement agency shall make the written report of its findings to the county board.

(K) Any person or any hospital, institution, school, health department, or agency participating in the making of reports pursuant to this section, any person participating as a witness in an administrative or judicial proceeding resulting from the reports, or any person or governmental entity that discharges responsibilities under sections 5126.31 to 5126.33 of the Revised Code shall be immune from any civil or criminal liability that might otherwise be incurred or imposed as a result of such actions except liability for perjury, unless the person or governmental entity has acted in bad faith or with malicious purpose.

(L) No employer or any person with the authority to do so shall discharge, demote, transfer, prepare a negative work performance evaluation, reduce pay or benefits, terminate work privileges, or take any other action detrimental to an employee or retaliate against an employee as a result of the employee's having made a report under this section. This division does not preclude an employer or person with authority from taking action with regard to an employee who has made a report under this section if there is another reasonable basis for the action.

(M) Reports made under this section are not public records as defined in section 149.43 of the Revised Code. Information contained in the reports on request shall be made available to the person who is the subject of the report, to the person's legal counsel, and to agencies authorized to receive information in the report by the department or by a county board of mental retardation and developmental disabilities.

(N) Notwithstanding section 4731.22 of the Revised Code, the physician-patient privilege shall not be a ground for excluding evidence regarding the injuries or physical neglect of a person with mental retardation or a developmental disability or the cause thereof in any judicial proceeding resulting from a report submitted pursuant to this section.

(2004 S 178, eff. 1–30–04; 2000 S 171, eff. 11–22–00; 1998 H 606, eff. 3–9–99; 1996 H 670, eff. 12–2–96; 1993 S 21, eff. 10–29–93; 1990 H 569; 1988 H 403; 1985 H 66; 1980 H 900)

Historical and Statutory Notes

Ed. Note: 5123.61 is former 5123.98 amended and recodified by 1980 H 900, eff. 7–1–80; 1977 H 219; 1974 S 336.

Ed. Note: Former 5123.61 repealed by 129 v 1448, eff. 10–25–61; 125 v 823; 1953 H 1; GC 1890–110.

Pre–1953 H 1 Amendments: 121 v 423; 119 v 616; 117 v 550

Library References

Asylums ⊜3 to 5.
Mental Health ⊜20, 52.1.
Westlaw Topic Nos. 43, 257A.
C.J.S. Asylums and Institutional Care Facilities § 5 to 12.
C.J.S. Insane Persons § 14 to 16, 102, 104, 106 to 107.

5123.611 Report of findings following review of report of abuse, neglect, or major unusual incident

(A) As used in this section, "MR/DD employee" means all of the following:

(1) An employee of the department of mental retardation and developmental disabilities;

(2) An employee of a county board of mental retardation and developmental disabilities;

(3) An employee in a position that includes providing specialized services, as defined in section 5123.50 of the Revised Code, to an individual with mental retardation or a developmental disability.

(B) At the conclusion of a review of a report of abuse, neglect, or a major unusual incident that is conducted by a review committee established pursuant to section 5123.61 of the Revised Code, the committee shall issue recommendations to the department. The department shall review the committee's recommendations and issue a report of its findings. The department shall make the report available to all of the following:

(1) The individual with mental retardation or a developmental disability who is the subject of the report;

(2) That individual's guardian or legal counsel;

(3) The licensee, as defined in section 5123.19 of the Revised Code, of a residential facility in which the individual resides;

(4) The employer of any MR/DD employee who allegedly committed or was responsible for the abuse, neglect, or major unusual incident.

(C) Except as provided in this section, the department shall not disclose its report to any person or government entity that is not authorized to investigate reports of abuse, neglect, or other major unusual incidents, unless the individual with mental retardation or a developmental disability who is the subject of the report or the individual's guardian gives the department written consent.

(2002 S 191, eff. 12–31–03; 2000 H 538, eff. 9–22–00)

Library References

Asylums ⊜4.
Mental Health ⊜20, 52.1.
Westlaw Topic Nos. 43, 257A.
C.J.S. Asylums and Institutional Care Facilities § 9 to 10.
C.J.S. Insane Persons § 14 to 16, 102, 104, 106 to 107.

5123.612 Rules regarding reporting of incidents

The director of mental retardation and developmental disabilities shall adopt rules in accordance with Chapter 119. of the Revised Code regarding the reporting of major unusual incidents and unusual incidents concerning persons with mental retardation or a developmental disability. The rules shall specify what constitutes a major unusual incident or an unusual incident.

(2000 H 538, eff. 9–22–00)

Library References

Mental Health ⊜20.
Westlaw Topic No. 257A.
C.J.S. Insane Persons § 14 to 16.

5123.613 Reports

(A) When a person who is the subject of a report under section 5123.61 of the Revised Code dies, the department of mental retardation and developmental disabilities or the county board of mental retardation and developmental disabilities, whichever is applicable, shall, on written request, provide to both of the following persons the report and any records relating to the report:

(1) If the report or records are necessary to administer the estate of the person who is the subject of the report, to the executor or administrator of the person's estate;

(2) To the guardian of the person who is the subject of the report or, if the individual had no guardian at the time of death, to a person in the first applicable of the following categories:

(a) The person's spouse;

(b) The person's children;

(c) The person's parents;

(d) The person's brothers or sisters;

(e) The person's uncles or aunts;

(f) The person's closest relative by blood or adoption;

(g) The person's closest relative by marriage.

(B) The department or county board shall provide the report and related records as required by this section not later than thirty days after receipt of the request." [1]

(2000 H 538, eff. 9–22–00)

[1] So in original.

Library References

Mental Health ⊜21, 52.1.
Westlaw Topic No. 257A.
C.J.S. Insane Persons § 17 to 20, 102, 104, 106 to 107.

5123.614 Reports; independent review or investigation

(A) Subject to division (B) of this section, on receipt of a report of a major unusual incident made pursuant to section 5123.61 or 5126.31 of the Revised Code or rules adopted under section 5123.612 of the Revised Code, the department of mental retardation and developmental disabilities may do either of the following:

(1) Conduct an independent review or investigation of the incident;

(2) Request that an independent review or investigation of the incident be conducted by a county board of mental retardation and developmental disabilities that is not implicated in the report, a regional council of government, or any other entity authorized to conduct such investigations.

(B) If a report described in division (A) of this section concerning the health or safety of a person with mental retardation or a developmental disability involves an allegation that an employee of a county board of mental retardation and developmental disabilities has created a substantial risk of serious physical harm to a person with mental retardation or a developmental disability, the department shall do one of the following:

(1) Conduct an independent investigation regarding the incident;

(2) Request that an independent review or investigation of the incident be conducted by a county board of mental retardation and developmental disabilities that is not implicated in the report, a regional council of government, or any other entity authorized to conduct such investigations.

(2004 S 178, eff. 1–30–04)

5123.62 Rights of persons with mental retardation or developmental disability

The rights of persons with mental retardation or a developmental disability include, but are not limited to, the following:

(A) The right to be treated at all times with courtesy and respect and with full recognition of their dignity and individuality;

(B) The right to an appropriate, safe, and sanitary living environment that complies with local, state, and federal standards and recognizes the persons' need for privacy and independence;

(C) The right to food adequate to meet accepted standards of nutrition;

(D) The right to practice the religion of their choice or to abstain from the practice of religion;

(E) The right of timely access to appropriate medical or dental treatment;

(F) The right of access to necessary ancillary services, including, but not limited to, occupational therapy, physical therapy, speech therapy, and behavior modification and other psychological services;

(G) The right to receive appropriate care and treatment in the least intrusive manner;

(H) The right to privacy, including both periods of privacy and places of privacy;

(I) The right to communicate freely with persons of their choice in any reasonable manner they choose;

(J) The right to ownership and use of personal possessions so as to maintain individuality and personal dignity;

(K) The right to social interaction with members of either sex;

(L) The right of access to opportunities that enable individuals to develop their full human potential;

(M) The right to pursue vocational opportunities that will promote and enhance economic independence;

(N) The right to be treated equally as citizens under the law;

(O) The right to be free from emotional, psychological, and physical abuse;

(P) The right to participate in appropriate programs of education, training, social development, and habilitation and in programs of reasonable recreation;

(Q) The right to participate in decisions that affect their lives;

(R) The right to select a parent or advocate to act on their behalf;

(S) The right to manage their personal financial affairs, based on individual ability to do so;

(T) The right to confidential treatment of all information in their personal and medical records, except to the extent that disclosure or release of records is permitted under sections 5123.89 and 5126.044 of the Revised Code;

(U) The right to voice grievances and recommend changes in policies and services without restraint, interference, coercion, discrimination, or reprisal;

(V) The right to be free from unnecessary chemical or physical restraints;

(W) The right to participate in the political process;

(X) The right to refuse to participate in medical, psychological, or other research or experiments.

(2000 H 538, eff. 9–22–00; 1996 H 629, eff. 3–13–97; 1993 S 21, eff. 10–29–93; 1986 S 322)

Historical and Statutory Notes

Ed. Note: Former 5123.62 amended and recodified as 5123.90 by 1980 H 900, eff. 7–1–80; 1977 H 725; 1972 H 494; 1970 H 970; 1953 H 1; GC 1890–106.

Pre–1953 H 1 Amendments: 117 v 550, § 106

Library References

Mental Health ⚖ 1, 31, 51.1, 331.
Westlaw Topic No. 257A.
C.J.S. Insane Persons § 2 to 3, 21, 45, 47, 53, 86 to 92, 209.

5123.63 Rights list to be furnished to providers; posting and distribution of list

Every state agency, county board of mental retardation and developmental disabilities, or political subdivision that provides services, either directly or through a contract, to persons with mental retardation or a developmental disability shall give each provider a copy of the list of rights contained in section 5123.62 of the Revised Code. Each public and private provider of services shall carry out the requirements of this section in addition to any other posting or notification requirements imposed by local, state, or federal law or rules.

The provider shall make copies of the list of rights and shall be responsible for an initial distribution of the list to each individual receiving services from the provider. If the individual is unable to read the list, the provider shall communicate the contents of the list to the individual to the extent practicable in a manner that the individual understands. The individual receiving services or the parent, guardian, or advocate of the individual shall sign an acknowledgement of receipt of a copy of the list of rights, and a copy of the signed acknowledgement shall be placed in the individual's file. The provider shall also be responsible for answering any questions and giving any explanations necessary to assist the individual to understand the rights enumerated. Instruction in these rights shall be documented.

Each provider shall make available to all persons receiving services and all employees and visitors a copy of the list of rights and the addresses and telephone numbers of the legal rights service, the department of mental retardation and developmental disabilities, and the county board of mental retardation and developmental disabilities of the county in which the provider provides services.

(2000 H 538, eff. 9–22–00; 1986 S 322, eff. 4–4–86)

Historical and Statutory Notes

Ed. Note: Former 5123.63 amended and recodified as 5119.50 by 1980 H 900, eff. 7-1-80; 1969 H 688; 128 v 333.

Library References

Mental Health ⇌1, 31, 51.1, 331.
Westlaw Topic No. 257A.
C.J.S. Insane Persons § 2 to 3, 21, 45, 47, 53, 86 to 92, 209.

5123.64 Familiarity and compliance with rights list; remedies for violations

(A) Every provider of services to persons with mental retardation or a developmental disability shall establish policies and programs to ensure that all staff members are familiar with the rights enumerated in section 5123.62 of the Revised Code and observe those rights in their contacts with persons receiving services. Any policy, procedure, or rule of the provider that conflicts with any of the rights enumerated shall be null and void. Every provider shall establish written procedures for resolving complaints of violations of those rights. A copy of the procedures shall be provided to any person receiving services or to any parent, guardian, or advocate of a person receiving services.

(B) Any person with mental retardation or a developmental disability who believes that the person's rights as enumerated in section 5123.62 of the Revised Code have been violated may:

(1) Bring the violation to the attention of the provider for resolution;

(2) Report the violation to the department of mental retardation and developmental disabilities, the ombudsperson section of the legal rights service, or the appropriate county board of mental retardation and developmental disabilities;

(3) Take any other appropriate action to ensure compliance with sections 5123.60 to 5123.64 of the Revised Code, including the filing of a legal action to enforce rights or to recover damages for violation of rights.

(2000 H 538, eff. 9-22-00; 1986 S 322, eff. 4-4-86)

Historical and Statutory Notes

Ed. Note: Former 5123.64 amended and recodified as 5119.51 by 1980 H 900, eff. 7-1-80; 1972 H 494; 128 v 333.

Library References

Asylums ⇌5, 6.
Westlaw Topic No. 43.
C.J.S. Asylums and Institutional Care Facilities § 11 to 13.

INSTITUTIONALIZATION OF MENTALLY RETARDED PERSONS

5123.67 Purposes of chapter

This chapter shall be liberally interpreted to accomplish the following purposes:

(A) To promote the human dignity and to protect the constitutional rights of persons with mental retardation or a developmental disability in the state;

(B) To encourage the development of the ability and potential of each person with mental retardation or a developmental disability in the state to the fullest possible extent, no matter how severe the degree of disability;

(C) To promote the economic security, standard of living, and meaningful employment of persons with mental retardation or a developmental disability;

(D) To maximize the assimilation of persons with mental retardation or a developmental disability into the ordinary life of the communities in which they live;

(E) To promote opportunities for persons with mental retardation or a developmental disability to live in surroundings or circumstances that are typical for other community members;

(F) To promote the right of persons with mental retardation or a developmental disability to speak and be heard about the desired direction of their lives and to use available resources in ways that further that direction.

(2000 H 538, eff. 9-22-00; 1990 H 569, eff. 7-1-91; 1974 S 336)

Library References

Mental Health ⇌2, 32.
Statutes ⇌184, 235.
Westlaw Topic Nos. 257A, 361.
C.J.S. Insane Persons § 22, 45 to 46, 49 to 50, 54, 60 to 64, 66.
C.J.S. Statutes § 306, 316, 376.

5123.69 Voluntary admission; discharge

(A) Except as provided in division (E) of this section, any person who is eighteen years of age or older and who is or believes self to be mentally retarded may make written application to the managing officer of any institution for voluntary admission. Except as provided in division (E) of this section, the application may be made on behalf of a minor by a parent or guardian, and on behalf of an adult adjudicated mentally incompetent by a guardian.

(B) The managing officer of an institution, with the concurrence of the chief program director, may admit a person applying pursuant to this section only after a comprehensive evaluation has been made of the person and only if the comprehensive evaluation concludes that the person is mentally retarded and would benefit significantly from admission.

(C) If application for voluntary admission of a minor or of a person adjudicated mentally incompetent is made by the parent or guardian of the minor or by the guardian of an incompetent and the minor or incompetent is admitted, the probate division of the court of common pleas shall determine, upon petition by the legal rights service, whether the voluntary admission or continued institutionalization is in the best interest of the minor or incompetent.

(D) The managing officer shall discharge any voluntary resident if, in the judgment of the chief program director, the results of a comprehensive examination indicate that institutionalization no longer is advisable. In light of the results of the comprehensive evaluation, the managing officer also may discharge any voluntary resident if, in the judgment of the chief program director, the discharge would contribute to the most effective use of the institution in the habilitation and care of the mentally retarded.

(E) A person who is found incompetent to stand trial or not guilty by reason of insanity and who is committed pursuant to section 2945.39, 2945.40, 2945.401, or 2945.402 of the Revised Code shall not voluntarily commit self pursuant to this section until after the final termination of the commitment, as described in division (J) of section 2945.401 of the Revised Code.

(1996 S 285, eff. 7-1-97; 1980 S 297, eff. 4-30-80; 1974 S 336)

Library References

Mental Health ⇌37.1, 38, 59.1.
Westlaw Topic No. 257A.
C.J.S. Insane Persons § 53, 58, 83.

5123.70 Request of voluntarily admitted resident for release

(A) A resident admitted pursuant to section 5123.69 of the Revised Code who requests his own release or whose release is requested in writing by his counsel, legal guardian, parent, spouse, or adult next of kin shall be released forthwith except that:

(1) If a resident was admitted on his own application and the request for release is made by a person other than the resident, release may be made conditional upon the agreement of the resident thereto if his continued institutionalization is supported by his most recent comprehensive evaluation;

(2) If, within three court days from the receipt of the request for release, the managing officer files an affidavit or causes an affidavit to be filed under section 5123.71 of the Revised Code with the probate division of the court of common pleas of the county where the resident has his residence or where he is institutionalized, release may be postponed until a hearing can be held pursuant to section 5123.76 of the Revised Code. In such case, the request for release shall substitute for the request for a probable cause hearing under section 5123.75 of the Revised Code.

A telephone communication to the probate division from the managing officer of the institution or his designee indicating that the required affidavit has been mailed by certified mail shall be sufficient compliance with division (A)(2) of this section.

(B) Judicial proceedings for instituionalization [1] shall not be commenced with respect to a voluntary resident except pursuant to division (A)(2) of this section.

(C) Sections 5121.01 to 5121.10 of the Revised Code shall apply to the persons received in a public institution on a voluntary application.

(D) The managing officer shall inform residents, parents, guardians, and custodians of the right to release as provided in this section and shall assist residents in making and presenting requests for release.

(1974 S 336, eff. 7–1–75)

[1] So in original; should this read "institutionalization"?

Library References

Mental Health ⇒59.1, 60.
Westlaw Topic No. 257A.
C.J.S. Insane Persons § 83 to 84.

5123.701 Person may apply for his admission for short-term care

(A) Except as provided in division (E) of this section, any person in the community who is eighteen years of age or older and who is or believes self to be mentally retarded may make written application to the managing officer of any institution for temporary admission for short-term care. The application may be made on behalf of a minor by a parent or guardian, and on behalf of an adult adjudicated mentally incompetent by a guardian.

(B) For purposes of this section, short-term care shall be defined to mean appropriate services provided to a person with mental retardation for no more than fourteen consecutive days and for no more than forty-two days in a fiscal year. When circumstances warrant, the fourteen-day period may be extended at the discretion of the managing officer. Short–term care is provided in a developmental center to meet the family's or caretaker's needs for separation from the person with mental retardation.

(C) The managing officer of an institution, with the concurrence of the chief program director, may admit a person for short-term care only after a medical examination has been made of the person and only if the managing officer concludes that the person is mentally retarded.

(D) If application for admission for short-term care of a minor or of a person adjudicated mentally incompetent is made by the minor's parent or guardian or by the incompetent's guardian and the minor or incompetent is admitted, the probate division of the court of common pleas shall determine, upon petition by the legal rights service, whether the admission for short-term care is in the best interest of the minor or the incompetent.

(E) A person who is found not guilty by reason of insanity shall not admit self to an institution for short-term care unless a hearing was held regarding the person pursuant to division (A) of section 2945.40 of the Revised Code and either of the following applies:

(1) The person was found at the hearing not to be a mentally retarded person subject to institutionalization by court order;

(2) The person was found at the hearing to be a mentally retarded person subject to institutionalization by court order, was involuntarily committed, and was finally discharged.

(F) The mentally retarded person, liable relatives, and guardians of mentally retarded persons admitted for respite care shall pay support charges in accordance with sections 5121.01 to 5121.21 of the Revised Code.

(G) At the conclusion of each period of short-term care, the person shall return to the person's family or caretaker. Under no circumstances shall a person admitted for short-term care according to this section remain in the institution after the period of short-term care unless the person is admitted according to section 5123.70, sections 5123.71 to 5123.76, or section 2945.38, 2945.39, 2945.40, 2945.401, or 2945.402 of the Revised Code.

(2005 H 66, eff. 1–1–06; 1996 S 285, eff. 7–1–97; 1981 H 694, eff. 11–15–81)

Library References

Mental Health ⇒36, 37.1, 73, 439.1.
Westlaw Topic No. 257A.
C.J.S. Insane Persons § 49 to 53, 203, 205, 207, 241 to 245.

5123.71 Involuntary institutionalization; procedure; rights of person detained

(A)(1) Proceedings for the involuntary institutionalization of a person pursuant to sections 5123.71 to 5123.76 of the Revised Code shall be commenced by the filing of an affidavit with the probate division of the court of common pleas of the county where the person resides or where the person is institutionalized, in the manner and form prescribed by the department of mental retardation and developmental disabilities either on information or actual knowledge, whichever is determined to be proper by the court. The affidavit may be filed only by a person who has custody of the individual as a parent, guardian, or service provider or by a person acting on behalf of the department or a county board of mental retardation and developmental disabilities. This section does not apply regarding the institutionalization of a person pursuant to section 2945.39, 2945.40, 2945.401, or 2945.402 of the Revised Code.

The affidavit shall contain an allegation setting forth the specific category or categories under division (O) of section 5123.01 of the Revised Code upon which the commencement of proceedings is based and a statement of the factual ground for the belief that the person is a mentally retarded person subject to institutionalization by court order. Except as provided in division (A)(2) of this section, the affidavit shall be accompanied by both of the following:

(a) A comprehensive evaluation report prepared by the person's evaluation team that includes a statement by the members of the team certifying that they have performed a comprehensive evaluation of the person and that they are of the opinion that the person is a mentally retarded person subject to institutionalization by court order;

(b) An assessment report prepared by the county board of mental retardation and developmental disabilities under section 5123.711 of the Revised Code specifying that the individual is in need of services on an emergency or priority basis.

(2) In lieu of the comprehensive evaluation report, the affidavit may be accompanied by a written and sworn statement that the person or the guardian of a person adjudicated incompetent has refused to allow a comprehensive evaluation and county board assessment and assessment reports. Immediately after accepting an affidavit that is not accompanied by the reports of a comprehensive evaluation and county board assessment, the court shall cause a comprehensive evaluation and county board assessment of the person named in the affidavit to be performed. The evaluation shall be conducted in the least restrictive environment possible and the assessment shall be conducted in the same manner as assessments conducted under section 5123.711 of the Revised Code. The evaluation and assessment must be completed before a probable cause hearing or full hearing may be held under section 5123.75 or 5123.76 of the Revised Code.

A written report of the evaluation team's findings and the county board's assessment shall be filed with the court. The reports shall, consistent with the rules of evidence, be accepted as probative evidence in any proceeding under section 5123.75 or 5123.76 of the Revised Code. If the counsel for the person who is evaluated or assessed is known, the court shall send to the counsel a copy of the reports as soon as possible after they are filed and prior to any proceedings under section 5123.75 or 5123.76 of the Revised Code.

(B) Any person who is involuntarily detained in an institution or otherwise is in custody under this chapter shall be informed of the right to do the following:

(1) Immediately make a reasonable number of telephone calls or use other reasonable means to contact an attorney, a physician, or both, to contact any other person or persons to secure representation by counsel, or to obtain medical assistance, and be provided assistance in making calls if the assistance is needed and requested;

(2) Retain counsel and have independent expert evaluation and, if the person is an indigent person, be represented by court-appointed counsel and have independent expert evaluation at court expense;

(3) Upon request, have a hearing to determine whether there is probable cause to believe that the person is a mentally retarded person subject to institutionalization by court order.

(C) No person who is being treated by spiritual means through prayer alone in accordance with a recognized religious method of healing may be ordered detained or involuntarily committed unless the court has determined that the person represents a very substantial risk of self-impairment, self-injury, or impairment or injury to others.

(2005 H 66, eff. 7–1–05; 2001 H 94, eff. 6–6–01; 1996 S 285, eff. 7–1–97; 1996 H 629, eff. 3–13–97; 1993 S 21, eff. 10–29–93; 1990 H 569; 1980 H 965, H 900, S 297; 1974 S 336)

Library References

Mental Health ⚖33, 38 to 43.
Westlaw Topic No. 257A.
C.J.S. Insane Persons § 48 to 49, 54 to 70.

5123.711 Assessment of an individual's needs; request for assessment

(A) As used in this section:

(1) "Emergency" means either of the following that creates a risk of substantial harm to an individual or others if action is not taken within thirty days:

(a) Health and safety conditions that pose a serious risk of immediate harm or death to the individual or others;

(b) Changes in the emotional or physical condition of an individual that necessitates substantial accommodation that cannot reasonably be provided by the individual's existing caretaker.

(2) "Priority" means a situation creating a risk of substantial harm to an individual or others, but for which action within thirty days is not necessary.

(3) "Resources" has the same meaning as in section 5126.01 of the Revised Code.

(B) Prior to filing an affidavit under section 5123.71 of the Revised Code for the involuntary institutionalization of an individual, a person who is eligible to file under that section and intends to do so shall request that the county board of mental retardation and developmental disabilities conduct an assessment of the individual's needs. Not later than thirty days after the date a request is received, the board shall complete the assessment and provide to the person a report of its findings and recommendations. The report shall be delivered by certified mail.

Within three working days after receiving a request for an assessment, the board shall notify the department of mental retardation and developmental disabilities that the request has been made and that there is the potential for court-ordered institutionalization of an individual. The department may provide assistance to the board in the performance of the assessment.

(C) The board's assessment of an individual's needs shall include the following:

(1) A determination of the current needs of the individual, including an appropriate plan for services;

(2) A determination of whether the community is the least restrictive environment in which the individual may be appropriately served;

(3) A determination of whether the individual meets the conditions for assistance on an emergency or priority basis;

(4) Identification of available resources to meet the individual's needs, including service providers with the capability of appropriately meeting those needs, special ancillary services, and moneys to pay for the services necessary to meet the individual's needs within the community rather than in a state institution.

(D) If the board's assessment of an individual identifies that county resources are available to meet the individual's needs in the community, the board shall provide services to the individual or arrange for the provision of services. If county resources are not available, the board shall petition the department of mental retardation and developmental disabilities for necessary resources that may be available from the department.

(1996 H 629, eff. 3–13–97)

Library References

Mental Health ⚖37.1, 38, 43.
Westlaw Topic No. 257A.
C.J.S. Insane Persons § 53, 58 to 59, 63, 70.

PRACTICE AND PROCEDURE

5123.72 Designee of director to present case for state

Except as provided in division (B) of this section, the director of mental retardation and developmental disabilities shall designate a person to present the case on behalf of the state at the hearings provided for in sections 5123.75 and 5123.76 of the Revised Code. The designee of the director also may present the case on behalf of the state in any other hearing provided for in this chapter.

(1996 S 285, eff. 7–1–97; 1980 H 965, eff. 4–9–81; 1980 H 900, S 297; 1974 S 336)

Library References

Mental Health ⚖=37.1, 41.
Westlaw Topic No. 257A.
C.J.S. Insane Persons § 49, 53 to 54, 59 to 64, 66 to 70.

5123.73 Notice of hearing

(A) After receipt of the affidavit required by section 5123.71 of the Revised Code, the court shall cause written notice, by mail or otherwise, of any hearing the court directs, to be given to all of the following persons:

(1) The respondent;

(2) The respondent's legal guardian, if any;

(3) The respondent's spouse, if address is known;

(4) The person filing the affidavit;

(5) Any one person designated by the respondent, except that if the respondent does not make a selection, the notice shall be sent to the adult next of kin other than the person who filed the affidavit, if that person's address is known to the court;

(6) The respondent's counsel;

(7) The director of mental retardation and developmental disabilities or the director's designee under section 5123.72 of the Revised Code.

(B) All persons entitled to notice under this section may waive that notice.

(C) A copy of the affidavit and of any temporary order shall be served with a notice under this section.

(1996 S 285, eff. 7–1–97; 1993 S 21, eff. 10–29–93; 1980 H 965, H 900, S 297; 1974 S 336)

Library References

Mental Health ⚖=39, 41.
Westlaw Topic No. 257A.
C.J.S. Insane Persons § 49, 54, 56, 59 to 64, 66 to 70.

5123.74 Procedures prior to emergency institutionalization; probable cause hearing

(A) On receipt of an affidavit under section 5123.71 of the Revised Code, the probate division of the court of common pleas may, if it has probable cause to believe that the person named in the affidavit is a mentally retarded person subject to institutionalization by court order and that emergency institutionalization is required, do any of the following:

(1) Issue a temporary order of detention ordering any health or police officer or sheriff to take into custody and transport such person to an institution or other place as designated in section 5123.77 of the Revised Code;

(2) Order the county board of mental retardation and developmental disabilities to provide services to the individual in the community if the board's assessment of the individual conducted under section 5123.711 of the Revised Code identifies that resources are available to meet the individual's needs in an appropriate manner within the community as an alternative to institutionalization;

(3) Set the matter for further hearing.

(B) A managing officer of a nonpublic institution may, and the managing officer of a public institution shall, receive for observation, diagnosis, habilitation, and care any person whose admission is ordered pursuant to division (A)(1) of this section.

The alternatives to institutionalization that may be ordered under division (A)(2) of this section are limited to those that are necessary to remediate the emergency condition; necessary for the person's health, safety or welfare; and necessary for the protection of society, if applicable.

(C) A person detained under this section may be observed and habilitated until the probable cause hearing provided for in section 5123.75 of the Revised Code. If no probable cause hearing is requested or held, the person may be evaluated and shall be provided with habilitative services until the full hearing is held pursuant to section 5123.76 of the Revised Code.

(1996 H 629, eff. 3–13–97; 1987 H 231, eff. 10–5–87; 1974 S 336)

Library References

Mental Health ⚖=37.1, 44.
Westlaw Topic No. 257A.
C.J.S. Insane Persons § 53, 66, 71 to 73.

5123.75 Probable cause hearing; procedure

A respondent who is involuntarily placed in an institution or other place as designated in section 5123.77 of the Revised Code or with respect to whom proceedings have been instituted under section 5123.71 of the Revised Code shall, on request of the respondent, his guardian, or his counsel, or upon the court's own motion, be afforded a hearing to determine whether there is probable cause to believe that the respondent is a mentally retarded person subject to institutionalization by court order.

(A) The probable cause hearing shall be conducted within two court days from the day on which the request is made. Failure to conduct the probable cause hearing within this time shall effect an immediate discharge of the respondent. If the proceedings are not reinstituted within thirty days, records of the proceedings shall be expunged.

(B) The respondent shall be informed that he may retain counsel and have independent expert evaluation and, if he is an indigent person, be represented by court appointed counsel and have independent expert evaluation at court expense.

(C) The probable cause hearing shall be conducted in a manner consistent with the procedures set forth in division (A) of section 5123.76 of the Revised Code, except divisions (A)(10) and (14) of that section, and the designee of the director of mental retardation and developmental disabilities shall present evidence for the state.

(D) If the court does not find probable cause to believe that the respondent is a mentally retarded person subject to institutionalization by court order, it shall order immediate release of the respondent and dismiss and expunge all record of the proceedings under this chapter.

(E) On motion of the respondent or his counsel and for good cause shown, the court may order a continuance of the hearing.

(F) If the court finds probable cause to believe that the respondent is a mentally retarded person subject to institutionalization by court order, the court may issue an interim order of placement and, where proceedings under section 5123.71 of the Revised Code have been instituted, shall order a full hearing as provided in section 5123.76 of the Revised Code to be held on the question of whether the respondent is a mentally retarded person subject to institutionalization by court order. Unless specifically waived by the respondent or the respondent's counsel, the court shall schedule said hearing to be held as soon as possible within ten days from the probable cause hearing. A waiver of such full hearing at this point shall not preclude the respondent from asserting the respondent's right to such hearing under section 5123.76 of the Revised Code at any time prior to the mandatory hearing provided in division (H) of section 5123.76 of the Revised Code. In any case, if the respondent has waived his right to the full hearing, a mandatory hearing shall be held under division (H) of section 5123.76 of the Revised Code between the ninetieth and the one hundredth day after the original involuntary detention of the person unless the respondent has been discharged.

(G) Whenever possible, the probable cause hearing shall be held before the respondent is taken into custody.

(1980 H 900, eff. 7–1–80; 1974 S 336)

Library References

Mental Health ⇐40, 41.
Westlaw Topic No. 257A.
C.J.S. Insane Persons § 48 to 49, 54, 59 to 64, 66 to 70.

5123.76 Conduct of hearing; respondent's rights; disposition; post–admission rights

(A) The full hearing shall be conducted in a manner consistent with the procedures outlined in this chapter and with due process of law. The hearing shall be held by a judge of the probate division or, upon transfer by the judge of the probate division, by another judge of the court of common pleas, or a referee designated by the judge of the probate division. Any referee designated by the judge of the probate division must be an attorney.

(1) The following shall be made available to counsel for the respondent:

(a) All relevant documents, information, and evidence in the custody or control of the state or prosecutor;

(b) All relevant documents, information, and evidence in the custody or control of the institution, facility, or program in which the respondent currently is held or in which the respondent has been held pursuant to these proceedings;

(c) With the consent of the respondent, all relevant documents, information, and evidence in the custody or control of any institution or person other than the state.

(2) The respondent has the right to be represented by counsel of the respondent's choice and has the right to attend the hearing except if unusual circumstances of compelling medical necessity exist that render the respondent unable to attend and the respondent has not expressed a desire to attend.

(3) If the respondent is not represented by counsel and the court determines that the conditions specified in division (A)(2) of this section justify the respondent's absence and the right to counsel has not been validly waived, the court shall appoint counsel forthwith to represent the respondent at the hearing, reserving the right to tax costs of appointed counsel to the respondent unless it is shown that the respondent is indigent. If the court appoints counsel, or if the court determines that the evidence relevant to the respondent's absence does not justify the absence, the court shall continue the case.

(4) The respondent shall be informed of the right to retain counsel, to have independent expert evaluation, and, if an indigent person, to be represented by court appointed counsel and have expert independent evaluation at court expense.

(5) The hearing may be closed to the public unless counsel for the respondent requests that the hearing be open to the public.

(6) Unless objected to by the respondent, the respondent's counsel, or the designee of the director of mental retardation and developmental disabilities, the court, for good cause shown, may admit persons having a legitimate interest in the proceedings.

(7) The affiant under section 5123.71 of the Revised Code shall be subject to subpoena by either party.

(8) The court shall examine the sufficiency of all documents filed and shall inform the respondent, if present, and the respondent's counsel of the nature of the content of the documents and the reason for which the respondent is being held or for which the respondent's placement is being sought.

(9) The court shall receive only relevant, competent, and material evidence.

(10) The designee of the director shall present the evidence for the state. In proceedings under this chapter, the attorney general shall present the comprehensive evaluation, assessment, diagnosis, prognosis, record of habilitation and care, if any, and less restrictive habilitation plans, if any. The attorney general does not have a similar presentation responsibility in connection with a person who has been found not guilty by reason of insanity and who is the subject of a hearing under section 2945.40 of the Revised Code to determine whether the person is a mentally retarded person subject to institutionalization by court order.

(11) The respondent has the right to testify and the respondent or the respondent's counsel has the right to subpoena witnesses and documents and to present and cross-examine witnesses.

(12) The respondent shall not be compelled to testify and shall be so advised by the court.

(13) On motion of the respondent or the respondent's counsel for good cause shown, or upon the court's own motion, the court may order a continuance of the hearing.

(14) To an extent not inconsistent with this chapter, the Rules of Civil Procedure shall be applicable.

(B) Unless, upon completion of the hearing, the court finds by clear and convincing evidence that the respondent named in the affidavit is a mentally retarded person subject to institutionalization by court order, it shall order the respondent's discharge forthwith.

(C) If, upon completion of the hearing, the court finds by clear and convincing evidence that the respondent is a mentally retarded person subject to institutionalization by court order, the court may order the respondent's discharge or order the respondent, for a period not to exceed ninety days, to any of the following:

(1) A public institution, provided that commitment of the respondent to the institution will not cause the institution to exceed its licensed capacity determined in accordance with section 5123.19 of the Revised Code and provided that such a placement is indicated by the comprehensive evaluation report filed pursuant to section 5123.71 of the Revised Code;

(2) A private institution;

(3) A county mental retardation program;

(4) Receive private habilitation and care;

(5) Any other suitable facility, program, or the care of any person consistent with the comprehensive evaluation, assessment, diagnosis, prognosis, and habilitation needs of the respondent.

(D) Any order made pursuant to division (C)(2), (4), or (5) of this section shall be conditional upon the receipt by the court of consent by the facility, program, or person to accept the respondent.

(E) In determining the place to which, or the person with whom, the respondent is to be committed, the court shall consider the comprehensive evaluation, assessment, diagnosis, and projected habilitation plan for the respondent, and shall order the implementation of the least restrictive alternative available and consistent with habilitation goals.

(F) If, at any time it is determined by the director of the facility or program to which, or the person to whom, the respondent is committed that the respondent could be equally well habilitated in a less restrictive environment that is available, the following shall occur:

(1) The respondent shall be released by the director of the facility or program or by the person forthwith and referred to the court together with a report of the findings and recommendations of the facility, program, or person.

(2) The director of the facility or program or the person shall notify the respondent's counsel and the designee of the director of mental retardation and developmental disabilities.

(3) The court shall dismiss the case or order placement in the less restrictive environment.

(G)(1) Except as provided in divisions (G)(2) and (3) of this section, any person who has been committed under this section may apply at any time during the ninety-day period for voluntary admission to an institution under section 5123.69 of the Revised Code. Upon admission of a voluntary resident, the managing officer immediately shall notify the court, the respondent's counsel, and the designee of the director in writing of that fact by mail or otherwise, and, upon receipt of the notice, the court shall dismiss the case.

(2) A person who is found incompetent to stand trial or not guilty by reason of insanity and who is committed pursuant to section 2945.39, 2945.40, 2945.401, or 2945.402 of the Revised Code shall not be voluntarily admitted to an institution pursuant to division (G)(1) of this section until after the termination of the commitment, as described in division (J) of section 2945.401 of the Revised Code.

(H) If, at the end of any commitment period, the respondent has not already been discharged or has not requested voluntary admission status, the director of the facility or program, or the person to whose care the respondent has been committed, shall discharge the respondent forthwith, unless at least ten days before the expiration of that period the designee of the director of mental retardation and developmental disabilities or the prosecutor files an application with the court requesting continued commitment.

(1) An application for continued commitment shall include a written report containing a current comprehensive evaluation and assessment, a diagnosis, a prognosis, an account of progress and past habilitation, and a description of alternative habilitation settings and plans, including a habilitation setting that is the least restrictive setting consistent with the need for habilitation. A copy of the application shall be provided to respondent's counsel. The requirements for notice under section 5123.73 of the Revised Code and the provisions of divisions (A) to (E) of this section apply to all hearings on such applications.

(2) A hearing on the first application for continued commitment shall be held at the expiration of the first ninety-day period. The hearing shall be mandatory and may not be waived.

(3) Subsequent periods of commitment not to exceed one hundred eighty days each may be ordered by the court if the designee of the director of mental retardation and developmental disabilities files an application for continued commitment, after a hearing is held on the application or without a hearing if no hearing is requested and no hearing required under division (H)(4) of this section is waived. Upon the application of a person involuntarily committed under this section, supported by an affidavit of a licensed physician alleging that the person is no longer a mentally retarded person subject to institutionalization by court order, the court for good cause shown may hold a full hearing on the person's continued commitment prior to the expiration of any subsequent period of commitment set by the court.

(4) A mandatory hearing shall be held at least every two years after the initial commitment.

(5) If the court, after a hearing upon a request to continue commitment, finds that the respondent is a mentally retarded person subject to institutionalization by court order, the court may make an order pursuant to divisions (C), (D), and (E) of this section.

(I) Notwithstanding the provisions of division (H) of this section, no person who is found to be a mentally retarded person subject to institutionalization by court order pursuant to division (O)(2) of section 5123.01 of the Revised Code shall be held under involuntary commitment for more than five years.

(J) The managing officer admitting a person pursuant to a judicial proceeding, within ten working days of the admission, shall make a report of the admission to the department.

(2005 H 66, eff. 7–1–05; 2001 H 94, eff. 6–6–01; 1996 S 285, eff. 7–1–97; 1996 H 629, eff. 3–13–97; 1996 H 567, eff. 10–29–96; 1993 S 21, eff. 10–29–93; 1987 H 231; 1980 H 965, H 900, S 297; 1974 S 336)

Library References

Mental Health ⚖︎33, 41, 42, 44.
Westlaw Topic No. 257A.
C.J.S. Insane Persons § 49, 54 to 55, 57, 59 to 73.

5123.77   Temporary detention

(A) Pending removal to an institution, a person taken into custody or ordered to be institutionalized pursuant to this chapter may be held in the person's home, a certified foster home, licensed [1] rest or nursing home, a county home, or a facility used for detention, but the person shall be kept separate from persons charged with or convicted of penal offenses.

(B) Whenever any person is taken into custody under this chapter, the person in charge of the institution or facility in which that person is temporarily held under division (A) of this section immediately shall notify that person's legal guardian, spouse, or next of kin and the person's counsel, if such can be ascertained.

(2000 H 332, eff. 1–1–01; 2000 H 448, eff. 10–5–00; 1993 H 152, eff. 7–1–93; 1974 S 336)

[1] Prior and current versions differ; although no amendment to this language appeared in 2000 H 332 or 2000 H 448, "foster home, licensed" appeared as "foster home, a licensed" in 1993 H 152.

Historical and Statutory Notes

Ed. Note: The amendment of this section by 2000 H 332, eff. 1–1–01, and 2000 H 448, eff. 10–5–00, was identical. See *Baldwin's Ohio Legislative Service Annotated*, 2000, pages 6/L–2181 and 6/L–2276, or the OH–LEGIS or OH–LEGIS–OLD database on WESTLAW, for original versions of these Acts.

Library References

Mental Health ⚖︎40.
Westlaw Topic No. 257A.
C.J.S. Insane Persons § 48.

MISCELLANEOUS PROVISIONS

5123.79   Administrative discharge; review of need for institutionalization

(A) Notwithstanding a finding pursuant to section 5123.76 of the Revised Code that a person is a mentally retarded person subject to institutionalization by court order, the managing officer of an institution, with the concurrence of the chief program director, shall, except as provided in division (C) of this section, grant a discharge without the consent or the authorization of any court upon a determination that institutionalization no longer is appropriate. Upon the discharge, the managing officer of the institution shall notify the probate division of the court of common pleas that made the involuntary commitment.

(B) Upon the request of the director of a private institution, program, facility, or person having custody of a resident institutionalized pursuant to section 5123.76 of the Revised Code, or on the order of the probate division of the court of common pleas, the resident may be called for a rehearing to determine the advisability of continued institutionalization at a place within the county of resident's residence or the county where the resident is institutionalized as the probate division designates. The hearing shall be held pursuant to section 5123.76 of the Revised Code.

(1996 S 285, eff. 7–1–97; 1980 H 965, eff. 4–9–81; 1980 S 297; 1974 S 336)

Library References

Mental Health ⚖=59.1, 60.
Westlaw Topic No. 257A.
C.J.S. Insane Persons § 83 to 84.

5123.80 Trial visits

(A) When the chief program director of an institution for the mentally retarded considers that it is in the best interest of a resident, the managing officer may permit the resident to leave the institution on a trial visit. The trial visit shall be for the period of time the managing officer determines.

(B) The managing officer, upon releasing a resident on trial visit, may impose such requirements and conditions upon the resident while the resident is absent from the institution as are consistent with the habilitation plan.

(C) The managing officer of the institution from which an involuntary resident is given trial visit status may at any time revoke the trial visit if there is reason to believe that it is in the best interests of the resident to be returned to the institution.

(D) If the revocation is not voluntarily complied with, the managing officer, within five days, shall authorize any health or police officer, or sheriff to take the resident into custody and transport the resident to the institution.

(E) An involuntarily committed resident who has successfully completed one year of continuous trial visit shall be automatically discharged.

(1996 S 285, eff. 7–1–97; 1980 S 297, eff. 4–30–80; 1974 S 336)

Library References

Mental Health ⚖=58.
Westlaw Topic No. 257A.
C.J.S. Insane Persons § 101.

5123.801 Trial visit or discharge visit expenses; clothing

If neither a discharged resident, nor a resident granted trial visit, nor the persons requesting the resident's trial visit or discharge are financially able to bear the expense of the resident's trial visit or discharge, the managing officer of an institution under the control of the department of mental retardation and developmental disabilities may then provide actual traveling and escort expenses to the township of which the resident resided at the time of institutionalization. The amount payable shall be charged to the current expense fund of the institution.

The expense of the return of a resident on trial visit from an institution, if it cannot be paid by the responsible relatives, shall be borne by the county of institutionalization.

The managing officer of the institution shall provide sufficient and proper clothing for traveling if neither the resident nor the persons requesting the resident's trial visit or discharge are financially able to provide that clothing.

(2003 H 95, eff. 9–26–03; 2000 H 538, eff. 9–22–00; 1980 H 900, eff. 7–1–80)

Historical and Statutory Notes

Ed. Note: 5123.801 is former 5123.53 amended and recodified by 1980 H 900, eff. 7–1–80; 1972 H 494; 1970 H 970; 129 v 1448; 1953 H 1; GC 1890–64.

Library References

Mental Health ⚖=58, 71 to 73.
Westlaw Topic No. 257A.
C.J.S. Insane Persons § 101, 203 to 207.

5123.81 Procedure on absence without leave

When an involuntarily committed resident of an institution for the mentally retarded is absent without leave, an order shall be issued within five days after his absence requiring the resident to be taken into custody by any health or police officer, or sheriff and transported to the institution from which the resident is absent. The order may be issued by the director of mental retardation and developmental disabilities, the managing officer of the institution from which the resident is absent, or the probate judge of the county from which the resident was ordered institutionalized or in which he is found. The officer who takes the resident into custody shall immediately notify the issuer of the order.

(1980 H 900, eff. 7–1–80; 1974 S 336)

Library References

Mental Health ⚖=31.
Westlaw Topic No. 257A.
C.J.S. Insane Persons § 45, 47, 53.

5123.811 Report of removal; death

The managing officer of an institution under the control of the department of mental retardation and developmental disabilities shall immediately report the removal, death, absence without leave, discharge, or trial visit of any resident, or return of an absent without leave or visiting resident to the department, the probate judge of the county from which such resident was institutionalized, and the probate judge of the county of the residence of such resident. In case of death, the managing officer shall also notify one or more of the nearest relatives of the deceased resident, if known to him, by letter, telegram, or telephone. If the place of residence of such relative is unknown to the managing officer, immediately upon receiving notification, the probate judge shall in the speediest manner possible notify such relatives, if known to him.

The managing officer of the institution shall, upon the request of the probate judge of the county from which such resident was institutionalized or the probate judge of the county of the residence of such resident, make a report to such judge of the condition of any resident under the care, treatment, custody, or control of such managing officer.

(1980 H 965, eff. 4–9–81; 1980 H 900)

Historical and Statutory Notes

Ed. Note: 5123.811 is former 5123.56 amended and recodified by 1980 H 900, eff. 7–1–80; 1972 H 494; 1970 H 970; 129 v 1448; 125 v 823; 1953 H 1; GC 1890–67.

Library References

Asylums ⟺5.
Mental Health ⟺31.
Westlaw Topic Nos. 43, 257A.
C.J.S. Asylums and Institutional Care Facilities § 11 to 12.
C.J.S. Insane Persons § 45, 47, 53.

5123.82 Application of discharged person for additional care; outpatient care

(A) Any person who has been institutionalized under this chapter may, at any time after discharge from such institution, make application to the managing officer of any public institution for habilitation and care if such person feels he is in need of such services. If the chief program director determines the applicant to be in need of such services, the managing officer may provide such services as are required by the applicant.

(B) Any person may apply to the managing officer of any public institution for habilitation and care if such person feels he is in need of such services. If his condition warrants, he may be enrolled as an outpatient and, during such enrollment, he may receive services subject to Chapter 5121. of the Revised Code.

(C) The application prescribed in division (A) or (B) of this section may also be made on behalf of a minor by a parent, guardian, or custodian of a minor, and on behalf of an adult adjudicated incompetent by the guardian or custodian of the adult.

(D) The managing officer of the public institution may refer any discharged resident who makes an application under this section to the director of any community mental retardation program serving the county in which such resident resides, or to such other facility as the director of mental retardation and developmental disabilities may designate. Upon notice of such referral, the director of such program may provide the services required by the applicant.

(1980 H 900, eff. 7–1–80; 1974 S 336)

Library References

Mental Health ⟺59.1, 61.
Westlaw Topic No. 257A.
C.J.S. Insane Persons § 83, 85.

5123.83 Civil and employment rights

No person shall be deprived of any civil right, or public or private employment, solely by reason of his having received services, voluntarily or involuntarily, for mental retardation or a developmental disability. Any person in custody, voluntarily or involuntarily, under the provisions of this chapter, retains all rights not specifically denied him under this or any other chapter of the Revised Code.

(1990 H 569, eff. 7–1–91; 1974 S 336)

Library References

Mental Health ⟺331.
Westlaw Topic No. 257A.
C.J.S. Insane Persons § 209.

5123.84 Freedom to communicate

All residents of institutions for the mentally retarded shall be allowed to communicate freely with others, including but not restricted to the following:

(A) Receiving visitors at reasonable times;

(B) Being visited by counsel or personal physician, or both, at any reasonable time;

(C) Having reasonable access to telephones to make and receive confidential calls, including a reasonable number of free calls if unable to pay for them and assistance in calling if requested and needed;

(D) Having ready access to letter writing materials and stamps, including a reasonable number without cost if the resident is unable to pay for them, to mailing and receiving unopened correspondence, and to receiving assistance in writing if requested and needed.

(1974 S 336, eff. 7–1–75)

Library References

Mental Health ⟺31.
Westlaw Topic No. 257A.
C.J.S. Insane Persons § 45, 47, 53.

5123.85 Plans for care required

(A) All residents institutionalized pursuant to this chapter shall receive, within thirty days of their admission, a comprehensive evaluation, a diagnosis, a prognosis, and a description of habilitation goals consistent therewith.

(B) All such residents shall have a written habilitation plan consistent with the comprehensive evaluation, diagnosis, prognosis, and goals which shall be provided, upon request of resident or resident's counsel, to resident's counsel and to any private physician designated by the resident or the resident's counsel.

(C) All such residents shall receive habilitation and care consistent with the habilitation plan. The department of mental retardation and developmental disabilities shall set standards for habilitation and care provided to such residents, consistent wherever possible with standards set by the joint commission on accreditation of facilities for the mentally retarded.

(D) All such residents shall receive periodic comprehensive re-evaluations of the habilitation plan by the professional staff of the institution at intervals not to exceed ninety days.

(E) All such residents shall be provided with prompt and adequate medical treatment for any physical or mental disease or injury.

(2000 H 538, eff. 9–22–00; 1980 H 900, eff. 7–1–80; 1974 S 336)

Library References

Mental Health ⟺51.1, 51.5.
Westlaw Topic No. 257A.
C.J.S. Insane Persons § 86 to 92.

5123.851 Personal effects of discharged resident

When a resident institutionalized pursuant to this chapter is discharged from the institution, the managing officer of the institution may provide the resident with all personal items that were purchased in implementing the resident's habilitation plan established pursuant to section 5123.85 of the Revised Code. The personal items may be provided to the resident, regardless of the source of the funds that were used to purchase the items.

(2003 H 95, eff. 9–26–03)

5123.86 Knowledge essential to informed consent to procedures; exceptions; procedure in medical emergency

(A) Except as provided in divisions (C), (D), (E), and (F) of this section, the chief medical officer shall provide all information, including expected physical and medical consequences, necessary to enable any resident of an institution for the mentally retarded to give a fully informed, intelligent, and knowing consent if any of the following procedures are proposed:

(1) Surgery;

(2) Convulsive therapy;

(3) Major aversive interventions;

(4) Sterilization;

(5) Experimental procedures;

(6) Any unusual or hazardous treatment procedures.

(B) No resident shall be subjected to any of the procedures listed in division (A)(4), (5), or (6) of this section without the resident's informed consent.

(C) If a resident is physically or mentally unable to receive the information required for surgery under division (A)(1) of this section, or has been adjudicated incompetent, the information may be provided to the resident's natural or court-appointed guardian, including an agency providing guardianship services under contract with the department of mental retardation and developmental disabilities under sections 5123.55 to 5123.59 of the Revised Code, who may give the informed, intelligent, and knowing written consent for surgery. Consent for surgery shall not be provided by a guardian who is an officer or employee of the department of mental health or the department of mental retardation and developmental disabilities.

If a resident is physically or mentally unable to receive the information required for surgery under division (A)(1) of this section and has no guardian, then the information, the recommendation of the chief medical officer, and the concurring judgment of a licensed physician who is not a full-time employee of the state may be provided to the court in the county in which the institution is located, which may approve the surgery. Before approving the surgery, the court shall notify the legal rights service created by section 5123.60 of the Revised Code, and shall notify the resident of the resident's rights to consult with counsel, to have counsel appointed by the court if the resident is indigent, and to contest the recommendation of the chief medical officer.

(D) If, in the judgment of two licensed physicians, delay in obtaining consent for surgery would create a grave danger to the health of a resident, emergency surgery may be performed without the consent of the resident if the necessary information is provided to the resident's guardian, including an agency providing guardianship services under contract with the department of mental retardation and developmental disabilities under sections 5123.55 to 5123.59 of the Revised Code, or to the resident's spouse or next of kin to enable that person or agency to give an informed, intelligent, and knowing written consent.

If the guardian, spouse, or next of kin cannot be contacted through exercise of reasonable diligence, or if the guardian, spouse, or next of kin is contacted, but refuses to consent, then the emergency surgery may be performed upon the written authorization of the chief medical officer and after court approval has been obtained. However, if delay in obtaining court approval would create a grave danger to the life of the resident, the chief medical officer may authorize surgery, in writing, without court approval. If the surgery is authorized without court approval, the chief medical officer who made the authorization and the physician who performed the surgery shall each execute an affidavit describing the circumstances constituting the emergency and warranting the surgery and the circumstances warranting their not obtaining prior court approval. The affidavit shall be filed with the court with which the request for prior approval would have been filed within five court days after the surgery, and a copy of the affidavit shall be placed in the resident's file and shall be given to the guardian, spouse, or next of kin of the resident, to the hospital at which the surgery was performed, and to the legal rights service created by section 5123.60 of the Revised Code.

(E)(1) If it is the judgment of two licensed physicians, as described in division (E)(2) of this section, that a medical emergency exists and delay in obtaining convulsive therapy creates a grave danger to the life of a resident who is both mentally retarded and mentally ill, convulsive therapy may be administered without the consent of the resident if the resident is physically or mentally unable to receive the information required for convulsive therapy and if the necessary information is provided to the resident's natural or court-appointed guardian, including an agency providing guardianship services under contract with the department of mental retardation and developmental disabilities under sections 5123.55 to 5123.59 of the Revised Code, or to the resident's spouse or next of kin to enable that person or agency to give an informed, intelligent, and knowing written consent. If neither the resident's guardian, spouse, nor next of kin can be contacted through exercise of reasonable diligence, or if the guardian, spouse, or next of kin is contacted, but refuses to consent, then convulsive therapy may be performed upon the written authorization of the chief medical officer and after court approval has been obtained.

(2) The two licensed physicians referred to in division (E)(1) of this section shall not be associated with each other in the practice of medicine or surgery by means of a partnership or corporate arrangement, other business arrangement, or employment. At least one of the physicians shall be a psychiatrist as defined in division (E) of section 5122.01 of the Revised Code.

(F) Major aversive interventions shall not be used unless a resident continues to engage in behavior destructive to self or others after other forms of therapy have been attempted. The director of the legal rights service created by section 5123.60 of the Revised Code shall be notified of any proposed major aversive intervention. Major aversive interventions shall not be applied to a voluntary resident without the informed, intelligent, and knowing written consent of the resident or the resident's guardian, including an agency providing guardianship services under contract with the department of mental retardation and developmental disabilities under sections 5123.55 to 5123.59 of the Revised Code.

(G)(1) This chapter does not authorize any form of compulsory medical or psychiatric treatment of any resident who is being treated by spiritual means through prayer alone in accordance with a recognized religious method of healing.

(2) For purposes of this section, "convulsive therapy" does not include defibrillation.

(1996 H 670, eff. 12–2–96; 1980 S 209, eff. 3–23–81; 1980 H 900; 1978 S 415; 1974 S 336)

Library References

Mental Health ⇐51.5, 51.15, 57.
Westlaw Topic No. 257A.
C.J.S. Insane Persons § 8 to 13, 86 to 90, 92 to 96, 98.

5123.87 Limits on labor required of residents

(A) No resident of an institution for the mentally retarded shall be compelled to perform labor which involves the operation, support, or maintenance of the institution or for which the institution is under contract with an outside organization. Privileges or release from the institution shall not be conditional upon the performance of such labor. Residents who volunteer to perform such labor shall be compensated at a rate derived from the value of the work performed, having reference to the prevailing wage rate for comparable work or wage rates established under section 4111.06 of the Revised Code.

(B) A resident may be required to perform habilitative tasks which do not involve the operation, support, or maintenance of the institution if those tasks are an integrated part of the resident's habilitation plan and supervised by a mental retardation professional designated by the chief program director.

(C) A resident may be required to perform tasks of a personal housekeeping nature.

(1974 S 336, eff. 7–1–75)

Library References

Mental Health ⚖51.5.
Westlaw Topic No. 257A.
C.J.S. Insane Persons § 86 to 90, 92.

5123.88 Petition for writ of habeas corpus

Any person detained pursuant to this chapter shall be entitled to the writ of habeas corpus upon proper petition by himself or a friend to any court generally empowered to issue the writ of habeas corpus in the county in which the person is detained.

No person may bring a petition for a writ of habeas corpus that alleges that a person involuntarily detained pursuant to this chapter is no longer mentally retarded subject to institutionalizaton by court order unless the person shows that the release procedures of division (H) of section 5123.76 of the Revised Code are inadequate or unavailable.

(1980 H 965, eff. 4–9–81; 1974 S 336)

Library References

Habeas Corpus ⚖233.
Westlaw Topic No. 197.
C.J.S. Habeas Corpus § 132 to 135.

5123.89 Confidentiality of records; exceptions

(A) All certificates, applications, records, and reports made for the purpose of this chapter, other than court journal entries or court docket entries, which directly or indirectly identify a resident or former resident of an institution for the mentally retarded or person whose institutionalization has been sought under this chapter shall be kept confidential and shall not be disclosed by any person except in the following situations:

(1) It is the judgment of the court for judicial records, and the managing officer for institution records, that disclosure is in the best interest of the person identified, and that person or that person's guardian or, if that person is a minor, that person's parent or guardian consents.

(2) Disclosure is provided for in other sections of this chapter.

(3) It is the judgment of the managing officer for institution records that disclosure to a mental health facility is in the best interest of the person identified.

(B) The department of mental retardation and developmental disabilities shall adopt rules with respect to the systematic and periodic destruction of residents' records.

(C)(1) As used in this division, "family" means a parent, brother, sister, spouse, son, daughter, grandparent, aunt, uncle, or cousin.

(2) Upon the death of a resident or former resident of an institution for the mentally retarded or a person whose institutionalization was sought under this chapter, the managing officer of an institution shall provide access to the certificates, applications, records, and reports made for the purposes of this chapter to the resident's, former resident's, or person's guardian if the guardian makes a written request. If a deceased resident, former resident, or person whose institutionalization was sought under this chapter did not have a guardian at the time of death, the managing officer shall provide access to the certificates, applications, records, and reports made for purposes of this chapter to a member of the person's family, upon that family member's written request.

(D) No person shall reveal the contents of a record of a resident except as authorized by this chapter.

(2000 H 538, eff. 9–22–00; 1981 H 694, eff. 11–15–81; 1980 H 900; 1974 S 336)

Library References

Mental Health ⚖21.
Westlaw Topic No. 257A.
C.J.S. Insane Persons § 17 to 20.

5123.90 Duty of attorney general

The attorney general shall attend to all suits instituted on behalf of or against any public institution under the jurisdiction of the department of mental retardation and developmental disabilities and the managing officer thereof.

If a writ of habeas corpus is applied for, the clerk of the court shall give notice of the time and place of hearing to the attorney general.

(1980 H 900, eff. 7–1–80)

Historical and Statutory Notes

Ed. Note: 5123.90 is former 5123.62 amended and recodified by 1980 H 900, eff. 7–1–80; 1977 H 725; 1972 H 494; 1970 H 970; 1953 H 1; GC 1890–106.

Ed. Note: Former 5123.90 repealed by 1980 H 900, eff. 7–1–80; 1974 S 336.

Library References

Attorney General ⚖6.
Westlaw Topic No. 46.
C.J.S. Attorney General § 7 to 15.

5123.91 Immunity from liability

All persons who are not subject to any criminal provisions and who act reasonably and in good faith, either upon actual knowledge or upon information reasonably thought by them to be reliable, shall be free from any liability to a person institutionalized in institutions for the mentally retarded or to any other person in their procedural or physical assistance administered in the course of the institutionalization or discharge of a person pursuant to the provisions of this chapter.

(1974 S 336, eff. 7–1–75)

Library References

Mental Health ⚖31, 51.20.
States ⚖112(1).
Westlaw Topic Nos. 257A, 360.
C.J.S. Insane Persons § 45, 47, 53, 93 to 99.
C.J.S. States § 126, 196 to 202.

5123.92 Venue

If an affidavit alleging that a person is mentally retarded and subject to institutionalization by court order is filed, according to the provisions of section 5123.71 of the Revised Code, in the probate division of a county within the institutional district but not in the county within which the institution is located, and if such person is detained in the institution, the probate division of the county in which the institution is located shall, upon the request of the probate division receiving the affidavit, hold a hearing and make a disposition of the person in accordance with the procedures prescribed by this chapter.

(1974 S 336, eff. 7–1–75)

Library References

Mental Health ⚖=33.
Westlaw Topic No. 257A.
C.J.S. Insane Persons § 57.

5123.93 Guardianships

Minors with mental retardation shall remain under the guardianship of their parents or of a guardian appointed pursuant to Chapter 2111. of the Revised Code, notwithstanding institutionalization pursuant to any section of this chapter, unless parental rights have been terminated pursuant to a court finding that the child is neglected, abused, or dependent pursuant to Chapter 2151. of the Revised Code. If a minor with mental retardation has been found to be dependent, abused, or neglected, the public children services agency to whom permanent custody has been assigned pursuant to Chapter 2151. of the Revised Code shall have the same authority and responsibility it would have if the child were not mentally retarded and were not institutionalized. In no case shall the guardianship of a person with mental retardation be assigned to the managing officer or any other employee of an institution in which the person is institutionalized, or be assigned, unless there is a relationship by blood or marriage or unless the service is a protective service as defined in section 5123.55 of the Revised Code, to a person or agency who provides services to the person with mental retardation.

(2000 H 538, eff. 9–22–00; 1997 H 408, eff. 10–1–97; 1975 H 85, eff. 11–28–75; 1974 S 336)

Library References

Mental Health ⚖=101, 102, 104.1, 116.1.
Westlaw Topic No. 257A.
C.J.S. Insane Persons § 108 to 111, 123 to 125, 128 to 129, 143.

5123.95 Transmittal of records; patient's clothing to be provided; patient's estate; special guardian

The probate judge, upon making an order institutionalizing a person under this chapter, shall forthwith transmit copies, under his official seal, of court papers in the case, including the certificate of the expert witnesses, and of his findings in the case to the managing officer of the institution for the mentally retarded.

If not otherwise furnished, the probate judge shall see that each person institutionalized under section 5123.76 of the Revised Code is properly attired for transportation and, in addition, the institution shall be furnished a complete change of clothing for such person, which shall be paid for on the certificate of the probate judge and the order of the county auditor from the county treasury. The clothing shall be new or as good as new. The managing officer of the institution need not receive the person without such clothing.

Upon institutionalization, the managing officer of the institution to which the individual is admitted shall take possession of all money and other valuables that may be upon the person of the individual and shall, within ten days, file a list thereof with the probate judge of the county of which the individual is a resident.

If the amount of money is fifty dollars or less it shall be retained and expended by the managing officer of the institution for the benefit of the individual. Unless a guardian of the estate of the individual has already been appointed, the probate judge may, upon his own motion and without notice, appoint a special guardian of the estate of the individual. Any special guardian, before being appointed, shall file a bond approved by the probate judge in the same amount as is required by section 2109.04 of the Revised Code. A special guardian as provided for in this section, and while acting as such, shall be governed by all laws applicable to guardians of the estates of incompetents. The special guardian shall be allowed such compensation for his services as the court thinks reasonable, providing he forthwith performs all the duties incumbent upon him.

(1993 S 21, eff. 10–29–93; 1980 H 900; 1974 S 336)

Library References

Mental Health ⚖=31, 211, 212.
Westlaw Topic No. 257A.
C.J.S. Insane Persons § 45, 47, 53, 165.

5123.96 Costs, fees, and expenses of proceedings

Costs, fees, and expenses of all proceedings held under this chapter shall be paid as follows:

(A) To police and health officers, other than sheriffs or their deputies, the same fees allowed to constables, to be paid upon the approval of the probate judge;

(B) To sheriffs or their deputies, the same fees allowed for similar services in the court of common pleas;

(C) To physicians or licensed clinical psychologists acting as expert witnesses and to other expert witnesses designated by the court, an amount determined by the court;

(D) To other witnesses, the same fees and mileage as for attendance at the court of common pleas, to be paid upon the approval of the probate judge;

(E) To a person, other than the sheriff or his deputies, for taking a mentally retarded person to an institution or removing a mentally retarded person from an institution, the actual necessary expenses incurred, specifically itemized, and approved by the probate judge;

(F) To assistants who convey mentally retarded persons to institutions when authorized by the probate judge, a fee set by the probate court, provided the assistants are not drawing a salary from the state or any political subdivision of the state, and their actual necessary expenses incurred, provided that the expenses are specifically itemized and approved by the probate judge;

(G) To an attorney appointed by the probate division for an indigent who allegedly is a mentally retarded person pursuant to any section of this chapter, the fees that are determined by the probate division. When those indigent persons are before the court, all filing and recording fees shall be waived.

(H) To a referee who is appointed to conduct proceedings under this chapter that involve a respondent whose domicile is or, before his institutionalization, was not the county in which the proceedings are held, compensation as fixed by the probate division, but not more than the compensation paid for similar proceedings for respondents whose domicile is in the county in which the proceedings are held;

(I) To a court reporter appointed to make a transcript of proceedings under this chapter, the compensation and fees allowed in other cases under section 2101.08 of the Revised Code.

All costs, fees, and expenses described in this section, after payment by the county from appropriations pursuant to section 2101.11 of the Revised Code, shall be certified by the county auditor to the department of mental retardation and developmental disabilities within two months of the date the costs, fees, and expenses are incurred by the county. Payment shall be provided for by the director of budget and management upon presentation of properly verified vouchers. The director of mental retardation and developmental disabilities may adopt rules in accordance with Chapter 119. of the Revised Code to implement the payment of costs, fees, and expenses under this section.

(1992 H 427, eff. 10-8-92; 1985 H 201; 1981 H 694; 1977 H 164; 1976 H 244; 1974 S 336)

Library References

Mental Health ⚖46, 158.1, 159.
Westlaw Topic No. 257A.
C.J.S. Insane Persons § 80 to 81.

5123.97 Preservation of case record

In cases of proceedings held under this chapter, the probate judge shall file and preserve all papers filed with him and make such entries upon his docket as, together with the papers so filed, will constitute a complete record of each case determined by him.

(1974 S 336, eff. 7-1-75)

Library References

Mental Health ⚖44.
Westlaw Topic No. 257A.
C.J.S. Insane Persons § 66, 71 to 73.

5123.99 Penalties

(A) Whoever violates section 5123.20 of the Revised Code is guilty of a misdemeanor of the first degree.

(B) Whoever violates division (C), (E), or (G)(3) of section 5123.61 of the Revised Code is guilty of a misdemeanor of the fourth degree or, if the abuse or neglect constitutes a felony, a misdemeanor of the second degree. In addition to any other sanction or penalty authorized or required by law, if a person who is convicted of or pleads guilty to a violation of division (C), (E), or (G)(3) of section 5123.61 of the Revised Code is an MR/DD employee, as defined in section 5123.50 of the Revised Code, the offender shall be eligible to be included in the registry regarding misappropriation, abuse, neglect, or other specified misconduct by MR/DD employees established under section 5123.52 of the Revised Code.

(C) Whoever violates division (A) of section 5123.604 of the Revised Code is guilty of a misdemeanor of the second degree.

(D) Whoever violates division (B) of section 5123.604 of the Revised Code shall be fined not more than one thousand dollars. Each violation constitutes a separate offense.

(2004 S 178, eff. 1-30-04; 1993 S 21, eff. 10-29-93; 1986 S 322; 1985 H 66; 1980 H 900; 1978 H 870; 1977 S 71; 1970 S 367; 129 v 1448; 1953 H 1)

Library References

Penalties ⚖2, 3.
Westlaw Topic No. 295.
C.J.S. Penalties § 4 to 5.

CHAPTER 5126

COUNTY BOARDS OF MENTAL RETARDATION AND DEVELOPMENTAL DISABILITIES

ABUSED OR NEGLECTED ADULTS

Section
5126.30 Definitions
5126.31 Review of reports of abuse and neglect; provision of services
5126.311 Review of reports of abuse or neglect by other governmental entity
5126.313 Investigation of abuse or neglect
5126.32 Injunctive relief against interference with review
5126.33 Order to arrange services; complaint; notice; modification; temporary orders
5126.331 Ex parte emergency orders; authorized actions; notice
5126.332 Ex parte emergency orders; hearings
5126.333 Ex parte emergency orders; failure to seek order; notice; investigation
5126.34 Rules establishing minimum standards for training

Uncodified Law

1993 H 152, § 68.01, eff. 7-1-93, reads, in part:

Community Residential

Notwithstanding Chapters 5123. and 5126. of the Revised Code, the Department of Mental Retardation and Developmental Disabilities may develop community programs that enable persons with mental retardation and developmental disabilities to live in the community. Notwithstanding Chapter 5121. and section 5123.122 of the Revised Code, the department may waive the support collection requirements of those statutes for persons in community programs developed by the department under this section. The department shall adopt rules or may use existing rules for the implementation of these programs.

Library References

Mental Health ⚖20, 36.
Westlaw Topic No. 257A.
C.J.S. Insane Persons §§ 3, 64.

ABUSED OR NEGLECTED ADULTS

5126.30 Definitions

As used in sections 5126.30 to 5126.34 of the Revised Code:

(A) "Adult" means a person eighteen years of age or older with mental retardation or a developmental disability.

(B) "Caretaker" means a person who is responsible for the care of an adult by order of a court, including an order of guardianship, or who assumes the responsibility for the care of an adult as a volunteer, as a family member, by contract, or by the acceptance of payment for care.

(C) "Abuse" has the same meaning as in section 5123.50 of the Revised Code, except that it includes a misappropriation, as defined in that section.

(D) "Neglect" has the same meaning as in section 5123.50 of the Revised Code.

(E) "Exploitation" means the unlawful or improper act of a caretaker using an adult or an adult's resources for monetary or personal benefit, profit, or gain, including misappropriation, as defined in section 5123.50 of the Revised Code, of an adult's resources.

(F) "Working day" means Monday, Tuesday, Wednesday, Thursday, or Friday, except when that day is a holiday as defined in section 1.14 of the Revised Code.

(G) "Incapacitated" means lacking understanding or capacity, with or without the assistance of a caretaker, to make and carry out decisions regarding food, clothing, shelter, health care, or other necessities, but does not include mere refusal to consent to the provision of services.

(H) "Emergency protective services" means protective services furnished to a person with mental retardation or a developmental disability to prevent immediate physical harm.

(I) "Protective services" means services provided by the county board of mental retardation and developmental disabilities to an adult with mental retardation or a developmental disability for the prevention, correction, or discontinuance of an act of as well as conditions resulting from abuse, neglect, or exploitation.

(J) "Protective service plan" means an individualized plan developed by the county board of mental retardation and developmental disabilities to prevent the further abuse, neglect, or exploitation of an adult with mental retardation or a developmental disability.

(K) "Substantial risk" has the same meaning as in section 2901.01 of the Revised Code.

(L) "Party" means all of the following:

(1) An adult who is the subject of a probate proceeding under sections 5126.30 to 5126.33 of the Revised Code;

(2) A caretaker, unless otherwise ordered by the probate court;

(3) Any other person designated as a party by the probate court including but not limited to, the adult's spouse, custodian, guardian, or parent.

(M) "Board" means a county board of mental retardation and developmental disabilities.

(2005 S 10, eff. 9–5–05; 2004 S 178, eff. 1–30–04; 2002 S 191, eff. 3–31–03; 2000 S 171, eff. 11–22–00; 1988 H 403, eff. 3–16–89)

Library References

Mental Health ⚖101, 102.
Statutes ⚖179.
Westlaw Topic Nos. 257A, 361.
C.J.S. Insane Persons § 108 to 110, 128, 143.
C.J.S. Statutes § 306, 309.

5126.31 Review of reports of abuse and neglect; provision of services

(A) A county board of mental retardation and developmental disabilities shall review reports of abuse and neglect made under section 5123.61 of the Revised Code and reports referred to it under section 5101.611 of the Revised Code to determine whether the person who is the subject of the report is an adult with mental retardation or a developmental disability in need of services to deal with the abuse or neglect. The board shall give notice of each report to the registry office of the department of mental retardation and developmental disabilities established pursuant to section 5123.61 of the Revised Code on the first working day after receipt of the report. If the report alleges that there is a substantial risk to the adult of immediate physical harm or death, the board shall initiate review within twenty-four hours of its receipt of the report. If the board determines that the person is sixty years of age or older but does not have mental retardation or a developmental disability, it shall refer the case to the county department of job and family services. If the board determines that the person is an adult with mental retardation or a developmental disability, it shall continue its review of the case.

(B) For each review over which the board retains responsibility under division (A) of this section, it shall do all of the following:

(1) Give both written and oral notice of the purpose of the review to the adult and, if any, to the adult's legal counsel or caretaker, in simple and clear language;

(2) Visit the adult, in the adult's residence if possible, and explain the notice given under division (B)(1) of this section;

(3) Request from the registry office any prior reports concerning the adult or other principals in the case;

(4) Consult, if feasible, with the person who made the report under section 5101.61 or 5123.61 of the Revised Code and with any agencies or persons who have information about the alleged abuse or neglect;

(5) Cooperate fully with the law enforcement agency responsible for investigating the report and for filing any resulting criminal charges and, on request, turn over evidence to the agency;

(6) Determine whether the adult needs services, and prepare a written report stating reasons for the determination. No adult shall be determined to be abused, neglected, or in need of services for the sole reason that, in lieu of medical treatment, the adult relies on or is being furnished spiritual treatment through prayer alone in accordance with the tenets and practices of a church or religious denomination of which the adult is a member or adherent.

(C) The board shall arrange for the provision of services for the prevention, correction or discontinuance of abuse or neglect or of a condition resulting from abuse or neglect for any adult who has been determined to need the services and consents to receive them. These services may include, but are not limited to, service and support administration, fiscal management, medical, mental health, home health care, homemaker, legal, and residential services and the provision of temporary accommodations and necessities such as food and clothing. The services do not include acting as a guardian, trustee, or protector as defined in section 5123.55 of the Revised Code. If the provision of residential services would require expenditures by the department of mental retardation and developmental disabilities, the board shall obtain the approval of the department prior to arranging the residential services.

To arrange services, the board shall:

(1) Develop an individualized service plan identifying the types of services required for the adult, the goals for the services, and the persons or agencies that will provide them;

(2) In accordance with rules established by the director of mental retardation and developmental disabilities, obtain the consent of the adult or the adult's guardian to the provision of any of these services and obtain the signature of the adult or guardian on the individual service plan. An adult who has been found incompetent under Chapter 2111. of the Revised Code may consent to services. If the board is unable to obtain consent, it may seek, if the adult is incapacitated, a court order pursuant to section 5126.33 of the Revised Code authorizing the board to arrange these services.

(D) The board shall ensure that the adult receives the services arranged by the board from the provider and shall have the services terminated if the adult withdraws consent.

(E) On completion of a review, the board shall submit a written report to the registry office established under section 5123.61 of the Revised Code. If the report includes a finding that a person with mental retardation or a developmental disability is a victim of action or inaction that may constitute a crime under federal law or the law of this state, the board shall submit the report to the law enforcement agency responsible for investigating the report. Reports prepared under this section are not public records as defined in section 149.43 of the Revised Code.

(2002 S 191, eff. 3–31–03; 2001 H 94, eff. 6–6–01; 2000 S 171, eff. 11–22–00; 1999 H 471, eff. 7–1–00; 1988 H 403, eff. 3–16–89)

Library References

Mental Health ⇐3.1, 20, 101 to 103.
Westlaw Topic No. 257A.
C.J.S. Insane Persons § 2, 6, 14 to 16, 108 to 110, 128, 143.

5126.311 Review of reports of abuse or neglect by other governmental entity

(A) Notwithstanding the requirement of section 5126.31 of the Revised Code that a county board of mental retardation and developmental disabilities review reports of abuse and neglect, one of the following government entities, at the request of the county board or the department of mental retardation and developmental disabilities, shall review the report instead of the county board if circumstances specified in rules adopted under division (B) of this section exist:

(1) Another county board of mental retardation and developmental disabilities;

(2) The department;

(3) A regional council of government established pursuant to Chapter 167. of the Revised Code;

(4) Any other government entity authorized to investigate reports of abuse and neglect.

(B) The director of mental retardation and developmental disabilities shall adopt rules in accordance with Chapter 119. of the Revised Code specifying circumstances under which it is inappropriate for a county board to review reports of abuse and neglect.

(2001 H 94, eff. 6–6–01; 2000 H 538, eff. 9–22–00)

Library References

Mental Health ⇐20.
Westlaw Topic No. 257A.
C.J.S. Insane Persons § 14 to 16.

5126.313 Investigation of abuse or neglect

(A) After reviewing a report of abuse or neglect under section 5126.31 of the Revised Code or a report of a major unusual incident made in accordance with rules adopted under section 5123.612 of the Revised Code, a county board of mental retardation and developmental disabilities shall conduct an investigation if circumstances specified in rules adopted under division (B) of this section exist. If the circumstances specified in the rules exist, the county board shall conduct the investigation in the manner specified by the rules.

(B) The director of mental retardation and developmental disabilities shall adopt rules in accordance with Chapter 119. of the Revised Code specifying circumstances under which a county board shall conduct investigations under division (A) of this section and the manner in which the county board shall conduct the investigation.

(2001 H 94, eff. 6–6–01)

5126.32 Injunctive relief against interference with review

If during the course of the review conducted under section 5126.31 of the Revised Code or the investigation conducted under section 5126.313 of the Revised Code, any person denies or obstructs the board's access to the residence of the adult who is the subject of the review or investigation, the board may file a petition with the probate court of the county in which the residence is located for a temporary restraining order, in accordance with Civil Rule 65, to prevent the denial or obstruction of access. If the court finds reasonable cause to believe that the adult is abused or neglected and that access to the adult's residence has been denied or obstructed, the court shall issue a temporary order restraining the interference or obstruction. After the order has been obtained, at the request of the board, an officer of the law enforcement agency investigating the report shall accompany representatives of the board to the adult's residence.

If a person refuses to allow or interferes with the provision of services described in division (C) of section 5126.31 of the Revised Code to an adult who has consented to them, the county board may file a petition with the probate court of the county in which the adult resides for appropriate injunctive relief in accordance with Civil Rule 65.

(2001 H 94, eff. 6–6–01; 1988 H 403, eff. 3–16–89)

Library References

Mental Health ⇐20, 101 to 103.
Westlaw Topic No. 257A.
C.J.S. Insane Persons § 14 to 16, 108 to 110, 128, 143.

5126.33 Order to arrange services; complaint; notice; modification; temporary orders

(A) A county board of mental retardation and developmental disabilities may file a complaint with the probate court of the county in which an adult with mental retardation or a developmental disability resides for an order authorizing the board to arrange services described in division (C) of section 5126.31 of the Revised Code for that adult if the adult is eligible to receive services or support under section 5126.041 of the Revised Code and the board has been unable to secure consent. The complaint shall include:

(1) The name, age, and address of the adult;

(2) Facts describing the nature of the abuse, neglect, or exploitation and supporting the board's belief that services are needed;

(3) The types of services proposed by the board, as set forth in the protective service plan described in division (J) of section 5126.30 of the Revised Code and filed with the complaint;

(4) Facts showing the board's attempts to obtain the consent of the adult or the adult's guardian to the services.

(B) The board shall give the adult notice of the filing of the complaint and in simple and clear language shall inform the adult of the adult's rights in the hearing under division (C) of this section and explain the consequences of a court order. This notice shall be personally served upon all parties, and also shall be given to the adult's legal counsel, if any, and the legal rights service. The notice shall be given at least twenty-four hours prior to the hearing, although the court may waive this requirement upon a showing that there is a substantial risk that the adult will suffer immediate physical harm in the twenty-four hour period and that the board has made reasonable attempts to give the notice required by this division.

(C) Upon the filing of a complaint for an order under this section, the court shall hold a hearing at least twenty-four hours and no later than seventy-two hours after the notice under division (B) of this section has been given unless the court has waived the notice. All parties shall have the right to be present at the hearing, present evidence, and examine and cross-examine witnesses. The Ohio Rules of Evidence shall apply to a hearing conducted pursuant to this division. The adult shall be represented by counsel unless the court finds that the adult has made a voluntary, informed, and knowing waiver of the right to counsel. If the adult is indigent, the court shall appoint counsel to represent the adult. The board shall be represented by the county prosecutor or an attorney designated by the board.

(D)(1) The court shall issue an order authorizing the board to arrange the protective services if it finds, on the basis of clear and convincing evidence, all of the following:

(a) The adult has been abused, neglected, or exploited;

(b) The adult is incapacitated;

(c) There is a substantial risk to the adult of immediate physical harm or death;

(d) The adult is in need of the services;

(e) No person authorized by law or court order to give consent for the adult is available or willing to consent to the services.

(2) The board shall develop a detailed protective service plan describing the services that the board will provide, or arrange for the provision of, to the adult to prevent further abuse, neglect, or exploitation. The board shall submit the plan to the court for approval. The protective service plan may be changed only by court order.

(3) In formulating the order, the court shall consider the individual protective service plan and shall specifically designate the services that are necessary to deal with the abuse, neglect, or exploitation or condition resulting from abuse, neglect, or exploitation and that are available locally, and authorize the board to arrange for these services only. The court shall limit the provision of these services to a period not exceeding six months, renewable for an additional six-month period on a showing by the board that continuation of the order is necessary.

(E) If the court finds that all other options for meeting the adult's needs have been exhausted, it may order that the adult be removed from the adult's place of residence and placed in another residential setting. Before issuing that order, the court shall consider the adult's choice of residence and shall determine that the new residential setting is the least restrictive alternative available for meeting the adult's needs and is a place where the adult can obtain the necessary requirements for daily living in safety. The court shall not order an adult to a hospital or public hospital as defined in section 5122.01 or a state institution as defined in section 5123.01 of the Revised Code.

(F) The court shall not authorize a change in an adult's placement ordered under division (E) of this section unless it finds compelling reasons to justify a change. The parties to whom notice was given in division (B) of this section shall be given notice of a proposed change at least five working days prior to the change.

(G) The adult, the board, or any other person who received notice of the petition may file a motion for modification of the court order at any time.

(H) The county board shall pay court costs incurred in proceedings brought pursuant to this section. The adult shall not be required to pay for court-ordered services.

(I)(1) After the filing of a complaint for an order under this section, the court, prior to the final disposition, may enter any temporary order that the court finds necessary to protect the adult with mental retardation or a developmental disability from abuse, neglect, or exploitation including, but not limited to, the following:

(a) A temporary protection order;

(b) An order requiring the evaluation of the adult;

(c) An order requiring a party to vacate the adult's place of residence or legal settlement, provided that, subject to division (K)(1)(d) of this section, no operator of a residential facility licensed by the department may be removed under this division;

(d) In the circumstances described in, and in accordance with the procedures set forth in, section 5123.191 of the Revised Code, an order of the type described in that section that appoints a receiver to take possession of and operate a residential facility licensed by the department.

(2) The court may grant an ex parte order pursuant to this division on its own motion or if a party files a written motion or makes an oral motion requesting the issuance of the order and stating the reasons for it if it appears to the court that the best interest and the welfare of the adult require that the court issue the order immediately. The court, if acting on its own motion, or the person requesting the granting of an ex parte order, to the extent possible, shall give notice of its intent or of the request to all parties, the adult's legal counsel, if any, and the legal rights service. If the court issues an ex parte order, the court shall hold a hearing to review the order within seventy-two hours after it is issued or before the end of the next day after the day on which it is issued, whichever occurs first. The court shall give written notice of the hearing to all parties to the action.

(2004 S 178, eff. 1–30–04; 2000 S 171, eff. 11–22–00; 1988 H 403, eff. 3–16–89)

Library References

Mental Health ⚖120 to 124, 137.1.
Westlaw Topic No. 257A.
C.J.S. Insane Persons § 130 to 132.

5126.331 Ex parte emergency orders; authorized actions; notice

(A) A probate court, through a probate judge or magistrate, may issue by telephone an ex parte emergency order authorizing any of the actions described in division (B) of this section if all of the following are the case:

(1) The court receives notice from the county board of mental retardation and developmental disabilities, or an authorized employee of the board, that the board or employee believes an emergency order is needed as described in this section.

(2) The adult who is the subject of the notice is eligible to receive services or support under section 5126.041 of the Revised Code.

(3) There is reasonable cause to believe that the adult is incapacitated.

(4) There is reasonable cause to believe that there is a substantial risk to the adult of immediate physical harm or death.

(B) An order issued under this section may authorize the county board of mental retardation and developmental disabilities to do any of the following:

(1) Provide, or arrange for the provision of, emergency protective services for the adult;

(2) Remove the adult from the adult's place of residence or legal settlement;

(3) Remove the adult from the place where the abuse, neglect, or exploitation occurred.

(C) A court shall not issue an order under this section to remove an adult from a place described in division (B)(2) or (3) of this section until the court is satisfied that reasonable efforts have been made to notify the adult and any person with whom the adult resides of the proposed removal and the reasons for it, except that, the court may issue an order prior to giving the notice if one of the following is the case:

(1) Notification could jeopardize the physical or emotional safety of the adult.

(2) The notification could result in the adult being removed from the court's jurisdiction.

(D) An order issued under this section shall be in effect for not longer than twenty-four hours, except that if the day following the day on which the order is issued is a weekend-day or legal holiday, the order shall remain in effect until the next business day.

5126.331

(E)(1) Except as provided in division (E)(2) of this section, not later than twenty-four hours after an order is issued under this section, the county board or employee that provided notice to the probate court shall file a complaint with the court in accordance with division (A) of section 5126.33 of the Revised Code.

(2) If the day following the day on which the order was issued is a weekend-day or a holiday, the county board or employee shall file the complaint with the probate court on the next business day.

(3) Except as provided in section 5126.332 of the Revised Code, proceedings on the complaint filed pursuant to this division shall be conducted in accordance with section 5126.33 of the Revised Code.

(2004 S 178, eff. 1–30–04)

5126.332 Ex parte emergency orders; hearings

(A) If an order is issued pursuant to section 5126.331 of the Revised Code, the court shall hold a hearing not later than twenty-four hours after the issuance to determine whether there is probable cause for the order, except that if the day following the day on which the order is issued is a weekend-day or legal holiday, the court shall hold the hearing on the next business day.

(B) At the hearing, the court:

(1) Shall consider the adult's choice of residence and determine whether protective services are the least restrictive alternative available for meeting the adult's needs;

(2) May issue temporary orders to protect the adult from immediate physical harm, including, but not limited to, temporary protection orders, evaluations, and orders requiring a party to vacate the adult's place of residence or legal settlement;

(3) May order emergency protective services.

(C) A temporary order issued pursuant to division (B)(2) of this section is effective for thirty days. The court may renew the order for an additional thirty-day period.

(2004 S 178, eff. 1–30–04)

5126.333 Ex parte emergency orders; failure to seek order; notice; investigation

Any person who has reason to believe that there is a substantial risk to an adult with mental retardation or a developmental disability of immediate physical harm or death and that the responsible county board of mental retardation and developmental disabilities has failed to seek an order pursuant to section 5126.33 or 5126.331 of the Revised Code may notify the department of mental retardation and developmental disabilities. Within twenty-four hours of receipt of such notice, the department shall cause an investigation to be conducted regarding the notice. The department shall provide assistance to the county board to provide for the health and safety of the adult as permitted by law.

(2004 S 178, eff. 1–30–04)

5126.34 Rules establishing minimum standards for training

Each county board of mental retardation and developmental disabilities shall provide comprehensive, formal training for county board employees and other persons authorized to implement sections 5126.30 to 5126.34 of the Revised Code.

The department of mental retardation and developmental disabilities shall adopt rules establishing minimum standards for the training provided by county boards pursuant to this section. The training provided by the county boards shall meet the minimum standards prescribed by the rules.

(2002 S 191, eff. 3–31–03)

Historical and Statutory Notes

Ed. Note: 5126.34 is former 5126.312, amended and recodified by 2002 S 191, eff. 3–31–03; 2000 H 538, eff. 9–22–00.

Library References

Mental Health ⬅20, 101 to 103.
Westlaw Topic No. 257A.
C.J.S. Insane Persons § 14 to 16, 108 to 110, 128, 143.

CHAPTER 5302

STATUTORY FORMS OF LAND CONVEYANCE

SURVIVORSHIP

Section
5302.17 Survivorship deed
5302.171 Successor trustee to file affidavit
5302.20 Survivorship tenancy; creation; effects; characteristics; termination; liens; change of tenants' relationship; former deeds unaffected
5302.21 Persons not required to create survivorship tenancy
5302.22 Transfer on death deed
5302.23 Characteristics and ramifications of real property subject to transfer on death beneficiary designation

SURVIVORSHIP

5302.17 Survivorship deed

A deed conveying any interest in real property to two or more persons, and in substance following the form set forth in this section, when duly executed in accordance with Chapter 5301. of the Revised Code, creates a survivorship tenancy in the grantees, and upon the death of any of the grantees, vests the interest of the decedent in the survivor, survivors, or the survivor's or survivors' separate heirs and assigns.

"SURVIVORSHIP DEED

_____ (marital status), of _____ County, _____ for valuable consideration paid, grant(s), (covenants, if any), to _____ (marital status) and _____ (marital status), for their joint lives, remainder to the survivor of them, whose tax-mailing addresses are _____, the following real property:

(description of land or interest therein and encumbrances, reservations, and exceptions, if any)

Prior Instrument Reference: _____

_____, wife (husband) of the grantor, releases all rights of dower therein.

Executed this ____ day of _____.

_____
(Signature of Grantor)

(Execution in accordance with Chapter 5301. of the Revised Code)"

Any persons who are the sole owners of real property, prior to April 4, 1985, as tenants with a right of survivorship under the common or statutory law of this state or as tenants in common may create in themselves and in any other person or persons a survivorship tenancy in the real property by executing a deed as provided in this section conveying their entire, separate interests in the real property to themselves and to the other person or persons.

Except as otherwise provided in this section, when a person holding real property as a survivorship tenant dies, the transfer of the interest of the decedent may be recorded by presenting to the county auditor and filing with the county recorder either a certificate of transfer as provided in section 2113.61 of the Revised Code, or an affidavit accompanied by a certified copy of a death certificate. The affidavit shall recite the names of the other survivorship tenant or tenants, the address of the other survivorship tenant or tenants, the date of death of the decedent, and a description of the real property. The county recorder shall make index reference to any certificate or affidavit so filed in the record of deeds. When a person holding real property as a survivorship tenant dies and the title to the property is registered pursuant to Chapter 5309. of the Revised Code, the procedure for the transfer of the interest of the decedent shall be pursuant to section 5309.081 of the Revised Code.

(2002 H 470, eff. 2–1–02; 2001 H 279, eff. 2–1–02; 1992 H 280, eff. 8–19–92; 1984 S 201; 1973 H 571; 1971 H 878)

Historical and Statutory Notes

Amendment Note: 2002 H 470 rewrote the execution clause of the form, which prior thereto read:

"Executed before me on ____ day of _____ by _____, who, under penalty of perjury in violation of section 2921.11 of the Revised Code, represented to me to be said person.

_____

(Signature of Judge or Officer

Taking the Acknowledgment)

"(Execution in accordance with Chapter 5301. of the Revised Code)"

Amendment Note: 2001 H 279 made changes to reflect gender neutral language; and rewrote the execution portion of the survivorship deed form, which prior thereto read:

"Witness ____ hand this ____ day of ____.

"(Execution in accordance with Chapter 5301. of the Revised Code)".

Library References

Deeds ⚖29.
Westlaw Topic No. 120.
C.J.S. Deeds § 22.

5302.171 Successor trustee to file affidavit

Upon the death, resignation, removal, or other event terminating the appointment of a trustee of a trust, which trustee holds title to real property, the successor trustee or any co-trustee of the trust shall file with the county auditor and the county recorder of the county in which the real property is located, as soon as is practical, an affidavit reciting the name of the immediately preceding trustee and any co-trustees, the addresses of all trustees, a reference to the deed or other instrument vesting title in the trustees, and a legal description of the real property. The affidavit shall be indexed and recorded in the record of deeds.

The affidavit described in this section shall not be required if the original trust instrument naming the trustees and successors and containing relevant facts pertaining to the succession of trustees, or if a memorandum of trust in compliance with section 5301.255 of the Revised Code that contains relevant facts pertaining to the succession of trustees, is recorded in the office of the county recorder.

Failure to file the affidavit required by this section does not affect title to real property in the one or more trustees.

(1996 S 262, eff. 3–18–97; 1996 S 158, eff. 5–8–96)

Historical and Statutory Notes

Amendment Note: 1996 S 262 rewrote this section, which prior thereto read:

"When a trustee of a trust that owns real property ceases to be a trustee of that trust due to death, resignation, or any other reason, the successor trustee or a co-trustee, within thirty days from the death, resignation, or other terminating event of the prior trustee, shall present to the county auditor and file with the county recorder an affidavit, accompanied by a certified copy of a death certificate in the case of death of the trustee. The affidavit shall recite the name of the trustee that served immediately prior to the successor trustee, the name of any other trustee or trustees, the addresses of all trustees, and a description of the real property. The county recorder shall make index reference to any affidavit so filed in the record of deeds."

5302.20 Survivorship tenancy; creation; effects; characteristics; termination; liens; change of tenants' relationship; former deeds unaffected

(A) Except as provided in section 5302.21 of the Revised Code, if any interest in real property is conveyed or devised to two or more persons for their joint lives and then to the survivor or survivors of them, those persons hold title as survivorship tenants, and the joint interest created is a survivorship tenancy. Any deed or will containing language that shows a clear intent to create a survivorship tenancy shall be liberally construed to do so. The use of the word "or" between the names of two or more grantees or devisees does not by itself create a survivorship tenancy but shall be construed and interpreted as if the word "and" had been used between the names.

(B) If two or more persons hold an interest in the title to real property as survivorship tenants, each survivorship tenant holds an equal share of the title during their joint lives unless otherwise provided in the instrument creating the survivorship tenancy. Upon the death of any of them, the title of the decedent vests proportionately in the surviving tenants as survivorship tenants. This is the case until only one survivorship tenant remains alive, at which time the survivor is fully vested with title to the real property as the sole title holder. If the last two or more survivorship tenants die under such circumstances that the survivor cannot be determined, title passes as if those last survivors had been tenants in common.

(C) A survivorship tenancy has the following characteristics or ramifications:

(1) Unless otherwise provided in the instrument creating the survivorship tenancy, each of the survivorship tenants has an equal right to share in the use, occupancy, and profits, and each of the survivorship tenants is subject to a proportionate share of the costs related to the ownership and use of the real property subject to the survivorship tenancy.

(2) A conveyance from all of the survivorship tenants to any other person or from all but one of the survivorship tenants to the remaining survivorship tenant terminates the survivorship tenancy and vests title in the grantee. A conveyance from any survivorship tenant, or from any number of survivorship tenants that is from less than all of them, to a person who is not a survivorship tenant vests the title of the grantor or grantors in the grantee, conditioned on the survivorship of the grantor or grantors of the conveyance, and does not alter the interest in the title of any of the other survivorship tenants who do not join in the conveyance.

(3) A fee simple title, leasehold interest, or land contract vendee's interest in real property or any fractional interest in any of these interests may be subjected to a survivorship tenancy.

(4) A creditor of a survivorship tenant may enforce a lien against the interest of one or more survivorship tenants by an action to marshall liens against the interest of the debtor or debtors. Every person with an interest in or lien against the interest of the debtor or debtors shall be made a party to the action. Upon a determination by the court that a party or cross-claimant has a valid lien against the interest of a survivorship tenant, the title to the real property ceases to be a survivorship tenancy and becomes a tenancy in common. Each tenant in common of that nature then holds an undivided share in the title. The interest of each tenant in common of that nature shall be equal unless otherwise provided in the instrument creating the survivorship tenancy. The court then may order the sale of the fractional interest of the lien debtor or debtors as on execution, and the proceeds of the sale shall be applied to pay the lien creditors in the order of their priority.

(5) If the entire title to a parcel of real property is held by two survivorship tenants who are married to each other and the marriage is terminated by divorce, annulment, or dissolution of marriage, the title, except as provided in this division, immediately ceases to be a survivorship tenancy and becomes a tenancy in common. Each tenant in common of that nature holds an undivided interest in common in the title to the real property, unless the judgment of divorce, annulment, or dissolution of marriage expressly states that the survivorship tenancy shall continue after termination of the marriage. The interest of each tenant in common of that nature shall be equal unless otherwise provided in the instrument creating the survivorship tenancy or in the judgment of divorce, annulment, or dissolution of marriage.

If a survivorship tenancy includes one or more survivorship tenants in addition to a husband and wife whose marriage is terminated by divorce, annulment, or dissolution of marriage, the survivorship tenancy is not affected by the divorce, annulment, or dissolution of marriage unless the court alters the interest of the survivorship tenants whose marriage has been terminated.

(1995 H 378, eff. 3–11–96; 1984 S 201, eff. 4–4–85)

Historical and Statutory Notes

Amendment Note: 1995 H 378 inserted "unless otherwise provided in the instrument creating the survivorship tenancy", "of the decedent", and "proportionately", in division (B); inserted "unless otherwise provided in the instrument creating the survivorship tenancy", and "of the survivorship tenants" before "is subject to", in division (C)(1); deleted "equal" before "undivided share" and added the fifth sentence in division (C)(4); substituted "undivided interest" for "equal undivided half interest", changed "dissolution" to "dissolution of marriage" throughout, and added the third sentence in division (C)(5); and made other nonsubstantive changes.

Library References

Tenancy in Common ⇒3.
Westlaw Topic No. 373.
C.J.S. Tenancy in Common §§ 7 to 10.

5302.21 Persons not required to create survivorship tenancy

(A) Sections 5302.17 to 5302.20 of the Revised Code do not affect deeds that were executed and recorded prior to the effective date of this section and that created a tenancy by the entireties in a husband and wife pursuant to section 5302.17 of the Revised Code as it existed prior to the effective date of this section. If spouses covered by such deeds are tenants by the entireties on the day prior to the effective date of this section, such deeds continue to be valid on and after such effective date, and, unless they choose to do so, the spouses do not have to prepare a deed, as described in section 5302.17 of the Revised Code as effective on the effective date of this section, creating in themselves a survivorship tenancy.

(B) Sections 5302.17 to 5302.20 of the Revised Code do not affect conveyances or devises of real property to two or more persons for their joint lives and then to the survivor or survivors of them, that occurred prior to the effective date of this section and that did not involve tenancies by the entireties. These conveyances and devises, if they are valid on the effective date of this section, continue to be valid on and after that date. Unless persons so holding property choose to do so, they do not have to prepare a deed, as described in section 5302.17 of the Revised Code as effective on the effective date of this section, creating in themselves a survivorship tenancy.

(1984 S 201, eff. 4–4–85)

Library References

Tenancy in Common ⇒2.
Westlaw Topic No. 373.
C.J.S. Tenancy in Common § 4 et seq.

5302.22 Transfer on death deed

(A) A deed conveying any interest in real property, and in substance following the form set forth in this division, when duly executed in accordance with Chapter 5301. of the Revised Code and recorded in the office of the county recorder, creates a present interest as sole owner or as a tenant in common in the grantee and creates a transfer on death interest in the beneficiary or beneficiaries. Upon the death of the grantee, the deed vests the interest of the decedent in the beneficiary or beneficiaries. The deed described in this division shall in substance conform to the following form:

"Transfer on Death Deed

_____ (marital status), of _____ County, _____ (for valuable consideration paid, if any), grant(s) (with covenants, if any), to _____ whose tax mailing address is _____, transfer on death to _____, beneficiary(s), the following real property:

(Description of land or interest in land and encumbrances, reservations, and exceptions, if any.)

Prior Instrument Reference: _____

_____, wife (husband) of the grantor, releases all rights of dower therein.

Executed this _____ day of _____.

_____

(Signature of Grantor)

(Execution in accordance with Chapter 5301. of the Revised Code)"

(B) Any person who, under the Revised Code or the common law of this state, owns real property or any interest in real property as a sole owner or as a tenant in common may create an interest in the real property transferable on death by executing and recording a deed as provided in this section conveying the person's entire, separate interest in the real property to one or more individuals, including the grantor, and designating one or more other persons, identified in the deed by name, as transfer on death beneficiaries.

A deed conveying an interest in real property that includes a transfer on death beneficiary designation need not be supported by consideration and need not be delivered to the transfer on death beneficiary to be effective.

(C) Upon the death of any individual who owns real property or an interest in real property that is subject to a transfer on death beneficiary designation made under a transfer on death deed as provided in this section, the deceased owner's interest shall be transferred only to the transfer on death beneficiaries who are identified in the deed by name and who survive the deceased owner or that are in existence on the date of death of the deceased owner. The transfer of the deceased owner's interest shall be recorded by presenting to the county auditor and filing with the county recorder an affidavit, accompanied by a certified copy of a death certificate for the deceased owner. The affidavit shall recite the name and address of each designated transfer on death beneficiary who survived the deceased owner or that is in existence on the date of the deceased owner's death, the date of the deceased owner's death, a description of the subject real property or interest in real property, and the names of each designated transfer on death beneficiary who has not survived the deceased owner or that is not in existence on the date of the deceased owner's death. The affidavit shall be accompanied by a certified copy of a death certificate for each designated transfer on death beneficiary who has not survived the deceased owner. The county recorder shall make an index reference to any affidavit so filed in the record of deeds.

Upon the death of any individual holding real property or an interest in real property that is subject to a transfer on death beneficiary designation made under a transfer on death deed as provided in this section, if the title to the real property is registered pursuant to Chapter 5309. of the Revised Code, the procedure for the transfer of the interest of the deceased owner shall be pursuant to section 5309.081 of the Revised Code.

(2002 H 470, eff. 2–1–02; 2001 H 279, eff. 2–1–02; 2000 H 313, eff. 8–29–00)

Historical and Statutory Notes

Amendment Note: 2002 H 470 rewrote the execution clause of the form, which prior thereto read:

"Executed before me on _____ day of _____ by _____, who, under penalty of perjury in violation of section 2921.11 of the Revised Code, represented to me to be said person.

_____

(Signature of Judge or Officer

Taking the Acknowledgment)

"(Execution in accordance with Chapter 5301. of the Revised Code)"

Amendment Note: 2001 H 279 rewrote the execution portion of the transfer on death deed form, which prior thereto read:

"Witness _____ hand this _____ day of _____.

"(Execution in accordance with Chapter 5301. of the Revised Code)".

5302.23 Characteristics and ramifications of real property subject to transfer on death beneficiary designation

(A) Any deed containing language that shows a clear intent to designate a transfer on death beneficiary shall be liberally construed to do so.

(B) Real property or an interest in real property that is subject to a transfer on death beneficiary designation as provided in section 5302.22 of the Revised Code or as described in division (A) of this section has all of the following characteristics and ramifications:

(1) An interest of a deceased owner shall be transferred to the transfer on death beneficiaries who are identified in the deed by name and who survive the deceased owner or that are in existence on the date of the deceased owner's death. If there is a designation of more than one transfer on death beneficiary, the beneficiaries shall take title in the interest in equal shares as tenants in common. If a transfer on death beneficiary does not survive the deceased owner or is not in existence on the date of the deceased owner's death, and the deceased owner has designated one or more persons as contingent transfer on death beneficiaries as provided in division (B)(2) of this section, the designated contingent transfer on death beneficiaries shall take the same interest that would have passed to the transfer on death beneficiary had that transfer on death beneficiary survived the deceased owner or been in existence on the date of the deceased owner's death. If none of the designated transfer on death beneficiaries survives the deceased owner or is in existence on the date of the deceased owner's death and no contingent transfer on death beneficiaries have been designated or have survived the deceased owner, the interest of the deceased owner shall be distributed as part of the probate estate of the deceased owner of the interest.

(2) A transfer on death deed may contain a designation of one or more persons as contingent transfer on death beneficiaries, who shall take the interest of the deceased owner that would otherwise have passed to the designated transfer on death beneficiary if that named designated transfer on death beneficiary does not survive the deceased owner or is not in existence on the date of death of the deceased owner. Persons designated as contingent transfer on death beneficiaries shall be identified in the deed by name.

(3) The designation of a transfer on death beneficiary has no effect on the present ownership of real property, and a person designated as a transfer on death beneficiary has no interest in the real property until the death of the owner of the interest.

(4) The designation in a deed of any transfer on death beneficiary may be revoked or changed at any time, without the consent of that designated transfer on death beneficiary, by the owner of the interest by executing in accordance with Chapter 5301. of the Revised Code and recording a deed conveying the grantor's entire, separate interest in the real property to one or more persons, including the grantor, with or without the designation of another transfer on death beneficiary.

(5) A fee simple title or any fractional interest in a fee simple title may be subjected to a transfer on death beneficiary designation.

(6) A designated transfer on death beneficiary takes only the interest that the deceased owner or owners held on the date of death, subject to all encumbrances, reservations, and exceptions.

(7) No rights of any lienholder, including, but not limited to, any mortgagee, judgment creditor, or mechanic's lien holder, shall be affected by the designation of a transfer on death beneficiary pursuant to this section and section 5302.22 of the Revised Code. If any lienholder takes action to enforce the lien, by foreclosure or otherwise through a court proceeding, it is not necessary to join the transfer on death beneficiary as a party defendant in the action unless the transfer on death beneficiary has another interest in the real property that is currently vested.

(8) Any transfer on death of real property or of an interest in real property that results from a deed designating a transfer on death beneficiary is not testamentary.

(2000 H 313, eff. 8–29–00)

CHAPTER 5305

DOWER

GENERAL PROVISIONS

Section
5305.01 Assignment of dower
5305.02 Petition for dower
5305.03 Encumbrances presented
5305.04 Land situated in different counties
5305.05 Death of plaintiff before assignment
5305.06 Appointment of commissioners to assign dower
5305.07 Proceedings upon return of assignment of dower
5305.08 Assignment of dower when estate indivisible
5305.09 Timberlands or other unimproved lands or lots
5305.10 Election by owner of lands to pay value of dower
5305.11 Dower during pendency of petition
5305.12 Exemptions in estimating yearly value of dower
5305.13 Minor heir not to be prejudiced by collusive assignment of dower
5305.14 Costs
5305.15 Surviving spouse may elect to be endowed out of proceeds of sale
5305.16 Election by answer is a release of dower

DOWER OF INSANE SPOUSE

5305.17 Guardian may elect for surviving spouse
5305.18 Petition to discharge land of dower of insane person
5305.19 Inquest of lunacy
5305.20 Proceedings on report of inquest of lunacy
5305.21 Dower of insane person may be barred
5305.22 Real estate may be conveyed free from dower if spouse insane

GENERAL PROVISIONS

5305.01 Assignment of dower

When the lands of a deceased person are not encumbered by mortgage, or by judgment obtained against such decedent during life, the heir, guardian of an heir, or other person having the next immediate estate of inheritance, may assign in writing to the surviving spouse, dower therein, particularly describing such estate, which, if approved in writing on the deed of assignment by the probate judge of the county, and also by the probate judge of the county appointing such guardian, and accepted by such spouse, in writing thereon, shall be a valid assignment.

(1953 H 1, eff. 10–1–53; GC 12004)

Historical and Statutory Notes

Pre–1953 H 1 Amendments: RS 5707

Library References

Dower and Curtesy ☞1, 65.
Westlaw Topic No. 136.
C.J.S. Curtesy §§ 1, 2.
C.J.S. Dower §§ 79 to 81.

5305.02 Petition for dower

A surviving spouse may file a petition for dower in the court of common pleas, against the heir, or other person having the next immediate estate of inheritance or other estate or interest therein, setting forth the right thereto, and describing the tracts of land in which dower is claimed. On the hearing the court shall render such judgment as appears just and consistent with the rights of the parties interested.

(1953 H 1, eff. 10–1–53; GC 12005)

Historical and Statutory Notes

Pre–1953 H 1 Amendments: RS 5708

Library References

Dower and Curtesy ☞70.1.
Westlaw Topic No. 136.

5305.03 Encumbrances presented

When the rights of a lessee or lienor are shown by cross-petition filed before judgment, such rights and liens shall be regarded by the court of common pleas, and no inequality shall be allowed or injustice done to such lessee or lienor.

(1953 H 1, eff. 10–1–53; GC 12006)

Historical and Statutory Notes

Pre–1953 H 1 Amendments: RS 5709

Library References

Dower and Curtesy ☞23.
Westlaw Topic No. 136.
C.J.S. Curtesy § 1.

5305.04 Land situated in different counties

When the lands in which dower is claimed lie in several counties, the petition for dower may be filed by the surviving spouse in any county in which a part of the estate is situated. The court of common pleas of such county has complete jurisdiction, and may order the whole dower of such spouse to be assigned in one or more of such counties, and out of one or more of such tracts of land, if it may be done without prejudice to the rights of any person claiming title to or holding a lien on the land.

(1953 H 1, eff. 10–1–53; GC 12007)

Historical and Statutory Notes

Pre–1953 H 1 Amendments: RS 5710

Library References

Dower and Curtesy ☞70.1.
Westlaw Topic No. 136.

5305.05 Death of plaintiff before assignment

When a plaintiff in an action to assign dower dies before the assignment, or before entry of the final judgment, the action may be revived in the name of the executor or administrator. The court of common pleas shall determine, if not before decided, whether the plaintiff was entitled to dower in such action. If the plaintiff was so entitled, the court shall adjudge in favor of such executor or administrator a sum equal to one third of the rental value of the real estate in which the plaintiff was entitled to dower, from the filing of the petition until death, after deducting one third of the necessary expenses. The sum so adjudged in favor of such executor or administrator is a lien upon such real estate, and its payment may be enforced by sale as upon execution.

(1953 H 1, eff. 10–1–53; GC 12008)

Historical and Statutory Notes

Pre–1953 H 1 Amendments: RS 5711

Library References

Abatement and Revival ⚖︎52.
Westlaw Topic No. 2.
C.J.S. Abatement and Revival §§ 130 to 154.

5305.06 Appointment of commissioners to assign dower

When dower is adjudged, the court of common pleas shall appoint three judicious, disinterested men of the county in which the action to assign dower is pending, who are not of kin to either of the parties interested, to be commissioners. The court shall issue its order to the sheriff of that county, commanding him that by the oaths of the commissioners which may be administered by him, he cause such dower to be set off and assigned to the plaintiff in the manner set forth in the judgment.

(1953 H 1, eff. 10–1–53; GC 12009)

Historical and Statutory Notes

Pre–1953 H 1 Amendments: RS 5712

Library References

Dower and Curtesy ⚖︎82.
Westlaw Topic No. 136.
C.J.S. Dower §§ 85, 97.

5305.07 Proceedings upon return of assignment of dower

The commissioners provided for in section 5305.06 of the Revised Code and the sheriff shall obey the order to assign dower, and return their proceedings thereon to the court of common pleas at such time as it appoints. If the court approves the assignment, it shall be entered on its records, and thenceforth the assignment is valid. Thereupon execution shall be issued, directing the sheriff to put the surviving spouse in full possession of the dower assigned.

(1953 H 1, eff. 10–1–53; GC 12010)

Historical and Statutory Notes

Pre–1953 H 1 Amendments: RS 5713

Library References

Dower and Curtesy ⚖︎97.
Westlaw Topic No. 136.
C.J.S. Dower § 105.

5305.08 Assignment of dower when estate indivisible

When an estate of which a surviving spouse is dowable is entire, and no division of it can be made by metes and bounds, dower shall be assigned as of a third part of the rents, issues, and profits thereof, to be computed and ascertained by the commissioners provided for in section 5305.06 of the Revised Code.

(1953 H 1, eff. 10–1–53; GC 12011)

Historical and Statutory Notes

Pre–1953 H 1 Amendments: RS 5714

Library References

Dower and Curtesy ⚖︎83.
Westlaw Topic No. 136.
C.J.S. Curtesy § 14.

5305.09 Timberlands or other unimproved lands or lots

When an estate of which a surviving spouse is dowable, or in which such spouse owns a dower interest assigned to or vested in such spouse, consists in whole or in part of timberlands or other unimproved lands or lots, the commissioners, appointed as provided in section 5305.06 of the Revised Code, shall return to the court of common pleas a true appraisement of such lands in money, and also a true appraisement of their annual rental value. Upon the hearing of such report, if it appears to the court that the assignment of dower in such lands, either by metes and bounds, or as of the rents, issues, and profits, cannot be or has not been made so as to provide such surviving spouse with an income from the lands or lots so charged commensurate with their value, as fixed by such commissioners, the court shall determine the value of such dower in money, and make an order directing the sheriff to advertise and sell such lands, or so much thereof as is necessary, as upon execution. The sheriff shall not cause the lands to be appraised, but their value as returned by the commissioners shall be the appraised value, and they shall not be sold for less than two thirds of that value. Upon the confirmation of such sale, the court shall order the payment to the surviving spouse out of the money arising therefrom the value of the dower so determined by it.

(1953 H 1, eff. 10–1–53; GC 12012)

Historical and Statutory Notes

Pre–1953 H 1 Amendments: RS 5714a

Library References

Dower and Curtesy ⚖︎83.
Westlaw Topic No. 136.
C.J.S. Curtesy § 14.

5305.10 Election by owner of lands to pay value of dower

The person owning lands or lots mentioned in section 5305.09 of the Revised Code, at the time the order for the sale of such lands is made, may elect to pay to the surviving spouse the value of the dower. If such payment is made within ten days or such further reasonable time as the court of common pleas grants not exceeding ninety days from such election, the court shall make a decree divesting such spouse of any interest by way of dower in such lands. A surviving spouse owning a dower interest in timber lands or other unimproved lots or lands assigned to or vested in such spouse may maintain an action for relief in accordance with section 5305.09 of the Revised Code.

(1953 H 1, eff. 10–1–53; GC 12013)

Historical and Statutory Notes

Pre–1953 H 1 Amendments: RS 5714a

Library References

Dower and Curtesy ⚖︎95.
Westlaw Topic No. 136.
C.J.S. Dower § 103.

5305.11 Dower during pendency of petition

When the commissioners provided for in section 5305.06 of the Revised Code have set off and assigned dower, they shall make a true appraisement of the yearly value, after deducting necessary expenses, of the real estate in which the surviving spouse is entitled to dower, estimating such value from the day of filing the petition for dower to the day of assigning dower, and return such appraisement and assignment. The court of common pleas shall adjudge the payment of one third of the whole sum so returned to the surviving spouse out of the real estate not covered by the dower, upon which judgment execution may issue. This section does not require execution to be issued against such of the defendants in dower as are minors. In such cases the dower shall operate as a lien upon the real estate, for their proportion of the judgment, until it is paid.

(1953 H 1, eff. 10–1–53; GC 12014)

Historical and Statutory Notes

Pre–1953 H 1 Amendments: RS 5715

5305.12 Exemptions in estimating yearly value of dower

In making the appraisement of the yearly value of the real estate provided for in section 5305.11 of the Revised Code, the commissioners must exclude all permanent or valuable improvements made thereon after the deceased consort of the surviving spouse ceased to be its owner.

(1953 H 1, eff. 10–1–53; GC 12015)

Historical and Statutory Notes

Pre–1953 H 1 Amendments: RS 5716

Library References

Dower and Curtesy ⚖104.
Westlaw Topic No. 136.
C.J.S. Curtesy § 13.

5305.13 Minor heir not to be prejudiced by collusive assignment of dower

During the minority of an heir, if dower is assigned to a surviving spouse not entitled thereto, or, if such dower was recovered by the default, fraud, or collusion of the guardian, such heir, on coming of age, may have an action against such spouse to recover the lands wrongfully awarded.

(1953 H 1, eff. 10–1–53; GC 12016)

Historical and Statutory Notes

Pre–1953 H 1 Amendments: RS 5717

Library References

Infants ⚖31(1).
Westlaw Topic No. 211.
C.J.S. Infants §§ 128 to 140.

5305.14 Costs

If the petition of a person claiming dower is contested, and the court of common pleas finds that such person is entitled to dower as claimed therein, the defendant so contesting shall pay all costs of the suit. If the petition is not contested, the plaintiff shall pay one third, and the legal owner of the real estate two thirds of the costs.

(1953 H 1, eff. 10–1–53; GC 12017)

Historical and Statutory Notes

Pre–1953 H 1 Amendments: RS 5718

Library References

Costs ⚖79, 102.
Westlaw Topic No. 102.
C.J.S. Costs § 46.

5305.15 Surviving spouse may elect to be endowed out of proceeds of sale

In actions for partition, when an estate cannot be divided, and is ordered to be sold, and in actions for the sale of real estate by executors, administrators, guardians, and assignees, acting under a general assignment for the benefit of creditors, and in all other actions and proceedings in which the court orders the sale of real estate to satisfy a judgment or decree, the surviving spouse who has a dower interest in such real estate, and is a party, may file an answer, waive the assignment of dower by metes and bounds, and ask to have the estate sold free of dower and to be allowed, in lieu thereof, such money out of the proceeds of sale as the court deems the just value of the dower interest therein.

(1953 H 1, eff. 10–1–53; GC 12018)

Historical and Statutory Notes

Pre–1953 H 1 Amendments: RS 5719

Library References

Dower and Curtesy ⚖100.
Westlaw Topic No. 136.
C.J.S. Dower §§ 101, 104.

5305.16 Election by answer is a release of dower

The answer of a surviving spouse under section 5305.15 of the Revised Code has the same effect, in all respects, as a deed of release to the purchaser of such estate of the dower interest therein of such spouse.

(1953 H 1, eff. 10–1–53; GC 12019)

Historical and Statutory Notes

Pre–1953 H 1 Amendments: RS 5720

Library References

Dower and Curtesy ⚖49.
Westlaw Topic No. 136.
C.J.S. Curtesy § 12.

DOWER OF INSANE SPOUSE

5305.17 Guardian may elect for surviving spouse

The guardian of a surviving spouse who has been adjudged insane may appear and answer for such insane person in an action under section 5305.15 of the Revised Code, subject to the approval of the court in which it is pending. Such answer has the same effect as if such spouse answered personally. The guardian shall be liable to such spouse, or the heirs, for all damage or loss sustained by his fraud or collusion, notwithstanding the approval of the court.

(1953 H 1, eff. 10–1–53; GC 12020)

Historical and Statutory Notes

Pre–1953 H 1 Amendments: RS 5721

Library References

Mental Health ⟶216, 236.
Westlaw Topic No. 257A.
C.J.S. Insane Persons § 85.

5305.18 Petition to discharge land of dower of insane person

A person owning real property in this state, encumbered by the contingent or vested right of dower of an insane person, may apply, by petition to the court of common pleas of the county in which the real estate, or any part thereof, is situated, making defendants thereto such insane person, and the spouse and guardian, if such insane person has either or both, for leave to sell any part of such real property, discharged and unencumbered of such contingent or vested right of dower. The position [1] must set forth the insanity of the person, together with a description of the land proposed to be sold. Thereupon the court shall appoint a committee of six competent men, of whom at least three are physicians, who, under oath, shall inquire into the insanity of such person, and hear testimony to be produced by the spouse or guardian, or, if there is no such guardian, by a guardian ad litem to be appointed in the action. The committee shall make a report, in writing, of the result of its investigation, signed by its members.

(1976 H 390, eff. 8–6–76; 1953 H 1; GC 12021)

[1] Prior and current versions differ although no amendment to this language was indicated in 1976 H 390; "position" appeared as "petition" in 1953 H 1.

Historical and Statutory Notes

Pre–1953 H 1 Amendments: RS 5722

Comparative Laws

Ind.—West's A.I.C. 32–1–17–1.
Iowa—I.C.A. § 597.6.
Minn.—M.S.A. § 507.04.
Mo.—V.A.M.S. § 451.300.

Library References

Dower and Curtesy ⟶118.
Westlaw Topic No. 136.
C.J.S. Curtesy §§ 1, 13, 21.

5305.19 Inquest of lunacy

If the committee provided for in section 5305.18 of the Revised Code unanimously reports that the person having a contingent or vested right of dower, in its opinion, is permanently insane, the court of common pleas shall appoint three judicious freeholders to appraise the real estate described in the petition mentioned in said section, whether or not such real estate is in one or several counties. Such freeholders shall report in writing the value of each tract.

(1953 H 1, eff. 10–1–53; GC 12022)

Historical and Statutory Notes

Pre–1953 H 1 Amendments: RS 5723

Library References

Dower and Curtesy ⟶82, 83.
Westlaw Topic No. 136.
C.J.S. Curtesy § 14.
C.J.S. Dower §§ 85, 97.

5305.20 Proceedings on report of inquest of lunacy

When the report provided for in section 5305.19 of the Revised Code is filed, the court of common pleas may direct the petitioner, by a sufficient deed of conveyance, to convey to the insane person, to be held by such person in fee, such proportion of the real estate described in the petition as seems just, or the court may assign to such insane person, to be held by him during life, after the death of the spouse of such person, such proportion of the real estate described in the petition as seems just, for his support, or the court may order the petitioner to invest an amount by it fixed, in the stock of a company, or stocks created by the laws of this state, as the court designates, the profits, and dividends or distributions, arising from such investment to be applied to the support and maintenance of the insane person after the death of the spouse of such person. The petitioner, upon his compliance with the order of the court, may sell all the real property he is possessed of, described in the petition, free and unencumbered of the contingent or vested right of dower of such insane person.

(1984 H 250, eff. 7–30–84; 1953 H 1; GC 12023)

Historical and Statutory Notes

Pre–1953 H 1 Amendments: RS 5724

Library References

Dower and Curtesy ⟶82.
Westlaw Topic No. 136.
C.J.S. Dower §§ 85, 97.

5305.21 Dower of insane person may be barred

When the spouse of an insane person conveys real estate in this state, in which such person has a contingent or vested right of dower, and the insane person does not join the spouse in the conveyance, the spouse may apply by petition to the court of common pleas of the county in which the insane person resides, or, if such insane person resides out of the state, then in the county in which the real estate is situated, for leave to have part or all of such real estate so conveyed, released of the dower right therein. Such petition shall set forth the insanity of the insane person, and a description of the land proposed to be affected. The insane person, guardian, if there is one, and all persons in interest, shall be made defendants, and the action shall be proceeded with as prescribed in sections 5305.18 to 5305.20, inclusive, of the Revised Code, except that instead of ordering the petitioner to sell the real estate or to convey or assign to such insane person any part of it, the court shall direct the petitioner to make such investment as is provided in section 5305.20 of the Revised Code, or require him to secure the amount to the use of the insane person by mortgage of unencumbered real estate of at least double the value thereof. Upon compliance by the petitioner with the order made, the court shall enter a judgment releasing and discharging the real estate from the encumbrance of such right of dower, and adjudge the holder of the legal title, or other party liable, to pay to the petitioner any sum withheld or retired [1] as indemnity against such dower right.

(1953 H 1, eff. 10–1–53; GC 12024)

[1] So in original; should this read "retained"?

Historical and Statutory Notes

Pre–1953 H 1 Amendments: RS 5725

Library References

Dower and Curtesy ⟶37.
Westlaw Topic No. 136.
C.J.S. Curtesy § 12.

5305.22 Real estate may be conveyed free from dower if spouse insane

Any real estate or interest therein coming to a person by purchase, inheritance, or otherwise, after the spouse of such person is adjudged insane, and is an inmate of a hospital for the insane in this state, or confined in the insane department of any epileptic hospital of this state, or any state of the United States, or is an inmate of a hospital for the insane, or confined in the insane department of any hospital of the United States, may be conveyed by such person while such insane spouse remains an inmate thereof, free and clear from any dower right or expectancy of such insane spouse. Dower shall not attach to any real estate so acquired and conveyed during the time described in this section in favor of such insane spouse. The indorsement upon the instrument of conveyance, by the superintendent of the hospital, that such spouse is an insane inmate thereof, stating when received therein and signed officially by him, shall be sufficient evidence of the fact that such spouse is such inmate. This indorsement shall be a part of the instrument of conveyance.

(1953 H 1, eff. 10–1–53; GC 12025)

Historical and Statutory Notes

Pre–1953 H 1 Amendments: 119 v 26; RS 5725a

Library References

Dower and Curtesy ⟶34.
Westlaw Topic No. 136.
C.J.S. Dower § 60.

CHAPTER 5731

ESTATE TAX

PRELIMINARY PROVISIONS

Section	
5731.01	Definitions
5731.011	Valuation of qualified farm property; election; additional tax upon certain dispositions of the property
5731.02	Estate tax; rates

VALUE OF GROSS ESTATE

Section	
5731.03	Interest of decedent
5731.04	Interest of surviving spouse
5731.05	Value of gross estate; transfers in contemplation of death; exceptions
5731.06	Value of gross estate; transfers with retention of life estate or power of appointment
5731.07	Value of gross estate; transfers conditioned on survivorship; reversionary interest
5731.08	Value of gross estate; transfers subject to power to alter, amend, revoke, or terminate
5731.09	Annuities; employer death benefit plans; exclusions
5731.10	Value of gross estate; joint and survivorship property
5731.11	Value of gross estate; interest subject to general power of appointment
5731.12	Value of gross estate
5731.13	Value of gross estate; transfers for less than adequate consideration
5731.131	Effect on life interest if subject to federal marital deduction

VALUE OF TAXABLE PROPERTY; EXEMPTIONS; DEDUCTIONS

Section	
5731.14	Determination of taxable estate
5731.15	Marital deduction; pay during missing in action status
5731.16	Deductions for funeral and administration expenses, debts, and mortgage debts
5731.161	Taxable estate of transferee spouse; value
5731.17	Deduction for charitable bequests and transfers

MISCELLANEOUS TAXES

Section	
5731.18	Additional estate tax; rates
5731.181	Generation–skipping transfers
5731.19	Nonresident estate tax

ESTATE TAX RETURN

Section	
5731.21	Returns; certificates
5731.22	Failure to file return; penalties; persons liable

RETURNS AND PAYMENTS; TIME REQUIREMENTS

Section	
5731.23	Time for payment of tax
5731.24	Time for return and payment of additional tax
5731.25	Extension of time for payment because of undue hardship; postponement of payment at election of executor or administrator; interest; bond

PROCEDURAL PROVISIONS

Section	
5731.26	Duties and powers of tax commissioner
5731.27	Certificate of determination of tax liability; deficiency; refund
5731.28	Refund; time for filing claim

APPEALS

Section	
5731.30	Appeal to probate court from determination of tax commissioner; notice; hearing
5731.31	Jurisdiction of probate court
5731.32	Appeal from final order of probate court

MISCELLANEOUS PROVISIONS

Section	
5731.33	Payment; receipts; duties of county treasurer; prohibitions
5731.34	Tax imposed on transfers of intangible personal property employed in business; reciprocity
5731.35	Foreign estate taxes; compromise
5731.36	Administrator of foreign death tax laws deemed creditor of decedent; reciprocity
5731.37	Estate tax lien and discharge, restriction, or transfer; personal liability of executor or administrator
5731.38	Limitation on time for determination of tax liability
5731.39	Release of assets; consent to transfer; exceptions; contents of safe deposit box
5731.40	Transfer of assets of nonresident decedent
5731.41	Appointment of agents by tax commissioner; compensation
5731.42	Collection of tax; proceedings; duties of attorney general
5731.43	Attorney general to represent the state; appointment of attorney employed by department of taxation
5731.44	County auditor; appointment of deputies
5731.45	Administration of tax; appointment of assistants by tax commissioner; regulations
5731.46	County treasurer to keep account of taxes received; duties of county treasurer and county auditor; fees

Section

5731.47 Fees of officers; approval; payment

DISTRIBUTION AND DETERMINATION OF TAX REVENUES

5731.48 Distribution of tax revenues

5731.49 Determination of tax revenues due political subdivisions; payment

ORIGIN OF TAX

5731.50 Origin of tax on transfer of realty and tangible personalty located in state

5731.51 Origin of tax on transfer of personalty not located in state

CONFIDENTIALITY OF INFORMATION

5731.90 Confidentiality of information

PENALTY

5731.99 Penalty

PRELIMINARY PROVISIONS

5731.01 Definitions

As used in this chapter:

(A) The "value of the gross estate" of the decedent shall include, to the extent provided in sections 5731.03 to 5731.131 of the Revised Code, the value, on the date of the decedent's death or on an alternate valuation date prescribed by division (D) of this section, of all property, real or personal, tangible or intangible, wherever situated, except real property situated and tangible personal property having an actual situs outside of this state.

(B) Subject to the provisions of section 5731.011 of the Revised Code that permit a valuation of qualified farm property at its value for its actual qualified use, the value of any property included in the gross estate shall be the price at which such property would change hands between a willing buyer and a willing seller, neither being under any compulsion to buy or sell and both having reasonable knowledge of relevant facts. All relevant facts and elements of value as of the valuation date shall be considered in determining such value.

The rulings and regulations of the internal revenue service and decisions of the federal courts defining the principles applicable in determining fair market value for purposes of the federal estate tax imposed by Subchapter A, Chapter 11 of the Internal Revenue Code shall be applied in determining fair market value for purposes of the estate taxes imposed by this chapter, to the extent that these rulings, regulations, and decisions are not inconsistent with the express provisions of this chapter, but the actual determination of the fair market value by the internal revenue service of any asset included in the gross estate is not controlling for purposes of the estate taxes imposed by this chapter, unless the person filing the estate tax return and the tax commissioner have agreed in writing to be bound by the federal determination, as provided in section 5731.26 of the Revised Code.

(C) In the case of stock and securities of a corporation the value of which, by reason of their not being listed on an exchange and by reason of the absence of sales of them, cannot be determined with reference to bid and asked prices, or with reference to sales prices, the value of them shall be determined by taking into consideration, in addition to all other factors, the value of stock or securities of corporations engaged in the same or a similar line of business which are listed on an exchange or which are traded actively in the over-the-counter market.

If a valuation of securities is undertaken by reference to market transactions and if the block of securities to be valued is so large in relation to actual sales on existing markets that it could not be liquidated in a reasonable time without depressing the market, the price at which the block could be sold, as such, outside the usual market, as through an underwriter, shall be considered in determining the value of such block of securities.

(D) "Alternate valuation date" means the date for valuation of a gross estate permitted by filing an election under this division. Whether or not an alternate valuation date election is available to an estate for federal estate tax purposes or, if available, is made for the estate, the value of the gross estate may be determined, if the person required to file the estate tax return so elects, by valuing all the property included in the gross estate on the alternate date, if any, provided in section 2032 (a) of the Internal Revenue Code as such section generally applies, for federal estate tax purposes, to the estates of persons dying on the decedent's date of death.

No deduction under this chapter of any item shall be allowed if allowance is, in effect, given by use of the alternate valuation date. In the determination of any tax liability of any estate in which an election is filed under this division, all provisions in this chapter that refer to value at the time of the decedent's death shall be construed for all purposes to mean the value of such property used in determining the value of the gross estate. For the purposes of the charitable deduction under section 5731.17 of the Revised Code, any bequest, legacy, devise, or transfer enumerated in it shall be valued as of the date of the decedent's death with adjustment for any difference in value, not due to mere lapse of time or the occurrence or nonoccurrence of a contingency, of the property as of the date six months after the decedent's death, or in case of its earlier disposition, on such date of disposition.

An election under this division shall be exercised on the estate tax return by the person required to file the return. When made, an election under this division is irrevocable. An election cannot be exercised under this division if a return is filed more than one year after the time prescribed, including any extensions of time granted, pursuant to law for filing the return.

(E) Unless otherwise indicated by the context, "county" means one of the following:

(1) The county in which the decedent's estate is administered;

(2) If no administration of the decedent's estate is being had, the county of residence of the decedent at the time of death;

(3) If the decedent dies a resident of another state, any county in which any property subject to tax is located.

(F) "Internal Revenue Code" means the "Internal Revenue Code of 1986," 100 Stat. 2085, 26 U.S.C. 1, as amended.

(2005 H 66, eff. 6–30–05; 1986 H 139, eff. 7–24–86; 1983 H 291; 1981 S 28; 1971 S 398; 132 v S 326)

Uncodified Law

2005 H 66, § 557.24, eff. 6–30–05, reads:

The amendment by this act of sections 5731.01, 5731.05, 5731.131, 5731.14, 5731.18, and 5731.181 of the Revised Code, and the repeal by this act of section 5731.20 of the Revised Code, applies to estates of decedents dying on or after the effective date of those sections as amended by this act.

1986 H 139, § 3: See Uncodified Law under 5731.12.

1983 H 291, § 127, eff. 7–1–83, reads: The amendment of sections 2117.06, 5731.01, 5731.011, 5731.02, 5731.05, 5731.09, 5731.14, 5731.15, 5731.16, 5731.18, 5731.21, 5731.22, 5731.26, 5731.42, and 5731.48, the enactment of sections 5731.131, 5731.181, 5731.231, and 5731.99, and the repeal of section 5731.20 of the Revised Code, all by this act, shall apply to the estate of any decedent whose death occurs on or after July 1, 1983.

1981 S 28, § 3, eff. 10–9–81, reads, in part: Sections 1 and 2 of this act do not apply to the estates of decedents who died prior to January 1, 1982.

Historical and Statutory Notes

Ed. Note: Former 5731.01 repealed by 132 v S 326, eff. 7–1–68; 132 v H 1; 131 v S 74; 1953 H 1; GC 5331.

Pre–1953 H 1 Amendments: 113 v 682; 108 v Pt 1, 562; 90 v 17, § 17

Amendment Note: 2005 H 66 corrected the spelling of "date" in division (A); deleted "of 1954, 26 U.S.C. 2001, as amended," in the second paragraph of division (B); deleted "of 1954, 26 U.S.C. 2032(a), as amended" in the first paragraph of division (D); substituted "that" for "which" in the second paragraph of division (D); deleted "his" in division (E)(2); added division (F); and made other nonsubstantive changes.

Library References

Taxation ⚖=856–906.
Westlaw Topic No. 371.
C.J.S. Taxation § 1073, 1111–1122, 1124, 1127–1128, 1131, 1133–1142, 1144- 1145, 1147–1153, 1157–1174, 1176–1181, 1183, 1185–1187, 1190, 1192, 1195–1196, 1198, 1200–1203, 1205, 1207, 1214–1223, 1225, 1228–1229.

5731.011 Valuation of qualified farm property; election; additional tax upon certain dispositions of the property

(A) As used in this section:

(1) "Adjusted value" means:

(a) In the case of the gross estate, the value of the gross estate as determined pursuant to section 5731.01 of the Revised Code and without regard to this section, reduced by any amounts allowable as a deduction under division (A)(4) of section 5731.16 of the Revised Code;

(b) In the case of any real or personal property, the value of the property as determined pursuant to section 5731.01 of the Revised Code and without regard to this section, reduced by any amounts allowable as a deduction in respect to such property under division (A)(4) of section 5731.16 of the Revised Code.

(2) "Member of the decedent's family" means, with respect to any decedent, only his ancestor or lineal descendant, a lineal descendant of any of his grandparents, his spouse, the spouse of any such descendant, or a step child or foster child of the decedent.

(3) "Qualified farm property" means real property that is located in this state, that is included in the gross estate of the decedent under this chapter, and that was acquired by, or passed to, a qualified heir, but only if both of the following apply:

(a) Fifty per cent or more of the adjusted value of the gross estate consists of the adjusted value of real or personal property which, on the date of the decedent's death, was being used for a qualified use;

(b) Twenty–five per cent or more of the adjusted value of the gross estate consists of the adjusted value of real property which, on the date of the decedent's death, was being used for a qualified use.

(4) "Qualified heir" means a member of the decedent's family who acquired qualified farm property, or to whom such property passed. If a qualified heir disposes of any interest in qualified farm property to any member of the decedent's family, that member shall thereafter be treated as the qualified heir with respect to the interest.

(5) "Qualified use" means the devotion of real property exclusively to agricultural use as described in the definition of "land devoted exclusively to agricultural use" contained in division (A) of section 5713.30 of the Revised Code, whether or not an application has been filed by the decedent or a qualified heir pursuant to section 5713.31 of the Revised Code.

(B)(1) For purposes of determining the value of property included in the gross estate, the value of qualified farm property is, subject to division (D) of this section, whichever of the following the person filing the estate tax return elects:

(a) Its fair market value, as determined pursuant to division (B) of section 5731.01 of the Revised Code;

(b) Its value for its actual qualified use, on the date of the decedent's death or on an alternate valuation date prescribed by division (D) of section 5731.01 of the Revised Code;

(c) Its value for its actual qualified use, as determined under section 5713.31 of the Revised Code.

(2) The election shall be made on or before the date by which the return is required to be filed, determined with regard to any extension of time granted pursuant to law for filing the return.

(C)(1) For purposes of this section, the existence of a qualified use may be established, but is not required to be established, by the filing of an application pursuant to section 5713.31 of the Revised Code and its approval by the county auditor.

(2) This section applies to any interest in qualified farm property that is held in a partnership, corporation, or trust, if the interest would qualify under this section if it were held directly by the decedent.

(D) If the person filing the estate tax return elects pursuant to division (B)(1)(b) or (c) of this section, to have qualified farm property valued at its value for its actual qualified use, and if the difference between the fair market value of the property as determined pursuant to division (B) of section 5731.01 of the Revised Code and the value for its actual qualified use under division (B)(1)(b) or (c) of this section, whichever was elected, exceeds five hundred thousand dollars, the property shall be valued at the amount that is five hundred thousand dollars less than the fair market value.

(E) If an election is made, pursuant to division (B)(1)(b) or (c) of this section, to have qualified farm property valued at its value for its actual qualified use, and if, within four years after the date of the decedent's death and before the death of the qualified heir, the qualified heir disposes of any interest in the property to a person other than a member of the decedent's family, or ceases to use any part of the property for a qualified use, a recapture tax shall be imposed. The recapture tax shall be equivalent to the estate tax savings realized in the decedent's estate by valuating the interest disposed of, or the part of the property that has ceased to be used for a qualified use, at its value for its actual qualified use, instead of at its fair market value pursuant to division (B) of section 5731.01 of the Revised Code. The recapture tax, plus interest computed at the rate per annum determined under section 5703.47 of the Revised Code, from nine months after the date of the decedent's death, is due and payable on the day that is nine months after the date of the disposition or cessation of use, and shall be paid by the qualified heir who disposed of the interest or ceased use of the part of the property for a qualified use.

(F) The tax commissioner shall prescribe rules and forms to implement this section. The rules may require, for purposes of division (E) of this section, that a qualified heir file an annual report with the commissioner, establishing that the qualified farm property has not been disposed of to a person other than a member of the decedent's family and that no part of it has ceased to be used for a qualified use.

(1986 H 139, eff. 7–24–86; 1983 H 291; 1981 S 28)

Uncodified Law

1986 H 139, § 3: See Uncodified Law under 5731.12.

1983 H 291, § 127, eff. 7–1–83, reads: The amendment of sections 2117.06, 5731.01, 5731.011, 5731.02, 5731.09, 5731.14, 5731.15, 5731.16, 5731.18, 5731.21, 5731.22, 5731.26, 5731.42, and 5731.48, the enactment of sections 5731.131, 5731.181, 5731.231, and 5731.99, and the repeal of section 5731.20 of the Revised Code, all by this act, shall apply to the estate of any decedent whose death occurs on or after July 1, 1983.

1981 S 28, § 3, eff. 10–9–81, reads, in part: Sections 1 and 2 of this act do not apply to the estates of decedents who died prior to January 1, 1982.

Library References

Taxation ⇔895.
Westlaw Topic No. 371.
C.J.S. Taxation § 1171.

5731.02 Estate tax; rates

(A) A tax is hereby levied on the transfer of the taxable estate, determined as provided in section 5731.14 of the Revised Code, of every person dying on or after July 1, 1968, who at the time of death was a resident of this state, as follows:

If the taxable estate is:	The tax shall be:
Not over $40,000	2% of the taxable estate
Over $40,000 but not over $100,000	$800 plus 3% of the excess over $40,000
Over $100,000 but not over $200,000	$2,600 plus 4% of the excess over $100,000
Over $200,000 but not over $300,000	$6,600 plus 5% of the excess over $200,000
Over $300,000 but not over $500,000	$11,600 plus 6% of the excess over $300,000
Over $500,000	$23,600 plus 7% of the excess over $500,000

(B) A credit shall be allowed against the tax imposed by division (A) of this section equal to the lesser of five hundred dollars or the amount of the tax for persons dying on or after July 1, 1968, but before January 1, 2001; the lesser of six thousand six hundred dollars or the amount of the tax for persons dying on or after January 1, 2001, but before January 1, 2002; or the lesser of thirteen thousand nine hundred dollars or the amount of the tax for persons dying on or after January 1, 2002.

(2000 S 108, eff. 9–29–00; 1983 H 291, eff. 7–1–83; 132 v S 326)

Uncodified Law

1983 H 291, § 127, eff. 7–1–83, reads: The amendment of sections 2117.06, 5731.01, 5731.011, 5731.02, 5731.05, 5731.09, 5731.14, 5731.15, 5731.16, 5731.18, 5731.21, 5731.22, 5731.26, 5731.42, and 5731.48, the enactment of sections 5731.131, 5731.181, 5731.231, and 5731.99, and the repeal of section 5731.20 of the Revised Code, all by this act, shall apply to the estate of any decedent whose death occurs on or after July 1, 1983.

Historical and Statutory Notes

Ed. Note: Former 5731.02 repealed by 132 v S 326, eff. 7–1–68; 129 v 582; 127 v 102, 128; 1953 H 1; GC 5332; see now 5731.06, 5731.07, 5731.08, and 5731.10 for provisions analogous to former 5731.02.

Pre–1953 H 1 Amendments: 108 v Pt 1, 562; 103 v 463; 94 v 101, § 1

Amendment Note: 2000 S 108 deleted "his" before "death" in division (A); and inserted "for persons dying on or after July 1, 1968, but before January 1, 2001; the lesser of six thousand six hundred dollars or the amount of the tax for persons dying on or after January 1, 2001, but before January 1, 2002; or the lesser of thirteen thousand nine hundred dollars or the amount of the tax for persons dying on or after January 1, 2002" in division (B).

Library References

Taxation ⇔863.
Westlaw Topic No. 371.
C.J.S. Taxation § 1115, 1138, 1140.

VALUE OF GROSS ESTATE

5731.03 Interest of decedent

The value of the gross estate shall include the value of all property, to the extent of the interest therein of the decedent on the date of the decedent's death.

(132 v S 326, eff. 7–1–68)

Historical and Statutory Notes

Ed. Note: Former 5731.03 repealed by 132 v S 326, eff. 7–1–68; 1953 H 1; GC 5332–1.

Pre–1953 H 1 Amendments: 108 v Pt 2, 1197

Library References

Taxation ⇔895.
Westlaw Topic No. 371.
C.J.S. Taxation § 1171.

5731.04 Interest of surviving spouse

The value of the gross estate shall include the value of all property, to the extent of any interest therein of the surviving spouse, existing on the date of the decedent's death as dower or curtesy or by virtue of a statute creating an estate in lieu of dower or curtesy.

(132 v S 326, eff. 7–1–68)

Historical and Statutory Notes

Ed. Note: Former 5731.04 repealed by 132 v S 326, eff. 7–1–68; 1953 H 1; GC 5332–2.

Pre–1953 H 1 Amendments: 110 v 26

Library References

Taxation ⇔875, 895.
Westlaw Topic No. 371.
C.J.S. Taxation § 1163, 1171.

5731.05 Value of gross estate; transfers in contemplation of death; exceptions

(A) Except as provided in divisions (B) and (C) of this section, the value of the gross estate shall include the value of all property, to the extent of any interest in property, of which the decedent has at any time made a transfer, by trust or otherwise, in contemplation of death.

(B) Any transfer, except as provided in division (C) of this section, by trust or otherwise, made within a period of three years ending with the date of the decedent's death shall be deemed to have been made in contemplation of death, unless the contrary is shown. No transfer made before that three-year period shall be treated as having been made in contemplation of death.

(C) This section does not apply to any of the following:

(1) A bona fide sale for an adequate and full consideration in money or money's worth;

(2) A transfer of property that would not be included in the decedent's gross estate if retained by the decedent until death;

(3) The first ten thousand dollars of the transfers that were made by the decedent to each transferee, other than the spouse of the decedent, in each calendar year, but only to the extent that those transfers qualify as present interests under section 2503(b) and (c) of the Internal Revenue Code. The exclusion provided by division (C)(3) of this section does not apply to any portion of a transfer that is treated as being made by the spouse of the decedent under section 2513 of the Internal Revenue Code.

(4) A transfer of property made to the spouse of the transferor, except as provided in section 5731.131 of the Revised Code;

(5) Federal or state gift taxes paid with respect to any includible transfer.

(2005 H 66, eff. 6–30–05; 1990 S 336, § 3, eff. 7–1–93; 1990 S 336, § 1; 1989 H 111, § 1, 3; 1986 H 139; 1984 H 794; 1983 H 291; 132 v S 326)

Uncodified Law

2005 H 66, § 557.24: See Uncodified Law under RC 5731.01.

1986 H 139, § 3: See Uncodified Law under 5731.12.

1983 H 291, § 127, eff. 7–1–83, reads: The amendment of sections 2117.06, 5731.01, 5731.011, 5731.02, 5731.05, 5731.09, 5731.14, 5731.15, 5731.16, 5731.18, 5731.21, 5731.22, 5731.26, 5731.42, and 5731.48, the enactment of sections 5731.131, 5731.181, 5731.231, and 5731.99, and the repeal of section 5731.20 of the Revised Code, all by this act, shall apply to the estate of any decedent whose death occurs on or after July 1, 1983.

Historical and Statutory Notes

Ed. Note: Memo, Department of Taxation, Estate Tax Division, July 6, 1984:

RC 5731.05(C)(3): The corrective language makes it explicit that only one $10,000 exemption per donee per year within the 3 year period of death is exempt. This will include transfers to spouses.

Contractual interests which are not present interests qualifying for the federal gift tax $10,000 exclusion will not qualify for the Ohio $10,000 exclusion. See I.R.S. Code Sec. 2503 and regulations.

Other transfers within three years of death are presumed to be in contemplation.

RC 5731.05(C)(5) has been repealed as superfluous because insurance and death benefits treatment are covered under RC 5731.09 and 5731.12.

Ed. Note: Former 5731.05 repealed by 132 v S 326, eff. 7–1–68; 1953 H 1; GC 5332–3.

Pre–1953 H 1 Amendments: 111 v 97

Amendment Note: 2005 H 66 deleted "of 1986,' 26 U.S.C. 2503, as amended" and "of 1986,' 26 U.S.C. 2513, as amended" in division (C)(3); deleted division (D); made changes to reflect gender neutral language; and made other nonsubstantive changes. Prior to amendment, division (D) read:

"(D) The amendments made to this section by Amended Substitute House Bill No. 111 and Substitute Senate Bill No. 336 of the 118th general assembly that are effective on July 1, 1993, shall apply only to the estates of decedents who die on or after that date."

Library References

Torts ⚖═879.
Westlaw Topic No. 379.
C.J.S. Torts § 90.

5731.06 Value of gross estate; transfers with retention of life estate or power of appointment

The value of the gross estate shall include the value of all property, to the extent of any interest therein of which the decedent has at any time made a transfer, except in the case of a bona fide sale for an adequate and full consideration in money or money's worth, by trust or otherwise, under which he has retained for his life or for any period not ascertainable without reference to his death or for any period which does not in fact end before his death the possession or enjoyment of, or the right to the income from, the property, or the right, either alone or in conjunction with any person, to designate the persons who shall possess or enjoy the property or the income therefrom.

(132 v S 326, eff. 7–1–68)

Historical and Statutory Notes

Ed. Note: 5731.06 contains provisions analogous to former 5731.02, repealed by 132 v S 326, eff. 7–1–68.

Ed. Note: Former 5731.06 repealed by 132 v S 326, eff. 7–1–68; 132 v H 6; 129 v 454; 1953 H 1; GC 5332–4.

Pre–1953 H 1 Amendments: 114 v 94

Library References

Taxation ⚖═877, 895.
Westlaw Topic No. 371.
C.J.S. Taxation § 1142, 1171.

5731.07 Value of gross estate; transfers conditioned on survivorship; reversionary interest

(A) The value of the gross estate shall include the value of all property, to the extent of any interest therein of which the decedent has at any time made a transfer, except in the case of a bona fide sale for an adequate and full consideration in money or money's worth, by trust or otherwise, if both of the following conditions exist:

(1) Possession or enjoyment of the property can, through ownership of such interest, be obtained only by surviving the decedent; and

(2) The decedent has retained a reversionary interest by the express terms of the instrument of transfer and the value of such reversionary interest immediately before the death of the decedent exceeds five per cent of the value of such property.

(B) "Reversionary interest" includes a possibility that property transferred by the decedent may return to him or to his estate or become subject to a power of disposition by him and its value shall be determined immediately before the death of the decedent by the usual methods of valuation, including the use of tables of mortality and actuarial principles, under rules and regulations prescribed by the tax commissioner.

(132 v S 326, eff. 7–1–68)

Historical and Statutory Notes

Ed. Note: 5731.07 contains provisions analogous to former 5731.02, repealed by 132 v S 326, eff. 7–1–68.

Ed. Note: Former 5731.07 repealed by 132 v S 326, eff. 7–1–68; 1953 H 1; GC 5332–5; see now 5731.34 for provisions analogous to former 5731.07.

Pre–1953 H 1 Amendments: 119 v 436

Library References

Taxation ⚖═877.
Westlaw Topic No. 371.
C.J.S. Taxation § 1142.

5731.08 Value of gross estate; transfers subject to power to alter, amend, revoke, or terminate

The value of the gross estate shall include the value of all property, to the extent of any interest therein of which the decedent has made a transfer except in the case of a bona fide sale for an adequate and full consideration in money or money's worth, by trust or otherwise, where the enjoyment thereof was subject on the date of the decedent's death to any change through the exercise of a power, in whatever capacity exercisable, by the decedent alone or by the decedent in conjunction with any other person to alter, amend, revoke or terminate.

(132 v S 326, eff. 7–1–68)

Historical and Statutory Notes

Ed. Note: 5731.08 contains provisions analogous to former 5731.02, repealed by 132 v S 326, eff. 7–1–68.

Ed. Note: Former 5731.08 repealed by 131 v H 663, eff. 10–8–65; 1953 H 1; GC 5333.

Pre–1953 H 1 Amendments: 111 v 97; 108 v Pt 2, 1193; 108 v Pt 1, 564; 103 v 463; 91 v 170, § 2

Library References

Taxation ⚖877.
Westlaw Topic No. 371.
C.J.S. Taxation § 1142.

5731.09 Annuities; employer death benefit plans; exclusions

(A) Except as provided in division (B) of this section, the value of the gross estate includes the value of an annuity or other payment receivable by a beneficiary by reason of surviving the decedent under any form of contract or agreement under which an annuity or similar payment was payable to the decedent, or the decedent possessed the right to receive such annuity or payment, either alone or in conjunction with another, for the decedent's life or for any period not ascertainable without reference to the decedent's death, or for any period which does not in fact end before the decedent's death.

However, the value of the gross estate includes only such part of the value of the annuity or other payment receivable under the contract or agreement as is proportionate to that part of the purchase price of the contract or agreement contributed by the decedent. The value of the gross estate does not include the part of the value of the annuity or other payment as is proportionate to the part of the purchase price of the contract or agreement contributed by the employer or former employer of the decedent, whether to an employee's trust or fund forming part of a pension, annuity, retirement, bonus, or profit-sharing plan or otherwise, if the contributions were made by reason of the decedent's employment.

(B) The value of the gross estate does not include the value of a pension or annuity accruing to any person under federal employment, including service in the armed forces, or the value of an annuity or other payment from the Ohio police and fire pension fund created by section 742.02 of the Revised Code, the Ohio public safety officers death benefit fund created by section 742.62 of the Revised Code, the state highway patrol retirement system created by section 5505.02 of the Revised Code, the public employees retirement system created by section 145.03 of the Revised Code, the state teachers retirement system created by section 3307.03 of the Revised Code, and the school employees retirement system created by section 3309.03 of the Revised Code.

(1999 H 222, eff. 11–2–99; 1998 H 648, eff. 9–16–98; 1996 S 224, eff. 3–7–97; 1984 H 794, eff. 7–6–84; 1983 H 291; 1976 H 1013; 1975 S 145; 1970 H 865; 1969 H 1; 132 v S 326)

Uncodified Law

1996 S 224, § 3, eff. 3–7–97, reads: Sections 1 and 2 of this act apply only to the estates of persons who die on or after the effective date of this act.

1983 H 291, § 127, eff. 7–1–83, reads: The amendment of sections 2117.06, 5731.01, 5731.011, 5731.02, 5731.05, 5731.09, 5731.14, 5731.15, 5731.16, 5731.18, 5731.21, 5731.22, 5731.26, 5731.42, and 5731.48; the enactment of sections 5731.131, 5731.181, 5731.231, and 5731.99, and the repeal of section 5731.20 of the Revised Code, all by this act, shall apply to the estate of any decedent whose death occurs on or after July 1, 1983.

Historical and Statutory Notes

Ed. Note: Former 5731.09 repealed by 132 v S 326, eff. 7–1–68; 132 v S 207; 131 v H 319; 128 v 125; 127 v 561; 1953 H 1; GC 5334.

Pre–1953 H 1 Amendments: 120 v 247; 118 v 365, § 1; 110 v 26; 108 v Pt 2, 1193; 108 v Pt 1, 564; 91 v 170, § 2; 90 v 15, § 3 et seq

Amendment Note: 1999 H 222 substituted "Ohio police and fire pension fund" for "police and firemen's disability and pension fund" and "Ohio public safety officers death benefit fund" for "firemen and policemen's death benefit fund" in division (B).

Amendment Note: 1998 H 648 substituted "742.62" for "742.61" in division (B); and made changes to reflect gender neutral language.

Amendment Note: 1996 S 224 rewrote this section, which prior thereto read:

"(A) The value of the gross estate shall include the value of an annuity or other payment receivable by a beneficiary by reason of surviving the decedent under any form of contract or agreement, including the value of an annuity or other payment receivable by any beneficiary under any form of contract or agreement as is proportionate to the purchase price contributed by an employer or former employer which is excludable from the gross estate by reason of subchapter A, Chapter 11, subtitle B, of the Internal Revenue Code of 1954, 26 U.S.C. 2039, if, under such contract or agreement, an annuity or similar payment was payable to the decedent or the decedent possessed the right to receive such annuity or payment, either alone or in conjunction with another, for his life or for any period not ascertainable without reference to his death or for any period which does not in fact end before his death.

"(B) Division (A) of this section applies to only such part of the value of the annuity or other payment receivable under the contract or agreement as is proportionate to that part of the purchase price therefor contributed by the decedent or the decedent's employer or former employer.

"(C) Notwithstanding divisions (A) and (B) of this section, the value of the gross estate does not include the value of a pension or annuity accruing to any person under federal employment, including service in the armed forces, or the value of an annuity or other payment from the police and firemen's disability and pension fund created by section 742.02 of the Revised Code, the firemen and policemen's death benefit fund created by section 742.61 of the Revised Code, the state highway patrol retirement system created by section 5505.02 of the Revised Code, the public employees retirement system created by section 145.03 of the Revised Code, the state teachers retirement system created by section 3307.03 of the Revised Code, and the school employees retirement system created by section 3309.03 of the Revised Code."

Library References

Taxation ⚖863, 896.
Westlaw Topic No. 371.
C.J.S. Taxation § 1118, 1177, 1179.

5731.10 Value of gross estate; joint and survivorship property

(A) The value of the gross estate shall include the value of all property, to the extent of the interest therein held by the decedent and any person jointly, so that upon the death of one of them, the survivor has or the survivors have a right to the immediate ownership or possession or enjoyment of the whole property, except such part thereof as may be shown to have originally belonged to such other person or persons and never to have been received or acquired by the latter from the decedent for less than an adequate and full consideration in money or money's worth.

(B) When the person [sic.] holding property jointly are a husband and wife, the amount includible in the gross estate shall be one-half the value of said property. When the property has been acquired by gift, bequest, devise, or inheritance by the decedent and any other person or persons as joint owners and their interests are not otherwise specified or fixed by law, the amount includible in the gross estate shall be the value of a fractional part of said property determined by dividing the value of the property by the number of joint owners.

(132 v S 326, eff. 7–1–68)

Historical and Statutory Notes

Ed. Note: 5731.10 contains provisions analogous to former 5731.02, repealed by 132 v S 326, eff. 7–1–68.

Ed. Note: Former 5731.10 repealed by 132 v S 326, eff. 7–1–68; 1953 H 1; GC 5334–1; see now 5731.19 for provisions analogous to former 5731.10.

Pre–1953 H 1 Amendments: 112 v 103; 111 v 97

Library References

Taxation ⚖=863–894.

Westlaw Topic No. 371.

C.J.S. Taxation § 1114–1119, 1138–1142, 1144–1145, 1147–1153, 1157–1171, 1181, 1190, 1192, 1229.

5731.11 Value of gross estate; interest subject to general power of appointment

(A) The value of the gross estate shall include the value of all property, to the extent of any interest with respect to which the decedent has on the date of the decedent's death a general power of appointment, or with respect to which the decedent has at any time exercised or released such a power of appointment by a disposition which is of such nature that if it were a transfer of property owned by the decedent, such property would be includible in the decedent's gross estate under sections 5731.05 to 5731.08, inclusive, of the Revised Code. A disclaimer or renunciation of such power of appointment shall not be deemed an exercise or a release of such power.

(B) For purposes of this section, "general power of appointment" means a power which is exercisable in favor of the decedent, his estate, his creditors, or the creditors of his estate.

(C) For the purposes of this section, if a general power of appointment created on or before October 21, 1942, has been partially or completely released so that it is no longer a general power of appointment, any such release of such power is neither the release nor the exercise of a general power of appointment if such release occurred before November 1, 1951, or the donee of such power was under a legal disability to release such power on October 21, 1942, and such release occurred not later than six months after the termination of such legal disability.

(1971 S 398, eff. 4–1–72; 132 v S 326)

Historical and Statutory Notes

Ed. Note: Former 5731.11 repealed by 132 v S 326, eff. 7–1–68; 1953 H 1; GC 5334–2; see now 5731.36 for provisions analogous to former 5731.11.

Pre–1953 H 1 Amendments: 115 v Pt 2, 69

Library References

Taxation ⚖=878(2).

Westlaw Topic No. 371.

C.J.S. Taxation § 1117, 1148.

5731.12 Value of gross estate

The value of the gross estate shall include the value of all property to the extent of the amount receivable by the decedent's estate as insurance under policies on the life of the decedent. The value of the gross estate shall not include any amount receivable as insurance under policies on the life of the decedent by beneficiaries other than the decedent's estate, whether paid directly to those beneficiaries, to a testamentary, inter vivos, or employee benefit trust for their benefit, or to a guardian or custodian for the benefit of an incompetent or minor.

(1986 H 139, eff. 7–24–86; 1984 H 794; 1980 S 317; 132 v S 326)

Uncodified Law

1986 H 139, § 3, eff. 7–24–86, reads, in part: Sections 1 and 2 of this act shall apply only to the estates of decedents whose death occurs on or after the effective date of this act.

Historical and Statutory Notes

Ed. Note: Former 5731.12 repealed by 132 v S 326, eff. 7–1–68; 129 v 582; 128 v 125; 127 v 126; 1953 H 1; GC 5335.

Pre–1953 H 1 Amendments: 113 v 512; 108 v Pt 1, 565

Library References

Taxation ⚖=863–894.

Westlaw Topic No. 371.

C.J.S. Taxation § 1114–1119, 1138–1142, 1144–1145, 1147–1153, 1157–1171, 1181, 1190, 1192, 1229.

5731.13 Value of gross estate; transfers for less than adequate consideration

(A) If any one of the transfers, trusts, interests, rights, or powers enumerated and described in sections 5731.05 to 5731.08, inclusive, and 5731.11 of the Revised Code, is made, created, exercised or relinquished for a consideration in money or money's worth, but is not a bona fide sale for an adequate and full consideration in money or money's worth, there shall be included in the gross estate only the excess of the fair market value of the property at the time of death otherwise to be included on account of such transaction, over the value of the consideration received therefor by the decedent.

(B) For purposes of Chapter 5731. of the Revised Code, a relinquishment or promised relinquishment of dower or curtesy, or of a statutory estate created in lieu of dower or curtesy, or of other marital rights in the decedent's property or estate, shall not be considered to any extent a consideration "in money or money's worth."

(132 v S 326, eff. 7–1–68)

Historical and Statutory Notes

Ed. Note: Former 5731.13 repealed by 132 v S 326, eff. 7–1–68; 128 v 991; 1953 H 1; GC 5335–1.

Pre–1953 H 1 Amendments: 112 v 421

Library References

Taxation ⚖=877.

Westlaw Topic No. 371.

C.J.S. Taxation § 1142.

5731.131 Effect on life interest if subject to federal marital deduction

The value of the gross estate shall include the value of any property in which the decedent had an income interest for life as follows:

(A) If a marital deduction was allowed with respect to the transfer of such property to the decedent under section 2523(f) of the Internal Revenue Code, in connection with the determination of the value of the taxable estate of the decedent's predeceasing spouse;

(B) If the decedent's predeceasing spouse was not a resident of this state at the time of death and if a marital deduction was allowed with respect to the transfer of such property to the decedent under section 2056(b)(7) of the Internal Revenue Code, in connection with the determination of the value of the taxable estate of the decedent's predeceasing spouse;

(C) If the decedent's predeceasing spouse died prior to July 1, 1993, and if a marital deduction was allowed with respect to the transfer of such property to the decedent under division (A)(1) of section 5731.15 of the Revised Code as it existed prior to July 1, 1993, in connection with the determination of the value of the taxable estate of the decedent's predeceasing spouse;

(D) If a qualified terminable interest property deduction was allowed with respect to the transfer of such property to the decedent under division (B) of section 5731.15 of the Revised Code, in connection with the determination of the value of the taxable estate of the decedent's predeceasing spouse.

(2005 H 66, eff. 6–30–05; 1990 S 336, § 3, eff. 7–1–93; 1990 S 336, § 1; 1989 H 111, § 1, 3; 1986 H 139; 1983 H 291)

Uncodified Law

2005 H 66, § 557.24: See Uncodified Law under RC 5731.01.

1986 H 139, § 5, eff. 7–24–86, reads: The provisions of section 5731.131 of the Revised Code as amended by this act apply to the estates of decedents who died on or after July 1, 1983, and prior to the effective date of this act, as well as to decedents who die on or after the effective date of this act. If an estate tax return for the estate of a decedent who had an income interest for life in property and who died on or after July 1, 1983 and prior to the effective date of this act, is filed pursuant to Chapter 5731. of the Revised Code prior to the effective date of this act, the executor, administrator, or other person responsible for filing the return may file an amended return to reflect the provisions of section 5731.131 of the Revised Code as revised by this act or, if applicable, may submit a claim for a refund of any estate tax paid that exceeds the estate tax payable after consideration of the revised provisions. An amended return or claim for refund shall be filed, within one year after the effective date of this act, in the same manner as is prescribed for the filing of an estate tax return under section 5731.21 of the Revised Code.

1983 H 291, § 127, eff. 7–1–83, reads: The amendment of sections 2117.06, 5731.01, 5731.011, 5731.02, 5731.05, 5731.09, 5731.14, 5731.15, 5731.16, 5731.18, 5731.21, 5731.22, 5731.26, 5731.42, and 5731.48, the enactment of sections 5731.131, 5731.181, 5731.231, and 5731.99, and the repeal of section 5731.20 of the Revised Code, all by this act, shall apply to the estate of any decedent whose death occurs on or after July 1, 1983.

Historical and Statutory Notes

Amendment Note: 2005 H 66 redesignated former divisions (A)(1) through (A)(4) as (A) through (D); deleted "of 1986,' 26 U.S.C. 2523(f), as amended" from newly redesignated division (A); deleted "of 1986,' 26 U.S.C. 2056(b)(7), as amended" in newly redesignated division (B); deleted former division (B); and made other nonsubstantive changes. Prior to amendment, former division (B) read:

"(B) The amendments made to this section by Amended Substitute House Bill No. 111 and substitute Senate Bill No. 336 of the 118th general assembly that are effective on July 1, 1993, shall apply only to the estates of decedents who die on or after that date."

Library References

Taxation ⚖866, 875(1).
Westlaw Topic No. 371.
C.J.S. Taxation § 1115, 1119, 1140, 1149, 1163.

VALUE OF TAXABLE PROPERTY; EXEMPTIONS; DEDUCTIONS

5731.14 Determination of taxable estate

For purposes of the tax levied by section 5731.02 of the Revised Code, the value of the taxable estate shall be determined by deducting from the value of the gross estate deductions provided for in sections 5731.15 to 5731.17 of the Revised Code.

(2005 H 66, eff. 6–30–05; 2000 S 108, eff. 9–29–00; 1983 H 291, eff. 7–1–83; 132 v S 452)

Uncodified Law

2005 H 66, § 557.24: See Uncodified Law under RC 5731.01.

1983 H 291, § 127, eff. 7–1–83, reads: The amendment of sections 2117.06, 5731.01, 5731.011, 5731.02, 5731.05, 5731.09, 5731.14, 5731.15, 5731.16, 5731.18, 5731.21, 5731.22, 5731.26, 5731.42, and 5731.48, the enactment of sections 5731.131, 5731.181, 5731.231, and 5731.99, and the repeal of section 5731.20 of the Revised Code, all by this act, shall apply to the estate of any decedent whose death occurs on or after July 1, 1983.

Historical and Statutory Notes

Ed. Note: Former 5731.14 repealed by 132 v S 452, eff. 7–1–68; 132 v S 326; prior 5731.14 repealed by 132 v S 326, eff. 7–1–68; 1953 H 1; GC 5335–2.

Pre–1953 H 1 Amendments: 112 v 422

Amendment Note: 2005 H 66 deleted "and 5731.20".

Amendment Note: 2000 S 108 inserted "and 5731.20".

Library References

Taxation ⚖895(6).
Westlaw Topic No. 371.
C.J.S. Taxation § 1183.

5731.15 Marital deduction; pay during missing in action status

For purposes of the tax levied by section 5731.02 of the Revised Code, the value of the taxable estate shall be determined by deducting from the value of the gross estate:

(A) If the decedent dies on or after July 1, 1993 and is survived by a spouse, a marital deduction which shall be allowed in an amount equal to the value of any interest in property that passes or has passed from the decedent to the surviving spouse, but only to the extent the interest is included in the value of the gross estate. For purposes of the marital deduction, an interest in property shall be considered as passing or as having passed from the decedent to the surviving spouse only if one or more of the following apply:

(1) The interest was bequeathed or devised to the surviving spouse in the will of the decedent;

(2) The interest was inherited by the surviving spouse through intestate succession from the decedent;

(3) The interest is a dower interest of the surviving spouse, or the interest is an estate of the surviving spouse that is authorized by the Revised Code and that is in lieu of dower;

(4) The decedent transferred the interest to the surviving spouse at any time;

(5) At the time of the death of the decedent, the interest was held by the decedent and the surviving spouse, or by the decedent, the surviving spouse, and one or more other persons, in any form of joint ownership with a right of survivorship;

(6) The decedent, alone or in conjunction with any other person, had a power to appoint the interest and the interest was so appointed to the surviving spouse, or the surviving spouse acquired the interest as a result of the release or the nonexercise of the power.

(B)(1) In addition to the marital deduction provided by division (A) of this section, if an election is made in accordance with division (B)(2) of this section and the decedent dies on or after July 1, 1993, a qualified terminable interest property deduction. This deduction shall be allowed in an amount equal to all or any specific portion of qualified terminable interest property treated as separate property, but only to the extent that the property is included in the value of the gross estate.

(2) An election to have property treated as qualified terminable interest property for purposes of the deduction provided by division (B)(1) of this section shall be made by the person filing the estate tax return under this chapter, in writing, on or before the date by which the return is required to be filed, determined with regard to any extension of time granted for the filing of the

return. The election shall specify whether all or only a specific portion of qualified terminable interest property treated as separate property shall be taken into account in determining the deduction. If an election as provided in this division is made, the election is irrevocable.

(3) As used in divisions (B)(1) and (2) of this section, "qualified terminable interest property" means property that satisfies all of the following:

(a) It is included in the value of the gross estate;

(b) It passes from the decedent to the surviving spouse of the decedent;

(c) It is property in which the surviving spouse of the decedent has a qualifying interest for life. For purposes of this division, the surviving spouse has a qualifying interest for life if both of the following apply:

(i) The surviving spouse is entitled to all income from the property, which income is payable annually or at more frequent intervals.

(ii) No person has a power to appoint any part of the property to any person other than the surviving spouse. This division shall not apply to a power that is exercisable only at or after the death of the surviving spouse.

(C) The pay and allowances determined by the United States to be due to a member of the armed forces for active duty in Vietnam service for the period between the date declared by the United States as the beginning of his missing in action status to the date of his death as determined by the United States. As used in this division, "Vietnam service" means military service within the Republic of Vietnam during the period between February 28, 1961, to July 1, 1973, or military service in southeast Asia for which hostile fire pay was awarded pursuant to 37 U.S.C. 310, during the period February 28, 1961, to July 1, 1973.

(1991 S 206, § 6, eff. 7–1–93; 1991 S 206, § 1; 1990 S 336, § 3; 1989 H 111, § 1, 3; 1988 S 386; 1987 H 231; 1986 H 139; 1983 H 291; 1981 S 28; 1979 H 26; 1975 S 145; 1973 S 1; 132 v S 326)

Uncodified Law

1991 S 206, § 5, eff. 6–29–91, reads: The version of section 5731.15 of the Revised Code that results from this act is hereby repealed, effective July 1, 1993. This repeal does not affect the version of section 5731.15 of the Revised Code that is scheduled to take effect on July 1, 1993.

1988 S 386, § 39, eff. 3–29–88, reads: The provisions of section 5731.15 of the Revised Code, as amended by this act, apply to the estates of decedents who died on or after July 1, 1983, and prior to the effective date of this act, as well as to decedents who die on or after the effective date of this act. If an estate tax return for the estate of a decedent who is survived by a spouse and who died on or after July 1, 1983, and prior to the effective date of this act, was or is filed pursuant to Chapter 5731. of the Revised Code prior to the effective date of this act, the executor, administrator, or other person responsible for filing the return may file an amended return to reflect the revised marital deduction provided by division (A) of section 5731.15 of the Revised Code or, if applicable, may submit a claim for a refund of any estate tax paid that exceeds the estate tax payable after a consideration of the revised marital deduction. An amended return or claim for refund shall be filed, within one year after the effective date of this act, in the same manner as is prescribed for the filing of an estate tax return under section 5731.21 of the Revised Code.

1987 H 231, § 32, eff. 10–5–87, reads: The provisions of section 5731.15 of the Revised Code, as amended by this act, apply to the estates of decedents who died on or after July 1, 1983, and prior to the effective date of this act, as well as to decedents who die on or after the effective date of this act. If an estate tax return for the estate of a decedent who is survived by a spouse and who died on or after July 1, 1983, and prior to the effective date of this act, was or is filed pursuant to Chapter 5731. of the Revised Code prior to the effective date of this act, the executor, administrator, or other person responsible for filing the return may file an amended return to reflect the revised marital deduction provided by division (A) of section 5731.15 of the Revised Code or, if applicable, may submit a claim for a refund of any estate tax paid that exceeds the estate tax payable after consideration of the revised marital deduction. An amended return or claim for refund shall be filed, within one year after the effective date of this act, in the same manner as is prescribed for the filing of an estate tax return under section 5731.21 of the Revised Code.

1986 H 139, § 4, eff. 7–24–86, reads: The provisions of section 5731.15 of the Revised Code as amended by this act apply to the estates of decedents who died on or after July 1, 1983, and prior to the effective date of this act, as well as to decedents who die on or after the effective date of this act. If an estate tax return for the estate of a decedent who is survived by a spouse and who died on or after July 1, 1983, and prior to the effective date of this act, is filed pursuant to Chapter 5731. of the Revised Code prior to the effective date of this act, the executor, administrator, or other person responsible for filing the return may file an amended return to reflect the revised deduction provided by division (A) of section 5731.15 of the Revised Code or, if applicable, may submit a claim for a refund of any estate tax paid that exceeds the estate tax payable after consideration of the revised deduction. An amended return or claim for refund shall be filed, within one year after the effective date of this act, in the same manner as is prescribed for the filing of an estate tax return under section 5731.21 of the Revised Code.

1983 H 291, § 127, eff. 7–1–83, reads: The amendment of sections 2117.06, 5731.01, 5731.011, 5731.02, 5731.05, 5731.09, 5731.14, 5731.15, 5731.16, 5731.18, 5731.21, 5731.22, 5731.26, 5731.42, and 5731.48, the enactment of sections 5731.131, 5731.181, 5731.231, and 5731.99, and the repeal of section 5731.20 of the Revised Code, all by this act, shall apply to the estate of any decedent whose death occurs on or after July 1, 1983.

1981 S 28, § 3, eff. 10–9–81, reads, in part: Sections 1 and 2 of this act do not apply to the estates of decedents who died prior to January 1, 1982.

Historical and Statutory Notes

Ed. Note: Former 5731.15 repealed by 132 v S 326, eff. 7–1–68; 1953 H 1; GC 5335–3.

Pre–1953 H 1 Amendments: 112 v 422

Library References

Taxation ⊜875, 895(6).
Westlaw Topic No. 371.
C.J.S. Taxation § 1163, 1183.

5731.16 Deductions for funeral and administration expenses, debts, and mortgage debts

(A) For purposes of the tax levied by section 5731.02 of the Revised Code, the value of the taxable estate shall be determined by deducting from the value of the gross estate amounts for the following:

(1) Funeral expenses;

(2) Administration expenses, excluding the value of any money or property set off and allowed under section 2106.13 of the Revised Code, to the extent that such expenses have been or will be actually paid;

(3) Claims against the estate that are outstanding and unpaid as of the date of decedent's death;

(4) Unpaid mortgages on, or any indebtedness in respect of, property if the value of the decedent's interest in the property, undiminished by the mortgage or indebtedness, is included in the value of the gross estate, as are allowable by the laws of this state.

(B) There shall be deducted in determining the taxable estate amounts representing expenses incurred in administering property not subject to claims which is included in the gross estate, to the same extent such amounts would be allowable as a deduction under division (A) of this section if such property were subject to claims and such amounts are paid before the expiration of the period of limitations provided for in section 5731.38 of the Revised Code.

(C) The deduction allowed by this section in the case of claims against the estate, unpaid mortgages, or any indebtedness, when founded on a promise or agreement, is limited to the extent that they were contracted bona fide and for an adequate and full consideration in money or money's worth, except that in any case in which any such claim is founded on a promise or agreement of the decedent to make a contribution or gift to or for the use of any donee described in section 5731.17 of the Revised Code for the purposes specified in that section, the deduction is not so limited, but is limited to the extent that it would be allowable as a deduction under section 5731.17 of the Revised Code if the promise or agreement constituted a bequest.

(D) Any income taxes on income received after the death of the decedent, or property taxes not accrued before his death, or any estate, succession, legacy, or inheritance taxes, shall not be deductible under this section.

(1990 H 346, eff. 5–31–90; 1983 H 291; 1975 S 145; 1971 S 398; 132 v S 326)

Uncodified Law

1990 H 346, § 3, eff. 5–31–90, reads, in part: (A) Sections 1 and 2 of this act shall apply only to the estates of decedents who die on or after the effective date of this act.

1983 H 291, § 127, eff. 7–1–83, reads: The amendment of sections 2117.06, 5731.01, 5731.011, 5731.02, 5731.05, 5731.09, 5731.14, 5731.15, 5731.16, 5731.18, 5731.21, 5731.22, 5731.26, 5731.42, and 5731.48, the enactment of sections 5731.131, 5731.181, 5731.231, and 5731.99, and the repeal of section 5731.20 of the Revised Code, all by this act, shall apply to the estate of any decedent whose death occurs on or after July 1, 1983.

Historical and Statutory Notes

Ed. Note: Former 5731.16 repealed by 132 v S 326, eff. 7–1–68; 1953 H 1; GC 5335–4; see now 5731.24 for provisions analogous to former 5731.16.

Pre–1953 H 1 Amendments: 114 v 597; 112 v 423

Library References

Taxation ⚯895(7).
Westlaw Topic No. 371.
C.J.S. Taxation § 1185, 1187.

Baldwin's Ohio Legislative Service, 1990 Laws of Ohio, H 346—LSC Analysis, p 5–87

5731.161 Taxable estate of transferee spouse; value

(A) As used in this section:

(1) "General power of appointment" has the same meaning as in division (B) of section 5731.11 of the Revised Code.

(2) "Property" means any beneficial interest in property, whether in trust or otherwise, other than a life estate, an estate for a term of years, an annuity, or other similar interest. "Property" includes property passing as a result of the exercise or failure to exercise a power of appointment and also includes a general power of appointment.

(3) "Spousal exemption" means the exemption that was allowed to a transferor spouse's estate and that was equal to the value of any interest in property included in the value of the transferor's gross estate and transferred to or for the benefit of, and vested in, the transferee spouse, but not to exceed either sixty thousand dollars or thirty thousand dollars, whichever amount was applicable.

(4) "Transferee spouse" means the spouse who died on or after July 1, 1983, but prior to July 1, 1986, and within three years of the transferor spouse's death.

(5) "Transferor spouse" means the spouse who died prior to July 1, 1983, and within three years of the transferee spouse's death.

(B) For purposes of the tax levied by section 5731.02 of the Revised Code, the value of the taxable estate of the transferee spouse shall be determined by deducting from the value of the gross estate the value, as specified in this division, of property that was transferred to the transferee spouse by the transferor spouse and that, because of the transfer, was taxed in the estate of the transferor spouse under this chapter. The value of the property for purposes of the deduction shall be the net value of the property actually transferred, as determined and taxed in the estate of the transferor spouse, reduced by the amount of the spousal exemption with respect to the transferee spouse that was allowed in the estate of the transferor spouse, but, in any event, the value of the property for purposes of the deduction shall not exceed the greater of the following:

(1) Five hundred thousand dollars;

(2) One–half of the difference between the value of the gross estate of the transferor spouse and the deductions allowed in the estate of the transferor spouse under section 5731.16 of the Revised Code.

The deduction otherwise allowable under this section shall be reduced by the amount of the marital deduction allowed in the estate of the transferee spouse under section 5731.15 of the Revised Code.

In determining the value of the property, the value of any remainder interest, power of appointment, or similar interest shall not be reduced by the value of any intervening interest that is not considered as property for purposes of this section.

(1984 H 70, eff. 3–28–85)

Library References

Taxation ⚯863–894.
Westlaw Topic No. 371.
C.J.S. Taxation § 1114–1119, 1138–1142, 1144–1145, 1147–1153, 1157–1171, 1181, 1190, 1192, 1229.

5731.17 Deduction for charitable bequests and transfers

(A) For purposes of the tax levied by section 5731.02 of the Revised Code, the value of the taxable estate shall be determined by deducting from the value of the gross estate the amount of all bequests, legacies, devises, or transfers, including the interest which falls into any such bequest, legacy, devise or transfer as a result of an irrevocable disclaimer of a bequest, legacy, devise, transfer or power, if the disclaimer is made before the date prescribed for the filing of the estate tax return:

(1) To or for the use of the United States, any state, territory, any political subdivision thereof, or the District of Columbia, for exclusively public purposes;

(2) To or for the use of any corporation organized and operated exclusively for religious, charitable, scientific, literary, or educational purposes, including the encouragement of art and the prevention of cruelty to children or animals, no part of the net earnings of which inures to the benefit of any private stockholder or individual, and no substantial part of the activities of which is carrying on propaganda or otherwise attempting to influence legislation;

(3) To a trustee or trustees, or a fraternal society, order, or association operating under the lodge system, but only if such contributions or gifts are to be used by such trustee or trustees, or by such fraternal society, order, or association, exclusively for religious, charitable, scientific, literary, or educational purposes, or for the prevention of cruelty to children or animals, and no substantial part of the activities of such trustee or trustees, or of such fraternal society, order, or association, is carrying on propaganda, or otherwise attempting to influence legislation;

(4) To or for the use of any veterans' organization incorporated by act of Congress, or of its departments or local chapters or posts, no part of the net earnings of which inures to the benefit of any private shareholder or individual.

If any estate, succession, or inheritance taxes are, either by the terms of the will, by the law of the jurisdiction under which the estate is administered, or by the law of the jurisdiction imposing the particular tax, payable in whole or in part out of the bequests, legacies, or devises otherwise deductible under this section, then the amount deductible under this section shall be the amount of such bequests, legacies, or devises unreduced by the amount of such taxes.

(B) If, as of the date of a decedent's death, any bequest, legacy, devise or transfer for any of the purposes specified in division (A) of this section is dependent upon the performance of some act or the happening of a precedent event in order that it might become effective, no deduction is allowable unless the possibility that such bequest, legacy, devise or transfer will not become effective is so remote as to be negligible. The present value of a remainder, deferred payment or other limited interest shall be determined by the usual methods of valuation, including the use of tables or mortality and actuarial principles, under rules and regulations prescribed by the tax commissioner.

(132 v S 326, eff. 7–1–68)

Historical and Statutory Notes

Ed. Note: Former 5731.17 repealed by 132 v S 326, eff. 7–1–68; 1953 H 1; GC 5336; see now 5731.37 for provisions analogous to former 5731.17.

Pre–1953 H 1 Amendments: 108 v Pt 2, 1194; 108 v Pt 1, 565; 94 v 101, § 1; 90 v 15, § 5 et seq

Library References

Taxation ⚖876.
Westlaw Topic No. 371.
C.J.S. Taxation § 1161.

MISCELLANEOUS TAXES

5731.18 Additional estate tax; rates

(A) In addition to the tax levied by section 5731.02 of the Revised Code, a tax is hereby levied upon the transfer of the estate of every person dying on or after July 1, 1968, who, at the time of death was a resident of this state, in an amount equal to the maximum credit allowable by subtitle B, Chapter 11 of the Internal Revenue Code, for any taxes paid to any state.

(B) The tax levied on any estate under this section shall be credited with the amount of the tax levied under section 5731.02 of the Revised Code and with the amount of any estate, inheritance, legacy, or succession taxes actually paid to any state or territory of the United States or to the District of Columbia on any property included in the decedent's gross estate for federal estate tax purposes.

(C) The additional tax levied under this section shall be administered, collected, and paid as provided in section 5731.24 of the Revised Code.

(2005 H 66, eff. 6–30–05; 1983 H 291, eff. 7–1–83; 132 v S 326)

Uncodified Law

2005 H 66, § 557.03, eff. 6–30–05, reads:

A credit is hereby allowed against the additional estate tax imposed by section 5731.18 of the Revised Code on the estate of a decedent who dies on or after January 1, 2002, but before the effective date of that section as amended by this act. The credit shall equal that portion of the additional estate tax imposed by section 5731.18 of the Revised Code that is over and above the additional estate tax that would have been imposed if the tax levied by division (A) of that section had been an amount equal to the maximum credit allowable by section 2011 of the Internal Revenue Code that was in effect and applicable on the date of such decedent's death for any taxes paid to any state.

2005 H 66, § 557.24: See Uncodified Law under RC 5731.01.

1983 H 291, § 127, eff. 7–1–83, reads: The amendment of sections 2117.06, 5731.01, 5731.011, 5731.02, 5731.05, 5731.09, 5731.14, 5731.15, 5731.16, 5731.18, 5731.21, 5731.22, 5731.26, 5731.42, and 5731.48, the enactment of sections 5731.131, 5731.181, 5731.231, and 5731.99, and the repeal of section 5731.20 of the Revised Code, all by this act, shall apply to the estate of any decedent whose death occurs on or after July 1, 1983.

Historical and Statutory Notes

Ed. Note: Former 5731.18 repealed by 132 v S 326, eff. 7–1–68; 1953 H 1; GC 5337.

Pre–1953 H 1 Amendments: 108 v Pt 1, 566; 90 v 16, § 6

Amendment Note: 2005 H 66 deleted "his" and "of 1954, 26 U.S.C. 2011, as amended" and made other nonsubstantive changes in division (A).

Library References

Taxation ⚖886.5.
Westlaw Topic No. 371.
C.J.S. Taxation § 1181.

5731.181 Generation–skipping transfers

(A) For purposes of this section, "generation-skipping transfer," "taxable distribution," and "taxable termination" have the same meaning as in Chapter 13 of subtitle B of the Internal Revenue Code.

(B) A tax is hereby levied upon every generation-skipping transfer of property having a situs in this state, that occurs at the same time as, and as a result of, the death of an individual, in an amount equal to the credit allowed by Chapter 13 of subtitle B of the Internal Revenue Code, for any taxes paid to any state in respect of any property included in the generation-skipping transfer.

For purposes of this division, "property having a situs in this state" includes all the following:

(1) Real property situated in this state;

(2) Tangible personal property having an actual situs in this state;

(3) Intangible personal property employed in carrying on a business in this state;

(4) Intangible personal property owned by a trust, the trustee of which resides in or has its principal place of business in this state, or, if there is more than one trustee of the trust, the principal place of administration of which is in this state.

(C) The return with respect to the generation-skipping tax levied by division (B) of this section shall be filed in the form that the tax commissioner shall prescribe, on or before the day prescribed by law, including extensions, for filing the generation-skipping transfer tax return under Chapter 13 of subtitle B of the Internal Revenue Code, for the same generation-skipping transfer. The return shall be filed by the distributee in the case of a taxable distribution and by the trustee in the case of a taxable termination.

(D) The generation-skipping tax levied by division (B) of this section shall be paid, without notice or demand by the tax commissioner, with the return, and shall be charged, collected, and administered in the same manner as estate taxes levied by this chapter. This chapter is generally applicable to, except to the extent it is inconsistent with the nature of, the generation-skipping tax.

(E) If another state levies a generation-skipping tax on a transfer described in division (B) of this section, the tax commissioner may enter into a compromise of the generation-skipping tax levied by division (B) of this section in the manner provided in section 5731.35 of the Revised Code, except that no approval of any probate court is required. If such a compromise agreement is made, no interest and penalties shall accrue for the period prior to the execution of the agreement and for sixty days after its execution.

(2005 H 66, eff. 6–30–05; 1990 H 286, eff. 11–8–90; 1983 H 291)

Uncodified Law

2005 H 66, § 557.24: See Uncodified Law under RC 5731.01.

1990 H 286, § 3, eff. 11–8–90, reads: Sections 1 and 2 of this act apply only to the estates of decedents who die on or after the effective date of this act.

1983 H 291, § 127, eff. 7-1-83, reads: The amendment of sections 2117.06, 5731.01, 5731.011, 5731.02, 5731.05, 5731.09, 5731.14, 5731.15, 5731.16, 5731.18, 5731.21, 5731.22, 5731.26, 5731.42, and 5731.48, the enactment of sections 5731.131, 5731.181, 5731.231, and 5731.99, and the repeal of section 5731.20 of the Revised Code, all by this act, shall apply to the estate of any decedent whose death occurs on or after July 1, 1983.

Historical and Statutory Notes

Amendment Note: 2005 H 66 deleted "of 1986, 100 Stat. 2718, 26 U.S.C. 2601 2624, as amended" in divisions (A),(B), and (C).

Library References

Taxation ⚖877.
Westlaw Topic No. 371.
C.J.S. Taxation § 1142.

5731.19 Nonresident estate tax

(A) A tax is hereby levied upon the transfer of so much of the taxable estate of every person dying on or after July 1, 1968, who, at the time of his death, was not a resident of this state, as consists of real property situated in this state, tangible personal property having an actual situs in this state, and intangible personal property employed in carrying on a business within this state unless exempted from tax under the provisions of section 5731.34 of the Revised Code.

(B) The amount of the tax on such real and tangible personal property shall be determined as follows:

(1) Determine the amount of tax which would be payable under Chapter 5731. of the Revised Code if the decedent had died a resident of this state with all his property situated or located within this state;

(2) Multiply the tax so determined by a fraction, the denominator of which shall be the value of the gross estate wherever situated and the numerator of which shall be the said gross estate value of the real property situated and the tangible personal property having an actual situs in this state and intangible personal property employed in carrying on a business within this state and not exempted from tax under section 5731.34 of the Revised Code. The product shall be the amount of tax payable to this state.

(C) In addition to the tax levied by division (A) of this section, an additional tax is hereby levied on such real and tangible personal property determined as follows:

(1) Determine the amount of tax which would be payable under division (A) of section 5731.18 of the Revised Code, if the decedent had died a resident of this state with all his property situated or located within this state;

(2) Multiply the tax so determined by a fraction, the denominator of which shall be the value of the gross estate wherever situated and the numerator of which shall be the said gross estate value of the real property situated and the tangible property having an actual situs in this state and intangible personal property employed in carrying on a business within this state and not exempted from tax under section 5731.34 of the Revised Code.

The product so derived shall be credited with the amount of the tax determined under division (B) of this section.

(132 v S 326, eff. 7–1–68)

Historical and Statutory Notes

Ed. Note: 5731.19 contains provisions analogous to former 5731.10, repealed by 132 v S 326, eff. 7–1–68.

Ed. Note: Former 5731.19 repealed by 132 v S 326, eff. 7–1–68; 126 v 814; 1953 H 1; GC 5338; see now 5731.23 for provisions analogous to former 5731.19.

Pre–1953 H 1 Amendments: 108 v Pt 2, 1194; 108 v Pt 1, 566; 91 v 170, § 4

Library References

Taxation ⚖867, 886.5.
Westlaw Topic No. 371.
C.J.S. Taxation § 1116, 1141, 1181.

ESTATE TAX RETURN

5731.21 Returns; certificates

(A)(1)(a) Except as provided under division (A)(3) of this section, the executor or administrator, or, if no executor or administrator has been appointed, another person in possession of property the transfer of which is subject to estate taxes under section 5731.02 or division (A) of section 5731.19 of the Revised Code, shall file an estate tax return, within nine months of the date of the decedent's death, in the form prescribed by the tax commissioner, in duplicate, with the probate court of the county. The return shall include all property the transfer of which is subject to estate taxes, whether that property is transferred under the last will and testament of the decedent or otherwise. The time for filing the return may be extended by the tax commissioner.

(b) The estate tax return described in division (A)(1)(a) of this section shall be accompanied by a certificate, in the form prescribed by the tax commissioner, that is signed by the executor, administrator, or other person required to file the return, and that states all of the following:

(i) The fact that the return was filed;

(ii) The date of the filing of the return;

(iii) The fact that the estate taxes under section 5731.02 or division (A) of section 5731.19 of the Revised Code, that are shown to be due in the return, have been paid in full;

(iv) If applicable, the fact that real property listed in the inventory for the decedent's estate is included in the return;

(v) If applicable, the fact that real property not listed in the inventory for the decedent's estate, including, but not limited to, survivorship tenancy property as described in section 5302.17 of the Revised Code or transfer on death property as described in sections 5302.22 and 5302.23 of the Revised Code, also is included in the return. In this regard, the certificate additionally shall describe that real property by the same description used in the return.

(2) The probate court shall forward one copy of the estate tax return described in division (A)(1)(a) of this section to the tax commissioner.

(3) A person shall not be required to file a return under division (A) of this section if the decedent was a resident of this state and the value of the decedent's gross estate is twenty-five thousand dollars or less in the case of a decedent dying on or after July 1, 1968, but before January 1, 2001; two hundred thousand dollars or less in the case of a decedent dying on or after January 1, 2001, but before January 1, 2002; or three hundred thirty-eight thousand three hundred thirty-three dollars

or less in the case of a decedent dying on or after January 1, 2002.

(4)(a) Upon receipt of the estate tax return described in division (A)(1)(a) of this section and the accompanying certificate described in division (A)(1)(b) of this section, the probate court promptly shall give notice of the return, by a form prescribed by the tax commissioner, to the county auditor. The auditor then shall make a charge based upon the notice and shall certify a duplicate of the charge to the county treasurer. The treasurer then shall collect, subject to division (A) of section 5731.25 of the Revised Code or any other statute extending the time for payment of an estate tax, the tax so charged.

(b) Upon receipt of the return and the accompanying certificate, the probate court also shall forward the certificate to the auditor. When satisfied that the estate taxes under section 5731.02 or division (A) of section 5731.19 of the Revised Code, that are shown to be due in the return, have been paid in full, the auditor shall stamp the certificate so forwarded to verify that payment. The auditor then shall return the stamped certificate to the probate court.

(5)(a) The certificate described in division (A)(1)(b) of this section is a public record subject to inspection and copying in accordance with section 149.43 of the Revised Code. It shall be kept in the records of the probate court pertaining to the decedent's estate and is not subject to the confidentiality provisions of section 5731.90 of the Revised Code.

(b) All persons are entitled to rely on the statements contained in a certificate as described in division (A)(1)(b) of this section if it has been filed in accordance with that division, forwarded to a county auditor and stamped in accordance with division (A)(4) of this section, and placed in the records of the probate court pertaining to the decedent's estate in accordance with division (A)(5)(a) of this section. The real property referred to in the certificate shall be free of, and may be regarded by all persons as being free of, any lien for estate taxes under section 5731.02 and division (A) of section 5731.19 of the Revised Code.

(B) An estate tax return filed under this section, in the form prescribed by the tax commissioner, and showing that no estate tax is due shall result in a determination that no estate tax is due, if the tax commissioner within three months after the receipt of the return by the department of taxation, fails to file exceptions to the return in the probate court of the county in which the return was filed. A copy of exceptions to a return of that nature, when the tax commissioner files them within that period, shall be sent by ordinary mail to the person who filed the return. The tax commissioner is not bound under this division by a determination that no estate tax is due, with respect to property not disclosed in the return.

(C) If the executor, administrator, or other person required to file an estate tax return fails to file it within nine months of the date of the decedent's death, the tax commissioner may determine the estate tax in that estate and issue a certificate of determination in the same manner as is provided in division (B) of section 5731.27 of the Revised Code. A certificate of determination of that nature has the same force and effect as though a return had been filed and a certificate of determination issued with respect to the return.

(2002 H 675, eff. 12-13-02; 2001 H 94, eff. 9-5-01; 2000 S 108, eff. 9-29-00; 2000 H 313, eff. 8-29-00; 1990 H 286, eff. 11-8-90; 1986 H 139; 1983 H 291; 1981 S 28; 1978 H 826; 1971 S 413; 132 v S 326)

Uncodified Law

1990 H 286, § 3, eff. 11-8-90, reads: Sections 1 and 2 of this act apply only to the estates of decedents who die on or after the effective date of this act.

1988 S 386, § 39: See Uncodified Law under 5731.15.

1986 H 139, § 3: See Uncodified Law under 5731.12.

1983 H 291, § 127, eff. 7-1-83, reads: The amendment of sections 2117.06, 5731.01, 5731.011, 5731.02, 5731.05, 5731.09, 5731.14, 5731.15, 5731.16, 5731.18, 5731.21, 5731.22, 5731.26, 5731.42, and 5731.48, the enactment of sections 5731.131, 5731.181, 5731.231, and 5731.99, and the repeal of section 5731.20 of the Revised Code, all by this act, shall apply to the estate of any decedent whose death occurs on or after July 1, 1983.

1981 S 28, § 3, eff. 10-9-81, reads, in part: Sections 1 and 2 of this act do not apply to the estates of decedents who died prior to January 1, 1982.

Historical and Statutory Notes

Ed. Note: Former 5731.21 repealed by 132 v S 326, eff. 7-1-68; 1953 H 1; GC 5340; see now 5731.31 for provisions analogous to former 5731.21.

Pre-1953 H 1 Amendments: 108 v Pt 1, 567

Amendment Note: 2002 H 675 deleted "may, but" after "A person" and the last sentence in division (A)(3). Prior to deletion the last sentence in division (A)(3) read:

"If a probate court issues an order that grants a summary release from administration in connection with a decedent's estate under section 2113.031 of the Revised Code, that order eliminates the duty of all persons to file an estate tax return and certificate under divisions (A)(1)(a) and (b) of this section with respect to the estate for which the order was granted."

Amendment Note: 2001 H 94 added "three hundred thirty-three" after "three hundred thirty-eight thousand" in paragraph (A)(3).

Amendment Note: 2000 S 108 rewrote division (A)(3), which prior thereto read:

"(3) If the value of the gross estate of the decedent is twenty-five thousand dollars or less and the decedent was a resident of this state, the person otherwise required to file a return may file a return, but shall not be required to do so. If a probate court issues an order that grants a summary release from administration in connection with a decedent's estate under section 2113.031 of the Revised Code, that order eliminates the duty of all persons to file an estate tax return and certificate under divisions (A)(1)(a) and (b) of this section with respect to the estate for which the order was granted."

Amendment Note: 2000 H 313 inserted "or transfer on death property as described in sections 5302.22 and 5302.23 of the Revised Code" in division (A)(1)(b)(v); inserted the last sentence in division (A)(3); and made other nonsubstantive changes.

Library References

Taxation ⚖893.
Westlaw Topic No. 371.
C.J.S. Taxation § 1190.

5731.22 Failure to file return; penalties; persons liable

If the executor, administrator, or other person required to file a return fails to file the return required by this chapter on the date prescribed therefor, determined with regard to any extension of time for filing, unless it is shown that such failure is due to reasonable cause and not due to willful neglect, there shall be added to the amount of tax as finally determined a penalty determined by the tax commissioner, in the amount of five per cent of the amount of that tax if the failure is not for more than one month, or, if the failure is for more than one month, in the amount of five per cent of the amount of that tax plus an additional five per cent for each additional month or fraction of a month during which the failure continues, not exceeding twenty-five per cent in the aggregate. If, due to fraud, there is a failure to file the return or an underpayment of tax due under this chapter, there shall be added to the amount of tax as finally determined a penalty determined by the tax commissioner, in an amount not to exceed ten thousand dollars. The penalties imposed by this section shall be collected at the same time and in the same manner as the tax itself.

The penalties shall be charged against the executor, administrator, or other person having custody or control of any property the transfer of which is subject to estate tax, and such executor, administrator, or other person is personally liable for the penalties. Such penalties shall be divided in the same manner prescribed for the division of the tax in sections 5731.50 and 5731.51 of the Revised Code.

(1983 H 291, eff. 7–1–83; 132 v S 326)

Uncodified Law

1983 H 291, § 127, eff. 7–1–83, reads: The amendment of sections 2117.06, 5731.01, 5731.011, 5731.02, 5731.05, 5731.09, 5731.14, 5731.15, 5731.16, 5731.18, 5731.21, 5731.22, 5731.26, 5731.42, and 5731.48, the enactment of sections 5731.131, 5731.181, 5731.231, and 5731.99, and the repeal of section 5731.20 of the Revised Code, all by this act, shall apply to the estate of any decedent whose death occurs on or after July 1, 1983.

Historical and Statutory Notes

Ed. Note: Former 5731.22 repealed by 132 v S 326, eff. 7–1–68; 1953 H 1; GC 5341.

Pre–1953 H 1 Amendments: 108 v Pt 1, 568; 90 v 16, § 12

Library References

Taxation ⚖️906.
Westlaw Topic No. 371.
C.J.S. Taxation § 1207.

RETURNS AND PAYMENTS; TIME REQUIREMENTS

5731.23 Time for payment of tax

Subject to division (A) of section 5731.25 of the Revised Code or any other statute extending the time for payment of an estate tax, the tax levied by section 5731.02 and division (A) of section 5731.19 of the Revised Code shall, without notice or demand by the tax commissioner, be due and payable by the person liable for it, at the expiration of nine months from the date of the decedent's death, to the treasurer of the county. If any amount of tax levied by section 5731.02 or division (A) of section 5731.19 of the Revised Code is not paid on or before nine months from the date of the decedent's death, interest on such amount shall be paid for the period from such date to the date paid, computed at the federal short-term rate determined by the tax commissioner under section 5703.47 of the Revised Code. Interest at the same rate shall be paid on any amount of tax determined to be due by way of deficiency from nine months from the date of the decedent's death to the date of payment thereof. Such interest shall be charged and collected in the same manner as the tax.

Interest computed at the federal short-term rate determined by the tax commissioner under section 5703.47 of the Revised Code shall be allowed and paid upon any overpayment of tax levied by section 5731.02 or division (A) of section 5731.19 of the Revised Code from nine months from the date of the decedent's death or the date of payment of the tax, whichever is later, to the date such overpayment is repaid.

At any time after nine months from the date of the decedent's death, payment of an estimated deficiency may be made and shall be credited against any deficiency of tax finally determined. Interest on any deficiency ultimately determined to be due shall be charged only upon the unpaid portion thereof.

(2005 H 66, eff. 6–30–05; 1986 H 139, eff. 7–24–86; 1982 S 530; 1971 S 413; 132 v S 452)

Uncodified Law

1986 H 139, § 3: See Uncodified Law under 5731.12.

Historical and Statutory Notes

Ed. Note: 5731.23 contains provisions analogous to former 5731.19, repealed by 132 v S 326, eff. 7–1–68.

Ed. Note: Former 5731.23 repealed by 132 v S 452, eff. 7–1–68; 132 v S 326; prior 5731.23 repealed by 132 v S 326, eff. 7–1–68; 1953 H 1; GC 5342.

Pre–1953 H 1 Amendments: 108 v Pt 2, 1195; 108 v Pt 1, 568; 90 v 16, § 11, 12

Amendment Note: 2005 H 66 substituted "federal short–term rate determined by the tax commissioner under" for "rate per annum prescribed by" in the first and second paragraph; and deleted the last sentence of the second paragraph, which prior thereto read: "Such payment may be made upon an estimated basis whether or not a return is filed, and shall be charged and collected in the same manner as provided in section 5731.21 of the Revised Code."

Library References

Taxation ⚖️903.
Westlaw Topic No. 371.
C.J.S. Taxation § 1220.

5731.24 Time for return and payment of additional tax

If an additional tax prescribed by section 5731.18 of the Revised Code is due, the executor, administrator, or other person required to file the estate tax return, within sixty days after the date of the final determination of the federal estate tax liability, shall file an additional tax return, in the form prescribed by the tax commissioner, in the same manner as is prescribed for the filing of the estate tax return. Subject to division (A) of section 5731.25 of the Revised Code or any other statue [*sic*] extending the time for payment of an estate tax, the additional tax shall be paid, without notice or demand by the tax commissioner, with the return, and shall be charged and collected in the same manner as the estate tax, except that no interest shall accrue until sixty days after the date of the final determination of the federal estate tax liability.

(1986 H 139, eff. 7–24–86; 132 v S 326)

Uncodified Law

1986 H 139, § 3: See Uncodified Law under 5731.12.

Historical and Statutory Notes

Ed. Note: 5731.24 contains provisions analogous to former 5731.16, repealed by 132 v S 326, eff. 7–1–68.

Ed. Note: Former 5731.24 repealed by 132 v S 326, eff. 7–1–68; 1953 H 1; GC 5342–1.

Pre–1953 H 1 Amendments: 110 v 26

Library References

Taxation ⚖️893, 903.
Westlaw Topic No. 371.
C.J.S. Taxation § 1190, 1220.

5731.25 Extension of time for payment because of undue hardship; postponement of payment at election of executor or administrator; interest; bond

(A)(1) As used in this division, "undue hardship" means that any of the following applies:

(a) There is difficulty in marshalling liquid assets of the gross estate that are located in several jurisdictions;

(b) A substantial portion of the assets of the gross estate consists of rights to receive payments in the future, including, but not limited to, annuities, copyright royalties, contingent fees, and accounts receivable;

(c) The size of the gross estate cannot be determined accurately because a claim to substantial assets of the decedent is subject to litigation;

(d) Despite reasonable efforts to convert assets of the gross estate into cash, there are not sufficient liquid funds in the gross estate to pay the entire amount of an estate tax imposed by this chapter when it is due, to provide for the reasonable needs of the widow and dependent children of the decedent during the remaining period of the administration of the estate, and to pay claims against the estate that are due and payable;

(e) A significant portion of the gross estate consists of a farm or a closely-held business, and there are not readily available, sufficient funds in the gross estate to pay an estate tax imposed by this chapter and any federal estate tax. For purposes of this division, funds shall not be considered readily available because the farm or closely-held business could be sold to persons who are not related by consanguinity or affinity to the decedent, at a price that equals the fair market value of the farm or closely-held business.

(f) Assets in the gross estate that would have to be liquidated to pay an estate tax imposed by this chapter when due, only could be sold at a price that is considered a sacrifice price or only could be sold in a depressed market.

(g) Other circumstances exist as specified by a rule of the tax commissioner. The tax commissioner may adopt rules that specify circumstances not described in divisions (A)(1)(a) to (f) of this section that he considers constitute undue hardship.

(2) If an estate tax return is filed pursuant to this chapter and estate tax due, including a deficiency in tax, cannot be paid in whole or in part because of undue hardship to the estate or a person required to pay tax, the tax commissioner shall extend the time for payment of the tax or a portion of it for a period or periods, subject to the limitations set forth in this division. The maximum time of one period of extension shall be one year, and the maximum time of all periods of extension shall be fourteen years. The tax commissioner shall prescribe rules that govern extensions authorized by this division.

(B) If the value of a reversionary or remainder interest in property is included under this chapter in the value of the gross estate, the payment of the part of the tax imposed by this chapter attributable to such interest may, at the election of the executor, administrator, or any other person liable for such tax, be postponed until six months after the termination of the precedent interest or interests in property. The amount, the payment of which is so postponed, shall bear interest at the rate of three per cent per annum from the date fixed for payment of the tax, which interest shall be paid by the person liable for the tax in addition to the tax. The postponement of such amount shall be under rules prescribed by the tax commissioner, and shall be upon condition that the executor, administrator, or any other person liable for the tax, gives bond to the county treasurer in such amount, and with such sureties as the tax commissioner considers necessary, conditioned upon the payment within six months after the termination of such precedent interest or interests of the amount, the payment of which is so postponed, together with interest on it, as provided in this division.

(1986 H 139, eff. 7–24–86; 132 v S 326)

Uncodified Law

1986 H 139, § 3: See Uncodified Law under 5731.12.

Historical and Statutory Notes

Ed. Note: Former 5731.25 repealed by 132 v S 326, eff 7–1–68; 1953 H 1; GC 5342–2.

Pre–1953 H 1 Amendments: 110 v 26

Library References

Taxation ⚖903.
Westlaw Topic No. 371.
C.J.S. Taxation § 1220.

PROCEDURAL PROVISIONS

5731.26 Duties and powers of tax commissioner

(A) The tax commissioner shall promptly determine the correctness of the return with respect to the includibility of property, the fair market value or, if applicable, the actual qualified use value of the assets included in the gross estate, the allowance of the credit against the tax and deductions, and all other matters necessary to determine the correct amount of the tax. For this purpose, he may issue subpoenas, compel the attendance of witnesses and the production of books and papers, examine the witnesses under oath concerning any relevant matter, and require the submission of affidavits and forms which he may deem necessary to determine the correct amount of the tax.

The tax commissioner may designate an employee or employees of the county auditor or of the probate court of any county, with the consent of the county auditor or of the probate judge of that county, as his agent or agents to assist him in accepting filings of returns in the county, in determining the correctness of the returns filed in the county, and in complying with this chapter. The employee or employees so designated shall have all of the powers granted to the tax commissioner for these purposes.

(B) The tax commissioner shall give notice to the person filing the return of any adjustments which he proposes to make, and, at the request of the person, shall set a time for an administrative conference on the notice in the county or, by agreement of the person filing the return and the tax commissioner, in Columbus. At the conclusion of such conference, or if the conference is waived by the person filing the return, the tax commissioner shall proceed with the final determination of the tax liability as provided in section 5731.27 of the Revised Code.

(C) At or before the time of the administrative conference, the person filing the return and the tax commissioner may agree in writing to have the correctness of the return as to any item determined in accordance with the final determination of such item for federal estate tax purposes. If such agreement is made, the person filing the return shall, within sixty days after the final determination of the federal estate tax liability, furnish to the tax commissioner such information as may be required to determine the tax in accordance with such agreement, and the tax commissioner shall make his final determination of tax liability in the same manner as is provided in section 5731.27 of the Revised Code.

(1983 H 291, eff. 7–1–83; 132 v S 326)

Uncodified Law

1983 H 291, § 127, eff. 7–1–83, reads: The amendment of sections 2117.06, 5731.01, 5731.011, 5731.02, 5731.05, 5731.09, 5731.14, 5731.15, 5731.16, 5731.18, 5731.21, 5731.22, 5731.26, 5731.42, and 5731.48, the enactment of sections 5731.131, 5731.181, 5731.231, and 5731.99, and the repeal of section 5731.20 of the Revised Code, all by this act, shall apply to the estate of any decedent whose death occurs on or after July 1, 1983.

Historical and Statutory Notes

Ed. Note: Former 5731.26 repealed by 132 v S 326, eff. 7–1–68; 1953 H 1; GC 5342–3.

Pre–1953 H 1 Amendments: 111 v 97

Library References

Taxation ⚖893.
Westlaw Topic No. 371.

5731.27 Certificate of determination of tax liability; deficiency; refund

(A) The tax commissioner shall, if he determines that a return indicating that a tax is due is correct as filed, issue a certificate of determination of final estate tax liability showing the amount of such liability, if any, in triplicate, one copy of which shall be sent by regular mail to the person filing the return, one copy of which shall be sent to the county auditor for the county in which the return was filed, and one copy of which shall be sent to the probate court of the county in which the return was filed if there is an administration of or other proceedings in the decedent's estate.

(B) The tax commissioner, if he determines a deficiency or refund of tax or penalty addition to tax, shall issue his certificate of determination stating the adjusted amount of the tax due and the amount of any refund, deficiency, or penalty. Such certificate also shall state whether or not any portion of the tax liability has been reserved for later determination in accordance with division (C) of section 5731.26 of the Revised Code. Such certificate shall be issued in triplicate, one copy of which shall be sent by certified mail, return receipt requested, to the person filing the return, or to the person required to file the return if no such return was filed, one copy of which shall be sent to the county auditor for the county in which the return was filed or was required to be filed, and one copy of which shall be sent to the probate court for the county in which the return was filed or required to be filed if there will be an administration of or other proceedings in the decedent's estate. The person required to file the return, or any interested party, shall have sixty days from the date of receipt of such certificate by the person required to file the return within which to file exceptions to such determination as provided in section 5731.30 of the Revised Code.

(C) The county auditor, if no exceptions have been filed within the time specified in division (B) of this section, or if the right to file exceptions has been waived by all interested parties by written waivers filed with the county auditor, shall:

(1) If the certificate of determination is for a refund, draw his warrant for the proper amount of the refund and interest on it, which warrant shall be paid by the county treasurer out of any money in his possession to the credit of estate taxes;

(2) If the certificate of determination is for a deficiency or penalty, make a charge based upon such determination, and certify a duplicate of it to the county treasurer, who shall collect, subject to division (A) of section 5731.25 of the Revised Code or any other statute extending the time for payment of an estate tax, the deficiency or penalty so charged.

(1986 H 139, eff. 7–24–86; 132 v S 326)

Uncodified Law

1986 H 139, § 3: See Uncodified Law under 5731.12.

Historical and Statutory Notes

Ed. Note: 5731.27 contains provisions analogous to former 5731.39, repealed by 132 v S 326, eff. 7–1–68.

Ed. Note: Former 5731.27 repealed by 132 v S 326, eff. 7–1–68; 1953 H 1; GC 5342–4.

Pre–1953 H 1 Amendments: 112 v 190

Library References

Taxation ⚖893, 904.
Westlaw Topic No. 371.
C.J.S. Taxation § 1190, 1222.

5731.28 Refund; time for filing claim

If any debts deductible under section 5731.16 of the Revised Code are proved against the gross estate after the tax levied by section 5731.02 or division (A) of section 5731.19 of the Revised Code has been determined, or if the determination of taxes so made is erroneous due to a mistake of fact or law, a claim for refund of tax may be filed by an executor, administrator, trustee, person in possession of property subject to tax, or any transferee thereof, within three years from the time the return was required to be filed (determined without regard to any extension of time for filing), in the form prescribed by the tax commissioner. The claim for refund shall be filed in the same manner as is prescribed for the filing of a return in section 5731.21 of the Revised Code and the determination of its correctness shall be made in the same manner as is provided for in the case of the return itself.

(1976 S 466, eff. 5–26–76; 132 v S 326)

Historical and Statutory Notes

Ed. Note: 5731.28 contains provisions analogous to former 5731.20, repealed by 132 v S 326, eff. 7–1–68.

Ed. Note: Former 5731.28 repealed by 132 v S 326, eff. 7–1–68; 1953 H 1; GC 5343.

Pre–1953 H 1 Amendments: 108 v Pt 1, 569

Library References

Taxation ⚖904.
Westlaw Topic No. 371.
C.J.S. Taxation § 1222.

APPEALS

5731.30 Appeal to probate court from determination of tax commissioner; notice; hearing

The tax commissioner, the person required to file the return, or any interested party may file exceptions in writing to the tax commissioner's final determination of taxes, with the probate court of the county. Exceptions shall be filed within sixty days from the receipt of the certificate of determination issued by the tax commissioner, stating the grounds upon which such exceptions are taken. The court shall, by order, fix a time, not less than ten days thereafter, for the hearing of such exceptions, and shall give such notice of that hearing as it considers necessary, provided, that a copy of such notice and of such exceptions shall be forthwith mailed to the tax commissioner. Upon the hearing of such exceptions, the court may make a just and proper order. No costs shall be allowed by the court on such exceptions.

In a like manner, exceptions may be filed to the disallowance or partial disallowance of any claim for refund of taxes filed pursuant to section 5731.28 of the Revised Code.

Upon redetermination of taxes pursuant to this section, if no appeal is taken from the redetermination, the tax commissioner shall issue his certificate of determination of taxes reflecting the corrected determination in the same manner as is provided in section 5731.27 of the Revised Code.

(1986 H 139, eff. 7–24–86; 132 v S 326)

Uncodified Law

1986 H 139, § 3: See Uncodified Law under 5731.12.

Historical and Statutory Notes

Ed. Note: 5731.30 contains provisions analogous to former 5731.38, repealed by 132 v S 326, eff. 7–1–68.

Ed. Note: Former 5731.30 repealed by 132 v S 326, eff. 7–1–68; 132 v S 321; 1953 H 1; GC 5343–2.

Pre–1953 H 1 Amendments: 121 v 319; 112 v 190

Library References

Taxation ⚖900(5).
Westlaw Topic No. 371.
C.J.S. Taxation § 1205.

5731.31 Jurisdiction of probate court

The probate court of the county has jurisdiction to determine all questions concerning the administration of the taxes levied by this chapter, and all questions concerning the proper determination of the amount of such taxes or penalties upon exceptions filed as provided in section 5731.30 of the Revised Code. Such jurisdiction shall exist not only as to the transfer of property which would otherwise invoke the jurisdiction of such court, but shall extend to all cases covered by this chapter, so that all transfers, taxable under this chapter, whether made under the last will and testament of the decedent or otherwise, shall be within such jurisdiction.

(1986 H 139, eff. 7–24–86; 132 v S 326)

Uncodified Law

1986 H 139, § 3: See Uncodified Law under 5731.12.

Historical and Statutory Notes

Ed. Note: 5731.31 contains provisions analogous to former 5731.21, repealed by 132 v S 326, eff. 7–1–68.

Ed. Note: Former 5731.31 repealed by 132 v S 326, eff. 7–1–68; 1953 H 1; GC 5344.

Pre–1953 H 1 Amendments: 108 v Pt 1, 570

Library References

Taxation ⚖900(5).
Westlaw Topic No. 371.
C.J.S. Taxation § 1205.

5731.32 Appeal from final order of probate court

An appeal may be taken by any party, including the tax commissioner, from the final order of the probate court under section 5731.30 of the Revised Code in the manner provided by law for appeals from orders of the probate court in other cases. An appeal by the tax commissioner may be perfected in the manner provided by law.

Upon redetermination of taxes pursuant to this section, the tax commissioner shall issue his certificate of determination of taxes reflecting the corrected determination thereof in the same manner as is provided in section 5731.27 of the Revised Code.

(132 v S 326, eff. 7–1–68)

Historical and Statutory Notes

Ed. Note: 5731.32 contains provisions analogous to former 5731.40, repealed by 132 v S 326, eff. 7–1–68.

Ed. Note: Former 5731.32 repealed by 132 v S 326, eff. 7–1–68; 1953 H 1; GC 5345.

Pre–1953 H 1 Amendments: 110 v 26; 108 v Pt 1, 570

Library References

Taxation ⚖900(5).
Westlaw Topic No. 371.
C.J.S. Taxation § 1205.

MISCELLANEOUS PROVISIONS

5731.33 Payment; receipts; duties of county treasurer; prohibitions

(A)(1) Upon the payment of [1] the county treasurer of any tax due under this chapter, the treasurer shall issue a receipt for the payment in triplicate. He shall deliver one copy to the person paying the taxes, and he immediately shall send the original receipt to the tax commissioner, who shall certify the original receipt and immediately transmit it to the probate court for the county in which the return has been filed if there is an administration of or other proceedings in the decedent's estate.

(2) Upon the payment to a county treasurer of all estate taxes due under section 5731.02 or division (A) of section 5731.19 of the Revised Code with respect to a particular decedent's estate, the treasurer, in order to assist the county auditor in performing his responsibility under division (A)(4)(b) of section 5731.21 of the Revised Code, also shall notify the auditor, in writing, of the full payment of those taxes.

(B) An executor, administrator, or testamentary trustee is not entitled to credits in his accounts and is not entitled to be discharged from liability for taxes due under this chapter, and the estate under his control shall not be distributed, unless a certified receipt has been filed with the probate court as described in division (A)(1) of this section.

(C) Any person, upon the payment of one dollar to a county treasurer issuing a receipt as described in division (A)(1) of this section, shall be entitled to a duplicate receipt, executed in the same manner as the original receipt.

(1990 H 286, eff. 11–8–90; 1986 H 139; 132 v S 326)

[1] Prior and current versions differ; although no amendment to this language was indicated in 1990 H 286, "of" appeared as "to" in 1986 H 139.

Uncodified Law

1990 H 286, § 3, eff. 11–8–90, reads: Sections 1 and 2 of this act apply only to the estates of decedents who die on or after the effective date of this act.

1986 H 139, § 3: See Uncodified Law under 5731.12.

Historical and Statutory Notes

Ed. Note: 5731.33 contains provisions analogous to former 5731.41, repealed by 132 v S 326, eff. 7–1–68.

Ed. Note: Former 5731.33 repealed by 132 v S 326, eff. 7–1–68; 1953 H 1; GC 5345–1.

Pre–1953 H 1 Amendments: 111 v 97

Library References

Taxation ⚖903.
Westlaw Topic No. 371.
C.J.S. Taxation § 1220.

5731.34 Tax imposed on transfers of intangible personal property employed in business; reciprocity

No estate or additional tax shall be imposed upon any transfer of intangible personal property by or from a person who was not legally domiciled in this state at the time of his death, or by reason of the death of such a person, whether such person was the legal or the beneficial owner of such property, and whether or not such property was held for him in this state or elsewhere by another, in trust or otherwise, unless such property was employed by such non-resident in carrying on business within this state. No estate or additional tax shall be imposed upon the transfer of intangible personal property in any case if the laws of the state, territory, or country of domicile of the transferor at the time of his death contained a reciprocal exemption provision under which non-residents were exempted from transfer or death taxes of every character on personal property, except tangible personal property having an actual situs therein, if the state, territory, or country of domicile of such non-resident allowed a similar exemption to residents of the state, territory, or country of domicile of such transferor.

(1969 H 1, eff. 3–18–69; 132 v S 326)

Historical and Statutory Notes

Ed. Note: 5731.34 contains provisions of former 5731.07, repealed by 132 v S 326, eff. 7–1–68.

Ed. Note: Former 5731.34 repealed by 132 v S 326, eff. 7–1–68; 1953 H 1; GC 5345–2.

Pre–1953 H 1 Amendments: 111 v 97

Library References

Taxation ⚖ 867(1).
Westlaw Topic No. 371.
C.J.S. Taxation § 1116, 1141.

5731.35 Foreign estate taxes; compromise

When a probate court or the tax commissioner determines or claims that a decedent was domiciled in this state at the date of decedent's death, and when the taxing authorities of another state, territory, or possession of the United States, or the District of Columbia, make a like claim on behalf of their state, territory, or possession of the United States, or the District of Columbia, the tax commissioner, with the approval of the probate court having jurisdiction of the estate, may enter into a written agreement or compromise with the taxing authorities of such other state, territory, or possession of the United States, or the District of Columbia, and the executor, administrator, or personal representatives of the estate, that a certain amount may be accepted in full satisfaction of any and all estate and additional taxes imposed under Chapter 5731. of the Revised Code, including any interest or penalties accruing to the date of the signing of the agreement. The agreement shall also fix the amount to be accepted by the taxing authorities of such other state, territory, or possession of the United States, or the District of Columbia, in full satisfaction of their inheritance, succession, and estate taxes. Unless the amount of the tax, so agreed upon, is paid within sixty days after the date of execution of the agreement, interest and penalties, as provided under Chapter 5731. of the Revised Code, shall thereafter accrue upon the amount fixed in the agreement, but the time between fifteen months from the date of decedent's death and the signing of such agreement, shall not be included in computing interest or penalties.

(132 v S 326, eff. 7–1–68)

Historical and Statutory Notes

Ed. Note: 5731.35 contains provisions analogous to former 5731.081, repealed by 132 v S 326, eff. 7–1–68.

Ed. Note: Former 5731.35 repealed by 132 v S 326, eff. 7–1–68; 1953 H 1; GC 5345–3.

Pre–1953 H 1 Amendments: 114 v 799

Library References

Taxation ⚖ 856.1, 868(2).
Westlaw Topic No. 371.
C.J.S. Taxation § 1111–1120, 1131, 1139.

5731.36 Administrator of foreign death tax laws deemed creditor of decedent; reciprocity

(A) The official or body charged with the administration of the estate of [1] other death tax laws of the domiciliary state of a nonresident decedent is deemed a creditor of the decedent and may sue in the courts of this state and enforce any claim for taxes, penalties, and interest due to that state or a political subdivision of that state. This section applies to the estate of a decedent not domiciled in this state only if the laws of his domicile state contain a provision, of any nature, by which this state is given reasonable assurance of the collection of its estate and other death taxes, interest, and penalties from the estates of decedents dying domiciled in this state.

(B) This section does not apply to the generation-skipping tax levied by division (B) of section 5731.181 of the Revised Code.

(C) This section shall be liberally construed in order to ensure that the state of domicile of a decedent receives any estate or other death taxes, interest, and penalties due it from the decedent's estate.

(D) As used in this section, "state" includes any state or territory of the United States, the District of Columbia, and Canada or any province of Canada.

(1990 H 286, eff. 11–8–90; 132 v S 326)

[1] So in original; 1990 H 286. Should this read "or"?

Uncodified Law

1990 H 286, § 3, eff. 11–8–90, reads: Sections 1 and 2 of this act apply only to the estates of decedents who die on or after the effective date of this act.

Historical and Statutory Notes

Ed. Note: 5731.36 contains provisions analogous to former 5731.11, repealed by 132 v S 326, eff. 7–1–68.

Ed. Note: Former 5731.36 repealed by 132 v S 326, eff. 7–1–68; 1953 H 1; GC 5345–4.

Pre–1953 H 1 Amendments: 114 v 799

5731.37 Estate tax lien and discharge, restriction, or transfer; personal liability of executor or administrator

(A) Taxes levied by this chapter shall be, until restricted, transferred, or discharged pursuant to this division, until paid, or unless division (A)(5)(b) of section 5731.21 of the Revised Code applies to them, a lien upon all property subject to the taxes. This lien:

(1) Is discharged, as to property applied to costs and expenses of administration, property constituting the allowance made to the surviving spouse, minor children, or surviving spouse and minor children of the decedent under section 2106.13 of the Revised Code for their support, and all of the property of a decedent that is subject to inclusion in the gross estate and that has been disclosed to the tax commissioner by the time a certificate of discharge is issued;

(2) Is transferred, to the extent of any such property sold by the executor, administrator, or trustee for the purpose of paying debts, administration expenses, or taxes of the estate, or for any purpose to a bona fide purchaser for an adequate and full consideration in money or money's worth, to the money or other property received from the purchaser. Knowledge that the property is being sold by a fiduciary and that it otherwise would be subject to the estate tax lien does not preclude the purchaser from being classified as a bona fide purchaser.

(3) May be, by written authorization of the tax commissioner, restricted to all property that is subject to such taxes, and not

specifically released, transferred to other property on conditions acceptable to the tax commissioner, or fully discharged, each upon conditions, including payment of a reasonable fee, prescribed by rules adopted under section 5703.14 of the Revised Code, when he determines that any of these actions will not jeopardize the collection of the taxes;

(4) Shall be restricted, transferred, or discharged, as authorized in division (A)(3) of this section, by the tax commissioner, upon order of the probate court after notice to the commissioner and any other person whose substantial rights may reasonably be affected by the lien and hearing on an application of the executor, administrator, trustee, or the owner of an interest in any property subject, or reasonably the object of a claim to be subject, to the lien, and proof that the collection of the taxes will not be jeopardized by the action, and that the tax commissioner failed to grant a reasonable request for the action within sixty days of his receipt of a written request.

(B) The executor, administrator, trustee, or other person in possession of property, the transfer of which is subject to the taxes, or any transferee of the property, except a bona fide purchaser for an adequate and full consideration in money or money's worth, is personally liable for all the taxes to the extent that their collection is reduced by his omission to perform a statutory duty, with interest as provided in section 5731.23 of the Revised Code, until they have been paid. An administrator, executor, or trustee of any property, the transfer of which is subject to the taxes shall deduct the taxes from the property, or collect them from any person entitled to the property. He shall not deliver or be compelled to deliver any property, the transfer of which is subject to the taxes, to any person, until the taxes on it have been collected, and on any other property of the same decedent that has been, or is to be, transferred to the person or his spouse or minor child. He may sell so much of the estate of the decedent as will enable him to pay the taxes in the same manner as for the payment of the debts of the decedent. Knowledge that the property is being sold by a fiduciary and that it otherwise would be subject to the estate tax lien does not preclude the purchaser from being classified as a bona fide purchaser.

(C) If an election is made, pursuant to division (B)(1)(b) or (c) of section 5731.011 of the Revised Code to have qualified farm property valued at its value for actual qualified use, an amount equivalent to the estate tax savings realized in the decedent's estate by valuating the property at its value for its actual qualified use, instead of at its fair market value pursuant to division (B) of section 5731.01 of the Revised Code, shall be a lien in favor of this state on the property for four years after the decedent's death, unless it is earlier discharged. The tax commissioner may issue a certificate of subordination of any lien imposed by this division upon any part of the property subject to the lien, if the tax commissioner determines that the state will be adequately secured after the subordination.

(1990 H 286, eff. 11–8–90; 1990 H 346; 1986 H 139; 1981 S 28; 1975 S 145; 1971 S 398; 132 v S 326)

Uncodified Law

1990 H 286, § 3, eff. 11–8–90, reads: Sections 1 and 2 of this act apply only to the estates of decedents who die on or after the effective date of this act.

1990 H 346, § 3, eff. 5–31–90, reads, in part: (A) Sections 1 and 2 of this act shall apply only to the estates of decedents who die on or after the effective date of this act.

1986 H 139, § 3: See Uncodified Law under 5731.12.

1981 S 28, § 3, eff. 10–9–81, reads, in part: Sections 1 and 2 of this act do not apply to the estates of decedents who died prior to January 1, 1982.

Historical and Statutory Notes

Ed. Note: 5731.37 contains provisions analogous to former 5731.17, repealed by 132 v S 326, eff. 7–1–68.

Ed. Note: Former 5731.37 repealed by 132 v S 326, eff. 7–1–68; 1953 H 1; GC 5345–5.

Pre–1953 H 1 Amendments: 114 v 800

Library References

Taxation ⚭890, 902.
Westlaw Topic No. 371.
C.J.S. Taxation § 1169, 1214–1219.
Baldwin's Ohio Legislative Service, 1990 Laws of Ohio, H 346—LSC Analysis, p 5–87

5731.38 Limitation on time for determination of tax liability

No liability for the payment of taxes levied under Chapter 5731. of the Revised Code, including all interest and penalties thereon, may be determined as to the return required to be filed under section 5731.21 of the Revised Code, subsequent to three years after such return is filed, and as to the return required to be filed under section 5731.24 of the Revised Code, subsequent to three years after such return is filed. Any lien in realty created under Chapter 5731. of the Revised Code shall become void upon the expiration of ten years after the date of decedent's death.

In the event there is litigation pending at the expiration of such three-year period for the determination or collection of any such tax, including interest or penalties thereon, the liability for the payment thereof continues until the expiration of one year after final determination of such litigation.

(1971 S 186, eff. 3–20–72; 132 v S 326)

Historical and Statutory Notes

Ed. Note: 5731.38 contains provisions analogous to former 5731.171, repealed by 132 v S 326, eff. 7–1–68.

Ed. Note: Former 5731.38 repealed by 132 v S 326, eff. 7–1–68; 1953 H 1; GC 5346; see now 5731.30 for provisions analogous to former 5731.38.

Pre–1953 H 1 Amendments: 108 v Pt 1, 570

Library References

Taxation ⚭893.
Westlaw Topic No. 371.
C.J.S. Taxation § 1190.

5731.39 Release of assets; consent to transfer; exceptions; contents of safe deposit box

(A) No corporation organized or existing under the laws of this state shall transfer on its books or issue a new certificate for any share of its capital stock registered in the name of a decedent, or in trust for a decedent, or in the name of a decedent and another person or persons, without the written consent of the tax commissioner.

(B) No safe deposit company, trust company, financial institution as defined in division (A) of section 5725.01 of the Revised Code or other corporation or person, having in possession, control, or custody a deposit standing in the name of a decedent, or in trust for a decedent, or in the name of a decedent and another person or persons, shall deliver or transfer an amount in excess of three-fourths of the total value of such deposit, including accrued interest and dividends, as of the date of decedent's death, without the written consent of the tax commissioner. The written consent of the tax commissioner need not be obtained prior to the delivery or transfer of amounts having a value of three-fourths or less of said total value.

(C) No life insurance company shall pay the proceeds of an annuity or matured endowment contract, or of a life insurance contract payable to the estate of a decedent, or of any other insurance contract taxable under Chapter 5731. of the Revised Code, without the written consent of the tax commissioner. Any life insurance company may pay the proceeds of any insurance contract not specified in this division (C) without the written consent of the tax commissioner.

(D) No trust company or other corporation or person shall pay the proceeds of any death benefit, retirement, pension or profit sharing plan in excess of two thousand dollars, without the written consent of the tax commissioner. Such trust company or other corporation or person, however, may pay the proceeds of any death benefit, retirement, pension, or profit-sharing plan which consists of insurance on the life of the decedent payable to a beneficiary other than the estate of the insured without the written consent of the tax commissioner.

(E) No safe deposit company, trust company, financial institution as defined in division (A) of section 5725.01 of the Revised Code, or other corporation or person, having in possession, control, or custody securities, assets, or other property (including the shares of the capital stock of, or other interest in, such safe deposit company, trust company, financial institution as defined in division (A) of section 5725.01 of the Revised Code, or other corporation), standing in the name of a decedent, or in trust for a decedent, or in the name of a decedent and another person or persons, and the transfer of which is taxable under Chapter 5731. of the Revised Code, shall deliver or transfer any such securities, assets, or other property which have a value as of the date of decedent's death in excess of three-fourths of the total value thereof, without the written consent of the tax commissioner. The written consent of the tax commissioner need not be obtained prior to the delivery or transfer of any such securities, assets, or other property having a value of three-fourths or less of said total value.

(F) No safe deposit company, financial institution as defined in division (A) of section 5725.01 of the Revised Code, or other corporation or person having possession or control of a safe deposit box or similar receptacle standing in the name of a decedent or in the name of the decedent and another person or persons, or to which the decedent had a right of access, except when such safe deposit box or other receptacle stands in the name of a corporation or partnership, or in the name of the decedent as guardian or executor, shall deliver any of the contents thereof unless the safe deposit box or similar receptacle has been opened and inventoried in the presence of the tax commissioner or the commissioner's agent, and a written consent to transfer issued; provided, however, that a safe deposit company, financial institution, or other corporation or person having possession or control of a safe deposit box may deliver wills, deeds to burial lots, and insurance policies to a representative of the decedent, but that a representative of the safe deposit company, financial institution, or other corporation or person must supervise the opening of the box and make a written record of the wills, deeds, and policies removed. Such written record shall be included in the tax commissioner's inventory records.

(G) Notwithstanding any provision of this section:

(1) The tax commissioner may authorize any delivery or transfer or waive any of the foregoing requirements under such terms and conditions as the commissioner may prescribe;

(2) An adult care facility, as defined in section 3722.01 of the Revised Code, or a home, as defined in section 3721.10 of the Revised Code, may transfer or use the money in a personal needs allowance account in accordance with section 5111.113 of the Revised Code without the written consent of the tax commissioner, and without the account having been opened and inventoried in the presence of the commissioner or the commissioner's agent.

Failure to comply with this section shall render such safe deposit company, trust company, life insurance company, financial institution as defined in division (A) of section 5725.01 of the Revised Code, or other corporation or person liable for the amount of the taxes and interest due under the provisions of Chapter 5731. of the Revised Code on the transfer of such stock, deposit, proceeds of an annuity or matured endowment contract or of a life insurance contract payable to the estate of a decedent, or other insurance contract taxable under Chapter 5731. of the Revised Code, proceeds of any death benefit, retirement, pension, or profit sharing plan in excess of two thousand dollars, or securities, assets, or other property of any resident decedent, and in addition thereto, to a penalty of not less than five hundred or more than five thousand dollars.

(2005 H 66, eff. 6–30–05; 1995 H 167, eff. 11–15–95; 1982 H 816, eff. 3–4–83; 132 v S 326)

Historical and Statutory Notes

Ed. Note: 5731.39 contains provisions analogous to former 5731.42, repealed by 132 v S 326, eff. 7–1–68.

Ed. Note: Former 5731.39 repealed by 132 v S 326, eff. 7–1–68; 1953 H 1; GC 5347; see now 5731.27 for provisions analogous to former 5731.39.

Pre–1953 H 1 Amendments: 108 v Pt 1, 571

Amendment Note: 2005 H 66 substituted "5111.113" for "5111.112" in division (G)(2).

Amendment Note: 1995 H 167 added division (G)(2); and made other changes to reflect gender neutral language.

5731.40 Transfer of assets of nonresident decedent

The consent of the tax commissioner is not required in the case of the issuance, transfer, or delivery of any intangible personal property specified in section 5731.39 of the Revised Code, when the decedent is not domiciled in this state or when the intangible personal property is issued, transferred, or delivered to the surviving spouse of the decedent.

In any action brought under section 5731.39 of the Revised Code, it shall be sufficient defense that the issuance, transfer, or delivery of the intangible personal property was made in good faith and without knowledge or circumstances sufficient to place the defendant on inquiry as to the domicile of the decedent or as to the identity of the surviving spouse of the decedent.

(1996 H 391, eff. 10–1–96; 132 v S 326, eff. 7–1–68)

Historical and Statutory Notes

Ed. Note: 5731.40 contains provisions analogous to former 5731.421, repealed by 132 v S 326, eff. 7–1–68.

Ed. Note: Former 5731.40 repealed by 132 v S 326, eff. 7–1–68; 1953 H 1; GC 5348; see now 5731.32 for provisions analogous to former 5731.40.

Pre–1953 H 1 Amendments: 108 v Pt 1, 571

Amendment Note: 1996 H 391 inserted "or when the intangible personal property is issued, transferred, or delivered to the surviving spouse of the decedent." at the end of the first paragraph and "or as to the identity of the surviving spouse of the decedent." at the end of the second paragraph; substituted "the intangible personal property" for "any such property" in the second paragraph; and made other nonsubstantive changes.

5731.41 Appointment of agents by tax commissioner; compensation

To enforce section 5731.39 of the Revised Code, and to administer Chapters 5713. and 4503. of the Revised Code the tax commissioner may appoint agents in the unclassified civil service who shall perform such duties as are prescribed by the commissioner. Such agents shall, as compensation, receive annually eight cents per capita for each full one thousand of the first twenty thousand of the population of the county and two cents per capita for each full one thousand over twenty thousand of the population of the county, as shown by the last federal census, which shall be paid in equal monthly installments from the undivided inheritance or estate tax in the county treasury on the warrant of the county auditor or from the county real estate assessment fund pursuant to division (B)(6) of section 325.31 of the Revised Code, any other provision of law to the contrary notwithstanding. The amount paid to any agent in the unclassified service for all of the duties performed under this section, as directed by the commissioner, shall not exceed three thousand nor be less than twelve hundred dollars in any calendar year.

(2005 H 66, eff. 6–30–05; 132 v S 326, eff. 12–1–67)

Historical and Statutory Notes

Ed. Note: Former 5731.41 repealed by 132 v S 326, eff. 7–1–68; 1953 H 1; GC 5348–1; see now 5731.33 for provisions analogous to former 5731.41.

Pre–1953 H 1 Amendments: 108 v Pt 1, 571

Amendment Note: 2005 H 66 inserted "and to administer Chapters 5713. and 4503. of the Revised Code" in the first sentence; inserted "or from the county real estate assessment fund pursuant to division (B)(6) of section 325.31 of the Revised Code" in the second sentence; inserted "all of the" and substituted "under this section" for "in estate tax matters" in the last sentence.

Library References

Taxation ⚖=893, 905.
Westlaw Topic No. 371.
C.J.S. Taxation § 1190, 1223.

5731.42 Collection of tax; proceedings; duties of attorney general

If, after the determination of any tax levied under this chapter, such tax remains unpaid, the tax commissioner shall notify the attorney general in writing of the nonpayment. The attorney general shall obtain from the tax commissioner a certified copy of the certificate of determination of the tax. Such certified copy of the certificate of determination of the tax shall be filed in the office of the clerk of the court of common pleas of the county, and the same proceedings shall be had with respect thereto as are provided by section 2329.04 of the Revised Code with respect to transcripts of judgments rendered by judges of the county courts, except that the attorney general shall not be required to pay the costs accruing at the time of filing the certified copy. The same effect shall be given to such certified copy of the certificate of determination of the tax for all purposes as is given to such transcripts of judgments of judges of the county courts filed in like manner. This section does not affect the date of the lien of such taxes on the property passing, or divest such lien before the payment of such tax in the event of failure to seek out execution within the period prescribed by section 2329.07 of the Revised Code.

(1983 H 291, eff. 7–1–83; 132 v S 326)

Uncodified Law

1983 H 291, § 127, eff. 7–1–83, reads: The amendment of sections 2117.06, 5731.01, 5731.011, 5731.02, 5731.05, 5731.09, 5731.14, 5731.15, 5731.16, 5731.18, 5731.21, 5731.22, 5731.26, 5731.42, and 5731.48, the enactment of sections 5731.131, 5731.181, 5731.231, and 5731.99, and the repeal of section 5731.20 of the Revised Code, all by this act, shall apply to the estate of any decedent whose death occurs on or after July 1, 1983.

Historical and Statutory Notes

Ed. Note: Former 5731.42 repealed by 132 v S 326, eff. 7–1–68; 129 v 428; 127 v 130; 1953 H 1; GC 5348–2, 5348–2a; see now 5731.39 for provisions analogous to former 5731.42.

Pre–1953 H 1 Amendments: 114 v 598; 108 v Pt 2, 1197; 108 v Pt 1, 572

Library References

Taxation ⚖=905(1).
Westlaw Topic No. 371.
C.J.S. Taxation § 1223.

5731.43 Attorney general to represent the state; appointment of attorney employed by department of taxation

The attorney general, when requested by the tax commissioner, shall represent the state, the tax commissioner, and the county auditor in any proceedings under Chapter 5731. of the Revised Code. The tax commissioner, with the consent of the attorney general, may designate any attorney assigned to or employed by the estate tax division of the Department of Taxation to represent the tax commissioner, and no additional compensation shall be paid to any attorney so designated for services performed in such capacity.

(132 v S 326, eff. 7–1–68)

Historical and Statutory Notes

Ed. Note: Former 5731.43 repealed by 132 v S 326, eff. 11–30–67; 1953 H 1; GC 5348–2b.

Pre–1953 H 1 Amendments: 124 v S 22; 122 v 749; 122 v S 345

Library References

Taxation ⚖=900, 904–906.
Westlaw Topic No. 371.
C.J.S. Taxation § 1201, 1207, 1222–1223, 1225, 1228.

5731.44 County auditor; appointment of deputies

The county auditor may, and when directed by the tax commissioner shall, appoint such number of deputies as the tax commissioner prescribes for him, who shall be qualified to assist him in the performance of his duties under Chapter 5731. of the Revised Code.

(132 v S 326, eff. 7–1–68)

Historical and Statutory Notes

Ed. Note: 5731.44 contains provisions analogous to former 5731.46, repealed by 132 v S 326, eff. 7–1–68.

Ed. Note: Former 5731.44 repealed by 132 v S 326, eff. 7–1–68; 129 v 582; 1953 H 1; GC 5348–3.

Pre–1953 H 1 Amendments: 108 v Pt 1, 572

Library References

Taxation ⚖=893, 895(3).
Westlaw Topic No. 371.
C.J.S. Taxation § 1190, 1196.

5731.45 Administration of tax; appointment of assistants by tax commissioner; regulations

The tax commissioner may designate such of his examiners, experts, accountants, and other assistants as he deems necessary for the purpose of aiding in the administration of taxes levied under Chapter 5731. of the Revised Code; and the provisions of Chapter 5731. of the Revised Code shall be deemed a law which the tax commissioner is required to administer for the purposes of sections 5703.17 to 5703.37, inclusive, 5703.39, and 5703.41 of the Revised Code. The tax commissioner shall in the administration of the taxes levied under Chapter 5731. of the Revised Code see that the proceedings are instituted and carried to determination in all cases in which a tax is due.

The tax commissioner may adopt and promulgate regulations not inconsistent with sections 5731.01 to 5731.52, inclusive, of the Revised Code.

(132 v S 326, eff. 7–1–68)

Historical and Statutory Notes

Ed. Note: 5731.45 contains provisions analogous to former 5731.47, repealed by 132 v S 326, eff. 7–1–68.

Ed. Note: Former 5731.45 repealed by 132 v S 326, eff. 7–1–68; 1953 H 1; GC 5348–4.

Pre–1953 H 1 Amendments: 108 v Pt 1, 573

Library References

Taxation ⇐893, 895(3).
Westlaw Topic No. 371.
C.J.S. Taxation § 1190, 1196.

5731.46 County treasurer to keep account of taxes received; duties of county treasurer and county auditor; fees

The county treasurer shall keep an account showing the amount of all taxes and interest received by him under Chapter 5731. of the Revised Code. On the twenty-fifth day of February and the twentieth day of August of each year he shall settle with the county auditor for all such taxes and interest so received at the time of making such settlement, not included in any preceding settlement, showing for what estate, by whom, and when paid. At each such settlement the auditor shall allow to the treasurer and himself, on the money so collected and accounted for by him, their respective fees, at the percentages allowed by law. The correctness thereof, together with a statement of the fees allowed at such settlement, and the fees and expenses allowed to the officers under such chapter shall be certified by the auditor.

(132 v S 326, eff. 7–1–68)

Historical and Statutory Notes

Ed. Note: 5731.46 contains provisions analogous to former 5731.57, repealed by 132 v S 326, eff. 7–1–68.

Ed. Note: Former 5731.46 repealed by 132 v S 326, eff. 7–1–68; 1953 H 1; GC 5348–5; see now 5731.44 for provisions analogous to former 5731.46.

Pre–1953 H 1 Amendments: 108 v Pt 1, 573

Library References

Taxation ⇐905.
Westlaw Topic No. 371.
C.J.S. Taxation § 1223.

5731.47 Fees of officers; approval; payment

The fees of the sheriff or other officers for services performed under this chapter and the expenses of the county auditor shall be certified by the county auditor by a report filed with the tax commissioner. If the tax commissioner finds that those fees and expenses are correct and reasonable in amount, the tax commissioner shall indicate approval of the fees and expenses in writing to the county auditor. The county auditor shall pay those fees and expenses out of the undivided estate tax fund. The county auditor then shall deduct, from the amount required to be credited to each of the funds or boards of education listed or referred to in division (A) of section 5731.48 of the Revised Code, a pro rata share of the amount so paid. The pro rata share shall be computed on the basis of the proportions of the gross taxes levied and paid under this chapter that are required to be credited to the funds or boards of education listed or referred to under that section. The county auditor shall draw warrants payable from those taxes on the county treasurer in favor of the fee funds or officers personally entitled to the fees and expenses.

(2004 S 189, eff. 6–29–04; 2000 S 108, eff. 9–29–00; 132 v S 326, eff. 7–1–68)

Historical and Statutory Notes

Ed. Note: 5731.47 contains provisions analogous to former 5731.52, repealed by 132 v S 326, eff. 7–1–68.

Ed. Note: Former 5731.47 repealed by 132 v S 326, eff. 7–1–68; 1953 H 1; GC 5348–6; see now 5731.45 for provisions analogous to former 5731.47.

Pre–1953 H 1 Amendments: 108 v Pt 1, 573

Amendment Note: 2004 S 189 substituted "undivided estate tax fund" for "state's share of the undivided inheritance taxes in the county treasury and" in the third sentence; inserted a new fourth and fifth sentences; inserted "The county auditor shall" in the sixth sentence; deleted the last two sentences; and made other nonsubstantive changes.

Amendment Note: 2000 S 108 added the fourth and fifth sentences; and made changes to reflect gender neutral language and other nonsubstantive changes.

Library References

Taxation ⇐905(3).
Westlaw Topic No. 371.
C.J.S. Taxation § 1228.

DISTRIBUTION AND DETERMINATION OF TAX REVENUES

5731.48 Distribution of tax revenues

(A) If a decedent dies on or after July 1, 1989, and before January 1, 2001, sixty-four per cent of the gross amount of taxes levied and paid under this chapter shall be for the use of the municipal corporation or township in which the tax originates, and shall be credited as provided in division (A)(1), (2), or (3) of this section:

(1) To the general revenue fund in the case of a city;

(2) To the general revenue fund of a village or to the board of education of a village, for school purposes, as the village council by resolution may approve;

(3) To the general revenue fund or to the board of education of the school district of which the township is a part, for school purposes, as the board of township trustees by resolution may approve, in the case of a township.

The remainder of the taxes levied and paid shall be for the use of the state and shall be credited to the general revenue fund.

(B) If a decedent dies on or after January 1, 2001, and before January 1, 2002, seventy per cent of the gross amount of taxes levied and paid under this chapter shall be for the use of the municipal corporation or township in which the tax originates and credited as provided in division (A)(1), (2), or (3) of this section, and the remainder shall be for the use of the state and credited to the general revenue fund.

(C) If a decedent dies on or after January 1, 2002, eighty per cent of the gross amount of taxes levied and paid under this chapter, less any deduction from the municipal corporation's or township's share of those taxes for fees or expenses charged under section 5731.47 of the Revised Code, shall be for the use of the municipal corporation or township in which the tax originates and credited as provided in division (A)(1), (2), or (3) of this section, and the remainder, less any deduction from the state's share of those taxes for fees or expenses charged under section 5731. 47 of the Revised Code, shall be for the use of the state and shall be credited to the general revenue fund.

(D) If a municipal corporation is in default with respect to the principal or interest of any outstanding notes or bonds, one half of the taxes distributed under this section shall be credited to the sinking or bond retirement fund of the municipal corporation, and the residue shall be credited to the general revenue fund.

(E) The council, board of trustees, or other legislative authority of a village or township may, by ordinance in the case of a village, or by resolution in the case of a township, provide that whenever there is money in the treasury of the village or township from taxes levied under this chapter, not required for immediate use, that money may be invested in federal, state, county, or municipal bonds, upon which there has been no default of the principal during the preceding five years.

(2004 S 189, eff. 6–29–04; 2000 S 108, eff. 9–29–00; 1991 H 298, eff. 7–26–91; 1991 S 206; 1989 H 111; 1983 H 291; 132 v S 326)

Uncodified Law

1983 H 291, § 127, eff. 7–1–83, reads: The amendment of sections 2117.06, 5731.01, 5731.011, 5731.02, 5731.05, 5731.09, 5731.14, 5731.15, 5731.16, 5731.18, 5731.21, 5731.22, 5731.26, 5731.42, and 5731.48, the enactment of sections 5731.131, 5731.181, 5731.231, and 5731.99, and the repeal of section 5731.20 of the Revised Code, all by this act, shall apply to the estate of any decedent whose death occurs on or after July 1, 1983.

Historical and Statutory Notes

Ed. Note: 5731.48 contains provisions analogous to former 5731.53, repealed by 132 v S 326, eff. 7–1–68.

Ed. Note: Former 5731.48 repealed by 129 v 373, eff. 9–7–61; 1953 H 1; GC 5348–7.

Pre–1953 H 1 Amendments: 108 v Pt 2, 1195; 108 v Pt 1, 573

Amendment Note: 2004 S 189 deleted "after any deduction for fees and costs charged under section 5731.47 of the Revised Code" in the last sentences of division (A)(3), (B), and (C); inserted "less any deduction from the municipal corporation's or township's share of those taxes for fees or expenses charged under section 5731.47 of the Revised Code" and "less any deduction from the state's share of those taxes for fees or expenses charged under section 5731.47 of the Revised Code" in division (C); and made other nonsubstantive changes.

Amendment Note: 2000 S 108 rewrote this section, which prior thereto read:

"If a decedent dies on or after July 1, 1989, sixty-four per cent of the gross amount of taxes levied and paid under this chapter shall be for the use of the municipal corporation or township in which the tax originates, and shall be credited as follows:

"(A) To the general revenue fund in the case of a city;

"(B) To the general revenue fund of a village or to the board of education of a village, for school purposes, as the village council by resolution may approve;

"(C) To the general revenue fund or to the board of education of the school district of which the township is a part, for school purposes, as the board of township trustees by resolution may approve, in the case of a township.

"Where a municipal corporation is in default with respect to the principal or interest of any outstanding notes or bonds, one half of the taxes distributed under this section shall be credited to the sinking or bond retirement fund of the municipal corporation, and the residue shall be credited to the general revenue fund.

"The council, board of trustees, or other legislative authority of a village or township may, by ordinance in the case of a village, or by resolution in the case of a township, provide that whenever there is money in the treasury of the village or township from taxes levied under this chapter, not required for immediate use, that money may be invested in federal, state, county, or municipal bonds, upon which there has been no default of the principal during the preceding five years.

"The remainder of the taxes levied and paid under this chapter, after deducting the fees and costs charged against the proceeds of the tax under this chapter, shall be for the use of the state, and shall be paid into the state treasury to the credit of the general revenue fund."

Library References

Taxation ⟐913.5.
Westlaw Topic No. 371.
C.J.S. Taxation § 1230.

5731.49 Determination of tax revenues due political subdivisions; payment

At each semiannual settlement provided for by section 5731.46 of the Revised Code, the county auditor shall certify to the county auditor of any other county in which is located in whole or in part any municipal corporation or township to which any of the taxes collected under this chapter and not previously accounted for, is due, a statement of the amount of such taxes due to each corporation or township in such county entitled to share in the distribution thereof. The amount due upon such settlement to each such municipal corporation or township, and to each municipal corporation and township in the county in which the taxes are collected, shall be paid upon the warrant of the county auditor to the county treasurer or other proper officer of such municipal corporation or township. The amount of any refund chargeable against any such municipal corporation or township at the time of making such settlement, shall be adjusted in determining the amount due to such municipal corporation or township at such settlement; provided that if the municipal corporation or township against which such refund is chargeable is not entitled to share in the fund to be distributed at such settlement, the auditor shall draw a warrant for the amount in favor of the treasurer payable from any undivided general taxes in the possession of such treasurer, unless such municipal corporation or township is located in another county, in which event the auditor shall issue a certificate for such amount to the auditor of the proper county, who shall draw a like warrant therefor payable from any undivided general taxes in the possession of the treasurer of such county. In either case at the next semiannual settlement of such undivided general taxes, the amount of such warrant shall be deducted from the distribution of taxes of such municipal corporation or township and charged against the proceeds of levies for the general fund of such municipal corporation or township, and a similar deduction shall be made at each next semiannual settlement of such undivided general taxes until such warrant has been satisfied in full.

If it is discovered that an amount of taxes collected under this chapter has been paid in error to a township or municipal corporation to which the taxes are not due under this chapter, the township or municipal corporation to which the amount was erroneously paid, when repaying that amount to any subdivision to which the taxes were due, shall not be required to pay interest on that amount.

(2002 H 301, eff. 5–30–02; 1989 H 230, eff. 10–30–89; 132 v S 326)

Historical and Statutory Notes

Ed. Note: 5731.49 is analogous to former 5731.54, repealed by 132 v S 326, eff. 7–1–68.

Ed. Note: Former 5731.49 repealed by 132 v S 326, eff. 7–1–68; 129 v 373; 1953 H 1; GC 5348–8.

Pre–1953 H 1 Amendments: 108 v Pt 2, 1196; 108 v Pt 1, 574

Amendment Note: 2002 H 301 added the second paragraph; made changes to reflect gender neutral language; and made other nonsubstantive changes.

Library References

Taxation ⇌913.5.
Westlaw Topic No. 371.
C.J.S. Taxation § 1230.
Baldwin's Ohio Legislative Service, 1989 Laws of Ohio, H 230—LSC Analysis, p 5–925

ORIGIN OF TAX

5731.50 Origin of tax on transfer of realty and tangible personalty located in state

When the property transferred is real estate or tangible personal property within this state, the tax on the transfer thereof shall be deemed to have originated in the municipal corporation or township in which such property is physically located. In case of real estate located in more than one municipal corporation or township, the tax on the transfer thereof, or of any interest therein, shall be apportioned between the municipal corporation or townships in which it is located in the proportions in which the tract is assessed for general property taxation in such townships or municipal corporations.

(132 v S 326, eff. 7–1–68)

Historical and Statutory Notes

Ed. Note: 5731.50 is analogous to former 5731.55, repealed by 132 v S 326, eff. 7–1–68.

Ed. Note: Former 5731.50 repealed by 126 v 65, eff. 7–7–55; 1953 H 1; GC 5348–8a.

Pre–1953 H 1 Amendments: 108 v Pt 2, 1197

5731.51 Origin of tax on transfer of personalty not located in state

The tax on the transfer of intangible property or tangible personal property not within this state from a resident of this state shall be deemed to have originated in the municipal corporation or township in which the decedent was domiciled.

The municipal corporation or township in which the tax on the transfer of the intangible property of a nonresident accruing under Chapter 5731. of the Revised Code shall be deemed to have originated, shall be determined as follows:

(A) As to bonds, notes, or other securities or assets, in the possession or in the control or custody of a corporation, institution, or person in this state, such tax shall be deemed to have originated in the municipal corporation or township in which such corporation, institution, or person had the same in possession, control, or custody at the time of the transfer.

(B) As to money on deposit with any corporation, bank, institution, or person, such tax shall be deemed to have originated in the municipal corporation or township in which such corporation, bank or other institution had its principal place of business, or in which such person resided at the time of such succession.

(1969 H 1, eff. 3–18–69; 132 v S 326)

Historical and Statutory Notes

Ed. Note: 5731.51 is analogous to former 5731.56, repealed by 132 v S 326, eff. 7–1–68.

Ed. Note: Former 5731.51 repealed by 132 v S 326, eff. 7–1–68; 1953 H 1; GC 5348–9; see now 5731.46 for provisions analogous to former 5731.51.

Pre–1953 H 1 Amendments: 108 v Pt 1, 574

CONFIDENTIALITY OF INFORMATION

5731.90 Confidentiality of information

(A)(1) Except as provided in division (A)(2) of this section, to the extent that any of the following are in the possession of a probate court, the department of taxation, a county auditor or county treasurer, the fiscal officer of a municipal corporation or township, the attorney general, or other authorized person as specified in this chapter, the following and any of their contents are confidential; are not subject to inspection or copying as public records pursuant to section 149.43 of the Revised Code; and may be inspected or copied by members of the general public only after the probate court of the county in which a return was filed pursuant to this chapter or, if none, another appropriate probate court, has issued an order, based on good cause shown, specifically authorizing the inspection or copying:

(a) An estate tax return, generation-skipping tax return, or other tax return filed pursuant to this chapter;

(b) All documents and other records that pertain to the determination of a decedent's taxable estate that is the subject of a return as described in division (A)(1)(a) of this section;

(c) The amount of the estate, generation-skipping, or other taxes paid or payable in connection with a decedent's taxable estate as described in division (A)(1)(b) of this section.

(2) Division (A)(1) of this section does not do any of the following:

(a) Preclude the inspection, copying, and use of an estate, generation-skipping, or other tax return filed pursuant to this chapter, documents and other records as described in division (A)(1)(b) of this section, and the amount of the estate, generation-skipping, or other taxes paid or payable in connection with a decedent's taxable estate as described in that division, by the tax commissioner, county auditors and treasurers, fiscal officers of municipal corporations or townships, probate judges, the attorney general, and other authorized persons as specified in this chapter, in connection with their duties and responsibilities as described in this chapter, including, but not limited to, the determination and collection of an estate, generation-skipping, or other tax;

(b) Preclude the tax commissioner from furnishing to the internal revenue service, in accordance with federal law and in connection with its official business, a copy of any estate, generation-skipping, or other tax return, any document or other record, or the amount of any estate, generation-skipping, or other tax paid or payable, as described in division (A)(2)(a) of this section;

(c) Apply to the certificates described in division (A)(1)(b) of section 5731.21 of the Revised Code that, pursuant to division (A)(5) of that section, are made public records subject to inspection and copying in accordance with section 149.43 of the Revised Code;

(d) Affect rights of inspection under Chapter 1347. of the Revised Code by persons who are the subject of personal information contained in an estate, generation-skipping, or other tax return, or any document or other record, as described in division (A)(2)(a) of this section.

(B) No person shall do any of the following:

(1) Permit the inspection or copying of an estate tax return, generation-skipping tax return, or other tax return filed pursuant to this chapter, or documents and other records that pertain to the determination of the decedent's taxable estate that is the subject of the return, except as provided in division (A) of this section;

(2) Otherwise divulge information contained in the return or the documents or other records, except as provided in division (A) of this section;

(3) Divulge the amount of the estate, generation-skipping, or other taxes paid or payable in connection with the decedent's

taxable estate that is the subject of the return, except as provided in division (A) of this section.

(1994 S 128, eff. 1–18–94; 1990 H 286)

Uncodified Law

1990 H 286, § 3, eff. 11–8–90, reads: Sections 1 and 2 of this act apply only to the estates of decedents who die on or after the effective date of this act.

Historical and Statutory Notes

Amendment Note: 1994 S 128 inserted "the fiscal officer of a municipal corporation or township" in division (A)(1); and inserted "fiscal officers of municipal corporations or townships" in division (A)(2)(a).

PENALTY

5731.99 Penalty

Whoever violates this chapter, or any lawful rule promulgated by the tax commissioner under authority of this chapter, for the violation of which no other penalty is provided in this chapter, shall be fined not less than one hundred or more than five thousand dollars.

(1983 H 291, eff. 7–1–83)

Uncodified Law

1983 H 291, § 127, eff. 7–1–83, reads: The amendment of sections 2117.06, 5731.01, 5731.011, 5731.02, 5731.05, 5731.09, 5731.14, 5731.15, 5731.16, 5731.18, 5731.21, 5731.22, 5731.26, 5731.42, and 5731.48, the enactment of sections 5731.131, 5731.181, 5731.231, and 5731.99, and the repeal of section 5731.20 of the Revised Code, all by this act, shall apply to the estate of any decedent whose death occurs on or after July 1, 1983.

Library References

Taxation ⊕906.
Westlaw Topic No. 371.
C.J.S. Taxation § 1207.

CHAPTER 5747

INCOME TAX

GENERAL PROVISIONS

Section	
5747.01	Definitions
5747.011	Definitions; limited application
5747.012	Definitions
5747.013	Determination of fraction used in calculating trust's modified taxable income; determination of property, payroll, and sales factors
5747.02	Rates of taxation; exemption
5747.022	Additional credit
5747.025	Personal exemption for taxpayer and spouse
5747.026	Extension for national guard and reservists called to active duty
5747.05	Credits
5747.056	Credit for exempted income

WITHHOLDING

5747.06	Withholding; exceptions; notification of amount withheld; liability of employer; provision of information by employee

RETURNS

5747.08	Individual returns; returns of nonresident pass-through entity investors; joint returns of husband and wife; attestation; filing extensions; interest payments
5747.09	Declaration of estimated tax; payment; required portion; interest charge for underpayment
5747.10	Amended return

REFUNDS

5747.11	Refunds; interest
5747.113	Tax refund contributions to specified funds
5747.12	Application of refund to satisfaction of other tax indebtedness

PRACTICE AND PROCEDURE

5747.121	Procedures for collection of overdue child support from state income tax refunds; child support intercept fund
5747.123	Overpaid child support
5747.13	Failure to file return or pay tax; assessment; notice; hearing; appeal; judgment; payment pending review

CALCULATION AND ALLOCATION OF INCOME AND DEDUCTIONS

Section	
5747.20	Allocation of nonbusiness income or deduction
5747.211	Apportionment of items of business income or deduction earned by financial institution
5747.221	Allocation or apportionment of income or deduction; investment pass-through entity
5747.231	Inclusion of distributive share of items of income, property, compensation and sales in computations

NONRESIDENT TAXPAYERS

5747.25	Election to be treated as nonresident taxpayer

CHILD DAY–CARE AND ADOPTION CREDITS

5747.37	Credit for legal adoption of minor child

QUALIFIED PASS–THROUGH ENTITIES OR TRUSTS

5747.39	Credit for employee training costs
5747.40	Use of terms; purpose and applicability of tax
5747.401	Investment pass-through entities
5747.41	Tax on qualifying pass-through entities with at least one individual qualifying investor or qualifying trusts with at least one individual qualifying beneficiary
5747.42	Returns; remittance of tax
5747.43	Estimated tax returns
5747.44	Payment by electronic funds transfer
5747.45	Qualifying taxable year; method of accounting; amended reports
5747.451	Effect of retirement, dissolution, or sale; tax liens; enforcement of judgments; quo warranto actions; settlements
5747.453	Personal liability for failure to file reports or pay tax

LOCAL GOVERNMENT FUNDS

5747.51	Allocation to county undivided local government funds
5747.53	Alternative method of apportioning fund by county budget commission
5747.54	Conditions upon payment of share to county from local government fund
5747.55	Appeal to board of tax appeals

ORDER OF CREDITS

5747.98	Priority of credits

GENERAL PROVISIONS

5747.01 Definitions

Except as otherwise expressly provided or clearly appearing from the context, any term used in this chapter that is not otherwise defined in this section has the same meaning as when used in a comparable context in the laws of the United States relating to federal income taxes or if not used in a comparable context in those laws, has the same meaning as in section 5733.40 of the Revised Code. Any reference in this chapter to the Internal Revenue Code includes other laws of the United States relating to federal income taxes.

As used in this chapter:

(A) "Adjusted gross income" or "Ohio adjusted gross income" means federal adjusted gross income, as defined and used in the Internal Revenue Code, adjusted as provided in this section:

(1) Add interest or dividends on obligations or securities of any state or of any political subdivision or authority of any state, other than this state and its subdivisions and authorities.

(2) Add interest or dividends on obligations of any authority, commission, instrumentality, territory, or possession of the United States to the extent that the interest or dividends are exempt from federal income taxes but not from state income taxes.

(3) Deduct interest or dividends on obligations of the United States and its territories and possessions or of any authority, commission, or instrumentality of the United States to the extent that the interest or dividends are included in federal adjusted gross income but exempt from state income taxes under the laws of the United States.

(4) Deduct disability and survivor's benefits to the extent included in federal adjusted gross income.

(5) Deduct benefits under Title II of the Social Security Act [1] and tier 1 railroad retirement benefits to the extent included in federal adjusted gross income under section 86 of the Internal Revenue Code [2].

(6) In the case of a taxpayer who is a beneficiary of a trust that makes an accumulation distribution as defined in section 665 of the Internal Revenue Code, add, for the beneficiary's taxable years beginning before 2002, the portion, if any, of such distribution that does not exceed the undistributed net income of the trust for the three taxable years preceding the taxable year in which the distribution is made to the extent that the portion was not included in the trust's taxable income for any of the trust's taxable years beginning in 2002 or thereafter. "Undistributed net income of a trust" means the taxable income of the trust increased by (a)(i) the additions to adjusted gross income required under division (A) of this section and (ii) the personal exemptions allowed to the trust pursuant to section 642(b) of the Internal Revenue Code, and decreased by (b)(i) the deductions to adjusted gross income required under division (A) of this section, (ii) the amount of federal income taxes attributable to such income, and (iii) the amount of taxable income that has been included in the adjusted gross income of a beneficiary by reason of a prior accumulation distribution. Any undistributed net income included in the adjusted gross income of a beneficiary shall reduce the undistributed net income of the trust commencing with the earliest years of the accumulation period.

(7) Deduct the amount of wages and salaries, if any, not otherwise allowable as a deduction but that would have been allowable as a deduction in computing federal adjusted gross income for the taxable year, had the targeted jobs credit allowed and determined under sections 38, 51, and 52 of the Internal Revenue Code [3] not been in effect.

(8) Deduct any interest or interest equivalent on public obligations and purchase obligations to the extent that the interest or interest equivalent is included in federal adjusted gross income.

(9) Add any loss or deduct any gain resulting from the sale, exchange, or other disposition of public obligations to the extent that the loss has been deducted or the gain has been included in computing federal adjusted gross income.

(10) Deduct or add amounts, as provided under section 5747.70 of the Revised Code, related to contributions to variable college savings program accounts made or tuition units purchased pursuant to Chapter 3334. of the Revised Code.

(11)(a) Deduct, to the extent not otherwise allowable as a deduction or exclusion in computing federal or Ohio adjusted gross income for the taxable year, the amount the taxpayer paid during the taxable year for medical care insurance and qualified long-term care insurance for the taxpayer, the taxpayer's spouse, and dependents. No deduction for medical care insurance under division (A)(11) of this section shall be allowed either to any taxpayer who is eligible to participate in any subsidized health plan maintained by any employer of the taxpayer or of the taxpayer's spouse, or to any taxpayer who is entitled to, or on application would be entitled to, benefits under part A of Title XVIII of the "Social Security Act," 49 Stat. 620 (1935), 42 U.S.C. 301, as amended. For the purposes of division (A)(11)(a) of this section, "subsidized health plan" means a health plan for which the employer pays any portion of the plan's cost. The deduction allowed under division (A)(11)(a) of this section shall be the net of any related premium refunds, related premium reimbursements, or related insurance premium dividends received during the taxable year.

(b) Deduct, to the extent not otherwise deducted or excluded in computing federal or Ohio adjusted gross income during the taxable year, the amount the taxpayer paid during the taxable year, not compensated for by any insurance or otherwise, for medical care of the taxpayer, the taxpayer's spouse, and dependents, to the extent the expenses exceed seven and one-half per cent of the taxpayer's federal adjusted gross income.

(c) For purposes of division (A)(11) of this section, "medical care" has the meaning given in section 213 of the Internal Revenue Code, subject to the special rules, limitations, and exclusions set forth therein, and "qualified long-term care" has the same meaning given in section 7702B(c) of the Internal Revenue Code [4].

(12)(a) Deduct any amount included in federal adjusted gross income solely because the amount represents a reimbursement or refund of expenses that in any year the taxpayer had deducted as an itemized deduction pursuant to section 63 of the Internal Revenue Code and applicable United States department of the treasury regulations. The deduction otherwise allowed under division (A)(12)(a) of this section shall be reduced to the extent the reimbursement is attributable to an amount the taxpayer deducted under this section in any taxable year.

(b) Add any amount not otherwise included in Ohio adjusted gross income for any taxable year to the extent that the amount is attributable to the recovery during the taxable year of any amount deducted or excluded in computing federal or Ohio adjusted gross income in any taxable year.

(13) Deduct any portion of the deduction described in section 1341(a)(2) of the Internal Revenue Code, for repaying previously reported income received under a claim of right, that meets both of the following requirements:

(a) It is allowable for repayment of an item that was included in the taxpayer's adjusted gross income for a prior taxable year and did not qualify for a credit under division (A) or (B) of section 5747.05 of the Revised Code for that year;

(b) It does not otherwise reduce the taxpayer's adjusted gross income for the current or any other taxable year.

(14) Deduct an amount equal to the deposits made to, and net investment earnings of, a medical savings account during the taxable year, in accordance with section 3924.66 of the Revised Code. The deduction allowed by division (A)(14) of this section

does not apply to medical savings account deposits and earnings otherwise deducted or excluded for the current or any other taxable year from the taxpayer's federal adjusted gross income.

(15)(a) Add an amount equal to the funds withdrawn from a medical savings account during the taxable year, and the net investment earnings on those funds, when the funds withdrawn were used for any purpose other than to reimburse an account holder for, or to pay, eligible medical expenses, in accordance with section 3924.66 of the Revised Code;

(b) Add the amounts distributed from a medical savings account under division (A)(2) of section 3924.68 of the Revised Code during the taxable year.

(16) Add any amount claimed as a credit under section 5747.059 of the Revised Code to the extent that such amount satisfies either of the following:

(a) The amount was deducted or excluded from the computation of the taxpayer's federal adjusted gross income as required to be reported for the taxpayer's taxable year under the Internal Revenue Code;

(b) The amount resulted in a reduction of the taxpayer's federal adjusted gross income as required to be reported for any of the taxpayer's taxable years under the Internal Revenue Code.

(17) Deduct the amount contributed by the taxpayer to an individual development account program established by a county department of job and family services pursuant to sections 329.11 to 329.14 of the Revised Code for the purpose of matching funds deposited by program participants. On request of the tax commissioner, the taxpayer shall provide any information that, in the tax commissioner's opinion, is necessary to establish the amount deducted under division (A)(17) of this section.

(18) Beginning in taxable year 2001 but not for any taxable year beginning after December 31, 2005, if the taxpayer is married and files a joint return and the combined federal adjusted gross income of the taxpayer and the taxpayer's spouse for the taxable year does not exceed one hundred thousand dollars, or if the taxpayer is single and has a federal adjusted gross income for the taxable year not exceeding fifty thousand dollars, deduct amounts paid during the taxable year for qualified tuition and fees paid to an eligible institution for the taxpayer, the taxpayer's spouse, or any dependent of the taxpayer, who is a resident of this state and is enrolled in or attending a program that culminates in a degree or diploma at an eligible institution. The deduction may be claimed only to the extent that qualified tuition and fees are not otherwise deducted or excluded for any taxable year from federal or Ohio adjusted gross income. The deduction may not be claimed for educational expenses for which the taxpayer claims a credit under section 5747.27 of the Revised Code.

(19) Add any reimbursement received during the taxable year of any amount the taxpayer deducted under division (A)(18) of this section in any previous taxable year to the extent the amount is not otherwise included in Ohio adjusted gross income.

(20)(a)(i) Add five-sixths of the amount of depreciation expense allowed by subsection (k) of section 168 of the Internal Revenue Code, including the taxpayer's proportionate or distributive share of the amount of depreciation expense allowed by that subsection to a pass-through entity in which the taxpayer has a direct or indirect ownership interest.

(ii) Add five-sixths of the amount of qualifying section 179 depreciation expense, including a person's proportionate or distributive share of the amount of qualifying section 179 depreciation expense allowed to any pass-through entity in which the person has a direct or indirect ownership. For the purposes of this division, "qualifying section 179 depreciation expense" means the difference between (I) the amount of depreciation expense directly or indirectly allowed to the taxpayer under section 179 of the Internal Revenue Code, and (II) the amount of depreciation expense directly or indirectly allowed to the taxpayer under section 179 of the Internal Revenue Code as that section existed on December 31, 2002.

The tax commissioner, under procedures established by the commissioner, may waive the add-backs related to a pass-through entity if the taxpayer owns, directly or indirectly, less than five per cent of the pass-through entity.

(b) Nothing in division (A)(20) of this section shall be construed to adjust or modify the adjusted basis of any asset.

(c) To the extent the add-back required under division (A)(20)(a) of this section is attributable to property generating nonbusiness income or loss allocated under section 5747.20 of the Revised Code, the add-back shall be sitused to the same location as the nonbusiness income or loss generated by the property for the purpose of determining the credit under division (A) of section 5747.05 of the Revised Code. Otherwise, the add-back shall be apportioned, subject to one or more of the four alternative methods of apportionment enumerated in section 5747.21 of the Revised Code.

(d) For the purposes of division (A) of this section, net operating loss carryback and carryforward shall not include five-sixths of the allowance of any net operating loss deduction carryback or carryforward to the taxable year to the extent such loss resulted from depreciation allowed by section 168(k) of the Internal Revenue Code and by the qualifying section 179 depreciation expense amount.

(21)(a) If the taxpayer was required to add an amount under division (A)(20)(a) of this section for a taxable year, deduct one-fifth of the amount so added for each of the five succeeding taxable years.

(b) If the amount deducted under division (A)(21)(a) of this section is attributable to an add-back allocated under division (A)(20)(c) of this section, the amount deducted shall be sitused to the same location. Otherwise, the add-back shall be apportioned using the apportionment factors for the taxable year in which the deduction is taken, subject to one or more of the four alternative methods of apportionment enumerated in section 5747.21 of the Revised Code.

(c) No deduction is available under division (A)(21)(a) of this section with regard to any depreciation allowed by section 168(k) of the Internal Revenue Code and by the qualifying section 179 depreciation expense amount to the extent that such depreciation resulted in or increased a federal net operating loss carryback or carryforward to a taxable year to which division (A)(20)(d) of this section does not apply.

(22) Deduct, to the extent not otherwise deducted or excluded in computing federal or Ohio adjusted gross income for the taxable year, the amount the taxpayer received during the taxable year as reimbursement for life insurance premiums under section 5919.31 of the Revised Code.

(23) Deduct, to the extent not otherwise deducted or excluded in computing federal or Ohio adjusted gross income for the taxable year, the amount the taxpayer received during the taxable year as a death benefit paid by the adjutant general under section 5919.33 of the Revised Code.

(24) Deduct, to the extent included in federal adjusted gross income and not otherwise allowable as a deduction or exclusion in computing federal or Ohio adjusted gross income for the taxable year, military pay and allowances received by the taxpayer during the taxable year for active duty service in the United States army, air force, navy, marine corps, or coast guard or reserve components thereof or the national guard. The deduction may not be claimed for military pay and allowances received by the taxpayer while the taxpayer is stationed in this state.

(B) "Business income" means income, including gain or loss, arising from transactions, activities, and sources in the regular course of a trade or business and includes income, gain, or loss from real property, tangible property, and intangible property if the acquisition, rental, management, and disposition of the property constitute integral parts of the regular course of a trade or business operation. "Business income" includes income, including gain or loss, from a partial or complete liquidation of a business, including, but not limited to, gain or loss from the sale or other disposition of goodwill.

(C) "Nonbusiness income" means all income other than business income and may include, but is not limited to, compensation, rents and royalties from real or tangible personal property, capital gains, interest, dividends and distributions, patent or copyright royalties, or lottery winnings, prizes, and awards.

(D) "Compensation" means any form of remuneration paid to an employee for personal services.

(E) "Fiduciary" means a guardian, trustee, executor, administrator, receiver, conservator, or any other person acting in any fiduciary capacity for any individual, trust, or estate.

(F) "Fiscal year" means an accounting period of twelve months ending on the last day of any month other than December.

(G) "Individual" means any natural person.

(H) "Internal Revenue Code" means the "Internal Revenue Code of 1986," 100 Stat. 2085, 26 U.S.C.A. 1, as amended.

(I) "Resident" means any of the following, provided that division (I)(3) of this section applies only to taxable years of a trust beginning in 2002 or thereafter:

(1) An individual who is domiciled in this state, subject to section 5747.24 of the Revised Code;

(2) The estate of a decedent who at the time of death was domiciled in this state. The domicile tests of section 5747.24 of the Revised Code are not controlling for purposes of division (I)(2) of this section.

(3) A trust that, in whole or part, resides in this state. If only part of a trust resides in this state, the trust is a resident only with respect to that part.

For the purposes of division (I)(3) of this section:

(a) A trust resides in this state for the trust's current taxable year to the extent, as described in division (I)(3)(d) of this section, that the trust consists directly or indirectly, in whole or in part, of assets, net of any related liabilities, that were transferred, or caused to be transferred, directly or indirectly, to the trust by any of the following:

(i) A person, a court, or a governmental entity or instrumentality on account of the death of a decedent, but only if the trust is described in division (I)(3)(e)(i) or (ii) of this section;

(ii) A person who was domiciled in this state for the purposes of this chapter when the person directly or indirectly transferred assets to an irrevocable trust, but only if at least one of the trust's qualifying beneficiaries is domiciled in this state for the purposes of this chapter during all or some portion of the trust's current taxable year;

(iii) A person who was domiciled in this state for the purposes of this chapter when the trust document or instrument or part of the trust document or instrument became irrevocable, but only if at least one of the trust's qualifying beneficiaries is a resident domiciled in this state for the purposes of this chapter during all or some portion of the trust's current taxable year. If a trust document or instrument became irrevocable upon the death of a person who at the time of death was domiciled in this state for purposes of this chapter, that person is a person described in division (I)(3)(a)(iii) of this section.

(b) A trust is irrevocable to the extent that the transferor is not considered to be the owner of the net assets of the trust under sections 671 to 678 of the Internal Revenue Code [5].

(c) With respect to a trust other than a charitable lead trust, "qualifying beneficiary" has the same meaning as "potential current beneficiary" as defined in section 1361(e)(2) of the Internal Revenue Code, and with respect to a charitable lead trust "qualifying beneficiary" is any current, future, or contingent beneficiary, but with respect to any trust "qualifying beneficiary" excludes a person or a governmental entity or instrumentality to any of which a contribution would qualify for the charitable deduction under section 170 of the Internal Revenue Code.

(d) For the purposes of division (I)(3)(a) of this section, the extent to which a trust consists directly or indirectly, in whole or in part, of assets, net of any related liabilities, that were transferred directly or indirectly, in whole or part, to the trust by any of the sources enumerated in that division shall be ascertained by multiplying the fair market value of the trust's assets, net of related liabilities, by the qualifying ratio, which shall be computed as follows:

(i) The first time the trust receives assets, the numerator of the qualifying ratio is the fair market value of those assets at that time, net of any related liabilities, from sources enumerated in division (I)(3)(a) of this section. The denominator of the qualifying ratio is the fair market value of all the trust's assets at that time, net of any related liabilities.

(ii) Each subsequent time the trust receives assets, a revised qualifying ratio shall be computed. The numerator of the revised qualifying ratio is the sum of (1) the fair market value of the trust's assets immediately prior to the subsequent transfer, net of any related liabilities, multiplied by the qualifying ratio last computed without regard to the subsequent transfer, and (2) the fair market value of the subsequently transferred assets at the time transferred, net of any related liabilities, from sources enumerated in division (I)(3)(a) of this section. The denominator of the revised qualifying ratio is the fair market value of all the trust's assets immediately after the subsequent transfer, net of any related liabilities.

(iii) Whether a transfer to the trust is by or from any of the sources enumerated in division (I)(3)(a) of this section shall be ascertained without regard to the domicile of the trust's beneficiaries.

(e) For the purposes of division (I)(3)(a)(i) of this section:

(i) A trust is described in division (I)(3)(e)(i) of this section if the trust is a testamentary trust and the testator of that testamentary trust was domiciled in this state at the time of the testator's death for purposes of the taxes levied under Chapter 5731. of the Revised Code.

(ii) A trust is described in division (I)(3)(e)(ii) of this section if the transfer is a qualifying transfer described in any of divisions (I)(3)(f)(i) to (vi) of this section, the trust is an irrevocable inter vivos trust, and at least one of the trust's qualifying beneficiaries is domiciled in this state for purposes of this chapter during all or some portion of the trust's current taxable year.

(f) For the purposes of division (I)(3)(e)(ii) of this section, a "qualifying transfer" is a transfer of assets, net of any related liabilities, directly or indirectly to a trust, if the transfer is described in any of the following:

(i) The transfer is made to a trust, created by the decedent before the decedent's death and while the decedent was domiciled in this state for the purposes of this chapter, and, prior to the death of the decedent, the trust became irrevocable while the decedent was domiciled in this state for the purposes of this chapter.

(ii) The transfer is made to a trust to which the decedent, prior to the decedent's death, had directly or indirectly transferred assets, net of any related liabilities, while the decedent was domiciled in this state for the purposes of this chapter, and prior to the death of the decedent the trust became irrevocable while the decedent was domiciled in this state for the purposes of this chapter.

(iii) The transfer is made on account of a contractual relationship existing directly or indirectly between the transferor and either the decedent or the estate of the decedent at any time prior to the date of the decedent's death, and the decedent was domiciled in this state at the time of death for purposes of the taxes levied under Chapter 5731. of the Revised Code.

(iv) The transfer is made to a trust on account of a contractual relationship existing directly or indirectly between the transferor and another person who at the time of the decedent's death was domiciled in this state for purposes of this chapter.

(v) The transfer is made to a trust on account of the will of a testator.

(vi) The transfer is made to a trust created by or caused to be created by a court, and the trust was directly or indirectly created in connection with or as a result of the death of an individual who, for purposes of the taxes levied under Chapter 5731. of the Revised Code, was domiciled in this state at the time of the individual's death.

(g) The tax commissioner may adopt rules to ascertain the part of a trust residing in this state.

(J) "Nonresident" means an individual or estate that is not a resident. An individual who is a resident for only part of a taxable year is a nonresident for the remainder of that taxable year.

(K) "Pass-through entity" has the same meaning as in section 5733.04 of the Revised Code.

(L) "Return" means the notifications and reports required to be filed pursuant to this chapter for the purpose of reporting the tax due and includes declarations of estimated tax when so required.

(M) "Taxable year" means the calendar year or the taxpayer's fiscal year ending during the calendar year, or fractional part thereof, upon which the adjusted gross income is calculated pursuant to this chapter.

(N) "Taxpayer" means any person subject to the tax imposed by section 5747.02 of the Revised Code or any pass-through entity that makes the election under division (D) of section 5747.08 of the Revised Code.

(O) "Dependents" means dependents as defined in the Internal Revenue Code and as claimed in the taxpayer's federal income tax return for the taxable year or which the taxpayer would have been permitted to claim had the taxpayer filed a federal income tax return.

(P) "Principal county of employment" means, in the case of a nonresident, the county within the state in which a taxpayer performs services for an employer or, if those services are performed in more than one county, the county in which the major portion of the services are performed.

(Q) As used in sections 5747.50 to 5747.55 of the Revised Code:

(1) "Subdivision" means any county, municipal corporation, park district, or township.

(2) "Essential local government purposes" includes all functions that any subdivision is required by general law to exercise, including like functions that are exercised under a charter adopted pursuant to the Ohio Constitution.

(R) "Overpayment" means any amount already paid that exceeds the figure determined to be the correct amount of the tax.

(S) "Taxable income" or "Ohio taxable income" applies only to estates and trusts, and means federal taxable income, as defined and used in the Internal Revenue Code, adjusted as follows:

(1) Add interest or dividends, net of ordinary, necessary, and reasonable expenses not deducted in computing federal taxable income, on obligations or securities of any state or of any political subdivision or authority of any state, other than this state and its subdivisions and authorities, but only to the extent that such net amount is not otherwise includible in Ohio taxable income and is described in either division (S)(1)(a) or (b) of this section:

(a) The net amount is not attributable to the S portion of an electing small business trust and has not been distributed to beneficiaries for the taxable year;

(b) The net amount is attributable to the S portion of an electing small business trust for the taxable year.

(2) Add interest or dividends, net of ordinary, necessary, and reasonable expenses not deducted in computing federal taxable income, on obligations of any authority, commission, instrumentality, territory, or possession of the United States to the extent that the interest or dividends are exempt from federal income taxes but not from state income taxes, but only to the extent that such net amount is not otherwise includible in Ohio taxable income and is described in either division (S)(1)(a) or (b) of this section;

(3) Add the amount of personal exemption allowed to the estate pursuant to section 642(b) of the Internal Revenue Code;

(4) Deduct interest or dividends, net of related expenses deducted in computing federal taxable income, on obligations of the United States and its territories and possessions or of any authority, commission, or instrumentality of the United States to the extent that the interest or dividends are exempt from state taxes under the laws of the United States, but only to the extent that such amount is included in federal taxable income and is described in either division (S)(1)(a) or (b) of this section;

(5) Deduct the amount of wages and salaries, if any, not otherwise allowable as a deduction but that would have been allowable as a deduction in computing federal taxable income for the taxable year, had the targeted jobs credit allowed under sections 38, 51, and 52 of the Internal Revenue Code not been in effect, but only to the extent such amount relates either to income included in federal taxable income for the taxable year or to income of the S portion of an electing small business trust for the taxable year;

(6) Deduct any interest or interest equivalent, net of related expenses deducted in computing federal taxable income, on public obligations and purchase obligations, but only to the extent that such net amount relates either to income included in federal taxable income for the taxable year or to income of the S portion of an electing small business trust for the taxable year;

(7) Add any loss or deduct any gain resulting from sale, exchange, or other disposition of public obligations to the extent that such loss has been deducted or such gain has been included in computing either federal taxable income or income of the S portion of an electing small business trust for the taxable year;

(8) Except in the case of the final return of an estate, add any amount deducted by the taxpayer on both its Ohio estate tax return pursuant to section 5731.14 of the Revised Code, and on its federal income tax return in determining federal taxable income;

(9)(a) Deduct any amount included in federal taxable income solely because the amount represents a reimbursement or refund of expenses that in a previous year the decedent had deducted as an itemized deduction pursuant to section 63 of the Internal Revenue Code and applicable treasury regulations. The deduction otherwise allowed under division (S)(9)(a) of this section shall be reduced to the extent the reimbursement is attributable to an amount the taxpayer or decedent deducted under this section in any taxable year.

(b) Add any amount not otherwise included in Ohio taxable income for any taxable year to the extent that the amount is attributable to the recovery during the taxable year of any amount deducted or excluded in computing federal or Ohio taxable income in any taxable year, but only to the extent such amount has not been distributed to beneficiaries for the taxable year.

(10) Deduct any portion of the deduction described in section 1341(a)(2) of the Internal Revenue Code, for repaying previously reported income received under a claim of right, that meets both of the following requirements:

(a) It is allowable for repayment of an item that was included in the taxpayer's taxable income or the decedent's adjusted gross income for a prior taxable year and did not qualify for a credit under division (A) or (B) of section 5747.05 of the Revised Code for that year.

(b) It does not otherwise reduce the taxpayer's taxable income or the decedent's adjusted gross income for the current or any other taxable year.

(11) Add any amount claimed as a credit under section 5747.059 of the Revised Code to the extent that the amount satisfies either of the following:

(a) The amount was deducted or excluded from the computation of the taxpayer's federal taxable income as required to be reported for the taxpayer's taxable year under the Internal Revenue Code;

(b) The amount resulted in a reduction in the taxpayer's federal taxable income as required to be reported for any of the taxpayer's taxable years under the Internal Revenue Code.

(12) Deduct any amount, net of related expenses deducted in computing federal taxable income, that a trust is required to report as farm income on its federal income tax return, but only if the assets of the trust include at least ten acres of land satisfying the definition of "land devoted exclusively to agricultural use" under section 5713.30 of the Revised Code, regardless of whether the land is valued for tax purposes as such land under sections 5713.30 to 5713.38 of the Revised Code. If the trust is a pass-through entity investor, section 5747.231 of the Revised Code applies in ascertaining if the trust is eligible to claim the deduction provided by division (S)(12) of this section in connection with the pass-through entity's farm income.

Except for farm income attributable to the S portion of an electing small business trust, the deduction provided by division (S)(12) of this section is allowed only to the extent that the trust has not distributed such farm income. Division (S)(12) of this section applies only to taxable years of a trust beginning in 2002 or thereafter.

(13) Add the net amount of income described in section 641(c) of the Internal Revenue Code [6] to the extent that amount is not included in federal taxable income.

(14) Add or deduct the amount the taxpayer would be required to add or deduct under division (A)(20) or (21) of this section if the taxpayer's Ohio taxable income were computed in the same manner as an individual's Ohio adjusted gross income is computed under this section. In the case of a trust, division (S)(14) of this section applies only to any of the trust's taxable years beginning in 2002 or thereafter.

(T) "School district income" and "school district income tax" have the same meanings as in section 5748.01 of the Revised Code.

(U) As used in divisions (A)(8), (A)(9), (S)(6), and (S)(7) of this section, "public obligations," "purchase obligations," and "interest or interest equivalent" have the same meanings as in section 5709.76 of the Revised Code.

(V) "Limited liability company" means any limited liability company formed under Chapter 1705. of the Revised Code or under the laws of any other state.

(W) "Pass–through entity investor" means any person who, during any portion of a taxable year of a pass-through entity, is a partner, member, shareholder, or equity investor in that pass-through entity.

(X) "Banking day" has the same meaning as in section 1304.01 of the Revised Code.

(Y) "Month" means a calendar month.

(Z) "Quarter" means the first three months, the second three months, the third three months, or the last three months of the taxpayer's taxable year.

(AA)(1) "Eligible institution" means a state university or state institution of higher education as defined in section 3345.011 of the Revised Code, or a private, nonprofit college, university, or other post-secondary institution located in this state that possesses a certificate of authorization issued by the Ohio board of regents pursuant to Chapter 1713. of the Revised Code or a certificate of registration issued by the state board of career colleges and schools under Chapter 3332. of the Revised Code.

(2) "Qualified tuition and fees" means tuition and fees imposed by an eligible institution as a condition of enrollment or attendance, not exceeding two thousand five hundred dollars in each of the individual's first two years of post-secondary education. If the individual is a part-time student, "qualified tuition and fees" includes tuition and fees paid for the academic equivalent of the first two years of post-secondary education during a maximum of five taxable years, not exceeding a total of five thousand dollars. "Qualified tuition and fees" does not include:

(a) Expenses for any course or activity involving sports, games, or hobbies unless the course or activity is part of the individual's degree or diploma program;

(b) The cost of books, room and board, student activity fees, athletic fees, insurance expenses, or other expenses unrelated to the individual's academic course of instruction;

(c) Tuition, fees, or other expenses paid or reimbursed through an employer, scholarship, grant in aid, or other educational benefit program.

(BB)(1) "Modified business income" means the business income included in a trust's Ohio taxable income after such taxable income is first reduced by the qualifying trust amount, if any.

(2) "Qualifying trust amount" of a trust means capital gains and losses from the sale, exchange, or other disposition of equity or ownership interests in, or debt obligations of, a qualifying investee to the extent included in the trust's Ohio taxable income, but only if the following requirements are satisfied:

(a) The book value of the qualifying investee's physical assets in this state and everywhere, as of the last day of the qualifying investee's fiscal or calendar year ending immediately prior to the date on which the trust recognizes the gain or loss, is available to the trust.

(b) The requirements of section 5747.011 of the Revised Code are satisfied for the trust's taxable year in which the trust recognizes the gain or loss.

Any gain or loss that is not a qualifying trust amount is modified business income, qualifying investment income, or modified nonbusiness income, as the case may be.

(3) "Modified nonbusiness income" means a trust's Ohio taxable income other than modified business income, other than the qualifying trust amount, and other than qualifying investment income, as defined in section 5747.012 of the Revised Code, to the extent such qualifying investment income is not otherwise part of modified business income.

(4) "Modified Ohio taxable income" applies only to trusts, and means the sum of the amounts described in divisions (BB)(4)(a) to (c) of this section:

(a) The fraction, calculated under section 5747.013, and applying section 5747.231 of the Revised Code, multiplied by the sum of the following amounts:

(i) The trust's modified business income;

(ii) The trust's qualifying investment income, as defined in section 5747.012 of the Revised Code, but only to the extent the qualifying investment income does not otherwise constitute modified business income and does not otherwise constitute a qualifying trust amount.

(b) The qualifying trust amount multiplied by a fraction, the numerator of which is the sum of the book value of the qualifying investee's physical assets in this state on the last day of the qualifying investee's fiscal or calendar year ending immediately prior to the day on which the trust recognizes the qualifying trust amount, and the denominator of which is the sum of the book value of the qualifying investee's total physical assets everywhere on the last day of the qualifying investee's fiscal or calendar year ending immediately prior to the day on which the trust recognizes the qualifying trust amount. If, for a taxable year, the trust recognizes a qualifying trust amount with respect to more than one qualifying investee, the amount described in division (BB)(4)(b) of this section shall equal the sum of the products so computed for each such qualifying investee.

(c)(i) With respect to a trust or portion of a trust that is a resident as ascertained in accordance with division (I)(3)(d) of this section, its modified nonbusiness income.

(ii) With respect to a trust or portion of a trust that is not a resident as ascertained in accordance with division (I)(3)(d) of this section, the amount of its modified nonbusiness income satisfying the descriptions in divisions (B)(2) to (5) of section 5747.20 of the Revised Code, except as otherwise provided in division (BB)(4)(c)(ii) of this section. With respect to a trust or portion of a trust that is not a resident as ascertained in accordance with division (I)(3)(d) of this section, the trust's portion of modified nonbusiness income recognized from the sale, exchange, or other disposition of a debt interest in or equity interest in a section 5747.212 entity, as defined in section 5747.212 of the Revised Code, without regard to division (A) of that section, shall not be allocated to this state in accordance with section 5747.20 of the Revised Code but shall be apportioned to this state in accordance with division (B) of section 5747.212 of the Revised Code without regard to division (A) of that section.

If the allocation and apportionment of a trust's income under divisions (BB)(4)(a) and (c) of this section do not fairly represent the modified Ohio taxable income of the trust in this state, the alternative methods described in division (C) of section 5747.21 of the Revised Code may be applied in the manner and to the same extent provided in that section.

(5)(a) Except as set forth in division (BB)(5)(b) of this section, "qualifying investee" means a person in which a trust has an equity or ownership interest, or a person or unit of government the debt obligations of either of which are owned by a trust. For the purposes of division (BB)(2)(a) of this section and for the purpose of computing the fraction described in division (BB)(4)(b) of this section, all of the following apply:

(i) If the qualifying investee is a member of a qualifying controlled group on the last day of the qualifying investee's fiscal or calendar year ending immediately prior to the date on which the trust recognizes the gain or loss, then "qualifying investee" includes all persons in the qualifying controlled group on such last day.

(ii) If the qualifying investee, or if the qualifying investee and any members of the qualifying controlled group of which the qualifying investee is a member on the last day of the qualifying investee's fiscal or calendar year ending immediately prior to the date on which the trust recognizes the gain or loss, separately or cumulatively own, directly or indirectly, on the last day of the qualifying investee's fiscal or calendar year ending immediately prior to the date on which the trust recognizes the qualifying trust amount, more than fifty per cent of the equity of a pass-through entity, then the qualifying investee and the other members are deemed to own the proportionate share of the pass-through entity's physical assets which the pass-through entity directly or indirectly owns on the last day of the pass-through entity's calendar or fiscal year ending within or with the last day of the qualifying investee's fiscal or calendar year ending immediately prior to the date on which the trust recognizes the qualifying trust amount.

(iii) For the purposes of division (BB)(5)(a)(iii) of this section, "upper level pass-through entity" means a pass-through entity directly or indirectly owning any equity of another pass-through entity, and "lower level pass-through entity" means that other pass-through entity.

An upper level pass-through entity, whether or not it is also a qualifying investee, is deemed to own, on the last day of the upper level pass-through entity's calendar or fiscal year, the proportionate share of the lower level pass-through entity's physical assets that the lower level pass-through entity directly or indirectly owns on the last day of the lower level pass-through entity's calendar or fiscal year ending within or with the last day of the upper level pass-through entity's fiscal or calendar year. If the upper level pass-through entity directly and indirectly owns less than fifty per cent of the equity of the lower level pass-through entity on each day of the upper level pass-through entity's calendar or fiscal year in which or with which ends the calendar or fiscal year of the lower level pass-through entity and if, based upon clear and convincing evidence, complete information about the location and cost of the physical assets of the lower pass-through entity is not available to the upper level pass-through entity, then solely for purposes of ascertaining if a gain or loss constitutes a qualifying trust amount, the upper level pass-through entity shall be deemed as owning no equity of the lower level pass-through entity for each day during the upper level pass-through entity's calendar or fiscal year in which or with which ends the lower level pass-through entity's calendar or fiscal year. Nothing in division (BB)(5)(a)(iii) of this section shall be construed to provide for any deduction or exclusion in computing any trust's Ohio taxable income.

(b) With respect to a trust that is not a resident for the taxable year and with respect to a part of a trust that is not a resident for the taxable year, "qualifying investee" for that taxable year does not include a C corporation if both of the following apply:

(i) During the taxable year the trust or part of the trust recognizes a gain or loss from the sale, exchange, or other disposition of equity or ownership interests in, or debt obligations of, the C corporation.

(ii) Such gain or loss constitutes nonbusiness income.

(6) "Available" means information is such that a person is able to learn of the information by the due date plus extensions, if any, for filing the return for the taxable year in which the trust recognizes the gain or loss.

(CC) "Qualifying controlled group" has the same meaning as in section 5733.04 of the Revised Code.

(DD) "Related member" has the same meaning as in section 5733.042 of the Revised Code.

(EE)(1) For the purposes of division (EE) of this section:

(a) "Qualifying person" means any person other than a qualifying corporation.

(b) "Qualifying corporation" means any person classified for federal income tax purposes as an association taxable as a corporation, except either of the following:

(i) A corporation that has made an election under subchapter S, chapter one, subtitle A, of the Internal Revenue Code for its taxable year ending within, or on the last day of, the investor's taxable year;

(ii) A subsidiary that is wholly owned by any corporation that has made an election under subchapter S, chapter one, subtitle A of the Internal Revenue Code for its taxable year ending within, or on the last day of, the investor's taxable year.

(2) For the purposes of this chapter, unless expressly stated otherwise, no qualifying person indirectly owns any asset directly or indirectly owned by any qualifying corporation.

(FF) For purposes of this chapter and Chapter 5751. of the Revised Code:

(1) "Trust" does not include a qualified pre-income tax trust.

(2) A "qualified pre-income tax trust" is any pre-income tax trust that makes a qualifying pre-income tax trust election as described in division (FF)(3) of this section.

(3) A "qualifying pre-income tax trust election" is an election by a pre-income tax trust to subject to the tax imposed by section 5751.02 of the Revised Code the pre-income tax trust and all pass-through entities of which the trust owns or controls, directly, indirectly, or constructively through related interests, five per cent or more of the ownership or equity interests. The trustee shall notify the tax commissioner in writing of the election on or before April 15, 2006. The election, if timely made, shall be effective on and after January 1, 2006, and shall apply for all tax periods and tax years until revoked by the trustee of the trust.

(4) A "pre-income tax trust" is a trust that satisfies all of the following requirements:

(a) The document or instrument creating the trust was executed by the grantor before January 1, 1972;

(b) The trust became irrevocable upon the creation of the trust; and

(c) The grantor was domiciled in this state at the time the trust was created.

(2006 H 73, eff. 4-4-07; 2006 H 530, eff. 3-30-06 (See Historical and Statutory Notes); 2005 H 66, eff. 6-30-05; 2004 H 362, eff. 12-30-04; 2003 H 127, eff. 12-11-03; 2003 H 95, eff. 9-26-03; 2002 H 675, eff. 12-13-02; 2002 S 266, eff. 4-3-03; 2002 S 261, eff. 6-5-02; 2000 S 161, § 3, eff. 7-1-00; 2000 S 161, § 1, eff. 6-8-00; 1999 H 471, eff. 7-1-00; 1999 H 4, eff. 10-14-99; 1999 H 282, eff. 9-28-99; 1998 H 770, eff. 9-16-98; 1997 H 408, eff. 10-1-97; 1997 H 215, eff. 9-29-97; 1996 H 627, eff. 12-2-96; 1996 H 179, eff. 10-1-96; 1994 S 74, eff. 7-1-94; 1993 S 123, eff. 10-29-93; 1993 H 152; 1992 H 478; 1990 S 223, H 286; 1989 H 111, H 61; 1988 S 386; 1987 H 171; 1986 H 428; 1985 S 121; 1984 S 307, H 250; 1983 H 291; 1981 H 694; 1980 H 653; 1974 H 971; 1973 H 95; 1972 S 464, S 472; 1971 H 475)

1 42 U.S.C.A. § 401 et seq.
2 26 U.S.C.A. § 86.
3 26 U.S.C.A. § 38, 51, 52.
4 26 U.S.C.A. § 7702(B)(c).
5 26 U.S.C.A. § 671 to 678.
6 26 U.S.C.A. § 641(c).

Uncodified Law

2006 H 73, § 3, eff. 4-4-07, reads:

Sections 1 and 2 of this act apply to taxable years beginning on or after January 1, 2007.

2005 H 66, § 553.01 and 553.02, eff. 6-30-05, read:

Sec. 553.01. (A) As used in this section:

(1) "Qualifying delinquent taxes" means any tax levied under Chapter 5733., 5739., 5741., 5747., or 5748. of the Revised Code, including the taxes levied under sections 5733.41 and 5747.41 of the Revised Code and taxes required to be withheld under Chapters 5747. and 5748. of the Revised Code, which were due and payable from any person as of May 1, 2005, were unreported or underreported, and remain unpaid.

(2) "Qualifying delinquent personal property taxes" means a tax for which a return is filed under section 5711.02 of the Revised Code.

(3) "Qualifying delinquent taxes" and "qualifying delinquent personal property taxes" do not include any tax for which a notice of assessment or audit has been issued, for which a bill has been issued, which relates to a tax period that ends after the effective date of this section, or for which an audit has been conducted or is currently being conducted.

(B) The Tax Commissioner shall establish and administer a tax amnesty program with respect to qualifying delinquent taxes and qualifying delinquent personal property taxes. The program shall commence on January 1, 2006, and shall conclude on February 15, 2006. The Tax Commissioner shall issue forms and instructions and take other actions necessary to implement the program. The Tax Commissioner shall publicize the program so as to maximize public awareness and participation in the program.

(C)(1) During the program, if a person pays the full amount of qualifying delinquent taxes owed by that person and one-half of any interest that has accrued as a result of the person failing to pay those taxes in a timely fashion, the Tax Commissioner shall waive or abate all applicable penalties and one-half of any interest that accrued on the qualifying delinquent taxes.

(2) During the program, if a person who owes qualifying delinquent personal property taxes files a return with the Tax Commissioner, in the form and manner prescribed by the Tax Commissioner, listing all taxable property that was required to be listed on the return required to be filed under section 5711.02 of the Revised Code, the Tax Commissioner shall issue a preliminary assessment certificate to the appropriate county auditor. Upon receiving a preliminary assessment certificate issued by the Tax Commissioner pursuant to this division, the county auditor shall compute the amount of qualifying delinquent personal property taxes owed by the person and shall add to that amount one-half of the interest prescribed under sections 5711.32 and 5719.041 of the Revised Code. The county treasurer shall collect the amount of tax and interest computed by the county auditor under this division by preparing and mailing a tax bill to the person as prescribed in section 5711.32 of the Revised Code. If the person pays the full amount of tax and interest thereon on or before the date shown on the tax bill all applicable penalties and one-half of any interest that accrued on the qualifying delinquent personal property taxes shall be waived.

(3) No payment required under division (G) of section 321.24 of the Revised Code shall be made with respect to any person who pays qualifying delinquent personal property taxes under division (C)(2) of this section.

(4) Notwithstanding any contrary provision of the Revised Code, the Tax Commissioner shall not furnish to the county auditor any information pertaining to the exemption from taxation under division (C)(3) of section 5709.01 of the Revised Code insofar as that information pertains to any person who pays qualifying delinquent personal property taxes under division (C)(2) of this section.

(D) The Tax Commissioner may require a person participating in the program to file returns or reports, including amended returns and reports, in connection with the person's payment of qualifying delinquent taxes or qualifying delinquent personal property taxes.

(E) A person who participates in the program and pays in full any outstanding qualifying delinquent tax or qualifying delinquent personal property tax and the interest payable on such tax in accordance with this section shall not be subject to any criminal prosecution or any civil action with respect to that tax, and no assessment shall thereafter be issued against that person with respect to that tax.

(F) Taxes and interest collected under the program shall be credited to the General Revenue Fund, except that:

(1) Qualifying delinquent personal property taxes and interest payable thereon shall be credited to the appropriate county undivided income tax fund, and the county auditor shall distribute the amount thereof among the various taxing districts in the county as if it had been levied, collected, and settled, as personal property taxes;

(2) Qualifying delinquent taxes levied under section 5739.021, 5739.023, or 5739.026 of the Revised Code shall be distributed to the appropriate counties and transit authorities in accordance with section 5739.21 of the Revised Code during the next distribution required under that section;

(3) Qualifying delinquent taxes levied under section 5741.021, 5741.022, or 5741.023 of the Revised Code shall be distributed to the appropriate counties and transit authorities in accordance with section 5741.03 of the Revised Code during the next distribution required under that section; and

(4) Qualifying delinquent taxes levied under Chapter 5748. of the Revised Code shall be credited to the school district income tax fund and then paid to the appropriate school district during the next payment required under division (D) of section 5747.03 of the Revised Code.

Sec. 553.02. Section 553.01 of this act is hereby repealed, effective February 16, 2006. The repeal of Section 553.01 of this act does not affect, after the effective date of the repeal, the rights, remedies, or actions authorized under that section.

2005 H 66, § 557.30, eff. 6-30-05, reads:

Except as otherwise provided in division (A)(18) of section 5747.01 and division (A) of section 5747.02 of the Revised Code, the amendment by this act of sections 5747.01 and 5747.02 of the Revised Code applies to taxable years ending on or after the effective date of this section.

2004 H 362, § 5, eff. 12–30–04, reads:

(A) Except as provided in division (B) of this section, the amendment by this act of sections 5733.04 and 5747.01 of the Revised Code, which updates references to federal income tax laws and thereby incorporates recent changes to those laws, first applies to taxable years ending on or after the effective date of those sections, as amended by this act.

(B) A taxpayer may irrevocably elect to apply section 5733.04 or 5747.01 of the Revised Code, as amended by this act, to the taxpayer's taxable year ending in 2004. The filing of a return or report by the taxpayer for that taxable year that incorporates the amendments to those sections by this act without adjustments to reverse the effects of those amendments constitutes the making of an irrevocable election under this section.

1999 H 4, § 5, eff. 10–14–99, reads:

The amendment by this act of section 5747.01 of the Revised Code applies to taxable years beginning on or after January 1, 1999.

1996 H 179, § 3, eff. 10–1–96, reads: Section 5747.01 of the Revised Code, as amended by this act, applies to taxable years ending on or after the effective date of this act.

1996 H 627, § 13, eff. 12–2–96, reads: The amendments in this act to division (A)(10) of section 5747.01 of the Revised Code first apply to taxable year 1996.

1993 H 152, § 135, eff. 7–1–93, reads: Section 5747.01 of the Revised Code, as amended by this act, first applies to taxable years ending on or after the effective date of this act.

1992 H 478, § 5, eff. 1–14–93, reads, in part: (D) Division (A)(11) of section 5747.01 of the Revised Code, as amended by this act, shall first apply to taxable years commencing on or after January 1, 1993.

1990 H 286, § 3, eff. 11–8–90, reads: Sections 1 and 2 of this act apply only to the estates of decedents who die on or after the effective date of this act.

Historical and Statutory Notes

Ed. Note: 2006 H 530 Effective Date Provision:

SECTION 821.06. (A) Except as otherwise provided in division (B) of this section, the amendments by this act to section 5747.01 of the Revised Code provide for or are essential to implementation of a tax levy. Therefore, under Ohio Constitution, Article II, Section 1d, the amendments are not subject to the referendum and go into immediate effect when this act becomes law.

(B) The amendments adding divisions (A)(22) and (23) to section 5747.01 of the Revised Code are subject to the referendum. Therefore, under Ohio Constitution, Article II, Section 1c, the amendments take effect on the ninety-first day after this act is filed with the Secretary of State. If, however, a referendum petition is filed against either amendment, the amendment, unless rejected at the referendum, takes effect at the earliest time permitted by law.

Ed. Note: 2005 H 66 Effective Date Provision:

SECTION 612.72. (A) Except as otherwise provided in division (B) of this section, the amendments by this act to section 5747.01 of the Revised Code provides for or is essential to implementation of a tax levy. Therefore, under Ohio Constitution, Article II, Section 1d, the amendments are not subject to the referendum and go into immediate effect when this act becomes law.

(B) The amendment to division (A)(10) of section 5747.01 of the Revised Code is subject to the referendum. Therefore, under Ohio Constitution, Article II, Section 1c and section 1.471 of the Revised Code, the amendment takes effect on the ninety-first day after this act is filed with the Secretary of State. If, however, a referendum petition is filed against the amendment, the amendment, unless rejected at the referendum, takes effect at the earliest time permitted by law.

Amendment Note: 2006 H 530 substituted "B(c)" for "(B)(b)" after "7702" in division (A)(11)(c); added divisions (A)(22) and (A)(23); added language in division (BB)(4)(c)(ii) after "Revised Code," beginning with ", except as otherwise provided"; added division (FF); corrected a typo in division (S)(12); and made other nonsubstantive changes.

Amendment Note: 2005 H 66 inserted "that is not otherwise defined in this section" and "or if not used in a comparable context in those laws, has the same meaning as in section 5733.40 of the Revised Code" in the first paragraph; deleted "or after 2004," after "before 2002" and deleted ", 2003," and substituted "thereafter" for "2004" in division (A)(6); substituted "units" for "credits" in division (A)(10); inserted "but not for any taxable year beginning after December 31, 2005" at the beginning of division (A)(18); deleted ", 2003," in divisions (I), the second paragraph of division (S)(12), and division (S)(14); substituted "thereafter" for "2004" in division (I); added the last sentence in division (I)(3)(a)(iii); added division (I)(3)(d)(iii); rewrote division (EE); and made other nonsubstantive changes. Prior to amendment, division (EE) read:

"(EE) Any term used in this chapter that is not otherwise defined in this section and that is not used in a comparable context in the Internal Revenue Code and other statutes of the United States relating to federal income taxes has the same meaning as in section 5733.40 of the Revised Code."

Amendment Note: 2004 H 362 substituted "laws" for "Internal Revenue Code, and all other statutes" and added the last sentence in the first paragraph.

Amendment Note: 2003 H 127 deleted "division (B)(2) of" and "as if the trust were a corporation subject to the tax imposed by section 5733.06 of the Revised Code," from subdivision (BB)(4)(a) and substituted "5747.013" for "5733.05" and "5747.231" for "5733.057" in the same subdivision.

Amendment Note: 2003 H 95 rewrote division (A)(20)(a), added division (A)(20)(d), added division (A)(21)(c). Prior to amendment, division (A)(20)(a) read:

"(20)(a)Add five-sixths of the amount of depreciation expense allowed by subsection (k) of section 168 of the Internal Revenue Code, including the taxpayer's proportionate or distributive share of the amount of depreciation expense allowed by that subsection to a pass-through entity in which the taxpayer has a direct or indirect ownership interest. The tax commissioner, under procedures established by the commissioner, may waive the add-back related to a pass-through entity if the taxpayer owns, directly or indirectly, less than five per cent of the pass-through entity."

Amendment Note: 2002 S 266 substituted "career colleges and schools" for "proprietary school registration" in division (AA)(1).

Amendment Note: 2002 H 675 inserted "federal" before "adjusted gross income" in division (A); inserted "to the extent" and "the interest or dividends" in division (A)(2); inserted "that the interest or dividends are" in division (A)(3); inserted "that the interest or interest equivalent" in division (A)(8); inserted "that the loss has been deducted or the gain has been" and "computing" in division (A)(9); inserted ", including gain or loss, after "means income" and ", gain, or loss" after "and includes income" in division (B); rewrote divisions (I), (S) and (BB); added new divisions (CC) and (DD); and redesignated former division (CC) as new division (EE). Prior to amendment divisions (I), (S), and (BB) read:

"(I) "Resident" means:

"(1) An individual who is domiciled in this state, subject to section 5747.24 of the Revised Code;

"(2) The estate of a decedent who at the time of death was domiciled in this state. The domicile tests of section 5747.24 of the Revised Code and any election under section 5747.25 of the Revised Code are not controlling for purposes of division (I)(2) of this section.

"(3) Division (I)(3) of this section applies only to taxable years of a trust beginning in 2002, 2003, or 2004.

"A trust that, in whole or part, resides in this state. If only part of a trust resides in this state, the trust is a resident only with respect to that part. For the purposes of division (I)(3) of this section, a trust resides in this state to the extent that it consists, directly or indirectly, in whole or in part, of the net current value, adjusted for any profits, gains, or losses, of assets or liabilities that were transferred to the trust by any of the following:

"(a) The will of a decedent who was domiciled in this state at the time of the decedent's death;

"(b) A person who is domiciled in this state if the trust or part of the trust is not irrevocable;

"(c) A person who was domiciled in this state when the trust or part of the trust became irrevocable, but only if, for all or some portion of the current taxable year of the trust, at least one beneficiary of the trust is a resident for the purposes of this chapter.

"For the purpose of divisions (I)(3)(b) and (c) of this section, the transfer of net assets to a trust is irrevocable to the extent that the transferor is not considered to be the owner of the net assets of the trust under sections 671 to 678 of the Internal Revenue Code.

"The tax commissioner may adopt rules to ascertain the part of a trust residing in this state under this division.

"(S) "Taxable income" applies only to estates and trusts, and means taxable income as defined and used in the Internal Revenue Code adjusted as follows:

"(1) Add interest or dividends on obligations or securities of any state or of any political subdivision or authority of any state, other than this state and its subdivisions and authorities;

"(2) Add interest or dividends on obligations of any authority, commission, instrumentality, territory, or possession of the United States that are exempt from federal income taxes but not from state income taxes;

"(3) Add the amount of personal exemption allowed to the estate pursuant to section 642(b) of the Internal Revenue Code;

"(4) Deduct interest or dividends on obligations of the United States and its territories and possessions or of any authority, commission, or instrumentality of the United States that are exempt from state taxes under the laws of the United States;

"(5) Deduct the amount of wages and salaries, if any, not otherwise allowable as a deduction but that would have been allowable as a deduction in computing federal taxable income for the taxable year, had the targeted jobs credit allowed under sections 38, 51, and 52 of the Internal Revenue Code not been in effect;

"(6) Deduct any interest or interest equivalent on public obligations and purchase obligations to the extent included in federal taxable income;

"(7) Add any loss or deduct any gain resulting from sale, exchange, or other disposition of public obligations to the extent included in federal taxable income;

"(8) Except in the case of the final return of an estate, add any amount deducted by the taxpayer on both its Ohio estate tax return pursuant to section 5731.14 of the Revised Code, and on its federal income tax return in determining either federal adjusted gross income or federal taxable income;

"(9)(a) Deduct any amount included in federal taxable income solely because the amount represents a reimbursement or refund of expenses that in a previous year the decedent had deducted as an itemized deduction pursuant to section 63 of the Internal Revenue Code and applicable treasury regulations. The deduction otherwise allowed under division (S)(9)(a) of this section shall be reduced to the extent the reimbursement is attributable to an amount the taxpayer or decedent deducted under this section in any taxable year.

"(b) Add any amount not otherwise included in Ohio taxable income for any taxable year to the extent that the amount is attributable to the recovery during the taxable year of any amount deducted or excluded in computing federal or Ohio taxable income in any taxable year.

"(10) Deduct any portion of the deduction described in section 1341(a)(2) of the Internal Revenue Code, for repaying previously reported income received under a claim of right, that meets both of the following requirements:

"(a) It is allowable for repayment of an item that was included in the taxpayer's taxable income or the decedent's adjusted gross income for a prior taxable year and did not qualify for a credit under division (A) or (B) of section 5747.05 of the Revised Code for that year.

"(b) It does not otherwise reduce the taxpayer's taxable income or the decedent's adjusted gross income for the current or any other taxable year.

"(11) Add any amount claimed as a credit under section 5747.059 of the Revised Code to the extent that the amount satisfies either of the following:

"(a) The amount was deducted or excluded from the computation of the taxpayer's federal taxable income as required to be reported for the taxpayer's taxable year under the Internal Revenue Code;

"(b) The amount resulted in a reduction in the taxpayer's federal taxable income as required to be reported for any of the taxpayer's taxable years under the Internal Revenue Code.

"(12) Deduct any amount that a trust is required to report as farm income on its federal income tax return, but only if the assets of the trust include at least ten acres of land satisfying the definition of "land devoted exclusively to agricultural use" under section 5713.30 of the Revised Code, regardless of whether the land is valued for tax purposes as such land under sections 5713.30 to 5713.38 of the Revised Code. Division (S)(12) of this section applies only to taxable years of a trust beginning in 2002, 2003, or 2004.

"(13) Add the net amount of income described in section 641(c) of the Internal Revenue Code to the extent that amount is not included in federal taxable income.

"(14) Add or deduct the amount the taxpayer would be required to add or deduct under division (A)(20) or (21) of this section if the taxpayer's taxable income were computed in the same manner as an individual's adjusted gross income is computed under this section. In the case of a trust, division (S)(14) of this section applies only to any of the trust's taxable years beginning in 2002, 2003, or 2004.

"(BB)(1) "Modified business income" means the business income included in a trust's taxable income after such taxable income is first reduced by the qualifying amount, if any.

"(2) "Qualifying amount" of a trust means capital gains and losses from the sale, exchange, or other disposition of equity or ownership interest in, or debt obligations of, a qualifying investee to the extent included in the trust's taxable income, but only if the location of the physical assets of the qualifying investee is available to the trust.

"(3) "Modified nonbusiness income" means a trust's taxable income other than modified business income and other than the qualifying amount.

"(4) "Modified taxable income" applies only to trusts and means the sum of the following:

"(a) Modified business income multiplied by the fraction calculated under division (B)(2) of section 5733.05, and applying section 5733.057 of the Revised Code, as if the trust were a corporation subject to the tax imposed by section 5733.06 of the Revised Code;

"(b) The qualifying amount multiplied by the ratio of the book value of the physical assets in this state of the qualifying investee to the book value of the total physical assets everywhere of the qualifying investee. If, for a taxable year, the trust recognizes a qualifying amount with respect to more than one qualifying investee, the amount described in division (BB)(4)(b) of this section shall equal the sum of the products so computed for each such qualifying investee.

"(c) Modified nonbusiness income to the extent produced by assets held by a trust or portion of a trust that is a resident for the purposes of this chapter.

"If the allocation and apportionment of a trust's income under divisions (BB)(4)(a) and (c) of this section do not fairly represent the modified taxable income of the trust in this state, the alternative methods described in division (C) of section 5747.21 of the Revised Code may be applied in the manner and to the same extent provided in that section.

"(5) "Qualifying investee" means a person in which a trust has an equity or ownership interest, or a person or unit of government the debt obligations of either of which are owned by a trust."

Amendment Note: 2002 S 261 inserted "add, for the beneficiary's taxable years beginning before 2002 or after 2004," and "to the extent that the portion was not included in the trust's taxable income for any of the trust's taxable years beginning in 2002, 2003, or 2004" in division (A)(6); added new division (A)(20); inserted "real property" before, and "property" after, "tangible", and added "Business income includes income, including gain or loss, from a partial or complete liquidation of a business, including, but not limited to, gain or loss from the sale or other disposition of good will." in division (B); added new division (I)(3); inserted "and trusts" in division (S); added new divisions (S)(12) to (S)(14); added new division (BB); redesignated former division (BB) as new division (CC); and made other nonsubstantive changes.

Amendment Note: 2000 S 161, § 3, rewrote division (A)(10), which prior thereto read:

"(10) Regarding tuition credits purchased under Chapter 3334. of the Revised Code:

"(a) Deduct the following:

"(i) For credits that as of the end of the taxable year have not been refunded pursuant to the termination of a tuition payment contract under section 3334.10 of the Revised Code, the amount of income related to the credits, to the extent included in federal adjusted gross income;

"(ii) For credits that during the taxable year have been refunded pursuant to the termination of a tuition payment contract under section 3334.10 of the Revised Code, the excess of the total purchase price of the tuition credits refunded over the amount of refund, to the extent the amount of the excess was not deducted in determining federal adjusted gross income.

"(b) Add the following:

"(i) For credits that as of the end of the taxable year have not been refunded pursuant to the termination of a tuition payment contract under section 3334.10 of the Revised Code, the amount of loss related to the credits, to the extent the amount of the loss was deducted in determining federal adjusted gross income;

"(ii) For credits that during the taxable year have been refunded pursuant to the termination of a tuition payment contract under section 3334.10 of the Revised Code, the excess of the amount of refund over the purchase price of each tuition credit refunded, to the extent not included in federal adjusted gross income."

Amendment Note: 2000 S 161, § 1, rewrote division (A)(10); and added the final paragraph. Prior to amendment, division (A)(10) read:

"(10) Regarding tuition credits purchased under Chapter 3334. of the Revised Code:

"(a) Deduct the following:

"(i) For credits that as of the end of the taxable year have not been refunded pursuant to the termination of a tuition payment contract under section 3334.10 of the Revised Code, the amount of income related to the credits, to the extent included in federal adjusted gross income;

"(ii) For credits that during the taxable year have been refunded pursuant to the termination of a tuition payment contract under section 3334.10 of the Revised Code, the excess of the total purchase price of the tuition credits refunded over the amount of refund, to the extent the amount of the excess was not deducted in determining federal adjusted gross income.

"(b) Add the following:

"(i) For credits that as of the end of the taxable year have not been refunded pursuant to the termination of a tuition payment contract under section 3334.10 of the Revised Code, the amount of loss related to the credits, to the extent the amount of the loss was deducted in determining federal adjusted gross income;

"(ii) For credits that during the taxable year have been refunded pursuant to the termination of a tuition payment contract under section 3334.10 of the Revised Code, the excess of the amount of refund over the purchase price of each tuition credit refunded, to the extent not included in federal adjusted gross income."

Amendment Note: 1999 H 471 substituted "job and family" for "human" in division (A)(17).

Amendment Note: 1999 H 4 rewrote divisions (A)(11), (A)(12), and (S)(9); and made other nonsubstantive changes. Prior to amendment, divisions (A)(11), (A)(12), and (S)(9) read:

"(11) Deduct, in the case of a self-employed individual as defined in section 401(c)(1) of the Internal Revenue Code and to the extent not otherwise allowable as a deduction in computing federal adjusted gross income for the taxable year, the amount paid during the taxable year for insurance that constitutes medical care for the taxpayer, the taxpayer's spouse, and dependents. No deduction under division (A)(11) of this section shall be allowed to any taxpayer who is eligible to participate in any subsidized health plan maintained by any employer of the taxpayer or of the spouse of the taxpayer. No deduction under division (A)(11) of this section shall be allowed to the extent that the sum of such deduction and any related deduction allowable in computing federal adjusted gross income for the taxable year exceeds the taxpayer's earned income, within the meaning of section 401(c) of the Internal Revenue Code, derived by the taxpayer from the trade or business with respect to which the plan providing the medical coverage is established.

"(12) Deduct any amount included in federal adjusted gross income solely because the amount represents a reimbursement or refund of expenses that in a previous year the taxpayer had deducted as an itemized deduction pursuant to section 63 of the Internal Revenue Code and applicable United States department of the treasury regulations."

"(9) Deduct any amount included in federal taxable income solely because the amount represents a reimbursement or refund of expenses that in a previous year the decedent had deducted as an itemized deduction pursuant to section 63 of the Internal Revenue Code and applicable treasury regulations;".

Amendment Note: 1999 H 282 added divisions (A)(18), (A)(19), and new division (AA); redesignated former division (AA) as division (BB); and made other nonsubstantive changes.

Amendment Note: 1998 H 770 substituted "(A)(17)" for "(A)(16)" in division (A); added the second sentence in division (A)(14); redesignated the former second occurrence of division (A)(16) as new division (A)(17)

and substituted "(A)(17)" for "(A)(16)" therein; and made other nonsubstantive changes.

Amendment Note: 1997 H 408 added division (A)(16); and made other nonsubstantive changes.

Amendment Note: 1997 H 215 added division (A)(16); rewrote division (K); inserted "or any pass-through entity that makes the election under division (D) of section 5747.08 of the Revised Code" in division (N); added divisions (S)(11) and (W) through (AA); and made other nonsubstantive changes. Prior to amendment, division (K) read:

"(K) 'Partnership' means any unincorporated business association and includes, but is not limited to, a syndicate, group, pool, or joint venture through or by means of which any business, financial operation, or venture is carried on, but does not include a trust, or estate within the meaning of this section."

Amendment Note: 1996 H 627 rewrote division (A)(10); and made changes to reflect gender neutral language. Prior to amendment, division (A)(10) read:

"(10) Deduct any increase during the taxable year in the value of tuition credits or supplemental tuition credits purchased pursuant to Chapter 3334. of the Revised Code in excess of their purchase price as established under division (B) of section 3334.07 of the Revised Code to the extent the increase is included in federal adjusted gross income, except that the total increase in the value of tuition credits that are refunded, and the total increase in the value of supplemental tuition credits that are used or refunded, pursuant to Chapter 3334. of the Revised Code in excess of their purchase price as established under division (B) of section 3334.07 of the Revised Code shall be added to adjusted gross income in the year that they are refunded or used to the extent that the increase is not included in federal adjusted gross income [.]"

Amendment Note: 1996 H 179 added divisions (A)(14) and (A)(15); and made changes to reflect gender neutral language.

Amendment Note: 1994 S 74 added division (V).

Amendment Note: 1993 S 123 inserted "or 'Ohio adjusted gross income'" in the first sentence of division (A); and rewrote division (I), which previously read:

"(I) 'Resident' means:

"(1) An individual who is domiciled in this state;

"(2) An individual who lives in and maintains a permanent place of abode in this state, and who does not maintain a permanent place of abode elsewhere, unless such individual, in the aggregate, lives more than three hundred thirty-five days of the taxable year outside this state; or

"(3) The estate of a decedent who at the time of his death was domiciled in this state."

Amendment Note: 1993 H 152 added divisions (A)(12), (A)(13), (S)(9), and (S)(10).

Library References

Taxation ⚖ 978–1049.
Westlaw Topic No. 371.
C.J.S. Taxation § 1092–1100.

Baldwin's Ohio Legislative Service Annotated, 1999 H 4—LSC Analysis, p 7/L–849

5747.011 Definitions; limited application

(A) As used in this section:

(1) "Qualifying closely-held C corporation" means a person classified for federal income tax purposes as an association taxed as a corporation and that has more than fifty per cent of the value of its outstanding stock or equity owned, directly or indirectly, by or for not more than five qualifying persons. For the purposes of this division, the ownership of stock shall be determined under the rules set forth in section 544 of the Internal Revenue Code.

(2) "Qualifying person" means an individual; an organization described in section 401(a), 501(c)(17), or 509(a) of the Internal Revenue Code; or a portion of a trust permanently set aside or to be used exclusively for the purposes described in section 642(c) of the Internal Revenue Code or a corresponding provision of a prior federal income tax law.

(3) "Qualifying limited liability company" means a limited liability company that is not classified for federal income tax purposes as an association taxed as a corporation.

(4) "Ownership interest" means the equity or ownership interest in, or debt obligation of, a "qualifying investee" as defined in section 5747.01 of the Revised Code.

(5) "Qualifying individual beneficiary" has the same meaning as qualifying beneficiary as used in division (I)(3)(c) of section 5747.01 of the Revised Code, but is limited to individuals.

(6) "Family" of an individual means only the individual's spouse; the individual's ancestors, limited to the individual's parents, grandparents, and great grandparents; the siblings of such ancestors, whether by the whole or half blood or by legal adoption; the lineal descendants of such ancestors and siblings; persons legally adopted by such ancestors or by such siblings; and the spouses of such ancestors, siblings, legally adopted persons, and lineal descendants.

(B) The requirements of this division apply for purposes of division (BB)(2)(b) of section 5747.01 of the Revised Code and for the purposes of division (D) of section 5747.012 of the Revised Code. Gain or loss included in a trust's Ohio taxable income is not a qualifying trust amount unless the trust's ownership interest in the qualifying investee is at least five per cent of the total outstanding ownership interests in such qualifying investee at any time during the ten-year period ending on the last day of the trust's taxable year in which the sale, exchange, or other disposition occurs. Nothing in this section negates the requirements in division (BB)(2) of section 5747.01 of the Revised Code.

For the purpose of ascertaining whether the trust's ownership interest in a qualifying investee is at least five per cent of the total outstanding ownership interests in such qualifying investee, the following apply:

(1) On each day, an ownership interest owned, directly or indirectly, by or for a qualifying closely-held C corporation, an S corporation, a partnership other than a publicly traded partnership, a qualifying limited liability company, an estate, or a trust that is irrevocable as defined in division (I)(3)(b) of section 5747.01 of the Revised Code is considered as being owned proportionately on the same day by the equity investors of such qualifying closely-held C corporation, S corporation, partnership, or qualifying limited liability company, or by the beneficiaries of such estate or trust, as the case may be. For the purposes of division (B)(1) of this section, a beneficiary's proportionate share of an ownership interest held by a trust shall be ascertained in accordance with section 544(a)(1) of the Internal Revenue Code.

(2) On each day, a trust, hereinafter referred to as the first trust, is considered as owning any ownership interest owned, directly or indirectly, by or for another trust, hereinafter referred to as the second trust, if on the same day the second trust has at least one individual trustee who is either (a) a trustee of the first trust, or (b) a member of a family that includes at least one of the trustees of the first trust.

(3) On each day, a trust, hereinafter referred to as the first trust, is considered as owning any ownership interest owned, directly or indirectly, by or for another trust, hereinafter referred to as the second trust, if on the same day the second trust has at least one qualifying individual beneficiary who is either (a) a qualifying individual beneficiary of the first trust or (b) a member of a family which includes a qualifying individual beneficiary of the first trust.

(4) An ownership interest constructively owned by a person by reason of the application of division (B)(1) of this section shall, for the purpose of applying divisions (B)(1) to (3) of this section, be treated as actually owned by that person.

(5) An ownership interest constructively owned by a trust by reason of the application of division (B)(2) or (3) of this section shall not be treated as actually owned by that trust for purposes of applying divisions (B)(1) to (3) of this section.

(6) If an ownership interest may be considered as owned by a trust under division (B)(1) or (2) of this section, the ownership interest shall be considered owned by that trust under division (B)(2) of this section.

(7) If an ownership interest may be considered as owned by a trust under division (B)(1) or (3) of this section, the ownership interest shall be considered owned by that trust under division (B)(3) of this section.

(2002 H 675, eff. 12–13–02)

5747.012 Definitions

This section applies for the purposes of divisions (BB)(3) and (BB)(4)(a)(ii) of section 5747.01 of the Revised Code.

(A) As used in this section:

(1)(a) Except as set forth in division (A)(1)(b) of this section, "qualifying investment income" means the portion of a qualifying investment pass-through entity's net income attributable to transaction fees in connection with the acquisition, ownership, or disposition of intangible property; loan fees; financing fees; consent fees; waiver fees; application fees; net management fees; dividend income; interest income; net capital gains from the sale or exchange or other disposition of intangible property; and all types and classifications of income attributable to distributive shares of income from other pass-through entities.

(b)(i) Notwithstanding division (A)(1)(a) of this section, "qualifying investment income" does not include any part of the qualifying investment pass-through entity's net capital gain which, after the application of section 5747.231 of the Revised Code with respect to a trust, would also constitute a qualifying trust amount.

(ii) Notwithstanding division (A)(1)(a) of this section, "qualifying investment income" does not include any part of the qualifying investment pass-through entity's net income attributable to the portion of a distributive share of income directly or indirectly from another pass-through entity to the extent such portion constitutes the other pass-through entity's net capital gain which, after the application of section 5747.231 of the Revised Code with respect to a trust, would also constitute a qualifying trust amount.

(2) "Qualifying investment pass-through entity" means an investment pass-through entity, as defined in section 5733.401 of the Revised Code, subject to the following qualifications:

(a) "Forty per cent" shall be substituted for "ninety per cent" wherever "ninety per cent" appears in section 5733.401 of the Revised Code.

(b) The pass-through entity must have been formed or organized as an entity prior to June 5, 2002, and must exist as a pass-through entity for all of the taxable year of the trust.

(c) The qualifying section 5747.012 trust or related persons to the qualifying section 5747.012 trust must directly or indirectly own at least five per cent of the equity of the investment pass-through entity each day of the entity's fiscal or calendar year ending within or with the last day of the qualifying section 5747.012 trust's taxable year;

(d) During the investment pass-through entity's calendar or fiscal year ending within or with the last day of the qualifying section 5747.012 trust's taxable year, the qualifying section 5747.012 trust or related persons of or to the qualifying section 5747.012 trust must, on each day of the investment pass-through entity's year, own directly, or own through equity investments in other pass-through entities, more than sixty per cent of the equity of the investment pass-through entity.

(B) "Qualifying section 5747.012 trust" means a trust satisfying one of the following:

(1) The trust was created prior to, and was irrevocable on, June 5, 2002; or

(2) If the trust was created after June 4, 2002, or if the trust became irrevocable after June 4, 2002, then at least eighty per cent of the assets transferred to the trust must have been previously owned by related persons to the trust or by a trust created prior to June 5, 2002, under which the creator did not retain the power to change beneficiaries, amend the trust, or revoke the trust. For purposes of division (B)(2) of this section, the power to substitute property of equal value shall not be considered to be a power to change beneficiaries, amend the trust, or revoke the trust.

(C) For the purposes of this section, "related persons" means the family of a qualifying individual beneficiary, as defined in division (A)(5) of section 5747.011 of the Revised Code. For the purposes of this division, "family" has the same meaning as in division (A)(6) of section 5747.011 of the Revised Code.

(D) For the purposes of applying divisions (A)(2)(c), (A)(2)(d), and (B)(2) of this section, the related persons or the qualifying section 5747.012 trust, as the case may be, shall be deemed to own the equity of the investment pass-through entity after the application of division (B) of section 5747.011 of the Revised Code.

(E) "Irrevocable" has the same meaning as in division (I)(3)(b) of section 5747.01 of the Revised Code.

(F) Nothing in this section requires any item of income, gain, or loss not satisfying the definition of qualifying investment income to be treated as modified nonbusiness income. Any item of income, gain, or loss that is not qualifying investment income is modified business income, modified nonbusiness income, or a qualifying trust amount, as the case may be.

(2006 H 530, eff. 3–30–06; 2005 H 66, eff. 6–30–05; 2002 H 675, eff. 12–13–02)

Historical and Statutory Notes

Amendment Note: 2006 H 530 inserted "the qualifying section 5747.012 trust or" in division (A)(2)(d).

Amendment Note: 2005 H 66 inserted "as an entity" and ", and must exist as a pass-through entity for all of the taxable year of the trust" in division (A)(2)(b).

5747.013 Determination of fraction used in calculating trust's modified taxable income; determination of property, payroll, and sales factors

(A) As used in this section:

(1) "Electric company," "combined company," and "telephone company" have the same meanings as in section 5727.01 of the Revised Code.

(2) "Qualified research" means laboratory research, experimental research, and other similar types of research; research in developing or improving a product; or research in developing or improving the means of producing a product. It does not include market research, consumer surveys, efficiency surveys, management studies, ordinary testing or inspection of material or products for quality control, historical research, or literary research. "Product," as used in this paragraph, does not include services or intangible property.

(B) The fraction to be used in calculating a trust's modified Ohio taxable income under division (BB)(4)(a) of section 5747.01 of the Revised Code shall be determined as follows: The numerator of the fraction is the sum of the following products: the property factor multiplied by twenty, the payroll factor multiplied by twenty, and the sales factor multiplied by sixty. The denominator of the fraction is one hundred, provided that the denominator shall be reduced by twenty if the property factor has a denominator of zero, by twenty if the payroll factor has a denominator of zero, and by sixty if the sales factor has a denominator of zero.

The property, payroll, and sales factors shall be determined as follows:

(1) The property factor is a fraction the numerator of which is the average value of the trust's real and tangible personal property owned or rented and used in the trade or business in this state during the taxable year, and the denominator of which is the average value of all the trust's real and tangible personal property owned or rented and used in the trade or business everywhere during such year. Real and tangible personal property that is owned but leased to a lessee to be used in the lessee's trade or business shall not be included in the property factor of the owner. There shall be excluded from the numerator and denominator of the fraction the original cost of all of the following property within Ohio: property with respect to which a "pollution control facility" certificate has been issued pursuant to section 5709.21 of the Revised Code; property with respect to which an "industrial water pollution control certificate" has been issued pursuant to that section or former section 6111.31 of the Revised Code; and property used exclusively during the taxable year for qualified research.

(a) Property owned by the trust is valued at its original cost. Property rented by the trust is valued at eight times the net annual rental rate. "Net annual rental rate" means the annual rental rate paid by the trust less any annual rental rate received by the trust from subrentals.

(b) The average value of property shall be determined by averaging the values at the beginning and the end of the taxable year, but the tax commissioner may require the averaging of monthly values during the taxable year, if reasonably required to reflect properly the average value of the trust's property.

(2) The payroll factor is a fraction the numerator of which is the total amount paid in this state during the taxable year by the trust for compensation, and the denominator of which is the total compensation paid everywhere by the trust during such year. There shall be excluded from the numerator and the denominator of the payroll factor the total compensation paid in this state to employees who are primarily engaged in qualified research.

(a) Compensation is paid in this state if: (i) the recipient's service is performed entirely within this state; (ii) the recipient's service is performed both within and without this state, but the service performed without this state is incidental to the recipient's service within this state; or (iii) some of the service is performed within this state and either the base of operations, or if there is no base of operations, the place from which the service is directed or controlled, is within this state, or the base of operations or the place from which the service is directed or controlled is not in any state in which some part of the service is performed, but the recipient's residence is in this state.

(b) Compensation is paid in this state to any employee of a common or contract motor carrier corporation, who performs the employee's regularly assigned duties on a motor vehicle in more than one state, in the same ratio by which the mileage traveled by such employee within the state bears to the total mileage traveled by such employee everywhere during the taxable year.

(3) The sales factor is a fraction the numerator of which is the total sales in this state by the trust during the taxable year, and the denominator of which is the total sales by the trust everywhere during such year. In determining the numerator and denominator of the fraction, receipts from the sale or other disposal of a capital asset or an asset described in section 1231 of the Internal Revenue Code shall be eliminated. Also, in determining the numerator and denominator of the sales factor, in the case of a trust owning at least eighty per cent of the issued and outstanding common stock of one or more insurance companies or public utilities, except an electric company and a combined company, and, for tax years 2005 and thereafter, a telephone

company, or owning at least twenty-five per cent of the issued and outstanding common stock of one or more financial institutions, receipts received by the trust from such insurance companies, utilities, and financial institutions shall be eliminated.

For the purpose of this section and section 5747.08 of the Revised Code, sales of tangible personal property are in this state where such property is received in this state by the purchaser. In the case of delivery of tangible personal property by common carrier or by other means of transportation, the place at which such property is ultimately received after all transportation has been completed shall be considered as the place at which such property is received by the purchaser. Direct delivery in this state, other than for purposes of transportation, to a person or firm designated by a purchaser constitutes delivery to the purchaser in this state, and direct delivery outside this state to a person or firm designated by a purchaser does not constitute delivery to the purchaser in this state, regardless of where title passes or other conditions of sale.

Sales, other than sales of tangible personal property, are in this state if either:

(a) The income-producing activity is performed solely in this state; or

(b) The income-producing activity is performed both within and without this state and a greater proportion of the seller's income-producing activity is performed within this state than in any other state, based on costs of performance.

(2003 H 127, eff. 12-11-03)

5747.02 Rates of taxation; exemption

(A) For the purpose of providing revenue for the support of schools and local government functions, to provide relief to property taxpayers, to provide revenue for the general revenue fund, and to meet the expenses of administering the tax levied by this chapter, there is hereby levied on every individual, trust, and estate residing in or earning or receiving income in this state, on every individual, trust, and estate earning or receiving lottery winnings, prizes, or awards pursuant to Chapter 3770. of the Revised Code, and on every individual, trust, and estate otherwise having nexus with or in this state under the Constitution of the United States, an annual tax measured in the case of individuals by Ohio adjusted gross income less an exemption for the taxpayer, the taxpayer's spouse, and each dependent as provided in section 5747.025 of the Revised Code; measured in the case of trusts by modified Ohio taxable income under division (D) of this section; and measured in the case of estates by Ohio taxable income. The tax imposed by this section on the balance thus obtained is hereby levied as follows:

(1) For taxable years beginning in 2004:

OHIO ADJUSTED GROSS INCOME LESS EXEMPTIONS (INDIVIDUALS) OR MODIFIED OHIO TAXABLE INCOME (TRUSTS) OR OHIO TAXABLE INCOME (ESTATES)	TAX
$5,000 or less	.743%
More than $5,000 but not more than $10,000	$37.15 plus 1.486% of the amount in excess of $5,000
More than $10,000 but not more than $15,000	$111.45 plus 2.972% of the amount in excess of $10,000
More than $15,000 but not more than $20,000	$260.05 plus 3.715% of the amount in excess of $15,000
More than $20,000 but not more than $40,000	$445.80 plus 4.457% of the amount in excess of $20,000
More than $40,000 but not more than $80,000	$1,337.20 plus 5.201% of the amount in excess of $40,000
More than $80,000 but not more than $100,000	$3,417.60 plus 5.943% of the amount in excess of $80,000
More than $100,000 but not more than $200,000	$4,606.20 plus 6.9% of the amount in excess of $100,000
More than $200,000	$11,506.20 plus 7.5% of the amount in excess of $200,000

(2) For taxable years beginning in 2005:

OHIO ADJUSTED GROSS INCOME LESS EXEMPTIONS (INDIVIDUALS) OR MODIFIED OHIO TAXABLE INCOME (TRUSTS) OR OHIO TAXABLE INCOME (ESTATES)	TAX
$5,000 or less	.712%
More than $5,000 but not more than $10,000	$35.60 plus 1.424% of the amount in excess of $5,000
More than $10,000 but not more than $15,000	$106.80 plus 2.847% of the amount in excess of $10,000
More than $15,000 but not more than $20,000	$249.15 plus 3.559% of the amount in excess of $15,000
More than $20,000 but not more than $40,000	$427.10 plus 4.27% of the amount in excess of $20,000
More than $40,000 but not more than $80,000	$1,281.10 plus 4.983% of the amount in excess of $40,000
More than $80,000 but not more than $100,000	$3,274.30 plus 5.693% of the amount in excess of $80,000
More than $100,000 but not more than $200,000	$4,412.90 plus 6.61% of the amount in excess of $100,000
More than $200,000	$11,022.90 plus 7.185% of the amount in excess of $200,000

(3) For taxable years beginning in 2006:

OHIO ADJUSTED GROSS INCOME LESS EXEMPTIONS (INDIVIDUALS) OR MODIFIED OHIO TAXABLE INCOME (TRUSTS) OR OHIO TAXABLE INCOME (ESTATES)	TAX
$5,000 or less	.681%
More than $5,000 but not more than $10,000	$34.05 plus 1.361% of the amount in excess of $5,000
More than $10,000 but not more than $15,000	$102.10 plus 2.722% of the amount in excess of $10,000
More than $15,000 but not more than $20,000	$238.20 plus 3.403% of the amount in excess of $15,000
More than $20,000 but not more than $40,000	$408.35 plus 4.083% of the amount in excess of $20,000
More than $40,000 but not more than $80,000	$1,224.95 plus 4.764% of the amount in excess of $40,000
More than $80,000 but not more than $100,000	$3,130.55 plus 5.444% of the amount in excess of $80,000
More than $100,000 but not more than $200,000	$4,219.35 plus 6.32% of the amount in excess of $100,000
More than $200,000	$10,539.35 plus 6.87% of the amount in excess of $200,000

(4) For taxable years beginning in 2007:

OHIO ADJUSTED GROSS INCOME LESS EXEMPTIONS (INDIVIDUALS) OR MODIFIED OHIO TAXABLE INCOME (TRUSTS) OR OHIO TAXABLE INCOME (ESTATES)	TAX
$5,000 or less	.649%
More than $5,000 but not more than $10,000	$32.45 plus 1.299% of the amount in excess of $5,000
More than $10,000 but not more than $15,000	$97.40 plus 2.598% of the amount in excess of $10,000
More than $15,000 but not more than $20,000	$227.30 plus 3.247% of the amount in excess of $15,000
More than $20,000 but not more than $40,000	$389.65 plus 3.895% of the amount in excess of $20,000
More than $40,000 but not more than $80,000	$1,168.65 plus 4.546% of the amount in excess of $40,000
More than $80,000 but not more than $100,000	$2,987.05 plus 5.194% of the amount in excess of $80,000
More than $100,000 but not more than $200,000	$4,025.85 plus 6.031% of the amount in excess of $100,000
More than $200,000	$10,056.85 plus 6.555% of the amount in excess of $200,000

(5) For taxable years beginning in 2008:

OHIO ADJUSTED GROSS INCOME LESS EXEMPTIONS (INDIVIDUALS) OR MODIFIED OHIO TAXABLE INCOME (TRUSTS) OR OHIO TAXABLE INCOME (ESTATES)	TAX
$5,000 or less	.618%
More than $5,000 but not more than $10,000	$30.90 plus 1.236% of the amount in excess of $5,000
More than $10,000 but not more than $15,000	$92.70 plus 2.473% of the amount in excess of $10,000
More than $15,000 but not more than $20,000	$216.35 plus 3.091% of the amount in excess of $15,000
More than $20,000 but not more than $40,000	$370.90 plus 3.708% of the amount in excess of $20,000
More than $40,000 but not more than $80,000	$1,112.50 plus 4.327% of the amount in excess of $40,000
More than $80,000 but not more than $100,000	$2,843.30 plus 4.945% of the amount in excess of $80,000
More than $100,000 but not more than $200,000	$3,832.30 plus 5.741% of the amount in excess of $100,000
More than $200,000	$9,573.30 plus 6.24% of the amount in excess of $200,000

(6) For taxable years beginning in 2009 or thereafter:

OHIO ADJUSTED GROSS INCOME LESS EXEMPTIONS (INDIVIDUALS) OR MODIFIED OHIO TAXABLE INCOME (TRUSTS) OR OHIO TAXABLE INCOME (ESTATES)	TAX
$5,000 or less	.587%
More than $5,000 but not more than $10,000	$29.35 plus 1.174% of the amount in excess of $5,000
More than $10,000 but not more than $15,000	$88.05 plus 2.348% of the amount in excess of $10,000
More than $15,000 but not more than $20,000	$205.45 plus 2.935% of the amount in excess of $15,000
More than $20,000 but not more than $40,000	$352.20 plus 3.521% of the amount in excess of $20,000
More than $40,000 but not more than $80,000	$1,056.40 plus 4.109% of the amount in excess of $40,000
More than $80,000 but not more than $100,000	$2,700.00 plus 4.695% of the amount in excess of $80,000
More than $100,000 but not more than $200,000	$3,639.00 plus 5.451% of the amount in excess of $100,000
More than $200,000	$9,090.00 plus 5.925% of the amount in excess of $200,000

In July of each year, beginning in 2010, the tax commissioner shall adjust the income amounts prescribed in this division by multiplying the percentage increase in the gross domestic product deflator computed that year under section 5747.025 of the Revised Code by each of the income amounts resulting from the adjustment under this division in the preceding year, adding the resulting product to the corresponding income amount resulting from the adjustment in the preceding year, and rounding the resulting sum to the nearest multiple of fifty dollars. The tax commissioner also shall recompute each of the tax dollar amounts to the extent necessary to reflect the adjustment of the income amounts. The rates of taxation shall not be adjusted.

The adjusted amounts apply to taxable years beginning in the calendar year in which the adjustments are made. The tax commissioner shall not make such adjustments in any year in which the amount resulting from the adjustment would be less than the amount resulting from the adjustment in the preceding year.

(B) If the director of budget and management makes a certification to the tax commissioner under division (B) of section 131.44 of the Revised Code, the amount of tax as determined under division (A) of this section shall be reduced by the percentage prescribed in that certification for taxable years beginning in the calendar year in which that certification is made.

(C) The levy of this tax on income does not prevent a municipal corporation, a joint economic development zone created under section 715.691, or a joint economic development district created under section 715.70 or 715.71 or sections 715.72 to 715.81 of the Revised Code from levying a tax on income.

(D) This division applies only to taxable years of a trust beginning in 2002 or thereafter.

(1) The tax imposed by this section on a trust shall be computed by multiplying the Ohio modified taxable income of the trust by the rates prescribed by division (A) of this section.

(2) A credit is allowed against the tax computed under division (D) of this section equal to the lesser of (1) the tax paid to another state or the District of Columbia on the trust's modified nonbusiness income, other than the portion of the trust's non-business income that is qualifying investment income as defined in section 5747.012 of the Revised Code, or (2) the effective tax rate, based on modified Ohio taxable income, multiplied by the trust's modified nonbusiness income other than the portion of trust's nonbusiness income that is qualifying investment income. The credit applies before any other applicable credits.

(3) The credits enumerated in divisions (A)(1) to (13) of section 5747.98 of the Revised Code do not apply to a trust subject to this division. Any credits enumerated in other divisions of section 5747.98 of the Revised Code apply to a trust subject to this division. To the extent that the trust distributes income for the taxable year for which a credit is available to the trust, the credit shall be shared by the trust and its beneficiaries. The tax commissioner and the trust shall be guided by applicable regulations of the United States treasury regarding the sharing of credits.

(E) For the purposes of this section, "trust" means any trust described in Subchapter J of Chapter 1 of the Internal Revenue

Code, excluding trusts that are not irrevocable as defined in division (I)(3)(b) of section 5747.01 of the Revised Code and that have no modified Ohio taxable income for the taxable year, charitable remainder trusts, qualified funeral trusts and preneed funeral contract trusts established pursuant to section 1111.19 of the Revised Code that are not qualified funeral trusts, endowment and perpetual care trusts, qualified settlement trusts and funds, designated settlement trusts and funds, and trusts exempted from taxation under section 501(a) of the Internal Revenue Code[1].

(2005 H 66, eff. 6–30–05; 2003 H 95, eff. 9–26–03; 2002 H 675, eff. 12–13–02; 2002 S 261, eff. 6–5–02; 1997 H 215, § 1, eff. 9–29–97; 1997 H 215, § 208, eff. 6–30–97; 1996 H 442, eff. 7–9–96; 1996 S 310, § 41, eff. 6–30–98; 1996 S 310, § 1, eff. 7–1–96; 1995 H 269, eff. 11–15–95; 1995 H 117, eff. 9–29–95; 1994 H 715, eff. 7–22–94; 1992 H 904, eff. 12–22–92; 1990 H 174; 1989 H 111; 1988 H 708; 1986 S 417; 1985 H 238; 1983 H 291, H 100; 1982 S 530; 1974 H 1476, H 1013; 1973 H 95; 1971 H 475)

[1] 26 U.S.C.A. § 501(a).

Uncodified Law

2005 H 66, § 557.30: See Uncodified Law under RC 5747.01.

1997 H 215, § 50.33, eff. 6–30–97, reads:

In fiscal year 1998 and fiscal year 1999, in addition to the limitation specified in division (B)(1) of section 5747.03 of the Revised Code requiring at least fifty per cent of the income tax collected by the state under section 5747.02 of the Revised Code be returned to certain subdivisions of the state pursuant to Section 9 of Article XII, Ohio Constitution, there shall also be a limitation that at least seventy-five per cent of the moneys deposited in the general revenue fund shall be expended for primary and secondary education, including vocational and special education, the Ohio School for the Deaf, and the Ohio School for the Blind and for the purpose of making payments to school districts as required by section 323.156 and divisions (F) and (G) of section 321.24 of the Revised Code.

1997 H 215, § 212, eff. 6–30–97, reads:

Sections 122.16, 122.17, 122.18, and 5709.66 of the Revised Code, as amended by this act, apply to tax years 1999 and thereafter in the case of persons subject to the tax imposed under section 5733.06 of the Revised Code, and apply to taxable years beginning in 1998 and thereafter for persons subject to the tax imposed by section 5747.02 of the Revised Code.

1995 H 117, § 184, eff. 6–30–95, reads:

(A) The Tax Commissioner shall not decrease the amount an employer is required to deduct and withhold from the compensation of an employee in the taxable year beginning in 1996 to reflect the increases in the personal income tax exemption provided for by this act. The Tax Commissioner may adjust the withholding amounts for the taxable year beginning in 1997 to reflect this act's personal income tax exemption increases.

(B) The amendment in this act to section 5747.02 of the Revised Code first applies to the taxable year beginning in 1996. For the preceding taxable year beginning before 1996, the personal exemption amount remains six hundred fifty dollars.

1992 H 904, § 143, eff. 12–22–92, reads: Section 5747.02 of the Revised Code, as amended by this act, applies to taxable years beginning on or after January 1, 1993.

1989 H 111, § 13, eff. 7–1–89, reads, in part: Sections 5747.01, 5747.02, 5747.022, 5747.05, 5747.13, 5747.15, and 5747.20 as amended and section 5733.053 of the Revised Code as enacted by this act shall take effect at the earliest time permitted by law, but shall first apply to a taxpayer's first taxable year ending on or after the effective date of those sections.

Historical and Statutory Notes

Ed. Note: The amendment of this section by 1996 S 310, § 41, eff. 6–30–98, was repealed by 1997 H 215, § 208, eff. 6–30–97. See *Baldwin's Ohio Legislative Service Annotated*, 1996, page 6/L–1353, and 1997, page 8/L–2236, or the OH–LEGIS or OH–LEGIS–OLD database on Westlaw.

Amendment Note: 2005 H 66 designated division (A)(1) and inserted "(1) For taxable years beginning in 2004:"; added division (A)(2) through (A)(6); substituted "2010" for "2005" in the first sentence of the second to the last paragraph of division (A); deleted ", 2003," and substituted "thereafter" for "2004" in the first sentence of division (D).

Amendment Note: 2003 H 95 inserted "and preneed funeral contract trusts established pursuant to section 1111.19 of the Revised Code that are not qualified funeral trusts," in Division (E).

Amendment Note: 2002 H 675 inserted "Ohio" throughout division (A); and rewrote divisions (D) and (E), which prior thereto read:

"(D) Division (D) of this section applies only to taxable years of a trust beginning in 2002, 2003, or 2004.

"The tax imposed by this section on a trust shall be computed by multiplying the modified taxable income of the trust by the rates prescribed by division (A) of this section.

"A credit is allowed against the tax computed under division (D) of this section equal to the lesser of (1) the tax paid to another state or the District of Columbia on modified nonbusiness income of a trust, or (2) the effective tax rate, based on modified taxable income, multiplied by the modified nonbusiness income of the trust. The credit applies before any other applicable credits. The credits enumerated in divisions (A)(1) to (13) of section 5747.98 of the Revised Code do not apply to a trust subject to this division.

"(E) For the purposes of this section, "trust" means any trust described in Subchapter J of the Internal Revenue Code, excluding a trust exempted from taxation under section 501(c)(3) of Internal Revenue Code."

Amendment Note: 2002 S 261 rewrote the section, which prior thereto read:

"(A) For the purpose of providing revenue for the support of schools and local government functions, to provide relief to property taxpayers, to provide revenue for the general revenue fund, and to meet the expenses of administering the tax levied by this chapter, there is hereby levied on every individual and every estate residing in or earning or receiving income in this state, on every individual and estate earning or receiving lottery winnings, prizes, or awards pursuant to Chapter 3770. of the Revised Code, and on every individual and estate otherwise having nexus with or in this state under the Constitution of the United States, an annual tax measured in the case of individuals by adjusted gross income less an exemption for the taxpayer, the taxpayer's spouse, and each dependent as provided in section 5747.025 of the Revised Code, and measured in the case of estates by taxable income. The tax imposed by this section on the balance thus obtained is hereby levied as follows:

OHIO ADJUSTED GROSS INCOME LESS EXEMPTIONS (INDIVIDUALS) OR MODIFIED OHIO TAXABLE INCOME (TRUSTS) OR OHIO TAXABLE INCOME (ESTATES)	TAX
$5,000 or less	.743%
More than $5,000 but not more than $10,000	$37.15 plus 1.486% of the amount in excess of $5,000
More than $10,000 but not more than $15,000	$111.45 plus 2.972% of the amount in excess of $10,000
More than $15,000 but not more than $20,000	$260.05 plus 3.715% of the amount in excess of $15,000
More than $20,000 but not more than $40,000	$445.80 plus 4.457% of the amount in excess of $20,000
More than $40,000 but not more than $80,000	$1,337.20 plus 5.201% of the amount in excess of $40,000
More than $80,000 but not more than $100,000	$3,417.60 plus 5.943% of the amount in excess of $80,000
More than $100,000 but not more than $200,000	$4,606.20 plus 6.9% of the amount in excess of $100,000
More than $200,000	$11,506.20 plus 7.5% of the amount in excess of $200,000

"(B) If the director of budget and management makes a certification to the tax commissioner under division (B) of section 131.44 of the Revised Code, the amount of tax as determined under division (A) of this section shall be reduced by the percentage prescribed in that certification for taxable years beginning in the calendar year in which that certification is made.

"(C) The levy of this tax on income does not prevent a municipal corporation, a joint economic development zone created under section 715.691, or a joint economic development district created under section 715.70 or 715.71 or sections 715.72 to 715.81 of the Revised Code from levying a tax on income."

Amendment Note: 1997 H 215 inserted "and on every individual and estate otherwise having nexus with or in this state under the Constitution of the United States," in division (A).

Amendment Note: 1996 H 442 inserted ", a joint economic development zone created under section 715.691," in the final paragraph.

Amendment Note: 1996 S 310, § 41, eff. 6–30–98, removed the designation from former division (A); deleted former division (B); and removed the designation from former division (C). Prior to amendment, former division (B) read:

"(B) If the director of budget and management makes a certification to the tax commissioner under division (B) of section 131.44 of the Revised Code, the amount of tax as determined under division (A) of this section shall be reduced by the percentage prescribed in that certification for taxable years beginning in the calendar year in which that certification is made."

Amendment Note: 1996 S 310, § 1, eff. 7–1–96, added division (B); and redesignated former division (B) as division (C).

Amendment Note: 1995 H 269 inserted "or sections 715.72 to 715.81"; and made changes to reflect gender neutral language.

Amendment Note: 1995 H 117 substituted "for the taxpayer, the taxpayer's spouse, and each dependent as provided in section 5747.025 of the Revised Code" for "of six hundred fifty dollars each for the the taxpayer, his spouse, and each dependent" in the first paragraph.

Amendment Note: 1994 H 715 inserted "or 715.71" in the final paragraph.

Library References

Taxation ⚖1031, 1047–1048, 1061.
Westlaw Topic No. 371.
C.J.S. Taxation § 1098–1099, 1101.

5747.022 Additional credit

An individual subject to the tax imposed by section 5747.02 of the Revised Code may claim a credit equal to twenty dollars times the number of exemptions allowed for the taxpayer, his spouse, and each dependent under section 5747.02 of the Revised Code. The credit shall be claimed in the order required under section 5747.98 of the Revised Code. The credit shall not be considered in determining the taxes required to be withheld under section 5747.06 of the Revised Code or the estimated taxes required to be paid under section 5747.09 of the Revised Code.

(1994 H 715, eff. 7–22–94; 1994 S 271, eff. 7–22–94; 1993 H 152, eff. 7–1–93; 1989 H 111; 1987 H 171; 1983 H 291)

Uncodified Law

1994 S 271, § 3: See Uncodified Law under 5747.98.

1989 H 111, § 13, eff. 7–1–89, reads, in part: Sections 5747.01, 5747.02, 5747.022, 5747.05, 5747.13, 5747.15, and 5747.20 as amended and section 5733.053 of the Revised Code as enacted by this act shall take effect at the earliest time permitted by law, but shall first apply to a taxpayer's first taxable year ending on or after the effective date of those sections.

Historical and Statutory Notes

Amendment Note: 1994 H 715 deleted certain provisions pertaining to tax credits and added provisions regarding the order of tax credits established in section 5747.98.

Amendment Note: 1994 S 271 deleted certain provisions pertaining to tax credits and added provisions regarding the order of tax credits established in section 5747.98.

Amendment Note: 1993 H 152 inserted "and section 5747.057".

Library References

Taxation ⚖1047.
Westlaw Topic No. 371.
C.J.S. Taxation § 1098.

5747.025 Personal exemption for taxpayer and spouse

(A) The personal exemption for the taxpayer and the taxpayer's spouse shall be seven hundred fifty dollars each for the taxable year beginning in 1996, eight hundred fifty dollars each for the taxable year beginning in 1997, nine hundred fifty dollars each for the taxable year beginning in 1998, and one thousand fifty dollars each for the taxable year beginning in 1999 and taxable years beginning after 1999. The personal exemption amount prescribed in this division for taxable years beginning after 1999 shall be adjusted each year in the manner prescribed in division (C) of this section.

(B) The personal exemption for each dependent shall be eight hundred fifty dollars for the taxable year beginning in 1996, and one thousand fifty dollars for the taxable year beginning in 1997 and taxable years beginning after 1997. The personal exemption amount prescribed in this division for taxable years beginning after 1999 shall be adjusted each year in the manner prescribed in division (C) of this section.

(C) In September of each year, beginning in 2000, the tax commissioner shall determine the percentage increase in the gross domestic product deflator determined by the bureau of economic analysis of the United States department of commerce from the first day of January of the preceding calendar year to the last day of December of the preceding year, and adjust the personal exemption amount for taxable years beginning in the current calendar year by multiplying that amount by the percentage increase in the gross domestic product deflator for that period; adding the resulting product to the personal exemption amount for taxable years beginning in the preceding calendar year; and rounding the resulting sum upward to the nearest multiple of fifty dollars. The commissioner shall not make such an adjustment in any calendar year in which the amount resulting from the adjustment would be less than the amount resulting from the adjustment in the preceding calendar year.

(2002 S 200, eff. 9–6–02; 1997 H 215, eff. 6–30–97; 1996 S 310, eff. 9–19–96; 1995 H 117, eff. 9–29–95)

Historical and Statutory Notes

Amendment Note: 2002 S 200 substituted "In September of each" for "each", "January" for "July", "December" for "June" and "preceding" for "current" in the first sentence of division (C); deleted "tax" before "commissioner" in the second sentence of division (C).

Amendment Note: 1997 H 215 added the second sentence in division (A), the second sentence in division (B), and division (C).

Amendment Note: 1996 S 310 inserted ", nine hundred fifty dollars each for the taxable year beginning in 1998, and one thousand fifty dollars each for the taxable year beginning in 1999" in, and substituted "1999" for "1997" at the end of, division (A); and made other nonsubstantive changes.

Library References

Taxation ⚖1031, 1048.
Westlaw Topic No. 371.
C.J.S. Taxation § 1098–1099.

5747.026 Extension for national guard and reservists called to active duty

(A) For taxable years beginning on or after January 1, 2002, each member of the national guard and each member of a reserve component of the armed forces of the United States called to active duty pursuant to an executive order issued by the president of the United States or an act of the congress of the United States may apply to the tax commissioner for both an extension for filing of the return and an extension of time for payment of taxes required under this chapter and under Chapter

5748. of the Revised Code during the period of the member's duty service and for sixty days thereafter. The application shall be filed on or before the sixtieth day after the member's duty terminates. An applicant shall provide such evidence as the tax commissioner considers necessary to demonstrate eligibility for the extension.

(B)(1) If the tax commissioner ascertains that an applicant is qualified for an extension under this section, the tax commissioner shall enter into a contract with the applicant for the payment of the tax in installments that begin on the sixty-first day after the applicant's active duty terminates. Except as provided in division (B)(3) of this section, the tax commissioner may prescribe such contract terms as the tax commissioner considers appropriate. If the amount owed is two thousand four hundred dollars or less, the contract shall be for not longer than twelve months. If the amount owed is more than two thousand four hundred dollars, the contract shall be for not longer than twenty-four months.

(2) If the tax commissioner ascertains that an applicant is qualified for an extension under this section, the applicant shall neither be required to file any return, report, or other tax document nor be required to pay any tax otherwise due under this chapter and Chapter 5748. of the Revised Code before the sixty-first day after the applicant's active duty terminates.

(3) Taxes paid pursuant to a contract entered into under division (B)(1) of this section are not delinquent. The tax commissioner shall not require any payments of penalties, interest penalties, or interest in connection with those taxes for the extension period.

(C)(1) Nothing in this division denies to any person described in this division the application of divisions (A) and (B) of this section.

(2)(a) A qualifying taxpayer who is eligible for an extension under the Internal Revenue Code shall receive both an extension of time in which to file any return, report, or other tax document described in this chapter and an extension of time in which to make any payment of taxes required under this chapter and Chapter 5748. of the Revised Code. The length of any extension granted under division (C)(2)(a) of this section shall be equal to the length of the corresponding extension that the taxpayer receives under the Internal Revenue Code. As used in this section, "qualifying taxpayer" means a member of the national guard, or a member of the reserve component of the armed forces of the United States, who is called to active duty pursuant to either an executive order issued by the president of the United States or an act of the congress of the United States.

(b) Taxes whose payment is extended in accordance with division (C)(2)(a) of this section are not delinquent during the extension period. The tax commissioner shall not require any payment of penalties, interest penalties, or interest in connection with those taxes for the extension period. The tax commissioner shall not include any period of extension granted under division (C)(2)(a) of this section in calculating the penalty, interest penalty, or interest due on any unpaid tax.

(D) For each taxable year to which division (A), (B), or (C) of this section applies to a taxpayer, the provisions of divisions (B)(2) and (3) or (C) of this section, as applicable, apply to the spouse of that taxpayer if the filing status of the spouse and the taxpayer is married filing jointly for that year.

(E) The tax commissioner may adopt rules necessary to administer this section, including rules establishing the following:

(1) Forms and procedures by which applicants may apply for extensions;

(2) Criteria for eligibility;

(3) A schedule for repayment of deferred taxes.

(2005 H 2, eff. 6–2–05; 2003 H 95, eff. 9–26–03)

Uncodified Law

2005 H 2, § 4, eff. 6–2–05, reads:

Sections 5747.026 and 5747.08 of the Revised Code, as amended by this act, shall apply to all years beginning on and after January 1, 2002.

Historical and Statutory Notes

Amendment Note: 2005 H 2 rewrote this section, which prior thereto read:

"(A) For taxable years beginning on or after January 1, 2002, a member of the national guard or a member of a reserve component of the armed forces of the United States called to active or other duty under operation Iraqi freedom may apply to the tax commissioner for an extension for filing of the return and payment of taxes required under this chapter during the period of the member's duty service and for sixty days thereafter. The application shall be filed on or before the sixtieth day after the member's duty terminates. An applicant shall provide such evidence as the commissioner considers necessary to demonstrate eligibility for the extension.

"(B)(1) If the commissioner determines that an applicant is qualified for an extension under this section, the commissioner shall enter into a contract with the applicant for the payment of the tax in installments that begin on the sixty-first day after the applicant's duty under operation Iraqi freedom terminates. Except as provided in division (B)(3) of this section, the commissioner may prescribe such contract terms as the commissioner considers appropriate.

"(2) If the commissioner determines that an applicant is qualified for an extension under this section, the applicant shall not be required to file any return, report, or other tax document before the sixty-first day after the applicant's duty under operation Iraqi freedom terminates.

"(3) Taxes paid pursuant to a contract entered into under division (B)(1) of this section are not delinquent. The tax commissioner shall not require any payments of penalties or interest in connection with such taxes.

"(C)(1) Divisions (A) and (B) of this section do not apply to any taxable year for which a taxpayer receives an extension of time in which to file a federal income tax return or pay federal income tax under the Internal Revenue Code.

"(2)(a) A taxpayer who is eligible for an extension under the Internal Revenue Code shall receive an extension of time in which to file any return, report, or other tax document described in this chapter and an extension of time in which to make any payment of taxes required under this chapter or Chapter 5748. of the Revised Code. The length of any extension granted under division (C)(2)(a) of this section shall be equal to the length of the corresponding extension that the taxpayer receives under the Internal Revenue Code.

"(b) Taxes paid in accordance with division (C)(2)(a) of this section are not delinquent. The tax commissioner shall not require any payment of penalties or interest in connection with such taxes. The tax commissioner shall not include any period of extension granted under division (C)(2)(a) of this section in calculating the interest due on any unpaid tax.

"(D) The tax commissioner shall adopt rules necessary to administer this section, including rules establishing the following:

"(1) Forms and procedures by which applicants may apply for extensions;

"(2) Criteria for eligibility;

"(3) A schedule for repayment of deferred taxes."

5747.05 Credits

As used in this section, "income tax" includes both a tax on net income and a tax measured by net income.

The following credits shall be allowed against the income tax imposed by section 5747.02 of the Revised Code on individuals and estates:

(A)(1) The amount of tax otherwise due under section 5747.02 of the Revised Code on such portion of the adjusted gross income of any nonresident taxpayer that is not allocable to this state pursuant to sections 5747.20 to 5747.23 of the Revised Code;

(2) The credit provided under this division shall not exceed the portion of the total tax due under section 5747.02 of the Revised Code that the amount of the nonresident taxpayer's adjusted

gross income not allocated to this state pursuant to sections 5747.20 to 5747.23 of the Revised Code bears to the total adjusted gross income of the nonresident taxpayer derived from all sources everywhere.

(3) The tax commissioner may enter into an agreement with the taxing authorities of any state or of the District of Columbia that imposes an income tax to provide that compensation paid in this state to a nonresident taxpayer shall not be subject to the tax levied in section 5747.02 of the Revised Code so long as compensation paid in such other state or in the District of Columbia to a resident taxpayer shall likewise not be subject to the income tax of such other state or of the District of Columbia.

(B) The lesser of division (B)(1) or (2) of this section:

(1) The amount of tax otherwise due under section 5747.02 of the Revised Code on such portion of the adjusted gross income of a resident taxpayer that in another state or in the District of Columbia is subjected to an income tax. The credit provided under division (B)(1) of this section shall not exceed the portion of the total tax due under section 5747.02 of the Revised Code that the amount of the resident taxpayer's adjusted gross income subjected to an income tax in the other state or in the District of Columbia bears to the total adjusted gross income of the resident taxpayer derived from all sources everywhere.

(2) The amount of income tax liability to another state or the District of Columbia on the portion of the adjusted gross income of a resident taxpayer that in another state or in the District of Columbia is subjected to an income tax. The credit provided under division (B)(2) of this section shall not exceed the amount of tax otherwise due under section 5747.02 of the Revised Code.

(3) If the credit provided under division (B) of this section is affected by a change in either the portion of adjusted gross income of a resident taxpayer subjected to an income tax in another state or the District of Columbia or the amount of income tax liability that has been paid to another state or the District of Columbia, the taxpayer shall report the change to the tax commissioner within sixty days of the change in such form as the commissioner requires.

(a) In the case of an underpayment, the report shall be accompanied by payment of any additional tax due as a result of the reduction in credit together with interest on the additional tax and is a return subject to assessment under section 5747.13 of the Revised Code solely for the purpose of assessing any additional tax due under this division, together with any applicable penalty and interest. It shall not reopen the computation of the taxpayer's tax liability under this chapter from a previously filed return no longer subject to assessment except to the extent that such liability is affected by an adjustment to the credit allowed by division (B) of this section.

(b) In the case of an overpayment, an application for refund may be filed under this division within the sixty day period prescribed for filing the report even if it is beyond the period prescribed in section 5747.11 of the Revised Code if it otherwise conforms to the requirements of such section. An application filed under this division shall only claim refund of overpayments resulting from an adjustment to the credit allowed by division (B) of this section unless it is also filed within the time prescribed in section 5747.11 of the Revised Code. It shall not reopen the computation of the taxpayer's tax liability except to the extent that such liability is affected by an adjustment to the credit allowed by division (B) of this section.

(4) No credit shall be allowed under division (B) of this section for income tax paid or accrued to another state or to the District of Columbia if the taxpayer, when computing federal adjusted gross income, has directly or indirectly deducted, or was required to directly or indirectly deduct, the amount of that income tax.

(C) For a taxpayer sixty-five years of age or older during the taxable year, a credit for such year equal to fifty dollars for each return required to be filed under section 5747.08 of the Revised Code.

(D) A taxpayer sixty-five years of age or older during the taxable year who has received a lump-sum distribution from a pension, retirement, or profit-sharing plan in the taxable year may elect to receive a credit under this division in lieu of the credit to which the taxpayer is entitled under division (C) of this section. A taxpayer making such election shall receive a credit for the taxable year equal to fifty dollars times the taxpayer's expected remaining life as shown by annuity tables issued under the provisions of the Internal Revenue Code and in effect for the calendar year which includes the last day of the taxable year. A taxpayer making an election under this division is not entitled to the credit authorized under division (C) of this section in subsequent taxable years except that if such election was made prior to July 1, 1983, the taxpayer is entitled to one-half the credit authorized under such division in subsequent taxable years but may not make another election under this division.

(E) A taxpayer who is not sixty-five years of age or older during the taxable year who has received a lump-sum distribution from a pension, retirement, or profit-sharing plan in a taxable year ending on or before July 31, 1991, may elect to take a credit against the tax otherwise due under this chapter for such year equal to fifty dollars times the expected remaining life of a taxpayer sixty-five years of age as shown by annuity tables issued under the provisions of the Internal Revenue Code and in effect for the calendar year which includes the last day of the taxable year. A taxpayer making an election under this division is not entitled to a credit under division (C) or (D) of this section in any subsequent year except that if such election was made prior to July 1, 1983, the taxpayer is entitled to one-half the credit authorized under division (C) of this section in subsequent years but may not make another election under this division. No taxpayer may make an election under this division for a taxable year ending on or after August 1, 1991.

(F) A taxpayer making an election under either division (D) or (E) of this section may make only one such election in the taxpayer's lifetime.

(G)(1) On a joint return filed by a husband and wife, each of whom had adjusted gross income of at least five hundred dollars, exclusive of interest, dividends and distributions, royalties, rent, and capital gains, a credit equal to the percentage shown in the table contained in this division of the amount of tax due after allowing for any other credit that precedes the credit under this division in the order required under section 5747.98 of the Revised Code.

(2) The credit to which a taxpayer is entitled under this division in any taxable year is the percentage shown in column B that corresponds with the taxpayer's adjusted gross income, less exemptions for the taxable year:

A. IF THE ADJUSTED GROSS INCOME, LESS EXEMPTIONS, FOR THE TAX YEAR IS:	B. THE CREDIT FOR THE TAXABLE YEAR IS:
$25,000 or less	20%
More than $25,000 but not more than $50,000	15%
More than $50,000 but not more than $75,000	10%
More than $75,000	5%

(3) The credit allowed under this division shall not exceed six hundred fifty dollars in any taxable year.

(H) No claim for credit under this section shall be allowed unless the claimant furnishes such supporting information as the tax commissioner prescribes by rules. Each credit under this section shall be claimed in the order required under section 5747.98 of the Revised Code.

(I) An individual who is a resident for part of a taxable year and a nonresident for the remainder of the taxable year is allowed the credits under divisions (A) and (B) of this section in accordance with rules prescribed by the tax commissioner. In no event shall the same income be subject to both credits.

(J) The credit allowed under division (A) of this section shall be calculated based upon the amount of tax due under section 5747.02 of the Revised Code after subtracting any other credits that precede the credit under that division in the order required under section 5747.98 of the Revised Code. The credit allowed under division (B) of this section shall be calculated based upon the amount of tax due under section 5747.02 of the Revised Code after subtracting any other credits that precede the credit under that division in the order required under section 5747.98 of the Revised Code.

(K) No credit shall be allowed under division (B) of this section unless the taxpayer furnishes such proof as the tax commissioner shall require that the income tax liability has been paid to another state or the District of Columbia.

(L) No credit shall be allowed under division (B) of this section for compensation that is not subject to the income tax of another state or the District of Columbia as the result of an agreement entered into by the tax commissioner under division (A)(3) of this section.

(2006 H 530, eff. 3–30–06; 2005 H 66, eff. 6–30–05; 2002 S 261, eff. 6–5–02; 1994 H 715, eff. 7–22–94; 1994 S 271, eff. 7–22–94; 1993 S 123, eff. 10–29–93; 1992 S 358, S 361; 1991 H 298; 1990 H 956; 1989 H 111; 1987 H 171; 1984 H 250; 1983 H 291; 1977 S 221; 1972 S 464, H 1203; 1971 H 475)

Uncodified Law

2005 H 66, § 557.33, eff. 6–30–05, reads:

The amendment by this act of section 5747.05 of the Revised Code applies to taxable years ending on or after the effective date of this section.

1994 S 271, § 3: See Uncodified Law under 5747.98.

1990 H 956, § 3, eff. 12–31–90, reads: Sections 5747.05, 5747.11, and 5747.13 of the Revised Code, as amended by this act, apply in taxable years ending on or after the effective date of this act.

Historical and Statutory Notes

Amendment Note: 2006 H 530 rewrote division (B)(4), which prior thereto read:

"(4) No credit shall be allowed under division (B) of this section to the extent that for any taxable year the taxpayer has directly or indirectly deducted, or was required to directly or indirectly deduct, the amount of income tax liability to another state or the District of Columbia in computing federal adjusted gross income."

Amendment Note: 2005 H 66 added division (B)(4).

Amendment Note: 2002 S 261 inserted "on individuals and estates" in the second introductory paragraph; and made changes to reflect gender neutral language.

Amendment Note: 1994 H 715 deleted certain provisions pertaining to tax credits and added provisions regarding the order of tax credits established in section 5747.98.

Amendment Note: 1994 S 271 deleted certain provisions pertaining to tax credits and added provisions regarding the order of tax credits established in section 5747.98.

Amendment Note: 1993 S 123 inserted "net" in the first sentence; and inserted "under this chapter" in division (G)(1).

Library References

Taxation ⇔1047.
Westlaw Topic No. 371.
C.J.S. Taxation § 1098.

5747.056 Credit for exempted income

For taxable years beginning in 2005 or thereafter, a credit shall be allowed per return against the tax imposed by section 5747.02 of the Revised Code for a return not filed by an estate or trust that indicates Ohio adjusted gross income less exemptions of ten thousand dollars or less. For taxable years beginning in 2005, the credit shall equal one hundred seven dollars. For taxable years beginning in 2006, the credit shall equal one hundred two dollars. For taxable years beginning in 2007, the credit shall equal ninety-eight dollars. For taxable years beginning in 2008, the credit shall equal ninety-three dollars. For taxable years beginning in 2009 or thereafter, the credit shall equal eighty-eight dollars. The credit shall be claimed in the order required under section 5747.98 of the Revised Code.

(2006 H 530, eff. 3–30–06; 2005 H 66, eff. 6–30–05)

Historical and Statutory Notes

Amendment Note: 2006 H 530 rewrote the first sentence, which prior thereto read: "For taxable years beginning in 2005 or thereafter, a credit shall be allowed against the tax imposed by section 5747.02 of the Revised Code for an individual whose Ohio adjusted gross income less exemptions is ten thousand dollars or less."

WITHHOLDING

5747.06 Withholding; exceptions; notification of amount withheld; liability of employer; provision of information by employee

(A) Except as provided in division (E)(3) of this section, every employer, including the state and its political subdivisions, maintaining an office or transacting business within this state and making payment of any compensation to an employee who is a taxpayer shall deduct and withhold from such compensation for each payroll period a tax computed in such manner as to result, as far as practicable, in withholding from the employee's compensation during each calendar year an amount substantially equivalent to the tax reasonably estimated to be due from the employee under this chapter and Chapter 5748. of the Revised Code with respect to the amount of such compensation included in the employee's adjusted gross income during the calendar year. The employer shall deduct and withhold the tax on the date that the employer directly, indirectly, or constructively pays the compensation to, or credits the compensation to the benefit of, the employee. The method of determining the amount to be withheld shall be prescribed by rule of the tax commissioner.

In addition to any other exclusions from withholding permitted under this section, no tax shall be withheld by an employer from the compensation of an employee when such compensation is paid for:

(1) Agricultural labor as defined in division G of section 3121 of Title 26 of the United States Code;

(2) Domestic service in a private home, local college club, or local chapter of a college fraternity or sorority;

(3) Service performed in any calendar quarter by an employee unless the cash remuneration paid for such service is three hundred dollars or more and such service is performed by an individual who is regularly employed by such employer to perform such service;

(4) Services performed for a foreign government or an international organization;

(5) Services performed by an individual under the age of eighteen in the delivery or distribution of newspapers or shopping news, not including delivery or distribution to any point for subsequent delivery or distribution, or when performed by such individual under the age of eighteen under an arrangement where

newspapers or magazines are to be sold by the individual at a fixed price, the individual's compensation being based on the retention of the excess of such price over the amount at which the newspapers or magazines are charged to the individual;

(6) Services not in the course of the employer's trade or business to the extent paid in any medium other than cash.

(B) Every employer required to deduct and withhold tax from the compensation of an employee under this chapter shall furnish to each employee, with respect to the compensation paid by such employer to such employee during the calendar year, on or before the thirty-first day of January of the succeeding year, or, if the employee's employment is terminated before the close of such calendar year, within thirty days from the date on which the last payment of compensation was made, a written statement as prescribed by the tax commissioner showing the amount of compensation paid by the employer to the employee, the amount deducted and withheld as state income tax, any amount deducted and withheld as school district income tax for each applicable school district, and any other information as the commissioner prescribes.

(C) The failure of an employer to withhold tax as required by this section does not relieve an employee from the liability for the tax. The failure of an employer to remit the tax as required by law does not relieve an employee from liability for the tax if the tax commissioner ascertains that the employee colluded with the employer with respect to the failure to remit the tax.

(D) If an employer fails to deduct and withhold any tax as required, and thereafter the tax is paid, the tax so required to be deducted and withheld shall not be collected from the employer, but the employer is not relieved from liability for penalties and interest otherwise applicable in respect to the failure to deduct and withhold the tax.

(E) To ensure that taxes imposed pursuant to Chapter 5748. of the Revised Code are deducted and withheld as provided in this section:

(1) An employer shall request that each employee furnish the name of the employee's school district of residence;

(2) Each employee shall furnish the employer with sufficient and correct information to enable the employer to withhold the taxes imposed under Chapter 5748. of the Revised Code. The employee shall provide additional or corrected information whenever information previously provided to the employer becomes insufficient or incorrect.

(3) If the employer complies with the requirements of division (E)(1) of this section and if the employee fails to comply with the requirements of division (E)(2) of this section, the employer is not required to withhold and pay the taxes imposed under Chapter 5748. of the Revised Code and is not subject to any penalties and interest otherwise applicable for failing to deduct and withhold such taxes.

(2002 S 200, eff. 9–6–02; 1993 H 152, eff. 7–1–93; 1989 S 28; 1981 H 694; 1978 H 619; 1973 H 95; 1971 H 475)

Uncodified Law

1993 H 152, § 188, eff. 7–1–93, reads: Sections 5747.06, 5747.07, 5747.072, 5747.13, and 5747.15 of the Revised Code as amended by this act and the amendment in this act to division (E) of section 1306.03 of the Revised Code first apply on January 1, 1994.

1986 S 417, § 7, eff. 12–13–87, reads: For the purpose of prescribing the method of determining the amount to be withheld by every employer under section 5747.06 of the Revised Code, the Tax Commissioner shall not reduce the amount or percentages of compensation deducted and withheld for taxable years ending on or after January 1, 1987, except as provided in Section 126 of Am. Sub. H.B. 238 of the 116th General Assembly.

Historical and Statutory Notes

Amendment Note: 2002 S 200 rewrote division (C); and made changes to reflect gender neutral language throughout the section. Prior to amendment division (C) read:

"(C) The failure of an employer to withhold tax as required by this section or to remit such tax as required by law does not relieve an employee from the liability for the tax."

Amendment Note: 1993 H 152 added the second last sentence of the first paragraph of division (A).

Library References

Taxation ⟸1100.
Westlaw Topic No. 371.
C.J.S. Taxation § 1107.

RETURNS

5747.08 Individual returns; returns of nonresident pass-through entity investors; joint returns of husband and wife; attestation; filing extensions; interest payments

An annual return with respect to the tax imposed by section 5747.02 of the Revised Code and each tax imposed under Chapter 5748. of the Revised Code shall be made by every taxpayer for any taxable year for which the taxpayer is liable for the tax imposed by that section or under that chapter, unless the total credits allowed under divisions (E), (F), and (G) of section 5747.05 of the Revised Code for the year are equal to or exceed the tax imposed by section 5747.02 of the Revised Code, in which case no return shall be required unless the taxpayer is liable for a tax imposed pursuant to Chapter 5748. of the Revised Code.

(A) If an individual is deceased, any return or notice required of that individual under this chapter shall be made and filed by that decedent's executor, administrator, or other person charged with the property of that decedent.

(B) If an individual is unable to make a return or notice required by this chapter, the return or notice required of that individual shall be made and filed by the individual's duly authorized agent, guardian, conservator, fiduciary, or other person charged with the care of the person or property of that individual.

(C) Returns or notices required of an estate or a trust shall be made and filed by the fiduciary of the estate or trust.

(D)(1)(a) Except as otherwise provided in division (D)(1)(b) of this section, any pass-through entity may file a single return on behalf of one or more of the entity's investors other than an investor that is a person subject to the tax imposed under section 5733.06 of the Revised Code. The single return shall set forth the name, address, and social security number or other identifying number of each of those pass-through entity investors and shall indicate the distributive share of each of those pass-through entity investor's income taxable in this state in accordance with sections 5747.20 to 5747.231 of the Revised Code. Such pass-through entity investors for whom the pass-through entity elects to file a single return are not entitled to the exemption or credit provided for by sections 5747.02 and 5747.022 of the Revised Code; shall calculate the tax before business credits at the highest rate of tax set forth in section 5747.02 of the Revised Code for the taxable year for which the return is filed; and are entitled to only their distributive share of the business credits as defined in division (D)(2) of this section. A single check drawn by the pass-through entity shall accompany the return in full payment of the tax due, as shown on the single return, for such investors, other than investors who are persons subject to the tax imposed under section 5733.06 of the Revised Code.

(b)(i) A pass-through entity shall not include in such a single return any investor that is a trust to the extent that any direct or indirect current, future, or contingent beneficiary of the trust is a person subject to the tax imposed under section 5733.06 of the Revised Code.

(ii) A pass-through entity shall not include in such a single return any investor that is itself a pass-through entity to the extent that any direct or indirect investor in the second pass-through entity is a person subject to the tax imposed under section 5733.06 of the Revised Code.

(c) Nothing in division (D) of this section precludes the tax commissioner from requiring such investors to file the return and make the payment of taxes and related interest, penalty, and interest penalty required by this section or section 5747.02, 5747.09, or 5747.15 of the Revised Code. Nothing in division (D) of this section shall be construed to provide to such an investor or pass-through entity any additional deduction or credit, other than the credit provided by division (J) of this section, solely on account of the entity's filing a return in accordance with this section. Such a pass-through entity also shall make the filing and payment of estimated taxes on behalf of the pass-through entity investors other than an investor that is a person subject to the tax imposed under section 5733.06 of the Revised Code.

(2) For the purposes of this section, "business credits" means the credits listed in section 5747.98 of the Revised Code excluding the following credits:

(a) The retirement credit under division (B) of section 5747.055 of the Revised Code;

(b) The senior citizen credit under division (C) of section 5747.05 of the Revised Code;

(c) The lump sum distribution credit under division (D) of section 5747.05 of the Revised Code;

(d) The dependent care credit under section 5747.054 of the Revised Code;

(e) The lump sum retirement income credit under division (C) of section 5747.055 of the Revised Code;

(f) The lump sum retirement income credit under division (D) of section 5747.055 of the Revised Code;

(g) The lump sum retirement income credit under division (E) of section 5747.055 of the Revised Code;

(h) The credit for displaced workers who pay for job training under section 5747.27 of the Revised Code;

(i) The twenty-dollar personal exemption credit under section 5747.022 of the Revised Code;

(j) The joint filing credit under division (G) of section 5747.05 of the Revised Code;

(k) The nonresident credit under division (A) of section 5747.05 of the Revised Code;

(*l*) The credit for a resident's out-of-state income under division (B) of section 5747.05 of the Revised Code;

(m) The low-income credit under section 5747.056 of the Revised Code.

(3) The election provided for under division (D) of this section applies only to the taxable year for which the election is made by the pass-through entity. Unless the tax commissioner provides otherwise, this election, once made, is binding and irrevocable for the taxable year for which the election is made. Nothing in this division shall be construed to provide for any deduction or credit that would not be allowable if a nonresident pass-through entity investor were to file an annual return.

(4) If a pass-through entity makes the election provided for under division (D) of this section, the pass-through entity shall be liable for any additional taxes, interest, interest penalty, or penalties imposed by this chapter if the tax commissioner finds that the single return does not reflect the correct tax due by the pass-through entity investors covered by that return. Nothing in this division shall be construed to limit or alter the liability, if any, imposed on pass-through entity investors for unpaid or underpaid taxes, interest, interest penalty, or penalties as a result of the pass-through entity's making the election provided for under division (D) of this section. For the purposes of division (D) of this section, "correct tax due" means the tax that would have been paid by the pass-through entity had the single return been filed in a manner reflecting the tax commissioner's findings. Nothing in division (D) of this section shall be construed to make or hold a pass-through entity liable for tax attributable to a pass-through entity investor's income from a source other than the pass-through entity electing to file the single return.

(E) If a husband and wife file a joint federal income tax return for a taxable year, they shall file a joint return under this section for that taxable year, and their liabilities are joint and several, but, if the federal income tax liability of either spouse is determined on a separate federal income tax return, they shall file separate returns under this section.

If either spouse is not required to file a federal income tax return and either or both are required to file a return pursuant to this chapter, they may elect to file separate or joint returns and, pursuant to that election, their liabilities are separate or joint and several. If a husband and wife file separate returns pursuant to this chapter, each must claim the taxpayer's own exemption, but not both, as authorized under section 5747.02 of the Revised Code on the taxpayer's own return.

(F) Each return or notice required to be filed under this section shall contain the signature of the taxpayer or the taxpayer's duly authorized agent and of the person who prepared the return for the taxpayer, and shall include the taxpayer's social security number. Each return shall be verified by a declaration under the penalties of perjury. The tax commissioner shall prescribe the form that the signature and declaration shall take.

(G) Each return or notice required to be filed under this section shall be made and filed as required by section 5747.04 of the Revised Code, on or before the fifteenth day of April of each year, on forms that the tax commissioner shall prescribe, together with remittance made payable to the treasurer of state in the combined amount of the state and all school district income taxes shown to be due on the form, unless the combined amount shown to be due is one dollar or less, in which case that amount need not be remitted.

Upon good cause shown, the tax commissioner may extend the period for filing any notice or return required to be filed under this section and may adopt rules relating to extensions. If the extension results in an extension of time for the payment of any state or school district income tax liability with respect to which the return is filed, the taxpayer shall pay at the time the tax liability is paid an amount of interest computed at the rate per annum prescribed by section 5703.47 of the Revised Code on that liability from the time that payment is due without extension to the time of actual payment. Except as provided in section 5747.132 of the Revised Code, in addition to all other interest charges and penalties, all taxes imposed under this chapter or Chapter 5748. of the Revised Code and remaining unpaid after they become due, except combined amounts due of one dollar or less, bear interest at the rate per annum prescribed by section 5703.47 of the Revised Code until paid or until the day an assessment is issued under section 5747.13 of the Revised Code, whichever occurs first.

If the tax commissioner considers it necessary in order to ensure the payment of the tax imposed by section 5747.02 of the Revised Code or any tax imposed under Chapter 5748. of the Revised Code, the tax commissioner may require returns and payments to be made otherwise than as provided in this section.

To the extent that any provision in this division conflicts with any provision in section 5747.026 of the Revised Code, the provision in that section prevails.

(H) If any report, claim, statement, or other document required to be filed, or any payment required to be made, within a prescribed period or on or before a prescribed date under this chapter is delivered after that period or that date by United States mail to the agency, officer, or office with which the report, claim, statement, or other document is required to be filed, or to which the payment is required to be made, the date of the postmark stamped on the cover in which the report, claim, statement, or other document, or payment is mailed shall be deemed to be the date of delivery or the date of payment.

If a payment is required to be made by electronic funds transfer pursuant to section 5747.072 of the Revised Code, the payment is considered to be made when the payment is received by the treasurer of state or credited to an account designated by the treasurer of state for the receipt of tax payments.

"The date of the postmark" means, in the event there is more than one date on the cover, the earliest date imprinted on the cover by the United States postal service.

(I) The amounts withheld by the employer pursuant to section 5747.06 of the Revised Code shall be allowed to the recipient of the compensation as credits against payment of the appropriate taxes imposed on the recipient by section 5747.02 and under Chapter 5748. of the Revised Code.

(J) If, in accordance with division (D) of this section, a pass-through entity elects to file a single return and if any investor is required to file the return and make the payment of taxes required by this chapter on account of the investor's other income that is not included in a single return filed by a pass-through entity, the investor is entitled to a refundable credit equal to the investor's proportionate share of the tax paid by the pass-through entity on behalf of the investor. The investor shall claim the credit for the investor's taxable year in which or with which ends the taxable year of the pass-through entity. Nothing in this chapter shall be construed to allow any credit provided in this chapter to be claimed more than once. For the purposes of computing any interest, penalty, or interest penalty, the investor shall be deemed to have paid the refundable credit provided by this division on the day that the pass-through entity paid the estimated tax or the tax giving rise to the credit.

(2005 H 66, eff. 6–30–05; 2005 H 2, eff. 6–2–05; 2002 S 200, eff. 9–6–02; 1999 H 99, eff. 9–29–99; 1998 H 770, eff. 9–16–98; 1997 H 215, eff. 9–29–97; 1996 S 310, eff. 9–19–96; 1994 S 74, eff. 7–1–94; 1992 H 740, eff. 3–19–93; 1982 H 366; 1981 H 694; 1979 S 59; 1975 H 1; 1974 S 402; 1973 H 95; 1972 S 464; 1971 H 475)

Uncodified Law

2005 H 2, § 4, eff. 6–2–05, reads:

Sections 5747.026 and 5747.08 of the Revised Code, as amended by this act, shall apply to all years beginning on and after January 1, 2002.

1999 H 99, § 3, eff. 9–29–99, reads:

The amendment or enactment by this act of sections 5733.26, 5733.261, 5747.08, and 5747.132 of the Revised Code shall be applied to prohibit the accrual of interest or penalty with respect to tax refund overpayment assessments received by taxpayers after the effective date of this act, regardless of the time of claim for the refund.

1997 H 215, § 211: See Baldwin's Ohio Revised Code Annotated, Uncodified Law under 5747.057.

1997 H 215, § 213: See Baldwin's Ohio Revised Code Annotated, Uncodified Law under 5747.07.

Historical and Statutory Notes

Amendment Note: 2005 H 66 added division (D)(2)(m) and made other nonsubstantive changes.

Amendment Note: 2005 H 2 inserted "tax" after "commissioner" in the first and third sentence of division (D)(4) and in the first sentence of the second and third paragraphs of division (G); and added the last paragraph of division (G).

Amendment Note: 2002 S 200 inserted "or other identi... number" after "social security number" in division (D)(1)(a); insert... as shown on the single return," in the last sentence of division (D)(1)(a); rewrote the phrase "tax commissioner determines" to read "commissioner finds" and substituted "the" for "nonresident" before "pass-through entity investors" in the first sentence of division (D)(4); deleted "and including" after "reflecting", and inserted "commissioner's" before, and deleted "and determinations made by the tax commissioner" after, "findings", in the second sentence of division (D)(4).

Amendment Note: 1999 H 99 redesignated former divisions (D)(2)(b) through (D)(2)(m) as new divisions (D)(2)(a) through (D)(2)(l); inserted "Except as provided in section 5747.132 of the Revised Code," in the second paragraph in division (G); separated out the third paragraph in division (G); and made other nonsubstantive changes.

Amendment Note: 1998 H 770 rewrote division (D)(1); deleted "Returns for taxable years for which a reduction in the tax due is made under division (B) of section 5747.02 of the Revised Code shall include the following statement: 'the tax on this line reflects a ____% (here enter the percentage reduction described in division (B) of section 5747.02 of the Revised Code) reduction under legislation enacted by the General Assembly requiring the return of excess state revenue to taxpayers.' The statement shall appear in boldface type and shall be placed in a prominent location on the return in the vicinity of the location where the amount of tax due, before any credits or amounts withheld, is entered." from the end of the first paragraph of division (G); deleted "by section 5747.02 of the Revised Code or" following "all taxes imposed" in the second paragraph in division (G); inserted "this chapter or" in the second paragraph in division (G); and added division (J). Prior to amendment, division (D)(1) read:

"(D)(1) Any pass-through entity having two or more nonresident pass-through entity investors who derive no taxable income from this state, other than a distributive share of the pass-through entity income, may file a single return on behalf of all or some of those pass-through entity investors who are individuals or estates. The single return shall set forth the name, address, and social security number of each pass-through entity investor of that nature and shall indicate the distributive share of each pass-through entity investor's income taxable in this state in accordance with sections 5747.20 to 5747.231 of the Revised Code. Such nonresident pass-through entity investors for whom the pass-through entity elects to file a single return are not entitled to the exemption or credit provided for by section 5747.02 and 5747.022 of the Revised code; shall calculate the tax before business credits at the highest rate of tax set forth in section 5747.02 of the Revised code for the taxable year for which the return is filed; and are entitled to only their distributive share of the business credits as defined in division (D)(2) of this section. A single check drawn by the pass-through entity shall accompany the return in full payment of the tax due. Such a pass-through entity also shall make the filing and payment of estimated taxes on behalf of those nonresident pass-through entity investors."

Amendment Note: 1997 H 215 rewrote this section; see Baldwin's Ohio Legislative Service Annotated, 1997, p 8/L–1985, or the OH–LEGIS or OH–LEGIS–OLD database on Westlaw, for text of previous version.

Amendment Note: 1996 S 310 deleted "written" before "declaration" and added the third sentence in division (F); substituted "postal service" for "post office" in the third paragraph in division (H); and made other nonsubstantive changes.

Amendment Note: 1994 S 74 added references to limited liability companies and members in division (D).

Library References

Taxation ⚖︎1079.
Westlaw Topic No. 371.
C.J.S. Taxation § 1102.

5747.09 Declaration of estimated tax; payment; required portion; interest charge for underpayment

(A) As used in this section:

(1) "Estimated taxes" means the amount that the taxpayer estimates to be the taxpayer's combined tax liability under this chapter and Chapter 5748. of the Revised Code for the current taxable year.

(2) "Tax liability" means the total taxes due for the taxable year, after allowing any credit to which the taxpayer is entitled, but prior to applying any estimated tax payment, withholding payment, or refund from another tax year.

(3) "Taxes paid" include payments of estimated taxes made under division (C) of this section, taxes withheld from the taxpayer's compensation, and tax refunds applied by the taxpayer in payment of estimated taxes.

(B) Every taxpayer shall make declaration of estimated taxes for the current taxable year, in the form that the tax commissioner shall prescribe, if the amount payable as estimated taxes, less the amount to be withheld from the taxpayer's compensation, is more than five hundred dollars. For purposes of this section, taxes withheld from compensation shall be considered as paid in equal amounts on each payment date unless the taxpayer establishes the dates on which all amounts were actually withheld, in which case the amounts withheld shall be considered as paid on the dates on which the amounts were actually withheld. Taxpayers filing joint returns pursuant to section 5747.08 of the Revised Code shall file joint declarations of estimated taxes. A taxpayer may amend a declaration under rules prescribed by the commissioner. A taxpayer having a taxable year of less than twelve months shall make a declaration under rules prescribed by the commissioner. The declaration of estimated taxes for an individual under a disability shall be made and filed by the person who is required to file the income tax return.

The declaration of estimated taxes shall be filed on or before the fifteenth day of April of each year or on or before the fifteenth day of the fourth month after the taxpayer becomes subject to tax for the first time.

Taxpayers reporting on a fiscal year basis shall file a declaration on or before the fifteenth day of the fourth month after the beginning of each fiscal year or period.

The declaration shall be filed upon a form prescribed by the commissioner and furnished by or obtainable from the commissioner.

The original declaration or any subsequent amendment may be increased or decreased on or before any subsequent quarterly payment day as provided in this section.

(C) The required portion of the tax liability for the taxable year that shall be paid through estimated taxes made payable to the treasurer of state, including the application of tax refunds to estimated taxes, and withholding on or before the applicable payment date shall be as follows:

(1) On or before the fifteenth day of the fourth month after the beginning of the taxable year, twenty-two and one-half per cent of the tax liability for the taxable year;

(2) On or before the fifteenth day of the sixth month after the beginning of the taxable year, forty-five per cent of the tax liability for the taxable year;

(3) On or before the fifteenth day of the ninth month after the beginning of the taxable year, sixty-seven and one-half per cent of the tax liability for the taxable year;

(4) On or before the fifteenth day of the first month of the following taxable year, ninety per cent of the tax liability for the taxable year.

When an amended return has been filed, the unpaid balance shown due on the amended return shall be paid in equal installments on or before the remaining payment dates.

On or before the fifteenth day of the fourth month of the year following that for which the declaration or amended declaration was filed, an annual return shall be filed and any balance which may be due shall be paid with the return in accordance with section 5747.08 of the Revised Code.

(D) In the case of any underpayment of estimated taxes, an interest penalty shall be added to the taxes for the tax year at the rate per annum prescribed by section 5703.47 of the Revised Code upon the amount of underpayment for the period of underpayment, unless the underpayment is due to reasonable cause as described in division (E) of this section. The amount of the underpayment shall be determined as follows:

(1) For the first payment of estimated taxes each year, twenty-two and one-half per cent of the tax liability, less the amount of taxes paid by the date prescribed for that payment;

(2) For the second payment of estimated taxes each year, forty-five per cent of the tax liability, less the amount of taxes paid by the date prescribed for that payment;

(3) For the third payment of estimated taxes each year, sixty-seven and one-half per cent of the tax liability, less the amount of taxes paid by the date prescribed for that payment;

(4) For the fourth payment of estimated taxes each year, ninety per cent of the tax liability, less the amount of taxes paid by the date prescribed for that payment.

The period of the underpayment shall run from the day the estimated payment was required to be made to the date on which the payment is made. For purposes of this section, a payment of estimated taxes on or before any payment date shall be considered a payment of any previous underpayment only to the extent the payment of estimated taxes exceeds the amount of the payment presently required to be paid to avoid any penalty.

The interest penalty imposed under division (D) of this section shall be in lieu of any other interest charge or penalty imposed for failure to file an estimated return and make estimated payments as required by this section.

(E) An underpayment of estimated taxes determined under division (D) of this section shall be due to reasonable cause and the interest penalty imposed by this section shall not be added to the taxes for the tax year if either of the following apply:

(1) The amount of tax that was paid equals at least ninety per cent of the tax liability for the current taxable year, determined by annualizing the income received during the year up to the end of the month immediately preceding the month in which the payment is due;

(2) The amount of tax that was paid equals at least one hundred per cent of the tax liability shown on the return of the taxpayer for the preceding taxable year, provided that the immediately preceding taxable year reflected a period of twelve months and the taxpayer filed a return under section 5747.08 of the Revised Code for that year.

The tax commissioner may waive the requirement for filing a declaration of estimated taxes for any class of taxpayers after finding that the waiver is reasonable and proper in view of administrative costs and other factors.

(2000 H 612, eff. 9–29–00; 1987 H 231, eff. 10–5–87; 1983 H 291; 1982 H 366; 1981 H 694; 1973 H 95; 1971 H 475)

Historical and Statutory Notes

Amendment Note: 2000 H 612 substituted "five" for "three" in the first paragraph of division (B); made changes to reflect gender neutral language; and made other nonsubstantive changes.

Library References

Taxation ⇔1079.1.
Westlaw Topic No. 371.
C.J.S. Taxation § 1102.

5747.10 Amended return

If any of the facts, figures, computations, or attachments required in a taxpayer's annual return to determine the tax charged by this chapter or Chapter 5748. of the Revised Code must be altered as the result of an adjustment to the taxpayer's federal income tax return, whether initiated by the taxpayer or the internal revenue service, and such alteration affects the taxpayer's tax liability under this chapter or Chapter 5748. of the Revised Code, the taxpayer shall file an amended return with the tax commissioner in such form as the commissioner requires. The amended return shall be filed not later than sixty days after the adjustment has been agreed to or finally determined for federal income tax purposes or any federal income tax deficiency or refund, or the abatement or credit resulting therefrom, has been assessed or paid, whichever occurs first.

(A) In the case of an underpayment, the amended return shall be accompanied by payment of any combined additional tax due together with interest thereon. If the combined tax shown to be due is one dollar or less, such amount need not accompany the amended return. An amended return required by this section is a return subject to assessment under section 5747.13 of the Revised Code for the purpose of assessing any additional tax due under this section, together with any applicable penalty and interest. It shall not reopen those facts, figures, computations, or attachments from a previously filed return no longer subject to assessment that are not affected, either directly or indirectly, by the adjustment to the taxpayer's federal income tax return.

(B) In the case of an overpayment, an application for refund may be filed under this division within the sixty-day period prescribed for filing the amended return even if it is filed beyond the period prescribed in section 5747.11 of the Revised Code if it otherwise conforms to the requirements of such section. An application filed under this division shall claim refund of overpayments resulting from alterations to only those facts, figures, computations, or attachments required in the taxpayer's annual return that are affected, either directly or indirectly, by the adjustment to the taxpayer's federal income tax return unless it is also filed within the time prescribed in section 5747.11 of the Revised Code. It shall not reopen those facts, figures, computations, or attachments that are not affected, either directly or indirectly, by the adjustment to the taxpayer's federal income tax return.

(1992 S 358, eff. 1–15–93; 1982 H 38; 1981 H 694; 1974 S 402; 1971 H 475)

Library References

Taxation ⚖1079.
Westlaw Topic No. 371.
C.J.S. Taxation § 1102.

REFUNDS

5747.11 Refunds; interest

(A) The tax commissioner shall refund to employers, qualifying entities, or taxpayers, with respect to any tax imposed under section 5733.41, 5747.02, or 5747.41, or Chapter 5748. of the Revised Code:

(1) Overpayments of more than one dollar;

(2) Amounts in excess of one dollar paid illegally or erroneously;

(3) Amounts in excess of one dollar paid on an illegal, erroneous, or excessive assessment.

(B) Except as otherwise provided under divisions (D) and (E) of this section, applications for refund shall be filed with the tax commissioner, on the form prescribed by the commissioner, within four years from the date of the illegal, erroneous, or excessive payment of the tax, or within any additional period allowed by division (B)(3)(b) of section 5747.05, division (B) of section 5747.10, division (A) of section 5747.13, or division (C) of section 5747.45 of the Revised Code.

On filing of the refund application, the commissioner shall determine the amount of refund due and certify such amount to the director of budget and management and treasurer of state for payment from the tax refund fund created by section 5703.052 of the Revised Code. Payment shall be made as provided in division (C) of section 126.35 of the Revised Code.

(C)(1) Interest shall be allowed and paid upon any illegal or erroneous assessment in excess of one dollar in respect of the tax imposed under section 5747.02 or Chapter 5748. of the Revised Code at the rate per annum prescribed by section 5703.47 of the Revised Code from the date of the payment of the illegal or erroneous assessment until the date the refund of such amount is paid. If such refund results from the filing of a return or report, or the payment accompanying such return or report, by an employer or taxpayer, rather than from an assessment by the commissioner, such interest shall run from a period ninety days after the final filing date of the annual return until the date the refund is paid.

(2) Interest shall be allowed and paid at the rate per annum prescribed by section 5703.47 of the Revised Code upon any overpayment in excess of one dollar in respect of the tax imposed under section 5747.02 or Chapter 5748. of the Revised Code from the date of the overpayment until the date of the refund of the overpayment, except that if any overpayment is refunded within ninety days after the final filing date of the annual return or ninety days after the return is filed, whichever is later, no interest shall be allowed on such overpayment. If the overpayment results from the carryback of a net operating loss or net capital loss to a previous taxable year, the overpayment is deemed not to have been made prior to the filing date, including any extension thereof, for the taxable year in which the net operating loss or net capital loss arises. For purposes of the payment of interest on overpayments, no amount of tax, for any taxable year, shall be treated as having been paid before the date on which the tax return for that year was due without regard to any extension of time for filing such return.

(3) Interest shall be allowed at the rate per annum prescribed by section 5703.47 of the Revised Code on amounts refunded with respect to the taxes imposed under sections 5733.41 and 5747.41 of the Revised Code. The interest shall run from whichever of the following days is the latest until the day the refund is paid: the day the illegal, erroneous, or excessive payment was made; the ninetieth day after the final day the annual report was required to be filed under section 5747.42 of the Revised Code; or the ninetieth day after the day that report was filed.

(D) "Ninety days" shall be substituted for "four years" in division (B) of this section if the taxpayer satisfies both of the following conditions:

(1) The taxpayer has applied for a refund based in whole or in part upon section 5747.059 of the Revised Code;

(2) The taxpayer asserts that either the imposition or collection of the tax imposed or charged by this chapter or any portion of such tax violates the Constitution of the United States or the Constitution of Ohio.

(E)(1) Division (E)(2) of this section applies only if all of the following conditions are satisfied:

(a) A qualifying entity pays an amount of the tax imposed by section 5733.41 or 5747.41 of the Revised Code;

(b) The taxpayer is a qualifying investor as to that qualifying entity;

(c) The taxpayer did not claim the credit provided for in section 5747.059 of the Revised Code as to the tax described in division (E)(1)(a) of this section;

(d) The four-year period described in division (B) of this section has ended as to the taxable year for which the taxpayer otherwise would have claimed that credit.

(2) A taxpayer shall file an application for refund pursuant to division (E) of this section within one year after the date the payment described in division (E)(1)(a) of this section is made. An application filed under division (E)(2) of this section shall

claim refund only of overpayments resulting from the taxpayer's failure to claim the credit described in division (E)(1)(c) of this section. Nothing in division (E) of this section shall be construed to relieve a taxpayer from complying with division (A)(16) of section 5747.01 of the Revised Code.

(2006 H 530, eff. 12–1–06; 1999 H 283, eff. 9–29–99; 1997 H 215, eff. 9–29–97; 1992 S 358, eff. 1–15–93; 1991 H 298; 1990 H 956; 1986 H 428; 1985 H 201, S 127; 1982 H 366, H 38; 1981 H 694; 1977 S 221; 1974 S 402; 1973 H 95; 1972 S 472; 1971 H 475)

Uncodified Law

1997 H 215, § 211: See Baldwin's *Ohio Revised Code Annotated*, Uncodified Law under 5747.057.

1991 H 298, § 166, eff. 7–26–91, reads: Sections 5733.26 and 5747.11 of the Revised Code as amended by this act shall take effect at the earliest time allowed by law, but shall first apply to net operating losses or net capital losses arising in taxable years ending on or after the effective date of this act.

1990 H 956, § 3, eff. 12–31–90, reads: Sections 5747.05, 5747.11, and 5747.13 of the Revised Code, as amended by this act, apply in taxable years ending on or after the effective date of this act.

Historical and Statutory Notes

Amendment Note: 2006 H 530 substituted "126.35" for "117.45" in the last sentence of the second paragraph of division (B); and made other nonsubstantive changes.

Amendment Note: 1999 H 283 added the final sentence in the second paragraph in division (B).

Amendment Note: 1997 H 215 designated division (A); inserted ", qualifying entities," and substituted "section 5733.41, 5747.02, or 5747.41," for "this chapter" in the first paragraph thereof; redesignated former divisions (A) through (C) as new divisions (A)(1) through (A)(3); designated division (B) and inserted "Except as otherwise provided under divisions (D) and (E) of this section," and added the reference to section 5747.45(C) therein; designated divisions (C)(1) and (C)(2) and changed references to Chapter 5747 to references to section 5747.02 therein; added divisions (C)(3), (D), and (E); and made changes to reflect gender neutral language and other nonsubstantive changes.

Library References

Taxation ⚖1097–1099.
Westlaw Topic No. 371.
C.J.S. Taxation § 1109.

5747.113 Tax refund contributions to specified funds

(A) Any taxpayer claiming a refund under section 5747.11 of the Revised Code for taxable years ending on or after October 14, 1983, who wishes to contribute any part of the taxpayer's refund to the natural areas and preserves fund created in section 1517.11 of the Revised Code, the nongame and endangered wildlife fund created in section 1531.26 of the Revised Code, the military injury relief fund created in section 5101.98 of the Revised Code, or all of those funds, may designate on the taxpayer's income tax return the amount that the taxpayer wishes to contribute to the fund or funds. A designated contribution is irrevocable upon the filing of the return and shall be made in the full amount designated if the refund found due the taxpayer upon the initial processing of the taxpayer's return, after any deductions including those required by section 5747.12 of the Revised Code, is greater than or equal to the designated contribution. If the refund due as initially determined is less than the designated contribution, the contribution shall be made in the full amount of the refund. The tax commissioner shall subtract the amount of the contribution from the amount of the refund initially found due the taxpayer and shall certify the difference to the director of budget and management and treasurer of state for payment to the taxpayer in accordance with section 5747.11 of the Revised Code. For the purpose of any subsequent determination of the taxpayer's net tax payment, the contribution shall be considered a part of the refund paid to the taxpayer.

(B) The tax commissioner shall provide a space on the income tax return form in which a taxpayer may indicate that the taxpayer wishes to make a donation in accordance with this section. The tax commissioner shall also print in the instructions accompanying the income tax return form a description of the purposes for which the natural areas and preserves fund , the nongame and endangered wildlife fund, and the military injury relief fund were created and the use of moneys from the income tax refund contribution system established in this section. No person shall designate on the person's income tax return any part of a refund claimed under section 5747.11 of the Revised Code as a contribution to any fund other than the natural areas and preserves fund, the nongame and endangered wildlife fund, the military injury relief fund or all of those funds.

(C) The money collected under the income tax refund contribution system established in this section shall be deposited by the tax commissioner into the natural areas and preserves fund, the nongame and endangered wildlife fund, and the military injury relief fund in the amounts designated on the tax returns.

(D) No later than the thirtieth day of September each year, the tax commissioner shall determine the total amount contributed to each fund under this section during the preceding eight months, any adjustments to prior months, and the cost to the department of taxation of administering the income tax refund contribution system during that eight-month period. The commissioner shall make an additional determination no later than the thirty-first day of January of each year of the total amount contributed to each fund under this section during the preceding four calendar months, any adjustments to prior years made during that four-month period, and the cost to the department of taxation of administering the income tax contribution system during that period. The cost of administering the income tax contribution system shall be certified by the tax commissioner to the director of budget and management, who shall transfer an amount equal to one-third of such administrative costs from the natural areas and preserves fund, one-third of such costs from the nongame and endangered wildlife fund, and one-third of such costs from the military injury relief fund to the litter control and natural resource tax administration fund, which is hereby created, provided that the moneys that the department receives to pay the cost of administering the income tax refund contribution system in any year shall not exceed two and one-half per cent of the total amount contributed under that system during that year.

(E)(1) The director of natural resources, in January of every odd- numbered year, shall report to the general assembly on the effectiveness of the income tax refund contribution system as it pertains to the natural areas and preserves fund and the nongame and endangered wildlife fund. The report shall include the amount of money contributed to each fund in each of the previous five years, the amount of money contributed directly to each fund in addition to or independently of the income tax refund contribution system in each of the previous five years, and the purposes for which the money was expended.

(2) The director of job and family services, in January of every odd- numbered year, shall report to the general assembly on the effectiveness of the income tax refund contribution system as it pertains to the military injury relief fund. The report shall include the amount of money contributed to the fund in each of the previous five years, the amount of money contributed directly to the fund in addition to or independently of the income tax refund contribution system in each of the previous five years, and the purposes for which the money was expended.

(2005 H 66, eff. 6–30–05; 1988 H 514, eff. 2–11–88; 1985 H 201; 1984 H 794; 1983 H 5)

Historical and Statutory Notes

Amendment Note: 2005 H 66 inserted references to the military injury relief fund throughout; designated divisions (A) through (E); substituted "all of those funds" for "both" before "may designate" in the first sentence of division (A); substituted "all" for "both" in the last sentence of division (B); substituted "one-third" for "one-half" and ", one-third" for "and one-half" after "transfer an amount equal to" in the last sentence of division (D); inserted "as it pertains to the natural areas and preserves fund and the nongame and endangered wildlife fund" after "system" in division (E)(1); substituted "each fund" for "the natural areas and preserves fund and the nongame and endangered wildlife fund" in the last sentence of division (E)(1); made changes to reflect gender neutral language; and made other nonsubstantive changes.

Library References

Taxation ⊙⊃1079, 1097.
Westlaw Topic No. 371.
C.J.S. Taxation § 1102, 1109.

5747.12 Application of refund to satisfaction of other tax indebtedness

If a person entitled to a refund under section 5747.11 or 5747.13 of the Revised Code is indebted to this state for any tax, workers' compensation premium due under section 4123.35 of the Revised Code, unemployment compensation contribution due under section 4141.25 of the Revised Code, certified claim under section 131.02 or 131.021 of the Revised Code, or fee that is paid to the state or to the clerk of courts pursuant to section 4505.06 of the Revised Code, or any charge, penalty, or interest arising from such a tax, workers' compensation premium, unemployment compensation contribution, certified claim, or fee, the amount refundable may be applied in satisfaction of the debt. If the amount refundable is less than the amount of the debt, it may be applied in partial satisfaction of the debt. If the amount refundable is greater than the amount of the debt, the amount remaining after satisfaction of the debt shall be refunded. If the person has more than one such debt, any debt subject to section 5739.33 or division (G) of section 5747.07 of the Revised Code shall be satisfied first. Except as provided in section 131.021 of the Revised Code, this section applies only to debts that have become final.

The tax commissioner may charge each respective agency of the state for the commissioner's cost in applying refunds to debts due to the state and may charge the attorney general for the commissioner's cost in applying refunds to certified claims. The commissioner may promulgate rules to implement this section. The rules may address, among other things, situations such as those where persons may jointly be entitled to a refund but do not jointly owe a debt or certified claim.

The tax commissioner may, with the consent of the taxpayer, provide for the crediting, against tax imposed under this chapter or Chapter 5748. of the Revised Code and due for any taxable year, of the amount of any refund due the taxpayer under this chapter or Chapter 5748. of the Revised Code, as appropriate, for a preceding taxable year.

(2005 H 16, eff. 5–6–05; 2003 H 95, eff. 9–26–03; 1997 H 215, eff. 9–29–97; 1985 H 201, eff. 7–1–85; 1982 H 38; 1981 H 694; 1972 S 472; 1971 H 475)

Historical and Statutory Notes

Amendment Note: 2005 H 16 inserted "certified claim under section 131.02 or 131.021 of the Revised Code," and "certified claim," in the first paragraph; inserted "Except as provided in section 131.021 of the Revised Code, this" in the last sentence of the first paragraph; added the second paragraph; and made other nonsubstantive changes.

Amendment Note: 2003 H 95 rewrote the first sentence of the section, which prior thereto read:

"If a person entitled to a refund under section 5747.11 or 5747.13 of the Revised Code is indebted to this state for any tax or fee administered by the tax commissioner that is paid to the state or to the clerk of courts pursuant to section 4505.06 of the Revised Code, or any charge, penalty, or interest arising from said tax or fee, the amount refundable may be applied in satisfaction of the debt."

Amendment Note: 1997 H 215 rewrote this section, which prior thereto read:

"Any refund, including interest thereon, that a person is entitled to under section 5747.11 or 5747.13 of the Revised Code shall be reduced by the amount of any tax indebtedness due the state from the person. The amount of such reduction shall be applied in satisfaction of such indebtedness. If the amount refundable is less than the amount of such indebtedness, it shall be applied in partial satisfaction of such indebtedness.

"The tax commissioner may, with the consent of the taxpayer, provide for the crediting, against tax imposed under this chapter or Chapter 5748. of the Revised Code and due for any taxable year, of the amount of any refund due the taxpayer under this chapter or Chapter 5748. of the Revised Code, as appropriate, for a preceding taxable year.

"As used in this section, 'tax indebtedness due the state' or 'such indebtedness' means the unpaid portion of an assessment for any tax, penalty, or interest payable to the general revenue fund or imposed under this chapter, to the extent such assessment has become conclusive and has been or otherwise would be brought to judgment, together with any additional penalties or interest accrued."

Library References

Taxation ⊙⊃1097.
Westlaw Topic No. 371.
C.J.S. Taxation § 1109.

PRACTICE AND PROCEDURE

5747.121 Procedures for collection of overdue child support from state income tax refunds; child support intercept fund

(A) In accordance with sections 3123.821 to 3123.823 of the Revised Code, the tax commissioner shall cooperate with the department of job and family services in establishing and then implementing procedures for the collection of overdue child support from refunds of paid state income taxes under this chapter that are payable to obligors. The tax commissioner shall deposit money collected from such refunds into the child support intercept fund.

(B) At the request of the department of job and family services in connection with the collection of overdue child support from a refund of paid state income taxes pursuant to sections 3123.821 to 3123.823 of the Revised Code and division (A) of this section, the tax commissioner shall release to the department the home address and social security number of any obligor whose overdue child support may be collected from a refund of paid state income taxes pursuant to sections 3123.821 to 3123.823 of the Revised Code and division (A) of this section.

(C) In the case of persons filing a joint income tax return, the amount of the refund available for the collection of overdue child support shall be based on the proportion of the refund due to the obligor only. Any obligor's spouse who objects to the amount of the refund to be used for the collection of overdue child support may file a complaint with the tax commissioner within twenty-one days after receiving notice of the collection. The commissioner shall afford a complainant an opportunity to be heard. The burden of proving an error by the commissioner in determining the amount of a refund to be used for the collection of overdue child support shall be on the complainant.

(D) There is hereby created in the state treasury the child support intercept fund, which shall consist of moneys paid into it by the tax commissioner under division (A) of this section. Moneys in the fund shall be disbursed pursuant to vouchers approved by the director of job and family services for use by the division of child support to meet the requirements of section 666 of Title IV–D of the "Social Security Act," 98 Stat. 1306 (1975), 42 U.S.C. 666, as amended, and any rules promulgated under Title IV–D. Moneys appropriated from the fund are not intended to replace other moneys appropriated for this purpose.

(E) As used in this section, "obligor" has the same meaning as in section 3123.82 of the Revised Code.

(2000 S 180, eff. 3–22–01; 1999 H 471, eff. 7–1–00; 1986 H 428, eff. 12–23–86; 1986 H 509; 1985 S 80)

Uncodified Law

2001 S 170, § 1, eff. 10–25–01, reads:

(A) As used in this section:

(1) "ADC assistance" means assistance provided pursuant to the former aid to dependent children program.

(2) "Assistance group" and "Ohio works first" have the same meanings as in section 5107.02 of the Revised Code.

(3) "Child support order" has the same meaning as in section 3119.01 of the Revised Code.

(4) "Support payee" means a person who is entitled to receive support payments made under a child support order and with respect to whom both of the following apply:

(a) The person is a member of an assistance group that applied for and began participating in Ohio works first on or after October 1, 1997.

(b) Prior to the person's application for participation in Ohio works first, a support arrearage accrued under the child support order to which all of the following apply:

(i) The support arrearage was collected from payments on the support arrearages and not payments of current support.

(ii) The support arrearage was not collected pursuant to section 464 of Title IV–D of the "Social Security Act," 95 Stat. 860 (1981), 42 U.S.C. 664, as amended.

(iii) The support arrearage was collected on and after the date the assistance group of which the person is a member ceased participating in Ohio works first.

(B)(1) Each county child support enforcement agency shall do the following:

(a) Conduct a review of all child support cases involving a support payee the agency is administering or has administered and apply, retroactive to October 1, 1997 through September 30, 2000, the provisions of section 457(a)(2)(B)(i)(II), (ii)(II), and (v) of Title IV–D of the "Social Security Act," 110 Stat. 2200 (1996), 42 U.S.C. 657(a)(2)(B)(i)(II), (ii)(II), and (v), as amended, to the support payees' child support orders to determine the amount of assigned support and the proper distribution of support arrearage payments;

(b) Conduct a review of all child support cases the agency administered during the years 1997 through 2000 to determine whether refunds of paid state income taxes collected pursuant to sections 3123.82 to 3123.823 and 5747.121 of the Revised Code on and after October 1, 1997, and before October 1, 2000, and distributed to the state to reimburse ADC assistance or Ohio works first assistance were collected and distributed in accordance with section 457 of Title IV–D of the "Social Security Act," 88 Stat. 2356 (1975), 42 U.S.C. 657, as amended.

(2) Agencies shall conduct the reviews in accordance with rules adopted by the Department pursuant to division (D) of this section.

(C)(1) Notwithstanding the Revised Code, any election made by the state pursuant to section 457(a)(6) of Title IV–D of the "Social Security Act," 111 Stat. 626 (1997), 42 U.S.C. 657(a)(6), as amended, or any court order establishing assigned support arrearage amounts, and based on reviews conducted under division (B)(1)(a) of this section, the Department shall distribute to support payees payments that represent the amount of child support arrearage payments that were distributed to the state instead of the support payees and that would have been distributed to the support payees if 42 U.S.C. 657(a)(2)(B)(i)(II), (ii)(II), and (v) had been applied retroactive to October 1, 1997, through September 30, 2000. The payments to the support payees shall not be reduced by the federal share of the arrearage amount collected as provided in section 457 of Title IV–D of the "Social Security Act," 88 Stat. 2356 (1975), 42 U.S.C. 657, as amended, regardless of whether the federal share is received by the state.

(2) If the review conducted pursuant to division (B)(1)(b) of this section reveals payments that were incorrectly distributed to the state, the Department shall redistribute the payments in accordance with section 457 of Title IV–D of the "Social Security Act," 88 Stat. 2356 (1975), 42 U.S.C. 657, as amended.

(3) Prior to completion of a case review under division (B)(1)(a) of this section, the Department shall distribute to support payees any assigned support collected and distributed to the state on and after October 1, 2000, other than amounts collected pursuant to section 464 of Title IV–D of the "Social Security Act," 95 Stat. 860 (1981), 42 U.S.C. 664, as amended. Support payees receiving the payments under division (C)(3) of this section shall not be required to repay those amounts to the state if it is determined later that the payments should have been retained by the state as assigned support.

(4) On completion of a case review under division (B)(1)(a) of this section and payment of the amounts required by divisions (C)(1) and (3) of this section, if a support arrearage amount is still subject to assignment, the Department shall collect and distribute all support arrearage amounts in accordance with section 457 of Title IV–D of the "Social Security Act," 88 Stat. 2356 (1975), 42 U.S.C. 657, as amended.

(5) The Department shall pay, pursuant to this section, interest at the rate of six and one half per cent per annum, if the interest amount exceeds ten dollars.

(6) To the extent permitted under federal law, receipt of a payment pursuant to this section shall not be treated as income to the recipient for purposes of determining eligibility for benefits from means-tested government administered programs, including Ohio Works First; Prevention, Retention, and Contingency; Food Stamps; Disability Assistance; or other assistance for which eligibility is based on income or assets.

(D) The Department shall adopt internal management rules pursuant to section 111.15 of the Revised Code to govern the conduct of agency reviews under division (B) of this section. The Department shall adopt rules pursuant to Chapter 119. of the Revised Code governing the calculation and payment distributions pursuant to division (C) of this section.

Historical and Statutory Notes

Amendment Note: 2000 S 180 substituted "sections 3123.821 to 3123.823" for "section 5101.321" twice in division (B); and deleted "division (D) of" after "meaning as in" and substituted "3123.82" for "5101.321" in division (E).

Amendment Note: 1999 H 471 substituted "job and family" for "human" in divisions (A), (B), and (D); and substituted "division" for "bureau" in division (D).

Library References

Child Support ⇌467, 495.
Taxation ⇌1097.
Westlaw Topic Nos. 76E, 371.
C.J.S. Taxation § 1109.

5747.123 Overpaid child support

(A) As used in this section:

(1) "Obligee" and "obligor" have the same meanings as in section 3119.01 of the Revised Code;

(2) "Overpaid child support" has the same meaning as in section 3123.82 of the Revised Code.

(B) In accordance with sections 3123.821 to 3123.823 of the Revised Code, the tax commissioner shall cooperate with the department of job and family services in establishing and implementing procedures for the collection of overpaid child support from refunds of paid state income taxes under this chapter that are payable to obligees. The tax commissioner shall collect the refunds and send the amounts to the department of job and family services for distribution to obligors who made the overpayment.

(C) In the case of persons filing a joint income tax return, the amount of the refund available for the collection of overpaid child support shall be based on the proportion of the refund due the obligee only. An obligee's spouse who objects to the amount of the refund to be used for the collection of overpaid child support may file a complaint with the tax commissioner within twenty-one days after receiving notice of the collection. The commissioner shall afford a complainant an opportunity to be heard. The burden of proving an error by the commissioner in determining the amount of the refund to be used for the collection of overpaid child support shall be on the complainant.

(2000 S 180, eff. 3–22–01)

5747.13 Failure to file return or pay tax; assessment; notice; hearing; appeal; judgment; payment pending review

(A) If any employer collects the tax imposed by section 5747.02 or under Chapter 5748. of the Revised Code and fails to remit the tax as required by law, or fails to collect the tax, the employer is personally liable for any amount collected that the employer fails to remit, or any amount that the employer fails to collect. If any taxpayer fails to file a return or fails to pay the tax imposed by section 5747.02 or under Chapter 5748. of the Revised Code, the taxpayer is personally liable for the amount of the tax.

If any employer, taxpayer, or qualifying entity required to file a return under this chapter fails to file the return within the time prescribed, files an incorrect return, fails to remit the full amount of the taxes due for the period covered by the return, or fails to remit any additional tax due as a result of a reduction in the amount of the credit allowed under division (B) of section 5747.05 of the Revised Code together with interest on the additional tax within the time prescribed by that division, the tax commissioner may make an assessment against any person liable for any deficiency for the period for which the return is or taxes are due, based upon any information in the commissioner's possession.

An assessment issued against either the employer or the taxpayer pursuant to this section shall not be considered an election of remedies or a bar to an assessment against the other for failure to report or pay the same tax. No assessment shall be issued against any person if the tax actually has been paid by another.

No assessment shall be made or issued against an employer, taxpayer, or qualifying entity more than four years after the final date the return subject to assessment was required to be filed or the date the return was filed, whichever is later. However, the commissioner may assess any balance due as the result of a reduction in the credit allowed under division (B) of section 5747.05 of the Revised Code, including applicable penalty and interest, within four years of the date on which the taxpayer reports a change in either the portion of the taxpayer's adjusted gross income subjected to an income tax or tax measured by income in another state or the District of Columbia, or the amount of liability for an income tax or tax measured by income to another state or the District of Columbia, as required by division (B)(3) of section 5747.05 of the Revised Code. Such time limits may be extended if both the employer, taxpayer, or qualifying entity and the commissioner consent in writing to the extension or if an agreement waiving or extending the time limits has been entered into pursuant to section 122.171 of the Revised Code. Any such extension shall extend the four-year time limit in division (B) of section 5747.11 of the Revised Code for the same period of time. There shall be no bar or limit to an assessment against an employer for taxes withheld from employees and not remitted to the state, against an employer, taxpayer, or qualifying entity that fails to file a return subject to assessment as required by this chapter, or against an employer, taxpayer, or qualifying entity that files a fraudulent return.

The commissioner shall give the party assessed written notice of the assessment in the manner provided in section 5703.37 of the Revised Code. With the notice, the commissioner shall provide instructions on how to petition for reassessment and request a hearing on the petition.

(B) Unless the party assessed files with the tax commissioner within sixty days after service of the notice of assessment, either personally or by certified mail, a written petition for reassessment, signed by the party assessed or that party's authorized agent having knowledge of the facts, the assessment becomes final, and the amount of the assessment is due and payable from the party assessed to the commissioner with remittance made payable to the treasurer of state. The petition shall indicate the objections of the party assessed, but additional objections may be raised in writing if received by the commissioner prior to the date shown on the final determination. If the petition has been properly filed, the commissioner shall proceed under section 5703.60 of the Revised Code.

(C) After an assessment becomes final, if any portion of the assessment remains unpaid, including accrued interest, a certified copy of the tax commissioner's entry making the assessment final may be filed in the office of the clerk of the court of common pleas in the county in which the employer's, taxpayer's, or qualifying entity's place of business is located or the county in which the party assessed resides. If the party assessed is not a resident of this state, the certified copy of the entry may be filed in the office of the clerk of the court of common pleas of Franklin county.

Immediately upon the filing of the entry, the clerk shall enter a judgment against the party assessed in the amount shown on the entry. The judgment shall be filed by the clerk in one of two loose-leaf books, one entitled "special judgments for state and school district income taxes," and the other entitled "special judgments for qualifying entity taxes." The judgment shall have the same effect as other judgments. Execution shall issue upon the judgment upon the request of the tax commissioner, and all laws applicable to sales on execution shall apply to sales made under the judgment.

The portion of the assessment not paid within sixty days after the assessment was issued shall bear interest at the rate per annum prescribed by section 5703.47 of the Revised Code from the day the tax commissioner issues the assessment until it is paid. Interest shall be paid in the same manner as the tax and may be collected by the issuance of an assessment under this section.

(D) All money collected under this section shall be considered as revenue arising from the taxes imposed by this chapter or Chapter 5733. or 5748. of the Revised Code, as appropriate.

(E) The portion of an assessment that must be paid upon the filing of a petition for reassessment shall be as follows:

(1) If the sole item objected to is the assessed penalty or interest, payment of the assessment, including interest but not penalty, is required;

(2) If the taxpayer or qualifying entity that is assessed failed to file, prior to the date of issuance of the assessment, the annual return or report required by section 5747.08 or 5747.42 of the Revised Code, any amended return or amended report required by section 5747.10 or 5747.45 of the Revised Code for the taxable year at issue, or any report required by division (B) of section 5747.05 of the Revised Code to indicate a reduction in the amount of the credit provided under that division, payment of the assessment, including interest but not penalty, is required, except as otherwise provided under division (E)(6) or (7) of this section;

(3) If the employer assessed had not filed, prior to the date of issuance of the assessment, the annual return required by division (E)(2) of section 5747.07 of the Revised Code covering the period at issue, payment of the assessment, including interest but not penalty, is required;

(4) If the taxpayer or qualifying entity that is assessed filed, prior to the date of issuance of the assessment, the annual return or report required by section 5747.08 or 5747.42 of the Revised Code, all amended returns or reports required by section 5747.10 or 5747.45 of the Revised Code for the taxable year at issue, and

all reports required by division (B) of section 5747.05 of the Revised Code to indicate a reduction in the amount of the credit provided under that division, and a balance of the taxes shown due on the returns or reports as computed on the returns or reports remains unpaid, payment of only that portion of the assessment representing the unpaid balance of tax and interest is required;

(5) If the employer assessed filed, prior to the date of issuance of the assessment, the annual return required by division (E)(2) of section 5747.07 of the Revised Code covering the period at issue, and a balance of the taxes shown due on the return as computed on the return remains unpaid, payment of only that portion of the assessment representing the unpaid balance of tax and interest is required;

(6) In the case of a party assessed as a qualifying entity subject to the tax levied under section 5733.41 or 5747.41 of the Revised Code, if the party does not dispute that it is a qualifying entity subject to that tax but claims the protections of section 101 of Public Law 86–272, 73 Stat. 555, 15 U.S.C.A. 381, as amended, no payment is required;

(7) In the case of a party assessed as a qualifying entity subject to the tax levied under section 5733.41 or 5747.41 of the Revised Code, if the party does dispute that it is a qualifying entity subject to that tax, no payment is required;

(8) If none of the conditions specified in divisions (E)(1) to (7) of this section apply, no payment is required.

(F) Notwithstanding the fact that a petition for reassessment is pending, the petitioner may pay all or a portion of the assessment that is the subject of the petition. The acceptance of a payment by the treasurer of state does not prejudice any claim for refund upon final determination of the petition.

If upon final determination of the petition an error in the assessment is corrected by the tax commissioner, upon petition so filed or pursuant to a decision of the board of tax appeals or any court to which the determination or decision has been appealed, so that the amount due from the party assessed under the corrected assessment is less than the portion paid, there shall be issued to the petitioner or to the petitioner's assigns or legal representative a refund in the amount of the overpayment as provided by section 5747.11 of the Revised Code, with interest on that amount as provided by such section, subject to section 5747.12 of the Revised Code.

(2002 S 200, eff. 9–6–02; 2001 H 405, eff. 12–13–01; 2000 H 612, eff. 9–29–00; 1997 H 215, eff. 9–29–97; 1993 H 152, eff. 7–1–93; 1992 S 358; 1990 H 956; 1989 H 111; 1987 H 231; 1983 H 291; 1982 H 366; 1981 H 694; 1971 H 475)

Uncodified Law

1997 H 215, § 213: See *Baldwin's Ohio Revised Code Annotated*, Uncodified Law under 5747.07.

1993 H 152, § 188, eff. 7–1–93, reads: Sections 5747.06, 5747.07, 5747.072, 5747.13, and 5747.15 of the Revised Code as amended by this act and the amendment in this act to division (E) of section 1306.03 of the Revised Code first apply on January 1, 1994.

1990 H 956, § 3, eff. 12–31–90, reads: Sections 5747.05, 5747.11, and 5747.13 of the Revised Code, as amended by this act, apply in taxable years ending on or after the effective date of this act.

Historical and Statutory Notes

Amendment Note: 2002 S 200 inserted "in the manner" and "With the notice, the commissioner shall provide instructions on how to petition for reassessment and request a hearing on the petition." in division (A); rewrote division (B); inserted "tax" before "commissioner" in the first paragraph of division (C) and in the second paragraph of division (F); and made other nonsubstantive changes throughout the section. Prior to amendment division (B) read:

"(B) Unless the party to whom the notice of assessment is directed files with the commissioner within sixty days after service of the notice of assessment, either personally or by certified mail, a petition for reassessment in writing, signed by the party assessed, or by the party's authorized agent having knowledge of the facts and makes payment of the portion of the assessment required by division (E) of this section, the assessment shall become final, and the amount of the assessment shall be due and payable from the party assessed to the commissioner with remittance made payable to the treasurer of state. The petition shall indicate the objections of the party assessed, but additional objections may be raised in writing if received prior to the date shown on the final determination by the commissioner.

"Unless the petitioner waives a hearing, the commissioner shall assign a time and place for the hearing on the petition and notify the petitioner of the time and place of the hearing by personal service or certified mail, but the commissioner may continue the hearing from time to time if necessary.

"The commissioner may make such correction to an assessment as the commissioner finds proper. The commissioner shall serve a copy of a final determination on the petitioner by personal service or certified mail, and the commissioner's decision in the matter shall be final, subject to appeal as provided in section 5717.02 of the Revised Code. Only objections decided on the merits by the board of tax appeals or a court shall be given collateral estoppel or res judicata effect in considering an application for refund of amounts paid pursuant to the assessment."

Amendment Note: 2001 H 405 inserted "or if an agreement waiving or extending the time limits has been entered into pursuant to section 122.171 of the Revised Code" at the end of the third sentence in the fourth paragraph of division (A).

Amendment Note: 2000 H 612 substituted "as provided in section 5703.37 of the Revised Code" for "by personal service or certified mail" in the last paragraph in division (A); substituted "sixty" for "thirty" in divisions (B) and (C); deleted "full" before "payment of the assessment" three times and "and interest" three times before "is required" three times in division (E); and inserted "interest but not" three times and "of tax and interest" twice in division (E).

Amendment Note: 1997 H 215 rewrote this section; see *Baldwin's Ohio Legislative Service Annotated*, 1997, p 8/L–1989, or the OH–LEGIS or OH–LEGIS–OLD database on Westlaw, for text of previous version.

Amendment Note: 1993 H 152 changed references to section 5747.07(D) to references to section 5747.07(E)(2) in divisions (E)(3) and (E)(5).

Library References

Taxation ⚖1071, 1100, 1103.
Westlaw Topic No. 371.
C.J.S. Taxation § 1103, 1107.

CALCULATION AND ALLOCATION OF INCOME AND DEDUCTIONS

5747.20 Allocation of nonbusiness income or deduction

This section applies solely for the purposes of computing the credit allowed under division (A) of section 5747.05 of the Revised Code and computing income taxable in this state under division (D) of section 5747.08 of the Revised Code.

All items of nonbusiness income or deduction shall be allocated in this state as follows:

(A) All items of nonbusiness income or deduction taken into account in the computation of adjusted gross income for the taxable year by a resident shall be allocated to this state.

(B) All items of nonbusiness income or deduction taken into account in the computation of adjusted gross income for the taxable year by a nonresident shall be allocated to this state as follows:

(1) All items of compensation paid to an individual for personal services performed in this state who was a nonresident at the time of payment and all items of deduction directly allocated thereto shall be allocated to this state.

(2) All gains or losses from the sale of real property, tangible personal property, or intangible property shall be allocated as follows:

(a) Capital gains or losses from the sale or other transfer of real property are allocable to this state if the property is located physically in this state.

(b) Capital gains or losses from the sale or other transfer of tangible personal property are allocable to this state if, at the time of such sale or other transfer, the property had its physical location in this state.

(c) Capital gains or losses from the sale or other transfer of intangible personal property are allocable to this state if the taxpayer's domicile was in this state at the time of such sale or other transfer.

(3) All rents and royalties of real or tangible personal property shall be allocated to this state as follows:

(a) Rents and royalties derived from real property are allocable to this state if the property is physically located in this state.

(b) Rents and royalties derived from tangible personal property are allocable to this state to the extent that such property is utilized in this state.

The extent of utilization of tangible personal property in a state is determined by multiplying the rents or royalties derived from such property by a fraction, the numerator of which is the number of days of physical location of the property in this state during the rental or royalty period in the taxable year and the denominator of which is the number of days of physical location of the property everywhere during all rental or royalty periods in the taxable year. If the physical location of the property during the rental or royalty period is unknown or unascertainable by the nonresident, tangible personal property is utilized in the state in which the property was located at the time the rental or royalty payor obtained possession.

(4) All patent and copyright royalties shall be allocated to this state to the extent the patent or copyright was utilized by the payor in this state.

A patent is utilized in a state to the extent that it is employed in production, fabrication, manufacturing, or other processing in the state, or to the extent that a patented product is produced in the state. If the basis of receipts from patent royalties does not permit allocation to states or if the accounting procedures do not reflect states of utilization, the patent is utilized in this state if the taxpayer's domicile was in this state at the time such royalties were paid or accrued.

A copyright is utilized in a state to the extent that printing or other publication originates in the state. If the basis of receipts from copyright royalties does not permit allocation to states or if the accounting procedures do not reflect states of utilization, the copyright is utilized in this state if the taxpayer's domicile was in this state at the time such royalties were paid or accrued.

(5)(a) All lottery prize awards paid by the state lottery commission pursuant to Chapter 3770. of the Revised Code shall be allocated to this state.

(b) All earnings, profit, income, and gain from the sale, exchange, or other disposition of lottery prize awards paid or to be paid to any person by the state lottery commission pursuant to Chapter 3770. of the Revised Code shall be allocated to this state.

(c) All earnings, profit, income, and gain from the direct or indirect ownership of lottery prize awards paid or to be paid to any person by the state lottery commission pursuant to Chapter 3770. of the Revised Code shall be allocated to this state.

(d) All earnings, profit, income, and gain from the direct or indirect interest in any right in or to any lottery prize awards paid or to be paid to any person by the state lottery commission pursuant to Chapter 3770. of the Revised Code shall be allocated to this state.

(6) Any item of income or deduction which has been taken into account in the computation of adjusted gross income for the taxable year by a nonresident and which is not otherwise specifically allocated or apportioned pursuant to sections 5747.20 to 5747.23 of the Revised Code, including, without limitation, interest, dividends and distributions, items of income taken into account under the provisions of sections 401 to 425 of the Internal Revenue Code, and benefit payments received by a beneficiary of a supplemental unemployment trust which is referred to in section 501(c)(17) of the Internal Revenue Code, shall not be allocated to this state unless the taxpayer's domicile was in this state at the time such income was paid or accrued.

(C) If an individual is a resident for part of the taxable year and a nonresident for the remainder of the taxable year, all items of nonbusiness income or deduction shall be allocated under division (A) of this section for the part of the taxable year that the individual is a resident and under division (B) of this section for the part of the taxable year that the individual is a nonresident.

(2002 S 226, eff. 9–17–02; 1997 H 215, eff. 9–29–97; 1989 H 111, eff. 7–1–89; 1987 H 171; 1984 H 250; 1973 H 95; 1971 H 475)

Uncodified Law

1997 H 215, § 211: See Baldwin's Ohio Revised Code Annotated, Uncodified Law under 5747.057.

1989 H 111, § 13, eff. 7–1–89, reads, in part: (A) Sections 5747.01, 5747.02, 5747.022, 5747.05, 5747.13, 5747.15, and 5747.20 as amended and section 5733.053 of the Revised Code as enacted by this act shall take effect at the earliest time permitted by law, but shall first apply to a taxpayer's first taxable year ending on or after the effective date of those sections.

Historical and Statutory Notes

Amendment Note: 2002 S 226 redesignated existing division (B)(5) as division (B)(5)(a); added new divisions (B)(5)(b), (c), and (d); and made other nonsubstantive changes.

Amendment Note: 1997 H 215 added the first paragraph; and made changes to reflect gender neutral language and other nonsubstantive changes.

Library References

Taxation ⚖1005, 1047, 1074.

Westlaw Topic No. 371.

C.J.S. Taxation § 1096, 1098, 1103.

5747.211 Apportionment of items of business income or deduction earned by financial institution

This section applies solely for the purpose of computing the credit allowed under division (A) of section 5747.05 of the Revised Code, computing income taxable in this state under division (D) of section 5747.08 of the Revised Code, and computing the credit allowed under section 5747.057 of the Revised Code. In lieu of sections 5747.20 and 5747.21 of the Revised Code, all items of business income or business deductions earned by a financial institution as defined in section 5725.01 of the Revised Code shall be apportioned to this state as required under section 5733.056 of the Revised Code.

(1997 H 215, eff. 6–30–97)

Library References

Taxation ⚖983, 1005, 1047.

Westlaw Topic No. 371.

C.J.S. Taxation § 1096, 1098.

5747.221 Allocation or apportionment of income or deduction; investment pass-through entity

(A) As used in this section, "investment pass-through entity" has the same meaning as in section 5733.401 of the Revised Code.

(B) Except as provided in division (C) of this section, for the purposes of sections 5747.20, 5747.21, and 5747.22 of the Revised Code, no item of income or deduction shall be allocated or apportioned to this state to the extent that such item represents the portion of an adjusted qualifying amount for which the withholding tax is not imposed under section 5747.41 of the Revised Code by reason of division (C) of section 5733.401 of the Revised Code. This section shall be applied without regard to division (I) of section 5733.40 of the Revised Code.

(C) If a taxpayer has a direct or indirect investment in an investment pass-through entity that has a direct or indirect investment in any other pass-through entity, division (B) of this section does not apply to any item of income, gain, deduction, or loss where, under section 5747.231 of the Revised Code, the item is directly or indirectly attributable to either of the following:

(1) A distributive share of income or gain from a pass-through entity that does not qualify as an investment pass-through entity;

(2) A pass-through entity's income or gain to which division (C) of section 5733.401 of the Revised Code does not apply.

An indirect investment includes any interest that a person constructively owns on account of the attribution rules set forth in section 267, 318, or 1563 of the Internal Revenue Code.

(2001 H 94, eff. 9-5-01; 2000 S 287, eff. 12-21-00)

Uncodified Law

2000 S 287, § 13, eff. 12-21-00, reads:

The amendment or enactment by this act of sections 5733.053, 5733.06, 5733.40, 5747.221, and 5747.24 of the Revised Code first applies to tax year 2002.

2000 S 180, § 6, eff. 3-22-01, reads:

Notwithstanding Section 13 of Am. Sub. S.B. 287 of the 123rd General Assembly, the amendment by that act of sections 5747.221 and 5747.24 of the Revised Code applies to taxable years beginning in 2001 or thereafter.

Historical and Statutory Notes

Amendment Note: 2001 H 94 rewrote this section which prior thereto read:

"For the purposes of sections 5747.20, 5747.21, and 5747.22 of the Revised Code, no item of income or deduction shall be allocated or apportioned to this state to the extent that such item represents or relates to the portion of an adjusted qualifying amount for which the withholding tax is not imposed under section 5747.41 of the Revised Code by reason of division (C) of section 5733.401 of the Revised Code. This section shall be applied without regard to division (I) of section 5733.40 of the Revised Code."

Library References

Taxation ⟲1005.
Westlaw Topic No. 371.
C.J.S. Taxation § 1096.

5747.231 Inclusion of distributive share of items of income, property, compensation and sales in computations

As used in this section, "adjusted qualifying amount" has the same meaning as in section 5733.40 of the Revised Code.

This section does not apply to division (BB)(5)(a)(ii) of section 5747.01 of the Revised Code.

Except as set forth in this section and except as otherwise provided in divisions (A) and (B) of section 5733.401 of the Revised Code, in making all apportionment, allocation, income, gain, loss, deduction, tax, and credit computations under this chapter, each person shall include in that person's items of business income, nonbusiness income, adjusted qualifying amounts, allocable income or loss, apportionable income or loss, property, compensation, and sales, the person's entire distributive share or proportionate share of the items of business income, nonbusiness income, adjusted qualifying amounts, allocable income or loss, apportionable income or loss, property, compensation, and sales of any pass-through entity in which the person has a direct or indirect ownership interest at any time during the person's taxable year. A pass-through entity's direct or indirect distributive share or proportionate share of any other pass-through entity's items of business income, nonbusiness income, adjusted qualifying amounts, allocable income or loss, apportionable income or loss, property, compensation, and sales shall be included for the purposes of computing the person's distributive share or proportionate share of the pass-through entity's items of business income, nonbusiness income, adjusted qualifying amounts, allocable income or loss, apportionable income or loss, property, compensation, and sales under this section. Those items shall be in the same form as was recognized by the pass-through entity.

(2002 H 675, eff. 12-13-02)

Historical and Statutory Notes

Ed. Note: Former 5747.231 repealed by 2002 H 675, eff. 12-13-02; 1997 H 215, eff. 6-30-07.

Library References

Taxation ⟲1005, 1074.
Westlaw Topic No. 371.
C.J.S. Taxation § 1096, 1103.

NONRESIDENT TAXPAYERS

5747.25 Election to be treated as nonresident taxpayer

Note: Repealed by 2006 H 73, eff. 4-4-07.

(A) An individual may elect to be treated as a nonresident taxpayer under this section for any taxable year. An individual who makes an election in accordance with this section shall be considered a nonresident for the entire taxable year with respect to the tax imposed by section 5747.02 of the Revised Code and the credits allowed against that tax. Except as provided in division (B) of this section, for an individual who makes and does not revoke an election under this section, the portion of Ohio adjusted gross income allocated or apportioned to this state for purposes of computing the nonresident taxpayer credit under division (A) of section 5747.05 of the Revised Code shall be the sum of the following:

(1) The individual's Ohio adjusted gross income allocated or apportioned to this state under sections 5747.20 to 5747.23 of the Revised Code for purposes of computing the nonresident taxpayer credit under division (A) of section 5747.05 of the Revised Code;

(2) The remaining amount of the individual's Ohio adjusted gross income, if any, multiplied by a fraction, the numerator of which is the number of contact periods in excess of one hundred twenty that the individual has in this state during the taxable year and the denominator of which is sixty-three. The numerator may be zero, but shall not exceed sixty-three.

(B)(1) This division applies to an individual who makes and does not revoke an election under this section and who meets both of the following conditions:

(a) The individual agrees that at least one other state that imposes an income tax has jurisdiction to impose that income tax on the individual for the taxable year. "Income tax" includes both a tax on net income and a tax measured by net income.

(b) No later than ninety days after the individual files the return required under section 5747.08 of the Revised Code for the taxable year, he also files with such other state or states the income tax returns or reports required for the same taxable year. For good cause shown, the tax commissioner may extend the ninety-day deadline.

(2) For an individual to whom this division applies, the portion of Ohio adjusted gross income allocated or apportioned to this state for purposes of computing the nonresident taxpayer credit under division (A) of section 5747.05 of the Revised Code shall be the sum of the following:

(a) The individual's Ohio adjusted gross income allocated or apportioned to this state under sections 5747.20 to 5747.23 of the Revised Code for purposes of computing the nonresident taxpayer credit under division (A) of section 5747.05 of the Revised Code;

(b) The included remaining amount of the individual's Ohio adjusted gross income, if any, multiplied by a fraction, the numerator of which is the number of contact periods in excess of one hundred twenty that the individual has in this state during the taxable year and the denominator of which is sixty-three. The numerator may be zero, but shall not exceed sixty-three.

As used in this division, "the included remaining amount of the individual's Ohio adjusted gross income" means the portion of the individual's Ohio adjusted gross income that is not allocated or apportioned to this state under sections 5747.20 to 5747.23 of the Revised Code for purposes of computing the nonresident taxpayer credit under division (A) of section 5747.05 of the Revised Code, minus the portion, if any, that would be allocated or apportioned to the other state or states that impose an income tax on the individual for the taxable year assuming, solely for the purposes of this division, that the other state or states have nonresident taxpayer credit apportionment and allocation provisions identical to sections 5747.20 to 5747.23 of the Revised Code.

(C)(1) An individual may make an election under this section by filing a written statement with the tax commissioner during the taxable year immediately preceding the taxable year to which the election applies. Except as provided in division (D) of this section, the tax commissioner has no authority to challenge or deny the nonresident status of the individual for the taxable year to which the election applies.

(2) An individual may revoke an election under this section by filing a written revocation with the tax commissioner before the first day of the taxable year to which the election would otherwise apply. Thereafter, the individual may revoke the election only by applying to the commissioner and presenting clear and convincing evidence showing good cause that the election should be revoked. The commissioner shall determine whether the individual shows such good cause and whether to permit the election to be revoked, and his decision shall be final subject to appeal under section 5717.02 of the Revised Code. The commissioner shall transmit a copy of his certificate of final determination to the individual, by personal service or certified mail.

(3) If an individual makes an election for a taxable year and dies during or after that year, the death does not affect the election, unless the personal representative of the estate of the deceased individual applies under division (C)(2) of this section to permit the election to be revoked and the commissioner determines to permit the revocation.

(D)(1) After the end of a taxable year to which an election applies, the tax commissioner, in writing and by personal service or certified mail, return receipt requested, may request an affidavit from the individual verifying the individual's election under this section. Within sixty days after receiving the commissioner's request, the individual shall submit a written affidavit to the commissioner stating both of the following:

(a) During the entire taxable year to which the election applies, the individual was not domiciled in this state;

(b) During the entire taxable year to which the election applies, the individual had at least one abode outside this state.

In the case of an individual who has died, the personal representative of the estate of the deceased individual may respond to the commissioner's request on behalf of the individual by making to the best of the representative's knowledge and belief the statement under this division with respect to the deceased individual and submitting the affidavit to the commissioner within sixty days after receiving the commissioner's request for it.

An individual or personal representative of an estate who knowingly makes a false statement under this division is guilty of perjury under section 2921.11 of the Revised Code.

(2) Except as provided in division (D)(3) of this section, if an individual or the personal representative of the estate of an individual does not submit within sixty days after receiving the commissioner's request the affidavit under division (D)(1) of this section, the individual shall be considered to be a resident taxpayer for the entire taxable year to which the election applies with respect to the taxes imposed by Chapters 5747. and 5748. of the Revised Code and the credits allowed against those taxes. The individual, or the personal representative of the estate of the individual, shall have no authority to challenge such resident status.

(3) If an individual or a personal representative of an estate does not submit within sixty days after receiving the commissioner's request the affidavit under division (D)(1) of this section, he still may apply to the commissioner under division (C)(2) of this section to permit the election to be revoked.

(E) With respect to a school district income tax imposed under Chapter 5748. of the Revised Code and any credit allowed against that tax, and to the extent the individual lives in and maintains a permanent place of abode in the school district as described in division (F)(1) of section 5748.01 of the Revised Code, an individual who makes an election under this section shall be considered to be a resident of this state and of the school district. However, for purposes of that tax and credit, the individual shall be considered to have earned and received only the amount of income arrived at by multiplying the amount of income allocated or apportioned to this state under division (A) or (B) of this section for the purpose of computing the nonresident taxpayer credit by a fraction, the numerator of which is the number of contact periods the individual has in the school district during the taxable year and the denominator of which is the number of contact periods the individual has in this state during the taxable year. The individual shall not challenge or deny his status as a resident for the purposes of this division or the taxation of the amount of income required under this division.

(F) An individual or personal representative of an estate shall not apply under division (C)(2) of this section to revoke an election under this section and the tax commissioner shall not request an affidavit under division (D) of this section after the expiration of the period, if any, within which the commissioner may make an assessment under section 5747.13 of the Revised Code against the individual for the taxable year in question.

(2006 H 73, eff. 4-4-07; 1993 S 123, eff. 10-29-93)

Uncodified Law

2006 H 73, § 3: See Uncodified Law under RC 5747.01.

1993 S 123, § 4, eff. 10-29-93, reads: This act applies to taxable years ending on and after its effective date. Notwithstanding any provision of section 5747.25 of the Revised Code to the contrary, an individual may make an election to be treated as a nonresident taxpayer under that section for the taxable year in which this act takes effect at any time within thirty days after the effective date of this act. The individual may revoke the election for that taxable year only by applying to the Tax Commissioner under division (C)(2) of section 5747.25 of the Revised Code and presenting clear and convincing evidence showing good cause that the election should be revoked.

Library References

Taxation ⚖1012.
Westlaw Topic No. 371.
C.J.S. Taxation § 1092.

CHILD DAY–CARE AND ADOPTION CREDITS

5747.37 Credit for legal adoption of minor child

As used in this section:

(A) "Minor child" means a person under eighteen years of age.

(B) "Legally adopt" means to adopt a minor child pursuant to Chapter 3107. of the Revised Code, or pursuant to the laws of any other state or nation if such an adoption is recognizable under section 3107.18 of the Revised Code. For the purposes of this section, a minor child is legally adopted when the final decree or order of adoption is issued by the proper court under the laws of the state or nation under which the child is adopted, or, in the case of an interlocutory order of adoption, when the order becomes final under the laws of the state or nation. "Legally adopt" does not include the adoption of a minor child by the child's stepparent.

There is hereby granted a credit against the tax imposed by section 5747.02 of the Revised Code for the legal adoption by a taxpayer of a minor child. The amount of the credit shall be five hundred dollars for each minor child legally adopted by the taxpayer during the taxable year. the credit shall be claimed in the order required under section 5747.98 of the Revised Code. For the purposes of making tax payments under this chapter, taxes equal to the amount of the credit shall be considered to be paid to this state on the first day of the taxable year.

(1999 S 4, eff. 8–19–99)

Uncodified Law

1999 S 4, § 3, eff. 8–19–99, reads:

Section 5747.37 of the Revised Code, as enacted by this act, applies to adoptions of minor children under final decrees or orders of adoption duly issued, or interlocutory orders of adoption that become final, during taxable years beginning on or after January 1, 1999.

Library References

Taxation ⚖1047.
Westlaw Topic No. 371.
C.J.S. Taxation § 1098.

QUALIFIED PASS–THROUGH ENTITIES OR TRUSTS

5747.39 Credit for employee training costs

(A) As used in this section, "eligible employee" and "eligible training costs" have the same meanings as in section 5733.42 of the Revised Code, and "pass-through entity" includes a sole proprietorship.

(B)(1) For taxable years beginning in 2003, 2004, 2005, 2006, and 2007 there is hereby allowed a nonrefundable credit against the tax imposed by section 5747.02 of the Revised Code for a taxpayer that is an investor in a pass-through entity for which a tax credit certificate is issued under section 5733.42 of the Revised Code. For the taxable year beginning in 2003, the amount of eligible training costs for which a credit may be claimed by all taxpayers that are investors in an entity shall equal one-half of the average of the eligible training costs incurred by the entity during calendar years 1999, 2000, and 2001, but shall not exceed one thousand dollars for each eligible employee on account of whom such costs were paid or incurred by the entity. The amount of a taxpayer's credit for the taxpayer's taxable year beginning in 2003 shall equal the taxpayer's interest in the entity on December 31, 2001, multiplied by the credit available to the entity as computed by the entity.

(2) For the taxable year beginning in 2004, the amount of the eligible training costs for which a credit may be claimed by all taxpayers that are investors in an entity shall equal one-half of the average of the eligible training costs incurred by the entity during calendar years 2002, 2003, and 2004, but shall not exceed one thousand dollars for each eligible employee on account of whom such costs were paid or incurred by the entity. The amount of a taxpayer's credit for the taxpayer's taxable year beginning in 2004 shall equal the taxpayer's interest in the entity on December 31, 2004, multiplied by the credit available to the entity as computed by the entity.

(3) For the taxable year beginning in 2005, the amount of the eligible training costs for which a credit may be claimed by all taxpayers that are investors in an entity shall equal one-half of the average of the eligible training costs incurred by the entity during calendar years 2003, 2004, and 2005, but shall not exceed one thousand dollars for each eligible employee on account of whom such costs were paid or incurred by the entity. The amount of a taxpayer's credit for the taxpayer's taxable year beginning in 2005 shall equal the taxpayer's interest in the entity on December 31, 2005, multiplied by the credit available to the entity as computed by the entity.

(4) For the taxable year beginning in 2006, the amount of the eligible training costs for which a credit may be claimed by all taxpayers that are investors in an entity shall equal one-half of the average of the eligible training costs incurred by the entity during calendar years 2004, 2005, and 2006, but shall not exceed one thousand dollars for each eligible employee on account of whom such costs were paid or incurred by the entity. The amount of a taxpayer's credit for the taxpayer's taxable year beginning in 2006 shall equal the taxpayer's interest in the entity on December 31, 2006, multiplied by the credit available to the entity as computed by the entity.

(5) For the taxable year beginning in 2007, the amount of the eligible training costs for which a credit may be claimed by all taxpayers that are investors in an entity shall equal one-half of the average of the eligible training costs incurred by the entity during calendar years 2005, 2006, and 2007, but shall not exceed one thousand dollars for each eligible employee on account of whom such costs were paid or incurred by the entity. The amount of a taxpayer's credit for the taxpayer's taxable year beginning in 2007 shall equal the taxpayer's interest in the entity on December 31, 2007, multiplied by the credit available to the entity as computed by the entity.

(6) The total amount of credits that may be claimed by all such taxpayers with respect to each pass-through entity for each taxable year shall not exceed one hundred thousand dollars.

(C) The credit shall be claimed in the order prescribed by section 5747.98 of the Revised Code. A taxpayer may carry forward the credit to the extent that the taxpayer's credit exceeds the taxpayer's tax due after allowing for any other credits that precede the credit allowed by this section in the order prescribed by section 5747.98 of the Revised Code. The taxpayer may carry the excess credit forward for three taxable years following the taxable year for which the taxpayer first claims the credit under this section.

(D) A pass-through entity shall apply to the director of job and family services for a tax credit certificate in the manner prescribed by division (C) of section 5733.42 of the Revised Code.

Divisions (C) to (H) of that section govern the tax credit allowed by this section, except that "taxable year" shall be substituted for "tax year" wherever that phrase appears in those divisions, and that "pass-through entity" shall be substituted for "taxpayer" wherever "taxpayer" appears in those divisions.

(2006 H 699, eff. 3–29–07; 2005 S 190, eff. 11–22–05; 2001 H 94, eff. 6–6–01; 2000 S 287, eff. 12–21–00)

Historical and Statutory Notes

Amendment Note: 2005 S 190 designated divisions (A) through (D); deleted "after" before "in 2003, 2004" and ", and the total amount of credits that may be claimed by all such taxpayers shall not exceed one hundred thousand dollars" and inserted "and 2006" in the first paragraph of division (B)(1); deleted ", and the total amount of credits that may be claimed by all such taxpayers shall not exceed one hundred thousand dollars" at the end of the first sentence in divisions (B)(2) and (B)(3); added new divisions (B)(4) and (B)(5); and made other nonsubstantive changes.

Amendment Note: 2001 H 94 rewrote this section which prior thereto read:

"As used in this section, 'eligible employee' and 'eligible training costs' have the same meanings as in section 5733.42 of the Revised Code, and 'pass-through entity' includes a sole proprietorship.

"For taxable years beginning after December 31, 2000 there is hereby allowed a nonrefundable credit against the tax imposed by section 5747.02 of the Revised Code for a taxpayer that is an investor in a pass-through entity for which a tax credit certificate is issued under section 5733.42 of the Revised Code. The amount of eligible training costs for which a credit may be claimed by all taxpayers that are investors in an entity shall equal one-half of the average of the eligible training costs incurred by the entity during the three calendar years that end in the taxable year for which the credit is claimed, but shall not exceed one thousand dollars for each eligible employee on account of whom such costs were paid or incurred by the entity, and the total amount of credits that may be claimed by all such taxpayers shall not exceed one hundred thousand dollars each year. Each taxpayer's credit shall be claimed for the taxpayer's taxable year that includes the last day of the third calendar year of the three-year period during which eligible training costs are paid or incurred by the entity. The credit may be claimed for eligible training costs paid or incurred on or before December 31, 2003. The amount of a taxpayer's credit shall equal the taxpayer's interest in the entity on the last day of the third calendar year of the three-year period ending in or with the last day of the taxpayer's taxable year, multiplied by the credit available to the entity as computed by the entity.

"The credit shall be claimed in the order prescribed by section 5747.98 of the Revised Code. A taxpayer may carry forward the credit to the extent that the taxpayer's credit exceeds the taxpayer's tax due after allowing for any other credits that precede the credit allowed by this section in the order prescribed by section 5747.98 of the Revised Code. The taxpayer may carry the excess credit forward for three taxable years following the taxable year for which the taxpayer first claims the credit under this section.

"A pass-through entity shall apply to the director of job and family services for a tax credit certificate in the manner prescribed by division (C) of section 5733.42 of the Revised Code. Divisions (C) to (H) of that section govern the tax credit allowed by this section, except that 'taxable year' shall be substituted for 'tax year' wherever that phrase appears in those divisions, and that 'pass-through entity' shall be substituted for 'taxpayer' wherever 'taxpayer' appears in those divisions."

Library References

Taxation ⚖1047.
Westlaw Topic No. 371.
C.J.S. Taxation § 1098.

5747.40 Use of terms; purpose and applicability of tax

Any term used in sections 5747.40 to 5747.43 of the Revised Code has the same meaning as defined in section 5733.40 of the Revised Code.

The purpose of sections 5747.40 to 5747.43 of the Revised Code is to complement and to reinforce the tax levied under section 5747.02 of the Revised Code. Those sections do not apply to a pass-through entity if all of the investors of the pass-through entity are resident taxpayers for the purposes of this chapter for the entire qualifying taxable year of the pass-through entity, or to a trust if all of the beneficiaries of the trust are resident taxpayers for the purposes of this chapter for the entire qualifying taxable year of the trust.

(1997 H 215, eff. 6–30–97)

Uncodified Law

1997 H 215, § 211: See *Baldwin's Ohio Revised Code Annotated*, Uncodified Law under 5747.057.

Library References

Taxation ⚖1015, 1021.
Westlaw Topic No. 371.
C.J.S. Taxation § 1093–1094.

5747.401 Investment pass-through entities

(A)(1) Except as otherwise provided in division (B) of this section, for the purposes of sections 5733.40, 5733.401, 5733.402, 5733.41, and 5747.40 to 5747.457 of the Revised Code, the investors in an investment pass-through entity as defined in section 5733.401 of the Revised Code, hereinafter the "deemed investors," shall be deemed to be investors in any other pass-through entity in which the investment pass-through entity is a direct investor without regard to sections 5733.057 or 5747.231 of the Revised Code. Each deemed investor's portion of such other pass-through entity's adjusted qualifying amount shall be the adjusted qualifying amount that, without regard to this section, passes through from such other pass-through entity to the investment pass-through entity multiplied by the percentage of the deemed investor's direct ownership in the investment pass-through entity without regard to sections 5733.057 or 5747.231 of the Revised Code.

(2) For the purposes of sections 5733.40, 5733.401, 5733.402, 5733.41, and 5747.40 to 5747.457 of the Revised Code, the investment pass-through entity shall not be deemed to be an investor in such other pass-through entity.

(3) If the taxable year of the investment pass-through entity ends on a day other than the last day of such other pass-through entity's taxable year, division (A)(1) of this section applies to those persons who are investors in the investment pass-through entity on the last day of such other pass-through entity's taxable year ending within the investment pass-through entity's taxable year.

(B) Division (A) of this section applies only to the extent to which the investment pass-through entity provides on a timely basis to such other pass-through entity the name, address, and social security number or federal identification number for each direct investor in the investment pass-through entity without regard to sections 5733.057 and 5747.231 of the Revised Code. Once such other pass-through entity receives such information from the investment pass-through entity, division (A) of this section applies for such other pass-through entity's taxable year unless the tax commissioner permits the investment pass-through entity to revoke the notice that the investment pass-through entity previously provided to such other pass-through entity.

(1998 H 770, eff. 9–16–98)

Library References

Taxation ⚖1015, 1021.
Westlaw Topic No. 371.
C.J.S. Taxation § 1093–1094.

5747.41 Tax on qualifying pass-through entities with at least one individual qualifying investor or qualifying trusts with at least one individual qualifying beneficiary

For the same purposes for which the tax is levied under section 5747.02 of the Revised Code, there is hereby levied a withholding tax on every qualifying pass-through entity having at least one qualifying investor who is an individual and on every qualifying trust having at least one qualifying beneficiary who is an individual. The withholding tax imposed by this section is imposed on the sum of the adjusted qualifying amounts of a qualifying pass-through entity's qualifying investors who are individuals and on the sum of the adjusted qualifying amounts of a qualifying trust's qualifying beneficiaries, at the rate of five per cent of that sum.

The tax imposed by this section applies only if the qualifying entity has nexus with this state under the Constitution of the United States for any portion of the qualifying entity's qualifying taxable year, and the sum of the qualifying entity's adjusted qualifying amounts exceeds one thousand dollars for the qualifying entity's qualifying taxable year.

The levy of the tax under this section does not prevent a municipal corporation or a joint economic development district created under section 715.70 or 715.71 or sections 715.72 to 715.81 of the Revised Code from levying a tax on income.

(1997 H 215, eff. 6–30–97)

Uncodified Law

1997 H 215, § 211: See *Baldwin's Ohio Revised Code Annotated*, Uncodified Law under 5747.057.

Library References

Taxation ⚖1015, 1021.
Westlaw Topic No. 371.
C.J.S. Taxation § 1093–1094.

5747.42 Returns; remittance of tax

(A) In addition to the other returns required to be filed and other remittances required to be made pursuant to this chapter, every qualifying entity that is subject to the tax imposed by section 5733.41 or 5747.41 of the Revised Code shall file an annual return on or before the fifteenth day of the fourth month following the end of the qualifying entity's qualifying taxable year, and remit to the tax commissioner, with the remittance made payable to the treasurer of state, the amount of the taxes shown to be due on the return, less the amount paid for the taxable year on a declaration of estimated tax report filed by the taxpayer as provided by section 5747.43 of the Revised Code. Remittance shall be made in the form prescribed by the tax commissioner, including electronic funds transfer if required by section 5747.44 of the Revised Code.

A domestic qualifying entity shall not dissolve, and a foreign qualifying entity shall not withdraw or retire from business in this state, without filing the tax returns and paying the taxes charged for the year in which such dissolution or withdrawal occurs.

(B) The tax commissioner shall furnish qualifying entities, upon request, copies of the forms prescribed by the commissioner for the purpose of making the returns required by sections 5747.42 to 5747.453 of the Revised Code.

(C) The annual return required by this section shall be signed by the qualifying entity's trustee or other fiduciary, or president, vice-president, secretary, treasurer, general manager, general partner, superintendent, or managing agent in this state. The annual return shall contain the facts, figures, computations, and attachments that result in the tax charged by section 5733.41 or 5747.41 of the Revised Code. Each qualifying entity also shall file with its annual return all of the following:

(1) The full name and address of each qualifying investor or qualifying beneficiary unless the qualifying entity submits such information in accordance with division (D) of this section;

(2) The social security number, federal employer identification number, or other identifying number of each qualifying investor or qualifying beneficiary, unless the taxpayer submits that information in accordance with division (D) of this section;

(3) The amount of tax imposed by sections 5733.41 and 5747.41 of the Revised Code, and the amount of the tax paid by the qualifying entity, for the qualifying taxable year covered by the annual return;

(4) The amount of tax imposed by sections 5733.41 and 5747.41 of the Revised Code that is attributable to each qualifying investor or qualifying beneficiary, unless the qualifying entity submits this information in accordance with division (D) of this section.

(D) On the date the annual return is due, including extensions of time, if any, the qualifying entity may be required by rule to transmit electronically or by magnetic media the information set forth in division (C) of this section. The tax commissioner may adopt rules governing the format for the transmission of such information. The tax commissioner may exempt a qualifying entity or a class of qualifying entities from the requirements imposed by this division.

(E) Upon good cause shown, the tax commissioner may extend the period for filing any return required to be filed under this section or section 5747.43 or 5747.44 of the Revised Code and for transmitting any information required to be transmitted under those sections. The tax commissioner may adopt rules relating to extensions of time to file and to transmit. At the time a qualifying entity pays any tax imposed under section 5733.41 or 5747.41 of the Revised Code or estimated tax as required under section 5747.43 of the Revised Code, the qualifying entity also shall pay interest computed at the rate per annum prescribed by section 5703.47 of the Revised Code on that tax or estimated tax, from the time the tax or estimated tax originally was required to be paid, without consideration of any filing extensions, to the time of actual payment. Nothing in this division shall be construed to abate, modify, or limit the imposition of any penalties imposed for the failure to timely pay taxes under this chapter or Chapter 5733. of the Revised Code without consideration of any filing extensions.

(1997 H 215, eff. 6–30–97)

Uncodified Law

1997 H 215, § 211: See *Baldwin's Ohio Revised Code Annotated*, Uncodified Law under 5747.057.

Library References

Taxation ⚖1079.
Westlaw Topic No. 371.
C.J.S. Taxation § 1102.

5747.43 Estimated tax returns

(A) As used in this section:

(1) "Estimated taxes" means the amount that a qualifying entity estimates to be the sum of its liability under sections 5733.41 and 5747.41 of the Revised Code for its current qualifying taxable year.

(2) "Tax liability" means the total of the taxes and withholding taxes due under sections 5733.41 and 5747.41 of the Revised Code for the qualifying taxable year prior to applying any estimated tax payment or refund from another year.

(3) "Taxes paid" includes payments of estimated taxes made under division (C) of this section and tax refunds applied by the qualifying entity in payment of estimated taxes.

(B) In addition to the return required to be filed pursuant to section 5747.42 of the Revised Code, each qualifying entity subject to the tax imposed under section 5733.41 and to the withholding tax imposed by section 5747.41 of the Revised Code shall file an estimated tax return and pay a portion of the qualifying entity's tax liability for its qualifying taxable year. The portion of those taxes required to be paid, and the last day prescribed for payment thereof, shall be as prescribed by divisions (B)(1), (2), (3), and (4) of this section:

(1) On or before the fifteenth day of the month following the last day of the first quarter of the qualifying entity's qualifying taxable year, twenty-two and one-half per cent of the qualifying entity's estimated tax liability for that taxable year;

(2) On or before the fifteenth day of the month following the last day of the second quarter of the qualifying entity's qualifying taxable year, forty-five per cent of the qualifying entity's estimated tax liability for that taxable year;

(3) On or before the fifteenth day of the month following the last day of the third quarter of the qualifying entity's qualifying taxable year, sixty-seven and one-half per cent of the qualifying entity's estimated tax liability for that taxable year;

(4) On or before the fifteenth day of the month following the last day of the fourth quarter of the qualifying entity's qualifying taxable year, ninety per cent of the qualifying entity's estimated tax liability for that taxable year.

Payments of estimated taxes shall be made payable to the treasurer of state.

(C) If a payment of estimated taxes is not paid in the full amount required under division (B) of this section, a penalty shall be added to the taxes charged for the qualifying taxable year unless the underpayment is due to reasonable cause as described in division (D) of this section. The penalty shall accrue at the rate per annum prescribed by section 5703.47 of the Revised Code upon the amount of underpayment from the day the estimated payment was required to be made to the day the payment is made.

The amount of the underpayment upon which the penalty shall accrue shall be determined as follows:

(1) For the first payment of estimated taxes each year, twenty-two and one-half per cent of the tax liability less the amount of taxes paid by the date prescribed for that payment;

(2) For the second payment of estimated taxes each year, forty-five per cent of the tax liability less the amount of taxes paid by the date prescribed for that payment;

(3) For the third payment of estimated taxes each year, sixty-seven and one-half per cent of the tax liability less the amount of taxes paid by the date prescribed for that payment;

(4) For the fourth payment of estimated taxes each year, ninety per cent of the tax liability less the amount of taxes paid by the date prescribed for that payment.

For the purposes of this section, a payment of estimated taxes on or before any payment date shall be considered a payment of a previous underpayment only to the extent the payment of estimated taxes exceeds the amount of the payment presently required to be paid to avoid any penalty.

The penalty imposed under division (C) of this section is in lieu of any other interest charge or penalty imposed for failure to file a declaration of estimated tax report and make estimated payments as required by this section.

(D) An underpayment of estimated taxes determined under division (C) of this section is due to reasonable cause if any of the following apply:

(1) The amount of tax that was paid equals at least ninety per cent of the tax liability for the current qualifying taxable year, determined by annualizing the income received during that year up to the end of the month immediately preceding the month in which the payment is due;

(2) The amount of tax liability that was paid equals at least ninety per cent of the tax liability for the current qualifying taxable year;

(3) The amount of tax liability that was paid equals at least one hundred per cent of the tax liability shown on the return of the qualifying entity for the preceding qualifying taxable year, provided that the immediately preceding qualifying taxable year reflected a period of twelve months and the qualifying entity filed a return under section 5747.42 of the Revised Code for that year.

(E)(1) Divisions (B) and (C) of this section do not apply for a taxable year if either of the following applies to the qualifying entity:

(a) For the immediately preceding taxable year, the entity computes in good faith and in a reasonable manner that the sum of its adjusted qualifying amounts is ten thousand dollars or less.

(b) For the taxable year the entity computes in good faith and in a reasonable manner that the sum of its adjusted qualifying amounts is ten thousand dollars or less.

(2) Notwithstanding any other provision of Title LVII of the Revised Code to the contrary, the entity shall establish by a preponderance of the evidence that its computation of the adjusted qualifying amounts for the immediately preceding taxable year and the taxable year was, in fact, made in good faith and in a reasonable manner.

(F) The tax commissioner may waive the requirement for filing a declaration of estimated taxes for any class of qualifying entities if the commissioner finds the waiver is reasonable and proper in view of administrative costs and other factors.

(1998 H 770, eff. 9–16–98; 1997 H 215, eff. 6–30–97)

Uncodified Law

1997 H 215, § 211: See *Baldwin's Ohio Revised Code Annotated*, Uncodified Law under 5747.057.

Historical and Statutory Notes

Amendment Note: 1998 H 770 added division (E); and designated division (F).

Library References

Taxation ⚯1079.
Westlaw Topic No. 371.
C.J.S. Taxation § 1102.

5747.44 Payment by electronic funds transfer

(A) If a qualifying entity's total liability for taxes imposed under sections 5733.41 and 5747.41 of the Revised Code exceeds one hundred eighty thousand dollars for the second preceding qualifying taxable year, the qualifying entity shall make all payments required under sections 5747.42 and 5747.43 of the Revised Code by electronic funds transfer as prescribed by this section and rules adopted by the treasurer of state under section 113.061 of the Revised Code.

The tax commissioner shall notify each qualifying entity required to remit taxes by electronic funds transfer of the entity's obligation to do so, shall maintain an updated list of those entities, and shall provide the list and any additions thereto or deletions therefrom to the treasurer of state. Failure by the tax commissioner to notify a qualifying entity subject to this section to remit taxes by electronic funds transfer does not relieve the qualifying entity of its obligation to remit taxes by electronic funds transfer.

(B) Except as otherwise provided in this division, the payment of taxes by electronic funds transfer does not affect a qualifying entity's obligation to file the returns required under sections 5747.42 and 5747.43 of the Revised Code. The treasurer of state, in consultation with the tax commissioner, may adopt rules in addition to the rules adopted under section 113.061 of the Revised Code governing the format for filing returns by qualifying entities that remit taxes by electronic funds transfer. The rules may provide for the filing of returns at less frequent intervals than otherwise required if the treasurer of state and the tax commissioner determine that remittance by electronic funds transfer warrants less frequent filing of returns.

(C) A qualifying entity required by this section to remit taxes by electronic funds transfer may apply to the treasurer of state in the manner prescribed by the treasurer of state to be excused from that requirement. The treasurer of state may excuse the qualifying entity from remittance by electronic funds transfer for good cause shown for the period of time requested by the qualifying entity or for a portion of that period. The treasurer of state shall notify the tax commissioner and the qualifying entity of the treasurer of state's decision as soon as is practicable.

(D) If a qualifying entity required by this section to remit taxes by electronic funds transfer remits those taxes by some means other than by electronic funds transfer as prescribed by this section and the rules adopted by the treasurer of state, and the treasurer of state determines that such failure was not due to reasonable cause or was due to willful neglect, the treasurer of state shall notify the tax commissioner of the failure to remit by electronic funds transfer and shall provide the commissioner with any information used in making that determination. The tax commissioner may collect an additional charge by assessment in the manner prescribed by section 5747.13 of the Revised Code. The additional charge shall equal five per cent of the amount of the taxes required to be paid by electronic funds transfer, but shall not exceed five thousand dollars. Any additional charge assessed under this section is in addition to any other penalty or charge imposed under this chapter or Chapter 5733. of the Revised Code, and shall be considered as revenue arising from the taxes imposed under sections 5733.41 and 5747.41 of the Revised Code. The tax commissioner may remit all or a portion of such a charge and may adopt rules governing such remission.

No additional charge shall be assessed under this division against a qualifying entity that has been notified of its obligation to remit taxes under this section and that remits its first two tax payments after such notification by some means other than electronic funds transfer. The additional charge may be assessed upon the remittance of any subsequent tax payment that the qualifying entity remits by some means other than electronic funds transfer.

(1997 H 215, eff. 6–30–97)

Uncodified Law

1997 H 215, § 211: See *Baldwin's Ohio Revised Code Annotated*, Uncodified Law under 5747.057.

Library References

Taxation ⚖︎1096.
Westlaw Topic No. 371.
C.J.S. Taxation § 1106.

5747.45 Qualifying taxable year; method of accounting; amended reports

(A) A qualifying entity's qualifying taxable year is the same as its taxable year for federal income tax purposes. If a qualifying entity's taxable year is changed for federal income tax purposes, the qualifying taxable year for purposes of this chapter and sections 5733.40 and 5733.41 of the Revised Code is changed accordingly.

(B) A qualifying entity's method of accounting shall be the same as its method of accounting for federal income tax purposes. In the absence of any method of accounting for federal income tax purposes, income shall be computed under such method as in the opinion of the tax commissioner clearly reflects income.

If a qualifying entity's method of accounting is changed for federal income tax purposes, its method of accounting for purposes of this chapter shall be changed accordingly.

(C) If any of the facts, figures, computations, or attachments required in a qualifying entity's annual report to determine the taxes imposed by section 5733.41 or 5747.41 of the Revised Code must be altered as the result of an adjustment to the qualifying entity's federal income tax return, whether the adjustment is initiated by the qualifying entity or the internal revenue service, and such alteration affects the qualifying entity's tax liability under one or both of those sections, the qualifying entity shall file an amended report with the tax commissioner in such form as the commissioner requires. The amended report shall be filed not later than one year after the adjustment has been agreed to or finally determined for federal income tax purposes or any federal income tax deficiency or refund, or the abatement or credit resulting therefrom, has been assessed or paid, whichever occurs first.

(1) In the case of an underpayment, the amended report shall be accompanied by payment of an additional tax and interest due and is a report subject to assessment under section 5747.13 of the Revised Code for the purpose of assessing any additional tax due under this division, together with any applicable penalty and interest. It shall not reopen those facts, figures, computations, or attachments from a previously filed report no longer subject to assessment that are not affected, either directly or indirectly, by the adjustment to the qualifying entity's federal income tax return.

(2) In the case of an overpayment, an application for refund may be filed under this division within the one-year period prescribed for filing the amended report even if it is filed beyond the period prescribed in division (B) of section 5747.11 of the Revised Code if it otherwise conforms to the requirements of that section. An application filed under this division shall claim refund of overpayments resulting from alterations to only those facts, figures, computations, or attachments required in the qualifying entity's annual report that are affected, either directly or indirectly, by the adjustment to the qualifying entity's federal income tax return unless it is also filed within the time prescribed in division (B) of section 5747.11 of the Revised Code. It shall not reopen those facts, figures, computations, or attachments that are not affected, either directly or indirectly, by the adjustment to the qualifying entity's federal income tax return.

(1997 H 215, eff. 6–30–97)

Uncodified Law

1997 H 215, § 211: See *Baldwin's Ohio Revised Code Annotated*, Uncodified Law under 5747.057.

Library References

Taxation ⚖︎982, 1078, 1079.
Westlaw Topic No. 371.
C.J.S. Taxation § 1100, 1102–1103.

5747.451 Effect of retirement, dissolution, or sale; tax liens; enforcement of judgments; quo warranto actions; settlements

(A) The mere retirement from business or voluntary dissolution of a domestic or foreign qualifying entity does not exempt it from the requirements to make reports as required under sections 5747.42 to 5747.44 or to pay the taxes imposed under section 5733.41 or 5747.41 of the Revised Code. If any qualifying entity subject to the taxes imposed under section 5733.41 or 5747.41 of the Revised Code sells its business or stock of merchandise or quits its business, the taxes required to be paid prior to that time, together with any interest or penalty thereon, become due and payable immediately, and the qualifying entity shall make a final return within fifteen days after the date of selling or quitting business. The successor of the qualifying entity shall withhold a sufficient amount of the purchase money to cover the amount of such taxes, interest, and penalties due and unpaid until the qualifying entity produces a receipt from the tax commissioner showing that the taxes, interest, and penalties have been paid, or a certificate indicating that no taxes are due. If the purchaser of the business or stock of goods fails to withhold purchase money, the purchaser is personally liable for the payment of the taxes, interest, and penalties accrued and unpaid during the operation of the business by the qualifying entity. If the amount of those taxes, interest, and penalty unpaid at the time of the purchase exceeds the total purchase money, the tax commissioner may adjust the qualifying entity's liability for those taxes, interest, and penalty, or adjust the responsibility of the purchaser to pay that liability, in a manner calculated to maximize the collection of those liabilities.

(B) Annually, on the last day of each qualifying taxable year of a qualifying entity, the taxes imposed under section 5733.41 or 5747.41 of the Revised Code, together with any penalties subsequently accruing thereon, become a lien on all property in this state of the qualifying entity, whether such property is employed by the qualifying entity in the prosecution of its business or is in the hands of an assignee, trustee, or receiver for the benefit of the qualifying entity's creditors and investors. The lien shall continue until those taxes, together with any penalties subsequently accruing, are paid.

Upon failure of such a qualifying entity to pay those taxes on the day fixed for payment, the treasurer of state shall thereupon notify the tax commissioner, and the commissioner may file in the office of the county recorder in each county in this state in which the qualifying entity owns or has a beneficial interest in real estate, notice of the lien containing a brief description of such real estate. No fee shall be charged for such a filing. The lien is not valid as against any mortgagee, purchaser, or judgment creditor whose rights have attached prior to the time the notice is so filed in the county in which the real estate which is the subject of such mortgage, purchase, or judgment lien is located. The notice shall be recorded in a book kept by the recorder, called the qualifying entity tax lien record, and indexed under the name of the qualifying entity charged with the tax. When the tax, together with any penalties subsequently accruing thereon, have been paid, the tax commissioner shall furnish to the qualifying entity an acknowledgment of such payment that the qualifying entity may record with the recorder of each county in which notice of such lien has been filed, for which recording the recorder shall charge and receive a fee of two dollars.

(C) In addition to all other remedies for the collection of any taxes or penalties due under law, whenever any taxes, interest, or penalties due from any qualifying entity under section 5733.41 of the Revised Code or this chapter have remained unpaid for a period of ninety days, or whenever any qualifying entity has failed for a period of ninety days to make any report or return required by law, or to pay any penalty for failure to make or file such report or return, the attorney general, upon the request of the tax commissioner, shall file a petition in the court of common pleas in the county of the state in which such qualifying entity has its principal place of business for a judgment for the amount of the taxes, interest, or penalties appearing to be due, the enforcement of any lien in favor of the state, and an injunction to restrain such qualifying entity and its officers, directors, and managing agents from the transaction of any business within this state, other than such acts as are incidental to liquidation or winding up, until the payment of such taxes, interest, and penalties, and the costs of the proceeding fixed by the court, or the making and filing of such report or return.

The petition shall be in the name of the state. Any of the qualifying entities having its principal places of business in the county may be joined in one suit. On the motion of the attorney general, the court of common pleas shall enter an order requiring all defendants to answer by a day certain, and may appoint a special master commissioner to take testimony, with such other power and authority as the court confers, and permitting process to be served by registered mail and by publication in a newspaper of general circulation published in the county, which publication need not be made more than once, setting forth the name of each delinquent qualifying entity, the matter in which the qualifying entity is delinquent, the names of its officers, directors, and managing agents, if set forth in the petition, and the amount of any taxes, fees, or penalties claimed to be owing by the qualifying entity.

All or any of the trustees or other fiduciaries, officers, directors, investors, beneficiaries, or managing agents of any qualifying entity may be joined as defendants with the qualifying entity.

If it appears to the court upon hearing that any qualifying entity that is a party to the proceeding is indebted to the state for taxes imposed under section 5733.41 or 5747.41 of the Revised Code, or interest or penalties thereon, judgment shall be entered therefor with interest; and if it appears that any qualifying entity has failed to make or file any report or return, a mandatory injunction may be issued against the qualifying entity, its trustees or other fiduciaries, officers, directors, and managing agents, enjoining them from the transaction of any business within this state, other than acts incidental to liquidation or winding up, until the making and filing of all proper reports or returns and until the payment in full of all taxes, interest, and penalties.

If the trustees or other fiduciaries, officers, directors, investors, beneficiaries, or managing agents of a qualifying entity are not made parties in the first instance, and a judgment or an injunction is rendered or issued against the qualifying entity, those officers, directors, investors, or managing agents may be made parties to such proceedings upon the motion of the attorney general, and, upon notice to them of the form and terms of such injunction, they shall be bound thereby as fully as if they had been made parties in the first instance.

In any action authorized by this division, a statement of the tax commissioner, or the secretary of state, when duly certified, shall be prima-facie evidence of the amount of taxes, interest, or penalties due from any qualifying entity, or of the failure of any qualifying entity to file with the commissioner or the secretary of state any report required by law, and any such certificate of the commissioner or the secretary of state may be required in evidence in any such proceeding.

On the application of any defendant and for good cause shown, the court may order a separate hearing of the issues as to any defendant.

The costs of the proceeding shall be apportioned among the parties as the court deems proper.

The court in such proceeding may make, enter, and enforce such other judgments and orders and grant such other relief as is necessary or incidental to the enforcement of the claims and lien of the state.

In the performance of the duties enjoined upon the attorney general by this division, the attorney general may direct any prosecuting attorney to bring an action, as authorized by this division, in the name of the state with respect to any delinquent qualifying entities within the prosecuting attorney's county, and like proceedings and orders shall be had as if such action were instituted by the attorney general.

(D) If any qualifying entity fails to make and file the reports or returns required under this chapter, or to pay the penalties provided by law for failure to make and file such reports or returns for a period of ninety days after the time prescribed by this chapter, the attorney general, on the request of the tax commissioner, shall commence an action in quo warranto in the court of appeals of the county in which that qualifying entity has its principal place of business to forfeit and annul its privileges and franchises. If the court is satisfied that any such qualifying entity is in default, it shall render judgment ousting such qualifying entity from the exercise of its privileges and franchises within this state, and shall otherwise proceed as provided in sections 2733.02 to 2733.39 of the Revised Code.

(2002 H 396, eff. 6–13–02; 1997 H 215, eff. 6–30–97)

Uncodified Law

1997 H 215, § 211: See *Baldwin's Ohio Revised Code Annotated*, Uncodified Law under 5747.057.

Historical and Statutory Notes

Ed. Note: Former RC 5747.451(E) contained provisions relating to compromise and settlement of tax claims by the attorney general of Ohio. See now RC 131.02(E) for provisions analogous to former RC 5747.451(E).

Amendment Note: 2002 H 396 deleted former division (E) which prior thereto read:

"(E) With the advice and consent of the tax commissioner, the attorney general may, before or after any action for the recovery of taxes imposed under section 5733.41 or 5747.41 of the Revised Code, or interest or penalties thereon and certified to the attorney general as delinquent, compromise or settle any claim for delinquent taxes, interest, or penalties so certified."

Library References

Taxation ⚖1015, 1021, 1079, 1090, 1100.
Westlaw Topic No. 371.
C.J.S. Taxation § 1093–1094, 1102, 1107.

5747.453 Personal liability for failure to file reports or pay tax

An employee or beneficiary of, or investor in, a qualifying entity having control or supervision of, or charged with the responsibility for, filing returns and making payments, or any trustee or other fiduciary, officer, member, or manager of the qualifying entity who is responsible for the execution of the qualifying entity's fiscal responsibilities, is personally liable for the failure to file any report or to pay any tax due as required by sections 5747.40 to 5747.453 of the Revised Code. The dissolution, termination, or bankruptcy of a qualifying entity does not discharge a responsible trustee's, fiduciary's, officer's, member's, manager's, employee's, investor's, or beneficiary's liability for failure of the qualifying entity to file any report or pay any tax due as required by those sections. The sum due for the liability may be collected by assessment in the manner provided in section 5747.13 of the Revised Code.

(1997 H 215, eff. 6–30–97)

Library References

Taxation ⚖1100.
Westlaw Topic No. 371.

C.J.S. Taxation § 1107.

LOCAL GOVERNMENT FUNDS

5747.51 Allocation to county undivided local government funds

(A) Within ten days after the fifteenth day of July of each year, the tax commissioner shall make and certify to the county auditor of each county an estimate of the amount of the local government fund to be allocated to the undivided local government fund of each county for the ensuing calendar year and the estimated amount to be received by the undivided local government fund of each county from the taxes levied pursuant to section 5707.03 of the Revised Code for the ensuing calendar year.

(B) At each annual regular session of the county budget commission convened pursuant to section 5705.27 of the Revised Code, each auditor shall present to the commission the certificate of the commissioner, the annual tax budget and estimates, and the records showing the action of the commission in its last preceding regular session. The estimates shown on the certificate of the commissioner of the amount to be allocated from the local government fund and the amount to be received from taxes levied pursuant to section 5707.03 of the Revised Code shall be combined into one total comprising the estimate of the undivided local government fund of the county. The commission, after extending to the representatives of each subdivision an opportunity to be heard, under oath administered by any member of the commission, and considering all the facts and information presented to it by the auditor, shall determine the amount of the undivided local government fund needed by and to be apportioned to each subdivision for current operating expenses, as shown in the tax budget of the subdivision. This determination shall be made pursuant to divisions (C) to (I) of this section, unless the commission has provided for a formula pursuant to section 5747.53 of the Revised Code.

Nothing in this section prevents the budget commission, for the purpose of apportioning the undivided local government fund, from inquiring into the claimed needs of any subdivision as stated in its tax budget, or from adjusting claimed needs to reflect actual needs. For the purposes of this section, "current operating expenses" means the lawful expenditures of a subdivision, except those for permanent improvements and except payments for interest, sinking fund, and retirement of bonds, notes, and certificates of indebtedness of the subdivision.

(C) The commission shall determine the combined total of the estimated expenditures, including transfers, from the general fund and any special funds other than special funds established for road and bridge; street construction, maintenance, and repair; state highway improvement; and gas, water, sewer, and electric public utilities operated by a subdivision, as shown in the subdivision's tax budget for the ensuing calendar year.

(D) From the combined total of expenditures calculated pursuant to division (C) of this section, the commission shall deduct the following expenditures, if included in these funds in the tax budget:

(1) Expenditures for permanent improvements as defined in division (E) of section 5705.01 of the Revised Code;

(2) In the case of counties and townships, transfers to the road and bridge fund, and in the case of municipalities, transfers to the street construction, maintenance, and repair fund and the state highway improvement fund;

(3) Expenditures for the payment of debt charges;

(4) Expenditures for the payment of judgments.

(E) In addition to the deductions made pursuant to division (D) of this section, revenues accruing to the general fund and any special fund considered under division (C) of this section from the following sources shall be deducted from the combined total of expenditures calculated pursuant to division (C) of this section:

(1) Taxes levied within the ten-mill limitation, as defined in section 5705.02 of the Revised Code;

(2) The budget commission allocation of estimated county library and local government support fund revenues to be distributed pursuant to section 5747.48 of the Revised Code;

(3) Estimated unencumbered balances as shown on the tax budget as of the thirty-first day of December of the current year in the general fund, but not any estimated balance in any special fund considered in division (C) of this section;

(4) Revenue, including transfers, shown in the general fund and any special funds other than special funds established for road and bridge; street construction, maintenance, and repair; state highway improvement; and gas, water, sewer, and electric public utilities, from all other sources except those that a subdivision receives from an additional tax or service charge voted by its electorate or receives from special assessment or revenue bond collection. For the purposes of this division, where the charter of a municipal corporation prohibits the levy of an income tax, an income tax levied by the legislative authority of such municipal corporation pursuant to an amendment of the charter of that municipal corporation to authorize such a levy represents an additional tax voted by the electorate of that municipal corporation. For the purposes of this division, any measure adopted by a board of county commissioners pursuant to section 322.02, 324.02, 4504.02, or 5739.021 of the Revised Code, including those measures upheld by the electorate in a referendum conducted pursuant to section 322.021, 324.021, 4504.021, or 5739.022 of the Revised Code, shall not be considered an additional tax voted by the electorate.

Subject to division (G) of section 5705.29 of the Revised Code, money in a reserve balance account established by a county, township, or municipal corporation under section 5705.13 of the Revised Code shall not be considered an unencumbered balance or revenue under division (E)(3) or (4) of this section. Money in a reserve balance account established by a township under section 5705.132 of the Revised Code shall not be considered an unencumbered balance or revenue under division (E)(3) or (4) of this section.

If a county, township, or municipal corporation has created and maintains a nonexpendable trust fund under section 5705.131 of the Revised Code, the principal of the fund, and any additions to the principal arising from sources other than the reinvestment of investment earnings arising from such a fund, shall not be considered an unencumbered balance or revenue under division (E)(3) or (4) of this section. Only investment earnings arising from investment of the principal or investment of such additions to principal may be considered an unencumbered balance or revenue under those divisions.

(F) The total expenditures calculated pursuant to division (C) of this section, less the deductions authorized in divisions (D) and (E) of this section, shall be known as the "relative need" of the subdivision, for the purposes of this section.

(G) The budget commission shall total the relative need of all participating subdivisions in the county, and shall compute a relative need factor by dividing the total estimate of the undivided local government fund by the total relative need of all participating subdivisions.

(H) The relative need of each subdivision shall be multiplied by the relative need factor to determine the proportionate share of the subdivision in the undivided local government fund of the county; provided, that the maximum proportionate share of a county shall not exceed the following maximum percentages of the total estimate of the undivided local government fund governed by the relationship of the percentage of the population of the county that resides within municipal corporations within the county to the total population of the county as reported in the reports on population in Ohio by the department of development as of the twentieth day of July of the year in which the tax budget is filed with the budget commission:

Percentage of municipal population within the county:	Percentage share of the county shall not exceed:
Less than forty-one per cent	Sixty per cent
Forty-one per cent or more but less than eighty-one per cent	Fifty per cent
Eighty-one per cent or more	Thirty per cent

Where the proportionate share of the county exceeds the limitations established in this division, the budget commission shall adjust the proportionate shares determined pursuant to this division so that the proportionate share of the county does not exceed these limitations, and it shall increase the proportionate shares of all other subdivisions on a pro rata basis. In counties having a population of less than one hundred thousand, not less than ten per cent shall be distributed to the townships therein.

(I) The proportionate share of each subdivision in the undivided local government fund determined pursuant to division (H) of this section for any calendar year shall not be less than the product of the average of the percentages of the undivided local government fund of the county as apportioned to that subdivision for the calendar years 1968, 1969, and 1970, multiplied by the total amount of the undivided local government fund of the county apportioned pursuant to former section 5735.23 of the Revised Code for the calendar year 1970. For the purposes of this division, the total apportioned amount for the calendar year 1970 shall be the amount actually allocated to the county in 1970 from the state collected intangible tax as levied by section 5707.03 of the Revised Code and distributed pursuant to section 5725.24 of the Revised Code, plus the amount received by the county in the calendar year 1970 pursuant to division (B)(1) of former section 5739.21 of the Revised Code, and distributed pursuant to former section 5739.22 of the Revised Code. If the total amount of the undivided local government fund for any calendar year is less than the amount of the undivided local government fund apportioned pursuant to former section 5739.23 of the Revised Code for the calendar year 1970, the minimum amount guaranteed to each subdivision for that calendar year pursuant to this division shall be reduced on a basis proportionate to the amount by which the amount of the undivided local government fund for that calendar year is less than the amount of the undivided local government fund apportioned for the calendar year 1970.

(J) On the basis of such apportionment, the county auditor shall compute the percentage share of each such subdivision in the undivided local government fund and shall at the same time certify to the tax commissioner the percentage share of the county as a subdivision. No payment shall be made from the undivided local government fund, except in accordance with such percentage shares.

Within ten days after the budget commission has made its apportionment, whether conducted pursuant to section 5747.51 or 5747.53 of the Revised Code, the auditor shall publish a list of the subdivisions and the amount each is to receive from the undivided local government fund and the percentage share of each subdivision, in a newspaper or newspapers of countywide circulation, and send a copy of such allocation to the tax commissioner.

The county auditor shall also send by certified mail, return receipt requested, a copy of such allocation to the fiscal officer of each subdivision entitled to participate in the allocation of the undivided local government fund of the county. This copy shall constitute the official notice of the commission action referred to in section 5705.37 of the Revised Code.

All money received into the treasury of a subdivision from the undivided local government fund in a county treasury shall be paid into the general fund and used for the current operating expenses of the subdivision.

If a municipal corporation maintains a municipal university, such municipal university, when the board of trustees so requests the legislative authority of the municipal corporation, shall participate in the money apportioned to such municipal corporation from the total local government fund, however created and constituted, in such amount as requested by the board of trustees, provided such sum does not exceed nine per cent of the total amount paid to the municipal corporation.

If any public official fails to maintain the records required by sections 5747.50 to 5747.55 of the Revised Code or by the rules issued by the tax commissioner, the auditor of state, or the treasurer of state pursuant to such sections, or fails to comply with any law relating to the enforcement of such sections, the local government fund money allocated to the county shall be withheld until such time as the public official has complied with such sections or such law or the rules issued pursuant thereto.

(2006 H 385, eff. 9–21–06; 1998 H 426, eff. 7–22–98; 1995 H 86, eff. 11–1–95; 1985 H 201, eff. 7–1–85; 1985 H 146; 1983 H 260; 1976 H 920; 1971 H 475)

Historical and Statutory Notes

Ed. Note: 5747.51 contains provisions analogous to former 5739.23, repealed by 1971 H 475, eff. 12–20–71.

Amendment Note: 2006 H 385 added the last sentence in the second paragraph of division (E)(4).

Amendment Note: 1998 H 426 rewrote the second and third paragraphs in division (E)(4); and made other nonsubstantive changes. Prior to amendment, the second and third paragraph in division (E)(4) read:

"Money in a reserve balance account established by a county or township under section 305.23, 505.83, or 505.831 of the Revised Code or by a municipal corporation pursuant to an ordinance or resolution that has been included as a reserve balance in the county's, township's, or municipal corporations's budget under section 5705.29 of the Revised Code shall not be considered an unencumbered balance or revenue under division (E)(3) or (4) of this section.

"If a municipal corporation has created an maintains a fund exclusively for the purpose of investing the principal of the fund and using the investment earnings to fund expenditures, the principal of the fund, and any additions to the principal arising from sources other than the reinvestment of investment earnings arising from such a fund, shall not be considered an unencumbered balance or revenue under division (E)(3) or (4) of this section. Only investment earnings arising from investment of the principal or additions to principal may be considered an unencumbered balance or revenue under those divisions."

Amendment Note: 1995 H 86 added the second and third paragraphs to (E)(4).

Library References

Counties ⚖=195.
Taxation ⚖=1104.
Westlaw Topic Nos. 104, 371.
C.J.S. Counties § 227.
C.J.S. Taxation § 1110.

5747.53 Alternative method of apportioning fund by county budget commission

(A) As used in this section:

(1) "City, located wholly or partially in the county, with the greatest population" means the city, located wholly or partially in the county, with the greatest population residing in the county; however, if the county budget commission on or before January 1, 1998, adopted an alternative method of apportionment that was approved by the legislative authority of the city, located partially in the county, with the greatest population but not the greatest population residing in the county, "city, located wholly or partially in the county, with the greatest population" means the city, located wholly or partially in the county, with the greatest population whether residing in the county or not, if this alternative meaning is adopted by action of the board of county commissioners and a majority of the boards of township trustees and legislative authorities of municipal corporations located wholly or partially in the county.

(2) "Participating political subdivision" means a municipal corporation or township that satisfies all of the following:

(a) It is located wholly or partially in the county.

(b) It is not the city, located wholly or partially in the county, with the greatest population.

(c) Undivided local government fund moneys are apportioned to it under the county's alternative method or formula of apportionment in the current calendar year.

(B) In lieu of the method of apportionment of the undivided local government fund of the county provided by section 5747.51 of the Revised Code, the county budget commission may provide for the apportionment of the fund under an alternative method or on a formula basis as authorized by this section.

Except as otherwise provided in division (C) of this section, the alternative method of apportionment shall have first been approved by all of the following governmental units: the board of county commissioners; the legislative authority of the city, located wholly or partially in the county, with the greatest population; and a majority of the boards of township trustees and legislative authorities of municipal corporations, located wholly or partially in the county, excluding the legislative authority of the city, located wholly or partially in the county, with the greatest population. In granting or denying approval for an alternative method of apportionment, the board of county commissioners, boards of township trustees, and legislative authorities of municipal corporations shall act by motion. A motion to approve shall be passed upon a majority vote of the members of a board of county commissioners, board of township trustees, or legislative authority of a municipal corporation, shall take effect immediately, and need not be published.

Any alternative method of apportionment adopted and approved under this division may be revised, amended, or repealed in the same manner as it may be adopted and approved. If an alternative method of apportionment adopted and approved under this division is repealed, the undivided local government fund of the county shall be apportioned among the subdivisions eligible to participate in the fund, commencing in the ensuing calendar year, under the apportionment provided in section 5747.52 of the Revised Code, unless the repeal occurs by operation of division (C) of this section or a new method for apportionment of the fund is provided in the action of repeal.

(C) This division applies only in counties in which the city, located wholly or partially in the county, with the greatest population has a population of twenty thousand or less and a population that is less than fifteen per cent of the total population of the county. In such a county, the legislative authorities or boards of township trustees of two or more participating political subdivisions, which together have a population residing in the county that is a majority of the total population of the county, each may adopt a resolution to exclude the approval otherwise required of the legislative authority of the city, located wholly or partially in the county, with the greatest population. All of the resolutions to exclude that approval shall be adopted not later than the first M onday of August of the year preceding the calendar year in which distributions are to be made under an alternative method of apportionment.

A motion granting or denying approval of an alternative method of apportionment under this division shall be adopted by a majority vote of the members of the board of county commissioners and by a majority vote of a majority of the boards of township trustees and legislative authorities of the municipal corporations located wholly or partially in the county, other than the city, located wholly or partially in the county, with the greatest population, shall take effect immediately, and need not be published. The alternative method of apportionment under this division shall be adopted and approved annually, not later than the first

Monday of August of the year preceding the calendar year in which distributions are to be made under it. A motion granting approval of an alternative method of apportionment under this division repeals any existing alternative method of apportionment, effective with distributions to be made from the fund in the ensuing calendar year. An alternative method of apportionment under this division shall not be revised or amended after the first Monday of August of the year preceding the calendar year in which distributions are to be made under it.

(D) In determining an alternative method of apportionment authorized by this section, the county budget commission may include in the method any factor considered to be appropriate and reliable, in the sole discretion of the county budget commission.

(E) The limitations set forth in section 5747.51 of the Revised Code, stating the maximum amount that the county may receive from the undivided local government fund and the minimum amount the townships in counties having a population of less than one hundred thousand may receive from the fund, are applicable to any alternative method of apportionment authorized under this section.

(F) On the basis of any alternative method of apportionment adopted and approved as authorized by this section, as certified by the auditor to the county treasurer, the county treasurer shall make distribution of the money in the undivided local government fund to each subdivision eligible to participate in the fund, and the auditor, when the amount of those shares is in the custody of the treasurer in the amounts so computed to be due the respective subdivisions, shall at the same time certify to the tax commissioner the percentage share of the county as a subdivision. All money received into the treasury of a subdivision from the undivided local government fund in a county treasury shall be paid into the general fund and used for the current operating expenses of the subdivision. If a municipal corporation maintains a municipal university, the university, when the board of trustees so requests the legislative authority of the municipal corporation, shall participate in the money apportioned to the municipal corporation from the total local government fund, however created and constituted, in the amount requested by the board of trustees, provided that amount does not exceed nine per cent of the total amount paid to the municipal corporation.

(G) The actions of the county budget commission taken pursuant to this section are final and may not be appealed to the board of tax appeals, except on the issues of abuse of discretion and failure to comply with the formula.

(2002 H 329, eff. 8-29-02; 1999 H 185, eff. 7-26-99; 1991 H 298, eff. 7-26-91; 1985 H 201; 1975 H 1; 1971 H 475)

Uncodified Law

2002 H 329, § 3 and 4, eff. 8-29-02, read:

Section 3. (A) Notwithstanding the date specified in division (C) of section 5705.321, division (C) of section 5747.53, or division (C) of section 5747.63 of the Revised Code, as amended by this act, an alternative method of apportionment may be adopted and approved as provided in one or more of those divisions not later than September 2, 2002, for distributions of County Library and Local Government Support Fund, Undivided Local Government Fund, or Undivided Local Government Revenue Assistance Fund moneys during 2003.

(B) Notwithstanding the completion date specified in section 5705.27 of the Revised Code, the day by which a county budget commission must complete its work in 2002 in a county in which an alternative method of apportionment is adopted and approved as provided in division (C) of section 5705.321, division (C) of section 5747.53, or division (C) of section 5747.63 of the Revised Code, as amended by this act, is hereby extended to October 1, 2002, unless the Tax Commissioner, for good cause, extends the time for completing the work to a later date.

Section 4. Section 3 of this act is hereby repealed, effective December 31, 2002.

Historical and Statutory Notes

Ed. Note: 5747.53 contains provisions analogous to former 5739.232, repealed by 1971 H 475, eff. 12-20-71.

Amendment Note: 2002 H 329 rewrote the section, which prior thereto read:

"(A) In lieu of the method of apportionment of the undivided local government revenue assistance fund of the county provided by section 5747.62 of the Revised Code, the county budget commission may provide for the apportionment of such fund under an alternative method or on a formula basis as authorized by this section. Such alternative method of apportionment shall have first been approved by all of the following governmental units: the board of county commissioners; the legislative authority of the city, located wholly or partially in the county, with the greatest population; and a majority of the boards of township trustees and legislative authorities of municipal corporations, located wholly or partially in the county, excluding the legislative authority of the city with the greatest population. In granting or denying such approval, the board of county commissioners, boards of township trustees, and legislative authorities of municipal corporations shall act by motion. A motion to approve shall be passed upon a majority vote of the members of a board of county commissioners, board of township trustees, or legislative authority of a municipal corporation, shall take effect immediately, and need not be published. Any method of apportionment adopted and approved under this section may be revised, amended, or repealed in the same manner as it may be adopted and approved. In the event a method of apportionment adopted and approved under this section is repealed, the undivided local government revenue assistance fund of the county shall be apportioned among the subdivisions eligible to participate therein, commencing in the ensuing fiscal year, under the apportionment provided in section 5747.62 of the Revised Code, unless a new method for apportionment of such fund is provided in the action of repeal.

"As used in this division, the term 'legislative authority of the city, located wholly or partially in the county, with the greatest population' means the legislative authority of the city, located wholly or partially in the county, with the greatest population residing in the county; however, if the county budget commission on or before January 1, 1998, adopted an alternative method of apportionment which was approved by the legislative authority of the city, located partially in the county, with the greatest population but not the greatest population residing in the county, the term shall be deemed to mean the legislative authority of the city, located wholly or partially in the county, with the greatest population whether residing in the county or not, if such alternative meaning is adopted by action of the board of county commissioners and a majority of the boards of township trustees and legislative authorities of municipal corporations located wholly or partially in the county.

"(B) In determining the alternative method of apportionment authorized by this section, the county budget commission may include in such method any factor considered to be appropriate and reliable, in the sole discretion of the county budget commission, but the commission shall give special consideration to the needs of villages incorporated after January 1, 1980.

"(C) The limitations set forth in section 5747.62 of the Revised Code, stating the maximum amount that the county may receive from such fund and the minimum amount the townships in counties having a population of less than one hundred thousand may receive from such fund, are applicable to any alternative apportionment authorized under this section.

"(D) On the basis of any alternative apportionment adopted and approved as authorized by this section, as certified by the auditor to the county treasurer, the county treasurer shall make distribution of the money in the undivided local government revenue assistance fund to each subdivision eligible to participate in such fund, and the auditor, when the amount of such shares is in the custody of the treasurer in the amounts so computed to be due the respective subdivisions, shall at the same time certify to the tax commissioner the percentage share of the county as a subdivision. All money received by a subdivision from the county undivided local government revenue assistance fund shall be paid into the subdivision's general fund and used for the current operating expenses.

"(E) The actions of the budget commission taken pursuant to this section are final and may not be appealed to the board of tax appeals, except on the issues of abuse of discretion and failure to comply with the formula."

Amendment Note: 1999 H 185 added the second paragraph in division (A).

Library References

Counties ⌾195.
Taxation ⌾1104.
Westlaw Topic Nos. 104, 371.
C.J.S. Counties § 227.
C.J.S. Taxation § 1110.

5747.54 Conditions upon payment of share to county from local government fund

The tax commissioner shall not distribute local government fund money to any county where the county auditor has failed to certify to the tax commissioner the percentage share of the undivided local government fund of the county as a subdivision for the year for which distribution is to be made. The director shall withhold from such county the percentage of the amount distributable thereto that constitutes the share of the county as a subdivision so long as such county is indebted or otherwise obligated to the state, until such indebtedness or other obligation has been duly paid, but no distribution of such percentage share of the local government fund shall be withheld unless an itemized statement of such indebtedness is furnished the county auditor of the county from which the indebtedness is due at least thirty days prior to the withholding of the distribution.

Any indebtedness or obligation of the state to a county shall be deducted from the amount owing to the state by such county in determining the indebtedness or obligation as to which distribution is withheld.

(1985 H 201, eff. 7–1–85; 1983 H 291; 1973 H 1; 1971 H 475)

Historical and Statutory Notes

Ed. Note: 5747.54 contains provisions analogous to former 5739.24, repealed by 1971 H 475, eff. 12–20–71.

5747.55 Appeal to board of tax appeals

The action of the county budget commission under sections 5747.51 and 5747.62 of the Revised Code may be appealed to the board of tax appeals in the manner and with the effect provided in section 5705.37 of the Revised Code, in accordance with the following rules:

(A) The notice of appeal shall be signed by the authorized fiscal officer and shall set forth in clear and concise language:

(1) A statement of the action of the budget commission appealed from, and the date of the receipt by the subdivision of the official certificate or notice of such action;

(2) The error or errors the taxing district believes the budget commission made;

(3) The specific relief sought by the taxing district.

(B) The notice of appeal shall have attached thereto:

(1) A certified copy of the resolution of the taxing authority authorizing the fiscal officer to file the appeal;

(2) An exact copy of the official certificate, or notice of the action of the budget commission appealed from;

(3) An exact copy of the budget request filed with the budget commission by the complaining subdivision, with the date of filing noted thereon.

(C) There shall also be attached to the notice of appeal a statement showing:

(1) The name of the fund involved, the total amount in dollars allocated, and the exact amount in dollars allocated to each participating subdivision;

(2) The amount in dollars which the complaining subdivision believes it should have received;

(3) The name of each participating subdivision, as well as the name and address of the fiscal officer thereof, that the complaining subdivision believes received more than its proper share of the allocation, and the exact amount in dollars of such alleged over-allocation.

(D) Only the participating subdivisions named pursuant to division (C) of this section are to be considered as appellees before the board of tax appeals and no change shall, in any amount, be made in the amount allocated to participating subdivisions not appellees.

(E) The total of the undivided local government fund or undivided local government revenue assistance fund to be allocated by the board of tax appeals upon appeal is the total of that fund allocated by the budget commission to those subdivisions which are appellants and appellees before the board of tax appeals.

(1989 H 111, eff. 7–1–89; 1971 H 475)

Historical and Statutory Notes

Ed. Note: 5747.55 contains provisions analogous to former 5739.25, repealed by 1971 H 475, eff. 12–20–71.

Library References

Counties ⌾159–161, 195.
Taxation ⌾1104.
Westlaw Topic Nos. 104, 371.
C.J.S. Counties § 194–196, 227.
C.J.S. Taxation § 1110.

ORDER OF CREDITS

5747.98 Priority of credits

(A) To provide a uniform procedure for calculating the amount of tax due under section 5747.02 of the Revised Code, a taxpayer shall claim any credits to which the taxpayer is entitled in the following order:

(1) The retirement income credit under division (B) of section 5747.055 of the Revised Code;

(2) The senior citizen credit under division (C) of section 5747.05 of the Revised Code;

(3) The lump sum distribution credit under division (D) of section 5747.05 of the Revised Code;

(4) The dependent care credit under section 5747.054 of the Revised Code;

(5) The lump sum retirement income credit under division (C) of section 5747.055 of the Revised Code;

(6) The lump sum retirement income credit under division (D) of section 5747.055 of the Revised Code;

(7) The lump sum retirement income credit under division (E) of section 5747.055 of the Revised Code;

(8) The low-income credit under section 5747.056 of the Revised Code;

(9) The credit for displaced workers who pay for job training under section 5747.27 of the Revised Code;

(10) The campaign contribution credit under section 5747.29 of the Revised Code;

(11) The twenty-dollar personal exemption credit under section 5747.022 of the Revised Code;

(12) The joint filing credit under division (G) of section 5747.05 of the Revised Code;

(13) The nonresident credit under division (A) of section 5747.05 of the Revised Code;

(14) The credit for a resident's out-of-state income under division (B) of section 5747.05 of the Revised Code;

(15) The credit for employers that enter into agreements with child day-care centers under section 5747.34 of the Revised Code;

(16) The credit for employers that reimburse employee child care expenses under section 5747.36 of the Revised Code;

(17) The credit for adoption of a minor child under section 5747.37 of the Revised Code;

(18) The credit for purchases of lights and reflectors under section 5747.38 of the Revised Code;

(19) The job retention credit under division (B) of section 5747.058 of the Revised Code;

(20) The credit for purchases of new manufacturing machinery and equipment under section 5747.26 or section 5747.261 of the Revised Code;

(21) The second credit for purchases of new manufacturing machinery and equipment and the credit for using Ohio coal under section 5747.31 of the Revised Code;

(22) The job training credit under section 5747.39 of the Revised Code;

(23) The enterprise zone credit under section 5709.66 of the Revised Code;

(24) The credit for the eligible costs associated with a voluntary action under section 5747.32 of the Revised Code;

(25) The credit for employers that establish on-site child day-care centers under section 5747.35 of the Revised Code;

(26) The ethanol plant investment credit under section 5747.75 of the Revised Code;

(27) The credit for purchases of qualifying grape production property under section 5747.28 of the Revised Code;

(28) The export sales credit under section 5747.057 of the Revised Code;

(29) The credit for research and development and technology transfer investors under section 5747.33 of the Revised Code;

(30) The enterprise zone credits under section 5709.65 of the Revised Code;

(31) The research and development credit under section 5747.331 of the Revised Code;

(32) The refundable credit for rehabilitating a historic building under section 5747.76 of the Revised Code;

(33) The refundable jobs creation credit under division (A) of section 5747.058 of the Revised Code;

(34) The refundable credit for taxes paid by a qualifying entity granted under section 5747.059 of the Revised Code;

(35) The refundable credits for taxes paid by a qualifying pass-through entity granted under division (J) of section 5747.08 of the Revised Code;

(36) The refundable credit for tax withheld under division (B)(1) of section 5747.062 of the Revised Code;

(37) The refundable credit under section 5747.80 of the Revised Code for losses on loans made to the Ohio venture capital program under sections 150.01 to 150.10 of the Revised Code.

(B) For any credit, except the credits enumerated in divisions (A)(32) to (37) of this section and the credit granted under division (I) of section 5747.08 of the Revised Code, the amount of the credit for a taxable year shall not exceed the tax due after allowing for any other credit that precedes it in the order required under this section. Any excess amount of a particular credit may be carried forward if authorized under the section creating that credit. Nothing in this chapter shall be construed to allow a taxpayer to claim, directly or indirectly, a credit more than once for a taxable year.

(2006 H 149, eff. 4–4–07; 2006 S 321, eff. 6–5–06; 2005 H 66, eff. 6–30–05; 2004 H 11, eff. 5–18–05; 2003 H 1, eff. 7–9–03; 2002 S 180, eff. 4–9–03; 2002 S 226, eff. 9–17–02; 2002 S 144, eff. 3–21–02; 2001 H 405, eff. 12–13–01; 2000 S 287, eff. 12–21–00; 2000 H 484, eff. 10–5–00; 1999 S 3, eff. 10–5–99; 1999 S 4, eff. 8–19–99; 1998 H 770, eff. 9–16–98; 1997 H 215, eff. 9–29–97; 1996 S 18, eff. 11–19–96; 1996 H 441, eff. 8–22–96; 1995 H 343, eff. 3–5–96; 1995 S 188, eff. 7–19–95; 1995 S 8, eff. 8–23–95; 1994 H 715, eff. 7–22–94; 1994 S 271, eff. 7–22–94)

Uncodified Law

2006 S 321, § 503.03: See *Baldwin's Ohio Revised Code Annotated*, Uncodified Law under RC 5747.80.

1999 S 3, § 12: See *Baldwin's Ohio Revised Code Annotated*, Uncodified Law under 5747.31.

1997 H 215, § 211: See *Baldwin's Ohio Revised Code Annotated*, Uncodified Law under 5747.057.

1995 S 8, § 10: See *Baldwin's Ohio Revised Code Annotated*, Uncodified Law under 5747.29.

1994 S 271, § 3, eff. 4–22–94, reads: Section 1 of this act first applies to taxable year 1994 for the state income tax.

Historical and Statutory Notes

Amendment Note: 2006 S 321 deleted text of division (A)(20); redesignated divisions (A)(21) through (A)(37) as divisions (A)(20) through (A)(36); rewrote former division (A)(37); and changed references in division (B) to reflect division redesignations. Prior to amendment, the text of former division (A)(20) and (A)(37) read:

"(20) The credit for losses on loans made under the Ohio venture capital program under sections 150.01 to 150.10 of the Revised Code if the taxpayer elected a nonrefundable credit under section 150.07 of the Revised Code;"

"(37) The refundable credit for losses on loans made to the Ohio venture capital program under sections 150.01 to 150.10 of the Revised Code if the taxpayer elected a refundable credit under section 150.07 of the Revised Code."

Amendment Note: 2005 H 66 inserted new text in division (A)(8); redesignated former divisions (A)(8) through (A)(36) as divisions (A)(9) through (A)(37); substituted "(A)(33)" for "(A)(32)" and "(37)" for "(36)" in the first sentence of division (B).

Amendment Note: 2004 H 11 substituted "care" for "day care" in division (A)(15).

Amendment Note: 2003 H 1 inserted new division (A)(31); redesignated former divisions (A)(31) through (A)(35) as new divisions (A)(32) through (A)(36) respectively; substituted "(32)" for "(31)" after "(A)" and "(36)" for "(35)" before "of this section" in division (B).

Amendment Note: 2002 S 180 deleted "manufacturing investments under section 5747.051" following "The credit for" in division (A)(19); added division (A)(35); and deleted "refundable" preceding "credits" in division (B).

Amendment Note: 2002 S 226 added new division (A)(34); and deleted "divisions (A)(31), (32), and (33) of" after "enumerated in" in the first sentence of division (B).

Amendment Note: 2002 S 144 added new division (A)(26) and redesignated prior divisions (A)(26) through (A)(32) as new divisions (A)(27) through (A)(33), respectively; and substituted "(31)" for "(30)" and inserted ", and (33)" after "(32)" in the first sentence of division (B).

Amendment Note: 2001 H 405 added new division (A)(18); redesignated former divisions (A)(18) through (A)(31) as new divisions (A)(19) through (A)(32); inserted "division (A) of" before "section 5747.058" in new division (A)(30); and deleted "29" before "30" and inserted "and 32" in the first sentence of division (B).

Amendment Note: 2000 S 287 added new division (A)(21); redesignated former divisions (A)(21) through (A)(30) as new divisions (A)(22) through (A)(31); and made corresponding corrective changes in division (B).

Amendment Note: 2000 H 484 added new division (A)(17) and redesignated former divisions (A)(17) to (A)(29) as new divisions (A)(18) to (A)(30); and deleted "(27)" before "(28)" and "and" before "(29)" and inserted "and (30)" in division (B).

Amendment Note: 1999 S 3 inserted "and the credit for using Ohio coal" in division (A)(19).

Amendment Note: 1999 S 4 renumbered former divisions (A)(2) through (A)(16) as new divisions (A)(1) through (A)(15); added new division (A)(16); and made other nonsubstantive changes.

Amendment Note: 1998 H 770 deleted "jobs creations credit and the refundable credit for taxes paid by a qualifying entity" following "except the refundable" in division (B); inserted "credits enumerated in divisions (A)(27), (28), and (29) of this section and the credit granted under division (I) of section 5747.08 of the Revised Code" in division (B); and added the third sentence in division (B).

Amendment Note: 1997 H 215 added divisions (A)(14) and (A)(15); redesignated former divisions (A)(14) through (A)(18) as new divisions (A)(16) through (A)(20); added division (A)(21); redesignated former divisions (A)(19) through (A)(22) as new divisions (A)(22) through (A)(26); added division (A)(27); and inserted "and the refundable credit for taxes paid by a qualifying entity" in division (B).

Amendment Note: 1996 S 18 added division (A)(20), and redesignated former divisions (A)(20) and (21) as (A)(21) and (22), respectively.

Amendment Note: 1996 H 441 added division (A)(19); and redesignated former divisions (A)(19) through (A)(21) as divisions (A)(20) through (A)(22).

Amendment Note: 1995 H 343 inserted "or section 5747.261" in division (A)(15).

Amendment Note: 1995 S 188 added divisions (A)(15) through (A)(17); and redesignated former divisions (A)(15) through (A)(18) as divisions (A)(18) through (A)(21), respectively.

Amendment Note: 1995 S 8 added division (A)(9); and renumbered the successive paragraphs in division (A) accordingly.

Library References

Taxation ⚖1047.
Westlaw Topic No. 371.
C.J.S. Taxation § 1098.

OHIO REVISED CODE
TITLE 58
TRUSTS

Complete to February 28, 2007

CHAPTER		CHAPTER	
5801	General Provisions	5812	Uniform Principal and Income Act (1997)
5802	Judicial Proceedings	5813	Institutional Trust Funds Act
5803	Representation	5814	Ohio Transfers to Minors Act
5804	Creation, Validity, Modification and Termination of Trust	5815	Fiduciary Law
5805	Spendthrift and Discretionary Trusts		
5806	Revocable Trusts		
5807	Office of Trustee		
5808	Powers and Duties of Trustee		
5809	Prudent Investor Act		
5810	Remedies for Breach of Trust		
5811	Miscellaneous Provisions		

Law Review and Journal Commentaries

The modification and termination of irrevocable trusts under the Ohio uniform trust code. Alan Newman, 16 Prob L J Ohio 1 (September/October 2005).

Treatment of supplemental needs trusts under the OUTC. Richard Davis, 16 Prob L J Ohio 17 (September/October 2005).

CHAPTER 5801

GENERAL PROVISIONS

Section
5801.01 Definitions
5801.011 Short title
5801.02 Applicability of title
5801.03 Notice or knowledge of fact defined
5801.04 Scope; mandatory rules; exceptions
5801.05 Applicability of common law of trusts and principles of equity
5801.06 Governing law
5801.07 Principal place of administration
5801.08 Notice; waiver of notice
5801.09 Notice to other beneficiaries; persons treated as beneficiaries
5801.10 Parties to agreements; effect on creditor rights

5801.01 Definitions

As used in Chapters 5801. to 5811. of the Revised Code:

(A) "Action," with respect to an act of a trustee, includes a failure to act.

(B) "Ascertainable standard" means a standard relating to an individual's health, education, support, or maintenance within the meaning of section 2041(b)(1)(A) or 2514(c)(1) of the Internal Revenue Code.

(C) "Beneficiary" means a person that has a present or future beneficial interest in a trust, whether vested or contingent, or that, in a capacity other than that of trustee, holds a power of appointment over trust property, or a charitable organization that is expressly designated in the terms of the trust to receive distributions. "Beneficiary" does not include any charitable organization that is not expressly designated in the terms of the trust to receive distributions, but to whom the trustee may in its discretion make distributions.

(D) "Beneficiary surrogate" means a person, other than a trustee, designated by the settlor in the trust instrument to receive notices, information, and reports otherwise required to be provided to a current beneficiary under divisions (B)(8) and (9) of section 5801.04 of the Revised Code.

(E) "Charitable trust" means a trust, or portion of a trust, created for a charitable purpose described in division (A) of section 5804.05 of the Revised Code.

(F) "Current beneficiary" means a beneficiary that, on the date the beneficiary's qualification is determined, is a distributee or permissible distributee of trust income or principal.

(G) "Environmental law" means a federal, state, or local law, rule, regulation, or ordinance relating to protection of the environment.

(H) "Guardian of the estate" means a guardian appointed by a court to administer the estate of any individual or to serve as conservator of the property of an individual eighteen years of age or older under section 2111.021 of the Revised Code.

(I) "Guardian of the person" means a guardian appointed by a court to make decisions regarding the support, care, education, health, and welfare of any individual or to serve as conservator of the person of an individual eighteen years of age or older under section 2111.021 of the Revised Code. "Guardian of the person" does not include a guardian ad litem.

(J) "Internal Revenue Code" means the "Internal Revenue Code of 1986," 100 Stat. 2085, 26 U.S.C. 1 et seq., as amended.

(K) "Interests of the beneficiaries" means the beneficial interests provided in the terms of the trust.

(L) "Jurisdiction," with respect to a geographic area, includes a state or country.

(M) "Mandatory distribution" means a distribution of income or principal, including a distribution upon termination of the trust, that the trustee is required to make to a beneficiary under the terms of the trust. Mandatory distributions do not include distributions that a trustee is directed or authorized to make pursuant to a support or other standard, regardless of whether the terms of the trust provide that the trustee "may" or "shall" make the distributions pursuant to a support or other standard.

(N) "Person" means an individual, corporation, business trust, estate, trust, partnership, limited liability company, association, joint venture, government, governmental agency or instrumentality, public corporation, or any other legal or commercial entity.

(O) "Power of withdrawal" means a presently exercisable general power of appointment other than a power exercisable by a trustee that is limited by an ascertainable standard or that is exercisable by another person only upon consent of the trustee or a person holding an adverse interest.

(P) "Property" means anything or any interest in anything that may be the subject of ownership.

(Q) "Qualified beneficiary" means a beneficiary to whom, on the date the beneficiary's qualification is determined, any of the following applies:

(1) The beneficiary is a distributee or permissible distributee of trust income or principal.

(2) The beneficiary would be a distributee or permissible distributee of trust income or principal if the interests of the distributees described in division (Q)(1) of this section terminated on that date, but the termination of those interests would not cause the trust to terminate.

(3) The beneficiary would be a distributee or permissible distributee of trust income or principal if the trust terminated on that date.

(R) "Revocable," as applied to a trust, means revocable at the time of determination by the settlor alone or by the settlor with the consent of any person other than a person holding an adverse interest. A trust's characterization as revocable is not affected by the settlor's lack of capacity to exercise the power of revocation, regardless of whether an agent of the settlor under a power of attorney, or a guardian of the person or estate of the settlor, is serving.

(S) "Settlor" means a person, including a testator, who creates, or contributes property to, a trust. If more than one person creates or contributes property to a trust, each person is a settlor of the portion of the trust property attributable to that person's contribution except to the extent another person has the power to revoke or withdraw that portion.

(T) "Spendthrift provision" means a term of a trust that restrains both voluntary and involuntary transfer of a beneficiary's interest.

(U) "State" means a state of the United States, the District of Columbia, the Commonwealth of Puerto Rico, a territory or possession of the United States, or an Indian tribe or band recognized by federal law or formally acknowledged by a state.

(V) "Terms of a trust" means the manifestation of the settlor's intent regarding a trust's provisions as expressed in the trust instrument or as may be established by other evidence that would be admissible in a judicial proceeding.

(W) "Trust instrument" means an instrument executed by the settlor that contains terms of the trust and any amendments to that instrument.

(X) "Trustee" includes an original, additional, and successor trustee and a cotrustee.

(Y)(1) "Wholly discretionary trust" means a trust to which all of the following apply:

(a) The trust is irrevocable.

(b) Distributions of income or principal from the trust may or shall be made to or for the benefit of the beneficiary only at the trustee's discretion.

(c) The beneficiary does not have a power of withdrawal from the trust.

(d) The terms of the trust use "sole," "absolute," "uncontrolled," or language of similar import to describe the trustee's discretion to make distributions to or for the benefit of the beneficiary.

(e) The terms of the trust do not provide any standards to guide the trustee in exercising its discretion to make distributions to or for the benefit of the beneficiary.

(f) The beneficiary is not the settlor, the trustee, or a cotrustee.

(g) The beneficiary does not have the power to become the trustee or a cotrustee.

(2) A trust may be a wholly discretionary trust with respect to one or more but less than all beneficiaries.

(3) If a beneficiary has a power of withdrawal, the trust may be a wholly discretionary trust with respect to that beneficiary during any period in which the beneficiary may not exercise the power. During a period in which the beneficiary may exercise the power, both of the following apply:

(a) The portion of the trust the beneficiary may withdraw may not be a wholly discretionary trust with respect to that beneficiary;

(b) The portion of the trust the beneficiary may not withdraw may be a wholly discretionary trust with respect to that beneficiary.

(4) If the beneficiary and one or more others have made contributions to the trust, the portion of the trust attributable to the beneficiary's contributions may not be a wholly discretionary trust with respect to that beneficiary, but the portion of the trust attributable to the contributions of others may be a wholly discretionary trust with respect to that beneficiary. If a beneficiary has a power of withdrawal, then upon the lapse, release, or waiver of the power, the beneficiary is treated as having made contributions to the trust only to the extent the value of the property affected by the lapse, release, or waiver exceeds the greatest of the following amounts:

(a) The amount specified in section 2041(b)(2) or 2514(e) of the Internal Revenue Code;

(b) If the donor of the property subject to the beneficiary's power of withdrawal is not married at the time of the transfer of the property to the trust, the amount specified in section 2503(b) of the Internal Revenue Code;

(c) If the donor of the property subject to the beneficiary's power of withdrawal is married at the time of the transfer of the property to the trust, twice the amount specified in section 2503(b) of the Internal Revenue Code.

(5) Notwithstanding divisions (Y)(1)(f) and (g) of this section, a trust may be a wholly discretionary trust if the beneficiary is, or has the power to become, a trustee only with respect to the management or the investment of the trust assets, and not with respect to making discretionary distribution decisions. With respect to a trust established for the benefit of an individual who is blind or disabled as defined in 42 U.S.C. 1382c(a)(2) or (3), as amended, a wholly discretionary trust may include either or both of the following:

(a) Precatory language regarding its intended purpose of providing supplemental goods and services to or for the benefit of the beneficiary, and not to supplant benefits from public assistance programs;

(b) A prohibition against providing food, clothing, and shelter to the beneficiary.

(2006 H 416, eff. 1-1-07)

Historical and Statutory Notes

Uniform Law: This section is analogous to § 103 of the Uniform Trust Code. See 7C Uniform Laws Annotated, Master Edition or ULA database on Westlaw.

Editor's Comment

2006:

RC 5801.01 includes four terms not found in the Uniform Trust Code, these being "beneficiary surrogate," "current beneficiary," "mandatory distribution," and "wholly discretionary trust."

RC 5801.01(C) also provides that the term "beneficiary" includes charitable trusts expressly designated to receive distributions.

Cross References

Application to existing relationships, 5811.03
Appointment of representative by court, 5803.05
Creation of oral trust, 5804.07
Duty to administer trust, 5808.01
Electronic records and signatures, 5811.02
General powers of trustee, 5808.15
Laws applicable to testamentary trusts, 2109.69
Modification or termination of noncharitable irrevocable trust by consent, 5804.11
Requirements for creation, 5804.02
Uniformity of application and construction, 5811.01

Library References

Baldwin's Ohio Legislative Service Annotated, 2006 H 416 LSC Analysis, p 3/L-1709

Law Review and Journal Commentaries

Beneficiary information and notices. Susan S. Locke, 17 Prob L J Ohio 5 (September/October 2006).

The evolution of Ohio trust law from the English common law to the Ohio trust code. Joanne E. Hindel, 17 Prob L J Ohio 1 (September/October 2006).

Ohio adopts new trust code—an overview of the new Ohio trust code and house bill 416. Alan Newman, 20 Ohio Law 9 (September/October 2006).

5801.011 Short title

Chapters 5801. to 5811. of the Revised Code may be cited as the Ohio trust code.

(2006 H 416, eff. 1–1–07)

Historical and Statutory Notes

Uniform Law: This section is analogous to § 101 of the Uniform Trust Code. See 7C Uniform Laws Annotated, Master Edition or ULA database on Westlaw.

Library References

Baldwin's Ohio Legislative Service Annotated, 2006 H 416 LSC Analysis, p 3/L-1709

5801.02 Applicability of title

Except as otherwise provided in any provision of Chapters 5801. to 5811. of the Revised Code, those chapters apply to charitable and noncharitable inter vivos express trusts and to trusts created pursuant to a statute, judgment, or decree that requires the trust to be administered in the manner of an express trust. Chapters 5801. to 5811. of the Revised Code apply to testamentary trusts to the extent provided by section 2109.69 of the Revised Code.

(2006 H 416, eff. 1–1–07)

Historical and Statutory Notes

Uniform Law: This section is analogous to § 102 of the Uniform Trust Code. See 7C Uniform Laws Annotated, Master Edition or ULA database on Westlaw.

Editor's Comment

2006:

RC 5801.02 differs from the Uniform Trust Code in part by its provision that its application to testamentary trusts is "to the extent provided by section 2109.69 of the Revised Code."

Library References

Baldwin's Ohio Legislative Service Annotated, 2006 H 416 LSC Analysis, p 3/L-1709

5801.03 Notice or knowledge of fact defined

(A) Subject to division (B) of this section, a person has knowledge of a fact if any of the following apply:

(1) The person has actual knowledge of the fact.

(2) The person has received notice or notification of the fact.

(3) From all the facts and circumstances known to the person at the time in question, the person has reason to know the fact.

(B) An organization that conducts activities through employees has notice or knowledge of a fact involving a trust only from the time an employee having responsibility to act for the trust received the information or the information would have been brought to the employee's attention if the organization had exercised reasonable diligence. An organization exercises reasonable diligence if it maintains reasonable routines for communicating significant information to the employee having responsibility to act for the trust and there is reasonable compliance with the routines. Reasonable diligence does not require an employee of the organization to communicate information unless the communication is part of the individual's regular duties or the individual knows a matter involving the trust would be materially affected by the information.

(2006 H 416, eff. 1–1–07)

Historical and Statutory Notes

Uniform Law: This section is analogous to § 104 of the Uniform Trust Code. See 7C Uniform Laws Annotated, Master Edition or ULA database on Westlaw.

Library References

Baldwin's Ohio Legislative Service Annotated, 2006 H 416 LSC Analysis, p 3/L-1709

5801.04 Scope; mandatory rules; exceptions

(A) Except as otherwise provided in the terms of the trust, Chapters 5801. to 5811. of the Revised Code govern the duties and powers of a trustee, relations among trustees, and the rights and interests of a beneficiary.

(B) The terms of a trust prevail over any provision of Chapters 5801. to 5811. of the Revised Code except the following:

(1) The requirements for creating a trust;

(2) The duty of a trustee to act in good faith and in accordance with the purposes of the trust;

(3) The requirement that the trust have a purpose that is lawful, not contrary to public policy, and possible to achieve;

(4) The power of the court to modify or terminate a trust under sections 5804.10 to 5804.16 of the Revised Code;

(5) The effect of a spendthrift provision and the rights of certain creditors and assignees to reach a trust as provided in Chapter 5805. of the Revised Code;

(6) The power of the court under section 5807.02 of the Revised Code to require, dispense with, or modify or terminate a bond;

(7) The power of the court under division (B) of section 5807.08 of the Revised Code to adjust a trustee's compensation specified in the terms of the trust which is unreasonably low or high;

(8) Subject to division (C) of this section, the duty under divisions (B)(2) and (3) of section 5808.13 of the Revised Code to notify current beneficiaries of an irrevocable trust who have attained twenty-five years of age of the existence of the trust, of the identity of the trustee, and of their right to request trustee's reports;

(9) Subject to division (C) of this section, the duty under division (A) of section 5808.13 of the Revised Code to respond to the request of a current beneficiary of an irrevocable trust for trustee's reports and other information reasonably related to the administration of a trust;

(10) The effect of an exculpatory term under section 5810.08 of the Revised Code;

(11) The rights under sections 5810.10 to 5810.13 of the Revised Code of a person other than a trustee or beneficiary;

(12) Periods of limitation for commencing a judicial proceeding;

(13) The power of the court to take any action and exercise any jurisdiction that may be necessary in the interests of justice;

(14) The subject-matter jurisdiction of the court for commencing a proceeding as provided in section 5802.03 of the Revised Code.

(C) With respect to one or more of the current beneficiaries, the settlor, in the trust instrument, may waive or modify the duties of the trustee described in divisions (B)(8) and (9) of this section. The waiver or modification may be made only by the settlor designating in the trust instrument one or more beneficiary surrogates to receive any notices, information, or reports otherwise required under those divisions to be provided to the current beneficiaries. If the settlor makes a waiver or modification pursuant to this division, the trustee shall provide the notices, information, and reports to the beneficiary surrogate or surrogates in lieu of providing them to the current beneficiaries. The beneficiary surrogate or surrogates shall act in good faith to protect the interests of the current beneficiaries for whom the notices, information, or reports are received. A waiver or modification made under this division shall be effective for so long as the beneficiary surrogate or surrogates, or their successor or successors designated in accordance with the terms of the trust instrument, act in that capacity.

(2006 H 416, eff. 1–1–07)

Historical and Statutory Notes

Uniform Law: This section is analogous to § 105 of the Uniform Trust Code. See 7C Uniform Laws Annotated, Master Edition or ULA database on Westlaw.

Editor's Comment

2006:

RC 5801.04 does not contain the Uniform Trust Code requirement that a trust and its terms be for the benefit of the beneficiaries. At RC 5804.04, the Ohio Trust Code does state that the trust and its assets are "for the benefit of its beneficiaries in accordance with the interests of the beneficiaries in the trust."

RC 5801.04 (B)(8) and (B)(9) alter the duties of the trustee under the Uniform Trust Code to inform and report to the beneficiaries.

Library References

Baldwin's Ohio Legislative Service Annotated, 2006 H 416 LSC Analysis, p 3/L-1709

Law Review and Journal Commentaries

Beneficiary information and notices. Susan S. Locke, 17 Prob L J Ohio 5 (September/October 2006).

Ohio adopts new trust code—an overview of the new Ohio trust code and house bill 416. Alan Newman, 20 Ohio Law 9 (September/October 2006).

5801.05 Applicability of common law of trusts and principles of equity

The common law of trusts and principles of equity continue to apply in this state, except to the extent modified by Chapters 5801. to 5811. or another section of the Revised Code.

(2006 H 416, eff. 1–1–07)

Historical and Statutory Notes

Uniform Law: This section is analogous to § 106 of the Uniform Trust Code. See 7C Uniform Laws Annotated, Master Edition or ULA database on Westlaw.

Library References

Baldwin's Ohio Legislative Service Annotated, 2006 H 416 LSC Analysis, p 3/L-1709

5801.06 Governing law

The law of the jurisdiction designated in the terms of a trust determines the meaning and effect of the terms unless the designation of that jurisdiction's law is contrary to a strong public policy of the jurisdiction having the most significant relationship to the matter at issue. In the absence of a controlling designation in the terms of the trust, the law of the jurisdiction having the most significant relationship to the matter at issue determines the meaning and effect of the terms.

(2006 H 416, eff. 1–1–07)

Historical and Statutory Notes

Uniform Law: This section is analogous to § 107 of the Uniform Trust Code. See 7C Uniform Laws Annotated, Master Edition or ULA database on Westlaw.

Library References

Baldwin's Ohio Legislative Service Annotated, 2006 H 416 LSC Analysis, p 3/L-1709

5801.07 Principal place of administration

(A) Without precluding other means for establishing a sufficient connection with the designated jurisdiction, the terms of a trust designating the principal place of administration of the trust are valid and controlling if a trustee's principal place of business is located in or a trustee is a resident of the designated jurisdiction or if all or part of the administration occurs in the designated jurisdiction.

(B) A trustee is under a continuing duty to administer the trust at a place appropriate to its purposes, its administration, and the interests of the beneficiaries.

(C) Without precluding the right of the court to order, approve, or disapprove a transfer, the trustee, in furtherance of the duty prescribed by division (B) of this section, may transfer the trust's principal place of administration to another state or to a jurisdiction outside of the United States.

(D) The trustee shall notify the current beneficiaries of a proposed transfer of a trust's principal place of administration not less than sixty days before initiating the transfer. The notice of a proposed transfer shall include all of the following:

(1) The name of the jurisdiction to which the principal place of administration is to be transferred;

(2) The address and telephone number at the new location at which the trustee can be contacted;

(3) An explanation of the reasons for the proposed transfer;

(4) The date on which the trustee expects the proposed transfer to occur.

(E) In connection with a transfer of the trust's principal place of administration, the trustee may transfer some or all of the trust property to a successor trustee designated in the terms of the trust or appointed pursuant to section 5807.04 of the Revised Code.

(2006 H 416, eff. 1-1-07)

Historical and Statutory Notes

Uniform Law: This section is analogous to § 108 of the Uniform Trust Code. See 7C Uniform Laws Annotated, Master Edition or ULA database on Westlaw.

Editor's Comment

2006:

Under RC 5801.07, unlike the Uniform Trust Code, only the current beneficiaries of a trust must be notified if the trustee proposes to change the principal place of administration of the trust. In addition, the Uniform provision that a principal beneficiary may prevent such a transfer by objecting has been removed in Ohio.

Library References

Baldwin's Ohio Legislative Service Annotated, 2006 H 416 LSC Analysis, p 3/L-1709

Law Review and Journal Commentaries

Setting your sights on trust situs. Joanne Hindel, 16 Prob L J Ohio 135 (May/June 2006).

The office of trustee and the duties and powers of the trustee under the Ohio trust code. Joanne E. Hindel, 17 Prob L J Ohio 10 (September/October 2006).

5801.08 Notice; waiver of notice

(A) Notice to a person or the sending of a document to a person under Chapters 5801. to 5811. of the Revised Code shall be accomplished in a manner reasonably suitable under the circumstances and likely to result in receipt of the notice or document. Permissible methods of notice or for sending a document include first-class mail, personal delivery, delivery to the person's last known place of residence or place of business, or a properly directed electronic message.

(B) Notice otherwise required or a document otherwise required to be sent under Chapters 5801. to 5811. of the Revised Code is not required to be provided to a person whose identity or location is unknown to and not reasonably ascertainable by the trustee.

(C) The person to be notified or sent a document may waive notice or the sending of a document under Chapters 5801. to 5811. of the Revised Code.

(D) Notice of a judicial proceeding must be given as provided in the applicable rules of civil procedure.

(2006 H 416, eff. 1-1-07)

Historical and Statutory Notes

Uniform Law: This section is analogous to § 109 of the Uniform Trust Code. See 7C Uniform Laws Annotated, Master Edition or ULA database on Westlaw.

Library References

Baldwin's Ohio Legislative Service Annotated, 2006 H 416 LSC Analysis, p 3/L-1709

Law Review and Journal Commentaries

Beneficiary information and notices. Susan S. Locke, 17 Prob L J Ohio 5 (September/October 2006).

The evolution of Ohio trust law from the English common law to the Ohio trust code. Joanne E. Hindel, 17 Prob L J Ohio 1 (September/October 2006).

5801.09 Notice to other beneficiaries; persons treated as beneficiaries

(A) Whenever Chapters 5801. to 5811. of the Revised Code require notice to current or qualified beneficiaries of a trust, the trustee shall also give notice to any other beneficiary who has sent the trustee a request for notice.

(B) A person appointed to enforce a trust created for the care of an animal or another noncharitable purpose as provided in section 5804.08 or 5804.09 of the Revised Code has the rights of a current beneficiary under Chapters 5801. to 5811. of the Revised Code.

(2006 H 416, eff. 1-1-07)

Historical and Statutory Notes

Uniform Law: This section is analogous to § 110 of the Uniform Trust Code. See 7C Uniform Laws Annotated, Master Edition or ULA database on Westlaw.

Editor's Comment

2006:

Uniform provisions that charitable trusts do not have beneficiaries in the usual sense, and that the attorney general has the rights of a qualified beneficiary as to charitable trusts, have not been adopted in RC 5801.09.

Library References

Baldwin's Ohio Legislative Service Annotated, 2006 H 416 LSC Analysis, p 3/L-1709

5801.10 Parties to agreements; effect on creditor rights

(A) As used in this section, "creditor" means any of the following:

(1) A person holding a debt or security for a debt entered into by a trustee on behalf of the trust;

(2) A person holding a debt secured by one or more assets of the trust;

(3) A person having a claim against the trustee or the assets of the trust under section 5805.06 of the Revised Code;

(4) A person who has attached through legal process a beneficiary's interest in the trust.

(B) The parties to an agreement under this section shall be all of the following, or their representatives under the representation provisions of Chapter 5803. of the Revised Code, except that only the settlor and any trustee are required to be parties to an amendment of any revocable trust:

(1) The settlor if living and if no adverse income or transfer tax results would arise from the settlor's participation;

(2) All beneficiaries;

(3) All currently serving trustees;

(4) Creditors, if their interest is to be affected by the agreement.

(C) The persons specified in division (B) of this section may by written instrument enter into an agreement with respect to any matter concerning the construction of, administration of, or distributions under the trust instrument, the investment of income or principal held by the trustee, or other matters. The agreement is valid only to the extent that it does not effect a termination of the trust before the date specified for the trust's termination in the trust instrument, does not change the interests of the beneficiaries in the trust except as necessary to effect a modification described in division (C)(5) or (6) of this section, and includes terms and conditions that could be properly approved by the court under Chapters 5801. to 5811. of the Revised Code or other applicable law. Matters that may be resolved by a private settlement agreement include, but are not limited to, all of the following:

(1) Determining classes of creditors, beneficiaries, heirs, next of kin, or other persons;

(2) Resolving disputes arising out of the administration or distribution under the trust instrument, including disputes over the construction of the language of the trust instrument or construction of the language of other writings that affect the trust instrument;

(3) Granting to the trustee necessary or desirable powers not granted in the trust instrument or otherwise provided by law, to the extent that those powers either are not inconsistent with the express provisions or purposes of the trust instrument or, if inconsistent with the express provisions or purposes of the trust instrument, are necessary for the due administration of the trust instrument;

(4) Modifying the trust instrument, if the modification is not inconsistent with any dominant purpose or objective of the trust;

(5) Modifying the trust instrument in the manner required to qualify the gift under the trust instrument for the charitable estate or gift tax deduction permitted by federal law, including the addition of mandatory governing instrument requirements for a charitable remainder trust as required by the Internal Revenue Code and regulations promulgated under it in any case in which all parties interested in the trust have submitted written agreements to the proposed changes or written disclaimer of interest;

(6) Modifying the trust instrument in the manner required to qualify any gift under the trust instrument for the estate tax marital deduction available to noncitizen spouses, including the addition of mandatory governing instrument requirements for a qualified domestic trust under section 2056A of the Internal Revenue Code [1] and regulations promulgated under it in any case in which all parties interested in the trust have submitted written agreements to the proposed changes or written disclaimer of interest;

(7) Resolving any other matter that arises under Chapters 5801. to 5811. of the Revised Code.

(D) No agreement shall be entered into under this section affecting the rights of a creditor without the creditor's consent or affecting the collection rights of federal, state, or local taxing authorities.

(E) Any agreement entered into under this section that complies with the requirements of division (C) of this section shall be final and binding on the trustee, the settlor if living, all beneficiaries, and their heirs, successors, and assigns.

(F) Notwithstanding anything in this section, in division (D) of section 5803.03 of the Revised Code, or in any other rule of law to the contrary, a trustee serving under the trust instrument shall only represent its own individual or corporate interests in negotiating or entering into an agreement subject to this section. No trustee serving under the trust instrument shall be considered to represent any settlor, beneficiary, or the interests of any settlor or beneficiary in negotiating or entering into an agreement subject to this section.

(G) Any party to a private settlement agreement entered into under this section may request the court to approve the agreement, to determine whether the representation as provided in Chapter 5803. of the Revised Code was adequate, and to determine whether the agreement contains terms and conditions the court could have properly approved.

(H) If an agreement entered into under this section contains a provision requiring binding arbitration of any disputes arising under the agreement, the provision is enforceable.

(I) Nothing in this section affects any of the following:

(1) The right of a beneficiary to disclaim under section 5815.36 of the Revised Code;

(2) The termination or modification of a trust under section 5804.10, 5804.11, 5804.12, 5804.13, 5804.14, 5804.15, or 5804.16 of the Revised Code;

(3) The ability of a trustee to divide or consolidate a trust under section 5804.17 of the Revised Code.

(J) Nothing in this section restricts or limits the jurisdiction of any court to dispose of matters not covered by agreements under this section or to supervise the acts of trustees appointed by that court.

(K) This section shall be liberally construed to favor the validity and enforceability of agreements entered into under it.

(L) A trustee serving under the trust instrument is not liable to any third person arising from any loss due to that trustee's actions or inactions taken or omitted in good faith reliance on the terms of an agreement entered into under this section.

(M) This section does not apply to any of the following:

(1) A charitable trust that has one or more charitable organizations as qualified beneficiaries;

(2) A charitable trust the terms of which authorize or direct the trustee to distribute trust income or principal to one or more charitable organizations to be selected by the trustee, or for one or more charitable purposes described in division (A) of section 5804.05 of the Revised Code, if any of the following apply:

(a) The distributions may be made on the date that an agreement under this section would be entered into.

(b) The distributions could be made on the date that an agreement under this section would be entered into if the interests of the current beneficiaries of the trust terminated on that date, but the termination of those interests would not cause the trust to terminate.

(c) The distributions could be made on the date that an agreement under this section would be entered into if the trust terminated on that date.

(2006 H 416, eff. 1–1–07)

[1] 26 U.S.C.A. § 2056a.

Editor's Comment

2006:

RC 5801.10 replaces the Uniform Trust Code's "nonjudicial settlement agreements" with "private settlement agreements," redefines potential parties to such agreements, and makes changes in the subject matter that may be covered by an agreement. The model for private settlement agreements was drafted by the Ohio Bankers League.

Cross References

Representation by fiduciaries and parents, 5803.03

Library References

Baldwin's Ohio Legislative Service Annotated, 2006 H 416 LSC Analysis, p 3/L-1709

Law Review and Journal Commentaries

Ohio adopts new trust code—an overview of the new Ohio trust code and house bill 416. Alan Newman, 20 Ohio Law 9 (September/October 2006).

Private settlement agreements, representation and court proceedings under the Ohio trust code. Tom Cummiskey, 17 Prob L J Ohio 21 (September/October 2006).

CHAPTER 5802

JUDICIAL PROCEEDINGS

Section
5802.01 Role of court in administration of trust
5802.02 Jurisdiction over trustee and beneficiary
5802.03 Concurrent jurisdiction

5802.01 Role of court in administration of trust

(A) A court may intervene in the administration of a trust to the extent its jurisdiction is invoked by an interested person or as provided by law.

(B) An inter vivos trust is not subject to continuing judicial supervision unless ordered by the court. Trusts created pursuant to a section of the Revised Code or a judgment or decree of a court are subject to continuing judicial supervision to the extent provided by the section, judgment, or decree or by court order.

(C) A judicial proceeding involving a trust may relate to any matter involving the trust's administration, including a request for instructions and an action to declare rights.

(2006 H 416, eff. 1–1–07)

Historical and Statutory Notes

Uniform Law: This section is analogous to § 201 of the Uniform Trust Code. See 7C Uniform Laws Annotated, Master Edition or ULA database on Westlaw.

Editor's Comment

2006:

In contrast to the Uniform Trust Code stance that trusts are not subject to continuing supervision by the court unless so ordered, RC 5802.01(B) provides that testamentary trusts remain under court supervision

Library References

Baldwin's Ohio Legislative Service Annotated, 2006 H 416 LSC Analysis, p 3/L-1709

5802.02 Jurisdiction over trustee and beneficiary

(A) By accepting the trusteeship of a trust having its principal place of administration in this state or by moving the principal place of administration to this state, the trustee submits personally to the jurisdiction of the courts of this state regarding any matter involving the trust.

(B) With respect to their interests in the trust, the beneficiaries of a trust having its principal place of administration in this state are subject to the jurisdiction of the courts of this state regarding any matter involving the trust. By accepting a distribution from the trust, the recipient submits personally to the jurisdiction of the courts of this state regarding any matter involving the trust.

(C) This section does not preclude other methods of obtaining jurisdiction over a trustee, beneficiary, or other person receiving property from the trust.

(2006 H 416, eff. 1–1–07)

Historical and Statutory Notes

Uniform Law: This section is analogous to § 202 of the Uniform Trust Code. See 7C Uniform Laws Annotated, Master Edition or ULA database on Westlaw.

Editor's Comment

2006:

In contrast to the Uniform Trust Code stance that trusts are not subject to continuing supervision by the court unless so ordered, RC 5802.01(B) provides that testamentary trusts remain under court supervision

Library References

Baldwin's Ohio Legislative Service Annotated, 2006 H 416 LSC Analysis, p 3/L-1709

5802.03 Concurrent jurisdiction

The probate division of the court of common pleas has concurrent jurisdiction with, and the same powers at law and in equity as, the general division of the court of common pleas to issue writs and orders and to hear and determine any action that involves an inter vivos trust.

(2006 H 416, eff. 1–1–07)

Editor's Comment

2006:

RC 5802.03 vests the probate division and general division of the probate court with concurrent powers over inter vivos trusts, rather than the division of jurisdiction proposed in the Uniform Trust Code.

Cross References

Scope, mandatory rules, exceptions, 5801.04

Library References

Baldwin's Ohio Legislative Service Annotated, 2006 H 416 LSC Analysis, p 3/L-1709

CHAPTER 5803

REPRESENTATION

Section
5803.01 Notice and consent regarding representation and binding another person
5803.02 Representation by holder of general testamentary power of appointment
5803.03 Representation by fiduciaries and parents
5803.04 Representation by person with substantially identical interest
5803.05 Appointment of representative by court

Law Review and Journal Commentaries

Private settlement agreements, representation and court proceedings under the Ohio trust code. Tom Cummiskey, 17 Prob L J Ohio 21 (September/October 2006).

5803.01 Notice and consent regarding representation and binding another person

(A) Notice to a person who may represent and bind another person under this chapter has the same effect as if notice were given directly to the other person.

(B) The consent of a person who may represent and bind another person under this chapter is binding on the person represented unless the person represented objects to the representation before the consent would otherwise have become effective.

(C) Except as otherwise provided in sections 5804.11 and 5806.02 of the Revised Code, a person who under this chapter may represent a settlor who lacks capacity may receive notice and give a binding consent on the settlor's behalf.

(D) A settlor may not represent and bind a beneficiary under this chapter with respect to the termination or modification of a trust under division (A) of section 5804.11 of the Revised Code.

(2006 H 416, eff. 1–1–07)

Historical and Statutory Notes

Uniform Law: This section is analogous to § 301 of the Uniform Trust Code. See 7C Uniform Laws Annotated, Master Edition or ULA database on Westlaw.

Cross References

Parties to agreements, effect on creditor rights, 5801.10

Library References

Baldwin's Ohio Legislative Service Annotated, 2006 H 416 LSC Analysis, p 3/L-1709

Law Review and Journal Commentaries

Private settlement agreements, representation and court proceedings under the Ohio trust code. Tom Cummiskey, 17 Prob L J Ohio 21 (September/October 2006).

5803.02 Representation by holder of general testamentary power of appointment

To the extent there is no conflict of interest between the holder of a general testamentary power of appointment and the persons represented with respect to the particular question or dispute, the holder may represent and bind persons whose interests, as permissible appointees, takers in default, or otherwise, are subject to the power.

(2006 H 416, eff. 1–1–07)

Historical and Statutory Notes

Uniform Law: This section is analogous to § 302 of the Uniform Trust Code. See 7C Uniform Laws Annotated, Master Edition or ULA database on Westlaw.

Library References

Baldwin's Ohio Legislative Service Annotated, 2006 H 416 LSC Analysis, p 3/L-1709

5803.03 Representation by fiduciaries and parents

To the extent there is no conflict of interest between the representative and the person represented or among those being represented with respect to a particular question or dispute, all of the following apply:

(A) A guardian of the estate may represent and bind the estate that the guardian of the estate controls.

(B) A guardian of the person may represent and bind the ward if a guardian of the estate has not been appointed.

(C) An agent having authority to act with respect to the particular question or dispute may represent and bind the principal.

(D) Except as provided in division (F) of section 5801.10 of the Revised Code, a trustee may represent and bind the beneficiaries of the trust.

(E) A personal representative of a decedent's estate may represent and bind persons interested in the estate.

(F) A parent may represent and bind the parent's minor or unborn child if neither a guardian for the child's estate or a guardian of the person has been appointed.

(2006 H 416, eff. 1–1–07)

Historical and Statutory Notes

Uniform Law: This section is analogous to § 303 of the Uniform Trust Code. See 7C Uniform Laws Annotated, Master Edition or ULA database on Westlaw.

Cross References

Parties to agreements, effect on creditor rights, 5801.10

Library References

Baldwin's Ohio Legislative Service Annotated, 2006 H 416 LSC Analysis, p 3/L-1709

Law Review and Journal Commentaries

Ohio adopts new trust code—an overview of the new Ohio trust code and house bill 416. Alan Newman, 20 Ohio Law 9 (September/October 2006).

5803.04 Representation by person with substantially identical interest

Unless otherwise represented, a minor, incapacitated individual, unborn individual, or person whose identity or location is unknown and not reasonably ascertainable may be represented by and bound by another having a substantially identical interest with respect to the particular question or dispute, but only to the extent there is no conflict of interest between the representative and the person represented.

(2006 H 416, eff. 1–1–07)

Historical and Statutory Notes

Uniform Law: This section is analogous to § 304 of the Uniform Trust Code. See 7C Uniform Laws Annotated, Master Edition or ULA database on Westlaw.

Library References

Baldwin's Ohio Legislative Service Annotated, 2006 H 416 LSC Analysis, p 3/L-1709

Law Review and Journal Commentaries

Ohio adopts new trust code—an overview of the new Ohio trust code and house bill 416. Alan Newman, 20 Ohio Law 9 (September/October 2006).

5803.05 Appointment of representative by court

(A) If the court determines that an interest is not represented under this chapter or that the otherwise available representation might be inadequate, the court may appoint a representative to receive notice, give consent, and otherwise represent, bind, and act on behalf of a minor, incapacitated individual, unborn individual, or person whose identity or location is unknown. A representative may be appointed to represent several persons or interests.

(B) A representative may act on behalf of the individual represented with respect to any matter arising under Chapters 5801. to 5811. of the Revised Code, whether or not a judicial proceeding concerning the trust is pending.

(C) In making decisions, a representative may consider general benefit accruing to the living members of the individual's family.

(2006 H 416, eff. 1–1–07)

Historical and Statutory Notes

Uniform Law: This section is analogous to § 305 of the Uniform Trust Code. See 7C Uniform Laws Annotated, Master Edition or ULA database on Westlaw.

Library References

Baldwin's Ohio Legislative Service Annotated, 2006 H 416 LSC Analysis, p 3/L-1709

CHAPTER 5804

CREATION, VALIDITY, MODIFICATION AND TERMINATION OF TRUST

Section
5804.01 Methods of creating trust
5804.02 Requirements for creation
5804.03 Trusts created in other jurisdictions
5804.04 Purposes of trust
5804.05 Charitable trusts
5804.06 Creation induced by fraud, duress, or undue influence
5804.07 Creation of oral trust
5804.08 Trust for care of animal
5804.09 Noncharitable trust without ascertainable beneficiary
5804.10 Modification or termination of trust
5804.11 Modification or termination of noncharitable irrevocable trust by consent
5804.12 Modification or termination because of unanticipated circumstances or inability to administer
5804.13 Application of cy pres
5804.14 Modification or termination of uneconomic trust
5804.15 Reformation to correct mistakes
5804.16 Modification to achieve settlor's tax objectives
5804.17 Combination or division of trusts
5804.18 Irrevocable trust

5804.01 Methods of creating trust

A trust may be created by any of the following methods:

(A) Transfer of property to another person as trustee during the settlor's lifetime or by will or other disposition taking effect upon the settlor's death;

(B) Declaration by the owner of property that the owner holds identifiable property as trustee;

(C) Exercise of a power of appointment in favor of a trustee;

(D) A court order.

(2006 H 416, eff. 1–1–07)

Historical and Statutory Notes

Uniform Law: This section is analogous to § 401 of the Uniform Trust Code. See 7C Uniform Laws Annotated, Master Edition or ULA database on Westlaw.

Editor's Comment

2006:

To the three methods for creating a trust in the Uniform Trust Code, RC 5804.01(D) adds the fourth, "by court order."

Library References

Baldwin's Ohio Legislative Service Annotated, 2006 H 416 LSC Analysis, p 3/L-1709

5804.02 Requirements for creation

(A) A trust is created only if all of the following apply:

(1) The settlor of the trust, other than the settlor of a trust created by a court order, has capacity to create a trust.

(2) The settlor of the trust, other than the settlor of a trust created by a court order, indicates an intention to create the trust.

(3) The trust has a definite beneficiary or is one of the following:

(a) A charitable trust;

(b) A trust for the care of an animal, as provided in section 5804.08 of the Revised Code;

(c) A trust for a noncharitable purpose, as provided in section 5804.09 of the Revised Code.

(4) The trustee has duties to perform.

(5) The same person is not the sole trustee and sole beneficiary.

(B) A beneficiary is definite if the beneficiary can be ascertained now or in the future, subject to any applicable rule against perpetuities.

(C) A power in a trustee to select a beneficiary from an indefinite class is valid. If the power is not exercised within a reasonable time, the power fails, and the property subject to the power passes to the persons who would have taken the property had the power not been conferred.

(D) A trust is valid regardless of the existence, size, or character of the corpus of the trust. This division applies to any trust that was executed prior to, or is executed on or after, the effective date of Chapters 5801. to 5811. of the Revised Code.

(E) A trust is not invalid because a person, including, but not limited to, the creator of the trust, is or may become the sole trustee and the sole holder of the present beneficial enjoyment of the corpus of the trust, provided that one or more other persons hold a vested, contingent, or expectant interest relative to the enjoyment of the corpus of the trust upon the cessation of the present beneficial enjoyment. A merger of the legal and equitable titles to the corpus of a trust described in this division does not occur in its creator, and, notwithstanding any contrary provision of Chapter 2107. of the Revised Code, the trust is not a testamentary trust that is required to comply with that chapter in order for its corpus to be legally distributed to other beneficiaries in accordance with the provisions of the trust upon the cessation of the present beneficial enjoyment. This division applies to any trust that satisfies the provisions of this division, whether the trust was executed prior to, on, or after October 10, 1991.

(2006 H 416, eff. 1–1–07)

Historical and Statutory Notes

Uniform Law: This section is analogous to § 402 of the Uniform Trust Code. See 7C Uniform Laws Annotated, Master Edition or ULA database on Westlaw.

Editor's Comment

2006:

RC 5804.02(A) contains an exception to the Uniform Trust Code requirements that a settlor must both have the capacity, and indicate an intention, to create a trust. The exception is for trusts created by court order for incapacitated individuals.

RC 5804.02(B) and (C) are also in addition to the Uniform Trust Code, and make a trust valid even where there is no trust corpus or the sole current beneficiary is the sole trustee.

Those provisions are also found in the Statute of Frauds at RC 1335.01(B) and (C).

Library References

Baldwin's Ohio Legislative Service Annotated, 2006 H 416 LSC Analysis, p 3/L-1709

5804.03 Trusts created in other jurisdictions

A trust not created by will is validly created if its creation complies with the law of the jurisdiction in which the trust instrument was executed or the law of the jurisdiction in which, at the time of creation, any of the following applies:

(A) The settlor was domiciled in, had a place of abode in, or was a national of the jurisdiction.

(B) A trustee was domiciled or had a place of business in the jurisdiction.

(C) Any trust property was located in the jurisdiction.

(2006 H 416, eff. 1–1–07)

Historical and Statutory Notes

Uniform Law: This section is analogous to § 403 of the Uniform Trust Code. See 7C Uniform Laws Annotated, Master Edition or ULA database on Westlaw.

Library References

Baldwin's Ohio Legislative Service Annotated, 2006 H 416 LSC Analysis, p 3/L-1709

5804.04 Purposes of trust

A trust may be created only to the extent that its purposes are lawful, not contrary to public policy, and possible to achieve. A trust exists, and its assets shall be held, for the benefit of its beneficiaries in accordance with the interests of the beneficiaries in the trust.

(2006 H 416, eff. 1–1–07)

Historical and Statutory Notes

Uniform Law: This section is analogous to § 404 of the Uniform Trust Code. See 7C Uniform Laws Annotated, Master Edition or ULA database on Westlaw.

Editor's Comment

2006:

In RC 5804.04, the Ohio Trust Code states that the trust and its assets are "for the benefit of its beneficiaries in accordance with the interests of the beneficiaries . . ."

In RC Chapter 5801, RC 5801.04 does not contain the Uniform Trust Code requirement that a trust and its terms be for the benefit of the beneficiaries.

Library References

Baldwin's Ohio Legislative Service Annotated, 2006 H 416 LSC Analysis, p 3/L-1709

5804.05 Charitable trusts

(A) A charitable trust may be created for the relief of poverty, the advancement of education or religion, the promotion of health, governmental or municipal purposes, or other purposes the achievement of which is beneficial to the community.

(B) If the terms of a charitable trust do not indicate a particular charitable purpose or beneficiary, the court may select one or more charitable purposes or beneficiaries. The selection must be consistent with the settlor's intention to the extent it can be ascertained.

(C) The settlor of a charitable trust, among others, may maintain a proceeding to enforce the trust.

(2006 H 416, eff. 1–1–07)

Historical and Statutory Notes

Uniform Law: This section is analogous to § 405 of the Uniform Trust Code. See 7C Uniform Laws Annotated, Master Edition or ULA database on Westlaw.

Cross References

Parties to agreements, effect on creditor rights, 5801.10

Library References

Baldwin's Ohio Legislative Service Annotated, 2006 H 416 LSC Analysis, p 3/L-1709

Law Review and Journal Commentaries

Ohio adopts new trust code—an overview of the new Ohio trust code and house bill 416. Alan Newman, 20 Ohio Law 9 (September/October 2006).

5804.06 Creation induced by fraud, duress, or undue influence

A trust is void to the extent its creation was induced by fraud, duress, or undue influence. As used in this section, "fraud," "duress," and "undue influence" have the same meanings for trust validity purposes as they have for purposes of determining the validity of a will.

(2006 H 416, eff. 1–1–07)

Historical and Statutory Notes

Uniform Law: This section is analogous to § 406 of the Uniform Trust Code. See 7C Uniform Laws Annotated, Master Edition or ULA database on Westlaw.

Editor's Comment

2006:

RC 5804.06 adopts the Uniform provision that a trust is void to the extent induced in its creation by undue influence, fraud or duress. The section then adds a sentence stating that those terms have the same meaning here with trusts as they do when applied in determining the validity of a will.

Library References

Baldwin's Ohio Legislative Service Annotated, 2006 H 416 LSC Analysis, p 3/L-1709

5804.07 Creation of oral trust

Except as required by any section of the Revised Code not in Chapters 5801. to 5811. of the Revised Code, a trust is not required to be evidenced by a trust instrument, but the creation of an oral trust and its terms may be established only by clear and convincing evidence.

(2006 H 416, eff. 1–1–07)

Historical and Statutory Notes

Uniform Law: This section is analogous to § 407 of the Uniform Trust Code. See 7C Uniform Laws Annotated, Master Edition or ULA database on Westlaw.

Library References

Baldwin's Ohio Legislative Service Annotated, 2006 H 416 LSC Analysis, p 3/L-1709

5804.08 Trust for care of animal

(A) A trust may be created to provide for the care of an animal alive during the settlor's lifetime. The trust terminates upon the death of the animal or, if the trust was created to provide for the care of more than one animal alive during the settlor's lifetime, upon the death of the last surviving animal.

(B) A person appointed in the terms of a trust or, if no person is so appointed, a person appointed by the court may enforce a trust authorized by this section. A person having an interest in the welfare of an animal that is provided care by a trust authorized by this section may request the court to appoint a person to enforce the trust or to remove a person appointed.

(C) The property of a trust authorized by this section may be applied only to its intended use, except to the extent the court determines that the value of the trust property exceeds the amount required for the intended use. Except as otherwise provided in the terms of the trust, property not required for the intended use must be distributed to the settlor if then living or to the settlor's successors in interest.

(2006 H 416, eff. 1–1–07)

Historical and Statutory Notes

Uniform Law: This section is analogous to § 408 of the Uniform Trust Code. See 7C Uniform Laws Annotated, Master Edition or ULA database on Westlaw.

Cross References

Notice to other beneficiaries, persons treated as beneficiaries, 5801.09

Library References

Baldwin's Ohio Legislative Service Annotated, 2006 H 416 LSC Analysis, p 3/L-1709

Law Review and Journal Commentaries

Ohio adopts new trust code—an overview of the new Ohio trust code and house bill 416. Alan Newman, 20 Ohio Law 9 (September/October 2006).

5804.09 Noncharitable trust without ascertainable beneficiary

Except as otherwise provided in section 5804.08 of the Revised Code or any other section of the Revised Code:

(A) A trust may be created for a noncharitable purpose without a definite or definitely ascertainable beneficiary or for a noncharitable but otherwise valid purpose to be selected by the trustee. A trust created for a noncharitable purpose may not be enforced for more than twenty-one years.

(B) A trust authorized by this section may be enforced by a person appointed in the terms of the trust or, if no person is so appointed, by a person appointed by the court.

(C) The property of a trust authorized by this section may be applied only to its intended use, except to the extent the court determines that the value of the trust property exceeds the amount required for the intended use. Except as otherwise provided in the terms of the trust, property not required for the intended use must be distributed to the settlor if then living or to the settlor's successors in interest.

(2006 H 416, eff. 1–1–07)

Historical and Statutory Notes

Uniform Law: This section is analogous to § 409 of the Uniform Trust Code. See 7C Uniform Laws Annotated, Master Edition or ULA database on Westlaw.

Cross References

Notice to other beneficiaries, persons treated as beneficiaries, 5801.09

Library References

Baldwin's Ohio Legislative Service Annotated, 2006 H 416 LSC Analysis, p 3/L-1709

5804.10 Modification or termination of trust

(A) In addition to the methods of termination prescribed by sections 5804.11 to 5804.14 of the Revised Code, a trust terminates to the extent the trust is revoked or expires pursuant to its terms, a court determines that no purpose of the trust remains to be achieved, or a court determines that the purposes of the trust have become unlawful or impossible to achieve.

(B) A trustee or beneficiary may commence a proceeding to approve or disapprove a proposed modification or termination under sections 5804.11 to 5804.16 of the Revised Code or to approve or disapprove a trust combination or division under section 5804.17 of the Revised Code. The settlor may commence a proceeding to approve or disapprove a proposed modification or termination under section 5804.11 of the Revised Code. The settlor of a charitable trust may maintain a proceeding to modify the trust under section 5804.13 of the Revised Code.

(2006 H 416, eff. 1–1–07)

Historical and Statutory Notes

Uniform Law: This section is analogous to § 410 of the Uniform Trust Code. See 7C Uniform Laws Annotated, Master Edition or ULA database on Westlaw.

Editor's Comment

2006:

While the Uniform Trust Code calls for termination of a trust when no purpose remains to be achieved, or the purpose has become unlawful, impossible, or contrary to public policy, the Ohio provision RC 5804.10 removes the provision concerning purposes contrary to public policy. In addition, the Ohio provision states that it is for the court to determine whether a trust purpose has become unlawful or impossible. The Uniform law does not state who is to make that determination.

Cross References

Parties to agreements, effect on creditor rights, 5801.10
Scope, mandatory rules, exceptions, 5801.04

Library References

Baldwin's Ohio Legislative Service Annotated, 2006 H 416 LSC Analysis, p 3/L-1709

5804.11 Modification or termination of noncharitable irrevocable trust by consent

(A) If upon petition the court finds that the settlor and all beneficiaries consent to the modification or termination of a noncharitable irrevocable trust, the court shall enter an order approving the modification or termination even if the modification or termination is inconsistent with a material purpose of the trust. An agent under a power of attorney may exercise a settlor's power to consent to a trust's modification or termination only to the extent expressly authorized by both the power of attorney and the terms of the trust. The settlor's guardian of the estate may exercise a settlor's power to consent to a trust's modification or termination with the approval of the court supervising the guardianship if an agent is not so authorized. The guardian of the settlor's person may exercise a settlor's power to consent to a trust's modification or termination with the approval of the court supervising the guardianship if an agent is not so authorized and a guardian of the estate has not been appointed. This division applies only to irrevocable trusts created on or after the effective date of Chapters 5801. to 5811. of the Revised Code and to revocable trusts that become irrevocable on or after the effective date of Chapters 5801. to 5811. of the Revised Code. This division does not apply to a noncharitable irrevocable trust described in 42 U.S.C. 1396p(d)(4).

(B) A noncharitable irrevocable trust may be terminated upon consent of all of the beneficiaries if the court concludes that continuance of the trust is not necessary to achieve any material purpose of the trust. A noncharitable irrevocable trust may be modified, but not to remove or replace the trustee, upon consent of all of the beneficiaries if the court concludes that modification is not inconsistent with a material purpose of the trust. A spendthrift provision in the terms of the trust may, but is not presumed to, constitute a material purpose of the trust.

(C) Upon termination of a trust under division (A) or (B) of this section, the trustee shall distribute the trust property as agreed by the beneficiaries.

(D) If not all of the beneficiaries consent to a proposed modification or termination of the trust under division (A) or (B) of this section, the court may approve the modification or termination if the court is satisfied of both of the following:

(1) That if all of the beneficiaries had consented, the trust could have been modified or terminated under this section;

(2) That the interests of a beneficiary who does not consent will be adequately protected.

(2006 H 416, eff. 1–1–07)

Historical and Statutory Notes

Uniform Law: This section is analogous to § 411 of the Uniform Trust Code. See 7C Uniform Laws Annotated, Master Edition or ULA database on Westlaw.

Editor's Comment

2006:

The Uniform Trust Code provision that all beneficiaries may agree to modify or terminate a noncharitable irrevocable trust, if the court concludes that this result is not inconsistent with a material term of the trust, has been altered in two respects by RC 5804.11(B). The Ohio law specifies that the power to modify may not be used to remove and replace the trustee. Second, regarding spendthrift provisions, the Uniform Trust Code states that these are not presumed to be a "material purpose" of the trust that cannot be changed by agreement. The Ohio provision says a spendthrift clause may, though is not presumed to, be a material purpose of the trust.

Cross References

Notice and consent regarding representation and binding another person, 5803.01
Parties to agreements, effect on creditor rights, 5801.10

Library References

Baldwin's Ohio Legislative Service Annotated, 2006 H 416 LSC Analysis, p 3/L-1709

5804.12 Modification or termination because of unanticipated circumstances or inability to administer

(A) The court may modify the administrative or dispositive terms of a trust or terminate the trust if because of circumstances not anticipated by the settlor modification or termination will further the purposes of the trust. To the extent practicable, the court shall make the modification in accordance with the settlor's probable intention.

(B) The court may modify the administrative terms of a trust if continuation of the trust on its existing terms would be impracticable or impair the trust's administration.

(C) Upon termination of a trust under this section, the trustee shall distribute the trust property in a manner consistent with the purposes of the trust.

(2006 H 416, eff. 1–1–07)

Historical and Statutory Notes

Uniform Law: This section is analogous to § 412 of the Uniform Trust Code. See 7C Uniform Laws Annotated, Master Edition or ULA database on Westlaw.

Editor's Comment

2006:

Unlike the Uniform Trust Code, RC 5804.12 does not recognize the fact a trust has become "wasteful" as a ground for its modification or termination.

Cross References

Parties to agreements, effect on creditor rights, 5801.10

Library References

Baldwin's Ohio Legislative Service Annotated, 2006 H 416 LSC Analysis, p 3/L-1709

Law Review and Journal Commentaries

Ohio adopts new trust code—an overview of the new Ohio trust code and house bill 416. Alan Newman, 20 Ohio Law 9 (September/October 2006).

5804.13 Application of cy pres

(A) Except as otherwise provided in division (B) of this section, if a particular charitable purpose becomes unlawful, impracticable, or impossible to achieve, all of the following apply:

(1) The trust does not fail in whole or in part.

(2) The trust property does not revert to the settlor or the settlor's successors in interest.

(3) The court may apply cy pres to modify or terminate the trust by directing that the trust property be applied or distributed, in whole or in part, in a manner consistent with the settlor's charitable purposes. In accordance with section 109.25 of the Revised Code, the attorney general is a necessary party to a judicial proceeding brought under this section.

(B) A provision in the terms of a charitable trust for the distribution of the trust property to a noncharitable beneficiary prevails over the power of the court under division (A) of this section to apply cy pres to modify or terminate the trust.

(2006 H 416, eff. 1–1–07)

Historical and Statutory Notes

Uniform Law: This section is analogous to § 413 of the Uniform Trust Code. See 7C Uniform Laws Annotated, Master Edition or ULA database on Westlaw.

Editor's Comment

2006:

Unlike the Uniform Trust Code, RC 5804.13 does not recognize the fact a trust has become "wasteful" as a ground for its modification or termination. RC 5804.13(A)(3) also provides that the attorney general is a necessary party to cy pres proceedings.

Cross References

Parties to agreements, effect on creditor rights, 5801.10

Library References

Baldwin's Ohio Legislative Service Annotated, 2006 H 416 LSC Analysis, p 3/L-1709

5804.14 Modification or termination of uneconomic trust

(A)(1) Except as provided in division (A)(2) of this section, after notice to the qualified beneficiaries, the trustee of an inter vivos trust consisting of trust property having a total value of less than one hundred thousand dollars may terminate the trust if the trustee concludes that the value of the trust property is insufficient to justify the cost of administration.

(2) Division (A)(1) of this section does not apply to any of the following:

(a) A charitable trust that has one or more charitable organizations as qualified beneficiaries;

(b) A charitable trust the terms of which authorize or direct the trustee to distribute trust income or principal to one or more charitable organizations to be selected by the trustee, or for one or more charitable purposes described in division (A) of section 5804.05 of the Revised Code, if any of the following apply:

(i) The distributions may be made on the date that the trust would be terminated under division (A)(1) of this section.

(ii) The distributions could be made on the date that the trust would be terminated under division (A)(1) of this section if the interests of the current beneficiaries of the trust terminated on that date, but the termination of those interests would not cause the trust to terminate.

(iii) The distributions could be made on the date that the trust would be terminated under division (A)(1) of this section, if the trust terminated on that date but not under that division.

(B) If an inter vivos trust consists of trust property having a total value of less than one hundred thousand dollars, the court may modify or terminate the trust or remove the trustee and appoint a different trustee if it determines that the value of the trust property is insufficient to justify the cost of administration.

(C) Upon the termination of a trust pursuant to division (A)(1) of this section, the trustee shall distribute the trust estate in accordance with any provision specified in the trust instrument for the premature termination of the trust. If there is no provision of that nature in the trust instrument, the trustee shall distribute the trust estate among the beneficiaries of the trust in accordance with their respective beneficial interests and in a manner that the trustee determines to be equitable. For purposes of distributing the trust estate among the beneficiaries of the trust under this division, the trustee shall consider all of the following:

(1) The existence of any agreement among the beneficiaries with respect to their beneficial interests;

(2) The actuarial values of the separate beneficial interests of the beneficiaries;

(3) Any expression of preference of the beneficiaries that is contained in the trust instrument.

(D) Upon the termination of a trust pursuant to division (B) of this section, the probate court shall order the distribution of the trust estate in accordance with any provision specified in the trust instrument for the premature termination of the trust. If there is no provision of that nature in the trust instrument, the probate court shall order the distribution of the trust estate among the beneficiaries of the trust in accordance with their respective beneficial interests and in a manner that the court determines to be equitable. For purposes of ordering the distribution of the trust estate among the beneficiaries of the trust under this division, the court shall consider the three factors listed in division (C) of this section.

(E) The existence of a spendthrift or similar provision in a trust instrument or will does not preclude the termination of a trust pursuant to this section.

(F) This section does not apply to an easement for conservation or preservation.

(2006 H 416, eff. 1–1–07)

Historical and Statutory Notes

Uniform Law: This section is analogous to § 414 of the Uniform Trust Code. See 7C Uniform Laws Annotated, Master Edition or ULA database on Westlaw.

Editor's Comment

2006:

The Uniform Trust Code provision on modifying or ending trusts, where the value of the property is insufficient to justify administration costs, has been modified in several particulars in RC 5804.14. The Ohio provision is made expressly applicable only to inter vivos trusts. The $50,000 maximum value in the Uniform provision is changed to $100,000. In addition, while the Uniform Trust Code gives courts power to modify or terminate trusts with a corpus exceeding $100,000, the Ohio provision does not. The Ohio provision also does not require the trustee to distribute the assets of the terminated trust "in a manner consistent with the purposes of the trust." Finally, RC 5804.14(E) provides that the existence of a spendthrift provision does not prevent termination of a trust on the grounds of it being uneconomic.

Cross References

Parties to agreements, effect on creditor rights, 5801.10

Library References

Baldwin's Ohio Legislative Service Annotated, 2006 H 416 LSC Analysis, p 3/L-1709

Law Review and Journal Commentaries

Beneficiary information and notices. Susan S. Locke, 17 Prob L J Ohio 5 (September/October 2006).

The evolution of Ohio trust law from the English common law to the Ohio trust code. Joanne E. Hindel, 17 Prob L J Ohio 1 (September/October 2006).

5804.15 Reformation to correct mistakes

The court may reform the terms of a trust, even if they are unambiguous, to conform the terms to the settlor's intention if it is proved by clear and convincing evidence that both the settlor's intent and the terms of the trust were affected by a mistake of fact or law, whether in expression or inducement.

(2006 H 416, eff. 1-1-07)

Historical and Statutory Notes

Uniform Law: This section is analogous to § 415 of the Uniform Trust Code. See 7C Uniform Laws Annotated, Master Edition or ULA database on Westlaw.

Cross References

Parties to agreements, effect on creditor rights, 5801.10

Library References

Baldwin's Ohio Legislative Service Annotated, 2006 H 416 LSC Analysis, p 3/L-1709

Law Review and Journal Commentaries

Ohio adopts new trust code—an overview of the new Ohio trust code and house bill 416. Alan Newman, 20 Ohio Law 9 (September/October 2006).

5804.16 Modification to achieve settlor's tax objectives

To achieve the settlor's tax objectives, the court may modify the terms of a trust in a manner that is not contrary to the settlor's probable intention. The court may provide that the modification has retroactive effect.

(2006 H 416, eff. 1-1-07)

Historical and Statutory Notes

Uniform Law: This section is analogous to § 416 of the Uniform Trust Code. See 7C Uniform Laws Annotated, Master Edition or ULA database on Westlaw.

Cross References

Parties to agreements, effect on creditor rights, 5801.10
Scope, mandatory rules, exceptions, 5801.04

Library References

Baldwin's Ohio Legislative Service Annotated, 2006 H 416 LSC Analysis, p 3/L-1709

Law Review and Journal Commentaries

Ohio adopts new trust code—an overview of the new Ohio trust code and house bill 416. Alan Newman, 20 Ohio Law 9 (September/October 2006).

5804.17 Combination or division of trusts

After notice to the qualified beneficiaries, a trustee may combine two or more trusts into a single trust or divide a trust into two or more separate trusts if the result does not impair the rights of any beneficiary or adversely affect achievement of the purposes of the trust.

(2006 H 416, eff. 1-1-07)

Historical and Statutory Notes

Uniform Law: This section is analogous to § 417 of the Uniform Trust Code. See 7C Uniform Laws Annotated, Master Edition or ULA database on Westlaw.

Cross References

Parties to agreements, effect on creditor rights, 5801.10

Library References

Baldwin's Ohio Legislative Service Annotated, 2006 H 416 LSC Analysis, p 3/L-1709

Law Review and Journal Commentaries

Beneficiary information and notices. Susan S. Locke, 17 Prob L J Ohio 5 (September/October 2006).

The evolution of Ohio trust law from the English common law to the Ohio trust code. Joanne E. Hindel, 17 Prob L J Ohio 1 (September/October 2006).

5804.18 Irrevocable trust

A trust described in 42 U.S.C. 1396p(d)(4) is irrevocable if the terms of the trust prohibit the settlor from revoking it, whether or not the settlor's estate or the settlor's heirs are named as the remainder beneficiary or beneficiaries of the trust upon the settlor's death.

(2006 H 416, eff. 1-1-07)

Library References

Baldwin's Ohio Legislative Service Annotated, 2006 H 416 LSC Analysis, p 3/L-1709

CHAPTER 5805

SPENDTHRIFT AND DISCRETIONARY TRUSTS

Section	
5805.01	Spendthrift provision
5805.02	Enforceability of spendthrift provision; exceptions
5805.03	Creditor or assignee claims against discretionary trust
5805.04	Effect of standard on discretionary trusts
5805.05	Rights of beneficiary's creditor or assignee
5805.06	Creditor's or assignee's claims against settlor

Section
5805.07 Personal obligations of trustee

5805.01 Spendthrift provision

(A) A spendthrift provision is valid only if it restrains both voluntary and involuntary transfer of a beneficiary's interest or if it restrains involuntary transfer of a beneficiary's interest and permits voluntary transfer of a beneficiary's interest only with the consent of a trustee who is not the beneficiary.

(B) A term of a trust providing that the interest of a beneficiary is held subject to a "spendthrift trust," or words of similar import, is sufficient to restrain both voluntary and involuntary transfer of the beneficiary's interest.

(C) A beneficiary may not transfer an interest in a trust in violation of a valid spendthrift provision and, except as otherwise provided in this chapter and in section 5810.04 of the Revised Code, a creditor or assignee of the beneficiary may not reach the interest or a distribution by the trustee before its receipt by the beneficiary. Real property or tangible personal property that is owned by the trust but that is made available for a beneficiary's use or occupancy in accordance with the trustee's authority under the trust instrument shall not be considered to have been distributed by the trustee or received by the beneficiary for purposes of allowing a creditor or assignee of the beneficiary to reach the property.

(2006 H 416, eff. 1-1-07)

Historical and Statutory Notes

Uniform Law: This section is analogous to § 502 of the Uniform Trust Code. See 7C Uniform Laws Annotated, Master Edition or ULA database on Westlaw.

Library References

Baldwin's Ohio Legislative Service Annotated, 2006 H 416 LSC Analysis, p 3/L-1709

Law Review and Journal Commentaries

Ohio adopts new trust code—an overview of the new Ohio trust code and house bill 416. Alan Newman, 20 Ohio Law 9 (September/October 2006).

5805.02 Enforceability of spendthrift provision; exceptions

(A) As used in this section, "child" includes any person for whom an order or judgment for child support has been entered in this or another state.

(B) Subject to section 5805.03 of the Revised Code, a spendthrift provision is unenforceable against either of the following:

(1) The beneficiary's child or spouse who has a judgment or court order against the beneficiary for support, but only if distributions can be made for the beneficiary's support or the beneficiary is entitled to receive mandatory distributions under the terms of the trust;

(2) A claim of this state or the United States to the extent provided by the Revised Code or federal law.

(C) A spendthrift provision is enforceable against the beneficiary's former spouse.

(D) A claimant described in division (B) of this section may obtain from the court an order attaching present or future distributions to or for the benefit of the beneficiary. The court may limit the award to the relief that is appropriate under the circumstances, considering among any other factors determined appropriate by the court the support needs of the beneficiary, the beneficiary's spouse, and the beneficiary's dependent children or, with respect to a beneficiary who is the recipient of public benefits, the supplemental needs of the beneficiary if the trust was not intended to provide for the beneficiary's basic support.

(E) The only exceptions to the effectiveness of a spendthrift provision are those described in divisions (B) and (D) of this section, in division (B) of section 5805.05 of the Revised Code, and in sections 5805.06 and 5810. 04 of the Revised Code.

(2006 H 416, eff. 1-1-07)

Historical and Statutory Notes

Uniform Law: This section is analogous to § 503 of the Uniform Trust Code. See 7C Uniform Laws Annotated, Master Edition or ULA database on Westlaw.

Library References

Baldwin's Ohio Legislative Service Annotated, 2006 H 416 LSC Analysis, p 3/L-1709

Law Review and Journal Commentaries

Ohio adopts new trust code—an overview of the new Ohio trust code and house bill 416. Alan Newman, 20 Ohio Law 9 (September/October 2006).

5805.03 Creditor or assignee claims against discretionary trust

Notwithstanding anything to the contrary in division (B) of section 5805.02 of the Revised Code, no creditor or assignee of a beneficiary of a wholly discretionary trust may reach the beneficiary's interest in the trust, or a distribution by the trustee before its receipt by the beneficiary, whether by attachment of present or future distributions to or for the benefit of the beneficiary, by judicial sale, by obtaining an order compelling the trustee to make distributions from the trust, or by any other means, regardless of whether the trust instrument includes a spendthrift provision.

(2006 H 416, eff. 1-1-07)

Library References

Baldwin's Ohio Legislative Service Annotated, 2006 H 416 LSC Analysis, p 3/L-1709

Law Review and Journal Commentaries

Ohio adopts new trust code—an overview of the new Ohio trust code and house bill 416. Alan Newman, 20 Ohio Law 9 (September/October 2006).

5805.04 Effect of standard on discretionary trusts

(A) As used in this section, "child" includes any person for whom an order or judgment for child support has been entered in this or any other state.

(B) Except as otherwise provided in divisions (C) and (D) of this section, whether or not a trust contains a spendthrift provision, a creditor of a beneficiary may not compel a distribution that is subject to the trustee's discretion, even if the discretion is expressed in the form of a standard of distribution or the trustee has abused the discretion.

(C) Division (B) of this section does not apply to this state for any claim for support of a beneficiary in a state institution if the terms of the trust do not include a spendthrift provision and do include a standard for distributions to or for the beneficiary under which the trustee may make distributions for the beneficiary's support.

(D) Unless the settlor has explicitly provided in the trust that the beneficiary's child or spouse or both are excluded from benefiting from the trust, to the extent a trustee of a trust that is not a wholly discretionary trust has not complied with a standard of distribution or has abused a discretion, both of the following apply:

(1) The court may order a distribution to satisfy a judgment or court order against the beneficiary for support of the beneficiary's child or spouse, provided that the court may order the distributions only if distributions can be made for the beneficiary's support under the terms of the trust and that the court may not order any distributions under this division to satisfy a judgment or court order against the beneficiary for support of the beneficiary's former spouse.

(2) The court shall direct the trustee to pay to the child or spouse the amount that is equitable under the circumstances but not more than the amount the trustee would have been required to distribute to or for the benefit of the beneficiary had the trustee complied with the standard or not abused the discretion.

(E) Even if a trust does not contain a spendthrift provision, to the extent a beneficiary's interest in a trust is subject to the exercise of the trustee's discretion, whether or not such discretion is subject to one or more standards of distribution, the interest may not be ordered sold to satisfy or partially satisfy a claim of the beneficiary's creditor or assignee.

(F) If the trustee's or cotrustee's discretion to make distributions for the trustee's or cotrustee's own benefit is limited by an ascertainable standard, a creditor may not reach or compel distribution of the beneficial interest except to the extent the interest would be subject to the creditor's claim if the beneficiary were not acting as trustee or cotrustee.

(2006 H 416, eff. 1–1–07)

Historical and Statutory Notes

Uniform Law: This section is analogous to § 504 of the Uniform Trust Code. See 7C Uniform Laws Annotated, Master Edition or ULA database on Westlaw.

Library References

Baldwin's Ohio Legislative Service Annotated, 2006 H 416 LSC Analysis, p 3/L-1709

Law Review and Journal Commentaries

Ohio adopts new trust code—an overview of the new Ohio trust code and house bill 416. Alan Newman, 20 Ohio Law 9 (September/October 2006).

5805.05 Rights of beneficiary's creditor or assignee

(A) To the extent that a trust that gives a beneficiary the right to receive one or more mandatory distributions does not contain a spendthrift provision, the court may authorize a creditor or assignee of the beneficiary to attach present or future mandatory distributions to or for the benefit of the beneficiary or to reach the beneficiary's interest by other means. The court may limit an award under this section to the relief that is appropriate under the circumstances, considering among any other factors determined appropriate by the court, the support needs of the beneficiary, the beneficiary's spouse, and the beneficiary's dependent children or, with respect to a beneficiary who is the recipient of public benefits, the supplemental needs of the beneficiary if the trust was not intended to provide for the beneficiary's basic support. If in exercising its power under this section the court decides to order either a sale of a beneficiary's interest or that a lien be placed on the interest, in deciding between the two types of action, the court shall consider among any other factors it considers relevant the amount of the claim of the creditor or assignee and the proceeds a sale would produce relative to the potential value of the interest to the beneficiary.

(B) Whether or not a trust contains a spendthrift provision, a creditor or assignee of a beneficiary may reach a mandatory distribution the beneficiary is entitled to receive if the trustee has not made the distribution to the beneficiary within a reasonable time after the designated distribution date.

(2006 H 416, eff. 1–1–07)

Historical and Statutory Notes

Uniform Law: This section is analogous, in part, to § 506 of the Uniform Trust Code. See 7C Uniform Laws Annotated, Master Edition or ULA database on Westlaw.

Library References

Baldwin's Ohio Legislative Service Annotated, 2006 H 416 LSC Analysis, p 3/L-1709

Law Review and Journal Commentaries

Ohio adopts new trust code—an overview of the new Ohio trust code and house bill 416. Alan Newman, 20 Ohio Law 9 (September/October 2006).

5805.06 Creditor's or assignee's claims against settlor

(A) Whether or not the terms of a trust contain a spendthrift provision, all of the following apply:

(1) During the lifetime of the settlor, the property of a revocable trust is subject to claims of the settlor's creditors.

(2) With respect to an irrevocable trust, a creditor or assignee of the settlor may reach the maximum amount that can be distributed to or for the settlor's benefit. If a trust has more than one settlor, the amount the creditor or assignee of a particular settlor may reach may not exceed the settlor's interest in the portion of the trust attributable to that settlor's contribution.

(3) With respect to a trust described in 42 U.S.C. section 1396p(d)(4)(A) or (C), the court may limit the award of a settlor's creditor under division (A)(1) or (2) of this section to the relief that is appropriate under the circumstances, considering among any other factors determined appropriate by the court, the supplemental needs of the beneficiary.

(B) For purposes of this section, all of the following apply:

(1) The holder of a power of withdrawal is treated in the same manner as the settlor of a revocable trust to the extent of the property subject to the power during the period the power may be exercised.

(2) Upon the lapse, release, or waiver of the power of withdrawal, the holder is treated as the settlor of the trust only to the extent the value of the property affected by the lapse, release, or waiver exceeds the greatest of the following amounts:

(a) The amount specified in section 2041(b)(2) or 2514(e) of the Internal Revenue Code;[1]

(b) If the donor of the property subject to the holder's power of withdrawal is not married at the time of the transfer of the property to the trust, the amount specified in section 2503(b) of the Internal Revenue Code;[2]

(c) If the donor of the property subject to the holder's power of withdrawal is married at the time of the transfer of the property to the trust, twice the amount specified in section 2503(b) of the Internal Revenue Code.

(2006 H 416, eff. 1–1–07)

[1] 26 U.S.C.A. §§ 2041(b)(2), 2514(e), respectively.
[2] 26 U.S.C.A. § 2503(b).

Historical and Statutory Notes

Uniform Law: This section is analogous to § 505 of the Uniform Trust Code. See 7C Uniform Laws Annotated, Master Edition or ULA database on Westlaw.

Library References

Baldwin's Ohio Legislative Service Annotated, 2006 H 416 LSC Analysis, p 3/L-1709

Law Review and Journal Commentaries

Ohio adopts new trust code—an overview of the new Ohio trust code and house bill 416. Alan Newman, 20 Ohio Law 9 (September/October 2006).

5805.07 Personal obligations of trustee

Trust property is not subject to personal obligations of the trustee, even if the trustee becomes insolvent or bankrupt.

(2006 H 416, eff. 1–1–07)

Historical and Statutory Notes

Uniform Law: This section is analogous to § 507 of the Uniform Trust Code. See 7C Uniform Laws Annotated, Master Edition or ULA database on Westlaw.

Library References

Baldwin's Ohio Legislative Service Annotated, 2006 H 416 LSC Analysis, p 3/L-1709

CHAPTER 5806

REVOCABLE TRUSTS

Section
5806.01 Capacity of settlor of revocable trust
5806.02 Revocation or amendment of revocable trust
5806.03 Powers of settlor; withdrawal
5806.04 Limitation of actions pertaining to revocable trusts made irrevocable by death of settlor

5806.01 Capacity of settlor of revocable trust

The capacity required to create, amend, revoke, or add property to a revocable trust, or to direct the actions of the trustee of a revocable trust, is the same as that required to make a will.

(2006 H 416, eff. 1–1–07)

Historical and Statutory Notes

Uniform Law: This section is analogous to § 601 of the Uniform Trust Code. See 7C Uniform Laws Annotated, Master Edition or ULA database on Westlaw.

Library References

Baldwin's Ohio Legislative Service Annotated, 2006 H 416 LSC Analysis, p 3/L-1709

Law Review and Journal Commentaries

Ohio adopts new trust code—an overview of the new Ohio trust code and house bill 416. Alan Newman, 20 Ohio Law 9 (September/October 2006).

5806.02 Revocation or amendment of revocable trust

(A) Unless the terms of a trust expressly provide that the trust is irrevocable, the settlor may revoke or amend the trust. This division does not apply to a trust created under an instrument executed before the effective date of this section.

(B) If a revocable trust is created or funded by more than one settlor, all of the following apply:

(1) To the extent the trust consists of community property, either spouse acting alone may revoke the trust, but the trust may be amended only by joint action of both spouses.

(2) To the extent the trust consists of property other than community property, each settlor may revoke or amend the trust with regard to the portion of the trust property attributable to that settlor's contribution.

(3) Upon the revocation or amendment of the trust by less than all of the settlors, the trustee shall promptly notify the other settlors of the revocation or amendment.

(C) The settlor may revoke or amend a revocable trust by substantial compliance with a method provided in the terms of the trust or, if the terms of the trust do not provide a method, by any other method manifesting clear and convincing evidence of the settlor's intent, provided that a revocable trust may not be revoked or amended by a will or codicil, regardless of whether it refers to the trust or specifically devises property that would otherwise have passed according to the terms of the trust unless the terms of the trust expressly allow it to be revoked or amended by a will or codicil.

(D) Upon revocation of a revocable trust, the trustee shall deliver the trust property as the settlor directs.

(E) An agent under a power of attorney may exercise a settlor's powers with respect to revocation, amendment, or distribution of trust property only to the extent expressly authorized by both the terms of the trust and the power.

(F) A guardian of the estate of the settlor or, if no guardian of the estate has been appointed, a guardian of the person of the settlor may exercise a settlor's powers with respect to revocation, amendment, or distribution of trust property only with the approval of the court supervising the guardianship.

(G) A trustee who does not know that a trust has been revoked or amended is not liable to the settlor or settlor's successors in interest for distributions made and other actions taken on the assumption that the trust had not been amended or revoked.

(2006 H 416, eff. 1–1–07)

Historical and Statutory Notes

Uniform Law: This section is analogous to § 602 of the Uniform Trust Code. See 7C Uniform Laws Annotated, Master Edition or ULA database on Westlaw.

Cross References

Notice and consent regarding representation and binding another person, 5803.01

Library References

Baldwin's Ohio Legislative Service Annotated, 2006 H 416 LSC Analysis, p 3/L-1709

Law Review and Journal Commentaries

Beneficiary information and notices. Susan S. Locke, 17 Prob L J Ohio 5 (September/October 2006).

The evolution of Ohio trust law from the English common law to the Ohio trust code. Joanne E. Hindel, 17 Prob L J Ohio 1 (September/October 2006).

Ohio adopts new trust code—an overview of the new Ohio trust code and house bill 416. Alan Newman, 20 Ohio Law 9 (September/October 2006).

5806.03 Powers of settlor; withdrawal

(A) During the lifetime of the settlor of a revocable trust, whether or not the settlor has capacity to revoke the trust, the rights of the beneficiaries are subject to the control of, and the duties of the trustee are owed exclusively to, the settlor. If the trustee breaches its duty during the lifetime of the settlor, any recovery obtained from the trustee after the settlor becomes incapacitated or dies shall be apportioned by the court. If the settlor is living when the recovery is obtained, the court shall apportion the recovery between the settlor and the trust, or allocate the entire recovery to the settlor or the trust, as it determines to be equitable under the circumstances. If the settlor is not living when the recovery is obtained, the court shall apportion the recovery between the settlor's estate and the trust, or allocate the entire recovery to the settlor's estate or the trust, as it determines to be equitable under the circumstances.

(B) During the period the power may be exercised, the holder of a power of withdrawal has the rights of a settlor of a revocable trust under this section to the extent of the property subject to the power.

(2006 H 416, eff. 1–1–07)

Historical and Statutory Notes

Uniform Law: This section is analogous to § 603 of the Uniform Trust Code. See 7C Uniform Laws Annotated, Master Edition or ULA database on Westlaw.

Library References

Baldwin's Ohio Legislative Service Annotated, 2006 H 416 LSC Analysis, p 3/L-1709

Law Review and Journal Commentaries

Ohio adopts new trust code—an overview of the new Ohio trust code and house bill 416. Alan Newman, 20 Ohio Law 9 (September/October 2006).

5806.04 Limitation of actions pertaining to revocable trusts made irrevocable by death of settlor

(A) Any of the following actions pertaining to a revocable trust that is made irrevocable by the death of the settlor of the trust shall be commenced within two years after the date of the death of the settlor of the trust:

(1) An action to contest the validity of the trust;

(2) An action to contest the validity of any amendment to the trust that was made during the lifetime of the settlor of the trust;

(3) An action to contest the revocation of the trust during the lifetime of the settlor of the trust;

(4) An action to contest the validity of any transfer made to the trust during the lifetime of the settlor of the trust.

(B) Upon the death of the settlor of a revocable trust that was made irrevocable by the death of the settlor, the trustee, without liability, may proceed to distribute the trust property in accordance with the terms of the trust unless either of the following applies:

(1) The trustee has actual knowledge of a pending action to contest the validity of the trust, any amendment to the trust, the revocation of the trust, or any transfer made to the trust during the lifetime of the settlor of the trust.

(2) The trustee receives written notification from a potential contestant of a potential action to contest the validity of the trust, any amendment to the trust, the revocation of the trust, or any transfer made to the trust during the lifetime of the settlor of the trust, and the action is actually filed within ninety days after the written notification was given to the trustee.

(C) If a distribution of trust property is made pursuant to division (B) of this section, a beneficiary of the trust shall return any distribution to the extent that it exceeds the distribution to which the beneficiary is entitled if the trust, an amendment to the trust, or a transfer made to the trust later is determined to be invalid.

(D) This section applies only to revocable trusts that are made irrevocable by the death of the settlor of the trust if the grantor dies on or after July 23, 2002.

(2006 H 416, eff. 1–1–07)

Historical and Statutory Notes

Ed. Note: RC 5806.04 is former RC 2305.121, amended and recodified by 2006 H 416, eff. 1–1–07; 2002 H 345, eff. 7–23–02.

Uniform Law: This section is analogous to § 604 of the Uniform Trust Code. See 7C Uniform Laws Annotated, Master Edition or ULA database on Westlaw.

Library References

Baldwin's Ohio Legislative Service Annotated, 2006 H 416 LSC Analysis, p 3/L-1709

Law Review and Journal Commentaries

New Ohio Statute Creates a Uniform Statute of Limitations in Ohio to Contest the Validity of an Inter Vivos Trust. Karen M. Moore, 12 Prob L J Ohio 84 (May/June 2002).

Ohio adopts new trust code—an overview of the new Ohio trust code and house bill 416. Alan Newman, 20 Ohio Law 9 (September/October 2006).

CHAPTER 5807

OFFICE OF TRUSTEE

Section
5807.01 Accepting or rejecting trusteeship
5807.02 Trustee's bond
5807.03 Cotrustees
5807.04 Vacancy in trusteeship; appointment of successor
5807.05 Resignation of trustee
5807.06 Removal of trustee
5807.07 Delivery of property by former trustee

Section
5807.08 Compensation of trustee
5807.09 Reimbursement of expenses

Law Review and Journal Commentaries

The office of trustee and the duties and powers of the trustee under the Ohio trust code. Joanne E. Hindel, 17 Prob L J Ohio 10 (September/October 2006).

5807.01 Accepting or rejecting trusteeship

(A) Except as otherwise provided in division (C) of this section, a person designated as trustee accepts the trusteeship by substantially complying with a method of acceptance provided in the terms of the trust or, if the terms of the trust do not provide a method or the method provided in the terms is not expressly made exclusive, by accepting delivery of the trust property, exercising powers or performing duties as trustee, or otherwise indicating acceptance of the trusteeship.

(B) A person designated as trustee who has not yet accepted the trusteeship may reject the trusteeship. A designated trustee who does not accept the trusteeship within a reasonable time after knowing of the designation is deemed to have rejected the trusteeship.

(C) A person designated as trustee, without accepting the trusteeship, may do either or both of the following:

(1) Act to preserve the trust property if, within a reasonable time after acting, the person sends a rejection of the trusteeship to the settlor or, if the settlor is dead or lacks capacity, to a qualified beneficiary;

(2) Inspect or investigate trust property to determine potential liability under environmental or other law or for any other purpose.

(2006 H 416, eff. 1–1–07)

Historical and Statutory Notes

Uniform Law: This section is analogous to § 701 of the Uniform Trust Code. See 7C Uniform Laws Annotated, Master Edition or ULA database on Westlaw.

Library References

Baldwin's Ohio Legislative Service Annotated, 2006 H 416 LSC Analysis, p 3/L-1709

Law Review and Journal Commentaries

The office of trustee and the duties and powers of the trustee under the Ohio trust code. Joanne E. Hindel, 17 Prob L J Ohio 10 (September/October 2006).

5807.02 Trustee's bond

(A) A trustee shall give bond to secure performance of the trustee's duties only if the court finds that a bond is needed to protect the interests of the beneficiaries or is required by the terms of the trust and the court has not dispensed with the requirement.

(B) The court may specify the amount of a bond, its liabilities, and whether sureties are necessary. The court may modify or terminate a bond at any time.

(C) A regulated financial-service institution qualified to do trust business in this state need not give bond, even if required by the terms of the trust.

(2006 H 416, eff. 1–1–07)

Historical and Statutory Notes

Uniform Law: This section is analogous to § 702 of the Uniform Trust Code. See 7C Uniform Laws Annotated, Master Edition or ULA database on Westlaw.

Cross References

Scope, mandatory rules, exceptions, 5801.04

Library References

Baldwin's Ohio Legislative Service Annotated, 2006 H 416 LSC Analysis, p 3/L-1709

5807.03 Cotrustees

(A) If there are three or more cotrustees serving, the cotrustees may act by majority decision.

(B) If a vacancy occurs in a cotrusteeship, the remaining cotrustees may act for the trust.

(C) A cotrustee must participate in the performance of a trustee's function unless the cotrustee is unavailable to perform the function because of absence, illness, disqualification under other law, or other temporary incapacity or the cotrustee has properly delegated the performance of the function to another trustee.

(D) If a cotrustee is unavailable to perform duties because of absence, illness, disqualification under other law, or other temporary incapacity and prompt action is necessary to achieve the purposes of the trust or to avoid injury to the trust property, the remaining cotrustee or a majority of the remaining cotrustees may act for the trust.

(E) A trustee may delegate to a cotrustee duties and powers that a prudent trustee of comparable skills could properly delegate under the circumstances. A delegation made under this division shall be governed by section 5808.07 of the Revised Code. Unless a delegation was irrevocable, a trustee may revoke a delegation previously made.

(F) Except as otherwise provided in division (G) of this section, and subject to divisions (C) and (E) of this section, a trustee who does not join in an action of another trustee is not liable for the action.

(G) Except as otherwise provided in this division, each trustee shall exercise reasonable care to prevent a cotrustee from committing a serious breach of trust and to compel a cotrustee to redress a serious breach of trust. A trustee is not required to exercise reasonable care of that nature under this division, and a trustee is not liable for resulting losses, when section 5815.25 of the Revised Code is applicable or there is more than one other trustee and the other trustees act by majority vote.

(H) A dissenting trustee who joins in an action at the direction of the majority of the trustees and who notified any cotrustee of the dissent at or before the time of the action is not liable for the action.

(2006 H 416, eff. 1–1–07)

Historical and Statutory Notes

Uniform Law: This section is analogous to § 703 of the Uniform Trust Code. See 7C Uniform Laws Annotated, Master Edition or ULA database on Westlaw.

Library References

Baldwin's Ohio Legislative Service Annotated, 2006 H 416 LSC Analysis, p 3/L-1709

Law Review and Journal Commentaries

The office of trustee and the duties and powers of the trustee under the Ohio trust code. Joanne E. Hindel, 17 Prob L J Ohio 10 (September/October 2006).

5807.04 Vacancy in trusteeship; appointment of successor

(A) A vacancy in a trusteeship occurs under any of the following circumstances:

(1) A person designated as trustee rejects the trusteeship;

(2) A person designated as trustee cannot be identified or does not exist;

(3) A trustee resigns;

(4) A trustee is disqualified or removed;

(5) A trustee dies;

(6) A guardian of the estate or person is appointed for an individual serving as trustee.

(B) If one or more cotrustees remain in office, a vacancy in a trusteeship need not be filled. A vacancy in a trusteeship must be filled if the trust has no remaining trustee.

(C) A vacancy in a trusteeship of a noncharitable trust that is required to be filled must be filled in the following order of priority:

(1) By a person designated in the terms of the trust to act as successor trustee;

(2) By a person appointed by someone designated in the terms of the trust to appoint a successor trustee;

(3) By a person appointed by unanimous agreement of the qualified beneficiaries;

(4) By a person appointed by the court.

(D) A vacancy in a trusteeship of a charitable trust that is required to be filled must be filled in the following order of priority:

(1) By a person designated in the terms of the trust to act as successor trustee;

(2) By a person appointed by someone designated in the terms of the trust to appoint a successor trustee;

(3) By a person selected by the charitable organizations expressly designated to receive distributions under the terms of the trust;

(4) By a person appointed by the court.

(E) Whether or not a vacancy in a trusteeship exists or is required to be filled, the court may appoint an additional trustee or special fiduciary whenever the court considers the appointment necessary for the administration of the trust.

(2006 H 416, eff. 1–1–07)

Historical and Statutory Notes

Uniform Law: This section is analogous to § 704 of the Uniform Trust Code. See 7C Uniform Laws Annotated, Master Edition or ULA database on Westlaw.

Library References

Baldwin's Ohio Legislative Service Annotated, 2006 H 416 LSC Analysis, p 3/L-1709

Law Review and Journal Commentaries

The office of trustee and the duties and powers of the trustee under the Ohio trust code. Joanne E. Hindel, 17 Prob L J Ohio 10 (September/October 2006).

Ohio adopts new trust code—an overview of the new Ohio trust code and house bill 416. Alan Newman, 20 Ohio Law 9 (September/October 2006).

5807.05 Resignation of trustee

(A) A trustee may resign upon at least thirty days' notice to the qualified beneficiaries, the settlor, if living, and all cotrustees or with the approval of the court.

(B) In approving a resignation of a trustee, the court may issue orders and impose conditions reasonably necessary for the protection of the trust property.

(C) Any liability of a resigning trustee or of any sureties on the trustee's bond for acts or omissions of the trustee is not discharged or affected by the trustee's resignation.

(2006 H 416, eff. 1–1–07)

Historical and Statutory Notes

Uniform Law: This section is analogous to § 705 of the Uniform Trust Code. See 7C Uniform Laws Annotated, Master Edition or ULA database on Westlaw.

Library References

Baldwin's Ohio Legislative Service Annotated, 2006 H 416 LSC Analysis, p 3/L-1709

Law Review and Journal Commentaries

Beneficiary information and notices. Susan S. Locke, 17 Prob L J Ohio 5 (September/October 2006).

The evolution of Ohio trust law from the English common law to the Ohio trust code. Joanne E. Hindel, 17 Prob L J Ohio 1 (September/October 2006).

5807.06 Removal of trustee

(A) The settlor, a cotrustee, or a beneficiary may request the court to remove a trustee, or the court may remove a trustee on its own initiative.

(B) The court may remove a trustee for any of the following reasons:

(1) The trustee has committed a serious breach of trust;

(2) Lack of cooperation among cotrustees substantially impairs the administration of the trust;

(3) Because of unfitness, unwillingness, or persistent failure of the trustee to administer the trust effectively, the court determines that removal of the trustee best serves the interests of the beneficiaries.

(C) Pending a final decision on a request to remove a trustee, or in lieu of or in addition to removing a trustee, the court may order any appropriate relief under division (B) of section 5810.01 of the Revised Code that is necessary to protect the trust property or the interests of the beneficiaries.

(2006 H 416, eff. 1–1–07)

Historical and Statutory Notes

Uniform Law: This section is analogous to § 706 of the Uniform Trust Code. See 7C Uniform Laws Annotated, Master Edition or ULA database on Westlaw.

Library References

Baldwin's Ohio Legislative Service Annotated, 2006 H 416 LSC Analysis, p 3/L-1709

Law Review and Journal Commentaries

The office of trustee and the duties and powers of the trustee under the Ohio trust code. Joanne E. Hindel, 17 Prob L J Ohio 10 (September/October 2006).

Ohio adopts new trust code—an overview of the new Ohio trust code and house bill 416. Alan Newman, 20 Ohio Law 9 (September/October 2006).

5807.07 Delivery of property by former trustee

(A) Unless a cotrustee remains in office or the court otherwise orders, and until the trust property is delivered to a successor trustee or other person entitled to it, a trustee who has resigned or been removed has the duties of a trustee and the powers necessary to protect the trust property.

(B) A trustee who has resigned or been removed shall proceed expeditiously to deliver the trust property within the trustee's possession to the cotrustee, successor trustee, or other person entitled to it.

(2006 H 416, eff. 1–1–07)

Historical and Statutory Notes

Uniform Law: This section is analogous to § 707 of the Uniform Trust Code. See 7C Uniform Laws Annotated, Master Edition or ULA database on Westlaw.

Library References

Baldwin's Ohio Legislative Service Annotated, 2006 H 416 LSC Analysis, p 3/L-1709

5807.08 Compensation of trustee

(A) If the terms of a trust do not specify the trustee's compensation, a trustee is entitled to compensation that is reasonable under the circumstances.

(B) If the terms of a trust specify the trustee's compensation, the trustee is entitled to be compensated as specified, but the court may allow more or less compensation if the duties of the trustee are substantially different from those contemplated when the trust was created or the compensation specified by the terms of the trust would be unreasonably low or high.

(2006 H 416, eff. 1–1–07)

Historical and Statutory Notes

Uniform Law: This section is analogous to § 708 of the Uniform Trust Code. See 7C Uniform Laws Annotated, Master Edition or ULA database on Westlaw.

Cross References

Scope, mandatory rules, exceptions, 5801.04

Library References

Baldwin's Ohio Legislative Service Annotated, 2006 H 416 LSC Analysis, p 3/L-1709

Law Review and Journal Commentaries

The office of trustee and the duties and powers of the trustee under the Ohio trust code. Joanne E. Hindel, 17 Prob L J Ohio 10 (September/October 2006).

5807.09 Reimbursement of expenses

(A) A trustee is entitled to be reimbursed out of the trust property, with interest as appropriate, for expenses that were properly incurred in the administration of the trust and, to the extent necessary to prevent unjust enrichment of the trust, expenses that were not properly incurred in the administration of the trust.

(B) An advance by the trustee of money for the protection of the trust gives rise to a lien against trust property to secure reimbursement with reasonable interest.

(2006 H 416, eff. 1–1–07)

Historical and Statutory Notes

Uniform Law: This section is analogous to § 709 of the Uniform Trust Code. See 7C Uniform Laws Annotated, Master Edition or ULA database on Westlaw.

Library References

Baldwin's Ohio Legislative Service Annotated, 2006 H 416 LSC Analysis, p 3/L-1709

CHAPTER 5808

POWERS AND DUTIES OF TRUSTEE

Section
5808.01 Duty to administer trust
5808.02 Duty of loyalty; conflict of interest
5808.03 Loyalty; impartiality
5808.04 Prudent administration
5808.05 Investment costs
5808.06 Trustee's skills or expertise
5808.07 Delegation of duties and powers
5808.08 Powers to direct
5808.09 Control and protection of trust property
5808.10 Recordkeeping and separation of trust property
5808.11 Enforcement and defense of claims
5808.12 Collection of trust property
5808.13 Duty to inform and report
5808.14 Discretionary powers
5808.15 General powers of trustee
5808.16 Specific powers of trustee
5808.17 Distribution upon termination

Law Review and Journal Commentaries

The office of trustee and the duties and powers of the trustee under the Ohio trust code. Joanne E. Hindel, 17 Prob L J Ohio 10 (September/October 2006).

5808.01 Duty to administer trust

Upon acceptance of a trusteeship, the trustee shall administer the trust in good faith, in accordance with its terms and purposes and the interests of the beneficiaries, and in accordance with Chapters 5801. to 5811. of the Revised Code.

(2006 H 416, eff. 1–1–07)

Historical and Statutory Notes

Uniform Law: This section is analogous to § 801 of the Uniform Trust Code. See 7C Uniform Laws Annotated, Master Edition or ULA database on Westlaw.

Library References

Baldwin's Ohio Legislative Service Annotated, 2006 H 416 LSC Analysis, p 3/L-1709

Law Review and Journal Commentaries

The office of trustee and the duties and powers of the trustee under the Ohio trust code. Joanne E. Hindel, 17 Prob L J Ohio 10 (September/October 2006).

5808.02 Duty of loyalty; conflict of interest

(A) A trustee shall administer the trust solely in the interests of the beneficiaries.

(B) Subject to the rights of persons dealing with or assisting the trustee as provided in section 5810.12 of the Revised Code, a sale, encumbrance, or other transaction involving the investment or management of trust property entered into by the trustee for the trustee's own personal account or that is otherwise affected by a conflict between the trustee's fiduciary and personal interests is voidable by a beneficiary affected by the transaction unless one of the following applies:

(1) The transaction was authorized by the terms of the trust or by other provisions of the Revised Code.

(2) The transaction was approved by the court.

(3) The beneficiary did not commence a judicial proceeding within the time allowed by section 5810.05 of the Revised Code.

(4) The beneficiary consented to the trustee's conduct, ratified the transaction, or released the trustee in compliance with section 5810.09 of the Revised Code.

(5) The transaction involves a contract entered into or claim acquired by the trustee before the person became or contemplated becoming trustee.

(C) A sale, encumbrance, or other transaction involving the investment or management of trust property is presumed to be affected by a conflict between personal and fiduciary interests if it is entered into by the trustee with one of the following:

(1) The trustee's spouse;

(2) The trustee's descendant, sibling, or parent or the spouse of a trustee's descendant, sibling, or parent;

(3) An agent or attorney of the trustee;

(4) A corporation or other person or enterprise in which the trustee, or a person that owns a significant interest in the trustee, has an interest that might affect the trustee's best judgment.

(D) A transaction not concerning trust property in which the trustee engages in the trustee's individual capacity involves a conflict between personal and fiduciary interests if the transaction concerns an opportunity properly belonging to the trust.

(E) An investment by a trustee that is permitted by other provisions of the Revised Code is not presumed to be affected by a conflict between personal and fiduciary interests if the investment otherwise complies with the prudent investor rule of Chapter 5809. of the Revised Code.

(F) In voting shares of stock or in exercising powers of control over similar interests in other forms of enterprise, the trustee shall act in the best interests of the beneficiaries. If the trust is the sole owner of a corporation or other form of enterprise, the trustee shall elect or appoint directors or other managers who will manage the corporation or enterprise in the best interests of the beneficiaries.

(G) This section does not preclude either of the following:

(1) Any transaction authorized by another section of the Revised Code;

(2) Unless the beneficiaries establish that it is unfair, any of the following transactions:

(a) An agreement between a trustee and a beneficiary relating to the appointment or compensation of the trustee;

(b) Payment of reasonable compensation to the trustee;

(c) A transaction between a trust and another trust, decedent's estate, or guardianship of which the trustee is a fiduciary or in which a beneficiary has an interest;

(d) A deposit of trust money in a regulated financial-services institution that is an affiliate of the trustee;

(e) An advance by the trustee of money for the protection of the trust.

(H) The court may appoint a special fiduciary to make a decision with respect to any proposed transaction that might violate this section if entered into by the trustee.

(2006 H 416, eff. 1–1–07)

Historical and Statutory Notes

Uniform Law: This section is analogous to § 802 of the Uniform Trust Code. See 7C Uniform Laws Annotated, Master Edition or ULA database on Westlaw.

Library References

Baldwin's Ohio Legislative Service Annotated, 2006 H 416 LSC Analysis, p 3/L-1709

Law Review and Journal Commentaries

The office of trustee and the duties and powers of the trustee under the Ohio trust code. Joanne E. Hindel, 17 Prob L J Ohio 10 (September/October 2006).

5808.03 Loyalty; impartiality

If a trust has two or more beneficiaries, the trustee shall act impartially in investing, managing, and distributing the trust property, giving due regard to the beneficiaries' respective interests.

(2006 H 416, eff. 1–1–07)

Uncodified Law

1998 H 701, § 3: See Uncodified Law under 5809.01.

Historical and Statutory Notes

Ed. Note: RC 5808.03 is former RC 1339.55, amended and recodified by 2006 H 416, eff. 1–1–07; 1998 H 701, eff. 3–22–99.

Uniform Law: This section is analogous to § 803 of the Uniform Trust Code. See 7C Uniform Laws Annotated, Master Edition or ULA database on Westlaw.

Uniform Law: This section is similar to § 5 and 6 of the Uniform Prudent Investor Act. See 7B, Uniform Laws Annotated, Master Edition.

Library References

Trusts ⚖ 179, 217.3(1).
Westlaw Topic No. 390.
C.J.S. Trusts §§ 321 to 324, 326, 482, 491, 493 to 494.

Baldwin's Ohio Legislative Service Annotated, 2006 H 416 LSC Analysis, p 3/L-1709

Baldwin's Ohio Legislative Service Annotated, 1998 H 701—LSC Analysis, p 12/L-2178

5808.04 Prudent administration

A trustee shall administer the trust as a prudent person would and shall consider the purposes, terms, distributional requirements, and other circumstances of the trust. In satisfying this standard, the trustee shall exercise reasonable care, skill, and caution.

(2006 H 416, eff. 1–1–07)

Historical and Statutory Notes

Uniform Law: This section is analogous to § 804 of the Uniform Trust Code. See 7C Uniform Laws Annotated, Master Edition or ULA database on Westlaw.

Library References

Baldwin's Ohio Legislative Service Annotated, 2006 H 416 LSC Analysis, p 3/L-1709

5808.05 Investment costs

Except as otherwise permitted by law, in administering a trust, a trustee may incur only costs that are appropriate and reasonable in relation to the assets, the purposes of the trust, and the skills of the trustee.

(2006 H 416, eff. 1–1–07)

Uncodified Law

1998 H 701, § 3: See Uncodified Law under 5809.01.

Historical and Statutory Notes

Ed. Note: RC 5808.05 is former RC 1339.57, amended and recodified by 2006 H 416, eff. 1–1–07; 1998 H 701, eff. 3–22–99.

Uniform Law: This section is analogous to § 805 of the Uniform Trust Code. See 7C Uniform Laws Annotated, Master Edition or ULA database on Westlaw.

Uniform Law: This section is similar to § 7 of the Uniform Prudent Investor Act. See 7B, Uniform Laws Annotated, Master Edition.

Library References

Trusts ⚖227.
Westlaw Topic No. 390.
C.J.S. Trusts §§ 383, 389 to 390, 395 to 400.

Baldwin's Ohio Legislative Service Annotated, 2006 H 416 LSC Analysis, p 3/L-1709
Baldwin's Ohio Legislative Service Annotated, 1998 H 701—LSC Analysis, p 12/L-2178

5808.06 Trustee's skills or expertise

A trustee who has special skills or expertise, or is named trustee in reliance upon the trustee's representation that the trustee has special skills or expertise, shall use those special skills or expertise.

(2006 H 416, eff. 1–1–07)

Historical and Statutory Notes

Uniform Law: This section is analogous to § 806 of the Uniform Trust Code. See 7C Uniform Laws Annotated, Master Edition or ULA database on Westlaw.

Library References

Baldwin's Ohio Legislative Service Annotated, 2006 H 416 LSC Analysis, p 3/L-1709

5808.07 Delegation of duties and powers

(A) A trustee may delegate duties and powers that a prudent trustee having comparable skills could properly delegate under the circumstances. In accordance with this division, a trustee shall exercise reasonable care, skill, and caution in doing all of the following:

(1) Selecting an agent, cotrustee, or other fiduciary to whom the delegation is made;

(2) Establishing the scope and terms of the delegation consistent with the purposes and terms of the trust;

(3) Periodically reviewing the agent's, cotrustee's, or other fiduciary's actions in order to monitor the agent's, cotrustee's, or other fiduciary's performance and compliance with the terms of the delegation.

(B) In performing a delegated function, an agent, cotrustee, or other fiduciary owes a duty to the trust to exercise reasonable care to comply with the terms of the delegation.

(C) A trustee who complies with division (A) of this section is not liable to the beneficiaries of the trust or to the trust for the decisions or actions of the agent, cotrustee, or other fiduciary to whom the function was delegated.

(D) By accepting the delegation of powers or duties from the trustee of a trust that is subject to the laws of this state, an agent, cotrustee, or other fiduciary submits to the jurisdiction of this state.

(2006 H 416, eff. 1–1–07)

Uncodified Law

1998 H 701, § 3: See Uncodified Law under 5809.01.

Historical and Statutory Notes

Ed. Note: RC 5808.07 is former RC 1339.59, amended and recodified by 2006 H 416, eff. 1–1–07; 1998 H 701, eff. 3–22–99.

Uniform Law: This section is analogous to § 807 of the Uniform Trust Code. See 7C Uniform Laws Annotated, Master Edition or ULA database on Westlaw.

Uniform Law: This section is similar to § 9 of the Uniform Prudent Investor Act. See 7B, Uniform Laws Annotated, Master Edition.

Cross References

Cotrustees, 5807.03
Delegation by trustee, 5809.06

Library References

Trusts ⚖176.
Westlaw Topic No. 390.
C.J.S. Trusts §§ 343 to 344.

Baldwin's Ohio Legislative Service Annotated, 2006 H 416 LSC Analysis, p 3/L-1709
Baldwin's Ohio Legislative Service Annotated, 1998 H 701—LSC Analysis, p 12/L-2178

Law Review and Journal Commentaries

The New Ohio Uniform Prudent Investor Act, Joanne E. Hindel. 9 Prob L J Ohio 38 (January/February 1999).

The office of trustee and the duties and powers of the trustee under the Ohio trust code. Joanne E. Hindel, 17 Prob L J Ohio 10 (September/October 2006).

5808.08 Powers to direct

(A) While a trust is revocable, the trustee may follow a direction of the settlor that is contrary to the terms of the trust.

(B) As provided in section 5815.25 of the Revised Code, a trustee is not liable for losses resulting from certain actions or failures to act when other persons are granted certain powers with respect to the administration of the trust.

(C) The terms of a trust may confer upon a trustee or other person a power to direct the modification or termination of the trust.

(D) A person other than a beneficiary who holds a power to direct is presumptively a fiduciary who, as a fiduciary, is required to act in good faith with regard to the purposes of the trust and the interests of the beneficiaries. The holder of a power to direct is liable for any loss that results from breach of a fiduciary duty.

(2006 H 416, eff. 1–1–07)

Historical and Statutory Notes

Uniform Law: This section is analogous to § 808 of the Uniform Trust Code. See 7C Uniform Laws Annotated, Master Edition or ULA database on Westlaw.

Library References

Baldwin's Ohio Legislative Service Annotated, 2006 H 416 LSC Analysis, p 3/L-1709

Law Review and Journal Commentaries

The office of trustee and the duties and powers of the trustee under the Ohio trust code. Joanne E. Hindel, 17 Prob L J Ohio 10 (September/October 2006).

5808.09 Control and protection of trust property

A trustee shall take reasonable steps to take control of and protect the trust property.

(2006 H 416, eff. 1–1–07)

Historical and Statutory Notes

Uniform Law: This section is analogous to § 809 of the Uniform Trust Code. See 7C Uniform Laws Annotated, Master Edition or ULA database on Westlaw.

Library References

Baldwin's Ohio Legislative Service Annotated, 2006 H 416 LSC Analysis, p 3/L-1709

5808.10 Recordkeeping and separation of trust property

(A) A trustee shall keep adequate records of the administration of the trust.

(B) A trustee shall keep trust property separate from the trustee's own property.

(C) Except as otherwise provided in division (D) of this section and in section 2131.21 of the Revised Code, a trustee not subject to federal or state banking regulation shall cause the trust property to be designated so that the interest of the trust, to the extent feasible, appears in records maintained by a party other than a trustee or beneficiary.

(D) If the trustee maintains records clearly indicating the respective interests, a trustee may invest as a whole the property of two or more separate trusts.

(2006 H 416, eff. 1–1–07)

Historical and Statutory Notes

Uniform Law: This section is analogous to § 810 of the Uniform Trust Code. See 7C Uniform Laws Annotated, Master Edition or ULA database on Westlaw.

Library References

Baldwin's Ohio Legislative Service Annotated, 2006 H 416 LSC Analysis, p 3/L-1709

5808.11 Enforcement and defense of claims

A trustee shall take reasonable steps to enforce claims of the trust and to defend claims against the trust.

(2006 H 416, eff. 1–1–07)

Historical and Statutory Notes

Uniform Law: This section is analogous to § 811 of the Uniform Trust Code. See 7C Uniform Laws Annotated, Master Edition or ULA database on Westlaw.

Library References

Baldwin's Ohio Legislative Service Annotated, 2006 H 416 LSC Analysis, p 3/L-1709

5808.12 Collection of trust property

A trustee shall take reasonable steps to collect trust property held by third persons. The responsibility of a successor trustee with respect to the administration of the trust by a prior trustee shall be governed by section 5815.24 of the Revised Code.

(2006 H 416, eff. 1–1–07)

Historical and Statutory Notes

Uniform Law: This section is analogous, in part, to § 812 of the Uniform Trust Code. See 7C Uniform Laws Annotated, Master Edition or ULA database on Westlaw.

Library References

Baldwin's Ohio Legislative Service Annotated, 2006 H 416 LSC Analysis, p 3/L-1709

5808.13 Duty to inform and report

(A) A trustee shall keep the current beneficiaries of the trust reasonably informed about the administration of the trust and of the material facts necessary for them to protect their interests. Unless unreasonable under the circumstances, a trustee shall promptly respond to a beneficiary's request for information related to the administration of the trust.

(B) A trustee shall do all of the following:

(1) Upon the request of a beneficiary, promptly furnish to the beneficiary a copy of the trust instrument. If the settlor of a revocable trust that has become irrevocable has completely restated the terms of the trust, the trust instrument furnished by the trustee shall be the restated trust instrument, including any amendments to the restated trust instrument. Nothing in division (B)(1) of this section limits the ability of a beneficiary to obtain a copy of the original trust instrument, any other restatements of the original trust instrument, or amendments to the original trust instrument and any other restatements of the original trust instrument in a judicial proceeding with respect to the trust.

(2) Within sixty days after accepting a trusteeship, notify the current beneficiaries of the acceptance and of the trustee's name, address, and telephone number;

(3) Within sixty days after the date the trustee acquires knowledge of the creation of an irrevocable trust, or the date the trustee acquires knowledge that a formerly revocable trust has become irrevocable, whether by the death of the settlor or otherwise, notify the current beneficiaries of the trust's existence, of the identity of the settlor or settlors, of the right to request a copy of the trust instrument, and of the right to a trustee's report as provided in division (C) of this section;

(4) Notify the current beneficiaries in advance of any change in the method or rate of the trustee's compensation.

(C) A trustee shall send to the current beneficiaries, and to other beneficiaries who request it, at least annually and at the termination of the trust, a report of the trust property, liabilities, receipts, and disbursements, including the source and amount of the trustee's compensation, a listing of the trust assets, and, if feasible, the trust assets' respective market values. Upon a vacancy in a trusteeship, unless a cotrustee remains in office, a report for the period during which the former trustee served must be sent to the current beneficiaries by the former trustee. A personal representative or guardian may send the current beneficiaries a report on behalf of a deceased or incapacitated trustee.

(D) A beneficiary may waive the right to a trustee's report or other information otherwise required to be furnished under this section. A beneficiary, with respect to future reports and other information, may withdraw a waiver previously given.

(E) The trustee may provide information and reports to beneficiaries to whom the provided information and reports are not required to be provided under this section.

(F) Divisions (B)(2) and (3) of this section apply only to a trustee who accepts a trusteeship on or after the effective date of this section, to an irrevocable trust created on or after the effective date of this section, and to a revocable trust that becomes irrevocable on or after the effective date of this section.

(2006 H 416, eff. 1–1–07)

Historical and Statutory Notes

Uniform Law: This section is analogous to § 813 of the Uniform Trust Code. See 7C Uniform Laws Annotated, Master Edition or ULA database on Westlaw.

Cross References

Laws applicable to testamentary trusts, 2109.69
Scope, mandatory rules, exceptions, 5801.04

Library References

Baldwin's Ohio Legislative Service Annotated, 2006 H 416 LSC Analysis, p 3/L-1709

Law Review and Journal Commentaries

Beneficiary information and notices. Susan S. Locke, 17 Prob L J Ohio 5 (September/October 2006).

The evolution of Ohio trust law from the English common law to the Ohio trust code. Joanne E. Hindel, 17 Prob L J Ohio 1 (September/October 2006).

The office of trustee and the duties and powers of the trustee under the Ohio trust code. Joanne E. Hindel, 17 Prob L J Ohio 10 (September/October 2006).

Ohio adopts new trust code—an overview of the new Ohio trust code and house bill 416. Alan Newman, 20 Ohio Law 9 (September/October 2006).

5808.14 Discretionary powers

(A) The judicial standard of review for discretionary trusts is that the trustee shall exercise a discretionary power reasonably, in good faith, and in accordance with the terms and purposes of the trust and the interests of the beneficiaries, except that a reasonableness standard shall not be applied to the exercise of discretion by the trustee of a wholly discretionary trust. The greater the grant of discretion by the settlor to the trustee, the broader the range of permissible conduct by the trustee in exercising it.

(B) Subject to division (D) of this section, and unless the terms of the trust expressly indicate that a rule in this division does not apply:

(1) A person other than a settlor who is a beneficiary and trustee of a trust that confers on the trustee a power to make discretionary distributions to or for the trustee's personal benefit may exercise the power only in accordance with an ascertainable standard.

(2) A trustee may not exercise a power to make discretionary distributions to satisfy a legal obligation of support that the trustee personally owes another person.

(C) A power whose exercise is limited or prohibited by division (B) of this section may be exercised by a majority of the remaining trustees whose exercise of the power is not so limited or prohibited. If the power of all trustees is so limited or prohibited, the court may appoint a special fiduciary with authority to exercise the power.

(D) Division (B) of this section does not apply to any of the following:

(1) A power held by the settlor's spouse who is the trustee of a trust for which a marital deduction, as defined in section 2056(b)(5) or 2523(e) of the Internal Revenue Code, was previously allowed;

(2) Any trust during any period that the trust may be revoked or amended by its settlor;

(3) A trust if contributions to the trust qualify for the annual exclusion under section 2503(c) of the Internal Revenue Code.[1]

(2006 H 416, eff. 1–1–07)

[1] 26 U.S.C.A. 2503(c).

Uncodified Law

2006 H 416, § 4, eff. 1–1–07, reads:

In enacting divisions (B) to (D) of section 5808.14 of the Revised Code in Section 1 of this act, the General Assembly hereby declares its intent to codify certain fiduciary and trust law principles, previously codified in sections 1340.21 and 1340.23 of the Revised Code, relating to a fiduciary's conflict of interests and, in general, to provide for the exercise of certain discretionary powers to distribute either principal or income to a beneficiary by a beneficially interested fiduciary for the beneficially interested fiduciary's own benefit to the extent of an ascertainable standard.

Historical and Statutory Notes

Uniform Law: This section is analogous to § 814 of the Uniform Trust Code. See 7C Uniform Laws Annotated, Master Edition or ULA database on Westlaw.

Library References

Baldwin's Ohio Legislative Service Annotated, 2006 H 416 LSC Analysis, p 3/L-1709

Law Review and Journal Commentaries

The office of trustee and the duties and powers of the trustee under the Ohio trust code. Joanne E. Hindel, 17 Prob L J Ohio 10 (September/October 2006).

5808.15 General powers of trustee

(A) A trustee, without authorization by the court, may exercise powers conferred by the terms of the trust and, except as limited by the terms of the trust, may exercise all of the following powers:

(1) All powers over the trust property that an unmarried competent owner has over individually owned property;

(2) Any other powers appropriate to achieve the proper investment, management, and distribution of the trust property;

(3) Any other powers conferred by Chapters 5801. to 5811. of the Revised Code.

(B) The exercise of a power is subject to the fiduciary duties prescribed by Chapter 5808. of the Revised Code.

(2006 H 416, eff. 1–1–07)

Historical and Statutory Notes

Uniform Law: This section is analogous to § 815 of the Uniform Trust Code. See 7C Uniform Laws Annotated, Master Edition or ULA database on Westlaw.

Library References

Baldwin's Ohio Legislative Service Annotated, 2006 H 416 LSC Analysis, p 3/L-1709

Law Review and Journal Commentaries

The office of trustee and the duties and powers of the trustee under the Ohio trust code. Joanne E. Hindel, 17 Prob L J Ohio 10 (September/October 2006).

Ohio adopts new trust code—an overview of the new Ohio trust code and house bill 416. Alan Newman, 20 Ohio Law 9 (September/October 2006).

5808.16 Specific powers of trustee

Without limiting the authority conferred by section 5808.15 of the Revised Code, a trustee may do all of the following:

(A) Collect trust property and accept or reject additions to the trust property from a settlor or any other person;

(B) Acquire or sell property, for cash or on credit, at public or private sale;

(C) Exchange, partition, or otherwise change the character of trust property;

(D) Deposit trust money in an account in a regulated financial-service institution;

(E) Borrow money, with or without security, and mortgage or pledge trust property for a period within or extending beyond the duration of the trust;

(F) With respect to an interest in a proprietorship, partnership, limited liability company, business trust, corporation, or other form of business or enterprise, continue the business or other enterprise and take any action that may be taken by shareholders, members, or property owners, including merging, dissolving, or otherwise changing the form of business organization or contributing additional capital;

(G) With respect to stocks or other securities, exercise the rights of an absolute owner, including the right to do any of the following:

(1) Vote, or give proxies to vote, with or without power of substitution, or enter into or continue a voting trust agreement;

(2) Hold a security in the name of a nominee or in other form without disclosure of the trust so that title may pass by delivery;

(3) Pay calls, assessments, and other sums chargeable or accruing against the securities and sell or exercise stock subscription or conversion rights;

(4) Deposit the securities with a depositary or other regulated financial-service institution.

(H) With respect to an interest in real property, construct, or make ordinary or extraordinary repairs to, alterations to, or improvements in, buildings or other structures, demolish improvements, raze existing or erect new party walls or buildings, subdivide or develop land, dedicate land to public use or grant public or private easements, and make or vacate plats and adjust boundaries;

(I) Enter into a lease for any purpose as lessor or lessee, including a lease or other arrangement for exploration and removal of natural resources, with or without the option to purchase or renew, for a period within or extending beyond the duration of the trust;

(J) Grant an option involving a sale, lease, or other disposition of trust property or acquire an option for the acquisition of property, including an option exercisable beyond the duration of the trust, and exercise an option so acquired;

(K) Insure the property of the trust against damage or loss and insure the trustee, the trustee's agents, and beneficiaries against liability arising from the administration of the trust;

(L) Abandon or decline to administer property of no value or of insufficient value to justify its collection or continued administration;

(M) With respect to possible liability for violation of environmental law, do any of the following:

(1) Inspect or investigate property the trustee holds or has been asked to hold, or property owned or operated by an organization in which the trustee holds or has been asked to hold an interest, for the purpose of determining the application of environmental law with respect to the property;

(2) Take action to prevent, abate, or otherwise remedy any actual or potential violation of any environmental law affecting property held directly or indirectly by the trustee, whether taken before or after the assertion of a claim or the initiation of governmental enforcement;

(3) Decline to accept property into trust or disclaim any power with respect to property that is or may be burdened with liability for violation of environmental law;

(4) Compromise claims against the trust that may be asserted for an alleged violation of environmental law;

(5) Pay the expense of any inspection, review, abatement, or remedial action to comply with environmental law.

(N) Pay or contest any claim, settle a claim by or against the trust, and release, in whole or in part, a claim belonging to the trust;

(O) Pay taxes, assessments, compensation of the trustee and of employees and agents of the trust, and other expenses incurred in the administration of the trust;

(P) Exercise elections with respect to federal, state, and local taxes;

(Q) Select a mode of payment under any employee benefit or retirement plan, annuity, or life insurance policy payable to the trustee, exercise rights under any employee benefit or retirement plan, annuity, or life insurance policy payable to the trustee, including the right to indemnification for expenses and against liabilities, and take appropriate action to collect the proceeds;

(R) Make loans out of trust property, including loans to a beneficiary on terms and conditions the trustee considers to be fair and reasonable under the circumstances, and the trustee has a lien on future distributions for repayment of those loans;

(S) Pledge the property of a revocable trust to guarantee loans made by others to the settlor of the revocable trust, or, if the settlor so directs, to guarantee loans made by others to a third party;

(T) Appoint a trustee to act in another jurisdiction with respect to trust property located in the other jurisdiction, confer upon the appointed trustee all of the powers and duties of the appointing trustee, require that the appointed trustee furnish security, and remove any trustee so appointed;

(U) Pay an amount distributable to a beneficiary who is under a legal disability or who the trustee reasonably believes is incapacitated, by paying it directly to the beneficiary or applying it for the beneficiary's benefit, or by doing any of the following:

(1) Paying it to the beneficiary's guardian of the estate, or, if the beneficiary does not have a guardian of the estate, the beneficiary's guardian of the person;

(2) Paying it to the beneficiary's custodian under sections 5814.01 to 5814.09 of the Revised Code and, for that purpose, creating a custodianship;

(3) If the trustee does not know of a guardian of the person or estate, or custodian, paying it to an adult relative or other person having legal or physical care or custody of the beneficiary, to be expended on the beneficiary's behalf;

(4) Managing it as a separate fund on the beneficiary's behalf, subject to the beneficiary's continuing right to withdraw the distribution.

(V) On distribution of trust property or the division or termination of a trust, make distributions in divided or undivided interests, allocate particular assets in proportionate or disproportionate shares, value the trust property for those purposes, and adjust for resulting differences in valuation;

(W) Resolve a dispute concerning the interpretation of the trust or its administration by mediation, arbitration, or other procedure for alternative dispute resolution;

(X) Prosecute or defend an action, claim, or judicial proceeding in any jurisdiction to protect trust property and the trustee in the performance of the trustee's duties;

(Y) Sign and deliver contracts and other instruments that are useful to achieve or facilitate the exercise of the trustee's powers;

(Z) On termination of the trust, exercise the powers appropriate to wind up the administration of the trust and distribute the trust property to the persons entitled to it.

(2006 H 416, eff. 1–1–07)

Historical and Statutory Notes

Uniform Law: This section is analogous to § 816 of the Uniform Trust Code. See 7C Uniform Laws Annotated, Master Edition or ULA database on Westlaw.

Library References

Baldwin's Ohio Legislative Service Annotated, 2006 H 416 LSC Analysis, p 3/L-1709

Law Review and Journal Commentaries

The office of trustee and the duties and powers of the trustee under the Ohio trust code. Joanne E. Hindel, 17 Prob L J Ohio 10 (September/October 2006).

Ohio adopts new trust code—an overview of the new Ohio trust code and house bill 416. Alan Newman, 20 Ohio Law 9 (September/October 2006).

5808.17 Distribution upon termination

(A) Upon termination or partial termination of a trust, the trustee may send to the beneficiaries a proposal for distribution. The right of any beneficiary to object to the proposed distribution terminates if the beneficiary does not notify the trustee of an objection within thirty days after the proposal was sent but only if the proposal informed the beneficiary of the right to object and of the time allowed for objection.

(B) Upon the occurrence of an event terminating or partially terminating a trust, the trustee shall proceed expeditiously to distribute the trust property to the persons entitled to it, subject to the right of the trustee to retain a reasonable reserve for the payment of debts, expenses, and taxes.

(C) A release by a beneficiary of a trustee from liability for breach of trust is invalid to the extent that it was induced by improper conduct of the trustee or that the beneficiary, at the time of the release, did not know of the beneficiary's rights or of the material facts relating to the breach.

(2006 H 416, eff. 1–1–07)

Historical and Statutory Notes

Uniform Law: This section is analogous to § 817 of the Uniform Trust Code. See 7C Uniform Laws Annotated, Master Edition or ULA database on Westlaw.

Library References

Baldwin's Ohio Legislative Service Annotated, 2006 H 416 LSC Analysis, p 3/L-1709

Law Review and Journal Commentaries

The office of trustee and the duties and powers of the trustee under the Ohio trust code. Joanne E. Hindel, 17 Prob L J Ohio 10 (September/October 2006).

CHAPTER 5809

PRUDENT INVESTOR ACT

Section
5809.01 Short title; prudent investor rule
5809.02 Standard of care; portfolio strategy; risk and return objectives
5809.03 Diversification
5809.04 Duties at inception of trusteeship
5809.05 Reviewing compliance
5809.06 Delegation by trustee
5809.07 Language invoking standard of Prudent Investor Act
5809.08 Uniformity of application and construction; application to existing trusts

5809.01 Short title; prudent investor rule

(A)(1) As used in the Revised Code, the "Ohio Uniform Prudent Investor Act" means sections 5809.01 to 5809.08, 5808.03, 5808.05, and 5808.06, division (A) of section 5808.02, and division (B) of section 5808.07 of the Revised Code, and those sections may be cited as the "Ohio Uniform Prudent Investor Act."

(2) As used in the Ohio Uniform Prudent Investor Act, "trustee" means a trustee under any testamentary, inter vivos, or other trust.

(B) Except as provided in division (C) or (D) of this section, a trustee who invests and manages trust assets under the Ohio Uniform Prudent Investor Act owes a duty to the beneficiaries of the trust to comply with the Ohio Uniform Prudent Investor Act.

(C) The Ohio Uniform Prudent Investor Act may be expanded, restricted, eliminated, or otherwise altered, without express reference by the instrument creating a trust to the Ohio Uniform Prudent Investor Act or any section of the Revised Code that is part of that act.

(D) A trustee is not liable to a beneficiary of a trust to the extent the trustee acted in reasonable reliance on the provisions of the trust.

(2006 H 416, eff. 1–1–07)

Uncodified Law

1998 H 701, § 3, eff. 3–22–99, reads:

If, on the effective date of this act, a trust meets all of the following conditions, it is not subject to this act until January 1, 2000:

(A) The trust assets are invested and managed by a non-corporate trustee.

(B) The trust cannot be terminated by the grantor.

(C) The value of the trust, as of December 31, 1998, is less than $100,000.

Historical and Statutory Notes

Ed. Note: RC 5809.01 is former RC 1339.52, amended and recodified by 2006 H 416, eff. 1–1–07; 1998 H 701, eff. 3–22–99.

Uniform Law: This section is similar to § 1 of the Uniform Prudent Investor Act. See 7B, Uniform Laws Annotated, Master Edition.

Cross References

Duty of loyalty, conflict of interest, 5808.02
Fiduciaries, investment powers, 2109.37
Trust companies, investment of trust funds, 1111.13
Trust company may purchase from itself or an affiliate, 1111.15

Library References

Trusts ⊕=217.3(5).
Westlaw Topic No. 390.
C.J.S. Trusts §§ 482, 491, 496.

Baldwin's Ohio Legislative Service Annotated, 2006 H 416 LSC Analysis, p 3/L-1709

Baldwin's Ohio Legislative Service Annotated, 1998 H 701—LSC Analysis, p 12/L-2178

Law Review and Journal Commentaries

Formal Recognition of Modern Portfolio Theory—Investing for Total Return in Personal Trusts, Michael S. Bailes. 10 Prob L J Ohio 49 (March/April 2000).

5809.02 Standard of care; portfolio strategy; risk and return objectives

(A) A trustee shall invest and manage trust assets as a prudent investor would, by considering the purposes, terms, distribution requirements, and other circumstances of the trust. In satisfying this requirement, the trustee shall exercise reasonable care, skill, and caution.

(B) A trustee shall make a reasonable effort to verify facts relevant to the investment and management of trust assets.

(C) A trustee's investment and management decisions respecting individual trust assets shall not be evaluated in isolation but in the context of the trust portfolio as a whole and as part of an overall investment strategy having risk and return objectives reasonably suited to the trust.

(D) Among circumstances that a trustee shall consider in investing and managing trust assets are the following as are relevant to the trust or its beneficiaries:

(1) The general economic conditions;

(2) The possible effect of inflation or deflation;

(3) The expected tax consequences of investment decisions or strategies;

(4) The role that each investment or course of action plays within the overall trust portfolio, which may include financial assets, interests in closely held enterprises, tangible and intangible personal property, and real property;

(5) The expected total return from income and appreciation of capital;

(6) Other resources of the beneficiaries;

(7) Needs for liquidity, regularity of income, and preservation or appreciation of capital;

(8) An asset's special relationship or special value, if any, to the purposes of the trust or to one or more of the beneficiaries.

(2006 H 416, eff. 1–1–07)

Uncodified Law

1998 H 701, § 3: See Uncodified Law under 5809.01.

Historical and Statutory Notes

Ed. Note: RC 5809.02 is former RC 1339.53, amended and recodified by 2006 H 416, eff. 1–1–07; 1998 H 701, eff. 3–22–99.

Amendment Note: 2006 H 416 deleted the text of division (C) and redesignated divisions (D) and (E) as divisions (C) and (D). Prior to deletion, division (C) read: "A trustee who has special skills or expertise, or is named trustee in reliance upon the trustee's representation that the trustee has special skills or expertise, has a duty to use those special skills or expertise."

Uniform Law: This section is similar to § 2 of the Uniform Prudent Investor Act. See 7B, Uniform Laws Annotated, Master Edition.

Library References

Trusts ⊕=217.3(5).
Westlaw Topic No. 390.
C.J.S. Trusts §§ 482, 491, 496.

Baldwin's Ohio Legislative Service Annotated, 2006 H 416 LSC Analysis, p 3/L-1709

Baldwin's Ohio Legislative Service Annotated, 1998 H 701—LSC Analysis, p 12/L-2178

Law Review and Journal Commentaries

The New Ohio Uniform Prudent Investor Act, Joanne E. Hindel. 9 Prob L J Ohio 38 (January/February 1999).

5809.03 Diversification

(A) A trustee may invest in any kind of property or type of investment provided that the investment is consistent with the requirements and standards of the Ohio Uniform Prudent Investor Act.

(B) A trustee shall diversify the investments of a trust unless the trustee reasonably determines that, because of special circumstances, the purposes of the trust are better served without diversifying.

(2006 H 416, eff. 1–1–07)

Uncodified Law

1998 H 701, § 3: See Uncodified Law under 5809.01.

Historical and Statutory Notes

Ed. Note: RC 5809.03 is former RC 1339.54, amended and recodified by 2006 H 416, eff. 1–1–07; 1998 H 701, eff. 3–22–99.

Amendment Note: 2006 H 416 substituted "sections 1339.52 to 1339.61 of the Revised Code" with "the Ohio Uniform Prudent Investor Act" in division (A).

Uniform Law: This section is similar to § 2 and 3 of the Uniform Prudent Investor Act. See 7B, Uniform Laws Annotated, Master Edition.

Library References

Trusts ⊕=217.3(6).
Westlaw Topic No. 390.
C.J.S. Trusts §§ 482, 491 to 492.

Baldwin's Ohio Legislative Service Annotated, 2006 H 416 LSC Analysis, p 3/L-1709

Baldwin's Ohio Legislative Service Annotated, 1998 H 701—LSC Analysis, p 12/L-2178

Law Review and Journal Commentaries

The New Ohio Uniform Prudent Investor Act, Joanne E. Hindel. 9 Prob L J Ohio 38 (January/February 1999).

5809.04 Duties at inception of trusteeship

Within a reasonable time after accepting a trusteeship or receiving trust assets, a trustee shall review the trust assets and make and implement decisions concerning the retention and disposition of trust assets in order to bring the trust portfolio into compliance with the purposes, terms, distribution requirements, and other circumstances of the trust, and in order to comply with the requirements and standards of the Ohio Uniform Prudent Investor Act.

(2006 H 416, eff. 1–1–07)

Uncodified Law

1998 H 701, § 3: See Uncodified Law under 5809.01.

Historical and Statutory Notes

Ed. Note: RC 5809.04 is former RC 1339.56, amended and recodified by 2006 H 416, eff. 1–1–07; 1998 H 701, eff. 3–22–99.

Amendment Note: 2006 H 416 substituted "sections 1339.52 to 1339.61 of the Revised Code" with "the Ohio Uniform Prudent Investor Act".

Uniform Law: This section is similar to § 4 of the Uniform Prudent Investor Act. See 7B, Uniform Laws Annotated, Master Edition.

Library References

Trusts ⚖171, 271.
Westlaw Topic No. 390.
C.J.S. Trusts §§ 318 to 320.
   Baldwin's Ohio Legislative Service Annotated, 2006 H 416 LSC Analysis, p 3/L-1709
   Baldwin's Ohio Legislative Service Annotated, 1998 H 701—LSC Analysis, p 12/L-2178

5809.05 Reviewing compliance

Compliance with the Ohio Uniform Prudent Investor Act shall be determined in light of the facts and circumstances existing at the time of a trustee's decision or action and not by hindsight.

(2006 H 416, eff. 1–1–07)

Uncodified Law

1998 H 701, § 3: See Uncodified Law under 5809.01.

Historical and Statutory Notes

Ed. Note: RC 5809.05 is former RC 1339.58, amended and recodified by 2006 H 416, eff. 1–1–07; 1998 H 701, eff. 3–22–99.

Amendment Note: 2006 H 416 substituted "sections 1339.52 to 1339.61 of the Revised Code" with "the Ohio Uniform Prudent Investor Act".

Uniform Law: This section is similar to § 8 of the Uniform Prudent Investor Act. See 7B, Uniform Laws Annotated, Master Edition.

Library References

Trusts ⚖4.
Westlaw Topic No. 390.
C.J.S. Trusts § 27.
   Baldwin's Ohio Legislative Service Annotated, 2006 H 416 LSC Analysis, p 3/L-1709
   Baldwin's Ohio Legislative Service Annotated, 1998 H 701—LSC Analysis, p 12/L-2178

5809.06 Delegation by trustee

(A) A trustee may delegate investment and management functions of a trust that a prudent trustee having comparable skills could properly delegate under the circumstances. A trustee that exercises its delegation authority under this division shall comply with the requirements of division (A) of section 5808.07 of the Revised Code.

(B) In performing investment or management functions of a trust that are delegated to an agent, an agent owes a duty to the trust to exercise reasonable care to comply with the terms of the delegation.

(C) A trustee who delegates a function to an agent in compliance with division (A) of this section is not liable to the beneficiaries of the trust or to the trust for the decisions or actions of the agent to whom the function was delegated.

(D) By accepting the delegation of investment or management functions of a trust that is subject to the laws of this state, an agent submits to the jurisdiction of this state.

(2006 H 416, eff. 1–1–07)

Library References

Baldwin's Ohio Legislative Service Annotated, 2006 H 416 LSC Analysis, p 3/L-1709

5809.07 Language invoking standard of Prudent Investor Act

The following terms or comparable language in the provisions of a trust, unless otherwise limited or modified, authorizes any investment or strategy permitted by the Ohio Uniform Prudent Investor Act: "investments permissible by law for investment of trust funds"; "legal investments"; "authorized investments"; "using the judgment and care under the circumstances then prevailing that persons of prudence, discretion, and intelligence exercise in the management of their own affairs, not in regard to speculation but in regard to the permanent disposition of their funds considering the probable income as well as the probable safety of their capital"; "prudent man rule"; "prudent trustee rule"; "prudent person rule"; and "prudent investor rule."

(2006 H 416, eff. 1–1–07)

Uncodified Law

1998 H 701, § 3: See Uncodified Law under 5809.01.

Historical and Statutory Notes

Ed. Note: RC 5809.07 is former RC 1339.60, amended and recodified by 2006 H 416, eff. 1–1–07; 1998 H 701, eff. 3–22–99.

Amendment Note: 2006 H 416 substituted "sections 1339.52 to 1339.61 of the Revised Code" with "the Ohio Uniform Prudent Investor Act".

Uniform Law: This section is similar to § 10 of the Uniform Prudent Investor Act. See 7B, Uniform Laws Annotated, Master Edition.

Library References

Trusts ⚖26.
Westlaw Topic No. 390.
C.J.S. Trusts §§ 40 to 41.
   Baldwin's Ohio Legislative Service Annotated, 2006 H 416 LSC Analysis, p 3/L-1709
   Baldwin's Ohio Legislative Service Annotated, 1998 H 701—LSC Analysis, p 12/L-2178

5809.08 Uniformity of application and construction; application to existing trusts

(A) The Ohio Uniform Prudent Investor Act shall be applied and construed to effectuate the general purpose to make uniform the law with respect to the subject of these sections among the states enacting it.

(B) The Ohio Uniform Prudent Investor Act applies to trusts existing on or created after March 22, 1999. As applied to trusts existing on March 22, 1999, the Ohio Uniform Prudent Investor Act governs only decisions or actions occurring after March 22, 1999.

(C) The temporary investment of cash or funds pursuant to section 5815.26 or 2109.372 of the Revised Code shall be considered a prudent investment in compliance with the Ohio Uniform Prudent Investor Act.

(2006 H 416, eff. 1–1–07)

Uncodified Law

1998 H 701, § 3: See Uncodified Law under 5809.01.

Historical and Statutory Notes

Ed. Note: RC 5809.08 is former RC 1339.61, amended and recodified by 2006 H 416, eff. 1–1–07; 1998 H 701, eff. 3–22–99.

Amendment Note: 2006 H 416 rewrote the section, which prior thereto read:

"(A) Sections 1339.52 to 1339.61 of the Revised Code shall be applied and construed to effectuate the general purpose to make uniform the law with respect to the subject of these sections among the states enacting it. These sections may be cited as the 'Ohio Uniform Prudent Investor Act.'

"(B) Sections 1339.52 to 1339.61 of the Revised Code apply to trusts existing on or created after the effective date of these sections. As applied to trusts existing on the effective date of these sections, sections 1339.52 to 1339.61 of the Revised Code govern only decisions or actions occurring after the effective date of these sections.

"(C) The temporary investment of cash or funds pursuant to section 1339.44 or 2109.372 of the Revised Code shall be considered a prudent investment in compliance with sections 1339.52 to 1339.61 of the Revised Code."

Uniform Law: This section is similar to § 11 and 12 of the Uniform Prudent Investor Act. See 7B, Uniform Laws Annotated, Master Edition.

Cross References

Trust company may purchase from itself or an affiliate, 1111.15

Library References

Trusts ⟷4.
Westlaw Topic No. 390.
C.J.S. Trusts § 27.

Baldwin's Ohio Legislative Service Annotated, 2006 H 416 LSC Analysis, p 3/L-1709
Baldwin's Ohio Legislative Service Annotated, 1998 H 701—LSC Analysis, p 12/L-2178

CHAPTER 5810

REMEDIES FOR BREACH OF TRUST

Section
5810.01 Remedies for breach of trust
5810.02 Damages for breach of trust
5810.03 Damages in absence of breach
5810.04 Attorney fees and costs
5810.05 Limitation of action against trustee
5810.06 Reliance on trust instrument
5810.07 Liability when event affecting administration or distribution
5810.08 Enforceability of trust terms relieving trustee of liability
5810.09 Beneficiary's consent, release, or ratification
5810.10 Limitation on personal liability of trustee
5810.11 Interest as general partner
5810.12 Protection of person dealing with trustee
5810.13 Certification of trust

Law Review and Journal Commentaries

Liability of trustees and rights of persons dealing with a trustee under the Ohio trust code. Edward J. Tognetti, 17 Prob L J Ohio 16 (September/October 2006).

5810.01 Remedies for breach of trust

(A) A violation by a trustee of a duty the trustee owes to a beneficiary is a breach of trust.

(B) To remedy a breach of trust that has occurred or may occur, the court may do any of the following:

(1) Compel the trustee to perform the trustee's duties;

(2) Enjoin the trustee from committing a breach of trust;

(3) Compel the trustee to redress a breach of trust by paying money, restoring property, or other means;

(4) Order a trustee to account;

(5) Appoint a special fiduciary to take possession of the trust property and administer the trust;

(6) Suspend the trustee;

(7) Remove the trustee as provided in section 5807.06 of the Revised Code;

(8) Reduce or deny compensation to the trustee;

(9) Subject to section 5810.12 of the Revised Code, void an act of the trustee, impose a lien or a constructive trust on trust property, or trace trust property wrongfully disposed of and recover the property or its proceeds;

(10) Order any other appropriate relief.

(2006 H 416, eff. 1–1–07)

Historical and Statutory Notes

Uniform Law: This section is analogous to § 1001 of the Uniform Trust Code. See 7C Uniform Laws Annotated, Master Edition or ULA database on Westlaw.

Cross References

Removal of trustee, 5807.06

Library References

Baldwin's Ohio Legislative Service Annotated, 2006 H 416 LSC Analysis, p 3/L-1709

Law Review and Journal Commentaries

Liability of trustees and rights of persons dealing with a trustee under the Ohio trust code. Edward J. Tognetti, 17 Prob L J Ohio 16 (September/October 2006).

5810.02 Damages for breach of trust

(A) A trustee who commits a breach of trust is liable to the beneficiaries affected for the greater of the following:

(1) The amount required to restore the value of the trust property and trust distributions to what they would have been had the breach not occurred;

(2) The profit the trustee made by reason of the breach.

(B) Except as otherwise provided in this division, if more than one trustee is liable to the beneficiaries for a breach of trust, a trustee is entitled to contribution from the other trustee or trustees. A trustee is not entitled to contribution if the trustee was substantially more at fault than another trustee or if the trustee committed the breach of trust in bad faith or with reckless indifference to the purposes of the trust or the interests of the beneficiaries. A trustee who received a benefit from the breach of trust is not entitled to contribution from another trustee to the extent of the benefit received.

(2006 H 416, eff. 1–1–07)

Historical and Statutory Notes

Uniform Law: This section is analogous to § 1002 of the Uniform Trust Code. See 7C Uniform Laws Annotated, Master Edition or ULA database on Westlaw.

Library References

Baldwin's Ohio Legislative Service Annotated, 2006 H 416 LSC Analysis, p 3/L-1709

Law Review and Journal Commentaries

Liability of trustees and rights of persons dealing with a trustee under the Ohio trust code. Edward J. Tognetti, 17 Prob L J Ohio 16 (September/October 2006).

5810.03 Damages in absence of breach

(A) Absent a breach of trust, a trustee is not accountable to a beneficiary for any profit made by the trustee arising from the administration of the trust.

(B) Absent a breach of trust, a trustee is not liable to a beneficiary for a loss or depreciation in the value of trust property or for not having made a profit.

(2006 H 416, eff. 1–1–07)

Historical and Statutory Notes

Uniform Law: This section is analogous to § 1003 of the Uniform Trust Code. See 7C Uniform Laws Annotated, Master Edition or ULA database on Westlaw.

Library References

Baldwin's Ohio Legislative Service Annotated, 2006 H 416 LSC Analysis, p 3/L-1709

Law Review and Journal Commentaries

Liability of trustees and rights of persons dealing with a trustee under the Ohio trust code. Edward J. Tognetti, 17 Prob L J Ohio 16 (September/October 2006).

5810.04 Attorney fees and costs

In a judicial proceeding involving the administration of a trust, including a trust that contains a spendthrift provision, the court, as justice and equity may require, may award costs, expenses, and reasonable attorney's fees to any party, to be paid by another party, from the trust that is the subject of the controversy, or from a party's interest in the trust that is the subject of the controversy.

(2006 H 416, eff. 1–1–07)

Historical and Statutory Notes

Uniform Law: This section is analogous to § 1004 of the Uniform Trust Code. See 7C Uniform Laws Annotated, Master Edition or ULA database on Westlaw.

Cross References

Enforceability of spendthrift provision, exceptions, 5805.02
Spendthrift provision, 5805.01

Library References

Baldwin's Ohio Legislative Service Annotated, 2006 H 416 LSC Analysis, p 3/L-1709

Law Review and Journal Commentaries

Liability of trustees and rights of persons dealing with a trustee under the Ohio trust code. Edward J. Tognetti, 17 Prob L J Ohio 16 (September/October 2006).

5810.05 Limitation of action against trustee

(A) A beneficiary may not commence a proceeding against a trustee for breach of trust more than two years after the date the beneficiary, a representative of the beneficiary, or a beneficiary surrogate is sent a report that adequately discloses the existence of a potential claim for breach of trust and informs the beneficiary, the representative of the beneficiary, or the beneficiary surrogate of the time allowed for commencing a proceeding against a trustee.

(B) A report adequately discloses the existence of a potential claim for breach of trust if it provides sufficient information so that the beneficiary or the representative of the beneficiary knows of the potential claim or should know of the existence of the potential claim.

(C) If division (A) of this section does not apply, notwithstanding section 2305.09 of the Revised Code, a judicial proceeding by a beneficiary against a trustee for breach of trust must be commenced within four years after the first of the following to occur:

(1) The removal, resignation, or death of the trustee;

(2) The termination of the beneficiary's interest in the trust;

(3) The termination of the trust;

(4) The time at which the beneficiary knew or should have known of the breach of trust.

(2006 H 416, eff. 1–1–07)

Historical and Statutory Notes

Uniform Law: This section is analogous to § 1005 of the Uniform Trust Code. See 7C Uniform Laws Annotated, Master Edition or ULA database on Westlaw.

Cross References

Duty of loyalty, conflict of interest, 5808.02

Library References

Baldwin's Ohio Legislative Service Annotated, 2006 H 416 LSC Analysis, p 3/L-1709

Law Review and Journal Commentaries

Beneficiary information and notices. Susan S. Locke, 17 Prob L J Ohio 5 (September/October 2006).

Liability of trustees and rights of persons dealing with a trustee under the Ohio trust code. Edward J. Tognetti, 17 Prob L J Ohio 16 (September/October 2006).

5810.06 Reliance on trust instrument

A trustee who acts in reasonable reliance on the terms of the trust as expressed in the trust instrument is not liable to a beneficiary for a breach of trust to the extent the breach resulted from the reliance.

(2006 H 416, eff. 1–1–07)

Historical and Statutory Notes

Uniform Law: This section is analogous to § 1006 of the Uniform Trust Code. See 7C Uniform Laws Annotated, Master Edition or ULA database on Westlaw.

Library References

Baldwin's Ohio Legislative Service Annotated, 2006 H 416 LSC Analysis, p 3/L-1709

Law Review and Journal Commentaries

Liability of trustees and rights of persons dealing with a trustee under the Ohio trust code. Edward J. Tognetti, 17 Prob L J Ohio 16 (September/October 2006).

5810.07 Liability when event affecting administration or distribution

If the happening of an event, including marriage, divorce, performance of educational requirements, or death, affects the administration or distribution of a trust, a trustee who has exercised reasonable care to ascertain the happening of the event is not liable for a loss resulting from the trustee's lack of knowledge.

(2006 H 416, eff. 1–1–07)

Historical and Statutory Notes

Uniform Law: This section is analogous to § 1007 of the Uniform Trust Code. See 7C Uniform Laws Annotated, Master Edition or ULA database on Westlaw.

Library References

Baldwin's Ohio Legislative Service Annotated, 2006 H 416 LSC Analysis, p 3/L-1709

Law Review and Journal Commentaries

Liability of trustees and rights of persons dealing with a trustee under the Ohio trust code. Edward J. Tognetti, 17 Prob L J Ohio 16 (September/October 2006).

5810.08 Enforceability of trust terms relieving trustee of liability

A term of a trust relieving a trustee of liability for breach of trust is unenforceable to the extent that it relieves the trustee of liability for breach of trust committed in bad faith or with reckless indifference to the purposes of the trust or the interests of the beneficiaries or was inserted as the result of an abuse by the trustee of a fiduciary or confidential relationship to the settlor.

(2006 H 416, eff. 1–1–07)

Historical and Statutory Notes

Uniform Law: This section is analogous to § 1008 of the Uniform Trust Code. See 7C Uniform Laws Annotated, Master Edition or ULA database on Westlaw.

Cross References

Scope, mandatory rules, exceptions, 5801.04

Library References

Baldwin's Ohio Legislative Service Annotated, 2006 H 416 LSC Analysis, p 3/L-1709

Law Review and Journal Commentaries

Liability of trustees and rights of persons dealing with a trustee under the Ohio trust code. Edward J. Tognetti, 17 Prob L J Ohio 16 (September/October 2006).

5810.09 Beneficiary's consent, release, or ratification

A trustee is not liable to a beneficiary for breach of trust if the beneficiary consented to the conduct constituting the breach, released the trustee from liability for the breach, or ratified the transaction constituting the breach, unless the consent, release, or ratification of the beneficiary was induced by improper conduct of the trustee or, at the time of the consent, release, or ratification, the beneficiary did not know of the beneficiary's rights or of the material facts relating to the breach.

(2006 H 416, eff. 1–1–07)

Historical and Statutory Notes

Uniform Law: This section is analogous to § 1009 of the Uniform Trust Code. See 7C Uniform Laws Annotated, Master Edition or ULA database on Westlaw.

Cross References

Duty of loyalty, conflict of interest, 5808.02

Library References

Baldwin's Ohio Legislative Service Annotated, 2006 H 416 LSC Analysis, p 3/L-1709

Law Review and Journal Commentaries

Liability of trustees and rights of persons dealing with a trustee under the Ohio trust code. Edward J. Tognetti, 17 Prob L J Ohio 16 (September/October 2006).

5810.10 Limitation on personal liability of trustee

(A) Except as otherwise provided in the contract, for contracts entered into on or after March 22, 1984, a trustee is not personally liable on a contract properly entered into in the trustee's fiduciary capacity in the course of administering the trust if the trustee in the contract disclosed the fiduciary capacity. The words "trustee," "as trustee," "fiduciary," or "as fiduciary," or other words that indicate one's trustee capacity, following the name or signature of a trustee are sufficient disclosure for purposes of this division.

(B) A trustee is personally liable for torts committed in the course of administering a trust or for obligations arising from ownership or control of trust property, including liability for violation of environmental law, only if the trustee is personally at fault.

(C) A claim based on a contract entered into by a trustee in the trustee's fiduciary capacity, on an obligation arising from ownership or control of trust property, or on a tort committed in the course of administering a trust may be asserted in a judicial proceeding against the trustee in the trustee's fiduciary capacity, whether or not the trustee is personally liable for the claim.

(2006 H 416, eff. 1–1–07)

Historical and Statutory Notes

Uniform Law: This section is analogous to § 1010 of the Uniform Trust Code. See 7C Uniform Laws Annotated, Master Edition or ULA database on Westlaw.

Library References

Baldwin's Ohio Legislative Service Annotated, 2006 H 416 LSC Analysis, p 3/L-1709

Law Review and Journal Commentaries

Liability of trustees and rights of persons dealing with a trustee under the Ohio trust code. Edward J. Tognetti, 17 Prob L J Ohio 16 (September/October 2006).

5810.11 Interest as general partner

(A)(1) Except as otherwise provided in division (C) of this section or unless personal liability is imposed in the contract, a trustee who holds an interest as a general partner in a general or limited partnership is not personally liable on a contract entered into by the partnership after the trust's acquisition of the interest if the fiduciary capacity was disclosed. A partnership certificate that is filed pursuant to Chapter 1777. or another chapter of the Revised Code and that indicates that a trustee holds a general partnership interest in a fiduciary capacity by the use following the name or signature of the trustee of the words "as trustee" or other words that indicate the trustee's fiduciary capacity constitutes a sufficient disclosure for purposes of this division.

(2) If a partnership certificate is not required to be filed pursuant to Chapter 1777. or another chapter of the Revised Code, a sufficient disclosure for purposes of division (A) of this

section can be made by a trustee if a certificate that is filed with the recorder of the county in which the partnership's principal office or place of business is situated and with the recorder of each county in which the partnership owns real estate satisfies all of the following requirements:

(a) The certificate states in full the names of all persons holding interests in the partnership and their places of residence.

(b) The certificate is signed by all persons who are general partners in the partnership and is acknowledged by a person authorized to take acknowledgements of deeds.

(c) The certificate uses the words "trustee under the (will or trust) of (name of decedent or settlor)," or other words that indicate the trustee's fiduciary capacity, following the trustee's name or signature.

(3) A contract or other written instrument that is delivered to a party that contracts with the partnership in which a trustee holds a general partnership interest in a fiduciary capacity and that indicates that the trustee so holds the interest constitutes a disclosure for purposes of division (A)(1) of this section with respect to transactions between the party and the partnership. If a disclosure has been made by a certificate in accordance with division (A) of this section, a disclosure for purposes of division (A) of this section with respect to such transactions exists regardless of whether a contract or other instrument indicates the trustee holds the general partnership interest in a fiduciary capacity.

(B) Except as otherwise provided in division (C) of this section, a trustee who holds an interest as a general partner in a general or limited partnership is not personally liable for torts committed by the partnership or for obligations arising from ownership or control of the interest unless the trustee is personally at fault.

(C) The immunity provided by this section does not apply if an interest in the partnership is held by the trustee in a capacity other than that of trustee or is held by the trustee's spouse or one or more of the trustee's descendants, siblings, or parents, or the spouse of any of them.

(D) If the trustee of a revocable trust holds an interest as a general partner in a general or limited partnership, the settlor is personally liable for contracts and other obligations of the partnership as if the settlor were a general partner.

(2006 H 416, eff. 1–1–07)

Historical and Statutory Notes

Uniform Law: This section is analogous, in part, to § 1011 of the Uniform Trust Code. See 7C Uniform Laws Annotated, Master Edition or ULA database on Westlaw.

Library References

Baldwin's Ohio Legislative Service Annotated, 2006 H 416 LSC Analysis, p 3/L-1709

Law Review and Journal Commentaries

Liability of trustees and rights of persons dealing with a trustee under the Ohio trust code. Edward J. Tognetti, 17 Prob L J Ohio 16 (September/October 2006).

5810.12 Protection of person dealing with trustee

(A) A person other than a beneficiary who in good faith assists a trustee, or who in good faith and for value deals with a trustee, without knowledge that the trustee is exceeding or improperly exercising the trustee's powers is protected from liability as if the trustee properly exercised the power.

(B) A person other than a beneficiary who in good faith deals with a trustee is not required to inquire into the extent of the trustee's powers or the propriety of their exercise.

(C) A person who in good faith delivers assets to a trustee is not required to ensure their proper application.

(D) A person other than a beneficiary who in good faith assists a former trustee, or who in good faith and for value deals with a former trustee, without knowledge that the trusteeship has terminated is protected from liability as if the former trustee were still a trustee.

(E) Comparable protective provisions of other laws relating to commercial transactions or transfer of securities by fiduciaries prevail over the protection provided by this section.

(2006 H 416, eff. 1–1–07)

Historical and Statutory Notes

Uniform Law: This section is analogous to § 1012 of the Uniform Trust Code. See 7C Uniform Laws Annotated, Master Edition or ULA database on Westlaw.

Cross References

Duty of loyalty, conflict of interest, 5808.02

Library References

Baldwin's Ohio Legislative Service Annotated, 2006 H 416 LSC Analysis, p 3/L-1709

Law Review and Journal Commentaries

Beneficiary information and notices. Susan S. Locke, 17 Prob L J Ohio 5 (September/October 2006).

The evolution of Ohio trust law from the English common law to the Ohio trust code. Joanne E. Hindel, 17 Prob L J Ohio 1 (September/October 2006).

Liability of trustees and rights of persons dealing with a trustee under the Ohio trust code. Edward J. Tognetti, 17 Prob L J Ohio 16 (September/October 2006).

5810.13 Certification of trust

(A) Instead of furnishing a copy of the trust instrument to a person other than a beneficiary, the trustee may furnish to the person a certification of trust containing all of the following information:

(1) A statement that the trust exists and the date the trust instrument was executed;

(2) The identity of the settlor;

(3) The identity and address of the currently acting trustee;

(4) The powers of the trustee;

(5) The revocability or irrevocability of the trust and the identity of any person holding a power to revoke the trust;

(6) The authority of cotrustees to sign or otherwise authenticate and whether all or less than all are required in order to exercise powers of the trustee;

(7) The trust's taxpayer identification number;

(8) The manner of taking title to trust property.

(B) Any trustee may sign or otherwise authenticate a certification of trust.

(C) A certification of trust shall state that the trust has not been revoked, modified, or amended in any manner that would cause the representations contained in the certification of trust to be incorrect.

(D) A certification of trust is not required to contain the dispositive terms of a trust.

(E) A recipient of a certification of trust may require the trustee to furnish copies of those excerpts from the original trust instrument and later amendments that designate the trustee and confer upon the trustee the power to act in the pending transaction.

(F) A person who acts in reliance upon a certification of trust without knowledge that the representations contained in the certification are incorrect is not liable to any person for so acting and may assume without inquiry the existence of the facts contained in the certification. Knowledge of the terms of the trust may not be inferred solely from the fact that a copy of all or part of the trust instrument is held by the person relying upon the certification.

(G) A person who in good faith enters into a transaction in reliance upon a certification of trust may enforce the transaction against the trust property as if the representations contained in the certification were correct.

(H) A person making a demand for the trust instrument in addition to a certification of trust or excerpts is liable for damages if the court determines that the person did not act in good faith in demanding the trust instrument.

(I) This section does not limit the right of a person to obtain a copy of the trust instrument in a judicial proceeding concerning the trust.

(2006 H 416, eff. 1–1–07)

Historical and Statutory Notes

Uniform Law: This section is analogous to § 1013 of the Uniform Trust Code. See 7C Uniform Laws Annotated, Master Edition or ULA database on Westlaw.

Cross References

Scope, mandatory rules, exceptions, 5801.04

Library References

Baldwin's Ohio Legislative Service Annotated, 2006 H 416 LSC Analysis, p 3/L-1709

Law Review and Journal Commentaries

Beneficiary information and notices. Susan S. Locke, 17 Prob L J Ohio 5 (September/October 2006).

The evolution of Ohio trust law from the English common law to the Ohio trust code. Joanne E. Hindel, 17 Prob L J Ohio 1 (September/October 2006).

Liability of trustees and rights of persons dealing with a trustee under the Ohio trust code. Edward J. Tognetti, 17 Prob L J Ohio 16 (September/October 2006).

CHAPTER 5811

MISCELLANEOUS PROVISIONS

Section
5811.01 Uniformity of application and construction
5811.02 Electronic records and signatures
5811.03 Application to existing relationships

5811.01 Uniformity of application and construction

In applying and construing Chapters 5801. to 5811. of the Revised Code, a court may consider the need to promote uniformity of the law with respect to the subject matter of those chapters among states that enact the uniform trust code.

(2006 H 416, eff. 1–1–07)

Historical and Statutory Notes

Uniform Law: This section is analogous to § 1101 of the Uniform Trust Code. See 7C Uniform Laws Annotated, Master Edition or ULA database on Westlaw.

Cross References

Applicability of common law of trusts and principles of equity, 5801.05
Applicability of title, 5801.02
Appointment of representative by court, 5803.05
Creation of oral trust, 5804.07
General powers of trustee, 5808.15
Laws applicable to testamentary trusts, 2109.69
Modification or termination of noncharitable irrevocable trust by consent, 5804.11
Notice to other beneficiaries, persons treated as beneficiaries, 5801.09
Notice, waiver of notice, 5801.08
Parties to agreements, effect on creditor rights, 5801.10
Requirements for creation, 5804.02
Scope, mandatory rules, exceptions, 5801.04

Library References

Baldwin's Ohio Legislative Service Annotated, 2006 H 416 LSC Analysis, p 3/L-1709

5811.02 Electronic records and signatures

The provisions of Chapters 5801. to 5811. of the Revised Code governing the legal effect, validity, or enforceability of electronic records or electronic signatures and of contracts formed or performed with the use of electronic records or electronic signatures conform to the requirements of section 102 of the Electronic Signatures in Global and National Commerce Act, 15 U.S.C. 7002, 114 Stat. 467, and supersede, modify, and limit the requirements of the Electronic Signatures in Global and National Commerce Act.

(2006 H 416, eff. 1–1–07)

Historical and Statutory Notes

Uniform Law: This section is analogous to § 1102 of the Uniform Trust Code. See 7C Uniform Laws Annotated, Master Edition or ULA database on Westlaw.

Library References

Baldwin's Ohio Legislative Service Annotated, 2006 H 416 LSC Analysis, p 3/L-1709

5811.03 Application to existing relationships

(A) Except as otherwise provided in Chapters 5801. to 5811. of the Revised Code, all of the following apply:

(1) Chapters 5801. to 5811. of the Revised Code apply to all trusts created before, on, or after their effective date.

(2) Chapters 5801. to 5811. of the Revised Code apply to all judicial proceedings concerning trusts commenced on or after their effective date.

(3) Chapters 5801. to 5811. of the Revised Code apply to judicial proceedings concerning trusts commenced before the effective date of those chapters unless the court finds that application of a particular provision of those chapters would substantially interfere with the effective conduct of the judicial proceedings or prejudice the rights of the parties, in which case

the particular provision does not apply, and the superseded law applies.

(4) Any rule of construction or presumption provided in Chapters 5801. to 5811. of the Revised Code applies to trust instruments executed before the effective date of those chapters unless there is a clear indication of a contrary intent in the terms of the trust.

(5) Chapters 5801. to 5811. of the Revised Code do not affect an act done before the effective date of those chapters.

(B) If a right is acquired, extinguished, or barred upon the expiration of a prescribed period that has commenced to run under any other statute before the effective date of Chapters 5801. to 5811. of the Revised Code, that statute continues to apply to the right even if it has been repealed or superseded.

(2006 H 416, eff. 1–1–07)

Historical and Statutory Notes

Uniform Law: This section is analogous to § 1106 of the Uniform Trust Code. See 7C Uniform Laws Annotated, Master Edition or ULA database on Westlaw.

Library References

Baldwin's Ohio Legislative Service Annotated, 2006 H 416 LSC Analysis, p 3/L-1709

Law Review and Journal Commentaries

Ohio adopts new trust code—an overview of the new Ohio trust code and house bill 416. Alan Newman, 20 Ohio Law 9 (September/October 2006).

CHAPTER 5812

UNIFORM PRINCIPAL AND INCOME ACT (1997)

Section
5812.01 Definitions
5812.02 Fiduciary duties; general principles
5812.03 Trustee's power to adjust
5812.07 Determination and distribution of net income
5812.08 Distribution to residuary and remainder beneficiaries
5812.12 When right to income begins and ends
5812.13 Apportionment of receipts and disbursements when decedent dies or income interest begins
5812.14 Apportionment when income interest ends
5812.18 Character of receipts
5812.19 Distribution from trust or estate
5812.20 Business and other activities conducted by trustee
5812.24 Principal receipts
5812.25 Rental property
5812.26 Obligation to pay money
5812.27 Insurance policies and similar contracts
5812.31 Insubstantial allocations not required
5812.32 Deferred compensation, annuities, and similar payments
5812.33 Liquidating asset
5812.34 Minerals, water, and other natural resources
5812.35 Timber
5812.36 Property not productive of income
5812.37 Derivatives and options
5812.38 Asset-backed securities
5812.42 Disbursements from income
5812.43 Disbursements from principal
5812.44 Transfers from income to principal for depreciation
5812.45 Transfers from income to reimburse principal
5812.46 Income taxes
5812.47 Adjustments between principal and income because of taxes
5812.51 Uniformity of application and construction
5812.52 Application to existing trust or decedent's estate

5812.01 Definitions

As used in sections 5812.01 to 5812.52 of the Revised Code:

(A) "Accounting period" means a calendar year unless another twelve-month period is selected by a fiduciary. "Accounting period" includes a portion of a calendar year or other twelve-month period that begins when an income interest begins or ends when an income interest ends.

(B) "Beneficiary" includes, in the case of a decedent's estate, an heir, legatee, and devisee and, in the case of a trust, an income beneficiary and a remainder beneficiary.

(C) "Fiduciary" means a personal representative or a trustee. The term includes an executor, administrator, successor personal representative, special administrator, and a person performing substantially the same function.

(D) "Income" means money or property that a fiduciary receives as current return from a principal asset. "Income" includes a portion of receipts from a sale, exchange, or liquidation of a principal asset, to the extent provided in sections 5812.18 to 5812.38 of the Revised Code.

(E) "Income beneficiary" means a person to whom net income of a trust is or may be payable.

(F) "Income interest" means the right of an income beneficiary to receive all or part of net income, whether the terms of the trust require or authorize it to be distributed in the trustee's discretion.

(G) "Mandatory income interest" means the right of an income beneficiary to receive net income that the terms of the trust require the fiduciary to distribute.

(H) "Net income" means the total receipts allocated to income during an accounting period minus the disbursements made from income during the period, plus or minus transfers under sections 5812. 01 to 5812.52 of the Revised Code to or from income during the period.

(I) "Person" means an individual, corporation, business trust, estate, trust, partnership, limited liability company, association, joint venture, or government; governmental subdivision, agency, or instrumentality; public corporation; or any other legal or commercial entity.

(J) "Principal" means property held in trust for distribution to a remainder beneficiary when the trust terminates.

(K) "Remainder beneficiary" means a person entitled to receive principal when an income interest ends.

(L) "Terms of a trust" means the manifestation of the intent of a settlor or decedent with respect to the trust, expressed in a manner that admits of its proof in a judicial proceeding, whether by written or spoken words or by conduct.

(M) "Trustee" includes an original, additional, or successor trustee, whether or not appointed or confirmed by a court.

(2006 H 416, eff. 1–1–07)

Historical and Statutory Notes

Ed. Note: RC 5812.01 is former RC 1340.40, amended and recodified by 2006 H 416, eff. 1–1–07; 2002 H 522, eff. 1–1–03.

Amendment Note: 2006 H 416 substituted "1340.40" with "5812.01", "1340.91" with "5812.52", "1340.57" with "5812.18", and "1340.77" with "5812.38".

Uniform Law: This section is analogous to §102 of the Uniform Principal and Income Act (1997 Act). See 7B Uniform Laws Annotated, Master Edition.

Cross References

Allocation by fiduciary, 2109.68
Restrictions on definition of income or on distributions, 5813.05

Library References

Baldwin's Ohio Legislative Service Annotated, 2006 H 416 LSC Analysis, p 3/L-1709

5812.02 Fiduciary duties; general principles

(A) In allocating receipts and disbursements to or between principal and income, and with respect to any matter within the scope of sections 5812.07 to 5812.14 of the Revised Code, all of the following apply:

(1) A fiduciary shall administer a trust or estate in accordance with the terms of the trust or the will, even if there is a different provision in sections 5812.01 to 5812.52 of the Revised Code.

(2) A fiduciary may administer a trust or estate by the exercise of a discretionary power of administration given to the fiduciary by the terms of the trust or the will, even if the exercise of the power produces a result different from a result required or permitted by any provision of sections 5812.01 to 5812.52 of the Revised Code.

(3) A fiduciary shall administer a trust or estate in accordance with sections 5812.01 to 5812.52 of the Revised Code if the terms of the trust or the will do not contain a different provision or do not give the fiduciary a discretionary power of administration.

(4) A fiduciary shall add a receipt, or charge a disbursement, to principal to the extent that the terms of the trust and any provision of sections 5812.01 to 5812.52 of the Revised Code do not provide for allocating the receipt or disbursement to or between principal and income.

(B) In exercising the power to adjust under division (A) of section 5812.03 of the Revised Code or a discretionary power of administration regarding a matter within the scope of sections 5812.01 to 5812.52 of the Revised Code, whether granted by the terms of a trust, a will, or a provision of any such section, a fiduciary shall administer a trust or estate impartially, based on what is fair and reasonable to all of the beneficiaries, except to the extent that the terms of the trust or the will clearly manifest an intention that the fiduciary shall or may favor one or more of the beneficiaries. A determination in accordance with sections 5812.01 to 5812.52 of the Revised Code is presumed to be fair and reasonable to all of the beneficiaries.

(C) In allocating receipts and disbursements to or between principal and income, a fiduciary may credit a receipt or charge an expenditure to income or principal with respect to a decedent's estate, a trust, or property passing to a trust, that is eligible for a federal estate tax marital deduction or Ohio estate tax marital deduction, or for a federal estate tax charitable deduction or Ohio estate tax charitable deduction, or for a federal gift tax marital deduction or federal gift tax charitable deduction only to the extent that the credit of the receipt or charge of the expenditure will not cause the reduction or loss of the deduction.

(D) As used in division (C) of this section:

(1) "Federal estate tax charitable deduction" means the estate tax charitable deduction allowed by subtitle B, Chapter 11 of the "Internal Revenue Code of 1986," 26 U.S.C.A. 2055, as amended.

(2) "Federal estate tax marital deduction" means the estate tax marital deduction allowed by subtitle B, Chapter 11 of the "Internal Revenue Code of 1986," 26 U.S.C.A. 2056, as amended.

(3) "Federal gift tax charitable deduction" means the gift tax charitable deduction allowed by subtitle B, Chapter 12 of the "Internal Revenue Code of 1986," 26 U.S.C.A. 2522, as amended.

(4) "Federal gift tax marital deduction" means the gift tax marital deduction allowed by subtitle B, Chapter 12 of the "Internal Revenue Code of 1986," 26 U.S.C.A. 2523, as amended.

(5) "Ohio estate tax charitable deduction" means the estate tax charitable deduction allowed by division (A) of section 5731.17 of the Revised Code.

(6) "Ohio estate tax marital deduction" means the estate tax marital deduction allowed by section 5731.15 of the Revised Code.

(2006 H 416, eff. 1–1–07)

Uncodified Law

2002 H 522, § 4, eff. 1–1–03, reads:

It is the intent of the General Assembly in enacting section 1340.41 of the Revised Code to limit the application of the holding in *Sherman v. Sherman* (1966), 5 Ohio St. 2d 27, relative to a trustee's allocation of receipts and disbursements between principal and income of a trust.

Historical and Statutory Notes

Ed. Note: RC 5812.02 is former RC 1340.41, amended and recodified by 2006 H 416, eff. 1–1–07; 2002 H 522, eff. 1–1–03.

Amendment Note: 2006 H 416 substituted "1340.46" with "5812.07", "1340.53" with "5812.14", "1340.40" with "5812.01", "1340.91" with "5812.52", and "1340.42" with "5812.03".

Uniform Law: This section is analogous to §103 of the Uniform Principal and Income Act (1997 Act). See 7B Uniform Laws Annotated, Master Edition.

Library References

Trusts ⟬177, 270, 271.
Westlaw Topic No. 390.
C.J.S. Trusts §§ 318 to 324, 330 to 331, 347 to 348, 350 to 360.

Baldwin's Ohio Legislative Service Annotated, 2006 H 416 LSC Analysis, p 3/L-1709

5812.03 Trustee's power to adjust

(A) A trustee may adjust between principal and income to the extent the trustee considers necessary if the trustee invests and manages the trust assets as a prudent investor, the terms of the trust describe the amount that may or must be distributed to a beneficiary by referring to the trust's income, and the trustee determines, after applying division (A) of section 5812.02 of the Revised Code, that the trustee is unable to comply with division (B) of that section.

(B) In deciding whether and to what extent to exercise the power conferred by division (A) of this section, a trustee shall consider all factors relevant to the trust and its beneficiaries, including all of the following factors to the extent they are relevant:

(1) The nature, purpose, and expected duration of the trust;

(2) The intent of the settlor;

(3) The identity and circumstances of the beneficiaries;

(4) The needs for liquidity, regularity of income, and preservation and appreciation of capital;

(5) The assets held in the trust; the extent to which they consist of financial assets, interests in closely held enterprises, tangible and intangible personal property, or real property; the

extent to which an asset is used by a beneficiary; and whether an asset was purchased by the trustee or received from the settlor;

(6) The net amount allocated to income under sections 5812.01, 5812.02, and 5812.07 to 5812.52 of the Revised Code; and the increase or decrease in the value of the principal assets, which the trustee may estimate as to assets for which market values are not readily available;

(7) Whether and to what extent the terms of the trust give the trustee the power to invade principal or accumulate income or prohibit the trustee from invading principal or accumulating income, and the extent to which the trustee has exercised a power from time to time to invade principal or accumulate income;

(8) The actual and anticipated effect of economic conditions on principal and income and effects of inflation and deflation;

(9) The anticipated tax consequences of an adjustment.

(C) A trustee shall not make an adjustment if any of the following applies:

(1) The adjustment diminishes the income interest in a trust that requires all of the income to be paid at least annually to a spouse and for which an estate tax or gift tax marital deduction would be allowed, in whole or in part, if the trustee did not have the power to make the adjustment.

(2) The adjustment reduces the actuarial value of the income interest in a trust to which a person transfers property with the intent to qualify for a gift tax exclusion.

(3) The adjustment changes the amount payable to a beneficiary as a fixed annuity or a fixed fraction of the value of the trust assets.

(4) The adjustment is from any amount that is permanently set aside for charitable purposes under a will or the terms of a trust unless both income and principal are so set aside.

(5) If possessing or exercising the power to make the adjustment causes an individual to be treated as the owner of all or part of the trust for income tax purposes, and the individual would not be treated as the owner if the trustee did not possess the power to make the adjustment;

(6) If possessing or exercising the power to make the adjustment causes all or part of the trust assets to be included for estate tax purposes in the estate of an individual who has the power to remove a trustee or appoint a trustee, or both, and the assets would not be included in the estate of the individual if the trustee did not possess the power to make the adjustment;

(7) If the trustee is a beneficiary of the trust;

(8) If the trustee is not a beneficiary, but the adjustment would benefit the trustee directly or indirectly.

(D) If division (C)(5), (6), (7), or (8) of this section applies to a trustee and there is more than one trustee, a cotrustee to whom the provision does not apply may make the adjustment unless the exercise of the power by the remaining trustee or trustees is not permitted by the terms of the trust.

(E) A trustee may release the entire power conferred by division (A) of this section or may release only the power to adjust from income to principal or the power to adjust from principal to income if the trustee is uncertain about whether possessing or exercising the power will cause a result described in division (C)(1), (2), (3), (4), (5), (6), or (8) of this section or if the trustee determines that possessing or exercising the power will or may deprive the trust of a tax benefit or impose a tax burden not described in division (C) of this section. The release may be permanent or for a specified period, including a period measured by the life of an individual.

(F) Terms of a trust that limit the power of a trustee to make an adjustment between principal and income do not affect the application of this section unless it is clear from the terms of the trust that the terms are intended to deny the trustee the power of adjustment conferred by division (A) of this section.

(G) The liability of a trustee relative to the exercise of adjustment authority conferred by divisions (A) to (F) of this section shall be limited in the following manner:

(1) Unless a court determines that a trustee has acted in bad faith, no trustee shall be held liable for damages for choosing not to make an adjustment.

(2) Unless a court determines that a trustee has acted in bad faith with respect to an adjustment, the sole remedy to be ordered by a court shall be a prospective correction of the adjustment.

(3) For purposes of this section, and subject to division (C) of this section, from time to time a trustee may make a safe-harbor adjustment to increase net trust accounting income up to and including an amount equal to four per cent of the trust's fair market value determined as of the first business day of the current year. If a trustee determines to make this safe-harbor adjustment, the propriety of this adjustment shall be conclusively presumed. Nothing in division (G)(3) of this section prohibits any other type of adjustment authorized under any provision of this section.

(2006 H 416, eff. 1–1–07)

Historical and Statutory Notes

Ed. Note: RC 5812.03 is former RC 1340.42, amended and recodified by 2006 H 416, eff. 1–1–07; 2002 H 522, eff. 1–1–03.

Amendment Note: 2006 H 416 substituted "1340.41" with "5812.02", "1340.40" with "5812.01", "1340.46" with "5812.07", and "1340.91" with "5812.52h".

Uniform Law: This section is analogous to §104 of the Uniform Principal and Income Act (1997 Act). See 7B Uniform Laws Annotated, Master Edition.

Library References

Trusts ⇐274.
Westlaw Topic No. 390.
C.J.S. Trusts §§ 391 to 400, 510 to 511.

Baldwin's Ohio Legislative Service Annotated, 2006 H 416 LSC Analysis, p 3/L-1709

5812.07 Determination and distribution of net income

After a decedent dies, in the case of an estate, or after an income interest in a trust ends, all of the following apply:

(A) The fiduciary of the estate or of the terminating income interest shall determine, under the provisions of sections 5812.12 to 5812.47 of the Revised Code that apply to trustees and under division (E) of this section, the amount of net income and net principal receipts received from property specifically given to a beneficiary. The fiduciary shall distribute the net income and net principal receipts to the beneficiary that is to receive the specific property.

(B) A fiduciary shall determine the remaining net income of a decedent's estate or a terminating income interest under the provisions of sections 5812.12 to 5812.47 of the Revised Code that apply to trustees and by doing all of the following:

(1) Including in net income all income from property used to discharge liabilities;

(2) Paying from income or principal, in the fiduciary's discretion, fees of attorneys, accountants, and fiduciaries; court costs and other expenses of administration; and interest on death taxes. However, the fiduciary may pay those expenses from income of property passing to a trust for which the fiduciary claims an estate tax marital or charitable deduction only to the

extent that the payment of those expenses from income will not cause the reduction or loss of the deduction.

(3) Paying from principal all other disbursements made or incurred in connection with the settlement of a decedent's estate or the winding up of a terminating income interest, including debts, funeral expenses, disposition of remains, family allowances, and death taxes and related penalties that are apportioned to the estate or terminating income interest by the will, the terms of the trust, or applicable law.

(C) A fiduciary shall distribute to a beneficiary that receives a pecuniary amount outright the interest or any other amount provided by the will, the terms of the trust, or applicable law from net income determined under division (B) of this section or from principal to the extent that net income is insufficient. If a beneficiary is to receive a pecuniary amount outright from a trust after an income interest ends and no interest or other amount is provided for by the terms of the trust or applicable law, the fiduciary shall distribute the interest or other amount to which the beneficiary would be entitled under applicable law if the pecuniary amount were required to be paid under a will.

(D) A fiduciary shall distribute the net income remaining after distributions required by division (C) of this section, in the manner described in section 5812.08 of the Revised Code, to all other beneficiaries, including a beneficiary that receives a pecuniary amount in trust, even if the beneficiary holds an unqualified power to withdraw assets from the trust or other presently exercisable, general power of appointment over the trust.

(E) A fiduciary shall not reduce principal or income receipts from property described in division (A) of this section because of a payment described in section 5812.42 or 5812.43 of the Revised Code to the extent that the will, the terms of the trust, or applicable law requires the fiduciary to make the payment from assets other than the property or to the extent that the fiduciary recovers or expects to recover the payment from a third party. The net income and principal receipts from the property are determined by including all of the amounts the fiduciary receives or pays with respect to the property, whether those amounts accrued or became due before, on, or after the date of a decedent's death or an income interest's terminating event, and by making a reasonable provision for amounts that the fiduciary believes the estate or terminating income interest may become obligated to pay after the property is distributed.

(2006 H 416, eff. 1–1–07)

Historical and Statutory Notes

Ed. Note: RC 5812.07 is former RC 1340.46, amended and recodified by 2006 H 416, eff. 1–1–07; 2002 H 522, eff. 1–1–03.

Amendment Note: 2006 H 416 substituted "1340.51" with "5812.12", "1340.86" with "5812.47", "1340.47" with "5812.08", "1340.81" with "5812.42", and "1340.82" with "5812.43".

Uniform Law: This section is analogous to §201 of the Uniform Principal and Income Act (1997 Act). See 7B Uniform Laws Annotated, Master Edition.

Library References

Trusts ⟾280.
Wills ⟾684.10.
Westlaw Topic Nos. 390, 409.
C.J.S. Trusts §§ 544 to 550.
C.J.S. Wills §§ 1463, 1483 to 1484, 1488 to 1489, 1492 to 1496.
Baldwin's Ohio Legislative Service Annotated, 2006 H 416 LSC Analysis, p 3/L-1709

5812.08 Distribution to residuary and remainder beneficiaries

(A) Each beneficiary described in division (D) of section 5812.07 of the Revised Code is entitled to receive a portion of the net income equal to the beneficiary's fractional interest in undistributed principal assets, using values as of the distribution date. If a fiduciary makes more than one distribution of assets to beneficiaries to whom this section applies, each beneficiary, including one that does not receive part of the distribution, is entitled, as of each distribution date, to the net income the fiduciary has received after the date of the decedent's death or terminating event or earlier distribution date but has not distributed as of the current distribution date.

(B) In determining a beneficiary's share of net income for the purpose of this section, all of the following apply:

(1) The beneficiary is entitled to receive a portion of the net income equal to the beneficiary's fractional interest in the undistributed principal assets immediately before the distribution date, including assets that later may be sold to meet principal obligations.

(2) The beneficiary's fractional interest in the undistributed principal assets must be calculated without regard to property specifically given to a beneficiary and property required to pay pecuniary amounts not in trust.

(3) The beneficiary's fractional interest in the undistributed principal assets must be calculated on the basis of the aggregate value of those assets as of the distribution date without reducing the value by any unpaid principal obligation.

(4) The distribution date for purposes of this section may be the date as of which the fiduciary calculates the value of the assets if that date is reasonably near the date on which assets are actually distributed.

(C) If a fiduciary does not distribute all of the collected but undistributed net income described in divisions (A) and (B) of this section to each person as of a distribution date, the fiduciary shall maintain appropriate records showing the interest of each.

(D) To the extent that a fiduciary considers it appropriate, the fiduciary may apply the provisions of divisions (A) to (C) of this section to any net gain or loss, realized after the date of the decedent's death or an income interest termination or earlier distribution date, from the disposition of a principal asset to which such provisions apply.

(2006 H 416, eff. 1–1–07)

Historical and Statutory Notes

Ed. Note: RC 5812.08 is former RC 1340.47, amended and recodified by 2006 H 416, eff. 1–1–07; 2002 H 522, eff. 1–1–03.

Amendment Note: 2006 H 416 substituted "1340.46" with "5812.07".

Uniform Law: This section is analogous to §202 of the Uniform Principal and Income Act (1997 Act). See 7B Uniform Laws Annotated, Master Edition.

Library References

Trusts ⟾280.
Wills ⟾684.9.
Westlaw Topic Nos. 390, 409.
C.J.S. Trusts §§ 544 to 550.
C.J.S. Wills §§ 1463, 1488 to 1489.
Baldwin's Ohio Legislative Service Annotated, 2006 H 416 LSC Analysis, p 3/L-1709

5812.12 When right to income begins and ends

(A) An income beneficiary is entitled to net income from the date on which the income interest begins. An income interest begins on the date specified in the terms of the trust or, if no date is specified, on the date an asset becomes subject to a trust or successive income interest.

(B) An asset becomes subject to a trust on any of the following dates:

(1) The date it is transferred to the trust, in the case of an asset that is transferred to a trust during the transferor's life;

(2) The date of a testator's death, in the case of an asset that becomes subject to a trust by reason of a will, even if there is an intervening period of administration of the testator's estate;

(3) The date of an individual's death, in the case of an asset that is transferred to a fiduciary by a third party because of the individual's death.

(C) An asset becomes subject to a successive income interest on the day after the preceding income interest ends, as determined under division (D) of this section, even if there is an intervening period of administration to wind up the preceding income interest.

(D) An income interest ends on the day before an income beneficiary dies or another terminating event occurs, or on the last day of a period during which there is no beneficiary to whom a trustee may distribute income.

(2006 H 416, eff. 1–1–07)

Historical and Statutory Notes

Ed. Note: RC 5812.12 is former RC 1340.51, recodified by 2006 H 416, eff. 1–1–07; 2002 H 522, eff. 1–1–03.

Uniform Law: This section is analogous to §301 of the Uniform Principal and Income Act (1997 Act). See 7B Uniform Laws Annotated, Master Edition.

Library References

Trusts ⚖ 273.
Wills ⚖ 684.7.
Westlaw Topic Nos. 390, 409.
C.J.S. Trusts §§ 542 to 550.
C.J.S. Wills §§ 1463, 1481.

Baldwin's Ohio Legislative Service Annotated, 2006 H 416 LSC Analysis, p 3/L–1709

5812.13 Apportionment of receipts and disbursements when decedent dies or income interest begins

(A) A trustee shall allocate to principal an income receipt or disbursement other than one to which division (A) of section 5812.07 of the Revised Code applies, if its due date occurs before a decedent dies in the case of an estate or before an income interest begins in the case of a trust or successive income interest.

(B) A trustee shall allocate an income receipt or disbursement to income if its due date occurs on or after the date on which a decedent dies or an income interest begins and if it is a periodic due date. An income receipt or disbursement shall be treated as accruing from day to day if its due date is not periodic or it has no due date. The portion of the receipt or disbursement accruing before the date on which a decedent dies or an income interest begins shall be allocated to principal, and the balance shall be allocated to income.

(C) For the purposes of this section, an item of income or an obligation is due on the date the payer is required to make a payment. If a payment date is not stated, there is no due date. Distributions to shareholders or other owners from an entity to which section 5812.18 of the Revised Code applies are deemed to be due on the date fixed by the entity for determining who is entitled to receive the distribution or, if no date is fixed, on the declaration date for the distribution. A due date is periodic for receipts or disbursements that must be paid at regular intervals under a lease or an obligation to pay interest or if an entity customarily makes distributions at regular intervals.

(2006 H 416, eff. 1–1–07)

Historical and Statutory Notes

Ed. Note: RC 5812.13 is former RC 1340.52, amended and recodified by 2006 H 416, eff. 1–1–07; 2002 H 522, eff. 1–1–03.

Amendment Note: 2006 H 416 substituted "1340.46" with "5812.07" and "1340.57" with "5812.18".

Uniform Law: This section is analogous to §302 of the Uniform Principal and Income Act (1997 Act). See 7B Uniform Laws Annotated, Master Edition.

Library References

Trusts ⚖ 274(1), 280.
Wills ⚖ 684.3(2).
Westlaw Topic Nos. 390, 409.
C.J.S. Trusts §§ 510, 544 to 550.
C.J.S. Wills §§ 1463, 1465 to 1466.

Baldwin's Ohio Legislative Service Annotated, 2006 H 416 LSC Analysis, p 3/L–1709

5812.14 Apportionment when income interest ends

(A) As used in this section, "undistributed income" means net income received before the date on which an income interest ends. "Undistributed income" excludes an item of income or expense that is due or accrued or net income that has been added or is required to be added to principal under the terms of the trust.

(B) When a mandatory income interest ends, the trustee shall pay to a mandatory income beneficiary that survives that date, or the estate of a deceased mandatory income beneficiary whose death causes the interest to end, the beneficiary's share of the undistributed income that is not disposed of under the terms of the trust, unless the beneficiary has an unqualified power to revoke more than five per cent of the trust immediately before the income interest ends. If the beneficiary has such power, the undistributed income from the portion of the trust that may be revoked shall be added to principal.

(C) When a trustee's obligation to pay a fixed annuity or a fixed fraction of the value of the trust's assets ends, the trustee shall prorate the final payment if and to the extent required by applicable law to accomplish a purpose of the trust or its settlor relating to income, gift, estate, or other tax requirements.

(2006 H 416, eff. 1–1–07)

Historical and Statutory Notes

Ed. Note: RC 5812.14 is former RC 1340.53, recodified by 2006 H 416, eff. 1–1–07; 2002 H 522, eff. 1–1–03.

Uniform Law: This section is analogous to §303 of the Uniform Principal and Income Act (1997 Act). See 7B Uniform Laws Annotated, Master Edition.

Library References

Trusts ⚖ 280, 274(1).
Wills ⚖ 684.6.
Westlaw Topic Nos. 390, 409.
C.J.S. Trusts §§ 510, 544 to 550.
C.J.S. Wills §§ 1463, 1471, 1478, 1490.

Baldwin's Ohio Legislative Service Annotated, 2006 H 416 LSC Analysis, p 3/L–1709

5812.18 Character of receipts

(A) As used in this section, "entity" means a corporation, partnership, limited liability company, regulated investment company, real estate investment trust, common trust fund, or any other organization in which a trustee has an interest other than a trust or estate to which section 5812.19 of the Revised Code applies, a business or activity to which section 5812.20 of the Revised Code applies, or an asset-backed security to which section 5812.38 of the Revised Code applies.

(B) Except as otherwise provided in this section, a trustee shall allocate to income money received from an entity.

(C) A trustee shall allocate all of the following receipts from an entity to principal:

(1) Property other than money;

(2) Money received in one distribution or a series of related distributions in exchange for part or all of a trust's interest in the entity;

(3) Money received in total or partial liquidation of the entity;

(4) Money received from an entity that is a regulated investment company or a real estate investment trust if the money distributed is a capital gain dividend for federal income tax purposes.

(D) Money is received in partial liquidation in either of the following circumstances:

(1) To the extent that the entity, at or near the time of a distribution, indicates that it is a distribution in partial liquidation;

(2) If the total amount of money and property received in a distribution or series of related distributions is greater than twenty per cent of the entity's gross assets, as shown by the entity's year-end financial statements immediately preceding the initial receipt.

(E) Money is not received in partial liquidation, nor shall it be taken into account under division (D)(2) of this section, to the extent that it does not exceed the amount of income tax that a trustee or beneficiary must pay on taxable income of the entity that distributes the money.

(F) A trustee may rely upon a statement made by an entity about the source or character of a distribution if the statement is made at or near the time of distribution by the entity's board of directors or other person or group of persons authorized to exercise powers to pay money or transfer property comparable to those of a corporation's board of directors.

(2006 H 416, eff. 1–1–07)

Historical and Statutory Notes

Ed. Note: RC 5812.18 is former RC 1340.57, amended and recodified by 2006 H 416, eff. 1–1–07; 2002 H 522, eff. 1–1–03.

Amendment Note: 2006 H 416 substituted "1340.58" with "5812.19", "1340.59" with "5812.20", and "1340.77" with "5812.38".

Uniform Law: This section is analogous to §401 of the Uniform Principal and Income Act (1997 Act). See 7B Uniform Laws Annotated, Master Edition.

Library References

Trusts ⚖=272.1.
Wills ⚖=684.3(2).
Westlaw Topic Nos. 390, 409.
C.J.S. Trusts §§ 551, 554.
C.J.S. Wills §§ 1463, 1465 to 1466.

Baldwin's Ohio Legislative Service Annotated, 2006 H 416 LSC Analysis, p 3/L-1709

5812.19 Distribution from trust or estate

A trustee shall allocate to income an amount received as a distribution of income from a trust or an estate in which the trust has an interest other than a purchased interest, and shall allocate to principal an amount received as a distribution of principal from such a trust or estate. If a trustee purchases an interest in a trust that is an investment entity, or a decedent or donor transfers an interest in such a trust to a trustee, section 5812.18 or 5812.38 of the Revised Code applies to a receipt from the trust.

(2006 H 416, eff. 1–1–07)

Historical and Statutory Notes

Ed. Note: RC 5812.19 is former RC 1340.58, amended and recodified by 2006 H 416, eff. 1–1–07; 2002 H 522, eff. 1–1–03.

Amendment Note: 2006 H 416 substituted "1340.57" with "5812.18" and "1340.77" with "5812.38".

Uniform Law: This section is analogous to §402 of the Uniform Principal and Income Act (1997 Act). See 7B Uniform Laws Annotated, Master Edition.

Library References

Trusts ⚖=272.1.
Wills ⚖=684.3(2).
Westlaw Topic Nos. 390, 409.
C.J.S. Trusts §§ 551, 554.
C.J.S. Wills §§ 1463, 1465 to 1466.

Baldwin's Ohio Legislative Service Annotated, 2006 H 416 LSC Analysis, p 3/L-1709

5812.20 Business and other activities conducted by trustee

(A) If a trust that conducts a business or other activity determines that it is in the best interest of all the beneficiaries to account separately for the business or activity instead of accounting for it as part of the trust's general accounting records, the trustee may maintain separate accounting records for its transactions, whether or not its assets are segregated from other trust assets.

(B) A trustee that accounts separately for a business or other activity may determine the extent to which its net cash receipts must be retained for working capital, the acquisition or replacement of fixed assets, and other reasonably foreseeable needs of the business or activity, and the extent to which the remaining net cash receipts are accounted for as principal or income in the trust's general accounting records. If a trustee sells assets of the business or other activity, other than in the ordinary course of the business or activity, the trustee shall account for the net amount received as principal in the trust's general accounting records to the extent the trustee determines that the amount received is no longer required in the conduct of the business.

(C) Activities for which a trustee may maintain separate accounting records under this section include all of the following:

(1) Retail, manufacturing, service, and other traditional business activities;

(2) Farming;

(3) Raising and selling livestock and other animals;

(4) Management of rental properties;

(5) Extraction of minerals and other natural resources;

(6) Timber operations;

(7) Activities to which section 5812.37 of the Revised Code applies.

(2006 H 416, eff. 1–1–07)

Historical and Statutory Notes

Ed. Note: RC 5812.20 is former RC 1340.59, amended and recodified by 2006 H 416, eff. 1–1–07; 2002 H 522, eff. 1–1–03.

Amendment Note: 2006 H 416 substituted "1340.76" with "5812.37".

Uniform Law: This section is analogous to §403 of the Uniform Principal and Income Act (1997 Act). See 7B Uniform Laws Annotated, Master Edition.

Library References

Trusts ⚖︎177.
Wills ⚖︎684.10(1).
Westlaw Topic Nos. 390, 409.
C.J.S. Trusts §§ 347 to 348, 350 to 360.
C.J.S. Wills §§ 1463, 1483 to 1484, 1488 to 1489.
  Baldwin's Ohio Legislative Service Annotated, 2006 H 416 LSC Analysis, p 3/L-1709

5812.24 Principal receipts

A trustee shall allocate to principal all of the following:

(A) To the extent not allocated to income under sections 5812.01 to 5812.52 of the Revised Code, assets received from a transferor during the transferor's lifetime, a decedent's estate, a trust with a terminating income interest, or a payer under a contract naming the trust or its trustee as beneficiary;

(B) Money or other property received from the sale, exchange, liquidation, or change in form of a principal asset, including realized profit, subject to sections 5812.18 to 5812.38 of the Revised Code;

(C) Amounts recovered from third parties to reimburse the trust because of disbursements described in division (A)(7) of section 5812.43 of the Revised Code or for other reasons to the extent not based on the loss of income;

(D) Proceeds of property taken by eminent domain, but a separate award made for the loss of income with respect to an accounting period during which a current income beneficiary had a mandatory income interest is income;

(E) Net income received in an accounting period during which there is no beneficiary to whom a trustee may or must distribute income;

(F) Other receipts as provided in sections 5812.31 to 5812.38 of the Revised Code.

(2006 H 416, eff. 1–1–07)

Historical and Statutory Notes

Ed. Note: RC 5812.24 is former RC 1340.63, amended and recodified by 2006 H 416, eff. 1–1–07; 2002 H 522, eff. 1–1–03.

Amendment Note: 2006 H 416 substituted "1340.40" with "5812.01", "1340.91" with "5812.52", "1340.57" with "5812.18", "1340.77" with "5812.38", "1340.82" with "5812.43", and "1340.70" with "5812.31".

Uniform Law: This section is analogous to §404 of the Uniform Principal and Income Act (1997 Act). See 7B Uniform Laws Annotated, Master Edition.

Library References

Trusts ⚖︎272.1.
Wills ⚖︎684.3(2).
Westlaw Topic Nos. 390, 409.
C.J.S. Trusts §§ 551, 554.
C.J.S. Wills §§ 1463, 1465 to 1466.
  Baldwin's Ohio Legislative Service Annotated, 2006 H 416 LSC Analysis, p 3/L-1709

5812.25 Rental property

To the extent that a trustee accounts for receipts from rental property pursuant to this section, the trustee shall allocate to income an amount received as rent of real or personal property, including an amount received for cancellation or renewal of a lease. An amount received as a refundable deposit, including a security deposit or a deposit that is to be applied as rent for future periods, shall be added to principal and held subject to the terms of the lease and shall not be available for distribution to a beneficiary until the trustee's contractual obligations have been satisfied with respect to that amount.

(2006 H 416, eff. 1–1–07)

Historical and Statutory Notes

Ed. Note: RC 5812.25 is former RC 1340.64, recodified by 2006 H 416, eff. 1–1–07; 2002 H 522, eff. 1–1–03.

Uniform Law: This section is analogous to §405 of the Uniform Principal and Income Act (1997 Act). See 7B Uniform Laws Annotated, Master Edition.

Library References

Trusts ⚖︎183.
Wills ⚖︎684.3(2).
Westlaw Topic Nos. 390, 409.
C.J.S. Trusts §§ 367 to 368.
C.J.S. Wills §§ 1463, 1465 to 1466.
  Baldwin's Ohio Legislative Service Annotated, 2006 H 416 LSC Analysis, p 3/L-1709

5812.26 Obligation to pay money

(A) An amount received as interest, whether determined at a fixed, variable, or floating rate, on an obligation to pay money to the trustee, including an amount received as consideration for prepaying principal, shall be allocated to income without any provision for amortization of premium.

(B) A trustee shall allocate to principal an amount received from the sale, redemption, or other disposition of an obligation to pay money to the trustee more than one year after the date it is purchased or acquired by the trustee, including an obligation whose purchase price or value when it is acquired is less than its value at maturity. If the obligation matures within one year after the date it is purchased or acquired by the trustee, an amount received in excess of its purchase price or its value when acquired by the trust shall be allocated to income.

(C) This section does not apply to an obligation to which section 5812.32, 5812.33, 5812.34, 5812.35, 5812.37, or 5812.38 of the Revised Code applies.

(2006 H 416, eff. 1–1–07)

Historical and Statutory Notes

Ed. Note: RC 5812.26 is former RC 1340.65, amended and recodified by 2006 H 416, eff. 1–1–07; 2002 H 522, eff. 1–1–03.

Amendment Note: 2006 H 416 substituted "1340.71" with "5812.32", "1340.72" with "5812.33", "1340.73" with "5812.34", "1340.74" with "5812.35", "1340.76" with "5812.37", and "1340.77" with "5812.38".

Uniform Law: This section is analogous to §406 of the Uniform Principal and Income Act (1997 Act). See 7B Uniform Laws Annotated, Master Edition.

Library References

Trusts ⚖︎219.
Wills ⚖︎684.3(2).
Westlaw Topic Nos. 390, 409.
C.J.S. Trusts §§ 512 to 524.
C.J.S. Wills §§ 1463, 1465 to 1466.
  Baldwin's Ohio Legislative Service Annotated, 2006 H 416 LSC Analysis, p 3/L-1709

5812.27 Insurance policies and similar contracts

(A) Except as otherwise provided in division (B) of this section, a trustee shall allocate to principal the proceeds of a life insurance policy or other contract in which the trust or its trustee is named as beneficiary, including a contract that insures the trust or its trustee against loss for damage to, destruction of, or loss of title to a trust asset. The trustee shall allocate dividends on an insurance policy to income if the premiums on the policy are paid from income, and to principal if the premiums are paid from principal.

(B) A trustee shall allocate to income proceeds of a contract that insures the trustee against loss of occupancy or other use by an income beneficiary, loss of income, or, subject to section 5812.20 of the Revised Code, loss of profits from a business.

(C) This section does not apply to a contract to which section 5812.32 of the Revised Code applies.

(2006 H 416, eff. 1–1–07)

Historical and Statutory Notes

Ed. Note: RC 5812.27 is former RC 1340.66, amended and recodified by 2006 H 416, eff. 1–1–07; 2002 H 522, eff. 1–1–03.

Amendment Note: 2006 H 416 substituted "1340.59" with "5812.20" and "1340.71" with "5812.32".

Uniform Law: This section is analogous to §407 of the Uniform Principal and Income Act (1997 Act). See 7B Uniform Laws Annotated, Master Edition.

Library References

Trusts ⚖ 210, 272.1.
Wills ⚖ 684.3(2).
Westlaw Topic Nos. 390, 409.
C.J.S. Trusts §§ 381 to 382, 551, 554.
C.J.S. Wills §§ 1463, 1465 to 1466.
Baldwin's Ohio Legislative Service Annotated, 2006 H 416 LSC Analysis, p 3/L-1709

Notes of Decisions

Ed. Note: This section contains annotations from former RC 1340.66.

Trustee powers and duties 1

---

1. **Trustee powers and duties**

Trial court order granting life insurance company a secured priority interest in trust beneficiary's year-end distributions, as a result of creditor's bill insurance company obtained to collect on payment on judgment against beneficiary, did not alter beneficiary's interest in the trust or give insurance company a greater interest in the trust than that held by the beneficiary, even though the order directed trustees not to make discretionary distributions to beneficiary until his debt was repaid and to apply nondiscretionary distributions to the reduction of beneficiary's debt; trust occupied position of unsecured creditor whose interest was subordinate to insurance company's. Great American Ins. Co. v. Thompson Trust (Ohio App. 1 Dist., Hamilton, 01-27-2006) No. C-040127, 2006-Ohio-304, 2006 WL 199751, Unreported, appeal not allowed 109 Ohio St.3d 1496, 848 N.E.2d 858, 2006-Ohio-2762. Trusts ⚖ 151.1

5812.31   Insubstantial allocations not required

If a trustee determines that an allocation between principal and income required by section 5812.32, 5812.33, 5812.34, 5812.35, or 5812.38 of the Revised Code is insubstantial, the trustee may allocate the entire amount to principal unless one of the circumstances described in division (C) of section 5812.03 of the Revised Code applies to the allocation. This power may be exercised by a cotrustee in the circumstances described in division (D) of that section and may be released for the reasons and in the manner described in division (E) of the section. An allocation is presumed to be insubstantial if either of the following applies:

(A) The amount of the allocation would increase or decrease net income in an accounting period, as determined before the allocation, by less than ten per cent.

(B) The value of the asset producing the receipt for which the allocation would be made is less than ten per cent of the total value of the trust's assets at the beginning of the accounting period.

(2006 H 416, eff. 1–1–07)

Historical and Statutory Notes

Ed. Note: RC 5812.31 is former RC 1340.70, amended and recodified by 2006 H 416, eff. 1–1–07; 2002 H 522, eff. 1–1–03.

Amendment Note: 2006 H 416 substituted "1340.71" with "5812.32", "1340.72" with "5812.33", "1340.73" with "5812.34", "1340.74" with "5812.35", "1340.77" with "5812.38", and "1340.42" with "5812.03".

Uniform Law: This section is analogous to §408 of the Uniform Principal and Income Act (1997 Act). See 7B Uniform Laws Annotated, Master Edition.

Library References

Trusts ⚖ 272.1.
Wills ⚖ 684.10(6).
Westlaw Topic Nos. 390, 409.
C.J.S. Trusts §§ 551, 554.
C.J.S. Wills §§ 1463, 1483 to 1484, 1488 to 1489.
Baldwin's Ohio Legislative Service Annotated, 2006 H 416 LSC Analysis, p 3/L-1709

5812.32   Deferred compensation, annuities, and similar payments

(A) As used in this section, "payment" means a payment that a trustee may receive over a fixed number of years or during the life of one or more individuals because of services rendered or property transferred to the payer in exchange for future payments. "Payment" includes a payment made in money or property from the payer's general assets or from a separate fund created by the payer, including a private or commercial annuity, an individual retirement account, or a pension, profit-sharing, stock-bonus, or stock-ownership plan.

(B) To the extent that a payment is characterized as interest or a dividend or a payment made in lieu of interest or a dividend, a trustee shall allocate it to income. The trustee shall allocate to principal the balance of the payment and any other payment received in the same accounting period that is not characterized as interest, a dividend, or an equivalent payment.

(C) If no part of a payment is characterized as interest, a dividend, or an equivalent payment, and all or part of the payment is required to be made, a trustee shall allocate to income ten per cent of the part that is required to be made during the accounting period and the balance to principal. If no part of a payment is required to be made or the payment received is the entire amount to which the trustee is entitled, the trustee shall allocate the entire payment to principal. For purposes of this division, a payment is not "required to be made" to the extent that it is made because the trustee exercises a right of withdrawal.

(D) If, to obtain an estate tax marital deduction for a trust, a trustee must allocate more of a payment to income than is provided for by this section, the trustee shall allocate to income the additional amount necessary to obtain the marital deduction.

(E) This section does not apply to payments to which section 5812.33 of the Revised Code applies.

(2006 H 416, eff. 1–1–07)

Historical and Statutory Notes

Ed. Note: RC 5812.32 is former RC 1340.71, amended and recodified by 2006 H 416, eff. 1–1–07; 2002 H 522, eff. 1–1–03.

Amendment Note: 2006 H 416 substituted "1340.72" with "5812.33".

Uniform Law: This section is analogous to §409 of the Uniform Principal and Income Act (1997 Act). See 7B Uniform Laws Annotated, Master Edition.

Library References

Trusts ⇌272.1.
Wills ⇌684.3(2).
Westlaw Topic Nos. 390, 409.
C.J.S. Trusts §§ 551, 554.
C.J.S. Wills §§ 1463, 1465 to 1466.

Baldwin's Ohio Legislative Service Annotated, 2006 H 416 LSC Analysis, p 3/L-1709

5812.33 Liquidating asset

(A) As used in this section, "liquidating asset" means an asset whose value will diminish or terminate because the asset is expected to produce receipts for a period of limited duration. "Liquidating asset" includes a leasehold, patent, copyright, royalty right, and right to receive payments during a period of more than one year under an arrangement that does not provide for the payment of interest on the unpaid balance. "Liquidating asset" excludes a payment subject to section 5812.32 of the Revised Code, resources subject to section 5812.34 of the Revised Code, timber subject to section 5812.35 of the Revised Code, an activity subject to section 5812.37 of the Revised Code, an asset subject to section 5812.38 of the Revised Code, or any asset for which the trustee establishes a reserve for depreciation under section 5812.44 of the Revised Code.

(B) A trustee shall allocate to income ten per cent of the receipts from a liquidating asset and the balance to principal.

(2006 H 416, eff. 1–1–07)

Historical and Statutory Notes

Ed. Note: RC 5812.33 is former RC 1340.72, amended and recodified by 2006 H 416, eff. 1–1–07; 2002 H 522, eff. 1–1–03.

Amendment Note: 2006 H 416 substituted "1340.71" with "5812.32", "1340.73" with "5812.34", "1340.74" with "5812.35", "1340.76" with "5812.37", "1340.77" with "5812.38", and "1340.83" with "5812.44".

Uniform Law: This section is analogous to §410 of the Uniform Principal and Income Act (1997 Act). See 7B Uniform Laws Annotated, Master Edition.

Library References

Trusts ⇌272.1.
Wills ⇌684.3(5).
Westlaw Topic Nos. 390, 409.
C.J.S. Trusts §§ 551, 554.
C.J.S. Wills § 1463.

Baldwin's Ohio Legislative Service Annotated, 2006 H 416 LSC Analysis, p 3/L-1709

5812.34 Minerals, water, and other natural resources

(A) To the extent that a trustee accounts for receipts from an interest in minerals or other natural resources pursuant to this section, the trustee shall allocate the receipts in accordance with all of the following:

(1) If received as nominal delay rental or nominal annual rent on a lease, a receipt shall be allocated to income.

(2) If received from a production payment, a receipt shall be allocated to income if and to the extent that the agreement creating the production payment provides a factor for interest or its equivalent. The balance shall be allocated to principal.

(3) If an amount received as a royalty, shut-in-well payment, take-or-pay payment, bonus, or delay rental is more than nominal, ninety per cent shall be allocated to principal and the balance to income.

(4) If an amount is received from a working interest or any other interest not provided for in division (A)(1), (2), or (3) of this section, ninety per cent of the net amount received shall be allocated to principal and the balance to income.

(B) An amount received on account of an interest in water that is renewable shall be allocated to income. If the water is not renewable, ninety per cent of the amount shall be allocated to principal and the balance to income.

(C) This section applies whether or not a decedent or donor was extracting minerals, water, or other natural resources before the interest became subject to the trust.

(D) If a trust owns an interest in minerals, water, or other natural resources on January 1, 2003, the trustee may allocate receipts from the interest as provided in this section or in the manner used by the trustee before that date. If the trust acquires an interest in minerals, water, or other natural resources after January 1, 2003, the trustee shall allocate receipts from the interest as provided in this section.

(2006 H 416, eff. 1–1–07)

Historical and Statutory Notes

Ed. Note: RC 5812.34 is former RC 1340.73, amended and recodified by 2006 H 416, eff. 1–1–07; 2002 H 522, eff. 1–1–03.

Amendment Note: 2006 H 416 substituted "the effective date of this section" with "January 1, 2003" in division (D).

Uniform Law: This section is analogous to §411 of the Uniform Principal and Income Act (1997 Act). See 7B Uniform Laws Annotated, Master Edition.

Library References

Trusts ⇌272.1.
Wills ⇌684.3(2).
Westlaw Topic Nos. 390, 409.
C.J.S. Trusts §§ 551, 554.
C.J.S. Wills §§ 1463, 1465 to 1466.

Baldwin's Ohio Legislative Service Annotated, 2006 H 416 LSC Analysis, p 3/L-1709

5812.35 Timber

(A) To the extent that a trustee accounts for receipts from the sale of timber and related products pursuant to this section, the trustee shall allocate the net receipts in accordance with all of the following:

(1) To income, to the extent that the amount of timber removed from the land does not exceed the rate of growth of the timber during the accounting periods in which a beneficiary has a mandatory income interest;

(2) To principal, to the extent that the amount of timber removed from the land exceeds the rate of growth of the timber or the net receipts are from the sale of standing timber;

(3) To or between income and principal, if the net receipts are from the lease of timberland or from a contract to cut timber from land owned by a trust, by determining the amount of timber removed from the land under the lease or contract and applying divisions (A)(1) and (2) of this section;

(4) To principal, to the extent that advance payments, bonuses, and other payments are not allocated pursuant to division (A)(1), (2), or (3) of this section.

(B) In determining net receipts to be allocated pursuant to division (A) of this section, a trustee shall deduct and transfer to principal a reasonable amount for depletion.

(C) This section applies whether or not a decedent or transferor was harvesting timber from the property before it became subject to the trust.

(D) If a trust owns an interest in timberland on January 1, 2003, the trustee may allocate net receipts from the sale of timber and related products as provided in this section or in the manner used by the trustee before that date. If the trust acquires an interest in timberland after January 1, 2003, the trustee shall allocate net receipts from the sale of timber and related products as provided in this section.

(2006 H 416, eff. 1–1–07)

Historical and Statutory Notes

Ed. Note: RC 5812.35 is former RC 1340.74, amended and recodified by 2006 H 416, eff. 1–1–07; 2002 H 522, eff. 1–1–03.

Amendment Note: 2006 H 416 substituted "the effective date of this section" with "January 1, 2003" in division (D).

Uniform Law: This section is analogous to §412 of the Uniform Principal and Income Act (1997 Act). See 7B Uniform Laws Annotated, Master Edition.

Library References

Trusts ⚖=272.1.
Wills ⚖=684.3(2).
Westlaw Topic Nos. 390, 409.
C.J.S. Trusts §§ 551, 554.
C.J.S. Wills §§ 1463, 1465 to 1466.
　Baldwin's Ohio Legislative Service Annotated, 2006 H 416 LSC Analysis, p 3/L-1709

5812.36　Property not productive of income

(A) If a marital deduction is allowed for all or part of a trust whose assets consist substantially of property that does not provide the spouse with sufficient income from or use of the trust assets, and if the amounts that the trustee transfers from principal to income under section 5812.03 of the Revised Code and distributes to the spouse from principal pursuant to the terms of the trust are insufficient to provide the spouse with the beneficial enjoyment required to obtain the marital deduction, the spouse may require the trustee to make property productive of income, convert property within a reasonable time, or exercise the power conferred by division (A) of that section. The trustee may decide which action or combination of actions to take.

(B) In cases not governed by division (A) of this section, proceeds from the sale or other disposition of an asset shall be principal without regard to the amount of income the asset produces during any accounting period.

(2006 H 416, eff. 1–1–07)

Uncodified Law

2002 H 522, § 3, eff. 1–1–03, reads:

Division (A) of section 1340.75 of the Revised Code relating to the duty of a trustee to make property productive of income, with respect to a trust for which a marital deduction is allowed, is intended to codify existing fiduciary and trust law principles.

Historical and Statutory Notes

Ed. Note: RC 5812.36 is former RC 1340.75, amended and recodified by 2006 H 416, eff. 1–1–07; 2002 H 522, eff. 1–1–03.

Amendment Note: 2006 H 416 substituted "1340.42" with "5812.03".

Uniform Law: This section is analogous to §413 of the Uniform Principal and Income Act (1997 Act). See 7B Uniform Laws Annotated, Master Edition.

Library References

Trusts ⚖=280.
Wills ⚖=684.3(7).
Westlaw Topic Nos. 390, 409.
C.J.S. Trusts §§ 544 to 550.
C.J.S. Wills §§ 1463, 1467 to 1470.
　Baldwin's Ohio Legislative Service Annotated, 2006 H 416 LSC Analysis, p 3/L-1709

5812.37　Derivatives and options

(A) As used in this section, "derivative" means a contract or financial instrument or a combination of contracts and financial instruments that gives a trust the right or obligation to participate in some or all changes in the price of a tangible or intangible asset or group of assets, or changes in a rate, an index of prices or rates, or other market indicator for an asset or a group of assets.

(B) To the extent that a trustee does not account under section 5812.20 of the Revised Code for transactions in derivatives, the trustee shall allocate to principal receipts from and disbursements made in connection with those transactions.

(C) If a trustee grants an option to buy property from the trust, whether or not the trust owns the property when the option is granted, grants an option that permits another person to sell property to the trust, or acquires an option to buy property for the trust or an option to sell an asset owned by the trust, and the trustee or other owner of the asset is required to deliver the asset if the option is exercised, an amount received for granting the option shall be allocated to principal. An amount paid to acquire the option shall be paid from principal. A gain or loss realized upon the exercise of an option, including an option granted to a settlor of the trust for services rendered, shall be allocated to principal.

(2006 H 416, eff. 1–1–07)

Historical and Statutory Notes

Ed. Note: RC 5812.37 is former RC 1340.76, amended and recodified by 2006 H 416, eff. 1–1–07; 2002 H 522, eff. 1–1–03.

Amendment Note: 2006 H 416 substituted "1340.59" with "5812.20".

Uniform Law: This section is analogous to §414 of the Uniform Principal and Income Act (1997 Act). See 7B Uniform Laws Annotated, Master Edition.

Library References

Trusts ⚖=272.1.
Wills ⚖=684.3(2).
Westlaw Topic Nos. 390, 409.
C.J.S. Trusts §§ 551, 554.
C.J.S. Wills §§ 1463, 1465 to 1466.
　Baldwin's Ohio Legislative Service Annotated, 2006 H 416 LSC Analysis, p 3/L-1709

5812.38　Asset-backed securities

(A) As used in this section, "asset-backed security" means an asset whose value is based upon the right it gives the owner to receive distributions from the proceeds of financial assets that provide collateral for the security. "Asset-backed security" includes an asset that gives the owner the right to receive from the collateral financial assets only the interest or other current return or only the proceeds other than interest or current return. "Asset-backed security" excludes an asset to which section 5812.18 or 5812.32 of the Revised Code applies.

(B) If a trust receives a payment from interest or other current return and from other proceeds of the collateral financial assets, the trustee shall allocate to income the portion of the payment that the payer identifies as being from interest or other current return and shall allocate the balance of the payment to principal.

(C) If a trust receives one or more payments in exchange for the trust's entire interest in an asset-backed security in one accounting period, the trustee shall allocate the payments to principal. If a payment is one of a series of payments that will result in the liquidation of the trust's interest in the security over more than one accounting period, the trustee shall allocate ten per cent of the payment to income and the balance to principal.

(2006 H 416, eff. 1–1–07)

Historical and Statutory Notes

Ed. Note: RC 5812.38 is former RC 1340.77, amended and recodified by 2006 H 416, eff. 1–1–07; 2002 H 522, eff. 1–1–03.

Amendment Note: 2006 H 416 substituted "1340.57" with "5812.18" and "1340.71" with "5812.32".

Uniform Law: This section is analogous to §415 of the Uniform Principal and Income Act (1997 Act). See 7B Uniform Laws Annotated, Master Edition.

Library References

Trusts ⚖272.1.
Wills ⚖684.3(2).
Westlaw Topic Nos. 390, 409.
C.J.S. Trusts §§ 551, 554.
C.J.S. Wills §§ 1463, 1465 to 1466.

Baldwin's Ohio Legislative Service Annotated, 2006 H 416 LSC Analysis, p 3/L-1709

5812.42 Disbursements from income

A trustee shall make all of the following disbursements from income to the extent that they are not disbursements to which division (B)(2) or (3) of section 5812.07 of the Revised Code applies:

(A) One–half of the regular compensation of the trustee and of any person providing investment advisory or custodial services to the trustee;

(B) One–half of all expenses for accountings, judicial proceedings, or other matters that involve both the income and remainder interests;

(C) All of the other ordinary expenses incurred in connection with the administration, management, or preservation of trust property and the distribution of income, including interest, ordinary repairs, regularly recurring taxes assessed against principal, and expenses of a proceeding or other matter that concerns primarily the income interest;

(D) Recurring premiums on insurance covering the loss of a principal asset or the loss of income from or use of the asset.

(2006 H 416, eff. 1–1–07)

Historical and Statutory Notes

Ed. Note: RC 5812.42 is former RC 1340.81, amended and recodified by 2006 H 416, eff. 1–1–07; 2002 H 522, eff. 1–1–03.

Amendment Note: 2006 H 416 substituted "1340.46" with "5812.07".

Uniform Law: This section is analogous to §501 of the Uniform Principal and Income Act (1997 Act). See 7B Uniform Laws Annotated, Master Edition.

Library References

Trusts ⚖280.
Wills ⚖684.2(1).
Westlaw Topic Nos. 390, 409.
C.J.S. Trusts §§ 544 to 550.
C.J.S. Wills §§ 1463, 1480 to 1481.

Baldwin's Ohio Legislative Service Annotated, 2006 H 416 LSC Analysis, p 3/L-1709

5812.43 Disbursements from principal

(A) A trustee shall make all of the following disbursements from principal:

(1) The remaining one-half of the disbursements described in divisions (A) and (B) of section 5812.42 of the Revised Code;

(2) All of the trustee's compensation calculated on principal as a fee for acceptance, distribution, or termination, and disbursements made to prepare property for sale;

(3) Payments on the principal of a trust debt;

(4) Expenses of a proceeding that concerns primarily principal, including a proceeding to construe the trust or to protect the trust or its property;

(5) Premiums paid on a policy of insurance not described in division (D) of section 5812.42 of the Revised Code of which the trust is the owner and beneficiary;

(6) Estate, inheritance, and other transfer taxes, including penalties, apportioned to the trust;

(7) Disbursements related to environmental matters, including reclamation, assessing environmental conditions, remedying and removing environmental contamination, monitoring remedial activities and the release of substances, preventing future releases of substances, collecting amounts from persons liable or potentially liable for the costs of those activities, penalties imposed under environmental laws or regulations and other payments made to comply with those laws or regulations, statutory or common law claims by third parties, and defending claims based on environmental matters.

(B) If a principal asset is encumbered with an obligation that requires income from that asset to be paid directly to the creditor, the trustee shall transfer from principal to income an amount equal to the income paid to the creditor in reduction of the principal balance of the obligation.

(2006 H 416, eff. 1–1–07)

Historical and Statutory Notes

Ed. Note: RC 5812.43 is former RC 1340.82, amended and recodified by 2006 H 416, eff. 1–1–07; 2002 H 522, eff. 1–1–03.

Amendment Note: 2006 H 416 substituted "1340.81" with "5812.42".

Uniform Law: This section is analogous to §502 of the Uniform Principal and Income Act (1997 Act). See 7B Uniform Laws Annotated, Master Edition.

Library References

Trusts ⚖276.
Wills ⚖684.2(3).
Westlaw Topic Nos. 390, 409.
C.J.S. Trusts §§ 539 to 541.
C.J.S. Wills §§ 1463 to 1464, 1480, 1486.

Baldwin's Ohio Legislative Service Annotated, 2006 H 416 LSC Analysis, p 3/L-1709

5812.44 Transfers from income to principal for depreciation

(A) As used in this section, "depreciation" means a reduction in value due to wear, tear, decay, corrosion, or gradual obsolescence of a fixed asset having a useful life of more than one year.

(B) A trustee may transfer to principal a reasonable amount of the net cash receipts from a principal asset that is subject to depreciation, but shall not transfer any amount for depreciation under any of the following circumstances:

(1) Any amount for depreciation of that portion of real property used or available for use by a beneficiary as a residence or of tangible personal property held or made available for the personal use or enjoyment of a beneficiary;

(2) Any amount for depreciation during the administration of a decedent's estate;

(3) Any amount for depreciation under this section if the trustee is accounting under section 5812.20 of the Revised Code for the business or activity in which the asset is used.

(C) An amount transferred to principal need not be held as a separate fund.

(2006 H 416, eff. 1–1–07)

Historical and Statutory Notes

Ed. Note: RC 5812.44 is former RC 1340.83, amended and recodified by 2006 H 416, eff. 1–1–07; 2002 H 522, eff. 1–1–03.

Amendment Note: 2006 H 416 substituted "1340.59" with "5812.20".

Uniform Law: This section is analogous to §503 of the Uniform Principal and Income Act (1997 Act). See 7B Uniform Laws Annotated, Master Edition.

Library References

Trusts ⚖218(1).
Wills ⚖684.10(6).
Westlaw Topic Nos. 390, 409.
C.J.S. Trusts §§ 482, 506 to 511.
C.J.S. Wills §§ 1463, 1483 to 1484, 1488 to 1489.

Baldwin's Ohio Legislative Service Annotated, 2006 H 416 LSC Analysis, p 3/L-1709

5812.45 Transfers from income to reimburse principal

(A) If a trustee makes or expects to make a principal disbursement described in this section, the trustee may transfer an appropriate amount from income to principal in one or more accounting periods to reimburse principal or to provide a reserve for future principal disbursements.

(B) Principal disbursements to which division (A) of this section applies include all of the following, but only to the extent that the trustee has not been and does not expect to be reimbursed by a third party:

(1) An amount chargeable to income but paid from principal because it is unusually large, including extraordinary repairs;

(2) A capital improvement to a principal asset, whether in the form of changes to an existing asset or the construction of a new asset, including special assessments;

(3) Disbursements made to prepare property for rental, including tenant allowances, leasehold improvements, and broker's commissions;

(4) Periodic payments on an obligation secured by a principal asset to the extent that the amount transferred from income to principal for depreciation is less than the periodic payments;

(5) Disbursements described in division (A)(7) of section 5812.43 of the Revised Code.

(C) If the asset whose ownership gives rise to the disbursements becomes subject to a successive income interest after an income interest ends, a trustee may continue to transfer amounts from income to principal as provided in division (A) of this section.

(2006 H 416, eff. 1–1–07)

Historical and Statutory Notes

Ed. Note: RC 5812.45 is former RC 1340.84, amended and recodified by 2006 H 416, eff. 1–1–07; 2002 H 522, eff. 1–1–03.

Amendment Note: 2006 H 416 substituted "1340.82" with "5812.43".

Uniform Law: This section is analogous to §504 of the Uniform Principal and Income Act (1997 Act). See 7B Uniform Laws Annotated, Master Edition.

Library References

Trusts ⚖280.
Wills ⚖684.10(6).
Westlaw Topic Nos. 390, 409.
C.J.S. Trusts §§ 544 to 550.
C.J.S. Wills §§ 1463, 1483 to 1484, 1488 to 1489.

Baldwin's Ohio Legislative Service Annotated, 2006 H 416 LSC Analysis, p 3/L-1709

5812.46 Income taxes

(A) A tax required to be paid by a trustee based on receipts allocated to income shall be paid from income.

(B) A tax required to be paid by a trustee based on receipts allocated to principal shall be paid from principal, even if the tax is called an income tax by the taxing authority.

(C) A tax required to be paid by a trustee on the trust's share of an entity's taxable income shall be paid proportionately as follows:

(1) From income, to the extent that receipts from the entity are allocated to income;

(2) From principal, as follows:

(a) To the extent that receipts from the entity are allocated to principal; and

(b) To the extent that the trust's share of the entity's taxable income exceeds the total receipts described in divisions (C)(1) and (2)(a) of this section.

(D) For purposes of this section, receipts allocated to principal or income shall be reduced by the amount distributed to a beneficiary from principal or income for which the trust receives a deduction in calculating the tax.

(2006 H 416, eff. 1–1–07)

Historical and Statutory Notes

Ed. Note: RC 5812.46 is former RC 1340.85, recodified by 2006 H 416, eff. 1–1–07; 2002 H 522, eff. 1–1–03.

Uniform Law: This section is analogous to §505 of the Uniform Principal and Income Act (1997 Act). See 7B Uniform Laws Annotated, Master Edition.

Library References

Trusts ⚖226.
Wills ⚖684.1.
Westlaw Topic Nos. 390, 409.
C.J.S. Trusts §§ 383, 389 to 390, 393 to 394.
C.J.S. Wills §§ 1463 to 1464.

Baldwin's Ohio Legislative Service Annotated, 2006 H 416 LSC Analysis, p 3/L-1709

5812.47 Adjustments between principal and income because of taxes

(A) A fiduciary may make adjustments between principal and income to offset the shifting of economic interests or tax benefits between income beneficiaries and remainder beneficiaries that arise from any of the following:

(1) Elections and decisions, other than those described in division (B) of this section, that the fiduciary makes from time to time regarding tax matters;

(2) An income tax or any other tax that is imposed upon the fiduciary or a beneficiary as a result of a transaction involving or a distribution from the estate or trust;

(3) The ownership by an estate or trust of an interest in an entity whose taxable income, whether or not distributed, is includable in the taxable income of the estate, trust, or beneficiary.

(B) If the amount of an estate tax marital deduction or charitable contribution deduction is reduced because a fiduciary deducts an amount paid from principal for income tax purposes instead of deducting it for estate tax purposes, and as a result estate taxes paid from principal are increased and income taxes paid by an estate, trust, or beneficiary are decreased, each estate, trust, or beneficiary that benefits from the decrease in income tax shall reimburse the principal from which the increase in estate tax is paid. The total reimbursement shall equal the increase in the estate tax to the extent that the principal used to pay the increase would have qualified for a marital deduction or charitable contribution deduction but for the payment. The proportionate share of the reimbursement for each estate, trust, or beneficiary whose income taxes are reduced shall be the same as its proportionate share of the total decrease in income tax. An estate or trust shall reimburse principal from income.

(2006 H 416, eff. 1–1–07)

Historical and Statutory Notes

Ed. Note: RC 5812.47 is former RC 1340.86, recodified by 2006 H 416, eff. 1–1–07; 2002 H 522, eff. 1–1–03.

Uniform Law: This section is analogous to §506 of the Uniform Principal and Income Act (1997 Act). See 7B Uniform Laws Annotated, Master Edition.

Library References

Trusts ⚖274(2).
Westlaw Topic No. 390.
C.J.S. Trusts §§ 391 to 394, 510.
  Baldwin's Ohio Legislative Service Annotated, 2006 H 416 LSC Analysis, p 3/L-1709

5812.51 Uniformity of application and construction

(A) Sections 5812.01 to 5812.52 of the Revised Code may be cited as the "uniform principal and income act (1997)."

(B) In applying and construing the "uniform principal and income act (1997)", consideration shall be given to the need to promote uniformity of the law with respect to its subject matter among states that enact the "uniform principal and income act (1997)".

(2006 H 416, eff. 1–1–07)

Historical and Statutory Notes

Ed. Note: RC 5812.51 is former RC 1340.90, amended and recodified by 2006 H 416, eff. 1–1–07; 2002 H 522, eff. 1–1–03.

Amendment Note: 2006 H 416 substituted "1340.40" with "5812.01" and "1340.91" with "5812.52".

Uniform Law: This section is analogous to §601 of the Uniform Principal and Income Act (1997 Act). See 7B Uniform Laws Annotated, Master Edition.

Library References

Baldwin's Ohio Legislative Service Annotated, 2006 H 416 LSC Analysis, p 3/L-1709

5812.52 Application to existing trust or decedent's estate

Sections 5812.01 to 5812.51 of the Revised Code apply to every trust or decedent's estate existing on January 1, 2003, except as otherwise expressly provided in the will or terms of the trust or in sections 5812.01 to 5812.51 of the Revised Code.

(2006 H 416, eff. 1–1–07)

Historical and Statutory Notes

Ed. Note: RC 5812.52 is former RC 1340.91, amended and recodified by 2006 H 416, eff. 1–1–07; 2002 H 522, eff. 1–1–03.

Amendment Note: 2006 H 416 substituted "1340.40" with "5812.01", "1340.90" with "5812.51", and substituted "the effective date of this section" with "January 1, 2003,".

Uniform Law: This section is analogous to §605 of the Uniform Principal and Income Act (1997 Act). See 7B Uniform Laws Annotated, Master Edition.

Cross References

Allocation by fiduciary, 2109.68

Library References

Trusts ⚖113.
Wills ⚖680.
Westlaw Topic Nos. 390, 409.
C.J.S. Trusts §§ 220 to 223.
C.J.S. Wills §§ 1425 to 1429, 1448 to 1452.
  Baldwin's Ohio Legislative Service Annotated, 2006 H 416 LSC Analysis, p 3/L-1709

CHAPTER 5813

INSTITUTIONAL TRUST FUNDS ACT

Section	
5813.01	Definitions
5813.02	Income defined
5813.03	Application of statutory definition of income when settlor expressly indicates intent
5813.04	Standard of care
5813.05	Restrictions on definition of income or on distributions
5813.06	Effect on uniform management of institutional funds act
5813.07	Citation of act

5813.01 Definitions

As used in sections 5813.01 to 5813.07 of the Revised Code:

(A) "Institution" means an incorporated or unincorporated organization that is organized and operated exclusively for educational, religious, charitable, or other eleemosynary purposes or a governmental organization to the extent that it holds funds exclusively for any of those purposes.

(B) "Governing board" means the body responsible for the management of an institution.

(C) "Institutional trust fund" means a trust fund, or a part of a trust fund, that is held by a trustee for the exclusive use, benefit, or purposes of one or more institutions and that is not wholly distributable to the institution or institutions on a current basis under the terms of the applicable trust instrument. "Institutional trust fund" does not include a fund in which a beneficiary that is not an institution has an interest other than a right that may arise upon a violation of a covenant under the terms of the applicable trust instrument or upon a violation of or the failure of the purposes of the fund.

(D) "Applicable fund value" means for any particular fiscal year the sum of the month-end values of the net assets of an institutional trust fund for the prior fiscal year for those months in which the institutional trust fund has been in existence during such prior fiscal year divided by the number of those months. The month-end values shall be determined by the trustee in accordance with the trustee's records, and any such determination made by a trustee in good faith is conclusive.

(E) "Trust instrument" means a testamentary or inter vivos trust under which the trustee of the trust holds an institutional trust fund.

(F) "Trustee" means an individual, corporation, institution, or organization, including, but not limited to, a bank, trust company, or other financial institution, serving as a trustee or as sole trustee under a trust instrument. "Trustee" includes an original trustee and any successor or added trustee.

(2006 H 416, eff. 1–1–07)

Historical and Statutory Notes

Ed. Note: RC 5813.01 is former RC 1340.31, amended and recodified by 2006 H 416, eff. 1–1–07; 1999 H 161, eff. 9–15–99.

Amendment Note: 2006 H 416 substituted "1340.31" with "5813.01" and "1340.37" with "5813.07".

Library References

Baldwin's Ohio Legislative Service Annotated, 2006 H 416 LSC Analysis, p 3/L-1709

Law Review and Journal Commentaries

Formal Recognition of Modern Portfolio Theory—Investing for Total Return in Personal Trusts, Michael S. Bailes. 10 Prob L J Ohio 49 (March/April 2000).

5813.02 Income defined

(A) Subject to division (D) of this section and section 5813.03 of the Revised Code, during any fiscal year in which income may be or is required to be distributed to an institution from an institutional trust fund, income means the greater of the following:

(1) The income from the assets of the institutional trust fund for the fiscal year as determined in accordance with the applicable trust instrument and applicable law without regard to sections 5813.01 to 5813.07 of the Revised Code;

(2) The amount requested by the institution's governing board for the fiscal year pursuant to division (B) of this section.

(B) An institution's governing board may request that an amount be distributed to the institution for the fiscal year, and that amount shall not exceed the sum of both of the following:

(1) Five per cent of the applicable fund value for the institutional trust fund for the fiscal year;

(2) If, in any prior fiscal year that is after September 15, 1999, the governing board requested less than five per cent of the applicable fund value for that prior fiscal year and if the amount the institution actually received from the institutional trust fund pursuant to division (A) of this section was less than five per cent for that prior fiscal year, the aggregate difference between five per cent of the applicable fund value with respect to each such prior fiscal year and the amount the institution actually received pursuant to division (A) of this section for each prior fiscal year.

(C) If, under a trust instrument, more than one institution is a beneficiary of an institutional trust fund, the trustee shall take such actions that the trustee determines appropriate or necessary to allow for the distributions of income as contemplated by division (A) of this section, which actions may include dividing the institutional trust fund into separate shares according to the interest that each institution has in the total institutional trust fund held under the trust instrument.

(D) This section does not limit the authority or obligation of a trustee to distribute, or the authority of a governing board to request, funds as permitted or required under the terms of the applicable trust instrument.

(2006 H 416, eff. 1–1–07)

Historical and Statutory Notes

Ed. Note: RC 5813.02 is former RC 1340.32, amended and recodified by 2006 H 416, eff. 1–1–07; 1999 H 161, eff. 9–15–99.

Amendment Note: 2006 H 416 substituted "1340.33" with "5813.03", "1340.31" with "5813.01", and "1340.37" with "5813.07" in division (A); substituted "the effective date of this section" with "September 15, 1999" and "such" with "each" preceding "prior fiscal year." in division (B)(2); and made other nonsubstantive changes.

Library References

Trusts ⟪126.
Westlaw Topic No. 390.
C.J.S. Trusts §§ 216 to 217.

Baldwin's Ohio Legislative Service Annotated, 2006 H 416 LSC Analysis, p 3/L-1709

5813.03 Application of statutory definition of income when settlor expressly indicates intent

(A) Division (A) of section 5813.02 of the Revised Code does not apply if the applicable trust instrument expressly indicates the settlor's intention that income is to be otherwise than as defined in division (A) of section 5813.02 of the Revised Code.

(B) A restriction upon the definition of income in division (A) of section 5813.02 of the Revised Code may not be inferred from a designation of an institutional trust fund as an endowment; a direction or authorization in the applicable trust instrument to use only "income," "interest," "dividends," or "rents, issues, or profits," or "to preserve the principal intact," or a direction that contains other words of a similar import; a direction in a trust instrument that income and principal are to be determined by reference to certain statutory provisions; or, subject to division (A) of this section, the inclusion of specified provisions in a trust instrument setting forth the way in which income and principal are to be determined.

(C) The rule of construction set forth in division (B) of this section applies to trust instruments executed or in effect before, on, or after September 15, 1999.

(2006 H 416, eff. 1–1–07)

Historical and Statutory Notes

Ed. Note: RC 5813.03 is former RC 1340.33, amended and recodified by 2006 H 416, eff. 1–1–07; 1999 H 161, eff. 9–15–99.

Amendment Note: 2006 H 416 substituted "1340.32" with "5813.02" and "the effective date of this section" with "September 15, 1999".

Library References

Trusts ⚖126.
Westlaw Topic No. 390.
C.J.S. Trusts §§ 216 to 217.
Baldwin's Ohio Legislative Service Annotated, 2006 H 416 LSC Analysis, p 3/L-1709

5813.04 Standard of care

(A) In administering the powers to request amounts from a trustee of an institutional trust fund in accordance with divisions (A) and (B) of section 5813.02 of the Revised Code, members of a governing board of an institution shall exercise ordinary business care and prudence under the facts and circumstances prevailing at the time of the action or decision and shall make requests for amounts under divisions (A) and (B) of section 5813.02 of the Revised Code only as is prudent under this standard. In so doing, the governing board shall consider the long- and short-term needs of the institution in carrying out its educational, religious, charitable, or other eleemosynary purposes; the institution's present and anticipated financial requirements; the expected total return on the investments held by the institution and held by the trustee under the applicable trust instrument; price level trends; and general economic conditions.

(B) In determining the expected total return on the investments held by a trustee of an institutional trust fund under the applicable trust instrument, the members of the governing board of an institution may follow, and are not required to examine independently, the determination of the trustee regarding the expected total return on the investments held by the trustee.

(C) A trustee of an institutional trust fund has no duty to inquire or ascertain whether the governing board of an institution has satisfied the standards set forth in divisions (A) and (B) of this section, and the trustee does not have any liability for the failure of the governing board to satisfy those standards.

(2006 H 416, eff. 1–1–07)

Historical and Statutory Notes

Ed. Note: RC 5813.04 is former RC 1340.34, amended and recodified by 2006 H 416, eff. 1–1–07; 1999 H 161, eff. 9–15–99.

Amendment Note: 2006 H 416 substituted "1340.32" with "5813.02".

Library References

Trusts ⚖179.
Westlaw Topic No. 390.
C.J.S. Trusts §§ 321 to 324, 326.
Baldwin's Ohio Legislative Service Annotated, 2006 H 416 LSC Analysis, p 3/L-1709

5813.05 Restrictions on definition of income or on distributions

Nothing in sections 5812.01 to 5812.52, or any other section of the Revised Code limits or restricts the definition of income in division (A) of section 5813.02 of the Revised Code or limits or restricts a governing board of an institution from requesting, or a trustee from making, distributions from an institutional trust fund in accordance with sections 5813.01 to 5813.07 of the Revised Code.

(2006 H 416, eff. 1–1–07)

Historical and Statutory Notes

Ed. Note: RC 5813.05 is former RC 1340.35, amended and recodified by 2006 H 416, eff. 1–1–07; 2002 H 522, eff. 1–1–03; 1999 H 161, eff. 9–15–99.

Amendment Note: 2006 H 416 substituted "1340.40" with "5812.01", "1340.91" with "5812.52", "1340.32" with "5813.02", "1340.31" with "5813.01", and "1340.37" with "5813.07".

Amendment Note: 2002 H 522 deleted "section 2109.67," following "Nothing in"; and substituted "1340.40" for "1340.01" and "1340.91" for "1340.13".

Library References

Trusts ⚖126.
Westlaw Topic No. 390.
C.J.S. Trusts §§ 216 to 217.
Baldwin's Ohio Legislative Service Annotated, 2006 H 416 LSC Analysis, p 3/L-1709

5813.06 Effect on uniform management of institutional funds act

(A) Nothing in sections 5813.01 to 5813.05 of the Revised Code affects the construction or interpretation of sections 1715.51 to 1715.59 of the Revised Code relating to the uniform management of institutional funds act. Specifically, neither the percentage set forth in division (B) of section 1340.32 of the Revised Code nor the amount actually requested by a governing board pursuant to section 5813.02 of the Revised Code shall be construed or interpreted to limit or expand what is a prudent amount that can be expended by a governing board of an institution under sections 1715.51 to 1715.59 of the Revised Code.

(B) If an institutional trust fund is also an institutional fund as defined in division (B) of section 1715.51 of the Revised Code with the result that sections 1715.51 to 1715.59 of the Revised Code also are applicable to the institutional trust fund, then sections 1715.51 to 1715.59 of the Revised Code apply to the institutional trust fund, and sections 5813.01 to 5813.07 of the Revised Code do not apply to the institutional trust fund.

(2006 H 416, eff. 1–1–07)

Historical and Statutory Notes

Ed. Note: RC 5813.06 is former RC 1340.36, amended and recodified by 2006 H 416, eff. 1–1–07; 1999 H 161, eff. 9–15–99.

Amendment Note: 2006 H 416 substituted "1340.31" with "5813.01", "1340.35" with "5813.05", "1340.32" with "5813.02", and "1340.37" with "5813.07".

Library References

Trusts ⚖4.
Westlaw Topic No. 390.
C.J.S. Trusts § 27.
Baldwin's Ohio Legislative Service Annotated, 2006 H 416 LSC Analysis, p 3/L-1709

5813.07 Citation of act

Sections 5813.01 to 5813.07 of the Revised Code may be cited as the "institutional trust funds act."

(2006 H 416, eff. 1–1–07)

Historical and Statutory Notes

Ed. Note: RC 5813.07 is former RC 1340.37, amended and recodified by 2006 H 416, eff. 1–1–07; 1999 H 161, eff. 9–15–99.

Amendment Note: 2006 H 416 substituted "1340.31" with "5813.01" and "1340.37" with "5813.07".

Library References

Baldwin's Ohio Legislative Service Annotated, 2006 H 416 LSC Analysis, p 3/L-1709

CHAPTER 5814

OHIO TRANSFERS TO MINORS ACT

Section
5814.01 Definitions
5814.02 Form of gift or transfer
5814.03 Effect of making a gift or transfer
5814.04 Powers and duties of custodians
5814.05 Reimbursement, compensation, and liability
5814.06 Third person's liability limited
5814.07 Registration or removal of custodian; successor custodian
5814.08 Accounting by custodian
5814.09 Effect of Ohio transfers to minors act

5814.01 Definitions

As used in sections 5814.01 to 5814.09 of the Revised Code, unless the context otherwise requires:

(A) "Benefit plan" means any plan of an employer for the benefit of any employee, any plan for the benefit of any partner, or any plan for the benefit of a proprietor, and includes, but is not limited to, any pension, retirement, death benefit, deferred compensation, employment agency, stock bonus, option, or profit-sharing contract, plan, system, account, or trust.

(B) "Broker" means a person that is lawfully engaged in the business of effecting transactions in securities for the account of others. A "broker" includes a financial institution that effects such transactions and a person who is lawfully engaged in buying and selling securities for the person's own account, through a broker or otherwise, as a part of a regular business.

(C) "Court" means the probate court.

(D) "The custodial property" includes:

(1) All securities, money, life or endowment insurance policies, annuity contracts, benefit plans, real estate, tangible and intangible personal property, proceeds of a life or endowment insurance policy, an annuity contract, or a benefit plan, and other types of property under the supervision of the same custodian for the same minor as a consequence of a transfer or transfers made to the minor, a gift or gifts made to the minor, or a purchase made by the custodian for the minor, in a manner prescribed in sections 5814.01 to 5814.09 of the Revised Code;

(2) The income from the custodial property;

(3) The proceeds, immediate and remote, from the sale, exchange, conversion, investment, reinvestment, or other disposition of the securities, money, life or endowment insurance policies, annuity contracts, benefit plans, real estate, tangible and intangible personal property, proceeds of a life or endowment insurance policy, an annuity contract, or a benefit plan, other types of property, and income.

(E) "Custodian" or "successor custodian" means a person so designated in a manner prescribed in sections 5814.01 to 5814.09 of the Revised Code.

(F) "Financial institution" means any bank, as defined in section 1101.01, any building and loan association, as defined in section 1151.01, any credit union as defined in section 1733.01 of the Revised Code, and any federal credit union, as defined in the "Federal Credit Union Act," 73 Stat. 628 (1959), 12 U.S.C.A. 1752, as amended.

(G) "Guardian of the minor" includes the general guardian, guardian, tutor, or curator of the property, estate, or person of a minor.

(H) "Issuer" means a person who places or authorizes the placing of the person's name on a security, other than as a transfer agent, to evidence that it represents a share, participation, or other interest in the person's property or in an enterprise, or to evidence the person's duty or undertaking to perform an obligation that is evidenced by the security, or who becomes responsible for or in place of any such person.

(I) "Legal representative" of a person means the executor, administrator, general guardian, guardian, committee, conservator, tutor, or curator of the person's property or estate.

(J) "Member of the minor's family" means a parent, stepparent, spouse, grandparent, brother, sister, uncle, or aunt of the minor, whether of the whole or half blood, or by adoption.

(K) "Minor" means a person who has not attained the age of twenty-one years.

(L) "Security" includes any note, stock, treasury stock, common trust fund, bond, debenture, evidence of indebtedness, certificate of interest or participation in an oil, gas, or mining title or lease or in payments out of production under an oil, gas, or mining title or lease, collateral trust certificate, transferable share, voting trust certificate, or, in general, any interest or instrument commonly known as a security, or any certificate of interest or participation in, any temporary or interim certificate, receipt or certificate of deposit for, or any warrant or right to subscribe to or purchase, any of the foregoing. A "security" does not include a security of which the donor or transferor is the issuer. A security is in "registered form" when it specifies a person who is entitled to it or to the rights that it evidences and its transfer may be registered upon books maintained for that purpose by or on behalf of the issuer.

(M) "Transfer" means a disposition, other than a gift, by a person who is eighteen years of age or older that creates custodial property under sections 5814.01 to 5814.09 of the Revised Code.

(N) "Transfer agent" means a person who acts as authenticating trustee, transfer agent, registrar, or other agent for an issuer in the registration of transfers of its securities, in the issue of new securities, or in the cancellation of surrendered securities.

(O) "Transferor" means a person who is eighteen years of age or older, who makes a transfer.

(P) "Trust company" means a financial institution that is authorized to exercise trust powers.

(Q) "Administrator" includes an "administrator with the will annexed."

(2006 H 416, eff. 1–1–07)

Historical and Statutory Notes

Ed. Note: RC 5814.01 is former RC 1339.31, amended and recodified by 2006 H 416, eff. 1–1–07; 1986 H 297, eff. 5–7–86; 1980 H 1007; 1976 S 166; 1973 S 1; 129 v 1550.

Amendment Note: 2006 H 416 substituted "1339.31" with "5814.01", substituted "1339.39" with "5814.09", and made changes to reflect gender neutral language.

Cross References

Annuities; nonforfeiture values, 3915.071
Executors and administrators, 2113.01
Guardians, 2111.01
How money may be handled for minor with no guardian of the estate, 2111.131
Life insurance, 3911.01, 3915.01, 3917.01
Securities, 1707.01
Specific powers of trustee, 5808.16
Termination of trust, 1339.66
Termination of trust, distribution, 2109.62
Trust companies, 1109.01

Library References

Baldwin's Ohio Legislative Service Annotated, 2006 H 416 LSC Analysis, p 3/L-1709

Law Review and Journal Commentaries

The Ohio Transfers to Minors Act—An Overlooked Tool For Probate Practitioners, Kirk T. Albrecht. 2 Ohio Law 10 (September/October 1988).

Property Transfers to Minors and Young Adults—Proposed Ohio Law Changes to Assist with Property Management, Karen M. Moore. 5 Prob L J Ohio 54 (March/April 1995).

5814.02 Form of gift or transfer

(A) A person who is eighteen years of age or older may, during the person's lifetime, make a gift or transfer of a security, money, a life or endowment insurance policy, an annuity contract, a benefit plan, real estate, tangible or intangible personal property, or any other property to, may designate as beneficiary of a life or endowment insurance policy, an annuity contract, or a benefit plan, or make a transfer by the irrevocable exercise of a power of appointment in favor of, a person who is a minor on the date of the gift or transfer:

(1) If the subject of the gift or transfer is a security in registered form, by registering it in the name of the donor or transferor, another person who is eighteen years of age or older, or a trust company, followed, in substance, by the words: "as custodian for .... (name of minor) under the Ohio Transfers to Minors Act";

(2) If the subject of the gift or transfer is a security not in registered form, by delivering it to the donor or transferor, another person who is eighteen years of age or older, or a trust company, accompanied by a statement of a gift or transfer in the following form, in substance, signed by the donor or transferor and the person or trust company designated as custodian:

"GIFT OR TRANSFER UNDER THE OHIO TRANSFERS TO MINORS ACT

I, ... (name of donor or transferor), hereby deliver to (name of custodian) as custodian for .... (name of minor) under the Ohio Transfers to Minors Act, the following security (ies): (insert an appropriate description of the security or securities delivered, sufficient to identify it or them).

....
(signature of donor or transferor)

.... (name of custodian) hereby acknowledges receipt of the above described security (ies) as custodian for the above minor under the Ohio Transfers to Minors Act.

Dated: ....
(signature of custodian)"

(3) If the subject of the gift or transfer is money, by paying or delivering it to a broker, or a financial institution for credit to an account in the name of the donor or transferor, another person who is eighteen years of age or older, or a trust company, followed, in substance, by the words: "as custodian for .... (name of minor) under the Ohio Transfers to Minors Act."

(4) If the subject of the gift or transfer is a life or endowment insurance policy, an annuity contract, or a benefit plan, by assigning the policy, contract, or plan to the donor or transferor, another person who is eighteen years of age or older, or a trust company, followed, in substance by the words: "as custodian for .... (name of minor) under the Ohio Transfers to Minors Act."

(5) If the subject of the gift or transfer is an interest in real estate, by executing and delivering in the appropriate manner a deed, assignment, or similar instrument in the name of the donor or transferor, another person who is eighteen years of age or older, or a trust company, followed, in substance, by the words: "as custodian for .... (name of minor) under the Ohio Transfers to Minors Act."

(6) If the subject of the gift or transfer is tangible personal property, by delivering it to the donor or transferor, another person who is eighteen years of age or older, or a trust company, accompanied by a statement of a gift or transfer in the following form, in substance, signed by the donor or transferor and the person or trust company designated as custodian:

"GIFT OR TRANSFER UNDER THE OHIO TRANSFERS TO MINORS ACT

I, ... (name of donor or transferor), hereby deliver to .... (name of custodian) as custodian for .... (name of minor) under the Ohio Transfers to Minors Act, the following property: (insert an appropriate description of the property delivered, sufficient to identify it).

....
(signature of donor or transferor)

.... (name of custodian) hereby acknowledges receipt of the above described property as custodian for the above minor under the Ohio Transfers to Minors Act.

Dated: ....
(signature of custodian)"

(7) If the subject of the gift or transfer is tangible personal property, title to which is evidenced by a certificate of title issued by a department or agency of a state or of the United States, by issuing title to the donor or transferor, another person who is eighteen years of age or older, or a trust company, accompanied by a statement of a gift or transfer in the following form, in substance: "as custodian for .... (name of minor) under the Ohio Transfers to Minors Act"; or by delivering the title to another person who is eighteen years of age or older or a trust company, endorsed to that person followed in substance by the following words: "as custodian for ....[1] under the Ohio Transfers to Minors Act."

(8) If the subject of the gift or transfer is the designation of a minor as beneficiary of a life or endowment insurance policy, an annuity contract, or a benefit plan, by designating as beneficiary of the policy, contract, or plan the donor or transferor, another person who is eighteen years of age or older, or a trust company, followed, in substance, by the words: "as custodian for .... (name of minor) under the Ohio Transfers to Minors Act."

(9) If the subject of the gift or transfer is an irrevocable exercise of a power of appointment in favor of a minor or is an interest in any property that is not described in divisions (A)(1) to (8) of this section, by causing the ownership of the property to be transferred by any written document in the name of the donor or transferor, another person who is eighteen years of age or older, or a trust company, followed, in substance, by the words: "as custodian for .... (name of minor) under the Ohio Transfers to Minors Act."

(B) Trustees, inter vivos or testamentary, executors, and administrators having authority to distribute or pay any trust or estate property to or for the benefit of a minor, or having authority to distribute or pay any trust or estate property to any other person for the benefit of a minor may, if authorized by a will or trust instrument, distribute or pay trust or estate property of any type mentioned in division (A) of this section in the manner and form provided in that division, and may name the custodian or successor custodian of the property if the will or trust instrument does not name an eligible custodian, or if the will or trust does not name an eligible successor custodian and the naming of a successor custodian is necessary. A person who is eighteen years of age or older, in the person's will or trust instrument, may provide that the fiduciary shall make any payment or distribution as provided in this division and may name the custodian and a successor custodian of the trust or estate property. As to any distribution or payment so made, the testator of a will, under the provisions of which a testamentary trust or estate is being administered, or the settlor of an inter vivos trust shall be deemed the donor or transferor.

(C) Any gift, transfer, payment, or distribution that is made in a manner prescribed in division (A), (B), or (E) of this section may be made to only one minor and only one person may be the custodian. All gifts, transfers, payments, and distributions made by a person in a manner prescribed in sections 5814.01 to 5814.09 of the Revised Code to the same custodian for the benefit of the same minor result in a single custodianship.

(D) A donor or transferor who makes a gift or transfer to a minor in a manner prescribed in division (A) of this section and a trustee, executor, or administrator acting under division (B) or (E) of this section shall promptly do all things within the donor's, transferor's, trustee's, executor's, or administrator's power to put the subject of the gift or transfer in the possession and control of the custodian, but neither the donor's, transferor's, trustee's, executor's, or administrator's failure to comply with this division, nor the designation by the donor, transferor, trustee, executor, or administrator of an ineligible custodian, nor the renunciation by the person or trust company designated as custodian, affects the consummation of the gift or transfer.

(E) If there is no will, or if a will, trust, or other governing instrument does not contain an authorization to make a transfer as described in this division, a trustee, executor, or administrator may make a transfer in a manner prescribed in division (A) of this section to self, another person who is eighteen years of age or older, or a trust company, as custodian, if all of the following apply:

(1) Irrespective of the value of the property, the trustee, executor, or administrator considers the transfer to be in the best interest of the minor;

(2) Irrespective of the value of the property, the transfer is not prohibited by or inconsistent with the applicable will, trust agreement, or other governing instrument;

(3) If the value of the property exceeds ten thousand dollars, the transfer is authorized by the appropriate court.

(2006 H 416, eff. 1–1–07)

[1] Prior and current versions differ; although no amendment to this text was indicated, the signature designation "(name of minor)" was not included by the 2006 H 416 amendment and recodification.

Historical and Statutory Notes

Ed. Note: RC 5814.02 is former RC 1339.32, amended and recodified by 2006 H 416, eff. 1–1–07; 1986 H 428, eff. 12–23–86; 1986 H 297; 1980 H 1007; 1976 S 166; 129 v 1550.

Amendment Note: 2006 H 416 substituted "1339.31" with "5814.01" and "1339.39" with "5814.09" in division (C); inserted "by the donor, transferor, trustee, executor, or administrator" and substituted "his" with "the donor's, transferor's, trustee's, executor's, or administrator's" in division (D); and made other changes to reflect gender neutral language.

Library References

Gifts ⚖︎29, 30(2), 31(3).
Westlaw Topic No. 191.
Baldwin's Ohio Legislative Service Annotated, 2006 H 416 LSC Analysis, p 3/L-1709

Law Review and Journal Commentaries

Features in Ohio Transfers to Minors Act [Amended R.C. §§ 1339.31 thru [sic] 1339.39 and 1733.24, effective May 7, 1986]. 55 Title Topics 7 (February 1988).

The Ohio Transfers to Minors Act—An Overlooked Tool For Probate Practitioners, Kirk T. Albrecht. 2 Ohio Law 10 (September/October 1988).

Notes of Decisions

Ed. Note: *This section contains annotations from former RC 1339.32.*

Bank accounts 2
Deeds 1

---

1. Deeds

A deed from a parent to a child reciting money consideration as well as love, affection and faithful service is not a deed of gift. Brown v. Whaley (Ohio 1898) 58 Ohio St. 654, 39 W.L.B. 129, 40 W.L.B. 130, 49 N.E. 479, 65 Am.St.Rep. 793.

2. Bank accounts

Judgment debtor's motion to set aside garnishment to extent that garnishment had been applied to custodial accounts that were controlled by debtor, and had been established for benefit of debtor's sons under Ohio Uniform Transfers to Minors Act (OTMA), was not rendered moot when executrix of judgment creditor's estate returned funds taken from custodial accounts to debtor's son, who had reached age of majority, and to mother of debtor's minor son; payment of funds to minor son's mother did not restore status quo, because debtor was divested of control over money. Tipton v. Tipton (Ohio App. 2 Dist., Greene, 07-08-2005) No. CIV.A.2004 CA 92, 2005-Ohio-3660, 2005 WL 1685048, Unreported. Garnishment ⚖︎ 194

Under the Uniform Gifts to Minors Act, a gift is not made without the requisite donative intent; the opening of a bank account demonstrates prima facie evidence of that intent, but withdrawal of money from that account by the purported donor indicates there was not the requisite intent to make an irrevocable gift of the money in the account. State v. Keith (Lorain 1991) 81 Ohio App.3d 192, 610 N.E.2d 1017.

Where a bank account was, as argued by the plaintiff, intended to be a gift to the plaintiff from her mother under the Uniform Gifts to Minors Act, the account can still be forfeited under the RICO statute even where there is no connection between the money in the account and the mother's illegal activities where the mother agreed to forfeit the account as a part of her plea bargain and the plaintiff daughter cannot prove a title or right to the account superior to that of her mother. State v. Keith (Lorain 1991) 81 Ohio App.3d 192, 610 N.E.2d 1017.

5814.03 Effect of making a gift or transfer

(A) A gift or transfer made in a manner prescribed in sections 5814.01 to 5814.09 of the Revised Code, is irrevocable and conveys to the minor indefeasibly vested legal title to the security, money, life or endowment insurance policy, annuity contract, benefit plan, real estate, tangible or intangible personal property, or other property given or, subject to the right of the owner of the policy, contract, or benefit plan to change the beneficiary if the custodian is not the owner, to the proceeds of a life or endowment insurance policy, an annuity contract, or a benefit plan given, but no guardian of the minor has any right, power, duty, or authority with respect to the custodial property except as provided in sections 5814.01 to 5814.09 of the Revised Code.

(B) By making a gift or transfer in a manner prescribed in sections 5814.01 to 5814.09 of the Revised Code, the donor or transferor incorporates in the gift or transfer all the provisions of these sections and grants to the custodian, and to any issuer, transfer agent, financial institution, broker, or third person dealing with a person or trust company designated as custodian, the respective powers, rights, and immunities provided in these sections.

(2006 H 416, eff. 1–1–07)

Historical and Statutory Notes

Ed. Note: RC 5814.03 is former RC 1339.33, amended and recodified by 2006 H 416, eff. 1–1–07; 1986 H 297, eff. 5–7–86; 1980 H 1007; 129 v 1550.

Amendment Note: 2006 H 416 substituted "1339.31" with "5814.01", "1339.39" with "5814.09", and made a change to reflect gender neutral language.

Library References

Gifts ⬩42.1.
Westlaw Topic No. 191.
Baldwin's Ohio Legislative Service Annotated, 2006 H 416 LSC Analysis, p 3/L-1709

5814.04 Powers and duties of custodians

(A) The custodian shall collect, hold, manage, invest, and reinvest the custodial property.

(B) The custodian shall pay over to the minor for expenditure by the minor, or expend for the use or benefit of the minor, as much of or all the custodial property as the custodian considers advisable for the use and benefit of the minor in the manner, at the time or times, and to the extent that the custodian in the custodian's discretion considers suitable and proper, with or without court order, with or without regard to the duty or ability of the custodian or of any other person to support the minor or the minor's ability to do so, and with or without regard to any other income or property of the minor that may be applicable or available for any purpose. Any payment or expenditure that is made under this division is in addition to, is not a substitute for, and does not affect the obligation of any person to support the minor for whom the payment or expenditure is made.

(C) The court, on the petition of a parent or guardian of the minor or of the minor, if the minor has attained the age of fourteen years, may order the custodian to pay over to the minor for expenditure by the minor or to expend as much of or all the custodial property as is necessary for the use and benefit of the minor.

(D)(1) Except as provided in division (D)(2) of this section, to the extent that the custodial property is not so expended, the custodian shall deliver or pay the custodial property over to the minor on the minor's attaining the age of twenty-one years or, if the minor dies before attaining the age of twenty-one years, shall, upon the minor's death, deliver or pay the custodial property over to the estate of the minor.

(2) If the donor or transferor, in the written instrument that makes or provides for the gift or transfer, directs the custodian to deliver or pay over the custodial property to the minor on the minor's attaining any age between eighteen and twenty-one, the custodian shall deliver or pay over the custodial property to the minor on the minor's attaining that age, or, if the minor dies before attaining that age, the custodian shall, upon the minor's death, deliver or pay the custodial property over to the estate of the minor.

(E) The custodian, notwithstanding statutes restricting investments by fiduciaries, shall invest and reinvest the custodial property as would a prudent person of discretion and intelligence dealing with the property of another, except that the custodian may, in the discretion of the custodian and without liability to the minor or the estate of the minor, retain any custodial property received in a manner prescribed in sections 5814.01 to 5814.09 of the Revised Code. If a custodian has special skills or is named custodian on the basis of representations of special skills or expertise, the custodian is under a duty to use those skills or that expertise.

(F) The custodian may sell, exchange, convert, or otherwise dispose of custodial property in the manner, at the time or times, for the price or prices, and upon the terms the custodian considers advisable. The custodian may vote in person or by general or limited proxy a security that is custodial property. The custodian may consent, directly or through a committee or other agent, to the reorganization, consolidation, merger, dissolution, or liquidation of an issuer of a security that is custodial property, and to the sale, lease, pledge, or mortgage of any property by or to such an issuer, and to any other action by such an issuer. The custodian may purchase any life or endowment insurance policy or annuity contract on the life of the minor or any member of the family of the minor and pay, from funds in the custodian's custody, any premiums on any life or endowment insurance policy or annuity contract held by the custodian as custodial property. The custodian may execute and deliver any and all instruments in writing that the custodian considers advisable to carry out any of the custodian's powers as custodian.

(G) The custodian shall register each security that is custodial property and in registered form in the name of the custodian, followed, in substance, by the words: "as custodian for............ (name of minor) under the Ohio Transfers to Minors Act," or shall maintain each security that is custodial property and in registered form in an account with a broker or in a financial institution in the name of the custodian, followed, in substance, by the words: "as custodian for............ (name of minor) under the Ohio Transfers to Minors Act." A security held in account with a broker or in a financial institution in the name of the custodian may be held in the name of the broker or financial institution. A security that is custodial property and in registered form and that is held by a broker or in a financial institution in which the broker or financial institution does not have a lien for indebtedness due to it from a custodial account may not be pledged, lent, hypothecated, or disposed of except upon the specific instructions of the custodian. The custodian shall hold all money that is custodial property in an account with a broker or in a financial institution in the name of the custodian, followed, in substance, by the words: "as custodian for............ (name of minor) under the Ohio Transfers to Minors Act." The custodian shall hold all life or endowment insurance policies, annuity contracts, or benefit plans that are custodial property in the name of the custodian, followed, in substance, by the words "as custodian for............... (name of minor) under the Ohio Transfers to Minors Act." The custodian shall take title to all real estate that is custodial property in the name of the custodian, followed, in substance, by the words: "as custodian for............ (name of minor) under the Ohio Transfers to Minors Act." The custodian shall keep all other custodial property separate and distinct from the custodian's own property in a manner to identify it clearly as custodial property.

(H) The custodian shall keep records of all transactions with respect to the custodial property and make the records available for inspection at reasonable intervals by a parent or legal representative of the minor or by the minor, if the minor has attained the age of fourteen years.

(I) A custodian has, with respect to the custodial property, in addition to the rights and powers provided in sections 5814.01 to 5814.09 of the Revised Code, all the rights and powers that a guardian has with respect to property not held as custodial property.

(J) The custodian may invest in or pay premiums on any life or endowment insurance policy or annuity contract on either of the following:

(1) The life of the minor, if the minor or the estate of the minor is the sole beneficiary under the policy or contract;

(2) The life of any person in whom the minor has an insurable interest, if the minor, the minor's estate, or the custodian in the custodian's capacity as custodian is the sole beneficiary.

(K) All of the rights, powers, and authority of the custodian over custodial property, including all of the incidents of ownership in any life or endowment insurance policy, annuity contract, or benefit plan, are held only in the capacity of the custodian as custodian.

(2006 H 416, eff. 1–1–07)

Historical and Statutory Notes

Ed. Note: RC 5814.04 is former RC 1339.34, amended and recodified by 2006 H 416, eff. 1–1–07; 1993 H 62, eff. 10–1–93; 1986 H 297; 1980 H 1007; 1977 H 1; 1976 S 166; 1973 S 1; 129 v 1550.

Amendment Note: 2006 H 416 substituted "1339.31" with "5814.01", "1339.39" with "5814.09", and made changes to reflect gender neutral language.

Amendment Note: 1993 H 62 inserted, in division (G), "or shall maintain each security that is custodial property and in registered form in an account with a broker or in a financial institution in the name of the custodian, followed, in substance, by the words: 'as custodian for _____ (name of minor) under the Ohio Transfers to Minors Act.' A security held in an account with a broker or in a financial institution in the name of the custodian may be held in the name of the broker or financial institution. A security that is custodial property and in registered form and that is held by a broker or in a financial institution in which the broker or financial institution does not have a lien for indebtedness due to it from a custodial account may not be pledged, lent, hypothecated, or disposed of except upon the specific instructions of the custodian.".

Cross References

Fiduciaries, 2109.01

Library References

Guardian and Ward ⬧57.
Westlaw Topic No. 196.
Baldwin's Ohio Legislative Service Annotated, 2006 H 416 LSC Analysis, p 3/L-1709

Law Review and Journal Commentaries

H. 297: Ohio's Transfers to Minors Act: A Resolution to Problems in Litigation and Taxation?, Note. 12 U Dayton L Rev 441 (Winter 1986).

5814.05 Reimbursement, compensation, and liability

(A) A custodian is entitled to reimbursement from the custodial property for reasonable expenses incurred in the performance of the custodian's duties.

(B) A custodian may act without compensation for the custodian's services.

(C) Unless the custodian is a donor or transferor, the custodian may receive from custodial property reasonable compensation for the custodian's services determined by one of the following standards in the order stated:

(1) A direction by the donor or transferor when the gift or transfer is made;

(2) A statute of this state applicable to custodians;

(3) The statute of this state applicable to guardians;

(4) An order of the court.

(D) Except as otherwise provided in sections 5814.01 to 5814.09 of the Revised Code, a custodian shall not be required to give a bond for the performance of the custodian's duties.

(E) A custodian not compensated for the custodian's services is not liable for losses to the custodial property unless they result from the custodian's bad faith, intentional wrongdoing, or gross negligence or from the custodian's failure to maintain the standard of prudence in investing the custodial property provided in sections 5814.01 to 5814.09 of the Revised Code.

(2006 H 416, eff. 1–1–07)

Historical and Statutory Notes

Ed. Note: RC 5814.05 is former RC 1339.35, amended and recodified by 2006 H 416, eff. 1–1–07; 1986 H 297, eff. 5–7–86; 129 v 1550.

Amendment Note: 2006 H 416 substituted "1339.31" with "5814.01", "1339.39" with "5814.09", made changes to reflect gender neutral language, and made other nonsubstantive changes.

Library References

Guardian and Ward ⬧68.
Westlaw Topic No. 196.
Baldwin's Ohio Legislative Service Annotated, 2006 H 416 LSC Analysis, p 3/L-1709

5814.06 Third person's liability limited

An issuer, transfer agent, financial institution, broker, life insurance company, or other person acting on the instructions of or otherwise dealing with any person purporting to act as a donor or transferor or dealing with any person or trust company purporting to act as a custodian is not required to do any of the following:

(A) Determine either of the following:

(1) Whether the person or trust company designated by the purported donor or transferor, or the person or trust company purporting to act as a custodian, has been duly designated;

(2) Whether any purchase, sale, or transfer to or by, or any other act of, any person or trust company purporting to act as a custodian is in accordance with or authorized by sections 5814.01 to 5814.09 of the Revised Code.

(B) Inquire into the validity or propriety under sections 5814.01 to 5814.09 of the Revised Code of any instrument or instructions executed or given by a person purporting to act as a donor or transferor or by a person or trust company purporting to act as a custodian;

(C) See to the application by any person or trust company purporting to act as a custodian of any money or other property paid or delivered to the person or trust company.

(2006 H 416, eff. 1–1–07)

Historical and Statutory Notes

Ed. Note: RC 5814.06 is former RC 1339.36, amended and recodified by 2006 H 416, eff. 1–1–07; 1986 H 297, eff. 5–7–86; 1980 H 1007; 129 v 1550.

Amendment Note: 2006 H 416 substituted "1339.31" with "5814.01" and "1339.39" with "5814.09".

Library References

Guardian and Ward ⬧17.
Westlaw Topic No. 196.
Baldwin's Ohio Legislative Service Annotated, 2006 H 416 LSC Analysis, p 3/L-1709

5814.07 Registration or removal of custodian; successor custodian

(A) Any person who is eighteen years of age or older or a trust company is eligible to become a successor custodian. A successor custodian has all the rights, powers, duties, and immunities of a custodian designated in a manner prescribed by sections 5814.01 to 5814.09 of the Revised Code.

(B) A custodian may resign and designate the custodian's successor by doing all of the following:

(1) Executing an instrument of resignation that designates the successor custodian;

(2) Causing each security that is custodial property and in registered form to be registered in the name of the successor custodian followed, in substance, by the words: "as custodian for ...(name of minor)... under the Ohio Transfers to Minors Act;"

(3) Executing in the appropriate manner a deed, assignment, or similar instrument for all interest in real estate that is custodial property in the name of the successor custodian, followed, in substance, by the words: "as custodian for ...(name of minor)... under the Ohio Transfers to Minors Act";

(4) Delivering to the successor custodian the instrument of resignation, each security registered in the name of the successor custodian, each deed, assignment, or similar instrument for all interest in real estate that is in the name of the successor custodian, and all other custodial property, together with any additional instruments that are required for the transfer of the custodial property.

(C) A custodian may petition the court for permission to resign and for the designation of a successor custodian.

(D) A custodian may designate by the custodian's will a successor custodian, which designation is effective at the custodian's death. Upon the custodian's death, the custodian's legal representative shall do each of the following:

(1) Cause each security that is custodial property and in registered form to be registered in the name of the successor custodian, followed, in substance, by the words: "as custodian for ...(name of minor)... under the Ohio Transfers to Minors Act";

(2) Execute in the appropriate manner a deed, assignment, or similar instrument for all interest in real estate that is custodial property in the name of the successor custodian, followed, in substance, by the words: "as custodian for ...(name of minor)... under the Ohio Transfers to Minors Act";

(3) Deliver to the successor custodian each security registered in the name of the successor custodian, each deed, assignment, or similar instrument for all interest in real estate that is in the name of the successor custodian, and all other custodial property, together with any additional instruments that are required for the transfer of the custodial property.

(E) If no eligible successor custodian is designated by the donor or transferor in the donor's or transferor's will or trust or by the custodian in the custodian's will, or if the custodian dies intestate or is adjudged to be an incompetent by a court, the legal representative of the custodian may designate a successor custodian. If the court in which the estate or guardianship proceedings relative to the custodian are pending approves the designation, the designation shall be regarded as having been effective as of the date of the death of the custodian or as of the date the custodian was adjudged to be an incompetent. Upon the approval of the court, the legal representative of the custodian shall cause the custodial property to be transferred or registered in the name of the successor custodian as provided in divisions (D)(1) to (3) of this section.

(F) If a person or entity designated as successor custodian is not eligible, or renounces or dies before the minor attains the age of twenty-one years, or if the custodian dies without designating a successor custodian and division (E) of this section does not apply because the custodian does not have a legal representative, the guardian of the minor shall be the successor custodian. If the minor does not have a guardian, a donor or transferor, the legal representative of the donor or transferor, the legal representative of the custodian, a member of the minor's family who is eighteen years of age or older, or the minor, if the minor has attained the age of fourteen years, may petition the court for the designation of a successor custodian.

(G) A donor or transferor, the legal representative of a donor or transferor, a member of the minor's family who is eighteen years of age or older, a guardian of the minor, or the minor, if the minor has attained the age of fourteen years, may petition the court that, for cause shown in the petition, the custodian be removed and a successor custodian be designated or, in the alternative, that the custodian be required to give bond for the performance of the custodian's duties.

(H) Upon the filing of a petition as provided in this section, the court shall grant an order, directed to the persons and returnable on any notice that the court may require, to show cause why the relief prayed for in the petition should not be granted and, in due course, grant any relief that the court finds to be in the best interests of the minor.

(2006 H 416, eff. 1–1–07)

Historical and Statutory Notes

Ed. Note: RC 5814.07 is former RC 1339.37, amended and recodified by 2006 H 416, eff. 1–1–07; 1986 H 297, eff. 5–7–86; 1980 H 1007; 1973 S 1; 129 v 1550.

Amendment Note: 2006 H 416 substituted "1339.31" with "5814.01", "1339.39" with "5814.09", and made changes to reflect gender neutral language.

Cross References

Conveyances, 5301.01

Library References

Guardian and Ward ⚖23, 27.
Westlaw Topic No. 196.
Baldwin's Ohio Legislative Service Annotated, 2006 H 416 LSC Analysis, p 3/L-1709

5814.08 Accounting by custodian

(A) The minor, if the minor has attained the age of fourteen years, or the legal representative of the minor, a member of the minor's family who is eighteen years of age or older, or a donor or transferor or the donor's or transferor's legal representative may petition the court for an accounting by the custodian or the custodian's legal representative. A successor custodian may petition the court for an accounting by the custodian that the successor custodian succeeded.

(B) The court, in a proceeding under sections 5814.01 to 5814.09 of the Revised Code, or otherwise, may require or permit the custodian or the custodian's legal representative to account and, if the custodian is removed, shall so require and order delivery of all custodial property to the successor custodian and the execution of all instruments required for the transfer of the custodial property.

(2006 H 416, eff. 1–1–07)

Historical and Statutory Notes

Ed. Note: RC 5814.08 is former RC 1339.38, amended and recodified by 2006 H 416, eff. 1–1–07; 1986 H 297, eff. 5–7–86; 129 v 1550.

Amendment Note: 2006 H 416 substituted "1339.31" with "5814.01", "1339.39" with "5814.09", and made changes to reflect gender neutral language.

Library References

Guardian and Ward ⚖138.
Westlaw Topic No. 196.
Baldwin's Ohio Legislative Service Annotated, 2006 H 416 LSC Analysis, p 3/L-1709

5814.09 Effect of Ohio transfers to minors act

(A) Sections 5814.01 to 5814.09 of the Revised Code shall be construed to effectuate their general purpose to make uniform the law of those states that enact similar provisions.

(B) Sections 5814.01 to 5814.09 of the Revised Code shall not be construed as providing an exclusive method for making gifts or transfers to minors.

(C) Nothing in sections 5814.01 to 5814.09 of the Revised Code, shall affect gifts made under former sections 1339.19 to

1339.28 of the Revised Code, nor the powers, duties, and immunities conferred by gifts in such manner upon custodians and persons dealing with custodians. Sections 5814.01 to 5814.09 of the Revised Code henceforth apply, however, to all gifts made in a manner and form prescribed in former sections 1339.19 to 1339.28 of the Revised Code, except insofar as the application impairs constitutionally vested rights. Sections 5814.01 to 5814.09 of the Revised Code shall be construed as a continuation of the provisions of former sections 1339.19 to 1339.28 of the Revised Code, according to the language employed, and not as a new enactment.

(D) Nothing in sections 5814.01 to 5814.09 of the Revised Code, as of May 7, 1986, shall affect gifts made under those sections as they existed prior to May 7, 1986, or the powers, duties, and immunities conferred by the gifts in any manner upon custodians and persons dealing with custodians. Sections 5814.01 to 5814.09 of the Revised Code, as of May 7, 1986, hereafter apply to all gifts made in a manner and form prescribed in those sections as they existed prior to May 7, 1986, except to the extent that the application of those sections, as of May 7, 1986, would impair constitutionally vested rights.

(2006 H 416, eff. 1–1–07)

Historical and Statutory Notes

Ed. Note: RC 5814.09 is former RC 1339.39, amended and recodified by 2006 H 416, eff. 1–1–07; 1986 H 297, eff. 5–7–86; 129 v 1550.

Amendment Note: 2006 H 416 substituted "1339.31" with "5814.01", "1339.39" with "5814.09", "the effective date of this amendment" with "May 7, 1986," and made a nonsubstantive change.

Cross References

How money may be handled for minor with no guardian of the estate, 2111.131
Retroactive laws, O Const Art II §28
Specific powers of trustee, 5808.16
Termination of trust, distribution, 2109.62

Library References

Gifts ⚖3.
Westlaw Topic No. 191.
Baldwin's Ohio Legislative Service Annotated, 2006 H 416 LSC Analysis, p 3/L-1709

CHAPTER 5815

FIDUCIARY LAW

UNIFORM FIDUCIARY ACT

Section
5815.01 Interpretation of terms
5815.02 Issuers of securities and holders of record
5815.03 Issuer of securities may treat holders of record as competent
5815.04 Definitions
5815.05 Transferee not responsible for proper application of money
5815.06 Deposit in name of fiduciary as such; liability of bank
5815.07 Check drawn by fiduciary upon account of principal; liability of bank
5815.08 Deposit to personal credit of fiduciary
5815.09 Deposit in name of two or more trustees; checks
5815.10 Interpretation and construction
5815.11 Rules of law and equity applicable

POWERS OF APPOINTMENT

5815.12 "Power of appointment" defined
5815.13 Power of appointment; age limit
5815.14 Release and disclaimer of a power
5815.15 Notice of release

DUTY TO THIRD PARTIES

5815.16 Fiduciary duties of attorney or fiduciary

INTER VIVOS OR TESTAMENTARY TRUSTS

5815.21 Distribution by fiduciary involving federal estate tax marital deduction
5815.22 Spendthrift provision not causing forfeiture or postponement of interest in property
5815.23 Accumulation for more than one year of income of property
5815.24 Transactions between fiduciaries; responsibilities; limitation of liability
5815.25 Limitation on liability of fiduciary when certain powers granted to other persons
5815.26 Temporary investments by fiduciary; procedure
5815.27 Provision for generation skipping transfer tax
5815.28 Trusts for supplemental services for disabled individuals

MISCELLANEOUS PROVISIONS

5815.31 Spouse granted power of appointment or nominated as trustee; termination of marriage as revocation

Section
5815.32 Revocation of spouse's power of attorney upon divorce, dissolution, or separation
5815.33 Spouse designated as beneficiary of death benefits, effect of termination of marriage
5815.34 Personal property held jointly by spouses; effect of termination of marriage
5815.35 Liability when acting as general partner; disclosures
5815.36 Disclaimers of successions to property

CONSIGNMENT OF ART WORKS TO DEALERS

5815.41 Definitions
5815.42 Consignment by artist of his work of art to a dealer; effects; trust
5815.43 Continuation of trust after purchase by dealer for own account
5815.44 Not subject to claims of dealer's creditors
5815.45 Written contract required of dealer
5815.46 Display requires consent of artist and notice to viewers as to artist's identity
5815.47 Waiver of statutory provisions void
5815.48 Special damages for certain violations by dealer

UNIFORM FIDUCIARY ACT

5815.01 Interpretation of terms

Except when the intent of the settlor clearly is to the contrary, the following rules of construction shall apply in interpreting the terms "inheritance" and "bequest":

(A) The term "inheritance," in addition to its meaning at common law or under any other section or sections of the Revised Code, includes any change of title to real property by reason of the death of the owner of that real property, regardless of whether the owner died testate or intestate.

(B) The term "bequest," in addition to its meaning at common law or under any other section or sections of the Revised Code, includes any disposition of real property that occurs as a result of the death of the settlor.

(2006 H 416, eff. 1–1–07)

Historical and Statutory Notes

Ed. Note: RC 5815.01 is former RC 1339.031, recodified by 2006 H 416, eff. 1–1–07; 1994 H 208, eff. 6–23–94.

Library References

Baldwin's Ohio Legislative Service Annotated, 2006 H 416 LSC Analysis, p 3/L-1709

5815.02 Issuers of securities and holders of record

As used in sections 5815.02 and 5815.03 of the Revised Code:

(A) "Fiduciary" includes a trustee under any trust, expressed, implied, resulting, or constructive; an executor, administrator, public administrator, guardian, committee, conservator, curator, receiver, trustee in bankruptcy, assignee for the benefit of creditors, partner, agent, officer of a public or private corporation, or public officer; or any other person acting in a fiduciary capacity for any person, trust, or estate.

(B) "Good faith" includes an act done honestly, whether it is done negligently or not.

(C) "Issuer" includes domestic corporations, companies, associations, and trusts; foreign corporations, companies, associations, and trusts, to the extent that securities issued by them are held of record by persons in this state or are held on deposit in this state, and to the extent that such foreign corporation, company, association, or trust is a holder of record of, or otherwise interested in, securities of domestic corporations, companies, associations, or trusts; and also the transfer agents and registrars of the issuer and the depositories for its securities.

(D) "Person" includes a corporation, partnership, association, or two or more persons having a joint or common interest.

(E) "Securities" includes the items in the following enumeration, which, however, is not exclusive:

(1) Shares, share certificates, and other certificates and evidences of ownership or participation in property, assets, or trust estate; bonds, notes, debentures, certificates, or evidences of indebtedness, certificates of interest or participation, collateral trust certificates, equipment-trust certificates, preorganization or subscription certificates or receipts, and voting-trust certificates; passbooks or certificates of deposit of money, securities, or other property; scrip certificates, fractional interests certificates, and, in general, interests or instruments commonly known as securities, and certificates of interest or participation in, temporary or interim certificates or receipts for, or warrants or rights to subscribe to, purchase, or receive, any of the foregoing, whether such securities were issued by the issuer in its corporate capacity, in its individual capacity, or in a fiduciary capacity;

(2) Securities that were issued originally by other corporations, companies, associations, or trusts, but have become the securities of the present issuer, individually or as a fiduciary.

(2006 H 416, eff. 1–1–07)

Historical and Statutory Notes

Ed. Note: RC 5815.02 is former RC 1339.01, amended and recodified by 2006 H 416, eff. 1–1–07; 1953 H 1, eff. 10–1–53; GC 8509–2.

Amendment Note: 2006 H 416 substituted "1339.01" with "5815.02", "1339.02" with "5815.03", and made a nonsubstantive change.

Cross References

Assignment for benefit of creditors, 1313.01
Corporations and nonprofit corporations, 1701.01, 1702.01
Executors and administrators, 2113.01
Foreign corporations, 1703.01
Guardians, 2111.01
Partnerships, 1775.01
Receivership, 2735.01
Securities, 1707.01

Library References

Baldwin's Ohio Legislative Service Annotated, 2006 H 416 LSC Analysis, p 3/L-1709

Notes of Decisions

Ed. Note: This section contains annotations from former RC 1339.01.

Bankruptcy 3
Defacto relationships 2
Fiduciary 1

---

1. Fiduciary

Whether debtor and creditor enjoy fiduciary relationship, within meaning of statutory exception to discharge, is one of federal rather than state law, but state law may be consulted. In re Steed (Bkrtcy.N.D.Ohio 1993) 157 B.R. 355. Bankruptcy ☞ 3376(3)

The traditional meaning of a fiduciary as someone standing in a special relation of good faith, trust, and confidence is held by a federal bankruptcy court to be far too broad for purposes of federal bankruptcy laws such as 11 USC 523(a)(4), which prevents a "fiduciary" from discharging a debt resulting from fraud or defalcation. In re Hiner (Bkrtcy.N.D.Ohio 1988) 94 B.R. 955.

A fiduciary relationship, for the purposes of RC section 102.02(A)(3), includes the relationship of director to a corporation and a trustee to a trust. Ethics Op 76–011.

2. Defacto relationships

A de facto fiduciary relationship can arise under Ohio law from a confidential relationship and the existence of such a relation is a question of fact for the jury. Hofstetter v. Fletcher (C.A.6 (Ohio) 1988) 905 F.2d 897. Fraud ☞ 7; Fraud ☞ 64(1)

3. Bankruptcy

Contingent claims of defendants, who were former officers and directors of debtor, for indemnification and contribution against the debtor were sufficient to create "related to" bankruptcy jurisdiction, and thus constitute basis for removal of investors' state law claims against them for fraud, breach of contract, breach of fiduciary duty, negligence, misrepresentation, and securities fraud; defendants showed that their claims had a basis in contract, statute, corporate bylaws, and insurance policies, and had filed proofs of claim in the bankruptcy proceedings. In re National Century Financial Enterprises, Inc., Inv. Litigation (S.D.Ohio, 06-10-2004) 323 F.Supp.2d 861. Bankruptcy ☞ 2053; Bankruptcy ☞ 2088

5815.03 Issuer of securities may treat holders of record as competent

Unless there has been delivered to an issuer a certified copy of an order, judgment, or decree of a court, judge, or administrative body or official, the legal effect of which is to restrict, suspend, or remove such capacity or authority, the issuer may treat all persons in whose names its securities are of record on its records as being of full age and competent and as having capacity and authority to exercise all rights of ownership in respect of the securities, including the right to receive and to give receipts for payments and distributions, the right to transfer the securities, and the right to vote or to give consent in person or by proxy, notwithstanding any description, limitation, or qualification appearing on the securities or on the records, any reference thereon to another instrument or to any fiduciary or pledgee or other relationship, or any knowledge or notice, actual or constructive, of the right, interest, or claim of any other person or of the infancy or lack of capacity or authority of the persons in whose names the securities are of record.

The issuer may treat a fiduciary as having capacity and authority to exercise all rights of ownership in respect of the securities that are of record in the name of a decedent holder, of a person in conservation, receivership, or bankruptcy, or of a minor, incompetent person, or person under disability, and the issuer shall be protected in any action taken or suffered by it in reliance upon any instrument showing the appointment of the fiduciary.

The issuer is not liable for loss caused by any act done or omitted by it under this section. The issuer need not see to the execution of any trust, or to the observance or performance of any obligation of a holder of record, a fiduciary, or a pledgee of the securities, and it need not inquire or inform itself concerning those matters.

This section does not enlarge the capacity, right, or authority of any holder of record of the securities as against any person other than the issuer, nor prevent any court of competent jurisdiction from enforcing or protecting any right, title, or interest in the securities in any person who is not a holder of record the securities.

This section does not protect any issuer who participates with a fiduciary in a breach of the fiduciary's trust with knowledge of such facts that the action of the issuer amounts to bad faith.

(2006 H 416, eff. 1–1–07)

Historical and Statutory Notes

Ed. Note: RC 5815.03 is former RC 1339.02, amended and recodified by 2006 H 416, eff. 1–1–07; 1953 H 1, eff. 10–1–53; GC 8509–1.

Amendment Note: 2006 H 416 made a change to reflect gender neutral language, and made other nonsubstantive changes.

Cross References

Guardianship, 2111.01
Instruction to issuer of uncertificated security to register transfer, pledge, or release from pledge of the security; fiduciary instructing, 1308.23

Library References

Securities Regulation ⚖247.
Westlaw Topic No. 349B.
C.J.S. Securities Regulation and Commodity Futures Trading Regulation § 372.
Baldwin's Ohio Legislative Service Annotated, 2006 H 416 LSC Analysis, p 3/L-1709

Law Review and Journal Commentaries

Further Remarks Concerning the Transfer of Corporate Securities in Ohio, Henry Pirtle. 14 Ohio St B Ass'n Rep 418 (September 29, 1941).

Modification in Ohio of Doctrine that Corporation is Trustee For its Shareholders, Henry Pirtle. 14 Ohio St B Ass'n Rep 295 (August 4, 1941).

Notes of Decisions

Ed. Note: This section contains annotations from former RC 1339.02.

In general 1

---

1. In general

A financial institution is not liable to an estate for disbursing funds of a decedent to a party presenting tax waiver forms incorrectly naming the financial institution by omitting the word "North" from the institution's name where the party presenting the forms (1) has applied for executrix status pursuant to a will but at the time of disbursement had not yet been appointed executrix by the probate court, (2) presented to the institution's employee a valid power of attorney, and (3) possesses tax consent forms. North Akron S. & L. Assn. v. Rondy (Summit 1990) 68 Ohio App.3d 518, 589 N.E.2d 82.

A savings institution, presented with letters of guardianship and a request to change the registration of a payable-on-death account owned by the ward of the presenting guardian, may substitute that guardian's name on the account without incurring any liability to the former beneficiaries of the account under RC 1339.02, and such former beneficiaries of a payable-on-death account may challenge the action of the savings institution with respect to changing the registration of such account only by complying with the provisions of RC 1151.192. Miller v. Peoples Federal Sav. & Loan Ass'n (Ohio 1981) 68 Ohio St.2d 175, 429 N.E.2d 439, 22 O.O.3d 406. Building And Loan Associations ⚖ 40

5815.04 Definitions

As used in sections 5815.04 to 5815.11 of the Revised Code:

(A) "Bank" includes any person, carrying on the business of banking and any financial institution defined in section 5725.01 of the Revised Code.

(B) "Fiduciary" includes a trustee under any trust, expressed, implied, resulting, or constructive, an executor, administrator, guardian, conservator, curator, receiver, trustee in bankruptcy, assignee for the benefit of creditors, partner, agent, officer of a corporation, public or private, public officer, or any other person acting in a fiduciary capacity for any person, trust, or estate.

(C) "Person" includes a corporation, partnership, association, or two or more persons having a joint or common interest.

(D) "Principal" includes any person to whom a fiduciary as such owes an obligation.

(E) "Good faith" includes an act when it is in fact done honestly.

(2006 H 416, eff. 1–1–07)

Historical and Statutory Notes

Ed. Note: RC 5815.04 is former RC 1339.03, amended and recodified by 2006 H 416, eff. 1–1–07; 1953 H 1, eff. 10–1–53; GC 8509–7.

Amendment Note: 2006 H 416 substituted "1339.03" with "5815.04", "1339.13, inclusive," with "5815.11", and "adminstrator" with "administrator".

Library References

Baldwin's Ohio Legislative Service Annotated, 2006 H 416 LSC Analysis, p 3/L-1709

Notes of Decisions

Ed. Note: This section contains annotations from former RC 1339.03.

Fiduciary 1

---

1. Fiduciary

Evidence supported conclusion that former employee breached fiduciary duty to former employer and tortiously interfered with business relations by forming competitor and soliciting customers; he presented himself as employer's corporate counsel after he had resigned that position, and he solicited customers for his new company while he was still employed. Holiday Properties Acquisition Corp. v. Lowrie (Ohio App. 9 Dist., Summit, 03-12-2003) No. 21055, No. 21133, 2003-Ohio-1136, 2003 WL 1040162, Unreported, appeal not allowed 99 Ohio St.3d 1467, 791 N.E.2d 983, 2003-Ohio-3669, reconsideration denied 99 Ohio St.3d 1548, 795 N.E.2d 685, 2003-Ohio-4671. Labor And Employment ⚖ 111; Torts ⚖ 241

Bank did not act in bad faith, in violation of Uniform Fiduciary Act (UFA), by allowing title corporation's principal to transfer escrow account funds, which represented disbursements from title insurer for loan borrowers, for improper purposes; bank was not responsible to track escrow account's declining average daily balance, principal's request for overdraft protection was reasonable, and bank's failure to investigate account activities was not a deliberate evasion of knowledge. Nations Title Ins. of New York, Inc. v. Bertram (Ohio App. 2 Dist., 06-09-2000) 140 Ohio App.3d 157, 746 N.E.2d 1145, appeal allowed 90 Ohio St.3d 1451, 737 N.E.2d 55, appeal dismissed as improvidently allowed 91 Ohio St.3d 1246, 745 N.E.2d 432, 2001-Ohio-246. Banks And Banking ⚖ 130(3); Deposits And Escrows ⚖ 24.1

Bank which had participated in placing and offering of senior subordinated notes by publicly traded corporation did not owe duty to disclose to purchasers of notes, as would allow bank's alleged failure to disclose information which contradicted that contained in corporation's financial statements to support fraud claim based on fraudulent concealment by purchasers, where no fiduciary relationship existed, and purchasers were not a known group possessed of vested rights and marked by a definable limit. Fed. Mgt. Co. v. Coopers & Lybrand (Ohio App. 10 Dist., 04-04-2000) 137 Ohio App.3d 366, 738 N.E.2d 842, appeal not allowed 90 Ohio St.3d 1424, 735 N.E.2d 902. Banks And Banking ⚖ 100

Uniform Fiduciaries Act does not protect bank if bank had actual knowledge of fiduciary's breach of fiduciary obligations, bank had knowledge of sufficient facts that its actions amounted to bad faith, or fiduciary was indebted to bank and funds were applied to that indebtedness. Savin v. Cent. Trust Co., N.A. (Ohio App. 1 Dist., 09-27-1995) 106 Ohio App.3d 465, 666 N.E.2d 332. Banks And Banking ⚖ 130(1)

Bank acts in bad faith and is not protected by Uniform Fiduciaries Act, where surrounding facts and circumstances are so cogent and obvious that to remain passive would amount to deliberate desire to evade knowledge because of a belief or fear that inquiry would disclose defect in the transaction. Savin v. Cent. Trust Co., N.A. (Ohio App. 1 Dist., 09-27-1995) 106 Ohio App.3d 465, 666 N.E.2d 332. Banks And Banking ⚖ 130(1)

Uniform Fiduciaries Act shields bank from liability when bank knows of existence of fiduciary relationship and when fiduciary in fact possesses authority to conduct transaction in question. Savin v. Cent. Trust Co., N.A. (Ohio App. 1 Dist., 09-27-1995) 106 Ohio App.3d 465, 666 N.E.2d 332. Banks And Banking ⚖ 130(1)

Treasurer who was authorized to withdraw funds from company's checking account and transact business on the account was a "fiduciary" of the company with respect to that account, for purposes of Uniform Fiduciaries Act. Savin v. Cent. Trust Co., N.A. (Ohio App. 1 Dist., 09-27-1995) 106 Ohio App.3d 465, 666 N.E.2d 332. Banks And Banking ⚖ 130(1)

Bookkeeper was not a "fiduciary" of company with respect to its checking account, for purposes of Uniform Fiduciaries Act, where bookkeeper was not an authorized signer. Savin v. Cent. Trust Co., N.A. (Ohio App. 1 Dist., 09-27-1995) 106 Ohio App.3d 465, 666 N.E.2d 332. Banks And Banking ⚖ 130(1)

Uniform Fiduciaries Act insulated bank from tort claims such as breach of fiduciary duty. Savin v. Cent. Trust Co., N.A. (Ohio App. 1 Dist., 09-27-1995) 106 Ohio App.3d 465, 666 N.E.2d 332. Banks And Banking ⚖ 130(1)

Person acting in "fiduciary" capacity is person having duty created by his or her undertaking to act primarily for benefit of another in matters connected with his or her undertaking. Savin v. Cent. Trust Co., N.A. (Ohio App. 1 Dist., 09-27-1995) 106 Ohio App.3d 465, 666 N.E.2d 332. Fraud ⚖ 7

Bank cannot contractually absolve itself from responsibility to act in good faith and exercise ordinary care. Master Chemical Corp. v. Inkrott (Ohio 1990) 55 Ohio St.3d 23, 563 N.E.2d 26. Banks And Banking ⚖ 96

Under Ohio law, bank upheld its narrow and primary fiduciary duty, arising from custody agreement for customer's investment assets, not to make unauthorized distributions; customer's account was administrative and nondiscretionary in that the bank would not distribute funds absent written direction from customer or an authorized third party, and all of bank's disbursements were directed by customer's investment advisor pursuant to her written authorization. Pavlovich v. National City Bank (C.A.6 (Ohio), 01-09-2006) 435 F.3d 560, redesignated as opinion and publication ordered. Banks And Banking ⚖ 130(1)

Under Ohio law, "fiduciary relationship" is one in which special confidence and trust is reposed in integrity and fidelity of another and there is a resulting position of superiority or influence, acquired by virtues of this special trust; in this context, fiduciary's rule can be assumed through formal appointment, or it may arise de facto through more informal confidential relationship. Anchor v. O'Toole (C.A.6 (Ohio), 09-09-1996) 94 F.3d 1014, rehearing denied. Fraud ⚖ 7

Under Ohio law, "confidential relationship" is one where person comes to rely on and trust another in his important affairs and relations there involved are not necessarily legal, but may be moral, social, domestic, or merely personal; such a confidential relationship cannot be unilateral. Anchor v. O'Toole (C.A.6 (Ohio), 09-09-1996) 94 F.3d 1014, rehearing denied. Fraud ⚖ 7

Under Ohio law, "fiduciary duty" need not arise out of contract but may arise out of informal relationship where both parties understand that special trust or confidence has been reposed. NPF IV, Inc. v. Transitional Health Services (S.D.Ohio, 04-04-1996) 922 F.Supp. 77. Fraud ⚖ 7

An individual's debt for fraud or defalcation while acting in a fiduciary capacity is excepted by 11 USC 523(a)(4) from debts the individual can discharge in bankruptcy proceedings; the definition of a "fiduciary" for purposes of this provision is a question of federal law but state law is considered relevant to the issue. In re Kern (Bkrtcy.S.D.Ohio 1989) 98 B.R. 321.

A fiduciary's inability, even if innocent or negligent, to account for a sum constitutes "defalcation" and renders the debt created by the breach of fiduciary duty nondischargeable under 11 USC 523(a)(4) in the fiduciary's bankruptcy proceedings. In re Kern (Bkrtcy.S.D.Ohio 1989) 98 B.R. 321.

5815.05 Transferee not responsible for proper application of money

A person who in good faith pays or transfers to a fiduciary any money or other property that the fiduciary as such is authorized to receive is not responsible for the proper application of the money or other property by the fiduciary. Any right or title acquired from the fiduciary in consideration of the payment or transfer is not invalid because of a misapplication by the fiduciary.

(2006 H 416, eff. 1–1–07)

Historical and Statutory Notes

Ed. Note: RC 5815.05 is former RC 1339.04, amended and recodified by 2006 H 416, eff. 1–1–07; 1953 H 1, eff. 10–1–53; GC 8509–8.

Amendment Note: 2006 H 416 made nonsubstantive changes.

Library References

Banks and Banking ⚖130.
Fraud ⚖7.
Guardian and Ward ⚖69.
Westlaw Topic Nos. 184, 196, 52.
C.J.S. Banks and Banking §§ 270, 280, 287 to 289, 327, 336.
   Baldwin's Ohio Legislative Service Annotated, 2006 H 416 LSC Analysis, p 3/L-1709

Notes of Decisions

   Ed. Note: This section contains annotations from former RC 1339.04.

In general 1

---

1. In general

Uniform Fiduciaries Act is designed to relieve those who deal with authorized fiduciaries from duty of insuring that entrusted funds are properly utilized for benefit of principal by fiduciary. Savin v. Cent. Trust Co., N.A. (Ohio App. 1 Dist., 09-27-1995) 106 Ohio App.3d 465, 666 N.E.2d 332. Fraud ⚖ 7

5815.06 Deposit in name of fiduciary as such; liability of bank

If a deposit is made in a bank to the credit of a fiduciary as such, the bank may pay the amount of the deposit or any part thereof upon the check of the fiduciary, signed with the name in which the deposit is entered, without being liable to the principal, unless the bank pays the check with actual knowledge that the fiduciary is committing a breach of the obligation as fiduciary in drawing the check or with knowledge of such facts that its action in paying the check amounts to bad faith.

If such a check is payable to the drawee bank and is delivered to it in payment of or as security for a personal debt of the fiduciary to it, the bank is liable to the principal if the fiduciary in fact commits a breach of the obligation as fiduciary in drawing or delivering the check.

(2006 H 416, eff. 1–1–07)

Historical and Statutory Notes

Ed. Note: RC 5815.06 is former RC 1339.08, amended and recodified by 2006 H 416, eff. 1–1–07; 1953 H 1, eff. 10–1–53; GC 8509–12.

Amendment Note: 2006 H 416 made a nonsubstantive change and a change to reflect gender neutral language.

Library References

Baldwin's Ohio Legislative Service Annotated, 2006 H 416 LSC Analysis, p 3/L-1709

Notes of Decisions

Ed. Note: This section contains annotations from former RC 1339.08.

Improper wire transfers 1

---

1. Improper wire transfers

Bank's policy of allowing wire transfers of funds from escrow account in unlimited amounts to any place was not commercially unjustifiable under Uniform Fiduciary Act (UFA). Nations Title Ins. of New York, Inc. v. Bertram (Ohio App. 2 Dist., 06-09-2000) 140 Ohio App.3d 157, 746 N.E.2d 1145, appeal allowed 90 Ohio St.3d 1451, 737 N.E.2d 55, appeal dismissed as improvidently allowed 91 Ohio St.3d 1246, 745 N.E.2d 432, 2001-Ohio-246. Banks And Banking ⬷ 130(3); Banks And Banking ⬷ 188.5; Deposits And Escrows ⬷ 24.1

Bank did not act in bad faith, in violation of Uniform Fiduciary Act (UFA), by allowing title corporation's principal to transfer escrow account funds, which represented disbursements from title insurer for loan borrowers, for improper purposes; bank was not responsible to track escrow account's declining average daily balance, principal's request for overdraft protection was reasonable, and bank's failure to investigate account activities was not a deliberate evasion of knowledge. Nations Title Ins. of New York, Inc. v. Bertram (Ohio App. 2 Dist., 06-09-2000) 140 Ohio App.3d 157, 746 N.E.2d 1145, appeal allowed 90 Ohio St.3d 1451, 737 N.E.2d 55, appeal dismissed as improvidently allowed 91 Ohio St.3d 1246, 745 N.E.2d 432, 2001-Ohio-246. Banks And Banking ⬷ 130(3); Deposits And Escrows ⬷ 24.1

Bank client's use of overdraft protection for escrow account did not qualify as indebtedness to bank on part of client's principal, for purposes of Uniform Fiduciary Act (UFA); application was signed on behalf of client, overdraft protection was not used for principal's personal account, and bank did not have actual knowledge of improper withdrawals at time that it repaid itself for amount of overdraft protection. Nations Title Ins. of New York, Inc. v. Bertram (Ohio App. 2 Dist., 06-09-2000) 140 Ohio App.3d 157, 746 N.E.2d 1145, appeal allowed 90 Ohio St.3d 1451, 737 N.E.2d 55, appeal dismissed as improvidently allowed 91 Ohio St.3d 1246, 745 N.E.2d 432, 2001-Ohio-246. Banks And Banking ⬷ 130(3); Deposits And Escrows ⬷ 24.1

Under Ohio law, bank's delay in instituting five-day rule, prohibiting bank from approving any wire transfers from customer's investment advisor that were dependent on funds that had been deposited by check less than five days earlier, was not a breach of custody agreement for customer's investment assets, which did not require the rule. Pavlovich v. National City Bank (C.A.6 (Ohio), 01-09-2006) 435 F.3d 560, redesignated as opinion and publication ordered. Banks And Banking ⬷ 188.5

5815.07 Check drawn by fiduciary upon account of principal; liability of bank

If a check is drawn upon the principal's account by a fiduciary who is empowered to do so, the bank may pay the check without being liable to the principal, unless the bank pays the check with actual knowledge that the fiduciary is committing a breach of the obligation as fiduciary in drawing the check or with knowledge of such facts that its action in paying the check amounts to bad faith.

If such a check is payable to the drawee bank and is delivered to it in payment of or as security for a personal debt of the fiduciary to it, the bank is liable to the principal if the fiduciary in fact commits a breach of the obligation as fiduciary in drawing or delivering the check.

(2006 H 416, eff. 1–1–07)

Historical and Statutory Notes

Ed. Note: RC 5815.07 is former RC 1339.09, amended and recodified by 2006 H 416, eff. 1–1–07; 1953 H 1, eff. 10–1–53; GC 8509–13.

Amendment Note: 2006 H 416 made nonsubstantive changes and changes to reflect gender neutral language.

Cross References

Commercial paper; unauthorized signature; imposters; effect of negligence, 1303.40, 1303.41, 1303.42

Library References

Banks and Banking ⬷ 130(1).
Westlaw Topic No. 52.
C.J.S. Banks and Banking §§ 270, 280, 287, 327, 336.

Baldwin's Ohio Legislative Service Annotated, 2006 H 416 LSC Analysis, p 3/L-1709

Notes of Decisions

Ed. Note: This section contains annotations from former RC 1339.09.

In general 1
Improper wire transfers 2

---

1. In general

Letters of guardianship issued by probate court, which sought to provide "notice to financial institutions" that funds being held in name of ward "shall not be released to" guardian without a court order directing release of a specific fund and amounts thereof, did not create duty on part of bank in which guardianship funds were held not to permit any withdrawals unless specifically authorized by court order. Rinehart v. Bank One, Columbus, N.A. (Ohio App. 10 Dist., 03-31-1998) 125 Ohio App.3d 719, 709 N.E.2d 559, dismissed, appeal not allowed 82 Ohio St.3d 1480, 696 N.E.2d 1087. Banks And Banking ⬷ 130(1); Mental Health ⬷ 215

Bank's issuance of debit card to guardian in connection with guardianship account, which guardian allegedly used to misappropriate guardianship funds, did not by itself establish liability on part of bank under Uniform Fiduciary Act. Rinehart v. Bank One, Columbus, N.A. (Ohio App. 10 Dist., 03-31-1998) 125 Ohio App.3d 719, 709 N.E.2d 559, dismissed, appeal not allowed 82 Ohio St.3d 1480, 696 N.E.2d 1087. Banks And Banking ⬷ 130(1)

Fact that guardian who had allegedly misappropriated funds from guardianship account had used debit card issued by bank in connection with misappropriations did not remove transactions from scope of Uniform Fiduciary Act. Rinehart v. Bank One, Columbus, N.A. (Ohio App. 10 Dist., 03-31-1998) 125 Ohio App.3d 719, 709 N.E.2d 559, dismissed, appeal not allowed 82 Ohio St.3d 1480, 696 N.E.2d 1087. Banks And Banking ⬷ 130(1)

Where a bank deals with a known fiduciary, in order to establish bank's liability under Uniform Fiduciary Act for misappropriations by the fiduciary, plaintiff must show that the bank had actual knowledge of the fiduciary's breach of the fiduciary obligation, or that the bank had knowledge of such facts that its actions in paying the checks amounted to bad faith, or that the fiduciary was indebted to the bank and the funds were applied to that indebtedness. Rinehart v. Bank One, Columbus, N.A. (Ohio App. 10 Dist., 03-31-1998) 125 Ohio App.3d 719, 709 N.E.2d 559, dismissed, appeal not allowed 82 Ohio St.3d 1480, 696 N.E.2d 1087. Banks And Banking ⬷ 130(1)

Bank did not act in commercially unjustifiable manner in failing to notify company that its treasurer, who was a fiduciary and had authority to cash checks, was withdrawing money from company's checking account, and therefore bank was protected under Uniform Fiduciaries Act; although bank ignored errors in corporate resolutions, treasurer's actions did not rise to level of being so obvious that for bank to remain silent amounted to deliberate desire to evade knowledge. Savin v. Cent. Trust Co., N.A. (Ohio App. 1 Dist., 09-27-1995) 106 Ohio App.3d 465, 666 N.E.2d 332. Banks And Banking ⬷ 130(1)

In an action against a bank for wrongful payment of a check deposited, where the payee-bank presents the defense that it dealt with an individual knowing him to be a fiduciary, the drawer-depositor, in order to successfully maintain such action, must show that the bank had actual knowledge of the fiduciary's breach of the fiduciary obligation, or that the bank had knowledge of such facts that its actions in paying the checks amounted to bad faith, or that the fiduciary was indebted to the bank and the funds were applied to that indebtedness. Master Chemical Corp. v. Inkrott (Ohio 1990) 55 Ohio St.3d 23, 563 N.E.2d 26. Banks And Banking ⇐ 130(1)

Under Ohio law, bank could not be held liable for aiding and abetting investment advisor's alleged fraud against customer, where bank was not aware that advisor breached any duties to customer, and bank employee responsible for administering account did not see anything to raise concern of possible fraud by advisor. Pavlovich v. National City Bank (N.D.Ohio, 09-30-2004) 342 F.Supp.2d 718, affirmed 435 F.3d 560, redesignated as opinion and publication ordered. Fraud ⇐ 30

Under Ohio law, bank had no independent duty of care to customer beyond its contractual duties under custody agreement, and thus economic loss rule barred customer's negligence claim against bank based on bank's transfers of funds pursuant to orders from customer's investment advisor, where extent and scope of bank's duties to customer were governed by custody agreement, and customer's losses were purely economic. Pavlovich v. National City Bank (N.D.Ohio, 09-30-2004) 342 F.Supp.2d 718, affirmed 435 F.3d 560, redesignated as opinion and publication ordered. Banks And Banking ⇐ 100; Banks And Banking ⇐ 130(1)

Under Ohio law, bank did not have fiduciary relationship with customer with regard to customer's account, where custody agreement gave bank no authority over how funds in account were to be disbursed, and bank's only duty was to execute written orders it received from customer or her designated agent. Pavlovich v. National City Bank (N.D.Ohio, 09-30-2004) 342 F.Supp.2d 718, affirmed 435 F.3d 560, redesignated as opinion and publication ordered. Banks And Banking ⇐ 119

Under Ohio law, bank was protected by Uniform Fiduciary Act (UFA) from liability arising from its honoring of withdrawal of funds by investment advisor from customer's account, where customer had explicitly designated advisor as her agent, customer's agreement with advisor gave it "complete discretion" over account, customer never informed bank of any limitations on advisor's authority, and there was no evidence that bank acted in bad faith. Pavlovich v. National City Bank (N.D.Ohio, 09-30-2004) 342 F.Supp.2d 718, affirmed 435 F.3d 560, redesignated as opinion and publication ordered. Banks And Banking ⇐ 130(1)

Under Ohio's Uniform Fiduciary Act (UFA), bank is shielded from liability for accepting instructions from customer's fiduciary who has authority to transact business in question. Pavlovich v. National City Bank (N.D.Ohio, 09-30-2004) 342 F.Supp.2d 718, affirmed 435 F.3d 560, redesignated as opinion and publication ordered. Banks And Banking ⇐ 130(1)

Under Ohio law, customer ratified investment advisor's authority to withdraw funds from her bank account to purchase debt instruments, and thus bank did not violate custody agreement with customer by permitting advisor to withdraw funds, despite customer's contentions that advisor's authority extended only to securities transactions, that she did not have full knowledge of material facts, and that her husband had objected to transfers, where customer received monthly statements detailing account activities, was aware of risks involved, and accepted benefits of allowing advisor to invest her money in debt instruments over period of several years, husband did not have authority over account, and customer never gave bank written instructions to reject further transfers or investment instructions from advisor. Pavlovich v. National City Bank (N.D.Ohio, 09-30-2004) 342 F.Supp.2d 718, affirmed 435 F.3d 560, redesignated as opinion and publication ordered. Banks And Banking ⇐ 130(1); Brokers ⇐ 36

Under Ohio law, bank did not breach custody agreement governing customer's account by executing trades ordered by customer's investment advisor, despite customer's contention that trades made by advisor exceeded its authority, where advisor's agreement with customer gave it "complete discretion" over account, bank genuinely believed that directions from advisor were made on customer's behalf, and custody agreement explicitly relieved bank of any duty to review investment made by advisor. Pavlovich v. National City Bank (N.D.Ohio, 09-30-2004) 342 F.Supp.2d 718, affirmed 435 F.3d 560, redesignated as opinion and publication ordered. Banks And Banking ⇐ 130(1)

Under Ohio law, bank could not be held liable for aiding and abetting investment advisor's alleged fraud against customer, where bank was not aware that advisor breached any duties to customer, and bank employee responsible for administering account did not see anything to raise concern of possible fraud by advisor. Sekerak v. National City Bank (N.D.Ohio, 09-30-2004) 342 F.Supp.2d 701. Fraud ⇐ 30

Under Ohio law, bank had no independent duty of care to customer beyond its contractual duties under custody agreement, and thus economic loss rule barred customer's negligence claim against bank based on bank's transfers of funds pursuant to orders from customer's investment advisor, where extent and scope of bank's duties to customer were governed by custody agreement, and customer's losses were purely economic. Sekerak v. National City Bank (N.D.Ohio, 09-30-2004) 342 F.Supp.2d 701. Banks And Banking ⇐ 100; Banks And Banking ⇐ 130(1)

Under Ohio law, bank did not have fiduciary relationship with customer with regard to customer's account, where custody agreement gave bank no authority over how funds in account were to be disbursed, and bank's only duty was to execute written orders it received from customer or her designated agent. Sekerak v. National City Bank (N.D.Ohio, 09-30-2004) 342 F.Supp.2d 701. Banks And Banking ⇐ 119

Under Ohio law, bank was protected by Uniform Fiduciary Act (UFA) from liability arising from its honoring of withdrawal of funds by investment advisor from customer's account, where customer had explicitly designated advisor as her agent, customer's agreement with advisor gave it "complete discretion" over account, customer never informed bank of any limitations on advisor's authority, and there was no evidence that bank acted in bad faith. Sekerak v. National City Bank (N.D.Ohio, 09-30-2004) 342 F.Supp.2d 701. Banks And Banking ⇐ 130(1)

Under Ohio's Uniform Fiduciary Act (UFA), bank is shielded from liability for accepting instructions from customer's fiduciary who has authority to transact business in question. Sekerak v. National City Bank (N.D.Ohio, 09-30-2004) 342 F.Supp.2d 701. Banks And Banking ⇐ 130(1)

Under Ohio law, customer ratified investment advisor's authority to withdraw funds from her bank account to purchase debt instruments, and thus bank did not violate custody agreement with customer by permitting advisor to withdraw funds, despite customer's contentions that advisor's authority extended only to securities transactions, and that she did not have full knowledge of material facts, where customer received monthly statements detailing account activities, was aware of risks involved, and accepted benefits of allowing advisor to invest her money in debt instruments by accepting interest that instruments paid over period of several years and reporting interest as income on her annual tax returns. Sekerak v. National City Bank (N.D.Ohio, 09-30-2004) 342 F.Supp.2d 701. Banks And Banking ⇐ 130(1); Brokers ⇐ 36

Under Ohio law, bank did not breach custody agreement governing customer's account by executing trades ordered by customer's investment advisor, despite customer's contention that trades made by advisor exceeded its authority, where advisor's agreement with customer gave it "complete discretion" over account, bank genuinely believed that directions from advisor were made on customer's behalf, and custody agreement explicitly relieved bank of any duty to review investment made by advisor. Sekerak v. National City Bank (N.D.Ohio, 09-30-2004) 342 F.Supp.2d 701. Banks And Banking ⇐ 130(1)

2. Improper wire transfers

Bank's policy of allowing wire transfers of funds from escrow account in unlimited amounts to any place was not commercially unjustifiable under Uniform Fiduciary Act (UFA). Nations Title Ins. of New York, Inc. v. Bertram (Ohio App. 2 Dist., 06-09-2000) 140 Ohio App.3d 157, 746 N.E.2d 1145, appeal allowed 90 Ohio St.3d 1451, 737 N.E.2d 55, appeal dismissed as improvidently allowed 91 Ohio St.3d 1246, 745 N.E.2d 432, 2001-Ohio-246. Banks And Banking ⇐ 130(3); Banks And Banking ⇐ 188.5; Deposits And Escrows ⇐ 24.1

Bank did not act in bad faith, in violation of Uniform Fiduciary Act (UFA), by allowing title corporation's principal to transfer escrow account funds, which represented disbursements from title insurer for loan borrowers, for improper purposes; bank was not responsible to track escrow account's declining average daily balance, principal's request for overdraft protection was reasonable, and bank's failure to investigate account activities was not a deliberate evasion of knowledge. Nations Title Ins. of New York, Inc. v. Bertram (Ohio App. 2 Dist., 06-09-2000) 140 Ohio App.3d 157, 746 N.E.2d 1145, appeal allowed 90 Ohio St.3d 1451, 737 N.E.2d 55, appeal dismissed as improvidently allowed 91 Ohio St.3d 1246, 745 N.E.2d 432, 2001-Ohio-246. Banks And Banking ⇐ 130(3); Deposits And Escrows ⇐ 24.1

Bank client's use of overdraft protection for escrow account did not qualify as indebtedness to bank on part of client's principal, for purposes of Uniform Fiduciary Act (UFA); application was signed on behalf of client, overdraft protection was not used for principal's personal account, and bank did not have actual knowledge of improper withdrawals at time that it repaid itself for amount of overdraft protection. Nations Title Ins. of New York, Inc. v. Bertram (Ohio App. 2 Dist., 06-09-2000) 140 Ohio App.3d 157, 746 N.E.2d 1145, appeal allowed 90 Ohio St.3d 1451, 737 N.E.2d 55, appeal dismissed as improvidently allowed 91 Ohio St.3d 1246, 745 N.E.2d 432, 2001-Ohio-246. Banks And Banking ⟶ 130(3); Deposits And Escrows ⟶ 24.1

Under Ohio law, payment orders from customer's investment advisor to bank were authorized orders, and thus bank was not subject to liability for making unauthorized wire transfers, despite customer's husband's allegation that he had ordered bank to stop making wire transfers, where advisor was customer's authorized agent for purposes of investing her money, husband did not have authority over customer's account, husband's order did not comply with agreement's requirement that such orders be in writing, and customer ratified advisor's actions by failing to object after she had notice of transactions. Pavlovich v. National City Bank (N.D.Ohio, 09-30-2004) 342 F.Supp.2d 718, affirmed 435 F.3d 560, redesignated as opinion and publication ordered. Banks And Banking ⟶ 188.5

Under Ohio law, payment orders from customer's investment advisor to bank were authorized orders, and thus bank was not subject to liability for making unauthorized wire transfers, where advisor was customer's authorized agent for purposes of investing her money, and customer ratified advisor's actions by failing to object after she had notice of transactions. Sekerak v. National City Bank (N.D.Ohio, 09-30-2004) 342 F.Supp.2d 701. Banks And Banking ⟶ 188.5

5815.08 Deposit to personal credit of fiduciary

If a fiduciary makes a deposit in a bank to the fiduciary's personal credit of checks drawn by the fiduciary upon an account in the fiduciary's own name as fiduciary, checks payable to the fiduciary as fiduciary, checks drawn by the fiduciary upon an account in the name of the principal if the fiduciary is empowered to draw checks thereon, checks payable to the principal and indorsed by the fiduciary if the fiduciary is empowered to indorse the checks, or if the fiduciary otherwise makes a deposit of funds held by the fiduciary as fiduciary, the bank receiving the deposit is not bound to inquire whether the fiduciary is committing a breach of the obligation as fiduciary.

The bank may pay the amount of the deposit or any part thereof upon the personal check of the fiduciary without being liable to the principal, unless the bank receives the deposit or pays the check with actual knowledge that the fiduciary is committing a breach of the obligation as fiduciary in making the deposit or in drawing the check, or with knowledge of such facts that the action of the bank in receiving the deposit or paying the check amounts to bad faith.

(2006 H 416, eff. 1–1–07)

Historical and Statutory Notes

Ed. Note: RC 5815.08 is former RC 1339.10, amended and recodified by 2006 H 416, eff. 1-1-07; 1953 H 1, eff. 10-1-53; GC 8509-14.

Amendment Note: 2006 H 416 made nonsubstantive changes and changes to reflect gender neutral language.

Library References

Banks and Banking ⟶130(3).
Westlaw Topic No. 52.
C.J.S. Banks and Banking §§ 270, 280, 287 to 289, 327, 336.

Baldwin's Ohio Legislative Service Annotated, 2006 H 416 LSC Analysis, p 3/L-1709

5815.09 Deposit in name of two or more trustees; checks

When a deposit is made in a bank in the name of two or more persons as trustees and a check is drawn upon the trust account by any trustee authorized to do so by the other, neither the payee or other holder nor the bank is bound to inquire whether it is a breach of trust to authorize the trustee to draw checks upon the trust account and neither is liable unless the circumstances are such that the action of the payee or other holder or the bank amounts to bad faith.

(2006 H 416, eff. 1–1–07)

Historical and Statutory Notes

Ed. Note: RC 5815.09 is former RC 1339.11, amended and recodified by 2006 H 416, eff. 1-1-07; 1953 H 1, eff. 10-1-53; GC 8509-15.

Amendment Note: 2006 H 416 made a nonsubstantive change.

Library References

Banks and Banking ⟶130(3).
Westlaw Topic No. 52.
C.J.S. Banks and Banking §§ 270, 280, 287 to 289, 327, 336.

Baldwin's Ohio Legislative Service Annotated, 2006 H 416 LSC Analysis, p 3/L-1709

5815.10 Interpretation and construction

Sections 5815.04 to 5815.11 of the Revised Code shall be construed to effectuate their general purpose of making the law of this state uniform with the law of those states that enact similar legislation.

(2006 H 416, eff. 1–1–07)

Historical and Statutory Notes

Ed. Note: RC 5815.10 is former RC 1339.12, amended and recodified by 2006 H 416, eff. 1-1-07; 1953 H 1, eff. 10-1-53; GC 8509-18.

Amendment Note: 2006 H 416 substituted "1339.03" with "5815.04", "1339.13, inclusive," with "5815.11", and made other nonsubstantive changes.

Library References

Baldwin's Ohio Legislative Service Annotated, 2006 H 416 LSC Analysis, p 3/L-1709

5815.11 Rules of law and equity applicable

In any case not provided for in sections 5815.04 to 5815.11 of the Revised Code, the rules of law and equity, including the law merchant and those rules of law and equity relating to trusts, agency, negotiable instruments, and banking apply.

(2006 H 416, eff. 1–1–07)

Historical and Statutory Notes

Ed. Note: RC 5815.11 is former RC 1339.13, amended and recodified by 2006 H 416, eff. 1-1-07; 1953 H 1, eff. 10-1-53; GC 8509-17.

Amendment Note: 2006 H 416 substituted "1339.03" with "5815.04" and "1339.13, inclusive," with "5815.11".

Cross References

Banking law, 1101.01, 1103.01, 1105.01, 1107.01
Commercial paper, 1303.01

Library References

Baldwin's Ohio Legislative Service Annotated, 2006 H 416 LSC Analysis, p 3/L-1709

POWERS OF APPOINTMENT

5815.12 "Power of appointment" defined

As used in sections 5815.13, 5815.14, and 5815.15 of the Revised Code, "power of appointment" means any power that is in effect a power to appoint, however created, regardless of nomenclature used in creating the power and regardless of connotations under the law of property, trusts, or wills. The power includes but is not limited to powers which are special, general, limited, absolute, in gross, appendant, appurtenant, or collateral.

(2006 H 416, eff. 1–1–07)

Historical and Statutory Notes

Ed. Note: RC 5815.12 is former RC 1339.15, amended and recodified by 2006 H 416, eff. 1–1–07; 131 v S 25, eff. 8–10–65; 1953 H 1; GC 8509–23.

Amendment Note: 2006 H 416 substituted "1339.151" with "5815.13", "1339.16" with "5815.14", "1339.17" with "5815.15", and made other nonsubstantive changes.

Library References

Guardian and Ward ⬢17.
Westlaw Topic No. 196.
Baldwin's Ohio Legislative Service Annotated, 2006 H 416 LSC Analysis, p 3/L-1709

Law Review and Journal Commentaries

Effective Use of Powers of Appointment: Tools of Flexibility, Robert K. Lease. 9 Prob L J Ohio 82 (May/June 1999).

Notes of Decisions

Ed. Note: *This section contains annotations from former RC 1339.15.*

In general 1
Choice of law 2
Judgments 3

---

1. In general

Father did not exceed his authority by disinheriting his daughter completely when he exercised his limited power of appointment in allocating the principal of her mother's trust, since he had been given the right to allocate among the class of his children in any way he wished. Cowden v. Huntington Natl. Bank (Ohio App. 2 Dist., Montgomery, 04-09-2004) No. 20027, 2004-Ohio-1813, 2004 WL 758390, Unreported. Wills ⬢ 589(1)

RC 2107.06 does not apply to the testamentary grant of a power of appointment or the testamentary exercise thereof. In re Lowe's Estate (Cuyahoga 1963) 119 Ohio App. 303, 191 N.E.2d 196, 92 Ohio Law Abs. 369, 27 O.O.2d 319.

A general testamentary power of appointment exercised in favor of a charitable organization is not rendered invalid by application of RC 2107.06 to the facts that the original donor of the power died within one year from the execution of his will plus the fact that the donee of the power died within one year of the execution of her will and there remain lineal descendants, or issue, of the original donor. In re Lowe's Estate (Cuyahoga 1963) 119 Ohio App. 303, 191 N.E.2d 196, 92 Ohio Law Abs. 369, 27 O.O.2d 319.

The appointment by will of one half of the balance of trust property to the executor was a valid exercise of the decedent's general power of appointment granted by her father's will. Fifth Third Bank v Montagu, No. C–820207 (1st Dist Ct App, Hamilton, 1–5–83).

2. Choice of law

The determination of whether a testamentary special power of appointment conferred by an Ohio trust has been effectively exercised by the donee is governed by the law of the jurisdiction wherein the donee was domiciled at the time of the power's purported exercise. Toledo Trust Co. v. Santa Barbara Foundation (Ohio 1987) 32 Ohio St.3d 141, 512 N.E.2d 664, certiorari denied 108 S.Ct. 1089, 485 U.S. 916, 99 L.Ed.2d 250.

3. Judgments

The determination of the intent of a donee in exercising a testamentary special power of appointment by a court of competent jurisdiction of the state within which the donee is domiciled at the time of the power's exercise is binding in any subsequent judicial proceedings in Ohio and entitled to full faith and credit. Toledo Trust Co. v. Santa Barbara Foundation (Ohio 1987) 32 Ohio St.3d 141, 512 N.E.2d 664, certiorari denied 108 S.Ct. 1089, 485 U.S. 916, 99 L.Ed.2d 250.

5815.13 Power of appointment; age limit

Any power of appointment that is not subject to an express condition that it may be exercised only by a donee or holder of a greater age may be exercised by any donee or holder of the age of eighteen years or over.

(2006 H 416, eff. 1–1–07)

Historical and Statutory Notes

Ed. Note: RC 5815.13 is former RC 1339.151, amended and recodified by 2006 H 416, eff. 1–1–07; 131 v S 25, eff. 8–10–65.

Amendment Note: 2006 H 416 made nonsubstantive changes.

Cross References

Age of majority, 3109.01

Library References

Guardian and Ward ⬢10.
Westlaw Topic No. 196.
Baldwin's Ohio Legislative Service Annotated, 2006 H 416 LSC Analysis, p 3/L-1709

Law Review and Journal Commentaries

Effective Use of Powers of Appointment: Tools of Flexibility, Robert K. Lease. 9 Prob L J Ohio 82 (May/June 1999).

5815.14 Release and disclaimer of a power

Any power of appointment may be released in whole or in part by the donee or holder of the power by an instrument in writing, signed and acknowledged in the manner prescribed for the execution of deeds. No such release is ineffective because it was given either for or without consideration, because it was signed and acknowledged before June 3, 1943, or because no delivery is made of a copy of the release as provided for in section 5815.15 of the Revised Code.

Sections 5815.14 and 5815.15 of the Revised Code do not affect the validity of a release of a power of appointment effected in any other form or manner.

A donee or holder of a power of appointment may disclaim the same at any time, wholly or in part, in the same manner and to the same extent as the donee or holder of the power might release it.

(2006 H 416, eff. 1–1–07)

Historical and Statutory Notes

Ed. Note: RC 5815.14 is former RC 1339.16, amended and recodified by 2006 H 416, eff. 1–1–07; 1953 H 1, eff. 10–1–53; GC 8509–22, 8509–24, 8509–27.

Amendment Note: 2006 H 416 substituted "1339.17" with "5815.15", "1339.16" with "5815.14", and made a change to reflect gender neutral language.

Cross References

Signing and acknowledgment of deeds, 5301.01

Library References

Guardian and Ward ⬢2.
Westlaw Topic No. 196.
Baldwin's Ohio Legislative Service Annotated, 2006 H 416 LSC Analysis, p 3/L-1709

5815.15 Notice of release

No fiduciary or other person having the possession or control of any property subject to a power of appointment, other than the donee or holder of such power, has notice of a release of the power until a copy of the release is delivered to the fiduciary or other person having possession or control.

No purchaser or mortgagee of real property subject to a power of appointment has notice of a release of the power until a copy of the release is delivered to the officer charged by law with the recording of deeds in the county in which the property is situated. If the property is in this state the county recorder to whom a release is delivered shall record the release in the record of powers of attorney and shall charge a fee computed in the same manner as the fee charged for recording deeds.

(2006 H 416, eff. 1–1–07)

Historical and Statutory Notes

Ed. Note: RC 5815.15 is former RC 1339.17, amended and recodified by 2006 H 416, eff. 1–1–07; 1953 H 1, eff. 10–1–53; GC 8509–25, 8509–26.

Amendment Note: 2006 H 416 made a nonsubstantive change and a change to reflect gender neutral language.

Cross References

Fees of county recorder, 317.32
Recording of instruments conveying land, 317.08, 5301.25

Library References

Guardian and Ward ⚖2.
Westlaw Topic No. 196.
Baldwin's Ohio Legislative Service Annotated, 2006 H 416 LSC Analysis, p 3/L-1709

DUTY TO THIRD PARTIES

5815.16 Fiduciary duties of attorney or fiduciary

(A) Absent an express agreement to the contrary, an attorney who performs legal services for a fiduciary, by reason of the attorney performing those legal services for the fiduciary, has no duty or obligation in contract, tort, or otherwise to any third party to whom the fiduciary owes fiduciary obligations.

(B) As used in this section, "fiduciary" means a trustee under an express trust or an executor or administrator of a decedent's estate.

(2006 H 416, eff. 1–1–07)

Uncodified Law

1998 H 701, § 3: See Uncodified Law under 5809.01.

Historical and Statutory Notes

Ed. Note: RC 5815.16 is former RC 1339.18, recodified by 2006 H 416, eff. 1–1–07; 1998 H 701, eff. 3–22–99.

Library References

Attorney and Client ⚖123(1).
Westlaw Topic No. 45.
C.J.S. Attorney and Client § 241.
Baldwin's Ohio Legislative Service Annotated, 2006 H 416 LSC Analysis, p 3/L-1709

Law Review and Journal Commentaries

Adoption of New Ethical Consideration Relating to Lawyer's Representation of a Trustee of an Express Trust, Executor, Administrator, or Personal Representative, Sidney Nudelman. 10 Prob L J Ohio 17 (November/December 1999).

Scope of Lawyer's Duties in Estates and Trusts Clarified, Robert G. Dykes. (Ed. Note: New RC 1339.18 is discussed.) 9 Prob L J Ohio 44 (January/February 1999).

INTER VIVOS OR TESTAMENTARY TRUSTS

5815.21 Distribution by fiduciary involving federal estate tax marital deduction

Whenever the executor of a will or the trustee of a testamentary or inter vivos trust is permitted or required to select assets in kind to satisfy a gift, devise, or bequest, whether outright or in trust, intended to qualify for the federal estate tax marital deduction prescribed by the United States "Internal Revenue Code of 1954," 68A Stat. 392, 26 U.S.C.A. 2056, or any comparable federal statute enacted after July 20, 1965, and the will or trust instrument empowers or requires the fiduciary to satisfy such gift, devise, or bequest by allocating assets thereto at any values other than market values at the date of satisfaction of such gift, devise, or bequest, the executor or trustee shall satisfy such gift, devise, or bequest by distribution of assets having a value fairly representative in the aggregate of appreciation or depreciation in the value of all property, including cash, available for distribution in satisfaction of such gift, devise, or bequest, unless the will or trust instrument expressly requires that distribution be made in a manner so as not to be fairly representative of such appreciation or depreciation.

(2006 H 416, eff. 1–1–07)

Historical and Statutory Notes

Ed. Note: RC 5815.21 is former RC 1339.41, recodified by 2006 H 416, eff. 1–1–07; 132 v H 1, eff. 2–21–67; 131 v S 18.

Cross References

Distribution by executor, 2113.53

Library References

Executors and Administrators ⚖288.
Internal Revenue ⚖4169(1).
Westlaw Topic Nos. 162, 220.
C.J.S. Executors and Administrators § 533.
C.J.S. Internal Revenue §§ 512, 525, 535.
Baldwin's Ohio Legislative Service Annotated, 2006 H 416 LSC Analysis, p 3/L-1709

Law Review and Journal Commentaries

A Scrivener's "Delight"—The Marital Deduction Formula Clause, John H. Minan. 37 Ohio St L J 81 (1976).

5815.22 Spendthrift provision not causing forfeiture or postponement of interest in property

(A)(1) Except as provided in divisions (A)(2), (3), and (4) of this section, a spendthrift provision in an instrument that creates an inter vivos or testamentary trust shall not cause any forfeiture or postponement of any interest in property that satisfies both of the following:

(a) It is granted to a surviving spouse of the testator or other settlor.

(b) It qualifies for the federal estate tax marital deduction allowed by Subtitle B, Chapter 11, of the "Internal Revenue Code of 1986," 26 U.S.C.A. 2056, as amended, the estate tax marital deduction allowed by division (A) of section 5731.15 of the Revised Code, or the qualified terminable interest property deduction allowed by division (B) of section 5731.15 of the Revised Code.

(2) Division (A)(1) of this section does not apply if an instrument that creates an inter vivos or testamentary trust expressly

states the intention of the testator or other settlor that obtaining a marital deduction or a qualified terminable interest property deduction as described in division (A)(1)(b) of this section is less important than enforcing the forfeiture or postponement of the interest in property in accordance with the spendthrift provision in the instrument.

(3) Division (A)(1) of this section applies only to the forfeiture or postponement portions of a spendthrift provision and does not apply to any portion of a spendthrift provision that prohibits a beneficiary from assigning, alienating, or otherwise disposing of any beneficial interest in a trust or prohibits a creditor of a beneficiary from attaching or otherwise encumbering the trust estate.

(4) Division (A)(1) of this section does not apply to any beneficiary of an inter vivos or testamentary trust other than the surviving spouse of the testator or other settlor or to any inter vivos or testamentary trust of which the surviving spouse of the testator or other settlor is a beneficiary if an interest in property does not qualify for a marital deduction or a qualified terminable interest property deduction as described in division (A)(1)(b) of this section.

(B)(1) Except as provided in divisions (B)(2) and (3) of this section, if an instrument creating an inter vivos or testamentary trust includes a spendthrift provision and the trust holds shares in an S corporation, the spendthrift provision shall not cause any forfeiture or postponement of any beneficial interest, income, principal, or other interest in the shares of the S corporation held by the trust. For purposes of division (B)(1) of this section, "S corporation" has the same meaning as in section 1361 of the "Internal Revenue Code of 1986," 26 U.S.C. 1361.

(2) Division (B)(1) of this section does not apply if an instrument that creates an inter vivos or testamentary trust expressly states the intention of the testator or other settlor that maintenance of the corporation's status as an S corporation is less important than enforcing the forfeiture or postponement of any beneficial interest, income, principal, or other interest in the S corporation shares in accordance with the spendthrift provision in the instrument.

(3) Division (B)(1) of this section applies only to the forfeiture or postponement portions of a spendthrift provision and does not apply to any portion of a spendthrift provision that prohibits a beneficiary from assigning, alienating, or otherwise disposing of any beneficial interest in a trust or prohibits a creditor of a beneficiary from attaching or otherwise encumbering the trust estate.

(C)(1) Except as provided in divisions (C)(2) and (3) of this section, a spendthrift provision in an instrument that creates an inter vivos or testamentary trust shall not cause any forfeiture or postponement of any interest in property that satisfies both of the following:

(a) It is granted to a person who is a skip person under the federal generation-skipping transfer tax imposed by Subtitle B, Chapter 13, of the "Internal Revenue Code of 1986," 26 U.S.C.A. 2601–2663, as amended.

(b) It qualifies as a nontaxable gift under section 2642(c) of the "Internal Revenue Code of 1986," 26 U.S.C.A. 2642(c).

(2) Division (C)(1) of this section does not apply if an instrument that creates an inter vivos or testamentary trust expressly states the intention of the testator or other settlor that qualifying as a nontaxable trust gift as described in division (C)(1)(b) of this section is less important than enforcing the forfeiture or postponement of the interest in property in accordance with the spendthrift provision in the instrument.

(3) Division (C)(1) of this section applies only to the forfeiture or postponement portions of a spendthrift provision and does not apply to any portion of a spendthrift provision that prohibits a beneficiary from assigning, alienating, or otherwise disposing of any beneficial interest in a trust or prohibits a creditor of a beneficiary from attaching or otherwise encumbering the trust estate.

(D) Divisions (A), (B), and (C) of this section are intended to codify certain fiduciary and trust law principles relating to the interpretation of a testator's or other settlor's intent with respect to the provisions of a trust. Divisions (A), (B), and (C) of this section apply to trust instruments executed prior to and existing on August 29, 2000, and to trust instruments executed on or after August 29, 2000.

(2006 H 416, eff. 1–1–07)

Historical and Statutory Notes

Ed. Note: RC 5815.22 is former RC 1339.411, recodified by 2006 H 416, eff. 1–1–07; 2003 S 64, eff. 10–21–03; 2000 H 313, eff. 8–29–00; 1996 H 391, eff. 10–1–96; 1992 H 427, eff. 10–8–92.

Amendment Note: 2003 S 64 inserted ", or the qualified terminable interest property deduction allowed by division (B) of section 5731.15 of the Revised Code" in division (A)(1)(b); inserted "or a qualified terminable interest property deduction" in divisions (A)(2) and (A)(4); substituted "August 29, 2000" for "the effective date of this amendment" twice in division (D); and made other nonsubstantive changes.

Amendment Note: 2000 H 313 rewrote this section, which prior thereto read:

"(A)(1) Except as provided in divisions (A)(2) and (3) of this section, a spendthrift provision in an instrument that creates an inter vivos or testamentary trust shall not cause any forfeiture or postponement of any interest in property that satisfies both of the following:

"(a) It is granted to a surviving spouse of the testator or other settlor.

"(b) It qualifies for the federal estate tax marital deduction allowed by subtitle B, Chapter 11 of the 'Internal Revenue Code of 1986,' 26 U.S.C.A. 2056, as amended, or the estate tax marital deduction allowed by division (A) of section 5731.15 of the Revised Code.

"(2) Division (A)(1) of this section does not apply if an instrument that creates an inter vivos or testamentary trust expressly states the intention of the testator or other settlor that obtaining a marital deduction as described in division (A)(1)(b) of this section is less important than enforcing the forfeiture or postponement of the interest in property in accordance with the spendthrift provision in the instrument.

"(3) Division (A)(1) of this section does not apply to any beneficiary of an inter vivos or testamentary trust other than the surviving spouse of the testator or other settlor or to any inter vivos or testamentary trust of which the surviving spouse of the testator or other settlor is a beneficiary if an interest in property does not qualify for a marital deduction as described in division (A)(1)(b) of this section.

"(B)(1) Except as provided in divisions (B)(2) and (3) of this section, if an instrument creating an inter vivos or testamentary trust includes a spendthrift provision and the trust holds shares in an S corporation, the spendthrift provision shall not cause any forfeiture or postponement of any beneficial interest, income, principal, or other interest in the shares of the S corporation held by the trust. For purposes of division (B)(1) of this section, 'S corporation' has the same meaning as in section 1361 of the 'Internal Revenue Code of 1986,' 26 U.S.C. 1361.

"(2) Division (B)(1) of this section does not apply if an instrument that creates an inter vivos or testamentary trust expressly states the intention of the testator or other settlor that maintenance of the corporation's status as an S corporation is less important than enforcing the forfeiture or postponement of any beneficial interest, income, principal, or other interest in the S corporation shares in accordance with the spendthrift provision in the instrument.

"(3) Division (B)(1) of this section applies only to the forfeiture or postponement portions of a spendthrift provision and does not apply to any portion of a spendthrift provision that prohibits a beneficiary from assigning, alienating, or otherwise disposing of any beneficial interest in a trust or prohibits a creditor of a beneficiary from attaching or otherwise encumbering the trust estate.

"(4) Divisions (B)(1), (2), and (3) of this section are intended to codify certain fiduciary and trust law principles relating to the interpretation of a testator's or other settlor's intent with respect to the provisions of a trust. Divisions (B)(1), (2), and (3) of this section apply to trust instruments executed prior to and existing on the effective date of this amendment, unless the trustee of a trust of that nature, in a written trust amendment, elects to do otherwise. Any election of that nature, when made, is irrevocable."

Amendment Note: 1996 H 391 substituted "divisions (A)(2) and (3)" for "division (B)(1)" in division (A)(1); deleted ", and shall not be construed as causing," following "shall not cause" in division (A)(1); designated division (A)(1); redesignated former divisions (A)(1), (A)(2), (B)(1) and (B)(2) as divisions (A)(1)(a), (A)(1)(b), (A)(2) and (A)(3), respectively, and made related numbering changes; deleted ", and shall not be construed as applying," in division (A)(3); and added division (B).

Library References

Trusts ⚖=141, 152.
Westlaw Topic No. 390.
C.J.S. Trusts §§ 251, 263, 269 to 272.
Baldwin's Ohio Legislative Service Annotated, 2006 H 416 LSC Analysis, p 3/L-1709

Law Review and Journal Commentaries

Generation–Skipping Transfer Tax Annual Exclusion, Robert M. Brucken. 10 Prob L J Ohio 75 (May/June 2000).

A Radical Theory of Jurisprudence: The "Decisionmaker" as the Source of Law—The Ohio Supreme Court's Adoption of the Spendthrift Trust Doctrine as a Model, Gerald P. Moran. 30 Akron L Rev 393 (Spring 1997).

Ohio Spendthrift Clauses, Wiley Dinsmore. 4 Prob L J Ohio 92 (September/October 1993).

Spendthrift Clauses and the Marital Deduction, Robert G. Dykes. 3 Prob L J Ohio 21 (November/December 1992).

Substitute House Bill 391—Omnibus Probate Bill, William B. McNeil. 7 Prob L J Ohio 2 (September/October 1996).

Notes of Decisions

Ed. Note: This section contains annotations from former RC 1339.411.

In general 1
Federal taxes 2

---

1. In general

Spendthrift provision in trust was invalid to protect beneficiary's interest in year-end distributions from his creditor, a life insurance company seeking creditor's bill to collect on prior judgment against beneficiary, where beneficiary had unconditional power to make annual withdrawals from the trust so long as he was alive at the end of each year. Great American Ins. Co. v. Thompson Trust (Ohio App. 1 Dist., Hamilton, 01-27-2006) No. C-040127, 2006-Ohio-304, 2006 WL 199751, Unreported, appeal not allowed 109 Ohio St.3d 1496, 848 N.E.2d 858, 2006-Ohio-2762. Trusts ⚖ 12

The court's purpose in interpreting a trust is to effectuate, within the legal parameters established by a court or by statute, the settlor's intent. Domo v. McCarthy (Ohio 1993) 66 Ohio St.3d 312, 612 N.E.2d 706. Trusts ⚖ 112

In Ohio, a spendthrift provision of a trust, when applicable, will be given full force and effect. Domo v. McCarthy (Ohio 1993) 66 Ohio St.3d 312, 612 N.E.2d 706. Trusts ⚖ 152

In Ohio, spendthrift provision of trust, when applicable, will be given full force and effect. Bank One Ohio Trust Co., N.A. v. U.S. (C.A.6 (Ohio), 04-04-1996) 80 F.3d 173. Trusts ⚖ 152

2. Federal taxes

Restraints on alienation effected by spendthrift provisions of trust are not effective to prevent federal tax lien from attaching. Bank One Ohio Trust Co., N.A. v. U.S. (C.A.6 (Ohio), 04-04-1996) 80 F.3d 173. Internal Revenue ⚖ 4778

5815.23 Accumulation for more than one year of income of property

(A) Except as provided in division (B) of this section, an instrument that creates an inter vivos or testamentary trust shall not require or permit the accumulation for more than one year of any income of property that satisfies both of the following:

(1) The property is granted to a surviving spouse of the testator or other settlor.

(2) The property qualifies for the federal estate tax marital deduction allowed by subtitle B, Chapter 11 of the "Internal Revenue Code of 1986," 26 U.S.C. 2056, as amended, the estate tax marital deduction allowed by division (A) of section 5731.15 of the Revised Code, or the qualified terminable interest property deduction allowed by division (B) of section 5731.15 of the Revised Code.

(B)(1) Division (A) of this section does not apply if an instrument that creates an inter vivos or testamentary trust expressly states the intention of the testator or other settlor that obtaining a marital deduction or a qualified terminable interest property deduction as described in division (A)(2) of this section is less important than requiring or permitting the accumulation of income of property in accordance with a provision in the instrument that requires or permits the accumulation for more than one year of any income of property.

(2) Division (A) of this section does not apply to any beneficiary of an inter vivos or testamentary trust other than the surviving spouse of the testator or other settlor or to any inter vivos or testamentary trust of which the surviving spouse of the testator or other settlor is a beneficiary if an interest in property does not qualify for a marital deduction or a qualified terminable interest property deduction as described in division (A)(2) of this section.

(C)(1) The trustee of a trust that qualifies for an estate tax marital deduction for federal or Ohio estate tax purposes and that is the beneficiary of an individual retirement account has a fiduciary duty, in regard to the income distribution provision of the trust, to withdraw and distribute the income of the individual retirement account, at least annually, to the surviving spouse of the testator or other settlor.

(2) A trustee's fiduciary duty as described in division (C)(1) of this section is satisfied if the terms of the trust instrument expressly provide the surviving spouse a right to withdraw all of the assets from the trust or a right to compel the trustee to withdraw and distribute the income of the individual retirement account to the surviving spouse.

(D) Divisions (A), (B), and (C)(1) of this section are intended to codify existing fiduciary and trust law principles relating to the interpretation of a testator's or other settlor's intent with respect to the income provisions of a trust. Divisions (A), (B), and (C) of this section apply to trust instruments executed prior to and existing on October 1, 1996, or executed thereafter. The trustee of a trust described in division (A) or (B) of this section, in a written trust amendment, may elect to not apply divisions (A) and (B) of this section to the trust. Any election of that nature, when made, is irrevocable.

(2006 H 416, eff. 1–1–07)

Historical and Statutory Notes

Ed. Note: RC 5815.23 is former RC 1339.412, recodified by 2006 H 416, eff. 1–1–07; 2003 S 64, eff. 10–21–03; 2000 S 108, eff. 9–29–00; 1996 H 391, eff. 10–1–96.

Amendment Note: 2003 S 64 inserted ",or the qualified terminable interest property deduction allowed by division (B) of section 5731.15 of the Revised Code" in division (A)(2); and inserted "or a qualified terminable interest property deduction" in divisions (B)(1) and (B)(2).

Amendment Note: 2000 S 108 added new division (C); and rewrote former division (C) and redesignated it as new division (D). Prior to amendment, former division (C) read:

"(C) Divisions (A) and (B) of this section are intended to codify certain fiduciary and trust law principles relating to the interpretation of a testator's or other settlor's intent with respect to the provisions of a trust. Divisions (A) and (B) of this section apply to trust instruments executed prior to and existing on the effective date of this section, unless the trustee of a trust of that nature, in a written trust amendment, elects to do otherwise. Any election of that nature, when made, is irrevocable."

Library References

Trusts ⚖140(2).
Westlaw Topic No. 390.
C.J.S. Trusts §§ 251, 254 to 258.

Baldwin's Ohio Legislative Service Annotated, 2006 H 416 LSC Analysis, p 3/L-1709

Law Review and Journal Commentaries

Recently Enacted Ohio Estate Tax Changes, Wayne A. Jenkins. 10 Prob L J Ohio 81 (July/August 2000).

Should Everyone Trust a Living Trust?, (Revisited), William A. Fields. 9 Prob L J Ohio 106 (July/August 1999).

Substitute House Bill 391—Omnibus Probate Bill, William B. McNeil. 7 Prob L J Ohio 2 (September/October 1996).

5815.24 Transactions between fiduciaries; responsibilities; limitation of liability

(A) As used in this section, "fiduciary" means a trustee under any expressed, implied, resulting, or constructive trust; an executor, administrator, public administrator, committee, guardian, conservator, curator, receiver, trustee in bankruptcy, or assignee for the benefit of creditors; a partner, agent, officer of a public or private corporation, or public officer; or any other person acting in a fiduciary capacity for any person, trust, or estate.

(B) A fiduciary, or a custodian, who is a transferee of real or personal property that is held by a fiduciary other than the person or entity serving as the transferee, is not required to inquire into any act, or audit any account, of the transferor fiduciary, unless the transferee is specifically directed to do so in the instrument governing the transferee or unless the transferee has actual knowledge of conduct of the transferor that would constitute a breach of the transferor's fiduciary responsibilities.

(C) If a trustee is authorized or directed in a trust instrument to pay or advance all or any part of the trust property to the personal representative of a decedent's estate for the payment of the decedent's legal obligations, death taxes, bequests, or expenses of administration, the trustee is not liable for the application of the trust property paid or advanced to the personal representative and is not liable for any act or omission of the personal representative with respect to the trust property, unless the trustee has actual knowledge, prior to the payment or advancement of the trust property, that the personal representative does not intend to use the trust property for such purposes.

(2006 H 416, eff. 1–1–07)

Historical and Statutory Notes

Ed. Note: RC 5815.24 is former RC 1339.42, amended and recodified by 2006 H 416, eff. 1–1–07; 1982 H 263, eff. 6–1–82.

Amendment Note: 2006 H 416 made a change to reflect gender neutral language.

Cross References

Assignment for benefit of creditors, 1313.01
Collection of trust property, 5808.12
Executors and administrators, 2113.01
Guardians, 2111.01

Library References

Guardian and Ward ⚖17.
Trusts ⚖280.
Westlaw Topic Nos. 196, 390.
C.J.S. Trusts §§ 544 to 550.

Baldwin's Ohio Legislative Service Annotated, 2006 H 416 LSC Analysis, p 3/L-1709

Law Review and Journal Commentaries

Liability of the Ohio Successor Fiduciary—Is a Sound Night's Sleep Now Possible?, C. Terry Johnson. 44 Ohio St L J 1027 (1983).

Notes of Decisions

Ed. Note: This section contains annotations from former RC 1339.42.

Bankruptcy 1

---

1. Bankruptcy

Even though RC 1339.42 implies that a guardian has fiduciary obligations, a federal bankruptcy court will not necessarily hold a guardian to be a fiduciary for purposes of 11 USC 523(a)(4), which prevents a fiduciary from discharging in bankruptcy a debt resulting from fraud or defalcation. In re Hiner (Bkrtcy.N.D.Ohio 1988) 94 B.R. 955.

5815.25 Limitation on liability of fiduciary when certain powers granted to other persons

(A) As used in this section, "fiduciary" means a trustee under any testamentary, inter vivos, or other trust, an executor or administrator, or any other person who is acting in a fiduciary capacity for any person, trust, or estate.

(B) When an instrument under which a fiduciary acts reserves to the grantor, or vests in an advisory or investment committee or in one or more other persons, including one or more fiduciaries, to the exclusion of the fiduciary or of one or more of several fiduciaries, any power, including, but not limited to, the authority to direct the acquisition, disposition, or retention of any investment or the power to authorize any act that an excluded fiduciary may propose, any excluded fiduciary is not liable, either individually or as a fiduciary, for either of the following:

(1) Any loss that results from compliance with an authorized direction of the grantor, committee, person, or persons;

(2) Any loss that results from a failure to take any action proposed by an excluded fiduciary that requires a prior authorization of the grantor, committee, person, or persons if that excluded fiduciary timely sought but failed to obtain that authorization.

(C) Any excluded fiduciary as described in division (B) of this section is relieved from any obligation to perform investment reviews and make recommendations with respect to any investments to the extent the grantor, an advisory or investment committee, or one or more other persons have authority to direct the acquisition, disposition, or retention of any investment.

(D) This section does not apply to the extent that the instrument under which an excluded fiduciary as described in division (B) of this section acts contains provisions that are inconsistent with this section.

(2006 H 416, eff. 1–1–07)

Uncodified Law

1988 S 228, § 3, eff. 3–22–89, reads: The amendments to sections 1339.43 and 2109.022 of the Revised Code contained in this act shall apply to all transactions that occur on or after the effective date of this act.

Historical and Statutory Notes

Ed. Note: RC 5815.25 is former RC 1339.43, recodified by 2006 H 416, eff. 1–1–07; 1988 S 228, eff. 3–22–89; 1985 S 129.

Cross References

Cotrustees, 5807.03
Executors and administrators, 2113.01
Fiduciaries, limitation on liability, 2109.022
Powers to direct, 5808.08

Library References

Trusts ⇒172.
Westlaw Topic No. 390.
C.J.S. Trusts §§ 318 to 320.
Baldwin's Ohio Legislative Service Annotated, 2006 H 416 LSC Analysis, p 3/L-1709
Baldwin's Ohio Legislative Service, 1988 Laws of Ohio, S 228—LSC Analysis, p 5–968

5815.26 Temporary investments by fiduciary; procedure

(A) As used in this section:

(1) "Fiduciary" means a trustee under any testamentary, inter vivos, or other trust, an executor or administrator, or any other person who is acting in a fiduciary capacity for a person, trust, or estate.

(2) "Short term trust-quality investment fund" means a short term investment fund that meets both of the following conditions:

(a) The fund may be either a collective investment fund established pursuant to section 1111.14 of the Revised Code or a registered investment company, including any affiliated investment company whether or not the fiduciary has invested other funds held by it in an agency or other nonfiduciary capacity in the securities of the same registered investment company or affiliated investment company.

(b) The fund is invested in any one or more of the following manners:

(i) In obligations of the United States or of its agencies;

(ii) In obligations of one or more of the states of the United States or their political subdivisions;

(iii) In variable demand notes, corporate money market instruments including, but not limited to, commercial paper rated at the time of purchase in either of the two highest classifications established by at least one nationally recognized standard rating service;

(iv) In deposits in banks or savings and loan associations whose deposits are insured by the federal deposit insurance corporation, if the rate of interest paid on such deposits is at least equal to the rate of interest generally paid by such banks or savings and loan associations on deposits of similar terms or amounts;

(v) In fully collateralized repurchase agreements or other evidences of indebtedness that are of trust quality and are payable on demand or have a maturity date consistent with the purpose of the fund and the duty of fiduciary prudence.

(3) "Registered investment company" means any investment company that is defined in and registered under sections 3 and 8 of the "Investment Company Act of 1940," 54 Stat. 789, 15 U.S.C.A. 80a–3 and 80a–8.

(4) "Affiliated investment company" has the same meaning as in division (E)(1) of section 1111.10 [1] of the Revised Code.

(B) A fiduciary is not required to invest cash that belongs to the trust and may hold that cash for the period prior to distribution if either of the following applies:

(1) The fiduciary reasonably expects to do either of the following:

(a) Distribute the cash to beneficiaries of the trust on a quarterly or more frequent basis;

(b) Use the cash for the payment of debts, taxes, or expenses of administration within the ninety-day period following the receipt of the cash by the fiduciary.

(2) Determined on the basis of the facilities available to the fiduciary and the amount of the income that reasonably could be earned by the investment of the cash, the amount of the cash does not justify the administrative burden or expense associated with its investment.

(C) If a fiduciary wishes to hold funds that belong to the trust in liquid form and division (B) of this section does not apply, the fiduciary may so hold the funds as long as they are temporarily invested as described in division (D) of this section.

(D)(1) A fiduciary may make a temporary investment of cash that may be held uninvested in accordance with division (B) of this section, and shall make a temporary investment of funds held in liquid form pursuant to division (C) of this section, in any of the following investments, unless the governing instrument provides for other investments in which the temporary investment of cash or funds is permitted:

(a) A short term trust-quality investment fund;

(b) Direct obligations of the United States or of its agencies;

(c) A deposit with a bank or savings and loan association, including a deposit with the fiduciary itself or any bank subsidiary corporation owned or controlled by the bank holding company that owns or controls the fiduciary, whose deposits are insured by the federal deposit insurance corporation, if the rate of interest paid on that deposit is at least equal to the rate of interest generally paid by that bank or savings and loan association on deposits of similar terms or amounts.

(2) A fiduciary that makes a temporary investment of cash or funds pursuant to division (D)(1) of this section may charge a reasonable fee for the services associated with that investment. The fee shall be in addition to the compensation to which the fiduciary is entitled for his ordinary fiduciary services.

(3) Fiduciaries that make one or more temporary investments of cash or funds pursuant to division (D)(1) of this section shall provide to the beneficiaries of the trusts involved, that are currently receiving income or have a right to receive income, a written disclosure of their temporary investment practices and, if applicable, the method of computing reasonable fees for their temporary investment services pursuant to division (D)(2) of this section. Fiduciaries may comply with this requirement in any appropriate written document, including, but not limited to, any periodic statement or account.

(4) A fiduciary that makes a temporary investment of cash or funds in an affiliated investment company pursuant to division (D)(1)(a) of this section shall, when providing any periodic account statements of its temporary investment practices, report the net asset value of the shares comprising the investment in the affiliated investment company.

(5) If a fiduciary that makes a temporary investment of cash or funds in an affiliated investment company pursuant to division (D)(1)(a) of this section invests in any mutual fund, the fiduciary shall provide to the beneficiaries of the trust involved, that are currently receiving income or have a right to receive income, a written disclosure, in at least ten-point boldface type, that the mutual fund is not insured or guaranteed by the federal deposit insurance corporation or by any other government agency or government-sponsored agency of the federal government or of this state.

(2006 H 416, eff. 1–1–07)

[1] So in original. RC 1111.10 repealed by 132 v S 97.

Uncodified Law

1987 H 287, § 3, eff. 10–20–87, reads: Sections 1109.10, 2109.371, 2109.38, 2109.41, 2109.42, and 5303.27 of the Revised Code, as amended by this act, and sections 1339.44 and 2109.372 of the Revised Code, as enacted by this act, are intended as a declaration and clarification of statutory authority that existed prior to the effective date of this act.

Historical and Statutory Notes

Ed. Note: RC 5815.26 is former RC 1339.44, amended and recodified by 2006 H 416, eff. 1–1–07; 1996 H 538, eff. 1–1–97; 1992 S 269, eff. 3–24–93; 1992 H 332; 1988 H 503; 1987 H 287.

Amendment Note: 2006 H 416 made a change to reflect gender neutral language.

Amendment Note: 1996 H 538 substituted "collective investment" for "common trust" and "1111.14" for "1109.20" in division (A)(2)(a).

Cross References

Calculating time, 1.14
Executors and administrators, Ch 2113
Fiduciary authority to invest, 2109.371, 2109.372
Investment of trust funds, 1111.13
Trust companies, investment of trust funds, 1111.13

Library References

Trusts ⚖=217.3(8).
Westlaw Topic No. 390.
C.J.S. Trusts §§ 482, 487, 491.

Baldwin's Ohio Legislative Service Annotated, 2006 H 416 LSC Analysis, p 3/L-1709

5815.27 Provision for generation skipping transfer tax

(A) A provision in a will or trust agreement, which provision pertains to the payment of any taxes that are imposed by reason of the testator's or trust creator's death, does not include the payment of any portion of any tax that is imposed on any transfer under any other will or trust agreement by Chapter 13 of subtitle B of the "Internal Revenue Code of 1986," 100 Stat. 2718, 26 U.S.C. 2601–2624, as amended, unless the provision of the will or trust agreement specifically states, using the words "generation-skipping transfer tax," that the payment of the tax imposed under that chapter is included within the provision of the will or trust agreement.

(B) This section applies to wills and trust agreements that are executed before or after March 14, 1979.

(2006 H 416, eff. 1–1–07)

Uncodified Law

1990 H 286, § 3, eff. 11–8–90, reads: Sections 1 and 2 of this act apply only to the estates of decedents who die on or after the effective date of this act.

Historical and Statutory Notes

Ed. Note: RC 5815.27 is former RC 1339.45, recodified by 2006 H 416, eff. 1–1–07; 1990 H 286, eff. 11–8–90; 1978 H 1127.

Cross References

Apportionment of generation-skipping transfer tax, 2113.861
Generation-skipping transfer tax, apportionment, 2113.861

Library References

Trusts ⚖=25(1).
Westlaw Topic No. 390.
C.J.S. Trusts §§ 39 to 41.

Baldwin's Ohio Legislative Service Annotated, 2006 H 416 LSC Analysis, p 3/L-1709

5815.28 Trusts for supplemental services for disabled individuals

(A) As used in this section:

(1) "Ascertainable standard" includes a standard in a trust instrument requiring the trustee to provide for the care, comfort, maintenance, welfare, education, or general well-being of the beneficiary.

(2) "Disability" means any substantial, medically determinable impairment that can be expected to result in death or that has lasted or can be expected to last for a continuous period of at least twelve months, except that "disability" does not include an impairment that is the result of abuse of alcohol or drugs.

(3) "Political subdivision" and "state" have the same meanings as in section 2744.01 of the Revised Code.

(4) "Supplemental services" means services specified by rule of the department of mental health under section 5119.01 of the Revised Code or the department of mental retardation and developmental disabilities under section 5123.04 of the Revised Code that are provided to an individual with a disability in addition to services the individual is eligible to receive under programs authorized by federal or state law.

(B) Any person may create a trust under this section to provide funding for supplemental services for the benefit of another individual who meets either of the following conditions:

(1) The individual has a physical or mental disability and is eligible to receive services through the department of mental retardation and developmental disabilities or a county board of mental retardation and developmental disabilities;

(2) The individual has a mental disability and is eligible to receive services through the department of mental health or a board of alcohol, drug addiction, and mental health services.

The trust may confer discretion upon the trustee and may contain specific instructions or conditions governing the exercise of the discretion.

(C) The general division of the court of common pleas and the probate court of the county in which the beneficiary of a trust authorized by division (B) of this section resides or is confined have concurrent original jurisdiction to hear and determine actions pertaining to the trust. In any action pertaining to the trust in a court of common pleas or probate court and in any appeal of the action, all of the following apply to the trial or appellate court:

(1) The court shall render determinations consistent with the testator's or other settlor's intent in creating the trust, as evidenced by the terms of the trust instrument.

(2) The court may order the trustee to exercise discretion that the trust instrument confers upon the trustee only if the instrument contains specific instructions or conditions governing the exercise of that discretion and the trustee has failed to comply with the instructions or conditions. In issuing an order pursuant to this division, the court shall require the trustee to exercise the trustee's discretion only in accordance with the instructions or conditions.

(3) The court may order the trustee to maintain the trust and distribute assets in accordance with rules adopted by the director of mental health under section 5119.01 of the Revised Code or the director of mental retardation and developmental disabilities under section 5123.04 of the Revised Code if the trustee has failed to comply with such rules.

(D) To the extent permitted by federal law and subject to the provisions of division (C)(2) of this section pertaining to the enforcement of specific instructions or conditions governing a trustee's discretion, a trust authorized by division (B) of this section that confers discretion upon the trustee shall not be considered an asset or resource of the beneficiary, the beneficiary's estate, the settlor, or the settlor's estate and shall be exempt from the claims of creditors, political subdivisions, the state, other governmental entities, and other claimants against the beneficiary, the beneficiary's estate, the settlor, or the settlor's estate, including claims based on provisions of Chapters 5111., 5121., or 5123. of the Revised Code and claims sought to be satisfied by way of a civil action, subrogation, execution, garnishment, attachment, judicial sale, or other legal process, if all of the following apply:

(1) At the time the trust is created, the trust principal does not exceed the maximum amount determined under division (E) of this section;

(2) The trust instrument contains a statement of the settlor's intent, or otherwise clearly evidences the settlor's intent, that the beneficiary does not have authority to compel the trustee under any circumstances to furnish the beneficiary with minimal or other maintenance or support, to make payments from the principal of the trust or from the income derived from the principal, or to convert any portion of the principal into cash, whether pursuant to an ascertainable standard specified in the instrument or otherwise;

(3) The trust instrument provides that trust assets can be used only to provide supplemental services, as defined by rule of the director of mental health under section 5119.01 of the Revised Code or the director of mental retardation and developmental disabilities under section 5123.04 of the Revised Code, to the beneficiary;

(4) The trust is maintained and assets are distributed in accordance with rules adopted by the director of mental health under section 5119.01 of the Revised Code or the director of mental retardation and developmental disabilities under section 5123.04 of the Revised Code;

(5) The trust instrument provides that on the death of the beneficiary, a portion of the remaining assets of the trust, which shall be not less than fifty per cent of such assets, will be deposited to the credit of the services fund for individuals with mental illness created by section 5119.17 of the Revised Code or the services fund for individuals with mental retardation and developmental disabilities created by section 5123.40 of the Revised Code.

(E) In 1994, the trust principal maximum amount for a trust created under this section shall be two hundred thousand dollars. The maximum amount for a trust created under this section prior to November 11, 1994, may be increased to two hundred thousand dollars.

In 1995, the maximum amount for a trust created under this section shall be two hundred two thousand dollars. Each year thereafter, the maximum amount shall be the prior year's amount plus two thousand dollars.

(F) This section does not limit or otherwise affect the creation, validity, interpretation, or effect of any trust that is not created under this section.

(G) Once a trustee takes action on a trust created by a settlor under this section and disburses trust funds on behalf of the beneficiary of the trust, then the trust may not be terminated or otherwise revoked by a particular event or otherwise without payment into the services fund created pursuant to section 5119.17 or 5123.40 of the Revised Code of an amount that is equal to the disbursements made on behalf of the beneficiary for medical care by the state from the date the trust vests but that is not more than fifty per cent of the trust corpus.

(2006 H 416, eff. 1–1–07)

Uncodified Law

1992 S 124, § 8, eff. 4–16–93, reads: In enacting sections 1339.51 and 5111.15 and in amending sections 2101.24, 5119.01, 5121.04, 5121.10, 5123,04, 5123.18, and 5123.28 of the Revised Code, the General Assembly hereby declares its intent to supersede the effect of the holding of the Ohio Supreme Court in the December 31, 1968, decision in *Bureau of Support v. Kreitzer* (1968), 16 Ohio St. 2d 147.

Historical and Statutory Notes

Ed. Note: RC 5815.28 is former RC 1339.51, recodified by 2006 H 416, eff. 1–1–07; 2001 H 178, eff. 10–26–01; 1994 H 694, eff. 11–11–94; 1992 S 124, eff. 4–16–93.

Amendment Note: 2001 H 178 deleted "testamentary" before "trust" in division (B); rewrote division (D); substituted "November 11, 1994" for "the effective date of this amendment"; added new division (G); and made changes to reflect gender neutral language. Prior to amendment division (D) read:

"(D) To the extent permitted by federal law and subject to the provisions of division (C)(2) of this section pertaining to the enforcement of specific instructions or conditions governing a trustee's discretion, a trust authorized by division (B) of this section that confers discretion upon the trustee shall not be considered an asset or resource of the beneficiary, his estate, or the testator's estate and shall be exempt from the claims of creditors, political subdivisions, the state, other governmental entities, and other claimants against the beneficiary, his estate, or the testator's estate, including claims based on provisions of Chapters 5111., 5121., or 5123. of the Revised Code and claims sought to be satisfied by way of a civil action, subrogation, execution, garnishment, attachment, judicial sale, or other legal process, if all of the following apply:

"(1) At the time the trust is created, the trust principal does not exceed the maximum amount determined under division (E) of this section;

"(2) The trust instrument contains a statement of the testator's intent, or otherwise clearly evidences his intent, that the beneficiary does not have authority to compel the trustee under any circumstances to furnish the beneficiary with minimal or other maintenance or support, to make payments from the principal of the trust or from the income derived from the principal, or to convert any portion of the principal into cash, whether pursuant to an ascertainable standard specified in the instrument or otherwise;

"(3) The testator is deceased;

"(4) The trust instrument provides that trust assets can be used only to provide supplemental services, as defined by rule of the director of mental health under section 5119.01 of the Revised Code or the director of mental retardation and developmental disabilities under section 5123.04 of the Revised Code, to the beneficiary;

"(5) The trust is maintained and assets are distributed in accordance with rules adopted by the director of mental health under section 5119.01 of the Revised Code or the director of mental retardation and developmental disabilities under section 5123.04 of the Revised Code;

"(6) The trust instrument provides that on the death of the beneficiary, a portion of the remaining assets of the trust, which shall be not less than fifty per cent of such assets, will be deposited to the credit of the services fund for individuals with mental illness created by section 5119.17 of the Revised Code or the services fund for individuals with mental retardation and developmental disabilities created by section 5123.40 of the Revised Code."

Amendment Note: 1994 H 694 substituted "director" for "department" throughout divisions (C) and (D); and rewrote division (E), which previously read:

"(E) In 1992, the trust principal maximum amount for a trust created under this section shall be fifty thousand dollars. Each year thereafter, the maximum amount shall be the prior year's amount plus two thousand dollars."

Cross References

Beneficiaries of trusts for disabled individuals, 5111.15
Care of residents' money and property, disposition on death, 5123.28
Claims against estate for support of patient or resident of institution, 5121.10
Claims against estate of deceased patient or relative, contracts for fixed annual payment on behalf of living patient, 5121.52
Cost for support of residents and relatives, determination of payments, agreements, 5121.04
Duties of director, 5123.04
Eligibility determinations regarding beneficiaries of trusts, medicaid qualifying trusts, self-settled trusts, exempt trusts, trust established for benefit of applicant or recipient, 5111.151
Institutions for mentally retarded and developmentally disabled, deposit of principal or income of trust not required, 5123.28
Investigation of financial condition of patient or resident of institution, 5121.04
Medical assistance recipients, 5111.15

Powers and duties of director, 5119.01
Probate court jurisdiction, 2101.24
Services fund for individuals with mental illness, 5119.17
Services fund for individuals with mental retardation and developmental disabilities, 5123.40
Services fund for individuals with mental retardation and developmental disabilities, 5123.40
Trusts for supplemental services for disabled individuals, 1339.51

Ohio Administrative Code References

Distribution of funds from the supplemental services fund, OAC 5123:2–18–02
Trusts for supplemental services, OAC 5122–22–01, 5123:2–18–01

Library References

Trusts ⚖9, 171.
Westlaw Topic No. 390.
C.J.S. Trusts §§ 20, 318 to 320.
Baldwin's Ohio Legislative Service Annotated, 2006 H 416 LSC Analysis, p 3/L-1709

Law Review and Journal Commentaries

Disability Trusts and Medicaid, Bryan L. Adamson and William J. Day. 5 Prob L J Ohio 4 (September/October 1994).

Disability Trusts in Ohio: A Look Now and Into the Future, Philip S. Kaufmann. 12 Prob L J Ohio 62 (March/April 2002).

Inter Vivos Supplemental Needs Trusts, Jacqueline L. Rogers. 12 Prob L J Ohio 13 (September/October 2001).

Statutory Disability Trust Limit Raised to $200,000: Is It Enough?, David F. Allen. 5 Prob L J Ohio 24 (November/December 1994).

Statutory Disability Trusts, Robert G. Dykes. 3 Prob L J Ohio 61 (May/June 1993).

MISCELLANEOUS PROVISIONS

5815.31 Spouse granted power of appointment or nominated as trustee; termination of marriage as revocation

Unless the trust or separation agreement provides otherwise, if, after executing a trust in which the grantor reserves to self a power to alter, amend, revoke, or terminate the provisions of the trust, a grantor is divorced, obtains a dissolution of marriage, has the grantor's marriage annulled, or, upon actual separation from the grantor's spouse, enters into a separation agreement pursuant to which the parties intend to fully and finally settle their prospective property rights in the property of the other, whether by expected inheritance or otherwise, the spouse or former spouse of the grantor shall be deemed to have predeceased the grantor and any provision in the trust conferring a general or special power of appointment on the spouse or former spouse or nominating the spouse or former spouse as trustee or trust advisor shall be revoked. If the grantor remarries the grantor's former spouse or if the separation agreement is terminated, the spouse shall not be deemed to have predeceased the grantor and any provision in the trust conferring a general or special power of appointment on the spouse or former spouse or nominating the spouse or former spouse as trustee or trust advisor shall not be revoked.

(2006 H 416, eff. 1–1–07)

Historical and Statutory Notes

Ed. Note: RC 5815.31 is former RC 1339.62, amended and recodified by 2006 H 416, eff. 1–1–07; 1986 S 248, eff. 12–17–86.

Amendment Note: 2006 H 416 made changes to reflect gender neutral language.

Cross References

Spouse granted power of appointment or nominated as trustee, termination of marriage as revocation, 1339.62
Wills, revocation of disposition or appointment of property to spouse upon termination of marriage, 2107.33

Library References

Husband and Wife ⚖279.
Trusts ⚖162.
Westlaw Topic Nos. 205, 390.
C.J.S. Trusts §§ 303 to 305.
Baldwin's Ohio Legislative Service Annotated, 2006 H 416 LSC Analysis, p 3/L-1709

Notes of Decisions

Ed. Note: This section contains annotations from former RC 1339.62.

Procedural issues 1

---

1. **Procedural issues**

Where a trust agreement states that the trust may be terminated upon the joint order of mother, father, and son, and a court in a previous action following the divorce of the mother and father ruled that the joint agreement of all three is necessary for termination regardless of the divorce, res judicata is inapplicable to a subsequent action in which the sole survivor of the three is seeking to terminate the trust since the subsequent action raises a different issue. Hobeck v. Society Nat. Bank (Ohio App. 8 Dist., Cuyahoga, 09-22-1994) No. 66029, 1994 WL 520890, Unreported.

5815.32 Revocation of spouse's power of attorney upon divorce, dissolution, or separation

If a principal executes a power of attorney designating the principal's spouse as the attorney in fact for the principal and if after executing the power of attorney, the principal and the principal's spouse are divorced, obtain a dissolution or annulment of their marriage, or enter into a separation agreement pursuant to which they intend to fully and finally settle each spouse's prospective property rights in the property of the other, the designation in the power of attorney of the spouse or former spouse of the principal to act as attorney in fact for the principal is revoked, unless the power of attorney provides otherwise. The subsequent remarriage of the principal to the principal's former spouse, or the termination of a separation agreement between the principal and the principal's spouse, does not revive a power of attorney that is revoked under this section.

(2006 H 416, eff. 1–1–07)

Historical and Statutory Notes

Ed. Note: RC 5815.32 is former RC 1339.621, recodified by 2006 H 416, eff. 1–1–07; 2003 S 64, eff. 10–21–03.

Library References

Baldwin's Ohio Legislative Service Annotated, 2006 H 416 LSC Analysis, p 3/L-1709

Law Review and Journal Commentaries

Former Spouse's Right to Act Under Power of Attorney Revoked Effective 10/21/2003, Nirakar Thakur. 14 Prob L J Ohio 4 (September/October 2003).

Revocation of Power of Attorney Upon Termination of Marriage, Nirakar Thakur. 13 Prob L J Ohio 100 (May/June 2003).

5815.33 Spouse designated as beneficiary of death benefits, effect of termination of marriage

(A) As used in this section:

(1) "Beneficiary" means a beneficiary of a life insurance policy, an annuity, a payable on death account, an individual retirement plan, an employer death benefit plan, or another right to death benefits arising under a contract.

(2) "Employer death benefit plan" means any funded or unfunded plan or program, or any fund, that is established to provide the beneficiaries of an employee participating in the plan, program, or fund with benefits that may be payable upon the death of that employee.

(3) "Individual retirement plan" means an individual retirement account or individual retirement annuity as defined in section 408 of the "Internal Revenue Code of 1986," 100 Stat. 2085, 26 U.S.C.A. 408, as amended.

(B)(1) Unless the designation of beneficiary or the judgment or decree granting the divorce, dissolution of marriage, or annulment specifically provides otherwise, and subject to division (B)(2) of this section, if a spouse designates the other spouse as a beneficiary or if another person having the right to designate a beneficiary on behalf of the spouse designates the other spouse as a beneficiary, and if, after either type of designation, the spouse who made the designation or on whose behalf the designation was made, is divorced from the other spouse, obtains a dissolution of marriage, or has the marriage to the other spouse annulled, then the other spouse shall be deemed to have predeceased the spouse who made the designation or on whose behalf the designation was made, and the designation of the other spouse as a beneficiary is revoked as a result of the divorce, dissolution of marriage, or annulment.

(2) If the spouse who made the designation or on whose behalf the designation was made remarries the other spouse, then, unless the designation no longer can be made, the other spouse shall not be deemed to have predeceased the spouse who made the designation or on whose behalf the designation was made, and the designation of the other spouse as a beneficiary is not revoked because of the previous divorce, dissolution of marriage, or annulment.

(C) An agent, bank, broker, custodian, issuer, life insurance company, plan administrator, savings and loan association, transfer agent, trustee, or other person is not liable in damages or otherwise in a civil or criminal action or proceeding for distributing or disposing of property in reliance on and in accordance with a designation of beneficiary as described in division (B)(1) of this section, if both of the following apply:

(1) The distribution or disposition otherwise is proper;

(2) The agent, bank, broker, custodian, issuer, life insurance company, plan administrator, savings and loan association, transfer agent, trustee, or other person did not have any notice of the facts that resulted in the revocation of the beneficiary designation by operation of division (B)(1) of this section.

(2006 H 416, eff. 1–1–07)

Uncodified Law

1990 H 346, § 3, eff. 5–31–90, reads, in part: (A) Sections 1 and 2 of this act shall apply only to the estates of decedents who die on or after the effective date of this act.

Historical and Statutory Notes

Ed. Note: RC 5815.33 is former RC 1339.63, recodified by 2006 H 416, eff. 1–1–07; 1990 H 346, eff. 5–31–90.

Library References

Divorce ⟲252.3(4).
Westlaw Topic No. 134.
C.J.S. Divorce §§ 508 to 511, 514, 553 to 560, 563 to 564, 571, 580 to 582.
Baldwin's Ohio Legislative Service Annotated, 2006 H 416 LSC Analysis, p 3/L-1709
Baldwin's Ohio Legislative Service, 1990 Laws of Ohio, H 346—LSC Analysis, p 5–87

Law Review and Journal Commentaries

Joint and Survivorship Accounts: A New Approach to an Old Problem, William B. McNeil. 13 Prob L J Ohio 26 (November/December 2002).

Joint and Survivorship Accounts: A New Era, William B. McNeil. 5 Prob L J Ohio 33 (January/February 1995).

Revocation–By–Divorce—Insurance Statute Held Unconstitutional, Sidney Nudelman. 4 Prob L J Ohio 101 (November/December 1993).

Statutory Provisions Controlling Beneficiary Designations Are of Limited Effect, John W. Eilers. 12 Prob L J Ohio 16 (September/October 2001).

Notes of Decisions

Ed. Note: This section contains annotations from former RC 1339.63.

In general 2
Constitutional issues 1
Federal preemption 3

---

1. Constitutional issues

Statute nullifying husband's designation of his spouse as beneficiary of death benefits payable under life insurance contract, if marital relationship was terminated after designation was made, applied to contract under which insured husband executed change of beneficiaries, revoking all previously named beneficiaries, after effective date of statute, even though insured did not in fact make any change in designation of beneficiaries; since change of beneficiaries contract was entered into after effective date of statute, statute did not unconstitutionally impair obligation of contracts. Western and Southern Life Ins. Co. v. Braun (Ohio App. 10 Dist., 12-05-1996) 116 Ohio App.3d 423, 688 N.E.2d 534, dismissed, appeal not allowed 78 Ohio St.3d 1425, 676 N.E.2d 531. Insurance ⟲ 3481(2)

Statute nullifying husband's or wife's designation of his or her spouse as beneficiary of death benefits payable under insurance contract if marital relationship was terminated after designation was made unconstitutionally impairs obligation of contracts, as applied to contracts entered into before effective date of statute. Aetna Life Ins. Co. v. Schilling (Ohio 1993) 67 Ohio St.3d 164, 616 N.E.2d 893, rehearing denied 67 Ohio St.3d 1468, 619 N.E.2d 701. Constitutional Law ⟲ 145; Insurance ⟲ 3481(2)

2. In general

Statute providing that a spouse's designation of the other spouse as a beneficiary is revoked as a result of their divorce could not be applied retroactively to revoke insured's first wife's status as beneficiary of life insurance policy, and thus first wife was entitled to proceeds of policy, even though insured did not divorce first wife until approximately three years after the effective date of statute, and divorce decree contained no provision with respect to the policy, where policy was executed and the beneficiary was designated prior to enactment of the statute. In re Estate of Holycross (Ohio App. 2 Dist., Champaign, 10-21-2005) No. 2005 CA 1, 2005-Ohio-5582, 2005 WL 2693587, Unreported, appeal allowed 108 Ohio St.3d 1487, 843 N.E.2d 793, 2006-Ohio-962. Insurance ⟲ 3481(2)

Former husband's designation of former wife as beneficiary of his life insurance proceeds was statutorily revoked at the time of their divorce, where divorce decree did not address policy. Aey v. Bargainer Ragland (Ohio App. 7 Dist., Mahoning, 12-17-2003) No. 03 MA 99, 2003-Ohio-7041, 2003 WL 22999370, Unreported, appeal not allowed 102 Ohio St.3d 1447, 808 N.E.2d 398, 2004-Ohio-2263. Insurance ⟲ 3481(2)

Statute which states that, if a spouse designates the other spouse as a beneficiary, the designation is revoked as result of dissolution of marriage, applied to life insurance policy and death benefit plan, even though the insured had designated his former wife as beneficiary before their marriage; thus, the dissolution revoked the designation. Ohio State Life Ins. Co. v. Garcia (Ohio App. 10 Dist., Franklin, 12-24-2002) No. 02AP-274,

2002-Ohio-7194, 2002 WL 31867906, Unreported, appeal not allowed 98 Ohio St.3d 1566, 787 N.E.2d 1231, 2003-Ohio-2242. Insurance ⇨ 3481(2)

Even if agreed divorce judgment were liberally construed in favor of individual retirement custodial account (IRA) owner's subsequent spouse, so as to eliminate ex-spouse as primary beneficiary of IRA, that elimination would not affect rights of contingent beneficiary, owner's child, given that contingent beneficiary's rights could not be affected by virtue of anything other than change in beneficiary, and owner's will, which was executed few days prior to owner's death, had no affect on change of beneficiary. Finch v. Key Bank Nat. Ass'n (Ohio App. 10 Dist., Franklin, 05-21-2002) No. 01AP-884, 2002-Ohio-3082, 2002 WL 1013011, Unreported. Banks And Banking ⇨ 153; Divorce ⇨ 254(1)

Right of owner of individual retirement custodial account (IRA) to change beneficiary or beneficiaries to IRA account terminated upon death. Finch v. Key Bank Nat. Ass'n (Ohio App. 10 Dist., Franklin, 05-21-2002) No. 01AP-884, 2002-Ohio-3082, 2002 WL 1013011, Unreported. Banks And Banking ⇨ 153

Pursuant to RC 1339.63, a dissolution of marriage revokes the designation of the former husband as primary beneficiary on the former wife's life insurance policy; the fact the dissolution occurred prior to the enactment of RC 1339.63 does not render the statute retroactive in effect because the death of the policyholder after enactment of the statute is the operative occurrence in this case. Prudential Insurance Co of America v Houk, No. CA–9093 (5th Dist Ct App, Stark, 3–22–93), reversed by 68 OS(3d) 108 (1993).

Although RC 1339.63 does not apply retroactively to life insurance contracts already in existence at the time of its enactment in 1990, a surviving ex-wife is not automatically entitled to death benefits under her ex-husband's life insurance policy, since she has no vested right in the policy but only an expectancy. Nationwide Insurance Co v Boes, No. 13–91–16 (3d Dist Ct App, Seneca, 1–29–93).

3. Federal preemption

Breach of contract claim in which widow of insured alleged that life insurer erroneously paid policy proceeds to insured's ex-wife was completely preempted by ERISA, and therefore, removal of claim was warranted, despite widow's contention that claim was based on state statute providing that decree of divorce operates as automatic revocation of ex-spouse as beneficiary; life insurance policy was provided through insured's employer. Dunson-Taylor v. Metropolitan Life Ins. Co. (S.D.Ohio, 04-24-2001) 164 F.Supp.2d 988. Insurance ⇨ 1117(1); Removal Of Cases ⇨ 25(1); States ⇨ 18.41

5815.34 Personal property held jointly by spouses; effect of termination of marriage

(A)(1) Unless the judgment or decree granting the divorce, dissolution of marriage, or annulment specifically provides otherwise, and subject to division (A)(2) of this section, if the title to any personal property is held by two persons who are married to each other, if the title is so held for the joint lives of the spouses and then to the survivor of them, and if the marriage of the spouses subsequently is terminated by a judgment or decree granting a divorce, dissolution of marriage, or annulment, then the survivorship rights of the spouses terminate, and each spouse shall be deemed the owner of an undivided interest in common in the title to the personal property, that is in proportion to the spouse's net contributions to the personal property.

(2) If the spouses described in division (A)(1) of this section remarry each other and the title to the personal property continues to be held by them in accordance with that division, then the survivorship rights of the spouses are not terminated, and the spouses again hold title in the personal property for their joint lives and then to the survivor of them.

(B)(1) Unless the judgment or decree granting the divorce, dissolution of marriage, or annulment specifically provides otherwise, and subject to division (B)(2) of this section, if the title to any personal property is held by more than two persons and at least two of the persons are married to each other, if the title is so held for the joint lives of the titleholders and then to the survivor or survivors of them, and if the marriage of any of the titleholders who are married to each other subsequently is terminated by a judgment or decree granting a divorce, dissolution of marriage, or annulment, then the survivorship rights of the titleholders who were married to each other terminate, the survivorship rights of the other titleholders are not affected, and each of the titleholders who were married to each other shall be deemed to be the owner of an undivided interest in common in the personal property, that is in proportion to the net contributions of the titleholders who were married to each other to the personal property.

(2) If the titleholders who were married to each other as described in division (B)(1) of this section remarry each other, and if the title to the personal property continues to be held by them, and the other titleholders whose survivorship rights continued unaffected, in accordance with that division, then the survivorship rights of the remarried titleholders are not terminated, and the remarried and other titleholders again hold title in the personal property for their joint lives and then to the survivor or survivors of them.

(C) An agent, bank, broker, custodian, issuer, life insurance company, plan administrator, savings and loan association, transfer agent, trustee, or other person is not liable in damages or otherwise in a civil or criminal action or proceeding for distributing or disposing of personal property in reliance on and in accordance with a registration in the form of a joint ownership for life, with rights of survivorship, as described in division (A)(1) or (B)(1) of this section, if both of the following apply:

(1) The distribution or disposition otherwise is proper;

(2) The agent, bank, broker, custodian, issuer, life insurance company, plan administrator, savings and loan association, transfer agent, trustee, or other person did not have any notice of the facts that resulted in the termination of the rights of survivorship by operation of division (A)(1) or (B)(1) of this section.

(2006 H 416, eff. 1–1–07)

Uncodified Law

1990 H 346, § 3: See Uncodified Law under 1339.63.

Historical and Statutory Notes

Ed. Note: RC 5815.34 is former RC 1339.64, amended and recodified by 2006 H 416, eff. 1–1–07; 1990 H 346, eff. 5–31–90.

Amendment Note: 2006 H 416 made changes to reflect gender neutral language.

Library References

Divorce ⇨252.3(2).
Westlaw Topic No. 134.
C.J.S. Divorce §§ 508 to 511, 514 to 520, 526, 538 to 543, 553 to 560, 563 to 564, 571, 580 to 582.
Baldwin's Ohio Legislative Service Annotated, 2006 H 416 LSC Analysis, p 3/L-1709
Baldwin's Ohio Legislative Service, 1990 Laws of Ohio, H 346—LSC Analysis, p 5–87

Notes of Decisions

Ed. Note: This section contains annotations from former RC 1339.64.

Judgments 2
Procedural issues 1

---

1. Procedural issues

Ex-wife was not entitled to withdraw money from parties' joint checking account, as to disposition of which divorce decree was silent, pursuant to statute governing effect of termination of marriage on personal property held jointly by spouses, even though ex-wife's name was listed on account, as ex-husband was sole contributor to funds of account, ex-wife had made no contribution of funds to account, and ex-wife withdrew money without ex-husband's permission. Justice v. Justice (Ohio App. 12 Dist., Butler,

Note 1

04-18-2005) No. CA2004-03-074, No. CA2004-04-084, 2005-Ohio-1802, 2005 WL 880234, Unreported. Divorce ⚖ 322

Issue of who contributed to joint accounts with a right of survivorship that decedent and his former wife held at time of their divorce and in what amounts was an element of estate's claim to accounts, not an affirmative defense to that claim which former wife was required to raise in a responsive pleading or motion. Aey v. Bargainer Ragland (Ohio App. 7 Dist., Mahoning, 12-17-2003) No. 03 MA 99, 2003-Ohio-7041, 2003 WL 22999370, Unreported, appeal not allowed 102 Ohio St.3d 1447, 808 N.E.2d 398, 2004-Ohio-2263. Executors And Administrators ⚖ 443(6)

2. Judgments

Absent any indication of how much either decedent or his former wife contributed to bank account with a right of survivorship that they jointly owned at time of their divorce, trial court's decision awarding all assets in account to decedent's estate was error, as former wife owned accounts in proportion to her net contribution to the account. Aey v. Bargainer Ragland (Ohio App. 7 Dist., Mahoning, 12-17-2003) No. 03 MA 99, 2003-Ohio-7041, 2003 WL 22999370, Unreported, appeal not allowed 102 Ohio St.3d 1447, 808 N.E.2d 398, 2004-Ohio-2263. Executors And Administrators ⚖ 55

5815.35 Liability when acting as general partner; disclosures

(A)(1) As used in this division, fiduciary" means any person, association, or corporation, other than a trustee of a testamentary trust, an assignee or trustee for an insolvent debtor, or a guardian under Chapter 5905. of the Revised Code, that is appointed by and accountable to the probate court, and that is acting in a fiduciary capacity for another or charged with duties in relation to any property, interest, or estate for another's benefit. A fiduciary also includes an agency under contract with the department of mental retardation and developmental disabilities for the provision of protective service under sections 5123.55 to 5123.59 of the Revised Code, when appointed by and accountable to the probate court as a guardian or trustee for a mentally retarded or developmentally disabled person.

(2) A fiduciary who enters a contract as fiduciary on or after March 22, 1984, is not personally liable on that contract, unless the contract otherwise specifies, if the contract is within the fiduciary's authority and the fiduciary discloses that the contract is being entered into in a fiduciary capacity. In a contract, the words "fiduciary" or "as fiduciary" or other words that indicate one's fiduciary capacity following the name or signature of a fiduciary are sufficient disclosure for purposes of this division.

(B)(1) As used in this division, "partnership" includes a partnership composed of only general partners and a partnership composed of general and limited partners.

(2) Subject to division (D) of this section, an executor or administrator who acquires, in a fiduciary capacity, a general partnership interest upon the death of a general partner of a partnership is not personally liable for any debt, obligation, or liability of the partnership that arises from the executor's or administrator's actions, except as provided in this division, as a general partner, or for any debt, obligation, or liability of the partnership for which the executor or administrator otherwise would be personally liable because the executor or administrator holds the general partnership interest, if the executor or administrator discloses that the general partnership interest is held by the executor or administrator in a fiduciary capacity. This immunity does not apply if an executor or administrator causes loss or injury to a person who is not a partner in the partnership by a wrongful act or omission. This immunity is not available to an executor or administrator who holds a general partnership interest in a fiduciary capacity if the spouse or any lineal descendants of the executor or administrator, or the executor or administrator other than in a fiduciary capacity, holds any interest in the partnership.

A partnership certificate that is filed pursuant to Chapter 1777. or another chapter of the Revised Code and that indicates that an executor or administrator holds a general partnership interest in a fiduciary capacity by the use following the name or signature of the executor or administrator of the words "executor under the will of (name of decedent)" or "administrator of the estate of (name of decedent)" or other words that indicate the executor's or administrator's fiduciary capacity constitutes a sufficient disclosure for purposes of this division.

If a partnership certificate is not required to be filed pursuant to Chapter 1777. or another chapter of the Revised Code, a sufficient disclosure for purposes of this division can be made by an executor or administrator if a certificate that satisfies the following requirements is filed with the recorder of the county in which the partnership's principal office or place of business is situated and with the recorder of each county in which the partnership owns real estate:

(a) The certificate shall state in full the names of all persons holding interests in the partnership and their places of residence;

(b) The certificate shall be signed by all persons who are general partners in the partnership, and shall be acknowledged by a person authorized to take acknowledgements of deeds;

(c) The certificate shall use the words "executor under the will of (name of decedent)" or "administrator of the estate of (name of decedent)" or other words that indicate the executor's or administrator's fiduciary capacity, following the name or signature of the executor or administrator.

A contract or other written instrument delivered to a party that contracts with the partnership in which an executor or administrator holds a general partnership interest in a fiduciary capacity, which indicates that the executor or administrator so holds the interest, constitutes a disclosure for purposes of this division with respect to transactions between the party and the partnership. If a disclosure has been made by a certificate in accordance with this division, a disclosure for purposes of this division with respect to such transactions exists regardless of whether a contract or other instrument indicates the executor or administrator holds the general partnership interest in a fiduciary capacity.

If an executor or administrator acquires, in a fiduciary capacity, a general partnership interest, the decedent's estate is liable for debts, obligations, or liabilities of the partnership.

(C) An estate that includes a general partnership interest is not liable for the debts, obligations, or liabilities of a partnership in which another estate has a general partnership interest, merely because the executor or administrator of the estates holds a general partnership interest in both of the partnerships in the executor's or administrator's fiduciary capacities.

(D) Divisions (B) and (C) of this section apply to general partnership interests held by executors or administrators in their fiduciary capacities prior to and on or after the effective date of this section. If an appropriate disclosure is made pursuant to division (B) of this section, the immunity acquired under that division extends only to debts, obligations, and liabilities of the partnership arising on and after the date of the disclosure and to debts, obligations, and liabilities of the partnership that arose prior to the acquisition of the general partnership interest by the executor or administrator becoming a general partner.

(2006 H 416, eff. 1–1–07)

Historical and Statutory Notes

Ed. Note: RC 5815.35 is former RC 1339.65, amended and recodified by 2006 H 416, eff. 1–1–07; 1989 S 46, eff. 1–1–90; 1983 H 288.

Amendment Note: 2006 H 416 rewrote this section. See *Baldwin's Ohio Legislative Service Annotated*, 2006, page 3/L–1879, or the OH–LEGIS or OH–LEGIS–OLD database on WESTLAW, for prior version of this section.

Cross References

Executors and administrators, Ch 2113

Laws applicable, status of existing contracts, 1775.03
Liability for false representation, 1775.15
Liability to partners for acts after dissolution, 1775.33
Probate court, Ch 2101
Records to be kept by county recorder, 317.08
Rights and powers of a general partner, 1782.24
Rules for determining rights and duties of partners, 1775.17
Uniform partnership law, liability for false representation, 1775.15
Uniform partnership law, liability of partners, 1775.14
Uniform partnership law, liability to partners for acts after dissolution, 1775.33
Uniform partnership law, rules for determining rights and duties of partners, 1775.17
Uniform partnership law, status of existing contracts when conflict between law of agency and RC 1339.65, 1775.03

Library References

Partnership ⚖170.
Trusts ⚖210.
Westlaw Topic Nos. 289, 390.
C.J.S. Partnership § 168.
C.J.S. Trusts §§ 381 to 382.

Baldwin's Ohio Legislative Service Annotated, 2006 H 416 LSC Analysis, p 3/L-1709

Law Review and Journal Commentaries

S 115 and H 288: Steps Toward Logic and Fairness in the Ohio Probate Law, Note. 10 U Dayton L Rev 213 (Fall 1984).

5815.36 Disclaimers of successions to property

(A) As used in this section:

(1) "Disclaimant" means any person, any guardian or personal representative of a person or estate of a person, or any attorney-in-fact or agent of a person having a general or specific authority to act granted in a written instrument, who is any of the following:

(a) With respect to testamentary instruments and intestate succession, an heir, next of kin, devisee, legatee, donee, person succeeding to a disclaimed interest, surviving joint tenant, surviving tenant by the entireties, surviving tenant of a tenancy with a right of survivorship, beneficiary under a testamentary instrument, or person designated to take pursuant to a power of appointment exercised by a testamentary instrument;

(b) With respect to nontestamentary instruments, a grantee, donee, person succeeding to a disclaimed interest, surviving joint tenant, surviving tenant by the entireties, surviving tenant of a tenancy with a right of survivorship, beneficiary under a nontestamentary instrument, or person designated to take pursuant to a power of appointment exercised by a nontestamentary instrument;

(c) With respect to fiduciary rights, privileges, powers, and immunities, a fiduciary under a testamentary or nontestamentary instrument. This section does not authorize a fiduciary to disclaim the rights of beneficiaries unless the instrument creating the fiduciary relationship authorizes such a disclaimer.

(d) Any person entitled to take an interest in property upon the death of a person or upon the occurrence of any other event.

(2) "Property" means all forms of property, real and personal, tangible and intangible.

(B)(1) A disclaimant, other than a fiduciary under an instrument who is not authorized by the instrument to disclaim the interest of a beneficiary, may disclaim, in whole or in part, the succession to any property by executing and by delivering, filing, or recording a written disclaimer instrument in the manner provided in this section.

(2) A disclaimant who is a fiduciary under an instrument may disclaim, in whole or in part, any right, power, privilege, or immunity, by executing and by delivering, filing, or recording a written disclaimer instrument in the manner provided in this section.

(3) The written instrument of disclaimer shall be signed and acknowledged by the disclaimant and shall contain all of the following:

(a) A reference to the donative instrument;

(b) A description of the property, part of property, or interest disclaimed, and of any fiduciary right, power, privilege, or immunity disclaimed;

(c) A declaration of the disclaimer and its extent.

(4) The guardian of the estate of a minor or an incompetent, or the personal representative of a deceased person, with the consent of the probate division of the court of common pleas, may disclaim, in whole or in part, the succession to any property, or interest in property, that the ward, if an adult and competent, or the deceased, if living, might have disclaimed. The guardian or personal representative, or any interested person may file an application with the probate division of the court of common pleas that has jurisdiction of the estate, asking that the court order the guardian or personal representative to execute and deliver, file, or record the disclaimer on behalf of the ward or estate. The court shall order the guardian or personal representative to execute and deliver, file, or record the disclaimer if the court finds, upon hearing after notice to interested parties and such other persons as the court shall direct, that:

(a) It is in the best interests of those interested in the estate of the person and of those who will take the disclaimed interest;

(b) It would not materially, adversely affect the minor or incompetent, or the beneficiaries of the estate of the decedent, taking into consideration other available resources and the age, probable life expectancy, physical and mental condition, and present and reasonably anticipated future needs of the minor or incompetent or the beneficiaries of the estate of the decedent.

A written instrument of disclaimer ordered by the court under this division shall be executed and be delivered, filed, or recorded within the time and in the manner in which the person could have disclaimed if the person were living, an adult, and competent.

(C) A partial disclaimer of property that is subject to a burdensome interest created by the donative instrument is not effective unless the disclaimed property constitutes a gift that is separate and distinct from undisclaimed gifts.

(D) The disclaimant shall deliver, file, or record the disclaimer, or cause the same to be done, not later than nine months after the latest of the following dates:

(1) The effective date of the donative instrument if both the taker and the taker's interest in the property are finally ascertained on that date;

(2) The date of the occurrence of the event upon which both the taker and the taker's interest in the property become finally ascertainable;

(3) The date on which the disclaimant attains twenty-one years of age or is no longer an incompetent, without tendering or repaying any benefit received while the disclaimant was under twenty-one years of age or an incompetent, and even if a guardian of a minor or incompetent had filed an application pursuant to division (B)(4) of this section and the probate division of the court of common pleas involved did not consent to the guardian executing a disclaimer.

(E) No disclaimer instrument is effective under this section if either of the following applies under the terms of the disclaimer instrument:

(1) The disclaimant has power to revoke the disclaimer.

(2) The disclaimant may transfer, or direct to be transferred, to self the entire legal and equitable ownership of the property subject to the disclaimer instrument.

(F)(1) Subject to division (F)(2) of this section, if the interest disclaimed is created by a nontestamentary instrument, the disclaimer instrument shall be delivered personally or by certified mail to the trustee or other person who has legal title to, or possession of, the property disclaimed.

(2) If the interest disclaimed is created by a testamentary instrument, by intestate succession, by a transfer on death deed pursuant to section 5302.22 of the Revised Code, or by a certificate of title to a motor vehicle, watercraft, or outboard motor that evidences ownership of the motor vehicle, watercraft, or outboard motor that is transferable on death pursuant to section 2131.13 of the Revised Code, the disclaimer instrument shall be filed in the probate division of the court of common pleas in the county in which proceedings for the administration of the decedent's estate have been commenced, and an executed copy of the disclaimer instrument shall be delivered personally or by certified mail to the personal representative of the decedent's estate.

(3) If no proceedings for the administration of the decedent's estate have been commenced, the disclaimer instrument shall be filed in the probate division of the court of common pleas in the county in which proceedings for the administration of the decedent's estate might be commenced according to law. The disclaimer instrument shall be filed and indexed, and fees charged, in the same manner as provided by law for an application to be appointed as personal representative to administer the decedent's estate. The disclaimer is effective whether or not proceedings thereafter are commenced to administer the decedent's estate. If proceedings thereafter are commenced for the administration of the decedent's estate, they shall be filed under, or consolidated with, the case number assigned to the disclaimer instrument.

(4) If an interest in real estate is disclaimed, an executed copy of the disclaimer instrument also shall be recorded in the office of the recorder of the county in which the real estate is located. The disclaimer instrument shall include a description of the real estate with sufficient certainty to identify it, and shall contain a reference to the record of the instrument that created the interest disclaimed. If title to the real estate is registered under Chapters 5309. and 5310. of the Revised Code, the disclaimer interest shall be entered as a memorial on the last certificate of title. A spouse of a disclaimant has no dower or other interest in the real estate disclaimed.

(G) Unless the donative instrument expressly provides that, if there is a disclaimer, there shall not be any acceleration of remainders or other interests, the property, part of property, or interest in property disclaimed, and any future interest that is to take effect in possession or enjoyment at or after the termination of the interest disclaimed, shall descend, be distributed, or otherwise be disposed of, and shall be accelerated, in the following manner:

(1) If intestate or testate succession is disclaimed, as if the disclaimant had predeceased the decedent;

(2) If the disclaimant is one designated to take pursuant to a power of appointment exercised by a testamentary instrument, as if the disclaimant had predeceased the donee of the power;

(3) If the donative instrument is a nontestamentary instrument, as if the disclaimant had died before the effective date of the nontestamentary instrument;

(4) If the disclaimer is of a fiduciary right, power, privilege, or immunity, as if the right, power, privilege, or immunity was never in the donative instrument.

(H) A disclaimer pursuant to this section is effective as of, and relates back for all purposes to, the date upon which the taker and the taker's interest have been finally ascertained.

(I) A disclaimant who has a present and future interest in property, and disclaims the disclaimant's present interest in whole or in part, is considered to have disclaimed the disclaimant's future interest to the same extent, unless a contrary intention appears in the disclaimer instrument or the donative instrument.

A disclaimant is not precluded from receiving, as an alternative taker, a beneficial interest in the property disclaimed, unless a contrary intention appears in the disclaimer instrument or in the donative instrument.

(J) The disclaimant's right to disclaim under this section is barred if, before the expiration of the period within which the disclaimant may disclaim the interest, the disclaimant does any of the following:

(1) Assigns, conveys, encumbers, pledges, or transfers, or contracts to assign, convey, encumber, pledge, or transfer, the property or any interest in it;

(2) Waives in writing the disclaimant's right to disclaim and executes and delivers, files, or records the waiver in the manner provided in this section for a disclaimer instrument;

(3) Accepts the property or an interest in it;

(4) Permits or suffers a sale or other disposition of the property pursuant to judicial action against the disclaimant.

(K) A fiduciary's application for appointment or assumption of duties as a fiduciary does not waive or bar the disclaimant's right to disclaim a right, power, privilege, or immunity.

(L) The right to disclaim under this section exists irrespective of any limitation on the interest of the disclaimant in the nature of a spendthrift provision or similar restriction.

(M) A disclaimer instrument or written waiver of the right to disclaim that has been executed and delivered, filed, or recorded as required by this section is final and binding upon all persons.

(N) The right to disclaim and the procedures for disclaimer established by this section are in addition to, and do not exclude or abridge, any other rights or procedures existing under any other section of the Revised Code or at common law to assign, convey, release, refuse to accept, renounce, waive, or disclaim property.

(O)(1) No person is liable for distributing or disposing of property in a manner inconsistent with the terms of a valid disclaimer if the distribution or disposition is otherwise proper and the person has no actual knowledge of the disclaimer.

(2) No person is liable for distributing or disposing of property in reliance upon the terms of a disclaimer that is invalid because the right of disclaimer has been waived or barred if the distribution or disposition is otherwise proper and the person has no actual knowledge of the facts that constitute a waiver or bar to the right to disclaim.

(P)(1) A disclaimant may disclaim pursuant to this section any interest in property that is in existence on September 27, 1976, if either the interest in the property or the taker of the interest in the property is not finally ascertained on that date.

(2) No disclaimer executed pursuant to this section destroys or diminishes an interest in property that exists on September 27, 1976, in any person other than the disclaimant.

(2006 H 416, eff. 1–1–07)

Uncodified Law

1998 H 701, § 3: See Uncodified Law under 5809.01.

Historical and Statutory Notes

Ed. Note: RC 5815.36 is former RC 1339.68, recodified by 2006 H 416, eff. 1–1–07; 2002 H 345, eff. 7–23–02; 2000 H 313, eff. 8–29–00; 1998 H 701, eff. 3–22–99.

Amendment Note: 2002 H 345 deleted "or" after "intestate succession" and inserted "or by a certificate of title to a motor vehicle, watercraft, or outboard motor that evidences ownership of the motor vehicle, watercraft, or outboard motor that is transferable on death pursuant to section 2131.13 of the Revised Code" in division (F)(2).

Amendment Note: 2000 H 313 inserted "Subject to division (F)(2) of this section, if" in division (F)(1); and deleted "or" after "testamentary instrument" and inserted "or by a transfer on death deed pursuant to section 5302.22 of the Revised Code," in division (F)(2).

Amendment Note: 1998 H 701 made changes to reflect gender neutral language.

Cross References

Executors and administrators; distribution; rejected claims, 2113.53
Fiduciaries, 2109.01
Guardians, 2111.01
Intestate succession, 2105.01
Parties to agreements, effect on creditor rights, 5801.10
Parties to agreements, effect on creditor rights, 5801.10
Powers of attorney, 1337.01
Probate court fees, 2101.16
Tenancy with right of survivorship, 5302.17, 5302.20
Wills, 2107.01

Library References

Wills ⇐717.
Westlaw Topic No. 409.
C.J.S. Wills §§ 1708 to 1710, 1713 to 1717.

Baldwin's Ohio Legislative Service Annotated, 2006 H 416 LSC Analysis, p 3/L-1709

Law Review and Journal Commentaries

Disclaimer Talk, Richard V. Wellman. 11 Prob L J Ohio 5 (September/October 2000).

New Uniform Act on Disclaimers Compared With Earlier Models and Ohio Legislation, Richard V. Wellman. 10 Prob L J Ohio 45 (March/April 2000).

Qualified Disclaimers of Joint Property in Ohio, M. Patricia Culler. 9 Prob L J Ohio 76 (May/June 1999).

Renunciation of Testamentary Benefit as Fraudulent Transfer, Note. 37 Case W Res L Rev 148 (1986–87).

Notes of Decisions

Ed. Note: This section contains annotations from former RC 1339.60, 1339.68, 2105.061, and 2113.60.

Acceleration of remainders 7
Age of disclaimant 6
Declaratory relief 4
Fraudulent conveyances 3
Joint tenancies 5
Judgments 2
Jurisdiction 1

---

1. Jurisdiction

The probate court has exclusive jurisdiction of an action to rescind a renunciation of intestate succession properly filed with it. Wolfrum v. Wolfrum (Ohio 1965) 2 Ohio St.2d 237, 208 N.E.2d 537, 31 O.O.2d 501. Courts ⇐ 472.4(2.1)

Cancellation by the probate court of a written renunciation of an interest in property through intestate succession is governed by general equitable procedures and principles, as in an equitable action for rescission or cancellation of a written instrument by reason of the mistake of the person executing the instrument. In re Wolfrum's Estate (Defiance 1963) 120 Ohio App. 379, 202 N.E.2d 631, 29 O.O.2d 244, reversed 2 Ohio St.2d 237, 208 N.E.2d 537, 31 O.O.2d 501. Descent And Distribution ⇐ 72

The probate court is without jurisdiction to cancel a written renunciation of interest in property through intestate succession where the court's jurisdiction is improperly invoked by the filing of a motion therefor. In re Wolfrum's Estate (Defiance 1963) 120 Ohio App. 379, 202 N.E.2d 631, 29 O.O.2d 244, reversed 2 Ohio St.2d 237, 208 N.E.2d 537, 31 O.O.2d 501.

2. Judgments

A determination of the disposition of a refused legacy under RC 2113.60 by a federal district court would not be binding on the probate court having jurisdiction over the administration of the estate. U.S. v. McCrackin (S.D.Ohio 1960) 189 F.Supp. 632, 85 Ohio Law Abs. 143.

3. Fraudulent conveyances

Where a will beneficiary seeks to disclaim an inheritance pursuant to RC 1339.60(B) with the actual intent to defraud a present or future creditor, the renunciation is a fraudulent conveyance under RC 1336.07. Stein v. Brown (Ohio 1985) 18 Ohio St.3d 305, 480 N.E.2d 1121, 18 O.B.R. 352. Fraudulent Conveyances ⇐ 64(1)

A debtor in bankruptcy is held unable to disclaim under RC 1339.60 an inheritance that will otherwise be used to pay his creditors, on the ground that the disclaimer would "defraud" the creditors and is thus a "conveyance made... with actual intent... to hinder, delay, or defraud creditors" in violation of RC 1336.07. In re Betz (Bkrtcy.N.D.Ohio 1987) 84 B.R. 470.

4. Declaratory relief

Parties desiring to determine their rights in the event they renounce legacies, and a surviving spouse desiring to determine her rights should she elect under the will of the decedent, may obtain declaratory relief. Abram v. Wilson (Ohio Prob. 1966) 8 Ohio Misc. 420, 220 N.E.2d 739, 37 O.O.2d 288, 37 O.O.2d 394.

5. Joint tenancies

Property held in joint tenancy with right of survivorship may be disclaimed by the survivor, whereupon such property will be subject to probate administration. In re Krakoff's Estate (Ohio Prob. 1961) 179 N.E.2d 566, 87 Ohio Law Abs. 387, 18 O.O.2d 116.

A renunciation by a surviving wife of her joint interest in bank accounts and stocks held jointly was ineffective where she had signed bank signature cards and indorsed dividend checks, and consequently where she purported to renounce so that two-thirds of the property passed to the children, a gift tax was properly imposed thereon. (See also 431 F(2d) 847, 31 Misc 252 (6th Cir Ohio 1970).) Krakoff v. U. S. (C.A.6 (Ohio) 1971) 439 F.2d 1023, 58 O.O.2d 381, 60 O.O.2d 417.

6. Age of disclaimant

Statute governing disclaimer of an interest in a trust did not require disclaimant to be at least 21 years old, and thus 18-year-old beneficiary could disclaim her interest in testamentary trust; statute simply required disclaimer to be filed by the latest of three dates, one of which was nine months after disclaimant attained 21 years of age, and beneficiary disclaimed her interest well before that date. In re Testamentary Trust of Flynn (Ohio App. 2 Dist., Montgomery, 08-05-2005) No. 20699, No. 20700, 2005-Ohio-4028, 2005 WL 1846520, Unreported. Trusts ⇐ 39

7. Acceleration of remainders

Trustee's failure to file motion to terminate testamentary trust did not preclude trial court from terminating trust after beneficiary disclaimed her interest in trust; statute governing termination of trust on motion by trustee was not the exclusive means of terminating trust, but rather trust could be terminated under doctrine of acceleration of remainders. In re Testamentary Trust of Flynn (Ohio App. 2 Dist., Montgomery, 08-05-2005) No. 20699, No. 20700, 2005-Ohio-4028, 2005 WL 1846520, Unreported. Trusts ⇐ 61(3)

CONSIGNMENT OF ART WORKS TO DEALERS

5815.41 Definitions

As used in sections 5815.41 to 5815.48 of the Revised Code:

(A) "Art dealer" means a person engaged in the business of selling works of art, other than a person exclusively engaged in the business of selling goods at public auction.

(B) "Artist" means the creator of a work of art.

(C) "On consignment" means delivered to an art dealer for the purpose of sale or exhibition, or both, to the public by the art dealer other than at a public auction.

(D) "Work of art" means an original art work that is any of the following:

(1) A visual rendition including, but not limited to, a painting, drawing, sculpture, mosaic, or photograph;

(2) A work of calligraphy;

(3) A work of graphic art, including, but not limited to, an etching, lithograph, offset print, or silk screen;

(4) A craft work in materials, including, but not limited to, clay, textile, fiber, wood, metal, plastic, or glass;

(5) A work in mixed media, including, but not limited to, a collage or a work consisting of any combination of the items listed in divisions (D)(1) to (4) of this section.

(2006 H 416, eff. 1–1–07)

Uncodified Law

1984 S 247, § 2: See *Baldwin's Ohio Revised Code Annotated*, Uncodified Law under 1339.72.

Historical and Statutory Notes

Ed. Note: RC 5815.41 is former RC 1339.71, amended and recodified by 2006 H 416, eff. 1–1–07; 1984 S 247, eff. 10–10–84.

Amendment Note: 2006 H 416 substituted "1339.71" with "5815.41" and "1339.78" with "5815.48".

Cross References

Auctions, 1318.01

Library References

Baldwin's Ohio Legislative Service Annotated, 2006 H 416 LSC Analysis, p 3/L-1709

Notes of Decisions

Ed. Note: This section contains annotations from former RC 1339.71.

Art dealer, defined 1

---

1. Art dealer, defined

Fact question as to whether zoo, which exhibited and sold artist's work, was "art dealer" under statute governing consignment of artworks to dealers precluded summary judgment in artist's strict liability action against zoo after sculpture was damaged. Eboigbe v. Zoological Soc. of Cincinnati (Ohio App. 1 Dist., 07-06-1994) 96 Ohio App.3d 102, 644 N.E.2d 693. Judgment ⇐ 181(15.1)

5815.42 Consignment by artist of his work of art to a dealer; effects; trust

If an art dealer accepts a work of art, on a fee, commission, or other compensation basis, on consignment from the artist who created the work of art, the following consequences attach:

(A) The art dealer is, with respect to that work of art, the agent of the artist.

(B) The work of art is trust property and the art dealer is a trustee for the benefit of the artist until the work of art is sold to a bona fide third party or returned to the artist.

(C) The proceeds of the sale of the work of art are trust property and the art dealer is a trustee for the benefit of the artist until the amount due the artist from the sale is paid.

(D) The art dealer is strictly liable for the loss of, or damage to, the work of art while it is in the art dealer's possession or control. The value of the work of art is, for the purpose of this division, the value established in the written contract between the artist and art dealer entered into pursuant to section 5815.45 of the Revised Code.

(2006 H 416, eff. 1–1–07)

Uncodified Law

1984 S 247, § 2, eff. 10–10–84, reads: Sections 1339.71 to 1339.78 of the Revised Code, as enacted by this act, apply only to a work of art accepted on consignment on or after the effective date of this act. If a work of art is accepted on consignment on or after the effective date of this act under a contract in existence prior to the effective date of this act, sections 1339.71 to 1339.78 of the Revised Code apply to the work of art, proceeds of sale, and art dealers only to the extent such sections do not conflict with an express provision of the contract.

Historical and Statutory Notes

Ed. Note: RC 5815.42 is former RC 1339.72, amended and recodified by 2006 H 416, eff. 1–1–07; 1984 S 247, eff. 10–10–84.

Amendment Note: 2006 H 416 substituted "1339.75" with "5815.45".

Library References

Factors ⇐ 1 to 66.
Guardian and Ward ⇐ 6.
Westlaw Topic Nos. 167, 196.
C.J.S. Agriculture §§ 163 to 174, 176 to 178.
Baldwin's Ohio Legislative Service Annotated, 2006 H 416 LSC Analysis, p 3/L-1709

Notes of Decisions

Ed. Note: This section contains annotations from former RC 1339.72.

Contract price, damages 1
Damages 1, 2
    Contract price 1
    Fair market value, determination 2
Fair market value, determination, Damages 2

---

1. Damages—Contract price

In action brought by artist, whose sculpture was damaged while being exhibited by zoo, for breach of contract, negligence and strict liability, trial court's failure to rule on contract claim was improper, where contract claim represented alternative theory of recovery of potentially higher amount than sculpture's fair market value, which was awarded under strict liability claim. Eboigbe v. Zoological Soc. of Cincinnati (Ohio App. 1 Dist., 07-06-1994) 96 Ohio App.3d 102, 644 N.E.2d 693. Trial ⇐ 397(1)

2. —— Fair market value, determination, Damages

Trial court's determination as to fair market value of wooden sculpture, which was damaged while being exhibited at zoo, was based upon sufficient evidence; although artist had not received offer to buy sculpture, there was substantial evidence that there was market for artist's artwork, and in determining fair market value, court was free to consider insurance figures, artist's asking and selling price, sales of lesser pieces, artist's reputation in art world and expert opinions. Eboigbe v. Zoological Soc. of Cincinnati (Ohio App. 1 Dist., 07-06-1994) 96 Ohio App.3d 102, 644 N.E.2d 693. Damages ⇐ 188(2)

5815.43 Continuation of trust after purchase by dealer for own account

(A) If a work of art is trust property under section 5815.42 of the Revised Code when it is initially received by the art dealer, it remains trust property, notwithstanding the subsequent purchase of the work of art by the art dealer directly or indirectly for the art dealer's own account, until the purchase price specified pursuant to division (A)(3) of section 5815.45 of the Revised Code is paid in full to the artist.

(B) If an art dealer resells a work of art that the art dealer purchased for the art dealer's own account to a bona fide third party before the artist has been paid in full, the work of art ceases to be trust property and the proceeds of the resale are trust funds in the possession or control of the art dealer for the benefit of the artist to the extent necessary to pay any balance still due to the artist. The trusteeship of the proceeds continues until the artist is paid in full under the contract entered into pursuant to section 5815.45 of the Revised Code.

(2006 H 416, eff. 1–1–07)

Uncodified Law

1984 S 247, § 2: See *Baldwin's Ohio Revised Code Annotated*, Uncodified Law under 1339.72.

Historical and Statutory Notes

Ed. Note: RC 5815.43 is former RC 1339.73, amended and recodified by 2006 H 416, eff. 1–1–07; 1984 S 247, eff. 10–10–84.

Amendment Note: 2006 H 416 substituted "1339.72" with "5815.42", "1339.75" with "5815.45", and made changes to reflect gender neutral language.

Library References

Factors ⇔1 to 66.
Westlaw Topic No. 167.
C.J.S. Agriculture §§ 163 to 174, 176 to 178.
Baldwin's Ohio Legislative Service Annotated, 2006 H 416 LSC Analysis, p 3/L-1709

5815.44 Not subject to claims of dealer's creditors

A work of art that is trust property under section 5815.42 or 5815.43 of the Revised Code is not subject to the claims, liens, or security interests of the creditors of the art dealer, notwithstanding Chapters 1301. to 1310. of the Revised Code.

(2006 H 416, eff. 1–1–07)

Uncodified Law

1984 S 247, § 2: See *Baldwin's Ohio Revised Code Annotated*, Uncodified Law under 1339.72.

Historical and Statutory Notes

Ed. Note: RC 5815.44 is former RC 1339.74, amended and recodified by 2006 H 416, eff. 1–1–07; 1992 H 693, eff. 11–6–92; 1984 S 247.

Amendment Note: 2006 H 416 substituted "1339.72" with "5815.42" and "1339.73" with "5815.43".

Library References

Factors ⇔1 to 66.
Westlaw Topic No. 167.
C.J.S. Agriculture §§ 163 to 174, 176 to 178.
Baldwin's Ohio Legislative Service Annotated, 2006 H 416 LSC Analysis, p 3/L-1709

5815.45 Written contract required of dealer

(A) An art dealer shall not accept a work of art, on a fee, commission, or other compensation basis, on consignment from the artist who created the work of art unless, prior to or at the time of acceptance, the art dealer enters into a written contract with the artist that contains all of the following:

(1) The value of the work of art and whether it may be sold;

(2) The time within which the proceeds of the sale are to be paid to the artist, if the work of art is sold;

(3) The minimum price for the sale of the work of art;

(4) The fee or percentage of the sale price that is to be paid to the art dealer for displaying or selling the work of art.

(B) If an art dealer violates this section, a court, at the request of the artist, may void the obligation of the artist to that art dealer or to a person to whom the obligation is transferred, other than a holder in due course.

(2006 H 416, eff. 1–1–07)

Uncodified Law

1984 S 247, § 2: See *Baldwin's Ohio Revised Code Annotated*, Uncodified Law under 1339.72.

Historical and Statutory Notes

Ed. Note: RC 5815.45 is former RC 1339.75, recodified by 2006 H 416, eff. 1–1–07; 1984 S 247, eff. 10–10–84.

Library References

Factors ⇔1 to 66.
Westlaw Topic No. 167.
C.J.S. Agriculture §§ 163 to 174, 176 to 178.
Baldwin's Ohio Legislative Service Annotated, 2006 H 416 LSC Analysis, p 3/L-1709

5815.46 Display requires consent of artist and notice to viewers as to artist's identity

An art dealer who accepts a work of art, on a fee, commission, or other compensation basis, on consignment from the artist who created the work of art shall not use or display the work of art or a photograph of the work of art, or permit the use or display of the work of art or a photograph of the work of art, unless both of the following occur:

(A) Notice is given to users or viewers that the work of art is the work of the artist;

(B) The artist gives prior written consent to the particular use or display.

(2006 H 416, eff. 1–1–07)

Uncodified Law

1984 S 247, § 2: See *Baldwin's Ohio Revised Code Annotated*, Uncodified Law under 1339.72.

Historical and Statutory Notes

Ed. Note: RC 5815.46 is former RC 1339.76, amended and recodified by 2006 H 416, eff. 1–1–07; 1984 S 247, eff. 10–10–84.

Amendment Note: 2006 H 416 redesignated divisions (1) and (2) as divisions (A) and (B).

Library References

Copyrights and Intellectual Property ⇔50.1(1).
Factors ⇔1 to 66.
Westlaw Topic Nos. 167, 99.
C.J.S. Agriculture §§ 163 to 174, 176 to 178.
C.J.S. Copyrights and Intellectual Property §§ 35, 95.
Baldwin's Ohio Legislative Service Annotated, 2006 H 416 LSC Analysis, p 3/L-1709

5815.47 Waiver of statutory provisions void

Any portion of an agreement that waives any provision of sections 5815.41 to 5815.48 of the Revised Code is void.

(2006 H 416, eff. 1–1–07)

Uncodified Law

1984 S 247, § 2: See *Baldwin's Ohio Revised Code Annotated*, Uncodified Law under 1339.72.

Historical and Statutory Notes

Ed. Note: RC 5815.47 is former RC 1339.77, amended and recodified by 2006 H 416, eff. 1–1–07; 1984 S 247, eff. 10–10–84.

Amendment Note: 2006 H 416 substituted "1339.71" with "5815.41" and "1339.78" with "5815.48".

Library References

Factors ⚖1 to 66.
Westlaw Topic No. 167.
C.J.S. Agriculture §§ 163 to 174, 176 to 178.
Baldwin's Ohio Legislative Service Annotated, 2006 H 416 LSC Analysis, p 3/L-1709

5815.48 Special damages for certain violations by dealer

Any art dealer who violates section 5815.45 or 5815.46 of the Revised Code is liable to the artist for the artist's reasonable attorney's fees and in an amount equal to the greater of either of the following:

(A) Fifty dollars;

(B) The actual damages, if any, including the incidental and consequential damages, sustained by the artist by reason of the violation.

(2006 H 416, eff. 1–1–07)

Uncodified Law

1984 S 247, § 2: See *Baldwin's Ohio Revised Code Annotated*, Uncodified Law under 1339.72.

Historical and Statutory Notes

Ed. Note: RC 5815.48 is former RC 1339.78, amended and recodified by 2006 H 416, eff. 1–1–07; 1984 S 247, eff. 10–10–84.

Amendment Note: 2006 H 416 substituted "1339.75" with "5815.45", "1339.76" with "5815.46", and made a change to reflect gender neutral language.

Cross References

Reasonable attorney fees; determination, DR 2–106

Library References

Copyrights and Intellectual Property ⚖90(2).
Factors ⚖1 to 66.
Westlaw Topic Nos. 167, 99.
C.J.S. Agriculture §§ 163 to 174, 176 to 178.
C.J.S. Copyrights and Intellectual Property §§ 79, 82, 98.
Baldwin's Ohio Legislative Service Annotated, 2006 H 416 LSC Analysis, p 3/L-1709

OHIO COURT RULES

Complete to February 1, 2007

RULES OF JUVENILE PROCEDURE
RULES OF SUPERINTENDENCE FOR THE COURTS OF OHIO

RULES OF JUVENILE PROCEDURE

Research Note

Consult Giannelli and Yeomans, *Ohio Juvenile Law,* for analysis, commentary, and annotations concerning Ohio juvenile law.

Use Westlaw® to find cases citing or applying specific rules. Westlaw may also be used to search for specific terms in court rules or to update court rules. See the OH–RULES and OH–ORDERS Scope Screens for detailed descriptive information and search tips.

Amendments to these rules are published, as received, in the advance sheets for Ohio Official Reports, North Eastern Reporter 2d and Ohio Cases, and in Baldwin's Ohio Legislative Service Annotated.

Publisher's Note: These Rules are published as they appear in the *Ohio Official Reports*.

Publisher's Note: Until 1968, when the Modern Courts Amendment to the Ohio Constitution was adopted, Ohio court procedure was governed entirely by statute and case law. The Modern Courts Amendment required the Supreme Court of Ohio, subject to the approval of the General Assembly, to "prescribe rules governing practice and procedure in all courts of the state." Rules of practice and procedure are the Civil, Criminal, Appellate, and Juvenile Rules, Rules of the Court of Claims, and the Ohio Rules of Evidence. Pursuant to Ohio Constitution Article IV, Section 5(B), such rules "shall not abridge, enlarge, or modify any substantive right," and " [a]ll laws in conflict with such rules shall be of no further force or effect."

Publisher's Note: The Supreme Court Rules Advisory Committee prepared Staff Notes for each of the substantive rule amendments. The Staff Note follows the applicable rule. Although the Supreme Court used the Staff Notes as background for its deliberations, the Staff Notes are not adopted by the Court and are not a part of the rule. Where they interpret the law, describe present conditions, or predict future practices, the Staff Notes represent the views of the Rules Advisory Committee and not necessarily the views of the Supreme Court. Each staff note should be read in light of the language of the rule at the time of its adoption or amendment.

Publisher's Note: Editor's Comments follow applicable rules and each should be read in light of the language of the rule at the time of its adoption.

Rule

1. Scope of rules: applicability; construction; exceptions
2. Definitions
3. Waiver of rights
4. Assistance of counsel; guardian ad litem
5. [Reserved]
6. Taking into custody
7. Detention and shelter care
8. Filing by electronic means
9. Intake
10. Complaint
11. Transfer to another county
12. [Reserved]
13. Temporary disposition; temporary orders; emergency medical and surgical treatment
14. Termination, extension or modification of temporary custody orders
15. Process: issuance, form
16. Process: service
17. Subpoena
18. Time
19. Motions
20. Service and filing of papers when required subsequent to filing of complaint
21. Preliminary conferences
22. Pleadings and motions; defenses and objections
23. Continuance
24. Discovery

Rule

25. Depositions
26. [Reserved]
27. Hearings: general
28. [Reserved]
29. Adjudicatory hearing
30. Relinquishment of jurisdiction for purposes of criminal prosecution
31. [Reserved]
32. Social history; physical examination; mental examination; investigation involving the allocation of parental rights and responsibilities for the care of children
33. [Reserved]
34. Dispositional hearing
35. Proceedings after judgment
36. Dispositional review
37. Recording of proceedings
38. Voluntary surrender of custody
39. Out of county removal hearings
40. Magistrates
41. [Reserved]
42. Consent to marry
43. Reference to Ohio Revised Code
44. Jurisdiction unaffected
45. Rules by juvenile courts; procedure not otherwise specified
46. Forms
47. Effective date
48. Title

Cross References

Cuyahoga county juvenile court, jurisdiction, 2153.16
Humane societies, protection of children, 1717.14
Judges of the court of domestic relations, juvenile court responsibility, 2301.03
Trial, magistrate courts, applicability of chapter, 2938.02
Youth commission, commitment of children, assignment to juvenile diagnostic center, 5139.05

Law Review and Journal Commentaries

An Answer to the Challenge of Kent, Daniels W. McLean. 53 A B A J 456 (May 1967).

Evidence in Cuyahoga County Juvenile Court, Elaine J. Columbro. 10 Clev–Marshall L Rev 524 (September 1961).

In re Gault, Juvenile Courts and Lawyers, Norman Lefstein. 53 A B A J 811 (September 1967).

The Juvenile Court—A Court of Law, Walter G. Whitlatch. 18 W Reserve U L Rev 1239 (May 1967).

The Juvenile Court: Effective Justice or Benevolent Despotism?, Bertram Polow. 53 A B A J 31 (January 1967).

Juvenile Court: "Neglected Child" of the Judiciary, Hon. Albert A. Woldman. 37 Clev B J 257 (September 1966).

Juvenile Court: Time for Change, Charles Auerbach. 37 Clev B J 179 (June 1966).

The Kent Case and the Juvenile Court: A Challenge to Lawyers, Robert Gardner. 52 A B A J 923 (October 1966).

A legal look at Juvenile Court, Paul W. Alexander. 27 Clev B J 171 (August 1956).

Rights of Children: The Legal Vacuum, Lois G. Forer. 55 A B A J 1151 (December 1969).

Role of the Attorney in Juvenile Court, Julian Greenspun. 18 Clev St L Rev 599 (September 1969).

Rules of the Juvenile Court of Cuyahoga County. Vol 33 Cuyahoga County B Ass'n Bull, No. 8.

A synopsis of Ohio Juvenile Court Law, Hon. Don J. Young, Jr. 31 U Cin L Rev 131 (Spring 1962).

A Way Out of Juvenile Delinquency, Roman C. Pucinski. 54 A B A J 33 (January 1968).

Juv R 1 Scope of rules: applicability; construction; exceptions

(A) Applicability

These rules prescribe the procedure to be followed in all juvenile courts of this state in all proceedings coming within the jurisdiction of such courts, with the exceptions stated in subdivision (C).

(B) Construction

These rules shall be liberally interpreted and construed so as to effectuate the following purposes:

(1) to effect the just determination of every juvenile court proceeding by ensuring the parties a fair hearing and the recognition and enforcement of their constitutional and other legal rights;

(2) to secure simplicity and uniformity in procedure, fairness in administration, and the elimination of unjustifiable expense and delay;

(3) to provide for the care, protection, and mental and physical development of children subject to the jurisdiction of the juvenile court, and to protect the welfare of the community; and

(4) to protect the public interest by treating children as persons in need of supervision, care and rehabilitation.

(C) Exceptions

These rules shall not apply to procedure (1) Upon appeal to review any judgment, order, or ruling; (2) Upon the trial of criminal actions; (3) Upon the trial of actions for divorce, annulment, legal separation, and related proceedings; (4) In proceedings to determine parent-child relationships, provided, however that appointment of counsel shall be in accordance with Rule 4(A) of the Rules of Juvenile Procedure; (5) In the commitment of the mentally ill and mentally retarded; (6) In proceedings under section 2151.85 of the Revised Code to the extent that there is a conflict between these rules and section 2151.85 of the Revised Code.

When any statute provides for procedure by general or specific reference to the statutes governing procedure in juvenile court actions, procedure shall be in accordance with these rules.

(Adopted eff. 7–1–72; amended eff. 7–1–91, 7–1–94, 7–1–95)

Historical and Statutory Notes

Amendment Note: The 7–1–95 amendment deleted "(4)" after "Rule 4(A)" in the first paragraph in division (C).

Amendment Note: The 7–1–94 amendment consolidated the first paragraph of division (C) and divisions (C)(1) through (C)(6) into a single paragraph; and inserted ", and related proceedings" and substituted "parent-child relationships, provided, however that appointment of counsel shall be in accordance with Rule 4(A)(4) of the Rules of Juvenile Procedure" for "the paternity of any child born out of wedlock" in the first paragraph of division (C).

Staff Notes

1995:

Rule 1(C) Exceptions

The amendment effective July 1, 1994 contained an error that is corrected by this revision. The 1994 amendment erroneously referred to division (A)(4) of Rule 4, when no division (A)(4) exists.

1994:

Rule 1(C) Exceptions

Juv. R. 1(C)(4) now reflects current terminology used in Revised Code Sections 3111.01 through 3111.19 regarding the establishment of the parent and child relationship. Additionally, the division clarifies that Juv. R. 4(A)(4), regarding appointment of counsel for certain parties, now applies in actions to establish the parent and child relationship.

Editor's Comment

Applicability   1
Construction   2
Exceptions   3

1. Applicability

Juv R 1(A) follows the format of both Civ R 1(A) and Crim R 1(A) and prescribes the procedure to be followed by all juvenile courts of Ohio and those exercising juvenile jurisdiction in all proceedings within their jurisdiction except those exceptions stated in Juv R 1(C). There are eight courts in Ohio exercising exclusively juvenile jurisdiction. These are the Butler, Cuyahoga, Hamilton, Lake, Lucas, Mahoning, Montgomery, and Summit county courts, which are now juvenile court divisions of their respective common pleas courts. Juvenile jurisdiction in all other counties in Ohio is exercised either by the probate division or the domestic relations division of the court of common pleas.

2. Construction

Juv R 1(B) restates the purposes of the Juvenile Court Act, Ch 2151, and follows the language used in 2151.01. Juv R 1(B)(1) adopts the language of 2151.01(D); Juv R 1(B)(2) follows the general format of Crim R 1(B) and Civ R 1(B) and clearly outlines the thrust of the rules to secure simplicity and uniformity, fairness in administration and the elimination of unjustifiable expense and delay. Juv R 1(B)(3) adopts the language of 2151.01(A) with the added phrase "to protect the welfare of the community". Juv R 1(B)(4) is a rephrasing of 2151.01(B) in that the language "removing the consequences of criminal behavior and the taint of criminality from children committing delinquent acts and to substitute therefor a program" has been deleted so as to make it clear that juvenile proceedings are not criminal actions. The language of 2151.01(C) has been deleted as being superfluous as the best interest of the child still permeates the entire juvenile proceeding with the protection of the community also a major consideration.

3. Exceptions

The Rules of Juvenile Procedure are clearly applicable to all juvenile proceedings except as stated herein to appeals which are governed by the Appellate Rules; criminal actions within the jurisdiction of juvenile courts pursuant to 2151.23(A)(5) and 2151.23(B)(1) which are governed by the Criminal Rules; divorce, annulment and alimony actions which are governed by Ch 3105 and the Civil Rules; paternity actions pursuant to 2151.23(B)(2) which are governed by the provisions of Ch 3111 and the Civil Rules, except that the appointment of counsel shall be in accordance with Juv R 4(A); and commitment proceedings regarding the mentally ill or mentally retarded which are governed by the provisions of Ch 5122 and 5125. In addition, proceedings under 2151.85 (minor female's complaint for abortion) are excepted from the applicability of the Rules of Juvenile Procedure to the extent that there is a conflict between the rules and the statute. For instance, a conflict exists between Juv R 15(A) and 2151.85(D) with respect to service of summons on a child's parents. As a result of Juv R 1(C)(6), the statute would control the issue.

Juv R 1(C) like Crim R 1(C) and Civ R 1(C) is both a rule of exclusion and a rule of inclusion. The rule states the general exclusions from applicability but also by stating "When any statute provides for procedure by general or specific reference to the statutes governing procedure in juvenile court actions such procedure shall be in accordance with these rules" it becomes a rule of inclusion. The Juvenile Rules apply not only because of this proviso but also because O Const Art IV, § 5(B) states "all laws in conflict with such rules shall be of no further force or effect after such rules have taken effect".

Juv R 1(C) makes it clear that when jurisdiction is transferred to the juvenile court by any other court pursuant to 2111.46, 3107.14, 3109.04 or 3109.06, these Rules of Juvenile Procedure apply.

Cross References

Powers and duties of supreme court, administrative director, rules, O Const Art IV §5
Rules of Criminal Procedure, application to juvenile proceedings limited, Crim R 1

Library References

Infants ⬥68.1, 68.2, 132, 191.
Westlaw Topic No. 211.
C.J.S. Infants §§ 32, 41 to 54, 95, 198, 199.

Research References

Encyclopedias

OH Jur. 3d Family Law § 1533, Construction.
OH Jur. 3d Family Law § 1655, Right to Attend; Public or Private Hearing.

Treatises and Practice Aids

Klein, Darling, & Terez, Baldwin's Ohio Practice Civil Practice § 1:25, Civ. R. 1(C)(1): Upon Appeal to Review Any Judgment, Order, or Ruling--Appeals in Supreme Court--Role of Supreme Court Rules of Practice.

Klein, Darling, & Terez, Baldwin's Ohio Practice Civil Practice § 24:2, Applicability of Civ. R. 24.

Giannelli and Snyder, Baldwin's Ohio Practice, Evidence, R 101, Scope of Rules: Applicability; Privileges; Exceptions.

Giannelli and Snyder, Baldwin's Ohio Practice, Evidence, § 102.3, History of Rule.

Carlin, Baldwin's Ohio Practice, Merrick-Rippner Probate Law § 104:3, Juvenile Court—Purpose and Function.

Carlin, Baldwin's Ohio Practice, Merrick-Rippner Probate Law § 106:4, Juvenile Court Jurisdiction—Delinquent Child—Non-Criminal Nature of Delinquency Proceedings.

Carlin, Baldwin's Ohio Practice, Merrick-Rippner Probate Law § 107:1, Intake.

Carlin, Baldwin's Ohio Practice, Merrick-Rippner Probate Law § 108:4, Juvenile Court—Criminal Jurisdiction—Applicability of Rules of Criminal Procedure.

Carlin, Baldwin's Ohio Practice, Merrick-Rippner Probate Law § 106:21, Juvenile Court Jurisdiction—Consent for Abortion—Minor Female's Complaint for Abortion.

Carlin, Baldwin's Ohio Practice, Merrick-Rippner Probate Law § 107:50, Adjudicatory Hearings—Applicability of Rules of Court.

Carlin, Baldwin's Ohio Practice, Merrick-Rippner Probate Law § 107:84, Disposition of Delinquent Children—Prior to January 1, 2002.

Giannelli & Yeomans, Ohio Juvenile Law § 1:8, Rules of Juvenile Procedure.

Giannelli & Yeomans, Ohio Juvenile Law § 12:6, Summons.

Giannelli & Yeomans, Ohio Juvenile Law § 15:3, Diversion, Youth Services Grant.

Giannelli & Yeomans, Ohio Juvenile Law § 32:3, Responsibilities to Victims and Others.

Giannelli & Yeomans, Ohio Juvenile Law § 34:5, Notice of Appeal.

Law Review and Journal Commentaries

Juvenile Delinquency, Hon. Richard L. Davis. (Ed. note: Observations from twenty-two years on the bench concerning the decline of family values as delinquency's cause.) 14 Ohio N U L Rev 195 (1987).

Notes of Decisions

Authority of judges 6
Constitutional issues 1
Exceptions 2
Jurisdiction 5
Liberal construction 4
Rules, applicability 3

---

1. Constitutional issues

A juvenile's Fifth and Sixth Amendment rights are the same as if she were an adult. In re M.H. (Ohio Com.Pl., 10-03-2003) 129 Ohio Misc.2d 5, 814 N.E.2d 1264, 2003-Ohio-7371. Infants ⬥ 174; Infants ⬥ 205; Infants ⬥ 207

A juvenile's right to be free from unreasonable search and seizure by law enforcement officers is the same as if she were an adult. In re M.H. (Ohio Com.Pl., 10-03-2003) 129 Ohio Misc.2d 5, 814 N.E.2d 1264, 2003-Ohio-7371. Searches And Seizures ⬥ 25.1

Traditional interests of confidentiality and rehabilitation prevent the public from having a qualified constitutional right of access to juvenile delinquency proceedings. State ex rel. Plain Dealer Publishing Co. v. Geauga Cty. Court of Common Pleas, Juv. Div. (Ohio, 08-11-2000) 90 Ohio St.3d 79, 734 N.E.2d 1214, 2000-Ohio-35. Constitutional Law ⬥ 90.1(3); Constitutional Law ⬥ 328

News media did not have qualified constitutional right of access to delinquency proceedings involving juvenile charged in connection with murder and robbery, including proceedings on motion to transfer case to adult court. State ex rel. Plain Dealer Publishing Co. v. Geauga Cty. Court of Common Pleas, Juv. Div. (Ohio, 08-11-2000) 90 Ohio St.3d 79, 734 N.E.2d 1214, 2000-Ohio-35. Constitutional Law ⬥ 90.1(3); Constitutional Law ⬥ 328; Infants ⬥ 203

When, in an adjudicatory hearing held pursuant to Juv R 29, the only evidence of guilt utilized by the court is testimony presented at the preliminary hearing, where the accused exercised adequate rights of cross-examination, he is denied no constitutional right. Matter of Gantt (Wood 1978) 61 Ohio App.2d 44, 398 N.E.2d 800, 15 O.O.3d 67.

2. Exceptions

Although a parentage action brought by a natural mother takes place in a juvenile division of the common pleas court, the civil rules apply rather than the juvenile rules; thus, a motion for judgment on the pleadings under Civ R 12(C) is permissible in a parentage action. Nelson v. Pleasant (Lawrence 1991) 73 Ohio App.3d 479, 597 N.E.2d 1137.

3. Rules, applicability

Juvenile was not entitled to acquittal in delinquency proceedings pursuant to rule of criminal procedure, because rules of criminal procedure did not apply to juvenile proceeding. In re Barchet (Ohio App. 3 Dist., Hancock, 10-09-2002) No. 5-02-27, No. 5-02-30, No. 5-02-28, No. 5-02-31, No. 5-02-29, No. 5-02-32, 2002-Ohio-5420, 2002 WL 31255290, Unreported. Infants ⬥ 195

A hearing on a complaint for permanent custody must be bifurcated according to Juv R 29 and 34 into separate adjudicatory and dispositional hearings, notwithstanding the contrary provisions of RC 2151.414, since Juv R 1(A) provides that all proceedings in a juvenile court are governed by the Rules of Juvenile Procedure. In re Vickers Children (Butler 1983) 14 Ohio App.3d 201, 470 N.E.2d 438, 14 O.B.R. 228.

4. Liberal construction

The juvenile statutes are designed primarily for the protection of dependent and reformation of delinquent children and must be given a liberal construction. (Annotation from former RC 2151.05.) In re Decker (Ohio Juv. 1930) 28 Ohio N.P.(N.S.) 433.

5. Jurisdiction

The juvenile and general divisions of a court of common pleas possess concurrent jurisdiction over a juvenile accused of a crime, and the juvenile division has not been divested of personal jurisdiction over one whose disposition is returned to it after the accused initially waived his right to be judged in that tribunal. State ex rel. Leis v. Black (Hamilton 1975) 45 Ohio App.2d 191, 341 N.E.2d 853, 74 O.O.2d 270. Infants ⬥ 68.5

6. Authority of judges

Mother's claim on appeal that trial court erred in determining child support when it failed to complete a child support computation worksheet was not waived by her failure to provide juvenile court with a transcript of the proceedings before magistrate which set father's child support obligation; issue was purely legal, the resolution of which did not require a review of the hearing transcript. Estes v. Smith (Ohio App. 12 Dist., Butler, 10-07-2002) No. CA2001-09-206, 2002-Ohio-5448, 2002 WL 31255745, Unreported. Child Support ⬥ 542

A juvenile judge has no authority to commit the trial of a criminal charge against an adult to a referee, and any proceedings so committed are null and void. State v. Eddington (Marion 1976) 52 Ohio App.2d 312, 369 N.E.2d 1054, 6 O.O.3d 317. Criminal Law ⬥ 254.1

Juv R 2 Definitions

As used in these rules:

(A) "Abused child" has the same meaning as in section 2151.031 of the Revised Code.

(B) "Adjudicatory hearing" means a hearing to determine whether a child is a juvenile traffic offender, delinquent, unruly, abused, neglected, or dependent or otherwise within the jurisdiction of the court.

(C) "Agreement for temporary custody" means a voluntary agreement that is authorized by section 5103.15 of the Revised Code and transfers the temporary custody of a child to a public children services agency or a private child placing agency.

(D) "Child" has the same meaning as in sections 2151.011 and 2152.02 of the Revised Code.

(E) "Chronic truant" has the same meaning as in section 2151.011 of the Revised Code.

(F) "Complaint" means the legal document that sets forth the allegations that form the basis for juvenile court jurisdiction.

(G) "Court proceeding" means all action taken by a court from the earlier of (1) the time a complaint is filed and (2) the time a person first appears before an officer of a juvenile court until the court relinquishes jurisdiction over such child.

(H) "Custodian" means a person who has legal custody of a child or a public children's services agency or private child-placing agency that has permanent, temporary, or legal custody of a child.

(I) "Delinquent child" has the same meaning as in section 2152.02 of the Revised Code.

(J) "Dependent child" has the same meaning as in section 2151.04 of the Revised Code.

(K) "Detention" means the temporary care of children in restricted facilities pending court adjudication or disposition.

(L) "Detention hearing" means a hearing to determine whether a child shall be held in detention or shelter care prior to or pending execution of a final dispositional order.

(M) "Dispositional hearing" means a hearing to determine what action shall be taken concerning a child who is within the jurisdiction of the court.

(N) "Guardian" means a person, association, or corporation that is granted authority by a probate court pursuant to Chapter 2111 of the Revised Code to exercise parental rights over a child to the extent provided in the court's order and subject to the residual parental rights of the child's parents.

(O) "Guardian ad litem" means a person appointed to protect the interests of a party in a juvenile court proceeding.

(P) "Habitual truant" has the same meaning as in section 2151.011 of the Revised Code.

(Q) "Hearing" means any portion of a juvenile court proceeding before the court, whether summary in nature or by examination of witnesses.

(R) "Indigent person" means a person who, at the time need is determined, is unable by reason of lack of property or income to provide for full payment of legal counsel and all other necessary expenses of representation.

(S) "Juvenile court" means a division of the court of common pleas, or a juvenile court separately and independently created, that has jurisdiction under Chapters 2151 and 2152 of the Revised Code.

(T) "Juvenile judge" means a judge of a court having jurisdiction under Chapters 2151 and 2152 of the Revised Code.

(U) "Juvenile traffic offender" has the same meaning as in section 2151.021 of the Revised Code.

(V) "Legal custody" means a legal status that vests in the custodian the right to have physical care and control of the child and to determine where and with whom the child shall live, and the right and duty to protect, train, and discipline the child and provide the child with food, shelter, education, and medical care, all subject to any residual parental rights, privileges, and responsibilities. An individual granted legal custody shall exercise the rights and responsibilities personally unless otherwise authorized by any section of the Revised Code or by the court.

(W) "Mental examination" means an examination by a psychiatrist or psychologist.

(X) "Neglected child" has the same meaning as in section 2151.03 of the Revised Code.

(Y) "Party" means a child who is the subject of a juvenile court proceeding, the child's spouse, if any, the child's parent or parents, or if the parent of a child is a child, the parent of that parent, in appropriate cases, the child's custodian, guardian, or guardian ad litem, the state, and any other person specifically designated by the court.

(Z) "Permanent custody" means a legal status that vests in a public children's services agency or a private child-placing agency, all parental rights, duties, and obligations, including the right to consent to adoption, and divests the natural parents or adoptive parents of any and all parental rights, privileges, and obligations, including all residual rights and obligations.

(AA) "Permanent surrender" means the act of the parents or, if a child has only one parent, of the parent of a child, by a voluntary agreement authorized by section 5103.15 of the Revised Code, to transfer the permanent custody of the child to a public children's services agency or a private child-placing agency.

(BB) "Person" includes an individual, association, corporation, or partnership and the state or any of its political subdivisions, departments, or agencies.

(CC) "Physical examination" means an examination by a physician.

(DD) "Planned permanent living arrangement" means an order of a juvenile court pursuant to which both of the following apply:

(1) The court gives legal custody of a child to a public children's services agency or a private child-placing agency without the termination of parental rights;

(2) The order permits the agency to make an appropriate placement of the child and to enter into a written planned permanent living arrangement agreement with a foster care provider or with another person or agency with whom the child is placed.

(EE) "Private child-placing agency" means any association, as defined in section 5103.02 of the Revised Code that is certified pursuant to sections 5103.03 to 5103.05 of the Revised Code to accept temporary, permanent, or legal custody of children and place the children for either foster care or adoption.

(FF) "Public children's services agency" means a children's services board or a county department of human services that has assumed the administration of the children's services function prescribed by Chapter 5153 of the Revised Code.

(GG) "Removal action" means a statutory action filed by the superintendent of a school district for the removal of a child in an out-of-county foster home placement.

(HH) "Residence or legal settlement" means a location as defined by section 2151.06 of the Revised Code.

(II) "Residual parental rights, privileges, and responsibilities" means those rights, privileges, and responsibilities remaining with the natural parent after the transfer of legal custody of the child, including but not limited to the privilege of reasonable visitation, consent to adoption, the privilege to determine the child's religious affiliation, and the responsibility for support.

(JJ) "Rule of court" means a rule promulgated by the Supreme Court or a rule concerning local practice adopted by another court that is not inconsistent with the rules promulgated by the Supreme Court and that is filed with the Supreme Court.

(KK) "Serious youthful offender" means a child eligible for sentencing as described in sections 2152.11 and 2152.13 of the Revised Code.

(LL) "Serious youthful offender proceedings" means proceedings after a probable cause determination that a child is eligible for sentencing as described in sections 2152.11 and 2152.13 of the Revised Code. Serious youthful offender proceedings cease to be serious youthful offender proceedings once a child has been determined by the trier of fact not to be a serious youthful offender or the juvenile judge has determined not to impose a serious youthful offender disposition on a child eligible for discretionary serious youthful offender sentencing.

(MM) "Shelter care" means the temporary care of children in physically unrestricted facilities, pending court adjudication or disposition.

(NN) "Social history" means the personal and family history of a child or any other party to a juvenile proceeding and may include the prior record of the person with the juvenile court or any other court.

(OO) "Temporary custody" means legal custody of a child who is removed from the child's home, which custody may be terminated at any time at the discretion of the court or, if the legal custody is granted in an agreement for temporary custody, by the person or persons who executed the agreement.

(PP) "Unruly child" has the same meaning as in section 2151.022 of the Revised Code.

(QQ) "Ward of court" means a child over whom the court assumes continuing jurisdiction.

(Adopted eff. 7–1–72; amended eff. 7–1–94, 7–1–98, 7–1–01, 7–1–02)

Historical and Statutory Notes

Amendment Note: The 7–1–02 amendment deleted former divisions (W), (W)(1) and (W)(2), relating to "Long term foster care" and redesignated former divisions (X) through (DD) as new divisions (W) through (CC), respectively; added new divisions (DD), (DD)(1) and (DD)(2).

Amendment Note: The 7–1–01 amendment substituted "2151.011 and 2152.02" for "2151.011(B)(1)" in division (D); created new divisions (E) and (P); made nonsubstantive changes to new divisions (F), (H), (W), (AA), (BB), (EE) and (FF); redesignated former divisions (E) through (N) as new divisions (F) through (O), respectively; redesignated former divisions (O) through (HH) as new divisions (Q) through (JJ); created new divisions (KK) and (LL); redesignated former divisions (II) through (MM) as new divisions (MM) through (QQ); substituted "2152.02" for "2151.02" in new division (I); and added "and 2152" after "2151" in new divisions (S) and (T).

Amendment Note: The 7–1–98 amendment deleted "or whether temporary legal custody should be converted to permanent custody" from the end of division (B); rewrote division (D); added new division (EE); and redesignated former divisions (EE) through (LL) as new divisions (FF) through (MM). Prior to amendment, division (D) read:

"(D) 'Child' means a person who is under the age of eighteen years except as it relates to transfer of jurisdiction pursuant to Juv. R. 30 for purposes of criminal prosecution. A child who violates a federal or state law or municipal ordinance prior to attaining eighteen years of age shall be considered a child irrespective of age at the time the complaint is filed or hearing is had."

Amendment Note: The 7–1–94 amendment added divisions (A), (C), (H), (I), (S), (T), (U), (W), (Y), (Z), (CC), (DD), (EE), (FF), (JJ), and (KK); redesignated former divisions (1) through (22) as divisions (B), (D), (E), (F), (G), (J), (K), (L), (M), (N), (O), (P), (Q), (R), (V), (X), (AA), (BB), (GG), (HH), (II), and (LL), respectively; inserted "abused," in division (B); inserted "except as it relates to transfer of jurisdiction pursuant to Juv. R. 30 for purposes of criminal prosecution" in division (D); substituted "legal custody of a child or a public children services agency or private child placing agency that has permanent, temporary, or legal custody of a child" for "been granted custody of a child by a court" in division (G); deleted ", or execution of a court order" from the end of division (J); substituted "person, association, or corporation that is granted authority by a probate court pursuant to Chapter 2111. of the Revised Code to exercise parental rights over a child to the extent provided in the court's order and subject to the residual parental rights of the child's parents" for "court appointed guardian of the person of a child" in division (M); and deleted ", or execution of a court order" from the end of division (HH).

Staff Notes

2002:

Juvenile Rule 2 Definitions

The July 1, 2002, amendments substituted the language of "planned permanent living arrangement" for the former language of "long term foster care," to conform to the new legislative designation for these child-placing arrangements. Former division (W), "Long term foster care," was deleted, a new division (DD), "Planned permanent living arrangement," was added, and other divisions were relettered accordingly.

The amendments to Juv. R. 2 conform to section 2151.011 of the Revised Code. Juvenile Rules 10, 15, and 34 also were amended effective July 1, 2002 to reflect this change in terminology.

2001:

Rule 2 Definitions

Several definitions in Rule 2 were amended to correct the language: Rules 2(F), (H), (W), (AA), (BB), (EE), and (FF).

Rule 2(D) was amended to reflect that the definition of "child" in the Revised Code had been placed into two new sections, i.e., R. C. 2151.011 and 2152.02.

Rules 2(E) and (P) were added to reflect the new categories of chronic truant [defined in Revised Code section 2151.011(B)(9)] and habitual truant [defined in Revised Code section 2151.011(B)(18)], added by Sub. Sen. Bill 181, which became effective September 4, 2000. Other rules that were amended to reflect changes necessitated by the chronic and habitual truancy bill are Rule 10(A), Rule 15(B), Rule 27(A), Rule 29(F), and Rule 37.

Rules 2(I), (S) and (T) were amended to reflect the reorganization of the Revised Code made by Sub. Sen. Bill 179, effective January 1, 2002. The reorganization moved delinquency into a new chapter, Chapter 2152 of the Revised Code, thus necessitating that "juvenile court" and "juvenile judge" be redefined to include those having jurisdiction under Chapter 2152 as well as under Chapter 2151, and that "delinquent child" be amended to reflect it is now defined in section 2152.02.

Rule 2(KK) was added to reflect the new category of "serious youthful offender" created by Sub. Sen. Bill 179. Although the Revised Code does not define serious youthful offender specifically, sections 2152.11 and 2152.13 describe in detail the predicate offenses and other predicates to treatment as a serious youthful offender, as well as the types of dispositional sentencing available for each. Other rules that were amended to reflect changes necessitated by the serious youthful offender bill are Rule 7(A), Rule 22(D) and (E), Rule 27(A), and Rule 29(A), (C) and (F).

Rule 2(LL) defines "serious youthful offender proceedings." The new category of serious youthful offender created by Sub. Sen. Bill 179 contemplates imposition of an adult sentence in addition to a juvenile disposition upon conviction. Therefore, serious youthful offenders have statutory and constitutional rights commensurate with those of adults. Some proceedings in juvenile court needed to be altered to ensure adult substantive and procedural protections where appropriate. The amendment makes clear that juvenile protections and confidentiality apply both before a probable cause determination that a child may be subject to serious youthful offender disposition, and after a determination that the child shall not be given a serious youthful offender disposition.

1998:

Rule 2 Definitions

Rule 2(B) Adjudicatory hearing

Included under the prior definition of "adjudicatory hearing" in Juv. R. 2(B) were proceedings in which "temporary legal custody should be converted to permanent custody." This provision, which had been included in Juv. R. 2 since its adoption in 1972, appeared to conflict with the 1994 enactment of Juv. R. 34(I), which provides, "Hearings to determine whether temporary orders regarding custody should be modified to orders for permanent custody shall be considered dispositional hearings and need not be bifurcated. The Rules of Evidence shall apply in hearings on motions for permanent custody." Similarly, section 2151.414(A) of the Revised Code provides, "The adjudication that the child is an abused, neglected, or dependent child and the grant of temporary custody to the agency that filed the motion or placement into long-term foster care shall not be readjudicated at the hearing and shall not be affected by a denial of the motion for permanent custody."

The case law on this issue is in conflict. Several pre–1994 cases have held that hearings on motions for permanent custody are adjudicatory in nature. See *In re Hopkins* (1992), 78 Ohio App. 3d 92; *In re Workman* (June 14, 1993), Tuscarawas App. No. 92 AP080055, unreported; *In re Davis* (July 21, 1993), Summit App. No. 16051, unreported. The most recent reported decision, *In re Duncan/Walker Children,* (1996), 109 Ohio App. 3d 841, held that a permanent custody hearing under R.C. 2151.414 is adjudicatory, and did not make reference to either Juv. R. 2(B) or Juv. R. 34(I).

By deleting the final phrase of Juv. R. 2(B) with this amendment, Juv. R. 34(I) becomes the sole authority on this issue with the Rules of Juvenile Procedure.

Rule 2(D) Child

The definition of "child" contained in Juv. R. 2(D) has been amended to conform to the definition of the term found in sections 2151.011(B)(1)(a) of the Revised Code, as amended by legislation (1996 H 124, eff. 3–31–97, and 1996 H 265, eff. 3–3–97). Because the definition of the term "child" appears to be a matter of substantive law since it deals with a jurisdiction issue, the amended definition of the term simply makes reference to the statutory definition.

Rule 2(EE) Removal action

The definition of the term "removal action" added as Juv. R. 2(EE) refers to the cause of action first created by section 2151.55 of the Revised Code (1996 H 215, eff. 9–29–97). This new cause of action applies exclusively to a child in out-of-county foster home placement who is alleged to be causing a significant and unreasonable disruption to the educational process in the school the child is attending.

The addition of division (EE) required the relettering of previous divisions (EE) through (LL) to divisions (FF) through (MM).

1994:

Rule 2 Definitions

Definitions in Juv. R. 2 have been amended or added to reflect definitions found in Revised Code 2151.011, as amended by legislation (Am. Sub. S.B. 89 of the 117th General Assembly and Am. Sub. S.B. 3 of the 118th General Assembly). Amended language exists for the following terms: adjudicatory hearing; child; custodian; guardian; shelter care.

New terms defined in accordance with new statutes are: agreement for temporary custody; delinquent child; dependent child; juvenile traffic offender; legal custody; long term foster care; neglected child; permanent custody; permanent surrender; private child placing agency; public children services agency; residence or legal settlement; residual parental rights, privileges and responsibilities; temporary custody; unruly child.

All other changes in the definitions are to assure gender neutral language.

Editor's Comment

Abused child   1
Adjudicatory hearing   2
Agreement for temporary custody   3
Child   4
Complaint   5
Court proceeding   6
Custodian   7
Delinquent child   8
Dependent child   9
Detention   10
Detention hearing   11
Dispositional hearing   12
Guardian   13
Guardian ad litem   14
Hearing   15
Indigent person   16
Juvenile court   17
Juvenile judge   18
Juvenile traffic offender   19
Legal custody   20
Long term foster care   21
Mental examination   22
Neglected child   23
Party   24
Permanent custody   25
Permanent surrender   26
Person   27
Physical examination   28
Private child placing agency   29
Public children services agency   30
Residence or legal settlement   31
Residual parental rights, privileges, and responsibilities   32
Rule of court   33
Shelter care   34
Social history   35
Temporary custody   36
Unruly child   37
Ward of court   38

Juv R 2 is the definitions rule. The inclusion of a definitions rule follows the pattern of Ch 2151 (2151.011), the Minnesota Rules and the National Council on Crime and Delinquency Model Rules. This departure from the pattern of the Ohio Civil Rules and Criminal Rules was adopted by the committee because a number of crucial terms occur throughout the Juvenile Rules. Once a definition rule was included for such terms, it made sense to include all definitions in the rule.

The definitions are organized alphabetically because of their number and the impossibility of finding any fully satisfactory conceptual order. In this regard, they follow the Minnesota Rules, but not the Model Rules or 2151.011.

1. Abused child

Because the definition of abused child is a substantive issue relating to the jurisdiction of the juvenile court under 2151.23(A)(1), Juv R 2(A) appropriately refers to the statutory definition of the term contained in 2151.031.

2. Adjudicatory hearing

This definition determines the scope of Juv R 29 (Adjudicatory hearing), so as to make it clear that the procedural safeguards connected with that type of hearing are applicable in the cases so defined. The definition includes any hearing to establish that a person is within the jurisdiction of the juvenile court, specifically mentioning six of the most typical types of cases: delinquency, unruliness, abuse, neglect, dependency, and juvenile traffic offender. The phrase "otherwise within the jurisdiction" would encompass other categories of cases over which the juvenile court has jurisdiction under 2151.23.

A significant part of the definition is the inclusion of hearings to determine whether a temporary legal custody commitment should be changed to permanent custody. This provision, which has been included in Juv R 2 since its adoption in 1972, appears to conflict with the 1994 enactment of Juv R 34(I), which provides that, "Hearings to determine whether temporary orders regarding custody should be modified to orders for permanent custody shall be considered dispositional hearings and need not be bifurcated. The Rules of Evidence shall apply in hearings on motions for permanent custody." Moreover, 2151.414(A) provides that the "adjudication that the child is an abused, neglected, or dependent child and the grant of temporary custody to the agency that filed the motion shall not be readjudicated at the hearing and shall not be affected by a denial of the motion for permanent custody."

The definition is adapted to the Ohio setting from Minnesota Rule 1–2(a).

3. Agreement for temporary custody

This definition repeats the statutory definition of the term contained in 2151.011(B)(17).

4. Child

The term "child" is used throughout the rules and so is defined here.

The definition differs from the definition of "child" contained in 2151.011(B)(1). The statute excludes from the definition of "child" any person who has been transferred for criminal prosecution pursuant to 2151.26, and convicted, and who thereafter is alleged to have committed murder or aggravated murder, an aggravated felony of the first or second degree, or a felony of the first or second degree.

5. Complaint

This definition provides that the document by which juvenile court proceedings are commenced is to be called a complaint. This term is more fully defined in Juv R 10.

The form of the definition is taken from Minnesota Rule 1–2(q) and NCCD Model Rule 1(7), although the term "complaint" is used in place of the term "petition" which is used in those rules, so as to conform to the terminology of the Civil Rules.

6. Court proceeding

The term "court proceeding" is used many places in the rules (see Juv R 3, 4, 37). The intent of the definition is to indicate that the term has a broad scope. A significant example of the effect of the definition is to be seen in conjunction with Juv R 4(A) on the time when the right to counsel arises.

7. Custodian

This term is used in many cases and is defined so as to clearly indicate the difference between one who has physical custody and one who has been granted legal custody by a court. The definition is taken from 2151.011(B)(26).

8. Delinquent child

Because the definition of delinquent child is a substantive issue relating to the jurisdiction of the juvenile court under 2151.23(A)(1), Juv R 2(H) appropriately refers to the statutory definition of the term contained in 2151.02.

9. Dependent child

Because the definition of dependent child is a substantive issue relating to the jurisdiction of the juvenile court under 2151.23(A)(1), Juv R 2(I) appropriately refers to the statutory definition of the term contained in 2151.04.

10. Detention

This definition, together with that of "shelter care" (Juv R 2(II)), defines the scope of Juv R 7 (Detention and shelter). In many respects, detention is treated differently from shelter care within that rule. Thus, the definitions of the two terms and the differences between them are important. The essence of detention is the presence of physically restrictive facilities for children found to be delinquent or unruly while the essence of shelter care is the absence of restrictive facilities and is designed for children found to be dependent or neglected.

The definition is taken from 2151.011(B)(3).

11. Detention hearing

Detention hearing is required by Juv R 7(F).

12. Dispositional hearing

This definition determines the scope of the hearing provided for in Juv R 34.

13. Guardian

The guardian is included as a party under Juv R 2(X). The definition is taken from 2151.011(B)(18).

14. Guardian ad litem

The appointment and functions of the guardian ad litem are dealt with in Juv R 4. The definition here indicates clearly that the "guardian ad litem" is conceptually different from the "guardian" as defined in Juv R 2(M).

This definition is consistent with the use of the term in 2151.281.

15. Hearing

This definition provides a general meaning for the term "hearing" as used in the rules. It should make it clear that the adjudicatory and dispositional hearings are not the only types of hearings in juvenile court. Some rules refer to all hearings (see, particularly, Juv R 27).

The definition is taken from the Minnesota Rules.

16. Indigent person

The definition provides that the court should look not only to the expense of employing counsel to determine indigency, but should also consider the other expenses of juvenile court proceedings, such as those involved in securing expert evaluations and testimony.

The juvenile court has a strong interest in having parties in juvenile court represented by counsel, and a more realistic flexible standard was thus required in the juvenile court. While one might assume that some adults can reasonably protect their own interests without counsel, that assumption clearly cannot be indulged with respect to a child.

17. Juvenile court

This definition must be seen in conjunction with the definition of "juvenile judge," from which it is distinguished. The latter term has been used whenever a particular rule applies only to a judge of the juvenile court, while the broader terms "juvenile court" and "court" are used when a rule applies to the court in general, judges and referees.

The definition is taken from 2151.011(A)(1).

18. Juvenile judge

The function of this definition is described in connection with the preceding definition.

The definition is taken from 2151.011(A)(2).

19. Juvenile traffic offender

Because the definition of juvenile traffic offender is a substantive issue relating to the jurisdiction of the juvenile court under 2151.23(A)(1), Juv R 2(S) appropriately refers to the statutory definition of the term contained in 2151.021.

20. Legal custody

This definition repeats the statutory definition of the term contained in 2151.011(B)(9).

21. Long term foster care

Long term foster care is one of the dispositional options listed in 2151.353.

The definition is taken from 2151.011(B)(24).

22. Mental examination

The definition is particularly important and relates to Juv R 30 dealing with transfer of jurisdiction for the purposes of criminal prosecution.

23. Neglected child

Because the definition of neglected child is a substantive issue relating to the jurisdiction of the juvenile court under 2151.23(A)(1), Juv R 2(W) appropriately refers to the statutory definition contained in 2151.03.

24. Party

The term "party" is used throughout the Juvenile Rules and so is a centrally important definition.

This definition creates two categories of parties. Persons in the first group are always parties in a juvenile proceeding covered by these rules. This includes the child who is the subject of the proceeding, his spouse, if any, and his parents. The second category consists of persons who may be parties in appropriate cases; they are a custodian, guardian or guardian ad litem for the child, the state, and any other person the court may designate.

The effect of the rule should be to erase any doubt that both parent and child are parties to all types of juvenile court proceedings covered by these rules. This is significant in that the various aspects of procedural due process are accorded to parties to juvenile court proceedings, but depend on the definition of this crucial term.

By indicating that where the state is involved in a juvenile court proceeding it too becomes a party, the rules make it clear that such mechanisms as juvenile court discovery are available against the state.

The flexibility provided in the last phrase in the rule is crucial in juvenile court, where the welfare of a child may be directly affected by the conduct of some person outside the legal family. The most obvious category of person the court might wish to make a party is a stepparent or person living with a parent of the child and contributing to his neglect. In some cases, the court might also wish to make a children's services board or other agency a party in order to facilitate the use of dispositional alternatives available only through such agency.

25. Permanent custody

Permanent custody is one of the dispositional options listed in 2151.353.

The definition is taken from 2151.011(B)(11).

26. Permanent surrender

This definition repeats the statutory definition of the term contained in 2151.011(B)(21).

27. Person

This definition indicates clearly that the term "person" as used in these rules is not limited to physical persons.

The definition is taken from the Minnesota Rules.

28. Physical examination

This definition determines the scope of part of Juv R 32 and is especially important in neglect and child abuse proceedings.

29. Private child placing agency

This definition repeats the statutory definition of the term contained in 2151.011(B)(8).

30. Public children services agency

In some counties, this agency is organized as a children services board, while in others it is a department of human services.

The definition is taken from 2151.011(B)(25).

31. Residence or legal settlement

The determination of a child's residence or legal settlement is important for various reasons, including venue and the educational support of a child in placement.

32. Residual parental rights, privileges, and responsibilities

This definition is taken from 2151.011(B)(10).

33. Rule of court

Local rules of court may be used to supplement these rules in such areas as that of intake procedure, which is only dealt with here in the most general terms (Juv R 9).

The definition is taken from Civ R 83.

34. Shelter care

The function of this definition is discussed in connection with Juv R 2(J) dealing with detention.

The definition is taken from 2151.011(B)(4). The term "shelter care" has been used here instead of the term "shelter" used in the Revised Code, as being more expressive of the concept involved.

35. Social history

This definition provides a broad scope for a term that is used extensively in Juv R 32. The social history provides the juvenile court with the basis for making a disposition in the best interest of a child found to be within the court's jurisdiction.

36. Temporary custody

Temporary custody is one of the dispositional options listed in 2151.353.

The definition is taken from 2151.011(B)(12).

37. Unruly child

Because the definition of unruly child is a substantive issue relating to the jurisdiction of the juvenile court under 2151.23(A)(1), Juv R 2(LL) appropriately refers to the statutory definition of the term contained in 2151.022.

38. Ward of court

This term is used in Juv R 42(G) and is used but not defined in Ch 2151.

Some terms defined in 2151.011 have not been defined in this rule as their meaning has been established in other statutes and case decisions. Terms which are used but not defined in this rule shall be given a meaning consistent with the purposes outlined in Juv R 1(B).

Library References

Infants ⚖68.1, 131.
Westlaw Topic No. 211.
C.J.S. Infants §§ 31 to 54, 198, 199.

Research References

Encyclopedias

OH Jur. 3d Criminal Law § 1970, Application of Procedural Rules and Statutes.
OH Jur. 3d Family Law § 904, Who May Adopt—Foster Parents.
OH Jur. 3d Family Law § 974, Necessary Parties.
OH Jur. 3d Family Law § 1500, Relating to Persons.
OH Jur. 3d Family Law § 1501, Relating to Control and Care.
OH Jur. 3d Family Law § 1502, Relating to Facilities.
OH Jur. 3d Family Law § 1503, Relating to Procedure.
OH Jur. 3d Family Law § 1535, Definitions.
OH Jur. 3d Family Law § 1626, Right Under Juvenile Court Law and Rules.
OH Jur. 3d Family Law § 1643, Motion and Order for Discovery.
OH Jur. 3d Family Law § 1731, Accelerated Appellate Procedure.

Treatises and Practice Aids

Klein, Darling, & Terez, Baldwin's Ohio Practice Civil Practice § 24:2, Applicability of Civ. R. 24.
Klein, Darling, & Terez, Baldwin's Ohio Practice Civil Practice § 24:12, Intervention of Right--Nonstatutory Intervention of Right--"The Applicant Claims an Interest Relating to the Property or Transaction Which is the Subject of the Action"--Interest...
Klein, Darling, & Terez, Baldwin's Ohio Practice Civil Practice § 24:21, Permissive Intervention--Nonstatutory Permissive Intervention--"Applicant's Claim or Defense and the Main Action Have a Question of Law or Fact in Common".
Katz, Giannelli, Blair and Lipton, Baldwin's Ohio Practice, Criminal Law, § 35:11, Juvenile Cases.
Carlin, Baldwin's Ohio Practice, Merrick-Rippner Probate Law § 19:8, Uniform Parentage Act—Support Order.
Carlin, Baldwin's Ohio Practice, Merrick-Rippner Probate Law § 105:8, Juvenile Court—Age Jurisdiction.
Carlin, Baldwin's Ohio Practice, Merrick-Rippner Probate Law § 107:9, Parties to Proceedings.
Carlin, Baldwin's Ohio Practice, Merrick-Rippner Probate Law § 105:10, Juvenile Court—Duration and Termination of Jurisdiction.
Carlin, Baldwin's Ohio Practice, Merrick-Rippner Probate Law § 107:45, Adjudicatory Hearings—Parties' Right to Counsel.
Carlin, Baldwin's Ohio Practice, Merrick-Rippner Probate Law § 107:48, Adjudicatory Hearings—Prosecuting Attorney's Assistance at Hearing.
Carlin, Baldwin's Ohio Practice, Merrick-Rippner Probate Law § 107:51, Adjudicatory Hearings—Applicability of Rules of Evidence.
Carlin, Baldwin's Ohio Practice, Merrick-Rippner Probate Law § 107:78, Disposition of Abused, Neglected, or Dependent Child—Temporary Custody.
Carlin, Baldwin's Ohio Practice, Merrick-Rippner Probate Law § 107:79, Disposition of Abused, Neglected, or Dependent Child—Legal Custody.
Carlin, Baldwin's Ohio Practice, Merrick-Rippner Probate Law § 107:110, Disposition of Juvenile Traffic Offender—Revocation of Probationary Operator's License by the Bureau of Motor Vehicles.
Carlin, Baldwin's Ohio Practice, Merrick-Rippner Probate Law § 107:114, Juvenile Court Records—Confidentiality.
Giannelli & Yeomans, Ohio Juvenile Law § 2:2, Age Jurisdiction.
Giannelli & Yeomans, Ohio Juvenile Law § 3:3, Concurrent Jurisdiction.
Giannelli & Yeomans, Ohio Juvenile Law § 5:6, Syo Adjudicatory Hearing.
Giannelli & Yeomans, Ohio Juvenile Law § 11:2, Jurisdiction for Custody Agreements.
Giannelli & Yeomans, Ohio Juvenile Law § 15:2, Intake.
Giannelli & Yeomans, Ohio Juvenile Law § 16:1, Introduction.
Giannelli & Yeomans, Ohio Juvenile Law § 16:2, Standing to File Complaint.
Giannelli & Yeomans, Ohio Juvenile Law § 16:5, Parental Identification.
Giannelli & Yeomans, Ohio Juvenile Law § 17:4, Transfer of Venue.

Giannelli & Yeomans, Ohio Juvenile Law § 18:2, Issuance of Summons: Proper Parties.
Giannelli & Yeomans, Ohio Juvenile Law § 19:2, Place of Detention.
Giannelli & Yeomans, Ohio Juvenile Law § 19:5, Detention Hearing.
Giannelli & Yeomans, Ohio Juvenile Law § 19:7, Time Requirements.
Giannelli & Yeomans, Ohio Juvenile Law § 23:1, Introduction.
Giannelli & Yeomans, Ohio Juvenile Law § 23:3, Right to Counsel.
Giannelli & Yeomans, Ohio Juvenile Law § 23:6, Guardian Ad Litem.
Giannelli & Yeomans, Ohio Juvenile Law § 25:2, Bifurcated Hearings.
Giannelli & Yeomans, Ohio Juvenile Law § 30:6, Temporary Custody.
Giannelli & Yeomans, Ohio Juvenile Law § 30:7, Legal Custody.
Giannelli & Yeomans, Ohio Juvenile Law § 30:8, Permanent Custody—Defined.
Giannelli & Yeomans, Ohio Juvenile Law § 31:4, Hearings on Permanent Custody Motions.
Giannelli & Yeomans, Ohio Juvenile Law § 31:5, Evidence.
Giannelli & Yeomans, Ohio Juvenile Law § 32:2, Jurisdiction Over Parents and Others.
Giannelli & Yeomans, Ohio Juvenile Law § 33:6, Revocation of Probation.
Giannelli & Yeomans, Ohio Juvenile Law § 33:9, Department of Youth Services.
Giannelli & Yeomans, Ohio Juvenile Law § 34:3, Standing.
Giannelli & Yeomans, Ohio Juvenile Law § 35:2, Confidentiality Requirement.
Giannelli & Yeomans, Ohio Juvenile Law App. D, Appendix D. Glossary.
Giannelli & Yeomans, Ohio Juvenile Law § 22:11, Right to Counsel.
Giannelli & Yeomans, Ohio Juvenile Law § 22:13, Rules of Evidence.
Giannelli & Yeomans, Ohio Juvenile Law § 23:17, Evidence—Separation of Witnesses.
Giannelli & Yeomans, Ohio Juvenile Law § 30:13, Planned Permanent Living Arrangement.

Notes of Decisions

Compatibility of offices 5
Delinquent child 3
Evidence 4
Final orders 2
Hearings 7
Jurisdiction 6
Parties 1

---

1. Parties

Juvenile court was required to hold in-camera interview of child to determine whether conflict existed between guardian ad litem's recommended disposition and child's wishes, such that appointment of separate counsel for child was required, in child protection proceeding in which county sought permanent custody of child; potential conflict between guardian ad litem's recommended disposition of adoption and child's wishes to maintain some contact with her father could not be avoided by guardian ad litem's mere expression of child's wishes to trial court. In re H.R. (Ohio App. 2 Dist., Montgomery, 03-31-2006) No. 21274, 2006-Ohio-1595, 2006 WL 827385, Unreported. Infants 205

Following mother's eighteenth birthday, any party could file motion with juvenile court to remove grandparents of mother's child as parties in proceeding in which county children services board sought permanent custody of mother's child; although grandparents were necessary parties to proceeding prior to mother's eighteenth birthday, they remained discretionary parties following mother's eighteenth birthday. In re Walker (Ohio App. 11 Dist., Ashtabula, 02-17-2006) No. 2005-A-0067, 2006-Ohio-739, 2006 WL 389596, Unreported, appeal allowed 109 Ohio St.3d 1506, 849 N.E.2d 1027, 2006-Ohio-2998. Infants 200

Burden fell on county children services board, as party seeking to remove grandparents of child from proceeding in which board sought permanent custody of child, to demonstrate why grandparents should no longer be parties; juvenile rules deemed inclusion of grandparents mandatory when respective parent was less than 18 years old, mother was 15 years old at time of child's birth, and, since grandparents were already parties, they had vested interest in proceedings. In re Walker (Ohio App. 11 Dist., Ashtabula, 02-17-2006) No. 2005-A-0067, 2006-Ohio-739, 2006 WL 389596, Unreported, appeal allowed 109 Ohio St.3d 1506, 849 N.E.2d 1027, 2006-Ohio-2998. Infants 200

Trial court abused its discretion in removing maternal grandmother of child as a party in proceeding in which county children services board sought permanent custody of child; court removed grandparents, who were opposed to granting of board's motion for permanent custody, and added foster parents, who were in favor of granting board's motion, court provided no reasoning in support of decision, and collective nature of court's decisions regarding grandparents and foster parents was arbitrary. In re Walker (Ohio App. 11 Dist., Ashtabula, 02-17-2006) No. 2005-A-0067, 2006-Ohio-739, 2006 WL 389596, Unreported, appeal allowed 109 Ohio St.3d 1506, 849 N.E.2d 1027, 2006-Ohio-2998. Infants 200

Factors in support of maternal grandparent of child remaining as a party outweighed those calling for her removal, in proceeding in which county children services board sought permanent custody of child; grandmother was significantly and actively involved in proceedings up to point board's motion to remove her was filed, and potential prejudice to mother and child weighed heavily in favor of keeping grandmother as a party to proceeding, since mother allegedly had developmental difficulties, court joined foster parents as parties to proceeding, and mother was facing permanent custody proceeding from the very beginning. In re Walker (Ohio App. 11 Dist., Ashtabula, 02-17-2006) No. 2005-A-0067, 2006-Ohio-739, 2006 WL 389596, Unreported, appeal allowed 109 Ohio St.3d 1506, 849 N.E.2d 1027, 2006-Ohio-2998. Infants 200

Failure to name child as a party was fault of claimant, rather than trial court, in proceeding in which claimant challenged administrative order establishing nonexistence of parent-child relationship and sought to establish parent-child relationship between himself and child; child was subject of proceeding and was required to be named as a party, claimant filed complaint and neither named nor served child with complaint. E.B. v. T.J. (Ohio App. 8 Dist., Cuyahoga, 02-02-2006) No. 86399, 2006-Ohio-441, 2006 WL 242507, Unreported, appeal not allowed 109 Ohio St.3d 1507, 849 N.E.2d 1028, 2006-Ohio-2998. Children Out-of-wedlock 41

Father had no standing to challenge trial court's grant of permanent custody of child to county department of children and family services; father did not allege to be putative father of child, and father was named as a party only for other two children. In re A.D. (Ohio App. 8 Dist., Cuyahoga, 10-13-2005) No. 85648, 2005-Ohio-5441, 2005 WL 2600638, Unreported. Infants 242

Finding that child's maternal grandparents were "parties," within meaning of juvenile procedure rule, who could file motions for emergency shelter care hearing and for child custody was not abuse of trial court's discretion, where mother had child custody until she died and, since grandparents spent significant amount of time with child since her birth, grandparents' presence was necessary to fully litigate issue of child's custody and to protect interests of child, who was too young to express her own wishes and concerns. Christopher A.L. v. Heather D.R. (Ohio App. 6 Dist., Huron, 08-13-2004) No. H-03-040, 2004-Ohio-4271, 2004 WL 1802987, Unreported. Child Custody 409; Infants 200

Trial court denial of maternal grandparents' motion to intervene in child dependency proceeding was an abuse of discretion; trial court had previously granted grandparents temporary custody of child, Juvenile Rule provided that temporary custody meant legal custody, and statute provided that a person with legal custody to a child should be joined in a dependency proceeding. In re Perez (Ohio App. 5 Dist., Tuscarawas, 05-24-2004) No. 2003AP120091, 2004-Ohio-2707, 2004 WL 1171689, Unreported. Infants 200

Rule of juvenile procedure was not unconstitutional in violation of due process for failure to give foster parents, who sought custody of foster children removed from their care and whose motion to join as parties in juvenile proceedings was denied, affirmative right to join as parties in proceedings. In re McDaniel (Ohio App. 11 Dist., Lake, 05-21-2004) No. 2002-L-158, No. 2002-L-159, 2004-Ohio-2595, 2004 WL 1144390, Unreported, appeal not allowed 103 Ohio St.3d 1465, 815 N.E.2d 680, 2004-Ohio-5056. Constitutional Law 274(5); Infants 132

Foster parents, who sought custody of foster children removed from their care and whose motion to join as parties in juvenile proceedings was denied, failed to preserve due process challenge to rule of juvenile procedure which did not give them affirmative right to join as parties in proceedings, since they did not raise issue in juvenile court. In re McDaniel (Ohio App. 11 Dist., Lake, 05-21-2004) No. 2002-L-158, No. 2002-L-159, 2004-Ohio-2595, 2004 WL 1144390, Unreported, appeal not allowed 103 Ohio St.3d 1465, 815 N.E.2d 680, 2004-Ohio-5056. Infants 243

Order which permitted maternal grandmother and great-grandmother to intervene in child dependency case was not an abuse of discretion; grandmother and great-grandmother exercised significant parental control over child, and child was placed in the home of great-grandmother. In re

C.M. (Ohio App. 9 Dist., Summit, 04-21-2004) No. 21720, 2004-Ohio-1984, 2004 WL 840112, Unreported. Infants ☞ 200

Grandparents were not prejudiced by denial of motion to intervene in dependency proceedings involving grandson; grandparents were not parties to juvenile proceeding under juvenile rule governing such proceedings, and there was no showing that grandparents had legally protectable interest in custody or visitation or that they acted in loco parentis with respect to child. In re Goff (Ohio App. 11 Dist., Portage, 12-12-2003) No. 2001-P-0144, 2003-Ohio-6768, 2003 WL 22952808, Unreported. Infants ☞ 200

Paternal grandparents of allegedly dependent child, who was born to underage mother who allegedly was artificially inseminated by step-father, were not entitled to intervene regarding motion for permanent custody of child that was filed by county department of job and family services, since grandparents were not parties for purposes of juvenile proceedings, grandparents did not state how their presence was necessary condition to court's determination of child's best interests, grandparents did not have right to custody or visitation, and trial court's determination that intervention in this case was against public policy was neither arbitrary nor unreasonable. In re Goff (Ohio App. 11 Dist., Portage, 11-14-2003) No. 2003-P-0068, 2003-Ohio-6087, 2003 WL 22697969, Unreported. Infants ☞ 200

Putative father had standing to file a motion to set aside judgment, in termination of parental rights case; father was named in the proceedings, he was served with pleading, and he was represented by counsel during the proceedings. In re Phillips (Ohio App. 12 Dist., Butler, 09-29-2003) No. CA2003-03-062, 2003-Ohio-5107, 2003 WL 22227364, Unreported. Infants ☞ 230.1

Dismissal of paternal grandmother's appeal was warranted, based on failure to demonstrate a final appealable order, of the trial court's denial of her motion to intervene in dependency proceeding; trial court permitted grandmother to have visitation with child and ordered county department of job and family services to investigate grandmother for possible relative placement. In re Cunningham (Ohio App. 5 Dist., Stark, 08-11-2003) No. 2003CA00161, 2003-Ohio-4271, 2003 WL 21919874, Unreported. Infants ☞ 247

Failing to appoint counsel to represent children in termination of parental rights proceeding involving allegations of child abuse was harmless error, where allegations of abuse were dismissed by agreement of parties and court attempted to determine each child's wishes by conducting in camera interview. In re Joshua B. (Ohio App. 6 Dist., Sandusky, 06-13-2003) No. S-02-018, No. S-02-021, No. S-02-019, No. S-02-020, 2003-Ohio-3096, 2003 WL 21384883, Unreported. Infants ☞ 253

Supreme Court decision in *In re Williams* that, pursuant to statute governing right to counsel in juvenile cases and juvenile rules, child who was subject of juvenile court proceeding to terminate parental rights was a party to that proceeding and, thus, was entitled to independent counsel in certain circumstances, had retroactive effect and applied to mother's case, in which permanent custody of her dependent children was being determined; *Williams* decision had been foreshadowed, and applying *Williams* decision retroactively would not produce injustice or hardship. In re Moore (Ohio App. 7 Dist., 08-24-2004) 158 Ohio App.3d 679, 821 N.E.2d 1039, 2004-Ohio-4544, supplemented 2005-Ohio-136, 2005 WL 78754. Courts ☞ 100(1)

Juvenile has a right to counsel in a proceeding to terminate parental rights, based on the juvenile's status as a party to the proceeding; courts should make a determination, on a case-by-case basis, whether the child actually needs independent counsel, taking into account the maturity of the child and the possibility of the child's guardian ad litem being appointed to represent the child. In re Williams (Ohio, 04-14-2004) 101 Ohio St.3d 398, 805 N.E.2d 1110, 2004-Ohio-1500. Infants ☞ 205

Any error was harmless as to trial court's failure to name child as party to paternity and child support action and its failure to appoint counsel for child, where child's interest did not appear to conflict with mother's interests. Still v. Hayman (Ohio App. 7 Dist., 07-30-2003) 153 Ohio App.3d 487, 794 N.E.2d 751, 2003-Ohio-4113. Child Support ☞ 558(1); Children Out-of-wedlock ☞ 72.1

A child's grandparents are necessary parties to a permanent custody proceeding only if they have obtained through statute, court order, or other means a legal right to custody or visitation with the child. In re Schmidt (Ohio 1986) 25 Ohio St.3d 331, 496 N.E.2d 952, 25 O.B.R. 386.

Permitting foster mother to become a party to action to terminate mother's parental rights was not an abuse of discretion; mother cared more for her own selfish interests than those of her child, repeatedly telling her doctors that she only took her psychotropic medication to get her child back and that, once reunified, she would discontinue her medication because she did not believe she suffered from any mental illness; mother showed an inability to perform rudimentary parenting skills; county contin-ued to advocate reunification, despite mother's discouraging lack of progress; and mother refused to fight for the child after child had been abducted to China. In re Zhang (Ohio App. 8 Dist., 06-10-1999) 135 Ohio App.3d 350, 734 N.E.2d 379, dismissed, appeal not allowed 87 Ohio St.3d 1417, 717 N.E.2d 1105, reconsideration stricken 87 Ohio St.3d 1437, 719 N.E.2d 2. Infants ☞ 200

Juvenile court has wide discretion in affording any individual party status in proceeding for custody. In re Hitchcock (Ohio App. 8 Dist., 11-21-1996) 120 Ohio App.3d 88, 696 N.E.2d 1090, stay granted 77 Ohio St.3d 1462, 672 N.E.2d 1119, stay denied 77 Ohio St.3d 1502, 673 N.E.2d 921, motion to vacate stay denied 77 Ohio St.3d 1521, 674 N.E.2d 373, appeal allowed 78 Ohio St.3d 1455, 677 N.E.2d 815, appeal dismissed as improvidently allowed 81 Ohio St.3d 1222, 689 N.E.2d 43, 1998-Ohio-653, stay denied 81 Ohio St.3d 1469, 690 N.E.2d 1288, stay denied 81 Ohio St.3d 1476, 691 N.E.2d 294. Child Custody ☞ 409

Juvenile court did not abuse its discretion by permitting couple legally ineligible to adopt children to remain as parties to post-dispositional custody proceeding while court examined merits of couple's motion for legal custody; motion presented additional disposition option, which court was required to consider as part of its obligation to consider best interests of children. In re Hitchcock (Ohio App. 8 Dist., 11-21-1996) 120 Ohio App.3d 88, 696 N.E.2d 1090, stay granted 77 Ohio St.3d 1462, 672 N.E.2d 1119, stay denied 77 Ohio St.3d 1502, 673 N.E.2d 921, motion to vacate stay denied 77 Ohio St.3d 1521, 674 N.E.2d 373, appeal allowed 78 Ohio St.3d 1455, 677 N.E.2d 815, appeal dismissed as improvidently allowed 81 Ohio St.3d 1222, 689 N.E.2d 43, 1998-Ohio-653, stay denied 81 Ohio St.3d 1469, 690 N.E.2d 1288, stay denied 81 Ohio St.3d 1476, 691 N.E.2d 294. Infants ☞ 230.1

Trial court's allowing state witness' mother, a nonparty witness, to communicate extensively out of presence of one of the parties, namely, accused delinquent minor, about referee's findings and recommendations raised questions regarding appearance of unfairness of proceedings and warranted vacation of adjudication of delinquency based upon attempted felonious assault finding and remand for hearing and ruling on objections to initial referee's report and recommendations. In re Ross (Ohio App. 10 Dist., 10-24-1995) 107 Ohio App.3d 35, 667 N.E.2d 1012. Infants ☞ 207; Infants ☞ 254

County child support enforcement agency (CSEA) had standing, as collecting agent of Department of Human Services (DHS), to bring action in juvenile court to determine child support and to make determination of reimbursement for amount of support already provided by DHS to children of mothers receiving public assistance who had assigned their rights to child support to DHS; even if statute authorizing only parent, guardian, or custodian of child to bring action in juvenile court requesting child support order did not authorize state to bring such action, Juvenile Rules of Procedure giving state or its agencies standing to file complaint to order child support payments controlled over statute. State ex rel. Lamier v. Lamier (Ohio App. 8 Dist., 09-05-1995) 105 Ohio App.3d 797, 664 N.E.2d 1384. Child Support ☞ 179

Question of standing, i.e., of who is proper party to bring complaint, is procedural matter governed by Rules of Juvenile Procedure; these rules control over inconsistent statute purporting to govern procedural matters. State ex rel. Lamier v. Lamier (Ohio App. 8 Dist., 09-05-1995) 105 Ohio App.3d 797, 664 N.E.2d 1384. Child Custody ☞ 409

Indigent father was entitled to have counsel appointed to represent him on custody and visitation issues in child support action under statute and juvenile court rules; both rule and statute guarantee right to appointed counsel for all indigent parties in juvenile court proceedings, father, being natural father and parent of children, was a party to juvenile court proceeding under juvenile court rules, and father was indigent as defined in rules. McKinney v. McClure (Ohio App. 12 Dist., 03-27-1995) 102 Ohio App.3d 165, 656 N.E.2d 1310. Children Out-of-wedlock ☞ 20.4

While statute regarding dispositional review hearings does not list a child's legal custodian at the time review hearing is ordered as an "interested party" entitled to notice of the review hearing, the list is not exhaustive. In re Bowman (Ohio App. 9 Dist., 03-08-1995) 101 Ohio App.3d 599, 656 N.E.2d 355. Infants ☞ 230.1

Grandmother became an "interested party," entitled to notice of dispositional hearing, when court awarded her legal custody of dependent child. In re Bowman (Ohio App. 9 Dist., 03-08-1995) 101 Ohio App.3d 599, 656 N.E.2d 355. Infants ☞ 230.1

Although individual party may represent himself, such right of self-representation does not extend to parties who are not natural persons. In re Lawson (Ohio App. 10 Dist., 11-08-1994) 98 Ohio App.3d 456, 648 N.E.2d 889. Attorney And Client ☞ 62

Foster parents were not entitled to party status, in proceedings by county childrens services board that had temporary custody of child to accept permanent voluntary surrender of natural mother's rights for purposes of adoption, by virtue of juvenile court rule defining party by virtue of rule's reference to "any other party specifically designated by court"; rule merely afforded procedural device permitting trial court to include individuals not specifically otherwise designated party but whose presence was necessary to fully litigate issue presented in action, and such action was within trial court's sound discretion. In re Franklin (Marion 1993) 88 Ohio App.3d 277, 623 N.E.2d 720. Infants ☞ 200

In a delinquency proceeding, a trial court does not err in ordering that the regional consortium for children be made a party following the final disposition hearing where (1) a representative for the consortium was given notice and appeared as a witness for the state, (2) the court asked whether the consortium was represented by counsel at the beginning of the second dispositional hearing, and (3) the consortium representative was given the opportunity to question other witnesses. In re Hoodlet (Athens 1991) 72 Ohio App.3d 115, 593 N.E.2d 478. Infants ☞ 253

A county children services agency may not appeal an order of a juvenile court finding two minors to be unruly because of habitual truancy and committing them to the agency's custody, as the agency is not a party to the litigation under Juv R 2(16). In re Blakey (Franklin 1989) 65 Ohio App.3d 341, 583 N.E.2d 1343.

A father is a party to proceedings in a juvenile court in which his children are found to be neglected and in which temporary custody is given to the mother; he is also a party to a subsequent proceeding in the same court modifying such temporary custody order and is entitled to appear in an appeal from such order and move to dismiss such appeal. In re Rule (Crawford 1963) 1 Ohio App.2d 57, 203 N.E.2d 501, 30 O.O.2d 76.

The father of a juvenile adjudged delinquent is a party as defined in Juv R 2(16) and is subject to orders of the court. In re Dague, No. 87–CA–12 (5th Dist Ct App, Delaware, 10–22–87).

Foster parents who had cared for a child for over two years are not parties in interest in a dependency case because they have no property or liberty rights which would require a juvenile court to permit their intervention. In re Palmer, No. CA–6026 (5th Dist Ct App, Stark, 4–12–83).

2. Final orders

A temporary order of a juvenile court changing custody under Juv R 13 or 29 is not a dispositional order under Juv R 34, and hence is not a final appealable order. Morrison v. Morrison (Summit 1973) 45 Ohio App.2d 299, 344 N.E.2d 144, 74 O.O.2d 441.

3. Delinquent child

A juvenile who has been placed in a residential treatment center by order of a juvenile court and who leaves such premises without permission may properly be adjudicated delinquent, as the act of leaving the center without permission constitutes escape. In re Wells, No. CA–8287, CA–8347, and CA–8307 (5th Dist Ct App, Stark, 3–18–91).

4. Evidence

In an adjudicatory hearing to convert temporary custody of a minor to permanent custody pursuant to Juv R 2(1), the trial court erred in admitting into evidence reports of a child welfare agency where no foundation was laid to admit such report as a business records exception or public records exception to hearsay. In re Knipp, No. 1388 (4th Dist Ct App, Scioto, 3–28–83).

Juvenile's plea of true to committing gross sexual imposition was knowing, intelligent, and voluntary, even though prosecutor failed to correctly read the statutory language of the complaint and trial court failed to specifically address juvenile's right to present evidence at adjudicatory hearing; juvenile was represented by defense counsel, juvenile has received copies of complaint, juvenile never contended that attorney failed to explain complaint or nature of the charges against him, neither juvenile nor defense counsel indicated any confusion when asked by the court if anything further should be added to information before the court, juvenile's admissions were the result of extensive plea negotiations, form signed by juvenile contained detailed recitation of constitutional rights, and juvenile indicated that he was aware of all rights contained in form. In re Argo (Ohio App. 5 Dist., Muskingum, 09-16-2004) No. CT2003-055, 2004-Ohio-4938, 2004 WL 2260701, Unreported. Infants ☞ 199

5. Compatibility of offices

The office of probate and juvenile judge is incompatible with the office of county court judge. (Annotation from former RC 2151.011.) 1957 OAG 880.

6. Jurisdiction

Trial court order denying maternal grandparents' motion to intervene in child dependency case was not an abuse of discretion; maternal grandparents were not within the scope of parties, as defined by the juvenile rules, and the trial court found that the delay that would be caused by allowing maternal grandparents to intervene would be detrimental to the children. In re Aasiyah T. (Ohio App. 6 Dist., Lucas, 02-18-2005) No. L-04-1235, 2005-Ohio-667, 2005 WL 388700, Unreported. Infants ☞ 200

Rule requiring the state to respond to discovery requests in juvenile matters applies to "mandatory bindover" or waiver of jurisdiction proceedings wherein the court determines whether probable cause exists to transfer the matter for prosecution of the juvenile as an adult. In re A.M. (Ohio Com.Pl., 05-28-1998) 92 Ohio Misc.2d 4, 699 N.E.2d 574, affirmed 139 Ohio App.3d 303, 743 N.E.2d 937, appeal not allowed 91 Ohio St.3d 1431, 741 N.E.2d 895. Infants ☞ 68.7(3)

Under authority of this act, juvenile court has exclusive jurisdiction of all persons under eighteen charged with arson or other burnings as contained in GC 12433 (RC 2907.02) and GC 12436 (RC 2907.07). (Annotation from former RC 2151.25.) 1939 OAG 726.

7. Hearings

Error cannot be predicated on the juvenile court's holding a dispositional hearing immediately following an adjudicatory hearing and its failure to continue the dispositional hearing for a reasonable time to enable the party to obtain or consult counsel, as prescribed by Juv R 34(A), unless it affirmatively appears in the record that the affected nonindigent party has requested such continuance. In re Bolden (Allen 1973) 37 Ohio App.2d 7, 306 N.E.2d 166, 66 O.O.2d 26.

Probable cause hearing in a "mandatory bindover" or waiver of jurisdiction proceeding is both an "adjudicatory hearing" and a "hearing" as those terms are used in the rules governing juvenile matters. In re A.M. (Ohio Com.Pl., 05-28-1998) 92 Ohio Misc.2d 4, 699 N.E.2d 574, affirmed 139 Ohio App.3d 303, 743 N.E.2d 937, appeal not allowed 91 Ohio St.3d 1431, 741 N.E.2d 895. Infants ☞ 68.7(3)

Juv R 3 Waiver of rights

A child's right to be represented by counsel at a hearing conducted pursuant to Juv. R. 30 may not be waived. Other rights of a child may be waived with the permission of the court.

(Adopted eff. 7–1–72; amended eff. 7–1–94)

Historical and Statutory Notes

Amendment Note: The 7-1-94 amendment rewrote this rule, which previously read:

"A child's right to be represented by counsel at a hearing to determine whether the juvenile court shall relinquish its jurisdiction for purposes of criminal prosecution may not be waived. No other right of a child may be waived without the permission of the court."

Staff Notes

1994:

Rule 3 Waiver of Rights

Prior to this revision, some courts had interpreted Juv. R. 3 to permit a juvenile to waive the right to counsel at the probable cause hearing phase of the bindover process. Juv. R. 3 now makes specific reference to bindover proceedings delineated in Juv. R. 30 to remind the court and practitioners that a juvenile cannot waive counsel at any stage of the bindover procedure.

Editor's Comment

Juv R 3 deals with basic rights in juvenile court and the waiver of those rights. The provision that the child's right to counsel may not be waived at a hearing under Juv R 30 dealing with relinquishment of jurisdiction for purposes of criminal prosecution is mandated by the ruling in *Kent v United States*, 383 US 541, 86 SCt 1045, 16 LEd(2d) 84 (1966), holding that at such a critical stage of the proceedings due process of law and fundamental fairness require that the child be represented by counsel. All other rights which come within the purview of the Juvenile Rules may be waived if the waiver is knowingly, intelligently, and voluntarily made. It should be noted, however, that 2151.28(H) prohibits a child from waiving the service of summons.

Both Juv R 29(B) and RC 2151.35(H) include the requirement of juvenile courts to inform children of certain rights, prior to the adjudicatory hearing.

Cross References

Relinquishment of jurisdiction for purpose of criminal prosecution, Juv R 30

Library References

Infants ⚖︎68.7(3), 191.
Westlaw Topic No. 211.
C.J.S. Infants §§ 42 to 54.

Research References

ALR Library
101 ALR 5th 351, Validity and Efficacy of Minor's Waiver of Right to Counsel--Cases Decided Since Application of Gault, 387 U.S. 1, 87 S. Ct. 1428, 18 L. Ed. 2d 527 (1967).

Encyclopedias
OH Jur. 3d Family Law § 1624, Waiver of Child's Rights; Double Jeopardy.

Treatises and Practice Aids
Carlin, Baldwin's Ohio Practice, Merrick-Rippner Probate Law § 104:5, Juvenile Courts—Constitutional Issues—Right to Notice, Counsel, and Trial.

Carlin, Baldwin's Ohio Practice, Merrick-Rippner Probate Law § 107:14, Police Investigation of Juveniles—Custodial Interrogation.

Carlin, Baldwin's Ohio Practice, Merrick-Rippner Probate Law § 107:45, Adjudicatory Hearings—Parties' Right to Counsel.

Carlin, Baldwin's Ohio Practice, Merrick-Rippner Probate Law § 107:67, Procedural Due Process Requirements in Transfer Proceedings.

Giannelli & Yeomans, Ohio Juvenile Law § 18:5, Waiver of Summons Requirements.

Giannelli & Yeomans, Ohio Juvenile Law § 22:4, Improper Transfer; Lack of Jurisdiction.

Giannelli & Yeomans, Ohio Juvenile Law § 22:9, Amenability Hearing Procedures.

Giannelli & Yeomans, Ohio Juvenile Law § 23:4, Waiver of Right to Counsel.

Giannelli & Yeomans, Ohio Juvenile Law § 14:10, Confessions—Miranda.

Giannelli & Yeomans, Ohio Juvenile Law § 22:11, Right to Counsel.

Law Review and Journal Commentaries

Do Juveniles Facing Civil Commitment Have a Right to Counsel? A Therapeutic Jurisprudence Brief. Bruce J. Winick and Ginger Lerner-Wren, 71 U Cin L Rev 115 (Fall 2002).

Notes of Decisions

Confessions, admissibility 2
Constitutional issues 1
Miranda warnings 3

---

1. Constitutional issues

Juvenile court's procedures in obtaining juvenile's waiver of right to counsel and admission to probation violation violated juvenile's rights to counsel and due process in probation revocation proceedings; court had minimal discussion with juvenile regarding his right to counsel and no discussion with juvenile's father, juvenile's decision to admit violation was made without counsel and after consultation with his father, juvenile's father's interests were adverse to juvenile's given that father acknowledged he could not control juvenile's behavior and father was not opposed to juvenile court's involvement, juvenile court never answered juvenile's main concern as to how long he would be committed to Department of Youth Services (DYS), trial court never explained that consecutive minimum sentences would need to be served before any release for good behavior, and trial court's explanation of rights was misleading. In re Poland (Ohio App. 5 Dist., Licking, 10-15-2004) No. 04CA18, 2004-Ohio-5693, 2004 WL 2391813, Unreported. Constitutional Law ⚖︎ 255(4); Infants ⚖︎ 225

Application of 180-day time period in which to file motion for postconviction relief to juvenile did not amount to a waiver of his right to file a motion for post-conviction relief in violation of rule requiring permission of court for waiver of rights; since juvenile had no constitutional right to post-conviction relief, and the legislature provided a time limitation for filing petitions for post-conviction relief, trial court did not violate rule by dismissing his motion as untimely filed. In re Snyder (Ohio App. 4 Dist., Highland, 06-26-2002) No. 01CA11, 2002-Ohio-6137, 2002 WL 31520119, Unreported, appeal not allowed 97 Ohio St.3d 1469, 779 N.E.2d 236, 2002-Ohio-6347. Infants ⚖︎ 230.1

Juvenile court's limited inquiry at dispositional hearing and 14-year-old juvenile's limited responses, including court's asking whether juvenile recalled the rights explained to him at adjudicatory hearing and juvenile's response, "Um-hum," were insufficient to establish valid admission or valid waiver of right to counsel under the federal and state due process clauses. In re Royal (Ohio App. 7 Dist., 03-01-1999) 132 Ohio App.3d 496, 725 N.E.2d 685. Constitutional Law ⚖︎ 43(1); Infants ⚖︎ 199; Infants ⚖︎ 205

Trial court accepted 13-year-old juvenile's waiver of counsel without proper assurances that waiver was knowing, intelligent and voluntary; referee gave basic explanation to juvenile on his right to counsel at initial hearing and adjudicatory hearing, and asked juvenile to sign waiver form, but failed to inquire into any circumstances that would demonstrate that juvenile knowingly, intelligently, and voluntarily waived his right to counsel, and trial judge did not address subject of right to counsel at dispositional hearing. In re Johnson (Ohio App. 1 Dist., 08-23-1995) 106 Ohio App.3d 38, 665 N.E.2d 247. Infants ⚖︎ 205

Where a juvenile has received the following essentials of due process and fair treatment: (1) written notice of the specific charge or factual allegations, given to the juvenile and his parents or guardian sufficiently in advance of the hearing to permit preparation; (2) notification to the juvenile and his parents of the juvenile's right to be represented by counsel retained by them, or, if they are unable to afford counsel, that counsel will be appointed to represent the juvenile; (3) application of the constitutional privileges against self-incrimination; and (4), absent a valid confession, a determination of delinquency and an order of commitment based only on sworn testimony subjected to the opportunity for cross-examination in accordance with constitutional requirements, such juvenile has not been deprived of due process under either the Constitution of the United States or the Constitution of the State of Ohio. (Annotation from former RC 2151.35.) In re Baker (Hocking 1969) 18 Ohio App.2d 276, 248 N.E.2d 620, 47 O.O.2d 411.

A trial court does not fulfill its duty to ascertain whether a juvenile knows of his right to be provided with counsel if he is indigent simply by asking the juvenile if he has received a copy of the statement of rights and whether he has any questions about those rights where (1) the statement of rights is two pages in length, (2) single-spaced, and (3) the right of counsel if indigent is not stated until near the top of the second page; under such circumstances, the juvenile even with a parent present, is likely to sign a form he has not fully read or does not fully understand while at the same time telling a judge otherwise. In re Shane (Ohio App. 2 Dist., Darke, 01-26-2001) No. 1523, 2001 WL 62550, Unreported.

Federal and state due process rights extend to juvenile court proceedings, so that a plea agreement may not be broken by refiling charges. In re Leonhardt (Ohio Com.Pl. 1993) 62 Ohio Misc.2d 783, 610 N.E.2d 1238.

A juvenile taken into custody as a delinquent has certain rights guaranteed by the Due Process Clause of the United States Constitution in delinquency proceedings by the state which include the following: (1) notice of the charge, (2) right to counsel, (3) right to confrontation and cross-examination, and (4) privilege against self incrimination. Application of Gault (U.S.Ariz. 1967) 87 S.Ct. 1428, 387 U.S. 1, 18 L.Ed.2d 527, 40 O.O.2d 378.

2. Confessions, admissibility

Juvenile's waiver of rights and statement to police implicating himself, made at correctional facility, were voluntary; juvenile was 15-years-old at time of incident, he could read, understand and write English, he was not handcuffed or under any other physical restraint, nor was he subject to any apparent coercion at time of questioning, and he was aware that he had right to remain silent and right to have attorney present. In re Hill (Ohio App. 10 Dist., Franklin, 11-20-2003) No. 03AP-82, 2003-Ohio-6185, 2003 WL 22725297, Unreported. Infants ⚖︎ 174

Neither juvenile's waiver of counsel nor his admission to charges against him were made in a knowing manner, for purposes of delinquency proceedings, where juvenile was never informed of nature of charges against him, trial court made no mention of possible defenses or mitigating circumstances that related to juvenile's situation, and juvenile was not informed that if he admitted to the charges he would be losing certain rights associated with trial. In re Styer (Ohio App. 3 Dist., Union, 11-19-2002) No. 14-02-12, 2002-Ohio-6273, 2002 WL 31555992, Unreported. Infants ⇔ 199; Infants ⇔ 205

A voluntary confession to the perpetration of murder obtained from a sixteen and three-fourths year old high school junior, which confession was made before indictment and while the accused was detained for investigation, is admissible in evidence (1) where the accused had been allowed to consult with an attorney prior to being questioned; (2) where the accused first was advised that he did not have to talk; (3) where the accused, when told that his parents and another attorney were there and waiting to see him, stated that he did not want to see them; and (4) where there is no showing that the confession was obtained by inquisitorial processes. (Annotation from former RC 2151.31.) State v. Carder (Fairfield 1965) 3 Ohio App.2d 381, 210 N.E.2d 714, 32 O.O.2d 524, affirmed 9 Ohio St.2d 1, 222 N.E.2d 620, 38 O.O.2d 1.

A voluntary confession to the perpetration of murder, obtained from a seventeen-year-old high school senior, which confession was made before indictment on said charge and while the accused was under arrest for a misdemeanor, is admissible in evidence where (1) the accused was first advised that "he would not be compelled to give a statement... if he wanted to give a statement it would be by his own free will and that statement would be used for or against him in court;" (2) the accused was further advised that "he could secure the services of an attorney;" and (3) there is no showing that the confession was obtained by inquisitorial processes, without the procedural safeguards of due process, and by such compulsion that the confession is irreconcilable with the possession of mental freedom. (Annotation from former RC 2151.31.) State v. Stewart (Summit 1963) 120 Ohio App. 199, 201 N.E.2d 793, 29 O.O.2d 4, affirmed 176 Ohio St. 156, 198 N.E.2d 439, 27 O.O.2d 42, certiorari denied 85 S.Ct. 443, 379 U.S. 947, 13 L.Ed.2d 544.

3. Miranda warnings

Juvenile court erred in delinquency proceeding by allowing prosecutor to prove elements of state's case by questioning juvenile, an unrepresented minor held in custody, without informing him of his *Miranda* rights against self-incrimination, where juvenile was asked to stipulate to prior theft offense needed for disposition chosen. In re Johnson (Ohio App. 1 Dist., 08-23-1995) 106 Ohio App.3d 38, 665 N.E.2d 247. Infants ⇔ 199; Infants ⇔ 207

Unrepresented juvenile who did not receive *Miranda* warning could not be bound to stipulation that he had committed prior offense. In re Johnson (Ohio App. 1 Dist., 08-23-1995) 106 Ohio App.3d 38, 665 N.E.2d 247. Infants ⇔ 199

Where a fourteen-year-old minor, without counsel, made a statement to police implicating herself in setting a fire which killed her father, and the court psychologist testified that such minor was of average intelligence, the minor's statement is properly admitted into evidence where the minor had waived her Miranda rights and during the course of such statement the minor answered intelligently, coherently, and gave no indication of undue influence. In re Hawkins, No. 3430 (9th Dist Ct App, Lorain, 5-11-83).

Juv R 4   Assistance of counsel; guardian ad litem

(A) Assistance of counsel

Every party shall have the right to be represented by counsel and every child, parent, custodian, or other person in loco parentis the right to appointed counsel if indigent. These rights shall arise when a person becomes a party to a juvenile court proceeding. When the complaint alleges that a child is an abused child, the court must appoint an attorney to represent the interests of the child. This rule shall not be construed to provide for a right to appointed counsel in cases in which that right is not otherwise provided for by constitution or statute.

(B) Guardian ad litem; when appointed

The court shall appoint a guardian *ad litem* to protect the interests of a child or incompetent adult in a juvenile court proceeding when:

(1) The child has no parents, guardian, or legal custodian;

(2) The interests of the child and the interests of the parent may conflict;

(3) The parent is under eighteen years of age or appears to be mentally incompetent;

(4) The court believes that the parent of the child is not capable of representing the best interest of the child.

(5) Any proceeding involves allegations of abuse or neglect, voluntary surrender of permanent custody, or termination of parental rights as soon as possible after the commencement of such proceeding.

(6) There is an agreement for the voluntary surrender of temporary custody that is made in accordance with section 5103.15 of the Revised Code, and thereafter there is a request for extension of the voluntary agreement.

(7) The proceeding is a removal action.

(8) Appointment is otherwise necessary to meet the requirements of a fair hearing.

(C) Guardian ad litem as counsel

(1) When the guardian ad litem is an attorney admitted to practice in this state, the guardian may also serve as counsel to the ward providing no conflict between the roles exist.

(2) If a person is serving as guardian ad litem and as attorney for a ward and either that person or the court finds a conflict between the responsibilities of the role of attorney and that of guardian ad litem, the court shall appoint another person as guardian ad litem for the ward.

(3) If a court appoints a person who is not an attorney admitted to practice in this state to be a guardian ad litem, the court may appoint an attorney admitted to pracice [sic.] in this state to serve as attorney for the guardian ad litem.

(D) Appearance of attorneys

An attorney shall enter appearance by filing a written notice with the court or by appearing personally at a court hearing and informing the court of said representation.

(E) Notice to guardian ad litem

The guardian ad litem shall be given notice of all proceedings in the same manner as notice is given to other parties to the action.

(F) Withdrawal of counsel or guardian ad litem

An attorney or guardian ad litem may withdraw only with the consent of the court upon good cause shown.

(G) Costs

The court may fix compensation for the services of appointed counsel and guardians ad litem, tax the same as part of the costs and assess them against the child, the child's parents, custodian, or other person in loco parentis of such child.

(Adopted eff. 7–1–72; amended eff. 7–1–76, 7–1–94, 7–1–95, 7–1–98)

Historical and Statutory Notes

Amendment Note: The 7–1–98 amendment added new division (B)(7); and redesignated former division (B)(7) as new division (B)(8).

Amendment Note: The 7–1–95 amendment rewrote the titles of this rule and of division (A), which previously read:

"Rule 4. Appointment of Counsel; Guardian Ad Litem

"(A) Right to counsel; when arises."

Amendment Note: The 7–1–94 amendment added the final sentence of division (A); added divisions (B)(4) through (B)(6); redesignated former division (B)(4) as division (B)(7); rewrote division (C); added division (E); redesignated former divisions (E) and (F) as divisions (F) and (G); and made changes to reflect gender-neutral language. Prior to amendment, division (C) read:

"(C) Guardian ad litem as counsel

When the guardian ad litem is an attorney admitted to practice in this state, he may also serve as counsel to his ward."

Staff Notes

1998:

Rule 4(B) Guardian ad litem; when appointed

The 1998 amendment added division (B)(7), requiring the appointment of a guardian *ad litem* for removal actions, as defined in Juv. R. 2(EE), also added in the amendments effective July 1, 1998. At the discretion of the court, the court may appoint the guardian *ad litem* initially appointed for the child by the court that entered the original dispositional placement order, with the consent of that guardian *ad litem*. Alternatively, the court may appoint a new guardian *ad litem*.

The addition of a new division (B)(7) required the renumbering of the former division to what is now division (B)(8).

1995:

Rule 4. Assistance of Counsel; Guardian Ad Litem

The 1995 amendment changed the title of this rule and of division (A) to more accurately reflect the substance of the rule. There were no changes to the text of the rule.

1994:

Rule 4 Right to Counsel; Guardian Ad Litem

Masculine references throughout Juv. R. 4 have been replaced by gender neutral language.

Rule 4(A) Right to counsel; when arises

The 1994 amendment added a new sentence to the end of division (A) to clarify that Juv. R. 4 does not create a right to court-appointed counsel, and that the right to appointed counsel arises from other sources of law.

Rule 4(B) Guardian ad litem; when appointed

Juv. R. 4(B) governs the appointment of a guardian ad litem (GAL). New sections specify the appointment of a GAL as required by section 2151.281 of the Revised Code.

Rule 4(C) Guardian ad litem as counsel

Juv. R. 4(C) requires the appointment of a new GAL when an attorney serving as GAL is also the child's attorney and a conflict of interest exists. (Revised Code 2151.281(H)).

Rule 4(E) Notice to guardian ad litem

Juv. R. 4(E) specifies notice requirements to GALs pursuant to section 2151.281(I) of the Revised Code.

Editor's Comment

Right to counsel; guardian ad litem 1
Right to counsel; when arises 2
Guardian ad litem; when appointed 3
Guardian ad litem as counsel 4
Appearance of attorneys 5
Notice to guardian ad litem 6
Withdrawal of counsel or guardian ad litem 7
Costs 8

1. Right to counsel; guardian ad litem

Juv R 4 governs the right to counsel and guardian ad litem and tries to coordinate the two more clearly than is done in Ch 2151.

2. Right to counsel; when arises

Juv R 4(A) first states the right of all parties to counsel and to appointed counsel if indigent. The terms "party" and "indigent person" are broadly defined in Juv R 2(X) and 2(P) respectively.

The rule then provides that these rights arise as soon as a person becomes a party to a juvenile court proceeding as defined in Juv R 2(F). These rights arise also whenever a child is taken into custody pursuant to Juv R 6. The rule is based on 2151.352.

Juv R 4(A) further provides that in child abuse cases (2151.031) the court must appoint an attorney to represent the interests of the child. When considering this provision in conjunction with the statutory requirement (2151.281(B)(1)) that a guardian ad litem be appointed to protect the interests of an alleged abused or neglected child, it appears that the proper procedure would be to appoint an attorney to act as both legal counsel and guardian ad litem for an alleged abused child. If the court finds that a conflict may exist between the attorney's dual role of legal counsel and guardian ad litem, 2151.281(H) and Juv R 4(C)(2) require the court to relieve the person of his duties as guardian ad litem and appoint someone else as guardian ad litem for the child.

The last sentence of Juv R 4(A), which was added in 1994, provides that the rule does not create a right to court-appointed counsel where that right is not provided for by constitution or statute. Many courts have held that the statutory equivalent to Juv R 4(A), 2151.352, provides for court-appointed counsel in all juvenile court proceedings. (See *Lowry v Lowry*, 48 App(3d) 184, 549 NE(2d) 176 (Ross 1988); *In re Kriak*, 30 App(3d) 83, 506 NE(2d) 556 (Medina 1986).) However, other courts have held that the statute is limited to delinquency, unruly, neglect, dependency, abuse, and juvenile traffic offender cases, and excludes from its purview "private" child custody proceedings initiated under 2151.23(A)(2). (See *Forntey v Hines*, No. 90AP020018 (5th Dist Ct App, Tuscarawas, 10–31–90); *In re Stover*, No. 92–CA–15 (5th Dist Ct App, Guernsey, 9–9–93).)

3. Guardian ad litem; when appointed

Juv R 4(B) continues Ohio practice, as represented by 2151.281, by handling the problem of conflict between interests of parents and their children through the appointment of a guardian ad litem rather than simply by appointment of a second counsel. The guardian ad litem can then act as counsel under Juv R 4(C) if he is an attorney or may ask the court to appoint a separate attorney for the child.

On the other hand, Juv R 4(B) expands the cases in which a guardian ad litem is to be appointed. The cases mentioned in Juv R 4(B)(1), 4(B)(3), 4(B)(4), 4(B)(5), and 4(B)(6) are already covered in 2151.281. The catch-all provision of Juv R 4(B)(7), however, is not covered in the statute, and Juv R 4(B)(2) is significantly broader than 2151.281(A)(2), which provides that a guardian ad litem shall be appointed where the court finds there *is* a conflict of interest. Juv R 4(B)(2) substitutes "may" for "is" on the theory that a possibility of conflict should be sufficient to appoint someone to insure that the child is adequately represented. The court should consider the appointment of a guardian ad litem whenever a child so requests, on the theory that when the child perceives a conflict of interest he is entitled to individual representation.

4. Guardian ad litem as counsel

Juv R 4(C) provides that a guardian ad litem may serve as counsel to his ward where he is an attorney admitted to practice in this state. Juv R 4(C)(3) and 2151.281(H) provide that if the guardian ad litem is not an attorney, the court may appoint an attorney to serve as attorney for the guardian ad litem. Moreover, 2151.281(B)(1) prohibits the court from appointing as guardian ad litem the attorney responsible for presenting the evidence alleging that the child is abused or neglected, or an employee of any party in the proceeding.

5. Appearance of attorneys

Juv R 4(D) provides the means by which an attorney is to enter his appearance in a case. The rule is taken from the Minnesota Rules and the National Council on Crime and Delinquency Model Rules.

6. Notice to guardian ad litem

Both Juv R 4(E) and 2151.352(I) require notice of all proceedings to be given to the guardian ad litem in the same manner as is given to other parties. These provisions are probably not necessary because the guardian ad litem is defined as a party in Juv R 2(X), and Juv R 15(A) requires service of summons on all parties.

7. Withdrawal of counsel or guardian ad litem

Juv R 4(F) gives the court discretion to disallow a request for withdrawal by an attorney or guardian ad litem unless there is good cause shown. The rule is consistent with 2151.281.

8. Costs

Juv R 4(G), which includes compensation for guardians ad litem and provides for assessment against other parties where appropriate, is consistent with 2151.281(D).

Cross References

Child, parents and custodian, right to legal counsel, 2151.352
Guardian ad litem to be appointed in proceeding concerning delinquent or unruly child, 2151.281
Paternity proceedings, representation of child's interests, 3111.07

Library References

Infants ⚖68.4, 68.7(3), 205.
Westlaw Topic No. 211.
C.J.S. Infants §§ 46 to 52, 62 to 67, 201, 202.

Research References

ALR Library

101 ALR 5th 351, Validity and Efficacy of Minor's Waiver of Right to Counsel--Cases Decided Since Application of Gault, 387 U.S. 1, 87 S. Ct. 1428, 18 L. Ed. 2d 527 (1967).

Encyclopedias

OH Jur. 3d Family Law § 961, Civil Nature of Proceedings—Indigent Defendants.
OH Jur. 3d Family Law § 969, Who May Bring an Action—Child Support Enforcement Agency.
OH Jur. 3d Family Law § 1626, Right Under Juvenile Court Law and Rules.
OH Jur. 3d Family Law § 1627, Procedure to Obtain Counsel.
OH Jur. 3d Family Law § 1628, Appearance by and Withdrawal of Counsel.
OH Jur. 3d Family Law § 1631, Withdrawal or Discharge of Guardian Ad Litem.
OH Jur. 3d Family Law § 1647, Proceedings Before Referee; Powers and Duties.
OH Jur. 3d Family Law § 1667, Admission or Denial of Allegations.
OH Jur. 3d Family Law § 1681, Conduct of Hearing; Advisement of Rights.
OH Jur. 3d Family Law § 1721, Appointed Counsel.
OH Jur. 3d Family Law § 1722, Guardian Ad Litem.
OH Jur. 3d Family Law § 1628.1, Ineffective Assistance of Counsel.
OH Jur. 3d Family Law § 1628.5, Waiver of Counsel.
OH Jur. 3d Family Law § 1629.5, in Delinquency Proceedings.

Treatises and Practice Aids

Klein, Darling, & Terez, Baldwin's Ohio Practice Civil Practice § 24:2, Applicability of Civ. R. 24.
Sowald & Morganstern, Baldwin's Ohio Practice Domestic Relations Law § 15:64, Guardian Ad Litem—Conflict of Interest.
Sowald & Morganstern, Baldwin's Ohio Practice Domestic Relations Law § 15:66, Guardian Ad Litem—Training.
Carlin, Baldwin's Ohio Practice, Merrick-Rippner Probate Law § 104:5, Juvenile Courts—Constitutional Issues—Right to Notice, Counsel, and Trial.
Carlin, Baldwin's Ohio Practice, Merrick-Rippner Probate Law § 107:9, Parties to Proceedings.
Carlin, Baldwin's Ohio Practice, Merrick-Rippner Probate Law § 104:10, Juvenile Court—Constitutional Issues—Due Process Rights in Actions to Terminate Parental Rights.
Carlin, Baldwin's Ohio Practice, Merrick-Rippner Probate Law § 107:45, Adjudicatory Hearings—Parties' Right to Counsel.
Carlin, Baldwin's Ohio Practice, Merrick-Rippner Probate Law § 107:46, Adjudicatory Hearings—Child's Right to Guardian Ad Litem.
Carlin, Baldwin's Ohio Practice, Merrick-Rippner Probate Law § 107:49, Adjudicatory Hearings—Conduct of Hearing by Magistrate.
Carlin, Baldwin's Ohio Practice, Merrick-Rippner Probate Law § 108:25, Juvenile Court—Parentage Act—Right to Counsel for Indigent Paternity Defendant.
Carlin, Baldwin's Ohio Practice, Merrick-Rippner Probate Law § 107:104, Requests to Invoke Adult Portion of Serious Youthful Offender disposition, Effective January 1, 2002.
Carlin, Baldwin's Ohio Practice, Merrick-Rippner Probate Law § 107:164, Waiver of Service of Summons—Form.
Giannelli & Yeomans, Ohio Juvenile Law § 1:8, Rules of Juvenile Procedure.
Giannelli & Yeomans, Ohio Juvenile Law § 15:2, Intake.
Giannelli & Yeomans, Ohio Juvenile Law § 18:2, Issuance of Summons: Proper Parties.
Giannelli & Yeomans, Ohio Juvenile Law § 18:3, Summons: Contents and Form.
Giannelli & Yeomans, Ohio Juvenile Law § 23:3, Right to Counsel.
Giannelli & Yeomans, Ohio Juvenile Law § 23:5, Ineffective Assistance of Counsel.
Giannelli & Yeomans, Ohio Juvenile Law § 23:6, Guardian Ad Litem.
Giannelli & Yeomans, Ohio Juvenile Law § 24:4, Pretrial Orders.
Giannelli & Yeomans, Ohio Juvenile Law § 32:2, Jurisdiction Over Parents and Others.
Giannelli & Yeomans, Ohio Juvenile Law App. D, Appendix D. Glossary.
Giannelli & Yeomans, Ohio Juvenile Law § 22:11, Right to Counsel.
Giannelli & Yeomans, Ohio Juvenile Law § 30:12, Permanent Custody—Procedural Issues.

Law Review and Journal Commentaries

The Criminal Defense Lawyer in the Juvenile Justice System, David A. Harris. 26 U Tol L Rev 751 (Summer 1995).

Do Juveniles Facing Civil Commitment Have a Right to Counsel? A Therapeutic Jurisprudence Brief. Bruce J. Winick and Ginger Lerner-Wren, 71 U Cin L Rev 115 (Fall 2002).

Lassiter v. Department of Social Services: The Due Process Right to Appointed Counsel Left Hanging Uneasily in the Mathews v. Eldrodge Balance, Jane E. Jackson. 8 N Ky L Rev 513 (1981).

Legal Representation Of A Fetus: The Mother And Child Disunion, Comment. 18 Cap U L Rev 591 (Winter 1989).

Manipulated by *Miranda*: A Critical Analysis of Bright Lines and Voluntary Confessions Under *United States v. Dickerson*, Casenote. 68 U Cin L Rev 555 (Winter 2000).

The Right to Remain Silent: The Use of Pre–Arrest Silence in *United States v. Oplinger*, 150 F.3d 1061 (5th Cir. 1998), Casenote. 68 U Cin L Rev 505 (Winter 2000).

Notes of Decisions

Cause of action 10
Constitutional issues 1
Damages 8
Effective assistance of counsel 4
Equitable actions 2
Fees and costs 5
Guardian ad litem 9
Jurisdiction 11
Persons represented 6
Right to counsel 7
Waiver of counsel 3

---

1. Constitutional issues

Defendant, who was convicted of burglary and committed to Department of Youth Services, did not validly waive his right to counsel; at adjudication hearing, trial court made no mention of counsel issue and merely asked whether defendant was ready to proceed, record was devoid of any evidence that court explained defendant's rights to him with respect to obtaining counsel, there was no evidence that defendant waived his right to counsel at any point prior to or during trial, and record did not disclose any attempt on part of court to explain defendant's right to counsel or waiver of that right at any time. In re L.E.P. (Ohio App. 2 Dist., Clark, 09-02-2005) No. 2004 CA 85, 2005-Ohio-4600, 2005 WL 2107854, Unreported. Criminal Law ⚖ 641.4(4)

There is no constitutional right to appointment of counsel for indigent parents in a hearing on a complaint by a county social services department for temporary custody of allegedly neglected children. (Annotation from former RC 2151.352.) In re Miller (Ohio 1984) 12 Ohio St.3d 40, 465 N.E.2d 397, 12 O.B.R. 35.

Juvenile court magistrate's judgment entry, indicating only a finding that "subject child, after first being advised of all procedural and constitutional rights, including the right to counsel and a continuance herein, asserts said rights and ADMITS the allegations as they appear in the complaint," did not establish under the federal and state due process clauses a valid waiver of counsel or that the admission was voluntarily, knowingly, and intelligently made. In re Royal (Ohio App. 7 Dist., 03-01-1999) 132 Ohio App.3d 496, 725 N.E.2d 685. Constitutional Law ⚖ 43(1); Infants ⚖ 199; Infants ⚖ 205

There is no material difference with respect to constitutional right to counsel between adult and juvenile proceedings. In re East (Ohio App. 8 Dist., 07-17-1995) 105 Ohio App.3d 221, 663 N.E.2d 983, dismissed, appeal not allowed 74 Ohio St.3d 1482, 657 N.E.2d 1375. Infants ⚖ 205

Where a juvenile has received the following essentials of due process and fair treatment: (1) written notice of the specific charge or factual allegations, given to the juvenile and his parents or guardian sufficiently in advance of the hearing to permit preparation; (2) notification to the juvenile and his parents of the juvenile's right to be represented by counsel retained by them, or, if they are unable to afford counsel, that counsel will be appointed to represent the juvenile; (3) application of the constitutional privileges against self-incrimination; and (4), absent a valid confession, a determination of delinquency and an order of commitment based only on sworn testimony subjected to the opportunity for cross-examination in accordance with constitutional requirements, such juvenile has not been deprived of due process under either the Constitution of the United States or the Constitution of the State of Ohio. (Annotation from former RC 2151.35.) In re Baker (Hocking 1969) 18 Ohio App.2d 276, 248 N.E.2d 620, 47 O.O.2d 411.

In a complaint against a juvenile for gross sexual imposition it is not necessary for the juvenile to be given Miranda rights during a noncustodial interview that takes place in the juvenile's home at the kitchen table. State v. Gray (Ohio App. 9 Dist., Lorain, 03-14-2001) No. 00CA007695, 2001 WL 251345, Unreported.

Appointment of the guardian ad litem for the children as counsel for child did not violate child's constitutional right to counsel, in termination of parental rights proceeding; there was no conflict of interest between counsel's roles as guardian ad litem and as attorney for child since the children both expressed a desire to remain with their foster mother. In re Legg (Ohio App. 8 Dist., Cuyahoga, 09-05-2002) No. 80542, No. 80543, 2002-Ohio-4582, 2002 WL 2027290, Unreported. Infants ⇐ 205

The trial court has the discretion to decide, in the interests of due process, whether there should be an appointment of counsel for the indigent in every parental status termination hearing, and the failure to appoint counsel does not presumptively deny the parent of constitutional rights where the presence of counsel could not have made a determinative difference. Lassiter v. Department of Social Services of Durham County, N. C. (U.S.N.C. 1981) 101 S.Ct. 2153, 452 U.S. 18, 68 L.Ed.2d 640, rehearing denied 102 S.Ct. 889, 453 U.S. 927, 69 L.Ed.2d 1023.

A juvenile taken into custody as a delinquent has certain rights guaranteed by the Due Process Clause of the United States Constitution in delinquency proceedings by the state which include the following: (1) notice of the charge, (2) right to counsel, (3) right to confrontation and cross-examination, and (4) privilege against self incrimination. Application of Gault (U.S.Ariz. 1967) 87 S.Ct. 1428, 387 U.S. 1, 18 L.Ed.2d 527, 40 O.O.2d 378.

2. Equitable actions

Indigent parent was entitled to writ of mandamus commanding juvenile court judge to appoint counsel for her in child custody action commenced by her; parent had a clear legal right to relief prayed for, judge was under clear legal duty to appoint counsel for mother, and mother had no plain and adequate remedy in the ordinary course of law. State ex rel. Lunsford v. Buck (Meigs 1993) 88 Ohio App.3d 425, 623 N.E.2d 1356. Mandamus ⇐ 29

3. Waiver of counsel

Juvenile did not have statutory right to appointed counsel in delinquency adjudication proceedings, where both juvenile and his mother chose to waive counsel. In re Spears (Ohio App. 5 Dist., Licking, 04-17-2006) No. 2005-CA-93, 2006-Ohio-1920, 2006 WL 1011201, Unreported. Infants ⇐ 205

Father could not be viewed as having waived his right to counsel, and thus trial court committed plain error in allowing father's counsel to withdraw her representation immediately prior to dispositional hearing at which father's parental rights were terminated; trial court could not have reasonably concluded that failure of counsel's communication with father resulted in inability of counsel to ascertain father's wishes because it was counsel who informed court that it was father's desire to have custody of child. In re Tyler S. (Ohio App. 6 Dist., Lucas, 03-18-2005) No. L-04-1294, 2005-Ohio-1225, 2005 WL 635029, Unreported. Infants ⇐ 243

Juvenile knowingly, voluntarily, and intelligently waived right to counsel at delinquency proceeding related to probation violation, where juvenile was 17 years old, possessed above-average intelligence, had extensive experience with juvenile court system, had his parents present to assist him, was advised of charge and possible punishments, was advised of right to counsel, and indicated that he did not want counsel to represent him. In re Estes (Ohio App. 4 Dist., Washington, 09-24-2004) No. 04CA11, 2004-Ohio-5163, 2004 WL 2260510, Unreported. Infants ⇐ 205

Mother's failure to cooperate with appointed counsel and court constituted waiver of her right to counsel in termination of parental rights proceeding; mother did not appear at disposition hearing in spite of receiving notice, counsel made continued attempts to contact mother without success, caseworker had not had recent contact with mother, other evidence showed that mother was disinterested in welfare of child since birth, and court permitted counsel to withdraw. In re Savanah M. (Ohio App. 6 Dist., Lucas, 10-31-2003) No. L-03-1112, 2003-Ohio-5855, 2003 WL 22462478, Unreported. Infants ⇐ 205

Neither juvenile's waiver of counsel nor his admission to charges against him were made in a knowing manner, for purposes of delinquency proceedings, where juvenile was never informed of nature of charges against him, trial court made no mention of possible defenses or mitigating circumstances that related to juvenile's situation, and juvenile was not informed that if he admitted to the charges he would be losing certain rights associated with trial. In re Styer (Ohio App. 3 Dist., Union, 11-19-2002) No. 14-02-12, 2002-Ohio-6273, 2002 WL 31555992, Unreported. Infants ⇐ 199; Infants ⇐ 205

Juvenile's waiver of right to counsel at probation violation hearing was not voluntary, knowing, and intelligent, where trial court did not engage juvenile in meaningful discussion to determine whether juvenile understood rights she was waiving. In re Vaughters (Ohio App. 8 Dist., Cuyahoga, 10-24-2002) No. 80650, 2002-Ohio-5843, 2002 WL 31401623, Unreported. Infants ⇐ 205

Juvenile, who had been adjudicated delinquent, did not knowingly, intelligently, and voluntarily waive his right to counsel, at show-cause hearing that state brought against juvenile for failing to follow all terms and conditions of treatment at Youth Treatment Center (YTC); juvenile was advised that in order to be afforded his constitutional rights, he would have to deny charges levied against him, juvenile had right to counsel at every stage of juvenile proceeding, including disposition, and statute governing right to counsel did not differentiate between juvenile who denied charge and juvenile who admitted charge. In re William B. (Ohio App. 6 Dist., 08-26-2005) 163 Ohio App.3d 201, 837 N.E.2d 414, 2005-Ohio-4428. Infants ⇐ 205

Mother waived her right to counsel in proceeding to terminate mother's parental rights; mother failed to maintain contact with and to cooperate with counsel, mother failed to appear at scheduled hearings even though she was present at hearing when county department of jobs and family services initially filed complaint alleging dependency, and counsel sent one letter and made numerous phone calls in attempt to contact mother. In re C.H. (Ohio App. 3 Dist., 08-15-2005) 162 Ohio App.3d 602, 834 N.E.2d 401, 2005-Ohio-4183. Infants ⇐ 205

Where a parent in proceeding to terminate parental rights fails to maintain contact with counsel, fails to appear for scheduled hearings despite receiving notice of such, and fails to cooperate with counsel and the court, the court may infer that the parent has waived his or her right to counsel and may grant counsel's request to withdraw. In re C.H. (Ohio App. 3 Dist., 08-15-2005) 162 Ohio App.3d 602, 834 N.E.2d 401, 2005-Ohio-4183. Infants ⇐ 205

Trial court abused its discretion in failing to either appoint counsel to represent indigent child in delinquency proceedings or to obtain a waiver of counsel from guardian ad litem, even though guardian had counsel; court could not presume dual appointment absent express dual appointment. In re Amos (Ohio App. 3 Dist., 09-22-2003) 154 Ohio App.3d 434, 797 N.E.2d 568, 2003-Ohio-5014. Infants ⇐ 205

To be effective, a waiver of a juvenile's right to counsel must be voluntary, knowing and intelligent. In re Johnston (Ohio App. 11 Dist., 04-30-2001) 142 Ohio App.3d 314, 755 N.E.2d 457. Infants ⇐ 205

Juvenile court's limited inquiry at dispositional hearing and 14-year-old juvenile's limited responses, including court's asking whether juvenile recalled the rights explained to him at adjudicatory hearing and juvenile's response, "Um-hum," were insufficient to establish valid admission or valid waiver of right to counsel under the federal and state due process clauses. In re Royal (Ohio App. 7 Dist., 03-01-1999) 132 Ohio App.3d 496, 725 N.E.2d 685. Constitutional Law ⇐ 43(1); Infants ⇐ 199; Infants ⇐ 205

Presence of 14-year-old juvenile's mother at the adjudicatory hearing did not provide dispositive proof that the juvenile waived his rights and gave his admission voluntarily, knowingly, and intelligently. In re Royal (Ohio App. 7 Dist., 03-01-1999) 132 Ohio App.3d 496, 725 N.E.2d 685. Infants ⇐ 199; Infants ⇐ 205

Since juvenile was advised of his right to counsel and waived it when he entered his admission to robbery charge, it was not necessary for court to again advise juvenile of his right at disposition hearing. In re East (Ohio App. 8 Dist., 07-17-1995) 105 Ohio App.3d 221, 663 N.E.2d 983, dismissed, appeal not allowed 74 Ohio St.3d 1482, 657 N.E.2d 1375. Infants ⇐ 203

Fact that juvenile's mother signed waiver of counsel form did not amount to waiver of juvenile's right to counsel, but fact that mother was present when waiver took place indicated that waiver was voluntary and knowing. In re East (Ohio App. 8 Dist., 07-17-1995) 105 Ohio App.3d 221, 663 N.E.2d 983, dismissed, appeal not allowed 74 Ohio St.3d 1482, 657 N.E.2d 1375. Infants ⚖ 205

Referee's report/journal entry and supplemental report, stating that juvenile was advised of his right to counsel and he chose to waive this right, were adequate to show juvenile's waiver of his right to counsel, absent request for transcript of admission hearing. In re East (Ohio App. 8 Dist., 07-17-1995) 105 Ohio App.3d 221, 663 N.E.2d 983, dismissed, appeal not allowed 74 Ohio St.3d 1482, 657 N.E.2d 1375. Infants ⚖ 246

An alleged delinquent's response of "don't think so" in response to the juvenile court judge's questions as to whether she desired the representation of counsel is insufficient to support the court's finding that the right to counsel was waived. In re Nation (Shelby 1989) 61 Ohio App.3d 763, 573 N.E.2d 1155.

Colloquy prior to juvenile's admission of delinquency allegations, in which trial court informed juvenile that she had the right to an attorney and that one would be appointed for her if she could not afford one, asked whether juvenile wished to have an attorney, and was told "no" by juvenile, was not sufficient to establish a knowing, voluntary, and intelligent waiver of juvenile's right to counsel. In re K.J. (Ohio App. 8 Dist., Cuyahoga, 05-23-2002) No. 79612, No. 79940, 2002-Ohio-2615, 2002 WL 1041818, Unreported. Infants ⚖ 174

A trial court does not fulfill its duty to ascertain whether a juvenile knows of his right to be provided with counsel if he is indigent simply by asking the juvenile if he has received a copy of the statement of rights and whether he has any questions about those rights where (1) the statement of rights is two pages in length, (2) single-spaced, and (3) the right of counsel if indigent is not stated until near the top of the second page; under such circumstances, the juvenile even with a parent present, is likely to sign a form he has not fully read or does not fully understand while at the same time telling a judge otherwise. In re Shane (Ohio App. 2 Dist., Darke, 01-26-2001) No. 1523, 2001 WL 62550, Unreported.

A juvenile does not knowingly and intelligently waive her right to counsel (1) in absence of any examination by the court regarding such right in deciding whether to admit or deny the complaint, (2) where the complaint states that the juvenile is a delinquent child by reason of committing an act that would constitute complicity to receiving stolen property if she were an adult, and (3) where the magistrate fails to ascertain whether the juvenile understands the charge against her or the possible length of any commitment in the custody of the Department of Youth Services. In re Doyle (App. 2 Dist., 10-03-1997) 122 Ohio App.3d 767, 702 N.E.2d 970.

4. Effective assistance of counsel

In proceeding in which county children services sought permanent custody of children, failure of mother's counsel to obtain an expert witness to rebut testimony of psychologist who testified on behalf of county did not result in prejudice to mother, and thus could not amount to ineffective assistance. In re Ohler (Ohio App. 4 Dist., Hocking, 03-24-2005) No. 04CA8, 2005-Ohio-1583, 2005 WL 737580, Unreported. Infants ⚖ 205

Failure of mother's appointed counsel to appear at hearing before juvenile court concerning mother's objections to magistrate's decision constituted ineffective assistance of counsel in dependency proceeding in which county jobs and family services sought permanent custody of child; counsel had not sought permission to withdraw, failure to appear constituted deficient performance, and mother was prejudiced by counsel's failure to appear. In re Walling (Ohio App. 1 Dist., Hamilton, 04-01-2005) No. C-040745, 2005-Ohio-1558, 2005 WL 736665, Unreported. Infants ⚖ 205

Putative father failed to establish that he was denied effective assistance of counsel in termination of parental rights proceeding, where, even if counsel had informed trial court that putative father wished to be reunited with son, there was no reasonable probability that court would not have granted permanent custody to county children services agency as there was ample evidence that putative father failed to meet requirements of case plan, including that putative father did not cooperate in paternity testing process and did not offer financial support for child. In re C.S. (Ohio App. 2 Dist., Montgomery, 10-22-2004) No. 20379, 2004-Ohio-5810, 2004 WL 2445238, Unreported. Infants ⚖ 205

Counsel's failure to object when guardian ad litem for the children questioned witnesses during termination of parental rights hearing did not constitute ineffective assistance; mother failed to overcome the strong presumption that counsel's failure to object was reasonable trial strategy, and mother failed to establish that counsel's failure to object to the questioning by guardian ad litem prejudiced mother or affected the outcome of trial. In re Curry (Ohio App. 4 Dist., Washington, 02-11-2004) No. 03CA51, 2004-Ohio-750, 2004 WL 307476, Unreported. Infants ⚖ 205

Father's counsel at termination of parental rights hearing was not ineffective for failing to ask questions on cross examination or present witnesses; failing to question witnesses on cross examination and choosing not to present witnesses fell within realm of trial strategy, and father failed to demonstrate how counsel's alleged deficient performance affected outcome of proceedings. In re Riley (Ohio App. 4 Dist., Washington, 07-25-2003) No. 03CA19, 2003-Ohio-4109, 2003 WL 21783373, Unreported. Infants ⚖ 205

Trial court's error in failing to either make express dual appointment of guardian ad litem to serve as dependent child's guardian and attorney, or to make separate appointments for child's guardian ad litem and child's attorney at outset of child dependency proceeding did not prejudice child; child's attorney and guardian ad litem entered her appearance at probable cause and dependency hearings, and no conflict existed, given that child asked to be placed in Planned Permanent Living Arrangement (PPLA), and attorney/guardian ad litem's recommendation as guardian was that court place child in PPLA. In re Beasley (Ohio App. 4 Dist., Scioto, 05-28-2003) No. 03CA2874, 2003-Ohio-2857, 2003 WL 21278912, Unreported, motion for delayed appeal denied 99 Ohio St.3d 1466, 791 N.E.2d 982, 2003-Ohio-3669, appeal not allowed 99 Ohio St.3d 1515, 792 N.E.2d 201, 2003-Ohio-3957. Infants ⚖ 253

Father failed to establish that he was prejudiced by his trial counsel's alleged failure to be more involved in the parental rights termination hearing, counsel's representation of mother and father and the same time, and counsel's failure to arrange for father's presence at the hearing; none of counsel's alleged deficiencies affected the outcome at trial. In re Joseph P. (Ohio App. 6 Dist., Lucas, 05-02-2003) No. L-02-1385, 2003-Ohio-2217, 2003 WL 2007268, Unreported. Infants ⚖ 205

Juvenile did not validly waive her right to counsel in delinquency proceeding; while juvenile court orally informed juvenile that she had a right to an attorney at date in which juvenile was not admit or deny guilt to delinquency charge, trial court made no mention of the counsel issue at adjudication hearing and merely asked whether juvenile was ready to proceed, and juvenile court never inquired whether juvenile was waiving her right to counsel. In re Bays (Ohio App. 2 Dist., Greene, 03-14-2003) No. 2002-CA-52, No. 2002-CA-56, 2003-Ohio-1256, 2003 WL 1193787, Unreported. Infants ⚖ 205

For purposes of ineffective assistance claim, minor mother and her parents did not make necessary showing that mother was prejudiced, in dependency proceeding that culminated in judgment terminating mother's parental rights to infant child, by failure of mother's counsel to appear at a pretrial hearing, where counsel made unsuccessful request for continuance of pretrial hearing, and all information shared at hearing was to be shared with mother's counsel. In re Baby Girl Doe (Ohio App. 6 Dist., 08-30-2002) 149 Ohio App.3d 717, 778 N.E.2d 1053, 2002-Ohio-4470, appeal not allowed 97 Ohio St.3d 1425, 777 N.E.2d 278, 2002-Ohio-5820. Infants ⚖ 205

Where the proceeding contemplates the loss of parents' essential and basic civil rights to raise their children, the test for ineffective assistance of counsel used in criminal cases is equally applicable to actions seeking to force the permanent, involuntary termination of parental custody. In re Baby Girl Doe (Ohio App. 6 Dist., 08-30-2002) 149 Ohio App.3d 717, 778 N.E.2d 1053, 2002-Ohio-4470, appeal not allowed 97 Ohio St.3d 1425, 777 N.E.2d 278, 2002-Ohio-5820. Infants ⚖ 205

Even assuming that testimony of protective services supervisor for county children's services agency, that child's maternal grandmother told on-call social worker and supervisor that she was upset that she could not have custody of child and that "she was just going to 'go' over and just take him," was inadmissible hearsay, any deficient performance of father's counsel in failing to object at the shelter care hearing was not prejudicial; court was not bound by formal rules of evidence at the hearing, and there was abundant evidence establishing that father's relatives were no longer able to care for child and that child should be placed in foster care. In re Wingo (Ohio App. 4 Dist., 06-01-2001) 143 Ohio App.3d 652, 758 N.E.2d 780, 2001-Ohio-2477. Infants ⚖ 173.1; Infants ⚖ 253

Even assuming father's counsel provided deficient performance by failing to object that testimony of protective services supervisor for county children's services agency involved events and statements outside her personal knowledge, father was not prejudiced at hearing on agency's motion to terminate parental rights; much of the information was also testified to by other witnesses who had firsthand knowledge of events. In re Wingo (Ohio App. 4 Dist., 06-01-2001) 143 Ohio App.3d 652, 758 N.E.2d 780, 2001-Ohio-2477. Infants ⚖ 205; Infants ⚖ 253

Assuming that father's counsel provided deficient performance by failing to submit written argument to court regarding whether child was dependent child and by failing to appear at the hearing extending temporary custody, father was not prejudiced; at that juncture of the case, county children's services agency was attempting to reunify child with mother and place him with a relative until such goal could be accomplished, father had expressed no desire to gain custody of child, and child's relatives were either not interested in custody or were considered improper placements by agency. In re Wingo (Ohio App. 4 Dist., 06-01-2001) 143 Ohio App.3d 652, 758 N.E.2d 780, 2001-Ohio-2477. Infants ⇒ 205; Infants ⇒ 253

Where proceeding contemplates loss of parents' essential and basic civil rights to raise their children, test for ineffective assistance of counsel used in criminal cases is equally applicable to actions seeking to force permanent, involuntary termination of parental custody. In re Heston (Ohio App. 1 Dist., 09-18-1998) 129 Ohio App.3d 825, 719 N.E.2d 93. Infants ⇒ 205

Statutory right to counsel in child protection proceedings includes right to effective assistance of counsel. In re Heston (Ohio App. 1 Dist., 09-18-1998) 129 Ohio App.3d 825, 719 N.E.2d 93. Infants ⇒ 205

The two-part test for ineffective assistance of counsel used in criminal cases, announced in Strickland v Washington, 466 US 668, 104 SCt 2052, 80 LEd(2d) 674 (1984), is equally applicable in actions by the state to force the permanent, involuntary termination of parental rights. Jones v. Lucas County Children Services Bd. (Lucas 1988) 46 Ohio App.3d 85, 546 N.E.2d 471. Infants ⇒ 205

5. Fees and costs

Fees and expenses of guardian ad litem appointed in proceeding to modify child support should have been divided equally between mother and father, since both parties equally caused the work of the guardian ad litem. Jarvis v. Witter (Ohio App. 8 Dist., Cuyahoga, 12-09-2004) No. 84128, 2004-Ohio-6628, 2004 WL 2830789, Unreported. Infants ⇒ 83

Ruling on motion for guardian ad litem fees without conducting evidentiary hearing was not error in proceeding for modification of child support, where ex-husband filed objections to fees prior to court's ruling on fees such that court had ample information to determine reasonableness of fees and court had great deal of experience with case and parties. Fox v. Fox (Ohio App. 3 Dist., Hancock, 06-28-2004) No. 5-03-42, 2004-Ohio-3344, 2004 WL 1433553, Unreported. Infants ⇒ 83

Trial court's approval of request of guardian ad litem for fees and equal division of fees between former husband and former wife in proceeding on former husband's motion for temporary custody of his and former wife's children did not constitute abuse of discretion; approval implicitly rejected husband's claim that guardian did not act in ward's best interest, notwithstanding husband's claims that guardian was biased against him. Beatley v. Beatley (Ohio App. 5 Dist., Delaware, 08-15-2003) No. 03CAF02010, 2003-Ohio-4375, 2003 WL 21962540, Unreported. Infants ⇒ 83

Court did not err in ruling on motion of guardian ad litem for fees in proceeding on former husband's motion for temporary custody of his and former wife's children, without holding evidentiary hearing on issue; record reflected parties were given opportunity to be heard on fee issue, former husband filed memorandum in opposition to fee request, parties were almost continuously in front of court on variety of issues, and the same judge had been involved with case since its inception. Beatley v. Beatley (Ohio App. 5 Dist., Delaware, 08-15-2003) No. 03CAF02010, 2003-Ohio-4375, 2003 WL 21962540, Unreported. Infants ⇒ 83

Parents should not have been ordered to pay bill prepared by Public Defender's Office for representation of their son in delinquency proceedings, where, at no time prior to dispositional hearing did court address parents, inform them of their status as parties to action, or advise them of their right to counsel. In re Hinko (Cuyahoga 1992) 84 Ohio App.3d 89, 616 N.E.2d 515. Infants ⇒ 205

In an action brought against a parent and his child for damages caused by a fire in a rental unit, where the court finds the child alone liable for such damages in that the child was responsible for starting the fire, the fees and expenses of a court-appointed guardian ad litem are properly charged to the indigent minor child and not to his parent, as part of the court costs. Nationwide Mut. Ins. Co. v. Wymer (Franklin 1986) 33 Ohio App.3d 318, 515 N.E.2d 987.

Pursuant to Juv R 4(F), the juvenile court is authorized to order a child's parents to pay the costs for the services of appointed counsel and guardians ad litem. In re Vaughn, No. 53462 (8th Dist Ct App, Cuyahoga, 10–15–87).

6. Persons represented

Juvenile court was not authorized to proceed with custody hearing and grant permanent and legal custody of children, where father, who had been represented by counsel during much of custody proceedings, was not represented by counsel at custody hearing, and juvenile court had not consented to withdrawal of father's attorney. In re B.P. (Ohio App. 8 Dist., Cuyahoga, 11-21-2002) No. 80659, 2002-Ohio-6318, 2002 WL 31619047, Unreported. Child Custody ⇒ 500

Parents are denied proper representation when the attorney for their children acts as both guardian ad litem and attorney in an action wherein custody is challenged by a county agency. In re Smith (Ottawa 1991) 77 Ohio App.3d 1, 601 N.E.2d 45.

Pursuant to RC 2151.352, a child, his parents, custodian, or other persons in loco parentis, if indigent, is entitled to be represented in all juvenile proceedings by a public defender in accordance with the comprehensive system set forth in RC Ch 120, regardless of whether the outcome of the proceeding could result in a loss of liberty. (Annotation from former RC 2151.352.) OAG 84–023, approved and followed by OAG 97–040.

7. Right to counsel

Dependent children were not deprived right to counsel in proceedings to terminate father's parental rights when guardians ad litem were appointed to also act as counsel for children, where there was no showing of either implied or actual conflict of interest in acting as their guardian ad litem or as counsel. In re McLean (Ohio App. 11 Dist., Trumbull, 05-25-2005) No. 2005-T-0018, 2005-Ohio-2576, 2005 WL 1231614, Unreported. Infants ⇒ 205

Record did not support finding that juvenile was represented by counsel at time of his commitment and sexual predator classification hearing that was held subsequent to juvenile's guilty plea to gross sexual imposition, even though trial court made two references to counsel and argument was made on juvenile's behalf urging the court not to impose a sexual predator classification; review of the record revealed that juvenile's probation officer argued in juvenile's defense, record indicated trial court's reference to "counsel" related to probation officer and the argument he made on juvenile's behalf, and transcript of the proceedings did not mention the name of defense counsel. In re C.F. (Ohio App. 8 Dist., Cuyahoga, 05-05-2005) No. 84434, 2005-Ohio-2190, 2005 WL 1048126, Unreported. Infants ⇒ 205

Grandmother whose minor daughter gave birth to child who was adjudicated dependent was not entitled to appointed counsel at dispositional hearing for the child, and thus trial court that appointed counsel for grandmother could permit such appointed counsel to withdraw at outset of the dispositional hearing, even though grandmother was party to the proceeding by virtue of her daughter's minor status, where there was no evidence that grandmother was ever a custodian of child or acted in loco parentis with respect to child. In re Denisha Michelle T. (Ohio App. 6 Dist., Lucas, 03-11-2005) No. L-04-1236, 2005-Ohio-1032, 2005 WL 567121, Unreported. Infants ⇒ 205

Magistrate erred in conducting hearing on father's motion to modify allocation of parental rights and responsibilities, which father brought following finding in paternity proceeding that he was child's natural father, without first informing mother of her statutory right to counsel or asking mother whether she wished to waive this right; magistrate further erred by conducting hearing despite mother's obvious unpreparedness and desire for counsel. Christopher V. v. Roxanne G. (Ohio App. 6 Dist., Lucas, 10-15-2004) No. L-03-1259, 2004-Ohio-5510, 2004 WL 2320336, Unreported. Children Out-of-wedlock ⇒ 20.10

Trial court was required to conduct investigation into whether dependent children were entitled to independent counsel in proceeding to determine their permanent custodian; guardian ad litem (GAL) who had been appointed for children was not a lawyer, and thus there was no possibility of court appointing him to represent children as their attorney, and, in GAL's report to court, in which he recommended that permanent custody of children be awarded to county, he made no mention of having talked with children about their feelings as to their permanent custodian, and whether children needed counsel was not discernable from record, given that, while court interviewed one child and was able to obtain some input from him as to his feelings about his mother, court failed to interview other child. In re Moore (Ohio App. 7 Dist., 08-24-2004) 158 Ohio App.3d 679, 821 N.E.2d 1039, 2004-Ohio-4544, supplemented 2005-Ohio-136, 2005 WL 78754. Infants ⇒ 205

Juvenile rule providing that, when complaint alleged that child was an abused child, court had to appoint attorney to represent interests of child, with respect to proceedings to determine permanent custodian for child, did not preclude appointment of independent counsel to represent children who had been adjudicated dependent rather than as abused. In re Moore (Ohio App. 7 Dist., 08-24-2004) 158 Ohio App.3d 679, 821 N.E.2d 1039, 2004-Ohio-4544, supplemented 2005-Ohio-136, 2005 WL 78754. Infants ⇨ 205

Mother did not waive on appeal issue of whether trial court should have appointed independent counsel for dependent children, in proceeding to determine whether county department of job and family services should be granted permanent custody of children, though mother did not raise issue in trial court; it would have been unfair to deny children their due process rights because mother failed to raise issue for children. In re Moore (Ohio App. 7 Dist., 08-24-2004) 158 Ohio App.3d 679, 821 N.E.2d 1039, 2004-Ohio-4544, supplemented 2005-Ohio-136, 2005 WL 78754. Infants ⇨ 243

Supreme Court decision in In re Williams that, pursuant to statute governing right to counsel in juvenile cases and juvenile rules, child who was subject of juvenile court proceeding to terminate parental rights was a party to that proceeding and, thus, was entitled to independent counsel in certain circumstances, had retroactive effect and applied to mother's case, in which permanent custody of her dependent children was being determined; Williams decision had been foreshadowed, and applying Williams decision retroactively would not produce injustice or hardship. In re Moore (Ohio App. 7 Dist., 08-24-2004) 158 Ohio App.3d 679, 821 N.E.2d 1039, 2004-Ohio-4544, supplemented 2005-Ohio-136, 2005 WL 78754. Courts ⇨ 100(1)

Trial court's decision during termination of parental rights proceedings to hold the dispositional hearing without the children's attorney/guardian ad litem did not amount to plain error; there was no evidence that the outcome of the trial would have been different if the attorney/guardian ad litem had not been absent. In re A.P. (Ohio App. 8 Dist., Cuyahoga, 08-05-2004) No. 83220, 2004-Ohio-4080, 2004 WL 1752941, Unreported. Infants ⇨ 243

Child's lack of attorney did not require reversal of order granting temporary custody of child to father and grandmother; order was interlocutory order subject to later modification, record reflected that mother, although informed of child's right to counsel, failed to request counsel, and record reflected that child was subsequently represented by counsel on appeal. In re S.M. (Ohio App. 8 Dist., Cuyahoga, 03-18-2004) No. 81566, 2004-Ohio-1243, 2004 WL 527925, Unreported. Child Custody ⇨ 923(1); Child Custody ⇨ 923(5)

Mother was not denied her right to counsel, in child dependency proceeding; trial court complied with the juvenile court rules when the notice of the permanent custody hearing informed mother of her right to counsel and explained how mother could request the appointment of counsel, and mother failed to pursue counsel. In re Williams (Ohio App. 10 Dist., Franklin, 02-12-2004) No. 03AP-1007, 2004-Ohio-678, 2004 WL 285560, Unreported. Infants ⇨ 205

Fact that incarcerated father did not face jail time was not a proper basis for denying him appointed counsel in child support arrearage proceedings. Jones v. Bowens (Ohio App. 11 Dist., Ashtabula, 09-26-2003) No. 2002-A-0034, 2003-Ohio-5224, 2003 WL 22235372, Unreported, appeal not allowed 101 Ohio St.3d 1423, 802 N.E.2d 154, 2004-Ohio-123. Child Support ⇨ 491

Incarcerated father had not been formally adjudicated indigent, for purposes of child support arrearage proceedings, and thus his right to appointed counsel had not been triggered. Jones v. Bowens (Ohio App. 11 Dist., Ashtabula, 09-26-2003) No. 2002-A-0034, 2003-Ohio-5224, 2003 WL 22235372, Unreported, appeal not allowed 101 Ohio St.3d 1423, 802 N.E.2d 154, 2004-Ohio-123. Child Support ⇨ 491

Juvenile court should have appointed juvenile, who had been adjudicated delinquent, counsel to protect his constitutional rights at show-cause hearing that state brought against him for failing to follow all terms and conditions of treatment at Youth Treatment Center (YTC); although state argued court was not required to appoint counsel for juvenile since he was represented by his mother at court proceedings, sufficient evidence demonstrated that, as one of juvenile's victims and custodian of another of juvenile's victims, juvenile's mother may have had interests adverse to juvenile's best interests and therefore was unable to fully represent his interests. In re William B. (Ohio App. 6 Dist., 08-26-2005) 163 Ohio App.3d 201, 837 N.E.2d 414, 2005-Ohio-4428. Infants ⇨ 205

Supreme Court decision in In re Williams that, pursuant to statute governing right to counsel in juvenile cases and juvenile rules, child who was subject of juvenile court proceeding to terminate parental rights was a party to that proceeding and, thus, was entitled to independent counsel in certain circumstances, had retroactive effect and applied to mother's case, in which permanent custody of her dependent children was being determined; Williams decision had been foreshadowed, and applying Williams decision retroactively would not produce injustice or hardship. In re Moore (Ohio App. 7 Dist., 08-24-2004) 158 Ohio App.3d 679, 821 N.E.2d 1039, 2004-Ohio-4544, supplemented 2005-Ohio-136, 2005 WL 78754. Courts ⇨ 100(1)

When a guardian ad litem who is also appointed as the juvenile's attorney in a proceeding for the termination of parental rights recommends a disposition that conflicts with the juvenile's wishes, the juvenile court must appoint independent counsel to represent the child. In re Williams (Ohio, 04-14-2004) 101 Ohio St.3d 398, 805 N.E.2d 1110, 2004-Ohio-1500. Infants ⇨ 205

Guardian ad litem can, in some situations, serve a dual role, in a proceeding for the termination of parental rights, as both the guardian ad litem and the juvenile's attorney, and thereby fulfill the juvenile's right to counsel, provided there has been an express dual appointment by the juvenile court. In re Williams (Ohio, 04-14-2004) 101 Ohio St.3d 398, 805 N.E.2d 1110, 2004-Ohio-1500. Infants ⇨ 205

Child who was subject of juvenile court proceeding to terminate parental rights was party to that proceeding, and entitled to independent counsel; abrogating In re Alfrey, Clark App. No. 01CA0083, 2003-Ohio-608, 2003 WL 262587. In re Williams (Ohio, 04-14-2004) 101 Ohio St.3d 398, 805 N.E.2d 1110, 2004-Ohio-1500. Infants ⇨ 200; Infants ⇨ 205

County child support enforcement agency (CSEA) lacked standing to appeal trial court's failure to appoint counsel for indigent mother in paternity and child support action, because agency was not prejudiced by any error; agency's ability to assert its claim that laches did not bar establishment of paternity or bar issuance of child support order was not affected, because agency could have subpoenaed mother to testify and because agency presented, without mother's testimony, her explanation for delay in revealing father's identity. Still v. Hayman (Ohio App. 7 Dist., 07-30-2003) 153 Ohio App.3d 487, 794 N.E.2d 751, 2003-Ohio-4113. Child Support ⇨ 538; Children Out-of-wedlock ⇨ 73

Indigent mother was entitled to have the trial court appoint counsel for her in paternity and child support action, even if funding in the account for payment of court-appointed counsel was lacking. Still v. Hayman (Ohio App. 7 Dist., 07-30-2003) 153 Ohio App.3d 487, 794 N.E.2d 751, 2003-Ohio-4113. Child Support ⇨ 210; Children Out-of-wedlock ⇨ 57

RC 120.33(B) does not impose a clear legal duty upon a judge to appoint as counsel of record the attorney personally selected by an indigent party. State ex rel. Butler v. Demis (Ohio 1981) 66 Ohio St.2d 123, 420 N.E.2d 116, 20 O.O.3d 121.

The trial court's failure to consider child's desire to reside with mother prejudiced mother, in permanent custody proceeding, and warranted remand for a new hearing; child had a right to be represented by counsel at the hearing, counsel for child had a duty to advocate for child's position, and mother was entitled to cross-examine the supplemental evidence concerning child's wishes. In re Williams (Ohio App. 11 Dist., Geauga, 07-03-2003) No. 2003-G-2498, No. 2003-G-2499, 2003-Ohio-3550, 2003 WL 21517986, Unreported, stay granted 99 Ohio St.3d 1526, 793 N.E.2d 496, 2003-Ohio-4303, motion to certify allowed 99 Ohio St.3d 1540, 795 N.E.2d 680, 2003-Ohio-4671, appeal not allowed 99 Ohio St.3d 1547, 795 N.E.2d 684, 2003-Ohio-4671, affirmed 101 Ohio St.3d 398, 805 N.E.2d 1110, 2004-Ohio-1500. Infants ⇨ 205; Infants ⇨ 207; Infants ⇨ 253; Infants ⇨ 254

Failing to appoint counsel to represent children in termination of parental rights proceeding involving allegations of child abuse was harmless error, where allegations of abuse were dismissed by agreement of parties and court attempted to determine each child's wishes by conducting in camera interview. In re Joshua B. (Ohio App. 6 Dist., Sandusky, 06-13-2003) No. S-02-018, No. S-02-021, No. S-02-019, No. S-02-020, 2003-Ohio-3096, 2003 WL 21384883, Unreported. Infants ⇨ 253

Mother of dependent children did not waive right to assert children's right to counsel in termination of parental rights proceeding, where mother filed motion raising issue of counsel one week after guardian ad litem (GAL) interviewed children and they indicated desire to reunify. In re Emery (Ohio App. 4 Dist., Lawrence, 04-25-2003) No. 02CA40, 2003-Ohio-2206, 2003 WL 2003811, Unreported. Infants ⇨ 200

Mother of dependent children was entitled to assert children's right to counsel in termination of parental rights proceeding, where both mother and children desired reunification. In re Emery (Ohio App. 4 Dist., Lawrence, 04-25-2003) No. 02CA40, 2003-Ohio-2206, 2003 WL 2003811, Unreported. Infants ⇨ 200

Dependent children were not represented by counsel in termination of parental rights proceeding; although individual appointed as guardian ad litem (GAL) was licensed attorney, there was nothing to indicate that court made dual appointment so that individual could also serve as children's attorney. In re Emery (Ohio App. 4 Dist., Lawrence, 04-25-2003) No. 02CA40, 2003-Ohio-2206, 2003 WL 2003811, Unreported. Infants ⇐ 205

Indigent dependent children were parties to termination of parental rights proceeding who had right to appointed counsel upon being name in complaints. In re Emery (Ohio App. 4 Dist., Lawrence, 04-25-2003) No. 02CA40, 2003-Ohio-2206, 2003 WL 2003811, Unreported. Infants ⇐ 205

Trial court's failure to inquire as to appointment of counsel for mother in father's proceeding to modify shared parenting plan was harmless error, where, at trial, mother admitted that she made too much money to be considered indigent, and thus, mother would not have been entitled to appointment of counsel. In re Lemon (Ohio App. 5 Dist., Stark, 11-12-2002) No. 2002 CA 00098, 2002-Ohio-6263, 2002 WL 31546216, Unreported. Child Custody ⇐ 923(4)

County child support enforcement agency (CSEA) lacked standing to appeal trial court's failure to appoint counsel for indigent mother in paternity and child support action, because agency was not prejudiced by any error; agency's ability to assert its claim that laches did not bar establishment of paternity or bar issuance of child support order was not affected, because agency could have subpoenaed mother to testify and because agency presented, without mother's testimony, her explanation for delay in revealing father's identity. Still v. Hayman (Ohio App. 7 Dist., 07-30-2003) 153 Ohio App.3d 487, 794 N.E.2d 751, 2003-Ohio-4113. Child Support ⇐ 538; Children Out-of-wedlock ⇐ 73

Indigent mother was entitled to have the trial court appoint counsel for her in paternity and child support action, even if funding in the account for payment of court-appointed counsel was lacking. Still v. Hayman (Ohio App. 7 Dist., 07-30-2003) 153 Ohio App.3d 487, 794 N.E.2d 751, 2003-Ohio-4113. Child Support ⇐ 210; Children Out-of-wedlock ⇐ 57

Parents were denied their statutory right to counsel in termination of parental rights proceedings, where father was never represented, mother's counsel withdrew at dispositional hearing for lack of contact with mother, and hearing continued ex parte. In re Alyssa C. (Ohio App. 6 Dist., 05-23-2003) 153 Ohio App.3d 10, 790 N.E.2d 803, 2003-Ohio-2673. Infants ⇐ 205

In order to sustain commitment of a juvenile offender to a state institution in a delinquency proceeding, where such commitment will deprive the child of his liberty, the alleged delinquent must have been afforded representation by counsel, appointed at state expense in case of indigency. (Annotation from former RC 2151.35.) In re Agler (Ohio 1969) 19 Ohio St.2d 70, 249 N.E.2d 808, 48 O.O.2d 85. Infants ⇐ 205

An adjudication proceeding cannot go forward unless the juvenile is represented by counsel or there has been a valid waiver of the right to counsel. In re Johnston (Ohio App. 11 Dist., 04-30-2001) 142 Ohio App.3d 314, 755 N.E.2d 457. Infants ⇐ 205

Juvenile was entitled to representation by counsel in adjudication for vandalism and criminal trespass, where juvenile did not waive his right to counsel, and conviction on charges could result in juvenile having his liberty curtailed. In re Johnston (Ohio App. 11 Dist., 04-30-2001) 142 Ohio App.3d 314, 755 N.E.2d 457. Infants ⇐ 205

Custodian's statement to court that she advised juvenile to admit to the charges if true or deny them if false did not urge juvenile to admit to something she did not do, nor did it recommend to the court any suggested disposition of the matter, and thus custodian did not act contrary to juvenile's best legal interests. In re Smith (Ohio App. 8 Dist., 03-26-2001) 142 Ohio App.3d 16, 753 N.E.2d 930. Infants ⇐ 205

Children who were subject of action to terminate parental rights had right to appointed counsel that attached when they were removed from the home. In re Stacey S. (Ohio App. 6 Dist., 12-30-1999) 136 Ohio App.3d 503, 737 N.E.2d 92, 1999-Ohio-989. Infants ⇐ 205

Complaint to terminate parental rights claiming that children were neglected and dependent, which included facts showing that both physical and sexual abuse were believed to be at issue, was sufficient to allege that children were "abused," such that children had right to appointed counsel. In re Stacey S. (Ohio App. 6 Dist., 12-30-1999) 136 Ohio App.3d 503, 737 N.E.2d 92, 1999-Ohio-989. Infants ⇐ 197; Infants ⇐ 205

Appointment of guardian ad litem and attorney for the guardian ad litem was not sufficient to satisfy children's right to counsel in action to terminate parental rights. In re Stacey S. (Ohio App. 6 Dist., 12-30-1999) 136 Ohio App.3d 503, 737 N.E.2d 92, 1999-Ohio-989. Infants ⇐ 205

Appointment of attorney for guardian ad litem as the substitute guardian ad litem in parental rights termination proceeding did not satisfy children's right to counsel, even though attorney claimed she performed as counsel to children, where court failed to make finding that there was no conflict between the attorney's dual roles as guardian ad litem and attorney for children and suggestions were raised during dispositional hearing that a conflict did exist. In re Stacey S. (Ohio App. 6 Dist., 12-30-1999) 136 Ohio App.3d 503, 737 N.E.2d 92, 1999-Ohio-989. Infants ⇐ 205

Child is entitled to counsel at all stages of juvenile proceedings. In re Solis (Ohio App. 8 Dist., 12-22-1997) 124 Ohio App.3d 547, 706 N.E.2d 839. Infants ⇐ 205

Juvenile adjudicated delinquent and provisionally placed in foster care was entitled to counsel at dispositional hearing, as provisional placement was not equivalent of probation and dispositional hearing was not equivalent of probation revocation hearing. In re Solis (Ohio App. 8 Dist., 12-22-1997) 124 Ohio App.3d 547, 706 N.E.2d 839. Infants ⇐ 205

Trial court failed to adequately advise juvenile of her right to counsel, where court did not conduct any meaningful colloquy with juvenile, made most of its remarks to juvenile's mother, who had filed unruly child complaint, and addressed child directly only briefly, almost as an afterthought. In re Rogers (Ohio App. 9 Dist., 12-10-1997) 124 Ohio App.3d 392, 706 N.E.2d 390. Infants ⇐ 205

Magistrate who presided over arraignment in juvenile proceeding failed to adequately inform juvenile of her right to counsel; magistrate discussed right to counsel only in terms of representation if she were to proceed to trial, and gave explanation of right to counsel that was confusing, if not misleading, and could have led juvenile to believe that she was not entitled to counsel while deciding whether to admit or deny complaint. In re Doyle (App. 2 Dist., 10-03-1997) 122 Ohio App.3d 767, 702 N.E.2d 970. Infants ⇐ 205

Prior to juvenile's admission to habitual truancy charge, trial court failed to adequately advise juvenile of his constitutional rights and of consequences of his admission and also failed to sufficiently ascertain whether juvenile's purported waiver of counsel was made knowingly and voluntarily; there was no indication in record that trial court ever made determination concerning juvenile's indigency or advised juvenile that he had right to appointed counsel based on his indigency; trial court had merely asked juvenile whether it could be assumed that juvenile wished to proceed without attorney since juvenile was there without attorney, and trial court had not advised juvenile of purpose of hearing, possible penalties for alleged truancy violation, ramifications of admission to charge or of juvenile's rights to remain silent, offer evidence, cross-examine witnesses and have record made of proceedings. In re Kimble (Ohio App. 3 Dist., 09-25-1996) 114 Ohio App.3d 136, 682 N.E.2d 1066. Infants ⇐ 199; Infants ⇐ 205

Indigent father was entitled to have counsel appointed to represent him on custody and visitation issues in child support action under statute and juvenile court rule; both rule and statute guarantee right to appointed counsel for all indigent parties in juvenile court proceedings, father, being natural father and parent of children, was a party to juvenile court proceeding under juvenile court rules, and father was indigent as defined in rules. McKinney v. McClure (Ohio App. 12 Dist., 03-27-1995) 102 Ohio App.3d 165, 656 N.E.2d 1310. Children Out-of-wedlock ⇐ 20.4

Right to appointed counsel for indigent parties applies to all matters properly brought before juvenile court, including custody and visitation issues. McKinney v. McClure (Ohio App. 12 Dist., 03-27-1995) 102 Ohio App.3d 165, 656 N.E.2d 1310. Child Custody ⇐ 500

Juvenile rule and statute guarantee right to counsel for all indigent parties in juvenile proceedings. Holley v. Higgins (Franklin 1993) 86 Ohio App.3d 240, 620 N.E.2d 251. Infants ⇐ 205

Indigent parties to juvenile court proceedings have a right to counsel under RC 2151.312 and Juv R 4(A). Lowry v. Lowry (Ross 1988) 48 Ohio App.3d 184, 549 N.E.2d 176.

The guarantee of the right to be represented by counsel set forth in Juv R 4(A) does not, as to a nonindigent party, require that trial be continued indefinitely until counsel can be obtained, but merely requires, if it does not appear that counsel could not be obtained through the exercise of reasonable diligence and a willingness to enter into reasonable contractual arrangements for counsel's services, that a reasonable opportunity be given to the party before trial to employ such counsel. In re Bolden (Allen 1973) 37 Ohio App.2d 7, 306 N.E.2d 166, 66 O.O.2d 26.

Trial court was not required to unilaterally appoint counsel for dependent child regarding action by county child services to modify disposition of child from temporary custody to permanent custody and to terminate father's parental rights, where no allegation of abuse was set forth in complaint. In re Graham (Ohio App. 4 Dist., Athens, 08-02-2002) No. 01CA57, 2002-Ohio-4411, 2002 WL 1978881, Unreported. Infants ⇐ 205

Juvenile court commits reversible error when it violates a parent's statutory right to be represented by counsel at a dispositional hearing to modify temporary custody of her son to long term foster care by failing to advise the parent of her right to counsel and her right to appointed counsel if she is indigent. In re Lander (Ohio App. 12 Dist., Butler, 06-26-2000) No. CA99-05-096, 2000 WL 819775, Unreported.

A child dependency proceeding invokes a parent's right to counsel under Juv R 4(A), and a court abuses its discretion in revoking the pro hac vice status of a parent's attorney without a hearing where there are only bald accusations that the attorney is engaging in egregious misconduct. In re N.B. (Ohio App. 12 Dist., Butler, 08-01-1994) No. CA93-09-183, No. CA93-09-184, 1994 WL 394972, Unreported.

Stepmother's and her allegedly abused stepson's interests were aligned and any error prejudicial to stepson was prejudicial to stepmother, and thus, stepmother had standing to raise as assignment of error whether stepson's right to be represented by counsel was violated, even though stepson did not appeal from judgment ordering protective supervision. (Per O'Neill, P.J., with one judge concurring in judgment only.) In re Calvin, Anthony, Alyshia (Ohio App. 11 Dist., Geauga, 11-22-2002) No. 2001-G-2379, 2002-Ohio-6468, 2002 WL 31663562, Unreported, stay granted 98 Ohio St.3d 1459, 783 N.E.2d 518, 2003-Ohio-644, appeal not allowed 98 Ohio St.3d 1513, 786 N.E.2d 63, 2003-Ohio-1572. Infants ⇔ 242

Allegedly abused child was entitled to have counsel appointed to represent his interests in dependency proceedings. (Per O'Neill, P.J., with one judge concurring in judgment only.) In re Calvin, Anthony, Alyshia (Ohio App. 11 Dist., Geauga, 11-22-2002) No. 2001-G-2379, 2002-Ohio-6468, 2002 WL 31663562, Unreported, stay granted 98 Ohio St.3d 1459, 783 N.E.2d 518, 2003-Ohio-644, appeal not allowed 98 Ohio St.3d 1513, 786 N.E.2d 63, 2003-Ohio-1572. Infants ⇔ 205

An indigent child is entitled pursuant to RC 2151.352 and Juv R 4(A) to be represented by the county public defender in all juvenile court proceedings pertaining to a complaint alleging the child to be a juvenile traffic offender, regardless of whether the outcome of the proceeding could result in a loss of liberty, except when the right to counsel is waived or the juvenile court pursuant to RC 120.16(E) appoints counsel other than the county public defender or allows an indigent child to select his own personal counsel to represent him. OAG 97-040.

8. Damages

Since the decision to appoint or refuse to appoint an attorney to represent indigent juvenile litigants rests entirely in the discretion of the juvenile court judge, it follows that neither the court administrator, county board of commissioners, nor the county juvenile court can be held liable for any damages suffered by the attorney when his name is removed by the juvenile court judge from the court-appointment list. Eichenberger v. Petree (Franklin 1992) 76 Ohio App.3d 779, 603 N.E.2d 366, motion overruled 64 Ohio St.3d 1409, 592 N.E.2d 846. Counties ⇔ 59; Courts ⇔ 55; Judges ⇔ 36

9. Guardian ad litem

Trial court was required to appoint a new guardian ad litem, who was also appointed as counsel, for ten-year-old child who lived with mother and was deemed dependent and whose father sought to be named as residential parent, when a contradiction became apparent between the testimony of the guardian ad litem, who stated that custody should be granted to father, and the in-camera testimony of the child, who stated she did not wish to live with father, warranting reversal of trial court's decision to name father as residential parent; the guardian ad litem failed to act as advocate for the child. In re Butler (Ohio App. 3 Dist., Logan, 09-05-2006) No. 8-06-03, 2006-Ohio-4547, 2006 WL 2533010, Unreported. Infants ⇔ 253

Trial court was not required to appoint an attorney as guardian ad litem (GAL) for children, in termination of parental rights proceeding, as there was no statutory requirement that a GAL also be a licensed attorney. In re D.R. (Ohio App. 2 Dist., Miami, 07-07-2006) No. 2005 CA 10, No. 2006 CA 7, 2006-Ohio-3513, 2006 WL 1868314, Unreported. Infants ⇔ 205

The juvenile court was not required to appoint a guardian ad litem for juvenile, in delinquency proceeding, even though juvenile alleged a conflict of interest existed between him and his parents; mother appeared with juvenile at each of the hearings, and mother spoke on juvenile's behalf at the dispositional hearing and urged the court not to commit juvenile to the Department of Youth Services (DYS). In re Smith (Ohio App. 3 Dist., Union, 06-05-2006) No. 14-05-33, 2006-Ohio-2788, 2006 WL 1519688, Unreported. Infants ⇔ 205

Attorney was permitted to act as guardian ad litem and as attorney for mother and father's ten children, in termination of parental rights proceeding; there was no evidence that the children expressed strong desires or interests that were inconsistent with the recommendations of the guardian ad litem, and when the guardian ad litem reported that one child had expressed an interest in living with a relative the court made an inquiry and determined that the child was not serious and was more concerned about staying in contact with her siblings. In re Hilyard (Ohio App. 4 Dist., Vinton, 04-13-2006) No. 05CA600, No. 05CA603, No. 05CA607, No. 05CA601, No. 05CA604, No. 05CA608, No. 05CA602, No. 05CA606, No. 05CA609, 2006-Ohio-1965, 2006 WL Infants ⇔ 205

Juvenile court was required to hold in-camera interview of child to determine whether conflict existed between guardian ad litem's recommended disposition and child's wishes, such that appointment of separate counsel for child was required, in child protection proceeding in which county sought permanent custody of child; potential conflict between guardian ad litem's recommended disposition of adoption and child's wishes to maintain some contact with her father could not be avoided by guardian ad litem's mere expression of child's wishes to trial court. In re H.R. (Ohio App. 2 Dist., Montgomery, 03-31-2006) No. 21274, 2006-Ohio-1595, 2006 WL 827385, Unreported. Infants ⇔ 205

Juvenile court abused its discretion by failing to appoint a guardian ad litem or further inquire into whether a guardian ad litem was necessary during delinquency proceeding in which juvenile was charged with felonious assault, domestic violence, and being an unruly child, where record demonstrated at least the strong possibility of a conflict between juvenile and his father, the victim. In re Cook (Ohio App. 11 Dist., Ashtabula, 09-30-2005) No. 2003-A-0132, 2005-Ohio-5288, 2005 WL 2416615, Unreported. Infants ⇔ 205

Juvenile court abused its discretion during delinquency proceeding by failing to appoint a guardian ad litem or to make further inquiry into whether a guardian ad litem was necessary, in light of father's statements against juvenile's penal interest. In re Bostwick (Ohio App. 4 Dist., Ross, 09-26-2005) No. 05CA2820, 2005-Ohio-5123, 2005 WL 2374933, Unreported. Infants ⇔ 205

Mother failed to demonstrate that trial court committed plain error by failing to appoint her guardian ad litem (GAL) and that her trial counsel was ineffective for failing to request that GAL be appointed on her behalf, in proceeding terminating parental rights; there was nothing in record to indicate extent to which, if at all, mother's mental health issues impeded her ability to understand and participate in proceedings, record demonstrated that mother appeared to understand nature of proceedings, and there was nothing to suggest that mother appeared incompetent at time she voluntarily relinquished her parental rights. In re D.C.H. (Ohio App. 9 Dist., Summit, 08-17-2005) No. 22648, 2005-Ohio-4257, 2005 WL 1962963, Unreported. Infants ⇔ 243

Trial court's accepting of guardian ad litem's report in termination of parental rights proceedings was not plain error, even if report was not filed in proper compliance with juvenile rules, where there was ample evidence to support the trial court's decision without the guardian ad litem's report. In re S.B. (Ohio App. 8 Dist., Cuyahoga, 06-23-2005) No. 85560, 2005-Ohio-3163, 2005 WL 1490128, Unreported. Infants ⇔ 243

Mother was not prejudiced by trial court's failure to appoint guardian ad litem for her, in permanent custody proceeding in which children had been removed from mother's custody; appointment of guardian ad litem would not have remedied mother's failure to comply with her case plan and would not have improved her parenting abilities or changed fact that children had special needs, and mother was adequately protected because she had been represented by counsel throughout dispositional hearing. In re McHugh Children (Ohio App. 5 Dist., Licking, 05-05-2005) No. 2004CA00091, 2005-Ohio-2345, 2005 WL 1125334, Unreported. Infants ⇔ 253

Trial court was not required to conduct independent examination as to whether children should have been appointed separate counsel in proceedings to terminate mother's and father's parental rights based on initial ambivalence by children regarding their wishes for placement; guardian ad litem subsequently determined that children expressed adamant desire to remain with foster family, and such wishes were not in conflict with those of guardian ad litem. In re Miller (Ohio App. 10 Dist., Franklin, 03-03-2005) No. 04AP-783, 2005-Ohio-897, 2005 WL 488396, Unreported. Infants ⇔ 205

Trial court was not required to appoint separate attorney and guardian at litem to represent child in child dependency proceeding, as there was no evidence to establish that conflict existed with respect to attorney's performance as child's guardian ad litem and attorney. In re Miller (Ohio App. 5 Dist., Licking, 02-24-2005) No. 04 CA 32, 2005-Ohio-856, 2005 WL 469260, Unreported. Infants ⇔ 205

Trial court had the duty to interview three-year-old child who was the subject of a termination of parental rights proceeding to determine if she wanted to live with her mother, which would require appointment of independent counsel, where guardian ad litem recommended that parental rights be terminated, but child's older sister had told the guardian ad litem she and her sister wanted to live with their mother. In re Wylie (Ohio App. 2 Dist., Greene, 12-14-2004) No. 2004CA0054, 2004-Ohio-7243, 2004 WL 3561213, Unreported. Infants ⇔ 207

Trial court committed prejudicial error in failing to appoint guardian ad litem for juvenile accused of raping family member and whose parents testified for prosecution and recommended that juvenile be placed in Department of Youth Services (DYS), even though juvenile was represented by competent counsel; task of guardian ad litem and attorney could conflict, and no one testified on juvenile's behalf at adjudicatory hearing. In re Wilson (Ohio App. 4 Dist., Washington, 12-22-2004) No. 04CA26, 2004-Ohio-7276, 2004 WL 3090235, Unreported. Infants ⇔ 253

Appointment of guardian ad litem was required for juvenile accused of rape for performing fellatio on his seven-year-old step-brother, where juvenile's victims in previous episodes of physical and sexual acting out were also family members, and juvenile's parents testified for prosecution and recommended that juvenile be placed in Department of Youth Services (DYS). In re Wilson (Ohio App. 4 Dist., Washington, 12-22-2004) No. 04CA26, 2004-Ohio-7276, 2004 WL 3090235, Unreported. Infants ⇔ 205

Closing argument and recommendation of guardian ad litem appointed in proceeding to modify child support were material and pertinent and thus not subject to being stricken. Jarvis v. Witter (Ohio App. 8 Dist., Cuyahoga, 12-09-2004) No. 84128, 2004-Ohio-6628, 2004 WL 2830789, Unreported. Child Support ⇔ 340

Guardian ad litem was properly appointed in proceeding to modify child support, since child's interests potentially conflicted with those of her parents, mother might not have been capable of representing child's best interests, and the appointment was necessary for a fair hearing and thorough review of the parties' financial circumstances. Jarvis v. Witter (Ohio App. 8 Dist., Cuyahoga, 12-09-2004) No. 84128, 2004-Ohio-6628, 2004 WL 2830789, Unreported. Infants ⇔ 78(7)

Any error in trial court's failure to appoint counsel to represent dependent child prior to hearing before magistrate in termination of parental rights proceeding was waived, where counsel, who was appointed to represent child before trial court adopted magistrate's recommendations, did not object to magistrate's recommendations for reason that child did not have counsel at hearing, as presumably counsel believed child's guardian ad litem adequately protected child's interest at that hearing. In re C.S. (Ohio App. 2 Dist., Montgomery, 10-22-2004) No. 20379, 2004-Ohio-5810, 2004 WL 2445238, Unreported. Infants ⇔ 243

Trial court's failure to appoint guardian ad litem for mother at child dependency hearing did not constitute plain error; although mother appeared to be mentally incompetent, mother was represented by appointed counsel throughout proceeding, and appointment of guardian ad litem would not have remedied mother's failure to comply with case plan or improved her parenting abilities, which resulted in termination of her parental rights. In re Amber G. & Josie G. (Ohio App. 6 Dist., Lucas, 10-22-2004) No. L-04-1091, 2004-Ohio-5665, 2004 WL 2384453, Unreported. Infants ⇔ 243

Mother waived for appellate review claim that guardian ad litem failed in her duty to make an independent investigation and failed to ask the court to do that which was in the children's best interest, in proceedings granting permanent custody of mother's five children to the Cuyahoga County Department of Children and Family Services (CCDCFS), where at no time prior to trial or during trial did mother object to the guardian ad litem's job performance or raise an issue that a conflict existed. In re C.C. (Ohio App. 8 Dist., Cuyahoga, 09-30-2004) No. 83793, 2004-Ohio-5213, 2004 WL 2340069, Unreported. Infants ⇔ 243

The trial court's failure to appoint a guardian ad litem for juvenile when a conflict of interest existed between juvenile and his parents constituted reversible error; the victim of juvenile's crime was his half-sister, juvenile's stepfather informed the court at juvenile's arraignment that they did not want juvenile to return to their home, juvenile's mother informed the court that she did not feel that she could make choices that were in juvenile's best interest, and juvenile was not represented by counsel at his probation revocation hearing. In re K.J.F. (Ohio App. 2 Dist., Clark, 01-23-2004) No. 2003 CA 41, 2004-Ohio-263, 2004 WL 102847, Unreported. Infants ⇔ 205; Infants ⇔ 253

Mother waived her appellate argument that the trial court erred when it failed to permit counsel for mother to examine the guardian ad litem with respect to the contents of his report submitted after the hearing, in child dependency proceeding, where mother failed to object to the manner in which guardian ad litem performed his duties, she did not object when the guardian ad litem failed to submit his report at the hearing, and she failed to object when the trial judge expressed an intention to receive and consider the guardian ad litem's report after the hearing. In re La.B. (Ohio App. 8 Dist., Cuyahoga, 12-18-2003) No. 81981, 2003-Ohio-6852, 2003 WL 22966171, Unreported, stay denied 101 Ohio St.3d 1453, 803 N.E.2d 401, 2004-Ohio-462, cause dismissed 101 Ohio St.3d 1458, 803 N.E.2d 830, 2004-Ohio-703, reconsideration granted 101 Ohio St.3d 1482, 805 N.E.2d 534, 2004-Ohio-1398, appeal not allowed 102 Ohio St.3d 1445, 808 N.E.2d 397, 2004-Ohio-2263. Infants ⇔ 243

Magistrate's failure to appoint guardian ad litem in delinquency proceeding, despite fact that minor's mother requested treatment for minor, while minor desired commitment to Department of Youth Services, was not plain error; transcript of proceeding revealed no anger or tension between minor and mother, which may have necessitated appointment of guardian ad litem. In re Harper (Ohio App. 2 Dist., Montgomery, 12-12-2003) No. 19948, 2003-Ohio-6666, 2003 WL 22927248, Unreported. Infants ⇔ 243

Trial court acted within its discretion in denying mother's motion for a separate guardian ad litem without a hearing, in proceedings in which mother sought to suspend father's visitation based on alleged sexual abuse, even though original guardian allegedly spent only an hour with family, where guardian ad litem's report revealed reasons for her recommendations and did not reveal bias, and mother did not show any other basis for appointment of separate guardian. Edwards v. Livingstone (Ohio App. 11 Dist., Ashtabula, 08-01-2003) No. 2001-A-0082, No. 2002-A-0060, 2003-Ohio-4099, 2003 WL 21782596, Unreported. Infants ⇔ 80(1)

Trial court should have either made express dual appointment of guardian ad litem to serve as dependent child's guardian and attorney, or should have made separate appointments for child's guardian ad litem and child's attorney at outset of child dependency proceeding. In re Beasley (Ohio App. 4 Dist., Scioto, 05-28-2003) No. 03CA2874, 2003-Ohio-2857, 2003 WL 21278912, Unreported, motion for delayed appeal denied 99 Ohio St.3d 1466, 791 N.E.2d 982, 2003-Ohio-3669, appeal not allowed 99 Ohio St.3d 1515, 792 N.E.2d 201, 2003-Ohio-3957. Infants ⇔ 205

Trial court was required to appoint a guardian ad litem for children in termination of parental rights case, whereas the court was not likewise required to appoint counsel to represent them. In re Alfrey (Ohio App. 2 Dist., Clark, 02-07-2003) No. 01CA0083, 2003-Ohio-608, 2003 WL 262587, Unreported. Infants ⇔ 205

Trial court committed reversible error when it failed to appoint guardian ad litem on behalf of juvenile, who had been adjudicated delinquent, at show-cause hearing that state brought against juvenile for failing to follow all terms and conditions of treatment at Youth Treatment Center (YTC); although juvenile's mother was present at court proceedings, as one of juvenile's victims, and as custodian of another of juvenile's victims, interests of juvenile's mother were in conflict with interests of juvenile. In re William B. (Ohio App. 6 Dist., 08-26-2005) 163 Ohio App.3d 201, 837 N.E.2d 414, 2005-Ohio-4428. Infants ⇔ 253

The trial court abused its discretion when it failed to appoint a guardian ad litem for juvenile, during delinquency proceeding charging juvenile with kidnapping, where juvenile and his legal guardians exhibited a conflict of interest since juvenile's victim was the daughter of his legal guardians, guardians refused to hire an attorney for juvenile, and guardians requested that the court institutionalize juvenile. In re Slider (Ohio App. 4 Dist., 03-23-2005) 160 Ohio App.3d 159, 826 N.E.2d 356, 2005-Ohio-1457. Infants ⇔ 205

Although an attorney may represent an indigent mother who is also incompetent as her counsel and as guardian ad litem, if he feels there is a conflict between the two roles of representing his client's wishes and asking the court to do what is in the best interests of his ward, he should withdraw so that the client/ward have proper representation at the hearing. In re Baby Girl Baxter (Ohio 1985) 17 Ohio St.3d 229, 479 N.E.2d 257, 17 O.B.R. 469.

Failure to appoint guardian at litem for juvenile or at least inquire further into whether guardian ad litem was necessary was reversible error in delinquency proceedings after juvenile's grandfather, his legal guardian, informed court that he had recently filed unruly charge against juvenile, thereby suggesting strong possibility of conflict of interest, particularly where grandfather apparently acted for purpose of ascertaining status of this additional charge rather than out of concern for juvenile's best interests, as evidenced by his refusal to explain circumstances surrounding charge. In re Spradlin (Ohio App. 4 Dist., 12-01-2000) 140 Ohio App.3d 402, 747 N.E.2d 877, 2000-Ohio-2003. Infants ⇔ 253

Permitting mother's counsel to withdraw from proceedings to terminate mother's parental rights was neither error nor an abuse of discretion; mother abducted child from foster parents' home in violation of existing court orders and voluntarily absconded from the court's jurisdiction to China, choosing not to contact either her counsel or the court, counsel advised the court that she did not know what her client wanted her to do and therefore could not zealously represent her client, and the Juvenile Court Rules authorized mother's guardian ad litem, also an attorney, to serve as her counsel. In re Zhang (Ohio App. 8 Dist., 06-10-1999) 135 Ohio App.3d 350, 734 N.E.2d 379, dismissed, appeal not allowed 87 Ohio St.3d 1417, 717 N.E.2d 1105, reconsideration stricken 87 Ohio St.3d 1437, 719 N.E.2d 2. Infants ⇐ 205

Strong possibility of conflict of interest between juvenile involved in delinquency adjudication proceeding and his father, who represented him in such proceeding, mandated appointment of guardian ad litem for juvenile; juvenile's parents had previously brought him before juvenile court on domestic violence charge, and father attempted to persuade juvenile court to act in manner which may have been against juvenile's interests and persuaded juvenile not to exercise his statutory right to attorney. In re Sappington (Ohio App. 2 Dist., 10-31-1997) 123 Ohio App.3d 448, 704 N.E.2d 339. Infants ⇐ 205

Failure of court to appoint guardian ad litem for juvenile, when such appointment is required under applicable rule or statute, constitutes reversible error. In re Sappington (Ohio App. 2 Dist., 10-31-1997) 123 Ohio App.3d 448, 704 N.E.2d 339. Infants ⇐ 205; Infants ⇐ 253

Appellate court should find reversible error in juvenile court's failure to appoint guardian ad litem for juvenile involved in proceedings before it when record from below reveals strong enough possibility of conflict of interest between parent and child to show that juvenile court abused its discretion by not so finding. In re Sappington (Ohio App. 2 Dist., 10-31-1997) 123 Ohio App.3d 448, 704 N.E.2d 339. Infants ⇐ 205; Infants ⇐ 253

Lawyer may, in proper circumstances, take on duties of both counsel for juvenile subjected to delinquency proceeding and juvenile's guardian ad litem; however, as lawyer's role is to represent client zealously within boundaries of law, and guardian's role is to investigate juvenile's situation and ask court to do what is in juvenile's best interest, duties of counsel and guardian may conflict to extent rendering lawyer incapable of performing both functions. In re Howard (Ohio App. 1 Dist., 04-16-1997) 119 Ohio App.3d 201, 695 N.E.2d 1. Infants ⇐ 205

In action to terminate parental rights, guardian ad litem's report was hearsay and could not be considered evidence, where report was not submitted under oath and guardian did not testify and was not subjected to direct or cross-examination. Matter of Duncan/Walker Children (Ohio App. 5 Dist., 03-18-1996) 109 Ohio App.3d 841, 673 N.E.2d 217. Infants ⇐ 174

Since guardian ad litem was not counsel for ward in action to terminate parental rights, guardian had no authority to file findings of fact and conclusions of law, and court should not have ordered guardian to do so. Matter of Duncan/Walker Children (Ohio App. 5 Dist., 03-18-1996) 109 Ohio App.3d 841, 673 N.E.2d 217. Infants ⇐ 210

For attorney to act as guardian ad litem and attorney for ward, there must be dual appointment, and finding that no conflict exists. Matter of Duncan/Walker Children (Ohio App. 5 Dist., 03-18-1996) 109 Ohio App.3d 841, 673 N.E.2d 217. Attorney And Client ⇐ 21.5(1); Infants ⇐ 81

Guardian ad litem has absolute immunity from actions arising out of performance of duties mandated by guardian's role as advocate for child in judicial proceedings. Penn v. McMonagle (Huron 1990) 60 Ohio App.3d 149, 573 N.E.2d 1234, motion overruled 58 Ohio St.3d 704, 569 N.E.2d 512. Infants ⇐ 85

Where an infant child has been in the custody of prospective adoptive parents as a result of a permanent order of custody in a dependency action and that permanent order is subsequently vacated and the parent moves to terminate temporary custody, it appears that the interests of the child and parent may conflict and a guardian ad litem must be appointed for the child pursuant to Juv R 4(B) prior to the hearing on the mother's motion to terminate custody. In re Christopher (Morrow 1977) 54 Ohio App.2d 137, 376 N.E.2d 603, 8 O.O.3d 271. Infants ⇐ 78(1)

The guardian ad litem appointed for a child in a dependency action where the interest of the child and the parent may conflict must have no ties or loyalties to anyone with an adversary interest in the outcome such as a natural parent or the prospective adoptive parents. In re Christopher (Morrow 1977) 54 Ohio App.2d 137, 376 N.E.2d 603, 8 O.O.3d 271. Infants ⇐ 81

Appointment of guardian ad litem (GAL) did not constitute an appointment to act as child's attorney in proceeding on father's motion which sought custody of child; there was no evidence of a dual appointment, such as mention on judgment entry that GAL was also acting as child's attorney or inclusion of an attorney number on documents bearing signature of GAL. Sabrina J. v Robbin C, No. L–00–1374, 2002–Ohio–2691, 2002 WL 1303148 (6th Dist Ct App, Lucas, 5–31–02).

The trial court errs in failing to inform the parent of her rights to remain silent, to cross-examine witnesses, and to offer evidence at the adjudicatory hearing and in granting permanent custody when no guardian ad litem's report is filed with the court. Matter of Eplin (Ohio App. 5 Dist., Stark, 06-29-1995) No. 94 CA 0311, 1995 WL 495451, Unreported.

10. Cause of action

Contempt judgment could not be entered for failure to pay court costs imposed in proceeding in which juvenile was found to be unruly child. In re Buffington (Ohio App. 6 Dist., 08-06-1993) 89 Ohio App.3d 814, 627 N.E.2d 1013, motion overruled 68 Ohio St.3d 1429, 624 N.E.2d 1066. Contempt ⇐ 20

In an attorney's action against a juvenile court administrative judge brought after the attorney's name is removed from the list of attorneys appointed to represent indigent clients appearing before the court, the attorney's allegation that the removal of his name prevented him from practicing law in the juvenile court is merely a conclusion about the consequences of the removal which need not be accepted as true for purposes of a motion to dismiss; the attorney failed to allege facts that the judge attempted to control the practice of law in juvenile court, and the removal of the attorney's name did not prevent him from representing indigent clients pro bono or from representing other clients. Eichenberger v. Petree (Franklin 1992) 76 Ohio App.3d 779, 603 N.E.2d 366, motion overruled 64 Ohio St.3d 1409, 592 N.E.2d 846. Pretrial Procedure ⇐ 652

Before withdrawing as appointed counsel in an appeal from a termination of parental rights on the ground that counsel finds the case wholly frivolous, the attorney should so advise the court, request permission to withdraw, and submit with the request a brief referring to anything in the record that might arguably support the appeal; a copy of the brief should be given the appellant and time allowed him to raise any points he chooses, after which the court will fully examine the proceedings to decide whether the case is wholly frivolous. Morris v. Lucas County Children Services Bd. (Lucas 1989) 49 Ohio App.3d 86, 550 N.E.2d 980.

11. Jurisdiction

Where a court, having acquired jurisdiction over a child by virtue of a divorce action between the child's parents, certifies the matter of the child's custody to a juvenile court, the consent of the juvenile court having been first obtained, the juvenile court has exclusive jurisdiction over the child's custody by virtue of RC 3109.06 and 2151.23(D) and a finding of unfitness of the parents or that there is no suitable relative to have custody is not a necessary prerequisite to such certification, and while such certification shall be deemed to be the complaint in the juvenile court, it does not constitute a complaint in the juvenile court that such child is dependent or neglected and those dispositions provided for under RC 2151.353, 2151.354, and 2151.355 are not applicable to the disposition of such a child, disposition thereof being subject to and controlled by RC 3109.04. In re Height (Van Wert 1975) 47 Ohio App.2d 203, 353 N.E.2d 887, 1 O.O.3d 279. Courts ⇐ 472.1

Juv R 5 [Reserved]

Juv R 6 Taking into custody

(A) A child may be taken into custody:

(1) pursuant to an order of the court;

(2) pursuant to the law of arrest;

(3) by a law enforcement officer or duly authorized officer of the court when any of the following conditions exist:

(a) There are reasonable grounds to believe that the child is suffering from illness or injury and is not receiving proper care, and the child's removal is necessary to prevent immediate or threatened physical or emotional harm;

(b) There are reasonable grounds to believe that the child is in immediate danger from the child's surroundings and that the child's removal is necessary to prevent immediate or threatened physical or emotional harm;

(c) There are reasonable grounds to believe that a parent, guardian, custodian, or other household member of the child has abused or neglected another child in the household, and that the child is in danger of immediate or threatened physical or emotional harm;

(d) There are reasonable grounds to believe that the child has run away from the child's parents, guardian, or other custodian;

(e) There are reasonable grounds to believe that the conduct, conditions, or surroundings of the child are endangering the health, welfare, or safety of the child;

(f) During the pendency of court proceedings, there are reasonable grounds to believe that the child may abscond or be removed from the jurisdiction of the court or will not be brought to the court;

(g) A juvenile judge or designated magistrate has found that there is probable cause to believe any of the conditions set forth in division (A)(3)(a), (b), or (c) of this rule are present, has found that reasonable efforts have been made to notify the child's parents, guardian ad litem or custodian that the child may be placed into shelter care, except where notification would jeopardize the physical or emotional safety of the child or result in the child's removal from the court's jurisdiction, and has ordered ex parte, by telephone or otherwise, the taking of the child into custody.

(4) By the judge or designated magistrate ex parte pending the outcome of the adjudicatory and dispositional hearing in an abuse, neglect, or dependency proceeding, where it appears to the court that the best interest and welfare of the child require the immediate issuance of a shelter care order.

(B) Probable cause hearing

When a child is taken into custody pursuant to an ex parte emergency order pursuant to division (A)(3)(g) or (A)(4) of this rule, a probable cause hearing shall be held before the end of the next business day after the day on which the order is issued but not later than seventy-two hours after the issuance of the emergency order.

(Adopted eff. 7–1–72; amended eff. 7–1–94, 7–1–96)

Historical and Statutory Notes

Amendment Note: The 7–1–96 amendment substituted "magistrate" for "referee" in divisions (A)(3)(g) and (A)(4).

Amendment Note: The 7–1–94 amendment rewrote this rule, which previously read:

"A child may be taken into custody: (1) pursuant to an order of the court, (2) pursuant to the law of arrest, (3) by a law enforcement officer or duly authorized officer of the court when there are reasonable grounds to believe that the child is suffering from illness or injury and is not receiving proper care, or is in immediate danger from his surroundings, and that his removal is necessary, (4) by a law enforcement officer or duly authorized officer of the court when there are reasonable grounds to believe that the child has run away from his parents, guardian, or other custodian, and (5) where, during the pendency of court proceedings, it appears to the court that the conduct, condition or surroundings of the child are endangering the health, welfare, person or property of himself or others, or that he may abscond or be removed from the jurisdiction of the court or will not be brought to the court."

Staff Notes

1996:

The amendment changed the rule's reference from "referee" to "magistrate" in divisions (A)(3)(G) [sic.] and (A)(4) in order to harmonize the rule with the language adopted in the 1995 amendments to Juv. R. 40. The amendment is technical only and no substantive change is intended.

1994:

Rule 6 Taking Into Custody

The 1994 amendment modified Juv. R. 6 to comply with section 2151.31 of the Revised Code, which requires particular conditions to exist to permit a law enforcement officer or a duly authorized officer of the court to take a child into emergency custody. Juv. R. 6(A)(3)(g) specifies when such taking into custody may be authorized by an ex parte telephone order pursuant to section 2151.31(D) of the Revised Code. Juv. R. 6(B) delineates time deadlines for a probable cause hearing to be held after the issuance of an emergency order.

Editor's Comment

Juv R 6 is similar to the procedural provisions of 2151.31 and 2151.28(G).

2151.28(G) provides that "If it appears from an affidavit filed or from sworn testimony before the court that the conduct, condition or surroundings of the child are endangering his health or welfare or those of others, that he may abscond or be removed from the jurisdiction of the court, or that will not be brought to the court, notwithstanding the service of the summons, the court may endorse upon the summons an order that a law enforcement officer serve the summons and take the child into immediate custody and bring him forthwith to the court."

Cross References

Custody of child by public agency, 2151.38
Disposition of abused, neglected, or dependent child, 2151.353
Disposition of unruly child, 2151.354

Ohio Administrative Code References

Authority to assume and retain custody of a child, OAC 5101:2–42–04

Library References

Infants ⚖68.3, 192.
Westlaw Topic No. 211.
C.J.S. Infants §§ 42, 53 to 55.

Research References

Encyclopedias

OH Jur. 3d Family Law § 1569, Ex Parte Order for Detention.
OH Jur. 3d Family Law § 1570, Apprehension.
OH Jur. 3d Family Law § 1647, Proceedings Before Referee; Powers and Duties.

Treatises and Practice Aids

Carlin, Baldwin's Ohio Practice, Merrick-Rippner Probate Law § 107:25, Juvenile Detention and Shelter Care—Grounds for Detention or Shelter Care.

Carlin, Baldwin's Ohio Practice, Merrick-Rippner Probate Law § 107:49, Adjudicatory Hearings—Conduct of Hearing by Magistrate.

Carlin, Baldwin's Ohio Practice, Merrick-Rippner Probate Law § 107:152, Motion for Temporary Custody Pending Hearing—Form.

Giannelli & Yeomans, Ohio Juvenile Law § 14:3, Custody, Arrests & Stops.

Giannelli & Yeomans, Ohio Juvenile Law § 19:6, Standard for Detention.

Giannelli & Yeomans, Ohio Juvenile Law § 20:4, Required Hearings.

Giannelli & Yeomans, Ohio Juvenile Law § 23:3, Right to Counsel.

Giannelli & Yeomans, Ohio Juvenile Law § 24:4, Pretrial Orders.

Law Review and Journal Commentaries

The Plight of the Interstate Child in American Courts, Leona Mary Hudak. 9 Akron L Rev 257 (Fall 1975).

Notes of Decisions

Confessions, admissibility 2
Hearings 1
Release from custody 3
Taking minor into custody 4
Waiver of Miranda rights 5

---

1. Hearings

RC 2151.28 and 2151.31 do not require a hearing as a condition precedent to the taking of a child into custody, pursuant to order of a juvenile court, during pendency of an action in such court. (Annotation from former RC 2151.31.) In re Jones (Allen 1961) 114 Ohio App. 319, 182 N.E.2d 631, 19 O.O.2d 286.

2. Confessions, admissibility

Juvenile's confessions at crime scene and at sheriff's office were voluntary; although juvenile was under 14 years of age and had no prior criminal experience, there was nothing to suggest that he was of insufficient intelligence to understand *Miranda* rights, juvenile was advised of such rights after pat down search and at sheriff's officer, police officers felt that juvenile understood his rights, juvenile waived such rights, and there was no evidence of physical deprivation, mistreatment, or threatening behavior by police. In re M.D. (Ohio App. 12 Dist., Madison, 11-08-2004) No. CA2003-12-038, 2004-Ohio-5904, 2004 WL 2505161, Unreported. Infants ⇐ 174

Three minors, suspected of murder, were apprehended; prior to their being taken before any court and before any charges were filed against them, signed confessions were obtained from each of them; they were then taken before juvenile court which conducted investigation, and nature of crime being apparent, cases were referred to common pleas court where accused were indicted, tried and convicted; in each instance confession obtained was used against one making it, in both juvenile court and court of common pleas; confessions were admissible in evidence, even though accused were not taken immediately before juvenile court as directed by this section; fact that confessions were used in juvenile court did not render them inadmissible in court of common pleas under GC 1639–30 (RC 2151.35) because there was but one case or proceeding. (Annotation from former RC 2151.31.) State v. Lowder (Stark 1946) 79 Ohio App. 237, 72 N.E.2d 785, 34 O.O. 568, appeal dismissed 147 Ohio St. 340, 70 N.E.2d 905, 34 O.O. 249, certiorari granted 67 S.Ct. 1728, 331 U.S. 803, 91 L.Ed. 1826, reversed 68 S.Ct. 302, 332 U.S. 596, 92 L.Ed. 224, 36 O.O. 530, appeal dismissed 147 Ohio St. 530, 72 N.E.2d 102, 34 O.O. 423, appeal dismissed 147 Ohio St. 531, 72 N.E.2d 81, 34 O.O. 423, appeal dismissed 151 Ohio St. 80, 84 N.E.2d 217, 38 O.O. 531, certiorari denied 69 S.Ct. 1501, 337 U.S. 945, 93 L.Ed. 1748.

3. Release from custody

A minor detained on delinquency charges is not charged with an offense and hence is not entitled to release on bail. (Annotation from former RC 2151.31.) State ex rel. Peaks v. Allaman (Montgomery 1952) 115 N.E.2d 849, 66 Ohio Law Abs. 403, 51 O.O. 321.

4. Taking minor into custody

Police officer's questioning of juvenile, who was detained in police cruiser while vandalism was being investigated, prior to pat-down for weapons did not constitute custodial interrogation, and thus, *Miranda* warnings were not required, where placement of juvenile in cruiser as part of investigation was not custodial placement and questions were merely on-the-scene inquiries done as part of normal fact-finding process. In re M.D. (Ohio App. 12 Dist., Madison, 11-08-2004) No. CA2003-12-038, 2004-Ohio-5904, 2004 WL 2505161, Unreported. Infants ⇐ 174

Search of juvenile's person was lawful, despite fact that he had already been detained in police cruiser for quite awhile without resistance while police officers investigated vandalism, where it was undisputed that inexperienced officer did not search juvenile before she put juvenile in cruiser and second officer testified that he patted juvenile down for weapons as safety precaution when he discovered that juvenile had not been patted down. In re M.D. (Ohio App. 12 Dist., Madison, 11-08-2004) No. CA2003-12-038, 2004-Ohio-5904, 2004 WL 2505161, Unreported. Infants ⇐ 192

Juvenile was not under arrest when he was placed in police cruiser, but was merely detained for investigation purposes, where juvenile was put in cruiser while police officers were performing on-scene inquiry into vandalism of home as part of normal fact-finding process and officers indicated that, until juvenile was subsequently patted down, he was not under arrest. In re M.D. (Ohio App. 12 Dist., Madison, 11-08-2004) No. CA2003-12-038, 2004-Ohio-5904, 2004 WL 2505161, Unreported. Infants ⇐ 192

Homeowner, who discovered that his home had recently been vandalized, did not conduct citizen's arrest of juvenile, where homeowner did not identify himself as off-duty police officer and did not tell juvenile he was under arrest, but simply detained and escorted juvenile to cruiser of police officer, whom homeowner had contacted regarding vandalism, which was parked in front of home and released juvenile to police officer. In re M.D. (Ohio App. 12 Dist., Madison, 11-08-2004) No. CA2003-12-038, 2004-Ohio-5904, 2004 WL 2505161, Unreported. Infants ⇐ 192

The warrantless arrest of a juvenile is on probable cause when the arresting officer has sufficient information, from the victim's description of the group responsible for a robbery and from a subsequent radio report concerning a disturbance created by a similar group in the same general area, to warrant a reasonable belief that a felony has been committed and that the arrestee is one of the perpetrators. In re Howard (Hamilton 1987) 31 Ohio App.3d 1, 508 N.E.2d 190, 31 O.B.R. 14.

Under RC 2151.14 and 2151.31 it is the manifest duty of enforcement officers to cooperate with and assist the juvenile authorities in the performance of their duties when such officers are specifically requested to do so by the juvenile authorities; and such officers may avoid liability in an action for false imprisonment by showing that they were justified in the detention or restraint of the juvenile made under the specific direction and order of the juvenile authorities. (Annotation from former RC 2151.31.) Garland v. Dustman (Portage 1969) 19 Ohio App.2d 292, 251 N.E.2d 153, 48 O.O.2d 408. False Imprisonment ⇐ 11; Infants ⇐ 192

Under Ohio law, unless matters of public safety are involved, a child alleged to be abused, neglected, or dependent may be removed from his home by court order only upon a judicial determination that continuation in the home would be contrary to the child's best interest. OAG 87–105.

5. Waiver of Miranda rights

Where police apprehended a fourteen-year-old minor for questioning following a fire, police may properly question such minor at the police station before delivering her to a place of detention or bringing her to court. In re Hawkins, No. 3430 (9th Dist Ct App, Lorain, 5–11–83).

Where a fourteen-year-old minor, without counsel, made a statement to police implicating herself in setting a fire which killed her father, and the court psychologist testified that such minor was of average intelligence, the minor's statement is properly admitted into evidence where the minor had waived her Miranda rights and during the course of such statement the minor answered intelligently, coherently, and gave no indication of undue influence. In re Hawkins, No. 3430 (9th Dist Ct App, Lorain, 5–11–83).

A juvenile's Fifth and Sixth Amendment rights are the same as if she were an adult. In re M.H. (Ohio Com.Pl., 10-03-2003) 129 Ohio Misc.2d 5, 814 N.E.2d 1264, 2003-Ohio-7371. Infants ⇐ 174; Infants ⇐ 205; Infants ⇐ 207

Juv R 7   Detention and shelter care

(A) Detention: standards

A child taken into custody shall not be placed in detention or shelter care prior to final disposition unless any of the following apply:

(1) Detention or shelter care is required:

(a) to protect the child from immediate or threatened physical or emotional harm; or

(b) to protect the person or property of others from immediate or threatened physical or emotional harm.

(2) The child may abscond or be removed from the jurisdiction of the court;

(3) The child has no parent, guardian, custodian or other person able to provide supervision and care for the child and return the child to the court when required;

(4) An order for placement of the child in detention or shelter care has been made by the court;

(5) Confinement is authorized by statute.

(B) Priorities in placement prior to hearing

A person taking a child into custody shall, with all reasonable speed, do either of the following:

(1) Release the child to a parent, guardian, or other custodian;

(2) Where detention or shelter care appears to be required under the standards of division (A) of this rule, bring the child to the court or deliver the child to a place of detention or shelter care designated by the court.

(C) Initial procedure upon detention

Any person who delivers a child to a shelter or detention facility shall give the admissions officer at the facility a signed report stating why the child was taken into custody and why the child was not released to a parent, guardian or custodian, and shall assist the admissions officer, if necessary, in notifying the parent pursuant to division (E)(3) of this rule.

(D) Admission

The admissions officer in a shelter or detention facility, upon receipt of a child, shall review the report submitted pursuant to division (C) of this rule, make such further investigation as is feasible and do either of the following:

(1) Release the child to the care of a parent, guardian or custodian;

(2) Where detention or shelter care is required under the standards of division (A) of this rule, admit the child to the facility or place the child in some appropriate facility.

(E) Procedure after admission

When a child has been admitted to detention or shelter care the admissions officer shall do all of the following:

(1) Prepare a report stating the time the child was brought to the facility and the reasons the child was admitted;

(2) Advise the child of the right to telephone parents and counsel immediately and at reasonable times thereafter and the time, place, and purpose of the detention hearing;

(3) Use reasonable diligence to contact the child's parent, guardian, or custodian and advise that person of all of the following:

(a) The place of and reasons for detention;

(b) The time the child may be visited;

(c) The time, place, and purpose of the detention hearing;

(d) The right to counsel and appointed counsel in the case of indigency.

(F) Detention hearing

(1) Hearing: time; notice. When a child has been admitted to detention or shelter care, a detention hearing shall be held promptly, not later than seventy-two hours after the child is placed in detention or shelter care or the next court day, whichever is earlier, to determine whether detention or shelter care is required. Reasonable oral or written notice of the time, place, and purpose of the detention hearing shall be given to the child and the parents, guardian, or other custodian, if that person or those persons can be found.

(2) Hearing: advisement of rights. Prior to the hearing, the court shall inform the parties of the right to counsel and to appointed counsel if indigent and the child's right to remain silent with respect to any allegation of a juvenile traffic offense, delinquency, or unruliness.

(3) Hearing procedure. The court may consider any evidence, including the reports filed by the person who brought the child to the facility and the admissions officer, without regard to formal rules of evidence. Unless it appears from the hearing that the child's detention or shelter care is required under division (A) of this rule, the court shall order the child's release to a parent, guardian, or custodian. Whenever abuse, neglect, or dependency is alleged, the court shall determine whether there are any appropriate relatives of the child who are willing to be temporary custodians and, if so, appoint an appropriate relative as the temporary custodian of the child. The court shall make a reasonable efforts determination in accordance with Juv. R. 27(B)(1).

(G) Rehearing

If a parent, guardian, or custodian did not receive notice of the initial hearing and did not appear or waive appearance at the hearing, the court shall rehear the matter promptly. After a child is placed in shelter care or detention care, any party and the guardian ad litem of the child may file a motion with the court requesting that the child be released from detention or shelter care. Upon the filing of the motion, the court shall hold a hearing within seventy-two hours.

(H) Separation from adults

No child shall be placed in or committed to any prison, jail, lockup, or any other place where the child can come in contact or communication with any adult convicted of crime, under arrest, or charged with crime.

(I) Physical examination

The supervisor of a shelter or detention facility may provide for a physical examination of a child placed in the shelter or facility.

(J) Telephone and visitation rights

A child may telephone the child's parents and attorney immediately after being admitted to a shelter or detention facility and at reasonable times thereafter.

The child may be visited at reasonable visiting hours by the child's parents and adult members of the family, the child's pastor, and the child's teachers. The child may be visited by the child's attorney at any time.

(Adopted eff. 7–1–72; amended eff. 7–1–94, 7–1–01)

Uncodified Law

2002 H 180, § 3, eff. 5–16–02, reads, in part:

The General Assembly further requests the Supreme Court to promptly modify Rule 7 of the Rules of Juvenile Procedure pursuant to its authority under the Ohio Constitution to make that rule consistent with the amendments of this act to section 2151.31 of the Revised Code.

Historical and Statutory Notes

Amendment Note: The 7–1–01 amendment redesignated former division (1) as divisions (1) and (1)(a); and added new division (1)(b) and new division (5).

Amendment Note: The 7–1–94 amendment designated divisions (A)(1) through (A)(3); inserted "shelter" and substituted "child from immediate or threatened physical or emotional harm" for "person and property of others or those of the child" in division (A)(1); added division (A)(4); added the final two sentences in division (F)(3); deleted "Any decision relating to detention or shelter care may be reviewed at any time upon motion of any party." from the beginning of, and added the final two sentences in, division (G); deleted the second and third paragraphs in division (H); substituted "Physical" for "Medical" in the title of division (I); and made changes to reflect gender-neutral language. Prior to amendment, the second and third paragraphs in division (H) read:

"A child may be detained in jail or other facility for detention of adults only if the child is alleged to be delinquent, there is no detention center for delinquent children under the supervision of the court or other agency approved by the court, and the detention is in a room separate and removed from those for adults. The court may order that a child over the age of fifteen years who is alleged to be delinquent be detained in a jail in a room separate and removed from adults if public safety or protection of the child or others reasonably requires such detention.

"A child alleged to be neglected or dependent shall not be detained in jail or other facility intended or used for detention of adults charged with criminal offenses or of children alleged to be delinquent unless upon order of the court."

Staff Notes

2001:

Rule 7(A) Detention: standards

Rule 7(A) was amended to add two rationales for placing a child in detention or shelter care: one, that the child is endangering the person or property of others [(A)(1)(b)] and two, that a statutory provision authorizes confinement [(A)(5)]. Rule 7(A)(1)(b) conforms to Sub. Sen. Bill 179 (January 1, 2002 effective date), Revised Code section 2151.31(A)(6)(b) and (d). Rule 7(A)(5) ensures that statutory provisions, i.e., Revised Code sections 2152.04 and 2151.31 (C)(2), that contemplate placing a child in detention are recognized as valid rationales by the Juvenile Rules.

1994:

Rule 7 Detention and Shelter Care

Am. Sub. S.B. 89, effective January 1, 1989, changed the parameters under which a child could be detained. The law removed the authority to detain a child to protect the person and property of others or to protect the property of the child, so such language in Juv. R. 7(A)(1) has been deleted. Juv. R. 7(A)(1) does define the right to place a child in shelter care because of immediate or threatened physical or emotional harm pursuant to Revised Code 2151.31.

Juv. R. 7(F)(3) requires the court to determine the issues of the opportunity for suitable placement with relatives and of reasonable efforts made by agencies to prevent removal or to return the child home, in accordance with Revised Code 2151.314(B)(2) and 2151.419. "Reasonable efforts" are further defined by amended Juv. R. 27(B)(1).

Juv. R. 7(G) has been modified to include the seventy-two hour shelter care hearing requirement imposed by Revised Code 2151.31(E).

The title for Juv. R. 7(I) was changed from "Medical Examination" to "Physical Examination" to conform it to the definition specified in Juv. R. 2.

Editor's Comment

Detention and shelter care   1
Detention: standards   2
Priorities in placement prior to hearing   3
Initial procedure upon detention   4
Admission   5
Procedure after admission   6
Detention hearing   7
Rehearing   8
Separation from adults   9
Physical examination   10
Telephone and visitation rights   11

1. Detention and shelter care

Juv R 7 governs detention and shelter care, which are defined in Juv R 2. Detention involves physically restricted facilities and shelter care involves physically unrestricted facilities. Generally, the rule is a restatement of present law and is drawn from 2151.31 through 2151.314.

The rule sets forth the standard to be employed in deciding whether detention or shelter care is required in Division (A). Subdivisions (B) through (C) provide the procedure through which the standards are to be implemented. Subdivision (G) provides for a rehearing at any time upon motion of any party and mandates a rehearing if a parent, guardian, or custodian failed to receive notice of the detention hearing and does not waive appearance. Subdivision (H) deals with the type of facilities required for detention. Subdivision (I) authorizes physical examinations for detained children. Subdivision (J) deals with a child's visitation and telephone rights while in detention.

The rule proceeds on the assumption, as does Ch 2151, that the state is empowered to provide interim shelter care or detention, prior to a hearing on the merits of the complaint, for a child who is not receiving adequate care in his home or who is accused of illegal behavior, without the right to bail normally available to adult defenders. The rule requires no finding of probable cause that an offense has been committed as a prerequisite to detention.

2. Detention: standards

Juv R 7(A) provides the standards that are to be employed in determining whether or not a child is to be held in detention or shelter care prior to final disposition. This standard is then employed by reference throughout Juv R 7 (See Juv R 7(B)(2), 7(D)(2) and 7(F)(3)).

Detention or shelter care in a pending case is permitted where (1) it is required to protect the child from immediate or threatened physical or emotional harm; (2) the child may leave or be removed from the jurisdiction; (3) the child has no parent, guardian, or custodian; and (4) an order for placement in detention or shelter care has been made by the court.

The standards are taken from 2151.31(C) and represent a continuation of present law.

3. Priorities in placement prior to hearing

Juv R 7(B) provides that an initial decision is to be made by the person taking the child into custody and that he is to release the child to his parent, guardian, or custodian unless detention or shelter care is justified and required under the standards provided in Division (A). Juv R 7(B) is taken from 2151.311(A)(1) and (A)(2).

4. Initial procedure upon detention

Juv R 7(C) requires the person delivering a child to a shelter or detention facility to give the admissions officer of the facility a written report of the reasons the child was taken into custody and the reasons he was not released to his parent, guardian, or custodian. It further requires such person to assist the admissions officer in informing parents of the child's detention under Division (E).

Juv R 7(C) is a modification of 2151.311(A)(2) in its procedure for notification. 2151.311(A)(2) places upon the person delivering the child to the facility the responsibility for notifying the parent. Juv R 7(C), with 7(E), places that responsibility on the admissions officer of the facility and only requires that the person delivering the child to the facility assist the admissions officer in a notification, which is broader than the notification under 2151.311(A)(2).

5. Admission

Juv R 7(D) is a restatement of 2151.314(A), and requires the admissions officer of a detention or shelter facility to make a determination of the appropriateness of detention or shelter care under the standards provided in Division (A). The only change from the Revised Code is the specification of the admissions officer as the person to make this determination, while the Revised Code refers to "the intake or other authorized officer of the court."

6. Procedure after admission

Juv R 7(E) provides that the admissions officer is to prepare a report on the reasons for admission when a child is admitted to the facility and to advise the child and his parents, if possible, of certain basic information. Under Division (C) the person delivering the child to the facility is to assist the admissions officer in advising the parent.

The requirement of a written report is not stated in the Revised Code, although it is standard practice in most courts of the state.

Juv R 7(E)(2) and (3) differ somewhat from 2151.314(A). Both the rule and the statute require that the child and parent be advised of the time, place, and purpose of the detention hearing, as well as their right to counsel and appointed counsel if indigent. In addition, the rule requires that they be notified of their telephone and visitation rights, which are further specified in Division (J), while the statute requires that the court inform the parties of the name and telephone number of a court employee who can be contacted during the normal business hours of the court to arrange for the prompt appointment of counsel for any indigent party.

7. Detention hearing

Juv R 7(F) provides the procedure by which the detention hearing is to be held. Although it is similar to 2151.314(A), there are some differences. Juv R 7(F)(3) makes it clear that the reports prepared by the person delivering the child and the admissions officer may be considered at the detention hearing. The rule also provides that the court may consider any evidence without regard to formal rules of evidence.

A change that the rule makes over present law is that 2151.314(A) provides that the hearing shall be held "promptly, not later than seventy-two hours after (the child) is placed in detention or shelter care." Juv R 7(F)(1) contains the same language, but adds the phrase "or the next court day, whichever is earlier." On the other hand, 2151.314(A) requires that the complaint be filed within the seventy-two hour period, while no such requirement is contained in the rule. The statutory requirement is preferable because it would be difficult to conduct a proper hearing without knowing the specifics of the complaint.

Juv R 7(F) provides that in abuse, neglect, or dependency cases, the court must determine whether there are any appropriate relatives who could take temporary custody of the child in lieu of detention or shelter care. This is preferable to a similar provision in 2151.314(B)(2), which requires this determination in any detention or shelter hearing, including delinquency cases.

8. Rehearing

Juv R 7(G) provides for rehearings on detention and shelter care decisions. It allows the court to rehear such matters upon motion of a party and requires a prompt rehearing where a parent, guardian, or custodian did not receive notice, appear or waive appearance at the hearing. Moreover, the rule requires a rehearing within seventy-two hours upon a motion filed by a party requesting the child's release.

9. Separation from adults

Juv R 7(H) places limitations on the type of facility within which a child may be detained. It requires separation from adults, and is taken from

2151.312(B). 2151.311(C) permits a person who takes a child into custody to hold that child only for processing purposes in an adult facility for a brief period of time subject to separation and supervision. Otherwise, 2151.312(B) prohibits holding children in adult facilities.

10. Physical examination

Juv R 7(I) authorizes the supervisor of a shelter or detention facility to provide for a physical examination of a child placed therein. The term physical examination is defined in Juv R 2 and requires that the examination be by a physician.

Juv R 7(I) outlines the authority of the supervisor of a detention or shelter facility to control health conditions within the facility. This is particularly important because of the incidence of drug problems, venereal disease and other infectious diseases of those persons who come into such facilities. While the supervisor is permitted to provide for an examination on his own authority, medical treatment is only authorized by court order under Juv R 13.

11. Telephone and visitation rights

Juv R 7(J) defines the telephone and visitation rights of a child held in detention or shelter care. The policy behind the rule is the need to have the incarceration of a child involve as little separation from his family as possible.

There is a slight distinction between the rule and 2151.352 with respect to the issue of visitation. Whereas the statute permits the attorney to visit the child "at any reasonable time," the rule permits such visitation "at any time."

Cross References

Detention or shelter care hearing, 2151.314

Ohio Administrative Code References

Operational procedures for detention centers to conform to Ohio Rules of Juvenile Procedure, OAC 5139-7-04
Standards for administration of detention center; confinement to be in accordance with Juv R 7, OAC 5139-37-03
Standards for admission to detention center, OAC 5139-37-17

Library References

Infants ⚖68.3, 192, 208.
Westlaw Topic No. 211.
C.J.S. Infants §§ 42, 51 to 85.

Research References

Encyclopedias

OH Jur. 3d Family Law § 1570, Apprehension.
OH Jur. 3d Family Law § 1574, Delivery of Child to Shelter or Detention Facility.
OH Jur. 3d Family Law § 1575, Delivery of Child to Shelter or Detention Facility—Telephone and Visitation Rights.
OH Jur. 3d Family Law § 1576, Detention Hearing; Notice.
OH Jur. 3d Family Law § 1578, Detention Hearing; Notice—Evidence and Order.
OH Jur. 3d Family Law § 1579, Detention Hearing; Notice—Rehearing.
OH Jur. 3d Family Law § 1583, Alleged Neglected, Abused, or Dependent Child.
OH Jur. 3d Family Law § 1584, Medical Examination.
OH Jur. 3d Family Law § 1637, Order for Social History or Physical or Mental Examination.
OH Jur. 3d Family Law § 1647, Proceedings Before Referee; Powers and Duties.
OH Jur. 3d Family Law § 1683, Conclusiveness; Collateral Attack.
OH Jur. 3d Family Law § 1709, Revocation of Probation on Hearing—Detention During Proceeding.

Treatises and Practice Aids

Katz, Giannelli, Blair and Lipton, Baldwin's Ohio Practice, Criminal Law, § 37:1, Introduction.
Giannelli and Snyder, Baldwin's Ohio Practice, Evidence, R 101, Scope of Rules: Applicability; Privileges; Exceptions.
Giannelli and Snyder, Baldwin's Ohio Practice, Evidence, § 101.13, Release on Bail.
Giannelli and Snyder, Baldwin's Ohio Practice, Evidence, § 101.16, Other Procedural Rules.
Carlin, Baldwin's Ohio Practice, Merrick-Rippner Probate Law § 104:9, Juvenile Court—Constitutional Issues—Pretrial Preventive Detention of Juveniles.
Carlin, Baldwin's Ohio Practice, Merrick-Rippner Probate Law § 107:25, Juvenile Detention and Shelter Care—Grounds for Detention or Shelter Care.
Carlin, Baldwin's Ohio Practice, Merrick-Rippner Probate Law § 107:26, Detention Prior to Hearing.
Carlin, Baldwin's Ohio Practice, Merrick-Rippner Probate Law § 107:27, Detention Separate from Adult Detainees.
Carlin, Baldwin's Ohio Practice, Merrick-Rippner Probate Law § 107:28, Children Subject to Detention.
Carlin, Baldwin's Ohio Practice, Merrick-Rippner Probate Law § 107:29, Admission and Release from Detention.
Carlin, Baldwin's Ohio Practice, Merrick-Rippner Probate Law § 107:30, Detention Hearing.
Carlin, Baldwin's Ohio Practice, Merrick-Rippner Probate Law § 107:36, Use of Social History and Investigation Report.
Carlin, Baldwin's Ohio Practice, Merrick-Rippner Probate Law § 107:49, Adjudicatory Hearings—Conduct of Hearing by Magistrate.
Carlin, Baldwin's Ohio Practice, Merrick-Rippner Probate Law § 107:117, Proceedings After Judgment—Continuing Jurisdiction of Juvenile Court.
Carlin, Baldwin's Ohio Practice, Merrick-Rippner Probate Law § 107:121, Custody Review Hearing—Revocation of Probation or Parole.
Carlin, Baldwin's Ohio Practice, Merrick-Rippner Probate Law § 107:125, Appeals—Availability of Habeas Corpus.
Carlin, Baldwin's Ohio Practice, Merrick-Rippner Probate Law § 107:152, Motion for Temporary Custody Pending Hearing—Form.
Carlin, Baldwin's Ohio Practice, Merrick-Rippner Probate Law § 107:172, Order Following Detention Hearing—Form.
Giannelli & Yeomans, Ohio Juvenile Law § 1:8, Rules of Juvenile Procedure.
Giannelli & Yeomans, Ohio Juvenile Law § 14:3, Custody, Arrests & Stops.
Giannelli & Yeomans, Ohio Juvenile Law § 14:9, Confessions—Due Process.
Giannelli & Yeomans, Ohio Juvenile Law § 19:1, Introduction.
Giannelli & Yeomans, Ohio Juvenile Law § 19:2, Place of Detention.
Giannelli & Yeomans, Ohio Juvenile Law § 19:3, Admissions Officer.
Giannelli & Yeomans, Ohio Juvenile Law § 19:4, Detention Hearing: Notice.
Giannelli & Yeomans, Ohio Juvenile Law § 19:5, Detention Hearing.
Giannelli & Yeomans, Ohio Juvenile Law § 19:6, Standard for Detention.
Giannelli & Yeomans, Ohio Juvenile Law § 19:7, Time Requirements.
Giannelli & Yeomans, Ohio Juvenile Law § 19:8, Motions for Release.
Giannelli & Yeomans, Ohio Juvenile Law § 19:9, Bail.
Giannelli & Yeomans, Ohio Juvenile Law § 21:6, Social History Report.
Giannelli & Yeomans, Ohio Juvenile Law § 24:4, Pretrial Orders.
Giannelli & Yeomans, Ohio Juvenile Law § 33:3, Detention.
Giannelli & Yeomans, Ohio Juvenile Law App. D, Appendix D. Glossary.
Giannelli & Yeomans, Ohio Juvenile Law § 19:10, Rights While Detained.
Giannelli & Yeomans, Ohio Juvenile Law § 19:11, Detention Facilities.
Giannelli & Yeomans, Ohio Juvenile Law § 34:12, Habeas Corpus.

Notes of Decisions

Constitutional issues 2
Employees' status 5
Fees and costs 6
Habeas corpus 1
Release from custody 3
Taking minor into custody 4

---

1. Habeas corpus

Habeas corpus will not lie at the request of the father of children found to be dependent and placed in the temporary care and custody of the county welfare department. Pettry v. McGinty (Ohio 1979) 60 Ohio St.2d 92, 397 N.E.2d 1190, 14 O.O.3d 331.

A parent, alleging that he failed to receive notice of a hearing concerning the shelter care of his child, must move the juvenile court for a rehearing, pursuant to Juv R 7(G), before seeking a writ of habeas corpus. Linger v. Weiss (Ohio 1979) 57 Ohio St.2d 97, 386 N.E.2d 1354, 11 O.O.3d 281, certiorari denied 100 S.Ct. 128, 444 U.S. 862, 62 L.Ed.2d 83. Habeas Corpus ⇌ 280

Habeas corpus relief was not available from decision of the juvenile court awarding temporary custody of father's children to county, which had alleged that one child was neglected; juvenile court had jurisdiction to make the award of temporary custody under applicable statutes, appeal provided an adequate remedy, and alleged errors actually attacked findings of the court. Rothacker v. McCafferty (Ohio App. 8 Dist., Cuyahoga, 09-19-2002) No. 81427, 2002-Ohio-4927, 2002 WL 31087671, Unreported. Habeas Corpus ⇌ 289; Habeas Corpus ⇌ 536

2. Constitutional issues

The due process clause of US Const Am 14 is not violated where a state statute provides for (1) the pretrial detention of a juvenile delinquent where there is a finding, following notice and a hearing, and a statement of reasons and facts, that there is a "serious risk" that the child might commit a crime before return date; and (2) a more formal hearing within a maximum of seventeen days where detention is ordered. (Ed. note: New York law construed in light of federal constitution.) Schall v. Martin (U.S.N.Y. 1984) 104 S.Ct. 2403, 467 U.S. 253, 81 L.Ed.2d 207.

Under the present Juvenile Code and Rules, a juvenile court cannot change a "temporary" commitment to the Ohio youth commission to an "permanent" commitment without hearing; further, the commitment of an unruly child, not declared "delinquent", is a violation of due process and any hearing held on the above matters requires the presence of the youth involved. OAG 72–071.

3. Release from custody

A minor detained on delinquency charges is not charged with an offense and hence is not entitled to release on bail. (Annotation from former RC 2151.27.) State ex rel. Peaks v. Allaman (Montgomery 1952) 115 N.E.2d 849, 66 Ohio Law Abs. 403, 51 O.O. 321.

RC 2151.311(A)(1), 2151.314(A), and Juv R 7(B) do not authorize the release of a child to the peace officer who took the child into custody. OAG 96–061.

4. Taking minor into custody

Statute and juvenile rule imposing duties on trial court in regard to shelter care hearings did not impose duties relative to permanent custody hearings. In re Speaks (Ohio App. 5 Dist., Licking, 06-20-2005) No. 2004 CA 0090, 2005-Ohio-3526, 2005 WL 1503572, Unreported. Infants ⇌ 203

Trial court fulfilled duty to investigate whether there were any relatives available to take custody of children, in proceeding in which permanent custody of children was granted to department; in its judgment entry granting department emergency shelter care of children, court stated that it had considered report of investigation, and report indicated that mother had stated that she was unable to name any relatives with whom children could be placed. In re Speaks (Ohio App. 5 Dist., Licking, 06-20-2005) No. 2004 CA 0090, 2005-Ohio-3526, 2005 WL 1503572, Unreported. Infants ⇌ 210

Where an allegedly neglected, dependent, or abused child is committed to the temporary, emergency custody of a children services board after a shelter care hearing under Juv R 7, the court need not order a reunification plan where it has not finally adjudged and disposed of the matter under RC 2151.353. In re Moloney (Ohio 1986) 24 Ohio St.3d 22, 492 N.E.2d 805, 24 O.B.R. 18.

Even assuming that testimony of protective services supervisor for county children's services agency, that child's maternal grandmother told on-call social worker and supervisor that she was upset that she could not have custody of child and that "she was just going to 'go' over and just take him," was inadmissible hearsay, any deficient performance of father's counsel in failing to object at the shelter care hearing was not prejudicial; court was not bound by formal rules of evidence at the hearing, and there was abundant evidence establishing that father's relatives were no longer able to care for child and that child should be placed in foster care. In re Wingo (Ohio App. 4 Dist., 06-01-2001) 143 Ohio App.3d 652, 758 N.E.2d 780, 2001-Ohio-2477. Infants ⇌ 173.1; Infants ⇌ 253

If a peace officer determines that the detention or shelter care of a child appears to be required as provided in RC 2151.31(C) and Juv R 7(A), the peace officer is required by RC 2151.311(A) and Juv R 7(B) to bring the child to the court or deliver the child to a place of detention or shelter care designated by the court. A peace officer who determines that the detention or shelter care of a child appears to be required may contact the juvenile court by telephone to determine the place of detention or shelter care to which to deliver the child. OAG 96–061.

Under Ohio law, unless matters of public safety are involved, a child alleged to be abused, neglected, or dependent may be removed from his home by court order only upon a judicial determination that continuation in the home would be contrary to the child's best interest. OAG 87–105.

The placement or detention of delinquent, dependent, neglected children, or juvenile traffic offenders, is upon final disposition of the juvenile court and does not include placement in a detention home provided under RC 2151.34. (Annotation from former RC 2151.35.) 1963 OAG 553.

5. Employees' status

Employees of a five-county joint juvenile detention center who are responsible for the supervision, education, and care of detained juveniles are not "officers of the [juvenile] courts" within the meaning of that term in RC 4117.01 where they have no independent authority to decide the disposition of juveniles but merely make recommendations; nor are these workers employees "of the courts" where the relations between the courts and the center are characterized by the following circumstances: (1) the juvenile court judges recommend and approve a list of potential trustees; (2) county commissioners then choose the trustees; (3) these trustees make all decisions about running the center, although the judges may give advice and recommend actions; (4) the trustees hire a superintendent, who in turn hires the other employees; (5) center employees are in the classified civil service; (6) the hours, duties, and schedules of employees are set by the trustees and superintendent; (7) employees often make daily reports to judges about admissions to and incidents at the center, and the superintendent reports to the courts each month; the relations between the courts and the center mandated by Juv R 7 are not enough standing alone to make center employees "court employees"; the employees are instead employees of a "public" or "special" district and are therefore covered by RC Ch 4117. Five–County Joint Juvenile Detention Center v SERB, 1989 SERB 4–81 (10th Dist Ct App, Franklin, 7–18–89), vacated by 57 OS(3d) 4 (1991).

6. Fees and costs

A judge of a juvenile court may not commit a child who has been found to be a delinquent child, or a juvenile traffic offender, to the county jail upon the failure, refusal, or inability of such child to pay a fine and court costs. (Annotation from former RC 2151.23.) OAG 70–143.

Juv R 8 Filing by electronic means

A court may provide, by local rules adopted pursuant to the Rules of Superintendence, for the filing of documents by electronic means. If the court adopts such local rules, they shall include all of the following:

(A) Any signature on electronically transmitted documents shall be considered that of the attorney or party it purports to be for all purposes. If it is established that the documents were transmitted without authority, the court shall order the filing stricken.

(B) A provision shall specify the days and hours during which electronically transmitted documents will be received by the court, and a provision shall specify when documents received electronically will be considered to have been filed.

(C) Any document filed electronically that requires a filing fee may be rejected by the clerk of court unless the filer has complied with the mechanism established by the court for the payment of filing fees.

(Adopted eff. 7–1–94, amended eff. 7–1–96, 7–1–01)

Historical and Statutory Notes

Amendment Note: The 7–1–01 amendment completely rewrote the section to bring it into conformity with the electronic filing procedures in place throughout the procedural rules of Ohio. See *Baldwin's Ohio Legislative Service Annotated*, 2001, page 6/R–64, or the OH–LEGIS or OH–LEGIS–OLD database on Westlaw, for prior version of this rule.

Amendment Note: The 7-1-96 amendment substituted "or magistrate, or both" for "and/or referee" and "this" for "such" in division (A)(2).

Staff Notes

2001:

Rule 8 Filing by Electronic Means

The amendments to this rule were part of a group of amendments that were submitted by the Ohio Courts Digital Signatures Task Force to establish minimum standards for the use of information systems, electronic signatures, and electronic filing. The substantive amendment to this rule was the addition of the first sentence of the rule and of divisions (B) and (C). The title of the rule was changed from "Filing by Facsimile Transmission." Comparable amendments were made to Civil Rule 5, Civil Rule 73 (for probate courts), Criminal Rule 12, and Appellate Rule 13.

As part of this electronic filing and signature project, the following rules were amended effective July 1, 2001: Civil Rules 5, 11, and 73; Criminal Rule 12; Juvenile Rule 8; and Appellate Rules 13 and 18. In addition, Rule 26 of the Rules of Superintendence for Courts of Ohio was amended and Rule of Superintendence 27 was added to complement the rules of procedure. Superintendence Rule 27 establishes a process by which minimum standards for information technology are promulgated, and requires that courts submit any local rule involving the use of information technology to a technology standards committee designated by the Supreme Court for approval.

1996:

The amendment changed the rule's reference from "referee" to "magistrate" in division (A)(2) in order to harmonize the rule with the language adopted in the 1995 amendments to Juv. R. 40. The amendment is technical only and no substantive change is intended.

1994:

Rule 8 Filing by Facsimile Transmission

Juv. R. 8 is an attempt to facilitate juvenile court filings by electronic means. Concerns about the reliability of facsimile transmission are addressed in several divisions. The rule sets forth the form and procedural requirements necessary for proper facsimile transmission in an effort to minimize unauthorized filings. Division 8(B) also requires the court to meet certain standards in paper and equipment in order to assure that the electronic filings will be able to be read and handled by court personnel.

Editor's Comment

Juv R 8, added in 1994, is not based on any statute or other rule, although Civ R 5(B) and (E) contain references to filing of pleadings by facsimile transmission and other electronic means.

Research References

Encyclopedias

OH Jur. 3d Family Law § 1608, Filing of Papers.

Juv R 9   Intake

(A) Court action to be avoided

In all appropriate cases formal court action should be avoided and other community resources utilized to ameliorate situations brought to the attention of the court.

(B) Screening; referral

Information that a child is within the court's jurisdiction may be informally screened prior to the filing of a complaint to determine whether the filing of a complaint is in the best interest of the child and the public.

(Adopted eff. 7-1-72)

Editor's Comment

Juv R 9 is a very general rule requiring juvenile courts to make every effort to avoid the use of formal court proceedings in cases involving children and to utilize alternative community resources to ameliorate situations brought to the attention of the court. The philosophy behind this rule is that formal court action should be a last resort in juvenile problems.

Pre-judicial screening of juvenile court cases was a primary recommendation of the Task Force Report on Juvenile Delinquency and Youth Crime to the President's Commission on Law Enforcement and the Administration of Justice (1967) and the National Council of Crime and Delinquency, Model Rules.

Most juvenile courts in the state have evolved and continue to experiment with procedures for the implementation of this principle of diversion.

Cross References

Scope of rules, applicability, construction, exceptions, Juv R 1

Library References

Infants ⬅191.
Westlaw Topic No. 211.
C.J.S. Infants §§ 42, 53, 54.

Research References

Treatises and Practice Aids

Carlin, Baldwin's Ohio Practice, Merrick-Rippner Probate Law § 107:1, Intake.

Giannelli & Yeomans, Ohio Juvenile Law § 2:6, Common Law Infancy Defense.

Giannelli & Yeomans, Ohio Juvenile Law § 15:2, Intake.

Giannelli & Yeomans, Ohio Juvenile Law § 15:3, Diversion, Youth Services Grant.

Giannelli & Yeomans, Ohio Juvenile Law § 15:4, Mediation.

Notes of Decisions

Constitutional issues   1
Formal court action   4
Juvenile considered "suspect"   2
Review of complaint   3

---

1. Constitutional issues

The prosecution of a twelve-year-old girl as a delinquent based on a charge of complicity to commit rape violates RC Ch 2151, Juv R 9(A), local court intake policy, public policy, and due process of law where such prosecution arises from an incident of three children "playing doctor," with the adjudicated delinquent directing a five-year-old boy to drop his pants and place his penis in a five-year-old girl's mouth in order to take her temperature, because no offense was actually committed and the failure to raise the issue of the constitutionality of applying the rape statute to children under the age of thirteen does not preclude consideration of the constitutional challenge on appeal. In re M.D. (Ohio 1988) 38 Ohio St.3d 149, 527 N.E.2d 286.

2. Juvenile considered "suspect"

For purposes of the confidential law enforcement investigatory records exception under RC 149.43(A), a juvenile may be considered a "suspect" when no charge, arrest, complaint, or referral to the juvenile court pursuant to Juv R 9 has been made. 1990 OAG 101.

For purposes of the confidential law enforcement investigatory records exception under RC 149.43(A), a juvenile ceases to be a "suspect" upon arrest, being charged, the filing of a complaint, or a referral to the juvenile court pursuant to Juv R 9. 1990 OAG 101.

A decision, at a particular point in time, not to charge, arrest, file a complaint with, or refer a juvenile to the juvenile court pursuant to Juv R 9 does not require disclosure or terminate the juvenile's status as a "suspect," pursuant to RC 149.43(A). 1990 OAG 101.

3. Review of complaint

Magistrate lacked authority to refer child protection proceeding to visiting judge, especially without judicial approval from sitting judge assigned to case. In re S.J. (Ohio App. 8 Dist., Cuyahoga, 04-21-2005) No. 84410, 2005-Ohio-1854, 2005 WL 914692, Unreported. Judges ⬅ 25(1)

The juvenile court is entitled to review the appropriateness of filing a complaint against a ten-year old boy for rape and to dismiss the complaint because it would not further the policies of the state. In re Smith (Hamilton 1992) 80 Ohio App.3d 502, 609 N.E.2d 1281, dismissed, jurisdictional motion overruled 65 Ohio St.3d 1441, 600 N.E.2d 683.

4. Formal court action

Formal court action is permissible in appropriate juvenile cases and it is within the discretion of the juvenile court to proceed in such a manner. In re Corcoran (Geauga 1990) 68 Ohio App.3d 213, 587 N.E.2d 957, dismissed 56 Ohio St.3d 702, 564 N.E.2d 703.

Complete lack of any record of adjudicatory and dispositional hearings before the magistrate required reversal of juvenile's delinquency adjudication; missing record concerned waiver of counsel and admission to complaint, and lack of record prevented finding that magistrate complied with juvenile procedure rule requiring courts to make every effort to avoid the use of formal court proceedings in cases involving children. In re L.B. (Ohio App. 8 Dist., Cuyahoga, 07-25-2002) No. 79370, No. 79942, 2002-Ohio-3767, 2002 WL 1729905, Unreported. Infants ⚖ 254

Juv R 10 Complaint

(A) Filing

Any person having knowledge of a child who appears to be a juvenile traffic offender, delinquent, unruly, neglected, dependent, or abused may file a complaint with respect to the child in the juvenile court of the county in which the child has a residence or legal settlement, or in which the traffic offense, delinquency, unruliness, neglect, dependency, or abuse occurred.

Persons filing complaints that a child appears to be an unruly or delinquent child for being an habitual or chronic truant and the parent, guardian, or other person having care of the child has failed to cause the child to attend school may also file the complaint in the county in which the child is supposed to attend public school.

Any person may file a complaint to have determined the custody of a child not a ward of another court of this state, and any person entitled to the custody of a child and unlawfully deprived of such custody may file a complaint requesting a writ of habeas corpus. Complaints concerning custody shall be filed in the county where the child is found or was last known to be.

Any person with standing may file a complaint for the determination of any other matter over which the juvenile court is given jurisdiction by the Revised Code. The complaint shall be filed in the county in which the child who is the subject of the complaint is found or was last known to be. In a removal action, the complaint shall be filed in the county where the foster home is located.

When a case concerning a child is transferred or certified from another court, the certification from the transferring court shall be considered the complaint. The juvenile court may order the certification supplemented upon its own motion or that of a party.

(B) Complaint: general form

The complaint, which may be upon information and belief, shall satisfy all of the following requirements:

(1) State in ordinary and concise language the essential facts that bring the proceeding within the jurisdiction of the court, and in juvenile traffic offense and delinquency proceedings, shall contain the numerical designation of the statute or ordinance alleged to have been violated;

(2) Contain the name and address of the parent, guardian, or custodian of the child or state that the name or address is unknown;

(3) Be made under oath.

(C) Complaint: juvenile traffic offense

A Uniform Traffic Ticket shall be used as a complaint in juvenile traffic offense proceedings.

(D) Complaint: permanent custody

A complaint seeking permanent custody of a child shall state that permanent custody is sought.

(E) Complaint: temporary custody

A complaint seeking temporary custody of a child shall state that temporary custody is sought.

(F) Complaint: planned permanent living arrangement

A complaint seeking the placement of a child into a planned permanent living arrangement shall state that placement into a planned permanent living arrangement is sought.

(G) Complaint: habeas corpus

Where a complaint for a writ of habeas corpus involving the custody of a child is based on the existence of a lawful court order, a certified copy of the order shall be attached to the complaint.

(Adopted eff. 7-1-72; amended eff. 7-1-75, 7-1-76, 7-1-94, 7-1-98, 7-1-01, 7-1-02)

Historical and Statutory Notes

Amendment Note: The 7-1-02 amendment substituted "a planned permanent living arrangement" for "long term foster care" throughout division (F).

Amendment Note: The 7-1-01 amendment added the second paragraph in division (A).

Amendment Note: The 7-1-98 amendment deleted "section 2151.23 of" before "the Revised Code" and added the third sentence in the third paragraph in division (A).

Amendment Note: The 7-1-94 amendment added the third paragraph in division (A) and divisions (E) and (F); and redesignated former division (E) as division (G).

Staff Notes

2002:

Juvenile Rule 10(F) Complaint: planned permanent living arrangement

The July 1, 2002, amendment to Juv. R. 10(F) substituted the language of "planned permanent living arrangement" for the former language of "long term foster care," to conform to the new legislative designation for these child-placing arrangements.

The amendment to Juv. R. 10(F) conforms to sections 2151.27(C) and 2151.353(B) of the Revised Code. Juvenile Rules 2, 15, and 34 also were amended effective July 1, 2002 to reflect this change in terminology.

2001:

Rule 10(A) Filing

Rule 10(A) was amended to conform to the Sub. Sen. Bill 181 (effective September 4, 2000) changes that provide in R. C. section 2151.27(A)(2) that chronic and habitual truancy complaints against both children and adults responsible for them may also be properly venued in the county in which the child is supposed to be attending public school.

1998:

Rule 10(A) Filing

The 1998 amendment revised the third paragraph of Juv. R. 10(A) by adding a reference to removal actions, which are defined in Juv. R. 2(EE), also added by the 1998 amendments. The provision that the complaint in removal actions must be filed in the county where the foster home is located clarifies the venue requirement where the boundaries of the school district extend beyond single county.

The 1998 amendment also deleted from the third paragraph a reference to section 2151.23 of Revised Code.

1994:

Rule 10 Complaint

Division (A) of Juv. R. 10 now includes a residual category of persons who may file a complaint in juvenile court. Juv. R. 10(E) and 10(F) have been modified to require that complainants specifically plead whether or not temporary custody or long term foster care is sought. All changes are pursuant to section 2151.27 of the Revised Code, as amended by S.B. 89.

Editor's Comment

Juv R 10 spells out the procedure to be followed in initiating a proceeding in the juvenile court and uses the same appellation for the formal filing as Crim R 3, i.e., complaint for uniformity.

The first paragraph of Division (A) is based on the first sentence of 2151.27(A), which defines venue in a juvenile proceeding. The second, third, and fourth paragraphs are similar to 2151.27(E), but provide more specific procedures for habeas corpus and custody cases, and cases transferred from another court to a juvenile court pursuant to 3109.04, 3109.06 (Domestic Relations) and 3107.12 (Probate). (*See* 2151.23(A)(2) and (3) and 2151.25.)

Venue in the custody and habeas corpus situation differs from the more typical delinquency, unruly, neglect, dependency, abuse, or juvenile traffic offender case because the matter does not involve conduct by a child. Rather, the concern is to find a proper place for a child who may be found without a legal custodian. Hence, the reference in this rule to venue being "where the child is found or was last known to be." When considering a child custody case in which a child from an Ohio county is removed to another state, the venue provisions of Juv R 10 should be read in conjunction with the Uniform Child Custody Jurisdiction Act (3109.21 et seq.) which, under certain circumstances, permits an Ohio court to assume jurisdiction even though the child is absent from this state. (Venue in abortion notification bypass cases is controlled by RC 2151.85(A).)

To avoid unnecessary delays and repetitious pleadings, the rule provides that the certification of the transferring court shall be the complaint in juvenile court, upon transfer of the case from a court without juvenile jurisdiction to the juvenile court.

The provision of Division (B) that the complaint may be on information and belief originates in 2151.27(A). The use of "ordinary and concise language" appears in Crim R 7(B), as does the requirement that the complaint include a reference to the statute or ordinance alleged to have been violated in delinquency cases. (*See* Crim R 3.)

A 1996 amendment to RC 2151.355(D)(2) provides that any prior delinquency adjudication shall be considered a conviction in determining the degree of offense for a new delinquent act. Due process concerns arguably require that reference to the prior adjudication be made in the new delinquency complaint.

The requirement of Division (B)(3) that the complaint be made under oath comes from 2151.27.

Divisions (D), (E), and (F), requiring that a complaint seeking permanent custody, temporary custody, or long term foster care must so state, follow 2151.27(C). However, there are some differences between the rule and the statute. Whereas the rule applies to any type of complaint, the statute requires the statement only in complaints which allege abuse, dependency, or neglect. Therefore, the rule, but not the statute, would apply to delinquency and unruly cases since it is legally possible for permanent custody to be ordered in such cases (2151.354(A), 2151.355(A)(1)).

The language of Division (F) requiring the attachment of a certified copy of an order which is the basis of a complaint for habeas corpus is similar to Civ R 10(D) and follows the holding in the case of *In re McTaggart*, 2 App(2d) 214, 207 NE(2d) 562 (1965).

Cross References

Adjudicatory hearing, Juv R 29
Complaint, Crim R 3
Complaint may be filed regarding a delinquent, unruly, abused, or neglected child in juvenile court, 2151.27
Warrant or summons, Crim R 7

Library References

Habeas Corpus ⚖︎670(10), 671.
Infants ⚖︎197, 200.
Westlaw Topic Nos. 197, 211.
C.J.S. Habeas Corpus §§ 167 to 169.
C.J.S. Infants §§ 42, 53 to 55.

Research References

Encyclopedias

OH Jur. 3d Family Law § 1586, County in Which to File Complaint.
OH Jur. 3d Family Law § 1590, Who May File Complaint.
OH Jur. 3d Family Law § 1594, Juvenile Traffic Offense.
OH Jur. 3d Family Law § 1595, Permanent Custody.
OH Jur. 3d Family Law § 1596, Habeas Corpus.
OH Jur. 3d Family Law § 1597, Case Transferred from Another Court.
OH Jur. 3d Family Law § 1603, Service of Motion; Notice of Hearing.

Treatises and Practice Aids

Carlin, Baldwin's Ohio Practice, Merrick-Rippner Probate Law § 104:5, Juvenile Courts—Constitutional Issues—Right to Notice, Counsel, and Trial.
Carlin, Baldwin's Ohio Practice, Merrick-Rippner Probate Law § 107:2, Types of Complaints.
Carlin, Baldwin's Ohio Practice, Merrick-Rippner Probate Law § 107:3, Contents of Juvenile Complaint—Facts Establishing Jurisdiction.
Carlin, Baldwin's Ohio Practice, Merrick-Rippner Probate Law § 107:4, Contents of Juvenile Complaint—Prayer for Disposition.
Carlin, Baldwin's Ohio Practice, Merrick-Rippner Probate Law § 107:7, Jurisdiction and Venue for Juvenile Proceedings.
Carlin, Baldwin's Ohio Practice, Merrick-Rippner Probate Law § 107:9, Parties to Proceedings.
Carlin, Baldwin's Ohio Practice, Merrick-Rippner Probate Law § 107:136, Complaint, Delinquent Child—Form.
Carlin, Baldwin's Ohio Practice, Merrick-Rippner Probate Law § 107:137, Complaint, Unruly Child—Form.
Carlin, Baldwin's Ohio Practice, Merrick-Rippner Probate Law § 107:138, Complaint, Abused, Neglected, or Dependent Child—Form.
Giannelli & Yeomans, Ohio Juvenile Law § 13:3, Venue.
Giannelli & Yeomans, Ohio Juvenile Law § 15:2, Intake.
Giannelli & Yeomans, Ohio Juvenile Law § 16:1, Introduction.
Giannelli & Yeomans, Ohio Juvenile Law § 16:2, Standing to File Complaint.
Giannelli & Yeomans, Ohio Juvenile Law § 16:3, Basis for Complaint.
Giannelli & Yeomans, Ohio Juvenile Law § 16:5, Parental Identification.
Giannelli & Yeomans, Ohio Juvenile Law § 16:6, Oath Requirement.
Giannelli & Yeomans, Ohio Juvenile Law § 16:7, Content of Complaint; Designating Type of Case.
Giannelli & Yeomans, Ohio Juvenile Law § 16:8, Delinquency Complaints.
Giannelli & Yeomans, Ohio Juvenile Law § 16:9, Traffic Offender Complaints.
Giannelli & Yeomans, Ohio Juvenile Law § 17:2, Proper Venue.
Giannelli & Yeomans, Ohio Juvenile Law App. D, Appendix D. Glossary.
Giannelli & Yeomans, Ohio Juvenile Law § 16:10, Unruly Complaints.
Giannelli & Yeomans, Ohio Juvenile Law § 16:11, Neglect & Abuse Complaints.
Giannelli & Yeomans, Ohio Juvenile Law § 16:12, Dependency Complaints.
Giannelli & Yeomans, Ohio Juvenile Law § 16:14, Permanent & Temporary Custody Complaints; Planned Permanent Living Arrangements.
Giannelli & Yeomans, Ohio Juvenile Law § 16:15, Certification or Transfer from Another Court.

Notes of Decisions

Constitutional issues 7
Evidence 6
Habeas corpus 4
Jurisdiction 3
Permanent custody 5
Procedural issues 2
Sufficiency of complaint 1

---

1. Sufficiency of complaint

Complaint filed against juvenile in juvenile court was not defective because it failed to plead that he had been charged with category two offense, making him eligible for mandatory transfer to Common Pleas Court, and thus, trial court had jurisdiction to try him as an adult; there was nothing in rule setting forth requirements for filing complaints against juvenile offenders that required juvenile be notified in complaint that the offense he had been charged with was category two offense, and juvenile did not cite any specific authority for proposition that complaint needed to inform juvenile of this fact, and juvenile did not suffer any prejudice as result of complaint not making this fact explicitly known. State v. Todd (Ohio App. 12 Dist., Butler, 05-09-2005) No. CA2004-06-123, 2005-Ohio-

2270, 2005 WL 1077179, Unreported, motion to certify allowed 106 Ohio St.3d 1502, 833 N.E.2d 1245, 2005-Ohio-4605, appeal allowed 106 Ohio St.3d 1505, 833 N.E.2d 1247, 2005-Ohio-4605. Infants ⚖ 68.7(1)

Child dependency complaint filed by the county department of children and family services was sufficient to put father on notice of the issues and did not deprive father of due process; complaint alleged that child was born while mother tested positive for drugs, mother's drug problem prevented her from caring for child, mother had other children that were not in her custody, mother failed to comply with her agency caseplan, father failed to provide care or support for child, and complaint sought an award of permanent custody to county department of children and family services. In re I.M. (Ohio App. 8 Dist., Cuyahoga, 12-24-2003) No. 82669, No. 82695, 2003-Ohio-7069, 2003 WL 23010024, Unreported. Infants ⚖ 197

Parents' complaint alleging that child suffered neglect while in foster care should not have been dismissed even though complaint incorrectly cited dependency statute, rather than child neglect statute, where complaint demonstrated good faith effort to comply with rules, and adequately notified opposing party of the claim; thus, dismissal of complaint would be reversed and cause remanded to allow parents opportunity to cure the defect. In re Fetters (Ohio App. 12 Dist., 04-22-1996) 110 Ohio App.3d 483, 674 N.E.2d 766, on reconsideration 1996 WL 280739. Infants ⚖ 17

A complaint to terminate parental custody in juvenile court is sufficient if the allegations therein notify the opposing party of the nature of the claim against her even if no specific facts or dates are mentioned. In re Pieper Children (Preble 1991) 74 Ohio App.3d 714, 600 N.E.2d 317, dismissed, jurisdictional motion overruled 66 Ohio St.3d 1410, 607 N.E.2d 9.

An allegation in a motion filed in juvenile court seeking to have that court "determine and award the future care and custody" of a child, that "neither parent is a suitable person to have the care and custody of said child," does not constitute a charge that such child is "neglected" or "dependent" and is not sufficiently definite to constitute the "complaint" necessitated by RC 2151.27. (Annotation from former RC 2151.03.) Union County Child Welfare Bd. v. Parker (Union 1964) 7 Ohio App.2d 79, 218 N.E.2d 757, 36 O.O.2d 162. Infants ⚖ 197

The recitation in the complaint of the numerical designations alone is insufficient to inform a defendant of the crime alleged even where the referee defines the statute enumerated in the complaint at the arraignment. Matter of Coen (Ohio App. 5 Dist., Tuscarawas, 06-14-1995) No. 94 AP 090060, 1995 WL 495384, Unreported.

2. Procedural issues

Juvenile court order dismissing father's complaint against child, which alleged child was an unruly child and sought to limit mother's parental involvement with child, was not an abuse of discretion; father's complaint was filed as a result of mother filing a child custody modification proceeding in a different county, father sought to stay the child custody modification proceedings, and father stated he believed child's behavior issues were a result of mother's efforts to gain custody of child. In re Brant (Ohio App. 11 Dist., Ashtabula, 12-09-2005) No. 2004-A-0074, 2005-Ohio-6577, 2005 WL 3367115, Unreported. Infants ⚖ 202

County in which unmarried father filed complaint for custody was proper venue for father's action, even though child moved to another state a few days before complaint was filed; all of child's connections with state prior to the move were in such county. Goeller v. Moore (Ohio App. 10 Dist., Franklin, 01-27-2005) No. 04AP-394, 2005-Ohio-292, 2005 WL 174809, Unreported. Children Out-of-wedlock ⚖ 20.13

Juvenile rule allowing "any person" to file for custody of a child did not override express statutory language precluding natural parent who lost permanent custody of child from filing nonparent custody petition, where right to file petition for custody was substantive right not subject to abridgment, enlargement, or modification by court rules. In re McBride (Ohio, 07-19-2006) 110 Ohio St.3d 19, 850 N.E.2d 43, 2006-Ohio-3454. Infants ⚖ 231

Biological mother, who had lost permanent custody of dependent child due to repeated incarcerations and her long-time addiction to cocaine, had standing to petition, as a legal stranger, for custody of child, who was still in custody of county family services agency, had not yet been placed in permanent family environment, and had no immediate likelihood of being adopted; juvenile rule provided that "any person" could file a petition for custody of a child. In re McBride (Ohio App. 1 Dist., 10-01-2004) 158 Ohio App.3d 572, 817 N.E.2d 459, 2004-Ohio-5269, stay denied 104 Ohio St.3d 1424, 819 N.E.2d 708, 2004-Ohio-6585, appeal allowed 105 Ohio St.3d 1451, 823 N.E.2d 456, 2005-Ohio-763. Infants ⚖ 231

RC 3109.27(A), which requires every party in a custody proceeding to give information in his first pleading as to the child's present and past addresses and custodians and as to any custody proceedings concerning the child pending in other jurisdictions, does not apply to a public agency that initiates a dependency complaint. In re Palmer (Ohio 1984) 12 Ohio St.3d 194, 465 N.E.2d 1312, 12 O.B.R. 259, certiorari denied 105 S.Ct. 918, 469 U.S. 1162, 83 L.Ed.2d 930.

Under RC 2151.353, the filing of a complaint containing a prayer requesting permanent custody of minor children, sufficiently apprising the parents of the grounds upon which the order is to be based, and the service of summons upon the parents, explaining that the granting of such an order permanently divests them of their parental rights, are prerequisite to a valid adjudication that a child is neglected or dependent for the purpose of obtaining an order for permanent custody divesting parental rights. In re Fassinger (Ohio 1975) 42 Ohio St.2d 505, 330 N.E.2d 431, 71 O.O.2d 503.

County child support enforcement agency (CSEA) had standing, as collecting agent of Department of Human Services (DHS), to bring action in juvenile court to determine child support and to make determination of reimbursement for amount of support already provided by DHS to children of mothers receiving public assistance who had assigned their rights to child support to DHS; even if statute authorizing only parent, guardian, or custodian of child to bring action in juvenile court requesting child support order did not authorize state to bring such action, Juvenile Rules of Procedure giving state or its agencies standing to file complaint to order child support payments controlled over statute. State ex rel. Lamier v. Lamier (Ohio App. 8 Dist., 09-05-1995) 105 Ohio App.3d 797, 664 N.E.2d 1384. Child Support ⚖ 179

Rules of Juvenile Procedure authorizing state or its agencies to file complaint in juvenile court to order child support payments was not inconsistent with statute authorizing only parent, guardian, or custodian of child to bring action in juvenile court requesting child support order, where statute, although specifying that parent, guardian, or custodian could bring support action, neither expressly authorized nor excluded state from bringing such action. State ex rel. Lamier v. Lamier (Ohio App. 8 Dist., 09-05-1995) 105 Ohio App.3d 797, 664 N.E.2d 1384. Child Support ⚖ 179

Question of standing, i.e., of who is proper party to bring complaint, is procedural matter governed by Rules of Juvenile Procedure; these rules control over inconsistent statute purporting to govern procedural matters. State ex rel. Lamier v. Lamier (Ohio App. 8 Dist., 09-05-1995) 105 Ohio App.3d 797, 664 N.E.2d 1384. Child Custody ⚖ 409

Where public children services agency did not have requisite grant of temporary custody, instead of filing post-dispositional motion for permanent custody, agency should have sought grant of temporary custody by asking court to modify its disposition terminating agency's grant of temporary custody or by filing a new complaint based on more recent allegations of abuse or on dependency theory. In re Miller (Ohio App. 2 Dist., 02-15-1995) 101 Ohio App.3d 199, 655 N.E.2d 252. Infants ⚖ 230.1

In accordance with Juv R 10(A), anyone who knows that a child is abused, neglected, or dependent may bring a complaint to the juvenile court. In re Dukes (Summit 1991) 81 Ohio App.3d 145, 610 N.E.2d 513, motion overruled 63 Ohio St.3d 1411, 585 N.E.2d 835.

A complaint filed with the juvenile court in a child abuse case must be made under oath and contain the facts of the abuse or neglect, sections of the Ohio Revised Code that have been violated, names and addresses of the parents, and a prayer for custody which must specifically indicate permanent custody, temporary custody, or long-term foster care. In re Dukes (Summit 1991) 81 Ohio App.3d 145, 610 N.E.2d 513, motion overruled 63 Ohio St.3d 1411, 585 N.E.2d 835.

A complaint which contains all the essential elements and facts but is not signed by the complainant under oath is defective, and the person who makes the complaint under oath must be the same person who signs the complaint. In re Dukes (Summit 1991) 81 Ohio App.3d 145, 610 N.E.2d 513, motion overruled 63 Ohio St.3d 1411, 585 N.E.2d 835.

A party must object to a defect in a complaint of child abuse by a prehearing motion before the adjudicatory hearing, within the time requirements of Juv R 22(E). In re Dukes (Summit 1991) 81 Ohio App.3d 145, 610 N.E.2d 513, motion overruled 63 Ohio St.3d 1411, 585 N.E.2d 835.

The juvenile court is entitled to review the appropriateness of filing a complaint against a ten-year old boy for rape and to dismiss the complaint because it would not further the policies of the state. In re Smith (Hamilton 1992) 80 Ohio App.3d 502, 609 N.E.2d 1281, dismissed, jurisdictional motion overruled 65 Ohio St.3d 1441, 600 N.E.2d 683.

A delinquency complaint which alleges that a juvenile "knowingly" aided another to commit robbery is sufficient to state a charge of complicity under Juv R 10(B). In re Howard (Hamilton 1987) 31 Ohio App.3d 1, 508 N.E.2d 190, 31 O.B.R. 14.

A properly served summons containing the "full explanation" required by RC 2151.353(B) must be accompanied by a copy of the complaint, amended or not, if the complaint seeks, temporarily or permanently, to divest a parent of his parental rights. In re Wilson (Huron 1984) 21 Ohio App.3d 36, 486 N.E.2d 152, 21 O.B.R. 38.

When a case concerning a child is transferred or certified from another court, such certification does not constitute a complaint in the juvenile court that such a child is neglected, dependent, or abused, and those dispositions provided for under RC 2151.353 pertaining to neglected, dependent, or abused children, including an award of permanent custody to a county welfare department which has assumed the administration of child welfare, are not applicable to such a child, disposition thereof being subject to and controlled by RC 3109.04. In re Snider (Defiance 1984) 14 Ohio App.3d 353, 471 N.E.2d 516, 14 O.B.R. 420. Infants ⇨ 197; Infants ⇨ 222

Even though a delinquency complaint designates a particular statute or statutes as being violated by a child, a juvenile court may find, on the basis of the facts alleged and proved, that the child is a delinquent child for the violation of an additional statute. In re Burgess (Preble 1984) 13 Ohio App.3d 374, 469 N.E.2d 967, 13 O.B.R. 456. Infants ⇨ 210

In a juvenile proceeding where a complaining witness designates two statutes she claims were violated, the court is free to find that the facts prove the violation of an additional statute and may find the accused to be a delinquent child. In re Burgess (Preble 1984) 13 Ohio App.3d 374, 469 N.E.2d 967, 13 O.B.R. 456. Infants ⇨ 210

Juv R 10(B) is not meant to force a complainant to state every fact surrounding every incident described in the complaint, and therefore, in proving its case in a neglect and dependency proceeding, the state need not limit its proof to the habits and faults of the custodial parent that are actually listed in the complaint. In re Sims (Preble 1983) 13 Ohio App.3d 37, 468 N.E.2d 111, 13 O.B.R. 40.

While the certification shall be deemed to be the complaint in the juvenile court, such certification does not constitute a complaint in the juvenile court that such child is dependent or neglected and those dispositions provided for under RC 2151.353, 2151.354, and 2151.355 pertaining to unruly, delinquent, dependent, or neglected children are not applicable to the disposition of such a child, disposition thereof being subject to and controlled by RC 3109.04. In re Height (Van Wert 1975) 47 Ohio App.2d 203, 353 N.E.2d 887, 1 O.O.3d 279. Courts ⇨ 488(1); Infants ⇨ 197

Proceedings, wherein the juvenile court determines in response to such motion that such child is a neglected and dependent child and orders such child placed in the temporary custody of the county welfare board, are void ab initio for want of a complaint filed as prescribed by RC 2151.27, and such proceedings cannot be the foundation for a determination of dependency or neglect necessary to support an order awarding custody of such child. (Annotation from former RC 2151.27.) Union County Child Welfare Bd. v. Parker (Union 1964) 7 Ohio App.2d 79, 218 N.E.2d 757, 36 O.O.2d 162. Infants ⇨ 197

Where an affidavit is filed in support of a motion for a new trial, alleging that the child was a neglected child within the meaning of this section, on which charges a hearing was had, the juvenile court has jurisdiction in such matter and may grant a motion for new trial. (Annotation from former RC 2151.27.) State ex rel. Sparto v. Williams (Darke 1949) 86 Ohio App. 377, 86 N.E.2d 501, 55 Ohio Law Abs. 341, 41 O.O. 474.

In complaint under this section, that a child of separated parents is dependent, a judgment of common pleas court that the child is dependent awarding its custody to its father "until further order of the court," is a final order from which appeal to the court of appeals may be taken. (Annotation from former RC 2151.27.) In re Anteau (Lucas 1941) 67 Ohio App. 117, 36 N.E.2d 47, 21 O.O. 129.

Any person has standing to bring an action for child custody under RC 2151.23; such a person need not be a parent, need not have established paternity and need not have legitimized the child. Harris v Hopper, No. L-81-187 (6th Dist Ct App, Lucas, 1-15-82).

There is a distinction between a "putative" father and a father who has been adjudicated as such by his own admission, in that a father adjudicated as such by his own admission has legal standing to seek custody of his illegitimate child against the world, including the mother. In re Wright (Ohio Com.Pl. 1977) 52 Ohio Misc. 4, 367 N.E.2d 931, 6 O.O.3d 31.

A certification by a common pleas court of its record to the juvenile court constitutes a filing of a complaint within the meaning of RC 2151.27.

(Annotation from former RC 2151.27.) Hartshorne v. Hartshorne (Columbiana 1959) 185 N.E.2d 329, 89 Ohio Law Abs. 243.

3. Jurisdiction

Trial court did not lack jurisdiction to preside over dependency proceedings based on father's claim that children were living in Pennsylvania and that he was not living in county where dependency complaint was filed, where complaint was filed in county where father's legal residence was listed and at which address father was receiving welfare benefits, and alleged acts constituting neglect or dependency occurred in county where complaint was filed. In re McLean (Ohio App. 11 Dist., Trumbull, 05-25-2005) No. 2005-T-0018, 2005-Ohio-2576, 2005 WL 1231614, Unreported, appeal not allowed 106 Ohio St.3d 1510, 833 N.E.2d 1251, 2005-Ohio-4605. Infants ⇨ 196

Trial court had subject matter jurisdiction over unmarried father's complaint for custody, even though child moved to another state a few days before complaint was filed, and juvenile rule required complaints to be filed in county where child "is found or was last known to be"; child lived in state all of his life before the move, and juvenile rule applied to venue, rather than subject matter jurisdiction. Goeller v. Moore (Ohio App. 10 Dist., Franklin, 01-27-2005) No. 04AP-394, 2005-Ohio-292, 2005 WL 174809, Unreported. Children Out-of-wedlock ⇨ 20.13

A complaint under Juv R 10 and RC 2151.27 alleging that a child is dependent must state the essential facts which bring the proceeding within the jurisdiction of the court. In re Hunt (Ohio 1976) 46 Ohio St.2d 378, 348 N.E.2d 727, 75 O.O.2d 450. Infants ⇨ 197

Where a court, having acquired jurisdiction over a child by virtue of a divorce action between the child's parents, certifies the matter of the child's custody to a juvenile court, the consent of the juvenile court having been first obtained, the juvenile court has exclusive jurisdiction over the child's custody by virtue of RC 3109.06 and 2151.23(D) and a finding of unfitness of the parents or that there is no suitable relative to have custody is not a necessary prerequisite to such certification, and while such certification shall be deemed to be the complaint in the juvenile court, it does not constitute a complaint in the juvenile court that such child is dependent or neglected and those dispositions provided for under RC 2151.353, 2151.354, and 2151.355 are not applicable to the disposition of such a child, disposition thereof being subject to and controlled by RC 3109.04. In re Height (Van Wert 1975) 47 Ohio App.2d 203, 353 N.E.2d 887, 1 O.O.3d 279. Courts ⇨ 472.1

An Ohio juvenile court, in a dependency proceeding pursuant to RC 2151.27 et seq., has no jurisdiction to interfere with a mother's legal custody of her children, in the absence of proof and a finding of unfitness of such parent, merely for the purpose of releasing such children to the officers of the court of a foreign state, and the court need not give full faith and credit to a Michigan decree where that decree was obtained by the husband in an ex parte custody determination, subsequent to a divorce decree, in which the Michigan court had no personal jurisdiction over the nonresident wife. (Annotation from former RC 2151.27.) In re Messner (Huron 1969) 19 Ohio App.2d 33, 249 N.E.2d 532, 48 O.O.2d 31.

Where a neglected child proceeding is instituted in the juvenile court by a parent of such child, and a divorce action is later instituted by such parent, the juvenile court has exclusive original jurisdiction to determine whether the child is neglected, the power to determine his custody and the authority to place the child with a relative. (Annotation from former RC 2151.27.) In re Small (Darke 1960) 114 Ohio App. 248, 181 N.E.2d 503, 19 O.O.2d 128.

The juvenile court of the county in which acts constituting neglect or dependency of a minor child occur has jurisdiction over complaints concerning such child whether or not the parent or minor child was a nonresident of such county. (Annotation from former RC 2151.27.) In re Belk (Crawford 1954) 97 Ohio App. 114, 123 N.E.2d 757, 55 O.O. 330. Infants ⇨ 196

The juvenile court is given original jurisdiction in a proper proceeding to determine the right of custody of any child where such child is not a ward of another court, and it is not necessary in the exercise of such jurisdiction that the juvenile court first determine that such child is a dependent, neglected or delinquent child. (Annotation from former RC 2151.27.) In re Lorok (Cuyahoga 1952) 93 Ohio App. 251, 114 N.E.2d 65, 51 O.O. 10. Child Custody ⇨ 920

Juvenile court has no jurisdiction to adjudicate a child as a dependent child until after filing of a complaint charging such dependency and notice given to the parent or parents. (Annotation from former RC 2151.27.) State ex rel. Clark v. Allaman (Montgomery 1950) 87 Ohio App. 101, 90 N.E.2d 394, 57 Ohio Law Abs. 17, 42 O.O. 330, affirmed 154 Ohio St. 296, 95 N.E.2d 753, 43 O.O. 190.

In an action to remove a child from her mother's custody, the mere allegation that such child is dependent, where the complaint fails to state the essential facts upon which the allegation of dependency is based and which allegations bring the proceeding within the jurisdiction of the court, such complaint is insufficient to confer jurisdiction upon the trial court. In re Baker, No. 6–81–12 (3d Dist Ct App, Hardin, 7–14–82).

The juvenile court has the authority to hear and determine the case of a "neglected child" notwithstanding the fact that the child is at the time within the continuing jurisdiction of the common pleas court by virtue of a divorce decree. (Annotation from former RC 2151.27.) In re L. (Ohio Juv. 1967) 12 Ohio Misc. 251, 231 N.E.2d 253, 41 O.O.2d 341. Courts ⚖ 475(15)

In order for a juvenile court to have jurisdiction to declare a child to be dependent, it must be shown that either the residence of the child is in the county or that the acts constituting neglect or dependency occurred in the county. (Annotation from former RC 2151.27.) State ex rel. Burchett v. Juvenile Court for Scioto County (Scioto 1962) 194 N.E.2d 912, 92 Ohio Law Abs. 357, 28 O.O.2d 116.

Where a juvenile court in the jurisdiction in which an offender resides waives jurisdiction so that the offender will be tried by a common pleas court, such defendant is entitled to a trial in the county where the offense occurred. (Annotation from former RC 2151.27.) In re Davis (Ohio Juv. 1961) 179 N.E.2d 198, 87 Ohio Law Abs. 222, 22 O.O.2d 108.

Where an affidavit was filed charging that children were neglected and dependent and the mother unfit, and such children were taken into custody by the county welfare department at a time when the mother and children were residents of the county, the juvenile court had jurisdiction of such proceedings even though citation was not served on the mother until after her removal to another county. (Annotation from former RC 2151.27.) In re Goshorn (Ohio Juv. 1959) 167 N.E.2d 148, 82 Ohio Law Abs. 599.

4. Habeas corpus

Mother had adequate remedy by appeal for any failure by father to comply with procedural rules in father's action to gain custody of child, and thus mother was not entitled to writ of habeas corpus. In re Complaint for Writ of Habeas Corpus for Goeller (Ohio, 11-03-2004) 103 Ohio St.3d 427, 816 N.E.2d 594, 2004-Ohio-5579. Habeas Corpus ⚖ 280

Mother waived claim concerning father's alleged failure to comply with rules regarding juvenile court complaints in connection with his child custody action by not raising the claim in her habeas corpus complaint or amending her complaint to add the claim, and thus Supreme Court would not consider claim. In re Complaint for Writ of Habeas Corpus for Goeller (Ohio, 11-03-2004) 103 Ohio St.3d 427, 816 N.E.2d 594, 2004-Ohio-5579. Habeas Corpus ⚖ 816

Habeas corpus relief is the exception rather than the general rule in child custody actions. Barnebey v. Zschach (Ohio, 03-08-1995) 71 Ohio St.3d 588, 646 N.E.2d 162. Habeas Corpus ⚖ 532(1)

Habeas corpus will not lie where a child has been adjudicated a neglected and dependent child and committed by a juvenile court. (Annotation from former RC 2151.23.) Byington v. Byington (Ohio 1964) 175 Ohio St. 513, 196 N.E.2d 588, 26 O.O.2d 176.

Habeas corpus in a court of competent jurisdiction as prescribed in RC Ch 2725 is the proper proceeding to raise the question of rightful custody of minor children, where it is alleged that the restraint is illegal, or where a parent or other person claims that he or she has been unlawfully deprived of custody of a minor child; and, as part of such proceedings, the best interests and welfare of the child is a primary question and determining factor, and all other matters must yield accordingly, including the comity existing between states. (Annotation from former RC 2151.23.) In re Messner (Huron 1969) 19 Ohio App.2d 33, 249 N.E.2d 532, 48 O.O.2d 31.

An application for a writ of habeas corpus will be denied where a complaint is duly filed in the county of legal residence, pursuant to RC 2151.27, charging a child with being a dependent or neglected child, notwithstanding the court of common pleas of another county in this state, as a result of a divorce action there heard, gave custody of the child to the mother who subsequently moved with the child to the county where the affidavit of dependency and neglect was filed. (Annotation from former RC 2151.27.) James v. Child Welfare Bd. (Summit 1967) 9 Ohio App.2d 299, 224 N.E.2d 358, 38 O.O.2d 347.

Where, in an action in habeas corpus instituted by the natural mother to gain custody of her minor child, the respondents, who have the child in their custody, are unable to show a valid judgment or order of the court that has jurisdiction to issue such order, it is error for the trial court to determine on the principle "what is for the best interests of the child" that the custody of such child should remain in the respondents and to deny custody to the natural mother. (Annotation from former RC 2151.23.) In re McTaggart (Cuyahoga 1965) 2 Ohio App.2d 214, 207 N.E.2d 562, 31 O.O.2d 336, on rehearing 4 Ohio App.2d 359, 212 N.E.2d 663, 33 O.O.2d 447.

An award of custody of a child in a divorce action is conclusive only as to the parties to such action, and the remedy of habeas corpus is available to obtain such child where a party other than the parties to the divorce action is involved; and it is not necessary to apply to the court which originally awarded custody of such child. (Annotation from former RC 3109.04.) In re Howland (Highland 1961) 115 Ohio App. 186, 184 N.E.2d 228, 20 O.O.2d 277.

Where a juvenile court assumes jurisdiction in a habeas corpus proceeding relating to the rights of a parent to custody of his children, it may exercise such further powers as are necessary to the complete resolution of the entire issue, including retention of continuing jurisdiction to make further orders, although the petition for writ of habeas corpus is denied. (Annotation from former RC 2151.23.) Baker v. Rose (Ohio Com.Pl. 1970) 28 Ohio Misc. 200, 270 N.E.2d 678, 57 O.O.2d 57, 57 O.O.2d 351.

Where a juvenile court has acquired jurisdiction over the question of custody of a child, the court of common pleas may not thereafter inquire into such custody in a habeas corpus proceeding. (Annotation from former RC 2151.23.) In re Ruth (Ohio Com.Pl. 1961) 176 N.E.2d 187, 88 Ohio Law Abs. 1, 16 O.O.2d 408.

On the evidence in a habeas corpus action the court will permit two boys to remain with their father rather than being given to their mother or separated. (Annotation from former RC 3109.04.) Trout v. Trout (Ohio Com.Pl. 1956) 136 N.E.2d 474, 73 Ohio Law Abs. 91, appeal dismissed 167 Ohio St. 476, 149 N.E.2d 728, 5 O.O.2d 156.

5. Permanent custody

Mother was required to state with particularity in her habeas corpus petition the extraordinary circumstances which entitled her to a writ of habeas corpus; mother's petition which alleged that she was entitled to custody of the children and that the trial court lacked jurisdiction to deprive mother of custody was insufficient to support her petition. Holloway v. Clermont Cty. Dept. of Human Serv. (Ohio, 08-15-2001) 92 Ohio St.3d 553, 751 N.E.2d 1055, 2001-Ohio-1282. Habeas Corpus ⚖ 670(10)

Res judicata barred mother from filing successive habeas corpus petitions to obtain custody of her children, where mother failed to allege any facts or circumstances which arose after she filed her second habeas corpus petition, and the allegations and attachments to mother's third habeas corpus petition restated the claims of her previous habeas corpus actions. Holloway v. Clermont Cty. Dept. of Human Serv. (Ohio, 08-15-2001) 92 Ohio St.3d 553, 751 N.E.2d 1055, 2001-Ohio-1282. Habeas Corpus ⚖ 897

A proceeding, instituted in the juvenile court under RC 2151.27 may not be used by the complainant either to force an adoption or as a substitute for an adoption proceeding. (Annotation from former RC 2151.27.) In re Minton (Darke 1960) 112 Ohio App. 361, 176 N.E.2d 252, 16 O.O.2d 283. Infants ⚖ 131

Court not bound to deliver a child to a parent upon the claim of mere legal right but should in the exercise of sound discretion and after careful consideration of the facts award custody to one other than the parent. (Annotation from former RC 2151.23.) Ex parte Justice (Ohio Com.Pl. 1956) 135 N.E.2d 285, 72 Ohio Law Abs. 323. Child Custody ⚖ 22; Child Custody ⚖ 76

6. Evidence

In a proceeding in the juvenile court, instituted by the filing of a complaint under RC 2151.27, a finding by the court that a child is "neglected," in that it "lacked proper parental care because of the faults and habits of his parents" and "dependent " in that its "condition and environment... is such as to warrant the court... in assuming his guardianship" must be based on evidence with respect to whether the child was receiving proper parental care in a proper environment in its home at the time of the hearing. (Annotation from former RC 2151.04.) In re Minton (Darke 1960) 112 Ohio App. 361, 176 N.E.2d 252, 16 O.O.2d 283. Infants ⚖ 156

7. Constitutional issues

While it was uncertain whether typed complaint which included firearm specification was ever prepared in juvenile delinquency case, record would have led reasonable person to believe that juvenile had prior notice of his alleged misconduct, and thus, there was no violation of juvenile's due process rights in finding that he violated statute prohibiting possession of firearm while committing felony. In re Good (Ohio App. 12 Dist., 02-24-1997) 118 Ohio App.3d 371, 692 N.E.2d 1072, dismissed, appeal not allowed 79 Ohio St.3d 1418, 680 N.E.2d 156. Constitutional Law ⚖ 255(4); Infants ⚖ 198

Due process requires that before being found delinquent, juvenile must be given written notice of alleged misconduct. In re Good (Ohio App. 12 Dist., 02-24-1997) 118 Ohio App.3d 371, 692 N.E.2d 1072, dismissed, appeal not allowed 79 Ohio St.3d 1418, 680 N.E.2d 156. Constitutional Law ⚖ 255(4)

Juv R 11   Transfer to another county

(A) Residence in another county; transfer optional

If the child resides in a county of this state and the proceeding is commenced in a court of another county, that court, on its own motion or a motion of a party, may transfer the proceeding to the county of the child's residence upon the filing of the complaint or after the adjudicatory or dispositional hearing for such further proceeding as required. The court of the child's residence shall then proceed as if the original complaint had been filed in that court. Transfer may also be made if the residence of the child changes.

(B) Proceedings in another county; transfer required

The proceedings, other than a removal action, shall be so transferred if other proceedings involving the child are pending in the juvenile court of the county of the child's residence.

(C) Adjudicatory hearing in county where complaint filed

Where either the transferring or receiving court finds that the interests of justice and the convenience of the parties so require, the adjudicatory hearing shall be held in the county wherein the complaint was filed. Thereafter the proceeding may be transferred to the county of the child's residence for disposition.

(D) Transfer of records

Certified copies of all legal and social records pertaining to the proceeding shall accompany the transfer.

(Adopted eff. 7–1–72; amended eff. 7–1–94, 7–1–98)

Historical and Statutory Notes

Amendment Note: The 7–1–98 amendment inserted ", other than a removal action," in division (B).

Amendment Note: The 7–1–94 amendment substituted "the child's" for "his" in division (B).

Staff Notes

1998:

Rule 11(B) Proceedings in another county; transfer required

An exception to the mandatory transfer provisions of Juv. R. 11(B) was added by this amendment to cover removal actions, which are defined in Juv. R. 2(EE), also added by the 1998 amendments. Mandatory transfer of the action to the county of the child's residence would be inconsistent with the purpose of a removal action.

1994:

Rule 11 Transfer to Another County

The 1994 amendments were made to reflect gender neutral language.

Editor's Comment

Residence in another county; transfer optional   1
Proceedings in another county; transfer required   2

1. Residence in another county; transfer optional

Division (A) is taken from the first two sentences of 2151.271.

2. Proceedings in another county; transfer required

Division (B) is the same as the fourth sentence of the first paragraph of 2151.271.

The rule clarifies the authority of the court having venue to transfer jurisdiction to the juvenile court of residence of the child at any stage of the proceedings. It also mandates transfer if proceedings are pending in the juvenile court of the child's residence.

Cross References

Transfer to juvenile court of another county, 2151.271

Library References

Infants ⚖196.
Westlaw Topic No. 211.
C.J.S. Courts §§ 249 et seq.
C.J.S. Infants §§ 42, 53, 54.

Research References

Encyclopedias

OH Jur. 3d Family Law § 1587, Transfer to County of Residence.
OH Jur. 3d Family Law § 1588, Transfer to County of Residence—Adjudicatory Hearing in County Where Complaint Filed.

Treatises and Practice Aids

Carlin, Baldwin's Ohio Practice, Merrick-Rippner Probate Law § 107:7, Jurisdiction and Venue for Juvenile Proceedings.

Carlin, Baldwin's Ohio Practice, Merrick-Rippner Probate Law § 108:13, Juvenile Court—Jurisdiction Over Child Custody Matters—Determination of Custody.

Giannelli & Yeomans, Ohio Juvenile Law § 13:3, Venue.

Giannelli & Yeomans, Ohio Juvenile Law § 17:2, Proper Venue.

Giannelli & Yeomans, Ohio Juvenile Law § 17:4, Transfer of Venue.

Giannelli & Yeomans, Ohio Juvenile Law § 16:15, Certification or Transfer from Another Court.

Notes of Decisions

County of residence   2
Transfer after adjudication   3
Venue   1

---

1. Venue

Venue was proper in permanent custody hearing; county agency's complaint was filed in same county in which children were removed from their home. In re S.V. (Ohio App. 9 Dist., Summit, 10-13-2004) No. 22116, 2004-Ohio-5445, 2004 WL 2292825, Unreported. Infants ⚖ 196

Pursuant to Juv R 11(A), a case may be transferred only to a court in the county of the child's residence; transfer to a court in the county of the parents' residence is improper. In re Smith (Lucas 1989) 61 Ohio App.3d 788, 573 N.E.2d 1170, reconsideration denied.

Proper venue for child custody dispute was a matter within discretion of trial court where no other proceedings were pending in juvenile court of county of child's legal residence. Ackerman v. Lucas County Children Services Bd. (Lucas 1989) 49 Ohio App.3d 14, 550 N.E.2d 549. Infants ⚖ 196

2. County of residence

Trial court was not required to transfer dependency case to county which had previously instigated investigation at request of Children Services, where complaint in other county had been dismissed on grounds father and children were not residing in that county prior to Children Services filing complaint in instant case. In re McLean (Ohio App. 11 Dist., Trumbull, 05-25-2005) No. 2005-T-0018, 2005-Ohio-2576, 2005 WL 1231614, Unreported. Infants ⚖ 196

Transfer of abused child case to county where child legally resided and matters were pending was mandatory despite court's failure to complete an adjudicatory hearing; child's parents resided in other county, and that county's children and family services agency held emergency temporary custody of the child pursuant to an order of the juvenile court. In re Don B. (Ohio App. 6 Dist., Huron, 03-21-2003) No. H-02-033, 2003-Ohio-1400, 2003 WL 1448059, Unreported. Venue ⚖ 45

Although parents and children had moved to Paulding County before complaint in neglect and dependency was filed, Defiance County common pleas court did not abuse its discretion in denying parents' motion to dismiss case, noting that alleged incidents of neglect occurred while children resided in Defiance County and that majority of witnesses resided in Defiance County. In re Meyer (Ohio App. 3 Dist., 10-25-1994) 98 Ohio App.3d 189, 648 N.E.2d 52, corrected. Infants ⇔ 196

Transfer of a permanent custody hearing from the county where the children have been found to be neglected and dependent and are the subjects of a temporary custody order to the county in which the children's parents currently reside is improper as the residency of the children, not the parents, controls jurisdiction. In re Smith (Lucas 1990) 64 Ohio App.3d 773, 582 N.E.2d 1117.

Forum county was proper venue in child custody dispute as both custodian in loco parentis and natural father of child were residents of that county, even though child's mother resided in another county. Ackerman v. Lucas County Children Services Bd. (Lucas 1989) 49 Ohio App.3d 14, 550 N.E.2d 549. Infants ⇔ 196

Venue in a custody proceeding in the juvenile division of common pleas court is governed by Juv R 11, which provides for an optional transfer of venue where the child resides in one county and the custody proceeding is brought in another county. Squires v. Squires (Preble 1983) 12 Ohio App.3d 138, 468 N.E.2d 73, 12 O.B.R. 460.

Proceedings declaring a child neglected by the juvenile court of another county do not prevent a child from thereafter becoming a school resident in a county to which he moves with his family. (Annotation from former RC 2151.27.) In re Laricchiuta (Preble 1968) 16 Ohio App.2d 164, 243 N.E.2d 111, 45 O.O.2d 456.

The juvenile court of the county in which acts constituting neglect or dependency of a minor child occur has jurisdiction over complaints concerning such child whether or not the parent or minor child was a nonresident of such county. (Annotation from former RC 2151.23.) In re Belk (Crawford 1954) 97 Ohio App. 114, 123 N.E.2d 757, 55 O.O. 330. Infants ⇔ 196

Where a case is pending against a juvenile in a foreign county, such case must be transferred to the juvenile's home county, if, at any time prior to dispositional order, proceedings against the juvenile are pending in his home county. Furthermore, such mandatory transfer may not be avoided by the foreign county through the use of a bindover proceeding. State v Payne, No. 81–CA–22 (4th Dist Ct App, Pickaway, 7–28–82).

A juvenile court has jurisdiction to declare any child dependent which is found within the county under facts and circumstances constituting dependency and the legal residence of the child or its parents, or those standing in loco parentis does not determine the jurisdiction of the court; the county in which such court assumes jurisdiction and declares such child to be dependent will be responsible for the support of such child. (Annotation from former RC 2151.23.) (See also 1929 OAG 755.) 1935 OAG 4172.

3. Transfer after adjudication

A juvenile court may not impose a fine and then transfer the case to another jurisdiction for further dispositional proceedings; once a final dispositional order is made, nothing remains to transfer to the other court. In re Sekulich (Ohio 1981) 65 Ohio St.2d 13, 417 N.E.2d 1014, 19 O.O.3d 192.

A juvenile court's erroneous transfer of a custodial proceeding subsequent to a dependency and neglect adjudication, but before a dispositional hearing, does not render subsequent collateral decisions by the receiving court null and void. In re Smith (Lucas 1990) 64 Ohio App.3d 773, 582 N.E.2d 1117.

Juv R 12   [Reserved]

Juv R 13   Temporary disposition; temporary orders; emergency medical and surgical treatment

(A) Temporary disposition

Pending hearing on a complaint, the court may make such temporary orders concerning the custody or care of a child who is the subject of the complaint as the child's interest and welfare may require.

(B) Temporary orders

(1) Pending hearing on a complaint, the judge or magistrate may issue temporary orders with respect to the relations and conduct of other persons toward a child who is the subject of the complaint as the child's interest and welfare may require.

(2) Upon the filing of an abuse, neglect, or dependency complaint, any party may by motion request that the court issue any of the following temporary orders to protect the best interest of the child:

(a) An order granting temporary custody of the child to a particular party;

(b) An order for the taking of the child into custody pending the outcome of the adjudicatory and dispositional hearings;

(c) An order granting, limiting, or eliminating visitation rights with respect to the child;

(d) An order for the payment of child support and continued maintenance of any medical, surgical, or hospital policies of insurance for the child that existed at the time of the filing of the complaint, petition, writ, or other document;

(e) An order requiring a party to vacate a residence that will be lawfully occupied by the child;

(f) An order requiring a party to attend an appropriate counseling program that is reasonably available to that party;

(g) Any other order that restrains or otherwise controls the conduct of any party which conduct would not be in the best interest of the child.

(3) The orders permitted by division (B)(2) of this rule may be granted ex parte if it appears that the best interest and welfare of the child require immediate issuance. If the court issues the requested ex parte order, the court shall hold a hearing to review the order within seventy-two hours after it is issued or before the end of the next court day after the day on which it is issued, whichever occurs first. The court shall appoint a guardian ad litem for the child prior to the hearing. The court shall give written notice of the hearing by means reasonably likely to result in the party's receiving actual notice and include all of the following:

(a) The date, time, and location of the hearing;

(b) The issues to be addressed at the hearing;

(c) A statement that every party to the hearing has a right to counsel and to court appointed counsel, if the party is indigent;

(d) The name, telephone number, and address of the person requesting the order;

(e) A copy of the order, except when it is not possible to obtain it because of the exigent circumstances in the case.

(4) The court may review any order under this rule at any time upon motion of any party for good cause shown or upon the motion of the court.

(5) If the court does not grant an ex parte order, the court shall hold a shelter care hearing on the motion within ten days after the motion is filed.

(C) Emergency medical and surgical treatment

Upon the certification of one or more reputable practicing physicians, the court may order such emergency medical and surgical treatment as appears to be immediately necessary for any child concerning whom a complaint has been filed.

(D) Ex parte proceedings

In addition to the ex parte proceeding described in division (B) of this rule, the court may proceed summarily and without notice under division (A), (B), or (C) of this rule, where it appears to the court that the interest and welfare of the child require that action be taken immediately.

(E) Hearing; notice

In addition to the procedures specified in division (B) of this rule and wherever possible, the court shall provide an opportunity for hearing before proceeding under division (D) of this rule. Where the court has proceeded without notice under division (D) of this rule, it shall give notice of the action it has taken to the parties and any other affected person and provide them an opportunity for a hearing concerning the continuing effects of the action.

(F) Probable cause finding

Upon the finding of probable cause at a shelter care hearing that a child is an abused child, the court may do any of the following:

(1) Upon motion by the court or of any party, issue reasonable protective orders with respect to the interviewing or deposition of the child;

(2) Order that the child's testimony be videotaped for preservation of the testimony for possible use in any other proceedings in the case;

(3) Set any additional conditions with respect to the child or the case involving the child that are in the best interest of the child.

(G) Payment

The court may order the parent, guardian, or custodian, if able, to pay for any emergency medical or surgical treatment provided pursuant to division (C) of this rule. The order of payment may be enforced by judgment, upon which execution may issue, and a failure to pay as ordered may be punished as contempt of court.

(Adopted eff. 7–1–72; amended eff. 7–1–94, 7–1–96)

Historical and Statutory Notes

Amendment Note: The 7–1–96 amendment substituted "magistrate" for "referee" in division (B)(1).

Amendment Note: The 7–1–94 amendment rewrote divisions (B), (D), and (E); added division (F); and redesignated former division (F) as division (G). Prior to amendment, divisions (B), (D), and (E) read:

"(B) Temporary orders. Pending hearing on a complaint, the court may issue such temporary orders with respect to the relations and conduct of other persons toward a child who is the subject of the complaint as the child's interest and welfare may require.

"(D) Ex parte proceedings. Where it appears to the court that the interest and welfare of the child require that action be taken immediately, the court may proceed summarily and without notice under subdivision (A), (B) or (C).

"(E) Hearing; notice. Wherever possible, the court shall provide an opportunity for hearing before proceeding under subdivision (A), (B) or (C) and shall give notice of the time and place of the hearing to the parties and any other person who may be affected by the proposed action. Where the court has proceeded without notice under subdivision (D), it shall give notice of the action it has taken to the parties and any other affected person and provide them an opportunity for a hearing concerning the continuing effects of such action."

Staff Notes

1996:

The amendment changed the rule's reference from "referee" to "magistrate" in division (B)(1) in order to harmonize the rule with the language adopted in the 1995 amendments to Juv. R. 40. The amendment is technical only and no substantive change is intended.

1994:

Rule 13 Temporary Disposition; Temporary Orders; Emergency Medical and Surgical Treatment

S.B. 89 amended section 2151.33 of the Revised Code to clarify the court's previously existing authority to issue emergency orders for children and Juv. R. 13 has been revised to reflect those amendments. Division (B) sets forth the type of temporary orders a court is authorized to make in an abuse, neglect or dependency case, as well as the procedure to be followed for notice and hearings when orders are made ex parte.

Division (D) clarifies that other kinds of ex parte hearings other than those specified in division (B) are still permitted, and division (E) emphasizes notice and hearing requirements where possible with hearings under division (D).

In accordance with section 2151.33(B) of the Revised Code, division (F)(1), (2), and (3) list the actions the court may take after finding, at a shelter care hearing, probable cause to believe that a child is an abused child.

Editor's Comment

Temporary disposition; temporary orders; emergency medical and surgical treatment 1
Ex parte proceedings 2
Hearing; notice 3
Payment 4

1. Temporary disposition; temporary orders; emergency medical and surgical treatment

Juv R 13 provides for temporary orders with respect to a child who is the subject of a juvenile court complaint. These temporary orders can deal with custody or care of the child (Division (A)), and the relations and conduct of other persons toward a child (Division (B)), and emergency medical and surgical treatment (Division (C)).

2. Ex parte proceedings

Divisions (B)(3) and (D) provide for summary procedure without notice in issuing such temporary orders, where required in the interest of the child.

3. Hearing; notice

Divisions (B)(3) and (E) provide that notice and hearing shall be given prior to the temporary order where possible and after the issuance of the order in all cases.

4. Payment

Division (G) provides a mechanism for getting reimbursement for medical and surgical treatment provided pursuant to Division (C).

This rule is taken from 2151.33.

Library References

Infants ⚖=68.3, 192, 228.
Westlaw Topic No. 211.
C.J.S. Infants §§ 42, 53 to 57, 69 to 85.

Research References

Encyclopedias

OH Jur. 3d Family Law § 1633, Emergency Medical Care.
OH Jur. 3d Family Law § 1634, Procedure.
OH Jur. 3d Family Law § 1724, Physicians, Psychologists, and Psychiatrists—Emergency Medical Treatment.
OH Jur. 3d Family Law § 1730, What is an Appealable Order.

Treatises and Practice Aids

Sowald & Morganstern, Baldwin's Ohio Practice Domestic Relations Law § 17:27, Icara—Petition for Return of Child—Form.

Carlin, Baldwin's Ohio Practice, Merrick-Rippner Probate Law § 107:36, Use of Social History and Investigation Report.

Carlin, Baldwin's Ohio Practice, Merrick-Rippner Probate Law § 107:41, Prehearing Procedures in Juvenile Court—Temporary Orders Pending Hearing.

Carlin, Baldwin's Ohio Practice, Merrick-Rippner Probate Law § 107:49, Adjudicatory Hearings—Conduct of Hearing by Magistrate.

Carlin, Baldwin's Ohio Practice, Merrick-Rippner Probate Law § 107:122, Appeals—Juvenile Court Judgments—Determination of Neglect, Dependency, Unruliness, Abuse, or Delinquency.

Carlin, Baldwin's Ohio Practice, Merrick-Rippner Probate Law § 107:152, Motion for Temporary Custody Pending Hearing—Form.

Carlin, Baldwin's Ohio Practice, Merrick-Rippner Probate Law § 107:153, Order Granting Temporary Custody Pending Hearing—Form.

Adrine & Ruden, Ohio Domestic Violence Law § 11:15, Remedies—Orders Allocating Parental Rights and Responsibilities.

Giannelli & Yeomans, Ohio Juvenile Law § 9:7, Neglect—Subsistence, Education & Medical Care.

Giannelli & Yeomans, Ohio Juvenile Law § 20:2, Temporary Care Orders.

Giannelli & Yeomans, Ohio Juvenile Law § 20:3, Emergency Medical Orders.

Giannelli & Yeomans, Ohio Juvenile Law § 20:4, Required Hearings.

Giannelli & Yeomans, Ohio Juvenile Law § 20:5, Notice of Hearing.

Giannelli & Yeomans, Ohio Juvenile Law § 20:6, Time Requirements.

Giannelli & Yeomans, Ohio Juvenile Law § 21:6, Social History Report.

Giannelli & Yeomans, Ohio Juvenile Law § 24:4, Pretrial Orders.

Giannelli & Yeomans, Ohio Juvenile Law § 34:4, Final Order Requirement.

Giannelli & Yeomans, Ohio Juvenile Law App. D, Appendix D. Glossary.

Giannelli & Yeomans, Ohio Juvenile Law § 19:11, Detention Facilities.

Law Review and Journal Commentaries

Consent to Medical Treatment for Minors Under Care of Children Services Board, Stephen D. Freedman. 10 Cap U L Rev 309 (Winter 1980).

Emergency Custody in Domestic Relations Court: A Proposed Procedural and Substantive Litmus Test, Hon. V. Michael Brigner. 49 Dayton B Briefs 19 (December 1999).

Rethinking The Relationship Between Juvenile Courts And Treatment Agencies—An Administrative Law Approach, Leslie J. Harris. 28 J Fam L 217 (1990).

Notes of Decisions

Constitutional issues 1
Emergency medical treatment 2
Final orders 3
Orders from other states 6
Removal of minor from home 5
Temporary custody 4

1. Constitutional issues

Due process is not denied to the parent of a severely abused child by a court holding a temporary custody hearing ex parte under Juv R 13 without appointing a guardian ad litem under RC 2151.281. Parker v. Children Services Bd. of Trumbull County (Trumbull 1984) 21 Ohio App.3d 115, 487 N.E.2d 341, 21 O.B.R. 123.

Under the present Juvenile Code and Rules, a juvenile court cannot change a "temporary" commitment to the Ohio youth commission to an "permanent" commitment without hearing; further, the commitment of an unruly child, not declared "delinquent", is a violation of due process and any hearing held on the above matters requires the presence of the youth involved. OAG 72–071.

2. Emergency medical treatment

Where an unemancipated child has been removed from the custody of his parents and placed in the temporary custody of a county department of human services, the department may properly consent to surgical treatment for the child without consulting with the parents. Kilgallion v Children's Hospital Medical Center, Nos. C–850644 and C–860342 (1st Dist Ct App, Hamilton, 4–15–87).

Juvenile court properly authorized hospital to administer blood transfusions to child over religious objections of parents. (Annotation from former RC 2151.33.) In re Clark (Ohio Com.Pl. 1962) 185 N.E.2d 128, 90 Ohio Law Abs. 21, 21 O.O.2d 86.

When a complaint or application for care concerning a child has been filed with the juvenile court, such court may, pending service of a citation on the child's parents, guardian or custodian, order the provision of emergency medical or surgical treatment. (Annotation from former RC 2151.33.) 1951 OAG 898.

Where a child has been permanently committed to a child welfare board by order of the juvenile court, such board may properly consent to medical and surgical treatment of such child; where a child has been temporarily so committed, the child remains a ward of juvenile court, and such court may properly consent to medical and surgical treatment of such child. (Annotation from former RC 2151.35.) 1951 OAG 898.

3. Final orders

A temporary order of a juvenile court changing custody under Juv R 13 or 29 is not a dispositional order under Juv R 34, and hence is not a final appealable order. Morrison v. Morrison (Summit 1973) 45 Ohio App.2d 299, 344 N.E.2d 144, 74 O.O.2d 441.

It is reversible error for a trial court to grant permanent custody of the parties' minor child to the father solely because the mother was incarcerated for child stealing at the time of the hearing and without first determining the best interest of the child. Dunn v. Martin (Ohio App. 2 Dist., Montgomery, 08-02-1996) No. 15208, 1996 WL 430867, Unreported.

4. Temporary custody

Trial court was required to determine whether child-support obligor was in default under temporary orders and, if so, whether such default was wilful, as would warrant assessment of interest on arrearage from date of default, when court modified temporary orders in judgment that established permanent child support obligation in parentage proceeding. Harbour v. Ridgeway (Ohio App. 10 Dist., Franklin, 05-26-2005) No. 04AP-350, 2005-Ohio-2643, 2005 WL 1252551, Unreported. Children Out-of-wedlock 69(6)

Trial court's temporary order granting unwed mother custody pending the judgment on mother's motion for parental rights ultimately merged with the final judgment of the court, which granted mother permanent residential and custodial parent status, and, because trial court's final order was proper, the issue as to whether trial court erred when it granted temporary order granting mother custody without holding a hearing, as required by law, was moot. Font v. Morris (Ohio App. 3 Dist., Mercer, 05-10-2004) No. 10-03-21, 2004-Ohio-2354, 2004 WL 1049130, Unreported. Children Out-of-wedlock 20.11

Court of Appeals was without jurisdiction to address mother's claim that trial court erred in awarding temporary custody of mother's child to child's father and grandmother because there was no motion pending and no finding of suitability was determined; order awarded temporary custody "until further order," and was thus not final, appealable order. In re S.M. (Ohio App. 8 Dist., Cuyahoga, 03-18-2004) No. 81566, 2004-Ohio-1243, 2004 WL 527925, Unreported. Child Custody 902

Agreed entry restoring custody of child to mother rendered moot any error or abuse of discretion in juvenile court's subsequent order approving magistrate's decision awarding temporary custody of child to paternal grandmother, from which order mother had appealed. In re Kepperling (Ohio App. 2 Dist., 04-14-2006) 166 Ohio App.3d 257, 850 N.E.2d 119, 2006-Ohio-1856. Child Custody 917

Magistrate was not prohibited from taking, without prior notice, evidence relating to the issue of temporary custody and child's best interest, which included evidence concerning mother's alleged refusal to allow visitation, on father's and guardian ad litem's contempt motions alleging mother had prevented father's visitation and counseling sessions with child, even though magistrate had granted mother's request for a continuance with respect to relief requested on the contempt charges due to short notice of hearing; magistrate was authorized by rule to take such evidence "summarily and without prior notice." In re Kepperling (Ohio App. 2 Dist., 04-14-2006) 166 Ohio App.3d 257, 850 N.E.2d 119, 2006-Ohio-1856. Child Custody 871

A comprehensive reunification plan need be prepared only when a child is committed to the temporary custody of the department of public welfare under RC 2151.353(A)(2) or 2151.353(A)(3); this is the plain meaning of RC 2151.412(C), which does not, it follows, require preparation of a plan when a temporary custody order is based on Juv R 13(A) and 13(D). In re Koballa, Nos. 48417 and 48480 (8th Dist Ct App, Cuyahoga, 1–24–85).

5. Removal of minor from home

Parents failed to demonstrate that fire occurring in residence of custodian affected interest and welfare of child, whom parents had voluntarily placed with custodian prior to court's award of custody to custodian due to parental unsuitability, so as to require immediate modification of custody, where nothing in parents' motion for modification or supporting affidavit showed that child's interest and welfare required immediate action, parents did not file motion until 20 days after fire, child's guardian ad litem and court were aware of fire, and fire did not constitute change of circumstances sufficient to warrant change of custody. In re Bailey (Ohio App. 1 Dist., Hamilton, 06-17-2005) No. C-040014, No. C-040479, 2005-Ohio-3039, 2005 WL 1413269, Unreported. Infants 231

Judgment entry following detention-shelter care hearing involving child did not constitute dependency adjudication, which was necessary step in process for county to gain permanent custody of child; trial court stated during hearing that proceedings were not "a hearing where...the dependency issue is being argued," but was hearing to determine whether county had sufficient evidence to base initial finding of dependency to remove child from mother's custody, evidence introduced at hearing did not support dependency determination, and trial court had granted ex parte order granting temporary emergency custody of child to county, thus indicating that hearing was that statutorily required to review ex parte order. In re Nibert (Ohio App. 4 Dist., Gallia, 05-24-2005) No. 04CA15, 2005-Ohio-2797, 2005 WL 1332019, Unreported. Infants ⇐ 222

Under Ohio law, unless matters of public safety are involved, a child alleged to be abused, neglected, or dependent may be removed from his home by court order only upon a judicial determination that continuation in the home would be contrary to the child's best interest. OAG 87–105.

6. Orders from other states

Where a court of another state has awarded custody of a minor child pursuant to a valid in personam order, and there is no evidence of a subsequent change in circumstances affecting the best interests of the child, the courts of this state will give full faith and credit to that order. Williams v. Williams (Ohio 1975) 44 Ohio St.2d 28, 336 N.E.2d 426, 73 O.O.2d 121.

Juv R 14 Termination, extension or modification of temporary custody orders

(A) Termination

Any temporary custody order issued shall terminate one year after the earlier of the date on which the complaint in the case was filed or the child was first placed into shelter care. A temporary custody order shall extend beyond a year and until the court issues another dispositional order, where any public or private agency with temporary custody, not later than thirty days prior to the earlier of the date for the termination of the custody order or the date set at the dispositional hearing for the hearing to be held pursuant to division (A) of section 2151.415 of the Revised Code, files a motion requesting that any of the following orders of disposition be issued:

(1) An order that the child be returned home with custody to the child's parents, guardian, or custodian without any restrictions;

(2) An order for protective supervision;

(3) An order that the child be placed in the legal custody of a relative or other interested individual;

(4) An order terminating parental rights;

(5) An order for long term foster care;

(6) An order for the extension of temporary custody.

(B) Extension

Upon the filing of an agency's motion for the extension of temporary custody, the court shall schedule a hearing and give notice to all parties in accordance with these rules. The agency shall include in the motion an explanation of the progress on the case plan and of its expectations of reunifying the child with the child's family, or placing the child in a permanent placement, within the extension period. The court may extend the temporary custody order for a period of up to six months. Prior to the end of the extension period, the agency may request one additional extension of up to six months. The court shall grant either extension upon finding that it is in the best interest of the child, that there has been significant progress on the case plan, and that there is reasonable cause to believe that the child will be reunited with one of the child's parents or otherwise permanently placed within the period of extension. Prior to the end of either extension, the agency that received the extension shall file a motion and the court shall issue one of the orders of disposition set forth in division (A) of this rule. Upon the agency's motion or upon its own motion, the court shall conduct a hearing and issue an appropriate order of disposition.

(C) Modification

The court, upon its own motion or that of any party, shall conduct a hearing with notice to all parties to determine whether any order issued should be modified or terminated, or whether any other dispositional order set forth in division (A) should be issued. The court shall so modify or terminate any order in accordance with the best interest of the child.

(Adopted eff. 7–1–94)

Staff Notes

1994:

Rule 14 Termination, Extension or Modification of Temporary Orders

S.B. 89 required new time periods to be established for the termination of abuse, neglect, and dependency cases; for the timing of possible final orders to terminate a case; and for the conditions, procedures, and limitations for seeking an extension. Juv. R. 14, previously reserved, has been written in accordance with the requirements of Revised Code 2151.353 and 2151.415.

Editor's Comment

Juv R 14(A), dealing with termination of temporary custody orders, is taken from 2151.353(F) and 2151.415(A).

Juv R 14(B), governing the procedures for extension of temporary custody orders, is taken from 2151.415(B) and (D).

Juv R 14(C), dealing with modification of dispositional orders, is taken from 2151.415(F).

Research References

Encyclopedias

OH Jur. 3d Family Law § 1647, Proceedings Before Referee; Powers and Duties.

Treatises and Practice Aids

Carlin, Baldwin's Ohio Practice, Merrick-Rippner Probate Law § 107:49, Adjudicatory Hearings—Conduct of Hearing by Magistrate.

Giannelli & Yeomans, Ohio Juvenile Law § 24:4, Pretrial Orders.

Giannelli & Yeomans, Ohio Juvenile Law § 30:6, Temporary Custody.

Giannelli & Yeomans, Ohio Juvenile Law § 33:4, Abuse, Neglect, and Dependency Proceedings.

Juv R 15 Process: issuance, form

(A) Summons: issuance

After the complaint has been filed, the court shall cause the issuance of a summons directed to the child, the parents, guardian, custodian, and any other persons who appear to the court to be proper or necessary parties. The summons shall require the parties to appear before the court at the time fixed to answer the allegations of the complaint. A child alleged to be abused, neglected, or dependent shall not be summoned unless the court so directs.

A summons issued for a child under fourteen years of age alleged to be delinquent, unruly, or a juvenile traffic offender shall be made by serving either the child's parents, guardian, custodian, or other person with whom the child lives or resides. If the person who has physical custody of the child or with whom the child resides is other than the parent or guardian, then the parents and guardian also shall be summoned. A copy of the complaint shall accompany the summons.

(B) Summons: form

The summons shall contain:

(1) The name of the party or person with whom the child may be or, if unknown, any name or description by which the party or person can be identified with reasonable certainty.

(2) A summary statement of the complaint and in juvenile traffic offense and delinquency proceedings the numerical designation of the applicable statute or ordinance.

(3) A statement that any party is entitled to be represented by an attorney and that upon request the court will appoint an attorney for an indigent party entitled to appointed counsel under Juv. R. 4(A).

(4) An order to the party or person to appear at a stated time and place with a warning that the party or person may lose

valuable rights or be subject to court sanction if the party or person fails to appear at the time and place stated in the summons.

(5) An order to the parent, guardian, or other person having care of a child alleged to be an unruly or delinquent child for being an habitual or chronic truant, to appear personally at the hearing and all proceedings, and an order directing the person having the physical custody or control of the child to bring the child to the hearing, with a warning that if the child fails to appear, the parent, guardian, or other person having care of the child may be subject to court sanction, including a finding of contempt.

(6) A statement that if a child is adjudicated abused, neglected, or dependent and the complaint seeks an order of permanent custody, an order of permanent custody would cause the parents, guardian, or legal custodian to be divested permanently of all parental rights and privileges.

(7) A statement that if a child is adjudicated abused, neglected, or dependent and the complaint seeks an order of temporary custody, an order of temporary custody will cause the removal of the child from the legal custody of the parents, guardian, or other custodian until the court terminates the order of temporary custody or permanently divests the parents of their parental rights.

(8) A statement that if the child is adjudicated abused, neglected, or dependent and the complaint seeks an order for a planned permanent living arrangement, an order for a planned permanent living arrangement will cause the removal of the child from the legal custody of the parent, guardian, or other custodian.

(9) A statement, in a removal action, of the specific disposition sought.

(10) The name and telephone number of the court employee designated by the court to arrange for the prompt appointment of counsel for indigent persons.

(C) Summons: endorsement

The court may endorse upon the summons an order directed to the parents, guardian, or other person with whom the child may be, to appear personally and bring the child to the hearing.

(D) Warrant: issuance

If it appears that the summons will be ineffectual or the welfare of the child requires that the child be brought forthwith to the court, a warrant may be issued against the child. A copy of the complaint shall accompany the warrant.

(E) Warrant: form

The warrant shall contain the name of the child or, if that is unknown, any name or description by which the child can be identified with reasonable certainty. It shall contain a summary statement of the complaint and in juvenile traffic offense and delinquency proceedings the numerical designation of the applicable statute or ordinance. A copy of the complaint shall be attached to the warrant. The warrant shall command that the child be taken into custody and be brought before the court that issued the warrant without unnecessary delay.

(Adopted eff. 7–1–72; amended eff. 7–1–94, 7–1–98, 7–1–01, 7–1–02)

Historical and Statutory Notes

Amendment Note: The 7–1–02 amendment substituted "a planned permanent living arrangement" for "long term foster care" throughout division (B)(8).

Amendment Note: The 7–1–01 amendment added new division (B)(5) and redesignated former divisions (B)(5) through (B)(9) as new divisions (B)(6) through (B)(10).

Amendment Note: The 7–1–98 amendment deleted "or other person with whom the child may be living" before "and any other person" in division (A).

Amendment Note: The 7–1–94 amendment rewrote divisions (A) and (B)(5); added divisions (B)(6) through (B)(8); substituted "parents, guardian, or other" for "party or" in division (C); and made changes to reflect gender-neutral language. Prior to amendment, divisions (A) and (B)(5) read:

"(A) Summons: issuance. After the complaint has been filed, the clerk shall promptly issue summons to the parties and to any person with whom the child may be, requiring the parties or person to appear before the court at the time fixed for hearing. A copy of the complaint shall accompany the summons.

"(5) If a complaint requests permanent custody a statement that the parent, guardian or other custodian may be permanently divested of all parental rights."

Staff Notes

2002:

Juvenile Rule 15(B) Summons: form

The July 1, 2002, amendment to Juv. R. 15(B)(8) substituted the language of "planned permanent living arrangement" for the former language of "long term foster care," to conform to the new legislative designation for these child-placing arrangements.

The amendment to Juv. R. 15(B)(8) conforms to sections 2151.28(D) and 2151.353(B) of the Revised Code. Juvenile Rules 2, 10, and 34 also were amended effective July 1, 2002 to reflect this change in terminology.

2001:

Rule 15(B) Summons: form

Rule 15(B) was amended to add new division (5), which deals with orders to be placed on a summons to parents or other responsible adults when a child or adult is summoned to court pursuant to a complaint of chronic or habitual truancy. The new section tracks the language of Revised Code section 2151.28 (E)(2), as amended by Sub. Sen. Bill 181 (effective September 4, 2000), and makes clear that the parent or responsible adult must bring the child to truancy hearings or be subject to court sanction, including a finding of contempt. Adding this language to the summons alerts responsible adults to the need to ensure not only his or her own appearance, but that of the child as well. Prior divisions (B)(5) through (B)(9) were renumbered (B)(6) through (B)(10) to reflect this interpolation.

1998:

Rule 15 Process: Issuance, Form

The 1998 amendment to the first paragraph of Juv. R. 15(A) was intended to clarify the requirement that summons must be issued to the child and to all of the following persons: the parents, guardian, custodian, and any other persons who appear to the court to be proper or necessary parties. Under the prior version of the rule, the use of the word "or" made it unclear whether summons was required to be issued to all of the listed persons. The 1998 amendment also deleted the phrase "other person with whom the child may be living," because this person would be covered by the remaining list of designated persons.

Pursuant to section 2151.55 of the Revised Code, which first created removal actions, the written notice issued to the school superintendent and to the entity that placed the child in the foster home must include an explanation of the purpose of the removal hearing. In furtherance of this notification objective, the 1998 addition of Juv. R. 15(B)(8) requires that those persons receiving a summons for the removal hearing also be notified of the purpose of the hearing and possible disposition.

1994:

Rule 15 Process: Issuance, Form

Pursuant to Revised Code 2151.28 (S.B. 89), Juv. R. 15 now sets forth the form of the summons issued in juvenile court. The revised statute requires the summons in an abuse, neglect, or dependency case to state precisely the potential consequences of an unfavorable adjudication, including permanent loss of parental rights. Therefore, those requirements are listed in divisions (B)(5), (6), (7), and (8).

Editor's Comment

Summons: issuance   1
Summons: form   2

Summons: endorsement 3
Warrant: issuance 4
Warrant: form 5

1. Summons: issuance

The requirements for issuance of summons are similar to those contained in 2151.28(C), the statutory equivalent of Juv R 15(A).

2. Summons: form

Juv R 15(B)(1) and 15(B)(2) "Summons: form," adopt the language of Crim R 4(C) and the provisions of 2935.18.

Juv R 15(B)(3) is a restatement of 2151.28(F). However, 2151.28(C) includes an additional requirement that the summons contain the name and telephone number of the court employee designated to arrange for the appointment of counsel for indigent persons.

Juv R 15(B)(4) follows Crim R 4(C)(2) but expands the warning beyond the arrest feature and adds to Ohio law language of Federal Rule 4.

Juv R 15(B)(5), (6), and (7) are similar to 2151.28(D).

Juv R 15(B)(9) is taken from 2151.28(C).

3. Summons: endorsement

Juv R 15(C) restates the provision of 2151.28(E).

4. Warrant: issuance

Juv R 15(D) is similar to 2151.28(G) and 2151.30, and adds the requirement that a copy of the complaint accompany the warrant.

5. Warrant: form

Juv R 15(E) is taken from Crim R 4(C)(1), substituting the word "custody" instead of "arrest" and "child" in lieu of "defendant." Juv R 6 states the other reasons in addition to the law of arrest for which a child can be deprived of his liberty and taken into custody. Juvenile proceedings are not criminal proceedings, and a child is never referred to as a defendant.

Cross References

Issuance of warrant against parent, custodian, guardian, or child, 2151.30
Summons on juvenile complaint, 2151.28
Warrant or summons, Crim R 4

Library References

Infants ⟫198.
Westlaw Topic No. 211.
C.J.S. Infants § 56.

Research References

Encyclopedias

OH Jur. 3d Family Law § 1610, Form and Contents.
OH Jur. 3d Family Law § 1611, Form and Contents—Orders Endorsed on Summons.
OH Jur. 3d Family Law § 1616, Form and Contents.
OH Jur. 3d Family Law § 1647, Proceedings Before Referee; Powers and Duties.

Treatises and Practice Aids

Carlin, Baldwin's Ohio Practice, Merrick-Rippner Probate Law § 106:21, Juvenile Court Jurisdiction—Consent for Abortion—Minor Female's Complaint for Abortion.
Carlin, Baldwin's Ohio Practice, Merrick-Rippner Probate Law § 107:10, Contents and Issuance of Summons.
Carlin, Baldwin's Ohio Practice, Merrick-Rippner Probate Law § 107:11, Service of Summons.
Carlin, Baldwin's Ohio Practice, Merrick-Rippner Probate Law § 107:13, Issuance of Warrant.
Carlin, Baldwin's Ohio Practice, Merrick-Rippner Probate Law § 107:49, Adjudicatory Hearings—Conduct of Hearing by Magistrate.
Carlin, Baldwin's Ohio Practice, Merrick-Rippner Probate Law § 107:127, Contempt of Court in Juvenile Proceedings.
Carlin, Baldwin's Ohio Practice, Merrick-Rippner Probate Law § 107:161, Summons to Parents, Guardian, or Person With Whom Child May be—Form.
Carlin, Baldwin's Ohio Practice, Merrick-Rippner Probate Law § 107:167, Warrant for Arrest of Child or Custodian—Form.
Giannelli & Yeomans, Ohio Juvenile Law § 1:8, Rules of Juvenile Procedure.
Giannelli & Yeomans, Ohio Juvenile Law § 13:4, Summons and Notice.
Giannelli & Yeomans, Ohio Juvenile Law § 14:3, Custody, Arrests & Stops.
Giannelli & Yeomans, Ohio Juvenile Law § 18:2, Issuance of Summons: Proper Parties.
Giannelli & Yeomans, Ohio Juvenile Law § 18:3, Summons: Contents and Form.
Giannelli & Yeomans, Ohio Juvenile Law § 23:3, Right to Counsel.
Giannelli & Yeomans, Ohio Juvenile Law § 24:4, Pretrial Orders.
Giannelli & Yeomans, Ohio Juvenile Law § 33:8, Contempt.
Giannelli & Yeomans, Ohio Juvenile Law App. D, Appendix D. Glossary.

Notes of Decisions

Constitutional issues 2
Hearings 8
Jurisdiction 3
Notice 4
Orders from other states 1
Parties 9
Right to counsel 5
Summons 7
Warrants 6

1. Orders from other states

Where a court of another state has awarded custody of a minor child pursuant to a valid in personam order, and there is no evidence of a subsequent change in circumstances affecting the best interests of the child, the courts of this state will give full faith and credit to that order. Williams v. Williams (Ohio 1975) 44 Ohio St.2d 28, 336 N.E.2d 426, 73 O.O.2d 121.

2. Constitutional issues

Due process entitles a party to reasonable notice of the setting of a trial date. Lowry v. Lowry (Ross 1988) 48 Ohio App.3d 184, 549 N.E.2d 176.

The notice provisions of RC 2151.85(D) violate the rulemaking authority of the Supreme Court, in O Const Art IV §5(B), as Juv R 15(A) requires that parents of a juvenile be notified of any proceedings involving the child; therefore, RC 2151.85 is unconstitutional. Further CP Sup R 76(H), promulgated in furtherance of RC 2151.85, conflicts with Juv R 15(A), and in such situations, the juvenile rule controls. In re Doe (Ohio Com.Pl. 1990) 57 Ohio Misc.2d 20, 565 N.E.2d 891.

3. Jurisdiction

In case of arrest of a minor, upon a warrant issued by a juvenile court, arising out of a complaint charging such minor with delinquency, the juvenile court has jurisdiction of the proceedings even though a citation has not been issued to the parents, guardian or other person having custody and control of such child. (Annotation from former RC 2151.28.) State ex rel. Heth v. Moloney (Ohio 1933) 126 Ohio St. 526, 186 N.E. 362.

Juvenile court has no jurisdiction to adjudicate a child as dependent until after filing of a complaint charging such dependency and notice given to the parent or parents. (Annotation from former RC 2151.28.) State ex rel. Clark v. Allaman (Montgomery 1950) 87 Ohio App. 101, 90 N.E.2d 394, 57 Ohio Law Abs. 17, 42 O.O. 330, affirmed 154 Ohio St. 296, 95 N.E.2d 753, 43 O.O. 190.

A juvenile court does not have jurisdiction to make commitments of children under former GC 1653 (Repealed) unless service, either actual or constructive, is first had on the father of such child or on the person having the custody of such child. (Annotation from former RC 2151.36.) 1929 OAG 281.

4. Notice

Under this section, the parents of a minor child or children are entitled to notice, actual or constructive, in a proceeding instituted in the juvenile court upon a complaint of dependency of such children; without such notice jurisdiction of the court does not attach and a judgment of commitment in proceeding is void. (Annotation from former RC 2151.28.) In re Corey (Ohio 1945) 145 Ohio St. 413, 61 N.E.2d 892, 31 O.O. 35. Infants ⇨ 198

Failure to serve a parent with a summons in a permanent custody action does not require dismissal of the action where the parent has actual notice of the action and has been served with a complaint. In re Webb (Hamilton 1989) 64 Ohio App.3d 280, 581 N.E.2d 570, dismissed, jurisdictional motion overruled 48 Ohio St.3d 704, 549 N.E.2d 1191.

Regular legal notice by service of process on the parent is an indispensable prerequisite to jurisdiction of juvenile court to make commitment of a minor child in delinquency cases. (Annotation from former RC 2151.28.) Ex parte Flickinger (Ohio Com.Pl. 1940) 5 Ohio Supp. 252, 33 Ohio Law Abs. 8, 20 O.O. 224.

5. Right to counsel

Juvenile rule and statute guarantee right to counsel for all indigent parties in juvenile proceedings. Holley v. Higgins (Franklin 1993) 86 Ohio App.3d 240, 620 N.E.2d 251. Infants ⇨ 205

6. Warrants

Under this section, a juvenile court may either issue a citation, requiring a minor charged with being dependent, neglected or delinquent and its parents or guardian or other person to appear, or the judge may in the first instance issue a warrant for the arrest of such minor. (Annotation from former RC 2151.28.) State ex rel. Heth v. Moloney (Ohio 1933) 126 Ohio St. 526, 186 N.E. 362.

7. Summons

A properly served summons containing the "full explanation" required by RC 2151.353(B) must be accompanied by a copy of the complaint, amended or not, if the complaint seeks, temporarily or permanently, to divest a parent of his parental rights. In re Wilson (Huron 1984) 21 Ohio App.3d 36, 486 N.E.2d 152, 21 O.B.R. 38.

The sheriff is required to serve summons, notices, and subpoenas which are directed to him by the juvenile court, and whether the juvenile court requests the summons, notices or subpoenas to be served personally or to be delivered by registered or certified mail, the sheriff's office is legally required to serve them in accordance with such directions of the juvenile court; and if the person to be served is out of the state and his address is known, service of summons may be made by the sheriff by delivering a copy to him personally or mailing a copy to him by registered or certified mail. (Annotation from former RC 2151.19.) OAG 70–130.

8. Hearings

RC 2151.28 and 2151.31 do not require a hearing as a condition precedent to the taking of a child into custody, pursuant to order of a juvenile court, during pendency of an action in such court. (Annotation from former RC 2151.28.) In re Jones (Allen 1961) 114 Ohio App. 319, 182 N.E.2d 631, 19 O.O.2d 286.

9. Parties

A father is a party to proceedings in a juvenile court in which his children are found to be neglected and in which temporary custody is given to the mother; and he is also a party to a subsequent proceeding in the same court modifying such temporary custody order and is entitled to appear in an appeal from such order and to move to dismiss such appeal. (Annotation from former RC 2151.28.) In re Rule (Crawford 1963) 1 Ohio App.2d 57, 203 N.E.2d 501, 30 O.O.2d 76.

Juv R 16 Process: service

(A) Summons: service, return

Except as otherwise provided in these rules, summons shall be served as provided in Civil Rules 4(A), (C) and (D), 4.1, 4.2, 4.3, 4.5 and 4.6. The summons shall direct the party served to appear at a stated time and place. Where service is by certified mail, the time shall not be less than seven days after the date of mailing.

Except as otherwise provided in this rule, when the residence of a party is unknown and cannot be ascertained with reasonable diligence, service shall be made by publication. Service by publication upon a non-custodial parent is not required in delinquent child or unruly child cases when the person alleged to have legal custody of the child has been served with summons pursuant to this rule, but the court may not enter any order or judgment against any person who has not been served with process or served by publication unless that person appears. Before service by publication can be made, an affidavit of a party or party's counsel shall be filed with the court. The affidavit shall aver that service of summons cannot be made because the residence of the person is unknown to the affiant and cannot be ascertained with reasonable diligence and shall set forth the last known address of the party to be served.

Service by publication shall be made by newspaper publication, by posting and mail, or by a combination of these methods. The court, by local rule, shall determine which method or methods of publication shall be used. If service by publication is made by newspaper publication, upon the filing of the affidavit, the clerk shall serve notice by publication in a newspaper of general circulation in the county in which the complaint is filed. If no newspaper is published in that county, then publication shall be in a newspaper published in an adjoining county. The publication shall contain the name and address of the court, the case number, the name of the first party on each side, and the name and last known address, if any, of the person or persons whose residence is unknown. The publication shall also contain a summary statement of the object of the complaint and shall notify the person to be served that the person is required to appear at the time and place stated. The time stated shall not be less than seven days after the date of publication. The publication shall be published once and service shall be complete on the date of publication.

After the publication, the publisher or the publisher's agent shall file with the court an affidavit showing the fact of publication together with a copy of the notice of publication. The affidavit and copy of the notice shall constitute proof of service.

If service by publication is made by posting and mail, upon the filing of the affidavit, the clerk shall cause service of notice to be made by posting in a conspicuous place in the courthouse in which the division of the common pleas court exercising jurisdiction over the complaint is located and in additional public places in the county that have been designated by local rule for the posting of notices pursuant to this rule. The number of additional public places to be designated shall be either two places or the number of state representative districts that are contained wholly or partly in the county in which the courthouse is located, whichever is greater. The notice shall contain the same information required to be contained in a newspaper publication. The notice shall be posted in the required locations for seven consecutive days. The clerk also shall cause the summons and accompanying pleadings to be mailed by ordinary mail, address correction requested, to the last known address of the party to be served. The clerk shall obtain a certificate of mailing from the United States Postal Service. If the clerk is notified of a corrected or forwarding address of the party to be served within the seven day period that notice is posted pursuant to this rule, the clerk shall cause the summons and accompanying pleadings to be mailed to the corrected or forwarding address. The clerk shall note the name, address, and date of each mailing in the docket.

After the seven days of posting, the clerk shall note on the docket where and when notice was posted. Service shall be complete upon the entry of posting.

(B) Warrant: execution; return

(1) By whom. The warrant shall be executed by any officer authorized by law.

(2) Territorial limits. The warrant may be executed at any place within this state.

(3) Manner. The warrant shall be executed by taking the party against whom it is issued into custody. The officer is not required to have possession of the warrant at the time it is executed, but in such case the officer shall inform the party of the

complaint made and the fact that the warrant has been issued. A copy of the warrant shall be given to the person named in the warrant as soon as possible.

(4) Return. The officer executing a warrant shall make return thereof to the issuing court. Unexecuted warrants shall upon request of the issuing court be returned to that court.

A warrant returned unexecuted and not cancelled or a copy thereof may, while the complaint is pending, be delivered by the court to an authorized officer for execution.

An officer executing a warrant shall take the person named therein without unnecessary delay before the court which issued the warrant.

(Adopted eff. 7–1–72; amended eff. 7–1–94, 7–1–98)

Historical and Statutory Notes

Amendment Note: The 7–1–98 amendment inserted "and shall set forth the last known address of the party to be served" at the end of the first paragraph in division (A); added the first two sentences, inserted "If service by publication is made by newspaper publication," and substituted "seven" for "fourteen" in the second paragraph in division (A); added the fourth and fifth paragraphs in division (A); and made other nonsubstantive changes.

Amendment Note: The 7–1–94 amendment rewrote the first two paragraphs in division (A); and made changes to reflect gender-neutral language. Prior to amendment, the first two paragraphs in division (A) read:

"(A) Summons: service, return. Summons shall be served as provided in Civil Rules 4(A), (C) and (D), 4.1, 4.2, 4.3, 4.5 and 4.6. The summons shall direct the party served to appear at a stated time and place; where service is by certified mail such time shall not be less than twenty-one days after the date of mailing.

"When the residence of a party is unknown, and cannot with reasonable diligence be ascertained, service shall be made by publication. Before service by publication can be made, an affidavit of a party or his counsel must be filed with the court. The affidavit shall aver that service of summons cannot be made because the residence of the defendant is unknown to the affiant and cannot with reasonable diligence be ascertained."

Staff Notes

1998:

Rule 16(A) Summons: service, return

The amendments to division (A) address the issue of service by publication where the residence of a party is unknown. Prior to the amendment, the rule only provided for publication in a newspaper of general circulation. This amendment changed the nature of service by publication in juvenile court cases.

Under this amendment, which is modeled partly on Civ. R. 4.4(A)(2), service by publication in all cases governed by the Juvenile Rules would be accomplished either by the traditional method of newspaper publication, by posting and mail, or by a combination of these methods. The court, by local rule, determines which method of service to select. Civ. R. 4.4(A)(2) mandates posting and mail publication in divorce, annulment, or legal separation actions where the plaintiff is proceeding *in forma pauperis.* Because most juvenile court cases are initiated by a complaint being filed by a parent (e.g., custody and unruly cases) or by an agency of the state (e.g., delinquency and unruly complaints filed by police departments and boards of education; neglect, dependency, and abuse complaints filed by children's services boards), the rationale which apparently supports Civ. R. 4.4(A)(2) would equally apply to juvenile court cases. Moreover, since the type of case and the status of the complainant should have no bearing on the method of service, the posting and mail form of publication should be permitted in all cases governed by the Juvenile Rules.

Another amendment relates to time frames. The prior rule provided that the publication had to occur not less than fourteen days prior to the scheduled hearing date. The amendment reduced the publication time frame to seven days. This amendment was based on several reasons. First, a 1994 amendment to Juv. R. 16(A) reduced the requisite waiting period for service by certified mail from twenty-one to seven days. Thus, the change to seven days for publication is consistent with the 1994 amendment. Second, Juv. R. 29(A) requires an adjudicatory hearing within ten days of the filing of a complaint when a child is in detention or shelter care. Although this hearing may be continued upon a showing of good cause, the amendment to Juv. R. 16(A) eliminated the potential conflict between the two rules. Third, Juv. R. 29(A) requires an adjudicatory hearing within thirty days after the filing of a complaint in all cases of abuse, neglect, or dependency. Although this hearing may be continued for a reasonable time beyond thirty days to obtain service on all parties, under no circumstances may the hearing be held later than sixty days after the complaint is filed. The condensed time frame for perfecting service by publication would facilitate conducting the hearing within the mandated time periods. Finally, section 2151.29 of the Revised Code, which has been in effect since 1969 (and which conflicts with both the prior and new versions of Juv. R. 16(A)), provides for a one week time frame for service by publication.

1994:

Rule 16 Process: Service

Juv. R. 29(A) requires that, when a child is in detention or shelter care, an adjudicatory hearing be set no later than ten days after the filing of the complaint. Certified mail service must, therefore, be completed prior to the ten day period. Juv. R. 16(A) now requires that a hearing shall be held not less than seven days after the date of mailing.

Service by publication permits fourteen days notice prior to the date of the hearing; however, new language has been added to Juv. R. 16(A) to eliminate the necessity of serving a non-custodial parent whose address is unknown, so long as the person with legal custody has been served with summons. Further safeguards have been added to the rule in that the court may not enter an order against any person who has not been served with process or served by publication unless that person appears.

Editor's Comment

Summons: service, return   1
Warrant: execution; return   2

1. Summons: service, return

Juv R 16(A) incorporates the provisions of Civ R 4 by reference, except as otherwise provided in the juvenile rules. Division (A) adds the requirement that the summons shall direct the party served to appear at a stated time and place. The main reason for adoption of this rule was the rationale that uniformity in the manner in which service of process was accomplished was desirable and in this respect juvenile procedure does not require any differentiation.

Juv R 16(A) provides that where service is made by certified mail, the hearing may not be held before seven days after the date of mailing.

The manner of perfecting service by publication adopts the language of 2151.29 with two important distinctions. Under the rule, service by publication upon a non-custodial parent is not required in delinquency and unruly cases when the legal custodian of the child has been served with summons. Secondly, the rule alters the time for hearing requirement from one week to fourteen days. When the child who is the subject of the complaint is in detention or shelter care, the rule conflicts with Juv R 29(A), which requires a hearing within ten days of the filing of the complaint.

Civ R 4.2(2), which requires that service of process upon a person under *sixteen* years of age be effected by serving a parent or guardian, would not apply to service of summons because Juv R 15(A) requires that summons issued for a child under *fourteen* years of age be served on the parent or guardian.

Civ R 4 through 4.6 cover, modify and expand the service of process principles generally set forth in Ch 2703. These are now the same principles applicable to a juvenile court proceeding which commences with the filing of the complaint pursuant to Juv R 10(A).

Refer to staff notes under Civ R 4 for further discussion of effect and clarification of the methods of service of process provided for by Juv R 16(A).

2. Warrant: execution; return

Juv R 16(B) dealing with the execution and return of warrants is identical with the provisions of Crim R 4(D).

Juv R 16(B)(2) adopts the provision of 2935.02 which permits a warrant to be executed at any place in the state.

Juv R 16(B)(3) providing that an officer need not have the warrant in his possession at the time he executes it is consistent with the provisions of 2151.14 and is similar to Crim R 4(D)(3).

Cross References

Issuance of warrant against parent, custodian, guardian, or child, 2151.30
Process: summons, Civ R 4 et seq.
Service of summons on juvenile complaint, 2151.29
Style of process, 7.01
Summons; expense, 2151.19
Summons on juvenile complaint, 2151.28
Warrant or summons, Crim R 4

Library References

Infants ⚖198.
Westlaw Topic No. 211.
C.J.S. Infants § 56.

Research References

Encyclopedias

OH Jur. 3d Family Law § 1610, Form and Contents.
OH Jur. 3d Family Law § 1613, Service; Proof of Service.
OH Jur. 3d Family Law § 1617, Execution and Return.
OH Jur. 3d Process § 86, Waiver of Objection to Process or Service.

Treatises and Practice Aids

Klein, Darling, & Terez, Baldwin's Ohio Practice Civil Practice § 4.1:6, Certified or Express Mail Service--Duties of the Clerk.
Klein, Darling, & Terez, Baldwin's Ohio Practice Civil Practice § 4.4:1, Process: Service by Publication--In General.
Klein, Darling, & Terez, Baldwin's Ohio Practice Civil Practice § 4.4:2, Process: Service by Publication--Service by Publication Authorized by Law--In General.
Klein, Darling, & Terez, Baldwin's Ohio Practice Civil Practice § 4.4:13, Process: Service by Publication--Effect of Noncompliance.
Carlin, Baldwin's Ohio Practice, Merrick-Rippner Probate Law § 107:11, Service of Summons.
Carlin, Baldwin's Ohio Practice, Merrick-Rippner Probate Law § 107:12, Service by Publication.
Carlin, Baldwin's Ohio Practice, Merrick-Rippner Probate Law § 107:13, Issuance of Warrant.
Carlin, Baldwin's Ohio Practice, Merrick-Rippner Probate Law § 107:50, Adjudicatory Hearings—Applicability of Rules of Court.
Carlin, Baldwin's Ohio Practice, Merrick-Rippner Probate Law § 107:117, Proceedings After Judgment—Continuing Jurisdiction of Juvenile Court.
Carlin, Baldwin's Ohio Practice, Merrick-Rippner Probate Law § 107:166, Summons on Parents, Guardian, or Custodian by Publication—Form.
Carlin, Baldwin's Ohio Practice, Merrick-Rippner Probate Law § 107:167, Warrant for Arrest of Child or Custodian—Form.
Giannelli & Yeomans, Ohio Juvenile Law § 1:8, Rules of Juvenile Procedure.
Giannelli & Yeomans, Ohio Juvenile Law § 13:4, Summons and Notice.
Giannelli & Yeomans, Ohio Juvenile Law § 18:2, Issuance of Summons: Proper Parties.
Giannelli & Yeomans, Ohio Juvenile Law § 18:4, Summons: Methods of Service.
Giannelli & Yeomans, Ohio Juvenile Law § 18:5, Waiver of Summons Requirements.

Notes of Decisions

Jurisdiction 3
Notice 2
Orders from other states 1
Service 4

1. Orders from other states

Where a court of another state has awarded custody of a minor child pursuant to a valid in personam order, and there is no evidence of a subsequent change in circumstances affecting the best interests of the child, the courts of this state will give full faith and credit to that order. Williams v. Williams (Ohio 1975) 44 Ohio St.2d 28, 336 N.E.2d 426, 73 O.O.2d 121.

2. Notice

Mother received adequate notice of final hearing in permanent custody case involving dependent children; mother was personally served with notice of the hearing, she failed to attend the hearing, her attorney informed her of the date of the final permanent custody hearing, and she failed to attend that hearing. In re Keith Lee P. (Ohio App. 6 Dist., Lucas, 04-16-2004) No. L-03-1266, 2004-Ohio-1976, 2004 WL 835989, Unreported. Infants ⚖ 198

Minor mother's legal guardian received sufficient notice of temporary custody hearing to provide court with jurisdiction in matter, even though mother claimed no notice was provided, where notice was endorsed and left at guardian's residence. In re D.H. (Ohio App. 8 Dist., Cuyahoga, 12-04-2003) No. 82533, 2003-Ohio-6478, 2003 WL 22861922, Unreported. Infants ⚖ 198

Mother received proper notice of motion filed by county department of children and family services seeking permanent custody of dependent child; record indicated that mother was personally served with notice some six months after filing of motion to modify temporary custody and seven months prior to the hearing for permanent custody. In re R.K. (Ohio App. 8 Dist., Cuyahoga, 11-26-2003) No. 82374, 2003-Ohio-6333, 2003 WL 22804937, Unreported. Infants ⚖ 198

Where only notice given mother of hearing to change child's temporary commitment to a permanent one was served on mother within an hour before such hearing, and she had no opportunity to either prepare for such hearing or to engage counsel to represent her, such notice is insufficient in law, and an order for permanent custody made at such hearing is void for want of jurisdiction of court in making it, even though mother was present at hearing; attack made upon it by an application for a writ of habeas corpus is proper even though judgment appears to be regular and valid upon its face. (Annotation from former RC 2151.29.) In re Frinzl (Ohio 1949) 152 Ohio St. 164, 87 N.E.2d 583, 39 O.O. 456.

The matters required to be shown under former GC 1648 (GC 1639–24; RC 2151.28) as a prerequisite to notice by publication of proceedings as to dependency of minor children were jurisdictional. In such case an attack upon a judgment for fraud in its procurement is direct, and is permitted, notwithstanding that the judgment questioned may appear on its face regular and valid. (Annotation from former RC 2151.29.) Lewis v. Reed (Ohio 1927) 117 Ohio St. 152, 157 N.E. 897, 5 Ohio Law Abs. 420, 25 Ohio Law Rep. 386.

Under GC 1648 (GC 1639–24; RC 2151.28), the mother of an illegitimate child is entitled to notice, actual or constructive, of proceedings upon a complaint of dependency instituted in the juvenile court in reference to such child; and until notice of such proceedings has been given to the mother, the jurisdiction of the juvenile court does not attach and a judgment of permanent commitment rendered in such dependency proceeding is void. (Annotation from former RC 2151.29.) Lewis v. Reed (Ohio 1927) 117 Ohio St. 152, 157 N.E. 897, 5 Ohio Law Abs. 420, 25 Ohio Law Rep. 386.

A published notice under Juv R 16 that lacks the last known address is defective as notice by publication; the requirements of Juv R 16 are mandatory and are to be strictly construed. In Matter of Holloway (Ohio App. 12 Dist., Clermont, 05-06-1996) No. CA95-09-064, 1996 WL 227481, Unreported.

Where a complaint for dependency is filed, an unknown father must be served by publication; even an apparently unconcerned putative father is entitled to notice by publication, and the mother's statement that she does not know who the father is does not justify dispensing with the notice. In re Ware, No. 79–03243 (8th Dist Ct App, Cuyahoga, 7–17–80).

The Common Pleas Court had jurisdiction to grant permanent custody of mother's two children to the county job and family services agency, even though notice to mother of the dispositional hearing was returned undeliverable; mother appeared with counsel at an earlier shelter-care hearing, at the shelter-care hearing the trial court noted the date of the adjudicatory hearing, counsel for mother appeared at the dispositional hearing, and neither mother or her counsel objected to the notice provided to mother. In re Billingsley (Ohio App. 3 Dist., Putnam, 01-28-2003) No. 12-02-07, No. 12-02-08, 2003-Ohio-344, 2003 WL 178661, Unreported. Infants ⚖ 198

Father waived on appeal in termination of parental rights proceeding issue of whether trial court lacked jurisdiction to enter order awarding permanent custody of children to county department of children and family services, based on his allegation that court did not provide proper notice to mother of proceedings, as he failed to raise issue in trial court. (Per O'Donnell, J., with two judges concurring in judgment only). In re Harlston (Ohio App. 8 Dist., Cuyahoga, 01-23-2003) No. 80672, 2003-

Ohio-282, 2003 WL 152939, Unreported, appeal not allowed 98 Ohio St.3d 1492, 785 N.E.2d 474, 2003-Ohio-1189. Infants ⇨ 243

Mother's absence at termination of parental rights hearing did not prejudice father's rights; not only was there no evidence that mother would have been awarded custody of children, but mother was in agreement with permanent custody of children being awarded to county department of children and family services. (Per O'Donnell, J., with two judges concurring in judgment only). In re Harlston (Ohio App. 8 Dist., Cuyahoga, 01-23-2003) No. 80672, 2003-Ohio-282, 2003 WL 152939, Unreported, appeal not allowed 98 Ohio St.3d 1492, 785 N.E.2d 474, 2003-Ohio-1189. Infants ⇨ 253

Daily legal newspaper that was designated as official law journal of county was "newspaper of general circulation" by special exemption of statutes defining publications that qualify as newspapers of general circulation, and thus, publication of notice of complaint and summons in official law journal to fathers of dependent children was sufficient for juvenile court to assert jurisdiction over fathers for hearing on state's motion for permanent custody. In re Starkey (Ohio App. 7 Dist., 12-11-2002) 150 Ohio App.3d 612, 782 N.E.2d 665, 2002-Ohio-6892. Infants ⇨ 198; Process ⇨ 105

3. Jurisdiction

Juvenile court is without jurisdiction to make permanent a temporary commitment of child unless notice of time and place of hearing is served on parent or guardian either by delivering a copy to the person to be notified, by leaving a copy at his usual place of residence, by service by registered mail, or by publication, as provided by this section; such notice must be served sufficiently in advance of hearing to allow reasonable time to obtain counsel and prepare for participation in such hearing. (Annotation from former RC 2151.29.) In re Frinzl (Ohio 1949) 152 Ohio St. 164, 87 N.E.2d 583, 39 O.O. 456. Infants ⇨ 198

4. Service

Trial court did not have jurisdiction to award permanent custody of child to Department of Children and Family Services, even though mother had notice of preliminary hearing, where service was not attempted on mother in regards to trial. In re D.H. (Ohio App. 8 Dist., Cuyahoga, 12-04-2003) No. 82533, 2003-Ohio-6478, 2003 WL 22861922, Unreported. Infants ⇨ 198

Service by publication, in child protection proceedings, was not rendered defective when affidavit incorrectly listed affiant, where affidavit contained a statement by the notary certifying that content was sworn to and it was subscribed in her presence. In re D.H. (Ohio App. 8 Dist., Cuyahoga, 12-04-2003) No. 82533, 2003-Ohio-6478, 2003 WL 22861922, Unreported. Infants ⇨ 198

Trial court lacked personal jurisdiction over father to enter child support order against him, due to defective service of process of motion to set support; docket sheet showed that father was served with motion to set child support by ordinary mail only, rather than by certified mail, or express mail, as required by rule, so continuing jurisdiction of juvenile court was not invoked, and, due to failure to provide notice, any subsequent order based on void order was nullity. In re Brandon P. (Ohio App. 6 Dist., Lucas, 04-11-2003) No. L-02-1230, 2003-Ohio-1861, 2003 WL 1861564, Unreported. Child Support ⇨ 180

An order of a juvenile court declaring a minor child to be a dependent child and awarding its custody to a stranger, obtained without service upon the parent, the guardian, or a person having the custody of such child by operation of law or awarded by a judicial order, judgment, or decree, confers upon such stranger no power to consent to the adoption of such child by any one. (Annotation from former RC 2151.29.) Rarey v. Schmidt (Ohio 1926) 115 Ohio St. 518, 154 N.E. 914, 5 Ohio Law Abs. 12, 25 Ohio Law Rep. 134.

Where a minor child has neither legal guardian nor custodian, other than a parent, and the residence of the parent is known, service, actual or constructive, must be had upon such parent before a juvenile court has jurisdiction to declare such child a dependent child. (Annotation from former RC 2151.29.) Rarey v. Schmidt (Ohio 1926) 115 Ohio St. 518, 154 N.E. 914, 5 Ohio Law Abs. 12, 25 Ohio Law Rep. 134.

Alleged father waived appellate review of sufficiency of service of process, through publication, for initial hearing regarding temporary custody of dependent, neglected, and abused child, where summons and complaint for permanent custody proceeding was properly served on alleged father once he was found in prison, alleged father was afforded an appointed attorney at hearing on permanent custody, and, at best, attorney referred only in passing, at hearing on permanent custody, to insufficiency of service of process for initial hearing on temporary custody. In re T.C. (Ohio App. 3 Dist., 12-13-2000) 140 Ohio App.3d 409, 747 N.E.2d 881, 2000-Ohio-1769. Infants ⇨ 243

Jurisdiction of juvenile court does not attach until notice of proceedings has been provided to parties; if parties do not receive notice of proceedings, judgment of court is void. In re Mullenax (Ohio App. 9 Dist., 01-03-1996) 108 Ohio App.3d 271, 670 N.E.2d 551. Infants ⇨ 198; Infants ⇨ 223.1

Social services organization which filed application for permanent custody of child demonstrated reasonable diligence in attempting to ascertain residence of child's biological father, and therefore service on child's biological father by publication was permissible, though child's putative father contended that child's mother lied about her inability to identify him and that someone on hospital staff would have identified him as child's father if inquiry had been made, where child's guardian ad litem testified that child's mother could not identify father or anyone else she had had sex with at time surrounding conception, caseworker for social services organization testified that child's mother and grandmother could not identify child's biological father, and putative father produced no evidence that inquiry of hospital staff would have had possibility of success. In re Mullenax (Ohio App. 9 Dist., 01-03-1996) 108 Ohio App.3d 271, 670 N.E.2d 551. Child Custody ⇨ 409

Service by publication is proper in a case in which a county children's services board files a motion for permanent custody of a mother's children where the board adequately establishes that it exercised reasonable diligence in attempting to locate the mother; the mother's history of sporadic contact coupled with her inability to obtain stable housing, ten addresses within one year, or provide the board with an address to send notices made it extremely impractical, if not impossible, to serve the mother in any other manner than by publication. In re Cowling (Summit 1991) 72 Ohio App.3d 499, 595 N.E.2d 470. Infants ⇨ 198

Service by publication pursuant to Juv R 16(A) is defective when the notice fails to include the last known address of the party to be served and where only minimal efforts are made discover the whereabouts of the party to be served. In re Miller (Cuyahoga 1986) 33 Ohio App.3d 224, 515 N.E.2d 635.

Where a challenge to a party's claim that reasonable diligence was exercised to locate a party served by publication under Juv R 16(A) is raised, the party claiming use of reasonable diligence must support such a claim. In re Miller (Cuyahoga 1986) 33 Ohio App.3d 224, 515 N.E.2d 635.

Service of summons by publication is defective if the published notice fails to include a last known address, when such an address is known, and fails to include a summary statement of the object of the complaint. In re Wilson (Huron 1984) 21 Ohio App.3d 36, 486 N.E.2d 152, 21 O.B.R. 38. Infants ⇨ 198

Service of a complaint alleging that children are dependent and neglected and notice of hearing by regular mail the day before the hearing and receipt of same the day after the hearing deprives the defending parent of sufficient notice and due process under the law; the report of the referee and judgment of the juvenile court are rendered a nullity, despite the fact that such service complies with the letter of the procedural rules. In re Marshall, No. C–830874 (1st Dist Ct App, Hamilton, 8–15–84).

The sheriff is required to serve summons, notices, and subpoenas which are directed to him by the juvenile court, and whether the juvenile court requests the summons, notices or subpoenas to be served personally or to be delivered by registered or certified mail, the sheriff's office is legally required to serve them in accordance with such directions of the juvenile court; and if the person to be served is out of the state and his address is known, service of summons may be made by the sheriff by delivering a copy to him personally or mailing a copy to him by registered or certified mail. (Annotation from former RC 2151.29.) OAG 70–130.

Preparing an envelope for certified mailing and then placing it into an "Express Mail" envelope is not the equivalent of actually sending the document by certified mail, but will instead be treated as an ordinary mailing, where the sender did not pay for certified mail delivery, did not have the post office affix a post mark to the envelope or a "domestic return receipt," and did not use the inner envelope in the mailing. It is unfortunate that the party was encouraged by the post office to use a form of delivery that resulted in the untimely filing. Little Tykes Co v Summit County Bd of Revision, BTA 96–T–1156, 1997 WL 39919 (1–24–97).

Juv R 17 Subpoena

(A) Form; issuance

(1) Every subpoena shall do all of the following:

(a) State the name of the court from which it is issued, the title of the action, and the case number;

(b) Command each person to whom it is directed, at a time and place specified in the subpoena, to do one or more of the following:

(i) Attend and give testimony at a trial, hearing, proceeding, or deposition;

(ii) Produce documents or tangible things at a trial, hearing, proceeding, or deposition;

(iii) Produce and permit inspection and copying of any designated documents that are in the possession, custody, or control of the person;

(iv) Produce and permit inspection and copying, testing, or sampling of any tangible things that are in the possession, custody, or control of the person.

(c) Set forth the text of divisions (D) and (E) of this rule.

A command to produce and permit inspection may be joined with a command to attend and give testimony, or may be issued separately.

(2) The clerk shall issue a subpoena, signed but otherwise in blank, to a party requesting it, who shall complete it before service. An attorney who has filed an appearance on behalf of a party in an action also may sign and issue a subpoena on behalf of the court in which the action is pending.

(3) If the issuing attorney modifies the subpoena in any way, the issuing attorney shall give prompt notice of the modifications to all other parties.

(B) Parties unable to pay

The court shall order at any time that a subpoena be issued for service on a named witness upon an ex parte application of a party and upon a satisfactory showing that the presence of the witness is necessary and that the party is financially unable to pay the witness fees required by division (C) of this rule. If the court orders the subpoena to be issued, the costs incurred by the process and the fees of the witness so subpoenaed shall be paid in the same manner that similar costs and fees are paid in case of a witness subpoenaed in behalf of the state in a criminal prosecution.

(C) Service

A subpoena may be served by a sheriff, bailiff, coroner, clerk of court, constable, probation officer, or a deputy of any, by an attorney or the attorney's agent, or by any person designated by order of the court who is not a party and is not less than eighteen years of age. Service of a subpoena upon a person named in the subpoena shall be made by delivering a copy of the subpoena to the person, by reading it to him or her in person, or by leaving it at the person's usual place of residence, and by tendering to the person upon demand the fees for one day's attendance and the mileage allowed by law. The person serving the subpoena shall file a return of the subpoena with the clerk. If the witness being subpoenaed resides outside the county in which the court is located, the fees for one day's attendance and mileage shall be tendered without demand. The return may be forwarded through the postal service or otherwise.

(D) Protection of persons subject to subpoenas

(1) A party or an attorney responsible for the issuance and service of a subpoena shall take reasonable steps to avoid imposing undue burden or expense on a person subject to that subpoena.

(2) (a) A person commanded to produce under division (A)(1)(b)(ii), (iii), or (iv) of this rule is not required to appear in person at the place of production or inspection unless commanded to attend and give testimony at a trial, hearing, proceeding, or deposition.

(b) Subject to division (E)(2) of this rule, a person commanded to produce under division (A)(1)(b)(ii), (iii), or (iv) of this rule may serve upon the party or attorney designated in the subpoena written objections to production. The objections must be served within fourteen days after service of the subpoena or before the time specified for compliance if that time is less than fourteen days after service. If objection is made, the party serving the subpoena shall not be entitled to production except pursuant to an order of the court that issued the subpoena. If objection has been made, the party serving the subpoena, upon notice to the person commanded to produce, may move at any time for an order to compel the production. An order to compel production shall protect any person who is not a party or an officer of a party from significant expense resulting from the production commanded.

(3) On timely motion, the court from which the subpoena was issued shall quash or modify the subpoena, or order appearance or production only under specified conditions, if the subpoena does any of the following:

(a) Fails to allow reasonable time to comply;

(b) Requires disclosure of privileged or otherwise protected matter and no exception or waiver applies;

(c) Requires disclosure of a fact known or opinion held by an expert not retained or specially employed by any party in anticipation of litigation or preparation for trial if the fact or opinion does not describe specific events or occurrences in dispute and results from study by that expert that was not made at the request of any party;

(d) Subjects a person to undue burden.

(4) Before filing a motion pursuant to division (D)(3)(d) of this rule, a person resisting discovery under this rule shall attempt to resolve any claim of undue burden through discussions with the issuing attorney. A motion filed pursuant to division (D)(3)(d) of this rule shall be supported by an affidavit of the subpoenaed person or a certificate of that person's attorney of the efforts made to resolve any claim of undue burden.

(5) If a motion is made under division (D)(3)(c) or (D)(3)(d) of this rule, the court shall quash or modify the subpoena unless the party in whose behalf the subpoena is issued shows a substantial need for the testimony or material that cannot be otherwise met without undue hardship and assures that the person to whom the subpoena is addressed will be reasonably compensated.

(E) Duties in responding to subpoena

(1) A person responding to a subpoena to produce documents shall, at the person's option, produce the documents as they are kept in the usual course of business or organized and labeled to correspond with the categories in the subpoena. A person producing documents pursuant to a subpoena for them shall permit their inspection and copying by all parties present at the time and place set in the subpoena for inspection and copying.

(2) When information subject to a subpoena is withheld on a claim that it is privileged or subject to protection as trial preparation materials, the claim shall be made expressly and shall be supported by a description of the nature of the documents, communications, or things not produced that is sufficient to enable the demanding party to contest the claim.

(F) Sanctions

Failure by any person without adequate excuse to obey a subpoena served upon that person may be a contempt of the court from which the subpoena issued. A subpoenaed person or that person's attorney who frivolously resists discovery under this rule may be required by the court to pay the reasonable expenses, including reasonable attorney's fees, of the party seeking the discovery. The court from which a subpoena was issued may impose upon a party or attorney in breach of the duty imposed by division (D)(1) of this rule an appropriate sanction, that may include, but is not limited to, lost earnings and reasonable attorney's fees.

(G) Privileges

Nothing in this rule shall be construed to authorize a party to obtain information protected by any privilege recognized by law or to authorize any person to disclose such information.

(H) Time

Nothing in this rule shall be construed to expand any other time limits imposed by rule or statute. All issues concerning subpoenas shall be resolved prior to the time otherwise set for hearing or trial.

(Adopted eff. 7–1–72; amended eff. 7–1–94)

Historical and Statutory Notes

Amendment Note: The 7–1–94 amendment rewrote division (A); substituted "(C)" for "(D)" in division (B); deleted former division (C); redesignated former division (D) as division (C); deleted former divisions (E) and (F); added divisions (D) and (E); redesignated former division (G) as division (F) and rewrote this division; added divisions (G) and (H); and made changes to reflect gender-neutral language. Prior to amendment, divisions (A), (C), (E), (F), and (G) read:

"(A) For attendance of witnesses; form; issuance. Every subpoena issued by the clerk shall be under the seal of the court, shall state the name of the court and the title of the action, and shall command each person to whom it is directed to attend and give testimony at a time and place therein specified. The clerk shall issue a subpoena, or a subpoena for the production of documentary evidence, signed and sealed but otherwise in blank, to a party requesting it, who shall fill it in and file a copy thereof with the clerk before service.

"(C) For production of documentary evidence. A subpoena may also command the person to whom it is directed to produce the books, papers, documents or other objects designated therein; but the court upon motion made promptly and in any event at or before the time specified in the subpoena for compliance therewith may quash or modify the subpoena if compliance would be unreasonable or oppressive. The court may direct that the books, papers, documents or other objects designated in the subpoena be produced before the court at a time prior to the hearing or prior to the time they are offered in evidence and may upon their production permit them or portions thereof to be inspected by the parties or their attorneys.

"(E) Subpoena for taking depositions; place of examination. When the attendance of a witness before an official authorized to take depositions is required, the subpoena shall be issued by such person and shall command the person to whom it is directed to attend and give testimony at a time and place specified therein. The subpoena may command the person to whom it is directed to produce designated books, papers, documents or tangible objects which constitute or contain evidence relating to any of the matters within the scope of the examination permitted by Rule 25.

"A person whose deposition is to be taken may be required to attend an examination in the county wherein he resides or is employed or transacts his business in person, or at such other convenient place as is fixed by an order of court.

"(F) Subpoena for a hearing. At the request of any party subpoenas for attendance at a hearing shall be issued by the clerk of the court in which the hearing is held. A subpoena requiring the attendance of a witness at a hearing may be served at any place within this state.

"(G) Contempt. Failure by any person without adequate excuse to obey a subpoena served upon him may be deemed a contempt of the court or officer issuing the subpoena."

Staff Notes

1994:

Rule 17 Subpoena

Juv. R. 17 has been revised to control the issuance and enforcement of subpoenas. Because of the special nature of juvenile proceedings, Juv. R. 17 must be read in conjunction with Juv. R. 24 and 25. Juv. R. 25 provides that the court may grant authority to take a deposition only upon good cause shown. Juv. R. 24 governs the scope of discovery, which is subject to the assertion of privilege.

Editor's Comment

For attendance of witnesses; form; issuance 1
Parties unable to pay 2
Service 3
Protection of persons subject to subpoenas; duties in responding to subpoena; sanctions; privileges 4

1. For attendance of witnesses; form; issuance

Juv R 17 follows closely the provisions of Civ R 45 and Crim R 17.

2. Parties unable to pay

Juv R 17(B) adopts the language of Crim R 17(B) as to parties unable to pay fees. There is no such provision in Civ R 45.

3. Service

Juv R 17(C) is similar to Crim R 17(D) and Civ R 45(D) and adds "probation officer" to those who may serve a subpoena as provided in 2151.14.

4. Protection of persons subject to subpoenas; duties in responding to subpoena; sanctions; privileges

Juv R 17(D), (E), (F), and (G) follow closely the provisions of Civ R 45(C), (D), (E), and (F), respectively.

The rule covers subpoenas for hearing, for production of materials and for depositions. The Ohio procedure closely follows Federal Rule 45 and is similar to 2317.11 through 2317.20. It provides for a uniform and flexible method for the issuance of subpoenas, changes and expands portions of the statutory law and supersedes 2317.11 through 2317.20.

Prior to the adoption of the rule there was no specific procedure for the issuance of subpoenas in the juvenile court except a reference in 2151.28(J).

(See Staff Notes under Civ R 45, *Baldwin's Ohio Revised Code Annotated*).

Cross References

Subpoena, Civ R 45; Crim R 17

Library References

Infants ⇌201, 207.
Witnesses ⇌16, 21.
Westlaw Topic Nos. 211, 410.
C.J.S. Infants §§ 42, 51 to 67.
C.J.S. Witnesses §§ 25, 27.

Research References

Encyclopedias

OH Jur. 3d Contempt § 19, Disobedience of Subpoena or Process.
OH Jur. 3d Family Law § 1545, Contempt.
OH Jur. 3d Family Law § 1619, Service and Return.
OH Jur. 3d Family Law § 1620, to Compel Attendance at Hearing.
OH Jur. 3d Family Law § 1621, to Take Deposition.
OH Jur. 3d Family Law § 1622, to Produce Documentary Evidence.
OH Jur. 3d Family Law § 1719, Service; Witness Fees.

Treatises and Practice Aids

Giannelli and Snyder, Baldwin's Ohio Practice, Evidence, § 804.8, Unavailability: Unable to Procure Testimony.

Giannelli and Snyder, Baldwin's Ohio Practice, Evidence, § 1004.4, Original Not Obtainable.

Carlin, Baldwin's Ohio Practice, Merrick-Rippner Probate Law § 107:162, Precipe for Subpoena—Form.

Carlin, Baldwin's Ohio Practice, Merrick-Rippner Probate Law § 107:163, Subpoena—Form.

Giannelli & Yeomans, Ohio Juvenile Law § 18:4, Summons: Methods of Service.

Giannelli & Yeomans, Ohio Juvenile Law § 21:5, Subpoenas.
Giannelli & Yeomans, Ohio Juvenile Law § 33:8, Contempt.
Giannelli & Yeomans, Ohio Juvenile Law App. D, Appendix D. Glossary.

Law Review and Journal Commentaries

White Collar Crime: Second Annual Survey of Law; Subpoena, Dona A. Nutini and Patricia J. Pannell. 19 Am Crim L Rev 173 (1981).

Notes of Decisions

Court costs 2
Service 1

___

1. Service

Court's refusal to grant juvenile's request for a continuance in aggravated burglary case, on grounds that subpoenas that defense counsel had filed with the clerk's office had not been served, did not violate juvenile's right to compel production of witnesses, where defense counsel did not explain why the witnesses were material, did not give any indication what the testimony would have been, and did not request continuance until shortly before trial was to begin. State v. K.W. (Ohio App. 8 Dist., Cuyahoga, 01-30-2003) No. 80951, 2003-Ohio-425, 2003 WL 194857, Unreported. Infants ⚖ 204

The sheriff is required to serve summons, notices, and subpoenas which are directed to him by the juvenile court, and whether the juvenile court requests the summons, notices or subpoenas to be served personally or to be delivered by registered or certified mail, the sheriff's office is legally required to serve them in accordance with such directions of the juvenile court; and if the person to be served is out of the state and his address is known, service of summons may be made by the sheriff by delivering a copy to him personally or mailing a copy to him by registered or certified mail. (Annotation from former RC 2151.19.) OAG 70–130.

2. Court costs

Trial court did not abuse its discretion by denying juvenile defendant's motion for appointment of an expert at State's expense in delinquency proceeding in order to rebut juvenile victim's statements to police of alleged sexual abuse; State presented no evidence as to what was said or displayed during victim's interviews, and thus, it was not relevant or reasonably necessary that an expert witness be appointed. In re Bright (Ohio App. 11 Dist., Trumbull, 05-23-2003) No. 2001-T-0095, No. 2001-T-0097, 2003-Ohio-2835, 2003 WL 21267810, Unreported. Infants ⚖ 212

In juvenile court cases in which the Ohio rules of juvenile procedure apply, Ohio Juv R 17(B) grants a juvenile court the authority to tax as costs and collect from a party the fees of the county sheriff in serving subpoenas issued by the court and the fees of witnesses subpoenaed by the court. However, pursuant to RC 2151.54, such fees may not be taxed as costs and collected by a juvenile court in cases of delinquent, unruly, dependent, abused, or neglected children except when specifically ordered by the court. OAG 98–021.

Juv R 18 Time

(A) Time: computation

In computing any period of time prescribed or allowed by these rules, by the local rules of any court, by order of court, or by any applicable statute, the date of the act or event from which the designated period of time begins to run shall not be included. The last day of the period so computed shall be included, unless it is a Saturday, a Sunday, or a legal holiday, in which event the period runs until the end of the next day that is not a Saturday, a Sunday or a legal holiday. Such extension of time includes, but is not limited to, probable cause, shelter care, and detention hearings.

Except in the case of probable cause, shelter care, and detention hearings when the period of time prescribed or allowed is less than seven days, intermediate Saturdays, Sundays, and legal holidays shall be excluded in computation.

(B) Time: enlargement

When an act is required or allowed to be performed at or within a specified time, the court for cause shown may at any time in its discretion (1) with or without motion or notice, order the period enlarged if application therefor is made before expiration of the period originally prescribed or of that period as extended by a previous order, or (2) upon motion permit the act to be done after expiration of the specified period if the failure to act on time was the result of excusable neglect or would result in injustice to a party, but the court may not extend the time for taking any action under Rule 7(F)(1), Rule 22(F), Rule 29(A) and Rule 29(F)(2)(b), except to the extent and under the conditions stated in them.

(C) Time: unaffected by expiration of term

The period of time provided for the doing of any act or the taking of any proceeding is not affected or limited by the expiration of a term of court. The expiration of a term of court in no way affects the power of a court to do any act in a juvenile proceeding.

(D) Time: for motions; affidavits

A written motion, other than one which may be heard ex parte, and notice of the hearing thereof, shall be served not later than seven days before the time specified for the hearing unless a different period is fixed by rule or order of the court. For cause shown such an order may be made on ex parte application. When a motion is supported by affidavit, the affidavit shall be served with the motion, and opposing affidavits may be served not less than one day before the hearing unless the court permits them to be served at a later time.

(E) Time: additional time after service by mail

Whenever a party has the right or is required to do an act within a prescribed period after the service of a notice or other paper upon the person and the notice or other paper is served upon the person by mail, three days shall be added to the prescribed period. This division does not apply to service of summons.

(Adopted eff. 7–1–72; amended eff. 7–1–94)

Historical and Statutory Notes

Amendment Note: The 7–1–94 amendment redesignated division (A) into two paragraphs; added the final sentence in the first paragraph of division (A); added "Except in the case of probable cause, shelter care, and detention hearings" at the beginning of the second paragraph of division (A); and made changes to reflect gender-neutral language.

Staff Notes

1994:

Rule 18 Time

Juv. R. 18(A) now clarifies that the computation of time allowed or prescribed by rules or statutes for probable cause, shelter care, and detention hearings shall not exclude intermediate Saturdays, Sundays, and legal holidays.

Editor's Comment

Juv R 18 is virtually identical to Civ R 6 and Crim R 45. Juv R 18 differs in that Juv R 18(B) provides that the court may not extend the time for taking any action under Juv R 7(F)(1) pertaining to a detention hearing; Juv R 22(F) pertaining to the time for filing pleadings; Juv R 29(A) pertaining to the adjudicatory hearing; and Juv R 29(F)(2)(b) pertaining to the dispositional hearing; except to the extent and under the conditions stated in them.

The rule is very similar in principle to Federal Rule 6 but does provide that computations of periods of time are unaffected by the expiration of a term of court. In the federal court system, terms of court have been abolished.

Computation of a period of time set forth in the rule varies slightly from 1.14 in that if the final day of the period falls on Saturday, that day shall be excluded in the computation of time unless otherwise provided. The term "legal holidays" refers to those legal holidays set forth in 1.14.

Under the rule the court has discretionary control over any time extensions provided request is made to the court before the expiration of the period originally prescribed or of that period as extended by a previous order. After the prescribed period of time the court may only extend the time required to perform an act if the party's failure was the result of excusable neglect or would result in an injustice to the party. The court may not extend the time in the instances enumerated in Juv R 18(B).

Cross References

Computation of time, 1.45
Standard time, official legal proceedings to be governed by, 1.04
Time, Civ R 6; Crim R 45

Library References

Infants ⊙152, 193, 204.
Westlaw Topic No. 211.
C.J.S. Infants §§ 31 to 91.

Research References

Encyclopedias

OH Jur. 3d Family Law § 1529, Computation of Time Allowed by Rules, Order, or Statute.
OH Jur. 3d Family Law § 1530, Computation of Time Allowed by Rules, Order, or Statute—Enlargement of Time.
OH Jur. 3d Family Law § 1603, Service of Motion; Notice of Hearing.
OH Jur. 3d Family Law § 1607, Service—by Mail.

Treatises and Practice Aids

Carlin, Baldwin's Ohio Practice, Merrick-Rippner Probate Law § 107:10, Contents and Issuance of Summons.
Carlin, Baldwin's Ohio Practice, Merrick-Rippner Probate Law § 107:30, Detention Hearing.
Carlin, Baldwin's Ohio Practice, Merrick-Rippner Probate Law § 107:42, Prehearing Motions in Juvenile Court.
Carlin, Baldwin's Ohio Practice, Merrick-Rippner Probate Law § 107:50, Adjudicatory Hearings—Applicability of Rules of Court.
Carlin, Baldwin's Ohio Practice, Merrick-Rippner Probate Law § 107:117, Proceedings After Judgment—Continuing Jurisdiction of Juvenile Court.
Giannelli & Yeomans, Ohio Juvenile Law § 19:7, Time Requirements.
Giannelli & Yeomans, Ohio Juvenile Law § 33:2, Motions.

Notes of Decisions

Constitutional issues 4
Discretion of court 2
Enlargement of time to file 3
Excusable neglect 1

---

1. Excusable neglect

Attorney ignorance as to the filing deadlines provided under juvenile court rules was insufficient to constitute excusable neglect under juvenile rule governing motion for extension of time to file. In re Malone (Ohio App. 10 Dist., Franklin, 12-30-2003) No. 03AP-489, 2003-Ohio-7156, 2003 WL 23024377, Unreported, appeal not allowed 102 Ohio St.3d 1423, 807 N.E.2d 367, 2004-Ohio-2003. Infants ⊙ 204

To determine whether a defendant's conduct constitutes "excusable neglect," for purposes of juvenile rule governing motion for extension of time to file, all of the surrounding facts and circumstances must be considered, and courts must be mindful of the admonition that cases should be decided on their merits where possible, rather than procedural grounds. In re Malone (Ohio App. 10 Dist., Franklin, 12-30-2003) No. 03AP-489, 2003-Ohio-7156, 2003 WL 23024377, Unreported, appeal not allowed 102 Ohio St.3d 1423, 807 N.E.2d 367, 2004-Ohio-2003. Infants ⊙ 204

Juvenile procedure rules, rather than civil procedure rules, governed motion for extension of time to file objections to magistrate's decision in juvenile dependency proceedings. In re Malone (Ohio App. 10 Dist., Franklin, 12-30-2003) No. 03AP-489, 2003-Ohio-7156, 2003 WL 23024377, Unreported, appeal not allowed 102 Ohio St.3d 1423, 807 N.E.2d 367, 2004-Ohio-2003. Infants ⊙ 204

2. Discretion of court

Court's determination under juvenile rule governing motion for extension of time to file rests within the sound discretion of the trial court and will not be disturbed on appeal absent a showing of an abuse of discretion. In re Malone (Ohio App. 10 Dist., Franklin, 12-30-2003) No. 03AP-489, 2003-Ohio-7156, 2003 WL 23024377, Unreported, appeal not allowed 102 Ohio St.3d 1423, 807 N.E.2d 367, 2004-Ohio-2003. Infants ⊙ 204

3. Enlargement of time to file

Juvenile court's failure to grant enlargement of time to mother to file objections to magistrate's decision in dependency proceedings did not result in an injustice to mother within meaning of juvenile rule governing enlargement of time to file; mother had a full and fair opportunity to litigate the matters before the magistrate, and failure to file resulted from attorney's ignorance as to filing deadlines. In re Malone (Ohio App. 10 Dist., Franklin, 12-30-2003) No. 03AP-489, 2003-Ohio-7156, 2003 WL 23024377, Unreported, appeal not allowed 102 Ohio St.3d 1423, 807 N.E.2d 367, 2004-Ohio-2003. Infants ⊙ 204

4. Constitutional issues

Mother failed to show prejudice resulting from attorney's failure to file timely objections to magistrate's decision in juvenile dependency proceedings, and thus such failure would not constitute ineffective assistance of counsel, where objections would have been without merit. In re Malone (Ohio App. 10 Dist., Franklin, 12-30-2003) No. 03AP-489, 2003-Ohio-7156, 2003 WL 23024377, Unreported, appeal not allowed 102 Ohio St.3d 1423, 807 N.E.2d 367, 2004-Ohio-2003. Infants ⊙ 205

Juv R 19 Motions

An application to the court for an order shall be by motion. A motion other than one made during trial or hearing shall be in writing unless the court permits it to be made orally. It shall state with particularity the grounds upon which it is made and shall set forth the relief or order sought. It shall be supported by a memorandum containing citations of authority and may be supported by an affidavit.

To expedite its business, unless otherwise provided by statute or rule, the court may make provision by rule or order for the submission and determination of motions without oral hearing upon brief written statements of reasons in support and opposition.

(Adopted eff. 7–1–72; amended eff. 7–1–94)

Historical and Statutory Notes

Amendment Note: The 7–1–94 amendment inserted "unless otherwise provided by statute or rule," in the second paragraph.

Staff Notes

1994:

Rule 19 Motions

Revised Code 2151.353, as amended by S.B. 89, mandates that an oral hearing be held, with notice to all parties and the guardian ad litem, on any motion to extend an original order for protective supervision. The language "unless otherwise provided by statute or law" is designed to prohibit the court from deciding, without an oral hearing, a motion for extension of protective supervision.

Editor's Comment

Juv R 19 adopts the language generally of Civ R 7(B) and differs only in providing that a motion shall be supported by a memorandum containing citations of authority. The court may by adoption of a local rule provide for the submission and determination of motions without oral hearing upon brief written statements of reasons in support and opposition and is based upon Federal Rule 78. This provision is consistent with Juv R 1(B)(2) pertaining to the elimination of unjustifiable expense and delay.

The authority of the court to determine motions without an oral hearing is qualified by the language "unless otherwise provided by statute or law." Thus, motions to extend original orders for protective supervision under 2151.353 and motions to release a child from shelter care under 2151.314(C) require the court to conduct a hearing.

The rule requires that an application to the court shall be by motion which unless made during the hearing shall be in writing and shall state the grounds with particularity.

The rule covers motion practice in juvenile court.

Cross References

Continuing jurisdiction to be invoked by motion, Juv R 35
Pleadings and motions, Civ R 7

Library References

Infants ⚖191.
Westlaw Topic No. 211.
C.J.S. Infants §§ 42, 53, 54.

Research References

Encyclopedias

OH Jur. 3d Family Law § 1604, Determination of Motion.

Treatises and Practice Aids

Carlin, Baldwin's Ohio Practice, Merrick-Rippner Probate Law § 107:42, Prehearing Motions in Juvenile Court.

Carlin, Baldwin's Ohio Practice, Merrick-Rippner Probate Law § 107:50, Adjudicatory Hearings—Applicability of Rules of Court.

Carlin, Baldwin's Ohio Practice, Merrick-Rippner Probate Law § 107:77, Disposition of Abused, Neglected, or Dependent Child—Protective Supervision.

Giannelli & Yeomans, Ohio Juvenile Law § 33:2, Motions.

Notes of Decisions

Constitutional issues 1
Procedural issues 2

---

1. Constitutional issues

Rules governing filing and service of motions in juvenile court are designed to safeguard due process rights of all litigants by creating orderly procedure to ensure adequate notice to all interested parties. In re Robert S. (Ohio App. 6 Dist., 12-09-1994) 98 Ohio App.3d 84, 647 N.E.2d 869. Infants ⚖ 132; Infants ⚖ 198

Huron County Department of Human Services (HCDHS) substantially complied with notice requirements of juvenile rule in filing motion seeking to require Cuyahoga County Department of Children and Family Services CCDCFS to contribute to support of adopted child; trial court erred in submission of postjudgment entry and supporting affidavits with recommendations for financial responsibility CCDCFS should bear for reimbursing HCDHS for past and future treatment of adopted child, HCDHS filed its motion to determine support obligations, and although HCDHS did not file supporting affidavits or memorandum, CCDCFS did not object. In re Robert S. (Ohio App. 6 Dist., 12-09-1994) 98 Ohio App.3d 84, 647 N.E.2d 869. Social Security And Public Welfare ⚖ 194.30

2. Procedural issues

Grandmother's letter to court requesting legal custody of mother's children was not substantive equivalent of motion to intervene, and thus, trial court's consideration of letter as basis for granting grandmother custody of mother's children was abuse of discretion, in proceedings brought by Department of Children and Family Services for permanent custody of children; letter was not in form of motion as required, letter was not served on any of parties involved, grandmother was never made party to proceedings, and she did not testify at trial. In re D.D. (Ohio App. 8 Dist., Cuyahoga, 08-12-2004) No. 83537, 2004-Ohio-4243, 2004 WL 1797186, Unreported. Infants ⚖ 200

Trial court denial of mother's motion to dismiss father's motion to modify visitation based on father's failure to include citations of authority within his motion was not an abuse of discretion; mother's motion was untimely since it was orally made at the hearing on father's motion to modify visitation, and father's motion provided adequate notice for mother to respond and defend herself. In re Lane (Ohio App. 4 Dist., Washington, 06-25-2003) No. 02CA61, 2003-Ohio-3755, 2003 WL 21652176, Unreported. Child Custody ⚖ 600; Child Custody ⚖ 609

Juv R 20 Service and filing of papers when required subsequent to filing of complaint

(A) Service: when required

Written notices, requests for discovery, designation of record on appeal and written motions, other than those which are heard ex parte, and similar papers shall be served upon each of the parties.

(B) Service: how made

Whenever under these rules or by an order of the court service is required or permitted to be made upon a party represented by an attorney, the service shall be made upon the attorney unless service is ordered by the court upon the party. Service upon the attorney or upon the party shall be made in the manner provided in Civ. R. 5(B).

(C) Filing

All papers required to be served upon a party shall be filed simultaneously with or immediately after service. Papers filed with the court shall not be considered until proof of service is endorsed thereon or separately filed. The proof of service shall state the date and the manner of service and shall be signed and filed in the manner provided in Civil Rule 5(D).

(Adopted eff. 7–1–72; amended eff. 7–1–94)

Historical and Statutory Notes

Amendment Note: The 7–1–94 amendment added "when required subsequent to filing of complaint" to the title of the rule; and made changes to reflect gender-neutral language.

Staff Notes

1994:

Rule 20 Service and Filing of Papers When Required Subsequent to Filing of Complaint

The words "when required subsequent to filing of complaint" have been added to the title of Juv. R. 20 to distinguish it from the requirements of initial service of process described under Juv. R. 16. Otherwise, the only changes to the rule are to render it gender neutral.

Editor's Comment

Juv R 20 is substantially like Crim R 49 and closely follows Civ R 5. Juv R 20(A) is more limited in the types of pleadings that may be filed in a juvenile proceeding and requires that necessary pleadings shall be served on each party. It follows the civil rule in providing for service upon an attorney of record unless service upon the party is ordered by the court. When service is upon the attorney it shall be made as provided in Civ R 5.

The rule differs from the civil rule in that it requires that all pleadings shall be filed simultaneously with or immediately after service rather than within three days after service.

Juv R 20 governs the filing with the court of pleadings and papers subsequent to the filing of the original complaint.

Cross References

Expense of service of process, 2151.19
Probation officer may serve process, 2151.14
Service and filing of papers, Crim R 49
Service and filing of pleadings and other papers subsequent to the original complaint, Civ R 5
Service of summons, 2151.29
Style of process, 7.01

Library References

Infants ⚖198, 201, 244.1.
Westlaw Topic No. 211.
C.J.S. Infants §§ 42, 53, 54, 56, 86 to 91.

Research References

Encyclopedias

OH Jur. 3d Family Law § 1606, Service.
OH Jur. 3d Family Law § 1608, Filing of Papers.

Treatises and Practice Aids

Klein, Darling, & Terez, Baldwin's Ohio Practice Civil Practice § 5:2, Service and Filing of Most Papers Subsequent to Original Complaint: Introduction Service as Prescribed by Civ. R. 5(B) and 5(C) Versus Service as Prescribed by Civ. R. 4 to 4.6.

Carlin, Baldwin's Ohio Practice, Merrick-Rippner Probate Law § 107:50, Adjudicatory Hearings—Applicability of Rules of Court.

Giannelli & Yeomans, Ohio Juvenile Law § 21:3, Discovery Procedure; Rule 24.

Juv R 21 Preliminary conferences

At any time after the filing of a complaint, the court upon motion of any party or upon its own motion may order one or more conferences to consider such matters as will promote a fair and expeditious proceeding.

(Adopted eff. 7–1–72)

Editor's Comment

This is a modification of Crim R 17.1, intended to encourage the expanded use of the preliminary conference technique in a manner appropriate to the purposes of the Juvenile Court Act. The requirement of the criminal rule that a memorandum be prepared and filed was deemed unwieldy and unnecessary in the juvenile setting.

Cross References

Indictment and information, Crim R 7

Library References

Infants ⊕191.
Westlaw Topic No. 211.
C.J.S. Infants §§ 42, 53, 54.

Research References

Encyclopedias
  OH Jur. 3d Family Law § 1640, Preliminary Conferences.
  OH Jur. 3d Family Law § 1647, Proceedings Before Referee; Powers and Duties.

Treatises and Practice Aids
Carlin, Baldwin's Ohio Practice, Merrick-Rippner Probate Law § 107:49, Adjudicatory Hearings—Conduct of Hearing by Magistrate.
Giannelli & Yeomans, Ohio Juvenile Law § 24:4, Pretrial Orders.

Juv R 22 Pleadings and motions; defenses and objections

(A) Pleadings and motions

Pleadings in juvenile proceedings shall be the complaint and the answer, if any, filed by a party. A party may move to dismiss the complaint or for other appropriate relief.

(B) Amendment of pleadings

Any pleading may be amended at any time prior to the adjudicatory hearing. After the commencement of the adjudicatory hearing, a pleading may be amended upon agreement of the parties or, if the interests of justice require, upon order of the court. A complaint charging an act of delinquency may not be amended unless agreed by the parties, if the proposed amendment would change the name or identity of the specific violation of law so that it would be considered a change of the crime charged if committed by an adult. Where requested, a court order shall grant a party reasonable time in which to respond to an amendment.

(C) Answer

No answer shall be necessary. A party may file an answer to the complaint, which, if filed, shall contain specific and concise admissions or denials of each material allegation of the complaint.

(D) Prehearing motions

Any defense, objection or request which is capable of determination without hearing on the allegations of the complaint may be raised before the adjudicatory hearing by motion. The following must be heard before the adjudicatory hearing, though not necessarily on a separate date:

(1) Defenses or objections based on defects in the institution of the proceeding;

(2) Defenses or objections based on defects in the complaint (other than failure to show jurisdiction in the court or to charge an offense which objections shall be noticed by the court at any time during the pendency of the proceeding);

(3) Motions to suppress evidence on the ground that it was illegally obtained;

(4) Motions for discovery;

(5) Motions to determine whether the child is eligible to receive a sentence as a serious youthful offender.

(E) Motion time

Except for motions filed under division (D)(5) of this rule, all prehearing motions shall be filed by the earlier of:

(1) seven days prior to the hearing, or

(2) ten days after the appearance of counsel.

Rule 22(D)(5) motions shall be filed by the later of:

(1) twenty days after the date of the child's initial appearance in juvenile court; or

(2) twenty days after denial of a motion to transfer.

The filing of the Rule 22(D)(5) motion shall constitute notice of intent to pursue a serious youthful offender disposition.

The court in the interest of justice may extend the time for making prehearing motions.

The court for good cause shown may permit a motion to suppress evidence under division (D)(3) of this rule to be made at the time the evidence is offered.

(F) State's right to appeal upon granting a motion to suppress

In delinquency proceedings the state may take an appeal as of right from the granting of a motion to suppress evidence if, in addition to filing a notice of appeal, the prosecuting attorney certifies that (1) the appeal is not taken for the purpose of delay and (2) the granting of the motion has rendered proof available to the state so weak in its entirety that any reasonable possibility of proving the complaint's allegations has been destroyed.

Such appeal shall not be allowed unless the notice of appeal and the certification by the prosecuting attorney are filed with the clerk of the juvenile court within seven days after the date of the entry of the judgment or order granting the motion. Any appeal which may be taken under this rule shall be diligently prosecuted.

A child in detention or shelter care may be released pending this appeal when the state files the notice of appeal and certification.

This appeal shall take precedence over all other appeals.

(Adopted eff. 7–1–72; amended eff. 7–1–77, 7–1–94, 7–1–01)

Historical and Statutory Notes

Amendment Note: The 7–1–01 amendment added new division (D)(5); and rewrote division (E), which prior thereto read:

"All prehearing motions shall be filed by the earlier of (1) seven days prior to hearing, or (2) ten days after the appearance of counsel. The court in the interest of justice may extend the time for making prehearing motions.

The court for good cause shown may permit a motion to suppress evidence under subsection (D)(3) to be made at the time such evidence is offered."

Amendment Note: The 7–1–94 amendment added the third sentence in division (B).

Staff Notes

2001:

Rule 22(D) Prehearing motions

Rule 22 (D) was amended to add a fifth category of prehearing motions, the motion of the prosecuting attorney to have the court hold a probable cause hearing to determine whether or not a child is eligible under Revised

Code sections 2152.11 or 2152.13 to receive a sentence as a serious youthful offender. These motions provide a timely opportunity for the needed probable cause determination of eligibility for treatment as a serious youthful offender, in circumstances in which the prosecuting attorney does not have sufficient time to seek a grand jury determination of such eligibility.

Rule 22(E) Motion time

Rule 22(E) was amended to conform to Sub. Sen. Bill 179 (effective date January 1, 2002) by reflecting that motions for determination of eligibility for treatment as a serious youthful offender are subject to a different time frame than other prehearing motions. It is important for the prosecuting attorney to have sufficient time to investigate before making the significant charging decision to pursue serious youthful offender sentencing. Revised Code section 2152.13(B) provides that the prosecuting attorney has twenty days after a child's initial appearance within which to file a notice of intent to pursue a serious youthful offender dispositional sentence. Juvenile rule time frames applicable in all other cases would truncate this statutory latitude. For instance, Juvenile Rule 29(A) contemplates that ordinarily the adjudicatory hearing of a child held in detention must occur within ten days. Since these are the most serious cases, it is not unlikely that the child will be in detention. Thus, the ordinary time frames of Rule 22(E) would require the motion to be filed well before the statutory period of twenty days has elapsed. Amended Rule 22(E) also clarifies that the prosecuting attorney has the statutory twenty-day time period for filing a notice of intent to pursue serious youthful offender dispositional sentencing after a transfer is denied.

Finally, Rule 22(E) as amended specifically provides that a Rule 22(D)(5) motion shall serve as the statutory "notice of intent" to pursue serious youthful offender dispositional sentencing. This serves to create a recognized procedural mechanism for the notice and to clarify that a motion is indeed the required notice. It also clarifies that the motion starts the speedy trial time clock running [see also Revised Code section 2152.13(D)(1)].

Other changes to Rule 22(E) were in form only, and were not intended to be substantive.

1994:

Rule 22 Pleadings and Motions; Defenses and Objections

The revision to Juv. R. 22(B) prohibits the amendment of a pleading after the commencement or termination of the adjudicatory hearing unless the amendment conforms to the evidence presented and also amounts to a lesser included offense of the crime charged. Because juveniles can be bound over as adults and become subject to the jurisdiction of the criminal division of the common pleas courts, it is important that Juv. R. 22(B) conform with Crim. R. 7(D), which similarly prohibits any amendment which would result in a change in the identity of the crime charged.

Editor's Comment

Pleadings and motions   1
Amendment of pleadings   2
Answer   3
Prehearing motions   4
Motion time   5
State's right to appeal upon granting a motion to suppress   6

1. Pleadings and motions

Division (A) is similar to Crim R 12(A), modified to conform with juvenile court practice.

2. Amendment of pleadings

Division (B) is an amalgamation of Crim R 7(D) and Civ R 15(B), and is intended to provide the parties with broad latitude in amending pleadings, while complying with the due process requirements of adequate notice. The prohibition contained in Crim R 7(D) against changing the name or identity of the crime charged is included in the juvenile rule with respect to delinquency complaints. The defense of variance is probably appropriate in delinquency cases, and the opportunity for a party to obtain time in which to respond to an amendment avoids due process complications in non-delinquency cases.

3. Answer

Division (C) conforms to present practice, in that no answer is required. If an answer is filed, the requirement of concise admissions or denials contained in Civ R 8(B) attaches.

4. Prehearing motions

Division (D) is basically Crim R 12(B), slightly modified grammatically and follows the holding in *State v Davis*, 1 OS(2d) 28, 203 NE(2d) 357 (1964).

5. Motion time

Division (E) adopts the structure of Crim R 12(C), but with time periods shortened to conform with the need for expeditious action in juvenile proceedings. Though it may appear to set extremely short periods, time extensions are available.

6. State's right to appeal upon granting a motion to suppress

Division (F) is basically Crim R 12(J) providing the right of appeal to the state. Also, the mandatory release of a criminal defendant required by Crim R 12(J) pending appeal has not been adopted. A child in detention or shelter care may be kept there pending the appellate decision.

The rule provides that appeal on the granting of a motion to suppress shall take precedence over all other appeals in order to avoid delay in prosecution of the matter.

Cross References

Amended and supplemental pleadings, Civ R 15
General rules of pleading, Civ R 8
Indictment and information, Crim R 7
Pleadings and motions before trial: defenses and objections, Crim R 12
Pleadings and motions, Civ R 7

Library References

Infants ⚖︎197, 242.
Westlaw Topic No. 211.
C.J.S.   Infants §§ 55, 86 to 91.

Research References

Encyclopedias
OH Jur. 3d Criminal Law § 3580, Notice of Appeal as of Right.
OH Jur. 3d Family Law § 1592, Amendment of Pleadings.
OH Jur. 3d Family Law § 1600, Prehearing Motions.
OH Jur. 3d Family Law § 1604, Determination of Motion.
OH Jur. 3d Family Law § 1728, State's Right of Appeal—Where Evidence Suppressed.

Treatises and Practice Aids
Baldwin's Ohio Handbook Series—Trial Handbook § 29:4, Motion to Suppress Evidence Illegally Seized.
Katz, Giannelli, Blair and Lipton, Baldwin's Ohio Practice, Criminal Law, § 80:10, Time Limit.
Carlin, Baldwin's Ohio Practice, Merrick-Rippner Probate Law § 106:3, Juvenile Court Jurisdiction—Delinquent Child—Proof of Age.
Carlin, Baldwin's Ohio Practice, Merrick-Rippner Probate Law § 107:6, Amendment of Juvenile Complaint.
Carlin, Baldwin's Ohio Practice, Merrick-Rippner Probate Law § 107:20, Unlawful Search and Seizure of Juveniles—Motion to Suppress Illegal Evidence.
Carlin, Baldwin's Ohio Practice, Merrick-Rippner Probate Law § 107:42, Prehearing Motions in Juvenile Court.
Carlin, Baldwin's Ohio Practice, Merrick-Rippner Probate Law § 107:122, Appeals—Juvenile Court Judgments—Determination of Neglect, Dependency, Unruliness, Abuse, or Delinquency.
Carlin, Baldwin's Ohio Practice, Merrick-Rippner Probate Law § 107:125, Appeals—Availability of Habeas Corpus.
Painter & Dennis, Ohio Appellate Practice § 3:6, Time for Filing Notice of Appeal-Appeal by State in Criminal Case.
Giannelli & Yeomans, Ohio Juvenile Law § 2:5, Proof of Age Jurisdiction.
Giannelli & Yeomans, Ohio Juvenile Law § 5:3, Syo Charging; Preliminary Hearing.
Giannelli & Yeomans, Ohio Juvenile Law § 14:2, Exclusionary Rule.
Giannelli & Yeomans, Ohio Juvenile Law § 21:3, Discovery Procedure; Rule 24.
Giannelli & Yeomans, Ohio Juvenile Law § 34:6, Stay of Proceedings.
Giannelli & Yeomans, Ohio Juvenile Law § 34:8, State Appeals.
Giannelli & Yeomans, Ohio Juvenile Law § 16:14, Permanent & Temporary Custody Complaints; Planned Permanent Living Arrangements.

Giannelli & Yeomans, Ohio Juvenile Law § 16:16, Amendment of Complaints.

Giannelli & Yeomans, Ohio Juvenile Law § 16:17, Objections to Complaints.

Giannelli & Yeomans, Ohio Juvenile Law § 22:15, Access to Reports & Discovery.

Giannelli & Yeomans, Ohio Juvenile Law § 23:14, Rules of Evidence.

Giannelli & Yeomans, Ohio Juvenile Law § 23:31, Double Jeopardy.

Giannelli & Yeomans, Ohio Juvenile Law § 34:11, Effect on Further Juvenile Court Proceedings.

Giannelli & Yeomans, Ohio Juvenile Law § 34:12, Habeas Corpus.

Law Review and Journal Commentaries

Access to "Confidential" Welfare Records in the Course of Child Protection Proceedings, Richard Steven Levine. 14 J Fam L 535 (1975–76).

The Fourth Amendment Exclusionary Rule: The Desirability of a Good Faith Exception, Donald L. Willits. 32 Case W Res L Rev 443 (1982).

Notes of Decisions

Appeals 8
Complaints 1
Constitutional issues 4
Jurisdiction 5
Miranda warnings 7
Prosecutions 6
Service, notice 3
Time limitations 2

---

1. Complaints

A complaint under Juv R 10 and RC 2151.27 alleging that a child is dependent must state the essential facts which bring the proceeding within the jurisdiction of the court. In re Hunt (Ohio 1976) 46 Ohio St.2d 378, 348 N.E.2d 727, 75 O.O.2d 450. Infants ⇆ 197

After adjudicatory hearing in juvenile delinquency proceeding, trial court could not amend original complaint charging acts constituting third-degree attempted felonious assault if committed by adult, so that juvenile could be found delinquent based on acts constituting second-degree felonious assault by means of deadly weapon; amended offense was not lesser included offense of originally charged offense, amendment made significant difference in juvenile's potential confinement if juvenile violated probation, and addition of "deadly weapon" element surprised juvenile. In re Reed (Ohio App. 8 Dist., 01-17-2002) 147 Ohio App.3d 182, 769 N.E.2d 412, 2002-Ohio-43. Infants ⇆ 197

Amended charge of acts constituting second-degree felonious assault by means of deadly weapon if committed by adult was not lesser included offense of original charge of third-degree attempted felonious assault, for purposes of amending the complaint after adjudicatory hearing in juvenile delinquency proceeding; second–degree felony adjudication carried longer minimum term of confinement for juvenile than third-degree felony adjudication, attempted felonious assault could be committed without felonious assault by means of deadly weapon also being committed, and attempted felonious assault did not contain deadly weapon element. In re Reed (Ohio App. 8 Dist., 01-17-2002) 147 Ohio App.3d 182, 769 N.E.2d 412, 2002-Ohio-43. Infants ⇆ 197

Court's decision to amend indictment to state juvenile's age and date of offenses did not prejudice the juvenile because it did not change the name or identity of the offenses. In re Smith (Ohio App. 8 Dist., 03-26-2001) 142 Ohio App.3d 16, 753 N.E.2d 930. Infants ⇆ 197

Referral for juvenile adjudication of parochial school student disciplined by school for sexual harassment and sexual violence did not amount to malicious civil prosecution, despite resolution of juvenile court complaint in student's favor, absent any allegation that student's person or body was seized. Iwenofu v. St. Luke School (Ohio App. 8 Dist., 02-16-1999) 132 Ohio App.3d 119, 724 N.E.2d 511, appeal not allowed 86 Ohio St.3d 1407, 711 N.E.2d 234. Malicious Prosecution ⇆ 11

Juvenile court properly amended complaint in delinquency adjudication proceeding to charge juvenile with unruliness as lesser included offense of charged conduct, which would, if committed by adult, have constituted third-degree misdemeanor sexual imposition; record of proceeding demonstrated that central issue of proceeding was whether juvenile grabbed a girl's breast, and amended complaint was based on same facts as original charge. In re Felton (Ohio App. 3 Dist., 12-19-1997) 124 Ohio App.3d 500, 706 N.E.2d 809, dismissed, appeal not allowed 81 Ohio St.3d 1497, 691 N.E.2d 1058. Infants ⇆ 197

A party must object to a defect in a complaint of child abuse by a prehearing motion before the adjudicatory hearing, within the time requirements of Juv R 22(E). In re Dukes (Summit 1991) 81 Ohio App.3d 145, 610 N.E.2d 513, motion overruled 63 Ohio St.3d 1411, 585 N.E.2d 835.

Juvenile court abused its discretion in modifying delinquency adjudication for robbery to misdemeanor theft after disposition, where rule cited by juvenile for amendment of pleading did not authorize the court to amend the complaint after the juvenile's adjudication and disposition, and no other rule authorized juvenile court to modify the adjudication. In re Harris (Ohio App. 11 Dist., Portage, 07-26-2002) No. 2001-P-0117, 2002-Ohio-3848, 2002 WL 1752261, Unreported. Infants ⇆ 230.1

A juvenile court may amend a complaint, after all the evidence has been submitted, from one of dependency to one of custody. In re Likens, No. 85 CA 80 (2d Dist Ct App, Greene, 10–24–86).

The juvenile court errs in permitting the county department of children and family services to orally amend its complaint for temporary custody to one which seeks permanent custody on the day of trial since the department has only been granted emergency temporary custody, and the court should proceed on the motion for temporary custody and provide the parents with an opportunity to prepare for a permanent custody hearing. In re Vandivner (Ohio App. 8 Dist., Cuyahoga, 02-22-2001) No. 77963, No. 77966, No. 77964, No. 77965, 2001 WL 175542, Unreported.

Trial court was authorized to amend murder charge at juvenile's dispositional hearing to murder by committing felonious assault to conform to the evidence, where amendment did not change the name or identity of the offense. In re B.M. (Ohio App. 8 Dist., Cuyahoga, 02-27-2003) No. 80909, 2003-Ohio-870, 2003 WL 548359, Unreported. Infants ⇆ 197

Juvenile waived error claim to trial court's amendment of complaint from murder to murder by committing felonious assault, where he failed to object to amendment at dispositional hearing. In re B.M. (Ohio App. 8 Dist., Cuyahoga, 02-27-2003) No. 80909, 2003-Ohio-870, 2003 WL 548359, Unreported. Infants ⇆ 243

2. Time limitations

Father's motion to dismiss dependency proceeding on basis of failure to hold adjudication and dispositional hearings within statutory time periods failed to comply with juvenile rule governing filing deadline for all prehearing motions; motion was filed on day of hearing. In re A.P. (Ohio App. 12 Dist., Butler, 05-30-2006) No. CA2005-10-425, 2006-Ohio-2717, 2006 WL 1493313, Unreported. Infants ⇆ 204

Any error arising from failure of magistrate to hold hearing on juvenile's motion to suppress prior to adjudicatory hearing did not prejudice juvenile, in delinquency proceeding, especially in light of fact that motion was technically not properly before the court, given its untimeliness. In re Hill (Ohio App. 10 Dist., Franklin, 11-20-2003) No. 03AP-82, 2003-Ohio-6185, 2003 WL 22725297, Unreported. Infants ⇆ 253

The time requirement for filing a prehearing motion in juvenile court is seven days prior to the hearing or ten days after the appearance of counsel, whichever is earlier. In re Dukes (Summit 1991) 81 Ohio App.3d 145, 610 N.E.2d 513, motion overruled 63 Ohio St.3d 1411, 585 N.E.2d 835. Infants ⇆ 203

The time requirement for filing a prehearing motion in juvenile court is not met when counsel makes his first appearance several months before the adjudicatory hearing where an objection is made to a defective complaint; thus, the objection is not timely. In re Dukes (Summit 1991) 81 Ohio App.3d 145, 610 N.E.2d 513, motion overruled 63 Ohio St.3d 1411, 585 N.E.2d 835.

3. Service, notice

Juvenile had sufficient notice of the complaint, although she first saw complaint at time of adjudicatory hearing, as her presence at hearing necessarily implied she had some notice of complaint. In re Smith (Ohio App. 8 Dist., 03-26-2001) 142 Ohio App.3d 16, 753 N.E.2d 930. Infants ⇆ 198

Mother was provided with adequate notice of hearing to place her two minor children in permanent custody of Department of Human Services (DHS), despite her claim that DHS's motion for permanent custody failed to meet statutory notice requirements, in view of fact that statutory notice must be provided by court, not DHS, that notice given to mother by trial court contained all information required by statute, that mother waived any objection to inadequacies of notice when she elected to appear and participate with counsel, and that she did not raise issue of adequacy of notice at trial level. In re Shaeffer Children (Van Wert 1993) 85 Ohio App.3d 683, 621 N.E.2d 426, dismissed, jurisdictional motion overruled 67 Ohio St.3d 1451, 619 N.E.2d 419. Infants ⇨ 198

Service of a complaint alleging that children are dependent and neglected and notice of hearing by regular mail the day before the hearing and receipt of same the day after the hearing deprives the defending parent of sufficient notice and due process under the law; the report of the referee and judgment of the juvenile court are rendered a nullity, despite the fact that such service complies with the letter of the procedural rules. In re Marshall, No. C–830874 (1st Dist Ct App, Hamilton, 8–15–84).

The Common Pleas Court had jurisdiction to grant permanent custody of mother's two children to the county job and family services agency, even though notice to mother of the dispositional hearing was returned undeliverable; mother appeared with counsel at an earlier shelter-care hearing, at the shelter-care hearing the trial court noted the date of the adjudicatory hearing, counsel for mother appeared at the dispositional hearing, and neither mother or her counsel objected to the notice provided to mother. In re Billingsley (Ohio App. 3 Dist., Putnam, 01-28-2003) No. 12-02-07, No. 12-02-08, 2003-Ohio-344, 2003 WL 178661, Unreported. Infants ⇨ 198

Father waived on appeal in termination of parental rights proceeding issue of whether trial court lacked jurisdiction to enter order awarding permanent custody of children to county department of children and family services, based on his allegation that court did not provide proper notice to mother of proceedings, as he failed to raise issue in trial court. (Per O'Donnell, J., with two judges concurring in judgment only). In re Harlston (Ohio App. 8 Dist., Cuyahoga, 01-23-2003) No. 80672, 2003-Ohio-282, 2003 WL 152939, Unreported, appeal not allowed 98 Ohio St.3d 1492, 785 N.E.2d 474, 2003-Ohio-1189. Infants ⇨ 243

Mother's absence at termination of parental rights hearing did not prejudice father's rights; not only was there no evidence that mother would have been awarded custody of children, but mother was in agreement with permanent custody of children being awarded to county department of children and family services. (Per O'Donnell, J., with two judges concurring in judgment only). In re Harlston (Ohio App. 8 Dist., Cuyahoga, 01-23-2003) No. 80672, 2003-Ohio-282, 2003 WL 152939, Unreported, appeal not allowed 98 Ohio St.3d 1492, 785 N.E.2d 474, 2003-Ohio-1189. Infants ⇨ 253

4. Constitutional issues

Minor's speedy trial rights were not violated by the fact that delinquency complaint was filed 17 months after the last act alleged in the complaint; minor was not in custody between the time police were contacted to conduct investigation and when the complaint was filed. In re N.K. (Ohio App. 8 Dist., Cuyahoga, 12-24-2003) No. 82332, 2003-Ohio-7059, 2003 WL 23009113, Unreported. Infants ⇨ 204

Notice to mother of adjudicatory hearing in dependency proceeding satisfied due process, where county children services agency filed amended complaint upon learning identities of child's birth parents, amended complaint that was served on mother included notices of pretrial hearing the next day and of adjudicatory hearing nine days later, mother's counsel filed entry of appearance five days before service on mother of amended complaint, mother did not object to any defects in complaint prior to adjudicatory hearing, and she did not challenge adequacy of notice at trial level. In re Baby Girl Doe (Ohio App. 6 Dist., 08-30-2002) 149 Ohio App.3d 717, 778 N.E.2d 1053, 2002-Ohio-4470, appeal not allowed 97 Ohio St.3d 1425, 777 N.E.2d 278, 2002-Ohio-5820. Constitutional Law ⇨ 274(5); Infants ⇨ 198

An appeal by the state from a finding of not guilty, on a charge of "delinquency by reason of murder," by the juvenile division of the court of common pleas is barred by the constitutional protection against former jeopardy. In re Gilbert (Summit 1974) 45 Ohio App.2d 308, 345 N.E.2d 79, 74 O.O.2d 480.

The matter of unlawful search and seizure under US Const Am 4 applies to juveniles. (Annotation from former RC 2151.01.) In re Morris (Ohio Com.Pl. 1971) 29 Ohio Misc. 71, 278 N.E.2d 701, 58 O.O.2d 126.

The federal courts will abstain from interfering in state proceedings where juveniles seek an injunction against the use of social histories in pre-adjudication instances, although they may hear an issue involving the constitutionality of post-adjudicatory dissemination of the social histories where state law is not clear and the proper factual issues were not decided; the dissemination of social histories compiled by probation officers during juvenile proceedings do not violate a constitutional right to privacy. J. P. v. DeSanti (C.A.6 (Ohio) 1981) 653 F.2d 1080.

5. Jurisdiction

Juvenile adjudicated delinquent waived any defense based upon of lack of personal jurisdiction by failing to challenge juvenile court's personal jurisdiction either before or at beginning of adjudicatory hearing. In re C.W. (Ohio App. 12 Dist., Butler, 08-01-2005) No. CA2004-12-312, 2005-Ohio-3905, 2005 WL 1799317, Unreported. Infants ⇨ 196

In a juvenile proceeding an objection, raised after trial and submission, based on a failure of the testimony to establish the age of the accused juvenile, relates to jurisdiction over the person and not to jurisdiction in the court, and is waived under Juv R 22(D)(2). In re Fudge (Clark 1977) 59 Ohio App.2d 129, 392 N.E.2d 1262, 13 O.O.3d 176.

The failure to include the particular facts in a permanent custody complaint is not a jurisdictional defect and may be waived if not timely objected to before the adjudicatory hearing pursuant to Juv R 22(D). In re Crose, No. 1055 (2d Dist Ct App, Darke, 10–18–82).

Juvenile waived all but plain error in trial court's alleged failure to establish jurisdiction over him in delinquency proceeding, where juvenile did not raise that objection below. In re Ball (Ohio App. 3 Dist., Allen, 01-30-2003) No. 1-02-72, 2003-Ohio-395, 2003 WL 193519, Unreported. Infants ⇨ 243

Trial court established proper jurisdiction in juvenile delinquency proceeding by eliciting testimony by subject of proceeding, at preliminary hearing, that he was 16 years old and by making a finding in judgment entry of commitment that subject of proceeding was born on a particular date and was therefore a juvenile. In re Ball (Ohio App. 3 Dist., Allen, 01-30-2003) No. 1-02-72, 2003-Ohio-395, 2003 WL 193519, Unreported. Infants ⇨ 196

6. Prosecutions

Magistrate's decision to hold suppression hearing simultaneously with adjudicatory hearing was not abuse of discretion, in delinquency proceeding; same or similar testimony was necessary for motion to suppress as well as adjudication, when magistrate considered motion, juvenile had full opportunity to have any concerns about confession and waiver addressed by the court, and magistrate ruled on motion prior to adjudication. In re Hill (Ohio App. 10 Dist., Franklin, 11-20-2003) No. 03AP-82, 2003-Ohio-6185, 2003 WL 22725297, Unreported. Criminal Law ⇨ 532(.5); Infants ⇨ 203

Even though a complaining witness may designate a particular statute or statutes as being violated by a child, a juvenile court is free to find, on the basis of the facts alleged and proved, a violation of an additional statute and that the accused is a delinquent child. In re Burgess (Preble 1984) 13 Ohio App.3d 374, 469 N.E.2d 967, 13 O.B.R. 456. Infants ⇨ 210

The state is not barred from prosecution following an unsuccessful appeal from the sustaining of a motion to suppress so long as the state's certification upon appeal pursuant to Juv R 22(F) or Crim R 12(J), that the evidence suppressed was of such nature that the prosecution could not be successful without it, was made in good faith; if such certification were not made in good faith, the time consumed in determining the appeal from the motion to suppress must be charged to the state as undue delay in prosecution of the accused with respect to a determination of whether there has been a violation of the accused's right to a speedy trial. In re Hester (Franklin 1982) 3 Ohio App.3d 458, 446 N.E.2d 202, 3 O.B.R. 539. Criminal Law ⇨ 577.12(1)

Complaint charging 13–year–old juvenile with aggravated burglary for entering unlocked door of friend's home and, after no one answered, taking pack of cigarettes from top of refrigerator would be amended, in interest of justice, to charge criminal trespass and petty theft; there was no evidence that intent to steal was formed prior to entry, and relative potential for harm to persons was minimal as result of juvenile's conduct. In re L.D. (Ohio Com.Pl., 11-09-1993) 63 Ohio Misc.2d 303, 626 N.E.2d 709. Infants ⇨ 197

7. Miranda warnings

Where a juvenile is asked to take a polygraph examination as a potential witness to a murder but is not charged, arrested, photographed, fingerprinted or considered a suspect, such juvenile is not in custody and Miranda has no application. In re Johnson, No. 7998 (2d Dist Ct App, Montgomery, 10–25–83).

8. Appeals

Juvenile, who was adjudicated a delinquent child, waived for appellate review claim that the juvenile court erred in admitting victim's in-court identification into evidence, where juvenile failed to file a motion to suppress the identification testimony, failed to object to the identification testimony at trial, and, more importantly, failed to file objections to the magistrate's decision adjudicating him a delinquent child. In re Carter (Ohio App. 4 Dist., Jackson, 12-30-2004) No. 04CA15, No. 04CA16, 2004-Ohio-7285, 2004 WL 3090250, Unreported. Infants ⇐ 243

Father waived his appellate argument that the complaint for permanent custody failed to set forth allegations in compliance with statute, in child dependency proceeding, where father failed to object to the sufficiency of the complaint until ten months after he was first served with the summons and complaint. In re I.M. (Ohio App. 8 Dist., Cuyahoga, 12-24-2003) No. 82669, No. 82695, 2003-Ohio-7069, 2003 WL 23010024, Unreported. Infants ⇐ 243

Juvenile's appeal of trial court's amendment of complaint after adjudicatory hearing in delinquency proceeding, to increase the level of the charged offense, was not "moot," though minimum confinement period for which juvenile could be sentenced had expired, where trial court had not stated a time limit for probation and trial court retained jurisdiction over the juvenile until he reached age of 21. In re Reed (Ohio App. 8 Dist., 01-17-2002) 147 Ohio App.3d 182, 769 N.E.2d 412, 2002-Ohio-43. Infants ⇐ 247

Trial court did not have authority to grant final verdict by dismissing charges in juvenile delinquency proceeding so as to defeat state's right to appeal granting of juveniles' motion to suppress evidence granted during trial; state could appeal from granting of motion to suppress as matter of right. In re Mojica (Ohio App. 8 Dist., 11-20-1995) 107 Ohio App.3d 461, 669 N.E.2d 35. Infants ⇐ 202; Infants ⇐ 242

Where the state has timely filed a notice of appeal from the granting of a motion to suppress, but has failed to make a proper certification as required by Juv R 22(F), a court of appeals may, pursuant to App R 3(E), allow the amendment of the timely filed notice of appeal and certification so that there may be full compliance with Juv R 22(F). In re Hester (Franklin 1981) 1 Ohio App.3d 24, 437 N.E.2d 1218, 1 O.B.R. 85.

Juvenile's appeal of delinquency adjudication and disposition was timely pursuant to rule of appellate procedure requiring filing of notice of appeal within thirty days of service of the notice of judgment and its entry, although notice of appeal was filed more than a year after disposition order was approved and journalized, and juvenile allegedly had actual notice of adjudication and disposition, where there was no evidence that juvenile court served or attempted to serve any of judge's or magistrate's journal entries on juvenile, or, on any other party. In re L.B. (Ohio App. 8 Dist., Cuyahoga, 07-25-2002) No. 79370, No. 79942, 2002-Ohio-3767, 2002 WL 1729905, Unreported. Infants ⇐ 241

Juv R 23 Continuance

Continuances shall be granted only when imperative to secure fair treatment for the parties.

(Adopted eff. 7–1–72)

Editor's Comment

This rule and 2151.22 state the policy that juvenile cases are to be heard and determined as expeditiously as possible. Juvenile courts are divisions of common pleas courts, and a conflicting engagement of counsel in a municipal court or other lower court is not an adequate basis for a continuance in juvenile court.

When a child is in detention or shelter care, Juv R 29(A) provides that the adjudicatory hearing may be continued and detention or shelter care extended upon a showing of good cause.

Juv R 34(A) provides that if the dispositional hearing is held immediately after the adjudicatory hearing, a party may request that the hearing be continued for a reasonable time to obtain or consult counsel.

Cross References

Actions pending at end of term automatically continued, 2151.22

Library References

Infants ⇐204.
Westlaw Topic No. 211.
C.J.S. Infants §§ 51, 52, 62 to 67.

Research References

Encyclopedias
OH Jur. 3d Family Law § 1647, Proceedings Before Referee; Powers and Duties.

Treatises and Practice Aids
Carlin, Baldwin's Ohio Practice, Merrick-Rippner Probate Law § 107:49, Adjudicatory Hearings—Conduct of Hearing by Magistrate.
Giannelli & Yeomans, Ohio Juvenile Law § 24:4, Pretrial Orders.

Notes of Decisions

Hearings 3
Right to counsel 2
Time limitations 1

---

1. Time limitations

Father was not entitled to reversal of trial court judgment terminating parental rights and granting permanent custody to county children services board based on time delay in case due to numerous continuances and extensions; services board was not responsible for all continuances, continuances were based on unavailability of key witnesses, father did not object to all continuances, and father did not file objection to the trial court from the magistrate's grant of continuances. In re Hess (Ohio App. 7 Dist., Jefferson, 03-21-2003) No. 02 JE 37, 2003-Ohio-1429, 2003 WL 1465190, Unreported. Infants ⇐ 243; Infants ⇐ 253

The ten-day period of limitations in Juv R 29(A) is procedural only and such rule confers no substantive right upon an accused to have his case dismissed if he is not tried within the designated time. In re Therklidsen (Franklin 1977) 54 Ohio App.2d 195, 376 N.E.2d 970, 8 O.O.3d 335.

Juvenile's request to call an additional witness at a later time in delinquency proceeding did not constitute a formal request for a continuance. In re Neff (Ohio App. 5 Dist., Tuscarawas, 02-04-2003) No. 2002AP080063, 2003-Ohio-569, 2003 WL 255739, Unreported. Infants ⇐ 204

Juvenile court was warranted in denying juvenile's motion for a continuance to call an additional witness at a later time in the delinquency proceeding, where juvenile did not subpoena witness until three days before trial, and entire trial was completed except for State's calling of the rape victim as a rebuttal witness when juvenile requested the continuance. In re Neff (Ohio App. 5 Dist., Tuscarawas, 02-04-2003) No. 2002AP080063, 2003-Ohio-569, 2003 WL 255739, Unreported. Infants ⇐ 204

Court's refusal to grant juvenile's request for a continuance in aggravated burglary case, on grounds that subpoenas that defense counsel had filed with the clerk's office had not been served, did not violate juvenile's right to compel production of witnesses, where defense counsel did not explain why the witnesses were material, did not give any indication what the testimony would have been, and did not request continuance until shortly before trial was to begin. State v. K.W. (Ohio App. 8 Dist., Cuyahoga, 01-30-2003) No. 80951, 2003-Ohio-425, 2003 WL 194857, Unreported. Infants ⇐ 204

Five and a half month delay between the finding of delinquency and the disposition did not divest the court of jurisdiction; juvenile rule provided that after adjudication a court may continue a matter for disposition for not more than six months, and juvenile did not object to the continuances entered by the court. In re Homan (Ohio App. 5 Dist., Tuscarawas, 01-27-2003) No. 2002AP080067, 2003-Ohio-352, 2003 WL 183811, Unreported. Infants ⇐ 223.1

Extending permanent custody proceedings so that county could present newly discovered evidence was consistent with juvenile code's purpose to provide for the care, protection, and mental and physical development of children, where evidence exposed fact that father had lied to county when he told county that he had no other children, when, in fact, he had another son who resided with him, allegedly had been victim of sexual abuse perpetrated by father and father's brother, and was also a perpetrator of sexual abuse. In re Sullivan (Ohio App. 12 Dist., Butler, 01-21-2003) No. CA2002-03-061, 2003-Ohio-195, 2003 WL 138665, Unreported. Infants ⇐ 207

2. Right to counsel

Denial of father's motion to continue trial on petition to terminate parental rights that was based on his inability to attend due to hospitalization was abuse of discretion, even though father was represented by counsel; much of testimony at trial dealt with issue whether father complied with case plan, and therefore, father's presence at trial was necessary to assist his attorney in cross-examination of witnesses, father's absence was due to matter beyond his control, and father had never before asked for continuance and had attended all other scheduled hearings. In re Edward M. (Ohio App. 6 Dist., Lucas, 06-30-2005) No. L-04-1282, No. L-04-1304, 2005-Ohio-3354, 2005 WL 1532715, Unreported. Infants ⇔ 204

Trial court was not required to continue dispositional hearing arising from minor's adjudication as delinquent to allow county children services board to have counsel present, as nonattorney caseworker could not properly request continuance on behalf of board. In re Lawson (Ohio App. 10 Dist., 11-08-1994) 98 Ohio App.3d 456, 648 N.E.2d 889. Infants ⇔ 204

The guarantee of the right to be represented by counsel set forth in Juv R 4(A) does not, as to a nonindigent party, require that trial be continued indefinitely until counsel can be obtained, but merely requires, if it does not appear that counsel could not be obtained through the exercise of reasonable diligence and a willingness to enter into reasonable contractual arrangements for counsel's services, that a reasonable opportunity be given to the party before trial to employ such counsel. In re Bolden (Allen 1973) 37 Ohio App.2d 7, 306 N.E.2d 166, 66 O.O.2d 26.

3. Hearings

Trial court was not required to continue dispositional hearing arising from minor's adjudication as delinquent at request of county children services board which sought to have expert prepare second psychological report; request for continuance was not properly made because board did not appear as party through counsel at hearing, and minor's need for treatment outweighed need for additional report. In re Lawson (Ohio App. 10 Dist., 11-08-1994) 98 Ohio App.3d 456, 648 N.E.2d 889. Infants ⇔ 204

Where the juvenile court (1) has gone through the process of hearing pursuant to RC 2151.417, (2) has reviewed placement of the child with his mother, and (3) has satisfied itself as to such placement, it is not an abuse of discretion for the court to deny a motion for continuance brought by the child's former custodian. In re Mull, No. 13–96–38, 1997 WL 155412 (3d Dist Ct App, Seneca, 3–24–97).

When a party does not request a continuance of a dispositional hearing which is to be held immediately after an adjudicatory hearing, the court may proceed immediately to disposition. In re Howell, No. 79–CA–16 (5th Dist Ct App, Coshocton, 1–31–80).

Juv R 24   Discovery

(A) Request for discovery

Upon written request, each party of whom discovery is requested shall, to the extent not privileged, produce promptly for inspection, copying, or photographing the following information, documents, and material in that party's custody, control, or possession:

(1) The names and last known addresses of each witness to the occurrence that forms the basis of the charge or defense;

(2) Copies of any written statements made by any party or witness;

(3) Transcriptions, recordings, and summaries of any oral statements of any party or witness, except the work product of counsel;

(4) Any scientific or other reports that a party intends to introduce at the hearing or that pertain to physical evidence that a party intends to introduce;

(5) Photographs and any physical evidence which a party intends to introduce at the hearing;

(6) Except in delinquency and unruly child proceedings, other evidence favorable to the requesting party and relevant to the subject matter involved in the pending action. In delinquency and unruly child proceedings, the prosecuting attorney shall disclose to respondent's counsel all evidence, known or that may become known to the prosecuting attorney, favorable to the respondent and material either to guilt or punishment.

(B) Order granting discovery: limitations; sanctions

If a request for discovery is refused, application may be made to the court for a written order granting the discovery. Motions for discovery shall certify that a request for discovery has been made and refused. An order granting discovery may make such discovery reciprocal for all parties to the proceeding, including the party requesting discovery. Notwithstanding the provisions of subdivision (A), the court may deny, in whole or part, or otherwise limit or set conditions on the discovery authorized by such subdivision, upon its own motion, or upon a showing by a party upon whom a request for discovery is made that granting discovery may jeopardize the safety of a party, witness, or confidential informant, result in the production of perjured testimony or evidence, endanger the existence of physical evidence, violate a privileged communication, or impede the criminal prosecution of a minor as an adult or of an adult charged with an offense arising from the same transaction or occurrence.

(C) Failure to comply

If at any time during the course of the proceedings it is brought to the attention of the court that a person has failed to comply with an order issued pursuant to this rule, the court may grant a continuance, prohibit the person from introducing in evidence the material not disclosed, or enter such other order as it deems just under the circumstances.

(Adopted eff. 7–1–72; amended eff. 7–1–94)

Historical and Statutory Notes

Amendment Note: The 7–1–94 amendment substituted "promptly" for "forthwith", inserted ", to the extent not privileged," and made changes to reflect gender-neutral language in the first paragraph of division (A); and added division (A)(6).

Staff Notes

1994:

Rule 24 Discovery

Juv. R. 24 governs the scope of discovery. It adds a new category under Juv. R. 24(A)(6) permitting the requesting party to discover relevant evidence which is favorable to the requesting party, except that in delinquency and unruly child proceedings, the requirement imposed upon prosecuting attorneys is to disclose only such favorable evidence which is material to guilt or punishment of the respondent. All categories of discovery are subject to the assertion of a privilege.

Editor's Comment

Request for discovery   1
Order granting discovery: limitations; sanctions   2
Failure to comply   3

1. Request for discovery

Juv R 24(A) establishes a procedure similar to that under Crim R 16(A), by which the discovery of non-privileged information, documents, and material authorized by the rule is to proceed upon request of one party upon another, without prior court order. Discovery of social histories prepared by the court is governed by Juv R 32.

Juv R 24(A)(1) is similar to Crim R 16(B)(1)(e), requiring the production of occurrence witnesses' names and addresses. The protection against witness harassment contained in Crim R 16(B)(1)(e) is provided in Division (B) of the Juvenile Rule.

Juv R 24(A)(2) and (3), requiring the production of transcriptions, recordings and summaries of witnesses' oral statements, authorizes broader discovery than would be available under Crim R 16(B)(1)(c). The scope of its coverage is similar to that contained in Civ R 34.

Juv R 24(A)(4) authorizes production of scientific reports, and is similar to the discovery allowed by Crim R 16(B)(1)(d).

Juv R 24(A)(5), authorizing discovery of photographs and physical evidence intended for use at a hearing, is similar to Crim R 16(B)(1)(c).

Juv R 24(A)(6), requiring the disclosure of all favorable evidence, is similar to Crim R 16(B)(1)(f).

2. Order granting discovery: limitations; sanctions

Juv R 24(B) regulates the procedure by which discovery can be obtained by court order, in the event that the person upon whom discovery is made refuses to comply with a request for discovery. It contains the restrictions of Crim R 16(B)(1)(e), which protects against witness harassment, and it provides additional protections against abuse of the discovery process. It is an effort to anticipate the main objections to broad discovery, and provide a procedure by which the discovery authorized in Division (A) can be effectuated fairly and expeditiously.

3. Failure to comply

Juv R 24(C) provides for remedies where an order for discovery has not been complied with.

The rule gives the court the power to deny in whole or in part or otherwise limit or set conditions regarding discovery either on its own motion or upon the motion of a party showing that the discovery requested may jeopardize the safety of a party, witness, or a confidential informant; result in production of perjured testimony or evidence; endanger the existence of physical evidence; violate a privileged communication; or impede the criminal prosecution of a minor or adult charged with an offense arising from the same transaction or occurrence.

The rule adopts the liberal discovery philosophy of the federal rules and is very similar to that expressed in *Ex Parte Oliver*, 173 OS 125, 180 NE(2d) 599 (1962). In this case the Supreme Court noted "any discovery proceeding... has inherent in it the possibility of revealing information or data helpful to one side or another even though such information or data would be inadmissible in a subsequent trial. Any disadvantage to one party from another's gaining such information is offset, however, by the possible advantage therefrom of arriving at the truth of the situation, which is, and must remain, the ultimate goal...." (*See* Civ R 26.)

Policies considered as supportive of the broad discovery of this rule include the following: the "open file" approach conforms to general, but informal practice in our juvenile courts; discovery along the lines suggested by the rule reduces the adversary quality of the hearings; the hearing process will be expedited; and regulation of discovery by rules will avoid litigation on the issue.

Cross References

Discovery and inspection, Crim R 16
General provisions governing discovery, Civ R 26
Production of documents and things for inspection, copying, testing and entry upon land for inspection and other purposes, Civ R 34

Library References

Infants ⇌201.
Westlaw Topic No. 211.
C.J.S. Infants §§ 42, 53, 54.

Research References

Encyclopedias

OH Jur. 3d Criminal Law § 368, Obtaining of Information; Disclosure and Discovery—Deliberate Suppression of Evidence; Loss or Destruction of Evidence Favorable to Defendant.
OH Jur. 3d Criminal Law § 2527, Discovery Under Discovery Rule.
OH Jur. 3d Family Law § 1562, Notice and Hearing.
OH Jur. 3d Family Law § 1642, Request for Discovery.
OH Jur. 3d Family Law § 1643, Motion and Order for Discovery.
OH Jur. 3d Family Law § 1644, Motion and Order for Discovery—Failure to Comply With Order for Discovery.
OH Jur. 3d Family Law § 1647, Proceedings Before Referee; Powers and Duties.

Treatises and Practice Aids

Katz, Giannelli, Blair and Lipton, Baldwin's Ohio Practice, Criminal Law, § 49:1, Introduction.
Carlin, Baldwin's Ohio Practice, Merrick-Rippner Probate Law § 107:32, Discovery in Juvenile Proceedings—Information in Possession of Adverse Party—Motion for Discovery.
Carlin, Baldwin's Ohio Practice, Merrick-Rippner Probate Law § 107:33, Restricting And/Or Enforcing Discovery.
Carlin, Baldwin's Ohio Practice, Merrick-Rippner Probate Law § 107:49, Adjudicatory Hearings—Conduct of Hearing by Magistrate.
Carlin, Baldwin's Ohio Practice, Merrick-Rippner Probate Law § 107:67, Procedural Due Process Requirements in Transfer Proceedings.
Carlin, Baldwin's Ohio Practice, Merrick-Rippner Probate Law § 107:156, Request for Discovery in Abuse, Neglect, or Dependency Case—Form.
Carlin, Baldwin's Ohio Practice, Merrick-Rippner Probate Law § 107:157, Motion for Discovery—Form.
Giannelli & Yeomans, Ohio Juvenile Law § 15:2, Intake.
Giannelli & Yeomans, Ohio Juvenile Law § 21:2, Scope of Discovery; Rule 24.
Giannelli & Yeomans, Ohio Juvenile Law § 21:3, Discovery Procedure; Rule 24.
Giannelli & Yeomans, Ohio Juvenile Law § 21:6, Social History Report.
Giannelli & Yeomans, Ohio Juvenile Law § 24:4, Pretrial Orders.
Giannelli & Yeomans, Ohio Juvenile Law App. D, Appendix D. Glossary.
Giannelli & Yeomans, Ohio Juvenile Law § 22:15, Access to Reports & Discovery.

Notes of Decisions

Access to records 4
Appeals 8
Failure to comply 5
Final orders 1
Limitations on discovery 2
Orders compelling discovery 7
Subpoenas 3
Witness' statement 6

---

1. Final orders

Under the discovery provisions of the Civil Rules, the court has a discretionary power, not a ministerial duty; an interlocutory order, overruling a motion to compel answers to interrogatories involving opinions, contentions, and legal conclusions, is not a final appealable order. State ex rel. Daggett v. Gessaman (Ohio 1973) 34 Ohio St.2d 55, 295 N.E.2d 659, 63 O.O.2d 88.

2. Limitations on discovery

A prosecutor is under a duty, imposed by the due process clauses of the state and federal constitutions and by the rule governing discovery in juvenile proceedings, to disclose to a juvenile respondent all evidence in the state's possession favorable to the juvenile respondent and material either to guilt or punishment that is known at the time of a mandatory bindover hearing and that may become known to the prosecuting attorney after the bindover. State v. Iacona (Ohio, 08-29-2001) 93 Ohio St.3d 83, 752 N.E.2d 937, 2001-Ohio-1292, on remand 2002 WL 208073. Constitutional Law ⇌ 255(4); Infants ⇌ 68.7(3)

The juvenile court is authorized, upon a proper showing, to limit discovery. In re A.M. (Ohio App. 8 Dist., 09-05-2000) 139 Ohio App.3d 303, 743 N.E.2d 937, appeal not allowed 91 Ohio St.3d 1431, 741 N.E.2d 895. Infants ⇌ 201

Juv R 24 does not permit discovery of police reports in delinquency cases. In re Hunter, No. 46019 (8th Dist Ct App, Cuyahoga, 4–5–84).

A social worker may not be compelled to reveal the name of the person who reported an instance of child abuse since such information is confidential under RC 2151.421. In re Hicks, No. H–78–7 (6th Dist Ct App, Huron, 11–17–78).

Justification existed for limiting juvenile's discovery on motion to transfer juvenile delinquency proceedings to criminal court for trial as adult, where five individuals had been formally charged with offenses arising from same transaction which formed basis of complaint filed against juvenile, two of whom were adults and two of whom had transfer proceedings pending, and granting full discovery might impede criminal prosecution of adult codefendants and potential criminal prosecution of child and his alleged codelinquent. In re Doss (Ohio Com.Pl., 05-11-1994) 65 Ohio Misc.2d 8, 640 N.E.2d 618. Infants ⇌ 68.7(1)

Although rule is generally move expansive than statute governing discovery in juvenile delinquency proceedings, nature of proceedings for which discovery is sought is relevant in determining extent to which discovery will be granted under rule. In re Doss (Ohio Com.Pl., 05-11-1994) 65 Ohio Misc.2d 8, 640 N.E.2d 618. Infants ⇌ 201

Order limiting scope of mother's discovery with respect to guardian ad litem did not deprive mother of right to prepare for trial, in proceedings to place mother's children in permanent custody of county children's services board; mother's discovery requests were overly broad and went beyond scope of allowable discovery, mother did not bring any discrepancies in guardian ad litem's information to court's attention, and mother never called guardian ad litem to testify at hearing. In re Adams (Ohio App. 2 Dist., Miami, 02-07-2003) No. 2002 CA 45, 2003-Ohio-618, 2003 WL 264357, Unreported. Infants ⇐ 201

3. Subpoenas

Where the parents of an alleged dependent child have filed a praecipe for a subpoena duces tecum of a children services board (the party filing the complaint) seeking to obtain or view the agency's records, it is error for the court to sustain a motion to quash the subpoena on the basis that the records are privileged and confidential; the court should allow counsel for the parents reasonable access to the files in order to use the parts which are relevant to the issues being presented to the court. In re Barzak (Trumbull 1985) 24 Ohio App.3d 180, 493 N.E.2d 1011, 24 O.B.R. 270.

4. Access to records

RC Ch 1347 and Ch 5153 do not conflict, and these chapters impose upon the keeper of the files of the county children services board an obligation to provide reasonable access to them for inspection by an involved party. In re Trumbull County Children Services Bd. (Ohio Com.Pl. 1986) 32 Ohio Misc.2d 11, 513 N.E.2d 360.

5. Failure to comply

Mother waived for appellate review issue as to whether County Children Services Board (CCSB) violated Americans with Disabilities Act (ADA) by failing to provide mother reasonable accommodations for her personality disorder throughout parental rights termination proceedings, where mother failed to raise issue at trial. In re Ratliff (Ohio App. 10 Dist., Franklin, 03-24-2005) No. 04AP-803, 2005-Ohio-1301, 2005 WL 675798, Unreported, appeal not allowed 106 Ohio St.3d 1417, 830 N.E.2d 348, 2005-Ohio-3154. Infants ⇐ 243

Children's treating therapist was properly allowed to testify at proceeding on county children services agency's motion to modify temporary custody to permanent custody, even though she was not on agency's witness list, since this list had been provided prior to her involvement in the case and included the name of the prior treating therapist. In re J.L. (Ohio App. 8 Dist., Cuyahoga, 11-10-2004) No. 84368, 2004-Ohio-6024, 2004 WL 2578874, Unreported, appeal not allowed 104 Ohio St.3d 1463, 821 N.E.2d 578, 2005-Ohio-204. Infants ⇐ 201

At mandatory bindover proceedings involving juvenile who allegedly murdered her newborn child, state committed *Brady* violation by not providing child's blood culture laboratory report, which indicated the presence of a potentially deadly bacterium, to the defense in time for use at the hearing. State v. Iacona (Ohio, 08-29-2001) 93 Ohio St.3d 83, 752 N.E.2d 937, 2001-Ohio-1292, on remand 2002 WL 208073. Infants ⇐ 68.7(3)

At mandatory bindover proceedings involving juvenile who allegedly murdered her newborn child, reversible error did not occur through state's committing *Brady* violation by not providing child's blood culture laboratory report, which indicated the presence of a potentially deadly bacterium, to the defense in time for use at the hearing, as trial court would have found probable cause even if juvenile possessed report. State v. Iacona (Ohio, 08-29-2001) 93 Ohio St.3d 83, 752 N.E.2d 937, 2001-Ohio-1292, on remand 2002 WL 208073. Infants ⇐ 68.8

In prosecution of defendant for involuntary manslaughter of her newborn child, state did not conceal significance of child's blood culture laboratory report, which indicated the presence of a potentially deadly bacterium, that it provided during pretrial discovery, even though faxed copy of report was unclear and hand-delivered copy was less-than-perfect. State v. Iacona (Ohio, 08-29-2001) 93 Ohio St.3d 83, 752 N.E.2d 937, 2001-Ohio-1292, on remand 2002 WL 208073. Criminal Law ⇐ 700(3)

Where a party fails to comply with a court order for discovery, the party seeking discovery must request the proper remedial order from the court in order to obtain such remedies. In re Hester (Franklin 1982) 3 Ohio App.3d 458, 446 N.E.2d 202, 3 O.B.R. 539.

In termination of parental rights case, juvenile court properly refused father's motion in limine to exclude testimony from clinical psychologist and case worker because state failed to respond to father's request for documents, as father never filed a motion to compel discovery, but instead waited until the day of the permanent custody hearing, which was nearly two weeks after the filing of his document request, to raise the issue with the court for the first time. In re Funk (Ohio App. 11 Dist., Portage, 09-20-2002) No. 2002-P-0035, No. 2002-P-0036, 2002-Ohio-4958, 2002 WL 31107531, Unreported. Infants ⇐ 173.1

Where discovery is not provided until immediately before the adjudicatory hearing and the party who requested it agrees to proceed with the hearing after reviewing the material, the party may not claim on appeal that he was denied discovery. In re Wyrock, Nos. 41827, 41828, and 41904 (8th Dist Ct App, Cuyahoga, 10–23–80).

6. Witness' statement

Under juvenile procedure rule and upon timely request, juvenile charged with rape was entitled to production of complaining witness' narrative to police on date of alleged offense, even though narrative was not signed by witness and was not taken verbatim. In re Johnson (Cuyahoga 1989) 61 Ohio App.3d 544, 573 N.E.2d 184. Infants ⇐ 201

There is nothing in Juv R 24 mandating the witness' signature on a narrative, nor does that rule specify that the statement must be taken verbatim. In re Johnson, No. 55204 (8th Dist Ct App, Cuyahoga, 3–23–89).

7. Orders compelling discovery

Juvenile court did not abuse its discretion in denying paternal uncle and aunt's motion to preclude witnesses and exclude evidence as discovery sanction in proceeding to determine legal custody of child who had been found dependent and removed from his biological parents' care, where uncle and aunt filed their discovery request 14 days before a scheduled hearing, never moved for a motion to compel the requested discovery, and never requested any sanction other than exclusion of the evidence subject to the discovery request. In re Halstead (Ohio App. 7 Dist., Columbiana, 01-27-2005) No. 04 CO 37, 2005-Ohio-403, 2005 WL 289576, Unreported. Infants ⇐ 201

Juvenile was entitled to discovery prior to hearing to determine whether juvenile would be tried in adult court, even though discovery available under juvenile rule was more expansive than that which was available to adult, as hearing was critically important, and juvenile had legitimate interest in discovering evidence that prosecutor would offer to establish probable cause mandating transfer. In re A.M. (Ohio App. 8 Dist., 09-05-2000) 139 Ohio App.3d 303, 743 N.E.2d 937, appeal not allowed 91 Ohio St.3d 1431, 741 N.E.2d 895. Infants ⇐ 68.7(3)

Because Juv R 24 contains no requirement that disclosures be updated, a party seeking current information must either repeat the discovery request or move for an order compelling discovery pursuant to Juv R 24(B). In re Gilbert, No. CA 86–10–144 (12th Dist Ct App, Butler, 9–28–87).

Rule requiring the state to respond to discovery requests in juvenile matters applies to "mandatory bindover" or waiver of jurisdiction proceedings wherein the court determines whether probable cause exists to transfer the matter for prosecution of the juvenile as an adult. In re A.M. (Ohio Com.Pl., 05-28-1998) 92 Ohio Misc.2d 4, 699 N.E.2d 574, affirmed 139 Ohio App.3d 303, 743 N.E.2d 937, appeal not allowed 91 Ohio St.3d 1431, 741 N.E.2d 895. Infants ⇐ 68.7(3)

8. Appeals

The failure to file a motion for discovery estops a party from thereafter raising the issue on appeal. State v Lee, No. 44902 (8th Dist Ct App, Cuyahoga, 2–10–83).

Juv R 25   Depositions

The court upon good cause shown may grant authority to take the deposition of a party or other person upon such terms and conditions and in such manner as the court may fix.

(Adopted eff. 7–1–72)

Editor's Comment

The rule provides that a request to take a deposition in a juvenile proceeding is within the sound discretion of the court and shall be granted only upon a showing of good cause. If the deposition is ordered, the court shall determine the procedure for notice, attendance, time and place. This rule has no statutory basis, though it is based generally on 2945.50 and Crim R 15. The authority of the court to take videotaped depositions in abuse cases is governed by 2151.35(G).

Cross References

Deposition, Crim R 15
Perpetuation of testimony, depositions before action or pending appeal, Civ R 27

Library References

Infants ⚖=201.
Westlaw Topic No. 211.
C.J.S. Infants §§ 42, 53, 54.

Research References

Encyclopedias

OH Jur. 3d Family Law § 1621, to Take Deposition.
OH Jur. 3d Family Law § 1641, Depositions.
OH Jur. 3d Family Law § 1647, Proceedings Before Referee; Powers and Duties.

Treatises and Practice Aids

Giannelli and Snyder, Baldwin's Ohio Practice, Evidence, § 804.8, Unavailability: Unable to Procure Testimony.
Giannelli and Snyder, Baldwin's Ohio Practice, Evidence, § 804.10, Former Testimony: Type of Proceeding.
Carlin, Baldwin's Ohio Practice, Merrick-Rippner Probate Law § 107:35, Depositions in Juvenile Proceedings.
Carlin, Baldwin's Ohio Practice, Merrick-Rippner Probate Law § 107:49, Adjudicatory Hearings—Conduct of Hearing by Magistrate.
Giannelli & Yeomans, Ohio Juvenile Law § 21:4, Depositions.
Giannelli & Yeomans, Ohio Juvenile Law § 24:4, Pretrial Orders.
Giannelli & Yeomans, Ohio Juvenile Law § 33:8, Contempt.

Notes of Decisions

Contempt of court 1
Procedures 2

1. Contempt of court

Where the mother of a child who is the subject of a dependency action fails to answer deposition questions after being granted immunity under RC 2945.44, she may be held in contempt of court. In re Poth (Huron 1981) 2 Ohio App.3d 361, 442 N.E.2d 105, 2 O.B.R. 417.

2. Procedures

The trial court has discretion to allow or disallow depositions and to control the manner and terms under which depositions are taken. In re Vaughn, No. CA89-11-162 (12th Dist Ct App, Butler, 8-13-90).

Admission of deposition of psychologist was not an abuse of discretion, in child dependency proceeding; psychologist qualified as a medical expert, the rules of civil procedure provided that the deposition of a medical expert was admissible as if the expert were present and testifying, defense counsel was present during psychologist's deposition and had an opportunity to cross-examine him, and defendant was not precluded from calling the psychologist to testify at the hearing. In re Mraz (Ohio App. 12 Dist., Brown, 12-30-2002) No. CA2002-05-011, No. CA2002-07-014, 2002-Ohio-7278, 2002 WL 31883343, Unreported. Infants ⚖= 173.1

Juv R 26 [Reserved]

Juv R 27 Hearings: general

(A) General provisions

Unless otherwise stated in this rule, the juvenile court may conduct its hearings in an informal manner and may adjourn its hearings from time to time.

The court may excuse the attendance of the child at the hearing in neglect, dependency, or abuse cases.

(1) Public access to hearings. In serious youthful offender proceedings, hearings shall be open to the public. In all other proceedings, the court may exclude the general public from any hearing, but may not exclude either of the following:

(a) persons with a direct interest in the case;

(b) persons who demonstrate, at a hearing, a countervailing right to be present.

(2) Separation of juvenile and adult cases. Cases involving children shall be heard separate and apart from the trial of cases against adults, except for cases involving chronic or habitual truancy.

(3) Jury trials. The court shall hear and determine all cases of children without a jury, except for the adjudication of a serious youthful offender complaint, indictment, or information in which trial by jury has not been waived.

Unless otherwise stated in this rule, the juvenile court may conduct its hearings in an informal manner and may adjourn its hearings from time to time.

The court may excuse the attendance of the child at the hearing in neglect, dependency, or abuse cases.

(B) Special provisions for abuse, neglect, and dependency proceedings

(1) In any proceeding involving abuse, neglect, or dependency at which the court removes a child from the child's home or continues the removal of a child from the child's home, or in a proceeding where the court orders detention, the court shall determine whether the person who filed the complaint in the case and removed the child from the child's home has custody of the child or will be given custody and has made reasonable efforts to do any of the following:

(a) Prevent the removal of the child from the child's home;

(b) Eliminate the continued removal of the child from the child's home;

(c) Make it possible for the child to return home.

(2) In a proceeding involving abuse, neglect, or dependency, the examination made by the court to determine whether a child is a competent witness shall comply with all of the following:

(a) Occur in an area other than a courtroom or hearing room;

(b) Be conducted in the presence of only those individuals considered necessary by the court for the conduct of the examination or the well being of the child;

(c) Be recorded in accordance with Juv. R. 37 or Juv. R. 40. The court may allow the prosecutor, guardian ad litem, or attorney for any party to submit questions for use by the court in determining whether the child is a competent witness.

(3) In a proceeding where a child is alleged to be an abused child, the court may order that the testimony of the child be taken by deposition in the presence of a judge or a magistrate. On motion of the prosecuting attorney, guardian ad litem, or a party, or in its own discretion, the court may order that the deposition be videotaped. All or part of the deposition is admissible in evidence where all of the following apply:

(a) It is filed with the clerk;

(b) Counsel for all parties had an opportunity and similar motive at the time of the taking of the deposition to develop the testimony by direct, cross, or redirect examination;

(c) The judge or magistrate determines there is reasonable cause to believe that if the child were to testify in person at the hearing, the child would experience emotional trauma as a result of the child's participation at the hearing.

(Adopted eff. 7-1-72; amended eff. 7-1-76, 7-1-94, 7-1-96, 7-1-01)

Historical and Statutory Notes

Amendment Note: The 7-1-01 amendment rewrote division (A), which prior thereto read:

"The juvenile court may conduct its hearings in an informal manner and may adjourn its hearings from time to time. In the hearing of any case the general public may be excluded and only persons admitted who have a direct interest in the case.

"All cases involving children shall be heard separate and apart from the trial of cases against adults. The court may excuse the attendance of the child at the hearing in neglect, dependency or abuse cases. The court shall hear and determine all cases of children without a jury."; the amendment further inserted "for abuse, neglect, and dependency proceedings" to the caption of division (B).

Amendment Note: The 7–1–96 amendment substituted "magistrate" for "referee" throughout division (B)(3).

Amendment Note: The 7–1–94 amendment designated division (A) and added division (B).

Staff Notes

2001:

Rule 27(A) General provisions

Rule 27(A) was completely rewritten and reorganized to conform to changes necessitated by Sub. Sen. Bill 179 (serious youthful offenders) (effective date January 1, 2002), and Sub. Sen. Bill 181 (chronic and habitual truants) (effective date September 4, 2000).

Rule 27(A) as amended deals separately with the informality of hearings [division (A)], public access to hearings [division (A)(1)], separation of juvenile and adult cases [division (A)(2)], and jury trials [division (A)(3)].

Division (A)(1) clarifies that in serious youthful offender proceedings, adult rules about public access shall apply, and thus a qualified presumption of public access is appropriate. The rule seeks to conform to the Supreme Court's ruling in *State ex rel. New World Communications of Ohio, Inc. v. Geauga County Court of Common Pleas, Juvenile Division* (2000), 90 Ohio St. 3d 79, 734 N.E.2d 1214. In juvenile proceedings, there is no qualified right of public access, and no presumption that the proceedings be either open or closed. The amended rule recognizes that the policies of confidentiality and rehabilitation important in juvenile proceedings may justify closure to those without a direct interest after a hearing. In that hearing, the party seeking closure bears the burden of proof, but Rule 27(A)(1)(b) clarifies that closure is justified unless there is a "comparable competing interest" for public access, which the rule describes as a countervailing right. The amendment also conforms to Revised Code section 2151.35 (A) as amended by Sub. Sen. Bill 179.

Rule 27(A)(2) conforms to Revised Code section 2151.35 (A)(1), which provides that in cases in which both a child and an adult are charged for chronic or habitual truancy, the cases need not be heard separately, while preserving separate proceedings in all other cases.

Rule 27(A)(3) conforms to Revised Code section 2152.13(D) providing for a jury determination in cases seeking a serious youthful offender dispositional sentence, while preserving nonjury proceedings in all other cases.

Rule 27(B) Special Provisions for Abuse, Neglect, and Dependency Proceedings

Rule 27(B) was not amended, but was recaptioned to clarify that its provisions apply to abuse, neglect and dependency proceedings.

1996:

The amendment changed the rule's reference from "referee" to "magistrate" in division (B)(3) and (B)(3)(c) in order to harmonize the rule with the language adopted in the 1995 amendments to Juv. R. 40. The amendment is technical only and no substantive change is intended.

1994:

Rule 27 Hearings: General

S.B. 89 set forth several additional criteria to be observed in the course of hearings in juvenile court. The revisions to Juv. R. 27 reflect the general policy of that legislation to protect children and to assure that all reasonable measures have been taken to keep children with their original families.

Juv. R. 27(B)(1) specifies the "reasonable efforts" determination necessary to assure that, as much as possible, children can remain with their families or return to them without undue trauma. Revised Code 2151.419.

Juv. R. 27(B)(1)[1] sets forth the requirements of the court's determination as to whether a child is a competent witness. Revised Code 2317.01.

[1] So in original; should this read "Juv. R. 27(B)(2)"?

Juv. R. 27(B)(3) details a procedure to permit a child's testimony to be taken by deposition in the presence of a judge or a referee. Revised Code 2151.35(G).

Editor's Comment

Juv R 27(A) is identical to the first two paragraphs of 2151.35(A) and provides for informal hearings and continuances of hearings. Continuances should only be granted for good cause shown. (*See* Juv R 23.) Privacy of the hearings is essential and in the best interest of the child, but the rule gives the court discretion in permitting persons admission to the hearing.

It is important to separate children's hearings from adult trials to avoid the taint of criminality and to serve the best interest of the child while still affording protection to the community.

The provision permitting the court to excuse the attendance of the child at neglect, dependency, and abuse hearings is advisable as many of the children involved are of tender age and unable to participate in the hearing. Where the child may be older, the question of disruption of the parental relationship is important and must be considered by the court.

The denial of the right to a jury in juvenile proceedings has been held to be constitutionally permissible by the U.S. Supreme Court. *See McKeiver, et al v Pennsylvania,* 403 US 528, 91 SCt 1976, 29 LEd(2d) 647 (1971). In this case, the U.S. Supreme Court held "the applicable due process standard in juvenile proceedings is fundamental fairness as developed in *In re Gault,* 387 US 1, 87 SCt 1428, 18 LEd(2d) 527 (1967), and *In re Winship,* 397 US 358, 90 SCt 1068, 25 LEd(2d) 368 (1970), which emphasized factfinding procedures, but in our legal system, the jury is not a necessary component of accurate fact finding." The court further stated: "Equating the adjudicative phase of the juvenile proceeding with a criminal trial ignores the aspect of fairness, concern, sympathy and paternal attention inherent in the juvenile court system."

Juv R 27(B) applies to abuse, neglect, and dependency proceedings. Division (B)(1), requiring a "reasonable efforts" determination, is taken from 2151.419. Division (B)(2), which deals with the competency of children as witnesses, is taken from 2317.01. Division (B)(3), permitting a child's testimony to be taken by deposition, is taken from 2151.35(G).

Cross References

Charges against adults, 2151.43
Hearing on abortion without parental consent, 2151.85
Hearing procedures; findings, record, 2151.35
Release of child from youth services department institution, 2151.38

Library References

Infants ⇔68.7(3), 203, 204.
Westlaw Topic No. 211.
C.J.S. Infants §§ 46 to 67.

Research References

ALR Library
39 ALR 5th 103, Propriety of Exclusion of Press or Other Media Representatives from Civil Trial.

Encyclopedias
OH Jur. 3d Courts & Judges § 18, Courts of Common Pleas—Juvenile Division and Juvenile Courts.
OH Jur. 3d Evidence & Witnesses § 723, Duty of Court; Determination of Competency.
OH Jur. 3d Family Law § 1578, Detention Hearing; Notice—Evidence and Order.
OH Jur. 3d Family Law § 1647, Proceedings Before Referee; Powers and Duties.
OH Jur. 3d Family Law § 1654, Determination of Reasonable Efforts.
OH Jur. 3d Family Law § 1655, Right to Attend; Public or Private Hearing.
OH Jur. 3d Family Law § 1656, Right to Jury Trial.
OH Jur. 3d Family Law § 1672, Testimony of Child.

Treatises and Practice Aids
Carlin, Baldwin's Ohio Practice, Merrick-Rippner Probate Law § 104:5, Juvenile Courts—Constitutional Issues—Right to Notice, Counsel, and Trial.
Carlin, Baldwin's Ohio Practice, Merrick-Rippner Probate Law § 107:47, Adjudicatory Hearings—Hearing Without a Jury.

Carlin, Baldwin's Ohio Practice, Merrick-Rippner Probate Law § 107:49, Adjudicatory Hearings—Conduct of Hearing by Magistrate.

Carlin, Baldwin's Ohio Practice, Merrick-Rippner Probate Law § 107:50, Adjudicatory Hearings—Applicability of Rules of Court.

Carlin, Baldwin's Ohio Practice, Merrick-Rippner Probate Law § 107:52, Adjudicatory Hearings—Confidentiality of Juvenile Court Proceedings.

Carlin, Baldwin's Ohio Practice, Merrick-Rippner Probate Law § 107:56, Adjudicatory Hearings—Attendance of Parties at Hearing.

Giannelli & Yeomans, Ohio Juvenile Law § 1:8, Rules of Juvenile Procedure.

Giannelli & Yeomans, Ohio Juvenile Law § 5:6, Syo Adjudicatory Hearing.

Giannelli & Yeomans, Ohio Juvenile Law § 18:2, Issuance of Summons: Proper Parties.

Giannelli & Yeomans, Ohio Juvenile Law § 19:6, Standard for Detention.

Giannelli & Yeomans, Ohio Juvenile Law § 21:4, Depositions.

Giannelli & Yeomans, Ohio Juvenile Law § 24:4, Pretrial Orders.

Giannelli & Yeomans, Ohio Juvenile Law § 25:5, Right to Attend Dispositional Hearing.

Giannelli & Yeomans, Ohio Juvenile Law § 25:6, Conduct of Hearing.

Giannelli & Yeomans, Ohio Juvenile Law § 35:2, Confidentiality Requirement.

Giannelli & Yeomans, Ohio Juvenile Law § 19:12, Closure of Hearing.

Giannelli & Yeomans, Ohio Juvenile Law § 22:19, Public Hearing; Victims; Gag Orders.

Giannelli & Yeomans, Ohio Juvenile Law § 23:10, Jury Trials.

Giannelli & Yeomans, Ohio Juvenile Law § 23:11, Public Trials; Gag Orders.

Giannelli & Yeomans, Ohio Juvenile Law § 23:18, Evidence—Competency of Witnesses.

Giannelli & Yeomans, Ohio Juvenile Law § 23:23, Confrontation—Face-To-Face Confrontation.

Giannelli & Yeomans, Ohio Juvenile Law § 23:24, Confrontation—Cross-Examination.

Giannelli & Yeomans, Ohio Juvenile Law § 23:32, Juvenile & Adult Cases; Truancy.

Giannelli & Yeomans, Ohio Juvenile Law § 25:14, Reasonable Efforts Determination; Abuse, Neglect & Dependency.

Law Review and Journal Commentaries

Confidentiality of Juvenile Court Proceedings, William A. Kurtz. 1 Prob L J Ohio 115 (May/June 1991).

The Effect of the Double Jeopardy Clause on Juvenile Proceedings, James G. Carr. 6 U Tol L Rev 1 (Fall 1974).

In re T.R.: Not In Front of the Children, Bill Dickhaut. 1 Ky Children's Rts J 10 (July 1991).

Interviewing Child Victims/Witnesses, Mary A. Lentz. 9 Baldwin's Ohio Sch L J 25 (July/August 1997).

Interviewing the child witness: Do's and don't's, how's and why's, Nancy E. Walker and Matthew Nguyen. 29 Creighton L Rev 1587 (1996).

Notes of Decisions

Constitutional issues 2
Discretion of court 4
Equitable actions 1
Public access 3

---

1. Equitable actions

It is within the discretion of a juvenile court judge to determine whether or not to close from the general public a hearing on the transfer of jurisdiction from the juvenile division to the court of common pleas, and thus a writ of prohibition to prevent the judge from conducting an open hearing will not lie. State ex rel. Fyffe v. Pierce (Ohio 1988) 40 Ohio St.3d 8, 531 N.E.2d 673.

2. Constitutional issues

Juvenile procedure rule that no public use shall be made by any person of any juvenile court record must yield when it impinges on the public's due process right to a meaningful hearing on a motion to close proceedings. State ex rel. Plain Dealer Publishing Co. v. Floyd (Ohio, 08-30-2006) 111 Ohio St.3d 56, 855 N.E.2d 35, 2006-Ohio-4437. Infants ⇌ 203

At closure hearing in juvenile proceeding, court may entertain summaries of testimony by witnesses who may subsequently testify at permanent commitment hearing, resolution of closure issues may be predicated upon those summaries, and the rules of evidence are necessarily relaxed to allow the presentation of the information in summary form. State ex rel. Dispatch Printing Co. v. Lias (Ohio, 03-23-1994) 68 Ohio St.3d 497, 628 N.E.2d 1368, 1994-Ohio-335. Infants ⇌ 203

Juvenile court did not violate double jeopardy principles when, after defendant began serving sentence, it issued amended sentencing entry and nunc pro tunc entry which corrected its original sentencing entry, which erroneously indicated that defendant's sentence had been suspended, to reflect juvenile court's actual decision at sentencing hearing that sentence was not suspended. State v. Parsons (Ohio App. 12 Dist., 08-04-1997) 122 Ohio App.3d 284, 701 N.E.2d 732. Double Jeopardy ⇌ 33

Due process clause of Fourteenth Amendment applies when child is charged with misconduct for which he may be incarcerated in institution, so child is entitled to notice of charges, counsel, confrontation and cross-examination, and privilege against self-incrimination. In re Jason R. (Ohio Com.Pl., 12-14-1995) 77 Ohio Misc.2d 37, 666 N.E.2d 666. Constitutional Law ⇌ 255(4)

Proceeding with dispositional hearing in juvenile's absence did not violate due process; juvenile effectively waived his right to be present, as he had notice of hearing but blatantly disregarded it. In re Jason R. (Ohio Com.Pl., 12-14-1995) 77 Ohio Misc.2d 37, 666 N.E.2d 666. Constitutional Law ⇌ 255(4); Infants ⇌ 203

Right to be present at every stage of trial, as encompassed by right of confrontation, applies to both adult criminal trials and juvenile proceedings. In re Jason R. (Ohio Com.Pl., 12-14-1995) 77 Ohio Misc.2d 37, 666 N.E.2d 666. Criminal Law ⇌ 662.70; Infants ⇌ 203; Infants ⇌ 207

Although juvenile's right to be present at dispositional hearing was implied by rule stating that court may excuse attendance of child at hearing in neglect, dependency, or abuse cases, and rule requiring court at conclusion of dispositional hearing to advise child of child's right to record expungement and right to appeal, juvenile nonetheless waived his right to be present at dispositional hearing by blatantly disregarding it after receiving adequate notice. In re Jason R. (Ohio Com.Pl., 12-14-1995) 77 Ohio Misc.2d 37, 666 N.E.2d 666. Infants ⇌ 203

Proceeding with dispositional hearing in juvenile's absence did not violate his right of allocution, as he waived his right to be present by blatantly disregarding hearing after receiving adequate notice, thus waiving his right to address court passing judgment upon him. In re Jason R. (Ohio Com.Pl., 12-14-1995) 77 Ohio Misc.2d 37, 666 N.E.2d 666. Infants ⇌ 203

Under the present Juvenile Code and Rules, a juvenile court cannot change a "temporary" commitment to the Ohio youth commission to an "permanent" commitment without hearing; further, the commitment of an unruly child, not declared "delinquent", is a violation of due process and any hearing held on the above matters requires the presence of the youth involved. OAG 72–071.

3. Public access

The press should not be expected to camp out in the hallway in order to ascertain whether evidentiary proceedings are being conducted in chambers on motions for closure of juvenile delinquency proceedings; instead, representatives of the press and general public must be given the opportunity to be heard on the question of exclusion. State ex rel. Plain Dealer Publishing Co. v. Floyd (Ohio, 08-30-2006) 111 Ohio St.3d 56, 855 N.E.2d 35, 2006-Ohio-4437. Infants ⇌ 203

Writ of mandamus would issue to compel juvenile court to release transcript of amenability hearing to determine whether juvenile should be tried as adult for murder after juvenile court denied juvenile's motion to close proceedings but refused to allow media to attend hearing after juvenile's mother testified. State ex rel. Plain Dealer Publishing Co. v. Floyd (Ohio, 08-30-2006) 111 Ohio St.3d 56, 855 N.E.2d 35, 2006-Ohio-4437. Mandamus ⇌ 60

Writ of mandamus would not issue to compel juvenile court to release transcript of arraignment hearing in delinquency proceedings based on court's failure to conduct evidentiary hearing to determine whether closure of hearing was appropriate when no party had filed motion to close proceedings; rather, mandamus would issue to compel juvenile court to conduct closure hearing, and then, if court decided that closure was unwarranted, to release transcript. State ex rel. Plain Dealer Publishing

Co. v. Floyd (Ohio, 08-30-2006) 111 Ohio St.3d 56, 855 N.E.2d 35, 2006-Ohio-4437. Mandamus ⇐ 60

Closure of delinquency proceedings for 17-year-old charged with aggravated murder, aggravated attempted murder, and aggravated robbery was abuse of discretion; public interest in proceedings outweighed bare assertion by juvenile's attorney that permitting access would not be in juvenile's best interest, in view of juvenile's near-adult age at time of alleged offenses, minimal likelihood that probable cause hearing would disclose confidential information, gravity of offenses, and fact that juvenile would be subject to mandatory bindover to adult court if probable cause was found. State ex rel. Plain Dealer Publishing Co. v. Geauga Cty. Court of Common Pleas, Juv. Div. (Ohio, 08-11-2000) 90 Ohio St.3d 79, 734 N.E.2d 1214, 2000-Ohio-35. Infants ⇐ 203

Decision to close juvenile proceedings to general public will be upheld unless juvenile court abused its discretion. State ex rel. Plain Dealer Publishing Co. v. Geauga Cty. Court of Common Pleas, Juv. Div. (Ohio, 08-11-2000) 90 Ohio St.3d 79, 734 N.E.2d 1214, 2000-Ohio-35. Infants ⇐ 251

Party seeking closure of juvenile proceedings bears burden of proof on relevant factors. State ex rel. Plain Dealer Publishing Co. v. Geauga Cty. Court of Common Pleas, Juv. Div. (Ohio, 08-11-2000) 90 Ohio St.3d 79, 734 N.E.2d 1214, 2000-Ohio-35. Infants ⇐ 172

Since juvenile proceedings to determine if child is abused, neglected, or dependent or to determine custody of minor child are neither presumptively open nor presumptively closed to public, juvenile court may restrict public access to those proceedings if it finds, after hearing evidence and argument on issue, that there exists reasonable and substantial basis for believing that public access could harm child or endanger fairness of adjudication, and that potential for harm outweighs benefits of public access. State ex rel. Scripps Howard Broadcasting Co. v. Cuyahoga Cty. Court of Common Pleas, Juv. Div. (Ohio, 07-13-1995) 73 Ohio St.3d 19, 652 N.E.2d 179. Constitutional Law ⇐ 90.1(3); Constitutional Law ⇐ 328

Those persons present and participating at in camera inspection held to determine whether closure hearing in juvenile proceeding should be closed are prohibited, under penalty of contempt, from disseminating any information determined by the juvenile court to be excluded from public disclosure, unless and until it is determined by competent authority that the information may be released to the public. State ex rel. Dispatch Printing Co. v. Lias (Ohio, 03-23-1994) 68 Ohio St.3d 497, 628 N.E.2d 1368, 1994-Ohio-335. Infants ⇐ 203

Proceedings in juvenile court to determine if a child is abused, neglected, or dependent, or to determine custody of a minor child, are neither presumptively open nor presumptively closed to the public; the juvenile court may restrict public access to these proceedings pursuant to Juv R 27 and RC 2151.35 if the court finds, after hearing evidence and argument on the issue, that (1) there exists a reasonable and substantial basis for believing that public access could harm the child or endanger the fairness of the adjudication, and (2) the potential for harm outweighs the benefits of public access. In re T.R. (Ohio 1990) 52 Ohio St.3d 6, 556 N.E.2d 439, certiorari denied 111 S.Ct. 386, 498 U.S. 958, 112 L.Ed.2d 396. Infants ⇐ 172; Infants ⇐ 203

Alleged falsity of news broadcast in suggesting that juvenile had prior record for rape and kidnapping did not require closing probable cause and amenability hearings in juvenile delinquency case, even though the broadcast would likely endanger fairness of trial as adult; state's agents and judge knew difference between facts of prior case and scenario presented in broadcast, and there was no reason to believe that any more harm would result from permitting public access to further proceedings. In re N.H. (Ohio Com.Pl., 06-09-1992) 63 Ohio Misc.2d 285, 626 N.E.2d 697. Infants ⇐ 203

Public had First Amendment right of access to probable cause hearing in juvenile delinquency case and to parts of amenability hearing involving prior juvenile record, but public had no right of access to portions of amenability hearing involving information about child's psychological, social, and family histories. In re N.H. (Ohio Com.Pl., 06-09-1992) 63 Ohio Misc.2d 285, 626 N.E.2d 697. Constitutional Law ⇐ 90.1(3); Infants ⇐ 203

Juvenile court proceedings in delinquency cases are not presumed to be opened or closed; rather, in each case juvenile court must weigh competing interests for and against public access. In re N.H. (Ohio Com.Pl., 06-09-1992) 63 Ohio Misc.2d 285, 626 N.E.2d 697. Infants ⇐ 203

4. Discretion of court

The trial court's denial of juvenile's request for a continuance to allow counsel for juvenile to determine whether the names provided by juvenile during the course of trial were individuals who could be viable witnesses was not an abuse of discretion; juvenile requested a continuance on the second day of the delinquency hearing at the close of the State's case, juvenile did not inform counsel of the names of the individuals until the second day of the hearing, and there was no evidence in the record as to the identity of the alleged witnesses or the content of their testimony. In re R.T. (Ohio App. 9 Dist., Lorain, 03-22-2006) No. 05CA008728, No. 05CA008742, 2006-Ohio-1311, 2006 WL 709057, Unreported. Infants ⇐ 204

"Evidence," for purposes of statute providing that juvenile court at dispositional hearing may admit any evidence that is material and relevant, contemplates sworn testimony, despite informal nature of such hearing. In re Ramsey Children (Ohio App. 5 Dist., 03-27-1995) 102 Ohio App.3d 168, 656 N.E.2d 1311. Infants ⇐ 173.1

Juvenile failed to show that he was prejudiced by juvenile court's refusal to conduct informal proceedings, rather than formal court proceedings, on charges of criminal mischief. In re Corcoran (Geauga 1990) 68 Ohio App.3d 213, 587 N.E.2d 957, dismissed 56 Ohio St.3d 702, 564 N.E.2d 703. Infants ⇐ 253

Juv R 28   [Reserved]

Juv R 29   Adjudicatory hearing

(A) Scheduling the hearing

The date for the adjudicatory hearing shall be set when the complaint is filed or as soon thereafter as is practicable. If the child is the subject of a complaint alleging a violation of a section of the Revised Code that may be violated by an adult and that does not request a serious youthful offender sentence, and if the child is in detention or shelter care, the hearing shall be held not later than fifteen days after the filing of the complaint. Upon a showing of good cause, the adjudicatory hearing may be continued and detention or shelter care extended.

The prosecuting attorney's filing of either a notice of intent to pursue or a statement of an interest in pursuing a serious youthful offender sentence shall constitute good cause for continuing the adjudicatory hearing date and extending detention or shelter care.

The hearing of a removal action shall be scheduled in accordance with Juv. R. 39(B).

If the complaint alleges abuse, neglect, or dependency, the hearing shall be held no later than thirty days after the complaint is filed. For good cause shown, the adjudicatory hearing may extend beyond thirty days either for an additional ten days to allow any party to obtain counsel or for a reasonable time beyond thirty days to obtain service on all parties or complete any necessary evaluations. However, the adjudicatory hearing shall be held no later than sixty days after the complaint is filed.

The failure of the court to hold an adjudicatory hearing within any time period set forth in this rule does not affect the ability of the court to issue any order otherwise provided for in statute or rule and does not provide any basis for contesting the jurisdiction of the court or the validity of any order of the court.

(B) Advisement and findings at the commencement of the hearing

At the beginning of the hearing, the court shall do all of the following:

(1) Ascertain whether notice requirements have been complied with and, if not, whether the affected parties waive compliance;

(2) Inform the parties of the substance of the complaint, the purpose of the hearing, and possible consequences of the hearing, including the possibility that the cause may be transferred to the appropriate adult court under Juv. R. 30 where the complaint alleges that a child fourteen years of age or over is delinquent by conduct that would constitute a felony if committed by an adult;

(3) Inform unrepresented parties of their right to counsel and determine if those parties are waiving their right to counsel;

(4) Appoint counsel for any unrepresented party under Juv. R. 4(A) who does not waive the right to counsel;

(5) Inform any unrepresented party who waives the right to counsel of the right: to obtain counsel at any stage of the proceedings, to remain silent, to offer evidence, to cross-examine witnesses, and, upon request, to have a record of all proceedings made, at public expense if indigent.

(C) Entry of admission or denial

The court shall request each party against whom allegations are being made in the complaint to admit or deny the allegations. A failure or refusal to admit the allegations shall be deemed a denial, except in cases where the court consents to entry of a plea of no contest.

(D) Initial procedure upon entry of an admission

The court may refuse to accept an admission and shall not accept an admission without addressing the party personally and determining both of the following:

(1) The party is making the admission voluntarily with understanding of the nature of the allegations and the consequences of the admission;

(2) The party understands that by entering an admission the party is waiving the right to challenge the witnesses and evidence against the party, to remain silent, and to introduce evidence at the adjudicatory hearing.

The court may hear testimony, review documents, or make further inquiry, as it considers appropriate, or it may proceed directly to the action required by division (F) of this rule.

(E) Initial procedure upon entry of a denial

If a party denies the allegations the court shall:

(1) Direct the prosecuting attorney or another attorney-at-law to assist the court by presenting evidence in support of the allegations of a complaint;

(2) Order the separation of witnesses, upon request of any party;

(3) Take all testimony under oath or affirmation in either question-answer or narrative form; and

(4) Determine the issues by proof beyond a reasonable doubt in juvenile traffic offense, delinquency, and unruly proceedings; by clear and convincing evidence in dependency, neglect, and abuse cases, and in a removal action; and by a preponderance of the evidence in all other cases.

(F) Procedure upon determination of the issues

Upon the determination of the issues, the court shall do one of the following:

(1) If the allegations of the complaint, indictment, or information were not proven, dismiss the complaint;

(2) If the allegations of the complaint, indictment, or information are admitted or proven, do any one of the following, unless precluded by statute:

(a) Enter an adjudication and proceed forthwith to disposition;

(b) Enter an adjudication and continue the matter for disposition for not more than six months and may make appropriate temporary orders;

(c) Postpone entry of adjudication for not more than six months;

(d) Dismiss the complaint if dismissal is in the best interest of the child and the community.

(3) Upon request make written findings of fact and conclusions of law pursuant to Civ. R. 52.

(4) Ascertain whether the child should remain or be placed in shelter care until the dispositional hearing in an abuse, neglect, or dependency proceeding. In making a shelter care determination, the court shall make written finding of facts with respect to reasonable efforts in accordance with the provisions in Juv. R. 27(B)(1) and to relative placement in accordance with Juv. R. 7(F)(3).

(Adopted eff. 7–1–72; amended eff. 7–1–76, 7–1–94, 7–1–98, 7–1–01, 7–1–04)

Uncodified Law

2002 H 180, § 3, eff. 5–16–02, reads, in part:

The General Assembly hereby requests the Supreme Court to promptly modify Rule 29 of the Rules of Juvenile Procedure pursuant to its authority under the Ohio Constitution to make that rule consistent with the amendments of this act to section 2151.28 of the Revised Code.

2000 S 179, § 6, eff. 4–9–01, reads:

The General Assembly hereby encourages the Supreme Court to amend the Juvenile Rules to be consistent with the changes in the Juvenile Laws pertaining to delinquent children, particularly the laws relating to serious youthful offender dispositional sentences.

The General Assembly hereby encourages the Supreme Court to amend Rule 29(C) to permit "no contest" pleas in juvenile traffic offender and non-traffic cases with the consent of the juvenile court in a manner similar to Criminal Rule 11. Children paying fines to juvenile traffic violations bureaus should be required to admit guilt, with parental knowledge.

The General Assembly hereby encourages the Supreme Court to amend the Rules for the Government of the Judiciary of Ohio or other appropriate rules, or to take other appropriate action, to encourage cooperation between divisions of the courts of common pleas to better implement this act, including, but not limited to, the provisions of this act authorizing, in specified circumstances, jury trials in juvenile courts.

Historical and Statutory Notes

Amendment Note: The 7–1–04 amendment rewrote the second sentence of the first paragraph of division (A) which previously read, "If the child who is the subject of a complaint that does not request a serious youthful offender sentence is in detention or shelter care, the hearing shall be held not later than ten days after the filing of the complaint."; substituted "fourteen" for "fifteen" in division (B)(2); and made other nonsubstantive changes.

Amendment Note: The 7–1–01 amendment inserted "that does not request a serious youthful offender sentence" between "complaint" and "is in detention" in the second sentence of the first paragraph of division (A); added the second paragraph of division (A); inserted the phrase "except in cases where the court consents to entry of a plea of no contest" at the end of division (C); substituted "proven" for "proved" throughout division (F); and substituted "complaint, indictment, or information" for "complaint" in divisions (F)(1) and (F)(2).

Amendment Note: The 7–1–98 amendment added the second paragraph in division (A); substituted "abuse cases, and in a removal action;" for "child abuse proceedings," in division (E)(4); substituted "entry" for "judgment" in division (F)(2)(c); and made other nonsubstantive changes.

Amendment Note: The 7–1–94 amendment added the second and third paragraphs in division (A), and division (F)(4); and made changes to reflect gender-neutral language.

Staff Notes

2004:

(A) Scheduling the hearing

Division (A) was amended to conform the language of the rule to R.C. 2151.28, as amended effective May 16, 2002.

(B) Advisement and findings at the commencement of the hearing

Division (C) was amended to conform the language of the rule to R.C. 2151.10 and 2151.12, which allow the transfer of juveniles age fourteen and over to adult court for trial.

2001:

Rule 29(A) Scheduling the hearing

Rule 29(A) was amended to conform to Revised Code section 2152.13(B), which provides that the prosecuting attorney has twenty days after a child's initial appearance in juvenile court within which to file a notice of intent to pursue a serious youthful offender dispositional sentence. The rule preserves the ten-day time period within which to hold an adjudicatory hearing for all other cases in which the child is in detention or shelter care. However, because the rule contemplates a hearing within ten days, but the statute grants a twenty-day time period for making the charging decision, the amended rule also provides a mechanism by which a prosecuting attorney can preserve the twenty-day time period by filing a "statement of interest in pursuing a serious youthful offender sentence." The amended rule states that either the notice of intent (i.e., a Rule 22(D)(5) motion) or a statement of interest shall be good cause for extending both the date for an adjudicatory hearing and detention or shelter care. If the prosecuting attorney does not file a notice of intent to pursue a serious youthful offender sentence before the twenty-day time period lapses, the ordinary juvenile time frames again become operative. If the prosecuting attorney does not obtain an indictment or information, or the court denies the Rule 22(D)(5) motion, the ordinary juvenile time frames will again become operative. If the child is determined to be eligible for a serious youthful offender sentence, the ordinary juvenile time frames do not apply. Instead, adult time frames, i.e., speedy trial provisions, become operative [Revised Code section 2152.13(D)(1)].

Rule 29(C) Entry of admission or denial

Rule 29(C) was amended in response to Section 3 of Sub. Sen. Bill 179 (effective January 1, 2002), in which the General Assembly encouraged the Supreme Court to amend Rule 29(C) to permit "no contest" pleas with the consent of the court, similar to the provisions in Criminal Rule 11.

Rule 29(F) Procedure upon determination of the issues

Rule 29(F) was amended in response to both the chronic and habitual truancy act and the serious youthful offender act. Divisions (F)(1) and (2) include recognition that a serious youthful offender case will proceed by indictment or information. Division (F)(2) also recognizes that certain dispositions within the power of the juvenile court may be precluded by statute for certain types of cases. The amendment removes any perception of conflict between statutorily authorized dispositions and those authorized in the rule. Specifically, the division conforms to Revised Code section 2152.13(E), which controls the dispositions in serious youthful offender cases. The division also recognizes that chronic or habitual truant dispositions are heavily regulated by statute.

1998:

Rule 29 Adjudicatory hearing

The 1998 amendment to Juv. R. 29(A) makes reference to Juv. R. 39(B), which governs service of process and the scheduling of hearings in removal actions.

The 1998 amendment to Juv. R. 29(E)(4) establishes a clear and convincing standard in removal actions for determining whether the child is causing a significant and unreasonable disruption to the educational process. This standard recognizes the significant consequences that will result if the allegations of the complaint are established.

1994:

Rule 29 Adjudicatory Hearing

The 1994 amendment revised Juv. R. 29(A) to require specific time deadlines for holding the adjudicatory hearing in abuse, neglect, and dependency cases. Specifically in abuse, neglect, and dependency cases, an adjudicatory hearing is to be conducted no later than thirty days after the complaint is filed, with the possibility of a ten day extension for obtaining counsel, and a reasonable time extension to perfect service of process. In any event, the time for the adjudicatory hearing is not to exceed ninety days from the filing of a complaint. Revised Code 2151.28 (amended by S.B. 89).

Masculine references have been replaced by gender neutral language.

Editor's Comment

Scheduling the hearing 1
Advisement and findings at the commencement of the hearing 2
Entry of admission or denial 3
Initial procedure upon entry of an admission 4
Initial procedure upon entry of denial 5
Procedure upon determination of the issues 6

1. Scheduling the hearing

The requirements for scheduling the adjudicatory hearing are governed by Juv R 29(A) and 2151.28(A). A 1996 amendment to 2151.28(A) requires that the date for the adjudicatory hearing be set "no later than seventy-two hours after the complaint is filed." Juv R 29(A) requires that the date for the adjudicatory hearing be set "when the complaint is filed or as soon thereafter as is practicable."

Both Juv R 29(A) and 2151.28(A)(2) establish the same time frames for scheduling the adjudicatory hearing in abuse, neglect, and dependency cases. The statute (2151.28(A)(1)) provides that the adjudicatory hearing in delinquency, unruly, and juvenile traffic offender cases shall be held in accordance with the Juvenile Rules. Juv R 29(A) requires that the hearing be held within ten days in such cases if the child is in detention, and that the hearing date be set in all cases as soon as practicable after the complaint is filed.

There is an apparent conflict between Juv R 29(A) and Juv R 16(A) in cases in which a child is in detention and a party needs to be served by publication (because the party's whereabouts is unknown). As indicated, Juv R 29(A) requires the adjudicatory hearing to be held within ten days if the child is detained. However, pursuant to Juv R 16(A), where service is by publication the hearing date shall not be less than fourteen days after the date of publication. (The fourteen day requirement where publication is required supersedes 2151.29, which requires only a one week period between publication and the hearing date.) Many courts resolve this conflict between the rules by providing a hearing for the child within ten days, at which time a determination may be made as to whether further detention is required pending the completion of service of process.

2. Advisement and findings at the commencement of the hearing

Juv R 29(B) repeats the format of other hearing provisions, by stating the specific advisements and findings required at the commencement of the hearing. This format follows the pattern of Crim R 10 and Minnesota Rule 5–1.

3. Entry of admission or denial

Juv R 29(C), which authorizes the court to call upon the parties to admit or deny the allegations of the complaint, is based on general practice. (See Crim R 10 and 11.) The major distinction between the juvenile rules and the criminal rules is that Juv R 29(C) permits the entry of either an admission or denial, whereas Crim R 11(A) permits the defendant to enter any one of four separate pleas: guilty, not guilty by reason of insanity, not guilty, or with the court's consent, no contest. Because the Traffic Rules apply in juvenile traffic offender cases (see Traf R 1), a child may plead no contest in such a case.

4. Initial procedure upon entry of an admission

Juv R 29(D), regulating the procedure upon entry of an admission, is based on Crim R 11. It differs from the criminal rule, however, in that it requires in all cases that the court determine that the party understands that his admission acts to waive the enumerated rights. Crim R 11 distinguishes among felony cases, serious misdemeanor cases, and petty misdemeanor cases. Only in felony cases is the court required to determine that the guilty plea results in a waiver of those rights.

2151.35(H)(1) includes additional information which must be provided to a child before the court may accept an admission to a category one or category two offense.

5. Initial procedure upon entry of denial

The structure of Juv R 29(E), regulating initial procedure upon entry of a denial, is based on Minnesota Juvenile Rule 5–2. Juv R 29(E)(1) requires participation of the prosecuting attorney or other attorney-at-law in contested cases. 2151.40 requires the prosecuting attorney to render "all assistance and cooperation within his jurisdictional power" to the juvenile court and to "assist the court in presenting the evidence at any hearing or proceeding concerning an alleged or adjudicated delinquent, unruly, abused, neglected, or dependent child or juvenile traffic offender." Appearance of the prosecutor in contested cases has been made mandatory by this rule.

Juv R 29(E)(2), which provides for the separation or exclusion of witnesses upon request, is similar to Evid R 615. However, Evid R 615 recognizes certain exceptions, including one for a party who is a natural person. Since parents are "parties" to juvenile court proceedings, Evid R 615 appears to supersede *State v Ostrowski*, 30 OS(2d) 34, 282 NE(2d) 359 (1972), which upheld the exclusion of parents who were also witnesses.

Division (E)(4), regulating the standard of proof, complies with *In re Winship*, 397 US 358, 90 SCt 1068, 25 LEd(2d) 368 (1970), which requires proof beyond a reasonable doubt in delinquency cases. The rule has expanded the requirements of *Winship* by providing for proof beyond a reasonable doubt in juvenile traffic offense and unruly proceedings as well. In dependency, neglect, and abuse proceedings, the standard of proof is clear and convincing evidence, which is in conformity with *Santosky v Kramer*, 455 US 745, 102 SCt 1388, 71 LEd(2d) 599 (1982). The same provisions are contained in 2151.35(A).

6. Procedure upon determination of the issues

Juv R 29(F), regulating procedure upon determination of the issues, provides a variety of alternatives, in conformity with present and preferred practice.

Division (F)(3) provides that written findings of fact and conclusions of law shall be prepared in accordance with Civ R 52 upon the request of a party. Civ R 52 provides that the court may in its discretion require the party to submit proposed findings of fact and conclusions of law which when made by the court shall form part of the record. This requirement may be satisfied by the filing of an opinion or memorandum of decision prior to entry of judgment. Since there is no jury in juvenile proceedings, findings of fact and conclusions of law are not mandatory, except as provided in 2151.33(C) and 2151.353(A).

The rule expands on the holding of the U.S. Supreme Court in *In re Gault*, 387 US 1, 87 SCt 1428, 18 LEd(2d) 527 (1967), in being more liberal and in meeting requirements of fundamental fairness and due process of law. In *In re Gault* although the issues of right to a record and right to appeal were raised, the court did not decide these questions. Right to a record in juvenile proceedings in Ohio is governed by both statute (2151.35(A)) and rule (Juv R 37(A)) as is the right to appeal (*See* 2505.17, Juv R 34(J), App R 7(C).)

Division (F)(4) is taken from 2151.28(B).

Cross References

Arraignment, Crim R 10
Hearing procedure; findings, record, 2151.35
Pleas, rights upon plea, Crim R 11

Library References

Infants ⚖199, 203.
Westlaw Topic No. 211.
C.J.S. Infants §§ 42 to 67.

Research References

ALR Library

101 ALR 5th 351, Validity and Efficacy of Minor's Waiver of Right to Counsel--Cases Decided Since Application of Gault, 387 U.S. 1, 87 S. Ct. 1428, 18 L. Ed. 2d 527 (1967).

Encyclopedias

OH Jur. 3d Family Law § 1624, Waiver of Child's Rights; Double Jeopardy.
OH Jur. 3d Family Law § 1626, Right Under Juvenile Court Law and Rules.
OH Jur. 3d Family Law § 1647, Proceedings Before Referee; Powers and Duties.
OH Jur. 3d Family Law § 1655, Right to Attend; Public or Private Hearing.
OH Jur. 3d Family Law § 1661, Advisement and Findings at Commencement of Hearing.
OH Jur. 3d Family Law § 1667, Admission or Denial of Allegations.
OH Jur. 3d Family Law § 1668, Initial Procedure—on Admission.
OH Jur. 3d Family Law § 1669, Initial Procedure—on Denial.
OH Jur. 3d Family Law § 1670, Required Degree of Proof.
OH Jur. 3d Family Law § 1681, Conduct of Hearing; Advisement of Rights.
OH Jur. 3d Family Law § 1730, What is an Appealable Order.
OH Jur. 3d Family Law § 1628.5, Waiver of Counsel.
OH Jur. 3d Family Law § 1670.5, Defenses.
OH Jur. 3d Family Law § 1676.5, Sufficiency.

Treatises and Practice Aids

Baldwin's Ohio Handbook Series—Trial Handbook § 4:24, Plea of Guilty or No Contest—Requirements for Valid Plea.
Klein, Darling, & Terez, Baldwin's Ohio Practice Civil Practice § 52:1, Findings by the Court--In General.
Katz, Giannelli, Blair and Lipton, Baldwin's Ohio Practice, Criminal Law, § 59:1, Introduction.

Giannelli and Snyder, Baldwin's Ohio Practice, Evidence, § 615.1, Introduction.
Giannelli and Snyder, Baldwin's Ohio Practice, Evidence, § 615.3, Sequestration; Policy & Application.
Carlin, Baldwin's Ohio Practice, Merrick-Rippner Probate Law § 104:1, Juvenile Court—Introduction.
Carlin, Baldwin's Ohio Practice, Merrick-Rippner Probate Law § 104:4, Juvenile Court—Constitutional Issues.
Carlin, Baldwin's Ohio Practice, Merrick-Rippner Probate Law § 106:2, Juvenile Court Jurisdiction—Delinquent Child—Quantum of Proof in Delinquency Hearings.
Carlin, Baldwin's Ohio Practice, Merrick-Rippner Probate Law § 106:4, Juvenile Court Jurisdiction—Delinquent Child—Non-Criminal Nature of Delinquency Proceedings.
Carlin, Baldwin's Ohio Practice, Merrick-Rippner Probate Law § 106:5, Juvenile Court Jurisdiction—Delinquent Child—Dna Testing of Certain Delinquent Children.
Carlin, Baldwin's Ohio Practice, Merrick-Rippner Probate Law § 106:9, Juvenile Court Jurisdiction—Unruly Child—Quantum of Proof in Unruly Child Hearing.
Carlin, Baldwin's Ohio Practice, Merrick-Rippner Probate Law § 104:15, Juvenile Court—Prosecuting Attorney's Role.
Carlin, Baldwin's Ohio Practice, Merrick-Rippner Probate Law § 106:12, Juvenile Court Jurisdiction—Neglected Child—Quantum of Proof in Neglect Hearings.
Carlin, Baldwin's Ohio Practice, Merrick-Rippner Probate Law § 106:15, Juvenile Court Jurisdiction—Dependent Child—Quantum of Proof in Dependency Hearings.
Carlin, Baldwin's Ohio Practice, Merrick-Rippner Probate Law § 106:18, Juvenile Court Jurisdiction—Abused Child—Quantum of Proof in Abuse Hearings.
Carlin, Baldwin's Ohio Practice, Merrick-Rippner Probate Law § 107:12, Service by Publication.
Carlin, Baldwin's Ohio Practice, Merrick-Rippner Probate Law § 107:20, Unlawful Search and Seizure of Juveniles—Motion to Suppress Illegal Evidence.
Carlin, Baldwin's Ohio Practice, Merrick-Rippner Probate Law § 107:41, Prehearing Procedures in Juvenile Court—Temporary Orders Pending Hearing.
Carlin, Baldwin's Ohio Practice, Merrick-Rippner Probate Law § 107:43, Scheduling Juvenile Court Hearing.
Carlin, Baldwin's Ohio Practice, Merrick-Rippner Probate Law § 107:48, Adjudicatory Hearings—Prosecuting Attorney's Assistance at Hearing.
Carlin, Baldwin's Ohio Practice, Merrick-Rippner Probate Law § 107:49, Adjudicatory Hearings—Conduct of Hearing by Magistrate.
Carlin, Baldwin's Ohio Practice, Merrick-Rippner Probate Law § 107:50, Adjudicatory Hearings—Applicability of Rules of Court.
Carlin, Baldwin's Ohio Practice, Merrick-Rippner Probate Law § 107:51, Adjudicatory Hearings—Applicability of Rules of Evidence.
Carlin, Baldwin's Ohio Practice, Merrick-Rippner Probate Law § 107:53, Adjudicatory Hearings—Mental Competency to Stand Trial.
Carlin, Baldwin's Ohio Practice, Merrick-Rippner Probate Law § 107:55, Adjudicatory Hearings—Procedure at Adjudicatory Hearing.
Carlin, Baldwin's Ohio Practice, Merrick-Rippner Probate Law § 107:56, Adjudicatory Hearings—Attendance of Parties at Hearing.
Carlin, Baldwin's Ohio Practice, Merrick-Rippner Probate Law § 107:57, Adjudicatory Hearings—Admission or Denial of Complaint.
Carlin, Baldwin's Ohio Practice, Merrick-Rippner Probate Law § 107:59, Adjudicatory Hearings—Proof Beyond a Reasonable Doubt.
Carlin, Baldwin's Ohio Practice, Merrick-Rippner Probate Law § 107:60, Adjudicatory Hearings—Right to Transcript of Proceedings.
Carlin, Baldwin's Ohio Practice, Merrick-Rippner Probate Law § 107:64, Mandatory Transfer.
Carlin, Baldwin's Ohio Practice, Merrick-Rippner Probate Law § 107:68, Retention of Jurisdiction by Juvenile Court.
Carlin, Baldwin's Ohio Practice, Merrick-Rippner Probate Law § 107:72, Dispositional Hearings—Procedure.
Carlin, Baldwin's Ohio Practice, Merrick-Rippner Probate Law § 107:79, Disposition of Abused, Neglected, or Dependent Child—Legal Custody.

Carlin, Baldwin's Ohio Practice, Merrick-Rippner Probate Law § 107:81, Disposition of Abused, Neglected, or Dependent Child—Permanent Custody—Best Interest Determination Factors.

Carlin, Baldwin's Ohio Practice, Merrick-Rippner Probate Law § 107:84, Disposition of Delinquent Children—Prior to January 1, 2002.

Carlin, Baldwin's Ohio Practice, Merrick-Rippner Probate Law § 108:14, Juvenile Court—Modification of Decree Allocating Parental Rights and Responsibilities for Care of Children.

Carlin, Baldwin's Ohio Practice, Merrick-Rippner Probate Law § 107:122, Appeals—Juvenile Court Judgments—Determination of Neglect, Dependency, Unruliness, Abuse, or Delinquency.

Carlin, Baldwin's Ohio Practice, Merrick-Rippner Probate Law § 107:173, Order Adjudging Child Dependent, Neglected, or Abused—Form.

Giannelli & Yeomans, Ohio Juvenile Law § 1:8, Rules of Juvenile Procedure.

Giannelli & Yeomans, Ohio Juvenile Law § 5:3, Syo Charging; Preliminary Hearing.

Giannelli & Yeomans, Ohio Juvenile Law § 8:6, Unruly—Status Offenses.

Giannelli & Yeomans, Ohio Juvenile Law § 13:5, Hearing.

Giannelli & Yeomans, Ohio Juvenile Law § 17:4, Transfer of Venue.

Giannelli & Yeomans, Ohio Juvenile Law § 18:2, Issuance of Summons: Proper Parties.

Giannelli & Yeomans, Ohio Juvenile Law § 18:4, Summons: Methods of Service.

Giannelli & Yeomans, Ohio Juvenile Law § 19:7, Time Requirements.

Giannelli & Yeomans, Ohio Juvenile Law § 20:2, Temporary Care Orders.

Giannelli & Yeomans, Ohio Juvenile Law § 20:6, Time Requirements.

Giannelli & Yeomans, Ohio Juvenile Law § 23:1, Introduction.

Giannelli & Yeomans, Ohio Juvenile Law § 23:3, Right to Counsel.

Giannelli & Yeomans, Ohio Juvenile Law § 23:4, Waiver of Right to Counsel.

Giannelli & Yeomans, Ohio Juvenile Law § 23:6, Guardian Ad Litem.

Giannelli & Yeomans, Ohio Juvenile Law § 23:8, Pleas.

Giannelli & Yeomans, Ohio Juvenile Law § 23:9, Uncontested Cases.

Giannelli & Yeomans, Ohio Juvenile Law § 24:4, Pretrial Orders.

Giannelli & Yeomans, Ohio Juvenile Law § 25:2, Bifurcated Hearings.

Giannelli & Yeomans, Ohio Juvenile Law § 25:4, Time Requirements.

Giannelli & Yeomans, Ohio Juvenile Law § 25:7, Advisement of Rights.

Giannelli & Yeomans, Ohio Juvenile Law § 25:8, Burden of Proof.

Giannelli & Yeomans, Ohio Juvenile Law § 27:2, Dispositional Alternatives.

Giannelli & Yeomans, Ohio Juvenile Law § 28:8, Revocation of Probationary Operator's License.

Giannelli & Yeomans, Ohio Juvenile Law § 33:6, Revocation of Probation.

Giannelli & Yeomans, Ohio Juvenile Law § 34:4, Final Order Requirement.

Giannelli & Yeomans, Ohio Juvenile Law App. D, Appendix D. Glossary.

Giannelli & Yeomans, Ohio Juvenile Law § 22:15, Access to Reports & Discovery.

Giannelli & Yeomans, Ohio Juvenile Law § 23:13, Burden of Proof.

Giannelli & Yeomans, Ohio Juvenile Law § 23:17, Evidence—Separation of Witnesses.

Giannelli & Yeomans, Ohio Juvenile Law § 23:24, Confrontation—Cross-Examination.

Giannelli & Yeomans, Ohio Juvenile Law § 23:27, Self-Incrimination.

Giannelli & Yeomans, Ohio Juvenile Law § 23:29, Speedy Trial.

Giannelli & Yeomans, Ohio Juvenile Law § 23:30, Right to a Transcript.

Giannelli & Yeomans, Ohio Juvenile Law § 30:11, Permanent Custody—"Best Interest" Factors.

Giannelli & Yeomans, Ohio Juvenile Law § 34:12, Habeas Corpus.

Law Review and Journal Commentaries

The Criminal Defense Lawyer in the Juvenile Justice System, David A. Harris. 26 U Tol L Rev 751 (Summer 1995).

Discrimination Perfected to a Science: The Evolution of the Supreme Court's War on Drugs, Note. 30 U Tol L Rev 677 (Summer 1999).

Juvenile Delinquency Proceedings in Ohio: Due Process and the Hearsay Dilemma, Comment. 24 Clev St L Rev 356 (Spring 1975).

Juvenile Delinquent and Unruly Proceedings in Ohio: Unconstitutional Adjudications, Note. 24 Clev St L Rev 602 (1975).

Notes of Decisions

Admissions 4
Best interest of child and community 18
Bifurcated hearings 5
Consequences of hearing 13
Constitutional issues 3
Delinquency not crime 10
Double jeopardy 8
Evidence and standards 6
Final orders 9
Insanity defense 14
Judge's duty to inform
    In general 15
    Right to counsel 2
Jurisdiction 1
No contest pleas 12
Notice 16
Preservation of error for review 17
Standing 19
Time limitations 7
Waiver of counsel 11

1. Jurisdiction

Trial court was without jurisdiction to accept juvenile's admission to aggravated robbery offense and adjudicate him as delinquent, where notice regarding juvenile delinquency proceedings was not given to juvenile's parents. In re Brunner (Ohio App. 4 Dist., Scioto, 03-10-2003) No. 02CA2865, 2003-Ohio-2590, 2003 WL 21152500, Unreported. Infants ⇔ 198

The juvenile court has exclusive original jurisdiction, pursuant to RC 2151.23(A), concerning any child who is alleged in a proper complaint to be neglected, and the court does not lose jurisdiction by failing to adhere to the time limits set forth in Juv R 29(A) and 34(A). Linger v. Weiss (Ohio 1979) 57 Ohio St.2d 97, 386 N.E.2d 1354, 11 O.O.3d 281, certiorari denied 100 S.Ct. 128, 444 U.S. 862, 62 L.Ed.2d 83.

2. —— Right to counsel, judge's duty to inform

Juvenile's constitutional right to counsel was violated during delinquency proceeding; juvenile indicated that he wanted an attorney at his arraignment, and there was no further discussion, either at the arraignment, or thereafter, of the matter of juvenile's legal representation. In re R.B. (Ohio App. 2 Dist., 01-13-2006) 2006-Ohio-264, 2006 WL 172367. Infants ⇔ 205

Record did not support finding that juvenile was represented by counsel at time of his commitment and sexual predator classification hearing that was held subsequent to juvenile's guilty plea to gross sexual imposition, even though trial court made two references to counsel and argument was made on juvenile's behalf urging the court not to impose a sexual predator classification; review of the record revealed that juvenile's probation officer argued in juvenile's defense, record indicated trial court's reference to "counsel" related to probation officer and the argument he made on juvenile's behalf, and transcript of the proceedings did not mention the name of defense counsel. In re C.F. (Ohio App. 8 Dist., Cuyahoga, 05-05-2005) No. 84434, 2005-Ohio-2190, 2005 WL 1048126, Unreported. Infants ⇔ 205

The trial court was not required to inform mother of her right to counsel at hearing to modify custody of child, in child dependency proceeding; Juvenile Rules required the trial court to inform parents of their right to counsel at the adjudicatory hearing, trial court informed mother of her right to counsel at the adjudicatory hearing, and there was no Juvenile Rule regarding counsel for modification of custody hearings. In re Williams (Ohio App. 10 Dist., Franklin, 02-12-2004) No. 03AP-1007, 2004-Ohio-678, 2004 WL 285560, Unreported. Infants ⇔ 203; Infants ⇔ 230.1

Mother in dependency proceedings was not prejudiced by juvenile court's alleged failure to inform parties of the substance of complaint, the purpose of hearing, the possible consequences of hearing prior to adjudicatory hearing, and the right to appeal after the dispositional hearing; mother contested the matter, was represented by counsel at trial, a full hearing was held on the merits, and mother appealed the juvenile court's judgment. In re Malone (Ohio App. 10 Dist., Franklin, 12-30-2003) No. 03AP-489, 2003-Ohio-7156, 2003 WL 23024377, Unreported, appeal not allowed 102 Ohio St.3d 1423, 807 N.E.2d 367, 2004-Ohio-2003. Infants ⇌ 198; Infants ⇌ 203

A juvenile's waiver of his constitutional right to counsel in a delinquency proceeding must be voluntarily, knowingly, and intelligently made; the court must fully and clearly explain to the juvenile his or her right to counsel, and the juvenile in turn must affirmatively waive that right on the record. In re R.B. (Ohio App. 2 Dist., 01-13-2006) 166 Ohio App.3d 626, 852 N.E.2d 1219, 2006-Ohio-264. Infants ⇌ 205

Juvenile's constitutional right to counsel was violated during delinquency proceeding; juvenile indicated that he wanted an attorney at his arraignment, and there was no further discussion, either at the arraignment, or thereafter, of the matter of juvenile's legal representation. In re R.B. (Ohio App. 2 Dist., 01-13-2006) 166 Ohio App.3d 626, 852 N.E.2d 1219, 2006-Ohio-264. Infants ⇌ 205

An indigent parent is entitled to a transcript and counsel on appeal from a judgment permanently terminating his parental rights. State ex rel. Heller v. Miller (Ohio 1980) 61 Ohio St.2d 6, 399 N.E.2d 66, 15 O.O.3d 3.

Juvenile court did not abuse its discretion by denying juvenile a continuance, and forcing him to go to trial on rape and attempted rape charges without the presence of his retained lawyer, where length of delay requested was open-ended in a case that had been on docket for almost a year and a half, court had granted other continuances, State would have been forced to subpoena its witnesses again, two of whom were minors who would have had to miss school, assigned visiting judge would have had to travel again from another county, juvenile contributed to need for request, having had at least a month to inform counsel of date of his final adjudicatory hearing, and case had been delayed due to fact that juvenile had changed lawyers four times between his first and last adjudicatory hearings. In re Daniel K. (Ohio App. 6 Dist., Ottawa, 03-14-2003) No. OT-02-025, No. OT-02-023, 2003-Ohio-1409, 2003 WL 1465043, Unreported. Infants ⇌ 204

Failure to advise juvenile, who was adjudicated delinquent by reason of rape and attempted rape, of his adjudicatory hearing rights until ultimate stage of his final hearing was reversible error. In re Daniel K. (Ohio App. 6 Dist., Ottawa, 03-14-2003) No. OT-02-025, No. OT-02-023, 2003-Ohio-1409, 2003 WL 1465043, Unreported. Infants ⇌ 203; Infants ⇌ 253

Juvenile court failed to substantially comply with rule requiring court to personally question juvenile defendant concerning voluntariness of admission and advise him of the rights he was waiving by entering admission; although court did question juvenile defendant as to the voluntariness of his admission, court failed to advise juvenile defendant that he was waiving his right to challenge witnesses and evidence against him, the right to remain silent, and the right to introduce evidence. In re Graham (Ohio App. 7 Dist., 05-17-2002) 147 Ohio App.3d 452, 770 N.E.2d 1123, 2002-Ohio-2407. Infants ⇌ 174

An adjudication proceeding cannot go forward unless the juvenile is represented by counsel or there has been a valid waiver of the right to counsel. In re Johnston (Ohio App. 11 Dist., 04-30-2001) 142 Ohio App.3d 314, 755 N.E.2d 457. Infants ⇌ 205

Juvenile was entitled to representation by counsel in adjudication for vandalism and criminal trespass, where juvenile did not waive his right to counsel, and conviction on charges could result in juvenile having his liberty curtailed. In re Johnston (Ohio App. 11 Dist., 04-30-2001) 142 Ohio App.3d 314, 755 N.E.2d 457. Infants ⇌ 205

Child is entitled to counsel at all stages of juvenile proceedings. In re Solis (Ohio App. 8 Dist., 12-22-1997) 124 Ohio App.3d 547, 706 N.E.2d 839. Infants ⇌ 205

Juvenile adjudicated delinquent and provisionally placed in foster care was entitled to counsel at dispositional hearing, as provisional placement was not equivalent of probation and dispositional hearing was not equivalent of probation revocation hearing. In re Solis (Ohio App. 8 Dist., 12-22-1997) 124 Ohio App.3d 547, 706 N.E.2d 839. Infants ⇌ 205

Magistrate who presided over arraignment in juvenile proceeding failed to adequately inform juvenile of her right to counsel; magistrate discussed right to counsel only in terms of representation if she were to proceed to trial, and gave explanation of right to counsel that was confusing, if not misleading, and could have led juvenile to believe that she was not entitled to counsel while deciding whether to admit or deny complaint. In re Doyle (App. 2 Dist., 10-03-1997) 122 Ohio App.3d 767, 702 N.E.2d 970. Infants ⇌ 205

Juvenile court failed to ascertain that juvenile understood charge against her, or possible consequences of admitting it, and thus failed to substantially comply with rule requiring it to make determination that admission by juvenile is being made voluntarily before accepting any admission; record was devoid of any indication that magistrate had determined whether juvenile had understanding of nature of allegations, and while juvenile was told that admission could result in her being placed in custody, no mention was made of possible length of any commitment. In re Doyle (App. 2 Dist., 10-03-1997) 122 Ohio App.3d 767, 702 N.E.2d 970. Infants ⇌ 199

Juvenile court failed to make sufficient inquiry, in delinquency proceeding, to determine whether juvenile's waiver of his right to counsel was knowing, intelligent and voluntary, though court addressed group of juveniles collectively as to their right to counsel, where court did not specifically mention in its group address the right to appointment of counsel, court only inquired of juvenile personally as to whether he heard and understood what court said earlier, and court simply gave juvenile and his mother "statement of rights and waiver form" to review and sign. In re Miller (Ohio App. 2 Dist., 04-04-1997) 119 Ohio App.3d 52, 694 N.E.2d 500. Infants ⇌ 205

County children services board was "party" to action in which minor was adjudicated delinquent when board was granted temporary custody of minor and board was thus entitled to appear at dispositional hearing through counsel. In re Lawson (Ohio App. 10 Dist., 11-08-1994) 98 Ohio App.3d 456, 648 N.E.2d 889. Infants ⇌ 200; Infants ⇌ 205

Juvenile rule and statute guarantee right to counsel for all indigent parties in juvenile proceedings. Holley v. Higgins (Franklin 1993) 86 Ohio App.3d 240, 620 N.E.2d 251. Infants ⇌ 205

The guarantee of the right to be represented by counsel set forth in Juv R 4(A) does not, as to a nonindigent party, require that trial be continued indefinitely until counsel can be obtained, but merely requires, if it does not appear that counsel could not be obtained through the exercise of reasonable diligence and a willingness to enter into reasonable contractual arrangements for counsel's services, that a reasonable opportunity be given to the party before trial to employ such counsel. In re Bolden (Allen 1973) 37 Ohio App.2d 7, 306 N.E.2d 166, 66 O.O.2d 26.

A trial court's failure to make a record of an adjudicatory hearing in a stolen car delinquency case in accordance with the mandates of Juv R 37(A) and Juv R 40(D)(2) prevents a finding that an affirmative waiver of the constitutional right to counsel took place, and the trial court magistrate's journal entry, which is the only record of the adjudicatory hearing in question, fails to even minimally satisfy the requirements of Juv R 29 since the magistrate did not check the box indicating whether the juvenile admitted or denied the allegations of the complaint and whether counsel was waived; although the informal detention hearing journal entry sets forth that an express waiver of counsel took place, the journal entry is not adequate evidence of a knowing, voluntary and intelligent waiver of counsel. In re Ward (Ohio App. 8 Dist., Cuyahoga, 06-12-1997) No. 71245, 1997 WL 321492, Unreported.

Juvenile court's failure to advise mother of her rights in dependency proceeding precluded it from accepting mother's plea of true to allegation that she repeatedly struck stepchild, where court did not inform mother of her right to counsel, to remain silent, to cross-examine witnesses, or to offer evidence, court did not inform her that she could request to have a record of the proceedings made at public expense if she were indigent, and court did not ascertain that mother understood consequences of making an admission. (Per O'Neill, P.J., with one judge concurring in judgment only.) In re Calvin, Anthony, Alyshia (Ohio App. 11 Dist., Geauga, 11-22-2002) No. 2001-G-2379, 2002-Ohio-6468, 2002 WL 31663562, Unreported, stay granted 98 Ohio St.3d 1459, 783 N.E.2d 518, 2003-Ohio-644, appeal not allowed 98 Ohio St.3d 1513, 786 N.E.2d 63, 2003-Ohio-1572. Infants ⇌ 199

3. Constitutional issues

Evidence was insufficient to establish that juvenile waived his right to counsel at the adjudicatory hearing or at the sexual predator classification hearing; at the adjudicatory hearing juvenile was never advised that he had the right to the assistance of legal counsel in connection with the hearing, he was never afforded the opportunity to request the assistance of counsel, and he never waived his right to counsel, and, at the sexual predator classification hearing, the court elicited a waiver from juvenile's mother but did not ascertain whether juvenile was willing to waive his right to counsel. In re C.A.C. (Ohio App. 2 Dist., Clark, 08-04-2006) No. 2005-CA-134, No. 2005-CA-135, 2006-Ohio-4003, 2006 WL 2219570, Unreported. Infants ⇌ 227(2)

Juvenile in delinquency proceedings failed to establish deficient assistance of counsel based on counsel's failure to impeach police witnesses with information contained in their personnel files that demonstrated police misconduct; there was no evidence of information in files alleging misconduct in the performance of officers' official duties, any extrinsic evidence would not have been admissible unless probative of character for truthfulness, and counsel properly cross-examined officers regarding the appropriateness of their provocative conduct in the instant case. In re D.B. (Ohio App. 2 Dist., Montgomery, 10-21-2005) No. 20979, 2005-Ohio-5583, 2005 WL 2697344, Unreported. Infants ⇐ 205

Juvenile in delinquency proceedings failed to establish deficient assistance of counsel based on counsel's failure to request a continuance in order to locate a particular witness; counsel made tactical decision not to continue proceedings in order to locate witness who was in another state and whose proposed testimony was somewhat inconsistent with the testimony of juvenile and defense witness but did not discredit in any way the identification or testimony by police officers. In re D.B. (Ohio App. 2 Dist., Montgomery, 10-21-2005) No. 20979, 2005-Ohio-5583, 2005 WL 2697344, Unreported. Infants ⇐ 205

Trial court's acceptance of juvenile's admissions to trafficking in drugs, corrupting another with drugs, and theft, without ever addressing juvenile personally regarding his admissions to offenses, violated juvenile procedure rule and required reversal of delinquency adjudication; trial court failed to inquire of juvenile whether he understood nature of allegations against him or consequences of his admissions, or to determine whether juvenile was aware that by admitting his actions, he waived right to challenge witnesses and evidence against him, right to remain silent, and right to introduce evidence at adjudicatory hearing. In re Phibbs (Ohio App. 7 Dist., Mahoning, 09-09-2005) No. 04-MA-113, 2005-Ohio-4761, 2005 WL 2206746, Unreported. Infants ⇐ 253

Defendant, who was convicted of burglary and committed to Department of Youth Services, did not validly waive his right to counsel; at adjudication hearing, trial court made no mention of counsel issue and merely asked whether defendant was ready to proceed, record was devoid of any evidence that court explained defendant's rights to him with respect to obtaining counsel, there was no evidence that defendant waived his right to counsel at any point prior to or during trial, and record did not disclose any attempt on part of court to explain defendant's right to counsel or waiver of that right at any time. In re L.E.P. (Ohio App. 2 Dist., Clark, 09-02-2005) No. 2004 CA 85, 2005-Ohio-4600, 2005 WL 2107854, Unreported. Criminal Law ⇐ 641.4(4)

Juvenile failed to establish that he was denied effective assistance of counsel during juvenile delinquency adjudication due to counsel's failure to timely file a motion to suppress statements juvenile provided to a detective during a custodial interrogation; trial court had discretion to admit the statements into evidence given the voluntarily nature of the same and detective's testimony regarding the nature of the interview. In re Taylor (Ohio App. 5 Dist., Licking, 08-26-2005) No. 04CA110, 2005-Ohio-4499, 2005 WL 2077936, Unreported. Infants ⇐ 205

Mother's stipulation agreeing to termination of her parental rights to child was not voluntary and knowing, in violation of her due process rights, as trial court failed to comply with procedural safeguards set forth in rule governing such stipulations; trial court addressed mother personally but failed to determine whether she understood nature of allegations against her and whether she was aware of consequences of stipulation, and trial court failed to advise mother that, by entering into stipulation, she was waiving her rights to challenge witnesses and evidence against her, to introduce evidence at adjudicatory hearing, and to remain silent should she so choose. In re Rock Children (Ohio App. 5 Dist., Stark, 05-23-2005) No. 2004CA00358, 2005-Ohio-2572, 2005 WL 1228036, Unreported. Infants ⇐ 199

Juvenile's admission to assault on school official was knowing, voluntary and intelligent; magistrate explained charge, possible punishment, juvenile's constitutional rights, and consequences admitting charges resulting in waiver of rights, and juvenile asserted that he understood his rights and consequences of admission and that he was satisfied with efforts of counsel. In re C.P. (Ohio App. 9 Dist., Lorain, 04-20-2005) No. 04CA008534, No. 04CA008535, 2005-Ohio-1819, 2005 WL 901209, Unreported. Infants ⇐ 199

Trial court's noncompliance with juvenile procedural rule governing constitutional rights a party waives upon entering an admission to allegations in parental rights termination proceeding rendered mother's admission invalid; trial court's colloquy was limited to determining whether mother understood the nature of the proceedings, without advising mother of any of the rights she would be waiving in exchange for her admission. In re S.G. (Ohio App. 8 Dist., Cuyahoga, 03-17-2005) No. 84228, 2005-Ohio-1163, 2005 WL 616115, Unreported. Infants ⇐ 199

Juvenile was adequately advised that he was waiving his right to present evidence at trial, as required for his admission to charge of rape to be knowing, intelligent and voluntary, where trial court informed him that he was giving up his right to question witnesses and juvenile indicated to court that his rights had previously been explained to him at hearing before magistrate. In re Wood (Ohio App. 9 Dist., Medina, 12-08-2004) No. 04CA0005-M, 2004-Ohio-6539, 2004 WL 2808913, Unreported, appeal not allowed 105 Ohio St.3d 1518, 826 N.E.2d 315, 2005-Ohio-1880. Infants ⇐ 199

Juvenile was adequately advised of the nature of the charge against him, as required for his admission to charge of rape to be knowing, intelligent and voluntary, where complaint was served on juvenile, he was represented by counsel, and he never alleged that he was unaware of the crime he was admitting to or the circumstances surrounding it. In re Wood (Ohio App. 9 Dist., Medina, 12-08-2004) No. 04CA0005-M, 2004-Ohio-6539, 2004 WL 2808913, Unreported, appeal not allowed 105 Ohio St.3d 1518, 826 N.E.2d 315, 2005-Ohio-1880. Infants ⇐ 199

Police officers had reasonable suspicion to conduct an investigatory detention of juvenile; the officers were in an area of high crime and drug activity, juvenile was observed standing with a group of juveniles point to or moving something in his hand, one juvenile nudged juvenile to alert him to the presence of the officers, once juvenile noticed the officers he quickly put his hand in his pocket and he appeared nervous, and officers stated that juvenile and his brothers were suspected crack cocaine dealers. In re Parks (Ohio App. 10 Dist., Franklin, 12-02-2004) No. 04AP-355, 2004-Ohio-6449, 2004 WL 2757852, Unreported. Infants ⇐ 192

Juvenile's consent to police officers' warrantless search of his person following investigatory stop was not voluntary; officers discovered no illegal activity as a result of their detention of juvenile, the officers continued to repeat their request to search juvenile, and the officers mentioned to juvenile that they could obtain a search warrant, even though the facts did not support the issuance of a warrant. In re Parks (Ohio App. 10 Dist., Franklin, 12-02-2004) No. 04AP-355, 2004-Ohio-6449, 2004 WL 2757852, Unreported. Infants ⇐ 192

Although trial court listed all of juvenile's rights for him in delinquency proceeding, trial court erred because it did not conduct a "dialogue" with juvenile before finding that juvenile had waived his rights knowingly, voluntarily, and intelligently; juvenile spoke once at end of the court's explanation of his rights to indicate he understood all the rights, juvenile did not have extensive familiarity with the juvenile court system, and juvenile pled "true" before the probation officer explained why juvenile was arrested. In re Christner (Ohio App. 5 Dist., Tuscarawas, 08-06-2004) No. 2004AP020014, 2004-Ohio-4252, 2004 WL 1802018, Unreported. Infants ⇐ 199

Trial court complied with juvenile procedure rule mandates when accepting mother's admissions at adjudication phase of procedure terminating her custody of her children, and thus did not violate mother's due process rights; record indicated mother acknowledged and fully comprehended that by admitting to allegations of abuse in amended complaint, she was waiving her right to challenge witnesses and evidence on that issue, waiving her right to remain silent, and waiving her right to introduce evidence on that issue, trial court read allegations of abuse to mother and asked her if she understood what each allegation and subsequent admission meant, and if mother stated that she did not understand, the trial court explained until mother stated that she understood. In re K.P. (Ohio App. 8 Dist., Cuyahoga, 03-25-2004) No. 82709, 2004-Ohio-1448, 2004 WL 583867, Unreported, as amended nunc pro tunc, stay denied 102 Ohio St.3d 1457, 809 N.E.2d 31, 2004-Ohio-2569, appeal not allowed 102 Ohio St.3d 1473, 809 N.E.2d 1159, 2004-Ohio-2830. Constitutional Law ⇐ 274(5); Infants ⇐ 199

Trial counsel's alleged failure to raise issue of juvenile's lack of competence did not establish ineffective assistance in delinquency proceeding in which juvenile admitted that he was guilty of rape, where court was made aware that juvenile was diagnosed as having bipolar disorder and attention deficit hyperactive disorder, record did not indicate and juvenile did not demonstrate that these disorders affected juvenile's understanding of issues involved in case, juvenile was properly informed of consequences of admission of guilt, and juvenile failed to show how he was prejudiced by counsel's actions. In re J. J. (Ohio App. 9 Dist., Summit, 03-24-2004) No. 21386, 2004-Ohio-1429, 2004 WL 574135, Unreported. Infants ⇐ 205

Minor's counsel in delinquency proceeding was not insufficient for failing to raise issue of negligent investigation into charges against minor in a motion to dismiss, where counsel raised the issue at trial by arguing that the investigation harmed the credibility of all of the State's evidence. In re N.K. (Ohio App. 8 Dist., Cuyahoga, 12-24-2003) No. 82332, 2003-Ohio-7059, 2003 WL 23009113, Unreported. Infants ⇐ 205

There was no evidence in the record that testimony from social worker would have aided minor during his delinquency proceeding, and thus, minor's counsel was not insufficient in failing to call social worker as a witness. In re N.K. (Ohio App. 8 Dist., Cuyahoga, 12-24-2003) No. 82332, 2003-Ohio-7059, 2003 WL 23009113, Unreported. Infants ⇐ 205

Mother waived her appellate argument that the trial court committed reversible error when it failed to comply with the Juvenile Procedural rule pertaining to the adjudicatory hearing, during adjudicatory hearing in child dependency proceeding, where mother failed to file a timely notice of appeal regarding any errors that occurred at the adjudicatory hearing. In re C.H. (Ohio App. 8 Dist., Cuyahoga, 12-18-2003) No. 82258, No. 82852, 2003-Ohio-6854, 2003 WL 22966248, Unreported. Infants ⚭ 244.1

Juvenile was not informed that by entering guilty plea to assault he would be waiving other constitutional rights, and thus his guilty plea was not voluntarily and intelligently made, where juvenile was only informed that if he entered plea he would not have the right to a trial. In re Adams (Ohio App. 7 Dist., Mahoning, 07-29-2003) No. 01 CA 237, No. 01 CA 238, No. 02 CA 120, 2003-Ohio-4112, 2003 WL 21783682, Unreported. Infants ⚭ 199

Juvenile understood constitutional rights he would be waiving by entering admission to charge of burglary, for purposes of determining whether his guilty plea was voluntarily and intelligently made, where court asked juvenile if he understood that he had right to trial, that he could make prosecutor prove case against him, that he could cross-examine and confront witnesses, and that he was giving up those rights by pleading, and juvenile said yes; trial court was not required to make additional inquiries following juvenile's affirmative responses. In re Adams (Ohio App. 7 Dist., Mahoning, 07-29-2003) No. 01 CA 237, No. 01 CA 238, No. 02 CA 120, 2003-Ohio-4112, 2003 WL 21783682, Unreported. Infants ⚭ 199

Juvenile had constitutional right to counsel in delinquency proceeding regardless of indigency; whether juvenile was indigent did not affect his right to counsel, but only whether he could require the state to underwrite the expense of legal counsel. In re R.B. (Ohio App. 2 Dist., 01-13-2006) 166 Ohio App.3d 626, 852 N.E.2d 1219, 2006-Ohio-264. Infants ⚭ 205

Juvenile court's conduct of dispositional hearing in delinquency proceedings in absence of juvenile's counsel, and without obtaining waiver of counsel from juvenile, violated juvenile's constitutional right to counsel and to due process of law. In re B.M.S. (Ohio App. 2 Dist., 03-03-2006) 165 Ohio App.3d 609, 847 N.E.2d 506, 2006-Ohio-981. Infants ⚭ 205

Juvenile court's failure to conduct competency hearing, after issue of juvenile's competency was raised and before adjudication hearing was commenced, in violation of juvenile's right to due process of law, was not harmless error and required reversal of juvenile's adjudication as delinquent on basis of his having committed rape, where court-appointed examiner found juvenile's competency "highly suspect." In re B.M.S. (Ohio App. 2 Dist., 03-03-2006) 165 Ohio App.3d 609, 847 N.E.2d 506, 2006-Ohio-981. Infants ⚭ 253

Admission of juvenile, who had been adjudicated delinquent, to violation of court order was not knowing, voluntary, and intelligent, at show-cause hearing that state brought against juvenile for failing to follow all terms and conditions of treatment at Youth Treatment Center (YTC); although juvenile was informed of nature of allegations against him and that, by entering admission, he was waiving his rights to challenge witnesses and evidence against him, to remain silent, and to introduce evidence at adjudicatory hearing, juvenile court failed to inform juvenile of consequences of his admission. In re William B. (Ohio App. 6 Dist., 08-26-2005) 163 Ohio App.3d 201, 837 N.E.2d 414, 2005-Ohio-4428. Infants ⚭ 199

A juvenile's Fifth and Sixth Amendment rights are the same as if she were an adult. In re M.H. (Ohio Com.Pl., 10-03-2003) 129 Ohio Misc.2d 5, 814 N.E.2d 1264, 2003-Ohio-7371. Infants ⚭ 174; Infants ⚭ 205; Infants ⚭ 207

Assuming that mother's counsel was derelict in failing to timely move for appointment of new counsel due to conflict of interest and in failing to follow up on motion, mother did not show prejudice, and thus, mother could not establish ineffective assistance of counsel in proceeding for permanent custody of dependent children; Montgomery County Children Services (MCCS) proved its case by clear and convincing evidence and nothing in record suggested any viable objections. In re Lakes (Ohio App. 2 Dist., 08-02-2002) 149 Ohio App.3d 128, 776 N.E.2d 510, 2002-Ohio-3917. Infants ⚭ 205

If the defendant, in seeking appointment of new counsel, alleges facts which, if true, would require relief, the trial court must inquire into the defendant's complaint and make the inquiry part of the record; the inquiry may be brief and minimal, but it must be made if the allegations are sufficiently specific. In re Lakes (Ohio App. 2 Dist., 08-02-2002) 149 Ohio App.3d 128, 776 N.E.2d 510, 2002-Ohio-3917. Criminal Law ⚭ 641.10(2)

Sixteen-year-old suspect was not in "custody" when he made videotaped confession at police station, as element for requiring *Miranda* warnings before interrogation, where suspect and his father voluntarily accompanied detective to the police station and suspect was not placed under arrest.

State v. Noggle (Ohio App. 3 Dist., 09-18-2000) 140 Ohio App.3d 733, 749 N.E.2d 309, 2000-Ohio-1927, appeal allowed 91 Ohio St.3d 1431, 741 N.E.2d 894, appeal dismissed as improvidently granted 91 Ohio St.3d 1280, 747 N.E.2d 827, 2001-Ohio-117. Criminal Law ⚭ 412.2(2); Infants ⚭ 174

Police, by telling 16-year-old suspect that suspect's father was his "legal advisor," did not mislead suspect into believing his right to counsel had been satisfied before he made videotaped confession; rather, police merely told suspect his father could act as his legal counsel if he desired. State v. Noggle (Ohio App. 3 Dist., 09-18-2000) 140 Ohio App.3d 733, 749 N.E.2d 309, 2000-Ohio-1927, appeal allowed 91 Ohio St.3d 1431, 741 N.E.2d 894, appeal dismissed as improvidently granted 91 Ohio St.3d 1280, 747 N.E.2d 827, 2001-Ohio-117. Infants ⚭ 174

Following juvenile's acquittal in delinquency proceeding, Court of Appeals exercised its discretion to review state's challenge to trial court's evidentiary ruling that identification of controlled substance had to be done in laboratory by a chemist, though principles of double jeopardy barred retrial, as issue was capable of repetition yet evading review. In re Bennett (Ohio App. 12 Dist., 09-20-1999) 134 Ohio App.3d 699, 731 N.E.2d 1226. Infants ⚭ 248.1

Guardian ad litem appointed for mother during dependency proceeding by reason of mother's diminished mental capacity lacked authority to consent to waiver of mother's fundamental constitutional rights, and guardian's indication that there was no objection to finding of dependency based upon complaint did not satisfy or lessen magistrate's obligation to ascertain that mother's waiver of her rights was knowing, intelligent and voluntary. In re Etter (Ohio App. 1 Dist., 06-12-1998) 134 Ohio App.3d 484, 731 N.E.2d 694. Infants ⚭ 205

Juvenile was deprived of constitutionally adequate representation on his appeal from his permanent commitment to Department of Youth Services following delinquency adjudication for domestic violence, where his appointed counsel filed *Anders* brief, setting forth conclusion that there was no infirmity in juvenile's adjudication for drug trafficking, but made no request to withdraw, did not refer to matters of record that might arguably support appeal, and failed to indicate that counsel consulted with, sought advice of, or notified juvenile regarding conclusion that appeal was frivolous. In re Booker (Ohio App. 1 Dist., 03-05-1999) 133 Ohio App.3d 387, 728 N.E.2d 405. Infants ⚭ 241

Dispositional hearing transcript's reference to juvenile court telling juvenile he had been advised of his right to trial at adjudicatory hearing at which his admission was accepted did not substantially comply with mandates of Juvenile Rule 29(D), requiring court to address juvenile personally and determine that admission was being made voluntarily and with understanding of juvenile's rights; it could not be presumed that 14-year-old juvenile would infer that trial encompassed the right to challenge witnesses and evidence against him. In re Royal (Ohio App. 7 Dist., 03-01-1999) 132 Ohio App.3d 496, 725 N.E.2d 685. Infants ⚭ 199

Juvenile court magistrate's judgment entry, indicating only a finding that "subject child, after first being advised of all procedural and constitutional rights, including the right to counsel and a continuance herein, asserts said rights and ADMITS the allegations as they appear in the complaint," did not establish under the federal and state due process clauses a valid waiver of counsel or that the admission was voluntarily, knowingly, and intelligently made. In re Royal (Ohio App. 7 Dist., 03-01-1999) 132 Ohio App.3d 496, 725 N.E.2d 685. Constitutional Law ⚭ 43(1); Infants ⚭ 199; Infants ⚭ 205

Juvenile court's limited inquiry at dispositional hearing and 14-year-old juvenile's limited responses, including court's asking whether juvenile recalled the rights explained to him at adjudicatory hearing and juvenile's response, "Um-hum," were insufficient to establish valid admission or valid waiver of right to counsel under the federal and state due process clauses. In re Royal (Ohio App. 7 Dist., 03-01-1999) 132 Ohio App.3d 496, 725 N.E.2d 685. Constitutional Law ⚭ 43(1); Infants ⚭ 199; Infants ⚭ 205

Minor's admission to offense of disorderly conduct was not entered knowingly, voluntarily, and intelligently, as necessary to comport with due process, where trial court did not apprise minor of the nature of charge against her, inform her of possible consequences of her admission, or advise her of rights she would waive by entering admission. In re Fulk (Ohio App. 3 Dist., 08-06-1999) 132 Ohio App.3d 470, 725 N.E.2d 357, 1999-Ohio-840. Constitutional Law ⚭ 255(4); Infants ⚭ 174

Required collection of blood sample for DNA identification purposes from juveniles who are adjudicated delinquent on certain charges does not constitute an unreasonable search and seizure under the Fourth Amendment; reasonable doubt standard for proof of delinquency imposes substantially greater burden than the probable cause standard required for a search warrant, and the minimal intrusion of taking a blood sample is outweighed by state's legitimate interest in recording the identity of a person who is lawfully incarcerated, committed to a secure care facility, or on probation. In re Nicholson (Ohio App. 8 Dist., 02-16-1999) 132 Ohio App.3d 303, 724 N.E.2d 1217, dismissed, appeal not allowed 86 Ohio St.3d 1403, 711 N.E.2d 231. Infants ⇐ 201; Searches And Seizures ⇐ 78

Counsel's examination of his juvenile client during admission colloquy in delinquency proceeding, in apparent attempt to establish juvenile's knowledge that car he had been driving at time of his arrest had been stolen, fell below objective standard of reasonableness and amounted to ineffective assistance, where juvenile had just contested knowledge element of crime of receiving stolen property. In re Terrance P. (Ohio App. 6 Dist., 08-14-1998) 129 Ohio App.3d 418, 717 N.E.2d 1160. Infants ⇐ 205

Juvenile who enters an admission of true to a delinquency count must be informed that he is waiving his right to remain silent at the adjudicatory hearing, in the same manner as an adult criminal defendant who enters guilty plea. In re Onion (Ohio App. 11 Dist., 06-22-1998) 128 Ohio App.3d 498, 715 N.E.2d 604. Infants ⇐ 199

Failure of trial court to address juvenile personally to determine whether he understood that he was waiving the privilege against self-incrimination, before accepting juvenile's admission of true on rape count, was reversible error. In re Onion (Ohio App. 11 Dist., 06-22-1998) 128 Ohio App.3d 498, 715 N.E.2d 604. Infants ⇐ 199; Infants ⇐ 253

Even if juvenile adjudicated delinquent was improperly denied counsel at dispositional hearing, such denial did not mandate or permit reversal of underlying adjudication, where juvenile's counsel was present at adjudication hearing. In re Solis (Ohio App. 8 Dist., 12-22-1997) 124 Ohio App.3d 547, 706 N.E.2d 839. Infants ⇐ 254

Trial court did not make determination that juvenile's admission to having received stolen vehicle was knowing, voluntary, and intelligent, as required by due process clause, prior to accepting admission and adjudicating juvenile delinquent; court did not conduct meaningful colloquy with juvenile to ensure that she understood consequences of plea, most of court's references to juvenile were in the third person, and court addressed juvenile directly concerning her rights only briefly, almost as an afterthought. In re Rogers (Ohio App. 9 Dist., 12-10-1997) 124 Ohio App.3d 392, 706 N.E.2d 390. Constitutional Law ⇐ 255(4); Infants ⇐ 199

Trial court failed to adequately advise juvenile of her right to counsel, where court did not conduct any meaningful colloquy with juvenile, made most of its remarks to juvenile's mother, who had filed unruly child complaint, and addressed child directly only briefly, almost as an afterthought. In re Rogers (Ohio App. 9 Dist., 12-10-1997) 124 Ohio App.3d 392, 706 N.E.2d 390. Infants ⇐ 205

Purpose of rule governing initial procedure upon juvenile's entry of admission to charge is to ensure that minors are afforded their due process right to fundamentally fair treatment in juvenile court proceedings. In re Miller (Ohio App. 2 Dist., 04-04-1997) 119 Ohio App.3d 52, 694 N.E.2d 500. Constitutional Law ⇐ 255(4)

Juvenile court erroneously adopted referee's report and proposed journal entry indicating that juvenile knowingly and voluntarily waived counsel and entered admission where there was no indication that referee addressed juvenile personally and determined that he understood nature of allegations and consequences of his admission, that juvenile knowingly and intelligently entered admission, or that he understood nature and ramifications of adjudicatory proceedings before he waived counsel and entered admission; referee's report and proposed journal entry consisted of one page with boilerplate language and check-off boxes to indicate proceedings. In re Montgomery (Ohio App. 8 Dist., 01-21-1997) 117 Ohio App.3d 696, 691 N.E.2d 349, dismissed, appeal not allowed 78 Ohio St.3d 1490, 678 N.E.2d 1228. Infants ⇐ 206

Trial court violated juvenile's constitutional rights to due process by accepting juvenile's admission to charge of rape without complying with statutory requirement that court personally address juvenile and determine whether juvenile understood nature of allegations made in complaint or consequences of entering admission to such allegations. In re Beechler (Ohio App. 4 Dist., 07-25-1996) 115 Ohio App.3d 567, 685 N.E.2d 1257. Constitutional Law ⇐ 255(4); Infants ⇐ 199

General statement that juvenile was waiving right to trial was insufficient to inform 15-year-old that, by entering admission, he was waiving his right to challenge adverse evidence and witnesses. In re Hendrickson (Ohio App. 2 Dist., 09-27-1996) 114 Ohio App.3d 290, 683 N.E.2d 76. Infants ⇐ 199

Prior to juvenile's admission to habitual truancy charge, trial court failed to adequately advise juvenile of his constitutional rights and of consequences of his admission and also failed to sufficiently ascertain whether juvenile's purported waiver of counsel was made knowingly and voluntarily; there was no indication in record that trial court ever made determination concerning juvenile's indigency or advised juvenile that he had right to appointed counsel based on his indigency; trial court had merely asked juvenile whether it could be assumed that juvenile wished to proceed without attorney since juvenile was there without attorney, and trial court had not advised juvenile of purpose of hearing, possible penalties for alleged truancy violation, ramifications of admission to charge or of juvenile's rights to remain silent, offer evidence, cross-examine witnesses and have record made of proceedings. In re Kimble (Ohio App. 3 Dist., 09-25-1996) 114 Ohio App.3d 136, 682 N.E.2d 1066. Infants ⇐ 199; Infants ⇐ 205

Rights dialogue in juvenile proceeding is mandatory, and failure to advise juvenile of constitutionally afforded protections constitutes reversible error. In re Kimble (Ohio App. 3 Dist., 09-25-1996) 114 Ohio App.3d 136, 682 N.E.2d 1066. Infants ⇐ 199; Infants ⇐ 253

Minor who entered plea of admission to delinquency by reason of rape was denied due process where, although trial court accepting plea established that minor made plea voluntarily, trial court did not substantially comply with rule requiring that court inquire as to whether minor understood nature of charges, consequences of plea, and that minor was waiving certain rights. In re Brooks (Ohio App. 9 Dist., 06-26-1996) 112 Ohio App.3d 54, 677 N.E.2d 1229. Constitutional Law ⇐ 255(4); Infants ⇐ 199

Juvenile court did not comply with rule setting forth duties to ensure that juveniles are afforded minimum protection under the Constitution; referee failed to ascertain whether notice requirements were met, failed to disclose either purpose of hearing or possible penalties, failed to determine whether juvenile waived his right to counsel voluntarily and failed to inform juvenile of his rights. In re Johnson (Ohio App. 1 Dist., 08-23-1995) 106 Ohio App.3d 38, 665 N.E.2d 247. Infants ⇐ 198; Infants ⇐ 199; Infants ⇐ 205

Representations by juvenile defendant's attorney that defendant understood rights waived and consequences of his plea are not sufficient to demonstrate knowing and voluntary waiver. In re McKenzie (Ohio App. 8 Dist., 03-30-1995) 102 Ohio App.3d 275, 656 N.E.2d 1377. Infants ⇐ 199

Acknowledgement on the record by juvenile's counsel that counsel had explained juvenile's rights to juvenile is insufficient to demonstrate knowing and voluntary waiver by juvenile, as the court itself must address juvenile. In re Flynn (Ohio App. 8 Dist., 05-25-1995) 101 Ohio App.3d 778, 656 N.E.2d 737. Infants ⇐ 199

Juvenile's signing of waiver of rights form does not constitute substitute for the court's duty to address the juvenile. In re Flynn (Ohio App. 8 Dist., 05-25-1995) 101 Ohio App.3d 778, 656 N.E.2d 737. Infants ⇐ 199

At hearing to accept juvenile's admission to charges of resisting arrest and unauthorized use of motor vehicle, juvenile court violated rule governing acceptance of juvenile admissions and denied juvenile due process, where juvenile court failed to determine whether juvenile was making admission voluntarily and failed to determine whether juvenile understood that by entering admission, he was waiving his right to challenge witnesses and evidence against him, his right to remain silent, and his right to introduce evidence. In re Christopher R. (Ohio App. 6 Dist., 06-16-1995) 101 Ohio App.3d 245, 655 N.E.2d 280. Constitutional Law ⇐ 255(4); Infants ⇐ 199

There are no constitutional violations in an adjudicatory hearing held pursuant to Juv R 29 when the court uses evidence of guilt that was presented at the preliminary hearing where the accused was afforded cross-examination of witnesses. Matter of Gantt (Wood 1978) 61 Ohio App.2d 44, 398 N.E.2d 800, 15 O.O.3d 67.

An alleged delinquent child should be specifically advised by the court concerning his right not to testify in his own behalf, that any statement made by him may be used against him, and that a refusal to testify may not be held against him. In re Collins (Cuyahoga 1969) 20 Ohio App.2d 319, 253 N.E.2d 824, 49 O.O.2d 448. Infants ⇐ 191

Where a juvenile has received the following essentials of due process and fair treatment: (1) written notice of the specific charge or factual allegations given to the juvenile and his parents or guardian sufficiently in advance of the hearing to permit preparation; (2) notification to the juvenile and his parents of the juvenile's right to be represented by counsel retained by them, or, if they are unable to afford counsel, that counsel will be appointed to represent the juvenile; (3) application of the constitutional privileges against self-incrimination; and (4), absent a valid confession, a determination of delinquency and an order of commitment based only on sworn testimony subjected to the opportunity for cross-examination in accordance with constitutional requirements, such juvenile has not been deprived of due process under either the Constitution of the United States or the Constitution of the State of Ohio. (Annotation from former RC

2151.35.) In re Baker (Hocking 1969) 18 Ohio App.2d 276, 248 N.E.2d 620, 47 O.O.2d 411.

Juvenile defendant waived any right to confront the witnesses against him when he entered an admission to raping his six year old half sister. In re Panko (Ohio App. 12 Dist., Brown, 05-13-2002) No. CA2001-05-008, 2002-Ohio-2306, 2002 WL 975135, Unreported. Infants ⇐ 174

Juvenile defendant, who admitted raping six year old half sister, waived his right to challenge on appeal evidentiary issues, including a motion to suppress. In re Panko (Ohio App. 12 Dist., Brown, 05-13-2002) No. CA2001-05-008, 2002-Ohio-2306, 2002 WL 975135, Unreported. Infants ⇐ 243

The trial court errs in failing to inform the parent of her rights to remain silent, to cross-examine witnesses, and to offer evidence at the adjudicatory hearing and in granting permanent custody when no guardian ad litem's report is filed with the court. Matter of Eplin (Ohio App. 5 Dist., Stark, 06-29-1995) No. 94 CA 0311, 1995 WL 495451, Unreported.

A juvenile court errs when it revokes a juvenile's probation status without affording the right to counsel at the dispositional hearing and by failing to provide the opportunity to secure counsel for the probation revocation hearing where (1) the juvenile pleads true at the adjudication hearing and is not informed of right to counsel, (2) there is no inquiry into the desire for counsel, and (3) there is no indication of a waiver of right to counsel. In re Sproule, Nos. 00CA007575 and 00CA007580, 2001 WL 39594 (9th Dist Ct App, Lorain, 1–17–01).

Juvenile who was adjudicated delinquent by reason of rape lacked standing to challenge constitutionality of juvenile sex offender registration and notification law on basis that law deprived juveniles of a jury trial for sexual offender designations, where the law was not applied to juvenile in case. In re Nooks (Ohio App. 2 Dist., Montgomery, 10-25-2002) No. 19374, 2002-Ohio-5824, 2002 WL 31398607, Unreported. Constitutional Law ⇐ 42.1(1)

Juvenile court's continued exercise of jurisdiction over juvenile regarding his parole violation in delinquency matter, when the parole violation was committed by juvenile when he was 19, was not an act of discrimination treating juvenile differently from other adults, but, rather, an act recognizing juvenile's ongoing status as a juvenile; pursuant to statute, juvenile court retained jurisdiction over the juvenile, who was adjudicated delinquent prior to age of 18, until he turned 21. In re Gillespie (Ohio App. 10 Dist., 12-19-2002) 150 Ohio App.3d 502, 782 N.E.2d 140, 2002-Ohio-7025, appeal not allowed 98 Ohio St.3d 1513, 786 N.E.2d 63, 2003-Ohio-1572. Infants ⇐ 281

Juvenile court's continued exercise of jurisdiction over juvenile in delinquency matter, after juvenile committed parole violation when he was 19 years old, did not arbitrarily or capriciously deny juvenile's right to bail in violation of due process, although common pleas court had released juvenile on bail on the adult charges underlying parole violation while juvenile court revoked juvenile's parole and returned him to custody; common pleas court's exercise of power over juvenile with respect to adult charges did not eviscerate juvenile court's coexisting power to hold juvenile pursuant to his parole violation, and juvenile had no absolute constitutional right to bail as a juvenile. In re Gillespie (Ohio App. 10 Dist., 12-19-2002) 150 Ohio App.3d 502, 782 N.E.2d 140, 2002-Ohio-7025, appeal not allowed 98 Ohio St.3d 1513, 786 N.E.2d 63, 2003-Ohio-1572. Constitutional Law ⇐ 255(4); Infants ⇐ 281

In delinquency matter, a juvenile is not entitled to indictment by grand jury, to a public trial, or to trial by jury. In re Gillespie (Ohio App. 10 Dist., 12-19-2002) 150 Ohio App.3d 502, 782 N.E.2d 140, 2002-Ohio-7025, appeal not allowed 98 Ohio St.3d 1513, 786 N.E.2d 63, 2003-Ohio-1572. Infants ⇐ 197; Infants ⇐ 203; Jury ⇐ 19.5

A juvenile has no absolute constitutional right to bail in a delinquency case. In re Gillespie (Ohio App. 10 Dist., 12-19-2002) 150 Ohio App.3d 502, 782 N.E.2d 140, 2002-Ohio-7025, appeal not allowed 98 Ohio St.3d 1513, 786 N.E.2d 63, 2003-Ohio-1572. Infants ⇐ 134

The exclusion on Fourth Amendment grounds of the contents of a fourteen-year-old schoolgirl's purse from delinquency proceedings is erroneous where a teacher discovered the pupil smoking in violation of school rules inasmuch as (1) the teacher's report supported a suspicion on the part of the principal that the pupil had violated school rules; (2) the principal's suspicion gave him reason to suspect the pupil had cigarettes in her purse, her denials notwithstanding, and a search of the purse for cigarettes was, therefore, proper; (3) the discovery in plain view of rolling papers on removal of the cigarette pack gave the principal reason to suspect the presence of marijuana; and (4) reasonable suspicion of the presence of marijuana justified a thorough search which turned up marijuana, letters implicating the pupil in dope dealing, and other evidence of drug-related activities. (Annotation from US Const Am 4.) New Jersey v. T.L.O. (U.S.N.J. 1985) 105 S.Ct. 733, 469 U.S. 325, 83 L.Ed.2d 720.

Juveniles who are charged with felony crimes are not entitled to a jury trial because the applicable due process standard for juvenile proceedings is fundamental fairness, and a jury, is not necessary for adequate factfinding. McKeiver v. Pennsylvania (U.S.Pa. 1971) 91 S.Ct. 1976, 403 U.S. 528, 29 L.Ed.2d 647.

A juvenile taken into custody as a delinquent has certain rights guaranteed by the Due Process Clause of the United States Constitution in delinquency proceedings by the state which include the following: (1) notice of the charge, (2) right to counsel, (3) right to confrontation and cross-examination, and (4) privilege against self incrimination. Application of Gault (U.S.Ariz. 1967) 87 S.Ct. 1428, 387 U.S. 1, 18 L.Ed.2d 527, 40 O.O.2d 378.

Under the present Juvenile Code and Rules, a juvenile court cannot change a "temporary" commitment to the Ohio youth commission to an "permanent" commitment without hearing; further, the commitment of an unruly child, not declared "delinquent", is a violation of due process and any hearing held on the above matters requires the presence of the youth involved. OAG 72–071.

4. Admissions

Juvenile's admissions to two counts of rape and to gross sexual imposition were not knowing, voluntary, or intelligent; at the initial hearing juvenile admitted to and entered a plea of guilty to the charged offenses, the court conducted a second hearing in which the court never referred to the fact that juvenile had already admitted and pled guilty to the charges, and during the second hearing the court never explained to juvenile that he had been incorrectly advised as to the potential dispositions and sentences for his offenses at the initial hearing. In re Smith (Ohio App. 3 Dist., Union, 06-05-2006) No. 14-05-33, 2006-Ohio-2788, 2006 WL 1519688, Unreported. Infants ⇐ 199

Mother's consent to adjudication of children as dependent and neglected was knowingly made; consent was decided by means of mediation, and thus only evidence in record reflecting mother's consent was in trial court's judgment entry, there was no evidence in record upon which it could be determined that mother's consent was not knowing or voluntary, and fact that mother was described as a "slow learner" did not establish that she did not understand consequences of her consent. In re Donell F. (Ohio App. 6 Dist., Lucas, 08-12-2005) No. L-04-1308, 2005-Ohio-4175, 2005 WL 1926512, Unreported. Infants ⇐ 199

Juvenile's admission to gross sexual imposition was knowing, voluntary, and intelligent; juvenile had declined offer to have complaint reread to him at plea hearing, trial court reminded juvenile of constitutional rights and that informed him that entering plea would result in waiver of rights, juvenile was informed of possible dispositions, and juvenile indicated that he understood all possibilities. In re J.F.F. (Ohio App. 2 Dist., Miami, 04-15-2005) No. 2004 CA 34, 2005-Ohio-1906, 2005 WL 937852, Unreported. Infants ⇐ 199

Mother's failure to object to trial court's adjudication order granting custody of children to Department of Children and Family Services (CCDCFS) did not waive for appellate review issue as to whether trial court complied with procedural rule governing acceptance of admissions to allegations in parental rights termination proceedings, where issue was subject to review under plain error doctrine. In re S.G. (Ohio App. 8 Dist., Cuyahoga, 03-17-2005) No. 84228, 2005-Ohio-1163, 2005 WL 616115, Unreported. Infants ⇐ 243

Juvenile court's admonishment with respect to potential penalty, prior to accepting juvenile's plea of true to allegation of disorderly conduct, substantially complied with requirements of applicable rule and was not reversible error in absence of prejudice to juvenile, where juvenile was adequately informed of more severe consequence of his admission to gross sexual imposition, and admissions were made in context of plea agreement in which two counts of violating past orders were dismissed, and count of domestic violence was reduced to disorderly conduct. In re Wisdom (Ohio App. 5 Dist., Stark, 02-28-2005) No. 2004CA00187, 2005-Ohio-930, 2005 WL 503407, Unreported. Infants ⇐ 253

Mother's appeal from denial of her motion to withdraw her admission that her child was a dependent child was moot, where trial court never adopted magistrate's recommendation but, rather, dismissed case, and mother never lost custody of her daughter. In re Johnson (Ohio App. 11 Dist., Ashtabula, 11-26-2004) No. 2004-A-0060, 2004-Ohio-6340, 2004 WL 2698031, Unreported. Infants ⇐ 247

Juvenile's adjudication as a delinquent child as a result of committing gross sexual imposition was not against the manifest weight of the evidence; witnesses testified that juvenile admitted putting five-year old victim's penis in his mouth, officer testified that juvenile admitted inappropriately touching and kissing victim, victim's mother testified that victim's behavior changed following the incident, and there was no innocent explanation for juvenile's placement of his mouth on the victim's mouth, chest, and penis. In re Higginbotham (Ohio App. 4 Dist., Lawrence, 10-27-2004) No. 04CA26, 2004-Ohio-6004, 2004 WL 2569446, Unreported. Infants ⇐ 176

State could indict juvenile for negligent homicide after juvenile had admitted to lesser charge of negligent assault at initial adjudicatory hearing (IAH), even though state chose not to be present at IAH and did not reserve any right to further charge juvenile in event victim died, where state did not enter into plea agreement with juvenile and, accordingly, admission to negligent assault was not part of any plea agreement with state. In Re J.A. P. (Ohio App. 2 Dist., Montgomery, 07-23-2004) No. 20058, 2004-Ohio-3918, 2004 WL 1662105, Unreported. Infants ⇐ 199

Juvenile court's statement at beginning of juvenile's amenability hearing, that disposition of matter depended upon whether juvenile was willing to plead to charged offenses, was not so coercive as to render juvenile's admissions involuntary; court had a right to consider whether juvenile was willing to accept responsibility for his delinquent conduct in determining whether he was amenable to treatment in the juvenile court system. In re S.H. (Ohio App. 2 Dist., Montgomery, 07-16-2004) No. 20107, 2004-Ohio-3779, 2004 WL 1587203, Unreported. Infants ⇐ 68.7(3); Infants ⇐ 199

The trial court's failure to personally address mother or father to determine whether they understood the nature of the allegations or the consequences of their admissions of dependency constituted plain error, in child dependency proceeding; the Juvenile Procedural Rules specifically required the trial court to directly address parents before accepting their admissions. In re Elliott (Ohio App. 4 Dist., Washington, 05-19-2004) No. 03CA65, No. 03CA66, 2004-Ohio-2770, 2004 WL 1189475, Unreported. Infants ⇐ 199; Infants ⇐ 243

Trial court substantially complied with requirements of rule related to acceptance of admission of guilt in juvenile delinquency proceeding, where court questioned juvenile concerning his awareness of charge against him, possible penalties stemming from admission, and rights he would be waiving by entering admission, and there was nothing to support contention that juvenile did not understand implications of entering guilty plea. In re J. J. (Ohio App. 9 Dist., Summit, 03-24-2004) No. 21386, 2004-Ohio-1429, 2004 WL 574135, Unreported. Infants ⇐ 199

Trial court order granting children services temporary custody of mother's two children was not an abuse of discretion; mother was a heavy prescription drug user, she had been arrested four times in the past three years, she missed several counseling appointments and was terminated from services, and she refused to comply with the case management plan. In re Barnosky (Ohio App. 4 Dist., Athens, 03-09-2004) No. 03CA32, 2004-Ohio-1127, 2004 WL 444527, Unreported. Infants ⇐ 154.1

Magistrate's acceptance of minor's admission to charge in delinquency complaint was not plain error; minor was represented by counsel when she entered her admission, no guardian ad litem was required, and minor agreed with magistrate's statements concerning minor's understanding of circumstances of her offense, consequences of an admission, and the voluntariness of her acceptance of responsibility without any apparent hesitation, confusion, or misgivings. In re Harper (Ohio App. 2 Dist., Montgomery, 12-12-2003) No. 19948, 2003-Ohio-6666, 2003 WL 22927248, Unreported. Infants ⇐ 243

Evidence supported trial court finding that juvenile's admission to gross sexual imposition and rape was knowing, intelligent, and voluntary; juvenile's responses to magistrate during plea colloquy were appropriate, and there was no evidence that juvenile's admission was other than knowing and voluntary. In re J.W. (Ohio App. 2 Dist., Montgomery, 09-26-2003) No. 19869, 2003-Ohio-5096, 2003 WL 22220345, Unreported. Infants ⇐ 199

Juvenile gained understanding of factual circumstances surrounding charges of burglary from juvenile's counsel, despite trial court's failure to explain elements of burglary, for purposes of determining whether his guilty plea was voluntarily and intelligently made, where counsel stated he had gone through the factual bases with juvenile, and juvenile stated he understood what his lawyer stated regarding the charges. In re Adams (Ohio App. 7 Dist., Mahoning, 07-29-2003) No. 01 CA 237, No. 01 CA 238, No. 02 CA 120, 2003-Ohio-4112, 2003 WL 21783682, Unreported. Infants ⇐ 199

Trial court adequately determined that juvenile entered admission voluntarily and with an understanding of the nature of the allegations against him and the consequences of the admission; juvenile heard from prosecutor all the charges for which the hearing was called, as well as the purpose of the proceedings, prosecutor then gave an extensive recitation of all the specifics of each offense before juvenile admitted them, and trial court verified that juvenile understood rights he was giving up, that his thinking was clear, and that he had no questions about the proceeding. State v. D.M. (Ohio App. 8 Dist., Cuyahoga, 06-19-2003) No. 81641, 2003-Ohio-3228, 2003 WL 21419595, Unreported. Infants ⇐ 199

Because hearing regarding motion to modify temporary custody to permanent custody was a dispositional hearing, rather than an adjudicatory hearing, juvenile court rule setting forth procedures to be followed by trial court upon filing of a complaint and its resolution by admission did not apply. In re L.D. (Ohio App. 8 Dist., Cuyahoga, 05-15-2003) No. 81397, 2003-Ohio-2471, 2003 WL 21101101, Unreported. Infants ⇐ 230.1

Complaint and summons in juvenile delinquency proceeding did not have to provide notice of potential disposition that juvenile could be placed in foster care; juvenile rule only required that trial court advise juvenile, prior to accepting an admission to complaint, of nature of allegations and consequences of admission, including possible dispositions. In re Hutzel (Ohio App. 5 Dist., Tuscarawas, 04-29-2003) No. 2002AP110087, 2003-Ohio-2288, 2003 WL 21025820, Unreported. Infants ⇐ 197; Infants ⇐ 198

Prior to accepting juvenile's admission to offense of gross sexual imposition, trial court failed to determine whether juvenile fully understood consequences of his admission, thus mandating reversal of delinquency adjudication, even though trial court asked juvenile if he understood that he would have been subject to a six-month minimum term of commitment and juvenile replied affirmatively, where court failed to inform him of any maximum potential term of commitment available, juvenile was not entering admission to avoid prosecution as an adult, he was only 16 at time of hearing, and proceeding was conducted in an abrupt manner. In re A.H. (Ohio App. 8 Dist., Cuyahoga, 04-17-2003) No. 81214, 2003-Ohio-1953, 2003 WL 1900952, Unreported. Infants ⇐ 199; Infants ⇐ 253

Revocation of juvenile's probation on two counts of raping his younger sister, following hearing at which juvenile moved unsuccessfully to withdraw his admission to those offenses based on allegations that his parents had coerced him into making admission, was not abuse of discretion; juvenile had repeatedly been brought back into court and warned that he would be sent to Department of Youth Services if his improper behavior did not cease, and he did not present adequate evidence to support allegations of coercion by parents. In re McElfresh (Ohio App. 7 Dist., Belmont, 03-07-2003) No. 02 BA 12, 2003-Ohio-1079, 2003 WL 932342, Unreported. Infants ⇐ 225

Denial of juvenile's motion to withdraw admission to two counts of raping his younger sister, brought on basis of allegation that juvenile's parents coerced him into making admission, was not abuse of discretion in view of insufficient supporting evidence; while juvenile testified that his parents were engaging in sexual activity with him and his siblings and that they advised him to enter an admission, he did not testify that they coerced into following that advice by engaging in sexual activity or any other means. In re McElfresh (Ohio App. 7 Dist., Belmont, 03-07-2003) No. 02 BA 12, 2003-Ohio-1079, 2003 WL 932342, Unreported. Infants ⇐ 199

Juvenile court failed to substantially comply with rule governing acceptance of admissions during neglected child proceedings, where it failed to question father in order to determine whether his admission was voluntary or inform him that by admitting to the neglect charge the court could terminate his parental rights. In re Aldridge (Ohio App. 4 Dist., Ross, 10-30-2002) No. 02CA2661, 2002-Ohio-5988, 2002 WL 31439807, Unreported. Infants ⇐ 199

Biological mother's surrender of parental rights over four of her children was voluntary, despite fact that she made it in return for dismissal of permanent custody motion as to one of her five children; trial court engaged in discussion with her concerning this promise, and mother indicated that she desired to surrender permanent custody as to other four children in exchange for this promise. In re White Children (Ohio App. 5 Dist., Stark, 10-28-2002) No. 2002CA00216, 2002-Ohio-5949, 2002 WL 31426250, Unreported. Infants ⇐ 157

Court complied with rule requiring it to address biological mother personally and to conduct discussion to determine whether her admission was entered knowingly and voluntarily prior to accepting stipulation regarding permanent custody of four of her children by county agency; record reflected court advised mother of options available to her, explained procedure, explained meaning of permanent custody, and mother acknowledged that she understood. In re White Children (Ohio App. 5 Dist., Stark, 10-28-2002) No. 2002CA00216, 2002-Ohio-5949, 2002 WL 31426250, Unreported. Infants ⇐ 199

Writ of mandamus could not be used as vehicle to require Ohio Department of Youth Services (ODYS) to conduct release review for juvenile who pled guilty to possession of over 250 grams of heroin and was ordered to be held by ODYS until her 21st birthday, as order apparently was entered as a result of a plea bargain in which state agreed to withdraw motion to bind juvenile over to adult court in return for juvenile receiving a maximum juvenile sentence of less than three years; if juvenile was dissatisfied with benefits she received as result of plea bargain she should ask to set aside admission she entered in juvenile court and again face risk of being incarcerated in adult prison for up to ten years. State ex rel. Delgado v. Thomas (Ohio App. 10 Dist., Franklin, 06-13-2002) No. 01AP-1449, 2002-Ohio-2930, 2002 WL 1291837, Unreported. Mandamus ⇐ 61

Juvenile's admission to rape was not knowingly, voluntarily, or intelligently made, where magistrate failed to determine whether juvenile understood nature of allegation and misinformed juvenile as to consequences of his admission; magistrate did not explain rape charge, and informed juvenile that he faced no more than 90 days in detention, when in fact juvenile was sentenced to one year in custody of Department of Youth Services (DYS) and placed on indefinite probation. In re B.M.S. (Ohio App. 2 Dist., 03-03-2006) 165 Ohio App.3d 609, 847 N.E.2d 506, 2006-Ohio-981. Infants ⇐ 199

A juvenile court errs in accepting a mother's admission of abuse or neglect without that courts' ensuring that the parent has a full understanding of her legal rights so that she may protect her custody of her child, and when that admission contributes to a finding of abuse and neglect and thus enables the court subsequently to award permanent custody to the county, the legitimacy of the underlying judicial process itself is challenged if mother is not permitted to appeal from the award on the basis of that admission. In re A.C. (Ohio App. 8 Dist., 04-14-2005) 160 Ohio App.3d 457, 827 N.E.2d 824, 2005-Ohio-1742. Infants ⇐ 199

Mother did not waive for appellate review claim that juvenile court committed prejudicial error by failing to substantially comply with the rules of juvenile procedure when it accepted mother's admission to county's complaint for permanent custody of her minor children, even though she failed to seek to withdraw her admissions at two different dispositional hearings; court's failure to determine that mother understood the consequences of her admission infected all that followed. In re A.C. (Ohio App. 8 Dist., 04-14-2005) 160 Ohio App.3d 457, 827 N.E.2d 824, 2005-Ohio-1742. Infants ⇐ 242

Before accepting mother's admission to county's complaint for permanent custody of her minor children, juvenile court was required, first, to ascertain that mother understood the allegations contained in the complaint and the consequences of her admission and, second, to inform her of the specific rights she was waiving by admitting to the complaint. In re A.C. (Ohio App. 8 Dist., 04-14-2005) 160 Ohio App.3d 457, 827 N.E.2d 824, 2005-Ohio-1742. Infants ⇐ 199

Juvenile procedural rule's mandate that a juvenile's failure or refusal to admit allegations shall be deemed a denial barred trial court from accepting juvenile's *Alford* plea, in delinquency proceeding in which it was alleged that juvenile had committed two counts of rape of a child under 13, as juvenile made no admission of culpability, which had to be deemed a denial. In re Kirby (Ohio, 03-17-2004) 101 Ohio St.3d 312, 804 N.E.2d 476, 2004-Ohio-970. Infants ⇐ 199

Waiver by minor mother's counsel of mother's appearance at adjudication hearing in child dependency proceeding did not involve an "admission" by mother and thus did not implicate juvenile procedure rule that prohibits a court from accepting an admission from a juvenile unless it addresses the party personally. In re Baby Girl Doe (Ohio App. 6 Dist., 08-30-2002) 149 Ohio App.3d 717, 778 N.E.2d 1053, 2002-Ohio-4470, appeal not allowed 97 Ohio St.3d 1425, 777 N.E.2d 278, 2002-Ohio-5820. Infants ⇐ 199

The best method for the trial court to comply with rule requiring court to personally question juvenile concerning voluntariness of admission and knowing waiver of rights is to use the language of the rule itself, carefully tailored to the child's level of understanding, stopping after each right and asking whether the child understands the right and knows that he is waiving it by entering an admission. In re Graham (Ohio App. 7 Dist., 05-17-2002) 147 Ohio App.3d 452, 770 N.E.2d 1123, 2002-Ohio-2407. Infants ⇐ 174

Juvenile court's attempt, at dispositional hearing, to remedy its failure at adjudication hearing to advise juvenile defendant of the rights he was waiving by entering admission, was inadequate; court was required to advise juvenile defendant of his rights before accepting his admission, not after. In re Graham (Ohio App. 7 Dist., 05-17-2002) 147 Ohio App.3d 452, 770 N.E.2d 1123, 2002-Ohio-2407. Infants ⇐ 174

To satisfy requirements of rule governing acceptance of juvenile admissions, court must address juvenile personally and conduct an on-the-record discussion to determine whether admission is being entered knowingly and voluntarily. In re Holcomb (Ohio App. 8 Dist., 02-04-2002) 147 Ohio App.3d 31, 768 N.E.2d 722, 2002-Ohio-2042. Infants ⇐ 174

Although strict compliance with rule governing acceptance of juvenile admissions is not required, courts must substantially comply with procedures specified therein. In re Holcomb (Ohio App. 8 Dist., 02-04-2002) 147 Ohio App.3d 31, 768 N.E.2d 722, 2002-Ohio-2042. Infants ⇐ 174

Fact that juvenile court intermingled acceptance of juvenile's plea with that of his brother did not mean that court failed to personally address juvenile, as required by rule governing acceptance of juvenile admissions, where court individually addressed each brother after each major component of its colloquy. In re Holcomb (Ohio App. 8 Dist., 02-04-2002) 147 Ohio App.3d 31, 768 N.E.2d 722, 2002-Ohio-2042. Infants ⇐ 174

Juvenile court properly determined whether juvenile made his admissions voluntarily by inquiring as to whether he was under influence of any alcohol or drugs that would cloud his judgment and whether anybody made any promises or threats to force either him to make admissions. In re Holcomb (Ohio App. 8 Dist., 02-04-2002) 147 Ohio App.3d 31, 768 N.E.2d 722, 2002-Ohio-2042. Infants ⇐ 174

Trial court properly made determination as to whether juvenile, who made an admission, understood charges against him, where state had read charges into record and provided detailed summary of evidence against juvenile. In re Holcomb (Ohio App. 8 Dist., 02-04-2002) 147 Ohio App.3d 31, 768 N.E.2d 722, 2002-Ohio-2042. Infants ⇐ 174

Juvenile court failed to substantially comply with rule governing acceptance of juvenile admissions, where it failed to inform juvenile of term of his possible commitment. In re Holcomb (Ohio App. 8 Dist., 02-04-2002) 147 Ohio App.3d 31, 768 N.E.2d 722, 2002-Ohio-2042. Infants ⇐ 174

The determination of whether a party's admission at a juvenile adjudicatory hearing complies with the governing juvenile rule is similar to that used in determining whether a criminal defendant's guilty plea complies with the governing criminal rule. In re Clark (Ohio App. 8 Dist., 01-29-2001) 141 Ohio App.3d 55, 749 N.E.2d 833, 2001-Ohio-4126. Infants ⇐ 174

Family court judge conducting proceedings on county Department of Child and Family Services' (DCFS) petition for permanent custody of mother's three children substantially complied with rule governing admissions at juvenile adjudicatory hearings; judge explained mother's rights at initial hearing, she was represented by lawyer throughout proceedings, when judge personally addressed mother at hearing at which she admitted allegations of amended complaint he asked her specifically, inter alia, whether she had discussed case with her attorney and whether she understood that her admission would result in finding of neglect, and mother indicated her understanding of these consequences in presence of attorney. In re Clark (Ohio App. 8 Dist., 01-29-2001) 141 Ohio App.3d 55, 749 N.E.2d 833, 2001-Ohio-4126. Infants ⇐ 174

Magistrate's questions to counsel for parties to dependency proceeding, asking whether modification of one word in complaint was acceptable, and then whether there was any objection to her making adjudication of dependency based upon stipulation to complaint as amended, did not satisfy her obligation to determine whether mother was making knowing, intelligent and voluntary admission to facts; magistrate never addressed mother personally, and made no real inquiry into whether mother understood nature of charges in complaint, consequences of making admission to facts, or rights she would be waiving as consequence of admission. In re Etter (Ohio App. 1 Dist., 06-12-1998) 134 Ohio App.3d 484, 731 N.E.2d 694. Infants ⇐ 199

Magistrate's failure, in dependency proceeding, to satisfy her obligation to determine whether mother was making knowing, intelligent and voluntary admission to facts in complaint was plain error, and mother's failure to object thereto did not waive appellate review of magistrate's failure to comply with applicable rule. In re Etter (Ohio App. 1 Dist., 06-12-1998) 134 Ohio App.3d 484, 731 N.E.2d 694. Infants ⇐ 243

Presence of 14-year-old juvenile's mother at the adjudicatory hearing did not provide dispositive proof that the juvenile waived his rights and gave his admission voluntarily, knowingly, and intelligently. In re Royal (Ohio App. 7 Dist., 03-01-1999) 132 Ohio App.3d 496, 725 N.E.2d 685. Infants ⇐ 199; Infants ⇐ 205

A waiver form is not a valid substitute for the court's duty to personally address the juvenile and determine that the admission is being made voluntarily and with an understanding of the juvenile's rights. In re Royal (Ohio App. 7 Dist., 03-01-1999) 132 Ohio App.3d 496, 725 N.E.2d 685. Infants ⇐ 199

Judgment entry of disposition, which merely stated that "upon inquiry, the 'Juvenile' Court finds said plea was entered voluntarily and intelligently and the Court accepts the same and affirms the decision submitted by the Magistrate," did not substantially comply with mandates of Juvenile Rule

29(D), requiring court to address juvenile personally and determine that admission was being made voluntarily and with understanding of juvenile's rights. In re Royal (Ohio App. 7 Dist., 03-01-1999) 132 Ohio App.3d 496, 725 N.E.2d 685. Infants ⇐ 199

Court would not presume regularity of adjudicatory hearing at which 14–year–old juvenile's admission was accepted, where juvenile was unrepresented by counsel at the hearing and nothing in the record indicated that juvenile court complied with the juvenile rules by informing juvenile of his rights if he waived counsel, including the right to request a transcript of any of the proceedings. In re Royal (Ohio App. 7 Dist., 03-01-1999) 132 Ohio App.3d 496, 725 N.E.2d 685. Infants ⇐ 250

If the juvenile court fails to substantially comply with Juvenile Rule 29(D), requiring the court to address the juvenile personally and determine that the admission is being made voluntarily and with an understanding of the juvenile's rights, the adjudication must be reversed so that the juvenile may plead anew. In re Royal (Ohio App. 7 Dist., 03-01-1999) 132 Ohio App.3d 496, 725 N.E.2d 685. Infants ⇐ 253

Requirement that juvenile who admitted delinquency on charge of gross sexual imposition provide a DNA sample was not a "consequence" of the admission of which trial court was obligated to inform him prior to accepting the admission; requirement was remedial and did not have a direct and immediate effect upon the range of juvenile's punishment. In re Nicholson (Ohio App. 8 Dist., 02-16-1999) 132 Ohio App.3d 303, 724 N.E.2d 1217, dismissed, appeal not allowed 86 Ohio St.3d 1403, 711 N.E.2d 231. Infants ⇐ 199

Whether State Department of Youth Services could properly require that juvenile provide blood sample for DNA identification, after failing to inform him of that requirement when he admitted his delinquency on charge of gross sexual imposition, was waived in proceeding to enjoin department from taking blood sample, where juvenile failed to seek a withdrawal of his admission. In re Nicholson (Ohio App. 8 Dist., 02-16-1999) 132 Ohio App.3d 303, 724 N.E.2d 1217, dismissed, appeal not allowed 86 Ohio St.3d 1403, 711 N.E.2d 231. Infants ⇐ 243

For purposes of determining voluntariness, juvenile's admission in delinquency proceeding is analogous to guilty plea made by adult in criminal proceeding and constitutes waiver of rights to challenge allegations in complaint. In re Terrance P. (Ohio App. 6 Dist., 08-14-1998) 129 Ohio App.3d 418, 717 N.E.2d 1160. Infants ⇐ 199

Court's initial questioning of juvenile concerning his understanding of charges against him in delinquency proceeding prior to explaining such charges was attempt to ascertain whether juvenile understood charges, rather than acceptance of his admissions to those charges, despite fact that juvenile's responses to questions were phrased as admissions, and juvenile's responses therefore did not amount to unknowing or involuntary waiver of his right to challenge allegations in complaint. In re Terrance P. (Ohio App. 6 Dist., 08-14-1998) 129 Ohio App.3d 418, 717 N.E.2d 1160. Infants ⇐ 199

Juvenile's challenge to knowledge element of crime of receiving stolen property with which he was charged in delinquency complaint invalidated his subsequent admission thereto; juvenile stated, in response to questioning by court, that he did not know car he had been driving at time of his arrest was stolen because insurance papers were in glove compartment. In re Terrance P. (Ohio App. 6 Dist., 08-14-1998) 129 Ohio App.3d 418, 717 N.E.2d 1160. Infants ⇐ 199

To comply with juvenile rule governing acceptance of admission by youth, court must address the youth personally and conduct an on-the-record discussion to determine whether the admission is being entered knowingly and voluntarily. In re West (Ohio App. 8 Dist., 06-15-1998) 128 Ohio App.3d 356, 714 N.E.2d 988. Infants ⇐ 199

Trial court improperly accepted juvenile's admission to burglary, even though court personally addressed juvenile, where there was only minimal discussion of charged offense and possible penalties, a cursory discussion of juvenile's right to counsel, and no discussion regarding the rights juvenile was waiving by entering admission. In re West (Ohio App. 8 Dist., 06-15-1998) 128 Ohio App.3d 356, 714 N.E.2d 988. Infants ⇐ 199

Absent a showing of prejudice, appellate court will not disturb admission by youth on appeal if trial court substantially complied with juvenile rule governing acceptance of admissions; test for prejudice is whether admission would otherwise have been made. In re West (Ohio App. 8 Dist., 06-15-1998) 128 Ohio App.3d 356, 714 N.E.2d 988. Infants ⇐ 253

Failure of juvenile court to substantially comply with rule requiring it to make determination that admission is being made voluntarily before accepting any admission has prejudicial effect necessitating reversal of adjudication, so that juvenile may plead anew. In re Doyle (App. 2 Dist., 10-03-1997) 122 Ohio App.3d 767, 702 N.E.2d 970. Infants ⇐ 205; Infants ⇐ 253

Juvenile court failed, during delinquency proceeding, to substantially comply with required procedures for accepting juvenile's admission to rape charge, where court only addressed group of juveniles regarding what rights they would be giving up if they entered admission to charge, no such colloquy was repeated when court addressed juvenile personally, and court merely asked whether juvenile had heard and understood what court previously said, asked both juvenile and his mother if juvenile understood his rights and knew what he was doing and provided juvenile and mother with "statement of rights and waiver form" which, while informing juvenile of his rights, did not specifically state that juvenile would waive those rights by entering admission. In re Miller (Ohio App. 2 Dist., 04-04-1997) 119 Ohio App.3d 52, 694 N.E.2d 500. Infants ⇐ 199

Best method for juvenile court to satisfy its obligations, in delinquency proceeding, under rule setting forth initial procedure upon entry of admission to charge is to use language contained in the rule, though carefully tailored to child's level of understanding, stopping after each right and asking whether child understands right and knows that he is waiving it by entering admission; absent that form of colloquy, substantial compliance with rule must be clearly demonstrated. In re Miller (Ohio App. 2 Dist., 04-04-1997) 119 Ohio App.3d 52, 694 N.E.2d 500. Infants ⇐ 199

Failure of juvenile court in delinquency proceeding to comply, at least substantially, with requirements of rule setting forth initial procedure upon entry of admission to charge constitutes reversible error. In re Miller (Ohio App. 2 Dist., 04-04-1997) 119 Ohio App.3d 52, 694 N.E.2d 500. Infants ⇐ 199; Infants ⇐ 253

Trial court violates rule governing adjudicatory hearings in delinquency proceedings if it accepts juvenile's admission of delinquency when trial court did not address juvenile personally to determine if he understood consequences of his admission and rights waived. In re Montgomery (Ohio App. 8 Dist., 01-21-1997) 117 Ohio App.3d 696, 691 N.E.2d 349, dismissed, appeal not allowed 78 Ohio St.3d 1490, 678 N.E.2d 1228. Infants ⇐ 199

Prior to accepting juvenile's admission to delinquency complaint, juvenile court must personally address actual juvenile before court and determine that juvenile, and not merely attorney, understands nature of allegations and consequences of entering admission, and test for accused delinquent's understanding of charges is subjective, such that juvenile must actually understand. In re Beechler (Ohio App. 4 Dist., 07-25-1996) 115 Ohio App.3d 567, 685 N.E.2d 1257. Infants ⇐ 199

Juvenile court's failure to substantially comply with statutory requirements for accepting juvenile's admission constitutes prejudicial error that requires reversal of adjudication in order to permit party to plead anew. In re Beechler (Ohio App. 4 Dist., 07-25-1996) 115 Ohio App.3d 567, 685 N.E.2d 1257. Infants ⇐ 199; Infants ⇐ 253

Lack of substantial compliance with requirements for accepting juvenile's admission requires reversal of delinquency adjudication and opportunity for juvenile to plead anew. In re Hendrickson (Ohio App. 2 Dist., 09-27-1996) 114 Ohio App.3d 290, 683 N.E.2d 76. Infants ⇐ 199; Infants ⇐ 253

Juvenile court was required, under rule requiring court to inform juvenile of "consequences" of admission, to tell juvenile that he faced potential commitment of up to six years in legal custody of Department of Youth Services. In re Hendrickson (Ohio App. 2 Dist., 09-27-1996) 114 Ohio App.3d 290, 683 N.E.2d 76. Infants ⇐ 199

Admission in delinquency case involves waiver of juvenile's right to challenge allegations of complaint and to confront witnesses. In re Brooks (Ohio App. 9 Dist., 06-26-1996) 112 Ohio App.3d 54, 677 N.E.2d 1229. Infants ⇐ 199

Before accepting admission of guilt to charge of delinquency, trial court must personally address juvenile on record with respect to areas of inquiry set forth in rule and may accept juvenile's admission only upon court's substantial compliance with rule; in absence of such compliance, adjudication must be reversed and juvenile permitted to plead again. In re Brooks (Ohio App. 9 Dist., 06-26-1996) 112 Ohio App.3d 54, 677 N.E.2d 1229. Infants ⇐ 199; Infants ⇐ 253

Trial court is required to substantially comply with juvenile rule setting forth procedure for acceptance of admission of criminal conduct, and strict scrutiny is not required. In re William H. (Ohio App. 6 Dist., 08-18-1995) 105 Ohio App.3d 761, 664 N.E.2d 1361. Infants ⇐ 199

Referee in juvenile delinquency proceeding erred when he failed to comply with juvenile rule stating that court shall not accept admission without determining if party understands that, by entering admission, party is waiving the right to challenge witnesses and evidence, to remain silent, and to introduce evidence at adjudicatory hearing, but this error was neither prejudicial nor plain since juvenile was given due process in these proceedings. In re Harris (Ohio App. 2 Dist., 05-05-1995) 104 Ohio App.3d 324, 662 N.E.2d 34. Constitutional Law ⇨ 255(4); Infants ⇨ 199; Infants ⇨ 253

Juvenile rule stating that court, in juvenile delinquency proceedings, shall not accept admission without determining that party understands that, by entering admission, party is waiving the right to challenge witnesses and evidence and to remain silent was drafted in order to satisfy due process and fairness requirements for juveniles in juvenile court proceedings. In re Harris (Ohio App. 2 Dist., 05-05-1995) 104 Ohio App.3d 324, 662 N.E.2d 34. Constitutional Law ⇨ 255(4); Infants ⇨ 199

Referee in juvenile delinquency hearing substantially complied with juvenile rule stating that court shall not accept admission without determining if party is making admission voluntarily with understanding of nature of the allegations and consequences of the admission; immediately after plea negotiation took place, referee asked juvenile "By admitting to these you are in fact stating you are responsible for these charges. Do you understand that?" and juvenile replied "yes" and later in the proceedings, juvenile's attorney stated that juvenile was "aware of the results of the plea." In re Harris (Ohio App. 2 Dist., 05-05-1995) 104 Ohio App.3d 324, 662 N.E.2d 34. Infants ⇨ 199

Trial court improperly accepted youth's admission to amended complaint alleging attempted receipt of stolen property without addressing him personally to ascertain whether he understood consequences of admission or rights he was waiving. In re McKenzie (Ohio App. 8 Dist., 03-30-1995) 102 Ohio App.3d 275, 656 N.E.2d 1377. Infants ⇨ 199

Prosecutor must affirmatively demonstrate that judge addressed youth personally and conducted on-the-record exchange to determine whether admission was knowing and voluntary. In re McKenzie (Ohio App. 8 Dist., 03-30-1995) 102 Ohio App.3d 275, 656 N.E.2d 1377. Infants ⇨ 199

As in criminal case in which defendant offers plea of guilty, juvenile court must make careful inquiry before accepting admission in juvenile case. In re Flynn (Ohio App. 8 Dist., 05-25-1995) 101 Ohio App.3d 778, 656 N.E.2d 737. Infants ⇨ 199

While admission in juvenile case is not deemed to be guilty plea under rules governing pleas in criminal cases, it is a waiver of the right to challenge the allegations raised in the complaint. In re Flynn (Ohio App. 8 Dist., 05-25-1995) 101 Ohio App.3d 778, 656 N.E.2d 737. Infants ⇨ 199

Court of Appeals' review of juvenile adjudication hearing is similar to its review of entry of guilty plea in criminal case. In re Flynn (Ohio App. 8 Dist., 05-25-1995) 101 Ohio App.3d 778, 656 N.E.2d 737. Infants ⇨ 248.1

Juvenile court's acceptance of juvenile's admission did not comply with rule governing entry of admissions at adjudicatory hearings where juvenile's counsel acknowledged on the record that he had explained to juvenile his rights, court asked juvenile if he understood that he was waiving his right to trial, court did not specifically ask juvenile about waiver of his rights to challenge witnesses and evidence, to remain silent, and to introduce evidence, and juvenile was only 14 years old and it was doubtful he understood that waiver of trial would encompass those other rights, even though juvenile signed waiver of rights form and clearly understood the charges against him. In re Flynn (Ohio App. 8 Dist., 05-25-1995) 101 Ohio App.3d 778, 656 N.E.2d 737. Infants ⇨ 199

Juvenile's failure to file objection to referee's recommendation did not prevent Court of Appeals from reviewing the voluntariness of juvenile's plea. In re Flynn (Ohio App. 8 Dist., 05-25-1995) 101 Ohio App.3d 778, 656 N.E.2d 737. Infants ⇨ 243

Trial court did not substantially comply with rule setting forth required colloquy with juvenile before acceptance of admission, necessitating reversal of delinquency adjudication, where there was no discussion by trial court to determine whether juvenile understood by entering his admission he was waiving his rights to challenge witnesses and evidence against him, to remain silent, and to introduce evidence at adjudicatory hearing. In re Jenkins (Ohio App. 12 Dist., 02-13-1995) 101 Ohio App.3d 177, 655 N.E.2d 238. Infants ⇨ 199

In a juvenile proceeding the trial court asks each party whether he admits or denies each allegation in the complaint to determine how the court will proceed, as the admission or denial of the allegations determines whether the court proceeds in accordance with Juv R 29(D) or 29(E). In re Dukes (Summit 1991) 81 Ohio App.3d 145, 610 N.E.2d 513, motion overruled 63 Ohio St.3d 1411, 585 N.E.2d 835.

While the trial court does not strictly follow the Juvenile Rules for an admission or denial to the allegations in the complaint, there is no prejudice against the parents where their behavior before the court indicates they will deny the allegations and the court proceeds in accordance with Juv R 29(E). In re Dukes (Summit 1991) 81 Ohio App.3d 145, 610 N.E.2d 513, motion overruled 63 Ohio St.3d 1411, 585 N.E.2d 835.

A parent's admission of neglect of the children in an action to terminate custody is invalid when the record shows that the parents were not personally addressed by the court, the court did not advise them of their rights, and there was no evidence their acts were voluntary. In re Smith (Ottawa 1991) 77 Ohio App.3d 1, 601 N.E.2d 45.

In a delinquency case, a juvenile's plea is an admission or denial of the facts contained in the complaint; an admission is not a guilty plea but a waiver of rights to challenge the allegations; a juvenile is not a delinquent child until so adjudicated; a denial is an assertion of the juvenile's right to challenge the allegations; if the allegations of the complaint are not proved, the complaint must be dismissed. State v. Penrod (Summit 1989) 62 Ohio App.3d 720, 577 N.E.2d 424, motion overruled 44 Ohio St.3d 715, 542 N.E.2d 1112.

Where a complaint alleges that a child is neglected or dependent within the meaning of RC 2151.03(B) and 2151.04(A), 2151.04(B), and 2151.04(C), the child's mother is not prohibited by Juv R 29(D)(2) from taking part in the adjudicatory hearing by the fact that she entered a plea of "admitted" to the allegations in the complaint. In re Sims (Preble 1983) 13 Ohio App.3d 37, 468 N.E.2d 111, 13 O.B.R. 40.

Juv R 29(C) provides that a failure or refusal to admit the allegations of the complaint shall be deemed a denial. In re Green (Franklin 1982) 4 Ohio App.3d 196, 447 N.E.2d 129, 4 O.B.R. 300.

Prosecutor's threat to file charges against complaining witness, if she were to testify to facts contrary to her signed affidavit, did not render involuntary juvenile's admission to charge that he was delinquent because he took a minivan without consent; during adjudicatory hearing, juvenile denied that anyone made threats or promises or otherwise forced him into admitting charge, juvenile, his father, and his guardian ad litem signed waiver that included a statement that no promises, threats, or inducements had been made to secure waiver, and prosecutor's statement was not related in any way to juvenile's admission. In re Hudnall (Ohio App. 4 Dist., Lawrence, 09-27-2002) No. 02CA21, 2002-Ohio-5364, 2002 WL 31230578, Unreported. Infants ⇨ 199

Trial court substantially complied with admissions rule, in accepting mother's admission that her two children were dependent, although court did not advise her of her right to remain silent and to introduce evidence at adjudicatory hearing; court held discussion with mother on the record, and determined that she entered admission knowingly and voluntarily. In re N.D. (Ohio App. 8 Dist., Cuyahoga, 07-25-2002) No. 80559, 2002-Ohio-3791, 2002 WL 1728880, Unreported. Infants ⇨ 199

At the time of a juvenile's "admit" plea where there is no record made of the proceeding there is no record for the judge to review in determining whether the juvenile's motion to withdraw his plea and vacate his sentence should be granted; as a result, a conviction for operating a motor vehicle under the influence of alcohol after underage consumption is vacated with instructions to conduct a new adjudicatory hearing which is properly recorded. In re L.D. (Ohio App. 8 Dist., Cuyahoga, 12-13-2001) No. 78750, 2001 WL 1612114, Unreported.

Juvenile court's failure to apprise a fourteen-year-old of the potential penalty which he faces in making an admission to the charge of burglary fails to comply with the requirements of Juv R 29(D). In re Gilbert (Ohio App. 7 Dist., Jefferson, 03-29-1999) No. 96-JE-34, 1999 WL 182526, Unreported.

A juvenile does not knowingly and intelligently waive her right to counsel (1) in absence of any examination by the court regarding such right in deciding whether to admit or deny the complaint, (2) where the complaint states that the juvenile is a delinquent child by reason of committing an act that would constitute complicity to receiving stolen property if she were an adult, and (3) where the magistrate fails to ascertain whether the juvenile understands the charge against her or the possible length of any commitment in the custody of the Department of Youth Services. In re Doyle (App. 2 Dist., 10-03-1997) 122 Ohio App.3d 767, 702 N.E.2d 970.

A homeowner's liability insurer has no duty to defend or indemnify its insured pursuant to the exclusion provision for expected or intentional injuries where the insured's son is adjudicated delinquent as a result of throwing a broken pool cue at another juvenile from a distance of fifteen feet with the intention of hurting him. Horace Mann Companies v. Harris (Ohio App. 12 Dist., Madison, 08-11-1997) No. CA96-11-051, 1997 WL 451371, Unreported.

Trial court adequately determined that juvenile entered plea voluntarily and with an understanding of the nature of the allegations against him and the consequences; the court advised juvenile that he was giving up his right to trial, his right to have the State prove he committed the offense beyond a reasonable doubt, his right to present his own defense, and his right to an appeal, and juvenile and his parents stated that they understood those rights. In re Homan (Ohio App. 5 Dist., Tuscarawas, 01-27-2003) No. 2002AP080067, 2003-Ohio-352, 2003 WL 183811, Unreported. Infants ⇨ 199

Juvenile court in dependency proceeding abused its discretion by denying mother's motion to withdraw her plea of true without conducting a hearing to determine whether there was a reasonable and legitimate basis for withdrawal. (Per O'Neill, P.J., with one judge concurring in judgment only.) In re Calvin, Anthony, Alyshia (Ohio App. 11 Dist., Geauga, 11-22-2002) No. 2001-G-2379, 2002-Ohio-6468, 2002 WL 31663562, Unreported, stay granted 98 Ohio St.3d 1459, 783 N.E.2d 518, 2003-Ohio-644, appeal not allowed 98 Ohio St.3d 1513, 786 N.E.2d 63, 2003-Ohio-1572. Infants ⇨ 199

5. Bifurcated hearings

Mother did not waive on appeal issue of whether trial court erred in failing to bifurcate permanent custody hearing into two separate adjudicatory and dispositional hearings, on basis that she failed to object to procedure during course of hearing and failed to request bifurcation of proceedings, as parties were not clearly put on notice that trial court intended to hold only a single evidentiary hearing simultaneously covering adjudication and disposition, and, as such, mother was not required to bring issue to attention of trial court or request bifurcation. In re J.H. (Ohio App. 12 Dist., Preble, 06-26-2006) No. CA2005-11-019, No. CA2005-11-020, 2006-Ohio-3237, 2006 WL 1726669, Unreported. Infants ⇨ 243

Fact that parents might have been served prior to permanent custody hearing with all documents required for hearing did not relieve trial court of requirement that it bifurcate hearing into two separate adjudicatory and dispositional hearings, in termination of parental rights proceeding, as juvenile rule required all parties to consent to dispositional hearing being held immediately after adjudicatory hearing, and there was no evidence that parents consented to a dispositional hearing being held immediately after adjudicatory hearing. In re J.H. (Ohio App. 12 Dist., Preble, 06-26-2006) No. CA2005-11-019, No. CA2005-11-020, 2006-Ohio-3237, 2006 WL 1726669, Unreported. Infants ⇨ 203

Trial court's failure to bifurcate permanent custody hearing into two separate adjudicatory and dispositional hearings, on county agency's original complaint for custody of child, as required by juvenile rules, was reversible error, in termination of parental rights proceeding; trial court made both an adjudicative finding, i.e., that child was dependent, and a dispositional finding, i.e., that it was in child's best interests to be placed in permanent custody of agency, following a single hearing. In re J.H. (Ohio App. 12 Dist., Preble, 06-26-2006) No. CA2005-11-019, No. CA2005-11-020, 2006-Ohio-3237, 2006 WL 1726669, Unreported. Infants ⇨ 253

Mother was entitled to adjudicatory hearing on her complaint alleging that father abused child and seeking order to protect child; trial court was not permitted to dismiss complaint without first conducting adjudicatory hearing. In re Robinson (Ohio App. 5 Dist., Perry, 11-02-2002) No. 02CA7, 2002-Ohio-6020, 2002 WL 31458237, Unreported. Breach Of The Peace ⇨ 20

In proceedings where parental rights are subject to termination, it is reversible error not to provide separate adjudicatory and dispositional hearings as required by RC 2151.35, Juv R 29(F)(2)(a), and 34. In re Baby Girl Baxter (Ohio 1985) 17 Ohio St.3d 229, 479 N.E.2d 257, 17 O.B.R. 469.

A bifurcated hearing on a permanent custody complaint is required due to the evidentiary and waiver requirements of Juv R 29 and due to the different standards of proof applicable to the adjudicatory and dispositional stages, and where the record does not reflect separate stages, a remand for further proceedings on the matter is proper. Elmer v. Lucas County Children Services Bd. (Lucas 1987) 36 Ohio App.3d 241, 523 N.E.2d 540.

In an action where the county files a motion for permanent custody of a child, the child's mother files a motion for permanent custody, and the court grants the county's motion at the close of the evidence, there is no requirement to bifurcate the permanent custody hearing into separate adjudicatory and dispositional stages since there is no dispositional option as either the mother's rights are terminated, or the motion is denied. In re Jones (Cuyahoga 1985) 29 Ohio App.3d 176, 504 N.E.2d 719, 29 O.B.R. 206.

A hearing on a complaint for permanent custody must be bifurcated according to Juv R 29 and 34 into separate adjudicatory and dispositional hearings, notwithstanding the contrary provisions of RC 2151.414, since Juv R 1(A) provides that all proceedings in a juvenile court are governed by the Rules of Juvenile Procedure. In re Vickers Children (Butler 1983) 14 Ohio App.3d 201, 470 N.E.2d 438, 14 O.B.R. 228.

6. Evidence and standards

State established when the alleged delinquent act of 14-year-old juvenile's rape of his five-year-old half-brother occurred by presenting evidence that delinquent act occurred shortly before father took half-brother to the hospital because he complained of discomfort in his anus. In re C.M. (Ohio App. 2 Dist., Montgomery, 07-21-2006) No. 21363, 2006-Ohio-3741, 2006 WL 2037185, Unreported. Infants ⇨ 176

Adjudication of delinquency for 14-year-old juvenile's rape of his five-year-old half-brother was against the manifest weight of the evidence; half-brother's testimony lacked coherence and included statements that he was "fully asleep" and "was dreaming" during alleged incident, there was a complete lack of physical evidence, and no expert testimony that half-brother exhibited behavior that was consistent with abuse. In re C.M. (Ohio App. 2 Dist., Montgomery, 07-21-2006) No. 21363, 2006-Ohio-3741, 2006 WL 2037185, Unreported. Infants ⇨ 176

Juvenile's delinquency adjudication by reason of having committed offense of receiving stolen property was not against the manifest weight of the evidence; officers identified juvenile as driver of vehicle discovered to be stolen from motel, steering column was damaged in a way consistent with the vehicle being started without a key, and juvenile's possession of stolen vehicle was completely unexplained. In re D.B. (Ohio App. 2 Dist., Montgomery, 10-21-2005) No. 20979, 2005-Ohio-5583, 2005 WL 2697344, Unreported. Infants ⇨ 176

Juvenile's delinquency adjudication by reason of having committed offense of complicity to commit felonious assault was not against the manifest weight of the evidence; officers identified juvenile as driver who was carrying a gun, shots were thereafter fired from passenger window as vehicle drove past officers, gun used in shooting was discovered in later traffic stop under seat where juvenile was sitting, juvenile's fingerprints were on magazine of gun, and, although officer's conduct in spitting on driver's vehicle and pointing gun at driver's head was seriously provocative, driver was no longer acting in sudden passion or rage when he returned to scene for retribution. In re D.B. (Ohio App. 2 Dist., Montgomery, 10-21-2005) No. 20979, 2005-Ohio-5583, 2005 WL 2697344, Unreported. Infants ⇨ 176

Juvenile's delinquency adjudication for committing offense of felony theft of a motor vehicle was not against the manifest weight of the evidence; although juvenile presented alibi evidence, credible witnesses testified regarding defendant's use and abandonment of stolen truck, and defendant implicated himself when he stated to police officer, "the most that you can get me for is joyriding." In re Travis L.H. (Ohio App. 6 Dist., Huron, 10-14-2005) No. H-05-001, 2005-Ohio-5571, 2005 WL 2694811, Unreported. Infants ⇨ 176

Juvenile procedure rule governing procedure for an adjudicatory hearing did not apply to juvenile's probation violation hearing. In re J.B. (Ohio App. 12 Dist., Brown, 09-26-2005) No. CA2004-09-024, No. CA2004-09-025, 2005-Ohio-5045, 2005 WL 2335314, Unreported. Infants ⇨ 225

Competent, credible evidence supported juvenile's adjudication of delinquency by reason of having committed the offenses of rape and gross sexual imposition; juvenile's admission that he engaged in sexual conduct with the victim was corroborated by witness testimony, including the testimony of the victim herself. In re Taylor (Ohio App. 5 Dist., Licking, 08-26-2005) No. 04CA110, 2005-Ohio-4499, 2005 WL 2077936, Unreported. Infants ⇨ 176

Delinquency adjudication for aggravated arson was supported by sufficient evidence and was not against manifest weight of evidence, even though juvenile claimed that his statements that he reached in through broken window, pulled out curtains, and set them on fire conflicted with fire investigator's testimony; fire investigator testified that fire started in area of couch in front of a window. State v. O'Brien (Ohio App. 5 Dist., Stark, 07-18-2005) No. 2004CA00370, 2005-Ohio-3765, 2005 WL 1713549, Unreported. Infants ⇨ 176

Evidence was sufficient to show that person other than accomplice was likely to be present in home at time of offense, so as to support delinquency adjudication for burglary; homeowner was temporarily living in domestic-violence shelter, had left all of her furniture and personal belongings in home, went back to her home to retrieve some items, always intended to return to home after her former husband was arrested, and stated that only time that she would not have returned to her home would have been in dark due to fear of her former husband. State v. O'Brien (Ohio App. 5 Dist., Stark, 07-18-2005) No. 2004CA00370, 2005-Ohio-3765, 2005 WL 1713549, Unreported. Infants ⇨ 176

Adjudication of delinquency based on knowingly causing a fire was against the manifest weight of the evidence; the State presented an improbable timeline that required juvenile to collect kerosene lamps from other rooms, return to her room and empty them on smoldering fire, grab her telephone, place an emergency call, and then walk outside the house within a span of 60-120 seconds, arson investigator never framed his opinions on the origins of the fire in terms of a reasonable degree of professional certainty, his conclusions were based on assumption that other witnesses proved to be false, and stepmother indicated that she awoke to crackling noises and her dogs barking, which would indicate an advanced fire. In re Horton (Ohio App. 4 Dist., Adams, 07-06-2005) No. 04CA794, 2005-Ohio-3502, 2005 WL 1595241, Unreported. Infants ⇒ 176

Evidence presented during delinquency proceeding was sufficient to support finding that juvenile "knowingly" caused fire in her room; juvenile repeatedly went in and out of her home before the fire, she placed several personal belongings, including make-up, a stereo, and clothing, in her stepmother's car before the fire, expert witness testified that the fire was not accidental in origin and kerosene lamps re-ignited the fire, stepmother testified that juvenile was the only person in the room when the fire started and that she had removed several kerosene lamps from the closet adjoining a wall in juvenile's room several weeks before the fire. In re Horton (Ohio App. 4 Dist., Adams, 07-06-2005) No. 04CA794, 2005-Ohio-3502, 2005 WL 1595241, Unreported. Infants ⇒ 176

Evidence was sufficient to support juvenile's delinquency conviction for aggravated riot; police detective testified that juvenile had been identified by police as a gang member, victim testified that when gang arrived at her house there were about 30 kids present, she could identify juvenile as being there, juvenile acted as an instigator, and she saw juvenile's lips move when he said "shoot the mother f***er." In re T.K. (Ohio App. 8 Dist., Cuyahoga, 05-12-2005) No. 84934, 2005-Ohio-2321, 2005 WL 1119807, Unreported, appeal allowed 106 Ohio St.3d 1543, 835 N.E.2d 726, 2005-Ohio-5343, stay granted 108 Ohio St.3d 1410, 841 N.E.2d 315, 2006-Ohio-179, reversed 109 Ohio St.3d 512, 849 N.E.2d 286, 2006-Ohio-3056. Infants ⇒ 176

Evidence was insufficient to support juvenile's delinquency convictions for two counts of felonious assault; trial judge found that juvenile's statement to "shoot the mother f***er" was directed at his brother, testimony at trial established that juvenile's brother handed his weapon to second juvenile and second juvenile fired weapon at victims, trial judge failed to find that juvenile's statement was directed at second juvenile in an attempt to cause harm, and juvenile's convictions could not stand under a theory of aiding and abetting since a principal could not be readily identified. In re T.K. (Ohio App. 8 Dist., Cuyahoga, 05-12-2005) No. 84934, 2005-Ohio-2321, 2005 WL 1119807, Unreported, appeal allowed 106 Ohio St.3d 1543, 835 N.E.2d 726, 2005-Ohio-5343, stay granted 108 Ohio St.3d 1410, 841 N.E.2d 315, 2006-Ohio-179, reversed 109 Ohio St.3d 512, 849 N.E.2d 286, 2006-Ohio-3056. Infants ⇒ 176

Trial court's employment of recording device in delinquency proceeding which left vast majority of juvenile's responses inaudible did not substantially comply with rule requiring record of adjudicatory and dispositional hearings, and left Court of Appeals unable to determine if trial court even minimally complied with requirements to ensure that juvenile's plea to inducing panic and violating probation was knowing, voluntary, and intelligent. In re Dawson (Ohio App. 11 Dist., Trumbull, 04-29-2005) No. 2004-T-0027, 2005-Ohio-2088, 2005 WL 1009834, Unreported. Infants ⇒ 203

Mother did not waive issues for review, that trial court did not comply with rule of juvenile procedure governing adjudicatory hearing, and that her admission was not made knowingly, intelligently and voluntarily, in proceeding in which permanent custody of her child was granted to county department of children and family services; time for appealing court's order adjudicating child as neglected and continuing its previous order placing child in temporary custody of department had been tolled since there was no notation on appearance docket that mother was served notice of order. In re M.C. (Ohio App. 8 Dist., Cuyahoga, 04-28-2005) No. 85054, No. 85108, 2005-Ohio-1968, 2005 WL 977832, Unreported. Infants ⇒ 244.1

Sentence to Department of Youth Services following delinquency adjudication for gross sexual imposition was supported by trial court's findings that juvenile was 14 years old at time of offense while victim was nine, juvenile had prior adjudication for assault which had been amended from charge of gross sexual imposition, that juvenile had not successfully completed court-ordered sex offender therapy, and that juvenile had reoffended after having completed only 23 sessions. In re J.F.F. (Ohio App. 2 Dist., Miami, 04-15-2005) No. 2004 CA 34, 2005-Ohio-1906, 2005 WL 937852, Unreported. Infants ⇒ 223.1

Adjudication as juvenile sex offender registrant following delinquency adjudication for gross sexual imposition was supported by findings that juvenile was 14 years old and victim was nine, offense involved juvenile placing hand inside victim's pants in vaginal region, prior assault charge had been amended from charge of gross sexual imposition, juvenile did not successfully complete court-ordered sex offender therapy, that juvenile reoffended after 23 sessions of treatment, and that juvenile appeared to view victims not as people, but as objects. In re J.F.F. (Ohio App. 2 Dist., Miami, 04-15-2005) No. 2004 CA 34, 2005-Ohio-1906, 2005 WL 937852, Unreported. Infants ⇒ 227(2)

Juvenile's delinquency adjudication based on chronic truancy was against the manifest weight of the evidence, where juvenile's absence was due to his father's refusal to allow him to attend school. In re Whittekind (Ohio App. 4 Dist., Washington, 12-17-2004) No. 04CA22, 2004-Ohio-7282, 2004 WL 3090246, Unreported. Infants ⇒ 153

Finding that juvenile was delinquent due to his commission of attempted burglary was not against manifest weight of evidence; juvenile's confession, and eyewitness testimony that juvenile attempted to break into residence, weighed heavily against juvenile's own testimony, and testimony of other juveniles, and, even without juvenile's confession, eyewitness testimony was competent, credible evidence of juvenile's guilt. In re Bays (Ohio App. 12 Dist., Warren, 03-01-2004) No. CA2003-02-026, 2004-Ohio-915, 2004 WL 369039, Unreported. Infants ⇒ 176

Admission of juvenile's confession in evidence at delinquency hearing, before state had established corpus delicti of crime, was not error; state presented strong evidence of guilt independent of juvenile's confession, and testimony of witness that she saw juvenile attempting to break into residence came immediately after testimony of deputy sheriff who testified that juvenile had confessed to offense. In re Bays (Ohio App. 12 Dist., Warren, 03-01-2004) No. CA2003-02-026, 2004-Ohio-915, 2004 WL 369039, Unreported. Infants ⇒ 174

Trial court adjudication of delinquency based on juvenile's commission of robbery was not against the manifest weight of the evidence; juvenile admitted that she hit and kicked the victim, victim's daughter testified that she saw juvenile kick and punch the victim, and victim testified that juvenile took her cigarette case, cigarettes, house keys, driver's license, and four dollars. In re J.G. (Ohio App. 2 Dist., Montgomery, 02-20-2004) No. 20074, 2004-Ohio-774, 2004 WL 316443, Unreported. Infants ⇒ 176

Minor who engaged in non-forcible sexual contact with a five-year-old girl was delinquent, even though girl consented to the conduct, where minor was nine or ten at the time of the offense, minor was presumably of greater physical and intellectual development, and evidence indicated that minor used manipulative threats to obtain compliance from other victim. In re N.K. (Ohio App. 8 Dist., Cuyahoga, 12-24-2003) No. 82332, 2003-Ohio-7059, 2003 WL 23009113, Unreported. Infants ⇒ 153

Evidence was sufficient to support trial court's finding that minor had forced sexual conduct with five-year-old girl so as to adjudicate minor delinquent; victim testified that minor threatened her by telling her he would tell her friends not to play with her if she did not perform oral sex, and that minor pushed her head down to gain compliance. In re N.K. (Ohio App. 8 Dist., Cuyahoga, 12-24-2003) No. 82332, 2003-Ohio-7059, 2003 WL 23009113, Unreported. Infants ⇒ 176

Trial court finding that child was a dependent child was not against the sufficiency of the evidence; mother had a history of being unable to provide for her children and for being unable to provide adequate housing, mother was unemployed, psychological testing of mother indicated a lack of efficacy and a lack of independence, and, at the hearing on mother's objections to dependency finding, the court found out that mother had moved out of the state and had not been in contact with child or inquired about child's welfare. In re Barker (Ohio App. 5 Dist., Stark, 11-24-2003) No. 03-CA-279, 2003-Ohio-6406, 2003 WL 22843907, Unreported. Infants ⇒ 155; Infants ⇒ 157; Infants ⇒ 158

Trial court finding of juvenile delinquency was not against the manifest weight of the evidence; police officers testified that, after they activated their lights and attempted to box in vehicle juvenile was driving, he drove vehicle at police officer, he rammed police vehicle, and he only stopped his vehicle after he was involved in another collision. In re B.B. (Ohio App. 8 Dist., Cuyahoga, 11-06-2003) No. 81948, 2003-Ohio-5920, 2003 WL 22510518, Unreported. Infants ⇒ 153

Evidence was sufficient to support juvenile's adjudication of delinquency based on the commission of felonious assault, and thus denial of juvenile's motion for judgment of acquittal was proper; defendant admitted that he punched the victim in the face, and the victim sustained a broken jaw as a result of the punch. In re D.P. (Ohio App. 8 Dist., Cuyahoga, 10-30-2003) No. 82151, 2003-Ohio-5821, 2003 WL 22456992, Unreported. Infants ⇒ 209

There was competent credible evidence to show that child suffered from acute pain of lasting duration, to support finding that child was abused; doctor testified that multiple bruises found on child's body were from one to five days old, were not in typical locations of common toddler bruises, and were in the outline of a hand. In re K.B. (Ohio App. 9 Dist., Summit, 07-16-2003) No. 21365, 2003-Ohio-3784, 2003 WL 21658319, Unreported. Infants ⇔ 179

Trial court's error in admitting hearsay testimony from officer in delinquency proceeding for assault offense, in which officer testified about what victim and witness told him about assault, did not result in prejudice to juvenile; trial judge made specific, detailed findings of fact, which focused less on the genesis of the assault, and more on the extent of juvenile's involvement once other individual and the victim fell to the ground. In re J.P. (Ohio App. 8 Dist., Cuyahoga, 07-03-2003) No. 81486, 2003-Ohio-3522, 2003 WL 21511316, Unreported. Infants ⇔ 253

Juvenile's placement of his hand in victim's pants would be sufficient to support delinquency adjudication for attempted rape if he commented, after victim removed his hand, that victim had "let other guys finger" her. In re Hardie (Ohio App. 4 Dist., Washington, 03-14-2003) No. 02CA55, 2003-Ohio-1388, 2003 WL 1423403, Unreported. Infants ⇔ 153

Delinquency adjudication for violating condition of parole for attempted gross sexual imposition that prohibited unsupervised contact with any individuals under age of 18 years was not against manifest weight of evidence, where social worker who had given juvenile permission to go to store with his 17-year-old girlfriend but had not given permission for contact with any other minors observed juvenile at store with girlfriend and with two persons under age of three. In re Raypole (Ohio App. 12 Dist., Fayette, 03-10-2003) No. CA2002-01-001, No. CA2002-01-002, 2003-Ohio-1066, 2003 WL 928976, Unreported. Infants ⇔ 225

Evidence that juvenile was at store with his 17-year-old girlfriend and with two persons under age of three supported a finding beyond a reasonable doubt that juvenile violated rule of parole on delinquency adjudication for attempted gross sexual imposition that prohibited any unsupervised contact with any individuals under age of 18 years; while social worker had given juvenile permission to go to store with girlfriend, juvenile had not sought permission to have contact with the other minors. In re Raypole (Ohio App. 12 Dist., Fayette, 03-10-2003) No. CA2002-01-001, No. CA2002-01-002, 2003-Ohio-1066, 2003 WL 928976, Unreported. Infants ⇔ 225

Offense of breaking and entering does not require specific proof of age, and thus state did not have to prove juvenile's age for court to have found that juvenile committed offense and to have adjudicated juvenile a delinquent. In re Tressler (Ohio App. 3 Dist., Paulding, 11-19-2002) No. 11-02-06, 2002-Ohio-6276, 2002 WL 31555996, Unreported. Burglary ⇔ 2; Infants ⇔ 153

Evidence existed that gas station was unoccupied, as required to support finding of juvenile delinquency based on offense of breaking and entering; evidence indicated that break-ins occurred after hours, owner's wife operated store by herself, and owner was with wife when wife closed store at night. In re Tressler (Ohio App. 3 Dist., Paulding, 11-19-2002) No. 11-02-06, 2002-Ohio-6276, 2002 WL 31555996, Unreported. Infants ⇔ 176

Adjudication of juvenile as delinquent for his involvement in burglary was not against the manifest weight of the evidence; although main evidence against defendant was testimony of co-defendant who testified as part of plea bargain, co-defendant's testimony was not inherently unreliable as a result of plea bargain, and his testimony about telephone call made to ensure that burglary victim was home was corroborated by telephone records. In re Barchet (Ohio App. 3 Dist., Hancock, 10-09-2002) No. 5-02-27, No. 5-02-30, No. 5-02-28, No. 5-02-31, No. 5-02-29, No. 5-02-32, 2002-Ohio-5420, 2002 WL 31255290, Unreported. Infants ⇔ 176

A juvenile court's determination of parental unsuitability for custody of minor children must be supported by a preponderance of the evidence. Reynolds v. Ross County Children's Services Agency (Ohio 1983) 5 Ohio St.3d 27, 448 N.E.2d 816, 5 O.B.R. 87.

In a neglect case, the juvenile court may proceed to find neglect at the adjudication stage upon the admission of the parent charged; no other evidence is required, even when the standard is clear and convincing evidence. In re Lakes (Ohio App. 2 Dist., 08-02-2002) 149 Ohio App.3d 128, 776 N.E.2d 510, 2002-Ohio-3917. Infants ⇔ 179

Uncontroverted evidence that juvenile and his sister, with whom juvenile resided, engaged in physical altercation over the issue of whether juvenile would be leaving the house, and that juvenile's sister sustained physical injuries as consequence of this encounter, was sufficient to support juvenile's adjudication as delinquent on basis of his commission of acts which, if committed by adult, would have constituted offense of domestic violence. In re Booker (Ohio App. 1 Dist., 03-05-1999) 133 Ohio App.3d 387, 728 N.E.2d 405. Infants ⇔ 176

Parochial school student disciplined by school officials for sexual harassment could also be referred for adjudication as delinquent for acts of sexual violence, consistent with student handbook, as disciplinary options available to school under sexual harassment and sexual violence provisions of handbook were not mutually exclusive and student's admissions and complaints of other students gave school reason to believe student had committed acts of sexual violence, triggering mandatory reporting requirement. Iwenofu v. St. Luke School (Ohio App. 8 Dist., 02-16-1999) 132 Ohio App.3d 119, 724 N.E.2d 511, appeal not allowed 86 Ohio St.3d 1407, 711 N.E.2d 234. Schools ⇔ 8

Trial court's erroneous admission, in delinquency adjudication proceeding, of hearsay statement of juvenile's adult codefendant, was prejudicial to juvenile and required reversal of adjudication, where evidence remaining after exclusion of hearsay statement was not overwhelming evidence of juvenile's guilt and reasonable probability existed that exclusion of statement from adjudication proceeding would have affected result. In re Carter (Ohio App. 4 Dist., 11-06-1997) 123 Ohio App.3d 532, 704 N.E.2d 625. Infants ⇔ 174; Infants ⇔ 253

Evidence that juvenile passenger in car stopped by police used alias upon being questioned, which was sole admissible evidence of guilt presented in delinquency adjudication proceeding, was insufficient to convince reasonable trier of fact, beyond reasonable doubt, that juvenile knowingly exercised dominion and control over cocaine found in purse of adult passenger, as required to support juvenile's adjudication as delinquent by reason of acts which would, if committed by adult, constituted felony drug abuse; only evidence that juvenile exerted actual control over purse at any time was improperly admitted hearsay. In re Carter (Ohio App. 4 Dist., 11-06-1997) 123 Ohio App.3d 532, 704 N.E.2d 625. Infants ⇔ 176

Credible evidence that juvenile was part of group of boys who attacked victim and shouted threats at him in attempt to steal money from him was sufficient to support adjudication of delinquency based upon finding that juvenile had committed what would be crime of robbery were he an adult. In re Howard (Ohio App. 1 Dist., 04-16-1997) 119 Ohio App.3d 201, 695 N.E.2d 1. Infants ⇔ 176

Adjudication of juvenile delinquency must be supported by proof beyond a reasonable doubt. In re Howard (Ohio App. 1 Dist., 04-16-1997) 119 Ohio App.3d 201, 695 N.E.2d 1. Infants ⇔ 176

Evidence that juvenile deliberately wrapped shirt around neck of her newborn son and tightened it supported adjudication of delinquency based upon commission of felony of murder. Matter of Chambers (Ohio App. 3 Dist., 12-13-1996) 116 Ohio App.3d 312, 688 N.E.2d 25, dismissed, appeal not allowed 78 Ohio St.3d 1464, 678 N.E.2d 221. Infants ⇔ 156

Issue of juvenile's sanity was properly reviewed at disposition hearing following her adjudication as delinquent for murder of her newborn son. Matter of Chambers (Ohio App. 3 Dist., 12-13-1996) 116 Ohio App.3d 312, 688 N.E.2d 25, dismissed, appeal not allowed 78 Ohio St.3d 1464, 678 N.E.2d 221. Infants ⇔ 203

"Clear and convincing evidence of dependency" is evidence by which trial court could form firm belief or conviction that essential statutory elements for dependency have been established. In re Tikyra A. (Ohio App. 6 Dist., 05-12-1995) 103 Ohio App.3d 452, 659 N.E.2d 867. Infants ⇔ 177

Because clear and convincing evidence standard must be met before permanent custody of children is granted to county and parental rights terminated, permanent custody hearing should be adjudicatory and not dispositional hearing; hearsay will not be admissible in adjudicatory proceedings unless exception is applicable. In re Brofford (Franklin 1992) 83 Ohio App.3d 869, 615 N.E.2d 1120. Infants ⇔ 173.1; Infants ⇔ 203

Although a finding of dependency may be made only upon the presentation of clear and convincing evidence, if the parties agree to waive such a hearing and stipulate to certain facts, then Juv R 29(D) must be fully complied with and the facts set forth in the record must sufficiently support a finding of dependency. Elmer v. Lucas County Children Services Bd. (Lucas 1987) 36 Ohio App.3d 241, 523 N.E.2d 540.

Although Juv R 29 provides for juvenile proceedings to be conducted in an informal manner, hearsay evidence that is otherwise inadmissible will not be admitted at the adjudicatory stage of a neglect and dependency proceeding since the importance of parental interests requires an accurate finding of the facts underlying a complaint which alleges neglect or dependency and requires substantial compliance with the Ohio Rules of Evidence. In re Sims (Preble 1983) 13 Ohio App.3d 37, 468 N.E.2d 111, 13 O.B.R. 40. Infants ⇔ 173.1

Proof of possession, use, or control by a juvenile of a hallucinogen is sufficient evidence upon which a juvenile court can find such juvenile a delinquent under RC Ch 2151. (Annotation from former RC 2151.35.) In re Baker (Hocking 1969) 18 Ohio App.2d 276, 248 N.E.2d 620, 47 O.O.2d 411.

In preliminary hearing on motion to transfer juvenile proceedings to criminal court, state need not provide as full discovery as that required for adjudicatory hearing in juvenile proceedings. In re Doss (Ohio Com.Pl., 05-11-1994) 65 Ohio Misc.2d 8, 640 N.E.2d 618. Infants ⇐ 68.7(1)

Evidence was sufficient to support adjudication of delinquency by reason of murder by committing felonious assault; juvenile made admissions to detectives, several members of his family, and infant's mother that he beat his infant son when the infant did not stop crying, and medical evidence showed that infant's death was a homicide and resulted from head and abdominal injuries inflicted within 24 hours prior to death. In re B.M. (Ohio App. 8 Dist., Cuyahoga, 02-27-2003) No. 80909, 2003-Ohio-870, 2003 WL 548359, Unreported. Infants ⇐ 176

Testimony by juvenile's companion at time of charged incident, who had previously entered admission in his own juvenile proceeding to his involvement in robbery, that he and juvenile approached victim as victim was playing basketball, asked him for his money and then slammed him to ground and kicked him when he resisted, removed victim's cash and pocket knife from victim's person, and fled the scene was sufficient to support delinquency adjudication for complicity to robbery. In re Ball (Ohio App. 3 Dist., Allen, 01-30-2003) No. 1-02-72, 2003-Ohio-395, 2003 WL 193519, Unreported. Infants ⇐ 176

Testimony against juvenile by his companion at time of charged incident was not so self-serving as to affect his credibility in delinquency proceeding involving charge of complicity to robbery, where companion had already entered an admission to involvement in robbery in his own delinquency proceeding complaint and was already in the custody of Department of Youth Services, and companion testified that he was not offered promises regarding his testimony and insisted that he made the decision to testify on his own. In re Ball (Ohio App. 3 Dist., Allen, 01-30-2003) No. 1-02-72, 2003-Ohio-395, 2003 WL 193519, Unreported. Infants ⇐ 176

Adjudication of delinquency for complicity to robbery was not against manifest weight of evidence; while two of juvenile's witnesses testified that juvenile's companion was victim's sole assailant, one of those witnesses admitted previously identifying juvenile to police as one of the assailants, victim and juvenile's companion presented similar versions of charged incident that both implicated juvenile, and investigating officer testified that victim immediately identified his assailants by name and positively identified juvenile and companion from photo line-up. In re Ball (Ohio App. 3 Dist., Allen, 01-30-2003) No. 1-02-72, 2003-Ohio-395, 2003 WL 193519, Unreported. Infants ⇐ 176

7. Time limitations

Appeal of alleged rule violation before magistrate at hearing over 18 months previously in action by county children services board (CSB) for protective supervision of appellant's daughter was untimely; magistrate's decision in that hearing became appealable eight months after it was rendered, when the trial court finally terminated the case. In re Johnson (Ohio App. 11 Dist., Ashtabula, 11-26-2004) No. 2004-A-0060, 2004-Ohio-6340, 2004 WL 2698031, Unreported. Infants ⇐ 244.1

Adjudicatory hearing held more than two weeks after complaint was filed against juvenile required dismissal of complaint with prejudice. In re Carlos O. (Ohio App. 6 Dist., 07-29-1994) 96 Ohio App.3d 252, 644 N.E.2d 1084. Infants ⇐ 204

Adjudicatory hearing that was held on December 14, 1993 and December 21, 1993 for complaint that was filed on December 13, 1993 was timely. In re Carlos O. (Ohio App. 6 Dist., 07-29-1994) 96 Ohio App.3d 252, 644 N.E.2d 1084. Infants ⇐ 204

The speedy trial provisions of RC 2945.71(C) do not apply to delinquency proceedings. In re Corcoran (Geauga 1990) 68 Ohio App.3d 213, 587 N.E.2d 957, dismissed 56 Ohio St.3d 702, 564 N.E.2d 703. Infants ⇐ 204

The ten-day period of limitations in Juv R 29(A) is procedural only and such rule confers no substantive right upon an accused to have his case dismissed if he is not tried within the designated time. In re Therklidsen (Franklin 1977) 54 Ohio App.2d 195, 376 N.E.2d 970, 8 O.O.3d 335.

Five and a half month delay between the finding of delinquency and the disposition did not divest the court of jurisdiction; juvenile rule provided that after adjudication a court may continue a matter for disposition for not more than six months, and juvenile did not object to the continuances entered by the court. In re Homan (Ohio App. 5 Dist., Tuscarawas, 01-27-2003) No. 2002AP080067, 2003-Ohio-352, 2003 WL 183811, Unreported. Infants ⇐ 223.1

8. Double jeopardy

Proceedings conducted in a juvenile court for the purpose of determining whether or not to bind over a juvenile defendant to be tried as an adult do not constitute an adjudicatory hearing in the sense that the evidence is put to the trier of fact or that jeopardy attaches. In re A.M. (Ohio App. 8 Dist., 09-05-2000) 139 Ohio App.3d 303, 743 N.E.2d 937, appeal not allowed 91 Ohio St.3d 1431, 741 N.E.2d 895. Infants ⇐ 68.7(3)

Jeopardy attached when juvenile's adjudicatory hearing began, for purposes of double jeopardy challenge to amendment of charge from unauthorized use of motor vehicle to robbery and transfer for prosecution as adult; because state failed to make transfer decision prior to adjudicatory hearing, juvenile's liberty was placed at risk when court proceeded with adjudicatory hearing. State v. Reddick (Ohio App. 9 Dist., 09-04-1996) 113 Ohio App.3d 788, 682 N.E.2d 38. Double Jeopardy ⇐ 62

Once a juvenile who has had complaints filed against him elects to proceed with an adjudicatory hearing, jeopardy attaches as to all the complaints so as to prevent the state from prosecuting him as an adult for acts underlying the complaints; the fact that the juvenile did not admit to all the allegations contained in the complaints and that no additional evidence was presented, does not prevent the attaching of jeopardy. State v. Penrod (Summit 1989) 62 Ohio App.3d 720, 577 N.E.2d 424, motion overruled 44 Ohio St.3d 715, 542 N.E.2d 1112.

Ohio juvenile adjudication of felonious assault and adult conviction of aggravated robbery did not violate double jeopardy clause; felonious assault contained element of knowledge in causing physical harm, and aggravated robbery contained element of theft. Robertson v. Morgan (C.A.6 (Ohio), 09-14-2000) 227 F.3d 589, rehearing denied. Double Jeopardy ⇐ 33

9. Final orders

Trial court's grant of permanent custody of child to county without first properly adjudicating child as a dependent child violated mother's right to due process, and required reversal of judgment entry granting permanent custody to county. In re Nibert (Ohio App. 4 Dist., Gallia, 05-24-2005) No. 04CA15, 2005-Ohio-2797, 2005 WL 1332019, Unreported. Infants ⇐ 253

Trial court's order in juvenile delinquency proceeding granting high school's motion to quash subpoena for school records of alleged assault victim was not final and appealable, despite fact that court indicated that order should be deemed final and appealable and that there was no just reason for delay, where order was provisional remedy and any mistake in granting motion could be remedied on appeal by ordering new trial. In re Tracy M. (Ohio App. 6 Dist., Huron, 10-20-2004) No. H-04-028, 2004-Ohio-5756, 2004 WL 2426243, Unreported. Infants ⇐ 242

Delinquency adjudication without disposition is not final appealable order. In re Solis (Ohio App. 8 Dist., 12-22-1997) 124 Ohio App.3d 547, 706 N.E.2d 839. Infants ⇐ 242

Order changing temporary custody of children, who had been adjudged neglected and dependent, pending final dispositional hearing was a "final, appealable order." In re Smith (Lucas 1989) 61 Ohio App.3d 788, 573 N.E.2d 1170, reconsideration denied. Infants ⇐ 242

A temporary order of a juvenile court changing custody under Juv R 13 or 29 is not a dispositional order under Juv R 34, and hence is not a final appealable order. Morrison v. Morrison (Summit 1973) 45 Ohio App.2d 299, 344 N.E.2d 144, 74 O.O.2d 441.

The finding of a juvenile court in an adjudicatory hearing is a final appealable order. In re Becker, No. 3301 (11th Dist Ct App, Trumbull, 3–9–84).

10. Delinquency not crime

Being found a juvenile delinquent is different from being found guilty of crime. In re Good (Ohio App. 12 Dist., 02-24-1997) 118 Ohio App.3d 371, 692 N.E.2d 1072, dismissed, appeal not allowed 79 Ohio St.3d 1418, 680 N.E.2d 156. Infants ⇐ 153

Juvenile court is neither criminal nor penal in nature, but is administrative police regulation of corrective nature. In re Good (Ohio App. 12 Dist., 02-24-1997) 118 Ohio App.3d 371, 692 N.E.2d 1072, dismissed, appeal not allowed 79 Ohio St.3d 1418, 680 N.E.2d 156. Infants ⇐ 194.1

Complaint in juvenile court alleging delinquency does not need to be read as strictly as criminal indictment. In re Good (Ohio App. 12 Dist., 02-24-1997) 118 Ohio App.3d 371, 692 N.E.2d 1072, dismissed, appeal not allowed 79 Ohio St.3d 1418, 680 N.E.2d 156. Infants ⇐ 197

As an adjudication of delinquency does not constitute a conviction for commission of a crime, RC 2941.25(A) does not apply to juvenile delinquency adjudications. In re Lugo, No. WD–90–38 (6th Dist Ct App, Wood, 6–14–91).

11. Waiver of counsel

Juvenile did not have statutory right to appointed counsel in delinquency adjudication proceedings, where both juvenile and his mother chose to waive counsel. In re Spears (Ohio App. 5 Dist., Licking, 04-17-2006) No. 2005-CA-93, 2006-Ohio-1920, 2006 WL 1011201, Unreported. Infants ⊕ 205

Record supported trial court's finding that 14-year-old defendant voluntarily waived his *Miranda* rights, even though defendant argued that his age and alleged mental deficiency of mild mental retardation prevented such voluntary waiver, where defendant told detectives, when shown copy of waiver form, that he had not taken alcohol or drugs in last 24 hours and that he had completed sixth grade, so he could read and write to some extent, defendant read waiver form to detectives and acknowledged that he understood his rights and had no questions about them, and detective testified, inter alia, that defendant's responses to questions during interview were appropriate. State v. Harris (Ohio App. 1 Dist., Hamilton, 02-17-2006) No. C-050160, 2006-Ohio-716, 2006 WL 367101, Unreported. Criminal Law ⊕ 412.2(5)

Under the totality of the circumstances, twelve-year-old juvenile's waiver of *Miranda* rights was not knowing, voluntary, and intelligent, and thus juvenile's confession was subject to suppression at trial in delinquency proceeding; no attorney or guardian was present to witness interrogation, juvenile had mental health and behavioral problems, juvenile could not read or write well, and officer could not recall whether officer explained rights to juvenile to ensure that juvenile understood the concept of waiver. In re Moyer (Ohio App. 5 Dist., Licking, 11-03-2004) No. 03CA116, 2004-Ohio-5882, 2004 WL 2496268, Unreported, appeal after new trial 2006-Ohio-85, 2006 WL 60685. Infants ⊕ 174

Because record did not demonstrate that juvenile waived his rights in delinquency proceeding, juvenile would not be held to the standard of being required to raise an objection to the complaint prior to pleading "true." In re Christner (Ohio App. 5 Dist., Tuscarawas, 08-06-2004) No. 2004AP020014, 2004-Ohio-4252, 2004 WL 1802018, Unreported. Infants ⊕ 243

Trial court failed to conduct a sufficient inquiry with juvenile during delinquency proceeding to determine whether juvenile knowingly, intelligently, and voluntarily waived her right to counsel; colloquy did not establish whether juvenile understood the nature of the right to counsel that she would be waiving, and there was no indication the trial court considered factors such as the juvenile's age, emotional stability, mental capacity, and prior criminal experience in making its determination. In re Kindred (Ohio App. 5 Dist., Licking, 07-02-2004) No. 04CA7, 2004-Ohio-3647, 2004 WL 1534135, Unreported. Infants ⊕ 205

Juvenile court's colloquy with 13-year-old juvenile, in which the court simply asked if juvenile had any questions and asked whether juvenile wanted to be represented by a lawyer in the juvenile delinquency proceeding, did not establish that juvenile knowingly waived his right to counsel before admitting to committing acts constituting burglary. In A.C. (Ohio App. 8 Dist., Cuyahoga, 10-16-2003) No. 82289, 2003-Ohio-5496, 2003 WL 22351114, Unreported. Infants ⊕ 199

Juvenile did not validly waive her right to counsel in delinquency proceeding; while juvenile court orally informed juvenile that she had a right to an attorney at date in which juvenile was not admit or deny guilt to delinquency charge, trial court made no mention of the counsel issue at adjudication hearing and merely asked whether juvenile was ready to proceed, and juvenile court never inquired whether juvenile was waiving her right to counsel. In re Bays (Ohio App. 2 Dist., Greene, 03-14-2003) No. 2002-CA-52, No. 2002-CA-56, 2003-Ohio-1256, 2003 WL 1193787, Unreported. Infants ⊕ 205

Juvenile's constitutional right to legal counsel, when faced with possible incarceration in delinquency proceeding, may be waived, and, under some circumstances, the waiver of the right to counsel may be inferred from circumstances. In re R.B. (Ohio App. 2 Dist., 01-13-2006) 166 Ohio App.3d 626, 852 N.E.2d 1219, 2006-Ohio-264. Infants ⊕ 205

To be effective, a waiver of a juvenile's right to counsel must be voluntary, knowing and intelligent. In re Johnston (Ohio App. 11 Dist., 04-30-2001) 142 Ohio App.3d 314, 755 N.E.2d 457. Infants ⊕ 205

Court's colloquy did not establish that juvenile fully understood nature of right that she was waiving when she entered admission, where court told juvenile, "you have the right to an attorney. If you cannot afford one, one will be appointed for you. Do you wish to have an attorney?" and when the juvenile replied, "No," the court said "the juvenile waives her right to an attorney." In re Smith (Ohio App. 8 Dist., 03-26-2001) 142 Ohio App.3d 16, 753 N.E.2d 930. Infants ⊕ 205

Sixteen-year-old suspect waived his right against self-incrimination and right to counsel knowingly, intelligently, and voluntarily before he made videotaped confession at police station, despite suspect's age and diminished IQ, where police made a thorough effort on three separate occasions to warn suspect of his *Miranda* rights and to obtain from him an acknowledgement that he understood and waived those rights. State v. Noggle (Ohio App. 3 Dist., 09-18-2000) 140 Ohio App.3d 733, 749 N.E.2d 309, 2000-Ohio-1927, appeal allowed 91 Ohio St.3d 1431, 741 N.E.2d 894, appeal dismissed as improvidently granted 91 Ohio St.3d 1280, 747 N.E.2d 827, 2001-Ohio-117. Criminal Law ⊕ 412.2(5); Infants ⊕ 174

At adjudicatory hearing, referee must personally address juvenile and ensure validity of waiver of right to counsel before accepting admission to charges. In re Montgomery (Ohio App. 8 Dist., 01-21-1997) 117 Ohio App.3d 696, 691 N.E.2d 349, dismissed, appeal not allowed 78 Ohio St.3d 1490, 678 N.E.2d 1228. Infants ⊕ 199

Journal entry indicating that juvenile waived his right to counsel in delinquency proceeding was not adequate to show that court explained juvenile's statutory right to counsel and informed him that counsel would be appointed if he was indigent. In re Montgomery (Ohio App. 8 Dist., 01-21-1997) 117 Ohio App.3d 696, 691 N.E.2d 349, dismissed, appeal not allowed 78 Ohio St.3d 1490, 678 N.E.2d 1228. Infants ⊕ 199

Trial court accepted 13–year–old juvenile's waiver of counsel without proper assurances that waiver was knowing, intelligent and voluntary; referee gave basic explanation to juvenile on his right to counsel at initial hearing and adjudicatory hearing, and asked juvenile to sign waiver form, but failed to inquire into any circumstances that would demonstrate that juvenile knowingly, intelligently, and voluntarily waived his right to counsel, and trial judge did not address subject of right to counsel at dispositional hearing. In re Johnson (Ohio App. 1 Dist., 08-23-1995) 106 Ohio App.3d 38, 665 N.E.2d 247. Infants ⊕ 205

In applying totality-of-the-circumstances test to waiver of counsel by juveniles, courts must give close scrutiny to factors such as juvenile's age, emotional stability, mental capacity, and prior criminal experience. In re Johnson (Ohio App. 1 Dist., 08-23-1995) 106 Ohio App.3d 38, 665 N.E.2d 247. Infants ⊕ 205

Valid waiver by juvenile may not be presumed from silent record. In re McKenzie (Ohio App. 8 Dist., 03-30-1995) 102 Ohio App.3d 275, 656 N.E.2d 1377. Infants ⊕ 250

Magistrate did not commit plain error in accepting juvenile's waiver of counsel before obtaining his admission to preparing crack cocaine for sale; magistrate informed juvenile of his right to counsel and made sufficient inquiry, employing informal language and encompassing the totality of the circumstances present, to determine whether juvenile knowingly, intelligently, and voluntarily waived his right to counsel, and juvenile and his mother additionally signed a waiver-of-counsel-and-rights form which the magistrate journalized in the court record. In re Sweeten (Ohio App. 1 Dist., Hamilton, 05-24-2002) No. C-010314, 2002-Ohio-2552, 2002 WL 1040229, Unreported. Infants ⊕ 243

Waiver of counsel will not be presumed from a silent record. In re Wilson, No. 11–80–28 (3d Dist Ct App, Paulding, 11–12–81).

12. No contest pleas

The trial court's refusal to accept juvenile's *Alford*-type plea was not an abuse of discretion, in juvenile delinquency proceeding; juvenile failed to admit the allegations in the complaint or a factual basis supporting the offense. In re Kirby (Ohio App. 12 Dist., Clinton, 12-16-2002) No. CA2002-03-015, 2002-Ohio-6881, 2002 WL 31798390, Unreported, appeal allowed 98 Ohio St.3d 1563, 787 N.E.2d 1229, 2003-Ohio-2242, affirmed 101 Ohio St.3d 312, 804 N.E.2d 476, 2004-Ohio-970. Infants ⊕ 199

Where a juvenile entered a no contest plea to a delinquency complaint apparently on the basis that she would be able to appeal the juvenile court's ruling on the pretrial motion to suppress, as would be true in an adult criminal case, the court erroneously disposed of the case on such a plea. In re Green (Franklin 1982) 4 Ohio App.3d 196, 447 N.E.2d 129, 4 O.B.R. 300. Infants ⊕ 199

The no contest plea in a juvenile proceeding is not the unequivocal admission of the allegations of the complaint contemplated by Juv R 29(D), and it must be construed as a denial and the prosecuting attorney must prove the issues of delinquency beyond a reasonable doubt. In re Green (Franklin 1982) 4 Ohio App.3d 196, 447 N.E.2d 129, 4 O.B.R. 300. Infants ⊕ 176; Infants ⊕ 199

There is no statement in Crim R 11 that a no contest plea results in a waiver of a defendant's right to challenge evidence against him as is specifically provided for by Juv R 29(D)(2) in relation to an admission of allegations of the complaint. In re Green (Franklin 1982) 4 Ohio App.3d 196, 447 N.E.2d 129, 4 O.B.R. 300.

13. Consequences of hearing

Once juvenile was placed on probation for criminal trespass and other crimes, trial court lacked authority, without conducting probation revocation hearing, to effectively revoke probation and order that juvenile be committed to Department of Youth Services for six months until 21st birthday after receiving information that juvenile violated terms of probation. In re Burner (Ohio App. 5 Dist., Stark, 10-31-2005) No. 2005 CA 00108, 2005-Ohio-5816, 2005 WL 2864706, Unreported. Infants ⇒ 225

Judgment entry following detention-shelter care hearing involving child did not constitute dependency adjudication, which was necessary step in process for county to gain permanent custody of child; trial court stated during hearing that proceedings were not "a hearing where...the dependency issue is being argued," but was hearing to determine whether county had sufficient evidence to base initial finding of dependency to remove child from mother's custody, evidence introduced at hearing did not support dependency determination, and trial court had granted ex parte order granting temporary emergency custody of child to county, thus indicating that hearing was that statutorily required to review ex parte order. In re Nibert (Ohio App. 4 Dist., Gallia, 05-24-2005) No. 04CA15, 2005-Ohio-2797, 2005 WL 1332019, Unreported. Infants ⇒ 222

Trial court's disposition of juvenile adjudicated delinquent for murder of her newborn son, suspending her commitment pending successful completion of probation and adherence to recommendations of mental health professionals, was necessary and appropriate. Matter of Chambers (Ohio App. 3 Dist., 12-13-1996) 116 Ohio App.3d 312, 688 N.E.2d 25, dismissed, appeal not allowed 78 Ohio St.3d 1464, 678 N.E.2d 221. Infants ⇒ 225

Juvenile was properly put on notice of a potential commitment to Department of Youth Services (DYS) for probation violation, even though at first adjudicatory hearing, court did not impose a suspended commitment to DYS; juvenile court informed juvenile during adjudicatory hearing that probation violation could have resulted in commitment to DYS. In re Rumph (Ohio App. 9 Dist., Summit, 09-04-2002) No. 20886, 2002-Ohio-4525, 2002 WL 2009212, Unreported. Infants ⇒ 223.1

In a juvenile traffic offender proceeding, failure to inform the child that a no contest plea could result in revocation of his driving privileges invalidated such plea. In re Kahan, No. L–82–170 (6th Dist Ct App, Lucas, 10–22–82).

14. Insanity defense

In juvenile proceedings, juvenile may not assert affirmative defense of insanity, although issue of sanity is factor to be considered during trial court's determination of delinquency; plea of not guilty by reason of insanity is feature of criminal cases, and child should not be dealt with on basis of criminal laws for felony out of which delinquency charge sprang. Matter of Chambers (Ohio App. 3 Dist., 12-13-1996) 116 Ohio App.3d 312, 688 N.E.2d 25, dismissed, appeal not allowed 78 Ohio St.3d 1464, 678 N.E.2d 221. Infants ⇒ 199

15. Judge's duty to inform—In general

Juvenile's waiver of objections to magistrate's decision in delinquency adjudication proceedings did not encompass imposition of court costs and restitution, where magistrate did not inform juvenile that he could be ordered to pay court costs and restitution. In re Spears (Ohio App. 5 Dist., Licking, 04-17-2006) No. 2005-CA-93, 2006-Ohio-1920, 2006 WL 1011201, Unreported. Infants ⇒ 243

Juvenile court substantially complied with advisement requirements of applicable rule in delinquency adjudication proceedings, where court advised juvenile of complaint filed against him, each charge therein, elements and category of each charge, possible consequences of being found delinquent on or admitting to each charge, his entitlement to counsel if he qualified under state guidelines, each of his constitutional rights, state's burden of proof, effect of his admission, and potential range of punishment, and juvenile indicated his understanding as to each advisement. In re Spears (Ohio App. 5 Dist., Licking, 04-17-2006) No. 2005-CA-93, 2006-Ohio-1920, 2006 WL 1011201, Unreported. Infants ⇒ 203

Juvenile's plea of admission and waiver of counsel were made voluntarily, knowingly, and intelligently, where juvenile court substantially complied with advisement requirements of applicable rule, juvenile was days short of his fourteenth birthday at time he entered plea and had previous record in juvenile court, juvenile's mother was present during court's explanation of rights and concurred with juvenile's decision to waive his right to counsel, juvenile and his mother acknowledged receipt of magistrate's decision and waived their rights to file written objections thereto, and juvenile and his mother signed written waiver of rights form prior to entry of plea. In re Spears (Ohio App. 5 Dist., Licking, 04-17-2006) No. 2005-CA-93, 2006-Ohio-1920, 2006 WL 1011201, Unreported. Infants ⇒ 205

Mother's admission that her children were neglected, during dependency proceeding, was not knowingly and voluntarily made, where the trial court failed to inform mother that by making an admission she was waiving her right to remain silent. In re A.A. (Ohio App. 8 Dist., Cuyahoga, 05-26-2005) No. 85002, 2005-Ohio-2618, 2005 WL 1245620, Unreported. Infants ⇒ 199

Juvenile's admission to inducing panic and violating probation was not knowing, intelligent, and voluntary, where magistrate completely failed to ask juvenile whether he understood he was waiving rights to remain silent, to present evidence, and to challenge adverse witnesses and evidence. In re Dawson (Ohio App. 11 Dist., Trumbull, 04-29-2005) No. 2004-T-0027, 2005-Ohio-2088, 2005 WL 1009834, Unreported. Infants ⇒ 199

Trial court did not sufficiently comply with requirements of juvenile rule governing initial procedure upon entry of admission in accepting admissions of mother and grandmother to amended complaint at adjudicatory hearing, thus requiring reversal of order adjudicating child as neglected; nothing in record indicated that court ascertained that parties understood that purpose of hearing was to determine whether child was neglected, and court did not inform parties that, by entering admission, they were admitting to truth of allegations in amended complaint and to finding of neglect, and thus, neither admission was made with understanding of nature of allegations and consequences of admission. In re M.C. (Ohio App. 8 Dist., Cuyahoga, 04-28-2005) No. 85054, No. 85108, 2005-Ohio-1968, 2005 WL 977832, Unreported. Infants ⇒ 253

Juvenile's admission to grand theft auto was not knowing, voluntary and intelligent, where trial court did not ensure that juvenile understood that, by admitting to offense, juvenile faced minimum commitment of six months and maximum period up to juvenile's 21st birthday. In re Stone (Ohio App. 5 Dist., Coshocton, 04-13-2005) No. 04-CA-013, 2005-Ohio-1831, 2005 WL 902026, Unreported. Infants ⇒ 199

Juvenile court was not required to inform juvenile that he might receive consecutive commitments to the Department of Youth Services prior to accepting admissions, but was only required to inform juvenile of the maximum penalty for each delinquent charge. In re S.H. (Ohio App. 2 Dist., Montgomery, 07-16-2004) No. 20107, 2004-Ohio-3779, 2004 WL 1587203, Unreported. Infants ⇒ 199

Trial court substantially complied with rule governing adjudicatory hearings, which required court to give juvenile certain advisements at beginning of juvenile's adjudicatory hearing, in delinquency proceeding; juvenile received detailed advisements required by rule at initial hearing, and, although court did not repeat advisements at adjudicatory hearing, both sides acknowledged that rape counts were being tried, full adversarial trial was conducted, and juvenile had opportunity to present and confront witnesses. In re Pyles (Ohio App. 2 Dist., Montgomery, 10-11-2002) No. 19354, 2002-Ohio-5539, 2002 WL 31317249, Unreported. Infants ⇒ 203

16. Notice

Statutory notice requirements of juvenile delinquency proceeding were met by providing juvenile's guardian with notice, instead of juvenile's father, where juvenile was in permanent county custody and had a guardian who was not his father. State v. D.M. (Ohio App. 8 Dist., Cuyahoga, 06-19-2003) No. 81641, 2003-Ohio-3228, 2003 WL 21419595, Unreported. Infants ⇒ 198

17. Preservation of error for review

Trial court acted within its discretion in committing juvenile to Department of Youth Services after he was adjudicated delinquent for burglary and aggravated arson, even though juvenile argued that his prior record suggested that alternative services were available; juvenile was adjudicated delinquent for two felony offenses, and trial court found that juvenile was menace to community and that community needed to be protected. State v. O'Brien (Ohio App. 5 Dist., Stark, 07-18-2005) No. 2004CA00370, 2005-Ohio-3765, 2005 WL 1713549, Unreported. Infants ⇒ 223.1

Juvenile failed to preserve for appellate review in juvenile delinquency case his claims that trial court failed to comply with requirements of rule governing admissions, where juvenile failed at any time before appeal to withdraw pleas admitting parole violation and failure to comply with order or signal of police officer. In re M.F. (Ohio App. 8 Dist., Cuyahoga, 09-

18. Best interest of child and community

Jeopardy attached when juvenile court dismissed rape charges in delinquency proceeding based on best interest of child and community so as to preclude initiation of any further criminal proceedings against juvenile based on allegations stated in complaint, where matter was submitted to court for adjudication on merits by joint stipulation of counsel and court accepted stipulation and made adjudication. In re Arnett (Ohio App. 3 Dist., Hancock, 11-01-2004) No. 5-04-20, 2004-Ohio-5766, 2004 WL 2426258, Unreported. Double Jeopardy ⇐ 62

Dismissal of charges in delinquency proceeding pursuant to rule addressing best interest of child and community is appealable by state and subject to evaluation as to double jeopardy implications when juvenile court bases dismissal on factors unrelated to rule's requirements and indicates that conduct of juvenile, accepted as true and proscribed by criminal statutes, does not constitute criminal or delinquency offense as matter of law. In re Arnett (Ohio App. 3 Dist., Hancock, 11-01-2004) No. 5-04-20, 2004-Ohio-5766, 2004 WL 2426258, Unreported. Double Jeopardy ⇐ 33; Infants ⇐ 242

Dismissing rape charges based on "best interest of child and community" was abuse of discretion in delinquency proceeding, where trial court focused on consensual and non-violent nature of acts at issue which were not defenses to charge and did not directly bear upon best interest of child and community, there was no impact evidence to assist court in determining whether dismissal was in best interest of child and community, and, given that case was submitted on joint stipulation of counsel, there were no relevant factual or legal determinations in record to distinguish dismissal of this case from every other delinquency case involving twelve-year-old victim and fifteen-year-old perpetrator. In re Arnett (Ohio App. 3 Dist., Hancock, 11-01-2004) No. 5-04-20, 2004-Ohio-5766, 2004 WL 2426258, Unreported. Infants ⇐ 202

19. Standing

City schools had standing to file motion to dismiss juvenile's appeal from trial court's grant in delinquency proceeding of high school's motion to quash subpoena for school records of alleged assault victim; city schools, as subpoenaed non-party, had to be able to defend in appellate court judgment entered in its favor in trial court. In re Tracy M. (Ohio App. 6 Dist., Huron, 10-20-2004) No. H-04-028, 2004-Ohio-5756, 2004 WL 2426243, Unreported. Infants ⇐ 242

Juv R 30 Relinquishment of jurisdiction for purposes of criminal prosecution

(A) Preliminary hearing

In any proceeding where the court considers the transfer of a case for criminal prosecution, the court shall hold a preliminary hearing to determine if there is probable cause to believe that the child committed the act alleged and that the act would be an offense if committed by an adult. The hearing may be upon motion of the court, the prosecuting attorney, or the child.

(B) Mandatory transfer

In any proceeding in which transfer of a case for criminal prosecution is required by statute upon a finding of probable cause, the order of transfer shall be entered upon a finding of probable cause.

(C) Discretionary transfer

In any proceeding in which transfer of a case for criminal prosecution is permitted, but not required, by statute, and in which probable cause is found at the preliminary hearing, the court shall continue the proceeding for full investigation. The investigation shall include a mental examination of the child by a public or private agency or by a person qualified to make the examination. When the investigation is completed, an amenability hearing shall be held to determine whether to transfer jurisdiction. The criteria for transfer shall be as provided by statute.

(D) Notice

Notice in writing of the time, place, and purpose of any hearing held pursuant to this rule shall be given to the state, the child's parents, guardian, or other custodian and the child's counsel at least three days prior to the hearing, unless written notice has been waived on the record.

(E) Retention of jurisdiction

If the court retains jurisdiction, it shall set the proceedings for hearing on the merits.

(F) Waiver of mental examination

The child may waive the mental examination required under division (C) of this rule. Refusal by the child to submit to a mental examination or any part of the examination shall constitute a waiver of the examination.

(G) Order of transfer

The order of transfer shall state the reasons for transfer.

(H) Release of child

With respect to the transferred case, the juvenile court shall set the terms and conditions for release of the child in accordance with Crim. R. 46.

(Adopted eff. 7–1–72; amended eff. 7–1–76, 7–1–94, 7–1–97)

Historical and Statutory Notes

Amendment Note: The 7–1–97 amendment substituted "considers the transfer of a case for criminal prosecution" for "may transfer a child fifteen or more years of age for prosecution as an adult" and "act would be an offense" for "act alleged would be a felony" in division (A); added division (B); redesignated former divisions (B), (C), (G), (H), and (I) as divisions (C), (D), (F), (G), and (H), respectively; deleted former divisions (D) and (F); substituted "Discretionary transfer. In any proceeding in which transfer of a case for criminal prosecution is permitted, but not required, by statute, and in which probable cause is found at the preliminary hearing, the court shall continue the proceeding for full investigation." for "Investigation. If the court finds probable cause it shall continue the proceedings for full investigation." and "an amenability hearing" for "a hearing" in division (C); added the last sentence in division (C); deleted "division (A) or (B) of" following "hearing held pursuant to" in division (D); deleted "and physical" in the caption and following "waive the mental" in division (F); substituted "(C)" for "(B)" in division (F); rewrote division (H); and made other nonsubstantive changes. Prior to deletion and amendment, former divisions (D), (F), and (H) read:

"(D) Prerequisites to transfer. The proceedings may be transferred if the court finds there are reasonable grounds to believe both of the following:

"(1) The child is not amenable to care or rehabilitation in any facility designed for the care, supervision, and rehabilitation of delinquent children;

"(2) The safety of the community may require that the child be placed under legal restraint for a period extending beyond the child's majority.

"(F) Determination of amenability to rehabilitation. In determining whether the child is amenable to the treatment or rehabilitative processes available to the juvenile court, the court shall consider the following relevant circumstances:

"(1) The child's age and mental and physical condition;

"(2) The child's prior juvenile record;

"(3) Efforts previously made to treat or rehabilitate the child;

"(4) The child's family environment;

"(5) The child's school record;

"(6) The specific facts relating to the offense for which probable cause was found, to the extent relevant to the child's physical or mental condition.

"(I) Release of transferred child. The juvenile court shall set terms and conditions for the release of the transferred child in accordance with Criminal Rule 46. The transfer abates the jurisdiction of the juvenile court with respect to the delinquent acts alleged in the complaint."

Amendment Note: The 7–1–94 amendment deleted "the Ohio Youth Commission" before "a public or private agency" in, and deleted "Written notice of the time, place and nature of the hearing shall be given to the parties at least three days prior to the hearing." from the end of, division

(B); added division (C); redesignated former divisions (C) through (H) as divisions (D) through (I), respectively; inserted "the following relevant circumstances" in the first paragraph of division (F); substituted "condition" for "health" in division (F)(1); inserted "child's" in division (F)(5); added division (F)(6); added the final sentence in division (I); and made changes to reflect gender-neutral language.

Staff Notes

1997:

With the passage of 1995 H1, effective January 1, 1996, major conflicts resulted between the statute governing bindover proceedings (Revised Code 2151.26) and the provisions of Juv.R. 30. The 1997 amendment to Juv.R. 30 eliminates these conflicts by removing from the rule all provisions governing substantive law, thus confining the rule to procedural matters. A significant amendment to Juv.R. 30(A) is the deletion of any reference to a minimum age at which a juvenile could be subject to bindover, since age jurisdiction is more appropriately covered by statute.

Revisions to Juv.R. 30(B) and (C) recognize the statutory distinctions between mandatory and discretionary bindover. Once probable cause has been established for mandatory bindover under Juv.R. 30(B), the only procedural step remaining is to enter the order of transfer. All references to the investigation contained in the former version of Juv.R. 30(B) have been removed from the current version. Similarly, Juv.R. 30(C) provides that the transfer of jurisdiction with respect to discretionary bindover shall be governed by statute.

The notice requirements of Juv.R. 30(D) (formerly Juv.R. 30(C)) have been changed to clarify that the three-day notice is required before any hearing held under Juv.R. 30. This language is consistent with similar language contained in Revised Code 2151.26(D).

In conformity with the decision to remove substantive law language from the rule, the amenability factors included in the former version of Juv.R. 30(F) have been deleted in their entirety, and the jurisdictional language in the former Juv.R. 30(I) has been eliminated from the new version of Juv.R. 30(H).

H. B. 1 also deleted the requirement for a physical examination of the juvenile as part of the background investigation in connection with a discretionary bindover. Accordingly, the requirement was deleted from divisions (C) and (F) of this rule (formerly divisions (B) and (G)).

1994:

Rule 30 Relinquishment of Jurisdiction for Purposes of Criminal Prosecution

Juv. R. 30 deals with bindover proceedings to determine whether or not to transfer a juvenile to the adult criminal justice system. The revision to Juv. R. 30(C) clarifies that written notice of the time, place, and purpose of any hearing under this rule be given in writing at least three days prior to the hearing to the state, the child's parents, guardian or other custodian, and the child's counsel, as required by Revised Code 2151.26(D), unless notice is waived on the record.

Revisions to Juv. R. 30(F) present an additional criterion for the court to consider in determining if the juvenile is amenable to rehabilitation. Juvenile courts may now consider the specific facts relating to the offense for which probable cause was found, to the extent relevant to the child's mental or physical condition, along with the other criteria specified in Juv. R. 30. While there is a danger that taking note of the facts surrounding a particularly heinous crime could prejudice a court's deliberations on the rehabilitation question, the Supreme Court of Ohio approved a court's ability to consider the totality of the circumstances which have brought the juvenile before the court in *State v. Watson* (1989), 47 Ohio St. 3d 93.

Editor's Comment

Introduction 1
Preliminary hearing 2
Investigation 3
Notice 4
Prerequisites to transfer 5
Determination of amenability to rehabilitation 6
Order of transfer; retention of jurisdiction 7

1. Introduction

Juv R 30 contains the procedural provisions governing the transfer of jurisdiction of cases of children alleged to have committed a felony to the appropriate court for criminal prosecution. The rule is substantially different from its statutory counterpart (2151.26) in several respects. Whereas Juv R 30(A) requires that the child be at least fifteen years of age at the time of the act charged, 2151.26(C)(1)(a) permits transfer of children age fourteen or older. Moreover, while Juv R 30 contemplates a process of discretionary bindover, 2151.26(B) mandates transfer under certain circumstances.

2. Preliminary hearing

Prior to making the transfer order, Division (A) requires the court to conduct a preliminary hearing to determine if there is probable cause to believe that the child committed the act alleged and that such act would be a felony if committed by an adult. This is in conformity with the U.S. Supreme Court decision in *Breed v Jones*, 421 US 519, 95 SCt 1779, 44 LEd(2d) 346 (1975) which held that the criminal prosecution of a juvenile in the adult court pursuant to an order of transfer made subsequent to an adjudicatory hearing in the juvenile court constitutes double jeopardy. Prior to *Breed* and the 1976 amendment to Juv R 30, the rule permitted the juvenile court to make the order of transfer at any time prior to the entry of an order of final disposition, even after adjudicatory hearing. *Breed* has been held to have retroactive application to pre-*Breed* cases in which an adjudicatory hearing was held prior to the order of transfer (*Sims v Engle*, 619 F(2d) 598 (6th Cir 1980), cert. denied, 101 SCt 1403, 67 LEd(2d) 372 (1981)).

3. Investigation

If probable cause is found at the preliminary hearing, Division (B) requires the court to continue the proceedings for further hearing and for a full investigation, including mental and physical examinations of the child. Pursuant to Division (G), the child may waive the mental and physical examinations. A child's refusal to submit to the examinations constitutes a waiver.

Unlike Juv R 30(B), 2151.26(B) mandates transfer under certain circumstances after the probable cause determination, without the subsequent investigation or mental and physical examinations.

4. Notice

Division (C) and 2151.26(D) require that written notice be given to the parties at least three days prior to any hearing, which would include the preliminary hearing, as well as the amenability hearing. The rule, but not the statute, adds that this notice may be waived on the record. This 1994 amendment to the rule overrules *State v Taylor*, 26 App(3d) 69, 26 OBR 243, 498 NE(2d) 211 (Auglaize 1985), which held these notice requirements to be mandatory and nonwaivable. Although 2151.28(H) prohibits a child from waiving service of summons, the rule apparently permits the child to waive the three-day notice.

5. Prerequisites to transfer

In order to transfer jurisdiction, Division (D) requires the court to find reasonable grounds to believe that the child is not amenable to care or rehabilitation in any facility designed for the care, supervision, and rehabilitation of delinquent children and that the safety of the community may require the minor's confinement beyond his majority.

This requirement is also contained in 2151.26(C)(1) relative to discretionary transfer. However, where transfer is mandated under 2151.26(B), no amenability hearing is conducted and no findings beyond probable cause are required.

6. Determination of amenability to rehabilitation

Division (F) lists the specific factors to be considered in determining whether the child is to be deemed amenable to rehabilitation. This is in conformity with the U.S. Supreme Court mandate. *See Kent v U.S.*, 383 US 541, 86 SCt 1045, 16 LEd(2d) 84 (1966). In this case, the court held that the transfer of jurisdiction was a critical stage of the proceedings, and that fundamental fairness and due process required representation by counsel (*See* Juv R 3) and opportunity to inspect all records considered by the court (*See* Juv R 32), and an examination by a psychiatrist or psychologist of his own choosing. The court also set down guidelines for the court to consider as a basis for transfer.

2151.26(C)(2) includes additional factors that the court must consider in favor of ordering the transfer of the case.

7. Order of transfer; retention of jurisdiction

If the court decides to transfer jurisdiction, Division (H) requires the court to recite the basis for transfer. If the court decides to retain jurisdiction, Division (E) requires the court to conduct a full hearing on the merits.

Library References

Infants ⇌68.7(1) to 68.7(5).
Westlaw Topic No. 211.
C.J.S. Infants §§ 45 to 48, 203.

Research References

ALR Library

101 ALR 5th 351, Validity and Efficacy of Minor's Waiver of Right to Counsel--Cases Decided Since Application of Gault, 387 U.S. 1, 87 S. Ct. 1428, 18 L. Ed. 2d 527 (1967).

Encyclopedias

OH Jur. 3d Criminal Law § 2013, Transfers from Juvenile Court for Criminal Prosecution; Relinquishment of Jurisdiction.

OH Jur. 3d Criminal Law § 2014, Transfers from Juvenile Court for Criminal Prosecution; Relinquishment of Jurisdiction—Notice and Hearing; Mental Examination.

OH Jur. 3d Family Law § 1562, Notice and Hearing.

OH Jur. 3d Family Law § 1563, Determination by Court.

OH Jur. 3d Family Law § 1564, Waiver of Mental or Physical Examination.

OH Jur. 3d Family Law § 1565, Order of Transfer; Resumption of Jurisdiction by Juvenile Court.

OH Jur. 3d Family Law § 1571, Apprehension—Release on Bail.

OH Jur. 3d Family Law § 1624, Waiver of Child's Rights; Double Jeopardy.

OH Jur. 3d Family Law § 1637, Order for Social History or Physical or Mental Examination.

OH Jur. 3d Family Law § 1640, Preliminary Conferences.

OH Jur. 3d Family Law § 1643, Motion and Order for Discovery.

OH Jur. 3d Family Law § 1655, Right to Attend; Public or Private Hearing.

OH Jur. 3d Family Law § 1661, Advisement and Findings at Commencement of Hearing.

Treatises and Practice Aids

Katz, Giannelli, Blair and Lipton, Baldwin's Ohio Practice, Criminal Law, § 91:6, Infancy.

Katz, Giannelli, Blair and Lipton, Baldwin's Ohio Practice, Criminal Law, § 128:2, Transfer to Criminal Courts.

Carlin, Baldwin's Ohio Practice, Merrick-Rippner Probate Law § 104:5, Juvenile Courts—Constitutional Issues—Right to Notice, Counsel, and Trial.

Carlin, Baldwin's Ohio Practice, Merrick-Rippner Probate Law § 105:9, Juvenile Court—Waiver of Jurisdiction.

Carlin, Baldwin's Ohio Practice, Merrick-Rippner Probate Law § 106:4, Juvenile Court Jurisdiction—Delinquent Child—Non-Criminal Nature of Delinquency Proceedings.

Carlin, Baldwin's Ohio Practice, Merrick-Rippner Probate Law § 107:33, Restricting And/Or Enforcing Discovery.

Carlin, Baldwin's Ohio Practice, Merrick-Rippner Probate Law § 107:36, Use of Social History and Investigation Report.

Carlin, Baldwin's Ohio Practice, Merrick-Rippner Probate Law § 107:45, Adjudicatory Hearings—Parties' Right to Counsel.

Carlin, Baldwin's Ohio Practice, Merrick-Rippner Probate Law § 107:50, Adjudicatory Hearings—Applicability of Rules of Court.

Carlin, Baldwin's Ohio Practice, Merrick-Rippner Probate Law § 107:52, Adjudicatory Hearings—Confidentiality of Juvenile Court Proceedings.

Carlin, Baldwin's Ohio Practice, Merrick-Rippner Probate Law § 107:63, Transfer of Jurisdiction to Criminal Court—Introduction.

Carlin, Baldwin's Ohio Practice, Merrick-Rippner Probate Law § 107:66, Discretionary Transfer.

Carlin, Baldwin's Ohio Practice, Merrick-Rippner Probate Law § 107:67, Procedural Due Process Requirements in Transfer Proceedings.

Carlin, Baldwin's Ohio Practice, Merrick-Rippner Probate Law § 107:69, Court's Discretion to Transfer or Retain Jurisdiction.

Carlin, Baldwin's Ohio Practice, Merrick-Rippner Probate Law § 107:70, Authority of Criminal Court Over Children.

Carlin, Baldwin's Ohio Practice, Merrick-Rippner Probate Law § 107:186, Order Transferring Action for Criminal Prosecution in Common Pleas Court—Form.

Giannelli & Yeomans, Ohio Juvenile Law § 1:8, Rules of Juvenile Procedure.

Giannelli & Yeomans, Ohio Juvenile Law § 2:3, Child Subject to Adult Prosecution.

Giannelli & Yeomans, Ohio Juvenile Law § 19:7, Time Requirements.

Giannelli & Yeomans, Ohio Juvenile Law § 21:6, Social History Report.

Giannelli & Yeomans, Ohio Juvenile Law § 22:1, Introduction.

Giannelli & Yeomans, Ohio Juvenile Law § 22:5, Transfer Age Requirement.

Giannelli & Yeomans, Ohio Juvenile Law § 22:6, Probable Cause Requirement.

Giannelli & Yeomans, Ohio Juvenile Law § 22:7, Mandatory Transfer.

Giannelli & Yeomans, Ohio Juvenile Law § 22:8, Discretionary Transfer.

Giannelli & Yeomans, Ohio Juvenile Law § 22:9, Amenability Hearing Procedures.

Giannelli & Yeomans, Ohio Juvenile Law § 32:3, Responsibilities to Victims and Others.

Giannelli & Yeomans, Ohio Juvenile Law App. D, Appendix D. Glossary.

Giannelli & Yeomans, Ohio Juvenile Law § 22:10, Mental Examination.

Giannelli & Yeomans, Ohio Juvenile Law § 22:11, Right to Counsel.

Giannelli & Yeomans, Ohio Juvenile Law § 22:12, Notice.

Giannelli & Yeomans, Ohio Juvenile Law § 22:17, Statement of Reasons.

Giannelli & Yeomans, Ohio Juvenile Law § 22:19, Public Hearing; Victims; Gag Orders.

Giannelli & Yeomans, Ohio Juvenile Law § 22:21, Retention of Jurisdiction.

Giannelli & Yeomans, Ohio Juvenile Law § 22:22, Transfer of Jurisdiction.

Giannelli & Yeomans, Ohio Juvenile Law § 27:19, Plural Dispositions.

Giannelli & Yeomans, Ohio Juvenile Law § 34:12, Habeas Corpus.

Law Review and Journal Commentaries

A Brief History of Ohio Gang Trends—Changes in Legislation as a Result of Gangs and Successful Prevention Methods, Linda M. Schmidt. 10 Baldwin's Ohio Sch L J 69 (November/December 1998).

The Effect of the Double Jeopardy Clause on Juvenile Proceedings, James G. Carr. 6 U Tol L Rev 1 (Fall 1974).

Judge's Column, Hon. William W. Weaver. (Ed. note: Judge Weaver of the Lake County Juvenile Court highlights the effects of 1995 H 1 on juvenile law and procedure and provides flow charts to explain the new procedures.) 19 Lake Legal Views 1 (January 1996).

Rights of passage: Analysis of waiver of juvenile court jurisdiction. 64 Fordham L Rev 2425 (1995).

Symposium: They Grow Up So Fast: When Juveniles Commit Adult Crimes, Hon. W. Don Reader, et al. 29 Akron L Rev 473 (Spring 1996).

Notes of Decisions

Adjudicatory hearing 13
Amenability to rehabilitation 5
Constitutional issues 9
County of transfer 11
Criminal charges and indictments 4
Final orders 1
Habeas corpus 15
Improper transfer 10
Investigation 8
Judge 12
Notice 6
Prerequisites to transfer 2
Sentences 14
Time limitations 3
Waiver of examination 7

---

1. Final orders

An order by a juvenile court pursuant to RC 2151.26 transferring a child to the court of common pleas for criminal prosecution is not a final appealable order. In re Becker (Ohio 1974) 39 Ohio St.2d 84, 314 N.E.2d 158, 68 O.O.2d 50. Infants ⇌ 68.8

In cases involving challenges to certification of juveniles to adult courts, counsel is required to include specific language in the text of the praecipe to the clerk of courts requesting all pertinent documents from both the juvenile division and the general division of the court of common pleas to establish that the case is a final appealable order. State v. Houston (Lucas 1990) 70 Ohio App.3d 152, 590 N.E.2d 839. Infants ⇐ 68.8

2. Prerequisites to transfer

At probable cause hearing to determine whether to bind over juvenile to be tried as adult for alleged criminal offense, discovery in juvenile court could be limited to evidence relevant to probable cause hearing, and thus trial court did not abuse its discretion at probable cause hearing when it deleted any request by juvenile for discovery of evidentiary materials and witnesses that prosecution intended to use at trial. State v. Gilbert (Ohio App. 6 Dist., Lucas, 05-13-2005) No. L-03-1273, 2005-Ohio-2350, 2005 WL 1125324, Unreported. Infants ⇐ 68.7(1)

Evidence was sufficient to support juvenile court's finding that probable cause existed that juvenile defendant committed aggravated robbery, thus supporting bindover to the court of common pleas; victim testified that defendant accosted him and placed a sawed-off shotgun to his back, victim saw a second person approach victim's vehicle, vehicle matching description of victim's vehicle was soon thereafter involved in police chase and crashed, defendant was one of the individuals apprehended after running from scene of crash, sawed-off shotgun was found in crashed vehicle, and defendant was found to have starter pistol in his pocket. State v. Goodwin (Ohio App. 8 Dist., 05-11-2006) 166 Ohio App.3d 709, 852 N.E.2d 1282, 2006-Ohio-2311. Infants ⇐ 68.7(3)

Juvenile court should have considered discretionary bindover factors in ruling on State's motion to bind over juveniles to common pleas court, where juveniles were age 14 or over at time of criminal acts, they were charged with engaging in pattern of criminal gang activity, a second-degree felony, and juvenile court had determined that there was probable cause to believe that juveniles had committed offense. In re Stanley (Ohio App. 7 Dist., 03-14-2006) 165 Ohio App.3d 726, 848 N.E.2d 540, 2006-Ohio-1279. Infants ⇐ 68.7(2)

Petitioner had adequate remedy at law by appeal to raise his claims that his convictions and sentence were void because his bindover from juvenile court was defective, and, as such, he was not entitled to habeas relief; juvenile court's bindover entry indicated that proper procedures were followed, probable cause finding regarding kidnapping charge was based in part on evidence presented to juvenile court and not solely on waiver of probable cause hearing that petitioner alleged was invalid, and petitioner had already unsuccessfully raised his claim concerning improper bindover based upon lack of a physical examination in his direct appeal. Smith v. Bradshaw (Ohio, 04-26-2006) 109 Ohio St.3d 50, 845 N.E.2d 516, 2006-Ohio-1829. Habeas Corpus ⇐ 291

Juvenile, who attempted to challenge his confinement at a juvenile detention center with a pending order to transfer him to the Division of Youth Services, was not entitled to a writ of mandamus to compel his release from the juvenile detention facility; juvenile had adequate remedies at law through an appeal and a motion for contempt to raise the issue of whether juvenile court judge, on remand, had violated a Court of Appeals mandate. State ex rel. Borden v. Hendon (Ohio, 07-24-2002) 96 Ohio St.3d 64, 771 N.E.2d 247, 2002-Ohio-3525. Mandamus ⇐ 3(3); Mandamus ⇐ 4(4)

Legislative elimination of requirement that allegedly delinquent child be given physical examination before juvenile court relinquishes jurisdiction could not be applied retroactively. State v. Golphin (Ohio, 04-29-1998) 81 Ohio St.3d 543, 692 N.E.2d 608, 1998-Ohio-336. Infants ⇐ 68.2

Under former versions of statute and rule governing bind-over procedures, juvenile court failed to properly relinquish jurisdiction over allegedly delinquent child where no physical examination was performed; thus, prosecution of child in common pleas court was void ab initio. State v. Golphin (Ohio, 04-29-1998) 81 Ohio St.3d 543, 692 N.E.2d 608, 1998-Ohio-336. Infants ⇐ 68.7(1)

Former rulings of a juvenile court judge demonstrating that the motion to transfer a youth for prosecution as an adult was granted in more than one-half of the cases in which the motion was considered are contrary to a claim that former rulings demonstrate a predisposition to deny such motions and therefore the rulings do not provide grounds for disqualification. In re Disqualification of Ruben (Ohio, 09-14-1995) No. 95-AP-109, No. 9536, 77 Ohio St.3d 1232, 674 N.E.2d 348, Unreported.

In deciding whether to relinquish jurisdiction over a child, a juvenile court may consider the seriousness of the alleged offense when determining pursuant to Juv R 30(C)(1) if the juvenile is "not amenable to care or rehabilitation" in the juvenile justice system. State v. Watson (Ohio 1989) 47 Ohio St.3d 93, 547 N.E.2d 1181. Infants ⇐ 68.7(2)

Where the record before a juvenile court contains sufficient credible evidence pertaining to each factor listed in Juv R 30(E), the court's determination to transfer the case for trial of the juvenile as an adult will be upheld, absent an abuse of discretion, even without any written statement of the court on those factors. State v. Douglas (Ohio 1985) 20 Ohio St.3d 34, 485 N.E.2d 711, 20 O.B.R. 282.

To bind juvenile over as an adult, it is not necessary that court resolve each of pertinent rule's factors against juvenile. State v. Lopez (Ohio App. 9 Dist., 07-17-1996) 112 Ohio App.3d 659, 679 N.E.2d 1155. Infants ⇐ 68.7(2)

Juvenile court enjoys wide latitude in determining whether to relinquish jurisdiction of juvenile, and its ultimate decision will not be reversed absent abuse of discretion. State v. Lopez (Ohio App. 9 Dist., 07-17-1996) 112 Ohio App.3d 659, 679 N.E.2d 1155. Infants ⇐ 68.7(2); Infants ⇐ 68.8

Juvenile court is not bound by expert opinions in determining whether juvenile is amenable to rehabilitation and should thus not be bound over as an adult. State v. Lopez (Ohio App. 9 Dist., 07-17-1996) 112 Ohio App.3d 659, 679 N.E.2d 1155. Infants ⇐ 68.7(3)

In deciding whether to relinquish its jurisdiction and permit state to prosecute child as adult, juvenile court enjoys wide latitude of discretion. State v. Hopfer (Ohio App. 2 Dist., 07-12-1996) 112 Ohio App.3d 521, 679 N.E.2d 321, dismissed, appeal not allowed 77 Ohio St.3d 1488, 673 N.E.2d 146, reconsideration denied 77 Ohio St.3d 1550, 674 N.E.2d 1187. Infants ⇐ 68.7(2)

In reviewing juvenile court's decision to permit state to prosecute child as adult, test is not whether appellate court would have reached same result upon evidence before juvenile court; test is whether juvenile court abused discretion confided in it. State v. Hopfer (Ohio App. 2 Dist., 07-12-1996) 112 Ohio App.3d 521, 679 N.E.2d 321, dismissed, appeal not allowed 77 Ohio St.3d 1488, 673 N.E.2d 146, reconsideration denied 77 Ohio St.3d 1550, 674 N.E.2d 1187. Infants ⇐ 68.8

In deciding whether juvenile court abused its discretion in permitting state to prosecute child as adult, appellate court had to determine whether juvenile court's decision was "unreasonable" (that is, without any reasonable basis), arbitrary, or unconscionable. State v. Hopfer (Ohio App. 2 Dist., 07-12-1996) 112 Ohio App.3d 521, 679 N.E.2d 321, dismissed, appeal not allowed 77 Ohio St.3d 1488, 673 N.E.2d 146, reconsideration denied 77 Ohio St.3d 1550, 674 N.E.2d 1187. Infants ⇐ 68.8

Any evidence that reasonably supports juvenile court's decision to relinquish jurisdiction over child and permit state to prosecute child as adult will suffice to sustain that court's judgment. State v. Hopfer (Ohio App. 2 Dist., 07-12-1996) 112 Ohio App.3d 521, 679 N.E.2d 321, dismissed, appeal not allowed 77 Ohio St.3d 1488, 673 N.E.2d 146, reconsideration denied 77 Ohio St.3d 1550, 674 N.E.2d 1187. Infants ⇐ 68.8

A juvenile court may consider the nature and seriousness of an alleged crime when deciding if the defendant, who struck the murder victim on the back of the head with a bat, should be tried as an adult. State v. Campbell (Hamilton 1991) 74 Ohio App.3d 352, 598 N.E.2d 1244, dismissed, jurisdictional motion overruled 62 Ohio St.3d 1431, 578 N.E.2d 823.

Possession of a loaded firearm while engaged in drug trafficking by a sixteen-year-old constitutes sufficient evidence that the juvenile poses a danger to the safety of the community to warrant his transfer to the general division of the court of common pleas. State v. Houston (Lucas 1990) 70 Ohio App.3d 152, 590 N.E.2d 839.

A juvenile faced with a bind-over attempt in juvenile court is not entitled to the appointment of a private psychiatric examiner, at the state's expense, instead of a court psychologist for purposes of determining whether juvenile court jurisdiction should be waived. State ex rel. A Juvenile v. Hoose (Lake 1988) 43 Ohio App.3d 109, 539 N.E.2d 704, cause dismissed 39 Ohio St.3d 713, 534 N.E.2d 94.

A minor does not have the right to be tried as an adult and there is no provision for bind-over upon motion of a minor. State v. Smith (Cuyahoga 1985) 29 Ohio App.3d 194, 504 N.E.2d 1121, 29 O.B.R. 237.

When there is sufficient evidence to show that a juvenile charged with murder is unresponsive to juvenile care or rehabilitation, the juvenile court has met its duty to find reasonable grounds for the relinquishment of jurisdiction to the county trial court, and the probable cause requirement of Juv R 30 is fulfilled. State v. Whiteside (Allen 1982) 6 Ohio App.3d 30, 452 N.E.2d 332, 6 O.B.R. 140.

Juvenile's case fell under statute governing requirements for a juvenile's transfer to adult court for criminal prosecution, thus meeting first requirement for case's mandatory transfer to adult court, where juvenile was charged with four category two offenses, was sixteen years old at the time of offenses, and complaint specifically alleged that juvenile had a firearm on his person and displayed such during the acts charged. State v. Fender

(Ohio App. 9 Dist., Lorain, 06-26-2002) No. 01CA007934, 2002-Ohio-3184, 2002 WL 1371090, Unreported. Infants ⇐ 68.7(2)

Evidence supported juvenile court's finding of probable cause that juvenile committed acts alleged in complaint, that is, two counts of aggravated robbery, two counts of kidnapping, and two counts of theft, and a gun specification on five of the six charges, as alleged in complaint, and thus, second requirement for mandatory transfer of case to adult court for criminal prosecution was met; juvenile knowingly and voluntarily waived probable cause hearing on charges, he stipulated to probable cause for all six offenses, and he did not dispute gun charges. State v. Fender (Ohio App. 9 Dist., Lorain, 06-26-2002) No. 01CA007934, 2002-Ohio-3184, 2002 WL 1371090, Unreported. Infants ⇐ 68.7(3)

Evidence that a juvenile was sixteen years and seven months old at the time of the murder and in seemingly satisfactory mental and physical health, his past adjudications as a delinquent, the juvenile's admission to selling drugs and using both drugs and alcohol, his association with friends with whom he had engaged in criminal behavior, and his expulsion from high school for setting fire to a trash can, supports a trial court decision to bind the juvenile over to be tried as an adult pursuant to Juv R 30(E) and RC 2151.26. State v Ruple, No. 15726, 1993 WL 290201 (9th Dist Ct App, Summit, 8–4–93).

Rule requiring the state to respond to discovery requests in juvenile matters applies to "mandatory bindover" or waiver of jurisdiction proceedings wherein the court determines whether probable cause exists to transfer the matter for prosecution of the juvenile as an adult. In re A.M. (Ohio Com.Pl., 05-28-1998) 92 Ohio Misc.2d 4, 699 N.E.2d 574, affirmed 139 Ohio App.3d 303, 743 N.E.2d 937, appeal not allowed 91 Ohio St.3d 1431, 741 N.E.2d 895. Infants ⇐ 68.7(3)

Juvenile who was almost 18 years old when he allegedly murdered 14-year-old girl after considering candidates for murder for approximately two months was not amenable to rehabilitation, and safety of community required that juvenile be placed under legal restrictions beyond age of majority despite fact that juvenile had no prior record, achieved above average grades in school, and worked steadily since junior high and, thus, jurisdiction of juvenile could be transferred for prosecution as adult. In re Snitzky (Ohio Com.Pl., 08-01-1995) 73 Ohio Misc.2d 52, 657 N.E.2d 1379. Infants ⇐ 68.7(2)

Justification existed for limiting juvenile's discovery on motion to transfer juvenile delinquency proceedings to criminal court for trial as adult, where five individuals had been formally charged with offenses arising from same transaction which formed basis of complaint filed against juvenile, two of whom were adults and two of whom had transfer proceedings pending, and granting full discovery might impede criminal prosecution of adult codefendants and potential criminal prosecution of child and his alleged codelinquent. In re Doss (Ohio Com.Pl., 05-11-1994) 65 Ohio Misc.2d 8, 640 N.E.2d 618. Infants ⇐ 68.7(1)

In preliminary hearing on motion to transfer juvenile proceedings to criminal court, state need not provide as full discovery as that required for adjudicatory hearing in juvenile proceedings. In re Doss (Ohio Com.Pl., 05-11-1994) 65 Ohio Misc.2d 8, 640 N.E.2d 618. Infants ⇐ 68.7(1)

3. **Time limitations**

If a juvenile is accused of committing a felony, the ninety-day period established by RC 2945.71(C)(2) and 2945.71(D) for commencing trial does not begin to run until the juvenile court relinquishes jurisdiction and transfers the accused to the "adult" court. State ex rel. Williams v. Court of Common Pleas of Lucas County (Ohio 1975) 42 Ohio St.2d 433, 329 N.E.2d 680, 71 O.O.2d 410.

4. **Criminal charges and indictments**

Juvenile court division did not have jurisdiction over defendant's case, where defendant was bound over and indicted in the general division after his eighteenth birthday. State v. Sherrills (Ohio App. 8 Dist., Cuyahoga, 05-19-2005) No. 85655, No. 85656, 2005-Ohio-2467, 2005 WL 1190729, Unreported. Infants ⇐ 68.7(3)

Evidence supported adjudication of juvenile as delinquent for carrying concealed weapon; though juvenile denied ownership of gun found in car he was driving, numerous witnesses had seen juvenile in possession of similar-looking gun. In re Merritt (Ohio App. 5 Dist., Richland, 01-19-2005) No. 2004CA0060, 2005-Ohio-222, 2005 WL 121718, Unreported. Infants ⇐ 176

Admission of evidence that juvenile, charged in delinquency proceeding with carrying concealed weapon, had been seen in possession of weapon on prior occasions was not abuse of discretion; juvenile had denied that gun was his, and prior bad acts evidence was thus probative on issues of knowledge and absence of mistake or accident. In re Merritt (Ohio App. 5 Dist., Richland, 01-19-2005) No. 2004CA0060, 2005-Ohio-222, 2005 WL 121718, Unreported. Infants ⇐ 173.1

Juvenile court considered relevant factors before allowing juvenile to be bound over for adult prosecution for murder and robbery offenses; stipulation existed that victims sustained physical harm to their persons during the robbery and that juvenile used a firearm to commit the robbery, record further demonstrated that both victims were over the age of five and under the age of sixty-five at the time of the robbery, evidence established that neither victim was disabled and that juvenile had never been committed to rehabilitation prior to the offense, and juvenile court appropriately considered the seriousness of the offense, as evidence was presented that revealed juvenile's actions were premeditated and occurred in a deliberate manner. State v. Moorer (Ohio App. 11 Dist., Geauga, 10-24-2003) No. 2001-G-2353, No. 2001-G-2354, 2003-Ohio-5698, 2003 WL 22427822, Unreported, appeal not allowed 101 Ohio St.3d 1489, 805 N.E.2d 539, 2004-Ohio-1293. Infants ⇐ 68.7(2)

Juvenile court did not abuse its discretion by ordering that juvenile defendant be bound over for adult prosecution for murder and robbery offenses; evidence at the amenability hearing established that defendant was manipulative and exploited the trust of those who cared for him, evidence indicated that even in the restricted setting of his foster home the criminal nature of juvenile's behavior was escalating, and psychological evaluation of court-appointed psychologist concluded that any behavioral improvements displayed by juvenile were superficial. State v. Moorer (Ohio App. 11 Dist., Geauga, 10-24-2003) No. 2001-G-2353, No. 2001-G-2354, 2003-Ohio-5698, 2003 WL 22427822, Unreported, appeal not allowed 101 Ohio St.3d 1489, 805 N.E.2d 539, 2004-Ohio-1293. Infants ⇐ 68.7(2)

Trial court did not abuse its discretion in relinquishing its jurisdiction of juvenile's case and transferring juvenile for prosecution as adult; several witnesses testified that juvenile was threat to community and himself and that juvenile had engaged in violent behavior which had escalated, and none of the witnesses was able to state that juvenile would be amenable to rehabilitation in juvenile justice system or that there would be no need for legal restraint beyond age of 21. State v. Shreves (Ohio App. 6 Dist., Lucas, 06-06-2003) No. L-02-1075, 2003-Ohio-2911, 2003 WL 21299925, Unreported. Infants ⇐ 68.7(3)

Once a juvenile is bound over in any county in Ohio pursuant to RC 2151.26 and Juv R 30, that juvenile is bound over for all felonies committed in other counties of this state, as well as for future felonies he may commit. State v. Adams (Ohio 1982) 69 Ohio St.2d 120, 431 N.E.2d 326, 23 O.O.3d 164. Infants ⇐ 68,7(4)

When a minor is transferred from the juvenile court to the court of common pleas on a charge which would constitute a felony if committed by an adult, the grand jury is empowered to return any indictment under the facts submitted to it and is not confined to returning indictments only on charges originally filed in the juvenile court. State v. Adams (Ohio 1982) 69 Ohio St.2d 120, 431 N.E.2d 326, 23 O.O.3d 164.

If a juvenile offender meets defined criteria, the juvenile court may, or in specific cases shall, transfer the case to the general division of the common pleas court; in specified situations, transfer to the general division is mandatory, one such mandatory transfer situation is where the juvenile is alleged to have used a firearm in commission of certain crimes. In re Graham (Ohio App. 7 Dist., 05-17-2002) 147 Ohio App.3d 452, 770 N.E.2d 1123, 2002-Ohio-2407. Infants ⇐ 68.7(1)

Statute requiring mandatory bindover to adult criminal court after a probable cause finding did not conflict with juvenile rule relating to bindover, as by its very language, juvenile rule was a discretionary provision and only affected discretionary bindovers, not those mandated by criminal statute. In re Langston (Ohio App. 5 Dist., 03-03-1997) 119 Ohio App.3d 1, 694 N.E.2d 468. Infants ⇐ 68.2

In determining whether juvenile could be bound over as an adult on charges of burglary and assault, juvenile court could consider testimony of arresting officer as to violent nature of crime. State v. Lopez (Ohio App. 9 Dist., 07-17-1996) 112 Ohio App.3d 659, 679 N.E.2d 1155. Infants ⇐ 68.7(3)

A juvenile court's bindover decision and conviction on two counts of murder are affirmed where at age fifteen defendant lures his girlfriend to a wooded area and drops a rock on her abdomen killing both her and the couple's unborn baby. State v. Steele (Ohio App. 10 Dist., Franklin, 06-28-2001) No. 00AP-499, 2001 WL 721806, Unreported, dismissed, appeal not allowed 93 Ohio St.3d 1459, 756 N.E.2d 1235.

The juvenile court was well within its discretion in determining that there were reasonable grounds to believe that a seventeen-year-old charged with aggravated murder was not amenable to rehabilitation in a juvenile treatment facility and in transferring jurisdiction to the general division after a full evidentiary hearing and careful examination of all the statutory factors showed that (1) the defendant was adjudicated delinquent in 1990 and 1991 for acts which if committed by an adult would be violent felonies, (2) rehabilitation after these offenses was not successful, (3) school officials were unsuccessful at disciplining him and his family was not cooperative in rectifying his disrespectful behavior, and (4) the murder victim was seventy-seven years old and was shot three times in the head at point-blank range while he was lying on the floor. State v. Metz (Ohio App. 4 Dist., Washington, 06-04-1997) No. 96CA03, 1997 WL 305220, Unreported, motion for delayed appeal granted 79 Ohio St.3d 1508, 684 N.E.2d 90, dismissed, appeal not allowed 81 Ohio St.3d 1413, 688 N.E.2d 1042, certiorari denied 119 S.Ct. 146, 525 U.S. 860, 142 L.Ed.2d 119.

In a felonious assault committed in a beating of a gang initiation member, where the initiate member cannot positively state whether the defendant-juvenile attacked him, there is sufficient evidence to conclude that the defendant's presence, companionship and conduct indicates his complicity where (1) the defendant is a member of the Folks gang and is seen riding his bicycle alongside the group of four members who were performing the initiation, (2) a detective sees the defendant confer with the four youths shortly before the attack, and (3) another gang member names the defendant as a participant in the assault. In re Meredith (Ohio App. 8 Dist., Cuyahoga, 02-22-1996) No. 68938, 1996 WL 75696, Unreported, dismissed, appeal not allowed 76 Ohio St.3d 1434, 667 N.E.2d 985.

5. Amenability to rehabilitation

Record supported juvenile court's conclusions that 17-year-old defendant charged with delinquency for aggravated robbery was not amenable to rehabilitation and that adult sanctions were necessary for community safety, as required for juvenile court to relinquish jurisdiction and transfer defendant to general division for prosecution as adult, even though defendant argued in part that there was evidence from psychological evaluation that he was both emotionally and psychologically immature; juvenile court expressly based its decision on defendant's prior conduct, failure of juvenile-justice system to rehabilitate him, and gravity of alleged crime. State v. Terrell (Ohio App. 6 Dist., Lucas, 09-16-2005) No. L-04-1131, 2005-Ohio-4871, 2005 WL 2249586, Unreported. Infants ⚖ 68.7(3)

Evidence was sufficient to support court finding that there were reasonable grounds to believe juvenile was not amenable to rehabilitation in the juvenile court, and thus order binding juvenile over to the general division was proper; juvenile was 17 years old when the offenses occurred, juvenile was charged with aggravated murder, which was a category one offense and had a mandatory bindover, and juvenile was in sole possession of the murder weapon for awhile on the date of the crime, she participated in the robbery, and she drove the car when the murder weapon was discarded. State v. Holder (Ohio App. 11 Dist., Geauga, 12-20-2002) No. 2001-G-2345, No. 2001-G-2350, 2002-Ohio-7124, 2002 WL 31862684, Unreported, appeal not allowed 98 Ohio St.3d 1513, 786 N.E.2d 63, 2003-Ohio-1572, denial of post-conviction relief affirmed 2003-Ohio-5860, 2003 WL 22470862, appeal not allowed 101 Ohio St.3d 1490, 805 N.E.2d 540, 2004-Ohio-1293. Infants ⚖ 68.7(3)

Juvenile defendant was not improperly denied amenability hearing following bindover from juvenile court; although hearing was brief, defendant stipulated to both his psychological evaluation and his family records, parties had opportunity to call witnesses and it was only after making inquiries to counsel regarding witnesses and final arguments that the juvenile court found that juvenile was not amenable to rehabilitation. State v. Goodwin (Ohio App. 8 Dist., 05-11-2006) 166 Ohio App.3d 709, 852 N.E.2d 1282, 2006-Ohio-2311. Infants ⚖ 68.7(3)

Court of Common Pleas had subject matter jurisdiction to hear defendant's case, following his bind-over from juvenile division, as juvenile division, in its bind-over entry, specifically stated that it found probable cause and that defendant was 17 years of age at time of conduct charged, and juvenile division went on to explain factors it considered in making its determination that defendant was not amenable to care or rehabilitation in the juvenile system, in compliance with provisions of statute and rule governing transfer of cases from juvenile court. State v. Mock (Ohio Com.Pl., 09-26-2005) 136 Ohio Misc.2d 21, 846 N.E.2d 108, 2005-Ohio-7142. Infants ⚖ 68.7(4)

Evidence in a juvenile murder suspect's bindover proceeding, including the gruesome facts of the murder, supported the conclusion that the suspect was not amenable to rehabilitation in the juvenile court, even though prior attempts at such rehabilitation had been limited to probation. State v. Whisenant (Ohio App. 11 Dist., 03-30-1998) 127 Ohio App.3d 75, 711 N.E.2d 1016, dismissed, appeal not allowed 83 Ohio St.3d 1416, 698 N.E.2d 1005. Infants ⚖ 68.7(3)

Juvenile court judge's personal opinion as to whether juvenile committed offenses alleged is not related to whether juvenile is amenable to rehabilitation, as will preclude transfer of juvenile to criminal court for prosecution as adult. State v. Payne (Ohio App. 3 Dist., 03-13-1997) 118 Ohio App.3d 699, 693 N.E.2d 1159. Infants ⚖ 68.7(3)

Juvenile court need not find that any of the statutory circumstances for determining child's amenability to care or rehabilitation within juvenile penal system specifically weighs against child before it relinquishes jurisdiction over child and permits state to prosecute child as adult, as long as totality of evidence supports finding that child is not amenable to treatment. State v. Hopfer (Ohio App. 2 Dist., 07-12-1996) 112 Ohio App.3d 521, 679 N.E.2d 321, dismissed, appeal not allowed 77 Ohio St.3d 1488, 673 N.E.2d 146, reconsideration denied 77 Ohio St.3d 1550, 674 N.E.2d 1187. Infants ⚖ 68.7(3)

Juvenile court did not abuse its discretion in relinquishing jurisdiction over 17-year-old child and permitting state to prosecute her as adult for murdering her newborn baby and grossly abusing its corpse, notwithstanding child's excellent academic record, lack of criminal history, clean disciplinary record, and previously stable family, where psychologist provided sufficient expert testimony about child's lack of remorse and skewed, self-focused value system to support conclusion that she would not be amenable to rehabilitation or treatment within juvenile penal system, child's age at time of hearing was only three months short of 18, and nature and severity of child's alleged act suggested callous indifference for human life which could pose threat to community even after she turned 21. State v. Hopfer (Ohio App. 2 Dist., 07-12-1996) 112 Ohio App.3d 521, 679 N.E.2d 321, dismissed, appeal not allowed 77 Ohio St.3d 1488, 673 N.E.2d 146, reconsideration denied 77 Ohio St.3d 1550, 674 N.E.2d 1187. Infants ⚖ 68.7(3)

In assessing probability of rehabilitating child within juvenile justice system, juvenile court enjoys wide latitude to entertain or relinquish jurisdiction, and ultimate decision lies within its sound discretion. In re Williams (Ohio App. 10 Dist., 05-14-1996) 111 Ohio App.3d 120, 675 N.E.2d 1254, dismissed, appeal not allowed 77 Ohio St.3d 1470, 673 N.E.2d 136. Infants ⚖ 68.7(2)

A sixteen-year-old in good physical and mental health and possessing above average intelligence who makes a conscious decision to terminate employment in order to traffic in drugs which pays more than his $4.50/hour job and who has previously been adjudicated a delinquent in another state due to drug trafficking is properly determined to be unamenable to rehabilitation in juvenile facilities. State v. Houston (Lucas 1990) 70 Ohio App.3d 152, 590 N.E.2d 839.

A prior rape adjudication should not be admitted in a rape prosecution where neither sentencing nor probation is involved; cross-examination of the juvenile about the inadmissible prior conviction is not prejudicial, however, where the judge is aware of it from the amenability hearing on the prosecutor's motion to bind the boy over for trial as an adult, there is no jury trial before laypersons, and the judge says that he put the adjudication out of his mind. In re Johnson (Cuyahoga 1989) 61 Ohio App.3d 544, 573 N.E.2d 184.

When a juvenile court determines whether a juvenile is amenable to rehabilitation, all five factors of Juv R 30(E) must be considered, but the court is not required to resolve all five factors against the juvenile in order to justify his transfer for prosecution as an adult. State v. Oviedo (Wood 1982) 5 Ohio App.3d 168, 450 N.E.2d 700, 5 O.B.R. 351.

A sixteen-year-old delinquent child who purposely causes the death of her father in violation of RC 2903.02 and 2151.02 is not amenable to rehabilitation within the juvenile system despite the lack of a physical examination where testimony and evidence coupled with the nature and severity of the act suggest a callous indifference for human life that could pose a threat to the community even beyond the juvenile's twenty-first birthday. State v Berenyi, No. 11–97–01, 1997 WL 576357 (3d Dist Ct App, Paulding, 9–18–97).

A penalty enhancement accompanying a prosecution of a juvenile as an adult, rather than in a juvenile delinquency proceeding, is not a factor to be considered by a juvenile court pursuant to Juv R 30(E) when determining whether the juvenile is amenable to rehabilitation. State v Ingram, No. CA–15049 (9th Dist Ct App, Summit, 12–26–91).

The decision to relinquish juvenile court jurisdiction rests with the juvenile court; expert testimony as to the amenability of a defendant to rehabilitation in juvenile facilities is not binding on the court. State v Dickens, No. 12967 (9th Dist Ct App, Summit, 9–23–87).

A judge is only required to find reasonable grounds to believe the accused would be amenable to rehabilitation, not that the accused cannot be rehabilitated. State v Barnum, No. 81–C–60 (7th Dist Ct App, Columbiana, 6–22–82).

Until juvenile court either begins to hear evidence in an adjudicatory hearing, or divests itself of jurisdiction by transferring child for prosecution as an adult, determination of child's amenability to care and rehabilitation in juvenile justice system is subject to reconsideration upon motion filed by party. In re K.W. (Ohio Com.Pl., 10-02-1995) 73 Ohio Misc.2d 20, 657 N.E.2d 611. Infants ☞ 68.7(4)

6. Notice

Where a grandmother states to a juvenile court that she has legal custody of a minor in a "bind-over" proceeding, the notice requirements of RC 2151.26 have been satisfied when the grandmother has been given proper notice. State v. Parks (Montgomery 1988) 51 Ohio App.3d 194, 555 N.E.2d 671.

7. Waiver of examination

Juvenile is not entitled to a court-appointed independent psychologist to assist him in determining whether to submit to or waive a mental examination in a bindover proceeding. State v. Whisenant (Ohio App. 11 Dist., 03-30-1998) 127 Ohio App.3d 75, 711 N.E.2d 1016, dismissed, appeal not allowed 83 Ohio St.3d 1416, 698 N.E.2d 1005. Infants ☞ 68.7(3)

According to RC 2151.26(C), the decision to submit to or waive the mental and physical examination authorized by RC 2151.26(A)(1)(c) rests ultimately with the child. The only requirement is that any waiver must be competently and intelligently made. State ex rel. Doe v. Tracy (Warren 1988) 51 Ohio App.3d 198, 555 N.E.2d 674, cause dismissed 39 Ohio St.3d 713, 534 N.E.2d 95.

8. Investigation

Pursuant to Juv R 30(G), an order of transfer is sufficient if it demonstrates that the statutory requirement of "full investigation" has been met and that the issue has received the full attention of the juvenile court. State v. Oviedo (Wood 1982) 5 Ohio App.3d 168, 450 N.E.2d 700, 5 O.B.R. 351. Infants ☞ 68.7(4)

9. Constitutional issues

Juvenile court did not err in determining that probable cause did not exist to support attempted murder charges against juvenile, as to which state sought relinquishment of jurisdiction, and thus dismissal of charges was proper; juvenile court determined that alleged victim's equivocations and inconsistencies between eyewitness's and alleged victim's testimony rendered victim's testimony not credible, and, if alleged victim's testimony was not credible, there was no other evidence to establish every element of the offense necessary to support a finding of probable cause. In re D.T.F. (Ohio App. 10 Dist., Franklin, 09-30-2005) No. 05AP-03, No. 05AP-04, 2005-Ohio-5245, 2005 WL 2403958, Unreported. Infants ☞ 68.7(3)

Statute providing for transfer of certain juveniles to General Division for criminal prosecution as an adult did not violate juvenile's due process or equal protection rights, nor did it conflict with juvenile procedure rule governing relinquishment of jurisdiction for purposes of criminal prosecution. State v. Agee (Ohio App. 2 Dist., 05-21-1999) 133 Ohio App.3d 441, 728 N.E.2d 442, dismissed, appeal not allowed 86 Ohio St.3d 1489, 716 N.E.2d 721, denial of habeas corpus affirmed 92 Ohio St.3d 540, 751 N.E.2d 1043, 2001-Ohio-1279. Constitutional Law ☞ 242.1(4); Constitutional Law ☞ 255(4); Infants ☞ 68.7(2)

Juvenile who was transferred to criminal court for prosecution as adult on assault charges received fair and impartial hearing, as required by due process clause, on his amenability for rehabilitation as juvenile, even though juvenile court judge had made statement during preliminary hearing that juvenile had, beyond a reasonable doubt, committed offense in question. State v. Payne (Ohio App. 3 Dist., 03-13-1997) 118 Ohio App.3d 699, 693 N.E.2d 1159. Constitutional Law ☞ 255(4); Infants ☞ 68.7(3)

Prosecutor's references to result of prior juvenile court hearing concerning defendant's amenability to treatment and rehabilitation within juvenile penal system were not improper and did not prejudice defendant's right to fair trial on charges of murdering her newborn baby and grossly abusing its corpse, where references were innocuous efforts to explain to potential jurors why state was prosecuting defendant as adult, to clarify one witness' comment that sheriff's deputy had called her before "first trial," and to establish chronological order of events in cross-examination of defendant, especially considering procedural nature of amenability hearings, which do not address merits of accusations against juvenile. State v. Hopfer (Ohio App. 2 Dist., 07-12-1996) 112 Ohio App.3d 521, 679 N.E.2d 321, dismissed, appeal not allowed 77 Ohio St.3d 1488, 673 N.E.2d 146, reconsideration denied 77 Ohio St.3d 1550, 674 N.E.2d 1187. Criminal Law ☞ 713

Jeopardy attached as to all four delinquency complaints filed against juvenile, so that juvenile could no longer be prosecuted as adult for acts underlying complaints, once juvenile requested that adjudicatory hearing proceed; fact that juvenile did not admit to all of the allegations contained in complaints and that no additional evidence was presented did not prevent attaching of jeopardy. State v. Penrod (Summit 1989) 62 Ohio App.3d 720, 577 N.E.2d 424, motion overruled 44 Ohio St.3d 715, 542 N.E.2d 1112. Double Jeopardy ☞ 33

When, in an adjudicatory hearing held pursuant to Juv R 29, the only evidence of guilt utilized by the court is testimony presented at the preliminary hearing, where the accused exercised adequate rights of cross-examination, he is denied no constitutional right. Matter of Gantt (Wood 1978) 61 Ohio App.2d 44, 398 N.E.2d 800, 15 O.O.3d 67.

Trial counsel did not render ineffective assistance by arranging plea agreement for juvenile, even though juvenile was committed to Department of Youth Services (DYS) for violating probation that resulted from plea agreement in which juvenile pled guilty to gross sexual imposition; plea agreement reduced juvenile's charge of first-degree felony rape to third-degree felony gross sexual imposition, counsel actively sought to obtain probation for juvenile rather than commitment to DYS when he negotiated plea bargain, and juvenile was aware when he pled guilty to gross sexual imposition that a possible disposition was that juvenile could have been sent to DYS. In re Staugler, No. 2001 CA 33, 2002–Ohio–2376, 2002 WL 1000602 (2d Dist Ct App, Miami, 5–17–02).

In a bindover proceeding a juvenile is denied effective assistance of counsel where his attorney fails to present any evidence in opposition to the prosecutor's bindover request and the record contains very little information concerning (1) the juvenile's prior offenses, (2) disposition of those offenses, (3) extent of the probation services offered, and (4) previous attempts to rehabilitate the juvenile. State v. Lett (Ohio App. 4 Dist., Ross, 09-04-1996) No. 95 CA 2094, 1996 WL 511732, Unreported.

Statutes are presumed constitutional and the burden is on a defendant to demonstrate the contrary; therefore, where a defendant alleges, without analysis, that RC 2151.26 and Juv R 30(E) are unconstitutionally void for vagueness, because they fail to provide a workable standard to insure equal treatment among juvenile defendants, that burden is not met. State v Brown, No. 52757 (8th Dist Ct App, Cuyahoga, 10–8–87).

While juvenile's probable cause hearing must measure up to essentials of due process and fair treatment, hearing need not conform with all requirements of criminal trial, adjudicatory hearing, or administrative hearing, and juvenile need not be afforded all rights that he or she may have for trial. In re Hunter (Ohio Com.Pl., 07-12-1999) 99 Ohio Misc.2d 107, 716 N.E.2d 802. Constitutional Law ☞ 255(4); Infants ☞ 203

Denial of juvenile's motion to compel discovery at probable cause hearing is not prejudicial to juvenile's right to fair trial. In re Hunter (Ohio Com.Pl., 07-12-1999) 99 Ohio Misc.2d 107, 716 N.E.2d 802. Infants ☞ 201

Juvenile court may, in its discretion, admit juvenile to bail in action wherein request for waiver of jurisdiction has been made seeking transfer of matter for prosecution as adult. In re K.G. (Ohio Com.Pl., 10-23-1997) 89 Ohio Misc.2d 16, 693 N.E.2d 1186. Infants ☞ 68.3

Jeopardy does not attach to probable cause determination made at preliminary hearing on motion to transfer juvenile to criminal court for trial as adult. In re Doss (Ohio Com.Pl., 05-11-1994) 65 Ohio Misc.2d 8, 640 N.E.2d 618. Double Jeopardy ☞ 33

There is a violation of the Double Jeopardy Clause of the US Constitution where a juvenile is subjected to a hearing at juvenile court where evidence is heard to determine if he committed acts that violated a criminal law, he is found unfit to be treated as a juvenile and then bound over to superior court for trial, because even though he was only subject to one punishment, he still faced the risk of two trials for the same offense. Breed v. Jones (U.S.Cal. 1975) 95 S.Ct. 1779, 421 U.S. 519, 44 L.Ed.2d 346, on remand 519 F.2d 1314.

Although a juvenile court has considerable latitude in determining whether it will retain or waive jurisdiction over a child, there must be sufficient procedural regularity to satisfy the requirements of due process, which include a full investigation, and where the judge fails to rule on various motions affecting the accused, fails to hold a hearing or confer with the accused, his parents, or counsel, and fails to recite any reasons for waiver of jurisdiction, the waiver order is invalid. Kent v. U. S. (U.S.Dist. Col. 1966) 86 S.Ct. 1045, 383 U.S. 541, 11 Ohio Misc. 53, 16 L.Ed.2d 84, 40 O.O.2d 270.

A decision of an Ohio juvenile court to transfer a fifteen-year-old to court because of deterrence and retribution rather than rehabilitation does not violate due process. Deel v. Jago (C.A.6 (Ohio) 1992) 967 F.2d 1079. Constitutional Law ☞ 255(4); Infants ☞ 68.7(2)

A juvenile who has been bound over to be tried as an adult for murder does not have his due process guarantees violated when the juvenile court considers the factors in Juv R 30(E) but does not formally receive the reports in evidence at the transfer hearing. Oviedo v. Jago (C.A.6 (Ohio) 1987) 809 F.2d 326.

Where the order of a juvenile court contained a finding only that there was probable cause to believe that the juvenile had committed an act which would be a felony if committed by an adult, the hearing in juvenile court was not an adjudicatory hearing and the subsequent trial of defendant as an adult in the court of common pleas did not subject him to double jeopardy. Johnson v. Perini (C.A.6 (Ohio) 1981) 644 F.2d 573. Double Jeopardy ☞ 33

A juvenile court proceeding to determine whether petitioner should be treated as a juvenile or transferred to the court of common pleas to be tried as an adult on a murder charge was not an adjudicatory proceeding to which double jeopardy attached and hence did not preclude a subsequent trial of petitioner as an adult, notwithstanding that the state presented evidence of probable cause in proceeding to believe that petitioner had committed the alleged offense, where probable cause evidence was heard solely for juvenile court to decide which judicial treatment of petitioner would serve his interests and those of the community, not for juvenile court to decide petitioner's guilt. Keener v. Taylor (C.A.6 (Ohio) 1981) 640 F.2d 839, 22 O.O.3d 248. Double Jeopardy ☞ 33

Where Ohio statute required full investigation of facts underlying charge of delinquency and finding of delinquency prior to bindover of juvenile for trial as an adult, once juvenile court, possessing jurisdiction and power to enter final orders levying a wide range of possible sanctions, began a hearing, not limited in scope by statute to preliminary or probable cause hearing, jeopardy attached, with the result that subsequent criminal prosecution for the same acts contravened his constitutional protection against double jeopardy. Sims v. Engle (C.A.6 (Ohio) 1980) 619 F.2d 598, certiorari denied 101 S.Ct. 1403, 450 U.S. 936, 67 L.Ed.2d 372. Double Jeopardy ☞ 33

10. Improper transfer

Absent proper bindover procedure pursuant to statute, jurisdiction of juvenile court is exclusive and cannot be waived. State ex rel. Harris v. Anderson (Ohio, 07-31-1996) 76 Ohio St.3d 193, 667 N.E.2d 1, 1996-Ohio-412. Infants ☞ 68.5

Juvenile court's failure to state with reasonable specificity the factual basis underlying its order to transfer a juvenile to common pleas court for prosecution as an adult renders the common pleas court without jurisdiction. State v Newton, No. F–82–17 (6th Dist Ct App, Fulton, 6–10–83).

11. County of transfer

Where a case is pending against a juvenile in a foreign county, such case must be transferred to the juvenile's home county, if, at any time prior to dispositional order, proceedings against the juvenile are pending in his home county. Furthermore, such mandatory transfer may not be avoided by the foreign county through the use of a bindover proceeding. State v Payne, No. 81–CA–22 (4th Dist Ct App, Pickaway, 7–28–82).

12. Judge

It would be apex juris and unreasonable to hold that every judge who presides over a preliminary hearing in a criminal or juvenile matter must thereafter disqualify himself because his impartiality might "reasonably" be questioned. In re Terry H, 1 OBR 377 (CP, Cuyahoga 1982).

13. Adjudicatory hearing

Closure of delinquency proceedings for 17–year-old charged with aggravated murder, aggravated attempted murder, and aggravated robbery was abuse of discretion; public interest in proceedings outweighed bare assertion by juvenile's attorney that permitting access would not be in juvenile's best interest, in view of juvenile's near-adult age at time of alleged offenses, minimal likelihood that probable cause hearing would disclose confidential information, gravity of offenses, and fact that juvenile would be subject to mandatory bindover result if probable cause was found. State ex rel. Plain Dealer Publishing Co. v. Geauga Cty. Court of Common Pleas, Juv. Div. (Ohio, 08-11-2000) 90 Ohio St.3d 79, 734 N.E.2d 1214, 2000-Ohio-35. Infants ☞ 203

Information which is normally considered confidential in juvenile court proceedings, such as a social history or mental examination, is not relevant to a juvenile court's probable cause determination at preliminary hearing. State ex rel. Plain Dealer Publishing Co. v. Geauga Cty. Court of Common Pleas, Juv. Div. (Ohio, 08-11-2000) 90 Ohio St.3d 79, 734 N.E.2d 1214, 2000-Ohio-35. Infants ☞ 203

Informal proceedings conducted in a juvenile court in 1962 for the purpose of determining whether or not to bind over a juvenile defendant to be tried as an adult do not constitute an "adjudicatory hearing" as described in Breed v Jones, 421 US 519, 95 SCt 1779, 44 LEd(2d) 346 (1975). (But see Sims v Engle, 619 F(2d) 598 (6th Cir Ohio 1980).) State v. Sims (Cuyahoga 1977) 55 Ohio App.2d 285, 380 N.E.2d 1350, 9 O.O.3d 417. Double Jeopardy ☞ 33

Preliminary hearing in delinquency adjudication proceeding to determine probable cause was not adjudicatory hearing for purposes of filing of discovery motions; juvenile's guilt or innocence was not at issue, and bindover to adult court was still possibility. In re Hunter (Ohio Com.Pl., 07-12-1999) 99 Ohio Misc.2d 107, 716 N.E.2d 802. Infants ☞ 201

General rule that court may deny or limit discovery in delinquency adjudication proceeding upon showing that granting discovery may impede criminal prosecution of minor as adult or of an adult charged with offense arising from same transaction, while applicable when there is adjudicatory hearing pending on juvenile and that juvenile has co-delinquent who has pending bindover hearing and/or adult co-defendant who has trial pending, is not applicable to preliminary probable cause hearings. In re Hunter (Ohio Com.Pl., 07-12-1999) 99 Ohio Misc.2d 107, 716 N.E.2d 802. Infants ☞ 201

Original determination, that child was amenable to care and rehabilitation in juvenile justice system, would be set aside prior to adjudicatory hearing and jurisdiction would be transferred to Common Pleas Court; child failed to appear for adjudicatory hearing and after turning age 18 was arrested as an adult for carrying concealed weapon, escaped from juvenile detention center one week after being placed there, and was rearrested for receiving stolen property and carrying concealed weapon. In re K.W. (Ohio Com.Pl., 10-02-1995) 73 Ohio Misc.2d 20, 657 N.E.2d 611. Infants ☞ 68.7(4)

Preliminary and amenability hearings in proceedings to transfer child for prosecution as adult are neither presumptively open nor presumptively closed. In re D.R. (Ohio Com.Pl. 1993) 63 Ohio Misc.2d 273, 624 N.E.2d 1120. Infants ☞ 68.7(3)

Preliminary hearing to determine whether 17–year-old juvenile should be transferred to be tried as adult for offenses of murder and felonious assault would be open to media and public; evidence did not indicate that there existed reasonable and substantial basis for believing that public access could harm child or endanger fairness of adjudication, or that potential for harm outweighed benefits of public access. In re D.R. (Ohio Com.Pl. 1993) 63 Ohio Misc.2d 273, 624 N.E.2d 1120. Infants ☞ 68.7(3)

14. Sentences

Defendant was not entitled to $30 per day credit towards his fine since defendant was not confined pursuant to statute providing that, if fine is imposed as part of sentence and if court determines that offender is able to pay but refuses to do so, court may order offender confined until fine is paid; time that defendant served in juvenile detention facility was prior to sentencing and, thus, he was not ordered to serve this time in satisfaction of his fine and even at time of sentencing, there was no issue raised as to defendant's ability or willingness to pay the $1,000 fine. State v. James (Ohio App. 9 Dist., 10-04-1995) 106 Ohio App.3d 686, 666 N.E.2d 1185. Fines ☞ 12

Trial court committed reversible error by failing to specify in defendant's record of conviction that he had served 179 days in juvenile detention facility or to order that defendant's sentence be reduced by the number of days he served in that facility. State v. James (Ohio App. 9 Dist., 10-04-1995) 106 Ohio App.3d 686, 666 N.E.2d 1185. Criminal Law ☞ 1177

Since defendant was unable to leave juvenile detention facility of his own volition, he was "confined" within meaning of statute stating that jailor shall reduce sentence of prisoner by the total number of days prisoner was "confined" for any reason, and, thus, defendant should have received credit for the 179 days that he served in juvenile detention facility. State v. James (Ohio App. 9 Dist., 10-04-1995) 106 Ohio App.3d 686, 666 N.E.2d 1185. Sentencing And Punishment ☞ 1157

Unless juvenile court exceeds statutory sentencing guidelines or abuses its discretion, Court of Appeals will not reverse decision of juvenile court. In re William H. (Ohio App. 6 Dist., 08-18-1995) 105 Ohio App.3d 761, 664 N.E.2d 1361. Infants ☞ 251; Infants ☞ 252

"Abuse of discretion" sufficient to overturn a sentencing decision by juvenile court, connotes more than an error of law of judgment; it implies that court's attitude is unreasonable, arbitrary or unconscionable. In re William H. (Ohio App. 6 Dist., 08-18-1995) 105 Ohio App.3d 761, 664 N.E.2d 1361. Infants ⚖ 251

An accused in a court of common pleas who has been bound over from a juvenile court is entitled to have his "jail time," service while under the jurisdiction of the latter, deducted from his sentence. State v. Young (Franklin 1975) 44 Ohio App.2d 387, 339 N.E.2d 668, 73 O.O.2d 462.

Trial court erred when it failed to credit days that juvenile was held in county juvenile detention center, and other facilities, toward the balance of his commitment to the Ohio Department of Youth Services after he violated probation. In re Keeran (Ohio App. 5 Dist., Licking, 03-28-2002) No. 01CA69, 2002-Ohio-1580, 2002 WL 1653799, Unreported, appeal not allowed 96 Ohio St.3d 1491, 774 N.E.2d 765, 2002-Ohio-4534. Infants ⚖ 69(7)

15. Habeas corpus

Doctrine of res judicata barred inmate from filing third petition for writ of habeas corpus, in which he claimed that his conviction and sentence were void due to fact he was never given physical examination before juvenile court bound him over for trial as an adult, where inmate could have raised such claim in his two prior habeas corpus actions. State ex rel. Childs v. Lazaroff (Ohio, 01-03-2001) 90 Ohio St.3d 519, 739 N.E.2d 802, 2001-Ohio-9. Habeas Corpus ⚖ 898(1)

Direct appeal of indictment and conviction provided defendant with adequate remedy for claim that he was improperly convicted of crimes for which he was never bound over from juvenile court, such that habeas relief was not available; petition challenged validity of subsequent indictment, conviction, and sentencing by common pleas court after a technically correct bindover on charges for which defendant was not prosecuted. State ex rel. Fryerson v. Tate (Ohio, 02-17-1999) 84 Ohio St.3d 481, 705 N.E.2d 353, 1999-Ohio-465, reconsideration denied 85 Ohio St.3d 1448, 708 N.E.2d 212. Habeas Corpus ⚖ 291

Habeas petition in which petitioner who alleged that conviction for which he was incarcerated occurred when he was 17 years old and that no bindover from juvenile court to adult court occurred stated potentially good cause of action in habeas corpus, even though petitioner may have possessed adequate remedy at law. State ex rel. Harris v. Anderson (Ohio, 07-31-1996) 76 Ohio St.3d 193, 667 N.E.2d 1, 1996-Ohio-412. Habeas Corpus ⚖ 291

Habeas corpus petition which alleges that court lacked jurisdiction over petitioner due to improper bindover from juvenile court states potentially good cause of action in habeas corpus. State ex rel. Harris v. Anderson (Ohio, 07-31-1996) 76 Ohio St.3d 193, 667 N.E.2d 1, 1996-Ohio-412. Habeas Corpus ⚖ 535

Contention by petitioner, who sought habeas corpus relief on basis that no proper bindover from juvenile court had occurred prior to his conviction, that he was 17 years old at time of commission of offenses was sufficient to meet particularity requirement to withstand dismissal, as petitioner was not required to provide supporting documentation of his age in petition in order to satisfy particularity requirement. State ex rel. Harris v. Anderson (Ohio, 07-31-1996) 76 Ohio St.3d 193, 667 N.E.2d 1, 1996-Ohio-412. Habeas Corpus ⚖ 670(10)

Juv R 31 [Reserved]

Juv R 32 Social history; physical examination; mental examination; investigation involving the allocation of parental rights and responsibilities for the care of children

(A) Social history and physical or mental examination: availability before adjudication

The court may order and utilize a social history or physical or mental examination at any time after the filing of a complaint under any of the following circumstances:

(1) Upon the request of the party concerning whom the history or examination is to be made;

(2) Where transfer of a child for adult prosecution is an issue in the proceeding;

(3) Where a material allegation of a neglect, dependency, or abused child complaint relates to matters that a history or examination may clarify;

(4) Where a party's legal responsibility for the party's acts or the party's competence to participate in the proceedings is an issue;

(5) Where a physical or mental examination is required to determine the need for emergency medical care under Juv. R. 13; or

(6) Where authorized under Juv. R. 7(I).

(B) Limitations on preparation and use

Until there has been an admission or adjudication that the child who is the subject of the proceedings is a juvenile traffic offender, delinquent, unruly, neglected, dependent, or abused, no social history, physical examination or mental examination shall be ordered except as authorized under subdivision (A) and any social history, physical examination or mental examination ordered pursuant to subdivision (A) shall be utilized only for the limited purposes therein specified. The person preparing a social history or making a physical or mental examination shall not testify about the history or examination or information received in its preparation in any juvenile traffic offender, delinquency, or unruly child adjudicatory hearing, except as may be required in a hearing to determine whether a child should be transferred to an adult court for criminal prosecution.

(C) Availability of social history or investigation report

A reasonable time before the dispositional hearing, or any other hearing at which a social history or physical or mental examination is to be utilized, counsel shall be permitted to inspect any social history or report of a mental or physical examination. The court may, for good cause shown, deny such inspection or limit its scope to specified portions of the history or report. The court may order that the contents of the history or report, in whole or part, not be disclosed to specified persons. If inspection or disclosure is denied or limited, the court shall state its reasons for such denial or limitation to counsel.

(D) Investigation: allocation of parental rights and responsibilities for the care of children; habeas corpus

On the filing of a complaint for the allocation of parental rights and responsibilities for the care of children or for a writ of habeas corpus to determine the allocation of parental rights and responsibilities for the care of a child, or on the filing of a motion for change in the allocation of parental rights and responsibilities for the care of children, the court may cause an investigation to be made as to the character, health, family relations, past conduct, present living conditions, earning ability, and financial worth of the parties to the action. The report of the investigation shall be confidential, but shall be made available to the parties or their counsel upon written request not less than three days before hearing. The court may tax as costs all or any part of the expenses of each investigation.

(Adopted eff. 7–1–72; amended eff. 7–1–73, 7–1–76, 7–1–91, 7–1–94)

Historical and Statutory Notes

Amendment Note: The 7–1–94 amendment made changes to reflect gender-neutral language.

Staff Notes

1994:

Rule 32 Social History; Physical Examination; Mental Examination; Investigation Involving the Allocation of Parental Rights and Responsibilities for the Care of Children

Masculine references were replaced by gender neutral language and other nonsubstantive grammatical changes were made.

Editor's Comment

Social history and physical or mental examination availability before adjudication 1
Limitations on preparation and use 2
Availability of social history or investigation report 3
Investigation: custody; habeas corpus 4

1. Social history and physical or mental examination availability before adjudication

Juv R 32(A) sets forth a list of situations in which the court may order a social history or physical or mental examination prior to an adjudication on the allegations of the complaint. These are all situations in which the history or examination is important to the proper resolution of issues that may arise prior to the adjudication.

2. Limitations on preparation and use

Juv R 32(B) specifies that the cases listed in Division (A) are the only cases in which a history or examination may be ordered prior to an adjudication and that even in those cases the history or report may be used prior to adjudication only for the purpose specified in Division (A).

3. Availability of social history or investigation report

Juv R 32(C) provides a general principle that the social history and reports on a physical or mental examination are to be available to counsel prior to their use. It also provides for limitations on that availability for good cause shown. The rule is drawn from 2151.352.

4. Investigation: custody; habeas corpus

Juv R 32(D) provides for an investigation very similar to those provided for in Divisions (A) through (C), but does so in language taken from Civ R 75(D), so that there will be no conflict in procedure in custody disputes depending on the court in which they are placed. A few minor modifications in the language of Civ R 75(D) have been made. These changes are:

(1) the addition of "health" and "present living conditions" to the items that may be included in the report;

(2) the statement that the report shall be confidential;

(3) the shortening of the time when a written request to see the report must be submitted from seven days to three days.

Jurisdiction in custody cases may be transferred from the domestic relations court to the juvenile court pursuant to 3109.04 where custody to neither parent is in the best interest of the child without the consent of the juvenile court, and pursuant to 3109.06 on motion of either party or the court with the consent of the juvenile court. Uniformity of procedure is desirable.

The juvenile court has exclusive original jurisdiction to determine the custody of a child not a ward of another court of this state pursuant to 2151.23(A)(2) and to hear and determine any application for a writ of habeas corpus involving the custody of a child pursuant to 2151.23(A)(3).

Cross References

Detention, and shelter care, Juv R 7
Divorce, annulment and alimony actions, Civ R 75
Relinquishment of jurisdiction for purposes of criminal prosecution, Juv R 30
Report concerning child in custody may be made available for good cause shown to attorney representing child, parents, or custodian, 2151.352
Temporary disposition, temporary orders, emergency medical and surgical treatment, Juv R 13

Library References

Habeas Corpus ⚖︎688.
Infants ⚖︎208.
Westlaw Topic Nos. 197, 211.
C.J.S. Habeas Corpus §§ 159, 207 to 220.
C.J.S. Infants §§ 51 to 85.

Research References

Encyclopedias

OH Jur. 3d Family Law § 1637, Order for Social History or Physical or Mental Examination.
OH Jur. 3d Family Law § 1638, Order for Social History or Physical or Mental Examination—Availability and Use of Results.
OH Jur. 3d Family Law § 1639, Custody Investigation.
OH Jur. 3d Family Law § 1647, Proceedings Before Referee; Powers and Duties.
OH Jur. 3d Family Law § 1720, Custody Investigation.

Treatises and Practice Aids

Carlin, Baldwin's Ohio Practice, Merrick-Rippner Probate Law § 107:36, Use of Social History and Investigation Report.
Carlin, Baldwin's Ohio Practice, Merrick-Rippner Probate Law § 107:49, Adjudicatory Hearings—Conduct of Hearing by Magistrate.
Carlin, Baldwin's Ohio Practice, Merrick-Rippner Probate Law § 107:53, Adjudicatory Hearings—Mental Competency to Stand Trial.
Carlin, Baldwin's Ohio Practice, Merrick-Rippner Probate Law § 107:66, Discretionary Transfer.
Carlin, Baldwin's Ohio Practice, Merrick-Rippner Probate Law § 107:114, Juvenile Court Records—Confidentiality.
Giannelli & Yeomans, Ohio Juvenile Law § 21:6, Social History Report.
Giannelli & Yeomans, Ohio Juvenile Law § 22:8, Discretionary Transfer.
Giannelli & Yeomans, Ohio Juvenile Law § 23:7, Mental Competency.
Giannelli & Yeomans, Ohio Juvenile Law § 24:4, Pretrial Orders.
Giannelli & Yeomans, Ohio Juvenile Law § 25:9, Evidence.
Giannelli & Yeomans, Ohio Juvenile Law § 35:2, Confidentiality Requirement.
Giannelli & Yeomans, Ohio Juvenile Law § 35:4, Expungement and Sealing.
Giannelli & Yeomans, Ohio Juvenile Law App. D, Appendix D. Glossary.
Giannelli & Yeomans, Ohio Juvenile Law § 22:10, Mental Examination.
Giannelli & Yeomans, Ohio Juvenile Law § 22:13, Rules of Evidence.
Giannelli & Yeomans, Ohio Juvenile Law § 22:14, Self-Incrimination.
Giannelli & Yeomans, Ohio Juvenile Law § 22:15, Access to Reports & Discovery.
Giannelli & Yeomans, Ohio Juvenile Law § 23:16, Evidence—Hearsay.
Giannelli & Yeomans, Ohio Juvenile Law § 23:28, Impartial Judge.
Giannelli & Yeomans, Ohio Juvenile Law § 25:10, Social History & Medical Examinations.

Law Review and Journal Commentaries

In re T.R.: Not In Front of the Children, Bill Dickhaut. I Ky Children's Rts J 10 (July 1991).

Juvenile Delinquency Proceedings in Ohio: Due Process and the Hearsay Dilemma, Comment. 24 Clev St L Rev 356 (Spring 1975).

Notes of Decisions

Confidentiality 1
Constitutional issues 2
Mental evaluation 3
Social history 4

---

1. Confidentiality

Good cause was demonstrated to release juvenile court records in action brought by tutor who was raped by juvenile placed in independent living facility and tutor's husband against county, its placement contractor, and facility owner, among others, for their alleged negligent supervision and placement of juvenile, where juvenile and his parent executed waivers permitting tutor and husband to access records. Grantz v. Discovery For Youth (Ohio App. 12 Dist., Butler, 02-22-2005) No. CA2004-09-216, No. CA2004-09-217, 2005-Ohio-680, 2005 WL 406211, Unreported. Records ⚖︎ 32

Application to the juvenile court was not only mechanism for obtaining confidential juvenile court records; rather, proper procedure for determining discoverability of confidential juvenile records required trial court to conduct in camera inspection to determine: (1) whether the records were necessary and relevant to the pending action; (2) whether good cause had been shown by the person seeking disclosure; and (3) whether their admission outweighed the statutory confidentiality considerations. Grantz v. Discovery For Youth (Ohio App. 12 Dist., Butler, 02-22-2005) No. CA2004-09-216, No. CA2004-09-217, 2005-Ohio-680, 2005 WL 406211, Unreported. Records ⚖︎ 32

Pursuant to Juv R 32(B), 37(B) and RC 2151.14, juvenile court records, the records of social, mental, and physical examinations pursuant to court order, and records of the juvenile court probation department are not public records under RC 149.43. OAG 90–101.

Under RC 1347.08 a juvenile court must permit a juvenile or a duly authorized attorney who represents the juvenile to inspect court records pertaining to the juvenile unless the records are exempt under RC 1347.04(A)(1)(e) (investigatory material compiled for law enforcement purposes) RC 1347.08(C) (certain medical, psychiatric, or psychological information), or RC 1347.08(E)(2) (confidential law enforcement investigatory records or trial preparation records). OAG 84–077.

2. Constitutional issues

The federal courts will abstain from interfering in state proceedings where juveniles seek an injunction against the use of social histories in pre-adjudication instances, although they may hear an issue involving the constitutionality of post-adjudicatory dissemination of the social histories where state law is not clear and the proper factual issues were not decided; the dissemination of social histories compiled by probation officers during juvenile proceedings do not violate a constitutional right to privacy. J. P. v. DeSanti (C.A.6 (Ohio) 1981) 653 F.2d 1080.

In proceedings to terminate father's parental rights and grant permanent custody to county children services board, father was not entitled, as a matter of due process, to appointment of a child psychologist at state expense to rebut the psychological finding of unsuitability made by the State's expert who evaluated mother; father was not faced with an allegation of a mental illness which he needed to counter, father's mental condition was not at issue, and father was not ordered to undergo psychological or psychiatric treatment. In re Hess (Ohio App. 7 Dist., Jefferson, 03-21-2003) No. 02 JE 37, 2003-Ohio-1429, 2003 WL 1465190, Unreported. Constitutional Law ⊱ 274(5); Infants ⊱ 212

3. Mental evaluation

Trial court's failure to hold competency hearing in delinquency proceeding was not harmless error, even though examiner's written report had concluded that juvenile was competent to proceed, since juvenile's counsel would have had an opportunity at competency hearing to cross-examine that examiner. In re B.M.R. (Ohio App. 2 Dist., Miami, 11-04-2005) No. 2005 CA 1, No. 2005 CA 18, 2005-Ohio-5911, 2005 WL 2978951, Unreported. Infants ⊱ 253

Juvenile's subsequent admission to rape charge did not constitute a waiver of his right to a competency determination in delinquency proceeding. In re B.M.R. (Ohio App. 2 Dist., Miami, 11-04-2005) No. 2005 CA 1, No. 2005 CA 18, 2005-Ohio-5911, 2005 WL 2978951, Unreported. Infants ⊱ 203

Trial court's failure to hold competency hearing in delinquency proceeding after juvenile's counsel raised the issue in a timely fashion, and its reliance instead on examiner's written report, violated state statute governing competence to stand trial as well as juvenile's due process rights. In re B.M.R. (Ohio App. 2 Dist., Miami, 11-04-2005) No. 2005 CA 1, No. 2005 CA 18, 2005-Ohio-5911, 2005 WL 2978951, Unreported. Infants ⊱ 203

Evidence supported trial court's determination that juvenile was competent to stand trial; although physician's conclusions as to juvenile's competency were mixed, she testified juvenile was not mentally ill and that he understood charge against him, and trial court properly evaluated juvenile's competency by juvenile norms, finding that juvenile's deficiencies in understanding nature of proceedings against him could be compensated for by special measures allowed by juvenile court. In re Stone (Ohio App. 12 Dist., Clinton, 06-16-2003) No. CA2002-09-035, 2003-Ohio-3071, 2003 WL 21373156, Unreported, appeal not allowed 100 Ohio St.3d 1432, 797 N.E.2d 512, 2003-Ohio-5396. Infants ⊱ 208

Trial court did not abuse its discretion in denying mother's request for independent psychiatric evaluation in proceedings to determine if her child was dependent; trial court had wide latitude in determining the need for a psychiatric examination, and court had granted state's motion for psychological evaluation. In re Fazio (Ohio App. 5 Dist., Licking, 10-11-2002) No. 2002CA0057, 2002-Ohio-5554, 2002 WL 31312276, Unreported. Infants ⊱ 208

Trial court was required to appoint an expert to evaluate juvenile's competency to participate in delinquency hearing; counsel for juvenile, guardian ad litem, and juvenile's aunt all expressed serious concerns as to whether juvenile understood the proceedings, and juvenile was enrolled in special education programs at her school. In re H. (Ohio App. 5 Dist., 10-24-2006) 2006-Ohio-5534, 2006 WL 3020293. Infants ⊱ 208

In order to find an abuse of the trial court's discretion in determining whether to appoint an expert to evaluate the competency of a juvenile, the Court of Appeals must determine the trial court's decision was unreasonable, arbitrary, or unconscionable, and not merely an error of law or judgment. In re H. (Ohio App. 5 Dist., 10-24-2006) 2006-Ohio-5534, 2006 WL 3020293. Infants ⊱ 251

Juvenile should have been afforded a hearing to assess his competence to stand trial for gross sexual imposition, as competency evaluation raised sufficient indicia of incompetence; report noted that juvenile had limited communication abilities due to his deafness, and psychologist concluded that juvenile was incompetent to stand trial because he was not able to aid his defense. In re Grimes (Ohio App. 7 Dist., 03-20-2002) 147 Ohio App.3d 192, 769 N.E.2d 420, 2002-Ohio-1547. Infants ⊱ 203

Juvenile court committed plain error by not holding hearing to assess juvenile's competence to be tried for gross sexual imposition, where psychologist concluded in competency evaluation that juvenile was incompetent because his deafness rendered him incapable of aiding his defense. In re Grimes (Ohio App. 7 Dist., 03-20-2002) 147 Ohio App.3d 192, 769 N.E.2d 420, 2002-Ohio-1547. Infants ⊱ 248.1

Rule prohibiting state from using any incriminating evidence obtained during court-ordered mental examination of juvenile defendant in any proceeding other than juvenile amenability hearing does not apply to mental examinations by persons hired by juvenile defendant to bolster defendant's case. State v. Hopfer (Ohio App. 2 Dist., 07-12-1996) 112 Ohio App.3d 521, 679 N.E.2d 321, dismissed, appeal not allowed 77 Ohio St.3d 1488, 673 N.E.2d 146, reconsideration denied 77 Ohio St.3d 1550, 674 N.E.2d 1187. Criminal Law ⊱ 393(1)

Addendum to psychological report offered by probation officer was admissible at dispositional hearing, though county children's services board with temporary custody of minor was not given opportunity to respond to report, as court was permitted to have psychological report conducted after adjudication of minor as delinquent, and addendum did not change recommendation of psychologist. In re Lawson (Ohio App. 10 Dist., 11-08-1994) 98 Ohio App.3d 456, 648 N.E.2d 889. Infants ⊱ 208

A juvenile faced with a bind-over attempt in juvenile court is not entitled to the appointment of a private psychiatric examiner, at the state's expense, instead of a court psychologist for purposes of determining whether juvenile court jurisdiction should be waived. State ex rel. A Juvenile v. Hoose (Lake 1988) 43 Ohio App.3d 109, 539 N.E.2d 704, cause dismissed 39 Ohio St.3d 713, 534 N.E.2d 94.

Where a court orders a psychological evaluation on the request of an indigent party, pursuant to Juv R 32(A)(1), the court may admit the evaluation into evidence over the objection of the party. In re Green (Montgomery 1984) 18 Ohio App.3d 43, 480 N.E.2d 492, 18 O.B.R. 155.

4. Social history

Admission of testimony from psychologist, who testified about mother's prior social history, was not an abuse of discretion in child dependency proceeding; dependency complaint made allegations regarding mother's past difficulties with parenting and stable housing, expert's testimony clarified the past issues for the court, and psychologist was permitted to testify as to issues that mother deemed were "confidential" since psychologist performed a competency examination of mother pursuant to a referral from the court. In re Barker (Ohio App. 5 Dist., Stark, 11-24-2003) No. 03-CA-279, 2003-Ohio-6406, 2003 WL 22843907, Unreported. Infants ⊱ 173.1

In a hearing to determine whether a child is dependent, hearsay evidence contained in a social history report may not be used as evidence of the truth of the complaint, although, pursuant to Juv R 32(A)(3), the report may be used to clarify allegations of the complaint. In re Barzak (Trumbull 1985) 24 Ohio App.3d 180, 493 N.E.2d 1011, 24 O.B.R. 270.

Juv R 33   [Reserved]

Juv R 34   Dispositional hearing

(A) Scheduling the hearing

Where a child has been adjudicated as an abused, neglected, or dependent child, the court shall not issue a dispositional order until after it holds a separate dispositional hearing. The dispositional hearing for an adjudicated abused, neglected, or dependent child shall be held at least one day but not more than thirty days after the adjudicatory hearing is held. The dispositional hearing may be held immediately after the adjudicatory hearing if all parties were served prior to the adjudicatory hearing with all documents required for the dispositional hearing and all parties consent to the dispositional hearing being held immediately after the adjudicatory hearing. Upon the request of any party or the guardian ad litem of the child, the court may continue a dispositional hearing for a reasonable time not to exceed the time limit set forth in this division to enable a party to obtain or consult counsel. The dispositional hearing shall not be held more than ninety days after the date on which the complaint in the case was filed. If the dispositional hearing is not held within this ninety day period of time, the court, on its own motion or the motion of any party or the guardian ad litem of the child, shall dismiss the complaint without prejudice.

In all other juvenile proceedings, the dispositional hearing shall be held pursuant to Juv. R. 29(F)(2)(a) through (d) and the ninety day requirement shall not apply. Where the dispositional hearing is to be held immediately following the adjudicatory hearing, the court, upon the request of any party, shall continue the hearing for a reasonable time to enable the party to obtain or consult counsel.

(B) Hearing procedure

The hearing shall be conducted in the following manner:

(1) The judge or magistrate who presided at the adjudicatory hearing shall, if possible, preside;

(2) Except as provided in division (I) of this rule, the court may admit evidence that is material and relevant, including, but not limited to, hearsay, opinion, and documentary evidence;

(3) Medical examiners and each investigator who prepared a social history shall not be cross-examined, except upon consent of all parties, for good cause shown, or as the court in its discretion may direct. Any party may offer evidence supplementing, explaining, or disputing any information contained in the social history or other reports that may be used by the court in determining disposition.

(C) Judgment

After the conclusion of the hearing, the court shall enter an appropriate judgment within seven days. A copy of the judgment shall be given to any party requesting a copy. In all cases where a child is placed on probation, the child shall receive a written statement of the conditions of probation. If the judgment is conditional, the order shall state the conditions. If the child is not returned to the child's home, the court shall determine the school district that shall bear the cost of the child's education and may fix an amount of support to be paid by the responsible parent or from public funds.

(D) Dispositional Orders

Where a child is adjudicated an abused, neglected, or dependent child, the court may make any of the following orders of disposition:

(1) Place the child in protective supervision;

(2) Commit the child to the temporary custody of a public or private agency, either parent, a relative residing within or outside the state, or a probation officer for placement in a certified foster home or approved foster care;

(3) Award legal custody of the child to either parent or to any other person who, prior to the dispositional hearing, files a motion requesting legal custody;

(4) Commit the child to the permanent custody of a public or private agency, if the court determines that the child cannot be placed with one of the child's parents within a reasonable time or should not be placed with either parent and determines that the permanent commitment is in the best interest of the child;

(5) Place the child in a planned permanent living arrangement with a public or private agency if the agency requests the court for placement, if the court finds that a planned permanent living arrangement is in the best interest of the child, and if the court finds that one of the following exists:

(a) The child because of physical, mental, or psychological problems or needs is unable to function in a family-like setting;

(b) The parents of the child have significant physical, mental or psychological problems and are unable to care for the child, adoption is not in the best interest of the child and the child retains a significant and positive relationship with a parent or relative;

(c) The child is sixteen years of age or older, has been counseled, is unwilling to accept or unable to adapt to a permanent placement and is in an agency program preparing the child for independent living.

(E) Protective supervision

If the court issues an order for protective supervision, the court may place any reasonable restrictions upon the child, the child's parents, guardian, or any other person including, but not limited to, any of the following:

(1) Ordering a party within forty-eight hours to vacate the child's home indefinitely or for a fixed period of time;

(2) Ordering a party, parent, or custodian to prevent any particular person from having contact with the child;

(3) Issuing a restraining order to control the conduct of any party.

(F) Case plan

As part of its dispositional order, the court shall journalize a case plan for the child. The agency required to maintain a case plan shall file the case plan with the court prior to the child's adjudicatory hearing but not later than thirty days after the earlier of the date on which the complaint in the case was filed or the child was first placed in shelter care. The plan shall specify what additional information, if any, is necessary to complete the plan and how the information will be obtained. All parts of the case plan shall be completed by the earlier of thirty days after the adjudicatory hearing or the date of the dispositional hearing for the child. If all parties agree to the content of the case plan and the court approves it, the court shall journalize the plan as part of its dispositional order. If no agreement is reached, the court, based upon the evidence presented at the dispositional hearing and the best interest of the child, shall determine the contents of the case plan and journalize it as part of the dispositional order for the child.

(G) Modification of temporary order

The department of human services or any other public or private agency or any party, other than a parent whose parental rights have been terminated, may at any time file a motion requesting that the court modify or terminate any order of disposition. The court shall hold a hearing upon the motion as if the hearing were the original dispositional hearing and shall give all parties and the guardian ad litem notice of the hearing pursuant to these rules. The court, on its own motion and upon proper notice to all parties and any interested agency, may modify or terminate any order of disposition.

(H) Restraining orders

In any proceeding where a child is made a ward of the court, the court may grant a restraining order controlling the conduct of any party if the court finds that the order is necessary to control any conduct or relationship that may be detrimental or harmful to the child and tend to defeat the execution of a dispositional order.

(I) Bifurcation; Rules of Evidence

Hearings to determine whether temporary orders regarding custody should be modified to orders for permanent custody shall be considered dispositional hearings and need not be bifurcated.

The Rules of Evidence shall apply in hearings on motions for permanent custody.

(J) Advisement of rights after hearing

At the conclusion of the hearing, the court shall advise the child of the child's right to record expungement and, where any part of the proceeding was contested, advise the parties of their right to appeal.

(Adopted eff. 7–1–72; amended eff. 7–1–94, 7–1–96, 7–1–02)

Historical and Statutory Notes

Amendment Note: The 7–1–02 amendment substituted "a planned permanent living arrangement" for "long term foster care" throughout division (D)(5).

Amendment Note: The 7–1–96 amendment substituted "magistrate" for "referee" in division (B)(1).

Amendment Note: The 7–1–94 amendment rewrote division (A); inserted "or referee" in division (B)(1); inserted "Except as provided in division (I) of this rule," and ", but not limited to," in division (B)(2); added divisions (D) through (G); redesignated former division (D) as division (H); added division (I); redesignated former division (E) as division (J); and made changed to reflect gender-neutral language. Prior to amendment, division (A) read:

"(A) Scheduling the hearing. The dispositional hearing may be held immediately following the adjudicatory hearing or at a later time fixed by the court. Where the dispositional hearing is to be held immediately following the adjudicatory hearing, the court, upon the request of a party shall continue the hearing for a reasonable time to enable the party to obtain or consult counsel."

Staff Notes

2002:

Juvenile Rule 34(D) Dispositional orders

The July 1, 2002, amendment to Juv. R. 34(D)(5) substituted the language of "planned permanent living arrangement" for the former language of "long term foster care," to conform to the new legislative designation for these child-placing arrangements.

The amendment to Juv. R. 34(D)(5) conforms to section 2151.353(A)(5) of the Revised Code. Juvenile Rules 2, 10, and 15 also were amended effective July 1, 2002 to reflect this change in terminology.

1996:

The amendment changed the rule's reference from "referee" to "magistrate" in division (B)(1) in order to harmonize the rule with the language adopted in the 1995 amendments to Juv. R. 40. The amendment is technical only and no substantive change is intended.

1994:

Rule 34 Dispositional Hearing

Changes in Juv. R. 34 now bring the rule into conformity with Revised Code 2151.35 as amended by S.B. 89.

Juv. R. 34(A) delineates the ninety day deadline for dispositional hearings in abuse, neglect, and dependency cases and clarifies that the ninety day rule does not apply in unruly and delinquency cases. Revised Code 2151.35(B)(1)

Juv. R. 34(B)(1) specifies that the judge or referee who presided at the adjudicatory hearing shall, if possible, preside at the dispositional hearing. Revised Code 2151.35(B)(2)(a).

Juv. R. 34(D) restates the dispositional alternatives for an adjudicated abused, neglected, or dependent child as set forth in Revised Code 2151.353(A)(1), (2), (3), (4), and (5).

Juv. R. 34(F) sets forth the utilization of the case plan as part of the dispositional order and restates the provisions of Revised Code 2151.353(D) and 2151.412.

Juv. R. 34(G) restates Revised Code 2151.353(E) regarding the procedure for modifying a temporary order.

Juv. R. 34(I) is new and attempts to eliminate the need to bifurcate a motion for permanent custody into adjudicatory and dispositional hearings. A good explanation of the state of current case law in appellate courts in

[1] Footnote 1: A motion to certify the record in *Lucas, supra*, to the

Ohio on the subject of bifurcation is found in *In the Matter of Amy Lyons, Alleged Dependent Child*, No. 1411 (4th District Court of Appeals of Ohio, Ross County, decided August 11, 1987). A concurring opinion states:

"There is a conflict in Ohio law as to whether hearings for permanent custody under Revised Code 2151.414 must be bifurcated into separate adjudicatory and dispositional stages. Kurtz and Giannelli, Ohio Juvenile Law (1985), T 13.04(D)(5). The Third and Twelfth District Courts of Appeals have held that Juv. R. 29 and Juv. R. 34 control over R.C. 2151.414 to require a bifurcated hearing. *In re Vickers Children* (1983), 14 Ohio App. 3d 210; *In re Lucas* (1985), 29 Ohio App. 3d 165.[1] However, the Eighth District Court of Appeals has held that only one hearing which is purely adjudicatory is required and that, contrary to *Vickers, supra*, there is no conflict between R.C. 2151.414 and the applicable Juvenile Rules.

"By contrast, however, in the case at bar, there is no dispositional option. Either the motion is granted, in which case the mother's parental rights are terminated, or else the motion is denied. The single hearing prescribed by R.C. 2151.414 is purely adjudicatory. The foregoing analysis is consistent with Juv. R. 2(1), which states:

"'Adjudicatory hearing' means a hearing to determine whether a child is a juvenile traffic offender, delinquent, unruly, neglected, or dependent or otherwise within the jurisdiction of the court or whether temporary legal custody should be converted to permanent custody.

"Consequently, this court holds that the juvenile court did not err in failing to bifurcate the permanent custody hearing into separate adjudicatory and dispositional stages." *In re Jones* (1985), 29 Ohio App. 3d 176, 179.

"Although permanent custody is clearly a dispositional order, Juv. R. 2(1)'s definition of "adjudicatory hearing" appears sufficiently broad to require only one hearing or one "stage". See Kurtz and Giannelli, Ohio Juvenile Law (1985), T 13.04, p. 164 at fn. 155. When a permanent custody motion is filed pursuant to R.C. 2151.414, unlike an original disposition pursuant to R.C. 2151.353(A), there is no dispositional option in that the trial court, as the majority opinion notes, can only either terminate parental rights by granting the permanent custody motion or not terminate parental rights by overruling the permanent custody motion. *Jones, supra*; Juv. R. 2(1).

"Assuming, arguendo, that pursuant to *Vickers* and *Lucas, supra*, a bifurcated hearing was required herein, any error was waived by the failure of appellate to object to the lack of such bifurcation below. *Jones, supra* at p. 179; *Vickers, supra*. Accordingly, I concur in the judgment."

Because the cases cited seemed to interpret the need for bifurcation based upon the current Juvenile Rules, Juv. R. 34(I) now seeks to clarify that the need to bifurcate a permanent custody hearing is unnecessary.

Editor's Comment

Dispositional hearing   1
Judgment   2
Dispositional orders   3
Restraining orders   4
Bifurcation; rules of evidence   5
Advisement of rights after hearing   6

1. Dispositional hearing

This rule follows the same structure as the rules regulating the detention and adjudicatory hearing. Until the adoption of this rule there was no uniform procedure to be followed by all courts. The rule is in conformity with Juv R 1(B)(2) to secure uniformity in procedure.

Division (A), which was amended in 1994 to conform with 2151.35 as amended by S.B. 89, is no longer in conformity with the statute due to 1996 amendments to the statute resulting from H.B. 274. RC 2151.35(B)(1) now permits the dispositional hearing in abuse, neglect, and dependency cases immediately after the adjudicatory if all parties have been served with requisite documents. The one-day delay, and the required consent of the parties, have been eliminated from the statute.

2. Judgment

Juv R 34(C) as to the requirement that a child placed on probation receive a written statement of the conditions of probation complements 2151.14 and 2151.355(A)(2).

Supreme Court of Ohio was overruled on May 21, 1986.

RC 2151.35(B)(3) and 2151.36 *require* the court to make an order of parental support if the child is not returned home, whereas Juv R 34(C) simply *permits* the court to make such an order.

3. Dispositional orders

Division (D) repeats the dispositional options provided for abused, neglected, and dependent children, as contained in 2151.353. Because the dispositional alternatives which a juvenile court may select constitute a legislative, not judicial, prerogative (see *State v Grady*, 3 App(3d) 174, 3 OBR 199, 444 NE(2d) 51 (Cuyahoga 1981)), it is not clear why the 1994 amendment to Juv R 34(D) added these alternatives.

4. Restraining orders

Division (E), which is taken from 2151.353(A)(6) and 2151.353(C), permits the court to enter restraining orders and other similar orders in cases where protective supervision has been granted. Division (H), taken from 2151.359, describes the more general authority of the court to issue restraining orders.

5. Bifurcation; rules of evidence

Juv R 34(I), which provides that hearings on motions for permanent custody shall be considered dispositional hearings, appears to conflict with the definition of adjudicatory hearing contained in Juv R 2(B). (See Editor's Comment to Juv R 2(B).)

6. Advisement of rights after hearing

Juv R 34(J) requires that a child adjudged delinquent, unruly, or a juvenile traffic offender shall be advised of the right to have his record expunged in accordance with 2151.358. Application to expunge a record shall not be made any sooner than two years after the termination of any order made by the court, or two years after his unconditional discharge from the Ohio Department of Youth Services or other institution or facility to which he may have been committed. (*See* 2151.358.)

Library References

Infants ⚖203, 204, 221, 223.1 to 225.
Westlaw Topic No. 211.
C.J.S. Infants §§ 51 to 85.

Research References

Encyclopedias

OH Jur. 3d Constitutional Law § 519, Evidence, Argument, and Witnesses.
OH Jur. 3d Evidence & Witnesses § 240, Generally; Purpose of Exclusion of Hearsay.
OH Jur. 3d Family Law § 1627, Procedure to Obtain Counsel.
OH Jur. 3d Family Law § 1668, Initial Procedure—on Admission.
OH Jur. 3d Family Law § 1681, Conduct of Hearing; Advisement of Rights.
OH Jur. 3d Family Law § 1690, Restraining Conduct of Party.
OH Jur. 3d Family Law § 1703, Generally; Continuing Jurisdiction.
OH Jur. 3d Family Law § 1718, Cost of Education.
OH Jur. 3d Family Law § 1730, What is an Appealable Order.

Treatises and Practice Aids

Giannelli and Snyder, Baldwin's Ohio Practice, Evidence, R 101, Scope of Rules: Applicability; Privileges; Exceptions.
Giannelli and Snyder, Baldwin's Ohio Practice, Evidence, R 802, Hearsay Rule.
Giannelli and Snyder, Baldwin's Ohio Practice, Evidence, § 802.7, Other Procedural Court Rules.
Giannelli and Snyder, Baldwin's Ohio Practice, Evidence, § 101.16, Other Procedural Rules.
Carlin, Baldwin's Ohio Practice, Merrick-Rippner Probate Law § 107:43, Scheduling Juvenile Court Hearing.
Carlin, Baldwin's Ohio Practice, Merrick-Rippner Probate Law § 107:50, Adjudicatory Hearings—Applicability of Rules of Court.
Carlin, Baldwin's Ohio Practice, Merrick-Rippner Probate Law § 107:51, Adjudicatory Hearings—Applicability of Rules of Evidence.
Carlin, Baldwin's Ohio Practice, Merrick-Rippner Probate Law § 107:72, Dispositional Hearings—Procedure.
Carlin, Baldwin's Ohio Practice, Merrick-Rippner Probate Law § 107:73, Alternatives for Disposition of Juvenile Cases.
Carlin, Baldwin's Ohio Practice, Merrick-Rippner Probate Law § 107:75, Case Plans.
Carlin, Baldwin's Ohio Practice, Merrick-Rippner Probate Law § 107:80, Disposition of Abused, Neglected, or Dependent Child—Permanent Custody.
Carlin, Baldwin's Ohio Practice, Merrick-Rippner Probate Law § 107:81, Disposition of Abused, Neglected, or Dependent Child—Permanent Custody—Best Interest Determination Factors.
Carlin, Baldwin's Ohio Practice, Merrick-Rippner Probate Law § 107:84, Disposition of Delinquent Children—Prior to January 1, 2002.
Carlin, Baldwin's Ohio Practice, Merrick-Rippner Probate Law § 107:85, Disposition of Delinquent Children—Mandatory Dispositions—Prior to January 1, 2002.
Carlin, Baldwin's Ohio Practice, Merrick-Rippner Probate Law § 107:106, Disposition of Juvenile Traffic Offender—Mandatory.
Carlin, Baldwin's Ohio Practice, Merrick-Rippner Probate Law § 107:111, Disposition of Unruly Children—Mandatory.
Carlin, Baldwin's Ohio Practice, Merrick-Rippner Probate Law § 107:113, Juvenile Court's Authority Over Parents.
Carlin, Baldwin's Ohio Practice, Merrick-Rippner Probate Law § 107:121, Custody Review Hearing—Revocation of Probation or Parole.
Carlin, Baldwin's Ohio Practice, Merrick-Rippner Probate Law § 107:122, Appeals—Juvenile Court Judgments—Determination of Neglect, Dependency, Unruliness, Abuse, or Delinquency.
Carlin, Baldwin's Ohio Practice, Merrick-Rippner Probate Law § 107:158, Motion for Expungement of Record—Form.
Carlin, Baldwin's Ohio Practice, Merrick-Rippner Probate Law § 107:159, Order Expunging Record—Form.
Carlin, Baldwin's Ohio Practice, Merrick-Rippner Probate Law § 107:180, Rules of Probation—Form.
Painter & Dennis, Ohio Appellate Practice § 2:5, Appealable Orders-Judgments-Juvenile Cases.
Giannelli & Yeomans, Ohio Juvenile Law § 1:8, Rules of Juvenile Procedure.
Giannelli & Yeomans, Ohio Juvenile Law § 20:2, Temporary Care Orders.
Giannelli & Yeomans, Ohio Juvenile Law § 23:1, Introduction.
Giannelli & Yeomans, Ohio Juvenile Law § 25:2, Bifurcated Hearings.
Giannelli & Yeomans, Ohio Juvenile Law § 25:3, Judge or Magistrate.
Giannelli & Yeomans, Ohio Juvenile Law § 25:4, Time Requirements.
Giannelli & Yeomans, Ohio Juvenile Law § 25:7, Advisement of Rights.
Giannelli & Yeomans, Ohio Juvenile Law § 25:9, Evidence.
Giannelli & Yeomans, Ohio Juvenile Law § 26:3, Time Requirements for Case Plans.
Giannelli & Yeomans, Ohio Juvenile Law § 26:4, Court Approval; Journalization.
Giannelli & Yeomans, Ohio Juvenile Law § 27:8, Probation.
Giannelli & Yeomans, Ohio Juvenile Law § 27:9, Drug & Alcohol Dispositions.
Giannelli & Yeomans, Ohio Juvenile Law § 28:2, Suspension or Revocation.
Giannelli & Yeomans, Ohio Juvenile Law § 29:4, Unruly—Drug & Alcohol Cases.
Giannelli & Yeomans, Ohio Juvenile Law § 30:3, Costs of Dispositions.
Giannelli & Yeomans, Ohio Juvenile Law § 30:4, Dispositional Alternatives for Abuse, Neglect or Dependency.
Giannelli & Yeomans, Ohio Juvenile Law § 30:5, Protective Supervision.
Giannelli & Yeomans, Ohio Juvenile Law § 30:6, Temporary Custody.
Giannelli & Yeomans, Ohio Juvenile Law § 31:4, Hearings on Permanent Custody Motions.
Giannelli & Yeomans, Ohio Juvenile Law § 31:5, Evidence.
Giannelli & Yeomans, Ohio Juvenile Law § 32:2, Jurisdiction Over Parents and Others.
Giannelli & Yeomans, Ohio Juvenile Law § 33:4, Abuse, Neglect, and Dependency Proceedings.
Giannelli & Yeomans, Ohio Juvenile Law § 33:6, Revocation of Probation.
Giannelli & Yeomans, Ohio Juvenile Law § 34:4, Final Order Requirement.
Giannelli & Yeomans, Ohio Juvenile Law App. D, Appendix D. Glossary.
Giannelli & Yeomans, Ohio Juvenile Law § 25:10, Social History & Medical Examinations.
Giannelli & Yeomans, Ohio Juvenile Law § 25:13, Judgment & Records.

Giannelli & Yeomans, Ohio Juvenile Law § 30:13, Planned Permanent Living Arrangement.

Law Review and Journal Commentaries

Access to "Confidential" Welfare Records in the Course of Child Protection Proceedings, Richard Steven Levine. 14 J Fam L 535 (1975–76).

Juvenile Delinquency Proceedings in Ohio: Due Process and the Hearsay Dilemma, Comment. 24 Clev St L Rev 356 (Spring 1975).

Navigating Between Scylla and Charybdis: Ohio's Efforts to Protect Children Without Eviscerating the Rights of Criminal Defendants–Evidentiary Considerations and the Rebirth of Confrontation Clause Analysis in Child Abuse Cases, Myrna S. Raeder. 25 U Tol L Rev 43 (1994).

Rethinking The Relationship Between Juvenile Courts And Treatment Agencies—An Administrative Law Approach, Leslie J. Harris. 28 J Fam L 217 (1990).

Notes of Decisions

Bifurcated hearings 1
Case plan 12
Dispositional hearing
 Timing 11
Dispositional orders 6
Evidence 9
Fees and costs 5
Final orders 4
Judgment 3
Jurisdiction 2
Probation 7
Right to counsel 8
Rights of juvenile 10

1. Bifurcated hearings

Trial court's failure to bifurcate permanent custody hearing into two separate adjudicatory and dispositional hearings, on county agency's original complaint for custody of child, as required by juvenile rules, was reversible error, in termination of parental rights proceeding; trial court made both an adjudicative finding, i.e., that child was dependent, and a dispositional finding, i.e., that it was in child's best interests to be placed in permanent custody of agency, following a single hearing. In re J.H. (Ohio App. 12 Dist., Preble, 06-26-2006) No. CA2005-11-019, No. CA2005-11-020, 2006-Ohio-3237, 2006 WL 1726669, Unreported. Infants ⇐ 253

Fact that parents might have been served prior to permanent custody hearing with all documents required for hearing did not relieve trial court of requirement that it bifurcate hearing into two separate adjudicatory and dispositional hearings, in termination of parental rights proceeding, as juvenile rule required all parties to consent to dispositional hearing being held immediately after adjudicatory hearing, and there was no evidence that parents consented to a dispositional hearing being held immediately after adjudicatory hearing. In re J.H. (Ohio App. 12 Dist., Preble, 06-26-2006) No. CA2005-11-019, No. CA2005-11-020, 2006-Ohio-3237, 2006 WL 1726669, Unreported. Infants ⇐ 203

Mother did not waive on appeal issue of whether trial court erred in failing to bifurcate permanent custody hearing into two separate adjudicatory and dispositional hearings, on basis that she failed to object to procedure during course of hearing and failed to request bifurcation of proceedings, as parties were not clearly put on notice that trial court intended to hold only a single evidentiary hearing simultaneously covering adjudication and disposition, and, as such, mother was not required to bring issue to attention of trial court or request bifurcation. In re J.H. (Ohio App. 12 Dist., Preble, 06-26-2006) No. CA2005-11-019, No. CA2005-11-020, 2006-Ohio-3237, 2006 WL 1726669, Unreported. Infants ⇐ 243

Dismissal of dependency complaint was warranted, where the Court of Appeals reversed the dependency finding based on the trial court's failure to conduct separate adjudicatory and dispositional hearings, a statute required that a dispositional order be entered within 90 days after the complaint was filed, and father filed a motion to dismiss the complaint on the 91st day due to the court's failure to conduct separate adjudicatory and dispositional hearings. In re Monroe (Ohio App. 7 Dist., Belmont, 09-17-2004) No. 03 BE 50, 2004-Ohio-4988, 2004 WL 2334358, Unreported. Infants ⇐ 202

The trial court committed reversible error when it failed to conduct separate adjudicatory and dispositional hearings, during child dependency proceedings; the parties were not served with all documents required for the dispositional hearing before the adjudicatory hearing, as required to conduct a dispositional hearing immediately after an adjudicatory hearing, and counsel for father twice objected to the court's failure to hold separate hearings. In re Monroe (Ohio App. 7 Dist., Belmont, 09-17-2004) No. 03 BE 50, 2004-Ohio-4988, 2004 WL 2334358, Unreported. Infants ⇐ 253

Mother in dependency proceedings was not prejudiced by juvenile court's alleged failure to inform parties of the substance of complaint, the purpose of hearing, the possible consequences of hearing prior to adjudicatory hearing, and the right to appeal after the dispositional hearing; mother contested the matter, was represented by counsel at trial, a full hearing was held on the merits, and mother appealed the juvenile court's judgment. In re Malone (Ohio App. 10 Dist., Franklin, 12-30-2003) No. 03AP-489, 2003-Ohio-7156, 2003 WL 23024377, Unreported, appeal not allowed 102 Ohio St.3d 1423, 807 N.E.2d 367, 2004-Ohio-2003. Infants ⇐ 198; Infants ⇐ 203

In proceedings where parental rights are subject to termination, it is reversible error not to provide separate adjudicatory and dispositional hearings as required by RC 2151.35, Juv R 29(F)(2)(a), and 34. In re Baby Girl Baxter (Ohio 1985) 17 Ohio St.3d 229, 479 N.E.2d 257, 17 O.B.R. 469.

In an action where the county files a motion for permanent custody of a child, the child's mother files a motion for permanent custody, and the court grants the county's motion at the close of the evidence, there is no requirement to bifurcate the permanent custody hearing into separate adjudicatory and dispositional stages since there is no dispositional option as either the mother's rights are terminated, or the motion is denied. In re Jones (Cuyahoga 1985) 29 Ohio App.3d 176, 504 N.E.2d 719, 29 O.B.R. 206.

A hearing on a complaint for permanent custody must be bifurcated according to Juv R 29 and 34 into separate adjudicatory and dispositional hearings, notwithstanding the contrary provisions of RC 2151.414, since Juv R 1(A) provides that all proceedings in a juvenile court are governed by the Rules of Juvenile Procedure. In re Vickers Children (Butler 1983) 14 Ohio App.3d 201, 470 N.E.2d 438, 14 O.B.R. 228.

2. Jurisdiction

The juvenile court has exclusive original jurisdiction, pursuant to RC 2151.23(A), concerning any child who is alleged in a proper complaint to be neglected, and the court does not lose jurisdiction by failing to adhere to the time limits set forth in Juv R 29(A) and 34(A). Linger v. Weiss (Ohio 1979) 57 Ohio St.2d 97, 386 N.E.2d 1354, 11 O.O.3d 281, certiorari denied 100 S.Ct. 128, 444 U.S. 862, 62 L.Ed.2d 83.

An Ohio juvenile court, in a dependency proceeding pursuant to RC 2151.27 et seq., has no jurisdiction to interfere with a mother's legal custody of her children, in the absence of proof and a finding of unfitness of such parent, merely for the purpose of releasing such children to the officers of the court of a foreign state, and the court need not give full faith and credit to a Michigan decree where that decree was obtained by the husband in an ex parte custody determination, subsequent to a divorce decree, in which the Michigan court had no personal jurisdiction over the nonresident wife. (Annotation from former RC 2151.35.) In re Messner (Huron 1969) 19 Ohio App.2d 33, 249 N.E.2d 532, 48 O.O.2d 31.

Where a defendant is a juvenile at the time he commits theft but is an adult at the time he receives the stolen property, the judgment of conviction for theft is vacated where no complaint for delinquency was ever brought against the defendant in juvenile court, there was no bindover from juvenile court to common pleas court, and the defendant was indicted, charged, and tried as an adult in common pleas court without subject matter jurisdiction for an offense committed while a juvenile. State v. Wilson (Ohio App. 1 Dist., Hamilton, 05-11-1994) No. C-930429, 1994 WL 176901, Unreported, motion to certify allowed 70 Ohio St.3d 1410, 637 N.E.2d 8, affirmed 73 Ohio St.3d 40, 652 N.E.2d 196, 1995-Ohio-217.

3. Judgment

Trial court's grant of permanent custody of child to county without first properly adjudicating child as a dependent child violated mother's right to due process, and required reversal of judgment entry granting permanent custody to county. In re Nibert (Ohio App. 4 Dist., Gallia, 05-24-2005) No. 04CA15, 2005-Ohio-2797, 2005 WL 1332019, Unreported. Infants ⇐ 253

During dispositional phase of dependency proceeding, lower court properly considered matters other than original violence allegations in the complaint. In re Pryor (Athens 1993) 86 Ohio App.3d 327, 620 N.E.2d 973. Infants ⇐ 197

While the seven-day requirement for filing a report is mandatory in a custody action, a trial court's failure to comply with the rule is not ground for reversal of its decision to terminate parental custody since the proper remedy would be for the complaining party to file a writ of procedendo compelling the court to finalize the decision. In re Galloway (Lucas 1991) 77 Ohio App.3d 61, 601 N.E.2d 83, motion overruled 62 Ohio St.3d 1503, 583 N.E.2d 974, denial of post-conviction relief affirmed.

The seven day time requirement of RC 2151.35(B)(3) and Juv R 34(C) is mandatory and must be applied as such and it may not be relaxed or eliminated. In re Fleming (Lucas 1991) 76 Ohio App.3d 30, 600 N.E.2d 1112.

The seven day rule of RC 2151.35(B)(3) and Juv R 34(C) can be applied consistently with Juv R 40(D), which (1) mandates the preparation and filing of findings of fact and recommendations by the referee; (2) provides an allowance of fourteen days from the filing of the referee's report for the filing of objections by the parties; and (3) provides for a hearing on the objections; when the dispositional hearing is conducted before a referee, the referee has seven days from the time the case becomes decisional in which to issue his findings of fact and recommendations and at the expiration of the fourteen day period for filing objections, if no objections are filed, the case is decisional and the trial court has seven days to issue its final judgment; however, if objections are filed pursuant to Juv R 40 and a hearing is held, the judge has seven days from the conclusion of the hearing to enter his final judgment. In re Fleming (Lucas 1991) 76 Ohio App.3d 30, 600 N.E.2d 1112.

In a proceeding to terminate a father's parental rights, a trial court's failure to comply with RC 2151.35(B)(3) and Juv R 34(C), which requires judgment to be entered within seven days of dispositional hearings, does not (1) result in a denial of the father's due process rights; (2) deprive the court of jurisdiction to enter a final determination; or (3) require reversal of the court's final judgment. In re Fleming (Lucas 1991) 76 Ohio App.3d 30, 600 N.E.2d 1112. Constitutional Law ⇨ 274(5); Infants ⇨ 221; Infants ⇨ 254

The proper remedy in cases where a trial court fails to meet the seven day requirement imposed by RC 2151.35(B)(3) and/or Juv R 34(C) is for counsel for the parents or county children services board to file, on expiration of the seven day time period, a petition for a writ of procedendo with the court of appeals requesting the court to direct the trial court to comply immediately with those requirements and proceed to final judgment. In re Fleming (Lucas 1991) 76 Ohio App.3d 30, 600 N.E.2d 1112. Courts ⇨ 207.1

When a child is placed in the permanent custody of the youth services department, the court shall determine the school district responsible for the costs of educating the child as provided by RC 2151.357; Juv R 34(C) is not inconsistent with RC 2151.357, and gives the court no discretion to determine such school district in any other manner. Christman v. Washington Court House (Fayette 1986) 30 Ohio App.3d 228, 507 N.E.2d 384, 30 O.B.R. 386.

Although RC 2151.35(B)(3) and Juv R 34(C) require that final judgment in the dispositional phase of an institutional child custody action be rendered within seven days of the dispositional hearing, failure to render judgment within seven days does not require reversal of the judgment ultimately rendered; procedendo is the proper remedy to compel a court to comply with the time limits. Galloway v Lucas County Children Services Bd, No. L–90–197 (6th Dist Ct App, Lucas, 9–6–91).

4. Final orders

Temporary custody orders entered pursuant to Juv R 34 are final, appealable orders when entered. Ackerman v. Lucas County Children Services Bd. (Lucas 1989) 49 Ohio App.3d 14, 550 N.E.2d 549.

A further dispositional order which continues an original order of temporary custody constitutes a final appealable order within the meaning of RC 2505.02. In re Patterson (Madison 1984) 16 Ohio App.3d 214, 475 N.E.2d 160, 16 O.B.R. 229. Infants ⇨ 242

A temporary order of a juvenile court changing custody under Juv R 13 or 29 is not a dispositional order under Juv R 34, and hence is not a final appealable order. Morrison v. Morrison (Summit 1973) 45 Ohio App.2d 299, 344 N.E.2d 144, 74 O.O.2d 441.

5. Fees and costs

Juvenile court was required to ascertain juvenile's ability to pay fine imposed following his adjudication as delinquent prior to imposing such fine. In re B.M.S. (Ohio App. 2 Dist., 03-03-2006) 165 Ohio App.3d 609, 847 N.E.2d 506, 2006-Ohio-981. Infants ⇨ 224

A court that commits a child to the custody of the youth services department is required to determine which school district shall bear the cost of educating the child. OAG 88–023.

Where a juvenile court commits a child to a specialized school in another state, the court must itself pay expenses occasioned by the commitment and authorized by the court at the time of commitment, which expenses are paid out of funds appropriated to the court by the board of county commissioners under RC 2151.10; and the court may order the parents, guardian, or person charged with the child's support to reimburse the court for such payments. (Annotation from former RC 2151.35.) 1962 OAG 2938.

6. Dispositional orders

Juvenile court's failure in dependency proceedings to wait at least one day between the adjudicatory and dispositional hearings was not improper, where parties consented to hold dispositional hearing immediately after adjudicatory hearing. In re Malone (Ohio App. 10 Dist., Franklin, 12-30-2003) No. 03AP-489, 2003-Ohio-7156, 2003 WL 23024377, Unreported, appeal not allowed 102 Ohio St.3d 1423, 807 N.E.2d 367, 2004-Ohio-2003. Infants ⇨ 210

Trial court lacked authority to place children in a Planned Permanent Living Arrangement (PPLA) as an alternative to terminating father's parental rights; there was no evidence to suggest that father or county department of children and family services sought a PPLA, and there was no evidence presented to establish any of the other statutory requirements necessary for court to place children in a PPLA. (Per O'Donnell, J., with two judges concurring in judgment only). In re Harlston (Ohio App. 8 Dist., Cuyahoga, 01-23-2003) No. 80672, 2003-Ohio-282, 2003 WL 152939, Unreported, appeal not allowed 98 Ohio St.3d 1492, 785 N.E.2d 474, 2003-Ohio-1189. Infants ⇨ 226

Compliance with procedural requirements set forth in statute and rule providing that, if a child is adjudicated an abused, neglected, or dependent child, the court may award legal custody of the child to either parent or to any person who, prior to the dispositional hearing, files a motion requesting legal custody of the child is mandatory. In re L.R.T. (Ohio App. 12 Dist., 01-23-2006) 165 Ohio App.3d 77, 844 N.E.2d 914, 2006-Ohio-207. Infants ⇨ 222

Trial court erred as a matter of law in awarding custody of dependent and neglected child to child's great-aunt when child's great-aunt had failed to file a motion for legal custody before the dispositional hearing; any person who sought an award of legal custody of a child had to file a motion, prior to the dispositional hearing, requesting such custody; abrogating In re Callier, 2002 WL 1010081 (Ohio App. 12 Dist.) In re L.R.T. (Ohio App. 12 Dist., 01-23-2006) 165 Ohio App.3d 77, 844 N.E.2d 914, 2006-Ohio-207. Infants ⇨ 222

A juvenile court may, upon finding that a child is neglected, dependent, or delinquent, commit the child to any person or institution meeting the requirements of RC 5103.02 and 5103.03, even though a county child welfare board exists and could provide care and support for the child; and the board of county commissioners has a duty to appropriate each year such sum as will provide the court with necessary funds for the care, maintenance, education, and support of neglected, dependent, and delinquent children. (Annotation from former RC 2151.10.) 1962 OAG 3489.

Juvenile court is empowered to commit a child to a foster home and to make such terms respecting such commitment as may be proper and suitable under the circumstances. (Annotation from former RC 2151.35.) 1941 OAG 3353.

7. Probation

The length of time for which a child is to remain on probation may be fixed at the dispositional hearing or at a later date and may extend until the time the child reaches age twenty-one. In re De Geronimo, No. 40089 (8th Dist Ct App, Cuyahoga, 6–28–79).

8. Right to counsel

The trial court was not required to inform mother of her right to counsel at hearing to modify custody of child, in child dependency proceeding; Juvenile Rules required the trial court to inform parents of their right to counsel at the adjudicatory hearing, trial court informed mother of her right to counsel at the adjudicatory hearing, and there was no Juvenile Rule regarding counsel for modification of custody hearings. In re Williams (Ohio App. 10 Dist., Franklin, 02-12-2004) No. 03AP-1007, 2004-Ohio-678, 2004 WL 285560, Unreported. Infants ⇨ 203; Infants ⇨ 230.1

Trial court committed reversible error in allowing father's attorney to withdraw at outset of dispositional hearing regarding termination of father's rights to minor child, on basis of father's tardiness at hearing and alleged failure to cooperate with attorney beforehand, where statute provided that parents were entitled to representation by legal counsel at all stages of such proceedings, father's attorney did not make requisite good cause showing to withdraw, from ethical perspective, attorney could not withdraw from employment until attorney had taken reasonable steps to avoid foreseeable prejudice to rights of client, and father could not have been deemed to have waived right to counsel. In re M.L.R. (Ohio App. 8 Dist., 10-31-2002) 150 Ohio App.3d 39, 779 N.E.2d 772, 2002-Ohio-5958. Infants ⇐ 205; Infants ⇐ 253.

Assuming that mother's counsel was derelict in failing to timely move for appointment of new counsel due to conflict of interest and in failing to follow up on motion, mother did not show prejudice, and thus, mother could not establish ineffective assistance of counsel in proceeding for permanent custody of dependent children; Montgomery County Children Services (MCCS) proved its case by clear and convincing evidence and nothing in record suggested any viable objections. In re Lakes (Ohio App. 2 Dist., 08-02-2002) 149 Ohio App.3d 128, 776 N.E.2d 510, 2002-Ohio-3917. Infants ⇐ 205.

If the defendant, in seeking appointment of new counsel, alleges facts which, if true, would require relief, the trial court must inquire into the defendant's complaint and make the inquiry part of the record; the inquiry may be brief and minimal, but it must be made if the allegations are sufficiently specific. In re Lakes (Ohio App. 2 Dist., 08-02-2002) 149 Ohio App.3d 128, 776 N.E.2d 510, 2002-Ohio-3917. Criminal Law ⇐ 641.10(2).

Error cannot be predicated on the juvenile court's holding a dispositional hearing immediately following an adjudicatory hearing and its failure to continue the dispositional hearing for a reasonable time to enable the party to obtain or consult counsel, as prescribed by Juv R 34(A), unless it affirmatively appears in the record that the affected nonindigent party has requested such continuance. In re Bolden (Allen 1973) 37 Ohio App.2d 7, 306 N.E.2d 166, 66 O.O.2d 26.

The guarantee of the right to be represented by counsel set forth in Juv R 4(A) does not, as to a nonindigent party, require that trial be continued indefinitely until counsel can be obtained, but merely requires, if it does not appear that counsel could not be obtained through the exercise of reasonable diligence and a willingness to enter into reasonable contractual arrangements for counsel's services, that a reasonable opportunity be given to the party before trial to employ such counsel. In re Bolden (Allen 1973) 37 Ohio App.2d 7, 306 N.E.2d 166, 66 O.O.2d 26.

9. Evidence

Trial court error in admitting guardian ad litem's report and considering it as substantive evidence, in termination of parental rights proceeding, was harmless and did not unfairly prejudice father; the court only referred to the guardian ad litem's report when it referred to the wishes of the four oldest children, and other admissible evidence supported the court's order terminating parental rights. In re Hilyard (Ohio App. 4 Dist., Vinton, 04-13-2006) No. 05CA600, No. 05CA603, No. 05CA607, No. 05CA601, No. 05CA604, No. 05CA608, No. 05CA602, No. 05CA606, No. 05CA609, 2006-Ohio-1965, 2006 WL Infants ⇐ 253.

Juvenile court improperly denied mother's request to introduce into evidence entire version of out-of-state human services interstate compact report after portions of it had been admitted through guardian ad litem's testimony, during legal custody proceeding in which dependent child's godmother was awarded legal custody of child. In re S.J. (Ohio App. 9 Dist., Summit, 09-21-2005) No. 22554, 2005-Ohio-4945, 2005 WL 2291892, Unreported. Infants ⇐ 173.1.

Report of child's guardian ad litem was properly considered by trial court, in termination of parental rights proceeding; rule governing dispositional hearing permitted evidence that was material and relevant, including hearsay, opinion, and documentary evidence, guardian was present at disposition, and mother chose not to examine or challenge guardian with respect to her recommendations. In re Erich L. (Ohio App. 6 Dist., Lucas, 06-10-2005) No. L-04-1340, 2005-Ohio-2945, 2005 WL 1389086, Unreported. Infants ⇐ 208.

Oral motion by guardian ad litem at dispositional hearing in child protection proceedings, seeking award of custody of subject child to child's maternal aunt, was insufficient basis upon which to award custody, where no motion for custody was filed by aunt or on her behalf prior to dispositional hearing, trial record contained no indication that child's mother consented to such award of custody, and mother's counsel explicitly argued against and objected to custody order on grounds that no motion for legal custody had been filed as required by statute. In re C.T. (Ohio App. 8 Dist., Cuyahoga, 03-03-2005) No. 84648, 2005-Ohio-887, 2005 WL 488914, Unreported. Infants ⇐ 222.

Rules of evidence applied to hearing to determine whether to grant permanent custody of mother's children to county agency. In re T.M., III (Ohio App. 8 Dist., Cuyahoga, 09-30-2004) No. 83933, 2004-Ohio-5222, 2004 WL 2340654, Unreported. Infants ⇐ 173.1; Infants ⇐ 207.

Videotaped statements that were made by mother during interrogations were admissible as admissions of a party opponent in state's proceeding to obtain permanent custody of allegedly dependent children; state offered statements against mother. In re K.W. (Ohio App. 12 Dist., Butler, 10-11-2004) No. CA2003-11-289, No. CA2003-11-291, 2004-Ohio-5406, 2004 WL 2272064, Unreported. Infants ⇐ 174.

Father's nonappearance at hearing on state's motion to obtain permanent custody of allegedly dependent children from mother and father did not preclude admission of father's videotaped statements as admissions of party-opponent; father was a party to proceeding. In re K.W. (Ohio App. 12 Dist., Butler, 10-11-2004) No. CA2003-11-289, No. CA2003-11-291, 2004-Ohio-5406, 2004 WL 2272064, Unreported. Infants ⇐ 174.

Mother's ongoing criminal legal problems (some involving dishonesty), her failure to provide stable housing, and her failure to financially support her children constituted clear and convincing evidence that county agency should be awarded permanent custody of dependent child. In re Ashley E.D. (Ohio App. 6 Dist., Huron, 11-15-2002) No. H-02-025, 2002-Ohio-6238, 2002 WL 31529030, Unreported. Infants ⇐ 155; Infants ⇐ 157.

Any error in admitting father's testimony was harmless at motion for permanent custody of dependent child, as there was more than sufficient evidence absent father's testimony to support trial court's findings. In re Ashley E.D. (Ohio App. 6 Dist., Huron, 11-15-2002) No. H-02-025, 2002-Ohio-6238, 2002 WL 31529030, Unreported. Infants ⇐ 253.

Lay opinions of social workers and dependent child's guardian ad litem were admissible on motion for permanent custody on issue of whether child's best interest was served by granting permanent custody to county department of jobs and family services. In re Ashley E.D. (Ohio App. 6 Dist., Huron, 11-15-2002) No. H-02-025, 2002-Ohio-6238, 2002 WL 31529030, Unreported. Infants ⇐ 173.1.

Rules of Evidence applied at motion for permanent custody of dependent child. In re Ashley E.D. (Ohio App. 6 Dist., Huron, 11-15-2002) No. H-02-025, 2002-Ohio-6238, 2002 WL 31529030, Unreported. Infants ⇐ 173.1.

Hearsay evidence was admissible at dispositional hearing in child dependency proceeding. In re Sean T. (Ohio App. 6 Dist., 10-28-2005) 164 Ohio App.3d 218, 841 N.E.2d 838, 2005-Ohio-5739. Infants ⇐ 174.

At dispositional hearing in child dependency proceeding, trial court should have considered both grandmother's motion for legal custody of dependent child and mother's motion for return of custody based on best interest standard, without requiring grandmother to establish that mother was unsuitable before her motion would be considered. In re D.R. (Ohio App. 9 Dist., 06-04-2003) 153 Ohio App.3d 156, 792 N.E.2d 203, 2003-Ohio-2852. Infants ⇐ 222; Infants ⇐ 231.

At the dispositional stage of a neglect case, evidence other than the parent's admission is required to determine whether a particular placement is in the child's best interest. In re Lakes (Ohio App. 2 Dist., 08-02-2002) 149 Ohio App.3d 128, 776 N.E.2d 510, 2002-Ohio-3917. Infants ⇐ 179.

In dispositional hearing related to permanent custody of neglected children, trial court was not required to engage in colloquy with mother similar to that required at adjudicatory hearing in determining whether mother knowingly, intelligently, and voluntarily relinquished custody of children. In re Lakes (Ohio App. 2 Dist., 08-02-2002) 149 Ohio App.3d 128, 776 N.E.2d 510, 2002-Ohio-3917. Infants ⇐ 203.

Mother whose children were subjects of county's motion for permanent custody had statutory right to rebut guardian ad litem's unsworn testimony concerning suitability of placement with mother's sister and condition of her home, as these matters were not contained in guardian ad litem's written report and were not previously addressed by sister in her earlier testimony; thus, refusal to permit such rebuttal evidence violated due process. In re Sadiku (Ohio App. 9 Dist., 11-22-2000) 139 Ohio App.3d 263, 743 N.E.2d 507. Constitutional Law ⇐ 274(5); Infants ⇐ 207.

The right of parents to raise their children is basic and essential, protected by due process of law. In re Sadiku (Ohio App. 9 Dist., 11-22-2000) 139 Ohio App.3d 263, 743 N.E.2d 507. Constitutional Law ⇐ 274(5).

Due process requires "fundamentally fair procedures" when a state attempts to terminate parental rights. In re Sadiku (Ohio App. 9 Dist., 11-

22-2000) 139 Ohio App.3d 263, 743 N.E.2d 507. Constitutional Law ⇐ 274(5)

The proper scope of rebuttal testimony in a parental rights termination case lies within the sound discretion of the trial court. In re Sadiku (Ohio App. 9 Dist., 11-22-2000) 139 Ohio App.3d 263, 743 N.E.2d 507. Infants ⇐ 207

A trial court's decision regarding the scope of rebuttal testimony in a parental rights termination case will not be reversed unless the trial court's decision was unreasonable, arbitrary, or unconscionable. In re Sadiku (Ohio App. 9 Dist., 11-22-2000) 139 Ohio App.3d 263, 743 N.E.2d 507. Infants ⇐ 252

"Evidence," for purposes of statute providing that juvenile court at dispositional hearing may admit any evidence that is material and relevant, contemplates sworn testimony, despite informal nature of such hearing. In re Ramsey Children (Ohio App. 5 Dist., 03-27-1995) 102 Ohio App.3d 168, 656 N.E.2d 1311. Infants ⇐ 173.1

Testimony regarding a child's home environment and parental care is admissible in an action to terminate parental custody, even if it is hearsay, so long as it is material and relevant to the best interest of the child. In re Smith (Ottawa 1991) 77 Ohio App.3d 1, 601 N.E.2d 45.

10. Rights of juvenile

Twenty-eight months of limbo in juvenile dispositional hearing is a per se due process violation, barring extraordinary circumstances. In re Omosun Children (Ohio App. 11 Dist., 10-16-1995) 106 Ohio App.3d 813, 667 N.E.2d 431. Constitutional Law ⇐ 274(5); Infants ⇐ 204

Juvenile court did not err by conducting dispositional hearing with judge after referee conducted adjudicatory hearing, absent showing that juvenile was prejudiced or that it was possible for referee to preside over both hearings. In re Johnson (Ohio App. 1 Dist., 08-23-1995) 106 Ohio App.3d 38, 665 N.E.2d 247. Infants ⇐ 253

Where no part of a proceeding conducted pursuant to Juv R 34(E) is contested, a juvenile court is not required to advise an accused of his right to appeal. In re Haas (Stark 1975) 45 Ohio App.2d 187, 341 N.E.2d 638, 74 O.O.2d 231.

Admission of reports of workers at juvenile rehabilitation center during dispositional hearing on revocation of juvenile's probation did not violate his right to due process, even though workers did not testify and were not subject to cross-examination, where program director of rehabilitation center and probation officer testified, and both were subject to cross-examination. In re Henderson (Ohio App. 12 Dist., Butler, 06-03-2002) No. CA2001-07-162, No. CA2001-09-228, 2002-Ohio-2575, 2002 WL 1160073, Unreported. Constitutional Law ⇐ 255(4); Infants ⇐ 225

Procedural rule that requires a criminal defendant to be present at sentencing is applicable to a delinquency adjudication. In re Sweeten (Ohio App. 1 Dist., Hamilton, 05-24-2002) No. C-010314, 2002-Ohio-2552, 2002 WL 1040229, Unreported. Infants ⇐ 203

Due process clause of Fourteenth Amendment applies when child is charged with misconduct for which he may be incarcerated in institution, so child is entitled to notice of charges, counsel, confrontation and cross-examination, and privilege against self-incrimination. In re Jason R. (Ohio Com.Pl., 12-14-1995) 77 Ohio Misc.2d 37, 666 N.E.2d 666. Constitutional Law ⇐ 255(4)

Proceeding with dispositional hearing in juvenile's absence did not violate due process; juvenile effectively waived his right to be present, as he had notice of hearing but blatantly disregarded it. In re Jason R. (Ohio Com.Pl., 12-14-1995) 77 Ohio Misc.2d 37, 666 N.E.2d 666. Constitutional Law ⇐ 255(4); Infants ⇐ 203

Right to be present at every stage of trial, as encompassed by right of confrontation, applies to both adult criminal trials and juvenile proceedings. In re Jason R. (Ohio Com.Pl., 12-14-1995) 77 Ohio Misc.2d 37, 666 N.E.2d 666. Criminal Law ⇐ 662.70; Infants ⇐ 203; Infants ⇐ 207

Although juvenile's right to be present at dispositional hearing was implied by rule stating that court may excuse attendance of child at hearing in neglect, dependency, or abuse cases, and rule requiring court at conclusion of dispositional hearing to advise child of child's right to record expungement and right to appeal, juvenile nonetheless waived his right to be present at dispositional hearing by blatantly disregarding it after receiving adequate notice. In re Jason R. (Ohio Com.Pl., 12-14-1995) 77 Ohio Misc.2d 37, 666 N.E.2d 666. Infants ⇐ 203

Proceeding with dispositional hearing in juvenile's absence did not violate his right of allocution, as he waived his right to be present by blatantly disregarding hearing after receiving adequate notice, thus waiving his right to address court passing judgment upon him. In re Jason R. (Ohio Com.Pl., 12-14-1995) 77 Ohio Misc.2d 37, 666 N.E.2d 666. Infants ⇐ 203

Variance between one year sentence in judgment entry, and six-month sentence pronounced at hearing in delinquency proceeding, required vacation of sentence and remand for resentencing, where juvenile was not present when trial court imposed one year confinement stated in judgment entry. State v. R.W. (Ohio App. 8 Dist., Cuyahoga, 01-30-2003) No. 80631, 2003-Ohio-401, 2003 WL 194771, Unreported, as amended nunc pro tunc. Infants ⇐ 254

11. ——— Timing, dispositional hearing

Juvenile court's decision to hold dispositional hearing 10 days after the adjudicatory hearing in which the court announced the judgment of dependency was within the timeframe required by the Juvenile Rules. In re Spangler (Ohio App. 3 Dist., Hardin, 07-05-2005) No. 6-04-15, 2005-Ohio-3450, 2005 WL 1545777, Unreported. Infants ⇐ 204

County children services' complaint for temporary custody of minor was statutorily required to be dismissed, where dispositional hearing was held some five months after date complaint was filed, rather than within mandated 90 days of filing. In re Olah (Ohio App. 9 Dist., 08-24-2000) 142 Ohio App.3d 176, 754 N.E.2d 1271, motion to certify allowed 90 Ohio St.3d 1491, 739 N.E.2d 816, appeal allowed 90 Ohio St.3d 1493, 739 N.E.2d 817, cause dismissed 93 Ohio St.3d 1404, 753 N.E.2d 208. Infants ⇐ 204

12. Case plan

Mother in dependency proceedings failed to show she was prejudiced by failure of county children services to file case plan prior to adjudicatory hearing; there was no evidence to demonstrate lack of action on behalf of county children services, any lack of action on behalf of county children services was not the result of any error by magistrate or trial court, and trial counsel's failure to raise issue with regard to such failure may have been result of strategy to avoid further delays. In re Malone (Ohio App. 10 Dist., Franklin, 12-30-2003) No. 03AP-489, 2003-Ohio-7156, 2003 WL 23024377, Unreported, appeal not allowed 102 Ohio St.3d 1423, 807 N.E.2d 367, 2004-Ohio-2003. Infants ⇐ 191

Juv R 35 Proceedings after judgment

(A) Continuing jurisdiction; invoked by motion

The continuing jurisdiction of the court shall be invoked by motion filed in the original proceeding, notice of which shall be served in the manner provided for the service of process.

(B) Revocation of probation

The court shall not revoke probation except after a hearing at which the child shall be present and apprised of the grounds on which revocation is proposed. The parties shall have the right to counsel and the right to appointed counsel where entitled pursuant to Juv. R. 4(A). Probation shall not be revoked except upon a finding that the child has violated a condition of probation of which the child had, pursuant to Juv. R. 34(C), been notified.

(C) Detention

During the pendency of proceedings under this rule, a child may be placed in detention in accordance with the provisions of Rule 7.

(Adopted eff. 7-1-72; amended eff. 7-1-94)

Historical and Statutory Notes

Amendment Note: The 7-1-94 amendment made changes to reflect gender-neutral language.

Staff Notes

1994:

Rule 35 Proceedings After Judgment

Masculine references were replaced by gender neutral language and other grammar changes were made; no substantive change was intended.

Editor's Comment

Continuing jurisdiction; invoked by motion   1
Revocation of probation   2

Detention 3

1. Continuing jurisdiction; invoked by motion

The rule states that the continuing jurisdiction of the court shall be invoked by motion filed in the original proceeding with notice of the filing being served as provided in Juv R 16. The rule is generally applicable to cases involving custody and allows the continuing jurisdiction of the court to be invoked without reference to a time limitation.

Division (A) is based on Civ R 75(I), and adopts a procedure similar to that in domestic relations cases.

2. Revocation of probation

Division (B) is based on Crim R 32.3, regulating probation revocation procedures. Case law clearly establishes the right of a person to proper notice, a hearing, representation by counsel and an opportunity to be heard on the issue of probation revocation.

3. Detention

Division (C) restates the requirement that placement of a child in detention or shelter care during the pendency of proceedings under this rule is governed by Juv R 7.

Cross References

Divorce, annulment and alimony actions, Civ R 75
Sentence, Crim R 32

Library References

Infants ⇐225, 230.1, 231.
Westlaw Topic No. 211.
C.J.S. Adoption of Persons §§ 10 to 12.
C.J.S. Infants §§ 57, 69 to 85.

Research References

Encyclopedias

OH Jur. 3d Family Law § 1549, Delinquent, Unruly, Abused, Neglected, or Dependent Children.
OH Jur. 3d Family Law § 1703, Generally; Continuing Jurisdiction.
OH Jur. 3d Family Law § 1708, Revocation of Probation on Hearing.
OH Jur. 3d Family Law § 1709, Revocation of Probation on Hearing—Detention During Proceeding.

Treatises and Practice Aids

Klein, Darling, & Terez, Baldwin's Ohio Practice Civil Practice § 4.1:5, Certified or Express Mail Service--In General.
Carlin, Baldwin's Ohio Practice, Merrick-Rippner Probate Law § 107:117, Proceedings After Judgment—Continuing Jurisdiction of Juvenile Court.
Carlin, Baldwin's Ohio Practice, Merrick-Rippner Probate Law § 107:121, Custody Review Hearing—Revocation of Probation or Parole.
Giannelli & Yeomans, Ohio Juvenile Law § 29:3, Unruly—Delinquency Dispositions.
Giannelli & Yeomans, Ohio Juvenile Law § 33:2, Motions.
Giannelli & Yeomans, Ohio Juvenile Law § 33:3, Detention.
Giannelli & Yeomans, Ohio Juvenile Law § 33:6, Revocation of Probation.
Giannelli & Yeomans, Ohio Juvenile Law § 33:7, Suspended Commitments.

Notes of Decisions

Constitutional issues
    Due process 3
Court's duty to inform 2
Jurisdiction 1
Procedural issues 4

---

1. Jurisdiction

Trial court lacked personal jurisdiction over father to enter child support order against him, due to defective service of process of motion to set support; docket sheet showed that father was served with motion to set child support by ordinary mail only, rather than by certified mail, or express mail, as required by rule, so continuing jurisdiction of juvenile court was not invoked, and, due to failure to provide notice, any subsequent order based on void order was nullity. In re Brandon P. (Ohio App. 6 Dist., Lucas, 04-11-2003) No. L-02-1230, 2003-Ohio-1861, 2003 WL 1861564, Unreported. Child Support ⇐ 180

Juvenile court's jurisdiction concerning any child who on or about date specified in complaint is alleged to be delinquent child is continuing and may be invoked at any time by motion before juvenile court. In re Bracewell (Ohio App. 1 Dist., 04-17-1998) 126 Ohio App.3d 133, 709 N.E.2d 938, dismissed, appeal not allowed 82 Ohio St.3d 1481, 696 N.E.2d 1087. Infants ⇐ 230.1

Juvenile court's jurisdiction to reinstate order of commitment upon juvenile adjudicated delinquent by reason of acts which, if committed by adult, would have constituted third-degree felony of carrying concealed weapon, continued after juvenile was released from official probation; at dispositional hearing, order of commitment was stayed, and juvenile was informed that he would not have to appear before court again unless he got himself into some "more difficulty" or violated his probation. In re Bracewell (Ohio App. 1 Dist., 04-17-1998) 126 Ohio App.3d 133, 709 N.E.2d 938, dismissed, appeal not allowed 82 Ohio St.3d 1481, 696 N.E.2d 1087. Infants ⇐ 230.1

The court's continuing jurisdiction may be invoked by the filing of a new complaint rather than a motion, as long as the parties are given notice and an opportunity to be heard. In re Luke, No. 83–CA–09 (5th Dist Ct App, Coshocton, 1–13–84).

2. Court's duty to inform

Trial court, in revoking juvenile's probation, complied with juvenile procedure rule governing probation revocation hearings, which granted trial court authority to revoke probation after hearing at which juvenile was present and apprised of grounds on which revocation was proposed, and advised that he had right to counsel. In re J.B. (Ohio App. 12 Dist., Brown, 09-26-2005) No. CA2004-09-024, No. CA2004-09-025, 2005-Ohio-5045, 2005 WL 2335314, Unreported. Infants ⇐ 225

Revocation of juvenile's probation violated due process notice rights, where juvenile was unrepresented by counsel and neither transcript of dispositional hearing, docket, nor judgment entry of disposition mentioned a probation violation or informed juvenile of the condition of probation that he was alleged to have violated, and juvenile court made no finding that juvenile violated a probation condition. In re Royal (Ohio App. 7 Dist., 03-01-1999) 132 Ohio App.3d 496, 725 N.E.2d 685. Constitutional Law ⇐ 255(4); Infants ⇐ 225

Juvenile court must give the minor notice as to why a previously suspended commitment is ordered reinstituted, if the court imposes a previously suspended commitment as a further disposition. In re Royal (Ohio App. 7 Dist., 03-01-1999) 132 Ohio App.3d 496, 725 N.E.2d 685. Infants ⇐ 198

Court of Common Pleas did not "reopen" juvenile's case at probation department's request; although court placed entry in docket sheet about "reopening" case, no journal entry supported notation, and nothing in record showed that probation department had terminated probation. In re Edwards (Ohio App. 8 Dist., 12-23-1996) 117 Ohio App.3d 108, 690 N.E.2d 22. Infants ⇐ 230.1

Court of Common Pleas never adequately determined that juvenile was probation violator after date on which it continued his probation; court in judgment entry neither identified condition allegedly violated, nor "found" juvenile had violated condition. In re Edwards (Ohio App. 8 Dist., 12-23-1996) 117 Ohio App.3d 108, 690 N.E.2d 22. Infants ⇐ 230.1

At hearing for probation violation, juvenile court was not required to inform juvenile of consequences of his plea and right to present evidence during hearing. In re Motley (Ohio App. 9 Dist., 05-01-1996) 110 Ohio App.3d 641, 674 N.E.2d 1268. Infants ⇐ 225

3. —— Due process, constitutional issues

Juvenile had due process right to be present at hearing in order to show cause why he should not be held in contempt for his alleged failure to complete treatment program into which he was ordered in delinquency adjudication proceeding, as such proceeding should have been treated as probation revocation hearing at which juvenile had statutory right to be present. In re Nowak (Ohio App. 11 Dist., 04-26-1999) 133 Ohio App.3d 396, 728 N.E.2d 411. Constitutional Law ⇐ 273; Infants ⇐ 230.1

Admission of reports of workers at juvenile rehabilitation center during dispositional hearing on revocation of juvenile's probation did not violate his right to due process, even though workers did not testify and were not subject to cross-examination, where program director of rehabilitation center and probation officer testified, and both were subject to cross-examination. In re Henderson (Ohio App. 12 Dist., Butler, 06-03-2002) No. CA2001-07-162, No. CA2001-09-228, 2002-Ohio-2575, 2002 WL 1160073, Unreported. Constitutional Law ⚖ 255(4); Infants ⚖ 225

Sentence entry informed juvenile of a suspended commitment to the Ohio Department of Youth Services, and thus there was no violation of due process and equal protection, and juvenile was not subjected to double jeopardy, when he was committed to the Ohio Department of Youth Services after he violated his probation. In re Keeran (Ohio App. 5 Dist., Licking, 03-28-2002) No. 01CA69, 2002-Ohio-1580, 2002 WL 1653799, Unreported, appeal not allowed 96 Ohio St.3d 1491, 774 N.E.2d 765, 2002-Ohio-4534. Constitutional Law ⚖ 242.1(4); Constitutional Law ⚖ 255(4); Double Jeopardy ⚖ 62; Infants ⚖ 69(7)

4. Procedural issues

Once juvenile was placed on probation for criminal trespass and other crimes, trial court lacked authority, without conducting probation revocation hearing, to effectively revoke probation and order that juvenile be committed to Department of Youth Services for six months until 21st birthday after receiving information that juvenile violated terms of probation. In re Burner (Ohio App. 5 Dist., Stark, 10-31-2005) No. 2005 CA 00108, 2005-Ohio-5816, 2005 WL 2864706, Unreported. Infants ⚖ 225

Revocation of juvenile's probation on two counts of raping his younger sister, following hearing at which juvenile moved unsuccessfully to withdraw his admission to those offenses based on allegations that his parents had coerced him into making admission, was not abuse of discretion; juvenile had repeatedly been brought back into court and warned that he would be sent to Department of Youth Services if his improper behavior did not cease, and he did not present adequate evidence to support allegations of coercion by parents. In re McElfresh (Ohio App. 7 Dist., Belmont, 03-07-2003) No. 02 BA 12, 2003-Ohio-1079, 2003 WL 932342, Unreported. Infants ⚖ 225

Court of Appeals could not address juvenile's challenges to actions taken and omissions made concerning original adjudication of delinquency, by reason of having committed burglary, and disposition, and juvenile's subsequent placement into custody of Department of Youth Services, where juvenile failed to file notices of appeal from juvenile court's orders; juvenile court's decision to suspend the commitment in order to permit juvenile to remain on probation did not affect its finality for purposes of appeal. In re R.M. (Ohio App. 8 Dist., Cuyahoga, 02-27-2003) No. 81085, 2003-Ohio-872, 2003 WL 549904, Unreported. Infants ⚖ 242; Infants ⚖ 244.1

Trial court, in delinquency proceeding, had authority to initiate contempt proceedings against juvenile's mother based on a violation of order that required mother to attend parenting classes, even though a stay of execution of such order on was issued next day; stay of execution only dealt with juvenile's ninety-day sentence to juvenile detention center, and thus order to attend parenting classes was still in effect at all times. In re Cunningham (Ohio App. 7 Dist., Harrison, 10-18-2002) No. 02-537-CA, 2002-Ohio-5875, 2002 WL 31412256, Unreported. Contempt ⚖ 22

Juvenile court improperly proceeded against juvenile in contempt for his alleged failure to complete treatment program into which he was ordered in delinquency adjudication proceeding, as such alleged failure, if proved, would have amounted to probation violation; proper action would have been probation violation proceeding rather than contempt of court hearing. In re Nowak (Ohio App. 11 Dist., 04-26-1999) 133 Ohio App.3d 396, 728 N.E.2d 411. Infants ⚖ 230.1

Trial court could not revoke juvenile's probation without notifying juvenile of grounds on which revocation was proposed and without finding that juvenile had violated a condition of probation. In re Lett (Ohio App. 7 Dist., Mahoning, 09-18-2002) No. 01 CA 222, 2002-Ohio-5023, 2002 WL 31115583, Unreported. Infants ⚖ 225

Juv R 36   Dispositional review

(A) Court review

A court that issues a dispositional order in an abuse, neglect, or dependency case may review the child's placement or custody arrangement, the case plan, and the actions of the public or private agency implementing that plan at any time. A court that issues a dispositional order shall hold a review hearing one year after the earlier of the date on which the complaint in the case was filed or the child was first placed into shelter care. The court shall schedule the review hearing at the time that it holds the dispositional hearing. The court shall hold a similar review hearing no later than every twelve months after the initial review hearing until the child is adopted, returned to the child's parents, or the court otherwise terminates the child's placement or custody arrangement. A hearing pursuant to section 2151.415 of the Revised Code shall take the place of the first review hearing. The court shall schedule each subsequent review hearing at the conclusion of the review hearing immediately preceding the review hearing to be scheduled. Review hearings may be conducted by a judge or magistrate.

(B) Citizens' review board

The court may appoint a citizens' review board to conduct review hearings, subject to the review and approval by the court.

(C) Agency review

Each agency required to prepare a case plan for a child shall complete a semiannual administrative review of the case plan no later than six months after the earlier of the date on which the complaint in the case was filed or the child was first placed in shelter care. After the first administrative review, the agency shall complete semiannual administrative reviews no later than every six months. The agency shall prepare and file a written summary of the semiannual administrative review that shall include an updated case plan. If the agency, parents, guardian, or custodian of the child and guardian ad litem stipulate to the revised case plan, the plan shall be signed by all parties and filed with the written summary of the administrative review no later than seven days after the completion of the administrative review. If the court does not object to the revised case plan, it shall journalize the case plan within fourteen days after it is filed with the court. If the court does not approve of the revised case plan or if the agency, parties, guardian ad litem, and the attorney of the child do not agree to the need for changes to the case plan and to all of the proposed changes, the agency shall file its written summary and request a hearing. The court shall schedule a review hearing to be held no later than thirty days after the filing of the case plan or written summary or both, if required. The court shall give notice of the date, time, and location of the hearing to all interested parties and the guardian ad litem of the child. The court shall take one of the following actions:

(1) Approve or modify the case plan based upon the evidence presented;

(2) Return the child home with or without protective supervision and terminate temporary custody or determine which agency shall have custody;

(3) If the child is in permanent custody determine what actions would facilitate adoption;

(4) Journalize the terms of the updated case plan.

(Adopted eff. 7–1–94; amended eff. 7–1–96)

Historical and Statutory Notes

Amendment Note: The 7–1–96 amendment deleted "also" after "may" and substituted "judge or magistrate" for "referee" in the last sentence in division (A).

Staff Notes

1996:

The amendment changed the rule's reference from "referee" to "magistrate" in division (A) in order to harmonize the rule with the language adopted in the 1995 amendments to Juv. R. 40. The amendment is technical only and no substantive change is intended.

1994:

Rule 36 Dispositional Review

Juv. R. 36 was previously reserved. The 1994 amendment was drafted to address requirements of dispositional review imposed by S.B. 89.

Revised Code 2151.353 and 2151.417(B) permit the court on its own motion or any public children's services agency or private child placing agency, the Department of Human Services, or any party at any time to move to modify or terminate any dispositional order on an abused, neglected, or dependent child.

Juv. R. 34 sets out the procedures for such a hearing to terminate or modify a dispositional order. Juv. R. 36(A) provides requirements for notice to all parties and the guardian ad litem.

Revised Code 2151.417(G) allows the appointment of a citizens' review board to review dispositional orders. Juv. R. 36(B) delineates that provision.

Juv. R. 36(C) delineates procedures for preparing case plans and conducting administrative reviews in accordance with Revised Code 2151.416(F).

Editor's Comment

Juv R 36, added in 1994, reiterates the statutory requirements for court and agency reviews of dispositional hearings. Division (C), which delineates the dispositional options which the court may select at the review hearing, is taken from 2151.417(F). Because the determination of dispositional options is a legislative function (see Editor's Comment to Juv R 34(D)), these provisions are more appropriate in the statutes rather than the rules.

Amendments to 2151.416(E) in 1996 regarding procedural aspects of the administrative review process have resulted in conflicts between the statute and the rule.

Research References

Encyclopedias

OH Jur. 3d Family Law § 1706, Modification or Vacation of Order.
OH Jur. 3d Family Law § 1711, Review Hearing.

Treatises and Practice Aids

Giannelli & Yeomans, Ohio Juvenile Law § 33:4, Abuse, Neglect, and Dependency Proceedings.

Giannelli & Yeomans, Ohio Juvenile Law § 33:10, Child Custody Agency Commitment—Semiannual Administrative Review.

Giannelli & Yeomans, Ohio Juvenile Law § 33:11, Child Custody Agency Commitment—Juvenile Court Dispositional Review.

Notes of Decisions

Court review 1

---

1. Court review

Trial court did not abuse its discretion when it found that continued placement with foster family was in best interests of child born to minor mother; placement of child and her mother with foster family had been successful, and mother's parenting skills had been called into question, raising issue of child's safety. In re M. (Ohio App. 6 Dist., Wood, 07-16-2004) No. WD-03-092, 2004-Ohio-3798, 2004 WL 1595006, Unreported. Infants ⇐ 226

While statute requires juvenile court to review dispositional order if any party files motion requesting modification or termination of order, statute and rule additionally allow juvenile court to review child's placement or custody arrangement at any time. In re Bowman (Ohio App. 9 Dist., 03-08-1995) 101 Ohio App.3d 599, 656 N.E.2d 355. Infants ⇐ 230.1

If a juvenile court, in making disposition of an unruly or delinquent child pursuant to RC 2151.354 or RC 2151.355, places the child into the temporary custody of the county department of human services in accordance with RC 2151.353, the juvenile court is required to hold periodic reviews pursuant to RC 2151.417 and Juv R 36(A). OAG 99–041.

Juv R 37   Recording of proceedings

(A) Record of proceedings

The juvenile court shall make a record of adjudicatory and dispositional proceedings in abuse, neglect, dependent, unruly, and delinquent cases; permanent custody cases; and proceedings before magistrates. In all other proceedings governed by these rules, a record shall be made upon request of a party or upon motion of the court. The record shall be taken in shorthand, stenotype, or by any other adequate mechanical, electronic, or video recording device.

(B) Restrictions on use of recording or transcript

No public use shall be made by any person, including a party, of any juvenile court record, including the recording or a transcript of any juvenile court hearing, except in the course of an appeal or as authorized by order of the court or by statute.

(Adopted eff. 7–1–72; amended eff. 7–1–96, 7–1–01)

Historical and Statutory Notes

Amendment Note: The 7–1–01 amendment inserted "or by statute" at the end of division (B).

Amendment Note: The 7–1–96 amendment rewrote this rule, which prior thereto read:

"(A) Recording of hearings.

"In all juvenile court hearings, upon request of a party, or upon the court's own motion, a complete record of all testimony, or other oral proceedings shall be taken in shorthand, stenotype or by any other adequate mechanical or electronic recording device.

"(B) Restrictions on use of recording or transcript.

"No public use shall be made by any person, including a party, of any juvenile court record, including the recording or a transcript thereof of any juvenile court hearing, except in the course of an appeal or as authorized by order of the court."

Staff Notes

2001:

Rule 37(B) Restrictions on use of recording or transcript

Division (B) of this rule was amended to conform the rule with Revised Code section 2151.358 (E)(2), which provides for law enforcement personnel to have access to certain juvenile court records. The amendment was not intended to designate juvenile court records as public documents or to enlarge access to juvenile records beyond that specifically designated by a statute directed at juvenile court records.

1996:

Division (A) of this rule was modified to require the making of a record in adjudication and dispositional proceedings in abuse, neglect, dependent, unruly, and delinquent cases; in permanent custody cases; and in all proceedings before magistrates. It should be noted that the making of a record is mandatory in adjudicatory and dispositional proceedings. "Proceedings" includes the receiving of any admission or denial, as well as evidentiary hearings. The rule is consistent with section 2151.35(A) of the Revised Code requiring a record of permanent custody proceedings.

Division (B), which was not changed by the 1996 amendment, further provides that no public use shall be made of a transcript except upon appeal or upon authorization of the court.

The preparation of a transcript shall be at public expense if the party is indigent, in accordance with Juvenile Rule 29(B)(5).

Editor's Comment

Juv R 37(A) was amended in 1996 to require the making of a record in virtually all children's cases. This amendment incorporates and expands upon 2151.35(A), which requires a record in all permanent custody proceedings, and Juv R 40(D)(2), which mandates it in all proceedings conducted by magistrates.

Juv R 37(B) further provides that no public use shall be made of a transcript except upon appeal or upon authorization of the court.

The preparation of a transcript shall be at public expense if the party is indigent in accordance with Juv R 29(B)(5).

Library References

Infants ⇐133, 203, 246.
Westlaw Topic No. 211.
C.J.S. Infants §§ 51 to 91.

Research References

ALR Library

101 ALR 5th 351, Validity and Efficacy of Minor's Waiver of Right to Counsel--Cases Decided Since Application of Gault, 387 U.S. 1, 87 S. Ct. 1428, 18 L. Ed. 2d 527 (1967).

Encyclopedias

OH Jur. 3d Family Law § 1549, Delinquent, Unruly, Abused, Neglected, or Dependent Children.

OH Jur. 3d Family Law § 1647, Proceedings Before Referee; Powers and Duties.

OH Jur. 3d Family Law § 1658, Restrictions on Use.

OH Jur. 3d Family Law § 1672, Testimony of Child.

OH Jur. 3d Family Law § 1628.5, Waiver of Counsel.

Treatises and Practice Aids

Giannelli and Snyder, Baldwin's Ohio Practice, Evidence, § 103.10, Record of Offer & Ruling.

Carlin, Baldwin's Ohio Practice, Merrick-Rippner Probate Law § 19:10, Uniform Parentage Act—Procedure in Action to Determine Father-Child Relationship.

Carlin, Baldwin's Ohio Practice, Merrick-Rippner Probate Law § 19:12, Uniform Parentage Act—Costs and Appointed Counsel.

Carlin, Baldwin's Ohio Practice, Merrick-Rippner Probate Law § 107:33, Restricting And/Or Enforcing Discovery.

Carlin, Baldwin's Ohio Practice, Merrick-Rippner Probate Law § 107:49, Adjudicatory Hearings—Conduct of Hearing by Magistrate.

Carlin, Baldwin's Ohio Practice, Merrick-Rippner Probate Law § 107:60, Adjudicatory Hearings—Right to Transcript of Proceedings.

Carlin, Baldwin's Ohio Practice, Merrick-Rippner Probate Law § 107:114, Juvenile Court Records—Confidentiality.

Giannelli & Yeomans, Ohio Juvenile Law § 34:9, Right to Transcript.

Giannelli & Yeomans, Ohio Juvenile Law § 35:2, Confidentiality Requirement.

Giannelli & Yeomans, Ohio Juvenile Law § 22:18, Right to a Transcript.

Giannelli & Yeomans, Ohio Juvenile Law § 23:11, Public Trials; Gag Orders.

Giannelli & Yeomans, Ohio Juvenile Law § 23:30, Right to a Transcript.

Giannelli & Yeomans, Ohio Juvenile Law § 25:12, Transcripts.

Notes of Decisions

Lack of record, effect 6
Method of recording 3
Motion for transcript 1
Public records 4
Retention of record; time limitations 7
Right to counsel 5
Right to transcript 2

---

1. Motion for transcript

In absence of motion by mother for transcript of oral proceedings on her motion to reopen custody cases of her two children, and to recover legal custody of those children, no transcript was required; it was not matter determining permanent custody, but only motion to change legal custody. In re Wright (Montgomery 1993) 88 Ohio App.3d 539, 624 N.E.2d 347. Child Custody ⚖ 907

2. Right to transcript

Father objecting to magistrate judge's resolution of child visitation dispute was not entitled to remand to magistrate for new hearing on ground that magistrate's failure to record initial hearing had preventing preparation of transcript; appropriate remedy, if transcript was unavailable, was filing of affidavit of evidence presented to magistrate. Wilms v. Herbert (Ohio App. 9 Dist., Lorain, 01-05-2005) No. 04CA008525, 2005-Ohio-2, 2005 WL 17901, Unreported. Child Custody ⚖ 504

Television station was entitled to purchase copy of transcript of contempt proceeding against family services director and attorney arising out of child custody case; court did not make requisite findings before denying public access to transcript, proceeding itself was open to press, and there was no evidence that child could be harmed by access to transcript. State ex rel. Scripps Howard Broadcasting Co. v. Cuyahoga Cty. Court of Common Pleas, Juv. Div. (Ohio, 07-13-1995) 73 Ohio St.3d 19, 652 N.E.2d 179. Constitutional Law ⚖ 90.1(9); Constitutional Law ⚖ 328; Records ⚖ 32

Juvenile court's order refusing to release transcript of contempt proceeding arising out of child custody case impinged on public's constitutional right of access and, as such, court was required to make findings that there existed reasonable and substantial basis for believing that public access could harm child or endanger fairness of adjudication, and that potential for harm outweighed benefits of public access. State ex rel. Scripps Howard Broadcasting Co. v. Cuyahoga Cty. Court of Common Pleas, Juv. Div. (Ohio, 07-13-1995) 73 Ohio St.3d 19, 652 N.E.2d 179. Constitutional Law ⚖ 328; Records ⚖ 32

Television station was entitled, under Public Records Act, to purchase copy of transcript of contempt proceeding against family services director and attorney arising out of child custody case, notwithstanding contention that release of transcript was prohibited by state law; juvenile court rule restricting access to transcripts did not prevent release of transcript, and that rule was sole basis for refusing to allow purchase of transcript. State ex rel. Scripps Howard Broadcasting Co. v. Cuyahoga Cty. Court of Common Pleas, Juv. Div. (Ohio, 07-13-1995) 73 Ohio St.3d 19, 652 N.E.2d 179. Records ⚖ 32

An indigent parent is entitled to a transcript and counsel on appeal from a judgment permanently terminating his parental rights. State ex rel. Heller v. Miller (Ohio 1980) 61 Ohio St.2d 6, 399 N.E.2d 66, 15 O.O.3d 3.

Requirement that juvenile must make request for recordation of juvenile proceeding is neither burdensome to juvenile nor unconstitutional under due process or equal protection clauses. In re Hannah (Ohio App. 8 Dist., 10-16-1995) 106 Ohio App.3d 766, 667 N.E.2d 76. Constitutional Law ⚖ 242.1(4); Constitutional Law ⚖ 255(4)

Failure of juvenile to request recordation of juvenile proceeding constitutes waiver. In re Hannah (Ohio App. 8 Dist., 10-16-1995) 106 Ohio App.3d 766, 667 N.E.2d 76. Infants ⚖ 203

Juvenile waived his right to recordation of his delinquency proceedings, so as to allow for production of verbatim transcript, by not timely requesting recording. In re Hannah (Ohio App. 8 Dist., 10-16-1995) 106 Ohio App.3d 766, 667 N.E.2d 76. Infants ⚖ 243; Infants ⚖ 246

An indigent juvenile offender is entitled to a record in a hearing conducted for the purpose of determining whether the juvenile court may waive jurisdiction and bind the offender over to the court of common pleas for criminal prosecution. (Annotation from former RC 2151.26.) State v. Ross (Greene 1970) 23 Ohio App.2d 215, 262 N.E.2d 427, 52 O.O.2d 311. Infants ⚖ 68.7(3)

Because the no contact order, prohibiting mother from contacting her child, was continued in a subsequent proceeding, the lack of a complete transcript of initial hearing did not render the order invalid; hearing transcript and the judge's subsequent order continuing the no contact restriction were adequate to show that it was imposed upon proper procedures and evidence that the restriction was in child's best interest. In re F.M. (Ohio App. 8 Dist., Cuyahoga, 08-01-2002) No. 80027, 2002-Ohio-3900, 2002 WL 1767396, Unreported, appeal not allowed 98 Ohio St.3d 1410, 781 N.E.2d 1019, 2003-Ohio-60. Infants ⚖ 221

Local rules conditioning right to a transcript upon prepayment of costs are not inconsistent with Juv R 37 where the local rules permit avoidance of costs by filing a poverty affidavit. In re Menich, No. 42727 (8th Dist Ct App, Cuyahoga, 3–26–81).

3. Method of recording

Trial court's employment of recording device in delinquency proceeding which left vast majority of juvenile's responses inaudible did not substantially comply with rule requiring record of adjudicatory and dispositional hearings, and left Court of Appeals unable to determine if trial court even minimally complied with requirements to ensure that juvenile's plea to inducing panic and violating probation was knowing, voluntary, and intelligent. In re Dawson (Ohio App. 11 Dist., Trumbull, 04-29-2005) No. 2004-T-0027, 2005-Ohio-2088, 2005 WL 1009834, Unreported. Infants ⚖ 203

Juvenile division's failure to record probable cause hearing in defendant's case, prior to binding him over to the general division, in violation of rule requiring it to do so, did not require remand to juvenile division so that another probable cause hearing could be held and properly recorded, as there was no requirement that trial court be provided with transcript of probable cause hearing as there was at the appellate level. State v. Mock (Ohio Com.Pl., 09-26-2005) 136 Ohio Misc.2d 21, 846 N.E.2d 108, 2005-Ohio-7142. Infants ⚖ 68.7(3)

Referee's report/journal entry and supplemental report, stating that juvenile was advised of his right to counsel and he chose to waive this right, were adequate to show juvenile's waiver of his right to counsel, absent request for transcript of admission hearing. In re East (Ohio App. 8 Dist., 07-17-1995) 105 Ohio App.3d 221, 663 N.E.2d 983, dismissed, appeal not allowed 74 Ohio St.3d 1482, 657 N.E.2d 1375. Infants ⚖ 246

It is within the trial court's discretion to determine which method of recording shall be used. In re Glenn, No. 35352 (8th Dist Ct App, Cuyahoga, 1–20–77).

4. Public records

Facts surrounding juvenile diver's juvenile delinquency proceeding were not "public information" for purposes of invasion of privacy action solely by virtue of the fact that juvenile court did not close hearings that occurred; records were public in the sense that they were kept by government entity, but records were shielded from inspection by general public. Roe ex rel. Roe v. Heap (Ohio App. 10 Dist., Franklin, 05-11-2004) No. 03AP-586, 2004-Ohio-2504, 2004 WL 1109849, Unreported, appeal not allowed 103 Ohio St.3d 1464, 815 N.E.2d 679, 2004-Ohio-5056. Torts ⇔ 393

Juvenile procedure rule that no public use shall be made by any person of any juvenile court record must yield when it impinges on the public's due process right to a meaningful hearing on a motion to close proceedings. State ex rel. Plain Dealer Publishing Co. v. Floyd (Ohio, 08-30-2006) 111 Ohio St.3d 56, 855 N.E.2d 35, 2006-Ohio-4437. Infants ⇔ 203

Even though an Oklahoma statute provides that juvenile proceedings are to be held in private and records opened only by order of court, the trial court may not enjoin a newspaper from publishing the name or picture of a juvenile charged with murder when the press was in fact present at the hearing with full knowledge of the judge, prosecutor, and defense counsel, and no objections were made to its presence or to the photographing when the child left the courthouse. Oklahoma Pub. Co. v. District Court In and For Oklahoma County (U.S.Okl. 1977) 97 S.Ct. 1045, 430 U.S. 308, 51 L.Ed.2d 355.

Pursuant to Juv R 32(B), 37(B) and RC 2151.14, juvenile court records, the records of social, mental, and physical examinations pursuant to court order, and records of the juvenile court probation department are not public records under RC 149.43. OAG 90–101.

Under RC 1347.08, a juvenile court must permit a juvenile or a duly authorized attorney who represents the juvenile to inspect court records pertaining to the juvenile unless the records are exempted under RC 1347.04(A)(1)(e), 1347.08(C), or 1347.08(E)(2). Under Juv R 37(B), the records may not, however, be put to any public use except in the course of an appeal or as authorized by order of the court. OAG 84–077.

5. Right to counsel

Journal entry with respect to disposition hearing following adjudication of delinquency, which stated that juvenile waived counsel after having been informed by judge of "legal rights, procedures and possible consequences of hearing," did not place waiver affirmatively in record and was therefore insufficient to establish knowing and voluntary waiver of counsel. In re Solis (Ohio App. 8 Dist., 12-22-1997) 124 Ohio App.3d 547, 706 N.E.2d 839. Infants ⇔ 205

Putative father validly waived his right to counsel at paternity hearing, despite the absence of a transcript, where magistrate made handwritten notation that putative father was advised of his right to counsel and blood testing and that he waived those rights, and putative father signed report. Douglas v. Boykin (Ohio App. 12 Dist., 07-07-1997) 121 Ohio App.3d 140, 699 N.E.2d 123. Children Out-of-wedlock ⇔ 57

Transcript of hearing at which putative father waived right to counsel was not mandatory requirement for a valid waiver of counsel in juvenile paternity proceeding, where putative father did not request transcript. Douglas v. Boykin (Ohio App. 12 Dist., 07-07-1997) 121 Ohio App.3d 140, 699 N.E.2d 123. Children Out-of-wedlock ⇔ 57

Failure to request recording device for verbatim transcript in juvenile delinquency proceeding is not per se ineffective assistance of counsel, even when juvenile's liberty is at issue. In re Hannah (Ohio App. 8 Dist., 10-16-1995) 106 Ohio App.3d 766, 667 N.E.2d 76. Infants ⇔ 205

Regardless of trial strategy or decision to waive recording device in juvenile delinquency proceeding, on claim of ineffective assistance of counsel, burden is on juvenile to show that lawyer breached his duty to provide reasonable representation and to show that outcome of case would have been different but for breach. In re Hannah (Ohio App. 8 Dist., 10-16-1995) 106 Ohio App.3d 766, 667 N.E.2d 76. Infants ⇔ 205

A trial court's failure to make a record of an adjudicatory hearing in a stolen car delinquency case in accordance with the mandates of Juv R 37(A) and Juv R 40(D)(2) prevents a finding that an affirmative waiver of the constitutional right to counsel took place, and the trial court magistrate's journal entry, which is the only record of the adjudicatory hearing in question, fails to even minimally satisfy the requirements of Juv R 29 since the magistrate did not check the box indicating whether the juvenile admitted or denied the allegations of the complaint and whether counsel was waived; although the informal detention hearing journal entry sets forth that an express waiver of counsel took place, the journal entry is not adequate evidence of a knowing, voluntary and intelligent waiver of counsel. In re Ward (Ohio App. 8 Dist., Cuyahoga, 06-12-1997) No. 71245, 1997 WL 321492, Unreported.

6. Lack of record, effect

Trial court was not required to make record of its in camera interview with child, in proceeding in which permanent custody of child was granted to county department of children and family services; although department made request for in camera interview, at no time did any party request that interview be recorded, and, given the lack of such a request, court did not violate any procedural requirements pursuant to juvenile rule governing recording of proceedings. In re T.W. (Ohio App. 8 Dist., Cuyahoga, 10-13-2005) No. 85845, 2005-Ohio-5446, 2005 WL 2600663, Unreported, appeal not allowed 108 Ohio St.3d 1418, 841 N.E.2d 321, 2006-Ohio-179, reconsideration denied 108 Ohio St.3d 1513, 844 N.E.2d 857, 2006-Ohio-1329. Infants ⇔ 207

Juvenile court failed to comply with rule requiring court to make record of adjudicatory and dispositional proceedings in permanent child custody case, where transcript of audiotape recording of permanent custody hearing contained thousands of indications that audiotape was inaudible and parties could not correct transcript. In re C.S. (Ohio App. 9 Dist., Medina, 11-17-2004) No. 04CA0044, No. 04CA0045, 2004-Ohio-6078, 2004 WL 2600442, Unreported. Child Custody ⇔ 500

Rule providing that it is appellant's duty to see that the record, including the transcript, is filed with the appellate court does not excuse juvenile court's obligation to provide for the recording of the transcript of delinquency adjudication proceeding. In re A.F. (Ohio App. 8 Dist., Cuyahoga, 03-11-2004) No. 82509, 2004-Ohio-1119, 2004 WL 443096, Unreported. Infants ⇔ 203

Juvenile court's failure to follow requirement to provide record of delinquency adjudication proceeding mandated appellate reversal of delinquency adjudication. In re A.F. (Ohio App. 8 Dist., Cuyahoga, 03-11-2004) No. 82509, 2004-Ohio-1119, 2004 WL 443096, Unreported. Infants ⇔ 246

Guardian ad litem for the children was not prejudiced by the trial court's alleged failure to properly record custody proceedings incident to a dependency action, based on the absence of the record of the in camera interview with the children and significant amounts of inaudible testimony from trial; juvenile court adequately complied with the Juvenile Rules for creation of a record since there was no difficulty in understanding the development of the proceedings regarding custody of the children, the trial judge stated information obtained during the in camera interview with the children in its judgment entry, both parties presented the court with recorded evidence for review, and guardian failed to allege with specificity what evidence or prejudicial errors were contained in the inaudible testimony. In re Mitchell (Ohio App. 11 Dist., Lake, 08-01-2003) No. 2002-L-078, No. 2002-L-079, 2003-Ohio-4102, 2003 WL 21782611, Unreported. Child Custody ⇔ 923(1); Infants ⇔ 253

Juvenile court's failure to follow requirement to provide record or termination of parental rights hearing mandated reversal; although court taped hearing, the tape ended in middle of direct examination of mother. In re B.E. (Ohio App. 8 Dist., Cuyahoga, 07-24-2003) No. 81781, 2003-Ohio-3949, 2003 WL 21710762, Unreported, appeal allowed 100 Ohio St.3d 1470, 798 N.E.2d 406, 2003-Ohio-5772, affirmed 102 Ohio St.3d 388, 811 N.E.2d 76, 2004-Ohio-3361. Infants ⇔ 203; Infants ⇔ 246

Mother was not prejudiced, and thus her due process rights were not violated, when the trial court failed to make a record of two hearings, in child dependency proceeding; no evidence was presented at either hearing in which the trial court failed to make a record, and each of the hearings were conducted in order to grant a continuance. In re D.F. (Ohio App. 8 Dist., Cuyahoga, 06-19-2003) No. 81613, 2003-Ohio-3221, 2003 WL 21419537, Unreported. Constitutional Law ⇔ 274(5); Infants ⇔ 203

Trial court made complete record of dispositional hearing, in which county child services agency was awarded permanent custody of children, even though testimony of foster mother of one of children was not recorded, where parents and agency prepared statements of evidence under rule of appellate procedure which allowed for statement of evidence in situations where no report of evidence or proceedings at hearing or trial was made, and trial court settled differences in statements by approving, in its entirety, agency's statement. In re Myers (Ohio App. 4 Dist., Athens, 05-23-2003) No. 02CA50, 2003-Ohio-2776, 2003 WL 21246432, Unreported. Infants ⇔ 246

Note 6

Juvenile court's failure to record adjudicatory and dispositional hearings in delinquency case justified reversal of juvenile's adjudication and disposition. In re Estep (Ohio App. 4 Dist., Meigs, 06-26-2002) No. 01CA2, 2002-Ohio-6141, 2002 WL 31520351, Unreported. Infants ⇔ 203; Infants ⇔ 246

Remand is not required in every case in which juvenile court fails to comply with requirement that it make a record of adjudicatory and dispositional proceedings; it may be appropriate for appellant to prepare a statement of the evidence or proceedings from the best available means, including appellant's recollection. In re B.E. (Ohio, 07-14-2004) 102 Ohio St.3d 388, 811 N.E.2d 76, 2004-Ohio-3361. Infants ⇔ 246; Infants ⇔ 254

Justice dictated remand of case in which trial court had granted permanent custody of children to county department of children and family services, where entire proceeding was not recorded and neither trial counsel recollected the missing testimony. In re B.E. (Ohio, 07-14-2004) 102 Ohio St.3d 388, 811 N.E.2d 76, 2004-Ohio-3361. Infants ⇔ 254

When a juvenile court fails to comply with the requirement that it make a record of adjudicatory and dispositional proceedings, and appellant attempts but is unable to submit a statement of evidence or proceedings from the best available means to correct or supplement the record, the matter must be remanded to the juvenile court for a rehearing. In re B.E. (Ohio, 07-14-2004) 102 Ohio St.3d 388, 811 N.E.2d 76, 2004-Ohio-3361. Infants ⇔ 254

Trial court abused its discretion when it failed to make a record of juvenile's adjudicatory proceedings, as required by juvenile rule. In re Amos (Ohio App. 3 Dist., 09-22-2003) 154 Ohio App.3d 434, 797 N.E.2d 568, 2003-Ohio-5014. Infants ⇔ 203

Although proceedings before magistrate, ancillary to delinquency complaint and involving alleged violation of court order, should have been recorded, failure to record did not cause juvenile prejudice, as magistrate's detention order would have expired on its own once court proceeded to disposition on delinquency complaint, and juvenile did not argue that her rights were violated in any respect before the magistrate. In re Smith (Ohio App. 8 Dist., 03-26-2001) 142 Ohio App.3d 16, 753 N.E.2d 930. Infants ⇔ 203

Trial court's failure to make record of adjudicatory proceedings in delinquency case, as mandated by rule, warranted reversal and remand for new adjudicatory hearing. In re Collins (Ohio App. 8 Dist., 04-20-1998) 127 Ohio App.3d 278, 712 N.E.2d 798. Infants ⇔ 246; Infants ⇔ 253; Infants ⇔ 254

At the time of a juvenile's "admit" plea where there is no record made of the proceeding there is no record for the judge to review in determining whether the juvenile's motion to withdraw his plea and vacate his sentence should be granted; as a result, a conviction for operating a motor vehicle under the influence of alcohol after underage consumption is vacated with instructions to conduct a new adjudicatory hearing which is properly recorded. In re L.D. (Ohio App. 8 Dist., Cuyahoga, 12-13-2001) No. 78750, 2001 WL 1612114, Unreported.

Juvenile courts must strictly comply with the requirement in amended Juv R 37 and failure to record adjudicatory or dispositional hearings contrary to that rule invalidates a juvenile's plea regardless of whatever information may be contained in the rest of the court's paperwork. Matter of Dikun (Ohio App. 11 Dist., Trumbull, 11-28-1997) No. 96-T-5558, 1997 WL 752630, Unreported.

Complete lack of any record of adjudicatory and dispositional hearings before the magistrate required reversal of juvenile's delinquency adjudication; missing record concerned waiver of counsel and admission to complaint, and lack of record prevented finding that magistrate complied with juvenile procedure rule requiring courts to make every effort to avoid the use of formal court proceedings in cases involving children. In re L.B. (Ohio App. 8 Dist., Cuyahoga, 07-25-2002) No. 79370, No. 79942, 2002-Ohio-3767, 2002 WL 1729905, Unreported. Infants ⇔ 254

7. Retention of record; time limitations

Delinquency proceeding would be remanded for limited purpose of findings of fact by juvenile court as to whether juvenile's waiver of his right to trial at the time of his admission to charged offense was knowingly, voluntarily, and intelligently given, where juvenile court made recording of proceeding in compliance with juvenile rule, that recording was subsequently destroyed after period of time prescribed by rule of superintendence had elapsed, and juvenile made no attempt on appeal to reconstruct the record. In re Raypole (Ohio App. 12 Dist., Fayette, 03-10-2003) No. CA2002-01-001, No. CA2002-01-002, 2003-Ohio-1066, 2003 WL 928976, Unreported. Infants ⇔ 254

Absence of a recording or transcript of delinquency adjudication did not require a reversal on appeal filed more than three years after that adjudication; court reporter's certificate indicated a recording was made of that proceeding in compliance with juvenile rule, and applicable rule of superintendence did not require retention of that recording for three years. In re Raypole (Ohio App. 12 Dist., Fayette, 03-10-2003) No. CA2002-01-001, No. CA2002-01-002, 2003-Ohio-1066, 2003 WL 928976, Unreported. Infants ⇔ 246

Juv R 38 Voluntary surrender of custody

(A) Temporary custody

(1) A person with custody of a child may enter into an agreement with any public or private children services agency giving the agency temporary custody for a period of up to thirty days without the approval of the juvenile court. The agency may request the court to grant a thirty day extension of the original agreement. The court may grant the original extension if it determines the extension to be in the best interest of the child. A case plan shall be filed at the same time the request for extension is filed. At the expiration of the original thirty day extension period, the agency may request the court to grant an additional thirty day extension. The court may grant the additional extension if it determines the extension is in the child's best interest. The agency shall file an updated case plan at the same time it files the request for additional extension. At the expiration of the additional thirty day extension period, or at the expiration of the original thirty day extension period if no additional thirty day extension was requested, the agency shall either return the child to the custodian or file a complaint requesting temporary or permanent custody and a case plan.

(2) Notwithstanding division (A)(1) of this rule, the agreement may be for a period of sixty days if executed solely for the purpose of obtaining the adoption of a child less than six months of age. The agency may request the court to extend the temporary custody agreement for thirty days. A case plan shall be filed at the same time the request for extension is filed. At the expiration of the thirty day extension, the agency shall either return the child to the child's custodian or file a complaint with the court requesting temporary or permanent custody and a case plan.

(B) Permanent custody

(1) A person with custody of a child may make an agreement with court approval surrendering the child into the permanent custody of a public children service agency or private child placing agency. A public children service agency shall request and a private child placing agency may request the juvenile court of the county in which the child had residence or legal settlement to approve the permanent surrender agreement. The court may approve the agreement if it determines it to be in the best interest of the child. The agency requesting the approval shall file a case plan at the same time it files its request for approval of the permanent surrender agreement.

(2) An agreement for the surrender of permanent custody of a child to a private service agency is not required to be approved by the court if the agreement is executed solely for the purpose of obtaining an adoption of a child who is less than six months of age on the date of the execution of the agreement.

One year after the agreement is entered and every subsequent twelve months after that date, the court shall schedule a review hearing if a final decree of adoption has not been entered for a child who is the subject of an agreement for the surrender of permanent custody.

(Adopted eff. 7–1–94)

Staff Notes

1994:

Rule 38 Voluntary Surrender of Custody

Prior to July 1, 1994, this rule was reserved. The 1994 amendment implements the provisions of Revised Code 5103.15 as amended by S.B. 89, regarding the procedure for making voluntary agreements of temporary custody to a public or private agency where extensions are requested.

Pursuant to the above-referenced statute, Juv. R. 38(A) provides that requests for extension of voluntary surrenders of custody must be accompanied by an updated case plan and the court may grant the extension if it determines the extension to be in the best interest of the child. Two such extensions may be granted for up to sixty days. If the agency desires a further extension, a new complaint for temporary or permanent custody must be filed. An agreement for temporary custody may be for sixty days if executed solely for the purpose of obtaining the adoption of a child less than six months of age.

Juv. R. 38(B) sets out procedures for the voluntary surrender of permanent custody. Agreements for permanent custody must have the approval of the juvenile court of the county in which the child resides or has legal settlement. Then, on an annual basis until a final decree of adoption is entered, the court must conduct a review hearing of the agreement.

Editor's Comment

Juv R 38, added to the Juvenile Rules in 1994, is taken from 5103.15.

Division (A) describes the process for entering into agreements for temporary custody. The term "agreement for temporary custody" is defined in Juv R 2(C) and 2151.011(B)(17).

Division (B) describes the process for entering into agreements for surrendering permanent custody. The term "permanent surrender" is defined in Juv R 2(Z) and 2151.011(B)(21).

Research References

Encyclopedias

OH Jur. 3d Family Law § 1431, Agreement for Temporary Custody—Extensions.

OH Jur. 3d Family Law § 1433, Agreement to Surrender Permanent Custody.

Treatises and Practice Aids

Giannelli & Yeomans, Ohio Juvenile Law § 11:3, Temporary Custody Agreements.

Giannelli & Yeomans, Ohio Juvenile Law § 11:4, Extension of Temporary Custody Agreements.

Giannelli & Yeomans, Ohio Juvenile Law § 11:5, Permanent Custody Agreements.

Giannelli & Yeomans, Ohio Juvenile Law § 33:11, Child Custody Agency Commitment—Juvenile Court Dispositional Review.

Juv R 39 Out of county removal hearings

(A) Notice of removal hearing

Upon the filing of a removal action, the court in which the complaint is filed shall immediately contact the court that issued the original dispositional order for information necessary for service of summons and issuance of notice of the removal hearing. The court that issued the original dispositional order shall respond within five days after receiving the request.

Summons shall issue pursuant to Juv. R. 15 and 16.

Notice of the removal hearing shall be sent by first class mail, as evidenced by a certificate of mailing filed with the clerk of court, to the following, not otherwise summoned, at least five days before the hearing:

(1) The court issuing the dispositional order;

(2) The guardian *ad litem* for the child;

(3) Counsel for the child;

(4) The placing entity;

(5) The custodial entity;

(6) The complainant;

(7) The guardian *ad litem* and counsel presently representing the child in the court that issued the original dispositional order;

(8) Any other persons the court determines to be appropriate.

(B) Removal hearing

The removal hearing shall be held not later than thirty days after service of summons is obtained. If, after the removal hearing, the court grants relief in favor of the complainant, the court shall send written notice of such relief to the juvenile court that issued the original dispositional order.

(Adopted eff. 7–1–98)

Staff Notes

1998:

Rule 39 Out-of-county removal hearings

The 1998 addition of Juv. R. 39 was intended to establish procedures for removal actions, as defined in Juv. R. 2(EE), which also was added by the 1998 amendments. Pursuant to Juv. R. 15(A), as in other cases within the purview of the Juvenile Rules, a summons must be issued to "the child, the parents, guardian, custodian, and any other persons who appear to the court to be proper or necessary parents." Juv. R. 39(A) includes a list of other entities and persons whose presence at the removal hearing may not be necessary, but who should be aware that the hearing will be conducted. This list includes, but is not limited to, the guardian *ad litem* and counsel for the child from the original proceeding in which the dispositional order was made, resulting in the child's out-of-county foster home placement.

Pursuant to Juv. R. 39(B), the time requirements for the scheduling of the hearing are predicated on service of summons.

Additional 1998 amendments governing removal actions were made to Juv. R. 2(EE), 4(B), 10(A), 11(B), 15(B), and 29(A) and (E).

Research References

Treatises and Practice Aids

Giannelli & Yeomans, Ohio Juvenile Law § 13:2, Jurisdictional Requirements.

Giannelli & Yeomans, Ohio Juvenile Law § 13:4, Summons and Notice.

Giannelli & Yeomans, Ohio Juvenile Law § 13:5, Hearing.

Juv R 40 Magistrates

(A) Appointment

The court may appoint one or more magistrates who shall be attorneys at law admitted to practice in Ohio. A magistrate appointed under this rule also may serve as a magistrate under Crim.R. 19. The court shall not appoint as a magistrate any person who has contemporaneous responsibility for working with, or supervising the behavior of, children who are subject to dispositional orders of the appointing court or any other juvenile court.

(B) Compensation

The compensation of magistrates shall be fixed by the court, and no part of the compensation shall be taxed as costs.

(C) Authority

(1) *Scope.* To assist juvenile courts of record and pursuant to reference under Juv.R. 40(D)(1), magistrates are authorized, subject to the terms of the relevant reference, to do any of the following:

(a) Determine any motion in any case, except a case involving the determination of a child's status as a serious youthful offender;

(b) Conduct the trial of any case that will not be tried to a jury, except the adjudication of a case against an alleged serious youthful offender;

(c) Upon unanimous written consent of the parties, preside over the trial of any case that will be tried to a jury; except the adjudication of a case against an alleged serious youthful offender;

(d) Exercise any other authority specifically vested in magistrates by statute and consistent with this rule.

(2) *Regulation of proceedings.* In performing the responsibilities described in Juv.R. 40(C)(1), magistrates are authorized, subject to the terms of the relevant reference, to regulate all proceedings as if by the court and to do everything necessary for the efficient performance of those responsibilities, including but not limited to, the following:

(a) Issuing subpoenas for the attendance of witnesses and the production of evidence;

(b) Ruling upon the admissibility of evidence;

(c) Putting witnesses under oath and examining them;

(d) Calling the parties to the action and examining them under oath;

(e) When necessary to obtain the presence of an alleged contemnor in cases involving direct or indirect contempt of court, issuing an attachment for the alleged contemnor and setting the type, amount, and any conditions of bail pursuant to Crim.R. 46;

(f) Imposing, subject to Juv.R. 40(D)(8), appropriate sanctions for civil or criminal contempt committed in the presence of the magistrate.

(D) Proceedings in matters referred to magistrates

(1) *Reference by court of record.*

(a) *Purpose and method* A court may, for one or more of the purposes described in Juv.R. 40(C)(1), refer a particular case or matter or a category of cases or matters to a magistrate by a specific or general order of reference or by rule.

(b) *Limitation.* A court may limit a reference by specifying or limiting the magistrate's powers, including but not limited to, directing the magistrate to determine only particular issues, directing the magistrate to perform particular responsibilities, directing the magistrate to receive and report evidence only, fixing the time and place for beginning and closing any hearings, or fixing the time for filing any magistrate's decision on the matter or matters referred.

(2) *Magistrate's order; motion to set aside magistrate's order.*

(a) *Magistrate's order.*

(i) *Nature of order.* Subject to the terms of the relevant reference, a magistrate may enter orders without judicial approval if necessary to regulate the proceedings and if not dispositive of a claim or defense of a party.

(ii) *Form, filing, and service of magistrate's order.* A magistrate's order shall be in writing, identified as a magistrate's order in the caption, signed by the magistrate, filed with the clerk, and served on all parties or their attorneys.

(iii) *Magistrate's order include.* A magistrate's order includes any of the following:

(A) Pretrial proceedings under Civ.R. 16;

(B) Discovery proceedings under Civ.R. 26 to 37, Juv.R. 24, and Juv.R. 25;

(C) Appointment of an attorney or guardian ad litem pursuant to Juv.R. 4 and Juv.R. 29(B)(4);

(D) Taking a child into custody pursuant to Juv.R. 6;

(E) Detention hearings pursuant to Juv.R. 7;

(F) Temporary orders pursuant to Juv.R. 13;

(G) Extension of temporary orders pursuant to Juv.R. 14;

(H) Summons and warrants pursuant to Juv.R. 15;

(I) Preliminary conferences pursuant to Juv.R. 21;

(J) Continuances pursuant to Juv.R. 23;

(K) Deposition orders pursuant to Juv.R. 27(B)(3);

(L) Orders for social histories, physical and mental examinations pursuant to Juv.R. 32;

(M) Proceedings upon application for the issuance of a temporary protection order as authorized by law;

(N) Other orders as necessary to regulate the proceedings.

(b) *Motion to set aside magistrate's order.* Any party may file a motion with the court to set aside a magistrate's order. The motion shall state the moving party's reasons with particularity and shall be filed not later than ten days after the magistrate's order is filed. The pendency of a motion to set aside does not stay the effectiveness of the magistrate's order, though the magistrate or the court may by order stay the effectiveness of a magistrate's order.

(3) *Magistrate's decision; objections to magistrate's decision.*

(a) *Magistrate's decision.*

(i) *When required.* Subject to the terms of the relevant reference, a magistrate shall prepare a magistrate's decision respecting any matter referred under Juv.R. 40(D)(1).

(ii) *Findings of fact and conclusions of law.* Subject to the terms of the relevant reference, a magistrate's decision may be general unless findings of fact and conclusions of law are timely requested by a party or otherwise required by law. A request for findings of fact and conclusions of law shall be made before the entry of a magistrate's decision or within seven days after the filing of a magistrate's decision. If a request for findings of fact and conclusions of law is timely made, the magistrate may require any or all of the parties to submit proposed findings of fact and conclusions of law.

(iii) *Form; filing, and service of magistrate's decision.* A magistrate's decision shall be in writing, identified as a magistrate's decision in the caption, signed by the magistrate, filed with the clerk, and served on all parties or their attorneys no later than three days after the decision is filed. A magistrate's decision shall indicate conspicuously that a party shall not assign as error on appeal the court's adoption of any factual finding or legal conclusion, whether or not specifically designated as a finding of fact or conclusion of law under Juv.R. 40(D)(3)(a)(ii), unless the party timely and specifically objects to that factual finding or legal conclusion as required by Juv.R. 40(D)(3)(b).

(b) *Objections to magistrate's decision.*

(i) *Time for filing.* A party may file written objections to a magistrate's decision within fourteen days of the filing of the decision, whether or not the court has adopted the decision during that fourteen-day period as permitted by Juv.R. 40(D)(4)(e)(i). If any party timely files objections, any other party may also file objections not later than ten days after the first objections are filed. If a party makes a timely request for findings of fact and conclusions of law, the time for filing objections begins to run when the magistrate files a decision that includes findings of fact and conclusions of law.

(ii) *Specificity of objection.* An objection to a magistrate's decision shall be specific and state with particularity all grounds for objection.

(iii) *Objection to magistrate's factual finding; transcript or affidavit.* An objection to a factual finding, whether or not specifically designated as a finding of fact under Juv.R. 40(D)(3)(a)(ii), shall be supported by a transcript of all the evidence submitted to the magistrate relevant to that finding or an affidavit of that evidence if a transcript is not available. With leave of court, alternative technology or manner of reviewing the relevant evidence may be considered. The objecting party shall file the transcript or affidavit with the court within thirty days after filing objections unless the court extends the time in writing for preparation of the transcript or other good cause. If a party files timely objections prior to the date on which a transcript is prepared, the party may seek leave of court to supplement the objections.

(iv) *Waiver of right to assign adoption by court as error on appeal.* Except for a claim of plain error, a party shall not assign as error on appeal the court's adoption of any factual finding or legal conclusion, whether or not specifically designated as a finding of fact or conclusion of law under Juv.R. 40(D)(3)(a)(ii), unless the party has objected to that finding or conclusion as required by Juv.R. 40(D)(3)(b).

(4) *Action of court on magistrate's decision and on any objections to magistrate's decision; entry of judgment or interim order by court.*

(a) *Action of court required.* A magistrate's decision is not effective unless adopted by the court.

(b) *Action on magistrate's decision.* Whether or not objections are timely filed, a court may adopt or reject a magistrate's decision in whole or in part, with or without modification. A court may hear a previously-referred matter, take additional evidence, or return a matter to a magistrate.

(c) *If no objections are filed.* If no timely objections are filed, the court may adopt a magistrate's decision, unless it determines that there is an error of law or other defect evident on the face of the magistrate's decision.

(d) *Action on objections.* If one or more objections to a magistrate's decision are timely filed, the court shall rule on those objections. In ruling on objections, the court shall undertake an independent review as to the objected matters to ascertain that the magistrate has properly determined the factual issues and appropriately applied the law. Before so ruling, the court may hear additional evidence but may refuse to do so unless the objecting party demonstrates that the party could not, with reasonable diligence, have produced that evidence for consideration by the magistrate.

(e) *Entry of judgment or interim order by court.* A court that adopts, rejects, or modifies a magistrate's decision shall also enter a judgment or interim order.

(i) *Judgment.* The court may enter a judgment either during the fourteen days permitted by Juv.R. 40(D)(3)(b)(i) for the filing of objections to a magistrate's decision or after the fourteen days have expired. If the court enters a judgment during the fourteen days permitted by Juv.R. 40(D)(3)(b)(i) for the filing of objections, the timely filing of objections to the magistrate's decision shall operate as an automatic stay of execution of the judgment until the court disposes of those objections and vacates, modifies, or adheres to the judgment previously entered.

(ii) *Interim order.* The court may enter an interim order on the basis of a magistrate's decision without waiting for or ruling on timely objections by the parties where immediate relief is justified. The timely filing of objections does not stay the execution of an interim order, but an interim order shall not extend more than twenty-eight days from the date of entry, subject to extension by the court in increments of twenty-eight additional days for good cause shown.

(5) *Extension of time.* For good cause shown, the court shall allow a reasonable extension of time for a party to file a motion to set aside a magistrate's order or file objections to a magistrate's decision. "Good cause" includes, but is not limited to, a failure by the clerk to timely serve the party seeking the extension with the magistrate's order or decision.

(6) *Disqualification of a magistrate.* Disqualification of a magistrate for bias or other cause is within the discretion of the court and may be sought by motion filed with the court.

(7) *Recording of proceedings before a magistrate.* Except as otherwise provided by law, all proceedings before a magistrate shall be recorded in accordance with procedures established by the court.

(8) *Contempt in the presence of a magistrate.*

(a) *Contempt order.* Contempt sanctions under Juv.R. 40(C)(2)(f) may be imposed only by a written order that recites the facts and certifies that the magistrate saw or heard the conduct constituting contempt.

(b) *Filing and provision of copies of contempt order.* A contempt order shall be filed and copies provided forthwith by the clerk to the appropriate judge of the court and to the subject of the order.

(c) *Review of contempt order by court; bail.* The subject of a contempt order may by motion obtain immediate review by a judge. A judge or the magistrate entering the contempt order may set bail pending judicial review of the order.

(Adopted eff. 7–1–72; amended eff. 7–1–75, 7–1–85, 7–1–92, 7–1–95, 7–1–98, 7–1–01, 7–1–03, 7–1–06)

Uncodified Law

2002 H 393, § 3, eff. 7–5–02, reads:

The General Assembly hereby encourages the Supreme Court to amend the Juvenile Rules to make clear that, while a magistrate may not try or sentence a case involving an alleged or adjudicated serious youthful offender, a magistrate may handle ministerial duties in that type of case, including arraignment and setting bail.

Historical and Statutory Notes

Amendment Note: The 7–1–06 amendment rewrote this rule, which prior thereto read:

"(A) Appointment

"The court may appoint one or more magistrates. Magistrates first appointed on or after the effective date of this amendment shall be attorneys admitted to practice in Ohio. A magistrate appointed under this rule also may serve as a magistrate under Crim. R. 19. The court shall not appoint as a magistrate any person who has contemporaneous responsibility for working with, or supervising the behavior of, children who are subject to dispositional orders of the appointing court or any other juvenile court.

"(B) Compensation

"The compensation of the magistrate shall be fixed by the court and no part of the compensation shall be taxed as costs.

"(C) Reference and powers

"(1) *Order of reference.*

"(a) The court by order may refer any of the following to a magistrate:

"(i) pretrial or post-judgment motion or proceeding in any case, except a case involving the determination of a child's status as a serious youthful offender;

"(ii) the trial of any case not to be tried to a jury, except the adjudication of a case against an alleged serious youthful offender;

"(iii) upon the unanimous written consent of the parties, the trial of any case to be tried to a jury, except the adjudication of a case against an alleged serious youthful offender.

"Except as provided in division (C)(1)(a)(iii) of this rule, the effect of a magistrate's order or decision is the same regardless of whether the parties have consented to the order of reference.

"(b) An order of reference may be specific to a particular case or proceeding or may refer categories of motions, cases, or proceedings.

"(c) The order of reference to a magistrate may do all of the following:

"(i) Specify the magistrate's powers;

"(ii) Direct the magistrate to report only upon particular issues, perform particular acts, or receive and report evidence only;

"(iii) Fix the time and place for beginning and closing the hearings and for the filing of the magistrate's decision or order.

"(2) *General powers*

"Subject to the specifications stated in the order of reference, the magistrate shall regulate all proceedings in every hearing as if by the court and do all acts and take all measures necessary or property for the efficient performance of the magistrate's duties under the order. The magistrate may do all of the following:

"(a) Issue subpoenas for the attendance of witnesses and the production of evidence;

"(b) Rule upon the admissibility of evidence, unless otherwise directed by the order of reference;

"(c) Put witnesses under oath and examine them;

"(d) Call the parties to the action and examine them under oath.

"(e) In cases involving direct or indirect contempt of court, when necessary to obtain the alleged contemnor's presence for hearing, issue an attachment for the alleged contemnor and set bail to secure the alleged contemnor's appearance. In determining bail, the magistrate shall consider the conditions of release prescribed in Crim. R. 46.

"(3) *Power to enter orders*

"(a) **Pretrial orders.** Unless otherwise specified in the order of reference, the magistrate may enter orders effective without judicial approval in pretrial proceedings under Civ. R. 16, in discovery proceedings under Civ. R. 26 to 37, Juv. R. 24 and 25, and in the following situations:

"(i) Appointment of an attorney or guardian ad litem pursuant to Juv. R. 4 and 29(B)(4);

"(ii) Taking a child into custody pursuant to Juv. R. 6;

"(iii) Detention hearings pursuant to Juv. R. 7;

"(iv) Temporary orders pursuant to Juv. R. 13;

"(v) Extension of temporary orders pursuant to Juv. R. 14;

"(vi) Summons and warrants pursuant to Juv. R. 15;

"(vii) Preliminary conferences pursuant to Juv. R. 21;

"(viii) Continuances pursuant to Juv. R. 23;

"(ix) Deposition orders pursuant to Juv. R. 27(B)(3);

"(x) Orders for social histories, physical and mental examinations pursuant to Juv. R. 32;

"(xi) Other orders as necessary to regulate the proceedings.

"(b) **Appeal of pretrial orders.** Any person may appeal to the court from any order of a magistrate entered under division (C)(3)(a) of this rule by filing a motion to set the order aside, stating the party's objections with particularity. The motion shall be filed no later than ten days after the magistrate's order is entered. The pendency of a motion to set aside does not stay the effectiveness of the magistrate's order unless the magistrate or the court grants a stay.

"(c) **Contempt in the magistrate's presence.** In cases of contempt in the presence of the magistrate, the magistrate may impose an appropriate civil or criminal contempt sanction. Contempt sanctions under division (C)(3)(c) of this rule may be imposed only by a written order that recites the facts and certifies that the magistrate saw or heard the conduct constituting contempt. The contempt order shall be filed and a copy provided by the clerk to the appropriate judge of the court forthwith. The contemnor may by motion obtain immediate review of the magistrate's contempt order by a judge, or the judge or magistrate may set bail pending judicial review.

"(d) **Other orders.** Unless prohibited by the order of reference, magistrates shall continue to be authorized to enter orders when authority to enter orders is specifically conveyed by statute or rule to magistrates or referees.

"(e) **Form of magistrate's orders.** All orders of a magistrate shall be in writing, signed by the magistrate, identified as a magistrate's order in the caption, filed with the clerk, and served on all parties or their attorneys.

"**(D) Proceedings**

"(1) All proceedings before the magistrate shall be in accordance with these rules and any applicable statutes, as if before the court.

"(2) Except as otherwise provided by law and notwithstanding the provisions of Juv. R. 37, all proceedings before magistrates shall be recorded in accordance with procedures established by the court.

"**(E) Decisions in referred matters.**

"Unless specifically required by the order of reference, a magistrate is not required to prepare any report other than the magistrate's decision. Except as to matters on which magistrates are permitted by division (C)(3) of this rule to enter orders without judicial approval, all matters referred to magistrates shall be decided as follows:

"(1) *Magistrate's decision.* The magistrate promptly shall conduct all proceedings necessary for decision of referred matters. The magistrate shall then prepare, sign, and file a magistrate's decision of the referred matter with the clerk, who shall serve copies on all parties or their attorneys.

"(2) *Findings of fact and conclusions of law.* If any party makes a request for findings of fact and conclusions of law under Civ. R. 52 or if findings and conclusions are otherwise required by law or by the order of reference, the magistrate's decision shall include findings of fact and conclusions of law. If the request under Civ. R. 52 is made after the magistrate's decision is filed, the magistrate shall include the findings of fact and conclusions of law in an amended magistrate's decision. A magistrate's findings of fact and conclusions of law shall indicate conspicuously that a party shall not assign as error on appeal the court's adoption of any finding of fact or conclusion of law unless the party timely and specifically objects to that finding or conclusion as required by Juv. R. 40(E)(3).

"(3) *Objections.*

"(a) **Time for filing.** A party may file written objections to a magistrate's decision within fourteen days of the filing of the decision, regardless of whether the court has adopted the decision pursuant to Juv. R. 40(E)(4)(c). If any party timely files objections, any other party also may file objections not later than ten days after the first objections are filed. If a party makes a request for findings of fact and conclusions of law under Civ. R. 52, the time for filing objections begins to run when the magistrate files a decision including findings of fact and conclusions of law.

"(b) **Form of objections.** Objections shall be specific and state with particularity the grounds of objection.

"(c) **Objections to magistrate's findings of fact.** If the parties stipulate in writing that the magistrate's findings of fact shall be final, they may only object to errors of law in the magistrate's decision. Any objection to a finding of fact shall be supported by a transcript of all the evidence submitted to the magistrate relevant to that fact or an affidavit of the evidence if a transcript is not available.

"(d) **Waiver of right to assign adoption by court as error on appeal.** A party shall not assign as error on appeal the court's adoption of any finding of fact or conclusion of law unless the party has objected to that finding or conclusion under this rule.

"(4) *Court's action on magistrate's decision.*

"(a) **When effective.** The magistrate's decision shall be effective when adopted by the court as noted in the journal record. The court may adopt the magistrate's decision if no written objections are filed unless it determines that there is an error of law or other defect on the face of the magistrate's decision.

"(b) **Disposition of objections.** The court shall rule on any objections. The court may adopt, reject, or modify the magistrate's decision, hear additional evidence, recommit the matter to the magistrate with instructions, or hear the matter itself. In delinquency, unruly, or juvenile traffic offender cases, the court may hear additional evidence or hear the matter itself only with the consent of the child. The court may refuse to consider additional evidence proffered upon objections unless the objecting party demonstrates that with reasonable diligence the party could not have produced that evidence for the magistrate's consideration.

"(c) **Permanent and interim orders.** The court may adopt a magistrate's decision and enter judgment without waiting for timely objections by the parties, but the filing of timely written objections shall operate as an automatic stay of execution of that judgment until the court disposes of those objections and vacates, modifies, or adheres to the judgment previously entered. The court may make an interim order on the basis of a magistrate's decision without waiting for or ruling on timely objections by the parties where immediate relief is justified. An interim order shall not be subject to the automatic stay caused by the filing of timely objections. An interim order shall not extend more than twenty-eight days from the date of its entry unless, within that time and for good cause shown, the court extends the interim order for an additional twenty-eight days."

Amendment Note: The 7-1-01 amendment inserted "except a case involving the determination of a child's status as a serious youthful offender;" at the end of division (C)(1)(a)(i); and inserted "except the adjudication of a case against an alleged serious youthful offender" at the end of divisions (C)(1)(a)(ii) and (C)(1)(a)(iii).

Amendment Note: The 7-1-98 amendment substituted "Disposition" for "Consideration" in the title of division (E)(4)(b); substituted the first sentence in division (E)(4)(b) for "Except as provided herein, upon consideration of any objections,"; and made other nonsubstantive changes.

Amendment Note: The 7-1-95 amendment substantially rewrote this rule to pertain to magistrates instead of referees; see *Baldwin's Ohio Legislative Service*, 1995, page 7/R-55.

Staff Notes

Rule 40 has been reorganized in an effort to make it more helpful to bench and bar and reflective of developments since the rule was last substantially revised effective July 1, 1995. The relatively-few significant changes included in the reorganization are noted below.

Rule 40(A) Appointment

Juv.R. 40(A) is similar to former Juv.R. 40(A), except that it now requires all magistrates appointed pursuant to the rule to be attorneys admitted to practice in Ohio. The former rule allowed magistrates first appointed prior to July 1, 1995 to be nonattorneys.

Rule 40(B) Compensation

Juv.R. 40(B) is the same as former Juv.R. 40(B).

Rule 40(C) Authority

Juv.R. 40(C) is drawn largely from former Juv.R. 40(C)(1) and (2) and reflects the admonition of the Supreme Court that "a [magistrate's] oversight of an issue or issues, or even an entire trial, is not a *substitute* for the judicial functions but only an *aid* to them." Hartt v. Munobe (1993), 67 Ohio St.3d 3, 6, 1993–Ohio–177, 615 N.E.2d 617 (emphases added). Juv.R. 40(C) specifies that juvenile court magistrates may determine motions and conduct trials but may not preside over the determination or trial of a serious youthful offender.

Rule 40(D) Proceedings in matters referred to magistrates

Juv.R. 40(D)(1) through (4) treat each of the steps that potentially occur if a magistrate participates: (1) reference to a magistrate; (2) magistrate's orders and motions to set aside magistrate's orders; (3) magistrate's decisions and objections to magistrate's decisions; and (4) action of the court on magistrate's decisions and on any objections to magistrate's decisions and entry of judgment or interim order by the court. Juv.R. 40(D)(5) through (8) deal with good cause extensions of time, disqualification of a magistrate, recording of proceedings before a magistrate, and contempt in the presence of a magistrate.

Reference by court of record

Juv.R. 40(D)(1), unlike former Juv.R. 40(C)(1)(b), specifically authorizes reference of types of matters by rule as well as by a specific or general order of reference. In so doing, it recognizes existing practice in some courts. See, e.g., Loc.R. 99.02, Franklin Cty. Ct. of Common Pleas; Loc. R. 23(B), Hamilton Cty. Ct. of Common Pleas; *State ex rel. Nalls v. Russo*, 96 Ohio St.3d 410, 412–13, 2002–Ohio–4907 at ¶¶ 20–24, 775 N.E. 2d 522; *Davis v. Reed* (Aug. 31, 2000), 8th Dist. App. No. 76712, 2000 WL 1231462 at *2 (citing *White v. White* (1977), 50 Ohio App.2d 263, 266–268, 362 N.E.2d 1013), and *Partridge v. Partridge* (Aug. 27, 1999), 2nd Dist. App. No. 98 CA 38, 1999 WL 945046 at *2, (treating a local rule of the Greene Cty. Ct. of Common Pleas, Dom. Rel. Div., as a standing order of reference).

Magistrate's order; motion to set aside magistrate's order

Juv.R. 40(D)(2)(a)(i) generally authorizes a magistrate to enter orders without judicial approval if necessary to regulate the proceedings and, adapting language from Crim.R. 19(B)(5)(a), if "not dispositive of a claim or defense of a party." The new language removes the arguably limiting title of former Juv.R. 40(C)(3)(a) ["Pretrial orders"] and is intended to more accurately reflect proper and existing practice. This language is not intended to narrow the power of a magistrate to enter orders without judicial approval. Juv.R. 40(D)(2)(a) lists certain actions that are included as magistrate orders. These are similar to those listed in former Juv.R. 40(C)(3), with the addition of division (D)(2)(a)(iii)(M) regarding the issuance of a temporary protection order. However, consistent with the admonition in *Hartt, supra*, any temporary protection order issued as a result of such proceedings must be signed by a judge.

Juv.R. 40(D)(2)(b) replaces language in former Juv.R. 40(C)(3)(b), which purported to authorize "[a]ny person" to "appeal to the court" from any order of a magistrate "by filing a motion to set the order aside." The new language refers to the appropriate challenge to a magistrate's order as solely a "motion to set aside" the order. Juv.R. 40(D)(2)(b) likewise limits the authorization to file a motion to "any *party*," though an occasional nonparty may be entitled to file a motion to set aside a magistrate's order. Sentence two of Juv.R. 40(D)(2)(b) changes the trigger for the ten days permitted to file a motion to set aside a magistrate's order from entry of the order to filing of the order, as the latter date is definite and more easily available to counsel. Juv.R. 40(D)(2)(b) retains the provision of former Juv.R. 40(C)(3)(b) that the pendency of a motion to set aside a magistrate's order does not stay the effectiveness of the magistrate's order, although the magistrate or the court, by order, may stay the magistrate's order.

Magistrate's decision; objections to magistrate's decision

Juv.R. 40(D)(3) prescribes procedures for preparation of a magistrate's decision and for any objections to a magistrate's decision.

Juv.R. 40(D)(3)(a)(ii), unlike former Juv.R. 40(E)(2), adapts language from Civ.R. 52 rather than simply referring to Civ.R. 52. The change is intended to make clear that, e.g., a request for findings of fact and conclusions of law in a referred matter should be directed to the magistrate rather than to the court. Juv.R. 40(D)(3)(a)(ii) explicitly authorizes a magistrate's decision, subject to the terms of the relevant reference, to be general absent a timely request for findings of fact and conclusions of law or a provision of law that provides otherwise. Occasional decisions under former Juv.R. 40 said as much. See, *e.g., In re Chapman* (Apr. 21, 1997), 12th Dist. App. No. CA96–07–127, 1997 WL 194879 at *2; *Burke v. Brown*, 4th Dist. App. No. 01CA731, 2002–Ohio–6164 at ¶ 21; and *Rush v. Schlagetter* (Apr. 15, 1997), 4th Dist. App. No. 96CA2215, 1997 WL 193169 at *3. For a table of sections of the Ohio Revised Code that purport to make findings of fact by judicial officers mandatory in specified circumstances, see 2 Klein–Darling, Ohio Civil Practice § 52–4, 2002 Pocket Part at 136 (West Group 1997).

Juv.R. 40(D)(3)(a)(iii) now requires that the magistrate's decision be served on the parties or their attorneys no later than three days after the decision was filed. The former rule contained no specific time requirement. The provision further requires that a magistrate's decision include a conspicuous warning of the waiver rule prescribed by amended Juv.R. 40(D)(3)(b)(iv). The latter rule now provides that a party shall not assign as error on appeal a court's adoption of any factual finding or legal conclusion of a magistrate, whether or not specifically designated as a finding of fact or conclusion of law under Juv.R. 40(D)(3)(a)(ii), unless that party has objected to that finding or conclusion as required by Juv.R. 40(D)(3)(b). While the prior waiver rule, prescribed by former Juv.R. 40(E)(3)(b) (effective July 1, 1995) and former Juv.R. 40(E)(3)(d) (effective July 1, 2003), arguably applied only to findings of fact or conclusions of law specifically designated as such, the amended waiver rule applies to any factual finding or legal conclusion in a magistrate's decision and the required warning is broadened accordingly.

Juv.R. 40(D)(3)(b)(i) retains the fourteen-day time for filing written objections to a magistrate's decision. While the rule continues to authorize filing of objections by a "party," it has been held that a non-party attorney can properly object to a magistrate's decision imposing sanctions on the attorney. *All Climate Heating & Cooling, Inc. v. Zee Properties, Inc.* (May 17, 2001), 10th Dist. App. No. 00AP–1141, 2001 WL 521408 at *3.

Sentence one of Juv.R. 40(D)(3)(b)(iii) requires that an objection to a factual finding in a magistrate's decision, whether or not specifically designated as a finding of fact under Juv.R. 40(D)(3)(a)(ii), be supported by a transcript of all the evidence submitted to the magistrate relevant to that fact or by an affidavit of that evidence if a transcript is not available. The Supreme Court has prescribed the consequences on appeal of failure to supply the requisite transcript or affidavit as follows: (1) "appellate review of the court's findings is limited to whether the trial court abused its discretion in adopting the [magistrate's decision]" and (2) "the appellate court is precluded from considering the transcript of the hearing submitted with the appellate record." *State ex rel. Duncan v. Chippewa Twp. Trustees* (1995), 73 Ohio St.3d 728, 730, 654 N.E.2d 1254.

Sentence two of Juv.R. 40(D)(3)(b)(iii) adds a new requirement, adapted from Loc.R. 99.05, Franklin Cty. Ct. of Common Pleas, that the requisite transcript or affidavit be filed within thirty days after filing objections unless the court extends the time in writing for preparation of the transcript or other good cause. The last sentence of Juv.R. 40(D)(3)(b)(iii) allows an objecting party to seek leave of court to supplement previously filed objections where the additional objections become apparent after a transcript has been prepared.

Juv.R. 40(D)(3)(b)(iv), as noted above, expands the "waiver rule" prescribed by former Juv.R. 40(E)(3)(b) (effective July 1, 1995) and former Juv.R. 40(E)(3)(d) (effective July 1, 2003) to include any factual finding or legal conclusion in a magistrate's decision, whether or not specifically designated as a finding of fact or conclusion of law under Juv.R. 40(D)(3)(a)(ii). The Rules Advisory Committee was unable to discern a principled reason to apply different requirements to, e.g., a factual finding depending on whether or not that finding is specifically designated as a finding of fact under Juv.R. 40(D)(3)(a)(ii). An exception to the "waiver rule" exists for plain error, which cannot be waived based on a party's failure to object to a magistrate's decision.

Action of court on magistrate's decision and on any objections to magistrate's decision; entry of judgment or interim order by the court

Juv.R. 40(D)(4)(a), like sentence one of former Juv.R. 40(E)(4)(a), confirms that a magistrate's decision is not effective unless adopted by the court.

Juv.R. 40(D)(4)(b) provides that a court may properly choose among a wide range of options in response to a magistrate's decision, whether or not objections are timely filed. See, e.g., *Johnson v. Brown* 2nd Dist. App. No. 2002 CA 76, 2003–Ohio–1257 at ¶ 12 (apparently concluding that former Civ.R. 53(E)(4)(b) permitted the trial court to modify an aspect of the magistrate's decision to which no objection had been made).

Juv.R. 40(D)(4)(c) provides that if no timely objections are filed, the court may adopt a magistrate's decision, unless the court determines that there is an error of law or other defect evident on the face of the decision. A similar result was reached under sentence two of former Civ.R. 53(E)(4)(a). See, e.g., *Perrine v. Perrine*, 9th Dist. App. No. 20923, 2002–Ohio–4351 at ¶ 9; *City of Ravenna Police Dept. v. Sicuro* (Apr. 30, 2002), 11th Dist. App. No. 2001–P–0037; and *In re Weingart* (Jan. 17, 2002), 8th Dist. App. No. 79489, 2002 WL 68204 at *4. The language of Juv.R. 40(D)(4)(c) has been modified in an attempt to make clear that the obligation of the court does not extend to any "error of law" whatever but is limited to errors of law that are evident on the face of the decision. To the extent that decisions such as *In re Kelley*, 11th Dist. App. No. 2002–A–0088, 2003–Ohio–194 at ¶ 8 suggest otherwise, they are rejected. The "evident on the face" standard does not require that the court conduct an independent analysis of the magistrate's decision. The amended rule does not speak to the effect, if any, on the waiver rule prescribed by amended Juv.R. 40(D)(3)(b)(iv) of the "evident on the face" requirement. At least two courts have explicitly held that the "evident on the face" standard generates an exception to the waiver rule. *Dean–Kitts v. Dean*, 2nd Dist. App. No. 2002CA18, 2002–Ohio–5590 at ¶ 13 and *Hennessy v. Hennessy* (Mar. 24, 2000), 6th Dist. App. No. L–99–1170, 2000 WL 299450 at *1. Other decisions have indicated that the standard may generate an exception to the waiver rule. *Ohlin v. Ohlin* (Nov. 12, 1999), 11th Dist. App. No. 98–PA–87, 1999 WL 1580977 at *2; *Group One Realty, Inc. v. Dixie Intl. Co.* (1998), 125 Ohio App.3d 767, 769, 709 N.E.2d 589; *In re Williams* (Feb. 25, 1997), 10th Dist. App. No. 96APF06–778, 1997 WL 84659 at *1. However, the Supreme Court applied the waiver rule three times without so much as referring to the "evident on the face" standard as a possible exception. *State ex rel. Wilson v. Industrial Comm'n.* (2003), 100 Ohio St.3d 23, 24, 2003–Ohio–4832 at ¶ 4, 795 N.E.2d 662; *State ex rel. Abate v. Industrial Comm'n.* (2002), 96 Ohio St.3d 343, 2002–Ohio–4796, 774 N.E.2d 1212; *State ex rel. Booher v. Honda of America Mfg. Co., Inc.* (2000), 88 Ohio St.3d 52, 2000–Ohio–269, 723 N.E.2d 571.

As noted above, even if no timely objection is made, a court may, pursuant to Juv.R. 40(D)(4)(b), properly choose a course of action other than adopting a magistrate's decision, even if there is no error of law or other defect evident on the face of the magistrate's decision.

Sentence one of Juv.R. 40(D)(4)(d), like sentence one of former Juv.R. 40(E)(4)(b), requires that the court rule on timely objections. Sentence two of Juv.R. 40(D)(4)(d) requires that, if timely objection is made to a magistrate's decision, the court give greater scrutiny than if no objections are made. The "independent review as to the objected matters" standard that applies if timely objection is made should be distinguished from the lesser scrutiny permitted if no objections to a magistrate's decision are timely filed, the latter standard having been first adopted by former Juv.R. 40(E)(4)(a), effective July 1, 1995, and retained by new Juv.R. 40(D)(4)(c), discussed above.

The "independent review as to the objected matters" standard is intended to exclude the more limited appellate standards of review and codify the practice approved by most courts of appeals. The Second District Court of Appeals has most clearly and consistently endorsed and explained that standard. See, e.g., *Crosby v. McWilliam*, 2nd Dist. App. No. 19856, 2003–Ohio–6063; *Quick v. Kwiatkowski* (Aug. 3, 2001), 2nd Dist. App. No. 18620, 2001 WL 871406 (acknowledging that "Magistrates truly do the 'heavy lifting' on which we all depend"); *Knauer v. Keener* (2001), 143 Ohio App.3d 789, 758 N.E.2d 1234. Other district courts of appeal have followed suit. *Reese v. Reese*, 3rd Dist. App. No. 14–03–42, 2004–Ohio–1395; *Palenshus v. Smile Dental Group, Inc.*, 3rd Dist. App. No. 3–02–46, 2003–Ohio–3095,; *Huffer v. Chafin*, 5th Dist. App. No. 01 CA 74, 2002–Ohio–356; *Rhoads v. Arthur* (June 30, 1999), 5th Dist. App. No. 98CAF10050, 1999 WL 547574; *Barker v. Barker* (May 4, 2001), 6th Dist. App. No. L–00–1346, 2001 WL 477267; *In re Day*, 7th Dist. App. No. 01 BA 28, 2003–Ohio–1215; *State ex rel. Ricart Auto. Personnel, Inc. v. Industrial Comm'n. of Ohio*, 10th Dist. App. No. 03AP–246, 2003–Ohio–7030; *Holland v. Holland* (Jan. 20, 1998), 10th Dist. App. No. 97APF08–974, 1998 WL 30179; *In re Gibbs* (Mar. 13, 1998), 11th Dist. App. No. 97–L–067, 1998 WL 257317.

Only one court of appeals appears consistently and knowingly to have taken a different approach. *Lowery v. Keystone Bd. of Ed.* (May 9, 2001), 9th Dist. App. No. 99CA007407, 2001 WL 490017; *Weber v. Weber* (June 30, 1999), 9th Dist. App. No. 2846–M, 1999 WL 459359; *Meadows v. Meadows* (Feb. 11, 1998), 9th Dist. App. No. 18382, 1998 WL 78686; *Rogers v. Rogers* (Dec. 17, 1997), 9th Dist. App. No. 18280, 1997 WL 795820.

The Rules Advisory Committee believes that the view adopted by the majority of courts of appeals is correct and that no change was made by the 1995 amendments to Juv.R. 40 in the review required of a trial judge upon the filing of timely objections to a magistrate's report.

The phrase "as to the objected matters" permits a court to choose to limit its independent review to those matters raised by proper objections. If a court need apply only the "defect evident on the face" standard if no objections are filed at all, then, if one or more objections *are* filed, a court logically need apply the more stringent independent review only to those aspects of the magistrate's decision that are challenged by that objection or those objections.

Sentence three of Juv.R. 40(D)(4)(d) provides that, before ruling on objections, a court may hear additional evidence and that it may refuse to hear additional evidence unless the objecting party demonstrates that the party could not, with reasonable diligence, have produced that evidence for consideration by the magistrate.

Juv.R. 40(D)(4)(e) is similar to former Juv.R. 40(D)(4)(c) and requires that a court that adopts, rejects, or modifies a magistrate's decision also enter a judgment or interim order. Juv.R. 40(D)(4)(e)(i) permits the court to enter a judgment during the fourteen days permitted for the filing of objections to a magistrate's decision but provides that the timely filing of objections operates as an automatic stay of execution of the judgment until the court disposes of those objections and vacates, modifies, or adheres to the judgment previously entered. Juv.R. 40(D)(4)(e)(ii) permits the court, if immediate relief is justified, to enter an interim order during the fourteen days permitted for the filing of objections to a magistrate's decision. The timely filing of objections does not stay such an interim order, but the order may not properly extend more than twenty-eight days from the date of entry, subject to extension by the court in increments of twenty-eight additional days for good cause shown. Juv.R. 40(D)(4)(e)(ii) allows multiple twenty-eight day extensions, whereas the former Juv.R. 40(D)(4)(c) allowed only one such extension.

Extension of time

Juv.R. 40(D)(5) is new and requires the court, for good cause shown, to provide an objecting party with a reasonable extension of time to file a motion to set aside a magistrate's order or file objections to a magistrate's decision. "Good cause" would include the failure of a party to receive timely service of the magistrate's order or decision.

Disqualification of a magistrate

Juv.R. 40(D)(6) has no counterpart in former Juv.R. 40. The statutory procedures for affidavits of disqualification apply to judges rather than magistrates. Rev. Code §§ 2101.39, 2501.13, 2701.03, 2701.131; *In re Disqualification of Light* (1988), 36 Ohio St.3d 604, 522 N.E.2d 458. The new provision is based on the observation of the Chief Justice of the Supreme Court that "[t]he removal of a magistrate is within the discretion of the judge who referred the matter to the magistrate and should be brought by a motion filed with the trial court." *In re Disqualification of Wilson* (1996), 77 Ohio St.3d 1250, 1251, 674 N.E.2d 260; see also *Mascorro v. Mascorro* (June 9, 2000), 2nd Dist. App. No. 17945, 2000 WL 731751 at *3 (citing *In re Disqualification of Wilson*); *Reece v. Reece* (June 22, 1994), 2nd Dist. App. No. 93–CA–45, 1994 WL 286282 at *2 ("Appointment of a referee is no different from any other process in which the trial court exercises discretion it is granted by statute or rule. * * * If the defect concerns possible bias or prejudice on the part of the referee, that may be brought to the attention of the court by motion."); *Moton v. Ford Motor Credit Co.*, 5th Dist. App. No. 01CA74, 2002–Ohio–2857, appeal not allowed (2002), 95 Ohio St.3d 1422, 2002–Ohio–1734, 766 N.E.2d 163, reconsideration denied (2002), 95 Ohio St.3d 1476, 2002–Ohio–244, 768 N.E.2d 1183; *Walser v. Dominion Homes, Inc.* (June 11, 2001), 5th Dist. App. No. 00–CA–G–11–035, 2001 WL 704408 at *5; *Unger v. Unger* (Dec. 29, 2000), 12th Dist. App. No. CA2000–04–009, 2000 WL 1902196 at *2 (citing *In re Disqualification of Wilson, supra*); *Jordan v. Jordan* (Nov. 15, 1996), 4th Dist. App. No. 1427, 1990 WL 178162 at *5 ("Although referees are not judges and arguably, are not bound by Canon 3(C)(1) of the Code of Judicial Conduct, it would appear axiomatic that a party should be able to petition the court to have a referee removed from the case if the referee is unable to render a fair and impartial decision."); *In re Reiner* (1991), 74 Ohio App.3d 213, 220, 598 N.E.2d 768 ("where a referee affirmatively states that he is biased on the matter before him, it is an abuse of the court's discretion to fail to recuse the referee"). Particularly because "a [magistrate's] oversight of an issue or issues, or even an entire trial, is not a *substitute* for the judicial functions but only an *aid* to them," *Hartt v. Munobe* (1993), 67 Ohio St.3d 3, 6, 1993–Ohio–177, 615 N.E.2d 617 (emphases added), Juv.R. 40(D)(6) contemplates that disqualification on a ground other than bias may sometimes be appropriate.

Recording of proceedings before a magistrate

Juv.R. 40(D)(7), generally requiring recording of proceedings before a magistrate, is taken verbatim from former Juv.R. 40(D)(2).

Contempt in the presence of a magistrate

Juv.R. 40(D)(8) is adapted from sentences two, three, and four of former Juv.R. 40(C)(3)(c). Juv.R. 40(D)(8)(b), unlike its predecessor, explicitly requires that the clerk provide a copy of a contempt order to the subject of the order.

2003:

Juvenile Rule 40(E) Decisions in referred matters

The amendment to this rule is identical to an amendment to Civ. R. 53(E), also effective July 1, 2003.

It was suggested to the Rules Advisory Committee that the waiver rule prescribed by sentence four of former Civ. R. 53(E)(3)(b) [identical to sentence four of former Juv.R. 40(E)(3)(b)] sometimes surprised counsel and *pro se* litigants because they did not expect to be required to object to a finding of fact or conclusion of law in a magistrate's decision in order to assign its adoption by the trial court as error on appeal. A review of relevant appellate decisions seemed to confirm that suggestion.

It was further suggested that counsel or a *pro se* litigant was particularly likely to be surprised by the waiver rule of sentence four of former Civ. R. 53(E)(3)(b) if a trial court, as authorized by sentence two of Civ. R. 53(E)(4)(a), adopted a magistrate's decision prior to expiration of the fourteen days permitted for the filing of objections. See, e.g., *Riolo v. Navin*, 2002 WL 502408, 2002–Ohio–1551, (8th Dist. Ct. App., 4–19–2002).

Since 1995, the potential for surprise posed by the waiver rule may have been exacerbated by the fact that, under the original versions of Juv. R. 40 and Civ. R. 53, a party did not, by failing to file an objection, waive the right to assign as error on appeal the adoption by the trial court of a finding or fact or conclusion of law of a referee. See 30 Ohio St. 3d xlii-xliii (1972) (original version of Juv. R. 40); *Normandy Place Associates v. Beyer*, 2 Ohio St.3d 102, 103 (1982) (syl. 1)(noting absence of waiver rule in original version of Civ. R. 53). As of July 1, 1985, sentence one of Juv. R. 40(E)(6) and sentence one of Civ. R. 53(E)(6) were amended to read "[a] party may not assign as error the court's adoption of a referee's *finding of fact* unless an objection to that finding is contained in that party's written objections to the referee's report" (emphasis added). See 18 Ohio St.2d xxxv (1985)(Juv. R. 40(E)(6)); *State ex rel. Donah v. Windham Exempted Village Sch Dist. Bd. of Ed.*, 69 Ohio St.3d 114, 118 (1994) (confirming that the waiver rule of sentence one of the 1985 version of Civ. R. 53 applied only to findings of fact by referee). The wording of the waiver rule of sentence one of Juv. R. 40(E)(6) was modified slightly effective July 1, 1992. See 64 Ohio St.3d cxlv (1992); *In re McClure*, 1995 WL 423391, No. 7–95–2 (3d Dist. Ct. App., 7–19–95) (applying 1992 version of the waiver rule of sentence one of Juv. R. 40(E)(6)). The present waiver rule, which applies to both findings of fact and conclusions of law, took effect July 1, 1995, and represents a complete reversal of the position of the original Juv. R. 40. See *State ex rel. Booher v. Honda of America Mfg., Inc.*, 88 Ohio St. 3d 52 (2000) (confirming that the waiver rule of sentence four of Civ.R. 53(E)(3)(b), which is identical to the waiver rule of sentence four of Juv. R. 40(E)(3)(b), now applies to conclusions of law as well as to findings of fact by a magistrate).

The amendment thus makes three changes in Juv. R. 40(E), none of which are intended to modify the substantive scope or effect of the waiver rule contained in sentence four of former Juv.R. 40(E)(3)(b) [now division (E)(3)(d)]. First, the amendment retains, but breaks into three appropriately-titled subdivisions, the four sentences which comprised former Juv. R. 40(E)(3)(b). Sentences two and three of former Juv.R. 40(E)(3)(b) are included in a new subdivision (c) entitled "Objections to magistrate's findings of fact." Sentence four of former Juv. R. 40(E)(3)(b), which prescribes the waiver rule, is a new subdivision (d) entitled "Waiver of right to assign adoption by court as error on appeal."

Second, new language is inserted at the beginning of Juv. R. 40(E)(3)(a) to make it more evident that a party may properly file timely objections to a magistrate's decision even if the trial court has previously adopted that decision as permitted by Juv. R. 40(E)(4)(c).

Third, the amendment adds a new sentence to Juv. R. 40(E)(2), which sentence requires that a magistrate who files a decision which includes findings of fact and conclusions of law also provide a conspicuous warning that timely and specific objection as required by Juv. R. 40(E)(3) is necessary to assign as error on appeal adoption by the trial court of any finding of fact or conclusion of law. It is ordinarily assumed that rule language which prescribes a procedural requirement (see, e.g., sentence six of Civ. R. 51(A), which is analogous to the waiver rule of sentence four of Juv. R. 40(E)(3)) constitutes sufficient notice to counsel and to *pro se* litigants of that requirement. The Committee nonetheless concluded that the additional provision requiring that a magistrate's decision that includes findings of fact and conclusions of law call attention of counsel and *pro se* litigants to the waiver rule is justified because, as noted above, the original version of Juv. R. 40 imposed no waiver at all and even the 1985 and 1992 versions imposed waiver only as to findings of fact by referees.

2001:

Rule 40(C) Reference and powers

Divisions (C)(1)(a)(i), (ii), and (iii) were amended to reflect that certain proceedings involving serious youthful offenders shall not be referred to a magistrate, i.e., the hearing on a motion to determine if there is probable cause to prosecute the child as a serious youthful offender, and the adjudication itself, whether to a jury or not. These restrictions recognize the seriousness of the charges and their determination, and are consistent with the restrictions upon the use of magistrates within the Criminal Rules.

Substitute Senate Bill 179, effective January 1, 2002, created the new category of serious youthful offender. Juv. R. 2(KK) was added effective July 1, 2001, defining serious youthful offender as "a child eligible for sentencing as described in sections 2152.11 and 2152.13 of the Revised Code."

1998:

Rule 40(E) Decisions in referred matters

The 1998 amendment was to division (E)(4)(b) of this rule. The amendment was made because some trial judges apparently had avoided ruling upon objections to magistrates' reports since the previous rule appeared to require only "consideration" of the objections. The amendment should clarify that the judge is to rule upon, not just consider, any objections.

An identical amendment was made to division (E)(4)(b) of Civ. R. 53, also effective July 1, 1998.

1995:

Rule 40. Magistrates

Juvenile Rule 40 has been extensively revised. to the extent possible the revisions mirror similar changes in Civ.R. 53 also effective July 1, 1995. For further clarification reference is made to those staff notes.

Rule 40(A) Appointment

Changes the title from referee to magistrate in juvenile court; requires all magistrates of juvenile courts to be attorneys; permits those who are not attorneys and are presently serving as referees (prior to July 1, 1995) to continue to serve as magistrates.

It is intended that this grandfather clause is personal to the non-attorney magistrate and is not extended to the position itself. Subsequent appointment of a non-attorney magistrate who otherwise qualifies under this rule will not affect the status of that non-attorney magistrate.

If otherwise applicable, this rule is intended to apply to "referees" as that term continues to exist in rule and statute.

Rule 40(B) Compensation

Clarifies that the compensation of magistrates shall be fixed by the court; eliminates language that allows compensation to be taxed as costs in certain situations.

Rule 40(C) Reference and Powers

(C)(1) Order of Reference. Division (C)(1)(a)(i) and (ii) set forth the subject matter and types of cases that may be referred to a magistrate by the court pursuant to an order of reference.

Division (C)(1)(a)(iii) adds specific language, consistent with the Court's ruling in *Hartt v. Munobe* (1993), 67 Ohio St.3d 3, that permits magistrates to conduct jury trials and, in order to obviate the consent issue in *Munobe*, requires that consent of the parties must be in writing.

Language is also added, as extracted from Civ.R. 53, which makes it clear that, except in cases under division (c)(1)(a)(iii), the consent of the parties to the order of reference is not required. This is consistent with the existing practice in the court.

Divisions (C)(1)(b) and (c) otherwise leave to the discretion of the court the form and contents of the order of reference and restates existing language in the rule.

(C)(2) General powers. Subpoena language is updated; unnecessary language describing the handling of account cases is deleted. Division (C)(2)(e) incorporates language adopted July 1, 1993 in Civ.R. 53 which permits magistrates to issue attachments.

(C)(3) Power to Enter Orders. Division (C)(3)(a) grants to magistrates the power to enter specified orders that are temporary or interlocutory in nature. Due process guarantees to the parties are preserved by allowing any party to file a timely motion to set the order aside and requiring the court itself to address that motion. This expansion of magistrate's power is consistent with similar provisions found elsewhere in rule and statute and is designed to expedite the processing of cases and the time limitations imposed by S.B. 89.

(C)(3)(c) Contempt in the Magistrate's Presence. Provides the magistrate with specific power to impose appropriate contempt sanctions where necessary and addresses conflicting case authority regarding the power of the magistrate to control the courtroom. Safeguards have been provided to assure due process guarantees.

(C)(3)(d) Other Orders. Clarifies that the amended rule is not intended to supersede existing authority which grants to magistrates or referees the power to enter certain orders but is designed to supplement that existing authority. As other rules and statutes continue to carry the term "referee," reference is also made to referees.

Rule 40(D) Proceedings

Prior division (C) is deleted; amended division (D) requires that all proceedings before a magistrate be recorded. If, due to the nature of the facility, the magistrate is not provided with a courtroom separate from chambers, those informal proceedings, such as conferences that would normally take place in chambers, need not be recorded.

Rule 40(E) Decisions in Referred Matters

Eliminates the report-writing requirement unless specifically required by the order of reference; substitutes the requirement that, except in situations in which the magistrate may issue an order, a magistrate issue a written decision, which does not become effective until approved by the court; requires a magistrate to issue findings of fact and conclusions of law in three specific situations: 1) where the order of reference requires them, 2) where otherwise required by law, 3) where findings and conclusions are requested by any party pursuant to Civ.R. 52; assures due process guarantees by retaining the right to file objections; adds to Juv.R. 40 a provision originally found in Civ.R. 53 that allows a party additional time to file counterobjections; and specifies the action to be taken by the court in acting upon a magistrate's decision.

Division (E)(4)(b) contains a new provision that limits the court's power to hear additional evidence or hear the matter itself in certain situations thereby eliminating the double jeopardy issues raised in *Swisher v. Brady* (1978), 438 U.S. 204.

Division (E)(4)(c) addresses the issue of permanent and interim orders. All of these provisions reflect what has been existing practice in many courts in response to increased pressure on the court system to process a burgeoning caseload efficiently and expeditiously. Due process considerations mandate that access to the court via the objection process be retained. Findings and conclusions are restricted to those situations where required by the court or by law or where, in fact, the parties themselves believe findings and conclusions to be necessary. The amendment is designed to facilitate the expeditious resolution of cases while preserving to the parties rights similar to those afforded previously by Juv.R. 40.

1992:

Rule 40(A) Appointment

Masculine references are replaced by gender-neutral language and surplus language is deleted; no substantive change is intended.

Rule 40(B) Powers

This division is completely restructured for clarity, masculine references are replaced by gender-neutral language, and surplus language is deleted; no substantive change is intended.

Rule 40(C) Proceedings

Grammatical changes are made, masculine references are replaced by gender-neutral language, surplus language is deleted, and the style used for rule references is revised. No substantive change is intended.

Rule 40(D) Report

The former reference in division (D)(3) to consent by the parties is deleted because there is no provision in the rule for consent by the parties to an order of reference.

Division (D)(7) was amended to clarify that an interim order shall not extend more than twenty-eight days from the date of its entry; the former rule did not specify when the twenty-eight day period commenced. This amendment makes the rule consistent with the comparable provision in Civ.R. 53(E)(7).

In addition, grammatical changes are made and surplus language is deleted throughout division (D); no substantive change is intended.

Editor's Comment

Referees: appointment; powers; duties 1
Appointment 2
Powers 3
Proceedings 4
Report 5

1. Referees: appointment; powers; duties

Juv R 40 governs the appointment, powers and duties of juvenile court magistrates. It is modeled very closely on Civ R 53, with modifications only to reflect the different use of magistrates in juvenile court.

2. Appointment

As a result of extensive amendments to Juv R 40 effective July 1, 1995, Juv R 40(A) now requires that all magistrates (formerly referees) appointed by a juvenile court be attorneys. However, those persons serving as referees prior to July 1, 1995, who are not attorneys may continue to serve as magistrates. Prior to this amendment, only those referees conducting hearings in juvenile traffic offender proceedings were required to be attorneys pursuant to Traf R 14. A magistrate appointed by a juvenile court may also serve as a magistrate under Crim R 19.

The last sentence of Juv R 40(A) was taken from Minnesota Rule 1–6. It requires that the functions of magistrates and probation officers or other court workers not be mingled in one person. A provision of 2151.16 that states a preference for female "referees" in cases involving female children is not included in this rule.

3. Compensation

Because the magistrate acts in a public capacity, Juv R 40(B) reflects the public policy that it would be inappropriate to tax the cost of the magistrate's service to the parties.

4. Reference and Powers

Juv R 40(C) sets forth the subject matter and types of cases that may be heard by a magistrate pursuant to an order of reference. Included is the authority to conduct jury trials, with the written consent of the parties. The utilization of this authority is questionable since Juv R 27(A) provides that, "The court shall hear and determine all cases of children without a jury," and pusuant to Juv R 1, there appear to be no cases governed by the Juvenile Rules which provide for the right of jury trial.

Juv R 40(C)(3) authorizes magistrates to enter certain temporary orders without judicial approval. Prior to the 1995 rule amendment, the only authority given to referees to enter orders applied to telephonic ex parte emergency custody orders under 2151.31(D).

5. Proceedings and Decisions

Juv R 40(D)(2) requires all proceedings before magistrates to be recorded, notwithstanding the provisions of Juv R 37.

One of the major amendments to Juv R 40 was the elimination of the report-writing requirement. Juv R 40(E) now requires a written report only if specifically required by the order of reference. Except in those situations governed by Juv R 40(C)(3) where a magistrate may enter orders, a magistrate's written decision does not become effective until approved by the court. Moreover, a magistrate's decision must include findings of fact and conclusions of law if requested by a party under Civ R 52, or if required by law (e.g., see 2151.33(C)(3)), or if required by the order of reference.

Juv R 40(E)(3), enacted in 1995, retains the right of the parties to file written objections within fourteen days of the filing of the magistrate's decision, but adds the right of other parties to file objections not later than ten days after the initial objections are filed. Although the form of objections is similar to that provided in the former Juv R 40(D)(2) and (3), an important addition is the provision prohibiting a party from assigning as error on appeal the court approval of a magistrate's finding of fact or conclusion of law unless a party has specifically objected to that finding or conclusion. This overrules the Supreme Court's holding in *Normandy Place Associates v Beyer*, 2 OS(3d) 102, 443 NE(2d) 161 (1982), at least as it applies to the decisions of juvenile court magistrates.

In accordance with the United States Supreme Court decision in *Swisher v Brady*, 438 US 204, (1978), dealing with double jeopardy concerns, Juv R 40(E)(4)(b) provides that if objections are filed with respect to a magistrate's report in delinquency, unruly, and juvenile traffic offender cases, the consent of the child is required in order for the court to hear additional evidence or hear the matter itself.

Cross References

Referees, Civ R 53
Referees, powers and duties, 2151.16

Library References

Infants ⚖ 206.
Westlaw Topic No. 211.
C.J.S. Infants §§ 63, 68.

Research References

Encyclopedias

OH Jur. 3d Appellate Review § 90, Child Custody.
OH Jur. 3d Appellate Review § 156, Rulings on Motions.
OH Jur. 3d Appellate Review § 202, Effect of Postjudgment Motion.
OH Jur. 3d Family Law § 1071, by Child's Unmarried Father.
OH Jur. 3d Family Law § 1646, Order of Reference.
OH Jur. 3d Family Law § 1647, Proceedings Before Referee; Powers and Duties.
OH Jur. 3d Family Law § 1648, Proceedings Before Referee; Powers and Duties—Rights of Parties; Action on Nonappearance of Party.
OH Jur. 3d Family Law § 1649, Proceedings Before Referee; Powers and Duties—Attendance of Witnesses.
OH Jur. 3d Family Law § 1650, Report of Referee.
OH Jur. 3d Family Law § 1651, Report of Referee—Draft Report; Stipulations and Objections.
OH Jur. 3d Family Law § 1652, Report of Referee—Constitutional Issues.
OH Jur. 3d Family Law § 1667, Admission or Denial of Allegations.
OH Jur. 3d Family Law § 1672, Testimony of Child.
OH Jur. 3d Habeas Corpus & Post Convict. Remedies § 3, Restrictions on Scope or Availability of Remedy; Strict Compliance With Statutory Procedures; Effect of Adequate Remedy at Law.
OH Jur. 3d Mandamus, Procedendo, & Prohibition § 199, Definition and General Nature.

Treatises and Practice Aids

Giannelli and Snyder, Baldwin's Ohio Practice, Evidence, R 101, Scope of Rules: Applicability; Privileges; Exceptions.
Giannelli and Snyder, Baldwin's Ohio Practice, Evidence, § 101.1, Introduction.
Giannelli and Snyder, Baldwin's Ohio Practice, Evidence, § 101.5, Magistrates & Referees.
Carlin, Baldwin's Ohio Practice, Merrick-Rippner Probate Law § 8:4, Appeal—Notice—Time for Filing.
Carlin, Baldwin's Ohio Practice, Merrick-Rippner Probate Law § 3:40, Appointment of Magistrate—Form.
Carlin, Baldwin's Ohio Practice, Merrick-Rippner Probate Law § 105:1, Juvenile Court—Exclusive Original Jurisdiction.
Carlin, Baldwin's Ohio Practice, Merrick-Rippner Probate Law § 107:2, Types of Complaints.
Carlin, Baldwin's Ohio Practice, Merrick-Rippner Probate Law § 107:41, Prehearing Procedures in Juvenile Court—Temporary Orders Pending Hearing.
Carlin, Baldwin's Ohio Practice, Merrick-Rippner Probate Law § 107:49, Adjudicatory Hearings—Conduct of Hearing by Magistrate.
Carlin, Baldwin's Ohio Practice, Merrick-Rippner Probate Law § 107:120, Custody Review Hearing—Juvenile Court Dispositional Review.
Carlin, Baldwin's Ohio Practice, Merrick-Rippner Probate Law § 107:122, Appeals—Juvenile Court Judgments—Determination of Neglect, Dependency, Unruliness, Abuse, or Delinquency.
Carlin, Baldwin's Ohio Practice, Merrick-Rippner Probate Law § 107:179, Findings and Decision of Magistrate; Child Placed on Probation; Approval by Judge—Form.
Carlin, Baldwin's Ohio Practice, Merrick-Rippner Probate Law § 107:181, Objections to Decision of Magistrate—Form.
Painter & Dennis, Ohio Appellate Practice § 3:4, Time for Filing Notice of Appeal-In General.
Painter & Dennis, Ohio Appellate Practice § 3:7, Time for Filing Notice of Appeal-Tolling the Time Limit.
Painter, Ohio Driving Under the Influence § 5:4, Appearance Before Magistrate—Criminal Magistrate's Powers.
Giannelli & Yeomans, Ohio Juvenile Law § 5:1, Introduction.
Giannelli & Yeomans, Ohio Juvenile Law § 5:3, Syo Charging; Preliminary Hearing.
Giannelli & Yeomans, Ohio Juvenile Law § 5:6, Syo Adjudicatory Hearing.
Giannelli & Yeomans, Ohio Juvenile Law § 20:4, Required Hearings.
Giannelli & Yeomans, Ohio Juvenile Law § 24:1, Introduction.
Giannelli & Yeomans, Ohio Juvenile Law § 24:2, Qualifications.
Giannelli & Yeomans, Ohio Juvenile Law § 24:3, Order of Reference.
Giannelli & Yeomans, Ohio Juvenile Law § 24:4, Pretrial Orders.
Giannelli & Yeomans, Ohio Juvenile Law § 24:5, Hearings.
Giannelli & Yeomans, Ohio Juvenile Law § 24:6, Recording of Proceedings.
Giannelli & Yeomans, Ohio Juvenile Law § 24:7, Magistrate's Decision.
Giannelli & Yeomans, Ohio Juvenile Law § 24:8, Objections.
Giannelli & Yeomans, Ohio Juvenile Law § 24:9, Court Action.
Giannelli & Yeomans, Ohio Juvenile Law § 34:4, Final Order Requirement.
Giannelli & Yeomans, Ohio Juvenile Law App. D, Appendix D. Glossary.
Giannelli & Yeomans, Ohio Juvenile Law § 23:31, Double Jeopardy.

Notes of Decisions

Constitutional issues 7
Findings of fact 1
Hearings 9
Invalid reports or judgments 5
Objections to report 2
Procedures 6
Referees, powers and duties 8
Time limitations 3
Transcripts 4

---

1. Findings of fact

Trial court did not commit plain error in finding mother in contempt of court when she claimed federal income tax exemption for child born out of wedlock in violation of order providing that mother could claim exemption only if her gross income exceeded $15,000; although "gross income" was not defined in agreed judgment entry, mother failed to draw court's attention to her claim on appeal that she interpreted "gross income" to mean "gross receipts" so as to include child support payments received. In re Moore (Ohio App. 10 Dist., Franklin, 02-24-2005) No. 04AP-299, 2005-Ohio-747, 2005 WL 449862, Unreported. Children Out-of-wedlock ⚖ 73

Magistrate was entitled to adopt guardian ad litem's proposed findings of fact and conclusions of law in proceeding to modify child support, since they were substantially similar to magistrate's decision, they were not factually inaccurate, and there was no evidence that magistrate did not thoroughly review them. Jarvis v. Witter (Ohio App. 8 Dist., Cuyahoga, 12-09-2004) No. 84128, 2004-Ohio-6628, 2004 WL 2830789, Unreported. Child Support ⚖ 341

Magistrate's findings of fact were sufficient for trial court to make independent analysis and to apply appropriate law in reaching its judgment, and thus trial court did not abuse its discretion when it adopted magistrate's decision, which ordered father to pay $1,167.22 per month in child support to mother of minor child; magistrate had found that father was voluntarily underemployed, that father claimed to earn $5.15 per hour, that father was earning $300,000 to $400,000 annually before parties' separation, that mother had received no child support for child since parties separated, and that father's testimony was incredible and led magistrate to believe that father was attempting to hide income and assets.

Howard v. Howard (Ohio App. 6 Dist., Lucas, 10-24-2003) No. L-02-1371, 2003-Ohio-5683, 2003 WL 22417178, Unreported. Child Support ⚖ 211

Mother waived challenge to magistrate's finding that change of circumstances warranted change of custody as to nonmarital child, where sole objection raised with trial court was finding that change of custody was in child's best interest. Noonan v. Edson (Ohio App. 12 Dist., Butler, 04-07-2003) No. CA2002-04-088, 2003-Ohio-1767, 2003 WL 1795576, Unreported. Children Out-of-wedlock ⚖ 20.11

In child custody matters, litigant must be given opportunity to object to referee's findings of fact. In re Wright (Montgomery 1993) 88 Ohio App.3d 539, 624 N.E.2d 347. Child Custody ⚖ 504

Order denying mother's motion to reopen custody cases of her two children, and to recover legal custody of those children from their paternal grandmother, was void due to referee's failure to prepare and file written report detailing findings of fact on which referee's recommendation was based; due to lack of written findings in record, there was no evidence that trial judge made independent analysis, and mother was never given opportunity to object to referee's findings of fact. In re Wright (Montgomery 1993) 88 Ohio App.3d 539, 624 N.E.2d 347. Child Custody ⚖ 659

Referee's report must contain sufficient facts for trial court to make independent analysis, and absent sufficient facts to make independent analysis, trial court cannot adopt referee's recommendation. Sharpe v. Sharpe (Lake 1993) 85 Ohio App.3d 638, 620 N.E.2d 916. Reference ⚖ 86

The requirement of Juv R 40(D)(1) that the report of the referee set forth his findings in the case is satisfied where a supplemental report provides necessary material lacking in the original. In re Weimer (Cuyahoga 1984) 19 Ohio App.3d 130, 483 N.E.2d 173, 19 O.B.R. 219.

A trial court's failure to make a record of an adjudicatory hearing in a stolen car delinquency case in accordance with the mandates of Juv R 37(A) and Juv R 40(D)(2) prevents a finding that an affirmative waiver of the constitutional right to counsel took place, and the trial court magistrate's journal entry, which is the only record of the adjudicatory hearing in question, fails to even minimally satisfy the requirements of Juv R 29 since the magistrate did not check the box indicating whether the juvenile admitted or denied the allegations of the complaint and whether counsel was waived; although the informal detention hearing journal entry sets forth that an express waiver of counsel took place, the journal entry is not adequate evidence of a knowing, voluntary and intelligent waiver of counsel. In re Ward (Ohio App. 8 Dist., Cuyahoga, 06-12-1997) No. 71245, 1997 WL 321492, Unreported.

Trial court was not precluded from rejecting findings of magistrate that mother did not abandon child, that mother did not relinquish custody of child to child's paternal grandparents, and that mother was able to provide support for child, on grandparents' timely-filed objection to magistrate's decision in proceedings to determine custody of child between mother and paternal grandparents. In re Ratliff (Ohio App. 11 Dist., Portage, 11-29-2002) No. 2001-P-0142, No. 2001-P-0143, 2002-Ohio-6586, 2002 WL 31716783, Unreported. Child Custody ⚖ 504

2. Objections to report

Trial court's finding that it did not have jurisdiction to consider father's objections to magistrate's interim order of visitation was proper, in proceeding in which father filed motion for shared parenting plan; interim order was only valid for 28 days, trial court did not extend order, and thus interim order expired, with trial court's subsequent judgment being final judgment of court. Steven D.C. v. Carrie Anne P. (Ohio App. 6 Dist., Huron, 07-29-2005) No. H-04-029, No. H-04-023, 2005-Ohio-3858, 2005 WL 1793770, Unreported. Child Custody ⚖ 504

Mother was not entitled to appellate review of claim that denial of continuance in proceedings to terminate parental rights violated constitutional right to parent children, where claim was not made subject of objection to magistrate's decision. In re Harris (Ohio App. 2 Dist., Montgomery, 07-15-2005) No. 20934, 2005-Ohio-3700, 2005 WL 1704920, Unreported. Infants ⚖ 243

Juvenile waived for appellate review claim that evidence adduced at magistrate hearing did not support trial court's decision imposing a term of commitment to the Department of Youth Services (DYS), where juvenile failed to file objections to the magistrate's decision along with a hearing transcript. In re J.H. (Ohio App. 9 Dist., Summit, 05-18-2005) No. 22384, 2005-Ohio-2398, 2005 WL 1163015, Unreported. Infants ⚖ 243

Trial court did not abuse its discretion in proceeding to determine custody of abused, dependent, and neglected child by overruling father's objections to magistrate's decision awarding permanent custody to maternal grandmother, even though trial court's order stated "No formal hearing was held"; record of dispositional hearing before magistrate showed that magistrate did conduct evidentiary hearing, and statement in trial court's order most likely referred to trial court's denial of father's objections without a hearing, rather than to the proceedings before the magistrate. In re Dorie F. (Ohio App. 6 Dist., Lucas, 03-31-2005) No. L-04-1097, 2005-Ohio-1551, 2005 WL 736992, Unreported. Infants ⚖ 206

Father waived on appeal issue of whether trial court had erred in determining that county had made reasonable efforts to reunify family, in child dependency proceeding, as he failed to challenge this determination by filing objections as required by rule. In re Miller (Ohio App. 5 Dist., Licking, 02-24-2005) No. 04 CA 32, 2005-Ohio-856, 2005 WL 469260, Unreported. Infants ⚖ 243

Putative father was required to include transcript of hearings on Department of Children Services' petition for permanent custody of children in support of objections to magistrate's decision, or, if no transcript was available, affidavit reflecting relevant evidence from hearing. In re Davis (Ohio App. 11 Dist., Ashtabula, 02-04-2005) No. 2004-A-0068, 2005-Ohio-411, 2005 WL 280507, Unreported. Infants ⚖ 206

Father challenging trial court's grant of legal custody of child to child's maternal grandmother could not argue on appeal that magistrate applied an improper burden of proof, where argument was not included in father's objections to decision of magistrate. In re M.O. (Ohio App. 9 Dist., Summit, 01-26-2005) No. 22177, 2005-Ohio-264, 2005 WL 159777, Unreported, appeal not allowed 106 Ohio St.3d 1414, 830 N.E.2d 346, 2005-Ohio-3154. Children Out-of-wedlock ⚖ 20.11

Father, whose objections to magistrate judge's decision placing restrictions on his child visitation rights did not specifically include contention that magistrate had failed to consider statutory factors, was precluded from asserting that ground on appeal from trial court's adoption of magistrate's decision. Wilms v. Herbert (Ohio App. 9 Dist., Lorain, 01-05-2005) No. 04CA008525, 2005-Ohio-2, 2005 WL 17901, Unreported. Child Custody ⚖ 904

Father objecting to magistrate judge's resolution of child visitation dispute was not entitled to remand to magistrate for new hearing on ground that magistrate's failure to record initial hearing had preventing preparation of transcript; appropriate remedy, if transcript was unavailable, was filing of affidavit of evidence presented to magistrate. Wilms v. Herbert (Ohio App. 9 Dist., Lorain, 01-05-2005) No. 04CA008525, 2005-Ohio-2, 2005 WL 17901, Unreported. Child Custody ⚖ 504

Court reviewing objections to magistrate judge's resolution of child visitation dispute was required to accept magistrate's fact findings as true, in absence of transcript or affidavit of evidence presented; party's memorandum, which merely recounted several factual assertions from party's perspective, was insufficient. Wilms v. Herbert (Ohio App. 9 Dist., Lorain, 01-05-2005) No. 04CA008525, 2005-Ohio-2, 2005 WL 17901, Unreported. Child Custody ⚖ 504

Refusing to hear additional testimony regarding paternal uncle's change in employment prior to ruling on objections to magistrate's decision awarding custody of orphaned children to paternal uncle and aunt was not abuse of trial court's discretion, where court was not required by rule to hear additional evidence prior to ruling on objections and court discussed supplemental report of guardian ad litem (GAL), which referred to paternal uncle's change in employment. In re R.N. (Ohio App. 10 Dist., Franklin, 08-24-2004) No. 04AP-130, 2004-Ohio-4420, 2004 WL 1879061, Unreported. Child Custody ⚖ 504

Father waived argument on appeal that trial court erred in finding him in contempt for failure to abide by order granting grandparents visitation rights, where father did not present argument to the trial court through properly filed objections to magistrate's decision finding him in contempt. Estate of Harrold v. Collier (Ohio App. 9 Dist., Wayne, 08-18-2004) No. 03CA0064, 2004-Ohio-4331, 2004 WL 1837186, Unreported, stay denied 103 Ohio St.3d 1457, 815 N.E.2d 674, 2004-Ohio-5076, motion to certify allowed 104 Ohio St.3d 1407, 818 N.E.2d 709, 2004-Ohio-6364, appeal allowed 104 Ohio St.3d 1408, 818 N.E.2d 710, 2004-Ohio-6364, affirmed 107 Ohio St.3d 44, 836 N.E.2d 1165, 2005-Ohio-5334, certiorari denied 126 S.Ct. 1474, 164 L.Ed.2d 248. Child Custody ⚖ 904

Minor's failure to object to magistrate's decision finding minor delinquent and ordering him committed to Department of Youth Services limited scope of appellate review to review for plain error. In re Harper (Ohio App. 2 Dist., Montgomery, 12-12-2003) No. 19948, 2003-Ohio-6666, 2003 WL 22927248, Unreported. Infants ⚖ 243

Mother failed to object before trial court to grounds for emergency custody order, removing her child from her home, and thus issue was waived for appeal. In re Lewis (Ohio App. 4 Dist., Athens, 09-25-2003) No. 03CA12, 2003-Ohio-5262, 2003 WL 22267129, Unreported. Infants ⚖ 243

After making independent review of magistrate's proposed modification of visitation schedule, juvenile court was free to disagree with magistrate's conclusions and to enter its own order, which it found to be in out-of-wedlock child's best interest. In re Ross (Ohio App. 1 Dist., 08-22-2003) 154 Ohio App.3d 1, 796 N.E.2d 6, 2003-Ohio-4419. Children Out-of-wedlock ⇐ 20.4

Mother was not entitled to extraordinary relief in habeas corpus to compel county children services executive director to release her dependent child from its temporary custody, as she had adequate legal remedies in the ordinary course of law to raise her claims; mother could have objected to magistrate's decision, raised issues regarding sufficiency of dependency complaint or constitutionality of child dependency statute in any subsequent hearing in case, or appealed any adverse judgment by the juvenile court. Rammage v. Saros (Ohio, 12-13-2002) 97 Ohio St.3d 430, 780 N.E.2d 278, 2002-Ohio-6669. Habeas Corpus ⇐ 280

Mother waived claim that magistrate should not have taken psychologist's testimony in child custody hearing after guardian ad litem withdrew, where objection to magistrate's findings at trial was limited to magistrate's finding that change of custody was in child's best interest. Noonan v. Edson (Ohio App. 12 Dist., Butler, 04-07-2003) No. CA2002-04-088, 2003-Ohio-1767, 2003 WL 1795576, Unreported. Children Out-of-wedlock ⇐ 20.11

Father was not entitled to reversal of trial court judgment terminating parental rights and granting permanent custody to county children services board based on time delay in case due to numerous continuances and extensions; services board was not responsible for all continuances, continuances were based on unavailability of key witnesses, father did not object to all continuances, and father did not file objection to the trial court from the magistrate's grant of continuances. In re Hess (Ohio App. 7 Dist., Jefferson, 03-21-2003) No. 02 JE 37, 2003-Ohio-1429, 2003 WL 1465190, Unreported. Infants ⇐ 243; Infants ⇐ 253

Trial court properly dismissed father's objections to magistrate's decision denying his motion for new genetic testing in order to determine paternity since father's objections were not accompanied by an evidentiary transcript; because father's objections were based on the magistrate's failure to take evidence, the trial court needed to have some way of knowing if and why the magistrate failed to do so in order to judge the propriety of the magistrate's actions. Milick v. Ciapala (Ohio App. 7 Dist., Mahoning, 03-19-2003) No. 02 CA 53, 2003-Ohio-1427, 2003 WL 1464400, Unreported, appeal not allowed 99 Ohio St.3d 1468, 791 N.E.2d 983, 2003-Ohio-3669. Children Out-of-wedlock ⇐ 57

Since mother filed no objections to the magistrate's report modifying father's child support obligation, mother waived, for purposes of appeal, her right to challenge the judgment of the trial court adopting magistrate's report. Dorothy P. v. Leo P. (Ohio App. 6 Dist., Sandusky, 08-30-2002) No. S-01-032, 2002-Ohio-4477, 2002 WL 1998448, Unreported. Child Support ⇐ 539

Parents waived right to appeal insufficiency of the evidence claim in termination of parental rights case, where parents failed to object to magistrate's decision regarding termination of parental rights. In re Alyssa C. (Ohio App. 6 Dist., 05-23-2003) 153 Ohio App.3d 10, 790 N.E.2d 803, 2003-Ohio-2673. Infants ⇐ 243

While trial court may enter judgment on referee's report without waiting for objections to be filed, it must make independent analysis of referee's report and it has responsibility to critically review and verify to its own satisfaction correctness of report. Sharpe v. Sharpe (Lake 1993) 85 Ohio App.3d 638, 620 N.E.2d 916. Reference ⇐ 100(7)

A trial court does not have discretion to overrule the objections and adopt the referee's report without reviewing and considering the transcript where a transcript has been ordered. In re Moorehead (Montgomery 1991) 75 Ohio App.3d 711, 600 N.E.2d 778.

Woman challenging permanent child custody award waived claim that trial court erred in failing to conduct in camera interview of dependent child, where woman failed to file objections when in camera interview was denied. In re Bradford (Ohio App. 10 Dist., Franklin, 08-08-2002) No. 01AP-1151, 2002-Ohio-4013, 2002 WL 1813406, Unreported, appeal not allowed 97 Ohio St.3d 1470, 779 N.E.2d 236, 2002-Ohio-6347. Infants ⇐ 243

Mother waived her appellate argument that the trial court erred when it determined that the county children's services board was not required to establish that reasonable efforts for reunification of mother and child had been made, in termination of parental rights proceeding, where mother failed to file any written objections to the trial court's decision to grant county's motion for a "reasonable efforts bypass," which excused county from making reasonable efforts to assist mother in reunification due to the prior involuntary termination of mother's parental rights to five of her other children. In re Pittman (Ohio App. 9 Dist., Summit, 05-08-2002) No. 20894, 2002-Ohio-2208, 2002 WL 987852, Unreported. Infants ⇐ 243

3. Time limitations

Juvenile court's failure to grant enlargement of time to mother to file objections to magistrate's decision in dependency proceedings did not result in an injustice to mother within meaning of juvenile rule governing enlargement of time to file; mother had a full and fair opportunity to litigate the matters before the magistrate, and failure to file resulted from attorney's ignorance as to filing deadlines. In re Malone (Ohio App. 10 Dist., Franklin, 12-30-2003) No. 03AP-489, 2003-Ohio-7156, 2003 WL 23024377, Unreported, appeal not allowed 102 Ohio St.3d 1423, 807 N.E.2d 367, 2004-Ohio-2003. Infants ⇐ 204

Juvenile procedure rules, rather than civil procedure rules, governed motion for extension of time to file objections to magistrate's decision in juvenile dependency proceedings. In re Malone (Ohio App. 10 Dist., Franklin, 12-30-2003) No. 03AP-489, 2003-Ohio-7156, 2003 WL 23024377, Unreported, appeal not allowed 102 Ohio St.3d 1423, 807 N.E.2d 367, 2004-Ohio-2003. Infants ⇐ 204

Court of Appeals lacked jurisdiction to review issue of whether magistrate erred in finding mother in direct contempt for failing to reveal child's location after being ordered to do so, as mother failed to file notice of appeal from contempt finding and jail sentence within 30 days after issuance of magistrate's contempt order, which order was reviewed and approved by juvenile court on same date, pursuant to rule. In re Kepperling (Ohio App. 2 Dist., 04-14-2006) 166 Ohio App.3d 257, 850 N.E.2d 119, 2006-Ohio-1856. Child Custody ⇐ 905

Mother was not prejudiced by short notice of hearing before magistrate to defend against indirect contempt allegations of father and child's guardian ad litem, who contended that mother had prevented father's visitation and counseling sessions with child, given that, when mother objected to short notice, magistrate continued proceedings on contempt allegations. In re Kepperling (Ohio App. 2 Dist., 04-14-2006) 166 Ohio App.3d 257, 850 N.E.2d 119, 2006-Ohio-1856. Child Custody ⇐ 923(1)

Mother did not establish an undue delay cognizable in procedendo, relating to magistrate's failure to issue a separate decision in child abuse and dependency proceeding, where the mother's action for extraordinary relief was filed three days after the juvenile court had made its journal entry adjudicating the child as dependent. State ex rel. Nalls v. Russo (Ohio, 10-02-2002) 96 Ohio St.3d 410, 775 N.E.2d 522, 2002-Ohio-4907. Prohibition ⇐ 5(3)

Father could not appeal juvenile court's adoption of magistrate's decisions granting temporary custody of unruly child to public children services agency, requiring psychological evaluation of child, and requiring anger risk assessment of family members, where father did not object to those decisions in the juvenile court within 14 days of the filing of the decisions. In re Kidd (Ohio App. 11 Dist., Lake, 12-27-2002) No. 2001-L-039, 2002-Ohio-7264, 2002 WL 31886759, Unreported. Infants ⇐ 243

The seven day rule of RC 2151.35(B)(3) and Juv R 34(C) can be applied consistently with Juv R 40(D), which (1) mandates the preparation and filing of findings of fact and recommendations by the referee; (2) provides an allowance of fourteen days from the filing of the referee's report for the filing of objections by the parties; and (3) provides for a hearing on the objections; when the dispositional hearing is conducted before a referee, the referee has seven days from the time the case becomes decisional in which to issue his findings of fact and recommendations and at the expiration of the fourteen day period for filing objections, if no objections are filed, the case is decisional and the trial court has seven days to issue its final judgment; however, if objections are filed pursuant to Juv R 40 and a hearing is held, the judge has seven days from the conclusion of the hearing to enter his final judgment. In re Fleming (Lucas 1991) 76 Ohio App.3d 30, 600 N.E.2d 1112.

Juvenile defendant, who had been adjudicated delinquent, waived her right to appeal the findings and conclusions contained in the magistrate's decision, where juvenile defendant failed to file written objections to the magistrate's decision within fourteen days after the filing of that decision. In re Stanford (Ohio App. 9 Dist., Summit, 07-24-2002) No. 20921, 2002-Ohio-3755, 2002 WL 1627917, Unreported. Infants ⇐ 243

4. Transcripts

Even assuming that transcript of juvenile's competency hearing was not available, State's affidavit fell short of requirement, in rule permitting objections to magistrate's decision to be supported with an affidavit in lieu of a transcript, that affidavit include all relevant evidence presented to magistrate; State's affidavit, which addressed only issue of magistrate's improperly placing burden of proof on State, described no relevant evidence. In re E.B. (Ohio App. 8 Dist., Cuyahoga, 02-03-2005) No. 85035, 2005-Ohio-401, 2005 WL 273028, Unreported. Infants ⇐ 203

Rejecting magistrate's decision which found eight-year-old juvenile incompetent to stand trial on statutory rape charge was abuse of juvenile court's discretion, where State, in submitting affidavit in support of its objections to magistrate's decision, failed to assert, much less demonstrate, that transcript of competency hearing was not available. In re E.B. (Ohio App. 8 Dist., Cuyahoga, 02-03-2005) No. 85035, 2005-Ohio-401, 2005 WL 273028, Unreported. Infants ⇐ 203

Trial court and appellate court were required to accept as true findings of fact supporting magistrate's decision granting legal custody of child to child's maternal grandmother, where father failed to submit the required transcript or affidavit when filing his objections to magistrate's decision. In re M.O. (Ohio App. 9 Dist., Summit, 01-26-2005) No. 22177, 2005-Ohio-264, 2005 WL 159777, Unreported, appeal not allowed 106 Ohio St.3d 1414, 830 N.E.2d 346, 2005-Ohio-3154. Children Out-of-wedlock ⇐ 20.11

Father was not required to file a transcript of the evidence submitted to magistrate in connection with his motion for reallocation of parental rights and responsibilities against mother, where father objected to magistrate's order concerning personal jurisdiction as a matter of law, not a finding of fact. Alestock v. Bomestar (Ohio App. 5 Dist., Stark, 11-08-2004) No. 2004CA00001, 2004-Ohio-7317, 2004 WL 3563903, Unreported. Child Custody ⇐ 907

Adjudicated father's failure to provide the juvenile court with a transcript of magistrate proceedings in paternity proceeding precluded him from raising factual objections on appeal from award of retroactive child support to mother. Pfeifer v. Shannon (Ohio App. 11 Dist., Portage, 12-23-2004) No. 2003-P-0117, 2004-Ohio-7241, 2004 WL 3090215, Unreported. Children Out-of-wedlock ⇐ 73

Mother's failure to provide juvenile court with transcript of magistrate hearing on father's motion to change child's surname following determination of paternity precluded her from raising factual objections on appeal. Cross v. Greaver (Ohio App. 11 Dist., Trumbull, 11-26-2004) No. 2003-T-0076, 2004-Ohio-6335, 2004 WL 2697273, Unreported. Children Out-of-wedlock ⇐ 1

Unwed mother's claim that the trial court erred in overruling her objection to the magistrate's decision to award the income tax dependency exemption to father because decision was not supported by the evidence was not preserved for appellate review, since mother failed to support her objections with a transcript of proceedings on father's motion to modify child support. Adkins v. Doss (Ohio App. 9 Dist., Medina, 12-31-2003) No. 03CA0046-M, 2003-Ohio-7174, 2003 WL 23094849, Unreported. Children Out-of-wedlock ⇐ 73

In reviewing trial court's adoption of magistrate's decision, which ordered father to pay child support to mother of minor child, magistrate's findings of fact would be considered established, because father failed to provide trial court with transcript to support father's contention that magistrate was in error. Howard v. Howard (Ohio App. 6 Dist., Lucas, 10-24-2003) No. L-02-1371, 2003-Ohio-5683, 2003 WL 22417178, Unreported. Child Support ⇐ 557(1)

Trial court had authority to disagree with a magistrate's best-interest determination, but it was inappropriate for court to do so without reviewing the transcript of the entire dispositional hearing in which magistrate granted Children Services Board permanent custody of dependent and neglected child; absent a review of all of the evidence presented to the magistrate, the trial court lacked a sufficient basis to disregard the magistrate's findings and to render its own. In re L.R.T. (Ohio App. 12 Dist., 01-23-2006) 165 Ohio App.3d 77, 844 N.E.2d 914, 2006-Ohio-207. Infants ⇐ 210

A trial court's refusal to grant a request for a transcript of proceedings concerning a change of child custody from the mother to the father on the mother's objections to the referee's report challenging the weight of the evidence is an abuse of discretion where the court fails to give a substantial reason for its refusal, particularly where the referee's report concerning custody was filed as a journal entry, which is an indicia of "rubber stamping," and the transcript is necessary to resolve manifest weight questions. In re Swain (Portage 1991) 68 Ohio App.3d 737, 589 N.E.2d 483. Divorce ⇐ 150.1(3)

At the time of a juvenile's "admit" plea where there is no record made of the proceeding there is no record for the judge to review in determining whether the juvenile's motion to withdraw his plea and vacate his sentence should be granted; as a result, a conviction for operating a motor vehicle under the influence of alcohol after underage consumption is vacated with instructions to conduct a new adjudicatory hearing which is properly recorded. In re L.D. (Ohio App. 8 Dist., Cuyahoga, 12-13-2001) No. 78750, 2001 WL 1612114, Unreported.

5. Invalid reports or judgments

Trial court decisions affirming magistrate's resolution of child support issues and attorney fee award were not final and appealable, where court merely stated that magistrate's decisions were correct, and did not order payment of modified child support or make any order with respect to attorney fees. Nickoloff v. Nickoloff (Ohio App. 9 Dist., Lorain, 08-18-2004) No. 03CA008415, 2004-Ohio-4327, 2004 WL 1842440, Unreported. Child Support ⇐ 537

Statements by parent of diving club member that other diver had been "convicted of sexual crimes" and was a "convicted sexual offender" were not substantially true, although magistrate had recommended that diver be adjudicated delinquent for assault and gross sexual imposition; juvenile justice system did not contemplate convictions, purpose of juvenile system was rehabilitation rather than punishment, magistrate's recommendation was not a decision, and diver was never adjudicated delinquent as to sexual offense but rather entered Alford plea to one count of disorderly conduct. Roe ex rel. Roe v. Heap (Ohio App. 10 Dist., Franklin, 05-11-2004) No. 03AP-586, 2004-Ohio-2504, 2004 WL 1109849, Unreported, appeal not allowed 103 Ohio St.3d 1464, 815 N.E.2d 679, 2004-Ohio-5056. Libel And Slander ⇐ 55

The magistrate and trial court's failure to comply with the Juvenile Rules for the issuance of a report and the entry of an order in dependency proceedings resulted in a void, and unappealable, judgment; the record did not contain a report with the magistrate's decision. In re D.N. (Ohio App. 8 Dist., Cuyahoga, 03-11-2004) No. 82708, 2004-Ohio-1106, 2004 WL 439965, Unreported, stay granted 102 Ohio St.3d 1520, 811 N.E.2d 547, 2004-Ohio-3579, appeal not allowed 103 Ohio St.3d 1462, 815 N.E.2d 678, 2004-Ohio-5056, reconsideration denied 104 Ohio St.3d 1411, 818 N.E.2d 712, 2004-Ohio-6364. Infants ⇐ 208; Infants ⇐ 242; Infants ⇐ 246

Magistrate's unauthorized assignment of child neglect case to visiting judge rendered judgment by visiting judge voidable, not void; error did not divest juvenile court of subject-matter jurisdiction over neglect and custody hearings. In re J.J. (Ohio, 11-08-2006) 111 Ohio St.3d 205, 855 N.E.2d 851, 2006-Ohio-5484. Infants ⇐ 221

Referee's report in delinquency proceedings must contain sufficient facts for trial court to make required independent analysis of law and issues; court cannot accept referee's recommendation absent sufficient facts to make independent analysis. In re Montgomery (Ohio App. 8 Dist., 01-21-1997) 117 Ohio App.3d 696, 691 N.E.2d 349, dismissed, appeal not allowed 78 Ohio St.3d 1490, 678 N.E.2d 1228. Infants ⇐ 206

Juvenile court erroneously adopted referee's report and proposed journal entry indicating that juvenile knowingly and voluntarily waived counsel and entered admission where there was no indication that referee addressed juvenile personally and determined that he understood nature of allegations and consequences of his admission, that juvenile knowingly and intelligently entered admission, or that he understood nature and ramifications of adjudicatory proceedings before he waived counsel and entered admission; referee's report and proposed journal entry consisted of one page with boilerplate language and check-off boxes to indicate proceedings. In re Montgomery (Ohio App. 8 Dist., 01-21-1997) 117 Ohio App.3d 696, 691 N.E.2d 349, dismissed, appeal not allowed 78 Ohio St.3d 1490, 678 N.E.2d 1228. Infants ⇐ 206

Evidence presented at competency hearing and experts' reports did not support finding that mentally retarded juvenile was competent to stand trial; experts' reports and testimony were irreparably muddled with incorrect standards of law and inappropriate judgments pertaining to moral responsibility, and evidence appeared to establish prima facie case that juvenile did not understand nature of proceedings against him and was incapable of assisting in his own defense. In re Williams (Ohio App. 2 Dist., 05-23-1997) 116 Ohio App.3d 237, 687 N.E.2d 507, appeal not allowed 80 Ohio St.3d 1415, 684 N.E.2d 706. Infants ⇐ 208

Defendant's appeal from speeding conviction was not moot after defendant paid $25 fine, where juvenile referee's instruction to defendant to pay, coupled with the threat of detention if defendant refused, established that fine was not voluntarily paid. In re Zindle (Ohio App. 9 Dist., 11-08-1995) 107 Ohio App.3d 342, 668 N.E.2d 969. Infants ⇐ 247

It is an abuse of discretion for a trial court to allow a referee to preside over a protracted child support and custody case after he petitioned the court for removal due to bias, and the subsequent order based on the referee's report is improper. In re Reiner (Cuyahoga 1991) 74 Ohio App.3d 213, 598 N.E.2d 768, dismissed, jurisdictional motion overruled 62 Ohio St.3d 1439, 579 N.E.2d 212.

Juv R 40(D) does not contemplate that a trial court rubber-stamp all reports by referees; thus, a court may, upon consideration of objections properly made, reject a referee's report. In re Bradford (Franklin 1986) 30 Ohio App.3d 87, 506 N.E.2d 925, 30 O.B.R. 185.

Juv R 40(D)(1), which requires copies of juvenile court referee reports to be furnished to the parties, comprehends a supplemental report filed at the request of the court to correct deficiencies in the original; approval of a supplemental report is prejudicial error where a copy of the supplement was not provided to the defending party. In re Weimer (Cuyahoga 1984) 19 Ohio App.3d 130, 483 N.E.2d 173, 19 O.B.R. 219.

A juvenile judge has no authority to commit the trial of a criminal charge against an adult to a referee and any proceedings so committed are null and void. State v. Eddington (Marion 1976) 52 Ohio App.2d 312, 369 N.E.2d 1054, 6 O.O.3d 317. Criminal Law ⇐ 254.1

A decision of the magistrate regarding child support is effective when adopted by the court and a nunc pro tunc order cannot be used to supply the omitted court approval and does not serve to make a child support order effective as of the date of the magistrate's decision; the order of support is ineffective during the period of time between the magistrate's decision and the trial court's signing and approval. No. CT 2001–0032, 2001 WL 950664 (5th Dist Ct App, Muskingum, 8–17–01), State v Tucker.

Where a referee fails to prepare a report upon matters submitted by an order of reference and fails to file such report with the judge and to provide copies to the parties as required under Juv R 40(D)(1), a trial court's denial of a motion to reopen a child custody case and to change custody from a paternal grandmother to the mother is error because a failure to make a referee's report, where a referee is required by statute or rule to make one, will render the ensuing judgment voidable on a timely objection of a party. In re Wright, Nos. 13372+, 1993 WL 257423 (2d Dist Ct App, Montgomery, 7–6–93).

A juvenile court's judgment entered before the filing of a referee's report is invalid. In re Langrehr, No. 2944 (11th Dist Ct App, Trumbull, 11–9–81).

A judgment of the juvenile court in the form of journalized recommendations of the referee is not rendered invalid because it was not immediately signed by the judge. (Annotation from former RC 2151.16.) Allstate Ins. Co. v. Cook (C.A.6 (Ohio) 1963) 324 F.2d 752, 26 O.O.2d 192.

6. Procedures

Unmarried mother was not harmed by any procedural errors in trial court's adoption of magistrate's decision awarding custody to father, or entry of interim order declaring father to be residential parent, even if such errors rendered the orders in question legal nullities; trial court previously entered temporary order naming father the temporary residential parent, and nullification of subsequent orders would therefore leave child in father's custody, rather than cause custody to revert to mother. Goeller v. Moore (Ohio App. 10 Dist., Franklin, 01-27-2005) No. 04AP-394, 2005-Ohio-292, 2005 WL 174809, Unreported. Children Out-of-wedlock ⇐ 20.11

Unmarried mother's arguments, on appeal from trial court's adoption of magistrate's decision awarding custody of child to father, that trial court lacked subject matter jurisdiction over father's complaint for custody were barred by doctrine of collateral estoppel, where mother raised identical arguments in her petition for writ of habeas corpus, and Supreme Court concluded in such habeas action that trial court had jurisdiction. Goeller v. Moore (Ohio App. 10 Dist., Franklin, 01-27-2005) No. 04AP-394, 2005-Ohio-292, 2005 WL 174809, Unreported. Habeas Corpus ⇐ 902

Juvenile, who was adjudicated a delinquent child, waived for appellate review claim that his conviction for breaking and entering was against the manifest weight of the evidence and not supported by sufficient evidence, where juvenile failed to file objections to the magistrate's decision adjudicating him a delinquent child. In re Carter (Ohio App. 4 Dist., Jackson, 12-30-2004) No. 04CA15, No. 04CA16, 2004-Ohio-7285, 2004 WL 3090250, Unreported. Infants ⇐ 243

Juvenile, who was adjudicated a delinquent child, waived for appellate review claim that the juvenile court erred in admitting victim's in-court identification into evidence, where juvenile failed to file a motion to suppress the identification testimony, failed to object to the identification testimony at trial, and, more importantly, failed to file objections to the magistrate's decision adjudicating him a delinquent child. In re Carter (Ohio App. 4 Dist., Jackson, 12-30-2004) No. 04CA15, No. 04CA16, 2004-Ohio-7285, 2004 WL 3090250, Unreported. Infants ⇐ 243

Trial court's failure to admit belt used to beat 11-year-old child at trial to determine whether he was an abused child did not constitute plain error, given that defendant in proceeding failed to subpoena the evidence or to make any attempt to arrange for the evidence to be present at trial. In re Horton (Ohio App. 10 Dist., Franklin, 11-23-2004) No. 03AP-1181, 2004-Ohio-6249, 2004 WL 2674562, Unreported. Infants ⇐ 243

Grandmother waived for appeal issue of whether her right to discovery was violated in child dependency proceedings, where grandmother made no objection at trial or written objection to magistrate's decision concerning discovery procedure. In re McCann (Ohio App. 12 Dist., Clermont, 01-26-2004) No. CA2003-02-017, 2004-Ohio-283, 2004 WL 111644, Unreported. Infants ⇐ 243

Grandmother waived for appeal issue of whether she was entitled to grant of her motion for new dispositional hearing in child dependency proceedings, where grandmother failed to object to magistrate's denial of her motion. In re McCann (Ohio App. 12 Dist., Clermont, 01-26-2004) No. CA2003-02-017, 2004-Ohio-283, 2004 WL 111644, Unreported. Infants ⇐ 243

Mother, appealing juvenile court's determination that child was a dependent child, waived for appeal irregularities during hearing before magistrate, where mother failed to object. In re Malone (Ohio App. 10 Dist., Franklin, 12-30-2003) No. 03AP-489, 2003-Ohio-7156, 2003 WL 23024377, Unreported, appeal not allowed 102 Ohio St.3d 1423, 807 N.E.2d 367, 2004-Ohio-2003. Infants ⇐ 243

Father's failure to object to magistrate's findings or conclusions in proceeding to terminate parental rights and to grant permanent custody of children to family services agency limited review on appeal to whether findings and conclusions adequately supported trial court's decision to grant permanent custody. In re Kincer (Ohio App. 5 Dist., Licking, 11-24-2003) No. 03-CA-43, 2003-Ohio-6356, 2003 WL 22828046, Unreported. Infants ⇐ 243

Trial court's decision not to specifically rule on child support obligor's objection to magistrate's decision, which found obligor to be in contempt for failure to pay child support, did not amount to reversible error regarding county child support enforcement agency's motion to show cause against obligor, since objection lacked specificity and did not state particular grounds, obligor failed to include transcript of magistrate's hearing, and trial court reviewed decision for errors of law and other facial defects. Heifner v. Bess (Ohio App. 5 Dist., Ashland, 11-13-2003) No. 03 COA 013, 2003-Ohio-6047, 2003 WL 22671565, Unreported. Child Support ⇐ 558(4)

Mother could not raise on appeal, from Juvenile Court's adoption of finding of facts and conclusion of law of magistrate in termination of parental rights proceeding, an objection to magistrate's decision, where objection was not raised in lower court. In re K.M. (Ohio App. 9 Dist., Summit, 10-29-2003) No. 21536, 2003-Ohio-5781, 2003 WL 22439756, Unreported. Infants ⇐ 243

Parents failed to preserve argument that there was conflict of interest in dual appointment of children's guardian ad litem as children's attorney when they failed to raise argument when objecting to magistrate's decision to grant permanent custody of children to county services. In re Sessoms (Ohio App. 12 Dist., Butler, 10-06-2003) No. CA2002-11-280, 2003-Ohio-5281, 2003 WL 22283495, Unreported. Infants ⇐ 243

Mother waived for appellate review claim that trial court decision adjudicating children dependent was against manifest weight of the evidence, where adjudication was originally made by a magistrate and later adopted by trial court, and mother failed to object to magistrate's adjudication. In re C.F. (Ohio App. 9 Dist., Lorain, 11-13-2002) No. 02CA008084, 2002-Ohio-6113, 2002 WL 31513423, Unreported. Infants ⇐ 243

Father waived for appeal issue of whether magistrate was authorized to assign child neglect case to visiting judge, where father failed to object, and alleged error did not divest juvenile court of subject matter jurisdiction. In re J.J. (Ohio, 11-08-2006) 111 Ohio St.3d 205, 855 N.E.2d 851, 2006-Ohio-5484. Infants ⇐ 243

A party in proceedings before the juvenile court may timely object to the authority of a visiting judge on the basis of an improper case transfer or assignment, but failure to timely enter such an objection waives the procedural error. In re J.J. (Ohio, 11-08-2006) 111 Ohio St.3d 205, 855 N.E.2d 851, 2006-Ohio-5484. Courts ⇐ 176.5

The juvenile court, when referring a matter to a magistrate, is not required to use any specified form of reference, nor is the juvenile court required to journalize an individual order of reference for each issue submitted. State ex rel. Nalls v. Russo (Ohio, 10-02-2002) 96 Ohio St.3d 410, 775 N.E.2d 522, 2002-Ohio-4907. Infants ⇐ 206

Juvenile court's journal entry was sufficient to refer a child abuse and dependency matter to a magistrate; the entry was titled in part an "Order of Reference," it expressly authorized the magistrate to "hear and recommend dispositions on official cases assigned to 'the magistrate' as the Court shall direct," and it directed the magistrate to preside over the child abuse and dependency proceeding. State ex rel. Nalls v. Russo (Ohio, 10-02-2002) 96 Ohio St.3d 410, 775 N.E.2d 522, 2002-Ohio-4907. Infants ⇔ 206

Mother's allegation that juvenile court's journal entry, which was signed by both magistrate and judge and which adjudicated the child as dependent, had failed to comply with the rule requiring the magistrate to prepare a separate decision did not establish that the magistrate and judge lacked jurisdiction over the child abuse and dependency proceeding. State ex rel. Nalls v. Russo (Ohio, 10-02-2002) 96 Ohio St.3d 410, 775 N.E.2d 522, 2002-Ohio-4907. Infants ⇔ 196

The language of the rule regarding the juvenile court's reference of a matter to a magistrate is discretionary rather than mandatory. State ex rel. Nalls v. Russo (Ohio, 10-02-2002) 96 Ohio St.3d 410, 775 N.E.2d 522, 2002-Ohio-4907. Infants ⇔ 206

Court of Appeals would not use abuse-of-discretion standard when reviewing trial court's decision to adopt magistrate's decision committing juvenile, who admitted to offenses of participation in a criminal gang and drug trafficking, to state Department of Youth Services (DYS) rather than releasing juvenile on community control, and review would be limited to errors of law or other defects on face of order, since juvenile failed to file objections to magistrate's decision. In re Harris (Ohio App. 10 Dist., Franklin, 05-15-2003) No. 02AP-1188, 2003-Ohio-2485, 2003 WL 21101271, Unreported. Infants ⇔ 243; Infants ⇔ 251

Mother was precluded from claiming that trial court erred by considering, in its ruling on magistrate's decision to award permanent custody of her four children to county, additional evidence after the conclusion of testimony in the initial hearing on the matter, where mother herself requested a further hearing so that she could testify. In re Pederson (Ohio App. 10 Dist., Franklin, 04-29-2003) No. 02AP-853, No. 02AP-856, No. 02AP-854, No. 02AP-855, 2003-Ohio-2138, 2003 WL 1962429, Unreported. Infants ⇔ 248.1

Trial court was authorized to hear additional evidence in ruling on mother's objections to magistrate's decision to grant permanent custody of mother's four children to county. In re Pederson (Ohio App. 10 Dist., Franklin, 04-29-2003) No. 02AP-853, No. 02AP-856, No. 02AP-854, No. 02AP-855, 2003-Ohio-2138, 2003 WL 1962429, Unreported. Infants ⇔ 206

Juvenile defendant failed to preserve for appeal any assignment of error challenging the weight and sufficiency of the evidence supporting his adjudication of delinquency; defense trial counsel never provided transcript of the proceedings, which prevented either the trial court or the appellate court from reviewing the factual findings of the magistrate, and moreover, counsel withdrew his objections to the magistrate's decision, affirmatively waiving any objection to factual findings. State v. Hughes (Ohio App. 1 Dist., Hamilton, 02-28-2003) No. C-020035, No. C-020088, 2003-Ohio-890, 2003 WL 554000, Unreported. Infants ⇔ 243; Infants ⇔ 246; Infants ⇔ 248.1

Mother waived her appellate argument that the trial court decision adjudication the children dependent was against the manifest weight of the evidence, in child dependency proceeding, where adjudication of dependency was originally made by a magistrate and later adopted by the trial court, and mother failed to object to the magistrate's adjudication. In re C.F. (Ohio App. 9 Dist., Lorain, 11-13-2002) No. 02CA008084, 2002-Ohio-6113, 2002 WL 31513423, Unreported. Infants ⇔ 243

Mother established entitlement to writ of mandamus compelling county child support enforcement agency to stop withholding child support from her wages, where trial court never ruled on mother's timely objections, and order issued by court was an interim order that was not final and appealable. State ex rel. Rangel v. Lucas County Child Support Enforcement Agency (Ohio App. 6 Dist., Lucas, 10-11-2002) No. L-02-1252, 2002-Ohio-5497, 2002 WL 31270279, Unreported. Mandamus ⇔ 105

Magistrate's failure, in dependency proceeding, to satisfy her obligation to determine whether mother was making knowing, intelligent and voluntary admission to facts in complaint was plain error, and mother's failure to object thereto did not waive appellate review of magistrate's failure to comply with applicable rule. In re Etter (Ohio App. 1 Dist., 06-12-1998) 134 Ohio App.3d 484, 731 N.E.2d 694. Infants ⇔ 243

Failure to draw juvenile court's attention to possible error, by objection or otherwise, when error could have been corrected, results in waiver of issue for purposes of appeal. In re Etter (Ohio App. 1 Dist., 06-12-1998) 134 Ohio App.3d 484, 731 N.E.2d 694. Infants ⇔ 243

Court of Appeals was precluded from considering any portion of the transcript of a magistrate's hearing on juvenile's motion to suppress, as the transcript was not provided to the trial court during earlier proceedings in the matter. In re Dengg (Ohio App. 11 Dist., 03-08-1999) 132 Ohio App.3d 360, 724 N.E.2d 1255. Infants ⇔ 246

Trial court's allowing state witness' mother, a nonparty witness, to communicate extensively out of presence of one of the parties, namely, accused delinquent minor, about referee's findings and recommendations raised questions regarding appearance of unfairness of proceedings and warranted vacation of adjudication of delinquency based upon attempted felonious assault finding and remand for hearing and ruling on objections to initial referee's report and recommendations. In re Ross (Ohio App. 10 Dist., 10-24-1995) 107 Ohio App.3d 35, 667 N.E.2d 1012. Infants ⇔ 207; Infants ⇔ 254

Because the no contact order, prohibiting mother from contacting her child, was continued in a subsequent proceeding, the lack of a complete transcript of initial hearing did not render the order invalid; hearing transcript and the judge's subsequent order continuing the no contact restriction were adequate to show that it was imposed upon proper procedures and evidence that the restriction was in child's best interest. In re F.M. (Ohio App. 8 Dist., Cuyahoga, 08-01-2002) No. 80027, 2002-Ohio-3900, 2002 WL 1767396, Unreported, appeal not allowed 98 Ohio St.3d 1410, 781 N.E.2d 1019, 2003-Ohio-60. Infants ⇔ 221

A trial court order entry that delineated basis of adjudication of dependency was not required, where neither party made such a request for findings and conclusions of law. In re Ware (Ohio App. 2 Dist., Montgomery, 09-06-2002) No. 19302, 2002-Ohio-4686, 2002 WL 31002612, Unreported, opinion modified on reconsideration 2002-Ohio-6086, 2002 WL 31492584. Infants ⇔ 210

Since mother filed no objections to the magistrate's report modifying father's child support obligation, mother waived, for purposes of appeal, her right to challenge the judgment of the trial court adopting magistrate's report. Dorothy P. v. Leo P. (Ohio App. 6 Dist., Sandusky, 08-30-2002) No. S-01-032, 2002-Ohio-4477, 2002 WL 1998448, Unreported. Child Support ⇔ 539

Notice required by this section to be given to parties must be in writing. (Annotation from former RC 2151.16.) In re Hobson (Franklin 1945) 62 N.E.2d 510, 44 Ohio Law Abs. 85, 44 Ohio Law Abs. 86.

7. Constitutional issues

Neither the magistrate's temporary no contact order, prohibiting mother from contacting her child, nor the judge's continuation of it required written findings of fact, even if mother had requested them, and lack of a decision with findings of fact did not deprive mother of due process; record contained enough facts to conclude that there was adequate basis for the order. In re F.M. (Ohio App. 8 Dist., Cuyahoga, 08-01-2002) No. 80027, 2002-Ohio-3900, 2002 WL 1767396, Unreported, appeal not allowed 98 Ohio St.3d 1410, 781 N.E.2d 1019, 2003-Ohio-60. Constitutional Law ⇔ 274(5); Infants ⇔ 221

A juvenile's double jeopardy protections are violated when the trial court reverses its own judgment entry dismissing the complaint and finding defendant delinquent of rape where the trial court has no remaining jurisdiction to reopen the decision, reverse an acquittal and find defendant delinquent where written objections to the magistrate's report and judgment entry dismissing rape charges against the juvenile are not timely filed within fourteen days. In re Donald Joseph M. (Ohio App. 6 Dist., Sandusky, 09-17-1999) No. S-98-058, 1999 WL 727168, Unreported.

An adjudication of delinquency following the court's initial finding that the state failed to prove beyond a doubt that the minor was guilty of carrying a concealed weapon violates his rights under the Double Jeopardy Clause. Matter of Phommarath (Ohio App. 10 Dist., Franklin, 11-14-1995) No. 95APF05-539, 1995 WL 681213, Unreported.

A juvenile is placed in jeopardy at a hearing before a master whose duty is to determine whether he has committed acts that violate a criminal law, and where the potential consequences are stigma and the deprivation of liberty. (Ed. note: Maryland law construed in light of federal constitution.) (See also United States v DiFrancesco, 449 US 117, 101 SCt 426, 66 LEd(2d) 328 (1980).) Swisher v. Brady (U.S.Md. 1978) 98 S.Ct. 2699, 438 U.S. 204, 57 L.Ed.2d 705.

8. Referees, powers and duties

Magistrate conducting delinquency adjudication hearing was required to prepare, sign and file a magistrate's decision of the matter. In re Deangelo M. (Ohio App. 6 Dist., Erie, 09-09-2005) No. E-04-049, 2005-Ohio-4726, 2005 WL 2174651, Unreported. Infants ⇔ 206

Magistrate lacked authority to refer child protection proceeding to visiting judge, especially without judicial approval from sitting judge assigned to case. In re S.J. (Ohio App. 8 Dist., Cuyahoga, 04-21-2005) No. 84410, 2005-Ohio-1854, 2005 WL 914692, Unreported. Judges ⇨ 25(1)

Although proceedings before magistrate, ancillary to delinquency complaint and involving alleged violation of court order, should have been recorded, failure to record did not cause juvenile prejudice, as magistrate's detention order would have expired on its own once court proceeded to disposition on delinquency complaint, and juvenile did not argue that her rights were violated in any respect before the magistrate. In re Smith (Ohio App. 8 Dist., 03-26-2001) 142 Ohio App.3d 16, 753 N.E.2d 930. Infants ⇨ 203

While the juvenile court has authority to appoint a referee with power of masters in chancery to hear a case and report his findings and recommendations to the judge, there is no such authority with reference to an investigating counselor, and the action and report of such counselor is ex parte and does not constitute the hearing of "additional testimony" by the judge under such statute. (Annotation from former RC 2151.16.) Dolgin v. Dolgin (Lucas 1965) 1 Ohio App.2d 430, 205 N.E.2d 106, 30 O.O.2d 435.

At present, referees are not required to comply with Gov Jud R IV, which mandates continuing legal education for judges. Both part-time and full-time referees are encouraged to participate in continuing legal education in order to increase their knowledge and understanding of their position as referees and their knowledge of the area of law over which they preside as referee. (Annotation from Gov Jud R IV.) Bd of Commrs on Grievances & Discipline Op 87-041 (9-25-87).

Members of a part-time referee's law firm may not appear before their colleague as referee, but may appear before another judge or referee in the same division. Bd of Commrs on Grievances & Discipline Op 87-036 (9-25-87).

A part-time referee is considered a part-time judge for purposes of the Code of Judicial Conduct and may serve as a member or officer of a local board of education, provided such activity does not reflect adversely upon his impartiality or interfere with the performance of his judicial duties. A part-time referee should not serve as a member or officer of a local board of education if it is likely that said board will be engaged in proceedings that would ordinarily come before him or will be regularly engaged in adversary proceedings in any court. Additionally, a part-time referee should disqualify himself in any case in which his decision could affect any organization which he serves as either an officer or member of its board and he should avoid even the appearance of impropriety in all his activities. (Annotation from Code of Jud Cond Canon 3.) Bd of Commrs on Grievances & Discipline Op 87-032 (6-22-87).

Referees are considered judges for purposes of complying with the Code of Judicial Conduct. In this regard, part-time referees may not practice before the court division on which they serve or before the judge or judges to whom they owe their appointment; however, part-time referees serving the domestic relations division of common pleas court may practice law before other judges in the general, probate, and juvenile divisions of that court so long as they avoid the appearance of impropriety. (Annotation from Code of Jud Cond Canon 2.) (See also Bd of Commrs on Grievances & Discipline Op 87-036 (9-25-87).) Bd of Commrs on Grievances & Discipline Op 87-014 (6-22-87).

9. Hearings

Trial court in termination of parental rights proceeding was not required to hold a hearing on mother's objections to magistrate's decision, which recommended termination of mother's parental rights. In re Goff (Ohio App. 11 Dist., Ashtabula, 12-23-2004) No. 2004-A-0051, 2004-Ohio-7235, 2004 WL 3090218, Unreported, appeal not allowed 105 Ohio St.3d 1473, 824 N.E.2d 542, 2005-Ohio-1186. Infants ⇨ 203

That magistrate in child custody hearing as to nonmarital child took testimony from psychologist after child's guardian ad litem withdrew was not plain error; magistrate continued hearing until after new guardian ad litem was appointed, psychologist's testimony was made available to new guardian ad litem, and guardian ad litem was allowed to call and question psychologist if necessary at subsequent hearing. Noonan v. Edson (Ohio App. 12 Dist., Butler, 04-07-2003) No. CA2002-04-088, 2003-Ohio-1767, 2003 WL 1795576, Unreported. Children Out-of-wedlock ⇨ 20.11

An evidentiary hearing before the juvenile court judge after a hearing before a juvenile court referee is not mandatory. In re Stall (Ohio 1973) 36 Ohio St.2d 139, 304 N.E.2d 596, 65 O.O.2d 338.

Rules governing objection to reports of juvenile referee do not require that trial court hold hearing when objections and affidavit about evidence have been filed; further consideration is required, but hearing is within discretion of court. In re Zindle (Ohio App. 9 Dist., 11-08-1995) 107 Ohio App.3d 342, 668 N.E.2d 969. Infants ⇨ 206

The action of a juvenile court in postponing a hearing on a matter submitted to a referee who failed to file findings and recommendations, and in rectifying such deficiency by taking additional testimony and, thereafter, rendering a decision constitutes a substantial compliance with 2151.16. (Annotation from former RC 2151.16.) In re Gutman (Hamilton 1969) 22 Ohio App.2d 125, 259 N.E.2d 128, 51 O.O.2d 252.

Juv R 41   [Reserved]

Juv R 42   Consent to marry

(A) Application where parental consent not required

When a minor desires to contract matrimony and has no parent, guardian, or custodian whose consent to the marriage is required by law, the minor shall file an application under oath in the county where the female resides requesting that the judge of the juvenile court give consent and approbation in the probate court for such marriage.

(B) Contents of application

The application required by division (A) of this rule shall contain all of the following:

(1) The name and address of the person for whom consent is sought;

(2) The age of the person for whom consent is sought;

(3) The reason why consent of a parent is not required;

(4) The name and address, if known, of the parent, where the minor alleges that parental consent is unnecessary because the parent has neglected or abandoned the child for at least one year immediately preceding the application.

(C) Application where female pregnant or delivered of child born out of wedlock

Where a female is pregnant or delivered of a child born out of wedlock and the parents of such child seek to marry even though one or both of them is under the minimum age prescribed by law for persons who may contract marriage, such persons shall file an application under oath in the county where the female resides requesting that the judge of the juvenile court give consent in the probate court to such marriage.

(D) Contents of application

The application required by subdivision (C) shall contain:

(1) The name and address of the person or persons for whom consent is sought;

(2) The age of such person;

(3) An indication of whether the female is pregnant or has already been delivered;

(4) An indication of whether or not any applicant under eighteen years of age is already a ward of the court; and

(5) Any other facts which may assist the court in determining whether to consent to such marriage.

If pregnancy is asserted, a certificate from a physician verifying pregnancy shall be attached to the application. If an illegitimate child has been delivered, the birth certificate of such child shall be attached.

The consent to the granting of the application by each parent whose consent to the marriage is required by law shall be indorsed on the application.

(E) Investigation

Upon receipt of an application under subdivision (C), the court shall set a date and time for hearing thereon at its earliest convenience and shall direct that an inquiry be made as to the circumstances surrounding the applicants.

(F) Notice

If neglect or abandonment is alleged in an application under subdivision (A) and the address of the parent is known, the court shall cause notice of the date and time of hearing to be served upon such parent.

(G) Judgment

If the court finds that the allegations stated in the application are true, and that the granting of the application is in the best interest of the applicants, the court shall grant the consent and shall make the applicant referred to in subdivision (C) a ward of the court.

(H) Certified copy

A certified copy of the judgment entry shall be transmitted to the probate court.

(Adopted eff. 7–1–72; amended eff. 7–1–80, 7–1–94)

Historical and Statutory Notes

Amendment Note: The 7–1–94 amendment made changes to reflect gender-neutral language.

Staff Notes

1994:

Rule 42 Consent to Marry

Masculine references in Juv. R. 42 were replaced by gender neutral language and nonsubstantive grammatical revisions were made.

Editor's Comment

Consent to marry   1
Application where parental consent not required   2
Contents of application   3
Application where minor female pregnant or delivered of a child born out of wedlock   4
Contents of application   5
Investigation   6
Notice   7
Judgment   8
Certified copy   9

1. Consent to marry

Juv R 42 was adopted pursuant to Juv R 1(B)(2) to provide for simplicity and uniformity in procedure. 3101.04 provides that when the juvenile court files a consent to marriage pursuant to the juvenile rules (i.e., Juv R 42), the probate court may thereupon issue a marriage license, notwithstanding either or both the contracting parties are under the minimum age prescribed in 3101.01. Pursuant to 3101.01, male persons of the age of eighteen and females of the age of sixteen, not nearer than second cousins, and not having a husband or wife living, may be joined in marriage. The statute requires that a minor must first obtain the consent of his parents, surviving parent, custodial parent, guardian, or a person or organization who has been awarded permanent custody of the child by a juvenile court.

2. Application where parental consent not required

Juv R 42(A) provides that an application under oath be filed in the juvenile court of the county where the female resides for consent to marry when parental consent is not required.

3. Contents of application

Juv R 42(B) sets forth what information shall be furnished the court in the application for consent to marry.

4. Application where minor female pregnant or delivered of a child born out of wedlock

Juv R 42(C) provides for the filing of an application for consent to marry when the female is under sixteen years of age and is pregnant or has been delivered of a child born out of wedlock.

5. Contents of application

Juv R 42(D) outlines what the application for consent to marry, where a female is under sixteen, is pregnant or has been delivered of an illegitimate child, shall contain.

6. Investigation

Juv R 42(E) requires that the court conduct an inquiry as to the circumstances and to set a date and time for the hearing.

7. Notice

Juv R 42(F) provides for notice to a parent whose address is known regarding the hearing when the application under Division (A) alleges that consent is not required because neglect for a period of one year or abandonment has occurred.

8. Judgment

Juv R 42(G) makes it clear that the court has discretionary authority to grant or deny the application. The best interests of the applicants is the determinative issue.

9. Certified copy

Juv R 42(H) requires that a certified copy of the judgment entry be furnished the probate court which may issue the marriage license upon the applicants' complying with the other provisions. (See Ch 3101 regarding marriage.)

Cross References

Abortion without parental consent, 2151.85
Persons who may marry, 3101.01
Probate court may issue license after juvenile court files consent to marriage, 3101.04

Library References

Marriage ⇐5, 12.1, 18, 19.
Westlaw Topic No. 253.
C.J.S. Marriage §§ 9 to 26, 36.

Research References

Encyclopedias

OH Jur. 3d Family Law § 20, Application for Consent by Juvenile Court.
OH Jur. 3d Family Law § 21, Application for Consent by Juvenile Court—Pregnancy of Underage Female.
OH Jur. 3d Family Law § 22, Hearing on Application for Consent.

Treatises and Practice Aids

Sowald & Morganstern, Baldwin's Ohio Practice Domestic Relations Law § 2:16, Capacity to Marry—Legal Age.
Carlin, Baldwin's Ohio Practice, Merrick-Rippner Probate Law § 106:20, Juvenile Court Jurisdiction—Consent for Child to Marry.
Carlin, Baldwin's Ohio Practice, Merrick-Rippner Probate Law § 106:27, Application for Consent to Marry—Juvenile Court—Form.

Notes of Decisions

Consent   1
Marriage without consent   2

1. Consent

A minor youth who has been committed to the youth services department pursuant to RC 2151.355 and 5139.05 and who wishes to get married must first obtain consent, as required by RC 3101.01 and Juv R 42, from one or both parents, from one of the alternative authorities named in RC 3101.01, or from the juvenile court as provided in Juv R 42(A). The youth services department has no authority to either consent or withhold consent to the marriage of a minor committed to its custody. OAG 89–046.

2. Marriage without consent

The marriage of a male person seventeen years of age is void except under the conditions provided for in section. (Annotation from former RC 3101.04.) Carlton v. Carlton (Wood 1945) 76 Ohio App. 338, 64 N.E.2d 428, 32 O.O. 82. Marriage ⇐ 5

Juv R 43   Reference to Ohio Revised Code

A reference in these rules to a section of the Revised Code shall mean the section as amended from time to time including the enactment of additional sections, the numbers of which are subsequent to the section referred to in the rules.

(Adopted eff. 7-1-94)

Staff Notes

1994:

Rule 43 Reference to Ohio Revised Code

Juv. R. 43 clarifies that any Revised Code section referred to in these rules shall mean the section as amended from time to time. This provision replicates Civ. R. 81.

Editor's Comment

Juv R 43, which was added in 1994, is significant because many of the Juvenile Rules refer to statutes contained in Chapter 2151. While the General Assembly frequently amends or enacts statutes, no comprehensive changes were made in the Juvenile Rules following their adoption in 1972 until 1994.

Juv R 44 Jurisdiction unaffected

These rules shall not be construed to extend or limit the jurisdiction of the juvenile court.

(Adopted eff. 7-1-72)

Editor's Comment

Juv R 44 makes it clear that the Rules of Juvenile Procedure do not affect the jurisdiction of the juvenile court. Jurisdiction is established by the Constitution of Ohio, 2151.23, and 2151.85.

Cross References

Scope of rules, exceptions, Juv R 1

Library References

Infants ⟐196.
Westlaw Topic No. 211.
C.J.S. Courts §§ 249 et seq.
C.J.S. Infants §§ 42, 53, 54.

Research References

Encyclopedias

OH Jur. 3d Family Law § 1533, Construction.

Treatises and Practice Aids

Giannelli & Yeomans, Ohio Juvenile Law § 1:8, Rules of Juvenile Procedure.

Giannelli & Yeomans, Ohio Juvenile Law § 19:7, Time Requirements.

Giannelli & Yeomans, Ohio Juvenile Law § 22:1, Introduction.

Giannelli & Yeomans, Ohio Juvenile Law § 25:4, Time Requirements.

Notes of Decisions

Constitutional issues 2
Jurisdiction 1

---

1. Jurisdiction

Because the Ohio Rules of Juvenile Procedure may not extend or limit the jurisdiction of the juvenile court, a procedural violation has no effect on jurisdictional issues, which are governed by statutory law. Linger v. Weiss (Ohio 1979) 57 Ohio St.2d 97, 386 N.E.2d 1354, 11 O.O.3d 281, certiorari denied 100 S.Ct. 128, 444 U.S. 862, 62 L.Ed.2d 83.

The juvenile court has exclusive original jurisdiction, pursuant to RC 2151.23(A), concerning any child who is alleged in a proper complaint to be neglected, and the court does not lose jurisdiction by failing to adhere to the time limits set forth in Juv R 29(A) and 34(A). Linger v. Weiss (Ohio 1979) 57 Ohio St.2d 97, 386 N.E.2d 1354, 11 O.O.3d 281, certiorari denied 100 S.Ct. 128, 444 U.S. 862, 62 L.Ed.2d 83.

2. Constitutional issues

A procedure which allows a juvenile court master to file written findings of fact with the juvenile court judge who may then make supplemental findings in response to the state's exceptions, the juvenile's exceptions or sua sponte, either on the record or a record supplemented by evidence to which the parties do not object, does not violate the Double Jeopardy Clause. (Ed. note: Maryland law construed in light of federal constitution.) (See also United States v DiFrancesco, 449 US 117, 101 SCt 426, 66 LEd(2d) 328 (1980).) Swisher v. Brady (U.S.Md. 1978) 98 S.Ct. 2699, 438 U.S. 204, 57 L.Ed.2d 705.

Juv R 45 Rules by juvenile courts; procedure not otherwise specified

(A) Local rules

The juvenile court may adopt rules concerning local practice that are not inconsistent with these rules. Local rules shall be adopted only after the court gives appropriate notice and an opportunity for comment. If the court determines that there is an immediate need for a rule, the court may adopt the rule without prior notice and opportunity for comment but promptly shall afford notice and opportunity for comment. Local rules shall be filed with the Supreme Court.

(B) Procedure not otherwise specified

If no procedure is specifically prescribed by these rules or local rule, the court shall proceed in any lawful manner not inconsistent with these rules or local rule.

(Adopted eff. 7-1-72; amended eff. 7-1-94)

Historical and Statutory Notes

Amendment Note: The 7-1-94 amendment added "Rules by juvenile courts;" to the title of the rule; added division (A); designated division (B); and added references to local rules in division (B).

Staff Notes

1994:

Rule 45 Rules by Juvenile Courts; Procedure Not Otherwise Specified

Division (A) has been added to permit juvenile courts to develop local rules not inconsistent with the Ohio Rules of Juvenile Procedure. This provision is consistent with similar changes in Civ. R. 83 and App. R. 31.

Editor's Comment

Juvenile court has jurisdiction over many different types of proceedings pursuant to 2151.23 for which no specific procedure has been provided in these rules, either because they are related to matters in the probate or domestic relations divisions of the common pleas court or the issue is seldom raised in the juvenile court.

Examples of this are transfer of jurisdiction from the probate division pursuant to 3107.12; transfer of jurisdiction from domestic relations division under 3109.04 and 3109.06; and the jurisdiction of the juvenile court to exercise the powers and jurisdiction of the probate division granted in Ch 5122 of the Ohio Revised Code, if a child is otherwise within the jurisdiction of the juvenile court. An example of seldom used procedure is proceedings under the Interstate Compact under 2151.56. Juv R 45 is designed to apply to these kinds of procedures.

Library References

Infants ⟐191.
Westlaw Topic No. 211.
C.J.S. Infants §§ 42, 53, 54.

Research References

Encyclopedias

OH Jur. 3d Family Law § 1533, Construction.

Treatises and Practice Aids

Klein, Darling, & Terez, Baldwin's Ohio Practice Civil Practice § 24:2, Applicability of Civ. R. 24.

Klein, Darling, & Terez, Baldwin's Ohio Practice Civil Practice § 24:12, Intervention of Right--Nonstatutory Intervention of Right--"The

Applicant Claims an Interest Relating to the Property or Transaction Which is the Subject of the Action"--Interest...

Carlin, Baldwin's Ohio Practice, Merrick-Rippner Probate Law § 107:50, Adjudicatory Hearings—Applicability of Rules of Court.

Carlin, Baldwin's Ohio Practice, Merrick-Rippner Probate Law § 107:117, Proceedings After Judgment—Continuing Jurisdiction of Juvenile Court.

Notes of Decisions
Constitutional issues   1

---

1. Constitutional issues

The federal courts will abstain from interfering in state proceedings where juveniles seek an injunction against the use of social histories in pre-adjudication instances, although they may hear an issue involving the constitutionality of post-adjudicatory dissemination of the social histories where state law is not clear and the proper factual issues were not decided; the dissemination of social histories compiled by probation officers during juvenile proceedings do not violate a constitutional right to privacy. J. P. v. DeSanti (C.A.6 (Ohio) 1981) 653 F.2d 1080.

Juv R 46   Forms

The forms contained in the Appendix of Forms which the supreme court from time to time may approve are illustrative and not mandatory.

(Adopted eff. 7–1–72)

Editor's Comment

Juv R 46 provides that forms approved by the Supreme Court are not mandatory. The rule permits local courts to devise forms to meet local conditions. However, pursuant to 2151.85(G), C P Sup R 76, and C P Sup R 77, certain forms developed by the Supreme Court with respect to abortion notification bypass proceedings must be utilized by the juvenile courts.

Juv R 47   Effective date

(A) Effective date of rules

These rules shall take effect on the first day of July, 1972. They govern all proceedings in actions brought after they take effect and also all further proceedings in actions then pending, except to the extent that their application in a particular action pending when the rules take effect would not be feasible or would work injustice, in which event the former procedure applies.

(B) Effective date of amendments

The amendments submitted by the Supreme Court to the general assembly on January 12, 1973, shall take effect on the first day of July, 1973. They govern all proceedings in actions brought after they take effect and also all further proceedings in actions then pending, except to the extent that their application in a particular action pending when the amendments take effect would not be feasible or would work injustice, in which event the former procedure applies.

(C) Effective date of amendments

The amendments submitted by the Supreme Court to the General Assembly on January 10, 1975, and on April 29, 1975, shall take effect on July 1, 1975. They govern all proceedings in actions brought after they take effect and also all further proceedings in actions then pending, except to the extent that their application in a particular action pending when the amendments take effect would not be feasible or would work injustice, in which event the former procedure applies.

(D) Effective date of amendments

The amendments submitted by the Supreme Court to the General Assembly on January 9, 1976 shall take effect on July 1, 1976. They govern all proceedings in actions brought after they take effect and also all further proceedings in actions then pending, except to the extent that their application in a particular action pending when the amendments take effect would not be feasible or would work injustice, in which event the former procedure applies.

(E) Effective date of amendments

The amendments submitted by the Supreme Court to the General Assembly on January 14, 1980, shall take effect on July 1, 1980. They govern all proceedings in actions brought after they take effect and also all further proceedings in actions then pending, except to the extent that their application in a particular action pending when the amendments take effect would not be feasible or would work injustice, in which event the former procedure applies.

(F) Effective date of amendments.

The amendments submitted by the Supreme Court to the General Assembly on December 24, 1984 and January 8, 1985 shall take effect on July 1, 1985. They govern all proceedings in actions brought after they take effect and also all further proceedings in actions then pending, except to the extent that their application in a particular action pending when the amendments take effect would not be feasible or would work injustice, in which event the former procedure applies.

(G) Effective date of amendments

The amendments submitted by the Supreme Court to the General Assembly on January 10, 1991 shall take effect on July 1, 1991. They govern all proceedings in actions brought after they take effect and also all further proceedings in actions then pending, except to the extent that their application in a particular action pending when the amendments take effect would not be feasible or would work injustice, in which event the former procedure applies.

(H) Effective date of amendments

The amendments filed by the Supreme Court with the General Assembly on January 14, 1992 and further filed on April 30, 1992, shall take effect on July 1, 1992. They govern all proceedings in actions brought after they take effect and also all future proceedings in actions then pending, except to the extent that their application in a particular action pending when the amendments take effect would not be feasible or would work injustice, in which event the former procedure applies.

(I) Effective date of amendments

The amendments filed by the Supreme Court with the General Assembly on January 14, 1994 and further revised and filed on April 29, 1994 shall take effect on July 1, 1994. They govern all proceedings in actions brought after they take effect and also all future proceedings in actions then pending, except to the extent that their application in a particular action pending when the amendments take effect would not be feasible or would work injustice, in which event the former procedure applies.

(J) Effective date of amendments

The amendments to Rules 1, 4, and 40 filed by the Supreme court [sic] with the General Assembly on January 11, 1995 and further revised and filed on April 25, 1995 shall take effect on July 1, 1995. They govern all proceedings in actions brought after they take effect and also all further proceedings in actions then pending, except to the extent that their application in a particular action pending when the amendments take effect would not be feasible or would work injustice, in which event the former procedure applies.

(K) Effective date of amendments

The amendments to Rules 6, 8, 13, 27, 34, 36, and 37 filed by the Supreme Court with the General Assembly on January 5, 1996 and refiled on April 26, 1996 shall take effect on July 1, 1996. They govern all proceedings in actions brought after they take effect and also all further proceedings in actions then pending, except to the extent that their application in a particular action pending when the amendments take effect would not be feasible or would work injustice, in which event the former procedure applies.

(L) Effective date of amendments

The amendments to Rule 30 filed by the Supreme Court with the General Assembly on January 10, 1997 and refiled on April 24, 1997 shall take effect on July 1, 1997. They govern all proceedings in actions brought after they take effect and also all further proceedings in actions then pending, except to the extent that their application in a particular action pending when the amendments take effect would not be feasible or would work injustice, in which event the former procedure applies.

(M) Effective date of amendments

The amendments to rules 2, 4, 10, 11, 15, 16, 29, 39, and 40 filed by the Supreme Court with the General Assembly on January 15, 1998 and further revised and refiled on April 30, 1998 shall take effect on July 1, 1998. They govern all proceedings in actions brought after they take effect and also all further proceedings in actions then pending, except to the extent that their application in a particular action pending when the amendments take effect would not be feasible or would work injustice, in which event the former procedure applies.

(N) Effective date of amendments

The amendments to Juvenile Rules 2, 7, 8, 10, 15, 22, 27, 29, 37, and 40 filed by the Supreme Court with the General Assembly on January 12, 2001, and revised and refiled on April 26, 2001, shall take effect on July 1, 2001. They govern all proceedings in actions brought after they take effect and also all further proceedings in actions then pending, except to the extent that their application in a particular action pending when the amendments take effect would not be feasible or would work injustice, in which event the former procedure applies.

(O) Effective date of amendments

The amendments to Juvenile Rules 2, 10, 15, and 34 filed by the Supreme Court with the General Assembly on January 11, 2002, and refiled on April 18, 2002 shall take effect on July 1, 2002. They govern all proceedings in actions brought after they take effect and also all further proceedings in actions then pending, except to the extent that their application in a particular action pending when the amendments take effect would not be feasible or would work injustice, in which event the former procedure applies.

(P) Effective date of amendments.

The amendments to Juvenile Rule 40 filed by the Supreme Court with the General Assembly on January 9, 2003 and refiled on April 28, 2003, shall take effect on July 1, 2003. They govern all proceedings in actions brought after they take effect and also all further proceedings in actions then pending, except to the extent that their application in a particular action pending when the amendments take effect would not be feasible or would work injustice, in which event the former procedure applies.

(Q) Effective date of amendments

The amendments to Juvenile Rule 29 filed by the Supreme Court with the General Assembly on January 7, 2004 and refiled on April 28, 2004 shall take effect on July 1, 2004. They govern all proceedings in actions brought after they take effect and also all further proceedings in actions then pending, except to the extent that their application in a particular action pending when the amendments take effect would not be feasible or would work injustice, in which event the former procedure applies.

(R) Effective date of amendments.

The amendments to Juvenile Rule 40 filed by the Supreme Court with the General Assembly on January 12, 2006 shall take effect on July 1, 2006. They govern all proceedings in actions brought after they take effect and also all further proceedings in actions then pending, except to the extent that their application in a particular action pending when the amendments take effect would not be feasible or would work injustice, in which event the former procedure applies.

(Adopted eff. 7–1–72; amended eff. 7–1–73, 7–1–75, 7–1–76, 7–1–80, 7–1–85, 7–1–91, 7–1–92, 7–1–94, 7–1–95, 7–1–96, 7–1–97, 7–1–98, 7–1–01, 7–1–02, 7–1–03, 7–1–04, 7–1–06)

Historical and Statutory Notes

Amendment Note: The 7–1–04 amendment added division (Q).
Amendment Note: The 7–1–03 amendment added division (P).
Amendment Note: The 7–1–02 amendment added division (O).
Amendment Note: The 7–1–01 amendment added division (N).
Amendment Note: The 7–1–98 amendment added division (M).
Amendment Note: The 7–1–97 amendment added division (L).
Amendment Note: The 7–1–96 amendment added division (K).
Amendment Note: The 7–1–95 amendment added division (J).
Amendment Note: The 7–1–94 amendment added division (I).

Editor's Comment

Juv R 47 is based upon O Const Art IV, § 5(B), which provides that rules approved by the Supreme Court and not disapproved by the legislature shall take effect on the first day of July in the year in which the rules were submitted to the legislature.

Library References

Infants ⇒132.
Westlaw Topic No. 211.
C.J.S. Infants §§ 32, 41, 43, 44, 95.

Research References

Treatises and Practice Aids
Giannelli & Yeomans, Ohio Juvenile Law § 1:8, Rules of Juvenile Procedure.

Juv R 48   Title

These rules shall be known as the Ohio Rules of Juvenile Procedure and may be cited as "Juvenile Rules" or "Juv. R. ___."

(Adopted eff. 7–1–72)

RULES OF SUPERINTENDENCE FOR THE COURTS OF OHIO
(Selected Provisions)

Research Note

Use Westlaw® *to find cases citing or applying specific rules. Westlaw may also be used to search for specific terms in court rules or to update court rules. See the OH–RULES and OH–ORDERS Scope Screens for detailed descriptive information and search tips.*

Amendments to these rules are published, as received, in the advance sheets for Ohio Official Reports, North Eastern Reporter 2d *and* Ohio Cases, *and in Baldwin's Ohio Legislative Service Annotated.*

These Rules are published as they appear in the *Ohio Official Reports*.

Rule
Sup R 11	Recording of proceedings
Sup R 12	Conditions for broadcasting and photographing court proceedings
Sup R 13	Videotaped testimony and evidence
Sup R 15	Arbitration
Sup R 16	Mediation
Sup R 23	Juvenile court procedures-complaint for abortion without parental notification
Sup R Form 23–A	Complaint for an order authorizing consent to an abortion without notification of a parent, guardian, or custodian
Sup R Form 23–A	Instructions Complaint for an order authorizing consent to an abortion without notification of a parent, guardian, or custodian
Sup R Form 23–B	Judgment
Sup R Form 23–C	Juvenile court
Sup R Form 23–D	Verification
Sup R 23.1	Juvenile court procedure—application for authorization to consent to an abortion or for judicial consent to an abortion (R.C. 2919.121)
Sup R Form 23.1–A	Petition for authorization to consent to an abortion or for judicial consent to an abortion (R.C. 2919.121)
Sup R Form 23.1–A	Instructions Petition for consent to an abortion or for judicial consent to an abortion (R.C. 2919.121)
Sup R Form 23.1–B	Judgment
Sup R Form 23.1–C	Notice of appeal
Sup R 24	Notifying physicians of affidavits alleging abuse under 2919.12
Sup R Form 24–A	Affidavit of minor
Sup R Form 24–B	Affidavit of recipient of notice of minor's intention to receive an abortion
Sup R Form 24–A and 24–B	Instructions Forms alleging abuse by parent and requesting that notification of abortion be provided to other relative
Sup R Form 24–C	Notice
Sup R 26	Court records management and retention
Sup R 26.01	Retention schedule for the administrative records of the courts
Sup R 26.04	Probate divisions of the courts of common pleas—records retention schedule
Sup R 36	Designation of trial attorney; assignment system
Sup R 36.1	Notice of appellate panels
Sup R 41	Conflict of trial court assignment dates, continuances and engaged counsel

Rule
PROBATE DIVISION
Sup R 50	Definitions
Sup R 51	Standard probate forms
Sup R 52	Specifications for printing probate forms
Sup R 53	Hours of the court
Sup R 54	Conduct in the court
Sup R 55	Examination of probate records
Sup R 56	Continuances
Sup R 57	Filings and judgment entries
Sup R 58	Deposit for court costs
Sup R 59	Wills
Sup R 60	Application for letters of authority to administer estate and notice of appointment
Sup R 61	Appraisers
Sup R 62	Claims against estate
Sup R 63	Application to sell personalty
Sup R 64	Accounts
Sup R 65	Land sales —R.C. Chapter 2127
Sup R 66	Guardianships
Sup R 67	Estates of minors of not more than ten thousand dollars
Sup R 68	Settlement of injury claims of minors
Sup R 69	Settlement of claims of or against adult wards
Sup R 70	Settlement of wrongful death and survival claims
Sup R 71	Counsel fees
Sup R 72	Executor's and administrator's commissions
Sup R 73	Guardian's compensation
Sup R 74	Trustee's compensation
Sup R 75	Local rules
Sup R 76	Exception to the rules
Sup R 77	Compliance
Sup R 78	Probate division of the court of common pleas—case management in decedent's estates, guardianship, and trusts
Sup R 99	Effective date
Sup R	Temp Prov Temporary provision (Hamilton County)
Sup R	Temp Prov Temporary provision (Trumbull County)
Sup R	Temp Prov Temporary provision (Cuyahoga County)

Sup R 11 Recording of proceedings

(A) Recording Devices

Proceedings before any court and discovery proceedings may be recorded by stenographic means, phonogramic means, photographic means, audio electronic recording devices, or video recording systems. The administrative judge may order the use of any method of recording authorized by this rule.

(B) Appeal

Transcripts of proceedings in electronic media shall be prepared in accordance with Rule 9(A) of the Rules of Appellate Procedure.

(C) Custody

Electronically recorded transcripts of proceedings shall be maintained and transcribed in the manner directed by the trial court.

(D) Inspection of Electronically Recorded Transcripts of Proceedings

A party may request a copy of an electronically recorded transcript of proceedings, or a portion of the transcript. The court may permit a party to view or hear the transcript of proceedings on file with the court.

(E) Reference to Electronically Recorded Transcripts of Proceedings

Reference to a particular portion of an electronically recorded transcript of proceedings shall be to the event, the number of the reel of tape on which it was recorded and the elapsed time counter reading.

(F) Expense of Electronically Recorded Transcripts of Proceedings

The expense of copies of electronically recorded transcripts of proceedings or such portions as are considered necessary by a party shall be borne by the requesting party or as provided by law. The expense of viewing or hearing an electronically recorded transcript of proceedings under division (D) of this rule shall be borne by the requesting party. All other expenses of electronically recorded transcripts of proceedings shall be costs in the action.

(Adopted eff. 7–1–97)

Historical and Statutory Notes

Ed. Note: Sup R 11 is analogous to former C P Sup R 10, adopted eff. 8–13–79; and former M C Sup R 8, adopted eff. 1–1–75; former C P Sup R 10 was analogous to former Sup R 10, adopted eff. 9–30–71.

Staff Notes

1997:

Rule 11 is analogous to former C.P.Sup.R. 10 and M.C.Sup.R. 8.

The rule authorizes the use of any one of several media in recording proceedings before a court.

In this comment and in the comment to Rule 12, the terms, "record," "transcript of proceedings," "transcribe," and "transcription" are used. As a preliminary consideration, the manner in which those terms are used in these comments is set forth.

The definition of "record" is the same as that contained in App.R. 9(A):

The original papers and exhibits thereto filed in the trial court, the transcript of proceedings, if any, including exhibits, and a certified copy of the docket and journal entries prepared by the clerk of the trial court shall constitute the record on appeal in all cases. * * *

The transcript of proceedings is the part of the record that reflects the events in the trial not represented by original papers. Essentially, it is the testimony of witnesses and the oral participation of counsel and of the trial judge, as recorded by the court reporter, and required for the purposes of appeal. The transcript of proceedings is the end product of whatever medium is used to record the proceedings. In traditional practice, the stenographic notes constituted a transcript of proceedings in that oral testimony was transcribed into stenographic notes. Of course, a second transcription into written form was necessary to put the proceedings into a form that could be readily used by all.

When the verb, transcribe, is used in these comments, it means preserving oral testimony by conversion to another medium. The other medium may be stenographic notes, videotape, motion picture sound track, or audio tape. It may also mean the conversion from one recorded medium to another.

When the noun, transcription, is used, it means the copy, either in the original medium or in the conversion medium.

Rule 11(A) Recording Devices. Recordation represents the best method of providing an accurate base for the creation of a transcript of proceedings required for an appeal under App.R. 9(A). In civil matters, there is no obligation to record the proceedings before the court. However, the court must provide a means of recording the proceedings in a civil matter upon the request of a party. R.C. 2301.20 requires the court of common pleas to provide a reporter on request of a party or their attorney. That provision applies to the municipal court by virtue of R.C. 1901.21(A).

Rule 11(A) authorizes stenographic means, which refers to shorthand in one of its forms. Phonogramic means refers to the use of a stenotype. Photographic means refers to sound motion pictures, the recording on photographic film. Audio electronic recording devices refers to the several systems for recording sound on magnetic tape, magnetic discs, or an impression disc or belt. A video recording system is one which records sound and picture on videotape.

Rule 11(A) directs that the choice of method of recording of proceedings is vested in the administrative judge rather than in the individual judge in a multi-judge court.

Rule 11(B) Appeal. A major source of delay in the appellate process is the transcribing from stenographic notes to written record. One of the advantages of recording proceedings on videotape is that there is an instant record prepared. The preparation of briefs can begin at the conclusion of the trial without a lengthy wait for the transcribing of the reporter's notes. Videotape has an advantage over the other electronic media in that it is easier to identify overlapping voices than it is in a pure audio recording.

On appeal, the record is composed of the original papers (pleadings, motions, depositions, exhibits, etc.), the transcript of proceedings, if any, including exhibits, and a certified copy of the docket and journal entries. The parties to the appeal have control over the extent of the transcript of proceedings under App.R. 9(B). The appellant selects the portions of the transcript that are necessary to the appeal. The appellee may require additional inclusions, if necessary to the resolution of the assignments of error. When the appellant intends to urge that a finding or conclusion is unsupported by the evidence or is contrary to the weight of the evidence, the appellant must include a transcript of all evidence relevant to the finding or conclusion. Even where it is claimed that a verdict is against the manifest weight of the evidence, it is not automatic that all evidence is relevant to that issue. For example, where a verdict finds no liability, evidence as to damages is not relevant to the issue of the verdict being against the manifest weight of the evidence. Appellants have followed a common practice of ordering the entire transcription of the proceedings for inclusion in the record on appeal, thus aggravating the problem of delay. The record on videotape negates the problem.

Rule 11(E) requires that the reference in a brief to a particular portion of a videotape recorded transcript of proceedings be to the event, the reel of videotape, and the elapsed time counter reading. For example: Testimony of Dr. Doug Ross, Reel 3, 1–06–55 to 1–14–23. The party would have the testimony within that time span transcribed into written form and append it to the brief to comply with Rule 11(B). The party may make the transcription from the videotape or from an audio tape recording furnished by the reporter, provided there is an accurate frame of reference to the elapsed time counter. The inclusion assists the reviewing court in that the court does not have to place the appropriate reel on the playback equipment, find the appropriate portion, and view the testimony, remembering it for the purposes of decision.

Rule 11(C) Custody. R.C. 2301.20 provides that the official shorthand reporter is required to retain and preserve the shorthand notes. The provision is necessary because the reporter may be called upon to transcribe the notes into written form. It is a difficult task for another person to transcribe a reporter's shorthand notes. In contrast, records made in electronic media are complete at the conclusion of the proceedings and do not require a reporter's transcription to be utilized by others.

The trial court has custody and control over the electronic recordings of proceedings, including the release of the videotape recording after it has served its function. Videotape is reusable and specific provision is made in Rule 13(E) for the disposition of videotape recordings filed with the court. The same standards serve to guide the court in releasing a videotape recording of proceedings under this rule.

Rule 11(D) Inspection of electronically recorded transcripts of proceedings. All electronically recorded transcripts of proceedings are required to be maintained in the manner directed by the trial court as provided in Rule 11(C).

Rule 11(D) provides that a party may view or hear the transcript of proceedings on file. Party is used as a simplified reference; the reference includes a party's counsel. There is a clear implication that electronic transcripts of proceedings are not available for indiscriminate public viewing, anymore than stenographic notes in the hands of the official court reporter are available for public inspection and reading. Rule 11(C) places the responsibility for custody and maintenance of the filed electronically recorded transcripts in the trial court. The court may entertain and dispose of requests to view the videotape record by persons other than parties or their counsel.

The important aspect of the rule is that a party does not have to order a copy of the videotape recording in videotape or in an audio recording for the purposes of preparing an appeal. The party may work from the original. As a practical matter, the inexpensive audio cassette recording made simultaneously with the videotape recording or made from the videotape sound track provides the information needed for brief preparation with the exception of the superimposed time readings.

Rule 11(E) References to electronically recorded transcripts of proceedings. The rule implements App.R. 16(D) and Rule VI, Section 1(B)(3) of the Rules of Practice of the Supreme Court. Those references contemplated written records and call for reference to the pages of the record. This rule adapts the reference system to the electronically recorded transcript of proceedings. The example used in the discussion above is repeated to illustrate the reference to videotape: Testimony of Dr. Doug Ross, Reel 3, 1–06–55 to 1–14–23.

Rule 11(F) Expense of electronically recorded transcripts of proceedings. The rule refers to three distinct areas of expense: (1) the recording of the proceedings themselves; (2) the securing of copies of the transcript of proceedings; and (3) the viewing of the transcript of proceedings.

The expense of recording the proceedings electronically may be made up of different items: the cost of the videotape used, a fee for personnel and equipment to make the recording, and a fee for renting equipment operated by court personnel. The rule provides that these expenses are costs in the action. The official shorthand reporter's services are paid for on an annual salary basis or, if the appointment is for less than one year, on a per diem fixed by the court. R.C. 2301.22. It is also provided that an $25.00 per diem fee be taxed as costs in each reported case and paid into the county general fund. R.C. 2301.21. The rule provision that the expenses of making the electronic recording of the proceedings be costs has the force of statute by virtue of Article IV, Section 5 of the Ohio Constitution and provides an equivalency to the statutory provision relating to an official shorthand reporter. The costs charged for electronic recording consist of the disbursements made by the court; the amounts applicable to the official shorthand reporter are not the amounts charged. Costs would not include allowances for regular court employees. The owner of the videotape is the party who pays the assessed costs, which include the price of the videotape used in the recording of the proceedings.

The rule provides that the cost of an electronically recorded transcript of proceedings shall be borne by the party requesting the copy or as provided by law. This is in contrast to the provisions made for copies of transcripts from the notes of the official shorthand reporter. R.C. 2301.24 provides that the requesting party pay the compensation specified directly to the reporter, and R.C. 2301.25 provides that the cost of the transcript shall be charged as costs in the case. The same statutes provide that the cost of copies ordered by the trial judge or the prosecuting attorney are to be paid from the public treasury and charged as costs in the case. The difference in treatment between an electronically recorded transcript and one recorded stenographically or phonogramically is that the electronic transcript is completed, accessible and usable at any given time without a transcription. A transcription is a convenience, not a necessity, in contrast to stenographic notes which must be transcribed to be useful. R.C. 2301.24 and 2301.25, relating to the provision of transcripts to indigent criminal defendants remain in effect, leaving the matter to the discretion of the trial court. Copies of the transcript may be whole or partial. It may be in the same medium or it may be transcribed into another medium. For example, videotape may be reproduced, the sound track alone may be reproduced as an audio tape recording, or the testimony may be transcribed into written form. Rule 13(A). The cited section applies in municipal courts by virtue of R.C. 1901.21. An example of a provision of law which would make the cost of a transcript recorded on videotape an item of costs in the case is App.R. 24.

Electronically recorded transcripts of proceedings introduce a new factor, viewing or hearing the original transcript of proceedings for brief preparation or the purposes of post-judgment motions. The rule provides that the expense of such viewing or hearing is an expense to be borne by the requesting party. The provision has no counterpart in the statutes by virtue of the nature of the reporter's notes. The provision is commensurate with the requirement that the requesting party bear the cost of a copy. It is a substitute for securing a copy. Viewing or hearing by the prosecuting attorney will be at public expense whether through the prosecuting attorney's budget or through the court's budget. The rule does not provide for that expense to be charged as costs in the case as was true of the expense of copies under the cited statutes.

Cross References

Court aides, 1901.33
Proceedings for serious offense shall be recorded, Crim R 22

Library References

Pretrial Procedure ⚖139.
Trial ⚖23.
Westlaw Topic No. 307A, 388.

C.J.S. Discovery §§ 30, 39, 51 to 53.
C.J.S. Trial § 41.

Research References

Encyclopedias

OH Jur. 3d Appellate Review § 240, Governing Law.
OH Jur. 3d Appellate Review § 260, Terminology.
OH Jur. 3d Appellate Review § 287, Review on Weight of Evidence.
OH Jur. 3d Appellate Review § 294, Recording of Proceedings.
OH Jur. 3d Appellate Review § 295, Duty of Parties to Order Transcript.
OH Jur. 3d Appellate Review § 298, Duty of Reporter—Form of Transcript Where Proceedings Were Recorded by Videotape.
OH Jur. 3d Appellate Review § 306, Videotape of Proceedings.
OH Jur. 3d Appellate Review § 363, Argument.
OH Jur. 3d Courts & Judges § 167, Courts of Common Pleas—Court Reporters or Stenographers.
OH Jur. 3d Courts & Judges § 352, Trial.

Forms

Ohio Jurisprudence Pleading and Practice Forms § 2:47, Media Request.
Ohio Jurisprudence Pleading and Practice Forms § 2:55, Entry—Media Permission.

Treatises and Practice Aids

Baldwin's Ohio Handbook Series—Trial Handbook § 2:16, Publicity Before and During Trial.
Carlin, Baldwin's Ohio Practice, Merrick-Rippner Probate Law § 107:60, Adjudicatory Hearings—Right to Transcript of Proceedings.

Notes of Decisions

In general 1
Appeal transcript 2
Expense 4
Recording devices 3
Videotape 5

---

1. In general

Parties bear responsibility of ensuring important bench conferences and other discussions of legal matters are properly recorded for use in event of appeal; therefore, when proceeding is being tape-recorded, party requesting conference should ask that jury be removed from courtroom in order to open discussion that will be recorded, rather than allowing jury to remain in courtroom and simply having hushed sidebar conference that is later discovered to be inaudible on court's tape recording. (Annotation from former C P Sup R 10.) State v. Gray (Allen 1993) 85 Ohio App.3d 165, 619 N.E.2d 460, dismissed, jurisdictional motion overruled 67 Ohio St.3d 1408, 615 N.E.2d 1043. Criminal Law ⚖ 643; Criminal Law ⚖ 853; Criminal Law ⚖ 1086.1

2. Appeal transcript

In a criminal appeal, audio tapes are not a proper substitute for a written transcript of the trial testimony. (Annotation from former C P Sup R 10.) State ex rel. Seigler v. Rone (Ohio 1975) 42 Ohio St.2d 361, 328 N.E.2d 811, 71 O.O.2d 328.

When the transcript of proceedings of a case involving disorderly conduct by intoxication is on videotape, a written transcript need not be provided when the issue on appeal is that there is no evidence to support a finding that the defendant committed the crime since that assignment of error is essentially one of the manifest weight of the evidence. (Annotation from former C P Sup R 10.) City of Lorain v. Wright (Lorain 1983) 11 Ohio App.3d 200, 463 N.E.2d 1298, 11 O.B.R. 296.

Where a proceeding was videotaped, it is not necessary to provide a written transcript on appeal where the issue is whether or not the judgment is against the manifest weight of the evidence. (Annotation from former MC Sup R 8.) City of Lorain v. Wright (Lorain 1983) 11 Ohio App.3d 200, 463 N.E.2d 1298, 11 O.B.R. 296. Criminal Law ⚖ 1104(3)

Where a record of proceedings in a trial is in the form of a videotape, and an indigent defendant is granted access to the tape pursuant to C P Sup R 15(D), he is not entitled to a written transcript of such proceedings. (Annotation from former C P Sup R 10.) State v. Lewis (Franklin 1973) 35 Ohio App.2d 218, 301 N.E.2d 568, 64 O.O.2d 325, certiorari denied 94 S.Ct. 546, 414 U.S. 1042, 38 L.Ed.2d 334.

3. Recording devices

A trial court may properly deny a capital defendant's request for a stenographic record in favor of mechanical recording devices, as Crim R 22 and C P Sup R 10 authorize the use of stenography or other adequate mechanical or electronic devices as the court determines is appropriate. (Annotation from former C P Sup R 10.) State, ex rel. Hurt, v. Kistler (Ohio 1992) 63 Ohio St.3d 307, 587 N.E.2d 298.

4. Expense

In the event that a municipal or county court chooses not to appoint its own reporter, for economic reasons or otherwise, or to tape record the proceedings upon a pretrial request by a party, the requesting party properly may be ordered by the court to procure its own reporter, whose expenses will be borne by the losing party. (Annotation from former MC Sup R 8.) State v. Dickard (Cuyahoga 1983) 10 Ohio App.3d 293, 462 N.E.2d 180, 10 O.B.R. 467. Criminal Law ⇔ 643

5. Videotape

Where a trial was recorded on videotape and the error assigned is that the judgment is against the manifest weight of the evidence, no transcript need be prepared from the tape and appended to the appellate brief; where specific rulings by the trial court are assigned as errors, however, the appellant must furnish a transcript demonstrating the errors. (Annotation from former MC Sup R 8.) City of Lorain v. Robertson (Lorain 1984) 21 Ohio App.3d 93, 487 N.E.2d 317, 21 O.B.R. 99.

A party's pretrial request for recordation gives notice to a municipal court that it must choose a method of recordation authorized by MC Sup R 8(A); where the court declines to appoint its own reporter, as provided by RC 1901.33, or to tape record the proceedings, the court may order the requesting party to obtain its own reporter, with costs to be taxed to the losing party. (Annotation from former MC Sup R 8.) State v. Dickard (Cuyahoga 1983) 10 Ohio App.3d 293, 462 N.E.2d 180, 10 O.B.R. 467.

In an action tried as a prerecorded videotape trial pursuant to Civ R 40, upon remand for a new trial, it is proper procedure to resubmit to a jury the prerecorded testimony when the prejudicial error occurred in the instructions to the jury only and not in the admission or rejection of evidence. (Annotation from former MC Sup R 8.) Lang v. Colonial Manor Nursing Home (Ohio Com.Pl. 1981) 4 Ohio Misc.2d 1, 446 N.E.2d 226, 4 O.B.R. 62. Appeal And Error ⇔ 1214

Sup R 12   Conditions for broadcasting and photographing court proceedings

(A) Presiding Judge

The judge assigned to the trial or hearing shall permit the broadcasting or recording by electronic means and the taking of photographs in court proceedings that are open to the public as provided by Ohio law. After consultation with the media, the judge shall specify the place or places in the courtroom where the operators and equipment are to be positioned. Requests for permission for the broadcasting, televising, recording, or taking of photographs in the courtroom shall be in writing and the written order of the judge shall be made a part of the record of the proceedings.

(B) Permissible Equipment and Operators

(1) Use of more than one portable television, videotape, or movie camera with one operator shall be allowed only with the permission of the judge.

(2) Not more than one still photographer shall be permitted to photograph trial proceedings without permission of the judge. Still photographers shall be limited to two cameras with two lenses for each camera.

(3) For radio broadcast purposes, not more than one audio system shall be permitted in court. Where available and suitable, existing audio pickup systems in the court facility shall be used by the media. If existing audio pickup systems are not available, microphones and other electronic equipment necessary for the audio pickup shall be as inconspicuous as possible but shall be visible.

(4) Visible audio recording equipment may be used by news media reporters with the prior permission of the judge.

(5) Arrangements between or among media for "pooling" of equipment shall be the responsibility of the media representative authorized to cover the proceeding. "Pooling" arrangements are to be made outside the courtroom and without imposing on the judge or court personnel. If disputes arise over arrangements between or among media representatives, the judge may exclude all contesting representatives from the proceedings.

(6) The judge shall prohibit the use of electronic or photographic equipment that produces distracting sound or light. No artificial lighting other than that normally used in the courtroom shall be employed, provided that, if the normal lighting in the courtroom can be improved without becoming obtrusive, the judge may permit modification.

(7) Still photographers and television and radio representatives shall be afforded a clear view but shall not be permitted to move about in the courtroom during court proceedings from the places where they have been positioned by the judge, except to leave or enter the courtroom.

(C) Limitations

(1) There shall be no audio pickup or broadcast of conferences conducted in a court facility between attorneys and clients or co-counsel or of conferences conducted at the bench between counsel and the judge.

(2) The judge shall inform victims and witnesses of their right to object to being filmed, videotaped, recorded, or photographed.

(3) This rule shall not be construed to grant media representatives any greater rights than permitted by law.

(4) Media representatives shall not be permitted to transmit or record anything other than the court proceedings from the courtroom while the court is in session.

(D) Revocation of Permission

Upon the failure of any media representative to comply with the conditions prescribed by this rule or the judge, the judge may revoke the permission to broadcast or photograph the trial or hearing.

(Adopted eff. 7–1–97)

Historical and Statutory Notes

Ed. Note: Sup R 12 is analogous to former C P Sup R 11, adopted eff. 8–13–79; and former M C Sup R 9, adopted eff. 1–1–75; former C P Sup R 11 was former Sup R 11, adopted eff. 9–30–71.

Staff Notes

1997:

Rule 12 is analogous to former C.P.Sup.R. 11 and M.C.Sup.R. 9. Division (A) was revised to include a reference to standards set forth in Ohio law, such as In re T.R. (1990), 52 Ohio St.3d 6, that govern public access to court proceedings. The 1997 amendments also eliminated the prohibition against changing film and videotape during court proceedings.

Rule 12(A) Presiding Judge. The judge assigned to the trial or hearing shall permit the broadcasting or recording by electronic means and the taking of photographs in court proceedings open to the public, upon request, if the judge determines that to do so would not distract the participants, impair the dignity of the proceedings or otherwise materially interfere with the achievement of a fair trial. Both the request for permission and the ruling on the request must be in writing and made a part of the record of the proceedings.

The filming, videotaping, recording, or taking of photographs of victims or witnesses who object shall not be permitted.

After consultation with the media the judge specifies the locations within the courtroom where operators and equipment may be located. However, still photographers and television and radio representatives must be given a clear view of the proceedings under division (B)(7).

Rule 12(B) Permissible Equipment and Operators. Not more than one portable television, videotape, or movie camera with one operator and not more than one still photographer with two cameras shall be allowed unless the judge presiding at the trial or hearing specifically permits additional cameras or operators. Each of the two still cameras permitted by the rule is limited to two lenses.

For purposes of radio broadcasting, not more than one audio system is permitted. If an existing audio system is available and suitable, it shall be used. If an audio system is not available, then microphones and other necessary equipment "shall be as inconspicuous as possible but must be visible."

Portable audio recording equipment may be used by reporters if it is visible and if the permission of the judge presiding at the trial or hearing is first obtained.

All pooling arrangements are the responsibility of the media representatives. Pooling arrangements must be made without involving the court. If any disputes arise, the judge may exclude all contesting media representatives.

Electronic or photographic equipment that produces distracting sound or light shall be prohibited by the judge. No artificial lighting, other than that normally used in the courtroom, is permitted unless the judge, upon request and after consultation with the media representatives, determines that the normal light can be improved without becoming obtrusive.

Still photographers and television and radio representatives shall not move about the courtroom from the place where they have been positioned by the judge, except to leave or enter the courtroom.

Rule 12(C) Limitations. Audio pickup or broadcast of conferences in a court facility between attorney and client or between counsel and the judge are prohibited.

The trial judge must advise victims and witnesses of their right to object to being filmed, videotaped, recorded, or photographed.

No part of Rule 12 gives authority for media coverage where it is otherwise limited or prohibited by law.

While the court is in session, media representatives are not permitted to either transmit or record anything from the courtroom other than court proceedings.

Rule 12(D) Revocation of Permission. If any media representative fails to comply with the conditions set by either the judge or this rule, the judge may revoke the permission to broadcast or photograph the trial or hearing.

Library References

Courts ⚖189(11 1/2).
Criminal Law ⚖635.
Municipal Corporations ⚖641.
Trial ⚖20.
Westlaw Topic Nos. 106, 110, 268, 388.
C.J.S. Criminal Law §§ 1134 to 1141.
C.J.S. Trial § 38.

Research References

Encyclopedias
OH Jur. 3d Trial § 89, Broadcasting or Photographing Trial.
OH Jur. 3d Trial § 117, Videotape Trial.

Treatises and Practice Aids
Katz, Giannelli, Blair and Lipton, Baldwin's Ohio Practice, Criminal Law, § 66:9, Televised Trials.

Law Review and Journal Commentaries

Constitutional Gag Orders Restricting Trial Participant's Speech: A Guide for Ohio Trial Judges, Elizabeth L. Hendershot. 56 Ohio St L J 1536 (1995).

Electronic Media in the Courtroom: Some Observations on Federalism and State Experimentation, Stephen G. Thompson. 9 Ohio N U L Rev 349 (1982).

Open Courts: How Cameras in Courts Help Keep the System Honest. Clara Tuma, 49 Clev St L Rev 417 (2001).

The Role of the Electronic Media in the Criminal Justice System, Note. 47 U Cin L Rev 417 (1978).

Struck by the Falling Bullet: The Continuing Need for Definitive Standards in Media Coverage of Criminal Proceedings. John A. Walton, 49 Clev St L Rev 407 (2001).

Witness to History: The Role of Legal Commentators in High Profile Trials. Laurie L. Levenson, 49 Clev St L Rev 439 (2001).

Notes of Decisions

In general 1
Disqualifying factors 4
Judicial discretion 3
Objection proceedings 5
Remedies for refusal 2

---

1. In general

Fact that defendant in murder trial might testify on his own behalf did not justify trial court's order that defendant not be photographed, filmed or taped while in courtroom; while witness may not be photographed while he is testifying, neither court rule nor Code of Judicial Conduct protected him when he was not testifying. (Annotation from former C P Sup R 11.) State ex rel. Nat. Broadcasting Co., Inc. v. Court of Common Pleas of Lake County (Ohio 1990) 52 Ohio St.3d 104, 556 N.E.2d 1120. Criminal Law ⚖ 633(1)

Broadcasting is permitted in a courtroom if the court determines that it would not distract participants, impair the dignity of proceedings, or otherwise materially interfere with the achievement of a fair trial or hearing. (Annotation from former C P Sup R 11.) (See also State v Rogers, 28 OS(3d) 427, 28 OBR 480, 504 NE(2d) 52 (1986).) State v. Rogers (Ohio 1985) 17 Ohio St.3d 174, 478 N.E.2d 984, 17 O.B.R. 414, vacated 106 S.Ct. 518, 474 U.S. 1002, 88 L.Ed.2d 452, on remand 28 Ohio St.3d 427, 504 N.E.2d 52, 28 O.B.R. 480. Criminal Law ⚖ 633(1)

Any error committed by trial court when it gave media oral, rather than written, permission to broadcast medical malpractice trial was harmless. (Annotation from former C P Sup R 11.) Stelma v. Juguilon (Cuyahoga 1992) 73 Ohio App.3d 377, 597 N.E.2d 523, motion overruled 64 Ohio St.3d 1408, 592 N.E.2d 846, appeal denied 64 Ohio St.3d 1444, 596 N.E.2d 474. Appeal And Error ⚖ 1046.1

Absent a clear and convincing evidentiary basis in the record for finding that one of the disqualifying factors stated in Canon 3A(7)(c)(ii) of Code of Judicial Conduct is present, electronic news coverage in a criminal case must be permitted, subject only to the conditions and limitations of C P Sup R 11 and Canon 3A(7)(c)(i), 3A(7)(c)(iii), and 3A(7)(c)(iv) of Code of Judicial Conduct. (Annotation from former C P Sup R 11.) State ex rel. Cosmos Broadcasting Corp. v. Brown (Lucas 1984) 14 Ohio App.3d 376, 471 N.E.2d 874, 14 O.B.R. 481. Criminal Law ⚖ 633(1)

CP Sup R 11 and Code of Jud Cond Canon 3A(7) require courts to permit the recording and broadcasting of criminal trials unless an adequate determination is made that one of the conditions in Code of Jud Cond Canon 3 renders such coverage improper. (Annotation from former MC Sup R 9.) State ex rel. Cosmos Broadcasting Corp. v. Brown (Lucas 1984) 14 Ohio App.3d 376, 471 N.E.2d 874, 14 O.B.R. 481.

2. Remedies for refusal

Mandamus will issue to compel a trial judge to permit radio and television coverage of a trial absent a determination by the judge of a disqualifying factor under Canon 3A(7)(c)(ii) or 3A(7)(iii). (Annotation from former C P Sup R 11.) State ex rel. Grinnell Communications Corp. v. Love (Ohio 1980) 62 Ohio St.2d 399, 406 N.E.2d 809, 16 O.O.3d 434.

3. Judicial discretion

C P Sup R 11 and Canon 3A(7) of the Code of Judicial Conduct require courts to permit the recording and broadcasting of criminal trials unless an adequate determination is made that one of the conditions in Canon 3 of the Code of Judicial Conduct renders such coverage improper. (Annotation from former C P Sup R 11.) State ex rel. Cosmos Broadcasting Corp. v. Brown (Lucas 1984) 14 Ohio App.3d 376, 471 N.E.2d 874, 14 O.B.R. 481.

4. Disqualifying factors

The fact that counsel to a defendant is, himself, under indictment for possession of cocaine allegedly accepted as payment for taking the case is insufficient reason, alone, to forbid telecasting of a trial. (Annotation from former C P Sup R 11.) State ex rel. Cosmos Broadcasting Corp. v. Brown (Lucas 1984) 14 Ohio App.3d 376, 471 N.E.2d 874, 14 O.B.R. 481.

5. Objection proceedings

A television station which seeks to broadcast a trial has the right to notice, adduce evidence and to cross-examine any witnesses testifying on behalf of those who object to broadcast coverage at the hearing on the issue of the coverage. (Annotation from former C P Sup R 11.) State ex rel. Miami Valley Broadcasting Corp. v. Kessler (Ohio 1980) 64 Ohio St.2d 165, 413 N.E.2d 1203, 18 O.O.3d 383.

The absolute prohibition of the photographing, broadcasting, and telecasting of judicial proceedings under local federal court rules and Fed Crim R 53 does not violate US Const Am 1 as an unreasonable restriction of access to the courtroom with respect to time, place, and manner; it is enough to satisfy US Const Am 1 that the journalists and photographers are permitted to simply enter the courtroom. (Annotation from former C P Sup R 11.) Conway v. U.S. (C.A.6 (Ohio) 1988) 852 F.2d 187, certiorari denied 109 S.Ct. 370, 488 U.S. 943, 102 L.Ed.2d 359.

Sup R 13 Videotaped testimony and evidence

(A) Videotape Depositions

(1) Authority. Videotape depositions are authorized by Civil Rule 30(B)(3).

(2) Notice. The notice requirements of Civil Rule 30(B)(3) regarding the manner of recording, preserving, and filing depositions apply to videotape depositions. Notice is sufficient if it specifies that the videotape deposition is to be taken pursuant to the provisions of this rule.

(3) Persons Authorized to Take Depositions. The officer before whom a videotape deposition is taken shall be one of those persons enumerated in Civil Rule 28.

(4) Date and Time Recording. A date and time generator shall be used to superimpose the year, month, day, hour, minute, and second over the video portion of the recording during the taking of the deposition. The total deposition time shall be noted on the outside of the videotape.

(5) Objections. The officer shall keep a log of objections referenced to the time of making each objection as superimposed on the video portion of the recording. If the deposition is transcribed, the log shall include the page of the transcript on which each objection occurs.

(6) Copies of the Deposition. Upon the request of a party, the officer shall provide an audio cassette recording of the deposition at the conclusion of its taking. Upon the request of a party, the officer shall provide a copy of the deposition in the medium of videotape or a written transcript of the deposition within a reasonable period of time. The requesting party shall bear the cost of the copy requested.

(7) Submission to Witness. After a videotape deposition is taken, the videotape shall be shown immediately to the witness for his examination, unless the examination is waived by the witness and the parties.

(8) Certification of Original Videotape Deposition. The officer before whom the videotape deposition is taken shall cause a written certification to be attached to the original videotape. The certification shall state that the witness was fully sworn or affirmed by the officer and that the videotape is a true record of the testimony given by the witness. If the witness has not waived his or her right to a showing and examination of the videotape deposition, the witness shall also sign the certification.

When an officer makes a copy or a transcription of the videotape deposition in any medium, he or she shall attach a written certification to the copy or transcription. The certification shall state that the copy is a true record of the videotape testimony of the witness.

(9) Certification of Edited Videotape Depositions. The officer who edits the original videotape deposition shall attach a written certification to the edited copy of the videotape deposition. The certification shall state that the editing complies with the rulings of the court and that the original videotape deposition has not been affected by the editing process.

(10) Filing Where Objections Not Made. Where objections are not made by a party or witness during the deposition and, if pursuant to Civil Rule 30(F)(1) a party requests, or the court orders, that the deposition be filed with the court, the officer shall file the deposition with the clerk of the court.

(11) Filing Where Objections Made. When a deposition containing objections is filed with the court pursuant to Civil Rule 30(F)(1), it shall be accompanied by the officer's log of objections. A party may request that the court rule upon the objections within fourteen days of the filing of the deposition or within a reasonable time as stipulated by the parties. In ruling upon objections, the court may view the videotape recording in its entirety or view only those parts of the videotape recording pertinent to the objections made. If the parties are not present at the time the court's rulings are made, the court shall provide the parties with copies of its rulings on the objections and his instructions as to editing.

(12) Editing Alternatives. The original videotape shall not be affected by any editing process.

(a) In its order and editing instructions the court may do any of the following:

(i) Release the videotape to the officer with instructions to keep the original videotape intact and make an edited copy of the videotape that deletes all references to objections and objectionable material;

(ii) Order the person showing the original videotape at trial to suppress the objectionable audio portions of the videotape;

(iii) Order the person showing the original videotape at trial to suppress the objectionable audio and video portions of the videotape.

(b) If the court uses alternative in division (A)(12)(a)(i) of this rule, the officer shall cause both the original videotape recording and the edited videotape recording, each clearly identified, to be filed with the clerk of the court. If the court uses the alternative in division (A)(12)(a)(ii) of this rule, it shall, in jury trials, instruct the jury to disregard the video portions of the presentation when the audio portion is suppressed. If the court uses the alternative in division (A)(12)(a)(iii) of this rule, it shall, in jury trials, instruct the jury to disregard any deletions apparent in the playing of the videotape.

(13) Storage. Each court shall provide secure and adequate facilities for the storage of videotape recordings.

(14) Inspection or Viewing. Except upon order of the court and upon such terms as it may provide, the videotape recordings on file with the clerk of the court shall not be available for inspection or viewing after filing and prior to use at trial or disposition in accordance with this rule. Upon the request of a party under division (A)(3) of this rule, the clerk, without court order, may release the videotape to the officer to allow the making of a copy of the videotape.

(15) Objections at Trial. Objections should be made prior to trial, and all objections shall be made before actual presentation of the videotape at trial. If an objection is made at trial that has not been waived pursuant to Civil Rule 32(D)(3) or previously raised and ruled upon, the objection shall be made before the videotape deposition is presented. The trial judge shall rule on objections prior to the presentation of the videotape. If an objection is sustained, that portion of the videotape containing the objectionable testimony shall not be presented.

(B) Videotape Trials

(1) Authority. Videotape trials are authorized by Civil Rule 40. In videotape trials, videotape is the exclusive medium of presenting testimony irrespective of the availability of the individual witness to testify in person. All testimony is recorded on videotape and the limitations of Civil Rule 32 upon the use of depositions shall not apply.

(2) Initiation of Videotape Trial. By agreement of the parties and with the consent of the trial judge all or a portion of testimony and appropriate evidence may be presented by videotape. The trial judge may order the recording of all or a portion of testimony and evidence on videotape in an appropriate case. In determining whether to order a videotape trial, the trial judge, after consultation with counsel, shall consider the costs involved, the nature of the action, and the nature and amount of testimony.

(3) Procedure. Divisions (A)(3) to (13) and (D) apply to videotape trials. The sequence of taking the testimony of individual witnesses and the sequence of presentation of that testimony shall be at the option of the proponent. In ordering or consenting to the recording of all of the testimony on videotape, the trial judge shall fix a date prior to the date of trial by which all recorded testimony shall be filed with the clerk of the court.

(4) Objections. All objections shall be made and ruled upon in advance of the trial. Objections may not be made during the presentation of the videotape evidence.

(5) Presence of Counsel and Trial Judge. In jury trials, counsel for the parties and the trial judge are not required to be present in the courtroom when the videotape testimony is played to the jury. If the trial judge leaves the courtroom during the playing of the videotape, the judge shall admonish the jurors regarding their duties and responsibilities. In the absence of the judge, a responsible officer of the court shall remain with the jury. The trial judge shall remain within such proximity to the courtroom that he or she can be readily summoned.

(C) Equipment

(1) Standard. There are several recording format standards used in the trial courts of this state. Proponents of videotape testimony or evidence shall determine the format utilized by the trial court in which the videotape is to be filed and shall make the videotape recording on the appropriate format machine. If a party records testimony or evidence on videotape that is not compatible with the trial court equipment, the party shall be responsible for the furnishing of reproduction equipment of institutional quality or for the conversion of the videotape to the standards used in trial court equipment, all of which shall be at the cost of the party and not chargeable as costs of the action.

Each court shall provide for the availability of playback equipment. As may be appropriate, the court may purchase or lease equipment or make contract for the equipment on occasions of need. The court shall provide for the adequate training of an operator from the personnel of the court or for the services of a competent operator to operate the equipment when videotape testimony or evidence is presented in court.

(2) Minimum Equipment. At a minimum, facilities for playback at trial shall consist of a videotape player and one monitor, having at least a fourteen-inch screen. Color facilities are not required.

(3) Maintenance. The trial court shall take reasonable steps to ensure that the equipment is maintained within operating tolerances. The trial court shall provide for competent regular maintenance of equipment that is owned or leased by the court.

(D) Costs; Videotape Depositions

(1) The expense of videotape as a material shall be borne by the proponent.

(2) The reasonable expense of recording testimony on videotape, the expense of playing the videotape recording at trial, and the expense of playing the videotape recording for the purpose of ruling upon objections shall be allocated as costs in the proceeding in accordance with Civil Rule 54.

(3) The expense of producing the edited version of the videotape recording shall be costs in the action, provided that the expense of the videotape, as a material, shall be borne by the proponent of the testimony.

(4) The expense of a copy of the videotape recording and the expense of an audio tape recording of the videotape sound track shall be borne by the party requesting the copy.

(E) Disposition of Videotape Filed With the Court

(1) Ownership. Videotape used in recording testimony shall remain the property of the proponent of the testimony. Videotape may be reused, but the proponent is responsible for submitting a recording of acceptable quality.

(2) Release of Videotape Recordings.

(a) The court may authorize the clerk of the court to release the original videotape recording and the edited videotape recording to the owner of the videotape upon any of the following:

(i) The final disposition of the cause where no trial occurs;

(ii) The expiration of the appeal period following trial, if no appeal is taken;

(iii) The final determination of the cause, if an appeal is taken.

If the testimony is recorded stenographically by a court reporter during the playing of the videotape at trial, the videotape may be returned to the proponent upon disposition of the cause following the trial.

(b) The court shall order release by journal entry.

(Adopted eff. 7-1-97)

Historical and Statutory Notes

Ed. Note: Sup R 13 is analogous to former C P Sup R 12, adopted eff. 8-13-79; and former M C Sup R 10, adopted eff. 1-1-75; former C P Sup R 12 was analogous to former Sup R 15, adopted eff. 9-1-72.

Staff Notes

1997:

Rule 13 is analogous to former C.P.Sup.R. 12 and M.C.Sup.R. 10. The rule is revised to require the exterior of the videotape to include the total deposition time [division (A)(4)]; to require objections to be noted on the log of transcripted depositions [division (A)(5)]; and to allow expenses associated with the use of videotape to be allocated as costs in the proceeding [division (D)(6)(b)].

In general, the rule implements Civ.R. 30(B)(3), which permits the recording of oral depositions by a means other than stenographic, and Civ.R. 40, which authorizes the prerecording of testimony on videotape for presentation at trial. The rule adapts the provisions developed in stenographic recording to use in electronic recording. Depositions in criminal cases are taken in the same manner as in civil cases. Crim.R. 15(E).

Rule 13(A) Videotape depositions.

Rule 13(A)(2) Notice. Civ.R. 30(B)(3) provides that the notice must specify the manner of recording, preserving, and filing of the deposition taken by other than stenographic means. A complete statement of notice would be lengthy, serve no useful purpose, refer to procedures within the control of the court, and not be uniform. Division (A) specifies the manner of recording, preserving and filing; thus it is necessary in the notice to merely make reference to Rule 13 to satisfy the requirements of Civ.R. 30(B)(3).

Rule 13(A)(3) Persons authorized to take depositions. R.C. 147.01 was amended in 1977 to provide that a notary public is appointed and commissioned as a notary public for the state. A videotape equipment operator need only be commissioned as a notary public to be an officer before whom a deposition may be taken anywhere in the state.

Rule 13(A)(4) Date and time recording. A date and time generator is required because it facilitates reference to any portion of the tape and provides an assurance that no material has been edited out of the tape.

Rule 13(A)(5) Objections. The officer before whom the deposition is taken is required to keep a log of objections and where recorded on the tape to facilitate reference to the objections. For the same purpose, the log must include the page of the transcript on which objections occur if the videotaped deposition is transcribed.

Rule 13(A)(6) Copies of the deposition. This provision was formerly a part of division (A)(3). It is more specific than its predecessor by providing for immediate delivery of an audio cassette recording and by placing the responsibility for the cost of copies on the requesting party.

Rule 13(A)(7) Submission to witnesses. Civ.R. 30(E) provides that an oral deposition, when fully transcribed, is to be submitted to the witness for examination and reading. The rule provides that changes in form or substance desired by the witness may be entered on the deposition with a statement as to the reasons the witness had for making the changes. The changes are not corrections. They are additions with explanations for the additions. When videotape is used, there is no necessity for waiting for a transcription into written form. As soon as the deposition is completed, it is ready for viewing by the witness. If there are changes desired, those additions may be made to the deposition, together with the reasons therefor, and recorded on the videotape in the same manner that the initial testimony was entered. The showing can be waived just as the reading can be waived.

In neither the stenographic method of recording nor in the videotape method of recording is the primary purpose of the review by the witness a check on the accuracy of the recording. It is intended to be an assurance that the final product is the testimony that the deponent wants used in the trial or proceeding.

Rule 13(A)(8) Certification of original videotape deposition. Civ.R. 30(F), relating to certification by the officer before whom the deposition was taken, was designed for the written deposition. Division (A)(8) allays confusion as to how a reel of videotape can be signed. It provides that a written certification be attached to the original videotape recording reel. The content of the certification is the same for either method. The rule also provides for adding the signature of the witness, if the witness' signing is not waived by the parties. Civ.R. 30(E) incorporates the requirement that the witness sign a written deposition.

The final paragraph of division (A)(8) provides for a different certification. It relates to the officer's certification as to the authenticity of a copy. It is applicable to every copy or transcription the officer makes.

Rule 13(A)(9) Certification of edited videotape depositions. When the court requires an edited copy of a videotape deposition pursuant to division (A)(12), the officer who makes the edited copy is required to certify the conformity of the edited copy to the rulings of the court. The officer also is required to certify that the integrity of the original videotape recording has not been breached.

Rule 13(A)(10) Filing where objections not made. The rule is the counterpart of a provision in Civ.R. 30(F)(1). Filing is not automatic in the case of a deposition irrespective of the medium in which it is recorded. Filing depends upon the request of the party or order of the court. When there are no objections interposed, there is no further step to be taken before the deposition is viewed by the trier of fact.

Civ.R. 30(F)(3) requires that the party requesting the filing of a deposition give notice of its filing to all other parties. Civ.R. 5(A). The modes of service are set forth in Civ.R. 5(B). Filing of the notice with proof of service is provided for in Civ.R. 5(D).

Rule 13(A)(11) Filing where objections made. The officer's log of objections is required by division (A)(5) and provides a means of easy reference to the location of the objections by listing the time of the objection as shown by the date and time generator's recording. When there are objections, a party may request the court to rule on the objections. The appropriate form of request would be a written motion. The rule has extended the period for filing the request to fourteen days from the filing of the deposition or such reasonable time as may be stipulated by the parties. Civ.R. 32(A) provides that a deposition need be filed only one day before trial to be used in the trial. In the event of late filing of a deposition, the disposition of the objections should be as the court directs.

Rarely does an objecting party urge all objections made. Good procedure requires the objecting party to indicate, by log reference, the objections no longer urged.

Rule 13(A)(12) Editing alternatives. It is vital to the use of videotape that the integrity of the original recording be maintained at every stage of the proceedings. No mode of editing may alter the original recording. The rule specifies three alternatives to be followed in the editing process, the choice among which lies with the court. The court, in an order to the officer, specifies the method desired.

One of the purposes of videotape usage is to provide an uninterrupted flow of admissible testimony. Editing serves to keep inadmissible testimony from the jurors.

The first alternative involves the making of a second tape, which is a copy of the original except that it omits all reference to inadmissible testimony. This method has the disadvantage of additional expense in material and time in creating the second tape, the one actually played to the jury.

The second alternative involves the use of the original videotape deposition. At the playing of the tape to the jury, the operator suppresses the sound where there is inadmissible testimony. A schedule of suppression, keyed to the time recorded on the videotape, is prepared in advance by the officer. The operator merely follows the directions of the schedule in playing the videotape recording. Editing for that mode consists of creating the suppression schedule in conformity to the court's rulings. Usage has demonstrated that the jury is not adversely affected by viewing the picture during the period of sound suppression. The method has the advantage of economy in preparation.

The third alternative involves the suppression of the picture as well as the sound.

The rule requires the court to instruct the jury against reading some meaning into the periods of suppression.

Rule 13(A)(13) Storage. The provision is necessitated by Civ.R. 30(B)(3), which requires the notice to contain information as to the method of preserving the recording. Rule 12(A)(2) permits compliance by a reference to Civ.R. 30(B)(3).

Rule 13(A)(14) Inspection or viewing. Former R.C. 2319.19 provided that a deposition, when sealed and filed, remained sealed until opened by the clerk for use, by order of the Court, or at the request of a party or counsel. Civ.R. 30(F)(1), which superseded the statute, provides that the deposition is sealed only upon request or upon court order with the implication of its unavailability to others until it is offered into evidence. The videotape medium requires mechanical aid in viewing that places an additional limitation upon inspection. Division (A)(14) limits inspection to that ordered by the court. Provision for copies of depositions in the form of videotape, audio recording, or written transcript is made in division (A)(6). The simplest and most economical copy is on audio tape and it obviates the necessity for viewing of the videotape deposition. To facilitate the making of a copy for a party, division (A)(14) provides for release of the original recording to the officer before whom the deposition was taken for the purpose of making a copy. Release may be by the clerk without a court order.

Rule 13(A)(15) Objections at trial. The rule recognizes that it is not possible for all objections to be ruled upon in advance of trial. For example, an objection to a hypothetical question propounded to a medical witness may be found to incorporate facts not established in the trial. Until the testimony relative to the facts has been introduced, the sufficiency of the question cannot be determined. In addition, it cannot be assumed that attorneys can foresee every valid objection, particularly when the testimony is being taken out of the normal sequence. The rule recognizes the possibility of a proper objection made at the trial for the first time. Two limitations are placed upon such objections. It cannot be the renewal of an objection previously ruled upon and it cannot be an objection waived under Civ.R. 32(D)(3). Under division (D)(3)(a) of that rule, objection to the competency of a witness or the competency, relevancy, or materiality of testimony is not waived by failure to raise at the deposition unless the ground might have been obviated or removed, if presented then. Errors and irregularities (e.g., form of question, which might be obviated), if raised, are waived unless objected to at the hearing. Division (A)(15) provides that objections raised at trial must be considered and ruled upon in advance of the playing of the recording. Testimony ruled inadmissible at that point poses no problem. The sound (and picture) may be suppressed for that testimony and thus not heard by the jury.

Rule 13(B) Videotape trials.

Rule 13(B)(1) Authority. Division (B) implements Civ.R. 40, which permits the presentation of the entire testimony and other appropriate evidence in a civil case by videotape. It does not authorize the use of videotape for the presentation of part of the testimony. If only part of the testimony is to be offered on videotape, then the deposition procedure of division (A) is to be followed. Division (B)(1) spells out the limitation of the concept to the entirety of the testimony in a civil trial and also provides that the limitations placed upon the use of depositions do not apply when Civ.R. 40 is invoked. The reason is that the deposition rule does not apply because depositions are not being offered.

In State v. Gettys (1976), 49 Ohio App.2d 241, a local rule of court required the prerecording of testimony on videotape in a criminal case for presentation to the jury without the intervention of testimony from the witness stand. The court of appeals held the rule to be unconstitutional as a violation of Article I, Section 10 of the Ohio Constitution, which limits depositions in criminal cases to situations of witness unavailability. The Court viewed the videotape recording of all testimony as a collection of depositions. The court also noted that the procedure was inconsistent with Crim.R. 15(A) and (F).

Rule 13(B)(2) Initiation of videotape trial. The procedure is to be invoked by agreement between the parties with the consent of the trial judge or upon the order of the trial judge in appropriate cases. The current application in municipal and county courts is more limited than in the common pleas court. Rising jurisdictional levels, refinements in docket control and scheduling, together with the development and usage of the medium, may increase the use of videotape prerecorded testimony in all courts. In its present form, agreement of the parties is necessary. A court is empowered to order the use of the procedure only after inquiry into the appropriateness of the measure.

Rule 13(B)(3) Procedure. The entire prerecording of testimony is distinguished from the taking of a deposition in division (B)(1). Although the concept is different, there are parallels. Division (B)(3) takes advantage of the similarity by making the procedures relative to the taking of depositions applicable to the taking of the entire testimony. If the parties do not simplify the procedure by stipulation pursuant to Civ.R. 29, the procedure of Civ.R. 30, as supplemented by division (A), is applicable. Division (B)(3) contains a very important reference to an inclusion in the order for prerecording of the entire testimony. That inclusion is the date for filing of all of the videotape. The trial judge must set a date that will permit him or her to rule on all objections before trial as required in division (B)(4).

The cost provisions for videotape trials parallel those for depositions. The proponent bears the cost of the videotape used to record the testimony because it is returned to the proponent for reuse when it has fulfilled its purpose. Requesting parties bear the cost of copies of the videotape or of transcriptions they have made in accordance with the basic rule practice expressed in Civ.R. 30(F)(2). For the same reasons expressed in the comment to division (D), the expense of the playback of the videotape trial is a general expense of the court not allocable as costs to the parties. All other expenses are costs to be charged or allocated as provided by law.

Rule 13(B)(4) Objections. The procedure differs significantly from the provision for objections relative to depositions as set forth in division (A). In a Civ.R. 40 proceeding, all objections must be ruled upon in advance of trial and no objections may be made at trial. With all of the evidence recorded, there is no development at trial that is not known upon the completion of the recording of all of the evidence. The videotape record played to the jury must exclude all nonadmissible testimony. The method of editing may be the creation of a second videotape or the suppression of the audio, or audio and video, relating to inadmissible evidence.

Rule 13(B)(5) Presence of counsel and trial judge. The provision clarifies the practice and answers the questions as to the obligations of the judge and counsel during the playing of the testimony.

Rule 13(C) Equipment.

Rule 13(C)(1) Standard. Compatibility of equipment is absolutely essential. Thus, the standard is set in the rule using the only existinga accepted standard in equipment of less than broadcast quality. A party deviates from the standard at the party's expense.

This provision affirms the obligation of the court to provide facilities for replay of videotape and indicates that the court may own or lease the necessary equipment or may contract with a service company where usage is infrequent. The purpose of the provision is to make clear that the furnishing of playback equipment is no different from the obligation to provide adequate furniture, supplies, and equipment for the conduct of the court. The cost of providing the videotape equipment is indistinguishable from the cost of providing a blackboard in terms of obligation.

It is incumbent upon counsel to determine what equipment the court has or can acquire and conform to that standard. If the proponent does not conform, the proponent has the obligation to provide equipment or pay the cost incurred in providing it.

Rule 13(C)(2) Minimum equipment. The rule specifies minimum facilities, but the specification does not foreclose the court from providing additional or more highly developed equipment utilizing the same standard.

Rule 13(C)(3) Maintenance. Compatibility relates to maintenance as well as to the size of the tape and the specifications for recorders and players. If either the recording equipment or the playback equipment is running at a speed outside the tolerances specified in the standard, the reproduction will be adversely affected. It is essential that the equipment be properly maintained whether leased or owned. The court shall take appropriate steps to maintain the equipment used.

Rule 13(D) Costs; videotape depositions.

Material. The proponent of a deposition must bear the cost of the videotape used to record the deposition. There is no provision that the amount be charged as costs in the action because, under Rule 13(E), the videotape is returned to the proponent after it has served its purpose.

Recording and playback expense. The reasonable expense of recording and playing a videotape deposition is charged as costs in the action pursuant to Civ.R. 54. "Reasonable" is inserted to make it clear that, for example, a color videotape of broadcast quality may not be used to increase the cost burden on a losing party.

Cost of copies. Under Civ.R. 30(F)(2), copies of depositions are the responsibility of the requesting party.

Rule 13(E) Disposition of videotape filed with the court.

Rule 13(E)(1) Ownership. The provision as to ownership is essential because the videotape has substantial value and may be reused.

Rule 13(E)(2) Release of videotape recording. The provisions are keyed to final disposition of the case except where the testimony is converted to stenographic recording during the presentation of the evidence in the trial, in which case the release may be made following the trial on the basis that the transcript of proceedings will be made up from the stenographic recording. The provision emerged in the early consideration of videotape applications when stenographic recording of the testimony as played at the trial was considered a safety factor. It is unlikely that the duplication would appear in current practice. When the trial is of a criminal matter rather than a civil matter, the finality of disposition of the case may be more difficult to establish. The testimony recorded on videotape may be converted to some other method of recording, audio or stenographic, upon the ostensible closing of the case. The videotape could then be released and reused. Should the testimony be essential to some post-judgment proceeding, it could be used in the converted form. Prudence would dictate the transcription of the stenographic recording into the written form at the time of the release. Release is to be by order, hence the provision for journalization.

Cross References

Composition of the record on appeal, App R 9

Library References

Courts ⚖189(8), 189(11 1/2).
Criminal Law ⚖627.2, 643.
Municipal Corporations ⚖641.
Pretrial Procedure ⚖139.
Trial ⚖23.
Witnesses ⚖228.
Westlaw Topic Nos. 106, 110, 268, 307A, 388, 410.
C.J.S. Criminal Law §§ 468, 1153.
C.J.S. Discovery §§ 30, 39, 51 to 53.
C.J.S. Trial § 41.
C.J.S. Witnesses § 322.

Research References

Encyclopedias

OH Jur. 3d Appellate Review § 294, Recording of Proceedings.
OH Jur. 3d Costs in Civil Actions § 8, Recovery of Judgment; "Prevailing Party".
OH Jur. 3d Costs in Civil Actions § 14, Depositions.
OH Jur. 3d Courts & Judges § 352, Trial.
OH Jur. 3d Discovery & Depositions § 50, Persons Before Whom Depositions May be Taken, Generally.
OH Jur. 3d Discovery & Depositions § 60, Notice.
OH Jur. 3d Discovery & Depositions § 64, Record of Examination—Videotaped Depositions.
OH Jur. 3d Discovery & Depositions § 65, Noting of Objections.
OH Jur. 3d Discovery & Depositions § 68, Submission of Testimony to Witness; Changes or Corrections; Signing.
OH Jur. 3d Discovery & Depositions § 69, Submission of Testimony to Witness; Changes or Corrections; Signing—Videotaped Deposition.

OH Jur. 3d Discovery & Depositions § 71, Certification and Filing of Deposition—Videotaped Deposition.

OH Jur. 3d Discovery & Depositions § 74, Copies of Testimony.

OH Jur. 3d Discovery & Depositions § 84, Presentation of Videotaped Deposition.

OH Jur. 3d Discovery & Depositions § 99, Objections to Videotaped Deposition.

OH Jur. 3d Discovery & Depositions § 105, Expenses Associated With Videotaped Depositions.

OH Jur. 3d Trial § 90, Presence of Judge.

OH Jur. 3d Trial § 94, Presence of Party by Counsel or Other Representative.

OH Jur. 3d Trial § 117, Videotape Trial.

OH Jur. 3d Trial § 146, Objection to Videotape Testimony.

Forms

Ohio Jurisprudence Pleading and Practice Forms § 45:2, Videotape Depositions.

Ohio Jurisprudence Pleading and Practice Forms § 45:3, Inspection or Viewing.

Ohio Jurisprudence Pleading and Practice Forms § 45:4, Objections at Trial.

Ohio Jurisprudence Pleading and Practice Forms § 45:5, Videotape Trials.

Ohio Jurisprudence Pleading and Practice Forms § 45:6, Equipment.

Ohio Jurisprudence Pleading and Practice Forms § 45:7, Costs.

Ohio Jurisprudence Pleading and Practice Forms § 45:8, Ownership and Release.

Ohio Jurisprudence Pleading and Practice Forms § 45:10, Stipulation—Another Form.

Treatises and Practice Aids

Baldwin's Ohio Handbook Series—Trial Handbook § 30:2, Deposition.

Klein, Darling, & Terez, Baldwin's Ohio Practice Civil Practice § 32:4, Restrictions on Use of Deposition--Admissibility Requirement.

Klein, Darling, & Terez, Baldwin's Ohio Practice Civil Practice § 40:1, Pre-Recorded Testimony.

Klein, Darling, & Terez, Baldwin's Ohio Practice Civil Practice § 54:5, Costs.

Giannelli and Snyder, Baldwin's Ohio Practice, Evidence, § 103.6, Objections: Timeliness.

Carlin, Baldwin's Ohio Practice, Merrick-Rippner Probate Law § 30:47, Drafting a Will—Mechanical Recording of Execution of Will—Purpose.

Ohio Personal Injury Practice § 5:7, Depositions Upon Oral Examination—Deposition Fees Taxed as Costs.

Ohio Personal Injury Practice § 7:13, United States Life Table.

Law Review and Journal Commentaries

The Dual Docket System, James L. McCrystal. 49 Ohio St B Ass'n Rep 51 (January 19, 1976).

Videotape: Prerecorded Trials—A Procedure for Judicial Expediency, Comment. 3 Ohio N U L Rev 849 (1976).

Notes of Decisions

In general 2
Constitutional issues 1
Costs 4
Error in entry, effect 7
Local rules 6
Objections 5
Videotaped trials 3

---

1. Constitutional issues

Rule establishing trial-by-videotape procedure, used to expedite large number of substantially identical claims involving issue of whether asbestosis claimant has right to participate in Workers' Compensation Fund, did not violate workers' compensation claimant's due process rights. Haught v. Chrysler Corp. (Ohio App. 9 Dist., Summit, 04-06-2005) No. 22286, 2005-Ohio-1631, 2005 WL 767109, Unreported. Workers' Compensation ⊙ 1703

Videotaped statements of defendant's girlfriend were not admissible as evidence in prosecution for possession of controlled substance, where statements lacked sufficient guarantees of trustworthiness to rebut their presumption of unreliability; law enforcement officers participated in conducting interviews of girlfriend, even though she was not in custody at time, she was asked leading questions, she made some inculpatory statements to establish defendant's guilt, questioning detective used girlfriend's fear of defendant to get her cooperation, and fact statements were made to defendant's attorney did not constitute rigorous testing in context of adversarial proceeding required by Confrontation Clause. State v. Lather (Ohio App. 6 Dist., Ottawa, 04-11-2003) No. OT-02-024, 2003-Ohio-1866, 2003 WL 1861415, Unreported. Criminal Law ⊙ 417(9); Criminal Law ⊙ 662.8

A defendant's rights to confrontation and cross examination of witnesses apply in the taking of a videotaped deposition to be used against the defendant in a criminal trial. (Annotation from former C P Sup R 12.) State v. Wilkinson (Ohio 1980) 64 Ohio St.2d 308, 415 N.E.2d 261, 18 O.O.3d 482. Criminal Law ⊙ 627.2; Criminal Law ⊙ 662.30

Where a record of proceedings in a trial is in the form of a videotape, and an indigent defendant is granted access to the tape pursuant to C P Sup R 15(D), he is not entitled to a written transcript of such proceedings. (Annotation from former C P Sup R 12.) State v. Lewis (Franklin 1973) 35 Ohio App.2d 218, 301 N.E.2d 568, 64 O.O.2d 325, certiorari denied 94 S.Ct. 546, 414 U.S. 1042, 38 L.Ed.2d 334.

Defendant's due process rights were not violated in dog-fighting prosecution by euthanasia, for cost-saving purposes, of dogs removed from property where they were allegedly being possessed for use in dog fighting; while better course of action would have been to preserve dogs until after trial, defense counsel failed to arrange for examination of dogs within a reasonable time, state preserved evidence by making a videotape of its expert examining and diagnosing dogs' injuries, and defendant was able to cross-examine state's expert and to rebut that testimony with testimony by his own expert. State v. Jones (Ohio App. 6 Dist., Lucas, 01-17-2003) No. L-00-1231, No. L-00-1232, No. L-00-1233, 2003-Ohio-219, 2003 WL 139762, Unreported. Constitutional Law ⊙ 268(5); Criminal Law ⊙ 700(9)

2. In general

In a criminal appeal, audio tapes are not a proper substitute for a written transcript of the trial testimony. (Annotation from former C P Sup R 12.) State ex rel. Seigler v. Rone (Ohio 1975) 42 Ohio St.2d 361, 328 N.E.2d 811, 71 O.O.2d 328.

3. Videotaped trials

Workers' compensation claimant's statutory right to jury trial did not encompass right to present his own testimony and that of his witnesses live, or right to have jury see him as case was presented, where case was otherwise appropriate for trial by video. Arrington v. DaimlerChrysler Corp. (Ohio, 07-12-2006) 109 Ohio St.3d 539, 849 N.E.2d 1004, 2006-Ohio-3257. Jury ⊙ 31.2(1)

It is reversible error for a trial court to order a prerecorded videotape trial over the objections of both parties unless the court reflects in a journal entry that it has, pursuant to C P Sup R 12(B), consulted with the attorneys and considered the costs involved, the nature of the action, the nature and amount of testimony, that these factors taken together indicate a compelling reason to conduct the trial by videotape, and that no cognizable prejudice will be suffered by the parties. (Annotation from former C P Sup R 12.) Fantozzi v. Sandusky Cement Prod. Co. (Ohio 1992) 64 Ohio St.3d 601, 597 N.E.2d 474. Appeal And Error ⊙ 1048(2); Witnesses ⊙ 228

Patient awarded judgment in medical malpractice suit was entitled to costs related to presentation of videotaped expert testimony, even if she was not entitled to cost of transcribing the depositions. Wilson v. Kenton Surgical Corp. (Ohio App. 3 Dist., 03-08-2001) 141 Ohio App.3d 702, 753 N.E.2d 233, 2001-Ohio-2166. Costs ⊙ 154

Objection to material within a videotaped deposition should be made before trial and shall be made before the videotape is presented. Zachariah v. Rockwell Internatl. (Ohio App. 3 Dist., 04-29-1998) 127 Ohio App.3d 298, 712 N.E.2d 811. Trial ⊙ 76

Trial court did not abuse its discretion in refusing to allow plaintiffs' pediatric expert, who had already testified, to present rebuttal testimony by live satellite or videotape; expert's rebuttal testimony mirrored that given by him at trial. (Annotation from former C P Sup R 12.) Sowers v. Middletown Hosp. (Ohio App. 12 Dist., 06-14-1993) 89 Ohio App.3d 572, 626 N.E.2d 968, motion overruled 68 Ohio St.3d 1409, 623 N.E.2d 566. Trial ⊙ 62(3)

In an action tried as a prerecorded videotape trial pursuant to Civ R 40, upon remand for a new trial, it is proper procedure to resubmit to a jury the prerecorded testimony when the prejudicial error occurred in the instructions to the jury only and not in the admission or rejection of evidence. (Annotation from former MC Sup R 10.) Lang v. Colonial Manor Nursing Home (Ohio Com.Pl. 1981) 4 Ohio Misc.2d 1, 446 N.E.2d 226, 4 O.B.R. 62. Appeal And Error ⇔ 1214

4. Costs

Driver who was sued by motorist for injuries allegedly sustained in an automobile accident waived, for purposes of appeal, any objection to trial court's award to motorist, as element of prevailing party costs, of the cost of a master videotape and a copy thereof for the deposition of motorist's medical expert, which were costs required to be borne by the proponent, where driver did not raise the issue in a cross-appeal. Wingfield v. Howe (Ohio App. 8 Dist., Cuyahoga, 01-26-2006) No. 85721, 2006-Ohio-276, 2006 WL 178563, Unreported. Appeal And Error ⇔ 878(6)

Motorist who prevailed in his personal injury action against driver whose vehicle collided with motorist was not entitled to recover, as elements of prevailing party costs, the amount spent on filing fees and subpoenas, or the cost to have a court reporter attend and transcribe the depositions of motorist's medical expert and of defendant; no statutory authority existed for the recovery of these expenses as costs. Wingfield v. Howe (Ohio App. 8 Dist., Cuyahoga, 01-26-2006) No. 85721, 2006-Ohio-276, 2006 WL 178563, Unreported. Automobiles ⇔ 361

Trial court did not abuse its discretion in declining to award fund-raising company that prevailed in action against former employee for breach of non-compete agreement litigation costs for videotaped depositions that were not used as evidence at trial but used instead for impeachment or cross-examination. QSP, Inc. v. Gibson (Ohio App. 8 Dist., Cuyahoga, 12-01-2005) No. 86054, No. 86457, 2005-Ohio-6346, 2005 WL 3219722, Unreported. Costs ⇔ 154

Trial court did not abuse its discretion in negligence action arising out of two motor vehicle accidents by refusing to award injured motorist, as part of its award of taxable costs following the entry of a jury verdict in motorist's favor, the cost of recording and playing videotaped deposition testimony; testimony in question was redundant, and motorist could have used trial court's video playback equipment rather than spending extra for a big-screen projection system. Falther v. Toney (Ohio App. 5 Dist., Fairfield, 11-01-2005) No. 05 CA 32, 2005-Ohio-5954, 2005 WL 2995161, Unreported. Automobiles ⇔ 251

Reasonable videotaped deposition expenses may be taxed as costs and awarded to a successful claimant on appeal from a decision of Industrial Commission, pursuant to statute governing the taxing of costs of legal proceeding establishing a claimant's right to participate in Worker's Compensation Fund. Cave v. Conrad (Ohio, 02-27-2002) 94 Ohio St.3d 299, 762 N.E.2d 991, 2002-Ohio-793. Workers' Compensation ⇔ 1988

Unsuccessful workers' compensation claimant was not entitled to payment from Industrial Commission for both stenographic and videotape reproductions of physician's deposition; former statute providing that claimant was entitled to cost of deposition did not obligate Industrial Commission to reimburse for multiple forms of deposition, abrogating Clark v Bur. of Workers' Comp. (1993), 88 Ohio App.3d 153, 623 N.E.2d 640. (Annotation from former C P Sup R 12.) State ex rel. Williams v. Colasurd (Ohio, 03-29-1995) 71 Ohio St.3d 642, 646 N.E.2d 830, 1995-Ohio-236. Workers' Compensation ⇔ 1987

Unsuccessful workers' compensation claimant was not entitled to reimbursement from Industrial Commission for cost of playing videotaped deposition at trial; former statute governing costs of workers' compensation appeal did not mandate that such costs be included as surplus fund payment, and rule provided that such costs be borne by court. (Annotation from former C P Sup R 12.) State ex rel. Williams v. Colasurd (Ohio, 03-29-1995) 71 Ohio St.3d 642, 646 N.E.2d 830, 1995-Ohio-236. Workers' Compensation ⇔ 1987

The expense of videotape depositions not used as evidence at trial is to be borne by the party taking such depositions and not taxed as costs in the action. (Annotation from former C P Sup R 12 and former MC Sup R 10.) Barrett v. Singer Co. (Ohio 1979) 60 Ohio St.2d 7, 396 N.E.2d 218, 14 O.O.3d 122. Costs ⇔ 154

Charges for videotape cassettes used to play depositions at trial were not taxable as costs. (Annotation from former C P Sup R 12.) Coleman v. Jagniszcak (Ohio App. 8 Dist., 06-12-1995) 104 Ohio App.3d 413, 662 N.E.2d 91. Costs ⇔ 154

Charges for expedited transcripts of video depositions of expert witnesses were not taxable as costs. (Annotation from former C P Sup R 12.) Coleman v. Jagniszcak (Ohio App. 8 Dist., 06-12-1995) 104 Ohio App.3d 413, 662 N.E.2d 91. Costs ⇔ 154

Charges for playing videotape recording of depositions of expert witnesses at trial were not taxable as costs. (Annotation from former C P Sup R 12.) Coleman v. Jagniszcak (Ohio App. 8 Dist., 06-12-1995) 104 Ohio App.3d 413, 662 N.E.2d 91. Costs ⇔ 154

Cost of deposition videotape playback at trial could not be awarded to prevailing party inasmuch as court rule mandated that expense of playing video recording at trial be borne by court. (Annotation from former C P Sup R 12.) Carr v. Lunney (Ohio App. 8 Dist., 05-30-1995) 104 Ohio App.3d 139, 661 N.E.2d 246. Costs ⇔ 193

Costs of play back and costs of videotape, as a material, were improperly allowed. (Annotation from former C P Sup R 12.) Siders v. Reynoldsburg School Dist. (Ohio App. 10 Dist., 12-13-1994) 99 Ohio App.3d 173, 650 N.E.2d 150. Costs ⇔ 193

Court of Common Pleas Superintendence Rule providing that reasonable expense of recording testimony on videotape shall be cost in action did not necessarily preclude also treating transcription expenses as "cost of the deposition" under statute requiring Bureau of Workers' Compensation to pay cost of physician depositions and cost of copies of such depositions in cases in which person claiming right to participate in Workers' Compensation Fund fails to establish that right on appeal; Superintendence Rule was silent as to that question. (Annotation from former C P Sup R 12.) Frawley v. Mihm (Ohio App. 2 Dist., 10-27-1993) 91 Ohio App.3d 275, 632 N.E.2d 573. Workers' Compensation ⇔ 1988

Where there is no evidence that a videotape transcript of an expert witness was required by the court in a negligence action wherein the plaintiffs suffered injuries in an automobile accident, the costs of such cannot be awarded. (Annotation from former C P Sup R 12.) Youssef v. Jones (Lucas 1991) 77 Ohio App.3d 500, 602 N.E.2d 1176, motion overruled 63 Ohio St.3d 1411, 585 N.E.2d 836.

In an employee's personal injury case against a third-party tortfeasor, a trial court errs in overruling an employee's entire motion to tax as costs the video deposition expenses of a physician because the cost of the videotape as material was not set forth separately since the court could have easily satisfied itself concerning the value of the blank tape and deducted that amount accordingly. (Annotation from former C P Sup R 12.) Jeffers v. Phillips Ready Mix (Greene 1991) 72 Ohio App.3d 62, 593 N.E.2d 443, motion overruled 59 Ohio St.3d 709, 571 N.E.2d 135. Costs ⇔ 198

Costs of court reporter's attendance to play videotape recording at trial was not properly taxable against losing party, where tape in question was never played at trial. (Annotation from former C P Sup R 12.) Shipman v. Alamo Rent–A–Car, Inc. (Cuyahoga 1990) 70 Ohio App.3d 333, 590 N.E.2d 1385. Costs ⇔ 184(3)

The expense of videotape depositions not used as evidence in an action which is settled without trial is to be borne by the party taking such depositions and not taxed as costs in the action. (Annotation from former C P Sup R 12 and former MC Sup R 10.) Dorko v. Woodruff (Medina 1988) 42 Ohio App.3d 13, 536 N.E.2d 56. Costs ⇔ 193

C P Sup R 12(D)(1)(c) provision that the expense of playing a videotaped deposition at trial shall be borne by the court does not conflict with the general language of Civ R 54(D) which grants a trial judge discretion in assessing costs deemed reasonable against parties to the action; thus, since C P Sup R 12 governs the assessment of costs of playing a videotape deposition during trial, an assessment of such costs against the party offering the videotape into evidence must be reversed. (Annotation from former C P Sup R 12 and former MC Sup R 10.) Friday v. Rice (Franklin 1987) 38 Ohio App.3d 113, 526 N.E.2d 1102.

A court is required to bear the expense of playing a videotape deposition for the purpose of ruling upon objections as well as the expense of playing the videotape recording at trial. (Annotation from former C P Sup R 12 and former MC Sup R 10.) Semenas v. Republic Steel Corp. (Cuyahoga 1985) 29 Ohio App.3d 237, 504 N.E.2d 1182, 29 O.B.R. 283.

The discretion of a trial court to tax as costs expenses of the prevailing party other than those traditionally allowed is limited and subject to careful scrutiny; taxing as costs the fee of an expert witness to testify on videotape is reversible error. (Annotation from former C P Sup R 12.) Gold v. Orr Felt Co. (Miami 1985) 21 Ohio App.3d 214, 487 N.E.2d 347, 21 O.B.R. 228.

Where editing of a videotaped deposition was done in court as it was being played back, this constituted playback as opposed to editing, and the expense should be borne by the court instead of being taxed as costs, under C P Sup R 12(D)(1)(c). (Annotation from former C P Sup R 12.) Szalay v Dupper, No. 11–175 (11th Dist Ct App, Lake, 3–13–87).

5. Objections

Court of Appeals would review for abuse of discretion trial court's admission of entire videotaped deposition of medical expert of Administrator of state Bureau of Workers' Compensation in claimant's appeal of Industrial Commission's denial of claim for benefits. Shrock v. Copperweld (Ohio App. 11 Dist., 04-22-2005) 160 Ohio App.3d 623, 828 N.E.2d 197, 2005-Ohio-1901. Workers' Compensation ⚖ 1967

Administrator of state Bureau of Workers' Compensation waived for appellate review his claim that trial court erred in admitting entire videotaped deposition of Administrator's medical expert in claimant's appeal of Industrial Commission's denial of claim for benefits, although Administrator served objections to portions of deposition to trial court on eve of trial; Administrator did not move court to rule on objections, never renewed objections when claimant presented deposition for admission into evidence, and did not object during trial. Shrock v. Copperweld (Ohio App. 11 Dist., 04-22-2005) 160 Ohio App.3d 623, 828 N.E.2d 197, 2005-Ohio-1901. Workers' Compensation ⚖ 1958

A party may object to the videotaped testimony of a cardiologist at trial in an action for obtaining insurance benefits upon the decedent's death since the grounds for the objections could not be removed at the deposition and objections were not waived. (Annotation from former C P Sup R 12.) Vargo v. Travelers Ins. Co., Inc. (Ohio 1987) 34 Ohio St.3d 27, 516 N.E.2d 226.

Objections to videotaped testimony should be made before trial and must be made before actual presentation of the videotape at trial. Sommer v. Conrad (Ohio App. 4 Dist., 09-07-1999) 134 Ohio App.3d 291, 730 N.E.2d 1058. Trial ⚖ 76

Bureau of Workers' Compensation and employer waived their objections to videotaped testimony of physicians, which they claimed was based upon vague hypothetical, though Bureau and employer objected at the physicians' depositions, where those objections were never communicated to trial court. Sommer v. Conrad (Ohio App. 4 Dist., 09-07-1999) 134 Ohio App.3d 291, 730 N.E.2d 1058. Workers' Compensation ⚖ 1855

Employer, in workers' compensation trial, waived its objections to doctors' videotaped deposition testimony by failing to object to admission of the depositions prior to playing of videotapes for jury. (Annotation from former C P Sup R 12.) Reed v. MTD Products, Inc., Midwest Industries (Ohio App. 6 Dist., 05-31-1996) 111 Ohio App.3d 451, 676 N.E.2d 576, dismissed, appeal not allowed 77 Ohio St.3d 1472, 673 N.E.2d 137. Workers' Compensation ⚖ 1855

Alleged disqualification of a notary at a deposition pursuant to Civ R 28(C) must be raised by objection on the record before the taking of the deposition begins or as soon thereafter as the disqualification becomes known or could be discovered with reasonable diligence, or that objection is waived. (Annotation from former C P Sup R 12.) Berwald v Ford Motor Co, No. 44064 (8th Dist Ct App, Cuyahoga, 5–6–82).

Objections to videotape deposition testimony must be raised prior to the deposition being offered into evidence and shown to the jury. Failure of counsel for the objecting party to ask the trial judge to rule before the presentation constitutes a waiver. (Annotation from former C P Sup R 12.) Berwald v Ford Motor Co, No. 44064 (8th Dist Ct App, Cuyahoga, 5–6–82).

6. Local rules

A local rule that requires objections to a videotaped trial deposition of a physician in a negligence action be made at the close of the question and answer period is proper as it affects procedural rather than substantive rights. (Annotation from former C P Sup R 12 and former MC Sup R 10.) Novak v. Lee (Wood 1991) 74 Ohio App.3d 623, 600 N.E.2d 260.

7. Error in entry, effect

Although sentencing court erred in capital murder case in making journal entry that imposed sentence of death five times, that is, one for aggravated murder charge and one for each aggravating circumstance, such error was cured by Supreme Court's independent review. State v. Reynolds (Ohio, 01-14-1998) 80 Ohio St.3d 670, 687 N.E.2d 1358, 1998-Ohio-171, certiorari denied 118 S.Ct. 2328, 524 U.S. 930, 141 L.Ed.2d 702, denial of post-conviction relief affirmed 1999 WL 980568, dismissed, appeal not allowed 88 Ohio St.3d 1425, 723 N.E.2d 1113. Sentencing And Punishment ⚖ 1789(9)

Sup R 15   Arbitration

(A) Arbitration in civil cases

(1) The judge or judges of general divisions of courts of common pleas, of municipal courts, or of county courts shall consider, and may adopt, a plan for the mandatory arbitration of civil cases. The plan shall specify the amount in controversy that will require submission of the case to arbitration and arbitration shall be required in cases where the amount in controversy does not exceed that specified sum. Arbitration shall be permitted in cases where the amount in controversy exceeds the sum specified in the plan for mandatory arbitration where all parties to the action agree to arbitration. The court shall determine at an appropriate pre-trial stage whether a case is to be referred to mandatory arbitration.

(2) Every plan for the mandatory arbitration of civil cases adopted pursuant to this rule shall be filed with the Supreme Court and shall include the following basic principles:

(a) Actions Excluded. Actions involving title to real estate, equitable relief and appeals shall be excluded.

(b) Arbitrators. The court shall establish a list of qualified attorneys who have consented to serve as arbitrators. The court shall appoint from the list an arbitrator who has no interest in the determination of the case or relationship with the parties or their counsel that would interfere with an impartial consideration of the case. Upon written request of a party, the court shall appoint a board of three arbitrators in the same manner as a single arbitrator is appointed.

(c) Report and Award. Within thirty days after the hearing, the board or the single arbitrator shall file a report and award with the clerk of the court and forward copies to all parties or their counsel. The report and award, unless appealed, shall be final and have the legal effect of a verdict upon which judgment shall be entered by the court.

(d) Appeals. Any party may appeal the award to the court if, within thirty days after the filing of the award with the clerk of court, the party does both of the following:

(i) Files a notice of appeal with the clerk of courts and serves a copy on the adverse party or parties accompanied by an affidavit that the appeal is not being taken for delay;

(ii) Reimburses the county or municipal corporation for all fees paid to the arbitrator or arbitrators in the case or pays the fees directly to the arbitrator or arbitrators, unless otherwise directed by the court.

All appeals shall be de novo proceedings at which members of the deciding board or the single arbitrator are barred as witnesses.

Exceptions to the decision of the board or single arbitrator based on either misconduct or corruption of the board or single arbitrator may also be filed by any party within thirty days after the filing of the report, and, if sustained, the report shall be vacated.

(B) Arbitration in Juvenile and Domestic Relations Cases

(1) The judge or judges of a division of a court of common pleas having domestic relations or juvenile jurisdiction may, at the request of all parties, refer a case or a designated issue to arbitration.

(2) The parties shall propose an arbitrator to the court and identify all issues to be resolved by the arbitrator. The arbitrator shall consent to serve and shall have no interest in the determination of the case or relationship with the parties or their counsel that would interfere with the impartial consideration of the case. An arbitrator selected pursuant to this section is not required to be an attorney.

(3) The request for arbitration submitted by the parties shall provide for the manner of payment of the arbitrator.

(4) The arbitrator shall file a report and award pursuant to division A)(2)(c) of this rule.

(5) Any party may appeal the report and award pursuant to division (A)(2)(d) of this rule.

(Adopted eff. 7–1–97)

Historical and Statutory Notes

Ed. Note: Sup R 15 is analogous to former C P Sup R 15, adopted eff. 8–13–79; and former M C Sup R 15, adopted eff. 1–1–75; former C P Sup R 15 was former Sup R 16, adopted eff. 7–2–73; amended eff. 10–22–73.

Staff Notes

1997:

The rule establishes guidelines for arbitration procedures. Adoption of a plan for the arbitration of cases is within the discretion of the court. Arbitration has been proven to be an effective method of case disposition.

Two changes are made from the former rule. The rule now permits the appointment of a single arbitrator or a panel of three arbitrators. This change was recommended by the Supreme Court Committee on Dispute Resolution. The amendment brings the rule into conformance with practice in several courts and provides a more cost effective route for litigants who seek arbitration services. Further, the use of a single, trusted, respected neutral should eliminate some advocacy that currently takes place when the three arbitrators engage in the decision-making aspect of the process. Also, as a cost savings measure, the rule provides for the direct payment of fees to the arbitrator or arbitrators.

Library References

Arbitration ⇐4.1.
Westlaw Topic No. 33.
C.J.S. Arbitration § 6.

Research References

Forms

Ohio Jurisprudence Pleading and Practice Forms § 109:9, Arbitration.

Ohio Jurisprudence Pleading and Practice Forms § 73:36, Reply to Motion to Vacate—Lack of Meritorious Defense—Failure to Respond to Requests for Admission—Failure to Appeal Within Presented Time.

Treatises and Practice Aids

Giannelli and Snyder, Baldwin's Ohio Practice, Evidence, R 101, Scope of Rules: Applicability; Privileges; Exceptions.

Giannelli and Snyder, Baldwin's Ohio Practice, Evidence, § 101.15, Arbitrations.

Ohio Consumer Law § 21:13, Arbitrability—Failure of Mutuality.

Giannelli & Yeomans, Ohio Juvenile Law § 15:5, Arbitration.

Notes of Decisions

Appeal
    In general 1
    Jurisdiction 3
    Notice; affidavit 2
    Review de novo 5
    Time 4
Referral to arbitration 6

---

1. —— In general, appeal

After motorist properly appealed award of court-ordered, non-binding arbitration, passenger's action for personal injuries sustain in automobile collision should have been returned to regular docket of the court and tried de novo as though the court ordered, non-binding arbitration had never happened; no "grounds" were required for motorist's exercise of the right to appeal, which was asserted by filing a timely notice of appeal and affidavit and reimbursement required. Rach ex rel. Rach v. DePasquale (Ohio App. 11 Dist., Trumbull, 12-15-2003) No. 2003-T-0006, 2003-Ohio-6738, 2003 WL 22941270, Unreported. Arbitration ⇐ 73.7(4)

It is not within a trial court's discretion to summarily dismiss an appeal from a decision of arbitrators simply because the trial court has determined that the appeal may lack merit; an appellant is entitled to a trial if he fully complies with all conditions set forth in a local rule which addresses the right of appeal de novo from the arbitrators' decision. (Annotation from former C P Sup R 15.) Buck v. Jarnigan (Lorain 1990) 67 Ohio App.3d 527, 587 N.E.2d 877. Arbitration ⇐ 73.8

Inadvertence and oversight do not constitute the type of excusable neglect which would justify departure from the procedural guidelines of C P Sup R 15(D). (Annotation from former C P Sup R 15.) Longhauser v. Beatty, Inc. (Clermont 1988) 55 Ohio App.3d 215, 563 N.E.2d 355.

RC 2711.21, relative to medical malpractice claims, takes precedence over any conflicting provisions of C P Sup R 15 or any local rule adopted pursuant to that rule; hence, in medical malpractice claims there is no requirement of an appeal from the arbitrators' decision, as required by C P Sup R 15(D) for other types of claims. (Annotation from former C P Sup R 15.) Krupansky v. Pascual (Lorain 1985) 27 Ohio App.3d 90, 499 N.E.2d 899, 27 O.B.R. 110.

Civ R 60(B) proceedings are not a substitute for appeal of an arbitration award, whether the arbitration agreement is consensual or not. (Annotation from former C P Sup R 15 and former MC Sup R 15.) Ruper v. Smith (Cuyahoga 1983) 12 Ohio App.3d 44, 465 N.E.2d 927, 12 O.B.R. 131.

Motion for relief from judgment is no substitute for appeal of arbitration award, whether or not arbitration agreement is consensual. (Annotation from former MC Sup R 15.) Ruper v. Smith (Cuyahoga 1983) 12 Ohio App.3d 44, 465 N.E.2d 927, 12 O.B.R. 131. Arbitration ⇐ 73.1

2. —— Notice; affidavit, appeal

The Rules of Superintendence for Courts of Common Pleas are procedural rather than jurisdictional, therefore it is erroneous for a trial court to rule that it lacked jurisdiction over a minimum wage case that had been referred to arbitration, due to the late filing of a notice of appeal from the arbitrator's award. (Annotation from former C P Sup R 15.) Was v. A.J.L.S., Inc. (Lorain 1985) 21 Ohio App.3d 280, 487 N.E.2d 918, 21 O.B.R. 352.

Requirement of local rule, following Superintendence Rule, of an affidavit with notice of appeal from arbitration proceedings is procedural rather than jurisdictional. (Annotation from former MC Sup R 15.) Richardson Bros., Inc. v. Dave's Towing Service (Medina 1983) 14 Ohio App.3d 1, 469 N.E.2d 850, 14 O.B.R. 3. Arbitration ⇐ 73.4

The affidavit requirement of C P Sup R 15(D)(1) is procedural rather than jurisdictional; therefore, a court of common pleas has discretion whether to use the sanction of dismissal for a failure to file such an affidavit with the notice of appeal. (Annotation from former C P Sup R 15.) Richardson Bros., Inc. v. Dave's Towing Service (Medina 1983) 14 Ohio App.3d 1, 469 N.E.2d 850, 14 O.B.R. 3.

A local court rule, which explicitly prohibits a party's attorney from filing the affidavit required to accompany a notice of appeal, under C P Sup R 15(D)(1), is void because C P Sup R 15(D)(1) does allow an attorney for a party to file the requisite affidavit. (Annotation from former C P Sup R 15.) Wilder v Ryce, No. 15633 (9th Dist Ct App, Summit, 1–13–93).

The affidavit accompanying a notice of appeal, pursuant to C P Sup R 15 (D)(1), may be signed by the appealing party or his attorney. (Annotation from former C P Sup R 15.) Medical Personnel Pool of Akron & Canton Inc v Ott, No. 13313 (9th Dist Ct App, Summit, 4–13–88).

3. —— Jurisdiction, appeal

A court of appeals lacks jurisdiction to hear an appeal directly from an arbitration board, which is not a court of record. (Annotation from former C P Sup R 15.) Holt v. Diamantopoulos (Summit 1989) 65 Ohio App.3d 723, 585 N.E.2d 453.

4. —— Time, appeal

Defendant failed to appeal arbitration award within 30 days of the filing of the award with the clerk of the courts as required by local rules, and thus, trial court was required to enter a judgment in accordance with the arbitration report. James v. Roadarmel (Ohio App. 9 Dist., Summit, 09-28-2005) No. 22630, 2005-Ohio-5107, 2005 WL 2372839, Unreported. Arbitration ⇐ 73.5

Local rule giving party 30 days in which to perfect appeal from arbitration decree gave rise to substantive right, precluding dismissal of complaint less than 30 days after arbitrator rendered decree for defendants, based on plaintiffs' failure to appear at previously scheduled, postarbitration trial. (Annotation from former C P Sup R 15.) Huffaker v. Ramella (Franklin 1991) 75 Ohio App.3d 836, 600 N.E.2d 1082. Arbitration ⇐ 73.1

The thirty-day requirement of C P Sup R 15(D) for filing an appeal from an arbitration award is a procedural rule that does not affect the trial court's jurisdiction. Thus, where a party fails to timely appeal an arbitration award, the common pleas court may, within its discretion, extend the thirty-day limit or dismiss the matter for failure to comply with the procedural requirements for filing the appeal. (Annotation from former C P Sup R 15.) Longhauser v. Beatty, Inc. (Clermont 1988) 55 Ohio App.3d 215, 563 N.E.2d 355. Arbitration ⇔ 73.5

5. —— Review de novo, appeal

Under local rule, trial court had to conduct trial de novo on all issues as to all parties after timely notice of appeal from arbitration award was filed, and trial court could not merely enter judgment on award. (Annotation from former C P Sup R 15.) Stevens v. Fentech Industries, Inc. (Franklin 1990) 66 Ohio App.3d 69, 583 N.E.2d 425. Arbitration ⇔ 73.7(4)

A trial court may not arbitrarily render judgment affirming an arbitration award where a party has appealed the award, thus entitling the party to a trial de novo. (Annotation from former C P Sup R 15.) Dupal v. Daedlow (Cuyahoga 1989) 61 Ohio App.3d 46, 572 N.E.2d 147.

6. Referral to arbitration

Absent a showing that a trial court has abused its discretion, the failure to insert into the record the reasons for referring a case to arbitration is not reversible error. (Annotation from former C P Sup R 15.) Kuenzer v. Teamsters Union Local 507 (Ohio 1981) 66 Ohio St.2d 201, 420 N.E.2d 1009, 20 O.O.3d 205.

When a case is erroneously referred to arbitration under a local rule which prohibits arbitration once a trial date is set, the substantive rights of the party who fails to object to the arbitration in a timely manner are not violated. (Annotation from former C P Sup R 15.) Cole v. Central Ohio Transit Authority (Franklin 1984) 20 Ohio App.3d 312, 486 N.E.2d 140, 20 O.B.R. 414.

Trial court's error in referring matter to arbitration in violation of its local rules was not a jurisdictional defect, but rather a procedural error. (Annotation from former MC Sup R 15.) Cole v. Central Ohio Transit Authority (Franklin 1984) 20 Ohio App.3d 312, 486 N.E.2d 140, 20 O.B.R. 414. Arbitration ⇔ 23.9

Erroneous referral of case to nonbinding arbitration pursuant to local rule does not affect substantive rights of party so as to require rejection of judgment based upon arbitration report and award, where full trial after arbitration was available upon request. (Annotation from former MC Sup R 15.) Cole v. Central Ohio Transit Authority (Franklin 1984) 20 Ohio App.3d 312, 486 N.E.2d 140, 20 O.B.R. 414. Arbitration ⇔ 82(3)

Sup R 16 Mediation

(A) General Provisions. A division of the court of common pleas, municipal court, and county court shall consider, and may adopt, a local rule providing for mediation.

(B) Content of Mediation Rule. A local rule providing for mediation shall include the applicable provisions set forth in this division, in addition to such other provisions as the court or division considers necessary and appropriate.

(1) *Required provisions for all mediation rules.* A local mediation rule shall include all of the following provisions:

(a) Procedures for ensuring that parties are allowed to participate in mediation, and if the parties wish, that their attorneys and other individuals they designate are allowed to accompany them and participate in mediation;

(b) Procedures for screening for domestic violence both before and during mediation;

(c) Procedures for encouraging appropriate referrals to legal counsel and other support services for all parties, including victims of and suspected victims of domestic violence;

(d) Procedures for prohibiting the use of mediation in any of the following:

1) as an alternative to the prosecution or adjudication of domestic violence;

2) in determining whether to grant, modify or terminate a protection order;

3) in determining the terms and conditions of a protection order; and

4) in determining the penalty for violation of a protection order.

Nothing in division (B)(1)(d) of this rule shall prohibit the use of mediation in a subsequent divorce or custody case even though that case may result in the termination of the provisions of a protection order.

(2) *Required provisions for domestic relations and juvenile court mediation rules.* A local rule for mediation of allocation of parental rights and responsibilities or the care of, or visitation with, minor children or delinquency or status offense cases shall include the provisions of division (B)(1) of this rule. The mediation rule shall include provisions that allow mediation to proceed, when violence or fear of violence is alleged, suspected, or present, only if the mediator has specialized training set forth in division (C)(2) of this rule and all of the following conditions are satisfied:

(a) The person who is or may be the victim of domestic violence is fully informed, both orally and in writing, about the mediation process, his or her right to decline participation in the mediation process, and his or her option to have a support person present at mediation sessions.

(b) The parties have the capacity to mediate without fear of coercion or control.

(c) Appropriate procedures are in place to provide for the safety of the person who is or may be the victim of domestic violence and all other persons present at the mediation.

(d) Procedures are in place for the mediator to terminate mediation if he or she believes there is continued threat of domestic violence or coercion between the parties.

(e) Procedures are in place for issuing written findings of fact, as required by R.C. 3109.052, to refer certain cases involving domestic violence to mediation.

(3) *Required provisions for child abuse, neglect, or dependency mediation rules.* A local rule for mediation in child abuse, neglect, or dependency cases shall include the provisions of division (B) (1) and (B)(2) of this rule and all of the following:

(a) A provision that allows mediation to proceed only if the mediator has specialized training set forth in division (C)(1), (C)(2), and (C)(3) of this rule.

(b) Procedures for ensuring that parties who are not represented by counsel attend mediation only if they have waived the right to counsel in open court, and that parties represented by counsel attend mediation without counsel only where the right to have counsel present at the mediation has been specifically waived. Waivers can be rescinded at any time.

(c) Procedures for the selection and referral of a case to mediation at any point after the case is filed.

(d) Procedures for notifying the parties and nonparty participants of the mediation.

(C) Qualification and Training for Domestic Relations and Juvenile Mediators. Each domestic relations and juvenile division of the court of common pleas that adopts a local rule providing for mediation shall include the following applicable provisions for the qualification and training of mediators.

(1) *General qualifications and training.* A mediator employed by the division or to whom the division makes referrals for mediation of allocation of parental rights and responsibilities, the care of, or visitation with, minor children, abuse, neglect, and dependency, or juvenile perpetrated domestic violence cases shall satisfy all of the following:

(a) Possess a bachelor's degree, or equivalent education experience as is satisfactory to the division, and at least two years of professional experience with families. "Professional experience with families" includes mediation, counseling, casework, legal representation in family law matters, or such other equivalent experience satisfactory to the division.

(b) Complete at least twelve hours of basic mediation training or equivalent experience as a mediator that is satisfactory to the division.

(c) After completing the training required by division (C)(1)(b) of this rule, complete at least forty hours of specialized family or divorce mediation training that is provided by a training program approved by the Dispute Resolution Section in accordance with standards established by the Supreme Court Advisory Committee on Dispute Resolution.

(2) *Specific qualifications and training; domestic abuse.* A mediator employed by the division or to whom the division makes referrals for mediation of any case shall complete at least fourteen hours of specialized training in domestic abuse and mediation through a training program approved by the Dispute Resolution Section in accordance with standards established by the Supreme Court Advisory Committee on Dispute Resolution. A mediator who has not completed this specialized training may mediate these cases only if he/she co-mediates with a mediator who has completed the specialized training.

(3) *Specific qualifications and training; abuse, neglect, and dependency cases.* In addition to satisfying the requirements of division (C)(1) and (C)(2) of this rule, a mediator employed by the division or to whom the division makes referrals for mediation of abuse, neglect, or dependency cases shall satisfy both of the following:

(a) Possess significant experience in mediating family disputes;

(b) Complete at least thirty-two hours of specialized child protection mediation training through either a formal training session or through a mentoring program approved by the Dispute Resolution Section in accordance with standards established by the Supreme Court Advisory Committee on Dispute Resolution.

(D) Aspirational Standards. Each division that adopts a local rule providing for mediation of family cases shall encourage mediators to comply with the Model Standards of Practice for Family and Divorce Mediation as set forth in Appendix F and the Special Policy Considerations for State Regulation of Family Mediators and Court Affiliated Programs as set forth in Appendix G to this rule. Wherever a conflict exists between the Model Standards of Practice for Family and Divorce Mediation set forth in Appendix F and the Special Policy Considerations for State Regulation of Family Mediators and Court Affiliated Programs in Appendix G and this rule, this rule shall control.

(Adopted eff. 7–1–97; amended eff. 11–24–97; 1–1–07)

Historical and Statutory Notes

Ed. Note: Sup R 16 is analogous to former C P Sup R 81, adopted eff. 9–7–92.

Amendment Note: The 11–24–97 amendment rewrote division (B); and substituted "Sup. R. 5" for "Rule 9 of the Rules of Superintendence for the Courts of Common Pleas" in division (C). Prior to amendment, division (B) read:

"(B) Pursuant to the plan, any mediator employed by the court, or to whom the court makes referrals, shall have the following minimum qualifications:

"(1) A bachelors degree or equivalent educational experience and at least two years of professional experience with families. 'Professional experience with families' includes counseling, casework, legal representation in family law matters, or equivalent experience that is satisfactory to the court.

"(2) Completion of at least forty hours of specialized family or divorce mediation training conducted in a program approved by the commission on continuing legal education in accordance with administrative guidelines established by the Committee on Dispute Resolution.

"(3) Adherence to the ethical standards of the mediator's profession.

"(4) Maintenance of appropriate liability insurance specifically covering the activities of the individual as a mediator."

Staff Notes

1997:

Interim Rule 81 of the Supreme Court Rules of Superintendence for Common Pleas Courts (now Rule 16 of the Rules of Superintendence for the Courts of Ohio) became effective on September 7, 1992, until July 1, 1994, or until a permanent rule was adopted by the Supreme Court. On October 13, 1994, the Supreme Court Committee on Dispute Resolution (Committee) conducted a public hearing concerning the qualifications necessary for mediators in the area of domestic relations, particularly relating to disputes over allocation of parental rights and responsibilities. Testimony was received, in written and oral form, from interested individuals and organizations. Following the October 13, 1994, public hearing, the Coordinator for Dispute Resolution Programs of the Supreme Court proposed modifications of interim Rule 81 based upon the comments received. The proposed modifications were presented to the Committee in January 1995. The Committee has reviewed the comments submitted by interested parties in 1994, 1995, and 1996 and has concluded that the interim rule should be modified. The comments received regarding the proposed amendments fall into several categories. Each category is reviewed separately.

A. *Qualifications.* Research is still not available that conclusively addresses the issue of mediator qualifications.

B. *Standards.* Some standards clearly are necessary to protect the public, particularly when the courts either employ the mediators or make referrals to private mediators.

C. *Monitoring and quality control.* Formal Education and Training Issues. Within comments received, there continued to be concern regarding the exclusion of otherwise qualified mediators, were a bachelor's degree to be minimally required. The majority of the comments urged the maintenance of the current rule's language allowing "equivalent educational experience" to satisfy the educational requirement. There is some limited research suggesting that experiential background is sufficient, in that reported mediation satisfaction rates do not vary significantly between mediators with higher education levels and mediation training and those with no higher education and mediation training and experience. The Committee continues to seek to balance the following concerns: 1) that court personnel qualified under the interim rule be permitted to mediate and 2) that unqualified mediators not be employed or retained to provide mediation services under the authority of a local court. The Committee strongly urges that the Supreme Court monitor the training and education of court-employed mediators to ensure high quality.

D. *Domestic violence.* Pursuant to O.R.C. § 3109.052, courts continue to effectively screen and assess for problems in referring parties with past domestic violence to mediation. The Committee believes that issues surrounding referral of cases are practice issues and are not appropriate for regulation in a qualifications rule.

E. The Committee considered whether to give courts any direction into establishing mediation programs. However, no such direction is given because the rule relates to the qualifications of a mediator rather than to the implementation of a program. Technical assistance and direction are available from both the Committee and the Supreme Court Coordinator for Dispute Resolution Programs.

F. *Training.* The Committee continues to view the issue of quality training of family mediators as a critical component of the success and quality of any program. The overwhelming majority of comments received favored increasing the amount of mediation training above the interim rule's stated minimum of forty hours. The Committee also recognized the need for a basic mediation training to be completed before the specialized family or divorce mediation training. Accordingly, the amendments adopted in 1997 amend Division (B) to require at least twelve hours of basic mediation training to be completed before the forty hours of specialized family or divorce mediation training required by the interim rule.

The Committee is also sensitive to the concerns of mediators providing mediation services to local courts on the effective date of this rule who are otherwise qualified, but will not have satisfied the twelve hours of basic training requirement. The Committee recognizes that many such mediators have provided high quality service to the courts under the interim rule and therefore each court may allow these mediators to continue mediating if they determine that an additional twelve hours of basic training is not needed. Mediators nominated to or applying for a local court panel or list after the effective date of this rule must meet the training standards of this rule. The Committee also strongly encourages the use of apprenticeship and mentoring for new mediators as implemented under several local court rules. The Committee also urges that significant attention be given to ethical considerations during mediation trainings. In order to ensure the quality of training programs, the Committee continues to require that training programs be accredited by the Supreme Court Commission on Continuing Legal Education, according to standards established by the Committee.

G. *Continuing education*. Although the overwhelming majority of comments received favored the addition of a yearly requirement of continuing mediation education, the Committee did not feel it necessary at this time to mandate it. There was concern about imposing additional financial hardships and the resulting exclusion of otherwise competent mediators. The Committee appreciates the value of continuing mediation training and strongly encourages local courts to provide opportunity for mediators to obtain additional training and to share learned experiences.

H. *Ethical standards*. The comments received regarding ethical standards expressed concern over the ambiguity of the language of the interim rule and resulting confusion as to which standards were to be followed. Most of the comments requested the creation of a specific set of standards unique for Ohio domestic mediators. Currently, there are no statewide ethical standards for Ohio domestic mediators to follow and no uniform standards for the mediation profession have been adopted by the Supreme Court of Ohio. The Committee agrees that ethical standards in mediation are important, but that vague standards are unenforceable, thus meaningless. The Academy of Family Mediators (AFM) has a comprehensive uniform set of ethical standards however the Committee is reluctant to place the responsibility of changing the standards for Ohio domestic mediators in a single professional organization. The Committee does not intend to imply that any other professional association is less qualified to set standards. Similarly, many of the AFM standards are unrelated to qualifications but are, rather, aspirational statements more appropriately addressed in a training program rather than in a minimum qualifications rule. Therefore, the Committee has amended the rule by deleting Division (B)(3). The Committee strongly urges the adherence to the ethical considerations provided in the accredited domestic mediation training, including but not limited to the maintenance of parties' reasonable expectations of confidentiality and the disclosure of conflicts of interest.

I. *Liability insurance*. Several comments favored the requirement of mediator professional liability insurance with a possible exemption for personnel of court in-house programs covered by county-wide risk management policies or willing to rely on county prosecutor opinions that extend existing immunities to court staff and volunteer mediators. The Committee is sensitive to the financial hardship and exclusionary result that a liability insurance requirement may present for otherwise qualified domestic mediators. While the Committee recognizes the possible threat of liability, the actual occurrence of malpractice suits against mediators has been extremely rare. Therefore, the Committee has amended the interim rule by deleting Division (B)(4). The Committee does not feel it necessary to mandate liability insurance in a minimum qualifications rule. Instead, the Committee encourages flexibility for local courts which may wish to consider the issue and retain the insurance requirement for their individual programs.

J. Finally, the Committee has amended the interim rule by deleting Division (D) thereby terminating the interim status of the rule. The Committee prefers the certainty of a permanent rule to be effective after adoption by the Supreme Court of Ohio.

1992:

This rule was proposed as part of the Preliminary Report of the Committee on Dispute Resolution. The text accompanying the proposed rule follows. The text gives the history of the proposal, as well as the Committee's rationale for the content of the rule.

On September 7, 1990, the Supreme Court Committee on Dispute Resolution conducted a public hearing concerning the qualifications necessary for mediators in the area of domestic relations, particularly relating to disputes over child custody or visitation. Testimony was received, in written and oral forms, from interested individuals and organizations.

As a result of this testimony, consensus was apparent in several areas, but some variation in perspective was indicated in others. These areas of consensus and concern are summarized as follows:

Areas of Consensus

A. No research currently is available that conclusively addresses the issues of mediator qualifications.

B. Rules or standards adopted at this time should be temporary and subject to review and revision as indicated.

C. Some standards clearly are necessary to protect the public, particularly when the courts either employ the mediators or make referrals to private mediators.

D. There was virtually unanimous agreement on certain basic requirements for mediators, including:

1. Adequate specialized training in mediation of custody and visitation disputes. This training should include general mediation training as well as family law, family dynamics, child development, and other relevant material.

2. Mediators should have liability insurance specifically covering their mediation activities.

Areas of Concern

A. Basic educational (degree requirements) or experiential background necessary prior to mediation training.

B. Additional components of mediation training:

1. Separate, basic mediation process training.
2. Supervised clinical component.
3. Completion of university-based curricula.

C. Philosophical concerns centering on the role of the mediator in relation to the children. Is the mediator a "pure" neutral, or does the mediator have an obligation to act as an advocate for the best interest of the children?

Thereafter, the Court published the rule recommended by the Committee in the *Ohio Advance Sheets*, Volume 59, No. 4, on May 13, 1991. The public was advised to submit any comments on the proposed rule by June 12, 1991. The Committee has reviewed the commentary submitted by interested parties and concluded that the original rule should be modified.

The commentary received regarding the proposed rule falls into several categories. Each category is reviewed separately:

1. *Education*. Several courts expressed concern that court personnel who had already received extensive training in family mediation did not possess a bachelor's degree, as required in Section (B)(1). Accordingly, the Committee has amended this section to permit a bachelor's degree or "equivalent educational experience." The Committee seeks to balance the concern of local courts that current court personnel be permitted to handle these responsibilities, when qualified, with the concern that unqualified mediators will be permitted to work under the authority of a local court. The Committee strongly urges that the Supreme Court monitor the training and education of court-employed mediators to ensure high quality.

2. *Domestic violence*. Some commentary was received regarding the concern that judges will refer spouses involved in domestic violence to mediation under the rule. First, the Committee notes that the rule discusses the qualifications of mediators in child custody and visitation issues, not which cases should be referred to mediation. Second, the Committee does not believe that this concern, while valid, is significant because it is unlikely that any court will submit a case involving domestic violence to mediation without careful and deliberate consideration. The very fact that domestic violence has occurred should routinely disqualify such cases from consideration for mediation.

3. *AFM standards*. Concern was expressed regarding the reference in the rule to the standards specifically established by the Academy of Family Mediators (AFM). The Committee initially referred to these standards because they were the most comprehensive, uniform, and well known. However, the Committee is sensitive to several concerns expressed by the use of these standards.

First, the Committee does not intend to imply that any other professional association is less qualified to set standards.

Second, many of the AFM Standards are not related to qualifications. Rather, these standards are aspirational statements that may be more appropriately addressed in a training program. The Committee is concerned that enacting such standards into a court rule would cause the mediation process to become a formal proceeding in which parties are required to acknowledge receiving a variety of warnings and explanations.

Third, the Committee considered whether to give courts any direction into establishing mediation programs. However, no such direction is given because the rule relates solely to the qualifications of a mediator rather than any rules for implementation of a program.

4. *Training*. The Committee continues to view the issue of quality training of family mediators as a critical component of the success and quality of any program. Therefore, the Committee makes it clear that training programs must be accredited by the Commission on Continuing Legal Education, according to the standards established by the Supreme

Court Committee on Dispute Resolution. The Committee does not intend to encourage one training program over another. However, there is a general consensus that a minimum level of training is necessary for a competent family mediator and the accreditation procedures would be designed to establish such an appropriate minimum level.

A post-graduate or professional degree is not required by the rule. Experience with the rule may dictate a modification; however, at this time, the Committee believes such a requirement would be too restrictive and would prevent the participation of many qualified individuals.

Finally, mediator professional liability insurance is available through the AFM. Mediators who are employed by the court may be exempted from this requirement if immune from liability.

The Committee urges the Court to adopt this rule on an interim basis. A final rule should be adopted only after a careful analysis and evaluation of needs.

ACCREDITATION GUIDELINES

The Supreme Court Commission on Continuing Legal Education Accreditation Standards for Mediator Training Programs Established by the Supreme Court Committee on Dispute Resolution Pursuant to Sup.R. 16.

Effective _____, any program seeking Sup.R. 16 accreditation as a mediator training program from the Commission on Continuing Legal Education must contain the following training components as part of a twelve (12) hour basic and forty (40) hour advanced minimum curriculum:

1. *Information gathering and communication skills*. Instruction in active listening skills, issue identification skills.

2. *Relationship skills*. Basic training: Instruction with a minimum of four hours supervised role play practice; Advanced Training: six hours of supervised role play practice, at least three of which the trainee acts as mediator.

3. *Problem solving skills*. Instruction in identifying and understanding factual problems, problem behaviors, recognizing and addressing impasse, brain-storming techniques.

4. *Conflict management skills*. Instruction in theories of conflict management and interest-based negotiation, mediation models, principles of neutrality, maintaining neutrality, dealing with power imbalances.

5. *Ethics*. Instruction in the role of mediator and other professionals in the mediation process, including but not limited to confidentiality, conflict of interest, dealing with legal issues, neutrality, cultural bias and sensitivity.

6. *Professional skills*. Instruction in interprofessional dynamics of divorce mediation, the effect of domestic violence on all aspects of mediation including, but not limited to, assessment, the role of advocates, ability to effectively mediate, bargaining imbalances, and psychological issues. Other issues to be covered include legal issues, financial issues, family dynamics, differences between mediation and therapeutic processes, drafting of agreements, and local court policies and procedures.

A program requesting accreditation must detail in a narrative that accompanies its proposed training agenda how each of these training components is addressed and how much time will be spent on each component. A statement of the goals and objectives for the training and description of the adult learning techniques to be used must also accompany the application.

1997:

Rule 16 is identical to former C.P.Sup.R. 81 except that former division (D), which identified the rule as an interim rule, is repealed.

Library References

Arbitration ⟐26.
Westlaw Topic No. 33.
C.J.S. Arbitration §§ 60, 62.

Research References

Encyclopedias

OH Jur. 3d Alternative Dispute Resolution § 129, Selecting a Mediator; Qualifications.

OH Jur. 3d Alternative Dispute Resolution § 131, Training and Education.

Forms

Ohio Jurisprudence Pleading and Practice Forms § 101:6, Conciliation and Mediation.

Treatises and Practice Aids

Giannelli & Yeomans, Ohio Juvenile Law § 15:4, Mediation.

Sup R 23 Juvenile court procedures-complaint for abortion without parental notification

(A) Complaint–Sealing Identifying Information

All actions pursuant to section 2151.85 of the Revised Code shall be commenced by filing a complaint on Form 23–A issued by the clerk of the Supreme Court of Ohio. A certified copy of the second page, with the case number noted on it, shall be given to the complainant after she signs it. The original second page shall be removed from the file jacket and filed under seal in a safe or other secure place where access is limited to essential court personnel. All index records shall be under, "In the Matter of Jane Doe."

Minors seeking to file an action under section 2151.85 of the Revised Code shall be given prompt assistance by the clerk in a private, confidential setting. Assistance shall include performing the notary services necessary to file the complaint and affidavits described in Sup.R. 23 and 24.

The complaint shall be filed promptly upon the request of the minor. The complaint and other forms described in these rules shall be provided without cost to the minor. No filing fees or court costs shall be imposed on the minor in connection with these proceedings or any notice of appeal filed in connection with these proceedings.

(B) Appointment of Counsel

Upon the filing of the complaint, the court shall appoint an attorney to represent the complainant if she is not represented by an attorney. Court–appointed attorneys shall be paid by the court without expense to the complainant.

(C) Appointment of Guardian Ad Litem

Upon the filing of the complaint the court shall also appoint a guardian ad litem. The court may appoint the same individual to serve as both the attorney and the guardian ad litem. If the court appoints an individual who volunteers to serve as a guardian for the complainant, that individual need not be paid. Other guardians shall be paid by the court without expense to the complainant.

(D) Hearing

A hearing shall be conducted promptly after the filing of the complaint, if possible within twenty-four hours. In no event shall the hearing be held later than five business days after the filing of the complaint. The court shall accommodate school hours if at all possible. The hearing shall be conducted by a judge and shall not be heard by a magistrate. Hearings must be closed to the public and exclude all persons except witnesses on behalf of the complainant, her attorney, her guardian ad litem, and essential court personnel. The hearing shall be conducted in a manner that will preserve the anonymity of the complainant. The complainant's name shall not appear on the record.

If both maturity and either abuse or best interest are alleged in the complaint, or if maturity, abuse, and best interest are alleged in the complaint, the court shall rule on the issue of maturity first. If the court finds against the complainant on the issue of maturity, it then shall determine the other issues alleged in the complaint.

(E) Judgment

The court shall enter judgment immediately after the conclusion of the hearing and a copy of the judgment shall be immediately provided to the complainant. If the court finds by clear and convincing evidence either that the complainant is sufficiently mature and well enough informed to decide intelligently; or that there is evidence of a pattern of physical, sexual, or emotional abuse by one or both of her parents, guardian, or custodian; or that notification is not in the best interest of the complainant, the court shall issue an order on Form 23–B authorizing the complainant to consent to the performance of an abortion without notice to a parent, guardian, or custodian.

If the court determines that the complainant has not established the allegations of the complaint by clear and convincing evidence, the court shall dismiss the complaint and notify the complainant that she has a right to appeal under section 2505.073 of the Revised Code. In that event the complainant shall be provided with a copy of the notice of appeal, Form 23–C.

(F) Appeals

(1) Immediately after the notice of appeal has been filed by the complainant, the clerk of the juvenile court shall notify the court of appeals. Within four days after the notice of appeal is filed in the juvenile court, the clerk of the juvenile court shall deliver a copy of the notice of appeal and the record, except page two of the complaint, to the clerk of the court of appeals who immediately shall place the appeal on the docket of the court of appeals.

(2) The juvenile court shall prepare a written transcript if possible. However, if a transcript cannot be prepared timely and if the testimony is on audio tape, the tape may be forwarded as part of the record in the case to the court of appeals without prior transcription and the court of appeals shall accept the audio tape as the transcript in the case without prior transcription. The juvenile court shall ensure that the court of appeals has the necessary equipment to listen to the audio tape.

(G) General Rule of Expedition

If a complainant files her notice of appeal on the same day as the dismissal of her complaint, the entire court process, including the juvenile court hearing, appeal, and decision, shall be completed in sixteen calendar days from the time the complaint was filed.

(H) Confidentiality

The court shall not notify the parents, guardian, or custodian of the complainant that she is pregnant, that she wants to have an abortion, or that the complaint was filed. All court papers and records that pertain to the action shall be kept confidential and are not public records under section 149.43 of the Revised Code.

(I) Verification Notice

Upon request of the complainant or her attorney, the clerk shall verify on Form 23–D the date the complaint was filed and whether a hearing has been held within five business days after the filing of the complaint. The form shall be filed and included as part of the record and a date-stamped copy shall be provided to the complainant or her attorney.

(Adopted eff. 7–1–97)

Historical and Statutory Notes

Ed. Note: Sup R 23 is analogous to former C P Sup R 76, adopted eff. 10–5–90.

Staff Notes

1997:

This rule and accompanying forms are identical to former C.P.Sup.R. 76.

Library References

Abortion and Birth Control ⟲.50.
Westlaw Topic No. 4.
C.J.S. Abortion and Birth Control; Family Planning §§ 4 to 8.

Research References

Treatises and Practice Aids

Giannelli & Yeomans, Ohio Juvenile Law § 12:3, Complaint.
Giannelli & Yeomans, Ohio Juvenile Law § 12:4, Attorney & Guardian Ad Litem.
Giannelli & Yeomans, Ohio Juvenile Law § 12:6, Summons.
Giannelli & Yeomans, Ohio Juvenile Law § 12:7, Scheduling the Hearing.
Giannelli & Yeomans, Ohio Juvenile Law § 12:8, Hearing.
Giannelli & Yeomans, Ohio Juvenile Law § 12:10, Appeals.

Law Review and Journal Commentaries

Update on Ohio Abortion Notification Law, William A. Kurtz. 1 Prob L J Ohio 36 (November/December 1990).

Notes of Decisions

Constitutional issues 1

---

1. Constitutional issues

The notice provisions of RC 2151.85(D) violate the rulemaking authority of the Supreme Court, in O Const Art IV §5(B), as Juv R 15(A) requires that parents of a juvenile be notified of any proceedings involving the child; therefore, RC 2151.85 is unconstitutional. Further CP Sup R 76(H), promulgated in furtherance of RC 2151.85, conflicts with Juv R 15(A), and in such situations, the juvenile rule controls. (Annotation from former C P Sup R 76.) In re Doe (Ohio Com.Pl. 1990) 57 Ohio Misc.2d 20, 565 N.E.2d 891.

Sup R Form 23–A Complaint for an order authorizing consent to an abortion without notification of a parent, guardian, or custodian

FORM 23–A. COMPLAINT FOR AN ORDER AUTHORIZING CONSENT TO AN ABORTION WITHOUT NOTIFICATION OF A PARENT, GUARDIAN, OR CUSTODIAN

JUVENILE COURT

_____ COUNTY, OHIO

In re complaint of Jane Doe   Case No. _____

COMPLAINT

Promulgated by the Clerk of the Supreme Court
of Ohio pursuant to R.C. 2151.85(G)

I swear or affirm that:

1. I am pregnant.

2. I am unmarried, under 18 years of age, and unemancipated.

3. I wish to have an abortion without notification of my parent, guardian, or custodian.

4. This complaint is being filed in the juvenile court of the county where I reside or have a legal settlement, in a county bordering the county where I reside or have a legal settlement, or in the county where the abortion will be performed.

[CHECK ONE OR MORE OF THE FOLLOWING STATEMENTS.]

5. ___ I am sufficiently mature and well enough informed to intelligently decide whether to have an abortion without the notification of my parent, guardian, or custodian.

    ___ One or both of my parents, my guardian, or my custodian has engaged in a pattern of physical, sexual, or emotional abuse against me.

    ___ Notification of my parent, guardian, or custodian of my desire to have an abortion is not in my best interest.

[CHECK ONE OF THE FOLLOWING STATEMENTS.]

6. ___ I do not have a lawyer.

    ___ I have a lawyer. The name, address, and telephone number of my lawyer are:

    Lawyer's Name: _____

    Lawyer's Address: _____

    _____

    Lawyer's Phone No: _____

THEREFORE, I request that this Court issue an order authorizing me to consent to an abortion without the notification of my parent, guardian, or custodian.

Page 2 of the complaint.   Case no. _____

THIS PAGE OF THE ORIGINAL MUST BE REMOVED AND PLACED UNDER SEAL IN A SAFE OR OTHER SECURE PLACE AS REQUIRED BY RULE 23(A) OF THE RULES OF SUPERINTENDENCE FOR OHIO COURTS.

I swear or affirm that the information in the attached complaint is true and accurate to the best of my knowledge and belief.

_____
Signature

Sworn to or affirmed in my presence this ____ day of ____, 19___.

_____
Notary Public

* *

PLEASE NOTE:

If you do not have a lawyer, please provide in the spaces below any address and phone number where the Court may contact you until a lawyer is appointed to represent you. You do not need to use your home address and phone number.

Address
_____

_____

Phone

Form 23–A

Revised 11/92

(Adopted eff. 7–1–97)

Research References

Treatises and Practice Aids
Carlin, Baldwin's Ohio Practice, Merrick-Rippner Probate Law § 107:147, Complaint for an Order Authorizing Consent to an Abortion Without Notification of a Parent, Guardian, or Custodian—Form.

Sup R Form 23–A Instructions Complaint for an order authorizing consent to an abortion without notification of a parent, guardian, or custodian

COMPLAINT FOR AN ORDER AUTHORIZING CONSENT TO AN ABORTION WITHOUT NOTIFICATION OF A PARENT, GUARDIAN, OR CUSTODIAN

INSTRUCTIONS

If you are pregnant, unmarried, under eighteen years old and unemancipated, and want to have an abortion without telling your parent, guardian, or custodian, you may ask a court for permission. The court will then decide whether your parent, guardian, or custodian must be told before you may have an abortion. The attached form, called a complaint, should be used to ask a court to let you have an abortion without telling your parent, guardian, or custodian.

If you are under 18 and not married, you are "unemancipated" if:

1. You have not entered the armed services of the United States or
2. You do not have a job and support yourself or
3. You are under the care and control of your parent, guardian, or custodian.

By law, you do not have to pay a filing fee or any court costs. If you do not have a lawyer, the court will appoint one for you free of charge.

The court is not allowed to tell your parent, guardian, or custodian that you are pregnant or that you want to have an abortion. The court must keep the complaint and all other papers in your case confidential.

The complaint must be filed in a juvenile court in the county where the abortion would be performed, in the county where you reside or have a legal settlement, or in any county that borders the county where you reside or have a legal settlement.

HOW TO FILL OUT THE FORM

Completing Statement # 5: Check one or more of the statements. If you check the first statement, the court will first consider if you are mature enough and well enough informed to intelligently decide whether to have an abortion without telling your parent, guardian, or custodian. If the court does not find that you are sufficiently mature and well enough informed to make the decision, and you have checked either or both of the remaining statements, the court will then consider:

___whether there is a pattern of physical, sexual, or emotional abuse of you by your parent, guardian, or custodian, or,

___whether telling your parent, guardian, or custodian is not in your best interest.

Completing Statement # 6: Check the statement that applies to you. If you have a lawyer, fill in the name, address and telephone number of your lawyer.

Completing the Top of Page 2: The law requires that the statements in the complaint be made under oath. This part of the form must be completed in the presence of a person who is allowed to administer oaths, such as a notary public, a lawyer, or a judge. After you sign your name on the signature line, that person should notarize the form.

Completing the Bottom of Page 2: Fill out the bottom of Page 2 only if you do not have a lawyer. Provide any address and phone number where you may be contacted about this matter. When the court appoints a lawyer for you, the lawyer will reach you at the address or phone number you provide. You do not have to complete the bottom of Page 2 until after the notary public signs the top of Page 2.

[Revised 11/92]

(Adopted eff. 7–1–97)

Research References

Treatises and Practice Aids
2 Carlin, Baldwin's Ohio Prac. Merrick-Rippner Probate Law § 107.147, Complaint for an Order Authorizing Consent to an Abortion Without Notification of a Parent, Guardian, or Custodian-Form.

Sup R Form 23–B Judgment

FORM 23–B. JUDGMENT

JUVENILE COURT

_____ COUNTY, OHIO

In re complaint of Jane Doe   Case No. _____

JUDGMENT

This matter came on for hearing on the _____ day of _____, 19___. Based upon the testimony and evidence presented, this court finds:

1. The complainant is an unemancipated minor.

2. The complainant is pregnant and she wishes to obtain an abortion.

3. No parent, legal guardian, or custodian of the complainant has been notified that she is seeking an abortion.

4. That clear and convincing evidence has been presented to support the following: [decide maturity issue first if pleaded]

___ Complainant is sufficiently mature and well enough informed to decide intelligently whether to have an abortion without notifying a parent, guardian, or custodian.

___ There is evidence of a pattern of physical, sexual, or emotional abuse of the complainant by one or both of her parents, her guardian, or her custodian.

___ Notification of a parent, guardian, or custodian would not be in complainant's best interest.

___ None of the criteria set forth in paragraph 4 has been established by clear and convincing evidence.

THEREFORE, IT IS ORDERED:

___ The complaint is granted and the complainant is hereby authorized to consent to the performance or inducement of an abortion without the notification of a parent, guardian, or custodian.

___ The complaint is dismissed. The Clerk is instructed to provide the complainant with the notice of appeal form and advise her of her right to an expedited appeal.

_____, OH   _____
                                                                               Judge

_____, 19___

[Effective: October 5, 1990; amended effective January 1, 1992.]

(Adopted eff. 7-1-97)

Research References

Treatises and Practice Aids

Carlin, Baldwin's Ohio Practice, Merrick-Rippner Probate Law § 107:151, Abortion Order—Form.

Sup R Form 23–C Juvenile court

FORM 23–C

JUVENILE COURT

_____ COUNTY, OHIO

In re complaint of Jane Doe   Case No. _____

NOTICE OF APPEAL

Promulgated by the Clerk of the Supreme Court of Ohio pursuant to R.C. 2151.85(G).

Notice is hereby given that the complainant appeals to the Court of Appeals for _____ County from the final order entered in the above-styled cause on _____, 19___, dismissing the complaint seeking an abortion without notification of complainant's parents, guardian or custodian.

_____
Signature of Attorney for Complainant

_____
Attorney Name

_____
Attorney Address

_____
Attorney Phone

[Effective: October 5, 1990.]

(Adopted eff. 7-1-97)

Sup R Form 23–D Verification

FORM 23–D. VERIFICATION

JUVENILE COURT

_____ COUNTY, OHIO

In re complaint of Jane Doe   Case No. _____

VERIFICATION

This will verify that on _____, 19___, Jane Doe filed her complaint for an order authorizing consent to an abortion without notification of a parent, guardian or custodian and as of _____, 19___, which is more than five business days after the filing of the complaint, the court has not held a hearing to consider her complaint.

Clerk

(Seal)

[Effective: October 5, 1990.]

(Adopted eff. 7–1–97)

Sup R 23.1 Juvenile court procedures—application for authorization to consent to an abortion or for judicial consent to an abortion (R.C. 2919.121)

(A) Petition; Filing; Sealing Identifying Information

(1) All actions pursuant to section 2919.121 of the Revised Code shall be commenced by filing a petition on Form 23.1–A issued by the clerk of the Supreme Court of Ohio. A certified copy of the second page, with the case number noted on it, shall be given to the petitioner after the petitioner or next friend signs it. The original second page shall be removed from the file jacket and filed under seal in a safe or other secure place where access is limited to essential court personnel. All index records shall be filed under, "In re the Petition of Jane Doe."

(2) Minors seeking to file an action under section 2919.121 of the Revised Code shall be given prompt assistance by the clerk in a private, confidential setting. Assistance shall include performing the notary services necessary to file the petition and affidavits described in this rule.

(3) The petition shall be filed promptly upon the request of the petitioner. The petition and other forms described in these rules shall be provided without cost to the petitioner. No filing fees or court costs shall be imposed on the petitioner in connection with these proceedings or any notice of appeal filed in connection with these proceedings.

(B) Appointment of Counsel

Upon the filing of the petition and at least twenty-four hours before the hearing scheduled pursuant to division (D) of this rule, the court shall appoint an attorney to represent the petitioner if she is not represented by an attorney. Court–appointed attorneys shall be paid by the court without expense to the petitioner.

(C) Appointment of Guardian Ad Litem

Upon the filing of the petition, the court shall appoint a guardian *ad litem* pursuant to Rule 4 of the Ohio Rules of Juvenile Procedure.

(D) Hearing

(1) A hearing shall be conducted promptly after the filing of the petition, if possible within twenty-four hours. In no event shall the hearing be held later than five calendar days after the filing of the petition. The court shall accommodate school hours if at all possible. The hearing shall be conducted by a judge and shall not be heard by a magistrate. Hearings shall be closed to the public and exclude all persons except witnesses on behalf of the petitioner, her attorney, her guardian *ad litem*, her next friend, if any, and essential court personnel. The hearing shall be conducted in a manner that will preserve the anonymity of the petitioner. The petitioner's name shall not appear on the record.

(2) If maturity and best interest are alleged in the petition, the court shall rule on the issue of maturity first. If the court finds against the petitioner on the issue of maturity, it then shall determine the issue of best interest.

(E) Judgment

(1) If the court finds that the petitioner is sufficiently mature and well enough informed to decide intelligently whether to consent to an abortion or that the abortion is in the best interests of the petitioner, the court shall issue an order on Form 23.1–B authorizing the petitioner to consent to the performance of an abortion or giving judicial consent to the abortion. If the court does not find that the petitioner is sufficiently mature and well enough informed to decide intelligently or that the abortion is in the best interests of the petitioner, or if the court finds that it does not have jurisdiction over the petition, the court shall issue an order on Form 23.1–B denying or dismissing the petition. The court shall enter judgment as soon as possible and no later than twenty-four hours after the conclusion of the hearing.

(2) If the judgment is entered immediately at the conclusion of the hearing, the court shall provide the petitioner and her attorney with a copy of the judgment. If the court denies or dismisses the petition, the court shall notify the petitioner that she has a right to appeal under division (C)(6) of section 2919.121 of the Revised Code and provide the petitioner and her attorney with a copy of the notice of appeal, Form 23.1–C.

(3) If the judgment is not entered immediately at the conclusion of the hearing, the court shall do all of the following:

(a) Inform the petitioner that the judgment will be entered within twenty-four hours;

(b) Inform the petitioner that the court will notify her attorney of the judgment upon its issuance;

(c) Inform the petitioner of the availability of other confidential procedures, which have been established by the court, to notify the petitioner of the court's judgment, including, but not limited to, providing the petitioner with the name of a designated court employee whom the petitioner may contact to obtain the judgment, arranging for the pick-up of the judgment at the court, or arranging for delivery of the judgment to an address designated by the petitioner;

(d) Notify the petitioner that, if the court denies or dismisses the petition, she has the right to appeal under division (D)(6) of section 2919.121 of the Revised Code;

(e) Provide the petitioner and her attorney with a copy of the notice of appeal, Form 23.1–C, and explain to the petitioner that the form may be filed only if the court denies or dismisses the petition.

(F) Appeals

(1) Immediately after the notice of appeal has been filed by the petitioner, the clerk of the juvenile court shall notify the court of appeals. Within four calendar days after the notice of appeal is filed in the juvenile court, the clerk of the juvenile court shall deliver a copy of the notice of appeal and the record, except page two of the petition, to the clerk of the court of appeals who immediately shall place the appeal on the docket of the court of appeals.

(2) The juvenile court shall prepare a written transcript if possible. If a transcript cannot be prepared timely and if the testimony is on audio tape, the tape may be forwarded as part of the record in the case to the court of appeals without prior transcription, and the court of appeals shall accept the audio tape as the transcript in the case without prior transcription. The juvenile court shall ensure that the court of appeals has the necessary equipment to listen to the audio tape.

(G) General Rule of Expedition

(1) If a petitioner files a notice of appeal on the same day as the denial or dismissal of her petition, the entire court process,

including the juvenile court hearing, appeal, and decision, shall be completed in sixteen calendar days from the time the petition was filed.

(2) If a petitioner files a notice of appeal after the day on which the court denies or dismisses her petition, the entire court process, including the juvenile court hearing, appeal, and decision, shall be completed in sixteen calendar days from the time the petition was filed, plus the number of calendar days that elapsed between the date on which the court's decision was issued and the date on which the notice of appeal was filed.

(H) Confidentiality

The court shall not notify the parents, guardian, or custodian of the petitioner that she is pregnant, that she wants to have an abortion, or that the petition was filed. All court papers and records that pertain to the action shall be kept confidential and are not public records under section 149.43 of the Revised Code.

(I) Definition

As used in this rule, Sup. R. 25, and Forms 23.1–A, 23.1–B, 23.1–C, and 25, "petitioner" means the minor female who is seeking consent to have an abortion regardless of whether the minor female or a next friend filed the petition.

(Adopted eff. 10–15–01)

Sup R Form 23.1–A Petition for authorization to consent to an abortion or for judicial consent to an abortion (R.C. 2919.121)

JUVENILE DIVISION
COURT OF COMMON PLEAS
_____COUNTY, OHIO

In re petition of Jane Doe.   Case No. _____

PETITION
Promulgated by the Supreme
Court of Ohio pursuant to R.C.
2919.121

I swear or affirm that:

1. I am pregnant.

2. I am unmarried, _____ years of age, and unemancipated.

3. I wish to have an abortion and have been fully informed of the risks and consequences of an abortion.

4. This petition is being filed in the juvenile court of the county where I reside, in a county bordering the county where I reside, or in the county where the abortion will be performed.

5. I have not previously filed a petition concerning the same pregnancy that has been denied on the merits.

[CHECK <u>ONE OR BOTH</u> OF THE FOLLOWING STATEMENTS.]

6. _____ I am of sound mind and have sufficient intellectual capacity to consent to an abortion.

   _____ The court should find that an abortion is in my best interests and give judicial consent to the abortion.

[CHECK <u>ONE</u> OF THE FOLLOWING STATEMENTS.]

7. _____ I do not have a lawyer and ask that the court appoint a lawyer free of charge.

   _____ I have a lawyer. The name, address, and telephone number of my lawyer are:

Lawyer's Name: _____

Lawyer's Address: _____

_____

Lawyer's Phone No: _____

Page 2 of the petition.   Case no. _____

THIS PAGE OF THE ORIGINAL MUST BE REMOVED AND PLACED UNDER SEAL IN A SAFE OR OTHER SECURE PLACE AS REQUIRED BY RULE 23.1 OF THE RULES OF SUPERINTENDENCE FOR THE COURTS OF OHIO.

8. The following is/are the name(s) and address(es) of my parent(s), guardian(s), custodian(s) or, if my parents are deceased and no guardian(s) is/are appointed, any person standing in place of my parent(s), guardian(s), or custodian(s):

Name(s):   _____

Address(es):   _____
               _____

THEREFORE, I request that this Court appoint a lawyer if I do not already have one, appoint a guardian *ad litem* to represent my best interests, and issue an order authorizing me to consent or granting judicial consent to an abortion without the consent of my parent, guardian, or custodian.

I swear or affirm that the information in the attached petition is true and accurate to the best of my knowledge and belief.

_____
Signature (Minor or Next Friend)

If this petition is being filed by a next friend on behalf of a minor, the minor's initials are: ____

Sworn to or affirmed in my presence this ____ day of ____, ____.

_____
Notary Public

* *

PLEASE NOTE:

If you do not have a lawyer, please provide in the spaces below any address and phone number where the Court may contact you until a lawyer is appointed to represent you. You do not need to use your home address and phone number.

Address: _____
            _____

Telephone: _____

Form 23.1–A

(Adopted eff. 10–15–01)

Sup R Form 23.1–A Instructions Petition for consent to an abortion or for judicial consent to an abortion (R.C. 2919.121)

INSTRUCTIONS

If you are pregnant, unmarried, under eighteen years old and unemancipated, and want to have an abortion without the consent of your parents, you may ask a court for permission. The court will then decide whether you are sufficiently mature and well-enough informed to decide intelligently to have an abortion or whether an abortion is in your best interests. The attached form, called a petition, should be used to ask a court to let you have an abortion without the consent of your parents.

If you are under 18 and not married, you are "unemancipated" if:

1. You have not entered the armed services of the United States or

2. You do not have a job and support yourself or

3. You are under the care and control of your parent, guardian, or custodian.

By law, you do not have to pay a filing fee or any court costs. If you do not have a lawyer, the court will appoint one for you free of charge. The court also will appoint a guardian *ad litem*, who is a person responsible for protecting your interests. The court may appoint your lawyer to be your guardian *ad litem*.

The court is not allowed to tell your parent, guardian, or custodian that you are pregnant or that you want to have an abortion. The court must keep the petition and all other papers in your case confidential.

The petition must be filed in a juvenile court in the county where the abortion would be performed, in the county where you reside, or in any county that borders the county where you reside.

HOW TO FILL OUT THE FORM

Completing Statement #5: "On the merits" means a court has heard testimony and has decided not to give you consent to have an abortion.

Completing Statement #6: Check one or both of the statements. If you check the first statement, the court will first consider if you are mature enough and well enough informed to intelligently decide whether to have an abortion. If the court does not find that you are sufficiently mature and well enough informed to make the decision, and you have checked the second statement, the court will then consider whether the abortion is in your best interest. If you are not sure which statement to check, you may check both and then discuss this with your lawyer.

Completing Statement #7: Check the statement that applies to you. If you have a lawyer, fill in the name, address and telephone number of your lawyer.

Completing Page 2: The law requires that the statements in the petition be made under oath. This part of the form must be completed by you or someone who is assisting you (called a "next friend") in the presence of a person who is allowed to administer oaths, such as a notary public, a lawyer, or a judge. After you or the person assisting you signs the petition, the person who administers oaths should sign the form.

Completing the Bottom of Page 2: Fill out the bottom of page 2 only if you do not have a lawyer. Provide any address and phone number where you may be contacted about this matter. When the court appoints a lawyer for you, the lawyer will reach you at the address or phone number you provide. You do not have to complete the bottom of page 2 until after the notary public signs on page 2.

(Adopted eff. 10-15-01)

Sup R Form 23.1-B Judgment

JUVENILE COURT
_____COUNTY, OHIO

In re petition of Jane Doe   Case No. _____

JUDGMENT

This matter came on for hearing on the _____ day of _____, _____. Based upon the testimony and evidence presented, this court finds:

1. The court:

    _____ Has jurisdiction over the petition.

    _____ Does not have jurisdiction over the petition for the following reasons:
    _____
    _____
    _____.

2. _____ The petitioner is an unemancipated minor.

3. _____ The petitioner is pregnant and she wishes to obtain an abortion.

4. _____ The petitioner has been fully informed of the risks and consequences of the abortion.

5. That evidence has been presented to support the following [decide maturity issue first if pleaded]:

    a. ____ Petitioner is sufficiently mature and well enough informed to decide intelligently whether to have an abortion without obtaining the consent of a parent, guardian, or custodian.

    b. ____ The abortion would be in petitioner's best interest for the following reasons:
    _____
    _____
    _____

    c. ____ Neither 5a. nor 5b. has been established for the following reasons:
    _____
    _____

THEREFORE, IT IS ORDERED:

_____ The petition is granted and the petitioner is hereby authorized to consent to the performance or inducement of an abortion.

_____ The court finds the abortion is in the best interest of the petitioner and judicial consent is hereby authorized.

_____ The petition is denied. The Clerk is instructed to provide the petitioner with the notice of appeal form and advise her of her right to an expedited appeal.

_____ The petition is dismissed for lack of jurisdiction. The Clerk is instructed to provide the petitioner with the notice of appeal form and advise her of her right to an expedited appeal.

_____, Ohio

_____
Judge

_____
Date

Form 23.1–B

(Adopted eff. 10-15-01)

Sup R Form 23.1–C Notice of appeal

JUVENILE COURT
_____ COUNTY, OHIO

In re petition of Jane Doe   Case No. _____

NOTICE OF APPEAL

Promulgated by the Supreme Court of Ohio pursuant to R.C. 2919.121

Notice is hereby given that the petitioner appeals to the Court of Appeals for _____ County from the final order entered in the above-styled cause on _____, _____, denying or dismissing the petition seeking an abortion.

_____
Signature of Attorney for Petitioner

_____
Attorney Name

_____
Attorney Address

_____
Attorney Phone

Form 23.1–C

(Adopted eff. 10-15-01)

Sup R 24 Notifying physicians of affidavits alleging abuse under 2919.12

(A) Filing Affidavits–Procedure

Pursuant to division (B)(1)(b) of section 2919.12 of the Revised Code, a minor may have notice of an intended abortion given to a specified adult instead of one of her parents, guardian, or custodian. Two affidavits must be filed with the clerk of the juvenile court by anyone seeking to invoke the notice provisions of the law. The first affidavit is executed by the minor and should be on Form 24–A. The second affidavit is executed by the specified adult and should be on Form 24–B. Anyone receiving these forms also shall be given the accompanying instruction sheet.

Upon the filing of both affidavits and upon the request of the minor, her attorney, or the person who will perform the abortion, the clerk of the juvenile court shall issue a notice on Form 24–C verifying that the affidavits have been filed with the court.

(B) Confidentiality

All affidavits filed and notices issued pursuant to this rule shall be placed under seal in a safe or other secure place where access is limited to essential court personnel.

Persons becoming aware of the contents of any affidavits prepared pursuant to this rule or section 2919.12 of the Revised Code are exempt from reporting such contents under section 2151.421 of the Revised Code. Any reporting by court personnel would breach the duty of confidentiality and is prohibited by section 102.03 of the Revised Code.

(Adopted eff. 7-1-97)

Historical and Statutory Notes

Ed. Note: Sup R 24 is analogous to former C P Sup R 77, adopted eff. 10–5–90.

Staff Notes

1997:

This rule and accompanying forms are identical to former C.P.Sup.R. 77.

Library References

Abortion and Birth Control ⇐.50.
Westlaw Topic No. 4.

C.J.S. Abortion and Birth Control; Family Planning §§ 4 to 8.

Research References

Treatises and Practice Aids

Giannelli & Yeomans, Ohio Juvenile Law § 12:2, Jurisdictional Requirements.

Giannelli & Yeomans, Ohio Juvenile Law § 12:8, Hearing.

Sup R Form 24–A Affidavit of minor

FORM 24–A. AFFIDAVIT OF MINOR

JUVENILE COURT

_____ COUNTY, OHIO

In re complaint of Jane Doe   Case No. _____

AFFIDAVIT
R.C. 2919.12(B)(1)(b)(ii)

STATE OF OHIO   )
)
COUNTY OF _____   )

I, _____, being duly sworn, state as follows:

1. I am pregnant, unmarried, under 18 years of age, and unemancipated.

2. I wish to have an abortion without notification of a parent, guardian, or custodian.

3. I request instead that notice of my intention to have the abortion be given to one of the following [Select One]:

    a. _____, a brother or sister twenty-one years
       Name   of age or older or.

    b. _____, a stepparent or grandparent.
       Name

4. I am in fear of physical, sexual, or severe emotional abuse from a parent, guardian, or custodian who otherwise would be notified of my intention to have an abortion under section 2919.12 of the Revised Code.

5. My fear is based on a pattern of physical, sexual, or severe emotional abuse exhibited by a parent, guardian, or custodian.

Page 1 of 2

6. I understand that upon the filing of this affidavit and an affidavit from the person specified above with the juvenile court, an officer of that court will prepare a notice verifying that the affidavits have been filed.

7. The person who intends to perform or induce my abortion and the address of that person are as follows:

_____
Name of Abortion Provider

_____
Address

_____
Signature

Before me appeared the above named person who under oath or by affirmation did sign this affidavit this _____ day of _____, 19___.

_____
Notary Public

Form 24–A

Revised 11/92

Page 2 of 2

(Adopted eff. 7-1-97)

Research References

Treatises and Practice Aids
Carlin, Baldwin's Ohio Practice, Merrick-Rippner Probate Law § 107:148, Affidavit of Minor—Form.

Sup R Form 24–B   Affidavit of recipient of notice of minor's intention to receive an abortion

FORM 24–B. AFFIDAVIT OF RECIPIENT OF NOTICE OF MINOR'S INTENTION TO RECEIVE AN ABORTION

JUVENILE COURT

_____ COUNTY, OHIO

In re complaint of Jane Doe   Case No. _____

AFFIDAVIT
R.C. 2919.12(B)(1)(b)(iii)

STATE OF OHIO   )
)
COUNTY OF   )

_____, being duly sworn, states as follows:
(Name)

1. I am [select appropriate one]

   ___ over twenty-one years of age and I am a brother or sister of

   ___ a stepparent or grandparent of

   _____, (hereafter, minor) who has name of pregnant minor filed an affidavit with the Juvenile Court under section 2919.12(B)(1)(b)(ii) of the Revised Code.

2. I have been specified in the minor's affidavit as the person to receive notice of the minor's intention to receive an abortion.

3. The minor has reason to fear physical, sexual, or severe emotional abuse from a parent, guardian, or custodian who otherwise would be notified of her intention to have an abortion under section 2919.12 of the Revised Code.

4. Her fear is based on a pattern of physical, sexual, or severe emotional abuse exhibited by a parent, guardian, or custodian.

_____
Signature

Before me appeared the above named person who under oath or by affirmation did sign this affidavit this _____ day of _____, 19___.

_____
Notary Public

Revised 11/92

(Adopted eff. 7–1–97)

Research References

Treatises and Practice Aids

Carlin, Baldwin's Ohio Practice, Merrick-Rippner Probate Law § 107:149, Affidavit of Recipient of Notice of Minor's Intention to Receive an Abortion—Form.

Sup R Form 24–A and 24–B Instructions Forms alleging abuse by parent and requesting that notification of abortion be provided to other relative

FORMS ALLEGING ABUSE BY PARENT AND REQUESTING THAT NOTIFICATION OF ABORTION BE PROVIDED TO OTHER RELATIVE

INSTRUCTIONS FOR FORMS 24–A and 24–B

If you use these forms, the person performing your abortion will not be required to give notice of your abortion to a parent, guardian, or custodian. Instead, you can choose to have notice provided to a brother or sister over twenty-one years of age or a stepparent or grandparent.

These forms are called affidavits. An affidavit is a sworn statement signed before a notary public or other person, such as a judge or attorney, authorized to administer oaths. The clerk's office will provide a notary public if you want to complete the forms in the clerk's office.

These forms may be used if <u>all</u> of the following apply.

You are:

1. pregnant;
2. unmarried;
3. under eighteen years old;
4. unemancipated, which means that:

you have not entered the armed forces of the United States, or

you do not have a job and support yourself, or

you are under the care and control of a parent, guardian, or custodian;

5. you fear, based on events that have happened in the past, physical, sexual, or severe emotional abuse if notice of the abortion is given to a parent, guardian, or custodian.

These forms will be filed with the juvenile court and kept confidential. The clerk of the juvenile court will provide notice to the abortion provider that the forms have been filed and the clerk will inform the abortion provider of the name of the person you have chosen to receive notice of your abortion. The forms will not be released by the juvenile court.

You do not have to pay any filing fee or court costs to the clerk for notarizing these forms, filing these forms, or issuing the notice to the abortion provider.

The affidavit must be filed in a juvenile court in the county where the abortion will be performed, in the county where you reside or have a legal settlement, or in any county that borders the county where you reside or have a legal settlement.

HOW TO FILL OUT THE FORMS

There are two forms. You complete one of them. The other form is completed by the person you select to receive notice of your abortion. That must be a brother or sister over twenty-one years old or a stepparent or grandparent.

Your form requires that you name the person to receive notice and provide the name and address of the person to perform the abortion.

Both of the forms must be signed in front of a notary public or other person, such as a judge or attorney, authorized to administer oaths.

WHAT TO DO AFTER FILLING OUT THE FORMS

After the forms are signed and notarized, give them to the juvenile court clerk who will file them in a confidential place within the clerk's office. Then the clerk will issue a notice that you may take to the abortion provider. With that notice the abortion provider will be authorized to provide notice of the abortion to the brother, sister, stepparent, or grandparent that you have selected.

Effective 11/92

(Adopted eff. 7–1–97)

Sup R Form 24–C   Notice

FORM 24–C. NOTICE

JUVENILE COURT

_____ COUNTY, OHIO

In re complaint of Jane Doe   Case No. _____

NOTICE

Notice is hereby given that on _____, 19___, **(minor's name)** filed affidavits pursuant to Section 2919.12(B)(1)(b)(ii) and (iii) of the Revised Code and may therefore proceed to have any notifications required by that statute issued to the following specified adult: _____

Clerk

(Seal)

(Adopted eff. 7–1–97)

Sup R 26   Court records management and retention

(A) Applicability

(1) This rule and Sup. R. 26.01 to 26.05 are intended to provide minimum standards for the maintenance, preservation, and destruction of records within the courts and to authorize alternative electronic methods and techniques. Implementation of this rule and Sup. R. 26.01 to 26.05 is a judicial, governmental function.

(2) This rule and Sup. R. 26.01 to 26.05 shall be interpreted to allow for technological advances that improve the efficiency of the courts and simplify the maintenance, preservation, and destruction of court records.

(B) Definitions

As used in this rule and Sup. R. 26.01 to 26.05:

(1) "Administrative record" means a record not related to cases of a court that documents the administrative, fiscal, personnel, or management functions of the court.

(2) "Case file" means the compendium of original documents filed in an action or proceeding in a court, including the pleadings, motions, orders, and judgments of the court on a case by case basis.

(3) "Index" means a reference record used to locate journal, docket, and case file records.

(4) "Journal" means a verbatim record of every order or judgment of a court.

(5) "OHS" means the Ohio Historical Society, State Archives Division.

(6) "Record" means any document, device, or item, regardless of physical form or characteristic, created or received by or coming under the jurisdiction of a court that serves to document the organization, functions, policies, decisions, procedures, operations, or other activities of the court.

(C) Combined records

Notwithstanding any other provision of the law, a court may combine indexes, dockets, journals, and case files provided that the combination contains the components of indexes, dockets, journals, and case files as defined in this rule and Sup. R. 26.01 to 26.05. A court may replace any paper bound books with an electronic medium or microfilm in accordance with this rule.

(D) Allowable record media

(1) A court may create, maintain, record, copy, or preserve a record on traditional paper media, electronic media, including text or digital images, or microfilm, including computer output to microfilm.

(2) A court may create, maintain, record, copy, or preserve a record using any nationally accepted records and information management process, including photography, microfilm, and electronic data processing, as an alternative to paper. The process may be used in regard to the original or a copy of a record if the process produces an accurate record or copy and the process complies with American National Standards Institute ("ANSI") standards and guidelines or, in the event that ANSI standards cease to exist, other nationally accepted records and information management process standards.

(a) If a court creates, maintains, records, copies, or preserves a record using a records and information management process in accordance with division (D)(2) of this rule and the record is required to be retained in accordance with the schedules set forth in Sup. R. 26.01 to 26.05, the court shall cause a back-up copy of the record to be made at periodic and reasonable times to insure the security and continued availability of the information. If Sup. R. 26.01 to 26.05 require the record to be retained permanently, the back-up copy shall be stored in a different building than the record it secures.

(b) Records shall be maintained in conveniently accessible and secure facilities, and provisions shall be made for inspecting and copying any public records in accordance with applicable statutes and rules. Machines and equipment necessary to allow inspection and copying of public records, including public records that are created, maintained, recorded, copied, or preserved by an alternative records and information management process in accordance with division (D)(2) of this rule, shall be provided.

(c) In accordance with applicable law and purchasing requirements, a court may acquire equipment, computer software, and related supplies and services for records and information management processes authorized by division (D)(2) of this rule.

(d) Paper media may be destroyed after it is converted to other approved media in accordance with division (D) of this rule.

(E) Destruction of records

(1) Subject to the notification and transfer requirements of divisions (E)(2) and (3) of this rule, a record and any back-up copy of a record produced in accordance with division (D)(2) of this rule may be destroyed after the record and its back-up copy have been retained for the applicable retention period set forth in Sup. R. 26.01 to 26.05.

(2) If Sup. R. 26.01 to 26.05 set forth a retention period greater than ten years for a record, or if a record was created prior to 1960, the court shall notify the OHS in writing of the court's intention to destroy the record at least sixty days prior to the destruction of the record.

(3) After submitting a written notice in accordance with division (E)(2) of this rule, the court shall, upon request of the OHS, cause the record described in the notice to be transferred to the OHS, or to an institution or agency that meets the criteria of the OHS, in the media and format designated by the OHS.

(F) Exhibits, depositions, and transcripts

At the conclusion of litigation, including times for direct appeal, a court or custodian of exhibits, depositions, or transcripts may destroy exhibits, depositions, and transcripts if all of the following conditions are satisfied:

(1) The court notifies the party that tendered the exhibits, depositions, or transcripts in writing that the party may retrieve the exhibits, depositions, or transcripts within sixty days from the date of the written notification;

(2) The written notification required in division (F)(1) of this rule informs the party that tendered the exhibits, depositions, or transcripts that the exhibits, depositions, or transcripts will be destroyed if not retrieved within sixty days of the notification;

(3) The written notification required in division (F)(1) of this rule informs the party that tendered the exhibits, depositions, or transcripts of the location for retrieval of the exhibits, depositions, or transcripts;

(4) The party that tendered the exhibits, depositions, or transcripts does not retrieve the exhibits, depositions, or transcripts within sixty days from the date of the written notification required in division (F)(1) of this rule.

(G) Local rules

By local rule, a court may establish retention schedules for any records not listed in Sup. R. 26.01 to 26.05 and may extend, but not limit, the retention schedule for any record listed in Sup. R. 26.01 to 26.05. Any record that is not listed in Sup. R. 26.01 to 26.05 but is listed in a general retention schedule established pursuant to section 149.331 of the Revised Code may be retained for the period of time set by the general retention schedule and then destroyed.

(H) Extension of retention period for individual case files

A court may order the retention period for an individual case file extended beyond the period specified in Sup. R. 26.02 to 26.05 for the case file.

(Adopted eff. 10–1–97; amended eff. 7–1–01)

Historical and Statutory Notes

Amendment Note: The 7–1–01 amendment deleted "production," before "maintenance" twice and substituted "advances" for "enhancements" in division (A); deleted "receive" after "maintain," in division (D)(2); deleted "receives" after "maintains," in division (D)(2)(a); and deleted "received" after "maintained" in the second sentence of division (D)(2)(b).

Staff Notes

2001:

The July 1, 2001 amendments to Sup. R. 26 removed the words "produce" and "production" from division (A) and the words "receive" and "receives" from division (D) for the purpose of restricting the scope of the rule to records management and retention. The word "advances" replaced the word "enhancements" in division (A)(2).

1997:

The Supreme Court's Task Force on Records Management recommended the substantive provisions of this rule and Sup. R. 26.01 to 26.05 after studying the records management procedures of Ohio courts for approximately eighteen months. This rule and Sup. R. 26.01 to 26.05 require courts to keep certain records and mandate minimum records retention schedules for administrative and case records of the courts. The rules also authorize the courts to maintain records in forms other than paper provided that when an alternative process is employed, it conforms to the standards established by the American National Standards Institute ("ANSI"). Courts are not required to use the alternative processes permitted by this rule.

To obtain information concerning ANSI standards, courts may contact the Ohio Historical Society, State Archives Division, 1982 Velma Avenue, Columbus, Ohio 43211–2497, (614) 297–2581.

Sup R 26.01 Retention schedule for the administrative records of the courts

The following retention schedule shall apply for the administrative records of the courts:

(A) Administrative journal

Administrative journals that consist of court entries, or a record of court entries, regarding policies and issues not related to cases shall be retained permanently.

(B) Annual reports

Two copies of each annual report shall be retained permanently.

(C) Bank records

Bank transaction records, whether paper or electronic, shall be retained for three years or until the issuance of an audit report by the Auditor of State, whichever is later.

(D) Cash books

Cash books, including expense and receipt ledgers, shall be retained for three years or until the issuance of an audit report by the Auditor of State, whichever is later.

(E) Communication records

Communication records, including routine telephone messages on any medium where official action will be recorded elsewhere, may be destroyed in the normal course of business as soon as they are considered to be of no value by the person holding the records.

(F) Correspondence and general office records

Correspondence and general office records, including all sent and received correspondence, in any medium, may be destroyed in the normal course of business as soon as they are considered to be of no value by the person holding the records.

(G) Drafts and informal notes

Drafts and informal notes consisting of transitory information used to prepare the official record in any other form may be destroyed in the normal course of business as soon as they are considered to be of no value by the person holding the drafts and informal notes.

(H) Employment applications for posted positions

Employment applications for posted or advertised positions shall be retained for two years.

(I) Employee benefit and leave records

Employee benefit and leave records, including court office copies of life and medical insurance records, shall be retained by the appropriate fiscal officer for three years or until the issuance of an audit report by the Auditor of State, whichever is later.

(J) Employee history and discipline records

Records concerning the hiring, promotion, evaluation, attendance, medical issues, discipline, termination, and retirement of court employees shall be retained for ten years after termination of employment.

(K) Fiscal records

Fiscal records, including copies of transactional budgeting and purchasing documents maintained by another office or agency, shall be retained for three years or until the issuance of an audit report by the Auditor of State, whichever is later.

(L) Grant records

Records of grants made or received by a court shall be retained for three years after expiration of the grant.

(M) Payroll records

Payroll records of personnel time and copies of payroll records maintained by another office or agency shall be retained for three years or until the issuance of an audit report by the Auditor of State, whichever is later.

(N) Publications received

Publications received by a court may be destroyed in the normal course of business as soon as they are considered to be of no value by the person holding the publications.

(O) Receipt records

Receipt and balancing records shall be retained for three years or until the issuance of an audit report by the Auditor of State, whichever is later.

(P) Requests for proposals, bids, and resulting contracts

Requests for proposals, bids received in response to a request for proposal, and contracts resulting from a request for proposal shall be retained for three years after the expiration of the contract that is awarded pursuant to the request for proposal.

(Adopted eff. 10–1–97)

Sup R 26.04 Probate divisions of the courts of common pleas—records retention schedule

(A) Definitions

As used in this rule:

(1) "Docket" means a reference record that provides the dates and a summary of all hearings, pleadings, filings, orders, and other matters that are essential to an action, proceeding, or other matter in the probate division.

(2) "Probate record" means a record that pertains to the duties of the probate division including, but not limited to, adoptions, marriage licenses, name changes, birth records, orders of civil commitment, the resolution of civil actions, and the appointment and supervision of fiduciaries.

(3) "Record of documents" means a collection of single or several page documents in which each document represents the probate division's action in a single incident of the same duty of the probate division, such as the issuance of marriage licenses.

(B) Closed probate record or case file

For purposes of this rule, a probate record or case file of an estate, trust, or other fiduciary relationship shall be considered closed when a final accounting has been filed and, if required by law at the time of the filing, the account has been approved and settled. All other probate records and case files shall be considered closed when the probate division orders the matter closed or there is a final disposition of the action or proceeding for which the probate record or case file is kept.

(C) Required records

(1) Dockets. (a) The probate division shall maintain all of the following dockets:

(i) An administration docket showing the name of the deceased;

(ii) A guardian's docket showing the name of each ward and, if the ward is a minor, the ward's age and name of the ward's parents and any limited powers or limited duration of powers;

(iii) A civil docket in which the names of the parties to actions and proceedings shall be noted;

(iv) A testamentary trust docket showing the names of the testator and trustee or trustees;

(v) A change of name docket showing the name of the petitioner and the present and proposed names of the person whose name is to be changed;

(vi) A birth registration and correction docket showing the name of the person whose birth certificate is being registered or corrected;

(vii) A civil commitment docket showing the name of the prospective patient;

(viii) A separate adoption docket, in accordance with section 3107.17 of the Revised Code, showing the name of the child as it would exist after finalization of the adoption and the name or names of the adoptive parent or parents;

(ix) A paternity docket showing the birth name of the child who is the subject of the petition, the name of the father, the name of the mother, and the name of the child after adjudication;

(x) A miscellaneous docket showing the names of parties or petitioners and the nature of the action or proceeding. The miscellaneous docket shall be limited to actions within the probate division's jurisdiction that are not kept in one of the other dockets described in division (C)(1) of this rule. If the number of filings warrants, a miscellaneous docket may be subdivided or grouped into sections containing files or records of similar content.

(b) All dockets of the probate division shall contain the dates of filing or occurrence and a brief description of any bond and surety, letter of authority, and each filing, order, or record of proceeding related to the case or action, with a reference to the file or record where the bond and surety, letter of authority, filing, order, or record of proceeding is to be found, and such other information as the court considers necessary.

(2) Records of documents. (a) The probate division shall maintain both of the following records of documents:

(i) A record of wills, if wills are not copied and permanently retained as part of an estate case file under division (D)(2) of this rule, in which the wills proved in the court shall be recorded with a certificate of the probate of the will, and wills proved elsewhere with the certificate of probate, authenticated copies of which have been admitted to record by the court;

(ii) A marriage record, in which shall be entered licenses, the names of the parties to whom the license is issued, the names of the persons applying for a license, a brief statement of the facts sworn to by the persons applying for a license, and the returns of the person solemnizing the marriage.

(b) Records of documents of the probate division shall contain documents, applications or affidavits, either original or copies, and information pertaining to those documents, as found in division (C)(2)(a) of this rule or as considered necessary by the court.

(3) Journal. The probate division shall maintain a journal for orders, entries, or judgments pertaining to the business and administration of the division, and other miscellaneous orders, entries, or judgments which the court may consider necessary to journalize, including all of the following:

(a) Orders of appointment and oaths of office pursuant to section 2101.11 of the Revised Code of court personnel and other nonfiduciary appointees;

(b) Orders of reference to magistrates;

(c) Changes of the local rules of the probate division;

(d) Orders changing the hours for the opening and closing of the probate court.

(4) Indexes. The probate division shall maintain an index for each docket, record of documents, and journal described in division (C) of this rule. Each index shall be kept current with names or captions of proceedings in alphabetical order and references to a docket, record or documents, journal, or case file where information pertaining to those names or proceedings may be found.

(5) Upon the filing of any paper or electronic entry permitted by the probate division, a stamp or entry shall be placed on the paper or electronic entry to indicate the day, month, and year of filing.

(D) Destruction and preservation of probate records

(1) The vouchers, proof, or other evidence filed with the probate division in support of the expenditures or distribution slated in an account, after review and reconciliation with the accounting and notation of reconciliation in the record or file, may be returned to the fiduciary or retained in accordance with divisions (D)(2) and (E) of this rule.

(2) All records, vouchers, inventories, accounts, pleadings, applications, petitions, records of adoptions, marriages, and mental health commitments, wills, trusts, journals, indexes, dockets, records or documents related to estate or inheritance taxes, and other papers and filings of the probate division, may be preserved using any nationally accepted records and information management process in accordance with Sup.R. 26(D).

(3) In the probate division's discretion, any nonessential note, notice, letter, form, or other paper, document, or memorandum in a case file that is not essential to providing a record of the case and the judgment of the probate division may be destroyed prior to, or after, the case is closed. For purposes of division (D)(3) of

this rule, evidence of service of notice of the initial complaint, petition, or application that establishes the probate division's jurisdiction is essential to providing a record of a probate case.

(4) Judge, magistrate, investigator, and clerk notes, drafts, and research prepared for the purpose of compiling a report, opinion, or other document or memorandum may be kept separate from the case file, retained in the case file, or destroyed at the discretion of the preparer.

(E) Case file and probate record retention schedule

(1) Adoption records. Adoption records shall be retained permanently.

(2) Birth and death registrations. Birth and death registrations dated prior to 1908 shall be retained permanently.

(3) Civil commitment records. Civil commitment records shall be retained for three years after the case is closed.

(4) Dockets, records of documents, journals and indexes. Dockets, records of documents, journals, and indexes shall be retained permanently.

(5) Evidence filed in support of expenditures or distributions. Vouchers, proof, or other evidence filed in support of expenditures or distributions stated in an account shall be retained for three years after the date of filing.

(6) Marriage license records. Marriage license records shall be retained permanently.

(7) Trust accountings. Trust accountings shall be retained for twelve years after the date the accounting was approved.

(8) All other records. All other records shall be retained for twelve years after the date the case, cause, proceeding, or matter is closed or completed.

(F) Temporary estate tax orders

Divisions (D) and (E) of this rule do not apply to records of estates in which temporary estate tax orders are pending.

(Adopted eff. 10–1–97; amended eff. 10–1–97)

Historical and Statutory Notes

Amendment Note: The 10–1–97 amendment substituted "a stamp" for "a time stamp" and deleted "time," preceding "day," in division (C)(5).

Sup R 36 Designation of trial attorney; assignment system

(A) Designation of Trial Attorney

In civil cases the attorney who is to try the case shall be designated as trial attorney on all pleadings. In criminal cases, except felonies, the attorney who is to try the case, upon being retained or appointed, shall notify the court that he or she is the trial attorney by filing a written statement with the clerk of the court.

(B) (1) Individual Assignment System

As used in these rules, "individual assignment system" means the system in which, upon the filing in or transfer to the court or a division of the court, a case immediately is assigned by lot to a judge of the division, who becomes primarily responsible for the determination of every issue and proceeding in the case until its termination. All preliminary matters, including requests for continuances, shall be submitted for disposition to the judge to whom the case has been assigned or, if the assigned judge is unavailable, to the administrative judge. The individual assignment system ensures all of the following:

(a) Judicial accountability for the processing of individual cases;

(b) Timely processing of cases through prompt judicial control over cases and the pace of litigation;

(c) Random assignment of cases to judges of the division through an objective and impartial system that ensures the equitable distribution of cases between or among the judges of the division.

(2) Each multi-judge general, domestic relations, and juvenile division of the court of common pleas shall adopt the individual assignment system for the assignment of all cases to judges of the division. Each multi-judge municipal or county court shall adopt the individual assignment system for the assignment of all cases to the judges of that court, except as otherwise provided in division (C) of this rule. Modifications to the individual assignment system may be adopted to provide for the redistribution of cases involving the same criminal defendant, parties, family members, or subject-matter. Any modifications shall satisfy divisions (B)(1)(a) to (c) of this rule and be adopted by local rule of court.

(C) Assignment System

In each multi-judge municipal or county court, cases may be assigned to an individual judge or to a particular session of court pursuant to the following system:

(1) Particular session. A particular session of court is one in which cases are assigned by subject category rather than by the individual assignment system. The following subject categories shall be disposed of by particular session:

(a) Civil cases in which a motion for default judgment is made;

(b) Criminal cases in which a plea of guilty or no contest is entered;

(c) Initial appearance in criminal cases;

(d) Preliminary hearings in criminal cases;

(e) Criminal cases in which an immediate trial is conducted upon initial appearance;

(f) Small claims cases;

(g) Forcible entry and detainer cases in which the right to trial by jury is waived or not demanded.

(h) Cases where a party has made application to, or has been accepted into, a specialized court or docket.

To guarantee a fair and equal distribution of cases, a judge who is assigned a case by subject matter pursuant to Sup. R. 36(B)(2), or by virtue of a specialized court or docket pursuant to Sup. R. 36(C)(1)(h), may request the administrative judge to reassign a similar case by lot to another judge in that multi-judge common pleas, municipal, or county court.

(2) Assignment. Cases not subject to assignment in a particular session shall be assigned using the individual assignment system. Civil cases shall be assigned under division (C)(2) of this rule when an answer is filed or when a motion, other than one for default judgment, is filed. Criminal cases shall be assigned under division (C)(2) of this rule when a plea of not guilty is entered.

(3) Duration of assignment to particular session. The administrative judge shall equally apportion particular session assignments among all judges. A judge shall not be assigned to a particular session of court for more than two consecutive weeks.

(D) Assignment of Refiled Cases

In any instance where a previously filed and dismissed case is refiled, that case shall be reassigned to the judge originally assigned by lot to hear it unless, for good cause shown, that judge is precluded from hearing the case.

(E) Assignment–New Judicial Positions

After the date of election, but prior to the first day of the term of a new judicial position, the administrative judge of a court or division through a random selection of pending cases shall equitably reassign cases pending in the court or division between or among the judges of the court or division and shall create a docket similar to a representative docket. Reassignment shall be completed in a manner consistent with this rule and may exclude criminal cases and cases scheduled for trial. Any matters arising in cases assigned to the docket for the new judicial position prior to the date on which the judge elected to that position takes office shall be resolved by the administrative judge or assigned to another judge.

(Adopted eff. 7–1–97; amended eff. 11–1–06)

Historical and Statutory Notes

Ed. Note: Sup R 36 is analogous to former C P Sup R 4, adopted eff. 8–13–79; and former M C Sup R 3, adopted eff. 1–1–75; former C P Sup R 4 was analogous to former Sup R 4, adopted eff. 9–30–71.

Staff Notes

2006:

Rule 36 (C)(1)(h). This amendment specifies that if a judge is assigned cases as a result of a specialized docket, that judge may request that the administrative judge of the court assign similar cases to another judge in order to ensure the fair and equitable distribution of cases within a court.

1997:

This rule merges the provisions of former C.P.Sup.R. 4 and M.C.Sup.R. 3 into a single rule governing the assignment of cases pursuant to the individual assignment system.

Rule 36(A) Designation of trial attorney. Rule 36(A) requires attorneys who are to serve as trial counsel in either civil or criminal cases to notify the court of that fact. Notification in civil cases is accomplished by designation of the trial attorney on all pleadings. In criminal cases, immediately upon being retained or appointed, the trial attorney is required to file a written notification of the attorney's retention or appointment with the clerk of court.

Rule 36(B)(1) Individual assignment. The individual assignment system is defined by the rule as a system whereby, upon the filing or transfer of a civil case, or upon arraignment in a criminal case, the case is immediately assigned to a judge of the court. The rule sets forth three purposes of the individual assignment system. All multi-judge divisions of the court of common pleas and all multi-judge municipal and county courts, except as provided in division (C)(2) of the rule, are required to adopt the individual assignment system. Courts or divisions are permitted to deviate from the individual assignment system only if the modifications satisfy the three stated purposes of the system and are adopted by local rule of court pursuant to Rule 5. Permissible modifications include the assignment and consideration of cases involving the same criminal defendant, parties, family members, or subject-matter.

The distinguishing feature of the individual assignment system is that it places responsibility upon one judge for the disposition of cases. Once a case is assigned to a judge under this system, all matters pertaining to the case are to be submitted to that judge for determination. An exception is made where that judge is unavailable. In that instance, the administrative judge may act in the assigned judge's absence.

Under Rule 36(B), the administrative judge is responsible for the assignment of cases to the individual judges of the court. Assignment may be made by the administrative judge personally or by court personnel at the administrative judge's direction. All assignments of cases to individual judges must be made by lot.

The purpose of the random assignment, by lot, of cases is to avoid judge-shopping on the part of counsel and to distribute the cases equitably among the judges. "Lot" mandates an assignment arbitrated by chance; the determination must be fortuitous, wholly uncontrolled.

Assignment to the judges of the division in an established order of rotation does not comply with the rule, even if the order of rotation is altered periodically.

An acceptable method of assignment is a form of drawing from a pool of the names of the judges, using paper, balls, or other objects as lots or counter. The pea pool system or the bingo cage are examples. To be an assignment by lot, the entire base of the number of judges in the division must be utilized in each assignment.

A computer may be used for lot selection as long as random assignment is maintained.

Assignment by lot can be systematized. Judges can be identified by number. Those numbers can then be arranged in random order by chance over any given range of numbers. The greater the range, the greater the validity of the arrangement. The range of numbers might well represent the total of three years or so of filings. Slips of paper are then printed with serial control numbers on the front and a line for writing in a case number upon assignment. The judges' numbers are printed in the order of their lot determination on the back of the serially arranged slips. The slips are then padded so that the judges' numbers may not be seen. The evidence of the selection or printing list shall not be revealed. When a case is to be assigned, a slip is removed, the case number written on it, the code number of an individual judge is revealed, and a control sheet maintained.

The practice of making no assignment until "X" number of cases have accumulated when there are "X" number of judges, merely provides for assignment by lot within a very small control and the operation of chance is minimized. That method is only a modified form of rotation and is not assignment by lot.

Once a case is assigned to an individual judge, by lot, it may be reassigned or transferred to another judge by order of the administrative judge. See the Instructions for Preparation concerning the proper use and reporting of transfers.

Although many ancillary matters, and in fact the entire case, frequently may be handled by a magistrate, the assignment system mandates responsibility for every case be affixed to a judge. The assigned judge's report form will reflect action taken by the magistrate.

See Rule 43(E) and its commentary concerning how the numbering system is geared to the record keeping requirements of the individual assignment system.

Rule 36(C) Assignment system. In multi-judge municipal and county courts, Rule 36(C) establishes a dual system for the assignment of cases. Under this system, certain types of cases are processed in a court session, designated particular session, presided over by a judge or magistrate for a specified period of time. Other types of cases are assigned to an individual judge pursuant to the individual assignment system.

Rule 36(C)(1) and (2) Particular session; assignment. The types of cases designated in division (C)(1) for disposition in particular sessions of court are high volume cases that may be processed by a judge or magistrate at a single session. The rule does not preclude the processing of types of cases, other than those listed, that are susceptible to disposition in particular sessions.

Cases that may not be processed by particular session are civil cases where an answer is filed or a motion, other than one for default judgment, is filed and criminal cases in which a plea of not guilty is entered. These cases are to be assigned pursuant to the individual assignment system at the time the answer, motion, or plea is filed or made.

Rule 36(C)(3) Duration of assignment to particular session. Assignments to particular session are to be equally divided among the judges of the court and are to be limited to two-week periods. The two week limitation accommodates the individual assignment system, and allows each judge adequate time to work on the cases individually assigned to the judge. Judges should not be assigned to a particular session or a series of particular sessions for more than two consecutive weeks.

Rule 36(D) Assignment of refiled cases. To promote judicial economy and discourage judge-shopping, this division mandates that all dismissed and subsequently refiled cases be reassigned to the originally assigned judge. An exception exists for circumstances in which the original judge is barred from hearing the refiled case.

Rule 36(E) Assignment-new judicial positions. This provision governs the reassignment of pending cases where a new judicial position is added to the court or division. Reassignment of cases must be random, equitable, and accomplished in a manner consistent with the principles set forth in division (B)(1) of the rule. In effect, a random selection system must be used, rather than culling cases from pending dockets. Certain dockets or portions of dockets may be created through the individual assignment system. This method may be particularly useful in assigning criminal cases. The process set forth in division (E) should facilitate the creation of a balanced docket with a minimum disruption of the pending caseload of the court or division.

Library References

Attorney and Client ⚖︎32(1).
Courts ⚖︎70.
Pleading ⚖︎42.
Westlaw Topic No. 45, 106, 302.
C.J.S. Attorney and Client § 43.
C.J.S. Courts § 123.
C.J.S. Pleading § 64.

Research References

Encyclopedias

OH Jur. 3d Courts & Judges § 61, Powers and Duties of Administrative Judge.

OH Jur. 3d Courts & Judges § 74, Municipal Court Judges; Presiding Judge—Acting Judge; Assignment of Judges.

OH Jur. 3d Courts & Judges § 227, Courts of Common Pleas; Individual Assignment System; Time for Determination; Statistical Reports.

OH Jur. 3d Courts & Judges § 228, Municipal and County Courts; Time for Disposition; Statistical Reports; Assignment of Cases.

OH Jur. 3d Courts & Judges § 323, Number of Judges Required to Render Judgment.

Treatises and Practice Aids

Klein, Darling, & Terez, Baldwin's Ohio Practice Civil Practice § 10:4, Case/File Number.

Carlin, Baldwin's Ohio Practice, Merrick-Rippner Probate Law § 108:9, Juvenile Court—Criminal Jurisdiction—Assignment of Case for Disposition.

Carlin, Baldwin's Ohio Practice, Merrick-Rippner Probate Law § 65:25, Application by Guardian for Authority to Settle Claim for Injury or Damage to Ward—Form.

Carlin, Baldwin's Ohio Practice, Merrick-Rippner Probate Law § 107:43, Scheduling Juvenile Court Hearing.

Law Review and Journal Commentaries

Spinning Cases, Mark A. Gamin. (Ed. note: The "spinning off" or reassignment of cases from a judge to a visiting or retired judge is discussed.) 67 Clev B J 8 (May 1996).

Notes of Decisions

In general 2
Assignment by lot 6
Constitutional issues 1
Extension of time 7
Procedural issues 5
Reassignment 4
Transfer of cases 3

---

1. Constitutional issues

A defendant in a federal prosecution has no right to have his case heard by a particular judge or a judge selected by random drawing; local rules governing case assignment are simply housekeeping rules that confer no rights upon defendants, and any error or violation of rules in assignment does not deny due process of law unless prejudice is shown to result. (Annotation from former C P Sup R 4.) Sinito v. U.S. (C.A.6 (Ohio) 1984) 750 F.2d 512.

2. In general

There is no error when a judge of a municipal court grants a motion to vacate judgment, and that judge is not the judge who granted the confessed judgment originally when no affirmative demonstration is shown that the court did not comply with MC Sup R 3(B). (Annotation from former MC Sup R 3.) Mancino v. Friedman (Cuyahoga 1980) 69 Ohio App.2d 30, 429 N.E.2d 1181, 23 O.O.3d 27.

3. Transfer of cases

Debtor's breach of contract and fraud defenses to judgment on cognovit note failed to address essential issue of whether debtor defaulted on note, and thus were not meritorious defenses required to obtain relief from default judgment. Saponari v. Century Limousine Service, Inc. (Ohio App. 8 Dist., Cuyahoga, 12-04-2003) No. 83018, 2003-Ohio-6501, 2003 WL 22862932, Unreported. Judgment ⇐ 68.2(5)

First common pleas court judge was not required to transfer to second common pleas court judge condominium unit association's action against condominium unit purchaser to foreclose lien on unit for delinquent maintenance fee, even though second judge had previously been assigned and had decided association's action against purchaser for declaration that transfer to purchaser was null and void and that association had right of first refusal; delinquent fee issue was independent and separate claim not litigated or raised in declaratory judgment action, and fee issue had nothing in common with association's first right of refusal. (Annotation from former C P Sup R 4.) Jamestown Village Condo. Owners Assn. v. Market Media Research, Inc. (Ohio App. 8 Dist., 08-04-1994) 96 Ohio App.3d 678, 645 N.E.2d 1265, dismissed, appeal not allowed 71 Ohio St.3d 1444, 644 N.E.2d 406. Courts ⇐ 486

An objection to the transfer of a case from one judge to another must be timely or it is waived; an objection to a reference order made by a judge to whom the case has been wrongly transferred is untimely when it is included with objections to the referee's report. (Annotation from former C P Sup R 4.) Brown v. Brown (Montgomery 1984) 15 Ohio App.3d 45, 472 N.E.2d 361, 15 O.B.R. 73.

Husband, who first objected to a second judge's involvement in proceedings subsequent to entry of original divorce decree several months after he was aware of second judge's involvement in the case, waived any objection he might have had to transfer of the case to second judge, particularly in light of fact that the "objection" to the transfer was embodied in a recommendation to the court as to how husband's counsel thought the court ought to rule on a referee's report and recommendations generally. (Annotation from former MC Sup R 3.) Brown v. Brown (Montgomery 1984) 15 Ohio App.3d 45, 472 N.E.2d 361, 15 O.B.R. 73. Judges ⇐ 51(2)

4. Reassignment

Judge had no duty to issue rulings in a case to which he was not assigned and, therefore, was not required to rule on motion to withdraw guilty plea; the case had never been reassigned from the original trial judge. State ex rel. Chavis v. Griffin (Ohio, 02-07-2001) 91 Ohio St.3d 50, 741 N.E.2d 130, 2001-Ohio-241. Judges ⇐ 25(1)

In a single divorce action wherein four different judges were assigned at various times to hear different matters, the rulings are voidable when the record fails to show proper reassignment of the case to the judge making the rulings unless the appealing party has waived his objections by failing to raise the issue in a timely manner. (Annotation from former C P Sup R 4.) Berger v. Berger (Cuyahoga 1981) 3 Ohio App.3d 125, 443 N.E.2d 1375, 3 O.B.R. 141, certiorari denied 103 S.Ct. 76, 459 U.S. 834, 74 L.Ed.2d 74.

Where plaintiff objects to the reassignment of his case to a different judge, and such reassignment is not accompanied by a journal entry executed by the administrative judge, the judge assuming to act without a formal assignment is without authority. (Annotation from former C P Sup R 4.) Zurowski v Cuyahoga County Bd of Revision, No. 44537 (8th Dist Ct App, Cuyahoga, 10–28–82).

5. Procedural issues

Wife's voluntary dismissal of divorce action filed in original county court divested such court of its priority jurisdiction, allowing wife to re-file divorce action in a second county, even if wife was engaging in forum shopping to avoid an unfavorable mediated settlement in original county; no final decree had been issued in original court before wife noticed her voluntary dismissal, wife had absolute right to dismiss her divorce action in original county, regardless of motive, and rule requiring that cases filed, dismissed and re-filed be heard by original judge did not apply to actions re-filed in a different county. Swearingen v. Swearingen (Ohio App. 10 Dist., Franklin, 12-22-2005) No. 05AP-657, 2005-Ohio-6809, 2005 WL 3494988, Unreported. Divorce ⇐ 139

Motion to transfer action to judge who had decided two cases arguably related to instant case could only be filed with administrative judge of multi-judge division in court of common pleas. (Annotation from former C P Sup R 4.) Jamestown Village Condo. Owners Assn. v. Market Media Research, Inc. (Ohio App. 8 Dist., 08-04-1994) 96 Ohio App.3d 678, 645 N.E.2d 1265, dismissed, appeal not allowed 71 Ohio St.3d 1444, 644 N.E.2d 406. Judges ⇐ 51(1)

A letter from a supreme court chief justice assigning a visiting judge to a case is valid even if that letter is not entered by the county clerk until the day after a motion is heard by that judge; further, a presiding judge may assign judges to another division temporarily without a reauthorization from the supreme court chief justice, but if the assigned judge is unavailable, preliminary matters may be decided by an administrative judge, who may then transfer the matter to a visiting judge. (Annotation from former C P Sup R 4.) Wissel v. Ohio High School Athletic Assn. (Hamilton 1992) 78 Ohio App.3d 529, 605 N.E.2d 458.

The administrative judge for a multi-judge division of the common pleas court has authority to determine preliminary matters in the case when the assigned judge is unavailable or to reassign any case to himself or any other judge of that court, by a journalized order stating a justifiable reason for transferring responsibility for the case to himself or to another judge. (Annotation from former C P Sup R 4.) Berger v. Berger (Cuyahoga 1981)

3 Ohio App.3d 125, 443 N.E.2d 1375, 3 O.B.R. 141, certiorari denied 103 S.Ct. 76, 459 U.S. 834, 74 L.Ed.2d 74. Courts ⟾ 70

The administrative judge in a multi-judge division of a common pleas court merely has authority and responsibility for control over the administration, docket and calendar of the division which he serves, and does not have authority to determine issues and proceedings in cases assigned to a trial judge, unless the issues and proceedings involve preliminary matters and the record before him affirmatively demonstrates that the judge to whom the case is assigned is unavailable, and that a delay in ruling on the matters until the trial judge is available would be prejudicial. (Annotation from former C P Sup R 4.) Rosenberg v. Gattarello (Cuyahoga 1976) 49 Ohio App.2d 87, 359 N.E.2d 467, 3 O.O.3d 151.

6. Assignment by lot

Neither mandamus nor prohibition will lie to challenge the assignment of a remanded case by lot. (Annotation from former C P Sup R 4.) State ex rel. Berger v. McMonagle (Ohio 1983) 6 Ohio St.3d 28, 451 N.E.2d 225, 6 O.B.R. 50, certiorari denied 104 S.Ct. 548, 464 U.S. 1017, 78 L.Ed.2d 723.

Where an indictment, properly assigned by lot to a judge, was dismissed after a second indictment was returned, differing from the first only in that it added specifications alleging physical harm, the trial court's failure to assign the second indictment by lot, whereby the judge assigned to the original indictment assumed authority over the disposition of the second indictment, did not result in prejudice to the defendant. (Annotation from former C P Sup R 4.) State v. Mahoney (Hamilton 1986) 34 Ohio App.3d 114, 517 N.E.2d 957.

7. Extension of time

When a court grants the defendant an extension of time to plead on the same day a motion for default judgment was filed, the case is ineligible for assignment under MC Sup R 3(B)(2) until the answer date set by the court. (Annotation from former MC Sup R 3.) State ex rel. Garnett v. Lyons (Ohio 1975) 44 Ohio St.2d 125, 339 N.E.2d 628, 73 O.O.2d 440.

Sup R 36.1 Notice of appellate panels

No later than fourteen days prior to the date on which oral argument will be heard, the court of appeals shall make available to the parties the names of the judges assigned to the three-judge panel that will hear the case. If the parties waive oral argument, the court of appeals shall make available to the parties the names of the judges assigned to the three-judge panel that will hear the case no later than fourteen days prior to the date on which the case is submitted to the panel. If the membership of the panel changes after the names of the judges are made available to the parties pursuant to this rule, the court of appeals shall immediately make the new membership of the panel available to the parties.

(Adopted eff. 7–1–02; amended eff. 11–1–06)

Sup R 41 Conflict of trial court assignment dates, continuances and engaged counsel

(A) Continuances; Granting Of

The continuance of a scheduled trial or hearing is a matter within the sound discretion of the trial court for good cause shown.

No party shall be granted a continuance of a trial or hearing without a written motion from the party or counsel stating the reason for the continuance, endorsed in writing by the party as well as counsel, provided that the trial judge may waive this requirement upon a showing of good cause. No court shall grant a continuance to any party at any time without first setting a definite date for the trial or hearing.

When a continuance is requested by reason of the unavailability of a witness at the time scheduled for trial or hearing, the court shall consider the feasibility of resorting to the several methods of recording testimony permitted by Civil Rule 30(B) and authorized for use by Civil Rule 32(A)(3).

(B) Conflict of Trial Date Assignments

(1) When a continuance is requested for the reasons that counsel is scheduled to appear in another case assigned for trial on the same date in the same or another trial court of this state, the case which was first set for trial shall have priority and shall be tried on the date assigned. Criminal cases assigned for trial have priority over civil cases assigned for trial. The court should not consider any motion for a continuance due to a conflict of trial assignment dates unless a copy of the conflicting assignment is attached to the motion and the motion is filed not less than thirty days prior to trial.

(2) Except as provided in division (B)(3) of this rule, a continuance shall be granted, upon request, under either of the following circumstances:

(a) A party, counsel, or witness under subpoena is scheduled to appear on the same date at a hearing before the Board of Commissioners on Grievances and Discipline of the Supreme Court as a member of the Board, as a party, as counsel for a party, or as a witness under subpoena for the hearing;

(b) Counsel requesting the continuance will be unavailable to participate in the judicial proceeding because counsel is a member of the General Assembly whose attendance is required at a scheduled voting session or committee meeting of the General Assembly.

(3) In considering a continuance requested pursuant to division (B)(2)(b) of this rule, the court may require counsel to obtain the consent of the client and provide notice to all other parties to the action. The court may deny the requested continuance if either or both of the following apply:

(a) Counsel has been granted prior continuances in the same case based on attendance at scheduled voting sessions or committee meetings of the General Assembly;

(b) The court determines that further delay in the proceeding would result in substantial prejudice to a party.

(C) Engaged Counsel

If a designated trial attorney has such a number of cases assigned for trial in courts of this state so as to cause undue delay in the disposition of such cases, the administrative judge may summon such trial attorney who persistently requests continuances and extensions to warn the attorney of the possibility of sanctions and to encourage the attorney to make necessary adjustments in the management of his or her practice. Where such measures fail, restrictions may properly be imposed by the administrative judge on the number of cases in which the attorney may participate at any one time.

(D) Continuances; Reporting

Trial continuances shall be reported on a monthly basis to the administrative judge. Where a judge is persistently and unreasonably indulgent in granting continuances or extensions, the administrative judge shall investigate the reasons for the excessive continuances and take appropriate corrective action at the local level. If corrective action at the local level is unsuccessful, the administrative judge shall report that fact to the Court Statistical Reporting Section of the Supreme Court. If it comes to the attention of the Court Statistical Reporting Section that the judge of a single-judge division is persistently and unreasonably indulgent in granting continuances, the Court Statistical Reporting Section shall report to the Chief Justice, who shall take appropriate corrective action.

(Adopted eff. 7–1–97; amended eff. 10–1–03)

Historical and Statutory Notes

Ed. Note: Sup R 41 is analogous to former C P Sup R 7, adopted eff. 8–13–79; and former M C Sup R 16, adopted eff. 1–1–75; former C P Sup R 7 was analogous to former Sup R 14, adopted eff. 9–1–72.

Amendment Note: The 10-1-03 amendment rewrote subdivision (B)(2) and added subdivision (B)(3). Prior to amendment, subdivision (B)(2) read:

"(2) A continuance shall be granted, upon request, when a party, counsel, or witness under subpoena is scheduled to appear on the same date at a hearing before the Board of Commissioners on Grievances and Discipline of the Supreme Court as a member of the Board, as a party, as counsel for a party, or as a witness under subpoena for the hearing."

Staff Notes

1997:

Rule 41 consolidates the provisions of former C.P.Sup.R. 7 and M.C.Sup.R. 16.

Rule 41(A) Continuances; granting of. Division (A) provides that the granting of a continuance is within the sound discretion of the court, and only upon a showing of good cause.

Written motion must be filed specifying the reason for the continuance. The motion must be signed by the party requesting the continuance, as well as their counsel. The requirement that the motion be signed by the party may be waived by the trial judge, for good cause. If a continuance is granted, the court shall, at that time, reset the trial or hearing for a definite date.

If a continuance is requested because of the unavailability of a witness, the court is required to consider the feasibility of recording testimony as permitted by Civ.R. 30(B).

The standards relating to court delay reduction adopted by the American Bar Association focus, to a great extent, upon the limitation of continuances as a means of expediting case dispositions.

Rule 41(B) Conflict of trial assignment dates. Division (B) sets priorities among all trial courts for resolution of conflicts when counsel is assigned for trial in more than one court on the same date.

When a continuance is requested by reason of conflict, the case first set for trial is to be given priority and tried on the date assigned. Priority is dependent on firm assignment for trial. Thus, a general policy of early assignment to achieve priority would be inconsistent with the purpose of this rule. Within this general system, criminal cases assigned for trial are to be accorded priority over civil cases.

Attached to the motion for a continuance should be a copy of the conflicting assignment, and the motion should be filed not less than thirty days prior to the trial sought to be continued. These provisions are not mandatory, and there may be situations where compliance with one or both is not possible.

Rule 41(C) Engaged counsel. Division (C) gives the administrative judge authority to restrict the number of cases that an attorney may handle at one time if trial counsel has so many cases assigned for trial that undue delay is caused in the disposition of those cases.

Rule 41(D) Continuances; reporting. Division (D) requires the administrative judge to take action if it appears that a judge grants an inappropriate number of continuances. The administrative judge shall first take corrective action at the local level. If that action is not successful, the administrative judge has the duty to refer the matter to the Court Statistical Reporting Section of the Supreme Court. The Court Statistical Reporting Section also has the responsibility to refer any matter to the Chief Justice for corrective action if it is brought to the Section's attention that the judge of a single-judge division or court appears to be granting an inappropriate number of continuances.

1975:

Rule 16(A)

Rule 16(A) sets forth procedures for the allowance of continuances of trials or hearings. Continuances are to be granted only upon written motion therefor. The motion must specify the reason the continuance is sought. Upon the granting of a motion for continuance, the court shall reset the trial or hearing for a definite date.

Rule 16(B)

Rule 16(B) sets priorities among *all trial courts* of the state for resolution of conflicts occurring when counsel is assigned for trial in more than one court on the same date. See Rule 1(A).

When a continuance is requested by reason of such conflict, the case first set for trial is to be given priority and tried on the date assigned. Priority is dependent on firm assignment for trial. Thus, a general policy of early assignment to achieve priority would be inconsistent with the purposes of this rule. Multiple assignment of cases for the same hour and date before an individual judge does not constitute firm assignment for purposes of priority determination.

Within this general priority system, criminal cases assigned for trial are to be accorded priority over civil cases. Priority for criminal cases is not new. R.C. 2938.03 and R.C. 2945.02 state "[c]riminal cases shall be given precedence over civil matters...." It is recognized that under the Rule 16(B) priority system civil cases may suffer delayed trial assignment, but priority is dictated by the statutory law, R.C. 2938.03 and R.C. 2945.02 (See Also R.C. 2945.71-73), and by the general principle that cases concerning individual liberty are more important than cases which involve other rights.

Rule 16(C)

Rule 16(C) is an adaptation of Sup. R. 14 and responds to a suggestion from the bar regarding the solution of the engaged counsel problem. The rule gives the administrative judge authority to order designated trial counsel to provide a substitute trial attorney where such counsel has so many cases assigned for trial that undue delay is caused in disposition of those cases. Upon failure of counsel to obey such an order, the administrative judge "shall remove him as counsel in the case." In the event the trial attorney was appointed by the court, the court "shall appoint a substitute trial attorney."

Rule 2(C)(8), which requires the administrative judge to keep records indicating the number of pending cases which counsel are designated to try, should be read in conjunction with Rule 16(C). See the Comment relating to Rule 2(C).

Cross References

Denial of continuance after grand jury discharged not reviewable in certain instances, Crim R 7
Forcible entry and detainer, eight day limit on continuances for defendant absent bond or plaintiff's consent, 1923.08

Library References

Courts ⚖189(10).
Criminal Law ⚖578 to 599.
Municipal Corporations ⚖637.
Pretrial Procedure ⚖711 to 726.
Westlaw Topic Nos. 106, 110, 268, 307A.
C.J.S. Criminal Law §§ 622 to 640.
C.J.S. Continuances §§ 2 to 133.
C.J.S. Municipal Corporations § 207.

Research References

Encyclopedias

OH Jur. 3d Actions § 148, Power and Discretion of Court, Generally.
OH Jur. 3d Actions § 158, Absence or Illness of Counsel—Counsel Engaged in Other Litigation.
OH Jur. 3d Actions § 159, Absence of Witnesses.
OH Jur. 3d Actions § 163, Generally; Motion for Continuance.
OH Jur. 3d Actions § 164, Hearing and Order.
OH Jur. 3d Courts & Judges § 349, Generally; Commencement of Action.
OH Jur. 3d Courts & Judges § 352, Trial.

Notes of Decisions

In general 1
Counsel exclusion or removal 14
Court's discretion 12
Good cause construed
    Appeal pending in related matter 8
    Counsel's unpreparedness 3
    Dilatory conduct 7
    Discovery 6
    Illness 5
    Party's absence 2
    Sua sponte orders 4
Trial assignment date conflict
    Disciplinary proceedings 13
    Motion requirements 11
    Priority of cases 10
    Reasonable time 9

Waiver of right to representation 15

---

1. In general

Trial court had rational basis to deny defendant's request for continuance to contact witnesses, where defendant had caused several delays in proceedings by failing to come to court, and value of witnesses was unsubstantiated. State v. Melvin (Ohio App. 2 Dist., Montgomery, 01-16-2004) No. 19900, 2004-Ohio-172, 2004 WL 67973, Unreported. Criminal Law ⚖ 594(1)

Defendant was not entitled to continuance in order to contact witness; trial court did allow time for defense counsel to contact witness, and defense counsel did not indicate how the testimony of witness would be favorable to the defense or give the amount of time that would be necessary to locate witness. State v. Komadina (Ohio App. 9 Dist., Lorain, 04-09-2003) No. 02CA008104, 2003-Ohio-1800, 2003 WL 1824923, Unreported, on subsequent appeal 2004-Ohio-4962, 2004 WL 2244368. Criminal Law ⚖ 594(1)

Party has right to reasonable opportunity to be present at trial and right to continuance for that purpose, but party does not have right to unreasonably delay trial. (Annotation from former C P Sup R 7.) Hartt v. Munobe (Ohio 1993) 67 Ohio St.3d 3, 615 N.E.2d 617, rehearing denied 67 Ohio St.3d 1457, 619 N.E.2d 424. Pretrial Procedure ⚖ 715; Trial ⚖ 21

Refusal to grant requests by bar patron's widow for continuance and to compel discovery prior to ruling on summary judgment motion was not abuse of discretion in negligence action against city and city-employed paramedics in connection with emergency medical services rendered to patron; any requested but not-yet-disclosed information from personnel files did not bear on legal question of whether paramedics acted wantonly and willfully so as to remove statutory immunity, and widow did not support continuance motion with an affidavit. Denham v. New Carlisle (Ohio App. 2 Dist., 06-30-2000) 138 Ohio App.3d 439, 741 N.E.2d 587, dismissed, appeal not allowed 90 Ohio St.3d 1449, 737 N.E.2d 53. Judgment ⚖ 186

Objective factors which may be considered by trial judge in determining whether to grant motion for continuance include length of delay requested, whether other continuances have been allowed, any inconvenience to litigants, court, and witnesses, whether requested delay is legitimate rather than dilatory, purposeful, or contrived, whether defendant contributed to circumstances underlying request, and other relevant factors based on unique aspects of each case. (Annotation from former C P Sup R 7.) Griffin v. Lamberjack (Ohio App. 6 Dist., 07-29-1994) 96 Ohio App.3d 257, 644 N.E.2d 1087. Pretrial Procedure ⚖ 711; Pretrial Procedure ⚖ 726

Journal entry by trial court constitutes reasonable, constructive notice that motion to continue hearing has been denied, especially since attorneys who have appeared in action are expected to keep themselves informed of progress of their case, and where local rule of court provides that if motion to continue is not granted, "case shall proceed as originally scheduled." (Annotation from former MC Sup R 16.) Holop v. Holop (Cuyahoga 1989) 59 Ohio App.3d 51, 570 N.E.2d 305. Pretrial Procedure ⚖ 725

A writ of procedendo will not issue to control or interfere with ordinary court procedures, such as the grant of a continuance pending the outcome of an appeal from a ruling on a motion. (Annotation from former C P Sup R 7.) State ex rel Swanson v Grigsby, No. L–85–316 (6th Dist Ct App, Lucas, 9–17–85).

2. —— Party's absence, good cause construed

Denial of tenant's motion for continuance on morning of trial was not abuse of discretion, in landlord's action to recover for damage to rental property, even though tenant's inability to attend trial was due to circumstances beyond his control when his vehicle broke down; tenant had already been granted one continuance, and inconvenience to court and landlord would have been great. Beard v. Rodriguez (Ohio App. 3 Dist., Seneca, 04-25-2005) No. 13-04-26, 2005-Ohio-1916, 2005 WL 941015, Unreported. Pretrial Procedure ⚖ 715

Granting continuance of trial date requested by physician and pain control center in medical negligence action was not abuse of discretion, where physician was deployed outside country for military service. Fernandez v. Ohio State Pain Control Ctr. (Ohio App. 10 Dist., Franklin, 12-14-2004) No. 03AP-1018, 2004-Ohio-6713, 2004 WL 2893402, Unreported, appeal not allowed 105 Ohio St.3d 1544, 827 N.E.2d 327, 2005-Ohio-2188. Pretrial Procedure ⚖ 715

Trial court denial of husband's motion for continuance, which husband alleged was required to obtain the presence of a witness, was not an abuse of discretion, in contempt proceeding after entry of divorce decree; trial court had previously granted husband a continuance, husband had no compelling explanation for his failure to produce the witness' testimony, and the trial court stated that it would delay journalizing the judgment entry for two weeks to allow husband to provide documentation from the witness. Byron v. Byron (Ohio App. 10 Dist., Franklin, 04-22-2004) No. 03AP-819, 2004-Ohio-2143, 2004 WL 894600, Unreported, appeal not allowed 103 Ohio St.3d 1462, 815 N.E.2d 678, 2004-Ohio-5056. Divorce ⚖ 269(12)

Inconvenience to the litigants, witnesses, opposing counsel, and the court, due to motorist's sole contribution to circumstances giving rise to need for the continuance in prosecution of motorist's accident claim, outweighed the prejudice caused to motorist by denial of the motion; trial court had rescheduled the trial date at least three times to allow motorist to obtain new counsel, his delay in retaining a new lawyer reduced amount of time his lawyer would have to prepare for trial, and although trial court warned motorist that he would be granted no further continuance, he and his new lawyer disregarded the court's orders when they failed to appear for trial. Felouzis v. Cochran (Ohio App. 8 Dist., Cuyahoga, 02-20-2003) No. 81457, 2003-Ohio-758, 2003 WL 360963, Unreported. Pretrial Procedure ⚖ 716

Denial of request for continuance, made after subpoenaed defense witness could not be located, was not abuse of discretion in murder prosecution; nothing in record suggested witness' attendance would have been secured if a continuance had been granted or that she would have been available to testify, defendant never indicated length of requested continuance, an open-ended continuance would have delayed conclusion of trial phase to the inconvenience of all involved with trial, and witness' anticipated testimony was not crucial to defense. State v. Jordan (Ohio, 03-10-2004) 101 Ohio St.3d 216, 804 N.E.2d 1, 2004-Ohio-783, stay granted 101 Ohio St.3d 1492, 805 N.E.2d 542, 2004-Ohio-1444, reconsideration denied 102 Ohio St.3d 1425, 807 N.E.2d 368, 2004-Ohio-2003, motion to reopen denied 103 Ohio St.3d 1423, 814 N.E.2d 488, 2004-Ohio-4524, certiorari dismissed 125 S.Ct. 439, 543 U.S. 952, 160 L.Ed.2d 314. Criminal Law ⚖ 594(3)

Continuance based on party's absence must be based on unavoidable, not voluntary, absence. (Annotation from former C P Sup R 7.) Hartt v. Munobe (Ohio 1993) 67 Ohio St.3d 3, 615 N.E.2d 617, rehearing denied 67 Ohio St.3d 1457, 619 N.E.2d 424. Pretrial Procedure ⚖ 715

Grounds for continuance due to absence of one party include the following factors: the absence is unavoidable and not voluntary; party's presence at trial is necessary; application is made in good faith; party probably will be able to attend court at some reasonable future time. (Annotation from former C P Sup R 7.) Sayre v. Hoelzle-Sayre (Ohio App. 3 Dist., 04-06-1994) 100 Ohio App.3d 203, 653 N.E.2d 712, appeal allowed 70 Ohio St.3d 1426, 638 N.E.2d 88, appeal dismissed as improvidently allowed 72 Ohio St.3d 1218, 651 N.E.2d 430, 1995-Ohio-274. Pretrial Procedure ⚖ 715

A party's absence is sufficient ground for a continuance only where the absence is unavoidable and not voluntary, the party's presence at trial is necessary, the application is made in good faith, and the party will be able to attend court at some reasonable future time. (Annotation from former C P Sup R 7.) Heard v. Sharp (Cuyahoga 1988) 50 Ohio App.3d 34, 552 N.E.2d 665.

3. —— Counsel's unpreparedness, good cause construed

Trial court abused its discretion in denying defendant's substitute counsel's request for a continuance; only reason for substitute counsel's request was his lack of preparation time due to his appointment the day before the trial. State v. Edwards (Ohio App. 4 Dist., Meigs, 12-18-2002) No. 01CA4, 2002-Ohio-7259, 2002 WL 31883967, Unreported. Criminal Law ⚖ 590(2)

Judge's denial of continuance because of counsel's unpreparedness is not abuse of discretion if unpreparedness was avoidable. (Annotation from former C P Sup R 7.) Hartt v. Munobe (Ohio 1993) 67 Ohio St.3d 3, 615 N.E.2d 617, rehearing denied 67 Ohio St.3d 1457, 619 N.E.2d 424. Pretrial Procedure ⚖ 721

Referee presiding over trial was not required to grant continuance on ground of defense counsel's unpreparedness; record did not show that unpreparedness could not have been avoided but, to contrary, record showed distinct lack of diligence on part of defendants throughout litigation, and defendants' mistaken belief that they could represent their respective corporations themselves should not have accrued to their benefit. (Annotation from former C P Sup R 7.) Hartt v. Munobe (Ohio 1993)

67 Ohio St.3d 3, 615 N.E.2d 617, rehearing denied 67 Ohio St.3d 1457, 619 N.E.2d 424. Pretrial Procedure ⚖ 721

Reviewing court would presume, based on alleged husband's failure to provide transcript of hearing on motion for continuance or otherwise to demonstrate that counsel's unpreparedness was unavoidable, that trial court did not abuse its discretion by denying request for continuance based on counsel's unpreparedness. (Annotation from former C P Sup R 7.) Ham v. Park (Ohio App. 8 Dist., 05-06-1996) 110 Ohio App.3d 803, 675 N.E.2d 505. Divorce ⚖ 184(4)

It is not an abuse of discretion to deny continuance requested based on counsel's unpreparedness if the unpreparedness was avoidable. (Annotation from former C P Sup R 7.) Ham v. Park (Ohio App. 8 Dist., 05-06-1996) 110 Ohio App.3d 803, 675 N.E.2d 505. Pretrial Procedure ⚖ 721

Trial court abused its discretion by denying adjoining landowner's motion for continuance after permitting counsel for adjoining landowner to withdraw on day before trial in action brought by landowners to quiet title to land claimed by both parties where court was aware that adjoining landowner was involved in federal bankruptcy proceedings in which his counsel was major creditor and that counsel and adjoining landowner had severed attorney-client relationship and court essentially forced adjoining landowner to retain counsel until morning of trial; no evidence indicated that request for continuance was dilatory, purposeful, or contrived, and length of requested 60—day continuance was reasonable in light of fact that new counsel would be required to familiarize himself or herself with case. (Annotation from former C P Sup R 7.) Griffin v. Lamberjack (Ohio App. 6 Dist., 07-29-1994) 96 Ohio App.3d 257, 644 N.E.2d 1087. Pretrial Procedure ⚖ 716

Trial court did not abuse its discretion in denying defendant's motion for continuance on ground that counsel would be on active duty within United States Army Reserve; counsel was not deprived of opportunity to prepare for trial, and his two-week period of active duty did not cause him to be unavailable for trial. (Annotation from former C P Sup R 7.) State v. Isreal (Butler 1993) 86 Ohio App.3d 696, 621 N.E.2d 793. Criminal Law ⚖ 593

Trial court did not err in denying a last-minute continuance on morning of disorderly conduct trial to allow defendant's expert to evaluate the answering machine tape which allegedly contained a threat from defendant to victim, where defendant had nearly two months from the discovery response until trial to have the expert authenticate the tape, yet failed to do so, and expert was not present to listen to the tape on the morning of trial; any problems in discovery should have been relayed to the court through an appropriate motion prior to the morning of trial. State v. Harris (Ohio App. 5 Dist., Stark, 09-16-2002) No. 2002CA00085, 2002-Ohio-4872, 2002 WL 31079591, Unreported, appeal not allowed 98 Ohio St.3d 1423, 782 N.E.2d 77, 2003-Ohio-259. Criminal Law ⚖ 590(1)

4. —— Sua sponte orders, good cause construed

A sua sponte continuance based on docket congestion will not be found reasonable absent a showing that the continued criminal case will take precedence over pending civil matters. (Annotation from former C P Sup R 7.) State v. Terra (Franklin 1991) 74 Ohio App.3d 189, 598 N.E.2d 753, dismissed, jurisdictional motion overruled 62 Ohio St.3d 1452, 579 N.E.2d 1391.

Rule relating to continuances does not prohibit a trial court from granting continuance sua sponte, but simply mandates that a party shall not be permitted any continuance without written motion stating reasons therefor. (Annotation from former MC Sup R 16.) Society Natl. Bank v. Kienzle (Cuyahoga 1983) 11 Ohio App.3d 178, 463 N.E.2d 1261, 11 O.B.R. 271. Pretrial Procedure ⚖ 711

While MC Sup R 16(A) requires a party to submit a written motion stating the reasons for a requested continuance, the trial court is not prohibited by the rule from granting a continuance sua sponte. (Annotation from former MC Sup R 16.) Society Natl. Bank v. Kienzle (Cuyahoga 1983) 11 Ohio App.3d 178, 463 N.E.2d 1261, 11 O.B.R. 271.

The granting of a sua sponte continuance may not be implied from the fact that the trial court originally set an accused's trial for a date beyond that permitted by RC 2945.71, and where the court's journal does not reflect that a continuance has been granted on or before the last day for trial permitted by RC 2945.71, the state may not rely upon RC 2945.72(H) to justify a delay in bringing the accused to trial. (Annotation from former C P Sup R 7.) Village of Oakwood v. Ferrante (Cuyahoga 1975) 44 Ohio App.2d 318, 338 N.E.2d 767, 73 O.O.2d 374.

5. —— Illness, good cause construed

Mother of deceased prisoner, acting pro se in action against Department of Rehabilitation and Correction to recover for prisoner's alleged wrongful death, was not entitled to grant of continuance on day of trial on grounds that she had been suffering from medical problems; mother had been informed on numerous occasions of the pending trial date, mother had had ample opportunity to inform the court of her medical issues and need for a continuance prior to day of trial, and Department's witnesses were inconvenienced because they were present to testify. Hudson v. Ohio Dept. of Rehab. and Corr. (Ohio App. 10 Dist., Franklin, 12-30-2004) No. 04AP-562, 2004-Ohio-7203, 2004 WL 3090258, Unreported. Pretrial Procedure ⚖ 715

Denying ex-husband's motion for continuance in proceeding to modify divorce decree was not abuse of discretion, where, except for oblique reference to being "overwhelmed," ex-husband failed to provide explanation for his inability to be present in court proceedings. Scott v. Scott (Ohio App. 10 Dist., Franklin, 03-23-2004) No. 03AP-411, 2004-Ohio-1405, 2004 WL 557316, Unreported. Divorce ⚖ 164

Alleged partner, who claimed that he was in ill health, was not entitled to continuance of trial in businessman's action against alleged partner that sought money damages regarding purported oral partnership, since length of requested delay was indefinite, businessman had already been inconvenienced, requested delay was contrived, and alleged partner contributed to situation alleged partner asserted gave rise to request for continuance. Samman v. Nukta (Ohio App. 8 Dist., Cuyahoga, 01-16-2003) No. 81156, 2003-Ohio-173, 2003 WL 132303, Unreported. Pretrial Procedure ⚖ 715

Trial court abused its discretion in denying defense counsel's motion for continuance, made after he suffered double fracture of his left forearm, which rendered him unable to write, and subsequent request for continuance by new defense counsel, on basis that new counsel was not prepared for trial, in prosecution for sexual battery and burglary; there were legitimate reasons for requested continuances, defendant in no way contributed to circumstances giving rise to need for continuances, there was no other competent counsel who was prepared to try case on scheduled trial date, and trial court, through its bailiff, pressured new counsel into stating that he was prepared to try case, despite his earlier admission to the contrary. State v. Wenzlick (Ohio App. 6 Dist., 10-28-2005) 2005-Ohio-5741, 2005 WL 2838607. Criminal Law ⚖ 590(1)

A trial court does not err in ordering counsel to proceed to trial and in denying a lead attorney's motion for continuance due to associate counsel's illness where the court determines that counsel is unprepared to proceed to trial due to a lack of preparation and that a continuance would cause great inconvenience to the court and witnesses. (Annotation from former C P Sup R 7.) State v. Christon (Montgomery 1990) 68 Ohio App.3d 471, 589 N.E.2d 53.

In an action involving a defendant real estate developer as president of three corporations against his accounting service, it is trial court error to deny the defendant's request for a continuance due to illness where the court, without further inquiry, terminates the trial and consequently denies the defendant's right to present all of its evidence. Pritchett, Dlusky & Saxe v. Pingue (Ohio App. 10 Dist., Franklin, 12-08-1994) No. 94APE04-516, 1994 WL 694996, Unreported.

Where a public defender assigned to represent a defendant takes ill and asks another public defender to take her place in court and requests either a dismissal of the case or a continuance, and where the substitute public defender asks for a continuance due to lack of preparation as well as lack of experience, it being the substitute counsel's first day with the public defender's office, the trial court's denial of a continuance is an abuse of discretion. (Annotation from former C P Sup R 7.) State v Beekman, No. 90AP-536 (10th Dist Ct App, Franklin, 1–7–92).

6. —— Discovery, good cause construed

Denying husband's motion for continuance to determine fair market value of horses purchased during marriage was abuse of discretion in divorce proceeding, where wife did not deny that she failed to produced certain discovery materials related to horses, wife did not deny that she was capable of producing such discovery materials, wife did not deny that such discovery materials were required in order to have horses appraised, there was no evidence that continuance would have inconvenienced parties or witnesses, and there was no evidence husband filed motion for illegitimate purpose. Schiesswohl v. Schiesswohl (Ohio App. 9 Dist., Summit, 03-31-2004) No. 21629, 2004-Ohio-1615, 2004 WL 626110, Unreported. Divorce ⚖ 253(1)

No continuance is required where a defendant discovers the identity of two confidential informants and receives transcripts of the tapes of certain transactions five days before the scheduled trial date where no prejudice is shown because defense counsel was able to develop for the jury (1) the paid nature of the informants' testimony, (2) the informant's crack use, (3) the male informant's earlier drug conviction, and (4) the female informant's motive of revenge. (Annotation from former C P Sup R 7.) State v. Taylor (Clark 1992) 76 Ohio App.3d 835, 603 N.E.2d 401.

A continuance upon proper motion is a favored method to avoid prejudice which may flow from a failure to provide discovery yet ensure that the charges against an accused are tried timely and fairly. (Annotation from former C P Sup R 7.) State v. Parks (Montgomery 1990) 69 Ohio App.3d 150, 590 N.E.2d 300.

Denial of a motion for continuance to secure the presence of a crucial defense witness denies the defendant of his constitutional due process rights to a fair trial and to compulsory process where a court does not even contemplate a short continuance of two days after learning that the defense witness is out of town and that the proffered testimony of the witness would impeach the credibility of the prosecution witnesses and would place defendant away from the scene of the crime at the time of its commission. State v. Hayes (Ohio App. 7 Dist., Mahoning, 12-27-1994) No. 92 C.A. 77, 1994 WL 718725, Unreported, motion for delayed appeal denied 72 Ohio St.3d 1407, 647 N.E.2d 495.

Where a case is set for trial only two days following pretrial, and a defendant is unable to subpoena a necessary witness within the two-day period prior to trial because of the sporadic nature of the witness' work hours, the denial of a continuance requested by the defense in order to secure the appearance of the witness constitutes an abuse of discretion. (Annotation from former C P Sup R 7.) State v Mularkey, Nos. 90AP–1377 and 90AP–1378 (10th Dist Ct App, Franklin, 5–30–91).

7. —— Dilatory conduct, good cause construed

Denying former husband's request for continuance so that he could obtain counsel was not an abuse of discretion in post-dissolution proceeding; husband became aware of hearing at least two months before it was to take place, but did not notify the court that he could no longer represent himself 26 days before hearing, and husband acted pro se, having terminated the services of his previous five attorneys. Unger v. Unger (Ohio App. 12 Dist., Brown, 12-30-2004) No. CA2003-10-013, 2004-Ohio-7136, 2004 WL 3015751, Unreported. Divorce ⚖ 145

Denial of theft defendant's motion for continuance was not an abuse of discretion, where this request was made on day of trial, defendant had previously received one continuance, and defendant contributed to the circumstances giving rise to the motion by failing to inform counsel of an alleged defense when counsel visited him in jail. State v. Aberle (Ohio App. 5 Dist., Fairfield, 12-20-2004) No. 03 CA 96, 2004-Ohio-7093, 2004 WL 2988299, Unreported. Criminal Law ⚖ 614(1)

Trial court was under no obligation to grant defendant's request for a third continuance to bring additional witnesses, in prosecution for operating a motorcycle without a motorcycle endorsement and having more passengers on a motorcycle than it was equipped for, since trial court had already afforded defendant two continuances prior to trial, and defendant requested the third continuance while the trial was in progress. State v. Davis (Ohio App. 1 Dist., Hamilton, 06-18-2004) No. C-030660, No. C-030661, 2004-Ohio-3134, 2004 WL 1363650, Unreported. Criminal Law ⚖ 614(1)

The denial of a continuance is neither unreasonable, arbitrary, nor unconscionable where (1) the defendant was present with appointed counsel on the date of trial; (2) the trial had been continued at defendant's request once before; (3) the state had been ready to proceed with its witnesses once before and this was the second time it was ready; (4) the request for a continuance did not reflect the specific time necessary for the delay; and (5) the need for the delay was attributable to the defendant (the defendant chose private counsel who was unavailable on the date of trial, knowing him to be unavailable). (Annotation from former C P Sup R 7.) State v. Jones (Wayne 1987) 42 Ohio App.3d 14, 535 N.E.2d 1372. Criminal Law ⚖ 593; Criminal Law ⚖ 614(1)

Trial court denial of father's motion for a continuance, in order to allow counsel time to prepare, on mother's and father's cross-motions for modification or termination of shared parenting plan, was not an abuse of discretion; father was on his third attorney, father had been aware of the hearing date for 47 days, and father had been aware that he needed new counsel for 14 days. In re Wright (Ohio App. 5 Dist., Stark, 02-03-2003) No. 2002CA00184, 2003-Ohio-546, 2003 WL 245677, Unreported. Child Custody ⚖ 651

8. —— Appeal pending in related matter, good cause construed

Stay or continuance of civil trial is not required pending appeal from conviction and sentence in criminal case merely because possibility exists that criminal case could be reversed and remanded for retrial. State ex rel. Verhovec v. Mascio (Ohio, 04-01-1998) 81 Ohio St.3d 334, 691 N.E.2d 282, 1998-Ohio-431. Action ⚖ 69(5)

9. —— Reasonable time, trial assignment date conflict

Defense counsel in a municipal court civil action had good cause for requesting continuance less than seven days before trial, and filed continuance motion when it was reasonably apparent that a conflict existed, and thus, court should have granted continuance under local rule; counsel was also representing a defendant in previously-filed federal criminal action, federal action was scheduled to end before start of municipal trial, it became clear by end of federal trial that federal trial was going to take more time, counsel then moved to continue municipal trial, and federal judge also notified municipal judge about federal trial taking longer than originally planned. Theis v. Hull (Ohio App. 3 Dist., Seneca, 12-06-2004) No. 13-04-20, 2004-Ohio-6494, 2004 WL 2785958, Unreported. Courts ⚖ 189(10)

Trial court did not act unreasonably in denying defendant's initial request for a continuance; defense counsel failed to file continuance request until five days before trial, even though he had prior knowledge of a conflict with the trial date, and defendant's failure to appear for final pretrial hearing already forced court to reschedule trial date. State v. Edwards (Ohio App. 4 Dist., Meigs, 12-18-2002) No. 01CA4, 2002-Ohio-7259, 2002 WL 31883967, Unreported. Criminal Law ⚖ 605

An attorney-defendant representing himself in a civil action is not denied due process by the denial of an oral motion for continuance made on the day of trial alleging that the attorney is unavailable due to participation in a criminal trial in another city where the attorney was aware of the conflicting trial dates when the trial notice was sent more than one month prior to trial, and the other parties and their attorneys are ready to go forward on the trial date. (Annotation from former MC Sup R 16.) Niam Investigations, Inc. v. Gilbert (Summit 1989) 64 Ohio App.3d 125, 580 N.E.2d 840.

Trial court did not abuse its discretion in denying motion for continuance, where counsel was aware of trial conflict more than one month prior to first scheduled trial, but failed to request continuance of either matter or to obtain new counsel until two days before scheduled trial date. (Annotation from former MC Sup R 16.) Touche Ross & Co. v. Landskroner (Cuyahoga 1984) 20 Ohio App.3d 354, 486 N.E.2d 850, 20 O.B.R. 459. Pretrial Procedure ⚖ 723.1

It is not an abuse of discretion to deny a continuance sought by new counsel where the original counsel knew he would be unavailable for trial for more than a month but failed to move for a continuance or to obtain new counsel in a timely manner. (Annotation from former C P Sup R 7.) Touche Ross & Co. v. Landskroner (Cuyahoga 1984) 20 Ohio App.3d 354, 486 N.E.2d 850, 20 O.B.R. 459.

A party has a duty to move for a continuance due to conflicting trial assignment dates of counsel within a reasonable time after such party's case is set for trial and the conflict thus created. A motion for continuance not made within a reasonable time is untimely, and the court does not abuse its discretion in overruling an untimely motion for continuance. (Annotation from former MC Sup R 16.) Alex N. Sill Co. v. Fazio (Cuyahoga 1981) 2 Ohio App.3d 65, 440 N.E.2d 807, 2 O.B.R. 72. Pretrial Procedure ⚖ 723.1

In a contract action which is replete with delays and continuances the trial court properly denies a motion for continuance claiming conflict of dates filed by the defendant one day before trial, since a party has the duty to move for a continuance due to conflicting trial assignment dates within a reasonable time after the party's case is set for trial and the conflict is created, and a court does not abuse its discretion in overruling an untimely motion for continuance. (Annotation from former C P Sup R 7.) Alex N. Sill Co. v. Fazio (Cuyahoga 1981) 2 Ohio App.3d 65, 440 N.E.2d 807, 2 O.B.R. 72.

A trial court abuses its discretion by denying a plaintiff's motion for a two day continuance due to scheduling conflict where (1) the defendant has no witnesses to call and would only testify in rebuttal and regarding attorney fees, (2) the record indicates that the defendant was granted numerous continuances, (3) the defendant's counsel's objections to the continuance seem both disingenuous and contrived, and (4) trial court leaves the decision to continue up to opposing counsel thereby abdicating its responsibility to conduct the proceedings. O'Neill v. O'Neill (Ohio

10. —— Priority of cases, trial assignment date conflict

Trial judge, who scheduled trial for same date that one party's lead counsel was scheduled to participate in trial in another case in which he was lead counsel, was required to grant a continuance of the trial date, and thus party whose attorney had the conflict was entitled to writ of mandamus compelling trial judge to grant the continuance, where other case was set for trial first. Smith v. Dartt (Ohio App. 6 Dist., Lucas, 04-15-2005) No. L-05-1124, 2005-Ohio-1885, 2005 WL 928157, Unreported. Pretrial Procedure ⇐ 716

A common pleas court does not err in denying a motion for continuance, based on the fact that counsel is scheduled for another trial on the same date, where the trial date in the instant case for which the continuance is requested was first set for trial. (Annotation from former C P Sup R 7.) State v. McLemore (Crawford 1992) 82 Ohio App.3d 541, 612 N.E.2d 795.

The case first scheduled for trial on a particular date has priority for trial on that date, and that date only, should a conflict of trial assignment dates occur. The case first set for trial is the case for which there exists the earliest docket entry selecting the conflicting trial date. (Annotation from former MC Sup R 16.) Alex N. Sill Co. v. Fazio (Cuyahoga 1981) 2 Ohio App.3d 65, 440 N.E.2d 807, 2 O.B.R. 72. Trial ⇐ 9(1)

Administrative hearings do not command priority when in conflict with a scheduled municipal court trial, and denial of a motion for a continuance made the day before trial for such reason is not an abuse of discretion. (Annotation from former MC Sup R 16.) Saddler v Vasi, No. 3612 (9th Dist Ct App, Lorain, 8–29–84).

11. —— Motion requirements, trial assignment date conflict

The trial court does not err in denying a motion for a continuance in a DWI action where the attorney for the defendant does not present to the judge a full explanation of his situation or a statement from the judge who is out to hear the conflicting case requesting accommodation and acknowledgment of priority under C P Sup R 7(B). (Annotation from former C P Sup R 7.) State v. Menucci (Ohio Com.Pl. 1986) 33 Ohio Misc.2d 15, 514 N.E.2d 758.

12. Court's discretion

Trial court did not abuse its discretion in denying incarcerated plaintiff's motion for continuance, in civil action, for purpose of retaining new counsel to replace counsel who withdrew, where trial court had granted plaintiff two continuances and two extensions, and held multiple pretrial conferences, plaintiff had approximately one month to retain new counsel, and original complaint was nearly three years old. Graham v. Audio Clinic (Ohio App. 3 Dist., Hancock, 03-14-2005) No. 5-04-35, 2005-Ohio-1088, 2005 WL 578999, Unreported. Pretrial Procedure ⇐ 726

Granting continuance of trial date requested by physician and pain control center in medical negligence action was not abuse of discretion, where counsel for physician and center was unavailable for trial on scheduled date due to vacation. Fernandez v. Ohio State Pain Control Ctr. (Ohio App. 10 Dist., Franklin, 12-14-2004) No. 03AP-1018, 2004-Ohio-6713, 2004 WL 2893402, Unreported, appeal not allowed 105 Ohio St.3d 1544, 827 N.E.2d 327, 2005-Ohio-2188. Pretrial Procedure ⇐ 716

Trial court was unreasonable and arbitrary in denying automobile buyer's request for continuance to retain counsel to defend against breach of contract claim and to represent buyer in counterclaim to recover for services provided to seller; although buyer's former attorney had withdrawn the day before trial on grounds that he had been terminated by buyer, delay would have been no greater than that required for new counsel to prepare for trial, there was no indication of any inconvenience a continuance would have caused, buyer indicated that he merely terminated attorney by attorney's request, buyer stated that attorney told him he would be present on day of trial, there was no indication that attorney had provided buyer notice of his request to withdraw the day before trial, and trial court would not permit buyer to explain why attorney had been terminated. Seget v. Seget (Ohio App. 8 Dist., Cuyahoga, 11-24-2004) No. 83905, 2004-Ohio-6289, 2004 WL 2677470, Unreported. Pretrial Procedure ⇐ 716

Refusal to lift stay of civil case pending resolution of defendant's appeal in related criminal matter, based on possibility that criminal conviction would be reversed and criminal action remanded for retrial, was abuse of discretion. State ex rel. Verhovec v. Mascio (Ohio, 04-01-1998) 81 Ohio St.3d 334, 691 N.E.2d 282, 1998-Ohio-431. Action ⇐ 69(5)

Failure to grant continuance when defendant appeared alone on morning of trial was abuse of discretion, where defense counsel earlier made timely request for continuance because of scheduling conflict and trial court indicated that defendant's trial would be continued if other trial went forward, but court made no offer at trial to continue and no inquiry into defendant's desire to proceed without counsel, instead accepting defendant's pleas of no contest. State v. Arcoria (Ohio App. 9 Dist., 08-12-1998) 129 Ohio App.3d 376, 717 N.E.2d 1131. Criminal Law ⇐ 593

On review of decision to grant or deny continuance, court balances trial court's interest in controlling its own docket, including facilitating and prompting an efficient dispatch of justice, versus any potential prejudice to movant. (Annotation from former C P Sup R 7.) Ham v. Park (Ohio App. 8 Dist., 05-06-1996) 110 Ohio App.3d 803, 675 N.E.2d 505. Appeal And Error ⇐ 863

Under *Unger*, objective factors that may be considered by trial court in determining whether to grant continuance include length of requested delay, whether other continuances have been requested and received, inconvenience to litigants, witnesses, opposing counsel, and court, whether requested delay is for legitimate reasons or is dilatory, purposeful, or contrived, whether movant contributed to circumstance which gives rise to request for continuance, and other relevant factors, depending on unique facts of the case. (Annotation from former C P Sup R 7.) Ham v. Park (Ohio App. 8 Dist., 05-06-1996) 110 Ohio App.3d 803, 675 N.E.2d 505. Pretrial Procedure ⇐ 711

In determining whether to grant continuance, trial judge may consider whether party contributed to the circumstance which gives rise to the request for continuance and may also consider such factors as amount of time requested, prior requests for continuances, inconvenience to parties, counsel and the court, legitimacy of request for delay, and other relevant factors depending on unique facts of each case. (Annotation from former C P Sup R 7.) Sayre v. Hoelzle-Sayre (Ohio App. 3 Dist., 04-06-1994) 100 Ohio App.3d 203, 653 N.E.2d 712, appeal allowed 70 Ohio St.3d 1426, 638 N.E.2d 88, appeal dismissed as improvidently allowed 72 Ohio St.3d 1218, 651 N.E.2d 430, 1995-Ohio-274. Pretrial Procedure ⇐ 711; Pretrial Procedure ⇐ 726

Refusal to grant continuance to defendant after subpoenaed defense witness failed to appear for trial did not prejudice defendant where defendant failed to reveal what nature of witness' testimony would have been, show whether it would have been relevant and material to defense, or give court any assurance that witness could be located within reasonable time. (Annotation from former C P Sup R 7.) State v. Clements (Ohio App. 2 Dist., 11-23-1994) 98 Ohio App.3d 797, 649 N.E.2d 912. Criminal Law ⇐ 649(2)

Where defendant had previously represented to the court that he was prepared to represent himself and that he was ready to go to trial on date and time originally scheduled, trial court did not abuse its discretion in conditioning grant of defendant's motion for continuance upon defendant's employment of court-appointed counsel. (Annotation from former C P Sup R 7.) State v. Butler (Ohio App. 10 Dist., 09-13-1994) 97 Ohio App.3d 322, 646 N.E.2d 856, dismissed, appeal not allowed 71 Ohio St.3d 1464, 644 N.E.2d 1387. Criminal Law ⇐ 590(1); Criminal Law ⇐ 593

In determining whether trial court abused its discretion in granting or denying motion for continuance, reviewing court must balance interests of judicial economy and justice against any potential prejudice to nonmoving party. (Annotation from former C P Sup R 7.) Griffin v. Lamberjack (Ohio App. 6 Dist., 07-29-1994) 96 Ohio App.3d 257, 644 N.E.2d 1087. Appeal And Error ⇐ 966(1)

Granting or denying of motion for continuance rests within sound discretion of trial court. (Annotation from former C P Sup R 7.) Holop v. Holop (Cuyahoga 1989) 59 Ohio App.3d 51, 570 N.E.2d 305. Pretrial Procedure ⇐ 713

The grant or denial of a continuance is a matter entrusted to the sound discretion of the trial judge; thus, the denial of a continuance due to the unavailability of the defendant's expert witness will be upheld absent a showing that the judge acted in a manner which was unreasonable, arbitrary, or unconscionable. (Annotation from former C P Sup R 7.) State v. Swisshelm (Wayne 1987) 40 Ohio App.3d 196, 532 N.E.2d 152.

Rulings on continuances and motions to dismiss for failure to prosecute are matters committed to sound discretion of the trial court, whose decision may be reversed only if record demonstrates that it abused its discretion, that is, that decision is arbitrary, unreasonable, or unconscionable. (Annotation from former C P Sup R 7.) Society Natl. Bank v. Kienzle (Cuyahoga 1983) 11 Ohio App.3d 178, 463 N.E.2d 1261, 11 O.B.R. 271. Appeal And Error ⇐ 962; Appeal And Error ⇐ 966(1); Pretrial Procedure ⇐ 583; Pretrial Procedure ⇐ 713

Trial court did not abuse its discretion in denying request for continuance; court had not been fully informed of circumstances underlying request for continuance. (Annotation from former MC Sup R 16.) State v. Menucci (Ohio Com.Pl. 1986) 33 Ohio Misc.2d 15, 514 N.E.2d 758. Criminal Law ⇔ 603.2

13. —— Disciplinary proceedings, trial assignment date conflict

While a trial court is generally vested with discretion to grant or deny a motion to vacate a trial date, when the motion is filed because of a conflict with a proceeding before the Board of Commissioners on Grievances and Discipline of the Supreme Court, the motion must be granted pursuant to C P Sup R 7(B)(2). (Annotation from former C P Sup R 7.) Pheils v Palmer, No. L-91-426, 1993 WL 155641 (6th Dist Ct App, Lucas, 5-14-93).

14. Counsel exclusion or removal

An attorney may be removed as counsel in a case under MC Sup R 16 when he has repeatedly requested continuances, failed to appear, and failed to provide substitute counsel as requested by the court over a period of several months. (Annotation from former MC Sup R 16.) State ex rel. Rose v. Garfield Heights Municipal Court (Ohio 1979) 57 Ohio St.2d 42, 385 N.E.2d 1314, 11 O.O.3d 156.

Trial court did not abuse its discretion by refusing to grant recycling corporation's motion for continuance to obtain new counsel to defend against metal processing company's suit on account, where court repeatedly warned recycling corporation that trial would proceed as scheduled, but corporation chose to fire counsel on the eve of trial. Cleveland Metal Processing of Ohio v. Precision Recycling Group Ltd. (Ohio App. 8 Dist., Cuyahoga, 12-05-2002) No. 81176, 2002-Ohio-6643, 2002 WL 31722916, Unreported. Pretrial Procedure ⇔ 716

Trial court's denial of wife's motion for continuance of final hearing in husband's action for divorce amounted to abuse of discretion, where court was on notice that wife would likely be without counsel at final hearing if continuance were not granted, matter was set for final hearing mere 65 days after complaint was filed, which time period included both the Thanksgiving and Christmas holidays, and neither party had previously requested continuance or issued subpoenas for witnesses who might have been inconvenienced by any delay in proceedings. Burton v. Burton (Ohio App. 3 Dist., 08-18-1999) 132 Ohio App.3d 473, 725 N.E.2d 359, 1999-Ohio-844. Divorce ⇔ 184(5)

A writ of prohibition will not issue to prohibit a municipal court judge from excluding the public defender's office from representing an indigent criminal defendant based on tardiness of the assigned public defender; appeal of the improper order is an adequate remedy. (Annotation from former MC Sup R 16.) State ex rel. Kura v. Sheward (Franklin 1992) 75 Ohio App.3d 244, 598 N.E.2d 1340.

When it appears to a party that removal of opposing counsel due to over-scheduling may be warranted, it is incumbent upon that party to move for an order from the administrative judge that substitute counsel be provided. Absent such a motion, the party may not later assert as prejudicial error the granting of a motion for continuance grounded upon a conflict of trial assignment dates of opposing counsel. (Annotation from former MC Sup R 16.) Alex N. Sill Co. v. Fazio (Cuyahoga 1981) 2 Ohio App.3d 65, 440 N.E.2d 807, 2 O.B.R. 72. Appeal And Error ⇔ 189(5); Attorney And Client ⇔ 75(1)

15. Waiver of right to representation

In inferring waiver of right to counsel when defendant refuses to take effective action to obtain counsel and on day of trial requests continuance in order to delay trial, court must consider total circumstances of case, including background, experience and conduct of defendant. (Annotation from former C P Sup R 7.) State v. Boone (Ohio App. 1 Dist., 12-29-1995) 108 Ohio App.3d 233, 670 N.E.2d 527. Criminal Law ⇔ 641.4(2)

Defendant charged with drug abuse, possession of drug paraphernalia and criminal trespass who failed to secure legal counsel despite being given ample time and opportunity to do so by trial court and who did not ask for continuance on day of trial in order to obtain counsel waived by inference his right to legal representation. (Annotation from former C P Sup R 7.) State v. Boone (Ohio App. 1 Dist., 12-29-1995) 108 Ohio App.3d 233, 670 N.E.2d 527. Criminal Law ⇔ 641.4(4)

Court may, under proper conditions, be permitted to infer waiver of right to counsel when defendant refuses to take effective action to obtain counsel and on day of trial requests continuance in order to delay trial. (Annotation from former C P Sup R 7.) State v. Boone (Ohio App. 1 Dist., 12-29-1995) 108 Ohio App.3d 233, 670 N.E.2d 527. Criminal Law ⇔ 641.4(2)

PROBATE DIVISION

Sup R 50 Definitions

As used in Sup. R. 50 to 82 "case" means any of the following when filed in the probate division of the court of common pleas:

(A) A civil complaint, petition, or administrative appeal;

(B) A decedent's estate; a testamentary, inter vivos or wrongful death trust; a guardianship, conservatorship or request for emergency orders pursuant to division (B)(3) of 2111.02 of the Revised Code; an adoption or name change. Each beneficiary of a wrongful death trust, each ward or conservatee, each adoptee and each individual requesting a change of name in those proceedings with multiple interested parties, shall be considered a separate "case."

(C) Any other proceeding for which a case number is assigned including but not limited to the following: tax filings, filings of wills for probate or record, real estate transfers, and filings of foreign records where an estate is not opened; release from administration; minor's settlements; birth corrections; delayed birth registrations; mental retardation or tuberculosis commitments; petition for protective services; petition to compel HIV testing; an application to appoint a guardian, trustee, protector, or conservator of a mentally retarded or developmentally disabled person; acknowledgment of paternity; a petition for release of adoption information; powers of attorney including those for health care; declarations concerning life-sustaining treatment; proceedings to designate heir; applications to disinter or to oppose disinterment; and voluntary assignment for the benefit of creditors.

(Adopted eff. 7–1–97; amended eff. 3–25–02)

Historical and Statutory Notes

Amendment Note: The 3–25–02 amendment deleted "recording of chiropractic licenses" and a second repetitive reference to adoption records from division (C).

Staff Notes

2002:

The March 25, 2002 amendment deleted an obsolete reference to the recording of chiropractic licenses in the probate division of the court of common pleas. See former R.C. 4734.08, repealed in H.B. 506 of the 123rd General Assembly.

Staff Notes

1997:

Rule 50 is a new rule that defines "case" as used in the rules applicable to the probate division of the court of common pleas.

Sup R 51 Standard probate forms

(A) Applicability

This rule prescribes the format, content, and use of standard forms for designated applications, pleadings, waivers, notices, entries, and other filings in certain proceedings in the probate division of the courts of common pleas.

Where a standard form has not been prescribed by this rule, the form used shall be that required by the Civil Rules, or prescribed or permitted by the probate division of the court of common pleas in which it is being filed.

(B) Effective date; use of standard and non-standard forms

(1) This rule takes effect July 1, 1977 and applies to proceedings had on and after that date, including proceedings in pending cases.

(2) The standard forms shall be used on and after January 1, 1978, and nonstandard forms shall be rejected for filing.

(C) Modification of standard forms; pleadings and filings prepared for particular cases

(1) A printed, blank standard form may be modified by deletion or interlineation to meet the circumstances of a particular case or proceeding, if the modification can be accomplished neatly and conveniently. No court shall require the modification of a standard form as a routine matter. If any allegation, statement, data, information, pleading, or filing is required by an appropriate local rule of court and a standard form does not make provision therefor, it shall be provided in a separate or supplemental filing.

(2) Even though a standard form is prescribed, an original instrument may be prepared for filing. Any such instrument shall be typed on eight and one-half by eleven inch paper. The caption prescribed in Sup. R. 52 shall be used, and the instrument shall follow the format prescribed for the standard forms. Any such instrument may modify the language of the standard form, omit inapplicable matter required by the standard form, and add matter not included in the standard form to the extent required by the circumstances of the particular case or proceeding.

(D) Standard probate forms

The standard forms prescribed for use in the probate division of the courts of common pleas are as follows. [omitted] [1]

(Adopted eff. 7-1-97; amended eff. 10-1-97)

[1] The Standard Probate Forms are available on WESTLAW and in Carlin, Baldwin's Ohio Practice, *Merrick-Rippner Probate Law*, Standard Probate Forms.

Historical and Statutory Notes

Ed. Note: Sup R 51 is analogous to former C P Sup R 16, adopted eff. 8-13-79; former C P Sup R 16 was former Sup R 17, adopted eff. 7-1-77.

Staff Notes

2000:

Scope of Forms:

The primary purpose of the standard probate forms has been to promote uniformity in probate practice throughout the state.

The Ohio Courts Summary 1998 reports there were 4553 change of name filings in the 88 counties. Each county had at least one filing (Jackson) and as many as 902 in Cuyahoga.

The majority of filings are by self-represented persons. The Ohio Association of Probate Judges' Forms committee believes that this is an area where we can improve the delivery of services by the Probate Courts to the general public and also assist the legal community in providing a set of standard forms. Currently, there are no standard probate forms for a change of name procedure.

The Forms Committee has also communicated to the Ohio Department of Health, Vital Statistics Division, to determine what information should be included in the Judgment Entry changing the name. As the result of these contacts the Judgment Entries now set forth not only the name of the person before and after the proceedings, but also the date of birth and place of birth of the applicant.

Form 21.0–Application for Change of Name of Adult–Standard Probate Form 21.0 sets forth the required statutory mandates of time and place of residence, the reason for the change of name and the direction to publish the notice. The contents of the standard probate form are verified by the applicant's signature thereby invoking falsification statutes for untrue information. The standard probate form concludes with a Judgment Entry setting hearing and ordering notice to interested parties.

Form 21.1–Judgment Entry–Change of Name of Adult–Standard Probate Form 21.1 orders the change of name from the present name to the requested name and also sets out information beneficial to the Ohio Department of Health to reference the Judgment Entry to the appropriate birth record. This form also contains a Certification of Judgment Entry so that the Court can provide certified copies of its order to the applicant.

Form 21.2–Application for Change of Name of Minor–Standard Probate Form 21.2 sets forth the required statutory mandates of time and place of residence, the reason for the change of name and the direction to publish the notice. For identification and notice purposes, the standard probate form also sets forth the name and address of the mother and father, alleged father, or statement that there is no alleged father. There is also an optional statement that the address of the mother, father, or alleged father is unknown and cannot with reasonable diligence be ascertained, which would alleviate the need for a separate affidavit. The contents of the form are verified by the applicant's signature thereby invoking falsification statutes for untrue information. The standard probate form concludes with a Judgement Entry setting hearing and ordering notice to interested persons.

Form 21.3–Judgment Entry–Change of Name of Minor–Standard Probate Form 21.3 orders the change of name from the present name to the requested name and also sets out information beneficial to the Ohio Department of Health to reference the Judgment Entry to the appropriate birth record. This form also contains a Certification of Judgment Entry so that the Court can provide certified copies of its order to the applicant.

Form 21.4–Consent to Change of Name–Standard Probate Form 21.4 sets forth the name and capacity in which the consent to change of name is given. The standard forms utilizes the check-off box system to indicate the identity of the person executing the consent. The standard form contains a jurat for those Courts that require a notarization for consents that are not executed in the presence of the Court.

Form 21.5–Notice of Hearing on Change of Name–Standard Probate Form 21.5 contains the required statutory information as to notice of the proceedings. The standard probate form sets forth the information required in the publication. The standard probate form also includes an optional specific notification to any person whose address is unknown, for those Courts that require a separate publication for parents whose residence is unknown, in addition to the general publication. The form also contains information to the Publisher regarding the frequency of the publication, the payment of its costs and the necessity of providing to the applicant an Affidavit of Publication.

1997:

This rule is identical to former C.P. Sup. R. 16.

This rule was amended effective December 13, 1989, to add a temporary provision suspending the use of Standard Probate Forms 15.0 through 17.5, the guardianship forms. This was necessitated by the revisions to the guardianship laws embodied in Substitute Senate Bill 46 of the 118th General Assembly, effective January 1, 1990. New guardianship forms were adopted effective September 1, 1991 and the temporary provision was repealed. In addition, additional estate forms were adopted as the result of Amended Substitute House Bill 346 of the 118th General Assembly, effective May 31, 1990. See R.C. 2113.03 and 2113.533.

The December 1989 amendment to this rule also added new Standard Probate Forms 18.0 through 19.1, which are used for adoptions.

Library References

Courts ⚖=202(1).
Westlaw Topic No. 106.

Research References

Treatises and Practice Aids

1 Carlin, Baldwin's Ohio Prac. Merrick-Rippner Probate Law Intro., Intro. Introduction.

Law Review and Journal Commentaries

Probate Rules of Superintendence Revised and Reorganized, David F. Allen. 9 Prob L J Ohio 21 (November/December 1998).

Sup R 52 Specifications for printing probate forms

(A) Applicability

(1) The specifications in this rule govern the reproduction of blank forms intended for, or used in, the administration of decedents' estates, guardianships, and adoptions in this state, including:

(a) Standard forms prescribed in Sup. R. 51;

(b) Commercially prepared blank forms, including standard and nonstandard forms, designed for use in any aspect of the administration of decedents' estates, guardianships, and adoptions;

(c) Blank forms prescribed by local rule of court for use in situations for which no standard form is prescribed.

(2) This rule does not apply to any of the following:

(a) Any pleading, application, entry, waiver, notice, or other filing that is prepared ad hoc for use in a particular case or proceeding, or that is not reproduced in any manner for use as a blank form;

(b) Any routing slip, memorandum index, cost bill, or other form designed solely for internal administrative or clerical use;

(c) Forms intended for use in matters other than the administration of decedents' estates, guardianships, or adoptions;

(d) Estate tax returns, reports, and other forms prescribed by the Department of Taxation.

(B) Size of forms; stock

All forms shall be on paper size eight and one-half by eleven inches, printed on twenty-four pound bond or heavier stock.

(C) Margins

Right and left margins shall be approximately one-half to three-quarters of one inch, and shall be justified. The top margin shall be approximately seven-eighths to one and one-eighth inches, measured from the top edge of the paper to the top of the first line of the caption. The distance between the bottom of the repeat of the main heading at the foot of the first page shall be as required by division (K) of this rule.

(D) Type styles

(1) All type shall be sans serif. Bold face type shall be used only as required or permitted by division (D)(2) of this rule. Italics shall not be used. Except as provided in division (D)(3) of this rule, all type shall be upper and lower case.

(2) Bold face type shall be used for the main heading immediately following the caption, and for the form number and repeat of the main heading at the foot of the first page. In addition bold face type may be used for:

(a) The caption;

(b) Subheadings;

(c) Directions enclosed in brackets;

(d) Instructions or identification under a blank line, indicating what is to be inserted in the line or identifying the office or status of a signer;

(e) Column headings;

(f) Any matter not covered in division (D)(2)(a) to (e) of this rule, for which the use of bold face type is expressly indicated on a standard form in Sup. R. 51.

(3) The following shall be printed in all capital letters:

(a) The first two lines of the caption;

(b) The main heading immediately following the caption;

(c) All subheadings;

(d) The form number and repeat of the main heading at the foot of the first page;

(e) Any matter not covered in division (D)(3)(a) to (d) of this rule, for which the use of all capital letters is expressly indicated on a standard form in Sup. R. 51.

(E) Type sizes

(1) The following type sizes shall be used:

(a) Main headings immediately following the caption shall use sixteen-point or larger type;

(b) The first line of the caption, and all subheadings, shall use not smaller than twelve-point nor larger than sixteen-point type;

(c) The last two lines of the caption, the body, and the form number and repeat of the main heading at the foot of the first page, shall use not smaller than eight-point nor larger than twelve-point type;

(d) Instructions or identification under a blank line, indicating what is to be inserted in the line or identifying the office or status of a signer, shall use not larger than eight-point type.

(2) Whatever type size is used within the limitations of division (E)(1) of this rule:

(a) The first line of the caption and all subheadings shall use type at least two points smaller than the main heading immediately following the caption;

(b) The last two lines of the caption, the body, and the form number and repeat of the main heading at the foot of the first page, shall use type at least two points smaller than the subheadings;

(c) Instructions or identification under a blank line, indicating what is to be inserted in the line or identifying the office or status of a signer, shall use type at least two points smaller than the body.

(F) Vertical spacing

(1) The vertical spacing on all forms shall be in units of one pica, to conform to standard typewriter vertical spacing.

(2) In order to permit optimum placement and promote visual appeal, the main heading and any subheading may be moved up or down within the available area without regard to the vertical spacing of the rest of the form, provided the rest of the form from head to foot maintains vertical spacing in units of one pica.

(G) Centering

The first line of the caption, the main heading, any explanatory information supplementing the main heading and appearing directly below it, subheadings, and the form number and repeat of the main heading at the foot of the first page of a form, shall be centered.

(H) Blank lines; length; vertical spacing in series

(1) Blanks to be filled in shall be indicated by a printed solid line. Wherever possible, such lines shall be of sufficient length to accommodate comfortably all characters included in any word, phrase, name, date, or other information that might reasonably be expected to be placed in the blank. Spaces and punctuation shall be included in counting characters. It shall be assumed that six pica will accommodate ten characters in calculating the length of a line.

(2) Wherever possible, blank lines shall be a minimum length of:

(a) Eight pica, when the name of a county is to be inserted;

(b) Eighteen pica, when a date is to be inserted;

(c) Twenty pica, when a name or signature is to be inserted;

(d) Eight pica, not counting the dollar sign, when a dollar amount is to be inserted.

(3) One, or two or more blank lines may be used for the insertion of an address. Wherever possible, such lines shall be a minimum length of:

(a) Forty pica when a single line is used;

(b) Twenty pica per line when two or more lines are used.

(4) When a series of signature lines, lines for tabulating particular information, or other blank lines in vertical series are called for in a form, then except where expressly indicated on a standard form in Sup. R. 51, the vertical spacing between lines shall be two pica. This spacing shall be maintained without regard to instructions or identification printed below a line.

(I) Boxes to be checked

(1) Where a form calls for a "check" or "X" to be inserted, a box shall be used for the purpose. The box shall precede the information to which it refers.

(2) When a series of "checks" or "X's" are called for in the same sentence or paragraph, each box and the information to which it refers shall be set apart visually from the preceding and following information in the same sentence or paragraph. Any device that provides visual separation and minimizes possible confusion may be used, including without limitation space-hyphen-space or a double or triple space, as in the following example:

"[check one of the following]—[☐] Decedent's will has been admitted to probate in this court—[☐] To applicant's knowledge decedent did not leave a will."

(J) Caption

(1) Except as provided in division (J)(3) of this rule, the following captions shall be used, respectively, on all forms for the administration of decedents' estates, guardianships, and adoptions:

PROBATE COURT OF _____ COUNTY, OHIO
ESTATE OF _____, DECEASED
Case No. ____;

PROBATE COURT OF _____ COUNTY, OHIO
GUARDIANSHIP OF _____
Case No. ____;

PROBATE COURT OF _____ COUNTY, OHIO
ADOPTION OF _____
_____
(Name after adoption)
Case No. ____

(2) The first line of the caption shall be centered. The second and third lines shall begin at the left margin and end at the right margin. The vertical space between the first and second lines may be two or three pica. The vertical space between the second and third lines shall be two pica.

(3) The following variations from the caption prescribed in division (J)(1) and (2) of this rule are permitted:

(a) The blank line in the first line of the caption may be replaced by the imprinted name of a particular county.

(b) The caption may be expanded to include the address of a particular court, using type of any suitable size. In such case, the blank lines intended for the court's address in the body of any form and introductory material for the address such as, "the court is located at _____," shall be omitted.

(c) In Standard Decedents' Estates Form 5.5, and in any other decedents' estates form dealing with two or more estates, the last two lines of the caption shall be omitted.

(K) Form number and repeat of main heading

(1) The main heading of a form, which appears immediately below the caption on the first page of a form, shall be repeated at the foot of the first page. If the form is a standard form, the repeat of the main heading shall be preceded on the same line by the form number.

(2) The form number and repeat of the main heading shall be centered, and located not higher than three-eighths inch above the bottom edge of the form.

(L) Printing front and back

When a standard probate form consists of more than one page, each page shall contain the case number in the upper portion of the page.

(M) Standard forms to govern; variations

(1) Matters not specifically covered in this rule are governed by the standard forms prescribed in Sup. R. 51. Overall, the format of all printed blank forms, whether standard or nonstandard, shall conform substantially to the standard forms. Except as provided in division (M)(2) of this rule, no additions to, deletions from, or changes in the form, content, or language of the standard forms are permitted when printing blank standard forms.

(2) The following variations from the standard forms in Sup. R. 51 are permitted:

(a) In any form calling for a court's address, the blank lines intended for the insertion of such information may be replaced by the imprinted information itself. If the court's address is imprinted in the caption, the blank lines in the body of the form for the address and introductory material for the address shall be omitted as provided in division (J)(3) of this rule.

(b) The name as well as the title of the probate judge may be imprinted below a judge's signature line on any form.

(c) In any form calling for the attorney's typed or printed name, address, telephone number, and attorney identification number, the blank lines intended for the insertion of that information may be replaced by the imprinted information itself. The signature line for the attorney shall be retained.

(d) In Standard Decedents' Estates Form 4.2, the portion of the form below the date line and principal's signature line, and above the repeat at the foot of the page, may be replaced by the imprinted name and address of a corporate surety, identified in some appropriate manner as the surety on the particular bond, and including a signature line for the attorney in fact. The last paragraph of the body of the form, relating to justification of personal sureties, shall be omitted.

(e) When standard forms are generated by computer, they shall conform to all specifications for standard forms stated in this rule. A court may accept for filing nonstandard computer generated forms for the receipts and disbursements attached to a standard account form or the schedule of assets attached to a standard inventory and appraisal form.

(f) All forms may include suitable coding for optical or magnetic scanning, or similar system designed to aid docketing, indexing, cost accounting, or other administrative or clerical activities.

(g) On all forms, the publisher may add its name, logotype, or other suitable identification. The size, style, and placement shall be such as not to detract from, interfere with, or overpower any part of the form.

(h) Wherever a form contains "19 ___" or "199 ___", a blank line shall be substituted to accommodate the correct year.

(N) Effective date

(1) This rule takes effect July 1, 1977.

(2) On and after January 1, 1978, any pleading, application, entry, waiver, notice, or other filing, prepared using a blank form to which this rule applies, shall not be accepted for filing by the probate division of a court of common pleas of this state unless such blank form complies with the specifications in this rule.

(3) The amendment to division M(2)(h) shall take effect on November 16, 1999.

(Adopted eff. 7–1–97; amended eff. 10–1–97, 11–16–99, 6–12–00, 12–1–02)

Historical and Statutory Notes

Ed. Note: Sup R 52 is analogous to former C P Sup R 17, adopted eff. 8–13–79; former C P Sup R 17 was former Sup R 18, adopted eff. 7–1–77.

Ed. Note: C P Sup R 17 is former Sup R 18, adopted eff. 7–1–77.

Ed. Note: See C P Sup R 16 for provisions of former Sup R 17, adopted eff. 7–1–77.

Amendment Note: The 12–1–02 amendment rewrote division (L) which prior thereto read:

"(L) Printing front and back. When a form requires more than one page, it shall be continued on the back of the same sheet and printed 'tumble' style, or it shall be printed on separate pages."

Amendment Note: The 6–12–00 amendment to division (L) inserted "or it shall be printed on separate pages."

Amendment Note: The 11–16–99 amendment added divisions (M)(2)(h) and (N)(3).

Staff Notes

1999:

This amendment permits the change of preprinted dates on existing standard probate forms.

1997:

This rule is unchanged substantively from former C.P. Sup. R. 17.

Library References

Courts ⚖202(1).
Westlaw Topic No. 106.

Research References

Treatises and Practice Aids

Carlin, Baldwin's Ohio Practice, Merrick-Rippner Probate Law App B SPF 2.0, Application to Probate Will.

Carlin, Baldwin's Ohio Practice, Merrick-Rippner Probate Law App B SPF 4.0, Application for Authority to Administer Estate.

Carlin, Baldwin's Ohio Practice, Merrick-Rippner Probate Law App B SPF 6.0, Inventory and Appraisal—Form.

Carlin, Baldwin's Ohio Practice, Merrick-Rippner Probate Law App B SPF 8.0, Citation to Surviving Spouse to Elect Exercise Elective Rights.

Carlin, Baldwin's Ohio Practice, Merrick-Rippner Probate Law App B SPF 13.0, Fiduciary's Account.

Carlin, Baldwin's Ohio Practice, Merrick-Rippner Probate Law App B SPF 14.0, Application to Approve Settlement and Distribution of Wrongful Death and Survival Claims—Form.

Carlin, Baldwin's Ohio Practice, Merrick-Rippner Probate Law App B SPF 18.0, Petition for Adoption of Minor—Form.

Carlin, Baldwin's Ohio Practice, Merrick-Rippner Probate Law App B SPF 18.1, Judgment Entry Setting Hearing and Ordering Notice—Form.

Carlin, Baldwin's Ohio Practice, Merrick-Rippner Probate Law App B SPF 18.3, Consent to Adoption—Form.

Carlin, Baldwin's Ohio Practice, Merrick-Rippner Probate Law App B SPF 18.4, Judgment Entry Finding Consent Not Required—Form.

Carlin, Baldwin's Ohio Practice, Merrick-Rippner Probate Law App B SPF 18.5, Interlocutory Order of Adoption—Form.

Carlin, Baldwin's Ohio Practice, Merrick-Rippner Probate Law App B SPF 18.6, Final Decree of Adoption (After Interlocutory Order)—Form.

Carlin, Baldwin's Ohio Practice, Merrick-Rippner Probate Law App B SPF 18.7, Final Decree of Adoption (Without Interlocutory Order)—Form.

Carlin, Baldwin's Ohio Practice, Merrick-Rippner Probate Law App B SPF 20.2, Letters of Conservatorship.

Sup R 53 Hours of the court

Each court shall establish hours for the transaction of business.

(Adopted eff. 7–1–97; amended eff. 10–1–97)

Historical and Statutory Notes

Ed. Note: Sup R 53 is analogous to former C P Sup R 18, adopted eff. 9–1–84.

Staff Notes

1997:

This rule is unchanged from former C.P. Sup. R. 18.

Library References

Courts ⚖75.
Westlaw Topic No. 106.

C.J.S. Courts § 120.

Research References

Encyclopedias

OH Jur. 3d Courts & Judges § 227, Courts of Common Pleas; Individual Assignment System; Time for Determination; Statistical Reports.

Sup R 54 Conduct in the court

(A) Proper decorum in the court is necessary to the administration of the court's function. Any conduct that interferes or tends to interfere with the proper administration of the court's business is prohibited.

(B) No radio or television transmission, voice recording device, other than a device used by a court reporter making a record in a proceeding, or the making or taking of pictures shall be permitted without the express consent of the court in advance and pursuant to Sup. R. 12.

(Adopted eff. 7–1–97; amended eff. 10–1–97)

Historical and Statutory Notes

Ed. Note: Sup R 54 is analogous to former C P Sup R 19, adopted eff. 9–1–84.

Staff Notes

1997:

This rule is identical to former C.P. Sup. R. 19.

Library References

Trial ⚖18, 20.
Westlaw Topic No. 388.
C.J.S. Trial §§ 36 to 38.

Sup R 55 Examination of probate records

(A) Records shall not be removed from the court, except when approved by the judge. Violation of this rule may result in the issuance of a citation for contempt.

(B) Copies of records may be obtained at a cost per page as authorized by the judge.

(C) Adoption, mental illness, and mental retardation proceedings are confidential. Records of those proceedings, and other records that are confidential by statute, may be accessed as authorized by the judge.

(D) A citation for contempt of court may be issued against anyone who divulges or receives information from confidential records without authorization of the judge.

(Adopted eff. 7–1–97; amended eff. 10–1–97)

Historical and Statutory Notes

Ed. Note: Sup R 55 is analogous to former C P Sup R 20, adopted eff. 9–1–84.

Staff Notes

1997:

This rule is analogous to former C.P. Sup. R. 20 and summarizes local practice and current law. In general, see R.C. 2101.11(A)(1), 2101.12, 2101.13, 3107.17, 5122.31, 5122.34.

Sup. R. 55 has been amended to make the rule grammatically correct and to make the rule applicable to all confidential records as opposed to specific enumerated confidential records.

Cross References

Adopted persons, release of information identifying biological relatives, 3107.39 to 3107.44

Library References

Mental Health ⚖21.

Records ⇨ 31, 32.
Westlaw Topic Nos. 257A, 326.
C.J.S. Criminal Law §§ 449, 450.
C.J.S. Mental Health §§ 17 to 20.
C.J.S. Records §§ 65 to 92.

Notes of Decisions

Adoption records 1

---

1. Adoption records

Contempt proceedings ex parte are a proper means for a court to protect the secrecy of adoption records. (Annotation from former C P Sup R 20.) State ex rel. Wolff v. Donnelly (Ohio 1986) 24 Ohio St.3d 1, 492 N.E.2d 810, 24 O.B.R. 1.

Sup R 56   Continuances

(A) Motions for continuance shall be submitted in writing with the proper caption and case number.

(B) Except on motion of the court, no continuance shall be granted in the absence of proof of reasonable notice to, or consent by, the adverse party or the party's counsel. Failure to object to the continuance within a reasonable time after receiving notice shall be considered consent to the continuance.

(C) A proposed entry shall be filed with a motion for continuance, leaving the time and date blank for the court to set a new date.

(Adopted eff. 7–1–97; amended eff. 10–1–97)

Historical and Statutory Notes

Ed. Note: Sup R 56 is analogous to former C P Sup R 23, adopted eff. 9–1–84.

Staff Notes

1997:

Sup. R. 56 is analogous to former C.P. Sup. R. 23 and is the basic continuance rule within Sup. R. 50 through Sup. R. 78.

Sup. R. 56 has been amended to be gender neutral and to require a "proposed" entry as opposed to a "judgment" entry to be submitted to the court with all motions for a continuance.

Library References

Pretrial Procedure ⇨723.
Westlaw Topic No. 307A.
C.J.S.   Continuances §§ 94 to 100.

Research References

Treatises and Practice Aids

Carlin, Baldwin's Ohio Practice, Merrick-Rippner Probate Law § 4:37, Notice of Hearing—Form.
Carlin, Baldwin's Ohio Practice, Merrick-Rippner Probate Law § 4:43, Personal Service—Form.
Carlin, Baldwin's Ohio Practice, Merrick-Rippner Probate Law § 4:53, Summons in Adversary Action—Form.

Notes of Decisions

Grounds   2
Judicial discretion   1

---

1. Judicial discretion

Unpreparedness of second cousins contesting will of testatrix for second trial on issue of testamentary capacity was avoidable and, thus, denial of continuance after trial counsel was permitted to withdraw 19 days before trial was not an abuse of discretion, where second cousins' attorney represented to court three months before trial that it was likely that trial counsel would withdraw and that delay in acquiring trial preparation materials was attributable to attorney's lack of diligence and not to conduct of withdrawing counsel. (Annotation from former C P Sup R 23.) Bland v. Graves (Ohio App. 9 Dist., 11-23-1994) 99 Ohio App.3d 123, 650 N.E.2d 117, dismissed, appeal not allowed 72 Ohio St.3d 1405, 647 N.E.2d 494. Pretrial Procedure ⇨ 716

Probate court abused its discretion by denying continuance in order to allow new counsel to prepare to litigate claim that decedent had fraudulently obtained and exercised predeceasing husband's power of attorney; motion for continuance was unopposed. (Annotation from former C P Sup R 23.) Carlin v. Mambuca (Ohio App. 8 Dist., 05-23-1994) 96 Ohio App.3d 500, 645 N.E.2d 737, motion to certify allowed 70 Ohio St.3d 1475, 640 N.E.2d 848, cause dismissed 71 Ohio St.3d 1441, 643 N.E.2d 1152. Pretrial Procedure ⇨ 723.1

Whether to grant a continuance is solely within the discretion of the trial court; absent an abuse of discretion, the trial court's decision will not be reversed. (Annotation from former C P Sup R 23.) State v. Lewis (Geauga 1990) 69 Ohio App.3d 318, 590 N.E.2d 805. Criminal Law ⇨ 586; Criminal Law ⇨ 1151

Trial court denial of father's motion for a continuance, in order to allow counsel time to prepare, on mother's and father's cross-motions for modification or termination of shared parenting plan, was not an abuse of discretion; father was on his third attorney, father had been aware of the hearing date for 47 days, and father had been aware that he needed new counsel for 14 days. In re Wright (Ohio App. 5 Dist., Stark, 02-03-2003) No. 2002CA00184, 2003-Ohio-546, 2003 WL 245677, Unreported. Child Custody ⇨ 651

2. Grounds

In a dispute over a tenant's rights involving rent in escrow, a continuance is warranted where (1) the motion is made by counsel for the landlord who states that his client's on-site manager, who is material to his claim for relief, is unable to attend due to illness, (2) hearings were set within the statutory sixty-day term but were continued on the motions of the tenant and the court and (3) the court is concerned about the age of the case. (Annotation from former C P Sup R 23.) Crease v Woods of Centerville, No. 14819, 1995 WL 632085 (2d Dist Ct App, Montgomery, 10–25–95).

Sup R 57   Filings and judgment entries

(A) All filings, except wills, shall be on eight and one-half by eleven inch paper, without backings, of stock that can be microfilmed.

(B) All filings shall contain the name, address, telephone number, and attorney registration number of the individual counsel representing the fiduciary and, in the absence of counsel, the name, address, and telephone number of the fiduciary. Any filing not containing the above requirements may be refused.

(C) Failure of the fiduciary to notify the court of the fiduciary's current address shall be grounds for removal. Not less than ten days written notice of the hearing to remove shall be given to the fiduciary by regular mail at the last address contained in the case file or by other method of service as the court may direct.

(D) Filings containing partially or wholly illegible signatures of counsel, parties or officers administering oaths may be refused, or, if filed, may be stricken, unless the typewritten or printed name of the person whose signature is purported to appear is clearly indicated on the filing.

(E) All pleadings, motions, or other filings are to be typed or printed in ink and correctly captioned.

(F) Unless the court otherwise directs, counsel for the party in whose favor a judgment is rendered, shall prepare the proposed judgment entry and submit the original to the court with a copy to counsel for the opposing party. The proposed judgment entry shall be submitted within seven days after the judgment is rendered. Counsel for the opposing party shall have seven days to object to the court. If the party in whose favor a judgment is rendered fails to comply with this division, the matter may be dismissed or the court may prepare and file the appropriate entry.

(G) When a pleading, motion, judgment entry or other filing consists of more than one page, each page shall contain the case number in the upper portion of the page.

(Adopted eff. 7–1–97; amended eff. 10–1–97, 12–1–02)

Historical and Statutory Notes

Ed. Note: Sup R 57 is analogous to former C P Sup R 24, adopted eff. 9–1–84.

Amendment Note: The 12–1–02 amendment added new division (G).

Staff Notes

1997:

Sup. R. 57 is analogous to former C.P. Sup. R. 24.

Sup. R. 57(A) is unchanged.

Sup. R. 57(B) has been amended to require the attorney's Supreme Court Registration Number on all filings in addition to the name, address and telephone number of the attorney.

Sup. R. 57(B) and (D) have been amended to substitute the term "filings" for "papers" as being more descriptive of the documents received by the court.

Sup. R. 57(C) has been amended to provide for removal of a fiduciary who fails to keep the court apprised of a current address. Sup. R. 57(C) has also been amended to reflect the notice requirements of R.C. 2109.24 requiring ten days notice upon the removal of the fiduciary. Sup. R. 57(C) has been amended to allow for service of notice to be by regular mail at the fiduciary's last known address instead of pursuant to Civil Rule 73(E). The amendment is to expedite the removal of dilatory fiduciaries and to timely complete the administration of estates by avoiding the eventual requirement of publication pursuant to Civil Rule 73(E)(6) and the requirement for certified mail notice when such notice is being given by the court.

See, generally R.C. 2109.02, 2109.06, 2109.18, 2109.19, 2109.24, 2109.31, 2109.53.

Sup. R. 57(E) has been amended to reflect recent case law that has noted a distinction between motions, pleadings and filings. The rule now requires all filings to be in ink.

Former C.P. Sup. R. 24(F) and (G) have been combined into new Sup. R. 57(F) since both matters were interrelated. There were no substantive changes made.

Library References

Jury ⚖25(8).
Westlaw Topic No. 230.
C.J.S. Federal Civil Procedure § 946.
C.J.S. Juries §§ 171 to 173.

Research References

Treatises and Practice Aids

Carlin, Baldwin's Ohio Practice, Merrick-Rippner Probate Law § 3:49, Demand for Jury—Form.

Carlin, Baldwin's Ohio Practice, Merrick-Rippner Probate Law § 38:21, Agreement and Release Before Filing of Will Contest—Form.

Sup R 58 Deposit for court costs

(A) Deposits in the amount set forth in a local rule shall be required upon the filing of any action or proceeding and additional deposits may be required.

(B) The deposit may be applied as filings occur.

(Adopted eff. 7–1–97; amended eff. 10–1–97)

Historical and Statutory Notes

Ed. Note: Sup R 58 is analogous to former C P Sup R 25, adopted eff. 9–1–84.

Staff Notes

1997:

Sup. R. 58 summarizes local practice and is analogous to former C.P. Sup. R. 25.

The reference to R.C. 2101.16 has been deleted as unnecessary in that the statute delegates the amount of the deposit to local rule.

Library References

Costs ⚖104.
Westlaw Topic No. 102.

Research References

Treatises and Practice Aids

Carlin, Baldwin's Ohio Practice, Merrick-Rippner Probate Law § 103:64, Motion for Continuance—Form.

Sup R 59 Wills

(A) Before an application is made to admit the will to probate, to appoint an estate fiduciary, or to relieve an estate from administration, each applicant or the applicant's attorney shall examine the index of wills deposited pursuant to section 2107.07 of the Revised Code. Wills deposited pursuant to section 2107.07 of the Revised Code previous to the will offered for probate shall be filed in the estate proceedings for record purposes only.

(B) Fiduciaries appointed to administer testate estates shall file a Certificate of Service of Notice of Probate of Will (Standard Probate Form 2. 4) within two months of their appointment or be subject to removal proceedings. If required by the court, proof of service shall consist of either waivers of notice of the probate of will or certified mail return receipt cards as provided under Civil Rule 73(E)(3), or if necessary, under Civil Rule 73(E)(4) and (5). A waiver of notice may not be signed by any minor, or on behalf of a minor sixteen or seventeen years of age. See Civil Rule 4.2.

(Adopted eff. 7–1–97; amended eff. 10–1–97, 12–1–02)

Uncodified Law

2001 H 85, § 3, eff. 10–31–01, reads:

The General Assembly hereby encourages the Supreme Court to amend Rule 59(B) of the Ohio Rules of Superintendence to require fiduciaries appointed to administer testate estates to file a Certificate of Service of Notice of Probate of Will within two weeks of the fiduciary's appointment.

Historical and Statutory Notes

Ed. Note: Sup R 59 is analogous to former C P Sup R 26, adopted eff. 9–1–84.

Amendment Note: The 12–1–02 amendment rewrote division (B) which prior thereto read:

"(B) Fiduciaries appointed to administer testate estates shall file a Certificate of Service of Notice of Probate of Will (Standard Probate Form 2.4) within one hundred twenty days of their appointment or be subject to removal proceedings. If required by the court, proof of service shall consist of either waivers of notice of the probate of the will or original certified mail return receipt cards as provided under Civil Rule 73(E)(3). A waiver of notice may not be signed by any minor, or on behalf of a minor sixteen or seventeen years of age. See Civil Rule 4.2."

Staff Notes

1997:

This rule substantially revises former C.P. Sup. R. 26. The title of Sup. R. 59 has been amended because the subject matter of the rule is more inclusive.

The provisions of former C.P. Sup. R. 26(A) and (D) have been deleted to reflect the repeal of R.C. 2107.13 and 2107.14 and reflect the revised method of admitting a will to probate effective May 31, 1990.

Sup. R. 59(A) has been amended to reflect wills in safekeeping pursuant to R.C. 2107.07. Sup. R. 59(A) imposes a duty upon the applicant or his or her attorney to ascertain before applying to administer an estate if a will is in safekeeping. The purpose of this division is to: (1) make certain that an estate is not administered intestate when a will in safekeeping does exist, (2) make certain the decedent's last will and testament has been offered for probate, and (3) remove all prior wills of a decedent from safekeeping.

Sup. R. 59(B) is amended to require a timely filing of the "Certificate of Service of Notice of Probate of Will" so that the will contest period will expire prior to the time for the filing of the account. The amended rule also confirms that waivers of notice of probate of wills shall conform to Civil Rule 4(D).

Former C.P. Sup. R. 26(C) has been entirely deleted. The requirement of R.C. 109.26 and 109.29 are adequately provided for in Standard Probate Form 2.0.

Library References

Courts ⇐202(1) to 202(5).
Executors and Administrators ⇐35(1).
Guardian and Ward ⇐25.
Mental Health ⇐175.
Westlaw Topic Nos. 106, 162, 196, 257A.
C.J.S. Appeal and Error § 14 et seq.
C.J.S. Executors and Administrators § 105.
C.J.S. Guardian and Ward §§ 41 to 52.
C.J.S. Mental Health § 149.

Sup R 60 Application for letters of authority to administer estate and notice of appointment

(A) Notice of an application for appointment of administrator shall be served at least seven days prior to the date set for hearing. If there is no known surviving spouse or next of kin resident of the state, the notice shall be served upon persons designated by the court.

(B) The administrator shall give notice of the appointment within seven days after the appointment to all persons entitled to inherit, including persons entitled to an allowance for support, unless those persons have been provided notice of the hearing on the appointment or have waived notice.

(C) The probate court shall serve by certified mail the spousal citation and summary of rights required by R.C. 2106.02 to the surviving spouse within 7 days of the initial appointment of the administrator or executor, unless a different time is established by local court rule.

(Adopted eff. 7–1–97; amended eff. 10–1–97, 12–1–02)

Historical and Statutory Notes

Ed. Note: Sup R 60 is analogous to former C P Sup R 27, adopted eff. 9–1–84.

Amendment Note: The 12–1–02 amendment added new division (C).

Staff Notes

1997:

This rule is analogous to former C.P. Sup. R. 27. The title to Sup. R. 60 has been amended to be more descriptive of the rule's requirements.

Former C.P. Sup. R. 27(A) and (B) have been joined and incorporated under amended Sup. R. 60(A). Any language changes were merely grammatical and not substantive.

Amended Sup. R. 60(B) is a new division that deals with notice of the appointment of a fiduciary. Sup. R. 60(B) reflects local practice requiring that notice of the appointment be given to all persons interested in the decedent's estate, so that they may properly monitor their particular interests.

Library References

Executors and Administrators ⇐20.
Westlaw Topic No. 162.
C.J.S. Executors and Administrators § 53.

Sup R 61 Appraisers

(A) Without special application to the court, a fiduciary may allow to the appraiser as compensation for services a reasonable amount agreed upon between the fiduciary and the appraiser, provided the compensation does not exceed the amount allowed by local court rule. If no local court rule exists, the compensation shall be subject to court approval.

(B) If, by reason of the special and unusual character of the property to be appraised, the fiduciary is of the opinion that the appraisal requires the services of persons qualified in the evaluation of that property, a qualified appraiser may be appointed and allowed compensation as provided in division (A) of this rule.

(Adopted eff. 7–1–97; amended eff. 10–1–97)

Historical and Statutory Notes

Ed. Note: Sup R 61 is analogous to former C P Sup R 28, adopted eff. 9–1–84.

Staff Notes

1997:

This rule is analogous to former C.P. Sup. R. 28. The title to Sup. R. 61 has been amended to be more inclusive and applies to appraisers in all probate matters. The term "appointment" in the title has been deleted since the rule no longer deals with this issue.

Former law required three disinterested appraisers. Former C.P. Sup. R. 28(A) was intended to clarify the transition from three appraisers to one appraiser. The rule is no longer needed and has been deleted.

Former divisions (B), (C), (D), and (F) attempted to set guidelines for appraiser fees when the court did not set forth a local rule. Division (A) now permits the compensation to be set by agreement of the fiduciary and appraiser unless set by local rule. All disputes shall be settled by the probate court.

Former C.P. Sup. R. 28(A), (B), (C), (D), and (F) are unnecessary since the appraiser's compensation is adequately addressed by R.C. 2115.06.

Former C.P. Sup. R. 28(E) has been redesignated as Sup. R. 61(B) without substantive changes.

Library References

Wills ⇐269, 272, 314.
Westlaw Topic No. 409.
C.J.S. Wills §§ 370, 373, 445.

Research References

Treatises and Practice Aids

Carlin, Baldwin's Ohio Practice, Merrick-Rippner Probate Law § 2:14, Probating the Will—Appeal—Will Contest.

Sup R 62 Claims against estate

(A) When a claim has been filed with the court pursuant to section 2117.06 of the Revised Code, the fiduciary shall file a copy of any rejection of the claim with the court.

(B) If the court requires a hearing on claims or the fiduciary requests a hearing on claims or insolvency, the fiduciary shall file a schedule of all claims against the estate with the court. The schedule of claims shall be filed with the fiduciary's application for hearing or within ten days after the court notifies the fiduciary of a court-initiated hearing.

(Adopted eff. 7–1–97; amended eff. 10–1–97)

Historical and Statutory Notes

Ed. Note: Sup R 62 is analogous to former C P Sup R 30, adopted eff. 9–1–84.

Staff Notes

1997:

The rule is analogous to former C.P. Sup. R. 30. The title of Sup. R. 62 has been amended to be more inclusive and descriptive. R.C. 2117.06 neither limits nor requires that claims be filed with the court. Filing with the court is merely one alternative pursuant to R.C. 2117.06(A)(2).

The last sentence of former C.P. Sup. R. 30(A) has been deleted because the issue is adequately addressed by R.C. 2117.06(I).

The statutory reference in Sup. R. 62(B) has been deleted as limiting the former rule. Insolvency hearings have been added to the requirement of Sup. R. 62(B). There is no statutory provisions regarding advising the court of the specific claims in an insolvent estate. The court requires this information and the rule supplements this void.

Library References

Executors and Administrators ⚖234, 251, 459.
Westlaw Topic No. 162.
C.J.S. Executors and Administrators §§ 455, 456, 483 to 485, 787.

Research References

Treatises and Practice Aids
Carlin, Baldwin's Ohio Practice, Merrick-Rippner Probate Law § 2:121, Administration of Decedent's Estate—Checklist.

Sup R 63   Application to sell personalty

An application to sell personal property shall include an adequate description of the property. Except for good cause shown, an order of sale shall not be granted prior to the filing of the inventory.

(Adopted eff. 7–1–97; amended eff. 10–1–97)

Historical and Statutory Notes

Ed. Note: Sup R 63 is analogous to former C P Sup R 31, adopted eff. 9–1–84.

Staff Notes

1997:

This rule is analogous to former C.P. Sup. R. 31. Sup. R. 63 has been amended to delete requirements that are currently required by statute. See, R.C. 2109.45.

The first and last sentences of former C.P. Sup. R. 31 have been deleted as they duplicate the requirements of the statute. The second sentence has been amended to permit an order of sale to issue upon the filing of the inventory as opposed to the previous version, which permitted the order to be granted upon the approval of the inventory. This would expedite the administration by permitting the order to be granted at an earlier date.

Cross References

Compensation of appraisers, 2127.25

Library References

Executors and Administrators ⚖67, 111(1), 193, 216(1), 353.
Guardian and Ward ⚖32, 93.
Mental Health ⚖219, 233, 264.
Westlaw Topic Nos. 162, 196, 257A.
C.J.S. Executors and Administrators §§ 157, 252 to 263, 376, 377, 414, 624.
C.J.S. Guardian and Ward §§ 74, 122.
C.J.S. Mental Health §§ 176, 180.

Research References

Treatises and Practice Aids
Carlin, Baldwin's Ohio Practice, Merrick-Rippner Probate Law § 2:18, Inventory and Appraisal—Appraisal of Assets.

Sup R 64   Accounts

(A) The vouchers or other proofs required by section 2109.302 and 2109.303 of the Revised Code and receipts filed or exhibited pursuant to section 2109.32(B)(1)(b) of the Revised Code, shall be referenced to the account by number, letter, or date.

(B) If land has been sold during the accounting period, the account shall show the gross amount of the proceeds and include a copy of the closing statement itemizing all of the disbursements.

(C) Receipts for distributive shares signed by persons holding power of attorney may be accepted, provided the power of attorney is recorded in the county in which the estate is being administered and a copy of the recorded power is attached to the account.

(D) Exhibiting assets.

(1) The court may require that all assets be exhibited at the time of filing a partial account.

(2) Cash balances may be verified by exhibiting a financial institution statement, passbook, or a current letter from the financial institution in which the funds are deposited certifying the amount of funds on deposit to the credit of the fiduciary. Assets held in a safe deposit box of a fiduciary or by a surety company on fiduciary's bond may be exhibited by filing a current inventory of the assets. The inventory shall be certified by the manager of the safe deposit box department of the financial institution leasing the safe deposit box or by a qualified officer of the surety company if the assets are held by a surety. If the assets are held by a bank, trust company, brokerage firm, or other financial institution, exhibition may be made by proper certification as to the assets so held. For good cause shown, the court may designate a deputy clerk of the court to make an examination of the assets located in the county, not physically exhibited to the court or may appoint a commissioner for that purpose if the assets are located outside the county. The commissioner appointed shall make a written report of findings to the court.

(E) A final or distributive account shall not be approved until all court costs have been paid.

(Adopted eff. 7–1–97; amended eff. 10–1–97, 4–8–04)

Historical and Statutory Notes

Ed. Note: Sup R 64 is analogous to former C P Sup R 32, adopted eff. 9–1–84.

Amendment Note: The 4–8–04 amendment rewrote division (A). Prior to amendment, division (A) read:

(A) The vouchers required by section 2109.30 of the Revised Code, shall be referenced to the account by number, letter or date.

Staff Notes

2004:

This Rule Amendment is necessary because of the adoption of Sub. H.B. 85, effective October 31, 2001.

1997:

This rule revises former C.P. Sup. R. 32.

Former C.P. Sup. R. 32(A) and (B) have been deleted. This subject matter is more appropriately addressed in proposed Sup. R. 78, the case management rule.

Former C.P. Sup. R. 32(C) has been changed grammatically and relettered as division (A). The substance has remained the same in that it requires the vouchers to be cross referenced to the account entries. Former divisions (A)(1) to (4) have been deleted in that they describe the parameters of the probate forms created under Sup. R. 52(D) and are therefore superfluous.

Former C.P. Sup. R. 32(D) has been relettered as division (B). The rule has been amended to require a closing statement to be submitted in lieu of the reporting requirements under the former rule.

Former C.P. Sup. R. 32(E) has been deleted to reflect local practice where each guardianship of a minor's estate is administered in a separate case file and a separate corresponding case number.

Former C.P. Sup. R. 32(F) has been relettered as division (C) and amended to require that when a power of attorney is used for the receipt of assets, the instrument must be recorded in the county of the court accepting the account. The previous rule required the instrument to be recorded in the State of Ohio.

Former C.P. Sup. R. 32(G) has been relettered as division (D). The term "safety deposit box" has been amended to "safe deposit box" to parallel Revised Code references. The term "financial institution" has been substituted for "bank" in order to be consistent with the terminology of Title XI of the Revised Code and to be more inclusive.

Former C.P. Sup. R. 32(H) has been relettered as division (E), and no amendments or language changes have been made.

Cross References

Newspaper of general circulation, 7.12

Library References

Executors and Administrators ⚖62, 64.
Guardian and Ward ⚖32.
Mental Health ⚖219.
Westlaw Topic Nos. 162, 196, 257A.
C.J.S. Executors and Administrators §§ 152, 153, 158.
C.J.S. Guardian and Ward § 74.
C.J.S. Mental Health § 180.

Research References

Treatises and Practice Aids

Carlin, Baldwin's Ohio Practice, Merrick-Rippner Probate Law § 2:17, Inventory and Appraisal—Ascertaining Assets.

Carlin, Baldwin's Ohio Practice, Merrick-Rippner Probate Law § 2:23, Inventory and Appraisal—Filing of Inventory.

Notes of Decisions

Notice 1

___

1. Notice

Notice of the filing of an estate inventory need not be by registered mail; notice of the filing of an estate inventory in a newspaper of general circulation is sufficient. (Annotation from former C P Sup R 29.) In re Estate of Sliwa (Medina 1989) 58 Ohio App.3d 82, 568 N.E.2d 741, dismissed 47 Ohio St.3d 702, 547 N.E.2d 986.

Sup R 65 Land sales —R.C. Chapter 2127

(A) In all land sale proceedings, the plaintiff, prior to the issuance of an order finding the sale necessary, shall file with the court evidence of title showing the record condition of the title to the premises described in the complaint and prepared by a title company licensed by the state of Ohio, an attorney's certificate, or other evidence of title satisfactory to the court. Evidence of title shall be to a date subsequent to the date on which the complaint was filed.

(B) The plaintiff shall give notice of the time and place of sale by regular mail at least three weeks prior to the date of a public sale to all defendants at their last known addresses. Prior to the public sale, the plaintiff shall file a certificate stating that the required notice was given to the defendants and the sale was advertised pursuant to section 2127.32 of the Revised Code.

(C) In all private land sale proceedings by civil action, the judgment entry confirming sale, ordering issuance of deed, and ordering distribution shall show the gross amount of the proceeds and include a copy of the proposed closing statement itemizing all of the proposed disbursements.

(D) The court may appoint a disinterested person, answerable to the court, who shall investigate the circumstances surrounding the proposed transaction, view the property, ascertain whether the proposed sale is justified and report findings in writing. The report shall be a part of the record. The compensation for the person performing these services shall be fixed by the court, according to the circumstances of each case, and shall be taxed as costs.

(Adopted eff. 7–1–97; amended eff. 10–1–97)

Historical and Statutory Notes

Ed. Note: Sup R 65 is analogous to former C P Sup R 33, adopted eff. 9–1–84.

Staff Notes

1997:

This rule is analogous to former C.P. Sup. R. 33 and has been amended to be inclusive and to apply to all land sale proceedings. Former C.P. Sup. R. 33(A) only applied to public land sale, and not private land sale proceedings. The rule has been amended to require that evidence of title prepared by a title company must be prepared by a title company that is licensed in the State of Ohio.

Former C.P. Sup. R. 33(B) has been amended to delete the requirement of giving notice by posting the notice of sale upon the premises. This appeared unnecessary since actual notice of the sale must be given to all defendants, and R.C. 2127.32 requires notice by publication to the general public.

Reference to the filing of an affidavit has been amended to refer to a "certificate," to reflect Civil Rule 73(H), which does not require certificates and pleadings to be under oath. An affidavit, by definition, is under oath. The content of the "certificate" has been amended to comply with the amended notice requirements of division (B).

Former C.P. Sup. R. 33(C) has been deleted in that the requirements are unnecessary and adequately covered by R.C. 2127.23 and 2127.35.

Amended division (C) requires that a proposed closing statement be attached to the order of confirmation of sale issued pursuant to R.C. 2127.35. The inclusion of the proposed closing statement provides the court with the details of the costs associated with the land sale proceedings.

Division (D) has been amended in order to be made gender neutral. No substantive changes have been made.

Library References

Executors and Administrators ⚖361 to 363.
Guardian and Ward ⚖94.1 to 97.
Mental Health ⚖264, 265.
Westlaw Topic Nos. 162, 196, 257A.
C.J.S. Executors and Administrators §§ 628 to 634.
C.J.S. Guardian and Ward §§ 124 to 126.

Research References

Treatises and Practice Aids

Carlin, Baldwin's Ohio Practice, Merrick-Rippner Probate Law § 91:2, Land Sale—Complaint.

Carlin, Baldwin's Ohio Practice, Merrick-Rippner Probate Law § 95:5, Public Sale—Notice.

Carlin, Baldwin's Ohio Practice, Merrick-Rippner Probate Law § 96:15, Mortgages, Judgments, and Liens.

Sup R 66 Guardianships

(A) All applications for the appointment of a guardian on the grounds of mental incompetency shall be accompanied by either a statement of a physician or clinical psychologist or a statement that the prospective ward has refused to submit to an examination.

(B) An Application for Authority to Expend Funds (Standard Probate Form 15.7) shall not be approved until an Inventory (Standard Probate Form 15.5) has been filed.

(C) An application for allowance of care and support of a minor shall allege, if such is the fact, that the father and mother are financially unable to provide the items for which the amount is sought.

(Adopted eff. 7–1–97; amended eff. 10–1–97)

Historical and Statutory Notes

Ed. Note: Sup R 66 is analogous to former C P Sup R 34, adopted eff. 9–1–84.

Staff Notes

1997:

This rule is analogous to former C.P. Sup. R. 34, and the title has been amended to be more inclusive in that the rule does not only apply to the guardian but also to all issues affecting the guardianship.

Division (A) has been deleted in that it described the parameters of the probate forms created under Sup. R. 51(D) and is therefore superfluous.

Former C.P. Sup. R. 34(B) has been relettered as division (A). The rule required the submission of a statement of a physician upon the filing of an application for guardianship or an application for dismissal of a guardianship or a declaration of competency. The rule has been amended to permit a clinical psychologist to complete the expert evaluation. This amendment recognizes that a psychologist's report is often more thorough than that of the physician and recognizes that the psychologist may complete the expert evaluation for the biennial report. The rule has not been expanded to permit the initial evaluation to be completed by a licensed clinical social worker.

The requirement for an expert evaluation for the dismissal or termination of a guardianship has been deleted due to statutory changes under R.C. 2111.49(C).

Former C.P. Sup. R. 34(C) has been deleted and incorporated in part in amended division (B), which continues the requirement to file an inventory prior to the authorization of any expenditure required in former C.P. Sup. R. 34(C).

Former C.P. Sup. R. 34(D) has been relettered as division (C). Division (C) has been amended to delete the term "parent-guardian" from the rule and to allow the application to be filed by the appointed guardian, who is not in all cases also the parent of the minor ward. With an application to expend funds for support of a minor ward, the rule formerly required a parent-guardian to state whether the parents had the ability to provide the support. The amendment expands the rule to require any guardian to state whether the parents can provide the support when requesting expenditure of the ward's funds for support.

Library References

Executors and Administrators ⚘346.
Guardian and Ward ⚘90.
Mental Health ⚘267.
Westlaw Topic Nos. 162, 196, 257A.
C.J.S. Executors and Administrators § 619, 620.
C.J.S. Guardian and Ward §§ 115, 120.

Research References

Treatises and Practice Aids

Carlin, Baldwin's Ohio Practice, Merrick-Rippner Probate Law § 62:17, Appointment of Guardian—Application—Contents.

Notes of Decisions

Physician's statement 1

---

1. Physician's statement

Physician who completed statement of expert evaluation regarding guardianship proceeding was engaged in role of independent evaluator, not proposed ward's doctor, and thus communications with proposed ward that were contained in statement were not protected by physician-patient privilege, since physician was appointed by court, and physician indicated in statement that proposed ward was not physician's patient. In re Guardianship and Conservatorship of Stancin (Ohio App. 10 Dist., Franklin, 03-11-2003) No. 02AP-637, 2003-Ohio-1106, 2003 WL 953840, Unreported, appeal not allowed 99 Ohio St.3d 1513, 792 N.E.2d 200, 2003-Ohio-3957. Witnesses ⚘ 209

Sup R 67 Estates of minors of not more than ten thousand dollars

(A) Each application relating to a minor shall be submitted by the parent or parents or by the person having custody of the minor and shall be captioned in the name of the minor.

(B) Each application shall indicate the amount of money or property to which the minor is entitled and to whom such money or property shall be paid or delivered. Unless the court otherwise orders, if no guardian has been appointed for either the receipt of an estate of a minor or the receipt of a settlement for injury to a minor, the attorney representing the interests of the minor shall prepare an entry that orders all of the following:

(1) The deposit of the funds in a financial institution in the name of the minor;

(2) Impounding the principal and interest;

(3) Releasing the funds only upon an order of the court or to the minor at the age of majority.

(C) The entry shall be presented at the time the entry dispensing with appointment of a guardian or approving settlement is approved. The attorney shall be responsible for depositing the funds and for providing the financial institution with a copy of the entry. The attorney shall obtain a Verification of Receipt and Deposit (Standard Probate Form 22.3) from the financial institution and file the form with the court within seven days from the issuance of the entry.

(Adopted eff. 7–1–97; amended eff. 10–1–97)

Historical and Statutory Notes

Ed. Note: Sup R 67 is analogous to former C P Sup R 35, adopted eff. 9–1–84.

Staff Notes

1997:

This rule is analogous to former C.P. Sup. R. 35. The title of the rule has been amended to include only the estates of minor wards, since the substantive rules even under former C.P. Sup. R. 35 only spoke of minors. The amended title is more descriptive of the subject matter covered by the rule.

Division (A) has been amended to delete any reference to one application being permitted to be filed on behalf of all minors of the same parent. This amendment is to reflect local practice whereby a separate application and corresponding case number is required for each minor ward. The rationale for the amendment is that the amount of funds received and the dates of majority are rarely the same for each ward. The remainder of the amendments to this division are grammatical and not substantive.

Divisions (B) and (C) set forth the requirements of the judgment entry counsel presents to the court for estates of minors less than $10,000. The words "unless the court otherwise orders" has [sic.] been added to alert counsel to the fact that specific circumstances or local court rule may alter these requirements. In addition, the former version of the rule required the attorney to deposit all funds within seven days of the approval of the entry and to obtain a receipt from the financial institution. As amended the rule requires the receipt to be filed with the court within seven days of the issuance of the entry and references the uniform form number of the receipt. The term "bank" has been changed to "financial institution" to reflect the term utilized in Title XI of the Revised Code and to recognize that funds are invested in institutions other than banks.

Library References

Executors and Administrators ⚘458 to 516(7).
Guardian and Ward ⚘137 to 165.
Mental Health ⚘291 to 313.
Westlaw Topic Nos. 162, 196, 257A.
C.J.S. Executors and Administrators §§ 785 to 899.
C.J.S. Guardian and Ward §§ 146 to 169, 196.
C.J.S. Mental Health §§ 183 to 202.

Research References

Treatises and Practice Aids

Carlin, Baldwin's Ohio Practice, Merrick-Rippner Probate Law § 67:5, Alternatives to Guardianship—Estate of Minor Not More Than $10,000.

Carlin, Baldwin's Ohio Practice, Merrick-Rippner Probate Law § 66:10, Termination of Guardianship—Minor.

Carlin, Baldwin's Ohio Practice, Merrick-Rippner Probate Law App B SPF 22.0, Application to Settle a Minor's Claim and Entry Setting Hearing—Form.

Sup R 68 Settlement of injury claims of minors

(A) An application for settlement of a minor's claim shall be brought by the guardian of the estate. If there is no guardian appointed and the court dispenses with the need for a guardian, the application shall be brought by the parents of the child or the parent or other individual having custody of the child. The noncustodial parent or parents shall be entitled to seven days notice of the application to settle the minor's claim which notice may be waived. The application shall be captioned in the name of the minor.

(B) The application shall be accompanied by a current statement of an examining physician in respect to the injuries sustained, the extent of recovery, and the permanency of any injuries. The application shall state what additional consideration, if any, is being paid to persons other than the minor as a result of the incident causing the injury to the minor. The application shall state what arrangement, if any, has been made with respect to counsel fees. Counsel fees shall be subject to approval by the court.

(C) The injured minor and the applicant shall be present at the hearing.

(Adopted eff. 7–1–97; amended eff. 10–1–97)

Historical and Statutory Notes

Ed. Note: Sup R 68 is analogous to former C P Sup R 36, adopted eff. 9–1–84.

Staff Notes

1997:

This rule is analogous to former C.P. Sup. R. 36 and 37. Former C.P. Sup. R. 36 and 37 dealt with claims to minors and bifurcated the claims into claims brought by the guardian and claims of less than $10,000 where there was no guardian. The former rules were virtually identical and thus the issues relating to minors have been consolidated into Sup. R. 68 to avoid duplication.

Division (A) has been amended to incorporate the provisions of former C.P. Sup. R. 37(A). In addition, the rule has been amended to require notice to the parents of the minor regardless of their county of residence and to increase the notice time requirement to the parents from three days to seven days in order that the notice is more meaningful.

Division (B) has been amended to provide that the statement of the examining physician is mandatory as opposed to discretionary. Former C.P. Sup. R. 36(D) and (E) have been consolidated into division (B).

Division (C) has been amended to make the applicant's and the minor's appearance at the hearing mandatory. This is to comply with prevailing local practice where the court wishes to view the minor in order to evaluate the nature of the injuries. Pursuant to Sup. R. 76, the court has the ability to waive the appearance of the minor for good cause.

Library References

Compromise and Settlement ⚖66.1.
Infants ⚖84.
Westlaw Topic Nos. 89, 211.
C.J.S. Compromise and Settlement § 2.
C.J.S. Infants §§ 234 to 236.

Research References

Treatises and Practice Aids

Carlin, Baldwin's Ohio Practice, Merrick-Rippner Probate Law App B SPF 22.0, Application to Settle a Minor's Claim and Entry Setting Hearing—Form.

Notes of Decisions

Counsel fees 1

---

1. Counsel fees

In light of counsel's failure to obtain court preapproval of contingent fee contract with regard to injured minors, as required by Rules of Superintendence and local court rule, there could be no contingent fee contract binding on children. (Annotation from former C P Sup R 36.) In re Settlements of Betts (Ohio Com.Pl. 1991) 62 Ohio Misc.2d 30, 587 N.E.2d 997. Attorney And Client ⚖ 147

Sup R 69 Settlement of claims of or against adult wards

(A) An application for settlement of a claim in favor of or against an adult ward shall be brought by the guardian of the estate. Notice of the hearing on the application shall be given to all persons who are interested parties to the proposed settlement, as determined by the court. The court may authorize or direct the guardian of the ward's estate to compromise and settle claims as the court considers to be in the best interest of the ward. The court may dispense with notice of hearing.

(B) The application for settlement of an injury claim shall be accompanied by a current statement of an examining physician describing the injuries sustained, the extent of recovery from those injuries, and permanency of any injuries. The application shall state what additional consideration, if any, is being paid to persons other than the ward as a result of the incident causing the injury to the ward. The application shall state what arrangement, if any, has been made with respect to counsel fees. Counsel fees shall be subject to approval by the court.

(Adopted eff. 7–1–97; amended eff. 10–1–97)

Staff Notes

1997:

This rule is not analogous to former C.P. Sup. R. 37, which has been incorporated in Sup. R. 68.

Sup. R. 69 is basically a new rule as it applies to all claims of incompetent adult wards. The purpose for the amended rule is to provide the court with information necessary to make an informed decision regarding a proposed settlement.

Division (A) provides for the application to settle a claim to be brought by the ward's guardian. Absent a guardianship, the "ward" is competent to settle the claim without court approval. Division (A) further gives the court discretion to require notice to interested parties or to dispense with notice with court approval.

Division (B) is similar to Sup. R. 68(B), which provides the court with adequate information to make an informed decision. Division (C) is similar to the last sentence of Sup. R. 68(B) and requires disclosure to the court and approval of the court of counsel fees in pursuing the adult ward's claim.

Cross References

Guardian, application for appointment of, 2111.03

Library References

Guardian and Ward ⚖13(3).
Mental Health ⚖126.
Westlaw Topic Nos. 196, 257A.
C.J.S. Guardian and Ward §§ 21 to 25.
C.J.S. Mental Health § 133.

Research References

Treatises and Practice Aids

Carlin, Baldwin's Ohio Practice, Merrick-Rippner Probate Law § 62:45, Guardianship Proceedings—Role of Physician or Investigators.

Sup R 70 Settlement of wrongful death and survival claims

(A) An application to approve settlement and Distribution of Wrongful Death and Survival Claims (Standard Probate Form 14.0) shall contain a statement of facts, including the amount to be allocated to the settlement of the claim and the amount, if any, to be allocated to the settlement of the survival claim. The application shall include the proposed distribution of the net proceeds allocated to the wrongful death claim.

(B) The fiduciary shall give written notice of the hearing and a copy of the application to all interested persons who have not waived notice of the hearing. Notwithstanding the waivers and consents of the interested persons, the court shall retain jurisdiction over the settlement, allocation, and distribution of the claims.

(C) The application shall state what arrangements, if any, have been made with respect to counsel fees. Counsel fees shall be subject to approval by the court.

(Adopted eff. 7–1–97; amended eff. 10–1–97)

Historical and Statutory Notes

Ed. Note: Sup R 70 is analogous to former C P Sup R 38, adopted eff. 9–1–84.

Staff Notes

1997:

This rule is analogous to former C.P. Sup. R. 38. The title has been amended to stress the existence and recognition of survival claims in a decedent's estate and to be in compliance with Standard Probate Forms Series 14.

Division (A) has been amended to incorporate the title of the uniform form as the description of the application to which the rule applies. The phase [sic.] "right of action for conscious pain and suffering" has been changed to "survival claim" as being a more complete description of the personal claim of the decedent. The remaining changes are grammatical and intended to stress the need for an allocation between the survival claim and the wrongful death claim.

Division (A) now requires a copy of the proposed distribution in addition to the notice of hearing to be served upon all interested persons who have not waived notice of the hearing. Those who have waived notice are required to receive a copy of the proposed distribution by the requirements of Form 14.1. The amended paragraph contains instructional language to remind interested persons and counsel that the court retains jurisdiction over the settlement notwithstanding an agreement by the parties as to the distribution.

Division (C) has been amended grammatically. There are no substantive changes.

Library References

Infants ⇌21, 84.
Westlaw Topic No. 211.
C.J.S. Infants §§ 120, 123, 234 to 236.

Research References

Treatises and Practice Aids

Carlin, Baldwin's Ohio Practice, Merrick-Rippner Probate Law § 67:10, Application for Release of Assets Without Appointment of Guardian—Minor—Form.

Carlin, Baldwin's Ohio Practice, Merrick-Rippner Probate Law App B SPF 14.0, Application to Approve Settlement and Distribution of Wrongful Death and Survival Claims—Form.

Carlin, Baldwin's Ohio Practice, Merrick-Rippner Probate Law App B SPF 22.3, Verification of Receipt and Deposit—Form.

Sup R 71 Counsel fees

(A) Attorney fees in all matters shall be governed by Rule 1.5 of the Ohio Rules of Professional Conduct.

(B) Attorney fees for the administration of estates shall not be paid until the final account is prepared for filing unless otherwise approved by the court upon application and for good cause shown.

(C) Attorney fees may be allowed if there is a written application that sets forth the amount requested and will be awarded only after proper hearing, unless otherwise modified by local rule.

(D) The court may set a hearing on any application for allowance of attorney fees regardless of the fact that the required consents of the beneficiaries have been given.

(E) Except for good cause shown, attorney fees shall not be allowed to attorneys representing fiduciaries who are delinquent in filing the accounts required by section 2109.30 of the Revised Code.

(F) If a hearing is scheduled on an application for the allowance of attorney fees, notice shall be given to all parties affected by the payment of fees, unless otherwise ordered by the court.

(G) An application shall be filed for the allowance of counsel fees for services rendered to a guardian, trustee, or other fiduciary. The application may be filed by the fiduciary or attorney. The application shall set forth a statement of the services rendered and the amount claimed in conformity with division (A) of this rule.

(H) There shall be no minimum or maximum fees that automatically will be approved by the court.

(I) Prior to a fiduciary entering into a contingent fee contract with an attorney for services, an application for authority to enter into the fee contract shall be filed with the court, unless otherwise ordered by local court rule. The contingent fee on the amount obtained shall be subject to approval by the court.

(Adopted eff. 7–1–97; amended eff. 10–1–97, 2–1–07)

Historical and Statutory Notes

Ed. Note: Sup R 71 is analogous to former C P Sup R 40, adopted eff. 9–1–84.

Staff Notes

1997:

This rule is analogous to former C.P. Sup. R. 40. Divisions (A), (B), (C), (D), (E), (F), and (G) have not been amended substantively.

The second sentence of division (H), pertaining to contingent fee contracts, has been transferred to a new division (I) where it has been combined with former C.P. Sup. R. 39.

Division (I) recognizes that unless a governing instrument has given the power to the fiduciary, the fiduciary has no inherent authority to enter into a contingent fee contract on behalf of the trust. Authority must be granted by the court. The rule as amended adopts the previous rule which required the fiduciary to file an application to enter into a contingent fee contract prior to the contract becoming enforceable. The rule has been amended to permit courts to establish their own procedure in the contingent fee approval process. The second sentence of division (I) was a portion of former C.P. Sup. R. 39 and restates the court's authority to review the contingent fee contract to ascertain whether it meets with the additional standards of this rule.

Library References

Executors and Administrators ⇌111(1), 216(2), 268.
Guardian and Ward ⇌162.
Mental Health ⇌309.
Westlaw Topic Nos. 162, 196, 257A.
C.J.S. Executors and Administrators §§ 252 to 263, 415, 516.
C.J.S. Guardian and Ward § 164.
C.J.S. Mental Health § 200.

Research References

Treatises and Practice Aids

Carlin, Baldwin's Ohio Practice, Merrick-Rippner Probate Law § 65:23, Settlement of Suits—Attorney Fees in Cases Where Court Approval is Required.

Carlin, Baldwin's Ohio Practice, Merrick-Rippner Probate Law App B SPF 22.0, Application to Settle a Minor's Claim and Entry Setting Hearing—Form.

Notes of Decisions

Approval 3
Cocounsel 2
Guardianship fees 1

---

1. Guardianship fees

Probate court did not abuse its discretion in guardianship proceeding by denying guardian's application for guardian fees; guardian filed inventory 15 months late, guardian's account was never approved by probate court, and guardian made expenditures for guardian fees and attorney fees without court approval. In re Guardianship of Papuska (Ohio App. 5 Dist., Stark, 02-22-2005) No. 2004-CA-00150, 2005-Ohio-741, 2005 WL 428031, Unreported. Guardian And Ward ⇐ 150

Attorney whose services resulted in establishment of guardianship is entitled to compensation. (Annotation from former C P Sup R 40.) In re Estate of Bickham (Logan 1993) 85 Ohio App.3d 634, 620 N.E.2d 913. Guardian And Ward ⇐ 162

An award to a guardian's attorney of $9,702 in attorney fees for services rendered in defending a claim against the estate by the former guardian is proper even though the balance of the estate is only $17,000 since (1) the ward was directly benefited by the legal expenses incurred because instead of the $25,000 paid for by the former guardian, only $1,050 was awarded; and (2) the fee charged by the attorney was reasonable under the Code of Professional Responsibility because the attorney actually worked 98.9 hours, but only billed the estate for 96 hours and $100 per hour rate charged was reasonable for services performed. (Annotation from former C P Sup R 40.) In re Guardianship of Rider (Huron 1990) 68 Ohio App.3d 709, 589 N.E.2d 465.

2. Cocounsel

An attorney who acts as cocounsel in a wrongful death action is entitled to recover his share of legal fees from the other attorney holding the proceeds of the action in trust for the clients who were vested beneficiaries, since the unpaid attorney was in privity with the clients, who were liable for his fees. (Annotation from former C P Sup R 40.) Weisberger v. Home Ins. Cos. (Cuyahoga 1991) 76 Ohio App.3d 391, 601 N.E.2d 660, dismissed, jurisdictional motion overruled 63 Ohio St.3d 1455, 590 N.E.2d 750.

An attorney who acts as cocounsel in a wrongful death action is not barred from bringing an action to recover his share of legal fees from another attorney holding the proceeds of the action in trust for the clients by virtue of an exclusionary provision in the attorney's legal malpractice policy since the exclusion means that damages did not include legal fees incurred by cocounsel in obtaining judgment against the attorney. (Annotation from former C P Sup R 40.) Weisberger v. Home Ins. Cos. (Cuyahoga 1991) 76 Ohio App.3d 391, 601 N.E.2d 660, dismissed, jurisdictional motion overruled 63 Ohio St.3d 1455, 590 N.E.2d 750.

3. Approval

Probate court did not abuse its discretion in guardianship proceedings and proceedings to administer ward's estate following ward's death by declining to award the full amount of attorney fees requested on behalf of attorney who represented guardian and estate; guardian and former administratrix of estate both were delinquent in filing their accounts. In re Guardianship of Papuska (Ohio App. 5 Dist., Stark, 02-22-2005) No. 2004-CA-00150, 2005-Ohio-741, 2005 WL 428031, Unreported. Guardian And Ward ⇐ 162

Trial court was required to consider successor attorneys' fee agreement and services, including time, effort, and skill of attorneys in representation, under standards set forth in rule governing counsel fees and rule of professional responsibility governing fees for legal services, before allocating fee award between clients' original and successor attorneys, in parents' litigation against amusement park arising out of child's accident in amusement park's swimming pool, in which successor attorneys negotiated partial settlement agreement of $200,000; trial court had engaged in analysis of valuation of original attorney's fees, but had failed to engage in analysis of valuation of successor attorneys' fees. In re J.F. (Ohio App. 9 Dist., 08-17-2005) 162 Ohio App.3d 716, 834 N.E.2d 876, 2005-Ohio-4258. Attorney And Client ⇐ 151

Rules requiring probate court's approval of fiduciary's application for authority to enter into contingency-fee agreement were not unconstitutional as applied to guardian of infant who brought action on infant's behalf. In re Thompson (Ohio App. 1 Dist., 11-08-2002) 150 Ohio App.3d 98, 779 N.E.2d 816, 2002-Ohio-6065. Guardian And Ward ⇐ 116(1)

Trial court was required to consider reasonableness of requested attorney fees before awarding fees from deceased ward's guardianship case in action regarding ward's estate. In re Estate of Waterman (Ohio App. 2 Dist., Champaign, 06-27-2003) No. 2002-CA-28, 2003-Ohio-3406, 2003 WL 21487863, Unreported. Executors And Administrators ⇐ 205

Reasonableness hearing was required to determine appropriate attorney fee for attorney who settled portion of wrongful death action brought on behalf of attorney's clients, where attorney sought approval of 40 percent fee under contingency agreement, but court approval of contingency fee contract had not been obtained as required by court rule in effect at time contract was entered; court could not mechanically limit attorney fees to 33 and 1/3 percent, which was percentage for which no prior court approval of contingency fee agreement was required under former local court rule. In re Thamann (Ohio App. 1 Dist., 04-25-2003) 152 Ohio App.3d 574, 789 N.E.2d 654, 2003-Ohio-2069. Attorney And Client ⇐ 147

Probate court had power to review contingency fee agreement between estate and estate attorney, even though agreement had been approved earlier and may have been fair, customary, and reasonable at that time, where it appeared that case pursued by attorney on behalf of estate had not required much preparation and had been settled without trial. In re Estate of York (Ohio App. 12 Dist., 03-15-1999) 133 Ohio App.3d 234, 727 N.E.2d 607, appeal not allowed 86 Ohio St.3d 1442, 713 N.E.2d 1052. Executors And Administrators ⇐ 216(2)

Probate court was required to thoroughly review time, effort and skill of estate's attorney in pursuing litigation on behalf of estate and to provide sufficient justification, supported by the evidence, for decision to reduce fee from that provided for in contingency fee agreement when litigation settled before trial. In re Estate of York (Ohio App. 12 Dist., 03-15-1999) 133 Ohio App.3d 234, 727 N.E.2d 607, appeal not allowed 86 Ohio St.3d 1442, 713 N.E.2d 1052. Executors And Administrators ⇐ 216(2)

Guardian was not required to obtain approval of probate court to hire legal counsel to represent him on ward's motion to terminate guardianship in order to bind ward or her estate to pay for legal services rendered on behalf of guardian. (Annotation from former C P Sup R 40.) Brown v. Haffey (Ohio App. 8 Dist., 09-06-1994) 96 Ohio App.3d 724, 645 N.E.2d 1295. Mental Health ⇐ 233

Probate court did not abuse its discretion in awarding attorney, who assisted guardian for infant in personal injury action, reasonable value of his services (60.95 hours times $150 per hour) rather than one-third of $90,000 settlement plus costs and expenses advanced, even though guardian and attorney had entered into contingent fee agreement, where agreement was not approved by court prior to guardian entering into agreement as required by statute. (Annotation from former C P Sup R 40.) In re Guardianship of Patrick (Huron 1991) 66 Ohio App.3d 415, 584 N.E.2d 86. Guardian And Ward ⇐ 58

Where a deceased child's parents entered into a contingent fee contract with an attorney on a wrongful death claim, the trial court properly held that without prior approval of the probate court as required by C P Sup R 40, the attorney fees must be paid on a hourly basis under the theory of quantum meruit. (Annotation from former C P Sup R 40.) Estate of Messner v Kaforey, No. 16270, 1993 WL 526683 (9th Dist Ct App, Summit, 12–15–93).

In light of counsel's failure to obtain court preapproval of contingent fee contract with regard to injured minors, as required by Rules of Superintendence and local court rule, there could be no contingent fee contract binding on children. (Annotation from former C P Sup R 40.) In re Settlements of Betts (Ohio Com.Pl. 1991) 62 Ohio Misc.2d 30, 587 N.E.2d 997. Attorney And Client ⇐ 147

Sup R 72 Executor's and administrator's commissions

(A) Additional compensation for extraordinary services may be allowed upon an application setting forth an itemized statement of the services rendered and the amount of compensation requested. The court may require the application to be set for hearing with notice given to interested persons in accordance with Civil Rule 73(E).

(B) The court may deny or reduce commissions if there is a delinquency in the filing of an inventory or an account, or if, after hearing, the court finds that the executor or administrator has not faithfully discharged the duties of the office.

(C) The commissions of co-executors or co-administrators in the aggregate shall not exceed the commissions that would have been allowed to one executor or administrator acting alone, except where the instrument under which the co-executors serve provides otherwise.

(D) Where counsel fees have been awarded for services to the estate that normally would have been performed by the executor or administrator, the executor or administrator commission, except for good cause shown, shall be reduced by the amount awarded to counsel for those services.

(Adopted eff. 7–1–97; amended eff. 10–1–97)

Historical and Statutory Notes

Ed. Note: Sup R 72 is analogous to former C P Sup R 41, adopted eff. 9–1–84.

Staff Notes

1997:

This rule is analogous to former C.P. Sup. R. 41. Division (A) has primarily been amended for grammatical purposes. The term "parties" has been replaced with the more descriptive term "interested person". The manner of service pursuant to Civil Rule 4.1 has been replaced with the more appropriate reference to Civil Rule 73(E), which incorporates by reference Civil Rule 4.1.

Division (B) has been amended to parallel R.C. 2113.35. The rule defines the delinquent filing of inventories and accounts as acts that are included within the phrase "not faithfully discharged the duties of the office."

Division (D) has been amended to be more inclusive and to apply to all counsel fees and not only extraordinary fees. The rule continues to allow the probate court discretion to reduce fiduciary fees by the amount of attorney fees charged in performing fiduciary services. The remaining language changes in the division are grammatical and not substantive.

Library References

Compromise and Settlement ⇐66.1
Westlaw Topic No. 89.
C.J.S. Compromise and Settlement § 2.

Research References

Treatises and Practice Aids

Carlin, Baldwin's Ohio Practice, Merrick-Rippner Probate Law § 67:10, Application for Release of Assets Without Appointment of Guardian—Minor—Form.

Sup R 73   Guardian's compensation

(A) Guardian's compensation shall be set by local rule.

(B) Additional compensation for extraordinary services, reimbursement for expenses incurred and compensation of a guardian of a person only may be allowed upon an application setting forth an itemized statement of the services rendered and expenses incurred and the amount for which compensation is applied. The court may require the application to be set for hearing with notice given to interested persons in accordance with Civil Rule 73(E).

(C) The compensation of co-guardians in the aggregate shall not exceed the compensation that would have been allowed to one guardian acting alone.

(D) The court may deny or reduce compensation if there is a delinquency in the filing of an inventory or account, or after hearing, the court finds the guardian has not faithfully discharged the duties of the office.

(Adopted eff. 7–1–97; amended eff. 10–1–97)

Historical and Statutory Notes

Ed. Note: Sup R 73 is analogous to former C P Sup R 42, adopted eff. 9–1–84.

Staff Notes

1997:

This rule is analogous to former C.P. Sup. R. 42. Division (A) has been amended to delete reference to Sup. R. 75.

Division (B) has been amended to clarify the requirements and procedure for extraordinary compensation of a guardian of the estate and for compensation of a guardian of a person who is not also the guardian of the estate. The procedure parallels the procedure that previously was in place for extraordinary compensation to an executor or administrator. Division (B) incorporates the requirements of former C.P. Sup. R. 42(C), which has been deleted. The reference to service in accordance with Civil Rule 4.1 has been deleted, since service is controlled by Civil Rule 73.

Division (C) has been relettered and amended grammatically.

Division (D) has been relettered. The first sentence, requiring a computation of the guardian fee to be attached to the account has been deleted in that the computation has often been previously filed thus causing a duplicity of filings. The second sentence has been deleted in that the compensation is set by local rule as required in division (A). The statement requiring the filing of the local rule with the Supreme Court has been deleted in that the filing is required by Sup. R. 5(A) and Sup. R. 75.

Cross References

Damages for wrongful death, O Const Art I §19a

Library References

Compromise and Settlement ⇐66.1
Westlaw Topic No. 89.
C.J.S. Compromise and Settlement § 2.

Research References

Encyclopedias

OH Jur. 3d Guardian & Ward § 26, Single or Multiple Guardians.

Treatises and Practice Aids

Carlin, Baldwin's Ohio Practice, Merrick-Rippner Probate Law App B SPF 14.0, Application to Approve Settlement and Distribution of Wrongful Death and Survival Claims—Form.

Carlin, Baldwin's Ohio Practice, Merrick-Rippner Probate Law App B SPF 14.1, Waiver and Consent Wrongful Death and Survival Claims—Form.

Carlin, Baldwin's Ohio Practice, Merrick-Rippner Probate Law App B SPF 22.3, Verification of Receipt and Deposit—Form.

Sup R 74   Trustee's compensation

(A) Trustee's compensation shall be set by local rule.

(B) Additional compensation for extraordinary services may be allowed upon application setting forth an itemized statement of the services rendered and the amount of compensation requested. The court may require that the application be set for hearing with notice given to interested parties in accordance with Civil Rule 73(E).

(C) The compensation of co-trustees in the aggregate shall not exceed the compensation that would have been allowed to one trustee acting alone, except where the instrument under which the co-trustees are acting provides otherwise.

(D) Except for good cause shown, neither compensation for a trustee nor fees to counsel representing the trustee shall be allowed while the trustee is delinquent in the filing of an account.

(E) The court may deny or reduce compensation if there is a delinquency in the filing of an inventory or account, or after hearing, the court finds the trustee has not faithfully discharged the duties of the office.

(Adopted eff. 7–1–97; amended eff. 10–1–97)

Historical and Statutory Notes

Ed. Note: Sup R 74 is analogous to former C P Sup R 43, adopted eff. 9–1–84.

Staff Notes

1997:

This rule is analogous to former C.P. Sup. R. 43. The statement requiring the filing of the local rule with the Supreme Court has been deleted from division (A) in that the filing is required by Sup. R. 5(A) and Sup. R. 75.

Former C.P. Sup. R. 43(C) has been deleted as being unnecessary.

Former C.P. Sup. R. 43(D) has been relettered division (C) and amended to clarify the requirements and procedure for extraordinary compensation for the trustee. The procedure parallels the procedure that was previously in place for extraordinary compensation to an executor or administrator. Division (C) incorporates the requirements of former C.P. Sup. R. 43(C), which has been deleted. The reference to service in accordance with Civil Rule 4.1 has been revised, since service is controlled by Civil Rule 73.

Former C.P. Sup. R. 43(E) has been relettered as division (D) and has been amended grammatically without substantive changes.

Division (E) is new and parallels R.C. 2113.35. It defines the delinquent filing of inventories and accounts as acts that are included within the phrase "not faithfully discharged other duties of the office".

Library References

Costs ⚖194.48.
Westlaw Topic No. 102.
C.J.S. Costs § 126.

Research References

Treatises and Practice Aids

Carlin, Baldwin's Ohio Practice, Merrick-Rippner Probate Law App B SPF 14.0, Application to Approve Settlement and Distribution of Wrongful Death and Survival Claims—Form.

Law Review and Journal Commentaries

More reflections on contingency fee contracts, Matt Kolb. 10 Ohio Law 8 (May/June 1996).

Notes of Decisions

Acquiescence of interested parties 1
Approval 2

1. Acquiescence of interested parties

Attorneys hired by administrator of estate for purposes of wrongful death action were entitled to contingency fee award based on amount of settlement, in light of settlement beneficiary's acquiescence in administrator's decision to employ counsel on contingency basis and in administrator's selection of counsel, and absent any evidence that administrator abused her discretion. (Annotation from former C P Sup R 39.) In re Estate of Craig (Butler 1993) 89 Ohio App.3d 80, 623 N.E.2d 620. Death ⚖ 109

2. Approval

Probate court's awarding trustee fees and expenses to trustee of testamentary trust during period in which proper distribution of deceased beneficiary's trust share was in dispute was not an abuse of discretion, where evidence supported a finding that trustee was reasonable in its refusal to distribute share. Natl. City Bank v. Beyer (Ohio, 06-21-2000) 89 Ohio St.3d 152, 729 N.E.2d 711, 2000-Ohio-126. Wills ⚖ 681(1)

Probate court, in order to maintain control over any personal injury settlement entered into on behalf of ward under its protection, has subject matter jurisdiction over entire amount of settlement funds, which includes attorney fees to be drawn therefrom. (Annotation from former C P Sup R 39.) In re Guardianship of Jadwisiak (Ohio 1992) 64 Ohio St.3d 176, 593 N.E.2d 1379. Guardian And Ward ⚖ 123

A probate court's finding that a contingent fee agreement regarding a personal injury claim of a minor ward under which an attorney would have received one-third of a $90,000 settlement, was not an enforceable contract because (1) it was signed only by the parents, (2) it was signed when the parents were under great mental stress, and (3) it was not approved by the court prior to the agreement being entered into by the guardian as required by statute, and in the place of the agreement, awarding the attorney $9,142.50, the reasonable value of his services (60.95 hours X $150 per hour), plus costs and expenses advanced of $423.50, does not constitute an abuse of discretion. (Annotation from former C P Sup R 39.) In re Guardianship of Patrick (Huron 1991) 66 Ohio App.3d 415, 584 N.E.2d 86.

A contingent fee contract is not binding on two children who were injured after being struck by an automobile driven by a drunk driver where counsel fails to obtain court preapproval of the contingent fee contract as required by CP Sup R 39 and local court rule; furthermore, even if the contingent fee contract was preapproved by the court, the court still has jurisdiction to look into the reasonableness of the approved fee. (Annotation from former C P Sup R 39.) In re Settlements of Betts (Ohio Com.Pl. 1991) 62 Ohio Misc.2d 30, 587 N.E.2d 997.

Sup R 75 Local rules

Local rules of the court shall be numbered to correspond with the numbering of these rules and shall incorporate the number of the rule it is intended to supplement. For example, a local rule that supplements Sup. R. 61 shall be designated County Local Rule 61.1.

(Adopted eff. 7–1–97; amended eff. 10–1–97)

Historical and Statutory Notes

Ed. Note: Sup R 75 is analogous to former C P Sup R 44, adopted eff. 9–1–84.

Staff Notes

1997:

This rule is analogous to former C.P. Sup. R. 44. Former C.P. Sup. R. 44(A) has been deleted entirely as its provisions are addressed adequately by Sup. R. 5.

Research References

Treatises and Practice Aids

Carlin, Baldwin's Ohio Practice, Merrick-Rippner Probate Law § 2:2, Explanation of Fees and Expenses.

Carlin, Baldwin's Ohio Practice, Merrick-Rippner Probate Law § 64:68, Application by Guardian for Authority to Pay Attorney Fees—Form.

Carlin, Baldwin's Ohio Practice, Merrick-Rippner Probate Law § 64:69, Entry for Guardian to Pay Attorney Fees—Form.

Carlin, Baldwin's Ohio Practice, Merrick-Rippner Probate Law § 80:26, Application for Authority to Pay Attorney Fees—Form.

Carlin, Baldwin's Ohio Practice, Merrick-Rippner Probate Law § 80:27, Entry for Payment of Attorney Fees—Form.

Sup R 76 Exception to the rules

Upon application, and for good cause shown, the probate division of the court of common pleas may grant exception to Sup. R. 53 to 79.

(Adopted eff. 7–1–97; amended eff. 10–1–97)

Historical and Statutory Notes

Ed. Note: Sup R 76 is analogous to former C P Sup R 45, adopted eff. 9–1–84.

Staff Notes

1997:

This rule is identical to former C.P. Sup. R. 45.

Library References

Executors and Administrators ⚖495(1), 497, 498.
Westlaw Topic No. 162.
C.J.S. Executors and Administrators §§ 252, 822, 827, 831.

Research References

Treatises and Practice Aids

Carlin, Baldwin's Ohio Practice, Merrick-Rippner Probate Law § 80:24, Application for Extraordinary Compensation—Form.

Carlin, Baldwin's Ohio Practice, Merrick-Rippner Probate Law § 80:25, Entry for Extraordinary Compensation—Form.

Carlin, Baldwin's Ohio Practice, Merrick-Rippner Probate Law § 30:169, Compensation: Specific Sum to Individual—Form.

Sup R 77 Compliance

Failure to comply with these rules may result in sanctions as the court may direct.

(Adopted eff. 7–1–97; amended eff. 10–1–97)

Historical and Statutory Notes

Ed. Note: Sup R 77 is analogous to former C P Sup R 46, adopted eff. 9–1–84.

Staff Notes

1997:

This rule is identical to former C.P. Sup. R. 46.

Library References

Guardian and Ward ⬅150.
Mental Health ⬅181 to 185.
Westlaw Topic Nos. 196, 257A.
C.J.S. Guardian and Ward §§ 162, 163.

Research References

Treatises and Practice Aids

Carlin, Baldwin's Ohio Practice, Merrick-Rippner Probate Law § 64:66, Application for Compensation—Guardian—Form.

Carlin, Baldwin's Ohio Practice, Merrick-Rippner Probate Law § 64:67, Order for Compensation—Guardian—Form.

Carlin, Baldwin's Ohio Practice, Merrick-Rippner Probate Law § 80:24, Application for Extraordinary Compensation—Form.

Carlin, Baldwin's Ohio Practice, Merrick-Rippner Probate Law § 80:25, Entry for Extraordinary Compensation—Form.

Carlin, Baldwin's Ohio Practice, Merrick-Rippner Probate Law App B SPF 14.0, Application to Approve Settlement and Distribution of Wrongful Death and Survival Claims—Form.

Carlin, Baldwin's Ohio Practice, Merrick-Rippner Probate Law App B SPF 14.1, Waiver and Consent Wrongful Death and Survival Claims—Form.

Sup R 78 Probate division of the court of common pleas—case management in decedent's estates, guardianship, and trusts

(A) Each fiduciary shall adhere to the statutory or court-ordered time period for filing the inventory, account, and, if applicable, guardian's report. The citation process set forth in section 2109.31 of the Revised Code shall be utilized to ensure compliance. The attorney of record and the fiduciary shall be subject to the citation process. The court may modify or deny fiduciary commissions or attorney fees, or both, to enforce adherence to the filing time periods.

(B)(1) If a decedent's estate must remain open more than six months pursuant to R.C. 2109.301(B)(1), the fiduciary shall file an application to extend administration (Standard Probate Form 13.8).

(2) An application to extend the time for filing an inventory, account, or guardian's report, shall not be granted unless the fiduciary has signed the application.

(C) The fiduciary and the attorney shall prepare, sign, and file a written status report with the court in all decedent's estates that remain open after a period of thirteen months from the date of the appointment of the fiduciary and annually thereafter. At the court's discretion, the fiduciary and the attorney shall appear for a status review.

(D) The court may issue a citation to the attorney of record for a fiduciary who is delinquent in the filing of an inventory, account, or guardian's report to show cause why the attorney should not be barred from being appointed in any new proceeding before the court or serving as attorney of record in any new estate, guardianship, or trust until all of the delinquent pleadings are filed.

(E) Upon filing of the exceptions to an inventory or to an account, the exceptor shall cause the exceptions to be set for a pretrial within thirty days. The attorneys and their clients, or individuals if not represented by an attorney, shall appear at the pretrial. The trial shall be set as soon as practical after pretrial. The court may dispense with the pretrial and proceed directly to trial.

(Adopted eff. 7–1–97; amended eff. 10–1–97, 12–1–02)

Historical and Statutory Notes

Amendment Note: The 12–1–02 amendment added divisions (B)(1) and (B)(2); substituted "thirteen months" for "one year" and inserted "and annually thereafter" in division (C).

Staff Notes

1997:

This rule imposes case management standards for actions filed in the probate division of the court of common pleas. In addition to establishing time periods for filing of documents and conducting pretrials and trials, the rule requires that an application for a continuance must be signed by the fiduciary and that written status reports be filed in estates that are open for more than one year. The rule also contains a citation procedure that may be employed to bar an attorney who is delinquent in the filing of an inventory, account, or guardian's report from being appointed or serving as attorney of record in any new proceeding until all delinquent pleadings have been filed.

Library References

Trusts ⬅315(1) to 321.
Westlaw Topic No. 390.
C.J.S. Trusts §§ 396 to 408.

Research References

Treatises and Practice Aids

Carlin, Baldwin's Ohio Practice, Merrick-Rippner Probate Law § 80:24, Application for Extraordinary Compensation—Form.

Carlin, Baldwin's Ohio Practice, Merrick-Rippner Probate Law § 80:25, Entry for Extraordinary Compensation—Form.

Carlin, Baldwin's Ohio Practice, Merrick-Rippner Probate Law App B SPF 13.8, Application and Entry to Extend Administration.

Carlin, Baldwin's Ohio Practice, Merrick-Rippner Probate Law App B SPF 13.10, Notice to Extend Administration.

Sup R 99 Effective date

(A) Except as otherwise provided in this rule, the Rules of Superintendence, adopted by the Supreme Court of Ohio on April 15, 1997, shall take effect on July 1, 1997. The rules govern all proceedings in actions brought on or after the effective date and to further proceedings in actions then pending, except to the extent that application in a particular pending action would not be feasible or would work an injustice, in which case the former procedure applies. Sup.R. 37(A)(4)(b) and (c) and 43(B)(2) shall take effect January 1, 1998.

(B) The amendments to Sup. R. 51 to 78, adopted by the Supreme Court of Ohio on July 7, 1997, shall take effect on October 1, 1997.

(C) Sup. R. 26 to 26.05, adopted by the Supreme Court of Ohio on July 7, 1997, shall take effect on October 1, 1997.

(D) The amendments to standard probate forms 18.0, 18.1, 18.2, 18.3, 18.4, 18.5, 18.6, 18.7, 18.8, and 18.9, adopted by the Supreme Court of Ohio on August 26, 1997, shall take effect on October 1, 1997.

(E) The amendments to Sup. R. 26.02 to 26.05 adopted by the Supreme Court of Ohio on September 9, 1997, shall take effect on October 1, 1997.

(F) Sup. R. 10.01 and 10.02 and standard domestic violence protection order forms 10.01–A to 10.01–J and 10.02–A, adopted by the Supreme Court of Ohio on October 7, 1997, shall take effect January 1, 1998.

(G) The amendments to standard domestic violence protection order form 10.02–A, adopted by the Supreme Court of Ohio on November 4, 1997, shall take effect on January 1, 1998.

(H) Effective date of amendments. The amendments to Rule 16, adopted by the Supreme Court of September 9, 1997, shall take effect on November 24, 1997.

(I) The amendments to Sup. R. 10 and 99 of the Rules of Superintendence for the Courts of Ohio, and Form 10–A adopted by the Supreme Court on March 24, 1998, shall take effect on March 24, 1998.

(J) The amendments to Sup. R. 9 of the Rules of Superintendence for the Courts of Ohio, adopted by the Supreme Court on May 12, 1998, shall take effect on May 12, 1998.

(K) The amendments to standard probate forms 6.1, 9.0, 9.1, 10.0, 10.1, 10.2, 12.0, 12.1, 14.0, 22.0, and 22.2 adopted by the Supreme Court of Ohio on August 19, 1998, shall take effect on October 1, 1998.

(K) [sic.] The amendments to Sup. R. 10, 10.03 and stalking protection order forms (Forms 10.03–A to 10.03–H), adopted by the Supreme Court of Ohio on December 14, 1999, shall take effect on March 1, 2000.

(L) The amendments to Sup. R. 10.01, Forms 10.01–A through 10.01–J, 10.02–A, and Form 10–A were adopted by the Supreme Court on April 10, 2000, shall take effect on June 1, 2000.

(M) The amendments Sup. R. 52(L) and to standard probate form 18.2, adopted by the Supreme Court of Ohio on May 9, 2000, shall take effect June 12, 2000.

(N) The amendments to Sup. R. 26 and 27 adopted by the Supreme Court on April 24, 2001, shall take effect on July 1, 2001.

(O) The amendments to Sup.R.23.1, Forms 23.1–A to 23.1–C, Sup.R.25 and Form 25–A adopted by the Supreme Court on September 18, 2001, shall take effect on October 15, 2001.

(P) The amendment to Sup R 50(C) adopted by the Supreme Court on February 26, 2002, shall take effect on March 25, 2002.

(Q) The amendments to Sup. R. 10, 10.01, 10.02, and 10.03 adopted by the Supreme Court on February 26, 2002, shall take effect on June 1, 2002.

(Q) [sic.] The amendment to Sup. R. 36.1 adopted by the Supreme Court on March 26, 2002, shall take effect on July 1, 2002.

(R) The amendments to Sup. R. 52(L), 57(G), 59(B), 60(C), 78(B) and (C) and Standard Probate Forms 1.0, 2.0, 2.1, 2.2, 4.0, 4.4, 6.0, 8.0, 8.1, 8.2, 8.3, 8.4, 8.5, 10.4A (eliminated), 13.0, 13.3, 13.8, 13.9, and 13.10 adopted by the Supreme Court on September 17, 2002, shall take effect on December 1, 2002.

(S) The amendment to Sup. R. 20 adopted by the Supreme Court on December 4, 2002, shall take effect January 6, 2003.

(T) The amendments to Sup. R. 41 adopted by the Supreme Court on June 24, 2003, shall take effect on October 1, 2003.

(U) The amendments to Sup. R. 64 and Standard Probate Forms 7.0 and 8.6 adopted by the Supreme Court on February 3, 2004, shall take effect on April 8, 2004.

(V) The amendments to Sup. R. 26.03 and 26.05 adopted by the Supreme Court on September 14, 2004, shall take effect on September 23, 2004.

(W) The amendments to Sup. R. 26.03 and 26.05 adopted by the Supreme Court on February 1, 2005, shall take effect on March 23, 2005.

(X) The amendments to Sup. R. 40 adopted by the Supreme Court on June 14, 2005, shall take effect on July 4, 2005.

(Y) The amendments to standard probate form 15.2, adopted by the Supreme Court of Ohio on June 14, 2005, shall take effect on July 4, 2005.

(Z) The amendments to Sup. R. 16 adopted by the Supreme Court on August 8, 2006 shall take effect on January 1, 2007.

(AA) The amendments to Sup. R. 36 adopted by the Supreme Court of Ohio on September 19, 2006, shall take effect on November 1, 2006.

(BB) The amendments to Sup. R. 71 adopted by the Supreme Court on January 23, 2007 shall take effect on February 1, 2007.

(Adopted eff. 7–1–97; amended eff. 10–1–97, 10–1–97, 10–1–97, 10–1–97, 11–24–97, 1–1–98, 1–1–98, 3–24–98, 5–12–98, 10–1–98, 3–1–00, 6–1–00, 6–12–00, 7–1–01, 10–15–01, 3–25–02, 6–1–02, 7–1–02, 12–1–02, 1–6–03, 10–1–03, 4–8–04, 9–23–04, 3–23–05, 7–4–05, 11–1–06, 1–1–07, 2–1–07)

Historical and Statutory Notes

Ed. Note: Sup R 99 is analogous to former C A Sup R 99, adopted eff. 1–1–90; former C P Sup R 99, adopted eff. 1–1–90; and M C Sup R 99, adopted eff. 1–1–90.

Amendment Note: The 9–23–04 amendment added new division (V).

Amendment Note: The 4–8–04 amendment added new division (U).

Amendment Note: The 10–1–03 amendment added new division (T).

Amendment Note: The 1–6–03 amendment added new division (S).

Amendment Note: The 7–1–02 amendment added new division (Q).

Amendment Note: The 6–1–02 amendment added new division (Q).

Amendment Note: The 3–25–02 amendment added new division (P).

Amendment Note: The 10–15–01 amendment added new division (O).

Amendment Note: The 7–1–01 amendment added new division (N).

Amendment Note: The 6–12–00 amendment added new division (M).

Amendment Note: The 3–1–00 amendment added division (K).

Amendment Note: The 10–1–98 amendment added division (K).

Amendment Note: The 5–12–98 amendment added division (J).

Amendment Note: The 3–24–98 amendment added division (I).

Amendment Note: The 1–1–98 amendments added divisions (F) and (G).

Amendment Note: The 11–24–97 amendment added division (H).

Amendment Note: The 10–1–97 amendments designated the first paragraph as division (A) and added divisions (B), (C), (D), and (E).

Sup R Temp Prov Temporary provision (Hamilton County)

(A) Notwithstanding any rule to the contrary, the Hamilton County Regional Crime Information Center and any courts, county or municipal agencies, and local law enforcement agencies in Hamilton County are authorized to use electronic forms and electronic signatures as necessary to implement the pilot project outlined in the May 10, 2000 letter submitted to the Supreme Court of Ohio. This Temporary Provision applies to all forms, and the signature requirements applicable to those forms, prescribed by or pursuant to rules adopted by the Supreme Court of Ohio.

(B) For purposes of this Temporary Provision:

(1) The filing requirement of any rule shall be considered satisfied if a form containing all information required by a rule is submitted to the proper authority in an electronic format;

(2) The signature requirement of any rule shall be considered satisfied if the individual who is required by rule to affix a signature to a document properly authorizes the use of his or her electronic signature on the document.

(C) The Center shall not materially modify the electronic signature and security aspects of this project, as described in the proposal submitted to the Supreme Court of Ohio on May 10, 2000, without first notifying the Court and obtaining advance approval of the modifications.

(D) Any printed, microfilmed, or imaged copies of electronic documents shall conform to the applicable rules of the Supreme Court and maintained in accordance with the Rules of Superintendence and local records retention rules.

(E) As used in this Temporary Provision:

(1) "Rule" means any provision of the Ohio Rules of Criminal Procedure, Ohio Rules of Civil Procedure, Ohio Rules of Juvenile Procedure, Ohio Rules of Evidence, Ohio Traffic Rules, or Rules of Superintendence of the Courts of Ohio.

(2) "Properly authorizes" means the person responsible for signing a form complies with the specifications prescribed by the Center relative to the use of electronic signatures.

(F) This Temporary Provision shall remain in effect through August 31, 2002.

(Adopted eff. 9–1–00)

Sup R Temp Prov   Temporary provision (Trumbull County)

(A) Notwithstanding any rule to the contrary, the Trumbull County Court of Common Pleas, Probate Division, is authorized to use electronic forms and electronic signatures as necessary to implement the pilot project outlined in the April 25, 2001 letter submitted to the Supreme Court of Ohio. This Temporary Provision applies to all forms, and the signature requirements applicable to those forms, prescribed by or pursuant to rules adopted by the Supreme Court of Ohio.

(B) For purposes of this Temporary Provision:

(1) The filing requirement of any rule shall be considered satisfied if a form containing all information required by a rule is submitted to the proper authority in an electronic format;

(2) The signature requirement of any rule shall be considered satisfied if the individual who is required by rule to affix a signature to a document properly authorizes the use of his or her electronic signature on the document.

(C) The Trumbull County Court of Common Pleas, Probate Division, shall not materially modify the electronic signature and security aspects of this project, as described in the proposal submitted to the Supreme Court of Ohio on April 25, 2001, without first notifying the Court and obtaining advance approval of the modifications.

(D) Any printed, microfilmed, or imaged copies of electronic documents shall conform to the applicable rules of the Supreme Court and maintained in accordance with the Rules of Superintendence and local records retention rules.

(E) As used in this Temporary Provision:

(1) "Rule" means any provision of the Ohio Rules of Criminal Procedure, Ohio Rules of Civil Procedure, Ohio Rules of Juvenile Procedure, Ohio Rules of Evidence, Ohio Traffic Rules, or Rules of Superintendence of the Courts of Ohio.

(2) "Properly authorizes" means the person responsible for signing a form complies with the specifications prescribed by the Trumbull County Court of Common Pleas, Probate Division, relative to the use of electronic signatures.

(F) This Temporary Provision shall remain in effect through June 30, 2003, unless modified or withdrawn by the Supreme Court of Ohio prior to that date.

(Adopted eff. 7–1–01)

Sup R Temp Prov   Temporary provision (Cuyahoga County)

(A) Notwithstanding any rule to the contrary, the Cuyahoga County Court of Common Pleas, General Division, is authorized to use electronic forms and electronic signatures as necessary to implement the pilot project outlined in the January 23, 2001 letter submitted to the Supreme Court of Ohio. This Temporary Provision applies to all forms, and the signature requirements applicable to those forms, prescribed by or pursuant to rules adopted by the Supreme Court of Ohio.

(B) For purposes of this Temporary Provision:

(1) The filing requirement of any rule shall be considered satisfied if a form containing all information required by a rule is submitted to the proper authority in an electronic format;

(2) The signature requirement of any rule shall be considered satisfied if the individual who is required by rule to affix a signature to a document properly authorizes the use of his or her electronic signature on the document.

(C) The Cuyahoga County Court of Common Pleas, General Division, shall not materially modify the electronic signature and security aspects of this project, as described in the proposal submitted to the Supreme Court of Ohio on January 23, 2001, without first notifying the Court and obtaining advance approval of the modifications.

(D) Any printed, microfilmed, or imaged copies of electronic documents shall conform to the applicable rules of the Supreme Court and maintained in accordance with the Rules of Superintendence and local records retention rules.

(E) As used in this Temporary Provision:

(1) "Rule" means any provision of the Ohio Rules of Criminal Procedure, Ohio Rules of Civil Procedure, Ohio Rules of Juvenile Procedure, Ohio Rules of Evidence, Ohio Traffic Rules, or Rules of Superintendence of the Courts of Ohio.

(2) "Properly authorizes" means the person responsible for signing a form complies with the specifications prescribed by the Cuyahoga County Court of Common Pleas, General Division, relative to the use of electronic signatures.

(F) This Temporary Provision shall remain in effect through June 30, 2003, unless modified or withdrawn by the Supreme Court of Ohio prior to that date.

(Adopted eff. 7–1–01)

COMMON PLEAS COURT LOCAL RULES
PROBATE DIVISION
(Selected Counties)

Includes all amendments received by the Publisher through February 1, 2007

Consult *Carlin*, Baldwin's Ohio Practice, Merrick-Rippner Probate Law (*three volumes*) for an in-depth analysis of Ohio probate law, author-drafted and standard probate forms and mortality tables.

CUYAHOGA COUNTY
FRANKLIN COUNTY
HAMILTON COUNTY
LUCAS COUNTY
MONTGOMERY COUNTY
STARK COUNTY
SUMMIT COUNTY

CUYAHOGA COUNTY COURT OF COMMON PLEAS

RULES OF THE PROBATE DIVISION

Rule
- 8.1 Court appointments
- 9.1 Security
- 9.2 Security policy/firearms and dangerous ordnance prohibition
- 11.1 Recording of proceedings
- 40.1 Hearing and submission of motions: objections to interrogatories
- 40.2 Reproduction of hospital records
- 53.1 Hours of the court
- 58.1 Court costs
- 64.1 Inventory
- 64.2 Accounts
- 64.3 Accounts
- 64.4 Accounts
- 66.1 Biennial report
- 66.2 Biennial report
- 66.3 Guardians of adult wards
- 71.1 Counsel fees
- 71.2 Counsel fees in connection with settlement of claims for wrongful death, conscious pain and suffering, claims for personal injuries to persons under guardianship, and settlement of personal injuries to minors under RC 2111.18
- 73.1 Guardian's compensation
- 74.1 Trustee's compensation
- 78.1 Case management
- 78.2 Fiduciary's certificate of notice of admission of will to probate
- 78.3 Jury management plan

Rule 8.1 Court appointments

Persons appointed by the Court to serve as appraisers, fiduciaries, attorneys, magistrates in Involuntary Psychiatric Commitment proceedings, investigators, guardians ad litem, and trustees for suit, shall be selected from lists maintained by the Court.

Appointments will be made from such lists taking into consideration the qualifications, skill, expertise and caseload of the appointee in addition to the type, complexity and requirements of the case.

Court appointees will be paid a reasonable fee with consideration given to the factors contained in DR–2–106 of the Code of Professional Responsibility, the Ohio Revised Code and the Local Rules of Court relating to fees.

The Court shall review Court appointment lists at least twice annually to ensure the equitable distribution of appointments.

(Amended effective November 10, 1997.)

Rule 9.1 Security

As required by Rule 9 of the Rules of Superintendence for Courts of Common Pleas, the Probate Division has adopted and implemented a local Security Policy and Procedures Plan/Manual.

(Adopted effective July 1, 1995.)

Rule 9.2 Security policy/firearms and dangerous ordnance prohibition

No person, including a judge of a court of record of this state, magistrate of a court of record of this state, employee of this court, bailiff or deputy bailiff of a court of record of this state, county prosecutor, assistant county prosecutor, or a secret service officer appointed by a county prosecutor shall knowingly possess, have under their control, convey, or attempt to convey a deadly weapon, firearm, or dangerous ordnance onto the premises of the Cuyahoga County Courthouse ("Court House").

Any person that possesses a valid license to carry a concealed firearm as issued under R.C. 2923.125 or the reciprocity provision contained in R.C. 109.69, and conveys or attempts to convey a firearm into the Court House, shall immediately inform the Cuyahoga County Sheriff ("Sheriff") of the individual's possession of a concealed firearm and shall be instructed by the Sheriff of the general prohibition against the possession of any deadly weapon, firearm, or dangerous ordnance within the Court House. The Sheriff shall not take possession of any firearm carried by a properly licensed person, but shall require that the licensee leave the Court House and further instruct the licensee to safely secure the firearm outside the Court House. Admittance of the licensee shall be permitted once the firearm has been safely secured outside the Court House and the licensee passes the security screening procedure as contained in the "Security Policy and Procedures Manual/Plan" as implemented by this court on June 29, 1995.

A peace officer or an officer of any law enforcement agency of the State of Ohio or another state, a peace officer or an officer of a political subdivision of the State of Ohio or another state, or an officer or agent of the United States of America, who is authorized to carry a deadly weapon, firearm, or dangerous ordnance, that possesses or has under that individual's control a deadly weapon, firearm, or ordnance, and who is acting within the scope of that individual's duties at the time of possession or control, shall immediately inform the Sheriff of the possession of the deadly weapon, firearm, or ordnance to the Sheriff prior to entering the Court House. The Sheriff shall secure the surrendered deadly weapon, firearm, or ordnance within the secured "gun lock boxes" located at the street level entrance and rear parking garage entrance to the Court House. The deadly weapon, firearm, or dangerous ordnance shall be returned to the individual upon leaving the Court House. This Local Rule of Court is not applicable to the Sheriff, Deputy Sheriffs, or a Cuyahoga County Central Services/Protective Services Officer while they are on official duty within the Court House.

The Sheriff shall post signs, at the street level entrance and the rear parking garage entrance to the Court House, which contain the following language: "Unless otherwise authorized by law pursuant to the Ohio Revised Code and Local Rule of Court, no person shall knowingly possess, have under the person's control, convey, or attempt to convey a deadly weapon, firearm, or dangerous ordnance onto the premises of the Cuyahoga County Court House. **THE CARRYING OF A CONCEALED FIREARM OR THE OPEN CARRY OF A FIREARM, WITHIN THE CUYAHOGA COUNTY COURT HOUSE, IS PROHIBITED BY LOCAL RULE OF COURT AS AUTHORIZED BY OHIO REVISED CODE § 2923.123 (C)(6)."**

(Adopted effective May 24, 2004.)

Rule 11.1   Recording of proceedings

Proceedings before a judge, magistrate, or referee may be recorded by stenographic means or other electronic means approved by the Court, provided that any party or counsel requesting such recording shall make satisfactory arrangements for payment of the costs.

(Adopted effective July 1, 1995.)

Rule 40.1   Hearing and submission of motions: objections to interrogatories

(A) Motions, in general, shall be submitted and determined upon the pleadings and motion papers. Oral arguments of motions may be permitted at the discretion of the Court.

(B) The moving party shall serve and file with the motion a brief written statement of reasons in support of the motion and a list of citations of authorities. If the motion requires consideration of facts not appearing of record, the movant shall serve and file copies of all affidavits, depositions, photographs or documentary evidence which the movant relies upon in support of the motion.

(C) Each party opposing the motion, except a motion for summary judgment, shall serve and file within seven (7) days thereafter, a brief written statement of reasons in opposition to the motion and a list of citations of the authorities which are relied upon. If the motion requires the consideration of facts not appearing of record, the respondent shall also serve and file copies of all affidavits, depositions, photographs or documentary evidence which the respondent relies upon.

(D) Reply or additional briefs upon motions and submissions may be filed with leave of the Court only upon a showing of good cause.

(E) Objections to interrogatories shall include, immediately preceding any discussions and citation of authority, the interrogatory in full to which objection is made.

(F) Counsel are encouraged to participate in pretrial discovery conferences to reduce the filing of unnecessary discovery procedures. To curtail undue delay in the administration of justice, no discovery procedure filed under Rule 26 through 37 of the Rules of Civil Procedure to which objection or opposition is made by the responding party shall be taken under consideration by the Court, unless the party seeking discovery shall first advise the Court in writing that after personal consultation and sincere attempts to resolve differences they are unable to reach an accord. This statement shall recite those matters which remain in dispute, and in addition, the date, time and place of such conference, and the names of all participating parties. It shall be the responsibility of counsel for the party seeking discovery to initiate such personal consultation.

(G) The presentation to the Court of unnecessary motions, and the unwarranted opposition of motions, which in either case unduly delay the course of an action through the Courts, subject an offender to appropriate sanctions including the imposition of costs.

(H) All pleadings and briefs containing references to statutes, or regulations, unpublished cases or cases from Courts outside of this state except U. S. Supreme Court decisions shall have attached a copy of the statute, regulations or case. A party who cites an unpublished opinion or case shall indicate any disposition by a superior appellate Court.

(I) Unless otherwise ordered by the Court,

(1) a party opposing a motion for summary judgment made pursuant to Civil Rule 56 may file a brief in opposition with accompanying evidentiary materials (as permitted by Civil Rule 56 (c)) within 30 days of service of the motion. The movant may file a reply brief in support of the motion within ten (10) days of service of the brief in opposition. The movant's reply brief shall not refer to or include any additional evidentiary materials without agreement of the parties or leave of Court.

(2) unless otherwise ordered by the Court, motions for summary judgment shall be heard on briefs and accompanying evidentiary materials (as permitted by Civil Rule 56 (c)) without oral argument.

(Adopted effective June 1, 2005.)

Rule 40.2   Reproduction of hospital records

(A) Upon motion of any party showing good cause and upon notice to all other parties and the individual who is the subject of the reports, the judge may order any hospital by any agent competent to act in its behalf, to reproduce all or any portion of designated hospital records, not privileged, which constitute or contain evidence pertinent to an action pending in this Court. The order shall direct the hospital to describe by cover letter the portion or portions of the records reproduced and any omissions and specify the usual and reasonable charges. The order shall designate the person or persons to whom such reproductions shall be delivered or made available.

(B) Objections to the admissibility of such reproduced hospital records on the grounds of materiality or competency shall be deemed reserved for ruling at the time of trial without specific reservation in the order to reproduce. Reproductions made pursuant to this procedure may be admitted in evidence without further identification or authentication but subject to rulings or objections impliedly or specifically reserved unless the order expressly provides otherwise.

(C) Charges for reproduction of its records shall be paid directly to the hospital by the movant or movants.

(D) Where original records are produced in Court and reproductions subsequently substituted by agreement of the parties or by order of the Court, the movant or movants shall be responsible for the cost. Unless otherwise ordered by the Court, all original records shall be returned by the Court reporter to the hospital upon entry of judgment in this Court.

(Adopted effective June 1, 2005.)

Rule 53.1   Hours of the court

The Probate Court and its offices shall be open for the transaction of business from 8:30 a.m. to 4:30 p.m. daily except Saturday, Sunday and legal holidays.

(Amended effective September 14, 1987.)

Rule 58.1   Court costs

Deposits in the amounts set forth below shall be required upon filing the following initial actions and proceedings:

INITIAL COURT COST DEPOSITS

Adoptions $135.00
  –Petitions for Release of Identifying Information . $ 50.00
  –Motions to Determine Suitability .... $ 20.00
  –Petitions for Foreign Adoptions .... $ 93.00
Adversary Cases $100.00
Birth Record Corrections .... $ 20.00
Birth Record Registrations .... $ 20.00
Conservatorships $100.00
Disinterment Applications .... $ 25.00
Estates $125.00

Guardianships	$100.00
Marriage Licenses	$ 40.00
Name Changes	$100.00
Pay or Deliver Applications	$ 27.00
Release of Assets Without Administration:	
- Without Wills	$ 60.00
- With Wills	$ 95.00
- With Wills and Publication	$122.00
- Supplemental Releases	$ 40.00
Settlement of Injury Claims	$ 22.00
Trusts	$ 75.00
Will Deposits	$ 5.00

Additional court costs for subsequent filings will be assessed in accordance with O.R.C. 2101.16

(Amended effective February 22, 1985; March 13, 1986; January 1, 1990; January 1, 1993; February 1, 1995; September 18, 1996; May 4, 2000.)

Rule 64.1 Inventory

Pursuant to O.R.C. 2115.16 and Civil Rule 73(E)(7) unless notice is waived, upon filing of an inventory as required by R.C. 2115.02, the executor or administrator shall serve the notice of the hearing by ordinary mail upon the surviving spouse and all next of kin in an intestate estate and to all beneficiaries in a testate estate.

Rule 64.2 Accounts

Pursuant to O.R.C. 2109.30, 2109.301–2109.303, 2109.32, 2109.33, and Civil Rule 73(E)(7) unless notice is waived, upon filing of final accounts, the fiduciary shall serve a copy of the account and notice of the hearing by certified mail as follows:

A. Decedent's Estates. To the surviving spouse and all next of kin in an intestate estate and to all residual beneficiaries in a testate estate.

B. Guardianships. To all next of kin of the ward.

C. Trusts. To all beneficiaries.

Any person entitled to notice who is under 16 years of age shall be served in accordance with Civil Rule 4.2(B).

The fiduciary shall file a certificate of service (Form 13.9) or an affidavit with his or her account indicating compliance with the requirements of this Rule. Proof of service by certified mail shall be retained by the fiduciary or counsel.

Rule 64.3 Accounts

In accordance with O.R.C. 2109.301(A) vouchers or proof of disbursements shall not be required to be filed by executors or administrators unless otherwise ordered by Court.

Original vouchers or receipts of disbursements must be filed with accounts of guardians, conservators or trustees.

Rule 64.4 Accounts

In accordance with O.R.C. 2109.301(B) the final account in estates shall be filed within six (6) months after appointment of the executor or administrator.

Upon motion of the fiduciary or counsel for the estate, the time for filing an account in an estate may be extended to thirteen (13) months from the date of appointment or other appropriate time for any of the reasons set forth in O.R.C. 2109.301(B).

Rule 66.1 Biennial report

Effective August 1, 1988 a Biennial Report of the mental and physical condition of the ward must be filed at the time of the filing of a partial account by the guardian of an incompetent person.

(Adopted effective August 1, 1988.)

Rule 66.2 Biennial report

Effective August 1, 1988 a Biennial Report of the mental and physical condition of an adult incompetent must be filed by the guardian of the person only.

(Adopted effective August 1, 1988.)

Rule 66.3 Guardians of adult wards

Guardians of adult wards shall deposit all wills of their wards, immediately following their appointment, with the Probate Court pursuant to Ohio Revised Code Section 2107.07.

(Adopted effective January 1, 1990.)

Rule 71.1 Counsel fees

(A) Counsel fees allowed as part of the expense for administering a decedent's estate, trust or guardianship, shall be based upon the actual services performed by the attorney and the reasonable value of the services.

(B) All applications for the allowance of attorney fees shall set forth an itemized statement of the services performed, the date services were performed, the time spent in rendering the services, and the rate charged per hour.

(C) Unless otherwise ordered by the Court, where all interested parties have consented in writing to the amount of counsel fees, an application need not be made for allowance, provided the consent is endorsed on the fiduciary account, or evidenced by a separate instrument filed with the account. This provision shall not apply to guardianships.

(D) Prior to a fiduciary entering into a contingent-fee contract with an attorney for services, an application for authority to enter into the contract shall be filed and approved by the Court.

(E) Any services provided by "paralegals" must be performed under the supervision of a licensed attorney who must verify such supervision on the application.

(Amended effective June 1, 1990; January 1, 1993.)

Rule 71.2 Counsel fees in connection with settlement of claims for wrongful death, conscious pain and suffering, claims for personal injuries to persons under guardianship, and settlement of personal injuries to minors under RC 2111.18

In cases where representation is on a contingent basis, counsel will be allowed fees on the amount obtained in accordance with the following schedule:

33 ⅓% of the first $100,000.00;

30% of the amount over $100,000.00.

Upon written application additional compensation may be granted if the applicant demonstrates and the court is satisfied that extraordinary services have been rendered.

Rule 73.1 Guardian's compensation

(A) Unless otherwise provided by law or ordered by the Court, a guardian may charge for ordinary services an amount computed in accordance with the following schedule:

(1) During each accounting period required by statute, 3% of the total income; and 3% of the total expenditures where total expenditures equal less than $200,000.00 or 2% of the total expenditures where total expenditures are equal to or greater than $200,000.00.

(2) An annual fee of $2.00 per $1,000.00 of the fair market value of the principal.

(3) Minimum compensation of $500.00 per year.

(4) Compensation computed on income will not be allowed on balances carried forward from one accounting period to another; nor will an investment of funds of the final distribution of unexpended balances to a ward at the close of a guardianship be considered as an expenditure.

(B) For the purpose of computing a guardian's compensation as herein provided, the fair market value of the principal shall be determined by the guardian as of the appointment date and as of each anniversary thereafter. The compensation so determined may be charged during the ensuing year. The annual principal valuation shall be adjusted from time to time to reflect additions to and withdrawals from the principal of the estate, and the compensation for the remaining portion of the annual period shall be similarly adjusted to reflect such revised valuation.

(C) Additional compensation, reimbursement for expenses incurred, and fees of a guardian of the person only may be fixed by the Court on application. The Court may require that applications for fees or compensation be set for hearing and that written notice of the time and place of the hearing and the amount applied for be given to interested parties, as required by the Court. A copy of the notice, with certified mail return receipt attached, together with an affidavit of the service of such notice, shall be filed prior to the hearing.

(D) The compensation of co-guardians in the aggregate shall not exceed the compensation which would have been payable if only one guardian had been acting.

(E) A separate schedule of the computation of the guardian's compensation shall be set forth in the guardian's account as a condition of its approval.

(F) Except for good cause shown, neither compensation for a guardian nor fees to the attorney representing the guardian, will be allowed when the guardian is delinquent in filing an account as required by RC 2109.30.

(Amended effective April 3, 2006.)

Rule 74.1 Trustee's compensation

(A) Except where the instrument creating the trust makes provision for compensation, a testamentary trustee may charge annually for ordinary services performed by the trustee in connection with the administration of each separate trust estate an amount to be computed on the fair market value of the principal of the trust property, in accordance with the following schedule, such compensation to be charged one-half to income and one-half to principal, unless otherwise provided in the instrument creating the trust:

(1) $12.00 per $1,000.00 on the first $1,000,000.00 of the fair market value of the principal;

$7.50 per $1,000.00 on the next $2,000,000.00 of the fair market value of the principal;

$5.50 per $1,000.00 on the next $2,000,000.00 of the fair market value of the principal;

$4.50 per $1,000.00 on the balance of the fair market value of the principal.

(2) The trustee may charge a minimum fee of $1,500.00.

(3) There may be allowed an amount equal to 1% of the fair market value of any distribution or payment from the principal of the trust property. This amount shall be charged against and deducted from the distribution or payment.

(4) A corporate trustee that proves a service which invests all available income and/or principal cash on a daily basis may be allowed an amount equal to one-half of one percent (0.5%), on an annual basis, of the amount invested, but not in excess of $100 per month.

(B) For the purpose of computing the trustee's compensation as herein provided, the fair market value of the principal of the trust property shall be determined by the trustee as of a date determined by the trustee, such date to commence during the month of the original receipt of trust property and each anniversary date thereafter. (At the option of the trustee, fee evaluations may be made on a quarterly basis, each evaluation to be coordinated with the original annual evaluation date as selected by the trustee—if this option is selected by the trustee, the trustee must continue to compute the fee on the quarterly valuation basis, unless upon application to the Probate Court, a change in fee valuation method is allowed.)

(C) Additional compensation for extraordinary services may be allowed upon application. The Court may require that the application be set for hearing and notice thereof be given to interested parties in accordance with Civil Rule 4.1. The notice shall contain a statement of amount of the compensation sought.

(D) The compensation of co-trustees in the aggregate shall not exceed the compensation which would have been payable if only one trustee had been acting, except in the following instances:

(1) Where the instrument under which the co-trustees are acting provides otherwise; or

(2) Where all the interested parties have consented in writing to the amount of the co-trustees' compensation, and the consent is endorsed on the trustees' account or evidenced by separate instrument filed therewith.

(E) A separate schedule of the computation of trustee's compensation shall be shown in the trustee's account as a condition of its approval.

(F) Except for good cause shown, neither compensation for a trustee nor fees to the counsel representing the trustee will be allowed while the trustee is delinquent in filing an account required by RC 2109.30.

(Amended effective September 30, 1986; March 1, 1988; September 15, 1999; April 3, 2006.)

Rule 78.1 Case management

I. Supervision of Estates, Trusts and Guardianships, Adoption and Psychiatric Proceedings.

A. The Court shall keep an inventory of all pending cases.

B. Each successive month, the Court shall make a report:

1. listing all new cases filed;

2. removing all cases where a final account has been approved or final judgment has been rendered;

3. listing the status of each open case.

II. Civil Actions.

A. The Court shall keep an inventory of all pending cases.

B. Each successive month, the Court shall make a report:

1. listing all new cases filed;

2. removing all cases where a final judgment has been rendered;
   3. listing the status of each open case.

C. A pretrial conference shall be conducted in all cases prior to trial except in land sale proceedings.

D. Within 30 days after the answer date, the case shall be set by the Court for a pretrial conference.

E. Notice of the pretrial conference shall be given to all parties or their counsel of record by certified mail not less than 14 days prior to the conference. Applications for continuance of the conference shall be in writing and filed with the Court in a timely manner.

F. At the conclusion of the pretrial conference, the Court shall prepare a pretrial order setting forth:
   1. discovery deadline date;
   2. exchange of witness list date;
   3. pleadings and briefing date;
   4. trial date.

III. Land Sales.

A. The Court shall keep an inventory of all pending cases.

B. All land sales which have not been concluded within one year from the date of filing shall be dismissed unless good cause is shown.

(Adopted effective July 1, 1991.)

Rule 78.2   Fiduciary's certificate of notice of admission of will to probate

Effective January 2, 2002, fiduciaries appointed to administer estates of decedents are required to file a Certificate of Notice of Admission of the Will to Probate within sixty (60) days of their appointment or be subject to removal proceedings.

Rule 78.3   Jury management plan

As required by Rule 9(C) of the Rules of Superintendence for Courts of Common Pleas, the Probate Division has adopted and implemented a Jury Management Plan which has been filed with the Supreme Court of Ohio.

(Adopted effective September 1, 1995.)

FRANKLIN COUNTY COURT OF COMMON PLEAS

RULES OF THE PROBATE DIVISION

Rule
Introduction

SUP R. 8. COURT APPOINTMENTS
Loc R. 8.1   Court appointments

SUP R. 9. SECURITY PLAN
Loc R. 9.1   Security plan

SUP R. 11. RECORDING OF PROCEEDINGS
Loc R. 11.1   Recording of proceedings

SUP R. 26. COURT RECORDS MANAGEMENT AND RETENTION
Loc R. 26.1   Court records management and retention
Loc R. 26.2   Disposition of exhibits

SUP R. 51. STANDARD PROBATE FORMS
Loc R. 51.1   Form availability

SUP R. 52. SPECIFICATIONS FOR PRINTING PROBATE FORMS
Loc R. 52.1   Computerized forms
Loc R. 52.2   Form specifications

SUP R. 53. HOURS OF THE COURT
Loc R. 53.1   Hours of the court

SUP R. 55. EXAMINATION OF PROBATE RECORDS
Loc R. 55.1   Withdrawal of files
Loc R. 55.2   Photocopies

SUP R. 57. FILINGS AND JUDGMENT ENTRIES
Loc R. 57.1   Facsimile filings
Loc R. 57.2   Court file
Loc R. 57.3   Complete street address
Loc R. 57.4   Case number
Loc R. 57.5   Original signatures
Loc R. 57.6   Fiduciary signature
Loc R. 57.7   Court filings
Loc R. 57.8   Forwarding copies
Loc R. 57.9   Issuance of summons
Loc R. 57.10   Computer disks
Loc R. 57.11   Death certificate to be exhibited
Loc R. 57.12   Certificate of notice of entry of judgment
Loc R. 57.13   Length of briefs
Loc R. 57.14   Social security numbers
Loc R. 57.15   Certificate of service
Loc R. 57.16   Filings for matters assigned to an acting judge

SUP R. 58. DEPOSIT FOR COURT COSTS
Loc R. 58.1   Deposits
Loc R. 58.2   Witness fees
Loc R. 58.3   Release of adoption information
Loc R. 58.4   Filing transcripts, exhibits, or foreign records

SUP R. 59. WILLS
Loc R. 59.1   Certificate of service of notice of probate of will

SUP R. 60. APPLICATION FOR LETTERS OF AUTHORITY TO ADMINISTER ESTATE AND NOTICE OF APPOINTMENT
Loc R. 60.1   Fiduciary's acceptance
Loc R. 60.2   Appointment of nonresident fiduciaries
Loc R. 60.3   Rule deleted
Loc R. 60.4   Identification with photograph required

Rule

SUP R. 61. APPRAISERS
Loc R. 61.1   Appraisers' fees
Loc R. 61.2   Appraiser self-dealing

SUP R. 62. CLAIMS AGAINST ESTATE
Loc R. 62.1   Deposit

SUP R. 64. ACCOUNTS
Loc R. 64.1   Fiduciary's signature
Loc R. 64.2   Delinquency in filing an account
Loc R. 64.3   Vouchers
Loc R. 64.4   Bond
Loc R. 64.5   Evidence of assets
Loc R. 64.6   Payment of debts
Loc R. 64.7   Time for filing
Loc R. 64.8   Certificate of service of notice to heirs

SUP R. 66. GUARDIANSHIPS
Loc R. 66.1   Guardianship of minors
Loc R. 66.2   Safe deposit box
Loc R. 66.3   Release of funds
Loc R. 66.4   Deposit of wills
Loc R. 66.5   Change of address
Loc R. 66.6   Guardian's report
Loc R. 66.7   Termination
Loc R. 66.8   Notice for guardianship of adults
Loc R. 66.9   Background Investigations
Loc R. 66.10   Indigent guardianships

SUP R. 67. ESTATES OF MINORS OF NOT MORE THAN TEN THOUSAND DOLLARS
Loc R. 67.1   Dispense with guardianship
Loc R. 67.2   Birth certificate
Loc R. 67.3   Attorney responsibility
Loc R. 67.4   Annual statements

SUP R. 68. SETTLEMENT OF INJURY CLAIMS OF MINORS
Loc R. 68.1   Birth certificate
Loc R. 68.2   Settlement conference
Loc R. 68.3   Deposit of proceeds
Loc R. 68.4   Structured settlements
Loc R. 68.5   Application to settle claim

SUP R. 70. SETTLEMENT OF WRONGFUL DEATH AND SURVIVAL CLAIMS
Loc R. 70.1   Settlement of claims
Loc R. 70.2   Wrongful death prototype trust
Loc R. 70.3   Wrongful death trust with multiple beneficiaries
Loc R. 70.4   Settlement conference

SUP R. 71. COUNSEL FEES
Loc R. 71.1   Attorney fees
Loc R. 71.2   Attorney serving as fiduciary
Loc R. 71.3   Early payment of attorney fees
Loc R. 71.4   Notice and consent for attorney fees in estates
Loc R. 71.5   Notice and consent for attorney fees in guardianships
Loc R. 71.6   Notice and consent for attorney fees in trusts
Loc R. 71.7   Contested fees
Loc R. 71.8   Contingent fees

SUP R. 73. GUARDIAN'S COMPENSATION
Loc R. 73.1   Guardian's compensation

Rule
Loc R. 73.2 Payments from the Indigent Guardianship Fund

SUP R. 74. TRUSTEE'S COMPENSATION
Loc R. 74.1 Trustee's compensation

SUP R. 75. LOCAL RULES
Loc R. 75.1 Guardian ad litem
Loc R. 75.2 Adoptions
Loc R. 75.3 Custodial deposits in lieu of bond
Loc R. 75.4 Surety bonds
Loc R. 75.5 Release of estates from administration
Loc R. 75.6 Pro hac vice
Loc R. 75.7 Additional fees
Loc R. 75.8 Registration of paralegals
Loc R. 75.9 Wills deposited for safekeeping
Loc R. 75.10 Applicants will exhibit photographic identification
Loc R. 75.11 Objections to magistrate's decision
Loc R. 75.12 Wills in safe deposit box
Loc R. 75.13 Service of summons
Loc R. 75.14 Marriage license applicants
Loc R. 75.15 Ohio estate tax return
Loc R. 75.16 Surviving spouse waiver of service of the citation to elect
Loc R. 75.17 Virtual service

SUP R. 78. CASE MANAGEMENT IN DECEDENT'S ESTATES, GUARDIANSHIPS, AND TRUSTS
Loc R. 78.1 Case management
Loc R. 78.2 Withdrawal of counsel
Loc R. 78.3 Inventory
Loc R. 78.4 Request for jury trial
Loc R. 78.5 Mediation
Loc R. 78.6 Extended administration
Loc R. 78.7 Special needs trusts

Introduction

The following rules are supplemental to the *Rules of Superintendence for the Courts of Ohio* and must be read in conjunction therewith.

SUP R. 8. COURT APPOINTMENTS

Loc. R. 8.1 Court appointments

Persons appointed by the Court to serve as appraisers, fiduciaries, attorneys, magistrates in Involuntary Psychiatric Commitment proceedings, investigators, guardians ad litem, and trustees for suit, shall be selected from lists maintained by the Court.

Appointments will be made from such lists taking into consideration the qualifications, skills, expertise, and caseload of the appointee in addition to the type, complexity, and requirements of the case.

Court appointees will be paid a reasonable fee with consideration given to the factors contained in DR 2–106 of the Code of Professional Responsibility, the Ohio Revised Code, and the Local Rules of Court relating to fees.

The Court will review Court appointment lists periodically to ensure the equitable distribution of appointments.

SUP R. 9. SECURITY PLAN

Loc. R. 9.1 Security plan

Pursuant to a Supreme Court of Ohio resolution dated July 26, 1995, the Franklin County Probate Court has determined the entire Security Plan as submitted to the Supreme Court of Ohio, effective January 1, 2001, be maintained as confidential and not a matter of public record.

SUP R. 11. RECORDING OF PROCEEDINGS

Loc. R. 11.1 Recording of proceedings

(A) The Court will make a digital recording of proceedings as the official record of the Court. Parties who desire to have a contemporaneous stenographic record of the proceedings must make their own arrangements, at least twenty-four (24) hours prior to the scheduled hearing, for a court reporter to appear at the hearing. The requesting party shall pay the costs associated with the stenographic record of the hearing unless otherwise ordered by the Court.

(B) Any interested person may request a recording of a hearing be transcribed by a stenographer approved by the Court. The person making the request shall pay the cost of transcription. A transcript filed with the Court under this paragraph shall supersede the digital recording as the official record of the Court.

(C) The Court will allow a person to listen to a recording of a hearing at the Court upon request made no less than twenty-four (24) hours in advance.

(D) An interested party will not be allowed to use the contents of a recording in subsequent pleadings filed with the Court or in argument before the Court unless a transcript of the entire hearing is filed with the Court as provided in paragraph (B) of this rule.

(E) All digital recorded proceedings will be maintained by the Court for three (3) years from the date of the hearing. Any interested person desiring to preserve the record beyond that period must arrange to have the record transcribed as provided by paragraph (B) of this rule and file the transcript in the underlying case. (Eff. 01/01/06)

SUP R. 26. COURT RECORDS MANAGEMENT AND RETENTION

Loc. R. 26.1 Court records management and retention

The Court has a Schedule of Records Retention and Disposition filed under case number 411,839, which will be followed in conjunction with the Rules of Superintendence for the Courts of Ohio.

Loc. R. 26.2 Disposition of exhibits

All exhibits offered for admission during a hearing or trial shall be labeled by party name and item identification. In a proceeding recorded by a Court stenographer, custody of exhibits admitted or proffered shall be given to the stenographer, unless otherwise ordered by the Court. If the proceeding is electronically recorded, exhibits shall be filed in the Court case file, unless otherwise ordered by the Court.

Upon agreement of the parties or by order of the Court, copies may be substituted for the original exhibit.

Disposal of exhibits shall be pursuant to Sup. R. 26. (Eff. 1/1/05)

SUP R. 51. STANDARD PROBATE FORMS

Loc. R. 51.1 Form availability

Forms for use in the Franklin County Probate Court are available at the Court and on the Court's website: www.co.franklin.oh.us/probate.

SUP R. 52. SPECIFICATIONS FOR PRINTING PROBATE FORMS

Loc. R. 52.1 Computerized forms

Computer generated forms must comply with the specifications and format outlined by the Rules of Superintendence. The signature of the applicant or attorney constitutes a certificate that the computer generated forms comply with the rules.

All computer forms presented for filing must be generated with the exact wording as well as blank lines as they appear in the uniform forms.

Loc. R. 52.2 Form specifications

The type size for the body of all forms filed in this Court cannot be less than ten (10) point, nor greater than twelve (12) point.

SUP R. 53. HOURS OF THE COURT

Loc. R. 53.1 Hours of the court

The Probate Court shall be open for the transaction of business from 8:00 a.m. to 5:00 p.m., Monday through Friday, except holidays. All pleadings requiring a new case number or the payment of Court costs shall be filed by 4:30 p.m.

SUP R. 55. EXAMINATION OF PROBATE RECORDS

Loc. R. 55.1 Withdrawal of files

Each Court file withdrawn from the Records Department must be accompanied by a withdrawal card. No person may withdraw more than six (6) files at a time from the Records Department.

Only attorneys and recognized title examiners are permitted to remove files from the Court. The removal of the file from the Court must be approved by the Judge or a Magistrate.

All files removed from the Court must be returned the following business day.

Loc. R. 55.2 Photocopies

Copies of any public record may be obtained at the cost of Five cents ($.05) per page.

SUP R. 57. FILINGS AND JUDGMENT ENTRIES

Loc. R. 57.1 Facsimile filings

The Court will not accept filings by facsimile transmission or electronic mail.

Loc. R. 57.2 Court file

All filings presented to the Court must be accompanied by the Court file.

Loc. R. 57.3 Complete street address

When required on a Court document, an address must be a street address and, if applicable, any post office box numbers used as a mailing address. The address of the fiduciary who is not an attorney at law must be the fiduciary's legal residence. A fiduciary who is an attorney at law may use an office address.

Reasonable diligence shall be exercised to obtain the complete street addresses of the surviving spouse, next of kin, legatees and devisees.

Loc. R. 57.4 Case number

All filings, including attachments, must have the case number on each page.

Loc. R. 57.5 Original signatures

All filings must contain original signatures. In all matters with multiple fiduciaries, the signature of all fiduciaries is required on all documents including fiduciary checks. Persons who are not an attorney may not sign on behalf of an attorney.

Loc. R. 57.6 Fiduciary signature

Any pleading, filing, or other document which by law or rule requires the fiduciary's signature, shall have the original signature of the fiduciary. The attorney for the fiduciary may not sign for the fiduciary.

Loc. R. 57.7 Court filings

All filings must be legible, on 8–1/2″ × 11″ paper and the type size for the body of the document be not less than ten (10) point or greater than twelve (12) point. The Court will accept for filing only those pleadings which are complete.

Loc. R. 57.8 Forwarding copies

The Court will not return file-stamped copies by mail unless submitted with a return, self-addressed, stamped envelope.

Loc. R. 57.9 Issuance of summons

A Request for Issuance of Summons (Form 1.P) shall be filed with all original and amended complaints or petitions in civil actions.

Loc. R. 57.10 Computer disks

In addition to filing written original documents, the parties may, or if the Court directs, shall submit proposed entries, briefs, memoranda, jury instructions, or other documents on a computer disk formatted in a manner which may be utilized by the Court's word processing system.

Loc. R. 57.11 Death certificate to be exhibited

Upon the initial filing of any matter captioned in the name of a deceased individual, or the termination of a guardianship due to the death of the ward, the applicant shall exhibit to the court a certified copy of the decedent's death certificate unless waived by the court for good cause shown. (Eff. 01/01/06)

Loc. R. 57.12 Certificate of notice of entry of judgment

Any proposed entry submitted to the Court which is subject to Civ. R. 58(B) as modified by Civ. R. 73(I) shall contain a certificate of service including the names and addresses of all parties and other interested persons required to be served.

Loc. R. 57.13 Length of briefs

Supporting, opposing, and memorandum briefs shall not exceed fifteen (15) pages exclusive of any supporting documents. Briefs exceeding fifteen (15) pages will not be accepted for filing without prior leave of Court.

Loc. R. 57.14 Social security numbers

Social security numbers are confidential and will not be required in any filing in this Court that is available for inspection by the general public. Applicants for guardianships will provide their social security number and the social security number for the proposed ward on a form that will not be disclosed to the general public.

Loc. R. 57.15 Certificate of service

The Certificate of Service shall identify by name all parties served.

Loc. R. 57.16 Filings for matters assigned to an acting judge

All filings in matters assigned to an Acting Judge are to be filed in duplicate with a deputy clerk of this Court and shall have the name of the Acting Judge shown in the caption. The deputy clerk receiving the filing is to be informed at the time of each filing that the matter has been assigned to an Acting Judge. The original filing shall be filed with the clerk of the Probate Court and the duplicate copy shall be submitted to the Acting Judge. (Eff. 01/01/06)

SUP R. 58. DEPOSIT FOR COURT COSTS

Loc. R. 58.1 Deposits

The business of this Court shall be conducted on a cash basis. The Court will not accept fiduciary or personal checks. The Court will only accept cash, money orders, cashier's checks, attorney, title company, or trust company checks.

(A) Filing an application for appointment of any estate fiduciary shall require a minimum deposit of One Hundred Twenty-five and No/100 Dollars ($125.00), however, the Court recommends a deposit of Two Hundred and No/100 Dollars ($200.00).

(B) Filing any complaint, except for the presentation of a claim or a land sale, shall require a minimum deposit of One Hundred Fifty and No/100 Dollars ($150.00).

(C) Filing a complaint for a land sale shall require a minimum deposit of One Hundred Seventy Five and No/100 Dollars ($175.00).

(D) Filing a presentation of a claim against an estate with the Court pursuant to Ohio R.C. 2117.06(A)(2) shall require the filing of a civil action and a minimum deposit of Seventy-five and No/100 Dollars ($75.00).

(E) Filing a subpoena shall require a minimum deposit of Thirty–Eight and No/100 ($38.00) for in county Sheriff service and Twelve and No/100 Dollars ($12.00) for the witness fee. Subpoenas served out of county may require additional deposits and shall include a check for witness and mileage fees made payable to the witness.

(F) In all cases of decedent's estates, civil actions and any other matters requiring a deposit, the fiduciary or plaintiff shall be required to maintain a positive balance in the deposit account.

The Daily Reporter, published by The Daily Reporter, Inc., is designated as the law journal in which the calendar of the Court, including such proceedings and notices as required by law or designated by the Judge, is published. These publication charges shall be charged as costs. (Eff. 01/01/06)

Loc. R. 58.2 Witness fees

Witness fees must be requested at the conclusion of the hearing for which the subpoena was issued. If not requested at that time, the fee is waived. All unused portions of the subpoena deposit will be refunded to the depositor.

Loc. R. 58.3 Release of adoption information

The fee for filing a petition for the release of adoption information pursuant to Ohio R.C. 2101.16(F) shall be Fifty and No/100 Dollars ($50.00).

Loc. R. 58.4 Filing transcripts, exhibits, or foreign records

The filing fee required by Ohio R.C. 2101.16(A)(57) shall be paid at the time of filing the transcript, exhibits, or foreign records.

SUP R. 59. WILLS

Loc. R. 59.1 Certificate of service of notice of probate of will

The applicant for the admission of a will to probate or other person listed in Ohio R.C. 2107.19(A)(4) shall file a Certificate of Service of Notice of Probate Of Will (Standard Probate Form 2.4) not later than two months after the appointment of the fiduciary or, if no fiduciary has been appointed, not later than two months after the admission of the will to probate. Proof of service shall consist of either waivers or notice of the probate of the will or original certified mail return receipt cards as provided under Civil Rule 73(E)(3). A waiver of notice may not be signed by any minor, or on behalf of a minor sixteen (16) or seventeen (17) years of age.

SUP R. 60. APPLICATION FOR LETTERS OF AUTHORITY TO ADMINISTER ESTATE AND NOTICE OF APPOINTMENT

Loc. R. 60.1 Fiduciary's acceptance

All executors and administrators shall personally sign and file the Fiduciary's Acceptance, Form 4.0A, prior to the issuance of the Letters of Authority.

Loc. R. 60.2 Appointment of nonresident fiduciaries

An applicant to be appointed fiduciary of a decedent's estate, or trust, who is not a resident of this state, must be in compliance with Ohio R.C. 2109.21 and use as the attorney of record an attorney licensed to practice law in this State. To assure the assets remain in Franklin County, Ohio, during the administration of the estate or trust, the applicant must meet one or more of the following criteria as required by the Court:

(A) Place a substantial amount of the decedent's personal assets in a custodial depository in this county, pursuant to Ohio R.C. 2109.13;

(B) Have a co-fiduciary who is a resident of this State;

(C) Post a bond in compliance with Ohio R.C. 2109.04.

Loc. R. 60.3 Rule deleted

Loc. R. 60.4 Identification with photograph required

Applicants for Authority to Administer a Decedent's Estate, who are not represented by an attorney, shall exhibit to the Court a picture identification and proof of a current address.

SUP R. 61. APPRAISERS

Loc. R. 61.1 Appraisers' fees

(A) Appraisers' fees for real estate shall be based upon the entire undivided value of the assets subject to appraisal (not the decedent's interest in the property which may be fractional). Fees shall be computed at the rate of:

(1) $1.50 per thousand for the first $200,000 of valuation;

(2) $1.00 per thousand in excess of $200,000 of valuation;

(3) The minimum appraiser fee shall be $100.

When an appraisal of multiple properties is performed, the above fee schedule shall apply to each property, not the aggregate value of all properties. Fees paid in compliance with this rule may be paid without application and entry.

(B) If a Franklin County appraiser is employed to appraise real estate located in another county, in addition to the fee calculation in paragraph (A) above, the appraiser may also charge a mileage fee.

(C) Any appraiser fee requested in excess of the above schedule and appraisals of personalty must either be by agreement between the fiduciary and the appraiser or must be approved by the Court prior to the appraisal being made.

(D) Unless there is a dispute, or an appraisal is required for other purposes, a Court-appointed appraiser shall not be necessary in the following situations:

(1) In estates relieved from administration, a statement attesting to the auditor's appraised value, signed by a representative of the County Auditor or a Deputy Clerk of the Probate Court, will be accepted as the appraised value of the real estate for Probate Court purposes and on the Ohio estate tax return.

(2) Where the estate is comprised of personal property of readily ascertainable value.

(E) All appraisers shall give to the fiduciary and the attorney of record a written appraisal of each property appraised on the appropriate form provided by the Court or a form which is in substantial compliance therewith. The signature of the appraiser shall constitute a certification that the appraisal was performed truly, honestly, and impartially.

(F) Appraisers' fees shall be paid within one (1) month after the filing of the inventory or sixty (60) days after the completion of the appraisal, which ever occurs first unless otherwise ordered by the Court. The proceedings shall remain open until the fiduciary has accounted for the payment of the appraisal fee. Should payment not be made pursuant to this rule, the fiduciary shall be held personally liable for the payment of the appraisers' fees.

Loc. R. 61.2   Appraiser self-dealing

During the administration of the estate or, if the estate is closed within twelve (12) months of the appointment of the appraiser, no appraiser shall directly or indirectly purchase or negotiate the purchase, sale, trade, or management of property that he or she has appraised. (Eff. 1/1/05)

SUP R. 62.   CLAIMS AGAINST ESTATE

Loc. R. 62.1   Deposit

Any claim against an estate filed with the Court pursuant to Ohio R.C. 2117.06(A)(1)(b) shall be in the form of a complaint, filed as a civil action, and heard not on its merits, but on whether the claim is accepted or rejected. A deposit of Seventy-five and No/100 ($75.00) is required. (Eff. 1/1/05)

SUP R. 64.   ACCOUNTS

Loc. R. 64.1   Fiduciary's signature

(A) All accounts must be personally signed by the fiduciary and contain the full name, current resident address, and telephone number of the fiduciary.

(B) All fiduciaries must sign the account when multiple fiduciaries have been appointed.

Loc. R. 64.2   Delinquency in filing an account

No expenditure, sale, distribution, or fee will be approved while the fiduciary is delinquent in filing an account. See also Sup. R. 78.

Loc. R. 64.3   Vouchers

When required by statute or court order, original vouchers are to be displayed when filing accounts. The Court will accept as a voucher a statement from a financial institution specifying the payee, check amount, and date of payment.

For decedent's estates where the date of death is prior to January 1, 2002, and the estate is solvent, in lieu of submitting vouchers, the fiduciary may file with the account, a waiver and consent from all the beneficiaries acknowledging each received a copy of the account, waives notice of the hearing on the account, and consents to the filing of the account. The signature of each beneficiary must be dated.

The Court may accept a combination of vouchers and consents. In lieu of receiving waivers and consents from all the beneficiaries, vouchers from specific and pecuniary beneficiaries may be submitted with consents from all remaining beneficiaries.

Upon request of the Court, adding machine tapes shall be provided which reflect receipts, disbursements, and balances.

Loc. R. 64.4   Bond

An account will not be accepted for filing unless the bond, when required, is sufficient to cover twice the sum of the value of the personal property assets on hand plus one (1) year's projected income.

Loc. R. 64.5   Evidence of assets

The Court requires that all assets be exhibited at the time of filing a partial account. The assets remaining in fiduciary's hands shall disclose the fair market value of the assets as of the last day covered by the account.

Loc. R. 64.6   Payment of debts

The fiduciary in a decedent's estate shall pay and disclose in the estate account all valid debts unless otherwise determined by law.

Loc. R. 64.7   Time for filing

(A) For decedents' estates, the final and distributive account due within six (6) months after appointment of the fiduciary may be extended by Motion to thirteen (13) months for the reasons enumerated in Ohio R.C. 2109.301(B)(1). All subsequent accounts must be filed on an annual basis unless the Court otherwise orders. Accounts not filed in compliance with this rule shall be subject to citation.

(B) For guardianships and trusts, the first account shall be filed not later than one (1) year following the date of the appointment of the fiduciary and all subsequent accounts shall be filed on an annual basis, unless otherwise ordered by the Court.

Loc. R. 64.8   Certificate of service of notice to heirs

For all estates of decedents with dates of death after December 31, 2001, a Certificate of Service of Account to Heirs or Beneficiaries (Standard Probate Form 13.9), shall be filed with the Court disclosing that the executor or administrator has provided a copy of the account to all persons entitled thereto under Ohio R.C. 2109.32(B)(1). This certificate shall be signed by the executor, administrator, or attorney of record, and shall be filed no later than three days after the filing of each account.

SUP R. 66.   GUARDIANSHIPS

Loc. R. 66.1   Guardianship of minors

(A) A certified copy of the minor's birth certificate must be filed with the guardian's application.

(B) The Court will not establish a guardianship for school purposes only. Custody for school purposes is a matter to be heard and determined by the Juvenile or Domestic Relations Divisions.

(C) The Court will not establish any guardianship over the person of a minor where another Court has jurisdiction over custody of the minor.

(D) Minors who are not U.S. citizens or resident aliens, are not considered by this Court to be residents or have legal settlement as set forth in Ohio R.C. 2111.02(A).

(E) No guardian of the person of a minor may create a power of attorney pursuant to Ohio R.C. 3109.52 transferring the guardian's rights and responsibilities without specific authority of the Court. (Eff. 1/1/05)

Loc. R. 66.2   Safe deposit box

Before making an appointment with the County Auditor to audit a ward's safe deposit box(es), the guardian shall deposit Ten and No/100 Dollars ($10.00) to the Probate Court cashier for each box to be audited. The contents of the ward's safe deposit box are not to be released without a specific court order.

Loc. R. 66.3   Release of funds

Funds in the name of the ward shall not be released to the guardian without a specific court order.

Loc. R. 66.4   Deposit of wills

The guardian must deposit with the Court any and all wills of the ward for safekeeping in accordance with Ohio R.C. 2107.07.

Loc. R. 66.5   Change of address

A guardian appointed by this Court shall inform the Court as to any change of address of the guardian or the ward. This notification must be made within thirty (30) days of the address change. Failure to notify the Court under this rule may result in the guardian being removed.

Loc. R. 66.6   Guardian's report

The guardian of the person shall file the guardian's report. If there is only a guardian of the estate, the guardian's report must be filed by this guardian.

Where a physician or clinical psychologist states on a Statement of Expert Evaluation that to a reasonable degree of medical certainty it is unlikely the ward's mental competence will improve, the Court may dispense with the filing of subsequent Statements of Expert Evaluation when filing their subsequent biennial guardian's reports.

Loc. R. 66.7   Termination

Applications to terminate a guardianship of a minor require notice to all persons designated in Ohio R.C. 2111.04 and any other individuals who received actual notice of the original appointment of the guardian.

Loc. R. 66.8   Notice for guardianship of adults

In addition to those entitled to notice of the hearing on the application for the appointment of a guardian of an adult under Ohio R.C. 2111.04, the applicant shall disclose to the Court the names and addresses of all adult children of the proposed ward known to reside in this state. The Court shall serve the adult children with notice of the time and date of the hearing, unless the notice is waived.

Loc. R. 66.9   Background Investigations

Any applicant for guardianship who is not an attorney at law licensed by the Supreme Court of Ohio and in good standing, or a state agency, must complete a criminal record check which is suitable to the Court. (Eff. 1–1–05)

Loc. R. 66.10   Indigent guardianships

For purposes of the indigent guardianship fund, an adult ward or alleged incompetent will be rebuttably presumed to be indigent if his or her personal property is less than One Thousand Five Hundred and No/100 Dollars ($1500.00) and his or her annual income is less than the U.S. Department of Health and Human Services poverty guidelines. (http://aspe.hhs.gov/poverty/figures–fedreg.shtml). Persons with greater resources are rebuttably presumed not to be indigent.

All adults qualified for Medicaid are rebuttably presumed to be indigent. (Eff. 01/01/06)

SUP R. 67.   ESTATES OF MINORS OF NOT MORE THAN TEN THOUSAND DOLLARS

Loc. R. 67.1   Dispense with guardianship

Applications to dispense with the appointment of a guardian shall follow the notice required in Ohio R.C. 2111.04.

Loc. R. 67.2   Birth certificate

A certified copy of the minor's birth certificate must be presented to the Court upon the filing of the application to dispense with guardianship.

Loc. R. 67.3   Attorney responsibility

The attorney representing the interests of the payor in a minor's settlement action shall not assume the duties imposed by Sup. R. 67.

Loc. R. 67.4   Annual statements

All institutions holding controlled accounts under Ohio R.C. 2111.05 shall annually file statements with the Court disclosing the year-end balance and all activity of each account. The statements shall be filed between January 1 and February 28 of each year. (Eff. 1/1/05)

SUP R. 68.   SETTLEMENT OF INJURY CLAIMS OF MINORS

Loc. R. 68.1   Birth certificate

A certified copy of the minor's birth certificate must be presented to the Court upon the filing of the application to settle a minor's claim.

Loc. R. 68.2   Settlement conference

It is suggested that the attorney, prior to bringing the clients to Court to settle a minor's claim, personally appear to discuss the settlement with the Court. At this conference, the matter may be set for hearing.

Loc. R. 68.3   Deposit of proceeds

Pursuant to Sup. R. 67(C) the attorney representing the applicants in the matter shall acknowledge responsibility for depositing the funds and providing the financial institution with a copy of the entry. If there is no attorney representing the applicants, the attorney for the payor shall acknowledge delivery of the funds to complete the delivery of consideration to effectuate the release.

The attorney shall obtain a Verification of Receipt and Deposit (Standard Probate Form 22.3) from the financial institution and file the form with the Court within seven (7) days of the issuance of the entry. (Eff. 1/1/05)

Loc. R. 68.4 Structured settlements

In the event that parties involved in claims for injuries to minors or incompetents desire to enter into a structured settlement, defined as a settlement wherein payments are made on a periodic basis, the following rules shall apply:

(A) The application shall include a signed statement from one of the following independent professionals, specifying the present value of the settlement, and the method of calculation of that value: an actuary, certified public accountant, certified financial planner, chartered life underwriter, chartered financial consultant, or an equivalent professional.

(B) If the settlement is to be funded by an annuity, the application shall include a signed statement by the annuity carrier or the broker procuring the policy stating:

(1) The annuity carrier is licensed to write annuities in Ohio.

(2) The annuity carrier's ratings from at least two of the following organizations, which meet the following criteria:

    a. **A.M. Best Company:** A++, A+, or A;

    b. **Fitch Ratings** (Financial Strength): AAA, AA+, or AA;

    c. **Moody's Investors Service** (Financial Strength): Aaa, Aa1, or Aa2;

    d. **Standard & Poor's Corporation** (Financial Strength): AAA, AA+, or AA;

    e. **Weiss Research Inc.:** A+ or A.

(C) In addition to the requirements of Paragraph (B) above, an annuity carrier must meet any other requirement the Court considers reasonably necessary to assure that funding to satisfy periodic payment settlements will be provided and maintained. (Eff. 1/1/05)

Loc. R. 68.5 Application to settle claim

When the net proceeds of a claim for the benefit of a minor is Ten Thousand and No/100 Dollars ($10,000.00) or less, an application may be filed with the Court to consider the approval of a settlement of the claim by a parent or other next friend of the minor. The Court will consider whether to dispense with the appointment of a guardian for the estate of the minor under the same case number.

When the net proceeds of the claim for the benefit of a minor is over Ten Thousand and No/100 Dollars ($10,000.00), an application shall be filed for the appointment of a guardian for the estate of that minor. The Court will consider the approval of the settlement of that claim under the guardianship case number.

SUP R. 70. SETTLEMENT OF WRONGFUL DEATH AND SURVIVAL CLAIMS

Loc. R. 70.1 Settlement of claims

The application to settle a claim for wrongful death and the apportionment of the proceeds are two distinct matters for which the Court may require separate hearings.

Loc. R. 70.2 Wrongful death prototype trust

The Court has adopted and filed a prototype Wrongful Death Trust under Case Number 424,500, which is available at the Court and on the Court's website: www.franklincountyohio.gov/probate. Attorneys who wish to use the prototype must file an acknowledgment that the trust conforms to the current prototype. An attorney who wishes to create his or her own form of trust must submit the form of trust to the Court at least seven (7) days prior to the hearing on the wrongful death settlement. (Eff. 1/1/05)

Loc. R. 70.3 Wrongful death trust with multiple beneficiaries

A separate wrongful death trust, with its own case number, shall be created for each trust beneficiary.

Loc. R. 70.4 Settlement conference

It is suggested that the attorneys, prior to bringing the clients to Court to settle the wrongful death and survival claims, discuss the settlement with the Court. At this conference, the matter may be set for hearing.

SUP R. 71. COUNSEL FEES

Loc. R. 71.1 Attorney fees

All fees charged by an attorney representing a fiduciary in matters before this Court, including but not limited to work on decedents' estates, guardianships, and trusts, must be disclosed on the fiduciary's account, regardless of the source of payment. If the source of payment is other than the fiduciary, the source of payment must be identified on the account. For the purpose of this rule, fiduciary includes commissioners and applicants for release from administration. If no account is to be filed, the payment must be disclosed on a consent to fees signed by the payor of the fees.

Attorneys are expected to be familiar with DR 2–106 of the Code of Professional Responsibility that governs the reasonableness of fees. Upon review of the records, the Court may set the fees for hearing, regardless of the submission of consent(s) to fees.

Loc. R. 71.2 Attorney serving as fiduciary

In all matters where an attorney is the fiduciary of the estate, guardianship, or trust, and that attorney or another is the attorney of record, detailed records shall be maintained describing time and services as fiduciary and as attorney, which records shall, upon request, be submitted to the Court for review. DR 2–106 of the Code of Professional Responsibility shall govern the reasonableness of all fees, notwithstanding statutory allowances. The Court assumes an attorney, appointed as fiduciary, has been selected due to the attorney's special knowledge and abilities resulting in a savings of fees to the estate, guardianship, or trust.

Upon review of the records, the Court may set the fees for hearing, regardless of the submission of consent(s) to fees.

Loc. R. 71.3 Early payment of attorney fees

Attorney fees for the administration of decedents' estates shall not be paid or advanced from any source until the final account or final closing documents are prepared for filing unless otherwise approved by the Court upon application. Such application shall contain a statement that the fee is being required in advance of the time permitted by Sup. R. 71(B) and shall set forth the reason for requesting the early payment of fees. The application shall be accompanied by a consent as to the amount and the timing of the fees by all beneficiaries who have yet to receive their complete distribution or shall be set for hearing with notice to the nonconsenting beneficiaries.

Loc. R. 71.4 Notice and consent for attorney fees in estates

Applications for attorney fees in estates shall include a statement of the amount of the fees and a statement of services rendered. The applicant shall give notice of the hearing on the fees to one hundred percent (100%) of the persons whose interests are affected by the payment of the fees, including creditors if the estate is insolvent.

Attorney fees may be paid upon the preparation of the final account, without application and entry, if persons entitled to greater than fifty percent (50%) of the assets used for the payment of the fees file their written consent to the fees, subject to any exceptions to the final account by nonconsenting beneficiaries or creditors.

Loc. R. 71.5 Notice and consent for attorney fees in guardianships

In guardianship administration, the Court shall consider applications for attorney fees for the establishment of the guardianship upon the filing of the inventory, and shall consider additional fees annually upon the filing of each account. Notice of the application shall be given to the guardian of the estate, and upon order by the Court, other interested persons. The guardian of the estate may waive notice of the hearing and consent to the payment of fees. All applications for attorney fees in guardianships shall be accompanied by a statement of all attorney and guardian fees approved by the Court in that guardianship in the last five (5) years.

After the death of the ward, the Court will consider attorney fees and guardian fees as liens on the ward's assets. If the fees are approved by the Court, the fees may be paid out of the guardianship assets and included in the final guardianship account.

The Court may require notice of the hearing on the fees be given to other interested persons, including the estate fiduciary of a deceased ward. (Eff. 1/1/05)

Loc. R. 71.6 Notice and consent for attorney fees in trusts

In trust administration, the Court shall consider applications for attorney fees for the establishment of the trust upon the filing of the inventory, and shall consider additional fees annually upon the filing of each account. All applications for attorney fees in trusts shall be accompanied by a statement of all attorney and trustee fees approved by the Court in that trust in the last five (5) years.

Notice of application shall be given to the trustee. The trustee may waive notice of the hearing and consent to payment of fees. The Court may require notice of the hearing on the payment of the fees be given to the trust beneficiaries who are affected by the payment of fees.

Loc. R. 71.7 Contested fees

The burden is upon the attorney to prove the reasonableness of the fee as governed by DR 2–106 of the Code of Professional Responsibility. A detailed fee statement may be required which includes the itemization and date of service performed, time expended, identification of the individual(s) performing the services, and the hourly rate charged.

Loc. R. 71.8 Contingent fees

All fiduciaries shall make written application to the Court for authority to enter into a contingent fee contract. The application must be accompanied by a case plan, time projection, and estimated costs, as available, which upon request of counsel, may be reviewed *in camera*. Upon review, the Court will either give preliminary approval or disapprove the request. Preliminary approval shall be subject to final review at the conclusion of the matter that is the subject of the contingent fee contract.

In minor settlement cases where no guardian has been appointed, the attorney shall make the above application, under Case Number 418,000. Before settlement may be approved, a guardianship must be established or dispensed with under its own case number.

In establishing an estate, guardianship, or dispensing with the appointment of a fiduciary for the primary purpose of settling or resolving a claim, the attorney fees associated with bringing the proceedings before this Court shall be assessed as a portion of the contingent fee, unless otherwise ordered by the Court for good cause shown. The Court may allocate the payment of this fee between the contingent fee and the beneficial interests.

SUP R. 73. GUARDIAN'S COMPENSATION

Loc. R. 73.1 Guardian's compensation

(A) Guardian's compensation for services as guardian of the estate shall be computed annually upon application and entry and shall be supported by calculations and documentation. The following fee schedule shall apply unless extraordinary fees are requested. Extraordinary fee applications shall be set for hearing unless hearing is waived by the Court.

(1) *Income/Expenditure Fee.* Excluding income from rental real estate, four percent (4%) of the first $10,000 of income received, plus three percent (3%) of the balance in excess of $10,000, and four percent (4%) of the first $10,000 of expenditures except expenditures pertaining to rental real estate, plus three percent (3%) of the balance in excess of such $10,000. If the guardian manages rental real estate, a fee amounting to ten percent (10%) of gross rental real estate income may be allowed. If the guardian receives net income from rental real estate actively managed by others, then the guardian shall treat such net income as ordinary income. No fee shall be allowed to the guardian on expenditures pertaining to rental real estate. As used in this rule, "income" shall mean the sum of income as defined in Ohio R.C. 1340.40(D), including pension benefits and net gains from the sale of principal. Assets held by the ward at the date of appointment are deemed to be principal and not income.

(2) *Principal Fee.* $3.00 per thousand for first $200,000 of fair market value, and $2.00 per thousand on the balance of the corpus, unless otherwise ordered.

(3) *Principal Distribution Fee.* $3.00 per thousand for the first $200,000 of fair market value of corpus distributed upon the termination of the guardianship, and $2.00 per thousand on the balance of the corpus distributed upon the termination of the guardianship, unless otherwise ordered.

(B) Compensation for services as guardian of the person only shall be set for hearing unless the hearing is waived by the Court.

(C) Compensation for corporate fiduciaries who are exempt from bond pursuant to Ohio R.C. 1111.21 shall be compensated pursuant to their published fee schedule if the fee schedule is filed in this Court under Case No. 368,530.

(D) All motions, including applications for compensation, by guardians of veterans must comply with Ohio R.C. Chapter 5905 and all other rules and regulations of the Department of Veterans Affairs. (Eff. 1/1/05)

Loc. R. 73.2 Payments from the Indigent Guardianship Fund

All services charged to the Indigent Guardianship Fund must be billed to the Court within twenty-five (25) months from the

SUP R. 74. TRUSTEE'S COMPENSATION

Loc. R. 74.1 Trustee's compensation

(A) Except where the instrument creating the trust makes provision for compensation, trustees subject to this Court's jurisdiction may, upon application and entry, be allowed compensation annually for ordinary services in connection with the administration of each separate trust in accordance with the following schedule.

(1) *Income Fee.* Six percent (6%) of the gross income received during the accounting period not exceeding $10,000 of gross income, five percent (5%) of the next $10,000 of gross income, and four percent (4%) of such gross income exceeding $20,000, chargeable to income unless otherwise ordered. As used in this rule, "income" shall mean the sum of income as defined in Ohio R.C. 1340.40(D), including pension benefits and net gains from the sale of principal accrued during the trust administration. Assets held by the trustee at the date of appointment are deemed to be principal and not income.

(2) *Principal Fee.* $5.00 per thousand for the first $200,000 of fair market value, and $4.00 per thousand on the next $200,000, and $3.00 per thousand on the balance of the corpus, chargeable to the principal, unless otherwise ordered.

(3) *Principal Distribution Fee.* $5.00 per thousand for the first $200,000 of fair market value of corpus distributed, and $4.00 per thousand of the next $200,000, and $3.00 per thousand of the corpus distributed, unless otherwise ordered.

(B) Compensation for corporate fiduciaries who are exempt from bond pursuant to Ohio R.C. 1111.21 may be compensated in accordance with their published fee schedule if the fee schedule is filed in this Court under Case No. 368,530. Vested trust beneficiaries affected by the payment of fees shall be notified by the trustee of any changes in its corporate fee schedule.

(C) Additional compensation for extraordinary services or allowance for expenses may be granted on application and entry, which shall be set for hearing unless waived by the Court. (Eff. 01/01/06)

SUP R. 75. LOCAL RULES

Loc. R. 75.1 Guardian ad litem

The Court shall select and appoint each guardian ad litem. In land sale proceedings, a minimum fee of Fifty and No/100 Dollars ($50.00) shall be assessed as costs for each guardian ad litem appointed, unless the circumstances warrant the payment of additional fees subject to Court approval. In all other proceedings, the amount of the guardian ad litem fee will be determined upon motion supported by a statement of services. The guardian ad litem's fees may be assessed as costs.

Loc. R. 75.2 Adoptions

(A) An original and a copy of all petitions, interlocutory decrees, and final decrees shall be filed in every adoption case. Additional copies of the petition shall be submitted as required for service.

(B) In private placement adoptions, a preplacement application in a form prescribed by the Court shall be filed by the proposed adopting parents not less than fifteen (15) days prior to placement if applicants are residents of Franklin County, Ohio, and not less than thirty (30) days prior to placement if applicants are not residents of Franklin County, Ohio.

(C) Once the applications have been approved by the Court, a hearing shall be held not less than seventy-two (72) hours after the birth of the child or after the parent(s) have met with the adoption assessor, whichever occurs later, for the placement and consent by the parents. Prior to the placement hearing, the Court shall be supplied with a statement from the child's physician as to the medical condition of the child to be placed. If the placement is approved, the adoption petition must be filed before the Court will issue a Hospital Release for the release of the child to the petitioners or the attorney for the petitioners. When the petitioner is the guardian of the minor to be adopted, the Court shall require a placement hearing. The adoption petition shall not be set for hearing until after the placement is complete.

(D) In all adoption cases, Court costs are required to be paid at the time of the filing. The Court should be consulted in advance for current deposit information.

(E) The criminal background checks pursuant to Ohio R.C. 2151.86(B) and petitioner's accounts shall be filed in all cases.

(F) In all adoptions, married petitioner(s) must be married for not less than one (1) year prior to the final approval of the adoption.

(G) In all placement hearings where a birth parent of the child to be adopted is a minor, that birth parent shall be represented by an attorney. The fees for the attorney for the birth parent will be assessed as costs to the petitioner.

(H) All adoption assessors who meet with the birth parent(s) in the course of preparing a report for an adoption proceeding in this Court, shall provide the birth parent(s) with a copy of the brochure prepared pursuant to Ohio R.C. 3107.082 and 3107.083.

Any adoption assessor providing the birth parent(s) with a copy of this brochure shall file a Certificate of Service by Adoption Assessor form prior to the first hearing in the adoption proceeding concerning the child of the birth parent(s) who received the brochure.

Loc. R. 75.3 Custodial deposits in lieu of bond

All custodial deposits of personal property, securities, and monies must comply with Ohio R.C. 2109.13. All institutions desiring to be a depository must satisfy the Court of their authorization and certification by the State of Ohio.

All custodial depositories shall annually file statements with the Court disclosing the year-end balance and all activity of each account. The statements shall be filed between January 1 and February 28 of each year.

Compensation for custodial depositories shall be in accordance with their published fee schedule if the fee schedule is filed in this Court under Case No. 368,530. (Eff. 1/1/05)

Loc. R. 75.4 Surety bonds

(A) A surety company, prior to executing a fiduciary bond, must register with the Court and file proof that the company is authorized to do business within this State. The Court will maintain a separate case file for each company to register the company and its agents. Agents must file a power of attorney from the company prior to executing bonds for that company.

(B) Attorneys shall not act as sureties in any case, nor shall they be permitted to become sureties on the bond of any fiduciary.

(C) The Court will not accept personal sureties.

(D) Bond required by law or court order shall be in an amount not less than double the probable value of the personal estate including all sources of income during the accounting period.

(E) The original bond must be approved in writing by a bonding agency prior to the issuance of Letters of Authority in all matters where a bond is required. Additional bonds must be approved by a bonding agency in writing before being approved by the Court.

(F) The bond premium shall be paid by the fiduciary within sixty (60) days of date of appointment. The premium for additional bond shall be paid by the fiduciary within sixty (60) days from the date the additional bond was approved by the Court. Should payment not be made pursuant to this rule, the fiduciary may be held personally liable for its payment and is subject to removal.

Loc. R. 75.5   Release of estates from administration

(A) The Court shall select and appoint Commissioners, when required, in estates released from administration.

(B) A short form release from administration may be filed when evidence is presented to establish:

(1) Gross assets are less than Two Thousand Two Hundred and No/100 Dollars ($2,200.00); or gross assets are less than Seven Thousand Two Hundred and No/100 Dollars ($7,200.00) and there is a surviving spouse and or minor children of the decedent, and;

(2) The funeral expenses to the extent of the estate priority pursuant to Ohio R.C. 2117.25(B) have been paid.

(C) The Court may waive a noticed hearing in those instances where it appears no beneficiaries or creditors will be prejudiced.

(D) Upon the filing of an Application to Relieve Estate from Administration, the applicant shall exhibit to the Court a certified copy of the decedent's death certificate.

(E) Any applicant to Relieve an Estate from Administration, not represented by an attorney shall present to the Court picture identification and proof of current address.

Loc. R. 75.6   *Pro hac vice*

(A) An attorney not licensed to practice law in the State of Ohio, but who is duly licensed to practice law in any other state or the District of Columbia, may, at the discretion of the Probate Judge, be permitted to represent a party or parties in any litigation pending or to be filed in this county after completion of all of the following conditions:

(1) File a written oath substantially in compliance with Rule I, Section 8A of the Supreme Court Rules for the Government of the Bar;

(2) The attorney must become familiar with Local Court Rules, Civil Rules, Rules of Evidence, and the Code of Professional Responsibility, and so certify to this Court in writing.

(3) Be sponsored in writing by an attorney licensed to practice law in the State of Ohio. The motion made by the licensed attorney shall certify such out-of-state attorney's compliance with this rule and the Supreme Court Rules for the Government of the Bar;

(4) The sponsoring attorney shall submit with the motion and certification an entry authorizing the approval of the motion;

(5) The sponsoring attorney, or any other attorney licensed to practice law in the State of Ohio, shall be co-counsel with the attorney admitted *pro hac vice*.

(B) The continuance of any scheduled trial or hearing date shall not be permitted solely because of the unavailability or inconvenience of the out-of-state attorney.

Loc. R. 75.7   Additional fees

(A) The fee for computerized legal research as authorized by Ohio R.C. 2101.162(A) shall be Three and No/100 Dollars ($3.00) per case, excluding marriage license applications.

(B) The fee for computerization as authorized by Ohio R.C. 2101.162(B) shall be Ten and No/100 Dollars ($10.00) per case and Nine and No/100 Dollars ($9.00) per marriage license application.

(C) The fee for dispute resolution as authorized by Ohio R.C. 2101.163(A) and 2101.163(B) shall be Ten and No/100 Dollars ($10.00) per case and Five and No/100 Dollars ($5.00) per marriage license application.

(D) The fee for a criminal records check completed by the Court shall be Fifteen and No/100 ($15.00) per record check.

(E) The fee for an investigation for a guardianship for an adult as authorized by Ohio R.C. 2101.16(B)(1) shall be Seventy-five and No/100 Dollars ($75.00).   (Eff.01/01/06)

Loc. R. 75.8   Registration of paralegals

(A) Paralegals performing services in matters before this Court must be registered with the Court under Case No. 461,100. The Court recognizes two (2) categories of paralegals: "employee paralegals," paralegals employed exclusively by and performing services for one law firm as an employee of that firm; and "independent paralegals," paralegals operating as free lance/independent contract paralegals or offering services to more than one law firm. Registration shall be on the forms prescribed by the Court.

(1) Employee paralegals need only be registered once, identifying the law firm and stating the paralegal services will be supervised by the attorney(s) of that law firm. An attorney from the firm and the paralegal shall sign the registration certifying that the paralegal is qualified through education, training, or work experience to assist an attorney in matters which will be filed in this Court and that an attorney from the law firm will supervise and be responsible for all services of the paralegal. In fee statements filed with the Court, services of the paralegal must be itemized separately from services performed by an attorney. The law firm shall notify the Court when the paralegal registered with the Court leaves the exclusive employment of the law firm.

(2) Independent paralegals shall be registered for each case in which the independent paralegal is performing services, identifying the case name, case number, and supervising attorney. The supervising attorney and the independent paralegal shall sign the registration certifying that the independent paralegal is qualified through education, training, or work experience to assist the supervising attorney in matters that will be filed in this Court and, as supervising attorney, he or she will supervise and be responsible for all services of the independent paralegal. In fee statements filed with the Court, services of the independent paralegal must be itemized separately from services performed by an attorney. Attorney fees reported in the account shall include a disclosure of the independent paralegal fees on the Receipts and Disbursements form.

(B) In conjunction with Civ. R. 11, a paralegal may not sign any document for the fiduciary, applicant, or supervising attorney.

(C) For purposes of this rule, the Court acknowledges the definition of "paralegal" adopted by the Columbus Bar Association. Registration with the Court does not constitute certification by the Court as to the qualifications of the paralegal.

(D) Failure to comply with this rule may result in the disallowance of the fees and such other action as the Court may deem appropriate.

Loc. R. 75.9   Wills deposited for safekeeping

Any person placing a will on deposit in this Court shall sign a written statement acknowledging the will is being placed on deposit at the request of the testator or guardian of the testator and identify the testator's current address and telephone number. When a will is being held by an attorney, and the address of the testator is unknown, that attorney must use reasonable diligence to locate the testator to sign the above statement. If the testator cannot be located after a diligent search the will may be placed on deposit with this Court on motion of the attorney on the form provided.

When an attorney who is holding wills for other persons dies, becomes disabled, or otherwise ceases to practice law, that attorney, or person who is handling the attorney's affairs must use due diligence to locate the testator and return the will. If a testator cannot be located after a diligent search, and the testator was last known to be a resident of this county, the will may be placed on deposit with this Court.

Any Order to Deliver a will previously deposited with this Court must be signed by the testator and the person to whom the will is to be delivered. The testator's signature must be notarized by a person other than the person to whom the will is to be delivered.

After the testator's death, wills deposited for safekeeping pursuant to Ohio R.C. 2107.07 shall only be released to a court of competent jurisdiction.

Loc. R. 75.10 Applicants will exhibit photographic identification

Applicants appearing before this Court for any matter may be required to exhibit a picture identification and proof of a current address.

Loc. R. 75.11 Objections to magistrate's decision

Upon filing objections to a magistrate's decision pursuant to Civ. R. 53, any party may cause the objections to be set for hearing and give notice to the remaining parties or attorneys of the date on which the matter is to be heard. If an entry setting hearing on the objections is not filed within twenty-eight (28) days of the filing, the objections shall be deemed submitted to the Court for consideration on the pleadings.

The objections shall be accompanied by a supporting memorandum. If required, the transcript shall be filed within thirty (30) days of the filing of the objections or two (2) days before the hearing, whichever occurs first. Failure to file a transcript when one is required by Civ. R. 53(E)(3)(c) is a basis for dismissal of the objections.

Memoranda contra to the objections may be filed by any party within ten (10) days of the filing of the objections, or two (2) days prior to the hearing, whichever occurs first. (Eff. 01/01/06)

Loc. R. 75.12 Wills in safe deposit box

The Court will appoint the attorney for a decedent's estate or a bailiff of this Court as a Commissioner to list the contents of the box and retrieve the decedent's will and codicils from the decedent's safe deposit box for delivery to the Court. A filing fee of Fifteen and No/100 Dollars ($15.00) must be paid and a case number assigned prior to the appointment of the Commissioner. If the Court bailiff is appointed as the Commissioner, an additional fee of Twenty and No/100 Dollars ($20.00) will be assessed.

Loc. R. 75.13 Service of summons

When the Court issues service of summons upon each defendant in a civil action pursuant to Civ. R. 4, the Court will only include the summons, a copy of the complaint, and when requested, an order to serve and an entry setting hearing.

Loc. R. 75.14 Marriage license applicants

Pursuant to Ohio R.C. 3101.05 any applicant for a marriage license who is a minor must provide proof of having had marriage counseling prior to applying for the license. The counseling can be provided by clergy or a person licensed by the State of Ohio to provide counseling. Proof of counseling may be in the form of a letter to this Court from the person who provided the counseling on his or her letterhead.

Loc. R. 75.15 Ohio estate tax return

In cases in which an Ohio estate tax return is not otherwise required to be filed, an Ohio estate tax form 22 shall be filed as described in Ohio R.C. 5731.21, if the value of the gross estate of the decedent, as defined in division (A) of Ohio R.C. 5731.01, includes any interest in real estate, and the decedent has been deceased for less than ten years.

Loc. R. 75.16 Surviving spouse waiver of service of the citation to elect

A surviving spouse may waive the service of the citation required under section 2106.01(A) of the Revised Code by filing in the probate court a written waiver of the citation. The waiver shall include an acknowledgement of receipt of the description of the general rights of the surviving spouse required by division (B) of section 2106.02 of the Revised Code.

Loc. R. 75.17 Virtual service

Effective November 1, 2004 the Court is participating in a pilot project under the direction of the Ohio Supreme Court to receive electronic receipts from the United States Postal Service for certified mail service. Therefore, electronic proof of service for certified or express mail sent by the Court pursuant to the virtual service program shall be deemed in compliance with the service requirements of Civil Rule 73. (Eff. 1/1/05)

SUP R. 78. CASE MANAGEMENT IN DECEDENT'S ESTATES, GUARDIANSHIPS, AND TRUSTS

Loc. R. 78.1 Case management

For the purpose of insuring the readiness of proceedings in the Franklin County Probate Court, the following procedure shall be in effect:

I. CIVIL ACTIONS: (Excluding Land Sales)

(A) All cases must have a general file number before a civil action may be filed.

(B) A status conference and a pretrial conference shall be conducted in all civil actions unless otherwise ordered by the Court.

(C) Within thirty (30) days after the final answer day, the case shall be set by plaintiff's counsel for a status conference.

(D) Plaintiff's counsel shall give not less than fourteen (14) days notice of the status conference to all counsel of record and/or all parties not represented by counsel who have entered an appearance.

(E) **Status Conference.** All counsel must have full authority to enter into binding orders. Unless otherwise ordered by the Court, the following matters and decisions shall be addressed at the status conference:

(1) the possibility of settlement of the action;

(2) a discovery schedule shall be agreed upon by all parties or set by the Court;

(3) a date of exchange of expert witness reports shall be determined;

(4) a final date for filing of all motions which shall not be later than twenty-eight (28) days before the pretrial conference. No

further motions shall be considered without good cause shown and leave of Court;

(5) the date for the pretrial conference shall be set by the Court and shall be no more than fourteen (14) days before the trial;

(6) the date for trial shall be set by the Court.

(F) Pretrial Conference. All counsel must have full authority to enter into binding orders. Unless otherwise ordered by the Court, the following matters and decisions shall be addressed at the pretrial conference:

(1) the Court may rule on any pending motions;

(2) the following shall be submitted:

   a. trial briefs;

   b. witness lists;

   c. exhibit lists;

   d. exhibits as ordered by the Court;

   e. proposed jury instructions;

   f. proposed jury interrogatories;

(3) Clients shall be present unless their presence has been excused by the Court.

(G) Witness lists exchanged between parties and/or presented to the Court are to provide the name and, if known, the address and telephone number of each person intended to be called as a witness.

(H) The trial date shall not be continued without good cause shown and order of the Court.

II. CIVIL ACTIONS: LAND SALES

(A) All cases must have a general file number before a civil action may be filed.

(B) All land sales which have not been concluded within one (1) year from the date of filing shall be set for status conference by plaintiff's counsel within thirty (30) days following the expiration of one (1) year.

(1) The fiduciary and the attorney must attend the status conference.

(2) A written status report shall be submitted to the Court at the status conference. The status report shall address pending issues and the efforts being made to conclude the land sale.

(3) The fiduciary shall show cause why the Court should not order public sale of the real estate.

(C) Motions for a fixed price shall be set for hearing with notice to all parties who have entered an appearance and all parties in default whose names and addresses are known or with reasonable diligence can be ascertained.

III. MOTIONS

(A) All motions filed in this Court shall be accompanied by a memorandum stating the grounds and citing the authorities relied upon. Opposing counsel or a party shall serve the response memorandum on or before the fourteenth (14th) day after the date of service as set forth on the certificate of service attached to the served copy of the motion. The moving party shall serve any reply memorandum on or before the seventh (7th) day after the date of service as set forth on the certificate of service attached to the served copy of the response memorandum. On the twenty-eighth (28th) day after the motion is filed, the motion shall be deemed submitted to the Court unless a prior written request for an oral hearing has been filed and approved by the Court. The time and length of any oral hearing shall be fixed by the Court. Except as otherwise provided, this rule shall apply to all motions.

(B) Motions for summary judgments are subject to the preceding Paragraph (A) and set for nonoral hearing on the twenty-eighth (28th) day following the filing of the motion for summary judgment. The filing of opposing affidavits and supporting documents are subject to Civ. R. 56.

(C) Motions for temporary restraining orders, preliminary injunctions, or similar urgent equitable relief, applications and motions relating to administrative matters, and appointments shall be submitted to the Court at a time set by the Court. When required, notice of the time and place of the hearing shall be served upon any adverse party or their counsel by the moving party.

(D) Interrogatories under Civ. R. 33, requests for production or inspection under Civ. R. 34, and requests for admissions under Civ. R. 36 shall be served upon other counsel or parties in accordance with these rules, but shall not be filed with the Court. The party responding may file with the Court interrogatories and requests together with any responses and objections. If relief is sought under Civ. R. 26(C) or Civ. R. 37 concerning any interrogatories, requests for production or inspection, and requests for admissions, copies of the portions of the documents which are in dispute shall be filed with the Court contemporaneously with any motion filed under Civ. R. 26(C) or Civ. R. 37.

IV. MENTAL ILLNESS AND MENTAL RETARDATION HEARINGS

All hearings shall comply with R.C. Chapters 5122 and 5123.

V. ADOPTIONS

The status of pending preplacement applications and adoption proceedings shall be reviewed annually and the Court may order further action as necessary. Additional rules on adoptions are located in Local Court Rule 75. 2.

VI. MISCELLANEOUS MATTERS

All miscellaneous matters shall be reviewed annually and the Court shall order further action as necessary.

VII. FAILURE TO COMPLY

Failure to comply with this Case Management Rule may result in dismissal pursuant to Civ. R. 41 and other sanctions, including but not limited to, payment of costs and attorney fees.

Loc. R. 78.2   Withdrawal of counsel

(A) An attorney desiring to withdraw shall file a motion to withdraw stating the reasons for withdrawal. The motion shall contain the last known address and telephone number of the client. The Court shall not issue an entry approving the withdrawal until the attorney has filed a certification that the following conditions have been fulfilled:

(1) Notice has been given to the client stating all filing deadlines affecting the client;

(2) Notice has been given to all attorneys, unrepresented parties, and interested persons;

(3) Attorneys withdrawing from representation of a fiduciary shall file the written acknowledgment of the withdrawal signed by the fiduciary or withdrawal shall be granted after a hearing with notice to the fiduciary. The attorney shall also notice any bonding agencies involved.

(B) No attorney shall be permitted to withdraw from a case sooner than twenty (20) days prior to a trial or dispositive hearing, except for extraordinary circumstances that require permission of the Court.

(C) Substitution of counsel shall be in writing but does not require approval of the Court. Notice shall be given to all attorneys, unrepresented parties, and interested persons.

Loc. R. 78.3 Inventory

(A) In lieu of the appraiser signing the estate inventory, the fiduciary may attach to the inventory the original appraisal(s) containing the signature of the appraiser(s).

(B) The inventory shall contain the address, legal description, and parcel number of the interest in the real estate of the decedent or ward.

(C) The inventory for a decedent's estate shall be filed in duplicate, the original and a copy.

(D) The inventory will not be accepted for filing unless the bond, when required, is sufficient pursuant to Loc. R. 75.4. A guardian's inventory shall include the projected annual income of the ward.

(E) The Court will not approve the distribution, sale, or expenditure of any estate or guardianship assets prior to the filing of the inventory.

(F) All fiduciaries must sign the inventory when multiple fiduciaries have been appointed.

Loc. R. 78.4 Request for jury trial

The Franklin County Common Pleas Court, General Division, Rule 27, as they relate to juries, shall apply to proceedings in the Probate Division, except to the extent that by their nature they would be clearly inapplicable.

Loc. R. 78.5 Mediation

(A) After the filing of an estate, guardianship application, trust, or any other action, the Court, on its own motion or the motion of any of the parties, may refer disputed issues to mediation.

(B) The mediation sessions may be held until all issues are resolved in a manner acceptable to the disputing parties, or until the mediator determines that continued mediation would not be productive.

(C) The Court may order parties to participate in or return to mediation at any time.

(D) Statements made during a mediation session shall be considered compromise negotiations and are not admissible as evidence pursuant to Evidence Rule 408. Mediators will not be permitted to testify regarding the substance of the mediation, including but not limited to, cooperation or noncooperation of the parties.

(E) To be accredited and appointed by the Court, a mediator shall possess the following qualifications:

(1) Be an attorney in good standing with the Supreme Court of Ohio;

(2) Have five (5) years of experience in handling probate matters; and,

(3) Have completed forty (40) hours of advanced mediation training, which has been approved for Continuing Legal Education and is approved by the Court.

(F) Referral to mediation by the Court shall be by "Notice of Mediation" which shall indicate the time, place of the mediation, and the name and telephone number of the mediator.

(G) The parties are equally responsible for paying one-half (1/2) of the mediator's fee for the first mediation session. The Court will pay the remaining one-half (1/2) of the fee for the first mediation session unless otherwise ordered. A mediation session is defined as a four (4) hour period. If continued mediation sessions are necessary, the mediator's fee shall be borne equally by the parties, unless otherwise ordered by the Court. The Court will determine the rate at which the mediator will be paid. The mediator's fee will be determined by the complexity of the issues in the matter being mediated. Any additional expenses associated with the mediation must be preapproved by the Court.

Loc. R. 78.6 Extended administration

All estates will initially be scheduled according to the six-month administration schedule of Ohio R.C. 2109.301(B). In those estates meeting the requirements for extended administration stated in Ohio R.C. 2109.30(B)(1)(a)–(f), the administrator or executor shall file a notice or application (Standard Probate Forms 13.8 or 13.10) to extend the filing deadlines.

Upon the appointment of a successor fiduciary, the estate will be rescheduled for a six-month administration unless the successor administrator or executor files a notice or Application to Extend Administration (Standard Probate Forms 13.8 or 13.10). (Eff. 1/1/05)

Loc. R. 78.7 Special needs trusts

In addition to the requirements of Ohio R.C. 5111.151(F)(1), all special needs trusts approved by this Court, or funded with Court approval, must have the following terms:

(A) No expenditures may be made without prior Court approval.

(B) Bond shall be posted unless all of the assets of the trust are in a custodial account under Ohio R.C. 2109.13, or the trustee is exempt from bond under Ohio R.C. 1111.21.

(C) The State of Ohio shall have all of the rights as a beneficiary of the trust.

(D) Annual accounts shall be filed unless all of the assets of the trust are in a custodial account under Ohio R.C. 2109.13.

(E) Distributions from the trust shall not discharge any duty of support owed to a beneficiary. (Eff. 01/01/06)

HAMILTON COUNTY COURT OF COMMON PLEAS

RULES OF THE PROBATE DIVISION

Rule
11.1   Record of proceedings
51.1   Standard probate forms
52.1   Specifications for printing probate forms (computer–generated forms)
53.1   Hours of the court
54.1   Court security plan
55.1   Probate files
57.1   Motions and entries
58.1   Court costs
58.2   Witness fees
59.1   Wills
59.2   Admission of wills with irregularities
60.1   Application for letters of authority to administer an estate and notice of appointment
61.1   Appraisals
61.2   Inventory and appraisal
62.1   Claims against an estate and bond premiums
64.1   Fiduciary accounts
64.2   Show cause hearings
65.1   Land sale proceedings
66.1   Guardianships
66.2   Emergency guardianships
67.1   Estates of minors not exceeding ten thousand dollars
68.1   Settlement of claims for injuries to minors
68.2   Structured settlements
70.1   Settlement of claims for wrongful death
71.1   Attorney fees
71.2   Contingent fee agreements
72.1   Executor's and administrator's commissions
73.1   Guardian's compensation
73.2   Veterans administration—guardianships
74.1   Trustee compensation
75.1   Local rules—special provisions
78.1   Case management in decedent's estates, guardianships and trusts
78.2   Case management and pre-trial procedure for civil actions

Appendix
A–1   Notice of hearing on application for attorney's fees
A–2   Waiver of notice of hearing on application for attorney fees and consent to payment of attorney fees
A–3   Waiver of notice of hearing on application for attorney fees and consent to payment of attorney fees
B   Guardian compensation form (Rule 73.1)
C   Trustees compensation form (Rule 74.1)
D   Deposits for court costs

Rule 11.1   Record of proceedings

A. Prior to any hearing, a party may submit an application for the Court to record the proceedings with its audio-electronic recording equipment. A nominal fee shall be charged and collected as costs in such case. Alternatively, any party may provide a record by a court reporter paid for by the party requesting that court reporter's attendance. The audio-electronic recording shall be the official record.

B. Upon filing a praecipe, transcription of the record shall be made at the expense of the person requesting such transcription unless otherwise ordered by the Court. The transcription shall be made by an agent of the Court. The agent shall charge the customary fee charged by a private reporter for services in this county for such transcription or as otherwise provided for by Hamilton County Common Pleas Local Rule.

C. For any matter in which the Court has received an application to record the proceedings, the original tape or tapes of the audio-electronic recording shall be maintained by the court for a period of sixty (60) days:

1. After journalization of a Decision of Magistrate adjudicating the recorded hearing; and/or,

2. Journalization of the final entry or judgment in the case.

If a written request for transcription has been made, the original tape shall become part of the record of proceedings.

(Amended eff. 9–1–98)

Rule 51.1   Standard probate forms

The applicable standard probate forms provided by the Hamilton County Probate Court shall be used for all filings in this court, except that computer-generated forms may be used subject to the limitations in Rule 52.1.

(Amended eff. 9–1–98)

Rule 52.1   Specifications for printing probate forms (computer–generated forms)

The Hamilton County Probate Court may accept computer-generated probate forms, provided the following conditions are met:

A. Such forms shall comply with the provisions of Rule 51 and Rule 52 of the Rules of Superintendence for the Probate Division of the Court of Common Pleas.

B. Such forms shall be in the same form as those provided by the Hamilton County Probate Court with respect to type-style, font, pitch, line spacing, 8 ½ × 11 page size, and twenty-four pound (24#) bond or heavier stock (70# bond preferred).

C. Counsel certifies to the Court that any computer-generated forms are in full compliance with the Rules of Superintendence and the Local Rules of Court. All printed material shall be in the same sequence and in the same location on the page as the Standard Form. In the event of multiple page forms or two-sided forms, the printed material shall be on the same side or same page as the Standard Form.

D. The Court shall reject such forms that deviate from the format of the standard probate forms provided by the Hamilton County Probate Court. Such forms may be rejected prior to filing or stricken from the record upon discovery and may subject the lawyer or law firm to such other sanctions as the Court deems appropriate.

(Amended eff. 9–1–98)

Rule 53.1   Hours of the court

Except as provided below, the Probate Court and its offices at 230 E. 9th Street shall be open for the transaction of business from 8:00 A.M. to 4:00 P.M. daily, except Saturday, Sunday and legal holidays. No filings are accepted after 3:45 P.M.

(Amended eff. 9-1-98)

Rule 54.1 Court security plan

The Court has developed and implemented a court security plan to help maintain the safety of those using the court's facilities.

(Amended eff. 9-1-98)

Rule 55.1 Probate files

The official Probate Court file must accompany all filings when any filing is presented to the Court for approval. Said files shall not be removed from the Court.

(Amended eff. 9-1-98)

Rule 57.1 Motions and entries

A. All motions shall be accompanied by a memorandum in support of the motion. Said memorandum shall include a brief statement of the grounds for the motion, with citations to authorities relied upon, and proof of service in accordance with Civil Rule 5.

B. Except for good cause, all motions shall be set for oral argument and shall be accompanied by an entry setting the same for hearing. The moving party shall consult with opposing counsel or the opposing party, if pro se, to set a hearing date that is mutually agreeable. In the absence of an agreed hearing date, the Court shall set a date for hearing within thirty days.

C. All entries and orders presented to the Court for approval shall include the date of the hearing, the names of those present, and the specific motion or application heard by the Court on that date. The caption shall state the Court's decision with specificity. The use of the terms "entry" or "order" without more specificity shall cause such proposed entry to be rejected.

D. All filings and entries which bear an endorsement of a party or counsel per telephone authorization shall state the date of said authorization and shall also contain a certificate of service by the attorney who prepared and filed the entry that notice has been given to the consenting party or counsel.

E. The Court reserves the right to reject any pleadings in which the text or the signatures are illegible. All pleadings, motions, applications and other filings presented to the Court shall be in typeface and correctly captioned. Any information interlineated on a court form shall be in ink.

F. All motions to withdraw as counsel shall be accompanied by an order compelling the attendance of the fiduciary. If the whereabouts of the fiduciary are unknown, counsel shall demonstrate due diligence in attempting to locate the fiduciary.

G. It is strongly recommended that black ink be used for all signatures appearing on any court filings and for the completion of any forms which are printed or hand written. Attorneys must type all forms. Applicants appearing pro se are encouraged to type all forms.

(Amended eff. 9-1-98)

Rule 58.1 Court costs

Deposits shall be required upon the initial filing of any action or proceeding. The deposit may be applied as filings occur and additional deposits may be required. The Court shall maintain and make available a current list of costs.

(Amended eff. 9-1-98)

Rule 58.2 Witness fees

Upon the filing of a praecipe for subpoena of witnesses, the party shall deposit, for each witness, an amount sufficient to pay the witness fee as prescribed by R.C. §2335.06.

(Amended eff. 9-1-98)

Rule 59.1 Wills

A. Before an application is made to admit a will to probate, to appoint an estate fiduciary, or to relieve an estate from administration, the applicant or the applicant's attorney shall examine the index of wills to determine if the decedent has deposited a prior will with the Court for safekeeping. Prior wills so deposited shall be filed in the estate proceedings for record purposes only.

B. Fiduciaries appointed to administer testate estates shall file a Certificate of Service of Notice of Probate of Will within one hundred twenty days of their appointment or be subject to removal.

C. One of the Court's Magistrates shall make the initial determination, upon presentation, whether a purported will shall be admitted to probate.

(Amended eff. 9-1-98)

Rule 59.2 Admission of wills with irregularities

A. If a will presented to probate contains alterations or extraneous markings and the original text remains *legible*, the admission of the will shall be set for hearing pursuant to R.C. §2107.181 and the witnesses to the will shall testify as to the execution of the will and the physical appearance or condition of the will at the time of execution.

B. If a will presented to probate contains alterations or extraneous markings and the original text is rendered *illegible*, the admission of the will shall be set for hearing pursuant to R.C. §2107.26 unless it clearly appears that the alterations or extraneous markings on the face of the will were made by the testator with the intent to void the will.

C. If a photocopy of an executed will is presented for probate, the admission of the will shall be set for hearing pursuant to R.C. §2107.26, except as provided below.

D. A photocopy of a will which is executed as an original may be admitted to probate without further hearing if:

1. the original unexecuted will is presented with the executed photocopy; or

2. upon affidavit by the witnesses to the will that the photocopy was executed as an original, and that the document so executed was the one and only will executed by the testator.

E. Any will presented for admission to probate under either R.C. §§2107.181 or 2107.26 shall be set for hearing and a record of the testimony shall be filed with the Court.

(Amended eff. 9-1-98)

Rule 60.1 Application for letters of authority to administer an estate and notice of appointment

A. Any person filing an Application for Letters of Administration who is not the surviving spouse or next of kin of the decedent shall give notice to the surviving spouse and next of kin of the decedent, including persons entitled to an allowance of support. Said notice shall be given regardless of the party's residency unless written waivers are obtained from said party. All written notices shall contain the date, time and place of the hearing and shall be served upon such persons at least seven (7) days prior to the date set for hearing. All such applications shall be set for hearing before the probate judge.

B. Before filing an Application for Letters of Administration, the attorney or the proposed fiduciary shall determine if there is a will of the decedent on deposit with the Court by checking the index of wills.

C. An applicant who has served as guardian of an estate shall not be granted letters of authority to administer the decedent's estate upon the death of the ward unless the guardian of the estate is also named as fiduciary in the ward's will, or upon a showing of good cause.

D. The Court reserves the right to deny appointment of a proposed fiduciary who fails to meet the Court's minimum competency standards for administering an estate.

(Amended eff. 9–1–98)

Rule 61.1   Appraisals

A. When required by law, there shall be suitable and disinterested appraiser(s) appointed by the executor or administrator of an estate, with court approval. The following persons shall be disqualified from being such an appraiser:

1. A person related by blood or marriage to the decedent;

2. A beneficiary of the estate;

3. A person related by blood, marriage or employment to the attorney of the estate; and

4. A person related by blood, marriage or employment to the fiduciary of the estate.

B. Real estate appraisals shall be made by licensed real estate appraisers or other such persons who by professional experience and training are qualified to make real estate appraisals.

C. As to all personal property with no reasonably ascertainable value, appraisals shall be made by licensed auctioneers, credentialed personal property appraisers, or such other persons who by experience and training are qualified to make such appraisals.

D. With regard to household goods and personal effects valued in excess of $2,000, the appraiser shall sign the standard probate appraisal form or a separate instrument that indicates the appraised value of said goods.

E. No appraiser or broker shall be permitted to purchase or acquire, directly or indirectly, any of the property he or she apprises, except at public auction.

F. The fiduciary or applicant shall certify on each appointment of appraiser (H.C. Form 3.0) that the appraiser is a qualified and suitable person in accordance with this rule.

(Amended eff. 9–1–98)

Rule 61.2   Inventory and appraisal

A. When an estate contains real estate, counsel shall examine record title to the real estate from the time it was acquired by the decedent. An inventory must be filed before consents to the sale of real estate may be filed.

B. Upon the filing of an inventory as required by R.C. §2115.02, the executor or administrator shall serve notice of the hearing by certified or express mail upon the surviving spouse, next of kin and any beneficiary named under the will, as well as any attorneys who represent the same, unless such notice is waived.

C. In order to perfect service upon any unknown next of kin in an intestate estate, the fiduciary shall publish notice of the filing of the inventory once each week for three consecutive weeks. For testate estates, this shall be accomplished when the will is filed.

D. The County Auditor's valuation may be used for the appraisal where an estate is being relieved from administration except as otherwise ordered by the Court.

(Amended eff. 9–1–98)

Rule 62.1   Claims against an estate and bond premiums

No estate, guardianship or trust shall be closed until all claims filed with the Court have been resolved, including claims for bond premiums. Bond premiums shall be regarded as administrative expenses and shall be paid when due. No application need be made for authority to pay bond premiums.

(Amended eff. 9–1–98)

Rule 64.1   Fiduciary accounts

A. All accounts shall be examined by an Account Review Officer. You may:

1. Make an appointment to personally present your account; or

2. May appear without an appointment and present your account on a first come/first served basis.

3. If you have three or more accounts to present, you must schedule an appointment; and

4. If you have more than one account to be presented the day before a citation docket, you must make an appointment.

B. Supporting documentation for the accounting period shall include:

1. Itemized statement of all receipts of the fiduciary;

2. Itemized statement of all disbursements and distributions verified by vouchers or proof, which shall be referenced to the account by number, letter or date;

3. Itemized statement of all funds, assets and investments;

4. Original or certified bank statement for each account on deposit.

5. Each bank account statement for the entire accounting period; and

6. Actual securities or a certificate of the person in possession of the same (R.C. §§2109.13 or 2131.21), except that if securities are in the process of transfer and are unavailable when the account is presented, the Court will accept:

   a. an itemized affidavit of the brokerage firm handling said transfer; or;

   b. an affidavit of the transfer agent of the corporation issuing said securities.

7. If real estate has been sold, the account shall include a copy of the closing statement itemizing all of the disbursements.

C. All corporate fiduciaries shall file a recapitulation of its accounts in conformity with standard probate Form 13.0.

D. Unless notice is waived in writing, upon the filing of a final account, the fiduciary shall serve notice of the hearing on the account, to the following, whose addresses are known:

1. Decedents Estates—to the surviving spouse and all next of kin in an intestate estate and to all residuary beneficiaries in a testate estate.

2. Guardianships

   (A). Minors—to the ward if the ward has reached the age of majority or to the next of kin if the ward is under 18 years old.

   (B). Incompetents—to all of the ward's next of kin

   3. Trusts—to all the trust beneficiaries.

   4. Regardless of the nature of the matter—to counsel of any represented party described above.

Unless notice is waived in writing, upon the filing of a **partial** or **current** account, the fiduciary shall serve notice of hearing on the account to the following:

   1. Charitable trusts—to the Ohio Attorney General, Charitable Trusts Division.

   2. Trusts—to all income beneficiaries of the trust.

   3. Veteran's Guardianships (R.C. 5905)—to the Veteran's Administration.

   E. 1. A waiver of partial or current account may be filed to prevent an estate from being reported delinquent pursuant to R.C. §2109.30(B)(1)(e). The waiver shall be signed by all necessary parties as required by law. The following certification of counsel may be filed in those instances where a partial accounting may be waived:

"The undersigned, counsel for the estate, hereby certifies that all the requirements of R.C. §2109.30(B)(1)(e) have been satisfied to permit the filing of a waiver of partial account."

   2. An affidavit and entry affirming that there are no assets in the hands of the fiduciary may be presented in lieu of a current account in wrongful death cases.

   3. Certificates of Termination may be filed as permitted by law.

   F. If an account is not timely filed and no arrangement has been made for an extension of the due date, a Notice to Appear shall be issued compelling the attendance of both the attorney and the fiduciary.

   G. A partial or current account shall have an accounting period which ends not more than six (6) months prior to the time it is presented and approved by the Court. The partial or current account shall specify the number of the account using ordinal numbers (e.g., Third Partial Account).

   H. No handwritten accounts are permitted.

(Amended eff. 9–1–98)

Rule 64.2 Show cause hearings

A fiduciary and attorney who have been cited for a show cause hearing shall personally appear. Counsel shall not appear in lieu of a cited fiduciary unless the Court grants leave for the attorney to appear in that capacity.

(Amended eff. 9–1–98)

Rule 65.1 Land sale proceedings

In land sales proceedings, the Court shall appoint one suitable and disinterested person as appraiser. Compensation for said appraiser shall be determined by the Court and shall not exceed $150.00, unless because of the special and unusual character of the property to be appraised, additional compensation shall be appropriate to reasonably compensate the appraiser.

(Amended eff. 9–1–98)

Rule 66.1 Guardianships

A. An application to expend funds shall not be granted if an inventory has not been filed or if an account is overdue.

B. The guardian of a minor ward's estate must demonstrate that the ward's parent(s) are unable to fulfill their responsibility to support the ward before the Court will consider allowing an expenditure from the ward's estate for the purpose of that ward's support, maintenance or education.

C. Attorney fees for establishing a guardianship (in non-contested cases) shall not be awarded until the filing of an annual account.

D. Funds shall not be released to a guardian except upon an order of the Court.

E. All applications for release of funds shall specify the exact amount to be released, the financial institution holding the fund, its address, and the person in whose name the fund is held.

F. None of a ward's assets may be accessed through an automated teller machine or debit card. Electronic payment of routine and recurring expenses is permitted with court approval.

(Amended eff. 9–1–98)

Rule 66.2 Emergency guardianships

A. For all applications for the appointment of an emergency guardian, a physician shall personally appear and testify why it is reasonably certain that immediate action is required to prevent significant injury to the person of the minor or alleged incompetent.

B. The applicant shall exercise due diligence in giving notice of hearing upon the proposed ward in all emergency guardianships.

(Amended eff. 9–1–98)

Rule 67.1 Estates of minors not exceeding ten thousand dollars

A. An application relating to funds of a minor shall be captioned in the name of the minor.

B. Unless otherwise ordered by the Court, funds of a minor shall be deposited in the sole name of the minor, with principal and interested compounded, until the minor attains the age of majority.

C. The attorney for said minor, or in case the applicant is not represented, the attorney for the payor, shall be responsible to immediately deposit said funds and thereafter file a completed Verification of Receipt of Deposit (Form 22.3) within seven (7) days of the issuance of the entry.

(Amended eff. 9–1–98)

Rule 68.1 Settlement of claims for injuries to minors

A. An application for settlement of a minor's claim that exceeds ten thousand (10,000) dollars shall be brought by the guardian of the estate. If the gross amount of the claim for injuries does not exceed ten thousand (10,000) dollars, the application shall be brought by the parent(s) of the child or the person having custody of the child.

B. An application for approval of settlement of claim for injuries to a minor shall be accompanied by a current statement of the examining physician with respect to the injuries sustained, the extent of the recovery, and the physician's prognosis.

C. The injured minor and the applicant shall be present at the hearing.

(Amended eff. 9-1-98)

Rule 68.2 Structured settlements

In the event that parties involved in claims for injuries to minors desire to enter into a structured settlement, defined as a settlement wherein payments are made on a periodic basis, the following rules shall also apply:

A. The application shall include an affidavit from an independent certified public accountant or equivalent professional, specifying the present value of the settlement and the method by which that value was calculated.

B. If the settlement is to be funded by an annuity, the annuity shall be provided by an annuity carrier who meets or exceeds the following criteria:

1. The annuity carrier must be licensed to write annuities in Ohio and, if affiliated with the liability carrier or the person or entity paying the settlement, must be separately capitalized, licensed and regulated and must have a separate financial rating.

2. The annuity carrier must have a minimum of $100,000,000.00 of capital and surplus, exclusive of any mandatory security valuation reserve.

3. The annuity carrier must have one of the following ratings from at least two of the following rating organizations:

   a. A.M. Best Company: A++, A+, or A.

   b. Moody's Investors Service (Financial Strength): Aaa, Aa1, or Aa2.

   c. Standard & Poor's Corporation (Claims Paying/Solvency): AAA or AA.

   d. Duff & Phelps Credit Rating Company (Claims Paying Ability Rating: AAA, AA+, or AA.

4. In addition to the requirement of subsection (3) immediately above, an annuity insurer must meet any other requirement the Court considers reasonably necessary to assure that funding to satisfy periodic-payment settlements will be provided and maintained.

5. A qualified insurer issuing an annuity contract pursuant to a qualified funding plan under these rules may not enter into an assumption reinsurance agreement for the annuity contract without the prior approval of the Court, the owner of the annuity contract and the claimant having the beneficial interest in the annuity contract. The Court shall not approve assumption reinsurance unless the re-insurer is also qualified under these rules.

6. The annuity insurance carrier and the broker procuring the policy shall each furnish the Court with an affidavit certifying that the carrier meets the criteria set forth in subsection (3) above as of the date of the settlement and that the qualification is not likely to change in the immediate future. The broker's affidavit shall state that the determination was made with due diligence based on rating information which was available or should have been available to an insurance broker in the structured settlement trade.

7. In the event the parties desire to place the annuity with a licensed insurer in Ohio that does not meet the above criteria, the Court may consider approving the same, but only if the annuity obligation is bonded by an independent insurance or bonding company, licensed in Ohio, in the full amount of the annuity obligation.

C. The application shall include a statement of the *actual cost* to the defendant of the settlement. The actual cost shall be used to fix and determine attorney's contingent fees.

(Amended eff. 9-1-98)

Rule 70.1 Settlement of claims for wrongful death

A. All applications to settle claims for wrongful death shall be set for hearing. All interested parties to the distribution of the net proceeds of the settlement shall be listed by name, residence, and relationship to the decedent on the proposed entry approving settlement or distributing wrongful death proceeds.

B. The term "interested parties" who are subject to notice as set forth in R.C. §2125.02, shall include the surviving spouse, the children and the parents of the decedent or other next of kin who claim to have suffered damages.

C. When the Court is called upon to endorse an agreed entry of distribution or to adjust the shares thereto, consents or notice from those "interested parties" designated above shall be required.

D. The applicant is required to appear at the hearing regarding an application to approve a wrongful death settlement or proposed distribution. An applicant shall have 30 days in which to file the report of distribution unless otherwise ordered by the Court.

E. A magistrate shall approve the report of distribution of the wrongful death proceeds only after appropriate vouchers are presented.

(Amended eff. 9-1-98)

Rule 71.1 Attorney fees

A. Counsel shall enter into a dated written fee agreement with the fiduciary for the estate by the time the inventory is filed. That agreement shall contain an estimate of the total fee and shall be provided to any residual beneficiary upon request. Attorney fees relative to all matters shall be governed by the Code of Professional Responsibility, DR 2-106. The Court has ultimate authority to set attorney fees in any matter.

B. Attorney fees for the administration of estates shall not be paid until the final account is prepared for filing unless otherwise approved by the Court upon application and for good cause shown.

C. Attorney fees may be allowed if there is a written application which sets forth the amount requested and will be awarded only after hearing, except as modified herein. Notice to parties affected by the payment of fees shall be in the form set forth in Appendix A-1.

1. If the requested fee is within the guideline fee set forth below in (H), the account is not delinquent, and *all* parties affected by the payment of fees have consented in writing to the payment of said fees, in the form set forth in Appendix A-2, a written fee application shall not be required.

2. If the requested fee is not within the guideline fee set forth below in (H), said application for attorney fees shall be set for hearing before the Probate Judge. Any party affected by payment of attorney fees may file a Waiver of Notice of Hearing on Application for Attorney Fees and Consent to Payment of Attorney Fees in the form set forth in Appendix A-3.

D. The Court may set a hearing on any application for allowance of attorney fees regardless of the fact that the beneficiaries have given their consent.

E. Except for good cause shown, attorney fees shall not be allowed to attorneys representing fiduciaries who are delinquent in filing the accounts required by R.C. §2109.30.

F. Where the attorney, law partner or firm associate is appointed as fiduciary, the total administration fee for ordinary administration may not exceed the statutory fiduciary commission plus one-half of the attorney fees.

G. As to all other matters, an application for the allowance of attorney fees shall have attached thereto an itemized statement of the services performed, the date services were performed, the time spent in rendering the services and the rate charged per hour.

H. Attorney fees for the administration of a decedent's estate as set forth below may serve as a guide in determining fees to be charged to the estate for legal services of an ordinary nature rendered as attorney for the fiduciary in the complete administration of a decedent's estate. The Court does not have, nor is there recognized, any minimum or maximum fees that will automatically be approved by the Court. The following is not to be considered or represented to clients as a schedule of minimum or maximum fees to be charged. Misrepresentation of this guideline may result in sanctions, including the partial or total disgorging of attorney fees.

1. On the personal property subject to administration and for which the fiduciary is charged and upon the gross proceeds of real estate that is sold under a power of sale under the will or by consent under R.C. § 2127.011 as follows:

a. For the first $50,000.00 at a rate of 5.5%;

b. All above $50,000.00 and not exceeding $100,000.00 at the rate of 4.5%;

c. All above $100,000.00 and not exceeding $400,000.00 at the rate of 3.5%;

d. All above $400,000.00 at the rate of 2.0%.

2. On real property that is not sold at a rate of 2%.

3. On all property not included above:

a. Joint and survivorship property between a husband and wife included in a federal estate tax return or an Ohio estate tax return at the rate of ½% of all such property;

b. All other non-probate property included in a federal estate tax return or an Ohio estate tax return at the rate of 1% of all such property.

4. On real estate sold by judicial proceedings, the guideline fee for attorney compensation shall set by the Court as follows:

a. The first $10,000.00 of the purchase price at the rate of 6%, and;

b. All above $10,000.00 at the rate of 2%.

I. Attorney fees for services rendered in a relief from administration shall be listed on the back of the schedule of assets to be relieved (Form 5.1) as a debt. For fees under $1,000, no application is required.

(Amended eff. 9-1-98)

Rule 71.2 Contingent fee agreements

Prior to an attorney entering into any contingent fee agreement with a fiduciary, an application for authority to enter into said agreement shall be approved by and filed with the Court. In all cases, there shall be a written fee agreement as required by R.C. §4705.15. The Court shall review the reasonableness of the attorney's fees and the itemized expenses of the litigation.

1. If the contingent fee agreement does not exceed 33 ⅓% of the recovery, or 40% if an appeal is taken, prior court approval is not required and the approval of the contingent fee agreement may be ratified at the time of settlement.

2. If the contingent fee agreement exceeds 33 ⅓% of the recovery or 40% if an appeal is taken, prior approval of the Court is required for the fiduciary to enter into such an agreement. Absent such prior approval, the maximum fee permitted shall not exceed 33 ⅓% of the recovery.

(Amended eff. 9-1-98)

Rule 72.1 Executor's and administrator's commissions

Unless otherwise authorized by the Court, extraordinary fiduciary commissions shall not be awarded for travel expenses that would not have been incurred but for the fact that the fiduciary resides outside of Hamilton County.

(Amended eff. 9-1-98)

Rule 73.1 Guardian's compensation

A. Guardians' compensation shall only be awarded after application. Compensation shall be allowed upon the same basis as that set forth for trustee's compensation (Rule 74.1) except that for accounts under $100,000.00 in market value, a maximum fee of ⁸⁄₁₀ of 1% of market valuation at the end of the accounting period shall be allowed with a minimum fee of $250.00 per year. A separate schedule of the guardian's computation, as set forth in Appendix B, shall be attached to said application.

B. Additional compensation, reimbursement for expenses incurred by a guardian and for fees of a guardian of the person only may be fixed by the Court on application. The Court may require that any application for fees or for compensation be set for hearing and that notice of the hearing be given to interested parties as ordered by the Court. A copy of such notice, together with an affidavit of the service of such notice, shall be filed prior to the hearing.

C. The compensation of co-guardians in the aggregate shall not exceed the compensation which would have been payable to only one guardian.

D. Except for good cause shown, neither compensation for a guardian nor fees to the attorney representing such guardian will be allowed while such guardian is delinquent in filing an inventory, account or Guardian's Report. The Court may deny or reduce compensation if there is such a delinquency or failure to faithfully discharge the duties of fiduciary.

(Amended eff. 9-1-98)

Rule 73.2 Veterans administration—guardianships

All applications for guardian compensation or attorney fees shall be set for hearing, and notice shall be given to the Veterans Administration Office, unless a waiver or consent is obtained from the Veterans Administration.

(Amended eff. 9-1-98)

Rule 74.1 Trustee compensation

A. Trustee's compensation shall be as follows:

1. *Corporate Trustees.*

a. Except where the instrument creating the trust provides for compensation, a testamentary trustee may charge fees on the same basis as it charges for living trusts.

b. When assets are invested in common trust funds (pooled funds), management fees may be charged within the fund rather than at the account level. However, a trust's portion of those fees may not exceed those that may have been charged to the trust had it not participated in the pooled funds.

c. On each accounting where fees have been taken, an affidavit is required which asserts that the fees charged and included in the accounting represent those charges for similar services in living trusts.

d. A separate schedule of the computations of the trustee's compensation shall be set forth in the trustee's account as a condition of its approval, in the form set forth in Appendix D.

   e. Corporate Trustees are to furnish their fee schedules to the Court on the 1st day of January of each year and whenever a change in fees is made within any calendar year.

2. *Individual Trustees.*

   a. Except where the instrument creating the trust makes provision for compensation, the trustee may charge fees on the same basis as is currently being charged by the banking institution with which the trust is doing business. However, an appropriate deduction on the trustee's fee must be made where the trustee has delegated any of his or her duties.

   b. Additional compensation, reimbursement for expenses incurred by a trustee may be fixed by the Court on application. The Court may require that any application for fees or for compensation be set for hearing and that notice of the hearing be given to interested parties as ordered by the Court. A copy of such notice, together with an affidavit of the service of such notice, shall be filed prior to the hearing.

   c. On each accounting where fees have been taken, an affidavit will be required setting forth that the fees charged are based on the schedules of the "name" bank.

   d. A separate schedule of the computations of the trustee's compensation shall be set forth in the trustee's account as a condition of its approval, in the form set forth in Appendix D.

(Amended eff. 9–1–98)

Rule 75.1 Local rules—special provisions

A. Civil Commitment of the Mentally Ill. When an affidavit of mental illness has been accepted and an order of detention issued, the Court shall immediately appoint an attorney to represent the respondent. The Court shall also appoint a qualified psychiatrist to act as an independent physician who may testify as to the respondent's psychiatric condition if called upon to do so.

While the patient/respondent is being held pursuant to the order of detention, a "voluntary" commitment shall not be accepted, unless the record or entry has been signed and approved by the patient/respondent's court-appointed counsel.

B. Joint Control of Assets. All bank accounts and brokerage accounts, including but not limited to checking accounts, money market accounts and certificates of deposit, shall remain in the joint control of the fiduciary and counsel for the estate or such other suitable person as the Court may approve in any of the following situations:

1. When the fiduciary is not a resident of Hamilton County, Ohio or any Ohio county contiguous to Hamilton County;

2. When the fiduciary is guardian of the estate of a ward; or

3. When the Court determines that the best interests of the estate will be served by the requirement of joint control.

The joint control requirement may be waived by the Court:

1. When the assets of the estate are held in a custodial depository account (R.C. §2109.13);

2. Upon written application and a showing of good cause by the fiduciary that said requirement should be waived. Good cause may include special training, education or experience that would demonstrate the fiduciary's understanding of fiduciary law and obligations.

C. Adoptions.

1. The attorney for the petitioner shall be responsible for all required notices in adoption proceedings.

2. If an adoption involves a child born before 1–01–97, the putative father, if applicable, shall be named and the petitioner shall exercise due diligence in providing notice to the putative father in all proceedings. If an adoption involves a child born after 1–01–97, petitioner's counsel shall request a search of the Putative Father's Registry and shall file the response to that request. The Court reserves the right to order additional notice to the putative father as deemed necessary.

3. Except in step-parent adoptions, a lawful placement must occur pursuant to R.C. §§5103.15, 5103.16 or 2111.06, prior to the filing of the Petition for Adoption.

4. In step-parent adoptions where the Domestic Relations Court, Juvenile Court or the Child Support Enforcement Agency has a pending case for child support, petitioner(s) or counsel shall notify said court or agency of the child's adoption to allow the support order to be terminated or reduced to a lump-sum judgment.

5. The petitioner is responsible for obtaining a new birth certificate from the Division of Vital Statistics once the adoption is finalized.

6. All surrogacy adoptions shall be treated as non-relative adoptions. All surrogacy contracts must be pre-approved as part of the pre-placement process. Any application or petition failing to comply with this requirement shall be dismissed.

7. The Court shall provide a list of qualified assessors. Petitioner's counsel shall inform the Court of the assessor so selected.

8. All contested adoptions shall be set for pretrial.

9. For all adoptions finalized out of state on children born in Ohio, where the consent hearing is performed by this court, the petitioners shall file ODHS Forms 1693 and 1616 (Release of Identifying Information and Social Medical History Forms).

10. Home Studies and Assessments, when not hand-delivered to the Court, shall be sent by certified or express mail.

D. Exhibits. Attachments to a pleading will remain with the pleading. Exhibits used by a party will be retained separately by either the Court or a court reporter. Any party introducing exhibits, whether introduced into evidence or not, must complete a List of Exhibits (H.C. Form 230.03) in duplicate. After the time for an appeal has expired and all costs have been paid, a party may petition the Court for the return of an original exhibit. Alternatively, the Court may destroy such exhibits pursuant to Sup.R. 26(F).

E. Miscellaneous.

1. Attorneys shall not act as sureties in any cause, nor shall they be permitted to become surety on the bond of any fiduciary. The surety or the surety's agent must personally appear to sign the fiduciary's bond.

2. No certified copies of Entries or Letters of Authority will be issued unless all required filings have been made.

3. When the Court determines that a guardian ad litem is necessary or appropriate, the Court shall appoint a suitable and disinterested person as guardian ad litem.

4. Trial Court Jury Use and Management Standards for the Probate Court shall be the same as those rules and regulations used by the Hamilton County Jury Commissioner, as set forth in the Hamilton County Common Pleas Court Local Rules.

(Amended eff. 9–1–98)

Rule 78.1 Case management in decedent's estates, guardianships and trusts

A. The guardian of an estate shall file an account at least once each year.

B. The fiduciary of every decedent's estate shall file a written Status Report (H.C. Form 113.46 or similar pleading) whenever a partial account, waiver of partial account, or affidavit and entry in lieu of a partial account is filed. If an estate is not fully administered within two years, the matter will be referred to a magistrate to determine whether court intervention is necessary.

C. A continuance to extend the time for filing an inventory, account, or Guardian's Report shall not be granted unless the fiduciary has signed the application for the continuance.

D. Upon citation to the attorney of record for a fiduciary who is delinquent in filing an inventory, account, or Guardian's Report, the Court may bar the attorney from opening any new cases in any new proceeding until all delinquent pleadings are filed.

E. Upon filing exceptions to the inventory or the account, the exceptor shall set said exceptions for a pretrial conference within thirty days. The Court may dispense with the pretrial conference and proceed directly to trial for good cause shown.

(Amended eff. 9–1–98)

Rule 78.2 Case management and pre-trial procedure for civil actions

A. In order to insure the readiness of civil cases in the Probate Division for scheduling conference, formal pretrial conference and trial, the following procedures shall be in effect:

1. A scheduling conference shall be conducted in all civil cases except land sale proceedings. A trial date will be set at said conference.

2. Within thirty (30) days after service has been perfected on all parties, the Court shall set a scheduling conference for the case.

3. Notice of the scheduling conference shall be given to all counsel of record by mail and/or telephone by the Court not less than fourteen (14) days prior to the conference. Any application for continuance of the conference shall be in writing and filed with the Court in a timely manner.

4. The following decisions shall be made at the scheduling conference and all counsel attending must have full authority to enter into a binding pretrial order.

   a. A definite discovery schedule shall be agreed upon by all parties for the completion of discovery.

   b. A definite date for exchange for expert witnesses shall be determined.

   c. A definite date for filing of all motions and pretrial statements which date shall not be later than seven (7) days before the formal pretrial. The date for the formal pretrial shall be set by the Court and shall be held approximately one week prior to the trial.

5. The following decisions shall be made at the formal pretrial and all counsel attending must have full authority to enter into a binding final pretrial order:

   a. Briefs on any legal issues shall be submitted.
   b. Proposed jury instructions shall be submitted.
   c. Proposed jury interrogatories shall be submitted.
   d. Clients shall be present or available by telephone.
   e. No motions shall be heard after the formal pretrial without leave of Court and without good cause being shown in writing.

6. The trial date shall not be changed nor shall the trial be continued without order of the Court and after the showing of good cause in writing.

B. All land sales which have not been concluded within nine (9) months from the date of filing shall be set for a status conference. The attorney of record and the fiduciary shall appear and describe the efforts being made to complete the case. A written status report shall be filed at least seven days prior to said status conference.

(Amended eff. 9–1–98)

Appendix A–1 Notice of hearing on application for attorney's fees

PROBATE COURT OF HAMILTON COUNTY, OHIO

TRUST OF
GUARDIANSHIP OF
ESTATE OF _____
CASE NO. _____

NOTICE OF HEARING ON APPLICATION FOR ATTORNEY'S FEES

To the following persons:

Name	Address
Name	Address
Name	Address

An application for allowance of attorney's fees in the within case has been filed with this Court. Said application requests approval of attorney's fees in the amount of $_____, extraordinary attorney's fee in the amount of $_____ and reimbursement of costs advanced in the amount of $_____. **A copy of the attorney's fee statement with a description of services rendered is attached to this notice.**

The hearing on the Application will be held on _____ at _____ o'clock ___.M. in this Court. The Court is located in Room Cincinnati, Ohio 45202–2145. You are one of those persons whose interests may be affected by the application, and if you know of any reason why such application should not be granted, you should appear and inform the Court.

[Check if applicable]
☐ **This application is for allowance of attorney fees in a decedent's estate, and the requested fees (are)(are not) within the Court's guideline fee.**

_____
Fiduciary/Deputy Clerk

(Amended eff. 9–1–98)

Appendix A–2 Waiver of notice of hearing on application for attorney fees and consent to payment of attorney fees

PROBATE COURT OF HAMILTON COUNTY, OHIO

ESTATE OF _____, DECEASED
CASE NO. _____

CONSENT TO PAYMENT OF ATTORNEY FEES
[This form to be used in a decedent's estate when the requested attorney fees are within the Court's guideline fee]

The undersigned, being a residuary beneficiary or other interested person in the above captioned estate, hereby consents to the payment of attorney fees in the amount of $_____ and costs in the amount of $_____.

In signing this consent, the undersigned hereby acknowledges:
(1) The receipt of the attorney's fee statement with a description of services rendered to the estate;
(2) The fee charged is within the Court's guideline and that said guideline fee has not been represented as a schedule of a minimum or a maximum fee to be charged.
(3) The Court need not make an independent determination that said services were reasonable, necessary and beneficial to the estate.

_____

(Amended eff. 9–1–98)

Appendix A–3 Waiver of notice of hearing on application for attorney fees and consent to payment of attorney fees

PROBATE COURT OF HAMILTON COUNTY, OHIO

ESTATE OF _____, DECEASED
CASE NO. _____

WAIVER OF NOTICE OF HEARING ON APPLICATION FOR ATTORNEY FEES AND CONSENT TO PAYMENT OF ATTORNEY FEES
[This form may only be used in a decedent's estate when the requested attorney fees are *not* within the Court's guideline fee]

The undersigned, being a residuary beneficiary or other interested person in the above captioned estate, hereby waives notice of hearing on application for attorney fees in the amount of $_____ and costs in the amount of $_____.

In signing this consent, the undersigned hereby acknowledges:
(1) The receipt of the attorney's fee statement with a description of services rendered to the estate.
(2) The fee charged is not within the Court's guideline and that said guideline fee has not been represented as a schedule of a minimum or a maximum fee to be charged.

_____

(Amended eff. 9–1–98)

Appendix B Guardian compensation form (Rule 73.1)

Appendix B GUARDIAN COMPENSATION FORM (RULE 73.1)

BASE OR ANNUAL FEE $ _____

PLUS
   MARKET VALUE FEE:

VALUATION   RATE

_____ × _____ = _____
_____ × _____ = _____
_____ × _____ = _____

INCOME FEE:

VALUATION   RATE

_____ × _____ = _____
_____ × _____ = _____
_____ × _____ = _____

EXTRAORDINARY FEES (ITEMIZE AND ATTACH TIME RECORDS)

_____
_____
_____

TOTAL EXTRAORDINARY FEES $ _____

(Amended eff. 9–1–98)

Appendix C Trustees compensation form (Rule 74.1)

Appendix C TRUSTEES COMPENSATION FORM (RULE 74.1)

BASE OR ANNUAL FEE $ _____

PLUS
   MARKET VALUE FEE:

VALUATION   RATE

_____ × _____ = _____
_____ × _____ = _____
_____ × _____ = _____

INCOME FEE:

VALUATION   RATE

_____ × _____ = _____
_____ × _____ = _____
_____ × _____ = _____

EXTRAORDINARY FEES (ITEMIZE AND ATTACH TIME RECORDS)

_____
_____

TOTAL EXTRAORDINARY FEES $ _____

(Amended eff. 9-1-98)

Appendix D Deposits for court costs

Appendix D. DEPOSITS FOR COURT COSTS

Note: THESE COSTS MAY BE CHANGED WITHOUT NOTICE. THE MOST CURRENT COST LIST MAY BE OBTAINED AT THE PROBATE COURT.

ESTATES
—WILL FOR RECORD ONLY	$ 15.00
—APPLICATION TO ADMIT WILL TO PROBATE AND RECORD	$ 30.00
—APPLICATION FOR APPOINTMENT OF EXECUTOR OR ADMINISTRATOR	$170.00
—APPLICATION FOR APPOINTMENT OF ADMINISTRATOR (WRONGFUL DEATH)	$125.00
—APPLICATION TO RELIEVE ESTATE FROM ADMINISTRATION	
$2,500.00 OR UNDER	$ 30.00
PUBLICATION NOT REQUIRED	$ 85.00
PUBLICATION REQUIRED	$125.00

GUARDIANSHIPS
—INCOMPETENT—PERSON ONLY	$145.00
—INCOMPETENT—PERSON AND ESTATE	$175.00
—MINOR—PERSON ONLY	$ 75.00
—MINOR—PERSON AND ESTATE	$100.00

ADOPTIONS
—AGENCY	$140.00
—STEP-PARENT	$120.00
—PRIVATE PLACEMENT	$140.00
—PETITION FOR RELEASE OF ADOPTION INFORMATION	$ 50.00
—PUBLICATION FEE, IF NECESSARY	$ 77.50

OTHER MATTERS
—CIVIL ACTION (LAND SALE, DETERMINATION OF HEIRSHIP, DECLARATORY JUDGMENT, ETC.)	$ 75.00
—NAME CHANGE	$ 75.00
—TESTAMENTARY TRUST	$ 90.00

ALL DEPOSITS WILL BE APPLIED TOWARDS FINAL COSTS. FINAL COSTS MAY VARY. PLEASE CALL FOR FINAL COSTS PRIOR TO THE FINAL ACCOUNT.

(Amended eff. 9–1–98)

LUCAS COUNTY COURT OF COMMON PLEAS

RULES OF THE PROBATE DIVISION

Rule
- Introduction [1]
- 9.1 Court security plan
- 26.1 Court records management and retention
- 53.1 Hours of the court
- 57.1 Filings and judgment entries
- 57.2 New case information sheet
- 57.3 Record checks
- 58.1 Court cost
- 59.1 Affidavit of giving notice of probate of will
- 59.2 Certificate of giving notice of probate of will
- 59.3 Certificate of giving notice of probate of will
- 61.1 Appraisers
- 62.1 Insolvency procedure
- 64.1 Accounts
- 65.1 Land sales
- 66.1 Guardians
- 68.1 Settlement of claims for injuries to minor
- 68.2 Settlement of claims for injuries to minor
- 70.1 Settlement of claims for wrongful death
- 71.1 Counsel fees
- 73.1 Guardian's compensation
- 74.1 Trustee's compensation
- 74.2 Corporate fiduciary compensation
- 75.1 Adoptions
- 78.1 Case management and pre-trial procedure
- 78.2 Jury management plan
- 78.3 Extension of time; continuance of hearing upon citation or removal
- 78.4 Certificate of transfer
- 78.5 Summons and notice
- 78.6 Inventory of decedent's estate

Introduction [1]

It is ordered that the following are adopted as the Local Rules of the Court of Common Pleas, Probate Division. These rules are supplemental to Rules 50–99 of the Rules of Superintendence and must be read in conjunction therewith. The Court of Common Pleas of Lucas County, Ohio, Probate Division, adopts the following rules effective June 21, 1999. Complete with amendments through July 1, 2005.

These rules supplement Rules 50–99 of the Rules of Superintendence for the Courts of Ohio and must be read in conjunction therewith.

[1] Suggested title added by Publisher.

Rule 9.1 Court security plan

The Court Security Plan for the Lucas County Probate Court shall be the same as the Court Security Plan for the General Division of the Lucas County Court of Common Pleas, set forth in Rule 2.01 of the Rules for the General Division of the Lucas County Common Pleas Court

Rule 26.1 Court records management and retention

Pursuant to Rule 26 (G) of the Rules of Superintendence for the Courts of Ohio, the Probate Division of the Court of Common Pleas, Lucas County, Ohio adopts the Court Records Management and Retention and schedules as set forth, and will be followed in conjunction with, the Rules of Superintendence for the Courts of Ohio.

Rule 53.1 Hours of the court

The Probate Court and its offices shall be open for the transaction of business from 8:30 a.m. to 4:30 p.m. daily except Saturday, Sunday, and legal holidays observed by the Court.

No court costs or accounts of fiduciaries shall be accepted after 4:15 p.m. Marriage applications shall not be accepted after 4:00 p.m. (Eff. 03–23–95)

Rule 57.1 Filings and judgment entries

A. WITHDRAWAL OF COUNSEL

An attorney of record on a matter pending in the Probate Court who wishes to withdraw as counsel shall obtain leave of the Probate Court. If the attorney of record is deceased or is permitted by the Court to withdraw from the case, the fiduciary shall promptly designate a new attorney and advise the Court in writing.

B. NOTICE OF NO FURTHER ADMINISTRATION

Where an estate is opened for purposes of admitting the will only, or filing an estate tax return only, or both, and no further administration is contemplated, the attorney shall so advise the Court in writing at the time of filing.

C. CERTIFICATION OF RELATED CASES:

Upon the filing of an application for the appointment of a fiduciary or the filing of a complaint or petition, the attorney of record shall certify that there is no related case on file in this Court. If there is a related case on file, the attorney shall certify the number, character and attorney of record of the related case. This shall be done on a form in the clerk's office.

D. CERTIFICATION–DEPOSITED WILLS

Upon the filing of an application for probate of a will, or an application to appoint a fiduciary for a decedent's intestate estate or relief therefrom, the deputy clerk shall certify that no will or later will is on deposit with the Court pursuant to R.C. 2107.07. A deputy clerk shall assist the attorney in searching for a deposited will.

E. ADDRESS CHANGE OF FIDUCIARY OR ATTORNEY OF RECORD

It is the responsibility of each attorney of record to advise the Court, in writing, and captioned in the particular matter, of any change in the mailing address of either the attorney or the fiduciary. It is the responsibility of each attorney of record to notify the Court, in writing, if a fiduciary dies, or moves out of the State of Ohio. Failure to comply with this rule may lead to the removal of the fiduciary and attorney of record and/or a disallowance of fiduciary and/or attorney fees.

F. ATTORNEY OF RECORD

At the time application is made to the Court of a fiduciary, that fiduciary shall file in the Court the name of the attorney who will represent the fiduciary and perform all legal services required of the fiduciary in all matters relating to the estate, trust, guardianship, or other proceeding. If the attorney is deceased, resigns or is no longer acting, the fiduciary shall promptly designate a new attorney and advise the Court in writing.

G. FILING OF PAPERS

Every filing shall be typewritten or computer generated, shall be prepared by the attorney or shall have endorsed thereon a certificate signed by the attorney certifying that the attorney has examined the pleading or other instrument and that it is correct and proper and shall obtain the original signature of the party submitting the pleading or other instrument. The Court may refuse all filings not so prepared or certified. (Eff. 04–01–92)

Every judgment entry submitted to the magistrate or judge for approval shall be typewritten or computer generated.

Rule 57.2   New case information sheet

Every new case filed shall contain a new case information sheet. The Case Information Sheet shall contain all information required, including, but not limited to a Certification of Related Cases, Certification of Deposited Wills, the Nature of the Case, a designation relating to the Citation of the Spouse and the Designation of an attorney.

Rule 57.3   Record checks

Unless otherwise ordered by the Probate Court, all applicants for appointment as a fiduciary must complete a criminal record check in the matter and form prescribed by the Probate Court, except for (1) applicants who are attorneys at law currently registered with the Ohio Supreme Court, (2) state agencies, and (3) corporate fiduciaries.

Rule 58.1   Court cost

A. Deposits in the amounts set forth below shall be required in the following actions and proceedings, including those where the fiduciary is bonded:

Estate (full administration)	$200.00
Guardianship of Adult Incompetent	$225.00
Conservatorship	$125.00
Guardianship of Minor-Person and Estate or Person only (Home Study Required)	$325.00
Guardianship of Minor-Estate only	$125.00
Emergency service of guardianship hearing	$ 25.00
Guardianship homestudy ordered by Court	$200.00
Testamentary trusts	$110.00
Civil Complaints (including Land Sale)	$110.00

Adoptions:

Agency	$136.00
Adult	$131.00
International	$186.00
Ohio Birth Certificate Only	$ 46.00
Independent/Out–of–State/Placement–Application Only	$ 75.00
Petition for Release of Information	$ 50.00
Independent/Private	$236.00

Homestudy costs are $1,220.00 (+ $50.00 per each extra child) to be paid directly to investigator.

Relative	$236.00

Homestudy costs are $400.00 (+ $50.00 per each extra child) to be paid directly to investigator.

Stepparent	$401.00

Homestudy costs are included in court costs (+ $50.00 per each extra child)

For all Adoptions–Each additional child $61.00 for court costs. Homestudy update	$325.00

No adoption shall be finalized until court costs are paid in full. If a birth parent requires counseling prior to or after the birth of the child, the cost of counseling shall be the responsibility of petitioners, up to the amount of $500.00.

The deposit shall be applied from time to time as filings occur and an additional deposit may be required by the Court if necessary.

B. Payment in full shall be required at the time of filing for relief from administration, minor settlement with no appointment of a guardian, application to probate will only, change of name, guardianship of person only, and other miscellaneous actions.

C. For the purpose of procuring and maintaining computerized legal research services, an additional fee of Three Dollars ($3.00) may be collected as costs in each cause filed in an estate, wrongful death, guardianships, trust, minor settlement, civil action, correction of birth record, registration of birth, change of name, or adoption. (eff. 1–1–93)

D. The Clerk of the Probate Court may charge an additional fee of up to $10.00 in each cause filed in an estate, wrongful death, guardianship, trust, minor settlement, civil action, correction of birth record, registration of birth, change of name, adoption or marriage license for the purpose of Court Computerization pursuant to H.B. 405. (eff. 1–1–93)

E. The Clerk of the Probate Court may retain up to $10.00 of every case where costs are paid in an estate, wrongful death, guardianship, trust, minor settlement, civil action, correction of birth record, registration of birth, change of name or adoption for the purpose of procuring and maintaining microfiche records.

F. The Clerk of the Probate Court may charge, in addition to fees and costs authorized under Section 2101.16 of the Revised Code, a reasonable fee not to exceed fifteen dollars that is to be collected on the filing of each action or proceeding including, but not limited to, an estate, wrongful death, guardianship, trust, minor settlement, civil action, correction of birth, registration of birth, change of name or adoption, and that is to be used to implement dispute resolution procedures.

G. The Clerk of the Probate Court may charge a fee of up to $30.00 for each Ohio Estate Tax Return or Form filed in the Probate Court.

Rule 59.1   Affidavit of giving notice of probate of will

For dates of death on or after 5–31–90, and before 6–23–94, every fiduciary (applicant/commissioner if the estate is relieved from administration) shall be required to file an affidavit of giving notice of the probate of the will within 90 days from the entry admitting said will to probate. The affidavit shall be supplemented by a copy of the form 1.0A (surviving spouse/next of kin) and waivers of notice, affidavit of no notice or a copy of the notice sent for all heirs at law and legatees and devisees of the will. Form 2.3A.

Failure to file the affidavit will forestall the commencement of the statutory period of time to contest the will and will delay the approval of an accounting or commissioner's report filed in said estate. (eff. 5–31–90)

Rule 59.2   Certificate of giving notice of probate of will

For dates of death occurring on or after 6–23–94, and before 1–1–02, every fiduciary (applicant/commissioner if the estate is relieved from administration or other interested person) in testate administration shall be required to file a certificate of giving notice of the probate of the will within 90 days from the entry admitting said will to probate. The certificate shall be supplemented by a copy of the form 1.0A (surviving spouse/next of kin) and waivers of notice, a copy of the notice sent by certified mail for all heirs at law and legatees and devisees of the will and the certified mail receipt for same. Form 2.4.

Failure to file the certificate will forestall the commencement of the statutory period of time to contest the will and will delay the approval of an accounting or commissioner's report filed in said estate. (Eff. 6-23-94)

Rule 59.3 Certificate of giving notice of probate of will

For dates of death occurring on or after 1-1-02, every fiduciary (applicant/commissioner if the estate is relieved from administration or other interested person) in testate administration shall be required to file a certificate of giving notice of the probate of will within two months after the appointment of a fiduciary, or two months after the will is admitted upon the application of an applicant/commissioner if the estate is relieved from administration or other interested person, unless the Court grants an extension of time. The certificate shall be supplemented by a copy of the form 1.0 (surviving spouse/children/next of kin) and waivers of notice, a copy of the notice sent by certified mail for all heirs at law and legatees and devisees of the will and the certified mail receipt for same. Form 2.4

Failure to file the certificate will forestall the commencement of the statutory period of time to contest the will and will delay the approval of an accounting or commissioner's report filed in said estate, and also be subject to citation and penalty provisions of 2109.31 of the Ohio Revised Code.

Rule 61.1 Appraisers

The following persons shall be approved by the Court as qualified appraisers of real estate:

1) State of Ohio licensed real estate brokers and similarly licensed real estate salesmen who are active in the trade or profession or

2) Members of National or State of Ohio recognized appraisal associations who are active in the trade or profession.

Real estate appraisers wishing to be on the Court's approved list of real estate appraisers shall submit a statement of qualifications for approval or non-approval by the Court, listing their:

a) home, business address, telephone numbers and occupation

b) educational background

c) details of familiarity with real estate evaluation

d) general resume of experience in the field of real estate, licenses held and appraisal society memberships.

Further, the following persons shall be approved by the Court as qualified appraisers of certain personal property, including but not limited to furniture, stamps, coins, books, art, boats, automobiles, guns, jewelry:

1) Members of national, state or local recognized appraisal associations who are active in appraising personal property.

Personal property appraisers wishing to be on the Court's approved list of personal property appraisers shall submit a statement of qualifications for approval or non-approval by the Court listing their:

a) home, business address, telephone numbers and occupation

b) educational background

c) details of familiarity with the particular property

d) general resume of experience in the field of their specialty, licenses held and society memberships.

Appraisers of closely held corporations and other business organizations may be selected for Court approval from the list of certified public accountants or public accountants.

The Court shall maintain alphabetical lists of all such approved persons available to the general public in the selection of appraisers for filings in this Court. The Court may, from time to time, add to and delete from this list in its discretion, based on above qualifications. All prior lists maintained by the Court shall be destroyed.

Effective 10-29-91 the Probate Court will no longer waive the required appraisal of real estate. All real estate in an estate must be appraised regardless of the value of the real estate unless a bona fide offer to sell the real estate was signed by the decedent not more than three (3) months prior to the date of death. The Court reserves the right to investigate the value of any real estate reported on an inventory of a fiduciary and may require a secondary appraisal of same.

Rule 62.1 Insolvency procedure

Insolvency hearings may be held in full administrations, reliefs from administration and guardianships (R.C. 2111.24). Insolvency proceedings shall be commenced by the fiduciary (applicant or commissioner if the estate has been relieved from administration) filing a representation of insolvency (LCPC form 7-A) accompanied by a schedule of claims (LCPC Form 7.0A). The attorney of record shall indicate on the schedule of claims in the footnote column the amount of the proposed payment to each creditor. Computer generated or self-drafted forms are permissible. The clerk shall set a hearing on the insolvency on a notice form (LCPC form 7-B) provided by the attorney. The attorney shall notify all creditors of said hearing by certified mail. At the hearing, counsel shall provide proof of notice by certified mail returns or a copy thereof. These returns shall be retained by the Court in the case file. Counsel shall also provide an affidavit of proof of service pursuant to R.C. 2117.17(B) which informs the Court what information was provided to the creditors. Upon receipt of the required certified mail returns and the affidavit of proof of service, the Court will approve the insolvency on the journal entry (LCPC form 7-C) provided by counsel, making any necessary changes and attaching an amended LCPC Form 7.0A only if needed. The Court reserves the right to require counsel to serve additional notice to creditors or submit a drafted journal entry if necessitated by a particular situation.

EXCEPTION TO INSOLVENCY PROCEDURE

No hearing is required and no insolvency forms need be filed if assets are valued at $4,000.00 or less. If a spouse or child(ren) claim a family allowance, then no hearing is required and no insolvency forms need be filed if the assets are valued at $27,000.00 or less for dates of death on or before March 17, 1999 or $42,000.00 or less for dates of death on or after March 18, 1999. In either situation, the estate may be relieved from administration with the creditors and amounts owed listed on the assets and liabilities form 5.1. The attorney shall add language to the form that the estate is insolvent and the estate is proceeding under this rule. Creditors shall be paid in accordance with R.C. 2117.25. It is suggested, as a courtesy only, that each creditor who has not received payment in full be notified accordingly by letter or otherwise; proof of such notification is not required.

This same exception applies in an estate where a full administration has been opened and the fiduciary has determined that the estate is insolvent. The fiduciary may either relieve the estate from further administration and proceed as set forth above or they may file a fiduciary's account indicating that the estate is insolvent and pay creditors pursuant to R.C. 2117.25. It is once again suggested as a courtesy that the fiduciary notify creditors when applying this exception to the insolvency proceeding.

Rule 64.1 Accounts

A. The time for filing fiduciary accounts shall be a follows:

1)(a) For estates, if the date of death is prior to January 1, 2002, the first account shall be due not later than nine months following the date of appointment of the fiduciary. All subsequent accounts must be filed on a yearly basis, unless the Court orders otherwise.

1)(b) For estates, if the date of death is on or after January 1, 2002, the final and distributive account shall be rendered within six months after appointment of the fiduciary unless extensions of administration and filing of account are ordered by the Court. See also Local Rule 78.3

After the initial account is rendered, every fiduciary shall render further accounts at least once each year.

2) For guardianships, the first account shall be due not later than one year following the date of appointment of the guardian. All subsequent accounts shall be due on a yearly basis, unless the Court orders otherwise.

3) For trusts, the first account shall be due not later than one year following the date of appointment of the trustee. All subsequent accounts shall be due on a yearly basis, unless the Court orders otherwise.

4)(a) In estates of decedents where R.C. 2109.301(A) waives the filing of a partial account, the administrator or executor shall file a waiver annually at least seven (7) days before the date the partial account would otherwise be due. Where applicable written consents must accompany each waiver.

4)(b) A Motion to waive the guardian's partial account(s) by Court order pursuant to R.C. 2109.302(B) shall be filed at least seven (7) days prior to the date the partial account(s) would otherwise be due.

5) With the exception of corporate fiduciaries subject to R.C. 1109.16, no fiduciary shall be permitted to file any account without first paying outstanding court costs due, or having an adequate deposit on file. Corporate fiduciaries must comply with this rule within 30 days of filing an account.

B. Compensation for fiduciaries whose fees are based on a computation schedule or on a percentage of assets that are managed, must submit the written computation for said fees simultaneously with the filing of the account.

C. The Lucas County Probate Court Accounting Procedures are hereby adopted by reference hereto. All accountings of fiduciaries shall comply with the accounting procedures adopted by the Lucas County Probate Court and shall be audited by the accounting staff prior to filing same to verify compliance thereto.

D. The Lucas County Probate Court shall publish notice of the hearing on the approval of the account of fiduciary in the Toledo Legal News and assess the publication fee accordingly. Waivers of notice of hearing are not required in the event of such publication. Notice by publication is not required if the Fiduciary submits to the Court proof of service of the hearing on approval for all heirs in an intestate estate and all residuary beneficiaries in a testate estate and/or waivers of such service.

Rule 65.1 Land sales

A. In a land sale proceeding involving a party defendant who is under legal disability, the Court shall appoint a guardian ad litem who shall be an attorney not associated with the attorney or law firm who filed the land sale complaint. The answer of the guardian ad litem shall set forth the facts involved in the sale of the real estate, the interests of the defendant who is under legal disability in the sale and recommendation to the Court as to what action is in the best interest of the defendant who is under legal disability. The Court shall have final approval for all fees submitted by the guardian ad litem.

B. In all land sale proceedings the Auditor and Treasurer of Lucas County shall be made party defendants.

Rule 66.1 Guardians

A. The Court will not accept for filing any guardianship for a minor where the only purpose of the guardianship is to establish a residency for school purpose, qualifying a minor for health/life insurance absent the written consent of the insurance company or to establish the placement for an adoption. The Court will not accept for filing any guardianship for an incompetent person where the sole purpose for the guardianship is to establish a no resuscitation code status for the proposed ward.

B. The Probate Court reserves the right to refer an applicant for guardianship of the person of a minor to the Juvenile Division of the Lucas County Court of Common Pleas. Should the Probate Court accept the application for filing, a home study will be required.

C. All guardians of an incompetent ward under the jurisdiction of the Probate Court who are in possession of any wills of their ward shall be required to deposit for safekeeping all of the wills of their ward in the Probate Court.

D. The Probate Court reserves the right to require any or all supporting documentation to be attached to a request for expenditure of funds in any guardianship proceeding under the jurisdiction of the Probate Court.

E. All reports of guardians as required by R.C. 2111.49 shall be accompanied by a statement of expert evaluation and shall be filed annually on the anniversary date of the appointment of the guardian. Failure to comply with this requirement may result in the removal of the guardian.

F. A Guardian of the person of an incompetent ward shall make at least two personal contacts with the ward on an annual basis. Failure to comply with this requirement may result in the removal of the guardian.

G. The Court will not accept for filing a motion to terminate the guardianship of the estate of an incompetent person in which the total assets of the estate of the ward exceed $1500.00.

Rule 68.1 Settlement of claims for injuries to minor

A. Prior to settling a claim, the attorney shall personally appear at the court to obtain preliminary approval of the completed Proposal for Minor Settlement (LCPC Form 22 MSP).

B. Rule 67 of the Rules of Superintendence for the Courts of Ohio shall apply to all settlements under $10,000.00.

C. When the minor and parents are unrepresented by counsel, the attorney drafting the pleadings and other instruments shall be responsible for depositing the funds and for providing the financial institution with a copy of the ENTRY DISPENSING WITH APPOINTMENT OF GUARDIAN AND ORDERING DEPOSIT (LCPC Form 16–A). This attorney shall obtain a receipt from the financial institution and deposit it with the Court within seven days of the approval of the ENTRY.

Rule 68.2 Settlement of claims for injuries to minor
UNDER $10,000.00

A. Unless otherwise ordered by the Court, all minor settlement applications must be accompanied by a current statement of the examining physician in respect to the injuries sustained, the extent of the recovery, and the physician's prognosis.

B. The injured minor and at least one custodial parent shall appear at the hearing on all applications unless presence of either is excused by the Court prior to the hearing for good cause shown.

C. The Court requires that the attorney, prior to settling a claim personally come to the Court to obtain preliminary approval of the settlement from the Court.

D. Superintendence Rule 67 shall apply to all settlements covered by this rule. In a situation where the minor and his parents are unrepresented by counsel, the attorney drafting the pleadings shall be responsible for depositing the funds and for providing the financial institution with a copy of the entry. Said attorney shall obtain a receipt from the bank and deposit it with the Court within seven days of the entry's approval.

Rule 70.1   Settlement of claims for wrongful death

The Court requires that the attorney, prior to settling a claim, personally come to the Court to obtain preliminary approval of the settlement and distribution of the proceeds of the claim from the Court.

Rule 71.1   Counsel fees

A. Attorney fees allowed as part of the expense for administering a decedent's estate, a trust or a guardianship, shall be based on actual services performed, the novelty and difficulty of the problem involved and the responsibility incurred by the attorney in relation to the amount of the assets. No retainer fees are permitted. Attorney fees and fiduciary fees for the administration of estates shall not be paid until the final account is prepared for filing unless otherwise approved by the Court upon application and for good cause shown. Attorney fees and fiduciary fees for services performed in connection with civil complaints shall not be paid until the matter is finalized unless otherwise approved by the Court upon application and for good cause shown.

B. Except as provided in paragraphs (C), (D) and (E) below, an application, signed by the fiduciary, must be filed for allowance of all attorney fees. Each application shall set forth: 1) an itemized statement of the services performed; 2) the date services were performed; 3) the time spent rendering the services; 4) the average rate charged per hour. If additional fees are claimed for extraordinary or unusual services, the application shall set forth details.

C. When Counsel and an Executor or Administrator have entered into a written contract for legal services to be performed for administering a decedent's estate, and an application to enter into that agreement has been filed with the Court no later than three months after the appointment of the fiduciary without relief from the Court, no application need be made for the allowance unless counsel intends to receive fees prior to the close of the administration of the estate [See 71.1(A)]. Contracts must set forth the method of calculation.

D. When payment of the attorney fee is included in the final account filed by the fiduciary, who is also the sole beneficiary of a solvent estate, no application need be made for the allowance. Counsel shall inform the Court when this circumstance exists by making a statement to that effect in the final account.

E. Any attorney fee, fiduciary fee or guardian's compensation based on a computation on the value of the assets in an estate involving real estate shall include the appraised value of the real estate listed in the inventory if the real estate is transferred and the sale price of the real estate if sold.

F. Except as provided in paragraph (G) below, no application need be made for the allowance of attorney fees if said fees are no greater than the sum of subparagraphs (1) and (2):

1) As to probate assets, including all real and personal property administered, as well as the income therefrom:

4 1/2 % of the first $100,000 thereof;

3 1/2 % of the next $300,000 thereof;

2 1/2 % of the balance thereof.

2) As to non-probate assets:

1 1/2 % of the non-probate assets listed on the Ohio Estate Tax Return;

1 1/2 % of the difference between the non-probate assets listed of the Federal and Ohio Estate Tax Returns

3) Asset values for this schedule shall be the value listed in the date of death column on the estate tax return(s).

4) If, in reliance on this paragraph, no application for attorney fees is filed, counsel shall complete form 13–C, "Computation of Attorney Fees", and attach it to the estate's final account.

G. When counsel and the fiduciary are the same individual, or when both are attorneys associated in the same firm, an application for attorney fees must be filed disclosing the amount of the fiduciary fee claimed. In addition, the options set forth in items (C) and (D) shall not be available for use if the fiduciary fee is taken on a percentage, the attorney fee must be requested at an hourly rate attached to an itemization which details the hours spent on the case, the work performed and the hourly rate of the attorney.

The court reserves the right to reduce the hourly rate if found excessive, or modify the number of hours requested if the interest of the case demands it. (eff. 1–23–92)

H. Application for attorney fees for services rendered to guardians and trustees in setting up the guardianship or trust in the probate court may initially be made after the inventory is filed with the court. Thereafter, application may be made annually when the account is being prepared for filing. (eff. 4–1–92)

Rule 73.1   Guardian's compensation

Unless otherwise provided by law or ordered by the Court, a guardian may charge for his ordinary services an amount computed in accordance with the following schedule during each accounting period required by statute or Court rule.

A. Excluding income from real estate, 4% of the first $3,000 of income, and 3% of the balance in excess of $3,000; and 4% of the first $3,000 of expenditures and 3% of the balance in excess of $3,000.

B. If the guardian manages real estate, a fee amounting to ten percent (10%) of gross rental real estate income may be allowed. If the guardian receives net income from real estate actively managed by others, the guardian shall treat such net income as ordinary income.

C. $2.50 per thousand for the first $100,000 of fair market value of the principal; $2.00 per thousand on the next $300,000 of fair market value of the principal; $1.50 per thousand of the fair market value of the balance.

D. A minimum annual fee of $250.00 will be allowed in each guardianship. (eff. 4–1–92)

Rule 74.1   Trustee's compensation

A. Except where the instrument creating the trust makes provision for compensation, a trustee who is accountable to the court, may charge annually for ordinary services performed by the trustee in connection with the administration of each separate trust estate:

1) An amount to be computed on the fair market value of the principal of the trust property, in accordance with the following schedule, such compensation to be charged one-half to income and one-half to principal, unless the beneficiary or beneficiaries have the power to invade the corpus in which case all compensation shall be paid out of income unless otherwise provided in the instrument creating the trust:

$8.50 per $1000 on the first $200,000 of the fair market value of the principal;

$7.50 per $1000 on the next $800,000 of the fair market value of the principal;

$5.00 per $1000 on the next $1,000,000 of the fair market value of the principal;

$2.50 per $1000 on any amount over $2,000,000.00 of the fair market value of the principal;

2) The trustee may charge a minimum fee of $1000 annually.

3) A separate fee, based upon the time expended, may be charged for the preparation and filing of fiduciary income tax returns. This fee may not exceed $500 except for just cause shown.

B) For the purpose of computing the trustee's compensation as herein provided, the fair market value of the principal of the trust property shall be determined by the trustee as of a date, determined by the trustee, such date to commence during the calendar quarter of the original receipt of trust property and each anniversary date thereafter.

(At the option of the trustee, fee evaluations may be made on a quarterly basis, each evaluation to be coordinated with the original annual evaluation date as selected by the trustee, if this option is selected by the trustee, the trustee must continue to compute such trustee's fee on the quarterly valuation basis, unless upon application to the Probate Court, a change in fee valuation method is allowed.)

C) Additional compensation for extraordinary services may be allowed upon application. The Court may require that the application be set for hearing and notice thereof be given to interested parties in accordance with Civil Rule 73(E). The notice shall contain a statement of amount of the compensation sought.

D) The compensation of co-trustees in the aggregate shall not exceed the compensation which would have been payable if only one trustee had been acting, except in the following instances:

1) Where the instrument under which the co-trustees are acting provided otherwise; or

2) Where all the interested parties have consented in writing to the amount of the co-trustees' compensation, and the consent is endorsed on the co-trustees' account or evidenced by separate instrument filed therewith.

Rule 74.2 Corporate fiduciary compensation

A) For purposes of this rule a Corporate Fiduciary shall be defined as a bank or trust company authorized to conduct a trust business under the laws of the State of Ohio or of the United States.

B) Except where the governing instrument makes a different provision for compensation, a corporate fiduciary, serving in the capacity of guardian or trustee who is accountable to the court may charge on a quarterly basis for ordinary services performed in connection with each separate guardian or trust estate:

1) An amount to be computed on the fair market value of the principal of the trust or guardianship property in accordance with the following schedule, such compensation to be charged one half to income and one half to principal, unless the beneficiary or beneficiaries have the power to invade corpus, in which case all compensation shall be paid out of income unless otherwise provided in the instrument creating the trust:

$10.00 per $1000 on the first $1,000,000 of the fair market value of principal;

$7.50 per $1000 on the next $1,000,000 of the fair market value of principal;

$5.00 per $1000 on any amount over $2,000,000.00 of the fair market value of principal;

2) The corporate fiduciary may charge a minimum fee of $2500 annually.

3) A separate fee, based upon time expended, may be charged for the preparation and filing of fiduciary income tax returns. This fee may not exceed $500 except for just cause shown.

C) For purposes of completing the trustee's and guardian's compensation as herein provided, the fair market value of the principal shall be determined on a quarterly basis.

D) Additional compensation for extraordinary services may be allowed upon application. The Court may require that the application be set for hearing and notice thereof be given to interested parties in accordance with Civil Rule 73(E). The notice shall contain a statement of the amount of the compensation sought.

E) The compensation of co-trustees in the aggregate shall not exceed the compensation which would have been payable if only one trustee had been acting, except in the following instances:

1) Where the instrument under which the co-trustees are acting provided otherwise; or

2) Where all the interested parties have consented in writing to the amount of the co-trustees' compensation, and the consent is endorsed on the co-trustees' account or evidenced by separate instrument filed therewith.

Rule 75.1 Adoptions

A) The Lucas County Probate Court Adoption Procedures are hereby adopted by reference hereto. Copies are available at the Probate Court.

B) If a birth parent requires counseling prior to or after the birth of the child, the cost of counseling shall be the responsibility of petitioners, up to the amount of $500.00.

Rule 78.1 Case management and pre-trial procedure

For the purpose of insuring the readiness of civil cases in the Probate Division for pre-trial, final pre-trial and trial, the following procedures shall be in effect:

I. CIVIL ACTIONS

A) A pre-trial conference shall be conducted in all civil cases prior to being scheduled for trial, including land sale proceedings.

B) Within forty-five (45) days after the answer date the case shall be set by the Court for a pre-trial conference.

C) Notice of the pre-trial conference shall be given to all counsel of record by mail and/or telephone by the court not less than fourteen (14) days prior to the conference. An application for continuance of the conference shall be in writing and filed with the Court in a timely manner.

D) The following decisions shall be made at the pre-trial conference and all counsel attending must have full authority to enter into a binding pre-trial order:

1) A definite discovery schedule shall be agreed upon by all parties for the completion of all discovery.

2) A definite date for exchange for expert witness reports shall be determined.

3) A definite date for filing of all motions which date shall not be later than seven (7) days before the final pre-trial. The date for the final pre-trial shall be set by the Court and shall be held approximately one week prior to the trial.

E) The following decisions shall be made at the final pre-trial and all counsel attending must have full authority to enter into a binding final pre-trial order:

1) The Court will rule on all pre-trial motions;

2) Briefs on any legal issues shall be submitted;

3) Proposed jury instructions shall be submitted;

4) Proposed jury interrogatories shall be submitted;

5) Clients shall be present;

6) No motions shall be heard after the final pre-trial without leave of Court and without good cause being shown.

F) The trial date shall not be changed nor shall the trial be continued without order of the Court and after showing of good cause.

G) The Probate Judge shall assign one or more deputy clerks to review and inventory all civil cases filed. The progress of each case will be noted on a case management worksheet that will be updated by the assigned clerk. In the event that any civil case is non-compliant with the case management plan, the clerk shall bring said case to the attention of the Probate judge.

H) The Lucas County Probate Court may refer any civil action or preceding that is within the jurisdiction of the Probate Court for dispute resolution, which shall include, but is not limited to, mediation.

The selection of the mediator, fees for mediator, and source of payment for mediator fees shall be within the sole discretion of the Probate Court Judge. Payment for any additional expenses associated with the resolution of disputes must have prior approval by the Probate Court.

I) Pursuant to Rule 53 of the Ohio Rules of Civil Procedure, the Probate Judge may assign any pending matter before the Court to a magistrate. This rule shall serve as an order of reference for any matter so assigned.

II. LAND SALES

All sale of lands actions which remain open after a period of twelve months from the date of the filing of the complaint shall be scheduled for a status conference. The following procedures shall be in effect for the status conference:

1) The attorney of record and fiduciary must attend the status conference;

2) A written status report shall be filed with the Court no later than seven (7) days prior to the status conference;

3) The status report shall address the issues as to the efforts being made to sell the real estate and when the case will be closed;

4) Failure to appear for this conference could result in the dismissal of the land sale complaint pursuant to Civ. R. 41(B)(1) and Superintendence Rule 40.

III. DECEDENT'S ESTATES

A. The statutory time for filing of an account (R.C. 2109.30 and R.C. 2109. 301) shall be adhered to and the citation procedure (R.C. 2109.31) shall be utilized if necessary to gain compliance.

B. RESERVED

IV. WRONGFUL DEATH SETTLEMENTS

All hearings shall be held within thirty (30) days after the proposal discussion with the magistrate.

V. GUARDIANSHIPS

Adequate statutory provisions exist to control timeliness of filings; however, each case shall be reviewed annually.

VI. TRUSTS

Adequate statutory provisions exist to control timeliness of filings; however, each case shall be reviewed annually.

VII. MOTIONS

All motions filed in this Court in a civil action or contested matter shall be accompanied by a memorandum stating the grounds and citing the authorities relied upon. Opposing counsel or a party shall serve the response memorandum on or before the fourteenth (14th) day after the date of service as set forth on the certificate of service attached to the served copy of the motion. The moving party shall serve any reply memorandum on or before the seventh (7th) day after the date of service as set forth on the certificate of service attached to the served copy of the response memorandum. The motion shall be deemed submitted to the Court upon the Court's determination but not later than the twenty-eighth (28th) day after the motion is filed unless the Court orders a hearing or a prior written request for oral hearing has been filed and approved by the Court. The time and length of any oral hearing shall be fixed by the Court.

Rule 78.2   Jury management plan

STANDARD 1

OPPORTUNITY FOR SERVICE

A. The opportunity for jury service is not to be denied or limited on the basis of race, national origin, gender, age, religious belief, income, occupation, disability, or any other factor that discriminates against a cognizable group in the jurisdiction.

B. Jury service is considered to be an obligation of all qualified citizens.

C. The Court shall make reasonable accommodations for those jurors having special needs due to a physical impairment.

STANDARD 2

JURY SOURCE LIST

A. The names of potential jurors are drawn from the most recent list of registered voters in Lucas County, Ohio. This list is maintained by the Lucas County Board of Elections.

B. The list of registered voters should be representative and should be as inclusive of the adult population in Lucas County as is feasible.

C. The Court will periodically request that the Lucas County Board of Elections review the Voter's Registration List to ensure that the list is representative and inclusive of the adult population in Lucas County.

D. Should the Court determine that improvement is needed in the representative or inclusive nature of the jury source list, appropriate corrective action will be taken. The Court may evaluate on a quarterly basis, the demographic profile of jurors reporting for service. This will be used as an indicator of the representative and inclusive nature of the jury source list.

STANDARD 3

STANDARD SELECTION PROCEDURES

A. Random selection procedures are used throughout the juror selection process. The method used provides each eligible and available person with an equal probability of selection. These methods are documented by the Annual Journal Entry of the court which outlines the selection process. The annual selection process, in compliance with Ohio Revised Code Section 2313.08, shall be as follows:

The record of registered voters shall be arranged alphabetically so far as practicable and under convenient divisions by precincts, districts and townships for all Lucas County.

The selections of the names for the annual jury list shall be as follows: The Jury Commissioners shall randomly draw a number from one (1) to ten (10). The number so drawn shall be the key number used to determine the first registered voter selected from the record to be a prospective juror. The same number shall be used to advance through the list of registered voters to select the remainder of the perspective jurors. This method shall be used until the list of registered voters is exhausted and the resulting list shall be the annual jury list.

B. The random order of selection shall be maintained throughout the jury service process to the greatest extent possible.

C. Departures from the principle of random selection are considered appropriate:

1. To exclude persons ineligible for service in accordance with Standard 4;

2. To excuse or defer prospective jurors in accordance with Standard 6;

3. To remove prospective jurors for cause or if challenged peremptorily in accordance with Standards 8 and 9, and;

4. To provide all prospective jurors with an opportunity to be called for jury service and to be assigned to a panel in accordance with Standard 13.

STANDARD 4
ELIGIBILITY FOR JURY SERVICE

All persons will be eligible for jury service except those who:

A. Are less than eighteen years of age;

B. Are not citizens of the United States;

C. Are not residents of the jurisdiction in which they have been summoned to serve;

D. Are not able to communicate in the English language; or

E. Have been convicted of a felony and have not had their civil rights restored.

STANDARD 5
TERM OF AND AVAILABILITY FOR JURY SERVICE

A. The time that persons are called upon to perform jury service and to be available is the shortest period consistent with the needs of justice.

B. A term of service for the Lucas County Common Pleas Court, Probate Division is two days or the completion of one trial, whichever is longer.

C. Persons are not required to maintain a status of availability for jury service for longer than two days.

STANDARD 6
EXEMPTION, EXCUSE AND DEFERRAL

A. There are no automatic excuses or exemptions, with the exception of statutory exemptions.

B. Eligible persons who are summoned may be excused from jury service only if:

1. Their ability to receive and evaluate information is so impaired that they are unable to perform their duties as jurors and they are excused for this reason, or

2. They request to be excused because their service would be continuing hardship to them or to members of the public and they are excused by the Court.

C. Deferrals for jury service for reasonable short periods of time may be permitted by the Court.

D. Requests for excuses, deferrals and disqualifications and their disposition are recorded. Specific uniform guidelines for determining such requests have been adopted by the Court.

STANDARD 7
VOIR DIRE

A. In civil cases the voir dire process shall be held on the record unless waived by the parties.

B. The Judge should ensure that the privacy of prospective jurors is reasonably protected and the questioning is consistent with purpose of the voir dire process.

C. Voir Dire examination should be limited to matters relevant to determine whether to remove a juror for cause and to determine the juror's fairness and impartiality.

D. The trial judge may conduct a preliminary voir dire examination. Counsel shall then be permitted to question panel members for a reasonable period of time.

STANDARD 8
REMOVAL FROM THE JURY PANEL FOR CAUSE

If the judge determines during the voir dire process that any individual is unable or unwilling to hear the particular case at issue fair and impartially, that individual should be removed from the panel. Such a determination may be made on a motion of counsel or by the Judge.

STANDARD 9
PEREMPTORY CHALLENGES

The exercise of Peremptory challenges shall be in accordance with the Ohio Revised Code, Civil Rules, and Criminal Rules.

STANDARD 10
ADMINISTRATION OF THE JURY SYSTEM

A. The responsibility for administration of the jury system is vested exclusively in Lucas County Common Pleas Court. Any administration of the jury system concerning Probate matters shall be handled in accordance with **Standard 10C**

B. All procedures concerning jury selection and service are governed by Ohio Rules of Court.

C. Responsibility for administering the jury system in the Probate Court is vested in the Assignment Commissioner of the Probate Court, acting under the supervision of the Probate Judge of the Lucas County Common Pleas Court, Probate Division.

STANDARD 11
NOTIFICATION AND SUMMONING PROCEDURES

A. The notice summoning a person to jury service and the questionnaire eliciting essential information regarding that person is:

1. Combined in a single document;

2. Phrased so as to be readily understood by an individual unfamiliar with the legal and jury systems; and

3. Delivered by ordinary mail.

B. The summons clearly explains how and when the recipient must respond and the consequences of failure to respond.

C. The questionnaire is phrased and organized so as to facilitate quick and accurate screening and request only that information essential for:

1. Determining whether a person meets the criteria for eligibility;

2. Providing basic background information ordinarily sought during voir dire examination; and

3. Efficiently managing the jury system.

D. Policies and procedures exist for monitoring failures to respond to a summons and for enforcing a summons to report for jury service.

STANDARD 12
MONITORING THE JURY SYSTEM

The Lucas County Common Pleas Court collects and analyzes information regarding the performance of the jury system on a regular basis in order to evaluate:

A. The representative and inclusive nature of the jury source list;

B. The effectiveness of qualification and summoning procedures;

C. The responsiveness of individual citizens to jury summonses;

D. The efficient use of jurors; and

E. The cost-effectiveness of the jury management system.

STANDARD 13
JUROR USE

A. The Lucas County Common Pleas Court employs the services of prospective jurors so as to achieve optimum use with a minimum inconvenience to jurors.

B. The Court determines the minimally sufficient number of jurors needed to accommodate anticipated trial activity. This information and appropriate techniques are used to adjust both the number of individuals summoned for jury duty and number assigned to jury panels. The Court makes every effort to ensure that each prospective juror who has reported to the Court is assigned for voir dire.

C. The Court coordinates jury management and calendar management to make effective use of jurors.

STANDARD 14
JURY FACILITIES

A. The Lucas County Common Please Court provides a separate room as a jury assembly and waiting area.

B. The entrance and registration area are clearly identified and appropriately designed to accommodate the daily flow of prospective jurors to the courthouse.

C. Jurors are accommodated in waiting facilities furnished with suitable amenities.

D. Jury deliberation rooms provide space, furnishings, and facilities conductive to reaching a fair verdict. The safety and security of the deliberation rooms are ensured.

E. To the extent feasible, juror facilities are arranged to minimize contact between jurors, parties, counsel, and the public.

STANDARD 15
JUROR COMPENSATION

A. Persons called for jury service will receive a reasonable fee for their service.

B. Such fees will be paid promptly.

C. Employers are prohibited from discharging, laying-off, denying advancement opportunities to, or otherwise penalizing employees who miss work because of jury service.

STANDARD 16
JUROR ORIENTATION AND INSTRUCTION

A. The orientation program is:

1. Designed to increase prospective jurors' understanding of the judicial system and prepare them to serve competently as jurors; and

2. Presented in a uniform and efficient manner using a combination of written, oral, and audiovisual materials.

B. The Court provides some form of orientation or instructions to persons called for jury service:

1. Upon initial contact prior to service;

2. Upon first appearance at the Court; and

3. Upon reporting to a courtroom for voir dire.

C. The trial judge shall within his or her discretion, give instructions deemed appropriate for each case.

D. The judge may instruct jurors as to the utilization of written instructions and note taking and questioning by jurors.

STANDARD 17
JURY SIZE AND UNANIMITY OF VERDICT

Jury size and unanimity in civil cases shall conform with existing Ohio law.

STANDARD 18
JURY DELIBERATIONS

A. Jury deliberations will take place under conditions and pursuant to procedures that are designed to ensure impartiality, secrecy, and enhance rational decision-making.

B. The judge will instruct the jury concerning appropriate procedures to be followed during deliberations in accordance with Standard 16C.

C. The deliberation room will conform to the recommendations set forth in Standard 14C.

D. The jury will not be sequestered except under the circumstances and procedures set forth in Standard 19.

E. A jury will not be required to deliberate after a reasonable hour unless the trial judge determines that evening or weekend deliberations would not impose an undue hardship upon the jurors and are required in the interest of justice.

F. Training is provided to personnel who escort and assist jurors during deliberation.

STANDARD 19
SEQUESTRATION OF JURORS

A. A jury will be sequestered only for good cause, including but not limited to insulating its members from improper information or influences.

B. The trial judge shall have the discretion to sequester a jury on the motion of counsel or on the judge's initiative and shall have the responsibility to oversee the conditions of sequestration.

C. Standard procedures will be promulgated to:

1. Achieve the purpose of sequestration; and

2. Minimize the inconvenience and discomfort of the sequestered jurors.

D. Training is provided to personnel who escort and assist jurors during sequestration.

Rule 78.3 Extension of time; continuance of hearing upon citation or removal

A. Requests for extensions of time for the filing of an account, inventory or commissioner's report which is not delinquent by six months or more may be submitted to the Court by facsimile without the requirement of filing a hard copy of same.

B. The probate court reserves the right to require the consent of the beneficiaries on any request for an extension of time.

C. Any request for a continuance of the hearing on a citation or removal of fiduciary shall be approved by the fiduciary and shall be filed in the account department to facilitate case tracking.

Rule 78.4 Certificate of transfer

A. In all administrations, reliefs, and no-administration estates, each certificate of transfer must be requested by the filing of an application and journal entry. (Form 12.0).

B. No certificate of transfer shall be issued by the Court unless the legal description listed on the certificate is the exact duplicate of that listed on the fiduciary's inventory excluding those certificates issued when an estate is relieved from administration. Whenever a certificate of transfer is issued by the Court, and it is later discovered that it is not needed or was issued in error, it shall be the responsibility of counsel to move the Court to cancel same; and where possible, tender any issued, but unrecorded, documents back to the Court. Any request to correct a certificate of transfer shall be made by an "Application for Amended Certificate of Transfer".

C. A request for a duplicate certificate of transfer may be made by an "Application for Alias Certificate of Transfer".

Rule 78.5 Summons and notice

A deposit of $10.00 is required for personal service upon each nonresident of the county or state.

Rule 78.6 Inventory of decedent's estate

The Lucas County Probate Court shall publish notice of the hearing on the approval of the inventory of fiduciary in the Toledo Legal News and assess the publication fee accordingly. Waivers of notice of hearing are not required in the event of such publication. Notice by publication is not required if the fiduciary submits to the Court proof of service of notice of the hearing on approval for any person interested in the decedent's estate and/or waivers of such service.

MONTGOMERY COUNTY COURT OF COMMON PLEAS

RULES OF THE PROBATE DIVISION

SUPERINTENDENCE RULE 5   LOCAL RULES
Rule
Local Rule 5.1   Adoption, scope and construction of rules

SUPERINTENDENCE RULE 6
Local Rule 6.1   Attorney registration number

SUPERINTENDENCE RULE 8
Local Rule 8.1   Court appointments

SUPERINTENDENCE RULE 9   SECURITY PLANS; CONFIDENTIALITY
Local Rule 9.1   Court security policy and procedures plan

SUPERINTENDENCE RULE 11
Local Rule 11.1   Recording of proceedings

SUPERINTENDENCE RULE 12
Local Rule 12.1   Conditions for broadcasting and photographing court proceedings

SUPERINTENDENCE RULE 26
Local Rule 26.1   Court records management and retention

SUPERINTENDENCE RULE 51
Local Rule 51.1   Standard probate forms

SUPERINTENDENCE RULE 52   SPECIFICATIONS FOR PRINTING PROBATE FORMS
Local Rule 52.1   Computerized forms

SUPERINTENDENCE RULE 53
Local Rule 53.1   Hours of the court
Local Rule 54.1   Conduct in the court

SUPERINTENDENCE RULE 55
Local Rule 55.1   Examination of probate records
Local Rule 56.1   Continuances

SUPERINTENDENCE RULE 57
Local Rule 57.1   Filings and judgment entries

SUPERINTENDENCE RULE 58
Local Rule 58.1   Deposit for court costs
Local Rule 59.1   Wills

SUPERINTENDENCE RULE 60
Local Rule 60.1   Application for letters of authority to administer estate and notice of appointment

SUPERINTENDENCE RULE 61
Local Rule 61.1   Appraisers

SUPERINTENDENCE RULE 62
Local Rule 62.1   Claims against estate
Local Rule 63.1   Application to sell personalty

SUPERINTENDENCE RULE 64
Local Rule 64.1   Accounts

SUPERINTENDENCE RULE 65
Local Rule 65.1   Land sales

SUPERINTENDENCE RULE 66
Local Rule 66.1   Guardianships

SUPERINTENDENCE RULE 67
Local Rule 67.1   Estates of minors of not more than $10,000.00

SUPERINTENDENCE RULE 68   SETTLEMENT OF INJURY CLAIMS OF MINORS
Rule
Local Rule 68.1   Settlement of minor's claims
Local Rule 69.1   Settlement of claims against adult ward

SUPERINTENDENCE RULE 70   SETTLEMENT OF WRONGFUL DEATH AND SURVIVAL CLAIMS
Local Rule 70.1   Settlement of wrongful death claims

SUPERINTENDENCE RULE 71
Local Rule 71.1   Counsel fees

SUPERINTENDENCE RULE 72   EXECUTOR'S AND ADMINISTRATOR'S COMMISSIONS
Local Rule 72.1   Executor's and administrator's compensation

SUPERINTENDENCE RULE 73
Local Rule 73.1   Guardian's compensation

SUPERINTENDENCE RULE 74
Local Rule 74.1   Trustee's compensation

SUPERINTENDENCE RULE 75
Local Rule 75.1   Guardian ad litem

SUPERINTENDENCE RULE 76
Local Rule 76.1   Exception to the rules
Local Rule 77.1   Compliance

SUPERINTENDENCE RULE 78   PROBATE DIVISION OF THE COURT OF COMMON PLEAS CASE MANAGEMENT IN DECEDENT'S ESTATES, GUARDIANSHIPS AND TRUSTS
Local Rule 78.1   Case management
Local Rule 79.1   Inventory
Local Rule 80.1   Employment of auctioneers and clerks
Local Rule 81.1   Qualification of guardian ad litem
Local Rule 82.1   Testamentary trustee must accept duties in person
Local Rule 83.1   Adoption
Local Rule 84.1   Court security
Local Rule 85.1   Jury management plan
Local Rule 86.1   Magistrates
Local Rule 87.1   Record
Local Rule 88.1   Relieving estate from administration
Local Rule 89.1   Disclaimers

APPENDICES
App A Attorney fees
App B Computation of attorney fees
App C Consent to payment fees
App D Computation of fiduciary fees in estate cases
App E Computation of guardian's fees
App F Computation of trustee's fees

SUPERINTENDENCE RULE 5   LOCAL RULES

Local Rule 5.1   **Adoption, scope and construction of rules**

The Probate Division of the Montgomery County Common Pleas Court adopts the following rules for the management of proceedings and other functions of the court pursuant to Rule 5 of the Rules of Superintendence for the Courts of Ohio. The court may amend these rules as needed or as required by law.

These rules are intended to supplement and complement the Ohio Rules of Civil Procedure, other applicable controlling statutes, and the Rules of Superintendence for the Courts of Ohio. (See www.sconet.state.oh.us/Rules/Superintendence/)

(Adopted eff. 2–1–05.)

SUPERINTENDENCE RULE 6

Local Rule 6.1 Attorney registration number

All attorneys who appear before this court or prepare documents for filing with this court shall include their attorney registration number issued by The Supreme Court of Ohio on all documents filed with the court.

(Adopted eff. 2–1–05.)

SUPERINTENDENCE RULE 8

Local Rule 8.1 Court appointments

(A) The court will maintain separate master lists of persons who may be appointed as attorneys, guardian ad litem, appraisers, commissioners, fiduciaries, investigators, mediators and trustees for suit. Appointees will be added to each list upon their request and a demonstration to the court that they possess the requisite skill, expertise and any required licensure pursuant to these rules and the laws of the State of Ohio.

(B) Appointments will be made from such lists taking into consideration the qualifications, skills, expertise, and caseload of the appointee, in addition to the type, complexity, and requirements of the case. The Court will periodically review the appointment lists to ensure the equitable distribution of appointments and that all potential appointees continue to meet the established qualifications.

(C) Court appointees will be paid a reasonable fee with consideration given to the factors contained in DR 2-106 of the Code of Professional Responsibility, the Ohio Revised Code, and the Local Rules of Court relating to fees except where otherwise noted.

(Adopted eff. 2–1–05.)

SUPERINTENDENCE RULE 9 SECURITY PLANS; CONFIDENTIALITY

Local Rule 9.1 Court security policy and procedures plan

The Court has adopted and implemented a Security Policy and Procedures Manual as required by Rule 9 of the Rules of Superintendence. This plan shall remain confidential and not be a matter of public record.

(Adopted eff. 2–1–05.)

SUPERINTENDENCE RULE 11

Local Rule 11.1 Recording of proceedings

(A) Proceedings before a judge or magistrate may be recorded by stenographic or other electronic means approved by the Court. The judge may order the use of any method of recording authorized by this rule.

(B) Any interested person may request a transcription of an electronic recording from the Court stenographer. The person making the request shall pay the cost of the transcription.

(C) The Court will maintain all electronically recorded proceedings for three (3) years from the date of the hearing. Any interested person desiring to preserve the record beyond that period must make arrangements to have the record transcribed.

(Adopted eff. 2–1–05.)

SUPERINTENDENCE RULE 12

Local Rule 12.1 Conditions for broadcasting and photographing court proceedings

In compliance with Rule 12 of the Rules of Superintendence, the court may permit the broadcasting, televising, recording or photographing of court proceedings. The term "proceedings" shall mean public hearings held by the court.

(A) The taking of photographs and/or making of sound or video recordings, or live broadcasting by radio or television of judicial proceedings in a courtroom or the adjacent corridors shall not be permitted unless authorized by the court in writing in advance.

(B) Request for permission to broadcast, televise, record or photograph shall be made in writing to the court administrator as far in advance as reasonably practicable but not later than twenty-four (24) hours prior to the proceeding, unless otherwise permitted by the judge. Request forms may be obtained form the court administrator's office.

(C) The court administrator shall immediately notify the judge, the attorneys for the parties, or the parties, if unrepresented of the media request. If the request is approved, the judge will file an entry setting forth the conditions of the broadcasting or photographing.

(D) If the proceeding is continued for a period of more than thirty (30) days, a new media request is required.

(E) In adoption hearings, the Court will allow the families to photograph the proceedings without advance written consent of the Court.

(Adopted eff. 2–1–05.)

SUPERINTENDENCE RULE 26

Local Rule 26.1 Court records management and retention

The court has a Schedule of Records Retention and Disposition filed under case number 2004MSC00404, which will be followed in conjunction with the Rules of Superintendence for the Courts of Ohio.

(Adopted eff. 2–1–05.)

SUPERINTENDENCE RULE 51

Local Rule 51.1 Standard probate forms

Forms approved for use in the Montgomery County Probate Court are available at the Court and on the Court's website: www.mcohio.org/probate

(Adopted eff. 9–20–99; amended eff. 4–20–2004; 2–1–05.)

SUPERINTENDENCE RULE 52 SPECIFICATIONS FOR PRINTING PROBATE FORMS

Local Rule 52.1 Computerized forms

(A) Computer generated forms must comply with the specifications and format outlined by the Rules of Superintendence. The signature of the applicant or attorney constitutes a certificate that the computer generated forms comply with the rules.

(B) All computer forms presented for filing must be generated with the exact wording as well as blank lines as they appear in the uniform forms.

(C) The type size for the body of all forms filed in this Court cannot be less than ten (10) point or greater than twelve (12) point.

(D) The Court may reject any forms that fail to comply with this rule.

(Adopted eff. 9–20–99; amended eff. 4–20–04; 2–1–05.)

SUPERINTENDENCE RULE 53

Local Rule 53.1   Hours of the court

The Probate Court shall be open for the transaction of business from 8:30 a.m. to 4:30 p.m., Monday through Friday except holidays. All pleadings requiring a new case number or the payment of Court costs shall be filed by 4:15 p.m.

(Adopted eff. 9–20–99; amended eff. 4–20–04; 2–1–05.)

Local Rule 54.1   Conduct in the court

(A) Proper conduct is required by all attorneys, parties, court personal, and all other persons who appear before this Court. Any conduct that interferes with the proper administration of justice is prohibited and will subject the offender to sanctions or removal from this Court.

(B) Proper attire is required of all parties who appear before this Court. Any party who does not appear in proper attire is subject to sanctions or removal from this Court.

(C) No radio, television, telephone, camera, video camera, or other audio or video recording device may be used in any proceeding or communication with this Court unless expressly permitted by this Court. Superintendence Rule 12 shall be followed to obtain the advance permission of this Court for the use of any of any audio or video recording device. In the case of adoptions, this Court will allow the use of cameras or video cameras without the advance consent of this Court. This Court will prepare and submit a list of adoption hearings to Court security personal in order to allow cameras or video cameras into the courthouse. The consent of the adoptive parents is required.

(Adopted eff. 9–20–99; amended eff. 4–20–04.)

SUPERINTENDENCE RULE 55

Local Rule 55.1   Examination of probate records

(A) Probate Court public records may be viewed at the Court's website: www.mcohio.org/probate. No records shall be removed from the court.

(B) Public records may be examined at the court and copies may be obtained at a reasonable cost.

(C) Adoption, mental illness, certain estate tax filings, and mental retardation proceedings are confidential. Records of these proceedings may be accessed only as allowed by law.

(Adopted eff. 9–20–99; amended eff. 4–20–04; 2–1–05.)

Local Rule 56.1   Continuances

(A) Continuances may be granted upon written or oral motions. In order to comply with the requirements of Rule 56 of the Rules of Superintendence, no continuance shall be granted without notice to, or the consent of, the adverse party or the adverse party's counsel of record.

(B) Absent special circumstance, all requests for continuances of hearing or trial dates shall be submitted to this Court at least ten (10) days before any scheduled trial or hearing.

(C) If the consent of all parties and or counsel for parties has been obtained, an agreed entry may be submitted to this Court. The parties or counsel for parties shall coordinate a new hearing date with the Clerk's Office and submit the new hearing date on the proposed entry. It is the responsibility of counsel to obtain the consent of their client before they consent to a continuance. It is also the responsibility of counsel to obtain the consent of their client before they request a continuance. All continuances will be made to a new hearing date.

(D) If the consent of all parties or counsel for all parties is not obtained, a written motion for continuance must be filed with this Court. Any motion for continuance shall set forth good cause for the requested continuance. Written notice of the motion shall be provided to all parties in interest. Failing to object to the requested continuance within seven (7) days after the motion if filed shall constitute consent to the continuance. The Court reserves the right to schedule any motion for continuance for hearing. The Court must find that the continuance serves the interests of justice.

(E) Any motions for leave to plead shall be made by written motion to the Court. The motion shall set forth any justification for the request and have attached to the motion a copy of any pleading that will be filed if the motion is granted.

(Adopted eff. 9–20–99; amended eff. 4–20–04.)

SUPERINTENDENCE RULE 57

Local Rule 57.1   Filings and judgment entries

(A) All filings, except wills, shall be on eight and one-half (8 1/2) by eleven (11) inch paper, without backings. All pleading, motions or other filings shall be typed or printed in ink and be sufficiently legible to meet the Court's criteria for imaging. The Court may refuse or strike any filings in which the text or the signatures are illegible. The court will accept for filing only those pleadings that are complete. <u>Filings that are not complete may be returned to counsel and/or the applicant.</u>

(B) When a filing consists of more than one page, the case number must appear in the upper portion of each page, including attachments.

(C) All filings shall contain the name, address, telephone number, and attorney registration number of the individual counsel representing the fiduciary or in the absence of counsel, the name address and telephone number of the fiduciary. The address of the fiduciary who is not an attorney must be the fiduciary's legal residence. A fiduciary who is an attorney may use an office address. Attorneys, fiduciaries, and pro se litigants shall notify the Court of any address changes.

Failure of the fiduciary to notify the court of the fiduciary's current address shall be grounds for removal. The fiduciary shall be given not less than ten days written notice of the hearing to remove. The notice shall be sent by regular mail to the last known address contained in the Court's case file.

(D) Unless otherwise ordered by the Court, the prevailing party shall prepare a proposed judgment entry and submit the original to the Court with a copy to Counsel for the opposing party or to the opposing party if there is no counsel. The proposed entry shall be submitted within seven (7) days after judgment. If the prevailing party fails to submit this entry, the matter may be dismissed or the Court may prepare and file the appropriate entry.

Any proposed entry submitted to the Court shall contain a certificate of service including the names and addresses of all parties and other interested persons required to be served.

(E) Social Security numbers are confidential and will not be required on any filing in this Court that is available for inspection by the public. Applicants for guardianships will provide their social security number and the social security number for the proposed ward on a form that will not be disclosed to the public.

(F) The Court will not accept filings by facsimile transmission or electronic mail.

(G) The court does not accept Power of Attorney signatures on pleadings or on any other documents except: (1) if there is specific language contained in the Power of Attorney authorizing the signature or (2) as authorized in Local Rule 64.1 (A)(2).

(Adopted eff. 9–20–99; amended eff. 4–20–04; 2–1–05.)

SUPERINTENDENCE RULE 58

Local Rule 58.1 Deposit for court costs

The business of this Court shall be conducted on a cash basis. The Court will only accept cash, money orders, cashier's checks, attorney, title company, or trust company checks.

(A) Deposits shall be required upon the initial filing of any action or proceeding. The deposit shall be applied as filings occur and additional deposits may be required. The Court shall maintain and make available a current list of costs.

(B) A minimum deposit of $25.00 shall be maintained in all pending estates, guardianships of estates, trusts and civil matters pending before this court. The Court may order additional deposits.

(C) Jury deposits shall be paid contemporaneously with the filing of a jury demand.

(Adopted eff. 9–20–99; amended eff. 4–20–04; 2–1–05.)

Local Rule 59.1 Wills

(A) Before an application is made to probate a will, to appoint an estate fiduciary, or to relieve an estate from administration, each applicant or the counsel for the applicant shall examine the index of wills deposited pursuant to R.C. 2107.07. If a will or wills are located on deposit, that were deposited previous to the will offered for probate, said will or wills shall be filed in the estate proceedings.

(B) In testate estates, the Certificate of Service, notices, affidavits, and waivers required by R.C. 2107.19 must be filed by the time of the filing of the Inventory, or within one hundred twenty (120) days of appointment of the fiduciary, whichever occurs first. Service of notice shall be made in accordance with Civil Rule 73(E)(3). Service on minors shall be made pursuant to Civil Rule 4.2.

(Adopted eff. 9–20–99; amended eff. 4–20–04.)

SUPERINTENDENCE RULE 60

Local Rule 60.1 Application for letters of authority to administer estate and notice of appointment

(A) Prior to the granting of an Application for Letters of Administration by a person who is not the nominated Executor, surviving spouse, next of kin, or legatee or devisee of the decedent, the Court shall give notice to the surviving spouse, next of kin or legatees and devisees of the decedent, including persons entitled to an allowance for support. Said notice shall be given regardless of the party's residence unless written waivers are submitted with the application. A written notice shall include the time, date and place of hearing and shall be served at least seven (7) days prior to the date set for hearing. Notice shall be given in the manner provided by Rule 73 of the Ohio Rules of Civil Procedure.

(B) Before filing an Application for Letters of Administration, the attorney or proposed fiduciary shall determine if there is a will of the decedent on deposit with this Court pursuant to Ohio R. C. 2107.07, if there is a will of the decedent on file with this Court pursuant to Ohio R.C. 2107. 084 or if there is a will of the decedent that has otherwise been filed with this Court.

(C) All executors or administrators shall sign and file the Fiduciary Acceptance Form that has been adopted for use by order of this Court. This form shall be signed and filed prior to the issuance of Letters of Authority.

(D) Non–resident executors shall keep all assets located in Montgomery County at the time of decedent's death in the County until final distribution or until further order of the Court.

(Adopted eff. 9–20–99; amended eff. 4–20–04; 2–1–05.)

SUPERINTENDENCE RULE 61

Local Rule 61.1 Appraisers

(A) When required by law, a suitable, disinterested appraiser may be appointed by the Court upon application of the fiduciary. This Court maintains a list of approved appraisers that shall be used by the fiduciary.

(B) In proceedings for release of estate from administration and summary release of estate from administration, a copy of the County Auditor's appraised value of the real estate may be used. The Court will use the one hundred percent (100%) figure in determining real estate value as maintained by the County Auditor at www.mcrealestate.org.

(C) Without application to the Court, fiduciaries may compensate the appraiser a reasonable agreed amount for the appraiser's services, or an amount computed on the gross value of the assets appraised in the estate (as set forth in the inventory) at a rate of $1.00 per thousand dollars of value with a minimum fee of $100.00. Fees for appraisals shall be computed on the full value of the property appraised even though the decedent's interest may be fractional.

(D) If the fiduciary and the appraiser cannot agree upon the amount of the appraiser's compensation, and the schedule set forth in paragraph C above is not used, the fiduciary shall file an application for allowance of compensation for each appraiser. Otherwise, no court order is necessary before payment of the appraisal fees, and credit may be taken for payment in the next accounting subject to exceptions allowed by law.

(E) During the administration of the estate, no appraiser or broker shall directly or indirectly purchase or negotiate the purchase or sale of property that the appraiser has appraised.

(Adopted eff. 9–20–99; amended eff. 4–20–04; 2–1–05.)

SUPERINTENDENCE RULE 62

Local Rule 62.1 Claims against estate

(A) When a claim has been filed with this Court pursuant to R.C. 2117.06, the fiduciary shall file a copy of any rejection of the claim with this Court.

(B) If the fiduciary requests a hearing on claims in an insolvency action, the fiduciary shall submit a schedule of claims or other similar form prioritizing the claims pursuant to R.C. 2117.25. The fiduciary shall serve notice of the hearing on all creditors, next of kin and/or legatees and devisees, who have not waived notice, pursuant to Civil Rule 73 and file proof of service with this Court within five (5) days of any hearing.

(C) No estate shall be closed until all claims filed with the Court have been rejected or accepted and resolved. Bond premiums shall be regarded as administration expenses and shall be paid when due.

(Adopted eff. 9–20–99; amended eff. 4–20–04; 2–1–05.)

Local Rule 63.1 Application to sell personalty

(A) In probate estates, no order of sale shall be granted before the inventory is filed except for good cause shown.

(Adopted eff. 9–20–99; amended eff. 4–20–04.)

SUPERINTENDENCE RULE 64

Local Rule 64.1 Accounts

All accounts must be signed by the fiduciary and contain the full name, current resident address, and telephone number of the fiduciary and counsel of record. If there are multiple fiduciaries, all fiduciaries must sign the account.

Delinquent Accounts

No expenditure, sale, distribution or fee will be approved while the fiduciary is delinquent in filing an account. No land sale actions will be confirmed in guardianship cases when accounts are delinquent.

(A) DECEDENT'S ESTATES:

(1) *Time for Filing*

For decedent's estates where the death occurred on or after January 1, 2002, the fiduciary's final distributive account is due within six (6) months after the appointment of the fiduciary as required by R.C. 2109.301. The time period may be extended by filing Form 13.10, Notice to Extend Administration or by filing Form 13.8, Application to Extend Administration and obtaining approval of the Court. Extensions beyond thirteen (13) months may only be obtained by filing Local Form 13.81 and obtaining the permission of the Court. If partial accounts are allowed, all subsequent accounts must be filed on an annual basis until the estate administration is completed, unless otherwise ordered by the Court.

For decedent's estates where the death occurred on or before December 31, 2001 the fiduciary shall file the first account with this Court within one (1) year from the appointment of the fiduciary. All subsequent accounts shall be filed on an annual basis, unless otherwise ordered by the Court.

(2) *Assets*

At the time of filing a partial account, all intangible personal assets remaining in the fiduciary's hands must be exhibited according to Rule 64 (D)(2) of the Rules of Superintendence.

If real property has been sold during an accounting period, under a power in a will or by consent, the gross proceeds from the sale and all costs of sale shall be accounted for on the fiduciary account and a copy of the closing statement shall be attached to and made a part of the fiduciary account.

If a distributive share is being received by a person holding a power of attorney, the attorney in fact must sign a receipt that is filed with the account and a copy of the recorded power of attorney for the attorney in fact must be submitted with the account.

(3) *Vouchers*

The fiduciary is required to present vouchers or receipts for all disbursements made on behalf of a minor and/or an incompetent. If the distribution has been made to a fiduciary appointed by another court, a certified copy of the fiduciary's letter of authority shall be submitted with the voucher or receipt.

Except as provided herein, the fiduciary of a decedent's estate is not required to submit to the Court vouchers to verify disbursements made from the estate. The fiduciary shall collect and retain vouchers for his or her records. If an interested party requests to view a voucher, the fiduciary shall provide a copy of the requested voucher to the interested party. If an interested party files exceptions to an account the fiduciary shall file any vouchers that relate to any exceptions with the Court at least five (5) days prior to any hearing on the exceptions.

(4) *Certificate of Service*

A Certificate of Service of Account to Heirs and Beneficiaries (Standard Probate Form 13.9) shall be signed by the fiduciary and filed with all accounts to certify that the fiduciary has provided a copy of the account to all persons entitled to a copy of the account pursuant to Section 2109.32(B)(1) of the Revised Code.

(5) *Final Accounts*

All final accounts shall be set for a hearing with notice. The fiduciary is required to file waivers of notice of hearing or serve notice of hearing on all next of kin or legatees and devisees of the estate. The fiduciary shall file proof of service of notice with this Court at least five (5) days prior to any hearing on the approval of the final account.

(B) GUARDIANSHIPS AND TRUSTS:

(1) *Time for Filing*

In guardianship and trust cases the fiduciary shall file the first account within twelve (12) months from the appointment of the fiduciary. All subsequent accounts shall be filed on an annual basis unless otherwise ordered by the Court. Accounts that are not timely filed are subject to citation.

(2) *Vouchers*

Vouchers shall be submitted for all disbursements in guardianship and trust cases. The vouchers will be retained for one year from the approval of the final account. The fiduciary and/or counsel of record may request the return of the vouchers at the end of this time period. If no request is made for the return of the vouchers, they will be destroyed.

(3) *Citations*

The Court will not issue citations on trust cases in January and February of each calendar year.

(Adopted eff. 9–20–99; amended eff. 7–3–00; amended eff. 4–20–04; 2–1–05.)

SUPERINTENDENCE RULE 65

Local Rule 65.1 Land sales

(A) No order confirming the sale of land by an executor, administrator, or guardian shall be approved by the Court until three (3) days after a written motion has been filed by the fiduciary requesting confirmation of the sale.

(B) Certification of title examination shall be included on all land sale complaints and motions or entry for the issuance of an order of sale pursuant to Local Rule 2.23 of the General Division of the Montgomery County Common Pleas Court.

(C) Any purchaser of real estate through a land sale proceeding shall have thirty (30) days from the date of sale to obtain an examination of title as allowed by Local Rule 2.23(VI) of the General Division of the Montgomery County Common Pleas Court. The purchaser may waive any or all of this thirty (30) day period by signing the Confirmation Entry.

(D) The distribution of sale proceeds must be included with any confirmation order. A proposed entry to confirm the sale and order of distribution must be submitted with all motions to confirm a sale.

(Adopted eff. 9–20–99; amended eff. 4–20–04; 2–1–05.)

SUPERINTENDENCE RULE 66
Local Rule 66.1 Guardianships

(A) All guardians of the person or estate shall receive a guardian's handbook issued by the Court. The guardian's handbook will provide the guardian with general information on the guardian's duties and responsibilities. The cost of the handbook will be assessed to the guardian or the estate of the ward.

(B) The biennial report required to be filed by R.C. 2111.49 shall be filed by the Guardian of the Person of the ward, except that if no Guardian of the Person was appointed then the report shall be filed by the Guardian of the Estate of the ward. The first biennial report is due two (2) years after the date of the appointment of the Guardian. Subsequent reports are due every two (2) years from the date of the filing of the last report.

(C) None of a ward's assets may be accessed through an automated teller machine or debit card. Electronic payment of routine and recurring expenses is permitted with court approval.

(D) An Application for Authority to Expend Funds shall not be approved until an Inventory has been filed in the case. All funds and assets held in the ward's name shall not be released to a guardian except upon order of the Court.

(E) Any expenditure for gifts from the ward's estate shall be made only with the approval of the Court pursuant to Ohio R.C. 2111.50.

(F) All guardians shall notify the Court of the death of the ward by written notice no later than sixty (60) days after the death of the ward. If the guardian does not notify the Court of the ward's death in the time prescribed, the guardian shall not be entitled to collect guardian fees from the ward's estate unless upon hearing the guardian can demonstrate good cause for the guardian's failure to comply with this rule. If the guardian is also the attorney for the estate, this rule shall also apply to attorney fees.

(G) All guardianship estate cases that involve Veterans' benefits are subject to and must comply with R.C. Chapter 5905 and all other rules and regulations of the Department of Veterans Affairs. All applications for authority to expend funds shall also be approved by the Department of Veterans Affairs or said application shall be set for hearing and notice given to the Department of Veterans Affairs.

(H) The guardian of the estate of an incompetent ward shall deposit the ward's will with the Court for safekeeping pursuant to Ohio R.C. 2107.07.

(I) The Court will grant an application for emergency guardianship only by testimony, affidavit or other evidence showing that immediate action is required to prevent significant injury to the alleged ward or the property of the alleged ward and that an application for the appointment of a guardian of the person or estate or both has been filed with the Court.

(J) (1) A certified copy of the minor's birth certificate must be filed with the Court with the application for guardianship of the minor.

(2) The Court will not accept for filing any guardianship of the person of a minor where another Court has prior jurisdiction over the custody of the minor unless the other Court consents to the guardianship or declines jurisdiction over the matter by Court order.

(3) The Court will not accept for filing any guardianship of the person of a minor where the sole purpose is to establish residency for school attendance purposes, qualify the minor for health/life insurance, or establish the placement for adoption.

(4) The Guardian of the person of a minor will be appointed with limited authority and shall not have the authority to create a power of attorney pursuant to R.C. 3109.52.

(Adopted eff. 9–20–99; amended eff. 4–20–04; 2–1–05.)

SUPERINTENDENCE RULE 67
Local Rule 67.1 Estates of minors of not more than $10,000.00

(A) Any application to dispense with a guardianship pursuant to R.C. 2111.05 shall be submitted by the parent or parents with whom the child resides or by the person who has custody of the child. The amount of funds involved must be $10,000.00 or less. The $10,000.00 limit refers to gross proceeds before any deductions for costs, fees, or other expenses.

(B) The application shall set forth the amount and source of any funds that will be distributed on behalf of the minor child. Unless otherwise ordered by the Court, the funds shall be ordered deposited in an interest bearing account in a financial institution approved by the Court in the name of the minor. The funds shall be impounded and shall be released to the child only when the child reaches the age of majority or as otherwise ordered by the Court.

(C) The attorney for the applicant or the attorney for the insurance company shall be responsible for depositing the funds in an approved financial institution. The attorney shall also obtain a verification of receipt and deposit (Local Probate Form 22.3) from the financial institution and file the verification with the Court within fourteen (14) days from the issuance of the entry unless otherwise ordered by this Court.

(Adopted eff. 9–20–99; amended eff. 4–20–04; 2–1–05.)

SUPERINTENDENCE RULE 68 SETTLEMENT OF INJURY CLAIMS OF MINORS
Local Rule 68.1 Settlement of minor's claims

(A) The Court will require the appointment of a guardian of the estate for all claims where the gross amount of the settlement is more than $10,000.00.

(B) A certified copy of the minor's birth certificate must be presented to the Court upon the filing of the application to settle a minor's claim.

(C) If the settlement of a minor's claim involves a structured settlement, the proposed structured settlement shall be reviewed with the Court before the application for settlement is filed. The application shall also include a statement of the total actual cost to the defendant of the settlement. This statement shall be used to fix and determine attorney fees.

(D) If the settlement is to be funded by an annuity, the annuity shall be provided by an annuity carrier that is licensed to write annuities in Ohio. The annuity carrier must have a minimum of $100,000.00 of capital and surplus, exclusive of any mandatory security valuation reserves. The annuity carrier must have one of the following ratings from the following rating organizations: A++, A+ or A from A.M. Best Company; AAA, Aa1 or Aa2 from Moody's Investors Service; or AAA or AA from Standard's & Poor's Corporation. The annuity insurer issuing an annuity contract may not enter into an assumption reinsurance agreement for the annuity contract without the prior approval of this Court, the owner of the annuity contract, and the claimant having the beneficial interest in the annuity. In all instances of reinsurance, the broker or the annuity insurance carrier shall provide the Court with an affidavit to certify that the carrier meets the standards set forth in this rule.

(E) The provisions of Local Rule 67.1 shall apply to the settlement of any minor's claim of $10,000.00 or less.

(Adopted eff. 9–20–99; amended eff. 4–20–04; 2–1–05.)

Local Rule 69.1 Settlement of claims against adult ward

(A) The guardian of the ward's estate shall bring an application for the settlement of a claim in favor of or against an adult ward. Notice of hearing on the application shall be given to all interested persons as ordered by the Court. The Court will authorize the guardian to compromise and settle claims the Court considers to be in the best interest of the ward.

(B) The application for settlement of an injury claim shall be accompanied by a current statement of an examining physician that lists the extent of the ward's injury, the extent of any recovery, and the physician's opinion on the permanency of any injuries. All counsel fees shall be set forth in the application. If the settlement of this claim will result in any payments to other parties, these payments shall be itemized on the application.

(Adopted eff. 9–20–99; amended eff. 4–20–04.)

SUPERINTENDENCE RULE 70 SETTLEMENT OF WRONGFUL DEATH AND SURVIVAL CLAIMS

Local Rule 70.1 Settlement of wrongful death claims

(A) All applications to settle wrongful death claims shall be set for hearing. The fiduciary shall serve written notice of the hearing and a copy of the application on all interested persons at least seven (7) day before the hearing.

(B) Interested persons who are subject to notice, as set forth in R.C. § 2125.02, shall include the surviving spouse, the children, the parents and other next of kin of the decedent.

(C) Interested persons may waive notice and consent to the settlement and allocation and distribution of proceeds in writing.

(D) The applicant must be present at the hearing.

(E) The report of distribution of wrongful death and survival claims shall be filed within thirty (30) days of the approval of the settlement unless otherwise ordered by the Court.

(F) If a wrongful death trust pursuant to R.C. § 2125.03 is to receive any settlement proceeds for a minor, approval of the trust must be obtained from the Court prior to filing the application to settle the claim.

(Adopted eff. 9–20–99; amended eff. 4–20–04; 2–1–05.)

SUPERINTENDENCE RULE 71

Local Rule 71.1 Counsel fees

Attorney fees in all matters shall be governed by DR 2–106 of the Code of Professional Responsibility. All attorney fees must be reasonable, and the services rendered must be necessary to the administration of the case. The Court may set any fee request for hearing.

(A) ESTATES

(1) Attorney fees, in decedent's estate cases, shall not be paid until the final account is prepared for filing unless otherwise approved by the Court upon application and for good cause shown. Any application for the payment of attorney fees, that is filed before the final account is filed, shall set forth the amount of fees requested and an hourly summary of work performed that justifies the requested fee. Applications for the payment of partial attorney fees will not be approved as a percentage of the attorney fees provided for under Appendix A of the Local Rules. In solvent estates, an application is not required if all of the beneficiaries consent in writing to the payment of the attorney fees on a partial account. Appendix C of the local rules of court shall be used for any written consents. The beneficiaries shall further acknowledge that they have been advised that the fees are not payable on a partial account without the approval of the beneficiaries or the consent of this Court upon application and good cause shown. The beneficiaries shall also be given, and acknowledge that they have been given, a good faith estimate of the percentage of the total attorney fees that will be paid as partial attorney fee.

(2) In a decedent's estate, no application for attorney fees is required on a final account in any of the following cases:

(a) Payment of the fee is included in an accounting or certificate of termination filed by the fiduciary who is also the sole beneficiary of a solvent estate.

(b) If all beneficiaries or creditors, whose share will be charged with the payment of any part of the fee, consent in writing to the specific dollar amount to be paid and the consent is filed with the account which claims credit for the fee paid. In such cases, a guardian may consent for the guardian's ward, the fiduciary of a deceased beneficiary's estate may consent on behalf of the deceased beneficiary, and a testamentary trustee or inter vivos trustee may consent on behalf of the trust beneficiaries.

(c) A calculation that reflects that the attorney fee taken is within the guidelines contained in Appendix A is attached to the account. Appendix A is merely a guideline and shall not be used by the attorney to receive a fee that would be unreasonable under DR 2–106.

(3) When an application for attorney fees that is signed by the fiduciary, contains an itemized description of the legal services performed, the court may approve the application without a hearing subject to the filing of any exceptions allowed by law.

(4) If the fiduciary is also the attorney for the estate, or if the attorney for the estate is a member of the fiduciary's law firm, the attorney may not use the guideline fees set forth in Appendix A if both attorney fees and fiduciary fees are taken. The attorney must submit an application for attorney fees showing time spent on the estate both as attorney and as fiduciary. If the attorney elects to take only one fee the attorney can use the full attorney fee allowed by Appendix A or the full fee allowed by R.C. 2113.35.

(5) The computation forms for attorney fees (Appendix B) and/or fiduciary fees (Appendix D) must be attached to all estate accounts when fiduciary fees or attorney fees are paid. Appendix B is only required when Appendix A is used to determine attorney fees.

(6) If Appendix A is used as a guide to compute attorney fees, no attorney fees shall be allowed on funds advanced to the estate.

(7) In release of administration cases, Appendix A may be used only as to the probate assets listed in the release. No fees are allowed on assets subject to Ohio or Federal estate tax that are not listed on the release forms.

(B) GUARDIANSHIPS AND TRUSTS

(1) In guardianship and trust cases, no hearing shall be required upon an application for attorney fees if all the following conditions are met:

(a) The application is signed by the fiduciary;

(b) The application contains an itemized statement of the legal services performed with the hourly rate charged;

(c) The order approving the fee requested contains a statement that a credit for the fee allowed may be taken in the next accounting and the attorney fees are subject to exception as provided by law.

(2) In cases where the attorney is also the guardian or trustee, the attorney shall set forth the time expended as both the guardian and attorney or as the trustee and attorney.

(3) All applications for attorney fees in guardianship cases that account for Veteran benefits shall be set for hearing and notice given to the Department of Veterans Affairs, unless a waiver or consent is obtained from the Department of Veterans Affairs.

(C) **WRONGFUL DEATHS**

A contingent fee agreement that does not exceed 33 1/3% of recovery in personal injury matters, 40% if an appeal is taken in personal injury matters, or 40% in a medical malpractice action may be approved by the Court at the settlement hearing without any prior approval of the Court. If the contingent fee agreement exceeds these guidelines prior approval must be obtained before the fiduciary may enter into the contract or fee agreement. In all cases, the Court will review the reasonableness of all fees and costs at the settlement hearing. The same contingent fee standards shall also apply to Local Rules 68.1 and 69.1.

(D) **COURT APPOINTED COUNSEL FEES**

(1) *Estates and Trusts*

See Local Rule 71.1 (A) (1–7).

(2) *Guardianships*

Whenever counsel is appointed pursuant to R.C. 2111.02, the following applies:

(a) Appointed counsel for an indigent ward or alleged ward shall be compensated for work performed out of Court at the rate of forty dollars ($40.00) per hour and for work performed in Court at the rate of fifty dollars ($50.00) per hour upon submission of an application for payment that sets forth the date, nature of the service and time expended. The application must be signed by the attorney and approved by the Court.

(b) Appointed counsel for a non-indigent ward or alleged ward shall be compensated for work performed at an approved reasonable hourly rate. The application must be signed by the attorney, the fiduciary and approved by the Court.

(3) *Mental Health*

(a) The Court will allow appointed counsel to be compensated for work performed out of Court at the rate of fifty dollars ($50.00) per hour and for work performed in Court at the rate of sixty dollars ($60.00) per hour upon submission of an application for payment that sets forth the date, nature of the service and time expended. The application must be signed by the attorney and approved by the Court.

(b) Counsel shall submit application for payment with in fourteen (14) days of services rendered. Untimely applications shall not be paid.

(Adopted eff. 9–20–99; amended eff. 4–20–04; 2–1–05.)

SUPERINTENDENCE RULE 72 EXECUTOR'S AND ADMINISTRATOR'S COMMISSIONS

Local Rule 72.1 Executor's and administrator's compensation

(A) Executor or administrator fees shall be allowed pursuant to R.C. 2113.35. A computation of fiduciary fees shall be filed with each account where fiduciary fees have been paid. Appendix D or a similar form shall be used to compute the allowed fiduciary fees.

(B) Extraordinary fees may be allowed in special circumstances upon application setting forth an itemized statement of all services rendered and the amount of compensation requested pursuant to R.C. 2113.36. Notice of the hearing on the application shall be given to all persons affected by the payment of these fees.

(C) The Court may reduce fiduciary commissions if the fiduciary is delinquent in filing an inventory, accounts, or if after hearing, the court finds that the fiduciary has not faithfully discharged the duties of the office.

(D) Co-Executor or Co-Administrator fees shall not exceed the amount that would have been allowed to one fiduciary.

(Adopted eff. 9–20–99; amended eff. 4–20–04; 2–1–05.)

SUPERINTENDENCE RULE 73

Local Rule 73.1 Guardian's compensation

(A) The compensation that may be taken by guardians as a credit in their accountings, without application and order first obtained, must be less than or equal to that provided by the following schedule:

(1) 5% of income from intangible investments and deposits and all installment receipts, such as Social Security or Veterans' benefits.

(2) 10% of gross rentals from real estate actually managed by the guardian (5% if proceeds of a net lease).

(3) $2.50 per thousand dollars of intangible personal property investments and deposits for each year of the accounting period.

(4) 1% of distribution of personal property corpus at conclusion of the guardianship.

(5) For corporate guardians: A fee may be charged on the same basis as the corporate guardian charges its clients as trustee of a living trust. Each corporate fiduciary shall file its current fee schedule with this Court. Any amendments to the schedule must be filed before a fee computed under the amended schedule is credited to an account. The fee schedule shall be limited to a maximum 1% fee for all guardianship estates with a market value of $75,000.00 or less.

(6) A computation of fiduciary fees shall be filed with each account where fiduciary fees have been paid. Appendix E or a similar form shall be used to compute the allowed fiduciary fees. Existence of the above schedule is not approval by the Court of the reasonableness of the fee so taken, and any credit for a fee in such amount shall be subject to exceptions to the account as provided by law.

(B) Additional compensation for extraordinary services, reimbursement for expenses incurred, and compensation of a guardian of the person only may be allowed upon application and hearing. Notice of the hearing on the application shall be given to interested persons as ordered by the Court.

(C) The compensation of co-guardians shall not exceed the compensation that would be allowed to one guardian.

(D) The Court may deny or reduce compensation if an inventory or account was delinquently filed, or after hearing, the court finds that the guardian has not faithfully discharged the guardian's duties.

(E) All applications for compensation of guardians of veterans must comply with Chapter 5905 of the Ohio Revised Code and all other rules and regulations of the Department of Veterans Affairs.

(Adopted eff. 9–20–99; amended eff. 4–20–04; 2–1–05.)

SUPERINTENDENCE RULE 74

Local Rule 74.1 Trustee's compensation

(A) The compensation that may be taken by trustees of testamentary trusts as a credit in their accountings, without application and order first obtained, must be less than or equal to that provided by the following schedule:

(1) 5% of income from intangible investments and deposits and all installment receipts, such as Social Security or Veterans' benefits.

(2) 10% of gross rentals from real estate actually managed by the guardian (5% if proceeds of a net lease).

(3) $2.50 per thousand dollars of intangible personal property investments and deposits for each year of the accounting period.

(4) 1% of distribution of personal property corpus at periodic distributions.

(5) For corporate guardians: A fee may be charged on the same basis as the corporate guardian charges its clients as trustee of a living trust. Each corporate fiduciary shall file its current fee schedule with this Court. Any amendments to the schedule must be filed before a fee computed under the amended schedule is credited to an account. The fee schedule shall be limited to a maximum 1% fee for all guardianship estates with a market value of $75,000.00 or less.

(6) A computation of fiduciary fees shall be filed with each account where fiduciary fees have been paid. Appendix F or a similar form shall be used to compute the allowed fiduciary fees. Existence of the above schedule is not approval by the Court of the reasonableness of the fee so taken, and any credit for a fee in such amount shall be subject to exceptions to the account as provided by law.

(B) Additional compensation for extraordinary services, reimbursement for expenses incurred, and compensation of a guardian of the person only may be allowed upon application and hearing. Notice of the hearing on the application shall be given to interested persons as ordered by the Court.

(C) The compensation of co-trustees shall not exceed the compensation that would be allowed to one trustee.

(D) The court may deny or reduce compensation if an inventory or account was delinquently filed, or after hearing, the Court finds that the trustee has not faithfully discharged the trustee's duties.

(Adopted eff. 9–20–99; amended eff. 4–20–04; 2–1–05.)

SUPERINTENDENCE RULE 75
Local Rule 75.1   Guardian ad litem

(A) GUARDIAN AD LITEM

(1) *Qualifications*

A guardian ad litem shall be an attorney who is not associated with an attorney of record for the proceeding in which the guardian ad litem has been appointed.

(2) *Appointment*

(a) Land Sales

Subject to approval by the Court, a guardian ad litem will be appointed on recommendation and entry of the attorney or record.

(b) All Other Matters

A guardian ad litem may be appointed without recommendation upon notification of the necessity for appointment.

(3) *Fees*

(a) Land Sales

Unless ordered by the Court, a fee shall be taxed in the costs of the case for each guardian ad litem in the amount of Ten Dollars ($10.00).

(b) All Other Matters

Unless ordered by the Court, upon application and entry, a fee based on a reasonable hourly rate for time expended shall be taxed in the costs of the case for each guardian ad litem.

(B) PRO HAC VICE

An attorney, who is not licensed to practice in Ohio, may upon order of this Court represent a party in a matter pending before this Court if the attorney complies with all of the following requirements:

(1) The attorney must be licensed and in good standing in another state or the District of Columbia;

(2) The attorney must submit a written oath that complies with Rule I, Section 8A of the Supreme Court Rules for Government of the Bar;

(3) The attorney must certify in writing that he is familiar with the Local Rules of Court, the Rules of Superintendence, the Civil Rules, the Rules of Evidence and the Code of Professional Responsibility;

(4) The attorney must be sponsored by an attorney licensed to practice in Ohio who is in good standing. Any motion to appear pro hac vice must be filed by an Ohio attorney who shall certify in the motion that the out-of-state attorney is in compliance with this rule of court. If permission is given for the out–of- state attorney to appear pro hac vice, the sponsoring attorney shall be co-counsel with the out-of-state attorney.

(5) The Court may withdraw permission to appear pro hac vice at any time.

(C) COMPLIANCE WITH AMERICANS WITH DISABILITIES ACT

(1) Individuals with disabilities, special needs or the need for an interpreter shall make requests to the Court Administrator for reasonable accommodations no later than seven (7) days prior to any scheduled hearing.

(2) If the interpreter service is no longer required or if the parties continue the hearing, the individual making the request shall immediately notify the Court Administrator to cancel or reschedule the service. Failure to notify the Court may result in the individual paying any cancellation fee for the interpreter service.

(Adopted eff. 2–1–05.)

SUPERINTENDENCE RULE 76
Local Rule 76.1   Exception to the rules

Upon application and for good cause shown, this Court may grant exceptions to the Local Rules and/ or to Rules of Superintendence.

(Adopted eff. 9–20–99; amended eff. 4–20–04; 2–1–05.)

Local Rule 77.1   Compliance

Failure to comply with these rules may result in sanctions as the Court may direct.

(Adopted eff. 9–20–99; amended eff. 4–20–04.)

SUPERINTENDENCE RULE 78   PROBATE DIVISION OF THE COURT OF COMMON PLEAS CASE MANAGEMENT IN DECEDENT'S ESTATES, GUARDIANSHIPS AND TRUSTS

Local Rule 78.1   Case management

For the purpose of insuring the readiness of proceedings in this Court, the following procedures shall be in effect and referred to as the "case management rule".

(A) DECEDENTS ESTATES

(1) All estate cases shall be assigned to a specific Magistrate. This Magistrate shall supervise the assigned case and will hear all related matters except civil actions unless otherwise referred by the Judge.

(2) All accounts shall be filed pursuant to R.C. 2109.301 as supplemented by Local Rule 64.1. The citation procedure set forth in R.C. 2109.31 shall be used to gain compliance.

(3) A hearing shall be scheduled on objections to inventories or accounts within sixty (60) days after the filing of objections unless otherwise extended by order of the Court.

(4) All decedent estates that remain open after a period of thirteen (13) months shall file a status report with this Court. The Court may order a status report at any time. The status report shall set forth the current status of the estate, list the steps remaining to complete the estate, and give an estimated time frame for completing the estate. A copy of this status report shall be served upon all persons or creditors that have an interest in completing the estate. The fiduciary shall file an annual status report on the anniversary date of the first status report until the estate is completed. Based upon a review of the status reports, the Court may require the fiduciary and counsel to attend a status conference.

(5) All fiduciaries appointed in estate proceedings shall sign and file a Fiduciary Acceptance Form, Montgomery County Probate Local Form 4.8.

(B) RELEASE OF ESTATE FROM ADMINISTRATION

(1) All release of estate from administration cases will be assigned to a specific Magistrate. This Magistrate shall supervise the assigned case and will hear all related matters unless otherwise referred by the Judge.

(2) Estates may be released from administration pursuant to R.C. 2113.03. The citation procedure set forth in R.C. 2109.31 shall apply to the filing of Commissioner Reports.

(3) The court shall select and appoint Commissioners, when required, in estates released from administration. Commissioner must be residents of the State of Ohio unless either of the following applies:

    (a) The proposed commissioner is named as executor in the decedent's will and is related to the decedent by blood or marriage; or

    (b) The proposed commissioner is the sole next of kin or legatee and devisee of the estate.

(4) The Commissioner shall be bonded unless one of the following applies:

    (a) Named as executor to serve without bond in the decedent's will

    (b) The proposed commissioner is the sole next of kin or legatee and devisee

    (c) The proposed commissioner is an attorney licensed in Ohio and in good standing

    (d) Except as otherwise ordered by the court.

(5) Publication of notice to creditors and interested parties shall be made in all cases except as otherwise ordered by the Court.

(C) INVENTORY

(1) Inventories in trust, guardianship and decedent's estate cases will be filed within ninety (90) days after the appointment of the fiduciary unless the Court otherwise extends this time period. The citation procedure under R.C. 2109.31 shall be utilized to gain compliance.

(2) On the Schedule of Assets (Form 6.1) to be filed in a decedent's estate, every itemized listing of corporate stock owned by a decedent must be preceded by one of the following symbols: If the stock is publicly traded and its valuation obtained from any recognized stock exchange or over-the-counter quotation, the listing shall be preceded by the symbol "X". If the stock is not publicly traded and represents an investment in what is commonly known as a closely held corporation, the listing must be preceded by the symbol "CC" and must be valued by a duly appointed and qualified appraiser.

(3) The Inventory shall be set for hearing no later than thirty-five (35) days after the Inventory is filed.

(4) The Schedule of Assets form in a decedent's estate case and the Inventory form in a guardianship case shall contain the legal description and parcel number of all real estate included in the estate.

(5) If multiple fiduciaries have been appointed by the court, all fiduciaries must sign the Inventory.

(6) In decedent estates, if an appraiser is used, the appraiser may sign a separate form that is attached to the inventory so long as this form has the same certification language set forth on the Inventory form.

(7) The Inventory of a ward shall include the expected annual income of the ward.

(8) The Inventory will not be accepted for filing unless the fiduciary has sufficient fiduciary bond posted, if required.

(9) If a partnership interest is listed as an asset of the decedent's estate on the Inventory, the fiduciary shall note on the Inventory if the value of the partnership interest was determined by the terms of the partnership agreement or by the provisions of R.C. § 1779.01.

(D) GUARDIANSHIPS

(1) All guardianship cases shall be assigned to a specific Magistrate. This Magistrate shall supervise the assigned case and will hear all related matters except for civil actions unless otherwise referred by the Judge.

(2) Guardianships are subject to R.C. 2109.032 and R.C. Chapter 2111 and Local Rules 66.1 and 73.1. The citation process set forth in R.C. 2109.31 will be utilized to insure compliance.

(E) TRUSTS

(1) All trust cases shall be assigned to a specific Magistrate. This Magistrate shall supervise the assigned case and will hear all related matters except for civil actions unless otherwise referred by the Judge.

(2) Trusts are subject to R.C. 2109.303 and Local Rule 74.1. The citation process set forth in R.C. 2109.31 will be utilized to insure compliance.

(3) The written acceptance of duties required by R.C. 2109.02 must be executed in the presence of the magistrate to be assigned to the case if the fiduciary is being appointed as a testamentary trustee, except as otherwise ordered by this Court. This rule shall not apply to attorneys or corporate fiduciaries.

(F) LAND SALES

(1) All land sales actions shall be assigned to a specific Magistrate. This Magistrate shall supervise the assigned case and will hear all related matters.

(2) All land sales that have not been concluded within one (1) year from the date of filing shall be set for status conference by plaintiff's counsel within thirty (30) days following the expiration of one (1) year anniversary of the filing of the land sale action. The fiduciary and the fiduciary's attorney must attend the status conference.

(3) A written status report shall be filed with the Court no later than seven (7) days before the status conference. The status report shall address the issue of the effort being made to complete the sale.

(4) At the status hearing, the fiduciary shall show cause why the Court should not order public sale of the real estate.

(G) ADOPTIONS

(1) The court shall be responsible for all required notices in adoption proceedings except for notices by publication.

(2) If an adoption involves a child born before 1–01–97 the putative father shall be named. If an adoption involves a child born after 1–01–97, petitioner's counsel or petitioner shall request a search of the Putative Father's Registry and shall file the response with the Court.

(3) An original and a copy of all pleadings shall be filed in every adoption case. Additional copies of the petition shall be submitted as required for service.

(4) Except in stepparent and grandparent adoptions, prior to the filing of the Petition for Adoption, a lawful placement must occur pursuant to R.C. 5103–5103.16.

(5) In all adoption cases, Court costs are required to be paid at the time of the filing. Before a hearing is set the petitioner must present all necessary documents to the Court for filing.

(6) Petitioner's accounts shall be filed in all cases except stepparent and adult adoptions.

(7) In all adoptions, married petitioner(s) must be married for not less than one (1) year prior to the final approval of the adoption.

(8) All adoption petitions and placement proceedings shall be reviewed annually, and the Court shall order further action as necessary.

(H) WRONGFUL DEATH SETTLEMENTS

All hearings shall be heard within sixty (60) days of the filing of any application for settlement. If a guardian or guardian ad litem is required, the hearing shall be held within thirty (30) days after the appointment of the guardian ad litem or within the original sixty (60) day period, whichever is greater, except as otherwise ordered by the court.

(I) MOTIONS

(1) The moving party shall, and the opposing party may, serve and file a brief written statement supporting or opposing the motion and include a list of citations of authorities in support or opposition to the motion.

(2) Unless otherwise disposed of by the Court, the moving party shall cause the motion to be set for hearing within sixty (60) days after the filing of the motion.

(3) The trial date shall be continued only upon motion demonstrating good cause and order of the Court.

(J) MENTAL ILLNESS AND MENTAL RETARDATION

All hearings pursuant to R.C. Chapter 5122 and R.C. Chapter 5123 shall be conducted pursuant to the standards and procedures set forth in these Chapters of the Revised Code.

(K) NAME CHANGES

All applications for a change of name shall be set for hearing at the time of filing. Upon failure to appear a notice of intention to dismiss shall be issued.

(L) CIVIL VERSUS ACTIONS (EXCLUDING LAND SALES)

(1) A pretrial conference shall be conducted in all cases prior to trial except land sale proceedings.

(2) Within thirty (30) days after the answer day, plaintiff or plaintiff's counsel shall request a pretrial conference.

(3) Plaintiff's counsel shall give not less than fourteen (14) days of the conference to all counsel of record and/or parties not represented by counsel who have entered an appearance. Requests for continuance of the conference shall be in writing and timely filed with the Court.

(4) All counsel must have full authority to enter into binding orders. Unless otherwise ordered by the court, the following matters and decisions shall be addressed at the pretrial conference:

(a) The possibility of settlement;

(b) Discovery deadline dates;

(c) A definite date for the exchange of expert witness reports;

(d) Pleadings, briefing and proposed jury instructions dates;

(e) Final pretrial date, if applicable;

(f) Trial date.

(5) All parties must be present unless their presence has been excused by the Court.

(M) FIDUCIARY BONDS

(1) A copy of the Power of Attorney for all bonding agents shall be attached to all bonds submitted to this Court. This Power of Attorney must have the name of the Attorney–In–Fact that has signed the bond and the bond amount limits, if any. The bond amount limits must be sufficient to cover the total bonded amount in the case. No bond will be accepted by this Court without an attached Power of Attorney.

(2) In guardianships of the estate, bond shall be posted in an amount of double the value of the personal assets from all sources plus double the amount of the ward's annual income. Real property is not bonded unless a land sale proceeding has been filed. All guardians of a ward's estate shall be required to post a minimum bond as determined by the Court.

(3) A fiduciary bond shall be filed by all fiduciaries appointed in decedent estate case unless waived by will or excused by law. The initial fiduciary bond shall be twice the value of any personal property assets in the estate. The amount of the fiduciary bond is subject to being adjusted upward or downward upon the filing of an inventory, consents to sell real estate, and/or upon the filing of any partial accounts. In all cases where the posting of a fiduciary bond is not waived or excused by law a minimum fiduciary bond shall be posted even if there are no personal property assets or other type of assets in the probate estate.

(4) In testamentary trust cases a fiduciary bond shall be posted unless waived by the decedent's will or by law. The initial fiduciary bond that is posted shall be double the value of the personal assets subject to the trust plus double the projected annual income of the trust.

(5) Fiduciary bond premiums must be paid when due. If the Court is notified that a fiduciary bond premium is delinquent, the Court may, on its own motion, file proceedings to remove the fiduciary.

(N) WITHDRAWAL OF COUNSEL

(1) Counsel who has entered an appearance in a case shall remain in the case until the case is concluded. The Court may permit counsel to withdraw if:

(a) Counsel files a motion to withdraw demonstrating good cause;

(b) The motion to withdraw is served on the client unless the client approved the motion in writing;

(c) Counsel lists in the motion all known filing deadlines; and

(d) Notice is given to all attorneys, unrepresented parties, and interested persons. Interested persons shall include next of kin, legatees and devisees, known creditors, trust beneficiaries and bonding agencies.

(2) The Court may schedule the motion to withdraw for hearing. If there is a pending hearing in the case, the motion to withdraw shall be set at that time.

(3) Substitution of counsel shall be in writing signed by the withdrawing counsel or the fiduciary and the substituting counsel.

Notice shall be served on all counsel, bonding agencies, and all other interested parties.

(O) JURY MANAGEMENT PLAN

The jury management plan for this Court shall be the same as the jury management plan for the General Division of the Montgomery County Common Pleas Court as set forth in Local Rule 1.23 of the Rules for the General Division of the Montgomery County Common Pleas Court, except to the extent the Rules of the General Division would be clearly inapplicable.

(P) MEDIATION

(1) Disputed issues in any civil case, estate, guardianship application, trust, or any other action, may be referred to mediation pursuant to a party's motion, by agreement of the parties, or on the Court's own motion. All referrals to mediation must be approved by the Court. Referral to mediation by the Court shall be by a "Notice of Mediation" which shall indicate the time and place of the mediation as well as the name and telephone number of the mediator.

(2) The mediator will be appointed from a list of qualified mediators maintained by the court. The list will contain the names of attorneys who meet certain qualifications set by the court. The Court will annually prepare and review this list.

(3) Qualified mediators shall receive a fee commensurate with those paid by the General Division of Montgomery County Common Pleas Court. Additional expenses must be approved by the Court.

(4) Compensation for qualified mediators shall be paid from the Mediation Fund funded by court costs dedicated to this fund.

(5) Written or oral statements made during a mediation session shall be considered confidential. Statements made during a mediation session shall be considered compromise negotiations and are not admissible as evidence pursuant to Evidence Rule 408. Mediators will not be permitted to testify regarding the substance of the mediation, including but not limited to, cooperation or non-cooperation of the parties.

(6) If a case is settled or dismissed prior to a scheduled mediation conference, the parties shall promptly file a settlement and conditional dismissal entry. Counsel for plaintiff shall immediately inform the mediation office by phone that the assigned mediation date is not needed.

(7) If a case is continued, settled, or dismissed more than seven (7) days prior to the scheduled mediation conference date, the qualified mediator shall not be entitled to compensation except in cases where the Court is not notified of the continuance, settlement, or dismissal by that date. If a case is continued, settled, or dismissed less than seven (7) days but more than (2) days prior to the scheduled mediation conference date, the qualified mediator shall be entitled to a cancellation fee in the amount of one-half of the compensation rate for conducting the mediation conference. If a case is continued, settled, or dismissed less than two (2) days prior to the scheduled mediation conference date, the qualified mediator shall be entitled to a cancellation fee in the amount of the full compensation rate for conducting the mediation conference.

(8) Upon reaching a settlement in mediation:

(a) The Mediator may immediately prepare a written memorandum memorializing the agreement reached by the parties. The parties and counsel shall sign the memorandum.

(b) Counsel shall be instructed to present a termination entry for approval within fourteen (14) days.

(c) The fact that a settlement has been reached shall be transmitted to a clerk who shall check for the filing of the termination entry at the end of the fourteen (14) day period;

(d) If the termination entry has not been filed, then a notice shall be sent to counsel informing them that they have fourteen (14) days to file a termination entry; and

(e) If no entry has been filed fourteen (14) days after notice has been sent to counsel, then an administrative dismissal entry shall be sent to the assigned Magistrate or Judge for approval.

(Q) MISCELLANEOUS MATTERS

All miscellaneous matters shall be reviewed annually, and the Court shall order further action as necessary.

(Adopted eff. 9–20–99; amended eff. 7–3–00; amended eff. 4–20–04; 2–1–05.)

Local Rule 79.1   Inventory

(A) Inventories will be filed within ninety (90) days after the appointment of the fiduciary unless the Court otherwise extends this time period. The citation procedure under R.C. 2109.31 shall be utilized to gain compliance.

(B) On the Schedule of Assets (Form 6.1) to be filed in a decedent's estate, every itemized listing of corporate stock owned by a decedent **MUST** be preceded by one of the following symbols: If the stock is publicly traded and its valuation obtained from any recognized stock exchange or over-the-counter quotation, the listing shall be preceded by the symbol X. If the stock is not publicly traded and represents an investment in what is commonly known as a close corporation, the listing **MUST** be preceded by the symbol *CC* and **MUST** be valued by a duly appointed and qualified appraiser.

(C) The Inventory of an Executor and Administrator shall be set for hearing no later than thirty-five days after the Inventory is filed.

(D) The Schedule of Assets shall contain the legal description and parcel number of all real estate included in the estate.

(Adopted eff. 9–20–99; amended eff. 4–20–04.)

Local Rule 80.1   Employment of auctioneers and clerks

(A) Whenever selling the personal property of a decedent, incompetent minor, or trust estate at public sale, whether by order of Court, or by authority contained in a last will and testament or by operation of law, the fiduciary may employ an auctioneer and clerk to assist the fiduciary without order of Court.

(B) Auctioneers and clerks, may be allowed the following fees without application:

(1) Household goods, small miscellaneous items, and business stock in trade, twelve per cent (12%) to auctioneer, including clerk hire.

(2) All other personal property, including motor vehicles, livestock, farm machinery, business fixtures and equipment:

(1) Up to two thousand dollars ($2,000.00), four per cent (4%) to auctioneer, including clerk hire.

(2) Two thousand dollars ($2,000.00) and over, three per cent (3%) to auctioneer, including clerk hire.

(3) This fee is for crying the sale and reasonable exhibition of the property to be sold. A reasonable amount may be expended by the fiduciary for special advertising. Which includes all forms of advertising other than the notices required by law.

(C) The fiduciary may without obtaining Court authority agree to a fee and expenses of sale in excess of this guideline and include the same in the fiduciary's accounting. Any agreed amounts so credited shall be subject to exceptions to the account as provided by law.

(Adopted eff. 9–20–99; amended eff. 4–20–04.)

Local Rule 81.1 Qualification of guardian ad litem

(A) Whenever a guardian ad litem or trustee for a suit is appointed by the Court, such person must be an attorney. The attorney shall not be associated in any business manner with any other attorney of record in the proceedings. A separate guardian ad litem shall be appointed for each necessary person.

(Adopted eff. 9–20–99; amended eff. 4–20–04.)

Local Rule 82.1 Testamentary trustee must accept duties in person

(A) The written acceptance of duties required by R.C. 2109.02 must be executed in the presence of the judge or a magistrate of this Court if the fiduciary being appointed is a testamentary trustee, except as otherwise ordered by this Court. This rule shall not apply to attorneys or corporate fiduciaries.

(Adopted eff. 9–20–99; amended eff. 4–20–04.)

Local Rule 83.1 Adoption

(A) Pursuant to R.C. 3101.16(D) the Court establishes the filing fee for a Petition for Release of Information Regarding an Adopted Person pursuant to R.C. 3107.41 to be $50.00.

(B) Putative fathers shall be named and due diligence made to provide notice to putative fathers in all adoption proceedings.

(C) Except in stepparent adoptions, prior to the filing of the Petition for Adoption, a lawful placement must occur pursuant to R.C. 5103.15 to R.C. 5103.16.

(D) A completed Form 1616 Social and Medical History Form shall be required in all cases except stepparent and grandparent adoptions. Petitioners must receive and receipt for Form 1616 at the time either an interlocutory or final order of adoption is granted, and the receipt shall be filed with the Court.

(E) In stepparent adoptions in which the Domestic Relations Court, Juvenile Court, or the Child Support Enforcement Agency has a pending case for support, petitioner(s) or counsel shall notify the court or agency of the child's adoption to allow the support order to be terminated or reduced to a lump-sum judgment.

(F) The attorney for the petitioner(s) or the petitioner shall procure a new birth certificate from the Division of Vital Statistics once the adoption is finalized.

(G) The court shall not set aside or rehear foreign final orders of adoption but shall give foreign decrees full faith and credit. (R.C. 3107.18).

(H) All surrogate adoptions shall be treated as non-relative adoptions unless the surrogate mother is a relative of the adopting parent or parents. All surrogate contracts must be pre-approved as part of the pre-placement process. Any application or petition failing to comply with this requirement shall be dismissed.

(I) The clerk shall collect the Next Friend Investigation Fee upon the filing of either the Petition for Adoption or an Application for Placement. The investigation fee shall be $1,501.50 for the placement or the adoption of a non-relative and $189.80 for a stepchild or relative. These fees are subject to change without notice.

(Adopted eff. 9–20–99; amended eff. 4–20–04.)

Local Rule 84.1 Court security

The Court Security Plan for the Court shall be the same as the Court Security Plan for the General Division of the Montgomery County Court of Common Pleas, as set forth in Local Rule 1.12 of the Rules for the General Division of the Montgomery County Common Pleas Court.

(Adopted eff. 9–20–99; amended eff. 4–20–04.)

Local Rule 85.1 Jury management plan

The jury management plan for the Court shall be the same as the Jury Management Plan for the General Division of the Montgomery County Common Pleas Court as set forth in Local Rule 1.23 of the Rules for the General Division of the Montgomery County Common Pleas Court, except to the extent the Rules of the General Division would be clearly inapplicable.

(Adopted eff. 9–20–99; amended eff. 4–20–04.)

Local Rule 86.1 Magistrates

(A) Magistrates may be appointed by the Probate Judge, and shall serve as full-time or part-time employees of the Court as provided in Civil Rule 53. Civil Magistrates shall have those powers as set forth in Civil Rules 53 and as set forth in any Order of Reference.

(B) The magistrates so appointed are hereby referred all matters, including pretrials, pertaining to estates, guardianships, trusts, adoptions civil commitments, and name changes. This reference includes all powers of the Court except as restricted by law.

(C) Before an appeal of, or objection to, a magistrate's decision, a request for findings of fact and conclusions of law shall be filed pursuant to Civil Rule 52 and Local Rule 57.1.

(Adopted eff. 9–20–99; amended eff. 4–20–04.)

Local Rule 87.1 Record

All matters occurring in open Court will be recorded by a court reporter or electronic recording devices. The party requesting a transcript must pay the costs of the preparation of the transcript.

(Adopted eff. 9–20–99; amended eff. 4–20–04.)

Local Rule 88.1 Relieving estate from administration

(A) Estates may be relieved from administration pursuant to R.C. 2113.03. In cases where a commissioner must be appointed to complete the administration of the estate, the Court shall appoint the commissioner and require any fiduciary bond as determined by the Court.

(B) The appraisal of assets shall be subject to Local Rule 61.1.

(C) Publication of notice to creditors and interested parties is not required for deaths before to March 18, 1999, where the personal assets are of less than $27,000.00 and the surviving spouse has paid the decedent's funeral expenses and is entitled to receive the entire support allowance allowed by R.C. 2106.13. For deaths after March 18, 1999, the same standards apply to estates of less than $42,000.00. Notice by publication will be provided for estates with real property unless otherwise ordered by this Court. If there is no surviving spouse and the estate assets are $2,000 or less, notice need not be published if the applicant has paid the decedent's funeral expenses of $2,000 or more.

(D) The Court may issue an order of distribution for a summary estate if the applicant paid the decedent's funeral expenses and the assets of the estate do not exceed $1,000.00. A summary estate proceeding may also be used if the decedent's funeral expenses were pre-paid and the applicant is entitled to receive the entire support allowance under R.C. 2106.13. Summary estate administration is limited to estates of $1,000 or less.

(Adopted eff. 9–20–99; amended eff. 4–20–04.)

Local Rule 89.1 Disclaimers

When any disclaimer is filed in this Court that modifies in any manner the persons listed on either the front or back of the form 1.0, the fiduciary shall file an amended form 1.0 that correctly reflects the heirs at law and devisees.

Any notices of the probate of will, that are necessitated by the filing of the disclaimer, shall be filed before the next account is filed. The account will not be accepted for filing unless the amended form 1.0 has been filed and any necessary notices are served or waived, and if necessary, a new certificate of service of notice of probate of will form has been filed.

(Adopted eff. 9–20–99; amended eff. 4–20–04.)

APPENDICES

App. A Attorney fees

The following schedule is merely a guide for determining attorney fees in an ordinary estate and shall not be considered to be a minimum or maximum fee schedule. The Law requires that attorney fees be reasonable in each case. Acceptance of an account for filing that reflects payment of attorney fees equal to or less than an amount computed upon the following basis **IS NOT APPROVAL OF THE REASONABLENESS OF THE FEE TAKEN**. The Court may review the fee on the Court's own motion or upon exceptions to the account as provided by law.

It is the responsibility of each fiduciary to review any and all attorney fee requests to determine if they are reasonable and are based upon necessary services for the estate. The fiduciary and/or beneficiaries of all estates have the right to object to any attorney fee that is not reasonable or necessary. If an objection to the attorney fee is filed with this Court the attorney must produce hourly time records of services provided to the estate. Any finding that the attorney fees exceed reasonable and necessary fees will be a finding against the fiduciary if the fiduciary has paid the attorney fees.

For transfer of real estate	2% of appraised value
For personal property accounted for including proceeds of real estate sold under a power in the will or by consent (R.C. 2127.011)	8% of 1st. $1000.00 6% of next $4000.00 4% of next $20,000.00 3% of next $125,000.00 2% of Balance
Proceeds of real estate sold in Land Sale	12% of 1st. $1,000.00 9% of next $3,500.00 7% of next $6,000.00 5% of next $5,000.00 3% of Balance

Fees for determination of estate tax upon non-probate property:

1% on joint and survivorship property between husband and wife.

2% on all other non-probate property included for Ohio estate tax determinations.

In release of administration cases the attorney fees are computed only on the assets of the probate estate. No fees are allowed on property subject to Ohio or Federal estate tax.

No fees are allowed on funds advanced to the estate.

NOTE: By having a fee guide for attorney fees for determination of tax upon non-probate property, the Court is **NOT** establishing that such fees are payable from the probate estate in all cases. Also, because of the wide variance in the amount of legal responsibility for determination of tax in such cases, the guide should be used in light of a careful view of the services actually performed in a given case; the nature of the assets included; and the potential amount of tax payable.

App. B Computation of attorney fees
PURSUANT TO APPENDIX A

Real Estate Transferred $ __ × 2% = __

Personal property and proceeds from the sale of real estate

Sold with consent or pursuant to power to sell in Will:

Total Value: __

8% of first $1000 (80) _____
6% of next $4000 (240) _____
4% of next $20,000 (800) _____
3% of next $125,000 (3750) _____
2% of balance _____ = _____

Proceeds sale of real estate in Land Sale:

12% of first $1000 (120) _____
9% of next $3,500 (315) _____
7% of next $6,000 (420) _____
5% of next $5,000 (250) _____
3% of balance _____

Estate Tax property:

1% of Joint and Survivorship property between spouses:
_____ × 1% _____ = _____

2% of all other taxable non-probate property:
_____ × 2% _____ = _____

TOTAL FEE = _____

DISCOUNT = (_____)

TOTAL FEE TAKEN = _____

App. C Consent to payment fees

Estate of _____

Case No. ___

CONSENT TO PAYMENT OF ATTORNEY FEES ON PARTIAL ACCOUNT

The undersigned, being an heir, devisee, or legatee of this estate has been advised by the attorney for the estate that the attorney is requesting the payment of _____ in attorney fees on a partial account.

The undersigned has further been advised that the above attorney fee represents payment for approximately __ % of total attorney work that will need to be performed in this estate. The undersigned acknowledges that he/she is aware that additional fees __ will be or _____ will not be requested at a later date.

The undersigned has been further advised that the Rules of Superintendence of the Ohio Supreme Court do not allow for the payment of attorney fees on a partial account unless the attorney obtains the approval of the Probate Court. In order to obtain the approval of the Probate Court, the attorney would have to file an itemized application for attorney fees with the Court. The application would have to set forth cause for this payment of these fees on a partial and not a final account.

The undersigned consents to the payment of attorney fees in the sum of $ __ and waives any requirement of a written application and approval of the Probate Court.

Date: _____   X _____

Witness: _____

App. D Computation of fiduciary fees in estate cases
R.C. 2113.35

Personal Property and Income (Including gross proceeds of real estate sold under authority of Will):

Personal Property _____
Income _____
TOTAL _____

4% of First $100,000.00 $_____
3% of Next $300,000.00 $_____
2% of Balance $_____

Real Estate Transferred (Not Sold)

1% of $_____ $_____

Non–Probate Assets (Subject to Ohio Estate Tax—Except Joint Survivorship Property):

1% of $_____ $_____

TOTAL ALLOWABLE FEE: $_____

TOTAL FEE TAKEN ON PRIOR ACCOUNTS: $_____

TOTAL FEE TAKEN ON THIS ACCOUNT: $_____

App. E Computation of guardian's fees
Local Rule 73.1

(1) Income from Investments:
    Installment Receipts: _____

    Total _____

    Total _____ × .05 = _____

And, if applicable:

(2) Total Rentals from Real Estate: _____

    Total _____ × 10% = _____

And, if applicable:

(3) Total Intangible Personal
    Property Invested: _____

    Total _____ divided by
    1000 = _____ × $2.50 = _____

And, if applicable:

(4) Total Final Distributions: _____

    Total _____ × 1% = _____

Equals:

Total Allowed Guardian Compensation: = _____

App. F Computation of trustee's fees
Local Rule 74.1

(1) Income from Investments:
    Installment Receipts: _____

    Total _____

    Total _____ × .05 = _____

And, if applicable:

(2) Total Rentals from Real Estate: _____

    Total _____ × 10% = _____

And, if applicable:

(3) Total Intangible Personal
    Property Invested: _____

    Total _____ divided by
    1000 = _____ × $2.50 = _____

And, if applicable:

(4) All Periodic Distributions of
    Personal Property Corpus: _____

    Total _____ × 1% = _____

Equals:

Total Allowed Trustee Compensation: = _____

Note: Per Local Rule 74.1 (A)(5), Corporate Trustee Fees can be determined as follows: A fee may be charged on the same basis as the corporate guardian charges its clients as trustee of a living trust. Each corporate fiduciary shall file its current fee schedule with this Court. Any amendments to the schedule must be filed before a fee computed under the amended schedule is credited to an account. **The fee schedule shall be limited to a maximum 1% fee for all guardianship estates with a market value of $75,000.00 or less.**

(Adopted eff. 7–3–00; amended eff. 4–20–04; 2–1–05.)

LOCAL RULES OF COURT, STARK COUNTY COURT OF COMMON PLEAS

RULES OF THE PROBATE DIVISION

SUP R. 8. COURT APPOINTMENTS
Rule
Local Rule 8.1 Court appointments

SUP R. 9. SECURITY PLANS
Local Rule 9.1 Security plans

SUP R. 11. RECORDING OF PROCEEDINGS
Local Rule 11.1 Recording of proceedings

SUP R. 26. COURT RECORDS MANAGEMENT AND RETENTION
Local Rule 26.1 Court records management and retention

SUP R. 27. STANDARDS RELATIVE TO THE USE OF ELECTRONIC DOCUMENTS AND RECORDS
Local Rule 27.1 Standards relative to the use of electronic documents and records

SUP R. 51. STANDARD PROBATE FORMS
Local Rule 51.1 Standard probate forms

SUP R. 52. SPECIFICATIONS FOR PRINTING PROBATE FORMS
Local Rule 52.1 Computer generated forms

SUP R. 53. HOURS OF THE COURT
Local Rule 53.1 Hours of the court

SUP R. 55. EXAMINATION OF PROBATE RECORDS
Local Rule 55.1 Case files
Local Rule 55.2 Photocopies

SUP R. 57. FILINGS AND JUDGMENT ENTRIES
Local Rule 57.1 Facsimile filings
Local Rule 57.2 Street address
Local Rule 57.3 Original signatures
Local Rule 57.4 Attorney signatures
Local Rule 57.5 Fiduciary signatures
Local Rule 57.6 Case number
Local Rule 57.7 Forwarding copies
Local Rule 57.8 Disposition of exhibits

SUP R. 58. DEPOSIT FOR COURT COSTS
Local Rule 58.1 Court costs

SUP R. 60. APPLICATION FOR LETTERS OF AUTHORITY TO ADMINISTER ESTATE AND NOTICE OF APPOINTMENT
Local Rule 60.1 Appointment of non resident fiduciaries

SUP R. 61. APPRAISERS
Local Rule 61.1 Appraisers and appraisals
Local Rule 61.2 Real estate appraisers
Local Rule 61.3 Self—dealing—appraiser
Local Rule 61.4 Readily ascertainable value of real property:
Local Rule 61.5 Readily ascertainable value of motor vehicle:
Local Rule 61.6 Household furnishings
Local Rule 61.7 Disputed appraisal

SUP R. 64. ACCOUNTS
Local Rule 64.1 Account timelines
Local Rule 64.2 Vouchers
Local Rule 64.3 Fiduciary's signature and address
Local Rule 64.4 Delinquency in filing an account

Rule
SUP R. 66. GUARDIANSHIPS
Local Rule 66.1 Guardianships of minors
Local Rule 66.2 Guardian's report
Local Rule 66.3 Sale of personal property
Local Rule 66.4 Deposit of wills
Local Rule 66.5 Change of address
Local Rule 66.6 Statement of expert evaluation

SUP R. 67. ESTATES OF MINOR'S OF NOT MORE THAN TEN THOUSAND DOLLARS
Local Rule 67.1 Representation of minor

SUP R. 68. SETTLEMENT OF INJURY CLAIMS OF MINORS
Local Rule 68.1 Separate case number
Local Rule 68.2 Structured settlements

SUP R. 70. SETTLEMENT OF WRONGFUL DEATH AND SURVIVAL CLAIMS
Local Rule 70.1 Wrongful death trusts
Local Rule 70.2 Wrongful death trust with multiple beneficiaries

SUP R. 71. COUNSEL FEES
Local Rule 71.1 Attorney serving as fiduciary
Local Rule 71.2 Counsel fees—decedent's estates
Local Rule 71.3 Counsel fees—guardianships

SUP R. 73. GUARDIAN'S COMPENSATION
Local Rule 73.1 Guardian's compensation

SUP R. 74. TRUSTEE'S COMPENSATION
Local Rule 74.1 Corporate trustees
Local Rule 74.2 Individual trustees

SUP R. 75. LOCAL RULES
Local Rule 75.1 Fiduciary bonds
Local Rule 75.2 Relieving estate from administration
Local Rule 75.3 Adoptions
Local Rule 75.4 Summary estate administration
Local Rule 75.5 Paralegals
Local Rule 75.6 Wills deposited for safekeeping
Local Rule 75.7 Objections to magistrate's decision

SUP R. 78. CASE MANAGEMENT IN DECEDENT'S ESTATES GUARDIANSHIPS AND TRUSTS
Local Rule 78.1 Civil actions
Local Rule 78.2 Land sales
Local Rule 78.3 Decedent's estates
Local Rule 78.4 Wrongful death settlements
Local Rule 78.5 Guardianships
Local Rule 78.6 Trusts
Local Rule 78.7 Motions
Local Rule 78.8 Adoptions

LOCAL RULE 79 MEDIATION
Local Rule 79.1 Purpose of mediation
Local Rule 79.2 Definitions
Local Rule 79.3 Mediation referral
Local Rule 79.4 Opposition to mediation referral
Local Rule 79.5 Attendance; authority to settle
Local Rule 79.6 Synopsis of dispute; agreement

Rule
Local Rule 79.7   Confidentiality
Local Rule 79.8   Outside referrals
Local Rule 79.9   Miscellaneous

SUP R. 8. COURT APPOINTMENTS

Local Rule 8.1   Court appointments

A. Persons appointed by the Court pursuant to constitutional or statutory authority, rule of court, or the inherent authority of the Court shall be selected from lists maintained by the Court. Such list will be maintained in Administrative Case File No. 167567.

B. Appointments will be made from such lists taking into consideration the qualifications, skill, expertise and caseload of the appointee in addition to the type, complexity and requirements of the case.

C. Court appointees will be paid a reasonable fee with consideration given to the factors contained in DR 2–106 of the Code of Professional Responsibility, the Ohio Revised Code and the Local Rules of Court relating to fees.

D. The Court shall review Court appointment lists at least annually to ensure the equitable distribution of appointments.

SUP R. 9.   SECURITY PLANS

Local Rule 9.1   Security plans

All persons shall be subject to the Stark County Security Policy and Procedure Manual, as adopted and as amended by the Court, in order that appropriate levels of security prevail in the Court to protect the integrity of Court procedures, to protect the rights of individuals before the Court, to deter those persons who would take violent action against the Court or litigants; to maintain the proper decorum and dignity of the Court, and to ensure that Court facilities are secure for all persons.

SUP R. 11. RECORDING OF PROCEEDINGS

Local Rule 11.1   Recording of proceedings

All hearings before the Court, if requested, will be recorded by audio-electronic recording devices and a fee in the amount $5.00 will be charged and collected as costs in such case. If any other recording procedure is desired, it must be provided by the requesting party, who shall make the necessary arrangements including the payment of costs. *The original audio electronic recording of the proceedings will not be made available to the parties.* All electronically recorded transcripts of proceedings and exhibits shall be maintained by the court for three (3) months from the date of the final appealable order in the case or final decision on appeal, whichever is later. Unless waived, a record in all jury trials will be taken by a court reporter.

SUP R. 26. COURT RECORDS MANAGEMENT AND RETENTION

Local Rule 26.1   Court records management and retention

The Court has established pursuant to Sup. R. 26(G), Schedules of Records Retention and Disposition which have been filed under administrative case file number 126131, and which schedules shall be followed in conjunction with the Rules of Superintendence for the Courts of Ohio.

SUP R. 27. STANDARDS RELATIVE TO THE USE OF ELECTRONIC DOCUMENTS AND RECORDS

Local Rule 27.1   Standards relative to the use of electronic documents and records

This Court submitted its proposed local rule to the Standards Subcommittee of the Supreme Court Advisory Committee on Technology and the Courts and received provisional approval on June 5, 2002. The local rule is set forth as Local Rule 57.1 herein.

SUP R. 51. STANDARD PROBATE FORMS

Local Rule 51.1   Standard probate forms

Forms for use in the Stark County Probate Court are available at the Court and on the Court's website: www.probate.co.stark.oh.us.

SUP R. 52. SPECIFICATIONS FOR PRINTING PROBATE FORMS

Local Rule 52.1   Computer generated forms

When standard forms are generated by computer, they shall conform to all specifications for standard forms stated in Sup. R. 52. The Court will accept for filing nonstandard computer generated forms for the receipts and disbursements attached to a standard account form or the schedule of assets attached to a standard inventory and appraisal form.

SUP R. 53. HOURS OF THE COURT

Local Rule 53.1   Hours of the court

The Probate Court and its offices shall be open for the transaction of business from 8:30 a.m. to 4:30 p.m. daily except Saturday, Sunday, and legal holidays. All pleadings requiring a new case number or the payment of court costs shall be filed by 4:15 p.m.

SUP R. 55. EXAMINATION OF PROBATE RECORDS

Local Rule 55.1   Case files

The Court's case files shall not be removed from the probate court. Individual pleadings shall not be removed from the retaining clips.

Local Rule 55.2   Photocopies

Copies of any public record may be obtained during regular court hours at the cost of five cents ($.05) per page with no charge for the first five (5) pages.

SUP R. 57. FILINGS AND JUDGMENT ENTRIES

Local Rule 57.1   Facsimile filings

Pursuant to Civil Rule 73(J) the Court in its discretion may allow facsimile filing during regular business hours of the Court as set forth in Local Rule 53.1 The area code and number of the receiving machine is 330.451.7040.

A. These rules only apply to civil proceedings and civil commitment proceedings in the Stark County Probate Court.

B. Any documents received after regular business hours shall be deemed filed the following business day.

C. Only documents subsequent to the initial document may be filed by facsimile.

D. A document filed by facsimile shall be accepted as the original and shall be filed by the attorney of record. All risks of transmission shall be borne by the sender.

E. All filings by facsimile shall be accompanied by a cover page that states all of the following information: (1) The date of transmission; (2) The name, telephone number, and facsimile number of the person transmitting the document; (3) The case number and caption of the case in which the document is to be filed; (4) The title of the document to be filed; (5) The number of pages being transmitted.

F. Any signature on documents transmitted by facsimile shall be considered that of the attorney or party that it purports to be for all purposes. If it is established that the documents were transmitted without authority, the Court may order the filing stricken.

G. The filing date of any documents transmitted by facsimile during regular business hours shall be the time and date the document was received by the probate court's facsimile machine.

H. No document filed by facsimile that requires a filing fee shall be accepted by the Clerk for filing until court costs and fees have been paid.

Local Rule 57.2   Street address

When required on a court document, the fiduciary's address must be a street address and, if applicable, any post office box number used as a mailing address. The address of the fiduciary must be the fiduciary's legal address. A fiduciary who is an attorney, may use an office address.

Local Rule 57.3   Original signatures

All filings must contain original signatures. In all matters with multiple fiduciaries, the signature of all fiduciaries is required.

Local Rule 57.4   Attorney signatures

A person who is not an attorney may not sign on behalf of an attorney.

Local Rule 57.5   Fiduciary signatures

The attorney for the fiduciary may not sign for the fiduciary.

Local Rule 57.6   Case number

All filings, including attachments, must have the case number on each page.

Local Rule 57.7   Forwarding copies

The Court will not return file-stamped copies by mail unless submitted with a return self-addressed stamped envelope.

Local Rule 57.8   Disposition of exhibits

All exhibits offered for admission during a hearing or trial shall be labeled by party name and item identification. In a proceeding recorded by a Court stenographer, custody of exhibits admitted or proffered shall be given to the stenographer, unless otherwise ordered by the Court. If the proceeding is electronically recorded, exhibits shall be retained separate from the case file, unless otherwise ordered by the Court.

Upon agreement of the parties or by order of the Court, copies may be substituted for the original exhibit. Disposal of exhibits shall be pursuant to Sup. R. 26.

SUP R. 58.   DEPOSIT FOR COURT COSTS

Local Rule 58.1   Court costs

A. Application to Admit Will to Probate $81.00

(when no administration necessary)

B. Application for Authority to Administer Testate Estate $125.00

C. Application for Authority to Administer Intestate Estate $125.00

D. Application to Relieve Estate From Administration *

* (varies as to statutory limits and dates of death)

1. Additional fee for certificate of transfer of real estate $ 7.00

E. Petition for Adoption, excepting independent adoptions*

(includes home study)

Effective July 1, 2005 through July 31, 2005 $316.00

Effective August 1, 2005 $416.00

(if more than one child is being adopted by the same adoptive parents each additional petition for adoption) $116.00 *

F. Application for Placement for Adoption $ 58.00

(attorney must make arrangements with qualified assessor for payment of fee)

G. Civil Actions $125.00

(Land sales, determination of heirs, etc.)

H. Application for Appointment of Guardian $151.00

Application for Appointment of Conservator $101.00

I. Estate Tax Return

(if filed without estate proceedings) $ 18.00

J. Exceptions to Inventory and Appraisal $ 23.00

K. Exceptions to Account $ 23.00

L. Petition for Release of Adoption Information $ 63.00

M. Application for Name Change $ 73.00

N. Minor's Settlement $ 66.00

O. Account $ 25.00

P. Testamentary Trust (extra Letters $1.00 each) $ 101.00

Q. Wrongful Death Trust $ 38.00

SUP R. 60.   APPLICATION FOR LETTERS OF AUTHORITY TO ADMINISTER ESTATE AND NOTICE OF APPOINTMENT

Local Rule 60.1   Appointment of non resident fiduciaries

An applicant to be appointed fiduciary of a decedent's estate, or trust, who is not a resident of this state, must be in compliance with Section 2109.21 of the Revised Code and use as the attorney of record an attorney licensed to practice law in this State. To assure the assets remain in Stark County, Ohio, during the administration of the estate or trust, the applicant must meet one or more of the following criteria as required by the Court:

A. Place a substantial amount of the assets in a custodial depository in this county, pursuant to Section 2109.13 of the Revised Code;

B. Have a co-fiduciary who is a resident of this State;

C. Post a bond in compliance with Section 2109.04 of the Revised Code.

SUP R. 61.   APPRAISERS

Local Rule 61.1   Appraisers and appraisals

When required by law, there shall be one suitable and disinterested appraiser appointed by the executor or administrator of an estate, with Court approval. The following persons shall be disqualified from being such an appraiser:

A. A person related by blood or marriage to the decedent;

B. A beneficiary of the estate;

C. A person related by blood, marriage or employment to the attorney for the estate;

D. A person related by blood, marriage or employment to the fiduciary for the estate, and

E. Real estate agents, and brokers who are or will be utilized to sell the assets which are to be appraised.

Local Rule 61.2 Real estate appraisers

Real estate appraisals shall be made by licensed real estate agents, brokers, auctioneers, credentialed real estate appraisers, or such other persons who by experience and training are qualified to make real estate appraisals.

Local Rule 61.3 Self—dealing—appraiser

No appraiser shall be permitted to directly or indirectly purchase or acquire any of the property he or she appraises, except at public auction.

Local Rule 61.4 Readily ascertainable value of real property:

Notwithstanding Local Rule 61.1 through Local Rule 61.3, the market value of real estate as found in the Stark County Auditor's property records may be accepted as the readily ascertainable value of the property and no further appraisal of such property shall be required except as provided under Local Rule 61.7. A copy of said evaluation shall be attached to Form 6.1—Schedule of Assets or Form 5.1—Assets and Liabilities of Estate to be Relieved from Administration, whichever is applicable.

Local Rule 61.5 Readily ascertainable value of motor vehicle:

Notwithstanding Local Rule 61.1 through Local Rule 61.3, the market value of any motor vehicle as found in the current N.A.D.A. Official Used Car Guide under the category "Av'g Retail" may be accepted as the readily ascertainable value of the property and no further appraisal of such property shall be required except as provided under Local Rule 61.7. A copy of the appropriate page from said booklet shall be attached to Form 6.1—Schedule of Assets or Form 5.1—Assets and Liabilities of Estate to be Relieved from Administration, whichever is applicable.

Local Rule 61.6 Household furnishings

All chattel property and household furnishings shall be appraised. If it all passes to the surviving spouse, it may be returned without an appraisal, subject to Court approval.

Local Rule 61.7 Disputed appraisal

A fiduciary, beneficiary, or creditor of a decedent's estate may file a written request with the Probate Court not later than five (5) days prior to the date set for hearing on the Inventory and Appraisal pursuant to Section 2115.16 of the Revised Code that any property deemed to be appraised by readily ascertainable value shall be appraised by a suitable and disinterested appraiser as provided in Local Rule 61.1 through Local Rule 61.3.

SUP R. 64. ACCOUNTS

Local Rule 64.1 Account timelines

A. For estates where the date of death is after January 1, 2002, the Final and Distributive Account or Certificate of Termination shall be due not later than six months following the date of the appointment of the estate fiduciary.

1. The time for filing the Final and Distributive Account may be extended to thirteen months by filing the notice or motion for the reasons enumerated in R.C. 2109.301(B)(1). (Use Standard Probate Forms 13.8 or 13.10)

B. For guardians, the first account shall be due not later than one year following the date of the appointment and each subsequent account shall be due on an annual basis, unless the court orders otherwise.

C. For trusts, the first account shall be due not later than two years following the date of the appointment and each subsequent account shall be due on a bi-annual basis, unless the court orders otherwise.

Local Rule 64.2 Vouchers

A. The Court requires copies of vouchers to be filed with estate accounts for decedent's dying on or before December 31, 2001, and all guardianship and trust accounts. The voucher copies will be kept by the Probate Court until the account is approved. After the account is approved, the vouchers may be destroyed by the Probate Court or if requested, returned to the Attorney for the Fiduciary.

B. Accounts requiring vouchers will not be approved without vouchers or other proof which verifies each disbursement. Copies of bank draft receipts and uncancelled checks will not satisfy R.C. 2109.302 and R.C. 2109.303.

C. The Court will accept as a voucher, a statement from a financial institution specifying the payee, check amount and date of payment on a bank statement that includes photo copies of cancelled checks.

Local Rule 64.3 Fiduciary's signature and address

A. All accounts must be personally signed by the fiduciary and contain the full name, current residence address and telephone number of the fiduciary.

B. All fiduciaries must sign the account when multiple fiduciaries have been appointed.

Local Rule 64.4 Delinquency in filing an account

No expenditure, sale, distribution or fee will be approved while the fiduciary is delinquent in filing an account. See also Sup. R. 78.

SUP R. 66. GUARDIANSHIPS

Local Rule 66.1 Guardianships of minors

A. A separate guardianship must be filed and a corresponding case file established for each proposed ward.

B. The Court will not accept for filing any guardianship for a minor where the sole purpose of the guardianship is to establish a residency for school purposes. Custody for school purposes is a matter to be heard and determined by the Juvenile Division of the Court of Common Pleas.

C. A certified copy of the minor's birth certificate shall be filed with every Form 16.0—Application for Appointment of a Guardian of a Minor.

D. Minor's who are not U.S. citizens or resident aliens, are not considered by this Court to be residents or have legal settlement as set forth in Section 2111.02(A) of the Revised Code.

Local Rule 66.2 Guardian's report

All guardians are required to file their Guardian's Report (Form 17.7) as detailed in Section 2111.49 of the Revised Code on the first anniversary after the date of the issuance of the Letters of Guardianship and annually thereafter.

Local Rule 66.3 Sale of personal property

A guardian may not sell any tangible personal property of the ward without prior Court approval. Every application to sell a ward's tangible personal property shall be supported by a written appraisal by a suitable and qualified appraiser.

Local Rule 66.4 Deposit of wills

The guardian must deposit with the Court any and all wills of the ward for safekeeping pursuant to Section 2107.07 of the Revised Code.

Local Rule 66.5 Change of address

A guardian shall inform the Court as to any change of address of the guardian or the ward within thirty (30) days of the address change. Failure to notify the Court under this rule may result in guardian being removed.

Local Rule 66.6 Statement of expert evaluation

Where a physician or clinical psychologist states on a Statement of Expert Evaluation that to a reasonable degree of medical certainty it is unlikely the ward's mental competence will improve, the Court may dispense with the filing of subsequent evaluations.

SUP R. 67. ESTATES OF MINOR'S OF NOT MORE THAN TEN THOUSAND DOLLARS

Local Rule 67.1 Representation of minor

A. If no attorney represents the interests of the minor, the attorney representing the interests of the payor shall assume the duties imposed by Sup. R. 67 (B) and (C).

B. Pursuant to Sup. R. 67(C), the attorney representing the applicants or the payor in the matter shall acknowledge responsibility for depositing the funds and providing the financial institution with a copy of the entry. The attorney shall obtain a Verification of Receipt and Deposit (Form 22.3) from the financial institution and file the form with the Court within seven (7) days of the issuance of the entry.

SUP R. 68. SETTLEMENT OF INJURY CLAIMS OF MINORS

Local Rule 68.1 Separate case number

Settlement of a minor's claim is a separate proceeding in this Court and shall not proceed under the case number assigned to the guardianship, if any.

Local Rule 68.2 Structured settlements

In the event that parties involved in claims for injuries to minors or incompetents desire to enter into a structured settlement, defined as a settlement wherein payments are made on a periodic basis, the following rules shall apply:

A. The application shall include a signed statement from one of the following independent professionals, specifying the present value of the settlement, and the method of calculation of that value: an actuary, certified public accountant, certified financial planner, chartered life underwriter, chartered financial consultant, or an equivalent professional.

B. If the settlement is to be funded by an annuity, the application shall include a signed statement by the annuity carrier or the broker procuring the policy stating:

(1) The annuity carrier is licensed to write annuities in Ohio.

(2) The annuity carrier's ratings from at least two of the following organizations, which meet the following criteria:

a. A.M. Best Company; A++, A+, or A;

b. Fitch Company (formerly Duff & Phelps Credit Rating Company (Claims Paying Ability Rating): AAA, AA+, or AA;

c. Moody's Investors Service (Financial Strength): Aaa, Aa1, or Aa2;

d. Standard & Poor's Corporation (Financial Strength): AAA, AA+, or AA;

e. Weiss Research Inc.: A+ or A.

C. In addition to the requirements of Paragraph (B) above, an annuity carrier must meet any other requirement the Court considers reasonably necessary to assure that funding to satisfy periodic payment settlements will be provided and maintained.

D. There shall be no premature withdrawals or hypothecation of the structure without prior Court approval.

SUP R. 70. SETTLEMENT OF WRONGFUL DEATH AND SURVIVAL CLAIMS

Local Rule 70.1 Wrongful death trusts

Any attorney who is submitting a wrongful death trust must submit the form of the trust to the Court at least seven (7) days prior to the hearing on the wrongful death settlement.

Local Rule 70.2 Wrongful death trust with multiple beneficiaries

A wrongful death trust with its own case number shall be created for each beneficiary.

SUP R. 71. COUNSEL FEES

Local Rule 71.1 Attorney serving as fiduciary

In all matters where an attorney is the fiduciary of the estate, guardianship, or trust, and that attorney is the attorney of record, detailed records shall be maintained describing time and services as fiduciary and as attorney, which records shall, upon request, be submitted to the Court for review. DR 2–106 of the Code of Professional Responsibility shall govern the reasonableness of all fees, notwithstanding statutory allowances. The Court assumes an attorney, appointed as fiduciary, has been selected due to the attorney's special knowledge and abilities resulting in a savings of fees to the estate, guardianship, or trust.

Upon review of the records, the Court may set the fees for hearing, regardless of the submission of consent(s) to fees.

Local Rule 71.2 Counsel fees—decedent's estates

A. Where the primary beneficiaries have consented in writing to the amount of counsel fees, an application need not be made for the allowance, provided the consent is endorsed on the fiduciary's account or evidenced by a separate instrument filed with the account.

B. Where the attorney on application to the court prior to or during administration requests a fixed fee, the court, if it deems appropriate and after appropriate notice to the interested parties, will then fix a reasonable fee for services beneficial to the administration of the estate.

C. Counsel fees for the administration of a decedent's estate shall be reasonable and beneficial to the estate. The application for fees shall be in writing which sets forth the details supporting the calculations on which the requested fees are based.

D. Counsel fees for the administration of a decedent's estate as set forth below may serve as a guide in determining fees to be charged to the estate for legal services of an ordinary nature rendered as attorney for the fiduciary in the complete administration of a decedent's estate.

E. Such schedules, however, are not to be considered or represented to clients as schedules of minimum or maximum fees to be charged.

1. On the personal property which is subject to administration and for which the fiduciary is charged and upon the proceeds of real estate that is sold under a power of will as follows:

    a. For the first $100,000.00 at a rate of 4.5%;

    b. All above $100,000.00 and not exceeding $400,000.00 at the rate of 3.5%;

    c. All above $400,000.00 at the rate of 2.5%.

2. On real property that is not sold at a rate of 2%.

3. On real estate sold by judicial proceedings according to the judgment entry confirming the proceedings.

4. On all other property not included in this rule:

    a. If a federal estate tax return is not required, 1 1/2% of all such property subject to Ohio estate tax.

    b. If a federal estate tax return is required, 2 1/2% of all such property subject to federal estate tax.

F. Where the attorney, law partner or firm associate is appointed as fiduciary, the total administration fee may not exceed the statutory fiduciary commission plus one half of the guideline counsel fee.

G. If by reason of the application of the above percentages to values of assets a disparity or injustice results, such disparity or injustice may be reviewed on the court's own motion in respect of any account reflecting such compensation or upon exceptions to such an account.

Local Rule 71.3 Counsel fees—guardianships

Counsel fees for the administration of a guardianship shall be those reasonable and beneficial to the guardianship. The application for fees shall be in writing which sets forth the details supporting the calculations on which the requested fees are based.

SUP R. 73. GUARDIAN'S COMPENSATION

Local Rule 73.1 Guardian's compensation

A. A guardian of the estate shall be allowed compensation for income and disbursements as follows:

1. Income and Disbursements:

4% of the first $5,000.00 of income

3% of the excess of $5,000.00 of income

4% of the first $5,000.00 of disbursements

3% of the excess of $5,000.00 of disbursements

2. Principal:

$3.00 per thousand on the first $250,000.00 of market value

$2.00 per thousand on excess of $250,000.00 of market value

B. For purposes of determining compensation based on income the following shall not be considered income:

1. Receipt of corpus by guardian

2. Balance carried forward from prior accountings

3. Investment and reinvestment of corpus

C. If by reason of the application of the above percentages a disparity or injustice results, such disparity or injustice may be reviewed on the court's own motion in respect of any account reflecting such compensation or upon exceptions to such an account.

D. Applications for compensation by guardians of veterans must comply with Chapter 5905 of the Ohio Revised Code and all other rules and regulations of the Department of Veterans Affairs.

SUP R. 74. TRUSTEE'S COMPENSATION

Local Rule 74.1 Corporate trustees

A. Except where the instrument creating the trust makes provisions for compensation, a testamentary trustee may charge fees on the same basis as it charges for living trusts.

B. Fee schedules are subject to prior Court approval and are to be furnished to the Court on the 1st day of January of each year and whenever a change in fees is made within any calendar year.

C. A separate schedule of the computation of the trustee's compensation shall be set forth in the trustee's account as a condition of its approval.

D. The trustee may charge its applicable "sweep fee" for the management of money market funds within testamentary trust accounts.

Local Rule 74.2 Individual trustees

A. Except where the instrument creating the trust makes provisions for compensation, the testamentary trustee may charge as follows:

(1) Principal Fee. A fee of $2.00 per $1,000 of the market value of the principal held by the trustee.

(2) Income Fee. A fee of six and one half percent (6.5%) of the total of the income for the accounting period.

(3) Principal Distribution Fee. A fee of one percent (1%) of the principal distributed during the accounting period.

B. If by reason of the application of the above percentages to values of assets a disparity or injustice results, such disparity or injustice may be reviewed on the Court's own motion in respect of any account reflecting such compensation or upon exceptions to such an account.

SUP R. 75. LOCAL RULES

Local Rule 75.1 Fiduciary bonds

A. When an instrument appointing an executor or testamentary trustee dispenses with the giving of bond, the Court will appoint the fiduciary without bond unless the Court is of the opinion that the best interest of the trust requires a bond.

B. A surety company, prior to executing a fiduciary bond, must register with the Court and file prior proof that the company is authorized to do business within Ohio.

C. The Court will not accept personal sureties.

Local Rule 75.2 Relieving estate from administration

A. Appraisal of assets:

1. The appraisal of assets shall be subject to Local Rule 61.1, "Appraisers and Appraisals".

2. Chattel property and household furnishings passing to the surviving spouse, may be returned without an appraisal, subject to court approval.

B. Publication of notice to creditors and all interested parties:

1. Publication of notice is not required if assets are less than the statutory limits and there is no surviving spouse and/or minor children of the decedent, and there is a paid funeral bill or waiver by the funeral director or a funeral payment agreement, and a Notice to Distributee (SCPC Form 10.4) is filed for each beneficiary.

2. Publication of notice is not required if assets are less than the statutory limits and the decedent is survived by minor children but no surviving spouse, and there is a paid funeral bill or waiver by the funeral director or funeral payment agreement, and a Notice to Distributee (SCPC Form 10.4) is filed for each beneficiary.

3. Publication of notice is not required if assets are less than $100,000. 00 and there is a surviving spouse who inherits the entire probate estate, and there is a paid funeral bill or waiver by the funeral director or funeral payment agreement and a Notice to Distributee (SCPC Form 10.4) is filed by the surviving spouse.

C. Commissioner—A commissioner shall be appointed:

1. To make distributions in kind;

2. To sell personal property;

3. To pay outstanding debts;

4. To execute documents to title personal property.

D. Every commissioner shall file a report of distribution within thirty (30) days of the appointment

Local Rule 75.3 Adoptions

A. In addition to the requirements of R.C. 3107.012, each person to be a qualified assessor, shall first have on file with the Court a copy of a current "Certificate of Completion".

B. Each assessor who is to perform a home study as provided in R.C. 3107.031 must first be approved and appointed by the Court.

C. The requirement of a pre-finalization assessment as provided in R.C. 3107.12 shall not be required in an adoption by a step-parent, unless the Court orders otherwise.

D. A final accounting in accordance with R.C. 3107.10 shall be filed in all public children services agency adoptions.

E. A preliminary estimate account and a final account as provided for in R.C. 3107.10 shall not be required in adoptions by a step-parent, unless the Court orders otherwise.

F. The application for search of the Ohio Putative Father Registry shall be filed by the mother of the child, the child welfare agency or the attorney for either of them.

G. There shall be separate legal counsel for the person(s) seeking to adopt and the parent(s) placing a child for adoption, pursuant to R.C. 5103.16.

H. In private placement adoptions, a pre-placement application in a form prescribed by the Court shall be filed by the prospective adopting parents not less than seven (7) days prior to the placement if the applicants are residents of Stark County, Ohio and not less than fourteen (14) days if the applicants are not residents of Stark County, Ohio.

I. In all adoptions, married petitioner(s) must be married for not less than one (1) year prior to the final approval of adoption.

Local Rule 75.4 Summary estate administration

A. The Court may issue an order of distribution for a summary estate administration, if the applicant satisfies all of the following requirements:

1. The applicant has paid, or is obligated in writing to pay the decedent's funeral expenses, and

2. The entire value of the decedent's estate, as verified by written documentation, does not exceed Two Thousand ($2,000.00) Dollars, and

3. The applicant is entitled to the entire estate to satisfy the claim for the decedent's funeral expenses or the family allowance.

B. If the applicant is not the decedent's surviving spouse or a next of kin, then notice must be given at the applicant's cost, to all next of kin before any order of distribution will issue.

Local Rule 75.5 Paralegals

In fee statements filed with the Court, services of the paralegal must be itemized separately from services performed by an attorney.

Local Rule 75.6 Wills deposited for safekeeping

After the testator's death, a will deposited for safekeeping pursuant to Section 2107.07 of the Revised Code shall only be released to a Court of probate jurisdiction.

Local Rule 75.7 Objections to magistrate's decision

Upon filing objections to a magistrate's decision pursuant to Civ. R. 53, the moving party shall cause the objections to be set for hearing and to give notice to the opposing party or attorney of the date on which the matter is to be heard or submitted for decision.

The objections must be accompanied by a supporting memorandum. If required, the transcript shall be filed within thirty (30) days of the filing of the objections or two (2) days before the hearing, whichever occurs first.

Failure to file a transcript when one is required by Civ. R. 53(E)(3)(b) is a basis for dismissal of the objections.

Memoranda contra to the objections may be filed by any party within ten (10) days of the filing of the objections, or two (2) days prior to the hearing, whichever occurs first.

SUP R. 78. CASE MANAGEMENT IN DECEDENT'S ESTATES GUARDIANSHIPS AND TRUSTS

Local Rule 78.1 Civil actions

A. A pre-trial conference shall be conducted in all civil cases, except in land sale proceedings, prior to being scheduled for trial.

B. Within thirty (30) days after the answer day the case shall be set by the Court for a pre-trial conference.

C. Not less than fourteen (14) days notice of the pre-trial conference shall be given by the Court to all counsel of record by mail and/or telephone. Any application for continuance of the conference shall be in writing and filed with the Court in a timely manner.

D. The following decisions shall be made at the pre-trial conference and all counsel attending must have full authority to enter into a binding pre-trial order;

1. A definite discovery schedule shall be agreed upon by all parties for the completion of all discovery.

2. A definite date for exchange of expert witness reports shall be determined.

3. A definite date for filing of all motions which date shall not be less than seven (7) days before the final pre-trial. The date for the final pre-trial shall be set by the Court and shall be held approximately one week prior to the trial.

4. The date for the trial shall be set by the Court.

E. The following decisions shall be made at the final pre-trial and all counsel attending must have full authority to enter into a binding final pre-trial order;

1. The Court will rule on all pre-trial motions.

2. Briefs on any legal issues, proposed jury instructions and proposed jury interrogatories shall be submitted to the Court.

3. Clients must attend the final pre-trial.

4. No motions shall be heard after the final pre-trial without leave of Court and without good cause being shown.

F. The trial date shall not be changed nor shall the trial be continued without order of the Court and after the showing of good cause.

Local Rule 78.2 Land sales

A. All land sales which have not been concluded within one (1) year from the date of filing the complaint shall be set for pre-trial conference within ten (10) days following the expiration of one year.

B. The following decisions shall be made at the pre-trial conference and all counsel attending must have full authority to enter into a binding pre-trial order;

1. The attorney of record and the fiduciary must attend the pre-trial conference.

2. A written status report shall be filed with the Court no later than seven (7) days prior to the pre-trial conference.

3. The status report shall address the efforts being made to sell the real estate and when the case will be closed.

Local Rule 78.3 Decedent's estates

A. The statutory time for filing of an inventory (R.C. 2115.02) and an account (R.C. 2109.30) shall be adhered to and the citation procedure (R.C. 2109.301) shall be utilized if necessary to gain compliance.

B. The Court shall set all exceptions to an inventory or an account for a pre-trial conference within thirty (30) days after exceptions are filed.

1. The Court at the pre-trial conference shall set the matter for an evidentiary hearing within thirty (30) days thereafter.

C. All decedent's estates, which are current as to filed accounts, that remain open after a period of thirteen months shall be subject to a status conference. The fiduciary and the attorney shall be present and a written status report shall be submitted to the Court at the time of the status conference.

Local Rule 78.4 Wrongful death settlements

All hearings shall be held within thirty (30) days of the filing of the Form 14.0, provided however, if either a guardian or guardian ad litem is required to be appointed the hearing shall be held within fifteen (15) days after the appointment.

Local Rule 78.5 Guardianships

A. The statutory time for filing of an account (R.C. 2109.30) shall be adhered to and the citation procedure (R.C. 2109.31) shall be utilized if necessary to gain compliance.

B. The statutory time for filing a guardian's report (R.C. 2111.49) shall be adhered to and the citation procedure (R.C. 2109.31) shall be utilized if necessary to gain compliance.

C. Each guardianship shall be reviewed not less than bi-annually, by the probate court investigator.

Local Rule 78.6 Trusts

The statutory time for filing of an account (R.C. 2109.30) shall be adhered to and the citation procedure (R.C. 2109.31) shall be utilized if necessary to gain compliance.

Local Rule 78.7 Motions

A. The moving party shall serve and file with the motion a brief written statement in support of the motion and a list of citations of authorities in support. Opposing counsel or a party shall serve the response memorandum on or before the fourteenth (14th) day after the date of service as set forth on the Certificate of Service attached to the served copy of the motion.

B. All motions shall be determined upon the pleadings and memorandum in support. Oral arguments upon motions may be permitted upon written application and after showing of good cause.

C. When a hearing is granted, the Court shall set the hearing within thirty (30) days after receipt of the request.

Local Rule 78.8 Adoptions

A. All hearings shall be held within seventy five (75) days of the filing of the Petition for Adoption.

B. All cases in which an Interlocutory Order of Adoption has been issued shall be reviewed six (6) months after the Interlocutory Order of Adoption is journalized and shall be finalized or set for further proceedings.

LOCAL RULE 79 MEDIATION

Local Rule 79.1 Purpose of mediation

The Court establishes mediation in order to increase access to justice; to increase parties participation in court processes and their satisfaction with the outcome; to allow cases to settle more quickly with less expense to the parties; and to expand dispute resolution resources available to the parties.

Local Rule 79.2 Definitions

(A) Mediation is a process whereby a mediator facilitates communication and negotiation between the parties to assist them in reaching a mutually acceptable agreement.

(B) Mediator means a neutral person who conducts the mediation.

(C) Party means a party who participates in a mediation and whose agreement is necessary to resolve the dispute.

Local Rule 79.3 Mediation referral

The Court may refer a case to mediation on the motion of any party, on the agreement of the parties, or on its own order.

Local Rule 79.4 Opposition to mediation referral

A party opposing either the mediation referral or the appointed mediator must file a written objection to the Court within ten days of receiving notice of the referral or mediator and explain the reason for any opposition.

Local Rule 79.5 Attendance; authority to settle

(A) Party representatives with authority to negotiate a settlement and all other persons necessary to negotiate a settlement, including insurance carriers, must attend the mediation session.

(B) In the event the parties and or their attorneys and or the insurance representatives do not attend the mediation session, the mediator shall report said con-compliance to the judge who shall impose appropriate sanctions, including but not limited to dismissal, default judgment, attorney fees and or costs.

Local Rule 79.6   Synopsis of dispute; agreement

(A) At least five (5) days before the mediation, the parties shall submit to the Mediator a short memorandum stating the legal and factual positions of each party, as well as other material as each party believes would be beneficial to the mediator, including but not limited to, the status of discovery, damages, injuries and or settlement attempts.

(B) In the event the parties come to terms, the agreement shall be reduced to writing and signed by the parties, and if the mediator deems it appropriate, the oral agreement will be recorded by a court reporter, tape recorder, or other reliable means of sound recording.

Local Rule 79.7   Confidentiality

(A) All communications, negotiations, or settlement discussions by and between participants in the course of a mediation are not subject to discovery or admissible in evidence; and shall remain confidential and are protected from disclosure, except as otherwise provided by law.

(B) The mediator shall be prohibited from being called as a witness in any subsequent legal proceeding. (Except as to the terms of the settlement agreement.)

Local Rule 79.8   Outside referrals

If a dispute involves such issues as mental health, mental retardation, developmental disability, or aging adults, but a guardianship case has not been filed, an agency may file a motion to refer the matter to mediation. A case shall be referred to mediation if mediation is likely to resolve the dispute as a less restrictive alternative to guardianship.

Local Rule 79.9   Miscellaneous

(A) The mediator shall provide a written report within ten days to the Court indicating the outcome of the mediation. If full agreement is reached, the report shall indicate the parties' agreement as to who shall be responsible for outstanding court costs and who will prepare any necessary journal entries.

SUMMIT COUNTY COURT OF COMMON PLEAS

RULES OF THE PROBATE DIVISION

SUP R. 26. COURT RECORDS MANAGEMENT AND RETENTION
Rule
26.1 Court records management and retention

SUP R. 53. HOURS OF THE COURT
53.1 Hours of the court

SUP R. 54. CONDUCT IN THE COURT
54.1 Magistrates
54.2 Record

SUP R. 55. EXAMINATION OF PROBATE RECORDS
55.1 Examination of probate records

SUP R. 56. CONTINUANCES
56.1 Continuances/leaves to plead

SUP R. 57. FILINGS AND JUDGMENT ENTRIES
57.1 Filings and judgment entries

SUP R. 58. DEPOSIT FOR COURT COSTS
58.1 Deposit for court costs

SUP R. 59. WILLS
59.1 Application to probate a will

SUP R. 60. APPLICATION FOR LETTERS OF AUTHORITY TO ADMINISTER ESTATE AND NOTICE OF APPOINTMENT
60.1 Application for letters of authority to administer estate and notice of appointment

SUP R. 61. APPRAISERS
61.1 Appraiser fees/compensation
61.2 Appraisal/full estate administrations, release and summary release from administration
61.3 Appraiser—Self Dealing

SUP R. 64. ACCOUNTS
64.1 Accounts

SUP R. 65. LAND SALES—R.C. CHAPTER 2127
65.1 Land sales

SUP R. 66. GUARDIANSHIPS
66.1 Guardianships

SUP R. 67. ESTATES OF MINORS OF NOT MORE THAN TEN THOUSAND DOLLARS
67.1 Minor settlement/net proceeds less than ten thousand dollars

SUP R. 68. SETTLEMENT OF INJURY CLAIMS OF MINORS
68.1 Settlement of injury claims of minors

SUP R. 70. SETTLEMENT OF WRONGFUL DEATH AND SURVIVAL CLAIMS
70.1 Wrongful death settlement

SUP R. 71. COUNSEL FEES
71.1 Counsel fees

SUP R. 72. EXECUTOR'S AND ADMINISTRATOR'S COMMISSIONS
72.1 Fiduciary computation

Rule
SUP R. 73. GUARDIAN'S COMPENSATION
73.1 Guardian's compensation

SUP R. 74. TRUSTEE'S COMPENSATION
74.1 Trustee's compensation

SUP R. 78. PROBATE DIVISION OF THE COURT OF COMMON PLEAS—CASE MANAGEMENT IN DECEDENT'S ESTATES, GUARDIANSHIPS, AND TRUSTS
78.1 Case management procedure

GENERAL PROVISIONS
86.1 Marriage license
87.1 Service by deputy clerk
88.1 Inventory/notice
88.2 Inventory/schedule of assets
89.1 Attorneys as sureties
90.1 Removal of will from safe deposit boxes
91.1 Guardian ad litem
92.1 Trusts
93.1 Change of name
94.1 Adoptions
95.1 Registration of birth/correction of birth
96.1 Concealment of assets
97.1 Appropriation of property
98.1 Mediation

APPENDICES
Section
App A Deposits for court costs
App B Adoption fees
App C Application—Computation of guardian fees
App D Application—Computation of fiduciary fees
App E Application for attorney fees
App F Notice of attorney fees
App G Application for attorney fees in land sale proceedings

Preface

Summit County Local Rules supplementing the Supreme Court Rules of Superintendence are numbered with a suffix. For example, a local rule which supplements Supreme Court Rule 53 is designated as Local Rule 53.1.

SUP R. 26. COURT RECORDS MANAGEMENT AND RETENTION

Rule 26.1 Court records management and retention

The Court has a Schedule of Records Retention and Disposition which will be followed in conjunction with The Rules of Superintendence for the Courts of Ohio.

(Adopted effective January 1, 2005.)

SUP R. 53. HOURS OF THE COURT

Rule 53.1 Hours of the court

The Probate Court shall be open for the transaction of business daily from 8:00 A.M. to 4:00 P.M., except Saturdays, Sundays, and legal holidays observed by the Court.

(Former Rule 18.1 amended and renumbered as Rule 53.1, effective June 10, 1998.)

SUP R. 54. CONDUCT IN THE COURT

Rule 54.1 Magistrates

(A) **Appointment/Powers.**

Magistrates may be appointed by the Common Pleas Court Probate Judge, and shall serve as full-time or part-time employees of the Court as provided in Civil Rule 53. Civil Magistrates shall have those powers as set out in Civil Rule 53 and as set out in any Order of Reference.

(B) **General Order of Reference.**

The Magistrates so appointed are hereby referred all matters, including pretrials, pertaining to estates, guardianships, trusts, adoptions, civil commitments, and name changes. This Reference includes all powers of the Court except as restricted by law.

(C) **Decisions.**

Prior to an objection to a Magistrate's Decision, a request for Findings of Fact and Conclusions of Law may be filed, pursuant to Civil Rule 52.

(Former Rule 19.1 amended and renumbered as Rule 54.1, effective June 10, 1998.)

Rule 54.2 Record

(A) **Matters Heard by the Judge.**

All matters occurring in open Court will be recorded on tape. A copy of the tape will be available at a cost set by the Court. Unless waived, a record in all jury trials will be taken by a court reporter. In all other matters, a record by a court reporter will be taken only upon written request.

(B) **Matters Heard by the Magistrate.**

All contested matters occurring in open Court will be recorded on tape. In all other matters, a record by the court reporter will be taken only upon written request.

(C) **Costs.**

Unless otherwise ordered, parties requesting a record by a court reporter will bear the cost of the reporter. The costs of taping a hearing shall be assessed to the case except where a party provides a court reporter, or by Order of the Court. Copies of the tape will be available at an additional cost set by the Court under Appendix A—Miscellaneous Court Costs.

(D) **Transcript.**

Preparations of transcripts are the responsibility of the requesting parties.

(Former Rule 19.2 amended and renumbered as Rule 54.2, effective June 10, 1998.)

SUP R. 55. EXAMINATION OF PROBATE RECORDS

Rule 55.1 Examination of probate records

(A) **Removal of Files.**

The Chief Magistrate, in addition to the Judge, may authorize removal of files. Prior to removal, a receipt shall be given containing the name, address, and telephone number of the person assuming responsibility for the documents. All items removed must be returned to the Court within five (5) working days of removal.

(Former Rule 20.1 amended and renumbered as Rule 55.1, effective June 10, 1998.)

SUP R. 56. CONTINUANCES

Rule 56.1 Continuances/leaves to plead

(A) **Continuances.**

(1) When a party fails to object within seven (7) days of the filing of a Motion to Continue, and the party has received notice of the Motion to Continue, such failure to object shall be considered as consent to the continuance.

(2) An attorney requesting a continuance in a civil action heard by the Judge shall serve a copy of the Motion upon opposing counsel, or upon the adverse party if not represented by counsel.

(B) **Leaves to Plead.**

The following procedures are applicable:

(1) Leaves to plead shall be by written application to the Court. The application shall set forth the number of leaves to plead previously obtained, and the total days of such leaves, and shall be served upon opposing counsel or upon the adverse party if not represented by counsel.

(2) Leaves Granted Without Order of Court

Unless the Court has, on its own Motion, limited leaves to plead, the following Motions for leave to plead are granted, without Order of the Court, for a period of twenty-one (21) days.

(a) First Leave to Plead

When a certification is filed that no previous leave to plead has been taken.

(b) Additional Leave to Plead with Consent

If the only leave to plead taken by a party is under the provision of paragraph (B)(2)(a), an additional leave may be taken by that party upon the filing of the written consent of opposing counsel.

(Former Rules 23.1 and 23.2 amended and renumbered as Rule 56.1, effective June 10, 1998.)

SUP R. 57. FILINGS AND JUDGMENT ENTRIES

Rule 57.1 Filings and judgment entries

(A) **Requirements for Acceptance.**

(1) The Court may, whenever it deems necessary, require the use of printed forms supplied by the Court.

(2) Upon filing a new case, or entering an appearance as substituted counsel or as co-counsel, each attorney shall provide the Court with their Attorney Registration Identification Number issued by the Supreme Court of Ohio. The number shall be conspicuously placed on an original filing or Order whenever an attorney first represents a fiduciary in any estate, trust, guardianship, or civil case.

(3) All filings, except Wills, shall be on white paper.

(B) **Approval by Attorney of Fiduciary Filings.**

Each document presented to the Court for filing on behalf of a fiduciary, if not otherwise required to be signed by the fiduciary's attorney, shall have endorsed thereon the approval of the attorney-at-law, if any, who represents the fiduciary, in the following form:

Approved:

_____

Attorney for Fiduciary

The signature of an attorney constitutes a certification that the attorney has read the pleadings; that to the attorney's best knowledge, information, and belief, there is good ground to support it; and that it is not interposed for delay.

(C) **Motions.**

Unless an oral hearing is requested, all Motions shall be submitted on memorandum or brief. Requests for hearing must be in writing, and filed with the Motion. A statement of the grounds upon which the Motion is based, together with a citation of authorities relied upon, shall be presented in the memorandum or brief.

Within ten (10) days after the receipt of a copy of a Motion, opposing counsel shall prepare and file a reply to the Motion, setting forth written statements of opposition to the Motion, together with a citation of authorities relied upon in opposition.

The Motion shall be ruled upon at any time after fourteen (14) days from the date of filing the Motion.

(Former Rule 24.1 amended and renumbered as Rule 57.1, effective June 10, 1998.)

SUP R. 58. DEPOSIT FOR COURT COSTS

Rule 58.1 Deposit for court costs

(A) **Deposits.**

Deposits in the amount set forth in Appendix A shall be required upon the filing of any action and proceeding listed therein.

(B) **Additional Deposits.**

Costs shall be updated, and a further deposit shall be required, when:

(1) An account is filed;

(2) Real estate is transferred;

(3) Requested by the Court to cover certified mail, publication, etc.;

(4) A wrongful death settlement is filed;

(5) An Entry confirming sale and ordering deed and distribution is filed in a Civil Land Sale proceeding.

(C) **Court Costs.**

For the purpose of procuring and maintaining computerized legal research services, an additional fee of Three Dollars ($3.00) shall be collected as costs in each cause filed in an estate, wrongful death, guardianship, trust, minor settlement, civil action, correction of birth record, registration of birth, change of name, or adoption.

(Former Rules 25.1, 25.2, and 25.3 amended and renumbered as Rule 58.1, effective June 10, 1998.)

SUP R. 59. WILLS

Rule 59.1 Application to probate a will

Before an Application to open an estate is filed, the proposed fiduciary shall review the indexes of Wills to determine if there is a Will of the decedent on file with the Court.

(Former Rule 26.1 amended and renumbered as Rule 59.1, effective June 10, 1998.)

SUP R. 60. APPLICATION FOR LETTERS OF AUTHORITY TO ADMINISTER ESTATE AND NOTICE OF APPOINTMENT

Rule 60.1 Application for letters of authority to administer estate and notice of appointment

(A) **Estate Administration.**

(1) Non-Resident Fiduciary

Upon Motion, the Court will appoint as executor a spouse or next of kin named in the Will who is a non-resident of the State of Ohio, provided that a resident of Ohio is also appointed as an Administrator with the Will Annexed.

(2) Notice of Application/Stepparent

If a surviving spouse files an application to be appointed as administrator of an intestate estate, and is:

(a) not the natural parent of the decedent's child or children, and is,

(b) entitled to a priority of appointment under R.C. 2113.06,

the surviving spouse shall, in accordance with Rule 73 of the Ohio Rules of Civil Procedure, cause to be served on all competent adult next of kin of the decedent who reside in the State of Ohio a notice containing the following:

(a) that an application has been filed for the appointment of the spouse as administrator, and

(b) time and place of the hearing for the application.

Notice may be waived, in writing, by the next of kin.

(3) Status Report by Fiduciary

The fiduciary of an estate, or the attorney of record, shall file an annual report with the Court on the anniversary date of the estate opening, explaining the status of the estate and why the case is not closed.

(B) **Qualification of Fiduciary.**

No person shall be appointed as an executor, administrator, guardian, receiver, trustee or assignee who cannot read, write and speak the English language, unless the Court, for good cause shown, directs otherwise. The Court may require a hearing with the applicant prior to allowing appointment as fiduciary.

(Former Rules 27.1 and 27.2 amended and renumbered as Rule 60.1, effective June 10, 1998.)

SUP R. 61. APPRAISERS

Rule 61.1 Appraiser fees/compensation

Appraisers' fees for real estate shall be based upon the entire value of the assets subject to appraisal (not the decedent's interest in the property which may be fractional). Fees shall be computed at the rate of:

(A) One Dollar ($1.00) per thousand on the first Thirty-Five Thousand Dollars ($35,000.00).

Minimum—Seventy-Five Dollars ($75.00)

(B) Two Dollars ($2.00) per thousand on the next Fifty Thousand Dollars ($50,000.00).

(C) One Dollar Fifty Cents ($1.50) per thousand on the next One Hundred Thousand Dollars ($100,000.00).

(D) One Dollar ($1.00) per thousand on the balance over One Hundred Eighty-Five Thousand Dollars ($185,000.00).

When an appraisal of multiple properties is performed, the above fee schedule shall apply to the aggregate value of all properties.

Ordinary fees under Five Hundred Dollars ($500.00), paid in compliance with this rule, may be paid without application and entry.

On tangible personal property subject to appraisal the value of which is not readily ascertainable, the appraiser's compensation shall be One Dollar ($1.00) per thousand of the total value.

If by reason of the application of such percentages to the value of assets of an estate, a disparity or injustice results, such disparity or injustice may be reviewed on the Court's own Motion or upon application of the fiduciary or any party in interest.

Additional compensation for extraordinary services performed may be allowed by the Court upon application filed by the fiduciary.

In land sale proceedings, the appraiser appointed by the Court may be compensated for services in the same manner as provided herein for estate appraisers, with a minimum fee of Seventy–Five Dollars ($75.00) per parcel, provided that the amount to be paid the appraiser shall be set forth in the entry of distribution and be subject to the approval of the Court.

An appraiser may waive entitlement to all or any part of the compensations allowable under this Rule.

Where any question arises in the interpretation of this Rule, or if the amount of compensation cannot be agreed upon, the executor or administrator shall file an application for allowance of compensation to each appraiser. Otherwise, no Court Order is necessary, and credit may be taken for payment in the next regular account as provided by law, subject to all exceptions which may be thereafter filed.

In the event the appraiser's fee exceeds Five Hundred Dollars ($500.00) when calculated in accordance with the above schedule, special approval must be obtained upon proper application to the Court.

(Former Rule 28.1 amended and renumbered as Rule 61.1, effective June 10, 1998; amended effective October 1, 2000; April 15, 2002; February 1, 2006.)

Rule 61.2 Appraisal/full estate administrations, release and summary release from administration

Unless there is a dispute, or an appraisal is required for other purposes, a Court-appointed appraiser shall not be necessary in estates filed as a Release, Summary Release from Administration, or Full Estate Administrations where the spouse inherits the entire estate.

A statement attesting to the auditor's appraisal value, signed by a representative of the County Auditor, will be accepted as the appraised value.

(Adopted effective November 1, 2001; amended effective February 1, 2006.)

Rule 61.3 Appraiser—Self Dealing

No appraiser shall directly or indirectly purchase, or negotiate the purchase, sale, trade, or management of the property that he or she has been appointed to appraise.

(Effective April 1, 2005.)

SUP R. 64.   ACCOUNTS

Rule 64.1 Accounts

(A) **All Accountings.**

(1) Partial Accounts.

The Court reserves the right to require a partial accounting where a waiver of partial accounting may be otherwise authorized.

(2) Notice of Filing.

The Court shall cause notice of the filing of an account and the time and place of the hearing thereon to be published once in a newspaper of general circulation in the County. The hearing shall be set at the discretion of the Court.

(3) Failure to File.

(a) Hearing/Fiduciary Must Appear.

Unless physically unable, a fiduciary who has been cited must appear in open Court for a show cause hearing. Counsel shall not appear in lieu of a cited fiduciary unless leave of Court to appear is granted.

(b) Continuance after Citation.

Upon issuance of a citation for failure to file an accounting, a continuance to file shall not be granted until the fiduciary has personally appeared at a show cause hearing.

(c) Appointment in Other Matters.

A fiduciary, including a corporate fiduciary, shall not be appointed as a fiduciary in other matters while under citation for failure to file an account.

(B) **Guardian's Accountings.**

(1) Guardian's Accountings shall be filed:

(a) on the first anniversary date of the appointment of the guardian, and

(b) annually thereafter on the anniversary date, except

(c) a qualified bank or trust shall file on a biennial basis.

(2) Period Covered.

Unless ordered otherwise, all guardian's accounts shall be for a period of twelve (12) months, except a final account may be for a period less than twelve (12) months.

(3) Continuances to File.

When granted, unless specifically ordered, a continuance to file shall not extend the period as required under Paragraphs (B)(1) and (B)(2) of this Rule.

(Former Rule 32.1 and 32.4 amended and renumbered as Rule 64.1, effective June 10, 1998; amended effective April 1, 2005.)

SUP R. 65.   LAND SALES—R.C. CHAPTER 2127

Rule 65.1 Land sales

(A) **Preliminary Judicial Title.**

Except for summary land sales, a preliminary judicial title shall be required in all actions filed for the sale of real estate by a fiduciary.

(B) **Real Estate Brokers' Commissions.**

(1) Real estate brokers' commissions are limited to seven percent (7%) of the sale price. No minimum fee shall be accepted by the Court.

(2) Commissions on commercial property (land only) are limited to ten percent (10%) of the sale price. No minimum fee shall be accepted by the Court.

(Former Rule 33.1 amended and renumbered as Rule 65.1, effective June 10, 1998; amended effective April 1, 2005.)

SUP R. 66.   GUARDIANSHIPS

Rule 66.1 Guardianships

(A) **Guardianships.**

(1) Bond.

Bond shall be posted in an amount of double the probable value of the personalty not in a custodial account or otherwise impounded according to law. However, all guardianships of the estate shall post a minimum bond as determined by the Court.

(2) Release of Funds and Assets.

Funds and assets held in the ward's name shall not be released to a guardian except upon Order of the Court. All Motions for release shall specify the exact amount to be released, the name and address of the financial institution holding the funds, and the person in whose name the funds are held. The Order releasing funds shall order the financial institution to hold all funds in excess of the amount to be released until further Order of the Court.

(3) Custodial Deposits.

Where found necessary, deposit of all, or a portion of, cash assets in a custodial account in a financial institution located in Summit County may be ordered by the Court. The deposit shall be made in the name of the fiduciary, and the personal property deposited shall not be withdrawn from the custody of the bank, association, or trust company, except upon the special Order of the Court.

(a) The custodial account shall be established by the filing of a Motion and Order to Create Accounts. A certified copy of this Motion and Order must be presented to the custodial depository.

(b) A verification of deposit signed by the custodial depository shall be filed within fourteen (14) days of the filing of the Motion and Order to Create Accounts.

(c) The Motion and Order to Create Accounts shall be filed prior to the filing of the Inventory. No Inventory will be accepted without the creation of the account.

(4) Investigation.

All applications for the appointment of a guardian for an adult incompetent shall be inquired into by a Court-appointed investigator, who shall also serve notice on the proposed ward according to law.

(5) School Guardianship.

The Court will not accept for filing any guardianship for a minor where the sole purpose of the guardianship is to establish a residency for school purposes.

(6) Voting.

No adult person adjudicated incompetent shall lose the right to vote, except upon motion, notice, and record hearing before the Court.

(7) Training Sessions.

All guardians of the person and estate, and all guardians of the estate only, shall, within six (6) months of the date of their appointment, attend one guardianship training session, as conducted and scheduled by this Court. This session need not be repeated upon subsequent appointments. Failure to attend a training session will subject the guardian to the Court's citation procedure.

(8) Guardian's Handbook.

Each guardian appointed after May 1, 1995, by this Court shall receive a guardian's handbook issued by the Court for the purpose of providing information as to a guardian's duties and responsibilities. At the time of appointment, the cost of the handbook shall be assessed to the guardian or the estate of the ward.

(9) Change of Residence of Ward.

All guardians must have the approval of Probate Court before transferring a ward out of Summit County or out of the State. A notice must be sent to the assigned Magistrate setting forth the transfer site, the reasons for the move, and alternatives available. The Court or Magistrate shall approve or disapprove the transfer.

(10) Personal Property.

Personal property of the ward, valued at $500.00 or less, may be sold without prior approval of the Court if the buyer is not a relative.

(11) Death of Ward.

A guardian shall notify the Court of the death of a ward by written notice no later than ninety (90) days after the date of death.

Failure to notify the Court within the prescribed time limits will be considered malfeasance, and will disqualify the guardian from collection of guardian's fees from the ward's estate, including any fees owing to the guardian but not collected or paid. If the guardian is also the attorney for the guardianship, the foregoing rule shall also apply to attorney's fees.

Upon hearing, and for good cause shown, the Court may award guardian's or attorney's fees otherwise denied by this Rule.

(12) Minors—Putative Fathers/Paternal Relatives.

As to all minors born on January 1, 1997, or thereafter, a putative father, as defined in R.C. 3107.01, is not entitled to notice of hearing on the Application for Guardianship of the minor unless any of the following applies:

(a) He has acknowledged paternity pursuant to R.C. 5101.314;

(b) An action under Chapter 3111 of the Revised Code has determined him to be the father; or

(c) He has registered with the Putative Father Registry in Columbus, pursuant to R.C. 3107.062.

The paternal (putative) relatives of a minor have no standing to apply for guardianship or request visitation/companionship (R.C. 3109.12) unless:

(a) The father has acknowledged paternity (R.C. 5101.314); or

(b) A Chapter 3111 action has determined him to be the father.

(B) **Guardian's Reports.**

Guardian Reports on all guardianships except Guardianship of a Minor's Estate only shall be filed annually on the anniversary of the appointment date.

(C) **Notice for Guardianship of Adult.**

In addition to those entitled to notice of the hearing on the application for appointment of a guardian of an adult under Ohio R.C. 2111.04, the applicant shall submit to the Court the names and addresses of all adult children of the proposed ward known to reside in this state. The Court shall serve the adult children with notice of the time and date of the hearing, unless the notice is waived.

(D) **Deposit of Wills.**

The guardian must deposit with the Court all Wills of the ward for safekeeping.

(Former Rules 34.1 and 34.2 amended and renumbered as Rule 66.1, effective June 10, 1998; amended effective April 1, 2001; October 1, 2001; December 31, 2001; April 1, 2005.)

SUP R. 67. ESTATES OF MINORS OF NOT MORE THAN TEN THOUSAND DOLLARS

Rule 67.1 Minor settlement/net proceeds less than ten thousand dollars

Unless otherwise provided for by Order of the Court, an applicant for release of assets pursuant to Section 2111.05 of the Ohio Revised Code shall:

(A) File an application for release of assets without appointment of a guardian. Upon approval of the application, the Order of Release shall state the institution acting as depository, shall state that the funds shall not be released until the ward reaches the age of 18, or the ward's death, or until further Order of the Court;

(B) Deposit funds in a bank or savings institution; and

(C) File a report within fourteen (14) days after deposit that the deposit was made with the same restrictions on withdrawal as cited in the Order of Release.

(Former Rule 37.1 amended and renumbered as Rule 67.1, effective June 10, 1998.)

SUP R. 68. SETTLEMENT OF INJURY CLAIMS OF MINORS

Rule 68.1 Settlement of injury claims of minors

(A) **Structured Payments.**

If the proposed settlement contains structured payments, counsel shall schedule a conference with the assigned Magistrate prior to setting the hearing date.

(B) **Record Hearing Required.**

Any settlement of a minor's claim where the parents/guardians are unrepresented by counsel, shall be scheduled for a hearing in open court and recorded on tape.

(Adopted effective June 10, 1998; amended effective April 1, 2001.)

SUP R. 70. SETTLEMENT OF WRONGFUL DEATH AND SURVIVAL CLAIMS

Rule 70.1 Wrongful death settlement

(A) **Conference.**

Upon filing of an estate, the assigned Magistrate shall hold a conference with counsel.

(B) **Notice.**

The Court shall publish notice to next of kin, pursuant to Civil Rule 73, at least seven (7) days prior to the hearing on settlement for wrongful death claims.

(C) **Hearing.**

If all beneficiaries are of an unequal degree of consanguinity, an evidentiary hearing shall be conducted at the discretion of the Magistrate.

(Former Rule 38.1 amended and renumbered as Rule 70.1, effective June 10, 1998.)

SUP R. 71. COUNSEL FEES

Rule 71.1 Counsel fees

(A) **Estate Administration.**

(1) Forms.

Forms as prescribed by the Court shall be used to make application for counsel fees. See Appendices E and F.

(2) When Paid.

Unless otherwise approved by the Court for good cause shown, attorney fees for the administration of decedents' estates shall not be paid until the final account is filed and attorney fees for services rendered to a guardian, trustee or other fiduciary shall not be paid until the annual or biennial account is filed.

(3) Application.

(a) When filed:

An application for counsel fees shall be filed when:

1) Counsel is unable to obtain consents as provided in Paragraph (A)(3)(b).

2) Counsel serves as both attorney for the estate and fiduciary.

3) An objection to counsel fees is filed, or an exception to an accounting based on fees is filed.

4) Counsel fees are requested in representing guardians and trustees.

(b) When Not Filed:

Application for fee approval is not required when:

1) Written consents are given by heirs at law or residuary beneficiaries, whose combined beneficial interests equal or exceed seventy-five percent (75%) of net distributable estate, are filed with the Court, and

2) Notice of consent is given to those not consenting, and whose beneficial interests would be affected.

3) Notice.

Notice, as required in Paragraph (A)(3)(b)(2) of this Rule, shall be sent by certified mail by the attorney of record, and shall be mailed thirty (30) days prior to the filing of an accounting upon which fees are based. Consents and proof of service shall be filed at the time of the required accounting.

(c) Attachment/Time Records:

All counsel fee applications shall be accompanied with itemized time records, which shall state the date and time expended, who performed the service, the nature of the service performed, the hourly rate requested, or the specific basis of the fee requested.

(4) Hearing/When Required:

A Magistrate may require a hearing on fees, or may approve an application for fees without hearing, except where an application is caused to be filed pursuant to Paragraph (A)(3)(a)(3) of this Rule. If application is filed under Paragraph (A)(3)(a)(3), a hearing is mandatory.

(B) **Insolvent Estates.**

A hearing will be held on counsel fees at the hearing on report of insolvency.

(C) **Land Sales.**

An application for counsel fees in a land sale shall be filed at the time that the judgment entry confirming sale, ordering deed and distribution, is filed. Fees shall be taken at this time. Notice and hearing shall be as the Court directs. See Appendix G.

(Former Rule 40.1 amended and renumbered as Rule 71.1, effective June 10, 1998; amended effective April 15, 2002.)

SUP R. 72. EXECUTOR'S AND ADMINISTRATOR'S COMMISSIONS

Rule 72.1 Fiduciary computation

A computation of fiduciary fees shall be filed on a form provided by the Court when the accounting upon which the fees are based is filed. See Appendix D.

(Former Rule 41.1 amended and renumbered as Rule 72.1, effective June 10, 1998.)

SUP R. 73. GUARDIAN'S COMPENSATION

Rule 73.1 Guardian's compensation

(A) **Application.**

Guardians shall file an application for allowance for fees at the time that the regular accounting is submitted to the Court. Such fees shall not be paid until authorized by the Court, and shall be accounted for in the next accounting period. Application forms shall be provided by the Court. See Appendix C.

(B) **Schedule.**

Guardian's compensation shall be based upon the following schedule:

5% of the first $100,000.00 of income

3% of all income over $100,000.00

5% of the authorized expenditures up to $100,000.00

3% of the authorized expenditures over $100,000.00

(C) **Extraordinary Fees.**

An application for extraordinary guardian's fees shall be accompanied with itemized time records. All time itemizations shall state the date and time expended, who performed the service, the nature of the service performed, the hourly rate requested, or the specific basis of the fee requested. A hearing shall be set with notice sent by the applicant to all interested parties as the Court so orders.

(D) **Authorized Expenditures.**

Conversion of assets to cash, reinvesting assets, distributions upon termination to another fiduciary, or the payment of guardian's fees shall not be deemed to be authorized expenditures or as income for purposes of computing compensation herein.

(E) **Minimum Fees.**

Minimum guardian's or trustee's fees shall be allowed in the amount of Three Hundred Dollars ($300.00) a year.

(Former Rule 42.1 amended and renumbered as Rule 73.1, effective June 10, 1998; amended effective July 1, 1999.)

SUP R. 74. TRUSTEE'S COMPENSATION

Rule 74.1 Trustee's compensation

(A) **Corporate Trustees.**

(1) Except where the instrument creating the trust makes provisions for compensation, a testamentary trustee may charge fees on the same basis as it charges for living trusts.

(2) On each accounting where fees have been taken, an affidavit will be required asserting that the fees charged and included in the accounting represent those charges for similar services in living trusts.

(3) A separate schedule of the computations of the trustee's compensation shall be set forth in the trustee's account as a condition of its approval.

(4) Fee schedules are to be furnished to the Court on the first day of January of each year, and whenever a change in fees is made within any calendar year.

(B) **Individual Trustees.**

(1) Except where the instrument creating the trust makes provisions for compensation, the trustee may charge fees on the same basis as is currently being charged by the banking institution with which the trust is doing business.

(2) On each accounting where fees have been taken, an affidavit will be required setting forth that the fees charged are based on the schedules of the "name" bank.

(3) A separate schedule of the computations of the trustee's compensation shall be set forth in the trustee's account as a condition of its approval.

(C) The Court reserves the right to determine the reasonableness of trustee's compensation in all cases.

(Former Rule 43.1 amended and renumbered as Rule 74.1, effective June 10, 1998.)

SUP R. 78. PROBATE DIVISION OF THE COURT OF COMMON PLEAS—CASE MANAGEMENT IN DECEDENT'S ESTATES, GUARDIANSHIPS, AND TRUSTS

Rule 78.1 Case management procedure

(A) **Inventory.**

(1) All pending cases shall be inventoried:

(a) Monthly by computer review.

(b) Yearly by physical review.

(2) The objective of an inventory shall be to obtain an accurate count of pending cases.

(3) All inventories are the responsibility of the Court Administrator.

(B) **Supervision of Estates and Guardianships.**

(1) Each estate and guardianship shall be assigned to a specific Magistrate.

(a) Assignment shall be made by the Chief Magistrate and the Magistrate in charge of Human Services.

(b) The Magistrate assigned shall be responsible for supervision of the assigned estate or guardianship.

(2) Monthly, the Court Administrator shall provide a summary of cases pending by Magistrate. Each summary shall indicate the number of cases assigned, completed, and pending at the end of the period, and any estates open for more than one (1) year.

(3) Estates open more than one year.

Each Magistrate shall, upon the anniversary of an estate that has been open for more than one year, cause to be sent to the fiduciary a letter of inquiry as to the reason/s for failure to close the estate.

(a) A standard letter shall be composed by the Chief Magistrate.

(b) All returned letters shall be made part of the case file, and shall be acted upon appropriately by the assigned Magistrate.

(C) **Supervision of Trusts, Adoptions, and Civil Commitments.**

(1) The Chief Magistrate shall have the responsibility for supervising trusts.

(2) The Magistrate in charge of Human Services shall be responsible for adoptions and civil commitments.

(D) **Overdue Accountings, Reports and Inventories.**

(1) Shall be cited pursuant to R.C. 2109.31.

(2) Citation shall be for appearance before the Court on a specified date known as Call Day, pursuant to Local Rule 64.1(A)(3)(a).

(E) **Civil Cases.**

(1) Shall be reviewed monthly to determine status.

(2) A pretrial shall be set in Will contests, concealment of assets, land appropriations, and all other matters upon request of either party.

(3) In all matters not set for pretrial, a hearing or trial date shall be set upon completion of service and pleadings.

(4) A pretrial shall determine:

(a) Discovery deadline date;

(b) Exchange of witness list date;

(c) Pleadings and briefing date; and

(d) Trial date.

(F) **Withdrawal of Counsel.**

It is contemplated that counsel who has entered an appearance in a case shall remain in the case until concluded. However, upon written motion for leave to withdraw from the action for good cause shown, the Court may permit counsel to withdraw. In such case, counsel shall certify that the client and all other counsel of record have been notified.

(Adopted effective June 10, 1998; amended effective February 28, 2002.)

GENERAL PROVISIONS

Rule 86.1 Marriage license

Pursuant to R.C. 3101.05, the five-day waiting period between marriage license application and issuance is hereby waived.

(Adopted effective January 1, 2000.)

Rule 87.1 Service by deputy clerk

Any deputy clerk of this Court who is not less than eighteen (18) years of age and not a party to the proceeding is hereby designated as an authorized person to make service of process or of any notice pursuant to the Ohio Rules of Civil Procedure.

(Adopted effective June 10, 1998.)

Rule 88.1 Inventory/notice

The notice of the filing of Inventory, in accordance with R.C. 2115.16, shall be by publication only. The publication required shall be issued by the Court.

(Adopted effective June 10, 1998.)

Rule 88.2 Inventory/schedule of assets

The Schedule of Assets shall contain the legal description and the parcel number of all real estate included in the Inventory of the Estate.

(Adopted effective June 10, 1998.)

Rule 89.1 Attorneys as sureties

Attorneys at law shall not act as sureties in any cause in this Court, nor shall they be permitted to become sureties on the bond of any fiduciary.

(Former Rule 47.1 renumbered as Rule 89.1, effective June 10, 1998.)

Rule 90.1 Removal of will from safe deposit boxes

Whenever the County Auditor, or his duly authorized representatives, in the course of conducting an inventory of a safe deposit box or similar receptacle standing in the name of a decedent or ward, locates a Will, or document purported to be the Will, of the decedent or ward, the County Auditor or his representative shall remove such Will or document, and deliver it immediately to a deputy clerk of the Probate Court, and shall receive a receipt therefore.

(Former Rule 48.1 amended and renumbered as Rule 90.1, effective June 10, 1998; amended effective April 15, 2002.)

Rule 91.1 Guardian ad litem

(A) **Qualifications.**

A guardian ad litem shall be an attorney who is not associated with an attorney of record for the proceeding in which the guardian ad litem has been appointed.

(B) **Appointment.**

(1) Land Sales

Subject to approval by the Court, a guardian ad litem will be appointed on recommendation and entry of the attorney of record.

(2) All Other Matters

A guardian ad litem will be appointed without recommendation upon notification of the necessity for appointment.

(C) **Fees.**

(1) Land Sales

A fee shall be taxed in the costs of the case for each guardian ad litem in the amount of Ten Dollars ($10.00).

(2) All Other Matters

Upon application and entry, a fee based on a reasonable hourly rate for time expended shall be taxed in the costs of the case for each guardian ad litem.

(Former Rule 49.1 renumbered as Rule 91.1, effective June 10, 1998; Amended effective April 1, 2005.)

Rule 92.1 Trusts

In cases where a trustee named in the Will is a non-resident of this State, the Court reserves the right to appoint a local resident co-trustee, with or without bond, who will insure that all assets pertaining to said trust remain in this County until distribution, or until the Court determines that the property may be removed from the County in accordance with R.C. 2109.21.

(Former Rule 50.1 amended and renumbered as Rule 92.1, effective June 10, 1998.)

Rule 93.1 Change of name

Whenever an application to change the name of a minor is filed without the consent of the natural parent/parents, a hearing shall be required before a Magistrate. Notice on such application shall be in accordance with Civil Rule 73 as the Court may require.

(Former Rule 51.1 amended and renumbered as Rule 93.1, effective June 10, 1998.)

Rule 94.1 Adoptions

(A) **Deposits.**

Deposits, costs, and fees required for the filing of adoptions are set forth in Appendix B.

(B) **Expense Hearing.**

In all adoptions, except by a stepparent or where the child was permanently surrendered and/or placed by an Ohio licensed adoption agency, the petitioners shall appear in open Court, before the Judge or Magistrate of the Probate Court, and swear under oath as to any and all expenses being incurred and paid by them to any party or parties involved in the adoption matter before the Court. Costs of the reporter to the petitioner.

(C) **Notice of Hearing on Petition for Adoption (R.C. 3107.11).**

Form 18.2 must be served not less than thirty (30) days prior to the date of the final adoption hearing. The failure to file an objection at least seven (7) days before the hearing may result in the termination of parental rights.

(D) All R.C. 3107.10 preliminary estimate accountings and R.C. 3107.083 birth parent forms shall be filed with the Court on or before the date of the scheduled placement hearing.

(E) Only forms currently in use by the Probate Court will be accepted.

(Former Rule 52.1 amended and renumbered as Rule 94.1, effective June 10, 1998; amended effective April 15, 2002.)

Rule 95.1   Registration of birth/correction of birth

(A) **Registration of Birth.**

(Reserved)

(B) **Correction of Birth.**

(1) An applicant residing in the State of Ohio shall make at least one (1) appearance in open Court before approval of a correction of birth.

(2) An applicant residing outside the State of Ohio must appear before a notary or other person able to administer an oath and complete a deposition as required by the Court.

(Former Rule 55.1 amended and renumbered as Rule 95.1, effective June 10, 1998.)

Rule 96.1   Concealment of assets

(A) **Examination before Magistrate.**

Pursuant to R.C. 2109.50, upon the filing of a complaint of concealment, the person or persons accused shall be examined before a Magistrate. The Magistrate, subject to objection, shall rule on all questions of evidence.

(B) **Reduction to Writing.**

Pursuant to R.C. 2109.50, reduction to writing shall be by a court reporter. A transcript of the examination shall be signed by the party examined, and submitted to the Court. The cost of the reporter and transcript shall be taxed to the complainant, except as provided by R.C. 2109.52.

(C) **Trial by the Court.**

Upon the filing of the transcript as provided in Paragraph (B), the concealment shall be set for pretrial to the Court or jury.

(Former Rule 56.1 renumbered as Rule 96.1, effective June 10, 1998.)

Rule 97.1   Appropriation of property

(A) **Filing of Petition and Service of Summons.**

Filing and service procedures shall be administered in accordance with R.C. 163.05, et seq..

(B) **Court Proceedings.**

(1) Hearing on Necessity:

If a property owner's Answer specifically challenges an Appropriation proceeding pursuant to R.C. 163.09(B), the Court shall set a hearing.

(2) Pretrial:

A pretrial shall be scheduled once all named parties are properly before the Court. Following the pretrial, an Order will be issued setting the date for trial and discovery schedule.

(3) Trial.

(C) **Award.**

The sum of money to be paid to the property owner(s), whether determined by trial or settlement, shall be deposited with the Court for distribution.

(D) **Distribution.**

Upon Motion for Distribution, the Court shall:

(1) Issue an Order of Distribution when the Motion is stipulated to by all interested parties, or

(2) Set the matter for hearing if distribution is not agreed upon by all interested parties.

(3) Issue checks per the Order of Distribution no sooner than two (2) weeks from date of Order.

(Former Rule 58.1 renumbered as Rule 97.1, effective June 10, 1998.)

Rule 98.1   Mediation

(A) Cases will be referred to mediation in one of two (2) ways:

(1) Voluntary referral by motion of all parties; or

(2) Selection by the Judge of this Court.

(B) Participation in mediation is voluntary unless referred by the Court, but the Court may not require that settlement be reached on any particular issue.

(C) Fees for the mediator shall be set by the Court Administrator.

(D) A mediator will be assigned by the Court to conduct the mediation and submit an agreement or report within ninety (90) days.

(E) Statements made during a mediation conference do not constitute admissions against interest, and cannot be used as evidence or for impeachment in any subsequent proceeding. If a final agreement is reached, that agreement may be filed under seal to preserve confidentiality, provided that the parties request that the agreement be sealed and the Court approves.

(F) If a dispute involves a matter under the jurisdiction of Probate Court, including a client with mental health, mental retardation and developmental disability, or aging adult issues, but a guardianship case has not been filed, an agency may file a motion with the Court to refer the matter to mediation. A case shall be referred if mediation is likely to resolve the dispute as a less restrictive alternative to guardianship.

(Adopted effective June 10, 1998; amended May 1, 2002.)

APPENDICES

App. A   Deposits for court costs

APPENDIX A
DEPOSITS FOR COURT COSTS

ESTATES—FULL ADMINISTRATION $200.00

ESTATES—RELEASE FROM ADMINISTRATION

    With or Without a Will (Deposit) $175.00
    Will Probated, Tax, Journal Entry .... $ 63.00
    Will Probated, Journal Entry .... $ 58.00
    Tax Only—Journal Entry .... $ 38.00
    Tax Only/Part B—Journal Entry .... $ 33.00
    Short–Form Release—W/Will .... $ 50.00
    Short–Form Release—W/O Will .... $ 25.00
    Summary Release—W/Will $101.15
    Summary Release—W/O Will .... $ 76.15

GUARDIANSHIPS

    Person and Estate $240.00
    Estate Only $240.00
    Person Only $240.00
    Each additional minor child $165.00
    Conservatorship $200.00
    Application to Dispense with Guardianship .... $ 48.00
    Minor Settlement/Dispense With Guardianship .... $ 68.00
    Successor Custodian .... $ 48.00

TRUSTS

    Application for Appointment of Trustee $200.00

CIVIL ACTIONS

    Complaint to Sell Real Estate $125.00
    Complaint—Appropriation $125.00
    Complaint—Concealment of Assets $225.00
    Complaint—Declaratory Judgment $125.00
    Complaint—Determination of Heirs $125.00
    Complaint—Presumption of Death $125.00
    Complaint—Will Construction $125.00
    Complaint—Will Contest $125.00

SUBPOENAS

    Witness subpoenaed—resident of county .... $ 20.00
    Witness subpoenaed—non–resident .... $ 30.00

MISCELLANEOUS COURT COSTS

Application to Correct Birth Record .... $ 18.00
Application for Registration of Birth .... $ 20.00
Certification of Document .... $ 1.00
Change of Name .... $ 84.00
    (Additional certified copies—$1.05 each)
Claims Against an Estate .... $ 20.00
Court Record—Taping per hearing session per day .... $ 8.00
Crossclaims/Counterclaims/Third–Party Claims .... $ 20.00
Deposit of Will .... $ 6.00
Exceptions/Objections (Accounts or Inventories) .... $ 30.00
Exceptions/Objections (All Others) .... $ 25.00
Fiduciary Claim .... $ 30.00
Motion to Remove Fiduciary .... $ 25.00
60(B) Motion (Relief from Judgment or Order) .... $ 25.00

In Re:
    APS Order/APS Emergency Order .... $ 0.00

Bureau of Worker's Compensation Subpoena	$ 75.00
Designation of an Heir at Law	$ 58.00
Disinterment	$ 48.00
Emergency Guardianship	$ 43.00
Emergency Order	$ 0.00
Enforcement of Out of State Orders	$ 75.00
Miscellaneous	$ 48.00
Paternity of Adult Child	$ 31.05
Transfer of Lottery Prize	$ 75.00
Transfer of Structured Settlement	$ 75.00
Marriage License	$ 40.00
Certified copy of Marriage License	$ 2.00

[Effective June 10, 1998; Amended November 4, 1998; December 1, 1999; October 1, 2000; October 1, 2001; December 31, 2001; February 28, 2002; amended effective April 1, 2005; amended effective October 1, 2005.]

App. B   Adoption fees

APPENDIX B
ADOPTION FEES

STEP–PARENT ADOPTION	
First Child	$561.00
Additional	$136.00
AGENCY ADOPTION	
First Child	$134.00
Additional	$ 96.00
PRIVATE ADOPTION	$689.00
INTERNATIONAL ADOPTION	$579.00
PRIVATE/INTERNATIONAL ADOPTION	
Additional Costs for Finalization	$220.00
FOREIGN READOPTION	
W/Prefinalization Assessment	$289.00
ADULT ADOPTION	$134.00
DISPENSE W/ADOPTION (Surrogacy) (Includes 2 Orders)	$ 35.00
PREFINALIZATION FEES (If Required)	$150.00
POST–PLACEMENT VISITS	$ 75.00
AMENDED PETITION	$ 30.00
HOME STUDY UPDATE	$100.00
OBJECTION TO ADOPTION	$ 25.00
MOTION TO VACATE ADOPTION (60–B)	$ 25.00
PETITION FOR RELEASE OF IDENTIFYING INFORMATION	$ 53.00
APPLICATION FOR FOREIGN BIRTH RECORD	$ 40.00
CERTIFIED COPY OF OHIO BIRTH CERTIFICATE	$ 16.50

[NOTE: Additional travel fee required if investigator travels outside Summit County.]

1957 SUMMIT COUNTY App. D

[Effective June 10, 1998; amended November 4, 1998; December 1, 1999; October 1, 2001; April 15, 2002; amended effective April 1, 2005; amended effective October 1, 2005.]

App. C Application—Computation of guardian fees

PROBATE COURT OF SUMMIT COUNTY, OHIO   Appendix C

GUARDIANSHIP OF: _____

CASE NO. _____

APPLICATION–COMPUTATION OF GUARDIAN FEES

ACCOUNTING PERIOD OF _____ 20 ___ TO _____ 20 ___

I. INCOME FOR ACCOUNTING PERIOD $_____
     5% of first $100,000   _____
     3% of balance   _____
     Total $_____

II. AUTHORIZED EXPENDITURES $_____
     5% of first $100,000   _____
     3% of balance   _____
     Total $_____

III. TOTAL ORDINARY FEES $_____

IV. EXTRAORDINARY FEES (Itemize and attach time records) $_____

V. TOTAL FEES REQUIRED $_____

VI. MINIMUM ANNUAL FEE $ $300.00

VII. GREATER OF "V" OR "VI" $_____

VIII. TOTAL FEES REQUESTED $_____

VIII. TOTAL FEES REQUESTED $_____

I have read and understand the above computation of fees, and submit they are necessary and reasonable for the administration of the guardianship for which I am guardian. I, therefore, request the Court's approval of payment of those fees from the assets of the said guardianship.

_____   _____
Attorney for Guardian   Guardian

_____   _____
MAGISTRATE   DISPOSITION

Form GA.1

App. D Application—Computation of fiduciary fees

PROBATE COURT OF SUMMIT COUNTY, OHIO   Appendix D

ESTATE OF _____ ,DECEASED

CASE NO. _____

APPLICATION–COMPUTATION OF FIDUCIARY FEES

I. ORDINARY FEES

<u>Personal Property and Income</u> (including gross proceeds of real estate sold under authority of Will)

    Personal Property $_____
    Income   _____
    TOTAL   _____

    Fees: 4% of first $100,000.00 $_____
    3% of next $300,000.00   _____
    2% of balance   _____

    TOTAL FEES (Personal Property and Income) $_____

<u>Transferred Real Estate (Unsold)</u>

    1% of $_____ Unsold Real Estate $_____

<u>Non–Probate Assets</u> (Subject to Ohio Estate Tax except Joint Survivorship Property)

    1% of $_____ Non–Probate Assets $_____

TOTAL ORDINARY FEES ALLOWABLE $_____

ORDINARY FEES REQUESTED $_____

II. EXTRAORDINARY FEES
<u>Extraordinary Fees Requested</u> (Attach itemized time records, and unless waived, a date for hearing should be requested when filing this form). $_____

III. TOTAL FEES TAKEN ON PRIOR ACCOUNTS $_____

IV. TOTAL FEES REQUESTED OR ALLOWABLE ON THIS
☐ Partial   ☐ Final   **ACCOUNT** $_____

I have read, and understand the above computation of fees, and submit they are necessary and reasonable for the administration of the estate for which I am fiduciary. I, therefore, request the Court's approval of payment of those fees from the assets of the said estate.

_____   _____
Attorney for Fiduciary   Fiduciary

_____   _____
Magistrate   DISPOSITION

Form ES.8

App. E Application for attorney fees

PROBATE COURT OF SUMMIT COUNTY, OHIO   Appendix E

ESTATE OF _____, DECEASED
CASE NO. _____

APPLICATION FOR ATTORNEY FEES

SUMMIT COUNTY App. E

DATE	SERVICE PERFORMED	BY WHOM	TIME EXPENDED	RATE	AMOUNT

RECAPITULATION: TOTAL HOURLY FEES $_____

$_____ Hourly Fees

$_____ TOTAL REQUESTED THIS APPLICATION

$_____ Prior Fees taken (includes fees from prior accounts, land sales, etc.)

$_____ TOTAL FEES

I have read and understand the Application for Attorney Fees, and I submit they are necessary and reasonable for the administration of the estate, and reflect a true and accurate accounting of the services I have performed.

_____
Attorney

Form ES.9

CASE NO. _____

CONSENT TO ATTORNEY FEES BY FIDUCIARY

I have read and understand the Application for Attorney Fees, and I submit they are necessary and reasonable for the administration of the estate, and reflect a true and accurate accounting of the services the attorney has performed.

_____
Fiduciary

NOTICE

TO THE FOLLOWING PERSONS:

YOU ARE HEREBY NOTIFIED THAT AN APPLICATION FOR ATTORNEY FEES was filed in this Court by _____, on _____, 20 ___.

The application will be for hearing before this Court, at the Summit County Court House, 209 S. High Street, Akron, Ohio, on _____, 20 ___, at _____ ___ M.

_____
Attorney

App. F Notice of attorney fees

PROBATE COURT OF SUMMIT COUNTY, OHIO   Appendix F

ESTATE OF _____, DECEASED
CASE NO. _____

NOTICE OF ATTORNEY FEES

TO THE FOLLOWING PERSONS:

Name	Address
Name	Address
Name	Address

YOU ARE HEREBY NOTIFIED THAT _____, ATTORNEY FOR THE ABOVE-CAPTIONED ESTATE, HAS CHARGED THE ESTATE THE SUM OF $ _____. This amount does not include prior fees taken of $ ___, which include fees from prior accounts, land sales, or other matters.

AN OBJECTION TO ATTORNEY FEES MUST BE FILED WITHIN THIRTY (30) DAYS OF RECEIPT OF THIS NOTICE AT:
Summit County Probate Court
209 S. High Street
Akron, Ohio 44308–1616

CONSENT TO ATTORNEY FEES

The undersigned hereby consents to the sum of $ _____, charged as attorney fees by _____, Attorney for the above-captioned estate.

Name	Address
Name	Address
Name	Address

Approved:

Form ES. 10

_____
Attorney

App. G Application for attorney fees in land sale proceedings

PROBATE COURT OF SUMMIT COUNTY, OHIO   Appendix G

_____ CASE _____
            Plaintiff(s)

V.   **APPLICATION FOR ATTORNEY FEES**
_____   **IN LAND SALE PROCEEDINGS**
            Defendant(s)

DATE	SERVICE PERFORMED	BY WHOM	TIME EXPENDED	RATE	AMOUNT

TOTAL HOURS _____
TOTAL HOURLY FEES $_____

_____   _____
Attorney for Fiduciary   Fiduciary

_____   _____
Magistrate   DISPOSITION

Form CV.16

INDEX

Revised Code sections are cited by number.

CuyR	Cuyahoga County Common Pleas Court Rules
FrankR	Franklin County Common Pleas Court Rules
HamR	Hamilton County Common Pleas Court Rules
JuvR	Ohio Rules of Juvenile Procedure
LucasR	Lucas County Common Pleas Court Rules
MontR	Montgomery County Common Pleas Court Rules
O Const	Ohio Constitution
ORC	Ohio Revised Code
SumR	Summit County Common Pleas Court Rules
SupR	Rules of Superintendence for the Courts of Ohio

Cross references to another main heading are in CAPITAL LETTERS.

ABANDONMENT
Children. See DEPENDENT AND NEGLECTED CHILDREN, generally
Divorce, grounds for, **ORC 3105.01(B)**
Eminent domain proceedings, **ORC 163.21**
Funds. See UNCLAIMED FUNDS
Legal separation, willful absence as grounds for, **ORC 3105.17(A)(2)**
Spouse, of. See SUPPORT AND MAINTENANCE

ABATEMENT
Actions by guardians, **ORC 2111.17**
Bequests or devises, **ORC 2107.34, ORC 2107.54 to 2107.59**

ABORTION
Complaints for in juvenile court
  Minor, by
    Juvenile procedure rules, applicability, **JuvR 1(C)**
  Parental consent, without. See Parental consent, complaint for abortion without, this heading
Definitions
  Person not to be defined so as to establish criminal liability, **ORC 2901.01**
Juvenile Court Procedures, Rules of Superintendence
  Application for authorization to consent, **SupR 23.1**
  Judicial consent, **SupR 23.1**
    Instructions, **SupR Form 23.1-A Instructions**
    Judgment, **SupR Form 23.1-B**
    Notice of appeal, **SupR Form 23.1-C**
    Petition, **SupR Form 23.1-A**
Parental consent, complaint for abortion without, **ORC 2151.85, SupR 23**
  Affidavit
    Minor, of, **SupR Form 24-A**
      Instructions, **SupR Forms 24-A and 24-B Instructions**
    Recipient of notice of minor's intent to receive abortion, **SupR Form 24-B**
      Instructions, **SupR Forms 24-A and 24-B Instructions**
  Appeal, notice of, **SupR Form 23-C**
  Appeal from denial, **SupR 23(F)**
  Confidentiality of records, **SupR 23(H)**
  Forms, **SupR Form 23-A to SupR Form 23-D**

ABORTION—Cont'd
Parental consent, complaint for abortion without, **ORC 2151.85, SupR 23**—Cont'd
  Instructions, **SupR Form 23-A Instructions**
  Judgment, **SupR Form 23-B**
  Notifying physicians of affidavits alleging abuse, **SupR 24**
  Verification, **SupR Form 23-D**

ABUSE
Adoption, abuse and neglect determination summary report, **ORC 3107.034**
Adults. See ABUSED OR NEGLECTED ADULTS
Aged persons, by caretakers, **ORC 5101.60 to 5101.71**
  See also PROTECTIVE SERVICES FOR ADULTS
Children. See CHILD ABUSE
Divorce, grounds for, **ORC 3105.01(D)**
Legal separation, grounds for, **ORC 3105.17(A)(4)**
Mentally retarded confined in state institution, reporting, **ORC 5123.093**

ABUSED OR NEGLECTED ADULTS
Generally, **ORC 5126.30-5126.34**
Complaint, **ORC 5126.33**
Definitions, **ORC 5126.30**
Ex parte emergency orders, **ORC 5126.331-5126.333**
Injunction against interference, **ORC 5126.32**
Investigation of abuse or neglect, **ORC 5126.313, ORC 5126.333**
Notice, **ORC 5126.33, ORC 5126.333**
Order to arrange services, **ORC 5126.33**
Orders
  Arranging services, orders for, **ORC 5126.33**
  Ex parte emergency orders, **ORC 5126.331-5126.333**
  Temporary orders, **ORC 5126.33**
Reports, **ORC 5126.31, ORC 5126.311**
Review
  Injunction against interference, **ORC 5126.32**
  Reports, **ORC 5126.31**
Rules establishing minimum standards for training, **ORC 5126.34**
Temporary orders, **ORC 5126.33**

ACCIDENTS
Mentally retarded suffering in institution, reporting, **ORC 5123.093**
Wrongful death. See WRONGFUL DEATH

ACCOUNTS AND ACCOUNTING
See also AUDITS
Administrators. See EXECUTORS AND ADMINISTRATORS
Adoption, by petitioner, **ORC 3107.055**
Annual, **SumR 64.1(B)**
Bank accounts. See BANKS AND BANKING
Cuyahoga county probate court, **CuyR 64.2 et seq.**
Estates. See ESTATES
Exceptions to, court costs, **Sup. R 58.1**
Executors. See EXECUTORS AND ADMINISTRATORS
Fiduciaries. See FIDUCIARIES
Franklin county probate court, **FrankR 64.1**
    Bond, **FrankR 64.4**
    Delinquent filing, **FrankR 64.2**
    Evidence of assets, **FrankR 64.5**
    Partial, filing, **FrankR 64.5**
    Payment of debts, **FrankR 64.5, FrankR 64.6**
    Signature of fiduciary, **FrankR 64.1**
    Vouchers, **FrankR 64.3**
Guardians. See GUARDIANSHIP
Hamilton county probate court, **HamR 64.1**
Lucas county probate court, **LucasR 64.1**
Mental retardation and developmental disabilities department, **ORC 5123.26, ORC 5123.30**
Minors, transfers to; uniform law, **ORC 5814.04**
Partial, **SumR 64.1(A)**
Probate courts, fees, **ORC 2101.15**
Show cause hearing
    Continuances, **SumR 64.1(A)**
    Fiduciary, appearance of, **SumR 64.1(A)**
Stark county probate court, **Sup. R 64.1 to Sup. R 64.4**
    Exceptions to account, court costs, **Sup. R 58.1**
Summit county probate court, **SumR 64.1**
    Guardians' accountings, **SumR 64.1(B)**
    Overdue, citations, **SumR 78.1(D)**
    Partial accounts, **SumR 64.1(A)**
Testamentary trustees, **ORC 2109.11**
Transfers to Minors Act, accounting by custodian, **ORC 5814.08**
Trustees. See TRUSTEES
Vouchers, **Sup. R 64.2**
Waiver, **HamR 64.1**

ACCUSED
Arrests. See ARRESTS
Defendants. See DEFENDANTS

ACKNOWLEDGMENTS
Paternity, **ORC 3111.03**
    Child support action subsequent to filing of, **ORC 2151.232**
    Consent to adoption, **ORC 3107.06**
    Court costs, **SumR Appx A, Sup. R 58.1**
    Duty to support child, **ORC 3103.031**
    Finality, **ORC 5101.314**
    Parent and child relationship, establishment, **ORC 3111.02**
    Rescission, **ORC 5101.314**
        Paternity action, **ORC 2151.232**
Power of attorney, **ORC Ch 1337**
    See also POWER OF ATTORNEY, generally
    Durable power of attorney for health care, **ORC 1337.12**
Will, **ORC 2107.03, ORC 2107.04**

ACT CHARGED
Defined, **ORC 2152.02**

ACTIONS
Administrators, by or against. See EXECUTORS AND ADMINISTRATORS
Adoption. See ADOPTION

ACTIONS—Cont'd
Antenuptial agreements, to set aside, **ORC 2106.22**
Appeals. See APPEALS
Artificial insemination, action for inspection of physicians files, **ORC 3111.94**
Assault by minor, liability, **ORC 3109.10**
Child support. See CHILD SUPPORT, generally
Civil procedure rules. See CIVIL RULES OF PROCEDURE
Claims against estates. See CLAIMS AGAINST ESTATES
Construction of wills, **ORC 2106.06**
Contest of will. See CONTEST OF WILL
Criminal prosecutions. See CRIMINAL PROSECUTIONS
Custody. See CUSTODY OF CHILDREN, DOMESTIC
Declaratory judgments. See CUSTODY OF CHILDREN
Destruction of property by minor, **ORC 3109.09**
Eminent domain. See EMINENT DOMAIN
Executors, by or against. See EXECUTORS AND ADMINISTRATORS
Fiduciaries
    Personal use of trust funds by, action against, **ORC 2109.43**
    Will construction, **ORC 2107.46**
Guardians, by or against. See GUARDIANSHIP
Habeas corpus. See HABEAS CORPUS
Heirs, by, **ORC 2107.46**
Illegitimate child, **ORC 3111.01 to 3111.19**
    See also PARENTAGE ACTIONS
Jurisdiction. See JURISDICTION
Juvenile proceedings. See JUVENILE COURTS
Land sale proceedings. See LAND SALE PROCEEDINGS
Limitation. See LIMITATION OF ACTIONS
Mother and child relationship, establishment, **ORC 3111.17**
Parentage, to establish. See PARENTAGE ACTIONS
Parties. See PARTIES TO ACTIONS
Paternity. See PARENTAGE ACTIONS
Probating wills. See PROBATE OF WILLS
Revivor
    Action pending against decedent at time of death, notice to fiduciary
    Equivalent to presentation of claim, **ORC 2117.25**
Rules of Civil Procedure. See CIVIL RULES OF PROCEDURE
Sale of land. See GUARDIANSHIP, at Sale of land by
Support and maintenance. See CHILD SUPPORT, generally
Support and maintenance. See SUPPORT AND MAINTENANCE
Survival, **ORC 2305.21**
Theft by minor, liability, **ORC 3109.09**
Trust for supplemental services for person with disabilities, **ORC 5815.28**
Will construction, for, **ORC 2106.06**
Will contests. See CONTEST OF WILL
Wills, probate. See PROBATE OF WILLS
Wrongful death, **ORC Ch 2125**
    See also WRONGFUL DEATH

ADEMPTION
Generally, **ORC 2107.33, ORC 2107.36**

ADJUSTED GROSS INCOME
Defined, **ORC 5747.01**

ADMINISTRATION OF ESTATES
Generally, **ORC Ch 2113**
See also ESTATES; EXECUTORS AND ADMINISTRATORS; NO ADMINISTRATION
Affidavit, estate recovery program, Medicaid expenses, **ORC 2113.041**
Ancillary administration. See ANCILLARY ADMINISTRATION
Attorney fees. See ATTORNEY FEES, at Estates, administration
Costs. See Expenses, this heading
Domiciliary, **ORC Ch 2113**
Expenses
    See also ESTATES, at Expenses
    Attorney fees. See ATTORNEY FEES, at Estates, administration
    Court costs, **SumR Appx A, Sup. R 58.1**

ADMINISTRATION OF ESTATES—continued
Expenses—continued
    Priority when paying claims against estates, **ORC 2117.25**
Heirs, determination. See HEIRS, at Determination proceedings
Heirs-at-law, determination. See DESIGNATED HEIRS
Joint control of assets, **HamR 75.1**
Letters of administration. See EXECUTORS AND ADMINISTRATORS
Letters testamentary, **ORC 2113.05**
    Court issuing, **ORC 2113.01**
Limited purpose, **LucasR 57.1**
Medicaid expenses and payments, estate recovery program, **ORC 2113.041**
Missing person's estate, **ORC Ch 2119**
    Presumed decedent, **ORC 2121.05**
        See also PRESUMED DECEDENTS, generally
No administration. See NO ADMINISTRATION
Notice, estate recovery program, **ORC 2113.041**
Perpetuities, rule against, **ORC 2131.08, ORC 2131.09**
Presumed decedent's estate, **ORC 2121.05**
    See also PRESUMED DECEDENTS, generally
Probate court jurisdiction. See PROBATE COURTS, at Estate administration proceedings
Real property. See ESTATES, at Real property
    Estate tax. See ESTATE TAX
    Land sale proceedings. See LAND SALE PROCEEDINGS
Recovery, estate recovery program
    Medicaid expenses, **ORC 2113.041**
    Notice, **ORC 2117.061**
Release from. See NO ADMINISTRATION, generally
Relief from. See NO ADMINISTRATION, generally
Special administration, **ORC 2113.15 to 2113.17**
Status reports, **SumR 60.1(A)**
Summary administration, **Sup. R 75.4**
Time limitation and extension, **ORC 2113.25 to 2113.29**

ADMINISTRATIVE AGENCIES AND PROCEDURE
Appeal of order or decision
    Appeals court jurisdiction, **O Const IV § 3**
    Common pleas court jurisdiction, **O Const IV § 4**
    Supreme court, jurisdiction, **O Const IV § 2**
Child support, administrative orders
    See also PARENTAGE ACTIONS, at Administrative support orders
Eminent domain. See EMINENT DOMAIN
Guardianship for mentally retarded and developmentally disabled persons provided by
    Bond, **ORC 5123.59**
Mentally retarded and developmentally disabled persons, guardianship provided by
    Bond, **ORC 5123.59**

ADMINISTRATORS
See EXECUTORS AND ADMINISTRATORS

ADMISSIBILITY OF EVIDENCE
See EVIDENCE, generally

ADMISSION TO PROBATE
See PROBATE OF WILLS

ADMISSIONS
Juvenile adjudicatory hearings, **JuvR 29(C), JuvR 29(D)**

ADOLESCENTS
See MINORS

ADOPTION
Generally, **HamR 75.1, ORC Ch 3107, Sup. R 75.3**
Abandoned children, **ORC 5103.16**
Abuse and neglect determination summary report, **ORC 3107.034**
Accounting by petitioner, **ORC 3107.055, Sup. R 75.3**

ADOPTION—continued
Adopted person
    Authorization of release form, notification of, **ORC 3107.47**
    Defined, **ORC 3107.45**
    Request for copy of contents of adoption file, **ORC 3107.47**
    Request to assist birth parent or birth sibling in locating adopted person's name by adoption, **ORC 3107.48**
    Form and contents, **ORC 3107.51**
    Notification of birth parent or birth sibling, **ORC 3107.49**
Adoption file, access to by adoptee, **ORC 3107.38 to 3107.44**
Adoptive parent
    Authorization of release form, notification of, **ORC 3107.47**
    Custody hearings, notice, **ORC 2151.424**
    Defined, **ORC 3107.45**
    Request for copy of contents of adoption file, **ORC 3107.47**
Agencies to arrange. See ADOPTION AGENCIES
Agreement, voluntary permanent custody surrender, **ORC 3107.071**
Amendment, Interstate Compact on Placement of Children, **ORC 5103.20**
Appeals, **ORC 3107.16**
Approved placement, defined under Interstate Compact on Placement of Children, **ORC 5103.20**
Assessments, Interstate Compact on Placement of Children, **ORC 5103.20**
Assessor
    Appointment, **Sup. R 75.3**
    Duties, **ORC 3107.082**
    Education programs, **ORC 3107.013 to 3107.016**
    Meeting with birth parent prior to adoption agreement, **ORC 3107.082, ORC 5103.152**
    Prefinalization assessment, **ORC 3107.12**
    Requirements, **ORC 3107.012, ORC 3107.014**
    Social and medical histories of birth parents, recording, **ORC 3107.09**
    Training programs, **ORC 3107.015**
Associations or organizations to arrange. See ADOPTION AGENCIES
Attorney or agency ceasing to arrange adoptions, transfer of adoption records, **ORC 3107.67**
Attorneys, **Sup. R 75.3**
    Representation of petitioner, **ORC 3107.011**
Best interest of child, consideration
    Contested adoption, **ORC 3107.161**
Birth certificate, **ORC 3107.05**
Birth parent
    Authorization of release form, **ORC 3107.46**
        Contents, **ORC 3107.50**
        Notification of adopted person or adoptive parent, **ORC 3107.47**
    Defined, **ORC 3107.45**
    Denial of release form, **ORC 3107.46**
        Contents, **ORC 3107.50**
        Effect on request for copy of contents of adoption file, **ORC 3107.47**
    Notification of adopted person's request to assist birth parent or birth sibling in locating name by adoption, **ORC 3107.49**
    Providing material to be given to adoptive child, **ORC 3107.68**
    Putative father registry, **ORC 3107.062**
    Request for assistance in locating adopted person's name by adoption, **ORC 3107.49**
    Requesting open adoption option, **ORC 3107.63**
Birth sibling
    Defined, **ORC 3107.45**
    Notification of adopted person's request to assist birth parent or birth sibling in locating name by adoption, **ORC 3107.49**
    Request for assistance in locating adopted person's name by adoption, **ORC 3107.49**
Charitable institution having custody of child, powers and duties, **ORC 5103.15**
Confidentiality, **ORC 3107.17, ORC 3107.52, SupR 55(C)**
    Penalties, **ORC 3107.43, ORC 3107.99**
    Unauthorized disclosure, contempt, **SupR 55(D)**

ADOPTION

ADOPTION—*continued*
Consent, **ORC 3107.05 to 3107.09**
    Assessor meeting with parent prior to consent, **ORC 3107.082**
    Conditions of court accepting parents' consent to minor's adoption, **ORC 3107.081**
    Execution, **ORC 3107.08**
    Failure to consent, persons listed, **ORC 3107.05(A)**
    Irrevocable, **ORC 3107.084**
    Putative father
        On notice that consent not required prior to adoption, **ORC 3107.061**
        Registry, establishment, **ORC 3107.062**
    Relinquishment, **ORC 3107.07**
    Voluntary permanent custody surrender agreement, **ORC 3107.071**
    Withdrawal, **ORC 3107.084**
Contested, **ORC 3107.161**
Costs, **ORC 3107.055, SumR Appx B**
    Children's assumption, **ORC 5103.16**
    Criminal record check, prospective parents, **ORC 2151.86**
    Deposits, **CuyR 58.1, SumR 94.1(A), Sup. R 58.1**
    Disclosure of adoption information, **ORC 3107.66**
    Home studies, **ORC 3107.031**
    Petitions
        Fees, **ORC 2101.16**
        Release of information, **FrankR 58.3, ORC 2101.16(F), ORC 3107.42**
Credits
    Personal income tax, **ORC 5747.37**
Criminal record check of prospective parents, **ORC 2151.86**
Custody hearings, notice to adoptive parents, **ORC 2151.424**
Custody proceedings, **ORC 3107.06**
    Hearings, notice to adoptive parents, **ORC 2151.424**
Cuyahoga county probate court
    Court costs, **CuyR 58.1**
    Supervision, case management, **CuyR 78.1**
Decree, final, **ORC 3107.14 to 3107.16**
    Foreign decrees, **ORC 3107.18**
    Forwarding to health department, **ORC 3107.19**
Default, defined under Interstate Compact on Placement of Children, **ORC 5103.20**
Definitions, **ORC 3107.01**
    Disclosure of adoption information, regarding, **ORC 3107.45**
    Open adoption, **ORC 3107.60**
Descent and distribution, **ORC 3107.15**
Disbursements, **ORC 3107.055**
Disclosure of adoption information, **ORC 3107.38 to 3107.44**
    Adopted person, request to assist birth parent or birth sibling in locating name by adoption, **ORC 3107.48, ORC 3107.51**
        Notification of birth parent or birth sibling, **ORC 3107.49**
    Agency or attorney ceasing to arrange adoptions, transfer of adoption records, **ORC 3107.67**
    Agency or attorney refusing to provide open adoption option, **ORC 3107.63**
    Authorization of release form, **ORC 3107.46**
        Contents, **ORC 3107.50**
        Notification of adopted person or adoptive parent, **ORC 3107.47**
    Birth parent completing and signing form, **ORC 5103.151**
    Birth parent or birth sibling, request for assistance in locating adopted person's name by adoption, **ORC 3107.49**
    Birth parent providing material to be given to adoptive child, **ORC 3107.68**
    Birth parents requesting open adoption option, **ORC 3107.63**
    Birth parents selecting adoptive parents from profile, **ORC 3107.61**
    Confidentiality, **ORC 3107.52**
    Definitions, **ORC 3107.39, ORC 3107.45**
    Denial of release form, **ORC 3107.46**
        Contents, **ORC 3107.50**

ADOPTION—*continued*
Disclosure of adoption information, **ORC 3107.38 to 3107.44** —*continued*
    Denial of release form, **ORC 3107.46**—*continued*
        Effect on request for copy of contents of adoption file, **ORC 3107.47**
    Duty of agency or attorney to inform parents of nonbinding open adoption option, **ORC 3107.62**
    File
        Adoptee, access to, **ORC 3107.38 to 3107.44**
    Health department
        Adopted person's request to assist birth parent or birth sibling in locating name by adoption, prescribing form, **ORC 3107.51**
        Authorization of release form, prescribing, **ORC 3107.40, ORC 3107.50**
        Denial of release form, prescribing, **ORC 3107.50**
        Immunity from liability of department personnel, **ORC 3107.53**
        Powers and duties, **ORC 3107.40**
        Records not deemed public records, **ORC 3107.52**
    Human services department, powers and duties, **ORC 3107.17**
    Identifying information about parent, form, **ORC 3107.083**
    Identifying information in profiles of adoptive parents, **ORC 3107.61**
    Immunity from liability of health department personnel, **ORC 3107.53**
    Inspection of social and medical histories, **ORC 3107.17**
    Liability, limitation, **ORC 3107.44**
    Open adoption, denial of access to information prohibited, **ORC 3107.65**
    Penalties, **ORC 3107.43, ORC 3107.99**
    Petition, **ORC 3107.41**
        Adoptee, by, **ORC 3107.38**
        Fee, **FrankR 58.3, ORC 2101.16(F), ORC 3107.42**
    Photographs of birth parents, **ORC 3107.68**
    Procedure, **ORC 3107.41**
    Prohibitions, **ORC 3107.43**
    Release by parent or sibling, **ORC 3107.40**
        Public records, not considered to be, **ORC 3107.42**
    Reporting after final decree, **ORC 3107.091**
    Request for copy of contents of adoption file, **ORC 3107.47**
    Request for information
        Adopted person or adoptive family, by, **ORC 3107.66**
        Birth parent, sibling, or family, by, **ORC 3107.66**
    Social and medical histories of birth parents, **ORC 3107.09**
    Social security number of child, **ORC 3107.68**
    Violations, **ORC 3107.43**
    Withdrawal of release, **ORC 3107.40**
    Withdrawal of request for open adoption, **ORC 3107.65**
Dismissal of petition, **ORC 3107.14**
Dispute resolution, Interstate Compact on Placement of Children, **ORC 5103.20, ORC 5103.20**
Dissolution, Interstate Compact on Placement of Children, **ORC 5103.20**
Duty to inform parents of nonbinding open adoption option, **ORC 3107.62**
Effective date, Interstate Compact on Placement of Children, **ORC 5103.20**
Eligibility, **ORC 3107.02, ORC 3107.03**
Failure to communicate, **ORC 3107.07(A)**
False statements
    Effect on, **ORC 3107.16**
    Representation by agency or attorney, **ORC 3107.011**
Fees. See Costs, this heading
File, access to by adoptee, **ORC 3107.38 to 3107.44**
Final decree. See Decree, final, this heading
Financing of Interstate Compact on Placement of Children, **ORC 5103.20**
Foreign children, **ORC 3107.07, ORC 5103.16**
Foreign decrees, **ORC 3107.18**
Forms, **SumR 94.1(E), SupR 51, SupR 52**
    Adopted person's request to assist birth parent or birth sibling in locating name by adoption, **ORC 3107.48, ORC 3107.51**

ADOPTION—*continued*
Forms, **SumR 94.1(E), SupR 51, SupR 52**—*continued*
    Authorization of release form, **ORC 3107.46, ORC 3107.50**
    Denial of release form, **ORC 3107.46, ORC 3107.50**
        Effect on request for copy of contents of adoption file, **ORC 3107.47**
    Release of adoption file, **ORC 3107.083**
        Birth parent completing and signing form, **ORC 5103.151**
    Release of identifying information, **ORC 3107.083**
        Birth parent completing and signing form, **ORC 5103.151**
    Social and medical histories of birth parents, **ORC 3107.09**
Foster child. See FOSTER HOMES
Franklin county probate court, **FrankR 75.2**
    Case management, **FrankR 78.1**
Fraud, effect on, **ORC 3107.16**
Grandparents, by, **ORC 5103.16**
Guardians, by, **ORC 5103.16**
Hamilton county probate court, **HamR 75.1**
    Court costs, deposit, **HamR Appx D**
Health department
    Adopted person's request to assist birth parent or birth sibling in locating name by adoption, prescribing form, **ORC 3107.51**
    Authorization of release form, prescribing, **ORC 3107.40, ORC 3107.50**
    Denial of release form, prescribing, **ORC 3107.50**
    Disclosure of adoption information, immunity from liability of department personnel, **ORC 3107.53**
    Records not deemed public records, **ORC 3107.52**
Hearing, **ORC 3107.11, ORC 3107.14, SumR 94.1(C)**
    Confidentiality, **ORC 3107.17**
    Expense, **SumR 94.1(B)**
    Filing required prior to, **SumR 94.1(D)**
    Withdrawal of consent, **ORC 3107.084(B)**
Home studies, **ORC 3107.031**
    Assessor. See Assessor, generally, this heading
    Foreign adoption, **ORC 5103.16**
    Prospective home visits, **ORC 3107.101**
    Qualifications and registry of assessor, **ORC 3107.014**
    Reassessment by order of court, **ORC 3107.141**
    Rules for conducting, **ORC 3107.033**
Illegitimate child, consent, **ORC 3107.06**
Income tax credit, **ORC 5747.37**
Independent placements, **SumR 94.1(B)**
Indians
    Child, compliance with federal requirements, **ORC 3107.12**
    Tribes, Interstate Compact on Placement of Children, **ORC 5103.20**
Information about biological parents and siblings, **ORC 3107.055, ORC 3107.17, ORC 3107.45 to 3107.53**
Institutions or associations to arrange
    Advertising, **ORC 5103.17**
Interlocutory order, **ORC 3107.14 to 3107.16**
    Legal effect, **ORC 3107.15**
Interstate Commission for the Placement of Children, **ORC 5103.20**
Interstate Compact for the Placement of Children, **ORC 5103.20**
Interview with birth parents, **ORC 3107.09**
Jurisdiction, Interstate Compact on Placement of Children, **ORC 5103.20, ORC 5103.20**
    Juvenile court
        Approval of adoption agreements, **ORC 5103.151**
        Case certified to, **ORC 3107.14**
        Consent to, **ORC 3107.06**
        Questioning of birth parent prior to adoption, **ORC 5103.151**
Lucas county probate court, **LucasR 75.1**
    Court costs, **LucasR 58.1(A)**
Married couples, by, **ORC 3107.03**
Medical history, **ORC 3107.17**
    Recording by assessor, **ORC 3107.09**
    Reporting after final decree, **ORC 3107.091**
Member states, Interstate Compact on Placement of Children, **ORC 5103.20**
Minors as natural parents, effect, **ORC 5103.16**

ADOPTION—*continued*
Minor's consent, **ORC 3107.06**
Multiple children assessment, **ORC 3107.032**
Neglect, determination summary report, **ORC 3107.034**
Non-custodial parent, defined under Interstate Compact on Placement of Children, **ORC 5103.20**
Non-member state, defined under Interstate Compact on Placement of Children, **ORC 5103.20**
Nonresident children, placement, **ORC 2151.39**
Notice, **ORC 3107.11**
    Social and medical histories, correction or expansion, **ORC 3107.17**
    Withdrawal of consent, hearing, **ORC 3107.084(B)**
Objections
    Eighteen-year-old child, by, **ORC 3107.02**
Open adoption
    Agency or attorney refusing to provide open adoption option, **ORC 3107.63**
    Birth parents requesting open adoption option, **ORC 3107.63**
    Birth parents selecting adoptive parents from profile, **ORC 3107.61**
    Denial of access to information prohibited, **ORC 3107.65**
    Duty of agency or attorney to inform parents of nonbinding open adoption option, **ORC 3107.62**
    Probate court refusing to approve, **ORC 3107.65**
    Profile of adoptive parents, selection of birth parents given priority, **ORC 3107.61**
    Prohibitions, **ORC 3107.65**
    Shared custody prohibited, **ORC 3107.65**
    Withdrawal of request for, **ORC 3107.65**
Orphaned children, **ORC 5103.16**
Parent and child relationship
    Definition, **ORC 3111.01**
    Establishment, **ORC 3111.02**
Parents' consent. See Consent, this heading
Penalties for breach of confidentiality, **ORC 3107.43, ORC 3107.99**
Personal income tax credit, **ORC 5747.37**
Petition
    Caption, **ORC 3107.04**
    Contents, **ORC 3107.05**
    Disclosure of information, **ORC 3107.41**
        Adoptee, by, **ORC 3107.38**
        Fee, **FrankR 58.3, ORC 2101.16(F), ORC 3107.42**
    Dismissal, **ORC 3107.14**
    Fees, **ORC 2101.16, ORC 3107.42**
    Filing procedure, **ORC 3107.05**
        Time for filing, **ORC 3107.051**
    Hearing on. See Hearing, this heading
    Jurisdiction, **ORC 3107.051**
    Release of adoption file, for
        Adoptee, by, **ORC 3107.38**
Photographs of birth parent provided to adoptive child, **ORC 3107.68**
Placement authority, Interstate Compact on Placement of Children, **ORC 5103.20**
Placement for adoption. See ADOPTION AGENCIES
Prefinalization assessment, **ORC 3107.12**
    Reassessment by order of court, **ORC 3107.141**
Pretermitted heir status, **ORC 2107.34**
    Debt payments, contributions by, **ORC 2107.55**
Private child placing agencies, notice of hearings to adoptive parents, **ORC 2151.424**
Probate court, **ORC Ch 3107**
Procedures, **LucasR 75.1**
Profile of prospective adoptive parents
    Selection by birth parents given priority, **ORC 3107.61**
Proof of parent-child relationship, **ORC 3111.02**
Prospective home visits, **ORC 3107.101**
Provisional placement, defined under Interstate Compact on Placement of Children, **ORC 5103.20**
Public children services agencies, notice of hearings to adoptive parents, **ORC 2151.424**
Public records, exclusions, **ORC 3107.42**

ADOPTION—*continued*
Putative father
    Consent to adoption, on notice that consent not required, **ORC 3107.061**
Putative father registry, **ORC 3107.062**
    Campaign to promote awareness, **ORC 3107.065**
    Rules, **ORC 3107.065**
    Search request, **ORC 3107.063**
        Certified document required prior to adoption, **ORC 3107.064**
        Certified documents in response to, **ORC 3107.063**
Receiving state, defined under Interstate Compact on Placement of Children, **ORC 5103.20**
Reciprocal recognition, **ORC 3107.18**
Records and reports, **ORC 3107.055, ORC 3107.17 to 3107.19**
    Abuse and neglect determination summary report, **ORC 3107.034**
    Confidentiality, **ORC 3107.17, ORC 3107.52, SupR 55(C)**
        Penalties for breach of, **ORC 3107.43, ORC 3107.99**
    Contempt, unauthorized disclosure, **SupR 55(D)**
    Criminal record check, **ORC 2151.86**
    Eligible children, **ORC 5103.16**
    Home studies, **ORC 3107.031**
        Rules for conducting, **ORC 3107.033**
    Identifying information about parent, **ORC 3107.082(B)**
    Investigatory reports
        Reporting after final decree, **ORC 3107.091**
    Prefinalization report, **ORC 3107.12**
    Probate court, in, **ORC 2101.12**
    Public records, not considered to be, **ORC 3107.42, ORC 3107.52**
    Releases of adoption information, **ORC 3107.40**
        Petition, **ORC 3107.41**
    Social and medical histories, **ORC 3107.091, ORC 3107.17**
Refusing to provide open adoption option, **ORC 3107.63**
Release for foreign children, **ORC 3107.07**
Release of adoption file
    Birth parent completing and signing form, **ORC 5103.151**
Representation of petitioner, **ORC 3107.011**
Request for information, **ORC 3107.66**
Requirements, **ORC 3107.05**
Residential facility, defined under Interstate Compact on Placement of Children, **ORC 5103.20**
Right to contest by natural parents, **ORC 5103.16**
Rules and rulemaking powers, Interstate Compact on Placement of Children, **5103.21, ORC 5103.20**
Schedule of training of assessors, **ORC 3107.016**
Sending state, defined under Interstate Compact on Placement of Children, **ORC 5103.20**
Severability and construction, Interstate Compact on Placement of Children, **ORC 5103.20**
Single adult, by, **ORC 3107.03**
Social history, **ORC 3107.17**
    Reassessment by order of court, **ORC 3107.141**
    Recording by assessor, **ORC 3107.09**
    Reporting after final decree, **ORC 3107.091**
Social security number of child provided to adoptive parent, **ORC 3107.68**
Special needs child
    Petition to adopt, **ORC 3107.051**
Stark county probate court, **Sup. R 75.3**
    Case management, **Sup. R 78.8**
    Court costs, **Sup. R 58.1**
State responsibility, Interstate Compact on Placement of Children, **ORC 5103.20**
Stepparents, by, **ORC 3107.02, ORC 3107.03, ORC 5103.16, Sup. R 75.3**
    Conditions of court accepting parent's consent to minor's adoption, **ORC 3107.081**
    Petition, certain requirements inapplicable, **ORC 3107.051**
Summit county probate court, **SumR 94.1**
    Fees, **SumR Appx B**
    Supervision, **SumR 78.1(C)**
Support, adoptive parents' duty, **ORC 3103.03(A), ORC 3103.031**

ADOPTION—*continued*
Temporary order regarding allocation of parental rights and responsibilities while action pending, **ORC 3109.043**
Temporary placement, **ORC 3107.13**
Time
    Before final, **ORC 3107.13**
    Prospective home visits, **ORC 3107.101**
Training
    Programs for assessors, **ORC 3107.015**
    Schedule of training of assessors, **ORC 3107.016**
Venue, **ORC 3107.04**
Voluntary permanent custody surrender agreements, **ORC 3107.071**
    Assessor meeting with birth parent prior to adoption agreement, **ORC 5103.152**
    Juvenile court approving, **ORC 5103.151**
    Requirements prior to approval, **ORC 5103.151**
Withdrawal
    Consent, **ORC 3107.084**
    Interstate Compact on Placement of Children, **ORC 5103.20**
    Release of adoption information, **ORC 3107.40**
Written materials required to be provided to birth parent, **ORC 3107.083**

ADOPTION AGENCIES
See also ADOPTION, generally
Assumption of responsibility for expenses, **ORC 5103.16**
Consent to adoption
    Conditions for juvenile court to approve parent's agreement with agency, **ORC 5103.151**
Disclosure of adoption information
    Agency or attorney ceasing to arrange adoptions, transfer of adoption records, **ORC 3107.67**
    Birth parent providing material to be given to adoptive child, **ORC 3107.68**
    Birth parents requesting open adoption option, **ORC 3107.63**
    Duty to inform parents of nonbinding open adoption option, **ORC 3107.62**
    Liability, limitation, **ORC 3107.44**
    Powers and duties, **ORC 3107.41**
    Refusing to provide open adoption option, **ORC 3107.63**
    Request for information by adopted person or adoptive family, **ORC 3107.66**
    Request for information by birth parent, sibling, or family, **ORC 3107.66**
    Social security number of child provided to adoptive parent, **ORC 3107.68**
    Violations, **ORC 3107.43**
Fees, **ORC 3107.055**
Information about biological parents, **ORC 3107.17**
Interstate Compact for the Placement of Children, **ORC 5103.20**
Open adoption
    Birth parents requesting open adoption option, **ORC 3107.63**
    Duty of agency or attorney to inform parents of nonbinding open adoption option, **ORC 3107.62**
    Profile of adoptive parents, selection of birth parents given priority, **ORC 3107.61**
    Refusing to provide open adoption option, **ORC 3107.63**
Records and reports
    Public records, not considered to be, **ORC 3107.42**
Representation of petitioner by, **ORC 3107.011**
Voluntary permanent custody surrender agreements, **ORC 3107.071**
    Juvenile court approving, **ORC 5103.151**
    Requirements prior to approval, **ORC 5103.151**

ADULT CHILD
Defined, **ORC 2105.25**

ADULT FOSTER CARE
See FOSTER HOMES

ADULT PAROLE AUTHORITY
Emergency hospitalization of mentally ill parolee, **ORC 5122.10**

ADULTERY
Divorce, grounds for, **ORC 3105.01(C)**
Dower interest, effect, **ORC 2103.05**

ADULTS
Abuse or neglect. See ABUSED OR NEGLECTED ADULTS

ADVANCEMENTS FROM ESTATES
Fiduciaries making, **ORC 2109.44**
Intestate succession, **ORC 2105.051**

ADVERSE PARTIES
See DEFENDANTS; PARTIES TO ACTIONS

ADVERSE POSSESSION
Recovery of title, limitation of actions, **ORC 2305.04**

ADVERTISING
See also NOTICE
Adoptions, **ORC 5103.17**
Highways, along
    Removal by order, compensation, **ORC 163.31 to 163.33**
Legal. See NOTICE
Outdoor
    Removal by order, compensation, **ORC 163.31 to 163.33**

AFFIDAVITS
Abortion for minor without parental consent, **SupR Form 24-A**
    Instructions, **SupR Forms 24-A and 24-B Instructions**
    Recipient of notice of minor's intent, **SupR Form 24-B**
        Instructions, **SupR Forms 24-A and 24-B Instructions**
Executors and administrators
    Estate recovery program, Medicaid expenses, **ORC 2113.041**
    Extension of time to administer estate, **ORC 2113.26**
    Notice to surviving spouse and heirs, **ORC 2107.19**
Grandparents. See GRANDPARENT POWER OF ATTORNEY OR CARETAKER AUTHORIZATION AFFIDAVIT
Hospitalization of mentally ill, **ORC 5122.11**
Judges, disqualification
    Probate court judges, **ORC 2101.39**
Mentally ill, hospitalization of mentally ill, **ORC 5122.11**
Mentally retarded, for institutionalization, **ORC 5123.71**
Paternity proceedings, **ORC 3109.27**
Power of attorney, **1337.01 et seq.**
Probate judge, to disqualify for prejudice, **ORC 2101.39**
Probate of wills, fiduciary filing affidavit of notice, **CuyR 34.4, LucasR 59.1**
    Additional notice, affidavit proving abolished, **ORC 2109.33**
Service, **JuvR 18(D)**
Survivorship tenancy, **ORC 5302.17**
Time for service, **JuvR 18(D)**

AFFIRMATIONS
See OATHS AND AFFIRMATIONS

AFFIRMATIVE DEFENSES
Generally, **ORC 2901.05(A), ORC 2901.05(C)**
See also DEFENSES, generally
Child abuse, permitting, **ORC 2903.15**

AFTERBORN CHILDREN
See PARENT AND CHILD; PRETERMITTED HEIRS

AGE REQUIREMENTS
Anatomical gifts, eligibility, **ORC 2108.02**
Blood donors, **ORC 2108.21**
Driver's license, **ORC 4507.08**
Fiduciaries, age limit on powers of appointment, **ORC 5815.13**
Majority, age of, **ORC 3109.01**
Testators, **ORC 2107.02**

AGED PERSONS
Abused, neglected, or exploited
    Probate courts referring information to law enforcement agencies, **ORC 2101.26, ORC 2151.421**
Caretaker abusing, neglecting, or exploiting, **ORC 5101.60 to 5101.71**
    See also PROTECTIVE SERVICES FOR ADULTS
Income tax credits, **ORC 5747.05(C), ORC 5747.05(D)**
Incompetence due to age, guardianship, **ORC Ch 2111**
    See also GUARDIANSHIP, generally
Legal disability. See DISABILITY, PERSONS UNDER, generally
Protective services, **ORC 5101.60 to 5101.71**
    See also PROTECTIVE SERVICES FOR ADULTS

AGREEMENT TO MAKE WILL
Generally, **ORC 2107.04**

AGREEMENTS
Generally, See CONTRACTS
Antenuptial. See ANTENUPTIAL AGREEMENTS
Interstate. See INTERSTATE AGREEMENTS
Separation. See SEPARATION AGREEMENTS

AGRICULTURAL LANDS
See FARMLANDS

AGRICULTURAL PRODUCTS
See CROPS

AGRICULTURAL SOCIETIES
Appropriations; escheat, proceeds from, **ORC 2105.09**

AGRICULTURE
See also FARMLANDS
Crops
    Estate assets, defined as, **ORC 2115.10**
Eminent domain, effect, **ORC Ch 163**

AIDS
Community alternative homes
    Aged persons suffering neglect, abuse, or exploitation; reporting, **ORC 5101.61**

ALCOHOL, DRUG ADDICTION, AND MENTAL HEALTH SERVICE DISTRICTS
Aftercare and outpatient services, **ORC 5122.231**

ALCOHOLISM
Divorce, grounds for, **ORC 3105.01(G)**
Incompetence due to, guardianship, **ORC Ch 2111**
    See also GUARDIANSHIP, generally
Legal disability, alcoholic considered to be under. See DISABILITY, PERSONS UNDER, generally
Legal separation, grounds for, **ORC 3105.17(A)(7)**
Parents
    Institutional custody of children based on, assessment and treatment requirement, **ORC 2151.3514**

ALCOHOLISM TREATMENT FACILITIES
Parents
    Institutional custody of children based on, assessment and treatment requirement, **ORC 2151.3514**

ALIENS
See also NONRESIDENTS
Adoption of foreign children, **ORC 3107.07**
Beneficiaries of trusts or estates, **ORC 2113.81, ORC 2113.82**
Death, notice to foreign consul, **ORC 2113.11**
Estates, administration, **ORC 2113.81, ORC 2113.82**
Property rights, **ORC 2105.16**
Testators, **ORC 2129.06**

ALIMONY
See SUPPORT AND MAINTENANCE, generally

ALTERNATIVE DISPUTE RESOLUTION
Juvenile courts establishing procedures, **ORC 2151.542**
Probate courts establishing procedures, **ORC 2101.163**

AMENDMENT OF PLEADINGS
Generally, **JuvR 22(B)**
Juvenile proceedings, **JuvR 22(B)**

AMENDMENTS
Interstate Compact on Placement of Children, **ORC 5103.20**
Pleadings, juvenile proceedings, **JuvR 22(B)**
Wills, **ORC 2107.084, ORC 2108.06**

AMERCEMENT OF OFFICIALS
Generally, **ORC 2101.10**
Constables, **ORC 2101.10**
Coroners, **ORC 2101.10**
Sheriffs, **ORC 2101.10**

AMUSEMENTS
Seasonal amusement or recreation establishments
    Age and schooling certificates, minors age sixteen and seventeen, exemption, **ORC 4109.02**

ANATOMICAL GIFTS
Generally, **ORC Ch 2108**
Acceptance, **ORC 2108.07**
Additional criteria for disqualification from serving as representative or successor representative, **ORC 2108.77**
Assignment
    Contents of declaration of assignment of right of disposition, **ORC 2108.72**
    Funeral, assignment of rights to direct disposition of remains after death and purchase goods and services related to, **ORC 2108.70**
    Priority of assignment of right of disposition, **ORC 2108.81**
    Probate court, assignment of disposition, **ORC 2108.82**
    Revocation of, **ORC 2108.80**
    Right of disposition relating to anatomical gifts, **ORC 2108.78**
    Vesting of assignment or reassignment of right of disposition, **ORC 2108.71**
Banks
    Eye banks, **ORC 2108.60**
Civil liability
    Failure to bring legal action, **ORC 2108.85**
    Right to good faith reliance on written declaration and instructions, **ORC 2108.86**
Contents of declaration of assignment of right of disposition, **ORC 2108.72**
Coroner's powers, **ORC 2108.02**
Costs
    Court costs, **ORC 2108.85**
    Goods and services, liability for cost of goods and services relating to exercise of right of disposition, **ORC 2108.89**
    Preservation of remains while dispute pending, **ORC 2108.84**
Court costs, **ORC 2108.85**
Criminal liability, right to good faith reliance on written declaration and instructions, **2108.86, ORC 2108.85**
Declarations
    Execution of written declaration, **ORC 2108.73**
    Form of written declaration, **ORC 2108.72**
    Good faith reliance on written declaration and instructions, right to, **ORC 2108.86**
    Truthfulness of declaration, **ORC 2108.74**
Definitions, **ORC 2108.01**
Disputes relating to right of disposition, immunity from liability, **ORC 2108.83**
Disqualification
    Additional criteria for disqualification from serving as representative or successor representative, **ORC 2108.77**
    Service as a representative or successor representative, **ORC 2108.75**
Donees
    Delivery of gift document to, **ORC 2108.05**

ANATOMICAL GIFTS—continued
Donees—continued
    Eligibility, **ORC 2108.03**
    Rights, **ORC 2108.02**
Donors
    Age, eligibility, **ORC 2108.02, ORC 2108.21**
    Eligible, **ORC 2108.02**
    Forms, **ORC 2108.10**
    Registry, **ORC 2108.18, ORC 2108.20**
    Toll-free telephone number, **ORC 2108.19**
Drivers' licenses, provision for, **ORC 2108.04, ORC 4507.06**
Effective date, **ORC 2108.04**
Examination to assure acceptability, **ORC 2108.02**
Exclusive jurisdiction, **ORC 2108.90**
Eyes, enucleation, **ORC 2108.071, ORC 2108.60**
Form for donor, **ORC 2108.10**
Former spouse as representative or successor representative, **ORC 2108.76**
Funeral, assignment of rights to direct disposition of remains after death and purchase goods and services related to, **ORC 2108.70**
Good faith reliance on written declaration and instructions, right to, **ORC 2108.86**
Goods and services, liability for cost of goods and services relating to exercise of right of disposition, **ORC 2108.89**
Grandparent, by, **ORC 2108.02**
Hospitals, anatomical gifts to facilitating procurement protocol, **ORC 2108.021**
Human tissue transactions, defined, **ORC 2108.11**
Identification cards, provisions for, **ORC 2108.04**
Immunity from liability, disputes relating to right of disposition, **ORC 2108.83**
Instrument of gift, **ORC 2108.04, ORC 2108.05**
    Amendment, **ORC 2108.06**
    Delivery or deposit, **ORC 2108.05**
    Driver's license or identification card, **ORC 4507.06**
    Forms, **ORC 2108.10**
    Living will, **ORC 2133.16**
    Revocation, **ORC 2108.06**
    Signature, **ORC 2108.04**
    Witnesses, **ORC 2108.04**
Investigation, duty to independently investigate existence of or locate representative or successor representative, **ORC 2108.87**
Legal action, criminal or civil liability for failure to bring, **ORC 2108.85**
Legal fees, **ORC 2108.85**
Liability, **2108.89, ORC 2108.08**
Living wills, **2133.16**
Majority vote prevailing when representative or successor representative is group or class of persons, **ORC 2108.79**
Minors, **ORC 2108.02, ORC 2108.04**
Motor Vehicles, Bureau of
    Registry of donors, **ORC 2108.18, ORC 2108.20**
    Toll-free telephone number, **ORC 2108.19**
Next of kin, by, **ORC 2108.02, ORC 2108.03**
Organ procurement organizations
    Agreements with hospitals, **ORC 2108.021**
Parent consenting to donation by child
    Probate court's powers, **ORC 2108.02**
Penalty for sale of human body parts, **ORC 2108.99**
Physician's duties, **ORC 2108.03, ORC 2108.04**
Pituitary glands, **ORC 2108.53**
Preservation of remains while dispute pending, cost of, **ORC 2108.84**
Priority of assignment of right of disposition, **ORC 2108.81**
Probate court to decide when no majority decision, **ORC 2108.79**
Protocols for facilitating procurement, **ORC 2108.021**
Recovery agencies, **ORC 2108.03**
Registry of donors, **ORC 2108.18, ORC 2108.20**
Renewal, **ORC 2108.04**
Representative
    Duty to independently investigate existence of or locate representative or successor representative, **ORC 2108.87**
    Majority vote prevailing when representative or successor repre-

ANATOMICAL GIFTS—continued
Representative—continued
    sentative is group or class of persons, **ORC 2108.79**
Representative or successor representative, former spouse as, **ORC 2108.76**
Representatives
    Additional criteria for disqualification from serving as representative or successor representative, **ORC 2108.77**
    Disqualification from serving as a representative or successor representative, **ORC 2108.75**
Resignation of right of disposition, **ORC 2108.88**
Revocation, **ORC 2108.06**
    Assignment, revocation of, **ORC 2108.80**
Sale of human body parts prohibited, **ORC 2108.12, ORC 2108.99**
Second chance trust fund, **ORC Ch 2108.15**
Second chance trust fund advisory committee, **ORC 2108.17**
Service, not sale transaction, **ORC 2108.11**
Signature to instrument, **ORC 2108.04**
Storage facilities, **ORC 2108.60**
Successor representative
    Additional criteria for disqualification from serving as representative or successor representative, **ORC 2108.77**
    Designation, **ORC 2108.70**
    Disqualification from serving as a representative or successor representative, **ORC 2108.75**
    Duty to independently investigate existence of or locate representative or successor representative, **ORC 2108.87**
    Former spouse as representative or, **ORC 2108.76**
    Majority vote prevailing when representative or successor representative is group or class of persons, **ORC 2108.79**
Telephone, toll-free telephone number, **ORC 2108.19**
Time of death, **ORC 2108.07**
Transplants, **ORC 2108.03**
Truthfulness of declaration, **ORC 2108.74**
Uniform Anatomical Gift Act, adoption, **ORC 2108.09**
Waiver by coroners, **ORC 2108.02**
Will, by, **ORC 2108.04**
    See also Instrument of gift, this heading
Witness to instrument, **ORC 2108.04**
Written declaration
    Execution of written declaration, **ORC 2108.73**
    Form of, **ORC 2108.72**

ANCILLARY ADMINISTRATION
Generally, **ORC Ch 2129**
Application, **ORC 2129.04**
Appointment, **ORC 2109.21, ORC 2129.08**
Assets, surrender of, **ORC 2129.03**
Bona fide purchaser protected, **ORC 2129.21**
Bond, **ORC 2129.08**
    Land sale, **ORC 2129.26**
Certificate of assets, liabilities to domiciliary, **ORC 2129.15, ORC 2129.16**
Certificate of transfer, **ORC 2113.61, ORC 2129.19**
Claims, **ORC 2129.12**
Clearing title to Ohio land, **ORC 2129.01, ORC 2129.02, ORC 2129.17**
Creditors' claims, **ORC 2129.12, ORC 2129.13, ORC 2129.16**
Debts owed to estate, **ORC 2129.20**
Distribution of estate, **ORC 2129.23**
Domiciliary administration
    Not commenced, **ORC 2129.11**
    Sale of land, **ORC 2129.14, ORC 2129.16**
Fees, **ORC 2129.24**
Foreign executor or administrator, **ORC 2129.02, ORC 2129.03, ORC 2129.25**
Foreign will, admitting to record, **ORC 2129.05 to 2129.07**
Heirship determination, **ORC 2129.18**
Jurisdiction, **ORC 2129.04**
Notice of appointment of administrator, **ORC 2129.08**

ANCILLARY ADMINISTRATION—continued
Payment of debts, **ORC 2129.12, ORC 2129.13, ORC 2129.16, ORC 2129.20**
    Land sold for, **ORC 2129.25, ORC 2129.26**
Personal property, delivery to foreign executor or administrator, **ORC 2129.03**
Presumed decedent's estate, **ORC 2121.02, ORC 2121.07**
Procedure same as for resident decedents, **ORC 2129.10**
Procedure when no domiciliary representative appointed, **ORC 2129.11**
Real property
    Certificate of transfer, **ORC 2129.19**
    Sale, **ORC 2129.13, ORC 2129.14, ORC 2129.16, ORC 2129.25, ORC 2129.26**
Records and reports, **ORC 2129.01, ORC 2129.17**
Sale of real estate, **ORC 2129.13, ORC 2129.14, ORC 2129.16**
    Foreign executor or administrator, by, **ORC 2129.25, ORC 2129.26**
Surplus assets, distribution, **ORC 2129.23**
Trusts under foreign will, **ORC 2129.27 to 2129.30**
Wills, foreign; admitting to record, **ORC 2129.05 to 2129.07**

ANIMALS
Gifts and grants for prevention of cruelty to, estate tax deductions, **ORC 5731.17**
Trust for care of animal, **ORC 5804.08**

ANNUITIES
Designation of spouse as beneficiary, effect of termination of marriage, **ORC 5815.33**
Estate tax, **ORC 5731.09**
Living wills, effect, **ORC 2133.12**
Uniform Principal and Income Act, **ORC 5812.32**

ANNULMENT OF MARRIAGE
Causes, **ORC 3105.31**
Custody of children. See CUSTODY OF CHILDREN, DOMESTIC
Designation of spouse as beneficiary, effect, **ORC 5815.33**
Grounds for, **ORC 3105.31**
Judgment, **ORC 3105.10(A)**
Juvenile procedure rules, applicability, **JuvR 1(C)**
Legal separation, counterclaim for not barred by complaint for, **ORC 3105.17(B)**
Minors due to age, **ORC 3105.31(A)**
Nonage marriage, **ORC 3105.31(A)**
Paternity, presumption, **ORC 3111.03**
Personal property held jointly by spouses, effect, **ORC 5815.34**
Service of process, **ORC 3105.06**
Wills, effect, **ORC 2107.33**

ANSWERS
See DEFENSES; PLEADINGS

ANTE MORTEM DECLARATION OF WILL VALIDITY
Generally, **ORC 2107.081 to 2107.085**
Appeal from, **ORC 2107.084**
Collateral attack, **ORC 2107.084**
Contest action, effect, **ORC 2107.71**
Declaratory judgments, **ORC 2107.081 to 2107.085**
Domicile of testator, defined, **ORC 2107.081**
Evidence, **ORC 2107.085**
Expenses and fees, **ORC 2107.62**
Failure to file not admission of improper execution, **ORC 2107.081, ORC 2107.085**
Hearing, **ORC 2107.083, ORC 2107.084**
    Revocation or modification of will, **ORC 2107.084**
Judgment, **ORC 2107.084**
Jurisdiction of probate court, **ORC 2107.081 to 2107.085**
Modification of will by testator subsequent to, **ORC 2107.084**
Other actions, applicability of proceedings to, **ORC 2107.085**
Parties defendant, **ORC 2107.081, ORC 2107.084**
Petition for declaratory judgment, **ORC 2107.081 to 2107.085**
Probate court jurisdiction, **ORC 2107.081 to 2107.085**
Revocation of will after, **ORC 2107.084**

ANTE MORTEM DECLARATION OF WILL VALIDITY
—continued
Service of process, **ORC 2107.082, ORC 2107.084**

ANTE MORTEM PROBATE OF WILL
See ANTE MORTEM DECLARATION OF WILL VALIDITY

ANTENUPTIAL AGREEMENTS
Action to set aside, **ORC 2106.22**

ANTI-LAPSE STATUTE
Generally, **ORC 2107.52**

APPEALS
See also COURTS OF APPEALS
Abortion, juvenile, notice of appeal, **SupR Form 23.1-C**
Abortion for minor without parental consent, **SupR 23(F)**
    Complaint, dismissal, **ORC 2151.85**
    Notice, **SupR Form 23-C, SupR Form 24-C**
Adoption, **ORC 3107.16**
Ante mortem declaration of will validity, **ORC 2107.084**
Arbitration award, from, **SupR 15**
Budget commission of county allocating income tax revenues, **ORC 5747.55**
Child day camp's criminal records checks violations, **ORC 2151.861**
Custody actions
    Priority on docket, **ORC 3109.04(H), ORC 3109.06**
Eminent domain, **ORC 163.09, ORC 163.19, ORC 163.58**
Estate tax, **ORC 5731.30 to 5731.32**
Evidence
    Returned or suppressed, from, **JuvR 22(F)**
Final orders. See DECREES; JUDGMENTS
Income tax, **ORC 5747.13(B) to 5747.13(E)**
Jurisdiction
    Appellate courts, **O Const IV § 3**
    Common pleas courts, **O Const IV § 4**
    Supreme court, **O Const IV § 2**
Juvenile cases
    Adult cases, **ORC 2151.52**
    Appropriations for, **ORC 2151.10**
    Juvenile procedure rules, applicability, **JuvR 1(C)**
    Right to appeal, **JuvR 34(E)**
Local government fund allocations, **ORC 5747.55**
Probate court, from. See PROBATE COURTS
Record on appeal
    Videotape, **SupR 11**
Right to
    Juvenile proceeding, from, **JuvR 34(E), JuvR 34(J)**
Suppression of evidence, from, **JuvR 22(F)**
Tax
    County undivided local government funds, estimate of revenues, **ORC 5747.51**
    Estate tax, **ORC 5731.30 to 5731.32**
    Income tax, **ORC 5747.13(B) to 5747.13(E)**
    Local government fund allocations, appeals, **ORC 5747.55**

APPEARANCE
Attorneys, **JuvR 4(D)**
Subpoena for. See SUBPOENAS
Summons. See SUMMONS

APPLICABLE FUND VALUE
Defined under Institutional Trust Funds Act, **ORC 5813.01**

APPOINTMENTS
Executors and administrators. See EXECUTORS AND ADMINISTRATORS
Fiduciaries. See FIDUCIARIES

APPORTIONMENT
Taxes. See particular tax concerned
Trust funds, between principal and income, **ORC Ch 1340**

APPRAISALS
Appraisers. See INVENTORY AND APPRAISAL OF ESTATES
Dower, **ORC 5305.11, ORC 5305.12**
Eminent domain proceedings, **ORC 163.06, ORC 163.09, ORC 163.59**
Estates. See INVENTORY AND APPRAISAL OF ESTATES
Guardians selling land. See GUARDIANSHIP, at Sale of land by
Land sale proceedings, **ORC 2127.22 to 2127.39**

APPROPRIATION OF PROPERTY
See EMINENT DOMAIN

APPROPRIATIONS
Counties. See COUNTIES
Detention homes, **ORC 2151.10, ORC 2151.34**
Family foster homes, **ORC 2151.331**
Juvenile courts, **ORC 2151.10**
Probate courts, **ORC 2101.11, ORC 2101.11(B)**

APPROVED PLACEMENT
Defined under Interstate Compact on Placement of Children, **ORC 5103.20**

ARBITRATION AND AWARD
Appeals, **SupR 15**
Arbitrators
    Appointment, **SupR 15**
Claims against estates, disputed, **ORC 2117.09**
Common pleas courts, procedure, **SupR 15**
County courts
    Procedure, **SupR 15**
Domestic relations cases, **SupR 15**
Excluded cases, **SupR 15**
Juvenile cases, **SupR 15**
Municipal courts, procedure, **SupR 15**
Records and reports, **SupR 15**

ARMED FORCES
See MILITARY SERVICE; VETERANS

ARRESTS
Child abuse offenders, **ORC 2151.43**
Children, of, **JuvR 6, ORC 2151.14, ORC 2151.27 to 2151.33**
    Fingerprinting, consent of juvenile court not required, **ORC 2151.313**
Contempt, parents failing to provide child support, **ORC 2151.43**
Contributing to delinquency, **ORC 2151.43**
Definitions, **ORC 2151.011**
Detention, defined, **ORC 2151.011**
Escapees from mental hospitals, **ORC 5122.26**
Mental retardation and developmental disabilities institutions' special police officers, by, **ORC 5123.13**
Photographing, consent of juvenile court not required, **ORC 2151.313**
Probation officers, by, **ORC 2151.14**
Warrantless, juveniles, **ORC 2151.14**

ART
Gifts, estate tax deductions, **ORC 5731.17**

ART DEALER
Defined, **ORC 5815.41**

ART GALLERIES AND MUSEUMS
Probate court's authorization to deposit works in, **ORC 2109.14**

ART WORKS
Consignment. See CONSIGNMENT OF ART WORKS TO DEALERS

ARTIFICIAL INSEMINATION, NONSPOUSAL
Generally, **ORC 3111.88 to 3111.96**
Action for inspection of physician's file, **ORC 3111.94**
Consents required, married woman, **ORC 3111.92**
Date, recording, **ORC 3111.93**
Definitions, **ORC 3111.88**

ARTIFICIAL INSEMINATION, NONSPOUSAL
—*continued*
Donor information, **ORC 3111.94**
Fresh semen, medical history of donor required for use of, **ORC 3111.91**
Frozen semen, medical history of donor and laboratory studies required for use of, **ORC 3111.91**
Husband regarded as natural father of child, **ORC 3111.95**
Married woman
    Consents required, **ORC 3111.92**
    Husband regarded as natural father of child, **ORC 3111.95**
Physicians
    Failure to comply with statutes, effect, **ORC 3111.96**
    Records and reports, **ORC 3111.93, ORC 3111.94**
    Supervision by, **ORC 3111.90**
Privileged information, **ORC 3111.94**
Recipient information and statements, **ORC 3111.93**
Semen
    Fresh, medical history of donor required for use, **ORC 3111.91**
    Frozen, medical history of donor and laboratory studies required for use of, **ORC 3111.91**
Spousal, laws inapplicable to, **ORC 3111.89**
Supervision by physician, **ORC 3111.90**
Surrogate motherhood, laws inapplicable to, **ORC 3111.89**

ASCERTAINABLE BENEFICIARY
Creation of noncharitable trust without ascertainable beneficiary, **ORC 5804.09**

ASCERTAINABLE STANDARD
Defined, **ORC 5801.01**

ASSAULT AND BATTERY
Juvenile offenders, liability of parents, **ORC 3109.10**
Mental patients, protected from, **ORC 5122.29**

ASSESSMENTS, REAL PROPERTY
See REAL PROPERTY, TAXATION, generally

ASSESSMENTS, SPECIAL
Detention homes, funding, **ORC 2152.43**
Juvenile rehabilitation facilities, to support, **ORC 2151.66, ORC 2151.78**

ASSETS OF ESTATES
See also ESTATES, generally
Allocation between income and principal, **ORC 2109.68**
Collection by executor or administrator, **ORC 2113.25 to 2113.29**
    Rents, **ORC 2113.311**
Concealed or embezzled, **ORC 2101.16, ORC 2109.50 to 2109.56**
    Trial and examination, **SumR 96.1**
Descent and distribution, **ORC Ch 2105**
    See also DESCENT AND DISTRIBUTION
Distribution, **ORC 2109.36, ORC 2113.53 to 2113.60**
    Ancillary administration, **ORC 2129.23**
    Application, **ORC 2113.54**
    Complaint to enforce, **ORC 2109.59**
    Devises, **ORC 2113.52**
    Fees, **ORC 2101.16**
    In kind, **ORC 2101.16, ORC 2113.40, ORC 2113.55**
        Intestate succession, **ORC 2106.11**
    Legacies, **ORC 2113.51**
    Liability of executor or administrator, **ORC 2113.53**
    Missing persons, **ORC 2101.24**
    No administration, **ORC 2113.03**
    Nonresident decedent's estate, **ORC 2129.23**
    Notice, **ORC 2113.533**
    Order, **ORC 2109.36**
    Presumed decedent's property, **ORC 2121.07**
    Principal and income, allocation, **ORC 2109.67**
    Real property, proceeds of sale, **ORC 2127.38**
    Recovery when will invalid, **ORC 2113.23**
    Rents collected by fiduciary, **ORC 2113.311**

ASSETS OF ESTATES—*continued*
Distribution, **ORC 2109.36, ORC 2113.53 to 2113.60**—*continued*
    Setting aside assets to satisfy claims, **ORC 2113.54**
    Settlement, after, **ORC 2113.57**
    Summary estate administration, **Sup. R 75.4**
Embezzled. See Concealed or embezzled, this heading
Escheat, **ORC 2105.07**
Inventory and appraisal. See INVENTORY AND APPRAISAL OF ESTATES
Joint control, **HamR 75.1**
Land sale proceedings. See LAND SALE PROCEEDINGS
Motor vehicles, watercraft or outboard motors
    Designation in beneficiary form, **ORC 2131.13**
Newly discovered, **ORC 2101.16, ORC 2113.69**
Personal property
    Escheat, **ORC 2105.07**
    Sale of, **ORC 2113.39 to 2113.52**
        See also Sale, generally, this heading
Real property
    See also LAND SALE PROCEEDINGS
    Ancestral, **ORC 2105.01**
    Certificates of transfer, **ORC 2113.61**
    Debts, liability, **ORC 2117.36**
    Escheat, **ORC 2105.09**
    Fraudulent transfers by decedent, **ORC 2127.40**
    Incomplete contracts, completion, **ORC 2113.48**
    Management, **ORC 2113.311**
    Missing person's estate, **ORC 2119.04**
    Mortgages
        Heirs' rights, **ORC 2117.29**
        Releases, **ORC 2127.19**
    Partition, **ORC 2127.41**
    Remainder, **ORC 2131.04 to 2131.07**
        Forfeiture for waste by life tenant, **ORC 2105.20**
        Protection of interest, **ORC 2113.58**
    Sale of, **ORC Ch 2127**
    Will contests, fiduciary's duty during, **ORC 2113.21**
Release by tax commissioner, **ORC 5731.39**
Sale, **ORC 2113.39 to 2113.52**
    Application for, **SupR 63**
    Authority
        Probate court, **ORC 2113.40 to 2113.52**
        Will, under, **ORC 2113.39**
    Credit, on
        Personal property, **ORC 2113.43**
        Real property, **ORC 2127.34, ORC 2127.35**
    Estate tax purposes, for, **ORC 5731.37**
    Land sale proceedings. See LAND SALE PROCEEDINGS
    Personal property, **ORC 2113.40 to 2113.52**
    Real property. See LAND SALE PROCEEDINGS
    Will authorizing, **ORC 2113.39**
Set aside for payment of rejected claims, **ORC 2113.54**
Transfers, **ORC 5731.05 to 5731.08**
    Transfer tax, situs, **ORC 5731.50**
Unclaimed funds, disposition, **ORC 2113.64 to 2113.68**
    Transfer to owner from county treasury, **ORC 2113.67**
Wages owed decedent, **ORC 2113.04**

ASSIGNMENT
Anatomical gifts. See ANATOMICAL GIFTS
Assignees, qualification by probate courts, **ORC 2101.24**
Court records, **ORC 2101.14**
Dower. See DOWER

ATTACHMENT
See also GARNISHMENT
Special administrators, against, **ORC 2113.16**
Wills, production, **ORC 2107.09**

ATTORNEY
See ATTORNEYS

ATTORNEY FEES

Adoption, **ORC 3107.055**
Application for, **CuyR 71.1, HamR 71.1, LucasR 71.1, SumR 71.1, SumR Appx E**
    Hearing on, notice, **HamR Appx A-1**
        Waiver, **HamR Appx A-3**
    Land sale proceedings, **SumR Appx G**
Child abuse, bad faith reporting of, **ORC 2151.421**
Child support, **ORC 3105.21(C)**
    Contempt for failure to pay, **ORC 3109.05(C)**
    Juvenile courts, **ORC 2151.23(G)**
    Parentage actions, **ORC 3111.13(F)**
Computation, **HamR 71.1**
Consent to payment of, **HamR Appx A-2, SumR Appx F**
    Waiver of notice of hearing, **HamR Appx A-3**
Contingent fees, **CuyR 71.2 et seq., HamR 71.2**
Court-appointed counsel, **JuvR 4(F)**
Custody action, **ORC 3109.32**
Cuyahoga county probate court, **CuyR 71.1**
    Contingent fees, **CuyR 71.2 et seq.**
    Personal injury claims, **CuyR 71.2 et seq.**
    Wrongful death settlements, **CuyR 71.2 et seq.**
Eminent domain, abandonment or disallowance of proceeding, **ORC 163.21**
Estates, administration, **CuyR 71.1, LucasR 71.1, ORC 2113.36, Sup. R 71.2, SupR 71**
    Management of real property, **ORC 2113.311**
    Probate court, jurisdiction, **ORC 2113.36**
    Sale of land, **ORC 2127.38**
Fiduciary, attorney for, **LucasR 71.1, SupR 71**
    Personal injury claims, settlement, **CuyR 71.2 et seq.**
    Representation of guardian, **SupR 71**
Franklin county probate court
    Code of Professional Responsibility, **FrankR 71.1**
    Contested fees, **FrankR 71.7**
    Contingent fees, **FrankR 71.8**
    Early payment, **FrankR 71.3**
    Fiduciary, attorney serving as, **FrankR 71.2**
    Notice and consent
        Estates, **FrankR 71.4**
        Guardianships, **FrankR 71.5**
        Trusts, **FrankR 71.6**
Guardianship, **CuyR 71.1, LucasR 71.1, Sup. R 71.3**
Hamilton county probate court, **HamR 71.1**
    Consent to payment of, **HamR Appx A-2**
        Waiver of notice of hearing on application, attached to, **HamR Appx A-3**
    Contingent fee agreements, **HamR 71.2**
    Notice of hearing on application for, **HamR Appx A-1**
        Waiver, **HamR Appx A-3**
Hearing on application for, notice, **HamR Appx A-1**
    Waiver, **HamR Appx A-3**
Hospitalization hearings for indigent mentally ill, **ORC 5122.43**
Insolvent estates, **SumR 71.1(B)**
Institutionalization hearings for indigent mentally retarded, **ORC 5123.96**
Land sale proceedings, **SumR 71.1(C), SumR Appx G**
Lucas county probate court, **LucasR 71.1**
Montgomery county probate court
    Schedule, **MontR Appx A**
Notice, **SumR Appx F**
    Hearing on application for, **HamR Appx A-1**
Paralegal fees, **Sup. R 75.5**
Paralegals, supervision, **CuyR 71.1**
Paternity proceedings, **ORC 3109.25, ORC 3109.26**
Payment, consent, **HamR Appx A-2**
    Waiver of notice of hearing, **HamR Appx A-3**
Personal injuries, settlement
    Minors' claims, **CuyR 71.2 et seq.**
    Wards' claims, **CuyR 71.2 et seq.**
Probate of will, **ORC 2113.36**

ATTORNEY FEES—continued

Stark county probate court
    Decedent's estates, **Sup. R 71.2**
    Estates, **Sup. R 71.2**
    Fiduciary, attorney serving as, **Sup. R 71.1**
    Guardianships, **Sup. R 71.3**
    Paralegal fees, **Sup. R 75.5**
Summit county probate court, **SumR 71.1, SumR Appx E**
    Land sale proceedings, **SumR 71.1(C), SumR Appx G**
    Notice, **SumR Appx F**
Support and maintenance actions. See Child support, this heading
Trust
    Administration of, **CuyR 71.1, LucasR 71.1**
    Remedies for breach of trust, **ORC 5810.04**
Will contests, **ORC 2107.75**
Wrongful death settlement, **CuyR 71.2 et seq.**

ATTORNEY GENERAL

Charitable trusts
    Representation of beneficiary by, **ORC 2109.34**
Child day camp's violation of criminal records check regulation, **ORC 2151.861**
Children's advocacy centers, annual registration, **ORC 2151.426**
Estate tax
    Collection, **ORC 5731.42, ORC 5731.43**
    Confidentiality of information, **ORC 5731.90**
Hospitalization of mentally ill, powers and duties, **ORC 5122.15**
Mental retardation and developmental disabilities institutions, duties, **ORC 5123.90**
Presumed decedents, complaint to establish presumption by, **ORC 2121.02**
Will contests, **ORC 2107.73**

ATTORNEY IN FACT

See POWER OF ATTORNEY

ATTORNEY-CLIENT PRIVILEGE

Child abuse reports, **ORC 2151.421**

ATTORNEYS

Address, notice of change, **LucasR 57.1**
Aged persons suffering neglect, abuse, or exploitation; report to county human services department, **ORC 5101.61**
Appointment, **CuyR 8.1, FrankR 8.1**
    Indigent persons, for. See INDIGENT PERSONS
Attorney general. See ATTORNEY GENERAL
Capital cases, appointment for indigents, **SupR 20**
Child abuse to be reported by, **ORC 2151.421**
Conflict of trial dates, **SupR 41(B)**
Court appointment, **JuvR 29(B), JuvR 4(A)**
    Abortion for minor without parental consent, **SupR 23(B)**
Disciplinary procedure, **O Const IV § 2, O Const IV § 5**
Entries, **HamR 57.1**
Estate, representing, **ORC 2109.03**
    Designation, **LucasR 57.1**
    Fees for administering estate. See ATTORNEY FEES, at Estates, administration
Ethics, **O Const IV § 5**
False statement, representation by agency or adoption attorney, **ORC 3107.011**
Fees. See ATTORNEY FEES
Fiduciary, for, **ORC 2109.03**
    Designation, **LucasR 57.1**
Fiduciary's filings, approval, **SumR 57.1(B)**
Filings, **HamR 57.1**
Guardian ad litem, serving as, **JuvR 4(C)**
Guardians, representation of, **ORC 2111.091**
    Prohibitions, **ORC 2111.091**
Indigents, appointment of counsel in capital cases, **SupR 20**
Juvenile courts. See JUVENILE COURTS
Mentally ill persons, appointment for, **HamR 75.1**

ATTORNEYS—continued
Notice
　Removal hearings, schools and school districts, **JuvR 39(A)**
Out-of-state, **FrankR 75.6**
Practice of law, **O Const IV § 2, O Const IV § 5**
　Probate court judges or clerks, by, **ORC 2101.41**
Pro hac vice, **FrankR 75.6**
Registration number on documents filed with probate court, **SupR 57(B)**
Right to
　Competence hearings, **ORC 2945.37(D)**
　Juvenile proceedings, **JuvR 29(B), JuvR 4(A), ORC 2151.28, ORC 2151.314, ORC 2151.352**
　　Waiver, **JuvR 3**
　Parental rights, termination by court, **ORC 2151.353, ORC 2151.353(B), ORC 2151.414(A)**
Service of process on, **JuvR 20(B)**
Show cause hearings, **HamR 64.2**
Signing of pleadings, **LucasR 57.1**
Sureties, not to act as, **HamR 75.1, SumR 89.1**
Tax department employing, **ORC 5731.43**
Trial attorneys, designation, **SupR 36**
Waiver of right to, juvenile proceedings, **JuvR 3**
Warning, persistent request of continuances, **SupR 41(C)**
Withdrawal, **FrankR 78.2, HamR 57.1**
　Juvenile proceedings, from, **JuvR 4(E)**
Workload
　Warning, **SupR 41(C)**

AUCTIONS
Escheated land, **ORC 2105.09**
Estate
　Personal property, **ORC 2113.40, ORC 2113.41**
　Real property, **ORC 2127.32**
Executors or administrators, by, **ORC 2127.32, ORC 2127.33**
Land sale, **ORC 2127.32**

AUDITORS, COUNTY
Deputies for estate tax matters, **ORC 5731.44**
Eminent domain transfer, journal entry, **ORC 163.15**
Escheat, powers and duties, **ORC 2105.07, ORC 2105.09**
Estate tax, powers and duties, **ORC 5731.44**
　See also ESTATE TAX, generally
　Audits by tax commissioner, assistance, **ORC 5731.26**
　Certificates of tax liability, filing, **ORC 5731.27**
　Certification of return to county treasurer, **ORC 5731.21**
　Collection, **ORC 5731.27**
　Confidentiality of information, **ORC 5731.90**
　Fees and expenses, certification, **ORC 5731.46, ORC 5731.47**
　Refunds, **ORC 5731.27**
　Return, notice, **ORC 5731.21**
　Revenue distribution, **ORC 5731.49**
Estates, fees for services concerning, **ORC 2129.24**
Fees and costs
　Estate tax duties, **ORC 5731.46**
　Estates, services for, **ORC 2129.24**
Income tax, powers and duties
　Estimates of revenues, **ORC 5747.51**
　Income tax, accounting to tax commissioner, **ORC 5747.54**
Juvenile rehabilitation facilities, powers and duties, **ORC 2151.79**
Personal property tax, powers and duties. See PERSONAL PROPERTY, TAXATION, generally
Probate judge's fees, accounting to auditor, **ORC 2101.15, ORC 2101.99**

AUDITS
Estate tax returns by tax commissioner. See ESTATE TAX
Mentally retarded and developmentally disabled persons
　Audits of contracts for residential services for, **ORC 5123.18**

AUTOMOBILES
See MOTOR VEHICLES

AUTOPSIES
Anatomical gifts, rights, **ORC 2108.02**
Consent, **ORC 2108.50 to 2108.52**
Eyes, enucleation during, **ORC 2108.60**
Liability, **ORC 2108.51**
Mentally retarded or developmentally disabled person, petition for post-mortem upon suspicious death, **ORC 2108.521**
Pituitary glands, removal during, **ORC 2108.53**

AWARDS
See DAMAGES

BABIES
See MINORS

BAIL
Generally, **O Const I § 9**
Hearing to deny, **ORC 2937.222**
Recognizance
　Juvenile delinquent, transfer from juvenile court, **ORC 2152.12(F)**

BAILIFFS
Juvenile courts, **ORC 2151.13**
　Cuyahoga county, **ORC 2153.11**
Probate courts, **ORC 2101.11(A)**
Service of process by, **JuvR 17(C)**

BALLOTS
Initiative and referendum, combining probate courts with common pleas courts, **ORC 2101.44**

BANKING DAY
Defined, **ORC 5747.01**

BANKS AND BANKING
Accounts
　Check drawn by fiduciary upon account of principal, liability of bank, **ORC 5815.07**
　Child support payments deducted from
　　Parentage actions, **ORC 3111.13(F)**
　Deposit in name of fiduciary as such, liability of bank, **ORC 5815.06**
　Deposits
　　Estate property, transfer and delivery, **ORC 5731.39**
　Fiduciary, **ORC 5815.04**
　Guardians, restrictions on attorneys representing, **ORC 2111.091**
　Payable on death accounts, **ORC 2131.10**
　Personal credit of fiduciary, deposit to, **ORC 5815.08**
　Transfer of estate property, release by tax commissioner, **ORC 5731.39**
Anatomical gifts, for
　Eye banks, **ORC 2108.60**
Definitions
　Payable on death, **ORC 2131.10, ORC 2131.11**
Deposits. See Accounts, this heading
Eye banks, **ORC 2108.60**
Fiduciary, bank as. See FIDUCIARIES, at Corporate
Fiduciary bank accounts, **ORC 5815.04**
Merger or consolidation, effect on fiduciary duties, **ORC 2109.28**
Safe deposit boxes. See SAFE DEPOSIT BOXES
Savings accounts. See Accounts, this heading
Securities, deposits in, **ORC 2131.21**
Trusts. See TRUST COMPANIES
Uniform Fiduciary Act, **ORC 5815.04**

BATTERED WOMAN SYNDROME
Expert testimony
　Not guilty by reason of insanity plea, **ORC 2945.392**
Not guilty by reason of insanity plea
　Expert testimony, **ORC 2945.392**
　Mental evaluation, **ORC 2945.371**

BATTERY, SEXUAL
DNA testing of prisoners, **ORC 2901.07**

BENEFICIARIES
See also HEIRS; LEGACIES AND DEVISES; NEXT OF KIN
Charitable bequests. See LEGACIES AND DEVISES
Gifts causa mortis. See GIFTS CAUSA MORTIS
Inter vivos gifts. See INTER VIVOS GIFTS, generally
Intestate succession. See DESCENT AND DISTRIBUTION
Trusts. See TRUSTS
Wrongful death actions, **ORC 2125.02, ORC 2125.03**

BENEFICIARY SURROGATE
Defined, **ORC 5801.01**

BEQUESTS
See LEGACIES AND DEVISES

BIDDING, COMPETITIVE
Mental retardation and developmental disabilities department contracts, **ORC 5123.25**

BIFURCATION
Dispositional custody hearing, **JuvR 34(D)**

BILLS OF EXCEPTIONS
Claims against estate, **ORC 2117.04**
Executor and administrator, accounting by, **ORC 2117.17**

BINDOVER ORDERS
Juvenile proceedings, **JuvR 30, ORC 2152.12**

BIRTH
Adoption expenses, **ORC 3107.055**
Certificates. See BIRTH CERTIFICATES
Correction, **CuyR 58.1, SumR 95.1(B)**
Out-of-state, recording, **ORC 3705.09**
Registration, **CuyR 58.1**
    Costs, **ORC 3705.15**
    Fees, **ORC 2101.16**
    Unrecorded birth, **ORC 3705.15**

BIRTH CERTIFICATES
Adoption petitions to include, **ORC 3107.05**
Correction of birth record, **ORC 3705.15**
    Costs, **ORC 3705.15**
    Fees, **ORC 2101.16**
    Parentage judgment, **ORC 3111.13, ORC 3111.58**
Fees, **ORC 2101.16**
Filing, **ORC 3705.09**
Illegitimate child
    Legitimized, **ORC 3705.09**
    New certificate, paternity judgment, **ORC 3111.18**
Legitimized child, **ORC 3705.09**
New
    Correction, **ORC 3705.15**
    Legitimized child, **ORC 3705.09**
Out-of-state birth, place of recording, **ORC 3705.09**
Paternity
    Correction based on judgment, **ORC 3111.13, ORC 3111.58**
    Duty to support child, **ORC 3103.031**
    Legitimized child, **ORC 3705.09**
    Proceedings
      Correction based on judgment, **ORC 3111.13, ORC 3111.58**
      New certificate, **ORC 3111.18**
Probate courts, record, **ORC 2101.12**
Social security numbers to accompany, **ORC 3705.09**
Unrecorded birth, **ORC 3705.15**

BLOOD
Donations
    Age requirement, **ORC 2108.21**
    Dissemination of information, **ORC 2108.21**

BLOOD—continued
Tests
    Alcoholic content analyses, **ORC 4511.19**
    Chemical, **ORC 4511.191**
    Drunk driving, **ORC 4511.19**
    Parentage action, **ORC 3111.09**
    Refusal, **ORC 4511.191**
Transactions, service not sale, **ORC 2108.11**

BOARDING HOMES
Placement of children in, **ORC 5103.16**

BOARDS
See ADMINISTRATIVE AGENCIES AND PROCEDURE

BOATS AND WATERCRAFT
Certificate of title
    Joint ownership with right of survivorship, **ORC 2131.12**
Designation of transfer on death beneficiary, **ORC 1548.072, ORC 2131.13**
Joint ownership with right of survivorship
    Designation in beneficiary form, **ORC 2131.13**
Transfer of ownership
    Joint ownership with right of survivorship, **ORC 2131.12**
    Surviving spouse, to, **ORC 2106.19**

BONA FIDE PURCHASERS
Estate property
    Ancillary administration, **ORC 2129.21**
    Debts, liability, **ORC 2117.36**
    Deed as evidence, **ORC 2127.35**
    Dower interest, **ORC 2103.021**
    Fraudulent transfers, **ORC 2127.40**
    Homicide, seller convicted of, **ORC 2105.19**
    Later will, protection, **ORC 2107.47**
    Pretermitted heir statute, effect, **ORC 2107.34**
    Will contest, effect, **ORC 2107.76**
Estate tax, liability, **ORC 5731.37**

BONDS, SURETY
Accounts
    Franklin county probate court, **FrankR 64.4**
Action on
    Limitation of action, **ORC 2305.12**
Administrative expenses as, **HamR 62.1**
Administrator. See EXECUTORS AND ADMINISTRATORS
Ancillary administration, **ORC 2129.08, ORC 2129.26**
Custodial deposits in lieu of, **FrankR 75.3**
Executors and administrators. See EXECUTORS AND ADMINISTRATORS
Fees, probate court, **ORC 2101.16**
Fiduciaries. See FIDUCIARIES
Forfeiture, adult offenders tried in juvenile courts, **ORC 2151.50**
Franklin county probate court, **FrankR 75.4**
    Accounts, **FrankR 64.4**
    Custodial deposits in lieu of, **FrankR 75.3**
Guardians. See GUARDIANSHIP
Heirs. See HEIRS
Juvenile court personnel, **ORC 2151.13**
    Cuyahoga county, **ORC 2153.08**
    Judges acting as clerks, **ORC 2151.12**
Juvenile proceedings, adult offenders for suspended sentences, **ORC 2151.50**
Juvenile rehabilitation facility superintendent, **ORC 2151.70**
Land sale proceedings, **ORC 2127.27**
    Foreign wards, **ORC 2127.42**
    Objecting party to give, **ORC 2127.31**
Master commissioners, **ORC 2101.06**
Mental retardation and developmental disabilities department, officers and employees, **ORC 5123.10**
Mentally retarded or developmentally disabled person's trustee, **ORC 5123.59**

BONDS, SURETY—continued
Premiums
    Unpaid, closure of estate, guardianship, or trusteeship prohibited, **HamR 62.1**
Presumed decedents' estate, beneficiaries, **ORC 2121.05**
Probate court personnel
    Appointees, **ORC 2101.11, ORC 2101.11(C)**
    Judges, **ORC 2101.03**
    Master commissioners, **ORC 2101.06**
    Record, **ORC 2101.12**
Probation officers, juvenile courts, **ORC 2151.13**
Support and maintenance, guarantee of payments
    Parentage actions, **ORC 3111.13(F)**
Testamentary trustees. See TESTAMENTARY TRUSTEES
Testator, by; effect on legacy or devise, **ORC 2107.33**

BONDS AND NOTES
See also SECURITIES, generally
Estate tax on, **ORC 5731.51**
Fiduciaries, investment powers, **ORC 2109.37**
Surety bonds. See BONDS, SURETY
Trustees, investment powers, **ORC 2109.37**

BROKERS
See REAL ESTATE BROKERS AND SALESPERSONS

BROTHERS
See also NEXT OF KIN
Descent and distribution, **ORC 2105.06**

BUDGET COMMISSIONS, COUNTY
Income tax revenues, powers and duties, **ORC 5747.51**
Tax budgets
    Local government fund revenues, apportionment, **ORC 5747.51 to 5747.55**
        Appeal, **ORC 5747.55**

BUDGETS
Estimates, apportionment of local government fund revenues, **ORC 5747.51 to 5747.55**
Tax, apportionment of local government fund revenues, **ORC 5747.51 to 5747.55**

BUILDING AND LOAN ASSOCIATIONS
Deposits, payable on death, **ORC 2131.10, ORC 2131.11**

BURGLARY
Aggravated, DNA testing of prisoners, **ORC 2901.07**

BURIALS
See FUNERALS AND BURIALS

BUSINESS
Continuation by executors or administrators, **ORC 2113.30**
Corporations. See CORPORATIONS
Eminent domain, effect, **ORC Ch 163**
Partnerships. See PARTNERSHIPS

BUSINESS INCOME
Defined, **ORC 5747.01**

CAMPS AND CAMPING
Child day camp
    Child abuse to be reported by administrators or employees, **ORC 2151.421**
    Criminal records checks, random sampling of registered day camps, **ORC 2151.861**
    Definitions, **ORC 2151.011**
Juvenile rehabilitation, **ORC 2151.65 to 2151.80**
    See also JUVENILE REHABILITATION
Residential camp administrators or employees, child abuse to be reported by, **ORC 2151.421**

CAPITAL IMPROVEMENTS
Eminent domain. See EMINENT DOMAIN, generally

CAPTIONS
Adoption, **ORC 3107.04**

CARETAKER AUTHORIZATION AFFIDAVIT
Grandparent. See GRANDPARENT POWER OF ATTORNEY OR CARETAKER AUTHORIZATION AFFIDAVIT

CARS
See MOTOR VEHICLES

CASE MANAGEMENT
Cuyahoga county probate court, **CuyR 78.1**
Franklin county probate court, **FrankR 78.1**
Hamilton county probate court, **HamR 78.1**
    Civil actions, **HamR 78.2**
Lucas county probate court, **LucasR 78.1**
Stark county probate court, **Sup. R 78.1**
Summit county probate court, **SumR 78.1**

CEMETERIES
Gravestones and monuments, powers of executors and administrators, **ORC 2113.37**
Perpetual care of graves, **ORC 2113.37**

CERTIFICATES
Birth. See BIRTH CERTIFICATES
Death certificate, record at probate court, **ORC 2101.12**
Licenses. See LICENSES AND PERMITS
Motor vehicles. See MOTOR VEHICLES
Notice, of, **LucasR 59.2, LucasR 59.3**
Tax. See particular tax concerned
Transfer, of, **LucasR 78.4**
Trusts, remedies for breach of trust, **ORC 5810.13**

CERTIFIED FOSTER HOME
Definitions, **ORC 2151.011**

CHANGE OF NAME
See NAMES

CHANGE OF VENUE
See VENUE

CHARITABLE CONTRIBUTIONS
See GIFTS AND GRANTS

CHARITABLE INSTITUTIONS
Children, for
    Adoption proceedings, powers and duties, **ORC 5103.15**
        See also ADOPTION AGENCIES
    Certification, **ORC 5103.03, ORC 5103.16**
    Human services department, powers and duties, **ORC 5103.03**
    Placement in, **ORC 5103.15 to 5103.16**
    Reports, **ORC 5103.03**
Patients, mental. See at Institutionalization
Patients, mental. See at Institutionalization. See MENTALLY RETARDED AND DEVELOPMENTALLY DISABLED PERSONS
Reporting requirements, **ORC 2151.37, ORC 2151.40**

CHARITABLE ORGANIZATIONS
Gifts and bequests to, estate tax deductions, **ORC 5731.17**
Institutional Trust Funds Act, **ORC 5813.01 to 5813.07**
    See also INSTITUTIONAL TRUST FUNDS ACT

CHARITABLE TRUSTS
Creation, **ORC 5804.05**
Defined, **ORC 5801.01**
Definitions, **ORC 2109.30**
Probate court jurisdiction, **ORC 2101.24**

CHARITABLE TRUSTS

CHARITABLE TRUSTS—*continued*
Qualified community foundation, merger with; fiduciary duties, **ORC 2109.30**
Service of process, hearing on accounts, **ORC 2109.34**

CHEATING
See FRAUD

CHILD
See MINORS

CHILD ABUSE
Adjudicatory hearing, **JuvR 29(E), ORC 2151.28**
    Findings, **ORC 2151.35**
Advocacy centers. See CHILDREN'S ADVOCACY CENTERS
Alcoholism of parent as grounds
    Assessment and treatment requirement, **ORC 2151.3514**
Attorney representing interests of child, **JuvR 4(A)**
Bad faith reporting of, liability for attorney fees and costs, **ORC 2151.421**
Case plans for children, **ORC 2151.412**
    Administrative review, **ORC 2151.416**
Charges, **ORC 2151.43**
Chemical dependency of parent as grounds
    Assessment and treatment requirement, **ORC 2151.3514**
Child custody jurisdiction based on, **ORC 3109.22(A)**
Children's advocacy centers. See CHILDREN'S ADVOCACY CENTERS
Commitment to custody of public or private agency, **ORC 2151.353(A)**
Complaints, **JuvR 10(A), ORC 2151.27, ORC 2151.44**
    Dismissal, **ORC 2151.35**
Court supervision of parental custody as disposition, **ORC 2151.353(A)**
Custody of child. See CUSTODY OF CHILDREN, INSTITUTIONAL
Defined, **ORC 2151.031**
Detention hearing, **ORC 2151.314**
Drug dependency of parent as grounds
    Assessment and treatment requirement, **ORC 2151.3514**
Emergency medical care, **JuvR 13(C), ORC 2151.33**
Emotional abuse, factor in determining lack of adequate parental care, **ORC 2151.414**
Factor in determining lack of adequate parental care, **ORC 2151.414**
Gifts and grants for prevention of, estate tax deductions, **ORC 5731.17**
Guardian ad litem, appointment, **ORC 2151.281**
Jurisdiction, **ORC 2151.23**
Medical care, emergency order, **ORC 2151.33**
Parental care, factor in determining lack of adequate, **ORC 2151.414**
Penalties, **ORC 2151.99**
Permitting, **ORC 2903.15**
Probable cause finding, **JuvR 13(F)**
Registries, central, **ORC 2151.421**
Removal of abusive person from child's home, **ORC 2151.353**
Report, duty to, **ORC 2151.421**
Report of sexual abuse. See CHILDREN'S ADVOCACY CENTERS
Reporting requirements, **ORC 2151.421**
    Homeless or domestic violence shelters, children living in, **ORC 2151.422**
    Penalties for violations, **ORC 2151.99**
Sexual abuse
    Advocacy center. See CHILDREN'S ADVOCACY CENTERS
    Factor in determining lack of adequate parental care, **ORC 2151.414**
Shelter care, **ORC 2151.28, ORC 2151.314**
Social history, court report, **JuvR 32**
Support of abused children by juvenile court, **ORC 2151.10**
Temporary care orders, **ORC 2151.33**
Unfit parents, **ORC 2151.05**

CHILD DAY CAMPS
See CAMPS AND CAMPING

CHILD STEALING
DNA testing of prisoners, **ORC 2901.07**

CHILD STEALING—*continued*
Uniform Child Custody Jurisdiction Act to prevent, **ORC 3109.21 to 3109.32**

CHILD SUPPORT
See also DEPENDENT AND NEGLECTED CHILDREN
Acknowledgment of paternity
    Filed with division of child support, **ORC 3705.091**
Action for, **ORC 2151.231**
    Parentage action, conversion into, **ORC 2151.232**
Action for order, **ORC 2151.231**
Adjudicatory hearing, **JuvR 29(E)**
Administrative orders
    Parentage actions. See PARENTAGE ACTIONS
    Parents of minor parents subject to, **ORC 3109.19**
Adopted child, **ORC 3103.03(A)**
Age of majority, orders in effect beyond for students or by court issue, **ORC 3103.03(B), ORC 3103.031, ORC 3105.21(D), ORC 3109.05(E), ORC 5101.314**
Allowance from estate of deceased parent, **ORC 2106.13**
Attorney fees, **ORC 3105.21(C)**
Commitment for rehabilitation or protection, **ORC 2151.36**
Complaint, **JuvR 10(A)**
Contempt proceedings to enforce
    Costs and attorney fees, **ORC 3105.21(C), ORC 3109.05(C)**
Divorce or annulment, following, **ORC 3105.21(A)**
Duties, **ORC 3103.031**
    Acknowledgment of paternity, upon, **ORC 5101.314**
    Husband and wife, **ORC 3103.03**
    Parents of minor parents, **ORC 3109.19**
Enforcement agencies. See CHILD SUPPORT ENFORCEMENT AGENCIES, generally
Estates, allowance from, **ORC 2106.13**
    Distribution under summary estate administration to pay, **Sup. R 75.4**
    Priority, **ORC 2117.25**
Failed divorce complaint, court's power to make orders as to children, **ORC 3105.21(B)**
Foster care facilities, in, **ORC 2151.34**
Grandparent power of attorney or caretaker authorization affidavit, effect on child support order, **ORC 3109.79**
Health care needs provided for, **ORC 3109.05(A)**
Hearings
    Parents of minor parents, duty of support imposed, **ORC 3109.19**
High school attendance, continuation during, **ORC 3103.03(B)**
Husband and wife, duties, **ORC 3103.03**
Income tax refunds collected to pay when past-due
    Overpaid child support, **ORC 5747.123**
    State taxes, **ORC 5747.121**
Intercept fund, **ORC 5747.121**
Jurisdiction, **ORC 2151.23, ORC 3109.05(B)**
Juvenile courts
    Actions, for
        Appropriations to provide for, **ORC 2151.10**
        Nonsupport charges, **ORC 2151.43**
        Orders, **ORC 2151.232**
    Certification of case to, **ORC 3109.06**
Marital misconduct, award made without regard to, **ORC 3109.05(A)**
Mental retardation and developmental disabilities department employees, certificates or registration, denial or suspension for noncompliance, **ORC 5123.083**
Notice
    Change in circumstances, parents of minor parents to report, **ORC 3109.19**
Orders
    Age of majority, in effect beyond for students or by court issue, **ORC 3103.03, ORC 3103.031, ORC 3105.21(D), ORC 3109.05(E), ORC 5101.314**
    Compliance, enforcing, **ORC 3105.21(C)**
    Duration, **ORC 3111.13(F)**
    Enforcing compliance, **ORC 2151.23(G)**

CHILD SUPPORT—continued
Orders—continued
> Grandparent power of attorney or caretaker authorization affidavit, effect on, **ORC 3109.79**
> Parents of minor parents subject to, **ORC 3109.19**

Parentage actions. See PARENTAGE ACTIONS, at Administrative support orders, and at Support orders
Parents of minor parents, duty of support imposed, **ORC 3109.19**
Paternity proceedings. See PARENTAGE ACTIONS, at Administrative support orders, and at Support orders
Putative father registry, **ORC 3107.062**
Separation agreements, **ORC 3105.10(B)**
Shared parenting, **ORC 3109.04(G)**
Social history or examination of child, **JuvR 32**
State tax refunds collected to pay when past-due, **ORC 5747.121**
Third party supplying, **ORC 3103.03(C), ORC 3103.03(D)**
Vacations, continuance during, **ORC 3103.03(B)**
Visitation rights
> Denial or interference
>> Escrowing, impoundment, or withholding of support, **ORC 3109.05(D)**
> Motion for visitation rights in action for support, **ORC 3109.051**
> Parents wishes to be considered, **ORC 3111.20 et seq.**

Withholding or deduction
> Child custody actions, **ORC 3105.21(C)**
> Divorce, dissolution, or legal separation actions, **ORC 3109.05(A)**

CHILD SUPPORT ENFORCEMENT AGENCIES
Genetic testing
> Providing, **ORC 3111.61**

Hearings
> Parents of minor parents, duty of support imposed, **ORC 3109.19**

Orders
> Filing with child support division of the human services department, **ORC 5101.314**

Parent and child relationship
> Action to establish brought by, **ORC 3111.04**
>> Parties to actions, **ORC 3111.07**

Paternity proceedings
> See also PARENTAGE ACTIONS, generally
> Genetic test results, disclosure, **ORC 3111.09**
> Liability for cost of genetic tests, **ORC 3111.09**
> Public assistance recipients, paternity determination, **ORC 3111.04, ORC 3111.07**

CHILDBIRTH
See BIRTH

CHILDREN
Generally, See MINORS
Abuse. See CHILD ABUSE
Adoption. See ADOPTION
Custody. See CUSTODY OF CHILDREN, DOMESTIC
Illegitimate. See ILLEGITIMATE CHILDREN
Interstate Compact for the Placement of Children, **ORC 5103.20**
Support. See CHILD SUPPORT

CHILDREN SERVICES BOARDS
Case plans, **ORC 2151.412**
Child abuse, reporting, **ORC 2151.421**
Children's advocacy center, **ORC 2151.426, ORC 2151.427**
Custody of children. See CUSTODY OF CHILDREN, INSTITUTIONAL, generally
Estate of ward, delivery to, **ORC 2111.05**
Grandparent power of attorney or caretaker authorization affidavit, report to public children services agency, **3109.74**
Trustees, as; bond, **ORC 2109.04**

CHILDREN'S ADVOCACY CENTERS
Attorney general, annual registration, **ORC 2151.426**
Counties, memorandum of understanding with other, **ORC 2151.426, ORC 2151.427**
Definitions, **ORC 2151.425**

CHILDREN'S ADVOCACY CENTERS—continued
Employment of staff, **ORC 2151.426**
Interagency agreements re child abuse, **ORC 2151.428**
Jurisdiction, **ORC 2151.426**
Memorandum of understanding with other entities re child abuse, **ORC 2151.426, ORC 2151.427**
Multidisciplinary team, powers and duties, **ORC 2151.427**
Public children services agency, members, **ORC 2151.426, ORC 2151.427**
Reports, generally, **ORC 2151.425**
"Sexual abuse of a child," defined, **ORC 2151.425**

CHIROPRACTORS
Aged persons suffering neglect, abuse, or exploitation; report to county human services department, **ORC 5101.61**

CHRONIC TRUANT
Definitions, **ORC 2151.011**

CHURCHES
See RELIGIOUS ORGANIZATIONS

CITATIONS
Probate court fees, **ORC 2101.16**
Surviving spouse, election. See SURVIVING SPOUSE, at Election by
Wills, production, **ORC 2107.09**

CITIES
See MUNICIPAL CORPORATIONS

CIVIL ACTIONS
See ACTIONS, generally

CIVIL RIGHTS
Mentally ill persons, **ORC 5122.301**
Mentally retarded or developmentally disabled persons, **ORC 5123.83**

CIVIL RULES OF PROCEDURE
Hospitalization hearings for mentally ill, applicability, **ORC 5122.15**
Mentally retarded persons, institutionalization hearings; applicability, **ORC 5123.76**
Paternity proceedings, applicability, **ORC 3111.08**
Will contests, applicability, **ORC 2107.72**

CIVIL SERVICE
See PUBLIC EMPLOYEES

CLAIMS
Complaints. See COMPLAINTS
Counterclaims and cross-claims. See COUNTERCLAIMS AND CROSS-CLAIMS
Estates, against. See CLAIMS AGAINST ESTATES
Pleadings. See PLEADINGS

CLAIMS AGAINST ESTATES
Generally, **ORC Ch 2117**
Acceleration of bar against, **ORC 2117.07, ORC 2129.02**
Actions, **ORC 2107.46, ORC 2117.30 to 2117.35**
> Joinder in one action, **ORC 2117.42**
> Rejected claims, **ORC 2117.12 to 2117.14**

Administrator
> Bringing claim, **ORC Ch 2117**
> Debts due, **ORC 2117.01**

Affidavit supporting, **ORC 2117.08**
Ancillary proceedings, **ORC 2129.04 to 2129.24**
Arbitration, **ORC 2117.09**
Authentication, **ORC 2117.08**
Bad debts, **ORC 2113.33**
Barred claim
> Nonresident executor or administrator, **ORC 2129.02**

Bill of exception, **ORC 2117.04**
Closing the administration prohibited, when, **ORC 2117.06**
Compromise, **ORC 2117.05**
Contingent claims, **ORC 2117.06, ORC 2117.37 to 2117.42**

CLAIMS AGAINST ESTATES—continued
Contributions by devisees and legatees, **ORC 2107.54**
    Insolvent devisee or legatee, effect, **ORC 2107.56**
Controversial, **ORC 2117.09**
Debts due executor or administrator, **ORC 2117.01**
Debts not due, **ORC 2117.28**
Deposit for costs, **FrankR 58.1, FrankR 62.1**
Discharge, **ORC 2115.11, ORC 2115.12**
Disinterested person to represent estate, **ORC 2117.03**
Disputed, **ORC 2117.09**
Distribution, complaint for, **ORC 2109.59**
Estate tax, **ORC Ch 5731**
    See also ESTATE TAX, generally
Executor, debts due, **ORC 2117.01**
Exemption of devises or bequests, **ORC 2107.54**
Filing
    Deposit for costs, **FrankR 58.1, FrankR 62.1**
Hearings and notices, **ORC 2117.02, ORC 2117.17, SupR 62(B)**
Insolvent devisee or legatee, effect, **ORC 2107.56**
Insolvent estate, **ORC 2117.15, ORC 2117.17**
Interest owed by decedent, **ORC 2117.06, ORC 2117.18**
    Sale proceeds to satisfy, **ORC 2127.38**
Joinder of actions, **ORC 2117.42**
Liability, **ORC 2107.54**
    Funeral expenses when irrevocable preneed funeral contract purchased, **ORC Ch 2117.251**
    Real property, **ORC 2117.36**
Liens, **ORC 2117.10**
Limitation of actions, **ORC 2113.17, ORC 2117.06, ORC 2117.12, ORC 2117.33**
    Acceleration of bar against, **ORC 2117.07, ORC 2129.02**
    Contingent claims, **ORC 2117.37 to 2117.42**
    Distribution of assets prior to expiration of filing period, notice, **ORC 2117.06**
    Foreign executor or administrator, **ORC 2129.02**
Mortgages, **ORC 2117.29**
    Debt payments, effect of contributions to, **ORC 2107.54**
    No right of exoneration, **ORC 2113.52**
Nonresident decedents, **ORC 2129.12**
Notice of rejection, **ORC 2117.11**
Order of payment, **ORC 2117.25**
Payment, **ORC 2113.25, ORC 2117.15**
    Complaint for, **ORC 2109.59**
    Contingent claims, **ORC 2117.38, ORC 2117.41**
    Contribution, **ORC 2107.54, ORC 2107.56**
    Priority, **ORC 2117.25**
    Residuary estate, from, **ORC 2127.38**
    Undevised real property, **ORC 2107.53**
Preneed funeral contract purchased, liability for funeral expenses when contract is irrevocable, **ORC Ch 2117.251**
Presentation, **ORC 2117.06**
Priority, **ORC 2117.25**
Probate court, filing claim with, **ORC 2117.06**
Proof, **ORC 2117.08**
Rejection, **ORC 2117.06, ORC 2117.11 to 2117.15, SupR 62(A)**
    Requisition of heir, devisee, or legatee, **ORC 2117.13**
Reserve funds to satisfy, **ORC 2113.53, ORC 2113.54**
Residuary estate, payable from, **ORC 2127.38**
Return of distributed assets to satisfy, **ORC 2113.53**
Schedule, **ORC 2115.09, SupR 62(B)**
Settlement, **ORC 2117.05**
Tax assessments, **ORC 2117.06, ORC 2117.18, ORC 2117.19**
United States, by
    Priority, **ORC 2117.25**
Will clause, **ORC 2127.39**

CLERGY
Aged persons suffering neglect, abuse, or exploitation; report to county human services department, **ORC 5101.61**
Mentally retarded and developmentally disabled persons, reporting abuse or neglect, **ORC 5123.61, ORC 5123.99**

CLERKS OF COURTS
Common pleas courts
    Juvenile court clerks, as, **ORC 2151.12**
Records
    Juvenile delinquency complaint, when victim 65 or older or disabled, **ORC 2152.71**

CODICILS
Contested, **ORC 2107.71 to 2107.77**
    See also CONTEST OF WILL, generally
Revocation of will by, **ORC 2107.33 to 2107.38**

COERCION
Marriage annulled due to, **ORC 3105.31(E)**
Trusts, creation induced by fraud, duress, or undue influence, **ORC 5804.06**

COGNOVIT NOTES
Claims against estate on, **ORC 2117.06**

COMMENCEMENT OF ACTIONS
See ACTIONS, generally

COMMERCIAL DRIVERS' LICENSES
Age requirement, **ORC 4507.08**
Anatomical gift, provision for, **ORC 2108.04**
Denial
    Convicted of certain violations, **ORC 4510.31, ORC 4510.33**
Suspension or revocation, **ORC 4510.31, ORC 4510.33**
    Drivers' licenses and temporary instruction permits, restrictions, **ORC 4507.08**

COMMERCIAL TRANSACTIONS
Fraudulent transfers, **ORC Ch 1336**

COMMITMENT
Children. See CUSTODY OF CHILDREN, INSTITUTIONAL
Jail, to. See IMPRISONMENT
Mentally ill. See MENTALLY ILL PERSONS, at Hospitalization
Mentally retarded. See MENTALLY RETARDED AND DEVELOPMENTALLY DISABLED PERSONS, at Institutionalization

COMMON LAW
Marriages. See COMMON LAW MARRIAGES
Perpetuities, rule against, **ORC 2131.08**
Survival of actions, **ORC 2305.21**

COMMON LAW MARRIAGES
Evidence of, **ORC 3105.12(A)**
Prohibition, **ORC 3105.12(B)**

COMMON LAW RULE AGAINST PERPETUITIES
Generally, **ORC 2131.08**

COMMON PLEAS COURTS
See COURTS OF COMMON PLEAS

COMMUNICABLE DISEASES
Sex offense victim, notice of accused's disease, **ORC 2151.14**

COMMUNITY CAPITAL REPLACEMENT FACILITIES FUND
Mental retardation and developmental disabilities boards, county, **ORC 5126.375**

COMMUNITY SERVICE
Parental liability for acts of child, community service in lieu of judgment in favor of school district, **ORC 3109.09**

COMMUNITY-BASED CORRECTIONAL FACILITIES AND PROGRAMS
DNA testing of prisoners, **ORC 2901.07**

COMPACTS, INTERSTATE
See INTERSTATE AGREEMENTS

COMPANIES
See BUSINESS; CORPORATIONS

COMPENSATION
Administrators. See EXECUTORS AND ADMINISTRATORS
Appraisers. See INVENTORY AND APPRAISAL OF ESTATES, at Appraisers
Attorneys. See ATTORNEY FEES
Decedent's wages, release by employer, **ORC 2113.04**
Detention home employees, **ORC 2151.34**
Eminent domain. See EMINENT DOMAIN
Executors. See EXECUTORS AND ADMINISTRATORS
Fiduciaries. See FIDUCIARIES
Guardians. See GUARDIANSHIP
Guardians ad litem, **JuvR 4(F), SumR 91.1(C)**
    Computation, **FrankR 73.1**
    Indigent Guardianship Fund, **FrankR 73.2**
Juvenile court employees, **ORC 2151.13**
    Detention home employees, **ORC 2151.34**
Juvenile rehabilitation facilities
    Boards of trustees, **ORC 2151.69, ORC 2151.80**
    Superintendent, **ORC 2151.70**
Mental retardation and developmental disabilities department
    Citizen's advisory councils, **ORC 5123.092**
Tax agents, estate tax matters, **ORC 5731.41**
Transfers to Minors Act, **ORC 5814.05**
Trustees. See TRUSTEES
Uniform Principal and Income Act, **ORC 5812.32**

COMPETENCY
Adjudication, probate court fee, **ORC 2101.16**
Defendants. See DEFENDANTS, at Incompetent to stand trial
Fiduciaries, issuer of securities may treat holders of record as competent, **ORC 5815.03**

COMPLAINTS
See also PETITIONS; PLEADINGS
Abortion for minor without parental consent, **ORC 2151.85, SupR 23(A), SupR Form 23-A to SupR Form 23-D**
    Instructions, **SupR Form 23-A Instructions**
Abused or neglected adult, **ORC 5126.33**
Child abuse, **JuvR 10(A), ORC 2151.27, ORC 2151.44**
    Dismissal, **ORC 2151.35**
Contents, **JuvR 10(B)**
Custody of child, **JuvR 10(A), JuvR 10(E), JuvR 10(F), JuvR 10(D), ORC 2151.27**
Defect in, **JuvR 22(D)**
Delinquent child, **JuvR 10(A), ORC 2151.27**
    Victim of delinquent 65 or older or disabled, record, **ORC 2151.27(D), ORC 2152.71**
Divorce, **ORC 3105.17**
Durable power of attorney for health care, decisions and determinations made under, **ORC 1337.16, ORC 2101.24**
Form, **JuvR 10(B)**
Incompetent to stand trial, complaint to restore heirship rights, **ORC 2105.19**
Inheritance from dead victim, complaint to restore right to, **ORC 2105.19**
Juvenile actions. See JUVENILE COURTS
Juvenile courts, **JuvR 10**
Land sale proceedings, **ORC 2127.10**
Legal separation, **ORC 3105.17**
Mental retardation and developmental disabilities department, administrative resolution procedures, **ORC 5123.043**
Neglect of child, **JuvR 10(A)**
Not guilty by reason of insanity, complaint to restore heirship rights, **ORC 2105.19**
Presumed decedent, establishment of presumption, **ORC 2121.02**
Related cases, certification of, **LucasR 57.1**
Removal action, **JuvR 10(A)**

COMPLAINTS—*continued*
Rules of juvenile procedure, **JuvR 10**
Unruly child, **JuvR 10(A)**

COMPROMISES
See SETTLEMENTS

COMPUTERS
Juvenile courts
    Computerization, costs applied to, **ORC 2151.541, ORC 2153.081**
Probate courts
    Computerization, costs applied to, **ORC 2101.162**

CONCEALMENT
Estate assets. See ASSETS OF ESTATES
Wills
    Withholding, **ORC 2107.09, ORC 2107.10**

CONCLUSIONS OF LAW
Juvenile court, **JuvR 29(F), ORC 2151.353(A)**
Visitation rights, **ORC 3109.051(F), ORC 3109.11, ORC 3109.12(B)**

CONCURRENT JURISDICTION
Judicial proceedings, **ORC 5802.03**
Marion County, probate court judges, concurrent jurisdiction with domestic relations-juvenile divisions, **ORC 2101.022**

CONDEMNATION OF PROPERTY
Generally, **ORC Ch 163**
See also EMINENT DOMAIN

CONFIDENTIAL INFORMATION
Abortion
    Minor without parental consent, **ORC 2151.85**
        Complaint, **SupR 23(H)**
        Notifying physicians of affidavits alleging abuse, **SupR 24**
Abortion without parental consent records, **ORC 2151.85**
Address, children services agency employee, residential address, **ORC 2151.142**
Adoption records, **ORC 3107.17, ORC 3107.52, SupR 55(C)**
    Penalties for breach of confidentiality, **ORC 3107.43, ORC 3107.99**
    Unauthorized disclosure, contempt, **SupR 55(D)**
Aged persons suffering neglect, abuse, or exploitation; reports to county human services department, **ORC 5101.61**
Artificial insemination records, **ORC 3111.94**
Child abuse reports, **ORC 2151.421**
Children services agency employee, residential address, **ORC 2151.142**
Disclosure
    Adoption records, **SupR 55(D)**
    Mental illness proceedings, **SupR 55(D)**
    Probate courts, **ORC 2151.423**
Estate tax documents, **ORC 5731.90**
Estate tax returns, **ORC 5731.90**
Incompetent to stand trial
    Evaluation of mental condition confidential, **ORC 2945.371**
Institutionalization of mentally retarded, records, **ORC 5123.89**
Mental illness proceedings, probate, **SupR 55(C)**
    Unauthorized disclosure, contempt, **SupR 55(D)**
Mental retardation proceedings, probate
    Unauthorized disclosure, contempt, **SupR 55(D)**
Not guilty by reason of insanity
    Evaluation of mental condition confidential, **ORC 2945.371**
Probation records of juveniles, **ORC 2151.14**
Protective orders limiting discovery, **JuvR 24(B)**
Residential address
    Children services agency employee, **ORC 2151.142**
Waiver, **ORC 2151.141**

CONFINEMENT
See IMPRISONMENT

CONFLICT OF INTEREST

CONFLICT OF INTEREST
Judges
    Probate courts, **ORC 2101.38, ORC 2101.39, ORC 2101.41**
        Penalties for violations, **ORC 2101.99**
Mentally retarded and developmentally disabled persons, providers of residential services for, **ORC 5123.042**
Parent and child, in juvenile proceedings, **JuvR 4(B)**
Probate court referees, **ORC 2101.41**
    Penalties for violations, **ORC 2101.99**

CONSANGUINITY
Equal degree of descendants, **ORC 2105.12**

CONSERVANCY DISTRICTS
Eminent domain, **ORC 163.02**

CONSERVATORS
Income tax, filing of state returns, **ORC 5747.08(B)**
Limitation on personal liability, **ORC 2111.151**

CONSERVATORSHIP
Generally, **ORC 2111.021**
Court costs, **Sup. R 58.1**
Defined, **ORC 2111.01**

CONSIGNMENT OF ART WORKS TO DEALERS
Continuation of trust after purchase by dealer for own account, **ORC 5815.43**
Creditors, not subject to claims of dealer's creditors, **ORC 5815.44**
Definitions, **ORC 5815.41**
Display required consent of artist and notice to viewers as to artist's identity, **ORC 5815.46**
Special damages for certain violations by dealers, **ORC 5815.48**
Trusts, **ORC 5815.42**
Waiver of statutory provisions void, **ORC 5815.47**
Work of art, defined, **ORC 5815.41**
Written contract required of dealer, **ORC 5815.45**

CONSOLIDATION
Trust companies, effect on fiduciary duties, **ORC 2109.28**

CONSTABLES
See also LAW ENFORCEMENT OFFICERS
Amercement, **ORC 2101.10**
Execution of judgment, collection of moneys for probate courts by, **ORC 2101.10**
Fees, service of process, **ORC 2101.16**
Liability
    Collection of moneys for probate courts, **ORC 2101.10**
    Penalties, **ORC 2101.99**
    Service of process, **ORC 2101.09**
Service of process by, **JuvR 17(C)**
    Fees, **ORC 2101.16**
    Probate courts, **ORC 2101.09**
        Fees, **ORC 2101.16**
        Penalties for violations, **ORC 2101.99**

CONSTITUTIONALITY
Appeals on questions of, jurisdiction, **O Const IV § 2**

CONSTRUCTION OF STATUTES
See STATUTORY CONSTRUCTION

CONSTRUCTION OF WILLS
Generally, **ORC 2101.24, ORC 2106.03, ORC 2107.46 to 2107.59**
Action for, **ORC 2106.06**
Fee, **ORC 2101.16**
Fiduciary, action by, **ORC 2106.06**

CONSULS
Death of alien, notice to, **ORC 2113.11**

CONTEMPT
Adoption records, unauthorized disclosure, **SupR 55(D)**

CONTEMPT—continued
Child support actions
    Costs and attorney fees, **ORC 3105.21(C), ORC 3109.05(C)**
Costs and attorney fees, **ORC 2151.23(G)**
    Paternity proceedings, **ORC 3111.13(F)**
Discovery, noncompliance, **JuvR 17(F)**
Executors and administrators. See EXECUTORS AND ADMINISTRATORS
Fiduciaries. See FIDUCIARIES
Genetic tests, failure to submit to, **ORC 3111.08, ORC 3111.09**
Juvenile courts. See JUVENILE COURTS
Paternity proceedings, enforcement of support orders, **ORC 3111.15**
Probate court, **ORC 2101.23**
    Adoption records, unauthorized disclosure, **SupR 55(D)**
    Fiduciary's embezzlement of trust assets, **ORC 2109.51**
    Mental illness proceedings, unauthorized disclosure, **SupR 55(D)**
    Mental retardation proceedings, unauthorized disclosure, **SupR 55(D)**
    Removal of records, **SupR 55(A)**
Support and maintenance action
    Costs and attorney fees, **ORC 2151.23(G)**
    Paternity proceedings, **ORC 3111.13(F)**
Visitation rights
    Interference with, **ORC 3109.051(K)**

CONTEST OF WILL
Generally, **ORC 2107.71 to 2107.77**
Attorney fees, **ORC 2107.75**
Court costs, **ORC 2107.75**
Destroyed records, effect, **ORC 2107.31**
Distribution, effect on, **ORC 2113.53**
Executors' and administrators' powers during, **ORC 2113.21**
Foreign will, **ORC 2107.48**
Jurisdiction, **ORC 2101.24, ORC 2107.12**
    See also PROBATE OF WILLS, at Jurisdiction
Jury trial, **ORC 2107.72**
Later wills, **ORC 2107.77**
Limitation of action, **ORC 2107.31, ORC 2107.76**
Parties, **ORC 2107.73**
Powers of fiduciaries during, **ORC 2113.21**
Prima facie evidence, **ORC 2107.74**
Probate court order, effect, **ORC 2107.74**
Rules of civil procedure to govern, **ORC 2107.72**
Venue, **ORC 2107.71**

CONTINUANCES
Common pleas court cases, **SupR 41**
Conflict of trial dates, due to, **SupR 41(B)**
Indulgent or excessive, investigation
    County courts, **SupR 41(D)**
    Courts of common pleas, **SupR 41(D)**
    Municipal courts, **SupR 41(D)**
Juvenile proceedings, **JuvR 23, JuvR 24(C)**
    Adjudicatory hearings, **JuvR 29(A)**
    Dispositional hearing, **JuvR 34(A)**
Motions for, **FrankR 78.1, HamR 78.1, LucasR 78.1, SumR 56.1, Sup. R 78.7, SupR 41**
Probate courts, **SupR 56**
Reporting, **SupR 41(D)**
Witness unavailable, due to, **SupR 41**

CONTRACTS
See also CONTRACTS, PUBLIC
Age of majority, **ORC 3109.01**
Agreement to make will, **ORC 2107.04**
Claims against estate arising out of, **ORC 2117.06**
Fiduciaries, liability, **ORC 5815.35**
Husband or wife entering into, **ORC 3103.05**
Legal age, **ORC 3109.01**
Mentally retarded and developmentally disabled persons, director to pay facility replacement costs, **ORC 5123.373**
Public. See CONTRACTS, PUBLIC

CONTRACTS—*continued*
Secured transactions. See SECURED TRANSACTIONS
Statute of frauds, **ORC 1335.05**
Testator, by; effect on legacy or devise, **ORC 2107.33**
Will
    Agreement to make, **ORC 2107.04**
    Execution, **ORC 2107.04**
Written, statute of frauds, **ORC 1335.05**

CONTRACTS, PUBLIC
Mental retardation and developmental disabilities department, **ORC 5123.25**
    Fiduciary capacity, liability, **ORC 5815.35**
    Residential services, **ORC 5123.18**
Statutes impairing obligations, **O Const II § 28**

CONTRIBUTION
Devisee or legatee, by, **ORC 2107.54 to 2107.57**
    Real property sale to satisfy, **ORC 2127.38**

CONTRIBUTIONS, CHARITABLE
See GIFTS AND GRANTS

CONTROLLED SUBSTANCES
Abuse. See DRUG OFFENSES

CONVERSION
Embezzlement. See EMBEZZLEMENT

CONVEYANCES
See also DEEDS; LEASES
Charge on title to property, intestate succession, **ORC 2106.11**
Dower interest
    Effect, **ORC 2103.02 to 2103.03**
    In lieu of, **ORC 2103.03**
Estate property, **ORC 2127.011, ORC 2127.35, ORC 2127.36**
    See also ASSETS OF ESTATES, at Sale; LAND SALE PROCEEDINGS
    Completion of contracts by fiduciaries
        Executors and administrators, **ORC 2113.48**
        Guardians, **ORC 2111.19**
    Debts, liability for, **ORC 2117.36**
    Nonresident decedent's, **ORC 2129.21**
    Released from administration, **ORC 2113.03**
    Vacation of order settling account, **ORC 2109.35**
    Validity, **ORC 2113.23**
Fraudulent, **ORC 2109.56**
Power of attorney, **1337.01 et seq., ORC Ch 1337**
Presumed decedent's property, **ORC 2121.05, ORC 2121.07**
Revocation of will, effect, **ORC 2107.33, ORC 2107.35**
Rule in Shelley's case, **ORC 2107.49**
Survivorship tenancy, **ORC 5302.17**
    Terminated when property conveyed, **ORC 5302.20**
Tax title to real property by guardian, **ORC 2111.22**
Transfer-on-death deeds, **ORC 5302.22 et seq.**
Trust assets
    Dishonest intent, **ORC 2109.56**
    Vacation of order settling account, **ORC 2109.35**
Will revocation, effect, **ORC 2107.33, ORC 2107.35**

CONVICTS
See PRISONERS

CORONERS
Aged persons suffering neglect, abuse, or exploitation; report to county human services department, **ORC 5101.61**
Amercement, **ORC 2101.10**
Anatomical gifts, powers and functions, **ORC 2108.02**
Child abuse, reporting, **ORC 2151.421**
Execution of judgment
    Collection of moneys for probate courts by, **ORC 2101.10**
    Enforcement for probate courts, **ORC 2101.35**
Failure to perform duty, **ORC 2101.10**

CORONERS—*continued*
Fees and costs
    Probate court, **ORC 2101.16**
Liability
    Collection of moneys for probate courts, **ORC 2101.10**
    Penalties, **ORC 2101.99**
    Service of process, **ORC 2101.09**
Probate court, duties, **ORC 2101.09, ORC 2101.10**
    Penalties for violations, **ORC 2101.99**
Service of process by, **JuvR 17(C)**
    Probate courts, **ORC 2101.09**
        Penalties for violations, **ORC 2101.99**

CORPORATIONS
Dissolution
    Fiduciary responsibilities, **ORC 2109.26**
Fiduciaries, as. See FIDUCIARIES
Guardianship of estates, **ORC 2111.10**
Legacies or devises to. See LEGACIES AND DEVISES, at Charitable bequests
Nonprofit. See NONPROFIT CORPORATIONS
Receivership, service of process on, **ORC 2305.19**
Securities. See SECURITIES
Service of process on, receivership, **ORC 2305.19**
Stock. See STOCK

CORPSES
Anatomical gifts, **ORC Ch 2108**
    See also ANATOMICAL GIFTS
Autopsies, **ORC 2108.50 to 2108.60**
Burials. See FUNERALS AND BURIALS

CORRECTIONAL INSTITUTIONS
Detention of minors in, **ORC 2152.26**
    Processing purposes, for, **ORC 2151.311**
DNA testing of prisoners, **ORC 2901.07**

CORRUPTION
Arbitrators of civil suits, **SupR 15**

CORRUPTION OF MINOR
DNA testing of prisoners, **ORC 2901.07**

COSTS
See FEES AND COSTS

COUNSELORS
Child abuse to be reported by, **ORC 2151.421**

COUNTERCLAIMS AND CROSS-CLAIMS
Divorce, **ORC 3105.17**
Legal separation, **ORC 3105.17**

COUNTIES
Administrative agencies. See particular agency or office
Appropriations
    Detention homes, **ORC 2151.34**
    Family foster homes, **ORC 2151.331**
    Juvenile courts, to, **ORC 2151.10**
    Juveniles, for
        Committed by court, support and maintenance, **ORC 2151.36**
        Rehabilitation facilities, **ORC 2151.77**
    Probate courts, to, **ORC 2101.11, ORC 2101.11(B)**
Assessments by, juvenile rehabilitation facilities, **ORC 2151.66, ORC 2151.78**
Auditors. See AUDITORS, COUNTY
Budgets
    Income tax revenues, inclusion, **ORC 5747.51**
Children's advocacy centers, **ORC 2151.426, ORC 2151.427**
Commissioners. See COUNTY COMMISSIONERS
Employees. See PUBLIC EMPLOYEES
Funds
    See also FUNDS, PUBLIC, for general provisions

COUNTIES—*continued*
Funds—*continued*
General fund
Escheat, proceeds from, **ORC 2105.09**
Income tax revenues, **ORC 5747.51 to 5747.55**
Marriage solemnization fees, probate judge collecting, **ORC 2101.27**
Local government fund
Income tax revenues credited to, **ORC 5747.51**
Undivided local government fund
Apportionment, **ORC 5747.51**
Alternative method, **ORC 5747.53**
Income tax revenues credited to, **ORC 5747.51**
Withholding of state revenues, **ORC 5747.54**
Gifts and bequests to, estate tax deductions, **ORC 5731.17**
Hospitalization and associated costs for mentally ill persons
Reimbursement by mental health department, **ORC 5122.43**
Juvenile proceedings, reimbursement to court, **ORC 2151.36**
Juvenile rehabilitation facilities, **ORC 2151.65 to 2151.80**
See also JUVENILE REHABILITATION
Police. See SHERIFFS
Prosecutors. See PROSECUTORS, COUNTY
Recorders. See RECORDERS, COUNTY
Securities
Juvenile courts, computerization, **ORC 2151.541, ORC 2153.081**
Probate courts, computerization, **ORC 2101.162**

COUNTRIES, FOREIGN
See FOREIGN COUNTRIES

COUNTY
See COUNTIES

COUNTY AUDITORS
See AUDITORS, COUNTY

COUNTY COMMISSIONERS
See also COUNTIES, generally
Courts of appeals, duties, **O Const IV § 3**
Detention homes
Establishment, **ORC 2151.34**
Funding, **ORC 2152.43**
Family foster homes, powers and duties, **ORC 2151.331**
Juvenile courts, appropriations, **ORC 2151.10**

COUNTY COURTS
Arbitration, **SupR 15**
Assignment of cases, **SupR 36**
Clerks, powers and duties. See CLERKS OF COURTS, generally
Continuances
Reporting, **SupR 41(D)**
Costs. See COURT COSTS
Court reporters, **SupR 11**
Destruction of court records, **SupR 26(E)**
Equipment and supplies
Videotaping, **SupR 13**
Judges
Assignment, temporary, **O Const IV § 5**
Assignment of cases, **SupR 36**
Cases, assignment of, **SupR 36**
Code of Judicial Conduct, **O Const IV § 5**
Records and reports
Continuances, **SupR 41(D)**
Court records, management and retention, **SupR 26**
Administrative records, retention schedule, **SupR 26.01**
Rules of superintendence. See RULES OF SUPERINTENDENCE
Sessions, **SupR 36**
Transcripts, delivery to appeals courts, **SupR 11**
Videotape recording of proceedings, **SupR 11**

COUNTY HOMES
Mentally retarded, temporary detention in, **ORC 5123.77**

COURT COSTS
Adoption fees, **SumR Appx B**
Disclosure of information petition, **ORC 2101.16(F)**
Anatomical gifts, **ORC 2108.85**
Assault by minor, **ORC 3109.10**
Child support actions, **ORC 3105.21(C), ORC 3109.05(C)**
Custody actions. See CUSTODY OF CHILDREN, DOMESTIC
Cuyahoga county probate court, **CuyR 58.1**
Deposits, **CuyR 58.1, HamR 58.1, HamR Appx D, LucasR 58.1, SumR 58.1, SumR Appx A, Sup. R 58.1**
Additional, **SumR 58.1**
Computerized research services, for, **SumR 58.1**
Destruction of property offense, minor defendant, **ORC 3109.09**
Dispute resolution procedures, implementation of
Juvenile courts, **ORC 2151.542**
Probate courts, **ORC 2101.163**
Dower actions, **ORC 5305.14**
Electronically recorded transcripts, **SupR 11**
Eminent domain proceedings, abandonment, **ORC 163.21**
Hamilton county probate court, **HamR 58.1**
Deposits, schedule, **HamR Appx D**
Schedule, **HamR Appx D**
Juvenile courts, **ORC 2151.54**
Lucas county probate court, **LucasR 58.1**
Parentage actions, **ORC 3111.14**
Genetic tests taxed as, **ORC 3111.09**
Inappropriate forum, party who commenced proceedings to pay, **ORC 3109.25(G)**
Violation necessitating action, out-of-state decree, **ORC 3109.26(C)**
Stark county probate court, **Sup. R 58.1**
Subpoenas
Juvenile proceedings, **JuvR 17(B)**
Summit county probate court, **SumR 58.1, SumR Appx A**
Support and maintenance actions, **ORC 2151.23(G)**
Paternity proceedings, **ORC 3111.13(F)**
Theft offense, minor defendant, **ORC 3109.09**
Videotape depositions and evidence, **SupR 13**
Visitation rights proceeding, waiver, **ORC 3109.051(L)**
Witnesses. See WITNESSES AND TESTIMONY, at Fees and costs

COURT REPORTERS
Compensation
Hospitalization hearings for mentally ill, **ORC 5122.43**
Institutionalization hearings for mentally retarded, **ORC 5123.96**
Costs, responsibility for, **SumR 54.2(C)**
County courts, **SupR 11**
Municipal courts, **SupR 11**
Probate courts, **ORC 2101.08, ORC 2101.11**
Appointment, **ORC 2101.11(A)**

COURT RULES
See RULES OF COURTS

COURTHOUSES
Juvenile courts, **ORC 2151.09**

COURTS
Generally, **O Const I § 16, O Const IV**
See also particular court by name
Actions. See ACTIONS
Administration, **O Const IV § 5**
Appellate. See APPEALS
Appellate. See APPEALS; COURTS OF APPEALS; SUPREME COURT
Clerks. See CLERKS OF COURTS
Common pleas. See COURTS OF COMMON PLEAS
Contempt. See CONTEMPT
Costs. See COURT COSTS
Judges. See JUDGES
Judgments. See JUDGMENTS
Jurisdiction. See JURISDICTION

COURTS—*continued*
Jury trials. See JURY TRIALS
Juvenile, **ORC Ch 2151**
    See also JUVENILE COURTS
Magistrates. See MAGISTRATES
Pleadings. See PLEADINGS
Powers, **O Const IV § 1**
Probate, **ORC Ch 2101**
    See also PROBATE COURTS
Records and reports, **O Const IV § 5**
Referees. See REFEREES
Reporters. See COURT REPORTERS
Rules. See RULES OF COURTS
Service of process. See SERVICE OF PROCESS
Supreme court. See SUPREME COURT, STATE
Term, expiration; effect on time computation, **JuvR 18(C)**
Trials. See TRIALS
Venue. See VENUE
Verdicts. See VERDICTS
Witnesses. See WITNESSES AND TESTIMONY

COURTS OF APPEALS
See also APPEALS, generally
Appropriations
    Probate courts, for; powers and duties, **ORC 2101.11(B)**
Case reporting, **O Const IV § 3**
Clerks. See CLERKS OF COURTS, generally
County commissioners, duties, **O Const IV § 3**
Courtroom, **O Const IV § 3**
Destruction of court records, **SupR 26(E)**
Districts, **O Const IV § 3**
Docket
    Custody appeals, priority, **ORC 3109.04(H), ORC 3109.06**
    Priority, actions concerning juvenile court appropriations, **ORC 2151.10**
Judges
    Assignment
        Another appeals court, temporary assignment to, **O Const IV § 2**
        Supreme court, temporary assignment to, **O Const IV § 2**
        Temporary, **O Const IV § 5**
    Code of Judicial Conduct, **O Const IV § 5**
    Disqualification, **O Const IV § 4, O Const IV § 5**
    Domestic relations division of common pleas court, **ORC 2301.03**
    Number, **O Const IV § 3**
    Supreme court, sitting in, **O Const IV § 2**
Judgments, **O Const IV § 3**
Jurisdiction, **O Const IV § 3**
Powers, **O Const IV § 1**
Records and reports
    Court records, management and retention, **SupR 26**
        Administrative records, retention schedule, **SupR 26.01**
Rules of superintendence. See RULES OF SUPERINTENDENCE
Terms, **O Const IV § 3**

COURTS OF COMMON PLEAS
See also PROBATE COURTS
Appointment powers
    Committee to investigate insanity of spouse, **ORC 5305.18, ORC 5305.19**
    Dower commissioners, **ORC 5305.06**
    Receivers
        Mentally retarded and developmentally disabled persons, facilities for, **ORC 5123.191**
    Appointments
        Attorneys, indigent defendants, capital cases, **SupR 20**
Arbitration, **SupR 15**
Capital cases, appointment of counsel for indigent defendants, **SupR 20**
Clerks
    See also CLERKS OF COURTS, generally
    Juvenile court clerks, as, **ORC 2151.12**
Confession of judgment, **ORC 2101.34**

COURTS OF COMMON PLEAS—*continued*
Contempt. See CONTEMPT, generally
Continuances in cases, **SupR 41**
Costs. See Fees and costs, this heading
Custody disputes, mediators, **SupR 16**
Destruction of court records, **SupR 26(E)**
Divisions, **O Const IV § 4**
    Domestic relations. See Domestic relations division, this heading
    Probate. See PROBATE COURTS
Divorce
    Hearing, **ORC 3105.10(A)**
Domestic relations division
    Child support, **ORC 3105.10(B)**
    Judges, **ORC 2301.03**
    Juvenile courts, **ORC Ch 2151**
        See also JUVENILE COURTS
    Referees. See REFEREES
Employees
    Operators for videotape equipment, **SupR 13**
Equipment and supplies
    Videotape, **SupR 13**
Estate taxes, delinquent, **ORC 5731.42**
Execution of judgment. See EXECUTION OF JUDGMENT
Fees and costs
    See also COURT COSTS, generally
    Eminent domain proceedings, **ORC 163.15, ORC 163.16**
        Abandonment, **ORC 163.21**
    Probate courts, applicability, **ORC 2101.15, ORC 2101.18**
Fiduciaries
    Payment or distribution by, complaint for, **ORC 2109.60**
Garnishment. See GARNISHMENT, generally
Income tax, powers and duties, **ORC 5747.13(C)**
Judges, **O Const IV § 4**
    Administrative judges
        Domestic relations division, **ORC 2301.03**
    Assignment, temporary, **O Const IV § 5**
    Code of Judicial Conduct, **O Const IV § 5**
    Compensation
        Probate judges, acting as, **ORC 2101.37**
    Disqualification, **O Const IV § 5**
    Domestic relations division, **ORC 2301.03**
    Juvenile courts. See JUVENILE COURTS
    Number of, **O Const IV § 4**
    Presiding judges, selection, **O Const IV § 4**
    Probate judges, as, **ORC 2101.37**
Judgments by confession, **ORC 2101.34**
Jurisdiction, **O Const IV § 4, ORC 2101.25**
    Paternity proceedings, **ORC 3111.06**
        Continuing jurisdiction, **ORC 3111.16**
Jury trials. See JURY TRIALS
Juvenile courts, **ORC Ch 2151**
    See also JUVENILE COURTS
Magistrates. See MAGISTRATES
Mediators, custody and visitation disputes, **SupR 16**
Powers, **O Const IV § 1**
Probate division. See PROBATE COURTS
Recorded transcripts, custody, **SupR 11**
Records and reports
    Arbitration, **SupR 15**
    Continuances, **SupR 41(D)**
    Court records, management and retention, **SupR 26**
        Administrative records, retention schedule, **SupR 26.01**
Referees. See REFEREES
Reporters. See COURT REPORTERS
Rulemaking powers
    Probate courts, applicability, **ORC 2101.32**
Rules of superintendence. See RULES OF SUPERINTENDENCE
Sentences. See SENTENCES
Separation agreements, enforcement, **ORC 3105.10(B)**
Sessions, **ORC 2301.05**
Special judgments for state, income tax, **ORC 5747.13(C)**

COURTS OF COMMON PLEAS   Index-24

COURTS OF COMMON PLEAS—*continued*
Terms of court, **ORC 2301.05**
Transcripts. See TRANSCRIPTS
Trials. See TRIALS
Videotape equipment, **SupR 13**
Visitation disputes, mediators, **SupR 16**
Witnesses. See WITNESSES AND TESTIMONY

COUSINS
See NEXT OF KIN

COVENANTS
See also CONTRACTS
Testator, by; effect on legacy or devise, remedies, **ORC 2107.33**

CREDIT
See also DEBTORS AND CREDITORS
Estates, real property deferred payments, **ORC 2113.43**

CREDIT UNIONS
Payable on death accounts, **ORC 2131.10, ORC 2131.11**

CREDITORS
See DEBTORS AND CREDITORS

CRIMES AND OFFENSES
Child abuse, permitting, **ORC 2903.15**
Conveyance or possession of deadly weapons or dangerous ordnance on school premises
 Drivers' license, denial or revocation of temporary instruction permit, **ORC 2923.122**
Definitions, **ORC 2901.01**
Drug offenses
 See DRUG OFFENSES
Embezzlement. See EMBEZZLEMENT
Felonies. See FELONIES
Fraud. See FRAUD
Homicide. See HOMICIDE
Homicide. See HOMICIDE; MURDER
Interfering with establishment of paternity, **ORC 3111.19, ORC 3111.99**
Permitting child abuse, **ORC 2903.15**
Person, defined, **ORC 2901.01**
Prosecution. See CRIMINAL PROSECUTIONS
Records, criminal
 Check, caring for minors; employment prerequisite, **ORC 2151.86, ORC 2151.861**
Sale of human body parts, **ORC 2108.99**
Sentences. See SENTENCES
Traffic offenses. See TRAFFIC OFFENSES
Victims. See VICTIMS OF CRIME

CRIMINAL IDENTIFICATION AND INVESTIGATION BUREAU
DNA testing of prisoners, **ORC 2901.07**
Records and reports
 Weekly report from juvenile courts, **ORC 2152.71**

CRIMINAL PROCEDURE
General provisions
 DNA testing of certain prisoners, **ORC 2901.07**
DNA testing of certain prisoners, **ORC 2901.07**
Indigent defendants, appointment of counsel, **SupR 20**

CRIMINAL PROSECUTIONS
Accused. See DEFENDANTS
Appeals. See APPEALS, generally
Arrests. See ARRESTS
Burden of proof, **ORC 2901.05(A)**
Child, of. See JUVENILE DELINQUENCY
Complaints. See COMPLAINTS
Costs. See COURT COSTS, generally
Defendants. See DEFENDANTS

CRIMINAL PROSECUTIONS—*continued*
Defenses. See DEFENSES
Jury trials. See JURY TRIALS, generally
Juvenile delinquency. See JUVENILE DELINQUENCY
Juvenile procedure rules, applicability, **JuvR 1(C)**
Presumption of innocence, **ORC 2901.05(A)**
Sentences. See SENTENCES
Venue, **O Const I § 12**

CRIMINAL RECORDS CHECK
Child day camp employees, **ORC 2151.861**
Defined, **ORC 5123.081**

CROPS
Estate assets, defined as, **ORC 2115.10**

CROSS-CLAIMS
See COUNTERCLAIMS AND CROSS-CLAIMS

CROSS-EXAMINATIONS
Juvenile proceedings, **JuvR 34(B)**

CRUELTY
Aged persons treated cruelly by caretakers, **ORC 5101.60 to 5101.71**
 See also PROTECTIVE SERVICES FOR ADULTS
Child. See CHILD ABUSE
Divorce, grounds for, **ORC 3105.01(D)**
Legal separation, grounds for, **ORC 3105.17**
Mentally retarded confined in state institution, reporting, **ORC 5123.093**

CURRENT BENEFICIARY
Defined, **ORC 5801.01**

CURTESY
Generally, **ORC 2103.09**
Gross estate of deceased spouse, inclusion, **ORC 5731.04, ORC 5731.13**
Relinquishment, effect on estate tax, **ORC 5731.13**

CUSTODIANS
See FIDUCIARIES, generally

CUSTODY OF CHILDREN, DOMESTIC
Affidavits, **ORC 3109.27**
Appeals
 Priority on docket, **ORC 3109.04(H), ORC 3109.06**
Attorney fees
 Inappropriate forum, party who commenced proceeding to pay, **ORC 3109.25(G)**
 Violation of order necessitating proceeding, violating party to pay, **ORC 3109.26(C), ORC 3109.32(B)**
 Wrongful removal of child, following, **ORC 3109.26(C)**
Award, **ORC 3109.04**
Best interests of child, **ORC 3109.04, ORC 3109.22(A)**
 Death of custodial parent, new custody order, **ORC 3109.06**
 Jurisdiction prerequisite, as, **ORC 3109.22(A)**
Certification of cases to juvenile court, **ORC 3109.04(D)(2), ORC 3109.06**
Costs
 Dismissal due to wrongful removal of child, **ORC 3109.26**
 Investigation, **JuvR 32(D), ORC 3109.04(C)**
 Medical or psychological examination, prior to award, **ORC 3109.04(C)**
 Violation necessitating action, out-of-state decree, **ORC 3109.32(B)**
Courts of common pleas, mediators, **SupR 16**
Criminal offense by parent, consideration, **ORC 3109.04(B)**
Custodial parent, defined, **ORC 3109.04(K)**
Death of custodial parent, effect, **ORC 3109.06**
Decree, **ORC 3105.21, ORC 3109.30, ORC 3109.32**
 Modification. See Modification of custody order, this heading
 Out-of-state court, **ORC 3109.30, ORC 3109.32**
 Reciprocity, **ORC 3109.30, ORC 3109.32**

CUSTODY OF CHILDREN, DOMESTIC—continued
Definitions
　　Shared parenting, **ORC 3109.04(I)**
Dismissal of actions
　　Inconvenient forum, **ORC 3109.25(E), ORC 3109.25(H)**
Divorce not granted, custody order still possible, **ORC 3105.21(B)**
Examinations of parents and children, **ORC 3109.04(C)**
Guardianship, **ORC Ch 2111**
　　See also GUARDIANSHIP
Habeas corpus writ, **JuvR 10(A), JuvR 10(G)**
Illegitimate child
　　Mother designated as sole residential parent and legal custodian, **ORC 3109.042**
Interference with, jurisdiction, **ORC 2151.23**
Interview of child, **ORC 3109.04(B)**
Investigations, **ORC 3109.04(C)**
Jurisdiction, **ORC 3109.04, ORC 3109.06**
　　Ancillary action to divorce, **ORC 3109.25(F)**
　　Certification to juvenile court, **ORC 3109.06**
　　Improperly obtained custody, effect, **ORC 3109.26(A)**
　　Prerequisites, **ORC 3109.22**
　　Uniform Child Custody Jurisdiction Act, **ORC 3109.21 to 3109.32**
Juvenile court, certification of cases to, **ORC 3109.04(D)(2), ORC 3109.06**
Mediators, courts of common pleas, **SupR 16**
Medical or mental examinations of parents and children, **ORC 3109.04(C)**
Modification of custody order, **ORC 3109.04(F)**
　　Appeal, priority on docket, **ORC 3109.04(H)**
　　Improperly obtained custody, **ORC 3109.26(B)**
　　Shared parenting, **ORC 3109.04(E)**
　　Wishes of child, **ORC 3109.04(F)(1)**
Move by residential parent, notice to court, **ORC 3109.051(G)**
Neglected child charge against parent, consideration, **ORC 3109.04(C)**
Neither parent fit, procedure, **ORC 3109.04(D)(2)**
Noncustodial parent, defined, **ORC 3109.04(K)**
Notice of proceedings, **ORC 3109.23**
Order. See Decree, this heading
Parent convicted of killing other parent, **ORC 3109.41 to 3109.48**
　　Best interest of child, **ORC 3109.47**
　　Definitions, **ORC 3109.41**
　　Notice of conviction, **ORC 3109.44**
　　　　Receipt deemed new complaint for custody, **ORC 3109.46**
　　　　Termination of custody upon receipt, **ORC 3109.46**
　　Unavailability, **ORC 3109.43**
Parent who is not the residential parent, defined, **ORC 3109.04(K)**
Paternity judgment, subsequent to, **ORC 3111.13**
Pleadings, **ORC 3109.27**
Records and reports, **ORC 3109.25**
　　Investigative reports, **JuvR 32(D), ORC 3109.04(C)**
　　Medical reports, **ORC 3109.04(C)**
　　Out-of-state decrees, **ORC 3109.32(A)**
　　Registry, **ORC 3109.24(B), ORC 3109.25(I)**
Registry, **ORC 3109.24(B), ORC 3109.25(I)**
　　Change of forum recorded in, **ORC 3109.25(I)**
Relatives receiving custody when neither parent fit, **ORC 3109.04(D)(2)**
Residential parent and legal custodian, defined, **ORC 3109.04(K)**
Service of process, **ORC 3109.23**
Shared parenting, **ORC 3109.04**
　　Child support, **ORC 3109.05(A)**
　　Modification, **ORC 3109.04(E)**
　　Termination, **ORC 3109.04(E)**
　　Visitation rights, **ORC 3109.04(G)**
Surrender of custody, voluntary, **JuvR 38**
　　Permanent custody, **JuvR 38(B)**
　　Temporary custody, **JuvR 38(A)**
Termination of custody order
　　Shared parenting, **ORC 3109.04(E)**

CUSTODY OF CHILDREN, DOMESTIC—continued
Unfit parent
　　Juvenile court, certification to, **ORC 3109.04(D)(2)**
　　Relative, placement with, **ORC 3109.04(D)(2)**
　　Third party, placement with, **ORC 3109.04(D)(2)**
Uniform Child Custody Jurisdiction Act, **ORC 3109.21 to 3109.32**
Unmarried mothers, designated as sole residential parent and legal custodian, **ORC 3109.042**
Venue, change for more convenient forum, **ORC 3109.24, ORC 3109.25**
Violations
　　Effect on jurisdiction, **ORC 3109.26(B)**
　　Out-of-state decrees, of, **ORC 3109.32(B)**
Visitation rights. See VISITATION RIGHTS
Voluntary surrender, **JuvR 38**
Wishes of child, **ORC 3109.04(B)**
Wrongful removal of child, **ORC 3109.26**

CUSTODY OF CHILDREN, INSTITUTIONAL
Generally, **ORC 2151.353 to 2151.40**
Adequate parental care lacking, disposition of child, **ORC 2151.353, ORC 2151.353(A), ORC 2151.414**
Adoption, placement for
　　Hearings, notice to adoptive parents, **ORC 2151.424**
　　Juvenile court approving adoption agreement, **ORC 5103.151**
　　Requirements prior to approval of adoption agreement, **ORC 5103.151**
Agencies for, powers and duties, **ORC 5103.15 to 5103.17**
Alcohol dependency of parent as grounds for placement, assessment and treatment requirement, **ORC 2151.3514**
Best interests of child
　　Modification or termination of permanent custody order, consideration, **ORC 2151.42**
　　Termination of parental rights, **ORC 2151.414(A)**
Case plans, **JuvR 34(F), ORC 2151.412**
　　Administrative review, **JuvR 36(C), ORC 2151.416**
Chemical dependency of parent as grounds for placement, assessment and treatment requirement, **ORC 2151.3514**
Child abuse, due to, **ORC 3109.22(A)**
Children services agency, commitment to, **ORC 2151.353**
Commitment, **ORC 2151.35 to 2151.353**
　　Approved institutions, **ORC 5103.03**
　　Children's services board, **ORC 2151.353**
　　Discharge. See Discharge, this heading
　　Youth services department. See YOUTH SERVICES DEPARTMENT
Complaints, **JuvR 10(A), JuvR 10(E), JuvR 10(F), ORC 2151.27**
　　Permanent custody, for, **JuvR 10(D)**
Comprehensive reunification plan, **ORC 2151.414(A)**
　　Mandatory counseling, **ORC 2151.412**
Definitions, **JuvR 2, ORC 2151.011**
Detention, **ORC 2151.31 to 2151.314**
　　Facilities, **ORC 2152.26**
　　Family foster homes, in, **ORC 2151.331, ORC 2152.26**
　　Hearing, **ORC 2151.314**
　　Jails, in, **ORC 2152.26**
　　Placement, **ORC 2152.26**
　　Release of child, **ORC 2151.311**
　　Time, length, **ORC 2151.34**
Determination, **ORC 2151.32**
Discharge
　　Early release, **ORC 2151.38(A), ORC 2151.38(B)**
　　Institution or agency applying for, **ORC 2151.38(B)**
　　Minimum term of institutionalization, **ORC 2151.38(A), ORC 2151.38(B)**
　　Multiple offenses, consecutive terms, **ORC 2151.38(B)**
　　Youth services department commitment, from. See YOUTH SERVICES DEPARTMENT, at Release of children
Disposition of child. See Placement, this heading
DNA testing, **ORC 2152.74**
Drug dependency of parent as grounds for placement, assessment and treatment requirement, **ORC 2151.3514**

CUSTODY OF CHILDREN, INSTITUTIONAL—continued

Emergency orders, ex parte, **ORC 2151.31**
Foster homes. See FOSTER HOMES
Grounds for court taking, **JuvR 6**
Guardianship, **ORC Ch 2111**
    See also GUARDIANSHIP
Habeas corpus writ, **JuvR 10(A), JuvR 10(G), JuvR 32(D)**
Hearings
    Foster parents, custodial relatives and adoptive parents, notice, **ORC 2151.424**
    Removal of children from homes, efforts of agencies to prevent, **ORC 2151.419**
Home studies, assessors
    Education programs, **ORC 3107.013 to 3107.016, ORC 3107.015**
    Requirements, **ORC 3107.012, ORC 3107.014**
Human services department, commitment to, **ORC 2151.414**
Institution or agency taking permanent custody, **ORC 2151.353**
Investigations, **JuvR 32(D)**
Jurisdiction, **ORC 2111.06**
    Certification to juvenile court, **ORC 3109.06**
    Juvenile courts, **ORC 2151.23**
Juvenile courts, powers and duties. See JUVENILE COURTS
Legal custody
    Defined, **ORC 2151.011**
Modification of order, **ORC 2151.42**
Nonresident children, **ORC 2151.39**
Notice
    Permanent custody motion by welfare agency, **ORC 2151.414(A)**
    Release of child, to committing court, **ORC 2151.38(B), ORC 2151.38(C)**
Parental rights, termination. See Permanent, this heading
Permanency plans
    Approval, **ORC 2151.419**
    Review, **ORC 2151.417**
Permanent, **ORC 2151.413, ORC 2151.414**
    Abandoned children
        Inability to locate parents, determination required for custody award, **ORC 2151.413(B)**
    Abuse of child, **ORC 2151.353**
    Adequate parental care lacking
        Definition, **ORC 2151.011**
        Determination, **ORC 2151.353(A), ORC 2151.414**
    Adjudicatory hearing, **ORC 2151.35**
    Best interests of child, determination, **ORC 2151.414(A)**
    Burden of proof, **ORC 2151.414(B)**
    Clear and convincing evidence standard, **ORC 2151.414(B)**
    Complaint for, **JuvR 10(D)**
    Counsel appointed for parents, **ORC 2151.414(A)**
    Definitions, **ORC 2151.011**
    Grounds, **ORC 2151.414**
    Hearing on motion, **ORC 2151.414**
    Human services department, state or county; commitment of child to
        Agreements, **ORC 5103.15**
        Medical and social histories of parents, **ORC 5103.15**
    Human services departments
        Commitment of child to, **ORC 2151.414**
    Institution or agency taking, **ORC 2151.353**
    Motion for, **ORC 2151.413**
        Hearing, **ORC 2151.414**
        Procedures, **ORC 2151.414**
    Notice, **ORC 2151.414(A)**
    Orphans, **ORC 2151.413**
    Parent's right to counsel, **ORC 2151.353**
    Presumption of permanency, **ORC 2151.42**
    Public children services agencies, children placed with, **ORC 2151.414(B)**
        Motion for, **ORC 2151.413(D)**
    Relatives
        Unavailable to take custody of orphaned child, determination required, **ORC 2151.413**

CUSTODY OF CHILDREN, INSTITUTIONAL—continued

Permanent, **ORC 2151.413, ORC 2151.414**—continued
    Right to counsel, **ORC 2151.353(B), ORC 2151.414(A)**
    Temporary custody awarded, motion for permanent custody filed following, **ORC 2151.353**
    Termination, **ORC 2151.38(A)**
    Transcripts of hearings, **ORC 2151.35**
    Unsuitability of parent, determination, **ORC 2151.353, ORC 2151.414(A)**
Placement, **ORC 2151.32, ORC 2151.353**
    See also CHILDREN'S SERVICES
    Alcohol or drug dependency of parent as grounds, assessment and treatment treatment requirement, **ORC 2151.3514**
    Boarding homes, **ORC 5103.16**
    Continuing jurisdiction, **ORC 2151.417**
    Detention, **ORC 2152.26**
    Judicial review of dispositional orders, **ORC 2151.417**
    Modification of order, **ORC 2151.42**
    Notice of intended, **ORC 2151.3510**
    Permanent. See Permanent, this heading
    Relatives, with, **ORC 5103.16**
    Temporary, **ORC 2151.33, ORC 2151.34, ORC 2151.353**
    Termination of order, **ORC 2151.42**
Planned permanent living arrangement
    Case plans for children, **ORC 2151.412**
    Long-term care, motions for, **ORC 2151.415**
Public children services agencies, permanent custody of children placed with, **ORC 2151.414(B)**
    Motion for, **ORC 2151.413(D)**
Records and reports
    Institutions and associations receiving children, **ORC 2151.37**
    Youth services department. See YOUTH SERVICES DEPARTMENT
Rehabilitation facilities, **ORC 2151.65 to 2151.80**
    See also JUVENILE REHABILITATION
Release of children. See Discharge, this heading
Religious considerations, **ORC 2151.32**
Restraining orders, **JuvR 34(H)**
Runaway child, **JuvR 6**
Surrender of custody, voluntary, **JuvR 38**
    Permanent custody, **JuvR 38(B)**
    Temporary custody, **JuvR 38(A)**
Temporary, **ORC 2151.34**
    Abandoned children, **ORC 2151.413(B)**
    Alcohol or drug dependency of parent as grounds, assessment and treatment treatment requirement, **ORC 2151.3514**
    Charitable institution or association, **ORC 5103.15**
    Commitment of child to, **ORC 2151.353(A)**
    Definitions, **ORC 2151.011**
    Dispositional hearings, **ORC 2151.415**
    Orders, **ORC 2151.415**
        Extension, **JuvR 14(B)**
        Modification, **JuvR 14(C)**
        Termination, **JuvR 14(A)**
    Permanent custody motion filed following award, **ORC 2151.413(A)**
    Welfare agency, **ORC 2151.353**
Termination of order, **ORC 2151.42**
Termination of parental rights. See Permanent, this heading
Transportation to places of commitment, expenses, **ORC 2151.54**
Visitation rights. See VISITATION RIGHTS
Voluntary permanent custody surrender agreement, **ORC 3107.071**
Warrant for court taking, **JuvR 15(E), JuvR 15(D), JuvR 16(B)**
Youth services department, commitment to. See YOUTH SERVICES DEPARTMENT, at Commitment of children to

CUYAHOGA COUNTY

See also COUNTIES, for general provisions
Court of common pleas. See COURTS OF COMMON PLEAS, generally
Juvenile court, **ORC 2151.07, ORC Ch 2153**
    See also JUVENILE COURTS, generally

CUYAHOGA COUNTY—*continued*
Probate court. See CUYAHOGA COUNTY PROBATE COURT
Probate court. See CUYAHOGA COUNTY PROBATE COURT; PROBATE COURT

CUYAHOGA COUNTY PROBATE COURT
Generally, **ORC 2101.021**
Accounts, **CuyR 64.2 et seq.**
Adoptions
    Court costs, **CuyR 58.1**
    Supervision, case management, **CuyR 78.1**
Affidavit of notice of admission of will to probate, **CuyR 34.4**
Appointments by court, **CuyR 8.1**
Appraisers, appointment, **CuyR 8.1**
Attorney fees, **CuyR 71.1**
    Contingent fees, **CuyR 71.2 et seq.**
    Personal injury claims, **CuyR 71.2 et seq.**
    Wrongful death settlements, **CuyR 71.2 et seq.**
Attorneys
    Appointment, **CuyR 8.1**
    Fees. See Attorney fees, this heading
Birth records, registration or correction, **CuyR 58.1**
Case management, **CuyR 78.1**
Civil actions, case management, **CuyR 78.1**
Compensation
    Attorney fees, **CuyR 71.1**
        Contingent fees, **CuyR 71.2 et seq.**
    Guardians, **CuyR 73.1**
    Trustees, **CuyR 74.1**
Court costs, **CuyR 58.1**
Estates
    Accounts, **CuyR 64.2 et seq.**
    Court costs, **CuyR 58.1**
    Supervision, case management, **CuyR 78.1**
Fees and costs
    Attorney fees, **CuyR 71.1**
        Contingent fees, **CuyR 71.2 et seq.**
    Court costs, deposit schedule, **CuyR 58.1**
    Recording of proceedings, **CuyR 11.1**
Fiduciaries, appointment, **CuyR 8.1**
Firearms and dangerous ordnance prohibition, **CuyR 9.2**
Guardians
    Compensation, **CuyR 73.1**
    Deposit of wills, **CuyR 66.3 et seq.**
    Reports
        Condition of incompetent adult, **CuyR 66.3 et seq.**
        Condition of ward, **CuyR 66.3 et seq.**
Guardians ad litem, appointment, **CuyR 8.1**
Guardianships
    Accounts, **CuyR 64.2 et seq.**
    Compensation of guardian, **CuyR 73.1**
    Court costs, **CuyR 58.1**
    Reports
        Condition of adult incompetent, **CuyR 66.3 et seq.**
        Condition of ward, **CuyR 66.3 et seq.**
    Supervision, case management, **CuyR 78.1**
    Wills, deposit with court, **CuyR 66.3 et seq.**
Hours of court, **CuyR 53.1**
Inventory, **CuyR 64.1**
Investigators, appointment, **CuyR 8.1**
Jury management plan, **CuyR 78.3**
Land sales, case management, **CuyR 78.1**
Magistrates, appointment, **CuyR 8.1**
Personal injury claims, attorney fees, **CuyR 71.2 et seq.**
Psychiatric proceedings
    Supervision, case management, **CuyR 78.1**
Recording proceedings, **CuyR 11.1**
Reports
    Condition of adult incompetent, **CuyR 66.3 et seq.**
    Condition of ward, **CuyR 66.3 et seq.**
Security, **CuyR 9.1, CuyR 9.2**

CUYAHOGA COUNTY PROBATE COURT—*continued*
Trustees
    Appointment, **CuyR 8.1**
    Compensation, **CuyR 74.1**
Trusts
    Accounts, **CuyR 64.2 et seq.**
    Supervision, case management, **CuyR 78.1**
Wills
    Affidavit of notice of admission to probate, **CuyR 34.4**
    Deposit with court, **CuyR 66.3 et seq.**
Wrongful death settlements, attorney fees, **CuyR 71.2 et seq.**

CY PRES DOCTRINE
Generally, **ORC 2131.08**
Trusts, application of cy pres, **ORC 5804.13**

DAMAGES
Assault by minors, **ORC 3109.10**
Consignment of art works to dealers, special damages for certain violations by dealers, **ORC 5815.48**
Destruction of property by minor, **ORC 3109.09**
Dower interest, waste by tenant in dower, **ORC 2103.07**
Embezzlement of trust funds, **ORC 2109.52**
Eminent domain surveys by state agencies, **ORC 163.03**
Juvenile delinquents, liability
    Assault by minor, **ORC 3109.10**
    Theft or destruction of property by minor, **ORC 3109.09**
Parental liability for children
    See also Juvenile delinquents, liability, this heading
Tenant for life damaging real property, **ORC 2105.20**
Theft by minor, **ORC 3109.09**
Trust funds, embezzlement, **ORC 2109.52**
Trusts. See TRUSTS
Wards, sustained by, **ORC 2111.18**
Waste, liability
    Tenant for life, **ORC 2105.20**
    Tenant in dower, **ORC 2103.07**
Will, concealing, **ORC 2107.09**
Wrongful death actions, **ORC 2125.02**
    See also WRONGFUL DEATH

DATA PROCESSING
Probate court records, **ORC 2101.121**

DAY CAMPS
See CAMPS AND CAMPING

DAY CARE CENTERS
Employees, reporting child abuse, **ORC 2151.421**
Noncustodial parent, access to, **ORC 3109.051(I)**

DEAD BODIES
See CORPSES

DEATH
See also DECEDENTS
Autopsies. See AUTOPSIES
Benefits. See DEATH BENEFITS
Burials. See FUNERALS AND BURIALS
Defined, **ORC 2108.30**
Descent and distribution,
    Establishment of death, **ORC 2105.35**
Devisees or legatees, **ORC 2107.52**
Dower actions, effect, **ORC 5305.05**
Employee, release of wages, **ORC 2113.04**
Executors and administrators, **ORC 2113.14, ORC 2113.19**
Fiduciaries
    Cofiduciary's death, effect on surviving fiduciaries, **ORC 2109.27**
Gifts in contemplation of. See GIFTS CAUSA MORTIS
Guardianship, notice of ward's death, **SumR 66.1(A)**
Heirs, **ORC 2107.52**
Legatees or devisees, **ORC 2107.52**
Life insurance. See LIFE INSURANCE

DEATH

Index-28

DEATH—continued

Mentally ill persons. See MENTALLY ILL PERSONS, at Hospitalization

Mentally retarded and developmentally disabled persons
    Autopsies, petition for post-mortem upon suspicious death, **ORC 2108.521**
    Reporting death of mentally retarded in state institution, **ORC 5123.093**

Parent
    Custodial parent, new custody order, **ORC 3109.06**
    Visitation by relatives after, **ORC 3109.11**

Parties to actions. See PARTIES TO ACTIONS

Paternity, presumption, **ORC 3111.03**

Power of attorney, effect, **ORC 1337.091**

Presumed decedents' law, **ORC Ch 2121**
    See also PRESUMED DECEDENTS

Property transfers in contemplation of, estate tax, **ORC 5731.05**

Revocable trusts, limitation of actions pertaining to revocable trusts made irrevocable by death of settlor, **ORC 5806.04**

Servicemen
    Presumed, when missing in action, **ORC Ch 2121**
    See also PRESUMED DECEDENTS

Surviving spouse. See SURVIVING SPOUSE

Transfer-on-death deed, **ORC 5302.22 et seq.**

Ward, notice to court, **SumR 66.1(A)**

Wrongful. See WRONGFUL DEATH

DEATH BENEFITS

Designation of spouse as beneficiary, effect of termination of marriage, **ORC 5815.33**

Estate tax, **ORC 5731.09, ORC 5731.12**

Transfer, estate property, **ORC 5731.39**

DEATH CERTIFICATES

County of residence, **ORC 3705.071**

Probate courts, record, **ORC 2101.12**

DEBTORS AND CREDITORS

See also CREDIT

Estates. See CLAIMS AGAINST ESTATES

Estates. See CLAIMS AGAINST ESTATES; DEBTS OWED TO ESTATES

Execution of judgment. See EXECUTION OF JUDGMENT

Fraudulent transfers, **ORC Ch 1336**
    Creditors with preexisting claims, **ORC 1336.05**
    Recovery by creditors, **ORC 1336.08**

Imprisonment for debt, **O Const I § 15**

Survivorship tenancies, effect, **ORC 5302.20(C)**

Trusts, parties to agreements and effect on creditor rights, **ORC 5801.10**

DEBTS OWED TO ESTATES

Ancillary administration, **ORC 2129.20**

Bad debts, **ORC 2113.33**

Beneficiary owing, set off, **ORC 2113.59**

Descent and distribution, effect, **ORC 2105.052**

Executor owing, **ORC 2115.12**

Settlement, **ORC 2117.05**

Wages, **ORC 2113.04**

Will discharging, **ORC 2115.11, ORC 2115.12**

DECEDENTS

See also CORPSES; DEATH

Administration. See ADMINISTRATION OF ESTATES

Alien, notice to surviving spouse and heirs, **ORC 2113.11**

Ancillary administration. See ANCILLARY ADMINISTRATION

Burial lots, **ORC 2113.37**
    See also FUNERALS AND BURIALS

Debts owed by. See CLAIMS AGAINST ESTATES

Debts owed to. See DEBTS OWED TO ESTATES

Docket, **ORC 2101.12**

Estates. See ESTATES

Estates. See ESTATES; EXECUTORS AND ADMINISTRATORS

DECEDENTS—continued

Fraudulent transfers by, **ORC 2127.40**

Funeral expenses. See FUNERALS AND BURIALS

Income tax liability, **ORC 5747.08(A)**

Intestate succession. See DESCENT AND DISTRIBUTION

Joint debtor, as; liability, **ORC 2117.31**

Judgments against, **ORC 2117.31**

Last illness. See LAST ILLNESS

Nonresident. See ESTATES

Presumed decedents' law, **ORC Ch 2121**
    See also PRESUMED DECEDENTS

Probate. See PROBATE OF WILLS

Real property contracts, incomplete, **ORC 2113.48**

Support and maintenance allowance for family of
    Distribution under summary estate administration to pay, **Sup. R 75.4**
    Priority, **ORC 2117.25**
    Surviving spouse, **ORC 2106.13**

Surviving spouse of. See SURVIVING SPOUSE

Tax. See ESTATE TAX; FEDERAL

Testators, as. See TESTATORS

Tombstones, **ORC 2113.37**

Wages, release of, **ORC 2113.04**

Wills. See WILLS

DECEPTION

See FALSE STATEMENTS; FRAUD

DECLARATIONS

Anatomical gifts. See ANATOMICAL GIFTS

Living wills. See LIVING WILLS, generally

Mental health treatment, declarations for. See MENTALLY ILL PERSONS

DECLARATORY JUDGMENTS

Executors and administrators seeking, **ORC 2107.46**

Fees and costs, **ORC 2101.16**

Fiduciaries, by, **ORC 2107.46**

Heirship determination, **ORC Ch 2123**
    Ancillary proceedings, **ORC 2129.18**

Probate courts, **ORC 2101.24**

Wills
    Ante mortem declaration of validity, **ORC 2107.081 to 2107.085**
    See also ANTE MORTEM DECLARATION OF WILL VALIDITY, generally

DECREES

See also JUDGMENTS

Adoption, **ORC 3107.14 to 3107.16**
    Foreign decrees, **ORC 3107.18**
    Forwarding to health department, **ORC 3107.19**

Custody action. See CUSTODY OF CHILDREN, DOMESTIC

Declaratory judgments. See DECLARATORY JUDGMENTS

Presumed death, **ORC 2121.04**
    Vacation, **ORC 2121.08**

Probate court, of; appeal, **ORC 2101.42**

DEEDS

See also CONVEYANCES, generally

Fraudulent conveyances, **ORC 2109.56**

Guardians selling real property, **ORC 2127.35**

Land sale proceedings, **ORC 2127.35**

Power of attorney, **1337.01 et seq.**

Survivorship tenancy, **ORC 5302.17**

Transfer-on-death deed, **ORC 5302.22 et seq.**

DEFAULT

Defined under Interstate Compact on Placement of Children, **ORC 5103.20**

DEFAULT JUDGMENTS

Parentage actions, **ORC 3111.08**

DEFENDANTS

See also PARTIES TO ACTIONS
Bail. See BAIL
Incompetent to stand trial, **ORC 2945.37 to 2945.402**
    Applicability of provisions, **ORC 5122.011**
    Commitment
        Civil commitment following maximum time for treatment, **ORC 2945.39**
        Conditional release, **ORC 2945.402**
        Least restrictive alternative, **ORC 2945.38(B)**
        Nonsecured status, **ORC 2945.38(E), ORC 2945.401**
        Records and reports, **ORC 2945.401(C)**
        Reduction of jail or workhouse time, **ORC 2945.38(I)**
        Short-term, **ORC 5123.701**
        Termination, **ORC 2945.401**
            Evidence, **ORC 2945.401(E)**
            Jurisdiction, **ORC 2945.401(J)**
            Recommendation of chief clinical officer, **ORC 2945.401(D)**
        Time limits, **ORC 2945.38(C)**
        Unsupervised on-grounds movement, supervised off-grounds movement or nonsecured status prohibited, **ORC 2945.38(E)**
        Voluntary commitment prohibited, **ORC 2945.38(D), ORC 5123.69**
    Conditional release, **ORC 2945.402**
    Definitions, **ORC 2945.37(A)**
    Determination not based on treatment for mental illness, **ORC 2945.37(F)**
    Discharge from hospital, **ORC 2945.38(C), ORC 5122.15, ORC 5122.21**
    Disclosure of information, **ORC 5122.31**
    Dismissal of action, **ORC 2945.38(H)**
    Escape, arrests, **ORC 5123.13**
    Evaluation, **ORC 2945.37(C), ORC 2945.371**
    Evidence, **ORC 2945.37(E)**
    Findings, **ORC 2945.38**
    Habeas corpus, **ORC 5122.30**
    Hearing, **ORC 2945.37(C), ORC 2945.38(F), ORC 2945.38(G), ORC 2945.401(B)**
        Burden of proof, **ORC 2945.401(G)**
        Defendant's rights, **ORC 2945.401(F)**
        Modification of recommendation, **ORC 2945.401(I)**
        Prosecutor's duties, **ORC 2945.401(H)**
    Institutionalization, applicability of provisions, **ORC 5123.011**
    Jurisdiction, **ORC 2945.401(A)**
    Municipal court procedures, **ORC 2945.37(H)**
    Presumption of competency, **ORC 2945.37(G)**
    Raising of issue, **ORC 2945.37(B)**
    Report by examiner, **ORC 2945.371, ORC 2945.38(F)**
    Treatment, **ORC 2945.38(A), ORC 2945.38(D)**
    Voluntary hospitalization, **ORC 5122.02**
Indigent, legal counsel. See INDIGENT PERSONS, at Attorney appointed for
Legal counsel for. See ATTORNEYS
Medication to maintain competence, **ORC 2945.38(A)**
    Involuntary administration, **ORC 2945.38(B)**
Pleadings. See PLEADINGS
Presumption of innocence, **ORC 2901.05(A)**

DEFENSES

See also PLEADINGS
Affirmative, **ORC 2901.05(A), ORC 2901.05(C)**
Battered woman syndrome, **ORC 2945.392**
Defect in complaint or indictment, **JuvR 22(D)**
Denials
    Juvenile adjudicatory hearings, **JuvR 29(E), JuvR 29(C)**
Fraudulent transfers, **ORC 1336.08**
Impairment of reason not constituting, **ORC 2945.391**
Juvenile proceedings, **JuvR 22(C) to JuvR 22(E)**
Nonresident decedent's property, transfer, **ORC 5731.40**
Prehearing motions, **JuvR 22(E), JuvR 22(D)**

DEFINITIONS

See also STATUTORY CONSTRUCTION
Abuse of aged persons, **ORC 5101.61**
Abused child, **JuvR 2, ORC 2151.031**
Act charged, **ORC 2152.02**
Adequate parental care, **ORC 2151.011**
Adjudicatory hearing, **JuvR 2**
Adjusted gross income, **ORC 5747.01**
Adoption, **ORC 3107.01**
    Criminal record check, **ORC 2151.86**
    Disclosure of adoption information
        Adoptee, access to file, **ORC 3107.39**
    Open adoption, **ORC 3107.60**
Adult, **ORC 5126.30**
Adult child, **ORC 2105.25**
Aged persons, protective services, **ORC 5101.60**
Agreement for temporary custody, **JuvR 2, ORC 2151.011**
Anatomical gifts, **ORC 2108.01**
Approved placement, **ORC 5103.20**
Artificial insemination, **ORC 3111.88**
Ascertainable standard, **ORC 5801.01**
Banking day, **ORC 5747.01**
Beneficiary form, **ORC 1709.01**
Beneficiary surrogate, **ORC 5801.01**
Bequest, **ORC 2107.011, ORC 5815.01**
Board, **ORC 5126.30**
Burial expenses, **ORC 2113.031**
Business, **ORC 163.51**
Business income, **ORC 5747.01**
Capacity to consent to mental health treatment decisions, **ORC 2135.01**
Caretaker, **ORC 5126.30**
Category one offense, **ORC 2152.02**
Category two offense, **ORC 2152.02**
Certified foster home, **ORC 2151.011**
Charitable trusts, **ORC 2109.30, ORC 5801.01**
Chemical dependency, **ORC 2151.3514**
Child, **JuvR 2, ORC 3109.51**
Child day camp, **ORC 2151.011**
Child day care provider, **ORC 2151.011**
Children, **JuvR 2, ORC 2151.011**
    Abuse, **ORC 2151.031**
    Custody, **JuvR 2, ORC 2151.011**
        Shared parenting, **ORC 3109.04(I)**
    Dependent, **ORC 2151.04**
    Neglected, **ORC 2151.03**
    Unruly, **ORC 2151.022**
Children's advocacy center, **ORC 2151.425**
Chronic truant, **JuvR 2, ORC 2151.011, ORC 2152.02**
Community corrections facility, **ORC 2152.02**
Compilation, **ORC 5122.44**
Complaint, **JuvR 2**
Conservator, **ORC 2111.01**
Co-owners with right of survivorship, **ORC 2105.31**
Court proceeding, **JuvR 2**
Crimes and offenses, **ORC 2901.01**
Criminal records check, **ORC 5123.081**
Current beneficiary, **ORC 5801.01**
Custodian, **JuvR 2, ORC 2151.011, ORC 3109.51**
Custody of child, **JuvR 2, ORC 2151.011**
Day camp, **ORC 2151.011**
Death, **ORC 2108.30**
    Presumption of, **ORC 2121.01**
Declaration for mental health treatment, **ORC 2135.01**
Delinquent child, **JuvR 2, ORC 2151.011, ORC 2152.02**
Dependent child, **JuvR 2**
Designated physician, **ORC 2135.01**
Detention, **JuvR 2, ORC 2151.011**
Detention of child, **JuvR 2**
Developmental center, **ORC 5123.032**
Developmental disability, **ORC 2151.011**
Disability, legal, **ORC 2131.02**

DEFINITIONS

DEFINITIONS—*continued*

Disclaimers of succession to property, **ORC 5815.36**
Discretionary serious youthful offender, **ORC 2152.02**
Discretionary SYO, **ORC 2152.02**
Discretionary transfer, **ORC 2152.02**
Displaced person, **ORC 163.51**
Dispositional hearing, **JuvR 2**
Dower interest, **ORC 2103.01**
Drug abuse offense, **ORC 2152.02**
Economic loss, **ORC 2152.02**
Electronic monitoring, **ORC 2152.02**
Eligible employee, **ORC 5747.39**
Emergency protective services, **ORC 5126.30**
Eminent domain, **ORC 163.01**
Essential local government purposes, **ORC 5747.01**
Estates, taxation, **ORC 2113.85, ORC 5731.01**
Event, **ORC 2105.31**
Exploitation, **ORC 5126.30**
Expunged or sealed records, **5122.01, ORC 2151.355**
Fiduciaries, **ORC 2109.01, ORC 5815.04**
Financial institution, **ORC 2113.031**
Firearm, **ORC 2152.02**
Fiscal year, **ORC 5747.01**
Forty per cent, **ORC 5747.012**
Foster caregiver, **ORC 2151.011**
Foster homes, **ORC 2151.011**
    Criminal record check, **ORC 2151.86**
Fraudulent transfers, **ORC 1336.01**
Funeral expenses, **ORC 2113.031**
Genetic test, **ORC 2105.25**
Genetic testing, **ORC 3111.09**
Good faith
    Fiduciary law, **ORC 5815.04**
    Uniform Fiduciary Act, **ORC 5815.04**
Governing instrument, **ORC 2105.31**
Guardian, **JuvR 2, ORC 2111.01, ORC 2135.01, ORC 2151.011, ORC 3109.51**
Guardian ad litem, **JuvR 2**
Guardian of the estate, **ORC 5801.01**
Guardian of the person, **ORC 5801.01**
Habitual truant, **JuvR 2, ORC 2151.011**
Health care, **ORC 2135.01**
Hearing, **JuvR 2**
Incapacitated, **ORC 5126.30**
Income tax, state, **ORC 5747.01, ORC 5747.011, ORC 5747.012**
Incompetent person, **ORC 2111.01**
Incompetent to stand trial, **ORC 2945.37(A)**
Indigent person, **JuvR 2**
Informed consent, **ORC 2135.01**
Inheritance, **ORC 2107.011, ORC 5815.01**
Insolvency, **ORC 1336.02**
Interests of the beneficiaries, **ORC 5801.01**
Interstate Compact for the Placement of Children, **ORC 5103.20**
Inventory, **ORC 2115.01**
Joint ownership with right of survivorship, **ORC 2131.12**
Jurisdiction, **ORC 5801.01**
Juvenile court, **JuvR 2**
Juvenile courts, **JuvR 2, ORC 2151.011 to 2151.06, ORC 2152.02**
Juvenile judge, **JuvR 2**
Juvenile traffic offender, **JuvR 2, ORC 2151.011, ORC 2152.02**
Juvenile traffic offenders, **JuvR 2**
Law enforcement officer, **ORC 2901.01**
Legal custody, **JuvR 2, ORC 2151.011**
Legal settlement, **JuvR 2**
Legitimate excuse for absence from public school the child is supposed to attend, **ORC 2151.011**
Legitimate excuse for absence from the public school the child is supposed to attend, **ORC 2152.02**
Limited liability company, **ORC 5747.01**
Living wills, **ORC 2133.01**
Long term foster care, **JuvR 2**

DEFINITIONS—*continued*

Mandatory distribution, **ORC 5801.01**
Mandatory serious youthful offender, **ORC 2152.02**
Mandatory SYO, **ORC 2152.02**
Mandatory transfer, **ORC 2152.02**
Mansion house, **ORC 2106.10(F)**
Medical record, **ORC 2135.01**
Mental examination, **JuvR 2**
Mental health treatment, **ORC 2135.01**
Mental health treatment decision, **ORC 2135.01**
Mental health treatment provider, **ORC 2135.01**
Mental illness, **ORC 2151.011, ORC 2152.02**
Mental injury, **ORC 2151.011**
Mentally ill, **ORC 5122.01**
Mentally retarded, **ORC 5123.011**
Mentally retarded or developmentally disabled persons, **ORC 2152.821, ORC 5123.01**
Mentally retarded person, **ORC 2152.02**
Minor drug possession offense, **ORC 5123.081**
Minors. See Children, this heading
Modified business income, **ORC 5747.01**
Modified nonbusiness income, **ORC 5747.01**
Monitored time, **ORC 2152.02**
Neglected child, **JuvR 2**
Next of kin, **ORC 2111.01**
Nonbusiness income, **ORC 5747.01**
Non-custodial parent, **ORC 5103.20**
Non-economic loss, **ORC 2152.02**
Non-member state, **ORC 5103.20**
Nonsecure care, supervision, or training, **ORC 2151.011**
Not guilty by reason of insanity, **ORC 2901.01**
Notice or knowledge of fact, defined, **ORC 5801.03**
    compulsory school age, **ORC 2152.02**
Of compulsory school age, **ORC 2151.011**
Out-of-home care, **ORC 2151.011**
Out-of-home care child abuse, **ORC 2151.011**
Out-of-home care child neglect, **ORC 2151.011**
Overpayment, **ORC 5747.01**
Parent, **ORC 3109.09**
Parent and child relationship, **ORC 3111.01**
Party, **JuvR 2, ORC 5126.30**
Pass-through entity, **ORC 5747.01**
Pass-through entity investor, **ORC 5747.01**
Patient, **ORC 5122.44**
Payor, **ORC 2105.31**
Permanent custody, **JuvR 2, ORC 2151.011**
Permanent surrender, **JuvR 2, ORC 2151.011**
Person, **JuvR 2, ORC 2901.01**
Person responsible for estate, **ORC 2117.061**
Physical examination, **JuvR 2**
Physician, **ORC 2135.01**
Placement for adoption, **ORC 2151.011**
Planned permanent living arrangement, **JuvR 2, ORC 2151.011**
Power of attorney
    Durable power of attorney for health care, **ORC 1337.11**
Power of withdrawal, **ORC 5801.01**
Powers of appointment, **ORC 5815.12**
Pre-income tax trust, **ORC 5747.01**
Principal and Income Act, **ORC 5812.01**
Principal county of employment, **ORC 5747.01**
Private child placing agencies, **JuvR 2, ORC 2151.011**
Private child placing agency, **JuvR 2**
Private noncustodial agency, **ORC 2151.011**
Probate court, **ORC 2101.01**
Probation, juveniles, **ORC 2151.011**
Professional disciplinary action, **ORC 2135.01**
Property, **ORC 2901.01**
    Dower interest, **ORC 2103.01**
Protective service plan, **ORC 5126.30**
Protective services, **ORC 5126.30**
Protective services for adults, **ORC 5101.60**

DEFINITIONS—Cont'd

Protective supervision, **ORC 2151.011**
Provisional placement, **ORC 5103.20**
Proxy, **ORC 2135.01**
Psychiatric nurse, **ORC 2135.01**
Public children's services agency, **JuvR 2**
Public record, **ORC 2152.02**
Qualified beneficiary, **ORC 5801.01**
Qualified research, **ORC 5747.013**
Qualified tuition and fees, **ORC 5747.01**
Qualifying investment pass-through entity, **ORC 5747.012**
Qualifying pre-income tax trust election, **ORC 5747.01**
Qualifying trust amount, **ORC 5747.01**
Receiving state, **ORC 5103.20**
Registering entity, **ORC 1709.01**
Relative of testator, **ORC 2107.52**
Relocation assistance under eminent domain, **ORC 163.51**
Removal action, **JuvR 2**
Removal actions, **JuvR 2**
Residence, **JuvR 2**
Residence or legal settlement, **JuvR 2**
Residential camp, **ORC 2151.011**
Residential care facility, **ORC 2151.011, ORC 5123.19**
Residential facility, **ORC 2151.011, ORC 5103.20**
Residential services, **ORC 5123.18**
Residual parental rights, privileges, and responsibilities, **JuvR 2, ORC 2151.011**
Rule of court, **JuvR 2**
Rules of superintendence
    Court records management and retention, **SupR 26**
    Probate, **SupR 50**
Sanction, service, or condition, **ORC 2151.011**
School activity, **ORC 2901.01(C)**
School safety zone, **ORC 2901.01(C)**
Secure correctional facility, **ORC 2151.011**
Security account, **ORC 1709.01**
Sending state, **ORC 5103.20**
Serious youthful offender, **ORC 2152.02**
Serious youthful offender proceedings, **JuvR 2**
Settlor, **ORC 5801.01**
Sexual abuse of a child, **ORC 2151.425**
Sexually oriented offense, **ORC 2152.02**
Shared parenting, **ORC 3109.04(I)**
Shelter care, **JuvR 2, ORC 2151.011**
Social history, **JuvR 2**
Spendthrift provision, **ORC 5801.01**
State agency, **ORC 5122.44**
State human services administration, **ORC 5103.22**
Taxable year, **ORC 5747.01**
Temporary custody, **JuvR 2, ORC 2151.011**
Terms of a trust, **ORC 5801.01**
Tort action, **ORC 2135.01**
Traditional juvenile, **ORC 2152.02**
Transfer, **ORC 2152.02**
Transfers to Minors Act, **ORC 5814.01**
Trust instrument, **ORC 5801.01**
Trusts
    Allocation between principal and income, **ORC 5812.02**
    Disabled persons, for supplemental services, **ORC 5815.28**
Uniform Principal and Income Act, **ORC 5812.01**
Uniform Transfer-on-Death Security Registration Act, **ORC 1709.01**
Unruly child, **JuvR 2, ORC 2151.022**
Value, **ORC 1336.03**
Ward, **ORC 2111.01**
Ward of court, **JuvR 2**
Wills, **ORC 2107.01**
Work of art, **ORC 5815.41**
Working day, **ORC 5126.30**

DEFRAUDING
See FRAUD

DELINQUENTS
See JUVENILE DELINQUENCY

DEMONSTRATIVE LEGACIES
See LEGACIES AND DEVISES, generally

DENTAL SCHOOLS
Anatomical gifts to, **ORC 2108.03**

DENTISTS AND DENTISTRY
Aged persons suffering neglect, abuse, or exploitation; report to county human services department, **ORC 5101.61**
Anatomical gifts, **ORC 2108.03**
Child abuse to be reported, **ORC 2151.421**
Mentally retarded and developmentally disabled persons, reporting abuse or neglect, **ORC 5123.61, ORC 5123.99**

DEPENDENT AND NEGLECTED CHILDREN
See also CHILD ABUSE; SUPPORT AND MAINTENANCE
Abandoned children
    Intestate succession to parent prohibited, **ORC 2105.10**
    Jurisdiction to determine custody, **ORC 3109.22(A)**
    Juvenile procedure rules, applicability, **JuvR 1(C)**
    Parent barred from recovery in wrongful death action, **ORC 2125.02, ORC 2125.03**
Adequate parental care lacking, **ORC 2151.414**
Adjudicatory hearing, **ORC 2151.28, ORC 2151.35**
Adoption, **ORC 5103.16**
Alcoholism of parent as grounds
    Assessment and treatment requirement, **ORC 2151.3514**
Apprehension, **ORC 2151.14, ORC 2151.31, ORC 2152.03**
    Ex parte emergency orders, **ORC 2151.31**
Case plans for children, **ORC 2151.412**
    Administrative review, **ORC 2151.416**
Chemical dependency of parent as grounds
    Assessment and treatment requirement, **ORC 2151.3514**
Complaints, **ORC 2151.27**
Court supervision of parental custody as disposition, **ORC 2151.353(A)**
Custody jurisdiction based on. See CUSTODY OF CHILDREN, INSTITUTIONAL
Defined, **ORC 2151.03, ORC 2151.04**
Detention or shelter hearing, **ORC 2151.314**
    See also CUSTODY OF CHILDREN, INSTITUTIONAL; DETENTION HOMES
Determination as, **ORC 2151.414**
    Temporary care orders, **ORC 2151.33**
Disposition, **ORC 2151.353**
Drug dependency of parent as grounds
    Assessment and treatment requirement, **ORC 2151.3514**
Expenses for care, funding by juvenile courts, **ORC 2151.10**
Foster home as place of detention, **ORC 2151.331**
Guardian ad litem, appointment, **ORC 2151.281**
Interstate agreements, **ORC 2151.56 to 2151.61**
Jurisdiction, **ORC 2151.23**
Mentally retarded, **ORC 5123.93**
Rehabilitation facilities, **ORC 2151.65 to 2151.80**
    See also JUVENILE REHABILITATION
Removal of neglectful person from child's home, **ORC 2151.353**
Shelter care, **ORC 2151.28, ORC 2151.314**
Support by juvenile court, **ORC 2151.10**
Temporary orders, **ORC 2151.33**
Unfit parents, **ORC 2151.05**

DEPOSITIONS
Certification, videotaped deposition, **SupR 13**
Copies, videotaped deposition, **SupR 13**
Eminent domain, **ORC 163.10**
Juvenile proceeding, **JuvR 25**
Notice, videotaping, **SupR 13**
Objections
    Videotaping, during, **SupR 13**
Paternity proceedings regarding unborn children, **ORC 3111.04**

DEPOSITIONS

DEPOSITIONS—*continued*
Probate courts, **ORC 2101.05**
Videotaping, **SupR 11, SupR 13**
    Child sex offense victims, **ORC 2152.81**
    Costs, **SupR 13**
    Notice, **SupR 13**
Wills, **ORC 2107.17, ORC 2107.181**

DEPOSITS
See BANKS AND BANKING, at Accounts

DEPRECIATION
Uniform Principal and Income Act, transfers from income to principal for depreciation, **ORC 5812.44**

DESCENT AND DISTRIBUTION
Generally, **ORC Ch 2105**
Abandoned children. See DEPENDENT AND NEGLECTED CHILDREN
Actions by, fiduciaries against distributees, **ORC 2107.46**
Adoption, effect on, **ORC 3107.15**
Advancements, **ORC 2105.051**
Aliens, rights, **ORC 2105.16**
Ancillary administration, **ORC 2129.04 to 2129.24**
    See also ANCILLARY ADMINISTRATION, generally
Appraisal. See INVENTORY AND APPRAISAL OF ESTATES
Automobiles, **ORC 2106.18**
Boats and watercraft, transfer to surviving spouse, **ORC 2106.19**
Construction of statute, **ORC Ch 2105**
    Died and living, construed, **ORC 2105.02**
Debts owed decedent, **ORC 2105.052**
Designation of heir. See DESIGNATED HEIRS
Devises after death of devisee, **ORC 2107.52**
Disclaimer of succession to property, **ORC 5815.36**
Distribution of assets, **ORC 2113.25, ORC 2113.53 to 2113.60**
Election to take under statute of, **ORC 2106.01 to 2106.08**
    See also SURVIVING SPOUSE, at Election by, and at Election against the will
Equal consanguinity of descendants, **ORC 2105.12**
    Wrongful death actions, apportionment of damages, **ORC 2125.03**
Escheat, **ORC 2105.06**
Estate, administration of, **ORC Ch 2113**
    See also EXECUTORS AND ADMINISTRATORS
Estate tax, apportionment, **ORC 2113.85 to 2113.88**
    See also ESTATE TAX
Future interests, **ORC 2131.04 to 2131.07**
Heirs, **ORC 2105.06, ORC 2105.11 to 2105.14**
    Action to determine, **ORC Ch 2123**
        Ancillary administration, **ORC 2129.18**
    At-law, designation, **ORC 2105.15**
        See also DESIGNATED HEIRS
    Unknown; escheat, relinquishment, **ORC 2105.08**
Homicide by heir, effect, **ORC 2105.19**
Illegitimate children, **ORC 2105.17**
Inheritance construed, **ORC 2107.011, ORC 5815.01**
Legacies after death of legatee, **ORC 2107.52**
Limitation of action, effect on paternity proceedings, **ORC 3111.05**
Motor vehicles, **ORC 2106.18**
Next of kin, **ORC 2105.03**
Outboard motors, transfer to surviving spouse, **ORC 2106.19**
Permanent leasehold estates, construed, **ORC 2105.04**
Posthumous children, **ORC 2105.14**
Presumed decedent's estate, **ORC 2121.06**
Real property
    Charged with debt, **ORC 2107.53**
    Election by surviving spouse, **ORC 2106.10, ORC 2106.11**
    Escheat, **ORC 2105.06**
    Presumed decedent's, **ORC 2121.06**
Statute, **ORC 2105.06**
Surviving spouse. See SURVIVING SPOUSE, generally
Survivorship
    Applicability, **ORC 2105.39**

DESCENT AND DISTRIBUTION—*continued*
Survivorship—*continued*
    Co-owners with right of survivorship, **ORC 2105.34**
    Definitions, **ORC 2105.31**
    Establishment of death, **ORC 2105.35**
    Exceptions, determination of survivorship, **ORC 2105.36**
    Liability of payor or other third party, **ORC 2105.37**
    Payor, liability of, **ORC 2105.37**
    Protected purchasers, **ORC 2105.38**
    Severability, **ORC 2105.39**
    Specified event, determination of survivorship with respect to, **ORC 2105.33**
    Specified person, determination of survivorship with respect to, **ORC 2105.32**
    Third party, liability of, **ORC 2105.37**
Watercraft or outboard motor
    Designation of transfer on death beneficiary, **ORC 1548.072, ORC 2131.13**

DESERTED CHILD
Generally, **ORC 2151.3515**
Anonymity of parent, **ORC 2151.3524**
Defined, **ORC 2151.3515**
Medical information forms, **ORC 2151.3525 to 2151.3530**
Temporary custody, **ORC 2151.3516 to 2151.3522**
Voluntarily delivering child not a criminal offense, **ORC 2151.3523**

DESIGNATED HEIRS
Generally, **ORC 2105.15**
Contributions to debt payments, **ORC 2107.55**
Fees, **ORC 2101.16**
Notice to release estate from administration, **ORC 2113.03**
Pretermitted, **ORC 2107.34**
    Debt payments, contributions by, **ORC 2107.55**

DESTITUTE PERSONS
See INDIGENT PERSONS

DESTROYED RECORDS
See LOST INSTRUMENTS AND RECORDS

DESTRUCTION OF PROPERTY
Minor committing, parental liability, **ORC 3109.09**

DETENTION
See ARRESTS

DETENTION FACILITIES
Juvenile courts, district detention facility trustees, **ORC 2152.44**

DETENTION HOMES
Generally, **JuvR 7, ORC 2152.26**
Admissions, **JuvR 7(C) to JuvR 7(E)**
Adults, separation from, **JuvR 7(H)**
Appropriations, **ORC 2151.10**
Definitions, **JuvR 2**
District homes
    Joint boards, **ORC 2152.43**
Family foster homes, **ORC 2151.331**
Funding, **ORC 2152.43**
Hearings, **JuvR 7(F)**
    Rehearings, **JuvR 7(G)**
Medical examination of child, **JuvR 7(I)**
Notice to parent of child's admission, **JuvR 7(E), JuvR 7(C)**
Placement of children in, **JuvR 7(A), JuvR 7(B), ORC 2152.26**
    Juvenile traffic offenders, **ORC 2151.34, ORC 2152.21**
    Temporary, **ORC 2151.33**
Probation or parole revocation hearing pending, **JuvR 35(C)**
Rehearings, **JuvR 7(G)**
Reports, **ORC 2151.37, ORC 2151.40**
    Admission, **JuvR 7(E), JuvR 7(C)**
Rights of child, **JuvR 7(E), JuvR 7(J)**
Schooling costs of children, **ORC 2151.362**

DETENTION HOMES—*continued*
Securities issue to finance, **ORC 2151.655**
Separation from adults, **JuvR 7(H)**
Telephone rights, **JuvR 7(J)**
Visitation rights, **JuvR 7(J)**

DEVELOPMENTALLY DISABLED PERSONS
See MENTALLY RETARDED AND DEVELOPMENTALLY DISABLED PERSONS

DEVISES
See LEGACIES AND DEVISES

DISABILITY
Powers of attorney, effect, **ORC 1337.091**

DISABILITY, PERSONS UNDER
Developmental. See MENTALLY RETARDED AND DEVELOPMENTALLY DISABLED PERSONS
Guardians. See GUARDIANSHIP, generally
Legal
    Defined, **ORC 2131.02**
    Heirs convicted of homicide, **ORC 2105.19**
    Surviving spouse under, **ORC 2106.08**
Mentally ill persons. See MENTALLY ILL PERSONS
Mentally retarded. See MENTALLY RETARDED AND DEVELOPMENTALLY DISABLED PERSONS
Physically disabled persons. See DISABLED PERSONS, generally

DISABLED PERSONS
Adoption of, **ORC 3107.02**
Children
    Mental retardation and developmental disabilities department making eligibility determinations, **ORC 5123.012**
Drivers' licenses, restrictions, **ORC 4507.08**
Jurisdiction, **ORC 2101.24**
Legal disability, considered to be under. See DISABILITY, PERSONS UNDER, generally
Supplemental services for disabled individuals, inter vivos and testamentary trusts, **ORC 5815.28**
Victims of crime
    Juvenile delinquency, disposition of case, **ORC 2152.12(C)**

DISCLAIMER OF SUCCESSION TO PROPERTY
Generally, **ORC 5815.36**
Charitable purpose, for; estate tax deduction, **ORC 5731.17**
Power of appointment, effect on estate tax, **ORC 5731.11**

DISCLAIMERS
Fiduciaries, release and disclaimer of a power of appointment, **ORC 5815.14**

DISCLOSURE
See CONFIDENTIAL INFORMATION, generally

DISCOVERY
Generally, **JuvR 24**
Commencement, **JuvR 24(A)**
Depositions. See DEPOSITIONS
Documents, production, **JuvR 24(A)**
Failure to comply, **JuvR 24(C)**
Juvenile proceedings, **JuvR 24**
Limitations, **JuvR 24(B)**
Motions to compel, hearing, **JuvR 22(D)**
Order granting, **JuvR 24(B)**
Privileged information, **JuvR 24(B)**
Production of documents, **JuvR 24(A)**
Reciprocal, **JuvR 24(B)**
Recording methods, **SupR 11, SupR 13**
Sanctions, **JuvR 24(B)**

DISCRETIONARY TRUSTS
See SPENDTHRIFT AND DISCRETIONARY TRUSTS

DISCRIMINATION
Generally, **O Const I § 2**
Mentally ill, against, **ORC 5122.301**
Mentally retarded or developmentally disabled persons, against, **ORC 5123.83**

DISINHERITANCE
Afterborn or pretermitted heirs, **ORC 2107.34**

DISMISSAL OF ACTIONS
Adoption, **ORC 3107.04**
Incompetent to stand trial, **ORC 2945.38(H)**
Juvenile proceedings, **JuvR 22(A), JuvR 29(F), ORC 2151.35**
Paternity proceedings, **ORC 3109.25**

DISOBEDIENCE
See CONTEMPT

DISPUTE RESOLUTION
Interstate Compact on Placement of Children, **ORC 5103.20**

DISSOLUTION
Interstate Compact on Placement of Children, **ORC 5103.20**

DISSOLUTION OF MARRIAGE
Children
    Care, custody, and control. See CHILD SUPPORT
    Care, custody, and control. See CHILD SUPPORT; CUSTODY OF CHILDREN
    Paternity, presumption, **ORC 3111.03**
    Shared parenting of, **ORC 3109.04**
Designation of spouse as beneficiary, effect, **ORC 5815.33**
Fiduciaries' responsibilities, **ORC 2109.26**
Jurisdiction, **ORC 2101.24**
    Paternity proceedings involved, **ORC 3109.25(F)**
Legal separation. See LEGAL SEPARATION
Paternity, presumption, **ORC 3111.03**
Personal property held jointly by spouses, effect, **ORC 5815.34**
Petition, shared parenting plan filed with, **ORC 3109.04(G)**
Power of attorney, revocation of spouse's power of attorney upon divorce, dissolution, or separation, **ORC 5815.32**
Separation, legal. See LEGAL SEPARATION
Separation agreements. See SEPARATION AGREEMENTS
Spouse presumed dead, **ORC 2121.04**
Wills, effect, **ORC 2107.33**

DISTRIBUTION AND DESCENT
See DESCENT AND DISTRIBUTION

DISTRIBUTION IN KIND
Generally, **ORC 2113.40, ORC 2113.55**

DISTRIBUTION OF ESTATE ASSETS
See ASSETS OF ESTATES

DISTRICT DETENTION FACILITY TRUSTEES
Juvenile courts, **ORC 2152.44**

DISTRICTS
Appeals courts, **O Const IV § 3**
Detention homes
    See also DETENTION HOMES
Taxing. See TAXING DISTRICTS

DIVORCE
Annulment of marriage. See ANNULMENT OF MARRIAGE
Answer, hearing and judgment, **ORC 3105.10(A)**
Children
    Care, custody, and control. See CHILD SUPPORT
    Care, custody, and control. See CHILD SUPPORT; CUSTODY OF CHILDREN
    Care, custody, and control. See CHILD SUPPORT; CUSTODY OF CHILDREN; DOMESTIC; VISITATION RIGHTS
    Paternity, presumption, **ORC 3111.03**

DIVORCE

DIVORCE—*continued*
Complaints, **ORC 3105.17**
Counterclaims, **ORC 3105.17**
Decree
    Shared parenting plan as final decree, **ORC 3109.04(D)(1)**
Designation of spouse as beneficiary, effect, **ORC 5815.33**
Domestic violence, grounds for divorce, **ORC 3105.01(D)**
Dower interest, termination, **ORC 2103.02, ORC 3105.10(D)**
Evidence of marriage, **ORC 3105.12**
Grounds, **ORC 3105.01**
Hearing, **ORC 3105.10(A)**
Judgment, **ORC 3105.10(A)**
Jurisdiction, paternity proceedings involved, **ORC 3109.25(F)**
Juvenile procedure rules, applicability, **JuvR 1(C)**
Legal separation. See LEGAL SEPARATION
Paternity, presumption, **ORC 3111.03**
Personal property held jointly by spouses, effect, **ORC 5815.34**
Power of appointment granted to spouse or nominated as trustee, termination of marriage as revocation, **ORC 5815.31**
Power of attorney, revocation of spouse's power of attorney upon divorce, dissolution, or separation, **ORC 5815.32**
Res judicata as defense
    Living separate and apart grounds, not bar to, **ORC 3105.01**
Separation, legalSee LEGAL SEPARATION
Service of process, **ORC 3105.06**
Trial, notice, **ORC 3105.06**
Wills, effect, **ORC 2107.33**

DNA
Database
    Records and reports, juvenile delinquents, **ORC 2152.74**
Prisoner testing, **ORC 2901.07**
Testing
    Juvenile delinquents, **ORC 2152.74**
    Prisoners, **ORC 2901.07**

DNR IDENTIFICATION
Generally, **ORC 2133.21 to 2133.26**
Advisory committee, representatives, **ORC 2133.25**
Clinical nurse specialist
    Approved actions by, **ORC 2133.211**
    Immunity, **ORC 2133.211, ORC 2133.22**
Concealment, **ORC 2133.26**
Defacement of, **ORC 2133.26**
Definitions, **ORC 2133.21**
Do-not-resuscitate protocol, **ORC 2133.25**
Durable power of attorney for health care, priority, **ORC 1337.12**
Falsification of, **ORC 2133.26**
Form, **ORC 2133.25**
Immunity, persons entitled to for actions taken following, **ORC 2133.22**
Informed consent, effect on right to, **ORC 2133.24**
Life insurance, effect on, **ORC 2133.24**
Living wills, superseding of, **ORC 2133.03**
Oral, compliance by emergency medical services personnel, **ORC 2133.23**
Physician or health care facility unable to comply, transfer to another facility, **ORC 2133.23**
Presumption concerning intent of those without, **ORC 2133.24**
Protocol, do-not-resuscitate, **ORC 2133.25**
Reduced to writing, **ORC 2133.23**
Rules, **ORC 2133.25**
Violations, **ORC 2133.26**
Written do-not-resuscitate order required, **ORC 2133.23**

DOCTORS
See PHYSICIANS

DOCUMENTS
See RECORDS AND REPORTS

DOMESTIC CORPORATIONS
See CORPORATIONS

DOMESTIC RELATIONS
Adoption. See ADOPTION
Alimony. See SUPPORT AND MAINTENANCE
Annulment. See ANNULMENT OF MARRIAGE
Child custody. See CUSTODY OF CHILDREN, DOMESTIC
Courts. See COURTS OF COMMON PLEAS, at Domestic relations division
Divorce. See DIVORCE
Husband and wife. See HUSBAND AND WIFE
Illegitimate children. See ILLEGITIMATE CHILDREN
Marriage. See MARRIAGE
Next of kin. See NEXT OF KIN
Parent and child. See PARENT AND CHILD

DOMESTIC RELATIONS COURTS
Arbitration, **SupR 15**
Destruction of court records, **SupR 26(E)**
Mediation, custody or visitation of children, **SupR 16**
Records and reports, management and retention, **SupR 26**
    Administrative records, retention schedule, **SupR 26.01**

DOMESTIC VIOLENCE
Child abuse. See CHILD ABUSE
Divorce, grounds for, **ORC 3105.01(D)**

DOMICILE
See RESIDENCY REQUIREMENTS

DOMICILIARY ADMINISTRATION
Generally, **ORC Ch 2113**
See also ADMINISTRATION OF ESTATES, generally

DONATIONS
See GIFTS AND GRANTS

DO-NOT-RESUSCITATE ORDERS
Generally, **ORC 2133.21 to 2133.26**

DOWER
Generally, **ORC Ch 2103, ORC Ch 5305**
Adultery, effect, **ORC 2103.05**
Affidavit of spouse, interest, **ORC 2103.021**
Aliens holding and acquiring land by, **ORC 2105.16**
Appraisement of yearly value, **ORC 5305.11**
    Exclusions, **ORC 5305.12**
Assignment, **ORC 2103.08, ORC 5305.01**
    Commissioners, **ORC 5305.06 to 5305.08**
    Death of plaintiff before, **ORC 5305.05**
    Fraud and collusion, effect on minor heir, **ORC 5305.13**
    Guardian's powers, **ORC 2111.21**
    Indivisible estate, **ORC 5305.08**
    Jurisdiction, **ORC 2101.24**
    Waiver, **ORC 5305.15, ORC 5305.16**
Claims, **ORC 2103.041**
Commissioners appointed to assign, **ORC 5305.06 to 5305.08**
Conveyances, **ORC 2103.02 to 2103.03**
    In lieu of, **ORC 2103.03, ORC 2103.04**
Costs, **ORC 5305.14**
Death
    Plaintiff's, effect on action, **ORC 5305.05**
    Termination, **ORC 2103.02**
Default, loss of property by; recovery, **ORC 2103.06**
Distributive share in lieu of, **ORC 2103.02**
Divorce, termination, **ORC 2103.02, ORC 3105.10(D)**
Election of owner to pay, **ORC 5305.10**
Election to be endowed out of sale proceeds, **ORC 5305.15, ORC 5305.16**
Encumbrances presented by cross-petition, **ORC 5305.03**
Eviction from premises conveyed in lieu of, **ORC 2103.04**
Execution of judgment, **ORC 2103.041**
Fraud
    Assignment, effect on minor heir, **ORC 5305.13**
    Recovery, **ORC 2103.06**

DOWER—continued

Gross estate of decedent spouse, inclusion, **ORC 5731.04, ORC 5731.13**
Guardianship, spouse under, **ORC 2111.21, ORC 2111.28, ORC 5305.17**
Incompetents. See Mentally ill persons, this heading
Judicial sale of property representing interest, **ORC 2103.041**
Land sale proceeding, **ORC 2127.16, ORC 2127.30**
Land situated in different counties, **ORC 5305.04**
Legal separation, termination, **ORC 3105.10(E)**
Lien presented by cross-petition, **ORC 5305.03**
Mentally ill persons, **ORC 5305.17 to 5305.22**
 Conveyance free from dower, **ORC 5305.22**
 Guardian, powers and duties, **ORC 5305.17**
 Inquest, **ORC 5305.18 to 5305.20**
 Petition to discharge land, **ORC 5305.18**
 Right of dower, barred, **ORC 5305.21**
Minor heirs, **ORC 2111.21, ORC 5305.11, ORC 5305.13**
Partition, **ORC 5305.15**
Payments in lieu of, **ORC 2127.16**
Pendency of action, during, **ORC 5305.11**
Petition, **ORC 5305.02**
 Discharge of land of mentally ill spouse, **ORC 5305.18**
Property, defined, **ORC 2103.01**
Real property
 Sale by fiduciary, effect on, **ORC 2127.16**
Recovery of interest, **ORC 2103.06**
Release, **ORC 2111.21, ORC 5305.16**
 Estate tax, effect, **ORC 5731.13**
 Spouse, mentally ill, **ORC 5305.22**
Termination, **ORC 2103.02**
 Divorce, by, **ORC 3105.10(D)**
 Legal separation, by, **ORC 3105.10(E)**
Timberlands, **ORC 5305.09, ORC 5305.10**
Waiver of assignment, **ORC 5305.15, ORC 5305.16**
Waste, **ORC 2103.07**

DRAFTING WILLS

Instruments, incorporation by reference, **ORC 2107.05**
Witnesses. See WITNESSES TO WILLS

DRIVERS' LICENSES

Age requirement, **ORC 4507.08**
Anatomical gift, provision for, **ORC 2108.04, ORC 4507.06**
Denial
 Convicted of certain violations, **ORC 4510.31, ORC 4510.33**
 Grounds for, **ORC 4507.08**
Durable power of attorney for health care, **ORC 4507.06**
Handicapped persons, restrictions, **ORC 4507.08**
Impounding plate, **ORC 4507.02**
Indigent driver's alcohol treatment funds, **ORC 4511.191**
Living wills, **ORC 4507.06**
Mentally ill or retarded persons, **ORC 4507.08**
Minors, **ORC 4507.07**
 Delinquent
  Denial, **ORC 4507.08**
  Suspension or revocation, **ORC 4510.31, ORC 4510.33**
 Denial for certain violations, **ORC 4510.31, ORC 4510.33**
 Juvenile driver improvement programs, **ORC 4510.31, ORC 4510.33**
 Juvenile traffic offenders
  Denial, **ORC 4507.08**
  Suspension or revocation, **ORC 2152.21, ORC 4510.31, ORC 4510.33**
  Suspension or revocation, **ORC 2151.354, ORC 2152.21, ORC 4507.021, ORC 4510.31, ORC 4510.33**
  Weapons, illegal conveyance or possession on school premises, **ORC 2923.122**
 Unruly
  Denial, **ORC 4507.08**
  Suspension or revocation, **ORC 2151.354, ORC 4510.31, ORC 4510.33**

DRIVERS' LICENSES—continued

Out-of-state license, surrender, **ORC 4507.02**
Plate, impounding, **ORC 4507.02**
Private property, **ORC 4507.02**
Probationary, **ORC 4507.07**
 Denial, minor convicted of certain violations, **ORC 4510.31, ORC 4510.33**
 Juvenile traffic offender, suspension or revocation, **ORC 2152.21**
 Restrictions, **ORC 4507.071**
 Suspension, **ORC 4510.31, ORC 4510.33**
 Unruly child, suspension or revocation, **ORC 2151.354**
Public property, **ORC 4507.02**
Reinstatement of suspended license, **ORC 4507.08**
Restricted licenses
 Denial, minor convicted of certain violations, **ORC 4510.31, ORC 4510.33**
 Plates, **ORC 4507.02**
 Suspension, **ORC 4510.31, ORC 4510.33**
Seizure, **ORC 4511.191**
Surrender, out-of-state license, **ORC 4507.02**
Suspension or revocation, **ORC 2152.21, ORC 4507.08, ORC 4510.31, ORC 4510.33**
 Unruly child, **ORC 2151.354, ORC 2151.355**
 Weapons, illegal conveyance or possession on school premises
  Drivers' license, denial or revocation of temporary instruction permit, **ORC 2923.122**
Temporary instruction permit
 Application, **ORC 4507.07**
 Juvenile traffic offender, suspension or revocation, **ORC 2152.21**
 Restrictions against issuance, **ORC 4507.08**
 Suspension or revocation, **ORC 4510.31, ORC 4510.33**
 Unruly child, suspension or revocation, **ORC 2151.354**

DRUG ABUSE

Juvenile courts, recovery of costs from juvenile drug abuse offenders, **ORC 2152.202**

DRUG OFFENSES

Abuse
 Parents
  Effect on adequate parental care determination, **ORC 2151.414(A)**
  Institutional custody of children based on, assessment and treatment requirement, **ORC 2151.3514**
Drivers' licenses, suspension or revocation, **ORC 4510.31, ORC 4510.33**
Driving while under the influence of drugs, **ORC 4511.19**
Minor drug possession offense, defined, **ORC 5123.081**

DRUG TREATMENT PROGRAMS

Parents
 Institutional custody of children based on, assessment and treatment requirement, **ORC 2151.3514**

DRUNK DRIVING

Generally, **ORC 4511.19, ORC 4511.191**
Blood or breath tests, **ORC 4511.19**
Chemical tests, **ORC 4511.191**
Criminal forfeiture of motor vehicles, **ORC 4507.021**
Drugs, driving under influence of, **ORC 4511.19**
Immunity for those withdrawing blood, **ORC 4511.19**
Minors, **ORC 4511.19**
Occupational driving privileges, **ORC 4510.31, ORC 4510.33**
Penalties, **ORC 4511.19**
Presumptions, **ORC 4511.19**
Refusal to submit to tests, **ORC 4511.191**
Tests, **4511.191, ORC 4511.19**

DRUNKENNESS

Fiduciary, removal grounds, **ORC 2109.24**

DUE PROCESS

Generally, **O Const I § 16**

DURABLE POWER OF ATTORNEY FOR HEALTH CARE
See POWER OF ATTORNEY

DURESS
See COERCION

EASEMENTS
Prescriptive rights, limitation of actions against, **ORC 2305.04**
Statute of frauds, **ORC 1335.04**

EDUCATION
See SCHOOLS AND SCHOOL DISTRICTS; UNIVERSITIES AND COLLEGES

EDUCATION, LOCAL BOARDS
Generally, See SCHOOLS AND SCHOOL DISTRICTS
Foster care, placement of children outside home county
    Notice to school boards, **ORC 2151.553**

EDUCATIONAL ORGANIZATIONS
See INSTITUTIONAL TRUST FUNDS ACT

ELDERLY
See AGED PERSONS

ELECTION BY SURVIVING SPOUSE
See SURVIVING SPOUSE

ELECTRONIC DATA PROCESSING
Probate court records, **ORC 2101.121**

ELECTRONIC RECORDS AND SIGNATURES
Existing relationships, application to, **ORC 5811.03**
Trusts, **ORC 5811.02**

ELECTRONIC TRANSFER OF FUNDS
Use and storage tax, remittance by, **ORC 5747.12**

ELEEMOSYNARY ORGANIZATIONS
See INSTITUTIONAL TRUST FUNDS ACT

EMBALMERS AND FUNERAL DIRECTORS
Eyes, enucleation, **ORC 2108.071, ORC 2108.60**

EMBEZZLEMENT
Fiduciaries, by, **ORC 2109.50 to 2109.56**
    See also ASSETS OF ESTATES, at Concealed or embezzled

EMERGENCY MEDICAL SERVICES
Child, for, **ORC 2151.33**
Do-not-resuscitate orders, compliance with, **ORC 2133.23**
Juveniles under court jurisdiction, **JuvR 13(C), ORC 2151.33**

EMERGENCY ORDERS
Mental retardation and developmental disabilities, county boards, ex parte emergency orders, **ORC 5126.331-5126.333**

EMINENT DOMAIN
Generally, **O Const I § 19, ORC Ch 163**
Abandonment of proceedings, **ORC 163.21**
Advertising devices, removal by order, **ORC 163.31 to 163.33**
Answer to petition, **ORC 163.08**
Appeals, **ORC 163.09, ORC 163.19**
    Compensation of owner, **ORC 163.58**
Application, review, **ORC 163.58**
Appraisals of property, **ORC 163.06, ORC 163.09, ORC 163.59**
Attorney fees, abandonment or disallowance of proceeding, **ORC 163.21**
Buildings and improvements on real property, **ORC 163.60**
Civil procedure rules, applicability, **ORC 163.22**
Compensation of owner, **O Const I § 19, ORC 163.09, ORC 163.60, ORC 163.61**
    Appeal, **ORC 163.58**
    Buildings and improvements, for, **ORC 163.60**

EMINENT DOMAIN—continued
Compensation of owner, **O Const I § 19, ORC 163.09, ORC 163.60, ORC 163.61**—continued
    Deposits. See Deposits of compensation, this heading
    Distribution, **ORC 163.18**
    Incidental expenses, **ORC 163.61**
    Judicial award, **ORC 163.62**
    Jury to determine, **O Const I § 19, ORC 163.09, ORC 163.10, ORC 163.12, ORC 163.14**
    Mortgage prepayment, penalty costs, **ORC 163.61**
    Offer, **ORC 163.59**
    Relocation assistance, **ORC 163.51 to 163.62**
Confession of judgment, **ORC 163.16**
Conservancy districts, powers, **ORC 163.02**
Consolidation of proceedings, **ORC 163.09**
Damages during surveys and inspections, **ORC 163.03**
Defect in proceedings, **ORC 163.12**
Definitions, **ORC 163.01**
Delay in proceedings, **ORC 163.13**
Depositions, use, **ORC 163.10**
Deposits of compensation, **ORC 163.06, ORC 163.59**
    Distribution, **O Const I § 19, ORC 163.18**
    Notice, **ORC 163.18**
    Retention when ownership disputed, **ORC 163.13**
Fees and costs, **ORC 163.15, ORC 163.16, ORC 163.61**
    Abandonment of proceedings, **ORC 163.21**
    Appropriation disallowed, **ORC 163.21**
    Relocation assistance, **ORC 163.53**
Guardian ad litem, appointment, **ORC 163.11**
Hearings, **ORC 163.10 to 163.14**
Joinder of parties, **ORC 163.12**
Jurisdiction, **ORC 163.01, ORC 2101.25**
Jury to determine compensation, **O Const I § 19, ORC 163.09, ORC 163.10, ORC 163.12, ORC 163.14**
Limitations, **ORC 163.04**
Mental retardation and developmental disabilities department, by, **ORC 5123.22**
Mentally ill persons, representation, **ORC 163.11**
Minors, representation, **ORC 163.11**
Municipal powers, **O Const XVIII § 10**
Notice, **ORC 163.59**
Orders of court, **ORC 163.09**
Owner of land
    Compensation. See Compensation of owner, this heading
    Unknown, **ORC 163.04**
Parties to actions in proceedings, **ORC 163.12**
Petition, **ORC 163.05 to 163.08**
    Answer, **ORC 163.08**
Policy, **ORC 163.04, ORC 163.59**
Possession of premises, **ORC 163.15**
    Notice, **ORC 163.59**
Public utility facility, relocation payments, **ORC 163.53**
Rail service, for, **ORC 163.06**
Relocation assistance, **ORC 163.51 to 163.62**
Right of entry, **ORC 163.03**
Rules, relocation assistance, **ORC 163.58**
Sanitary districts, powers, **ORC 163.02**
Service of process, **ORC 163.07**
Signs, removal by order, **ORC 163.31 to 163.33**
Summit county probate court, **SumR 97.1**
Surveys and inspections, **ORC 163.03**
Title to property, perfection, **ORC 163.20**
Trial date, advancement, **ORC 163.22**
Utility facility, relocation payment, **ORC 163.53**
Validity of acquisition, **ORC 163.52**
Verdict, **ORC 163.14**

EMOTIONALLY DISTURBED PERSONS
See MENTALLY ILL PERSONS

EMPLOYER AND EMPLOYEE
Caring for minors, criminal record check as prerequisite, **ORC 2151.86, ORC 2151.861**
Children's advocacy centers, **ORC 2151.426**
Compensation. See COMPENSATION
Death of employee
    Wages, release, **ORC 2113.04**
Garnishment of employee's wage. See GARNISHMENT
Training costs, state income tax, credit for employee training costs, **ORC 5747.39**
Witness at juvenile proceeding, employee as; penalization by employer prohibited, **ORC 2151.211**
Wrongful death actions, **ORC Ch 2125**
    See also WRONGFUL DEATH, generally

ENCUMBRANCES
See also LIENS
Dower, **ORC 5305.03**
Estate, against; will not revoked, **ORC 2107.35**
Leases. See LEASES
Liens. See LIENS

ENDANGERING CHILDREN
See also CHILD ABUSE; DEPENDENT AND NEGLECTED CHILDREN
Custody of child, **ORC 2151.31**
Jurisdiction, **ORC 2151.23**

ENTERING
See RIGHT OF ENTRY

EQUAL CONSANGUINITY
Descent, **ORC 2105.12**

EQUITY
Trusts, applicability, **ORC 5801.05**
Uniform Fiduciary Act
    Rules of law and equity applicable, **ORC 5815.11**

ERIE COUNTY
Probate courts, jurisdictional responsibilities of additional judge, **ORC 2101.023**

ERRORS
See APPEALS, generally

ESCAPE
Incompetent to stand trial, arrests, **ORC 5123.13**
Mentally ill, from hospital, **ORC 5122.26**
Not guilty by reason of insanity, arrests, **ORC 5123.13**

ESCHEAT
Estates, under intestate succession, **ORC 2105.06**

ESTATE BY THE ENTIRETIES
Generally, **ORC 5302.21**

ESTATE TAX
Generally, **O Const XII § 3, ORC Ch 5731**
Additional, **ORC 5731.18**
    Nonresidents, **ORC 5731.19**
    Payment, **ORC 5731.24**
Administration of estate, deductions, **ORC 5731.16**
Administrative conferences, **ORC 5731.26**
Agents, **ORC 5731.41**
Alternate valuation date, defined, **ORC 5731.01**
Annuities, **ORC 5731.09, ORC 5731.39**
Appeals, **ORC 5731.30 to 5731.32**
Apportionment among interested persons, **ORC 2113.85 to 2113.88**
    Actions by fiduciary to recover, **ORC 2113.89**
    Bond of fiduciary, **ORC 2113.88**
    Definitions, **ORC 2113.85**
    Exemptions, deductions, or credits; effect, **ORC 2113.86**
    Generation-skipping transfer tax, **ORC 2113.861**

ESTATE TAX—*continued*
Apportionment among interested persons, **ORC 2113.85 to 2113.88**—*continued*
    Nonresidents, **ORC 2113.90**
    Notice, **ORC 2113.87**
    Objections, **ORC 2113.87**
    Penalties, **ORC 2113.86**
    Probate courts determining, **ORC 2113.86, ORC 2113.87**
    Uncollectible amounts, reapportionment, **ORC 2113.89**
    Withholding taxes from distribution, **ORC 2113.88**
Apportionment of revenues, **ORC 5731.48**
Attorney general's duties, **ORC 5731.42, ORC 5731.43**
Audit by tax commissioner, **ORC 5731.21, ORC 5731.26**
    Amended returns, **ORC 5731.28**
    Appeal, **ORC 5731.30 to 5731.32**
    Exceptions to, **ORC 5731.27**
        Probate court, filing with, **ORC 5731.30, ORC 5731.31**
Auditors, county. See AUDITORS, COUNTY
Blockage rule, **ORC 5731.01**
Bonds and notes, **ORC 5731.51**
Certificate of determination, **ORC 5731.27**
Certificates, **ORC 5731.21**
Certificates of liability, **ORC 5731.27**
Charitable bequests, deductions, **ORC 5731.17**
Claims against estate, deductions, **ORC 5731.16**
    Late filing, amending return, **ORC 5731.28**
Collection, **ORC 5731.21**
    Additional estate tax, **ORC 5731.18**
Compromise, foreign estate taxes, **ORC 5731.35**
Computation, **ORC 5731.02**
Condition precedent, effect, **ORC 5731.17**
Confidentiality of information, **ORC 5731.90**
Contemplation of death, transfer, **ORC 5731.05**
County auditors. See AUDITORS, COUNTY
County of decedent, defined, **ORC 5731.01(E)**
County treasurers. See TREASURERS, COUNTY
Credits, **ORC 5731.02**
    Additional tax, **ORC 5731.18**
    Apportionment among interested persons, **ORC 2113.86**
Curtesy, **ORC 5731.04, ORC 5731.13**
Death benefit plans, proceeds, **ORC 5731.09**
Deductions, **ORC 5731.14 to 5731.17**
    Charitable, **ORC 5731.17**
    Claims against estate, **ORC 5731.16**
        Late filing, amending return, **ORC 5731.28**
    Death benefit plan annuities, **ORC 5731.09**
    Funeral expenses, **ORC 5731.16**
    Life insurance, **ORC 5731.12**
    Lobbying, effect, **ORC 5731.17**
    Marital, **ORC 5731.15**
        Trusts, charges to principal or income to preserve deduction, **ORC 5812.36**
    Missing-in-action pay, **ORC 5731.15**
    Mortgages, **ORC 5731.16**
    Qualified terminable interest property, **ORC 5731.15**
    Straddling estates, **ORC 5731.161**
Definitions, **ORC 2113.85, ORC 5731.01**
Determination by tax commissioner. See Audit by tax commissioner, this heading
Disclaimer of bequest, **ORC 5731.17**
Distribution of revenues, **ORC 5731.48**
Dower, **ORC 5731.04, ORC 5731.13**
Due date, **ORC 5731.23**
Estimates
    Tax commissioner to make when not filed by fiduciary, **ORC 5731.21**
Exceptions to tax commissioner's audit, **ORC 5731.27**
    Probate court, filing with, **ORC 5731.30, ORC 5731.31**
Exemptions
    Annuities, **ORC 5731.09**
    Gross estate of § 25,000 or less, **ORC 5731.21**

ESTATE TAX

ESTATE TAX—*continued*
Exemptions—*continued*
    Highway patrol retirement system benefits, **ORC 5731.09**
    Intangible property employed in business, **ORC 5731.34**
    Municipal retirement system benefits, **ORC 5731.09**
    Police and fire pension fund benefits, **ORC 5731.09**
    Public employees retirement system benefits, **ORC 5731.09**
    Reciprocal, **ORC 5731.34**
    School employees retirement system benefits, **ORC 5731.09**
    Teachers retirement system benefits, **ORC 5731.09**
Extension of filing time, **ORC 5731.21**
    Administration of estate, **ORC 2113.28, ORC 2115.17**
Farmland, valuation, **ORC 5731.011**
    Lien in favor of state, **ORC 5731.37**
Federal. See ESTATE TAX, FEDERAL
Fees and costs, **ORC 5731.47**
    County auditor and treasurer, **ORC 5731.46**
    Deduction from revenues before distribution, **ORC 5731.48**
    Sheriffs, **ORC 5731.47**
Filing
    Certificate, **ORC 5731.21**
    Failure to file, **ORC 5731.21**
    Return, with probate court, **FrankR 75.15, ORC 5731.21**
Foreign states, compromise, **ORC 5731.35**
Fraud, **ORC 5731.22**
Funeral expenses, deductions, **ORC 5731.16**
Generation-skipping transfer tax, **ORC 5731.181**
    Apportionment among interested persons, **ORC 2113.861**
Gifts. See Transfers, this heading
Gross estate, **ORC 5731.03 to 5731.131**
    Defined, **ORC 5731.01**
    Estimates to be filed
        Failure to file, **ORC 5731.22**
    Fair market value, determination, **ORC 5731.01**
    Insurance, **ORC 5731.12**
    Life interest subject to federal marital deduction, **ORC 5731.131**
    Life interest subject to qualified terminable interest property deduction, **ORC 5731.131**
    Payments made on, **ORC 5731.23**
    Transfers to be included, **ORC 5731.05, ORC 5731.08**
    § 25,000 or less, **ORC 5731.21**
Hearings
    Administrative conferences, **ORC 5731.26**
    Appeals, **ORC 5731.30**
Highway patrol retirement system benefits exempt, **ORC 5731.09**
Insurance
    Federal civil service, **ORC 5731.09**
    Life insurance, **ORC 5731.12**
    Military service, **ORC 5731.09**
Inter vivos trusts, distribution by fiduciary involving federal estate tax marital deduction, **ORC 5815.21**
Interest, **ORC 5731.23**
    Additional tax, **ORC 5731.24**
    Fiduciaries' liability, **ORC 2113.87**
    Postponed payments, **ORC 5731.25**
IRS regulations, applicability, **ORC 5731.18**
Joint tenancy, **ORC 5731.10**
Jurisdiction, **ORC 5731.31**
Liability, **ORC 5731.37, ORC 5731.38**
    Fiduciaries, **ORC 5731.22**
    Interest, **ORC 2113.87**
Liens, **ORC 5731.37, ORC 5731.38**
Life estates, **ORC 5731.06**
Life insurance proceeds, **ORC 5731.12**
Life interest subject to federal marital deduction, **ORC 5731.131**
Life interest subject to qualified terminable interest property deduction, **ORC 5731.131**
Limitation of actions
    Estate tax return, filing, **ORC 5731.21**
    Exception to estimate by tax commissioner, **ORC 5731.21**
    Liability subsequent to filing of return, **ORC 5731.38**

ESTATE TAX—*continued*
Limitation of actions—*continued*
    Refund claims, **ORC 5731.28**
Marital deduction, **ORC 5731.15**
    Inter vivos trusts or testamentary trust, distribution by fiduciary involving federal estate tax marital deduction, **ORC 5815.21**
    Trust interest qualifying for, spendthrift provision not causing forfeiture or postponement, **ORC 5815.22**
    Trust not to require or permit accumulation for more than one year of property subject to, **ORC 5815.23**
    Trusts, charges to principal or income to preserve deduction, **ORC 5812.36**
Missing-in-action pay, deduction, **ORC 5731.15**
Mortgages, deductions, **ORC 5731.16**
Municipal retirement system benefits exempt, **ORC 5731.09**
Nonresident decedent, **ORC 5731.19, ORC 5731.36**
    Apportionment of tax, **ORC 2113.90**
    Transfer of assets, **ORC 5731.40**
Notice
    Appeal of tax commissioner's audit, **ORC 5731.30**
    County officials, to, **ORC 5731.21**
    Exception to return, **ORC 5731.21**
    Failure to file, **ORC 5731.21**
    Hearing before tax commissioner, **ORC 5731.27**
    Payment, of, **ORC 5731.33**
Payments, **ORC 5731.23, ORC 5731.33**
    Additional tax, **ORC 5731.24**
    Deficient, **ORC 5731.23, ORC 5731.27, ORC 5731.42**
    Due date, **ORC 5731.23, ORC 5731.27, ORC 5731.42**
        Extension for undue hardship, **ORC 5731.25**
    Generation-skipping transfers, **ORC 5731.181**
    Postponement, **ORC 5731.25**
    Undue hardship, extension of time, **ORC 5731.25**
Penalties, **ORC 5731.22, ORC 5731.99**
    Apportionment among interested persons, **ORC 2113.86**
    Collection, **ORC 5731.27**
    Fiduciaries' liability, **ORC 2113.87**
Pension, **ORC 5731.09**
Police and fire pension fund benefits exempt, **ORC 5731.09**
Power of appointment, **ORC 5731.06, ORC 5731.11**
Probate courts. See PROBATE COURTS
Profit sharing plans, **ORC 5731.09**
Public employees retirement system benefits exempt, **ORC 5731.09**
Qualified farm use, **ORC 5731.011**
    Lien in favor of state, **ORC 5731.37**
Qualified terminable interest property deduction, **ORC 5731.15**
Qualified use, establishment, **ORC 5731.011**
Rates, **ORC 5731.02**
    Additional tax, **ORC 5731.18**
        Nonresident estate tax, **ORC 5731.19**
    Nonresident estate tax, **ORC 5731.19**
Real property
    Appraisals, conclusiveness, **ORC 2115.17**
Receipts, **ORC 5731.33**
Refunds, **ORC 5731.27, ORC 5731.28**
    Adjustments in distribution of revenues due to, **ORC 5731.49**
    Amended return, due to, **ORC 5731.28**
    Certification, **ORC 5731.27**
    Interest, **ORC 5731.23**
Release of assets, **ORC 5731.39**
Remaindermen, **ORC 5731.25**
Retirement plans, **ORC 5731.09**
Returns, **ORC 5731.21 to 5731.25**
    Additional estate tax, **ORC 5731.24**
    Amending due to error, **ORC 5731.28**
    Audit by tax commissioner. See Audit by tax commissioner, this heading
    Confidentiality, **ORC 5731.90**
    Exceptions, **ORC 5731.21**
    Extension of filing time, **ORC 5731.21**
    Failure to file, **ORC 5731.21, ORC 5731.22**

ESTATE TAX—continued
Returns, **ORC 5731.21 to 5731.25**—continued
  False statements, **ORC 5731.22**
  Franklin County Probate Court, **FrankR 75.15**
  Generation-skipping transfers, **ORC 5731.181**
  Time for filing, **ORC 5731.21**
Reversionary interests, **ORC 5731.07, ORC 5731.25**
Rulemaking power, **ORC 5731.45**
  IRS regulations, applicability, **ORC 5731.18**
Safe deposit box, limitation on opening, **ORC 5731.39**
School employees retirement system benefits exempt, **ORC 5731.09**
Statutes of limitations. See Limitation of actions, this heading
Straddling estates, deduction, **ORC 5731.161**
Tax commissioner, powers and duties. See Audit by tax commissioner, this heading
Taxable estate, determination, **ORC 5731.14 to 5731.17**
Teachers retirement system benefits exempt, **ORC 5731.09**
Testamentary trusts, distribution by fiduciary involving federal estate tax marital deduction, **ORC 5815.21**
Transfers, **ORC 5731.05 to 5731.08**
  In contemplation of death, **ORC 5731.05**
  Life estates, **ORC 5731.06**
  Nonresident decedents, **ORC 5731.40**
  Situs regarding transfer tax, **ORC 5731.50**
  Straddling estates deduction, **ORC 5731.161**
Treasurers, county. See TREASURERS, COUNTY
Underpayment, **ORC 5731.23**
  Certification, **ORC 5731.27**
Undue hardship, extension of time for payment, **ORC 5731.25**
Valuation. See Gross estate, generally, this heading
Verification, **ORC 5731.26**
Veterans' organizations, gifts to, **ORC 5731.17**
Violations
  Financial institutions and life insurance companies, **ORC 5731.39**
  Penalties, **ORC 5731.22, ORC 5731.99**

ESTATE TAX, FEDERAL
Apportionment among interested persons, **ORC 2113.85 to 2113.88**
  See also ESTATE TAX
Inter vivos trusts, distribution by fiduciary involving federal estate tax marital deduction, **ORC 5815.21**
Liability, effect, **ORC 5731.18, ORC 5731.24**
  Used to determine Ohio estate tax, **ORC 5731.26**
Payment, liability for, **ORC 5731.18, ORC 5731.24**
Testamentary trusts, distribution by fiduciary involving federal estate tax marital deduction, **ORC 5815.21**

ESTATES
Accounts and accounting
  Final account, notice, **CuyR 64.2 et seq.**
  Medicaid expenses, estate recovery program, **ORC 2113.041**
  Notice of hearing on approval, **LucasR 64.1**
  Time for filing, **LucasR 64.1**
  Vouchers, **Sup. R 64.2**
Actions. See PROBATE COURTS, at Estate administration proceedings
Administration, **ORC Ch 2113**
  See also ADMINISTRATION OF ESTATES; EXECUTORS AND ADMINISTRATORS
  No administration. See NO ADMINISTRATION
Advancements from
  Fiduciaries making, **ORC 2109.44**
  Intestate succession, **ORC 2105.051**
Ancillary administration, **ORC 2129.04 to 2129.24**
  See also ANCILLARY ADMINISTRATION
Arbitration of claims against, **ORC 2117.09**
Assets. See ASSETS OF ESTATES
Attorney fees. See ATTORNEY FEES, at Estates, administration
Attorney to represent, **ORC 2109.03**
  Designation, **LucasR 57.1**
  Fees. See ATTORNEY FEES, at Estates, administration
Automobiles, transfer, **ORC 2106.18, ORC 4505.10**

ESTATES—continued
Beneficiaries. See HEIRS
Beneficiaries. See HEIRS; LEGACIES AND DEVISES
Boats and watercraft, transfer to surviving spouse, **ORC 2106.19**
Case management, probate court, **SupR 78**
Claims against, **ORC Ch 2117**
  See also CLAIMS AGAINST ESTATES
Concealed assets. See ASSETS OF ESTATES
Contingent claims. See CLAIMS AGAINST ESTATES
Contingent claims against, **ORC 2117.06**
Conveyance of whole interest, **ORC 2107.51**
Convicted criminal's, **O Const I § 12**
Court records, **ORC 2101.14**
Cuyahoga county probate court
  Accounts, **CuyR 64.2 et seq.**
  Court costs, **CuyR 58.1**
  Supervision, case management, **CuyR 78.1**
Debts owed by. See CLAIMS AGAINST ESTATES
Debts owed to. See DEBTS OWED TO ESTATES
Defensible fee, **ORC 2131.07**
Descent and distribution, **ORC Ch 2105**
  See also DESCENT AND DISTRIBUTION
Disclaimer of succession to property, **ORC 5815.36**
Distribution
  Prior to expiration of time for filing claims, notice, **ORC 2117.06**
Distributions. See ASSETS OF ESTATES
Election of surviving spouse. See SURVIVING SPOUSE
Embezzled assets. See ASSETS OF ESTATES, at Concealed or embezzled
Emblements, **ORC 2115.10**
Entireties, estate by the, **ORC 5302.21**
Escheat, **ORC 2105.06**
  See also ESCHEAT, generally
Estate recovery program
  Medicaid expenses, **ORC 2113.041**
  Notice, **ORC 2117.061**
Estate tax. See ESTATE TAX
Estate tax. See ESTATE TAX; FEDERAL
Execution of judgment, **ORC 2117.31, ORC 2117.34, ORC 2117.35**
Executors and administrators, **ORC Ch 2113**
  See also EXECUTORS AND ADMINISTRATORS
Executors' and administrators'. See EXECUTORS AND ADMINISTRATORS, at Compensation
Exempt from administration. See NO ADMINISTRATION
Expenses
  See also ADMINISTRATION OF ESTATES, at Expenses
  Appraiser's fee, **ORC 2115.06, SupR 61**
    Land sale proceeds, **ORC 2127.25, SupR 61**
  Estate tax deduction, **ORC 5731.16**
  Funeral expenses, **ORC 2106.20, ORC 2113.031**
    Distribution under summary estate administration to pay, **Sup. R 75.4**
  Improper filings, **ORC 2109.021**
  Land sale proceedings, **ORC 2127.08, ORC 2127.25, ORC 2127.37**
  Medicaid expenses, estate recovery program, **ORC 2113.041**
  Principal and income, allocation, **ORC 2109.67**
  Probate of wills, **ORC 2107.62**
  Real property sale, **ORC 2127.28**
    Distribution of proceeds, **ORC 2127.38**
  Will contest actions, **ORC 2107.75**
Family allowance, **ORC 2106.13**
  Distribution under summary estate administration to pay, **Sup. R 75.4**
  Priority, **ORC 2117.25**
Federal estate tax. See ESTATE TAX, FEDERAL
Fee simple
  Defensible, **ORC 2131.07**
  Survivorship tenancy, applicability, **ORC 5302.20**
Fiduciaries. See EXECUTORS AND ADMINISTRATORS

ESTATES

Index-40

ESTATES—*continued*
Fiduciaries. See EXECUTORS AND ADMINISTRATORS; FIDUCIARIES
Forfeiture due to conviction, **O Const I § 12**
Forms for administration, **SupR 51, SupR 52**
Franklin county probate court
    Case management, **FrankR 78.1**
Future interests, **ORC 2131.04 to 2131.07**
Guardianship. See GUARDIANSHIP
Hamilton county probate court
    Case management, **HamR 78.1**
    Court costs, deposit, **HamR Appx D**
Hearings
    Claims, **ORC 2117.17, SupR 62(B)**
    Insolvent estates, on claims, **ORC 2117.17**
    Inventory and appraisal, **ORC 2115.16**
Heirs. See HEIRS
Income
    Allocation between income and principal, **ORC 2109.68**
Income tax, federal. See INCOME TAX, FEDERAL
Insolvent, **ORC 2117.15**
    Attorney fees, **SumR 71.1(B)**
    Claims, hearing on allowance of, **ORC 2117.17**
    Ward's estate, **ORC 2111.24**
Interest owed by decedent, **ORC 2117.18**
Intestate succession, **ORC Ch 2105**
    See also DESCENT AND DISTRIBUTION
Inventory and appraisal, **ORC Ch 2115**
    See also INVENTORY AND APPRAISAL OF ESTATES
    Present values, determination, **ORC 2131.01**
Joint debtor, liability, **ORC 2117.31**
Judgments against, liability, **ORC 2117.31, ORC 2117.34, ORC 2117.35**
Land sale proceedings, **ORC Ch 2127**
    See also LAND SALE PROCEEDINGS
Leasehold, descent, **ORC 2105.04**
Legacies. See LEGACIES AND DEVISES
Liens. See LIENS
Life estates. See LIFE ESTATES
Life insurance proceeds
    Estate tax, **ORC 5731.12**
    Testamentary trustee as beneficiary, **ORC 2107.64**
Lucas county probate court
    Case management, **LucasR 78.1**
    Court costs, **LucasR 58.1(A)**
    Inventory, **LucasR 78.6**
Mansion house, defined, **ORC 2106.10(F)**
Medicaid expenses, estate recovery program, **ORC 2113.041**
Missing persons, **ORC 2119.01**
    Disposition, **ORC 2101.24**
Mortgages. See MORTGAGES
Motor vehicles, transfer, **ORC 2106.18, ORC 2113.031, ORC 4505.10**
Newly discovered assets, disposition, **ORC 2101.16, ORC 2113.69**
No administration. See NO ADMINISTRATION
Nonresident decedent
    Ancillary administration, **ORC Ch 2129**
        See also ANCILLARY ADMINISTRATION
    Estate tax, **ORC 5731.19, ORC 5731.36**
        Apportionment, **ORC 2113.90**
        Transfer of assets, **ORC 5731.40**
Notice. See EXECUTORS AND ADMINISTRATORS, at Notice
Outboard motors, transfer to surviving spouse, **ORC 2106.19**
Perpetuities, rule against, **ORC 2131.09**
Personal property. See ASSETS OF ESTATES, generally
Present values, determination, **ORC 2131.01**
Presumed decedent, **ORC 2121.05**
Probate court. See PROBATE COURTS, generally
Property taxes owed by decedent, **ORC 2117.18, ORC 2117.19**
Real property
    See also ASSETS OF ESTATES, generally
    Ancestral, **ORC 2105.01**

ESTATES—*continued*
Real property—*continued*
    Certificates of transfer, **ORC 2113.61**
    Debts, liability, **ORC 2117.36**
    Descent and distribution, **ORC Ch 2105**
    Escheat, **ORC 2105.09**
    Fraudulent transfers by decedent, **ORC 2127.40**
    Incomplete contracts, completion, **ORC 2113.48**
    Management, **ORC 2113.311**
    Mansion house, **ORC 2106.05, ORC 2106.10, ORC 2106.15**
    Missing person's estate, **ORC 2119.04**
    Mortgages
        Heirs' rights, **ORC 2117.29**
        Releases, **ORC 2127.19**
    Partition, **ORC 2127.41**
    Remainder, **ORC 2131.04 to 2131.07**
        Forfeiture for waste by life tenant, **ORC 2105.20**
        Protection of interest, **ORC 2113.58**
    Sale of, **ORC Ch 2127**
        See also LAND SALE PROCEEDINGS
    Surviving spouse's rights. See SURVIVING SPOUSE
    Will contests, fiduciary's duty during, **ORC 2113.21**
Records of court, **ORC 2101.14**
    Extracounty and extrastate proceedings, **ORC 2129.01**
Recovery, estate recovery program
    Medicaid expenses, **ORC 2113.041**
    Notice, **ORC 2117.061**
Remaindermen. See REMAINDERMEN
Residuary
    Death of devisee or legatee, effect, **ORC 2107.52**
    Distribution by ancillary administrator, **ORC 2129.22**
    Undevised real estate, disposition, **ORC 2107.53**
Reversion, forfeiture, **ORC 2105.20**
Settlement
    Distribution after final, **ORC 2113.57**
    Probate courts, jurisdiction, **ORC 2101.24**
    Termination, time of, **ORC 2101.141**
Stark county probate court
    Attorney fees, **Sup. R 71.2**
    Case management, **Sup. R 78.3**
    Court costs, **Sup. R 58.1**
    Relief from administration, **Sup. R 75.2**
    Summary administration, **Sup. R 75.4**
Summary estate administration, **Sup. R 75.4**
Summit county probate court
    Administration, **SumR 60.1**
        Attorney fees, **SumR 71.1(A)**
        Court costs, **SumR Appx A**
    Supervision, **SumR 78.1(B)**
Surviving spouse. See SURVIVING SPOUSE
Survivorship. See SURVIVORSHIP
Taxation
    See also EXECUTORS AND ADMINISTRATORS, at Tax returns, duties
    Estate tax, **ORC Ch 5731**
        See also ESTATE TAX
    Federal estate tax. See ESTATE TAX, FEDERAL
    Federal income tax. See INCOME TAX, FEDERAL
    Property taxes owed by decedent, **ORC 2117.18, ORC 2117.19**
Theft from
    Probate courts referring information to law enforcement agencies, **ORC 2101.26**
Transfers of assets, **ORC 5731.05 to 5731.08**
    Transfer tax, situs, **ORC 5731.50**
Trucks, transfer, **ORC 2106.18(D)**
Trust, in
    Lease of, **ORC 2101.24**
    Sale of, **ORC 2101.24**
Trustees, constructive; convicted murderer, **ORC 2105.19**
Unclaimed funds, disposition, **ORC 2113.64 to 2113.68**
    Transfer to owner from county treasury, **ORC 2113.67**

ESTATES—Cont'd
Uniform Principal and Income Act, application to existing decedent's estate, **ORC 5812.52**
Wages owed decedent, **ORC 2113.04**
Wills. See WILLS

EUTHANASIA
Living will not authorizing, **ORC 2133.12**

EVIDENCE
Admissibility
    Costs of pregnancy, confinement, and genetic testing; parentage action, **ORC 3111.12**
    Paternity proceedings, **ORC 3111.10, ORC 3111.12**
Burden of proof, **ORC 2901.05(A)**
Competence to stand trial, **ORC 2945.37(E), ORC 2945.37(H)**
Drunk driving, **ORC 4511.19**
Heirship determination, **ORC 2123.05**
Highways and roads, presumptive evidence for appropriation, **ORC 163.08**
Judgment against weight of
    Transcript required on appeal, **SupR 11**
Juvenile proceedings. See JUVENILE COURTS
Marriage, **ORC 3105.12**
Mental illness, of, **ORC 5122.13 to 5122.15**
Mental retardation, of, **ORC 5123.76**
Paternity presumption, rebuttal, **ORC 3111.03**
Paternity proceedings, **ORC 3111.10, ORC 3111.12**
Power of attorney, **ORC 1337.06**
Presumed decedents' law, **ORC 2121.03**
Testimony. See WITNESSES AND TESTIMONY
Transcripts. See TRANSCRIPTS
Wills
    Validity petition, failure to file, **ORC 2107.081, ORC 2107.085**
Witnesses and testimony. See WITNESSES AND TESTIMONY

EVIDENCE RULES
Juvenile court, applicability, **JuvR 34(I)**

EX PARTE EMERGENCY ORDERS
Mental retardation and developmental disabilities, county boards, **ORC 5126.331-5126.333**

EX PARTE PROCEEDINGS
Juvenile court, **JuvR 13(D)**

EX POST FACTO LAWS
Enactment prohibited, **O Const II § 28**

EXAMINATIONS
Mental. See MEDICAL AND MENTAL EXAMINATIONS
Witnesses. See WITNESSES AND TESTIMONY

EXCISE TAXES
Generally, **O Const XII § 3**

EXCLUSIVE JURISDICTION
Anatomical gifts, **ORC 2108.90**
Probate courts, **ORC 2101.24**

EXECUTION OF JUDGMENT
Adult cases tried in juvenile courts, **ORC 2151.50**
Claims against estate on, **ORC 2117.06**
Disabled persons, trust for supplemental services for; exemption, **ORC 5815.28**
Docket for execution, probate court, **ORC 2101.12**
Dower interest, **ORC 2103.041**
Embezzlement of trust assets, **ORC 2109.54, ORC 2109.55**
Estate assets, **ORC 2117.34, ORC 2117.35**
Exemptions
    Trust for supplemental services for person with disabilities, **ORC 5815.28**
Income tax, default, **ORC 5747.13(C)**
Judicial sales. See JUDICIAL SALES

EXECUTION OF JUDGMENT—Cont'd
Probate courts
    Collection, **ORC 2101.09, ORC 2101.10**
    Docket, **ORC 2101.12**
    Enforcement, **ORC 2101.35**
    Fees, **ORC 2101.16**
Stay
    Magistrate's decision, filing of objections to Juvenile court, **JuvR 40(E)**
Support of juveniles committed in juvenile proceedings, **ORC 2151.36**
Tax default
    Income tax, **ORC 5747.13(C)**
Trust for supplemental services for person with disabilities, exemption, **ORC 5815.28**

EXECUTORS AND ADMINISTRATORS
Generally, **ORC Ch 2109, ORC Ch 2113**
See also FIDUCIARIES, for general provisions
Accounts and accounting, **ORC 2109.24, ORC 2109.26, ORC 2109.30 to 2109.36, ORC 2113.25**
    See also FIDUCIARIES
    Bond conditions, **ORC 2109.07 to 2109.12**
    Business of decedent, continuation by, **ORC 2113.30**
    Case management, **SupR 78**
    Citation to file, **ORC 2109.31**
    Deceased fiduciary, on behalf of, **ORC 2109.26**
    Estate recovery program, Medicaid expenses, **ORC 2113.041**
    Exhibiting assets, **SupR 64**
    Final account, notice, **CuyR 64.2 et seq.**
    Foreign fiduciaries, by, **ORC 2113.72**
    Hearings, **ORC 2109.33**
    Itemized statement, **ORC 2109.301**
    Medicaid expenses, estate recovery program, **ORC 2113.041**
    Newly discovered assets, **ORC 2113.69**
    Notice of filing, **ORC 2109.32**
    Sale of personal property, **ORC 2113.42**
    Successors, by, **ORC 2113.29**
    Time for filing, **ORC 2113.28, ORC 2113.301**
    Uniform Fiduciary Act, **ORC 5815.04**
    Unsettled claims, **ORC 2113.18**
    Wasteful or unfaithful administration, **ORC 2109.19**
Actions by, **ORC 2107.46**
    Extracounty and extrastate proceedings, **ORC Ch 2129**
    Foreign fiduciaries, **ORC 2113.75**
    Fraudulent transfers, **ORC 2127.40**
    Guardianship, **ORC 2111.17**
    Heirship, determination, **ORC Ch 2123**
        See also HEIRS, at Determination proceedings
    Predecessor, against, **ORC 2113.22**
    Real property sale, **ORC Ch 2127**
    Special administrators, **ORC 2113.15, ORC 2113.16**
    Successor administrator or executor, **ORC 2113.20**
Administrators
    Appointment
        Minority of named executor, during, **ORC 2113.13**
        Notice, **SupR 60**
    Bond, conditions, **ORC 2109.07**
    De bonis non
        Actions against former by, **ORC 2113.22**
        Appointment, **ORC 2113.13, ORC 2113.19**
        Discovery of will after administration of intestate estate commenced, **ORC 2113.20**
        Duties, **ORC 2113.13, ORC 2113.19**
        Letters of administration, **ORC 2113.06**
        Liability, **ORC 2113.29, ORC 2117.33**
    Letters of administration
        Notice, **SupR 60**
    Special, **ORC 2113.15 to 2113.17**
        Bond, conditions, **ORC 2109.08**
    With will annexed, **ORC 2113.05, ORC 2113.19**

EXECUTORS AND ADMINISTRATORS—*continued*
Affidavits
- Estate recovery program, Medicaid expenses, **ORC 2113.041**
- Extension of time to administer estate, **ORC 2113.26**
- Notice to surviving spouse and heirs, **ORC 2107.19**

Ancillary administration, **ORC Ch 2129**
- See also ANCILLARY ADMINISTRATION

Appointment, **ORC 2109.02, ORC Ch 2113**
- Application, **ORC 2113.031, ORC 2113.07**
- Conflict of interest, **ORC 2101.38**
- Delay, **ORC 2113.15 to 2113.17**
- Discovery of will after administration of intestate estate commenced, **ORC 2113.20**
- Docket, **ORC 2101.12**
- Fees, **ORC 2101.16**
- Funeral and burial expenses of decedent, application for summary release, **ORC 2113.031**
- Illegal, **ORC 2109.15**
- Informal, **ORC 2109.15**
- Jurisdiction, **ORC 2101.24**
- Letters, **ORC Ch 2113**
    - Application, **HamR 60.1**
    - Notice, **SupR 60**
- Limitations, **ORC 2113.02**
- Minority of named executor, **ORC 2113.13**
- Notice. See Notice, this heading
- Prepayment of fees and costs prior to, **ORC 2101.21**
- Renunciation, **ORC 2113.07, ORC 2113.12**
    - Surviving spouse or next of kin, by, **ORC 2113.06**
- Revocation due to divorce, dissolution, separation or annulment, **ORC 2107.33**
- Summary release, decedent's funeral and burial expenses, **ORC 2113.031**

Appraisals by. See INVENTORY AND APPRAISAL OF ESTATES
Appraisers, appointment by, **ORC 2115.06**
Assets, deposit of, **ORC 2109.41**
Attorney for, **ORC 2109.03**
- Designation, **LucasR 57.1**

Bank accounts, **ORC 5815.04**
Beneficiaries, as, **ORC 2109.39**
Bonds, **ORC 2109.04 to 2109.20, ORC 2113.05, Sup. R 75.1**
- See also FIDUCIARIES
- Additional, **ORC 2109.06, ORC 2127.06**
    - Will contest, during, **ORC 2113.21**
- Art objects, effect on amount, **ORC 2109.14**
- Conditions, **ORC 2109.07 to 2109.12**
- Distribution prior to estate tax apportionment, **ORC 2113.88**
- Docket, **ORC 2101.12**
- Estate tax, postponement of payment, **ORC 5731.25**
- Minor upon becoming eligible as executor, **ORC 2113.13**
- Parties to action, **ORC 2109.61**
- Personal property deposited in lieu of, **ORC 2109.13**
- Real property
    - Management, **ORC 2113.311**
    - Sale, **ORC 2127.27**
- Reduction, **ORC 2109.14**
- Securities in lieu of, **ORC 2109.13**
- Successor corporate fiduciary, **ORC 2109.28**
- Sureties, **ORC 2109.17 to 2109.19**
    - Indemnity bond to surety, **ORC 2109.19**
    - Joint control of funds, **ORC 2109.41**
    - Parties to action, **ORC 2109.59**
- Waiver, **ORC 2107.65, ORC 2109.07**

Business of decedent, continuation by, **ORC 2113.30**
Claims against estates, **ORC Ch 2117**
- See also CLAIMS AGAINST ESTATES

Coexecutors, power to nominate, **ORC 2107.65**
Collection of assets by, **ORC 2113.25 to 2113.29**
- Rents, **ORC 2113.311**

Commissions, **ORC 2113.35, SupR 72**

EXECUTORS AND ADMINISTRATORS—*continued*
Compensation, **ORC 2101.16, ORC 2113.35, ORC 2113.36, SupR 72**
- Embezzlement of funds, guilty of, **ORC 2109.53**
- Estate tax deduction, **ORC 5731.16**
- Failure to file account, inventory, or report; effect, **ORC 2109.31**
- Real property
    - Land sale proceeding, **ORC 2127.08, ORC 2127.28, ORC 2127.37**
    - Management, **ORC 2113.311**
- Special administrators, **ORC 2113.15**
- Will establishing, **ORC 2113.36**

Concealing assets, **ORC 2109.50 to 2109.56**
- See also ASSETS OF ESTATES

Conflict of interest, **ORC 2101.38**
Contempt of court, **ORC 2101.23**
- Embezzlement proceedings, failure to cooperate, **ORC 2109.51**
- Failure to file account, inventory, or report, **ORC 2109.31**

Counsel to, **ORC 2109.03**
- Designation, **LucasR 57.1**

De bonis non. See Administrators, this heading
Death of, **ORC 2113.14, ORC 2113.19**
Debts owed by testator. See CLAIMS AGAINST ESTATES
Debts owed to testator. See DEBTS OWED TO ESTATES
Declaratory judgments sought by, **ORC 2107.46**
Definitions, **ORC 2109.01, ORC 5815.04**
Denial of commissions by probate court, **ORC 2113.35**
Disabled, **ORC 2109.26**
Distributees, residuary; bond, **ORC 2109.10**
Distribution of assets by
- Prior to expiration of time for filing claims, notice, **ORC 2117.06**

Distribution of assets by. See ASSETS OF ESTATES
Dower interest, waste, **ORC 2103.07**
Duties. See Powers and duties, this heading
Eligibility, **ORC 2109.21, ORC 2109.22**
Embezzlement of assets, **ORC 2109.50 to 2109.56**
- See also ASSETS OF ESTATES, at Concealed or embezzled

Escheat, powers and duties, **ORC 2105.09**
Estate recovery program
- Medicaid expenses, **ORC 2113.041**
- Notice, **ORC 2117.061**

Estate tax, duties, **ORC 5731.21 to 5731.25**
- See also ESTATE TAX

Execution of judgment, **ORC 2117.34, ORC 2117.35**
Executors
- Bond, conditions, **ORC 2109.09**

Expenses. See ESTATES
Extension of time, application for, **ORC 2113.25, ORC 2113.26**
Failure to perform duties, commissions denied, **ORC 2113.35**
Fees. See Compensation, this heading
Fines and forfeitures, use of trust funds, **ORC 2109.43**
Foreign, **ORC 2113.70 to 2113.75**
- Real property, sale by, **ORC 2129.25**
    - Bond, **ORC 2129.26**

Fraud
- Accounting, **ORC 2109.35**
- Concealment of assets. See ASSETS OF ESTATES, at Concealed or embezzled
- Grounds for removal, **ORC 2109.24**
- Orders by probate court, remedies, **ORC 2109.34, ORC 2109.35**
- Remedies, **ORC 2109.34, ORC 2109.35**

Funds
- Concealment or embezzlement, **ORC 2109.50 to 2109.56**
    - See also ASSETS OF ESTATES, at Concealed or embezzled
- Deposit, **ORC 2109.41, ORC 2109.42**
- Interest, accounting, **ORC 2109.42**
- Investment. See Investments by, this heading
- Personal use, **ORC 2109.43**
- Unclaimed, **ORC 2109.57**

Funeral and burial expenses of decedent
- Application for summary release, **ORC 2113.031**

Funeral expenses of deceased, payment, **ORC 2113.37**

EXECUTORS AND ADMINISTRATORS

EXECUTORS AND ADMINISTRATORS—*continued*
Good faith, defined, **ORC 5815.04**
    Uniform fiduciary act, **ORC 5815.04**
Guardianship, eligibility, **ORC 2111.09**
Hearing, accounts, **ORC 2109.33**
Heirship, petition for proceedings to determine, **ORC Ch 2123**
    See also HEIRS, at Determination proceedings
Income, allocation between principal and income, **ORC 2109.68**
Income tax, state
    Returns, **ORC 5747.08(A)**
Inventory and appraisal. See INVENTORY AND APPRAISAL OF ESTATES
Investigation of, **ORC 2109.49**
Investments by, **ORC 2109.37 to 2109.38**
    Liability, **ORC 2109.42**
    Temporary, **ORC 2109.372**
    Unclaimed funds, **ORC 2113.64 to 2113.68**
Land sale proceedings. See LAND SALE PROCEEDINGS
Legal advertising by. See Notice, this heading
Legatees, residuary; as, **ORC 2109.10**
Letters of administration
    Application, **HamR 60.1**
    Court issuing, **ORC 2113.01**
    Stepparents, **SumR 60.1(A)**
Letters of appointment. See Appointment, this heading
Letters testamentary, **ORC 2113.05**
    Court issuing, **ORC 2113.01**
Liability, **ORC 1335.05, ORC 2109.02, ORC 2109.53, ORC 2113.22, ORC 2113.32**
    Business of decedent continued by, **ORC 2113.30**
    Claims against estate, **ORC 2113.33, ORC 2113.53, ORC 2117.30 to 2117.35**
        Bad debts, **ORC 2113.33**
    Devisee or legatee
        Insolvent, when contribution due estate, **ORC 2107.56**
    Distribution of assets, **ORC 2113.53, ORC 2113.56**
        Heirship determination, after, **ORC 2123.07**
    Estate tax, **ORC 5731.37**
        Discharge, **ORC 5731.33**
        Late filing, **ORC 2113.87**
        Penalties, **ORC 5731.22**
    Fines and forfeitures, **ORC 2113.34**
    Foreign fiduciaries, **ORC 2113.70, ORC 2113.73, ORC 2113.74**
    Insolvent devisee or legatee, when contribution due estate, **ORC 2107.56**
    Investment or deposit, failure to, **ORC 2109.42**
    Limitation, certain powers granted to other persons, **ORC 2109.022**
    Partnership interest, **ORC 5815.35**
    Special administration, **ORC 2113.17**
    Successor administrators, **ORC 2113.29**
    Surviving spouse, to, **ORC 2113.53**
    Trust funds, use of, **ORC 2109.43**
Loans, **ORC 2109.46 to 2109.48**
Mansion house, application for transfer by, **ORC 2106.10(C)**
Medicaid expenses and payments, estate recovery program, **ORC 2113.041**
Military service, effect, **ORC 2109.25**
Mineral rights, powers, **ORC 2127.07**
Minor as, **ORC 2113.13**
Mortgages, **ORC 2109.46 to 2109.48, ORC 2113.44 to 2113.47**
Newly discovered assets, disposition, **ORC 2113.69**
Nonresident, **ORC 2113.70 to 2113.75, SumR 60.1(A)**
    Extracounty and extrastate proceedings, **ORC Ch 2129**
    Powers and duties, **ORC 2109.21**
    Probate court fee, **ORC 2101.16**
    Property delivered to, **ORC 2129.03**
Notice
    Accounts and accounting, **LucasR 64.1**
    Alien, deceased; for, **ORC 2113.11**
    Ancillary proceedings, **ORC 2129.02**

EXECUTORS AND ADMINISTRATORS—*continued*
Notice—*continued*
    Appointment, **ORC Ch 2113, SupR 60**
        Ancillary, **ORC 2129.02, ORC 2129.08**
        Estate tax, **ORC 2113.87**
        Foreign, **ORC 2129.02**
    Citation to surviving spouse regarding election, **ORC 2106.02**
    Claim against estate; hearing, **ORC 2117.02**
    Distribution of assets, **ORC 2109.36, ORC 2113.533**
    Distribution of assets prior to expiration of time for filing claims, **ORC 2117.06**
    Estate recovery program, **ORC 2117.061**
    Filing of account, **ORC 2109.32**
    Hearing, account, **ORC 2109.33**
    Inventory
        Hearing on, **ORC 2115.16**
        Notice of hearing by certified mail, **ORC 2115.16**
        Taking, **ORC 2115.04**
    Pending action against decedent, **ORC 2117.06**
    Probate, denial, **ORC 2107.181**
    Real estate, sale of, **ORC 2127.32, SupR 65, SupR 65(B)**
    Spouse, sale of personal property, **ORC 2113.40**
    Wills, custody of, **ORC 2107.08**
Oaths by, inventories, **ORC 2115.15**
Parties plaintiff. See Actions by, this heading
Partnership, deceased member's estate
    Liability for debt or obligation of partnership, **ORC 5815.35**
Penalties, embezzlement of funds, **ORC 2109.52**
Perpetual care grave, authority, **ORC 2113.37**
Personal property
    See also ASSETS OF ESTATES
    Sale, **SupR 63**
        Credit, **ORC 5731.37**
        Estate tax purposes, for, **ORC 5731.37**
Personal use of assets, **ORC 2109.43**
Power to nominate, **ORC 2107.65**
    Letters testamentary issued to nominee, **ORC 2113.05**
    Notice to persons holding
        Custody of wills, of, **ORC 2107.08**
        Denial of admission to probate, **ORC 2107.181**
    Renunciation of nominee, **ORC 2113.12**
Powers and duties, **ORC 2109.02, ORC 2109.39 to 2109.45, ORC 2113.30 to 2113.34**
    See also particular subject concerned, this heading
    Enforcement by probate courts, **ORC 2101.23**
    Jurisdiction of probate courts, **ORC 2101.24**
    Prior to appointment, **ORC 2109.02**
    Will contests, during, **ORC 2113.21**
Presumed decedent's estate, **ORC 2121.08**
Pretermitted heir statute, effect on powers, **ORC 2107.34**
Principal and income, allocation, **ORC 2109.68**
Profits from administration of estate, **ORC 2113.32, ORC 2113.34**
Promissory notes, authority to sell, **ORC 2113.44**
Prudent person standard, **ORC 2109.371**
Real property
    See also ASSETS OF ESTATES
    Certificates of transfer
        Application for, intestate succession, **ORC 2106.10(C)**
    Contracts, completion by, **ORC 2113.48**
    Management by, **ORC 2113.311**
    Partition
        Remaindermen, protection of interest by, **ORC 2113.58**
        Rights of fiduciaries, **ORC 2127.41**
    Sale, **ORC 2107.58, ORC 2107.59, ORC Ch 2127**
        See also LAND SALE PROCEEDINGS
Records and reports
    Accounting. See Accounts and accounting, this heading
    Filing requirements, **ORC 2109.021**
    Fines for improper, **ORC 2109.021**
Recovery, estate recovery program, **ORC 2113.041, ORC 2117.061**

EXECUTORS AND ADMINISTRATORS

EXECUTORS AND ADMINISTRATORS—*continued*
Removal, **ORC 2109.02, ORC 2109.24, ORC 2109.25, ORC 2113.18 to 2113.23, ORC 2113.27**
    Embezzlement of funds, **ORC 2109.53**
    Failure to execute indemnity bond to surety, **ORC 2109.19**
    Failure to file account, inventory, or report, **ORC 2109.31**
    Failure to furnish additional bond, **ORC 2109.06**
    Failure to give bond, **ORC 2109.18**
Renunciation, **ORC 2113.07, ORC 2113.12**
    Surviving spouse or next of kin, by, **ORC 2113.06**
Requalification, fee, **ORC 2101.16**
Residency requirements, **ORC 2109.21, ORC 2113.05**
    See also Nonresident, this heading
Resignation, **ORC 2109.24**
Sale of assets, authority, **ORC 2113.39 to 2113.52**
    See also ASSETS OF ESTATES
    Nonresident decedent's estate, payment by domiciliary administrator in lieu of, **ORC 2129.16**
    Private sale, **ORC 2109.45**
    Real property. See LAND SALE PROCEEDINGS
Securities transactions by
    Investment powers, **ORC 2109.37**
Self-dealing, **ORC 2109.44**
Special administrators, **ORC 2113.15 to 2113.17**
    Bond, conditions, **ORC 2109.08**
Statements, private sale of property, **ORC 2109.45**
Status reports on administration of estates, **SumR 60.1(A)**
Statute of frauds, applicability, **ORC 1335.05**
Substitute
    Military service, during, **ORC 2109.25**
Successors, **ORC 2109.26**
    Bond, **ORC 2109.05**
    Corporate bond, **ORC 2109.28**
    Power to nominate, **ORC 2107.65**
    Real property, sale of, **ORC 2121.06**
Sureties. See Bonds, this heading
Survivorship, multiple fiduciaries, **ORC 2109.27**
Tax returns, duties
    Estate tax, **ORC 5731.21 to 5731.25**
    Income tax, **ORC 5731.16, ORC 5747.08(A)**
Termination. See Removal, this heading
Transactions by, validity, **ORC 2113.23**
Unclaimed funds, disposition, **ORC 2113.64 to 2113.68**
Uniform Fiduciary Act, **ORC 5815.04**
Use of assets by, **ORC 2109.43**
Vacancy, **ORC 2109.26**
Violations, embezzlement, **ORC 2109.50 to 2109.56**
    See also ASSETS OF ESTATES, at Concealed or embezzled
Wills
    Contests
        Parties to, **ORC 2107.73**
        Powers during, **ORC 2113.21**
    Enforcement, **ORC 2107.09**
    Notice of custody of, **ORC 2107.08**
    Power to nominate conferred in, **ORC 2107.65**
With will annexed, **ORC 2113.05, ORC 2113.19**
Wrongful death action, refusal to file, **ORC 2113.18**

EXPENSES
Generally, See FEES AND COSTS
Court actions. See COURT COSTS

EXPERT WITNESSES
Battered woman syndrome, **ORC 2945.392**
Fees and costs
    Parentage actions, **ORC 3111.14**
Not guilty by reason of insanity, appointment, **ORC 2945.40(C)**
Parentage actions, **ORC 3111.09, ORC 3111.12**
    Fees, **ORC 3111.14**

EXPERTS
Stark County probate court, guardianships, statement of expert evaluation, **Sup. R 66.6**
Trustees' skills or expertise, **ORC 5808.06**

EXPLOITATION
Aged persons exploited by caretakers, **ORC 5101.60 to 5101.71**
    See also PROTECTIVE SERVICES FOR ADULTS

EXPUNGEMENT OF RECORDS
Child's right to, **JuvR 34(J), ORC 2151.358**
Defined, **5122.01, ORC 2151.355**
Hospitalization of mentally ill
    Discharge when no probable cause for hospitalization, **ORC 5122.141**
    Emergency hospitalization, **ORC 5122.09**
Juvenile offenders, **JuvR 34(J), ORC 2151.358**
Juvenile records, **ORC 2151.313(B)**

EYES
Enucleation, **ORC 2108.071, ORC 2108.60**
    See also ANATOMICAL GIFTS, generally
Eye banks, **ORC 2108.60**

FACSIMILES
Filing of documents, **JuvR 8**
    Court record, not acceptable for, **FrankR 57.1, Sup. R 57.1**
Unacceptable for pleadings, **FrankR 57.1**

FALSE STATEMENTS
Adoption
    Effect on, **ORC 3107.16**
    Representation by agency or attorney, **ORC 3107.011**
Annulment, grounds for, **ORC 3105.31(D)**
Creditors, defrauding
    Imprisonment, **O Const I § 15**
Divorce, fraudulent contract as grounds, **ORC 3105.01(E)**
Dower
    Assignment, **ORC 5305.13**
    Interest, recovery, **ORC 2103.06**
Fiduciaries, accounting, **ORC 2109.35**
Limitation of actions, **ORC 2305.09**
Survival of actions, **ORC 2305.21**
Tax
    Estate tax returns, **ORC 5731.22**

FAMILY ALLOWANCE
Child support, **ORC 2106.13**
Priority when paying claims against estates, **ORC 2117.25**
Surviving spouse, **ORC 2106.13**

FARMLANDS
Estate tax valuation, **ORC 5731.011**
    Lien in favor of state, **ORC 5731.37**
Mental retardation and developmental disabilities department, **ORC 5123.221**

FATHERS
Generally, See PARENT AND CHILD
Paternity proceedings. See PARENTAGE ACTIONS

FEDERAL ESTATE TAX
See ESTATE TAX, FEDERAL

FEDERAL GOVERNMENT
See UNITED STATES

FEDERAL INCOME TAX
See INCOME TAX, FEDERAL

FEE SIMPLE ESTATES
See ESTATES

FEES AND COSTS
Administration of estates. See ADMINISTRATION OF ESTATES, at Expenses
Administrators. See EXECUTORS AND ADMINISTRATORS, at Compensation
Adoption. See ADOPTION, at Costs
Anatomical gifts. See ANATOMICAL GIFTS
Appraisers, **SumR 61.1**
Attorney fees. See ATTORNEY FEES
Child abuse, bad faith reporting of, **ORC 2151.421**
Computerized legal research
    Juvenile courts, **ORC 2151.541, ORC 2153.081**
Court costs. See COURT COSTS
Dispute resolution, implementation of procedures, **ORC 2101.163**
Eminent domain, **ORC 163.15, ORC 163.16**
    Abandonment of proceedings, **ORC 163.21**
    Appropriation disallowed, **ORC 163.21**
Executors. See EXECUTORS AND ADMINISTRATORS, at Compensation
Foster care
    Criminal record check, prospective parents, **ORC 2151.86**
Funerals and burials. See FUNERALS AND BURIALS, at Expenses
Genetic tests, paternity proceedings, **ORC 3111.09, ORC 3111.14**
Guardianship of incompetent, examination, **ORC 2111.031**
Juvenile courts. See JUVENILE COURTS
Juvenile courts, criminal provisions, **ORC 2152.20**
Juvenile courts, recovery of costs from juvenile drug abuse offenders, **ORC 2152.202**
Paternity proceedings, **ORC 3111.09, ORC 3111.14**
Probate courts. See PROBATE COURTS
Wills, **ORC 2107.62**
    Deposit with court, **ORC 2107.07**
Witness fees, **HamR 58.2**

FELONIES
Appeals, jurisdiction, **O Const IV § 2**
Juvenile courts, felony specifications, **ORC 2152.17**
Minor charged with, transfer of case, **JuvR 30**

FELONIOUS SEXUAL PENETRATION
DNA testing of prisoners, **ORC 2901.07**

FEMALES
Artificial insemination, **ORC 3111.88 to 3111.96**
Juvenile delinquent
    See also JUVENILE DELINQUENCY, generally
    Trials, **ORC 2151.16**
Widow. See SURVIVING SPOUSE
Wife. See HUSBAND AND WIFE

FIDUCIARIES
Generally, **ORC Ch 1339, ORC Ch 2109**
See also EXECUTORS AND ADMINISTRATORS; GUARDIANSHIP; TESTAMENTARY TRUSTEES; TRUSTEES
Accounts and accounting, **ORC 2109.24, ORC 2109.26, ORC 2109.30 to 2109.36**
    Case management, **SupR 78**
    Citation to file, **ORC 2109.31**
        Continuance following, **SumR 64.1(A)**
    Delinquent fiduciary, appointment of, **SumR 64.1(A)**
    Exhibiting assets, **SupR 64**
    Extension of time to file, **LucasR 78.3**
    Final account
        Notice, **CuyR 64.2 et seq.**
    Guardians and conservators, **ORC 2109.302**
    Review, **HamR 64.1**
    Show cause hearing, appearance at, **SumR 64.1(A)**
    Time for filing, **LucasR 64.1**
    Uniform Fiduciary Act, **ORC 5815.04**
    Wasteful or unfaithful administration, **ORC 2109.19**
Actions against
    Limitation. See LIMITATION OF ACTIONS

FIDUCIARIES—continued
Actions against—continued
    Personal use of trust funds by, **ORC 2109.43**
Actions by
    Will construction, **ORC 2107.46**
Address, notice of change, **LucasR 57.1**
Administrators. See EXECUTORS AND ADMINISTRATORS
Age limit, powers of appointment, **ORC 5815.13**
Appointment, **CuyR 8.1, FrankR 8.1, ORC 2109.02**
    Delinquent, **SumR 64.1(A)**
    Deposited wills
        Certification of, **LucasR 57.1**
    Fees, **ORC 2101.16**
    Illegal, **ORC 2109.15**
    Informal, **ORC 2109.15**
    Nonresident, **Sup. R 60.1**
    Notice, estate administration, **SupR 59**
    Prepayment of fees and costs prior to, **ORC 2101.21**
    Related cases, certification of, **LucasR 57.1**
    Successor, to fill vacancy, **ORC 2109.26**
Approval of third-party distribution, **ORC 2109.361**
Art. See CONSIGNMENT OF ART WORKS TO DEALERS
Assets, deposit of, **ORC 2109.41**
Attorney fees, **LucasR 71.1, SupR 71**
Attorney for
    Designation, **LucasR 57.1**
    Fiduciary duties of attorney of fiduciary, **ORC 2109.03, ORC 5815.16**
Bank accounts, **ORC 5815.04**
Beneficiaries, as, **ORC 2109.39**
Bond, **ORC 2109.04 to 2109.20, Sup. R 75.1**
    Actions on, **ORC 2109.59 to 2109.62**
        Limitation, **ORC 2305.12**
    Additional, **ORC 2109.06, ORC 2127.06**
        Will contest, during, **ORC 2113.21**
    Art objects, effect on amount, **ORC 2109.14**
    Deposit in lieu of, **ORC 2109.13**
    Estate tax, postponement of payment, **ORC 5731.25**
    Informal or illegal appointment, effect, **ORC 2109.15**
        Informality not to void, **ORC 2109.15**
    Joint fiduciaries, **ORC 2109.04**
    Parties to action, **ORC 2109.61**
    Personal property deposited in lieu of, **ORC 2109.13**
    Probate court jurisdiction, **ORC 2101.24**
    Reduction, **ORC 2109.04, ORC 2109.14**
    Securities in lieu of, **ORC 2109.13**
    Successor corporate fiduciary, **ORC 2109.28**
    Sureties, **ORC 2109.17 to 2109.19**
        Indemnity bond to surety, **ORC 2109.19**
        Joint control of funds, **ORC 2109.41**
        Parties to actions, **ORC 2109.59**
    Waiver, **ORC 2109.04**
Charitable trusts. See CHARITABLE TRUSTS
Checks
    Liability of bank, checks drawn by fiduciary upon account of principal, **ORC 5815.07**
    Two or more trustees, checks deposited in name of, **ORC 5815.09**
Claims, refusal to pay, **ORC 2109.59 to 2109.62**
Cofiduciaries
    Bond, **ORC 2109.05**
    Removal or resignation, **ORC 2109.27**
Compensation, **ORC 2101.16**
    Application, **SumR Appx D**
    Computation, **SumR 72.1**
        Estates involving real estate, **LucasR 71.1**
        Schedule, **LucasR 64.1**
    Corporate fiduciaries, **LucasR 74.2**
    Embezzlement of funds, guilty of, **ORC 2109.53**
    Failure to file account, inventory, or report; effect, **ORC 2109.31**
Competent, issuer of securities may treat holders of record as, **ORC 5815.03**

FIDUCIARIES

FIDUCIARIES—*continued*
Concealing of assets, **ORC 2109.50 to 2109.56**
    See also ASSETS OF ESTATES, at Concealed or embezzled
Consignment of art. See CONSIGNMENT OF ART WORKS TO DEALERS
Contempt of court, **ORC 2101.23**
    Embezzlement proceedings, failure to cooperate, **ORC 2109.51**
    Failure to file account, inventory, or report, **ORC 2109.31**
Contracts, liability, **ORC 5815.35**
Corporate
    Compensation, **LucasR 74.2**
    Deposit of funds, **ORC 2109.41**
    Dissolution, **ORC 2109.26**
    Merger and consolidation, effect, **ORC 2109.28**
    Transactions of trust assets, **ORC 2109.44**
Counsel to, **ORC 2109.03**
    Attorney fees, **LucasR 71.1, SupR 71**
    Designation, **LucasR 57.1**
Cuyahoga county probate court, appointment, **CuyR 8.1**
De bonis non. See EXECUTORS AND ADMINISTRATORS, at Administrators
Death
    Cofiduciary's death, effect on surviving fiduciaries, **ORC 2109.27**
Declaratory judgments sought by, **ORC 2107.46**
    See also DECLARATORY JUDGMENTS, generally
Definitions, **ORC 2109.01, ORC 5815.04**
Disabled, **ORC 2109.26**
Distribution of assets, **ORC 2109.36**
    Fees, **ORC 2101.16**
    Refusal to distribute, **ORC 2109.59 to 2109.62**
Dower interest, waste, **ORC 2103.07**
Eligibility, **ORC 2109.21, ORC 2109.22, SumR 60.1(B)**
Embezzlement of assets, **ORC 2109.50 to 2109.56**
    See also ASSETS OF ESTATES, at Concealed or embezzled
English proficiency requirement, **SumR 60.1(B)**
Estate administration, **ORC Ch 2113**
    See also EXECUTORS AND ADMINISTRATORS
Fees. See Compensation, this heading
Filings, approval by attorney, **SumR 57.1(B)**
Fines and forfeitures, use of trust funds, **ORC 2109.43**
Franklin county probate court
    Appointment, **FrankR 8.1**
Fraud by
    Accounting, **ORC 2109.35**
    Grounds for removal, **ORC 2109.24**
    Remedies, **ORC 2109.34, ORC 2109.35**
Funds
    Concealment, **ORC 2109.50 to 2109.56**
        See also ASSETS OF ESTATES, at Concealed or embezzled
    Deposit, **ORC 2109.41, ORC 2109.42**
    Interest, accounting, **ORC 2109.42**
    Personal use, **ORC 2109.43**
    Unclaimed, **ORC 2109.57**
Good faith, defined, **ORC 5815.04**
    Uniform Fiduciary Act, **ORC 5815.04**
Grandparents. See GRANDPARENT POWER OF ATTORNEY OR CARETAKER AUTHORIZATION AFFIDAVIT
Guardianship, **ORC Ch 2111**
    See also GUARDIANSHIP
Incapacity, final account of trust to be filed by, **ORC 2109.26**
Income tax, state returns, **ORC 5747.08(A) to 5747.08(C)**
Inter vivos trusts, transactions between fiduciaries, **ORC 5815.24**
Interpretation and construction, **ORC 5815.09**
Inventory. See INVENTORY AND APPRAISAL OF ESTATES, generally
Investigation of, **ORC 2109.49**
Investments by, **ORC 2109.29, ORC 2109.37 to 2109.38, ORC 5809.01 to 5809.08**
    See also UNIFORM PRUDENT INVESTOR ACT
    Affiliated investment companies, investments in, **ORC 2109.371**
    Liability, **ORC 2109.42**

FIDUCIARIES—*continued*
Investments by, **ORC 2109.29, ORC 2109.37 to 2109.38, ORC 5809.01 to 5809.08**—*continued*
    Temporary, **ORC 2109.372**
Joint fiduciaries. See Cofiduciaries, this heading
Land sale proceedings. See LAND SALE PROCEEDINGS
Letters of administration, application for, **HamR 60.1**
Liability, **ORC 2109.02, ORC 2109.53**
    Contracts, **ORC 5815.35**
    Estate tax, **ORC 5731.37**
        Discharge, **ORC 5731.33**
        Penalties, **ORC 5731.22**
    Investment or deposit, failure to make, **ORC 2109.42**
    Limitation, certain powers granted to other persons, **ORC 2109.022**
    Trust funds, use of, **ORC 2109.43**
Loans, **ORC 2109.46 to 2109.48**
Lucas county probate court
    Address change, notice to court, **LucasR 57.1**
    Attorney, designating, **LucasR 57.1**
Mental retardation and developmental disabilities department as, **ORC 2111.01**
Military service, effect, **ORC 2109.25**
Mortgages, **ORC 2109.46 to 2109.48**
Neglect of duty, removal for, **ORC 2109.24**
Nonresident, appointment, **Sup. R 60.1**
Notice
    Account, filing of, **ORC 2109.32, ORC 2109.33, ORC 2109.35**
    Attorney, **ORC 2109.03**
    Bond, **ORC 2109.06**
    Creditor, nonpayment, **ORC 2109.59**
    Distribution of assets, **ORC 2109.36**
        Not made, **ORC 2109.59**
    Estate administration, appointment, **SupR 59**
    Hearing on account, **ORC 2109.33**
    Release of power of appointment, **ORC 5815.15**
    Removal, of, **ORC 2109.24**
    Surety, for release of, **ORC 2109.18**
Penalties for embezzlement of funds, **ORC 2109.52**
Personal credit of fiduciary, deposit to, **ORC 5815.08**
Personal property, sale, **ORC 2109.45**
    Estate tax purposes, for, **ORC 5731.37**
Personal use of assets, **ORC 2109.43**
Powers and duties, **ORC 2109.02, ORC 2109.39 to 2109.45**
    Enforcement by probate courts, **ORC 2101.23**
Powers of appointment
    generally, **ORC 5815.12 to 5815.15**
    Age limit, **ORC 5815.13**
    Definition of power of appointment, **ORC 5815.12**
    Notice of release, **ORC 5815.15**
    Release and disclaimer of a power, **ORC 5815.14**
Pretermitted heir statute, effect on powers, **ORC 2107.34**
Principal and Income Act, **ORC 5812.01 to 5812.52**
    See also UNIFORM PRINCIPAL AND INCOME ACT
Probate of wills. See PROBATE OF WILLS, generally
Prudent Investor Act, **ORC 5809.01 to 5809.08**
    See also UNIFORM PRUDENT INVESTOR ACT
Prudent person standard, **ORC 2109.371**
Real property, sale, **ORC 2109.45**
    See also LAND SALE PROCEEDINGS
    Estate tax purposes, for, **ORC 5731.37**
    Successor, by, **ORC 2121.06**
Records and reports
    Accounts. See Accounts and accounting, this heading
    Filing requirements, **ORC 2109.021**
    Fines for improper, **ORC 2109.021**
Releases
    Notice of release of power of appointment, **ORC 5815.15**
    Power of appointment, **ORC 5815.14**
Removal, **ORC 2109.02, ORC 2109.24, ORC 2109.25**
    Cofiduciary, effect, **ORC 2109.27**

FIDUCIARIES—*continued*
Removal, **ORC 2109.02, ORC 2109.24, ORC 2109.25**—*continued*
    Concealing or embezzling assets, **ORC 2109.53**
    Failure to execute indemnity bond to surety, **ORC 2109.19**
    Failure to file account, inventory, or report, **ORC 2109.31**
    Failure to furnish additional bond, **ORC 2109.06**
    Failure to give bond, **ORC 2109.18, ORC 2109.24**
    Fees, **ORC 2101.16**
    Final account, **ORC 2109.36**
Residency requirements, **ORC 2109.21**
Resignation, **ORC 2109.24**
    Cofiduciary, effect, **ORC 2109.27**
    Fees, **ORC 2101.16**
Rules of law and equity applicable under Uniform Fiduciary Act, **ORC 5815.11**
Sale of assets
    Estate tax purposes, for, **ORC 5731.37**
    Private sale, **ORC 2109.45**
    Successor, sale of real property, **ORC 2121.06**
Securities
    Deposit, **ORC 2131.21**
    Investment powers, **ORC 2109.37**
Self-dealing by, **ORC 2109.44**
Show cause hearings, **HamR 64.2**
Spouse granted power of appointment or nominated as trustee, termination of marriage as revocation, **ORC 5815.31**
Stark county probate court
    Bonds, **Sup. R 75.1**
Statements for private sale of property, **ORC 2109.45**
Stock ownership, **ORC 2109.40**
Substitute
    Military service, during, **ORC 2109.25**
Successor, **ORC 2109.26**
    Bond, **ORC 2109.05**
    Corporate, bond, **ORC 2109.28**
    Real property, sale of, **ORC 2121.06**
Summit county probate court
    Compensation, **SumR 72.1, SumR Appx D**
    Qualifications, **SumR 60.1**
Sureties, **ORC 2109.17 to 2109.19**
    See also Bond, this heading
Survivorship, multiple fiduciaries, **ORC 2109.27**
Tax returns, duties
    Estate tax, **ORC 5731.21 to 5731.25**
    Income tax, **ORC 5747.08(A) to 5747.08(C)**
Testamentary charitable trusts, merger, **ORC 2109.30**
Testamentary trustees. See TESTAMENTARY TRUSTEES
Third parties
    Approval of third-party distribution, **ORC 2109.361**
    Duty to, **ORC 5815.16**
Transferee not responsible for proper application of money, **ORC 5815.05**
Transfers to Minors Act. See TRANSFERS TO MINORS ACT
Trustees. See TRUSTEES
Trusts, representation by fiduciaries and parents, **ORC 5803.03**
Two or more trustees, deposit in name of, **ORC 5815.09**
Unclaimed funds, **ORC 2109.57**
Uniform Fiduciary Act
    generally, **ORC 5815.04**
    Check drawn by fiduciary upon account of principal, liability of bank, **ORC 5815.07**
    Competent, issuers of securities may trust holders of record as, **ORC 5815.03**
    Definitions, **ORC 5815.04**
    Deposit in name of fiduciary as such, liability of bank, **ORC 5815.06**
    Interpretation and construction, **ORC 5815.10**
    Interpretation of terms, **ORC 5815.01**
    Personal credit of fiduciary, deposit to, **ORC 5815.08**
    Rules of law and equity applicable, **ORC 5815.11**
    Securities issuers and holders of record, **ORC 5815.02**

FIDUCIARIES—*continued*
Uniform Fiduciary Act—*continued*
    Transferee not responsible for proper application of money, **ORC 5815.05**
    Two or more trustees, deposit in name of, **ORC 5815.09**
Uniform Principal and Income Act, **ORC 5812.01 to 5812.52**
    See also UNIFORM PRINCIPAL AND INCOME ACT
Uniform Prudent Investor Act, **ORC 5809.01 to 5809.08**
    See also UNIFORM PRUDENT INVESTOR ACT
Use of assets by, **ORC 2109.43**
Vacancy, **ORC 2109.26**
Violations, embezzlement. See ASSETS OF ESTATES, at Concealed or embezzled
Will contest, powers during, **ORC 2113.21**
    See also CONTEST OF WILL, generally
With will annexed, **ORC 2113.05, ORC 2113.19**

FINAL ORDERS
See DECREES; JUDGMENTS

FINANCIAL INSTITUTIONS
Deposits of estate property, transfer and delivery, **ORC 5731.39**
Fiduciaries, as. See FIDUCIARIES, at Corporate
Uniform fiduciary act, **ORC 5815.04**

FINANCIAL RESPONSIBILITY, MOTOR VEHICLE
Juvenile traffic offenders subject to, **ORC 2152.21**
Minor, by, **ORC 4507.07**

FINDINGS OF FACT
Children, removal from homes, **ORC 2151.419**
Juvenile court, **JuvR 29(F)**
    Magistrate's decision, **JuvR 40(E)**
Magistrate's decision, juvenile court, **JuvR 40(E)**
Visitation rights, **ORC 3109.051(F), ORC 3109.11, ORC 3109.12(B)**

FINES
Juvenile courts, criminal provisions, **ORC 2152.20**

FINES AND FORFEITURES
Generally, **O Const I § 9**
See also particular subject concerned
Amercement of probate court officers, **ORC 2109.10, ORC 2109.11**
Child day camp's violation of criminal records check regulation, **ORC 2151.861**
Collection. See EXECUTION OF JUDGMENT
Concealment of assets, penalty, **ORC 2109.52**
Constables, collection of moneys for probate courts, **ORC 2101.10**
Coroners, collection of moneys for probate courts, **ORC 2101.10**
Dower, forfeiture, **ORC 2103.07**
Drunk driving, **ORC 4511.19**
Estates, forfeiture due to conviction, **O Const I § 12**
Executors and administrators, **ORC 2113.34**
Fiduciaries
    Improper filings, **ORC 2109.021**
    Trust funds, use of, **ORC 2109.43**
Juvenile delinquents
    Traffic offenses, **ORC 2152.21**
Motor vehicles, criminal forfeiture, **ORC 4507.021**
Sheriffs
    Collection of moneys for probate courts, **ORC 2101.10**
    Failure to serve and return process, **ORC 2101.09**
Tenants for life, forfeiture, **ORC 2105.20**

FINGERPRINTS
Juveniles, **ORC 2151.313**

FISCAL YEAR
Defined, **ORC 5747.01**

FOOD
Nutrition or hydration
    Refusal of or withdrawal of consent to under durable power of attorney for health care, **ORC 1337.13**

FOOD—*continued*
Nutrition or hydration—*continued*
    Withholding or withdrawal of under living will, **ORC 2133.09**
Sales tax, **O Const XII § 3**

FORCIBLE ENTRY AND DETAINER
Dower, premises conveyed in lieu of, **ORC 2103.04**

FORECLOSURE
Estate property, **ORC 2113.47**
    Surviving spouse, intestate share; enforcement, **ORC 2106.11**

FOREIGN COUNTRIES
Adoption of children from, **ORC 3107.07, ORC 5103.16**
Aliens. See ALIENS
Children, adoption, **ORC 3107.07, ORC 5103.16**
Income tax withholding exclusions for services to, **ORC 5747.06(A)**
Juvenile delinquents domiciled in, criminal prosecution, **ORC 2152.12(C)**
Legacies or devises. See LEGACIES AND DEVISES, at Charitable bequests
Wills made in, **ORC 2129.06**

FOREIGN STATES
Custody proceedings, jurisdiction, **ORC 3109.21 to 3109.32**
Interstate agreements. See INTERSTATE AGREEMENTS
Juvenile delinquents domiciled in, criminal prosecution, **ORC 2152.12(C)**
Residents of. See NONRESIDENTS

FOREIGN WILLS
Admission to record, **ORC 2129.05 to 2129.07**
Contests, **ORC 2107.48**
Fee, **ORC 2101.16**
Testamentary trusts, creation by, **ORC 2129.27 to 2129.30**

FOREIGNERS
See ALIENS; NONRESIDENTS

FORESTRY CAMPS
Juveniles, for, **ORC 2151.65 to 2151.80**
    See also JUVENILE REHABILITATION
Securities issue to finance, **ORC 2151.655**

FORESTS AND FORESTRY
Timberlands, dower estate, **ORC 5305.09, ORC 5305.10**

FORFEITURE
Limitation of actions, **ORC 2305.11**

FORFEITURES
See FINES AND FORFEITURES
Juvenile courts, criminal provisions, **ORC 2152.20**

FORMS
See also LEGAL INSTRUMENTS
Abortion for minor without parental consent
    Complaint for, **SupR Form 23-A to SupR Form 23-D**
    Instructions, **SupR Form 23-A Instructions**
Adoption, **SumR 94.1(E), SupR 51, SupR 52**
    Adopted person's request to assist birth parent or birth sibling in locating name by adoption, **ORC 3107.48, ORC 3107.51**
    Authorization of release form, **ORC 3107.46, ORC 3107.50**
    Denial of release form, **ORC 3107.46, ORC 3107.50**
        Effect on request for copy of contents of adoption file, **ORC 3107.47**
    Release of adoption file, **ORC 3107.083**
        Birth parent completing and signing form, **ORC 5103.151**
        Social and medical histories of birth parents, **ORC 3107.09**
Anatomical gifts, **ORC 2108.10**
Complaints, **JuvR 10(B)**
Court supplying, **SumR 57.1(A)**
Durable power of attorney for health care, **ORC 1337.17, ORC 1337.18**

FORMS—*continued*
Estates
    Administration, **SupR 51, SupR 52**
    No administration, application and order, **ORC 2113.03**
Grandparent power of attorney, **3109.53**
Grandparent's caretaker authorization affidavit, **3109.66**
Guardianship, **SupR 51, SupR 52**
Living will, declaration, **ORC 2133.07**
Mental retardation and developmental disabilities department, **ORC 5123.031**
Power of attorney, health care, **ORC 1337.18**
Printing specifications, probate court, **FrankR 52.1, FrankR 52.2**
    Computer-generated forms, **HamR 52.1**
Probate, **SupR 51, SupR 52**
Probate courts. See PROBATE COURTS
Standard forms, probate court, **HamR 51.1**
Subpoena, **JuvR 17(A)**
Summons, **JuvR 15(B)**
Warrant against child, **JuvR 15(E)**

FOSTER CAREGIVER
Definitions, **ORC 2151.011**

FOSTER HOMES
Adoption of child
    After adulthood, **ORC 3107.02**
    Caregiver, application for adoption by, **ORC 3107.014**
Adult facilities
    Aged persons suffering neglect, abuse, or exploitation; report to county human services department, **ORC 5101.61**
Case plans for children, administrative review, **ORC 2151.416**
Costs of foster care, juvenile courts reimbursed for, **ORC 2151.152**
Criminal records check, parenting prerequisite, **ORC 2151.86**
Custody hearings, notice, **ORC 2151.424**
Defined, **ORC 2151.011**
Detention, as place of, **ORC 2151.331**
Education, local boards
    Notification of placement of children outside home county, **ORC 2151.553**
Human services department, delegation of duties, **ORC 5103.03**
Immunity from liability, **ORC 5103.162**
Juvenile court, cost reimbursement, **ORC 2151.152**
Juvenile courts
    Notification of placement of children outside home county, **ORC 2151.554**
    Reimbursed for costs of foster care, **ORC 2151.152**
Juvenile delinquents
    Disclosure of status, **ORC 2152.72**
    Psychological examinations, **ORC 2152.72**
Juvenile facilities
    Case plans, **ORC 2151.416**
    Detention, as place of, **ORC 2151.331, ORC 2152.26**
    Mentally retarded, temporary detention in, **ORC 5123.77**
    Nonresident children, **ORC 2151.39**
    Temporary placement in, **ORC 2151.34**
Nonresident children
    Complaint by superintendent of schools of unruly child, **ORC 2151.55**
    Hearing on complaint by superintendent of schools, **ORC 2151.55**
    Notification of placement outside home county, **ORC 2151.55**
        Juvenile courts, to, **ORC 2151.554**
        Oral communication, requirements, **ORC 2151.551**
        Persons entitled to, **ORC 2151.55**
        School boards, to, **ORC 2151.553**
        Written information, time, **ORC 2151.552**
    Out of county removal hearings, **JuvR 39**
Notice of custody hearings, **ORC 2151.424**
Private child placing agencies
    Juvenile delinquents, placement, **ORC 2152.72**

FOUNDATIONS
See CHARITABLE ORGANIZATIONS; CHARITABLE TRUSTS

FRANCHISE TAX
Generally, **O Const XII § 3**
See also PERSONAL PROPERTY, TAXATION
Pass-through entities
    Accounting method, **ORC 5747.45**
    Collection actions by state, **ORC 5747.451**
    Electronic funds transfer, payments by, **ORC 5747.44**
    Estimated tax return, filing requirement, **ORC 5747.43**
    Liens, **ORC 5747.451**
    Overpayments, **ORC 5747.45**
    Quo warranto proceedings, **ORC 5747.451**
    Returns, **ORC 5747.42**
        Amended, **ORC 5747.45**
        Liability for failure to file, **ORC 5747.453**
    Taxable year, **ORC 5747.45**
    Underpayments, **ORC 5747.45**

FRANKLIN COUNTY
See COUNTIES, generally
Court of common pleas. See COURTS OF COMMON PLEAS, generally
Probate court. See FRANKLIN COUNTY PROBATE COURT
Probate court. See FRANKLIN COUNTY PROBATE COURT; PROBATE COURTS

FRANKLIN COUNTY PROBATE COURT
Accounts, **FrankR 64.1**
    Bond, **FrankR 64.4**
    Delinquent filing, **FrankR 64.2**
    Evidence of assets, **FrankR 64.5**
    Partial, filing, **FrankR 64.5**
    Payment of debts, **FrankR 64.6**
    Signature of fiduciary, **FrankR 64.1**
    Vouchers, **FrankR 64.3**
Adoption, **FrankR 75.2**
    Case management, **FrankR 78.1**
    Release of information, petition for
        Fees, **FrankR 58.3**
Adult protective services, **FrankR 75.10**
Appointments by court, **FrankR 8.1**
Appraisers
    Appointment by court, **FrankR 8.1**
    Exceptions, **FrankR 61.1**
    Fees, **FrankR 61.1**
    Self-dealing prohibited, **FrankR 61.2**
Attorney fees, **CuyR 71.2 et seq.**
    Code of Professional Responsibility, **FrankR 71.1**
    Contested fees, **FrankR 71.7**
    Contingent fees, **FrankR 71.8**
    Early payment, **FrankR 71.3**
    Fiduciary, attorney serving as, **FrankR 71.2**
    Notice and consent
        Estates, **FrankR 71.4**
        Guardianships, **FrankR 71.5**
        Trusts, **FrankR 71.6**
Attorney-in-fact, adult protective services, **FrankR 75.10**
Attorneys
    Appointment by court, **FrankR 8.1**
    Fees. See Attorney fees, this heading
    Pro hac vice, **FrankR 75.6**
    Withdrawal, **FrankR 78.2**
Bonds, surety, **FrankR 75.4**
    Accounts, **FrankR 64.4**
    Custodial deposits in lieu of, **FrankR 75.3**
Briefs
    Limitations, **FrankR 57.13**
Case management, **FrankR 78.1**
Certified mail deliveries, electronic receipts from US Postal Service, **FrankR 75.17**
Civil actions, case management, **FrankR 78.1**

FRANKLIN COUNTY PROBATE COURT—continued
Claims against estate
    Deposit for costs, **FrankR 58.1, FrankR 62.1**
Compensation
    Guardians, **FrankR 73.1, FrankR 73.2**
    Trustees, **FrankR 74.1**
Complaints
    Deposit for costs, **FrankR 58.1**
Court costs
    Deposits, **FrankR 58.1**
Deposit for court costs, **FrankR 58.1**
Electronic receipts from US Postal Service, certified mail deliveries, **FrankR 75.17**
Estate tax return, filing, **FrankR 57.15**
Estates
    Case management, **FrankR 78.1**
    Minors, § 10,000 or less; application to dispense with guardianship, **FrankR 67.1**
        Attorneys, responsibility, **FrankR 67.3**
        Birth certificate required, **FrankR 67.2**
    Release from administration, **FrankR 75.5**
Exhibits, **FrankR 57.11**
    Filing fee, **FrankR 58.4**
Fees
    Adoption information, petition for release, **FrankR 58.3**
    Computerization, additional fee, **FrankR 75.7**
    Computerized legal research, additional fee, **FrankR 75.7**
    Copies of court records, **FrankR 55.2**
    Court costs, deposits, **FrankR 58.1**
    Dispute resolution, additional fee, **FrankR 75.7**
    Exhibits, filing fee, **FrankR 58.4**
    Foreign records, filing fee, **FrankR 58.4**
    Transcripts, filing fee, **FrankR 58.4**
    Witnesses, **FrankR 58.2**
Fiduciaries
    Acceptance form, signing and filing, **FrankR 60.1**
    Accounts. See Accounts, this heading
    Application for appointment
        Deposit for costs, **FrankR 58.1**
    Appointment by court, **FrankR 8.1**
        Nonresident fiduciaries, **FrankR 60.2**
    Guardianships. See Guardianships, this heading
    Nonresident fiduciaries, **FrankR 60.2**
Files
    Accompanying filings with court, **FrankR 57.2**
    Copies of records, fees, **FrankR 55.2**
    Removal from court, **FrankR 55.1**
    Withdrawal from records room, **FrankR 55.1**
Filings with court
    Address of attorney or fiduciary, **FrankR 57.3**
    Briefs, limitations, **FrankR 57.13**
    Case numbers to be included, **FrankR 57.4**
    Certificate of notice of entry of judgment, **FrankR 57.12**
    Computer disks, submissions on, **FrankR 57.10**
    Electronic mail transmission, unacceptable, **FrankR 57.1**
    Exhibits, **FrankR 57.11**
    Facsimile transmission, unacceptable, **FrankR 57.1**
    Forwarding copies, **FrankR 57.8**
    Print specifications, **FrankR 57.7**
    Proposed judgment entries, **FrankR 57.12**
    Request for issuance of summons, **FrankR 57.9**
    Signatures, **FrankR 57.5, FrankR 57.6**
    Social Security numbers, **FrankR 57.14**
Forms, **FrankR 51.1**
    Computer generated forms, **FrankR 52.1**
Guardians
    Compensation, **FrankR 73.1, FrankR 73.2**
    Indigent Guardianship Fund, compensation of guardians, **FrankR 73.2**
Guardians ad litem
    Appointment by court, **FrankR 75.1, FrankR 8.1**

FRANKLIN COUNTY PROBATE COURT—*continued*
Guardians ad litem—*continued*
    Fees, **FrankR 75.1**
Guardianships
    Address, notice of change, **FrankR 66.5**
    Background investigation, **FrankR 66.9**
    Case management, **FrankR 78.1**
    Change of address, notice to court, **FrankR 66.5**
    Deposit of wills, **FrankR 66.4**
    Funds, release, **FrankR 66.3**
    Minors, of, **FrankR 66.1**
      Termination, notice, **FrankR 66.7**
    Notice for guardianship of adults, **FrankR 66.8**
    Release of funds, **FrankR 66.3**
    Report, filing, **FrankR 66.6**
    Safe deposit box audits, deposit with court, **FrankR 66.2**
    Termination of guardianship of minor, **FrankR 66.7**
    Wills, deposit with court, **FrankR 66.4**
Hours of court, **FrankR 53.1**
Inventory, **FrankR 78.3**
Investigators
    Appointment by court, **FrankR 8.1**
Jury trial, request for, **FrankR 78.4**
Land sale proceedings
    Case management, **FrankR 78.1**
Legal notice, publication charges, **FrankR 58.1**
Magistrates
    Appointment by court, **FrankR 8.1**
    Decisions, objections, **FrankR 75.11**
Management and retention of records, **FrankR 26.1**
Marriage license applicants
    Counseling required, **FrankR 75.14**
Mediation, **FrankR 78.5**
Minors
    Estates of § 10,000 or less, application to dispense with guardianship, **FrankR 67.1**
      Attorneys, responsibility, **FrankR 67.3**
      Birth certificate required, **FrankR 67.2**
    Guardianships. See Guardianships, generally, this heading
    Injury claims of, settlement, **FrankR 68.1**
      Birth certificate required, **FrankR 68.1**
      Conference, **FrankR 68.2**
      Separate case number, **FrankR 68.3**
      Structured settlements, **FrankR 68.4**
Motions, case management, **FrankR 78.1**
Nonresident fiduciaries, **FrankR 60.2**
Objections to magistrate's decision, **FrankR 75.11**
Paralegals, registration, **FrankR 75.8**
Power of attorney, adult protective services, **FrankR 75.10**
Psychiatric hearings, case management, **FrankR 78.1**
Recording proceedings, **FrankR 11.1**
Registration of paralegals, **FrankR 75.8**
Reports
    Guardians, by, **FrankR 66.6**
Safe deposit box audits, deposit with court
    Attorney-in-fact, adult protective services, **FrankR 75.10**
    Guardians, **FrankR 66.2**
Security plan, **FrankR 9.1**
Settlements
    Injury claims of minors, **FrankR 68.1**
      Birth certificate required, **FrankR 68.1**
      Conference, **FrankR 68.2**
      Separate case number, **FrankR 68.3**
      Structured settlements, **FrankR 68.4**
    Wrongful death and survival claims, **FrankR 70.1**
      Conference, **FrankR 70.4**
    Wrongful death prototype trust, **FrankR 70.2**
      Multiple beneficiaries, **FrankR 70.3**
Signatures, **FrankR 57.5, FrankR 57.6**
    Accounts, fiduciaries, **FrankR 64.1**

FRANKLIN COUNTY PROBATE COURT—*continued*
Social Security numbers
    Filings with court, **FrankR 57.14**
Subpoenas
    Deposit for costs, **FrankR 58.1**
Summons
    Request for issuance, **FrankR 57.9**
    Service, **FrankR 75.13**
Surviving spouse waiver of service of citation to elect, **FrankR 75.16**
Transcripts, **FrankR 11.1**
    Filing fee, **FrankR 58.4**
Trustees
    Appointment by court, **FrankR 8.1**
    Compensation, **FrankR 74.1**
Trusts, case management, **FrankR 78.1**
Wills, deposit with court
    Guardians, **FrankR 66.4**
    Release upon death of testator, **FrankR 75.9**
Wills in safe deposit box, **FrankR 75.12**
Withdrawal of attorney, **FrankR 78.2**
Witnesses
    Fees, **FrankR 58.2**
Wrongful death and survival claims, **FrankR 70.1**
    Conference, **FrankR 70.4**
Wrongful death prototype trust, **FrankR 70.2**
    Multiple beneficiaries, **FrankR 70.3**

FRATERNAL ORGANIZATIONS
Gifts and grants to, estate tax deductions, **ORC 5731.17**

FRAUD
See also FALSE STATEMENTS
Adoption, effect on, **ORC 3107.16**
Annulment, grounds for, **ORC 3105.31(D)**
Conveyances, **ORC 2109.56**
Creditors, defrauding
    Imprisonment, **O Const I § 15**
Divorce, fraudulent contract as grounds, **ORC 3105.01(E)**
Dower
    Assignment, **ORC 5305.13**
    Interest, recovery, **ORC 2103.06**
Estate tax returns, **ORC 5731.22**
Executors and administrators. See EXECUTORS AND ADMINISTRATORS
Fiduciaries. See FIDUCIARIES
Identity of another, taking, **ORC 2913.49**
Limitation of actions, **ORC 2305.09**
Personal identifying information, taking of another's, **ORC 2913.49**
Statute of frauds. See STATUTE OF FRAUDS
Survival of actions, **ORC 2305.21**
Taking identity of another, **ORC 2913.49**
Transfers, **ORC 2127.40**
Trusts, creation induced by fraud, duress, or undue influence, **ORC 5804.06**

FRAUDULENT CONTRACTS
Legal separation, grounds for, **ORC 3105.17(A)(5)**

FRAUDULENT CONVEYANCES
Generally, **ORC 2109.56**

FRAUDULENT TRANSFERS
Generally, **ORC 2127.40, ORC Ch 1336**
Creditors with preexisting claims, **ORC 1336.05**
Defenses, **ORC 1336.08**
Definitions, **ORC 1336.01**
Effect of other laws, **ORC 1336.10**
Effectiveness of transfer, **ORC 1336.06**
Good faith transferees and obligees, rights, **ORC 1336.08**
Insolvency, **ORC 1336.02**
Intent, **ORC 1336.04**
Limitation of actions, **ORC 1336.09**

FRAUDULENT TRANSFERS—*continued*
Partnerships, **ORC 1336.02**
Recovery by creditors, **ORC 1336.08**
Remedies, **ORC 1336.07**
Short title of act, **ORC 1336.11**
Value, **ORC 1336.03**

FREEWAYS
See HIGHWAYS AND ROADS

FUNDS
See also FUNDS, PUBLIC
Executors and administrators. See EXECUTORS AND ADMINISTRATORS
Gifts. See GIFTS AND GRANTS
Institutional Trust Funds Act, **ORC 5813.01 to 5813.07**
See also INSTITUTIONAL TRUST FUNDS ACT
Investments. See INVESTMENTS
Unclaimed. See UNCLAIMED FUNDS

FUNDS, PUBLIC
Accounts and accounting. See ACCOUNTS AND ACCOUNTING, generally
Agro Ohio fund
   Escheat, proceeds from, **ORC 2105.09**
Child support intercept fund, **ORC 5747.121**
Community mental retardation and developmental disabilities trust fund, **ORC 5123.352**
Counties
   General fund
      Escheat, proceeds from, **ORC 2105.09**
      Income tax revenues, **ORC 5747.51 to 5747.55**
      Marriage solemnization fees, probate judge collecting, **ORC 2101.27**
   Local government fund
      Income tax revenues credited to, **ORC 5747.51**
   Undivided local government fund
      Apportionment, **ORC 5747.51**
         Alternative method, **ORC 5747.53**
      Income tax revenues credited to, **ORC 5747.51**
      Withholding of state revenues, **ORC 5747.54**
Deposits and depositories
   Fees, computerized legal services; juvenile courts, **ORC 2151.541, ORC 2153.081**
   Probate courts, prepaid and unearned costs, **ORC 2101.161**
General revenue fund
   Estate tax revenues credited to, **ORC 5731.48**
   Income tax revenues, **ORC 5747.02**
   Mental retardation and developmental disabilities department lands
      Mineral rights, leases, **ORC 5123.23**
      Mineral rights, proceeds from sale to, **ORC 5123.23**
Indigent guardianship fund, **ORC 2111.51**
   Deposits into, **ORC 2101.16(C)**
Mental retardation and developmental disabilities department, **ORC 5123.26**
Military injury relief fund
   Income tax refunds contributed to, **ORC 5747.113**
Natural areas and preserves fund
   Income tax refunds contributed to, **ORC 5747.113**
Nongame and endangered wildlife fund
   Income tax refunds contributed to, **ORC 5747.113**
Probate court conduct of business fund, **ORC 2101.19**
Purchase of service fund, **ORC 5123.051**
Services fund for individuals with mental retardation and developmental disabilities, **ORC 5123.40**
Tax refund fund, income tax refunds, **ORC 5747.11**

FUNERALS AND BURIALS
See also CEMETERIES

FUNERALS AND BURIALS—*continued*
Anatomical gifts, assignment of rights to direct disposition of remains after death and purchase goods and services related to funeral, **ORC 2108.70**
Claims against estate, **ORC 2117.25**
Claims against estates, **2117.251, ORC 2117.25**
Executors and administrators, duties, **ORC 2113.37**
   Expenses, **ORC 2106.20, ORC 2109.02, ORC 2113.031, ORC 2117.25**
Expenses
   Application for summary release from administration by obligee, **ORC 2113.031**
   Defined, **ORC 2113.031**
   Estate tax deduction, **ORC 5731.16**
   Executors and administrators, duties, **ORC 2106.20, ORC 2109.02, ORC 2113.031, ORC 2117.25**
   Summary estate administration, order of distribution to pay, **Sup. R 75.4**
   Wrongful death, reimbursed from damages, **ORC 2125.02, ORC 2125.03**
Preneed funeral contracts
   Duty of surviving spouse, effect on, **ORC 3103.03(E)**

FUTURE INTERESTS
Generally, **ORC 2131.04 to 2131.07**

GARNISHMENT
Support and maintenance action
   Parentage actions, **ORC 3111.13(F)**

GENERAL ASSEMBLY
Powers, **O Const I § 2**

GENERATION SKIPPING TRANSFER TAX
Generally, **ORC 5731.181**
Apportionment among interested persons, **ORC 2113.861**

GENETIC TESTS
Adult child, fatherhood established, **ORC 2105.25**
Child support enforcement agencies providing, **ORC 3111.61**
Contempt for failure to submit to, **ORC 3111.08, ORC 3111.09**
Defined, **ORC 2105.25**
DNA testing of prisoners, **ORC 2901.07**
Parentage actions, **ORC 3111.08, ORC 3111.09, ORC 3111.14**
   Probability of ninety-five per cent or greater, presumption of paternity, **ORC 3111.03**

GIFTS AND GRANTS
Advancements from estates, **ORC 2105.051**
Aliens, rights, **ORC 2105.16**
Anatomical gifts. See ANATOMICAL GIFTS
Bequests. See LEGACIES AND DEVISES
Causa mortis, estate tax, **ORC 5731.05**
Counties, to, estate tax deduction, **ORC 5731.17**
Delinquency prevention, for, **ORC 2152.73**
Developmentally disabled persons, for, **ORC 5123.35**
Devises. See LEGACIES AND DEVISES
Disclaimer of succession to, **ORC 5815.36**
   See also DISCLAIMER OF SUCCESSION TO PROPERTY
Estate tax deductions, **ORC 5731.17**
Expectation of death, made in
   Estate tax, **ORC 5731.05**
Fraternal organizations, estate tax deductions, **ORC 5731.17**
Gift causa mortis, estate tax, **ORC 5731.05**
Gifts inter vivos. See INTER VIVOS GIFTS
Governmental grants. See APPROPRIATIONS
In contemplation of death, estate tax, **ORC 5731.05**
Inter vivos
   Advancements from estates, **ORC 2105.051**
      Fiduciaries making, **ORC 2109.44**
Juvenile courts, to, **ORC 2152.73**
Juvenile rehabilitation facilities, to, **ORC 2151.67**
Legacies. See LEGACIES AND DEVISES

GIFTS AND GRANTS—continued
Legal rights service, to, **ORC 5123.60**
Lodges, estate tax deductions, **ORC 5731.17**
Mental retardation and developmental disabilities department, to, **ORC 5123.27**
 State planning council, **ORC 5123.35**
Military injury relief fund
 Income tax refund contributions, **ORC 5747.113**
Mortmain statute. See LEGACIES AND DEVISES, at Charitable bequests
Natural areas and preserves fund, to
 Income tax refund contributions, **ORC 5747.113**
Nongame and endangered wildlife fund, to
 Income tax refund contributions, **ORC 5747.113**
Trusts incorporated to receive. See CHARITABLE TRUSTS

GIFTS CAUSA MORTIS
Estate tax, **ORC 5731.05**

GIFTS INTER VIVOS
Advancement from estate, **ORC 2105.051**
 Fiduciaries making, **ORC 2109.44**

GOOD FAITH
Anatomical gifts, right to good faith reliance on written declaration and instructions, **ORC 2108.86**
Fraudulent transfers, rights of good faith transferees and obligees, **ORC 1336.08**
Grandparent power of attorney or caretaker authorization affidavit, good faith reliance, **ORC 3109.61 3109.73**
Purchasers in good faith. See BONA FIDE PURCHASERS

GRAND JURIES
Juvenile proceedings with adult defendants transferred to, **ORC 2151.43**

GRANDPARENT POWER OF ATTORNEY OR CARETAKER AUTHORIZATION AFFIDAVIT
Generally, **3109.51-3109.80**
Academic or interscholastic programs, creation for participation in, **3109.78**
Best interest of child, hearing, **3109.77**
Care, physical custody and control of child, generally, **3109.52**
Caretaker authorization affidavit
 Generally, **3109.65**
 Execution, **3109.65, 3109.67, 3109.69**
 Filing with juvenile court, **3109.74**
 Form, **3109.66**
 Good faith reliance, immunity from liability, **3109.73**
 Negation, reversal, or disapproval of action taken pursuant to affidavit, **3109.72**
 Notice of hearing, best interest of child, **3109.77**
 Notice upon termination, **3109.71**
 Pending proceedings, effect of, **3109.68**
 Report to public children services agency, **3109.74**
 Subsequent or second affidavits, **3109.76**
 Termination, **3109.70, 3109.71**
 Verification, **3109.75**
Child support order, effect of, **3109.79**
Conditions precedent, **3109.56-3109.58**
De novo review, **3109.77**
Definitions, **3109.51**
Filing with juvenile court, **3109.74**
Form, **3109.53**
Good faith reliance, immunity from liability, **3109.61, 3109.73**
Military power of attorney, **3109.62**
Nonresidential parent, notice to, **3109.55**
Notarization, **3109.54**
Notice
 Hearing, best interest of child, **3109.77**
 Nonresidential parent and legal custodian, **3109.55**
 Termination of power of attorney, **3109.60**
One power of attorney or affidavit in effect per child, **3109.80**

GRANDPARENT POWER OF ATTORNEY OR CARETAKER AUTHORIZATION AFFIDAVIT
 —continued
Report to public children services agency, **3109.74**
Signature, **3109.54**
Subsequent or second powers of attorney or affidavits, **3109.76**
Termination or revocation, **3109.59, 3109.60**
Verification, **3109.75**

GRANDPARENTS
See also NEXT OF KIN
Adoption by grandparents, **ORC 5103.16**
Anatomical gifts, **ORC 2108.02**
Descent and distribution, **ORC 2105.06**
Power of attorney. See GRANDPARENT POWER OF ATTORNEY OR CARETAKER AUTHORIZATION AFFIDAVIT
Visitation rights, **ORC 3109.051(B)**
 Deceased parent, **ORC 3109.11**
 Illegitimate child, **ORC 3109.12**

GRANTS
See GIFTS AND GRANTS

GRAVES AND GRAVEYARDS
See CEMETERIES

GUARDIAN OF THE ESTATE
Defined, **ORC 5801.01**

GUARDIAN OF THE PERSON
Defined, **ORC 5801.01**

GUARDIANS
Ad Litem. See GUARDIANS AD LITEM

GUARDIANS AD LITEM
Generally, **JuvR 4**
Abortion for minor without parental consent complaint, **ORC 2151.85, SupR 23(C)**
Appointment, **CuyR 8.1, FrankR 75.1, FrankR 8.1, HamR 75.1, JuvR 4(B), LucasR 65.01, ORC 2111.23, SumR 91.1(B)**
Compensation, **JuvR 4(F), SumR 91.1(C)**
 Computation, **FrankR 73.1**
 Indigent Guardianship Fund, **FrankR 73.2**
Counsel for ward, as, **JuvR 4(C), ORC 2151.281**
Defined, **JuvR 2**
Delinquent or unruly juveniles, **ORC 2151.281**
Eminent domain proceedings, **ORC 163.11**
Fees, **FrankR 75.1**
Notice given to
 Removal hearings, schools and school districts, **JuvR 39(A)**
Powers and duties, **ORC 2151.281**
Qualifications, **SumR 91.1(A)**
Volunteers, **ORC 2151.281**
Withdrawal, **JuvR 4(E)**

GUARDIANSHIP
Generally, **ORC Ch 2111**
See also FIDUCIARIES, for general provisions
Accounts and accounting, **ORC 2101.24, ORC 2109.12, ORC 2109.30 to 2109.36, ORC 2111.16**
 See also FIDUCIARIES
 Annual, **SumR 64.1(B)**
 Case management, **SupR 78**
 Compensation, separate schedule of computation set forth in, **CuyR 73.1, HamR 73.1**
 Delinquent in filing, compensation, **CuyR 73.1, HamR 73.1**
 Exhibiting assets, **SupR 64**
 Final account, notice, **CuyR 64.2 et seq.**
 Improvements of real property, **ORC 2111.36**
 Incompetent ward, biennial report on mental and physical condition of, **CuyR 66.3 et seq.**
 Notice of hearing on approval, **LucasR 64.1**

GUARDIANSHIP—*continued*
Accounts and accounting, **ORC 2101.24, ORC 2109.12, ORC 2109.30 to 2109.36, ORC 2111.16**—*continued*
    Partial, **SumR 64.1(A)**
    Resident guardian of nonresident ward, by, **ORC 2111.40**
    Time for filing, **LucasR 64.1**
    Vouchers, **Sup. R 64.2**
    Waiver, **ORC 2109.30(C)**
Actions by guardian, **ORC 2111.17 to 2111.181**
    Juvenile proceedings. *See* JUVENILE COURTS, at particular subject concerned
    Leasing authority of guardian, **ORC 2111.25 to 2111.32**
    Parties to, **ORC 2111.28**
    Real property
        Improvements, **ORC 2111.33 to 2111.36**
        Sale, **ORC 2127.01, ORC 2127.05, ORC 2127.42**
Ad litem. *See* GUARDIANS AD LITEM
Administrators as, **ORC 2111.09**
Adoption by guardian, **ORC 5103.16**
Adult wards
    Settlement of damage claims, **SupR 69**
Anatomical gifts
    Authorization, **ORC 2108.02**
Application for appointment. *See* Appointment, this heading
Appointment, **ORC 2101.24, ORC 2111.02 to 2111.031, Sup. R 66.1**
    Application, **ORC 2111.03, SupR 66(A)**
        Investigation, **SumR 66.1(A)**
    Choice of minor, **ORC 2111.12**
    Conflict of interest, **ORC 2101.38**
    Establishing residency for school purposes improper purpose, **LucasR 66.1, SumR 66.1(A)**
    Fees, **ORC 2101.16**
    Improper, incompetent person, **ORC 2111.47**
    Juvenile courts, **ORC 2151.32**
    Nomination in writing, **ORC 2111.121**
    Nonresidency, effect. *See* Nonresidency, this heading
    Nonresident ward, **ORC 2111.37**
    Notice, **FrankR 66.8, ORC 2111.04**
    Qualifications, **ORC 2111.121(B)**
    Selection by minor ward, **ORC 2111.46**
    Several siblings as wards, **ORC 2109.16**
    Time of, **ORC 2111.06**
    Will, by, **ORC 2111.12**
        Revocation, **ORC 2107.33**
Appraisal, new appraisal ordered, **ORC 2127.32**
Attorney fees, **CuyR 71.1, FrankR 71.5, LucasR 71.1, Sup. R 71.3**
    Personal injury claims, settlement, **CuyR 71.2 et seq.**
    Representation of guardian, **SupR 71**
Attorneys for guardians of minors, prohibitions, **ORC 2111.091**
Bond, **ORC 2109.04 to 2109.20, SumR 66.1(A)**
    Action on, limitation, **ORC 2305.12**
    Conditions, **ORC 2109.12**
    Exemption, **ORC 2109.04(A)**
    Mortgage in lieu of, **ORC 2109.20**
    Nonresident ward, **ORC 2111.38**
    Real property sale by, **ORC 2127.27**
    Several siblings as wards, **ORC 2109.16**
    Sureties. *See* FIDUCIARIES
    Waiver in nomination, **ORC 2111.121**
Case management, probate court, **SupR 78**
Claims against estate or trust, **ORC 2109.59, ORC 2111.18**
Compensation, **Sup. R 73.1, SupR 73**
    Accounts, separate schedules of computation set forth in, **CuyR 73.1, HamR 73.1**
    Additional, **CuyR 73.1, FrankR 73.1, HamR 73.1**
    Application, **SumR 73.1(A), SumR Appx C**
    Authorized expenditures, **SumR 73.1(D)**
    Co-guardians, **CuyR 73.1, HamR 73.1**
    Computation, **CuyR 73.1, FrankR 73.1, HamR 73.1, LucasR 73.1**
        Estates involving real estate, **LucasR 71.1**

GUARDIANSHIP—*continued*
Compensation, **Sup. R 73.1, SupR 73**—*continued*
    Delinquent in filing account, **CuyR 73.1, HamR 73.1**
    Denied, **ORC 2109.24**
    Extraordinary fees, **SumR 73.1(C)**
    Form, **HamR Appx D**
    Hearings on applications, **CuyR 73.1, HamR 73.1**
    Indigent Guardianship Fund, **FrankR 73.2**
    Minimum fees, **SumR 73.1(E)**
        Annual, **LucasR 73.1**
    Sale of land by, **ORC 2127.08, ORC 2127.37**
        Commission, **ORC 2127.28**
    Schedule, **SumR 73.1(B)**
Conflict of interest, **ORC 2101.38**
Consent
    Adoption, to, **ORC 3107.06**
    Sale of real property, **ORC 2127.04**
Conservatorship, **ORC 2111.021**
Continued necessity, hearing to evaluate, **ORC 2111.49**
Corporation as, **ORC 2111.10**
Court costs, **CuyR 58.1, SumR Appx A, Sup. R 58.1**
Custodial deposits, **SumR 66.1(A)**
Custody by one parent, **ORC 2111.08**
Cuyahoga county probate court
    Accounts, **CuyR 64.2 et seq.**
    Compensation of guardian, **CuyR 73.1**
    Court costs, **CuyR 58.1**
    Reports
        Condition of adult incompetent, **CuyR 66.3 et seq.**
        Condition of ward, **CuyR 66.3 et seq.**
    Supervision, case management, **CuyR 78.1**
    Wills, deposit with court, **CuyR 66.3 et seq.**
Death
    Sale of land, effect, **ORC 2127.06**
    Ward, notice to court, **SumR 66.1(A)**
Declaratory judgments sought by. *See* DECLARATORY JUDGMENTS, generally
Definitions, **JuvR 2, ORC 2101.01, ORC 2111.01, ORC 3109.51**
Disabled fiduciary, duties, **ORC 2109.26**
Disclaimer of succession to property, **ORC 5815.36**
    See also DISCLAIMER OF SUCCESSION TO PROPERTY
Dower interest of ward, **ORC 2111.21, ORC 5305.17**
Durable power of attorney, nomination pursuant to
    Residency requirements, **ORC 2109.21**
Eligibility, **ORC 2111.08 to 2111.11**
Emancipation of ward, settlement of claims, **ORC 2111.181**
Emergency guardian, **HamR 66.2, ORC 2111.02**
Endangering children. *See* ENDANGERING CHILDREN
Estate, of, **ORC 2111.06, ORC 2111.07, ORC 2111.14**
    Accounting, waiver, **ORC 2109.30(C)**
    Corporation as guardian, **ORC 2111.10**
    Marriage of ward, effect, **ORC 2111.45**
    Nonresident ward, **ORC 2111.37 to 2111.40**
    Valued under § 10,000, **ORC 2111.05, SupR 67**
    Waiver when annual payments under § 5000, **ORC 2111.131(A)**
Executor as, **ORC 2111.09**
Expenditure of funds
    Procedural prerequisites, **HamR 66.1, SumR 66.1(A)**
Fees. *See* Compensation, this heading
Fiduciaries
    See also FIDUCIARIES, for general provisions
    Duties, **ORC Ch 2109**
Forms, **SupR 51, SupR 52**
Franklin county probate court
    Address, notice of change, **FrankR 66.5**
    Background investigation, **FrankR 66.9**
    Case management, **FrankR 78.1**
    Change of address, notice to court, **FrankR 66.5**
    Deposit of wills, **FrankR 66.4**
    Funds, release, **FrankR 66.3**

GUARDIANSHIP

GUARDIANSHIP—*continued*
  Franklin county probate court—*continued*
    Minors, of, **FrankR 66.1**
      Termination, notice, **FrankR 66.7**
    Notice for guardianship of adults, **FrankR 66.8**
    Release of funds, **FrankR 66.3**
    Report, filing, **FrankR 66.6**
    Safe deposit box audits, deposit with court, **FrankR 66.2**
    Termination of guardianship of minor, **FrankR 66.7**
    Wills, deposit with court, **FrankR 66.4**
  Funds
    Deposit upon termination of guardianship, **ORC 2111.05**
    Investment powers, **ORC 2109.37 to 2109.38**
  Hamilton county probate court
    Case management, **HamR 78.1**
    Court costs, deposit, **HamR Appx D**
    Emergency guardianship, **HamR 66.2**
    Funds, release and order to expend, **HamR 66.1**
  Handbook, **SumR 66.1(A)**
  Health care treatment for ward, authorizing, **ORC 2111.13(C)**
  Hearings
    Continued necessity, evaluation, **ORC 2111.49**
  Income tax returns, duties, **ORC 5747.08(B)**
  Incompetent, of
    See also Mentally ill persons, for, and Mentally retarded or developmentally disabled persons, for, this heading
    Adult, biennial report on mental and physical condition of, **CuyR 66.3 et seq.**
    Appointment, **LucasR 66.1**
    Emergency guardian, **HamR 66.2**
    Partial account, biennial report on mental and physical condition of ward, **CuyR 66.3 et seq.**
    Personal contact with ward twice a year required, **LucasR 66.1**
    Reports, **LucasR 66.1**
    Wills, deposit with court, **LucasR 66.1**
  Indigent guardianship fund, **ORC 2111.51**
    Deposits into, **ORC 2101.16(C)**
  Insolvency of estate of ward, **ORC 2111.24**
  Interim guardian, **ORC 2111.02**
  Inventory
    Evidence to support, **ORC 2111.141**
    Verification, **ORC 2111.141**
  Investigation
    Probate court investigator, by, **ORC 2111.042**
  Investment powers, **ORC 2109.37 to 2109.38**
    Temporary investments, **ORC 2109.372**
  Jurisdiction, **ORC 2111.46**
    Transfer of, **ORC 2111.471**
  Juvenile courts, supervision, **ORC 2151.359**
  Land contracts, completing, **ORC 2111.19**
  Land sale by. See Sale of land by, this heading
  Leases, **ORC 2111.25 to 2111.32**
  Legal disability, defined, **ORC 2131.02**
  Legal rights service serving as, **ORC 5123.60**
  Limitation on personal liability, **ORC 2111.151**
  Limited guardian, **ORC 2111.02**
  Lucas county probate court, **LucasR 66.1**
    Case management, **LucasR 78.1**
    Court costs, **LucasR 58.1(A)**
  Marriage of ward, effect, **ORC 2111.45**
  Mediation, **SumR 98.1**
  Mental retardation and developmental disabilities department as, **ORC 2111.01**
  Mentally ill persons, for, **ORC 5122.41**
    See also Incompetent, of, this heading
    Abuse or exploitation, probate courts referring information to law enforcement agencies, **ORC 2101.26, ORC 2151.421**
    Application, **SupR 66(A)**
    Children, **ORC 5122.39**
    Examination, **ORC 2111.031**
    Investigation of incompetency by probate court investigator, **ORC 2111.041**

GUARDIANSHIP—*continued*
  Mentally ill persons, for, **ORC 5122.41**—*continued*
    Real property transactions by guardians, validity, **ORC 2111.48**
    Report, **ORC 2111.49**
      Contents, **ORC 2111.49**
      Review by probate court, **ORC 2111.49**
    Spouse, **ORC 5305.17**
    Termination of guardianship, **ORC 2111.47**
  Mentally retarded or developmentally disabled persons, for, **ORC 5123.55 to 5123.59, ORC 5123.93, ORC 5123.95**
    See also Incompetent, of, this heading
    Real property transactions by guardians, validity, **ORC 2111.48**
    Termination of guardianship, **ORC 2111.47**
  Mineral rights. See MINERAL RIGHTS
  Minors, **ORC 2111.46**
    Abuse or exploitation, probate courts referring information to law enforcement agencies, **ORC 2101.26, ORC 2151.421**
    Adoption, consent to, **ORC 3107.06**
    Application, **SupR 67**
    Appointment, **LucasR 66.1**
    Attorneys for guardians of, prohibitions, **ORC 2111.091**
    Delivery of estate to, upon termination of guardianship, **SupR 67**
    Duties, **ORC 2111.06**
    Emergency guardian, **HamR 66.2**
    Investigation by probate court investigator, **ORC 2111.042**
    Mentally ill, **ORC 5122.39**
    Notice to putative father/paternal relatives, **SumR 66.1(A)**
    Person and estate, **ORC 2111.06**
    Reports, **LucasR 66.1**
    Selection by, **ORC 2111.12**
    Settlement of damage claims, **SupR 68**
  Modification
    Review of report, upon, **ORC 2111.49**
  More than one ward
    Sale of real property jointly owned, **ORC 2117.05**
    Siblings, **ORC 2109.16**
  Nomination, **ORC 2111.121**
    Successor guardian, **ORC 2111.121(A)**
  Nonresidency
    Guardians, of, **ORC 2109.21, ORC 2111.41 to 2111.44**
      Collection of money by, **ORC 2111.39**
      Payment of money to, **ORC 2111.42**
      Sale of realty for foreign ward, **ORC 2127.42**
    Wards, of, **ORC 2111.37 to 2111.40**
      Real property sale for benefit of, **ORC 2127.42**
      Removal from state, **ORC 2111.471**
  Notice
    Accounts and accounting, **LucasR 64.1**
    Adult, hearing as to appointment of guardian for, **FrankR 66.8**
    Appointment
      Adult, for, **FrankR 66.8**
      Incompetent, for, **ORC 2111.04**
      Minor, for, **ORC 2111.04**
    Death of ward, **SumR 66.1(A)**
    Incompetent
      Appointment, **ORC 2111.04**
      Termination, **ORC 2111.47**
    Minor, appointment, **ORC 2111.04**
      Putative father/paternal relatives, to, **SumR 66.1(A)**
    Nonresident appointed after removal of resident, **ORC 2111.41**
    Real estate
      Lease of, **ORC 2111.29**
      Sale of, **ORC 2127.13, ORC 2127.18, ORC 2127.32**
    Resident removed after appointment of nonresident, **ORC 2111.41**
    Termination of guardianship, **FrankR 66.7, ORC 2111.47**
  Objections by ward or interested party to guardian's authorizing of health or professional care, **ORC 2111.13(C)**
  Parental care, defined, **ORC 2151.05**
  Parents as, **ORC 2111.08**
  Person, of, **ORC 2111.13, ORC 2111.15**

GUARDIANSHIP

GUARDIANSHIP—*continued*
Personal injury claims
    Settlement, attorney fees, **CuyR 71.2 et seq.**
Personal property
    Sale, **ORC 2109.45, SumR 66.1(A)**
    Transactions, **ORC 2111.20**
Power of attorney
    Person nominated for as guardian also, **ORC 2111.02**
Powers and duties, **ORC 2111.06, ORC 2111.07, ORC 2111.13 to 2111.24, ORC 2111.131**
    Estate, of, **ORC 2111.13**
        Nonresident ward, **ORC 2111.38**
    Person, of, **ORC 2111.13, ORC 2111.15**
    Probate courts, jurisdiction, **ORC 2101.24**
Probate courts
    Case management, **SupR 78**
    Intervention by, **ORC 2111.49**
    Jurisdiction, **ORC 2101.24**
    Powers and duties, **ORC 2111.50**
Professional care for ward, authorizing, **ORC 2111.13(C)**
Real property
    Appraisal
        Lease of mineral rights, **ORC 2111.30**
        Sale of property, **ORC 2127.22 to 2127.39**
    Improvements, **ORC 2111.33 to 2111.36**
    Leases, **ORC 2111.25 to 2111.32**
    Releases and quitclaim, tax title, **ORC 2111.22**
    Sale of. See Sale of land by, this heading
    Transactions, **ORC 2111.19**
        Validation, **ORC 2111.48**
Records and reports
    Accounts. See Accounts and accounting, this heading
    Annual report, **SumR 66.1(B)**
    Biennial report
        Incompetent adult, **CuyR 66.3 et seq.**
        Incompetent ward, **CuyR 66.3 et seq.**
    Court records, **ORC 2101.14**
    Fees, **ORC 2101.16**
    Probate court docket, case management, **SupR 78**
Release of funds and assets
    Court order, **HamR 66.1, SumR 66.1(A)**
    Inventory filed or approved, **HamR 66.1**
Removal of guardian, **ORC 2101.24, ORC 2109.21**
    Nonresident ward, **ORC 2111.41**
Residency requirements, **ORC 2109.21**
    See also Nonresidency, this heading
Sale of land by, **ORC 2127.05**
    Appraisal, **ORC 2127.22 to 2127.39**
    Appraisers
        Appointment, **ORC 2127.22**
        Compensation, **ORC 2127.25**
        Report, **ORC 2127.23**
        Vacancy, **ORC 2127.24**
    Bond, **ORC 2127.27**
    Compensation, **ORC 2127.08, ORC 2127.37**
    Complaint, **ORC 2127.10**
    Confirmation, **ORC 2127.35**
    Death of guardian, effect, **ORC 2127.06**
    Deferred payments, **ORC 2127.34, ORC 2127.36**
    Dower interest, **ORC 2111.21**
    Expenses
        Proceeds distributed for, **ORC 2127.38**
        Realtor's commission, **ORC 2127.28**
    Foreign guardian, by, **ORC 2111.44**
    Fractional interest, **ORC 2127.08**
        Compensation of guardian, **ORC 2127.08**
    Joint wards, **ORC 2127.05**
    Jurisdiction, **ORC 2101.24**
    Liens, release, **ORC 2127.19**
    Mortgages, **ORC 2127.20**
        Release, **ORC 2127.19**

GUARDIANSHIP—*continued*
Sale of land by, **ORC 2127.05**—*continued*
    Nonresident ward, for, **ORC 2127.42**
    Notice of sale, **ORC 2127.13, ORC 2127.18, ORC 2127.32**
    Objections to, **ORC 2127.17**
    Parties to actions, **ORC 2127.13**
    Platting, **ORC 2127.21**
    Pleadings and procedure, **ORC 2127.15**
    Private, **ORC 2109.45, ORC 2127.32**
    Proceeds, **ORC 2127.38**
    Public, **ORC 2127.32**
    Purposes, **ORC 2127.05**
    Realtor's commission, **ORC 2127.28**
    Release and satisfaction of liens, **ORC 2127.19**
    Report of appraisers, **ORC 2127.23**
    Security for deferred payments, **ORC 2127.36**
    Several wards' interests joined, **ORC 2127.05**
    Successor guardian, by, **ORC 2127.06**
    Summary proceeding, **ORC 2127.11**
    Taxes, distribution of proceeds for, **ORC 2127.38**
    Terms of sale, **ORC 2127.34**
    Value of property less than § 3000, **ORC 2127.11**
    Venue of action, **ORC 2127.09**
Spouse as guardian, **ORC 2111.11**
Stark county probate court, **Sup. R 66.1 to Sup. R 66.6**
    Attorney fees, **Sup. R 71.3**
    Case management, **Sup. R 78.5**
Successor, **ORC 2111.46**
    Appointment, **ORC 2111.121(A)**
    Sale of land by, **ORC 2127.06**
Summary proceeding, sale of land by guardian, **ORC 2127.11**
Summit county probate court, **SumR 66.1**
    Accounting by guardian, **SumR 64.1(B)**
    Adults, mediation, **SumR 98.1**
    Bonds of guardian, **SumR 66.1(A)**
    Court costs, **SumR Appx A**
    Mediation, adult guardianships, **SumR 98.1**
    Reports, **SumR 66.1(B)**
    Supervision, **SumR 78.1(B)**
Support and maintenance of ward, **ORC 2111.13**
    Application for, **SupR 66(C)**
    Commitment of ward, after, **ORC 2151.36**
    Leases of mineral rights for, **ORC 2111.26**
    Monies paid to ward, **ORC 2111.131(B)**
Surety bond. See Bond, this heading
Tax returns, duties
    Income tax, state returns, **ORC 5747.08(B)**
Termination, **ORC 2111.45 to 2111.471**
    Estate valued under § 10,000, **ORC 2111.05**
    Fee, **ORC 2101.16**
    Incompetent ward, **ORC 2111.47**
    Minor's guardianship, notice of termination, **FrankR 66.7**
    Resident guardian of nonresident ward, **ORC 2111.40**
    Review of report, upon, **ORC 2111.49**
Testamentary guardians, **ORC 2107.33, ORC 2111.12**
Training sessions, **SumR 66.1(A)**
Unfit, **ORC 2151.05**
Veterans, **ORC Ch 2111**
Veterans administration, **HamR 73.2**
Voting, **SumR 66.1(A)**
Vouchers signed by wards, **ORC 2111.16**
Wards
    Change of residence, **SumR 66.1(A)**
    Claims, **ORC 2111.181**
    Death, notice to court, **SumR 66.1(A)**
    Defined, **ORC 2111.01**
    Delivery of estate to, upon termination of guardianship, **ORC 2111.05**
    Incompetent, of. See Incompetent, of, this heading
    Joint, sale of real property, **ORC 2127.05**

GUARDIANSHIP

GUARDIANSHIP—*continued*
Wards—*continued*
 Legal disability, considered to be under. See DISABILITY, PERSONS UNDER, generally
 Marriage, **ORC 2111.45**
 Mentally ill. See Mentally ill persons, for, this heading
 Mentally retarded. See Mentally retarded or developmentally disabled persons, for, this heading
 Minors. See Minors, this heading
 Nonresident. See Nonresidency, this heading
 Objections by, guardian's authorizing of health or professional care, **ORC 2111.13(C)**
 Personal injury settlements, attorney fees for, **CuyR 71.2 et seq.**
 Probate court jurisdiction, **ORC 2101.24**
 Real property, guardian selling. See Sale of land by, this heading
 Wills, deposit with court, **CuyR 66.3 et seq.**
Wills, deposit with court, **CuyR 66.3 et seq.**

HABEAS CORPUS
Custody of child, **JuvR 10(A), JuvR 10(G)**
 Investigation, **JuvR 32(D)**
Jurisdiction, **O Const IV § 2, O Const IV § 3**
 Juvenile court, **ORC 2151.23**
 Probate court, **ORC 2101.24**
Juvenile courts, jurisdiction, **ORC 2151.23**
Mentally ill patients, rights, **ORC 5122.30**
Mentally retarded residents of institutions, rights, **ORC 5123.88**
 Notice to attorney general, **ORC 5123.90**
Probate courts, jurisdiction, **ORC 2101.24**

HABITUAL TRUANT
Defined, **ORC 2151.011**

HAIR
Anatomical gifts, exemption from uniform act, **ORC 2108.11**

HAMILTON COUNTY
See also COUNTIES, generally
Court of common pleas. See COURTS OF COMMON PLEAS, generally
Juvenile court, **ORC 2151.07, ORC 2151.08**
Probate court. See generally
Probate court. See HAMILTON COUNTY PROBATE COURT
Probate court. See HAMILTON COUNTY PROBATE COURT; PROBATE COURTS

HAMILTON COUNTY PROBATE COURT
Accounts and accounting, **HamR 64.1**
Adoptions, **HamR 75.1**
 Court costs, deposit, **HamR Appx D**
Appraisers and appraisals, **HamR 61.1**
 Land sale proceedings, appointment, **HamR 65.1**
Assets, joint control, **HamR 75.1**
Attorney fees, **HamR 71.1**
 Consent to payment of, **HamR Appx A-2**
  Waiver of notice of hearing on application, attached to, **HamR Appx A-3**
 Contingent fee agreements, **HamR 71.2**
 Notice of hearing on application for, **HamR Appx A-1**
  Waiver, **HamR Appx A-3**
 Veterans' guardianship, **HamR 73.2**
Attorneys
 Show cause hearings, **HamR 64.2**
 Sureties, not to act as, **HamR 75.1**
 Withdrawal, **HamR 57.1**
Audio-electronic record of proceedings, **HamR 11.1**
Bond premiums as administrative expenses, **HamR 62.1**
Case management, **HamR 78.1**
 Civil actions, **HamR 78.2**
Civil actions
 Case management, **HamR 78.1**
 Court costs, deposits, **HamR Appx D**
Civil commitment of mentally ill persons, **HamR 75.1**

HAMILTON COUNTY PROBATE COURT—*continued*
Claims, **HamR 62.1**
Compensation
 Guardians, **HamR 73.1, HamR Appx D**
  Veterans' guardianships, **HamR 73.2**
 Trustees, **HamR 74.1, HamR Appx C**
Computer-generated forms
 Specifications, **HamR 52.1**
 Use, **HamR 51.1**
Consent to payment of attorney fees, **HamR Appx A-2**
 Waiver of notice of hearing, attached to, **HamR Appx A-3**
Contingent fee agreements, **HamR 71.2**
Corporate trustees, compensation, **HamR 74.1**
Court costs, **HamR 58.1**
 Deposits, schedule, **HamR Appx D**
Deposits for court costs, schedule, **HamR Appx D**
Emergency guardianships, **HamR 66.2**
Estates
 Case management, **HamR 78.1**
 Court costs, deposit, **HamR Appx D**
Exhibits, **HamR 75.1**
Fees and costs
 Attorney fees, **HamR 71.1**
  Contingent fee agreements, **HamR 71.2**
  Notice of hearing on application for, **HamR Appx A-1**
  Veterans' guardianships, **HamR 73.2**
  Waiver of notice of hearing and consent to payment, **HamR Appx A-3**
 Court costs, **HamR 58.1, HamR Appx D**
 Record of proceedings, **HamR 11.1**
 Witness fees, **HamR 58.2**
Fiduciaries
 Show cause hearings, **HamR 64.2**
Filings with court, **HamR 57.1**
 Official file to accompany, **HamR 55.1**
Forms, **HamR 51.1**
 Attorney fees
  Consent to payment of, **HamR Appx A-2**
  Notice of hearing on application for, **HamR Appx A-1**
   Waiver of notice and consent to payment, **HamR Appx A-3**
 Computer-generated, specifications, **HamR 52.1**
 Guardians, compensation, **HamR Appx D**
 Trustees, compensation, **HamR Appx C**
Guardian ad litem, appointment, **HamR 75.1**
Guardians
 Compensation, **HamR 73.1, HamR Appx D**
  Veterans' guardianships, **HamR 73.2**
Guardianships
 Case management, **HamR 78.1**
 Court costs, deposit, **HamR Appx D**
 Emergency guardianship, **HamR 66.2**
 Funds, release and order to expend, **HamR 66.1**
Hearings
 Notice
  Attorney fees, application for, **HamR Appx A-1**
   Waiver, **HamR Appx A-3**
  Final account hearing, **HamR 64.1**
Hours of court, **HamR 53.1**
Individual trustees, compensation, **HamR 74.1**
Inventory and appraisal, **HamR 61.2**
Joint control of assets, **HamR 75.1**
Judgment entries, **HamR 57.1**
Jury use and management standards, **HamR 75.1**
Land sale proceedings
 Appraisers, appointment, **HamR 65.1**
 Case management, **HamR 78.2**
 Court costs, deposits, **HamR Appx D**
Letters of administration, application, **HamR 60.1**
Letters of authority, issuance, **HamR 75.1**
Mentally ill persons, civil commitment, **HamR 75.1**

HAMILTON COUNTY PROBATE COURT—*continued*
Minors
    Personal injury claims, settlement, **HamR 68.1**
        Structured settlements, **HamR 68.2**
        § 10,000 or less, **HamR 67.1**
Motions, **HamR 57.1**
    Case management, **HamR 78.2**
Notice
    Appearance, to compel; delinquent accounts, **HamR 64.1**
    Hearings
        Attorney fees, application for, **HamR Appx A-1**
        Waiver, **HamR Appx A-3**
    Final accounts, **HamR 64.1**
Official record, **HamR 11.1(A)**
Personal injury claims of minors, settlement, **HamR 68.1**
    Structured settlements, **HamR 68.2**
    § 10,000 or less, **HamR 67.1**
Pretrial procedure, **HamR 78.2**
Record of proceedings, **HamR 11.1**
Security plan, **HamR 54.1**
Settlements
    Personal injury claims, minors, **HamR 68.1**
        Structured settlements, **HamR 68.2**
        § 10,000 or less, **HamR 67.1**
    Wrongful death, **HamR 70.1**
Show cause hearings, **HamR 64.2**
Signatures on court filings, black ink, **HamR 57.1**
Standard forms, **HamR 51.1**
    Computer-generated forms to comply with, **HamR 52.1**
Structured settlements, minors, **HamR 68.2**
Sureties, attorneys not to act as, **HamR 75.1**
Transcripts, **HamR 11.1**
Trustees, compensation, **HamR 74.1, HamR Appx C**
Trusts
    Case management, **HamR 78.1**
    Court costs, deposits, **HamR Appx D**
Wills
    Admission to probate, **HamR 59.1**
        Irregularities, wills containing, **HamR 59.2**
Witness fees, **HamR 58.2**
Wrongful death settlements, **HamR 70.1**

HANDICAPPED CHILDREN
See DISABLED PERSONS

HANDICAPPED PERSONS
Generally, See DISABLED PERSONS
Drivers' licenses, restrictions, **ORC 4507.08**
Legal disability, considered to be under. See DISABILITY, PERSONS UNDER, generally
Mental retardation and developmental disabilities department making eligibility determinations, **ORC 5123.012**
Victims of crime
    Juvenile delinquency, disposition of case, **ORC 2152.12(C)**

HEALTH
Examination. See MEDICAL AND MENTAL EXAMINATIONS
Hospitals. See HOSPITALS
Mental. See MENTALLY RETARDED AND DEVELOPMENTALLY DISABLED PERSONS
Mental. See MENTALLY RETARDED AND DEVELOPMENTALLY DISABLED PERSONS; See MENTALLY ILL PERSONS
Physicians. See PHYSICIANS

HEALTH AND HOSPITALIZATION INSURANCE
Child
    Divorced parents, for, **ORC 3109.05(A)**

HEALTH CARE SERVICES AND FACILITIES
See also HOSPITALS
Durable power of attorney for, **ORC 1337.11 to 1337.20**
Juvenile proceedings, **JuvR 13(C), ORC 2151.53**

HEALTH DEPARTMENT, STATE
Acknowledgment of paternity statements
    Agreements with human services department regarding, **ORC 3705.091**
    Storage of, **ORC 3705.091, ORC 5101.314**
Adoption records
    Petition for release, **ORC 3107.41**
    Public records, not considered to be, **ORC 3107.42**
    Releases, **ORC 3107.40**
Mental retardation and developmental disabilities institutions engaged in farming, assistance, **ORC 5123.221**
Reimbursement to counties for cost of care of mentally ill persons, **ORC 5122.43**
Second chance trust fund advisory committee, **ORC 2108.17**

HEARINGS
See also ACTIONS
Abortion for minor without parental consent complaint, **SupR 23(D)**
Abused or neglected adults, ex parte emergency orders, **ORC 5126.332**
Administrators, accounts, **ORC 2109.33**
Adoption, **ORC 3107.11, ORC 3107.14**
    Confidentiality, **ORC 3107.17**
    Withdrawal of consent, **ORC 3107.084(B)**
Bail
    Denial, **ORC 2937.222**
Bifurcation, juvenile court, **JuvR 34(I)**
Budgets, **ORC 5747.51(B)**
Complaints. See COMPLAINTS
Definitions, **JuvR 2**
Detention of child, **JuvR 7(F)**
Discovery motion, on, **JuvR 22(D)**
Eminent domain, **ORC 163.10 to 163.14**
Estate tax returns, on, **ORC 5731.26**
Estates. See ESTATES
Executors, accounts, **ORC 2109.33**
Grandparent power of attorney or caretaker authorization affidavit, best interest of child, **ORC 3109.77**
Hospitalization of mentally ill, **ORC 5122.12, ORC 5122.12 to 5122.15**
Institutionalization of mentally retarded, **ORC 5123.701 to 5123.77**
Juvenile procedure, rules of, **JuvR 34**
Mentally ill, hospitalization, **ORC 5122.12 to 5122.15**
Mentally ill persons, medication of, **ORC 2101.24**
Mentally retarded, institutionalization, **ORC 5123.701 to 5123.77**
Protective services for adults. See PROTECTIVE SERVICES FOR ADULTS
Summons to appear, **JuvR 15(A) to JuvR 15(C), JuvR 16(A)**
Tax budgets and estimates, **ORC 5747.51(B)**
Wills, on validity, **ORC 2107.083, ORC 2107.084**

HEIR-AT-LAW
See DESIGNATED HEIRS

HEIRS
Absent, pretermitted heir status, **ORC 2107.34**
    Debt payments, contributions by, **ORC 2107.55**
Actions by, **ORC 2107.46**
    Contributions to debt payments, enforcement, **ORC 2107.57**
Advancement of inheritance, **ORC 2105.051**
    See also ADVANCEMENTS FROM ESTATES
Afterborn, **ORC 2107.34**
    Debt payments, contributions by, **ORC 2107.55**
Alienation of property by, **ORC 2109.35, ORC 2117.36**
Ante mortem declaration of will validity, parties defendant, **ORC 2107.081, ORC 2107.084**
At-law. See DESIGNATED HEIRS
Bond
    Claims against estate, to secure, **ORC 2113.54**
    Executor or administrator, acting as, **ORC 2109.10**
    Presumed decedent's estate, distribution, **ORC 2121.07**
    Rejection on requisition by, **ORC 2117.13, ORC 2117.14**
Concealment of existing wills by, **ORC 2107.10**

HEIRS

HEIRS—*continued*
Consanguinity, **ORC 2105.12, ORC 2105.13**
Consent
    Distribution in kind, **ORC 2113.55**
    Real property sale, **ORC 2127.011, ORC 2127.04**
Contest of will. See CONTEST OF WILL
Contributions to debt payments, **ORC 2107.54 to 2107.57**
    Mortgage lien, effect, **ORC 2107.54, ORC 2113.52**
Death of
    Legacy or devise, effect, **ORC 2107.52**
Declaratory judgments sought by. See DECLARATORY JUDGMENTS, generally
Descent and distribution, **ORC Ch 2105**
    See also DESCENT AND DISTRIBUTION
Designation. See DESIGNATED HEIRS
Determination proceedings, **ORC Ch 2123**
    Fees, **ORC 2101.16**
    Nonresident decedent's estate, **ORC 2129.18**
Disabilities, **ORC 2105.19**
Distributions to, **ORC 2109.36**
    Application, **ORC 2113.54**
    Fees, **ORC 2101.16**
Estate tax apportioned among, **ORC 2113.85 to 2113.88**
Executors and administrators as, bond, **ORC 2109.10**
Fees, **ORC 2101.16**
Fiduciaries as, **ORC 2109.39**
Foreign, disposition of property, **ORC 2113.81**
Homicide convictions, effect on right to inherit, **ORC 2105.19**
Illegitimate children, descent and distribution, **ORC 2105.17**
Indebtedness to estate, **ORC 2113.59**
Intestate succession, **ORC Ch 2105**
    See also DESCENT AND DISTRIBUTION
Land sale proceedings. See LAND SALE PROCEEDINGS, generally
Liability, **ORC 2109.35**
    Decedent's debts, **ORC 2107.54**
Liens on share of estate, **ORC 2113.59**
Limitation of actions, paternity proceedings, **ORC 3111.05**
Minors, effect on land sale, **ORC 2127.011**
Mortgages
    Contributions to debt payments, effect, **ORC 2107.54**
    No right of exoneration, **ORC 2113.52**
    Rights, **ORC 2117.29**
Next of kin. See NEXT OF KIN
Not guilty by reason of insanity adjudication, effect on inheritance from victim, **ORC 2105.19**
Notice
    Inventory and appraisement hearing, **ORC 2115.16**
    Probate of will, **ORC 2107.19**
        Denial, **ORC 2107.181**
        Lost, spoliated, or destroyed will, **ORC 2107.27**
Posthumous children, **ORC 2105.14**
Presumed decedent, of, **ORC Ch 2121**
Pretermitted, **ORC 2107.34**
    Debt payments, contributions by, **ORC 2107.55**
Probate court's jurisdiction to determine. See Determination proceedings, this heading
Probate judges as, **ORC 2101.38**
Real property
    See also LEGACIES AND DEVISES
    Alienation or encumbrances by, **ORC 2117.36**
    Management, **ORC 2113.311**
    Sale
        Consent. See Consent, this heading
        Demand for, **ORC 2127.04**
Remaindermen, protection of interest, **ORC 2113.58**
Rents, collection, **ORC 2113.311**
Surviving spouse. See SURVIVING SPOUSE
Testate successor. See LEGACIES AND DEVISES
Unborn, representation in hearings, **ORC 2109.34**
Will contests, **ORC 2107.71 to 2107.77**
    See also CONTEST OF WILL

HEIRS—*continued*
Witnesses to will, as
    Contributions to debt payments, **ORC 2107.55**
    Effect, **ORC 2107.15**

HEIRS-AT-LAW
See HEIRS; DESIGNATED HEIRS

HIGHER EDUCATION
See UNIVERSITIES AND COLLEGES

HIGHWAY PATROL RETIREMENT SYSTEM
Benefits, estate tax, **ORC 5731.09**

HIGHWAYS AND ROADS
Eminent domain actions. See EMINENT DOMAIN
Evidence of intention to construct, **ORC 163.08**
Improvements, plans
    Presumptive evidence of intention to construct, **ORC 163.08**

HISTORICAL SOCIETY OF OHIO
Mentally-ill persons buried in cemeteries on or adjacent to grounds of mental institution, compilations, **5122.47**

HOLIDAYS
Time computation, effect on, **JuvR 18(A)**

HOLOGRAPHIC WILLS
Generally, **ORC 2107.03**

HOME HEALTH AGENCIES
Aged persons suffering neglect, abuse, or exploitation; report to county human services department, **ORC 5101.61**

HOME RULE
Generally, **O Const XVIII § 3**

HOME STUDIES
Adoption. See ADOPTION

HOMELESS PERSONS
Shelters, reporting of child abuse, **ORC 2151.422**

HOMES
Detention. See DETENTION HOMES
Foster. See FOSTER HOMES
Private. See MANSION HOUSE

HOMESTEADS
See MANSION HOUSE

HOMICIDE
Descent and distribution, effect, **ORC 2105.19**
Living wills, death as result of withdrawal or withholding life-sustaining equipment not constituting, **ORC 2133.12**
Parent convicted of killing other parent, **ORC 3109.41 to 3109.48**
Wrongful death actions, **ORC Ch 2125**
    See also WRONGFUL DEATH, generally

HOSPITALIZATION OF MENTALLY ILL
See MENTALLY ILL PERSONS

HOSPITALS
Administrators
    Mentally retarded and developmentally disabled persons, reporting abuse or neglect, **ORC 5123.61, ORC 5123.99**
Anatomical gifts to, **ORC 2108.03**
    Facilitating procurement protocol, **ORC 2108.021**
Definitions
    Mental hospitals, **ORC 5122.01**
Fees, payment by adoptive parents, **ORC 3107.055**
Liability
    Blood tests for alcohol content, **ORC 4511.19**
Mental. See MENTALLY ILL PERSONS, at Hospitalization
Organ procurement organizations, agreements with, **ORC 2108.021**

HOURS OF COURT
Cuyahoga county probate court, **CuyR 53.1**
Franklin county probate court, **FrankR 53.1**
Hamilton county probate court, **HamR 53.1**
Lucas county probate court, **LucasR 53.1**
Stark county probate court, **Sup. R 53.1**
Summit county probate court, **SumR 53.1**

HOUSE
See MANSION HOUSE

HOUSEHOLD GOODS
See PERSONAL PROPERTY

HOUSING
Eminent domain. See EMINENT DOMAIN
Mansion house. See MANSION HOUSE
Minor's residence, defined, **ORC 2151.06**

HUMAN SERVICES DEPARTMENT, STATE
Acknowledgment of paternity statement, filed with, **ORC 3705.091, ORC 5101.314**
Adoptions
    Advertising prohibited, legal action taken by department, **ORC 5103.17**
    Written materials
        Forms for social and medical histories of birth parents, **ORC 3107.09**
        Provided to birth parent, **ORC 3107.083**
        Provided to parent consenting to adoption, **ORC 3107.082(A)**
Agreements with health department regarding paternity records, **ORC 3705.091**
Birth registry, **ORC 5101.314**
Case plans for children, rulemaking powers, **ORC 2151.412**
Child abuse registry, **ORC 2151.421**
Child support
    Acknowledgment of paternity filed with, **ORC 3705.091, ORC 5101.314**
Custody of children
    Permanent, **ORC 2151.353, ORC 2151.413, ORC 2151.414**
    Temporary, **ORC 2151.353**
Double billings for care of mentally retarded, **ORC 5123.181**
Foster care
    Juvenile courts, reimbursed for costs, **ORC 2151.152**
Foster homes, delegation of duties, **ORC 5103.03**
Putative father registry
    Campaign to promote awareness, **ORC 3107.065**
    Establishment, **ORC 3107.062**
    Rules, **ORC 3107.065**
    Search request, **ORC 3107.063**
        Certified document required prior to adoption, **ORC 3107.064**
        Certified documents in response to, **ORC 3107.063**
Rulemaking powers
    Case plans, **ORC 2151.412**

HUMAN SERVICES DEPARTMENTS, COUNTY
Child abuse
    Filing of charges by, **ORC 2151.43**
    Reports, **ORC 2151.421**
Child support
    Actions to collect, **ORC 2151.43**
    Payments to, **ORC 2151.49**
Contributing to delinquency of juveniles, filing of charges by, **ORC 2151.43**
Custody of children
    Permanent, **ORC 2151.353**
    Temporary, **ORC 2151.353**
Protective services for aged. See PROTECTIVE SERVICES FOR ADULTS

HUSBAND AND WIFE
See also MARRIAGE; SURVIVING SPOUSE
Adoption by, **ORC 3107.03**

HUSBAND AND WIFE—continued
Anatomical gifts, former spouse as representative or successor representative, **ORC 2108.76**
Artificial insemination of married woman, nonspousal, **ORC 3111.92 to 3111.96**
Contracts
    Affecting status of marriage, **ORC 3103.06**
    Power to enter into, **ORC 3103.05**
    Separation agreements, **ORC 3103.06**
Death of spouse. See SURVIVING SPOUSE
Divorce. See DIVORCE
Dower interest, **ORC Ch 2103, ORC Ch 5305**
Duties
    Preneed funeral contract, effect on, **ORC 3103.03(E)**
Estates by the entireties, **ORC 5302.21**
Guardianship of spouse. See GUARDIANSHIP
Income tax, state, **ORC 5747.05(G), ORC 5747.08(E)**
    Personal exemption, **ORC 5747.025**
Legal separation. See LEGAL SEPARATION
Loss of consortium, wrongful death action, **ORC 2125.02**
Missing spouse's estate, **ORC Ch 2119**
Nonsupport. See SUPPORT AND MAINTENANCE, at Abandonment and neglect
Power of appointment granted to spouse or nominated as trustee, termination of marriage as revocation, **ORC 5815.31**
Property, dower rights. See DOWER
Separation, legal. See LEGAL SEPARATION
Surviving spouse. See SURVIVING SPOUSE
Tax returns, income tax, **ORC 5747.05(G), ORC 5747.08(E)**

IDENTIFICATION
Consignment of art works to dealers, display required consent of artist and notice to viewers as to artist's identity, **ORC 5815.46**
Personal identifying information, taking of another's, **ORC 2913.49**
Taking identity of another, **ORC 2913.49**

ILLEGITIMATE CHILDREN
Adoption, consent requirements, **ORC 3107.06**
    Putative father, on notice that consent not required, **ORC 3107.061**
    Putative father registry, **ORC 3107.062**
Artificial insemination, non-spousal
    Semen, medical history of donor, **ORC 3111.91**
Birth certificate, **ORC 3705.09**
    New, following paternity judgment, **ORC 3111.18**
Inheritance, descent and distribution, **ORC 2105.17**
Legitimation
    See also PARENTAGE ACTIONS
    Birth certificate, **ORC 3705.09**
    Consent of mother, **ORC 2105.08**
Minor delivered of, marriage application, **JuvR 42(G), JuvR 42(H), JuvR 42(C) to JuvR 42(E)**
Parentage action, **ORC 3111.01 to 3111.19**
    See also PARENTAGE ACTIONS
Parent-child relationship
    Definition, **ORC 3111.01**
    Establishment, **ORC 3111.02 to 3111.19**
        See also Legitimation, this heading; PARENTAGE ACTIONS
    Maternity proceedings, **ORC 3111.17**
        See also PARENTAGE ACTIONS, for general provisions
Presumptions as to father-child relationship, **ORC 3111.03**
Putative father registry, **ORC 3107.062**
    Campaign to promote awareness, **ORC 3107.065**
    Rules, **ORC 3107.065**
    Search request, **ORC 3107.063**
        Certified document required prior to adoption, **ORC 3107.064**
        Certified documents in response to, **ORC 3107.063**
Putative fathers
    Consent for adoption
        Father on notice that consent not required, **ORC 3107.061**
    Guardianship of minor, notice to, **SumR 66.1(A)**

ILLEGITIMATE CHILDREN

Index-60

ILLEGITIMATE CHILDREN—*continued*
Uniform Parentage Act, **ORC 3111.01 to 3111.19**
    See also PARENTAGE ACTIONS, generally
Visitation rights, **ORC 5101.314**
    Relatives, **ORC 3109.12**

ILLNESS, LAST
See LAST ILLNESS

IMMIGRATION AND NATURALIZATION
Adoption, effect of federal law, **ORC 3107.07**
Records in probate court, **ORC 2101.12**

IMMUNITY FROM PROSECUTION
Aged persons subject to abuse, neglect, or exploitation; reporting, **ORC 5101.61**
Child abuse, persons reporting, **ORC 2151.421**
DNR identifications, actions taken pursuant to, **ORC 2133.22**
Mentally retarded, abuse of; persons reporting, **ORC 5123.61**
Paternity actions, immunity from future criminal prosecution, **ORC 3111.12**
Physicians
    Durable power of attorney for health care, acts in reliance on, **ORC 1337.15**
    Living will, acts in compliance with, **ORC 2133.11**
State, **O Const I § 16**

IMPEACHMENT
Juvenile delinquency adjudication, by
    Prohibition, **ORC 2152.21**

IMPOUNDMENT
Child support, **ORC 3109.05(D)**
Drivers' license plate, **ORC 4507.02**

IMPRISONMENT
See also PRISONERS
Disability, prisoner considered to be under. See DISABILITY, PERSONS UNDER, generally
Divorce, grounds for, **ORC 3105.01(H)**
Fiduciaries, contempt of court, **ORC 2109.51**
Legal disability, prisoner considered to be under. See DISABILITY, PERSONS UNDER, generally
Legal separation, grounds for, **ORC 3105.17(A)(8)**
Prisoners. See PRISONERS

INCOME TAX
Definitions, **ORC 5747.011, ORC 5747.012**
Principal and Income Act, **ORC 5812.46, ORC 5812.47**
Uniform Principal and Income Act, **ORC 5812.46, ORC 5812.47**

INCOME TAX, FEDERAL
Estate tax, effect, **ORC 5731.16**
Joint return by husband and wife, effect on state return, **ORC 5747.08(E)**

INCOME TAX, MUNICIPAL
Estate tax, effect, **ORC 5731.16**

INCOME TAX, STATE
Generally, **O Const XII § 3**
Additional
    Credit reduction, due to, **ORC 5747.13(A)**
        Assessment by commissioner, limitation of actions, **ORC 5747.13(A)**
        Interest penalty, **ORC 5747.13(A)**
Adjusted gross income, **ORC 5747.02**
    Definition, **ORC 5747.05**
    Determination, **ORC 5747.05**
Aged persons, income tax credit, **ORC 5747.05(C), ORC 5747.05(D)**
Amended returns, **ORC 5747.10**
    Estimated tax, **ORC 5747.09**
    Pass-through entities, **ORC 5747.45**
Appeals, income tax in default, **ORC 5747.13(B) to 5747.13(E)**

INCOME TAX, STATE—*continued*
Assessment by tax commissioner
    Delinquent payments, **ORC 5747.13(A)**
    Limitation of actions, **ORC 5747.13(A)**
Business income, calculation, **ORC 5747.211**
Capital gains or losses, **ORC 5747.20(B)**
Child support
    Refunds collected to pay past-due support, **ORC 5747.121**
Claim of additional credit, **ORC 5747.022**
Credits, **ORC 5747.05**
    Additional, for individual, **ORC 5747.022**
    Adoption of minor child, **ORC 5747.37**
        Priority, **ORC 5747.98**
    Amounts withheld from compensation, **ORC 5747.08(I)**
    Calculation, **ORC 5747.05(J), ORC 5747.211**
    Changes in adjusted gross income, effect on, **ORC 5747.05(B)**
    Disallowances, **ORC 5747.05(K), ORC 5747.05(L)**
    Displaced workers, priority, **ORC 5747.98**
    Employee training costs, **ORC 5747.39**
    Enterprise zones, priority, **ORC 5747.98**
    Exempted income, **ORC 5747.056**
    Income, exempted, **ORC 5747.056**
    Manufacturing machinery or equipment, priority, **ORC 5747.98**
    Maximum, **ORC 5747.05(B)**
    Minor child, legal adoption of, **ORC 5747.37**
    Nonrefundable credit, **ORC 5747.39**
    Nonresidents, **ORC 5747.05(I)**
    Order for claiming, **ORC 5747.98**
    Personal exemption, priority, **ORC 5747.98**
    Political contributions, priority, **ORC 5747.98**
    Priority, **ORC 5747.98**
    Proof requirement, **ORC 5747.05(H)**
    Reduction, failure to pay additional tax, **ORC 5747.13(A)**
    Refunds, **ORC 5747.12**
    Residents, **ORC 5747.05(I)**
        Payment of another state's tax, **ORC 5747.05(B)**
    Retirement income, priority, **ORC 5747.98**
    Voluntary environmental cleanup, **ORC 5747.98**
Declaration of estimated, **ORC 5747.09(A)**
Deductions, allocation to state, **ORC 5747.20**
    Nonresidents, **ORC 5747.20(C)**
    Residents, **ORC 5747.20(C)**
Definitions, **ORC 5747.01, ORC 5747.013, ORC 5747.11**
Distributive share, inclusion of, **ORC 5747.231**
Due dates, **ORC 5747.08(G)**
    Estimated tax, **ORC 5747.09(A)**
    Extension of time, **ORC 5747.08(G)**
    Individual returns, **ORC 5747.08(G)**
Employee training costs, credit for, **ORC 5747.39**
Employer deducting from wages, **ORC 5747.06(A)**
Estate tax, effect, **ORC 5731.16**
Estimated, **ORC 5747.09**
    Interest penalty, **ORC 5747.09(E), ORC 5747.09(D)**
    Pass-through entities, required to file, **ORC 5747.43**
    Underpayment, **ORC 5747.09(E), ORC 5747.09(D)**
Execution of judgment, **ORC 5747.13(C)**
Exemptions, **ORC 5747.01, ORC 5747.02**
    Income, credit, **ORC 5747.056**
    Personal exemption, **ORC 5747.025**
Extension of filing time, **ORC 5747.08(G)**
    National guard, **ORC 5747.026**
    Participants in operation Iraqi freedom, **ORC 5747.026**
    Reservists, **ORC 5747.026**
Federal income tax adjustments, effect, **ORC 5747.10**
Fraction used in calculating trust's modified taxable income, **ORC 5747.013**
Interest. See Penalties and interest, this heading
Internal Revenue Code, applicability, **ORC 5747.01**
Iraqi freedom
    Extension of filing time for participants in operation Iraqi freedom, **ORC 5747.026**

Index-61

INCOME TAX, STATE—*continued*
Joint return, **ORC 5747.08**
    Credit, **ORC 5747.05(G)**
    Estimated tax, **ORC 5747.09(A)**
Liability
    Refund, application to liability for preceding years, **ORC 5747.12**
    Withholding tax, **ORC 5747.06(C)**
Limitation of actions
    Assessment by tax commissioner, **ORC 5747.13(A)**
National guard, extension of filing time, **ORC 5747.026**
Nonbusiness income, allocation, **ORC 5747.20(A)**
Nonrefundable credit, **ORC 5747.39**
Nonresident taxpayers, **ORC 5747.01, ORC 5747.05(A)**
    Adjusted gross income, **ORC 5747.05(A)**
        Changes in, **ORC 5747.05(B)**
    Credit, **ORC 5747.05(I)**
    Assessment on failure to file return, **ORC 5747.13(A)**
    Partnerships, joint returns of nonresident partners, **ORC 5747.08(D)**
    Pass-through entity investors, **ORC 5747.08(D)**
Notice of assessment by tax commissioner, **ORC 5747.13(A)**
Operation Iraqi freedom
    Extension of filing time for participants in, **ORC 5747.026**
Order for claiming credits, **ORC 5747.98**
Overpaid child support, refunds, **ORC 5747.123**
Partnerships
    Joint returns of nonresident partners, **ORC 5747.08(D)**
Pass-through entities, **ORC 5747.40**
    Accounting method, **ORC 5747.45**
    Adjusted qualifying amount, **ORC 5747.401**
    Collection actions by state, **ORC 5747.451**
    Distributive share, inclusion of, **ORC 5747.231**
    Electronic funds transfer, payments by, **ORC 5747.44**
    Estimated tax return, filing requirement, **ORC 5747.43**
    Investors, **ORC 5747.401**
    Liens, **ORC 5747.451**
    Nonrefundable credit, **ORC 5747.39**
    Quo warranto proceedings, **ORC 5747.451**
    Returns, **ORC 5747.42**
        Liability for failure to file, **ORC 5747.453**
    Taxable year, **ORC 5747.45**
    Withholding, applicability, **ORC 5747.41**
Pass-through entity investors
    Joint returns of nonresident members, **ORC 5747.08(D)**
Payments
    Additional tax and interest due to credit reduction
        Failure to make, **ORC 5747.13(A)**
    Credit reduction, additional tax and interest
        Failure to make, **ORC 5747.13(A)**
    Estimated tax, **ORC 5747.09(B)**
        Failure to make, **ORC 5747.13**
    Interest, **ORC 5747.08(G)**
    Overpayments, **ORC 5747.11**
        Refund applications, **ORC 5747.11**
    Pass-through entities
        Electronic funds transfer, by, **ORC 5747.44**
        Over or underpayments, **ORC 5747.45**
    Reassessment pending, **ORC 5747.13(E)**
        Failure to file report of changed circumstances, **ORC 5747.13(E)**
    Time of, **ORC 5747.08(G)**
    When deemed made, **ORC 5747.08(H)**
Payroll deductions, **ORC 5747.06(A)**
Payroll factor, trust's modified taxable income, **ORC 5747.013**
Penalties and interest, **ORC 5747.13**
    Additional tax, **ORC 5747.13(A)**
        Assessment by commissioner, **ORC 5747.13(A)**
        Limitation of actions, **ORC 5747.13(A)**
    Delinquent payments, **ORC 5747.13**
    Estimated tax, **ORC 5747.09(C)**
    Extension of filing and payment time, **ORC 5747.08(G)**

INCOME TAX, STATE—*continued*
Penalties and interest, **ORC 5747.13**—*continued*
    Failure to withhold, **ORC 5747.06(C)**
    Refunds, **ORC 5747.11, ORC 5747.13(C)**
        Application to other tax liabilities, **ORC 5747.12**
Percentage reduction in tax rates, **ORC 5747.02**
Postmark date, **ORC 5747.08(H)**
Priority of credits, **ORC 5747.98**
Property factor, trust's modified taxable income, **ORC 5747.013**
Purpose, **ORC 5747.02**
Rates, **ORC 5747.02**
    Estimated tax, **ORC 5747.09**
Reassessment, petition for, **ORC 5747.13(B)**
Reciprocal agreements, **ORC 5747.05(A)**
    Credits, disallowances, **ORC 5747.05(L)**
Records and reports
    Adjusted gross income change, taxpayer reporting, **ORC 5747.05(B)**
    Out-of-state tax liability change, taxpayer reporting, **ORC 5747.05(B)**
Reduction in tax rate, **ORC 5747.02**
Refunds, **ORC 5747.10, ORC 5747.13(F)**
    Application to other tax liabilities, **ORC 5747.12**
    Child support, collected to pay past-due, **ORC 5747.121**
    Contribution to natural areas and preserves or nongame and endangered wildlife fund, **ORC 5747.113**
    Erroneous assessments, **ORC 5747.13(C)**
    Interest, **ORC 5747.11, ORC 5747.13(C)**
    Military injury relief fund, **ORC 5747.113**
    Overpaid child support, **ORC 5747.123**
Reservists, extension of filing time, **ORC 5747.026**
Returns
    Amended, **ORC 5747.10**
        Estimated tax, **ORC 5747.09**
        Pass-through entities, **ORC 5747.45**
    Declaration of estimated, **ORC 5747.09(A)**
    Estimated tax, **ORC 5747.09**
    Failure to file, **ORC 5747.13**
    Individuals, by, **ORC 5747.08**
    Joint filing, **ORC 5747.08**
        Credit, **ORC 5747.05(G)**
        Estimated tax, **ORC 5747.09(A)**
    Pass-through entities, **ORC 5747.42**
        Liability for failure to file, **ORC 5747.453**
    Pass-through entity investors, nonresident, **ORC 5747.08(D)**
Revenues, distribution
    Withholding by state, **ORC 5747.51(J), ORC 5747.54**
Sales factor, trust's modified taxable income, **ORC 5747.013**
Trust's modified taxable income, fraction used in calculating, **ORC 5747.013**
Unemployment rate, effect, **ORC 5747.02**
Waiver of declaration of estimated tax, **ORC 5747.09(C)**
Withholding from paycheck, **ORC 5747.221**
    Employers, by, **ORC 5747.06(A)**
    Pass-through entities, applicability, **ORC 5747.41**

INCOMPETENT PERSONS
Generally, See MENTALLY ILL PERSONS
Guardians for. See GUARDIANSHIP

INCORPORATION BY REFERENCE
Generally, **ORC 2107.05**

INDEBTEDNESS
See DEBTORS AND CREDITORS

INDEXES
Probate court records, **ORC 2101.12 to 2101.13**

INDIANS
Adoption. See ADOPTION

INDIGENT PERSONS

INDIGENT PERSONS
Alcohol treatment funds, operation of motor vehicles, **ORC 4511.191**
Attorney appointed for, **JuvR 15(B), JuvR 29(B), JuvR 4(A)**
    Compensation, **JuvR 4(F)**
    Competency, to determine, **ORC 2945.371**
    Not guilty by reason of insanity plea, **ORC 2945.371, ORC 2945.40(C)**
Capital cases, appointment of counsel, **SupR 20**
Counsel, appointment of, **SupR 20**
Defined, **JuvR 2**
Guardianship for, **ORC Ch 2111**
    See also GUARDIANSHIP, generally
Juvenile proceedings
    Counsel appointed, **JuvR 15(B), JuvR 29(B), JuvR 4(A)**
    Compensation, **JuvR 4(F)**
Parentage actions, liability for cost of genetic tests, **ORC 3111.09**

INDUSTRY
See BUSINESS

INFANTS
See MINORS

INFORMATION, CONFIDENTIAL
See CONFIDENTIAL INFORMATION

INHERITANCE TAX
See ESTATE TAX

INITIATIVE AND REFERENDUM
Probate courts combined with common pleas courts, **ORC 2101.43 to 2101.46**

INJUNCTIVE RELIEF
Abused or neglected adult, relief against interference with review, **ORC 5126.32**
Parental control of child, restraining order, **ORC 2151.359**
Probate court
    Fees, **ORC 2101.16**
Restraining orders, **JuvR 34(H)**
    See also PROTECTIVE SERVICES FOR ADULTS

INJURIES
See DAMAGES; PERSONAL INJURIES

INMATES
See PRISONERS

INSANITY
See MENTALLY ILL PERSONS; NOT GUILTY BY REASON OF INSANITY

INSOLVENCY
Definitions, **ORC 1336.02**
Devisee or legatee, when contribution due estate, **ORC 2107.56**
Estates, **ORC 2117.17**
    Attorney fees, **SumR 71.1(B)**
    Claims, hearing on allowance, **ORC 2117.17**
    Ward's estate, **ORC 2111.24**
Exceptions to procedure, **LucasR 62.1**
Partnerships, **ORC 1336.02**
Procedure, **LucasR 62.1**

INSPECTIONS
Accounts. See AUDITS
Mental hospitals, **ORC 5122.301**
Mental retardation and developmental disabilities department institutions, **ORC 5123.031**
Residential care facilities, **ORC 5123.19**

INSTITUTIONAL TRUST FUNDS ACT
Generally, **ORC 5813.01 to 5813.07**
Applicable fund value, defined, **ORC 5813.01**
Citation of act, **ORC 5813.07**

INSTITUTIONAL TRUST FUNDS ACT—continued
Definitions, **ORC 5813.01**
Distributions
    Restrictions on, **ORC 5813.05**
Income
    Defined, **ORC 5813.02**
        Restrictions on definition, **ORC 5813.05**
    Settlor expressly indicating intent, **ORC 5813.03**
Short title, **ORC 5813.07**
Standard of care, **ORC 5813.04**
Trust instrument, defined, **ORC 5813.01**
Uniform Management of Institutional Funds Act, effect on, **ORC 5813.06**

INSTITUTIONS, PUBLIC
See CHARITABLE INSTITUTIONS; HOSPITALS

INSURANCE
Estate tax
    Federal civil service, **ORC 5731.09**
    Gross estate determination, **ORC 5731.12**
    Military service, **ORC 5731.09**
Gross estate determination for tax purposes, **ORC 5731.12**
Interest on proceeds, **ORC 3923.061**
Life insurance. See LIFE INSURANCE

INTANGIBLE PROPERTY TAX
See PERSONAL PROPERTY, TAXATION

INTER VIVOS GIFTS
Advancement from estate, **ORC 2105.051**
    Fiduciaries making, **ORC 2109.44**

INTER VIVOS TRUSTS
See also TRUSTS, generally
Accumulation for more than one year of property granted to surviving spouse and qualifying for marital deduction not required or permitted, **ORC 5815.23**
Allocation between income and principal, **ORC Ch 1340**
Contracts, liability of trustee, **ORC 5815.35**
Disabled individuals, supplemental services for, **ORC 5815.28**
Distribution by fiduciary involving federal estate tax marital deduction, **ORC 5815.21**
Limitation of liability of fiduciaries, **ORC 5815.24**
Other persons, limitation on liability of fiduciaries when certain powers granted to, **ORC 5815.25**
Probate court jurisdiction, **ORC 2101.24**
Responsibilities of fiduciaries, **ORC 5815.24**
Spendthrift provision not causing forfeiture or postponement of interest granted to surviving spouse and qualifying for marital deduction, **ORC 5815.22**
Supplemental services for disabled individuals, **ORC 5815.28**
Temporary investments by fiduciary, procedure, **ORC 5815.26**
Termination, **ORC 2109.62**
Transactions between fiduciaries, **ORC 5815.24**

INTEREST
Dower, **ORC Ch 2103**
    See also DOWER
Estate tax, **ORC 5731.23**
    Additional tax, **ORC 5731.24**
    Fiduciary's liability, **ORC 2113.87**
    Postponed payments, **ORC 5731.25**
Estates, claims against, **ORC 2117.06, ORC 2117.18**
    Sale proceeds to satisfy, **ORC 2127.38**
Fiduciaries accounting for, **ORC 2109.42**
Future, **ORC 2131.04 to 2131.07**
Insurance proceeds, **ORC 3923.061**
Probate courts, deposited prepaid and unearned costs, **ORC 2101.161**
Trust funds held by county treasurer, **ORC 2113.81**

INTERESTS OF THE BENEFICIARIES
Defined, **ORC 5801.01**

INTERLOCUTORY ORDERS
Adoption, **ORC 3107.14 to 3107.16**
    Legal effect, **ORC 3107.15**
Probate of will, **ORC 2107.181**

INTERMENT
See FUNERALS AND BURIALS

INTERNAL REVENUE CODE
Income tax, state; applicability, **ORC 5747.01**

INTERNAL REVENUE SERVICE
See also INCOME TAX, FEDERAL
Federal estate tax returns, liability used to determine Ohio estate tax, **ORC 5731.26**

INTERSTATE AGREEMENTS
Income tax exemption, **ORC 5747.05(A)**
Jurisdiction of juvenile courts, **ORC 2151.23**
Juveniles, **2151.56 to 2151.61, ORC 2151.23**

INTERSTATE COMMISSION FOR THE PLACEMENT OF CHILDREN
Generally, **ORC 5103.20**

INTERSTATE COMPACT ON JUVENILES
See INTERSTATE AGREEMENTS, generally

INTERVENTION
Paternity proceedings, **ORC 3111.07**

INTESTATE SUCCESSION
Generally, **ORC Ch 2105**
See also DESCENT AND DISTRIBUTION

INTOXICATION
Divorce, grounds for, **ORC 3105.01(G)**
Fiduciary, removal grounds, **ORC 2109.24**

INVENTORIES
Appraisals. See APPRAISALS
Defined, **ORC 2115.01**
Estates. See INVENTORY AND APPRAISAL OF ESTATES

INVENTORY AND APPRAISAL OF ESTATES
Generally, **ORC 2109.58, ORC Ch 2115**
Advancements from estate, **ORC 2105.051**
    See also ADVANCEMENTS FROM ESTATES
Appraisers, **ORC 2115.05, SupR 61**
    Appointment, **CuyR 8.1, FrankR 8.1, HamR 61.1, LucasR 61.1, Sup. R 61.1**
        Exceptions, **FrankR 61.1**
        Fees, **FrankR 61.1**
        Land sale proceedings, **HamR 65.1**
        Self-dealing prohibited, **FrankR 61.2**
    Compensation
        Computation, **SumR 61.1**
        Land sale proceedings, **HamR 65.1, ORC 2127.25**
    Qualifications, **HamR 61.1, LucasR 61.1**
    Real property sales
        Appointment, **HamR 65.1**
        Compensation, **HamR 65.1, ORC 2127.25**
    Signing appraisal, **ORC 2115.15**
Bond conditions, **ORC 2109.06 to 2109.20**
Certificate of nonresident decedent's debts and liabilities, **ORC 2129.15**
Contents, **ORC 2115.07, ORC 2115.09**
Cuyahoga county probate court, **CuyR 64.1**
Definition of inventory, **ORC 2115.01**
Exceptions
    Court costs, **Sup. R 58.1**
Exclusions, **ORC 2113.31**
Extensions, **LucasR 78.3**

INVENTORY AND APPRAISAL OF ESTATES
—*continued*
Failure to file, **ORC 2109.18, ORC 2109.24, ORC 2115.03**
Fees, **ORC 2101.16, SupR 61**
Filing, **ORC 2115.02, ORC 2115.03, ORC 2115.15 to 2115.17**
    Case management, **SupR 78**
    Extension of time, **LucasR 78.3**
    Predecessors filing, **ORC 2115.02**
Franklin county probate court, **FrankR 78.3**
Guardianship, under, **ORC 2111.14**
    Real property, **ORC 2111.29 to 2111.32**
Hamilton county probate court, **HamR 61.2**
Hearing on, **ORC 2115.16**
    Notice, **CuyR 64.1, HamR 61.2, LucasR 78.6**
Intestate succession, **ORC 2106.10(C), ORC 2106.11**
Items, separate inclusion, **ORC 2115.07**
Lucas county probate court, **LucasR 78.6**
Mansion house, **ORC 2106.10(C)**
Motor vehicles or watercraft passing to joint owner with right of survivorship exempt, **ORC 2131.12**
Newly discovered assets, **ORC 2101.16, ORC 2113.69**
Notice, **ORC 2115.04**
    Filing inventory, **SumR 88.1**
    Hearing, **CuyR 64.1, HamR 61.2, LucasR 78.6**
Present values, determination, **ORC 2131.01**
Real property, **ORC 2115.02, ORC 2115.17, ORC 2127.22 to 2127.39**
    Guardianship, under, **ORC 2111.29 to 2111.32**
    Mansion house, **ORC 2106.10(C)**
    Sales, appraisers to aid in
        Appointment, **HamR 65.1**
        Compensation, **HamR 65.1**
    Waiver prohibited, exceptions, **LucasR 61.1**
Release from administration, **ORC 2113.03**
Reopening estate, **ORC 2113.69**
Schedule of assets, contents, **SumR 88.2**
Signing, **ORC 2115.15**
Stark county probate court
    Appraisal, request for, **Sup. R 61.7**
    Exceptions, court costs, **Sup. R 58.1**
Summit county probate court
    Case management, **SumR 78.1(A)**
    Notice, **SumR 88.1**
    Overdue, citations, **SumR 78.1(D)**
    Schedule of assets, **SumR 88.2**
Time for filing
    Extension, **LucasR 78.3**

INVESTIGATIONS
Abuse or neglect of adults, **ORC 5126.313, ORC 5126.333**
County courts, continuances, **SupR 41(D)**
Criminal identification and investigation bureau. See CRIMINAL IDENTIFICATION AND INVESTIGATION BUREAU
Custody of children, **JuvR 32(D), ORC 3109.04(C)**
Executors and administrators, **ORC 2109.49**
Fiduciaries, investigation of, **ORC 2109.49**
Guardianship
    Appointment application, **SumR 66.1(A)**
    Mentally ill persons, investigation of incompetency by probate court investigator, **ORC 2111.041**
    Minors, investigation by probate court investigator, **ORC 2111.042**
Habeas corpus, custody of child, **JuvR 32(D)**
Juvenile courts
    Criminal identification records, weekly report to criminal identification and investigation bureau, **ORC 2152.71**
    Custody, **JuvR 32(D)**
    Discretionary transfer for criminal prosecution, **JuvR 30(C)**
    Transfer for criminal prosecution, **JuvR 30(B)**
Land sale proceedings, investigation by court, **SupR 65(D)**
Law enforcement officers
    Criminal identification and investigation of juveniles, **ORC 2151.313**

INVESTIGATIONS

INVESTIGATIONS—*continued*
Legal rights service, Ombudsman section, notice of investigations, **ORC 5123.604**
Mental retardation and developmental disabilities department
    Notice to legal rights service ombudsman section, **ORC 5123.604**
    Registry of abusive or neglectful employees, **ORC 5123.51**
    Reports of incidents of neglect or abuse, independent review or investigation, **ORC 5123.614**
Mentally ill persons, hospitalization, **ORC 5122.13, ORC 5122.33**
Motor vehicles sales, investigations by taxation department, **ORC 4505.06**
Probate courts
    Fiduciaries, fees and costs, **ORC 2109.49**
    Guardianship, appointment, **ORC 2111.042**
    Incompetency, investigation of, **ORC 2111.041**
Protective services for adults, **ORC 5101.62 to 5101.64**
Trusts, investigation of fiduciary, **ORC 2109.49**

INVESTIGATORS
Appointment, **FrankR 8.1**

INVESTMENT BONDS
See BONDS AND NOTES

INVESTMENTS
Affiliated investment companies
    Fiduciaries investing in, **ORC 2109.371**
Deposits payable on death, **ORC 2131.10, ORC 2131.11**
Executors and administrators, by, **ORC 2109.37 to 2109.38**
    Liability, **ORC 2109.42**
    Temporary investments, **ORC 2109.372**
    Unclaimed funds, **ORC 2113.64 to 2113.68**
Fee for investment services, fiduciary may charge, **ORC 2109.371**
Fiduciary's powers, **ORC 2109.29, ORC 2109.37 to 2109.38**
    Liability, **ORC 2109.42**
    Temporary investments, **ORC 2109.372**
Fiduciary's powers and duties
    Affiliated investment companies, **ORC 2109.371**
Guardians, by, **ORC 2109.37 to 2109.38**
    Temporary investments, **ORC 2109.372**
Prudent Investor Act, **ORC 5809.01 to 5809.08**
    See also UNIFORM PRUDENT INVESTOR ACT
Prudent person rule, **ORC 2109.371**
Records and reports
    Affiliated investment company securities, **ORC 2109.371**
Securities, fiduciary's powers and duties
    Fee for investment services, **ORC 2109.371**
    Records and reports, **ORC 2109.371**
Trust funds, powers of fiduciary, **ORC 2109.37, ORC 2109.371**
    Temporary investments, **ORC 2109.372**
Trustees
    Powers and duties, investment costs, **ORC 5808.05**
Trustees, by, **ORC 5809.01 to 5809.08**
    See also UNIFORM PRUDENT INVESTOR ACT
Uniform Prudent Investor Act, **ORC 5809.01 to 5809.08**
    See also UNIFORM PRUDENT INVESTOR ACT

IRON CURTAIN ACT
Generally, **ORC 2113.81, ORC 2113.82**

IRREVOCABLE TRUSTS
Generally, **ORC 5804.18**
Noncharitable irrevocable trust by consent, **ORC 5804.11**

ISSUE
See HEIRS

JAILS
Detention of minors in, **JuvR 7(H), ORC 2151.34, ORC 2152.26**
    Processing purposes, for, **ORC 2151.311**
DNA testing of prisoners, **ORC 2901.07**
Inmates
    See also PRISONERS

JAILS—*continued*
Inmates—*continued*
    Children, **JuvR 7(H), ORC 2151.34, ORC 2152.26**

JOBS
See EMPLOYER AND EMPLOYEE

JOINDER OF ACTIONS
Claims against estates, **ORC 2117.42**

JOINDER OF PARTIES
Eminent domain, **ORC 163.12**

JOINT BANK ACCOUNTS
See BANKS AND BANKING, at Accounts

JOINT DEBTORS
Child support, **ORC 3109.05(A)**
Decedent, liability, **ORC 2117.31**

JOINT TENANCY
Estate tax, **ORC 5731.10**
Estates by the entireties, **ORC 5302.21**
Transfer-on-death securities held in, **ORC 1709.02**

JUDGES
Appeals courts. See COURTS OF APPEALS
Common pleas courts. See COURTS OF COMMON PLEAS
Domestic relations division of common pleas court, **ORC 2301.03**
Juvenile courts. See JUVENILE COURTS
Magistrates. See MAGISTRATES
Probate courts. See PROBATE COURTS
Referees. See REFEREES

JUDGMENT, EXECUTION OF
See EXECUTION OF JUDGMENT

JUDGMENT BY CONFESSION
Generally, **ORC 2101.34**
Eminent domain, **ORC 163.16**
Paternity proceedings, **ORC 3111.08**

JUDGMENT DEBTORS
Arrest, **O Const I § 15**
Garnishment
    Parentage actions, support, **ORC 3111.13(F)**

JUDGMENT ENTRIES
Franklin county probate court
    File to accompany, **FrankR 57.2**
Hamilton county probate court, **HamR 57.1**
Lucas county probate court, **LucasR 57.1**
Probate courts, **SupR 57**
    Fee, **ORC 2101.16**
Stark county probate court, **Sup. R 57.1**
Summit county probate court, **SumR 57.1**

JUDGMENTS
See also SENTENCES; VERDICTS
Abortion. See ABORTION
Abortion for minor without parental consent, **SupR Form 23-B**
Annulment, **ORC 3105.10(A)**
Appeals. See APPEALS
Child, disposition by juvenile court, **JuvR 34(C)**
Contempt. See CONTEMPT, generally
Cuyahoga county juvenile court, vacating and modifying, **ORC 2153.15**
Declaratory. See DECLARATORY JUDGMENTS
Decrees. See DECREES
Divorce, **ORC 3105.10(A)**
Enforcement. See EXECUTION OF JUDGMENT
Entries. See JUDGMENT ENTRIES
Evidence, against weight of
    Transcript for appeal, **SupR 11**

JUDGMENTS—continued
Legal separation, **ORC 3105.10(E)**
Manifest weight of evidence, against
    Transcript for appeal, **SupR 11**
Modification. See APPEALS
Paternity proceedings, **ORC 3111.08**
    Genetic test results, based on, **ORC 3111.09**
Settlements. See SETTLEMENTS
Weight of evidence, against
    Transcript for appeal, **SupR 11**

JUDICIAL SALES
See also EXECUTION OF JUDGMENT
Dower interest, property representing, **ORC 2103.041**

JUDICIARY
See COURTS

JURIES
See JURY TRIALS

JURISDICTION
Abused children, **ORC 2151.23**
Appeals. See APPEALS, generally
Child abuse, **ORC 2151.23**
Child support, **ORC 3109.05(A)**, **ORC 3109.05(B)**
Children, **ORC 2151.23**
    Certification to juvenile court, **ORC 3109.06**
    Custody. See at Jurisdiction
    Custody. See CUSTODY OF CHILDREN
Children's advocacy center, memorandum of understanding, **ORC 2151.426**
Commitment of mentally ill, **ORC 5122.35**
Competency to stand trial, **ORC 2945.401(A)**
Continuing, juvenile court, **JuvR 35(A)**
Contributing to dependency, neglect, unruliness or delinquency of minor, **ORC 2151.23**
Courts of common pleas. See COURTS OF COMMON PLEAS
Custody action. See CUSTODY OF CHILDREN
Defined, **ORC 5801.01**
Dissolution of marriage, **ORC 2101.24**
    Paternity proceeding involved, **ORC 3109.25(F)**
Divorce proceedings
    Paternity proceeding involved, **ORC 3109.25**
Eminent domain, **ORC 2101.25**, **ORC Ch 163**
    See also EMINENT DOMAIN, generally
Endangering children, **ORC 2151.23**
Estate tax, **ORC 5731.31**
Estates. See PROBATE COURTS
Habeas corpus, **O Const IV § 2**, **O Const IV § 3**
Interference with custody, **ORC 2151.23**
Interstate Compact on Placement of Children, **ORC 5103.20**
Juvenile courts. See JUVENILE COURTS
Land sale proceedings, **ORC 2101.24**
Mandamus, **O Const IV § 2**, **O Const IV § 3**
Marriage by juveniles, **ORC 2151.23**
Mentally ill, hospitalization, **ORC 5122.35**
    Children, **ORC 2151.23**
Nonsupport, **ORC 2151.23**
Not guilty by reason of insanity, **ORC 2945.401(A)**
Original
    Appeals courts, **O Const IV § 3**
    Common pleas courts, **O Const IV § 4**
    Supreme court, **O Const IV § 2**
Parentage actions, **ORC 3111.381**
Paternity proceedings, **ORC 2151.23**, **ORC 2301.03**, **ORC 3111.06**
    Continuing jurisdiction, **ORC 3111.16**
Probate courts. See PROBATE COURTS, generally
Probating will, **ORC 2107.11**
Procedendo, **O Const IV § 2**, **O Const IV § 3**
Prohibition writs, **O Const IV § 2**, **O Const IV § 3**
Protective services for adults, **ORC 5101.60**

JURISDICTION—continued
Quo warranto actions, **O Const IV § 2**, **O Const IV § 3**
Relinquishment by juvenile court, **JuvR 30**
Support and maintenance action, **ORC 2151.23**
Trusts. See TRUSTS
Uniform Child Custody Jurisdiction Act, **ORC 3109.21 to 3109.32**
Venue. See VENUE

JURY DUTY
See JURY TRIALS, generally

JURY MANAGEMENT
Cuyahoga county probate court, **CuyR 78.3**
Hamilton county probate court, **HamR 75.1**
Lucas county probate court, **LucasR 78.2**

JURY TRIALS
Generally, **O Const I § 5**
Eminent domain
    Jury to determine compensation, **O Const I § 19**, **ORC 163.09**, **ORC 163.10**, **ORC 163.12**, **ORC 163.14**
Instructions to jurors
    Reasonable doubt, explaining, **ORC 2901.05(B)**, **ORC 2901.05(D)**
Jury management. See JURY MANAGEMENT
Juvenile courts, **ORC 2151.35**, **ORC 2152.67**
    Adults, proceedings against, **ORC 2152.67**
Probate courts, **ORC 2101.30**
Request for, **FrankR 78.4**
Right to, **O Const I § 5**
Will contests, **ORC 2107.72**

JUVENILE COURTS
Generally, **ORC Ch 2151**
Abortion, complaint for. See ABORTION, at Parental consent, complaint for abortion without
Abused child. See CHILD ABUSE, generally
Action to be avoided, **JuvR 9(A)**
Actions for child support orders, **ORC 2151.232**
Adjudicatory hearings, **JuvR 29**, **ORC 2151.35**, **ORC 2151.35 to 2151.353**, **ORC 2151.353 to 2151.40**
    See also Hearings, generally, this heading
    Admissions
        Acceptance, **JuvR 29(D)**
        Entry, **JuvR 29(C)**
    Advisement and findings, **JuvR 29(B)**
    Amendment of pleading, **JuvR 22(B)**
    Commitment to rehabilitation facility, **ORC 2151.65 to 2151.80**
    Continuance, **JuvR 29(A)**
    Definition, **JuvR 2**
    Denials
        Entry, **JuvR 29(C)**
        Procedure following, **JuvR 29(E)**
    Determination of issues, **JuvR 29(F)**, **ORC 2151.353(A)**
    Entry of adjudication, **JuvR 29(F)**
    Location, **JuvR 11(C)**
    Prehearing motions, **JuvR 22(D)**
    Scheduling, **JuvR 29(A)**
Adoption
    See also ADOPTION, generally
    Approval of adoption agreements, **ORC 5103.151**
    Case certified to, **ORC 3107.14**
    Consent to, **ORC 3107.06**
    Questioning of birth parent prior to adoption, **ORC 5103.151**
Adult cases
    See also particular offense concerned
    Appeals, **ORC 2151.52**
    Bonds for suspended sentences, **ORC 2151.50**
    Charges, **ORC 2151.43**
    Child abuse case. See CHILD ABUSE, generally
    Complaint, **ORC 2151.44**
        See also Complaints, generally, this heading

JUVENILE COURTS—continued
Adult cases—continued
Hearing charges against, **JuvR 27, ORC 2151.43**
    See also Hearings, generally, this heading
Jurisdiction, **ORC 2151.23**
Jury trials, **ORC 2152.67**
Rules of procedure, applicability, **JuvR 1(A)**
Sentences, **ORC 2151.49**
    Suspension, **ORC 2151.49**
Summons. See Summons, generally, this heading
Warrant or summons, issuance, **ORC 2151.43**

Amendment of pleadings, **JuvR 22(B)**
Annual reports, **ORC 2152.71**
Appeals from, **ORC 2151.52**
    Abortion without parental consent complaint dismissed, **ORC 2151.85**
    Revised Code sections governing common pleas appeals applicable to, **ORC 2153.17**
    Right to, **JuvR 34(J)**
Appearance
    Attorney, **JuvR 4(D)**
    Child, **ORC 2151.311, ORC 2151.35**
    Excusing attendance, **ORC 2151.35**
    Summons, **JuvR 16(A)**
Appropriations, **ORC 2151.10**
    Education of children committed to welfare agencies, **ORC 2151.362**
Arbitration, **SupR 15**
Attendance of juvenile, **ORC 2151.35**
Attorneys, **ORC 2151.28, ORC 2151.314, ORC 2151.352**
    Appearance, **JuvR 4(D)**
    Appointment by court, **JuvR 29(B), JuvR 4(A)**
        Compensation, **JuvR 4(F)**
    Detention or shelter hearing, **JuvR 7(F)**
    Permanent custody hearings, **ORC 2151.353, ORC 2151.414(A)**
    Right to, **JuvR 29(B), JuvR 4(A)**
    Waiver of right to, **JuvR 3**
    Withdrawal, **JuvR 4(E)**
Bailiffs, **ORC 2151.13**
    Cuyahoga county, **ORC 2153.11**
Bifurcation, **JuvR 34(I)**
Binding over. See Transfer of cases, this heading
Buildings and facilities, **ORC 2151.09**
Case plan, **JuvR 34(F)**
    Agency review, **JuvR 36(C)**
Cashbooks, **ORC 2152.71**
Child abuse. See CHILD ABUSE, generally
Child support. See CHILD SUPPORT, generally
Clerks, **ORC 2151.12**
    Computerization of offices, costs applied to, **ORC 2151.541, ORC 2153.081**
    Cuyahoga county, **ORC 2153.08 to 2153.10**
Commitment of children by, **ORC 2151.35 to 2151.353, ORC 2151.353 to 2151.40**
    See also CUSTODY OF CHILDREN, INSTITUTIONAL, generally
Complaints, **JuvR 10, ORC 2151.27, ORC 2152.021**
    Abortion without parental consent. See ABORTION, at Parental consent, complaint for abortion without
    Adults, against; for child abuse or contributing to delinquency, **ORC 2151.44**
    Answers, **JuvR 22(C) to JuvR 22(E)**
    Contents, **JuvR 10(B)**
    Custody of child, **JuvR 10(A), JuvR 10(E), JuvR 10(F), JuvR 10(D)**
    Defect in, defense or objection based on, **JuvR 22(D)**
    Definition, **JuvR 2**
    Detention hearings, **ORC 2151.314**
    Dismissal, **ORC 2151.35**
    Filing, **JuvR 10(A)**
    Form, **JuvR 10(B)**
    Screening prior to filing, **JuvR 9(B)**

JUVENILE COURTS—continued
Complaints, **JuvR 10, ORC 2151.27, ORC 2152.021**—continued
    Service of process, **ORC 2151.28**
    Traffic offender, juvenile, **JuvR 10(A), JuvR 10(C), ORC 2151.27**
    Victim of delinquent 65 or older or disabled, record, **ORC 2151.27(D), ORC 2152.71**
Computerization, costs applied to, **ORC 2151.541, ORC 2153.081**
Conclusions of law, **JuvR 29(F)**
Contempt, **ORC 2151.21, ORC 2151.359**
    Appropriations, insufficient, **ORC 2151.10**
    Cuyahoga county, **ORC 2153.13**
    Failure to answer service, **JuvR 17(F), ORC 2151.28**
    Reimbursement for emergency medical treatment, failure, **ORC 2151.33**
Continuances, **JuvR 23**
    Adjudicatory hearing, **JuvR 29(A)**
    Dispositional hearing, **JuvR 34(A)**
    Failure to comply with discovery order, **JuvR 24(C)**
Continuing jurisdiction, **JuvR 35(A)**
Cooperation of private and public agencies, **ORC 2151.40**
Court or child welfare agency, notification to institution or association of adjudication of child as delinquent for committing sexually oriented offense, **ORC 2152.192**
Courthouse building and sites, **ORC 2151.09, ORC 2151.24**
Courtrooms, Cuyahoga county court, **ORC 2153.07**
Creation, **ORC 2151.07**
Criminal court, transfer of child to. See Transfer of cases, this heading
Criminal identification records
    Weekly report to criminal identification and investigation bureau, **ORC 2152.71**
Criminal provisions
    Costs, **ORC 2152.20**
    Definitions, **ORC 2152.02**
    Detention
        Facilities, **ORC 2152.41**
    Dispositional orders, **ORC 2152.19**
    Felony specifications, **ORC 2152.17**
    Fines, **ORC 2152.20**
    Forfeitures, **ORC 2152.20**
    Institutionalization, place and duration, **ORC 2152.18**
    Release, **ORC 2152.22**
    Relinquishment of control, **ORC 2152.22**
    Restitution, **ORC 2152.20**
    Serious youthful offender, dispositional sentence, **JuvR 2, ORC 2152.13**
        Adult portion, invoking, **ORC 2152.14**
    Sex offenders
        Hearings, **ORC 2152.84**
        Orders, **ORC 2152.83, ORC 2152.84**
    Traffic offender, **JuvR 2**
    Transfer, mandatory and discretionary, **ORC 2152.10**
    Youth Services Department, child custody, **ORC 2152.16**
Criteria for sealing records, **ORC 2151.356**
Cross-examinations, **JuvR 34(B)**
Custody
    Youth Services Department, **ORC 2152.16**
Custody of child, powers and duties
    See also CUSTODY OF CHILDREN
    Complaint, **JuvR 10**
    Detention and shelter care, **JuvR 7**
    Grounds for, **JuvR 6**
    Jurisdiction, **ORC 2151.23**
    Restraining orders, **JuvR 34(H)**
    Temporary disposition pending hearing, **JuvR 13**
    Warrant for, **JuvR 15(E), JuvR 15(D), JuvR 16(B)**
Cuyahoga county, **ORC 2151.07, ORC Ch 2153**
Decrees. See Judgments, this heading
Defenses, **JuvR 22(C) to JuvR 22(E)**
Definitions, **JuvR 2, ORC 2151.011, ORC 2151.011 to 2151.06**
Delinquency. See JUVENILE DELINQUENCY

JUVENILE COURTS—continued
Dependent children. See DEPENDENT AND NEGLECTED CHILDREN, generally
Depositions, **JuvR 25**
    Minor victims of sex offenses, videotaped, **ORC 2152.81**
Destruction of court records, **SupR 26(E)**
Detention, **JuvR 2**
    Hearing, **ORC 2151.314**
Detention homes. See DETENTION HOMES
Detention or shelter hearings, **JuvR 7(F), ORC 2151.34**
    See also Hearings, generally, this heading
    Complaint, **ORC 2151.314**
    Definition, **JuvR 2**
    Rehearing, **JuvR 7(G)**
Discovery, **JuvR 24**
    Hearing on motion, **JuvR 22(D)**
Discretionary transfer of case for criminal prosecution, **JuvR 30(C)**
Dismissal of actions, **JuvR 22(A), JuvR 29(F), ORC 2151.35**
Disposition of children, **ORC 2151.35 to 2151.353**
Dispositional hearings, **JuvR 34, ORC 2151.35, ORC 2151.353 to 2151.40**
    See also Hearings, generally, this heading
    Abused children, **ORC 2151.353**
    Appeal, **JuvR 34(J)**
    Bifurcation, **JuvR 34(I)**
    Commitment of child, **ORC 2151.353**
    Continuances, **JuvR 34(A)**
    Definition, **JuvR 2**
    Dependent and neglected children, **ORC 2151.353**
    Family foster care, temporary custody granted for placement, **ORC 2151.353**
    Guardian, placing child with, **ORC 2151.353**
    Judgment, **JuvR 34(C)**
    Orders. See Dispositional orders, this heading
    Parents, placing child with, **ORC 2151.353**
    Procedure, **JuvR 34(B)**
    Protective supervision, orders, **JuvR 34(E)**
    Relatives, commitment to temporary custody of, **ORC 2151.353(A)**
    Removal of abusive or neglectful person from child's home, **ORC 2151.353**
    Restraining order, **JuvR 34(H)**
    Review hearings, **JuvR 36**
    Rights, advisement of, **JuvR 34(J)**
    Scheduling, **JuvR 34(A)**
    Sexually oriented offense, child adjudicated delinquent child for committing, **ORC 2152.191, ORC 2152.811**
    Social histories, cross-examinations, **JuvR 34(B)**
    Supervision of placement by court, **ORC 2151.353(A)**
Dispositional orders, **JuvR 34(D)**
    Case plan, **JuvR 34(F)**
    Notice of intended, **ORC 2151.3510**
    Review, hearings, **JuvR 36**
Dispositional review, **JuvR 36**
    Agency review, **JuvR 36(C)**
    Citizens' review board, **JuvR 36(B)**
    Court review, **JuvR 36(A)**
Dispute resolution procedures, **ORC 2151.542**
District detention facility trustees, **ORC 2152.44**
Dockets, **ORC 2152.71**
    See also Records and reports, this heading
    Traffic offenses, **ORC 2152.71**
Drunk driving proceedings, **ORC 4511.19**
Emergency medical treatment for child, **JuvR 13**
Employees, **ORC 2151.13**
    Rules, **ORC 2151.17**
Equipment and supplies, Cuyahoga county court, **ORC 2153.07**
Evidence
    Detention or shelter hearing, **JuvR 7(F)**
    Dispositional hearing, **JuvR 34(B)**
    Motion to suppress, **JuvR 22(D) to JuvR 22(F)**
Evidence Rules, **JuvR 34(I)**

JUVENILE COURTS—continued
Ex parte proceedings, **JuvR 13(D)**
Examination of child, **JuvR 32, ORC 2151.53**
    Definitions, **JuvR 2**
    Discretionary transfer for criminal prosecution, **JuvR 30(C)**
    Transfer for criminal prosecution, **JuvR 30(B), JuvR 30(F), JuvR 30(G), ORC 2152.12**
        Category one and two offenses, **ORC 2152.12(B)**
    Waiver, **JuvR 30(F), JuvR 30(G)**
Expenses, **ORC 2151.10**
Expunged or sealed records, defined, **ORC 2151.355**
Fees and costs, **ORC 2151.54**
    Appropriations, **ORC 2151.10**
    Assessment, **JuvR 4(F)**
    Clerks' offices, computerization; for, **ORC 2151.541, ORC 2153.081**
    Computerized legal services, **ORC 2151.541, ORC 2153.081**
    Counties, reimbursement by, **ORC 2151.36**
    Custody investigation, **JuvR 32(D)**
    Dispute resolution procedures, implementation of, **ORC 2151.542**
    Service of process, **ORC 2151.19**
    Waiver, **ORC 2151.54**
    Witness, **JuvR 17(B), JuvR 17(C), ORC 2151.28**
Felony cases, transfer to adult court. See Transfer of cases, this heading
Findings of fact, **JuvR 29(F), ORC 2151.35**
    Magistrate's decision, **JuvR 40(E)**
Forms, **JuvR 46**
    Complaint, **JuvR 10(B)**
    Subpoena, **JuvR 17(A)**
    Summons, **JuvR 15(B)**
    Warrant against child, **JuvR 15(E)**
Foster care
    Complaint by superintendent of schools of unruly child, **ORC 2151.55**
    Court reimbursed for costs, **ORC 2151.152**
    Placement of children outside home county, notice to courts, **ORC 2151.554**
Foster care costs, reimbursement, **ORC 2151.152**
Guardians ad litem. See GUARDIANS AD LITEM
Hamilton county, **ORC 2151.07, ORC 2151.08**
Hearing and deposition
    Detention, **ORC 2151.314**
Hearings, **JuvR 27, ORC 2151.35**
    Adjudicatory. See Adjudicatory hearings, this heading
    Adults, charges against, **JuvR 27, ORC 2151.43**
    Bifurcation, **JuvR 34(I)**
    Child's right to counsel, **JuvR 3**
    Citizens' review board, **JuvR 36(B)**
    Definition, **JuvR 2**
    Detention. See Detention or shelter hearings, this heading
    Discovery motion, on, **JuvR 22(D)**
    Dispositional. See Dispositional hearings, this heading
    Early release from youth services department custody, **ORC 2151.38(B), ORC 2151.38(C)**
    Exclusion from, **JuvR 27**
    Jurisdiction, **JuvR 30(E)**
    Magistrate's powers, **JuvR 40**
    Notice, **JuvR 30(D)**
    Placement of child prior to, **JuvR 7(B)**
    Proposed actions, **JuvR 13(E)**
    Recording, **JuvR 37, ORC 2151.35**
    Referee's powers, **ORC 2151.16**
    Release of child from youth services department institution, **ORC 2151.38(A), ORC 2151.38(A) to 2151.38(C), ORC 2151.38(B)**
    Review hearing, **JuvR 36(A)**
    Revocation of probation, **JuvR 35(B)**
    Revocation of probation or parole, **JuvR 35(B)**
    Right of child to counsel, **JuvR 3**
    Separation of children and adults, **JuvR 27**
    Summons to appear, **JuvR 15(A) to JuvR 15(C), JuvR 16(A)**
    Temporary orders prior to, **JuvR 13**

JUVENILE COURTS

JUVENILE COURTS—*continued*
Hearings, **JuvR 27, ORC 2151.35**—*continued*
   Transfer for criminal prosecution, **JuvR 30(A)**
     See also Transfer of cases, this heading
   Violations by child released from youth services department institution, **ORC 2151.38(B), ORC 2151.38(C), ORC 2151.38(D)**
   Waiver of rights, **JuvR 3**
Human services department, reimbursement of courts for foster care costs, **ORC 2151.152**
Indictment, **ORC 2152.021**
Indigent persons
   Counsel appointed, **JuvR 29(B), JuvR 4(A)**
     Compensation, **JuvR 4(F)**
   Definition, **JuvR 2**
Injury, duty to report, **ORC 2151.421**
Investigations
   Custody, **JuvR 32(D)**
   Discretionary transfer for criminal prosecution, **JuvR 30(C)**
   Transfer for criminal prosecution, **JuvR 30(B)**
Journal, **ORC 2152.71**
Judges
   Assignment, **ORC 2151.07**
     Temporary, **O Const IV § 5**
   Bond when acting as clerk, **ORC 2151.12**
   Clerk, as, **ORC 2151.12**
   Code of judicial conduct, **O Const IV § 5**
   Compensation, **ORC 2151.13**
   Cuyahoga county, **ORC 2153.02 to 2153.06**
   Defined, **ORC 2151.011**
   Disqualification, **O Const IV § 5**
   Expenses, **ORC 2151.13**
   Hamilton county, **ORC 2151.08**
Judgments, **JuvR 34(C)**
   Cuyahoga county, vacating and modifying, **ORC 2153.15**
Jurisdiction, **JuvR 44, ORC 2151.07, ORC 2151.23**
   Child support, **ORC 3109.05(B)**
   Contempt of court, **ORC 2151.21**
   Continuing, **JuvR 35(A)**
   Custody action, **ORC 3109.04(D)(2)**
     See also CUSTODY OF CHILDREN, DOMESTIC; CUSTODY OF CHILDREN, INSTITUTIONAL, generally
   Cuyahoga county, **ORC 2153.16**
   Guardianship of minor, **ORC 2111.46**
   Minor offender not taken into custody until after 21 years of age, **ORC 2151.23(I), ORC 2152.12(G)**
   Paternity proceedings, **ORC 3111.06**
   Person not taken into custody until after 21 years of age, **ORC 2151.23(I), ORC 2152.12(G)**
   Relinquishment, **JuvR 30**
     Child's right to counsel, **JuvR 3**
   Retention, **JuvR 30(E)**
   Termination, **ORC 2151.38(A)**
   Transfer for criminal prosecution, **ORC 2151.23(H)**
   Transfer to another county, **JuvR 11**
   Visitation rights, **ORC 3109.051(M)**
Jury trials, **ORC 2152.67**
   Not held, **ORC 2151.35**
Juvenile delinquency. See JUVENILE DELINQUENCY
Juvenile rehabilitation. See JUVENILE REHABILITATION
Magistrates, **JuvR 40**
Mandatory transfer of case for criminal prosecution, **JuvR 30(B)**
Marriage of minor, consent, **JuvR 42**
Mediation, **ORC 2151.542**
   Custody or visitation of children, **SupR 16**
Medical treatment for child, **JuvR 13**
Mental examination. See Examination of child, this heading
Mentally retarded or developmentally disabled victim, testimony of, **ORC 2152.821**
Motions, **JuvR 19**
   Continuing jurisdiction, for, **JuvR 35(A)**

JUVENILE COURTS—*continued*
Motions, **JuvR 19**—*continued*
   Prehearing, **JuvR 22(E), JuvR 22(D)**
   Time extension, for, **JuvR 18(B)**
   Time for making, **JuvR 18(D)**
     Extension, **JuvR 22(E)**
Murder cases, transfer to adult court. See Transfer of cases, this heading
Neglected children. See DEPENDENT AND NEGLECTED CHILDREN, generally
Notice, **ORC 2151.29**
   Attorney of record, **JuvR 4(D)**
   Continuing jurisdiction, **JuvR 35(A)**
   Detention or shelter hearing, **JuvR 7(F), ORC 2151.314**
   Dispositional orders, **ORC 2151.3510**
   Proceeding without, **JuvR 13(D)**
   Proposed actions, **JuvR 13(E)**
   Removal hearings, schools and school districts, **JuvR 39(A)**
   Sealing records, **ORC 2151.356**
   Sexually oriented offense, notice to institution or association of adjudication of child as delinquent for committing, **ORC 2152.192**
   Transfer for criminal prosecution, hearing on, **JuvR 30(C)**
Orders
   Bindover, **ORC 2152.12**
     Category one and two offenses, **ORC 2152.12(B)**
   Discovery, granting, **JuvR 24(B)**
     Failure to comply, **JuvR 24(C)**
   Dispositional. See Dispositional orders, this heading
   Emergency medical treatment of child, **JuvR 13(C)**
     Payment, **JuvR 13(C)**
   Mental or physical examination of child, **JuvR 32**
   Protective supervision, **JuvR 34(E)**
   Release of transferred child, **JuvR 30(H)**
   Restraining orders, **JuvR 34(H), ORC 2151.359**
   Social history of child, **JuvR 13**
   Temporary, **JuvR 13**
     Extension, **JuvR 14(B)**
     Modification, **JuvR 14(C), JuvR 34(G)**
     Termination, **JuvR 14(A)**
   Transfer for criminal prosecution, **JuvR 30(G), JuvR 30(H)**
Parties to actions, **ORC 2151.28**
   Definition, **JuvR 2**
   Right to counsel, **JuvR 4(A)**
Paternity action, **ORC 3111.01 to 3111.19**
   See also PARENTAGE ACTIONS
Physical examination. See Examination of child, this heading
Placement of child, detention or shelter care, **JuvR 7**
Pleadings, **JuvR 22**
   Amendment, **JuvR 22(B)**
   Service, **JuvR 20**
Powers and duties, **ORC 2151.07**
Prehearing motions, **JuvR 22(E), JuvR 22(D)**
Preliminary conferences, **JuvR 21**
Preliminary hearings, transfer for criminal prosecution, **JuvR 30(A)**
   Notice, **JuvR 30(C), JuvR 30(D)**
   Release of transferred child, **JuvR 30(H)**
Prevention of delinquency, participation, **ORC 2152.73**
Probation of child. See PROBATION
Probation officers, **ORC 2151.13, ORC 2151.14**
   Appointment, **ORC 2151.13**
   Arrest powers, **ORC 2151.14**
   Assistance of law enforcement officers, **ORC 2151.14**
   Powers and duties, **ORC 2151.14**
Proceedings, recording, **JuvR 37**
Prosecuting attorney, duties, **ORC 2151.40**
Protective supervision, **JuvR 34(E)**
Recording proceedings, **JuvR 37**
Records and reports, **ORC 2151.12, ORC 2151.35, ORC 2152.71**
   Attorney's access, **ORC 2151.352**
   Child abuse, **ORC 2151.421**

JUVENILE COURTS—continued

Records and reports, **ORC 2151.12, ORC 2151.35, ORC 2152.71** —continued
- Confidentiality, **ORC 2151.14**
- Copies, providing, **ORC 2151.14, ORC 2151.141**
- Court records, management and retention, **SupR 26**
  - Administrative records, retention schedule, **SupR 26.01**
- Criminal identification records, weekly report to criminal identification and investigation bureau, **ORC 2152.71**
- Criteria for sealing records, **ORC 2151.356**
- Custody investigation, **JuvR 32(D)**
- Disposition of fingerprints and photographs, **ORC 2151.313**
- Duty to report injury, **ORC 2151.421**
- Expungement, **JuvR 34(J), ORC 2151.358**
- Hearings, **ORC 2151.35**
- Injury, duty to report, **ORC 2151.421**
- Investigative reports, public inspection, **JuvR 32(C)**
- Magistrate's decision, **JuvR 40(E)**
- Proceedings, **JuvR 37**
- Referee's report, **ORC 2151.16**
- Sealing of records, **JuvR 34(J), ORC 2151.358**
- Sexual abuse of child. See CHILDREN'S ADVOCACY CENTERS
- Summons, **ORC 2151.19, ORC 2151.28**
- Transfer of case, **JuvR 11(D)**
- Youth services department, to, **ORC 2152.71**

Recovery of costs from juvenile drug abuse offenders, **ORC 2152.202**
Referees, **ORC 2151.16**
Referral of child to, screening, **JuvR 9(B)**
Release of child
- Criminal prosecution, for, **JuvR 30(I)**
- Parent or guardian, to, **JuvR 7(B), JuvR 7(F), JuvR 7(D)**

Restraining orders, **JuvR 34(H), ORC 2151.359**
Revised Code, reference to in Juvenile Procedure Rules, **JuvR 43**
Rights of child
- Adjudicatory hearing, **JuvR 29(B)**
- Appeal, to, **JuvR 34(J)**
- Attorney representing, **JuvR 29(B), JuvR 4(A)**
- Detention hearing, **JuvR 7(F)**
- Expungement of record, **JuvR 34(J), ORC 2151.358**
- Transcript of proceedings, **JuvR 37, ORC 2151.35**
- Waiver, **JuvR 3**

Rules of procedure, **JuvR 1 to JuvR 48, ORC 2151.17**
- See also particular subject concerned
- Applicability, **JuvR 1(A)**
- Construction, **JuvR 1(B)**
- Effective date, **JuvR 47**
- Exceptions, **JuvR 1(C)**
- Jurisdiction, effect on, **JuvR 44**
- Local rules, adoption, **JuvR 45(A)**
- Procedure not specified, **JuvR 45**
- Revised Code, referenced in, **JuvR 43**
- Title, **JuvR 48**

Seal, **ORC 2151.20**
- Cuyahoga county, **ORC 2153.14**

Sealing records, criteria and notice, **ORC 2151.356**
Sentencing adults, **ORC 2151.49**
Service of process, **JuvR 16, JuvR 20, ORC 2151.14, ORC 2151.19, ORC 2151.29**
- Mail, by; additional time allowed, **JuvR 18(E)**
- Motions and affidavits, **JuvR 18(D)**
- Permanent custody, **ORC 2151.414(A)**
- Subpoena, **JuvR 17(C)**
- Summons, **JuvR 16(A), ORC 2151.19, ORC 2151.28**

Sessions, **ORC 2151.22**
Sexual abuse of child. See CHILDREN'S ADVOCACY CENTERS
Sexually oriented offense
- Child adjudicated delinquent child for committing, **ORC 2152.191, ORC 2152.811**
- Notice to institution or association of adjudication of child as delinquent for committing sexually oriented offense, **ORC 2152.192**

JUVENILE COURTS—continued

Social history of child, **JuvR 32**
- Cross-examination at dispositional hearing, **JuvR 34(B)**
- Definition, **JuvR 2**

Statutory construction, **ORC 2151.01**
Subpoenas, **JuvR 17**
Summons, **ORC 2151.19, ORC 2151.28**
- Issuance, form, and endorsement, **JuvR 15(A) to JuvR 15(C)**
- Service and return, **JuvR 16(A)**
- Temporary custody, **ORC 2151.353(C)**

Support and maintenance, **ORC 2151.361**
Surrender of custody, voluntary, **JuvR 38**
- Agreement for surrender of permanent custody, court approval, **JuvR 38(B)**
- Permanent custody, **JuvR 38(B)**
- Temporary custody, **JuvR 38(A)**

Temporary orders, **JuvR 13**
- Extension, **JuvR 14(B)**
- Magistrate's decision, based on, **JuvR 40(E)**
- Modification, **JuvR 14(C), JuvR 34(G)**
- Termination, **JuvR 14(A)**

Termination of parental rights. See CUSTODY OF CHILDREN, INSTITUTIONAL, at Permanent
Terms of courts, **ORC 2151.22**
- Cuyahoga county, **ORC 2153.12**

Testimony. See Witnesses, this heading
Time, **JuvR 18**
- Extension, **JuvR 22(E)**

Traffic cases. See TRAFFIC OFFENSES, at Juveniles, by
Transcripts, **JuvR 37, ORC 2151.35**
Transfer of cases, **JuvR 11, ORC 2151.18, ORC 2152.01 et seq.**
- Certification as complaint, **JuvR 10(A)**
- Criminal prosecution, for, **JuvR 30**
  - Child's right to counsel, **JuvR 3**
  - Prerequisites to transfer, **JuvR 30(D)**

Unruly children. See UNRULY CHILDREN
Venue, **ORC 2151.271**
Videotaped testimony, minor victims of sex offenses, **ORC 2152.81**
Visitation rights, jurisdiction, **ORC 3109.051(M)**
Waiver
- Examination of child, **JuvR 30(F), JuvR 30(G)**
- Rights, **JuvR 3**

Warrant against child, **JuvR 15(E), JuvR 15(D), JuvR 16(B), ORC 2151.30**
Witnesses, **ORC 2151.28**
- Fees and costs, **JuvR 17(B), JuvR 17(C)**
- Mentally retarded or developmentally disabled victim, **ORC 2152.821**
- Penalization by employer prohibited, **ORC 2151.211**
- Separation, **JuvR 29(E)**
- Subpoena, **JuvR 17(A)**
- Videotaped testimony, minor victims of sex offenses, **ORC 2152.81**

JUVENILE DELINQUENCY

See also UNRULY CHILDREN
Adjudication, **JuvR 29(E)**
- Hearing, **ORC 2151.28**

Adult
- Treatment as, in criminal prosecutions. See Criminal prosecution, this heading

Amenability to rehabilitation, determination, **JuvR 30(A), ORC 2152.12(C)**
Apprehension, **ORC 2151.14, ORC 2151.31, ORC 2152.03**
Bail. See Recognizance, this heading
Case history, **ORC 2151.34**
Commitment of children
- See also CUSTODY OF CHILDREN, INSTITUTIONAL, generally
- Commitment to youth services department
  - Early release, **ORC 2151.38(A), ORC 2151.38(B)**

JUVENILE DELINQUENCY—continued
Commitment of children—continued
  Discharge
    Minimum term of institutionalization, **ORC 2151.38(A), ORC 2151.38(B)**
    Multiple offenses, consecutive terms, **ORC 2151.38(B)**
  Youth services department, institutionalization
    Early release, **ORC 2151.38(A), ORC 2151.38(B)**
Complaints, **JuvR 10(A), ORC 2151.27**
  Victim of delinquent 65 or older or disabled, record, **ORC 2151.27(D), ORC 2152.71**
Contributing to
  Charges, **ORC 2151.43**
  Complaints, **ORC 2151.44**
  Jurisdiction of juvenile court, **ORC 2151.23**
Criminal prosecution, **JuvR 30, ORC 2152.12**
  Category one and two offenses, **ORC 2152.12(B)**
    Repeat offenders, **ORC 2152.12(C)**
  Discretionary transfer, **JuvR 30(C)**
  Firearm, offense committed with, factor to consider, **ORC 2152.12(B), ORC 2152.12(C)**
  Mandatory transfer, **JuvR 30(B)**
  Right to counsel, **JuvR 3**
  Violent crime, factor to consider, **ORC 2152.12(C)**
Custody. See CUSTODY OF CHILDREN, INSTITUTIONAL
Damages, liability. See DAMAGES
Delinquent child, defined, **ORC 2151.011**
Detention, **ORC 2151.31 to 2151.314**
  See also CUSTODY OF CHILDREN, INSTITUTIONAL, at Detention
  Homes. See DETENTION HOMES
DNA testing of delinquents, **ORC 2152.74**
Driver's license suspension, **ORC 2151.354, ORC 2151.355**
Expenses for care, funding from juvenile courts, **ORC 2151.10**
Expungement of records, **JuvR 34(J), ORC 2151.358**
Females
  Trials, **ORC 2151.16**
Fingerprints, **ORC 2151.313**
Foreign jurisdiction, juvenile domiciled in, criminal prosecution, **ORC 2152.12(C)**
Foster care facility, commitment to
  Disclosure of delinquency status, **ORC 2152.72**
Guardian ad litem, appointment, **ORC 2151.281**
Impeachment by delinquency adjudication, prohibition, **ORC 2152.21**
Inheritance from dead victim prohibited, **ORC 2105.19**
Institutionalization
  Commitment to youth services department, early release, **ORC 2151.38(A), ORC 2151.38(B)**
  Discharge
    Minimum term, **ORC 2151.38(A), ORC 2151.38(B)**
    Multiple offenses, consecutive terms, **ORC 2151.38(B)**
Interstate agreements, **ORC 2151.56 to 2151.61**
Jurisdiction of juvenile courts, **ORC 2151.23**
Jail confinement, **JuvR 7(H)**
Jurisdiction, **ORC 2151.23**
Medical and mental examinations, **ORC 2152.12(C)**
Not guilty child, expungement of records, **JuvR 34(J)**
Notice of intended dispositional orders, **ORC 2151.3510**
Photographs, **ORC 2151.313**
Prevention programs; juvenile courts, participation, **ORC 2152.73**
Probation. See PROBATION
Recognizance
  Transfer of case from juvenile court, **ORC 2152.12(F)**
Records and reports
  Annual report by juvenile court, **ORC 2152.71**
  Complaints, filing of; notice to school superintendents, **ORC 2151.27**
  Copies, providing, **ORC 2151.141**
  Expungement of records, **JuvR 34(J), ORC 2151.358**
  Physical and mental examinations, **ORC 2151.53**
  Sealing of records, **ORC 2151.358**

JUVENILE DELINQUENCY—continued
Rehabilitation, **ORC 2151.65 to 2151.80**
  See also JUVENILE REHABILITATION
Repeat offender
  Category one and two offenses, transfer to adult court, **ORC 2152.12(C)**
Runaways. See RUNAWAYS
Sealing of records, **JuvR 34(J), ORC 2151.358**
Sex offenses
  Registry, juvenile sex offender, **ORC 2152.82 to 2152.851**
  Sexually oriented offense, child adjudicated delinquent child for committing, **ORC 2152.191, ORC 2152.811**
Shelter care, **ORC 2151.28**
Statute violated, providing to youth services department upon commitment, **ORC 2151.38(C), ORC 2151.38(D)**
Unfit parents, **ORC 2151.05**
Warrant against, **JuvR 15(E)**

JUVENILE PROCEDURE RULES
Generally, **JuvR 1 to JuvR 48, ORC 2151.17**
See also JUVENILE COURTS, at Rules of procedure

JUVENILE PROCEEDINGS
See JUVENILE COURTS

JUVENILE REHABILITATION
Generally, **ORC 2151.65 to 2151.80**
Accounts and accounting by facilities, **ORC 2151.75, ORC 2151.79**
Admission, **ORC 2151.65**
  Nonresident juveniles, **ORC 2151.654**
Amenability to, determination, **JuvR 30(F), ORC 2152.12(C)**
Boards of trustees, **ORC 2151.68 to 2151.78**
County auditor, powers and duties, **ORC 2151.79**
Detention homes, **ORC 2152.26**
  See also DETENTION HOMES
Districts, **ORC 2151.65**
  Withdrawal, **ORC 2151.78**
Education, cost, **ORC 2151.362**
Eligibility, **ORC 2152.12(C)**
Facilities, **ORC 2151.76**
  Acquisition, **ORC 2151.65**
  Appraisal, **ORC 2151.77**
  Detention homes. See DETENTION HOMES
  Financing, **ORC 2151.651**
  Site selection, **ORC 2151.72**
Funding, **ORC 2151.66, ORC 2151.77**
  Gifts and bequests, **ORC 2151.67**
  Youth services department, from, **ORC 2151.651, ORC 2151.652**
Gifts and bequests for, **ORC 2151.67**
Management of facilities, **ORC 2151.71**
Programs, **ORC 2151.653**
School boards, agreements, **ORC 2151.653**
Superintendents of facilities, **ORC 2151.70**
Taxes to support, **ORC 2151.66, ORC 2151.78**
Teachers, **ORC 2151.653**
Termination of commitment, **ORC 2151.65**
Transfer of juveniles, **ORC 2151.18, ORC 2151.65, ORC 2152.01 et seq.**
Trustees of facilities, **ORC 2151.68 to 2151.78**
  Expenses, **ORC 2151.80**

JUVENILE RULES OF PROCEDURE
Generally, **JuvR 1 to JuvR 48, ORC 2151.17**
See also JUVENILE COURTS, at Rules of procedure

JUVENILE TRAFFIC OFFENDERS
See TRAFFIC OFFENSES, at Juveniles, by

KEOGH PLANS
Testamentary trustees, **ORC 2107.64**

KIDNAPPING
Custody of child improperly obtained, **ORC 3109.26**

KIDNAPPING—continued
Parent, by
    Uniform Child Custody Jurisdiction Act to prevent, **ORC 3109.21 to 3109.32**

KILLING
See MURDER

KIN
See NEXT OF KIN

KNOWLEDGE
See NOTICE

LABOR
Generally, See EMPLOYER AND EMPLOYEE
Salary. See COMPENSATION; WAGES AND HOURS

LAND
Generally, See REAL PROPERTY
Conveyances. See CONVEYANCES
Deeds. See DEEDS
Eminent domain. See EMINENT DOMAIN
Estates
    See also ESTATES
    Sale. See LAND SALE PROCEEDINGS
Public. See LANDS, PUBLIC
Taxation. See REAL PROPERTY, TAXATION

LAND CONTRACTS
Death of purchaser before conveyance, **ORC 2113.50**
Survivorship tenancy, applicability, **ORC 5302.20**

LAND SALE PROCEEDINGS
Generally, **ORC 2107.58, ORC 2107.59, ORC Ch 2127**
Ancillary administration, **ORC 2129.13, ORC 2129.14, ORC 2129.16**
Appraisement, **ORC 2127.22 to 2127.39**
Appraisers
    Appointment, **HamR 65.1**
    Compensation, **HamR 65.1, ORC 2127.25**
    Fee, **SupR 61**
Attorney fees, **SumR 71.1(C)**
    Application, **SumR Appx G**
Auction, **ORC 2127.32**
Bond, **ORC 2127.27**
    Foreign wards, **ORC 2127.42**
    Objecting party to give, **ORC 2127.31**
Cash payment, **ORC 2127.36**
Commencement, **ORC 2127.04**
Commissions, real estate brokers, **SumR 65.1**
Complaint, **ORC 2127.10**
Confirmation of sale, **ORC 2127.35**
Consent, surviving spouse and heirs, **ORC 2127.011, ORC 2127.04**
Costs, **ORC 2127.04**
Court ordering, **ORC 2127.04**
Cuyahoga county probate court, case management, **CuyR 78.1**
Deed, **ORC 2127.35**
Deferred payments, **ORC 2127.34, ORC 2127.36**
Distribution of proceeds, **ORC 2127.03, ORC 2127.38**
Dower, **ORC 2127.16, ORC 2127.30**
Entire interest. See Interest in real property, sale, this heading
Equitable interest, **ORC 2127.30**
Escheated property, **ORC 2105.09**
Estate tax purposes, for, **ORC 5731.37**
Executors and administrators. See Fiduciary, this heading
Expenses, **ORC 2127.04**
Fees, **ORC 2127.08, ORC 2127.25, ORC 2127.37**
Fiduciary
    Foreign, by, **ORC 2129.25**
Foreign fiduciary, by, **ORC 2129.25**
Fractional interests, **ORC 2127.08, ORC 2127.10**
Franklin county probate court, case management, **FrankR 78.1**

LAND SALE PROCEEDINGS—continued
Guardian, consent to or demand for
    Sale of ward's land. See GUARDIANSHIP, at Sale of land by
Guardians ad litem, appointment, **LucasR 65.01**
Hamilton county probate court
    Appraisers, appointment, **HamR 65.1**
    Case management, **HamR 78.2**
    Court costs, deposits, **HamR Appx D**
Hearings, **ORC 2127.18**
Interest in real property, sale, **ORC 2127.07**
    Dower, **ORC 2127.16, ORC 2127.30**
    Entire interest, **ORC 2127.08**
    Equitable interest, **ORC 2127.30**
    Fractional interests, **ORC 2127.08, ORC 2127.10**
Investigation by court, **SupR 65(D)**
Jurisdiction, **ORC 2101.24**
Lucas county probate court, **LucasR 65.01**
    Case management, **LucasR 78.1**
Minor heirs, effect, **ORC 2127.011**
Nonresident decedent's property, **ORC 2129.13, ORC 2129.14, ORC 2129.16**
Objections to, **ORC 2127.04, ORC 2127.17, ORC 2127.31**
Order of, by court, **ORC 2127.29, ORC 2127.30**
Parties, **ORC 2127.12, ORC 2127.13**
Pleadings and procedure, **ORC 2127.15**
Power of sale, **ORC 2127.011**
Prevention, **ORC 2127.31**
Price, **ORC 2127.011, ORC 2127.33**
Private sale, **ORC 2127.32**
Public sale, **ORC 2127.32, SupR 65**
Purchasers, surviving spouse as, **ORC 2127.04**
Purposes, **ORC 2127.02, ORC 2127.03, ORC 2127.05**
Real estate brokers' commissions, **SumR 65.1**
Stark county probate court
    Case management, **Sup. R 78.2**
    Court costs, **Sup. R 58.1**
Summary order, **ORC 2127.11**
Summit county probate court, **SumR 65.1**
    Appraisers, compensation, **SumR 61.1**
    Attorney fees, **SumR 71.1(C), SumR Appx G**
    Preliminary judicial title, **SumR 65.1(A)**
    Real estate brokers' commissions, **SumR 65.1(B)**
Surviving spouse as purchaser, **ORC 2127.04**
Terms of sale, **ORC 2127.34**
Title
    Evidence of, **SupR 65(A)**
Title, preliminary judicial, **SumR 65.1**
Venue, **ORC 2127.09**
Will authorizing, **ORC 2113.39, ORC 2127.01**
Written consent, **ORC 2127.011**

LANDLORD AND TENANT
Statute of frauds, **ORC 1335.04**

LANDS, PUBLIC
Acquisition
    Purchase, by, **ORC 163.04, ORC 163.59**
Appropriation, **ORC Ch 163**
Eminent domain. See EMINENT DOMAIN

LAPSE STATUTE
Generally, **ORC 2107.52**

LAST ILLNESS
Expenses as claim against estate
    Priority, **ORC 2117.25**

LAW ENFORCEMENT OFFICERS
See also CONSTABLES; POLICE; SHERIFFS
Aged persons suffering neglect, abuse, or exploitation; report to county human services department, **ORC 5101.61**
Children's advocacy center, memorandum of understanding, **ORC 2151.426**

LAW ENFORCEMENT OFFICERS

Index-72

LAW ENFORCEMENT OFFICERS—*continued*
Criminal identification and investigation of juveniles, **ORC 2151.313**
Definition, **ORC 2901.01**
Records and reports of juveniles, **ORC 2151.313**
Special
    Mental retardation and developmental disabilities department, **ORC 5123.13**

LAW MERCHANT
Fraudulent transfers, applicability, **ORC 1336.10**

LAWS
See STATUTES

LAWSUITS
See ACTIONS

LAWYERS
See ATTORNEYS

LEASEHOLD ESTATES
Descent and distribution statute, construction, **ORC 2105.04**

LEASES
Estate or trust, lease from; vacated order of settlement of account, **ORC 2109.35**
Fees, probate court, **ORC 2101.16**
Guardians, by, **ORC 2111.25 to 2111.32**
Mineral rights, **ORC 2111.30**
Oil and gas lands, probate court fee, **ORC 2101.16**
Power of attorney, **1337.01 et seq., ORC Ch 1337**
Probate court fees, **ORC 2101.16**
Statute of frauds, **ORC 1335.04**

LEGACIES AND DEVISES
Abatement, **ORC 2107.34, ORC 2107.54**
Action against legatee, **ORC 2117.41**
Advancements, **ORC 2105.051, ORC 2109.44**
Agreement to make, **ORC 2107.04**
Aliens, rights, **ORC 2105.16**
Alteration of property bequeathed, effect, **ORC 2107.36**
Anti-lapse statute, **ORC 2107.52**
Assessments, liability for, **ORC 2113.52**
Automobile title, transfer to surviving spouse, **ORC 2106.18, ORC 4505.10**
Bequest construed, **ORC 2107.011, ORC 5815.01**
Boat or watercraft title, transfer to surviving spouse, **ORC 2106.19**
Bonds, contracts or covenants by testator, effect, **ORC 2107.33**
Charitable bequests
    Attorney general as party, will contest, **ORC 2107.73**
    Estate tax deduction, **ORC 5731.17**
Concealment of existing will, effect, **ORC 2107.10**
Conditional
    Estate tax deductions, effect, **ORC 5731.17**
Contributions to debt payments, **ORC 2107.54 to 2107.57**
    Mortgage lien, effect, **ORC 2107.54, ORC 2113.52**
    Real property sale to satisfy, **ORC 2127.38**
Death of legatees, **ORC 2107.52**
Debt payments, contributions to, **ORC 2107.54 to 2107.57**
    Mortgage lien, effect, **ORC 2107.54, ORC 2113.52**
    Real property sale to satisfy, **ORC 2127.38**
Declaratory judgments regarding. See DECLARATORY JUDGMENTS
Descent and distribution. See DESCENT AND DISTRIBUTION
Disclaimers of succession to, **ORC 5815.36**
    See also DISCLAIMER OF SUCCESSION TO PROPERTY
Distribution, **ORC 2113.25, ORC 2113.51**
    Application for, **ORC 2113.54**
    Recovery, **ORC 2113.23**
    Return of, **ORC 2113.51, ORC 2113.53**
Estate tax
    Apportionment, **ORC 2113.85 to 2113.88**
    Deductions, **ORC 5731.17**

LEGACIES AND DEVISES—*continued*
Future interests, **ORC 2131.04 to 2131.07**
General legacies, interest, **ORC 2113.531**
Inheritance construed, **ORC 2107.011, ORC 5815.01**
Interest, **ORC 2113.52, ORC 2113.531**
Intestate succession. See DESCENT AND DISTRIBUTION
Juvenile courts, to, **ORC 2152.73**
Land sale proceedings
    Proceeds distributed for, **ORC 2127.03, ORC 2127.38**
    See also LAND SALE PROCEEDINGS, generally
Lapsing, anti-lapse statute, **ORC 2107.52**
Liens against, **ORC 2113.52**
Limitation of actions, effect on paternity proceedings, **ORC 3111.05**
Mental retardation and developmental disabilities department, to, **ORC 5123.27**
Mortgage lien, no right of exoneration, **ORC 2113.52**
    Contributions to debt payments, effect, **ORC 2107.54**
Motor vehicles, odometer information not required, **ORC 4505.06**
Motorcycle title, transfer to surviving spouse, **ORC 2106.18(D)**
Notice to beneficiaries, **ORC 2107.08**
Outboard motor title, transfer to surviving spouse, **ORC 2106.19**
Probate judges, **ORC 2101.38**
Property disposition during guardianship, **ORC 2107.501**
Public authorities, to. See Charitable bequests, this heading
Real estate, charge on, **ORC 2127.03**
Recorded in counties where real estate is located, **ORC 2107.21**
Recovery, invalidity of will, **ORC 2113.23**
Remaindermen, **ORC 2131.04 to 2131.07**
Residuary legacy, **ORC 2109.10**
Revocation, **ORC 2107.33 to 2107.38**
Specific bequests and devises, **ORC 2113.51**
Surviving spouse. See SURVIVING SPOUSE
Taxes, liability for, **ORC 2113.52**
Truck title, transfer to surviving spouse, **ORC 2106.18(D)**
Trust estate, to, **ORC 2107.63**
Unclaimed, **ORC 2113.64 to 2113.68**
Void, **ORC 2107.15**
Whole estate, **ORC 2107.51**
Witnesses to will, bequests or devises to, **ORC 2107.15**

LEGAL ADVERTISING
See NOTICE

LEGAL AGE
See AGE REQUIREMENTS

LEGAL COUNSEL
See ATTORNEYS

LEGAL CUSTODY
Defined, **ORC 2151.011**

LEGAL DISABILITY
See DISABILITY, PERSONS UNDER

LEGAL INSTRUMENTS
Deeds. See DEEDS
Disclaimer of succession to property, contents, **ORC 5815.36**
Leases. See LEASES
Lost. See LOST INSTRUMENTS AND RECORDS
Wills, **ORC Ch 2107**
Wills. See also WILLS

LEGAL RIGHTS SERVICE
Administrator, **ORC 5123.60**
Advocacy services, **ORC 5123.60**
Commission, **ORC 5123.60**
Complaints to, procedures, **ORC 5123.601**
Crimes, reporting, **ORC 5123.601**
Guardianship, **ORC Ch 2111**
Malpractice actions, **ORC 5123.60**
Mentally ill and mentally retarded or developmentally disabled persons, for, **ORC 5123.60**

LEGAL RIGHTS SERVICE—continued
Ombudsman section, **ORC 5123.601 to 5123.604**
    Access to information, **ORC 5123.602**
    Creation, **ORC 5123.601**
    Disclosures to, retaliation prohibited, **ORC 5123.604, ORC 5123.99**
    Interference with, **ORC 5123.604, ORC 5123.99**
    Notice of investigations, **ORC 5123.604**
    Powers and duties, **ORC 5123.603**
    Services, **ORC 5123.60**
Powers and duties, **ORC 5123.60**

LEGAL SEPARATION
Generally, **ORC 3105.17, ORC 3105.21**
Agreements. See SEPARATION AGREEMENTS
Annulment, complaint not barring counterclaim for, **ORC 3105.17(B)**
Complaint, **ORC 3105.17**
Counterclaim, **ORC 3105.17**
Custody order, **ORC 3105.21**
Divorce, complaint not barring counterclaim for, **ORC 3105.17(B)**
Dower rights barred, **ORC 3105.10(E)**
Grounds for, **ORC 3105.17**
Judgment, **ORC 3105.10(E)**
Jurisdiction, **ORC 3105.17**
Notice, **ORC 3105.06**
Power of attorney, revocation of spouse's power of attorney upon divorce, dissolution, or separation, **ORC 5815.32**
Service of process, **ORC 3105.06**

LEGATEES
See HEIRS

LEGITIMATION
See ILLEGITIMATE CHILDREN

LETTERS OF ADMINISTRATION
Application, **HamR 60.1**
Court issuing, **ORC 2113.01**
Stepparents, **SumR 60.1(A)**

LETTERS OF APPOINTMENT
See EXECUTORS AND ADMINISTRATORS

LETTERS TESTAMENTARY
Generally, **ORC 2113.05**

LIBEL
Limitation of actions, **ORC 2305.11**

LICENSES AND PERMITS
Drivers'. See DRIVERS' LICENSES
Marriage. See MARRIAGE
Residential care facilities, **ORC 5123.99**
    Mentally retarded or developmentally disabled persons, for, **ORC 5123.19, ORC 5123.192, ORC 5123.20**

LIENS
Dower, **ORC 5305.03**
Estate property, on, **ORC 2113.59**
    Actions, **ORC 2117.30, ORC 2127.08**
    Failure to present, **ORC 2117.10**
    Fractional interest, sale of, **ORC 2127.08**
    Mansion house, **ORC 2106.10(A)**
    Mortgages, **ORC 2117.29**
    Priority, **ORC 2127.18, ORC 2127.19, ORC 2127.38**
    Release, real property, **ORC 2127.19**
    Vendor's lien, **ORC 2117.27**
Estate tax, **ORC 5731.37, ORC 5731.38**
Sales to enforce. See JUDICIAL SALES
Tax
    Estate tax, **ORC 5731.37, ORC 5731.38**

LIFE ESTATES
Dower, **ORC Ch 2103**

LIFE ESTATES—continued
Estate tax, effect, **ORC 5731.06**
Remaindermen, **ORC 2113.58, ORC 2131.04 to 2131.07**
    Protection of interest, **ORC 2105.20, ORC 2113.58**
Rule in Shelley's case, **ORC 2107.49**
Waste by tenant, **ORC 2103.07, ORC 2105.20**

LIFE INSURANCE
See also INSURANCE, generally
Beneficiaries
    Designation of spouse as, effect of termination of marriage, **ORC 5815.33**
    Trustee named in will, **ORC 2107.64**
Estate tax, **ORC 5731.09, ORC 5731.12**
Fiduciaries, investment powers, **ORC 2109.37**
Living wills, effect, **ORC 2133.12**
Presumed decedent's, **ORC 2121.05, ORC 2121.08**
Principal and Income Act, **ORC 5812.27**
Proceeds payable to estate, **ORC 5731.09, ORC 5731.12**
    Release by tax commissioner, **ORC 5731.39**
Uniform Principal and Income Act, **ORC 5812.27**

LIFE TENANTS
See LIFE ESTATES

LIMITATION OF ACTIONS
Adoption
    Appeal, **ORC 3107.16**
    Consent requirements, **ORC 3107.07**
Adverse possession, recovery of title, **ORC 2305.04**
Antenuptial agreements, action to set aside, **ORC 2106.22**
Bodily injuries, **ORC 2305.10**
Bond actions, **ORC 2305.12**
Civil actions, generally, **ORC 2305.11**
Claims against estates. See CLAIMS AGAINST ESTATES
Contesting wills, **ORC 2107.31, ORC 2107.76**
Descent and distribution, effect on paternity proceedings, **ORC 3111.05**
Disability of party, effect, **ORC 2305.04**
Easements, prescriptive rights, **ORC 2305.04**
Election by surviving spouse, **ORC 2101.16**
Estate tax. See ESTATE TAX
Estates, claims against, **ORC 2117.06**
    Distribution of assets prior to expiration of filing period, notice, **ORC 2117.06**
Estates, claims against. See CLAIMS AGAINST ESTATES
Executors and administrators, actions against, **ORC 2113.24**
    Investment of unclaimed funds, **ORC 2113.66**
Fiduciaries, actions against
    Accounting, fraud by, **ORC 2109.35**
    Executors and administrators, **ORC 2113.24**
    Use of trust funds by, **ORC 2109.43**
Forfeiture, **ORC 2305.11**
Fraud, **ORC 2305.09**
Fraudulent transfers, **ORC 1336.09**
    Estate property, **ORC 2127.40**
Heirship, determination; effect of paternity proceedings, **ORC 3111.05**
Income tax, **ORC 5747.13(A)**
    State, refund applications, **ORC 5747.11**
Legacies and devices, effect of paternity proceedings, **ORC 3111.05**
Libel, **ORC 2305.11**
Malicious prosecution, **ORC 2305.11**
Malpractice, **ORC 2305.11**
Negligence, **ORC 2305.09**
Paternity proceedings, **ORC 3111.05**
Personal property, recovery, **ORC 2305.09, ORC 2305.10**
Product liability, **ORC 2305.10**
Real property, recovery of title, **ORC 2305.04**
Replevin, **ORC 2305.09**
Revocable trusts, limitation of actions pertaining to revocable trusts made irrevocable by death of settlor, **ORC 5806.04**
Separation agreement, action to set aside, **ORC 2106.22**
Slander, **ORC 2305.11**

LIMITATION OF ACTIONS

LIMITATION OF ACTIONS—*continued*
Surviving spouse, election, **ORC 2101.16**
Title to property, **ORC 2305.04**
Torts, **ORC 2305.09**
Trespassing, **ORC 2305.09**
Trusts
    Breach of trust, remedies, **ORC 5810.05**
    Claim by nonresident or unknown beneficiary of trust fund, **ORC 2109.57**
    Revocable, **ORC 5806.04**
Veterans, exposure to chemical agents, **ORC 2305.10**
Will contests, **ORC 2107.31, ORC 2107.76**
Wrongful death, **ORC 2125.02**

LIMITED LIABILITY COMPANY
Defined, **ORC 5747.01**

LIMITED PARTNERSHIPS
See PARTNERSHIPS, generally

LIMITED PRACTITIONERS
Mentally retarded and developmentally disabled persons, reporting abuse or neglect, **ORC 5123.61, ORC 5123.99**

LIVING WILLS
Generally, **ORC 2133.01 to 2133.16**
Anatomical gifts, **ORC 2133.16**
Annuities, effect, **ORC 2133.12**
Comfort care, actions for, **ORC 2133.12**
Definitions, **ORC 2133.01, ORC 2133.16**
DNR identification, priority, **ORC 2133.03**
Drivers' licenses, applications, **ORC 4507.06**
Durable power of attorney for health care, **ORC 2133.03**
Euthanasia not authorized by, **ORC 2133.12**
Execution, **ORC 2133.02**
    Foreign states, **ORC 2133.14**
    Former law, **ORC 2133.15**
Foreign declaration, effect, **ORC 2133.14**
Forms, **ORC 2133.07**
Grandfather clause, **ORC 2133.15**
Homicide, death as result of withholding or withdrawal of life-sustaining equipment not constituting, **ORC 2133.12**
Immunity of physician acting under, **ORC 2133.11**
Informed decisions by patient, **ORC 2133.06**
Life insurance, effect, **ORC 2133.12**
Life-sustaining equipment, withholding or withdrawal, **ORC 2133.08**
Mercy killing not authorized by, **ORC 2133.12**
Notice, determinations made under, **ORC 2133.05**
Nutrition or hydration, withholding or withdrawal of, **ORC 2133.09**
Objections to determinations made under, **ORC 2133.05**
Operation of declaration, prerequisites, **ORC 2133.03**
Pre-dating effective date of act, **ORC 2133.15**
Pregnant patients, effect, **ORC 2133.06**
Presumption of validity, **ORC 2133.13**
Printed forms, **ORC 2133.07**
Priority, **ORC 2133.03**
Records and reports, **ORC 2133.05**
Refusal to comply, **ORC 2133.02**
Revocation, **ORC 2133.04**
Suicide
    Assisting, not authorized by, **ORC 2133.12**
    Death as result of withholding or withdrawal of life-sustaining equipment not constituting, **ORC 2133.12**
Transfer of patient to complying provider, **ORC 2133.10**
Treatment to diminish pain and discomfort, **ORC 2133.11, ORC 2133.12**
Validity, presumption of, **ORC 2133.13**
When operative, **ORC 2133.03**
Withholding or withdrawal of life-sustaining equipment, **ORC 2133.08, ORC 2133.09**
Witnesses, **ORC 2133.02**

LOANS
Statute of frauds, **ORC 1335.02**
Writing requirement, **ORC 1335.02**

LOBBYING
Estate tax deduction, effect, **ORC 5731.17**

LOGAN COUNTY
Probate courts judges, powers and jurisdiction, **ORC 2101.024**

LORD CAMPBELL'S ACT
Generally, **ORC Ch 2125**
See also WRONGFUL DEATH

LOSS OF SERVICES
Wrongful death action for compensation, **ORC 2125.02**

LOST INSTRUMENTS AND RECORDS
Wills, **ORC 2107.26 to 2107.28**
    See also PROBATE OF WILLS

LUCAS COUNTY
See COUNTIES, for general provisions
Probate court. . See LUCAS COUNTY PROBATE COURT; PROBATE COURTS

LUCAS COUNTY PROBATE COURT
Accounts and accounting, **LucasR 64.1**
Address change of fiduciary or attorney of record, **LucasR 57.1**
Adoptions, **LucasR 75.1**
    Court costs, **LucasR 58.1(A)**
Affidavit of giving notice, **LucasR 59.1**
Appraisers, **LucasR 61.1**
Attorney fees, **LucasR 71.1**
Attorneys
    Address change, notice to court, **LucasR 57.1**
    Designation, **LucasR 57.1**
Case management, **LucasR 78.1**
Certificate of giving notice, **LucasR 59.2, LucasR 59.3**
Certificates of transfer, **LucasR 78.4**
Certification of related cases and deposited wills, **LucasR 57.1**
Civil actions, case management, **LucasR 78.1**
Compensation
    Attorney fees, **LucasR 71.1**
    Corporate fiduciaries, **LucasR 74.2**
    Guardians, **LucasR 73.1**
    Trustees, **LucasR 74.1**
Computerization of court, additional fees charged for, **LucasR 58.1(D)**
Computerized legal research, additional fees charged for, **LucasR 58.1(C)**
Continuances, request for, **LucasR 78.3**
Corporate fiduciaries, compensation, **LucasR 74.2**
Court costs, **LucasR 58.1**
Dispute resolution, additional fees, **LucasR 58.1(F)**
Estate tax returns, additional fees, **LucasR 58.1(G)**
Estates
    Case management, **LucasR 78.1**
    Court costs, **LucasR 58.1(A)**
    Inventory, **LucasR 78.6**
Extensions of time, requests for, **LucasR 78.3**
Fees
    Attorney fees, **LucasR 71.1**
    Continuances, request for, **LucasR 78.3**
    Personal service of summons, **LucasR 78.5**
Fiduciaries
    Address change, notice to court, **LucasR 57.1**
    Attorney, designating, **LucasR 57.1**
    Corporate, compensation, **LucasR 74.2**
Filing with court, **LucasR 57.1**
Guardians, compensation, **LucasR 73.1**
Guardianships, **LucasR 66.1**
    Case management, **LucasR 78.1**
    Court costs, **LucasR 58.1(A)**

LUCAS COUNTY PROBATE COURT—*continued*
Hours of court, **LucasR 53.1**
Insolvency proceedings, **LucasR 62.1**
Inventory of decedent's estate, **LucasR 78.6**
Judgment entries, **LucasR 57.1**
Jury management plan, **LucasR 78.2**
Land sales, **LucasR 65.01**
    Case management, **LucasR 78.1**
Management and retention of records, **LucasR 26.1**
Microfiche records, additional fees charged for, **LucasR 58.1(E)**
Minors
    Personal injuries, settlement of claims for, **LucasR 68.1**
    § 10,000 or less, **LucasR 68.2**
Motions, case management, **LucasR 78.1**
New case information sheet, **LucasR 57.2**
Notice
    Affidavit of giving, **LucasR 59.1**
    Certificate of giving, **LucasR 59.2, LucasR 59.3**
Personal injury claims of minors, settlement, **LucasR 68.1**
    § 10,000 or less, **LucasR 68.2**
Pleadings, **LucasR 57.1**
Pretrial procedure, **LucasR 78.1**
Records, management and retention of, **LucasR 26.1**
Related cases, certification, **LucasR 57.1**
School residency, guardianships for purpose of prohibited, **LucasR 66.1(A)**
Security plan, **LucasR 9.1**
Settlements
    Personal injury claims of minors, **LucasR 68.1**
    § 10,000 or less, **LucasR 68.2**
    Wrongful death claims, **LucasR 70.1**
Summons
    Personal service, deposit required, **LucasR 78.5**
Tax returns, additional fees, **LucasR 58.1(G)**
Trustees, compensation, **LucasR 74.1**
Trusts, case management, **LucasR 78.1**
Wills
    Deposited wills, certification, **LucasR 57.1**
Wrongful death settlements, **LucasR 70.1**
    Case management, **LucasR 78.1**

MAGISTRATES
Appointment, **CuyR 8.1, FrankR 8.1, JuvR 40(A), SumR 54.1**
Compensation, **JuvR 40(B)**
    Hospitalization proceedings for mentally ill, **ORC 5122.43**
    Institutionalization proceedings for mentally retarded, **ORC 5123.96**
Decisions, **JuvR 40(E), SumR 54.1**
    Objections, **FrankR 75.11**
    Objections to, **Sup. R 75.7**
Findings of fact by
    Juvenile courts, **JuvR 40(E)**
General order of reference, **SumR 54.1**
Institutionalization hearings for mentally retarded, conducted by, **ORC 5123.76**
Involuntary psychiatric commitment proceedings, appointment, **FrankR 8.1**
Juvenile courts, **JuvR 40**
Objections to decision, **FrankR 75.11, Sup. R 75.7**
    Court ruling on, **JuvR 40(E)**
Powers and duties, **JuvR 40(C), SumR 54.1**
Proceedings before, **JuvR 40(D)**
Recordings, **SumR 54.2(B)**

MAINTENANCE
See SUPPORT AND MAINTENANCE

MAJORITY VOTE
Anatomical gifts, majority vote prevailing when representative or successor representative is group or class of persons, **ORC 2108.79**

MALICIOUS PROSECUTION
Limitation of actions, **ORC 2305.11**

MALPRACTICE
Legal rights service, **ORC 5123.60**
Limitation of actions, **ORC 2305.11**

MANDAMUS
Jurisdiction, **O Const IV § 2, O Const IV § 3**

MANDATORY DISTRIBUTION
Defined, **ORC 5801.01**

MANSION HOUSE
Surviving spouse
    Right to remain in, **ORC 2106.05, ORC 2106.10, ORC 2106.15**

MANSLAUGHTER
See MURDER, generally

MANUFACTURED HOMES
Brokers
    Certificates of title, **ORC 4505.06**
Sales tax
    Casual sales, determination of purchase price, **ORC 4505.06**
    Penalty for returned or dishonored payment, **ORC 4505.06**

MARION COUNTY
Probate court judges, concurrent jurisdiction with domestic relations-juvenile divisions, **ORC 2101.022**

MARRIAGE
See also HUSBAND AND WIFE
Alimony. See SUPPORT AND MAINTENANCE
Annulment. See ANNULMENT OF MARRIAGE
Antenuptial agreements, action to set aside, **ORC 2106.22**
Attempted, presumption of paternity, **ORC 3111.03**
Common law marriages, **ORC 3105.12**
Consent to minor's marriage
    Jurisdiction, **JuvR 42, ORC 2151.23**
Dissolution. See DISSOLUTION OF MARRIAGE
Divorce. See DIVORCE
Evidence of, in divorce action, **ORC 3105.12**
Fees
    Probate judges, **ORC 2101.27**
Invalid, presumption of paternity, **ORC 3111.03**
Legal separation. See LEGAL SEPARATION
License
    Fees, **ORC 2101.16**
    Franklin county probate court, counseling required for applicants, **FrankR 75.14**
    Granting of, **ORC 2101.24**
    Summit county probate court, waiting period waived, **SumR 86.1**
Minor, by, **ORC 2151.23**
    Annulment due to age, **ORC 3105.31(A)**
    Consent, jurisdiction, **JuvR 42, ORC 2151.23**
    Juvenile court consenting to, **JuvR 42**
    Pregnancy, due to, **JuvR 42(C) to JuvR 42(E)**
Premarital agreements, action to set aside, **ORC 2106.22**
Presumption of spouse's death, dissolution, **ORC 2121.04**
Probate judge solemnizing, fees, **ORC 2101.27**
Promise, enforcement, **ORC 1335.05**
Records in probate court, **ORC 2101.12**
Remarriage, revival of property rights under will, **ORC 2107.33**
Same sex marriage prohibited, **O Const XV § 11**
Separation, legal. See LEGAL SEPARATION
Statute of frauds, applicable to promises of, **ORC 1335.05**
Ward, effect on guardianship, **ORC 2111.45**
Wills, effect, **ORC 2107.37**

MATERNITY PROCEEDINGS
Generally, **ORC 3111.17**
See also PARENTAGE ACTIONS, for general provisions

MEDIATION
Franklin county probate court, **FrankR 78.5**
Guardianship, **SumR 98.1**
Juvenile courts establishing procedures, **ORC 2151.542**
Probate courts establishing procedures, **ORC 2101.163**

MEDIATORS
Courts of common pleas, custody and visitation disputes, **SupR 16**

MEDICAID EXPENSES AND PAYMENTS
Estate recovery program, **ORC 2113.041**
Mental retardation and developmental disabilities boards, county, **ORC 5123.0411, ORC 5123.0412**
Mental retardation and developmental disabilities department, **ORC 5123.047**

MEDICAL AND MENTAL EXAMINATIONS
Child
    Order for pursuant to juvenile court proceeding, **JuvR 32**
    Transfer for criminal prosecution, **JuvR 30(B), JuvR 30(F), JuvR 30(G), JuvR 30(C), ORC 2152.12**
Child custody, parties and children, **ORC 3109.04(C)**
Competency, to determine
    Defendant awaiting trial, **ORC 2945.371**
    Fees for evaluation, **ORC 2945.371**
Court ordering, **JuvR 32, ORC 2152.12**
Defendants
    Competence to stand trial, **ORC 2945.371**
Definition, **JuvR 2**
Detention home residents, **JuvR 7(I)**
Fees, competency examination, **ORC 2945.371**
    Prior to appointment of guardian, **ORC 2111.031**
Incompetent person, prior to guardian's appointment, **ORC 2111.031**
Juvenile proceedings, **ORC 2151.53**
Transfer of juvenile for criminal prosecution, **JuvR 30(B), JuvR 30(F), JuvR 30(G), JuvR 30(C), ORC 2152.12**
Waiver, **ORC 2152.12(C)**

MEDICAL SCHOOLS
Corpses, dissection; consent requirement, **ORC 2108.52**
Mental retardation and developmental disabilities department, agreements with, **ORC 5123.11**

MEDICINE
Practice of. See PHYSICIANS

MEMBER STATES
Interstate Compact on Placement of Children, **ORC 5103.20**

MENTAL ANGUISH
Wrongful death action to recover damages for, **ORC 2125.02**

MENTAL EXAMINATIONS
See MEDICAL AND MENTAL EXAMINATIONS

MENTAL HEALTH DEPARTMENT
Institutions
    See also at Hospitalization
    See also CHARITABLE INSTITUTIONS
    See also MENTALLY ILL PERSONS
    Inspections, **ORC 5122.301**
Patients. See MENTALLY ILL PERSONS, at Hospitalization
Quality assurance records, confidentiality and disclosure, **ORC 5122.32**
    Penalty, **ORC 5122.99**
Records and reports
    Quality assurance, **ORC 5122.32**
        Penalty, **ORC 5122.99**

MENTAL HEALTH TREATMENT
Declarations for mental health treatment. See MENTALLY ILL PERSONS

MENTAL INJURY
Defined, **ORC 2151.011**

MENTAL RETARDATION AND DEVELOPMENTAL DISABILITIES BOARDS, COUNTY
Abused or neglected adults, reports as to, **ORC 5126.31, ORC 5126.311**
Application to sell facility to acquire replacement facility, **ORC 5126.37**
Appropriations, **ORC 5123.351**
Assessment of institutionalized individuals, **ORC 5123.711**
Autopsies, mentally retarded or developmentally disabled person, petition for post-mortem upon suspicious death, **ORC 2108.521**
Community capital replacement facilities fund, **ORC 5126.375**
Compliance, **ORC 5123.044**
Construction of facilities by, **ORC 5123.36**
Deadline for notification of readiness to acquire replacement facility, **ORC 5126.372**
Definitions, **ORC 5126.30**
Director, agreement to pay percentage of cost of replacement facility, **ORC 5126.373**
Employees
    Mentally retarded and developmentally disabled persons, reporting abuse or neglect, **ORC 5123.61, ORC 5123.99**
    Qualifications, **ORC 5123.351**
Extraordinary costs, **ORC 5123.0413**
Medicaid expenses, **ORC 5123.0411, ORC 5123.0412**
Members
    Mentally retarded and developmentally disabled persons, reporting abuse or neglect, **ORC 5123.61, ORC 5123.99**
Orders
    Ex parte emergency orders, **ORC 5126.331-5126.333**
    Services, orders to arrange, **ORC 5126.33**
Payment of proceeds after sale of facility to acquire replacement facility, **ORC 5126.371**
Plans, review of, **ORC 5123.046**
Real property sales
    Application to sell facility to acquire replacement facility, **ORC 5126.37**
    Payment of proceeds after sale of facility to acquire replacement facility, **ORC 5126.371**
Reimbursement by state, **ORC 5123.351**
Replacement facilities
    Application to sell facility to acquire, **ORC 5126.37**
    Deadline for notification of readiness to acquire replacement facility, **ORC 5126.372**
    Payment of proceeds after sale of facility to acquire replacement facility, **ORC 5126.371**
    Percentage of cost of replacement facility, agreement for director to pay, **ORC 5126.373**
    Rescission of approval to sell facility, **ORC 5126.374**
Rescission of approval to sell facility to acquire replacement facility, **ORC 5126.374**
Residential services
    Comprehensive service plan, **ORC 5123.042**
    Development goals, **ORC 5123.042**
    Patient moving from county-to-county, **ORC 5123.0410**
    Payment for providing services, **ORC 5123.045, ORC 5123.049**
    Recommendation of providers, **ORC 5123.042**
Rules, **ORC 5123.351, ORC 5126.34**
Superintendent
    Mentally retarded and developmentally disabled persons, reporting abuse or neglect, **ORC 5123.61, ORC 5123.99**
Training, minimum standards, **ORC 5126.34**
Units, programs, and services; certification and funding, **ORC 5123.351, ORC 5123.36**

MENTAL RETARDATION AND DEVELOPMENTAL DISABILITIES DEPARTMENT
Accounts and accounting, **ORC 5123.26, ORC 5123.30**
Administrative complaint resolution procedures, **ORC 5123.043**
Agreement by director to pay replacement costs, **ORC 5123.373**
Alternative facilities, **ORC 5123.032**
Annual report, **ORC 5123.33**

MENTAL RETARDATION AND DEVELOPMENTAL DISABILITIES DEPARTMENT—continued

Application to sell facility to acquire replacement facility, **ORC 5123.37**
Appropriation of real property, **ORC 5123.22**
Audits of contracts for residential services, **ORC 5123.18**
Audits of services and programs funded by, **ORC 5123.02, ORC 5123.06**
Autopsies, petition for post-mortem upon suspicious death of mentally retarded or developmentally disabled person, **ORC 2108.521**
Beds in residential facility beds, maximum number, **ORC 5123.26**
Branch institutions, **ORC 5123.092**
Buildings. See Institutions, this heading
Citizen's advisory councils, **ORC 5123.092, ORC 5123.093**
Closure commission, **ORC 5123.032**
Closure of developmental centers, **ORC 5123.032**
Colleges and universities, agreements for residency training programs with, **ORC 5123.12**
Community mental retardation and developmental disabilities trust fund, **ORC 5123.352**
Compliance, **ORC 5123.044**
Contracts
    Equipment and supplies, purchase, **ORC 5123.25**
    Fiduciary capacity, liability, **ORC 5815.35**
    Residential services, **ORC 5123.18**
County board workers
    Immunity, **ORC 5123.422**
    Medication, assisting patients in administration of, **ORC 5123.651**
Criminal records check of applicants and employees, **ORC 5123.081**
Definitions
    Adoption of rules establishing, **ORC 5123.011**
    Developmental center, **ORC 5123.032**
    Residential services, **ORC 5123.18**
Deputy director, **ORC 5123.05**
Director, **ORC 5123.04**
    Appointment powers
        Citizen's advisory councils, **ORC 5123.092**
        Deputy director, **ORC 5123.05**
        Divisions, **ORC 5123.05**
        Institution management officers, **ORC 5123.09**
Discharged resident, personal effects of, **ORC 5123.851**
Divisions, **ORC 5123.05, ORC 5123.06**
Double billings for care of mentally retarded, **ORC 5123.181**
Eligibility determinations, **ORC 5123.012**
Employees, **ORC 5123.06, ORC 5123.08 to 5123.09**
    Bonds, **ORC 5123.10**
    Certification or registration, **ORC 5123.082**
        Child support noncompliance, denial or suspension for, **ORC 5123.083**
        Crimes and offenses; denial, suspension, or revocation, **ORC 5123.082**
        Criminal records check of applicants and employees, **ORC 5123.081**
    Removal, **ORC 5123.031**
Equipment and supplies, purchasing, **ORC 5123.25**
Federal aid, **ORC 5123.35**
Fiduciary, agency under contract with as, **ORC 2109.01**
    Bond, **ORC 2109.04**
Fiduciary, as
    Liability, **ORC 5815.35**
Forms, **ORC 5123.031**
Funds, **ORC 5123.26**
    Institutions, **ORC 5123.29**
Gifts or bequests to, **ORC 5123.27**
Guardian, as, **ORC 2111.01**
    Liability, **ORC 5815.35**
Immunity, county board workers, **ORC 5123.422**
Independent study of closure of developmental centers, **ORC 5123.032**
Institutions, **ORC 5123.03**
    See also CHARITABLE INSTITUTIONS; MENTALLY RETARDED AND DEVELOPMENTALLY DISABLED

MENTAL RETARDATION AND DEVELOPMENTAL DISABILITIES DEPARTMENT—continued

Institutions, **ORC 5123.03**—continued
    PERSONS, at Institutionalization
    Abuse of residents or staff, reporting, **ORC 5123.093, ORC 5123.51 to 5123.54**
    Accidents, reporting, **ORC 5123.093**
    Attorney general's duties, **ORC 5123.90**
    Branch institutions, **ORC 5123.092**
    Citizen's advisory council, **ORC 5123.092, ORC 5123.093**
        Mentally retarded and developmentally disabled persons, reporting abuse or neglect, **ORC 5123.61, ORC 5123.99**
    Closure of developmental centers, **ORC 5123.032**
    Commissary fund, **ORC 5123.29**
    Deaths, reporting, **ORC 5123.093**
    Diseases, reporting, **ORC 5123.093**
    Drugs
        Administration errors, reporting, **ORC 5123.093**
    Funds, **ORC 5123.29, ORC 5123.30**
    Independent study of closure of developmental centers, **ORC 5123.032**
    Industrial and entertainment fund, **ORC 5123.29**
    Inspections
        Department director, by, **ORC 5123.031**
    Location of businesses near, **ORC 5123.24**
    Management, economic, **ORC 5123.34**
    Managing officers, **ORC 5123.09**
    Nonpartisan management, **ORC 5123.031**
    Notice of closure of developmental centers, **ORC 5123.032**
    Police officers, special, **ORC 5123.13**
    Purposes, **ORC 5123.34**
        Change, **ORC 5123.091**
    Reports, **ORC 5123.031**
    Residential services, provision after closure of, **ORC 5123.182**
    Residents. See MENTALLY RETARDED AND DEVELOPMENTALLY DISABLED PERSONS, at Institutionalization
    Respite care services, **ORC 5123.171**
    Suicides, reporting, **ORC 5123.093**
    Superintendents, **ORC 5123.09**
    Theft, reporting, **ORC 5123.093**
Investigating powers, **ORC 5123.14**
Investigations
    Notice to legal rights service ombudsman section, **ORC 5123.604**
    Reports of incidents of neglect or abuse, independent review or investigation, **ORC 5123.614**
Investigators, appointment, **ORC 5123.15**
Licensing
    Home care workers, unlicensed, **ORC 5123.47**
Managing officers of institutions, **ORC 5123.09**
Maximum number of residential facility beds, **ORC 5123.26**
Medicaid payments, **ORC 5123.047**
Medical schools, agreements with, **ORC 5123.11**
Medication, county board worker assisting patient in administration of, **ORC 5123.651**
Minors, powers and duties, **ORC 5123.122**
MR/DD Community capital replacement facilities fund, **ORC 5123.375**
Nonpartisan management of institutions, **ORC 5123.031**
Notice
    Closure of developmental centers, **ORC 5123.032**
    Entities required to give notice of conduct causing possible inclusion in registry of abusive or neglectful employees, **ORC 5123.542**
Notification deadline, sale of facility to acquire replacement, **ORC 5123.372**
Oil and gas leases, **ORC 5123.23**
Payment agreements, **ORC 5123.047, ORC 5123.051**
Payment of proceeds after sale of facility, **ORC 5123.371**
Personal effects of discharged resident, **ORC 5123.851**
Plans, review of, **ORC 5123.046**
Powers and duties, **ORC 5123.02, ORC 5123.03**
Protective service system, **ORC 5123.55 to 5123.58**

MENTAL RETARDATION AND DEVELOPMENTAL DISABILITIES DEPARTMENT

Index-78

MENTAL RETARDATION AND DEVELOPMENTAL DISABILITIES DEPARTMENT—continued

Providers, residential care
    Reimbursement of expenses, **ORC 5123.172**
    Reports by, **ORC 5123.172**
Psychological residency training programs, agreements with, **ORC 5123.11**
Purchase of service fund, **ORC 5123.051**
Purchasing of supplies and equipment, **ORC 5123.25**
Real property
    Appropriation, **ORC 5123.22**
    Farming, **ORC 5123.221**
    Oil and gas leases, **ORC 5123.23**
Reassignment of employees, **ORC 5123.08**
Receivership petitions, residential care facilities, **ORC 5123.191**
Records and reports, **ORC 5123.31, ORC 5123.613**
    See also MENTALLY RETARDED AND DEVELOPMENTALLY DISABLED PERSONS, at Institutionalization
    Abuse and neglect, **ORC 5123.51 to 5123.54**
    Annual report, **ORC 5123.33**
    Incidents of neglect or abuse, **ORC 5123.611 et seq.**
    Independent review or investigation, **ORC 5123.614**
    Institutions, **ORC 5123.031**
    Providers of residential care, by, **ORC 5123.172**
    Rules regarding reporting of incidents, **ORC 5123.612**
Registry of abusive or neglectful employees
    Generally, **ORC 5123.50 et seq.**
    Creation, **ORC 5123.52**
    Definitions, **ORC 5123.50**
    Entities required to give notice of conduct causing possible inclusion in registry, **ORC 5123.542**
    Hearings and notice, **ORC 5123.51**
    Investigations, **ORC 5123.51**
    Notice, entities required to give notice of conduct causing possible inclusion in registry, **ORC 5123.542**
    Removal from registry, **ORC 5123.53**
    Reporting of violations, **ORC 5123.541**
    Review of reports, **ORC 5123.51**
    Rules, **ORC 5123.54**
    Sexual conduct, prohibited, **ORC 5123.541**
Registry office, **ORC 5123.61**
Reinstatement rights of employees, **ORC 5123.08**
Rescission of approval to sell facility, **ORC 5123.374**
Research bureau, **ORC 5123.07**
Residential services
    Adoption of rules, **ORC 5123.04**
    Closing of facility, provision of after, **ORC 5123.182**
    Contracts, **ORC 5123.18**
    Development goals, **ORC 5123.042**
    Former residents of closed institutions, **ORC 5123.211**
    Maximum number of residential facility beds, **ORC 5123.26**
    Minors, **ORC 5123.122**
    Payment for providing services, **ORC 5123.045**
    Powers and duties, **ORC 5123.18 to 5123.19**
    Provision after closure of institution, **ORC 5123.182**
    Rulemaking powers, **ORC 5123.042**
Respite care services, **ORC 5123.171**
Rulemaking powers
    Definitions, **ORC 5123.011**
    Employees, certification or registration, **ORC 5123.082**
    Residential services, **ORC 5123.042, ORC 5123.18**
    Trusts for disabled persons, **ORC 5123.04**
Sale of facility to acquire replacement
    Generally, **ORC 5123.37**
    Agreement by director to pay replacement costs, **ORC 5123.373**
    Application to sell facility to acquire replacement facility, **ORC 5123.37**
    MR/DD Community capital replacement facilities fund, **ORC 5123.375**
    Notification deadline, **ORC 5123.372**
    Payment of proceeds after sale, **ORC 5123.371**

MENTAL RETARDATION AND DEVELOPMENTAL DISABILITIES DEPARTMENT—continued

Sale of facility to acquire replacement—continued
    Rescission of approval to sell facility, **ORC 5123.374**
Special police officers, **ORC 5123.13**
Specialized services for mentally retarded persons, determination by, **ORC 5123.021**
State planning council, **ORC 5123.35**
Superintendents of institutions, **ORC 5123.09**
Support payments for patients, collection by
    Waiver, **ORC 5123.194**
Supported living, **ORC 5123.182**
Trustee, as. See Fiduciary, as, this heading
Universities and colleges, agreements for residency training programs with, **ORC 5123.12**
Unlicensed in-home care workers, **ORC 5123.47**
Waiver of of collection of support payments, transition to independent living, **ORC 5123.194**

MENTALLY ILL PERSONS

Actions for commitment. See Hearings on hospitalization, this heading
Aftercare and outpatient services, **ORC 5122.231**
Annulment, grounds for, **ORC 3105.31(C)**
Attorney for, when . See Hearings on hospitalization, this heading
Child, jurisdiction, **ORC 2151.23**
Consent to treatment
    Declarations for treatment. See Declarations for mental health treatment, this heading
    Medication, informed consent hearing, **ORC 2101.24**
Death during hospitalization. See Hospitalization, this heading
Declarations for mental health treatment
    Alternate proxy, **ORC 2135.02**
    Appointment of proxy, **ORC 2135.13**
    Compliance with declaration by provider, **ORC 2135.07**
    Definitions, **ORC 2135.01**
    Designation of proxy, **ORC 2135.05**
    Dispute resolution, **ORC 2135.13**
    Execution of declaration governing treatment, **ORC 2135.02**
    Form of declaration, **ORC 2135.14**
    Informed consent, **ORC 2135.02**
    Insurance issues, prohibited conduct, **ORC 2135.11**
    Liability of care provider, **ORC 2135.10**
    Liability of proxy, **ORC 2135.08**
    Operation of declaration, **ORC 2135.04**
    Priority of declarations, **ORC 2135.12**
    Prohibited conduct, **ORC 2135.11**
    Provider unwilling to comply with declaration, **ORC 2135.07**
    Proxy
        Alternate, **ORC 2135.02**
        Appointment, **ORC 2135.13**
        Designation, **ORC 2135.05**
        Liability, **ORC 2135.08**
    Renewal of declaration, **ORC 2135.02**
    Revocation of declaration, **ORC 2135.02, ORC 2135.09**
    Time period for validity of declaration, **ORC 2135.02**
    Validity of declaration, **ORC 2135.02, ORC 2135.06**
Defendants. See DEFENDANTS, at Incompetent to stand trial
Definitions, **ORC 2135.01, ORC 2151.011, ORC 5122.01**
    Legal disability, **ORC 2131.02**
    Patient, **ORC 5122.44**
Disability, considered to be under. See DISABILITY, PERSONS UNDER
Discharge from hospital, **ORC 5122.02, ORC 5122.21**
    Hearing on commitment not held, **ORC 5122.15**
    Hospital failing to meet standards of care and failing to transfer patient, following, **ORC 5122.27**
    Probable cause for hospitalization lacking, **ORC 5122.141**
    Refusal to accept treatment, as grounds, **ORC 5122.02**
Disclosure of information, **ORC 5122.31**
Dower rights, **ORC 5305.17 to 5305.22**
    See also DOWER
Drivers' licenses, restrictions, **ORC 4507.08**

MENTALLY ILL PERSONS—continued

Emergency hospitalization, **ORC 5122.09, ORC 5122.10**
Eminent domain proceedings, representation, **ORC 163.11**
Estate, probate court fee, **ORC 2101.16**
Evidence to determine mental status, **ORC 5122.13 to 5122.15**
Full hearing, **ORC 5122.141, ORC 5122.15**
    See also Hearings on hospitalization, this heading, for general provisions
Guardianship, **ORC Ch 2111**
    See also GUARDIANSHIP
Hearings on hospitalization, **ORC 5122.12, ORC 5122.12 to 5122.15, ORC 5122.38**
    Attorney for respondent, **HamR 75.1, ORC 5122.15**
        Fees, **ORC 5122.43**
        Legal rights service, **ORC 5123.60**
    Closed to public, when, **ORC 5122.15**
    Continuing hospitalization, **ORC 5122.15**
    Expenses, **ORC 5122.36, ORC 5122.43**
    Full hearing, **ORC 5122.141, ORC 5122.15**
    Investigation by court, **ORC 5122.13**
    Juvenile procedure rules, applicability, **JuvR 1(C)**
    Magistrates, appointment, **FrankR 8.1**
    Notice, **ORC 5122.12**
    Open to public, when, **ORC 5122.15**
    Prehearing medical examination, **ORC 5122.14**
    Probable cause hearing, **ORC 5122.12**
    Records and reports, confidentiality, **SupR 55(C)**
        Contempt, unauthorized disclosure, **SupR 55(D)**
    Referees, powers to conduct, **ORC 5122.15**
    Rehearings, **ORC 5122.25**
    Review hearings, **ORC 5122.15**
    Rules of Civil Procedure, applicability, **ORC 5122.15**
    Rules of Juvenile Procedure, applicability, **JuvR 1(C)**
    Testimony, respondent's right to provide or withhold, **ORC 5122.15**
    Time limitations, **ORC 5122.141**
    Transcript, **ORC 5122.36**
    Transcripts, **ORC 5122.15**
    Transfer of patients, **ORC 5122.15**
    Waiver, **ORC 5122.141**
Hospitalization, **ORC 5122.05 to 5122.19**
    Absent without leave patients, **ORC 5122.26**
    Affidavit, filing in probate court, **ORC 5122.11**
    Assault and battery, protection during, **ORC 5122.29**
    Attorney's role. See Hearings on hospitalization, this heading
    Burial, lists. See Compilations, persons buried in cemeteries on or adjacent to grounds, this heading
    Certification of mental illness by head of hospital, **ORC 5122.19**
    Civil rights, **ORC 5122.301**
    Clothing, **ORC 5123.39**
    Compilations, persons buried in cemeteries on or adjacent to grounds
        Generally, **5122.44-5122.47**
        Access to records of Department of Mental Health, **5122.46**
        Definitions, **5122.44**
        Historical society, copies to be deposited with, **5122.47**
        State library, copies to be deposited with, **5122.47**
    Complaints of patients during, investigations, **ORC 5122.33**
    Consent to medical treatment, **ORC 5122.271**
    Court ordering. See Hearings on hospitalization, this heading
    Death during
        Burial, lists. See Compilations, persons buried in cemeteries on or adjacent to grounds, this heading
        Notice to family, **ORC 5122.23**
    Declarations for treatment. See Declarations for mental health treatment, this heading
    Defendant in criminal prosecution, **ORC 2945.38(C), ORC 2945.38(D)**
    Discharge. See Discharge from hospital, this heading
    Emergency, **ORC 5122.09, ORC 5122.10**
    Escape, apprehension, **ORC 5122.26**

MENTALLY ILL PERSONS—continued

Hospitalization, **ORC 5122.05 to 5122.19**—continued
    Federal facility, in, **ORC 5122.16**
    Habeas corpus, **ORC 5122.30**
    Hearings. See Hearings on hospitalization, this heading
    Involuntary, **ORC 5122.05 to 5122.19**
    Judicial, **ORC 5122.11, ORC 5122.11 to 5122.19**
    Juvenile procedure rules, applicability, **JuvR 1(C)**
    Labor performed during, **ORC 5122.28**
    Legal rights service, **ORC 5123.60**
    Liability for assisting, **ORC 5122.34**
    Medical examination after admission, **ORC 5122.19**
    Not guilty by reason of insanity. See NOT GUILTY BY REASON OF INSANITY
    Notice to family, **ORC 5122.18**
    Patients
        Definitions, **ORC 5122.44**
        Rights, **ORC 5122.05**
    Privacy during, **ORC 5122.29**
    Probable cause hearing, **ORC 5122.12**
    Purpose of laws, **ORC 5122.42**
    Records and reports, **ORC 5122.33, ORC 5122.36, ORC 5122.41**
        Access to burial records, **ORC 5122.46**
        Disclosure of information, **ORC 5122.31**
        Expungement, **ORC 5122.141**
        Legal rights service, access, **ORC 5123.60**
    Religious healing, involuntary commitment, **ORC 5122.05**
    Religious services during, **ORC 5122.29**
    Review hearings. See Review hearings, this heading
    Rights of patients, **ORC 5122.27 to 5122.31, ORC 5122.42**
        Treatment, refusing, **ORC 5122.271**
    Standards of care, **ORC 5122.27**
    Statutory construction, **ORC 5122.42**
    Temporary, **ORC 5122.17**
    Transfer between institutions, **ORC 5122.20**
    Treatment
        Consent, **ORC 5122.271**
        Declarations for treatment. See Declarations for mental health treatment, this heading
        Refusal, **ORC 5122.271**
    Visiting rights, **ORC 5122.29**
Involuntary hospitalization, **ORC 5122.05 to 5122.19**
    See also Hospitalization, generally, this heading
Judicial hospitalization, **ORC 5122.11, ORC 5122.11 to 5122.19**
    See also Hearings on hospitalization, this heading
Jurisdiction, **ORC 2101.24**
Legal disability, under, **ORC 2131.02**
    See also DISABILITY, PERSONS UNDER, generally
Legal rights service, **ORC 5123.60**
Medical aid. See Hospitalization, this heading
Medication, informed consent hearings, **ORC 2101.24**
Minors, outpatient mental health services for, **ORC 5122.04**
Not guilty by reason of insanity. See NOT GUILTY BY REASON OF INSANITY
Outpatient mental health services for minors, **ORC 5122.04**
Parole
    Discharge from hospital, **ORC 5122.21**
Probable cause hearing, **ORC 5122.12**
    See also Hearings on hospitalization, this heading, for general provisions
Probationer
    Discharge from hospital, **ORC 5122.21**
Psychiatrist, appointment, **HamR 75.1**
Quality assurance records, confidentiality and disclosure, **ORC 5122.32**
    Penalty, **ORC 5122.99**
Real property, sale by trustee of nonresident, **ORC 2127.43**
Records and reports, **ORC 5122.33, ORC 5122.36, ORC 5122.41**
    Disclosure of information, **ORC 5122.31**
    Expungement, **ORC 5122.141**
    Legal rights service, annual report, **ORC 5123.60**

MENTALLY ILL PERSONS—Cont'd
Records and reports, ORC 5122.33, ORC 5122.36, ORC 5122.41—Cont'd
    Probate court records, confidentiality, **SupR 55(C)**
    Contempt, unauthorized disclosure, **SupR 55(D)**
    Quality assurance, **ORC 5122.32**
    Penalty, **ORC 5122.99**
Review hearings, **ORC 5122.15**
    See also Hearings on hospitalization, this heading, for general provisions
Supplemental services
    Definitions, **ORC 5815.28**
Support. See Hospitalization, this heading
Surviving spouse, effect on election, **ORC 2106.08**
Temporary hospitalization, **ORC 5122.17**
Transfer of mental patients, **ORC 5122.20**
Transfer of patients, hearings, **ORC 5122.15**
Treatment. See Hospitalization, this heading
Trial visits, **ORC 5122.22**
Vital statistics, **ORC 5122.23**
Voluntary commitment, **HamR 75.1**
Voluntary hospitalization, **ORC 5122.02, ORC 5122.03**
    See also Hospitalization, generally, this heading
    Declarations for treatment. See Declarations for mental health treatment, this heading
    Notice to family, **ORC 5122.18**
    Release rights, **ORC 5122.03**
    Transfer to another hospital, **ORC 5122.20**

MENTALLY RETARDED AND DEVELOPMENTALLY DISABLED PERSONS
Abuse or neglect to be reported, **ORC 5123.61, ORC 5126.31, ORC 5126.311**
Adoption of, **ORC 3107.02**
Annulment, grounds for, **ORC 3105.31(C)**
Autopsies, petition for post-mortem upon suspicious death, **ORC 2108.521**
Bill of rights, **ORC 5123.62**
Biological risk, definition, **ORC 5123.011**
Community mental retardation and developmental disabilities trust fund, **ORC 5123.352**
Definitions, **ORC 2151.011, ORC 5123.01, ORC 5123.011**
    Residential services, **ORC 5123.18**
Developmental delay, definition, **ORC 5123.011**
Disability, considered to be under. See DISABILITY, PERSONS UNDER, generally
Discharge from institution, **ORC 5123.79**
    Aftercare and outpatient services, **ORC 5123.82**
    Expenses, **ORC 5123.801**
    Money and property, disposition, **ORC 5123.28**
    Probable cause for institutionalization found lacking, **ORC 5123.76**
    Records and reports, **ORC 5123.31, ORC 5123.811**
    Voluntarily institutionalized persons, **ORC 5123.69, ORC 5123.70**
Drivers' licenses, restrictions, **ORC 4507.08**
Eligibility for services
    Continuation, **ORC 5123.012**
    Determination, **ORC 5123.012**
Environmental risk, definition, **ORC 5123.011**
Established risk, definition, **ORC 5123.011**
Evidence of mental retardation, **ORC 5123.76**
Federal aid, **ORC 5123.35**
Fiduciaries for, **ORC 2127.43, ORC Ch 2109, ORC Ch 2111**
    See also FIDUCIARIES; GUARDIANSHIP, generally
Guardianship, **ORC 2109.01, ORC 5123.55 to 5123.59, ORC 5123.93, ORC 5123.95, ORC Ch 2111**
    See also GUARDIANSHIP, generally
Hearings on institutionalization, **ORC 5123.701 to 5123.77**
    Attorney for respondent, **ORC 5123.75, ORC 5123.76**
    Civil Procedure Rules, applicability, **ORC 5123.76**
    Costs, **ORC 5123.96**

MENTALLY RETARDED AND DEVELOPMENTALLY DISABLED PERSONS—continued
Hearings on institutionalization, **ORC 5123.701 to 5123.77**—continued
    Evaluation of mental status, **ORC 5123.74**
    Juvenile procedure rules, applicability, **JuvR 1(C)**
    Notice, **ORC 5123.73**
    Observation and habilitation prior to, **ORC 5123.74**
    Recommendations of board, **ORC 5123.74**
    Records and reports, **ORC 5123.97**
    Referees, powers to conduct, **ORC 5123.76**
    Time limitations, **ORC 5123.75**
Institutionalization
    Absence without leave, **ORC 5123.81**
        Apprehension, **ORC 5123.801**
        Money and property, disposition, **ORC 5123.28**
        Report, **ORC 5123.811**
    Assessment by county board of mental retardation and developmental disabilities, **ORC 5123.711**
    Capacity of institution not to be exceeded, **ORC 5123.76**
    Care outside state institution, **ORC 5123.17 to 5123.21**
    Civil rights, **ORC 5123.83**
    Clothing, **ORC 5123.39**
    Communication rights, **ORC 5123.84**
    Consent to medical procedures, **ORC 5123.86**
    Continuing periods of commitment, **ORC 5123.76**
    Death during, **ORC 5123.811**
        Money and property, disposition, **ORC 5123.28**
        Records, **ORC 5123.31**
    Defendant in criminal prosecution, **ORC 2945.38(C), ORC 2945.38(D)**
    Determinations by mental retardation and developmental disabilities department, **ORC 5123.012**
    Discharge. See Discharge from institution, this heading
    Habeas corpus
        Notice to attorney general, **ORC 5123.90**
        Rights, **ORC 5123.88**
    Habilitation goals, **ORC 5123.85**
    Hearings. See Hearings on institutionalization, this heading
    Involuntary, **ORC 5123.71 to 5123.77**
        Affidavits, **ORC 5123.71**
        Assessment by county board of mental retardation and developmental disabilities, **ORC 5123.711**
        Report, **ORC 5123.71**
        Evaluation report, **ORC 5123.71**
        Rights of involuntarily detained person, **ORC 5123.71**
        Temporary detention, court order for, **ORC 5123.74**
        Time limit, **ORC 5123.76**
    Juvenile procedure rules, applicability, **JuvR 1(C)**
    Labor performed during, **ORC 5123.87**
    Legal rights service, **ORC 5123.60**
    Liability for assisting in institutionalization proceedings, **ORC 5123.91**
    Maximum number of residential facility beds, **ORC 5123.196**
    Medical procedures, consent, **ORC 5123.86**
    Money and property, disposition, **ORC 5123.28**
    Plans for care, **ORC 5123.85**
    Probable cause hearings, **ORC 5123.71 to 5123.76**
    Purposes, **ORC 5123.67**
    Records and reports, **ORC 5123.89, ORC 5123.95**
        Admission, upon, **ORC 5123.76**
        Citizen's advisory council to have access, **ORC 5123.092**
        Evaluation and annual review, **ORC 5123.57**
        Legal rights service, **ORC 5123.60**
        Mental retardation and developmental disabilities department, to, **ORC 5123.31**
        Probate court records, confidentiality, **SupR 55(C)**
        Contempt, unauthorized disclosure, **SupR 55(D)**
    Religious healing, **ORC 5123.86**
    Rights during and after, **ORC 5123.83 to 5123.89**
    Short-term, **ORC 5123.701**

MENTALLY RETARDED AND DEVELOPMENTALLY DISABLED PERSONS—*continued*
Institutionalization—*continued*
  Support
    Minors, **ORC 5123.122**
  Temporary
    Detention prior to, **ORC 5123.77**
    Voluntary, **ORC 5123.701**
  Transfer between institutions, **ORC 5123.21**
  Trial visits, **ORC 5123.80**
    Reports, **ORC 5123.811**
  Visiting rights, **ORC 5123.84**
  Voluntary, **ORC 5123.69**
    Release, **ORC 5123.70**
    Short-term care, **ORC 5123.701**
Institutions
  Construction, reimbursement, **ORC 5123.36**
  State-supported. See MENTAL RETARDATION AND DEVELOPMENTAL DISABILITIES DEPARTMENT, at Institutions
Intermediate care facilities
  Respite care services, **ORC 5123.171**
Involuntary institutionalization, **ORC 5123.71 to 5123.77**
  See also Institutionalization, this heading, for general provisions
Jurisdiction, **ORC 2101.24**
Juvenile courts, testimony of, **ORC 2152.821**
Legal disability, considered to be under, **ORC 2131.02**
  See also DISABILITY, PERSONS UNDER
Legal rights service, **ORC 5123.60**
Minors. See MINORS
Not guilty by reason of insanity, **ORC 5123.76**
Nursing and rest homes
  Determination of need for specialized services, **ORC 5123.021**
    Prior to admission, **ORC 5123.021(B)**
    Significant change in resident's physical or mental condition, following, **ORC 5123.021(C)**
Outpatient care, insurance coverage, **ORC 5123.82**
Petition for post-mortem upon suspicious death, **ORC 2108.521**
Protective service system, **ORC 5123.55 to 5123.58**
Records of institutionalization. See Institutionalization, this heading
Residential care facilities for, **ORC 5123.18 to 5123.20**
  Closing, provision of residential services after, **ORC 5123.182**
  Contracts, **ORC 5123.18**
  Former residents of closed institutions, **ORC 5123.211**
  Minors, for, **ORC 5123.122**
Rights list, **ORC 5123.62**
  Compliance by providers, **ORC 5123.64**
  Distribution, **ORC 5123.63**
  Violations, remedies, **ORC 5123.64**
Services provided by county board of mental retardation and developmental disabilities, court order for, **ORC 5123.74**
Short-term institutionalization, **ORC 5123.701**
State planning council, **ORC 5123.35**
Substantial functional limitation, definition, **ORC 5123.011**
Support. See Institutionalization, this heading
Supported living for, **ORC 5123.182**
Suspicious death, petition for post-mortem upon suspicious death, **ORC 2108.521**
Testimony of, juvenile courts, **ORC 2152.821**
Trial visits, **ORC 5123.80**
  Reports, **ORC 5123.811**
Trustees, **ORC 2109.01, ORC 5123.55 to 5123.59**
  See also FIDUCIARIES
Venue for institutionalization proceedings, **ORC 5123.92**
Voluntary institutionalization, **ORC 5123.69**
  See also Institutionalization, this heading
  Release, **ORC 5123.70**
  Short-term, **ORC 5123.701**

MERCY KILLING
Living will not authorizing, **ORC 2133.12**

MERGER AND CONSOLIDATION
Trust companies, effect on fiduciary duties, **ORC 2109.28**

MILITARY SERVICE
Death of servicemen, presumed decedents' law, **ORC Ch 2121**
  See also PRESUMED DECEDENTS
Fiduciary duties, effect, **ORC 2109.25**
Income tax
  Extensions, state, **ORC 5747.026**
  Refunds, military injury relief fund, **ORC 5747.113**
Missing servicemen
  Estate tax exemption on pay, **ORC 5731.15**
  Presumed decedents' law, **ORC Ch 2121**
    See also PRESUMED DECEDENTS
Veterans. See VETERANS

MINERAL RIGHTS
Fiduciaries, powers, **ORC 2127.07**
Guardians
  Leases by, **ORC 2111.26**
    Appraisal, **ORC 2111.30**
  Sale, **ORC 2127.07**
Lease of real property for
  Mental retardation and developmental disabilities department, by, **ORC 5123.23**
Trust property, as
  Royalties, allocation between income and principal, **ORC 5812.34**

MINORS
See also PARENT AND CHILD
Abandoned. See DEPENDENT AND NEGLECTED CHILDREN, generally
Abortion. See ABORTION, at Parental consent, complaint for abortion without
Abuse. See CHILD ABUSE
Actions involving, **ORC Ch 2151**
  See also JUVENILE COURTS
Adoption, **ORC Ch 3107**
  See also ADOPTION
Afterborn. See PARENT AND CHILD, at Posthumous children
Afterborn. See PARENT AND CHILD, at Posthumous children; PRETERMITTED HEIRS
Age of majority, **ORC 3109.01**
Alternative diversion programs, **ORC 2151.331**
Anatomical gifts, **ORC 2108.02, ORC 2108.04**
Application for finding of emancipation, **ORC 2111.181**
Arrest, **JuvR 6, ORC 2151.27 to 2151.33**
  Fingerprinting, **ORC 2151.313**
  Photographs, **ORC 2151.313**
Assault by, parental liability, **ORC 3109.10**
Camps for. See CAMPS AND CAMPING
Care of, criminal record check as prerequisite, **ORC 2151.86, ORC 2151.861**
Change of name, **ORC 2717.01**
Charitable institutions for. See CHARITABLE INSTITUTIONS, at Children, for
Commitment to public or private agency, **ORC 2151.353(A)**
Condominium owners, dower action, **ORC 5305.11, ORC 5305.13**
Consent to marriage
  Jurisdiction, **ORC 2151.23**
  Juvenile court, by, **JuvR 42**
Correctional institutions housing, **ORC 2151.311(C), ORC 2152.26(C)**
Crimes and offenses by, liability of parent
  Assault, **ORC 3109.10**
  Theft or destruction of property, **ORC 3109.09**
Criminal prosecution, transfer from juvenile court, **JuvR 30**
Cruelty to. See CHILD ABUSE
Custody. See CUSTODY OF CHILDREN, DOMESTIC
Custody. See CUSTODY OF CHILDREN, DOMESTIC; CUSTODY OF CHILDREN
Damages, liability. See DAMAGES, at Juvenile delinquents, liability
Dangerous surroundings, removal from, **JuvR 6**

MINORS

MINORS—*continued*
Definitions. See DEFINITIONS, at Children
Delinquents. See JUVENILE DELINQUENCY
Dependent. See DEPENDENT AND NEGLECTED CHILDREN
Descent and distribution, **ORC 2105.06**
    See also DESCENT AND DISTRIBUTION
Deserted child, **ORC 2151.3515 to 2151.3530**
Destruction of property, liability, **ORC 3109.09**
Detention. See CUSTODY OF CHILDREN, INSTITUTIONAL
Disability, considered to be under. See DISABILITY, PERSONS UNDER
Divorce of parents. See CUSTODY OF CHILDREN, DOMESTIC
Driver's license
    Suspension, unruly child, **ORC 2151.354, ORC 2151.355**
Drivers' licenses, **ORC 4507.07**
    Juvenile driver improvement programs, **ORC 4510.31, ORC 4510.33**
    Occupational driving privileges, **ORC 4510.31, ORC 4510.33**
    Probationary
        Restrictions, **ORC 4507.071**
    Suspension or revocation, **ORC 4507.021, ORC 4510.31, ORC 4510.33**
Drunk driving, **ORC 4511.19**
Education. See SCHOOLS AND SCHOOL DISTRICTS
Emancipation, application to probate court, **ORC 2111.181**
Emergency medical treatment, court order, **JuvR 13(C)**
Eminent domain proceedings, representation, **ORC 163.11**
Estates of
    Deposit of funds on behalf of, **SupR 67**
    Probate court fee, **ORC 2101.16**
    Trustees' bond, **ORC 2109.05**
Executor, as, **ORC 2113.13**
Expungement of records, right to, **JuvR 34(J)**
Felonies committed by. See JUVENILE DELINQUENCY
Female
    Pregnant, consent of juvenile court for marriage, **JuvR 42**
Female, pregnant; consent of juvenile court for marriage, **JuvR 42(C) to JuvR 42(E)**
Foster homes. See FOSTER HOMES, at Juvenile facilities
Guardians. See GUARDIANS AD LITEM
Hamilton county probate court
    Personal injury claims, settlement, **HamR 68.1**
        Structured settlements, **HamR 68.2**
        § 10,000 or less, **HamR 67.1**
Ill or injured, taking custody of, **JuvR 6**
Illegitimate, **ORC 3111.01 to 3111.19**
    See also ILLEGITIMATE CHILDREN; PARENTAGE ACTIONS
Interstate compacts, **ORC 2151.56 to 2151.61**
    Jurisdiction of juvenile courts, **ORC 2151.23**
Intestate succession, **ORC 2105.06**
    See also DESCENT AND DISTRIBUTION
Jail confinement, **JuvR 7(H)**
Juvenile courts, **ORC Ch 2151**
    See also JUVENILE COURTS
Legal disability, considered to be under. See DISABILITY, PERSONS UNDER
Legitimacy. See ILLEGITIMATE CHILDREN; PARENTAGE ACTIONS
Liability
    Damages. See DAMAGES, at Juvenile delinquents, liability
    Destruction of property, **ORC 3109.09**
    Parental. See Crimes and offenses by, liability of parent, this heading
    Theft, **ORC 3109.09**
Lucas county probate court
    Personal injuries, settlement of claims for, **LucasR 68.1**
        § 10,000 or less, **LucasR 68.2**
Marriage
    Annulment due to age, **ORC 3105.31(A)**

MINORS—*continued*
Marriage—*continued*
    Consent
        Jurisdiction, **ORC 2151.23**
        Juvenile court, by, **JuvR 42**
Mental or physical examination
    Court order, **JuvR 32**
    Detention, during, **JuvR 7(I)**
    Transfer for criminal prosecution, **JuvR 30(B), JuvR 30(F), JuvR 30(G), JuvR 30(C)**
Mentally ill
    Guardianship, **ORC 5122.39**
    Outpatient mental health services for, **ORC 5122.04**
Mentally ill, jurisdiction, **ORC 2151.23**
Mentally retarded or developmentally disabled
    Guardianship, **ORC 5123.93**
    Short-term institutionalization, **ORC 5123.701**
    Support when institutionalized, **ORC 5123.122**
Motor vehicles
    Negligent operation, parental liability, **ORC 4507.07**
    Traffic offenses. See TRAFFIC OFFENSES, at Juveniles, by
Name change, **ORC 2717.01**
    Parental consent lacking, hearings, **SumR 93.1**
Neglected. See DEPENDENT AND NEGLECTED CHILDREN
Negligence in motor vehicle operation, parental liability, **ORC 4507.07**
Nonsupport. See DEPENDENT AND NEGLECTED CHILDREN
Orphans. See ORPHANS
Outpatient mental health services for, **ORC 5122.04**
Parents. See PARENT AND CHILD
Parents, as
    Adoption, legal rights, **ORC 5103.16**
    Parents of minor parents, duty of support imposed, **ORC 3109.19**
Paternity, presumption, **ORC 3111.03**
Paternity proceedings. See PARENTAGE ACTIONS
Payors
    Delivery of monies to person specified by probate court order, **ORC 2111.131(A)**
    Liability, disposition of monies, **ORC 2111.131(C)**
Personal injury settlements, **LucasR 68.1, ORC 2111.18, ORC 2111.181, SumR 68.1**
    Approval, **HamR 68.1**
    Separate case number, **Sup. R 68.1**
    Structured settlements, **HamR 68.2, Sup. R 68.2**
    Ten thousand dollars or less, **HamR 67.1**
    Under § 10,000, **LucasR 68.2, SumR 67.1**
Posthumous. See PARENT AND CHILD
Posthumous. See PARENT AND CHILD; PRETERMITTED HEIRS
Pregnant, consent of juvenile court for marriage, **JuvR 42(C) to JuvR 42(E)**
Probation. See PROBATION, at Juveniles
Proceedings against. See JUVENILE COURTS
Records, expungement, **JuvR 34(J)**
Residence, legal, **ORC 2151.06**
Runaways. See RUNAWAYS
Runaways. See RUNAWAYS; UNRULY CHILDREN
Schools for. See SCHOOLS AND SCHOOL DISTRICTS
Securities, transfers to, **ORC 5814.04**
Service of process on, **ORC 2151.28**
Settlement of damage claims, **ORC 2111.18, ORC 2111.181, SupR 68**
Shelter care. See CUSTODY OF CHILDREN, INSTITUTIONAL
Shelter care. See CUSTODY OF CHILDREN, INSTITUTIONAL; DETENTION HOMES
Social history, court order, **JuvR 32**
Stark county probate court
    Birth certificate filed with application for appointment, **Sup. R 66.1**
    Estates of § 10,000 or less, **Sup. R 67.1**
    Personal injury claims, settlement
        Separate case number, **Sup. R 68.1**
        Structured settlements, **Sup. R 68.2**
    Settlements, court costs, **Sup. R 58.1**

MINORS—continued
Summit county probate court
    Settlement of injury claims, **SumR 68.1**
    § 10,000 or less, **SumR 67.1**
Support. See CHILD SUPPORT
Surrender of custody, voluntary, **JuvR 38**
    Permanent custody, **JuvR 38(B)**
    Temporary custody, **JuvR 38(A)**
Termination of parental rights. See CUSTODY OF CHILDREN, INSTITUTIONAL, at Permanent
Theft, liability, **ORC 3109.09**
Traffic offenders. See TRAFFIC OFFENSES, at Juveniles, by
Transfers to. See TRANSFERS TO MINORS ACT
Transfers to, securities, **ORC 5814.04**
Trusts for. See TRUSTS, generally
Unborn. See UNBORN CHILDREN
Uniform Child Custody Jurisdiction Act, **ORC 3109.21 to 3109.32**
Unruly. See UNRULY CHILDREN
Visitation rights. See VISITATION RIGHTS, generally
Warrant against, **JuvR 15(E), JuvR 15(D), JuvR 16(B)**
Youth services department. See YOUTH SERVICES DEPARTMENT

MISCONDUCT IN OFFICE
Probate court appointees
    Liability of judge, **ORC 2101.11(C)**

MISDEMEANORS
Sentences. See SENTENCES

MISJOINDER
See JOINDER OF PARTIES

MISREPRESENTATION
See FRAUD

MISSING PERSONS
Estates, **ORC Ch 2119**
    Disposition, **ORC 2101.24**
Presumption of death, **ORC Ch 2121**
    See also PRESUMED DECEDENTS
Servicemen. See PRESUMED DECEDENTS
Trusts and trustees for absentee, **ORC Ch 2119**

MODIFIED BUSINESS INCOME
Defined, **ORC 5747.01**

MODIFIED NONBUSINESS INCOME
Defined, **ORC 5747.01**

MONEY, PUBLIC
See FUNDS, PUBLIC

MONTGOMERY COUNTY PROBATE COURT
Accounts, **MontR 64.1**
Adoption, **MontR 83.1**
Application for letter of authority, **MontR 60.1**
Application to sell property, **MontR 63.1**
Appraisers, **MontR 61.1**
Attorney fees
    Schedule, **MontR Appx A**
Auctioneers and clerks, employment of, **MontR 80.1**
Case management, **MontR 78.1**
Certificate, attorney's, **MontR Appx F**
Claims against estate, **MontR 62.1**
Compliance, **MontR 77.1**
Computation of fees
    Attorneys, **MontR Appx D**
    Fiduciaries, **MontR Appx C**
Conduct of court, **MontR 54.1**
Consent to payment of attorneys' fees, **MontR Appx E**
Continuances, **MontR 56.1**
Counsel fees, **MontR 71.1**
Court security, **MontR 84.1**

MONTGOMERY COUNTY PROBATE COURT
—continued
Deposits, **MontR Appx B**
Deposits for court costs, **MontR 58.1**
Disclaimers, **MontR 89.1**
Estates of minors, small, **MontR 67.1**
Examination of probate records, **MontR 55.1**
Exceptions, **MontR 76.1**
Executor's and administrator's compensation, **MontR 72.1**
Filings and judgment entries, **MontR 57.1**
Forms
    Generally, **MontR 51.1**
    Computer generated, **MontR 52.1**
Guardian ad litem, qualification of, **MontR 81.1**
Guardian's compensation, **MontR 73.1**
Guardianships, **MontR 66.1**
Hours of court, **MontR 53.1**
Inventory, **MontR 79.1**
Jury management plan, **MontR 85.1**
Land sales, **MontR 65.1**
Magistrates, **MontR 86.1**
Record, **MontR 87.1**
Relieving estate from administration, **MontR 88.1**
Settlement of claims against adult ward, **MontR 69.1**
Settlement of minor's claims, **MontR 68.1**
Settlement of wrongful death claims, **MontR 70.1**
Testamentary trustee, acceptance of duties, **MontR 82.1**
Trustee's compensation, **MontR 74.1**
Wills, **MontR 59.1**

MORTGAGES
Estate tax deductions, **ORC 5731.16**
Estates
    Claims against, **ORC 2117.29**
    Debt payments, effect of contributions to, **ORC 2107.54**
    Fiduciary's power, **ORC 2109.46 to 2109.48, ORC 2113.44 to 2113.47**
    No right of exoneration, **ORC 2113.52**
    Sale of, security, **ORC 2127.36**
Fees, probate court, **ORC 2101.16**
Foreclosure. See FORECLOSURE
Guardian selling land subject to, **ORC 2127.20**
    Release, **ORC 2127.19**
Missing person's estate, **ORC 2119.04**
Power of attorney, **1337.01 et seq., ORC Ch 1337**
Prepayment, eminent domain as reason for, **ORC 163.61**
Probate court fee, **ORC 2101.16**

MORTICIANS
Eyes, enucleation, **ORC 2108.071, ORC 2108.60**

MORTMAIN STATUTE
See LEGACIES AND DEVISES, at Charitable bequests

MOTIONS
Continuing jurisdiction, **JuvR 35(A)**
Custody of children, for permanent custody by welfare agency, **ORC 2151.413, ORC 2151.414**
Discovery, compelling; hearing, **JuvR 22(D)**
Extension of time to make, **JuvR 18(B), JuvR 22(E)**
Facsimile transmission, by, **JuvR 8**
Franklin county probate court, **FrankR 78.1**
Hamilton county probate court, **HamR 57.1, HamR 78.2**
Jurisdiction, continuing, **JuvR 35(A)**
Juvenile proceedings. See JUVENILE COURTS
Lucas county probate court, **LucasR 78.1**
Prehearing, **JuvR 22(E), JuvR 22(D)**
Procedural requirements, **SumR 57.1(C)**
Service of process, **JuvR 18(D)**
Stark county probate court, **Sup. R 78.7**
Summit county probate court, **SumR 57.1**

MOTIONS

MOTIONS—*continued*
Time for making, **JuvR 18(D)**
  Extensions, **JuvR 18(B), JuvR 22(E)**

MOTOR VEHICLE INSURANCE
Operation of vehicle without
  Criminal forfeiture of motor vehicles, **ORC 4507.021**

MOTOR VEHICLES
Certificates of title. See Transfer of ownership, this heading
Criminal forfeiture, **ORC 4507.021**
Drivers' licenses. See DRIVERS' LICENSES
Forfeiture, **ORC 4507.021**
Joint ownership with right of survivorship, **ORC 2131.12**
  Certificates of title, **ORC 4505.06**
  Designation in beneficiary form, **ORC 2131.13**
  Transfer of ownership, **ORC 4505.10**
Negligent operation by minor, parental liability, **ORC 4507.07**
Odometer reading statement on certificate of title, **ORC 4505.06**
Ownership
  Joint ownership with right of survivorship, **ORC 2131.12**
  Transfer. See Transfer of ownership, this heading
Sales
  Audit by taxation department, **ORC 4505.06**
  Dealers, certificates of title, **ORC 4505.06**
  Investigations by taxation department, **ORC 4505.06**
  Unpaid sales tax, certificate of title denied, **ORC 4505.06**
Serial number, estate inventory to include, **ORC 2115.09**
Traffic offenses. See TRAFFIC OFFENSES
Transfer of ownership
  Certificates of title, **ORC 4505.06**
    Issuance, **ORC 4505.10**
  Decedent's vehicle, **ORC 2106.18, ORC 4505.10**
  Joint ownership with right of survivorship, **ORC 2131.12, ORC 4505.10**
Unauthorized use, permitting
  Criminal forfeiture of motor vehicles, **ORC 4507.021**

MOTOR VEHICLES BUREAU
Anatomical gifts
  Second chance trust fund, **ORC 2108.17**

MUNICIPAL CORPORATIONS
Charitable institutions. See CHARITABLE INSTITUTIONS
Eminent domain. See EMINENT DOMAIN, generally
Escheated property, powers and duties, **ORC 2105.09**
  See also ESCHEAT
Funds, estate tax revenue distribution, **ORC 5731.48**
Gifts and bequests to, estate tax deductions, **ORC 5731.17**
Home rule, **O Const XVIII § 3**
Ordinances, **O Const XVIII § 3**
Powers and duties, **O Const XVIII § 3**
Resolutions, **O Const XVIII § 3**

MUNICIPAL COURTS
Arbitration, **SupR 15**
Assignment of cases, **SupR 36**
Competency of defendant, procedure to determine, **ORC 2945.37(H)**
Continuances
  Reporting, **SupR 41(D)**
Costs. See COURT COSTS
Court reporters, **SupR 11**
Criminal prosecutions
  Competency of defendant, procedure to determine, **ORC 2945.37(H)**
Destruction of court records, **SupR 26(E)**
Equipment and supplies
  Videotaping, **SupR 13**
Incompetency of defendant, procedure to determine, **ORC 2945.37(H)**
Judges, **O Const IV § 5**
  Assignment of cases, **SupR 36**

MUNICIPAL COURTS—*continued*
Records and reports
  Continuances, **SupR 41(D)**
  Court records, management and retention, **SupR 26**
    Administrative records, retention schedule, **SupR 26.01**
Rules of superintendence. See RULES OF SUPERINTENDENCE
Sessions, **SupR 36**
Videotape recording of proceedings, **SupR 11**

MUNICIPAL FINANCE
Generally, **O Const XVIII § 10**

MUNICIPAL ORDINANCES AND RESOLUTIONS
Generally, **O Const XVIII § 3**

MURDER
Parent convicted of killing other parent, **ORC 3109.41 to 3109.48**
Person convicted of not to benefit from death, **ORC 2105.19**

MUSEUMS
Art galleries and museums, probate court's authorization to deposit works in, **ORC 2109.14**

NAMES
Change, **ORC 2717.01, SumR 93.1**
  Court costs, **Sup. R 58.1**
  Fees, **CuyR 58.1, ORC 2101.16**
  Minors
    Parental consent lacking, hearing, **SumR 93.1**
  Notice, **ORC 2717.01**
  Persons, **ORC 2717.01**
Mental retardation and developmental disabilities institutions, **ORC 5123.03**
Notice of change, **ORC 2717.01**

NATIONAL GUARD
See MILITARY SERVICE

NATIVE AMERICANS
Adoption requirements, **ORC 3107.12**

NEEDY PERSONS
See INDIGENT PERSONS

NEGLECT
See also ABANDONMENT
Adoption, abuse and neglect determination summary report, **ORC 3107.034**
Adults. See ABUSED OR NEGLECTED ADULTS
Aged persons, **ORC 5101.60 to 5101.71**
  See also PROTECTIVE SERVICES FOR ADULTS
Children. See CHILD ABUSE
Children. See CHILD ABUSE; DEPENDENT AND NEGLECTED CHILDREN
Fiduciaries, removal for neglect of duty, **ORC 2109.24**

NEGLIGENCE
See also TORTS
Child's operation of motor vehicle, parental liability, **ORC 4507.07**
Death caused by, **ORC Ch 2125**
Death caused by.
  See also WRONGFUL DEATH
Limitation of actions, **ORC 2305.09**
Wrongful death resulting from, **ORC Ch 2125**
  See also WRONGFUL DEATH

NEWBORNS
See MINORS, generally
Birth certificates. See BIRTH CERTIFICATES
Deserted children. See DESERTED CHILD
Illegitimate children. See ILLEGITIMATE CHILDREN

NEWSPAPERS
See INDIGENT PERSONS

NEWSPAPERS—continued
Service by publication. See SERVICE OF PROCESS, at Publication, by
Trials, recording and photographing, **SupR 12**

NEXT OF KIN
Anatomical gifts by, **ORC 2108.02**
    Eyes, objection to removal, **ORC 2108.60**
    Pituitary glands, objection to removal, **ORC 2108.53**
Autopsies, consent by, **ORC 2108.50**
Construed, **ORC 2105.03**
Declaratory judgments sought by. See DECLARATORY JUDGMENTS
Defined, **ORC 2105.02, ORC 2111.01**
Descent and distribution, **ORC 2105.06**
    See also DESCENT AND DISTRIBUTION
Heirs. See HEIRS
Intestate succession, **ORC 2105.06**
    See also DESCENT AND DISTRIBUTION
Visitation rights to child's relative
    Illegitimate child, **ORC 3109.12**
Wrongful death actions, beneficiaries, **ORC 2125.02**

NO ADMINISTRATION
Generally, **ORC 2113.03, ORC 2113.04**
Commissioner, appointment, **Sup. R 75.2**
Court costs, **CuyR 58.1, SumR Appx A**
Election to receive mansion house, **ORC 2106.10(D)**
Fees, **ORC 2101.16**
Forms, **ORC 2105.03**
Franklin county probate court, **FrankR 75.5**
Notice, **Sup. R 75.2**
Wages, release of, **ORC 2113.04**

NONBUSINESS INCOME
Defined, **ORC 5747.01**

NONCHARITABLE IRREVOCABLE TRUSTS
Modification or termination of noncharitable irrevocable trust by consent, **ORC 5804.11**

NONCHARITABLE TRUSTS
Ascertainable beneficiary, creation of noncharitable trust without, **ORC 5804.09**

NON-CUSTODIAL PARENT
Defined under Interstate Compact on Placement of Children, **ORC 5103.20**

NON-MEMBER STATE
Defined under Interstate Compact on Placement of Children, **ORC 5103.20**

NONPROFIT CORPORATIONS
See also CORPORATIONS
Charitable trusts. See CHARITABLE TRUSTS
Gifts and bequests to
    Estate tax deduction, **ORC 5731.17**
Guardianship, eligibility, **ORC 2111.10**
Mentally retarded or developmentally disabled persons, protective services, **ORC 2111.10**

NONRESIDENTS
Administration of estate, **ORC Ch 2129**
    See also ANCILLARY ADMINISTRATION
Annulment action, notice by publication, **ORC 3105.06**
Beneficiaries of trust funds, **ORC 2109.57**
Correction of birth, **SumR 95.1(B)**
Divorce action, notice by publication, **ORC 3105.06**
Estate tax, **ORC 5731.19, ORC 5731.36**
    Apportionment of tax, **ORC 2113.90**
    Transfer of assets, **ORC 5731.40**
Estates of nonresident decedents. See ESTATES
Executors. See EXECUTORS AND ADMINISTRATORS

NONRESIDENTS—continued
Fiduciaries, appointment, **Sup. R 60.1**
Guardians as. See GUARDIANSHIP
Income tax liability, **ORC 5747.01, ORC 5747.05(A)**
    Adjusted gross income, changes, **ORC 5747.05(B)**
    Assessment upon failure to file return, **ORC 5747.13(A)**
    Nonresident pass-through entity investors, **ORC 5747.08(D)**
    Nonresident taxpayer credit, **ORC 5747.05(I)**
Juvenile rehabilitation facilities, admittance to, **ORC 2151.654**
Juveniles, placement, **ORC 2151.39, ORC 2151.654**
Legal separation action, notice by publication, **ORC 3105.06**
Minors, **ORC 2151.39, ORC 2151.654**
Service of process on. See SERVICE OF PROCESS
Wards. See GUARDIANSHIP, at Nonresidency
Witnesses to will, **ORC 2107.17**

NONSECURE CARE, SUPERVISION, OR TRAINING
Definitions, **ORC 2151.011**

NOT GUILTY BY REASON OF INSANITY
Applicability of provisions, **ORC 5122.011**
Battered woman syndrome, **ORC 2945.392**
Commitment, **ORC 2945.40**
    Conditional release, **ORC 2945.402**
    Hearing, **ORC 2945.401(B)**
        Burden of proof, **ORC 2945.401(G)**
        Defendant's rights, **ORC 2945.401(F)**
        Modification of recommendation, **ORC 2945.401(I)**
        Prosecutor's duties, **ORC 2945.401(H)**
    Least restrictive alternative, **ORC 2945.40(F)**
    Nonsecured status, **ORC 2945.401**
    Prosecutor's duties, **ORC 2945.40(G)**
    Records and reports, **ORC 2945.401(C)**
    Termination, **ORC 2945.401**
        Evidence, **ORC 2945.401(E)**
        Jurisdiction, **ORC 2945.401(J)**
        Recommendation of chief clinical officer, **ORC 2945.401(D)**
    Voluntary commitment prohibited, **ORC 2945.40(H), ORC 5123.69**
Conditional release, **ORC 2945.402**
    Return to more restrictive setting, **ORC 5123.76**
Definition, **ORC 2901.01**
Discharge following verdict, **ORC 2945.40(A), ORC 2945.40(E)**
Discharge from hospital, **ORC 5122.21**
Disclosure of information, **ORC 5122.31**
Escape, arrests, **ORC 5123.13**
Evaluation of defendant
    Battered woman syndrome, **ORC 2945.371**
    Confidential information, **ORC 2945.371**
Expert witnesses, appointment, **ORC 2945.40(C)**
Habeas corpus, **ORC 5122.30**
Hearings on hospitalization or institutionalization, **ORC 2945.40(A), ORC 2945.401(B)**
    Burden of proof, **ORC 2945.401(G)**
    Court's duty to inform defendant of rights, **ORC 2945.40(C)**
    Defendant's attendance, **ORC 2945.40(C)**
    Defendant's rights, **ORC 2945.401(F)**
    Modification of recommendation, **ORC 2945.401(I)**
    Open to the public, **ORC 2945.40(D)**
    Prosecutor's duties, **ORC 2945.401(H)**
    Record of proceedings, **ORC 2945.40(D)**
    Time limits, **ORC 2945.40(B)**
Impairment of reason not defense, **ORC 2945.391**
Inheritance from dead victim prohibited, **ORC 2105.19**
Institutionalization
    Applicability of provisions, **ORC 5123.011**
    Hearings on. See Hearings on hospitalization or institutionalization, this heading
Jurisdiction, **ORC 2945.401(A)**
Mentally retarded persons, **ORC 5123.76**
    Short-term institutionalization, **ORC 5123.701**

NOT GUILTY BY REASON OF INSANITY—continued
Transfer to another institution, ORC 5122.20
Verdict, ORC 2945.40(A)
Voluntary commitment prohibited, ORC 2945.40(H), ORC 5123.69
Voluntary hospitalization, ORC 5122.02

NOTARY PUBLIC
Grandparent power of attorney, 3109.54

NOTES
Generally, See BONDS AND NOTES
Promissory. See PROMISSORY NOTES

NOTICE
See also SERVICE OF PROCESS
Abortion for minor without parental consent, SupR Form 24-C
    Appeals, SupR Form 23-C
    Notifying physicians of affidavits alleging abuse, SupR 24
Abused or neglected adult, ORC 5126.33, ORC 5126.333
Admission to probate. See PROBATE OF WILLS
Adoption, ORC 3107.11
    Hearing on withdrawal of consent, ORC 3107.084(B)
    Social and medical histories, correction or expansion, ORC 3107.17
Ancillary administrators, appointment, ORC 2129.08
Annulment action, ORC 3105.06
Attorney of record, juvenile proceedings, JuvR 4(D)
Closure of developmental centers, mental retardation and developmental disabilities department, ORC 5123.032
Communicable disease of accused sex offender, notice to victim, ORC 2151.14
Continuing jurisdiction, JuvR 35(A)
Criminal prosecutions
    Delinquents, ORC 2152.12(D)
Default judgment, paternity proceedings, ORC 3111.08
Definitions, ORC 5801.03
Detention of child, JuvR 7(E), JuvR 7(C)
    Hearing, JuvR 7(F)
Distribution of assets of estate prior to expiration of time period for filing claims against estate, ORC 2117.06
Divorce action, ORC 3105.06
Durable power of attorney for health care, decisions and determinations made under, ORC 1337.16
Eminent domain proceedings, ORC 163.59
Estate tax. See ESTATE TAX
Estates
    See also EXECUTORS AND ADMINISTRATORS
    Distribution of assets, ORC 2113.533
    Public sales, ORC 2113.41
    Release from administration, ORC 2113.03
Executors and administrators. See EXECUTORS AND ADMINISTRATORS
Fiduciaries. See FIDUCIARIES
Foster care, placement of children outside home county, ORC 2151.55 to 2151.554
Grandparent power of attorney. See GRANDPARENT POWER OF ATTORNEY OR CARETAKER AUTHORIZATION AFFIDAVIT
Grandparent's caretaker authorization affidavit. See GRANDPARENT POWER OF ATTORNEY OR CARETAKER AUTHORIZATION AFFIDAVIT
Guardians. See GUARDIANSHIP
Hamilton county probate court
    Appearance, to compel; delinquent accounts, HamR 64.1
    Hearings
        Attorney fees, application for, HamR Appx A-1
            Waiver, HamR Appx A-3
        Final accounts, HamR 64.1
Heirs. See HEIRS
Hospitalization of mentally ill, ORC 5122.18
    Hearings, ORC 5122.12
Income tax, delinquent payments, ORC 5747.13(A)

NOTICE—continued
Inventory
    Notice of filing, SumR 88.1
Jurisdiction, continuing, JuvR 35(A)
Juvenile courts. See JUVENILE COURTS
Juvenile delinquency, intended dispositional orders, ORC 2151.3510
Legal separation action, ORC 3105.06
Letters of administration, SupR 60
Living wills, determinations made under, ORC 2133.05
Local government fund allocations, ORC 5747.51 to 5747.55
Lucas county probate court
    Affidavit of giving, LucasR 59.1
    Certificate of giving, LucasR 59.2
Mental retardation and developmental disabilities boards, deadline for notification of readiness to acquire replacement facility, ORC 5126.372
Mental retardation and developmental disabilities department
    Closure of developmental centers, ORC 5123.032
    Entities required to give notice of conduct causing possible inclusion in registry of abusive or neglectful employees, ORC 5123.542
Mentally ill, hospitalization, ORC 5122.18
    Hearings, ORC 5122.12
Mentally retarded, hearings on institutionalization, ORC 5123.73
Mentally retarded and developmentally disabled persons, deadline on sale of facility to acquire replacement, ORC 5123.372
Name change, ORC 2717.01
Out of county removal hearings
    Schools and school districts, JuvR 39(A)
Paternity proceedings, ORC 3109.23, ORC 3111.07
    Default judgment, ORC 3111.08
Permanent custody proceedings, ORC 2151.414
Possession of property under eminent domain, ORC 163.59
Probate. See PROBATE OF WILLS
Probate courts. . See SERVICE OF PROCESS
Probate courts. See at Probate courts
Protective services for adults. See PROTECTIVE SERVICES FOR ADULTS
Residential care facilities, proposed facility, ORC 5123.19
Service. See SERVICE OF PROCESS, generally
Stark county probate court
    Estates, relief from administration, Sup. R 75.2(B)
Summit county probate court
    Administrator of will, appointment, SumR 60.1
    Adoption hearings, SumR 94.1(C)
    Attorney fees, SumR Appx F
    Inventory, filing, SumR 88.1
    Wrongful death settlement hearings, SumR 70.1(B)
Surviving spouse. See SURVIVING SPOUSE
Taxes
    Estate tax. See ESTATE TAX
    Income tax, delinquent payments, ORC 5747.13(A)
Transfer for criminal prosecution, hearing, ORC 2152.12(D)
Trustee for missing person's estate, appointment, ORC 2119.02
Trusts. See TRUSTS
Unruly children, intended dispositional orders, ORC 2151.3510
Wills, admission to probate. See PROBATE OF WILLS

NUNCUPATIVE WILLS
Generally, ORC 2107.60, ORC 2107.61

NURSES AND NURSING
Aged persons suffering neglect, abuse, or exploitation; report to county human services department, ORC 5101.61
Child abuse to be reported, ORC 2151.421
Clinical nurse specialists
    DNR identifications, authority to act and immunity, ORC 2133.211, ORC 2133.22
Database, collection of specimen, ORC 2152.74
Liability, blood tests for alcohol content, ORC 4511.19

NURSING AND REST HOMES
Aged persons suffering neglect, abuse, or exploitation; reporting, **ORC 5101.61**
Intermediate care facility for mentally retarded or developmentally disabled persons
    Licensing, **ORC 5123.19, ORC 5123.192**
Mentally retarded or developmentally disabled persons
    Determination of need for specialized services, **ORC 5123.021**
        Prior to admission, **ORC 5123.021(B)**
        Significant change in resident's physical or mental condition, following, **ORC 5123.021(C)**
    Intermediate care facility for
        Licensing, **ORC 5123.19, ORC 5123.192**
    Temporary detention in, **ORC 5123.77**

OATHS AND AFFIRMATIONS
Accounts, fiduciary; abolishment of requirement, **ORC 2109.30**
    Resigned fiduciaries, **ORC 2109.54**
Administration
    Master commissioners, by, **ORC 2101.17**
    Probate court employees, by, **ORC 2101.11(A)**
    Probate judges, by, **ORC 2101.05**
Paternity, acknowledgment, **ORC 3111.03**
Probate court employees, administration by, **ORC 2101.11(A)**
Probate court master commissioners, administration by, **ORC 2101.07**
Probate judges, **ORC 2101.03**

OBJECTIONS
See also DEFENSES; MOTIONS
Adoption, **ORC 3107.06**
    Eighteen-year-old child, by, **ORC 3107.02**
Durable power of attorney for health care, decisions and determinations made under, **ORC 1337.16**
Filmed court proceedings, to, **SupR 12**
Living wills, determinations made under, **ORC 2133.05**
Magistrate's decision, court ruling on, **JuvR 40(E)**
Videotaped court proceedings, to, **SupR 12**
Videotaped evidence, to, **SupR 13**

OFFICE OF TRUSTEE
See TRUSTEES

OHIO
See STATE

OIL AND GAS
Leases
    Mental retardation and developmental disabilities department, by, **ORC 5123.23**

OPEN ADOPTION
See ADOPTION

ORAL TRUST
Creation, **ORC 5804.07**

ORAL WILLS
Generally, **ORC 2107.60, ORC 2107.61**

ORDERS
Abused or neglected adults. See ABUSED OR NEGLECTED ADULTS
Attachment. See ATTACHMENT
Child support. See CHILD SUPPORT
Contempt. See CONTEMPT
Criminal forfeiture orders, **ORC 4507.021**
Criminal prosecution of minor, transfer, **JuvR 30(G), JuvR 30(H)**
Discovery, compelling, **JuvR 24(B)**
    Failure to comply, **JuvR 24(C)**
Garnishment. See GARNISHMENT
Juvenile courts. See JUVENILE COURTS
Medical treatment of minor, **JuvR 13(C)**
    Payment, **JuvR 13(G)**

ORDERS—continued
Mental examination of child, **JuvR 32, ORC 3109.04(C)**
Mental retardation. See MENTAL RETARDATION AND DEVELOPMENTAL DISABILITIES BOARDS, COUNTY
Paternity, declaration of fatherhood of adult child, **ORC 2105.26**
Physical examination of child, **JuvR 32**
Social history of child, **JuvR 32**
Support orders. See SUPPORT AND MAINTENANCE, generally
Temporary, **JuvR 13**
    Extension, **JuvR 14(B)**
    Modification, **JuvR 14(C)**
    Termination, **JuvR 14(A)**
Transfer of minor for criminal prosecution, **JuvR 30(G), JuvR 30(H)**
    Release of transferred child, **JuvR 30(H)**

ORDINANCES, MUNICIPAL
Generally, **O Const XVIII § 3**

ORPHANS
Adoption, **ORC 5103.16**
Permanent custody by welfare agency, **ORC 2151.414(B)**

OSTEOPATHS
Aged persons suffering neglect, abuse, or exploitation; report to county human services department, **ORC 5101.61**
Statute of frauds, medical prognosis, **ORC 1335.05**

OUT-OF-HOME CARE
Defined, **ORC 2151.011**

OUT-OF-HOME CARE CHILD ABUSE
Defined, **ORC 2151.011**

OUT-OF-HOME CARE CHILD NEGLECT
Defined, **ORC 2151.011**

PARALEGALS
Fees, **Sup. R 75.5**
Registration, **FrankR 75.8**

PARENT AND CHILD
See also MINORS, generally
Abandonment and neglect of child. See DEPENDENT AND NEGLECTED CHILDREN
Abuse of child. See CHILD ABUSE
Acknowledgment of paternity, **ORC 3111.03**
    Finality, **ORC 5101.314**
    Rescission, **ORC 5101.314**
Adequate parental care
    Defined, **ORC 2151.011**
    Disposition of child deemed without, **ORC 2151.353, ORC 2151.414**
Adoption, **ORC Ch 3107**
    See also ADOPTION
Anatomical gifts, **ORC 2108.02, ORC 2108.04**
Artificial insemination, **ORC 3111.88 to 3111.96**
Artificial insemination, non-spousal
    Semen, medical history of donor, **ORC 3111.91**
Assault by child, parental liability, **ORC 3109.10**
Child custody. See CUSTODY OF CHILDREN, DOMESTIC
Death of father, presumption of paternity, **ORC 3111.03**
Definition, **ORC 3109.09, ORC 3111.01**
Dependent and neglected children. See DEPENDENT AND NEGLECTED CHILDREN
Descent and distribution, **ORC 2105.06**
    See also DESCENT AND DISTRIBUTION
Destruction of property by child, parental liability, **ORC 3109.09**
Duty to support
    Acknowledgment of parentage, upon, **ORC 5101.314**
    Parents of minor parents, **ORC 3109.19**
Establishment of relationship, **ORC 3111.02 to 3111.19**
    Acknowledgment of paternity, **ORC 5101.314**

PARENT AND CHILD

PARENT AND CHILD—*continued*
  Establishment of relationship, **ORC 3111.02 to 3111.19**—*continued*
    Parents of minor parents requesting determination, duty of support imposed, **ORC 3109.19**
  Grandparents. See GRANDPARENTS
  Guardianship, eligibility, **ORC 2111.08**
  Illegitimate child, **ORC 2105.17, ORC 3111.01 to 3111.19**
    See also ILLEGITIMATE CHILDREN; PARENTAGE ACTIONS
  Intestate succession, **ORC 2105.06**
    See also DESCENT AND DISTRIBUTION
  Juvenile proceedings. See JUVENILE COURTS
  Liability of parent
    Assault by child, **ORC 3109.10**
    Community service in lieu of judgment in favor of school district, **ORC 3109.09**
    Destruction of property by child, **ORC 3109.09**
    Motor vehicle operation by child, **ORC 4507.07**
    Theft by child, **ORC 3109.09**
  Minor as parent
    Parents of minor parents, duty of support imposed, **ORC 3109.19**
  Mother and child relationship, action to determine, **ORC 3111.17**
    See also PARENTAGE ACTIONS, for general provisions
  Motor vehicle operation by child, parental liability, **ORC 4507.07**
  Parent convicted of killing other parent, **ORC 3109.41 to 3109.48**
  Parentage actions. See PARENTAGE ACTIONS, generally
  Parental rights and duties
    Care, defined, **ORC 2151.05**
    Court supervision, **ORC 2151.359**
    Residual rights, defined, **ORC 2151.011**
    Schooling costs, **ORC 2151.362**
    Termination. See CUSTODY OF CHILDREN, INSTITUTIONAL, at Permanent
  Paternity proceedings. See PARENTAGE ACTIONS
  Posthumous children
    Hearing on account of fiduciary, representation, **ORC 2109.34**
    Intestate succession, **ORC 2105.14**
    Pretermitted heir status, **ORC 2107.34**
      Debt payments, contributions by, **ORC 2107.55**
    Termination; adoption, effect on, **ORC 3107.07, ORC 3107.15**
  Power of attorney
    Generally, **ORC 3109.56-3109.59**
    Grandparents, by. See GRANDPARENT POWER OF ATTORNEY OR CARETAKER AUTHORIZATION AFFIDAVIT
  Presumption of paternity, **ORC 3111.03**
  Relationship
    Definition, **ORC 3111.01**
    Establishment, **ORC 3111.02 to 3111.19**
  Residence, **ORC 2151.06**
  Stepchildren, descent and distribution, **ORC 2105.06**
    See also DESCENT AND DISTRIBUTION, generally
  Support and maintenance. See CHILD SUPPORT
  Termination of parental rights. See CUSTODY OF CHILDREN, INSTITUTIONAL, at Permanent
  Theft by child, parental liability, **ORC 3109.09**
  Transfers to minors. See TRANSFERS TO MINORS ACT
  Trusts, representation by fiduciaries and parents, **ORC 5803.03**
  Unborn children. See Posthumous children, this heading
  Unfit parent, **ORC 2151.05**
  Uniform Parentage Act, **ORC 3111.01 to 3111.19**
  Visitation rights after divorce or separation, **ORC 3109.051**
    See also VISITATION RIGHTS
  Will contests. See CONTEST OF WILL
  Wrongful death action, **ORC 2125.02**

PARENTAGE ACTIONS
  Generally, **ORC 3111.01 to 3111.19**
  See also ILLEGITIMATE CHILDREN
  Acknowledgment of paternity, **ORC 3111.03**
    Child support actions subsequent to filing of, **ORC 2151.232**
    Consent to adoption, **ORC 3107.06**

PARENTAGE ACTIONS—*continued*
  Acknowledgment of paternity, **ORC 3111.03**—*continued*
    Court costs, **Sup. R 58.1**
    Duty to support child, **ORC 3103.031**
    Finality, **ORC 5101.314**
    Parent and child relationship, establishment, **ORC 3111.02**
    Rescission, **ORC 2151.232, ORC 5101.314**
  Actions, priority by juvenile court, **ORC 3111.12**
  Agreements
    Compromise agreements, **ORC 3111.19**
  Alleged father to pay child support pending determination, **ORC 3111.111**
  Attorney for child, **ORC 3111.07**
  Birth mother regarded as natural mother, effect of husband's consent, **ORC 3111.97**
  Birth records
    Corrections, **ORC 3111.13, ORC 3111.58**
    New, issuance, **ORC 3111.18**
  Bond
    Child support payments, to enforce, **ORC 3111.13(F)**
  Child support
    Action for converted into, **ORC 2151.232**
    Administrative support orders. See Administrative support orders, this heading
    Alleged father to pay pending court determination, **ORC 3111.111**
    Garnishment of wages to pay, **ORC 3111.13(F)**
  Civil rules, applicability, **ORC 3111.08**
  Compromise agreements, **ORC 3111.19**
  Confession of judgment, **ORC 3111.08**
  Conflicting presumptions, **ORC 3111.03**
  Consent, birth mother regarded as natural mother, effect of husband's consent, **ORC 3111.97**
  Costs. See Fees and costs, this heading
  Costs of pregnancy, confinement, and genetic testing, **ORC 3111.12**
  Counsel for child, **ORC 3111.07**
  Custody action following judgment, **ORC 3111.13**
  Default judgments, **ORC 3111.08**
  Depositions concerning unborn children, **ORC 3111.04**
  Duty to support child, **ORC 3103.031**
  Evidence
    Admissibility, **ORC 3111.10**
    Costs of pregnancy, confinement, and genetic testing, **ORC 3111.12**
    Experts, **ORC 3111.09, ORC 3111.12**
    Rebuttal, **ORC 3111.03**
  Expert witnesses, **ORC 3111.09, ORC 3111.12**
    Fees, **ORC 3111.14**
  Fees and costs, **ORC 3111.14**
    Expert witnesses, **ORC 3111.09, ORC 3111.14**
    Genetic tests, **ORC 3111.09, ORC 3111.14**
  Genetic tests, **ORC 3111.08, ORC 3111.09**
    Child support enforcement agencies providing, **ORC 3111.61**
    Probability of ninety-five per cent or greater, presumption of paternity, **ORC 3111.03**
    Public assistance recipients, **ORC 3111.04, ORC 3111.07**
  HLA tests. See Genetic tests, this heading
  Husband, birth mother regarded as natural mother, effect of husband's consent, **ORC 3111.97**
  Immunity from criminal prosecution, **ORC 3111.12**
  Interference with, **ORC 3111.19**
    Penalties, **ORC 3111.99**
  Intervenors, **ORC 3111.07**
  Judgments, **ORC 3111.08, ORC 3111.13**
    Genetic test results, based on, **ORC 3111.09**
  Jurisdiction, **ORC 2151.23, ORC 2301.03, ORC 3111.06, ORC 3111.381**
    Continuing jurisdiction, **ORC 3111.16**
  Juvenile procedure rules, applicability, **JuvR 1(C)**
  Knowledge of impossibility of paternity
    Action barred, **ORC 3111.07**
  Limitation of actions, **ORC 3111.05**

PARENTAGE ACTIONS—*continued*
Mother and child relationship, applicability of proceedings to determine, **ORC 3111.17**
Natural mother, birth mother regarded as natural mother, effect of husband's consent, **ORC 3111.97**
Notice to parties, **ORC 3111.07**
Parents of minor parents bringing, duty of support imposed, **ORC 3109.19**
Parties to action, **ORC 3111.04, ORC 3111.07**
Physician-patient privilege, applicability, **ORC 3111.12**
Pregnancy-related expenses, liability, **ORC 3111.13, ORC 3111.15**
Presumption, **ORC 3111.03**
    Nonspousal artificial insemination of married woman, **ORC 3111.95**
Pretrial procedure, **ORC 3111.01 to 3111.19**
Requirements to bring actions, **ORC 3111.381**
Self-incrimination, **ORC 3111.12**
Service of process, nonresident defendant, **ORC 3111.06**
Settlement, **ORC 3111.19**
Standing to sue, **ORC 3111.04**
Stay of proceedings, **ORC 3111.04**
Subpoenas, **ORC 3111.12**
Support orders, **ORC 3111.13, ORC 3111.13(F), ORC 3111.15**
    Administrative orders. See Administrative support orders, this heading
    Continuing jurisdiction, **ORC 3111.16**
    Enforcement, **ORC 3111.13(F)**
    Out-of-court settlement in lieu of, **ORC 3111.19**
Unborn children, stay of proceedings, **ORC 3111.04**
Venue, **ORC 3111.06**
Verdicts, **ORC 3111.12**
Visitation rights, **ORC 3111.13**
Witnesses and testimony, **ORC 3111.12**
    Expert witnesses, **ORC 3111.09**
    Fees, **ORC 3111.14**

PARKING VIOLATIONS
Municipal facilities, escheated property, **ORC 2105.09**

PARKS AND RECREATION
Seasonal amusement or recreation establishments
    Age and schooling certificates, minors age sixteen and seventeen, exemption, **ORC 4109.02**

PAROLE
DNA testing of prisoners, **ORC 2901.07**
Mentally ill or retarded parolee
    Discharge from hospital, **ORC 5122.21**
Officers
    Emergency hospitalization of mentally ill, **ORC 5122.10**
Youth services department releasing child on, **ORC 2151.38**

PARTIES TO ACTIONS
See also ACTIONS, generally
Contest of will, **ORC 2107.73**
Death, survival of plaintiff's action, **ORC 2305.21**
Defendants. See DEFENDANTS
Defined, **JuvR 2**
Eminent domain proceedings, **ORC 163.12**
Estates, land sale proceedings, **ORC 2127.12, ORC 2127.13**
Heirship determination, **ORC 2123.02, ORC 2123.06**
Joinder. See JOINDER OF PARTIES
Juvenile proceedings, **ORC 2151.28**
    Definition, **JuvR 2**
    Right to counsel, **JuvR 4(A)**
Land sale proceedings, **ORC 2127.12, ORC 2127.13**
Mental examinations, **JuvR 32**
Paternity proceedings, **ORC 3111.04, ORC 3111.07**
Physical examinations, **JuvR 32**
Presumed decedents' law, **ORC 2121.09**
    Establishment of presumption, **ORC 2121.02**
Service of process on. See SERVICE OF PROCESS

PARTIES TO ACTIONS—*continued*
Wills
    Contests, **ORC 2107.73**
    Petition for declaratory judgment as to validity, **ORC 2107.081**

PARTITION
Dower, **ORC 5305.15**

PARTNERSHIPS
Death of partner
    Liability of executor or administrator for debt or obligation of partnership, **ORC 5815.35**
Executor, administrator or trustee acquiring interest; liability, **ORC 5815.35**
Fraudulent transfers, **ORC 1336.02**
Insolvency, **ORC 1336.02**
Liability
    Executor, administrator or trustee, **ORC 5815.35**
Limited
    Executor, administrator or trustee acquiring interest; liability, **ORC 5815.35**
Trust property, allocation between income and principal, **ORC 5812.18**

PASS-THROUGH ENTITY
Defined, **ORC 5747.01**

PASS-THROUGH ENTITY INVESTOR
Defined, **ORC 5747.01**

PATERNITY PRESUMPTION
Generally, **ORC 3111.03**
Declaration of fatherhood of adult child, **ORC 2105.25, ORC 2105.26**
Nonspousal artificial insemination of married woman, **ORC 3111.95**

PATIENT ABUSE, CRIMINAL
Mentally retarded and developmentally disabled persons, reports of abuse or neglect, **ORC 5123.99**

PATIENTS
Mentally ill. See MENTALLY ILL PERSONS, at Hospitalization
Mentally retarded. See MENTALLY RETARDED AND DEVELOPMENTALLY DISABLED PERSONS, at Institutionalization

PAYMENTS
Claims against estates. See CLAIMS AGAINST ESTATES
Debtors. See DEBTORS AND CREDITORS
Mentally retarded and developmentally disabled persons, sale of facility to acquire replacement, **ORC 5123.371**
Tax. See particular tax concerned

PENAL INSTITUTIONS
Generally, See CORRECTIONAL INSTITUTIONS
Inmates. See IMPRISONMENT
Inmates. See IMPRISONMENT; PRISONERS

PENALTIES
See FINES AND FORFEITURES; SENTENCES

PENITENTIARY
Minors housed in, **ORC 2151.311(C), ORC 2152.26(C)**

PER STIRPES
See DESCENT AND DISTRIBUTION, generally

PERMANENT CUSTODY
Defined, **ORC 2151.011**

PERMANENT SURRENDER
Defined, **ORC 2151.011**

PERPETUITIES, RULE AGAINST
Generally, **ORC 2131.08, ORC 2131.09**

PERSONAL IDENTIFYING INFORMATION
Taking of another's, **ORC 2913.49**

PERSONAL INJURIES
Adult wards, settlement of claims, **SupR 69**
Attorney fees, **CuyR 71.2 et seq.**
Cuyahoga county probate court
    Attorney fees, **CuyR 71.2 et seq.**
Hamilton county probate court
    Minors, settlement, **HamR 68.1**
        Structured settlements, **HamR 68.2**
        § 10,000 or less, **HamR 67.1**
Lucas county probate court
    Minors, settlement, **LucasR 68.1**
        § 10,000 or less, **LucasR 68.2**
Minors, settlement of claims, **HamR 68.1, LucasR 68.1, ORC 2111.18, ORC 2111.181, SumR 68.1, SupR 68**
    Separate case number, **Sup. R 68.1**
    Structured settlements, **HamR 68.2, Sup. R 68.2**
    Under § 10,000, **HamR 67.1, LucasR 68.2, SumR 67.1**
Settlements
    Minors, for, **HamR 68.1, LucasR 68.1, ORC 2111.18, ORC 2111.181, SumR 68.1, SupR 68**
        Separate case number, **Sup. R 68.1**
        Structured settlements, **HamR 68.2, Sup. R 68.2**
        § 10,000 or less, **HamR 67.1, LucasR 68.2, SumR 67.1**
Stark county probate court
    Personal injury claims of minors, settlements
        Separate case number, **Sup. R 68.1**
        Structured settlements, **Sup. R 68.2**
Summit county probate court
    Minors, injury claims, **SumR 68.1**
        § 10,000 or less, **SumR 67.1**
Survival of actions, **ORC 2305.21**
Wards, to, **ORC 2111.18, ORC 2111.181**

PERSONAL PROPERTY
Ancestral, descent and distribution statutes; construction, **ORC 2105.01**
    See also DESCENT AND DISTRIBUTION
Application to sell, executors and administrators, **SupR 63**
Bequests. See LEGACIES AND DEVISES
Damage to
    Survival of actions, **ORC 2305.21**
Descent and distribution, **ORC Ch 2105**
    See also DESCENT AND DISTRIBUTION
Disclaimers of succession to, **ORC 5815.36**
    See also DISCLAIMER OF SUCCESSION TO PROPERTY
Distribution. See DESCENT AND DISTRIBUTION
Estate property. See ASSETS OF ESTATES, generally
Estate tax, **ORC Ch 5731**
Estates. See ASSETS OF ESTATES, generally
Garnishment. See GARNISHMENT, generally
Gifts. See GIFTS AND GRANTS
Legacies. See LEGACIES AND DEVISES
Power of attorney, **ORC 1337.06 et seq.**
Recovery, limitation of actions, **ORC 2305.09**
Sale. See ASSETS OF ESTATES, at Sale
Spouses holding jointly, effect of termination of marriage, **ORC 5815.34**
Succession to, disclaimers, **ORC 5815.36**
    See also DISCLAIMER OF SUCCESSION TO PROPERTY
Taxation. See PERSONAL PROPERTY, TAXATION
Transfer tax. See ESTATE TAX

PERSONAL PROPERTY, TAXATION
Claims against estates to collect, **ORC 2117.18, ORC 2117.19**
Estate tax, **ORC Ch 5731**
    See also ESTATE TAX
Estates owing, **ORC 2117.18, ORC 2117.19**

PETITIONS
See also COMPLAINTS

PETITIONS—*continued*
Adoption. See ADOPTION
Autopsies, mentally retarded or developmentally disabled person, petition for post-mortem upon suspicious death, **ORC 2108.521**
Discharge of land of mentally ill persons, **ORC 5305.18**
Dower, **ORC 5305.02, ORC 5305.18**
Eminent domain, **ORC 163.05 to 163.08**

PHILANTHROPY
See CHARITABLE INSTITUTIONS; CHARITABLE TRUSTS

PHOTOGRAPHS
Juveniles, **ORC 2151.313**
Probate court proceedings, **SupR 54(B)**
Trials, of, **SupR 12**

PHYSICAL EXAMINATIONS
See MEDICAL AND MENTAL EXAMINATIONS

PHYSICIANS
Abortion. See ABORTION, generally
Aged persons suffering neglect, abuse, or exploitation; report to county human services department, **ORC 5101.61**
Anatomical gifts, duties, **ORC 2108.03, ORC 2108.04**
    Eyes, enucleation, **ORC 2108.60**
Artificial insemination
    Failure to comply with statutes, effect, **ORC 3111.96**
    Records and reports, **ORC 3111.93, ORC 3111.94**
    Supervision, **ORC 3111.90**
Autopsies, **ORC 2108.50 to 2108.60**
Child, treatment of; emergency, **JuvR 13(C)**
    Payment, **JuvR 13(G)**
Child abuse to be reported by, **ORC 2151.421**
Death determined by, **ORC 2108.30**
DNA database
    Collection of specimen, **ORC 2152.74**
Emergency hospitalization of mentally ill, **ORC 5122.10**
Emergency treatment of child, **JuvR 13(C), ORC 2151.33**
    Payment, **JuvR 13(G)**
Fees, adoption, **ORC 3107.055**
Immunity
    Acts in reliance on decision under durable power of attorney for health care, **ORC 1337.15**
    Living wills, acts in compliance with, **ORC 2133.11**
Liability
    Blood tests for alcohol content, **ORC 4511.19**
    Determination of death, **ORC 2108.30**
Mentally retarded and developmentally disabled persons, reporting abuse or neglect, **ORC 5123.61, ORC 5123.99**
Physician-patient privilege
    Child abuse reports, **ORC 2151.421**
Privileged communications, parentage actions, **ORC 3111.12**
Prognosis by, **ORC 1335.05**
Statute of frauds, applicability, **ORC 1335.05**

PITUITARY GLANDS
Removal during autopsy, **ORC 2108.53**

PLAINTIFFS
See PARTIES TO ACTIONS

PLANNED PERMANENT LIVING ARRANGEMENT
Defined, **ORC 2151.011**

PLATES
Impounding driver's license plates, **ORC 4507.02**

PLATS AND PLATTING
Real property sale by guardian, **ORC 2127.21**

PLEADINGS
See also COMPLAINTS
Captions. See CAPTIONS

PLEADINGS—*continued*
Counterclaims and cross-claims. See COUNTERCLAIMS AND CROSS-CLAIMS
Filing
    Extension of time, **LucasR 78.3**
    Facsimile transmission, by, **JuvR 8**
Juvenile proceedings, **JuvR 22**
    Service, **JuvR 20**
Leave of court, **SumR 56.1**
Paternity proceedings, **ORC 3109.27**
Service of process, **JuvR 20**
Signing, **LucasR 57.1**

PLEAS
Not guilty by reason of insanity, **ORC 2945.37 to 2945.402**

PODIATRISTS
Aged persons suffering neglect, abuse, or exploitation; report to county human services department, **ORC 5101.61**
Mentally retarded and developmentally disabled persons, reporting abuse or neglect, **ORC 5123.61, ORC 5123.99**
Prognosis by, **ORC 1335.05**
Statute of frauds, applicability, **ORC 1335.05**

POLICE
See also LAW ENFORCEMENT OFFICERS
Emergency hospitalization of mentally ill, **ORC 5122.10**
Fees
    Hospitalization of mentally ill, **ORC 5122.43**
    Institutionalization of mentally retarded, **ORC 5123.96**
Hospitalization of mentally ill by, **ORC 5122.10, ORC 5122.11, ORC 5122.141**
Institutionalization of mentally retarded by, **ORC 5123.81**

POLICE AND FIRE PENSION FUND
Benefits, estate tax, **ORC 5731.09**

POLITICAL SUBDIVISIONS
See COUNTIES; MUNICIPAL CORPORATIONS; TOWNSHIPS

POOR PERSONS
See INDIGENT PERSONS

POST MORTEM EXAMINATIONS
See AUTOPSIES

POSTHUMOUS CHILDREN
See PARENT AND CHILD

POUR-OVER TRUST
Generally, **ORC 2107.63**

POVERTY
See INDIGENT PERSONS

POWER OF APPOINTMENT
Annulment of marriage, effect, **ORC 2107.33**
Disclaimer
    Estate tax, effect on, **ORC 5731.11**
Dissolution of marriage, effect, **ORC 2107.33**
Divorce, effect, **ORC 2107.33**
Estate tax, **ORC 5731.06**
    Disclaimer of interest, **ORC 5731.11**
Fiduciaries. See FIDUCIARIES
Pretermitted heir statute, effect, **ORC 2107.34**
Release
    Partial, effect on estate tax, **ORC 5731.11**
Separation agreement, effect, **ORC 2107.33**
Trusts, representation by holder of general testamentary power of appointment, **ORC 5803.02**
Will to specifically state, **ORC 2107.521**

POWER OF ATTORNEY
Generally, **1337.01 et seq., ORC Ch 1337**

POWER OF ATTORNEY—*continued*
Affidavit, **1337.01**
Creation, **ORC 1337.12, ORC 1337.18**
Death or incompetency of principal, **ORC 1337.091**
Durable power of attorney for health care, **ORC 1337.11 to 1337.20**
    Acknowledgment, **ORC 1337.12**
    Attorney-in-fact, **ORC 1337.13, ORC 1337.19, ORC 1337.20**
    Complaint, decisions and determinations made under, **ORC 1337.16, ORC 2101.24**
    Creation, **ORC 1337.12, ORC 1337.18**
    Definitions, **ORC 1337.11**
    DNR identification, priority, **ORC 1337.12**
    Drivers' licenses, applications, **ORC 4507.06**
    Form, **ORC 1337.17, ORC 1337.18**
    Immunity of physicians, **ORC 1337.15**
    Life-sustaining treatment, refusal of or withdrawal of informed consent to, **ORC 1337.13**
    Living will, priority, **ORC 2133.03**
    May not be required or prohibited, **ORC 1337.16**
    Notice of decisions and determinations made under, **ORC 1337.16**
    Nutrition or hydration, refusal of or withdrawal of informed consent to, **ORC 1337.13**
    Objections to decisions and determinations made under, **ORC 1337.16**
    Probate court, jurisdiction, **ORC 2101.24**
    Records and reports, **ORC 1337.16**
    Transfer of principal, **ORC 1337.16**
    Witnesses, **ORC 1337.12**
Evidence, **ORC 1337.06**
Fees
    County recorder, **ORC 1337.10**
    Probate court, **ORC 2101.16**
Form, durable power of attorney for health care, **ORC 1337.18**
Grandparents. See GRANDPARENT POWER OF ATTORNEY OR CARETAKER AUTHORIZATION AFFIDAVIT
Grandparents, by. See GRANDPARENT POWER OF ATTORNEY OR CARETAKER AUTHORIZATION AFFIDAVIT
Guardian
    Person nominated for power of attorney as guardian also, **ORC 2111.02**
Health care, for. See Durable power of attorney for health care, this heading
Parent, generally. See PARENT AND CHILD
Probate court fee, **ORC 2101.16**
Revocation, **ORC 1337.091**
    Spouse, revocation of spouse's power of attorney upon divorce, dissolution, or separation, **ORC 5815.32**
Revocation, fee, **ORC 2101.16**

POWER OF WITHDRAWAL
Defined, **ORC 5801.01**

POWERS
Appointment, of. See POWER OF APPOINTMENT
Attorney, of. See POWER OF ATTORNEY
Courts. See JURISDICTION
Courts. See particular court concerned

PRACTICE OF MEDICINE
See PHYSICIANS

PRAECIPES
See NOTICE; SUMMONS

PREGNANCY
Artificial insemination, **ORC 3111.88 to 3111.96**
Living will, effect, **ORC 2133.06**
Minor, marriage application, **JuvR 42(G), JuvR 42(H), JuvR 42(C) to JuvR 42(E)**
Paternity proceedings, **ORC 3111.01 to 3111.19**
    See also PARENTAGE ACTIONS
Termination
    See also ABORTION

PREGNANCY

PREGNANCY—*continued*
Termination—*continued*
    Person not to be defined so as to establish criminal liability for abortion or acts or omissions of mother, **ORC 2901.01**

PREHEARING CONFERENCES
Juvenile proceedings, **JuvR 21**

PRELIMINARY HEARINGS
Juvenile courts
    Jurisdiction, **JuvR 30(E)**
    Transfer for criminal prosecution, **JuvR 30(A)**
    Notice, **JuvR 30(D)**

PREMARITAL AGREEMENTS
Action to set aside, **ORC 2106.22**

PRENEED FUNERAL CONTRACT
Estates, liability for funeral expenses when contract purchased is irrevocable, **ORC Ch 2117.251**

PRESUMED DECEDENTS
Generally, **ORC Ch 2121**
Administration of estate, **ORC 2121.05**
Complaint, **ORC 2121.02**
Decree, **ORC 2121.04**
    Vacation, **ORC 2121.08**
Evidence, **ORC 2121.03**
Federal missing persons act, **ORC 2121.01**
Insurance benefits, **ORC 2121.05**
Jurisdiction, **ORC 2101.24**
Marriage, effect, **ORC 2121.04**
Notice of action, **ORC 2121.02**
Parties to action, **ORC 2121.02**
Personal property, distribution, **ORC 2121.07**
Substitution as party to action, erroneously presumed decedent, **ORC 2121.09**
Title to property, effect, **ORC 2121.06**
When presumption arises, **ORC 2121.01**

PRESUMPTION OF DEATH
See PRESUMED DECEDENTS

PRESUMPTION OF VALIDITY OF LIVING WILL
Generally, **ORC 2133.13**

PRESUMPTIONS OF PATERNITY
Generally, **ORC 3111.03**
Nonspousal artificial insemination of married woman, **ORC 3111.95**

PRETERMITTED HEIRS
Generally, **ORC 2107.34**
Debt payments, contributions to by, **ORC 2107.55**

PRETRIAL OR PREHEARING CONFERENCES
Juvenile proceedings, **JuvR 21**

PRETRIAL PROCEDURE
Cuyahoga county probate court, **CuyR 78.1**
Franklin county probate court, **FrankR 78.1**
Hamilton county probate court, **HamR 78.2**
Lucas county probate court, **LucasR 78.1**
Paternity proceedings, **ORC 3111.11**
Stark county probate court, **Sup. R 78.1**
Summit county probate court, **SumR 78.1**

PRIMA-FACIE EVIDENCE
See EVIDENCE, generally

PRINCIPAL AND AGENT
Husband and wife. See HUSBAND AND WIFE, generally
Power of attorney, **ORC Ch 1337**
    See also POWER OF ATTORNEY
Property interests, grants, **ORC 1335.04**

PRINCIPAL AND AGENT—*continued*
Written agreements, **ORC 1335.05**

PRINCIPAL COUNTY OF EMPLOYMENT
Defined, **ORC 5747.01**

PRISONERS
See also IMPRISONMENT
Children as, **ORC 2151.34, ORC 2152.26**
Disclosure of information
    Mentally ill or retarded prisoners transferred to psychiatric hospitals, **ORC 5122.31**
Divorce based on imprisonment, **ORC 3105.01(H)**
DNA testing, **ORC 2901.07**
Guardianship, **ORC Ch 2111**
    See also GUARDIANSHIP, generally
Legal disability, considered to be under, **ORC 2131.02**
    See also DISABILITY, PERSONS UNDER, generally
Probation. See PROBATION

PRIVACY
See CONFIDENTIAL INFORMATION, generally

PRIVATE FOUNDATIONS
See CHARITABLE TRUSTS, for general provisions

PRIVILEGED INFORMATION
See CONFIDENTIAL INFORMATION

PRIVILEGES AND IMMUNITIES
DNR identifications, actions taken pursuant to, **ORC 2133.22**

PROBATE
See PROBATE OF WILLS

PROBATE COURTS
Generally, **O Const IV § 4, ORC Ch 2101**
Accounting of fees, **ORC 2101.15**
Actions
    Directions, for, **ORC 2106.06**
Administration
    Forms, **SupR 51(D)**
Adoption
    Disclosure of adoption information
        Agency or attorney ceasing to arrange adoptions, transfer of adoption records, **ORC 3107.67**
        Request for information by adopted person or adoptive family, **ORC 3107.66**
        Request for information by birth parent, sibling, or family, **ORC 3107.66**
    Open adoption, refusing to approve, **ORC 3107.65**
    Powers and duties, **ORC Ch 3107**
Adult wards
    Settlement of personal injury claims, **SupR 69**
Aged persons, alleged abuse or exploitation
    Referral of information to law enforcement agencies, **ORC 2101.26, ORC 2151.421**
Ante mortem declaration of will validity, jurisdiction, **ORC 2107.081 to 2107.085**
Appeals from, **ORC 2101.42**
    Claims against estate, **ORC 2117.04**
    Estate tax, **ORC 5731.32**
    Probate divisions, **ORC 2101.45**
    Wills
        Contested jurisdiction, **ORC 2107.12**
        Denial of admission to probate, **ORC 2107.181**
        Validity of declaratory judgment, **ORC 2107.084**
Appointment powers, **CuyR 8.1, Sup. R 8.1**
    Appraisers, **ORC 2115.06**
    Land sales, for, **ORC 2127.24**
    Receivers
        Mentally retarded and developmentally disabled persons, facilities for, **ORC 5123.191**

PROBATE COURTS—continued
Appropriations for administrative costs, **ORC 2101.11, ORC 2101.11(B)**
Assessors
    Appointment by judge, **ORC 2101.11**
    Contracted by judge, **ORC 2101.11**
    Judges, supervision by, **ORC 2101.01, ORC 2101.11**
Attorney fees allowed during administration of estate, jurisdiction, **ORC 2113.36**
Attorney registration number, **SupR 57(B)**
Bailiffs, **ORC 2101.11**
    Appointment, **ORC 2101.11(A)**
Birth records
    Correcting, **ORC 3705.15**
    Costs, **ORC 3705.15**
Bonds. See Surety bonds, this heading
Books. See Records and reports, this heading
Case management, **CuyR 78.1, FrankR 78.1, HamR 78.1, LucasR 78.1, SumR 78.1, Sup. R 78.1 to Sup. R 78.8, SupR 78**
    Civil actions, **HamR 78.2**
Certificates
    Fee exemptions, **ORC 2101.18**
    Real property, transfer, of, **ORC 2113.61**
        Intestate succession, **ORC 2105.061**
    Wills
        Copies, **ORC 2107.20**
        Deposit, **ORC 2107.07**
Citation. See SERVICE OF PROCESS, at Probate courts
Clerks, **ORC 2101.11**
    See also CLERKS OF COURTS, generally
    Appointment, **ORC 2101.11(A)**
    Computerization of offices, costs applied to, **ORC 2101.162**
Combining with common pleas court, **ORC 2101.43 to 2101.46**
Commitment of mentally ill by. See MENTALLY ILL PERSONS, at Hearings on hospitalization
Computerization, costs applied to, **ORC 2101.162**
Conduct, prohibited, **SupR 54**
Conduct of business fund, **ORC 2101.19**
Confidential information disclosure, **ORC 2151.423**
Conservatorship, powers and duties, **ORC 2111.021**
Construction of wills. See CONSTRUCTION OF WILLS
Contempt of court, **ORC 2101.23**
    Adoption records, unauthorized disclosure, **SupR 55(D)**
    Fiduciary's embezzlement of trust assets, **ORC 2109.51**
    Limitation of contempt power, **ORC 2101.11**
    Mental illness proceedings, unauthorized disclosure, **SupR 55(D)**
    Mental retardation proceedings, unauthorized disclosure, **SupR 55(D)**
    Removal of records, **SupR 55(A)**
Continuances, **SupR 56**
Costs. See Fees and costs, this heading
County taxing authority, submission of securities issues to electors, **ORC 2151.655**
Court reporters
    Appointment, **ORC 2101.11(A)**
Courts of common pleas
    Combining with, **ORC 2101.43 to 2101.46**
    Division of, as, **ORC 2101.45**
Custody of files, **ORC 2101.11**
Cuyahoga county judges, **ORC 2101.021**
Cuyahoga county probate court. See CUYAHOGA COUNTY PROBATE COURT
Decrees
    Appeal, **ORC 2101.42**
    Presumption of death, **ORC 2121.04, ORC 2121.08**
Defined, **ORC 2101.01**
Depositions, **ORC 2101.05**
Deposits, **SupR 58**
Destruction of court records, **SupR 26.04, SupR 26(E)**
Dispute resolution procedures, **ORC 2101.163**

PROBATE COURTS—continued
Dockets, **ORC 2101.12, ORC 2101.121**
    Extracounty and extrastate proceedings, **ORC 2129.01**
    Omission of entries, remedy, **ORC 2101.13**
    Probate division of common pleas courts, **ORC 2101.45**
Durable power of attorney for health care, decisions and determinations made under, **ORC 1337.16, ORC 2101.24**
Election by surviving spouse. See SURVIVING SPOUSE
Eminent domain proceedings, **ORC Ch 163**
    See also EMINENT DOMAIN
Employees, **O Const IV § 4**
Equipment, **ORC 2101.01**
Erie county judges, jurisdictional responsibilities of additional judge, **ORC 2101.023**
Escheat, powers and duties, **ORC 2105.09**
    See also ESCHEAT
Establishment, **ORC 2101.45**
Estate administration proceedings
    See also SURVIVING SPOUSE, at Election by
    Ancillary administration, **ORC 2129.04 to 2129.24**
    Attorney fees, **SupR 71**
    Claims against estate, **ORC Ch 2117**
        See also CLAIMS AGAINST ESTATES
    Executors and administrators, by, **ORC Ch 2113**
        See also EXECUTORS AND ADMINISTRATORS
        Denial of commissions, **ORC 2113.35**
        Foreign, jurisdiction, **ORC 2113.71**
    Extracounty and extrastate proceedings, **ORC Ch 2129**
    Heirship, determination; nonresident decedent's estate, **ORC 2129.18**
    Inventories and appraisals, **ORC Ch 2115**
        Hearings, **ORC 2115.16**
    Missing person's estate, **ORC Ch 2119**
    Real estate
        See also ESTATES, at Real property
        Fraudulent transfers by decedents, **ORC 2127.40**
        Sale of, **ORC 2127.02 to 2127.04**
        Transfer of, **ORC 2113.61**
    Tax. See Estate tax, powers and duties, this heading
    Trust funds held for benefit of foreign beneficiary or heir, **ORC 2113.81, ORC 2113.82**
    Unclaimed funds, **ORC 2113.64 to 2113.68**
Estate tax, powers and duties
    Apportionment among interested persons, **ORC 2113.86, ORC 2113.87**
    Audit by tax commissioner
        Assistance, **ORC 5731.26**
    Certificate of tax liability, filing, **ORC 5731.27**
    Confidentiality of information, **ORC 5731.90**
    Exceptions filed with, **ORC 5731.30, ORC 5731.30 to 5731.32**
    Jurisdiction, **ORC 5731.31**
    Receipts of payment, filing, **ORC 5731.33**
    Tax return filed with, **ORC 5731.21**
Estates, alleged theft from
    Referral of information to law enforcement agencies, **ORC 2101.26**
Exceptions, rules of superintendence, **SupR 76**
Exclusive jurisdiction, **ORC 2101.24**
Executors and administrators, powers and duties, **ORC Ch 2113**
    Denial of commissions, **ORC 2113.35**
    Foreign, jurisdiction, **ORC 2113.71**
Expenses. See Fees and costs, this heading
Extension of time, **ORC 2113.25 to 2113.29**
    Documents and records incorporated by reference, production of, **ORC 2107.05**
    Election by surviving spouse, **ORC 2106.01(E)**
    Hearing on account, **ORC 2109.33**
Fees and costs, **ORC 2101.15 to 2101.21**
    See also COURT COSTS, generally
    Accounting by judges, **ORC 2101.15**
        Penalties for violations, **ORC 2101.99**

PROBATE COURTS

PROBATE COURTS—*continued*
Fees and costs, **ORC 2101.15 to 2101.21**—*continued*
   Additional fees, **LucasR 58.1**
   Adoption, disclosure of information petition, **ORC 2101.16(F)**
   Advance deposits, **ORC 2101.15, SupR 58**
     Appointment of fiduciaries, **ORC 2101.21**
   Clerks' offices, computerization; for, **ORC 2101.162**
   Copies of records, **SupR 55(B)**
   Costs, prepaid and unearned; deposit with, **ORC 2101.161**
   Dispute resolution
     Additional fees charged for, **LucasR 58.1**
     Procedures, implementation of, **ORC 2101.163**
   Eminent domain proceedings, **ORC 163.15, ORC 163.16**
     Abandonment, **ORC 163.21**
   Estates, ancillary administration, **ORC 2129.24**
   Fiduciaries
     Investigation, **ORC 2109.49**
     Proceedings against, **ORC 2109.50**
   Guardianship, **ORC 2109.16**
     Veterans, of, **ORC 2111.02**
   Jury trials, **ORC 2152.67**
   Limitations, **ORC 2101.19**
   Marriages, solemnization, **ORC 2101.27**
   Nonresident guardians and wards, security deposits for actions, **ORC 2111.43**
   Oaths, administration, **ORC 2101.18**
   Payment, **LucasR 58.1**
   Permanent improvements of districts, permissible agreements to pay costs of, **ORC 2151.655**
   Proceedings and actions, **ORC 2101.32**
   Real property transfer, **ORC 2113.63, ORC 2127.17**
   Records, return to parties, **ORC 2101.141**
   Reduction, **ORC 2101.20**
   Schedule, **ORC 2101.16, ORC 2101.17**
   Wills deposited with judges, **ORC 2107.07**
Fiduciaries, jurisdiction, **ORC Ch 2109**
Files, examination by attorneys and title examiners, **FrankR 55.1**
Filing requirements, **SupR 57**
Forms, **SupR 51, SupR 52**
   Applicability, **SupR 51(A), SupR 52(A)**
   Blank lines, **SupR 52(H)**
   Boxes to be checked, **SupR 52(I)**
   Caption, **ORC 2101.01, SupR 52(J)**
   Centering, **SupR 52(G)**
   Computer-generated, **HamR 52.1**
   Effective date, **SupR 51(B)**
   Form number, **SupR 52(K)**
   Main heading, repeat at foot of first page, **SupR 52(K)**
   Margins, **SupR 52(C)**
   Modification, **SupR 51(C)**
   Original instrument, **SupR 51(C)**
   Paper, size and stock, **SupR 52(B)**
   Printing front and back, **SupR 52(L)**
   Printing specifications, **FrankR 52.1, FrankR 52.2, SupR 52**
     Computer-generated forms, **HamR 52.1**
   Sale of, limitations, **ORC 2101.19**
   Size of paper, **SupR 52(B)**
   Standard probate, **HamR 51.1**
   Stock, paper, **SupR 52(B)**
   Tumble style, **SupR 52(L)**
   Type sizes, **SupR 52(E)**
   Type styles, **SupR 52(D)**
   Variations from standard forms, **SupR 52(M)**
   Vertical spacing, **SupR 52(F)**
Franklin county probate court. *See* FRANKLIN COUNTY PROBATE COURT
Funds
   Probate court conduct of business fund, **ORC 2101.19**
Guardianship, supervision of, **ORC Ch 2111**
   See also GUARDIANSHIP

PROBATE COURTS—*continued*
Hamilton county probate court. *See* HAMILTON COUNTY PROBATE COURT
Health care, decisions and determinations made under durable power of attorney, **ORC 1337.16, ORC 2101.24**
Hearings, **FrankR 78.1, HamR 78.2, LucasR 78.1**
Heirs-at-law, designation, **ORC 2105.15**
Heirship, determination; jurisdiction, **ORC Ch 2123**
Hospitalization of mentally ill by. *See* MENTALLY ILL PERSONS, at Hearings on hospitalization
Hours of business, **CuyR 53.1, FrankR 53.1, HamR 53.1, LucasR 53.1, SumR 53.1, Sup. R 53.1, SupR 53**
Improvements, permissible agreements to pay costs of permanent improvements of districts, **ORC 2151.655**
Indigent guardianship fund, declaration of surplus, **ORC 2111.51**
Injunctive relief, jurisdiction. *See* INJUNCTIVE RELIEF, generally
Inquests, **ORC 2101.24**
Institutionalization of mentally retarded, **ORC 5123.701 to 5123.77**
Inter vivos trusts, jurisdiction, **ORC 2101.24**
Intestate succession, **ORC Ch 2105**
   See also DESCENT AND DISTRIBUTION
Investigators, **ORC 2101.11**
   Appointment, **CuyR 8.1, ORC 2101.11**
   Guardianship, appointment
     Minors, for; investigations, **ORC 2111.042**
     Notice of appointment, **ORC 2111.04**
   Incompetency, investigation of, **ORC 2111.041**
   Judges, supervision by, **ORC 2101.01**
   Temporary, **ORC 2111.04**
Journals, **ORC 2101.12**
Judges, **O Const IV § 4**
   See also COURTS OF COMMON PLEAS
   Appointment powers
     Bailiffs and deputy clerks, **ORC 2101.11(A)**
     Stenographic reporters, **ORC 2101.11(A)**
   Assessors
     Supervision, **ORC 2101.01**
   Assignment
     Juvenile court, to, **ORC 2151.07**
     Temporary, **O Const IV § 5**
   Bond, surety, **ORC 2101.03**
   Clerks of court, as, **ORC 2101.11, ORC 2101.11(A)**
   Code of Judicial Conduct, **O Const IV § 5**
   Common pleas judges as, **ORC 2101.37**
   Conflict of interest, **ORC 2101.38, ORC 2101.39**
     Penalties for violations, **ORC 2101.99**
     Practice of law, **ORC 2101.41**
   Cuyahoga county, **ORC 2101.021**
   Defined, **ORC 2101.01**
     Lunacy proceedings, **ORC 2101.36**
   Disqualification, **O Const IV § 5, ORC 2101.39**
   Election and term of office, **ORC 2101.02**
     Cuyahoga county, **ORC 2101.021**
   Estate assets, dealing in by, **ORC 2101.40**
   Forfeiture of office, **ORC 2101.41**
   Investigators, appointment and supervision, **ORC 2101.01**
   Liability
     Appointees' misconduct, for, **ORC 2101.11, ORC 2101.11(C)**
     Employees, for, **ORC 2151.13**
     Fees charged, default, **ORC 2101.15**
     Penalties for violations, **ORC 2101.15**
   Marion county, exercise of concurrent jurisdiction with domestic relations-juvenile division, **ORC 2101.022**
   Marriages, solemnization fees, **ORC 2101.27**
   Oath of office, **ORC 2101.03**
   Oaths, administration, **ORC 2101.05**
     Fees, exemptions, **ORC 2101.18**
   Powers and duties, **ORC 2101.22**
   Practice of law by, **ORC 2101.42**
   Qualifications, **ORC 2101.02**

Index-95   PROBATE COURTS

PROBATE COURTS—*continued*
Judges, **O Const IV § 4**—*continued*
    Terms of office, **ORC 2101.02**
        Cuyahoga county, **ORC 2101.021**
Judgment entries, **SupR 57**
Judgments
    Appeal, **ORC 2101.42**
    Declaratory, validity of will, **ORC 2107.33**
    Entry, **SupR 57**
    Execution, **ORC 2101.35**
    Modifying of, **ORC 2101.33**
    Vacating of, **ORC 2101.33**
    Validity of will, **ORC 2107.081 to 2107.085**
Judgments by confession in common pleas courts, **ORC 2101.34**
Juries, **ORC 2101.30**
Jurisdiction, **ORC 2101.24, ORC 2107.11, ORC 2107.12**
    See also particular subject, this heading
    Contested, admission of will to probate, **ORC 2107.12**
        See also PROBATE OF WILLS, at Jurisdiction
    Durable power of attorney for health care, **ORC 2101.24**
    Exclusive, **ORC 2101.24**
    Mentally ill, hospitalization, **ORC 5122.35**
    Optional, **ORC 2101.25**
Jury management plan, **CuyR 78.3, LucasR 78.2**
Juvenile divisions, **ORC Ch 2151**
    See also JUVENILE COURTS
Land sale proceedings. See LAND SALE PROCEEDINGS, generally
Life-sustaining equipment, withholding or withdrawal, **ORC 2133.08**
Limitation of contempt power, **ORC 2101.11**
Living wills, jurisdiction, **ORC 2101.24**
Local rules of courts, adoption, **SupR 75**
Location, **ORC 2101.01**
Logan county judges, powers and jurisdiction, **ORC 2101.024**
Lucas county probate court. See LUCAS COUNTY PROBATE COURT
Marion county
    Concurrent jurisdiction of judge with domestic relations-juvenile division, **ORC 2101.022**
Master commissioners, **ORC 2101.06, ORC 2101.07**
Mediation, **ORC 2101.163, SumR 98.1**
    Custody or visitation of children, **SupR 16**
Mentally ill and mentally retarded persons
    See also MENTALLY RETARDED AND DEVELOPMENTALLY DISABLED PERSONS, at Hearings on institutionalization
    Guardianship, under; alleged abuse or exploitation
        Referral of information to law enforcement agencies, **ORC 2101.26**
    Hospitalization of mentally ill. See MENTALLY ILL PERSONS, at Hearings on hospitalization
    Medication; informed consent, **ORC 2101.24**
Mentally ill persons under guardianship, alleged abuse or exploitation
    Referral of information to law enforcement agencies, **ORC 2151.421**
Minors
    Guardianship, alleged abuse or exploitation
        Referral of information to law enforcement agencies, **ORC 2101.26**
    Settlement of personal injury claims, **SupR 68**
    Under guardianship, alleged abuse or exploitation
        Referral of information to law enforcement agencies, **ORC 2151.421**
Missing persons, disposition of assets, **ORC Ch 2119**
Name changes, **ORC 2717.01**
Notices. See SERVICE OF PROCESS
Nutrition or hydration, withholding or withdrawal, **ORC 2133.09**
Oaths
    Administration of
        Employees of court, by, **ORC 2101.11(A)**
Oaths, administration of, **ORC 2101.05**
    Employees of court, by, **ORC 2101.11**

PROBATE COURTS—*continued*
Orders, **ORC 2101.22**
    Appeal, **ORC 2101.42**
    Modifying, **ORC 2101.33**
    Vacating, **ORC 2101.33**
Parties to action, affidavits; prejudice of judge, **ORC 2101.39**
Permanent improvements of districts, permissible agreements to pay costs, **ORC 2151.655**
Photographs of proceedings, **SupR 54(B)**
Practice and procedure, **ORC 2101.22 to 2101.42**
Presumed decedents, **ORC Ch 2121**
Pretrial procedure, **FrankR 78.1, HamR 78.2, LucasR 78.1, Sup. R 78.1**
Probate court conduct of business fund, **ORC 2101.19**
Proceedings before, recording, **CuyR 11.1, FrankR 11.1, HamR 11.1, Sup. R 11.1**
    Judges, matters heard by, **SumR 54.2(A)**
    Magistrates, matters heard by, **SumR 54.2(B)**
Process. See SERVICE OF PROCESS
Prohibited conduct, **SupR 54**
Protective services for adults, powers and duties, **ORC 5101.60 to 5101.71**
    See also PROTECTIVE SERVICES FOR ADULTS
Questions of fact, determination, **ORC 2101.31**
Radio broadcasts of proceedings, **SupR 54(B)**
Records and reports, **ORC 2101.01, ORC 2101.11 to 2101.141**
    Accounting for fees by judges, **ORC 2101.15**
        Penalties for violations, **ORC 2101.99**
    Admission of foreign wills to record, **ORC 2129.05 to 2129.07**
    Adoptions, **ORC 3107.17**
        Confidentiality, **SupR 55(C), SupR 55(D)**
    Conflict of interest, in case of, **ORC 2101.38**
    Copies, fees, **FrankR 55.2, SupR 55(B)**
    Court records, management and retention, **SupR 26**
        Administrative records, retention schedule, **SupR 26.01**
        Definitions, **SupR 26.04**
        Retention schedule, **SupR 26.04**
    Cuyahoga county, **ORC 2101.021**
    Destruction, **ORC 2101.141**
    Electronic, photographic, tape reproductions, **ORC 2101.121**
    Examination by attorneys and title examiners, **FrankR 55.1**
    Examination of, **SumR 55.1**
    Fees
        Copies, **FrankR 55.2, SupR 55(B)**
        Limitations, **ORC 2101.19**
    Forms, printing specifications, **FrankR 52.1, FrankR 52.2**
    Indexes, **ORC 2101.12, ORC 2101.121, ORC 2101.13**
    Limitation on number of files withdrawn, **FrankR 55.1**
    Mental illness proceedings, **SupR 55(C)**
        Unauthorized disclosure, contempt, **SupR 55(D)**
    Microfilming, **ORC 2101.141**
    Omissions, **ORC 2101.13**
    Proceedings, **FrankR 11.1**
    Proceedings, of, **CuyR 11.1, FrankR 11.1, HamR 11.1, Sup. R 11.1**
        Judges, matters heard by, **SumR 54.2(A)**
        Magistrates, matters heard by, **SumR 54.2(B)**
    Removal, **SumR 55.1, SupR 55(A)**
    Requests for, **HamR 11.1**
    Retention, **ORC 2101.14, ORC 2101.141**
Re-establishment, **ORC 2101.46**
Referees, **ORC 2101.06, ORC 2101.07, ORC 2117.09**
    Practice of law by, **ORC 2101.41**
Rules of Civil Procedure, applicability, **ORC 2101.32**
Rules of practice, **ORC 2101.04**
    Local, adoption, **SupR 75**
Rules of superintendence, **SupR 51 to SupR 78**
    Compliance, **SupR 77**
    Effective dates, **SupR 99**
    Exceptions, **SupR 76**
    Sanctions, **SupR 77**

PROBATE COURTS—continued
Security, **CuyR 9.1, FrankR 9.1, HamR 54.1, LucasR 9.1, Sup. R 9.1**
Service of process. See SERVICE OF PROCESS
Standard probate forms, **HamR 51.1**
Stark county probate court. See STARK COUNTY PROBATE COURT
Stenographic reporters, **ORC 2101.08, ORC 2101.11**
    Appointment, **ORC 2101.11(A)**
Summit county probate court. See SUMMIT COUNTY PROBATE COURT
Surety bonds
    Appointees, **ORC 2101.11, ORC 2101.11(C)**
    Judges, **ORC 2101.03**
    Master commissioners, **ORC 2101.06**
    Record, **ORC 2101.12**
Surviving spouse under legal disability
    Making election for, **ORC 2106.08**
Tape recordings, **SupR 54(B)**
Television broadcasts of proceedings, **SupR 54(B)**
Trusts, missing person's estate, **ORC Ch 2119**
Unclaimed funds, **ORC 2113.64 to 2113.68**
Venue
    Ancillary proceedings, **ORC 2129.04**
    Real property contracts, completion by executor or administrator, **ORC 2113.49**
    Real property sale by fiduciaries, **ORC 2127.08**
    Will contests, **ORC 2107.71**
Vital statistics, **ORC 2101.12**
Wills. See WILLS, generally
    Probating. See PROBATE OF WILLS, generally
Witnesses. See WITNESSES AND TESTIMONY

PROBATE OF WILLS
Generally, **ORC 2107.11 to 2107.22**
Admission, **HamR 59.1, ORC 2107.11 to 2107.22**
    Court costs, **Sup. R 58.1**
    Destruction of record of will, after, **ORC 2107.30**
    Foreign wills, **ORC 2129.07**
    Irregularities, wills containing, **HamR 59.1**
    Jurisdiction, **ORC 2101.24**
    Lost, spoliated, or destroyed wills, **ORC 2107.26 to 2107.28**
        See also Lost, spoliated, or destroyed wills, this heading
    Notice. See Notice, this heading
    Recording, **ORC 2101.12, ORC 2107.29 to 2107.32**
    Refusal to admit to, **ORC 2107.181**
    Revocation, **ORC 2107.22**
Affidavit of giving notice, **CuyR 34.4, LucasR 59.1**
Application, **SumR 59.1**
Binding, when, **ORC 2107.76**
Certificates
    Notice of probate of will, **LucasR 59.2, LucasR 59.3**
Construction. See CONSTRUCTION OF WILLS
Contested jurisdiction. See Jurisdiction, this heading
Cuyahoga county probate court
    Affidavit of giving notice, **CuyR 34.4**
Deposited wills, certification of, **LucasR 57.1**
Depositions, **ORC 2107.17, ORC 2107.181**
Directions, action for, **ORC 2106.06**
Failure to offer for, **ORC 2107.10**
Fees, **ORC 2101.16**
Filing and recording, **ORC 2107.20, ORC 2107.21**
    Destroyed wills, **ORC 2107.29 to 2107.32**
Hamilton county probate court
    Admission to probate, **HamR 59.1**
    Irregularities, wills containing, **HamR 59.2**
Interlocutory orders, **ORC 2107.181**
Jurisdiction, **ORC 2107.11, ORC 2107.12**
    Contested, **ORC 2107.12**
Legal advertising. See Notice, this heading
Lost, spoliated, or destroyed wills, **ORC 2107.26 to 2107.28**
    New records, **ORC 2107.29 to 2107.32**

PROBATE OF WILLS—continued
Lucas county probate court
    Affidavit of giving notice, **LucasR 59.1**
    Certificate of notice, **LucasR 59.2, LucasR 59.3**
    Deposited wills, certification of, **LucasR 57.1**
Noncompliance, probate court to treat document as will despite, **ORC 2107.24**
Notice, **ORC 2107.19, ORC 2107.32, SupR 59**
    Affidavit of, **LucasR 59.1**
    Certificate of, **LucasR 59.2, LucasR 59.3**
    Fiduciary filing affidavit of, **CuyR 34.4**
    Foreign wills, **ORC 2129.07**
    Hearing
        Additional notice, affidavit proving abolished, **ORC 2109.33**
    Lost, spoliated, or destroyed wills, **ORC 2107.27**
    Waiver, **ORC 2107.19**
Proof, **ORC 2107.16**
Refusal to admit to probate, **ORC 2107.181**
Subsequent will, **ORC 2107.22**
Summit county probate court, applications, **SumR 59.1**
Withholding will, **ORC 2107.10**

PROBATION
Juveniles, **JuvR 34(C)**
    Defined, **ORC 2151.011**
    Delinquents, **ORC 2152.21**
        County departments, powers and duties, **ORC 2151.15**
        Department powers and duties, **ORC 2151.14**
        Interstate compact, **ORC 2151.56 to 2151.61**
        Records, **ORC 2151.14**
            Copies, providing, **ORC 2151.141**
    Revocation, **JuvR 35(B), JuvR 35(C)**
    Services for, juvenile judges contracting for, **ORC 2151.151**
    Traffic offenses, **ORC 2152.21**
    Unruly children, **ORC 2151.354**
Mentally ill or mentally retarded probationer
    Discharge from hospital, **ORC 5122.21**
Officers
    Appointment by juvenile courts, **ORC 2151.13**
    County department of probation, **ORC 2151.15**
    Emergency hospitalization of mentally ill probationer, **ORC 5122.10**
    Juvenile courts. See JUVENILE COURTS, at Probation officers
Records and reports, juveniles, **ORC 2151.14**
    Copies, providing, **ORC 2151.141**
Revocation, **JuvR 35(B), JuvR 35(C)**

PROCEDENDO
Jurisdiction, **O Const IV § 2, O Const IV § 3**

PROCESS
See SERVICE OF PROCESS

PRODUCT LIABILITY
Limitation of actions, **ORC 2305.10**

PRODUCTION OF DOCUMENTS
Generally, **JuvR 24(A)**

PROFIT-SHARING PLANS
See also RETIREMENT PLANS
Estate tax, **ORC 5731.09**
Rule against perpetuities, exemption from, **ORC 2131.09**

PROHIBITION
Jurisdiction, **O Const IV § 2, O Const IV § 3**

PROMISSORY NOTES
See also SECURITIES
Estate property, sale by fiduciaries, **ORC 2113.44**

PROOF
See EVIDENCE

PROPERTY
Appropriation of property. See APPROPRIATION OF PROPERTY
Definition, **ORC 2901.01**
Eminent domain. See EMINENT DOMAIN
Estates. See ESTATES
Land sale proceedings. See LAND SALE PROCEEDINGS
Personal property. See PERSONAL PROPERTY
    Taxation. See PERSONAL PROPERTY, TAXATION
Real property. See REAL PROPERTY
    Taxation. See REAL PROPERTY, TAXATION
Trust property, trustee's control and protection of, **ORC 5808.09**

PROSECUTION
Civil. See ACTIONS
Criminal. See CRIMINAL PROSECUTIONS

PROSECUTOR, STATE
See ATTORNEY GENERAL

PROSECUTORS, COUNTY
Children's advocacy center, memorandum of understanding, **ORC 2151.426**
Escheat, collection and payment to treasurer, **ORC 2105.07**

PROTECTIVE ORDERS
See also INJUNCTIVE RELIEF
Discovery procedure, **JuvR 24(B)**

PROTECTIVE SERVICES FOR ADULTS
Generally, **ORC 5101.60 to 5101.71**
Abuse by caretaker, duty to report, **ORC 5101.61**
Consent to, **ORC 5101.64**
County human services department, report to, **ORC 5101.61**
    Investigation, **ORC 5101.62**
Court-ordered implementation of plan, **ORC 5101.65 to 5101.67**
    Expenses, **ORC 5101.70**
Definitions, **ORC 5101.60, ORC 5101.61**
Emergency services, **ORC 5101.69**
    Defined, **ORC 5101.60**
    Duration of emergency order, **ORC 5101.69**
    Limits on emergency orders, **ORC 5101.69**
Expenses, **ORC 5101.70**
Hearings
    Court-ordered services, **ORC 5101.67**
        Rights of elderly persons, **ORC 5101.67**
        Standard of proof, **ORC 5101.67**
        Time for, **ORC 5101.67**
    Emergency services, **ORC 5101.69**
        Notice, **ORC 5101.69**
        Rights of elderly adults, **ORC 5101.69**
        Standard of proof, **ORC 5101.69**
        Time for, **ORC 5101.69**
    Petition, prevention of interference with voluntary services, **ORC 5101.68**
Human services departments, county
    Powers and duties, **ORC 5101.71**
    Training, **ORC 5101.71**
Investigation, **ORC 5101.62 to 5101.64**
    Interviews, **ORC 5101.62**
    Notice, **ORC 5101.62**
    Obstructing, **ORC 5101.63**
Jurisdiction, **ORC 5101.60**
Notice
    Court-ordered services, **ORC 5101.66**
    Investigation, **ORC 5101.62**
    Petition, prevention of interference with voluntary services, **ORC 5101.68**
    Transfer of placement, **ORC 5101.67**
Obstructing investigation, **ORC 5101.63**
Order for nonvoluntary services, **ORC 5101.67**
Petition
    Court-ordered services, **ORC 5101.65**

PROTECTIVE SERVICES FOR ADULTS—continued
Petition—continued
    Emergency services, **ORC 5101.69**
    Voluntary services, to restrain interference, **ORC 5101.68**
Placement of adult, **ORC 5101.67**
    Appeal from, **ORC 5101.67**
    Duration of order, **ORC 5101.67**
    Modification of order, **ORC 5101.67**
Plan, **ORC 5101.65**
    Court-ordered implementation, **ORC 5101.65 to 5101.67**
    Voluntary implementation, **ORC 5101.64**
Reporting abuse by caretaker, **ORC 5101.61**
Right of entry, **ORC 5101.63**
Temporary restraining order
    Interference with voluntary services, **ORC 5101.68**
    Obstruction of investigation, to prevent, **ORC 5101.63**
Voluntary implementation of plan, **ORC 5101.64**
    Expenses, **ORC 5101.70**

PROTECTIVE SERVICES FOR MENTALLY RETARDED AND DEVELOPMENTALLY DISABLED PERSONS
Generally, **ORC 5123.55 to 5123.58**
See also GUARDIANSHIP
Eligibility determinations by mental retardation and developmental disabilities department, **ORC 5123.012**

PROTECTIVE SUPERVISION
Defined, **ORC 2151.011**

PROVISIONAL PLACEMENT
Defined under Interstate Compact on Placement of Children, **ORC 5103.20**

PRUDENT INVESTOR ACT
Generally, **ORC 5809.01 to 5809.08**
See also UNIFORM PRUDENT INVESTOR ACT

PRUDENT PERSON STANDARD
Fiduciaries, **ORC 2109.371**

PSYCHIATRIC EXAMINATIONS
See MEDICAL AND MENTAL EXAMINATIONS

PSYCHIATRISTS
See also PHYSICIANS, generally
Appointment, **HamR 75.1**
Emergency hospitalization of mentally ill, **ORC 5122.10**

PSYCHOLOGISTS
Aged persons suffering neglect, abuse, or exploitation; report to county human services department, **ORC 5101.61**
Child abuse, reporting, **ORC 2151.421**
Emergency hospitalization of mentally ill, **ORC 5122.10**
Residency training programs, agreements with mental retardation and developmental disabilities department, **ORC 5123.11**

PUBLIC AUCTIONS
See AUCTIONS

PUBLIC CHILDREN SERVICES AGENCIES
Adoption, powers and duties
    Hearings, notice to adoptive parents, **ORC 2151.424**
Child abuse, reporting
    Children living in homeless or domestic violence shelters, **ORC 2151.422**
Hearings, notice to adoptive parents, **ORC 2151.424**
Permanency plans
    Development, **ORC 2151.417**
Permanent custody of children placed with, **ORC 2151.414(B)**
    Adoption, notice of hearings to adoptive parents, **ORC 2151.424**
    Motion for, **ORC 2151.413(D)**

PUBLIC CONTRACTS
See CONTRACTS, PUBLIC

PUBLIC DEFENDERS
Juvenile proceedings, duties, **ORC 2151.352**

PUBLIC EMPLOYEES
Agents, estate tax matters, **ORC 5731.41**
Estate tax on death benefits, **ORC 5731.09**
Mental retardation and developmental disabilities department employees, **ORC 5123.06, ORC 5123.08**
Retirement system. See PUBLIC EMPLOYEES RETIREMENT SYSTEM
Tax personnel agents, estate tax matters, **ORC 5731.41**

PUBLIC EMPLOYEES RETIREMENT SYSTEM
Benefits, estate tax, **ORC 5731.09**

PUBLIC FUNDS
See FUNDS, PUBLIC

PUBLIC OFFICIALS
Records and reports
    Tax records, withholding of local government funds for failure to maintain, **ORC 5747.51(J)**
Retirement system. See PUBLIC EMPLOYEES RETIREMENT SYSTEM

PUBLIC SCHOOLS
See SCHOOLS AND SCHOOL DISTRICTS

PUBLIC UTILITIES
Eminent domain, relocation payments, **ORC 163.53**

PUBLIC WORKS
Eminent domain, **ORC Ch 163**
Municipal, **O Const XVIII § 10**

PUBLICATION, SERVICE BY
See SERVICE OF PROCESS, at Publication, by

PUNISHMENT
See FINES AND FORFEITURES; SENTENCES

PURCHASERS IN GOOD FAITH
See BONA FIDE PURCHASERS

QUALIFIED BENEFICIARY
Defined, **ORC 5801.01**

QUALIFIED TUITION AND FEES
Defined, **ORC 5747.01**

QUALIFYING INVESTMENT PASS-THROUGH ENTITY
Defined, **ORC 5747.012**

QUALIFYING PRE-INCOME TAX TRUST ELECTION
Defined, **ORC 5747.01**

QUALIFYING TRUST AMOUNT
Defined, **ORC 5747.01**

QUO WARRANTO
Jurisdiction, **O Const IV § 2, O Const IV § 3**

RADIO
Probate court proceeding, broadcasting, **SupR 54(B)**
Trials, broadcasting, **SupR 12**

RAIL SERVICE
Eminent domain, value of property deposited with court, **ORC 163.06**

RATES
See FEES AND COSTS

REAL ACTIONS
See REAL PROPERTY

REAL ESTATE
Generally, See REAL PROPERTY
Taxation. See REAL PROPERTY, TAXATION

REAL ESTATE BROKERS AND SALESPERSONS
Commissions
    Estates, land sale proceedings, **ORC 2127.28**
    Guardian's sale of ward's realty, **ORC 2127.28**

REAL PROPERTY
See also LAND SALE PROCEEDINGS
Ancillary administration. See ANCILLARY ADMINISTRATION
Appraisals. See APPRAISALS
Appropriation, **ORC Ch 163**
    See also EMINENT DOMAIN
Attachment. See ATTACHMENT
Auctions. See AUCTIONS
Brokers. See REAL ESTATE BROKERS AND SALESPERSONS
Conveyances. See CONVEYANCES
Deeds. See DEEDS
Descent and distribution, **ORC Ch 2105**
    See also DESCENT AND DISTRIBUTION
Devises. See LEGACIES AND DEVISES
Disclaimers of succession to, **ORC 5815.36**
    See also DISCLAIMER OF SUCCESSION TO PROPERTY
Dower, **ORC Ch 5305**
Eminent domain. See EMINENT DOMAIN
Encumbrances. See ENCUMBRANCES, generally
    Leases. See LEASES
    Liens. See LIENS
    Mortgages. See MORTGAGES
Escheat. See ESCHEAT
Estate property. See ESTATES
Estate property. See LAND SALE PROCEEDINGS; LEGACIES AND DEVISES
Estate tax, **ORC Ch 5731**
    See also ESTATE TAX
Fees, probate court, **ORC 2101.16**
Fiduciaries, investment powers, **ORC 2109.37**
    Fees, probate court, **ORC 2101.16**
Foreclosure. See FORECLOSURE
Fraud. See FRAUD
Guardians. See GUARDIANSHIP
Improvements by guardians, **ORC 2111.33 to 2111.36**
Intestate succession, **ORC Ch 2105**
    See also DESCENT AND DISTRIBUTION
Judicial sales. See JUDICIAL SALES
Land sale proceedings. See LAND SALE PROCEEDINGS
Legal separation, dower barred, **ORC 3105.10(E)**
Missing person's estate, **ORC 2119.04**
Mortgages. See MORTGAGES
Power of attorney, **1337.01 et seq., ORC Ch 1337**
Presumed decedent, **ORC 2121.05**
    Decree vacated, **ORC 2121.08**
Probate court fees, **ORC 2101.16**
Recovery action, limitation of actions, **ORC 2305.04**
Remaindermen. See REMAINDERMEN
Rental, Uniform Principal and Income Act, **ORC 5812.25**
Right of entry. See RIGHT OF ENTRY
Rule against perpetuities, **ORC 2131.08, ORC 2131.09**
Sales
    See also CONVEYANCES
    Completion by fiduciaries, **ORC 2113.48**
    Foreclosure. See FORECLOSURE
    Land sale proceedings. See LAND SALE PROCEEDINGS
    Mental retardation and developmental disabilities boards, county, **ORC 5126.37, ORC 5126.371**
    Salespersons. See REAL ESTATE BROKERS AND SALESPERSONS

REAL PROPERTY—continued
Succession to, disclaimer, **ORC 5815.36**
    See also DISCLAIMER OF SUCCESSION TO PROPERTY
Taxation. See REAL PROPERTY, TAXATION
    Estates. See ESTATE TAX
Tenancy, life. See LIFE ESTATES
Transfer. See CONVEYANCES
Transfer tax. See ESTATE TAX
Trusts, **ORC 2107.63**
    Foreign will creating, **ORC 2129.27 to 2129.30**

REAL PROPERTY, TAXATION
Claims against estates to collect, **ORC 2117.18, ORC 2117.19**
Estate tax, **ORC Ch 5731**
    See also ESTATE TAX, FEDERAL; ESTATE TAX
Estates owing, **ORC 2117.18, ORC 2117.19**
Improvements by guardian, **ORC 2111.33**
Transfer tax, situs regarding estate property, **ORC 5731.50**

REASSIGNMENT
Anatomical gifts, vesting of assignment or reassignment of right of disposition, **ORC 2108.71**
Mental retardation and developmental disabilities department employees, **ORC 5123.08**

REBUTTALS
Paternity, presumption, **ORC 3111.03**

RECEIVERSHIP
Mentally retarded and developmentally disabled persons, facilities for, **ORC 5123.191**
Residential care facilities, **ORC 5123.191**
Service of process on receiver, **ORC 2305.19**

RECEIVING STATE
Defined under Interstate Compact on Placement of Children, **ORC 5103.20**

RECIPROCITY
Adoption decrees, **ORC 3107.18**
Estate tax, **ORC 5731.34**
Juvenile rehabilitation facilities, admittance to, **ORC 2151.654**
Paternity decree, **ORC 3109.30(B)**

RECORDERS, COUNTY
Certificate of transfer, recording
    Survivorship tenancy, **ORC 5302.17**
Eminent domain transfer, recording, **ORC 163.15**
Fees
    Powers of attorney, recording, **ORC 1337.10**
    Real property transfers, decedent's property, **ORC 2113.63, ORC 2129.24**
Inherited property, recording, **ORC 2113.62**
Survivorship tenancy, transfer upon death, **ORC 5302.17**
Trust
    Memoranda of successor trustee, recording, **ORC 5302.171**

RECORDS AND REPORTS
Abused or neglected adults, **ORC 5126.31, ORC 5126.311**
Accounts. See ACCOUNTS AND ACCOUNTING
Administrators. See EXECUTORS AND ADMINISTRATORS
Adoption. See ADOPTION
Aged persons subject to abuse, neglect, or exploitation, **ORC 5101.61**
Birth certificates. See BIRTH CERTIFICATES
Child abuse. See CHILD ABUSE
Child custody. See CUSTODY OF CHILDREN, DOMESTIC
Criminal records
    Check, caring for minors; employment prerequisite, **ORC 2151.86, ORC 2151.861**
Cuyahoga county probate court
    Condition of adult incompetent, **CuyR 66.3 et seq.**
    Condition of ward, **CuyR 66.3 et seq.**
    Recording proceedings, **CuyR 11.1**

RECORDS AND REPORTS—continued
Delinquent children. See JUVENILE DELINQUENCY
Detention of child, **JuvR 7(E), JuvR 7(C), ORC 2151.37**
Durable power of attorney for health care, **ORC 1337.16**
Estate tax documents, **ORC 5731.90**
Executors. See EXECUTORS AND ADMINISTRATORS
Expungement. See EXPUNGEMENT OF RECORDS
Fiduciaries, **ORC 2109.021**
Franklin county probate court
    Guardian's report, **FrankR 66.6**
    Management and retention of records, **FrankR 26.1**
    Recording proceedings, **FrankR 11.1**
Grandparent power of attorney or caretaker authorization affidavit, report to public children services agency, **3109.74**
Investments, affiliated investment company securities, **ORC 2109.371**
Judge, matters heard by, **SumR 54.2(A)**
Juvenile courts. See JUVENILE COURTS
Juvenile delinquency. See JUVENILE DELINQUENCY
Living wills, **ORC 2133.05**
Lucas county probate court, management and retention of records, **LucasR 26.1**
Magistrates
    Decisions, **JuvR 40(E)**
    Matters heard by, **SumR 54.2(B)**
Mentally ill, hospitalization. See MENTALLY ILL PERSONS, at Hospitalization
Mentally ill persons
    Disclosure of information, **ORC 5122.31**
Mentally retarded and developmentally disabled persons
    Audits of contracts for residential services for, **ORC 5123.18**
    Institutionalization. See MENTALLY RETARDED AND DEVELOPMENTALLY DISABLED PERSONS, at Institutionalization
Minors, expungement of record, **JuvR 34(J)**
Proceedings before the court, stenographic record of, **FrankR 11.1**
Sexual abuse of children. See CHILDREN'S ADVOCACY CENTERS
Stark county probate court
    Guardians' reports, **Sup. R 66.2**
    Recording of proceedings, **Sup. R 11.1**
Summit county probate court
    Management and retention, **SumR 26.1**
    Record of proceedings, **SumR 54.2**
    Records of court, removal and examination, **SumR 55.1**
Traffic offenses, **ORC 4507.021**
Wills. See WILLS

RECOVERY
Damages. See DAMAGES
Dower interest, **ORC 2103.06**
Estate recovery program
    Medicaid expenses, **ORC 2113.041**
    Notice, **ORC 2117.061**
Legacies and devises, invalidity of will, **ORC 2113.23**

REFEREES
Hospitalization hearings for mentally ill, conducted by, **ORC 5122.15**
Juvenile courts, **ORC 2151.16**
Prisoners. See PRISONERS, generally

REFORMATORIES
See also CORRECTIONAL INSTITUTIONS
Detention of minors in, **ORC 2152.26**
Minors housed in, **ORC 2151.311(C), ORC 2152.26(C)**

REGIONAL COUNCILS OF GOVERNMENTS
Mental retardation and developmental disabilities boards creating, **ORC 5123.13**

REGISTRIES AND LISTINGS
Abusive or neglectful employees. See MENTAL RETARDATION AND DEVELOPMENTAL DISABILITIES DEPARTMENT
Custody of children, domestic, **ORC 3109.24(B), ORC 3109.25(I)**

REGISTRIES AND LISTINGS

REGISTRIES AND LISTINGS—*continued*
Sex offenses
    Juvenile sex offender registry, **ORC 2152.82 to 2152.851**

REHABILITATION
Juvenile. See JUVENILE REHABILITATION

REINSTATEMENT
Mental retardation and developmental disabilities department employees, rights to reinstatement, **ORC 5123.08**

RELATIVES
See NEXT OF KIN

RELEASES
Administration of estate, **ORC 2113.03**
Adoption, **ORC 3107.07**
Claims for injury or property damage to ward, **ORC 2111.18, ORC 2111.181**
Decedent's wages, **ORC 2113.04**
Deposits payable on death, **ORC 2131.11**
Dower rights, spouse under guardianship, **ORC 2111.28**
Estate administration, **ORC 2113.03, ORC 2113.041**
Estate recovery program, Medicaid expenses, **ORC 2113.041**
Estate tax, **ORC 5731.39**
Fiduciaries
    Notice of release of power of appointment, **ORC 5815.15**
    Release and disclaimer of a power of appointment, **ORC 5815.14**
Real property, sale by fiduciaries, **ORC 2127.19, ORC 2127.20**
Tax title, deed of release or quitclaim by guardian, **ORC 2111.22**
Trust funds, foreign beneficiaries or heirs, to, **ORC 2113.82**
Trusts, beneficiary's consent, release, or ratification, **ORC 5810.09**

RELIEF
Generally, See REMEDIES
Injunctive. See INJUNCTIVE RELIEF

RELIEF FROM ADMINISTRATION
See NO ADMINISTRATION

RELIGION
See also RELIGIOUS ORGANIZATIONS
Custody or placement of children, consideration, **ORC 2151.32**
Guardianship of children, consideration, **ORC 2151.32**
Mental illness, religious healing, **ORC 5122.05**
Mental patients, right to religious worship, **ORC 5122.29**
Mentally retarded, treatment by religious healing, **ORC 5123.86**

RELIGIOUS ORGANIZATIONS
Institutional Trust Funds Act, **ORC 5813.01 to 5813.07**
    See also INSTITUTIONAL TRUST FUNDS ACT
Pituitary glands, removal during autopsies; objections by, **ORC 2108.53**

RELOCATION ASSISTANCE
Eminent domain, under, **ORC 163.51 to 163.62**

REMAINDERMEN
Generally, **ORC 2131.04 to 2131.07**
Protection of interest, **ORC 2113.58**
Rule in Shelley's case abolished, **ORC 2107.49**
Surviving spouse's right, **ORC 2106.05**
Waste by life tenant, **ORC 2105.20**

REMEDIES
Generally, **O Const I § 16**
See also DAMAGES; particular type concerned
Injunctions. See INJUNCTIVE RELIEF

REMOVAL ACTIONS
Schools and school districts
    Hearings
        Out of county removal hearings, **JuvR 39(B)**
        Notice, **JuvR 39(A)**

RENT
Heirs, paid to, **ORC 2113.311**

RENTAL PROPERTY
Uniform Principal and Income Act, **ORC 5812.25**

RENUNCIATION OF INTESTATE SUCCESSION
See DISCLAIMER OF SUCCESSION TO PROPERTY

REPEAT OFFENDERS
Juvenile delinquents
    Category one and two offenses, transfer to adult court, **ORC 2152.12(C)**

REPLEVIN
Limitation of actions, **ORC 2305.09**

REPORTS
See RECORDS AND REPORTS

RES JUDICATA
Divorce, defense to
    Living separate and apart grounds, not bar to, **ORC 3105.01**

RESERVISTS
See MILITARY SERVICE

RESIDENCY REQUIREMENTS
See also NONRESIDENTS
Administrators, **ORC 2109.21, ORC 2113.05**
Death certificates, county of residence, **ORC 3705.071**
Executors, **ORC 2109.21**
Fiduciaries, **ORC 2109.21**
Guardians, **ORC 2109.21**
    School districting, for; prohibition, **LucasR 66.1, SumR 66.1, Sup. R 66.1**
Minor's residence, defined, **ORC 2151.06**
Testators, **ORC 2107.11**

RESIDENTIAL CAMPS
Child abuse to be reported by administrators or employees, **ORC 2151.421**
Defined, **ORC 2151.011**

RESIDENTIAL CARE FACILITIES
Audits of contracts, **ORC 5123.18**
Bill of rights, distribution, **ORC 5123.63**
Closing, provision of residential services after, **ORC 5123.182**
Complaints against, **ORC 5123.19**
Contracts, **ORC 5123.18**
Dangerous conditions, receivership, **ORC 5123.191**
Definitions, **ORC 2151.011, ORC 5123.19**
    Residential services, **ORC 5123.18**
Expenses, reimbursement, **ORC 5123.172**
Former residents of closed institutions, **ORC 5123.211**
Funding needs, **ORC 5123.18**
Inspections
    Mental retardation and developmental disabilities department, by, **ORC 5123.19**
Interim licenses, **ORC 5123.19**
Licensing, **ORC 5123.19, ORC 5123.20, ORC 5123.99**
Maximum efficiency incentive, **ORC 5123.18**
Mentally retarded and developmentally disabled, for, **ORC 5123.18 to 5123.20**
    Reporting abuse or neglect, **ORC 5123.61, ORC 5123.99**
Minors, for, **ORC 5123.122**
Notice of proposed facility, **ORC 5123.19**
Ownership changes, notices, **ORC 5123.19**
Purchase of service fund, **ORC 5123.051**
Receivership, appointment and duties, **ORC 5123.191**
Records and reports, **ORC 5123.172**
Reimbursement of expenses, **ORC 5123.172**
Violations, correction, **ORC 5123.19**

RESIDENTIAL FACILITY
Defined under Interstate Compact on Placement of Children, **ORC 5103.20**

RESIDUARY ESTATES
See ESTATES

RESIGNATION
Anatomical gifts, resignation of right of disposition, **ORC 2108.88**
Cofiduciaries, **ORC 2109.27**
Executors and administrators, **ORC 2109.24**
Fees, **ORC 2101.16**
Fiduciaries, **ORC 2109.24**
Sex offenses by juvenile delinquents, effect on existing order of resignation of offense, **ORC 2152.851**
Trustees, **ORC 5807.05**

RESOLUTIONS, MUNICIPAL
Generally, **O Const XVIII § 3**

RESTITUTION
Juvenile courts, criminal provisions, **ORC 2152.20**

RESTRAINING ORDERS
See INJUNCTIVE RELIEF

RETIREMENT PLANS
Actions in probate court, fees, **ORC 2101.18**
Benefits
    Estate tax, release by tax commissioner, **ORC 5731.39**
    Income tax credit, **ORC 5747.05(D) to 5747.05(F)**
Estate tax, **ORC 5731.09, ORC 5731.39**
Income tax credit, **ORC 5747.05(D) to 5747.05(F)**
    Priority, **ORC 5747.98**
Individual retirement accounts
    Designation of spouse as beneficiary, effect of termination of marriage, **ORC 5815.33**
    Testamentary trustees, **ORC 2107.64**
Public employees. See PUBLIC EMPLOYEES RETIREMENT SYSTEM
Rule against perpetuities, exemption from, **ORC 2131.09**
School employees. See SCHOOL EMPLOYEES RETIREMENT SYSTEM
Teachers retirement system. See TEACHERS RETIREMENT SYSTEM
Testamentary trustees, **ORC 2107.64**

RETURN OF SERVICE
See SERVICE OF PROCESS

REVENUES
Appropriations. See APPROPRIATIONS
Fees. See FEES AND COSTS
Fines. See FINES AND FORFEITURES
Public funds. See FUNDS, PUBLIC
Taxes. See particular tax by name

REVERSALS OF JUDGMENTS
See APPEALS

REVERSIONARY INTERESTS
Dower, **ORC 2103.07**
Estate tax, **ORC 5731.07, ORC 5731.25**

REVISED CODE
See STATUTES

REVOCABLE TRUSTS
Generally, **ORC 5806.01 to 5806.04**
Capacity of settlor of revocable trust, **ORC 5806.01**
Limitation of actions pertaining to revocable trusts made irrevocable by death of settlor, **ORC 5806.04**
Powers of settlor, **ORC 5806.03**
Revocation or amendment of revocable trust, **ORC 5806.02**

REVOCABLE TRUSTS—*continued*
Withdrawal of powers of settlor, **ORC 5806.03**

REVOCATION OF WILLS
Generally, **ORC 2107.33 to 2107.38**
Declaration of validity, effect, **ORC 2107.084**
Marriage, **ORC 2107.37**
Subsequent wills, effect, **ORC 2107.22**
Will previously declared valid by probate court, effect, **ORC 2107.084**

RICHLAND COUNTY
See COUNTIES, for general provisions

RIGHT OF ENTRY
Eminent domain proceedings, **ORC 163.03**
Protective services investigation of abuse or neglect of aged, **ORC 5101.63**
Residential care facilities, inspections, **ORC 5123.19**

ROADS
See HIGHWAYS AND ROADS

ROYALTIES
Mineral rights
    Leased by guardians, **ORC 2111.31, ORC 2111.32**
    Trusts, allocation between principal and income, **ORC 5812.34**
Trusts, allocation between principal and income, **ORC 5812.34**

RULE AGAINST PERPETUITIES
Generally, **ORC 2131.08, ORC 2131.09**

RULE IN SHELLEY'S CASE
Abolished, **ORC 2107.49**

RULES AND RULEMAKING POWERS
Eminent domain, relocation assistance, **ORC 163.58**
Estate tax, **ORC 5731.45**
    IRS regulations, applicability, **ORC 5731.18**
Interstate Compact on Placement of Children, **5103.21, ORC 5103.20**
Mentally retarded and developmentally disabled persons
    Residential services for, **ORC 5123.18**
Relocation assistance for eminent domain, **ORC 163.58**
Tax, estate tax, **ORC 5731.45**
    IRS regulations, applicability, **ORC 5731.18**
Trusts, supplemental services for disabled persons
    Mental retardation and development disabilities director, **ORC 5123.04**

RULES OF CIVIL PROCEDURE
Probate courts, applicability, **ORC 2101.32**

RULES OF COURTS
Adoption, **O Const IV § 5**
Construction
    Juvenile procedure rules, **JuvR 1(B)**
Local courts, **O Const IV § 5**
    Probate division adopting, **SupR 75**
Superintendence rules. See RULES OF SUPERINTENDENCE

RULES OF JUVENILE PROCEDURE
Complaint, **JuvR 10**
Date, effective, **JuvR 47**
Definitions, **JuvR 2**
Dispositional hearing, **JuvR 34**
Hearing, dispositional, **JuvR 34**
Process: issuance, form, **JuvR 15**

RULES OF SUPERINTENDENCE
Abortion, Juvenile Court procedures
    Application for authorization to consent, **SupR 23.1**
    Judicial consent, **SupR 23.1**
        Instructions, **SupR Form 23.1-A Instructions**
        Judgment, **SupR Form 23.1-B**
        Notice of appeal, **SupR Form 23.1-C**

RULES OF SUPERINTENDENCE

Index-102

RULES OF SUPERINTENDENCE—*continued*
Abortion, Juvenile Court procedures—*continued*
    Judicial consent, **SupR 23.1**—*continued*
        Petition, **SupR Form 23.1-A**
Appellate panels, notice of, **SupR 36.1**
Attorney registration number, **SupR 57(B)**
Capital cases, appointment of counsel for indigent defendants, **SupR 20**
Definitions
    Court records management and retention, **SupR 26**
    Probate, **SupR 50**
Effective dates, **SupR 99**
Exceptions
    Probate courts, **SupR 76**
Notice of appellate panels, **SupR 36.1**
Probate courts, **SupR 51 to SupR 78**
    Compliance, **SupR 77**
    Effective dates, **SupR 99**
    Exceptions, **SupR 76**
    Sanctions, **SupR 77**
    Temporary provisions, electronic filing
        Hamilton County, **SupR Temp Prov**

RUNAWAYS
See also UNRULY CHILDREN
Apprehension and custody, **ORC 2151.31**
Court taking custody, **JuvR 6**
Interstate agreement on, **ORC 2151.56**
Rehabilitation facilities, **ORC 2151.65 to 2151.80**
    See also JUVENILE REHABILITATION

SAFE DEPOSIT BOXES
Audits
    Attorney-in-fact, adult protective services, **FrankR 75.10**
    Guardians, **FrankR 66.2**
Inventory by tax commissioner upon death of owner, **ORC 5731.39**
Opening by guardian, **ORC 2111.14**
Release of contents by tax commissioner, **ORC 5731.39**
Wills in, removal, **SumR 90.1**

SALARIES
See COMPENSATION; WAGES AND HOURS

SALE OF GOODS
Anatomical gifts
    Sale of human body parts prohibited, **ORC 2108.12, ORC 2108.99**
    Service, not sale transaction, **ORC 2108.11**

SALE OF PROPERTY
See MENTAL RETARDATION AND DEVELOPMENTAL DISABILITIES DEPARTMENT

SAME SEX MARRIAGE
Prohibition, **O Const XV § 11**

SANCTIONS
Rules of superintendence
    Probate courts, **SupR 77**

SANITARY DISTRICTS
Eminent domain, **ORC 163.02**

SAVINGS AND LOAN ASSOCIATIONS
Deposits, payable on death, **ORC 2131.10, ORC 2131.11**

SCHOOL BOARDS
See SCHOOLS AND SCHOOL DISTRICTS, generally

SCHOOL BUILDINGS AND LANDS
Weapons
    Illegal conveyance or possession on school premises
        Drivers' license, denial or revocation of temporary instruction permit, **ORC 2923.122**

SCHOOL BUILDINGS AND LANDS—*continued*
Weapons—*continued*
    Possession of object indistinguishable from firearm on school premises
        Drivers' license, denial or revocation of temporary instruction permit, **ORC 2923.122**

SCHOOL BUSES
Weapons
    Illegal conveyance or possession on
        Drivers' license, denial or revocation of temporary instruction permit, **ORC 2923.122**
    Possession of object indistinguishable from firearm on
        Drivers' license, denial or revocation of temporary instruction permit, **ORC 2923.122**

SCHOOL EMPLOYEES RETIREMENT SYSTEM
Benefits, estate tax, **ORC 5731.09**

SCHOOL FINANCE
Expenses
    Educating child, for; court order, **JuvR 34(C)**
Funds, income tax revenues credited to, **ORC 5747.02**
Income tax
    Amended returns, **ORC 5747.10**
    Employer withholding from paycheck, **ORC 5747.06**
        Provision of information by employees, **ORC 5747.06(E)**

SCHOOLS AND SCHOOL DISTRICTS
Activities, weapons
    Illegal conveyance or possession of
        Drivers' license, denial or revocation of temporary instruction permit, **ORC 2923.122**
    Possession of object indistinguishable from firearm at
        Drivers' license, denial or revocation of temporary instruction permit, **ORC 2923.122**
Blood donation programs, information concerning, **ORC 2108.21**
Custody for districting purposes, prohibition, **LucasR 66.1, SumR 66.1, Sup. R 66.1**
Definitions, **ORC 2901.01(C)**
Employees
    Child abuse, reporting, **ORC 2151.421**
    Retirement system. See SCHOOL EMPLOYEES RETIREMENT SYSTEM
    Teachers. See TEACHERS
Escheat for benefit of, **ORC 2105.07**
Estate tax distribution to, **ORC 5731.48**
Expenses
    Educating child, for; court order, **JuvR 34(C)**
Expenses of educating child, court order, **JuvR 34(C)**
Finance. See SCHOOL FINANCE
High schools
    Child support orders in effect beyond age of majority for students, **ORC 3103.031, ORC 3105.21(D), ORC 3109.05(E)**
Institutionalized children, schooling costs, **ORC 2151.362**
Juvenile rehabilitation facilities, agreements with, **ORC 2151.653**
Parental liability for acts of child, community service in lieu of judgment in favor of, **ORC 3109.09**
Parent's access to, noncustodial parent, **ORC 3109.051(J)**
Psychologists
    Child abuse, reporting, **ORC 2151.421**
Rehabilitation facilities, **ORC 2151.65 to 2151.80**
School activity
    Definitions, **ORC 2901.01(C)**
School safety zone
    Definitions, **ORC 2901.01(C)**
Superintendents
    Juvenile delinquency, notice. See JUVENILE DELINQUENCY, at Records and reports
Teachers. See TEACHERS
Tuition, institutionalized children, **ORC 2151.362**

SCHOOLS AND SCHOOL DISTRICTS—*continued*
Weapons
    Illegal conveyance or possession of on school premises
        Drivers' license, denial or revocation of temporary instruction permit, **ORC 2923.122**
    Possession of object indistinguishable from firearm on school premises
        Drivers' license, denial or revocation of temporary instruction permit, **ORC 2923.122**

SEALING RECORDS
Definitions, **ORC 2151.355**
Juvenile courts, criteria for and notice of sealing records, **ORC 2151.356**
Juvenile records, **ORC 2151.358**

SEALS
Juvenile courts, **ORC 2151.20**
    Cuyahoga county, **ORC 2153.14**

SEAT BELTS
Operators and passengers required to wear
    Juveniles, violations by, **ORC 2152.21**

SECOND CHANCE TRUST FUND ADVISORY COMMITTEE
Department of health, **ORC 2108.17**

SECURE CORRECTIONAL FACILITY
Defined, **ORC 2151.011**

SECURED TRANSACTIONS
See also LIENS, generally
Real property sale by fiduciaries, **ORC 2127.36**

SECURITIES
See also BONDS AND NOTES; STOCK
Blockage rule, **ORC 5731.01**
Competency, issuer of securities may treat holders of record as competent, **ORC 5815.03**
Deposit by fiduciaries and custodians, **ORC 2131.21**
Detention homes, to finance, **ORC 2151.655**
Estate tax, valuation, **ORC 5731.01**
Fiduciaries, transactions by
    Investment powers
        Fees, **ORC 2109.371**
Fiduciary's duties. See FIDUCIARIES
Forestry camps, to finance, **ORC 2151.655**
Holders of record, **ORC 5815.02**
Issuance, **ORC 5815.02**
Principal and Income Act, **ORC 5812.38**
Registration
    Custodian, by; under Uniform Transfers to Minor Act, **ORC 5814.04**
Transfer, release by tax commissioner, **ORC 5731.39**
Trustees, bond of trustee, **ORC 5807.02**
Types of, **ORC 5815.02**
Uniform Principal and Income Act, **ORC 5812.38**
Value, estate tax, **ORC 5731.01**

SECURITY, COURTS
Cuyahoga county probate court, **CuyR 9.1, CuyR 9.2**
Franklin county probate court, **FrankR 9.1**
Hamilton county probate court, **HamR 54.1**
Lucas county probate court, **LucasR 9.1**
Stark county probate court, **Sup. R 9.1**

SELF-EMPLOYMENT
Decedent's business, continuation by fiduciary, **ORC 2113.30**

SELF-INCRIMINATION
Competence to stand trial
    Statements during mental evaluation confidential, **ORC 2945.371**

SELF-INCRIMINATION—*continued*
Not guilty by reason of insanity plea
    Statements during mental evaluation confidential, **ORC 2945.371**
Paternity proceedings, **ORC 3111.12**

SENATE, STATE
President, appointment powers
    Legal rights service commission members, **ORC 5123.60**

SENDING STATE
Defined under Interstate Compact on Placement of Children, **ORC 5103.20**

SENIOR CITIZENS
See AGED PERSONS

SENTENCES
Adult cases tried in juvenile court, **ORC 2151.49**
Cruel and unusual punishment, **O Const I § 9**
Imprisonment. See IMPRISONMENT
Imprisonment. See PRISONERS
Juvenile proceedings, adult offenders, **ORC 2151.49**
Suspension, adult cases tried in juvenile courts, **ORC 2151.49, ORC 2151.50**

SEPARATION, LEGAL
See LEGAL SEPARATION

SEPARATION AGREEMENTS
Action to set aside, **ORC 2106.22**
Children
    Care, custody, and control. See CUSTODY OF CHILDREN, DOMESTIC
    Care, custody, and control. See VISITATION RIGHTS
    Paternity, presumption, **ORC 3111.03**
    Support, **ORC 3105.10(B)**
Enforcement, **ORC 3105.10(B)**
Paternity, presumption, **ORC 3111.03**
Power to make, **ORC 3103.06**
Wills, effect, **ORC 2107.33**

SERVICE OF PROCESS
Generally, **JuvR 16, JuvR 20**
See also NOTICE; SUBPOENAS; SUMMONS
Affidavits, time, **JuvR 18(D)**
Annulment of marriage, **ORC 3105.06**
Ante mortem declaration of will validity, action for, **ORC 2107.082, ORC 2107.084**
Attorneys, on, **JuvR 20(B)**
Certified mail, by, **JuvR 16(A)**
    Ante mortem declaration of will validity, action for, **ORC 2107.082**
    Electronic receipts from US Postal Service, **FrankR 75.17**
Clerks of courts, by, **JuvR 17(C)**
Constables, by, **JuvR 17(C)**
    Fees, **ORC 2101.16**
Coroners, by, **JuvR 17(C)**
Deputy court clerk, by, **SumR 87.1**
Divorce, **ORC 3105.06**
Electronic receipts from US Postal Service, certified mail deliveries, **FrankR 75.17**
Eminent domain, **ORC 163.07**
Guardians
    Application, notice to interested parties, **ORC 2111.04**
Heirship determination, **ORC 2123.03, ORC 2123.04**
Income tax assessment
    Delinquent payer, **ORC 5747.13(A)**
Juvenile courts. See JUVENILE COURTS, at Service of process
Legal separation, **ORC 3105.06**
Mail, by
    Answer time after, **JuvR 18(E)**
    Certified mail. See Certified mail, by, this heading

SERVICE OF PROCESS

SERVICE OF PROCESS—*continued*
Methods, **JuvR 16(A)**
    See also particular method, this heading
Minors, **JuvR 16, ORC 2151.28**
Motions, time for, **JuvR 18(D)**
Newspaper publication, by. See Publication, by, this heading
Nonresidents, **JuvR 16(A)**
    Paternity proceedings, **ORC 3111.06**
Notice. See NOTICE, generally
Paternity proceedings, **ORC 3109.23**
    Nonresident defendants, **ORC 3111.06**
    Unborn children, concerning, **ORC 3111.04**
Personal service, **JuvR 16(A)**
    Deposit required, **LucasR 78.5**
Probate courts, **ORC 2101.22**
    Avoidance by parties, **ORC 2101.23**
    Fiduciaries, **ORC 2109.03**
        Embezzlement of assets, **ORC 2109.50**
        Hearing on accounts, filed by, **ORC 2109.32**
    Franklin county probate court, **FrankR 75.13**
    Master commissioners, powers, **ORC 2101.07**
    Penalties for violations, **ORC 2101.99**
    Sheriffs, constables and coroners; duties, **ORC 2101.09**
Production of documents, for. See SUBPOENAS
Proof of service, **JuvR 20(C)**
    Paternity proceedings, **ORC 3109.23**
    Publication affidavit, **JuvR 16(A)**
Publication, by, **JuvR 16(A)**
    See also NOTICE
    Ante mortem declaration of will validity, action for, **ORC 2107.082**
    Divorce, annulment, or legal separation action, **ORC 3105.06**
    Heirship determination, **ORC 2123.04**
    Paternity proceedings, **ORC 3109.23**
Real property sale by fiduciaries, **ORC 2127.14**
Residence service, **JuvR 16(A)**
    Residence unknown, **JuvR 16(A)**
Subpoenas. See SUBPOENAS
Summons. See SUMMONS
Surviving spouse waiver of citation of service to elect, **FrankR 75.16**
Time requirements, **JuvR 18(D)**
Warrant for custody of child, **JuvR 16(B)**
Wills
    Fees, **ORC 2107.62**
    Petition for declaratory judgment of validity, **ORC 2107.082**
    Production, **ORC 2107.09**

SETTLEMENTS
Adult wards, damage claims for injuries, **SupR 69**
Cuyahoga county probate court
    Wrongful death settlements, attorney fees, **CuyR 71.2 et seq.**
Estate tax due Ohio and other states, **ORC 5731.35**
Estates. See EXECUTORS AND ADMINISTRATORS, at Accounts and accounting
Hamilton county probate court
    Personal injury claims, settlement, **HamR 68.1**
        Structured settlements, **HamR 68.2**
        § 10,000 or less, **HamR 67.1**
    Wrongful death settlements, **HamR 70.1**
Lucas county probate court
    Personal injuries, settlement of claims for, **LucasR 68.1**
        § 10,000 or less, **LucasR 68.2**
    Wrongful death settlements, **LucasR 70.1**
        Case management, **LucasR 78.1**
Minors, damage claims for injuries. See Personal injury, minors, this heading
Paternity proceedings, **ORC 3111.19**
Personal injury, minors, **HamR 68.1, ORC 2111.18, ORC 2111.181, SumR 68.1, SupR 68**
    Application, **LucasR 68.1**
    Attorney fees, **CuyR 71.2 et seq.**

SETTLEMENTS—*continued*
Personal injury, minors, **HamR 68.1, ORC 2111.18, ORC 2111.181, SumR 68.1, SupR 68**—*continued*
    Hearings, **LucasR 68.1**
    Structured settlements, **HamR 68.2**
    Ten thousand dollars or less, **HamR 67.1, LucasR 68.2, SumR 67.1**
Personal injury claims, minors
    Franklin county probate court, **FrankR 68.1**
        Birth certificate required, **FrankR 68.1**
        Conference, **FrankR 68.2**
        Separate case number, **FrankR 68.3**
        Structured settlements, **FrankR 68.4**
Stark county probate court
    Birth certificate filed with application for appointment, **Sup. R 66.1**
    Settlements, court costs, **Sup. R 58.1**
    Wrongful death settlements, case management, **Sup. R 78.4**
Structured settlements, **HamR 68.2**
Summit county probate court
    Settlement of injury claims, **SumR 68.1**
        § 10,000 or less, **SumR 67.1**
    Wrongful death settlements, **SumR 70.1**
Wrongful death actions, **FrankR 70.1, LucasR 70.1, ORC 2125.02, SumR 70.1, SupR 70**
    See also WRONGFUL DEATH, at Damages
    Attorney fees, **CuyR 71.2 et seq.**
    Conference, **FrankR 70.4**
    Distribution, **HamR 70.1**
    Wrongful death prototype trust, **FrankR 70.2**
        Multiple beneficiaries, **FrankR 70.3**

SETTLOR
Defined, **ORC 5801.01**

SEX OFFENSES
Child victim
    Generally, See CHILD ABUSE
    Televised or recorded testimony, **ORC 2152.81**
    Videotaped depositions, **ORC 2152.81**
Communicable disease of accused, notice to victim, **ORC 2151.14**
DNA testing of prisoners, **ORC 2901.07**
Juvenile courts, notice to institution or association of adjudication of child as delinquent for committing sexually oriented offense, **ORC 2152.192**
Juvenile delinquents
    Registry, juvenile sex offender, **ORC 2152.82 to 2152.851**
    Resignation of offense, effect on existing order, **ORC 2152.851**
    Sexually oriented offense, child adjudicated delinquent child for committing, **ORC 2152.191, ORC 2152.811**
Mental retardation and developmental disabilities department
    Prohibition of sexual conduct, **ORC 5123.541**

SHARED PARENTING
Generally, **ORC 3109.04**
Modification, **ORC 3109.04(E)**
Termination, **ORC 3109.04(E)**
Visitation rights, **ORC 3109.04(G)**

SHAREHOLDERS
See STOCK

SHARES
See STOCK

SHELLEY'S RULE
Abolished, **ORC 2107.49**

SHELTER CARE
Abused children
    Determination, **ORC 2151.28, ORC 2151.314**
    Release, **ORC 2151.314**

SHELTER CARE—*continued*
Children, **ORC 2151.31**
    See also CUSTODY OF CHILDREN, INSTITUTIONAL; DETENTION HOMES
    Placement in, **JuvR 7(A)**
Defined, **ORC 2151.011**
Delinquent children, **ORC 2151.28**
Dependent and neglected children
    Determination, **ORC 2151.28, ORC 2151.314**
    Release, **ORC 2151.314**
Unruly children, **ORC 2151.28**

SHERIFFS
See also LAW ENFORCEMENT OFFICERS
Accounts and accounting
    Moneys collected, probate courts, **ORC 2101.10**
Amercement, **ORC 2101.10**
Dower judgments, powers and duties, **ORC 5305.06**
Emergency hospitalization of mentally ill, **ORC 5122.10**
Execution of judgment by. See EXECUTION OF JUDGMENT, generally
Fees
    Estate tax matters, **ORC 5731.47**
    Hospitalization of mentally ill, **ORC 5122.43**
    Institutionalization of mentally retarded, **ORC 5123.96**
Hospitalization of mentally ill by, **ORC 5122.10, ORC 5122.11, ORC 5122.141**
Institutionalization of mentally retarded by, **ORC 5123.81**
Judicial sales, powers. See JUDICIAL SALES, generally
Liability
    Collection of moneys for probate courts, **ORC 2101.10**
    Penalties, **ORC 2101.99**
    Service of process, **ORC 2101.09**
Moneys collected by probate courts, **ORC 2101.10**
Probate court duties
    Collection of moneys, **ORC 2101.10**
    Penalties for violations, **ORC 2101.99**
    Service of process, **ORC 2101.09**
Service of process by, **JuvR 17(C)**
    Probate courts, **ORC 2101.09**
        Penalties for violations, **ORC 2101.99**

SHERIFF'S SALE
See JUDICIAL SALES

SHORTHAND REPORTERS
See COURT REPORTERS

SHOW CAUSE HEARINGS
Hamilton county probate court, **HamR 64.2**

SIBLINGS
See also NEXT OF KIN
Descent and distribution, **ORC 2105.06**
    See also DESCENT AND DISTRIBUTION, generally

SIGNATURES
Anatomical gifts, **ORC 2108.04**
Computer-generated probate forms, certification of compliance with rules, **FrankR 52.1**
Franklin county probate court
    Accounts, fiduciaries, **FrankR 64.1**
    Filings with court, **FrankR 57.5, FrankR 57.6**
Grandparent power of attorney, **3109.54**
Loan agreements, **ORC 1335.02**
Trusts, electronic records and signatures, **ORC 5811.02**
Wills, **ORC 2107.03, ORC 2107.04**

SIGNS
Removal by order, compensation, **ORC 163.31 to 163.33**

SINKING FUNDS, MUNICIPAL
Estate tax distribution to, **ORC 5731.48**

SISTERS
See also NEXT OF KIN
Descent and distribution, **ORC 2105.06**
    See also DESCENT AND DISTRIBUTION, generally

SLANDER
Limitation of actions, **ORC 2305.11**

SOCIAL SECURITY NUMBERS
Adopted child, number provided to adoptive parent, **ORC 3107.68**
Birth certificates, accompanying, **ORC 3705.09**
Franklin County Probate Court
    Filings with court, **FrankR 57.14**

SOCIAL WORKERS
Aged persons suffering neglect, abuse, or exploitation; report to county human services department, **ORC 5101.61**
Mentally retarded and developmentally disabled persons, reporting abuse or neglect, **ORC 5123.61, ORC 5123.99**

SOLDIERS
See MILITARY SERVICE; VETERANS

SOLE PROPRIETORSHIP
Decedent's business, continuation by fiduciary, **ORC 2113.30**

SOVEREIGN IMMUNITY
Generally, **O Const I § 16**

SPECIAL ADMINISTRATORS
Generally, **ORC 2113.15 to 2113.17**
See also EXECUTORS AND ADMINISTRATORS

SPECIAL ASSESSMENTS
See ASSESSMENTS, SPECIAL

SPECIAL DAMAGES
Consignment of art works to dealers, special damages for certain violations by dealers, **ORC 5815.48**

SPECIAL EDUCATION
Mental retardation and developmental disabilities department, powers and duties
    Eligibility determinations, **ORC 5123.012**

SPEECH PATHOLOGISTS
Child abuse, reporting, **ORC 2151.421**

SPENDTHRIFT AND DISCRETIONARY TRUSTS
Generally, **ORC 5805.01 to 5805.07**
Beneficiary's creditor or assignee, rights of, **ORC 5805.05**
Creditor or assignee claims against discretionary trust, **ORC 5805.03**
Definition of spendthrift provision, **ORC 5801.01**
Enforceability of spendthrift provision, **ORC 5805.02**
Exceptions, enforceability of spendthrift provision, **ORC 5805.02**
Personal obligations of trustee, **ORC 5805.07**
Settlor, creditor's or assignee's claims against, **ORC 5805.06**
Spendthrift provision, **ORC 5805.01**
Standard, effect on discretionary trusts, **ORC 5805.04**

SPOUSE
See HUSBAND AND WIFE

STANDING
Will contests, **ORC 2107.71**

STARK COUNTY
See COUNTIES, for general provisions
Probate court. See PROBATE COURTS, generally

STARK COUNTY PROBATE COURT
Accounts and accounting
    Address of fiduciary, **Sup. R 64.3**
    Delinquency in filing account, **Sup. R 64.4**

STARK COUNTY PROBATE COURT

Index-106

STARK COUNTY PROBATE COURT—*continued*
Accounts and accounting—*continued*
  Exceptions
    Court costs, **Sup. R 58.1**
  Filing, **Sup. R 64.1**
  Signature of fiduciary, **Sup. R 64.3**
  Vouchers, **Sup. R 64.2**
Acknowledgment of paternity
  Court costs, **Sup. R 58.1**
Adoptions, **Sup. R 75.3**
  Case management, **Sup. R 78.8**
  Court costs, **Sup. R 58.1**
Appointments by court, **Sup. R 8.1**
Appraisals, **Sup. R 61.1 to Sup. R 61.7**
  Estates, relief from administration, **Sup. R 75.2(A)**
  Exceptions, court costs, **Sup. R 58.1**
  Request for, **Sup. R 61.7**
Appraisers
  Appointment, **Sup. R 61.1**
  Real estate appraisers, **Sup. R 61.2**
  Self-dealing prohibited, **Sup. R 61.3**
Attorney fees
  Decedent's estates, **Sup. R 71.2**
  Estates, **Sup. R 71.2**
  Fiduciary, attorney serving as, **Sup. R 71.1**
  Guardianships, **Sup. R 71.3**
  Paralegal fees, **Sup. R 75.5**
Bonds, fiduciaries, **Sup. R 75.1**
Case management, **Sup. R 78.1 to Sup. R 78.8**
Civil actions
  Case management, **Sup. R 78.1**
  Court costs, **Sup. R 58.1**
Compensation
  Appointees, **Sup. R 8.1**
  Guardians, **Sup. R 73.1**
  Trustees
    Corporate trustees, **Sup. R 74.1**
    Individual trustees, **Sup. R 74.2**
Corporate trustees, compensation, **Sup. R 74.1**
Court costs, **Sup. R 58.1**
Disputed appraisals, **Sup. R 61.7**
Electronic mail filings with court not acceptable, **Sup. R 57.1**
Estates
  Attorney fees, **Sup. R 71.2**
  Case management, **Sup. R 78.3**
  Court costs, **Sup. R 58.1**
  Minors, § 10,000 or less, **Sup. R 67.1**
  Relief from administration, **Sup. R 75.2**
  Summary administration, **Sup. R 75.4**
Exhibits, disposition, **Sup. R 57.8**
Facsimile filings with court not acceptable, **Sup. R 57.1**
Fees and costs
  Attorney fees
    Decedent's estates, **Sup. R 71.2**
    Guardianships, **Sup. R 71.3**
  Court costs, **Sup. R 58.1**
Fiduciaries
  Bonds, **Sup. R 75.1**
  Nonresident, appointment, **Sup. R 60.1**
Filings with court
  Address of fiduciary to be included, **Sup. R 57.2**
  Case number to be included, **Sup. R 57.6**
  Electronic mail, not acceptable, **Sup. R 57.1**
  Exhibits, disposition, **Sup. R 57.8**
  Facsimile transmission, not acceptable, **Sup. R 57.1**
  Forwarding copies, **Sup. R 57.7**
  Signatures required
    Attorney signatures, **Sup. R 57.4**
    Fiduciary signatures, **Sup. R 57.5**
    Original signatures, **Sup. R 57.3**
Guardians, compensation, **Sup. R 73.1**

STARK COUNTY PROBATE COURT—*continued*
Guardianships, **Sup. R 66.1 to Sup. R 66.6**
  Address, notice of change, **Sup. R 66.5**
  Attorney fees, **Sup. R 71.3**
  Case management, **Sup. R 78.5**
  Expert evaluation, statement of, **Sup. R 66.6**
  Personal property, sale, **Sup. R 66.3**
  Reports, guardians, **Sup. R 66.2**
  Wills, deposit of, **Sup. R 66.4**
Hours of the court, **Sup. R 53.1**
Household furnishings, appraisal, **Sup. R 61.6**
Individual trustees, compensation, **Sup. R 74.2**
Inventory
  Appraisal, request for, **Sup. R 61.7**
  Exceptions, court costs, **Sup. R 58.1**
Land sales
  Case management, **Sup. R 78.2**
  Court costs, **Sup. R 58.1**
Magistrates
  Objections to decisions, **Sup. R 75.7**
Minors
  Birth certificate filed with application for appointment, **Sup. R 66.1**
  Estates of § 10,000 or less, **Sup. R 67.1**
  Personal injury claims, settlement
    Separate case number, **Sup. R 68.1**
    Structured settlements, **Sup. R 68.2**
  Settlements, court costs, **Sup. R 58.1**
Motions, case management, **Sup. R 78.7**
Motor vehicles, readily ascertainable value, **Sup. R 61.5**
Name change, court costs, **Sup. R 58.1**
No administration, **Sup. R 75.2**
Nonresident fiduciaries, appointment, **Sup. R 60.1**
Notice
  Estates, relief from administration, **Sup. R 75.2(B)**
Objections to magistrate's decision, **Sup. R 75.7**
Paralegal fees, **Sup. R 75.5**
Paternity, acknowledgement
  Court costs, **Sup. R 58.1**
Personal injury claims of minors, settlement
  Separate case number, **Sup. R 68.1**
  Structured settlements, **Sup. R 68.2**
Personal property, appraisal, **Sup. R 61.6**
Pretrial procedure, **Sup. R 78.1**
Real property
  Readily ascertainable value, **Sup. R 61.4**
Recording of proceedings, **Sup. R 11.1**
Reports
  Guardians, **Sup. R 66.2**
Security plans, **Sup. R 9.1**
Settlements
  Minors, court costs, **Sup. R 58.1**
  Personal injury claims of minors, settlement
    Separate case number, **Sup. R 68.1**
    Structured settlements, **Sup. R 68.2**
  Wrongful death trust, **Sup. R 70.1**
    Multiple beneficiaries, **Sup. R 70.2**
Signatures
  Accounts, fiduciary signature, **Sup. R 64.3**
  Filings with court
    Attorney signatures, **Sup. R 57.4**
    Fiduciary signatures, **Sup. R 57.5**
    Original signatures, **Sup. R 57.3**
Subpoenas, court costs, **Sup. R 58.1**
Testamentary trusts, court costs, **Sup. R 58.1**
Trustees, compensation
  Corporate trustees, **Sup. R 74.1**
  Individual trustees, **Sup. R 74.2**
Trusts, case management, **Sup. R 78.6**
Wills
  Guardianships, deposit with court, **Sup. R 66.4**

STARK COUNTY PROBATE COURT—*continued*
Wills deposited with court, **Sup. R 75.6**
Wrongful death settlements, case management, **Sup. R 78.4**
Wrongful death trust, court costs, **Sup. R 58.1**
Wrongful death trusts, **Sup. R 70.1**
 Multiple beneficiaries, **Sup. R 70.2**

STATE
Actions involving, **O Const I § 16**
Aid. See APPROPRIATIONS
Appropriation of property by. See EMINENT DOMAIN
Attorney general. See ATTORNEY GENERAL
Employees. See PUBLIC EMPLOYEES
Escheat to. See ESCHEAT
Gifts and bequests to
 Estate tax deduction, **ORC 5731.17**
Institutions. See CHARITABLE INSTITUTIONS
Institutions. See CORRECTIONAL INSTITUTIONS
Institutions. See CORRECTIONAL INSTITUTIONS; MENTALLY ILL PERSONS
Records and reports. See RECORDS AND REPORTS, generally
Rights and privileges, **O Const I § 2**
Sovereign immunity, **O Const I § 16**

STATE HUMAN SERVICES ADMINISTRATION
Defined, **ORC 5103.22**

STATES OTHER THAN OHIO
See FOREIGN STATES

STATUTE AGAINST PERPETUITIES
Generally, **ORC 2131.08, ORC 2131.09**

STATUTE OF FRAUDS
Leases, **ORC 1335.04**
Loan agreements, **ORC 1335.02**

STATUTE OF LIMITATIONS
See LIMITATION OF ACTIONS

STATUTES
Construction. See DEFINITIONS
Construction. See STATUTORY CONSTRUCTION
Court rules, effect on, **O Const IV § 5**
Descent and distribution, **ORC 2105.06**
 See also DESCENT AND DISTRIBUTION
Retroactive, **O Const II § 28**

STATUTORY AGENTS
Income tax, state
 Returns by, **ORC 5747.08(F)**

STATUTORY CONSTRUCTION
Bequest, definition, **ORC 2107.011, ORC 5815.01**
Inheritance, definition, **ORC 2107.011, ORC 5815.01**
Juvenile courts, laws governing, **ORC 2151.01**

STEPCHILDREN
Adoption by stepparents, **ORC 3107.02, ORC 3107.03, ORC 5103.16**
 Parents' consent to minor's adoption, **ORC 3107.081**
Intestate succession, **ORC 2105.06**
 See also DESCENT AND DISTRIBUTION, generally

STERILIZATION
Mentally retarded, consent, **ORC 5123.86**

STOCK
See also SECURITIES
Fiduciaries, powers, **ORC 2109.09, ORC 2109.37, ORC 2109.40**
Fiduciary's powers and duties
 Affiliated investment companies, **ORC 2109.371**
Transfer of estate property, release by tax commissioner, **ORC 5731.39**

STOCK BONUS PLANS
Rule against perpetuities, exemption from, **ORC 2131.09**

STOCKHOLDERS
See also STOCK
Custodians of securities, under uniform transfers to minors act, **ORC 5814.04**

STREETS
See HIGHWAYS AND ROADS

SUBPOENAS
Generally, **JuvR 17**
See also SERVICE OF PROCESS, generally; SUMMONS
Contempt for noncompliance, **JuvR 17(G)**
Costs, **SumR Appx A, Sup. R 58.1**
 Juvenile proceeding, **JuvR 17(B)**
Duties in responding to, **JuvR 17(E)**
Failure to obey, **JuvR 17(G)**
 See also CONTEMPT, generally
Format, **JuvR 17(A)**
Juvenile proceedings. See JUVENILE COURTS, at Service of process
Paternity proceedings, **ORC 3111.12**
Persons subject to, protection, **JuvR 17(D)**
Protection of persons subject to, **JuvR 17(D)**
Responding to, duties, **JuvR 17(E)**
Service, **JuvR 17(D)**
 See also SERVICE OF PROCESS, generally
Under burden of, effect, **JuvR 17(D)**
Witnesses, juvenile proceeding, **JuvR 17(A)**

SUBSTANTIALLY IDENTICAL INTEREST
Trusts, **ORC 5803.04**

SUCCESSION, INTESTATE
Generally, **ORC Ch 2105**
See also DESCENT AND DISTRIBUTION

SUCCESSION TO PROPERTY, DISCLAIMER OF
See DISCLAIMER OF SUCCESSION TO PROPERTY

SUCCESSOR REPRESENTATIVES
Anatomical gifts. See ANATOMICAL GIFTS

SUICIDE
Assisting, living will not authorizing, **ORC 2133.12**
Living wills, death as result of withdrawal or withholding life-sustaining equipment not constituting, **ORC 2133.12**
Mentally retarded in state institution, reporting, **ORC 5123.093**

SUITS
Generally, See ACTIONS
Criminal. See CRIMINAL PROSECUTIONS

SUMMARY REPORTS
Adoption, abuse and neglect determination summary report, **ORC 3107.034**

SUMMIT COUNTY
See COUNTIES, for general provisions
Probate court. See SUMMIT COUNTY PROBATE COURT

SUMMIT COUNTY PROBATE COURT
Accounts and accounting, **SumR 64.1**
 Guardians' accountings, **SumR 64.1(B)**
 Overdue, citations, **SumR 78.1(D)**
 Partial accounts, **SumR 64.1(A)**
Adoptions, **SumR 94.1**
 Fees, **SumR Appx B**
 Supervision, **SumR 78.1(C)**
Appraisers, compensation, **SumR 61.1**
Appropriation of property, **SumR 97.1**
Assets, concealment, **SumR 96.1**

SUMMIT COUNTY PROBATE COURT

SUMMIT COUNTY PROBATE COURT—*continued*

Attorney fees, **SumR 71.1, SumR Appx E**
    Land sale proceedings, **SumR 71.1(C), SumR Appx G**
    Notice, **SumR Appx F**
Attorneys
    Sureties, not to act as, **SumR 89.1**
    Withdrawal, **SumR 78.1(F)**
Birth, correction, **SumR 95.1(B)**
Bonds, guardians, **SumR 66.1(A)**
Case management, **SumR 78.1**
Change of name, **SumR 93.1**
Citations for overdue accounts, reports, or inventories, **SumR 78.1(D)**
Civil cases
    Case management, **SumR 78.1(E)**
    Court costs, **SumR Appx A**
Civil commitments, supervision, **SumR 78.1(C)**
Compensation
    Appraisers, **SumR 61.1**
    Fiduciaries, **SumR 72.1, SumR Appx D**
    Guardians, **SumR 73.1, SumR Appx C**
    Guardians ad litem, **SumR 91.1(C)**
    Trustees, **SumR 74.1**
Concealment of assets, **SumR 96.1**
Continuances, **SumR 56.1(A)**
Corporate trustees, compensation, **SumR 74.1(A)**
Correction of birth, **SumR 95.1(B)**
Court costs, deposits, **SumR 58.1, SumR Appx A**
Decisions of magistrates, **SumR 54.1**
Estates
    Administration, **SumR 60.1**
        Attorney fees, **SumR 71.1(A)**
        Court costs, **SumR Appx A**
        Supervision, **SumR 78.1(B)**
Examination of probate records, **SumR 55.1**
Expense hearings, adoptions, **SumR 94.1(B)**
Fees and costs
    Adoptions, **SumR 94.1(A), SumR Appx B**
    Appraiser fees, **SumR 61.1**
    Court costs, **SumR 58.1, SumR Appx A**
    Fiduciaries, **SumR 72.1**
    Guardians ad litem, **SumR 91.1(C)**
    Record of proceedings, **SumR 54.2(C)**
Fiduciaries
    Compensation, **SumR 72.1, SumR Appx D**
    Qualifications, **SumR 60.1**
Filings with court, **SumR 57.1**
Guardians, compensation, **SumR 73.1, SumR Appx C**
Guardians ad litem, **SumR 91.1**
Guardianships, **SumR 66.1**
    Accounting by guardian, **SumR 64.1(B)**
    Adults, mediation, **SumR 98.1**
    Bonds of guardian, **SumR 66.1(A)**
    Court costs, **SumR Appx A**
    Mediation, adult guardianships, **SumR 98.1**
    Reports, **SumR 66.1(B)**
    Supervision, **SumR 78.1(B)**
Hearings
    Adoptions
        Expenses, **SumR 94.1(B)**
        Notice, **SumR 94.1(C)**
    Wrongful death settlements, **SumR 70.1(C)**
Hours of court, **SumR 53.1**
Individual trustees, compensation, **SumR 74.1(B)**
Insolvent estates, attorney fees, **SumR 71.1(B)**
Inventory
    Case management, **SumR 78.1(A)**
    Notice, **SumR 88.1**
    Overdue, citations, **SumR 78.1(D)**
    Schedule of assets, **SumR 88.2**
Judges, record of proceedings before, **SumR 54.2(A)**
Judgment entries, **SumR 57.1**

SUMMIT COUNTY PROBATE COURT—*continued*

Land sales, **SumR 65.1**
    Appraisers, compensation, **SumR 61.1**
    Attorney fees, **SumR 71.1(C), SumR Appx G**
    Preliminary judicial title, **SumR 65.1(A)**
    Real estate brokers' commissions, **SumR 65.1(B)**
Leaves to plead, **SumR 56.1(B)**
Letters of authority to administer estate, application, **SumR 60.1**
Magistrates, **SumR 54.1**
    Record of proceedings before, **SumR 54.2(B)**
Management and retention of records, **SumR 26.1**
Marriage license waiting period waived, **SumR 86.1**
Mediation, adult guardianships or alternatives, **SumR 98.1**
Minors
    Settlement of injury claims, **SumR 68.1**
        § 10,000 or less, **SumR 67.1**
Motions, **SumR 57.1**
Name, change of, **SumR 93.1**
Notice
    Administrator of will, appointment, **SumR 60.1**
    Adoption hearings, **SumR 94.1(C)**
    Attorney fees, **SumR Appx F**
    Inventory, filing, **SumR 88.1**
    Wrongful death settlement hearings, **SumR 70.1(B)**
Orders of reference, **SumR 54.1**
Personal injuries
    Minors, injury claims, **SumR 68.1**
        § 10,000 or less, **SumR 67.1**
    Wrongful death, **SumR 70.1**
Probate of will, applications, **SumR 59.1**
Real estate brokers' commissions, land sales, **SumR 65.1(B)**
Record of proceedings, **SumR 54.2**
Records of court, removal and examination, **SumR 55.1**
Removal of files, **SumR 55.1**
Reports
    Guardians, **SumR 66.1(B)**
    Overdue, citations, **SumR 78.1(D)**
Safe deposit box, removal of will from, **SumR 90.1**
Schedule of assets, **SumR 88.2**
School residency, guardianships for purpose of prohibited, **SumR 66.1(A)**
Service of process or notice, **SumR 87.1**
Settlements
    Minors, injury claims, **SumR 68.1**
        § 10,000 or less, **SumR 67.1**
    Wrongful death, **SumR 70.1**
Subpoenas, court costs, **SumR Appx A**
Sureties, attorneys not to act as, **SumR 89.1**
Title to property
    Preliminary judicial title, land sales, **SumR 65.1(A)**
Transcripts, **SumR 54.2(D)**
Trustees, compensation, **SumR 74.1**
Trusts, **SumR 92.1**
    Court costs, **SumR Appx A**
    Supervision, **SumR 78.1(C)**
Wills
    Probate of will, applications, **SumR 59.1**
    Removal from safe deposit boxes, **SumR 90.1**
Withdrawal of counsel, **SumR 78.1(F)**
Wrongful death settlements, **SumR 70.1**

SUMMONS

See also SERVICE OF PROCESS; SUBPOENAS
Costs, **LucasR 78.5**
Eminent domain, **ORC 163.07**
Form, **JuvR 15(A)**
Issuance, **JuvR 15(A)**
Juvenile proceedings. See JUVENILE COURTS, at Service of process, and at Summons
Service, **JuvR 16(A)**
    See also SERVICE OF PROCESS, generally

SUPPORT AND MAINTENANCE
Abandonment and neglect
    Affidavit for adoption, **ORC 3107.07(A)**
    Divorce, grounds for, **ORC 3105.01(B)**
    Legal separation, grounds for, **ORC 3105.17(A)(2)**
Child support
    Administrative order, health care, **ORC 3111.81**
    Agency, parental payment to, **ORC 2151.361**
    Health care, administrative order, **ORC 3111.81**
    Juvenile courts and delinquent and dependent children, **ORC 2151.361**
Child support. See CHILD SUPPORT
Guardianship, duties, **ORC 2111.13**
    Leases of mineral rights by guardians, to secure, **ORC 2111.26**
    Monies paid to ward, **ORC 2111.131(B)**
Minors. See CHILD SUPPORT
Missing person's estate needed for, **ORC Ch 2119**
Nonsupport. See Abandonment and neglect, this heading
Paternity proceedings. See PARENTAGE ACTIONS, at Administrative support orders, and at Support orders
Wrongful death action to recover loss of support, **ORC 2125.02**

SUPREME COURT, STATE
Administrative director, **O Const IV § 5**
Appeals to. See APPEALS, generally
Appointment powers
    Legal rights service commission chairman, **ORC 5123.60**
Case reporting, **O Const IV § 2**
Chief justice, absence or disability of, **O Const IV § 2**
Clerk
    See also CLERKS OF COURTS, generally
Judges, **O Const IV § 2**
Jurisdiction, **O Const IV § 2**
Juvenile courts, assignment of judges to, **ORC 2151.07**
Powers and duties, **O Const IV § 1**, **O Const IV § 5**
Probate courts, assignment of judges to, **ORC 2101.37**
Rulemaking powers
    Bar of Ohio, for, **O Const IV § 5**
    Codes of ethics, **O Const IV § 5**
    Juvenile courts, for, **ORC 2151.17**
    Probate court, **ORC 2101.04**
    State courts, procedure, **O Const IV § 5**

SURETIES
Attorneys not to act as, **HamR 75.1**, **SumR 89.1**
Bail. See BAIL
Bonds. See BONDS, SURETY
Fiduciary's bond. See FIDUCIARIES
Statute of frauds, applicability, **ORC 1335.05**

SURETY BONDS
See BONDS, SURETY

SURVEYS
Eminent domain, under
    State agencies, by, **ORC 163.03**

SURVIVING SPOUSE
Administrator, as. See EXECUTORS AND ADMINISTRATORS, generally
Allowance for support, **ORC 2106.13**
Anatomical gifts by, **ORC 2108.02**
Annulment of marriage, effect
    Property rights after, **ORC 2107.33**
Automobile, transfer to, **ORC 2106.18(A)**, **ORC 4505.10**
Automobiles
    Joint ownership with right of survivorship
        Designation in beneficiary form, **ORC 2131.13**
Boats and watercraft, transfer of title to, **ORC 2106.19**
Construction of will, complaint, **ORC 2106.03**
Curtesy, estate tax, **ORC 5731.04**, **ORC 5731.13**

SURVIVING SPOUSE—continued
Death
    Effect on election, **ORC 2106.04**
        Mansion house election, **ORC 2106.10(E)**
Descent and distribution, **ORC 2105.06**
    Method of payment, **ORC 2106.11**
    Share of estate not passed under will, **ORC 2106.05**
Disability, legal; effect, **ORC 2106.08**
Distribution in kind, **ORC 2106.11**
Divorce, dissolution, annulment, separation
    Property rights after, **ORC 2107.33**
Dower, **ORC Ch 2103**, **ORC Ch 5305**
    See also DOWER
Election against the will, **ORC 2106.01**, **ORC 2106.06**
    See also Election by, this heading
    Executors' and administrators' liability, **ORC 2113.53**
    Mansion home, **ORC 2106.05**, **ORC 2106.10**, **ORC 2106.15**
    Remainder
        Effect, **ORC 2106.01(D)**
Election by, **ORC 2106.01 to 2106.08**, **ORC 2106.16**
    Citation to, **ORC 2106.01**, **ORC 2106.02**
    Death, effect, **ORC 2106.04**, **ORC 2106.10(E)**
    Extension of time, **ORC 2106.01(E)**
    Failure to make, **ORC 2106.04**
        Legal disability, **ORC 2106.08**
    Fees, **ORC 2101.16**
    Inter vivos trust
        Addition to by testator; effect, **ORC 2107.63**
    Mansion house, **ORC 2106.05**, **ORC 2106.10**, **ORC 2106.15**
    Presumption, failure to make election, **ORC 2106.24**
    Rights explained, **ORC 2106.07**
    Sale of personal property, exceptions, **ORC 2113.40**
    Taking against the will. See Election against the will, this heading
    Time limit, **ORC 2106.01(E)**
Election under the will, **ORC 2106.05**
    See also Election by, this heading
Estate tax
    See also DOWER
    Deduction for property interests, **ORC 5731.15**
Executor, as. See EXECUTORS AND ADMINISTRATORS, generally
Exercising of rights, **ORC 2106.25**
Fees, probate court, **ORC 2101.16**
Fiduciary, as. See EXECUTORS AND ADMINISTRATORS, generally
Homestead, **ORC 2106.05**, **ORC 2106.10**, **ORC 2106.15**
Incompetent, effect on election, **ORC 2106.08**
Inter vivos trust, election
    Addition to by testators, effect, **ORC 2107.63**
Intestate succession, **ORC 2105.06**
    Method of payment, **ORC 2106.11**
    Share of estate not passed under will, **ORC 2106.05**
Land sale proceedings, surviving spouse as purchaser, **ORC 2127.04**
Mansion house, rights, **ORC 2106.05**, **ORC 2106.10**, **ORC 2106.15**
Monetary share, intestate succession, **ORC 2105.06**
    Method of payment, **ORC 2106.11**
Motor vehicles
    Joint ownership with right of survivorship
        Designation in beneficiary form, **ORC 2131.13**
Motorcycles
    Transfer to, **ORC 2106.18(D)**
Notice
    Election, **ORC 2106.02**
    Inventory and appraisement, **ORC 2115.04**
        Hearing on, **ORC 2115.16**
    Probate of will
        Admission of will, **ORC 2107.19**
        Lost, spoliated, or destroyed will, **ORC 2107.27**
        Release of estate from administration, **ORC 2113.03**
Outboard motors, transfer of title to, **ORC 2106.19**
Preneed funeral contract, effect of on duties, **ORC 3103.03(E)**
Probate court fees, **ORC 2101.16**

SURVIVING SPOUSE—continued
Probate court making election, legal disability, **ORC 2106.08**
Purchases from estate, rights, **ORC 2106.16**
　　See also Election by, this heading
　　Fees, **ORC 2101.16**
　　Real property, **ORC 2127.04**
Retention of other rights, **ORC 2106.24**
Revocation of will, effect, **ORC 2107.33**
Rights, exercising of, **ORC 2106.25**
Separation, effect
　　Property rights after, **ORC 2107.33**
Service of process, waiver, **FrankR 75.16**
Sole heir, as, **ORC 2106.01(F)**
Straddling estates, tax deduction, **ORC 5731.161**
Survivorship, right of
　　Motor vehicle, watercraft or outboard motor
　　　　Designation in beneficiary form, **ORC 2131.13**
Survivorship tenancy
　　Recording, **ORC 5302.17**
Taking against the will. See Election against the will, this heading
Taking under the will. See Election under the will, this heading
Transfer of property to, administration, **ORC 2113.03**
Trucks
　　Transfer to, **ORC 2106.18(D)**
Trust
　　Interest granted to, spendthrift provision not causing forfeiture or postponement, **ORC 5815.22**
Trust not to require or permit accumulation for more than one year of property granted to, **ORC 5815.23**
Watercraft or outboard motor, transfer to
　　Designation of transfer on death beneficiary, **ORC 1548.072**, **ORC 2131.13**
Will contest, effect on election, **ORC 2106.01(E)**
Wrongful death actions on behalf of, **ORC Ch 2125**

SURVIVORSHIP
Accounts. See BANKS AND BANKING, at Accounts
Descent and distribution
　　Applicability, **ORC 2105.39**
　　Co-owners with right of survivorship, **ORC 2105.34**
　　Definitions, **ORC 2105.31**
　　Establishment of death, **ORC 2105.35**
　　Exceptions, determination of survivorship, **ORC 2105.36**
　　Liability of payor or other third party, **ORC 2105.37**
　　Payor, liability of, **ORC 2105.37**
　　Protected purchasers, **ORC 2105.38**
　　Severability, **ORC 2105.39**
　　Specified event, determination of survivorship with respect to, **ORC 2105.33**
　　Specified person, determination of survivorship with respect to, **ORC 2105.32**
　　Third party, liability of, **ORC 2105.37**
Estate tax, **ORC 5731.07**, **ORC 5731.10**
Right of
　　Jointly owned motor vehicle, watercraft or outboard motor
　　　　Designation of transfer on death beneficiary, **ORC 1548.072**, **ORC 2131.13**
Transfers conditioned on, estate tax, **ORC 5731.07**

SURVIVORSHIP TENANCIES
Generally, **ORC 5302.17**, **ORC 5302.20**
Creditors' powers, **ORC 5302.20(C)**
Deed, form, **ORC 5302.17**
Defined, **ORC 5302.20(A)**
Marriage termination, effect, **ORC 5302.20(C)**
Termination upon conveyance to another, **ORC 5302.20(C)**
Transfer of interest upon death, recording, **ORC 5302.17**
Transfer-on-death securities held in, **ORC 1709.02**

SWINDLING
See FRAUD

TAPE RECORDINGS
Judge, matters heard by, **SumR 54.2(A)**
Probate court proceedings, **SupR 54(B)**
Probate court records, **ORC 2101.121**

TAX APPEALS
See APPEALS

TAX LIENS
See LIENS

TAXATION
Department. See TAXATION DEPARTMENT
Estate tax
　　Federal. See ESTATE TAX, FEDERAL
　　Ohio, **ORC Ch 5731**
　　　　See also ESTATE TAX
Income tax
　　Federal. See INCOME TAX, FEDERAL
　　State. See INCOME TAX, STATE
Inheritance tax. See ESTATE TAX
Personal property. See PERSONAL PROPERTY, TAXATION
Real property. See REAL PROPERTY, TAXATION
Refund. See particular tax concerned
Returns. See particular tax concerned
Revenues. See FUNDS, PUBLIC
Securities, county taxing authority's submission of securities issues to electors, **ORC 2151.655**
Trusts. See TRUSTS

TAXATION DEPARTMENT
Agents, appointment; estate tax, **ORC 5731.41**
Attorneys employed for estate tax matters, **ORC 5731.43**
Commissioner
　　Estate tax documents, confidentiality, **ORC 5731.90**
Estate tax, **ORC Ch 5731**
Safe deposit boxes, inventory and release after death of owner, **ORC 5731.39**

TAXING DISTRICTS
Gifts and bequests to, estate tax deduction, **ORC 5731.17**

TEACHERS
Child abuse, reporting, **ORC 2151.421**
Juvenile rehabilitation facilities, **ORC 2151.653**
Mentally retarded and developmentally disabled persons, reporting abuse or neglect, **ORC 5123.61**, **ORC 5123.99**

TEACHERS RETIREMENT SYSTEM
Benefits, estate tax, **ORC 5731.09**

TELEVISION
Closed circuit monitor
　　Child sex offense victim's testimony, used for, **ORC 2152.81**
Trials, broadcasting, **SupR 12**
　　Probate courts, **SupR 54(B)**

TEMPORARY CUSTODY
Defined, **ORC 2151.011**

TEMPORARY ORDERS
Adoption, temporary order regarding allocation of parental rights and responsibilities while action pending, **ORC 3109.043**

TENANCY
Common. See TENANTS IN COMMON
Joint. See JOINT TENANCY
Life estates. See LIFE ESTATES

TENANCY IN TAIL
Generally, **ORC 2131.09**

TENANTS IN COMMON
Estates by the entireties, **ORC 5302.21**

TENANTS IN COMMON—*continued*
Transfer-on-death securities, tenancy in common precluded, **ORC 1709.02**

TERMINATION OF GRANDPARENT'S CARETAKER AUTHORIZATION AFFIDAVIT
Generally, 3109.70

TERMINATION OF PARENTAL RIGHTS
See CUSTODY OF CHILDREN, INSTITUTIONAL, at Permanent

TERMINATION OF POWER OF ATTORNEY
Grandparent power of attorney, 3109.59, 3109.60

TERMS OF A TRUST
Defined, **ORC 5801.01**

TESTAMENTARY TRUSTEES
See also TESTAMENTARY TRUSTS, generally
Accounts and accounting, **ORC 2109.11**
Appointment, **ORC 2101.24**
Bond, **ORC 2109.05**
    Conditions, **ORC 2109.11**
    Foreign will, **ORC 2129.28 to 2129.30**
    Real estate trusts, **ORC 2129.28 to 2129.30**
Eligibility, **ORC 2109.21**
Foreign will, **ORC 2129.28 to 2129.30**
Funds, allocation between principal and income, **ORC Ch 1340**
Laws applicable, **ORC 2109.69**
Life insurance proceeds, disposition, **ORC 2107.64**
Nonresident, powers and duties, **ORC 2109.21**
Probate courts, jurisdiction, **ORC 2101.24**
Real estate trusts, **ORC 2129.28 to 2129.30**
Records and reports, accounting duties, **ORC 2101.24**
Remainderman's interest, protection by, **ORC 2113.58**
Removal, **ORC 2101.24**
Residency requirements, **ORC 2109.21**
Retirement benefit plans, **ORC 2107.64**
Revocation due to divorce, annulment, separation, or dissolution, **ORC 2107.33**
Sale of assets by, **ORC 2113.39**
Transactions between fiduciaries, **ORC 5815.24**
Will contests, powers during, **ORC 2113.21**

TESTAMENTARY TRUSTS
See also TESTAMENTARY TRUSTEES, generally
Accumulation for more than one year of property granted to surviving spouse and qualifying for marital deduction not required or permitted, **ORC 5815.23**
Allocation between income and principal, **ORC 2109.68, ORC Ch 1340**
Disabled individuals, supplemental services for, **ORC 5815.28**
Federal estate tax marital deduction, distribution by fiduciary involving, **ORC 5815.21**
Foreign will creating, **ORC 2129.27 to 2129.30**
Life insurance proceeds, disposition, **ORC 2107.64**
Limitation of liability of fiduciaries, **ORC 5815.24**
Other persons, limitation on liability of fiduciaries when certain powers granted to, **ORC 5815.25**
Responsibilities of fiduciaries, **ORC 5815.24**
Spendthrift provision not causing forfeiture or postponement of interest granted to surviving spouse and qualifying for marital deduction, **ORC 5815.22**
Temporary investments by fiduciary, procedure, **ORC 5815.26**
Termination, **ORC 2101.24, ORC 2109.62**
Transactions between fiduciaries, **ORC 5815.24**

TESTAMENTS
See WILLS

TESTATORS
See also WILLS
Acknowledgment of will, **ORC 2107.03**

TESTATORS—*continued*
Aliens as, **ORC 2129.06**
Charitable bequests, validity. See LEGACIES AND DEVISES, at Charitable bequests
Eligibility, **ORC 2107.02**
Petition for declaratory judgment on validity of will, **ORC 2107.081**
Residency requirements, **ORC 2107.11**
Signatures, **ORC 2107.03, ORC 2107.04**
Wills. See WILLS

TESTIMONY
See WITNESSES AND TESTIMONY

TESTS
Blood. See BLOOD
Drunk driving, **ORC 4511.19**
Genetic. See GENETIC TESTS

THEFT
Identity of another, taking, **ORC 2913.49**
Mental institutions, reporting occurrences, **ORC 5123.093**
Minor committing, parental liability, **ORC 3109.09**
Personal identifying information, taking of another's, **ORC 2913.49**
Taking identity of another, **ORC 2913.49**

THIRD PARTIES
Fiduciaries
    Approval of third-party distribution, **ORC 2109.361**
    Duty to third parties, **ORC 5815.16**
Transfers to Minors Act, limitation on third person's liability, **ORC 5814.06**

TIMBER
Trust property consisting of timber rights
    Receipts, allocation between income and principal, **ORC 5812.35**

TIME
Generally, **JuvR 18**
See also particular subject concerned
Additional, after service by mail, **JuvR 18(E)**
Computation, **JuvR 18(A)**
Extension, **JuvR 18(B), JuvR 22(E)**
    Service by mail, after, **JuvR 18(E)**
Juvenile proceedings, **JuvR 18**
Limitation of actions. See LIMITATION OF ACTIONS
Mail service, additional time allowed, **JuvR 18(E)**
Motions. See MOTIONS
Statute of limitations. See LIMITATION OF ACTIONS
Term of court, effect of expiration, **JuvR 18(C)**

TITLE TO PROPERTY
Acquisition from person convicted of homicide or adjudicated not guilty by reason of insanity, effect, **ORC 2105.19**
Actions involving
    Estate assets. See Estate assets, actions, this heading
    Recovering, limitation of actions, **ORC 2305.04**
Aliens, rights, **ORC 2105.16**
Deeds. See DEEDS
Descent and distribution, **ORC 2105.06**
    See also DESCENT AND DISTRIBUTION
Dower interest, **ORC 2103.021**
    Waiver of title in favor of dower, **ORC 2103.03**
Eminent domain, **ORC Ch 163**
    See also EMINENT DOMAIN
Escheat, **ORC 2105.09**
Estate assets, actions, **ORC 2117.30**
    Intestate succession, **ORC 2105.061**
    Land sale proceedings, **SupR 65(A)**
    Nonresident decedent's, **ORC 2129.21**
    Presumed decedent's estate, **ORC 2121.06, ORC 2121.07**
    Purchase from, vacated order of settlement of account, **ORC 2109.35**
    Unclaimed, **ORC 2113.65, ORC 2113.68**

TITLE TO PROPERTY

Index-112

TITLE TO PROPERTY—continued
Estates by the entireties, **ORC 5302.21**
Evidence, as, **ORC 2127.35**
Pretermitted heir statute, effect, **ORC 2107.34**
    Debt payments, contributions by, **ORC 2107.55**
Trust, purchase from; vacated order of settlement of account, **ORC 2109.35**
Wills, subsequent; effect on conveyance, **ORC 2107.47**

TOMBSTONES
See also CEMETERIES
Probate court allowance for, **ORC 2113.37**

TORTS
See also NEGLIGENCE
Claims against estate arising out of, **ORC 2117.06**
    Proof, **ORC 2117.08**
    Wrongful death, **ORC Ch 2125**
      See also WRONGFUL DEATH
Limitation of actions, **ORC 2305.09**
Survival of actions, **ORC 2305.21**

TOWNSHIPS
Funds
    Estate tax distribution to, **ORC 5731.48**
    General fund
      Income tax revenues from state, allocation, **ORC 5747.51 to 5747.55**
Gifts and grants to, estate tax deductions, **ORC 5731.17**

TRAFFIC OFFENSES
Complaint, **JuvR 10(C)**
Court records, **ORC 4507.021**
Dismissal of action
    Juvenile offender, **ORC 2151.35**
Financial Responsibility Act, juvenile offenders subject to, **ORC 2152.21**
Fines, juvenile offenders, **ORC 2152.21**
Jurisdiction, juveniles, **ORC 2151.23**
Juveniles, by, **ORC 4510.31, ORC 4510.33**
    Adjudication, **JuvR 29(E), ORC 2152.21**
    Complaint, **JuvR 10(A), ORC 2151.27**
      Uniform traffic ticket used as, **JuvR 10(C)**
    Defined, **JuvR 2**
    Definition of juvenile traffic offender, **ORC 2151.011**
    Detention homes, placement in, **ORC 2151.34, ORC 2152.21**
    Detention of child. See CUSTODY OF CHILDREN, INSTITUTIONAL, at Detention
    Dismissal of complaint, **ORC 2151.35**
    Dockets of juvenile courts, **ORC 2152.71**
    Driver's license, suspension or revocation, **ORC 2152.21, ORC 4507.021**
    Drug abuse or alcohol abuse education, intervention, or treatment program, reports, **ORC 4507.021**
    Emergency medical care, **ORC 2151.33**
    Financial responsibility act applicable, **ORC 2152.21**
    Fines, **ORC 2152.21**
    Foster homes as place of detention, **ORC 2151.331**
    Jurisdiction, **ORC 2151.23**
    Probation, **ORC 2152.21**
    Records and reports, **ORC 2151.141**
    Rehabilitation. See JUVENILE REHABILITATION
    Seat belt law, violations of, **ORC 2152.21**
    Unruly or delinquent child or juvenile traffic offender, reports, **ORC 4507.021**
    Warrant, **JuvR 15(E)**
Point system, **ORC 4507.021**
Proceedings, **ORC 4507.021**
Records and reports, **ORC 4507.021**
Repeat offenders, **ORC 4507.021**
School bus, stopping for, **ORC 4511.75**
Tickets as complaints, **JuvR 10(C)**

TRAFFIC SIGNS AND SIGNALS
Flashing, **ORC 4511.15**
Obeying, **ORC 4511.12**
School bus, stopping for, **ORC 4511.75**
Signal lights, **ORC 4511.13**

TRAINING
Adoption, training programs for assessors, **3107.016, ORC 3107.015**

TRANSCRIPTS
Common pleas court trials, **SupR 11**
County court, **SupR 11**
Court reporters. See COURT REPORTERS
Custody actions, institutional proceedings, **ORC 2151.35**
Discovery proceedings, **SupR 11**
Electronically recorded, **SupR 11**
Franklin county probate court, **FrankR 11.1**
    Filing fee, **FrankR 58.4**
Hamilton county probate court, **HamR 11.1**
Juvenile proceedings, **JuvR 37, ORC 2151.35**
Mentally ill persons, hearings on hospitalization, **ORC 5122.15**
Municipal court, **SupR 11**
Permanent custody proceedings, **ORC 2151.35**
Request for, **ORC 2151.35**
Summit county probate court, **SumR 54.2(D)**
Written form, when required, **SupR 11**

TRANSFER
Certificates of, **LucasR 78.4**
Conveyances. See CONVEYANCES
Estate property, fraudulent transfers, **ORC 2127.40**
Fraudulent, **ORC 2127.40**
Tax. See ESTATE TAX

TRANSFERS TO MINORS ACT
Generally, **ORC 5814.01 to 5814.09**
Accounting by custodian, **ORC 5814.08**
Benefit plan, defined, **ORC 5814.01**
Custodians
    Powers and duties, **ORC 5814.04**
    Registration or removal, **ORC 5814.07**
Definitions, **ORC 5814.01**
Effect of Act, **ORC 5814.09**
Effect of gift or transfer, **ORC 5814.03**
Form of transfer, **ORC 5814.02**
Registration of custodian, **ORC 5814.07**
Reimbursement, compensation, and liability, **ORC 5814.05**
Removal of custodian, **ORC 5814.07**
Third person's liability limited, **ORC 5814.06**

TRANSITIONAL CONTROL
DNA testing of prisoners, **ORC 2901.07**

TRANSPLANTS
Eligibility of donee, **ORC 2108.03**

TRANSPORTATION DEPARTMENT
Eminent domain powers, **ORC 163.02**

TREASURERS, COUNTY
Escheat, powers and duties, **ORC 2105.07, ORC 2105.09**
    Foreign heir's share in trust, **ORC 2113.81**
    Unclaimed funds, receipt by, **ORC 2113.65**
Estate tax, powers and duties
    Accounting for taxes received, **ORC 5731.46**
    Collection, **ORC 5731.21, ORC 5731.27**
    Confidentiality of information, **ORC 5731.90**
    Notice of payment, **ORC 5731.33**
    Receipts for payments, **ORC 5731.33**
    Refunds, **ORC 5731.27**
    Revenue distribution, **ORC 5731.49**
Fees, estate tax duties, **ORC 5731.46**

Index-113 TRUSTEES

TREASURERS, COUNTY—*continued*
Trust funds, foreign beneficiaries or heirs, **ORC 2113.81, ORC 2113.82**

TRESPASS
Limitation of actions, **ORC 2305.09**

TRIALS
See also JURY TRIALS
Appeals. See APPEALS
Competence to stand trial. See DEFENDANTS, at Incompetent to stand trial
Electronically recording, **SupR 11, SupR 12, SupR 54(B)**
Injunctions during. See INJUNCTIVE RELIEF
Juvenile courts. See JUVENILE COURTS
Photographing, **SupR 12, SupR 54(B)**
Recording electronically, **SupR 11, SupR 12, SupR 54(B)**
Testimony. See WITNESSES AND TESTIMONY
Videotaping, **SupR 11, SupR 13**
Witnesses. See WITNESSES AND TESTIMONY

TRUCKS
Generally, See MOTOR VEHICLES
Surviving spouse's right to. See SURVIVING SPOUSE

TRUST COMPANIES
See also BANKS AND BANKING, generally
Merger and consolidation, effect on fiduciary responsibilities, **ORC 2109.28**
Securities, deposit, **ORC 2131.21**
Succession to property, disclaimer, **ORC 5815.36**
  See also DISCLAIMER OF SUCCESSION TO PROPERTY

TRUSTEES
See also FIDUCIARIES; TESTAMENTARY TRUSTEES; TRUST COMPANIES; TRUSTS
Accounts and accounting, **ORC 2109.26, ORC 2109.30 to 2109.36**
    See also FIDUCIARIES
        Compensation, separate schedule of computation set forth in, **CuyR 74.1, HamR 74.1**
        Final account, notice, **CuyR 64.2 et seq.**
Appointment, **CuyR 8.1, FrankR 8.1**
        Court appointment of representative, **ORC 5803.05**
        Holder of general testamentary power of appointment, representation by, **ORC 5803.02**
        Vacancy in trusteeship and appointment of successor, **ORC 5807.04**
Attorney fees, **LucasR 71.1, SupR 71**
Bond, **ORC 5807.02, Sup. R 75.1**
        Actions on, limitations, **ORC 2305.12**
Collection of trust property, **ORC 5808.12**
Compensation, **ORC 5807.08, SupR 74**
        Accounts, separate schedules of computation set forth in, **CuyR 74.1, HamR 74.1**
        Additional, **CuyR 74.1, FrankR 74.1, LucasR 74.1(C)**
        Computation, **CuyR 74.1, FrankR 74.1, HamR 74.1, LucasR 74.1**
        Corporate trustees, **HamR 74.1, SumR 74.1(A), Sup. R 74.1**
        Co-trustees, **CuyR 74.1, LucasR 74.1(D)**
        Delinquent in filing account, **CuyR 74.1**
        Form, **HamR Appx C**
        Individual trustees, **HamR 74.1, SumR 74.1(B), Sup. R 74.2**
Conflict of interest and duty of loyalty, **ORC 5808.02**
Constructive
        Convicted murderer, **ORC 2105.19**
Contracts made in trustee capacity, liability, **ORC 5815.35**
Control and protection of trust property, **ORC 5808.09**
Cotrustees, office of trustee, **ORC 5807.03**
Cuyahoga county probate court
        Appointment, **CuyR 8.1**
        Compensation, **CuyR 73.1, CuyR 74.1**
Declaratory judgments sought by. See DECLARATORY JUDGMENTS

TRUSTEES—Cont'd
Deposit in name of two or more trustees, **ORC 5815.09**
Disabled persons, trust for supplemental services; actions, **ORC 5815.28**
Discretionary powers, property of trust, **ORC 5808.14**
Distribution of trust upon termination, **ORC 5808.17**
District detention facility trustees, **ORC 2152.44**
Divorce, spouse granted power of appointment or nominated as trustee, termination of marriage as revocation, **ORC 5815.31**
Dower interest, grantee, **ORC 2103.021**
Enforcement and defense of claims, **ORC 5808.11**
Fiduciary powers and duties, **ORC Ch 2109**
        See also FIDUCIARIES
Former trustee, delivery of property by, **ORC 5807.07**
Franklin county probate court
        Appointment, **FrankR 8.1**
        Compensation, **FrankR 74.1**
General powers, **ORC 5808.15**
Hamilton county probate court
        Compensation, **HamR 74.1, HamR Appx C**
Impartiality, **ORC 5808.03**
Income and principal, allocation, **ORC Ch 1340**
Institutional Trust Funds Act, **ORC 5813.01**
        See also INSTITUTIONAL TRUST FUNDS ACT
Inter vivos trusts. See INTER VIVOS TRUSTS
Investment costs, powers and duties, **ORC 5808.05**
Investment of assets, **ORC 2109.37 to 2109.38**
        Temporary, **ORC 2109.372**
Jurisdiction over trustee and beneficiary, **ORC 5802.02**
Juvenile courts, district detention facility trustees, **ORC 2152.44**
Juvenile rehabilitation facilities, **ORC 2151.68 to 2151.78**
Liability limitation, certain powers granted to other persons, **ORC 2109.022**
Loyalty and impartiality, **5808.03, ORC 5808.02**
Lucas County probate court, compensation, **LucasR 74.1**
Mentally retarded or developmentally disabled persons, for, **ORC 5123.55 to 5123.59**
Missing person's estate, for, **ORC 2119.01**
        Final account, **ORC 2119.05**
        Powers, **ORC 2119.03**
Nonresident
        Court appointing resident co-trustee, **SumR 92.1**
Notice
        Probate of will, denied, **ORC 2107.181**
Office of trustee
        generally, **ORC 5807.01 to 5807.09**
        Accepting or rejecting trusteeship, **ORC 5807.01**
        Bond of trustee, **ORC 5807.02**
        Compensation of trustee, **ORC 5807.08**
        Cotrustees, **ORC 5807.03**
        Delivery of property by former trustee, **ORC 5807.07**
        Reimbursement of expenses, **ORC 5807.09**
        Removal of trustee, **ORC 5807.06**
        Resignation of trustee, **ORC 5807.05**
        Vacancy in trusteeship and appointment of successor, **ORC 5807.04**
Powers and duties
        generally, **ORC 5808.01 to 5808.17**
        Conflict of interest and duty of loyalty, **ORC 5808.02**
        Control and protection of trust property, **ORC 5808.09**
        Delegation of powers and duties, **ORC 5808.07**
        Direct, powers to, **ORC 5808.08**
        Duty to administer trust, **ORC 5808.01**
        Investment costs, **ORC 5808.05**
        Loyalty and impartiality, **5808.03, ORC 5808.02**
        Prudent administration, **ORC 5808.04**
        Recordkeeping and separation of trust property, **ORC 5808.10**
        Skills or expertise of trustee, **ORC 5808.06**
Principal and income, allocation, **ORC Ch 1340**
Property of trust
        Collection of trust property, **ORC 5808.12**
        Control and protection of trust property, **ORC 5808.09**

TRUSTEES

Index-114

TRUSTEES—*continued*
Property of trust—*continued*
    Delivery by former trustee, **ORC 5807.07**
    Discretionary powers, **ORC 5808.14**
    Duty to inform and report, **ORC 5808.13**
    Enforcement and defense of claims, **ORC 5808.12**
    Recordkeeping and separation of trust property, **ORC 5808.10**
Prudent administration, powers and duties, **ORC 5808.04**
Prudent Investor Act, **ORC 5809.01 to 5809.08**
    See also UNIFORM PRUDENT INVESTOR ACT
Real estate of nonresident minor, mentally ill, or disabled person; sale by, **ORC 2127.43**
Real property
    Successor trustee's duties, **ORC 5302.171**
Recordkeeping and separation of trust property, **ORC 5808.10**
Reimbursement of expenses, office of trustee, **ORC 5807.09**
Removal, **ORC 2109.24, ORC 5807.06**
Resignation of trustee, **ORC 5807.05**
Sale of assets
    Private sale, **ORC 2109.45**
Skills or expertise of trustee, **ORC 5808.06**
Specific powers of trustee, **ORC 5808.16**
Stark county probate court
    Compensation
        Corporate trustees, **Sup. R 74.1**
        Individual trustees, **Sup. R 74.2**
Successor, **ORC 2109.26**
    Duties, **ORC 5302.171**
Summit county probate court
    Compensation, **SumR 74.1**
Tax returns, duties
    Estate tax. See FIDUCIARIES
Termination
    Successor trustee's duties, **ORC 5302.171**
Testamentary. See TESTAMENTARY TRUSTEES
Two or more trustees, deposit in name of, **ORC 5815.09**
Uniform Prudent Investor Act, **ORC 5809.01 to 5809.08**
    See also UNIFORM PRUDENT INVESTOR ACT
Uniform Prudent Investor Act, delegation by trustee, **ORC 5809.06**
Unknown or nonresident persons, funds of, **ORC 2109.57**
Vacancy in trusteeship and appointment of successor, **ORC 5807.04**

TRUSTS
Generally, **SumR 92.1**
See also GIFTS AND GRANTS; TRUSTEES
Accounts and accounting
    Notice of hearing on approval, **LucasR 64.1**
    Time for filing, **LucasR 64.1**
    Vouchers, **Sup. R 64.2**
Additions to, **ORC 2107.63**
Administration
    Attorney fees, **CuyR 71.1, LucasR 71.1**
Animal, trust for care of, **ORC 5804.08**
Applicability of title, **ORC 5801.02**
Appointment
    Representation by holder of general testamentary power of appointment, **ORC 5803.02**
    Representative by court, **ORC 5803.05**
Art, consignment of art works to dealers, **ORC 5815.42**
Ascertainable standard, defined, **ORC 5801.01**
Assets, distribution
    Complaint to enforce, **ORC 2109.59**
    Order, **ORC 2109.36**
Attorney fees, **FrankR 71.5**
    Remedies for breach of trust, **ORC 5810.04**
Beneficiaries
    Fiduciaries as, **ORC 2109.39**
    Foreign, disposition of property, **ORC 2113.81, ORC 2113.82**
    Jurisdiction over trustee and beneficiary, **ORC 5802.02**
    Liability, alienated property; vacated order of settlement of account, **ORC 2109.35**
    Notice to, denial of probate, **ORC 2107.181**

TRUSTS—Cont'd
Beneficiaries—Cont'd
    Persons treated as, **ORC 5801.09**
    Unborn, representation in account hearing, **ORC 2109.34**
    Unknown or nonresident, **ORC 2109.57**
Beneficiary surrogate, defined, **ORC 5801.01**
Case management, probate court, **SupR 78**
Certification of trust, remedies for breach of trust, **ORC 5810.13**
Charitable. See CHARITABLE TRUSTS
Claims against, complaint for payment, **ORC 2109.59**
Combination or division of trusts, **ORC 5804.17**
Common law of trusts and principles of equity, applicability, **ORC 5801.05**
Concurrent jurisdiction, **ORC 5802.03**
Consent, release, or ratification of beneficiary, **ORC 5810.09**
Consignment of art works to dealers, **ORC 5815.42**
Correction of mistakes, reformation for, **ORC 5804.15**
Court appointment of representative, **ORC 5803.05**
Court costs, **SumR Appx A**
Court records, **ORC 2101.14**
Creation of trust
    generally, **ORC 5804.01 to 5804.09**
    Animal, trust for care of, **ORC 5804.08**
    Charitable trusts, **ORC 5804.05**
    Fraud, duress, or undue influence, creation induced by, **ORC 5804.06**
    Methods of creating trust, **ORC 5804.01**
    Noncharitable trust without ascertainable beneficiary, **ORC 5804.09**
    Oral trust, **ORC 5804.07**
    Other jurisdictions, trusts created in, **ORC 5804.03**
    Purposes of trust, **ORC 5804.04**
    Requirements, **ORC 5804.02**
Current beneficiary, defined, **ORC 5801.01**
Cuyahoga county probate court
    Accounts, **CuyR 64.2 et seq.**
    Supervision, case management, **CuyR 78.1**
Cy pres, application of, **ORC 5804.13**
Damages
    Breach of trust, **ORC 5810.02**
    In absence of breach of trust, **ORC 5810.03**
Death benefit plans. See DEATH BENEFITS
Declaratory judgments. See DECLARATORY JUDGMENTS
Definitions, **ORC 5801.01**
Disabled persons, for supplemental services, **ORC 5815.28**
    Actions pertaining to, **ORC 5815.28**
    Death of beneficiary, disposition of proceeds
        Services fund for individuals with mental retardation and developmental disabilities, to, **ORC 5123.40**
    Definitions, **ORC 5815.28**
    Eligible conditions of beneficiary, **ORC 5815.28**
    Execution of judgment, exempt from, **ORC 5815.28**
    Maximum amount, **ORC 5815.28**
    Rules for
        Mental retardation and developmental disabilities director, by, **ORC 5123.04**
Disclaimer of succession to property, **ORC 5815.36**
Distribution of assets
    Complaint to enforce, **ORC 2109.59**
    Order, **ORC 2109.36**
Electronic records and signatures, **ORC 5811.02**
Enforceability of trust terms relieving trustee of liability, **ORC 5810.08**
Equity principles, applicability, **ORC 5801.05**
Estate tax, **ORC 5731.05**
Exceptions to mandatory rules, **ORC 5801.04**
Expenses
    Court costs, **SumR Appx A**
    Improper filings, **ORC 2109.021**
    Investigation of fiduciary, **ORC 2109.49**
Fiduciaries, duties, **ORC Ch 2109**
    See also FIDUCIARIES; TRUSTEES

TRUSTS—continued
Franklin county probate court
    Case management, **FrankR 78.1**
Fraud, duress, or undue influence, creation induced by, **ORC 5804.06**
General partner, interest as, remedies for breach of trust, **ORC 5810.11**
Generation skipping transfer tax, **ORC 5815.27**
Gifts and grants to, estate tax deductions, **ORC 5731.17**
Governing law, **ORC 5801.06**
Guardian of the estate, defined, **ORC 5801.01**
Guardian of the person, defined, **ORC 5801.01**
Hamilton county probate court
    Case management, **HamR 78.1**
    Court costs, deposits, **HamR Appx D**
Income
    Allocation between income and principal, **ORC Ch 1340**
    Defined, **ORC 5812.01**
Income tax, state returns, **ORC 5747.08(C)**
Inter vivos. See INTER VIVOS TRUSTS
Interests of the beneficiaries, defined, **ORC 5801.01**
Irrevocable trust, **ORC 5804.18**
Judicial proceedings
    Concurrent jurisdiction, **ORC 5802.03**
    Role of court in administration of trust, **ORC 5802.01**
Jurisdiction
    Defined, **ORC 5801.01**
    Trustee and beneficiary, jurisdiction over, **ORC 5802.02**
    Trusts created in other jurisdictions, **ORC 5804.03**
Liability
    Event affecting administration or distribution, remedies for breach of trust, **ORC 5810.07**
    Trustee capacity, contract made in, **ORC 5815.35**
Limitation of actions
    Claim by nonresident or unknown beneficiary of trust fund, **ORC 2109.57**
    Remedies for breach of trust, **ORC 5810.05**
    Revocable trust, **ORC 5806.04**
Limitation on personal liability of trustee, remedies for breach of trust, **ORC 5810.10**
Lucas county probate court
    Case management, **LucasR 78.1**
Mandatory distribution, defined, **ORC 5801.01**
Mandatory rules, **ORC 5801.04**
Missing person's estate, **ORC Ch 2119**
Mistakes, reformation to correct mistakes, **ORC 5804.15**
Modification or termination, **ORC 2109.62, ORC 2131.09, ORC 5804.10**
    Distribution of trust upon termination, **ORC 5808.17**
    Noncharitable irrevocable trust by consent, **ORC 5804.11**
    Uneconomic trust, **ORC 5804.14**
Noncharitable irrevocable trust by consent, modification or termination of, **ORC 5804.11**
Noncharitable trust without ascertainable beneficiary, **ORC 5804.09**
Notice
    Accounts and accounting, **LucasR 64.1**
    Other beneficiaries, notice to, **ORC 5801.09**
    Other person, notice and consent regarding representation and binding, **ORC 5803.01**
    Representation and binding another person, **ORC 5803.01**
    Waiver of notice, **ORC 5801.08**
Notice or knowledge of fact, defined, **ORC 5801.03**
Oral trust, creation, **ORC 5804.07**
Parents, representation by fiduciaries and, **ORC 5803.03**
Parties to agreements, effect on creditor rights, **ORC 5801.10**
Pension funds. See RETIREMENT PLANS, generally
Persons treated as beneficiaries, **ORC 5801.09**
Power of appointment, representation by holder of general testamentary power of appointment, **ORC 5803.02**
Power of withdrawal, defined, **ORC 5801.01**
Principal and income, allocation, **ORC Ch 1340**
    Administration, **ORC 5812.02**
    Definitions, **ORC 5812.01**
    Discretion of trustee, **ORC 5812.03**

TRUSTS—continued
Principal and income, allocation, **ORC Ch 1340**—continued
    Estate tax marital or charitable deduction, charges to principal or income to preserve, **ORC 5812.36**
    Fiduciary duties, **ORC 5812.02**
    Partnership net profits, **ORC 5812.18**
    Principal, definition, **ORC 5812.01**
    Timber rights, **ORC 5812.35**
Principal place of administration, **ORC 5801.07**
Principles of equity, applicability, **ORC 5801.05**
Probate court, case management, **SupR 78**
Protection of person dealing with trustee, remedies for breach of trust, **ORC 5810.12**
Qualified beneficiary, defined, **ORC 5801.01**
Records, electronic records and signatures, **ORC 5811.02**
Reformation to correct mistakes, **ORC 5804.15**
Remedies for breach of trust
    generally, **ORC 5810.01 to 5801.13**
    Attorney fees and costs, **ORC 5810.04**
    Certification of trust, **ORC 5810.13**
    Consent, release, or ratification of beneficiary, **ORC 5810.09**
    Damages for breach of trust, **ORC 5810.02**
    Damages in absence of breach, **ORC 5810.03**
    Enforceability of trust terms relieving trustee of liability, **ORC 5810.08**
    Interest as general partner, **ORC 5810.11**
    Liability when event affecting administration or distribution, **ORC 5810.07**
    Limitation of action against trustee, **ORC 5810.05**
    Limitation on personal liability of trustee, **ORC 5810.10**
    Protection of person dealing with trustee, **ORC 5810.12**
    Reliance on trust instrument, **ORC 5810.06**
Representation by holder of general testamentary power of appointment, **ORC 5803.02**
Revocable Trusts. See REVOCABLE TRUSTS
Role of court in administration of trust, **ORC 5802.01**
Rule against perpetuities, **ORC 2131.08, ORC 2131.09**
Settlement, time of termination, **ORC 2101.141**
Settlor, defined, **ORC 5801.01**
Settlor's tax objectives, modification to achieve, **ORC 5804.16**
Short title, **ORC 5801.011**
Spendthrift trusts. See SPENDTHRIFT AND DISCRETIONARY TRUSTS
Stark county probate court
    Case management, **Sup. R 78.6**
Substantially identical interest, representation by, **ORC 5803.04**
Succession to property, disclaimer. See DISCLAIMER OF SUCCESSION TO PROPERTY
Summit county probate court
    Court costs, **SumR Appx A**
    Supervision, **SumR 78.1(C)**
Taxation
    Estate tax, **ORC 5731.05 to 5731.08**
    Income tax returns, **ORC 5747.08(C)**
    Modification to achieve settlor's tax objectives, **ORC 5804.16**
    Personal property tax. See PERSONAL PROPERTY, TAXATION
Terms of a trust, defined, **ORC 5801.01**
Testamentary. See TESTAMENTARY TRUSTS
Transfer of property to, estate tax, **ORC 5731.05 to 5731.08**
Trust instrument, defined, **ORC 5801.01**
Unanticipated circumstances or inability to administer, modification or termination because of, **ORC 5804.12**
Uneconomic trust, modification or termination, **ORC 5804.14**
Uniformity of application and construction, **ORC 5811.01**
Waiver of notice, **ORC 5801.08**
Wrongful death damages deposited in, **ORC 2125.03**

TRUTH
Anatomical gifts, truthfulness of declaration, **ORC 2108.74**

UNBORN CHILDREN
Beneficiaries of estates or trusts, representation, **ORC 2109.34**
Intestate succession, **ORC 2105.14**
Paternity, presumption, **ORC 3111.03**
Paternity proceedings, stay, **ORC 3111.04**
Pretermitted heir statute, **ORC 2107.34**
    Debt payments, contributions by, **ORC 2107.55**

UNCLAIMED FUNDS
Legacies and devises, **ORC 2113.64 to 2113.68**

UNDUE INFLUENCE
Trusts, creation induced by fraud, duress, or undue influence, **ORC 5804.06**

UNECONOMIC TRUST
Modification or termination, **ORC 5804.14**

UNIFORM CHILD CUSTODY JURISDICTION ACT
Generally, **ORC 3109.21 to 3109.32**
Abandoned child, jurisdiction, **ORC 3109.22(A)**
Abused child, jurisdiction, **ORC 3109.22(A)**
Affidavits, **ORC 3109.27**
Appropriate forum, determination, **ORC 3109.25**
Attorney fees
    Dismissal of action due to wrongful removal of child, **ORC 3109.26(C)**
    Inappropriate forum, party who commenced proceedings to pay, **ORC 3109.25(G)**
    Violation of foreign decree, **ORC 3109.32(B)**
Best interests of child
    Jurisdiction prerequisite, as, **ORC 3109.22(A)**
Court costs
    Dismissal of action due to wrongful removal of child, **ORC 3109.26(C)**
    Inappropriate forum, party who commenced proceedings to pay, **ORC 3109.25(G)**
    Violation necessitating action, violating party to pay, **ORC 3109.26(C), ORC 3109.32(B)**
Decree, **ORC 3109.30, ORC 3109.32**
    Out-of-state court, **ORC 3109.30, ORC 3109.32**
    Reciprocity, **ORC 3109.30, ORC 3109.32**
    Treatment of foreign decree in same manner as Ohio decree, **ORC 3109.32(A)**
Dependent child, jurisdiction, **ORC 3109.22(A)**
Emergency jurisdiction, **ORC 3109.22(A)**
Enforcement of foreign decree in same manner as Ohio decree, **ORC 3109.32**
Foreign court not having or declining jurisdiction, prerequisite to Ohio jurisdiction, **ORC 3109.22(A)**
Home state
    Jurisdiction prerequisite, as, **ORC 3109.22(A)**
Inconvenient forum, determination, **ORC 3109.25**
Modification decree
    Improperly obtained custody, **ORC 3109.26(B)**
Neglected child, jurisdiction, **ORC 3109.22(A)**
Notice of proceedings, **ORC 3109.23**
Physical presence of child
    Insufficient to confer jurisdiction, **ORC 3109.22(B)**
    Prerequisite for jurisdiction, not considered as, **ORC 3109.22(C)**
Pleadings, **ORC 3109.27**
Prerequisites to jurisdiction, **ORC 3109.22**
Proceedings
    Pending in another state, **ORC 3109.24**
        Continuing duty to inform court, **ORC 3109.27(C)**
    Stay, **ORC 3109.24(C), ORC 3109.25(E), ORC 3109.25(H)**
Records and reports, **ORC 3109.25**
Registry, **ORC 3109.24(B), ORC 3109.25(I)**
    Change of forum recorded in, **ORC 3109.25(I)**
Service of process, **ORC 3109.23**
Significant connection with state, prerequisite to jurisdiction, **ORC 3109.22(A)**

UNIFORM CHILD CUSTODY JURISDICTION ACT
—continued
Stay of proceedings, **ORC 3109.24(C), ORC 3109.25(E), ORC 3109.25(H)**
Unclean hands, **ORC 3109.26**
Venue, change for more convenient forum, **ORC 3109.24, ORC 3109.25**
Violations
    Court costs, violating party to pay, **ORC 3109.26(C)**
    Effect on jurisdiction, **ORC 3109.26(B)**
    Out-of-state decrees, of, **ORC 3109.32(B)**
Wrongful removal of child, **ORC 3109.26**

UNIFORM FIDUCIARY ACT
Generally, **ORC 5815.04**
Check drawn by fiduciary upon account of principal, liability of bank, **ORC 5815.07**
Competent, issuers of securities may trust holders of record as, **ORC 5815.03**
Definitions, **ORC 5815.04**
Deposit in name of fiduciary as such, liability of bank, **ORC 5815.06**
Interpretation and construction, **ORC 5815.10**
Interpretation of terms, **ORC 5815.01**
Personal credit of fiduciary, deposit to, **ORC 5815.08**
Rules of law and equity applicable, **ORC 5815.11**
Securities issuers and holders of record, **ORC 5815.02**
Transferee not responsible for proper application of money, **ORC 5815.05**
Two or more trustees, deposit in name of, **ORC 5815.09**

UNIFORM LAWS
Anatomical gift act, **ORC 2108.09**
    See also ANATOMICAL GIFTS
Child custody jurisdiction law, **ORC 3109.21 to 3109.32**
    See also UNIFORM CHILD CUSTODY JURISDICTION ACT
Fiduciary bank accounts, **ORC 5815.04**
Fiduciary law. See UNIFORM PRINCIPAL AND INCOME ACT
Fraudulent Transfers Act, **ORC Ch 1336**
Parentage act, **ORC 3111.01 to 3111.19**
    See also PARENTAGE ACTIONS, generally
Prudent Investor Act, **ORC 5809.01 to 5809.08**
    See also UNIFORM PRUDENT INVESTOR ACT

UNIFORM PARENTAGE ACT
Generally, **ORC 3111.01 to 3111.19**
See also PARENTAGE ACTIONS, generally

UNIFORM PRINCIPAL AND INCOME ACT
Generally, **ORC 5812.01 to 5812.52**
Accounting period, **ORC 5812.01**
Adjustment by trustee, **ORC 5812.03**
Allocations, insubstantial, **ORC 5812.31**
Annuities, **ORC 5812.32**
Application and construction, **ORC 5812.51, ORC 5812.52**
Apportionment
    Decedent dies or income interest begins, **ORC 5812.13**
    Income interest ends, **ORC 5812.14**
Asset-backed securities, **ORC 5812.38**
Beneficiary
    Defined, **ORC 5812.01**
    Distribution to, **ORC 5812.08**
Business conducted by trustee, **ORC 5812.20**
Common trust fund, allocation between income and principal, **5812.18**
Compensation, deferred, **ORC 5812.32**
Construction and application, **ORC 5812.51, ORC 5812.52**
Corporation, allocation between income and principal, **5812.18**
Decedent's estate, application to existing, **ORC 5812.52**
Deferred compensation, **ORC 5812.32**
Definitions, **ORC 5812.01**
Depreciation, transfers from income to principal for, **ORC 5813.44**
Derivatives and options, **ORC 5812.37**

UNIFORM PRINCIPAL AND INCOME ACT—*continued*
Disbursements
    Income, **ORC 5812.42**
    Principal, **ORC 5812.43**
Distribution
    Residuary and remainder beneficiaries, **ORC 5812.08**
    Trust or estate, **ORC 5812.19**
Entity, **ORC 5812.18**
Existing decedent's estate, application to, **ORC 5812.52**
Fiduciary
    Defined, **ORC 5812.01**
    Duties, **ORC 5812.02**
Income
    Beneficiary, **ORC 5812.01**
    Defined, **ORC 5812.01**
    Interest, **ORC 5812.01**
    Right to, **ORC 5812.12**
    Undistributed, **ORC 5812.14**
Income taxes, **ORC 5812.46**
    Adjustments between principal and income, **ORC 5812.47**
Insubstantial allocations, **ORC 5812.31**
Insurance policies, **ORC 5812.27**
Investment company, allocation between income and principal, **5812.18**
Life insurance, **ORC 5812.27**
Limited liability company, allocation between income and principal, **5812.18**
Liquidating asset, **ORC 5812.33**
Mandatory income interest, **ORC 5812.01**
Marital deduction, **ORC 5812.36**
Minerals, **ORC 5812.34**
Money, obligation to pay, **ORC 5812.26**
Natural resources, **ORC 5812.34**
Net income
    Defined, **ORC 5812.01**
    Determination and distribution of, **ORC 5812.07**
    When right begins and ends, **ORC 5812.12**
Options and derivatives, **ORC 5812.37**
Partnership, allocation between income and principal, **ORC 5812.18**
Payments, **ORC 5812.32**
Person, **ORC 5812.01**
Principal
    Defined, **ORC 5812.01**
    Receipts, **ORC 5812.24**
Property not productive of income, **ORC 5812.36**
Real estate investment trust, allocation between income and principal, **5812.18**
Receipts
    Character of, **ORC 5812.18**
    Principal, **ORC 5812.24**
Reimburse principal, transfers to, **ORC 5812.45**
Remainder beneficiary, **ORC 5812.01**
Rental property, **ORC 5812.25**
Securities, asset-backed, **ORC 5812.38**
Taxes, **ORC 5812.46**
    Adjustments between principal and income, **ORC 5812.47**
Terms of trust, **ORC 5812.01**
Timber, **ORC 5812.35**
Transfers
    Income to principal for depreciation, **ORC 5813.44**
    Income to reimburse principal, **ORC 5812.45**
Trustee
    Defined, **ORC 5812.01**
    Power to adjust principal and income, **ORC 5812.03**
Undistributed income, **ORC 5812.14**
Water, **ORC 5812.34**

UNIFORM PRUDENT INVESTOR ACT
Generally, **ORC 5809.01 to 5809.08**
Application to existing trusts, **ORC 5809.08**
Compliance, reviewing, **ORC 5809.05**
Delegation by trustee, **ORC 5809.06**
Delegation of investment and management functions, **ORC 5808.07**

UNIFORM PRUDENT INVESTOR ACT—*continued*
Diversification, **ORC 5809.03**
Duties at inception of trusteeship, **ORC 5809.04**
Existing trusts, application to, **ORC 5809.08**
Impartiality, duty of, **ORC 5808.03**
Inception of trusteeship, duties at, **ORC 5809.04**
Investment costs, **ORC 5808.05**
Language invoking standard of act, **ORC 5809.07**
Language invoking standard of Prudent Investor Act, **ORC 5809.07**
Loyalty, duty of, **5808.03**, **ORC 5808.02**
Portfolio strategy, **ORC 5809.02**
Prudent investor rule, **ORC 5809.01**
Risk and return objectives, **ORC 5809.02**
Standard of care, **ORC 5809.02**
Uniformity of application and construction, **ORC 5809.08**

UNIFORM TRANSFER-ON-DEATH SECURITY REGISTRATION ACT
Definitions, **ORC 1709.01**
Joint tenancy, securities held in, **ORC 1709.02**
Security account, defined, **ORC 1709.01**
Tenancy in common precluded, **ORC 1709.02**

UNITED STATES
Charitable contributions to, estate tax deduction, **ORC 5731.17**
Claims against estates, priority, **ORC 2117.25**
Estate tax. See ESTATE TAX, FEDERAL
Hospitals for mentally ill operated by, **ORC 5122.16**
Income tax. See INCOME TAX, FEDERAL

UNIVERSITIES AND COLLEGES
Charitable contributions to, estate tax deductions, **ORC 5731.17**
Eligible institution, definition
    Income tax, state, **ORC 5747.01**
Mental retardation and developmental disabilities department, agreements with, **ORC 5123.12**
Psychology departments
    Mental retardation and developmental disabilities department, agreements with, **ORC 5123.11**
Qualified tuition and fees, definition
    Income tax, state, **ORC 5747.01**

UNRULY CHILDREN
See also RUNAWAYS
Adjudicatory hearing, **JuvR 29(E)**, **ORC 2151.28**
Alternative diversion programs, **ORC 2151.331**
Appeal pending, provision for, **ORC 2151.31**
Apprehension, **ORC 2151.14**, **ORC 2152.03**
Complaints, **JuvR 10(A)**, **ORC 2151.27**
Contributing to, jurisdiction, **ORC 2151.23**
Defined, **ORC 2151.022**
Detention. See CUSTODY OF CHILDREN, INSTITUTIONAL; DETENTION HOMES
Disposition as delinquent, **ORC 2151.354**
    Notice of intended orders, **ORC 2151.3510**
Driver's license, suspension or revocation, **ORC 2151.354**
Drug abuse or alcohol abuse counseling programs, **ORC 2151.354**
Expungement of record, **ORC 2151.358**
Foster homes as place of detention, **ORC 2151.331**
Fostered children
    Complaint by superintendent of schools, **ORC 2151.55**
Guardian ad litem, appointment, **ORC 2151.281**
Interstate agreements, **ORC 2151.56**
Jurisdiction, **ORC 2151.23**
Notice of intended dispositional orders, **ORC 2151.3510**
Records and reports, **ORC 2151.141**
Rehabilitation. See JUVENILE REHABILITATION
Shelter care, **ORC 2151.28**

VACANCY IN OFFICE
Trusteeship, vacancy in trusteeship and appointment of successor, **ORC 5807.04**

VALIDITY OF WILLS
Generally, See WILLS
Ante mortem declaration. See ANTE MORTEM DECLARATION OF WILL VALIDITY

VALUATION OF PROPERTY
Appraisals. See APPRAISALS
Estate property. See INVENTORY AND APPRAISAL OF ESTATES

VEHICLES
See MOTOR VEHICLES

VEHICULAR ASSAULT
Aggravated
    Driver's license, suspension at initial appearance or arraignment, **ORC 4511.196**

VEHICULAR HOMICIDE
Aggravated
    Driver's license, suspension at initial appearance or arraignment, **ORC 4511.196**

VENUE
Generally, **O Const I § 12**
Adoption, **ORC 3107.04**
Change of
    Juvenile proceedings, **ORC 2151.271**
    Paternity proceedings, **ORC 3109.24, ORC 3109.25**
Criminal prosecutions, **O Const I § 12**
Estates, sale of real property, **ORC 2127.09**
Guardians
    Selling real property, action, **ORC 2127.09**
Institutionalization proceedings for mentally retarded, **ORC 5123.92**
Paternity proceedings, **ORC 3111.06**
    Change of, **ORC 3109.24, ORC 3109.25**
Presumed decedents, complaint to establish presumption, **ORC 2121.02**
Will contest actions, **ORC 2107.71**

VERBAL WILLS
Generally, **ORC 2107.60, ORC 2107.61**

VERDICTS
Generally, **O Const I § 5**
See also JUDGMENTS; JURY TRIALS
Eminent domain, **ORC 163.14**
Majority verdicts, **O Const I § 5**
Not guilty by reason of insanity, **ORC 2945.40(A)**
Paternity proceedings, **ORC 3111.12**

VETERANS
Guardianship, **ORC Ch 2111**
    Notice to Veterans Administration office, **HamR 73.2**

VETERANS' ORGANIZATIONS
Gifts and bequests to, estate tax deduction, **ORC 5731.17**

VICTIMS OF CRIME
Age 65 or over
    Effect in cases of juvenile delinquents, **ORC 2152.12(C)**
        Statistics, **ORC 2152.71**
Age 5 or under
    Effect in cases of juvenile delinquents, **ORC 2152.12(C)**
Handicapped persons, juvenile delinquency cases, **ORC 2152.12(C)**
Juvenile delinquents committing crimes, **ORC 2152.12(C)**
Physical harm, juvenile delinquents committing crimes, **ORC 2152.12(C)**
Sex offense victim
    Communicable disease of accused, notice to, **ORC 2151.14**
    Minor, videotaped or televised testimony, **ORC 2152.81**

VIDEOTAPE RECORDING
Appeals, record on, **SupR 11**
Common pleas courts, **SupR 11**

VIDEOTAPE RECORDING—continued
Costs for trials, **SupR 13**
County courts, **SupR 11**
Depositions, **SupR 13**
    Costs, **SupR 13**
    Notice, **SupR 13**
Discovery proceedings, **SupR 11**
Juvenile proceedings, **JuvR 37**
Minor sex offense victim, testimony, **ORC 2152.81**
Municipal courts, **SupR 11**
Ownership of videotapes, **SupR 13**
Release by court, **SupR 13**
Transcript, as, **SupR 11**
Trials, **SupR 13**

VIETNAM CONFLICT
Missing in action servicemen, estate tax exemption on pay, **ORC 5731.15**

VI/FORM ALL

VILLAGES
See MUNICIPAL CORPORATIONS, for general provisions

VIOLENCE
Child abuse. See CHILD ABUSE

VIOLENCE, OFFENSES OF
Juvenile delinquents committing, **ORC 2152.12(C)**

VISITATION RIGHTS
Child support
    Denial of or interference with visitation, escrowing, impoundment, or withholding of support, **ORC 3109.05(D)**
    Motion for visitation rights in action for support, **ORC 3109.051**
    Parents wishes to be considered, **ORC 3111.20 et seq.**
Child's wishes, consideration, **ORC 3109.051(C), ORC 3109.051(D)**
Compensatory visitation, **ORC 3109.051(K)**
Contempt for failure to comply or interference with, **ORC 3109.051(K)**
Cost of proceeding, waiver, **ORC 3109.051(L)**
Courts of common pleas, mediators, **SupR 16**
Crime committed by parent, effect, **ORC 3109.051(G)**
Day care centers, at, **ORC 3109.051(I)**
Deceased parent, relatives to be granted visitation, **ORC 3109.11**
Denial by court, **ORC 3109.051(F)**
    Deceased parent, **ORC 3109.11**
    Illegitimate child, **ORC 3109.12(B)**
Dissolution of marriage pending, motion for rights, **ORC 3109.051**
Divorce pending, motion for rights, **ORC 3109.051**
Factors considered, **ORC 3109.051(D)**
    Deceased parent, **ORC 3109.11**
    Illegitimate child, **ORC 3109.12(B)**
Findings of fact and conclusions of law, **ORC 3109.051(F)**
    Deceased parent, **ORC 3109.11**
    Illegitimate child, **ORC 3109.12(B)**
Grandparents, **ORC 3109.051(B)**
    Death of parent, following, **ORC 3109.11**
    Unmarried woman, child born to, **ORC 3109.12**
Illegitimate children, **ORC 5101.314**
    Relatives to be granted visitation, **ORC 3109.12**
Interference with, **ORC 3109.051(K)**
Interview with child, **ORC 3109.051(C), ORC 3109.051(D)**
Jurisdiction, juvenile court, **ORC 3109.051(M)**
Juvenile detention or shelter facilities, **JuvR 7(J)**
Mediators, courts of common pleas, **SupR 16**
Mentally ill during hospitalization, **ORC 5122.29**
Mentally retarded, during institutionalization, **ORC 5123.84**
Move by residential parent, notice to court, **ORC 3109.051(G)**
Parent convicted of killing other parent, **ORC 3109.41 to 3109.48**
    Best interest of child, **ORC 3109.47**
    Consent of custodial parent required, **ORC 3109.48**
    Court order required, **ORC 3109.48**
    Definitions, **ORC 3109.41**

Index-119   WILLS

VISITATION RIGHTS—*continued*
Parent convicted of killing other parent, **ORC 3109.41 to 3109.48**
—*continued*
    Notice of conviction, **ORC 3109.44**
        Termination of rights upon receipt, **ORC 3109.45**
    Unavailability, **ORC 3109.43**
Parents, **ORC 3109.051**
    Wishes of parents to be considered in determination, **ORC 3111.20 et seq.**
Paternity judgment, subsequent to, **ORC 3111.13**
Records concerning child, access by noncustodial parent, **ORC 3109.051(H)**
Relatives, **ORC 3109.051(B)**
    Death of parent, following, **ORC 3109.11**
    Illegitimate child, **ORC 3109.12**
    Unmarried woman, child born to, **ORC 3109.12**
Remarriage of custodial parent, effect, **ORC 3109.051(E)**
    Deceased parent, **ORC 3109.11**
    Illegitimate child, **ORC 3109.12(B)**
Schools, access to, **ORC 3109.051(J)**
Shared parenting, **ORC 3109.04(G)**
Spousal support pending, motion for rights, **ORC 3109.051**
Statutory factors, **ORC 3109.051**

VITAL STATISTICS
Acknowledgment of paternity statements, filing with human services department, **ORC 3705.091**
Mental hospitals, **ORC 5122.23**
Minor, duties of registrar of vital statistics in event of death of, **ORC 3705.071**

WAGES AND HOURS
See also COMPENSATION
Child support payments withheld, **ORC 2151.23(G)**
    Paternity proceedings, **ORC 3111.13(F)**

WAIT AND SEE ACT
Generally, **ORC 2131.08**

WAIVER
Anatomical gift, donee's rights to, **ORC 2108.02**
Consignment of art works to dealers, waiver of statutory provisions void, **ORC 5815.47**
Coroners, by; donee's rights to anatomical gift, **ORC 2108.02**
Disclaimer of succession to property, **ORC 5815.36**
    See also DISCLAIMER OF SUCCESSION TO PROPERTY
Dower, assignment, **ORC 5305.15, ORC 5305.16**
Estate, administration
    Appointment as executor or administrator, **ORC 2113.07**
    Bonds, **ORC 2109.07**
Juvenile courts
    Examination of child, **JuvR 30(F), JuvR 30(G)**
    Rights of child, **JuvR 3**
Title to property, in favor of dower interest, **ORC 2103.03**
Trusts, waiver of notice, **ORC 5801.08**

WARDS
See GUARDIANSHIP

WARRANTS
Custody of child, court taking, **JuvR 15(E), JuvR 15(D), JuvR 16(B)**
Juvenile delinquency or traffic offense, for, **JuvR 15(E)**
Juvenile proceedings against parents or guardians, **ORC 2151.30**
Wills, production, **ORC 2107.09**

WEAPONS
Dangerous ordnances
    School activities, illegal conveyance or possession at
        Drivers' license, denial or revocation of temporary instruction permit, **ORC 2923.122**
    School buses, illegal conveyance or possession on
        Drivers' license, denial or revocation of temporary instruction permit, **ORC 2923.122**

WEAPONS—*continued*
Dangerous ordnances—*continued*
    School premises, illegal conveyance or possession on
        Drivers' license, denial or revocation of temporary instruction permit, **ORC 2923.122**
Possession
    Object indistinguishable from firearm, possession of on school premises or buses, or at school activities
        Drivers' license, denial or revocation of temporary instruction permit, **ORC 2923.122**
    School activities, illegal conveyance or possession at
        Drivers' license, denial or revocation of temporary instruction permit, **ORC 2923.122**
    School buses, illegal conveyance or possession on
        Drivers' license, denial or revocation of temporary instruction permit, **ORC 2923.122**
    School premises, illegal conveyance or possession on
        Drivers' license, denial or revocation of temporary instruction permit, **ORC 2923.122**
School activities
    Illegal conveyance or possession at
        Drivers' license, denial or revocation of temporary instruction permit, **ORC 2923.122**
    Possession of object indistinguishable from firearm at
        Drivers' license, denial or revocation of temporary instruction permit, **ORC 2923.122**
School buses
    Illegal conveyance or possession on
        Drivers' license, denial or revocation of temporary instruction permit, **ORC 2923.122**
    Possession of object indistinguishable from firearm on
        Drivers' license, denial or revocation of temporary instruction permit, **ORC 2923.122**
School premises
    Illegal conveyance or possession on
        Drivers' license, denial or revocation of temporary instruction permit, **ORC 2923.122**
    Possession of object indistinguishable from firearm on
        Drivers' license, denial or revocation of temporary instruction permit, **ORC 2923.122**

WELFARE
See INDIGENT PERSONS

WIDOW OR WIDOWER
See SURVIVING SPOUSE

WIFE
See HUSBAND AND WIFE

WILL CONTESTS
See CONTEST OF WILL

WILLS
Generally, **ORC Ch 2107**
See also PROBATE OF WILLS
Acknowledgment, **ORC 2107.03, ORC 2107.04**
Actions
    Construction, **ORC 2106.06**
    Contest. See CONTEST OF WILL
    Heirship, to determine, **ORC Ch 2123**
Administrators. See EXECUTORS AND ADMINISTRATORS
Admission to probate. See PROBATE OF WILLS
Adopted children, **ORC 2107.34**
    Debt payments, contributions by, **ORC 2107.55**
Afterborn children, rights, **ORC 2107.34**
    Debt payments, contributions by, **ORC 2107.55**
Age requirement of testator, **ORC 2107.02**
Age requirements
    Witness, **ORC 2107.06**
Agreement to make, **ORC 2107.04**
Alteration of property, effect, **ORC 2107.36**

WILLS

WILLS—*continued*
Amendment
    Anatomical gift clause, **ORC 2108.06**
    Declaration of validity, effect, **ORC 2107.084**
Anatomical gifts, **ORC 2108.04**
Annulment of marriage, effect, **ORC 2107.33**
Ante mortem declaration of validity, **ORC 2107.081 to 2107.085**
    See also ANTE MORTEM DECLARATION OF WILL VALIDITY
Anti-lapse statute, **ORC 2107.52**
Attestation, **ORC 2107.03, ORC 2107.04**
Attestation by minors, **2107.06**
Beneficiaries. See HEIRS
Bequests. See LEGACIES AND DEVISES
Cancellation. See REVOCATION OF WILLS
Charitable bequest. See LEGACIES AND DEVISES, at Charitable bequests
Codicils. See CODICILS
Concealment, **ORC 2107.09, ORC 2107.10**
    See also Production, this heading
Construction. See CONSTRUCTION OF WILLS
Contests. See CONTEST OF WILL
Contract to make will, **ORC 2107.04**
Copies
    Certified, **ORC 2107.20**
    Records in counties where real property is located, **ORC 2107.21**
Corrections. See Amendment, this heading
Custody of, **ORC 2107.08**
    See also Deposit of, this heading
    Delivery, **ORC 2107.08**
    Liability and penalties, **ORC 2107.09**
Cuyahoga county probate court
    Affidavit of notice of admission to probate, **CuyR 34.4**
    Deposit with court, **CuyR 66.3 et seq.**
Declaratory judgments, **ORC 2107.081 to 2107.085**
Definitions, **ORC 2107.01**
Delivery, **ORC 2107.08**
Deposit
    Guardians, **FrankR 66.4, Sup. R 66.4**
    Release to probate court, **Sup. R 75.6**
    Release upon death of testator, **FrankR 75.9**
Deposit of, **ORC 2107.07**
    Fee, **ORC 2101.16, ORC 2107.07**
    Guardians, **CuyR 66.3 et seq.**
Depositions, **ORC 2107.17, ORC 2107.181**
Destroyed, **ORC 2107.26 to 2107.28**
    New records, **ORC 2107.29 to 2107.32**
    Revocation, for purpose of, **ORC 2107.33 to 2107.38**
    Subsequent wills, **ORC 2107.38**
Devises. See LEGACIES AND DEVISES
Disclaimer of succession to property, **ORC 5815.36**
    See also DISCLAIMER OF SUCCESSION TO PROPERTY
Disclosure, **ORC 2107.08, ORC 2107.084**
Discovery after administration of intestate estate commenced, **ORC 2113.20**
Dissolution of marriage, effect, **ORC 2107.33**
Divorce, effect, **ORC 2107.33**
Documents and records, incorporation by reference, **ORC 2107.05**
Drafting. See DRAFTING WILLS
Election to take under or against. See SURVIVING SPOUSE
Encumbrances, effect, **ORC 2107.35**
Estate tax, provision for, **ORC 2113.85**
Execution, **ORC 2107.02 to 2107.05**
Executors and administrators. See EXECUTORS AND ADMINISTRATORS
Fees, **ORC 2107.62**
    Deposit with court, **ORC 2101.16, ORC 2107.07**
    Probate court, **ORC 2101.16**
Fiduciary, action for construction, **ORC 2106.06**
Filing and recording, **ORC 2107.20, ORC 2107.21**
    Destroyed wills, **ORC 2107.29 to 2107.32**

WILLS—*continued*
Foreign. See FOREIGN WILLS
Generation skipping transfer tax, **ORC 5815.27**
Guardian, deposit with court, **CuyR 66.3 et seq., Sup. R 66.4**
Hearings on validity, **ORC 2107.083, ORC 2107.084**
Heirs. See HEIRS
Holographic, **ORC 2107.03**
Incorporation by reference, **ORC 2107.05**
Ineffectual, **ORC 2107.61**
Interpretation, **ORC 2106.03**
    See also CONSTRUCTION OF WILLS
Jurisdiction to probate, **ORC 2107.11, ORC 2107.12**
Language. See CONSTRUCTION OF WILLS, generally
Later wills. See Subsequent, this heading
Legacies. See LEGACIES AND DEVISES
Legal advertising. See Notice, this heading
Living wills, **ORC 2133.01 to 2133.16**
    See also LIVING WILLS
Lost, **ORC 2107.26 to 2107.28**
    New records, **ORC 2107.29 to 2107.32**
Lucas county probate court
    Deposited wills, certification, **LucasR 57.1**
Marriage, effect, **ORC 2107.37**
Most recent, **ORC 2107.22**
Notice
    Deposit of, **ORC 2107.08**
    Foreign, **ORC 2129.07**
    Opening of will, **ORC 2107.08**
    Probate. See PROBATE OF WILLS
Nuncupative, **ORC 2107.60, ORC 2107.61**
Opening, when, **ORC 2107.08**
Oral, **ORC 2107.60, ORC 2107.61**
Perpetuities, statute against, **ORC 2131.09**
Power of appointment by, **ORC 2107.521**
Power to nominate executor, **ORC 2107.65**
Presumed decedents, of, **ORC 2121.05**
Pretermitted heir status, **ORC 2107.34**
    Debt payments, contributions by, **ORC 2107.55**
Probate. See PROBATE OF WILLS
Production, **ORC 2107.09, ORC 2107.10**
    Will of later date after admission to probate, **ORC 2107.22**
Property acquired subsequent to, **ORC 2107.50**
Publication, **ORC 2107.08, ORC 2107.38**
Recording, **ORC 2107.20, ORC 2107.21**
Remainder interest, surviving spouse's rights, **ORC 2106.05**
Renunciation by heir, **ORC 5815.36**
Revocation. See REVOCATION OF WILLS
Rule in Shelley's case, **ORC 2107.49**
Safe deposit boxes, in, **ORC 5731.39**
    Access after death of testator, **ORC 5731.39**
    Franklin County, **FrankR 75.12**
    Removal, **SumR 90.1**
Second will. See Subsequent, this heading
Separation agreements, effect, **ORC 2107.33**
Service of process
    Petition for declaration of validity of will, **ORC 2107.082**
    Production, **ORC 2107.09**
Signatures, **ORC 2107.03, ORC 2107.04**
    Acknowledgment, **ORC 2107.03**
Spoliated, **ORC 2107.26 to 2107.28**
    New records, **ORC 2107.29 to 2107.32**
Stark county probate court
    Wills deposited with court, **Sup. R 75.6**
Statute of frauds, **ORC 2107.04**
Subsequent, **ORC 2107.22**
    Contests, **ORC 2107.77**
    Destruction, **ORC 2107.38**
    Purchaser of property, protection against, **ORC 2107.47**
Summit county probate court
    Probate of will, applications, **SumR 59.1**
    Removal from safe deposit boxes, **SumR 90.1**

WILLS—*continued*
Surviving spouse, election. See SURVIVING SPOUSE
Testators. See TESTATORS
Trust estates, **ORC 2107.63**
Trusts. See TRUSTS
Unclaimed, opening, **ORC 2107.08**
Validity, **ORC 2107.16, ORC 2107.18, ORC 2107.22, ORC 2107.33**
    Anatomical gifts, effect, **ORC 2108.04**
    Ante mortem determination, **ORC 2107.081 to 2107.085**
        See also ANTE MORTEM DECLARATION OF WILL VALIDITY
    Contests. See CONTEST OF WILL
    Evidence, **ORC 2107.081**
    Nuncupative, **ORC 2107.60**
Verbal, **ORC 2107.60, ORC 2107.61**
Withholding, **ORC 2107.09, ORC 2107.10**
Witnesses
    Age, **ORC 2107.06**
    Minors as, **ORC 2107.06**
Witnesses. See WITNESSES TO WILLS

WITHDRAWAL
Adoption. See ADOPTION
Revocable trusts, withdrawal of powers of settlor, **ORC 5806.03**

WITNESSES AND TESTIMONY
See also WITNESSES TO WILLS
Continuances when witness unavailable, **SupR 41**
Cross-examinations. See CROSS-EXAMINATIONS
Custody actions
    Reimbursement of expenses
        Inappropriate forum, party who commenced proceeding to pay, **ORC 3109.25(G)**
        Violation of order, proceeding due to, **ORC 3109.32(B)**
Depositions. See DEPOSITIONS
Expert witnesses. See EXPERT WITNESSES
Fees and costs, **HamR 58.2, JuvR 17(C)**
    See also COURT COSTS, generally
    Party unable to pay, **JuvR 17(B)**
Hamilton county probate court, fees, **HamR 58.2**
Heirs-at-law, designation, **ORC 2105.15**
Juvenile courts. See JUVENILE COURTS
Living wills, **ORC 2133.02**
Mentally ill persons, hearings on hospitalization, **ORC 5122.15**
Paternity proceedings, **ORC 3111.12**
    Depositions, **ORC 3111.04**
        Experts, **ORC 3111.09**
    Fees, **ORC 3111.14**
    Reimbursement of expenses
        Violation of order, proceeding due to, **ORC 3109.26(C)**
        Wrongful removal of child, proceeding following, **ORC 3109.26(C)**
Power of attorney
    Durable power of attorney for health care, **ORC 1337.12**
Probate courts
    Master commissioners, powers, **ORC 2101.06**
    Summons, **ORC 2101.07**
Recording
    Witness unavailable, when, **SupR 41**
Sequestration, juvenile proceeding, **JuvR 29(E)**
Sex offenses, child victim
    Videotaped or televised testimony, **ORC 2152.81**
Subpoenas. See SUBPOENAS, generally
Unavailable witnesses
    Continuances due to, **SupR 41**
Unavailable witnesses, depositions used in place of. See DEPOSITIONS
Videotape testimony, **SupR 13**
Wills. See WITNESSES TO WILLS

WITNESSES TO INSTRUMENT
Anatomical gifts, **ORC 2108.04**

WITNESSES TO WILLS
Generally, **ORC 2107.03, ORC 2107.15**
See also WITNESSES AND TESTIMONY, generally
Conflict of interest of probate judges, **ORC 2101.38**
Contests, **ORC 2107.74**
Depositions, **ORC 2107.17, ORC 2107.181**
Devisee or legatee, as, **ORC 2107.15**
    Contributions to debt payments, **ORC 2107.55**
Examination, **ORC 2107.17, ORC 2107.181**
Fees for attendance, **ORC 2107.62**
Heirs as, **ORC 2107.15**

WORDS AND PHRASES
See DEFINITIONS

WORK
See EMPLOYER AND EMPLOYEE

WORK OF ART
Defined, **ORC 5815.41**

WORKERS' COMPENSATION
Child support withheld or deducted from payments
    Paternity proceedings, **ORC 3111.13(F)**

WORKHOUSES
Detention of minors in, **ORC 2152.26**
    Processing purposes, for, **ORC 2151.311**
DNA testing of prisoners, **ORC 2901.07**
Minors housed in, **ORC 2152.26(C)**

WRITS
Fees of probate court, **ORC 2101.16**

WRITTEN INSTRUMENTS
See LEGAL INSTRUMENTS

WRONGFUL DEATH
Generally, **O Const I § 19a, ORC Ch 2125**
Administrator failing or refusing to file, **ORC 2113.18**
Annuities, consideration, **ORC 2125.02**
Compensatory damages, **ORC 2125.02**
Cuyahoga county probate court
    Settlements, attorney fees, **CuyR 71.2 et seq.**
Damages, **O Const I § 19a, ORC Ch 2125**
    Apportionment among beneficiaries, **ORC 2125.03**
    Attorney fees, **CuyR 71.2 et seq.**
    Distribution, **HamR 70.1**
Date of death, effect on determination, **ORC 2125.02**
Executor failing to file, **ORC 2113.18**
Funeral expenses, **ORC 2125.02**
Hamilton county probate court
    Settlements, **HamR 70.1**
Hearing, settlements, **LucasR 78.1, Sup. R 78.4**
Limitation of actions, **ORC 2125.02**
Loss of support, services, or consortium; damages, **ORC 2125.02**
Lucas county probate court
    Settlements, **LucasR 70.1**
        Case management, **LucasR 78.1**
Mental anguish, damages, **ORC 2125.02**
Minor beneficiaries, trusts created for, **ORC 2125.03**
New action, **ORC 2125.04**
Personal representative bringing action, **ORC 2125.02**
Probate court
    Fee, **ORC 2101.16**
Prohibitions, **ORC 2125.02, ORC 2125.03**
Settlements, **FrankR 70.1, LucasR 70.1, ORC 2125.02, SumR 70.1, SupR 70**
    See also Damages, this heading
    Attorney fees, **CuyR 71.2 et seq.**
    Conference, **FrankR 70.4**
    Distribution, **HamR 70.1**

WRONGFUL DEATH—continued
Settlements, **FrankR 70.1, LucasR 70.1, ORC 2125.02, SumR 70.1, SupR 70**—continued
    Wrongful death prototype trust, **FrankR 70.2**
        Multiple beneficiaries, **FrankR 70.3**
Stark county probate court
    Settlements, case management, **Sup. R 78.4**
Summit county probate court
    Wrongful death settlements, **SumR 70.1**
Surviving spouse, remarriage; consideration, **ORC 2125.02**
Trusts, **Sup. R 70.1**
    Court costs, **Sup. R 58.1**
    Multiple beneficiaries, **Sup. R 70.2**
Trusts created for minor beneficiaries, **ORC 2125.03**

YEAR'S ALLOWANCE
See FAMILY ALLOWANCE

YOUTH COMMISSION
See YOUTH SERVICES DEPARTMENT

YOUTH SERVICES DEPARTMENT
Generally, **ORC 2151.38**
Commitment of children to
    Discharge. See Release of children, this heading
    Juveniles guilty of felonies or murders
        Early release, **ORC 2151.38(B)**
    Mental retardation and developmental disabilities department, transfer to, **ORC 5123.03**
    Minimum period, **ORC 2151.38(A), ORC 2151.38(B)**
    Termination, **ORC 2151.38**
Degree of violation
    Providing to department upon commitment of child, **ORC 2151.38(C)**
Detention homes
    See also DETENTION HOMES
    Funding, **ORC 2152.43**
Felony committed by juvenile, institutionalization due to
    Early release, **ORC 2151.38(A), ORC 2151.38(B)**
Foster care placement of children
    Early release, following, **ORC 2151.38(B)**
    Minimum time for commitment served, following, **ORC 2151.38(C)**
Hearings on release, **ORC 2151.38(B), ORC 2151.38(C)**
    Request for early release, **ORC 2151.38(C)**
Institutions. See CHARITABLE INSTITUTIONS, for general provisions
Juvenile rehabilitation facilities, **ORC 2151.651, ORC 2151.652**
    See also JUVENILE REHABILITATION

YOUTH SERVICES DEPARTMENT—continued
Minimum period of commitment, **ORC 2151.38(A), ORC 2151.38(B)**
Notice to committing court
    Termination of department custody, **ORC 2151.38(C)**
Parents, release of child to, **ORC 2151.38(A), ORC 2151.38(B), ORC 2151.38(C)**
    Minimum time for commitment served, following, **ORC 2151.38(C)**
Parole, releasing child on
    Early release, following, **ORC 2151.38(B)**
    Minimum time for commitment served, following, **ORC 2151.38(C)**
Records and reports
    Progress reports on children released from custody, **ORC 2151.38(E), ORC 2151.38(F)**
    Rehabilitation plan of children released from custody, **ORC 2151.38(C), ORC 2151.38(C) to 2151.38(E), ORC 2151.38(D)**
Release authority, **ORC 2151.38**
    Defined, **ORC 2151.38(G)**
    Hearing on judicial release, **ORC 2151.38(B)**
    Request for early release
        Hearings, **ORC 2151.38(C)**
    Terms and conditions of release, **ORC 2151.38(B)**
        Copy to court in child's new locale, **ORC 2151.38(B)**
Release of children, **ORC 2151.38(A), ORC 2151.38(B), ORC 2151.38(C)**
    Early release
        Juveniles guilty of felonies or murder, **ORC 2151.38(B)**
    Juvenile court hearing, **ORC 2151.38(B), ORC 2151.38(C)**
    Minimum term of institutionalization, **ORC 2151.38(A), ORC 2151.38(B)**
    Multiple offenses, consecutive terms, **ORC 2151.38(B)**
    Notice to committing court, **ORC 2151.38(B), ORC 2151.38(C)**
    Rehabilitation plan, **ORC 2151.38(C), ORC 2151.38(C) to 2151.38(E), ORC 2151.38(D)**
    Violation of terms of release, **ORC 2151.38(B), ORC 2151.38(C), ORC 2151.38(D)**
Return to custody due to violation of terms of release, **ORC 2151.38(B), ORC 2151.38(C), ORC 2151.38(D)**
Statute violated by delinquent child, providing to department upon commitment of child, **ORC 2151.38(C)**
Sua sponte motion for early release of child, **ORC 2151.38(B)**
Supervised release
    Defined, **ORC 2151.38(G)**
Treatment plan for child pursuant to release, **ORC 2151.38(B), ORC 2151.38(E), ORC 2151.38(C)**
Violation of terms of release, **ORC 2151.38(B), ORC 2151.38(C), ORC 2151.38(D)**